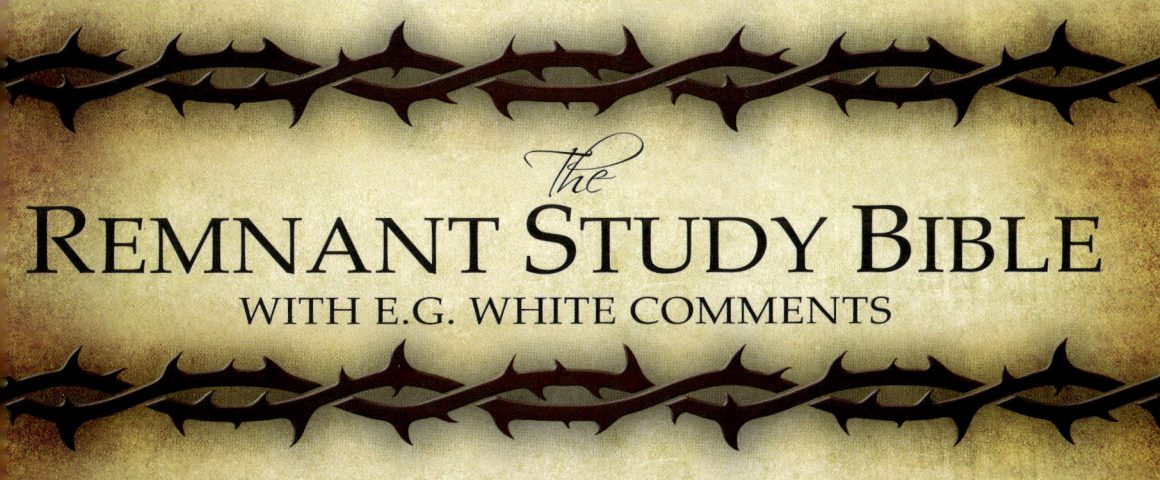

The REMNANT STUDY BIBLE
WITH E.G. WHITE COMMENTS

This Bible Belongs To:

_____

Name

_____

Given by

_____

Date and Occasion

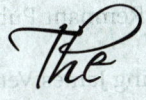

REMNANT STUDY BIBLE

WITH E. G. WHITE COMMENTS

KING JAMES VERSION

WORDS OF CHRIST IN RED

Table of Contents

CONTENTS

As the publisher of *The Remnant Study Bible*, we want to share with our readers some background on how this Bible was developed—and to offer suggestions on how to use its many features.

How This Bible Began
The idea for this Bible arose in conjunction with another Bible project—Remnant's "Bibles for Africa" project. At press time, this effort has already achieved the sending and distribution of nearly a million Bibles to many of Africa's nations.

As we explored other ways to make the Bible and its teachings accessible to people, the works of Ellen G. White came to mind. Because Remnant has printed so many Bible-based books by this prolific and well-respected author, a Bible featuring notes by her in the King James Version seemed a natural. Remnant Publications has as its mission to print and publish books that help people understand their Bibles, and so we are delighted to present to you this Bible you are now reading.

How the Comments Were Selected
Though approximately 120 books by E. G. White are in print today, for this special Bible, Remnant chose to focus on 10 of her best-known and most-loved books from which to draw her comments.

The actual selection of those comments was accomplished by an all-volunteer team of contributors from all walks of life. Our goal for *The Remnant Study Bible* was to make it as useful as possible for a maximum number of people. So we wanted it to appeal not only to scholars and those with great Bible knowledge but also to everyone else—those new in the faith, young people, both blue-collar and white-collar workers, homemakers, and many others—to a full cross-section of those interested in learning more from God's Word.

So in seeking those to help select comments from E. G. White, we purposely chose contributors with varying backgrounds and life pursuits: theologians and housewives, pastors and laymen, older Christians and younger ones—people of many viewpoints and at various stages in their spiritual experiences.

We believe this approach has produced a Bible that can be used by anyone and everyone.

A User-Friendly Bible
Many study Bibles available today include comments by a Christian leader or scholar but also offer a wide variety of study helps. Likewise, we at Remnant wanted *The Remnant Study Bible* to offer not only every useful feature such Bibles typically include but also as many additional features as we could reasonably add. Our goal has been to produce the best all-around study Bible possible.

This study Bible is unique, of course, in that it includes the illuminating comments of E. G. White. And we are so pleased to offer her comments for the first time ever in this King James Bible. But while her comments are a significant contribution to this Bible, they are only a part of a complete package of study aids that includes not only helps common to most study Bibles—a concordance, cross-references, and book outlines, for example—but also such added features as a full set of chain-reference studies, a section of prophetic symbols, a one-year Bible reading program, and so much more.

We've done our best to make this a user-friendly, accessible Bible that can be used in many ways. We think readers will enjoy doing just that—reading it. It's also replete with a wide array of study helps that will prove a powerful assist to anyone wishing to dig deep in personally searching the Word. And for those who find opportunities to share with others what they discover, *The Remnant Study Bible* provides topical Bible studies as an invaluable tool to open God's truth-filled messages.

The Bible Comes Alive!
As president of Remnant Publications, let me share with you my own experience with this Bible while it was still being developed. I wanted to review the good work our contributors

had done in selecting the comments from E. G. White to be included in our study Bible, so I committed to something that turned out to be one of the most wonderful spiritual journeys of my life.

I went through the Bible, book by book, and personally read each selected comment of E. G. White, and with them, the verses on which she commented. I can only say that doing this opened the Bible to me in a profoundly new way—it truly came alive as I continued reading. In reading just the comments and the verses linked to them, I enjoyed a quick overview of God's amazing grace, mercy, and love. In a powerful way, I saw more clearly than ever how He wants so much to restore His image in us and save us to live with Him forever.

Please let me invite you to consider beginning your use of this Bible by doing what I did: go through it and read just the comments by E. G. White and their associated verses. I'm certain you will find yourself as spiritually energized by this as I was.

I would encourage you, though, not to stop with just reading the comments by E. G. White in this Bible. Take a moment and go to page ix, where you'll find a list of those books and information on how you can order any or all of them for yourself. If you purchase all 10, my suggestion would be that you begin your reading with her masterpiece on living the Christian life—*Steps to Christ*. But I know that reading any of these books will be a spiritually transforming experience. You'll be blessed beyond measure.

With the world around us in increasing chaos, we each need something strong and solid to "hang onto." Nothing can offer that to us but God and His Word. So our prayer at Remnant Publications is that you will find in this study Bible what your deepest soul wants and needs—your strong shelter, your safe place, your anchor, your only security, your hope and joy, and your greatest Friend.

Dwight Hall, President/CEO
Remnant Publications
Coldwater, Michigan

Throughout *The Remnant Study Bible* are found—interspersed with the text of the King James Version—brief, illuminating comments by E. G. White.

Born Ellen Gould Harmon on November 26, 1827, she would—during the course of her lifetime (she died July 16, 1915)—become not only a Christian leader of remarkable accomplishments, but also one of the most prolific writer-authors of all time.

She wrote more than 5,000 periodical articles and 40 books during her lifetime. But today—including compilations from her 50,000 pages of manuscript—more than 120 titles are available in English.

She is the most-translated female nonfiction writer in the entire history of literature and also the most-translated American nonfiction author of either gender. One title alone—her masterpiece on Christian living entitled *Steps to Christ*—has been published in more than 140 languages. Her writings cover a broad range of subjects, including religion, education, health, social and family relationships, prophecy, publishing, and Christian leadership.

In her youth, Ellen would marry a young minister named James White, and together with a retired sea captain named Joseph Bates, the three of them founded a movement committed to sharing with the world the good and urgent news of the nearness of Christ's second coming to this earth.

Ellen G. White would become not only a noted speaker and writer but also the founder of schools, hospitals, and publishing houses both in North America and around the world. Most of these institutions continue their Christian ministry to this day.

Many of her contemporaries, as well as millions today, believe that her ministry and writings were abundantly and uniquely blessed with the spiritual gift of prophecy. Though she personally never claimed to be a prophet, she did see herself as a "messenger" and her writings as a "lesser light to lead to the greater light"—meaning the Bible.

Though her writings should therefore not be seen as taking the place of the Bible or adding to it, the publishers of *The Remnant Study Bible* invite you to read her comments to discover the same spiritual inspiration her words have already brought to countless of her readers for more than a century.

As Ellen G. White herself noted: "The fact that God has revealed His will to men through His Word, has not rendered needless the continued presence and guiding of the Holy Spirit. On the contrary, the Spirit was promised by our Saviour to open the Word to His servants, to illuminate and apply its teachings" (The Great Controversy, p. vii).

The late broadcaster Paul Harvey was deeply impressed by the lifework and writings of Mrs. White. In one of his broadcasts, he said: "I can name an American woman author [whose] . . . writings have been translated into 148 languages. More than Marx or Tolstoy, more than Agatha Christie, more than William Shakespeare. Only now is the world coming to appreciate her recommended prescription for optimum spiritual and physical health. Ellen White: You don't know her? Get to know her!"

In this special edition of the KJV, we echo that invitation!

Contributors to *The Remnant Study Bible*

The publisher of this special study Bible wishes to acknowledge the invaluable contribution of the following volunteers who invested their time and care in selecting the most outstanding comments of E. G. White to be interspersed throughout the text of the King James Version.

These contributors represent a wide cross-section of committed Christians from all walks of life: scholars and laymen, men and women, young and not-so-young. Without their assistance, this project could never have been completed:

Jim Aldrich—Director of Budget and Reimbursement, Adventist Health

Ann Anderson—Editor-Researcher, Creative Media Ministries

Jim Ayer—Vice President for Advancement, Adventist World Radio

Doug Batchelor—President/Speaker, Amazing Facts

Emma Cameron—Editor-Researcher, Creative Media Ministries

Kenneth Cox—Evangelist, Kenneth Cox Ministries

Herbert E. Douglass, Th.D.—Theologian

Melvyn Douglass—Executive Director, Scottish Clan Council of Houston

Jonathan D. Gibbs, Ph.D, M.Div.—President, Advent International Ministries

Clifford Goldstein—Editor, Adult Sabbath School Quarterlies

Joyce Griffith—Owner, Griffith Publishing

Blake Hall—Pastor

Dan Hall—Vice President, Remnant Publications

Dwight Hall—President, Remnant Publications

Glenn Hill—Pastor/Evangelist

Mark Howard—Pastor / Director of Emmanuel Institute of Evangelism

David Kang—President, Light for Life Ministries

Young Kim—Researcher and Homemaker

Kevin Longo—Director of Corporate Compliance, Adventist Health

Laurie Longo—Homemaker

Lindsey Longo—Student

Samuel Koranteng-Pipim, Ph.D.—Director of Public Campus Ministries

Dale Martin—Development, Amazing Facts

Ken McFarland—Owner, Page One Communications

Lonnie Mixon—Manufacturer's Representative, Nuclear Medicine

Terry Nelson—Pastor

Mark A. Swearingen—Pastor

Curtis Wiltse, Ph.D.—Researcher, Lilly Research Laboratories

Steven Winn—Freelance Editor

Judy Wright—Homemaker

By E. G. White, As Used in This Bible

Though more than 120 of her books are currently in print, in creating *The Remnant Study Bible*, the publisher chose to draw her comments from 10 that are the best-known and most-loved.

Following are the names and abbreviations of these books, as used in this Bible:

PP — *Patriarchs and Prophets*

PK — *Prophets and Kings*

DA — *The Desire of Ages*

AA — *The Acts of the Apostles*

GC — *The Great Controversy*

COL — *Christ's Object Lessons*

Ed — *Education*

MB — *Thoughts From the Mount of Blessing*

MH — *The Ministry of Healing*

SC — *Steps to Christ*

If you are interested in ordering books from this list or obtaining a full list of Remnant's books by E. G. White, please contact:

Remnant Publications
649 E. Chicago Road
Coldwater, Michigan 49036
Web site: www.remnantpublications.com

ITALIC TYPE in the Bible text indicates words that are not in the original languages of Hebrew, Aramaic, or Greek but have been supplied by the translators for clarity in English.

CAPS AND SMALL CAPS are used to identify places where the covenant name of God, *YHWH*, appears in the text (translated as "LORD" or "GOD").

CROSS-REFERENCES fall at the end of verses and mark other verses that will help explain the verse or passage.

Isaiah 19:5   **744**

rule over them, saith the Lord, the LORD of hosts.   Is. 20:4; Jer. 46:26; Ezek. 29:19
5 And the waters shall fail from the sea, and the river shall be wasted and dried up. Jer. 51:36
6 And they shall turn the rivers far away; *and* the brooks of defence shall be emptied and dried up: the reeds and flags shall wither.
7 The paper reeds by the brooks, by the mouth of the brooks, and every thing sown by the brooks, shall wither, be driven away, and be no *more.*
8 The fishers also shall mourn, and all they that cast ᵀangle into the brooks shall lament, and they that spread nets upon the waters shall ᵀlanguish.   Ezek. 47:10 ◆ *fish hook* ◆ *weaken*
9 Moreover they that work in fine flax, and they that weave networks, shall be confounded.   Prov. 7:16; Ezek. 27:7
10 And they shall be broken in the purposes thereof, all that make sluices *and* ponds for fish.
11 Surely the princes of Zoan *are* fools, the counsel of the wise counsellors of Pharaoh is become ᵀbrutish: how say ye unto Pharaoh, I *am* the son of the wise, the son of ancient kings?   Num. 13:22; 1 Kin. 4:30; Ps. 78:43 ◆ *dumb*
12 Where *are* they? where *are* thy wise *men*? and let them tell thee now, and let them know what the LORD of hosts hath purposed upon Egypt.   1 Cor. 1:20
13 The princes of Zoan are become fools, the princes of Noph are deceived; they have also seduced Egypt, *even they that are* the stay of the tribes thereof.   Jer. 2:16; 46:14; Ezek. 30:13
14 The LORD hath mingled a perverse spirit in the midst thereof: and they have caused Egypt to ᵀerr in every work thereof, as a drunken *man* staggereth in his vomit.   *stray*
15 Neither shall there be *any* work for Egypt, which the head or tail, branch or ᵀrush, may do.   Is. 9:14-15 ◆ *reed*
16 In that day shall Egypt be like unto women: and it shall be afraid and fear because of the shaking of the hand of the LORD of hosts, which he shaketh over it.   Is. 11:15
17 And the land of Judah shall be a terror unto Egypt, every one that maketh mention thereof shall be afraid in himself, because of the counsel of the LORD of hosts, which he hath determined against it.   Is. 14:24
18 In that day shall five cities in the land of Egypt speak the language of Canaan, and swear to the LORD of hosts; one shall be called, The city of destruction.   Zeph. 3:9
19 In that day shall there be an altar to the LORD in the midst of the land of Egypt, and a pillar at the border thereof to the LORD.
20 And it shall be for a sign and for a witness unto the LORD of hosts in the land of Egypt: for they shall cry unto the LORD because of the oppressors, and he shall send

them a saviour, and a great one, and he shall deliver them.
21 And the LORD shall be known to Egypt, and the Egyptians shall know the LORD in that day, and shall do sacrifice and ᵀoblation; yea, they shall vow a vow unto the LORD, and perform *it.*   Is. 11:9 ◆ *offering*
22 And the LORD shall ᵀsmite Egypt: he shall smite and heal *it*: and they shall return *even* to the LORD, and he shall be ᵀintreated of them, and shall heal them.   *strike* ◆ *pled with*
23 In that day shall there be a highway out of Egypt to Assyria, and the Assyrian shall come into Egypt, and the Egyptian into Assyria, and the Egyptians shall serve with the Assyrians.   Is. 11:16
24 In that day shall Israel be the third with Egypt and with Assyria, *even* a blessing in the midst of the land: Is. 65:8
25 Whom the LORD of hosts shall bless, saying, Blessed *be* Egypt my people, and Assyria the work of my hands, and Israel mine inheritance.   Ps. 100:3; Is. 29:23; Hos. 2:23

The Shame of Those Allied with Egypt

20 In the year that Tartan came unto Ashdod, (when Sargon the king of Assyria sent him,) and fought against Ashdod, and took it;   2 Kin. 18:17
2 At the same time spake the LORD by Isaiah the son of Amoz, saying, Go and loose the sackcloth from off thy loins, and put off thy shoe from thy foot. And he did so, walking naked and barefoot.   1 Sam. 19:24; Mic. 1:8 ◆ *waist*
3 And the LORD said, Like as my servant Isaiah hath walked naked and barefoot three years *for* a sign and wonder upon Egypt and upon Ethiopia;   Is. 8:18
4 So shall the king of Assyria lead away the Egyptians prisoners, and the Ethiopians captives, young and old, naked and barefoot, even with *their* buttocks uncovered, to the shame of Egypt.   Is. 19:4; Jer. 13:22, 26
5 And they shall be afraid and ashamed of Ethiopia their expectation, and of Egypt their glory.   Is. 30:3
6 And the inhabitant of this isle shall say in that day, Behold, such *is* our expectation, whither we flee for help to be delivered from the king of Assyria: and how shall we escape?   Matt. 23:33

The Fall of Babylon

21 The burden of the desert of the sea. As whirlwinds in the south pass through; *so* it cometh from the desert, from a terrible land.   Is. 13:1
2 A grievous vision is declared unto me; the treacherous dealer dealeth treacherously, and the spoiler spoileth. Go up, O Elam: be-

---

The superior "T" and italic type in its related reference indicate an EQUIVALENT TRANSLATION.

E. G. White Notes—See page vii for an article about E. G. White, whose notes appear in this Bible.

Judas Betrays Jesus

14 Then one of the twelve, called Judas Iscariot, went unto the chief priests, Luke 22:3-6
15 And said *unto them*, What will ye give me, and I will deliver him unto you? And they covenanted with him for thirty pieces of silver. Ex. 21:32
16 And from that time he sought opportunity to betray him.

> **26:14–16 One Little Sin Can Destroy Us**
>
> The history of Judas presents the sad ending of a life that might have been honored of God. . . .
>
> Judas had naturally a strong love for money; but he had not always been corrupt enough to do such a deed as this. . . . The love of mammon overbalanced his love for Christ. Through becoming the slave of one vice he gave himself to Satan, to be driven to any lengths in sin. DA 716

Jesus and the Disciples Eat the Passover

17 Now the first *day* of the *feast of* unleavened bread the disciples came to Jesus, saying unto him, Where wilt thou that we prepare for thee to eat the passover? Ex. 12:18-20
18 And he said, Go into the city to such a man, and say unto him, The Master saith, My time is at hand; I will keep the passover at thy house with my disciples. John 7:6, 30; 13:1
19 And the disciples did as Jesus had appointed them; and they made ready the passover.
20 Now when the even was come, he sat down with the twelve. Mark 14:17-21
21 And as they did eat, he said, Verily I say unto you, that one of you shall betray me. John 13:21
22 And they were exceeding sorrowful, and began every one of them to say unto him, Lord, is it I?
23 And he answered and said, He that dippeth *his* hand with me in the dish, the same shall betray me. Ps. 41:9; John 13:18
24 The Son of man goeth as it is written of him: but woe unto that man by whom the Son of man is betrayed! it had been good for that man if he had not been born. Mark 9:12; Luke 24:46
25 Then Judas, which betrayed him, answered and said, Master, is it I? He said unto him, Thou hast said. Matt. 26:64

Jesus Institutes His Holy Supper

26 And as they were eating, Jesus took bread, and blessed *it*, and brake *it*, and gave *it* to the disciples, and said, Take, eat; this is my body. Matt. 14:19

> **26:26–28 The Reason for Communion**
>
> As the Lord's disciples gather about His table, they are not to remember and lament their shortcomings. They are not to dwell upon their past religious experience, whether that experience has been elevating or depressing. They are not to recall the differences between them and their brethren. The preparatory service has embraced all this. . . .
>
> The love of Jesus, with its constraining power, is to be kept fresh in our memory. Christ has instituted this service that it may speak to our senses of the love of God that has been expressed in our behalf. DA 659, 660

27 And he took the cup, and gave thanks, and gave *it* to them, saying, Drink ye all of it;
28 For this is my blood of the new† testament, which is shed for many for the remission of sins. Ex. 24:7-8; Lev. 17:11; Matt. 20:28 ✦ covenant
Baptism/Lord's Supper   See John 13:12-15.

29 But I say unto you, I will not drink †henceforth of this fruit of the vine, until that day when I drink it new with you in my Father's kingdom. Matt. 13:43 ✦ *from this time forward*
30 And when they had sung an hymn, they went out into the mount of Olives. Matt. 21:1

Jesus Predicts Peter's Denial

31 Then saith Jesus unto them, All ye shall be offended because of me this night: for it is written, I will †smite the shepherd, and the sheep of the flock shall be scattered abroad. Zech. 13:7; Matt. 11:6; John 16:32 ✦ *strike*
32 But after I am risen again, I will go before you into Galilee. Matt. 28:10, 16; Mark 16:7
33 Peter answered and said unto him, Though all *men* shall be offended because of thee, *yet* will I never be offended. Luke 22:33
34 Jesus said unto him, Verily I say unto thee, That this night, before the cock crow, thou shalt deny me thrice. Luke 22:34; John 13:38
35 Peter said unto him, Though I should die with thee, yet will I not deny thee. Likewise also said all the disciples. John 13:37

Jesus Prays in Gethsemane

36 Then cometh Jesus with them unto a place called Gethsemane, and saith unto the disciples, Sit ye here, while I go and pray yonder. Matt. 26:39
37 And he took with him Peter and the two sons of Zebedee, and began to be sorrowful and very heavy. Matt. 4:21; 17:1; Mark 5:37
38 Then saith he unto them, My soul is exceeding sorrowful, even unto death: tarry ye here, and watch with me. John 12:27
39 And he went a little further, and fell on his face, and prayed, saying, O my Father,

See page ix for the E. G. White Books (and Their Abbreviations) used in this Bible. The numbers following the abbreviations refer to page numbers from the resources.

Topical Chain Topic—go to page 1468 for a complete list of the topics, which are covered by the chains.

Red Letter Type is used in the New Testament to signify words of Jesus Christ.

Subject Heads have been added to assist in identifying main subjects of the text that follows.

Topical Chain References—Passages that speak to some of the most important teachings from God's Word. Go to page 1468 for a listing of chains and how to use this feature.

The format of this volume is designed to enhance the vividness and devotional quality of the Holy Scriptures and to assist the reader in personal study. To this end, special features have been incorporated in the text of the Bible and in special study aids on each page.

Study Aids

The cross-references at the end of a verse point out verses that will enhance the reader's understanding of the text.

Superior T's indicate translation notes, which appear in italic type at the end of the verse. These notes clarify archaic words or phrases in the King James text. They are explanatory only and are not translated from the original languages.

Subject headings indicate the main subjects of the section of text that follow them. These headings are not found in the original Hebrew, Aramaic, or Greek, but have been added to assist the reader in identifying topics and transitions in the biblical content.

The Text

Italic type in the text (example: God saw that *it was* good) indicates words that are not found in the original languages but that are needed for clarity in English.

Paragraph breaks are indicated by verse numbers in bold type (example: see Genesis 1:6).

The covenant name of God in the Old Testament, represented by the Hebrew consonants *YHWH*, is translated "Lord" or "God" (using capital letters as shown), as it has been throughout the history of the King James Bible. In this edition the capitalized form is also used whenever the covenant name is quoted in the New Testament from a passage in the Old Testament.

Books of the Old and New Testaments

The Old Testament

One Year Reading Plan

This reading plan takes you through every chapter in the Bible during one year.

JANUARY

Day	Passage
1	Genesis 1:1–3:24
2	Genesis 4:1–5:32
3	Genesis 6:1–8:22
4	Genesis 9:1–11:32
5	Genesis 12:1–14:24
6	Genesis 15:1–17:27
7	Genesis 18:1–20:18
8	Genesis 21:1–23:20
9	Genesis 24:1–28:9
10	Genesis 28:10–30:43
11	Genesis 31:1–36:43
12	Genesis 37:1–41:57
13	Genesis 42:1–45:28
14	Genesis 46:1–50:26
15	Exodus 1:1–4:31
16	Exodus 5:1–7:13
17	Exodus 7:14–12:30
18	Exodus 12:31–18:27
19	Exodus 19:1–24:18
20	Exodus 25:1–31:18
21	Exodus 32:1–34:35
22	Exodus 35:1–40:38
23	Leviticus 1:1–7:38
24	Leviticus 8:1–10:20
25	Leviticus 11:1–17:16
26	Leviticus 18:1–22:33
27	Leviticus 23:1–25:55
28	Leviticus 26:1–27:34
29	Numbers 1:1–4:49
30	Numbers 5:1–10:10
31	Numbers 10:11–14:45

FEBRUARY

Day	Passage
1	Numbers 15:1–21:35
2	Numbers 22:1–25:18
3	Numbers 26:1–31:54
4	Numbers 32:1–34:29
5	Numbers 35:1–36:13
6	Deuteronomy 1:1–5:33
7	Deuteronomy 6:1–11:32
8	Deuteronomy 12:1–16:17
9	Deuteronomy 16:18–20:20
10	Deuteronomy 21:1–26:19
11	Deuteronomy 27:1–30:20
12	Deuteronomy 31:1–34:12
13	Joshua 1:1–5:12
14	Joshua 5:13–8:35
15	Joshua 9:1–12:24
16	Joshua 13:1–19:51
17	Joshua 20:1–24:33
18	Judges 1:1–3:6
19	Judges 3:7–8:35
20	Judges 9:1–12:15
21	Judges 13:1–16:31
22	Judges 17:1–21:25
23	Ruth 1:1–4:22
24	1 Samuel 1:1–3:21
25	1 Samuel 4:1–7:17
26	1 Samuel 8:1–12:25
27	1 Samuel 13:1–15:35
28	1 Samuel 16:1–17:58

MARCH

Day	Passage
1	1 Samuel 18:1–20:42
2	1 Samuel 21:1–26:25
3	1 Samuel 27:1–31:13
4	2 Samuel 1:1–4:12
5	2 Samuel 5:1–7:29
6	2 Samuel 8:1–10:19
7	2 Samuel 11:1–12:31
8	2 Samuel 13:1–14:33
9	2 Samuel 15:1–20:26
10	2 Samuel 21:1–24:25
11	1 Kings 1:1–4:34
12	1 Kings 5:1–8:66
13	1 Kings 9:1–11:43
14	1 Kings 12:1–16:34
15	1 Kings 17:1–19:21
16	1 Kings 20:1–22:53
17	2 Kings 1:1–8:15
18	2 Kings 8:16–10:36
19	2 Kings 11:1–13:25
20	2 Kings 14:1–17:41
21	2 Kings 18:1–21:26
22	2 Kings 22:1–25:30
23	1 Chronicles 1:1–9:44
24	1 Chronicles 10:1–12:40
25	1 Chronicles 13:1–17:27
26	1 Chronicles 18:1–22:1
27	1 Chronicles 22:2–27:34
28	1 Chronicles 28:1–29:30
29	2 Chronicles 1:1–5:1
30	2 Chronicles 5:2–9:31
31	2 Chronicles 10:1–14:1

APRIL		MAY		JUNE	
Day	Passage	Day	Passage	Day	Passage
1	2 Chronicles 14:2–16:14	1	Psalms 17:1–20:9	1	Psalms 120:1–124:8
2	2 Chronicles 17:1–20:37	2	Psalms 21:1–24:10	2	Psalms 125:1–129:8
3	2 Chronicles 21:1–24:27	3	Psalms 25:1–28:9	3	Psalms 130:1–134:3
4	2 Chronicles 25:1–28:27	4	Psalms 29:1–32:11	4	Psalms 135:1–137:9
5	2 Chronicles 29:1–32:33	5	Psalms 33:1–36:12	5	Psalms 138:1–140:13
6	2 Chronicles 33:1–35:27	6	Psalms 37:1–41:13	6	Psalms 141:1–144:15
7	2 Chronicles 36:1–23	7	Psalms 42:1–45:17	7	Psalms 145:1–150:6
8	Ezra 1:1–2:70	8	Psalms 46:1–49:20	8	Proverbs 1:1-33
9	Ezra 3:1–6:22	9	Psalms 50:1–53:6	9	Proverbs 2:1-22
10	Ezra 7:1–8:36	10	Psalms 54:1–56:13	10	Proverbs 3:1-35
11	Ezra 9:1–10:44	11	Psalms 57:1–59:17	11	Proverbs 4:1-27
12	Nehemiah 1:1–2:10	12	Psalms 60:1–62:12	12	Proverbs 5:1-23
13	Nehemiah 2:11–3:32	13	Psalms 63:1–65:13	13	Proverbs 6:1-35
14	Nehemiah 4:1–7:73	14	Psalms 66:1–68:35	14	Proverbs 7:1-27
15	Nehemiah 8:1–10:39	15	Psalms 69:1–72:20	15	Proverbs 8:1-36
16	Nehemiah 11:1–13:31	16	Psalms 73:1–75:10	16	Proverbs 9:1-18
17	Esther 1:1–2:23	17	Psalms 76:1–78:72	17	Proverbs 10:1-32
18	Esther 3:1–4:17	18	Psalms 79:1–81:16	18	Proverbs 11:1-31
19	Esther 5:1–10:3	19	Psalms 82:1–84:12	19	Proverbs 12:1-28
20	Job 1:1–2:13	20	Psalms 85:1–89:52	20	Proverbs 13:1-25
21	Job 3:1–14:22	21	Psalms 90:1–92:15	21	Proverbs 14:1-35
22	Job 15:1–21:34	22	Psalms 93:1–95:11	22	Proverbs 15:1-33
23	Job 22:1–31:40	23	Psalms 96:1–98:9	23	Proverbs 16:1-33
24	Job 32:1–37:24	24	Psalms 99:1–101:8	24	Proverbs 17:1-28
25	Job 38:1–41:34	25	Psalms 102:1–104:35	25	Proverbs 18:1-24
26	Job 42:1-17	26	Psalms 105:1–106:48	26	Proverbs 19:1-29
27	Psalms 1:1–4:8	27	Psalms 107:1–109:31	27	Proverbs 20:1-30
28	Psalms 5:1–8:9	28	Psalms 110:1–112:10	28	Proverbs 21:1-31
29	Psalms 9:1–12:8	29	Psalms 113:1–115:18	29	Proverbs 22:1-29
30	Psalms 13:1–16:11	30	Psalms 116:1–118:29	30	Proverbs 23:1-35
		31	Psalm 119:1-176		

JULY	AUGUST	SEPTEMBER
JULY	**AUGUST**	**SEPTEMBER**
Day *Passage*	*Day* *Passage*	*Day* *Passage*
1 Proverbs 24:1-34	*1* Jeremiah 25:1–29:32	*1* Nahum 1:1–3:19
2 Proverbs 25:1-28	*2* Jeremiah 30:1–33:26	*2* Habakkuk 1:1–3:19
3 Proverbs 26:1-28	*3* Jeremiah 34:1–38:28	*3* Zephaniah 1:1–3:20
4 Proverbs 27:1-27	*4* Jeremiah 39:1–45:5	*4* Haggai 1:1–2:23
5 Proverbs 28:1-28	*5* Jeremiah 46:1–52:34	*5* Zechariah 1:1–8:23
6 Proverbs 29:1-27	*6* Lamentations 1:1–5:22	*6* Zechariah 9:1–14:21
7 Proverbs 30:1-33	*7* Ezekiel 1:1–3:27	*7* Malachi 1:1–4:6
8 Proverbs 31:1-31	*8* Ezekiel 4:1–11:25	*8* Matthew 1:1–4:25
9 Ecclesiastes 1:1–2:26	*9* Ezekiel 12:1–17:24	*9* Matthew 5:1-48
10 Ecclesiastes 3:1–5:20	*10* Ezekiel 18:1–24:27	*10* Matthew 6:1-34
11 Ecclesiastes 6:1–8:17	*11* Ezekiel 25:1–32:32	*11* Matthew 7:1-29
12 Ecclesiastes 9:1–12:14	*12* Ezekiel 33:1–39:29	*12* Matthew 8:1–10:42
13 Song of Solomon 1:1–8:14	*13* Ezekiel 40:1–48:35	*13* Matthew 11:1–13:53
14 Isaiah 1:1–6:13	*14* Daniel 1:1–3:30	*14* Matthew 13:54–15:39
15 Isaiah 7:1–12:6	*15* Daniel 4:1–6:28	*15* Matthew 16:1–18:35
16 Isaiah 13:1–18:7	*16* Daniel 7:1–12:13	*16* Matthew 19:1–20:34
17 Isaiah 19:1–23:18	*17* Hosea 1:1–3:5	*17* Matthew 21:1–23:39
18 Isaiah 24:1–27:13	*18* Hosea 4:1–5:15	*18* Matthew 24:1–25:46
19 Isaiah 28:1–31:9	*19* Hosea 6:1–10:10	*19* Matthew 26:1–28:20
20 Isaiah 32:1–35:10	*20* Hosea 10:11–14:9	*20* Mark 1:1–3:35
21 Isaiah 36:1–39:8	*21* Joel 1:1–2:27	*21* Mark 4:1–7:23
22 Isaiah 40:1–48:22	*22* Joel 2:28–3:21	*22* Mark 7:24–9:1
23 Isaiah 49:1–52:12	*23* Amos 1:1–2:16	*23* Mark 9:2–10:52
24 Isaiah 52:13–55:13	*24* Amos 3:1–6:14	*24* Mark 11:1–12:44
25 Isaiah 56:1–59:21	*25* Amos 7:1–9:15	*25* Mark 13:1-37
26 Isaiah 60:1–66:24	*26* Obadiah 1:1–21	*26* Mark 14:1–16:20
27 Jeremiah 1:1–6:30	*27* Jonah 1:1–2:10	*27* Luke 1:1–4:13
28 Jeremiah 7:1–10:25	*28* Jonah 3:1–4:11	*28* Luke 4:14–6:49
29 Jeremiah 11:1–15:21	*29* Micah 1:1–3:12	*29* Luke 7:1–9:50
30 Jeremiah 16:1–20:18	*30* Micah 4:1–5:15	*30* Luke 9:51–10:42
31 Jeremiah 21:1–24:10	*31* Micah 6:1–7:20	

OCTOBER		NOVEMBER		DECEMBER	
Day	*Passage*	*Day*	*Passage*	*Day*	*Passage*
1	Luke 11:1-54	*1*	1 Corinthians 1:1 – 4:21	*1*	Titus 1:1-16
2	Luke 12:1-59	*2*	1 Corinthians 5:1–6:20	*2*	Titus 2:1-15
3	Luke 13:1–14:35	*3*	1 Corinthians 7:1–40	*3*	Titus 3:1–15
4	Luke 15:1–16:31	*4*	1 Corinthians 8:1–11:1	*4*	Philemon 1:1–25
5	Luke 17:1–19:27	*5*	1 Corinthians 11:2–14:40	*5*	Hebrews 1:1–2:18
6	Luke 19:28–21:38	*6*	1 Corinthians 15:1–16:24	*6*	Hebrews 3:1–4:13
7	Luke 22:1-71	*7*	2 Corinthians 1:1–2:11	*7*	Hebrews 4:14–7:28
8	Luke 23:1-56	*8*	2 Corinthians 2:12–7:16	*8*	Hebrews 8:1–10:23
9	Luke 24:1-53	*9*	2 Corinthians 8:1–9:15	*9*	Hebrews 10:24–13:25
10	John 1:1–2:12	*10*	2 Corinthians 10:1–13:14	*10*	James 1:1-27
11	John 2:13–3:36	*11*	Galatians 1:1–2:21	*11*	James 2:1–3:12
12	John 4:1–42	*12*	Galatians 3:1–4:31	*12*	James 3:13–5:20
13	John 4:43–6:71	*13*	Galatians 5:1–6:18	*13*	1 Peter 1:1–2:12
14	John 7:1–10:42	*14*	Ephesians 1:1–3:21	*14*	1 Peter 2:13–4:19
15	John 11:1–12:50	*15*	Ephesians 4:1–6:24	*15*	1 Peter 5:1-14
16	John 13:1–14:31	*16*	Philippians 1:1-30	*16*	2 Peter 1:1-21
17	John 15:1–17:26	*17*	Philippians 2:1-30	*17*	2 Peter 2:1-22
18	John 18:1–19:42	*18*	Philippians 3:1-21	*18*	2 Peter 3:1-18
19	John 20:1–21:25	*19*	Philippians 4:1-23	*19*	1 John 1:1–2:27
20	Acts 1:1–4:37	*20*	Colossians 1:1–2:23	*20*	1 John 2:28–4:21
21	Acts 5:1–8:3	*21*	Colossians 3:1–4:18	*21*	1 John 5:1-21
22	Acts 8:4–12:24	*22*	1 Thessalonians 1:1–3:13	*22*	2 John 1:1—3 John 1:15
23	Acts 12:25–15:35	*23*	1 Thessalonians 4:1–5:28	*23*	Jude 1:1-25
24	Acts 15:36–18:14	*24*	2 Thessalonians 1:1–2:17	*24*	Revelation 1:1–3:22
25	Acts 18:15–21:14	*25*	2 Thessalonians 3:1-18	*25*	Revelation 4:1–5:14
26	Acts 21:15–28:30	*26*	1 Timothy 1:1-17	*26*	Revelation 6:1–8:6
27	Romans 1:1–3:20	*27*	1 Timothy 1:18–3:16	*27*	Revelation 8:7–11:19
28	Romans 3:21–5:21	*28*	1 Timothy 4:1–6:21	*28*	Revelation 12:1–14:20
29	Romans 6:1–8:39	*29*	2 Timothy 1:1–2:26	*29*	Revelation 15:1–16:21
30	Romans 9:1–11:36	*30*	2 Timothy 3:1–4:22	*30*	Revelation 17:1–20:15
31	Romans 12:1–16:27			*31*	Revelation 21:1–22:21

THE OLD TESTAMENT

THE FIRST BOOK OF MOSES CALLED

GENESIS

"In the beginning God . . . ." The phrase is both simple and profound. In these four words are enveloped an entire worldview. In the beginning not *chance*, not *randomness*, not a god by another name. No, in the beginning *God* created the heaven and the earth. God alone took what was nothing and made something—the planets, the sun, our earth, then placed our earth exactly the right distance from the sun. Any closer, we would burn up. Any farther away, we'd freeze. Instead, we are granted the beauty of the seasons, the warmth of sun on our faces, the growth of plants for our food and enjoyment.

Before we even came to be, God created for us a place of beauty for our enjoyment, a fruitful place to sustain us.

In the beginning God...

The book is about beginnings—all of creation, humanity, sin, and even the story of redemption find their beginnings in the pages of this book. Here we read about the first marriage, the first lie, the first sin, the first consequences of sin, the first sacrifice, the first children, the first murder, the first flood, and the first rainbow, along with descriptions of early occupations (shepherd, musician, soldier, city builder). Here we read how God's people Israel became a nation.

Beyond that, of course, Genesis is the beginning of the story of the *redemption* of humanity from the curse of sin and death. The book is not meant to give the history of the world; instead, it is a selective spiritual interpretation of history focusing on God's plan for bestowing salvation.

Dates

The Book of Genesis spans from the unknown date of creation through to the death of Joseph (recorded in Genesis 50:26), occurring around 1589 B.C.

Using the divisions noted above, the dates fall roughly as follows:
(1) *Genesis 1—11, 4000 to 1875 B.C.*
Creation dated c. 4000 B.C. or earlier; death of Terah (11:32) dated c. 1875 B.C.
(2) *Genesis 12—36, 1875 to 1682 B.C.*
Death of Terah dated c. 1875 B.C.; Joseph taken to Egypt (37:28) dated c. 1682 B.C.
(3) *Genesis 37—50, 1682 to 1589 B.C.*
Joseph taken to Egypt dated c. 1682 B.C.; death of Joseph (50:26) dated at 1589 B.C.

Author

Even though the Book of Genesis ends a few centuries before Moses was born, Moses has widely been considered the author—by the early church, in the writings of the first-century Jewish historian Josephus, and in the Jerusalem Talmud. Moses, raised in Egypt and trained as a prince, was used by God to record not only the account of the history of which he was a part—the Exodus from Egypt, the wilderness wanderings, receiving God's laws—but he also recorded the history of creation and humanity under God's inspiration. The history of God's people Israel, collated from oral accounts and other available records, rounds out the book.

Although the Book of Genesis itself doesn't mention an author's name, the Bible offers the information throughout the Old and New Testaments, giving both direct and indirect testimonies to Moses' authorship (see Exodus 17:14; Leviticus 1:1, 2; Numbers 33:2; Deuteronomy 1:1; Joshua 1:7; 1 Kings 2:3; 2 Kings 14:6; Ezra 6:18; Nehemiah 13:1; Daniel 9:11–13; Malachi 4:4; Matthew 8:4; Mark 12:26; Luke 16:29; John 7:19; Acts 15:1; 26:22; Romans 10:19; 1 Corinthians 9:9; 2 Corinthians 3:15).

Meaning of the Name

The word "genesis" comes from the Greek word *geneseos*, which means "beginnings" or "birth" and refers to an origin or a source. In Hebrew, the title is *Bereshith*, which means "in the beginning."

Christ in Genesis

Predictions of the coming Messiah find their beginnings also in the Book of Genesis. With the creation of Adam, the New Testament calls him the "figure of him that was to come" (Romans 5:14), revealing Adam as the head of the old creation, while Jesus would come as head of the new creation.

Christ's sacrifice for sin is foreshadowed in God's words to the serpent, "It shall bruise thy head, and thou shalt bruise his heel" (Genesis 3:15). Jesus would have His "heel" bruised, for He would be wounded and killed, but death would not hold Him; however, Jesus would inflict a mortal wound on Satan—a blow to the head.

Jesus came from the line of Seth (4:25; Luke 3:38), and was the promised descendant of Abraham through whom "all families of the earth [would] be blessed" (Genesis 12:3).

Jesus' role or "type" (a historical fact that reveals a spiritual truth) is seen in the humanity of Adam, the blood sacrifice made by Abel—both in his sacrifice of animals and in his death at the hands of his brother (4:8), the King of Salem, Melchizedek, described as "like unto the Son of God" (Hebrews 7:3), and Joseph—raised from condemnation to great power by God Himself (Genesis 41:37–45).

Perhaps the most touching picture that foreshadows the Messiah's coming sacrifice is Abraham's willingness to sacrifice his only son, Isaac, at God's command (chapter 22). This pictures the day when God would give "his only begotten Son, that whosoever believeth in him should not perish, but have everlasting life" (John 3:16).

Overview

Genesis falls into three main parts which correspond to three geographical locations.

(1) *Genesis 1—11, The Fertile Crescent*: The beginning of the world, and the stories of Adam and Eve all the way through Noah occur in the Fertile Crescent area along the Tigris and Euphrates Rivers. This is the supposed location of the Garden of Eden, the beginnings of the Tower of Babel, and the location where Noah's ark landed after the Flood.

(2) *Genesis 12—36, Canaan*: The focus is on one faithful man, Abraham, who at God's command leaves his home in Haran and goes to the land of Canaan where he is promised to become a great nation. This section follows his descendants—his son Isaac, the rivalry between Isaac's sons Esau and Jacob, and ultimately the promise of salvation carried through Jacob's line.

(3) *Genesis 37—50, Egypt*: Jacob's sons attack their younger brother Joseph and sell him to slave traders bound for Egypt. A famine brings Jacob's sons to Egypt to purchase grain where they encounter their brother Joseph, who has become a mighty leader in the land. Jacob's family moves to Egypt where they are allowed to grow and prosper, setting the stage for the coming story in the Book of Exodus. Jacob's sons become the fathers of the twelve tribes of Israel.

Unlocking Genesis

KEY PEOPLE:
Adam, Eve, Noah, Abraham, Sarah, Isaac, Jacob, Joseph

KEY EVENTS:
Creation; the Fall; sacrifice; the great Flood; the dividing of nations and languages; the beginning of the nation of Israel

KEY WORD:
Beginnings. Genesis offers us the story of beginnings of the world, humanity, sin, the story of redemption, and the nation of Israel through whom redemption would come.

KEY VERSE:
"And I will put enmity between thee and the woman, and between thy seed and her seed; it shall bruise thy head, and thou shalt bruise his heel" (Genesis 3:15).

KEY CHAPTER:
Genesis 15 tells the story of God's covenant with Abraham, given in 12:1–3 and then ratified between God and Abraham in 15:1–21. God promises to Abraham a land (15:18), a great nation that will descend from him (13:16), and that the entire world will be blessed through his descendants (12:2, 3).

Creation of Heaven and Earth

1 In the beginning God created the heaven and the earth.   Job 38:4; Heb. 11:3; Rev. 4:11

2 And the earth was without form, and void; and darkness *was* upon the face of the deep. And the Spirit of God moved upon the face of the waters.   Ps. 104:30; Is. 45:18; Jer. 4:23

Creation of the Light

3 And God said, Let there be light: and there was light.   Ps. 33:6, 9; 2 Cor. 4:6

4 And God saw the light, that *it was* good: and God divided the light from the darkness.

5 And God called the light Day, and the darkness he called Night. And the evening and the morning were the first day.   Ps. 74:16

Creation of the Firmament

6 And God said, Let there be a firmament in the midst of the waters, and let it divide the waters from the waters.   Job 37:18

7 And God made the firmament, and divided the waters which *were* under the firmament from the waters which *were* above the firmament: and it was so.   Ps. 148:4; Prov. 8:28-29

8 And God called the firmament Heaven. And the evening and the morning were the second day.   Gen. 1:5

The Earth Separated from the Waters

9 And God said, Let the waters under the heaven be gathered together unto one place, and let the dry *land* appear: and it was so.

10 And God called the dry *land* Earth; and the gathering together of the waters called he Seas: and God saw that *it was* good.

11 And God said, Let the earth bring forth grass, the herb yielding seed, *and* the fruit tree yielding fruit after his kind, whose seed *is* in itself, upon the earth: and it was so.

12 And the earth brought forth grass, *and* herb yielding seed after his kind, and the tree yielding fruit, whose seed *was* in itself, after his kind: and God saw that *it was* good.

13 And the evening and the morning were the third day.

Creation of the Sun, Moon, and Stars

14 And God said, Let there be lights in the firmament of the heaven to divide the day from the night; and let them be for signs, and for seasons, and for days, and years:

15 And let them be for lights in the ᵀfirmament of the heaven to give light upon the earth: and it was so.   sky

16 And God made two great lights; the greater light to rule the day, and the lesser light to rule the night: *he made* the stars also.

17 And God set them in the firmament of the heaven to give light upon the earth,

18 And to rule over the day and over the night, and to divide the light from the darkness: and God saw that *it was* good.   Jer. 31:35

19 And the evening and the morning were the fourth day.

Creation of Fish, Fowl, Beasts, and Cattle

20 And God said, Let the waters bring forth abundantly the moving creature that hath life, and fowl *that* may fly above the earth in the open firmament of heaven.

21 And God created great whales, and every living creature that moveth, which the waters brought forth abundantly, after their kind, and every winged fowl after his kind: and God saw that *it was* good.

22 And God blessed them, saying, Be fruitful, and multiply, and fill the waters in the seas, and let fowl multiply in the earth.

23 And the evening and the morning were the fifth day.

24 And God said, Let the earth bring forth the living creature after his kind, cattle, and creeping thing, and beast of the earth after his kind: and it was so.   Gen. 6:20

25 And God made the beast of the earth after his kind, and cattle after their kind,

---

Creation Days: Evening and Morning

Genesis 1

Millions of years, it is claimed, were required for the evolution of the earth from chaos; and in order to accommodate the Bible to this supposed revelation of science, the days of creation are assumed to have been vast, indefinite periods, covering thousands or even millions of years.

Such a conclusion is wholly uncalled for. The Bible record is in harmony with itself and with the teaching of nature. Of the first day employed in the work of creation is given the record, "The evening and the morning were the first day" (Genesis 1:5). And the same in substance is said of each of the first six days of creation week. Each of these periods Inspiration declares to have been a day consisting of evening and morning, like every other day since that time. In regard to the work of creation itself the divine testimony is, "He spake, and it was done; He commanded, and it stood fast" (Psalm 33:9). With Him who could thus call into existence unnumbered worlds, how long a time would be required for the evolution of the earth from chaos? In order to account for His works, must we do violence to His word? *Ed 128, 129*

and every thing that creepeth upon the earth after his kind: and God saw that *it was* good.

Creation of Man in the Image of God

26 And God said, Let us make man in our image, after our likeness: and let them have dominion over the fish of the sea, and over the fowl of the air, and over the cattle, and over all the earth, and over every creeping thing that creepeth upon the earth. Gen. 9:6

> **1:26, 27 Man Created to Continually Develop**
>
> When Adam came from the Creator's hand, he bore, in his physical, mental, and spiritual nature, a likeness to his Maker. "God created man in His own image" (Genesis 1:27), and it was His purpose that the longer man lived the more fully he should reveal this image—the more fully reflect the glory of the Creator. All his faculties were capable of development; their capacity and vigor were continually to increase. *Ed 15*

27 So God created man in his *own* image, in the image of God created he him; male and female created he them. Ps. 139:14; Matt. 19:4

28 And God blessed them, and God said unto them, Be fruitful, and multiply, and replenish the earth, and subdue it: and have dominion over the fish of the sea, and over the fowl of the air, and over every living thing that moveth upon the earth. Lev. 26:9

Provision for Food

29 And God said, Behold, I have given you every herb bearing seed, which *is* upon the face of all the earth, and every tree, in the which *is* the fruit of a tree yielding seed; to you it shall be for meat. Gen. 9:3

> Health See Genesis 7:2.

30 And to every beast of the earth, and to every fowl of the air, and to every thing that creepeth upon the earth, wherein *there is* life,

I have given every green herb for meat: and it was so. Ps. 147:9

31 And God saw every thing that he had made, and, behold, *it was* very good. And the evening and the morning were the sixth day.

The First Sabbath

2 Thus the heavens and the earth were finished, and all the host of them.

2 And on the seventh day God ended his work which he had made; and he rested on the seventh day from all his work which he had made. Ex. 31:17; Deut. 5:14; Heb. 4:4

3 And God blessed the seventh day, and ᵀsanctified it: because that in it he had rested from all his work which God created and made. Lev. 23:3 ◆ *made it holy*

> The Sabbath See Exodus 20:8–11.

> **2:2, 3 The Sabbath Essential to Man**
>
> God saw that a Sabbath was essential for man, even in Paradise. He needed to lay aside his own interests and pursuits for one day of the seven, that he might more fully contemplate the works of God and meditate upon His power and goodness. He needed a Sabbath to remind him more vividly of God and to awaken gratitude because all that he enjoyed and possessed came from the beneficent hand of the Creator. *PP 48*

The Manner of the Creation

4 These *are* the generations of the heavens and of the earth when they were created, in the day that the LORD God made the earth and the heavens, Gen. 1:4

5 And every plant of the field before it was in the earth, and every herb of the field before it grew: for the LORD God had not caused it to rain upon the earth, and *there was* not a man to till the ground. Gen. 1:11-12

6 But there went up a mist from the earth, and watered the whole face of the ground.

The Harmony of Science and Scripture

Genesis 1:26, 27

When consideration is given to man's opportunities for research; how brief his life; how limited his sphere of action; how restricted his vision; how frequent and how great the errors in his conclusions, especially as concerns the events thought to antedate Bible history; how often the supposed deductions of science are revised or cast aside; with what readiness the assumed period of the earth's development is from time to time increased or diminished by millions of years; and how the theories advanced by different scientists conflict with one another—considering all this, shall we, for the privilege of tracing our descent from germs and mollusks and apes, consent to cast away that statement of Holy Writ, so grand in its simplicity, "God created man in His own image, in the image of God created He him"? (Genesis 1:27). Shall we reject that genealogical record—prouder than any treasured in the courts of kings—"which was the son of Adam, which was the son of God"? (Luke 3:38).

Rightly understood, both the revelations of science and the experiences of life are in harmony with the testimony of Scripture to the constant working of God in nature. *Ed 130*

7 And the LORD God formed man *of* the dust of the ground, and breathed into his nostrils the breath of life; and man became a living soul.   Gen. 3:19; Ps. 103:14; 1 Cor. 15:45

> After Death See Ecclesiastes 12:7.

The Garden of Eden

8 And the LORD God planted a garden eastward in Eden; and there he put the man whom he had formed.   Gen. 13:10
9 And out of the ground made the LORD God to grow every tree that is pleasant to the sight, and good for food; the tree of life also in the midst of the garden, and the tree of knowledge of good and evil. Rev. 2:7; 22:2
10 And a river went out of Eden to water the garden; and from thence it was parted, and became into four heads.   Ps. 46:4
11 The name of the first *is* Pison: that *is* it which compasseth the whole land of Havilah, where *there is* gold;   Gen. 25:18
12 And the gold of that land *is* good: there *is* bdellium and the onyx stone.
13 And the name of the second river *is* Gihon: the same *is* it that ᵀcompasseth the whole land of Ethiopia.   *surrounds*
14 And the name of the third river *is* Hiddekel: that *is* it which goeth toward the east of Assyria. And the fourth river *is* Euphrates.
15 And the LORD God took the man, and put him into the garden of Eden to dress it and to keep it.   Gen. 2:8
16 And the LORD God commanded the man, saying, Of every tree of the garden thou mayest freely eat:
17 But of the tree of the knowledge of good and evil, thou shalt not eat of it: for in the day that thou eatest thereof thou shalt surely die. Gen. 3:19; Rom. 6:23; James 1:15

> Salvation From Sin See Genesis 3:6.

2:17 Obey and Live

Like the angels, the dwellers in Eden had been placed upon probation; their happy estate could be retained only on condition of fidelity to the Creator's law. They could obey and live, or disobey and perish. God had made them the recipients of rich blessings; but should they disregard His will, He who spared not the angels that sinned, could not spare them; transgression would forfeit His gifts and bring upon them misery and ruin. *PP 53*

18 And the LORD God said, *It is* not good that the man should be alone; I will make him an help meet for him. Gen. 3:12
19 And out of the ground the LORD God formed every beast of the field, and every fowl of the air; and brought *them* unto Adam to see what he would call them: and whatsoever Adam called every living creature, that *was* the name thereof.   Gen. 1:28
20 And Adam gave names to all cattle, and to the fowl of the air, and to every beast of the field; but for Adam there was not found an help meet for him.

God Creates Woman as a Helper for the Man

21 And the LORD God caused a deep sleep to fall upon Adam, and he slept: and he took one of his ribs, and closed up the flesh instead thereof;   Gen. 15:12
22 And the rib, which the LORD God had taken from man, made he a woman, and brought her unto the man.
23 And Adam said, This *is* now bone of my bones, and flesh of my flesh: she shall be called Woman, because she was taken out of Man. Gen. 29:14; Judg. 9:2; 2 Sam. 5:1
24 Therefore shall a man leave his father

The First Marriage

Genesis 2:21–25

God Himself gave Adam a companion. He provided "an help meet for him"—a helper corresponding to him—one who was fitted to be his companion, and who could be one with him in love and sympathy. Eve was created from a rib taken from the side of Adam, signifying that she was not to control him as the head, nor to be trampled under his feet as an inferior, but to stand by his side as an equal, to be loved and protected by him. A part of man, bone of his bone, and flesh of his flesh, she was his second self, showing the close union and the affectionate attachment that should exist in this relation. "For no man ever yet hated his own flesh; but nourisheth and cherisheth it" (Ephesians 5:29). "Therefore shall a man leave his father and his mother, and shall cleave unto his wife; and they shall be one."

God celebrated the first marriage. Thus the institution has for its originator the Creator of the universe. "Marriage is honorable" (Hebrews 13:4); it was one of the first gifts of God to man, and it is one of the two institutions that, after the Fall, Adam brought with him beyond the gates of Paradise. When the divine principles are recognized and obeyed in this relation, marriage is a blessing; it guards the purity and happiness of the race, it provides for man's social needs, it elevates the physical, the intellectual, and the moral nature. *PP 46*

and his mother, and shall cleave unto his wife: and they shall be one flesh. 　Ps. 45:10

Marriage　See John 2:1–10.

25 And they were both naked, the man and his wife, and were not ashamed. 　Gen. 3:10-11

The Serpent's Deception and Man's Shameful Fall

3 Now the serpent was more subtil than any beast of the field which the LORD God had made. And he said unto the woman, Yea, hath God said, Ye shall not eat of every tree of the garden? 2 Cor. 11:3; Rev. 12:9
2 And the woman said unto the serpent, We may eat of the fruit of the trees of the garden:
3 But of the fruit of the tree which is in the midst of the garden, God hath said, Ye shall not eat of it, neither shall ye touch it, lest ye die.

3:4 The First False Sermon

The only one who promised Adam life in disobedience was the great deceiver. And the declaration of the serpent to Eve in Eden— "Ye shall not surely die"—was the first sermon ever preached upon the immortality of the soul. Yet this declaration, resting solely upon the authority of Satan, is echoed from the pulpits of Christendom, and is received by the majority of mankind as readily as it was received by our first parents. GC 533

4 And the serpent said unto the woman, Ye shall not surely die: 　John 8:44; 2 Cor. 11:3

After Death　See Job 4:17.

5 For God doth know that in the day ye eat thereof, then your eyes shall be opened, and ye shall be as gods, knowing good and evil.
6 And when the woman saw that the tree was good for food, and that it was pleasant to the eyes, and a tree to be desired to make one wise, she took of the fruit thereof, and did eat, and gave also unto her husband with her; and he did eat. 　Josh. 7:21; 1 Tim. 2:14

Salvation From Sin　See Genesis 3:19.

7 And the eyes of them both were opened, and they knew that they were naked; and they sewed fig leaves together, and made themselves aprons. 　Gen. 2:25
8 And they heard the voice of the LORD God walking in the garden in the cool of the day: and Adam and his wife hid themselves from the presence of the LORD God amongst the trees of the garden. 　Job 31:33

God Questions Adam and Eve

9 And the LORD God called unto Adam, and said unto him, Where art thou? 　Gen. 4:9

10 And he said, I heard thy voice in the garden, and I was afraid, because I was naked; and I hid myself. 　Gen. 2:25; 3:7
11 And he said, Who told thee that thou wast naked? Hast thou eaten of the tree, whereof I commanded thee that thou shouldest not eat?
12 And the man said, The woman whom thou gavest to be with me, she gave me of the tree, and I did eat. 　Job 31:33

3:12 Shifting Blame

Adam could neither deny nor excuse his sin; but instead of manifesting penitence, he endeavored to cast the blame upon his wife, and thus upon God Himself. . . . He who, from love to Eve, had deliberately chosen to forfeit the approval of God, his home in Paradise, and an eternal life of joy, could now, after his fall, endeavor to make his companion, and even the Creator Himself, responsible for the transgression. So terrible is the power of sin. PP 57, 58

13 And the LORD God said unto the woman, What is this that thou hast done? And the woman said, The serpent Tbeguiled me, and I did eat. 　2 Cor. 11:3; 1 Tim. 2:14 ◆ deceived

The Serpent Is Cursed

14 And the LORD God said unto the serpent, Because thou hast done this, thou art cursed above all cattle, and above every beast of the field; upon thy belly shalt thou go, and dust shalt thou eat all the days of thy life: 　Is. 65:25
15 And I will put Tenmity between thee and the woman, and between thy seed and her seed; it shall bruise thy head, and thou shalt bruise his heel. 　Is. 7:14; Rom. 16:20 ◆ hostility

Jesus　See Isaiah 7:14.

The Punishment God Promises for Mankind

16 Unto the woman he said, I will greatly multiply thy sorrow and thy conception; in sorrow thou shalt bring forth children; and thy desire shall be to thy husband, and he shall rule over thee. 　John 16:21; 1 Cor. 11:3; 14:34
17 And unto Adam he said, Because thou hast hearkened unto the voice of thy wife, and hast eaten of the tree, of which I commanded thee, saying, Thou shalt not eat of it: cursed is the ground for thy sake; in sorrow shalt thou eat of it all the days of thy life; 　Gen. 5:29; Job 14:1; Rom. 8:20-22
18 Thorns also and thistles shall it bring forth to thee; and thou shalt eat the herb of the field;

Health　See Genesis 9:2–4.

3:19

19 In the sweat of thy face shalt thou eat bread, till thou return unto the ground; for out of it wast thou taken: for dust thou *art,* and unto dust shalt thou return.   Ps. 104:29

Salvation From Sin   See Romans 3:23.

20 And Adam called his wife's name Eve; because she was the mother of all living.
21 Unto Adam also and to his wife did the LORD God make coats of skins, and clothed them.
22 And the LORD God said, Behold, the man is become as one of us, to know good and evil: and now, lest he put forth his hand, and take also of the tree of life, and eat, and live for ever: Gen. 1:26
23 Therefore the LORD God sent him forth from the garden of Eden, to till the ground from whence he was taken.   Gen. 2:5
24 So he drove out the man; and he placed at the east of the garden of Eden Cherubims, and a flaming sword which turned every way, to keep the way of the tree of life.

Cain and Abel

4 And Adam knew Eve his wife; and she conceived, and bare Cain, and said, I have gotten a man from the LORD.   Gen. 3:15
2 And she again bare his brother Abel. And Abel was a keeper of sheep, but Cain was a tiller of the ground.   Gen. 47:3
3 And in process of time it came to pass, that Cain brought of the fruit of the ground an offering unto the LORD.   Num. 18:12
4 And Abel, he also brought of the firstlings of his flock and of the fat thereof. And the LORD had respect unto Abel and to his offering: Ex. 13:12; Num. 18:17; Heb. 11:4
5 But unto Cain and to his offering he had not respect. And Cain was very wroth, and his ᵀcountenance fell.   *appearance*

4:1–5 Two Kinds of Sacrifice

Cain and Abel represent two classes that will exist in the world till the close of time. One class avail themselves of the appointed sacrifice for sin; the other venture to depend upon their own merits; theirs is a sacrifice without the virtue of divine mediation, and thus it is not able to bring man into favor with God. It is only through the merits of Jesus that our transgressions can be pardoned. *PP 72, 73*

---

6 And the LORD said unto Cain, Why art thou ᵀwroth? and why is thy countenance fallen?   *angered*
7 If thou doest well, shalt thou not be accepted? and if thou doest not well, sin lieth at the door. And unto thee *shall be* his desire, and thou shalt rule over him.

Cain Murders Abel

8 And Cain talked with Abel his brother: and it came to pass, when they were in the field, that Cain rose up against Abel his brother, and slew him.   Matt. 23:35; Jude 11

The Lord Places a Curse upon Cain

9 And the LORD said unto Cain, Where *is* Abel thy brother? And he said, I know not: *Am* I my brother's keeper?   John 8:44
10 And he said, What hast thou done? the voice of thy brother's blood crieth unto me from the ground.   Heb. 12:24
11 And now *art* thou cursed from the earth, which hath opened her mouth to receive thy brother's blood from thy hand;   Gen. 3:14
12 When thou tillest the ground, it shall not ᵀhenceforth yield unto thee her strength; a fugitive and a ᵀvagabond shalt thou be in the earth.   Lev. 26:36 ◆ *from this time forward* ◆ *wanderer*
13 And Cain said unto the LORD, My punishment *is* greater than I can bear.

Hope and Promise of Redemption

Genesis 3:15

But man was not abandoned to the results of the evil he had chosen. In the sentence pronounced upon Satan was given an intimation of redemption. . . . This sentence, spoken in the hearing of our first parents, was to them a promise. Before they heard of the thorn and the thistle, of the toil and sorrow that must be their portion, or of the dust to which they must return, they listened to words that could not fail of giving them hope. All that had been lost by yielding to Satan could be regained through Christ.

This intimation also nature repeats to us. Though marred by sin, it speaks not only of creation but of redemption. Though the earth bears testimony to the curse in the evident signs of decay, it is still rich and beautiful in the tokens of life-giving power. The trees cast off their leaves, only to be robed with fresher verdure; the flowers die, to spring forth in new beauty; and in every manifestation of creative power is held out the assurance that we may be created anew in "righteousness and holiness of truth" (Ephesians 4:24, margin). Thus the very objects and operations of nature that bring so vividly to mind our great loss become to us the messengers of hope.

As far as evil extends, the voice of our Father is heard, bidding His children see in its results the nature of sin, warning them to forsake the evil, and inviting them to receive the good. *Ed 27*

14 Behold, thou hast driven me out this day from the face of the earth; and from thy face shall I be hid; and I shall be a fugitive and a vagabond in the earth; and it shall come to pass, *that* every one that findeth me shall slay me.   Num. 35:19; Job 15:20-24; Prov. 28:1

15 And the LORD said unto him, Therefore whosoever slayeth Cain, vengeance shall be taken on him sevenfold. And the LORD set a mark upon Cain, lest any finding him should kill him.   Gen. 4:24; Ezek. 9:4, 6

16 And Cain went out from the presence of the LORD, and dwelt in the land of Nod, on the east of Eden.   Gen. 4:14

17 And Cain knew his wife; and she conceived, and bare Enoch: and he builded a city, and called the name of the city, after the name of his son, Enoch.   Ps. 49:11

18 And unto Enoch was born Irad: and Irad begat Mehujael: and Mehujael begat Methusael: and Methusael begat Lamech.

Lamech and His Two Wives

19 And Lamech took unto him two wives: the name of the one *was* Adah, and the name of the other Zillah.   Gen. 2:24

20 And Adah bare Jabal: he was the father of such as dwell in tents, and *of such as have* cattle.

21 And his brother's name *was* Jubal: he was the father of all such as handle the harp and organ.

22 And Zillah, she also bare Tubal-cain, an instructer of every artificer in brass and iron: and the sister of Tubal-cain *was* Naamah.

23 And Lamech said unto his wives, Adah and Zillah, Hear my voice; ye wives of Lamech, hearken unto my speech: for I have slain a man to my wounding, and a young man to my hurt.

24 If Cain shall be avenged sevenfold, truly Lamech seventy and sevenfold.   Gen. 4:15

Births of Seth and Enos

25 And Adam knew his wife again; and she bare a son, and called his name Seth: For God, *said she,* hath appointed me another seed instead of Abel, whom Cain slew.

26 And to Seth, to him also there was born a son; and he called his name Enos: then began men to call upon the name of the LORD.

Genealogy of the Patriarchs

5 This *is* the book of the generations of Adam. In the day that God created man, in the likeness of God made he him;

2 Male and female created he them; and blessed them, and called their name Adam, in the day when they were created. Gen. 1:27

3 And Adam lived an hundred and thirty years, and begat *a son* in his own likeness, after his image; and called his name Seth:

4 And the days of Adam after he had †begotten Seth were eight hundred years: and he begat sons and daughters: † brought forth

5 And all the days that Adam lived were nine hundred and thirty years: and he died.

6 And Seth lived an hundred and five years, and begat Enos: Gen. 4:26

7 And Seth lived after he †begat Enos eight hundred and seven years, and begat sons and daughters: † brought forth

8 And all the days of Seth were nine hundred and twelve years: and he died.

9 And Enos lived ninety years, and begat Cainan:

10 And Enos lived after he begat Cainan eight hundred and fifteen years, and begat sons and daughters:

11 And all the days of Enos were nine hundred and five years: and he died.

12 And Cainan lived seventy years, and begat Mahalaleel:

13 And Cainan lived after he begat Mahalaleel eight hundred and forty years, and begat sons and daughters:

14 And all the days of Cainan were nine hundred and ten years: and he died.

15 And Mahalaleel lived sixty and five years, and begat Jared:

16 And Mahalaleel lived after he begat Jared eight hundred and thirty years, and begat sons and daughters:

17 And all the days of Mahalaleel were eight hundred ninety and five years: and he died.

18 And Jared lived an hundred sixty and two years, and he begat Enoch:

19 And Jared lived after he begat Enoch eight hundred years, and begat sons and daughters:

20 And all the days of Jared were nine hundred sixty and two years: and he died.

21 And Enoch lived sixty and five years, and begat Methuselah:

22 And Enoch walked with God after he begat Methuselah three hundred years, and begat sons and daughters: Mic. 6:8; Mal. 2:6

23 And all the days of Enoch were three hundred sixty and five years:

24 And Enoch walked with God: and he *was* not; for God took him.   2 Kin. 2:11; 1 John 1:7

5:24 How Enoch Walked With God

Enoch's walk with God was not in a trance or a vision, but in all the duties of his daily life. He did not become a hermit, shutting himself entirely from the world; for he had a work to do for God in the world. In the family and in his intercourse with men, as a husband and father, a friend, a citizen, he was the steadfast, unwavering servant of the Lord. *PP 85*

25 And Methuselah lived an hundred eighty and seven years, and begat Lamech:
26 And Methuselah lived after he begat Lamech seven hundred eighty and two years, and begat sons and daughters:
27 And all the days of Methuselah were nine hundred sixty and nine years: and he died.
28 And Lamech lived an hundred eighty and two years, and begat a son:
29 And he called his name Noah, saying, This *same* shall comfort us concerning our work and toil of our hands, because of the ground which the LORD hath cursed.
30 And Lamech lived after he begat Noah five hundred ninety and five years, and begat sons and daughters:
31 And all the days of Lamech were seven hundred seventy and seven years: and he died.
32 And Noah was five hundred years old: and Noah begat Shem, Ham, and Japheth.

The Wickedness of the World

6 And it came to pass, when men began to multiply on the face of the earth, and daughters were born unto them,   Gen. 1:28
2 That the sons of God saw the daughters of men that they *were* fair; and they took them wives of all which they chose.
3 And the LORD said, My spirit shall not always strive with man, for that he also *is* flesh: yet his days shall be an hundred and twenty years.   Neh. 9:30; Ps. 78:39
4 There were giants in the earth in those days; and also after that, when the sons of God came in unto the daughters of men, and they bare *children* to them, the same *became* mighty men which *were* of old, men of renown.   Num. 13:33; Deut. 3:11
5 And GOD saw that the wickedness of man *was* great in the earth, and *that* every imagination of the thoughts of his heart *was* only evil continually.   Gen. 8:21; Prov. 6:18; Matt. 15:19

6:5 Wicked World—Then and Now

The inhabitants of the antediluvian world turned from Jehovah, refusing to do His holy will. They followed their own unholy imagination and perverted ideas. It was because of their wickedness that they were destroyed; and today the world is following the same way. It presents no flattering signs of millennial glory. The transgressors of God's law are filling the earth with wickedness. Their betting, their horse racing, their gambling, their dissipation, their lustful practices, their untamable passions, are fast filling the world with violence. *DA 633*

6 And it repented the LORD that he had made man on the earth, and it grieved him at his heart.   1 Sam. 15:11; 2 Sam. 24:16; Is. 63:10

7 And the LORD said, I will destroy man whom I have created from the face of the earth; both man, and beast, and the creeping thing, and the fowls of the air; for it repenteth me that I have made them.

Noah Finds Grace in God's Eyes

8 But Noah found grace in the eyes of the LORD.   Gen. 19:19; Luke 1:30; Acts 7:46
9 These *are* the generations of Noah: Noah was a just man *and* perfect in his generations, *and* Noah walked with God.   Luke 1:6
10 And Noah ᵀbegat three sons, Shem, Ham, and Japheth.   Gen. 5:32 ◆ brought forth
11 The earth also was corrupt before God, and the earth was filled with violence.
12 And God looked upon the earth, and, behold, it was corrupt; for all flesh had corrupted his way upon the earth.   Job 22:15-17

Building the Ark

13 And God said unto Noah, The end of all flesh is come before me; for the earth is filled with violence through them; and, behold, I will destroy them with the earth.
14 Make thee an ark of gopher wood; rooms shalt thou make in the ark, and shalt pitch it within and without with pitch.   Ex. 2:3
15 And this *is the fashion* which thou shalt make it *of*: The length of the ark *shall be* three hundred cubits, the breadth of it fifty cubits, and the height of it thirty cubits.
16 A window shalt thou make to the ark, and in a ᵀcubit shalt thou finish it above; and the door of the ark shalt thou set in the side thereof; *with* lower, second, and third *stories* shalt thou make it.   linear measurement

6:14–16 Designer and Builder

God gave Noah the exact dimensions of the ark and explicit directions in regard to its construction in every particular. Human wisdom could not have devised a structure of so great strength and durability. God was the designer, and Noah the master builder. *PP 92*

17 And, behold, I, even I, do bring a flood of waters upon the earth, to destroy all flesh, wherein *is* the breath of life, from under heaven; *and* every thing that *is* in the earth shall die.   Gen. 7:4, 21-23; 2 Pet. 2:5
18 But with thee will I establish my covenant; and thou shalt come into the ark, thou, and thy sons, and thy wife, and thy sons' wives with thee.   Gen. 7:7
19 And of every living thing of all flesh, two of every *sort* shalt thou bring into the ark, to keep *them* alive with thee; they shall be male and female.
20 Of fowls after their kind, and of cattle after their kind, of every creeping thing of

the earth after his kind, two of every *sort* shall come unto thee, to keep *them* alive.

21 And take thou unto thee of all food that is eaten, and thou shalt gather *it* to thee; and it shall be for food for thee, and for them.

22 Thus did Noah; according to all that God commanded him, so did he.   Gen. 7:5

Noah, His Family, and the Creatures Enter the Ark

7 And the LORD said unto Noah, Come thou and all thy house into the ark; for thee have I seen righteous before me in this generation.   Gen. 6:9; 7:7, 13

2 Of every clean beast thou shalt take to thee by sevens, the male and his female: and of beasts that *are* not clean by two, the male and his female.   Gen. 8:20

> Health   See Genesis 3:18.

3 Of fowls also of the air by sevens, the male and the female; to keep seed alive upon the face of all the earth.

4 For yet seven days, and I will cause it to rain upon the earth forty days and forty nights; and every living substance that I have made will I destroy from off the face of the earth.   Gen. 6:17; 7:12, 17

> **7:4 Two Possible Outcomes**
>
> Had the antediluvians believed the warning, and repented of their evil deeds, the Lord would have turned aside His wrath, as He afterward did from Nineveh. But by their obstinate resistance to the reproofs of conscience and the warnings of God's prophet, that generation filled up the measure of their iniquity, and became ripe for destruction. *PP 97*

5 And Noah did according unto all that the LORD commanded him.   Gen. 6:22

6 And Noah *was* six hundred years old when the flood of waters was upon the earth.

7 And Noah went in, and his sons, and his wife, and his sons' wives with him, into the ark, because of the waters of the flood.

8 Of clean beasts, and of beasts that *are* not clean, and of fowls, and of every thing that creepeth upon the earth,

9 There went in two and two unto Noah into the ark, the male and the female, as God had commanded Noah.

10 And it came to pass after seven days, that the waters of the flood were upon the earth.

11 In the six hundredth year of Noah's life, in the second month, the seventeenth day of the month, the same day were all the fountains of the great deep broken up, and the windows of heaven were opened.   2 Kin. 7:19

12 And the rain was upon the earth forty days and forty nights.   Gen. 7:4

13 In the selfsame day entered Noah, and Shem, and Ham, and Japheth, the sons of Noah, and Noah's wife, and the three wives of his sons with them, into the ark; Gen. 6:18

14 They, and every beast after his kind, and all the cattle after their kind, and every creeping thing that creepeth upon the earth after his kind, and every fowl after his kind, every bird of every sort.

15 And they went in unto Noah into the ark, two and two of all flesh, wherein *is* the breath of life.

16 And they that went in, went in male and female of all flesh, as God had commanded him: and the LORD shut him in.   Gen. 7:2-3

The Flood

17 And the flood was forty days upon the earth; and the waters increased, and bare up the ark, and it was lift up above the earth.

> ## Scoffing at a Warning
>
> ### Genesis 6:14–17
>
> "By faith Noah, being warned of God of things not seen as yet, moved with fear, prepared an ark to the saving of his house; by the which he condemned the world, and became heir of the righteousness which is by faith" (Hebrews 11:7). While Noah was giving his warning message to the world, his works testified of his sincerity. It was thus that his faith was perfected and made evident. He gave the world an example of believing just what God says. All that he possessed, he invested in the ark. As he began to construct that immense boat on dry ground, multitudes came from every direction to see the strange sight and to hear the earnest, fervent words of the singular preacher. Every blow struck upon the ark was a witness to the people.
>
> Many at first appeared to receive the warning; yet they did not turn to God with true repentance. They were unwilling to renounce their sins. During the time that elapsed before the coming of the Flood, their faith was tested, and they failed to endure the trial. Overcome by the prevailing unbelief, they finally joined their former associates in rejecting the solemn message. Some were deeply convicted, and would have heeded the words of warning; but there were so many to jest and ridicule, that they partook of the same spirit, resisted the invitations of mercy, and were soon among the boldest and most defiant scoffers; for none are so reckless and go to such lengths in sin as do those who have once had light, but have resisted the convicting Spirit of God. *PP 95*

18 And the waters prevailed, and were increased greatly upon the earth; and the ark went upon the face of the waters.
19 And the waters prevailed exceedingly upon the earth; and all the high hills, that *were* under the whole heaven, were covered.
20 Fifteen cubits upward did the waters prevail; and the mountains were covered.
21 And all flesh died that moved upon the earth, both of fowl, and of cattle, and of beast, and of every creeping thing that creepeth upon the earth, and every man:
22 All in whose nostrils *was* the breath of life, of all that *was* in the dry *land*, died.
23 And every living substance was destroyed which was upon the face of the ground, both man, and cattle, and the creeping things, and the fowl of the heaven; and they were destroyed from the earth: and Noah only remained *alive*, and they that *were* with him in the ark.   Heb. 11:7; 1 Pet. 3:20; 2 Pet. 2:5
24 And the waters prevailed upon the earth an hundred and fifty days.

The Waters Subside

8 And God remembered Noah, and every living thing, and all the cattle that *was* with him in the ark: and God made a wind to pass over the earth, and the waters ᵀasswaged;   Gen. 19:29; Ex. 2:24; 14:21 ◆ subsided
2 The fountains also of the deep and the windows of heaven were stopped, and the rain from heaven was restrained;   Gen. 7:11
3 And the waters returned from off the earth continually: and after the end of the hundred and fifty days the waters were abated.

The Ark Rests on Ararat

4 And the ark rested in the seventh month, on the seventeenth day of the month, upon the mountains of Ararat.
5 And the waters decreased continually until the tenth month: in the tenth *month*, on the first *day* of the month, were the tops of the mountains seen.
6 And it came to pass at the end of forty days, that Noah opened the window of the ark which he had made: Gen. 6:16
7 And he sent forth a raven, which went forth to and fro, until the waters were dried up from off the earth.
8 Also he sent forth a dove from him, to see if the waters were ᵀabated from off the face of the ground;   *diminished*
9 But the dove found no rest for the sole of her foot, and she returned unto him into the ark, for the waters *were* on the face of the whole earth: then he put forth his hand, and took her, and pulled her in unto him into the ark.

10 And he stayed yet other seven days; and again he sent forth the dove out of the ark;
11 And the dove came in to him in the evening; and, lo, in her mouth *was* an olive leaf pluckt off: so Noah knew that the waters were abated from off the earth.
12 And he stayed yet other seven days; and sent forth the dove; which returned not again unto him any more.
13 And it came to pass in the six hundredth and first year, in the first *month*, the first *day* of the month, the waters were dried up from off the earth: and Noah removed the covering of the ark, and looked, and, behold, the face of the ground was dry.
14 And in the second month, on the seven and twentieth day of the month, was the earth dried.

Noah Leaves the Ark

15 And God spake unto Noah, saying,
16 Go forth of the ark, thou, and thy wife, and thy sons, and thy sons' wives with thee.
17 Bring forth with thee every living thing that *is* with thee, of all flesh, *both* of fowl, and of cattle, and of every creeping thing that creepeth upon the earth; that they may breed abundantly in the earth, and be fruitful, and multiply upon the earth.   Gen. 1:22
18 And Noah went forth, and his sons, and his wife, and his sons' wives with him:
19 Every beast, every creeping thing, and every fowl, *and* whatsoever creepeth upon the earth, after their kinds, went forth out of the ark.

Noah Builds an Altar and Offers Sacrifices

20 And Noah builded an altar unto the LORD; and took of every clean beast, and of every clean fowl, and offered burnt offerings on the altar.   Gen. 12:7-8
21 And the LORD smelled a sweet savour; and the LORD said in his heart, I will not again curse the ground any more for man's sake; for the imagination of man's heart *is* evil from his youth; neither will I again ᵀsmite any more every thing living, as I have done.   Gen. 3:17; 6:5; Jer. 17:9 ◆ strike
22 While the earth remaineth, seedtime and harvest, and cold and heat, and summer and winter, and day and night shall not cease.

God Blesses Noah

9 And God blessed Noah and his sons, and said unto them, Be fruitful, and multiply, and replenish the earth.   Gen. 1:28
2 And the fear of you and the dread of you shall be upon every beast of the earth, and upon every fowl of the air, upon all that moveth *upon* the earth, and upon all the

fishes of the sea; into your hand are they delivered.   James 3:7

3 Every moving thing that liveth shall be meat for you; even as the green herb have I given you all things.   Deut. 12:15

4 But flesh with the life thereof, *which is the* blood thereof, shall ye not eat.   Acts 15:20

Health   See Leviticus 11:1–31.

9:3, 4 The Entrance of Animals As Food

The diet appointed man in the beginning did not include animal food. Not till after the Flood, when every green thing on the earth had been destroyed, did man receive permission to eat flesh. *MH 311*

5 And surely your blood of your lives will I require; at the hand of every beast will I require it, and at the hand of man; at the hand of every man's brother will I require the life of man.   Ex. 21:28-29

6 Whoso sheddeth man's blood, by man shall his blood be shed: for in the image of God made he man.   Lev. 24:17; Matt. 26:52

7 And you, be ye fruitful, and multiply; bring forth abundantly in the earth, and multiply therein.   Gen. 9:1

8 And God spake unto Noah, and to his sons with him, saying,

9 And I, behold, I establish my covenant with you, and with your seed after you;

10 And with every living creature that *is* with you, of the fowl, of the cattle, and of every beast of the earth with you; from all that go out of the ark, to every beast of the earth.

11 And I will establish my covenant with you; neither shall all flesh be cut off any more by the waters of a flood; neither shall there any more be a flood to destroy the earth.   Gen. 8:21-22; Is. 54:9

12 And God said, This *is* the token of the covenant which I make between me and you and every living creature that *is* with you, for perpetual generations: Gen. 17:11

13 I do set my bow in the cloud, and it shall be for a token of a covenant between me and the earth.   Ezek. 1:28

14 And it shall come to pass, when I bring a cloud over the earth, that the bow shall be seen in the cloud:

15 And I will remember my covenant, which *is* between me and you and every living creature of all flesh; and the waters shall no more become a flood to destroy all flesh.

16 And the bow shall be in the cloud; and I will look upon it, that I may remember the everlasting covenant between God and every living creature of all flesh that *is* upon the earth.   Gen. 17:13, 19; 2 Sam. 23:5

9:16 Promise of the Rainbow

The Lord declares that when He looks upon the bow, He will remember His covenant. . . . It was God's purpose that as the children of after generations should ask the meaning of the glorious arch which spans the heavens, their parents should repeat the story of the Flood, and tell them that the Most High had bended the bow and placed it in the clouds as an assurance that the waters should never again overflow the earth. *PP 106*

17 And God said unto Noah, This *is* the token of the covenant, which I have established between me and all flesh that *is* upon the earth.

18 And the sons of Noah, that went forth of the ark, were Shem, and Ham, and Japheth: and Ham *is* the father of Canaan.   Gen. 10:1, 6

19 These *are* the three sons of Noah: and of them was the whole earth overspread.

20 And Noah began *to be* an ᵀhusbandman, and he planted a vineyard: farmer

21 And he drank of the wine, and was drunken; and he was uncovered within his tent.   Prov. 20:1

22 And Ham, the father of Canaan, saw the nakedness of his father, and told his two brethren without.

23 And Shem and Japheth took a garment, and laid *it* upon both their shoulders, and went backward, and covered the nakedness of their father; and their faces *were* backward, and they saw not their father's nakedness.

24 And Noah awoke from his wine, and knew what his younger son had done unto him.

25 And he said, Cursed *be* Canaan; a servant of servants shall he be unto his brethren.

26 And he said, Blessed *be* the LORD God of Shem; and Canaan shall be his servant.

27 God shall enlarge Japheth, and he shall dwell in the tents of Shem; and Canaan shall be his servant.

28 And Noah lived after the flood three hundred and fifty years.

29 And all the days of Noah were nine hundred and fifty years: and he died.

The Generations of Noah

10 Now these *are* the generations of the sons of Noah, Shem, Ham, and Japheth: and unto them were sons born after the flood.   Gen. 2:4

2 The sons of Japheth; Gomer, and Magog, and Madai, and Javan, and Tubal, and Meshech, and Tiras.   1 Chr. 1:5-7; Ezek. 38:2, 6

3 And the sons of Gomer; Ashkenaz, and Riphath, and Togarmah.

4 And the sons of Javan; Elishah, and Tarshish, Kittim, and Dodanim.   Num. 24:24

5 By these were the isles of the Gentiles divided in their lands; every one after his tongue, after their families, in their nations.

The Sons of Ham
6 And the sons of Ham; Cush, and Mizraim, and Phut, and Canaan.
7 And the sons of Cush; Seba, and Havilah, and Sabtah, and Raamah, and Sabtecha: and the sons of Raamah; Sheba, and Dedan.
8 And Cush ᵀbegat Nimrod: he began to be a mighty one in the earth.   *brought forth*
9 He was a mighty hunter before the LORD: wherefore it is said, Even as Nimrod the mighty hunter before the LORD.
10 And the beginning of his kingdom was Babel, and Erech, and Accad, and Calneh, in the land of Shinar.   Gen. 11:2, 9; 14:1
11 Out of that land went forth Asshur, and builded Nineveh, and the city Rehoboth, and Calah,   Mic. 5:6
12 And Resen between Nineveh and Calah: the same *is* a great city.
13 And Mizraim begat Ludim, and Anamim, and Lehabim, and Naphtuhim,   1 Chr. 1:11-12
14 And Pathrusim, and Casluhim, (out of whom came Philistim,) and Caphtorim.
15 And Canaan begat Sidon his firstborn, and Heth,   Gen. 15:18-21
16 And the Jebusite, and the Amorite, and the Girgasite,
17 And the Hivite, and the Arkite, and the Sinite,
18 And the Arvadite, and the Zemarite, and the Hamathite: and afterward were the families of the Canaanites spread abroad.
19 And the border of the Canaanites was from Sidon, as thou comest to Gerar, unto Gaza; as thou goest, unto Sodom, and Gomorrah, and Admah, and Zeboim, even unto Lasha.   Gen. 14:2
20 These *are* the sons of Ham, after their families, after their tongues, in their countries, *and* in their nations.

The Sons of Shem
21 Unto Shem also, the father of all the children of Eber, the brother of Japheth the elder, even to him were *children* born.
22 The children of Shem; Elam, and Asshur, and Arphaxad, and Lud, and Aram.   Is. 66:19
23 And the children of Aram; Uz, and Hul, and Gether, and Mash.   Job 1:1
24 And Arphaxad begat Salah; and Salah begat Eber.
25 And unto Eber were born two sons: the name of one *was* Peleg; for in his days was the earth divided; and his brother's name *was* Joktan.   1 Chr. 1:19
26 And Joktan begat Almodad, and Sheleph, and Hazar-maveth, and Jerah,

27 And Hadoram, and Uzal, and Diklah,
28 And Obal, and Abimael, and Sheba,
29 And Ophir, and Havilah, and Jobab: all these *were* the sons of Joktan.   1 Kin. 9:28
30 And their dwelling was from Mesha, as thou goest unto Sephar a mount of the east.
31 These *are* the sons of Shem, after their families, after their tongues, in their lands, after their nations.   Gen. 10:5
32 These *are* the families of the sons of Noah, after their generations, in their nations: and by these were the nations divided in the earth after the flood.   Gen. 9:19; 10:1

One Language in the World
11 And the whole earth was of one language, and of one speech.
2 And it came to pass, as they journeyed from the east, that they found a plain in the land of Shinar; and they dwelt there.   Dan. 1:2

> **11:2 Post-Flood Apostasy**
>
> For a time the descendants of Noah continued to dwell among the mountains where the ark had rested. As their numbers increased, apostasy soon led to division. Those who desired to forget their Creator and to cast off the restraint of His law felt a constant annoyance from the teaching and example of their God-fearing associates, and after a time they decided to separate from the worshipers of God. *PP 118*

3 And they said one to another, Go to, let us make brick, and burn them throughly. And they had brick for stone, and slime had they for morter.   Gen. 14:10; Ex. 1:14; 2:3
4 And they said, Go to, let us build us a city and a tower, whose top *may reach* unto heaven; and let us make us a name, lest we be scattered abroad upon the face of the whole earth.   Deut. 1:28; 9:1; 2 Sam. 8:13

> **11:4 Scoffers and Rebels**
>
> The dwellers on the plain of Shinar disbelieved God's covenant that He would not again bring a flood upon the earth. Many of them denied the existence of God and attributed the Flood to the operation of natural causes. Others believed in a Supreme Being, and that it was He who had destroyed the antediluvian world; and their hearts, like that of Cain, rose up in rebellion against Him. One object before them in the erection of the tower was to secure their own safety in case of another deluge. *PP 119*

The Confusion of Languages
5 And the LORD came down to see the city and the tower, which the children of men builded.   Gen. 18:21; Ex. 19:11

6 And the LORD said, Behold, the people *is* one, and they have all one language; and this they begin to do: and now nothing will be restrained from them, which they have imagined to do.   Gen. 11:1

7 Go to, let us go down, and there confound their language, that they may not understand one another's speech.   Deut. 28:49

8 So the LORD scattered them abroad from thence upon the face of all the earth: and they left off to build the city.   Luke 1:51

9 Therefore is the name of it called Babel; because the LORD did there confound the language of all the earth: and from thence did the LORD scatter them abroad upon the face of all the earth.   Gen. 10:5, 10, 20

The Generations of Shem, the Ancestor of Abram

10 These *are* the generations of Shem: Shem *was* an hundred years old, and begat Arphaxad two years after the flood:

11 And Shem lived after he ᵀbegat Arphaxad five hundred years, and begat sons and daughters.   *brought forth*

12 And Arphaxad lived five and thirty years, and begat Salah:

13 And Arphaxad lived after he begat Salah four hundred and three years, and begat sons and daughters.

14 And Salah lived thirty years, and begat Eber:

15 And Salah lived after he begat Eber four hundred and three years, and begat sons and daughters.

16 And Eber lived four and thirty years, and begat Peleg:

17 And Eber lived after he begat Peleg four hundred and thirty years, and begat sons and daughters.

18 And Peleg lived thirty years, and begat Reu:

19 And Peleg lived after he begat Reu two hundred and nine years, and begat sons and daughters.

20 And Reu lived two and thirty years, and begat Serug: Luke 3:35

21 And Reu lived after he begat Serug two hundred and seven years, and begat sons and daughters.

22 And Serug lived thirty years, and begat Nahor:

23 And Serug lived after he begat Nahor two hundred years, and begat sons and daughters.

24 And Nahor lived nine and twenty years, and begat Terah: Luke 3:34

25 And Nahor lived after he begat Terah an hundred and nineteen years, and begat sons and daughters.

26 And Terah lived seventy years, and begat Abram, Nahor, and Haran.   Josh. 24:2

27 Now these *are* the generations of Terah: Terah begat Abram, Nahor, and Haran; and Haran begat Lot.   Gen. 11:31

28 And Haran died before his father Terah in the land of his nativity, in Ur of the Chaldees.   Gen. 15:7

29 And Abram and Nahor took them wives: the name of Abram's wife *was* Sarai; and the name of Nahor's wife, Milcah, the daughter of Haran, the father of Milcah, and the father of Iscah.   Gen. 17:15; 20:12; 22:20

30 But Sarai was barren; she *had* no child.

31 And Terah took Abram his son, and Lot the son of Haran his son's son, and Sarai his daughter in law, his son Abram's wife; and they went forth with them from Ur of the Chaldees, to go into the land of Canaan; and they came unto Haran, and dwelt there.

32 And the days of Terah were two hundred and five years: and Terah died in Haran.

God Calls Abram; Blesses Him with a Promise of Christ

12 Now the LORD had said unto Abram, Get thee out of thy country, and from thy kindred, and from thy father's house, unto a land that I will shew thee: Heb. 11:8

The High Stakes at Babel

Genesis 11:4–6

The men of Babel had determined to establish a government that should be independent of God. There were some among them, however, who feared the Lord, but who had been deceived by the pretensions of the ungodly and drawn into their schemes. For the sake of these faithful ones the Lord delayed His judgments and gave the people time to reveal their true character. As this was developed, the sons of God labored to turn them from their purpose; but the people were fully united in their Heaven-daring undertaking. Had they gone on unchecked, they would have demoralized the world in its infancy. Their confederacy was founded in rebellion; a kingdom established for self-exaltation, but in which God was to have no rule or honor. Had this confederacy been permitted, a mighty power would have borne sway to banish righteousness—and with it peace, happiness, and security—from the earth. For the divine statutes, which are "holy and just and good" (Romans 7:12), men were endeavoring to substitute laws to suit the purpose of their own selfish and cruel hearts. *PP 123*

2 And I will make of thee a great nation, and I will bless thee, and make thy name great; and thou shalt be a blessing: Deut. 26:5

3 And I will bless them that bless thee, and curse him that curseth thee: and in thee shall all families of the earth be blessed.

12:1–3 Abraham's High Honor

It was for the purpose of bringing the best gifts of Heaven to all the peoples of earth that God called Abraham out from his idolatrous kindred and bade him dwell in the land of Canaan. . . . It was a high honor to which Abraham was called—that of being the father of the people who for centuries were to be the guardians and preservers of the truth of God to the world, the people through whom all the nations of the earth should be blessed in the advent of the promised Messiah. *PK 15*

Abram Departs with Lot from Haran

4 So Abram departed, as the LORD had spoken unto him; and Lot went with him: and Abram *was* seventy and five years old when he departed out of Haran.   Gen. 11:27

5 And Abram took Sarai his wife, and Lot his brother's son, and all their substance that they had gathered, and the souls that they had gotten in Haran; and they went forth to go into the land of Canaan; and into the land of Canaan they came.   Gen. 14:14

Abram Journeys through Canaan

6 And Abram passed through the land unto the place of Sichem, unto the plain of Moreh. And the Canaanite *was* then in the land.   Gen. 35:4; Deut. 11:30; Heb. 11:9

7 And the LORD appeared unto Abram, and said, Unto thy seed will I give this land: and there builded he an altar unto the LORD, who appeared unto him.   Gen. 13:15; 17:1, 8

8 And he removed from thence unto a mountain on the east of Beth-el, and pitched his tent, *having* Beth-el on the west, and Hai on the east: and there he builded an altar unto the LORD, and called upon the name of the LORD.   Gen. 4:26

9 And Abram journeyed, going on still toward the south.   Gen. 13:3

Abram Is Driven by a Famine into Egypt

10 And there was a famine in the land: and Abram went down into Egypt to sojourn there; for the famine *was* grievous in the land.   Gen. 43:1

11 And it came to pass, when he was come near to enter into Egypt, that he said unto Sarai his wife, Behold now, I know that thou *art* a fair woman to look upon: Gen. 26:7

12 Therefore it shall come to pass, when the Egyptians shall see thee, that they shall say, This *is* his wife: and they shall kill me, but they will save thee alive.   Gen. 20:11

13 Say, I pray thee, thou *art* my sister: that it may be well with me for thy sake; and my soul shall live because of thee.   Gen. 20:2

Sarai Is Taken by Pharaoh

14 And it came to pass, that, when Abram was come into Egypt, the Egyptians beheld the woman that she *was* very fair.

15 The princes also of Pharaoh saw her, and commended her before Pharaoh: and the woman was taken into Pharaoh's house.

16 And he entreated Abram well for her sake: and he had sheep, and oxen, and he asses, and menservants, and maidservants, and she asses, and camels.   Gen. 13:2

17 And the LORD plagued Pharaoh and his house with great plagues because of Sarai Abram's wife.   Gen. 20:18; 1 Chr. 16:21

18 And Pharaoh called Abram, and said,

Abraham's Lack of Faith

Genesis 12:11–20

During his stay in Egypt, Abraham gave evidence that he was not free from human weakness and imperfection. In concealing the fact that Sarah was his wife, he betrayed a distrust of the divine care, a lack of that lofty faith and courage so often and nobly exemplified in his life. Sarah was fair to look upon, and he doubted not that the dusky Egyptians would covet the beautiful stranger, and that in order to secure her, they would not scruple to slay her husband. He reasoned that he was not guilty of falsehood in representing Sarah as his sister, for she was the daughter of his father, though not of his mother. But this concealment of the real relation between them was deception. No deviation from strict integrity can meet God's approval. Through Abraham's lack of faith, Sarah was placed in great peril. The king of Egypt, being informed of her beauty, caused her to be taken to his palace, intending to make her his wife. But the Lord, in His great mercy, protected Sarah by sending judgments upon the royal household. By this means the monarch learned the truth in the matter, and, indignant at the deception practiced upon him, he reproved Abraham and restored to him his wife, saying, "What is this that thou hast done unto me? . . . Why saidst thou, She is my sister? So I might have taken her to me to wife. Now therefore behold thy wife, take her, and go thy way." *PP 130*

What *is* this *that* thou hast done unto me? why didst thou not tell me that she *was* thy wife?   Gen. 20:9-10

19 Why saidst thou, She *is* my sister? so I might have taken her to me to wife: now therefore behold thy wife, take *her*, and go thy way.

20 And Pharaoh commanded *his* men concerning him: and they sent him away, and his wife, and all that he had.

Abram and Lot Return out of Egypt and Agree to Separate

13 And Abram went up out of Egypt, he, and his wife, and all that he had, and Lot with him, into the south.

2 And Abram *was* very rich in cattle, in silver, and in gold.   Gen. 24:35

3 And he went on his journeys from the south even to Beth-el, unto the place where his tent had been at the beginning, between Beth-el and Hai;

4 Unto the place of the altar, which he had made there at the first: and there Abram called on the name of the LORD.   Gen. 12:7-8

5 And Lot also, which went with Abram, had flocks, and herds, and tents.

6 And the land was not able to bear them, that they might dwell together: for their substance was great, so that they could not dwell together.   Gen. 36:6-7

7 And there was a strife between the herdmen of Abram's cattle and the herdmen of Lot's cattle: and the Canaanite and the Perizzite dwelled then in the land. Gen. 12:6; 26:20

8 And Abram said unto Lot, Let there be no strife, I pray thee, between me and thee, and between my herdmen and thy herdmen; for we *be* brethren.   Ps. 133:1

9 *Is* not the whole land before thee? separate thyself, I pray thee, from me: if *thou wilt take* the left hand, then I will go to the right; or if *thou depart* to the right hand, then I will go to the left.   Gen. 20:15

13:8, 9 We Are All One Family

Here the noble, unselfish spirit of Abraham was displayed. How many under similar circumstances would, at all hazards, cling to their individual rights and preferences! How many households have thus been rent asunder! How many churches have been divided, making the cause of truth a byword and a reproach among the wicked! "Let there be no strife between me and thee," said Abraham, "for we be brethren;" not only by natural relationship, but as worshipers of the true God. *PP 132*

Lot Goes to Sodom

10 And Lot lifted up his eyes, and beheld all the plain of Jordan, that it *was* well watered every where, before the LORD destroyed Sodom and Gomorrah, *even as* the garden of the LORD, like the land of Egypt, as thou comest unto Zoar.   Gen. 14:2, 8; Deut. 34:3

11 Then Lot chose him all the plain of Jordan; and Lot journeyed east: and they separated themselves the one from the other.

13:10, 11 A Selfish Choice

Dazzled with visions of worldly gain, Lot overlooked the moral and spiritual evils that would be encountered there. The inhabitants of the plain were "sinners before the Lord exceedingly;" but of this he was ignorant, or, knowing, gave it but little weight. He "chose him all the plain of Jordan," and "pitched his tent toward Sodom." How little did he foresee the terrible results of that selfish choice! *PP 133*

---

12 Abram dwelled in the land of Canaan, and Lot dwelled in the cities of the plain, and pitched *his* tent toward Sodom.

13 But the men of Sodom *were* wicked and sinners before the LORD exceedingly.

God Renews the Promise to Abram

14 And the LORD said unto Abram, after that Lot was separated from him, Lift up now thine eyes, and look from the place where thou art northward, and southward, and eastward, and westward: Is. 49:18

15 For all the land which thou seest, to thee will I give it, and to thy seed for ever.

16 And I will make thy seed as the dust of the earth: so that if a man can number the dust of the earth, *then* shall thy seed also be numbered.   Gen. 28:14

17 Arise, walk through the land in the length of it and in the breadth of it; for I will give it unto thee.

18 Then Abram removed *his* tent, and came and dwelt in the plain of Mamre, which *is* in Hebron, and built there an altar unto the LORD.   Gen. 8:20; 14:13; 35:27

The Battle of Four Kings against Five

14 And it came to pass in the days of Amraphel king of Shinar, Arioch king of Ellasar, Chedorlaomer king of Elam, and Tidal king of nations;   Gen. 10:10, 22; 11:2

2 *That these* made war with Bera king of Sodom, and with Birsha king of Gomorrah, Shinab king of Admah, and Shemeber king of Zeboiim, and the king of Bela, which is Zoar.   Gen. 10:19; 13:10; Deut. 29:23

3 All these were joined together in the vale of Siddim, which is the salt sea.   Josh. 3:16

4 Twelve years they served Chedorlaomer, and in the thirteenth year they rebelled.
5 And in the fourteenth year came Chedorlaomer, and the kings that *were* with him, and smote the Rephaims in Ashteroth Karnaim, and the Zuzims in Ham, and the Emims in Shaveh Kiriathaim,   Gen. 15:20
6 And the Horites in their mount Seir, unto El-paran, which *is* by the wilderness.
7 And they returned, and came to En-mishpat, which *is* Kadesh, and smote all the country of the Amalekites, and also the Amorites, that dwelt in Hazezon-tamar.
8 And there went out the king of Sodom, and the king of Gomorrah, and the king of Admah, and the king of Zeboiim, and the king of Bela (the same *is* Zoar;) and they joined battle with them in the ᵀvale of Siddim;   Gen. 13:10 ◆ *valley*
9 With Chedorlaomer the king of Elam, and with Tidal king of nations, and Amraphel king of Shinar, and Arioch king of Ellasar; four kings with five.
10 And the vale of Siddim *was full of* slime-pits; and the kings of Sodom and Gomorrah fled, and fell there; and they that remained fled to the mountain.   Gen. 11:3; 19:17, 30
11 And they took all the goods of Sodom and Gomorrah, and all their ᵀvictuals, and went their way.   Gen. 14:16 ◆ *food*
12 And they took Lot, Abram's brother's son, who dwelt in Sodom, and his goods, and departed.   Gen. 11:27
13 And there came one that had escaped, and told Abram the Hebrew; for he dwelt in the plain of Mamre the Amorite, brother of Eshcol, and brother of Aner: and these *were* confederate with Abram. Gen. 13:18; 14:24; 40:15
14 And when Abram heard that his brother was taken captive, he armed his trained *servants*, born in his own house, three hundred and eighteen, and pursued *them* unto Dan.
15 And he divided himself against them, he and his servants, by night, and smote them, and pursued them unto Hobah, which *is* on the left hand of Damascus.
16 And he brought back all the goods, and also brought again his brother Lot, and his goods, and the women also, and the people.
17 And the king of Sodom went out to meet him after his return from the slaughter of Chedorlaomer, and of the kings that *were* with him, at the valley of Shaveh, which *is* the king's dale.   2 Sam. 18:18
18 And Melchizedek king of Salem brought forth bread and wine: and he *was* the priest of the most high God.   Ps. 110:4; Heb. 5:6, 10
19 And he blessed him, and said, Blessed *be* Abram of the most high God, possessor of heaven and earth: Gen. 14:22
20 And blessed be the most high God, which

hath delivered thine enemies into thy hand. And he gave him tithes of all.   Gen. 28:22
21 And the king of Sodom said unto Abram, Give me the persons, and take the goods to thyself.
22 And Abram said to the king of Sodom, I have lift up mine hand unto the LORD, the most high God, the possessor of heaven and earth,   Ex. 6:8
23 That I will not *take* from a thread even to a shoelatchet, and that I will not take any thing that *is* thine, lest thou shouldest say, I have made Abram rich: 2 Kin. 5:16
24 Save only that which the young men have eaten, and the portion of the men which went with me, Aner, Eshcol, and Mamre; let them take their portion.

God Encourages Abram

15 After these things the word of the LORD came unto Abram in a vision, saying, Fear not, Abram: I *am* thy shield, *and* thy exceeding great reward.   Ps. 3:3; Is. 41:10

Abram Complains for Lack of an Heir

2 And Abram said, Lord GOD, what wilt thou give me, seeing I go childless, and the steward of my house *is* this Eliezer of Damascus?   Acts 7:5
3 And Abram said, Behold, to me thou hast given no seed: and, lo, one born in my house is mine heir.   Gen. 14:14
4 And, behold, the word of the LORD *came* unto him, saying, This shall not be thine heir; but he that shall come forth out of thine own bowels shall be thine heir.
5 And he brought him forth abroad, and said, Look now toward heaven, and tell the stars, if thou be able to number them: and he said unto him, So shall thy seed be.
6 And he believed in the LORD; and he counted it to him for righteousness. Rom. 4:9

Canaan Promised Again

7 And he said unto him, I *am* the LORD that brought thee out of Ur of the Chaldees, to give thee this land to inherit it.   Gen. 12:1
8 And he said, Lord GOD, whereby shall I know that I shall inherit it?   Luke 1:18
9 And he said unto him, Take me an heifer of three years old, and a she goat of three years old, and a ram of three years old, and a turtledove, and a young pigeon.
10 And he took unto him all these, and divided them in the midst, and laid each piece one against another: but the birds divided he not.   Lev. 1:17; Jer. 34:18-19
11 And when the fowls came down upon the carcases, Abram drove them away.
12 And when the sun was going down,

a deep sleep fell upon Abram; and, lo, an horror of great darkness fell upon him.
13 And he said unto Abram, Know of a surety that thy seed shall be a stranger in a land *that is* not theirs, and shall serve them; and they shall afflict them four hundred years; Gal. 3:17
14 And also that nation, whom they shall serve, will I judge: and afterward shall they come out with great substance.
15 And thou shalt go to thy fathers in peace; thou shalt be buried in a good old age.
16 But in the fourth generation they shall come ᵀhither again: for the iniquity of the Amorites *is* not yet full. 1 Kin. 21:26 ◆ *here*
17 And it came to pass, that, when the sun went down, and it was dark, behold a smoking furnace, and a burning lamp that passed between those pieces. Jer. 34:18-19
18 In the same day the LORD made a covenant with Abram, saying, Unto thy seed have I given this land, from the river of Egypt unto the great river, the river Euphrates: Gen. 12:7
19 The Kenites, and the Kenizzites, and the Kadmonites,
20 And the Hittites, and the Perizzites, and the Rephaims,
21 And the Amorites, and the Canaanites, and the Girgashites, and the Jebusites.

Sarai, Being Barren, Gives Hagar to Abram

16 Now Sarai Abram's wife bare him no children: and she had an handmaid, an Egyptian, whose name *was* Hagar. Gal. 4:24
2 And Sarai said unto Abram, Behold now, the LORD hath restrained me from bearing: I pray thee, go in unto my maid; it may be that I may obtain children by her. And Abram hearkened to the voice of Sarai.

16:1, 2 Abraham Fails Another Test

Abraham had accepted without question the promise of a son, but he did not wait for God to fulfill His word in His own time and way. A delay was permitted, to test his faith in the power of God; but he failed to endure the trial. *PP 145*

---

3 And Sarai Abram's wife took Hagar her maid the Egyptian, after Abram had dwelt ten years in the land of Canaan, and gave her to her husband Abram to be his wife.

Hagar Runs Away

4 And he went in unto Hagar, and she conceived: and when she saw that she had conceived, her mistress was despised in her eyes.

5 And Sarai said unto Abram, My wrong *be* upon thee: I have given my maid into thy bosom; and when she saw that she had conceived, I was despised in her eyes: the LORD judge between me and thee. Ex. 5:21
6 But Abram said unto Sarai, Behold, thy maid *is* in thy hand; do to her as it pleaseth thee. And when Sarai dealt hardly with her, she fled from her face.

An Angel Sends Hagar Back, Telling Her She Will Bear a Child

7 And the angel of the LORD found her by a fountain of water in the wilderness, by the fountain in the way to Shur. Gen. 25:18
8 And he said, Hagar, Sarai's maid, whence camest thou? and whither wilt thou go? And she said, I flee from the face of my mistress Sarai. Gen. 3:9
9 And the angel of the LORD said unto her, Return to thy mistress, and submit thyself under her hands.
10 And the angel of the LORD said unto her, I will multiply thy seed exceedingly, that it shall not be numbered for multitude.
11 And the angel of the LORD said unto her, Behold, thou *art* with child, and shalt bear a son, and shalt call his name Ishmael; because the LORD hath heard thy affliction.
12 And he will be a wild man; his hand *will be* against every man, and every man's hand against him; and he shall dwell in the presence of all his brethren. Gen. 21:20; Job 39:5-8
13 And she called the name of the LORD that spake unto her, Thou God seest me: for she said, Have I also here looked after him that seeth me? Gen. 32:30; Ps. 139:1-12
14 Wherefore the well was called Beer-lahai-roi; behold, *it is* between Kadesh and Bered.

Hagar Bears a Son Who Is Named Ishmael

15 And Hagar bare Abram a son: and Abram called his son's name, which Hagar bare, Ishmael. Gen. 25:12
16 And Abram *was* fourscore and six years old, when Hagar bare Ishmael to Abram.

God Renews the Covenant with Abram

17 And when Abram was ninety years old and nine, the LORD appeared to Abram, and said unto him, I *am* the Almighty God; walk before me, and be thou perfect. Gen. 6:9; 28:3; Deut. 18:13
2 And I will make my covenant between me and thee, and will multiply thee exceedingly.
3 And Abram fell on his face: and God talked with him, saying, Gen. 17:17
4 As for me, behold, my covenant *is* with thee, and thou shalt be a father of many nations. Gen. 35:11

5 Neither shall thy name any more be called Abram, but thy name shall be Abraham; for a father of many nations have I made thee.
6 And I will make thee exceeding fruitful, and I will make nations of thee, and kings shall come out of thee.   Gen. 17:16; 35:11
7 And I will establish my covenant between me and thee and thy seed after thee in their generations for an everlasting covenant, to be a God unto thee, and to thy seed after thee.   Gen. 26:24; 28:13; Heb. 11:16
8 And I will give unto thee, and to thy seed after thee, the land wherein thou art a stranger, all the land of Canaan, for an everlasting possession; and I will be their God.
9 And God said unto Abraham, Thou shalt keep my covenant therefore, thou, and thy seed after thee in their generations.
10 This is my covenant, which ye shall keep, between me and you and thy seed after thee; Every man child among you shall be circumcised.   Acts 7:8
11 And ye shall circumcise the flesh of your foreskin; and it shall be a token of the covenant ᵀbetwixt me and you.   between
12 And he that is eight days old shall be circumcised among you, every man child in your generations, he that is born in the house, or bought with money of any stranger, which is not of thy seed.
13 He that is born in thy house, and he that is bought with thy money, must needs be circumcised: and my covenant shall be in your flesh for an everlasting covenant.
14 And the uncircumcised man child whose flesh of his foreskin is not circumcised, that soul shall be cut off from his people; he hath broken my covenant.   Ex. 4:24-26

Sarai's Name Is Changed, and She Is Blessed

15 And God said unto Abraham, As for Sarai thy wife, thou shalt not call her name Sarai, but Sarah shall her name be.
16 And I will bless her, and give thee a son also of her: yea, I will bless her, and she shall be a mother of nations; kings of people shall be of her.   Gen. 35:11
17 Then Abraham fell upon his face, and laughed, and said in his heart, Shall a child be born unto him that is an hundred years old? and shall Sarah, that is ninety years old, bear?   Gen. 17:3; 18:12; 21:6
18 And Abraham said unto God, O that Ishmael might live before thee!
19 And God said, Sarah thy wife shall bear thee a son indeed; and thou shalt call his name Isaac: and I will establish my covenant with him for an everlasting covenant, and with his seed after him.   Gen. 21:2-3
20 And as for Ishmael, I have heard thee:

Behold, I have blessed him, and will make him fruitful, and will multiply him exceedingly; twelve princes shall he ᵀbeget, and I will make him a great nation.   bring forth

17:17–19 A Promise Misunderstood

When Abraham was nearly one hundred years old, the promise of a son was repeated to him, with the assurance that the future heir should be the child of Sarah. But Abraham did not yet understand the promise. His mind at once turned to Ishmael. . . . Again the promise was given, in words that could not be mistaken: "Sarah thy wife shall bear thee a son indeed; and thou shalt call his name Isaac: and I will establish My covenant with him." PP 146

21 But my covenant will I establish with Isaac, which Sarah shall bear unto thee at this set time in the next year.   Gen. 18:10
22 And he left off talking with him, and God went up from Abraham.   Gen. 18:33

Abraham and Ishmael Are Circumcised

23 And Abraham took Ishmael his son, and all that were born in his house, and all that were bought with his money, every male among the men of Abraham's house; and circumcised the flesh of their foreskin in the selfsame day, as God had said unto him.
24 And Abraham was ninety years old and nine, when he was circumcised in the flesh of his foreskin.   Rom. 4:11
25 And Ishmael his son was thirteen years old, when he was circumcised in the flesh of his foreskin.
26 In the selfsame day was Abraham circumcised, and Ishmael his son.
27 And all the men of his house, born in the house, and bought with money of the stranger, were circumcised with him.

The Lord Appears to Abraham

18 And the LORD appeared unto him in the plains of Mamre: and he sat in the tent door in the heat of the day;   Gen. 13:18
2 And he lift up his eyes and looked, and, lo, three men stood by him: and when he saw them, he ran to meet them from the tent door, and bowed himself toward the ground,
3 And said, My Lord, if now I have found favour in thy sight, pass not away, I pray thee, from thy servant:
4 Let a little water, I pray you, be fetched, and wash your feet, and rest yourselves under the tree: Gen. 19:2; 24:32; 43:24
5 And I will fetch a morsel of bread, and comfort ye your hearts; after that ye shall pass on: for therefore are ye come to your servant. And they said, So do, as thou hast said.   Judg. 13:15

6 And Abraham hastened into the tent unto Sarah, and said, Make ready quickly three measures of fine meal, knead *it*, and make cakes upon the hearth.

7 And Abraham ran unto the herd, and fetcht a calf tender and good, and gave *it* unto a young man; and he hasted to dress it.

8 And he took butter, and milk, and the calf which he had dressed, and set *it* before them; and he stood by them under the tree, and they did eat.   Gen. 19:3

Sarah Is Reproved for Laughing at the Strange Promise

9 And they said unto him, Where *is* Sarah thy wife? And he said, Behold, in the tent.

10 And he said, I will certainly return unto thee according to the time of life; and, lo, Sarah thy wife shall have a son. And Sarah heard *it* in the tent door, which *was* behind him.   Gen. 17:19, 21; 21:2

11 Now Abraham and Sarah *were* old *and* well stricken in age; *and* it ceased to be with Sarah after the manner of women. Gen. 17:17

12 Therefore Sarah laughed within herself, saying, After I am ᵀwaxed old shall I have pleasure, my lord being old also?   become

13 And the Lord said unto Abraham, Wherefore did Sarah laugh, saying, Shall I of a surety bear a child, which am old?

14 Is any thing too hard for the Lord? At the time appointed I will return unto thee, according to the time of life, and Sarah shall have a son.   Jer. 32:17; Zech. 8:6; Matt. 19:26

15 Then Sarah denied, saying, I laughed not; for she was afraid. And he said, Nay; but thou didst laugh.

16 And the men rose up from thence, and looked toward Sodom: and Abraham went with them to bring them on the way.

17 And the Lord said, Shall I hide from Abraham that thing which I do;   Amos 3:7

18 Seeing that Abraham shall surely become a great and mighty nation, and all the nations of the earth shall be blessed in him? Gal. 3:8

19 For I know him, that he will command his children and his household after him, and they shall keep the way of the Lord, to do justice and judgment; that the Lord may bring upon Abraham that which he hath spoken of him.

18:19 God's Law in Our Homes

The father is the lawmaker of the household; and, like Abraham, he should make the law of God the rule of his home. God said of Abraham, "I know him, that he will command his children and his household" (Genesis 18:19). . . . God has given rules for our guidance. Children should not be left to wander away from the safe path marked out in God's word, into ways leading to danger, which are open on every side. *MH 390, 391*

18:19 Parental Authority

Like Abraham, parents should command their households after them. Let obedience to parental authority be taught and enforced as the first step in obedience to the authority of God. *PP 142, 143*

20 And the Lord said, Because the cry of Sodom and Gomorrah is great, and because their sin is very grievous;   Gen. 19:13

21 I will go down now, and see whether they have done altogether according to the cry of it, which is come unto me; and if not, I will know.   Gen. 11:5; Ex. 3:8; 33:5

22 And the men turned their faces from thence, and went toward Sodom: but Abraham stood yet before the Lord.   Jer. 18:20

Abraham Intercedes for the People of Sodom

23 And Abraham drew near, and said, Wilt thou also destroy the righteous with the wicked?   Gen. 20:4; Num. 16:22; 2 Sam. 24:17

24 Peradventure there be fifty righteous within the city: wilt thou also destroy and not spare the place for the fifty righteous that *are* therein?   Jer. 5:1

25 That be far from thee to do after this manner, to slay the righteous with the wicked: and that the righteous should be as the wicked, that be far from thee: Shall not the Judge of all the earth do right?

26 And the Lord said, If I find in Sodom fifty righteous within the city, then I will spare all the place for their sakes.   Is. 65:8

27 And Abraham answered and said, Behold now, I have taken upon me to speak unto the Lord, which *am but* dust and ashes: Gen. 3:19

28 Peradventure there shall lack five of the fifty righteous: wilt thou destroy all the city for *lack of* five? And he said, If I find there forty and five, I will not destroy *it.*

29 And he spake unto him yet again, and said, Peradventure there shall be forty found there. And he said, I will not do *it* for forty's sake.

30 And he said *unto him*, Oh let not the Lord be angry, and I will speak: Peradventure there shall thirty be found there. And he said, I will not do *it*, if I find thirty there.

31 And he said, Behold now, I have taken upon me to speak unto the Lord: Peradventure there shall be twenty found there. And he said, I will not destroy *it* for twenty's sake.

32 And he said, Oh let not the Lord be angry, and I will speak yet but this once: Peradventure ten shall be found there. And he said, I will not destroy *it* for ten's sake.   Judg. 6:39

33 And the Lord went his way, as soon as

he had left communing with Abraham: and Abraham returned unto his place.

Lot Entertains Two Angels

19 And there came two angels to Sodom at even; and Lot sat in the gate of Sodom: and Lot seeing them rose up to meet them; and he bowed himself with his face toward the ground;   Gen. 18:1-5, 22
2 And he said, Behold now, my lords, turn in, I pray you, into your servant's house, and tarry all night, and wash your feet, and ye shall rise up early, and go on your ways. And they said, Nay; but we will abide in the street all night.   Gen. 18:4
3 And he pressed upon them greatly; and they turned in unto him, and entered into his house; and he made them a feast, and did bake unleavened bread, and they did eat.

The Vicious Sodomites Stricken with Blindness

4 But before they lay down, the men of the city, *even* the men of Sodom, ᵀcompassed the house round, both old and young, all the people from every quarter: Gen. 13:13 ◆ *surrounded*
5 And they called unto Lot, and said unto him, Where *are* the men which came in to thee this night? bring them out unto us, that we may know them.   Is. 3:9; Rom. 1:26-27
6 And Lot went out at the door unto them, and shut the door after him,   Judg. 19:23
7 And said, I pray you, brethren, do not so wickedly.
8 Behold now, I have two daughters which have not known man; let me, I pray you, bring them out unto you, and do ye to them as *is* good in your eyes: only unto these men do nothing; for therefore came they under the shadow of my roof.   Judg. 19:24
9 And they said, Stand back. And they said *again*, This one *fellow* came in to sojourn, and he will needs be a judge: now will we deal worse with thee, than with them. And they pressed sore upon the man, *even* Lot, and came near to break the door.   Ex. 2:14
10 But the men put forth their hand, and pulled Lot into the house to them, and shut to the door.
11 And they smote the men that *were* at the door of the house with blindness, both small and great: so that they wearied themselves to find the door.   2 Kin. 6:18; Acts 13:11

Lot Is Sent into the Mountains for Safety

12 And the men said unto Lot, Hast thou here any besides? son in law, and thy sons, and thy daughters, and whatsoever thou hast in the city, bring *them* out of this place:
13 For we will destroy this place, because the cry of them is ᵀwaxen great before the face of the LORD; and the LORD hath sent us to destroy it.   Gen. 18:20 ◆ *become*
14 And Lot went out, and spake unto his sons in law, which married his daughters, and said, Up, get you out of this place; for the LORD will destroy this city. But he seemed as one that mocked unto his sons in law.   Ex. 9:21; Num. 16:21, 45

19:14 The Tragedy of Warnings Dismissed

[Here Lot] repeated the words of the angels. . . . But he seemed to [his sons-in-law] as one that mocked. They laughed at what they called his superstitious fears. His daughters were influenced by their husbands. They were well enough off where they were. They could see no evidence of danger. Everything was just as it had been. They had great possessions, and they could not believe it possible that beautiful Sodom would be destroyed. *PP 160*

---

15 And when the morning arose, then the angels hastened Lot, saying, Arise, take thy wife, and thy two daughters, which are here; lest thou be consumed in the iniquity of the city.   Rev. 18:4
16 And while he lingered, the men laid hold upon his hand, and upon the hand of his wife, and upon the hand of his two daughters; the LORD being merciful unto him: and they brought him forth, and set him without the city.
17 And it came to pass, when they had brought them forth abroad, that he said, Escape for thy life; look not behind thee, neither stay thou in all the plain; escape to the mountain, lest thou be consumed.
18 And Lot said unto them, Oh, not so, my Lord:
19 Behold now, thy servant hath found grace in thy sight, and thou hast magnified thy mercy, which thou hast shewed unto me in saving my life; and I cannot escape to the mountain, lest some evil take me, and I die:
20 Behold now, this city *is* near to flee unto, and it *is* a little one: Oh, let me escape thither, (*is* it not a little one?) and my soul shall live.
21 And he said unto him, See, I have accepted thee concerning this thing also, that I will not overthrow this city, for the which thou hast spoken.
22 Haste thee, escape thither; for I cannot do any thing till thou be come thither. Therefore the name of the city was called Zoar.   Gen. 14:2
23 The sun was risen upon the earth when Lot entered into Zoar.

Sodom and Gomorrah Are Destroyed

24 Then the LORD rained upon Sodom and upon Gomorrah ᵀbrimstone and fire from the LORD out of heaven;   2 Pet. 2:6 ◆ *sulphur*

25 And he overthrew those cities, and all the plain, and all the inhabitants of the cities, and that which grew upon the ground.

Lot's Wife Becomes a Pillar of Salt

26 But his wife looked back from behind him, and she became a pillar of salt. Gen. 19:17

27 And Abraham gat up early in the morning to the place where he stood before the LORD:

28 And he looked toward Sodom and Gomorrah, and toward all the land of the plain, and beheld, and, lo, the smoke of the country went up as the smoke of a furnace.

29 And it came to pass, when God destroyed the cities of the plain, that God remembered Abraham, and sent Lot out of the midst of the overthrow, when he overthrew the cities in the which Lot dwelt.   Gen. 8:1

Beginnings of Moab and Ammon

30 And Lot went up out of Zoar, and dwelt in the mountain, and his two daughters with him; for he feared to dwell in Zoar: and he dwelt in a cave, he and his two daughters.

31 And the firstborn said unto the younger, Our father *is* old, and *there is* not a man in the earth to come in unto us after the manner of all the earth: Gen. 16:2

32 Come, let us make our father drink wine, and we will lie with him, that we may preserve seed of our father.

33 And they made their father drink wine that night: and the firstborn went in, and lay with her father; and he perceived not when she lay down, nor when she arose.

34 And it came to pass on the morrow, that the firstborn said unto the younger, Behold, I lay yesternight with my father: let us make him drink wine this night also; and go thou in, *and* lie with him, that we may preserve seed of our father.

35 And they made their father drink wine that night also: and the younger arose, and lay with him; and he perceived not when she lay down, nor when she arose.

36 Thus were both the daughters of Lot with child by their father.

37 And the firstborn bare a son, and called his name Moab: the same *is* the father of the Moabites unto this day.   Deut. 2:9

38 And the younger, she also bare a son, and called his name Ben-ammi: the same *is* the father of the children of Ammon unto this day.   Deut. 2:19

Abraham at Gerar

20 And Abraham journeyed from thence toward the south country, and dwelled between Kadesh and Shur, and sojourned in Gerar.   Gen. 18:1; 26:1, 6

2 And Abraham said of Sarah his wife, She *is* my sister: and Abimelech king of Gerar sent, and took Sarah.   Gen. 12:11-13, 15; 26:7

Abimelech Is Reproved by God for Taking Sarah

3 But God came to Abimelech in a dream by night, and said to him, Behold, thou *art but* a dead man, for the woman which thou hast taken; for she *is* a man's wife.   Job 33:15

4 But Abimelech had not come near her: and he said, Lord, wilt thou slay also a righteous nation?   Gen. 18:23-25

5 Said he not unto me, She *is* my sister? and she, even she herself said, He *is* my brother: in the integrity of my heart and innocency of my hands have I done this.   1 Kin. 9:4

6 And God said unto him in a dream, Yea, I know that thou didst this in the integrity of thy heart; for I also withheld thee from sinning against me: therefore suffered I thee not to touch her.   1 Sam. 25:26

7 Now therefore restore the man his wife; for he *is* a prophet, and he shall pray for

---

Doubt and Delay

Genesis 19:26

If Lot himself had manifested no hesitancy to obey the angels' warning, but had earnestly fled toward the mountains, without one word of pleading or remonstrance, his wife also would have made her escape. The influence of his example would have saved her from the sin that sealed her doom. But his hesitancy and delay caused her to lightly regard the divine warning. While her body was upon the plain, her heart clung to Sodom, and she perished with it. She rebelled against God because His judgments involved her possessions and her children in the ruin. Although so greatly favored in being called out from the wicked city, she felt that she was severely dealt with, because the wealth that it had taken years to accumulate must be left to destruction. Instead of thankfully accepting deliverance, she presumptuously looked back to desire the life of those who had rejected the divine warning. Her sin showed her to be unworthy of life, for the preservation of which she felt so little gratitude. *PP 161, 162*

thee, and thou shalt live: and if thou restore *her* not, know thou that thou shalt surely die, thou, and all that *are* thine.   Job 42:8

8 Therefore Abimelech rose early in the morning, and called all his servants, and told all these things in their ears: and the men were sore afraid.

9 Then Abimelech called Abraham, and said unto him, What hast thou done unto us? and what have I offended thee, that thou hast brought on me and on my kingdom a great sin? thou hast done deeds unto me that ought not to be done.   Gen. 12:18

10 And Abimelech said unto Abraham, What sawest thou, that thou hast done this thing?

11 And Abraham said, Because I thought, Surely the fear of God *is* not in this place; and they will slay me for my wife's sake.

12 And yet indeed *she is* my sister; she *is* the daughter of my father, but not the daughter of my mother; and she became my wife.

13 And it came to pass, when God caused me to wander from my father's house, that I said unto her, This *is* thy kindness which thou shalt shew unto me; at every place whither we shall come, say of me, He *is* my brother.   Gen. 12:1

Abimelech Restores Sarah

14 And Abimelech took sheep, and oxen, and menservants, and womenservants, and gave *them* unto Abraham, and restored him Sarah his wife.   Gen. 12:16

15 And Abimelech said, Behold, my land *is* before thee: dwell where it pleaseth thee.

16 And unto Sarah he said, Behold, I have given thy brother a thousand *pieces* of silver: behold, he *is* to thee a covering of the eyes, unto all that *are* with thee, and with all *other*: thus she was reproved.   Gen. 20:5

17 So Abraham prayed unto God: and God healed Abimelech, and his wife, and his maidservants; and they bare *children*.

18 For the LORD had fast closed up all the wombs of the house of Abimelech, because of Sarah Abraham's wife.   Gen. 12:17

Isaac Is Born

21 And the LORD visited Sarah as he had said, and the LORD did unto Sarah as he had spoken.   Gen. 18:10

2 For Sarah conceived, and bare Abraham a son in his old age, at the set time of which God had spoken to him.   Gal. 4:22; Heb. 11:11

3 And Abraham called the name of his son that was born unto him, whom Sarah bare to him, Isaac.   Gen. 17:19

4 And Abraham circumcised his son Isaac being eight days old, as God had commanded him.   Acts 7:8

5 And Abraham was an hundred years old, when his son Isaac was born unto him.

6 And Sarah said, God hath made me to laugh, *so that* all that hear will laugh with me.   Gen. 17:17; Ps. 126:2; Is. 54:1

7 And she said, Who would have said unto Abraham, that Sarah should have given children suck? for I have born *him* a son in his old age.   Gen. 18:11-12

8 And the child grew, and was weaned: and Abraham made a great feast the *same* day that Isaac was weaned.

Hagar and Ishmael Are Expelled

9 And Sarah saw the son of Hagar the Egyptian, which she had born unto Abraham, mocking.   Gen. 16:1, 15; Gal. 4:29

10 Wherefore she said unto Abraham, Cast out this bondwoman and her son: for the son of this bondwoman shall not be heir with my son, *even* with Isaac.   John 8:35

11 And the thing was very grievous in Abraham's sight because of his son.   Gen. 17:18

12 And God said unto Abraham, Let it not be grievous in thy sight because of the lad, and because of thy bondwoman; in all that Sarah hath said unto thee, hearken unto her voice; for in Isaac shall thy seed be called.

13 And also of the son of the bondwoman will I make a nation, because he *is* thy seed.

14 And Abraham rose up early in the morning, and took bread, and a bottle of water, and gave *it* unto Hagar, putting it on her shoulder, and the child, and sent her away: and she departed, and wandered in the wilderness of Beer-sheba.

15 And the water was spent in the bottle, and she cast the child under one of the shrubs.

16 And she went, and sat her down over against *him* a good way off, as it were a bowshot: for she said, Let me not see the death of the child. And she sat over against *him*, and lift up her voice, and wept.

17 And God heard the voice of the lad; and the angel of God called to Hagar out of heaven, and said unto her, What aileth thee, Hagar? fear not; for God hath heard the voice of the lad where he *is*.   Gen. 16:11

18 Arise, lift up the lad, and hold him in thine hand; for I will make him a great nation.   Gen. 16:10; 17:20; 21:13

19 And God opened her eyes, and she saw a well of water; and she went, and filled the bottle with water, and gave the lad drink.

20 And God was with the lad; and he grew, and dwelt in the wilderness, and became an archer.   Gen. 28:15

21 And he dwelt in the wilderness of Paran: and his mother took him a wife out of the land of Egypt.

Abimelech and Abraham Make a Covenant

22 And it came to pass at that time, that Abimelech and Phichol the chief captain of his host spake unto Abraham, saying, God *is* with thee in all that thou doest: Gen. 20:2
23 Now therefore swear unto me here by God that thou wilt not deal falsely with me, nor with my son, nor with my son's son: *but* according to the kindness that I have done unto thee, thou shalt do unto me, and to the land wherein thou hast sojourned.   Josh. 2:12
24 And Abraham said, I will swear.
25 And Abraham reproved Abimelech because of a well of water, which Abimelech's servants had violently taken away.
26 And Abimelech said, I ᵀwot not who hath done this thing: neither didst thou tell me, neither yet heard I *of it*, but to day.   know
27 And Abraham took sheep and oxen, and gave them unto Abimelech; and both of them made a covenant.
28 And Abraham set seven ewe lambs of the flock by themselves.
29 And Abimelech said unto Abraham, What *mean* these seven ewe lambs which thou hast set by themselves?
30 And he said, For *these* seven ewe lambs shalt thou take of my hand, that they may be a witness unto me, that I have digged this well.   Gen. 31:52
31 Wherefore he called that place Beersheba; because there they sware both of them.   Gen. 21:14; 26:33
32 Thus they made a covenant at Beer-sheba: then Abimelech rose up, and Phichol the chief captain of his host, and they returned into the land of the Philistines.
33 And *Abraham* planted a ᵀgrove in Beersheba, and called there on the name of the Lord, the everlasting God.   Gen. 4:26 ◆ *tree*
34 And Abraham sojourned in the Philistines' land many days.

God Asks Abraham to Sacrifice His Son

22 And it came to pass after these things, that God did tempt Abraham, and said unto him, Abraham: and he said, Behold, *here* I am.   Gen. 22:11; Deut. 8:2; Heb. 11:17
2 And he said, Take now thy son, thine only *son* Isaac, whom thou lovest, and get thee into the land of Moriah; and offer him there for a burnt offering upon one of the mountains which I will tell thee of.   Heb. 11:17

Abraham Gives Proof of Faith and Obedience

3 And Abraham rose up early in the morning, and saddled his ass, and took two of his young men with him, and Isaac his son, and ᵀclave the wood for the burnt offering, and rose up, and went unto the place of which God had told him.   *split*

> **22:1, 2 Abraham Tested Again**
>
> God had called Abraham to be the father of the faithful, and his life was to stand as an example of faith to succeeding generations. But his faith had not been perfect. He had shown distrust of God in concealing the fact that Sarah was his wife, and again in his marriage with Hagar. That he might reach the highest standard, God subjected him to another test, the closest which man was ever called to endure. *PP 147*

4 Then on the third day Abraham lifted up his eyes, and saw the place afar off.
5 And Abraham said unto his young men, Abide ye here with the ass; and I and the lad will go yonder and worship, and come again to you.
6 And Abraham took the wood of the burnt offering, and laid *it* upon Isaac his son; and he took the fire in his hand, and a knife; and they went both of them together.   John 19:17
7 And Isaac spake unto Abraham his father, and said, My father: and he said, Here *am* I, my son. And he said, Behold the fire and the wood: but where *is* the lamb for a burnt offering?
8 And Abraham said, My son, God will provide himself a lamb for a burnt offering: so they went both of them together.   John 1:36
9 And they came to the place which God had told him of; and Abraham built an altar there, and laid the wood in order, and bound Isaac his son, and laid him on the altar upon the wood.   James 2:21
10 And Abraham stretched forth his hand, and took the knife to slay his son.

The Angel Stops Abraham

11 And the angel of the Lord called unto him out of heaven, and said, Abraham, Abraham: and he said, Here *am* I.   Gen. 16:7
12 And he said, Lay not thine hand upon the lad, neither do thou any thing unto him: for now I know that thou fearest God, seeing thou hast not withheld thy son, thine only *son* from me.   Gen. 26:5; 1 Sam. 15:22; James 2:21-22
13 And Abraham lifted up his eyes, and looked, and behold behind *him* a ram caught in a thicket by his horns: and Abraham went and took the ram, and offered him up for a burnt offering in the stead of his son.
14 And Abraham called the name of that place Jehovah-jireh: as it is said *to* this day, In the mount of the Lord it shall be seen.

Abraham Is Again Blessed

15 And the angel of the LORD called unto Abraham out of heaven the second time,

16 And said, By myself have I sworn, saith the LORD, for because thou hast done this thing, and hast not withheld thy son, thine only *son*: Ps. 105:9; Luke 1:73; Heb. 6:13-14

17 That in blessing I will bless thee, and in multiplying I will multiply thy seed as the stars of the heaven, and as the sand which *is* upon the sea shore; and thy seed shall possess the gate of his enemies; Jer. 33:22

18 And in thy seed shall all the nations of the earth be blessed; because thou hast obeyed my voice. Gen. 12:3; 18:18; Acts 3:25

19 So Abraham returned unto his young men, and they rose up and went together to Beer-sheba; and Abraham dwelt at Beer-sheba. Gen. 21:31

The Generations of Nahor to Rebekah

20 And it came to pass after these things, that it was told Abraham, saying, Behold, Milcah, she hath also born children unto thy brother Nahor; Gen. 11:29; 24:24

21 Huz his firstborn, and Buz his brother, and Kemuel the father of Aram, Job 1:1

22 And Chesed, and Hazo, and Pildash, and Jidlaph, and Bethuel.

23 And Bethuel ^Tbegat Rebekah: these eight Milcah did bear to Nahor, Abraham's brother. Gen. 24:15 ◆ *brought forth*

24 And his ^Tconcubine, whose name *was* Reumah, she bare also Tebah, and Gaham, and Thahash, and Maachah. *less important wife*

The Age and Death of Sarah

23 And Sarah was an hundred and seven and twenty years old: *these were* the years of the life of Sarah.

2 And Sarah died in Kirjath-arba; the same *is* Hebron in the land of Canaan: and Abraham came to mourn for Sarah, and to weep for her. Gen. 23:19

The Purchase of Machpelah, Where Sarah Is Buried

3 And Abraham stood up from before his dead, and spake unto the sons of Heth, saying, Gen. 10:15

4 I *am* a stranger and a sojourner with you: give me a possession of a buryingplace with you, that I may bury my dead out of my sight. Gen. 17:8; 1 Chr. 29:15; Heb. 11:9

5 And the children of Heth answered Abraham, saying unto him,

6 Hear us, my lord: thou *art* a mighty prince among us: in the choice of our sepulchres bury thy dead; none of us shall withhold from thee his sepulchre, but that thou mayest bury thy dead. Gen. 14:14; 24:35

7 And Abraham stood up, and bowed himself to the people of the land, *even* to the children of Heth.

8 And he communed with them, saying, If it be your mind that I should bury my dead out of my sight; hear me, and ^Tintreat for me to Ephron the son of Zohar, *plead*

9 That he may give me the cave of Machpelah, which he hath, which *is* in the end of his field; for as much money as it is worth he shall give it me for a possession of a buryingplace amongst you.

Abraham Passes the Test

Genesis 22:1–12

Abraham's great act of faith stands like a pillar of light, illuminating the pathway of God's servants in all succeeding ages. Abraham did not seek to excuse himself from doing the will of God. During that three days' journey he had sufficient time to reason, and to doubt God, if he was disposed to doubt. He might have reasoned that the slaying of his son would cause him to be looked upon as a murderer, a second Cain; that it would cause his teaching to be rejected and despised; and thus destroy his power to do good to his fellow men. He might have pleaded that age should excuse him from obedience. But the patriarch did not take refuge in any of these excuses. Abraham was human; his passions and attachments were like ours; but he did not stop to question how the promise could be fulfilled if Isaac should be slain. He did not stay to reason with his aching heart. He knew that God is just and righteous in all His requirements, and he obeyed the command to the very letter.

"Abraham believed God, and it was imputed unto him for righteousness: and he was called the friend of God" (James 2:23). And Paul says, "They which are of faith, the same are the children of Abraham" (Galatians 3:7). But Abraham's faith was made manifest by his works. "Was not Abraham our father justified by works, when he had offered Isaac his son upon the altar? Seest thou how faith wrought with his works, and by works was faith made perfect?" (James 2:21, 22). There are many who fail to understand the relation of faith and works. They say, "Only believe in Christ, and you are safe. You have nothing to do with keeping the law." But genuine faith will be manifest in obedience. Said Christ to the unbelieving Jews, "If ye were Abraham's children, ye would do the works of Abraham" (John 8:39). *PP 153, 154*

10 And Ephron dwelt among the children of Heth: and Ephron the Hittite answered Abraham in the audience of the children of Heth, *even* of all that went in at the gate of his city, saying, Gen. 23:18; 34:20, 24

11 Nay, my lord, hear me: the field give I thee, and the cave that *is* therein, I give it thee; in the presence of the sons of my people give I it thee: bury thy dead.

12 And Abraham bowed down himself before the people of the land.

13 And he spake unto Ephron in the audience of the people of the land, saying, But if thou *wilt give it*, I pray thee, hear me: I will give thee money for the field; take *it* of me, and I will bury my dead there.

14 And Ephron answered Abraham, saying unto him,

15 My lord, hearken unto me: the land *is worth* four hundred shekels of silver; what *is* that ⸤betwixt me and thee? bury therefore thy dead. Ezek. 45:12 ◆ *between*

16 And Abraham hearkened unto Ephron; and Abraham weighed to Ephron the silver, which he had named in the audience of the sons of Heth, four hundred shekels of silver, current *money* with the merchant. Jer. 32:9

17 And the field of Ephron, which *was* in Machpelah, which *was* before Mamre, the field, and the cave which *was* therein, and all the trees that *were* in the field, that *were* in all the borders round about, were made sure Gen. 23:20; 25:9; 50:13

18 Unto Abraham for a possession in the presence of the children of Heth, before all that went in at the gate of his city.

19 And after this, Abraham buried Sarah his wife in the cave of the field of Machpelah before Mamre: the same *is* Hebron in the land of Canaan.

20 And the field, and the cave that *is* therein, were made sure unto Abraham for a possession of a buryingplace by the sons of Heth.

Abraham's Servant Swears an Oath

24 And Abraham was old, *and* well stricken in age: and the LORD had blessed Abraham in all things. Gen. 13:2

2 And Abraham said unto his eldest servant of his house, that ruled over all that he had, Put, I pray thee, thy hand under my thigh:

3 And I will make thee swear by the LORD, the God of heaven, and the God of the earth, that thou shalt not take a wife unto my son of the daughters of the Canaanites, among whom I dwell: Gen. 26:34-35

4 But thou shalt go unto my country, and to my kindred, and take a wife unto my son Isaac. Gen. 28:2

5 And the servant said unto him, Peradventure the woman will not be willing to follow me unto this land: must I needs bring thy son again unto the land from whence thou camest?

6 And Abraham said unto him, Beware thou that thou bring not my son thither again.

7 The LORD God of heaven, which took me from my father's house, and from the land of my kindred, and which spake unto me, and that sware unto me, saying, Unto thy seed will I give this land; he shall send his angel before thee, and thou shalt take a wife unto my son from thence. Gen. 13:15

8 And if the woman will not be willing to follow thee, then thou shalt be clear from this my oath: only bring not my son thither again. Josh. 2:17-20

9 And the servant put his hand under the thigh of Abraham his master, and sware to him concerning that matter. Gen. 24:2

> **24:1–9 Divine Guidance Before Marriage**
>
> If there is any subject which should be carefully considered and in which the counsel of older and more experienced persons should be sought, it is the subject of marriage; if ever the Bible was needed as a counselor, if ever divine guidance should be sought in prayer, it is before taking a step that binds persons together for life. *PP 175*

The Servant's Journey

10 And the servant took ten camels of the camels of his master, and departed; for all the goods of his master *were* in his hand: and he arose, and went to Mesopotamia, unto the city of Nahor. Gen. 11:31

11 And he made his camels to kneel down without the city by a well of water at the time of the evening, *even* the time that women go out to draw *water*. John 4:7

12 And he said, O LORD God of my master Abraham, I pray thee, send me good speed this day, and shew kindness unto my master Abraham. Gen. 24:27; 26:24; Ex. 3:6

13 Behold, I stand *here* by the well of water; and the daughters of the men of the city come out to draw water: Gen. 24:43

14 And let it come to pass, that the damsel to whom I shall say, Let down thy pitcher, I pray thee, that I may drink; and she shall say, Drink, and I will give thy camels drink also: *let the same be* she *that* thou hast appointed for thy servant Isaac; and thereby shall I know that thou hast shewed kindness unto my master. Gen. 15:8; Judg. 6:17, 37

15 And it came to pass, before he had done speaking, that, behold, Rebekah came out, who was born to Bethuel, son of Milcah, the wife of Nahor, Abraham's brother, with her pitcher upon her shoulder. Gen. 11:29; 24:45

16 And the damsel *was* very fair to look upon, a virgin, neither had any man known her: and she went down to the well, and filled her pitcher, and came up.   Gen. 26:7

17 And the servant ran to meet her, and said, Let me, I pray thee, drink a little water of thy pitcher.   John 4:7

18 And she said, Drink, my lord: and she hasted, and let down her pitcher upon her hand, and gave him drink.

19 And when she had done giving him drink, she said, I will draw *water* for thy camels also, until they have done drinking.

20 And she hasted, and emptied her pitcher into the trough, and ran again unto the well to draw *water*, and drew for all his camels.

21 And the man wondering at her held his peace, to ᵀwit whether the Lᴏʀᴅ had made his journey prosperous or not. Gen. 24:12 ◆ *know*

22 And it came to pass, as the camels had done drinking, that the man took a golden earring of half a shekel weight, and two bracelets for her hands of ten *shekels* weight of gold;   Ex. 32:2-3

23 And said, Whose daughter *art* thou? tell me, I pray thee: is there room *in* thy father's house for us to lodge in?

24 And she said unto him, I *am* the daughter of Bethuel the son of Milcah, which she bare unto Nahor.   Gen. 22:23; 24:15

25 She said moreover unto him, We have both straw and ᵀprovender enough, and room to lodge in.   *food for livestock*

26 And the man bowed down his head, and worshipped the Lᴏʀᴅ.   Gen. 24:48, 52; Ex. 4:31

27 And he said, Blessed *be* the Lᴏʀᴅ God of my master Abraham, who hath not left destitute my master of his mercy and his truth: I *being* in the way, the Lᴏʀᴅ led me to the house of my master's brethren.   Gen. 24:12, 48

28 And the damsel ran, and told *them of* her mother's house these things.

29 And Rebekah had a brother, and his name *was* Laban: and Laban ran out unto the man, unto the well.   Gen. 29:5

30 And it came to pass, when he saw the earring and bracelets upon his sister's hands, and when he heard the words of Rebekah his sister, saying, Thus spake the man unto me; that he came unto the man; and, behold, he stood by the camels at the well.

31 And he said, Come in, thou blessed of the Lᴏʀᴅ; wherefore standest thou without? for I have prepared the house, and room for the camels.   Gen. 26:29; Ruth 3:10; Ps. 115:15

32 And the man came into the house: and he ungirded his camels, and gave straw and provender for the camels, and water to wash his feet, and the men's feet that *were* with him.   Gen. 18:4; 43:24; Judg. 19:21

33 And there was set *meat* before him to eat: but he said, I will not eat, until I have told mine errand. And he said, Speak on.

34 And he said, I *am* Abraham's servant.

35 And the Lᴏʀᴅ hath blessed my master greatly; and he is become great: and he hath given him flocks, and herds, and silver, and gold, and menservants, and maidservants, and camels, and asses.   Gen. 13:2; 24:1

36 And Sarah my master's wife bare a son to my master when she was old: and unto him hath he given all that he hath.   Gen. 21:1-7, 10

37 And my master made me swear, saying, Thou shalt not take a wife to my son of the

Parental Influence on Children

Genesis 24:1–9

Parents should never lose sight of their own responsibility for the future happiness of their children. Isaac's deference to his father's judgment was the result of the training that had taught him to love a life of obedience. While Abraham required his children to respect parental authority, his daily life testified that that authority was not a selfish or arbitrary control, but was founded in love, and had their welfare and happiness in view.

Fathers and mothers should feel that a duty devolves upon them to guide the affections of the youth, that they may be placed upon those who will be suitable companions. They should feel it a duty, by their own teaching and example, with the assisting grace of God, to so mold the character of the children from their earliest years that they will be pure and noble and will be attracted to the good and true. Like attracts like; like appreciates like. Let the love for truth and purity and goodness be early implanted in the soul, and the youth will seek the society of those who possess these characteristics.

Let parents seek, in their own character and in their home life, to exemplify the love and beneficence of the heavenly Father. Let the home be full of sunshine. This will be worth far more to your children than lands or money. Let the home love be kept alive in their hearts, that they may look back upon the home of their childhood as a place of peace and happiness next to heaven. The members of the family do not all have the same stamp of character, and there will be frequent occasion for the exercise of patience and forbearance; but through love and self-discipline all may be bound together in the closest union. *PP 175, 176*

daughters of the Canaanites, in whose land I dwell:

38 But thou shalt go unto my father's house, and to my kindred, and take a wife unto my son. Gen. 24:4

39 And I said unto my master, Peradventure the woman will not follow me.

40 And he said unto me, The LORD, before whom I walk, will send his angel with thee, and prosper thy way; and thou shalt take a wife for my son of my kindred, and of my father's house: Gen. 17:1

41 Then shalt thou be clear from *this* my oath, when thou comest to my kindred; and if they give not thee *one*, thou shalt be clear from my oath. Gen. 24:8

42 And I came this day unto the well, and said, O LORD God of my master Abraham, if now thou do prosper my way which I go:

43 Behold, I stand by the well of water; and it shall come to pass, that when the virgin cometh forth to draw *water*, and I say to her, Give me, I pray thee, a little water of thy pitcher to drink; Gen. 24:13-14

44 And she say to me, Both drink thou, and I will also draw for thy camels: *let* the same *be* the woman whom the LORD hath appointed out for my master's son. Gen. 24:14

45 And before I had done speaking in mine heart, behold, Rebekah came forth with her pitcher on her shoulder; and she went down unto the well, and drew *water*: and I said unto her, Let me drink, I pray thee.

46 And she made haste, and let down her pitcher from her *shoulder*, and said, Drink, and I will give thy camels drink also: so I drank, and she made the camels drink also.

47 And I asked her, and said, Whose daughter *art* thou? And she said, The daughter of Bethuel, Nahor's son, whom Milcah bare unto him: and I put the earring upon her face, and the bracelets upon her hands.

48 And I bowed down my head, and worshipped the LORD, and blessed the LORD God of my master Abraham, which had led me in the right way to take my master's brother's daughter unto his son. Gen. 22:23

49 And now if ye will deal kindly and truly with my master, tell me: and if not, tell me; that I may turn to the right hand, or to the left. Gen. 47:29; Josh. 2:14

50 Then Laban and Bethuel answered and said, The thing proceedeth from the LORD: we cannot speak unto thee bad or good.

51 Behold, Rebekah *is* before thee, take *her*, and go, and let her be thy master's son's wife, as the LORD hath spoken. Gen. 24:15

52 And it came to pass, that, when Abraham's servant heard their words, he worshipped the LORD, *bowing himself* to the earth. Gen. 24:26

53 And the servant brought forth jewels of silver, and jewels of gold, and raiment, and gave *them* to Rebekah: he gave also to her brother and to her mother precious things.

54 And they did eat and drink, he and the men that *were* with him, and tarried all night; and they rose up in the morning, and he said, Send me away unto my master.

55 And her brother and her mother said, Let the damsel abide with us *a few* days, at the least ten; after that she shall go.

56 And he said unto them, Hinder me not, seeing the LORD hath prospered my way; send me away that I may go to my master.

57 And they said, We will call the damsel, and enquire at her mouth.

58 And they called Rebekah, and said unto her, Wilt thou go with this man? And she said, I will go.

59 And they sent away Rebekah their sister, and her nurse, and Abraham's servant, and his men. Gen. 35:8

60 And they blessed Rebekah, and said unto her, Thou *art* our sister, be thou *the mother* of thousands of millions, and let thy seed possess the gate of those which hate them.

61 And Rebekah arose, and her damsels, and they rode upon the camels, and followed the man: and the servant took Rebekah, and went his way.

The Meeting of Isaac and Rebekah

62 And Isaac came from the way of the well Lahai-roi; for he dwelt in the south country.

63 And Isaac went out to meditate in the field at the ^Teventide: and he lifted up his eyes, and saw, and, behold, the camels *were* coming. Ps. 1:2 ◆ *evening*

64 And Rebekah lifted up her eyes, and when she saw Isaac, she lighted off the camel.

65 For she *had* said unto the servant, What man *is* this that walketh in the field to meet us? And the servant *had* said, It *is* my master: therefore she took a ^Tvail, and covered herself. *veil*

66 And the servant told Isaac all things that he had done.

67 And Isaac brought her into his mother Sarah's tent, and took Rebekah, and she became his wife; and he loved her: and Isaac was comforted after his mother's *death*.

The Sons of Abraham by Keturah

25 Then again Abraham took a wife, and her name *was* Keturah.

2 And she bare him Zimran, and Jokshan, and Medan, and Midian, and Ishbak, and Shuah. 1 Chr. 1:32-33

3 And Jokshan ^Tbegat Sheba, and Dedan.

And the sons of Dedan were Asshurim, and Letushim, and Leummim. *brought forth*
4 And the sons of Midian; Ephah, and Epher, and Hanoch, and Abida, and Eldaah. All these *were* the children of Keturah.
5 And Abraham gave all that he had unto Isaac. *Gen. 24:36*
6 But unto the sons of the concubines, which Abraham had, Abraham gave gifts, and sent them away from Isaac his son, while he yet lived, eastward, unto the east country. *Gen. 21:14; Judg. 6:3*
7 And these *are* the days of the years of Abraham's life which he lived, an hundred ᵀthreescore and fifteen years. *Gen. 12:4 ◆ sixty*
8 Then Abraham gave up the ghost, and died in a good old age, an old man, and full *of years*; and was gathered to his people.
9 And his sons Isaac and Ishmael buried him in the cave of Machpelah, in the field of Ephron the son of Zohar the Hittite, which *is* before Mamre; *Gen. 35:29*
10 The field which Abraham purchased of the sons of Heth: there was Abraham buried, and Sarah his wife. *Gen. 23:16; 49:31*
11 And it came to pass after the death of Abraham, that God blessed his son Isaac; and Isaac dwelt by the well Lahai-roi.
12 Now these *are* the generations of Ishmael, Abraham's son, whom Hagar the Egyptian, Sarah's handmaid, bare unto Abraham:
13 And these *are* the names of the sons of Ishmael, by their names, according to their generations: the firstborn of Ishmael, Nebajoth; and Kedar, and Adbeel, and Mibsam,
14 And Mishma, and Dumah, and Massa,
15 Hadar, and Tema, Jetur, Naphish, and Kedemah: *1 Chr. 5:19*
16 These *are* the sons of Ishmael, and these *are* their names, by their towns, and by their castles; twelve princes according to their nations. *Gen. 17:20*
17 And these *are* the years of the life of Ishmael, an hundred and thirty and seven years: and he gave up the ghost and died; and was gathered unto his people.
18 And they dwelt from Havilah unto Shur, that *is* before Egypt, as thou goest toward Assyria: *and* he died in the presence of all his brethren. *Gen. 16:12; 20:1*

Rebekah Gives Birth to Esau and Jacob
19 And these *are* the generations of Isaac, Abraham's son: Abraham begat Isaac:
20 And Isaac was forty years old when he took Rebekah to wife, the daughter of Bethuel the Syrian of Padan-aram, the sister to Laban the Syrian. *Gen. 22:23; 24:29, 67*
21 And Isaac ᵀintreated the LORD for his wife, because she *was* barren: and the LORD

was intreated of him, and Rebekah his wife conceived. *2 Chr. 33:13; Ezra 8:23 ◆ pled with*
22 And the children struggled together within her; and she said, If *it be* so, why *am* I thus? And she went to enquire of the LORD.
23 And the LORD said unto her, Two nations *are* in thy womb, and two manner of people shall be separated from thy bowels; and *the one* people shall be stronger than *the other* people; and the elder shall serve the younger. *Gen. 17:16; 27:29, 40*
24 And when her days to be delivered were fulfilled, behold, *there were* twins in her womb.
25 And the first came out red, all over like an hairy garment; and they called his name Esau. *Gen. 27:11, 16, 23*
26 And after that came his brother out, and his hand took hold on Esau's heel; and his name was called Jacob: and Isaac *was* threescore years old when she bare them.
27 And the boys grew: and Esau was a cunning hunter, a man of the field; and Jacob *was* a plain man, dwelling in tents. *Heb. 11:9*
28 And Isaac loved Esau, because he did eat of *his* venison: but Rebekah loved Jacob.

Esau Sells His Birthright
29 And Jacob ᵀsod pottage: and Esau came from the field, and he *was* faint: *cooked*
30 And Esau said to Jacob, Feed me, I pray thee, with that same red *pottage*; for I *am* faint: therefore was his name called Edom.
31 And Jacob said, Sell me this day thy birthright.
32 And Esau said, Behold, I *am* at the point to die: and what profit shall this birthright do to me?
33 And Jacob said, Swear to me this day; and he sware unto him: and he sold his birthright unto Jacob. *Gen. 27:36; Heb. 12:16*
34 Then Jacob gave Esau bread and pottage of lentiles; and he did eat and drink, and rose up, and went his way: thus Esau despised *his* birthright.

25:29–34 A Fateful Trade

And for a dish of red pottage [Esau] parted with his birthright, and confirmed the transaction by an oath. A short time at most would have secured him food in his father's tents, but to satisfy the desire of the moment he carelessly bartered the glorious heritage that God Himself had promised to his fathers. His whole interest was in the present. He was ready to sacrifice the heavenly to the earthly, to exchange a future good for a momentary indulgence. *PP 179*

Isaac Goes to Gerar

26 And there was a famine in the land, beside the first famine that was in the days of Abraham. And Isaac went unto Abimelech king of the Philistines unto Gerar. Gen. 12:10

2 And the LORD appeared unto him, and said, Go not down into Egypt; dwell in the land which I shall tell thee of: Gen. 12:1, 7; 17:1

3 Sojourn in this land, and I will be with thee, and will bless thee; for unto thee, and unto thy seed, I will give all these countries, and I will perform the oath which I sware unto Abraham thy father; Gen. 12:7; 13:15; 28:15

4 And I will make thy seed to multiply as the stars of heaven, and will give unto thy seed all these countries; and in thy seed shall all the nations of the earth be blessed; Gal. 3:8

5 Because that Abraham obeyed my voice, and kept my charge, my commandments, my statutes, and my laws. Gen. 22:16

God's Law   See Exodus 16:24–30.

6 And Isaac dwelt in Gerar:

7 And the men of the place asked *him* of his wife; and he said, She *is* my sister: for he feared to say, *She is* my wife; lest, *said he*, the men of the place should kill me for Rebekah; because she *was* fair to look upon. Gen. 12:13

8 And it came to pass, when he had been there a long time, that Abimelech king of the Philistines looked out at a window, and saw, and, behold, Isaac *was* sporting with Rebekah his wife.

9 And Abimelech called Isaac, and said, Behold, of a surety she *is* thy wife: and how saidst thou, She *is* my sister? And Isaac said unto him, Because I said, Lest I die for her.

10 And Abimelech said, What *is* this thou hast done unto us? one of the people might lightly have lien with thy wife, and thou shouldest have brought guiltiness upon us.

11 And Abimelech charged all *his* people, saying, He that toucheth this man or his wife shall surely be put to death.

Isaac Grows Rich

12 Then Isaac sowed in that land, and received in the same year an hundredfold: and the LORD blessed him. Gen. 24:1; Job 42:12

13 And the man waxed great, and went forward, and grew until he became very great:

14 For he had possession of flocks, and possession of herds, and great store of servants: and the Philistines envied him. Gen. 37:11

15 For all the wells which his father's servants had digged in the days of Abraham his father, the Philistines had stopped them, and filled them with earth. Gen. 21:30

16 And Abimelech said unto Isaac, Go from us; for thou art much mightier than we.

17 And Isaac departed thence, and pitched his tent in the valley of Gerar, and dwelt there.

18 And Isaac digged again the wells of water, which they had digged in the days of Abraham his father; for the Philistines had stopped them after the death of Abraham: and he called their names after the names by which his father had called them. Gen. 21:31

19 And Isaac's servants digged in the valley, and found there a well of springing water.

20 And the herdmen of Gerar did strive with Isaac's herdmen, saying, The water *is* ours: and he called the name of the well Esek; because they strove with him. Gen. 21:25

21 And they digged another well, and strove for that also: and he called the name of it Sitnah.

22 And he removed from thence, and digged another well; and for that they strove not: and he called the name of it Rehoboth; and he said, For now the LORD hath made room for us, and we shall be fruitful in the land.

23 And he went up from thence to Beersheba.

24 And the LORD appeared unto him the same night, and said, I *am* the God of Abraham thy father: fear not, for I *am* with thee, and will bless thee, and multiply thy seed for my servant Abraham's sake. Gen. 15:1; 24:12

25 And he builded an altar there, and called upon the name of the LORD, and pitched his tent there: and there Isaac's servants digged a well. Gen. 12:7-8; 13:18; Ps. 116:17

26 Then Abimelech went to him from Gerar, and Ahuzzath one of his friends, and Phichol the chief captain of his army.

27 And Isaac said unto them, Wherefore come ye to me, seeing ye hate me, and have sent me away from you? Gen. 26:16

28 And they said, We saw certainly that the LORD was with thee: and we said, Let there be now an oath ᵀbetwixt us, *even* betwixt us and thee, and let us make a covenant with thee; Gen. 21:22-23 ♦ *between*

29 That thou wilt do us no hurt, as we have not touched thee, and as we have done unto thee nothing but good, and have sent thee away in peace: thou *art* now the blessed of the LORD. Gen. 24:31; Ps. 115:15

30 And he made them a feast, and they did eat and drink. Gen. 19:3

31 And they rose up ᵀbetimes in the morning, and sware one to another: and Isaac sent them away, and they departed from him in peace. *early*

32 And it came to pass the same day, that Isaac's servants came, and told him concerning the well which they had digged, and said unto him, We have found water.

33 And he called it Shebah: therefore the name of the city *is* Beer-sheba unto this day.

Esau's Wives

34 And Esau was forty years old when he took to wife Judith the daughter of Beeri the Hittite, and Bashemath the daughter of Elon the Hittite: Gen. 36:2
35 Which were a grief of mind unto Isaac and to Rebekah.

Isaac Sends Esau for Venison

27 And it came to pass, that when Isaac was old, and his eyes were dim, so that he could not see, he called Esau his eldest son, and said unto him, My son: and he said unto him, Behold, *here am* I.
2 And he said, Behold now, I am old, I know not the day of my death:
3 Now therefore take, I pray thee, thy weapons, thy quiver and thy bow, and go out to the field, and take me *some* venison;
4 And make me savoury meat, such as I love, and bring *it* to me, that I may eat; that my soul may bless thee before I die.   Gen. 27:25
5 And Rebekah heard when Isaac spake to Esau his son. And Esau went to the field to hunt *for* venison, *and* to bring *it*.

Rebekah and Jacob Conspire to Obtain Isaac's Blessing

6 And Rebekah spake unto Jacob her son, saying, Behold, I heard thy father speak unto Esau thy brother, saying,
7 Bring me venison, and make me savoury meat, that I may eat, and bless thee before the LORD before my death.
8 Now therefore, my son, obey my voice according to that which I command thee.
9 Go now to the flock, and fetch me from thence two good kids of the goats; and I will make them savoury meat for thy father, such as he loveth:
10 And thou shalt bring *it* to thy father, that he may eat, and that he may bless thee before his death.
11 And Jacob said to Rebekah his mother, Behold, Esau my brother *is* a hairy man, and I *am* a smooth man: Gen. 25:25
12 My father peradventure will feel me, and I shall seem to him as a deceiver; and I shall bring a curse upon me, and not a blessing.
13 And his mother said unto him, Upon me *be* thy curse, my son: only obey my voice, and go fetch me *them*.   Matt. 27:25
14 And he went, and fetched, and brought *them* to his mother: and his mother made savoury meat, such as his father loved.
15 And Rebekah took goodly ᵀraiment of her eldest son Esau, which *were* with her

in the house, and put them upon Jacob her younger son: Gen. 27:27 ◆ *clothing*
16 And she put the skins of the kids of the goats upon his hands, and upon the smooth of his neck:
17 And she gave the savoury meat and the bread, which she had prepared, into the hand of her son Jacob.
18 And he came unto his father, and said, My father: and he said, Here *am* I; who *art* thou, my son?
19 And Jacob said unto his father, I *am* Esau thy firstborn; I have done according as thou badest me: arise, I pray thee, sit and eat of my venison, that thy soul may bless me.
20 And Isaac said unto his son, How *is* it that thou hast found *it* so quickly, my son? And he said, Because the LORD thy God brought *it* to me.
21 And Isaac said unto Jacob, Come near, I pray thee, that I may feel thee, my son, whether thou *be* my very son Esau or not.
22 And Jacob went near unto Isaac his father; and he felt him, and said, The voice *is* Jacob's voice, but the hands *are* the hands of Esau.
23 And he discerned him not, because his hands were hairy, as his brother Esau's hands: so he blessed him.   Gen. 27:16
24 And he said, *Art* thou my very son Esau? And he said, I *am*.
25 And he said, Bring *it* near to me, and I will eat of my son's venison, that my soul may bless thee. And he brought *it* near to him, and he did eat: and he brought him wine, and he drank.
26 And his father Isaac said unto him, Come near now, and kiss me, my son.
27 And he came near, and kissed him: and he smelled the smell of his raiment, and blessed him, and said, See, the smell of my son *is* as the smell of a field which the LORD hath blessed: Heb. 11:20

27:1–29 The Fruit of Deception

Jacob and Rebekah succeeded in their purpose, but they gained only trouble and sorrow by their deception. God had declared that Jacob should receive the birthright, and His word would have been fulfilled in His own time had they waited in faith for Him to work for them. But like many who now profess to be children of God, they were unwilling to leave the matter in His hands. *PP 180*

---

28 Therefore God give thee of the dew of heaven, and the fatness of the earth, and plenty of corn and wine: Deut. 33:13, 28
29 Let people serve thee, and nations bow down to thee: be lord over thy brethren, and let thy mother's sons bow down to thee:

cursed *be* every one that curseth thee, and blessed *be* he that blesseth thee.   Num. 24:9

Esau Brings Venison to His Father

30 And it came to pass, as soon as Isaac had made an end of blessing Jacob, and Jacob was yet scarce gone out from the presence of Isaac his father, that Esau his brother came in from his hunting.

31 And he also had made savoury meat, and brought it unto his father, and said unto his father, Let my father arise, and eat of his son's venison, that thy soul may bless me.

32 And Isaac his father said unto him, Who *art* thou? And he said, I *am* thy son, thy first-born Esau.

33 And Isaac trembled very exceedingly, and said, Who? where *is* he that hath taken venison, and brought *it* me, and I have eaten of all before thou camest, and have blessed him? yea, *and* he shall be blessed.   Gen. 28:3-4

34 And when Esau heard the words of his father, he cried with a great and exceeding bitter cry, and said unto his father, Bless me, *even* me also, O my father.   Heb. 12:17

35 And he said, Thy brother came with sub-tilty, and hath taken away thy blessing.

36 And he said, Is not he rightly named Jacob? for he hath supplanted me these two times: he took away my birthright; and, behold, now he hath taken away my blessing. And he said, Hast thou not reserved a blessing for me?   Gen. 25:26

37 And Isaac answered and said unto Esau, Behold, I have made him thy lord, and all his brethren have I given to him for servants; and with corn and wine have I sustained him: and what shall I do now unto thee, my son?   Gen. 27:28-29

38 And Esau said unto his father, Hast thou but one blessing, my father? bless me, *even* me also, O my father. And Esau lifted up his voice, and wept.   Heb. 12:17

39 And Isaac his father answered and said unto him, Behold, thy dwelling shall be the fatness of the earth, and of the dew of heaven from above;   Gen. 27:28; Heb. 11:20

40 And by thy sword shalt thou live, and shalt serve thy brother; and it shall come to pass when thou shalt have the dominion, that thou shalt break his yoke from off thy neck.   Gen. 25:23; 2 Sam. 8:14; 2 Kin. 8:20-22

Esau Threatens to Kill Jacob

41 And Esau hated Jacob because of the blessing wherewith his father blessed him: and Esau said in his heart, The days of mourning for my father are at hand; then will I slay my brother Jacob.   1 John 3:12-15

42 And these words of Esau her elder son were told to Rebekah: and she sent and called Jacob her younger son, and said unto him, Behold, thy brother Esau, as touching thee, doth comfort himself, *purposing* to kill thee.

43 Now therefore, my son, obey my voice; and arise, flee thou to Laban my brother to Haran;   Gen. 11:31

44 And tarry with him a few days, until thy brother's fury turn away;   Gen. 31:38

45 Until thy brother's anger turn away from thee, and he forget *that* which thou hast done to him: then I will send, and fetch thee from thence: why should I be deprived also of you both in one day?

46 And Rebekah said to Isaac, I am weary of my life because of the daughters of Heth: if Jacob take a wife of the daughters of Heth, such as these *which are* of the daughters of the land, what good shall my life do me?

Isaac Blesses Jacob and Sends Him to Padan-aram

28 And Isaac called Jacob, and blessed him, and charged him, and said unto him, Thou shalt not take a wife of the daughters of Canaan.   Gen. 24:3

2 Arise, go to Padan-aram, to the house of Bethuel thy mother's father; and take thee a wife from thence of the daughters of Laban thy mother's brother.   Gen. 25:20

3 And God Almighty bless thee, and make thee fruitful, and multiply thee, that thou mayest be a multitude of people;   Gen. 35:11

4 And give thee the blessing of Abraham, to thee, and to thy seed with thee; that thou mayest inherit the land wherein thou art a stranger, which God gave unto Abraham.

5 And Isaac sent away Jacob: and he went to Padan-aram unto Laban, son of Bethuel the Syrian, the brother of Rebekah, Jacob's and Esau's mother.

28:5 Jacob, Deeply Troubled

Threatened with death by the wrath of Esau, Jacob went out from his father's home a fugitive; but he carried with him the fa-ther's blessing; Isaac had renewed to him the covenant promise. . . . Yet it was with a deeply troubled heart that Jacob set out on his lonely journey. . . . He feared that he had lost forever the blessing that God had pur-posed to give him; and Satan was at hand to press temptations upon him. *PP 183*

Esau Marries Mahalath, Daughter of Ishmael

6 When Esau saw that Isaac had blessed Jacob, and sent him away to Padan-aram, to take him a wife from thence; and that as he blessed him he gave him a charge, saying,

Thou shalt not take a wife of the daughters of Canaan;

7 And that Jacob obeyed his father and his mother, and was gone to Padan-aram;

8 And Esau seeing that the daughters of Canaan pleased not Isaac his father;

9 Then went Esau unto Ishmael, and took unto the wives which he had Mahalath the daughter of Ishmael Abraham's son, the sister of Nebajoth, to be his wife.   Gen. 36:3

Jacob's Vision of a Ladder

10 And Jacob went out from Beer-sheba, and went toward Haran.   Gen. 11:31

11 And he lighted upon a certain place, and tarried there all night, because the sun was set; and he took of the stones of that place, and put *them for* his pillows, and lay down in that place to sleep.

12 And he dreamed, and behold a ladder set up on the earth, and the top of it reached to heaven: and behold the angels of God ascending and descending on it.   John 1:51

> **28:12 Christ the Ladder**
>
> Christ is the ladder that Jacob saw, the base resting on the earth, and the topmost round reaching to the gate of heaven, to the very threshold of glory. If that ladder had failed by a single step of reaching the earth, we should have been lost. But Christ reaches us where we are. He took our nature and overcame, that we through taking His nature might overcome. *DA 311, 312*

13 And, behold, the Lord stood above it, and said, I *am* the Lord God of Abraham thy father, and the God of Isaac: the land whereon thou liest, to thee will I give it, and to thy seed;   Gen. 12:7; 13:15; 26:24

14 And thy seed shall be as the dust of the earth, and thou shalt spread abroad to the west, and to the east, and to the north, and to the south: and in thee and in thy seed shall all the families of the earth be blessed.

15 And, behold, I *am* with thee, and will keep thee in all *places* whither thou goest, and will bring thee again into this land; for I will not leave thee, until I have done *that* which I have spoken to thee of.   Gen. 26:24

16 And Jacob awaked out of his sleep, and he said, Surely the Lord is in this place; and I knew *it* not.   Ex. 3:5

17 And he was afraid, and said, How dreadful *is* this place! this *is* none other but the house of God, and this *is* the gate of heaven.

18 And Jacob rose up early in the morning, and took the stone that he had put *for* his pillows, and set it up *for* a pillar, and poured oil upon the top of it.   Gen. 31:13, 45; 35:14

19 And he called the name of that place

Beth-el: but the name of that city *was called* Luz at the first.   Gen. 48:3

20 And Jacob vowed a vow, saying, If God will be with me, and will keep me in this way that I go, and will give me bread to eat, and Traiment to put on,   1 Tim. 6:8 ◆ *clothing*

21 So that I come again to my father's house in peace; then shall the Lord be my God:

22 And this stone, which I have set *for* a pillar, shall be God's house: and of all that thou shalt give me I will surely give the tenth unto thee.   Gen. 14:20

> **28:22 Responding to Love**
>
> Said Jacob, "I will surely give the tenth unto Thee." Shall we who enjoy the full light and privileges of the gospel be content to give less to God than was given by those who lived in the former, less favored dispensation? . . . But how small the estimate; how vain the endeavor to measure with mathematical rules, time, money, and love, against a love so immeasurable and a gift of such inconceivable worth. *PP 188*

Jacob Comes to the Well of Haran

29 Then Jacob went on his journey, and came into the land of the people of the east.   Num. 23:7; Judg. 6:3, 33

2 And he looked, and behold a well in the field, and, lo, there *were* three flocks of sheep lying by it; for out of that well they watered the flocks: and a great stone *was* upon the well's mouth.   Gen. 24:11

3 And thither were all the flocks gathered: and they rolled the stone from the well's mouth, and watered the sheep, and put the stone again upon the well's mouth in his place.

4 And Jacob said unto them, My brethren, whence *be* ye? And they said, Of Haran *are* we.   Gen. 28:10

5 And he said unto them, Know ye Laban the son of Nahor? And they said, We know him.   Gen. 24:24

6 And he said unto them, *Is* he well? And they said, *He is* well: and, behold, Rachel his daughter cometh with the sheep.

7 And he said, Lo, *it is* yet high day, neither *is it* time that the cattle should be gathered together: water ye the sheep, and go *and* feed *them*.

8 And they said, We cannot, until all the flocks be gathered together, and *till* they roll the stone from the well's mouth; then we water the sheep.

Jacob Meets Rachel by the Well

9 And while he yet spake with them, Rachel came with her father's sheep: for she kept them.

10 And it came to pass, when Jacob saw Rachel the daughter of Laban his mother's brother, and the sheep of Laban his mother's brother, that Jacob went near, and rolled the stone from the well's mouth, and watered the flock of Laban his mother's brother.
11 And Jacob kissed Rachel, and lifted up his voice, and wept.   Gen. 33:4; 43:30; 45:2
12 And Jacob told Rachel that he *was* her father's brother, and that he *was* Rebekah's son: and she ran and told her father.
13 And it came to pass, when Laban heard the tidings of Jacob his sister's son, that he ran to meet him, and embraced him, and kissed him, and brought him to his house. And he told Laban all these things. Gen. 24:29
14 And Laban said to him, Surely thou *art* my bone and my flesh. And he abode with him the space of a month.   2 Sam. 19:12-13
15 And Laban said unto Jacob, Because thou *art* my brother, shouldest thou therefore serve me for ᵀnought? tell me, what *shall* thy wages *be?*   nothing
16 And Laban had two daughters: the name of the elder *was* Leah, and the name of the younger *was* Rachel.
17 Leah *was* tender eyed; but Rachel was beautiful and well favoured.   Gen. 12:11
18 And Jacob loved Rachel; and said, I will serve thee seven years for Rachel thy younger daughter.   Gen. 31:41; Hos. 12:12
19 And Laban said, *It is* better that I give her to thee, than that I should give her to another man: abide with me.
20 And Jacob served seven years for Rachel; and they seemed unto him *but* a few days, for the love he had to her.   Hos. 12:12
21 And Jacob said unto Laban, Give *me* my wife, for my days are fulfilled, that I may go in unto her.   Judg. 15:1
22 And Laban gathered together all the men of the place, and made a feast.
23 And it came to pass in the evening, that he took Leah his daughter, and brought her to him; and he went in unto her.
24 And Laban gave unto his daughter Leah Zilpah his maid *for* an handmaid. Gen. 30:9-12
25 And it came to pass, that in the morning, behold, it *was* Leah: and he said to Laban, What *is* this thou hast done unto me? did not I serve with thee for Rachel? wherefore then hast thou ᵀbeguiled me?   deceived
26 And Laban said, It must not be so done in our country, to give the younger before the firstborn.
27 Fulfil her week, and we will give thee this also for the service which thou shalt serve with me yet seven other years.   Judg. 14:12
28 And Jacob did so, and fulfilled her week: and he gave him Rachel his daughter to wife also.

29 And Laban gave to Rachel his daughter Bilhah his handmaid to be her maid.
30 And he went in also unto Rachel, and he loved also Rachel more than Leah, and served with him yet seven other years.
31 And when the LORD saw that Leah *was* hated, he opened her womb: but Rachel *was* barren.   Deut. 21:15
32 And Leah conceived, and bare a son, and she called his name Reuben: for she said, Surely the LORD hath looked upon my affliction; now therefore my husband will love me.   Ex. 3:7; 4:31; Deut. 26:7
33 And she conceived again, and bare a son; and said, Because the LORD hath heard that I *was* hated, he hath therefore given me this *son* also: and she called his name Simeon.
34 And she conceived again, and bare a son; and said, Now this time will my husband be joined unto me, because I have born him three sons: therefore was his name called Levi.   Gen. 49:5-7
35 And she conceived again, and bare a son: and she said, Now will I praise the LORD: therefore she called his name Judah; and left bearing.   Matt. 1:2

Rachel Gives Bilhah to Jacob

30 And when Rachel saw that she bare Jacob no children, Rachel envied her sister; and said unto Jacob, Give me children, or else I die.   Gen. 29:31; 37:11
2 And Jacob's anger was kindled against Rachel: and he said, Am I in God's stead, who hath withheld from thee the fruit of the womb?   Gen. 16:2
3 And she said, Behold my maid Bilhah, go in unto her; and she shall bear upon my knees, that I may also have children by her.
4 And she gave him Bilhah her handmaid to wife: and Jacob went in unto her.
5 And Bilhah conceived, and bare Jacob a son.
6 And Rachel said, God hath judged me, and hath also heard my voice, and hath given me a son: therefore called she his name Dan.
7 And Bilhah Rachel's maid conceived again, and bare Jacob a second son.
8 And Rachel said, With great wrestlings have I wrestled with my sister, and I have prevailed: and she called his name Naphtali.
9 When Leah saw that she had left bearing, she took Zilpah her maid, and gave her Jacob to wife.   Gen. 30:4
10 And Zilpah Leah's maid bare Jacob a son.
11 And Leah said, A troop cometh: and she called his name Gad.   Gen. 49:19
12 And Zilpah Leah's maid bare Jacob a second son.
13 And Leah said, Happy am I, for the

daughters will call me blessed: and she called his name Asher.　　Prov. 31:28; Luke 1:48

Reuben Finds Mandrakes
14 And Reuben went in the days of wheat harvest, and found mandrakes in the field, and brought them unto his mother Leah. Then Rachel said to Leah, Give me, I pray thee, of thy son's mandrakes.　　Song 7:13
15 And she said unto her, *Is it* a small matter that thou hast taken my husband? and wouldest thou take away my son's mandrakes also? And Rachel said, Therefore he shall lie with thee to night for thy son's mandrakes.
16 And Jacob came out of the field in the evening, and Leah went out to meet him, and said, Thou must come in unto me; for surely I have hired thee with my son's mandrakes. And he lay with her that night.
17 And God hearkened unto Leah, and she conceived, and bare Jacob the fifth son.
18 And Leah said, God hath given me my hire, because I have given my maiden to my husband: and she called his name Issachar.
19 And Leah conceived again, and bare Jacob the sixth son.
20 And Leah said, God hath endued me *with* a good dowry; now will my husband dwell with me, because I have born him six sons: and she called his name Zebulun.
21 And afterwards she bare a daughter, and called her name Dinah.
22 And God remembered Rachel, and God hearkened to her, and opened her womb.
23 And she conceived, and bare a son; and said, God hath taken away my reproach:
24 And she called his name Joseph; and said, The LORD shall add to me another son.

Jacob Is Denied Permission to Depart
25 And it came to pass, when Rachel had born Joseph, that Jacob said unto Laban, Send me away, that I may go unto mine own place, and to my country.　　Gen. 24:54
26 Give *me* my wives and my children, for whom I have served thee, and let me go: for thou knowest my service which I have done thee.　　Gen. 29:30
27 And Laban said unto him, I pray thee, if I have found favour in thine eyes, *tarry: for* I have learned by experience that the LORD hath blessed me for thy sake.　　Gen. 26:24
28 And he said, Appoint me thy wages, and I will give *it*.　　Gen. 29:15
29 And he said unto him, Thou knowest how I have served thee, and how thy cattle was with me.　　Gen. 31:6, 38-40
30 For *it was* little which thou hadst before I *came*, and it is *now* increased unto a multitude; and the LORD hath blessed thee since

my coming: and now when shall I provide for mine own house also?　　1 Tim. 5:8
31 And he said, What shall I give thee? And Jacob said, Thou shalt not give me any thing: if thou wilt do this thing for me, I will again feed *and* keep thy flock:
32 I will pass through all thy flock to day, removing from thence all the speckled and spotted cattle, and all the brown cattle among the sheep, and the spotted and speckled among the goats: and *of such* shall be my hire.　　Gen. 31:8
33 So shall my righteousness answer for me in time to come, when it shall come for my hire before thy face: every one that *is* not speckled and spotted among the goats, and brown among the sheep, that shall be counted stolen with me.
34 And Laban said, Behold, I would it might be according to thy word.
35 And he removed that day the he goats that were ringstraked and spotted, and all the she goats that were speckled and spotted, *and* every one that had *some* white in it, and all the brown among the sheep, and gave *them* into the hand of his sons.
36 And he set three days' journey ᵀbetwixt himself and Jacob: and Jacob fed the rest of Laban's flocks.　　*between*

Jacob's Policy, Whereby He Becomes Rich
37 And Jacob took him rods of green poplar, and of the hazel and chesnut tree; and pilled white ᵀstrakes in them, and made the white appear which *was* in the rods.　　*stripes*
38 And he set the rods which he had ᵀpilled before the flocks in the gutters in the watering troughs when the flocks came to drink, that they should conceive when they came to drink.　　*stripped off the bark*
39 And the flocks conceived before the rods, and brought forth cattle ringstraked, speckled, and spotted.
40 And Jacob did separate the lambs, and set the faces of the flocks toward the ringstraked, and all the brown in the flock of Laban; and he put his own flocks by themselves, and put them not unto Laban's cattle.
41 And it came to pass, whensoever the stronger cattle did conceive, that Jacob laid the rods before the eyes of the cattle in the gutters, that they might conceive among the rods.
42 But when the cattle were feeble, he put *them* not in: so the feebler were Laban's, and the stronger Jacob's.
43 And the man increased exceedingly, and had much cattle, and maidservants, and menservants, and camels, and asses.

Jacob Leaves Laban Secretly

31 And he heard the words of Laban's sons, saying, Jacob hath taken away all that *was* our father's; and of *that* which *was* our father's hath he gotten all this glory.

2 And Jacob beheld the ᵀcountenance of Laban, and, behold, it *was* not toward him as before.   Gen. 4:5 ◆ *appearance*

3 And the LORD said unto Jacob, Return unto the land of thy fathers, and to thy kindred; and I will be with thee.   Gen. 28:15; 31:13

4 And Jacob sent and called Rachel and Leah to the field unto his flock,

5 And said unto them, I see your father's countenance, that it *is* not toward me as before; but the God of my father hath been with me.   Gen. 31:2-3

6 And ye know that with all my power I have served your father.   Gen. 30:29

7 And your father hath deceived me, and changed my wages ten times; but God suffered him not to hurt me.   Gen. 31:29

8 If he said thus, The speckled shall be thy wages; then all the cattle bare speckled: and if he said thus, The ringstraked shall be thy hire; then bare all the cattle ringstraked.

9 Thus God hath taken away the cattle of your father, and given *them* to me.

10 And it came to pass at the time that the cattle conceived, that I lifted up mine eyes, and saw in a dream, and, behold, the rams which leaped upon the cattle *were* ringstraked, speckled, and ᵀgrisled.   *spotted*

11 And the angel of God spake unto me in a dream, *saying,* Jacob: And I said, Here *am* I.

12 And he said, Lift up now thine eyes, and see, all the rams which leap upon the cattle *are* ringstraked, speckled, and grisled: for I have seen all that Laban doeth unto thee.

13 I *am* the God of Beth-el, where thou anointedst the pillar, *and* where thou vowedst a vow unto me: now arise, get thee out from this land, and return unto the land of thy kindred.   Gen. 28:12-22; 31:3; 32:9

14 And Rachel and Leah answered and said unto him, *Is there* yet any portion or inheritance for us in our father's house?

15 Are we not counted of him strangers? for he hath sold us, and hath quite devoured also our money.   Gen. 29:15-20

16 For all the riches which God hath taken from our father, that *is* ours, and our children's: now then, whatsoever God hath said unto thee, do.

17 Then Jacob rose up, and set his sons and his wives upon camels;

18 And he carried away all his cattle, and all his goods which he had gotten, the cattle of his getting, which he had gotten in Padanaram, for to go to Isaac his father in the land of Canaan.

31:13–18 A Sad Journey

Though Jacob had left Padan-aram in obedience to the divine direction, it was not without many misgivings that he retraced the road which he had trodden as a fugitive twenty years before. His sin in the deception of his father was ever before him. He knew that his long exile was the direct result of that sin, and he pondered over these things day and night, the reproaches of an accusing conscience making his journey very sad. *PP 195*

---

19 And Laban went to shear his sheep: and Rachel had stolen the images that *were* her father's.   Gen. 31:30; 1 Sam. 19:13; Hos. 3:4

20 And Jacob stole away unawares to Laban the Syrian, in that he told him not that he fled.

21 So he fled with all that he had; and he rose up, and passed over the river, and set his face *toward* the mount Gilead.   2 Kin. 12:17

22 And it was told Laban on the third day that Jacob was fled.

23 And he took his brethren with him, and pursued after him seven days' journey; and they overtook him in the mount Gilead.

24 And God came to Laban the Syrian in a dream by night, and said unto him, Take heed that thou speak not to Jacob either good or bad.   Gen. 20:3; 24:50; 31:29

25 Then Laban overtook Jacob. Now Jacob had pitched his tent in the mount: and Laban with his brethren pitched in the mount of Gilead.

26 And Laban said to Jacob, What hast thou done, that thou hast stolen away unawares to me, and carried away my daughters, as captives *taken* with the sword?   1 Sam. 30:2

27 Wherefore didst thou flee away secretly, and steal away from me; and didst not tell me, that I might have sent thee away with ᵀmirth, and with songs, with ᵀtabret, and with harp?   Ex. 15:20 ◆ *gladness* ◆ *tambourine*

28 And hast not suffered me to kiss my sons and my daughters? thou hast now done foolishly in *so* doing.   Gen. 31:55; Ruth 1:9, 14

29 It is in the power of my hand to do you hurt: but the God of your father spake unto me yesternight, saying, Take thou heed that thou speak not to Jacob either good or bad.

30 And now, *though* thou wouldest needs be gone, because thou sore longedst after thy father's house, *yet* wherefore hast thou stolen my gods?   Gen. 31:19; Judg. 18:24

31 And Jacob answered and said to Laban, Because I was afraid: for I said, Peradventure thou wouldest take by force thy daughters from me.

32 With whomsoever thou findest thy gods, let him not live: before our brethren discern thou what *is* thine with me, and take *it* to

thee. For Jacob knew not that Rachel had stolen them.

33 And Laban went into Jacob's tent, and into Leah's tent, and into the two maidservants' tents; but he found them not. Then went he out of Leah's tent, and entered into Rachel's tent.

34 Now Rachel had taken the images, and put them in the camel's furniture, and sat upon them. And Laban searched all the tent, but found them not.

35 And she said to her father, Let it not displease my lord that I cannot rise up before thee; for the custom of women is upon me. And he searched, but found not the images.

Jacob's Complaint against Laban

36 And Jacob was wroth, and chode with Laban: and Jacob answered and said to Laban, What is my trespass? what is my sin, that thou hast so hotly pursued after me?

37 Whereas thou hast searched all my stuff, what hast thou found of all thy household stuff? set it here before my brethren and thy brethren, that they may judge Tbetwixt us both.   *between*

38 This twenty years have I been with thee; thy ewes and thy she goats have not cast their young, and the rams of thy flock have I not eaten.

39 That which was torn of beasts I brought not unto thee; I bare the loss of it; of my hand didst thou require it, whether stolen by day, or stolen by night.

40 Thus I was; in the day the drought consumed me, and the frost by night; and my sleep departed from mine eyes.

41 Thus have I been twenty years in thy house; I served thee fourteen years for thy two daughters, and six years for thy cattle: and thou hast changed my wages ten times.

> **31:41 Jacob's Amazing Service**
>
> For twenty years Jacob remained in Mesopotamia, laboring in the service of Laban, who, disregarding the ties of kinship, was bent upon securing to himself all the benefits of their connection. Fourteen years of toil he demanded for his two daughters; and during the remaining period, Jacob's wages were ten times changed. Yet Jacob's service was diligent and faithful. *PP 190*

42 Except the God of my father, the God of Abraham, and the fear of Isaac, had been with me, surely thou hadst sent me away now empty. God hath seen mine affliction and the labour of my hands, and rebuked thee yesternight.   Gen. 29:32; 31:29, 53

Jacob and Laban Make a Covenant

43 And Laban answered and said unto Jacob, These daughters are my daughters, and these children are my children, and these cattle are my cattle, and all that thou seest is mine: and what can I do this day unto these my daughters, or unto their children which they have born?

44 Now therefore come thou, let us make a covenant, I and thou; and let it be for a witness between me and thee.

45 And Jacob took a stone, and set it up for a pillar.

46 And Jacob said unto his brethren, Gather stones; and they took stones, and made an heap: and they did eat there upon the heap.

47 And Laban called it Jegar-sahadutha: but Jacob called it Galeed.

48 And Laban said, This heap is a witness between me and thee this day. Therefore was the name of it called Galeed;   Josh. 24:27

49 And Mizpah; for he said, The LORD watch between me and thee, when we are absent one from another.   Judg. 11:29

50 If thou shalt afflict my daughters, or if thou shalt take other wives beside my daughters, no man is with us; see, God is witness betwixt me and thee.   Judg. 11:10; Jer. 29:23; 42:5

51 And Laban said to Jacob, Behold this heap, and behold this pillar, which I have cast betwixt me and thee;

52 This heap be witness, and this pillar be witness, that I will not pass over this heap to thee, and that thou shalt not pass over this heap and this pillar unto me, for harm.

53 The God of Abraham, and the God of Nahor, the God of their father, judge betwixt us. And Jacob sware by the fear of his father Isaac.   Gen. 16:5; 31:42

54 Then Jacob offered sacrifice upon the mount, and called his brethren to eat bread: and they did eat bread, and tarried all night in the mount.   Ex. 18:12

55 And early in the morning Laban rose up, and kissed his sons and his daughters, and blessed them: and Laban departed, and returned unto his place. Gen. 18:33; 30:25; 31:28

Jacob Calls the Place of His Vision Mahanaim

32 And Jacob went on his way, and the angels of God met him.   Ps. 91:11

2 And when Jacob saw them, he said, This is God's host: and he called the name of that place Mahanaim.   Josh. 5:14; 21:38; 2 Sam. 2:8

Jacob's Message to Esau

3 And Jacob sent messengers before him to Esau his brother unto the land of Seir, the country of Edom.   Gen. 25:30

4 And he commanded them, saying, Thus

shall ye speak unto my lord Esau; Thy servant Jacob saith thus, I have sojourned with Laban, and stayed there until now:

5 And I have oxen, and asses, flocks, and menservants, and womenservants: and I have sent to tell my lord, that I may find grace in thy sight. *Gen. 33:8, 15*

6 And the messengers returned to Jacob, saying, We came to thy brother Esau, and also he cometh to meet thee, and four hundred men with him. *Gen. 33:1*

7 Then Jacob was greatly afraid and distressed: and he divided the people that *was* with him, and the flocks, and herds, and the camels, into two bands; *Gen. 35:3*

8 And said, If Esau come to the one company, and ᵀsmite it, then the other company which is left shall escape. *strike*

Jacob Prays for Deliverance

9 And Jacob said, O God of my father Abraham, and God of my father Isaac, the LORD which saidst unto me, Return unto thy country, and to thy kindred, and I will deal well with thee: *Gen. 28:13; 31:13, 42*

10 I am not worthy of the least of all the mercies, and of all the truth, which thou hast shewed unto thy servant; for with my staff I passed over this Jordan; and now I am become two bands. *2 Sam. 7:18; Ps. 18:35*

11 Deliver me, I pray thee, from the hand of my brother, from the hand of Esau: for I fear him, lest he will come and smite me, *and* the mother with the children. *Ps. 59:1-2*

12 And thou saidst, I will surely do thee good, and make thy seed as the sand of the sea, which cannot be numbered for multitude. *Gen. 28:13-15*

Jacob Sends a Present to Esau

13 And he lodged there that same night; and took of that which came to his hand a present for Esau his brother; *Prov. 18:16*

14 Two hundred she goats, and twenty he goats, two hundred ewes, and twenty rams,

15 Thirty ᵀmilch camels with their colts, forty ᵀkine, and ten bulls, twenty she asses, and ten foals. *nursing ◆ cattle*

16 And he delivered *them* into the hand of his servants, every drove by themselves; and said unto his servants, Pass over before me, and put a space betwixt drove and drove.

17 And he commanded the foremost, saying, When Esau my brother meeteth thee, and asketh thee, saying, Whose *art* thou? and whither goest thou? and whose *are* these before thee?

18 Then thou shalt say, *They be* thy servant Jacob's; it *is* a present sent unto my lord Esau: and, behold, also he *is* behind us.

19 And so commanded he the second, and the third, and all that followed the droves, saying, On this manner shall ye speak unto Esau, when ye find him.

20 And say ye moreover, Behold, thy servant Jacob *is* behind us. For he said, I will appease him with the present that goeth before me, and afterward I will see his face; ᵀperadventure he will accept of me. *Job 42:8-9 ◆ maybe*

21 So went the present over before him: and himself lodged that night in the company.

22 And he rose up that night, and took his two wives, and his two womenservants, and his eleven sons, and passed over the ford Jabbok. *Deut. 2:37; 3:16; Josh. 12:2*

23 And he took them, and sent them over the brook, and sent over that he had.

Jacob's Name Is Changed to Israel

24 And Jacob was left alone; and there wrestled a man with him until the breaking of the day.

25 And when he saw that he prevailed not against him, he touched the hollow of his thigh; and the hollow of Jacob's thigh was out of joint, as he wrestled with him.

26 And he said, Let me go, for the day breaketh. And he said, I will not let thee go, except thou bless me. *Hos. 12:4*

27 And he said unto him, What *is* thy name? And he said, Jacob.

28 And he said, Thy name shall be called no more Jacob, but Israel: for as a prince hast thou power with God and with men, and hast prevailed. *Gen. 17:5; 35:10*

32:28 Jacob Becomes Israel

As an evidence that [Jacob] had been forgiven, his name was changed from one that was a reminder of his sin, to one that commemorated his victory. *PP 198*

29 And Jacob asked *him*, and said, Tell *me*, I pray thee, thy name. And he said, Wherefore *is* it *that* thou dost ask after my name? And he blessed him there.

30 And Jacob called the name of the place Peniel: for I have seen God face to face, and my life is preserved. *Ex. 24:10-11; Num. 12:8*

31 And as he passed over Penuel the sun rose upon him, and he ᵀhalted upon his thigh. *limped*

32 Therefore the children of Israel eat not *of* the ᵀsinew which shrank, which *is* upon the hollow of the thigh, unto this day: because he touched the hollow of Jacob's thigh in the sinew that shrank. *tissue connecting muscle to bone*

Jacob and Esau Meet

33 And Jacob lifted up his eyes, and looked, and, behold, Esau came, and with him four hundred men. And he divided

the children unto Leah, and unto Rachel, and unto the two handmaids.

33:1 The Peace of Reconciliation

Jacob had received the blessing for which his soul had longed. His sin as a supplanter and deceiver had been pardoned. The crisis in his life was past. Doubt, perplexity, and remorse had embittered his existence, but now all was changed; and sweet was the peace of reconciliation with God. Jacob no longer feared to meet his brother. God, who had forgiven his sin, could move the heart of Esau also to accept his humiliation and repentance. *PP 198*

---

2 And he put the handmaids and their children foremost, and Leah and her children after, and Rachel and Joseph hindermost.
3 And he passed over before them, and bowed himself to the ground seven times, until he came near to his brother.   Gen. 18:2
4 And Esau ran to meet him, and embraced him, and fell on his neck, and kissed him: and they wept.   Gen. 45:14-15
5 And he lifted up his eyes, and saw the women and the children; and said, Who *are* those with thee? And he said, The children which God hath graciously given thy servant.   Gen. 48:9; Ps. 127:3; Is. 8:18
6 Then the handmaidens came near, they and their children, and they bowed themselves.
7 And Leah also with her children came near, and bowed themselves: and after came Joseph near and Rachel, and they bowed themselves.
8 And he said, What *meanest* thou by all this drove which I met? And he said, *These are* to find grace in the sight of my lord.   Gen. 32:5

9 And Esau said, I have enough, my brother; keep that thou hast unto thyself.   Gen. 27:39
10 And Jacob said, Nay, I pray thee, if now I have found grace in thy sight, then receive my present at my hand: for therefore I have seen thy face, as though I had seen the face of God, and thou wast pleased with me.
11 Take, I pray thee, my blessing that is brought to thee; because God hath dealt graciously with me, and because I have enough. And he urged him, and he took *it*. 1 Sam. 25:27
12 And he said, Let us take our journey, and let us go, and I will go before thee.
13 And he said unto him, My lord knoweth that the children *are* tender, and the flocks and herds with young *are* with me: and if men should overdrive them one day, all the flock will die.
14 Let my lord, I pray thee, pass over before his servant: and I will lead on softly, according as the cattle that goeth before me and the children be able to endure, until I come unto my lord unto Seir.   Gen. 32:3
15 And Esau said, Let me now leave with thee *some* of the folk that *are* with me. And he said, What needeth it? let me find grace in the sight of my lord.   Gen. 47:25; Ruth 2:13
16 So Esau returned that day on his way unto Seir.
17 And Jacob journeyed to Succoth, and built him an house, and made booths for his cattle: therefore the name of the place is called Succoth.   Josh. 13:27; Judg. 8:5; Ps. 60:6
18 And Jacob came to Shalem, a city of Shechem, which *is* in the land of Canaan, when he came from Padan-aram; and pitched his tent before the city.   Judg. 9:1; Acts 7:16
19 And he bought a parcel of a field, where he had spread his tent, at the hand of the

---

Time of Jacob's Trouble

Genesis 32:24–30

In his night of anguish beside the Jabbok, when destruction seemed just before him, Jacob had been taught how vain is the help of man, how groundless is all trust in human power. He saw that his only help must come from Him against whom he had so grievously sinned. Helpless and unworthy, he pleaded God's promise of mercy to the repentant sinner. That promise was his assurance that God would pardon and accept him. Sooner might heaven and earth pass than that word could fail; and it was this that sustained him through that fearful conflict.

Jacob's experience during that night of wrestling and anguish represents the trial through which the people of God must pass just before Christ's second coming. . . .

Such will be the experience of God's people in their final struggle with the powers of evil. God will test their faith, their perseverance, their confidence in His power to deliver them. Satan will endeavor to terrify them with the thought that their cases are hopeless; that their sins have been too great to receive pardon. They will have a deep sense of their shortcomings, and as they review their lives their hopes will sink. But remembering the greatness of God's mercy, and their own sincere repentance, they will plead His promises made through Christ to helpless, repenting sinners. Their faith will not fail because their prayers are not immediately answered. They will lay hold of the strength of God, as Jacob laid hold of the Angel, and the language of their souls will be, "I will not let Thee go, except Thou bless me." *PP 198–202*

children of Hamor, Shechem's father, for an hundred pieces of money. Josh. 24:32; Acts 7:16
20 And he erected there an altar, and called it El-elohe-Israel.

Dinah Is Ravished by Shechem

34 And Dinah the daughter of Leah, which she bare unto Jacob, went out to see the daughters of the land. Gen. 30:21

34:1 On Satan's Ground

The one daughter [Dinah] of [Jacob's] household had been brought to shame and sorrow, two brothers were involved in the guilt of murder, a whole city had been given to ruin and slaughter, in retaliation for the lawless deed of one rash youth. The beginning that led to results so terrible was the act of Jacob's daughter, who "went out to see the daughters of the land," thus venturing into association with the ungodly. *PP 204*

2 And when Shechem the son of Hamor the Hivite, prince of the country, saw her, he took her, and lay with her, and defiled her.
3 And his soul ᵀclave unto Dinah the daughter of Jacob, and he loved the damsel, and spake kindly unto the damsel.   *clung*
4 And Shechem spake unto his father Hamor, saying, Get me this damsel to wife.
5 And Jacob heard that he had defiled Dinah his daughter: now his sons were with his cattle in the field: and Jacob held his peace until they were come.
6 And Hamor the father of Shechem went out unto Jacob to commune with him.
7 And the sons of Jacob came out of the field when they heard *it*: and the men were grieved, and they were very ᵀwroth, because he had ᵀwrought folly in Israel in lying with Jacob's daughter; which thing ought not to be done. Josh. 7:15; Judg. 20:6 ◆ *angered* ◆ *made*
8 And Hamor communed with them, saying, The soul of my son Shechem longeth for your daughter: I pray you give her him to wife.
9 And make ye marriages with us, *and* give your daughters unto us, and take our daughters unto you.
10 And ye shall dwell with us: and the land shall be before you; dwell and trade ye therein, and get you possessions therein.
11 And Shechem said unto her father and unto her brethren, Let me find grace in your eyes, and what ye shall say unto me I will give. Gen. 33:15
12 Ask me never so much dowry and gift, and I will give according as ye shall say unto me: but give me the damsel to wife.
13 And the sons of Jacob answered Shechem and Hamor his father deceitfully, and said, because he had defiled Dinah their sister:
14 And they said unto them, We cannot do this thing, to give our sister to one that is uncircumcised; for that *were* a reproach unto us:
15 But in this will we consent unto you: If ye will be as we *be*, that every male of you be circumcised;
16 Then will we give our daughters unto you, and we will take your daughters to us, and we will dwell with you, and we will become one people.
17 But if ye will not hearken unto us, to be circumcised; then will we take our daughter, and we will be gone.
18 And their words pleased Hamor, and Shechem Hamor's son.
19 And the young man deferred not to do the thing, because he had delight in Jacob's daughter: and he *was* more honourable than all the house of his father.   1 Chr. 4:9
20 And Hamor and Shechem his son came unto the gate of their city, and communed with the men of their city, saying, Ruth 4:1
21 These men *are* peaceable with us; therefore let them dwell in the land, and trade therein; for the land, behold, *it is* large enough for them; let us take their daughters to us for wives, and let us give them our daughters.
22 Only herein will the men consent unto us for to dwell with us, to be one people, if every male among us be circumcised, as they *are* circumcised.
23 *Shall* not their cattle and their substance and every beast of theirs *be* ours? only let us consent unto them, and they will dwell with us.
24 And unto Hamor and unto Shechem his son hearkened all that went out of the gate of his city; and every male was circumcised, all that went out of the gate of his city.

Jacob's Sons Kill the Men of Shechem

25 And it came to pass on the third day, when they were sore, that two of the sons of Jacob, Simeon and Levi, Dinah's brethren, took each man his sword, and came upon the city boldly, and slew all the males.
26 And they slew Hamor and Shechem his son with the edge of the sword, and took Dinah out of Shechem's house, and went out.
27 The sons of Jacob came upon the slain, and spoiled the city, because they had defiled their sister.
28 They took their sheep, and their oxen, and their asses, and that which *was* in the city, and that which *was* in the field,

29 And all their wealth, and all their little ones, and their wives took they captive, and spoiled even all that *was* in the house.

30 And Jacob said to Simeon and Levi, Ye have troubled me to make me to stink among the inhabitants of the land, among the Canaanites and the Perizzites: and I *being* few in number, they shall gather themselves together against me, and slay me; and I shall be destroyed, I and my house.   1 Sam. 13:4

31 And they said, Should he deal with our sister as with an harlot?

God Sends Jacob to Beth-el

35 And God said unto Jacob, Arise, go up to Beth-el, and dwell there: and make there an altar unto God, that appeared unto thee when thou fleddest from the face of Esau thy brother.

2 Then Jacob said unto his household, and to all that *were* with him, Put away the strange gods that *are* among you, and be clean, and change your garments: Gen. 18:19; Ex. 19:10

3 And let us arise, and go up to Beth-el; and I will make there an altar unto God, who answered me in the day of my distress, and was with me in the way which I went.

4 And they gave unto Jacob all the strange gods which *were* in their hand, and *all their* earrings which *were* in their ears; and Jacob hid them under the oak which *was* by Shechem.   Josh. 24:25-26

5 And they journeyed: and the terror of God was upon the cities that *were* round about them, and they did not pursue after the sons of Jacob.   Ex. 23:27

Jacob Builds an Altar to God at Beth-el

6 So Jacob came to Luz, which *is* in the land of Canaan, that *is*, Beth-el, he and all the people that *were* with him.   Gen. 28:19

7 And he built there an altar, and called the place El-beth-el: because there God appeared unto him, when he fled from the face of his brother.   Gen. 28:13

8 But Deborah Rebekah's nurse died, and she was buried beneath Beth-el under an oak: and the name of it was called Allonbachuth.

9 And God appeared unto Jacob again, when he came out of Padan-aram, and blessed him.

10 And God said unto him, Thy name *is* Jacob: thy name shall not be called any more Jacob, but Israel shall be thy name: and he called his name Israel.   Gen. 17:5, 15

11 And God said unto him, I *am* God Almighty: be fruitful and multiply; a nation and a company of nations shall be of thee, and kings shall come out of thy loins;

12 And the land which I gave Abraham and Isaac, to thee I will give it, and to thy seed after thee will I give the land.   Gen. 12:7; 26:3-4

13 And God went up from him in the place where he talked with him.   Gen. 17:22; 18:33

14 And Jacob set up a pillar in the place where he talked with him, *even* a pillar of stone: and he poured a drink offering thereon, and he poured oil thereon.

15 And Jacob called the name of the place where God spake with him, Beth-el.

Rachel Bears Benjamin and Dies

16 And they journeyed from Beth-el; and there was but a little way to come to Ephrath: and Rachel travailed, and she had hard labour.   Mic. 5:2

17 And it came to pass, when she was in hard labour, that the midwife said unto her, Fear not; thou shalt have this son also.

18 And it came to pass, as her soul was in departing, (for she died) that she called his name Ben-oni: but his father called him Benjamin.

19 And Rachel died, and was buried in the way to Ephrath, which *is* Beth-lehem. Mic. 5:2

20 And Jacob set a pillar upon her grave: that *is* the pillar of Rachel's grave unto this day.   1 Sam. 10:2

21 And Israel journeyed, and spread his tent beyond the tower of Edar.   Mic. 4:8

22 And it came to pass, when Israel dwelt in that land, that Reuben went and lay with Bilhah his father's concubine: and Israel heard *it*. Now the sons of Jacob were twelve:

23 The sons of Leah; Reuben, Jacob's firstborn, and Simeon, and Levi, and Judah, and Issachar, and Zebulun: Gen. 29:32-35

24 The sons of Rachel; Joseph, and Benjamin: Gen. 30:22-24

25 And the sons of Bilhah, Rachel's handmaid; Dan, and Naphtali:

26 And the sons of Zilpah, Leah's handmaid; Gad, and Asher: these *are* the sons of Jacob, which were born to him in Padan-aram.

27 And Jacob came unto Isaac his father unto Mamre, unto the city of Arbah, which *is* Hebron, where Abraham and Isaac sojourned.   Gen. 13:18; 18:1; 23:19

28 And the days of Isaac were an hundred and ᵀfourscore years.   Gen. 25:7 ◆ *eighty*

29 And Isaac gave up the ghost, and died, and was gathered unto his people, *being* old and full of days: and his sons Esau and Jacob buried him.   Gen. 15:15; 49:31, 33

Esau's Three Wives

36 Now these *are* the generations of Esau, who *is* Edom.

2 Esau took his wives of the daughters of Canaan; Adah the daughter of Elon the Hittite, and Aholibamah the daughter of Anah the daughter of Zibeon the Hivite;   Gen. 36:25

3 And Bashemath Ishmael's daughter, sister of Nebajoth.   Gen. 28:9

4 And Adah bare to Esau Eliphaz; and Bashemath bare Reuel;   1 Chr. 1:35

5 And Aholibamah bare Jeush, and Jaalam, and Korah: these *are* the sons of Esau, which were born unto him in the land of Canaan.

6 And Esau took his wives, and his sons, and his daughters, and all the persons of his house, and his cattle, and all his beasts, and all his substance, which he had got in the land of Canaan; and went into the country from the face of his brother Jacob.

7 For their riches were more than that they might dwell together; and the land wherein they were strangers could not bear them because of their cattle.   Gen. 13:6; 17:8; 28:4

8 Thus dwelt Esau in mount Seir: Esau *is* Edom.   Gen. 32:3

Esau's Sons

9 And these *are* the generations of Esau the father of the Edomites in mount Seir:

10 These *are* the names of Esau's sons; Eliphaz the son of Adah the wife of Esau, Reuel the son of Bashemath the wife of Esau.

11 And the sons of Eliphaz were Teman, Omar, Zepho, and Gatam, and Kenaz.

12 And Timna was concubine to Eliphaz Esau's son; and she bare to Eliphaz Amalek: these *were* the sons of Adah Esau's wife.

13 And these *are* the sons of Reuel; Nahath, and Zerah, Shammah, and Mizzah: these were the sons of Bashemath Esau's wife.

14 And these were the sons of Aholibamah, the daughter of Anah the daughter of Zibeon, Esau's wife: and she bare to Esau Jeush, and Jaalam, and Korah.   Gen. 36:2

15 These *were* dukes of the sons of Esau: the sons of Eliphaz the firstborn *son* of Esau;

duke Teman, duke Omar, duke Zepho, duke Kenaz,   Gen. 36:11-12

16 Duke Korah, ᵀduke Gatam, *and* duke Amalek: these *are* the dukes *that came* of Eliphaz in the land of Edom; these *were* the sons of Adah.   *chief*

17 And these *are* the sons of Reuel Esau's son; duke Nahath, duke Zerah, duke Shammah, duke Mizzah: these *are* the dukes *that came* of Reuel in the land of Edom; these *are* the sons of Bashemath Esau's wife.

18 And these *are* the sons of Aholibamah Esau's wife; duke Jeush, duke Jaalam, duke Korah: these *were* the dukes *that came* of Aholibamah the daughter of Anah, Esau's wife.

19 These *are* the sons of Esau, who *is* Edom, and these *are* their dukes.

The Children of Seir

20 These *are* the sons of Seir the Horite, who inhabited the land; Lotan, and Shobal, and Zibeon, and Anah,   Gen. 14:6; Deut. 2:12, 22

21 And Dishon, and Ezer, and Dishan: these *are* the dukes of the Horites, the children of Seir in the land of Edom.

22 And the children of Lotan were Hori and Hemam; and Lotan's sister *was* Timna.

23 And the children of Shobal *were* these; Alvan, and Manahath, and Ebal, Shepho, and Onam.   1 Chr. 1:40

24 And these *are* the children of Zibeon; both Ajah, and Anah: this *was that* Anah that found the mules in the wilderness, as he fed the asses of Zibeon his father.

25 And the children of Anah *were* these; Dishon, and Aholibamah the daughter of Anah.   Gen. 36:2

26 And these *are* the children of Dishon; Hemdan, and Eshban, and Ithran, and Cheran.   1 Chr. 1:41

God's Election

Genesis 36:6, 7

Esau and Jacob had alike been instructed in the knowledge of God, and both were free to walk in His commandments and to receive His favor; but they had not both chosen to do this. The two brothers had walked in different ways, and their paths would continue to diverge more and more widely.

There was no arbitrary choice on the part of God by which Esau was shut out from the blessings of salvation. The gifts of His grace through Christ are free to all. There is no election but one's own by which any may perish. God has set forth in His word the conditions upon which every soul will be elected to eternal life—obedience to His commandments, through faith in Christ. God has elected a character in harmony with His law, and anyone who shall reach the standard of His requirement will have an entrance into the kingdom of glory. Christ Himself said, "He that believeth on the Son hath everlasting life: and he that believeth not the Son shall not see life" (John 3:36). "Not everyone that saith unto Me, Lord, Lord, shall enter into the kingdom of heaven; but he that *doeth the will of* My Father which is in heaven" (Matthew 7:21). And in the Revelation He declares, "Blessed are they that do His commandments, that they may have right to the tree of life, and may enter in through the gates into the city" (Revelation 22:14). As regards man's final salvation, this is the only election brought to view in the word of God. *PP 207, 208*

27 The children of Ezer *are* these; Bilhan, and Zaavan, and Akan.

28 The children of Dishan *are* these; Uz, and Aran.

29 These *are* the dukes *that came* of the Horites; duke Lotan, duke Shobal, duke Zibeon, duke Anah,   Gen. 36:20

30 Duke Dishon, duke Ezer, duke Dishan: these *are* the dukes *that came* of Hori, among their dukes in the land of Seir.

The Kings of Edom

31 And these *are* the kings that reigned in the land of Edom, before there reigned any king over the children of Israel.   Gen. 17:6

32 And Bela the son of Beor reigned in Edom: and the name of his city *was* Dinhabah.

33 And Bela died, and Jobab the son of Zerah of Bozrah reigned in his stead.

34 And Jobab died, and Husham of the land of Temani reigned in his stead.

35 And Husham died, and Hadad the son of Bedad, who smote Midian in the field of Moab, reigned in his stead: and the name of his city *was* Avith.

36 And Hadad died, and Samlah of Masrekah reigned in his stead.

37 And Samlah died, and Saul of Rehoboth *by* the river reigned in his stead.

38 And Saul died, and Baal-hanan the son of Achbor reigned in his stead.

39 And Baal-hanan the son of Achbor died, and Hadar reigned in his stead: and the name of his city *was* Pau; and his wife's name *was* Mehetabel, the daughter of Matred, the daughter of Mezahab.

40 And these *are* the names of the dukes *that came* of Esau, according to their families, after their places, by their names; duke Timnah, duke Alvah, duke Jetheth,

41 Duke Aholibamah, duke Elah, duke Pinon,

42 Duke Kenaz, duke Teman, duke Mibzar,

43 Duke Magdiel, duke Iram: these *be* the dukes of Edom, according to their habitations in the land of their possession: he *is* Esau the father of the Edomites.

Jacob in Canaan

37 And Jacob dwelt in the land wherein his father was a stranger, in the land of Canaan.   Gen. 17:8

2 These *are* the generations of Jacob. Joseph, *being* seventeen years old, was feeding the flock with his brethren; and the lad *was* with the sons of Bilhah, and with the sons of Zilpah, his father's wives: and Joseph brought unto his father their evil report. Gen. 35:25-26

3 Now Israel loved Joseph more than all his children, because he *was* the son of his old age: and he made him a coat of *many* colours.

4 And when his brethren saw that their father loved him more than all his brethren, they hated him, and could not speak peaceably unto him.   Gen. 27:41

37:3, 4 Parental Favoritism

[Joseph's] mother being dead, his affections clung the more closely to the father, and Jacob's heart was bound up in this child of his old age. He "loved Joseph more than all his children."

But even this affection was to become a cause of trouble and sorrow. Jacob unwisely manifested his preference for Joseph, and this excited the jealousy of his other sons. *PP 209*

Joseph's Two Dreams

5 And Joseph dreamed a dream, and he told *it* his brethren: and they hated him yet the more.   Gen. 28:12

6 And he said unto them, Hear, I pray you, this dream which I have dreamed:

7 For, behold, we *were* binding sheaves in the field, and, lo, my ᵀsheaf arose, and also stood upright; and, behold, your sheaves stood round about, and made obeisance to my sheaf.   Gen. 42:6, 9; 43:26 ◆ *bundle of cut grain*

8 And his brethren said to him, Shalt thou indeed reign over us? or shalt thou indeed have dominion over us? And they hated him yet the more for his dreams, and for his words.

9 And he dreamed yet another dream, and told it his brethren, and said, Behold, I have dreamed a dream more; and, behold, the sun and the moon and the eleven stars made ᵀobeisance to me.   *homage*

10 And he told *it* to his father, and to his brethren: and his father rebuked him, and said unto him, What *is* this dream that thou hast dreamed? Shall I and thy mother and thy brethren indeed come to bow down ourselves to thee to the earth?   Gen. 27:29

11 And his brethren envied him; but his father observed the saying. Luke 2:19, 51; Acts 7:9

12 And his brethren went to feed their father's flock in Shechem.   Gen. 33:18

13 And Israel said unto Joseph, Do not thy brethren feed *the flock* in Shechem? come, and I will send thee unto them. And he said to him, Here *am* I.

14 And he said to him, Go, I pray thee, see whether it be well with thy brethren, and well with the flocks; and bring me word again. So he sent him out of the ᵀvale of Hebron, and he came to Shechem.   *valley*

15 And a certain man found him, and,

behold, *he was* wandering in the field: and the man asked him, saying, What seekest thou?

16 And he said, I seek my brethren: tell me, I pray thee, where they feed *their flocks*.

17 And the man said, They are departed hence; for I heard them say, Let us go to Dothan. And Joseph went after his brethren, and found them in Dothan. 2 Kin. 6:13

18 And when they saw him afar off, even before he came near unto them, they conspired against him to slay him. Ps. 37:12

19 And they said one to another, Behold, this dreamer cometh.

20 Come now therefore, and let us slay him, and cast him into some pit, and we will say, Some evil beast hath devoured him: and we shall see what will become of his dreams.

21 And Reuben heard *it*, and he delivered him out of their hands; and said, Let us not kill him. Gen. 42:22

22 And Reuben said unto them, Shed no blood, *but* cast him into this pit that *is* in the wilderness, and lay no hand upon him; that he might rid him out of their hands, to deliver him to his father again.

23 And it came to pass, when Joseph was come unto his brethren, that they stript Joseph out of his coat, *his* coat of *many* colours that *was* on him; Gen. 37:3

24 And they took him, and cast him into a pit: and the pit *was* empty, *there was* no water in it. Jer. 38:6

25 And they sat down to eat bread: and they lifted up their eyes and looked, and, behold, a company of Ishmeelites came from Gilead with their camels bearing spicery and balm and myrrh, going to carry *it* down to Egypt.

26 And Judah said unto his brethren, What profit *is it* if we slay our brother, and conceal his blood? Gen. 4:10; 37:20

27 Come, and let us sell him to the Ishmeelites, and let not our hand be upon him; for he *is* our brother *and* our flesh. And his brethren were content. Gen. 42:21

37:28 Joseph's Accelerated Learning

But, in the providence of God, even this experience was to be a blessing to [Joseph]. He had learned in a few hours that which years might not otherwise have taught him, . . .

He would serve the Lord with undivided heart; he would meet the trials of his lot with fortitude and perform every duty with fidelity. One day's experience had been the turning point in Joseph's life. Its terrible calamity had transformed him from a petted child to a man, thoughtful, courageous, and self-possessed. *PP 213, 214*

---

28 Then there passed by Midianites merchantmen; and they drew and lifted up Joseph out of the pit, and sold Joseph to the Ishmeelites for twenty *pieces* of silver: and they brought Joseph into Egypt. Acts 7:9

29 And Reuben returned unto the pit; and, behold, Joseph *was* not in the pit; and he ᵀrent his clothes. Gen. 37:34 ◆ *tore apart*

30 And he returned unto his brethren, and said, The child *is* not; and I, whither shall I go? Gen. 42:13, 32; Jer. 31:15

Jacob Deceived, Mourns for Joseph

31 And they took Joseph's coat, and killed a kid of the goats, and dipped the coat in the blood; Gen. 37:3, 23

32 And they sent the coat of *many* colours, and they brought *it* to their father; and said, This have we found: know now whether it *be* thy son's coat or no.

33 And he knew it, and said, *It is* my son's coat; an evil beast hath devoured him; Joseph is without doubt rent in pieces.

34 And Jacob rent his clothes, and put sackcloth upon his ᵀloins, and mourned for his son many days. Gen. 37:29 ◆ *waist*

35 And all his sons and all his daughters rose up to comfort him; but he refused to be comforted; and he said, For I will go down into the grave unto my son mourning. Thus his father wept for him. Gen. 42:38

36 And the Midianites sold him into Egypt unto Potiphar, an officer of Pharaoh's, *and* captain of the guard. Gen. 37:28

Judah Begets Er, Onan, and Shelah

38 And it came to pass at that time, that Judah went down from his brethren, and turned in to a certain Adullamite, whose name *was* Hirah. 1 Sam. 22:1

2 And Judah saw there a daughter of a certain Canaanite, whose name *was* Shuah; and he took her, and went in unto her. 1 Chr. 2:3

3 And she conceived, and bare a son; and he called his name Er. Gen. 46:12; Num. 26:19

4 And she conceived again, and bare a son; and she called his name Onan. Gen. 46:12

5 And she yet again conceived, and bare a son; and called his name Shelah: and he was at Chezib, when she bare him. Num. 26:20

6 And Judah took a wife for Er his firstborn, whose name *was* Tamar.

7 And Er, Judah's firstborn, was wicked in the sight of the LORD; and the LORD slew him. Gen. 46:12; Num. 26:19; 1 Chr. 2:3

8 And Judah said unto Onan, Go in unto thy brother's wife, and marry her, and raise up seed to thy brother. Deut. 25:5-10

9 And Onan knew that the seed should not be his; and it came to pass, when he went in unto his brother's wife, that he spilled *it* on

the ground, lest that he should give seed to his brother. Deut. 25:6

10 And the thing which he did displeased the LORD: wherefore he slew him also.

11 Then said Judah to Tamar his daughter in law, Remain a widow at thy father's house, till Shelah my son be grown: for he said, Lest ᵀperadventure he die also, as his brethren *did*. And Tamar went and dwelt in her father's house. Lev. 22:13 ◆ *maybe*

12 And in process of time the daughter of Shuah Judah's wife died; and Judah was comforted, and went up unto his sheepshearers to Timnath, he and his friend Hirah the Adullamite. Josh. 15:10

13 And it was told Tamar, saying, Behold thy father in law goeth up to Timnath to shear his sheep.

14 And she put her widow's garments off from her, and covered her with a ᵀvail, and wrapped herself, and sat in an open place, which *is* by the way to Timnath; for she saw that Shelah was grown, and she was not given unto him to wife. Gen. 38:26 ◆ *veil*

15 When Judah saw her, he thought her *to be* an harlot; because she had covered her face.

16 And he turned unto her by the way, and said, Go to, I pray thee, let me come in unto thee; (for he knew not that she *was* his daughter in law.) And she said, What wilt thou give me, that thou mayest come in unto me?

17 And he said, I will send *thee* a kid from the flock. And she said, Wilt thou give *me* a pledge, till thou send *it*? Gen. 38:20

18 And he said, What pledge shall I give thee? And she said, Thy signet, and thy bracelets, and thy staff that *is* in thine hand. And he gave *it* her, and came in unto her, and she conceived by him. Gen. 38:25-26

19 And she arose, and went away, and laid by her vail from her, and put on the garments of her widowhood. Gen. 38:14

20 And Judah sent the kid by the hand of his friend the Adullamite, to receive *his* pledge from the woman's hand: but he found her not.

21 Then he asked the men of that place, saying, Where *is* the harlot, that *was* openly by the way side? And they said, There was no harlot in this *place*.

22 And he returned to Judah, and said, I cannot find her; and also the men of the place said, *that* there was no harlot in this *place*.

23 And Judah said, Let her take *it* to her, lest we be shamed: behold, I sent this kid, and thou hast not found her.

24 And it came to pass about three months after, that it was told Judah, saying, Tamar thy daughter in law hath played the harlot; and also, behold, she *is* with child by ᵀwhoredom. And Judah said, Bring her forth, and let her be burnt. *prostitution*

25 When she *was* brought forth, she sent to her father in law, saying, By the man, whose these *are, am* I with child: and she said, Discern, I pray thee, whose *are* these, the ᵀsignet, and bracelets, and staff. *identifying seal*

26 And Judah acknowledged *them*, and said, She hath been more righteous than I; because that I gave her not to Shelah my son. And he knew her again no more.

27 And it came to pass in the time of her travail, that, behold, twins *were* in her womb.

28 And it came to pass, when she travailed, that *the one* put out *his* hand: and the midwife took and bound upon his hand a scarlet thread, saying, This came out first.

29 And it came to pass, as he drew back his hand, that, behold, his brother came out:

Bible Records Faults, Not Just Virtues

Genesis 38

Inspiration faithfully records the faults of good men, those who were distinguished by the favor of God; indeed, their faults are more fully presented than their virtues. This has been a subject of wonder to many, and has given the infidel occasion to scoff at the Bible. But it is one of the strongest evidences of the truth of Scripture, that facts are not glossed over, nor the sins of its chief characters suppressed. The minds of men are so subject to prejudice that it is not possible for human histories to be absolutely impartial. Had the Bible been written by uninspired persons, it would no doubt have presented the character of its honored men in a more flattering light. But as it is, we have a correct record of their experiences.

Men whom God favored, and to whom He entrusted great responsibilities, were sometimes overcome by temptation and committed sin, even as we at the present day strive, waver, and frequently fall into error. Their lives, with all their faults and follies, are open before us, both for our encouragement and warning. If they had been represented as without fault, we, with our sinful nature, might despair at our own mistakes and failures. But seeing where others struggled through discouragements like our own, where they fell under temptation as we have done, and yet took heart again and conquered through the grace of God, we are encouraged in our striving after righteousness. *PP 238*

and she said, How hast thou broken forth? *this* breach *be* upon thee: therefore his name was called Pharez. Num. 26:20; 1 Chr. 2:4

30 And afterward came out his brother, that had the scarlet thread upon his hand: and his name was called Zarah.

Joseph Is Promoted in Potiphar's House

39 And Joseph was brought down to Egypt; and Potiphar, an officer of Pharaoh, captain of the guard, an Egyptian, bought him of the hands of the Ishmeelites, which had brought him down thither.

2 And the LORD was with Joseph, and he was a prosperous man; and he was in the house of his master the Egyptian. Gen. 21:22

3 And his master saw that the LORD *was* with him, and that the LORD made all that he did to prosper in his hand. Ps. 1:3

4 And Joseph found grace in his sight, and he served him: and he made him overseer over his house, and all *that* he had he put into his hand. Gen. 19:19

5 And it came to pass from the time *that* he had made him overseer in his house, and over all that he had, that the LORD blessed the Egyptian's house for Joseph's sake; and the blessing of the LORD was upon all that he had in the house, and in the field.

6 And he left all that he had in Joseph's hand; and he knew not ought he had, save the bread which he did eat. And Joseph was *a* goodly *person,* and well favoured.

Joseph Resists the Temptation of Potiphar's Wife

7 And it came to pass after these things, that his master's wife cast her eyes upon Joseph; and she said, Lie with me. 2 Sam. 13:11

8 But he refused, and said unto his master's wife, Behold, my master ᵀwotteth not what *is* with me in the house, and he hath committed all that he hath to my hand; *knows*

9 *There is* none greater in this house than I; neither hath he kept back any thing from me but thee, because thou *art* his wife: how then can I do this great wickedness, and sin against God? Gen. 20:6; 42:18; 2 Sam. 12:13

39:7–10 We Cannot Hide From God

Let the young ever remember that wherever they are, and whatever they do, they are in the presence of God. No part of our conduct escapes observation. We cannot hide our ways from the Most High. . . . The very motives of his heart are open to divine inspection. Every act, every word, every thought, is as distinctly marked as though there were only one person in the whole world, and the attention of heaven were centered upon him. *PP 217, 218*

---

10 And it came to pass, as she spake to Joseph day by day, that he hearkened not unto her, to lie by her, *or* to be with her.

11 And it came to pass about this time, that *Joseph* went into the house to do his business; and *there was* none of the men of the house there within.

12 And she caught him by his garment, saying, Lie with me: and he left his garment in her hand, and fled, and got him out.

Joseph Is Falsely Accused

13 And it came to pass, when she saw that he had left his garment in her hand, and was fled forth,

14 That she called unto the men of her house, and spake unto them, saying, See, he hath brought in an Hebrew unto us to mock us; he came in unto me to lie with me, and I cried with a loud voice:

15 And it came to pass, when he heard that I lifted up my voice and cried, that he left his garment with me, and fled, and got him out.

16 And she laid up his garment by her, until his lord came home.

17 And she spake unto him according to these words, saying, The Hebrew servant, which thou hast brought unto us, came in unto me to mock me: Ex. 23:1

18 And it came to pass, as I lifted up my voice and cried, that he left his garment with me, and fled out.

Joseph in Prison

19 And it came to pass, when his master heard the words of his wife, which she spake unto him, saying, After this manner did thy servant to me; that his wrath was kindled.

20 And Joseph's master took him, and put him into the prison, a place where the king's prisoners *were* bound: and he was there in the prison. Gen. 40:15

21 But the LORD was with Joseph, and shewed him mercy, and gave him favour in the sight of the keeper of the prison. Ex. 11:3

22 And the keeper of the prison committed to Joseph's hand all the prisoners *were* in the prison; and whatsoever they did there, he was the doer *of it.* Gen. 39:4

23 The keeper of the prison looked not to any thing *that was* under his hand; because the LORD was with him, and *that* which he did, the LORD made *it* to prosper. Gen. 39:2-3

The Butler and the Baker of Pharaoh Are with Joseph in Prison

40 And it came to pass after these things, *that* the butler of the king of Egypt and *his* baker had offended their lord the king of Egypt. Gen. 40:13

2 And Pharaoh was ᵀwroth against two *of*

his officers, against the chief of the butlers, and against the chief of the bakers.   *angered*

3 And he put them in ward in the house of the captain of the guard, into the prison, the place where Joseph *was* bound.

4 And the captain of the guard charged Joseph with them, and he served them: and they continued a season in ward.

Joseph Interprets the Prisoners' Dreams

5 And they dreamed a dream both of them, each man his dream in one night, each man according to the interpretation of his dream, the butler and the baker of the king of Egypt, which *were* bound in the prison.   Gen. 41:11

6 And Joseph came in unto them in the morning, and looked upon them, and, behold, they *were* sad.

7 And he asked Pharaoh's officers that *were* with him in the ward of his lord's house, saying, Wherefore look ye *so* sadly to day?

8 And they said unto him, We have dreamed a dream, and *there is* no interpreter of it. And Joseph said unto them, *Do* not interpretations *belong* to God? tell me *them*, I pray you.

9 And the chief butler told his dream to Joseph, and said to him, In my dream, behold, a vine *was* before me;

10 And in the vine *were* three branches: and it *was* as though it budded, *and* her blossoms shot forth; and the clusters thereof brought forth ripe grapes:

11 And Pharaoh's cup *was* in my hand: and I took the grapes, and pressed them into Pharaoh's cup, and I gave the cup into Pharaoh's hand.

12 And Joseph said unto him, This *is* the interpretation of it: The three branches *are* three days: Gen. 41:12

13 Yet within three days shall Pharaoh lift up thine head, and restore thee unto thy place: and thou shalt deliver Pharaoh's cup into his hand, after the former manner when thou wast his butler.   2 Kin. 25:27

14 But think on me when it shall be well with thee, and shew kindness, I pray thee, unto me, and make mention of me unto Pharaoh, and bring me out of this house:

15 For indeed I was stolen away out of the land of the Hebrews: and here also have I done nothing that they should put me into the dungeon.   Gen. 39:20

16 When the chief baker saw that the interpretation was good, he said unto Joseph, I also *was* in my dream, and, behold, *I had* three white baskets on my head:

17 And in the uppermost basket *there was* of all manner of ᵀbakemeats for Pharaoh; and the birds did eat them out of the basket upon my head.   *things made by a baker*

18 And Joseph answered and said, This *is* the interpretation thereof: The three baskets *are* three days: Gen. 40:12

19 Yet within three days shall Pharaoh lift up thy head from off thee, and shall hang thee on a tree; and the birds shall eat thy flesh from off thee.   Gen. 40:22

The Dreams Come to Pass according to Joseph's Interpretation

20 And it came to pass the third day, *which was* Pharaoh's birthday, that he made a feast unto all his servants: and he lifted up the head of the chief butler and of the chief baker among his servants.   Gen. 40:13; Matt. 14:6

21 And he restored the chief butler unto his butlership again; and he gave the cup into Pharaoh's hand: Gen. 40:13; Neh. 2:1

22 But he hanged the chief baker: as Joseph had interpreted to them.   Gen. 40:19

23 Yet did not the chief butler remember Joseph, but forgat him.   Job 19:14

Joseph's Character and Integrity

Genesis 39:20–23

But Joseph's real character shines out, even in the darkness of the dungeon. He held fast his faith and patience; his years of faithful service had been most cruelly repaid, yet this did not render him morose or distrustful. He had the peace that comes from conscious innocence, and he trusted his case with God. He did not brood upon his own wrongs, but forgot his sorrow in trying to lighten the sorrows of others. He found a work to do, even in the prison. God was preparing him in the school of affliction for greater usefulness, and he did not refuse the needful discipline. In the prison, witnessing the results of oppression and tyranny and the effects of crime, he learned lessons of justice, sympathy, and mercy, that prepared him to exercise power with wisdom and compassion.

Joseph gradually gained the confidence of the keeper of the prison, and was finally entrusted with the charge of all the prisoners. It was the part he acted in the prison—the integrity of his daily life and his sympathy for those who were in trouble and distress—that opened the way for his future prosperity and honor. Every ray of light that we shed upon others is reflected upon ourselves. Every kind and sympathizing word spoken to the sorrowful, every act to relieve the oppressed, and every gift to the needy, if prompted by a right motive, will result in blessings to the giver. *PP 218*

Pharaoh's Dreams

41 And it came to pass at the end of two full years, that Pharaoh dreamed: and, behold, he stood by the river.   Gen. 20:3
2 And, behold, there came up out of the river seven well favoured ᵀkine and fatfleshed; and they fed in a meadow.   cattle
3 And, behold, seven other kine came up after them out of the river, ill favoured and leanfleshed; and stood by the *other* kine upon the brink of the river.
4 And the ill favoured and leanfleshed kine did eat up the seven well favoured and fat kine. So Pharaoh awoke.
5 And he slept and dreamed the second time: and, behold, seven ears of corn came up upon one stalk, rank and good.
6 And, behold, seven thin ears and blasted with the east wind sprung up after them.
7 And the seven thin ears devoured the seven rank and full ears. And Pharaoh awoke, and, behold, *it was* a dream.
8 And it came to pass in the morning that his spirit was troubled; and he sent and called for all the magicians of Egypt, and all the wise men thereof: and Pharaoh told them his dream; but *there was* none that could interpret them unto Pharaoh.   Dan. 1:20

Joseph Interprets Pharaoh's Dreams

9 Then spake the chief butler unto Pharaoh, saying, I do remember my faults this day:
10 Pharaoh was wroth with his servants, and put me in ward in the captain of the guard's house, *both* me and the chief baker:
11 And we dreamed a dream in one night, I and he; we dreamed each man according to the interpretation of his dream.
12 And *there was* there with us a young man, an Hebrew, servant to the captain of the guard; and we told him, and he interpreted to us our dreams; to each man according to his dream he did interpret.   Gen. 37:36
13 And it came to pass, as he interpreted to us, so it was; me he restored unto mine office, and him he hanged.
14 Then Pharaoh sent and called Joseph, and they brought him hastily out of the dungeon: and he shaved *himself,* and changed his ᵀraiment, and came in unto Pharaoh.   clothing
15 And Pharaoh said unto Joseph, I have dreamed a dream, and *there is* none that can interpret it: and I have heard say of thee, *that* thou canst understand a dream to interpret it.   Dan. 5:16
16 And Joseph answered Pharaoh, saying, *It is* not in me: God shall give Pharaoh an answer of peace.   Gen. 40:8; Dan. 2:47; Acts 3:12
17 And Pharaoh said unto Joseph, In my dream, behold, I stood upon the bank of the river:

18 And, behold, there came up out of the river seven kine, fatfleshed and well favoured; and they fed in a meadow:
19 And, behold, seven other kine came up after them, poor and very ill favoured and leanfleshed, such as I never saw in all the land of Egypt for ᵀbadness: inferiority
20 And the lean and the ill favoured kine did eat up the first seven fat kine:
21 And when they had eaten them up, it could not be known that they had eaten them; but they *were* still ill favoured, as at the beginning. So I awoke.
22 And I saw in my dream, and, behold, seven ears came up in one stalk, full and good:
23 And, behold, seven ears, withered, thin, *and* blasted with the east wind, sprung up after them:
24 And the thin ears devoured the seven good ears: and I told *this* unto the magicians; but *there was* none that could declare *it* to me.   Gen. 41:8
25 And Joseph said unto Pharaoh, The dream of Pharaoh *is* one: God hath shewed Pharaoh what he *is* about to do.   Rev. 4:1
26 The seven good kine *are* seven years; and the seven good ears *are* seven years: the dream *is* one.   Gen. 41:2
27 And the seven thin and ill favoured kine that came up after them *are* seven years; and the seven empty ears blasted with the east wind shall be seven years of famine. 2 Kin. 8:1
28 This *is* the thing which I have spoken unto Pharaoh: What God *is* about to do he sheweth unto Pharaoh.   Gen. 41:25
29 Behold, there come seven years of great plenty throughout all the land of Egypt:
30 And there shall arise after them seven years of famine; and all the plenty shall be forgotten in the land of Egypt; and the famine shall consume the land;   Ps. 105:16
31 And the plenty shall not be known in the land by reason of that famine following; for it *shall be* very grievous.
32 And for that the dream *was* doubled unto Pharaoh twice; *it is* because the thing *is* established by God, and God will shortly bring it to pass.   Num. 23:19

Joseph Gives Pharaoh Counsel

33 Now therefore let Pharaoh look out a man discreet and wise, and set him over the land of Egypt.

34 Let Pharaoh do *this*, and let him appoint officers over the land, and take up the fifth part of the land of Egypt in the seven plenteous years.

35 And let them gather all the food of those good years that come, and lay up corn under the hand of Pharaoh, and let them keep food in the cities.

36 And that food shall be for store to the land against the seven years of famine, which shall be in the land of Egypt; that the land perish not through the famine.

37 And the thing was good in the eyes of Pharaoh, and in the eyes of all his servants.

38 And Pharaoh said unto his servants, Can we find *such a one* as this *is*, a man in whom the Spirit of God *is*?   Dan. 4:18; 5:11, 14

39 And Pharaoh said unto Joseph, Forasmuch as God hath shewed thee all this, *there is* none so discreet and wise as thou *art*:

40 Thou shalt be over my house, and according unto thy word shall all my people be ruled: only in the throne will I be greater than thou.   Ps. 105:21-22

41 And Pharaoh said unto Joseph, See, I have set thee over all the land of Egypt.

42 And Pharaoh took off his ring from his hand, and put it upon Joseph's hand, and arrayed him in ᵀvestures of fine linen, and put a gold chain about his neck;   *clothing*

43 And he made him to ride in the second chariot which he had; and they cried before him, Bow the knee: and he made him *ruler* over all the land of Egypt.   Gen. 42:6; 45:8, 26

44 And Pharaoh said unto Joseph, I *am* Pharaoh, and without thee shall no man lift up his hand or foot in all the land of Egypt.

45 And Pharaoh called Joseph's name Zaphnath-paaneah; and he gave him to wife Asenath the daughter of Poti-pherah priest of On. And Joseph went out over *all* the land of Egypt.   Gen. 46:20

46 And Joseph *was* thirty years old when he stood before Pharaoh king of Egypt. And Joseph went out from the presence of Pharaoh, and went throughout all the land of Egypt.   Gen. 37:2

47 And in the seven plenteous years the earth brought forth by handfuls.

48 And he gathered up all the food of the seven years, which were in the land of Egypt, and laid up the food in the cities: the food of the field, which *was* round about every city, laid he up in the same.

49 And Joseph gathered corn as the sand of the sea, very much, until he left numbering; for *it was* without number.   Gen. 22:17

50 And unto Joseph were born two sons before the years of famine came, which Asenath the daughter of Poti-pherah priest of On bare unto him.   Gen. 46:20; 48:5

51 And Joseph called the name of the firstborn Manasseh: For God, *said he*, hath made me forget all my toil, and all my father's house.

52 And the name of the second called he Ephraim: For God hath caused me to be fruitful in the land of my affliction.

53 And the seven years of plenteousness, that was in the land of Egypt, were ended.

54 And the seven years of ᵀdearth began to come, according as Joseph had said: and the dearth was in all lands; but in all the land of Egypt there was bread.   Acts 7:11 ♦ *scarcity*

Little Things and Character

Genesis 41:38–41

How was Joseph enabled to make such a record of firmness of character, uprightness, and wisdom?—In his early years he had consulted duty rather than inclination; and the integrity, the simple trust, the noble nature, of the youth bore fruit in the deeds of the man. A pure and simple life had favored the vigorous development of both physical and intellectual powers. . . . Faithful attention to duty in every station, from the lowliest to the most exalted, had been training every power for its highest service. . . . "The fear of the Lord, that is wisdom; and to depart from evil is understanding" (Job 28:28).

There are few who realize the influence of the little things of life upon the development of character. Nothing with which we have to do is really small. The varied circumstances that we meet day by day are designed to test our faithfulness and to qualify us for greater trusts. . . . By faithfulness in that which is least they acquire strength to be faithful in greater matters.

An upright character is of greater worth than the gold of Ophir. Without it none can rise to an honorable eminence. But character is not inherited. It cannot be bought. Moral excellence and fine mental qualities are not the result of accident. The most precious gifts are of no value unless they are improved. The formation of a noble character is the work of a lifetime and must be the result of diligent and persevering effort. God gives opportunities; success depends upon the use made of them. *PP 222, 223*

55 And when all the land of Egypt was famished, the people cried to Pharaoh for bread: and Pharaoh said unto all the Egyptians, Go unto Joseph; what he saith to you, do.

56 And the famine was over all the face of the earth: And Joseph opened all the storehouses, and sold unto the Egyptians; and the famine waxed sore in the land of Egypt.

57 And all countries came into Egypt to Joseph for to buy *corn*; because that the famine was *so* sore in all lands.   Gen. 41:54

Jacob Sends His Ten Sons to Buy Corn in Egypt

42 Now when Jacob saw that there was corn in Egypt, Jacob said unto his sons, Why do ye look one upon another?

2 And he said, Behold, I have heard that there is corn in Egypt: get you down thither, and buy for us from thence; that we may live, and not die.   Gen. 43:8

3 And Joseph's ten brethren went down to buy corn in Egypt.

4 But Benjamin, Joseph's brother, Jacob sent not with his brethren; for he said, Lest ᵀperadventure mischief befall him.   *maybe*

5 And the sons of Israel came to buy *corn* among those that came: for the famine was in the land of Canaan.   Gen. 12:10

6 And Joseph *was* the governor over the land, *and he* *it was* that sold to all the people of the land: and Joseph's brethren came, and bowed down themselves before him *with* their faces to the earth.

7 And Joseph saw his brethren, and he knew them, but made himself strange unto them, and spake roughly unto them; and he said unto them, Whence come ye? And they said, From the land of Canaan to buy food.

8 And Joseph knew his brethren, but they knew not him.

9 And Joseph remembered the dreams which he dreamed of them, and said unto them, Ye *are* spies; to see the nakedness of the land ye are come.   Gen. 37:5-9

10 And they said unto him, Nay, my lord, but to buy food are thy servants come.

11 We *are* all one man's sons; we *are* true *men*, thy servants are no spies.   Gen. 42:19

12 And he said unto them, Nay, but to see the nakedness of the land ye are come.

13 And they said, Thy servants *are* twelve brethren, the sons of one man in the land of Canaan; and, behold, the youngest *is* this day with our father, and one *is* not.

14 And Joseph said unto them, That *is it* that I spake unto you, saying, Ye *are* spies:

15 Hereby ye shall be proved: By the life of Pharaoh ye shall not go forth hence, except your youngest brother come ᵀhither.   *here*

16 Send one of you, and let him fetch your brother, and ye shall be kept in prison, that your words may be proved, whether *there be any* truth in you: or else by the life of Pharaoh surely ye *are* spies.

17 And he put them all together into ᵀward three days.   Gen. 40:4 ◆ *prison or guard*

42:17 Sorrow in Prison

The three days in the Egyptian prison were days of bitter sorrow as [Joseph's] brothers reflected upon their past sins. ᵖᵖ 225

18 And Joseph said unto them the third day, This do, and live; *for* I fear God: Lev. 25:43

19 If ye *be* true *men*, let one of your brethren be bound in the house of your prison: go ye, carry corn for the famine of your houses:

20 But bring your youngest brother unto me; so shall your words be verified, and ye shall not die. And they did so.   Gen. 42:34

The Sons Have Remorse for Joseph

21 And they said one to another, We *are* verily guilty concerning our brother, in that we saw the anguish of his soul, when he besought us, and we would not hear; therefore is this distress come upon us.

22 And Reuben answered them, saying, Spake I not unto you, saying, Do not sin against the child; and ye would not hear? therefore, behold, also his blood is required.

23 And they knew not that Joseph understood *them*; for he spake unto them by an interpreter.

24 And he turned himself about from them, and wept; and returned to them again, and communed with them, and took from them Simeon, and bound him before their eyes.

25 Then Joseph commanded to fill their sacks with corn, and to restore every man's money into his sack, and to give them provision for the way: and thus did he unto them.

26 And they ᵀladed their asses with the corn, and departed thence.   *loaded*

27 And as one of them opened his sack to give his ass ᵀprovender in the inn, he espied his money; for, behold, it *was* in his sack's mouth.   Ex. 4:24 ◆ *food for livestock*

28 And he said unto his brethren, My money is restored; and, lo, *it is* even in my sack: and their heart failed *them*, and they were afraid, saying one to another, What *is* this *that* God hath done unto us?

29 And they came unto Jacob their father unto the land of Canaan, and told him all that befell unto them; saying,

30 The man, *who is* the lord of the land, spake roughly to us, and took us for spies of the country.   Gen. 42:7

31 And we said unto him, We *are* true *men*; we are no spies:

32 We *be* twelve brethren, sons of our father; one *is* not, and the youngest *is* this day with our father in the land of Canaan.
33 And the man, the lord of the country, said unto us, Hereby shall I know that ye *are* true *men*; leave one of your brethren *here* with me, and take *food for* the famine of your households, and be gone: Gen. 42:15, 19-20
34 And bring your youngest brother unto me: then shall I know that ye *are* no spies, but *that* ye *are* true *men: so* will I deliver you your brother, and ye shall ᵀtraffick in the land. Gen. 34:10, 21 ◆ *trade*
35 And it came to pass as they emptied their sacks, that, behold, every man's bundle of money *was* in his sack: and when *both* they and their father saw the bundles of money, they were afraid. Gen. 43:21
36 And Jacob their father said unto them, Me have ye bereaved *of my children*: Joseph *is* not, and Simeon *is* not, and ye will take Benjamin *away*: all these things are against me. Gen. 43:14
37 And Reuben spake unto his father, saying, Slay my two sons, if I bring him not to thee: deliver him into my hand, and I will bring him to thee again. Gen. 46:9
38 And he said, My son shall not go down with you; for his brother is dead, and he is left alone: if mischief befall him by the way in the which ye go, then shall ye bring down my gray hairs with sorrow to the grave.

Jacob Is Persuaded to Send Benjamin

43 And the famine *was* sore in the land.
2 And it came to pass, when they had eaten up the corn which they had brought out of Egypt, their father said unto them, Go again, buy us a little food.
3 And Judah spake unto him, saying, The man did solemnly protest unto us, saying, Ye shall not see my face, except your brother *be* with you. Gen. 43:5; 44:23
4 If thou wilt send our brother with us, we will go down and buy thee food:
5 But if thou wilt not send *him*, we will not go down: for the man said unto us, Ye shall not see my face, except your brother *be* with you.
6 And Israel said, Wherefore dealt ye *so* ill with me, *as* to tell the man whether ye had yet a brother?
7 And they said, The man asked us ᵀstraitly of our state, and of our kindred, saying, *Is* your father yet alive? have ye *another* brother? and we told him according to the tenor of these words: could we certainly know that he would say, Bring your brother down? Gen. 43:3 ◆ *with strictness*
8 And Judah said unto Israel his father, Send the lad with me, and we will arise and go;

that we may live, and not die, both we, and thou, *and* also our little ones. Gen. 42:2
9 I will be surety for him; of my hand shalt thou require him: if I bring him not unto thee, and set him before thee, then let me bear the blame for ever: Gen. 42:37; Philem. 18-19
10 For except we had lingered, surely now we had returned this second time.
11 And their father Israel said unto them, If *it must be* so now, do this; take of the best fruits in the land in your vessels, and carry down the man a present, a little ᵀbalm, and a little honey, spices, and myrrh, nuts, and almonds: Gen. 37:25; Prov. 18:16; Jer. 8:22 ◆ *medicine*
12 And take double money in your hand; and the money that was brought again in the mouth of your sacks, carry *it* again in your hand; ᵀperadventure it *was* an oversight: *maybe*
13 Take also your brother, and arise, go again unto the man:
14 And God Almighty give you mercy before the man, that he may send away your other brother, and Benjamin. If I be bereaved *of my children*, I am bereaved. Neh. 1:11; Esth. 4:16

Joseph Entertains His Brothers

15 And the men took that present, and they took double money in their hand, and Benjamin; and rose up, and went down to Egypt, and stood before Joseph.
16 And when Joseph saw Benjamin with them, he said to the ruler of his house, Bring *these* men home, and slay, and make ready; for *these* men shall dine with me at noon.
17 And the man did as Joseph bade; and the man brought the men into Joseph's house.
18 And the men were afraid, because they were brought into Joseph's house; and they said, Because of the money that was returned in our sacks at the first time are we brought in; that he may seek occasion against us, and fall upon us, and take us for bondmen, and our asses. Gen. 42:35
19 And they came near to the steward of Joseph's house, and they communed with him at the door of the house,
20 And said, O sir, we came indeed down at the first time to buy food: Gen. 42:3
21 And it came to pass, when we came to the inn, that we opened our sacks, and, behold, *every* man's money *was* in the mouth of his sack, our money in full weight: and we have brought it again in our hand. Gen. 43:12
22 And other money have we brought down in our hands to buy food: we cannot tell who put our money in our sacks.
23 And he said, Peace *be* to you, fear not: your God, and the God of your father, hath given you treasure in your sacks: I had your

money. And he brought Simeon out unto them. Gen. 42:24

24 And the man brought the men into Joseph's house, and gave *them* water, and they washed their feet; and he gave their asses ᵀprovender. Gen. 18:4; 19:2 ◆ *food for livestock*

25 And they made ready the present against Joseph came at noon: for they heard that they should eat bread there. Gen. 43:11

26 And when Joseph came home, they brought him the present which *was* in their hand into the house, and bowed themselves to him to the earth. Gen. 37:7-10

27 And he asked them of *their* welfare, and said, Is your father well, the old man of whom ye spake? *Is* he yet alive? Gen. 42:11

28 And they answered, Thy servant our father *is* in good health, he *is* yet alive. And they bowed down their heads, and made ᵀobeisance. Gen. 37:7 ◆ *homage*

29 And he lifted up his eyes, and saw his brother Benjamin, his mother's son, and said, *Is* this your younger brother, of whom ye spake unto me? And he said, God be gracious unto thee, my son. Gen. 42:13

30 And Joseph made haste; for his bowels did yearn upon his brother: and he sought *where* to weep; and he entered into *his* chamber, and wept there. 1 Kin. 3:26; Jer. 31:20

31 And he washed his face, and went out, and refrained himself, and said, Set on bread. Gen. 45:1

32 And they set on for him by himself, and for them by themselves, and for the Egyptians, which did eat with him, by themselves: because the Egyptians might not eat bread with the Hebrews; for that *is* an abomination unto the Egyptians. Gen. 46:34; Ex. 8:26

33 And they sat before him, the firstborn according to his birthright, and the youngest according to his youth: and the men marvelled one at another.

34 And he took *and sent* messes unto them from before him: but Benjamin's mess was five times so much as any of theirs. And they drank, and were merry with him.

43:34 Joseph Tests His Brothers

Joseph "sent messes unto them from before him;" but Benjamin's was five times as much as any of [his brothers']. By this token of favor to Benjamin [Joseph] hoped to ascertain if the youngest brother was regarded with the envy and hatred that had been manifested toward himself. *PP 228*

Joseph's Policy to Delay His Brothers

44 And he commanded the steward of his house, saying, Fill the men's sacks *with* food, as much as they can carry, and put every man's money in his sack's mouth. Gen. 42:25; 43:16

2 And put my cup, the silver cup, in the sack's mouth of the youngest, and his corn money. And he did according to the word that Joseph had spoken.

3 As soon as the morning was light, the men were sent away, they and their asses.

4 *And* when they were gone out of the city, *and* not *yet* far off, Joseph said unto his steward, Up, follow after the men; and when thou dost overtake them, say unto them, Wherefore have ye rewarded evil for good?

5 *Is* not this *it* in which my lord drinketh, and whereby indeed he ᵀdivineth? ye have done evil in so doing. Lev. 19:26 ◆ *reads the future*

6 And he overtook them, and he spake unto them these same words.

7 And they said unto him, Wherefore saith my lord these words? God forbid that thy servants should do according to this thing:

8 Behold, the money, which we found in our sacks' mouths, we brought again unto thee out of the land of Canaan: how then should we steal out of thy lord's house silver or gold?

9 With whomsoever of thy servants it be found, both let him die, and we also will be my lord's bondmen. Gen. 31:32

10 And he said, Now also *let* it *be* according unto your words: he with whom it is found shall be my servant; and ye shall be blameless.

11 Then they speedily took down every man his sack to the ground, and opened every man his sack.

12 And he searched, *and* began at the eldest, and left at the youngest: and the cup was found in Benjamin's sack.

13 Then they rent their clothes, and laded every man his ass, and returned to the city.

14 And Judah and his brethren came to Joseph's house; for he *was* yet there: and they fell before him on the ground.

15 And Joseph said unto them, What deed *is* this that ye have done? ᵀwot ye not that such a man as I can certainly divine? *know*

16 And Judah said, What shall we say unto my lord? what shall we speak? or how shall we clear ourselves? God hath found out the iniquity of thy servants: behold, we *are* my lord's servants, both we, and *he* also with whom the cup is found. Num. 32:23; Dan. 9:7

17 And he said, God forbid that I should do so: *but* the man in whose hand the cup is found, he shall be my servant; and as for you, get you up in peace unto your father.

18 Then Judah came near unto him, and said, Oh my lord, let thy servant, I pray thee, speak a word in my lord's ears, and let

not thine anger burn against thy servant: for thou *art* even as Pharaoh.   Gen. 18:30; Ex. 32:22

19 My lord asked his servants, saying, Have ye a father, or a brother?   Gen. 43:7

20 And we said unto my lord, We have a father, an old man, and a child of his old age, a little one; and his brother is dead, and he alone is left of his mother, and his father loveth him.   Gen. 37:3; 42:38

21 And thou saidst unto thy servants, Bring him down unto me, that I may set mine eyes upon him.   Gen. 42:15, 20

22 And we said unto my lord, The lad cannot leave his father: for *if* he should leave his father, *his father* would die.

23 And thou saidst unto thy servants, Except your youngest brother come down with you, ye shall see my face no more.

24 And it came to pass when we came up unto thy servant my father, we told him the words of my lord.

25 And our father said, Go again, *and* buy us a little food.   Gen. 43:2

26 And we said, We cannot go down: if our youngest brother be with us, then will we go down: for we may not see the man's face, except our youngest brother *be* with us.

27 And thy servant my father said unto us, Ye know that my wife bare me two *sons*:

28 And the one went out from me, and I said, Surely he is torn in pieces; and I saw him not since: Gen. 37:33

29 And if ye take this also from me, and mischief befall him, ye shall bring down my gray hairs with sorrow to the grave.   Gen. 42:36, 38

30 Now therefore when I come to thy servant my father, and the lad *be* not with us; seeing that his life is bound up in the lad's life;   1 Sam. 18:1

31 It shall come to pass, when he seeth that the lad *is* not *with us*, that he will die: and thy servants shall bring down the gray hairs of thy servant our father with sorrow to the grave.   Gen. 37:35; 44:29

32 For thy servant became surety for the lad unto my father, saying, If I bring him not unto thee, then I shall bear the blame to my father for ever.

33 Now therefore, I pray thee, let thy servant abide instead of the lad a bondman to my lord; and let the lad go up with his brethren.

34 For how shall I go up to my father, and the lad *be* not with me? lest peradventure I see the evil that shall come on my father.

Joseph Makes Himself Known

45 Then Joseph could not refrain himself before all them that stood by him; and he cried, Cause every man to go out from me. And there stood no man with

him, while Joseph made himself known unto his brethren.

2 And he wept aloud: and the Egyptians and the house of Pharaoh heard.

3 And Joseph said unto his brethren, I *am* Joseph; doth my father yet live? And his brethren could not answer him; for they were troubled at his presence.   Acts 7:13

45:3 Joseph Reveals Himself

Joseph was satisfied. He had seen in his brothers the fruits of true repentance. Upon hearing Judah's noble offer he gave orders that all but these men should withdraw; then, weeping aloud, he cried, "I am Joseph; doth my father yet live?" *PP 230*

4 And Joseph said unto his brethren, Come near to me, I pray you. And they came near. And he said, I *am* Joseph your brother, whom ye sold into Egypt.   Gen. 37:28

5 Now therefore be not grieved, nor angry with yourselves, that ye sold me hither: for God did send me before you to preserve life.

6 For these two years *hath* the famine *been* in the land: and yet *there are* five years, in the which *there shall* neither *be* ᵀearing nor harvest.   Ex. 34:21 ◆ *plowing*

7 And God sent me before you to preserve you a posterity in the earth, and to save your lives by a great deliverance.

8 So now *it was* not you *that* sent me hither, but God: and he hath made me a father to Pharaoh, and lord of all his house, and a ruler throughout all the land of Egypt.

9 Haste ye, and go up to my father, and say unto him, Thus saith thy son Joseph, God hath made me lord of all Egypt: come down unto me, tarry not:

10 And thou shalt dwell in the land of Goshen, and thou shalt be near unto me, thou, and thy children, and thy children's children, and thy flocks, and thy herds, and all that thou hast: Ex. 8:22

11 And there will I nourish thee; for yet *there are* five years of famine; lest thou, and thy household, and all that thou hast, come to poverty.   Gen. 47:12

12 And, behold, your eyes see, and the eyes of my brother Benjamin, that *it is* my mouth that speaketh unto you.   Gen. 42:23

13 And ye shall tell my father of all my glory in Egypt, and of all that ye have seen; and ye shall haste and bring down my father ᵀhither.   Acts 7:14 ◆ *here*

14 And he fell upon his brother Benjamin's neck, and wept; and Benjamin wept upon his neck.

15 Moreover he kissed all his brethren, and wept upon them: and after that his brethren talked with him.   Luke 15:20

Pharaoh Is Pleased

16 And the fame thereof was heard in Pharaoh's house, saying, Joseph's brethren are come: and it pleased Pharaoh well, and his servants.

17 And Pharaoh said unto Joseph, Say unto thy brethren, This do ye; ᵀlade your beasts, and go, get you unto the land of Canaan; *load*

18 And take your father and your households, and come unto me: and I will give you the good of the land of Egypt, and ye shall eat the fat of the land.   Gen. 27:28

19 Now thou art commanded, this do ye; take you wagons out of the land of Egypt for your little ones, and for your wives, and bring your father, and come.   Gen. 45:27; 46:5

20 Also regard not your stuff; for the good of all the land of Egypt *is* yours.

21 And the children of Israel did so: and Joseph gave them wagons, according to the commandment of Pharaoh, and gave them provision for the way.   Gen. 45:19

22 To all of them he gave each man changes of ᵀraiment; but to Benjamin he gave three hundred *pieces* of silver, and five changes of raiment.   Gen. 43:34; 2 Kin. 5:5, 22-23 ◆ *clothing*

23 And to his father he sent after this *manner*; ten asses laden with the good things of Egypt, and ten she asses laden with corn and bread and meat for his father by the way.

24 So he sent his brethren away, and they departed: and he said unto them, See that ye fall not out by the way.   Gen. 42:21-22

Jacob Learns that Joseph Is Alive

25 And they went up out of Egypt, and came into the land of Canaan unto Jacob their father,

26 And told him, saying, Joseph *is* yet alive, and he *is* governor over all the land of Egypt. And Jacob's heart fainted, for he believed them not.   Gen. 37:35

45:26–28 Confession—and Forgiveness

Another act of humiliation remained for [Joseph's] ten brothers. They now confessed to their father the deceit and cruelty that for so many years had embittered his life and theirs. Jacob had not suspected them of so base a sin, but he saw that all had been overruled for good, and he forgave and blessed his erring children. *PP 232*

---

27 And they told him all the words of Joseph, which he had said unto them: and when he saw the wagons which Joseph had sent to carry him, the spirit of Jacob their father revived: Gen. 45:19

28 And Israel said, *It is* enough; Joseph my son *is* yet alive: I will go and see him before I die.

Jacob Is Comforted by God at Beersheba

46 And Israel took his journey with all that he had, and came to Beer-sheba, and offered sacrifices unto the God of his father Isaac.   Gen. 21:33; 28:10, 13

2 And God spake unto Israel in the visions of the night, and said, Jacob, Jacob. And he said, Here *am* I.   Gen. 15:1; 22:1; Job 33:14-15

3 And he said, I *am* God, the God of thy father: fear not to go down into Egypt; for I will there make of thee a great nation:

4 I will go down with thee into Egypt; and I will also surely bring thee up *again*: and Joseph shall put his hand upon thine eyes.

Jacob Journeys to Egypt

5 And Jacob rose up from Beer-sheba: and the sons of Israel carried Jacob their father, and their little ones, and their wives, in the wagons which Pharaoh had sent to carry him.   Gen. 45:19

6 And they took their cattle, and their goods, which they had gotten in the land of Canaan, and came into Egypt, Jacob, and all his seed with him: Josh. 24:4; Ps. 105:23; Is. 52:4

7 His sons, and his sons' sons with him, his daughters, and his sons' daughters, and all his seed brought he with him into Egypt.

8 And these *are* the names of the children of Israel, which came into Egypt, Jacob and his sons: Reuben, Jacob's firstborn.   Ex. 1:1-5

9 And the sons of Reuben; Hanoch, and Phallu, and Hezron, and Carmi.

10 And the sons of Simeon; Jemuel, and Jamin, and Ohad, and Jachin, and Zohar, and Shaul the son of a Canaanitish woman.

11 And the sons of Levi; Gershon, Kohath, and Merari.   Gen. 29:34

12 And the sons of Judah; Er, and Onan, and Shelah, and Pharez, and Zerah: but Er and Onan died in the land of Canaan. And the sons of Pharez were Hezron and Hamul.

13 And the sons of Issachar; Tola, and Phuvah, and Job, and Shimron.

14 And the sons of Zebulun; Sered, and Elon, and Jahleel.

15 These *be* the sons of Leah, which she bare unto Jacob in Padan-aram, with his daughter Dinah: all the souls of his sons and his daughters *were* thirty and three.   Gen. 29:32-35

16 And the sons of Gad; Ziphion, and Haggi, Shuni, and Ezbon, Eri, and Arodi, and Areli.

17 And the sons of Asher; Jimnah, and Ishuah, and Isui, and Beriah, and Serah their sister: and the sons of Beriah; Heber, and Malchiel.   Gen. 30:13

18 These *are* the sons of Zilpah, whom Laban gave to Leah his daughter, and these she bare unto Jacob, *even* sixteen souls.

19 The sons of Rachel Jacob's wife; Joseph, and Benjamin. Gen. 44:27
20 And unto Joseph in the land of Egypt were born Manasseh and Ephraim, which Asenath the daughter of Poti-pherah priest of On bare unto him. Gen. 41:45, 50-52
21 And the sons of Benjamin *were* Belah, and Becher, and Ashbel, Gera, and Naaman, Ehi, and Rosh, Muppim, and Huppim, and Ard.
22 These *are* the sons of Rachel, which were born to Jacob: all the souls *were* fourteen.
23 And the sons of Dan; Hushim.
24 And the sons of Naphtali; Jahzeel, and Guni, and Jezer, and Shillem. 1 Chr. 7:13
25 These *are* the sons of Bilhah, which Laban gave unto Rachel his daughter, and she bare these unto Jacob: all the souls *were* seven. Gen. 29:29
26 All the souls that came with Jacob into Egypt, which came out of his ᵀloins, besides Jacob's sons' wives, all the souls *were* ᵀthreescore and six; Ex. 1:5 ◆ *body* ◆ *sixty*
27 And the sons of Joseph, which were born him in Egypt, *were* two souls: all the souls of the house of Jacob, which came into Egypt, *were* threescore and ten. Deut. 10:22; Acts 7:14

Joseph Comes to Meet His Father

28 And he sent Judah before him unto Joseph, to direct his face unto Goshen; and they came into the land of Goshen. Gen. 45:10
29 And Joseph made ready his chariot, and went up to meet Israel his father, to Goshen, and presented himself unto him; and he fell on his neck, and wept on his neck a good while. Luke 15:20
30 And Israel said unto Joseph, Now let me die, since I have seen thy face, because thou *art* yet alive. Luke 2:29-30
31 And Joseph said unto his brethren, and unto his father's house, I will go up, and shew Pharaoh, and say unto him, My brethren, and my father's house, which *were* in the land of Canaan, are come unto me;
32 And the men *are* shepherds, for their trade hath been to feed cattle; and they have brought their flocks, and their herds, and all that they have. Gen. 47:3
33 And it shall come to pass, when Pharaoh shall call you, and shall say, What *is* your occupation? Gen. 46:32
34 That ye shall say, Thy servants' trade hath been about cattle from our youth even until now, both we, *and* also our fathers: that ye may dwell in the land of Goshen; for every shepherd *is* an abomination unto the Egyptians. Gen. 37:12; 43:32; Ex. 8:26

Joseph Presents Five of His Brothers

47 Then Joseph came and told Pharaoh, and said, My father and my brethren, and their flocks, and their herds, and all that they have, are come out of the land of Canaan; and, behold, they *are* in the land of Goshen. Gen. 45:10; 46:28, 31
2 And he took some of his brethren, *even* five men, and presented them unto Pharaoh.
3 And Pharaoh said unto his brethren, What *is* your occupation? And they said unto Pharaoh, Thy servants *are* shepherds, both we, *and* also our fathers. Gen. 46:33-34
4 They said moreover unto Pharaoh, For to sojourn in the land are we come; for thy servants have no pasture for their flocks; for the famine *is* sore in the land of Canaan: now therefore, we pray thee, let thy servants dwell in the land of Goshen. Deut. 26:5
5 And Pharaoh spake unto Joseph, saying, Thy father and thy brethren are come unto thee:
6 The land of Egypt *is* before thee; in the best of the land make thy father and brethren to dwell; in the land of Goshen let them dwell: and if thou knowest *any* men of activity among them, then make them rulers over my cattle. Gen. 47:4, 11; Ex. 18:21
7 And Joseph brought in Jacob his father, and set him before Pharaoh: and Jacob blessed Pharaoh. Gen. 47:10
8 And Pharaoh said unto Jacob, How old *art* thou?
9 And Jacob said unto Pharaoh, The days of the years of my pilgrimage *are* an hundred and thirty years: few and evil have the days of the years of my life been, and have not attained unto the days of the years of the life of my fathers in the days of their pilgrimage.
10 And Jacob blessed Pharaoh, and went out from before Pharaoh. Gen. 47:7
11 And Joseph placed his father and his brethren, and gave them a possession in the land of Egypt, in the best of the land, in the land of Rameses, as Pharaoh had commanded. Gen. 47:6; Ex. 1:11; 12:37
12 And Joseph nourished his father, and his brethren, and all his father's household, with bread, according to *their* families.

Joseph Collects the Egyptians' Money

13 And *there was* no bread in all the land; for the famine *was* very sore, so that the land of Egypt and *all* the land of Canaan fainted by reason of the famine. Acts 7:11
14 And Joseph gathered up all the money that was found in the land of Egypt, and in the land of Canaan, for the corn which they bought: and Joseph brought the money into Pharaoh's house. Gen. 41:56
15 And when money failed in the land of

Egypt, and in the land of Canaan, all the Egyptians came unto Joseph, and said, Give us bread: for why should we die in thy presence? for the money faileth.

16 And Joseph said, Give your cattle; and I will give you for your cattle, if money fail.

17 And they brought their cattle unto Joseph: and Joseph gave them bread *in exchange* for horses, and for the flocks, and for the cattle of the herds, and for the asses: and he fed them with bread for all their cattle for that year.

18 When that year was ended, they came unto him the second year, and said unto him, We will not hide *it* from my lord, how that our money is spent; my lord also hath our herds of cattle; there is not ought left in the sight of my lord, but our bodies, and our lands:

19 Wherefore shall we die before thine eyes, both we and our land? buy us and our land for bread, and we and our land will be servants unto Pharaoh: and give *us* seed, that we may live, and not die, that the land be not desolate.   Neh. 5:2-3

20 And Joseph bought all the land of Egypt for Pharaoh; for the Egyptians sold every man his field, because the famine prevailed over them: so the land became Pharaoh's.

21 And as for the people, he removed them to cities from *one* end of the borders of Egypt even to the *other* end thereof.

22 Only the land of the priests bought he not; for the priests had a portion *assigned them* of Pharaoh, and did eat their portion which Pharaoh gave them: wherefore they sold not their lands.   Ezra 7:24

23 Then Joseph said unto the people, Behold, I have bought you this day and your land for Pharaoh: lo, *here is* seed for you, and ye shall sow the land.

24 And it shall come to pass in the increase, that ye shall give the fifth *part* unto Pharaoh, and four parts shall be your own, for seed of the field, and for your food, and for them of your households, and for food for your little ones.   Gen. 41:34

25 And they said, Thou hast saved our lives: let us find grace in the sight of my lord, and we will be Pharaoh's servants.   Gen. 33:15

26 And Joseph made it a law over the land of Egypt unto this day, *that* Pharaoh should have the fifth *part*; except the land of the priests only, *which* became not Pharaoh's.

27 And Israel dwelt in the land of Egypt, in the country of Goshen; and they had possessions therein, and grew, and multiplied exceedingly.   Gen. 46:3

28 And Jacob lived in the land of Egypt seventeen years: so the whole age of Jacob was an hundred forty and seven years.

29 And the time drew nigh that Israel must die: and he called his son Joseph, and said unto him, If now I have found grace in thy sight, put, I pray thee, thy hand under my thigh, and deal kindly and truly with me; bury me not, I pray thee, in Egypt:

30 But I will lie with my fathers, and thou shalt carry me out of Egypt, and bury me in their buryingplace. And he said, I will do as thou hast said.   Gen. 49:29-32

31 And he said, Swear unto me. And he sware unto him. And Israel bowed himself upon the bed's head.   1 Kin. 1:47; Heb. 11:21

Joseph Brings His Sons to Jacob

48 And it came to pass after these things, that *one* told Joseph, Behold, thy father *is* sick: and he took with him his two sons, Manasseh and Ephraim.

2 And *one* told Jacob, and said, Behold, thy son Joseph cometh unto thee: and Israel strengthened himself, and sat upon the bed.

3 And Jacob said unto Joseph, God Almighty appeared unto me at Luz in the land of Canaan, and blessed me,   Gen. 17:1

4 And said unto me, Behold, I will make thee fruitful, and multiply thee, and I will make of thee a multitude of people; and will give this land to thy seed after thee *for* an everlasting possession.   Gen. 17:8

5 And now thy two sons, Ephraim and Manasseh, which were born unto thee in the land of Egypt before I came unto thee into Egypt, *are* mine; as Reuben and Simeon, they shall be mine.   Gen. 41:50-52; 46:20; Josh. 14:4

48:5 A Birthright Double Portion

Said Jacob, "Thy two sons, Ephraim, and Manasseh, which were born unto thee in the land of Egypt, before I came unto thee into Egypt, are mine; as Reuben and Simeon, they shall be mine." They were to be adopted as his own, and to become the heads of separate tribes. Thus one of the birthright privileges, which Reuben had forfeited, was to fall to Joseph—a double portion in Israel. *PP 234*

6 And thy issue, which thou ᵀbegettest after them, shall be thine, *and* shall be called after the name of their brethren in their inheritance.   *bring forth*

7 And as for me, when I came from Padan, Rachel died by me in the land of Canaan in the way, when yet *there was* but a little way to come unto Ephrath: and I buried her there in the way of Ephrath; the same *is* Bethlehem.   Gen. 35:9

8 And Israel beheld Joseph's sons, and said, Who *are* these?

9 And Joseph said unto his father, They *are* my sons, whom God hath given me in this

place. And he said, Bring them, I pray thee, unto me, and I will bless them.   Heb. 11:21

10 Now the eyes of Israel were dim for age, *so that* he could not see. And he brought them near unto him; and he kissed them, and embraced them.   Gen. 27:1, 27

11 And Israel said unto Joseph, I had not thought to see thy face: and, lo, God hath shewed me also thy seed.   Gen. 37:33

12 And Joseph brought them out from between his knees, and he bowed himself with his face to the earth.   Gen. 42:6

13 And Joseph took them both, Ephraim in his right hand toward Israel's left hand, and Manasseh in his left hand toward Israel's right hand, and brought *them* near unto him.

14 And Israel stretched out his right hand, and laid *it* upon Ephraim's head, who *was* the younger, and his left hand upon Manasseh's head, guiding his hands wittingly; for Manasseh *was* the firstborn.   Gen. 41:51

15 And he blessed Joseph, and said, God, before whom my fathers Abraham and Isaac did walk, the God which fed me all my life long unto this day,   Gen. 17:1

16 The Angel which redeemed me from all evil, bless the lads; and let my name be named on them, and the name of my fathers Abraham and Isaac; and let them grow into a multitude in the midst of the earth.

17 And when Joseph saw that his father laid his right hand upon the head of Ephraim, it displeased him: and he held up his father's hand, to remove it from Ephraim's head unto Manasseh's head.   Gen. 48:14

18 And Joseph said unto his father, Not so, my father: for this *is* the firstborn; put thy right hand upon his head.

19 And his father refused, and said, I know *it*, my son, I know *it*: he also shall become a people, and he also shall be great: but truly his younger brother shall be greater than he, and his seed shall become a multitude of nations.   Deut. 33:17

20 And he blessed them that day, saying, In thee shall Israel bless, saying, God make thee as Ephraim and as Manasseh: and he set Ephraim before Manasseh.   Ruth 4:11-12

21 And Israel said unto Joseph, Behold, I die: but God shall be with you, and bring you again unto the land of your fathers.

22 Moreover I have given to thee one portion above thy brethren, which I took out of the hand of the Amorite with my sword and with my bow.   Josh. 24:32; John 4:5

Jacob Calls His Sons to Bless Them

49 And Jacob called unto his sons, and said, Gather yourselves together, that I may tell you *that* which shall befall you in the last days.   Num. 24:14; Deut. 4:30; Jer. 23:20

2 Gather yourselves together, and hear, ye sons of Jacob; and hearken unto Israel your father.   Ps. 34:11

3 Reuben, thou *art* my firstborn, my might, and the beginning of my strength, the excellency of dignity, and the excellency of power:

4 Unstable as water, thou shalt not excel; because thou wentest up to thy father's bed; then defiledst thou *it*: he went up to my couch.   Deut. 27:20; 1 Chr. 5:1

5 Simeon and Levi *are* brethren; instruments of cruelty *are in* their habitations.

6 O my soul, come not thou into their secret; unto their assembly, mine honour, be not thou united: for in their anger they slew a man, and in their selfwill they digged down a wall.   Gen. 34:30; Ps. 16:9; 26:9

7 Cursed *be* their anger, for *it was* fierce; and their wrath, for it was cruel: I will divide them in Jacob, and scatter them in Israel.

8 Judah, thou *art he* whom thy brethren shall praise: thy hand *shall be* in the neck of thine enemies; thy father's children shall bow down before thee.   Gen. 27:29; 1 Chr. 5:2; Heb. 7:14

9 Judah *is* a lion's whelp: from the prey, my son, thou art gone up: he stooped down, he couched as a lion, and as an old lion; who shall rouse him up?   Num. 23:24; 24:9; Rev. 5:5

10 The sceptre shall not depart from Judah, nor a lawgiver from between his feet, until Shiloh come; and unto him *shall* the gathering of the people *be*.   Num. 24:17; Ps. 60:7; Is. 42:1

11 Binding his foal unto the vine, and his ass's colt unto the choice vine; he washed his garments in wine, and his clothes in the blood of grapes: 2 Kin. 18:32

12 His eyes *shall be* red with wine, and his teeth white with milk.   Prov. 23:29

13 Zebulun shall dwell at the haven of the sea; and he *shall be* for an haven of ships; and his border *shall be* unto Zidon.   Deut. 33:18-19

14 Issachar *is* a strong ass couching down between two burdens: Gen. 30:18

15 And he saw that rest *was* good, and the land that *it was* pleasant; and bowed his shoulder to bear, and became a servant unto tribute.

16 Dan shall judge his people, as one of the tribes of Israel.   Gen. 30:6; Deut. 33:22

17 Dan shall be a serpent by the way, an adder in the path, that biteth the horse heels, so that his rider shall fall backward.

18 I have waited for thy salvation, O LORD.

19 Gad, a troop shall overcome him: but he shall overcome at the last.   Gen. 30:11

20 Out of Asher his bread *shall be* fat, and he shall yield royal dainties.   Gen. 30:13

21 Naphtali *is* a hind let loose: he giveth goodly words.   Gen. 30:8; Deut. 33:23

22 Joseph *is* a fruitful bough, *even* a fruitful

bough by a well; *whose* branches run over the wall: Gen. 41:52

23 The archers have sorely grieved him, and shot *at him*, and hated him: Gen. 37:24

24 But his bow abode in strength, and the arms of his hands were made strong by the hands of the mighty *God* of Jacob; (from thence *is* the shepherd, the stone of Israel:)

25 *Even* by the God of thy father, who shall help thee; and by the Almighty, who shall bless thee with blessings of heaven above, blessings of the deep that lieth under, blessings of the breasts, and of the womb:

26 The blessings of thy father have prevailed above the blessings of my ᵀprogenitors unto the utmost ᵀbound of the everlasting hills: they shall be on the head of Joseph, and on the crown of the head of him that was separate from his brethren.   ancestors ◆ landmark

27 Benjamin shall ravin *as* a wolf: in the morning he shall devour the prey, and at night he shall divide the ᵀspoil.   plunder

28 All these *are* the twelve tribes of Israel: and this *is it* that their father spake unto them, and blessed them; every one according to his blessing he blessed them.

29 And he charged them, and said unto them, I am to be gathered unto my people: bury me with my fathers in the cave that *is* in the field of Ephron the Hittite,

30 In the cave that *is* in the field of Machpelah, which *is* before Mamre, in the land of Canaan, which Abraham bought with the field of Ephron the Hittite for a possession of a buryingplace.

31 There they buried Abraham and Sarah his wife; there they buried Isaac and Rebekah his wife; and there I buried Leah.   Gen. 25:9

32 The purchase of the field and of the cave that *is* therein *was* from the children of Heth.

33 And when Jacob had made an end of commanding his sons, he gathered up his feet into the bed, and yielded up the ghost, and was gathered unto his people.   Gen. 25:8

The Mourning for Jacob

50 And Joseph fell upon his father's face, and wept upon him, and kissed him.   Gen. 46:4

2 And Joseph commanded his servants the physicians to embalm his father: and the physicians embalmed Israel.   2 Chr. 16:14

3 And forty days were fulfilled for him; for so are fulfilled the days of those which are embalmed: and the Egyptians mourned for him ᵀthreescore and ten days.   sixty

4 And when the days of his mourning were past, Joseph spake unto the house of Pharaoh, saying, If now I have found grace in your eyes, speak, I pray you, in the ears of Pharaoh, saying,

5 My father made me swear, saying, Lo, I die: in my grave which I have digged for me in the land of Canaan, there shalt thou bury me. Now therefore let me go up, I pray thee, and bury my father, and I will come again.

6 And Pharaoh said, Go up, and bury thy father, according as he made thee swear.

7 And Joseph went up to bury his father: and with him went up all the servants of Pharaoh, the elders of his house, and all the elders of the land of Egypt,

---

Joseph—and Jesus

Genesis 50:22–26

The life of Joseph illustrates the life of Christ. It was envy that moved the brothers of Joseph to sell him as a slave; they hoped to prevent him from becoming greater than themselves. And when he was carried to Egypt, they flattered themselves that they were to be no more troubled with his dreams, that they had removed all possibility of their fulfillment. . . . So the Jewish priests and elders were jealous of Christ, fearing that He would attract the attention of the people from them. They put Him to death, to prevent Him from becoming king, but they were thus bringing about this very result.

Joseph, through his bondage in Egypt, became a savior to his father's family; yet this fact did not lessen the guilt of his brothers. So the crucifixion of Christ by His enemies made Him the Redeemer of mankind, the Saviour of the fallen race, and Ruler over the whole world; but the crime of His murderers was just as heinous as though God's providential hand had not controlled events for His own glory and the good of man.

As Joseph was sold to the heathen by his own brothers, so Christ was sold to His bitterest enemies by one of His disciples. Joseph was falsely accused and thrust into prison because of his virtue; so Christ was despised and rejected because His righteous, self-denying life was a rebuke to sin; and though guilty of no wrong, He was condemned upon the testimony of false witnesses. And Joseph's patience and meekness under injustice and oppression, his ready forgiveness and noble benevolence toward his unnatural brothers, represent the Saviour's uncomplaining endurance of the malice and abuse of wicked men, and His forgiveness, not only of His murderers, but of all who have come to Him confessing their sins and seeking pardon. *PP 239, 240*

8 And all the house of Joseph, and his brethren, and his father's house: only their little ones, and their flocks, and their herds, they left in the land of Goshen.

9 And there went up with him both chariots and horsemen: and it was a very great company.

10 And they came to the threshingfloor of Atad, which *is* beyond Jordan, and there they mourned with a great and very sore lamentation: and he made a mourning for his father seven days.   2 Sam. 1:17; Acts 8:2

11 And when the inhabitants of the land, the Canaanites, saw the mourning in the floor of Atad, they said, This *is* a grievous mourning to the Egyptians: wherefore the name of it was called Abel-mizraim, which *is* beyond Jordan.

12 And his sons did unto him according as he commanded them:

13 For his sons carried him into the land of Canaan, and buried him in the cave of the field of Machpelah, which Abraham bought with the field for a possession of a burying-place of Ephron the Hittite, before Mamre.

14 And Joseph returned into Egypt, he, and his brethren, and all that went up with him to bury his father, after he had buried his father.

Joseph Comforts His Brothers

15 And when Joseph's brethren saw that their father was dead, they said, Joseph will ᵀperadventure hate us, and will certainly ᵀrequite us all the evil which we did unto him.   *maybe ◆ repay*

16 And they sent a messenger unto Joseph, saying, Thy father did command before he died, saying,

17 So shall ye say unto Joseph, Forgive, I pray thee now, the ᵀtrespass of thy brethren, and their sin; for they did unto thee evil: and now, we pray thee, forgive the trespass of the servants of the God of thy father. And Joseph wept when they spake unto him.   *sin*

18 And his brethren also went and fell down before his face; and they said, Behold, we *be* thy servants.

19 And Joseph said unto them, Fear not: for *am* I in the place of God?   Gen. 30:2

20 But as for you, ye thought evil against me; *but* God meant it unto good, to bring to pass, as *it is* this day, to save much people alive.   Rom. 8:28

21 Now therefore fear ye not: I will nourish you, and your little ones. And he comforted them, and spake kindly unto them. Gen. 47:12

Joseph's Age and Death

22 And Joseph dwelt in Egypt, he, and his father's house: and Joseph lived an hundred and ten years.

23 And Joseph saw Ephraim's children of the third *generation*: the children also of Machir the son of Manasseh were brought up upon Joseph's knees.   Gen. 30:3

24 And Joseph said unto his brethren, I die: and God will surely visit you, and bring you out of this land unto the land which he sware to Abraham, to Isaac, and to Jacob.

25 And Joseph took an oath of the children of Israel, saying, God will surely visit you, and ye shall carry up my bones from hence.

26 So Joseph died, *being* an hundred and ten years old: and they embalmed him, and he was put in a coffin in Egypt.

THE SECOND BOOK OF MOSES CALLED

EXODUS

Exodus continues the story from the end of Genesis. Jacob's family had moved from Canaan to Egypt for relief from the famine. Jacob's son Joseph had become a powerful leader. As centuries passed, the Hebrew people grew from the original seventy to several million.

As the days of Joseph passed into history, the days of ease for the Hebrews in Egypt ended. Power-hungry Pharaohs, fearful of such a vast group of people inside their borders, forced the Hebrews into centuries of slavery and toil. Many of the great monuments of Egypt may be testaments to the greatness of an empire, but they also testify to the forced servitude of a nation.

The deliverance of the Hebrews from slavery by God demonstrates the nature of God as liberator, protector, and guide. He keeps His people safe through all manner of dangers and is faithful to the covenant that He made with Abraham (Genesis 15:13–16).

We also see the role of God as law-giver. In Exodus, God issues the first anti-slavery law (see 21:16), a social precept that leads to the notion that people should be ruled by laws rather than masters. God provides the laws that formed legal thought not only for the Hebrews but also for much of our modern-day jurisprudence.

God is the source of true freedom, and His laws provide the light that keeps us safe. These laws become written on the hearts of all who accept His Son, Jesus.

Dates

Exodus begins after the death of Joseph and extends to the building of God's tabernacle in the wilderness of Sinai. The two sections of Exodus fall approximately around the following dates:

(1) *Exodus 1—18, 1660 to 1445 B.C.*

The entrance of Jacob into Egypt dated c. 1660 B.C.; the arrival of the Hebrews at Mount Sinai dated c. 1445 B.C.

(2) *Exodus 19—40, 1445 B.C.*

The encampment of the Hebrews at Mount Sinai, dated c. 1445 B.C., culminating with the building of God's tabernacle.

Author

Moses is widely accepted as the author of Exodus. Testimonies to the Mosaic authorship come from Joshua (Joshua 8:30–32), Malachi (Malachi 4:4), the disciples (John 1:45), and Paul (Romans 10:5). Jesus also testifies to Moses' authorship (Mark 7:10; 12:26; Luke 20:37; John 5:46, 47; 7:19, 22, 23).

An analysis of the Book of Exodus reveals a consistent writing style throughout, suggesting a single author who was highly educated for his time and familiar with the customs and climate of Egypt. Moses, educated in the royal house of Pharaoh, is an ideal candidate. Moreover, several parts of Exodus indicate Moses as the author (Exodus 17:8–14; 24:4, 7, 12; 31:18; 34:1–27). The details of Exodus lend themselves to a first-hand account, while the book's literary constructs are consistent with similar ancient texts, testifying to its historical authenticity.

Meaning of the Name

"Exodus" comes from the Greek *exodos*, which means "the going out" or "departure." The Hebrews simply call this book *We'elleh Shemot*, "Now these are the names," which are the first words of the Book of Exodus. The book begins with the word "now," indicating that it is a continuation of the Book of Genesis.

Christ in Exodus

The redemption of the Hebrews from Egypt is a foreshadowing of Jesus' redemption of the world. Moses' escape as an infant from the Pharaoh's edict to kill all the male Hebrew children directly parallels Jesus' similar escape from Herod's edict (Matthew 2:16). Jesus and Moses were both prophets and priests, leaders and redeemers, deliverers and lawgivers.

The symbology of the Passover unmistakably points to Jesus. When God commanded Moses to have the Hebrews put lamb's blood on their door posts (Exodus 12:7), this is a

symbol of the blood of the Lamb of God (John 1:29). Paul writes, "Christ our passover is sacrificed for us" (1 Corinthians 5:7). Also worthy of note, when the Hebrews paint the sides and top of their doors with the blood, drawing a line between the side marks and from top to bottom forms the shape of the cross.

God also tells the Hebrews to keep seven holy feast days, each of which corresponds to an aspect of Jesus' ministry on earth.

The Exodus event itself has a symbolic link to Jesus. As the Hebrews pass through the waters of the Red Sea, it symbolizes the purification of baptism (Romans 6:2, 3; 1 Corinthians 10:1, 2) and renewal. The manna and water that God provides to sustain the Hebrews in the desert also are references to Jesus (John 6:31–35, 48–63; 1 Corinthians 10:3, 4).

The tabernacle that God instructs the Hebrews to build is a direct visual aid to understanding the role of Jesus. The thick veil around the entrance to the most holy place, the innermost part of the tabernacle, represents the separation between a sinful people and their holy God. This place can only be entered by the high priest, who brings the sacrificial blood with him for the atonement of sins. Jesus is our High Priest (Hebrews 9:11–15) and He brought the only blood that could atone for our sins—His own. When He died, the veil of the most holy place was torn (Matthew 27:51), meaning that He had made it possible for God to dwell among us again for all time (Revelation 21:3).

Overview

Exodus can be divided into two thematical sections:

(1) *Exodus 1—18, The Redemption from Egypt:* This is a story of freedom, of how a slave nation throws off the yoke of bondage and defeats the most powerful force on the planet at that time. The Hebrews know that only God can deliver them, and God hears their cries for deliverance, redeeming them "with a stretched out arm, and with great judgments" (6:6). At the center of the deliverance stands Moses, the man chosen by God to demand His people's freedom. God breaks the power of Pharaoh, miraculously saves His people, and institutes the Passover celebration for God's people to always remember what He did for them in setting them free. The Hebrews journey from Egypt to Mount Sinai to receive the laws of God that they might live in God's blessings.

(2) *Exodus 19—40, Revelation from God:* God gives Moses His Ten Commandments, laws and regulations for the people to follow, and instructions for how to worship Him. While Moses speaks with God on Mount Sinai for forty days, the people grow weary of waiting and decide to make their own god. God is angry with the people and wants to destroy them, but Moses pleads for God's mercy. God agrees. God tells Moses that He will bring the Hebrews to a land flowing with milk and honey where the people will dwell safely, and He will drive out all enemies before them.

Unlocking Exodus

KEY PEOPLE:
Moses; Joshua, the Pharaoh, Amram, Jochebed, Pharaoh's daughter, Aaron, Jethro, Miriam, Bezalel

KEY EVENTS:
Moses' birth; the plagues of Egypt; institution of the Passover; parting of the Red Sea; Moses receiving the Ten Commandments; building the tabernacle

KEY WORD:
Freedom. The theme of freedom in Exodus resonates with us today. Every freedom-loving government finds its origin in God's plan for the Hebrews.

KEY VERSE:
"Now therefore, if ye will obey my voice indeed, and keep my covenant, then ye shall be a peculiar treasure unto me above all people: for all the earth *is* mine" (Exodus 19:5).

KEY CHAPTER:
Exodus 20, wherein Moses gives the people the Ten Commandments (20:2–17). God knows that the Hebrews' hearts are sinful and stiff-necked (32:9), so He gives them laws to follow to constrain them until Jesus' sacrifice makes it possible for people's hearts to be changed in God's love (Romans 13:8–10).

The Israelites Increase

1 Now these *are* the names of the children of Israel, which came into Egypt; every man and his household came with Jacob. Gen. 46:8-26

2 Reuben, Simeon, Levi, and Judah,

3 Issachar, Zebulun, and Benjamin,

4 Dan, and Naphtali, Gad, and Asher.

5 And all the souls that came out of the loins of Jacob were seventy souls: for Joseph was in Egypt *already*. Gen. 46:26-27

6 And Joseph died, and all his brethren, and all that generation. Gen. 50:26

7 And the children of Israel were fruitful, and increased abundantly, and multiplied, and waxed exceeding mighty; and the land was filled with them. Gen. 12:2; 46:3; Deut. 26:5

A New King, Who Knew Not Joseph, Arises

8 Now there arose up a new king over Egypt, which knew not Joseph. Acts 7:18

9 And he said unto his people, Behold, the people of the children of Israel *are* more and mightier than we: Ps. 105:24-25

10 Come on, let us deal wisely with them; lest they multiply, and it come to pass, that, when there falleth out any war, they join also unto our enemies, and fight against us, and *so* get them up out of the land. Ps. 83:3-4; 105:25

11 Therefore they did set over them taskmasters to afflict them with their burdens. And they built for Pharaoh treasure cities, Pithom and Raamses. Gen. 15:13; 47:11; Ex. 2:11

12 But the more they afflicted them, the more they multiplied and grew. And they were grieved because of the children of Israel.

13 And the Egyptians made the children of Israel to serve with rigour:

14 And they made their lives bitter with hard bondage, in morter, and in brick, and in all manner of service in the field: all their service, wherein they made them serve, *was* with rigour. Ex. 2:23; 6:9; Num. 20:15

The Midwives Save the Male Children

15 And the king of Egypt spake to the Hebrew midwives, of which the name of the one *was* Shiphrah, and the name of the other Puah:

16 And he said, When ye do the office of a midwife to the Hebrew women, and see *them* upon the stools; if it *be* a son, then ye shall kill him: but if it *be* a daughter, then she shall live.

17 But the midwives feared God, and did not as the king of Egypt commanded them, but saved the men children alive. Prov. 16:6; Acts 5:29

18 And the king of Egypt called for the midwives, and said unto them, Why have ye done this thing, and have saved the men children alive?

19 And the midwives said unto Pharaoh, Because the Hebrew women *are* not as the Egyptian women; for they *are* lively, and are delivered ᵀere the midwives come in unto them. before

20 Therefore God dealt well with the midwives: and the people multiplied, and ᵀwaxed very mighty. Ex. 1:12 ◆ *became*

21 And it came to pass, because the midwives feared God, that he made them houses. 1 Sam. 2:35; 1 Kin. 2:24; 11:38

22 And Pharaoh charged all his people, saying, Every son that is born ye shall cast into the river, and every daughter ye shall save alive. Acts 7:19

Moses Is Born

2 And there went a man of the house of Levi, and took *to wife* a daughter of Levi. Num. 26:59

2 And the woman conceived, and bare a son: and when she saw him that he *was a* goodly *child*, she hid him three months. Acts 7:20

3 And when she could not longer hide him, she took for him an ark of bulrushes, and daubed it with slime and with pitch, and put the child therein; and she laid *it* in the flags by the river's brink. Is. 18:2

Influence of Praying Mothers

Exodus 2:2–9

Parents should direct the instruction and training of their children while very young, to the end that they may be Christians. They are placed in our care to be trained, not as heirs to the throne of an earthly empire, but as kings unto God, to reign through unending ages.

Let every mother feel that her moments are priceless; her work will be tested in the solemn day of accounts. Then it will be found that many of the failures and crimes of men and women have resulted from the ignorance and neglect of those whose duty it was to guide their childish feet in the right way. Then it will be found that many who have blessed the world with the light of genius and truth and holiness, owe the principles that were the mainspring of their influence and success to a praying, Christian mother. *PP 244*

4 And his sister stood afar off, to ᵀwit what would be done to him. Ex.15:20; Num. 26:59 ◆*know*

Moses Is Found, and Brought up by Pharaoh's Daughter

5 And the daughter of Pharaoh came down to wash *herself* at the river; and her maidens walked along by the river's side; and when she saw the ark among the ᵀflags, she sent her maid to fetch it.   *marsh reeds*
6 And when she had opened *it*, she saw the child: and, behold, the babe wept. And she had compassion on him, and said, This *is one* of the Hebrews' children.
7 Then said his sister to Pharaoh's daughter, Shall I go and call to thee a nurse of the Hebrew women, that she may nurse the child for thee?
8 And Pharaoh's daughter said to her, Go. And the maid went and called the child's mother.
9 And Pharaoh's daughter said unto her, Take this child away, and nurse it for me, and I will give *thee* thy wages. And the woman took the child, and nursed it.

> **2:9 Work of Christian Mothers**
>
> How far-reaching in its results was the influence of that one Hebrew woman, and she an exile and a slave! The whole future life of Moses, the great mission which he fulfilled as the leader of Israel, testifies to the importance of the work of the Christian mother. There is no other work that can equal this. To a very great extent the mother holds in her own hands the destiny of her children. *PP 244*

10 And the child grew, and she brought him unto Pharaoh's daughter, and he became her son. And she called his name Moses: and she said, Because I drew him out of the water.   Heb. 11:24

Moses Kills an Egyptian

11 And it came to pass in those days, when Moses was grown, that he went out unto his brethren, and looked on their burdens: and he spied an Egyptian smiting an Hebrew, one of his brethren.   Ex. 1:11; Heb. 11:24-26
12 And he looked this way and that way, and when he saw that *there was* no man, he slew the Egyptian, and hid him in the sand.

> **2:11, 12 Moses Falls Into Error**
>
> In slaying the Egyptian, Moses had fallen into the same error so often committed by his fathers, of taking into their own hands the work that God had promised to do. It was not God's will to deliver His people by warfare, as Moses thought, but by His own mighty power, that the glory might be ascribed to Him alone. *PP 247*

13 And when he went out the second day, behold, two men of the Hebrews strove together: and he said to him that did the wrong, Wherefore ᵀsmitest thou thy fellow?   *strikes*
14 And he said, Who made thee a prince and a judge over us? intendest thou to kill me, as thou killedst the Egyptian? And Moses feared, and said, Surely this thing is known.   Gen. 19:9
15 Now when Pharaoh heard this thing, he sought to slay Moses. But Moses fled from the face of Pharaoh, and dwelt in the land of Midian: and he sat down by a well. Heb. 11:27
16 Now the priest of Midian had seven daughters: and they came and drew *water*, and filled the troughs to water their father's flock.   Gen. 24:11; Ex. 3:1; 1 Sam. 9:11
17 And the shepherds came and drove them away: but Moses stood up and helped them, and watered their flock.   Gen. 29:10
18 And when they came to Reuel their father, he said, How *is it that* ye are come so soon to day?   Ex. 3:1
19 And they said, An Egyptian delivered us out of the hand of the shepherds, and also drew *water* enough for us, and watered the flock.
20 And he said unto his daughters, And where *is* he? why *is* it *that* ye have left the man? call him, that he may eat bread.   Gen. 31:54
21 And Moses was content to dwell with the man: and he gave Moses Zipporah his daughter.
22 And she bare *him* a son, and he called his name Gershom: for he said, I have been a stranger in a strange land.   Acts 7:29

God Hears the Complaints of the Israelites

23 And it came to pass in process of time, that the king of Egypt died: and the children of Israel sighed by reason of the bondage, and they cried, and their cry came up unto God by reason of the bondage.   Acts 7:30; James 5:4
24 And God heard their groaning, and God remembered his covenant with Abraham, with Isaac, and with Jacob. Gen. 26:3; Ps. 105:42
25 And God looked upon the children of Israel, and God had respect unto *them*. Luke 1:25

Moses Keeps Jethro's Flock

3 Now Moses kept the flock of Jethro his father in law, the priest of Midian: and he led the flock to the backside of the desert, and came to the mountain of God, *even* to Horeb.   Ex. 17:6; Num. 10:29; 1 Kin. 19:8
2 And the angel of the LORD appeared unto him in a flame of fire out of the midst of a bush: and he looked, and, behold, the

bush burned with fire, and the bush *was* not consumed.   Deut. 33:16

3 And Moses said, I will now turn aside, and see this great sight, why the bush is not burnt.   Acts 7:31

3:1 Moses, Alone With God

Shut in by the bulwarks of the mountains, Moses was alone with God. The magnificent temples of Egypt no longer impressed his mind with their superstition and falsehood. In the solemn grandeur of the everlasting hills he beheld the majesty of the Most High, and in contrast realized how powerless and insignificant were the gods of Egypt. Everywhere the Creator's name was written. *PP 248–251*

4 And when the LORD saw that he turned aside to see, God called unto him out of the midst of the bush, and said, Moses, Moses. And he said, Here *am* I.   Deut. 33:16

5 And he said, Draw not nigh ᵀhither: put off thy shoes from off thy feet, for the place whereon thou standest *is* holy ground.   here

3:5 Holy Ground

Moses at the burning bush was directed to put off his sandals, for the ground whereon he stood was holy. . . . Thus was constantly taught the lesson that all defilement must be put away from those who would approach into the presence of God. *PP 350*

6 Moreover he said, I *am* the God of thy father, the God of Abraham, the God of Isaac, and the God of Jacob. And Moses hid his face; for he was afraid to look upon God.   Ex. 4:5; Matt. 22:32; Mark 12:26

7 And the LORD said, I have surely seen the affliction of my people which *are* in Egypt, and have heard their cry by reason of their taskmasters; for I know their sorrows;   Ps. 106:44

8 And I am come down to deliver them out of the hand of the Egyptians, and to bring them up out of that land unto a good land and a large, unto a land flowing with milk and honey; unto the place of the Canaanites, and the Hittites, and the Amorites, and the Perizzites, and the Hivites, and the Jebusites.   Gen. 15:18-21; 50:24; Ex. 13:5

9 Now therefore, behold, the cry of the children of Israel is come unto me: and I have also seen the oppression wherewith the Egyptians oppress them.   Ex. 1:11; 2:23; 3:7

10 Come now therefore, and I will send thee unto Pharaoh, that thou mayest bring forth my people the children of Israel out of Egypt.   Ps. 105:26; Mic. 6:4

11 And Moses said unto God, Who *am* I, that I should go unto Pharaoh, and that I should bring forth the children of Israel out of Egypt?   Ex. 6:12; 1 Sam. 18:18; Jer. 1:6

12 And he said, Certainly I will be with thee; and this *shall be* a token unto thee, that I have sent thee: When thou hast brought forth the people out of Egypt, ye shall serve God upon this mountain.   Gen. 31:3; Ex. 4:12; Josh. 1:5

13 And Moses said unto God, Behold, *when* I come unto the children of Israel, and shall say unto them, The God of your fathers hath sent me unto you; and they shall say to me, What *is* his name? what shall I say unto them?   Ex. 3:14

14 And God said unto Moses, I AM THAT I AM: and he said, Thus shalt thou say unto the children of Israel, I AM hath sent me unto you.   Ex. 6:3; John 8:58; Heb. 13:8

15 And God said moreover unto Moses, Thus shalt thou say unto the children of Israel, The LORD God of your fathers, the God of Abraham, the God of Isaac, and the God of Jacob, hath sent me unto you: this *is* my name for ever, and this *is* my memorial unto all generations.   Ex. 3:6; Ps. 135:13; Hos. 12:5

Preparing to Be a Shepherd

Exodus 2:11—3:10

Yet even this rash act [by Moses] was overruled by God to accomplish His purposes. Moses was not prepared for his great work. He had yet to learn the same lesson of faith that Abraham and Jacob had been taught—not to rely upon human strength or wisdom, but upon the power of God for the fulfillment of His promises. And there were other lessons that, amid the solitude of the mountains, Moses was to receive. In the school of self-denial and hardship he was to learn patience, to temper his passions. Before he could govern wisely, he must be trained to obey. His own heart must be fully in harmony with God before he could teach the knowledge of His will to Israel. By his own experience he must be prepared to exercise a fatherly care over all who needed his help.

Man would have dispensed with that long period of toil and obscurity, deeming it a great loss of time. But Infinite Wisdom called him who was to become the leader of his people to spend forty years in the humble work of a shepherd. The habits of caretaking, of self-forgetfulness and tender solicitude for his flock, thus developed, would prepare him to become the compassionate, longsuffering shepherd of Israel. No advantage that human training or culture could bestow, could be a substitute for this experience. *PP 247, 248*

16 Go, and gather the elders of Israel together, and say unto them, The Lord God of your fathers, the God of Abraham, of Isaac, and of Jacob, appeared unto me, saying, I have surely visited you, and *seen* that which is done to you in Egypt: Gen. 50:24; Ex. 4:29, 31

17 And I have said, I will bring you up out of the affliction of Egypt unto the land of the Canaanites, and the Hittites, and the Amorites, and the Perizzites, and the Hivites, and the Jebusites, unto a land flowing with milk and honey.   Gen. 15:13-21

18 And they shall hearken to thy voice: and thou shalt come, thou and the elders of Israel, unto the king of Egypt, and ye shall say unto him, The Lord God of the Hebrews hath met with us: and now let us go, we ᵀbeseech thee, three days' journey into the wilderness, that we may sacrifice to the Lord our God.   Ex. 7:16 ◆ *beg*

19 And I am sure that the king of Egypt will not let you go, no, not by a mighty hand.

20 And I will stretch out my hand, and ᵀsmite Egypt with all my wonders which I will do in the midst thereof: and after that he will let you go.   Ex. 9:15; Deut. 6:22; Neh. 9:10 ◆ *strike*

21 And I will give this people favour in the sight of the Egyptians: and it shall come to pass, that, when ye go, ye shall not go empty: Ex. 11:3; 12:36; Ps. 106:46

22 But every woman shall borrow of her neighbour, and of her that sojourneth in her house, jewels of silver, and jewels of gold, and ᵀraiment: and ye shall put *them* upon your sons, and upon your daughters; and ye shall ᵀspoil the Egyptians.   Ezek. 39:10 ◆ *clothing* ◆ *plunder*

Moses' Rod Is Turned into a Serpent as a Sign

4 And Moses answered and said, But, behold, they will not believe me, nor hearken unto my voice: for they will say, The Lord hath not appeared unto thee.   Ex. 3:18

2 And the Lord said unto him, What *is* that in thine hand? And he said, A rod. Ex. 4:17, 20

3 And he said, Cast it on the ground. And he cast it on the ground, and it became a serpent; and Moses fled from before it.

4 And the Lord said unto Moses, Put forth thine hand, and take it by the tail. And he put forth his hand, and caught it, and it became a rod in his hand:

5 That they may believe that the Lord God of their fathers, the God of Abraham, the God of Isaac, and the God of Jacob, hath appeared unto thee.   Gen. 12:7; 18:1; Ex. 19:9

6 And the Lord said furthermore unto him, Put now thine hand into thy bosom. And he put his hand into his bosom: and when he took it out, behold, his hand *was* leprous as snow.   Num. 12:10; 2 Kin. 5:27

7 And he said, Put thine hand into thy bosom again. And he put his hand into his bosom again; and plucked it out of his bosom, and, behold, it was turned again as his *other* flesh.   Deut. 32:39; 2 Kin. 5:14; Matt. 8:3

8 And it shall come to pass, if they will not believe thee, neither hearken to the voice of the first sign, that they will believe the voice of the latter sign.

9 And it shall come to pass, if they will not believe also these two signs, neither hearken unto thy voice, that thou shalt take of the water of the river, and pour *it* upon the dry *land*: and the water which thou takest out of the river shall become blood upon the dry *land*.

Moses' Brother, Aaron, Joins Him

10 And Moses said unto the Lord, O my Lord, I *am* not eloquent, neither ᵀheretofore, nor since thou hast spoken unto thy servant: but I *am* slow of speech, and of a slow tongue.   Ex. 4:1; 6:12; Jer. 1:6 ◆ *before*

4:10–17 Trusting in Divine Strength

A man will gain power and efficiency as he accepts the responsibilities that God places upon him, and with his whole soul seeks to qualify himself to bear them aright. However humble his position or limited his ability, that man will attain true greatness who, trusting to divine strength, seeks to perform his work with fidelity. *PP 255*

11 And the Lord said unto him, Who hath made man's mouth? or who maketh the ᵀdumb, or deaf, or the seeing, or the blind? have not I the Lord?   Ps. 94:9 ◆ *mute*

12 Now therefore go, and I will be with thy mouth, and teach thee what thou shalt say.   Is. 50:4; Jer. 1:9; Matt. 10:19-20

13 And he said, O my Lord, send, I pray thee, by the hand *of him whom* thou wilt send.

14 And the anger of the Lord was kindled against Moses, and he said, *Is* not Aaron the Levite thy brother? I know that he can speak well. And also, behold, he cometh forth to meet thee: and when he seeth thee, he will be glad in his heart.   Ex. 4:27

15 And thou shalt speak unto him, and put words in his mouth: and I will be with thy mouth, and with his mouth, and will teach you what ye shall do.   Num. 23:5, 12; Is. 51:16

16 And he shall be thy spokesman unto the people: and he shall be, *even* he shall be to thee instead of a mouth, and thou shalt be to him instead of God.   Ex. 7:1-2

17 And thou shalt take this rod in thine hand, wherewith thou shalt do signs. Ex. 4:2

Moses Departs from Jethro

18 And Moses went and returned to Jethro his father in law, and said unto him, Let me go, I pray thee, and return unto my brethren which *are* in Egypt, and see whether they be yet alive. And Jethro said to Moses, Go in peace. Ex. 3:1

19 And the Lord said unto Moses in Midian, Go, return into Egypt: for all the men are dead which sought thy life. Ex. 2:15, 23; Matt. 2:20

20 And Moses took his wife and his sons, and set them upon an ass, and he returned to the land of Egypt: and Moses took the rod of God in his hand. Ex. 4:17; 17:9; Num. 20:8-9

21 And the Lord said unto Moses, When thou goest to return into Egypt, see that thou do all those wonders before Pharaoh, which I have put in thine hand: but I will harden his heart, that he shall not let the people go. Ex. 3:20; 7:13; 9:12

4:21 Results of Stubbornness

God had declared concerning Pharaoh, "I will harden his heart, that he shall not let the people go" (Exodus 4:21). There was no exercise of supernatural power to harden the heart of the king. . . . Every display of infinite power rejected by him, rendered him the more determined in his rebellion. . . . As he continued to venture on in his own course, going from one degree of stubbornness to another, his heart became more and more hardened. . . . *PP 268*

---

22 And thou shalt say unto Pharaoh, Thus saith the Lord, Israel *is* my son, *even* my firstborn: Jer. 31:9; Hos. 11:1; Rom. 9:4

23 And I say unto thee, Let my son go, that he may serve me: and if thou refuse to let him go, behold, I will slay thy son, *even* thy firstborn. Ex. 11:5; 12:29; Ps. 105:36

Zipporah Circumcises Her Son

24 And it came to pass by the way in the inn, that the Lord met him, and sought to kill him. Gen. 17:14; 1 Chr. 21:16

25 Then Zipporah took a sharp stone, and cut off the foreskin of her son, and cast *it* at his feet, and said, Surely a bloody husband *art* thou to me. Josh. 5:2-3

26 So he let him go: then she said, A bloody husband *thou art*, because of the circumcision.

27 And the Lord said to Aaron, Go into the wilderness to meet Moses. And he went, and met him in the mount of God, and kissed him. Ex. 3:1

28 And Moses told Aaron all the words of the Lord who had sent him, and all the signs which he had commanded him. Ex. 4:8-9

29 And Moses and Aaron went and gathered together all the elders of the children of Israel: Ex. 3:16

30 And Aaron spake all the words which the Lord had spoken unto Moses, and did the signs in the sight of the people.

31 And the people believed: and when they heard that the Lord had visited the children of Israel, and that he had looked upon their affliction, then they bowed their heads and worshipped. Gen. 24:26; Ex. 2:25; 3:18

Pharaoh Chides Moses and Aaron for Their Message

5 And afterward Moses and Aaron went in, and told Pharaoh, Thus saith the Lord God of Israel, Let my people go, that they may hold a feast unto me in the wilderness. Ex. 10:9

2 And Pharaoh said, Who *is* the Lord, that I should obey his voice to let Israel go? I know not the Lord, neither will I let Israel go. Ex. 3:19; 2 Kin. 18:35; Job 21:15

3 And they said, The God of the Hebrews

No Protection for the Disobedient

Exodus 4:24-26

On the way from Midian, Moses received a startling and terrible warning of the Lord's displeasure. An angel appeared to him in a threatening manner, as if he would immediately destroy him. No explanation was given; but Moses remembered that he had disregarded one of God's requirements; yielding to the persuasion of his wife, he had neglected to perform the rite of circumcision upon their youngest son. He had failed to comply with the condition by which his child could be entitled to the blessings of God's covenant with Israel; and such a neglect on the part of their chosen leader could not but lessen the force of the divine precepts upon the people. Zipporah, fearing that her husband would be slain, performed the rite herself, and the angel then permitted Moses to pursue his journey. In his mission to Pharaoh, Moses was to be placed in a position of great peril; his life could be preserved only through the protection of holy angels. But while living in neglect of a known duty, he would not be secure; for he could not be shielded by the angels of God.

In the time of trouble just before the coming of Christ, the righteous will be preserved through the ministration of heavenly angels; but there will be no security for the transgressor of God's law. Angels cannot then protect those who are disregarding one of the divine precepts. *PP 255, 256*

hath met with us: let us go, we pray thee, three days' journey into the desert, and sacrifice unto the LORD our God; lest he fall upon us with pestilence, or with the sword.   Ex. 3:18

4 And the king of Egypt said unto them, Wherefore do ye, Moses and Aaron, let the people from their works? get you unto your burdens.   Ex. 1:11

5 And Pharaoh said, Behold, the people of the land now *are* many, and ye make them rest from their burdens.

6 And Pharaoh commanded the same day the taskmasters of the people, and their officers, saying,   Ex. 5:10

7 Ye shall no more give the people straw to make brick, as ᵀheretofore: let them go and gather straw for themselves.   *before*

8 And the ᵀtale of the bricks, which they did make heretofore, ye shall lay upon them; ye shall not diminish *ought* thereof: for they *be* idle; therefore they cry, saying, Let us go *and* sacrifice to our God.   *counted number*

9 Let there more work be laid upon the men, that they may labour therein; and let them not regard vain words.

10 And the taskmasters of the people went out, and their officers, and they spake to the people, saying, Thus saith Pharaoh, I will not give you straw.   Ex. 1:11

11 Go ye, get you straw where ye can find it: yet not ought of your work shall be diminished.

12 So the people were scattered abroad throughout all the land of Egypt to gather stubble instead of straw.

13 And the taskmasters hasted *them*, saying, Fulfil your works, *your* daily tasks, as when there was straw.

14 And the officers of the children of Israel, which Pharaoh's taskmasters had set over them, were beaten, *and* demanded, Wherefore have ye not fulfilled your task in making brick both yesterday and to day, as heretofore?

Pharaoh Opposes Their Complaints

15 Then the officers of the children of Israel came and cried unto Pharaoh, saying, Wherefore dealest thou thus with thy servants?

16 There is no straw given unto thy servants, and they say to us, Make brick: and, behold, thy servants *are* beaten; but the fault *is* in thine own people.

17 But he said, Ye *are* idle, *ye are* idle: therefore ye say, Let us go *and* do sacrifice to the LORD.

18 Go therefore now, *and* work; for there shall no straw be given you, yet shall ye deliver the tale of bricks.

19 And the officers of the children of Israel did see *that* they *were* in evil *case*, after it was said, Ye shall not ᵀminish *ought* from your bricks of your daily task.   *diminish*

20 And they met Moses and Aaron, who stood in the way, as they came forth from Pharaoh:

21 And they said unto them, The LORD look upon you, and judge; because ye have made our savour to be abhorred in the eyes of Pharaoh, and in the eyes of his servants, to put a sword in their hand to slay us.

5:21 Why Some Preferred Bondage

The Hebrews had expected to obtain their freedom without any special trial of their faith or any real suffering or hardship. But they were not yet prepared for deliverance. . . . Many were content to remain in bondage rather than meet the difficulties attending removal to a strange land; and the habits of some had become so much like those of the Egyptians that they preferred to dwell in Egypt. *PP 260*

22 And Moses returned unto the LORD, and said, Lord, wherefore hast thou *so* evil entreated this people? why *is* it *that* thou hast sent me?

23 For since I came to Pharaoh to speak in thy name, he hath done evil to this people; neither hast thou delivered thy people at all.

God Renews His Promise by His Name Jehovah

6 Then the LORD said unto Moses, Now shalt thou see what I will do to Pharaoh: for with a strong hand shall he let them go, and with a strong hand shall he drive them out of his land.   Ex. 3:19-20; 12:33, 39

2 And God spake unto Moses, and said unto him, I *am* the LORD: Is. 42:8

3 And I appeared unto Abraham, unto Isaac, and unto Jacob, by *the name of* God Almighty, but by my name JEHOVAH was I not known to them.   Gen. 17:1; Ps. 68:4; 83:18

4 And I have also established my covenant with them, to give them the land of Canaan, the land of their pilgrimage, wherein they were strangers.   Gen. 15:18; 17:7-8; 28:4

5 And I have also heard the groaning of the children of Israel, whom the Egyptians keep in bondage; and I have remembered my covenant.   Ex. 2:24

6 Wherefore say unto the children of Israel, I *am* the LORD, and I will bring you out from under the burdens of the Egyptians, and I will rid you out of their bondage, and I will redeem you with a stretched out arm, and with great judgments: Deut. 7:8; 26:8; 1 Chr. 17:21

7 And I will take you to me for a people,

and I will be to you a God: and ye shall know that I *am* the LORD your God, which bringeth you out from under the burdens of the Egyptians.   Deut. 4:20; 7:6; 29:13
8 And I will bring you in unto the land, concerning the which I did swear to give it to Abraham, to Isaac, and to Jacob; and I will give it you for an heritage: I *am* the LORD.   Gen. 14:22; 15:18; 26:3
9 And Moses spake so unto the children of Israel: but they hearkened not unto Moses for anguish of spirit, and for cruel bondage.   Ex. 5:21
10 And the LORD spake unto Moses, saying,
11 Go in, speak unto Pharaoh king of Egypt, that he let the children of Israel go out of his land.
12 And Moses spake before the LORD, saying, Behold, the children of Israel have not hearkened unto me; how then shall Pharaoh hear me, who *am* of uncircumcised lips?   Ex. 4:10; 6:30; Jer. 1:6
13 And the LORD spake unto Moses and unto Aaron, and gave them a charge unto the children of Israel, and unto Pharaoh king of Egypt, to bring the children of Israel out of the land of Egypt.

The Genealogy of Reuben

14 These *be* the heads of their fathers' houses: The sons of Reuben the firstborn of Israel; Hanoch, and Pallu, Hezron, and Carmi: these *be* the families of Reuben.   Num. 26:5-7; 1 Chr. 5:3
15 And the sons of Simeon; Jemuel, and Jamin, and Ohad, and Jachin, and Zohar, and Shaul the son of a Canaanitish woman: these *are* the families of Simeon.   Gen. 46:10; 1 Chr. 4:24
16 And these *are* the names of the sons of Levi according to their generations; Gershon, and Kohath, and Merari: and the years of the life of Levi *were* an hundred thirty and seven years.   Gen. 46:11; Num. 3:17; 1 Chr. 6:1
17 The sons of Gershon; Libni, and Shimi, according to their families. Num. 3:18; 1 Chr. 6:17
18 And the sons of Kohath; Amram, and Izhar, and Hebron, and Uzziel: and the years of the life of Kohath *were* an hundred thirty and three years.   Num. 3:19; 1 Chr. 6:2, 18
19 And the sons of Merari; Mahali and Mushi: these *are* the families of Levi according to their generations.   Num. 3:20; 1 Chr. 6:19
20 And Amram took him Jochebed his father's sister to wife; and she bare him Aaron and Moses: and the years of the life of Amram *were* an hundred and thirty and seven years.   Ex. 2:1-2
21 And the sons of Izhar; Korah, and Nepheg, and Zichri.   Num. 16:1
22 And the sons of Uzziel; Mishael, and Elzaphan, and Zithri.   Lev. 10:4; Num. 3:30
23 And Aaron took him Elisheba, daughter

of Amminadab, sister of Naashon, to wife; and she bare him Nadab, and Abihu, Eleazar, and Ithamar.   Num. 1:7; 2:3; Ruth 4:19-20
24 And the sons of Korah; Assir, and Elkanah, and Abiasaph: these *are* the families of the Korhites.   1 Chr. 6:22-23
25 And Eleazar Aaron's son took him *one* of the daughters of Putiel to wife; and she bare him Phinehas: these *are* the heads of the fathers of the Levites according to their families.   Num. 25:7-13; Josh. 24:33
26 These *are* that Aaron and Moses, to whom the LORD said, Bring out the children of Israel from the land of Egypt according to their armies.   Ex. 7:4; 12:17, 51
27 These *are* they which spake to Pharaoh king of Egypt, to bring out the children of Israel from Egypt: these *are* that Moses and Aaron.
28 And it came to pass on the day *when* the LORD spake unto Moses in the land of Egypt,
29 That the LORD spake unto Moses, saying, I *am* the LORD: speak thou unto Pharaoh king of Egypt all that I say unto thee. Ex. 6:2, 11; 7:2
30 And Moses said before the LORD, Behold, I *am* of uncircumcised lips, and how shall Pharaoh hearken unto me?   Ex. 4:10; 6:12

Moses Is Encouraged to Go to Pharaoh

7 And the LORD said unto Moses, See, I have made thee a god to Pharaoh: and Aaron thy brother shall be thy prophet.
2 Thou shalt speak all that I command thee: and Aaron thy brother shall speak unto Pharaoh, that he send the children of Israel out of his land.   Ex. 4:15
3 And I will harden Pharaoh's heart, and multiply my signs and my wonders in the land of Egypt.   Ex. 4:21; 11:9; Ps. 78:43-51

> **7:2–5 To Humble a Proud Heart**
>
> Before the infliction of each plague, Moses was to describe its nature and effects, that the king might save himself from it if he chose. Every punishment rejected would be followed by one more severe, until his proud heart would be humbled, and he would acknowledge the Maker of heaven and earth as the true and living God. *PP 263*

4 But Pharaoh shall not hearken unto you, that I may lay my hand upon Egypt, and bring forth mine armies, *and* my people the children of Israel, out of the land of Egypt by great judgments.   Ex. 6:6
5 And the Egyptians shall know that I *am* the LORD, when I stretch forth mine hand upon Egypt, and bring out the children of Israel from among them.   Ex. 3:20; 7:17; 8:22
6 And Moses and Aaron did as the LORD commanded them, so did they.   Ex. 7:2

7 And Moses *was* ᵀfourscore years old, and Aaron fourscore and three years old, when they spake unto Pharaoh. Deut. 31:2; 34:7 ◆ *eighty*

Moses' Rod Is Turned into a Serpent

8 And the LORD spake unto Moses and unto Aaron, saying,

9 When Pharaoh shall speak unto you, saying, Shew a miracle for you: then thou shalt say unto Aaron, Take thy rod, and cast *it* before Pharaoh, *and* it shall become a serpent. Ex. 4:2; Is. 7:11; John 2:18

10 And Moses and Aaron went in unto Pharaoh, and they did so as the LORD had commanded: and Aaron cast down his rod before Pharaoh, and before his servants, and it became a serpent. Ex. 4:3

11 Then Pharaoh also called the wise men and the sorcerers: now the magicians of Egypt, they also did in like manner with their enchantments. Gen. 41:8; Ex. 7:22; 8:7

12 For they cast down every man his rod, and they became serpents: but Aaron's rod swallowed up their rods.

> **7:12 No Power to Give Life**
>
> The magicians did not really cause their rods to become serpents; but by magic, aided by the great deceiver, they were able to produce this appearance. It was beyond the power of Satan to change the rods to living serpents. The prince of evil, though possessing all the wisdom and might of an angel fallen, has not power to create, or to give life; this is the prerogative of God alone. *PP 264*

13 And he hardened Pharaoh's heart, that he hearkened not unto them; as the LORD had said. Ex. 4:21

The Plague of Water Turned to Blood

14 And the LORD said unto Moses, Pharaoh's heart *is* hardened, he refuseth to let the people go. Ex. 8:15

15 Get thee unto Pharaoh in the morning; lo, he goeth out unto the water; and thou shalt stand by the river's brink against he come; and the rod which was turned to a serpent shalt thou take in thine hand. Ex. 8:20

16 And thou shalt say unto him, The LORD God of the Hebrews hath sent me unto thee, saying, Let my people go, that they may serve me in the wilderness: and, behold, ᵀhitherto thou wouldest not hear. Ex. 3:12, 18 ◆ *up to now*

17 Thus saith the LORD, In this thou shalt know that I *am* the LORD: behold, I will ᵀsmite with the rod that *is* in mine hand upon the waters which *are* in the river, and they shall be turned to blood. Ex. 4:9; 5:2; 7:5 ◆ *strike*

18 And the fish that *is* in the river shall die, and the river shall stink; and the Egyptians shall lothe to drink of the water of the river. Ex. 7:21, 24

19 And the LORD spake unto Moses, Say unto Aaron, Take thy rod, and stretch out thine hand upon the waters of Egypt, upon their streams, upon their rivers, and upon their ponds, and upon all their pools of water, that they may become blood; and *that* there may be blood throughout all the land of Egypt, both in *vessels of* wood, and in *vessels of* stone. Ex. 8:5-6, 16; 10:12

20 And Moses and Aaron did so, as the LORD commanded; and he lifted up the rod, and smote the waters that *were* in the river, in the sight of Pharaoh, and in the sight of his servants; and all the waters that *were* in the river were turned to blood. Ps. 78:44; 105:29

21 And the fish that *was* in the river died; and the river stank, and the Egyptians could not drink of the water of the river; and there was blood throughout all the land of Egypt. Ex. 7:18

22 And the magicians of Egypt did so with their ᵀenchantments: and Pharaoh's heart was hardened, neither did he hearken unto them; as the LORD had said. Ex. 7:11 ◆ *secret arts*

23 And Pharaoh turned and went into his house, neither did he set his heart to this also.

24 And all the Egyptians digged round about the river for water to drink; for they could not drink of the water of the river.

25 And seven days were fulfilled, after that the LORD had smitten the river.

The Plague of Frogs

8 And the LORD spake unto Moses, Go unto Pharaoh, and say unto him, Thus saith the LORD, Let my people go, that they may serve me. Ex. 3:12, 18; 5:1

2 And if thou refuse to let *them* go, behold, I will smite all thy borders with frogs: Ex. 7:14

3 And the river shall bring forth frogs abundantly, which shall go up and come into thine house, and into thy bedchamber, and upon thy bed, and into the house of thy servants, and upon thy people, and into thine ovens, and into thy kneadingtroughs:

4 And the frogs shall come up both on thee, and upon thy people, and upon all thy servants.

> **8:2–4 A Plague of Slimy Pests**
>
> The frog was regarded as sacred by the Egyptians, and they would not destroy it; but the slimy pests had now become intolerable. They swarmed even in the palace of the Pharaohs, and the king was impatient to have them removed. The magicians had appeared to produce frogs, but they could not remove them. *PP 265*

5 And the Lord spake unto Moses, Say unto Aaron, Stretch forth thine hand with thy rod over the streams, over the rivers, and over the ponds, and cause frogs to come up upon the land of Egypt.   Ex. 7:19

6 And Aaron stretched out his hand over the waters of Egypt; and the frogs came up, and covered the land of Egypt.   Ps. 78:45; 105:30

7 And the magicians did so with their ᵀenchantments, and brought up frogs upon the land of Egypt.   Ex. 7:11, 22 ◆ secret arts

8 Then Pharaoh called for Moses and Aaron, and said, Intreat the Lord, that he may take away the frogs from me, and from my people; and I will let the people go, that they may do sacrifice unto the Lord. Ex. 9:28; 10:17; Num. 21:7

9 And Moses said unto Pharaoh, Glory over me: when shall I ᵀintreat for thee, and for thy servants, and for thy people, to destroy the frogs from thee and thy houses, *that* they may remain in the river only?   plead

10 And he said, To morrow. And he said, *Be it* according to thy word: that thou mayest know that *there is* none like unto the Lord our God.   Ex. 9:14; Deut. 33:26; 2 Sam. 7:22

11 And the frogs shall depart from thee, and from thy houses, and from thy servants, and from thy people; they shall remain in the river only.

12 And Moses and Aaron went out from Pharaoh: and Moses cried unto the Lord because of the frogs which he had brought against Pharaoh.   Ex. 8:30

13 And the Lord did according to the word of Moses; and the frogs died out of the houses, out of the villages, and out of the fields.

14 And they gathered them together upon heaps: and the land stank.

15 But when Pharaoh saw that there was respite, he hardened his heart, and hearkened not unto them; as the Lord had said. Ex. 7:4

The Plague of Lice

16 And the Lord said unto Moses, Say unto Aaron, Stretch out thy rod, and ᵀsmite the dust of the land, that it may become lice throughout all the land of Egypt.   strike

17 And they did so; for Aaron stretched out his hand with his rod, and smote the dust of the earth, and it became lice in man, and in beast; all the dust of the land became lice throughout all the land of Egypt.   Ps. 105:31

18 And the magicians did so with their enchantments to bring forth lice, but they could not: so there were lice upon man, and upon beast.   Ex. 7:11; 9:11; Dan. 5:8

19 Then the magicians said unto Pharaoh, This *is* the finger of God: and Pharaoh's heart was hardened, and he hearkened not unto them; as the Lord had said.   Ps. 8:3; Luke 11:20

The Plague of Swarms of Flies That Cover the Land

20 And the Lord said unto Moses, Rise up early in the morning, and stand before Pharaoh; lo, he cometh forth to the water; and say unto him, Thus saith the Lord, Let my people go, that they may serve me.   Ex. 7:15

21 Else, if thou wilt not let my people go, behold, I will send swarms *of flies* upon thee, and upon thy servants, and upon thy people, and into thy houses: and the houses of the Egyptians shall be full of swarms *of flies*, and also the ground whereon they *are*.

22 And I will sever in that day the land of Goshen, in which my people dwell, that no swarms *of flies* shall be there; to the end thou mayest know that I *am* the Lord in the midst of the earth.   Ex. 9:4, 6; 10:23

23 And I will put a division between my people and thy people: to morrow shall this sign be.

24 And the Lord did so; and there came a grievous swarm *of flies* into the house of Pharaoh, and *into* his servants' houses, and into all the land of Egypt: the land was corrupted by reason of the swarm *of flies*. Ps. 78:45; 105:31

25 And Pharaoh called for Moses and for Aaron, and said, Go ye, sacrifice to your God in the land.   Ex. 8:8

26 And Moses said, It is not meet so to do; for we shall sacrifice the abomination of the Egyptians to the Lord our God: lo, shall we sacrifice the abomination of the Egyptians before their eyes, and will they not stone us?   Gen. 43:32; 46:34

27 We will go three days' journey into the wilderness, and sacrifice to the Lord our God, as he shall command us.   Ex. 3:12, 18

28 And Pharaoh said, I will let you go, that ye may sacrifice to the Lord your God in the wilderness; only ye shall not go very far away: intreat for me.   Ex. 8:8; 9:28; 1 Kin. 13:6

29 And Moses said, Behold, I go out from thee, and I will intreat the Lord that the swarms *of flies* may depart from Pharaoh, from his servants, and from his people, to morrow: but let not Pharaoh deal deceitfully any more in not letting the people go to sacrifice to the Lord.   Ex. 8:8, 15; Jer. 42:20-21

30 And Moses went out from Pharaoh, and ᵀintreated the Lord.   Ex. 8:12 ◆ pled with

31 And the Lord did according to the word of Moses; and he removed the swarms *of flies* from Pharaoh, from his servants, and from his people; there remained not one.

32 And Pharaoh hardened his heart at this time also, neither would he let the people go.   Ex. 4:21; 8:15

The Plague of Death on the Beasts

9 Then the LORD said unto Moses, Go in unto Pharaoh, and tell him, Thus saith the LORD God of the Hebrews, Let my people go, that they may serve me.   Ex. 8:1
2 For if thou refuse to let *them* go, and wilt hold them still,   Ex. 8:2
3 Behold, the hand of the LORD is upon thy cattle which *is* in the field, upon the horses, upon the asses, upon the camels, upon the oxen, and upon the sheep: *there shall be* a very grievous ᵀmurrain.   Ex. 7:4; Acts 13:11 ◆ *plague*
4 And the LORD shall sever between the cattle of Israel and the cattle of Egypt: and there shall nothing die of all *that is* the children's of Israel.   Ex. 8:22
5 And the LORD appointed a set time, saying, To morrow the LORD shall do this thing in the land.
6 And the LORD did that thing on the morrow, and all the cattle of Egypt died: but of the cattle of the children of Israel died not one.   Ps. 78:48
7 And Pharaoh sent, and, behold, there was not one of the cattle of the Israelites dead. And the heart of Pharaoh was hardened, and he did not let the people go.   Ex. 7:14; 8:32

The Plague of Boils and Blisters

8 And the LORD said unto Moses and unto Aaron, Take to you handfuls of ashes of the furnace, and let Moses sprinkle it toward the heaven in the sight of Pharaoh.
9 And it shall become small dust in all the land of Egypt, and shall be a boil breaking forth *with* blains upon man, and upon beast, throughout all the land of Egypt. Deut. 28:27, 35
10 And they took ashes of the furnace, and stood before Pharaoh; and Moses sprinkled it up toward heaven; and it became a boil breaking forth *with* ᵀblains upon man, and upon beast.   *skin tumors*
11 And the magicians could not stand before Moses because of the boils; for the boil was upon the magicians, and upon all the Egyptians.
12 And the LORD hardened the heart of Pharaoh, and he hearkened not unto them; as the LORD had spoken unto Moses. Ex. 4:21

Moses Warns about the Coming Hail

13 And the LORD said unto Moses, Rise up early in the morning, and stand before Pharaoh, and say unto him, Thus saith the LORD God of the Hebrews, Let my people go, that they may serve me.   Ex. 7:15; 8:20
14 For I will at this time send all my plagues upon thine heart, and upon thy servants, and upon thy people; that thou mayest know that *there is* none like me in all the earth. Ex. 8:10
15 For now I will stretch out my hand, that I may ᵀsmite thee and thy people with pestilence; and thou shalt be cut off from the earth.   Ex. 3:20 ◆ *strike*
16 And in very deed for this *cause* have I raised thee up, for to shew *in* thee my power; and that my name may be declared throughout all the earth. Ps. 83:17-18; Prov. 16:4; Rom. 9:17
17 As yet exaltest thou thyself against my people, that thou wilt not let them go?
18 Behold, to morrow about this time I will cause it to rain a very grievous hail, such as hath not been in Egypt since the foundation thereof even until now.
19 Send therefore now, *and* gather thy cattle, and all that thou hast in the field; *for upon* every man and beast which shall be found in the field, and shall not be brought home, the hail shall come down upon them, and they shall die.
20 He that feared the word of the LORD among the servants of Pharaoh made his servants and his cattle flee into the houses:
21 And he that regarded not the word of the LORD left his servants and his cattle in the field.

The Plague of Hail

22 And the LORD said unto Moses, Stretch forth thine hand toward heaven, that there may be hail in all the land of Egypt, upon man, and upon beast, and upon every herb of the field, throughout the land of Egypt. Rev. 16:21
23 And Moses stretched forth his rod toward heaven: and the LORD sent thunder and hail, and the fire ran along upon the ground; and the LORD rained hail upon the land of Egypt.   Josh. 10:11; Ps. 18:13; Is. 30:30
24 So there was hail, and fire mingled with the hail, very grievous, such as there was none like it in all the land of Egypt since it became a nation.
25 And the hail smote throughout all the land of Egypt all that *was* in the field, both man and beast; and the hail smote every herb of the field, and brake every tree of the field.
26 Only in the land of Goshen, where the children of Israel *were*, was there no hail.
27 And Pharaoh sent, and called for Moses and Aaron, and said unto them, I have sinned this time: the LORD *is* righteous, and I and my people *are* wicked. Ex. 10:16; 2 Chr. 12:6; Ps. 129:4

9:27 Sorry, But Only for Sin's Results

Pharaoh, when suffering under the judgments of God, acknowledged his sin in order to escape further punishment, but returned to his defiance of Heaven as soon as the plagues were stayed. These all lamented the results of sin, but did not sorrow for the sin itself. *SC 24*

28 Intreat the LORD (for *it is* enough) that there be no *more* mighty thunderings and hail; and I will let you go, and ye shall stay no longer.   Ex. 8:8, 28; 10:17

29 And Moses said unto him, As soon as I am gone out of the city, I will spread abroad my hands unto the LORD; *and* the thunder shall cease, neither shall there be any more hail; that thou mayest know how that the earth *is* the LORD's.   1 Kin. 8:22, 38; Ps. 143:6

30 But as for thee and thy servants, I know that ye will not yet fear the LORD God. Is. 26:10

31 And the flax and the barley was smitten: for the barley *was* in the ear, and the flax *was* ᵀbolled.   Ruth 1:22 ◆ *blossomed*

32 But the wheat and the ᵀrie were not smitten: for they *were* not grown up.   *rye*

33 And Moses went out of the city from Pharaoh, and spread abroad his hands unto the LORD: and the thunders and hail ceased, and the rain was not poured upon the earth.   Ex. 9:29

34 And when Pharaoh saw that the rain and the hail and the thunders were ceased, he sinned yet more, and hardened his heart, he and his servants.   Ex. 7:14

35 And the heart of Pharaoh was hardened, neither would he let the children of Israel go; as the LORD had spoken by Moses.   Ex. 4:21

God Threatens to Send Locusts

10 And the LORD said unto Moses, Go in unto Pharaoh: for I have hardened his heart, and the heart of his servants, that I might shew these my signs before him: Ex. 4:21

2 And that thou mayest tell in the ears of thy son, and of thy son's son, what things I have ᵀwrought in Egypt, and my signs which I have done among them; that ye may know how that I *am* the LORD.   Deut. 4:9; Joel 1:3 ◆ *done*

3 And Moses and Aaron came in unto Pharaoh, and said unto him, Thus saith the LORD God of the Hebrews, How long wilt thou refuse to humble thyself before me? let my people go, that they may serve me.   1 Kin. 21:29; James 4:10; 1 Pet. 5:6

4 Else, if thou refuse to let my people go, behold, to morrow will I bring the locusts into thy coast: Rev. 9:3

5 And they shall cover the face of the earth, that one cannot be able to see the earth: and they shall eat the residue of that which is escaped, which remaineth unto you from the hail, and shall eat every tree which groweth for you out of the field: Ex. 9:32

6 And they shall fill thy houses, and the houses of all thy servants, and the houses of all the Egyptians; which neither thy fathers, nor thy fathers' fathers have seen, since the day that they were upon the earth unto this day. And he turned himself, and went out from Pharaoh.   Ex. 8:3

7 And Pharaoh's servants said unto him, How long shall this man be a snare unto us? let the men go, that they may serve the LORD their God: knowest thou not yet that Egypt is destroyed?   Ex. 23:33

8 And Moses and Aaron were brought again unto Pharaoh: and he said unto them, Go, serve the LORD your God: *but* who *are* they that shall go?   Ex. 10:24

9 And Moses said, We will go with our young and with our old, with our sons and with our daughters, with our flocks and with our herds will we go; for we *must hold* a feast unto the LORD.   Ex. 3:18

10 And he said unto them, Let the LORD be so with you, as I will let you go, and your little ones: look *to it*; for evil *is* before you.

11 Not so: go now ye *that are* men, and serve the LORD; for that ye did desire. And they were driven out from Pharaoh's presence.   Ex. 10:28

The Plague of Locusts

12 And the LORD said unto Moses, Stretch out thine hand over the land of Egypt for the locusts, that they may come up upon the land of Egypt, and eat every herb of the land, *even* all that the hail hath left.   Ex. 7:19; 10:4-5

13 And Moses stretched forth his rod over the land of Egypt, and the LORD brought an east wind upon the land all that day, and all *that* night; *and* when it was morning, the east wind brought the locusts.

14 And the locusts went up over all the land of Egypt, and rested in all the coasts of Egypt: very grievous *were they*; before them there were no such locusts as they, neither after them shall be such.   Ps. 78:46

15 For they covered the face of the whole earth, so that the land was darkened; and they did eat every herb of the land, and all the fruit of the trees which the hail had left: and there remained not any green thing in the trees, or in the herbs of the field, through all the land of Egypt.   Ex. 10:5

16 Then Pharaoh called for Moses and Aaron in haste; and he said, I have sinned against the LORD your God, and against you.   Ex. 9:27

17 Now therefore forgive, I pray thee, my sin only this once, and ᵀintreat the LORD your God, that he may take away from me this death only.   Ex. 8:8; 9:28; 1 Kin. 13:6 ◆ *plead with*

18 And he went out from Pharaoh, and ᵀintreated the LORD.   *pled with*

19 And the LORD turned a mighty strong west wind, which took away the locusts, and cast them into the Red sea; there

remained not one locust in all the coasts of Egypt.   Joel 2:20
20 But the LORD hardened Pharaoh's heart, so that he would not let the children of Israel go.   Ex. 4:21; 11:10

The Plague of Darkness

21 And the LORD said unto Moses, Stretch out thine hand toward heaven, that there may be darkness over the land of Egypt, even darkness *which* may be felt.   Ex. 9:22
22 And Moses stretched forth his hand toward heaven; and there was a thick darkness in all the land of Egypt three days: Ps. 105:28
23 They saw not one another, neither rose any from his place for three days: but all the children of Israel had light in their dwellings.   Ex. 8:22; 9:4

10:21–23 An Oppressive Darkness

Suddenly a darkness settled upon the land, so thick and black that it seemed a "darkness which may be felt." Not only were the people deprived of light, but the atmosphere was very oppressive, so that breathing was difficult. "They saw not one another, neither rose any from his place for three days: but all the children of Israel had light in their dwellings." The sun and moon were objects of worship to the Egyptians; in this mysterious darkness the people and their gods alike were smitten by the power that had undertaken the cause of the bondmen. *PP 272*

---

24 And Pharaoh called unto Moses, and said, Go ye, serve the LORD; only let your flocks and your herds be ᵀstayed: let your little ones also go with you. Ex. 10:8-10 ◆ *held back*
25 And Moses said, Thou must give us also sacrifices and burnt offerings, that we may sacrifice unto the LORD our God.
26 Our cattle also shall go with us; there shall not an hoof be left behind; for thereof must we take to serve the LORD our God; and we know not with what we must serve the LORD, until we come thither.
27 But the LORD hardened Pharaoh's heart, and he would not let them go.   Ex. 4:21; 14:4
28 And Pharaoh said unto him, Get thee from me, take heed to thyself, see my face no more; for in *that* day thou seest my face thou shalt die.
29 And Moses said, Thou hast spoken well, I will see thy face again no more.   Heb. 11:27

God's Message to the Israelites

11 And the LORD said unto Moses, Yet will I bring one plague *more* upon Pharaoh, and upon Egypt; afterwards he will let you go hence: when he shall let *you*

go, he shall surely thrust you out hence altogether.
2 Speak now in the ears of the people, and let every man borrow of his neighbour, and every woman of her neighbour, jewels of silver, and jewels of gold.   Ex. 3:22; 12:35-36
3 And the LORD gave the people favour in the sight of the Egyptians. Moreover the man Moses *was* very great in the land of Egypt, in the sight of Pharaoh's servants, and in the sight of the people.   Ex. 3:21

Moses Threatens Pharaoh with the Death of the Firstborn

4 And Moses said, Thus saith the LORD, About midnight will I go out into the midst of Egypt: Ex. 12:29; Job 34:20; Amos 4:10
5 And all the firstborn in the land of Egypt shall die, from the firstborn of Pharaoh that sitteth upon his throne, even unto the firstborn of the maidservant that *is* behind the mill; and all the firstborn of beasts. Ps. 78:51
6 And there shall be a great cry throughout all the land of Egypt, such as there was none like it, nor shall be like it any more. Ex. 12:30
7 But against any of the children of Israel shall not a dog move his tongue, against man or beast: that ye may know how that the LORD doth put a difference between the Egyptians and Israel.   Ex. 8:22
8 And all these thy servants shall come down unto me, and bow down themselves unto me, saying, Get thee out, and all the people that follow thee: and after that I will go out. And he went out from Pharaoh in a great anger.   Ex. 12:31-33
9 And the LORD said unto Moses, Pharaoh shall not hearken unto you; that my wonders may be multiplied in the land of Egypt.   Ex. 7:3-4
10 And Moses and Aaron did all these wonders before Pharaoh: and the LORD hardened Pharaoh's heart, so that he would not let the children of Israel go out of his land.   Ex. 4:21

The Beginning of the Year Is Changed, and the Passover Is Instituted

12 And the LORD spake unto Moses and Aaron in the land of Egypt, saying,
2 This month *shall be* unto you the beginning of months: it *shall be* the first month of the year to you.   Ex. 13:4; 23:15; Deut. 16:1
3 Speak ye unto all the congregation of Israel, saying, In the tenth *day* of this month they shall take to them every man a lamb, according to the house of *their* fathers, a lamb for an house:
4 And if the household be too little for the lamb, let him and his neighbour next unto his house take *it* according to the number of

the souls; every man according to his eating shall make your count for the lamb.

5 Your lamb shall be without blemish, a male of the first year: ye shall take *it* out from the sheep, or from the goats: Lev. 23:12

6 And ye shall keep it up until the fourteenth day of the same month: and the whole assembly of the congregation of Israel shall kill it in the evening.   Ex. 16:12; Lev. 23:5; Num. 28:16

7 And they shall take of the blood, and strike *it* on the two side posts and on the upper door post of the houses, wherein they shall eat it.

12:7 Christ Died for Us Individually

It was not enough that the paschal lamb be slain; its blood must be sprinkled upon the doorposts; so the merits of Christ's blood must be applied to the soul. We must believe, not only that He died for the world, but that He died for us individually. We must appropriate to ourselves the virtue of the atoning sacrifice. *PP 277*

---

8 And they shall eat the flesh in that night, roast with fire, and unleavened bread; *and* with bitter *herbs* they shall eat it. Ex. 13:3; 34:25

9 Eat not of it raw, nor sodden at all with water, but roast *with* fire; his head with his legs, and with the purtenance thereof. Ex. 12:8

10 And ye shall let nothing of it remain until the morning; and that which remaineth of it until the morning ye shall burn with fire.   Ex. 23:18; 29:34; 34:25

11 And thus shall ye eat it; *with* your ᵀloins girded, your shoes on your feet, and your staff in your hand; and ye shall eat it in haste: it *is* the LORD's passover.   Lev. 23:5; Eph. 6:15 ◆ *waist*

12:8–11 Nourished by the Word

The flesh was to be eaten. It is not enough even that we believe on Christ for the forgiveness of sin; we must by faith be constantly receiving spiritual strength and nourishment from Him through His word. Said Christ, "Except ye eat the flesh of the Son of man, and drink His blood, ye have no life in you. Whoso eateth My flesh, and drinketh My blood, hath eternal life" (John 6:53, 54). *PP 277*

---

12 For I will pass through the land of Egypt this night, and will smite all the firstborn in the land of Egypt, both man and beast; and against all the gods of Egypt I will execute judgment: I *am* the LORD. Ex. 6:2; 12:23; Num. 33:4

13 And the blood shall be to you for a token upon the houses where ye *are*: and when I see the blood, I will pass over you, and the plague shall not be upon you to destroy *you*, when I ᵀsmite the land of Egypt.   Heb. 11:28 ◆ *strike*

14 And this day shall be unto you for a memorial; and ye shall keep it a feast to the LORD throughout your generations; ye shall keep it a feast by an ordinance for ever.   Ex. 12:17, 24; 13:9-10

15 Seven days shall ye eat unleavened bread; even the first day ye shall put away leaven out of your houses: for whosoever eateth leavened bread from the first day until the seventh day, that soul shall be cut off from Israel.   Gen. 17:14; Ex. 23:15; Deut. 16:3

16 And in the first day *there shall be* an holy convocation, and in the seventh day there shall be an holy convocation to you; no manner of work shall be done in them, save *that* which every man must eat, that only may be done of you.   Lev. 23:7-8

17 And ye shall observe *the feast of* unleavened bread; for in this selfsame day have I brought your armies out of the land of Egypt: therefore shall ye observe this day in your generations by an ordinance for ever.   Ex. 13:3

18 In the first *month*, on the fourteenth day of the month at even, ye shall eat unleavened bread, until the one and twentieth day of the month at even.   Ex. 12:15

19 Seven days shall there be no leaven found in your houses: for whosoever eateth that which is leavened, even that soul shall be cut off from the congregation of Israel, whether he be a stranger, or born in the land.   Ex. 12:15, 43, 48

20 Ye shall eat nothing leavened; in all your habitations shall ye eat unleavened bread.

21 Then Moses called for all the elders of Israel, and said unto them, Draw out and take you a lamb according to your families, and kill the passover.   Ex. 12:3; Mark 14:12-16

22 And ye shall take a bunch of ᵀhyssop, and dip *it* in the blood that *is* in the bason, and strike the ᵀlintel and the two side posts with the blood that *is* in the bason; and none of you shall go out at the door of his house until the morning.   Heb. 11:28 ◆ *bitter herbs* ◆ *top of the door frame*

23 For the LORD will pass through to smite the Egyptians; and when he seeth the blood upon the lintel, and on the two side posts, the LORD will pass over the door, and will not suffer the destroyer to come in unto your houses to smite *you*.   Ex. 12:12-13; Heb. 11:28; Rev. 7:3

24 And ye shall observe this thing for an ordinance to thee and to thy sons for ever.

25 And it shall come to pass, when ye be come to the land which the LORD will give you, according as he hath promised, that ye shall keep this service.   Ex. 3:8

26 And it shall come to pass, when your children shall say unto you, What mean ye by this service?   Ex. 13:14-15

27 That ye shall say, It *is* the sacrifice of the LORD's passover, who passed over the

houses of the children of Israel in Egypt, when he smote the Egyptians, and delivered our houses. And the people bowed the head and worshipped.   Ex. 4:31; 12:11

28 And the children of Israel went away, and did as the LORD had commanded Moses and Aaron, so did they.

12:21-28 Pointing Back—and Forward

The Passover was to be both commemorative and typical [symbolic], not only pointing back to the deliverance from Egypt, but forward to the greater deliverance which Christ was to accomplish in freeing His people from the bondage of sin. The sacrificial lamb represents "the Lamb of God," in whom is our only hope of salvation. Says the apostle, "Christ our Passover is sacrificed for us" (1 Corinthians 5:7). *PP 277*

The Firstborn Are Slain

29 And it came to pass, that at midnight the LORD smote all the firstborn in the land of Egypt, from the firstborn of Pharaoh that sat on his throne unto the firstborn of the captive that *was* in the dungeon; and all the firstborn of cattle.   Ex. 4:23; 11:4-5; Ps. 78:51

30 And Pharaoh rose up in the night, he, and all his servants, and all the Egyptians; and there was a great cry in Egypt; for *there was* not a house where *there was* not one dead.   Ex. 11:6; Amos 5:17

31 And he called for Moses and Aaron by night, and said, Rise up, *and* get you forth from among my people, both ye and the children of Israel; and go, serve the LORD, as ye have said.   Ex. 10:9

32 Also take your flocks and your herds, as ye have said, and be gone; and bless me also.   Ex. 10:26

33 And the Egyptians were urgent upon the people, that they might send them out of the land in haste; for they said, We *be* all dead *men*.   Ex. 11:1; Ps. 105:38

34 And the people took their dough before it

was leavened, their kneadingtroughs being bound up in their clothes upon their shoulders.

35 And the children of Israel did according to the word of Moses; and they borrowed of the Egyptians jewels of silver, and jewels of gold, and ᵀraiment: Ex. 3:21-22 ◆ *clothing*

36 And the LORD gave the people favour in the sight of the Egyptians, so that they lent unto them *such things as they required.* And they spoiled the Egyptians.   Gen. 15:14

37 And the children of Israel journeyed from Rameses to Succoth, about six hundred thousand on foot *that were* men, beside children.   Ex. 38:26; Num. 1:46; 11:21

38 And a mixed multitude went up also with them; and flocks, and herds, *even* very much cattle.   Num. 11:4

12:37, 38 The Mixed Multitude

And they went out, "about six hundred thousand on foot that were men, beside children. And a mixed multitude went up also with them." In this multitude were not only those who were actuated by faith in the God of Israel, but also a far greater number who desired only to escape from the plagues, or who followed in the wake of the moving multitudes merely from excitement and curiosity. This class were ever a hindrance and a snare to Israel. *PP 281*

---

39 And they baked unleavened cakes of the dough which they brought forth out of Egypt, for it was not leavened; because they were thrust out of Egypt, and could not tarry, neither had they prepared for themselves any victual.   Ex. 6:1

40 Now the sojourning of the children of Israel, who dwelt in Egypt, *was* four hundred and thirty years.   Gen. 15:13

41 And it came to pass at the end of the four hundred and thirty years, even the selfsame day it came to pass, that all the hosts of the LORD went out from the land of Egypt.

42 It *is* a night to be much observed unto the

God's Purpose Through Israel

Exodus 12:31, 32

It was in order that the Israelites might be a blessing to the nations, and that God's name might be made known "throughout all the earth" (Exodus 9:16), that they were delivered from Egyptian bondage. If obedient to His requirements, they were to be placed far in advance of other peoples in wisdom and understanding; but this supremacy was to be reached and maintained only in order that through them the purpose of God for "all nations of the earth" might be fulfilled.

The marvelous providences connected with Israel's deliverance from Egyptian bondage and with their occupancy of the Promised Land led many of the heathen to recognize the God of Israel as the Supreme Ruler. "The Egyptians shall know," had been the promise, "that I am the Lord, when I stretch forth Mine hand upon Egypt, and bring out the children of Israel from among them" (Exodus 7:5). Even proud Pharaoh was constrained to acknowledge Jehovah's power. "Go, serve the Lord," he urged Moses and Aaron, "and bless me also" (Exodus 12:31, 32). *PK 368, 369*

LORD for bringing them out from the land of Egypt: this *is* that night of the LORD to be observed of all the children of Israel in their generations. Deut. 16:1-6

The Ordinance of the Passover

43 And the LORD said unto Moses and Aaron, This *is* the ordinance of the passover: There shall no stranger eat thereof: Lev. 22:10; Num. 9:14

44 But every man's servant that is bought for money, when thou hast circumcised him, then shall he eat thereof. Gen. 17:12-13

45 A foreigner and an hired servant shall not eat thereof. Lev. 22:10

46 In one house shall it be eaten; thou shalt not carry forth ought of the flesh abroad out of the house; neither shall ye break a bone thereof. Num. 9:12; John 19:33, 36

47 All the congregation of Israel shall keep it. Ex. 12:6

48 And when a stranger shall sojourn with thee, and will keep the passover to the LORD, let all his males be circumcised, and then let him come near and keep it; and he shall be as one that is born in the land: for no uncircumcised person shall eat thereof. Num. 9:14

49 One law shall be to him that is home-born, and unto the stranger that sojourneth among you. Lev. 24:22; Num. 15:15-16, 29

50 Thus did all the children of Israel; as the LORD commanded Moses and Aaron, so did they.

51 And it came to pass the selfsame day, *that* the LORD did bring the children of Israel out of the land of Egypt by their armies. Ex. 12:41

The Firstborn Are Sanctified to God

13 And the LORD spake unto Moses, saying,

2 Sanctify unto me all the firstborn, whatsoever openeth the womb among the children of Israel, *both* of man and of beast: it *is* mine. Num. 3:13; Deut. 15:19; Luke 2:23

3 And Moses said unto the people, Remember this day, in which ye came out from Egypt, out of the house of bondage; for by strength of hand the LORD brought you out from this *place*: there shall no leavened bread be eaten. Ex. 6:1; 12:8; Deut. 16:3

4 This day came ye out in the month Abib.

5 And it shall be when the LORD shall bring thee into the land of the Canaanites, and the Hittites, and the Amorites, and the Hivites, and the Jebusites, which he sware unto thy fathers to give thee, a land flowing with milk and honey, that thou shalt keep this service in this month. Ex. 3:8; 6:8; 12:25-26

6 Seven days thou shalt eat unleavened bread, and in the seventh day *shall be* a feast to the LORD. Ex. 12:15-20

7 Unleavened bread shall be eaten seven days; and there shall no leavened bread be seen with thee, neither shall there be leaven seen with thee in all thy quarters. Ex. 12:19

8 And thou shalt shew thy son in that day, saying, *This is done* because of that *which* the LORD did unto me when I came forth out of Egypt. Ex. 13:14

9 And it shall be for a sign unto thee upon thine hand, and for a memorial between thine eyes, that the LORD's law may be in thy mouth: for with a strong hand hath the LORD brought thee out of Egypt. Ex. 12:14; Deut. 6:8

10 Thou shalt therefore keep this ordinance in his season from year to year. Ex. 12:14

The Firstborn of Beasts Are Set Apart

11 And it shall be when the LORD shall bring thee into the land of the Canaanites, as he sware unto thee and to thy fathers, and shall give it thee,

12 That thou shalt set apart unto the LORD all that openeth the matrix, and every firstling that cometh of a beast which thou hast; the males *shall be* the LORD's. Lev. 27:26; Num. 18:15

13 And every ᵀfirstling of an ass thou shalt redeem with a lamb; and if thou wilt not redeem it, then thou shalt break his neck: and all the firstborn of man among thy children shalt thou redeem. Num. 18:15-17 ♦ *firstborn*

14 And it shall be when thy son asketh thee in time to come, saying, What *is* this? that thou shalt say unto him, By strength of hand the LORD brought us out from Egypt, from the house of bondage: Ex. 13:3; Josh. 4:6

15 And it came to pass, when Pharaoh would hardly let us go, that the LORD slew all the firstborn in the land of Egypt, both the firstborn of man, and the firstborn of beast: therefore I sacrifice to the LORD all that openeth the ᵀmatrix, being males; but all the firstborn of my children I redeem. Ex. 12:29 ♦ *womb*

16 And it shall be for a token upon thine hand, and for ᵀfrontlets between thine eyes: for by strength of hand the LORD brought us forth out of Egypt. Ex. 13:9, 14 ♦ *a case worn on one's forehead*

The Israelites Go out of Egypt, and Carry Joseph's Bones with Them

17 And it came to pass, when Pharaoh had let the people go, that God led them not *through* the way of the land of the Philistines, although that *was* near; for God said, Lest ᵀperadventure the people repent when they see war, and they return to Egypt: *maybe*

18 But God led the people about, *through* the way of the wilderness of the Red sea: and the children of Israel went up harnessed out of the land of Egypt. Ex. 14:2

19 And Moses took the bones of Joseph with him: for he had ᵀstraitly sworn the children of Israel, saying, God will surely visit you; and ye shall carry up my bones away hence with you. Gen. 50:24-25; Josh. 24:32; Acts 7:16 ♦ *with strictness*

20 And they took their journey from Succoth, and encamped in Etham, in the edge of the wilderness.

21 And the LORD went before them by day in a pillar of a cloud, to lead them the way; and by night in a pillar of fire, to give them light; to go by day and night: Neh. 9:12; Ps. 78:14

22 He took not away the pillar of the cloud by day, nor the pillar of fire by night, *from* before the people.

God Instructs the Israelites in Their Journey

14 And the LORD spake unto Moses, saying,

2 Speak unto the children of Israel, that they turn and encamp before Pi-hahiroth, between Migdol and the sea, over against Baal-zephon: before it shall ye encamp by the sea.   Num. 33:7-8; Jer. 44:1

3 For Pharaoh will say of the children of Israel, They *are* entangled in the land, the wilderness hath shut them in.

4 And I will harden Pharaoh's heart, that he shall follow after them; and I will be honoured upon Pharaoh, and upon all his host; that the Egyptians may know that I *am* the LORD. And they did so.   Ex. 7:5; Rom. 9:17, 22-23

5 And it was told the king of Egypt that the people fled: and the heart of Pharaoh and of his servants was turned against the people, and they said, Why have we done this, that we have let Israel go from serving us?   Ps. 105:25

6 And he made ready his chariot, and took his people with him:

7 And he took six hundred chosen chariots, and all the chariots of Egypt, and captains over every one of them.   Ex. 15:4

8 And the LORD hardened the heart of Pharaoh king of Egypt, and he pursued after the children of Israel: and the children of Israel went out with an high hand.   Num. 33:3

9 But the Egyptians pursued after them, all the horses *and* chariots of Pharaoh, and his horsemen, and his army, and overtook them encamping by the sea, beside Pi-hahiroth, before Baal-zephon.   Ex. 15:9; Josh. 24:6

The Israelites Murmur

10 And when Pharaoh drew nigh, the children of Israel lifted up their eyes, and, behold, the Egyptians marched after them; and they were sore afraid: and the children of Israel cried out unto the LORD.   Neh. 9:9; Ps. 34:17

11 And they said unto Moses, Because *there were* no graves in Egypt, hast thou taken us away to die in the wilderness? wherefore hast thou dealt thus with us, to carry us forth out of Egypt?   Ps. 106:7-8

12 *Is* not this the word that we did tell thee in Egypt, saying, Let us alone, that we may serve the Egyptians? For *it had been* better for us to serve the Egyptians, than that we should die in the wilderness.   Ex. 5:21

13 And Moses said unto the people, Fear ye not, stand still, and see the salvation of the LORD, which he will shew to you to day: for the Egyptians whom ye have seen to day, ye shall see them again no more for ever.   Ex. 14:30; 2 Chr. 20:15, 17

14 The LORD shall fight for you, and ye shall hold your peace.   Ex. 14:25; Deut. 1:30; 3:22

God Instructs Moses

15 And the LORD said unto Moses, Wherefore criest thou unto me? speak unto the children of Israel, that they go forward:

Walking by Faith, Not Sight

Exodus 14:13–16

God in His providence brought the Hebrews into the mountain fastnesses before the sea, that He might manifest His power in their deliverance and signally humble the pride of their oppressors. He might have saved them in any other way, but He chose this method in order to test their faith and strengthen their trust in Him. The people were weary and terrified, yet if they had held back when Moses bade them advance, God would never have opened the path for them. It was "by faith" that "they passed through the Red Sea as by dry land" (Hebrews 11:29). In marching down to the very water, they showed that they believed the word of God as spoken by Moses. They did all that was in their power to do, and then the Mighty One of Israel divided the sea to make a path for their feet.

The great lesson here taught is for all time. Often the Christian life is beset by dangers, and duty seems hard to perform. The imagination pictures impending ruin before and bondage or death behind. Yet the voice of God speaks clearly, "Go forward." We should obey this command, even though our eyes cannot penetrate the darkness, and we feel the cold waves about our feet. The obstacles that hinder our progress will never disappear before a halting, doubting spirit. Those who defer obedience till every shadow of uncertainty disappears and there remains no risk of failure or defeat, will never obey at all. Unbelief whispers, "Let us wait till the obstructions are removed, and we can see our way clearly;" but faith courageously urges an advance, hoping all things, believing all things. *PP 290*

16 But lift thou up thy rod, and stretch out thine hand over the sea, and divide it: and the children of Israel shall go on dry *ground* through the midst of the sea.   Ex. 4:17

14:15, 16 Faith Demonstrated

It was "by faith" that "they passed through the Red Sea as by dry land" (Hebrews 11:29). In marching down to the very water, they showed that they believed the word of God as spoken by Moses. They did all that was in their power to do, and then the Mighty One of Israel divided the sea to make a path for their feet. *PP 290*

---

17 And I, behold, I will harden the hearts of the Egyptians, and they shall follow them: and I will get me honour upon Pharaoh, and upon all his host, upon his chariots, and upon his horsemen.   Ex. 14:4

18 And the Egyptians shall know that I *am* the LORD, when I have gotten me honour upon Pharaoh, upon his chariots, and upon his horsemen.   Ex. 7:5

19 And the angel of God, which went before the camp of Israel, removed and went behind them; and the pillar of the cloud went from before their face, and stood behind them;   Ex. 13:21-22

20 And it came between the camp of the Egyptians and the camp of Israel; and it was a cloud and darkness *to them*, but it gave light by night *to these*: so that the one came not near the other all the night.

The Israelites Pass through the Red Sea

21 And Moses stretched out his hand over the sea; and the LORD caused the sea to go *back* by a strong east wind all that night, and made the sea dry *land*, and the waters were divided.   Ex. 15:8; Ps. 74:13; Is. 63:12

22 And the children of Israel went into the midst of the sea upon the dry *ground*: and the waters *were* a wall unto them on their right hand, and on their left.   Ps. 66:6; Heb. 11:29

23 And the Egyptians pursued, and went in after them to the midst of the sea, *even* all Pharaoh's horses, his chariots, and his horsemen.   Ex. 14:17

24 And it came to pass, that in the morning watch the LORD looked unto the host of the Egyptians through the pillar of fire and of the cloud, and troubled the host of the Egyptians,

25 And took off their chariot wheels, that they ᵀdrave them heavily: so that the Egyptians said, Let us flee from the face of Israel; for the LORD fighteth for them against the Egyptians.   Ex. 14:14 ❖ *drove*

26 And the LORD said unto Moses, Stretch out thine hand over the sea, that the waters may come again upon the Egyptians, upon their chariots, and upon their horsemen.

27 And Moses stretched forth his hand over the sea, and the sea returned to his strength when the morning appeared; and the Egyptians fled against it; and the LORD overthrew the Egyptians in the midst of the sea.   Josh. 4:18; Ps. 78:53

28 And the waters returned, and covered the chariots, and the horsemen, *and* all the host of Pharaoh that came into the sea after them; there remained not so much as one of them.   Ps. 78:53

29 But the children of Israel walked upon dry *land* in the midst of the sea; and the waters *were* a wall unto them on their right hand, and on their left.   Ex. 14:22

30 Thus the LORD saved Israel that day out of the hand of the Egyptians; and Israel saw the Egyptians dead upon the sea shore.   Ex. 14:13; Ps. 106:8, 10

31 And Israel saw that great work which the LORD did upon the Egyptians: and the people feared the LORD, and believed the LORD, and his servant Moses.   Ex. 4:31; John 2:11; 11:45

Moses' Song

15 Then sang Moses and the children of Israel this song unto the LORD, and spake, saying, I will sing unto the LORD, for he hath triumphed gloriously: the horse and his rider hath he thrown into the sea.   Ex. 15:21; Ps. 106:12; Rev. 15:3

15:1–18 A Precious Gift of God

The history of the songs of the Bible is full of suggestion as to the uses and benefits of music and song. Music is often perverted to serve purposes of evil, and it thus becomes one of the most alluring agencies of temptation. But, rightly employed, it is a precious gift of God, designed to uplift the thoughts to high and noble themes, to inspire and elevate the soul. . . . There are few means more effective for fixing His words in the memory than repeating them in song. *Ed 167*

---

2 The LORD *is* my strength and song, and he is become my salvation: he *is* my God, and I will prepare him an habitation; my father's God, and I will exalt him.   Is. 12:2; 25:1

3 The LORD *is* a man of war: the LORD *is* his name.   Ex. 3:15; Ps. 24:8; 83:18

4 Pharaoh's chariots and his host hath he cast into the sea: his chosen captains also are drowned in the Red sea.

5 The depths have covered them: they sank into the bottom as a stone.   Ex. 14:28; Neh. 9:11

6 Thy right hand, O LORD, is become glorious in power: thy right hand, O LORD, hath dashed in pieces the enemy.   Ps. 118:15-16

7 And in the greatness of thine excellency thou hast overthrown them that rose up against thee: thou sentest forth thy wrath, *which* consumed them as stubble.   Is. 5:24
8 And with the blast of thy nostrils the waters were gathered together, the floods stood upright as an heap, *and* the depths were congealed in the heart of the sea.   Job 4:9; Ps. 78:13
9 The enemy said, I will pursue, I will overtake, I will divide the ᵀspoil; my lust shall be satisfied upon them; I will draw my sword, my hand shall destroy them.   Is. 53:12 ♦ *plunder*
10 Thou didst blow with thy wind, the sea covered them: they sank as lead in the mighty waters.   Ex. 14:21
11 Who *is* like unto thee, O Lᴏʀᴅ, among the gods? who *is* like thee, glorious in holiness, fearful *in* praises, doing wonders?   Deut. 3:24
12 Thou stretchedst out thy right hand, the earth swallowed them.
13 Thou in thy mercy hast led forth the people *which* thou hast redeemed: thou hast guided *them* in thy strength unto thy holy habitation.   Ps. 77:20
14 The people shall hear, *and* be afraid: sorrow shall take hold on the inhabitants of Palestina.   Num. 14:14
15 Then the dukes of Edom shall be amazed; the mighty men of Moab, trembling shall take hold upon them; all the inhabitants of Canaan shall melt away.   Josh. 2:9, 11; 5:1
16 Fear and dread shall fall upon them; by the greatness of thine arm they shall be *as* still as a stone; till thy people pass over, O Lᴏʀᴅ, till the people pass over, *which* thou hast purchased.   Deut. 2:25; Josh. 2:9; Ps. 74:2
17 Thou shalt bring them in, and plant them in the mountain of thine inheritance, *in* the place, O Lᴏʀᴅ, *which* thou hast made for thee to dwell in, *in* the Sanctuary, O Lord, *which* thy hands have established. Ps. 44:2; 78:68-69; 80:8
18 The Lᴏʀᴅ shall reign for ever and ever.
19 For the horse of Pharaoh went in with his chariots and with his horsemen into the sea, and the Lᴏʀᴅ brought again the waters of the sea upon them; but the children of Israel went on dry *land* in the midst of the sea.   Ex. 14:28-29
20 And Miriam the prophetess, the sister of Aaron, took a ᵀtimbrel in her hand; and all the women went out after her with timbrels and with dances. Judg. 11:34; 1 Sam. 18:6 ♦ *tambourine*
21 And Miriam answered them, Sing ye to the Lᴏʀᴅ, for he hath triumphed gloriously; the horse and his rider hath he thrown into the sea.   Ex. 15:1

The People Want Water, but the Waters at Marah Are Bitter

22 So Moses brought Israel from the Red sea, and they went out into the wilderness of Shur; and they went three days in the wilderness, and found no water.   Gen. 16:7
23 And when they came to Marah, they could not drink of the waters of Marah, for they *were* bitter: therefore the name of it was called Marah.   Num. 33:8
24 And the people murmured against Moses, saying, What shall we drink?   Ex. 14:11; 16:2
25 And he cried unto the Lᴏʀᴅ; and the Lᴏʀᴅ shewed him a tree, *which* when he had cast into the waters, the waters were made sweet: there he made for them a statute and an ordinance, and there he proved them,   Ex. 14:10; 16:4; Judg. 3:4

15:26 Obedience Brings Health

Christ had been the guide and teacher of ancient Israel, and He taught them that health is the reward of obedience to the laws of God. The Great Physician who healed the sick in Palestine had spoken to His people from the pillar of cloud, telling them what they must do, and what God would do for them. . . . When they fulfilled the conditions, the promise was verified to them. DA 824

---

26 And said, If thou wilt diligently hearken to the voice of the Lᴏʀᴅ thy God, and wilt do that which is right in his sight, and wilt give ear to his commandments, and keep all his statutes, I will put none of these diseases upon thee, which I have brought upon the Egyptians: for I *am* the Lᴏʀᴅ that healeth thee.   Ex. 23:25; Deut. 7:15; 28:60

15:26

Health   See 1 Corinthians 10:31.

27 And they came to Elim, where *were* twelve wells of water, and ᵀthreescore and ten palm trees: and they encamped there by the waters.   Num. 33:9 ♦ *sixty*

God Sends Quail and Manna

16 And they took their journey from Elim, and all the congregation of the children of Israel came unto the wilderness of Sin, which *is* between Elim and Sinai, on the fifteenth day of the second month after their departing out of the land of Egypt.
2 And the whole congregation of the children of Israel murmured against Moses and Aaron in the wilderness: Ex. 15:24; Ps. 106:25; 1 Cor. 10:10
3 And the children of Israel said unto them, Would to God we had died by the hand of the Lᴏʀᴅ in the land of Egypt, when we sat by the flesh pots, *and* when we did eat bread to the full; for ye have brought us forth into this wilderness, to kill this whole assembly with hunger.   Ex. 17:3; Num. 11:4-5; Lam. 4:9
4 Then said the Lᴏʀᴅ unto Moses, Behold, I will rain bread from heaven for you; and the people shall go out and gather a certain rate

every day, that I may prove them, whether they will walk in my law, or no.   Ex. 15:25

5 And it shall come to pass, that on the sixth day they shall prepare *that* which they bring in; and it shall be twice as much as they gather daily.

6 And Moses and Aaron said unto all the children of Israel, At even, then ye shall know that the LORD hath brought you out from the land of Egypt: Ex. 6:7

7 And in the morning, then ye shall see the glory of the LORD; for that he heareth your murmurings against the LORD: and what *are* we, that ye murmur against us?   Num. 16:11

8 And Moses said, *This shall be,* when the LORD shall give you in the evening flesh to eat, and in the morning bread to the full; for that the LORD heareth your murmurings which ye murmur against him: and what *are* we? your murmurings *are* not against us, but against the LORD. 1 Sam. 8:7; Luke 10:16; Rom. 13:2

9 And Moses spake unto Aaron, Say unto all the congregation of the children of Israel, Come near before the LORD: for he hath heard your murmurings.   Num. 16:16

10 And it came to pass, as Aaron spake unto the whole congregation of the children of Israel, that they looked toward the wilderness, and, behold, the glory of the LORD appeared in the cloud.   Ex. 16:7; Num. 16:19, 42

11 And the LORD spake unto Moses, saying,

12 I have heard the murmurings of the children of Israel: speak unto them, saying, At even ye shall eat flesh, and in the morning ye shall be filled with bread; and ye shall know that I *am* the LORD your God.   Ex. 6:7

13 And it came to pass, that at even the quails came up, and covered the camp: and in the morning the dew lay round about the host.   Num. 11:9; Ps. 78:27-28; 105:40

14 And when the dew that lay was gone up, behold, upon the face of the wilderness *there lay* a small round thing, *as* small as the hoar frost on the ground.   Num. 11:7-9

15 And when the children of Israel saw *it,* they said one to another, It *is* manna: for they ᵀwist not what it *was.* And Moses said unto them, This *is* the bread which the LORD hath given you to eat.   Ex. 16:4, 31; Deut. 8:3 ◆ *knew*

16 This *is* the thing which the LORD hath commanded, Gather of it every man according to his eating, an omer for every man, *according to* the number of your persons; take ye every man for *them* which *are* in his tents.   Ex. 16:36

17 And the children of Israel did so, and gathered, some more, some less.

18 And when they did ᵀmete *it* with an omer, he that gathered much had nothing over, and he that gathered little had no lack; they gathered every man according to his eating.   *measure*

19 And Moses said, Let no man leave of it till the morning.   Ex. 12:10

20 Notwithstanding they hearkened not unto Moses; but some of them left of it until the morning, and it bred worms, and stank: and Moses was ᵀwroth with them.   *angry*

21 And they gathered it every morning, every man according to his eating: and when the sun ᵀwaxed hot, it melted.   *became*

22 And it came to pass, *that* on the sixth day they gathered twice as much bread, two omers for one *man:* and all the rulers of the congregation came and told Moses.   Ex. 16:5

23 And he said unto them, This *is that* which the LORD hath said, To morrow *is* the rest of the holy sabbath unto the LORD: bake *that* which ye will bake *to* day, and ᵀseethe that ye will seethe; and that which

16:22, 23

His People Forgot

Exodus 16:2, 3

   God had promised to be [Israel's] God, to take them to Himself as a people, and to lead them to a large and good land; but they were ready to faint at every obstacle encountered in the way to that land. In a marvelous manner He had brought them out from their bondage in Egypt, that He might elevate and ennoble them and make them a praise in the earth. But it was necessary for them to encounter difficulties and to endure privations. . . . Had they possessed faith in Him, in view of all that He had wrought for them, they would cheerfully have borne inconvenience, privation, and even real suffering; but they were unwilling to trust the Lord any further than they could witness the continual evidences of His power. They forgot their bitter service in Egypt. They forgot the goodness and power of God displayed in their behalf in their deliverance from bondage. They forgot how their children had been spared when the destroying angel slew all the first-born of Egypt. They forgot the grand exhibition of divine power at the Red Sea. They forgot that while they had crossed safely in the path that had been opened for them, the armies of their enemies, attempting to follow them, had been overwhelmed by the waters of the sea. They saw and felt only their present inconveniences and trials; and instead of saying, "God has done great things for us; whereas we were slaves, He is making of us a great nation," they talked of the hardness of the way, and wondered when their weary pilgrimage would end. *PP 292, 293*

remaineth over lay up for you to be kept until the morning.   Ex. 20:8-11; Lev. 23:3 ◆ *boil*

The Sabbath   See Luke 4:16.

24 And they laid it up till the morning, as Moses bade: and it did not stink, neither was there any worm therein.   Ex. 16:20
25 And Moses said, Eat that to day; for to day *is* a sabbath unto the LORD: to day ye shall not find it in the field.   Ex. 16:23
26 Six days ye shall gather it; but on the seventh day, *which is* the sabbath, in it there shall be none.
27 And it came to pass, *that* there went out *some* of the people on the seventh day for to gather, and they found none.
28 And the LORD said unto Moses, How long refuse ye to keep my commandments and my laws?   2 Kin. 17:14; Ps. 78:10; 106:13
29 See, for that the LORD hath given you the sabbath, therefore he giveth you on the sixth day the bread of two days; abide ye every man in his place, let no man go out of his place on the seventh day.
30 So the people rested on the seventh day.

God's Law   See Psalm 111:7–9.

31 And the house of Israel called the name thereof Manna: and it *was* like coriander seed, white; and the taste of it *was* like wafers *made* with honey.   Ex. 16:15

16:16–31 A Threefold Weekly Miracle

Every week during their long sojourn in the wilderness the Israelites witnessed a threefold miracle, designed to impress their minds with the sacredness of the Sabbath: a double quantity of manna fell on the sixth day, none on the seventh, and the portion needed for the Sabbath was preserved sweet and pure, when if any were kept over at any other time it became unfit for use. *PP 296*

An Omer of Manna Is Preserved

32 And Moses said, This *is* the thing which the LORD commandeth, Fill an omer of it to be kept for your generations; that they may see the bread wherewith I have fed you in the wilderness, when I brought you forth from the land of Egypt.
33 And Moses said unto Aaron, Take a pot, and put an omer full of manna therein, and lay it up before the LORD, to be kept for your generations.   Heb. 9:4
34 As the LORD commanded Moses, so Aaron laid it up before the Testimony, to be kept.   Ex. 25:16, 21; 27:21
35 And the children of Israel did eat manna forty years, until they came to a land inhabited; they did eat manna, until they came unto the borders of the land of Canaan.

36 Now an omer *is* the tenth *part* of an ephah.   Ex. 16:16

The People Murmur for Water at Rephidim

17 And all the congregation of the children of Israel journeyed from the wilderness of Sin, after their journeys, according to the commandment of the LORD, and pitched in Rephidim: and *there was* no water for the people to drink.   Ex. 16:1; 19:2
2 Wherefore the people did chide with Moses, and said, Give us water that we may drink. And Moses said unto them, Why chide ye with me? wherefore do ye tempt the LORD?
3 And the people thirsted there for water; and the people murmured against Moses, and said, Wherefore *is* this *that* thou hast brought us up out of Egypt, to kill us and our children and our cattle with thirst?   Ex. 16:2-3

17:3–7 Criminal Unbelief

In their thirst the people had tempted God, saying, "Is the Lord among us, or not?"—"If God has brought us here, why does He not give us water as well as bread?" The unbelief thus manifested was criminal, and Moses feared that the judgments of God would rest upon them. And he called the name of the place Massah, "temptation," and Meribah, "chiding," as a memorial of their sin. *PP 298*

4 And Moses cried unto the LORD, saying, What shall I do unto this people? they be almost ready to stone me.   1 Sam. 30:6; John 8:59
5 And the LORD said unto Moses, Go on before the people, and take with thee of the elders of Israel; and thy rod, wherewith thou smotest the river, take in thine hand, and go.
6 Behold, I will stand before thee there upon the rock in Horeb; and thou shalt smite the rock, and there shall come water out of it, that the people may drink. And Moses did so in the sight of the elders of Israel.   1 Cor. 10:4
7 And he called the name of the place Massah, and Meribah, because of the chiding of the children of Israel, and because they tempted the LORD, saying, Is the LORD among us, or not?   Num. 20:13; Ps. 81:7; 95:8

Amalek Is Conquered

8 Then came Amalek, and fought with Israel in Rephidim.   Gen. 36:12
9 And Moses said unto Joshua, Choose us out men, and go out, fight with Amalek: to morrow I will stand on the top of the hill with the rod of God in mine hand.   Ex. 4:20
10 So Joshua did as Moses had said to him,

and fought with Amalek: and Moses, Aaron, and Hur went up to the top of the hill.

11 And it came to pass, when Moses held up his hand, that Israel prevailed: and when he let down his hand, Amalek prevailed. 1 Tim. 2:8

12 But Moses' hands *were* heavy; and they took a stone, and put *it* under him, and he sat thereon; and Aaron and Hur ᵀstayed up his hands, the one on the one side, and the other on the other side; and his hands were steady until the going down of the sun.   held

13 And Joshua discomfited Amalek and his people with the edge of the sword.

17:11–13 Divine Strength Plus Human Effort

As the Hebrews triumphed when Moses was reaching his hands toward heaven and interceding in their behalf, so the Israel of God prevail when they by faith take hold upon the strength of their mighty Helper. Yet divine strength is to be combined with human effort. Moses did not believe that God would overcome their foes while Israel remained inactive. While the great leader was pleading with the Lord, Joshua and his brave followers were putting forth their utmost efforts to repulse the enemies of Israel and of God. *PP 299*

---

14 And the LORD said unto Moses, Write this *for* a memorial in a book, and rehearse *it* in the ears of Joshua: for I will utterly put out the remembrance of Amalek from under heaven.   Ex. 34:27

15 And Moses built an altar, and called the name of it Jehovah-nissi: Gen. 22:14

16 For he said, Because the LORD hath sworn *that* the LORD *will have* war with Amalek from generation to generation.

Jethro Brings to Moses His Wife and Two Sons

18 When Jethro, the priest of Midian, Moses' father in law, heard of all that God had done for Moses, and for Israel his people, *and* that the LORD had brought Israel out of Egypt;   Ex. 2:16; 3:1; Ps. 77:14-15

2 Then Jethro, Moses' father in law, took Zipporah, Moses' wife, after he had sent her back,   Ex. 2:21

3 And her two sons; of which the name of the one *was* Gershom; for he said, I have been an alien in a strange land: Ex. 2:22; 4:20; Acts 7:29

4 And the name of the other *was* Eliezer; for the God of my father, *said he, was* mine help, and delivered me from the sword of Pharaoh:

5 And Jethro, Moses' father in law, came with his sons and his wife unto Moses into the wilderness, where he encamped at the mount of God: Ex. 3:1, 12

6 And he said unto Moses, I thy father in law Jethro am come unto thee, and thy wife, and her two sons with her.

Moses Entertains Jethro

7 And Moses went out to meet his father in law, and did ᵀobeisance, and kissed him; and they asked each other of *their* welfare; and they came into the tent. Gen. 14:17; 18:2 ◆ *homage*

8 And Moses told his father in law all that the LORD had done unto Pharaoh and to the Egyptians for Israel's sake, *and* all the travail that had come upon them by the way, and *how* the LORD delivered them.   Num. 20:14

9 And Jethro rejoiced for all the goodness which the LORD had done to Israel, whom he had delivered out of the hand of the Egyptians.

10 And Jethro said, Blessed *be* the LORD, who hath delivered you out of the hand of the Egyptians, and out of the hand of Pharaoh, who hath delivered the people from under the hand of the Egyptians. 2 Sam. 18:28; Luke 1:68

11 Now I know that the LORD *is* greater than all gods: for in the thing wherein they dealt proudly *he was* above them. 2 Chr. 2:5; Luke 1:51

12 And Jethro, Moses' father in law, took a burnt offering and sacrifices for God: and Aaron came, and all the elders of Israel, to eat bread with Moses' father in law before God.

Moses Judges the People

13 And it came to pass on the morrow, that Moses sat to judge the people: and the people stood by Moses from the morning unto the evening.

14 And when Moses' father in law saw all that he did to the people, he said, What *is* this thing that thou doest to the people? why sittest thou thyself alone, and all the people stand by thee from morning unto even?

15 And Moses said unto his father in law, Because the people come unto me to enquire of God: Num. 15:34

16 When they have a matter, they come unto me; and I judge between one and another, and I do make *them* know the statutes of God, and his laws.   Ex. 24:14

17 And Moses' father in law said unto him, The thing that thou doest *is* not good.

18 Thou wilt surely wear away, both thou, and this people that *is* with thee: for this thing *is* too heavy for thee; thou art not able to perform it thyself alone.

19 Hearken now unto my voice, I will give thee counsel, and God shall be with thee: Be thou for the people to God-ward, that thou mayest bring the causes unto God:

20 And thou shalt teach them ordinances and laws, and shalt shew them the way

wherein they must walk, and the work that they must do. Deut. 1:18; 5:1; Ps. 143:8

21 Moreover thou shalt provide out of all the people able men, such as fear God, men of truth, hating covetousness; and place *such* over them, *to be* rulers of thousands, *and* rulers of hundreds, rulers of fifties, and rulers of tens: Deut. 16:18-19; 2 Chr. 19:5-10; Acts 6:3

22 And let them judge the people at all seasons: and it shall be, *that* every great matter they shall bring unto thee, but every small matter they shall judge: so shall it be easier for thyself, and they shall bear *the burden* with thee. Ex. 18:26; Lev. 24:11; Num. 11:17

23 If thou shalt do this thing, and God command thee *so*, then thou shalt be able to endure, and all this people shall also go to their place in peace. Ex. 18:18

24 So Moses hearkened to the voice of his father in law, and did all that he had said.

25 And Moses chose able men out of all Israel, and made them heads over the people, rulers of thousands, rulers of hundreds, rulers of fifties, and rulers of tens. Ex. 18:21; Deut. 1:15

26 And they judged the people at all seasons: the hard causes they brought unto Moses, but every small matter they judged themselves. Ex. 18:22

27 And Moses let his father in law depart; and he went his way into his own land.

The People Come to Sinai

19 In the third month, when the children of Israel were gone forth out of the land of Egypt, the same day came they *into* the wilderness of Sinai.

2 For they were departed from Rephidim, and were come *to* the desert of Sinai, and had pitched in the wilderness; and there Israel camped before the mount. Ex. 3:1, 12; 17:1

3 And Moses went up unto God, and the LORD called unto him out of the mountain, saying, Thus shalt thou say to the house of Jacob, and tell the children of Israel; Acts 7:38

4 Ye have seen what I did unto the Egyptians, and *how* I bare you on eagles' wings, and brought you unto myself. Is. 63:9; Rev. 12:14

5 Now therefore, if ye will obey my voice indeed, and keep my covenant, then ye shall be a ᵀpeculiar treasure unto me above all people: for all the earth *is* mine: Ex. 9:29 ◆ *special*

6 And ye shall be unto me a kingdom of priests, and an holy nation. These *are* the words which thou shalt speak unto the children of Israel. Deut. 7:6; 26:19; Is. 62:12

7 And Moses came and called for the elders of the people, and laid before their faces all these words which the LORD commanded him. Ex. 4:29-30

8 And all the people answered together, and said, All that the LORD hath spoken we will

do. And Moses returned the words of the people unto the LORD. Ex. 24:3, 7

> **19:3–8 A Covenant Relationship**
>
> God's favor toward Israel had always been conditional on their obedience. At the foot of Sinai they had entered into covenant relationship with Him as His "peculiar treasure . . . above all people." Solemnly they had promised to follow in the path of obedience. "All that the Lord hath spoken we will do," they had said (Exodus 19:5, 8). *PK 293*

9 And the LORD said unto Moses, Lo, I come unto thee in a thick cloud, that the people may hear when I speak with thee, and believe thee for ever. And Moses told the words of the people unto the LORD. Ex. 24:15-16; Deut. 4:36

10 And the LORD said unto Moses, Go unto the people, and sanctify them to day and to morrow, and let them wash their clothes,

11 And be ready against the third day: for the third day the LORD will come down in the sight of all the people upon mount Sinai. Ex. 19:16

12 And thou shalt set bounds unto the people round about, saying, Take heed to yourselves, *that ye* go *not* up into the mount, or touch the border of it: whosoever toucheth the mount shall be surely put to death:

13 There shall not an hand touch it, but he shall surely be stoned, or shot through; whether *it be* beast or man, it shall not live: when the trumpet soundeth long, they shall come up to the mount. Ex. 19:16

14 And Moses went down from the mount unto the people, and ᵀsanctified the people; and they washed their clothes. *made the people holy*

15 And he said unto the people, Be ready against the third day: come not at *your* wives. Ex. 19:11

The Awe-inspiring Presence of God on Mount Sinai

16 And it came to pass on the third day in the morning, that there were thunders and lightnings, and a thick cloud upon the mount, and the voice of the trumpet exceeding loud; so that all the people that *was* in the camp trembled. Ex. 19:9; Heb. 12:18-19, 21

17 And Moses brought forth the people out of the camp to meet with God; and they stood at the ᵀnether part of the mount. *lower*

18 And mount Sinai was altogether on a smoke, because the LORD descended upon it in fire: and the smoke thereof ascended as the smoke of a furnace, and the whole mount quaked greatly. Ex. 24:17; Judg. 5:5; Ps. 144:5

19 And when the voice of the trumpet sounded long, and ᵀwaxed louder and louder,

Moses spake, and God answered him by a voice.   Ex. 19:16; Ps. 81:7 ✧ *became*

20 And the Lord came down upon mount Sinai, on the top of the mount: and the Lord called Moses *up* to the top of the mount; and Moses went up.   Neh. 9:13

21 And the Lord said unto Moses, Go down, charge the people, lest they break through unto the Lord to gaze, and many of them perish.   Ex. 3:5; 1 Sam. 6:19

22 And let the priests also, which come near to the Lord, ᵀsanctify themselves, lest the Lord break forth upon them. *make themselves holy*

23 And Moses said unto the Lord, The people cannot come up to mount Sinai: for thou chargedst us, saying, Set bounds about the mount, and sanctify it.   Ex. 19:12

24 And the Lord said unto him, Away, get thee down, and thou shalt come up, thou, and Aaron with thee: but let not the priests and the people break through to come up unto the Lord, lest he break forth upon them.

25 So Moses went down unto the people, and spake unto them.

The Ten Commandments

20 And God spake all these words, saying,   Deut. 5:22

2 I *am* the Lord thy God, which have brought thee out of the land of Egypt, out of the house of bondage. Ex. 13:3; Lev. 26:1; Ps. 81:10

3 Thou shalt have no other gods before me.

4 Thou shalt not make unto thee any ᵀgraven image, or any likeness *of any thing* that *is* in heaven above, or that *is* in the earth beneath, or that *is* in the water under the earth.   Lev. 19:4; 26:1; Deut. 27:15 ✧ *engraved* or *cut out*

5 Thou shalt not bow down thyself to them, nor serve them: for I the Lord thy God *am* a jealous God, visiting the iniquity of the fathers upon the children unto the third and fourth *generation* of them that hate me;   Ex. 34:14; Num. 14:18; Deut. 4:24

6 And shewing mercy unto thousands of them that love me, and keep my commandments.   Deut. 7:9

7 Thou shalt not take the name of the Lord thy God in vain; for the Lord will not hold him guiltless that taketh his name in vain.   Lev. 19:12; James 5:12

8 Remember the sabbath day, to keep it holy.   Lev. 19:3

20:8–11 The Seal of God

The fourth commandment is the only one of all the ten in which are found both the name and the title of the Lawgiver. It is the only one that shows by whose authority the law is given. Thus it contains the seal of God, affixed to His law as evidence of its authenticity and binding force. *PP 307*

9 Six days shalt thou labour, and do all thy work: Ex. 23:12; 34:21; Luke 13:14

10 But the seventh day *is* the sabbath of the Lord thy God: *in it* thou shalt not do any work, thou, nor thy son, nor thy daughter, thy manservant, nor thy maidservant, nor thy cattle, nor thy stranger that *is* within thy gates: Ex. 34:21

11 For *in* six days the Lord made heaven and earth, the sea, and all that in them *is*, and rested the seventh day: wherefore the Lord blessed the sabbath day, and hallowed it.   Gen. 2:2-3; Ex. 31:17; Acts 20:7

The Sabbath   See Exodus 31:12–17.

12 Honour thy father and thy mother: that thy days may be long upon the land which the Lord thy God giveth thee.   Mark 7:10

13 Thou shalt not kill.   Gen. 9:5-6; Rom. 13:9

14 Thou shalt not commit adultery. Lev. 18:20

15 Thou shalt not steal. Lev. 19:11, 13; Matt. 19:18

The Law for Our Happiness

Exodus 20:1–17

God has given us His holy precepts, because He loves mankind. To shield us from the results of transgression, He reveals the principles of righteousness. . . . God desires us to be happy, and He gave us the precepts of the law that in obeying them we might have joy. . . .

Since "the law of the Lord is perfect," every variation from it must be evil. Those who disobey the commandments of God, and teach others to do so, are condemned by Christ. The Saviour's life of obedience maintained the claims of the law; it proved that the law could be kept in humanity, and showed the excellence of character that obedience would develop. All who obey as He did are likewise declaring that the law is "holy, and just, and good" (Romans 7:12). On the other hand, all who break God's commandments are sustaining Satan's claim that the law is unjust, and cannot be obeyed. Thus they second the deceptions of the great adversary, and cast dishonor upon God. They are the children of the wicked one, who was the first rebel against God's law. To admit them into heaven would again bring in the elements of discord and rebellion, and imperil the well-being of the universe. No man who willfully disregards one principle of the law shall enter the kingdom of heaven. *DA 308, 309*

16 Thou shalt not bear false witness against thy neighbour.   Ex. 23:1

17 Thou shalt not ᵀcovet thy neighbour's house, thou shalt not covet thy neighbour's wife, nor his manservant, nor his maidservant, nor his ox, nor his ass, nor any thing that *is* thy neighbour's.   Jer. 5:8; Rom. 7:7 ◆ *desire*

> **God's Law**   See Romans 3:20.

The People Are Afraid and Stand Far Away

18 And all the people saw the thunderings, and the lightnings, and the noise of the trumpet, and the mountain smoking: and when the people saw *it*, they removed, and stood afar off.   Ex. 19:16-18

19 And they said unto Moses, Speak thou with us, and we will hear: but let not God speak with us, lest we die.   Deut. 18:16

20 And Moses said unto the people, Fear not: for God is come to prove you, and that his fear may be before your faces, that ye sin not.   Deut. 13:3

21 And the people stood afar off, and Moses drew near unto the thick darkness where God *was*.   1 Kin. 8:12

The People Are Forbidden to Make Images

22 And the LORD said unto Moses, Thus thou shalt say unto the children of Israel, Ye have seen that I have talked with you from heaven.   Deut. 4:36; Neh. 9:13

23 Ye shall not make with me gods of silver, neither shall ye make unto you gods of gold.   Ex. 20:3-5

24 An altar of earth thou shalt make unto me, and shalt sacrifice thereon thy burnt offerings, and thy peace offerings, thy sheep, and thine oxen: in all places where I record my name I will come unto thee, and I will bless thee.   Deut. 12:5; 16:11; 26:2

25 And if thou wilt make me an altar of stone, thou shalt not build it of ᵀhewn stone: for if thou lift up thy tool upon it, thou hast polluted it.   Deut. 27:5-6 ◆ *cut*

26 Neither shalt thou go up by steps unto mine altar, that thy nakedness be not discovered thereon.

Laws for Servants

21 Now these *are* the judgments which thou shalt set before them.   Ex. 24:3-4

2 If thou buy an Hebrew servant, six years he shall serve: and in the seventh he shall go out free for nothing.   Deut. 15:12-15

3 If he came in by himself, he shall go out by himself: if he were married, then his wife shall go out with him.

> **21:1 The Laws Called Judgments**
>
> That the obligations of the Decalogue might be more fully understood and enforced, additional precepts were given, illustrating and applying the principles of the Ten Commandments. These laws were called judgments, both because they were framed in infinite wisdom and equity and because the magistrates were to give judgment according to them. Unlike the Ten Commandments, they were delivered privately to Moses, who was to communicate them to the people. *PP 310*

4 If his master have given him a wife, and she have born him sons or daughters; the wife and her children shall be her master's, and he shall go out by himself.

5 And if the servant shall plainly say, I love my master, my wife, and my children; I will not go out free: Deut. 15:16-17

6 Then his master shall bring him unto the judges; he shall also bring him to the door, or unto the door post; and his master shall bore his ear through with an aul; and he shall serve him for ever.   Ex. 22:8-9

> **End of Sin/Hell**   See 1 Samuel 1:22.

7 And if a man sell his daughter to be a maidservant, she shall not go out as the menservants do.   Neh. 5:5

8 If she please not her master, who hath ᵀbetrothed her to himself, then shall he let her be redeemed: to sell her unto a strange nation he shall have no power, seeing he hath dealt deceitfully with her.   *engaged*

9 And if he have betrothed her unto his son, he shall deal with her after the manner of daughters.

10 If he take him another *wife*; her food, her ᵀraiment, and her duty of marriage, shall he not diminish.   *clothing*

11 And if he do not these three unto her, then shall she go out free without money.

Laws about Manslaughter

12 He that smiteth a man, so that he die, shall be surely put to death.   Gen. 9:6; Lev. 24:17

13 And if a man lie not in wait, but God deliver *him* into his hand; then I will appoint thee a place whither he shall flee.   Josh. 20:2-9

14 But if a man come presumptuously upon his neighbour, to slay him with ᵀguile; thou shalt take him from mine altar, that he may die.   1 Kin. 2:28-34; Heb. 10:26 ◆ *deceit*

15 And he that ᵀsmiteth his father, or his mother, shall be surely put to death.   *strikes*

16 And he that stealeth a man, and selleth him, or if he be found in his hand, he shall surely be put to death.   Gen. 37:28; Deut. 24:7

17 And he that curseth his father, or his mother, shall surely be put to death. Prov. 20:20

18 And if men strive together, and one smite another with a stone, or with *his* fist, and he die not, but keepeth *his* bed: Ex. 21:20
19 If he rise again, and walk abroad upon his staff, then shall he that smote *him* be ᵀquit: only he shall pay *for* the loss of his time, and shall cause *him* to be thoroughly healed. *innocent*
20 And if a man ᵀsmite his servant, or his maid, with a rod, and he die under his hand; he shall be surely punished. *strike*
21 Notwithstanding, if he continue a day or two, he shall not be punished: for he *is* his money.

Laws about Those Hurt Accidentally

22 If men strive, and hurt a woman with child, so that her fruit depart *from her*, and yet no mischief follow: he shall be surely punished, according as the woman's husband will lay upon him; and he shall pay as the judges *determine*. Ex. 21:30; Deut. 22:18-19
23 And if *any* mischief follow, then thou shalt give life for life, Deut. 19:21
24 Eye for eye, tooth for tooth, hand for hand, foot for foot, Deut. 19:21
25 Burning for burning, wound for wound, stripe for stripe.
26 And if a man smite the eye of his servant, or the eye of his maid, that it perish; he shall let him go free for his eye's sake.
27 And if he smite out his manservant's tooth, or his maidservant's tooth; he shall let him go free for his tooth's sake.
28 If an ox gore a man or a woman, that they die: then the ox shall be surely stoned, and his flesh shall not be eaten; but the owner of the ox *shall be* quit. Ex. 21:32
29 But if the ox were ᵀwont to push with his horn in time past, and it hath been testified to his owner, and he hath not kept him in, but that he hath killed a man or a woman; the ox shall be stoned, and his owner also shall be put to death. *accustomed to*
30 If there be laid on him a sum of money, then he shall give for the ransom of his life whatsoever is laid upon him. Ex. 21:22
31 Whether he have gored a son, or have gored a daughter, according to this judgment shall it be done unto him.
32 If the ox shall push a manservant or a maidservant; he shall give unto their master thirty shekels of silver, and the ox shall be stoned. Zech. 11:12-13; Matt. 26:15
33 And if a man shall open a pit, or if a man shall dig a pit, and not cover it, and an ox or an ass fall therein;
34 The owner of the pit shall make *it* good, *and* give money unto the owner of them; and the dead *beast* shall be his.
35 And if one man's ox hurt another's, that

he die; then they shall sell the live ox, and divide the money of it; and the dead *ox* also they shall divide.
36 Or if it be known that the ox hath used to push in time past, and his owner hath not kept him in; he shall surely pay ox for ox; and the dead shall be his own.

Laws about Theft

22 If a man shall steal an ox, or a sheep, and kill it, or sell it; he shall restore five oxen for an ox, and four sheep for a sheep. 2 Sam. 12:6; Prov. 6:31; Luke 19:8
2 If a thief be found breaking up, and be smitten that he die, *there shall* no blood *be shed* for him. Num. 35:27; Matt. 6:19-20; 24:43
3 If the sun be risen upon him, *there shall be* blood *shed* for him; *for* he should make full restitution; if he have nothing, then he shall be sold for his theft. Ex. 21:2
4 If the theft be certainly found in his hand alive, whether it be ox, or ass, or sheep; he shall restore double. Ex. 21:16
5 If a man shall cause a field or vineyard to be eaten, and shall put in his beast, and shall feed in another man's field; of the best of his own field, and of the best of his own vineyard, shall he make restitution.
6 If fire break out, and catch in thorns, so that the stacks of corn, or the standing corn, or the field, be consumed *therewith*; he that kindled the fire shall surely make restitution. Ex. 22:9
7 If a man shall deliver unto his neighbour money or stuff to keep, and it be stolen out of the man's house; if the thief be found, let him pay double.
8 If the thief be not found, then the master of the house shall be brought unto the judges, *to see* whether he have put his hand unto his neighbour's goods. Ex. 21:6
9 For all manner of ᵀtrespass, *whether it be* for ox, for ass, for sheep, for raiment, *or* for any manner of lost thing, which *another* challengeth to be his, the cause of both parties shall come before the judges; *and* whom the judges shall condemn, he shall pay double unto his neighbour. Deut. 25:1 ◆ *sin*
10 If a man deliver unto his neighbour an ass, or an ox, or a sheep, or any beast, to keep; and it die, or be hurt, or driven away, no man seeing *it*:
11 *Then* shall an oath of the Lord be between them both, that he hath not put his hand unto his neighbour's goods; and the owner of it shall accept *thereof*, and he shall not make *it* good. Heb. 6:16
12 And if it be stolen from him, he shall make restitution unto the owner thereof.
13 If it be torn in pieces, *then* let him bring it

for witness, *and* he shall not make good that which was torn.

14 And if a man borrow *ought* of his neighbour, and it be hurt, or die, the owner thereof *being* not with it, he shall surely make *it* good. **15** *But* if the owner thereof *be* with it, he shall not make *it* good: if it *be* an hired *thing,* it came for his hire.

Laws about Fornication

16 And if a man entice a maid that is not ᵀbetrothed, and lie with her, he shall surely endow her to be his wife. Deut. 22:28-29 ◆ *engaged*
17 If her father utterly refuse to give her unto him, he shall pay money according to the ᵀdowry of virgins.   Gen. 34:12 ◆ *price paid for a wife*
18 Thou shalt not suffer a witch to live.
19 Whosoever lieth with a beast shall surely be put to death.   Lev. 18:23; 20:15-16; Deut. 27:21
20 He that sacrificeth unto *any* god, save unto the LORD only, he shall be utterly destroyed.   Deut. 17:2-5
21 Thou shalt neither ᵀvex a stranger, nor oppress him: for ye were strangers in the land of Egypt.   Ex. 23:9; Lev. 19:33; Deut. 10:19 ◆ *trouble*
22 Ye shall not afflict any widow, or fatherless child.   Deut. 24:17; 27:19; Is. 1:17
23 If thou afflict them in any wise, and they cry at all unto me, I will surely hear their cry;   Deut. 15:9; Ps. 18:6; Luke 18:7
24 And my wrath shall ᵀwax hot, and I will kill you with the sword; and your wives shall be widows, and your children fatherless.   Ps. 69:24; 109:9; Lam. 5:3 ◆ *become*

Laws about Usury

25 If thou lend money to *any of* my people *that is* poor by thee, thou shalt not be to him as an usurer, neither shalt thou lay upon him ᵀusury.   Lev. 25:35-37; Deut. 23:19-20 ◆ *interest charged*
26 If thou at all take thy neighbour's ᵀraiment to pledge, thou shalt deliver it unto him by that the sun goeth down: Deut. 24:6 ◆ *clothing*
27 For that *is* his covering only, it *is* his raiment for his skin: wherein shall he sleep? and it shall come to pass, when he crieth unto me, that I will hear; for I *am* gracious.
28 Thou shalt not ᵀrevile the gods, nor curse the ruler of thy people.   *attack the gods with words*
29 Thou shalt not delay *to offer* the first of thy ripe fruits, and of thy liquors: the firstborn of thy sons shalt thou give unto me.
30 Likewise shalt thou do with thine oxen, *and* with thy sheep: seven days it shall be with his ᵀdam; on the eighth day thou shalt give it me.   Lev. 22:27; Deut. 15:19 ◆ *mother*
31 And ye shall be holy men unto me: neither shall ye eat *any* flesh *that is* torn of beasts in the field; ye shall cast it to the dogs.   Deut. 14:21

22:29 God the Owner of Everything

By this system of benevolence the Lord sought to teach Israel that in everything He must be first. Thus they were reminded that God was the proprietor of their fields, their flocks, and their herds; that it was He who sent them the sunshine and the rain that developed and ripened the harvest. Everything that they possessed was His; they were but the stewards of His goods. *AA 337*

Laws about Slander and False Witness

23 Thou shalt not raise a false report: put not thine hand with the wicked to be an unrighteous witness. Ex. 20:16; Ps. 35:11; 101:5
2 Thou shalt not follow a multitude to *do* evil; neither shalt thou speak in a cause to decline after many to ᵀwrest *judgment*: Ex. 23:6-7 ◆ *twist*
3 Neither shalt thou ᵀcountenance a poor man in his cause.   *favor*
4 If thou meet thine enemy's ox or his ass going astray, thou shalt surely bring it back to him again.   Deut. 22:1-4
5 If thou see the ass of him that hateth thee lying under his burden, and wouldest forbear to help him, thou shalt surely help with him.
6 Thou shalt not wrest the judgment of thy poor in his cause.   Ex. 23:2-3
7 Keep thee far from a false matter; and the innocent and righteous slay thou not: for I will not justify the wicked.   Ex. 23:1; 34:7; Deut. 27:25
8 And thou shalt take no gift: for the gift blindeth the wise, and perverteth the words of the righteous.   Deut. 16:19; Prov. 15:27; 17:23
9 Also thou shalt not oppress a stranger: for ye know the heart of a stranger, seeing ye were strangers in the land of Egypt. Ex. 22:21

Laws about Rest for Land and People

10 And six years thou shalt sow thy land, and shalt gather in the fruits thereof:
11 But the seventh *year* thou shalt let it rest and lie still; that the poor of thy people may eat: and what they leave the beasts of the field shall eat. In like manner thou shalt deal with thy vineyard, *and* with thy oliveyard.

23:11 Law Concerning the Poor

The law of God gave the poor a right to a certain portion of the produce of the soil. When hungry, a man was at liberty to go to his neighbor's field or orchard or vineyard, and eat of the grain or fruit to satisfy his hunger. It was in accordance with this permission that the disciples of Jesus plucked and ate of the standing grain as they passed through a field upon the Sabbath day. *PP 531*

---

12 Six days thou shalt do thy work, and on the seventh day thou shalt rest: that thine

ox and thine ass may rest, and the son of thy handmaid, and the stranger, may be refreshed.   Ex. 20:8-11

13 And in all *things* that I have said unto you be circumspect: and make no mention of the name of other gods, neither let it be heard out of thy mouth.   Deut. 4:9

14 Three times thou shalt keep a feast unto me in the year.   Deut. 16:16

15 Thou shalt keep the feast of unleavened bread: (thou shalt eat unleavened bread seven days, as I commanded thee, in the time appointed of the month Abib; for in it thou camest out from Egypt: and none shall appear before me empty:)   Num. 28:16-25; Deut. 16:16

16 And the feast of harvest, the firstfruits of thy labours, which thou hast sown in the field: and the feast of ingathering, *which is* in the end of the year, when thou hast gathered in thy labours out of the field.   Ex. 34:22

17 Three times in the year all thy males shall appear before the Lord God.   Deut. 16:16

18 Thou shalt not offer the blood of my sacrifice with leavened bread; neither shall the fat of my sacrifice remain until the morning.   Ex. 34:25; Lev. 2:11; Deut. 16:4

19 The first of the firstfruits of thy land thou shalt bring into the house of the Lord thy God. Thou shalt not ᵀseethe a kid in his mother's milk.   Ex. 34:26; Deut. 14:21; 26:10 ◆ boil

An Angel Is Promised

20 Behold, I send an Angel before thee, to keep thee in the way, and to bring thee into the place which I have prepared.   Ex. 14:19; 33:2

21 Beware of him, and obey his voice, provoke him not; for he will not pardon your transgressions: for my name *is* in him.

22 But if thou shalt indeed obey his voice, and do all that I speak; then I will be an enemy unto thine enemies, and an adversary unto thine adversaries.   Num. 24:9; Deut. 30:7

23 For mine Angel shall go before thee, and bring thee in unto the Amorites, and the Hittites, and the Perizzites, and the Canaanites, the Hivites, and the Jebusites: and I will cut them off.   Ex. 23:20

24 Thou shalt not bow down to their gods, nor serve them, nor do after their works: but thou shalt utterly overthrow them, and quite break down their images.   Num. 33:52; Deut. 7:5

25 And ye shall serve the Lord your God, and he shall bless thy bread, and thy water; and I will take sickness away from the midst of thee.   Ex. 15:26; Deut. 6:13; 7:15

26 There shall nothing cast their young, nor be barren, in thy land: the number of thy days I will fulfil.   Deut. 7:14; Job 5:26; Ps. 55:23

27 I will send my fear before thee, and will destroy all the people to whom thou shalt come, and I will make all thine enemies turn their backs unto thee.   Gen. 35:5; Deut. 2:25; 7:23

28 And I will send hornets before thee, which shall drive out the Hivite, the Canaanite, and the Hittite, from before thee.   Deut. 7:20

29 I will not drive them out from before thee in one year; lest the land become desolate, and the beast of the field multiply against thee.   Deut. 7:22

30 By little and little I will drive them out from before thee, until thou be increased, and inherit the land.

31 And I will set thy bounds from the Red sea even unto the sea of the Philistines, and from the desert unto the river: for I will deliver the inhabitants of the land into your hand; and thou shalt drive them out before thee.   Gen. 15:18; Deut. 11:24; Josh. 21:44

32 Thou shalt make no covenant with them, nor with their gods.   Ex. 34:12, 15; Deut. 7:2

33 They shall not dwell in thy land, lest they make thee sin against me: for if thou serve their gods, it will surely be a snare unto thee.   Ex. 34:12; Deut. 7:16; Ps. 106:36

Moses Is Called up into the Mountain

24 And he said unto Moses, Come up unto the Lord, thou, and Aaron, Nadab, and Abihu, and seventy of the elders of Israel; and worship ye afar off.   Ex. 6:23; 28:1

2 And Moses alone shall come near the Lord: but they shall not come nigh; neither shall the people go up with him.   Ex. 24:13

3 And Moses came and told the people all the words of the Lord, and all the judgments: and all the people answered with one voice, and said, All the words which the Lord hath said will we do.   Ex. 19:8; 24:7

24:3–7 Israel to Remain Separate

"All that the Lord hath said will we do, and be obedient" (Exodus 24:3, 7). God had chosen Israel as His people, and they had chosen Him as their King. . . . Through Moses they were warned against the temptations that would assail them in the future; and they were earnestly exhorted to remain separate from the surrounding nations and to worship God alone. *PK 293, 294*

---

4 And Moses wrote all the words of the Lord, and rose up early in the morning, and builded an altar under the hill, and twelve pillars, according to the twelve tribes of Israel.   Gen. 28:18; 31:45; Deut. 31:9

5 And he sent young men of the children of Israel, which offered burnt offerings, and sacrificed peace offerings of oxen unto the Lord.   Ex. 18:12

6 And Moses took half of the blood, and

put *it* in basons; and half of the blood he sprinkled on the altar. Heb. 9:18

7 And he took the book of the covenant, and read in the audience of the people: and they said, All that the LORD hath said will we do, and be obedient. Ex. 24:3-4

8 And Moses took the blood, and sprinkled *it* on the people, and said, Behold the blood of the covenant, which the LORD hath made with you concerning all these words. Matt. 26:28

The Glory of God Appears

9 Then went up Moses, and Aaron, Nadab, and Abihu, and seventy of the elders of Israel: Ex. 24:1

10 And they saw the God of Israel: and *there was* under his feet as it were a paved work of a sapphire stone, and as it were the body of heaven in *his* clearness. John 1:18; Rev. 4:3

11 And upon the nobles of the children of Israel he laid not his hand: also they saw God, and did eat and drink. Gen. 16:13

12 And the LORD said unto Moses, Come up to me into the mount, and be there: and I will give thee tables of stone, and a law, and commandments which I have written; that thou mayest teach them. Ex. 31:18

13 And Moses rose up, and his minister Joshua: and Moses went up into the mount of God. Ex. 33:11

24:14-16 Preparing to Meet With God

This period of waiting was to [Moses] a time of preparation, of close self-examination. Even this favored servant of God could not at once approach into His presence and endure the exhibitions of His glory. Six days must be employed in devoting himself to God by searching of heart, meditation, and prayer before he could be prepared for direct communication with his Maker. *PP 313*

14 And he said unto the elders, Tarry ye here for us, until we come again unto you: and, behold, Aaron and Hur *are* with you: if any man have any matters to do, let him come unto them. Ex. 17:10

15 And Moses went up into the mount, and a cloud covered the mount. Ex. 19:9; Matt. 17:5

16 And the glory of the LORD abode upon mount Sinai, and the cloud covered it six days: and the seventh day he called unto Moses out of the midst of the cloud. Lev. 9:23

17 And the sight of the glory of the LORD *was* like devouring fire on the top of the mount in the eyes of the children of Israel. Ex. 3:2

18 And Moses went into the midst of the cloud, and gat him up into the mount: and Moses was in the mount forty days and forty nights. Ex. 34:28; Deut. 9:9; 10:10

Offerings for the Tabernacle

25 And the LORD spake unto Moses, saying,

2 Speak unto the children of Israel, that they bring me an offering: of every man that giveth it willingly with his heart ye shall take my offering. Ezra 1:6; 2:68; 2 Cor. 9:7

25:1-9 Funding the Sanctuary

For the building of the sanctuary great and expensive preparations were necessary; a large amount of the most precious and costly material was required; yet the Lord accepted only freewill offerings. "Of every man that giveth it willingly with his heart ye shall take My offering" was the divine command repeated by Moses to the congregation. Devotion to God and a spirit of sacrifice were the first requisites in preparing a dwelling place for the Most High. *PP 343*

3 And this *is* the offering which ye shall take of them; gold, and silver, and brass,

4 And blue, and purple, and scarlet, and fine linen, and goats' *hair*,

5 And rams' skins dyed red, and badgers' skins, and shittim wood,

6 Oil for the light, spices for anointing oil, and for sweet incense, Ex. 27:20

7 Onyx stones, and stones to be set in the ᵀephod, and in the breastplate. *priestly garment*

8 And let them make me a sanctuary; that I may dwell among them. 1 Kin. 6:13; 2 Cor. 6:16

25:8 God Dwelt With Us

God commanded Moses for Israel, "Let them make Me a sanctuary; that I may dwell among them" (Exodus 25:8), and He abode in the sanctuary, in the midst of His people. Through all their weary wandering in the desert, the symbol of His presence was with them. So Christ set up His tabernacle in the midst of our human encampment. He pitched His tent by the side of the tents of men, that He might dwell among us, and make us familiar with His divine character and life. *DA 23*

9 According to all that I shew thee, *after* the pattern of the tabernacle, and the pattern of all the instruments thereof, even so shall ye make *it*. Ex. 25:40; Heb. 8:5

The Form of the Ark of the Testimony

10 And they shall make an ark *of* shittim wood: two cubits and a half *shall be* the length thereof, and a cubit and a half the breadth thereof, and a cubit and a half the height thereof. Ex. 37:1-3; Deut. 10:1-3; Heb. 9:4

11 And thou shalt overlay it with pure gold, within and without shalt thou overlay

it, and shalt make upon it a crown of gold round about. _{Ex. 25:24}

12 And thou shalt cast four rings of gold for it, and put *them* in the four corners thereof; and two rings *shall be* in the one side of it, and two rings in the other side of it.

13 And thou shalt make ᵀstaves *of* shittim wood, and overlay them with gold. *clubs* or *rods*

14 And thou shalt put the staves into the rings by the sides of the ark, that the ark may be borne with them.

15 The staves shall be in the rings of the ark: they shall not be taken from it. _{1 Kin. 8:8}

16 And thou shalt put into the ark the testimony which I shall give thee. 1 Kin. 8:9; Heb. 9:4

17 And thou shalt make a mercy seat *of* pure gold: two cubits and a half *shall be* the length thereof, and a cubit and a half the breadth thereof. _{Ex. 37:6}

18 And thou shalt make two cherubims *of* gold, *of* beaten work shalt thou make them, in the two ends of the mercy seat.

19 And make one cherub on the one end, and the other cherub on the other end: *even* of the mercy seat shall ye make the cherubims on the two ends thereof.

20 And the cherubims shall stretch forth *their* wings on high, covering the mercy seat with their wings, and their faces *shall look* one to another; toward the mercy seat shall the faces of the cherubims be.   1 Chr. 28:18; Heb. 9:5

21 And thou shalt put the mercy seat above upon the ark; and in the ark thou shalt put the testimony that I shall give thee. _{Ex. 26:34}

22 And there I will meet with thee, and I will commune with thee from above the mercy seat, from between the two cherubims which *are* upon the ark of the testimony, of all *things* which I will give thee in commandment unto the children of Israel. Ex. 29:42-43; 30:6; Num. 7:89

The Table and Its Furniture

23 Thou shalt also make a table *of* shittim wood: two cubits *shall be* the length thereof, and a cubit the breadth thereof, and a cubit and a half the height thereof. _{Ex. 37:10-16}

24 And thou shalt overlay it with pure gold, and make thereto a crown of gold round about. _{Ex. 25:11}

25 And thou shalt make unto it a border of an hand breadth round about, and thou shalt make a golden crown to the border thereof round about.

26 And thou shalt make for it four rings of gold, and put the rings in the four corners that *are* on the four feet thereof.

27 Over against the border shall the rings be for places of the staves to bear the table.

28 And thou shalt make the staves *of* shittim wood, and overlay them with gold, that the table may be borne with them.

29 And thou shalt make the dishes thereof, and spoons thereof, and covers thereof, and bowls thereof, to cover ᵀwithal: *of* pure gold shalt thou make them. _{Num. 4:7 ◆ *with*}

30 And thou shalt set upon the table shewbread before me alway. _{Ex. 39:36}

The Candlestick and Its Instruments

31 And thou shalt make a candlestick *of* pure gold: *of* beaten work shall the candlestick be made: his shaft, and his branches, his bowls, his knops, and his flowers, shall be of the same. Ex. 37:17-24; 1 Kin. 7:49; Zech. 4:2

32 And six branches shall come out of the sides of it; three branches of the candlestick out of the one side, and three branches of the candlestick out of the other side:

33 Three bowls made like unto almonds, *with* a knop and a flower in one branch; and three bowls made like almonds in the other branch, *with* a knop and a flower: so in the six branches that come out of the candlestick.

34 And in the candlestick *shall be* four bowls made like unto almonds, *with* their knops and their flowers.

35 And *there shall be* a knop under two branches of the same, and a knop under two branches of the same, and a knop under two branches of the same, according to the six branches that proceed out of the candlestick.

36 Their ᵀknops and their branches shall be of the same: all it *shall be* one beaten work *of* pure gold. _{*architectural ornament*}

37 And thou shalt make the seven lamps thereof: and they shall light the lamps thereof, that they may give light over against it.

38 And the tongs thereof, and the snuffdishes thereof, *shall be of* pure gold.

39 *Of* a talent of pure gold shall he make it, with all these vessels.

40 And look that thou make *them* after their pattern, which was shewed thee in the mount. _{Ex. 26:30; Num. 8:4; Acts 7:44}

25:40 The Original—and the Copy

Moses made the earthly sanctuary, "according to the fashion that he had seen." Paul declares that "the tabernacle, and all the vessels of the ministry," when completed, were "the patterns of things in the heavens" (Acts 7:44; Hebrews 9:21, 23). And John says that he saw the sanctuary in heaven. That sanctuary, in which Jesus ministers in our behalf, is the great original, of which the sanctuary built by Moses was a copy. *PP 357*

The Ten Curtains of the Tabernacle

26 Moreover thou shalt make the tabernacle *with* ten curtains *of* fine twined linen, and blue, and purple, and scarlet: *with* cherubims of cunning work shalt thou make them. _{Ex. 26:36}

2 The length of one curtain *shall be* eight and twenty cubits, and the breadth of one curtain four cubits: and every one of the curtains shall have one measure.

3 The five curtains shall be coupled together one to another; and *other* five curtains *shall be* coupled one to another.

4 And thou shalt make loops of blue upon the edge of the one curtain from the selvedge in the coupling; and likewise shalt thou make in the uttermost edge of *another* curtain, in the coupling of the second.

5 Fifty loops shalt thou make in the one curtain, and fifty loops shalt thou make in the edge of the curtain that *is* in the coupling of the second; that the loops may take hold one of another.

6 And thou shalt make fifty ᵀtaches of gold, and couple the curtains together with the taches: and it shall be one tabernacle.   *hooks for curtains*

The Eleven Curtains of Goats' Hair

7 And thou shalt make curtains *of* goats' *hair* to be a covering upon the tabernacle: eleven curtains shalt thou make.

8 The length of one curtain *shall be* thirty cubits, and the breadth of one curtain four cubits: and the eleven curtains *shall be all* of one measure.

9 And thou shalt couple five curtains by themselves, and six curtains by themselves, and shalt double the sixth curtain in the forefront of the tabernacle.

10 And thou shalt make fifty loops on the edge of the one curtain *that is* outmost in the coupling, and fifty loops in the edge of the curtain which coupleth the second.

11 And thou shalt make fifty taches of brass, and put the taches into the loops, and couple the tent together, that it may be one.

12 And the remnant that remaineth of the curtains of the tent, the half curtain that remaineth, shall hang over the backside of the tabernacle.

13 And a cubit on the one side, and a cubit on the other side of that which remaineth in the length of the curtains of the tent, it shall hang over the sides of the tabernacle on this side and on that side, to cover it.

14 And thou shalt make a covering for the tent *of* rams' skins dyed red, and a covering above *of* badgers' skins.   Ex. 25:5; 36:19

The Boards of the Tabernacle, with Their Sockets and Bars

15 And thou shalt make boards for the tabernacle *of* shittim wood standing up. Ex. 36:20-33

16 Ten cubits *shall be* the length of a board, and a cubit and a half *shall be* the breadth of one board.

17 Two tenons *shall there be* in one board, set in order one against another: thus shalt thou make for all the boards of the tabernacle.

18 And thou shalt make the boards for the tabernacle, twenty boards on the south side southward.

19 And thou shalt make forty sockets of silver under the twenty boards; two sockets under one board for his two tenons, and two sockets under another board for his two tenons.   Ex. 38:27

20 And for the second side of the tabernacle on the north side *there shall be* twenty boards:

21 And their forty sockets *of* silver; two sockets under one board, and two sockets under another board.

22 And for the sides of the tabernacle westward thou shalt make six boards.

23 And two boards shalt thou make for the corners of the tabernacle in the two sides.

24 And they shall be coupled together beneath, and they shall be coupled together above the head of it unto one ring: thus shall it be for them both; they shall be for the two corners.

25 And they shall be eight boards, and their sockets *of* silver, sixteen sockets; two sockets under one board, and two sockets under another board.

26 And thou shalt make bars *of* shittim wood; five for the boards of the one side of the tabernacle,

27 And five bars for the boards of the other side of the tabernacle, and five bars for the boards of the side of the tabernacle, for the two sides westward.

28 And the middle bar in the midst of the boards shall reach from end to end.

29 And thou shalt overlay the boards with gold, and make their rings *of* gold *for* places for the bars: and thou shalt overlay the bars with gold.

30 And thou shalt rear up the tabernacle according to the fashion thereof which was shewed thee in the mount. Ex. 25:9, 40; Acts 7:44

The Veil for the Ark

31 And thou shalt make a vail *of* blue, and purple, and scarlet, and fine twined linen of cunning work: with cherubims shall it be made: Ex. 36:35; 2 Chr. 3:14; Matt. 27:51

32 And thou shalt hang it upon four pillars of shittim *wood* overlaid with gold: their hooks *shall be of* gold, upon the four sockets of silver.

33 And thou shalt hang up the ᵀvail under the taches, that thou mayest bring in thither within the vail the ark of the testimony: and the vail shall divide unto you between the holy *place* and the most holy.   Ex. 40:21 ◆ *veil*

34 And thou shalt put the mercy seat upon the ark of the testimony in the most holy *place*.   Ex. 25:21; 40:20; Heb. 9:5

26:33 The Ark of the Covenant

In this apartment was the ark, a chest of acacia wood, overlaid within and without with gold, and having a crown of gold about the top. It was made as a depository for the tables of stone, upon which God Himself had inscribed the Ten Commandments. Hence it was called the ark of God's testament, or the ark of the covenant, since the Ten Commandments were the basis of the covenant made between God and Israel. *PP 348*

---

35 And thou shalt set the table without the vail, and the candlestick over against the table on the side of the tabernacle toward the south: and thou shalt put the table on the north side.   Ex. 40:22, 24; Heb. 9:2

36 And thou shalt make an hanging for the door of the tent, *of* blue, and purple, and scarlet, and fine twined linen, ᵀwrought with needlework.   Ex. 36:37 ◆ *made*

37 And thou shalt make for the hanging five pillars *of* shittim *wood*, and overlay them with gold, *and* their hooks *shall be of* gold: and thou shalt cast five sockets of brass for them.   Ex. 36:38

The Altar of Burnt Offering with Its Vessels

27 And thou shalt make an altar *of* shittim wood, five cubits long, and five cubits broad; the altar shall be foursquare: and the height thereof *shall be* three cubits.   Ex. 38:1-7

2 And thou shalt make the horns of it upon the four corners thereof: his horns shall be of the same: and thou shalt overlay it with brass.   Ex. 29:12; Lev. 4:7; Ps. 118:27

3 And thou shalt make his pans to receive his ashes, and his shovels, and his basons, and his fleshhooks, and his firepans: all the vessels thereof thou shalt make *of* brass.   1 Kin. 7:45

4 And thou shalt make for it a grate of network *of* brass; and upon the net shalt thou make four brasen rings in the four corners thereof.

5 And thou shalt put it under the ᵀcompass of the altar beneath, that the net may be even to the midst of the altar.   *rim*

6 And thou shalt make ᵀstaves for the altar, staves *of* shittim wood, and overlay them with brass.   *clubs* or *rods*

7 And the staves shall be put into the rings, and the staves shall be upon the two sides of the altar, to bear it.

8 Hollow with boards shalt thou make it: as it was shewed thee in the mount, so shall they make *it*.   Ex. 25:9, 40; Heb. 8:5

The Court of the Tabernacle

9 And thou shalt make the court of the tabernacle: for the south side southward *there shall be* hangings for the court *of* fine twined linen of an hundred cubits long for one side: Ex. 38:9-20

10 And the twenty pillars thereof and their twenty sockets *shall be of* brass; the hooks of the pillars and their ᵀfillets *shall be of* silver.   *rods for curtains between columns*

11 And likewise for the north side in length *there shall be* hangings of an hundred *cubits* long, and his twenty pillars and their twenty sockets *of* brass; the hooks of the pillars and their fillets *of* silver.

12 And *for* the breadth of the court on the west side *shall be* hangings of fifty cubits: their pillars ten, and their sockets ten.

13 And the breadth of the court on the east side eastward *shall be* fifty cubits.

14 The hangings of one side *of the gate shall be* fifteen cubits: their pillars three, and their sockets three.

15 And on the other side *shall be* hangings fifteen *cubits*: their pillars three, and their sockets three.

16 And for the gate of the court *shall be* an hanging of twenty cubits, *of* blue, and purple, and scarlet, and fine twined linen, ᵀwrought with needlework: *and* their pillars *shall be* four, and their sockets four.   Ex. 26:36 ◆ *made*

17 All the pillars round about the court *shall be* filleted with silver; their hooks *shall be of* silver, and their sockets *of* brass.

18 The length of the court *shall be* an hundred cubits, and the breadth fifty every where, and the height five cubits *of* fine twined linen, and their sockets *of* brass.

19 All the vessels of the tabernacle in all the service thereof, and all the pins thereof, and all the pins of the court, *shall be of* brass.

The Oil for the Lamp

20 And thou shalt command the children of Israel, that they bring thee pure oil olive beaten for the light, to cause the lamp to burn always.

21 In the tabernacle of the congregation without the ᵀvail, which *is* before the testimony, Aaron and his sons shall order it from evening to morning before the Lᴏʀᴅ: *it shall be* a statute for ever unto their generations on the behalf of the children of Israel.   Ex. 28:43; Num. 18:23; 19:21 ◆ *veil*

Aaron and His Sons Are Set Apart for the Priest's Office

28 And take thou unto thee Aaron thy brother, and his sons with him, from among the children of Israel, that he may minister unto me in the priest's office, *even* Aaron, Nadab and Abihu, Eleazar and Ithamar, Aaron's sons.   Ex. 6:23; 24:1; Num. 18:7

2 And thou shalt make holy garments for Aaron thy brother for glory and for beauty.

3 And thou shalt speak unto all *that are* wise hearted, whom I have filled with the spirit of wisdom, that they may make Aaron's garments to ᵀconsecrate him, that he may minister unto me in the priest's office.   *set him apart*

4 And these *are* the garments which they shall make; a breastplate, and an ephod, and a robe, and a broidered coat, a mitre, and a girdle: and they shall make holy garments for Aaron thy brother, and his sons, that he may minister unto me in the priest's office.   Ex. 28:39-40

5 And they shall take gold, and blue, and purple, and scarlet, and fine linen.

The Ephod

6 And they shall make the ᵀephod *of* gold, *of* blue, and *of* purple, *of* scarlet, and fine twined linen, with cunning work.   *priestly garment*

7 It shall have the two shoulderpieces thereof joined at the two edges thereof; and *so* it shall be joined together.

8 And the curious girdle of the ephod, which *is* upon it, shall be of the same, according to the work thereof; *even of* gold, *of* blue, and purple, and scarlet, and fine twined linen.   Ex. 28:27-28

9 And thou shalt take two onyx stones, and grave on them the names of the children of Israel:

10 Six of their names on one stone, and *the other* six names of the rest on the other stone, according to their birth.

11 With the work of an engraver in stone, *like* the engravings of a ᵀsignet, shalt thou engrave the two stones with the names of the children of Israel: thou shalt make them to be set in ᵀouches of gold.   *identifying seal* ◆ *settings*

12 And thou shalt put the two stones upon the shoulders of the ephod *for* stones of memorial unto the children of Israel: and Aaron shall bear their names before the LORD upon his two shoulders for a memorial.   Ex. 28:29

28:9–12 Our Names on Christ's Heart

Like Aaron, who symbolized Christ, our Saviour bears the names of all His people on His heart in the holy place. Our great High Priest remembers all the words by which He has encouraged us to trust. He is ever mindful of His covenant.

All who seek of Him shall find. All who knock will have the door opened to them. *COL 148*

---

13 And thou shalt make ouches *of* gold;

14 And two chains *of* pure gold at the ends; *of* wreathen work shalt thou make them, and fasten the wreathen chains to the ouches.

The Breastplate, with Twelve Precious Stones

15 And thou shalt make the breastplate of judgment with cunning work; after the work of the ephod thou shalt make it; *of* gold, *of* blue, and *of* purple, and *of* scarlet, and *of* fine twined linen, shalt thou make it.

16 Foursquare it shall be *being* doubled; a span *shall be* the length thereof, and a span *shall be* the breadth thereof.

17 And thou shalt set in it settings of stones, *even* four rows of stones: *the first* row *shall be* a sardius, a topaz, and a ᵀcarbuncle: *this shall be* the first row.   Ezek. 28:13 ◆ *reddish precious stone*

18 And the second row *shall be* an emerald, a sapphire, and a diamond.

19 And the third row a ligure, an agate, and an amethyst.

20 And the fourth row a ᵀberyl, and an onyx, and a jasper: they shall be set in gold in their inclosings.   *precious stone*

21 And the stones shall be with the names of the children of Israel, twelve, according to their names, *like* the engravings of a signet; every one with his name shall they be according to the twelve tribes.   Rev. 7:4-8

28:15–21 The Priest's Breastplate

Over the ephod was the breastplate, the most sacred of the priestly vestments. This was of the same material as the ephod. It was in the form of a square, measuring a span, and was suspended from the shoulders by a cord of blue from golden rings. The border was formed of a variety of precious stones, the same that form the twelve foundations of the City of God. *PP 351*

---

22 And thou shalt make upon the breastplate chains at the ends *of* wreathen work *of* pure gold.

23 And thou shalt make upon the breastplate two rings of gold, and shalt put the two rings on the two ends of the breastplate.

24 And thou shalt put the two wreathen *chains* of gold in the two rings *which are* on the ends of the breastplate.

25 And *the other* two ends of the two wreathen *chains* thou shalt fasten in the two ouches, and put *them* on the shoulderpieces of the ephod before it.

26 And thou shalt make two rings of gold, and thou shalt put them upon the two ends of the breastplate in the border thereof, which *is* in the side of the ephod inward.

27 And two *other* rings of gold thou shalt make, and shalt put them on the two sides of the ephod underneath, toward the forepart thereof, over against the *other* coupling thereof, above the ᵀcurious girdle of the ephod.   *intricately detailed*

28 And they shall bind the breastplate by the rings thereof unto the rings of the ephod with a lace of blue, that *it* may be above the curious girdle of the ephod, and that the breastplate be not loosed from the ephod.   Num. 15:38

29 And Aaron shall bear the names of the children of Israel in the breastplate of judgment upon his heart, when he goeth in unto the holy *place*, for a memorial before the LORD continually.   Ex. 28:12, 30

30 And thou shalt put in the breastplate of judgment the Urim and the Thummim; and they shall be upon Aaron's heart, when he goeth in before the LORD: and Aaron shall bear the judgment of the children of Israel upon his heart before the LORD continually.   Lev. 8:8; Num. 27:21; Deut. 33:8

28:30 The Two Token Stones

At the right and left of the breastplate were two large stones of great brilliancy. These were known as the Urim and Thummim. . . . When questions were brought for decision before the Lord, a halo of light encircling the precious stone at the right was a token of the divine consent or approval, while a cloud shadowing the stone at the left was an evidence of denial or disapprobation. *PP 351*

The Robe of the Ephod and the Plate of the Mitre

31 And thou shalt make the robe of the ephod all *of* blue.

32 And there shall be an hole in the top of it, in the midst thereof: it shall have a binding of woven work round about the hole of it, as it were the hole of an ᵀhabergeon, that it be not ᵀrent.   *military garment ◆ torn apart*

33 And *beneath* upon the hem of it thou shalt make pomegranates *of* blue, and *of* purple, and *of* scarlet, round about the hem thereof; and bells of gold between them round about:

34 A golden bell and a pomegranate, a golden bell and a pomegranate, upon the hem of the robe round about.

35 And it shall be upon Aaron to minister: and his sound shall be heard when he goeth in unto the holy *place* before the LORD, and when he cometh out, that he die not.

36 And thou shalt make a plate *of* pure gold, and grave upon it, *like* the engravings of a signet, HOLINESS TO THE LORD. Zech. 14:20

37 And thou shalt put it on a blue lace, that it may be upon the ᵀmitre; upon the forefront of the mitre it shall be.   *turban*

38 And it shall be upon Aaron's forehead, that Aaron may bear the iniquity of the holy things, which the children of Israel shall ᵀhallow in all their holy gifts; and it shall be always

upon his forehead, that they may be accepted before the LORD. Lev. 10:17; Heb. 9:28 ◆ *render as sacred*

28:37, 38 The Priestly Apparel

The miter of the high priest consisted of the white linen turban, having attached to it by a lace of blue, a gold plate bearing the inscription, "Holiness to Jehovah." Everything connected with the apparel and deportment of the priests was to be such as to impress the beholder with a sense of the holiness of God, the sacredness of His worship, and the purity required of those who came into His presence. *PP 351*

---

39 And thou shalt embroider the coat of fine linen, and thou shalt make the mitre *of* fine linen, and thou shalt make the ᵀgirdle *of* needlework.   *belt*

The Garments for Aaron's Sons

40 And for Aaron's sons thou shalt make coats, and thou shalt make for them girdles, and bonnets shalt thou make for them, for glory and for beauty.   Ex. 28:2, 4; 39:41

41 And thou shalt put them upon Aaron thy brother, and his sons with him; and shalt anoint them, and consecrate them, and ᵀsanctify them, that they may minister unto me in the priest's office. Ex. 29:7, 9; 40:15 ◆ *make them holy*

42 And thou shalt make them linen ᵀbreeches to cover their nakedness; from the ᵀloins even unto the thighs they shall reach: Lev. 6:10; 16:4; Ezek. 44:18 ◆ *trousers ◆ waist*

43 And they shall be upon Aaron, and upon his sons, when they come in unto the tabernacle of the congregation, or when they come near unto the altar to minister in the holy *place*; that they bear not iniquity, and die: *it shall be* a statute for ever unto him and his seed after him.   Ex. 20:26; 27:21; Lev. 5:1

The Ceremonies of Consecrating the Priests

29 And this *is* the thing that thou shalt do unto them to ᵀhallow them, to minister unto me in the priest's office: Take one young bullock, and two rams without blemish,   *render them as sacred*

2 And unleavened bread, and cakes unleavened tempered with oil, and wafers unleavened anointed with oil: *of* wheaten flour shalt thou make them.   Num. 6:15

3 And thou shalt put them into one basket, and bring them in the basket, with the ᵀbullock and the two rams.   *bull*

4 And Aaron and his sons thou shalt bring unto the door of the tabernacle of the congregation, and shalt wash them with water.

5 And thou shalt take the garments, and put upon Aaron the coat, and the robe of the

ᵀephod, and the ephod, and the breastplate, and ᵀgird him with the ᵀcurious ᵀgirdle of the ephod: *priestly garment ♦ equip ♦ intricately detailed ♦ belt*

6 And thou shalt put the ᵀmitre upon his head, and put the holy crown upon the mitre.   Lev. 8:9 ♦ *turban*

7 Then shalt thou take the anointing oil, and pour *it* upon his head, and anoint him.

8 And thou shalt bring his sons, and put coats upon them.   Lev. 8:13

9 And thou shalt gird them with girdles, Aaron and his sons, and put the bonnets on them: and the priest's office shall be theirs for a perpetual statute: and thou shalt consecrate Aaron and his sons. Lev. 8:22-28; Num. 18:7

10 And thou shalt cause a bullock to be brought before the tabernacle of the congregation: and Aaron and his sons shall put their hands upon the head of the bullock.   Lev. 1:4

11 And thou shalt kill the bullock before the Lord, *by* the door of the tabernacle of the congregation.

12 And thou shalt take of the blood of the bullock, and put *it* upon the horns of the altar with thy finger, and pour all the blood beside the bottom of the altar.   Ex. 27:2; Lev. 8:15; 9:9

13 And thou shalt take all the fat that covereth the inwards, and the caul *that is* above the liver, and the two kidneys, and the fat that *is* upon them, and burn *them* upon the altar.   Lev. 3:3-4

14 But the flesh of the bullock, and his skin, and his dung, shalt thou burn with fire without the camp: it *is* a sin offering.   Ex. 30:10

15 Thou shalt also take one ram; and Aaron and his sons shall put their hands upon the head of the ram.   Ex. 29:19

16 And thou shalt slay the ram, and thou shalt take his blood, and sprinkle *it* round about upon the altar.

17 And thou shalt cut the ram in pieces, and wash the inwards of him, and his legs, and put *them* unto his pieces, and unto his head.

18 And thou shalt burn the whole ram upon the altar: it *is* a burnt offering unto the Lord: it *is* a sweet savour, an offering made by fire unto the Lord.   Gen. 8:21

19 And thou shalt take the other ram; and Aaron and his sons shall put their hands upon the head of the ram.   Ex. 29:3

20 Then shalt thou kill the ram, and take of his blood, and put *it* upon the tip of the right ear of Aaron, and upon the tip of the right ear of his sons, and upon the thumb of their right hand, and upon the great toe of their right foot, and sprinkle the blood upon the altar round about.

21 And thou shalt take of the blood that *is* upon the altar, and of the anointing oil, and sprinkle *it* upon Aaron, and upon his garments, and upon his sons, and upon the

garments of his sons with him: and he shall be hallowed, and his garments, and his sons, and his sons' garments with him.   Ex. 29:1

22 Also thou shalt take of the ram the fat and the rump, and the fat that covereth the inwards, and the ᵀcaul *above* the liver, and the two kidneys, and the fat that *is* upon them, and the right shoulder; for it *is* a ram of consecration: Ex. 29:13 ♦ *membrane*

23 And one loaf of bread, and one cake of oiled bread, and one wafer out of the basket of the unleavened bread that *is* before the Lord: Ex. 29:2-3

24 And thou shalt put all in the hands of Aaron, and in the hands of his sons; and shalt wave them *for* a wave offering before the Lord.   Lev. 7:30

25 And thou shalt receive them of their hands, and burn *them* upon the altar for a burnt offering, for a sweet savour before the Lord: it *is* an offering made by fire unto the Lord.   Lev. 8:28

26 And thou shalt take the breast of the ram of Aaron's ᵀconsecration, and wave it *for* a wave offering before the Lord: and it shall be thy part.   Lev. 8:29 ♦ *act of setting apart*

27 And thou shalt sanctify the breast of the wave offering, and the shoulder of the heave offering, which is waved, and which is heaved up, of the ram of the consecration, *even* of *that* which *is* for Aaron, and of *that* which is for his sons: Lev. 10:15

28 And it shall be Aaron's and his sons' by a statute for ever from the children of Israel: for it *is* an heave offering: and it shall be an heave offering from the children of Israel of the sacrifice of their peace offerings, *even* their heave offering unto the Lord.

29 And the holy garments of Aaron shall be his sons' after him, to be anointed therein, and to be ᵀconsecrated in them.   *set apart*

30 *And* that son that is priest in his stead shall put them on seven days, when he cometh into the tabernacle of the congregation to minister in the holy *place*.   Num. 20:28

31 And thou shalt take the ram of the consecration, and ᵀseethe his flesh in the holy place.   Lev. 8:31 ♦ *boil*

32 And Aaron and his sons shall eat the flesh of the ram, and the bread that *is* in the basket, *by* the door of the tabernacle of the congregation.   Matt. 12:4

33 And they shall eat those things wherewith the atonement was made, to consecrate *and* to ᵀsanctify them: but a stranger shall not eat *thereof,* because they *are* holy.   *make them holy*

34 And if ought of the flesh of the ᵀconsecrations, or of the bread, remain unto the morning, then thou shalt burn the remainder with fire: it shall not be eaten, because it *is* holy.   Ex. 12:10 ♦ *acts of setting apart*

35 And thus shalt thou do unto Aaron, and to his sons, according to all *things* which I have commanded thee: seven days shalt thou ᵀconsecrate them. *set them apart*

36 And thou shalt offer every day a bullock *for* a sin offering for atonement: and thou shalt cleanse the altar, when thou hast made an atonement for it, and thou shalt anoint it, to sanctify it. *Heb. 10:11*

37 Seven days thou shalt make an atonement for the altar, and sanctify it; and it shall be an altar most holy: whatsoever toucheth the altar shall be holy. *Ex. 40:10*

The Continual Burnt Offering

38 Now this *is that* which thou shalt offer upon the altar; two lambs of the first year day by day continually. *Num. 28:3-8*

39 The one lamb thou shalt offer in the morning; and the other lamb thou shalt offer at even: *2 Kin. 16:15; Ezek. 46:13-15*

40 And with the one lamb a tenth deal of flour mingled with the fourth part of an hin of beaten oil; and the fourth part of an hin of wine *for* a drink offering.

41 And the other lamb thou shalt offer at even, and shalt do thereto according to the meat offering of the morning, and according to the drink offering thereof, for a sweet savour, an offering made by fire unto the LORD.

42 *This shall be* a continual burnt offering throughout your generations *at* the door of the tabernacle of the congregation before the LORD: where I will meet you, to speak there unto thee. *Ex. 25:22*

43 And there I will meet with the children of Israel, and *the tabernacle* shall be ᵀsanctified by my glory. *1 Kin. 8:11 ◆ made holy*

44 And I will sanctify the tabernacle of the congregation, and the altar: I will sanctify also both Aaron and his sons, to minister to me in the priest's office. *Lev. 21:15*

45 And I will dwell among the children of Israel, and will be their God. *Ex. 25:8; Lev. 26:12*

46 And they shall know that I *am* the LORD their God, that brought them forth out of the land of Egypt, that I may dwell among them: I *am* the LORD their God. *Ex. 20:2*

Directions for Making the Altar of Incense

30 And thou shalt make an altar to burn incense upon: *of* shittim wood shalt thou make it. *Ex. 37:25-28*

2 A cubit *shall be* the length thereof, and a cubit the breadth thereof; foursquare shall it be: and two cubits *shall be* the height thereof: the horns thereof *shall be* of the same. *Ex. 27:2*

3 And thou shalt overlay it with pure gold, the top thereof, and the sides thereof round about, and the horns thereof; and thou shalt make unto it a crown of gold round about.

4 And two golden rings shalt thou make to it under the crown of it, by the two corners thereof, upon the two sides of it shalt thou make *it*; and they shall be for places for the staves to bear it withal. *Ex. 25:27*

5 And thou shalt make the ᵀstaves *of* shittim wood, and overlay them with gold. *clubs or rods*

6 And thou shalt put it before the ᵀvail that *is* by the ark of the testimony, before the mercy seat that *is* over the testimony, where I will meet with thee. *Ex. 25:21-22 ◆ veil*

7 And Aaron shall burn thereon sweet incense every morning: when he dresseth the lamps, he shall burn incense upon it. *1 Sam. 2:28*

8 And when Aaron lighteth the lamps at even, he shall burn incense upon it, a per-

---

By Blood and Incense

Exodus 30:1-10

In the offering of incense the priest was brought more directly into the presence of God than in any other act of the daily ministration. As the inner veil of the sanctuary did not extend to the top of the building, the glory of God, which was manifested above the mercy seat, was partially visible from the first apartment. When the priest offered incense before the Lord, he looked toward the ark; and as the cloud of incense arose, the divine glory descended upon the mercy seat and filled the most holy place, and often so filled both apartments that the priest was obliged to retire to the door of the tabernacle. As in that typical service the priest looked by faith to the mercy seat which he could not see, so the people of God are now to direct their prayers to Christ, their great High Priest, who, unseen by human vision, is pleading in their behalf in the sanctuary above.

The incense, ascending with the prayers of Israel, represents the merits and intercession of Christ, His perfect righteousness, which through faith is imputed to His people, and which can alone make the worship of sinful beings acceptable to God. Before the veil of the most holy place was an altar of perpetual intercession, before the holy, an altar of continual atonement. By blood and by incense God was to be approached—symbols pointing to the great Mediator, through whom sinners may approach Jehovah, and through whom alone mercy and salvation can be granted to the repentant, believing soul. *PP 353*

petual incense before the LORD throughout your generations.

9 Ye shall offer no strange incense thereon, nor burnt sacrifice, nor meat offering; neither shall ye pour drink offering thereon.   Lev. 10:1

10 And Aaron shall make an atonement upon the horns of it once in a year with the blood of the sin offering of atonements: once in the year shall he make atonement upon it throughout your generations: it *is* most holy unto the LORD.   Lev. 16:18; 23:27

The Ransom of Souls

11 And the LORD spake unto Moses, saying,

12 When thou takest the sum of the children of Israel after their number, then shall they give every man a ransom for his soul unto the LORD, when thou numberest them; that there be no plague among them, when *thou* numberest them. Ex. 38:25-26; Num. 31:50; Ps. 49:7

13 This they shall give, every one that passeth among them that are numbered, half a shekel after the shekel of the sanctuary: (a shekel *is* twenty gerahs:) an half shekel *shall be* the offering of the LORD. Lev. 27:25; Num. 3:47

14 Every one that passeth among them that are numbered, from twenty years old and above, shall give an offering unto the LORD.

15 The rich shall not give more, and the poor shall not give less than half a shekel, when *they* give an offering unto the LORD, to make an atonement for your souls.   Prov. 22:2

16 And thou shalt take the atonement money of the children of Israel, and shalt appoint it for the service of the tabernacle of the congregation; that it may be a memorial unto the children of Israel before the LORD, to make an atonement for your souls.   Ex. 38:25-31

The Brasen Laver

17 And the LORD spake unto Moses, saying,

30:17–21 The Laver

Between the altar and the door of the tabernacle was the laver, which was also of brass, made from the mirrors that had been the freewill offering of the women of Israel. At the laver the priests were to wash their hands and their feet whenever they went into the sacred apartments, or approached the altar to offer a burnt offering unto the Lord. PP 347, 348

18 Thou shalt also make a laver *of* brass, and his foot *also of* brass, to wash ᵀ*withal*: and thou shalt put it between the tabernacle of the congregation and the altar, and thou shalt put water therein.   Ex. 38:8 ◆ *with*

19 For Aaron and his sons shall wash their hands and their feet thereat: Ps. 26:6; Is. 52:11

20 When they go into the tabernacle of the congregation, they shall wash with water, that they die not; or when they come near to the altar to minister, to burn offering made by fire unto the LORD:

21 So they shall wash their hands and their feet, that they die not: and it shall be a statute for ever to them, *even* to him and to his seed throughout their generations.   Ex. 28:43

The Holy Anointing Oil

22 Moreover the LORD spake unto Moses, saying,

23 Take thou also unto thee principal spices, of pure myrrh five hundred *shekels*, and of sweet cinnamon half so much, *even* two hundred and fifty *shekels*, and of sweet calamus two hundred and fifty *shekels*,   Song 4:14

24 And of cassia five hundred *shekels*, after the shekel of the sanctuary, and of oil olive an hin: Ex. 29:40

25 And thou shalt make it an oil of holy ointment, an ointment compound after the art of the apothecary: it shall be an holy anointing oil.   Ex. 37:29; Num. 35:25; Ps. 89:20

26 And thou shalt anoint the tabernacle of the congregation therewith, and the ark of the testimony,   Num. 7:1

27 And the table and all his vessels, and the candlestick and his vessels, and the altar of incense,

28 And the altar of burnt offering with all his vessels, and the laver and his foot.

29 And thou shalt ᵀsanctify them, that they may be most holy: whatsoever toucheth them shall be holy.   Ex. 29:37 ◆ *make them holy*

30 And thou shalt anoint Aaron and his sons, and ᵀconsecrate them, that *they* may minister unto me in the priest's office. Lev. 8:12 ◆ *set apart*

31 And thou shalt speak unto the children of Israel, saying, This shall be an holy anointing oil unto me throughout your generations.

32 Upon man's flesh shall it not be poured, neither shall ye make *any other* like it, after the composition of it: it *is* holy, *and* it shall be holy unto you.   Ex. 30:25

33 Whosoever compoundeth *any* like it, or whosoever putteth *any* of it upon a stranger, shall even be cut off from his people. Gen. 17:14

34 And the LORD said unto Moses, Take unto thee sweet spices, stacte, and onycha, and galbanum; *these* sweet spices with pure frankincense: of each shall there be a like weight: Ex. 25:6

35 And thou shalt make it a perfume, a confection after the art of the ᵀapothecary, tempered together, pure *and* holy: *maker of perfumes*

36 And thou shalt beat *some* of it very small, and put of it before the testimony in the tabernacle of the congregation, where I will

meet with thee: it shall be unto you most holy.   Ex. 25:22

37 And *as for* the perfume which thou shalt make, ye shall not make to yourselves according to the composition thereof: it shall be unto thee holy for the LORD.

38 Whosoever shall make like unto that, to smell thereto, shall even be cut off from his people.   Ex. 30:33

Bezaleel and Aholiab Are Called for the Work of the Tabernacle

31 And the LORD spake unto Moses, saying,

2 See, I have called by name Bezaleel the son of Uri, the son of Hur, of the tribe of Judah: Ex. 36:1

3 And I have filled him with the spirit of God, in wisdom, and in understanding, and in knowledge, and in all manner of workmanship,   Ex. 35:31; 1 Kin. 7:14

4 To devise cunning works, to work in gold, and in silver, and in brass,

5 And in cutting of stones, to set *them*, and in carving of timber, to work in all manner of workmanship.

6 And I, behold, I have given with him Aholiab, the son of Ahisamach, of the tribe of Dan: and in the hearts of all that are wise hearted I have put wisdom, that they may make all that I have commanded thee; Ex. 28:3

31:1–6 Labor for Brain and Hand

What an industrial school was that in the wilderness, having for its instructors Christ and His angels!

In the preparation of the sanctuary and in its furnishing, all the people were to co-operate. There was labor for brain and hand. . . .

Thus in labor and in giving they were taught to co-operate with God and with one another. And they were to co-operate also in the preparation of the spiritual building—God's temple in the soul. *Ed 37*

---

7 The tabernacle of the congregation, and the ark of the testimony, and the mercy seat that *is* thereupon, and all the furniture of the tabernacle,   Ex. 36:8–37:9

8 And the table and his furniture, and the pure candlestick with all his furniture, and the altar of incense,   Ex. 37:10-28

9 And the altar of burnt offering with all his furniture, and the laver and his foot, Ex. 38:1-8

10 And the cloths of service, and the holy garments for Aaron the priest, and the garments of his sons, to minister in the priest's office,

11 And the anointing oil, and sweet incense for the holy *place*: according to all that I have commanded thee shall they do.   Ex. 37:29

The Observation of the Sabbath Is Commanded Again

12 And the LORD spake unto Moses, saying,

13 Speak thou also unto the children of Israel, saying, Verily my sabbaths ye shall keep: for it *is* a sign between me and you throughout your generations; that *ye* may know that I *am* the LORD that doth ᵀsanctify you.   Ezek. 20:12 ◆ *make you holy*

14 Ye shall keep the sabbath therefore; for it *is* holy unto you: every one that defileth it shall surely be put to death: for whosoever doeth *any* work therein, that soul shall be cut off from among his people.

31:12–17 The Sabbath a Sign

The Sabbath is a sign of creative and redeeming power; it points to God as the source of life and knowledge; it recalls man's primeval glory, and thus witnesses to God's purpose to re-create us in His own image.

The Sabbath and the family were alike instituted in Eden, and in God's purpose they are indissolubly linked together. On this day more than on any other, it is possible for us to live the life of Eden. *Ed 250*

---

15 Six days may work be done; but in the seventh *is* the sabbath of rest, holy to the LORD: whosoever doeth *any* work in the sabbath day, he shall surely be put to death. Gen. 2:2; Lev. 23:3

16 Wherefore the children of Israel shall keep the sabbath, to observe the sabbath throughout their generations, *for* a perpetual covenant.

17 It *is* a sign between me and the children of Israel for ever: for *in* six days the LORD made heaven and earth, and on the seventh day he rested, and was refreshed.   Gen. 1:31; 2:2-3

The Sabbath   See Ezekiel 20:12.

18 And he gave unto Moses, when he had made an end of communing with him upon mount Sinai, two tables of testimony, tables of stone, written with the finger of God.   Ex. 24:12; 32:15-16; Deut. 4:13

The Golden Calf

32 And when the people saw that Moses delayed to come down out of the mount, the people gathered themselves together unto Aaron, and said unto him, Up, make us gods, which shall go before us; for *as for* this Moses, the man that brought us up out of the land of Egypt, we wot not what is become of him.   Ex. 24:18; Deut. 9:9; Acts 7:40

2 And Aaron said unto them, Break off the golden earrings, which *are* in the ears of your wives, of your sons, and of your daughters, and bring *them* unto me.   Ex. 12:35-36

3 And all the people brake off the golden earrings which *were* in their ears, and brought *them* unto Aaron.

4 And he received *them* at their hand, and fashioned it with a graving tool, after he had made it a molten calf: and they said, These *be* thy gods, O Israel, which brought thee up out of the land of Egypt. Deut. 9:16; Neh. 9:18; Acts 7:41

5 And when Aaron saw *it*, he built an altar before it; and Aaron made proclamation, and said, To morrow *is* a feast to the LORD.

6 And they rose up early on the morrow, and offered burnt offerings, and brought peace offerings; and the people sat down to eat and to drink, and rose up to play. Num. 25:2; 1 Cor. 10:7

32:1–6 Pliant Leaders

How often, in our own day, is the love of pleasure disguised by a "form of godliness"! A religion that permits men, while observing the rites of worship, to devote themselves to selfish or sensual gratification, is as pleasing to the multitudes now as in the days of Israel. And there are still pliant Aarons, who, while holding positions of authority in the church, will yield to the desires of the unconsecrated, and thus encourage them in sin. *PP 317*

God Is Angered

7 And the LORD said unto Moses, Go, get thee down; for thy people, which thou broughtest out of the land of Egypt, have corrupted *themselves*: Gen. 6:11-12; Ex. 32:11; Deut. 9:12

8 They have turned aside quickly out of the way which I commanded them: they have made them a molten calf, and have worshipped it, and have sacrificed thereunto, and said, These *be* thy gods, O Israel, which have brought thee up out of the land of Egypt.

9 And the LORD said unto Moses, I have seen this people, and, behold, it *is* a stiffnecked people: Ex. 33:3, 5; 34:9

10 Now therefore let me alone, that my wrath may wax hot against them, and that I may consume them: and I will make of thee a great nation. Num. 14:12; Deut. 9:14, 19

11 And Moses ᵀbesought the LORD his God, and said, LORD, why doth thy wrath wax hot against thy people, which thou hast brought forth out of the land of Egypt with great power, and with a mighty hand? *begged*

32:11–14 An Unselfish Prayer

As Moses interceded for Israel, his timidity was lost in his deep interest and love for those for whom he had, in the hands of God, been the means of doing so much. The Lord listened to his pleadings, and granted his unselfish prayer. God had proved His servant; He had tested his faithfulness and his love for that erring, ungrateful people, and nobly had Moses endured the trial. His interest in Israel sprang from no selfish motive. *PP 319*

12 Wherefore should the Egyptians speak, and say, For mischief did he bring them out, to slay them in the mountains, and to consume them from the face of the earth? Turn from thy fierce wrath, and repent of this evil against thy people. Ex. 32:14; Num. 14:13-16; Deut. 9:28

13 Remember Abraham, Isaac, and Israel, thy servants, to whom thou swarest by thine own self, and saidst unto them, I will multiply your seed as the stars of heaven, and all this land that I have spoken of will I give unto your seed, and they shall inherit *it* for ever. Gen. 12:7; 22:16; Heb. 6:13

14 And the LORD repented of the evil which he thought to do unto his people. 2 Sam. 24:16

A Timid, Fearful Leader

Exodus 32:1–6

In the absence of Moses, the judicial authority had been delegated to Aaron, and a vast crowd gathered about his tent, with the demand, "Make us gods, which shall go before us; for as for this Moses, the man that brought us up out of the land of Egypt, we wot not what is become of him." . . .

Such a crisis demanded a man of firmness, decision, and unflinching courage; one who held the honor of God above popular favor, personal safety, or life itself. But the present leader of Israel was not of this character. Aaron feebly remonstrated with the people, but his wavering and timidity at the critical moment only rendered them the more determined. . . . There were some who remained true to their covenant with God, but the greater part of the people joined in the apostasy. . . .

Aaron feared for his own safety; and instead of nobly standing up for the honor of God, he yielded to the demands of the multitude. His first act was to direct that the golden earrings be collected from all the people and brought to him, hoping that pride would lead them to refuse such a sacrifice. But they willingly yielded up their ornaments; and from these he made a molten calf, in imitation of the gods of Egypt. . . . Seeing with what satisfaction the golden god was received, he built an altar before it, and made proclamation, "Tomorrow is a feast to the Lord." . . . "And they rose up early on the morrow, and offered burnt offerings, and brought peace offerings; and the people sat down to eat and to drink and rose up to play." Under the pretense of holding "a feast to the Lord," they gave themselves up to gluttony and licentious reveling. *PP 316, 317*

Moses Comes down with the Tablets

15 And Moses turned, and went down from the mount, and the two tables of the testimony *were* in his hand: the tables *were* written on both their sides; on the one side and on the other *were* they written.   Deut. 9:15

16 And the tables *were* the work of God, and the writing *was* the writing of God, ᵀgraven upon the tables.   Ex. 31:18 ◆ *engraved or cut out*

17 And when Joshua heard the noise of the people as they shouted, he said unto Moses, *There is* a noise of war in the camp.   Ex. 17:9

18 And he said, *It is* not the voice of *them that* shout for mastery, neither *is it* the voice of *them that* cry for being overcome: *but* the noise of *them that* sing do I hear.

19 And it came to pass, as soon as he came nigh unto the camp, that he saw the calf, and the dancing: and Moses' anger ᵀwaxed hot, and he cast the tables out of his hands, and brake them beneath the mount.   *became*

20 And he took the calf which they had made, and burnt *it* in the fire, and ground *it* to powder, and strawed *it* upon the water, and made the children of Israel drink *of it*.   Deut. 9:21

32:20 A Worthless God

Entering the camp, Moses passed through the crowds of revelers, and seizing upon the idol, cast it into the fire. He afterward ground it to powder, and having strewed it upon the stream that descended from the mount, he made the people drink of it. Thus was shown the utter worthlessness of the god which they had been worshiping. *PP 320*

---

21 And Moses said unto Aaron, What did this people unto thee, that thou hast brought so great a sin upon them?   Gen. 20:9

22 And Aaron said, Let not the anger of my lord ᵀwax hot: thou knowest the people, that they *are set* on mischief.   Deut. 9:24 ◆ *become*

23 For they said unto me, Make us gods, which shall go before us: for *as for* this Moses, the man that brought us up out of the land of Egypt, we ᵀwot not what is become of him.   Ex. 32:1-4 ◆ *know*

24 And I said unto them, Whosoever hath any gold, let them break *it* off. So they gave *it* me: then I cast it into the fire, and there came out this calf.   Ex. 32:4

25 And when Moses saw that the people *were* naked; (for Aaron had made them naked unto *their* shame among their enemies:)

26 Then Moses stood in the gate of the camp, and said, Who *is* on the LORD's side? *let him come* unto me. And all the sons of Levi gathered themselves together unto him.

27 And he said unto them, Thus saith the LORD God of Israel, Put every man his sword by his side, *and* go in and out from gate to gate throughout the camp, and slay every man his brother, and every man his companion, and every man his neighbour.   Num. 25:5

28 And the children of Levi did according to the word of Moses: and there fell of the people that day about three thousand men.

32:21–28 If Only . . .

If Aaron had had courage to stand for the right, irrespective of consequences, he could have prevented that apostasy. If he had unswervingly maintained his own allegiance to God, if he had cited the people to the perils of Sinai, and had reminded them of their solemn covenant with God to obey His law, the evil would have been checked. *PP 323*

---

29 For Moses had said, Consecrate yourselves to day to the LORD, even every man upon his son, and upon his brother; that he may ᵀbestow upon you a blessing this day.   Num. 25:11-13 ◆ *grant*

Moses Prays for the People

30 And it came to pass on the morrow, that Moses said unto the people, Ye have sinned a great sin: and now I will go up unto the LORD; ᵀperadventure I shall make an atonement for your sin.   Num. 25:13; 1 Sam. 12:20, 23 ◆ *maybe*

31 And Moses returned unto the LORD, and said, Oh, this people have sinned a great sin, and have made them gods of gold.   Ex. 20:23

32 Yet now, if thou wilt forgive their sin—; and if not, blot me, I pray thee, out of thy book which thou hast written.Ps. 69:28; Dan. 12:1

33 And the LORD said unto Moses, Whosoever hath sinned against me, him will I blot out of my book.   Ezek. 18:4

34 Therefore now go, lead the people unto *the place* of which I have spoken unto thee: behold, mine Angel shall go before thee: nevertheless in the day when I visit I will visit their sin upon them.   Ex. 23:20

35 And the LORD plagued the people, because they made the calf, which Aaron made.

The Lord Refuses to Go with the People

33 And the LORD said unto Moses, Depart, *and* go up hence, thou and the people which thou hast brought up out of the land of Egypt, unto the land which I sware unto Abraham, to Isaac, and to Jacob, saying, Unto thy seed will I give it: Gen. 12:7

2 And I will send an angel before thee; and I will drive out the Canaanite, the Amorite, and the Hittite, and the Perizzite, the Hivite, and the Jebusite: Ex. 32:34

3 Unto a land flowing with milk and honey: for I will not go up in the midst of thee; for

thou *art* a stiffnecked people: lest I consume thee in the way.   Ex. 3:8; 32:9-10; 33:15-17
4 And when the people heard these evil tidings, they mourned: and no man did put on him his ornaments.   Num. 14:1, 39; Ezek. 24:17
5 For the Lord had said unto Moses, Say unto the children of Israel, Ye *are* a stiffnecked people: I will come up into the midst of thee in a moment, and consume thee: therefore now put off thy ornaments from thee, that I may know what to do unto thee.
6 And the children of Israel stripped themselves of their ornaments by the mount Horeb.   Ex. 33:4

The Tabernacle Is Removed out of the Camp

7 And Moses took the tabernacle, and pitched it without the camp, afar off from the camp, and called it the Tabernacle of the congregation. And it came to pass, *that* every one which sought the Lord went out unto the tabernacle of the congregation, which *was* without the camp.   Ex. 29:42-43
8 And it came to pass, when Moses went out unto the tabernacle, *that* all the people rose up, and stood every man *at* his tent door, and looked after Moses, until he was gone into the tabernacle.   Num. 16:27
9 And it came to pass, as Moses entered into the tabernacle, the cloudy pillar descended, and stood *at* the door of the tabernacle, and *the* Lord talked with Moses.   Ps. 99:7
10 And all the people saw the cloudy pillar stand *at* the tabernacle door: and all the people rose up and worshipped, every man *in* his tent door.
11 And the Lord spake unto Moses face to face, as a man speaketh unto his friend. And he turned again into the camp: but his servant Joshua, the son of Nun, a young man, departed not out of the tabernacle.   Gen. 32:30

Moses Desires to See the Glory of God

12 And Moses said unto the Lord, See, thou sayest unto me, Bring up this people: and thou hast not let me know whom thou wilt send with me. Yet thou hast said, I know thee by name, and thou hast also found grace in my sight.   Ex. 32:34; 33:17; John 10:14-15
13 Now therefore, I pray thee, if I have found grace in thy sight, shew me now thy way, that I may know thee, that I may find grace in thy sight: and consider that this nation *is* thy people.   Deut. 9:26, 29; Ps. 25:4
14 And he said, My presence shall go *with* thee, and I will give thee rest.   Josh. 21:44; 22:4
15 And he said unto him, If thy presence go not *with me*, carry us not up hence.   Ex. 33:3
16 For wherein shall it be known here that I and thy people have found grace in thy

sight? *is it* not in that thou goest with us? so shall we be separated, I and thy people, from all the people that *are* upon the face of the earth.   Num. 14:14
17 And the Lord said unto Moses, I will do this thing also that thou hast spoken: for thou hast found grace in my sight, and I know thee by name.   Gen. 19:21
18 And he said, I ᵀbeseech thee, shew me thy glory.   Ex. 33:20 ◆ *beg*
19 And he said, I will make all my goodness pass before thee, and I will proclaim the name of the Lord before thee; and will be gracious to whom I will be gracious, and will shew mercy on whom I will shew mercy.   Ex. 34:5-7

> **33:18, 19 God's Character Revealed**
>
> It is our privilege to reach higher and still higher for clearer revealings of the character of God. When Moses prayed, "I beseech Thee, show me Thy glory," the Lord did not rebuke him, but He granted his prayer. God declared to His servant, "I will make all My goodness pass before thee, and I will proclaim the name of the Lord before thee" (Exodus 33:18, 19). *MH 464*

20 And he said, Thou canst not see my face: for there shall no man see me, and live.
21 And the Lord said, Behold, *there is* a place by me, and thou shalt stand upon a rock:
22 And it shall come to pass, while my glory passeth by, that I will put thee in a ᵀclift of the rock, and will cover thee with my hand while I pass by: Ps. 91:1, 4; Is. 2:21 ◆ *split or opening*
23 And I will take away mine hand, and thou shalt see my back parts: but my face shall not be seen.   Ex. 33:20

The Tablets Are Renewed

34 And the Lord said unto Moses, Hew thee two tables of stone like unto the first: and I will write upon *these* tables the words that were in the first tables, which thou brakest.   Ex. 31:18; 32:16, 19
2 And be ready in the morning, and come up in the morning unto mount Sinai, and present thyself there to me in the top of the mount.   Ex. 19:20
3 And no man shall come up with thee, neither let any man be seen throughout all the mount; neither let the flocks nor herds feed before that mount.   Ex. 19:12-13, 21
4 And he ᵀhewed two tables of stone like unto the first; and Moses rose up early in the morning, and went up unto mount Sinai, as the Lord had commanded him, and took in his hand the two tables of stone.   *cut*
5 And the Lord descended in the cloud, and stood with him there, and proclaimed the name of the Lord.   Ex. 33:19

6 And the LORD passed by before him, and proclaimed, The LORD, The LORD God, merciful and gracious, longsuffering, and abundant in goodness and truth, Neh. 9:17; Rom. 2:4
7 Keeping mercy for thousands, forgiving iniquity and ᵀtransgression and sin, and that will by no means clear *the guilty*; visiting the iniquity of the fathers upon the children, and upon the children's children, unto the third and to the fourth *generation.*　　*violation of a law*

34:6, 7 The Source of All Mercy

[God] does not ask if we are worthy of His love, but He pours upon us the riches of His love, to make us worthy. He is not vindictive. He seeks not to punish, but to redeem. Even the severity which He manifests through His providences is manifested for the salvation of the wayward. . . . It is true that God "will by no means clear the guilty" (Exodus 34:7), but He would take away the guilt. *MB 22*

---

8 And Moses made haste, and bowed his head toward the earth, and worshipped.　　Ex. 4:31
9 And he said, If now I have found grace in thy sight, O Lord, let my Lord, I pray thee, go among us; for it *is* a stiffnecked people; and pardon our iniquity and our sin, and take us for thine inheritance. Ex. 32:9; Deut. 32:9; Ps. 33:12

God Makes a Covenant with His People
10 And he said, Behold, I make a covenant: before all thy people I will do marvels, such as have not been done in all the earth, nor in any nation: and all the people among which thou *art* shall see the work of the LORD: for it *is* a terrible thing that I will do with thee.　　Deut. 5:2-3
11 Observe thou that which I command thee this day: behold, I drive out before thee the Amorite, and the Canaanite, and the Hittite, and the Perizzite, and the Hivite, and the Jebusite.　　Ex. 33:2
12 Take heed to thyself, lest thou make a covenant with the inhabitants of the land whither thou goest, lest it be for a snare in the midst of thee:　　Ex. 23:32-33; Deut. 7:2; Josh. 23:12-13
13 But ye shall destroy their altars, break their images, and cut down their ᵀgroves:　　*idols*
14 For thou shalt worship no other god: for the LORD, whose name *is* Jealous, *is* a jealous God:　　Ex. 20:3-5
15 Lest thou make a covenant with the inhabitants of the land, and they go a whoring after their gods, and do sacrifice unto their gods, and *one* call thee, and thou eat of his sacrifice;　　Num. 25:2; Judg. 2:17; 1 Cor. 8:4
16 And thou take of their daughters unto thy sons, and their daughters go a ᵀwhoring after their gods, and make thy sons go a whoring after their gods.　　Deut. 7:3-4 ◆ *prostituting*

17 Thou shalt make thee no molten gods.
18 The feast of unleavened bread shalt thou keep. Seven days thou shalt eat unleavened bread, as I commanded thee, in the time of the month Abib: for in the month Abib thou camest out from Egypt.　　Ex. 13:4
19 All that openeth the ᵀmatrix *is* mine; and every ᵀfirstling among thy cattle, *whether* ox or sheep, *that is male.*　　Ex. 13:2 ◆ *womb* ◆ *firstborn*
20 But the firstling of an ass thou shalt redeem with a lamb: and if thou redeem *him* not, then shalt thou break his neck. All the firstborn of thy sons thou shalt redeem. And none shall appear before me empty.　　Ex. 13:15
21 Six days thou shalt work, but on the seventh day thou shalt rest: in ᵀearing time and in harvest thou shalt rest.　　Ex. 23:12 ◆ *plowing*
22 And thou shalt observe the feast of weeks, of the firstfruits of wheat harvest, and the feast of ingathering at the year's end.
23 Thrice in the year shall all your men children appear before the Lord GOD, the God of Israel.　　Ex. 23:14, 17; Deut. 16:16
24 For I will cast out the nations before thee, and enlarge thy borders: neither shall any man desire thy land, when thou shalt go up to appear before the LORD thy God ᵀthrice in the year.　　Ex. 23:27-31; Ps. 78:55 ◆ *three times*
25 Thou shalt not offer the blood of my sacrifice with leaven; neither shall the sacrifice of the feast of the passover be left unto the morning.　　Ex. 12:10; 23:18
26 The first of the firstfruits of thy land thou shalt bring unto the house of the LORD thy God. Thou shalt not ᵀseethe a kid in his mother's milk.　　Ex. 23:19; Deut. 14:21; 26:2 ◆ *boil*
27 And the LORD said unto Moses, Write thou these words: for after the tenor of these words I have made a covenant with thee and with Israel.　　Ex. 17:14

Moses Returns from the Mountain
28 And he was there with the LORD forty days and forty nights; he did neither eat bread, nor drink water. And he wrote upon the tables the words of the covenant, the ten commandments.　　Ex. 24:18; 31:18; 34:1

34:29, 30 Guilt Brings Fear

Too awed to speak, [Aaron] silently pointed to the countenance of Moses, and then toward heaven. The great leader understood his meaning. In their conscious guilt, feeling themselves still under the divine displeasure, [the children of Israel] could not endure the heavenly light, which, had they been obedient to God, would have filled them with joy. There is fear in guilt. The soul that is free from sin will not wish to hide from the light of heaven. *PP 329, 330*

29 And it came to pass, when Moses came down from mount Sinai with the two tables of testimony in Moses' hand, when he came down from the mount, that Moses ᵀwist not that the skin of his face shone while he talked with him.   Ex. 32:15; Matt. 17:2; 2 Cor. 3:13 ◆ *knew*
30 And when Aaron and all the children of Israel saw Moses, behold, the skin of his face shone; and they were afraid to come nigh him.
31 And Moses called unto them; and Aaron and all the rulers of the congregation returned unto him: and Moses talked with them.
32 And afterward all the children of Israel came nigh: and he gave them in commandment all that the LORD had spoken with him in mount Sinai.
33 And *till* Moses had done speaking with them, he put a ᵀvail on his face.   *veil*
34 But when Moses went in before the LORD to speak with him, he took the vail off, until he came out. And he came out, and spake unto the children of Israel *that* which he was commanded.   2 Cor. 3:16
35 And the children of Israel saw the face of Moses, that the skin of Moses' face shone: and Moses put the vail upon his face again, until he went in to speak with him.

The Sabbath

35 And Moses gathered all the congregation of the children of Israel together, and said unto them, These *are* the words which the LORD hath commanded, that *ye* should do them.   Ex. 34:32
2 Six days shall work be done, but on the seventh day there shall be to you an holy day, a sabbath of rest to the LORD: whosoever doeth work therein shall be put to death.   Ex. 20:9-10
3 Ye shall kindle no fire throughout your habitations upon the sabbath day.   Ex. 12:16
4 And Moses spake unto all the congregation of the children of Israel, saying, This *is* the thing which the LORD commanded, saying,
5 Take ye from among you an offering unto the LORD: whosoever *is* of a willing heart, let him bring it, an offering of the LORD; gold, and silver, and brass,   Ex. 25:2-7
6 And blue, and purple, and scarlet, and fine linen, and goats' *hair*,
7 And rams' skins dyed red, and badgers' skins, and shittim wood,
8 And oil for the light, and spices for anointing oil, and for the sweet incense,
9 And onyx stones, and stones to be set for the ephod, and for the breastplate.
10 And every wise hearted among you shall come, and make all that the LORD hath commanded;
11 The tabernacle, his tent, and his covering, his ᵀtaches, and his boards, his bars, his pillars, and his sockets,   Ex. 26 ◆ *hooks for curtains*
12 The ark, and the staves thereof, *with* the mercy seat, and the ᵀvail of the covering, *veil*
13 The table, and his staves, and all his vessels, and the shewbread,   Ex. 25:23-30; Lev. 24:5-6
14 The candlestick also for the light, and his furniture, and his lamps, with the oil for the light,   Ex. 25:31-39
15 And the incense altar, and his ᵀstaves, and the anointing oil, and the sweet incense, and the hanging for the door at the entering in of the tabernacle,   Ex. 30:1-10 ◆ *clubs or rods*
16 The altar of burnt offering, with his brasen grate, his staves, and all his vessels, the ᵀlaver and his foot,   Ex. 27:1-8; 30:18-21 ◆ *basin for washing*
17 The hangings of the court, his pillars, and their sockets, and the hanging for the door of the court,
18 The pins of the tabernacle, and the pins of the court, and their cords,   Ex. 27:19
19 The cloths of service, to do service in the holy *place*, the holy garments for Aaron the priest, and the garments of his sons, to minister in the priest's office.   Ex. 31:10

The Readiness of the People to Make Offerings

20 And all the congregation of the children of Israel departed from the presence of Moses.
21 And they came, every one whose heart stirred him up, and every one whom his spirit made willing, *and* they brought the LORD's offering to the work of the tabernacle of the congregation, and for all his service, and for the holy garments.   Ex. 25:2
22 And they came, both men and women, as many as were willing hearted, *and* brought bracelets, and earrings, and rings, and tablets, all jewels of gold: and every man that offered *offered* an offering of gold unto the LORD.
23 And every man, with whom was found blue, and purple, and scarlet, and fine linen, and goats' *hair*, and red skins of rams, and badgers' skins, brought *them*.   1 Chr. 29:8
24 Every one that did offer an offering of silver and brass brought the LORD's offering: and every man, with whom was found shittim wood for any work of the service, brought *it*.
25 And all the women that were wise hearted did spin with their hands, and brought that which they had spun, *both* of blue, and of purple, *and* of scarlet, and of fine linen.   Ex. 28:3
26 And all the women whose heart stirred them up in wisdom spun goats' *hair*. Ex. 35:21

27 And the rulers brought onyx stones, and stones to be set, for the ᵀephod, and for the breastplate;   1 Chr. 29:6 ◆ *priestly garment*
28 And spice, and oil for the light, and for the anointing oil, and for the sweet incense.
29 The children of Israel brought a willing offering unto the LORD, every man and woman, whose heart made them willing to bring for all manner of work, which the LORD had commanded to be made by the hand of Moses.   Ex. 35:4

Bezaleel and Aholiab Are Called to the Work

30 And Moses said unto the children of Israel, See, the LORD hath called by name Bezaleel the son of Uri, the son of Hur, of the tribe of Judah;
31 And he hath filled him with the spirit of God, in wisdom, in understanding, and in knowledge, and in all manner of workmanship;
32 And to devise ᵀcurious works, to work in gold, and in silver, and in brass, *intricately detailed*
33 And in the cutting of stones, to set *them*, and in carving of wood, to make any manner of cunning work.
34 And he hath put in his heart that he may teach, *both* he, and Aholiab, the son of Ahisamach, of the tribe of Dan.   Ex. 31:6
35 Them hath he filled with wisdom of heart, to work all manner of work, of the engraver, and of the cunning workman, and of the embroiderer, in blue, and in purple, in scarlet, and in fine linen, and of the weaver, *even* of them that do any work, and of those that devise cunning work.   Ex. 31:3, 6; 35:31

The Offerings Are Delivered to the Workmen

36 Then wrought Bezaleel and Aholiab, and every wise hearted man, in whom the LORD put wisdom and understanding to know how to work all manner of work for the service of the sanctuary, according to all that the LORD had commanded.   Ex. 28:3
2 And Moses called Bezaleel and Aholiab, and every wise hearted man, in whose heart the LORD had put wisdom, *even* every one whose heart stirred him up to come unto the work to do it: Ex. 31:6
3 And they received of Moses all the offering, which the children of Israel had brought for the work of the service of the sanctuary, to make it ᵀwithal. And they brought yet unto him free offerings every morning.   *with*
4 And all the wise men, that ᵀwrought all the work of the sanctuary, came every man from his work which they made;   *made*
5 And they spake unto Moses, saying, The people bring much more than enough for the service of the work, which the LORD commanded to make.   2 Chr. 24:14
6 And Moses gave commandment, and they caused it to be proclaimed throughout the camp, saying, Let neither man nor woman make any more work for the offering of the sanctuary. So the people were restrained from bringing.
7 For the stuff they had was sufficient for all the work to make it, and too much.

The Curtains of the Cherubim

8 And every wise hearted man among them that wrought the work of the tabernacle made ten curtains *of* fine twined linen, and blue, and purple, and scarlet: *with* cherubims of cunning work made he them.
9 The length of one curtain *was* twenty and eight cubits, and the breadth of one curtain four cubits: the curtains *were* all of one size.
10 And he coupled the five curtains one unto another: and *the other* five curtains he coupled one unto another.
11 And he made loops of blue on the edge of one curtain from the selvedge in the coupling: likewise he made in the uttermost side of *another* curtain, in the coupling of the second.
12 Fifty loops made he in one curtain, and fifty loops made he in the edge of the curtain which *was* in the coupling of the second: the loops held one *curtain* to another.   Ex. 26:5
13 And he made fifty taches of gold, and coupled the curtains one unto another with the taches: so it became one tabernacle.

The Curtains of Goats' Hair

14 And he made curtains *of* goats' *hair* for the tent over the tabernacle: eleven curtains he made them.   Ex. 26:7-13
15 The length of one curtain *was* thirty cubits, and four cubits *was* the breadth of one curtain: the eleven curtains *were* of one size.
16 And he coupled five curtains by themselves, and six curtains by themselves.
17 And he made fifty loops upon the uttermost edge of the curtain in the coupling, and fifty loops made he upon the edge of the curtain which coupleth the second.
18 And he made fifty taches *of* brass to couple the tent together, that it might be one.
19 And he made a covering for the tent *of* rams' skins dyed red, and a covering *of* badgers' skins above *that*.
20 And he made boards for the tabernacle *of* shittim wood, standing up.   Ex. 25:5
21 The length of a board *was* ten cubits, and the breadth of a board one cubit and a half.
22 One board had two tenons, equally

distant one from another: thus did he make for all the boards of the tabernacle.

23 And he made boards for the tabernacle; twenty boards for the south side southward:

24 And forty sockets of silver he made under the twenty boards; two sockets under one board for his two tenons, and two sockets under another board for his two tenons.

25 And for the other side of the tabernacle, which is toward the north corner, he made twenty boards,

26 And their forty sockets of silver; two sockets under one board, and two sockets under another board.

27 And for the sides of the tabernacle westward he made six boards.

28 And two boards made he for the corners of the tabernacle in the two sides.

29 And they were coupled beneath, and coupled together at the head thereof, to one ring: thus he did to both of them in both the corners.

30 And there were eight boards; and their sockets were sixteen sockets of silver, under every board two sockets.

31 And he made bars of shittim wood; five for the boards of the one side of the tabernacle,   Ex. 26:26-29

32 And five bars for the boards of the other side of the tabernacle, and five bars for the boards of the tabernacle for the sides westward.

33 And he made the middle bar to shoot through the boards from the one end to the other.

34 And he overlaid the boards with gold, and made their rings of gold to be places for the bars, and overlaid the bars with gold.

The Veil

35 And he made a ᵀvail of blue, and purple, and scarlet, and fine twined linen: with cherubims made he it of cunning work.   veil

36 And he made thereunto four pillars of shittim wood, and overlaid them with gold: their hooks were of gold; and he cast for them four sockets of silver.

37 And he made an hanging for the tabernacle door of blue, and purple, and scarlet, and fine twined linen, of needlework;

38 And the five pillars of it with their hooks: and he overlaid their ᵀchapiters and their ᵀfillets with gold: but their five sockets were of brass.   tops of columns ◆ rods for curtains between columns

The Ark

37 And Bezaleel made the ark of shittim wood: two cubits and a half was the length of it, and a cubit and a half the breadth of it, and a cubit and a half the height of it:

2 And he overlaid it with pure gold within and without, and made a crown of gold to it round about.

3 And he cast for it four rings of gold, to be set by the four corners of it; even two rings upon the one side of it, and two rings upon the other side of it.

4 And he made ᵀstaves of shittim wood, and overlaid them with gold.   clubs or rods

5 And he put the staves into the rings by the sides of the ark, to bear the ark.

6 And he made the mercy seat of pure gold: two cubits and a half was the length thereof, and one cubit and a half the breadth thereof.   Heb. 9:5

7 And he made two cherubims of gold, beaten out of one piece made he them, on the two ends of the mercy seat;

8 One cherub on the end on this side, and another cherub on the other end on that side: out of the mercy seat made he the cherubims on the two ends thereof.

9 And the cherubims spread out their wings on high, and covered with their wings over the mercy seat, with their faces one to another; even to the mercy seatward were the faces of the cherubims.

The Table with Its Vessels

10 And he made the table of shittim wood: two cubits was the length thereof, and a cubit the breadth thereof, and a cubit and a half the height thereof:

11 And he overlaid it with pure gold, and made thereunto a crown of gold round about.

12 Also he made thereunto a border of an ᵀhandbreadth round about; and made a crown of gold for the border thereof round about.   about four inches

13 And he cast for it four rings of gold, and put the rings upon the four corners that were in the four feet thereof.

14 Over against the border were the rings, the places for the staves to bear the table.

15 And he made the staves of shittim wood, and overlaid them with gold, to bear the table.

16 And he made the vessels which were upon the table, his dishes, and his spoons, and his bowls, and his covers to cover ᵀwithal, of pure gold.   with

17 And he made the candlestick of pure gold: of beaten work made he the candlestick; his shaft, and his branch, his bowls, his knops, and his flowers, were of the same: Ex. 25:31-39

18 And six branches going out of the sides thereof; three branches of the candlestick out of the one side thereof, and three branches of the candlestick out of the other side thereof:

19 Three bowls made after the fashion of almonds in one branch, a ᵀknop and a flower; and three bowls made like almonds in another branch, a knop and a flower: so throughout the six branches going out of the candlestick.   *architectural ornament*

20 And in the candlestick *were* four bowls made like almonds, his knops, and his flowers:

21 And a knop under two branches of the same, and a knop under two branches of the same, and a knop under two branches of the same, according to the six branches going out of it.

22 Their knops and their branches were of the same: all of it *was* one beaten work *of* pure gold.

23 And he made his seven lamps, and his snuffers, and his snuffdishes, *of* pure gold.

24 *Of* a talent of pure gold made he it, and all the vessels thereof.

The Altar of Incense

25 And he made the incense altar *of* shittim wood: the length of it *was* a cubit, and the breadth of it a cubit; *it was* foursquare; and two cubits *was* the height of it; the horns thereof were of the same.   Ex. 30:1-5

26 And he overlaid it with pure gold, *both* the top of it, and the sides thereof round about, and the horns of it: also he made unto it a crown of gold round about.

27 And he made two rings of gold for it under the crown thereof, by the two corners of it, upon the two sides thereof, to be places for the staves to bear it withal.

28 And he made the staves *of* shittim wood, and overlaid them with gold.

29 And he made the holy anointing oil, and the pure incense of sweet spices, according to the work of the ᵀapothecary. *maker of perfumes*

The Altar of Burnt Offering

38 And he made the altar of burnt offering *of* shittim wood: five cubits *was* the length thereof, and five cubits the breadth thereof; *it was* foursquare; and three cubits the height thereof.   Ex. 27:1-8

2 And he made the horns thereof on the four corners of it; the horns thereof were of the same: and he overlaid it with brass.

3 And he made all the vessels of the altar, the pots, and the shovels, and the basons, *and* the fleshhooks, and the firepans: all the vessels thereof made he *of* brass.

4 And he made for the altar a brasen grate of network under the ᵀcompass thereof beneath unto the midst of it.   *rim*

5 And he cast four rings for the four ends of the grate of brass, *to be* places for the ᵀstaves.   *clubs* or *rods*

6 And he made the staves *of* shittim wood, and overlaid them with brass.

7 And he put the staves into the rings on the sides of the altar, to bear it ᵀwithal; he made the altar hollow with boards.   *with*

8 And he made the ᵀlaver *of* brass, and the foot of it *of* brass, of the lookingglasses of *the women* assembling, which assembled *at* the door of the tabernacle of the congregation.   Ex. 40:7 ◆ *basin for washing*

The Court

9 And he made the court: on the south side southward the hangings of the court *were of* fine twined linen, an hundred cubits:

10 Their pillars *were* twenty, and their brasen sockets twenty; the hooks of the pillars and their fillets *were of* silver.

11 And for the north side *the hangings were* an hundred cubits, their pillars *were* twenty, and their sockets of brass twenty; the hooks of the pillars and their fillets *of* silver.

12 And for the west side *were* hangings of fifty cubits, their pillars ten, and their sockets ten; the hooks of the pillars and their fillets *of* silver.

13 And for the east side eastward fifty cubits.

14 The hangings of the one side *of the gate were* fifteen cubits; their pillars three, and their sockets three.

15 And for the other side of the court gate, on this hand and that hand, *were* hangings of fifteen cubits; their pillars three, and their sockets three.

16 All the hangings of the court round about *were* of fine twined linen.

17 And the sockets for the pillars *were of* brass; the hooks of the pillars and their fillets *of* silver; and the overlaying of their ᵀchapiters *of* silver; and all the pillars of the court *were* filleted with silver.   *tops of columns*

18 And the hanging for the gate of the court *was* needlework, *of* blue, and purple, and scarlet, and fine twined linen: and twenty cubits *was* the length, and the height in the breadth *was* five cubits, answerable to the hangings of the court.

19 And their pillars *were* four, and their sockets *of* brass four; their hooks *of* silver, and the overlaying of their chapiters and their fillets *of* silver.

20 And all the pins of the tabernacle, and of the court round about, *were of* brass.

The People's Offering

21 This is the sum of the tabernacle, *even of* the tabernacle of testimony, as it was counted, according to the commandment of Moses, *for* the service of the Levites, by the hand of Ithamar, son to Aaron the priest.   Num. 1:50

22 And Bezaleel the son of Uri, the son of

Hur, of the tribe of Judah, made all that the LORD commanded Moses.

23 And with him was Aholiab, son of Ahisamach, of the tribe of Dan, an engraver, and a cunning workman, and an embroiderer in blue, and in purple, and in scarlet, and fine linen.   Ex. 35:34

24 All the gold that was occupied for the work in all the work of the holy *place*, even the gold of the offering, was twenty and nine talents, and seven hundred and thirty shekels, after the shekel of the sanctuary.   Lev. 27:25

25 And the silver of them that were numbered of the congregation was an hundred talents, and a thousand seven hundred and ᵀthreescore and fifteen shekels, after the shekel of the sanctuary: sixty

26 A bekah for every man, *that is,* half a shekel, after the shekel of the sanctuary, for every one that went to be numbered, from twenty years old and upward, for six hundred thousand and three thousand and five hundred and fifty *men*.   Ex. 12:37; 30:13; Num. 1:46

27 And of the hundred talents of silver were cast the sockets of the sanctuary, and the sockets of the ᵀvail; an hundred sockets of the hundred talents, a talent for a socket.   Ex. 26:19 ◆ veil

28 And of the thousand seven hundred seventy and five shekels he made hooks for the pillars, and overlaid their chapiters, and filleted them.

29 And the brass of the offering was seventy talents, and two thousand and four hundred shekels.

30 And therewith he made the sockets to the door of the tabernacle of the congregation, and the brasen altar, and the brasen grate for it, and all the vessels of the altar,   Ex. 26:37

31 And the sockets of the court round about, and the sockets of the court gate, and all the pins of the tabernacle, and all the pins of the court round about.

The Cloths of Service and Holy Garments

39 And of the blue, and purple, and scarlet, they made cloths of service, to do service in the holy *place*, and made the holy garments for Aaron; as the LORD commanded Moses.   Ex. 31:10; 35:19, 23

2 And he made the ephod *of* gold, blue, and purple, and scarlet, and fine twined linen.

3 And they did beat the gold into thin plates, and cut it *into* wires, to work it in the blue, and in the purple, and in the scarlet, and in the fine linen, *with* cunning work.

4 They made shoulderpieces for it, to couple *it* together: by the two edges was it coupled together.

5 And the ᵀcurious girdle of his ephod, that

was upon it, was of the same, according to the work thereof; *of* gold, blue, and purple, and scarlet, and fine twined linen; as the LORD commanded Moses.   *intricately detailed*

6 And they ᵀwrought onyx stones inclosed in ᵀouches of gold, ᵀgraven, as signets are graven, with the names of the children of Israel.   Ex. 28:9 ◆ *made* ◆ *settings* ◆ *engraved or cut out*

7 And he put them on the shoulders of the ephod, *that they should be* stones for a memorial to the children of Israel; as the LORD commanded Moses.   Ex. 28:12

8 And he made the breastplate *of* cunning work, like the work of the ephod; *of* gold, blue, and purple, and scarlet, and fine twined linen.

9 It was foursquare; they made the breastplate double: a span was the length thereof, and a span the breadth thereof, *being* doubled.

10 And they set in it four rows of stones: *the first* row was a sardius, a topaz, and a ᵀcarbuncle: this was the first row.   *reddish precious stone*

11 And the second row, an emerald, a sapphire, and a diamond.

12 And the third row, a ligure, an agate, and an amethyst.

13 And the fourth row, a ᵀberyl, an onyx, and a jasper: *they were* inclosed in ouches of gold in their inclosings.   *precious stone*

14 And the stones were according to the names of the children of Israel, twelve, according to their names, *like* the engravings of a signet, every one with his name, according to the twelve tribes.   Rev. 21:12

15 And they made upon the breastplate chains at the ends, *of* wreathen work *of* pure gold.

16 And they made two ᵀouches *of* gold, and two gold rings; and put the two rings in the two ends of the breastplate. *settings for precious stones*

17 And they put the two wreathen chains of gold in the two rings on the ends of the breastplate.

18 And the two ends of the two wreathen chains they fastened in the two ouches, and put them on the shoulderpieces of the ᵀephod, before it.   *priestly garment*

19 And they made two rings of gold, and put *them* on the two ends of the breastplate, upon the border of it, which was on the side of the ephod inward.

20 And they made two *other* golden rings, and put them on the two sides of the ephod underneath, toward the forepart of it, over against the *other* coupling thereof, above the curious ᵀgirdle of the ephod.   *belt*

21 And they did bind the breastplate by his rings unto the rings of the ephod with a lace of blue, that it might be above the curious girdle of the ephod, and that the breastplate

might not be loosed from the ephod; as the LORD commanded Moses.

22 And he made the robe of the ephod *of* woven work, all *of* blue.

23 And *there was* an hole in the midst of the robe, as the hole of an ᵀhabergeon, *with* a band round about the hole, that it should not ᵀrend.   *military garment ◆ tear apart*

24 And they made upon the hems of the robe pomegranates *of* blue, and purple, and scarlet, *and* twined *linen.*

25 And they made bells *of* pure gold, and put the bells between the pomegranates upon the hem of the robe, round about between the pomegranates;

26 A bell and a pomegranate, a bell and a pomegranate, round about the hem of the robe to minister *in;* as the LORD commanded Moses.

27 And they made coats *of* fine linen *of* woven work for Aaron, and for his sons,   Ezek. 44:18

28 And a mitre *of* fine linen, and goodly bonnets *of* fine linen, and linen ᵀbreeches *of* fine twined linen,   Ex. 28:4 ◆ *trousers*

29 And a girdle *of* fine twined linen, and blue, and purple, and scarlet, *of* needlework; as the LORD commanded Moses.

30 And they made the plate of the holy crown *of* pure gold, and wrote upon it a writing, *like to* the engravings of a ᵀsignet, HOLINESS TO THE LORD.   *identifying seal*

31 And they tied unto it a lace of blue, to fasten *it* on high upon the ᵀmitre; as the LORD commanded Moses.   *turban*

All Is Viewed and Approved by Moses

32 Thus was all the work of the tabernacle of the tent of the congregation finished: and the children of Israel did according to all that the LORD commanded Moses, so did they.   Ex. 39:42-43

33 And they brought the tabernacle unto Moses, the tent, and all his furniture, his ᵀtaches, his boards, his bars, and his pillars, and his sockets,   *hooks for curtains*

34 And the covering of rams' skins dyed red, and the covering of badgers' skins, and the ᵀvail of the covering,   *veil*

35 The ark of the testimony, and the ᵀstaves thereof, and the mercy seat,   *clubs or rods*

36 The table, *and* all the vessels thereof, and the shewbread,

37 The pure candlestick, *with* the lamps thereof, *even with* the lamps to be set in order, and all the vessels thereof, and the oil for light,

38 And the golden altar, and the anointing oil, and the sweet incense, and the hanging for the tabernacle door,   Ex. 30:7

39 The brasen altar, and his grate of brass, his staves, and all his vessels, the ᵀlaver and his foot,   *basin for washing*

40 The hangings of the court, his pillars, and his sockets, and the hanging for the court gate, his cords, and his pins, and all the vessels of the service of the tabernacle, for the tent of the congregation,

41 The cloths of service to do service in the holy *place,* and the holy garments for Aaron the priest, and his sons' garments, to minister in the priest's office.

42 According to all that the LORD commanded Moses, so the children of Israel made all the work.   Ex. 35:10

43 And Moses did look upon all the work, and, behold, they had done it as the LORD had commanded, even so had they done it: and Moses blessed them. Num. 6:23-27; 2 Sam. 6:18

The Sanctuary Completed

Exodus 39:32–43

No language can describe the glory of the scene presented within the sanctuary—the gold-plated walls reflecting the light from the golden candlestick, the brilliant hues of the richly embroidered curtains with their shining angels, the table, and the altar of incense, glittering with gold; beyond the second veil the sacred ark, with its mystic cherubim, and above it the holy Shekinah, the visible manifestation of Jehovah's presence; all but a dim reflection of the glories of the temple of God in heaven, the great center of the work for man's redemption.

A period of about half a year was occupied in the building of the tabernacle. When it was completed, Moses examined all the work of the builders, comparing it with the pattern shown him in the mount and the directions he had received from God. "As the Lord had commanded, even so had they done it: and Moses blessed them." With eager interest the multitudes of Israel crowded around to look upon the sacred structure. While they were contemplating the scene with reverent satisfaction, the pillar of cloud floated over the sanctuary and, descending, enveloped it. "And the glory of the Lord filled the tabernacle." There was a revealing of the divine majesty, and for a time even Moses could not enter. With deep emotion the people beheld the token that the work of their hands was accepted. There were no loud demonstrations of rejoicing. A solemn awe rested upon all. But the gladness of their hearts welled up in tears of joy, and they murmured low, earnest words of gratitude that God had condescended to abide with them. PP 349, 350

The Erection of the Tabernacle, with Its Anointing, Is Commanded

40 And the Lord spake unto Moses, saying,

2 On the first day of the first month shalt thou set up the tabernacle of the tent of the congregation.   Ex. 13:4

3 And thou shalt put therein the ark of the testimony, and cover the ark with the vail.

4 And thou shalt bring in the table, and set in order the things that are to be set in order upon it; and thou shalt bring in the candlestick, and light the lamps thereof.

5 And thou shalt set the altar of gold for the incense before the ark of the testimony, and put the hanging of the door to the tabernacle.

6 And thou shalt set the altar of the burnt offering before the door of the tabernacle of the tent of the congregation.   Ex. 40:29

7 And thou shalt set the ᵀlaver between the tent of the congregation and the altar, and shalt put water therein.   *basin for washing*

8 And thou shalt set up the court round about, and hang up the hanging at the court gate.

9 And thou shalt take the anointing oil, and anoint the tabernacle, and all that *is* therein, and shalt ᵀhallow it, and all the vessels thereof: and it shall be holy.   Lev. 8:10 ◆ *render it as sacred*

10 And thou shalt anoint the altar of the burnt offering, and all his vessels, and sanctify the altar: and it shall be an altar most holy.   Ex. 29:36-37

11 And thou shalt anoint the laver and his foot, and ᵀsanctify it.   *make it holy*

12 And thou shalt bring Aaron and his sons unto the door of the tabernacle of the congregation, and wash them with water. Lev. 8:1-13

13 And thou shalt put upon Aaron the holy garments, and anoint him, and sanctify him; that he may minister unto me in the priest's office.   Ex. 28:41

14 And thou shalt bring his sons, and clothe them with coats:

15 And thou shalt anoint them, as thou didst anoint their father, that they may minister unto me in the priest's office: for their anointing shall surely be an everlasting priesthood throughout their generations.   Num. 25:13

16 Thus did Moses: according to all that the Lord commanded him, so did he.

17 And it came to pass in the first month in the second year, on the first *day* of the month, *that* the tabernacle was reared up.   Num. 7:1

18 And Moses reared up the tabernacle, and fastened his sockets, and set up the boards thereof, and put in the bars thereof, and reared up his pillars.

19 And he spread abroad the tent over the tabernacle, and put the covering of the tent above upon it; as the Lord commanded Moses.

20 And he took and put the testimony into the ark, and set the ᵀstaves on the ark, and put the mercy seat above upon the ark: *clubs or rods*

21 And he brought the ark into the tabernacle, and set up the vail of the covering, and covered the ark of the testimony; as the Lord commanded Moses.   Ex. 26:33

22 And he put the table in the tent of the congregation, upon the side of the tabernacle northward, without the vail.   Ex. 26:35

23 And he set the bread in order upon it before the Lord; as the Lord had commanded Moses.   Ex. 25:30

24 And he put the candlestick in the tent of the congregation, over against the table, on the side of the tabernacle southward.

25 And he lighted the lamps before the Lord; as the Lord commanded Moses.   Ex. 25:37

26 And he put the golden altar in the tent of the congregation before the vail: Ex. 40:5

27 And he burnt sweet incense thereon; as the Lord commanded Moses.   Ex. 30:7

28 And he set up the hanging *at* the door of the tabernacle.   Ex. 40:5

29 And he put the altar of burnt offering *by* the door of the tabernacle of the tent of the congregation, and offered upon it the burnt offering and the meat offering; as the Lord commanded Moses.   Ex. 40:6

30 And he set the laver between the tent of the congregation and the altar, and put water there, to wash ᵀ*withal*. Ex. 40:7 ◆ *with*

31 And Moses and Aaron and his sons washed their hands and their feet thereat:

32 When they went into the tent of the congregation, and when they came near unto the altar, they washed; as the Lord commanded Moses.

33 And he reared up the court round about the tabernacle and the altar, and set up the hanging of the court gate. So Moses finished the work.   Ex. 27:9-16; 40:8

A Cloud Covers the Tabernacle

34 Then a cloud covered the tent of the congregation, and the glory of the Lord filled the tabernacle.   Num. 9:15-23

35 And Moses was not able to enter into the tent of the congregation, because the cloud abode thereon, and the glory of the Lord filled the tabernacle.   1 Kin. 8:11

36 And when the cloud was taken up from over the tabernacle, the children of Israel went onward in all their journeys: Num. 9:17; Neh. 9:19

37 But if the cloud were not taken up, then they journeyed not till the day that it was taken up.   Num. 9:19-22

38 For the cloud of the Lord *was* upon the tabernacle by day, and fire was on it by night, in the sight of all the house of Israel, throughout all their journeys.   Ex. 13:21

THE THIRD BOOK OF MOSES CALLED

LEVITICUS

As the newly-freed Hebrew people travel from slavery in Egypt toward the Promised Land, God gives His people rules to help them successfully navigate life under His kingly rule. Leviticus is a book of laws that shows God's people how to live, how to serve, and how to obey.

The center of worship is the tabernacle with an emphasis on perfection (perfect animals for sacrifices; the exclusion from worship of those with skin ailments until those ailments are treated; priests without physical challenges chosen to serve). The system of sacrifices and worship ordinances points to God's holiness. The consequences of disobedience are necessarily severe, for the people of Israel are called to be His priests (Exodus 19:6) and commanded to "be holy: for I the LORD your God am holy" (Leviticus 19:2). The people of Israel are to honor their God rightly through their daily behavior and through their worship. This book shows them how to do that.

Dates

Moses probably wrote Leviticus around 1405 B.C. The book begins in the second year—a year after the first Passover (Exodus 12). Only one month passes; the people of Israel are encamped around Mount Sinai for the duration of the book.

Author

Moses is generally viewed as the author of Leviticus and the other books of the Pentateuch. The Ras Shema Tablets found off the coast of northern Syria contain the same trespass offerings as mentioned in Leviticus. Also, about fifty-six times in Leviticus, God is described as giving the law to Moses (see, for example, 1:1; 4:1; 6:1; 8:1; 11:1; 12:1; 13:1).

Meaning of the Name

The Hebrew title for Leviticus is *Wayyiqra*, the first word in the book, which means "And He Called." But Leviticus is named in the Talmud as the "Law of the Priests" or the "Law of the Offerings." In the Septuagint, the Greek title *Leuitikon*, or "That Which Pertains to the Priests," led to the Latin Vulgate title, *Leviticus*.

Christ in Leviticus

The system of offerings and the duties of the high priest can be seen as allusions to the work of Christ. The burnt offering, grain offering, peace offering, sin offering, and trespass offering foreshadow Christ's submission, sinless nature, the peace with God brought about through the cross, and His atonement for sin. He also is the ultimate High Priest, one with whom Israel's first high priest Aaron is compared and contrasted in Hebrews 5:1–4.

The required feasts described in Leviticus 23 (Passover, Unleavened Bread, Firstfruits, Pentecost, Trumpets, Day of Atonement, and Tabernacles) also point to the work of Christ. Just as the best of the harvest or the "firstfruits" is required to represent the whole harvest (Exodus 23:19; Leviticus 2:12), Christ's resurrection is the "firstfruits"—a representation—of the promised resurrection of believers (1 Corinthians 15:20). His death was an atoning sacrifice made for all. Christ promised that the Holy Spirit would arrive around the time of the feast of Pentecost (Acts 1:4–5; 2:1–4). The feasts of Trumpets and Tabernacles foreshadow the second coming of Christ.

Overview

The wilderness becomes God's training ground for shaping His people. While their sanctification is His goal, the discipline of making sacrifices for sins is a necessary requirement. Thus, Leviticus is divided into two main sections:

(1) *Leviticus 1—17, Sacrifice:* The priests become the central figures in offering sacrifices to a holy God (chapters 1—7). Priests also determine whether or not a person is clean or unclean for worship (chapters 12—15; 22) in order to stay the spread of disease. The rule of clean and unclean also applies to food (chapter 11).

(2) *Leviticus 18—27, Sanctification:* God wants His people to be different from other nations. To keep His people from being defiled, God puts a system of government into place, rules are instituted for daily life (chapters 18—20), priests (chapter 21), festivals (chapters 23), the year of Jubilee (chapter 25), and other aspects of daily life, including vows (chapter 27).

Unlocking Leviticus

KEY PEOPLE:
Moses, Aaron, Nadab, Abihu, other priests

KEY EVENTS:
The institution of the five offerings; ordination of Aaron and his sons as priests; deaths of Nadab and Abihu for unlawful fire; health principles; the Day of Atonement; the establishment of the major feasts

KEY WORD:
Holiness. How to approach a holy God is a theme throughout Leviticus. God wants His people to be holy, hence the requirements for blood sacrifices. The feasts are to remember and celebrate the great acts of a holy God.

KEY VERSE:
"Speak unto all the congregation of the children of Israel, and say unto them, Ye shall be holy: for I the LORD your God am holy" (Leviticus 19:2).

KEY CHAPTER:
Leviticus 16, institutes the Day of Atonement and the sacrifices on behalf of Aaron the high priest and the people of Israel. While a bull is offered for the sins of the high priest and his family, a goat is sacrificed for the sins of the people of Israel. Another goat however—the scapegoat—bears the sins of the people and is released to symbolize their release from sin.

The Burnt Offerings

1 And the LORD called unto Moses, and spake unto him out of the tabernacle of the congregation, saying, *Ex. 19:3; 25:22; 40:34-35* 2 Speak unto the children of Israel, and say unto them, If any man of you bring an offering unto the LORD, ye shall bring your offering of the cattle, *even* of the herd, and of the flock. *Lev. 22:18-19*

1:1, 2 God Clears Things Up

The sacrificial system, committed to Adam, was also perverted by his descendants. Superstition, idolatry, cruelty, and licentiousness corrupted the simple and significant service that God had appointed. Through long intercourse with idolaters the people of Israel had mingled many heathen customs with their worship; therefore the Lord gave them at Sinai definite instruction concerning the sacrificial service. *PP 364*

The Burnt Offering of the Herd

3 If his offering *be* a burnt sacrifice of the herd, let him offer a male without blemish: he shall offer it of his own voluntary will at the door of the tabernacle of the congregation before the LORD. *Ex. 12:5; Lev. 6:9-13; Deut. 15:21* 4 And he shall put his hand upon the head of the burnt offering; and it shall be accepted for him to make atonement for him. *Lev. 3:2* 5 And he shall kill the ᵀbullock before the LORD: and the priests, Aaron's sons, shall bring the blood, and sprinkle the blood round about upon the altar that *is by* the door of the tabernacle of the congregation. *Lev. 3:2, 8 ◆ bull* 6 And he shall flay the burnt offering, and cut it into his pieces. *Lev. 7:8* 7 And the sons of Aaron the priest shall put fire upon the altar, and lay the wood in order upon the fire: *Gen. 22:9* 8 And the priests, Aaron's sons, shall lay the parts, the head, and the fat, in order upon the wood that *is* on the fire which *is* upon the altar: 9 But his inwards and his legs shall he wash in water: and the priest shall burn all on the altar, *to be* a burnt sacrifice, an offering made by fire, of a sweet savour unto the LORD. *Gen. 8:21; Lev. 1:13; Eph. 5:2*

The Burnt Offering of Flocks or Fowls

10 And if his offering *be* of the flocks, *namely*, of the sheep, or of the goats, for a burnt sacrifice; he shall bring it a male without blemish. 11 And he shall kill it on the side of the altar northward before the LORD: and the priests, Aaron's sons, shall sprinkle his blood round about upon the altar. *Lev. 1:5* 12 And he shall cut it into his pieces, with his head and his fat: and the priest shall lay them in order on the wood that *is* on the fire which *is* upon the altar: 13 But he shall wash the inwards and the legs with water: and the priest shall bring *it* all, and burn *it* upon the altar: it *is* a burnt sacrifice, an offering made by fire, of a sweet savour unto the LORD. 14 And if the burnt sacrifice for his offering to the LORD *be* of fowls, then he shall bring his offering of turtledoves, or of young pigeons. *Lev. 5:7; 12:8; Luke 2:24* 15 And the priest shall bring it unto the altar, and wring off his head, and burn *it* on the altar; and the blood thereof shall be wrung out at the side of the altar: 16 And he shall pluck away his crop with his feathers, and cast it beside the altar on the east part, by the place of the ashes: 17 And he shall cleave it with the wings thereof, *but* shall not divide *it* ᵀasunder: and the priest shall burn it upon the altar, upon the wood that *is* upon the fire: it *is* a burnt sacrifice, an offering made by fire, of a sweet savour unto the LORD. *Gen. 15:10 ◆ apart*

The Sacrificial System

Leviticus 1

Adam and Eve, at their creation, had a knowledge of the law of God; they were acquainted with its claims upon them; its precepts were written upon their hearts. When man fell by transgression the law was not changed, but a remedial system was established to bring him back to obedience. The promise of a Saviour was given, and sacrificial offerings pointing forward to the death of Christ as the great sin offering were established. But had the law of God never been transgressed, there would have been no death, and no need of a Saviour; consequently there would have been no need of sacrifices. . . .

The sacrificial system, committed to Adam, was also perverted by his descendants. Superstition, idolatry, cruelty, and licentiousness corrupted the simple and significant service that God had appointed. Through long intercourse [association] with idolaters the people of Israel had mingled many heathen customs with their worship; therefore the Lord gave them at Sinai definite instruction concerning the sacrificial service. *PP 363, 364*

The Meat (Meal) Offering of Flour with Oil and Incense

2 And when any will offer a meat offering unto the LORD, his offering shall be of fine flour; and he shall pour oil upon it, and put frankincense thereon: Lev. 6:14-18
2 And he shall bring it to Aaron's sons the priests: and he shall take thereout his handful of the flour thereof, and of the oil thereof, with all the frankincense thereof; and the priest shall burn the memorial of it upon the altar, *to be* an offering made by fire, of a sweet savour unto the LORD: Lev. 2:9; 5:12; 6:15
3 And the remnant of the meat offering *shall be* Aaron's and his sons': *it is* a thing most holy of the offerings of the LORD made by fire. Lev. 6:16-17; 10:12-13; 21:22

> **2:2, 3 Gifts and Offerings**
>
> As an acknowledgment that all things came from Him, the Lord directed that a portion of His bounty should be returned to Him in gifts and offerings to sustain His worship. *PP 525*

4 And if thou bring an oblation of a meat offering baken in the oven, *it shall be* unleavened cakes of fine flour mingled with oil, or unleavened wafers anointed with oil. Ex. 29:2
5 And if thy ᵀoblation *be* a meat offering *baken* in a pan, it shall be *of* fine flour unleavened, mingled with oil.   *offering*
6 Thou shalt part it in pieces, and pour oil thereon: *it is* a meat offering.
7 And if thy oblation *be* a meat offering *baken* in the fryingpan, it shall be made of fine flour with oil.
8 And thou shalt bring the meat offering that is made of these things unto the LORD: and when it is presented unto the priest, he shall bring it unto the altar.
9 And the priest shall take from the meat offering a memorial thereof, and shall burn *it* upon the altar: *it is* an offering made by fire, of a sweet savour unto the LORD. Lev. 2:2; 6:15
10 And that which is left of the meat offering *shall be* Aaron's and his sons': *it is* a thing most holy of the offerings of the LORD made by fire. Lev. 2:3
11 No meat offering, which ye shall bring unto the LORD, shall be made with leaven: for ye shall burn no leaven, nor any honey, in any offering of the LORD made by fire. Ex. 12:19-20
12 As for the oblation of the firstfruits, ye shall offer them unto the LORD: but they shall not be burnt on the altar for a sweet savour. Ex. 23:19
13 And every oblation of thy meat offering shalt thou season with salt; neither shalt thou suffer the salt of the covenant of thy God to be lacking from thy meat offering:

with all thine offerings thou shalt offer salt. Num. 18:19; 2 Chr. 13:5; Ezek. 43:24

> **2:13 Saving Salt of Righteousness**
>
> In the ritual service, salt was added to every sacrifice. This, like the offering of incense, signified that only the righteousness of Christ could make the service acceptable to God. Referring to this practice, Jesus said, "Every sacrifice shall be salted with salt." "Have salt in yourselves, and have peace one with another." All who would present themselves "a living sacrifice, holy, acceptable unto God" (Romans 12:1), must receive the saving salt, the righteousness of our Saviour. Then they become "the salt of the earth," restraining evil among men, as salt preserves from corruption. *DA 439*

14 And if thou offer a meat offering of thy firstfruits unto the LORD, thou shalt offer for the meat offering of thy firstfruits green ears of corn dried by the fire, *even* corn beaten out of full ears. Lev. 23:10
15 And thou shalt put oil upon it, and lay frankincense thereon: it *is* a meat offering.
16 And the priest shall burn the memorial of it, *part* of the beaten corn thereof, and *part* of the oil thereof, with all the frankincense thereof: it *is* an offering made by fire unto the LORD.

The Peace Offering of the Herd

3 And if his ᵀoblation *be* a sacrifice of peace offering, if he offer *it* of the herd; whether it *be* a male or female, he shall offer it without blemish before the LORD. Lev. 1:3 ◆ *offering*

> **3:1 Heavenly Peace**
>
> Christ is "the Prince of Peace" (Isaiah 9:6), and it is His mission to restore to earth and heaven the peace that sin has broken. "Being justified by faith, we have peace with God through our Lord Jesus Christ" (Romans 5:1). Whoever consents to renounce sin and open his heart to the love of Christ, becomes a partaker of this heavenly peace.
>
> There is no other ground of peace than this. *MB 27*

2 And he shall lay his hand upon the head of his offering, and kill it *at* the door of the tabernacle of the congregation: and Aaron's sons the priests shall sprinkle the blood upon the altar round about. Ex. 29:10
3 And he shall offer of the sacrifice of the peace offering an offering made by fire unto the LORD; the fat that covereth the inwards, and all the fat that *is* upon the inwards, Ex. 29:13
4 And the two kidneys, and the fat that *is* on them, which *is* by the flanks, and the caul

above the liver, with the kidneys, it shall he take away.   Lev. 3:10
5 And Aaron's sons shall burn it on the altar upon the burnt sacrifice, which *is* upon the wood that *is* on the fire: *it is* an offering made by fire, of a sweet savour unto the LORD.   Ex. 29:13; Lev. 6:12

The Peace Offering of the Flock
6 And if his offering for a sacrifice of peace offering unto the LORD *be* of the flock; male or female, he shall offer it without blemish.
7 If he offer a lamb for his offering, then shall he offer it before the LORD.   1 Kin. 8:62
8 And he shall lay his hand upon the head of his offering, and kill it before the tabernacle of the congregation: and Aaron's sons shall sprinkle the blood thereof round about upon the altar.   Lev. 1:5
9 And he shall offer of the sacrifice of the peace offering an offering made by fire unto the LORD; the fat thereof, *and* the whole rump, it shall he take off hard by the backbone; and the fat that covereth the inwards, and all the fat that *is* upon the inwards,   Ex. 29:22
10 And the two kidneys, and the fat that *is* upon them, which *is* by the flanks, and the ᵀcaul above the liver, with the kidneys, it shall he take away.   *membrane*
11 And the priest shall burn it upon the altar: *it is* the food of the offering made by fire unto the LORD.   Lev. 3:5; 21:6, 17
12 And if his offering *be* a goat, then he shall offer it before the LORD.
13 And he shall lay his hand upon the head of it, and kill it before the tabernacle of the congregation: and the sons of Aaron shall sprinkle the blood thereof upon the altar round about.   Lev. 3:8
14 And he shall offer thereof his offering, *even* an offering made by fire unto the LORD; the fat that covereth the inwards, and all the fat that *is* upon the inwards,
15 And the two kidneys, and the fat that *is* upon them, which *is* by the flanks, and the caul above the liver, with the kidneys, it shall he take away.
16 And the priest shall burn them upon the altar: *it is* the food of the offering made by fire for a sweet savour: all the fat *is* the LORD's.   Lev. 7:23-25
17 *It shall be* a perpetual statute for your generations throughout all your dwellings, that ye eat neither fat nor blood.   Gen. 9:4

3:17 Life in the Blood

God had given these injunctions to the Jews for the purpose of preserving their health. The Jews regarded it as sinful to use blood as an article of diet. They held that the blood was the life, and that the shedding of blood was in consequence of sin. *AA 191*

The Sin Offering of Ignorance
4 And the LORD spake unto Moses, saying,
2 Speak unto the children of Israel, saying, If a soul shall sin through ignorance against any of the commandments of the LORD *concerning things* which ought not to be done, and shall do against any of them: Lev. 4:27
3 If the priest that is anointed do sin according to the sin of the people; then let him bring for his sin, which he hath sinned, a young bullock without blemish unto the LORD for a sin offering.   Lev. 4:14
4 And he shall bring the bullock unto the door of the tabernacle of the congregation before the LORD; and shall lay his hand upon the bullock's head, and kill the bullock before the LORD.   Lev. 1:3-4
5 And the priest that is anointed shall take of the bullock's blood, and bring it to the tabernacle of the congregation: Lev. 16:14
6 And the priest shall dip his finger in the blood, and sprinkle of the blood seven times before the LORD, before the ᵀvail of the sanctuary.   *veil*
7 And the priest shall put *some* of the blood upon the horns of the altar of sweet incense before the LORD, which *is* in the tabernacle of the congregation; and shall pour all the blood of the bullock at the bottom of the altar of the burnt offering, which *is at* the door of the tabernacle of the congregation.   Lev. 8:15; 9:9; 16:18
8 And he shall take off from it all the fat of the bullock for the sin offering; the fat that covereth the inwards, and all the fat that *is* upon the inwards,   Lev. 3:3-5
9 And the two kidneys, and the fat that *is* upon them, which *is* by the flanks, and the ᵀcaul above the liver, with the kidneys, it shall he take away,   Lev. 3:4 ◆ *membrane*
10 As it was taken off from the ᵀbullock of the sacrifice of peace offerings: and the priest shall burn them upon the altar of the burnt offering.   *bull*
11 And the skin of the bullock, and all his flesh, with his head, and with his legs, and his inwards, and his dung,   Ex. 29:14; Num. 19:5
12 Even the whole bullock shall he carry forth without the camp unto a clean place, where the ashes are poured out, and burn him on the wood with fire: where the ashes are poured out shall he be burnt.   Heb. 13:11

The Sin Offering for the Congregation
13 And if the whole congregation of Israel sin through ignorance, and the thing be hid from the eyes of the assembly, and they have done *somewhat against* any of the commandments of the LORD *concerning things* which should not be done, and are guilty;   Lev. 5:2-5, 17
14 When the sin, which they have sinned

against it, is known, then the congregation shall offer a young bullock for the sin, and bring him before the tabernacle of the congregation.   Lev. 4:3

15 And the elders of the congregation shall lay their hands upon the head of the bullock before the LORD: and the bullock shall be killed before the LORD.   Lev. 1:4

16 And the priest that is anointed shall bring of the bullock's blood to the tabernacle of the congregation: Lev. 4:5-12

17 And the priest shall dip his finger *in some* of the blood, and sprinkle *it* seven times before the LORD, *even* before the vail.

18 And he shall put *some* of the blood upon the horns of the altar which *is* before the LORD, that *is* in the tabernacle of the congregation, and shall pour out all the blood at the bottom of the altar of the burnt offering, which *is at* the door of the tabernacle of the congregation.

19 And he shall take all his fat from him, and burn *it* upon the altar.

20 And he shall do with the bullock as he did with the bullock for a sin offering, so shall he do with this: and the priest shall make an atonement for them, and it shall be forgiven them.   Num. 15:25; Heb. 10:10-12

21 And he shall carry forth the bullock without the camp, and burn him as he burned the first bullock: it *is* a sin offering for the congregation.   Lev. 16:15

The Sin Offering for the Ruler

22 When a ruler hath sinned, and done *somewhat* through ignorance *against* any of the commandments of the LORD his God *concerning things* which should not be done, and is guilty;   Lev. 4:2, 13

23 Or if his sin, wherein he hath sinned, come to his knowledge; he shall bring his offering, a kid of the goats, a male without blemish: Lev. 4:14

24 And he shall lay his hand upon the head of the goat, and kill it in the place where they kill the burnt offering before the LORD: it *is* a sin offering.

25 And the priest shall take of the blood of the sin offering with his finger, and put *it* upon the horns of the altar of burnt offering, and shall pour out his blood at the bottom of the altar of burnt offering.   Lev. 4:7, 18, 30

26 And he shall burn all his fat upon the altar, as the fat of the sacrifice of peace offerings: and the priest shall make an atonement for him as concerning his sin, and it shall be forgiven him.   Lev. 4:20

The Sin Offering for Other Individuals

27 And if any one of the common people sin through ignorance, while he doeth *somewhat against* any of the commandments of the LORD *concerning things* which ought not to be done, and be guilty; Lev. 4:2, 13; Num. 15:27

28 Or if his sin, which he hath sinned, come to his knowledge: then he shall bring his offering, a kid of the goats, a female without blemish, for his sin which he hath sinned.   Lev. 4:3, 23, 32

29 And he shall lay his hand upon the head of the sin offering, and slay the sin offering in the place of the burnt offering.   Lev. 1:4; 4:4, 24

4:29 Symbolic Transfer of Sins

The most important part of the daily ministration was the service performed in behalf of individuals. The repentant sinner brought his offering to the door of the tabernacle, and, placing his hand upon the victim's head, confessed his sins, thus in figure transferring them from himself to the innocent sacrifice. *PP 354*

30 And the priest shall take of the blood thereof with his finger, and put *it* upon the horns of the altar of burnt offering, and shall pour out all the blood thereof at the bottom of the altar.   Lev. 4:7

31 And he shall take away all the fat thereof, as the fat is taken away from off the sacrifice of peace offerings; and the priest shall burn *it* upon the altar for a sweet savour unto the LORD; and the priest shall make an

Reconciled by Love

Leviticus 4

Upon Mount Moriah, Abraham had heard the question of his son, "My father, . . . where is the lamb for a burnt offering?" The father answered, "My son, God will provide Himself a lamb for a burnt offering" (Genesis 22:7, 8). And in the ram divinely provided in the place of Isaac, Abraham saw a symbol of Him who was to die for the sins of men. The Holy Spirit through Isaiah, taking up the illustration, prophesied of the Saviour, "He is brought as a lamb to the slaughter," "and the Lord hath laid on Him the iniquity of us all" (Isaiah 53:7, 6); but the people of Israel had not understood the lesson. Many of them regarded the sacrificial offerings much as the heathen looked upon their sacrifices—as gifts by which they themselves might propitiate the Deity. God desired to teach them that from His own love comes the gift which reconciles them to Himself. *DA 112, 113*

atonement for him, and it shall be forgiven him.   Lev. 1:9; 4:26, 35

32 And if he bring a lamb for a sin offering, he shall bring it a female without blemish.

33 And he shall lay his hand upon the head of the sin offering, and slay it for a sin offering in the place where they kill the burnt offering.

34 And the priest shall take of the blood of the sin offering with his finger, and put *it* upon the horns of the altar of burnt offering, and shall pour out all the blood thereof at the bottom of the altar: Lev. 4:7

35 And he shall take away all the fat thereof, as the fat of the lamb is taken away from the sacrifice of the peace offerings; and the priest shall burn them upon the altar, according to the offerings made by fire unto the LORD: and the priest shall make an atonement for his sin that he hath committed, and it shall be forgiven him.   Lev. 4:20, 26

The Sin of Concealing Knowledge of Guilt or of Unintended Transgression

5 And if a soul sin, and hear the voice of swearing, and *is* a witness, whether he hath seen or known *of it*; if he do not utter *it*, then he shall bear his iniquity.   Lev. 5:17; 7:18

2 Or if a soul touch any unclean thing, whether *it be* a carcase of an unclean beast, or a carcase of unclean cattle, or the carcase of unclean creeping things, and *if* it be hidden from him; he also shall be unclean, and guilty.   Lev. 5:17

3 Or if he touch the uncleanness of man, whatsoever uncleanness *it be* that a man shall be defiled ᵀwithal, and it be hid from him; when he knoweth *of it*, then he shall be guilty.   Lev. 12 ♦ with

4 Or if a soul swear, pronouncing with *his* lips to do evil, or to do good, whatsoever *it be* that a man shall pronounce with an oath, and it be hid from him; when he knoweth *of it*, then he shall be guilty in one of these.   Judg. 11:31

5 And it shall be, when he shall be guilty in one of these *things*, that he shall confess that he hath sinned in that *thing*: Lev. 16:21; Num. 5:7

6 And he shall bring his trespass offering unto the LORD for his sin which he hath sinned, a female from the flock, a lamb or a kid of the goats, for a sin offering; and the priest shall make an atonement for him concerning his sin.   Lev. 4:28, 32

The Sin Offering of Fowls

7 And if he be not able to bring a lamb, then he shall bring for his trespass, which he hath committed, two turtledoves, or two young pigeons, unto the LORD; one for a sin offering, and the other for a burnt offering.   Lev. 12:8; 14:21-22, 31

8 And he shall bring them unto the priest, who shall offer *that* which *is* for the sin offering first, and wring off his head from his neck, but shall not divide *it* ᵀasunder: Lev. 1:15 ♦ apart

9 And he shall sprinkle of the blood of the sin offering upon the side of the altar; and the rest of the blood shall be wrung out at the bottom of the altar: it *is* a sin offering.   Lev. 4:18

10 And he shall offer the second *for* a burnt offering, according to the manner: and the priest shall make an atonement for him for his sin which he hath sinned, and it shall be forgiven him.   Lev. 1:14-17; 4:20, 26

11 But if he be not able to bring two turtledoves, or two young pigeons, then he that sinned shall bring for his offering the tenth part of an ephah of fine flour for a sin offering; he shall put no oil upon it, neither shall he put *any* frankincense thereon: for it *is* a sin offering.   Num. 5:15

12 Then shall he bring it to the priest, and the priest shall take his handful of it, *even* a memorial thereof, and burn *it* on the altar, according to the offerings made by fire unto the LORD: it *is* a sin offering.   Lev. 2:9

13 And the priest shall make an atonement for him as touching his sin that he hath sinned in one of these, and it shall be forgiven him: and *the remnant* shall be the priest's, as a meat offering.   Lev. 2:3

The Trespass Offering

14 And the LORD spake unto Moses, saying,

15 If a soul commit a trespass, and sin through ignorance, in the holy things of the LORD; then he shall bring for his trespass unto the LORD a ram without blemish out of the flocks, with thy estimation by shekels of silver, after the shekel of the sanctuary, for a trespass offering: Ex. 30:13; Lev. 4:2; 6:6

16 And he shall make amends for the harm that he hath done in the holy thing, and shall add the fifth part thereto, and give it unto the priest: and the priest shall make an atonement for him with the ram of the trespass offering, and it shall be forgiven him.   Lev. 5:10; 22:14; Num. 5:7

17 And if a soul sin, and commit any of these things which are forbidden to be done by the commandments of the LORD; though he ᵀwist *it* not, yet is he guilty, and shall bear his iniquity.   Lev. 4:13 ♦ knew

---

5:17, 18 We're Not Forsaken

If in our ignorance we make missteps, the Saviour does not forsake us. We need never feel that we are alone. . . . There is not a sorrow, not a grievance, not a human weakness, for which He has not provided a remedy. *MH 249*

18 And he shall bring a ram without blemish out of the flock, with thy estimation, for a ᵀtrespass offering, unto the priest: and the priest shall make an atonement for him concerning his ignorance wherein he erred and wist *it* not, and it shall be forgiven him.   Lev. 5:15-16 ◆ *sin*
19 It *is* a trespass offering: he hath certainly ᵀtrespassed against the LORD.   *sinned*

The Trespass Offering for Sins Done Knowingly

6 And the LORD spake unto Moses, saying,
2 If a soul sin, and commit a trespass against the LORD, and lie unto his neighbour in that which was delivered him to keep, or in fellowship, or in a thing taken away by violence, or hath deceived his neighbour;   Ex. 22:7-10
3 Or have found that which was lost, and lieth concerning it, and sweareth falsely; in any of all these that a man doeth, sinning therein: Ex. 23:4
4 Then it shall be, because he hath sinned, and is guilty, that he shall restore that which he took violently away, or the thing which he hath deceitfully gotten, or that which was delivered him to keep, or the lost thing which he found,
5 Or all that about which he hath sworn falsely; he shall even restore it in the principal, and shall add the fifth part more thereto, *and* give it unto him to whom it ᵀappertaineth, in the day of his trespass offering.   Lev. 5:16 ◆ *belongs*
6 And he shall bring his trespass offering unto the LORD, a ram without blemish out of the flock, with thy estimation, for a trespass offering, unto the priest: Lev. 5:15, 18
7 And the priest shall make an atonement for him before the LORD: and it shall be forgiven him for any thing of all that he hath done in ᵀtrespassing therein. Lev. 4:26 ◆ *sinning*

> **6:5-7 Repentance and Reformation**
>
> There is no evidence of genuine repentance unless it works reformation. If he restore the pledge, give again that he had robbed, confess his sins, and love God and his fellow men, the sinner may be sure that he has found peace with God. *GC 462, 463*

The Law of the Burnt Offering

8 And the LORD spake unto Moses, saying,
9 Command Aaron and his sons, saying, This *is* the law of the burnt offering: It *is* the burnt offering, because of the burning upon the altar all night unto the morning, and the fire of the altar shall be burning in it.   Num. 28:3
10 And the priest shall put on his linen garment, and his linen ᵀbreeches shall he put upon his flesh, and take up the ashes which the fire hath consumed with the burnt offering on the altar, and he shall put them beside the altar.   Ex. 28:39-43 ◆ *trousers*
11 And he shall put off his garments, and put on other garments, and carry forth the ashes without the camp unto a clean place.
12 And the fire upon the altar shall be burning in it; it shall not be put out: and the priest shall burn wood on it every morning, and lay the burnt offering in order upon it; and he shall burn thereon the fat of the peace offerings.
13 The fire shall ever be burning upon the altar; it shall never go out.

The Law of the Meat (Meal) Offering

14 And this *is* the law of the meat offering: the sons of Aaron shall offer it before the LORD, before the altar.   Num. 15:4
15 And he shall take of it his handful, of the flour of the meat offering, and of the oil thereof, and all the frankincense which *is* upon the meat offering, and shall burn *it* upon the altar *for* a sweet savour, *even* the memorial of it, unto the LORD.   Lev. 2:2, 9
16 And the remainder thereof shall Aaron and his sons eat: with unleavened bread shall it be eaten in the holy place; in the court of the tabernacle of the congregation they shall eat it.   Lev. 2:3; 10:12-13; Ezek. 44:29
17 It shall not be baken with leaven. I have given it *unto them for* their portion of my offerings made by fire; it *is* most holy, as *is* the sin offering, and as the ᵀtrespass offering.   Lev. 2:11 ◆ *sin*
18 All the males among the children of Aaron shall eat of it. *It shall be* a statute for ever in your generations concerning the offerings of the LORD made by fire: every one that toucheth them shall be holy.   Lev. 6:29
19 And the LORD spake unto Moses, saying,
20 This *is* the offering of Aaron and of his sons, which they shall offer unto the LORD in the day when he is anointed; the tenth part of an ephah of fine flour for a meat offering perpetual, half of it in the morning, and half thereof at night.   Ex. 16:36
21 In a pan it shall be made with oil; *and when it is* baken, thou shalt bring it in: *and* the baken pieces of the meat offering shalt thou offer *for* a sweet savour unto the LORD.   Lev. 2:5; 7:9
22 And the priest of his sons that is anointed in his stead shall offer it: *it is* a statute for ever unto the LORD; it shall be wholly burnt.
23 For every meat offering for the priest shall be wholly burnt: it shall not be eaten.

The Law of the Sin Offering

24 And the LORD spake unto Moses, saying,
25 Speak unto Aaron and to his sons, saying, This is the law of the sin offering: In the place where the burnt offering is killed shall the sin offering be killed before the LORD: it is most holy.   Lev. 1:3, 11; 4:24
26 The priest that offereth it for sin shall eat it: in the holy place shall it be eaten, in the court of the tabernacle of the congregation.
27 Whatsoever shall touch the flesh thereof shall be holy: and when there is sprinkled of the blood thereof upon any garment, thou shalt wash that whereon it was sprinkled in the holy place.   Ex. 29:37
28 But the earthen vessel wherein it is sodden shall be broken: and if it be sodden in a brasen pot, it shall be both scoured, and rinsed in water.   Lev. 11:33; 15:12
29 All the males among the priests shall eat thereof: it is most holy.
30 And no sin offering, whereof any of the blood is brought into the tabernacle of the congregation to reconcile ᵀwithal in the holy place, shall be eaten: it shall be burnt in the fire.   Lev. 4:3-21 ◆ with

---

6:29, 30 Symbolic Ceremonies

In some cases the blood was not taken into the holy place; but the flesh was then to be eaten by the priest, as Moses directed the sons of Aaron, saying: "God hath given it you to bear the iniquity of the congregation" (Leviticus 10:17). Both ceremonies alike symbolized the transfer of the sin from the penitent to the sanctuary. *GC 418*

The Laws of the Trespass Offering and of the Peace Offering

7 Likewise this is the law of the trespass offering: it is most holy.   Lev. 5:1-6
2 In the place where they kill the burnt offering shall they kill the trespass offering: and the blood thereof shall he sprinkle round about upon the altar.   Lev. 1:5
3 And he shall offer of it all the fat thereof; the rump, and the fat that covereth the inwards,   Ex. 29:13
4 And the two kidneys, and the fat that is on them, which is by the flanks, and the ᵀcaul that is above the liver, with the kidneys, it shall he take away: membrane
5 And the priest shall burn them upon the altar for an offering made by fire unto the LORD: it is a ᵀtrespass offering.   sin
6 Every male among the priests shall eat thereof: it shall be eaten in the holy place: it is most holy.   Lev. 6:29
7 As the sin offering is, so is the trespass offering: there is one law for them: the priest

that maketh atonement therewith shall have it.   Lev. 6:25-26
8 And the priest that offereth any man's burnt offering, even the priest shall have to himself the skin of the burnt offering which he hath offered.
9 And all the meat offering that is baken in the oven, and all that is dressed in the fryingpan, and in the pan, shall be the priest's that offereth it.   Lev. 2:10
10 And every meat offering, mingled with oil, and dry, shall all the sons of Aaron have, one as much as another.
11 And this is the law of the sacrifice of peace offerings, which he shall offer unto the LORD.
12 If he offer it for a thanksgiving, then he shall offer with the sacrifice of thanksgiving unleavened cakes mingled with oil, and unleavened wafers anointed with oil, and cakes mingled with oil, of fine flour, fried. Num. 6:15
13 Besides the cakes, he shall offer for his offering leavened bread with the sacrifice of thanksgiving of his peace offerings. Amos 4:5
14 And of it he shall offer one out of the whole oblation for an heave offering unto the LORD, and it shall be the priest's that sprinkleth the blood of the peace offerings.
15 And the flesh of the sacrifice of his peace offerings for thanksgiving shall be eaten the same day that it is offered; he shall not leave any of it until the morning.
16 But if the sacrifice of his offering be a vow, or a voluntary offering, it shall be eaten the same day that he offereth his sacrifice: and on the morrow also the remainder of it shall be eaten: Lev. 19:5-8

7:15, 16 Directed to the Sacrifice

The peace offerings were especially an expression of thanksgiving to God. In these offerings the fat alone was to be burned upon the altar; a certain specified portion was reserved for the priests, but the greater part was returned to the offerer, to be eaten by him and his friends in a sacrificial feast. Thus all hearts were to be directed, in gratitude and faith, to the great Sacrifice that was to take away the sin of the world. *PP 576*

---

17 But the remainder of the flesh of the sacrifice on the third day shall be burnt with fire.   Ex. 12:10
18 And if any of the flesh of the sacrifice of his peace offerings be eaten at all on the third day, it shall not be accepted, neither shall it be imputed unto him that offereth it: it shall be an abomination, and the soul that eateth of it shall bear his iniquity. Lev. 11:41; 19:7-8; 22:25
19 And the flesh that toucheth any unclean thing shall not be eaten; it shall be burnt

with fire: and as for the flesh, all that be clean shall eat thereof.

20 But the soul that eateth *of* the flesh of the sacrifice of peace offerings, that *pertain* unto the Lord, having his uncleanness upon him, even that soul shall be cut off from his people.

21 Moreover the soul that shall touch any unclean *thing, as* the uncleanness of man, or *any* unclean beast, or any abominable unclean *thing,* and eat of the flesh of the sacrifice of peace offerings, which *pertain* unto the Lord, even that soul shall be cut off from his people.   Lev. 5:2-3

22 And the Lord spake unto Moses, saying, 23 Speak unto the children of Israel, saying, Ye shall eat no manner of fat, of ox, or of sheep, or of goat.   Lev. 3:16-17

7:23–27 About Meats for Food

Of the meats permitted, the eating of the fat and the blood was strictly forbidden.

Only such animals could be used for food as were in good condition. No creature that was torn, that had died of itself, or from which the blood had not been carefully drained, could be used as food. *MH 312*

24 And the fat of the beast that dieth of itself, and the fat of that which is torn with beasts, may be used in any other use: but ye shall in no wise eat of it. Ex. 22:31; Lev. 17:15; 22:8

25 For whosoever eateth the fat of the beast, of which men offer an offering made by fire unto the Lord, even the soul that eateth *it* shall be cut off from his people.

26 Moreover ye shall eat no manner of blood, *whether it be* of fowl or of beast, in any of your dwellings.   Gen. 9:4

27 Whatsoever soul *it be* that eateth any manner of blood, even that soul shall be cut off from his people.

28 And the Lord spake unto Moses, saying, 29 Speak unto the children of Israel, saying, He that offereth the sacrifice of his peace offerings unto the Lord shall bring his ˥oblation unto the Lord of the sacrifice of his peace offerings.   *offering*

30 His own hands shall bring the offerings of the Lord made by fire, the fat with the breast, it shall he bring, that the breast may be waved *for* a wave offering before the Lord.   Num. 6:20

31 And the priest shall burn the fat upon the altar: but the breast shall be Aaron's and his sons'.   Lev. 3:5

32 And the right shoulder shall ye give unto the priest *for* an heave offering of the sacrifices of your peace offerings.   Lev. 7:34

33 He among the sons of Aaron, that offereth the blood of the peace offerings, and the fat, shall have the right shoulder for *his* part.

34 For the wave breast and the heave shoulder have I taken of the children of Israel from off the sacrifices of their peace offerings, and have given them unto Aaron the priest and unto his sons by a statute for ever from among the children of Israel.   Num. 18:18-19

35 This *is the portion* of the anointing of Aaron, and of the anointing of his sons, out of the offerings of the Lord made by fire, in the day *when* he presented them to minister unto the Lord in the priest's office;

36 Which the Lord commanded to be given them of the children of Israel, in the day that he anointed them, *by* a statute for ever throughout their generations.   Lev. 8:12, 30

37 This *is* the law of the burnt offering, of the meat offering, and of the sin offering, and of the trespass offering, and of the

Perversion of the Sacrifices

Leviticus 7

The sacrifices and offerings of the Mosaic ritual were ever pointing toward a better service, even a heavenly. The earthly sanctuary was "a figure for the time then present," in which were offered both gifts and sacrifices; its two holy places were "patterns of things in the heavens;" for Christ, our great High Priest, is today "a minister of the sanctuary, and of the true tabernacle, which the Lord pitched, and not man" (Hebrews 9:9, 23; 8:2).

From the day the Lord declared to the serpent in Eden, "I will put enmity between thee and the woman, and between thy seed and her seed" (Genesis 3:15), Satan has known that he can never hold absolute sway over the inhabitants of this world. When Adam and his sons began to offer the ceremonial sacrifices ordained by God as a type of the coming Redeemer, Satan discerned in these a symbol of communion between earth and heaven. During the long centuries that have followed, it has been his constant effort to intercept this communion. Untiringly has he sought to misrepresent God and to misinterpret the rites pointing to the Saviour, and with a great majority of the members of the human family he has been successful.

While God has desired to teach men that from His own love comes the Gift which reconciles them to Himself, the archenemy of mankind has endeavored to represent God as one who delights in their destruction. Thus the sacrifices and the ordinances designed of Heaven to reveal divine love have been perverted to serve as means whereby sinners have vainly hoped to propitiate, with gifts and good works, the wrath of an offended God. *PK 685, 686*

^Tconsecrations, and of the sacrifice of the peace offerings;   Ex. 29:1 ◆ *acts of setting apart*
38 Which the LORD commanded Moses in mount Sinai, in the day that he commanded the children of Israel to offer their oblations unto the LORD, in the wilderness of Sinai.   Lev. 1:1-2

Moses Consecrates Aaron and His Sons

8 And the LORD spake unto Moses, saying,
2 Take Aaron and his sons with him, and the garments, and the anointing oil, and a ^Tbullock for the sin offering, and two rams, and a basket of unleavened bread;   Ex. 28:2-4 ◆ *bull*
3 And gather thou all the congregation together unto the door of the tabernacle of the congregation.
4 And Moses did as the LORD commanded him; and the assembly was gathered together unto the door of the tabernacle of the congregation.
5 And Moses said unto the congregation, This *is* the thing which the LORD commanded to be done.
6 And Moses brought Aaron and his sons, and washed them with water.   Ex. 29:4
7 And he put upon him the coat, and girded him with the ^Tgirdle, and clothed him with the robe, and put the ^Tephod upon him, and he girded him with the ^Tcurious girdle of the ephod, and bound *it* unto him therewith.   *belt* ◆ *priestly garment* ◆ *intricately detailed*
8 And he put the breastplate upon him: also he put in the breastplate the Urim and the Thummim.   Ezra 2:63
9 And he put the ^Tmitre upon his head; also upon the mitre, *even* upon his forefront, did he put the golden plate, the holy crown; as the LORD commanded Moses.   *turban*

8:9 The Holiness of God

The miter of the high priest consisted of the white linen turban, having attached to it by a lace of blue, a gold plate bearing the inscription, "Holiness to Jehovah." Everything connected with the apparel and deportment of the priests was to be such as to impress the beholder with a sense of the holiness of God, the sacredness of His worship, and the purity required of those who came into His presence. *PP 351*

10 And Moses took the anointing oil, and anointed the tabernacle and all that *was* therein, and ^Tsanctified them.   *made them holy*
11 And he sprinkled thereof upon the altar seven times, and anointed the altar and all his vessels, both the ^Tlaver and his foot, to ^Tsanctify them.   *basin for washing* ◆ *make them holy*
12 And he poured of the anointing oil upon

Aaron's head, and anointed him, to sanctify him.   Ex. 29:7; 30:30; Ps. 133:2

8:12 Our Great High Priest

The blood drops of agony that from [Christ's] wounded temples flowed down His face and beard were the pledge of His anointing with "the oil of gladness" (Hebrews 1:9) as our great high priest. *DA 734*

13 And Moses brought Aaron's sons, and put coats upon them, and girded them with girdles, and put bonnets upon them; as the LORD commanded Moses.   Ex. 29:8-9

A Sin Offering for Aaron and His Sons

14 And he brought the bullock for the sin offering: and Aaron and his sons laid their hands upon the head of the bullock for the sin offering.   Ezek. 43:19
15 And he slew *it*; and Moses took the blood, and put *it* upon the horns of the altar round about with his finger, and purified the altar, and poured the blood at the bottom of the altar, and sanctified it, to make reconciliation upon it.   Lev. 4:7
16 And he took all the fat that *was* upon the inwards, and the caul *above* the liver, and the two kidneys, and their fat, and Moses burned *it* upon the altar.   Ex. 29:13
17 But the bullock, and his hide, his flesh, and his dung, he burnt with fire without the camp; as the LORD commanded Moses.
18 And he brought the ram for the burnt offering: and Aaron and his sons laid their hands upon the head of the ram.   Lev. 8:2
19 And he killed *it*; and Moses sprinkled the blood upon the altar round about.
20 And he cut the ram into pieces; and Moses burnt the head, and the pieces, and the fat.
21 And he washed the inwards and the legs in water; and Moses burnt the whole ram upon the altar: it *was* a burnt sacrifice for a sweet savour, *and* an offering made by fire unto the LORD; as the LORD commanded Moses.   Ex. 29:18
22 And he brought the other ram, the ram of consecration: and Aaron and his sons laid their hands upon the head of the ram.   Lev. 8:2
23 And he slew *it*; and Moses took of the blood of it, and put *it* upon the tip of Aaron's right ear, and upon the thumb of his right hand, and upon the great toe of his right foot.   Ex. 29:20
24 And he brought Aaron's sons, and Moses put of the blood upon the tip of their right ear, and upon the thumbs of their right hands, and upon the great toes of their right feet: and Moses sprinkled the blood upon the altar round about.

25 And he took the fat, and the rump, and all the fat that *was* upon the inwards, and the ᵀcaul *above* the liver, and the two kidneys, and their fat, and the right shoulder: *membrane*
26 And out of the basket of unleavened bread, that *was* before the Lᴏʀᴅ, he took one unleavened cake, and a cake of oiled bread, and one wafer, and put *them* on the fat, and upon the right shoulder: Ex. 29:23
27 And he put all upon Aaron's hands, and upon his sons' hands, and waved them *for a* wave offering before the Lᴏʀᴅ.
28 And Moses took them from off their hands, and burnt *them* on the altar upon the burnt offering: they were ᵀconsecrations for a sweet savour: it *is* an offering made by fire unto the Lᴏʀᴅ. Ex. 29:25 ◆ *setting apart*
29 And Moses took the breast, and waved it *for* a wave offering before the Lᴏʀᴅ: *for* of the ram of ᵀconsecration it was Moses' part; as the Lᴏʀᴅ commanded Moses. *act of setting apart*
30 And Moses took of the anointing oil, and of the blood which *was* upon the altar, and sprinkled *it* upon Aaron, *and* upon his garments, and upon his sons, and upon his sons' garments with him; and sanctified Aaron, *and* his garments, and his sons, and his sons' garments with him. Num. 3:3

The Place and Time of the Priests' Consecration

31 And Moses said unto Aaron and to his sons, Boil the flesh *at* the door of the tabernacle of the congregation: and there eat it with the bread that *is* in the basket of consecrations, as I commanded, saying, Aaron and his sons shall eat it. Ex. 29:31-32
32 And that which remaineth of the flesh and of the bread shall ye burn with fire. Ex. 29:34
33 And ye shall not go out of the door of the tabernacle of the congregation *in* seven days, until the days of your consecration be at an end: for seven days shall he ᵀconsecrate you. Ex. 29:35 ◆ *set you apart*
34 As he hath done this day, *so* the Lᴏʀᴅ hath commanded to do, to make an atonement for you. Heb. 7:16
35 Therefore shall ye abide *at* the door of the tabernacle of the congregation day and night seven days, and keep the charge of the Lᴏʀᴅ, that ye die not: for so I am commanded. Num. 3:7; 9:19; Deut. 11:1
36 So Aaron and his sons did all things which the Lᴏʀᴅ commanded by the hand of Moses.

Aaron's First Offerings

9 And it came to pass on the eighth day, *that* Moses called Aaron and his sons, and the elders of Israel;

2 And he said unto Aaron, Take thee a young calf for a sin offering, and a ram for a burnt offering, without blemish, and offer *them* before the Lᴏʀᴅ. Lev. 4:3
3 And unto the children of Israel thou shalt speak, saying, Take ye a kid of the goats for a sin offering; and a calf and a lamb, *both* of the first year, without blemish, for a burnt offering; Lev. 4:23
4 Also a bullock and a ram for peace offerings, to sacrifice before the Lᴏʀᴅ; and a meat offering mingled with oil: for to day the Lᴏʀᴅ will appear unto you. Ex. 29:43; Lev. 9:6, 23
5 And they brought *that* which Moses commanded before the tabernacle of the congregation: and all the congregation drew near and stood before the Lᴏʀᴅ.
6 And Moses said, This *is* the thing which the Lᴏʀᴅ commanded that ye should do: and the glory of the Lᴏʀᴅ shall appear unto you. Ex. 24:16
7 And Moses said unto Aaron, Go unto the altar, and offer thy sin offering, and thy burnt offering, and make an atonement for thyself, and for the people: and offer the offering of the people, and make an atonement for them; as the Lᴏʀᴅ commanded. Heb. 5:1, 3

Aaron's Sin Offering and Burnt Offering for Himself

8 Aaron therefore went unto the altar, and slew the calf of the sin offering, which *was* for himself.
9 And the sons of Aaron brought the blood unto him: and he dipped his finger in the blood, and put *it* upon the horns of the altar, and poured out the blood at the bottom of the altar: Lev. 4:6-7
10 But the fat, and the kidneys, and the ᵀcaul above the liver of the sin offering, he burnt upon the altar; as the Lᴏʀᴅ commanded Moses. *membrane*
11 And the flesh and the hide he burnt with fire without the camp. Lev. 4:11-12; 8:17
12 And he slew the burnt offering; and Aaron's sons presented unto him the blood, which he sprinkled round about upon the altar.
13 And they presented the burnt offering unto him, with the pieces thereof, and the head: and he burnt *them* upon the altar.

14 And he did wash the inwards and the legs, and burnt *them* upon the burnt offering on the altar.   Lev. 8:21

15 And he brought the people's offering, and took the goat, which *was* the sin offering for the people, and slew it, and offered it for sin, as the first.   Lev. 4:27-31

16 And he brought the burnt offering, and offered it according to the manner.

17 And he brought the meat offering, and took an handful thereof, and burnt *it* upon the altar, beside the burnt sacrifice of the morning.   Lev. 2:1-2

18 He slew also the ᵀbullock and the ram *for* a sacrifice of peace offerings, which *was* for the people: and Aaron's sons presented unto him the blood, which he sprinkled upon the altar round about,   *bull*

19 And the fat of the bullock and of the ram, the rump, and that which covereth *the inwards*, and the kidneys, and the caul *above* the liver:

20 And they put the fat upon the breasts, and he burnt the fat upon the altar:

21 And the breasts and the right shoulder Aaron waved *for* a wave offering before the LORD; as Moses commanded.   Lev. 7:30-34

22 And Aaron lifted up his hand toward the people, and blessed them, and came down from offering of the sin offering, and the burnt offering, and peace offerings. Deut. 21:5; Luke 24:50

9:23, 24 Sacrifice on the Altar

All had been done as God commanded, and He accepted the sacrifice, and revealed His glory in a remarkable manner; fire came from the Lord and consumed the offering upon the altar. The people looked upon this wonderful manifestation of divine power with awe and intense interest. They saw in it a token of God's glory and favor, and they raised a universal shout of praise and adoration and fell on their faces as if in the immediate presence of Jehovah. *PP 359*

---

23 And Moses and Aaron went into the tabernacle of the congregation, and came out, and blessed the people: and the glory of the LORD appeared unto all the people. Lev. 9:6; Num. 16:19

24 And there came a fire out from before the LORD, and consumed upon the altar the burnt offering and the fat: *which* when all the people saw, they shouted, and fell on their faces.   Judg. 6:21

Nadab and Abihu Are Killed

10 And Nadab and Abihu, the sons of Aaron, took either of them his censer, and put fire therein, and put incense thereon, and offered strange fire before the LORD, which he commanded them not.   Ex. 24:1

10:1 Strange Fire

At the hour of worship, as the prayers and praise of the people were ascending to God, two of the sons of Aaron took each his censer and burned fragrant incense thereon, to rise as a sweet odor before the Lord. But they transgressed His command by the use of "strange [profane] fire." For burning the incense they took common instead of the sacred fire which God Himself had kindled, and which He had commanded to be used for this purpose. *PP 359*

---

2 And there went out fire from the LORD, and devoured them, and they died before the LORD.   Lev. 9:24; Num. 16:35; 26:61

3 Then Moses said unto Aaron, This *is it* that the LORD spake, saying, I will be ᵀsanctified in them that come nigh me, and before all the people I will be glorified. And Aaron held his peace.   Ex. 19:22; Lev. 21:6; Ezek. 28:22 ◆ *made holy*

4 And Moses called Mishael and Elzaphan, the sons of Uzziel the uncle of Aaron, and said unto them, Come near, carry your brethren from before the sanctuary out of the camp.   Ex. 6:18, 22; Num. 3:19

5 So they went near, and carried them in

No License to Sin

Leviticus 10

Next to Moses and Aaron, Nadab and Abihu had stood highest in Israel. They had been especially honored by the Lord, having been permitted with the seventy elders to behold His glory in the mount. But their transgression was not therefore to be excused or lightly regarded. All this rendered their sin more grievous. Because men have received great light, because they have, like the princes of Israel, ascended to the mount, and been privileged to have communion with God, and to dwell in the light of His glory, let them not flatter themselves that they can afterward sin with impunity, that because they have been thus honored, God will not be strict to punish their iniquity. This is a fatal deception. The great light and privileges bestowed require returns of virtue and holiness corresponding to the light given. Anything short of this, God cannot accept. Great blessings or privileges should never lull to security or carelessness. They should never give license to sin or cause the recipients to feel that God will not be exact with them. All the advantages which God has given are His means to throw ardor into the spirit, zeal into effort, and vigor into the carrying out of His holy will. *PP 359, 360*

their coats out of the camp; as Moses had said.

6 And Moses said unto Aaron, and unto Eleazar and unto Ithamar, his sons, Uncover not your heads, neither ᵀrend your clothes; lest ye die, and lest wrath come upon all the people: but let your brethren, the whole house of Israel, ᵀbewail the burning which the LORD hath kindled.   Josh. 7:1; 22:18 ◆ tear apart ◆ lament

7 And ye shall not go out from the door of the tabernacle of the congregation, lest ye die: for the anointing oil of the LORD is upon you. And they did according to the word of Moses.   Ex. 28:41; Lev. 8:30; 21:12

The Priests Are Forbidden to Drink Wine before Serving in the Tabernacle

8 And the LORD spake unto Aaron, saying,

9 Do not drink wine nor strong drink, thou, nor thy sons with thee, when ye go into the tabernacle of the congregation, lest ye die: it shall be a statute for ever throughout your generations: Is. 28:7; Luke 1:15; 1 Tim. 3:3

10:9 Drunken Priests

Nadab and Abihu would never have committed that fatal sin had they not first become partially intoxicated by the free use of wine. They understood that the most careful and solemn preparation was necessary before presenting themselves in the sanctuary, where the divine Presence was manifested; but by intemperance they were disqualified for their holy office. Their minds became confused and their moral perceptions dulled so that they could not discern the difference between the sacred and the common. PP 361, 362

10 And that ye may put difference between holy and unholy, and between unclean and clean;   Lev. 11:47; Ezek. 22:26; 44:23

11 And that ye may teach the children of Israel all the statutes which the LORD hath spoken unto them by the hand of Moses.

10:10, 11 No Partial Obedience

God designed to teach the people that they must approach Him with reverence and awe, and in His own appointed manner. He cannot accept partial obedience. It was not enough that in this solemn season of worship nearly everything was done as He had directed. God has pronounced a curse upon those who depart from His commandments, and put no difference between common and holy things. PP 360

The Law of Eating the Holy Things

12 And Moses spake unto Aaron, and unto Eleazar and unto Ithamar, his sons that were left, Take the meat offering that remaineth of the offerings of the LORD made by fire,

and eat it without leaven beside the altar: for it is most holy: Lev. 21:22; Num. 18:9-10

13 And ye shall eat it in the holy place, because it is thy due, and thy sons' due, of the sacrifices of the LORD made by fire: for so I am commanded.   Lev. 2:3

14 And the wave breast and heave shoulder shall ye eat in a clean place; thou, and thy sons, and thy daughters with thee: for they be thy due, and thy sons' due, which are given out of the sacrifices of peace offerings of the children of Israel.   Num. 18:11

15 The heave shoulder and the wave breast shall they bring with the offerings made by fire of the fat, to wave it for a wave offering before the LORD; and it shall be thine, and thy sons' with thee, by a statute for ever; as the LORD hath commanded.   Lev. 7:34

16 And Moses diligently sought the goat of the sin offering, and, behold, it was burnt: and he was angry with Eleazar and Ithamar, the sons of Aaron which were left alive, saying,   Lev. 9:3, 15

17 Wherefore have ye not eaten the sin offering in the holy place, seeing it is most holy, and God hath given it you to bear the iniquity of the congregation, to make atonement for them before the LORD?   Ex. 28:38

18 Behold, the blood of it was not brought in within the holy place: ye should indeed have eaten it in the holy place, as I commanded.   Lev. 6:26, 30

19 And Aaron said unto Moses, Behold, this day have they offered their sin offering and their burnt offering before the LORD; and such things have befallen me: and if I had eaten the sin offering to day, should it have been accepted in the sight of the LORD?   Lev. 9:8, 12

20 And when Moses heard that, he was content.

What Beasts May Be Eaten

11 And the LORD spake unto Moses and to Aaron, saying unto them,

2 Speak unto the children of Israel, saying, These are the beasts which ye shall eat among all the beasts that are on the earth.   Matt. 15:11

11:2 Clean and Unclean Food

The distinction between articles of food as clean and unclean was not a merely ceremonial and arbitrary regulation, but was based upon sanitary principles. . . . There are few who realize as they should how much their habits of diet have to do with their health, their character, their usefulness in this world, and their eternal destiny. The appetite should ever be in subjection to the moral and intellectual powers. The body should be servant to the mind, and not the mind to the body. PP 562

3 Whatsoever parteth the hoof, and is clovenfooted, *and* cheweth the cud, among the beasts, that shall ye eat.

4 Nevertheless these shall ye not eat of them that chew the cud, or of them that divide the hoof: *as* the camel, because he cheweth the cud, but divideth not the hoof; he *is* unclean unto you.

5 And the coney, because he cheweth the cud, but divideth not the hoof; he *is* unclean unto you.   Ps. 104:18

6 And the hare, because he cheweth the cud, but divideth not the hoof; he *is* unclean unto you.   Deut. 14:7

7 And the swine, though he divide the hoof, and be clovenfooted, yet he cheweth not the cud; he *is* unclean to you.   Is. 65:4

8 Of their flesh shall ye not eat, and their carcase shall ye not touch; they *are* unclean to you.   Is. 52:11

What Fishes May Be Eaten

9 These shall ye eat of all that *are* in the waters: whatsoever hath fins and scales in the waters, in the seas, and in the rivers, them shall ye eat.

10 And all that have not fins and scales in the seas, and in the rivers, of all that move in the waters, and of any living thing which *is* in the waters, they *shall be* an abomination unto you: Lev. 7:18

11 They shall be even an abomination unto you; ye shall not eat of their flesh, but ye shall have their carcases in abomination.

12 Whatsoever hath no fins nor scales in the waters, that *shall be* an abomination unto you.

13 And these *are they which* ye shall have in abomination among the fowls; they shall not be eaten, they *are* an abomination: the eagle, and the ossifrage, and the ospray,

14 And the vulture, and the kite after his kind;

15 Every raven after his kind;

16 And the owl, and the night hawk, and the cuckow, and the hawk after his kind,

17 And the little owl, and the cormorant, and the great owl,

18 And the swan, and the pelican, and the gier eagle,

19 And the stork, the heron after her kind, and the lapwing, and the bat.

20 All fowls that creep, going upon *all* four, *shall be* an abomination unto you.

21 Yet these may ye eat of every flying creeping thing that goeth upon *all* four, which have legs above their feet, to leap ᵀwithal upon the earth;   *with*

22 *Even* these of them ye may eat; the locust after his kind, and the bald locust after his kind, and the beetle after his kind, and the grasshopper after his kind.   Matt. 3:4

23 But all *other* flying creeping things, which have four feet, *shall be* an abomination unto you.

24 And for these ye shall be unclean: whosoever toucheth the carcase of them shall be unclean until the even.

25 And whosoever beareth *ought* of the carcase of them shall wash his clothes, and be unclean until the even.   Lev. 11:40

26 *The carcases* of every beast which divideth the hoof, and *is* not clovenfooted, nor cheweth the cud, *are* unclean unto you: every one that toucheth them shall be unclean.

27 And whatsoever goeth upon his paws, among all manner of beasts that go on *all* four, those *are* unclean unto you: whoso

The Best Diet

Leviticus 11

In choosing man's food in Eden, the Lord showed what was the best diet; in the choice made for Israel He taught the same lesson. He brought the Israelites out of Egypt and undertook their training, that they might be a people for His own possession. Through them He desired to bless and teach the world. He provided them with the food best adapted for this purpose, not flesh, but manna, "the bread of heaven." It was only because of their discontent and their murmuring for the fleshpots of Egypt that animal food was granted them, and this only for a short time. Its use brought disease and death to thousands. Yet the restriction to a nonflesh diet was never heartily accepted. It continued to be the cause of discontent and murmuring, open or secret, and it was not made permanent.

Upon their settlement in Canaan, the Israelites were permitted the use of animal food, but under careful restrictions which tended to lessen the evil results. The use of swine's flesh was prohibited, as also of other animals and of birds and fish whose flesh was pronounced unclean. Of the meats permitted, the eating of the fat and the blood was strictly forbidden.

Only such animals could be used for food as were in good condition. No creature that was torn, that had died of itself, or from which the blood had not been carefully drained, could be used as food.

By departing from the plan divinely appointed for their diet, the Israelites suffered great loss.
MH 311, 312

toucheth their carcase shall be unclean until the even.

28 And he that beareth the carcase of them shall wash his clothes, and be unclean until the even: they *are* unclean unto you.

29 These also *shall be* unclean unto you among the creeping things that creep upon the earth; the weasel, and the mouse, and the tortoise after his kind, Lev. 11:41-42

30 And the ferret, and the chameleon, and the lizard, and the snail, and the mole.

31 These *are* unclean to you among all that creep: whosoever doth touch them, when they be dead, shall be unclean until the even.

> Health   See Judges 13:4.

32 And upon whatsoever *any* of them, when they are dead, doth fall, it shall be unclean; whether *it be* any vessel of wood, or ᵀrai-ment, or skin, or sack, whatsoever vessel *it be*, wherein *any* work is done, it must be put into water, and it shall be unclean until the even; so it shall be cleansed. Lev. 15:12 ♦ *clothing*

33 And every earthen vessel, whereinto *any* of them falleth, whatsoever *is* in it shall be unclean; and ye shall break it.   Lev. 6:28

34 Of all meat which may be eaten, *that* on which *such* water cometh shall be unclean: and all drink that may be drunk in every *such* vessel shall be unclean.

35 And every *thing* whereupon *any part* of their carcase falleth shall be unclean; *whether it be* oven, or ranges for pots, they shall be broken down: *for* they *are* unclean, and shall be unclean unto you.

36 Nevertheless a fountain or pit, *wherein there is* plenty of water, shall be clean: but that which toucheth their carcase shall be unclean.

37 And if *any part* of their carcase fall upon any sowing seed which is to be sown, it *shall be* clean.

38 But if *any* water be put upon the seed, and *any part* of their carcase fall thereon, it *shall be* unclean unto you.

39 And if any beast, of which ye may eat, die; he that toucheth the carcase thereof shall be unclean until the even.

40 And he that eateth of the carcase of it shall wash his clothes, and be unclean until the even: he also that beareth the carcase of it shall wash his clothes, and be unclean until the even.   Lev. 22:8; Deut. 14:21; Ezek. 44:31

41 And every creeping thing that creepeth upon the earth *shall be* an abomination; it shall not be eaten.   Lev. 11:29

42 Whatsoever goeth upon the belly, and whatsoever goeth upon *all* four, or whatsoever hath more feet among all creeping things that creep upon the earth, them ye shall not eat; for they *are* an abomination.

43 Ye shall not make yourselves abominable with any creeping thing that creepeth, neither shall ye make yourselves unclean with them, that ye should be defiled thereby.   Lev. 11:41-42; 20:25

44 For I *am* the LORD your God: ye shall therefore ᵀsanctify yourselves, and ye shall be holy; for I *am* holy: neither shall ye defile yourselves with any manner of creeping thing that creepeth upon the earth. Ex. 19:6; Lev. 19:2; 20:7 ♦ *make holy*

45 For I *am* the LORD that bringeth you up out of the land of Egypt, to be your God: ye shall therefore be holy, for I *am* holy.   Ex. 6:7; 20:2

46 This *is* the law of the beasts, and of the fowl, and of every living creature that moveth in the waters, and of every creature that creepeth upon the earth:

47 To make a difference between the unclean and the clean, and between the beast that may be eaten and the beast that may not be eaten.   Lev. 10:10; Ezek. 44:23

> **11:46, 47 A Reason Some Foods Unclean**
>
> Many articles of food eaten freely by the heathen about them were forbidden to the Israelites. It was no arbitrary distinction that was made. The things prohibited were unwholesome. And the fact that they were pronounced unclean taught the lesson that the use of injurious foods is defiling. That which corrupts the body tends to corrupt the soul. It unfits the user for communion with God, unfits him for high and holy service. *MH 280*

The Purification of Women after Childbirth

12 And the LORD spake unto Moses, saying,

2 Speak unto the children of Israel, saying, If a woman have conceived seed, and born a man child: then she shall be unclean seven days; according to the days of the separation for her infirmity shall she be unclean.   Gen. 1:28; Lev. 15:19; 18:19

3 And in the eighth day the flesh of his foreskin shall be circumcised. Luke 1:59; John 7:22-23

> **12:3 Spirit of the Law**
>
> According to the law, every child must be circumcised on the eighth day. Should the appointed time fall upon the Sabbath, the rite must then be performed. How much more must it be in harmony with the spirit of the law to make a man "every whit whole on the Sabbath day." And [Jesus] warned [the Jews] to "judge not according to the appearance, but judge righteous judgment." *DA 456, 457*

4 And she shall then continue in the blood of her purifying three and thirty days; she shall touch no hallowed thing, nor come

into the sanctuary, until the days of her purifying be fulfilled.

5 But if she bear a maid child, then she shall be unclean two weeks, as in her separation: and she shall continue in the blood of her purifying [T]threescore and six days.   *sixty*

A Woman's Purification Offerings

6 And when the days of her purifying are fulfilled, for a son, or for a daughter, she shall bring a lamb of the first year for a burnt offering, and a young pigeon, or a turtledove, for a sin offering, unto the door of the tabernacle of the congregation, unto the priest: Luke 2:22

7 Who shall offer it before the LORD, and make an atonement for her; and she shall be cleansed from the issue of her blood. This *is* the law for her that hath born a male or a female.

8 And if she be not able to bring a lamb, then she shall bring two turtles, or two young pigeons; the one for the burnt offering, and the other for a sin offering: and the priest shall make an atonement for her, and she shall be clean.   Lev. 1:14; 4:26; 5:7

12:8 Offerings by the Poor

As an offering for the mother, the law required a lamb of the first year for a burnt offering, and a young pigeon or a turtledove for a sin offering. But the law provided that if the parents were too poor to bring a lamb, a pair of turtledoves or two young pigeons, one for a burnt offering, the other for a sin offering, might be accepted. *DA 50*

Guidance for the Priests in Discerning Leprosy

13 And the LORD spake unto Moses and Aaron, saying,

2 When a man shall have in the skin of his flesh a rising, a scab, or bright spot, and it be in the skin of his flesh *like* the plague of leprosy; then he shall be brought unto Aaron the priest, or unto one of his sons the priests: Lev. 14:3, 56; Deut. 24:8

13:2, 3 Law Concerning Lepers

By the ritual law, the leper was pronounced unclean. Like one already dead, he was shut out from the habitations of men. Whatever he touched was unclean. The air was polluted by his breath. One who was suspected of having the disease must present himself to the priests, who were to examine and decide his case. If pronounced a leper, he was isolated from his family, cut off from the congregation of Israel, and was doomed to associate with those only who were similarly afflicted. *DA 262*

3 And the priest shall look on the plague in the skin of the flesh: and *when* the hair in the plague is turned white, and the plague in sight *be* deeper than the skin of his flesh, it *is* a plague of leprosy: and the priest shall look on him, and pronounce him unclean.

4 If the bright spot *be* white in the skin of his flesh, and in sight *be* not deeper than the skin, and the hair thereof be not turned white; then the priest shall shut up *him that hath* the plague seven days: Num. 12:15

5 And the priest shall look on him the seventh day: and, behold, *if* the plague in his sight be at a stay, *and* the plague spread not in the skin; then the priest shall shut him up seven days more:

6 And the priest shall look on him again the seventh day: and, behold, *if* the plague *be* somewhat dark, *and* the plague spread not in the skin, the priest shall pronounce him clean: it *is but* a scab: and he shall wash his clothes, and be clean.   Lev. 11:25; 14:8

7 But if the scab spread much abroad in the skin, after that he hath been seen of the priest for his cleansing, he shall be seen of the priest again:

8 And *if* the priest see that, behold, the scab spreadeth in the skin, then the priest shall pronounce him unclean: it *is* a leprosy.

9 When the plague of leprosy is in a man, then he shall be brought unto the priest;

10 And the priest shall see *him*: and, behold, *if* the rising *be* white in the skin, and it have turned the hair white, and *there be* quick raw flesh in the rising;   2 Kin. 5:27

11 It *is* an old leprosy in the skin of his flesh, and the priest shall pronounce him unclean, and shall not shut him up: for he *is* unclean.

12 And if a leprosy break out abroad in the skin, and the leprosy cover all the skin of *him that hath* the plague from his head even to his foot, wheresoever the priest looketh;

13 Then the priest shall consider: and, behold, *if* the leprosy have covered all his flesh, he shall pronounce *him* clean *that hath* the plague: it is all turned white: he *is* clean.

14 But when raw flesh appeareth in him, he shall be unclean.

15 And the priest shall see the raw flesh, and pronounce him to be unclean: *for* the raw flesh *is* unclean: it *is* a leprosy.

16 Or if the raw flesh turn again, and be changed unto white, he shall come unto the priest;

17 And the priest shall see him: and, behold, *if* the plague be turned into white; then the priest shall pronounce *him* clean *that hath* the plague: he *is* clean.

18 The flesh also, in which, *even* in the skin thereof, was a boil, and is healed,   Ex. 9:9

19 And in the place of the boil there be a

white rising, or a bright spot, white, and somewhat reddish, and it be shewed to the priest;

20 And if, when the priest seeth it, behold, it *be* in sight lower than the skin, and the hair thereof be turned white; the priest shall pronounce him unclean: it *is* a plague of leprosy broken out of the boil.

21 But if the priest look on it, and, behold, *there be* no white hairs therein, and *if* it *be* not lower than the skin, but *be* somewhat dark; then the priest shall shut him up seven days:

22 And if it spread much abroad in the skin, then the priest shall pronounce him unclean: it *is* a plague.

23 But if the bright spot stay in his place, *and* spread not, it *is* a burning boil; and the priest shall pronounce him clean.

24 Or if there be *any* flesh, in the skin whereof *there is* a hot burning, and the ᵀquick *flesh* that burneth have a white bright spot, somewhat reddish, or white;   living

25 Then the priest shall look upon it: and, behold, *if* the hair in the bright spot be turned white, and it *be in* sight deeper than the skin; it *is* a leprosy broken out of the burning: wherefore the priest shall pronounce him unclean: it *is* the plague of leprosy.

26 But if the priest look on it, and, behold, *there be* no white hair in the bright spot, and it *be* no lower than the *other* skin, but *be* somewhat dark; then the priest shall shut him up seven days:

27 And the priest shall look upon him the seventh day: *and* if it be spread much abroad in the skin, then the priest shall pronounce him unclean: it *is* the plague of leprosy.

28 And if the bright spot stay in his place, *and* spread not in the skin, but it *be* somewhat dark; it *is* a rising of the burning, and the priest shall pronounce him clean: for it *is* an inflammation of the burning.

29 If a man or woman have a plague upon the head or the beard;

30 Then the priest shall see the plague: and, behold, if it *be* in sight deeper than the skin; *and there be* in it a yellow thin hair; then the priest shall pronounce him unclean: it *is* a dry ᵀscall, *even* a leprosy upon the head or beard.   scab on the skin

31 And if the priest look on the plague of the scall, and, behold, it *be* not in sight deeper than the skin, and *that there is* no black hair in it; then the priest shall shut up *him that hath* the plague of the scall seven days:

32 And in the seventh day the priest shall look on the plague: and, behold, *if* the scall spread not, and there be in it no yellow hair, and the scall *be* not in sight deeper than the skin;

33 He shall be shaven, but the scall shall he not shave; and the priest shall shut up *him that hath* the scall seven days more:

34 And in the seventh day the priest shall look on the scall: and, behold, *if* the scall be not spread in the skin, nor *be* in sight deeper than the skin; then the priest shall pronounce him clean: and he shall wash his clothes, and be clean.

35 But if the scall spread much in the skin after his cleansing;

36 Then the priest shall look on him: and, behold, if the scall be spread in the skin, the priest shall not seek for yellow hair; he *is* unclean.

37 But if the scall be in his sight at a stay, and *that* there is black hair grown up therein; the scall is healed, he *is* clean: and the priest shall pronounce him clean.

38 If a man also or a woman have in the skin of their flesh bright spots, *even* white bright spots;

39 Then the priest shall look: and, behold, *if* the bright spots in the skin of their flesh *be* darkish white; it *is* a freckled spot *that* groweth in the skin; he *is* clean.

40 And the man whose hair is fallen off his head, he *is* bald; *yet is* he clean.

41 And he that hath his hair fallen off from the part of his head toward his face, he *is* forehead bald: *yet is* he clean.

42 And if there be in the bald head, or bald forehead, a white reddish sore; it *is* a leprosy sprung up in his bald head, or his bald forehead.

43 Then the priest shall look upon it: and, behold, *if* the rising of the sore *be* white reddish in his bald head, or in his bald forehead, as the leprosy appeareth in the skin of the flesh;

44 He is a leprous man, he *is* unclean: the priest shall pronounce him utterly unclean; his plague *is* in his head.

45 And the leper in whom the plague *is*, his clothes shall be ᵀrent, and his head bare, and he shall put a covering upon his upper lip, and shall cry, Unclean, unclean. Ezek. 24:17 ♦ *torn apart*

46 All the days wherein the plague *shall be* in him he shall be defiled; he *is* unclean: he shall dwell alone; without the camp *shall* his habitation *be*.   2 Kin. 7:3

13:44–46 The Curse of Leprosy

Away from his friends and his kindred, the leper must bear the curse of his malady. He was obliged to publish his own calamity, to rend his garments, and sound the alarm, warning all to flee from his contaminating presence. The cry, "Unclean! unclean!" coming in mournful tones from the lonely exile, was a signal heard with fear and abhorrence. DA 262

47 The garment also that the plague of leprosy is in, *whether it be* a woollen garment, or a linen garment;   Jude 23

48 Whether *it be* in the warp, or woof; of linen, or of woollen; whether in a skin, or in any thing made of skin;

49 And if the plague be greenish or reddish in the garment, or in the skin, either in the warp, or in the woof, or in any thing of skin; it *is* a plague of leprosy, and shall be shewed unto the priest:

50 And the priest shall look upon the plague, and shut up *it that hath* the plague seven days:

51 And he shall look on the plague on the seventh day: if the plague be spread in the garment, either in the warp, or in the woof, or in a skin, *or* in any work that is made of skin; the plague *is* a fretting leprosy; it *is* unclean.   Lev. 14:44

52 He shall therefore burn that garment, whether warp or woof, in woollen or in linen, or any thing of skin, wherein the plague is: for it *is* a ᵀfretting leprosy; it shall be burnt in the fire.   corrosive

53 And if the priest shall look, and, behold, the plague be not spread in the garment, either in the warp, or in the woof, or in any thing of skin;

54 Then the priest shall command that they wash *the thing* wherein the plague *is,* and he shall shut it up seven days more:

55 And the priest shall look on the plague, after that it is washed: and, behold, *if* the plague have not changed his colour, and the plague be not spread; it *is* unclean; thou shalt burn it in the fire; it *is* ᵀfret inward, *whether* it be bare within or without.   corroded

56 And if the priest look, and, behold, the plague *be* somewhat dark after the washing of it; then he shall ᵀrend it out of the garment, or out of the skin, or out of the warp, or out of the woof: tear

57 And if it appear still in the garment, either in the warp, or in the woof, or in any thing of skin; it *is* a spreading *plague*: thou shalt burn that wherein the plague *is* with fire.

58 And the garment, either warp, or woof, or whatsoever thing of skin it *be,* which thou shalt wash, if the plague be departed from them, then it shall be washed the second time, and shall be clean.

59 This *is* the law of the plague of leprosy in a garment of woollen or linen, either in the warp, or woof, or any thing of skins, to pronounce it clean, or to pronounce it unclean.

The Rites and Sacrifices in Cleansing of a Leper

14 And the LORD spake unto Moses, saying,

2 This shall be the law of the leper in the day of his cleansing: He shall be brought unto the priest: Num. 6:9; Matt. 8:2-4; Luke 17:14

3 And the priest shall go forth out of the camp; and the priest shall look, and, behold, *if* the plague of leprosy be healed in the leper;   Lev. 13:46

4 Then shall the priest command to take for him that is to be cleansed two birds alive *and* clean, and cedar wood, and scarlet, and hyssop: Ex. 12:22; Lev. 14:6; Num. 19:6

5 And the priest shall command that one of the birds be killed in an earthen vessel over running water:

6 As for the living bird, he shall take it, and the cedar wood, and the scarlet, and the ᵀhyssop, and shall dip them and the living bird in the blood of the bird *that was* killed over the running water: bitter herb

7 And he shall sprinkle upon him that is to be cleansed from the leprosy seven times, and shall pronounce him clean, and shall let the living bird loose into the open field.   2 Kin. 5:10

8 And he that is to be cleansed shall wash his clothes, and shave off all his hair, and

---

wash himself in water, that he may be clean: and after that he shall come into the camp, and shall tarry abroad out of his tent seven days.   Lev. 11:25; Num. 8:7

9 But it shall be on the seventh day, that he shall shave all his hair off his head and his beard and his eyebrows, even all his hair he shall shave off: and he shall wash his clothes, also he shall wash his flesh in water, and he shall be clean.   Num. 6:9

10 And on the eighth day he shall take two he lambs without blemish, and one ewe lamb of the first year without blemish, and three tenth deals of fine flour *for* a meat offering, mingled with oil, and one log of oil.   Lev. 2:1; 14:12, 15

11 And the priest that maketh *him* clean shall present the man that is to be made clean, and those things, before the LORD, *at* the door of the tabernacle of the congregation:

12 And the priest shall take one he lamb, and offer him for a trespass offering, and the log of oil, and wave them *for* a wave offering before the LORD: Ex. 29:24; Lev. 6:6-7

13 And he shall slay the lamb in the place where he shall kill the sin offering and the burnt offering, in the holy place: for as the sin offering *is* the priest's, *so is* the trespass offering: it *is* most holy: Ex. 29:11

14 And the priest shall take *some* of the blood of the trespass offering, and the priest shall put *it* upon the tip of the right ear of him that is to be cleansed, and upon the thumb of his right hand, and upon the great toe of his right foot: Ex. 29:20; Lev. 8:23-24

15 And the priest shall take *some* of the log of oil, and pour *it* into the palm of his own left hand:

16 And the priest shall dip his right finger in the oil that *is* in his left hand, and shall sprinkle of the oil with his finger seven times before the LORD:

17 And of the rest of the oil that *is* in his hand shall the priest put upon the tip of the right ear of him that is to be cleansed, and upon the thumb of his right hand, and upon the great toe of his right foot, upon the blood of the ᵀtrespass offering: *sin*

18 And the remnant of the oil that *is* in the priest's hand he shall pour upon the head of him that is to be cleansed: and the priest shall make an atonement for him before the LORD.   Lev. 4:26

19 And the priest shall offer the sin offering, and make an atonement for him that is to be cleansed from his uncleanness; and afterward he shall kill the burnt offering: Lev. 14:12

20 And the priest shall offer the burnt offering and the meat offering upon the altar: and the priest shall make an atonement for him, and he shall be clean.   Lev. 14:10

14:2–32 Christ and the Law

The Pharisees had asserted that Christ's teaching was opposed to the law which God had given through Moses; but His direction to the cleansed leper to present an offering according to the law disproved this charge. It was sufficient testimony for all who were willing to be convinced. *DA 265*

---

21 And if he *be* poor, and cannot get so much; then he shall take one lamb *for* a trespass offering to be waved, to make an atonement for him, and one tenth deal of fine flour mingled with oil for a meat offering, and a log of oil;   Lev. 5:7; 12:8

22 And two turtledoves, or two young pigeons, such as he is able to get; and the one shall be a sin offering, and the other a burnt offering.

23 And he shall bring them on the eighth day for his cleansing unto the priest, unto the door of the tabernacle of the congregation, before the LORD.   Lev. 14:10-11

24 And the priest shall take the lamb of the trespass offering, and the log of oil, and the priest shall wave them *for* a wave offering before the LORD:

25 And he shall kill the lamb of the trespass offering, and the priest shall take *some* of the blood of the trespass offering, and put *it* upon the tip of the right ear of him that is to be cleansed, and upon the thumb of his right hand, and upon the great toe of his right foot:

26 And the priest shall pour of the oil into the palm of his own left hand:

27 And the priest shall sprinkle with his right finger *some* of the oil that *is* in his left hand seven times before the LORD:

28 And the priest shall put of the oil that *is* in his hand upon the tip of the right ear of him that is to be cleansed, and upon the thumb of his right hand, and upon the great toe of his right foot, upon the place of the blood of the trespass offering:

29 And the rest of the oil that *is* in the priest's hand he shall put upon the head of him that is to be cleansed, to make an atonement for him before the LORD.   Lev. 14:18

30 And he shall offer the one of the turtledoves, or of the young pigeons, such as he can get;   Lev. 14:22

31 *Even* such as he is able to get, the one *for* a sin offering, and the other *for* a burnt offering, with the meat offering: and the priest shall make an atonement for him that is to be cleansed before the LORD.

32 This *is* the law *of him* in whom *is* the plague of leprosy, whose hand is not able to get *that which pertaineth* to his cleansing.   Lev. 14:10

The Signs of Leprosy in a House, and the Cleansing Thereof

33 And the LORD spake unto Moses and unto Aaron, saying,

34 When ye be come into the land of Canaan, which I give to you for a possession, and I put the plague of leprosy in a house of the land of your possession;　　Gen. 17:8; Num. 32:22

35 And he that owneth the house shall come and tell the priest, saying, It seemeth to me *there is* as it were a plague in the house:

36 Then the priest shall command that they empty the house, before the priest go *into it* to see the plague, that all that *is* in the house be not made unclean: and afterward the priest shall go in to see the house:

37 And he shall look on the plague, and, behold, *if* the plague *be* in the walls of the house with ᵀhollow ᵀstrakes, greenish or reddish, which in sight *are* lower than the wall;　　recessed ◆ stripes

38 Then the priest shall go out of the house to the door of the house, and shut up the house seven days:

39 And the priest shall come again the seventh day, and shall look: and, behold, *if* the plague be spread in the walls of the house;

40 Then the priest shall command that they take away the stones in which the plague *is*, and they shall cast them into an unclean place without the city:

41 And he shall cause the house to be scraped within round about, and they shall pour out the dust that they scrape off without the city into an unclean place:

42 And they shall take other stones, and put *them* in the place of those stones; and he shall take other morter, and shall plaister the house.

43 And if the plague come again, and break out in the house, after that he hath taken away the stones, and after he hath scraped the house, and after it is plaistered;

44 Then the priest shall come and look, and, behold, *if* the plague be spread in the house, it *is* a ᵀfretting leprosy in the house: it *is* unclean.　　Lev. 13:51-52 ◆ corrosive

45 And he shall break down the house, the stones of it, and the timber thereof, and all the morter of the house; and he shall carry *them* forth out of the city into an unclean place.

46 Moreover he that goeth into the house all the while that it is shut up shall be unclean until the even.　　Num. 19:21-22

47 And he that lieth in the house shall wash his clothes; and he that eateth in the house shall wash his clothes.

48 And if the priest shall come in, and look *upon it*, and, behold, the plague hath not spread in the house, after the house was plaistered: then the priest shall pronounce the house clean, because the plague is healed.

49 And he shall take to cleanse the house two birds, and cedar wood, and scarlet, and hyssop:　　Lev. 14:4

50 And he shall kill the one of the birds in an earthen vessel over running water:

51 And he shall take the cedar wood, and the hyssop, and the scarlet, and the living bird, and dip them in the blood of the slain bird, and in the running water, and sprinkle the house seven times:

52 And he shall cleanse the house with the blood of the bird, and with the running water, and with the living bird, and with the cedar wood, and with the hyssop, and with the scarlet:

53 But he shall let go the living bird out of the city into the open fields, and make an atonement for the house: and it shall be clean.

54 This *is* the law for all manner of plague of leprosy, and ᵀscall,　　scabs on the skin

55 And for the leprosy of a garment, and of a house,

56 And for a rising, and for a scab, and for a bright spot:　　Lev. 13:2

57 To teach when *it is* unclean, and when *it is* clean: this *is* the law of leprosy.　　Lev. 10:10

Discharges and Uncleanness

15 And the LORD spake unto Moses and to Aaron, saying,

2 Speak unto the children of Israel, and say unto them, When any man hath a running issue out of his flesh, *because of* his issue he *is* unclean.　　Lev. 22:4; Num. 5:2; 2 Sam. 3:29

3 And this shall be his uncleanness in his issue: whether his flesh run with his issue, or his flesh be stopped from his issue, it *is* his uncleanness.

4 Every bed, whereon he lieth that hath the issue, is unclean: and every thing, whereon he sitteth, shall be unclean.

5 And whosoever toucheth his bed shall wash his clothes, and bathe *himself* in water, and be unclean until the even.　　Lev. 11:25

6 And he that sitteth on *any* thing whereon he sat that hath the issue shall wash his clothes, and bathe *himself* in water, and be unclean until the even.

7 And he that toucheth the flesh of him that hath the issue shall wash his clothes, and bathe *himself* in water, and be unclean until the even.

8 And if he that hath the issue spit upon him that is clean; then he shall wash his clothes, and bathe *himself* in water, and be unclean until the even.

9 And what saddle soever he rideth upon that hath the issue shall be unclean.

10 And whosoever toucheth any thing that was under him shall be unclean until the even: and he that beareth *any of* those things shall wash his clothes, and bathe *himself* in water, and be unclean until the even.

11 And whomsoever he toucheth that hath the issue, and hath not rinsed his hands in water, he shall wash his clothes, and bathe *himself* in water, and be unclean until the even.

12 And the vessel of earth, that he toucheth which hath the issue, shall be broken: and every vessel of wood shall be rinsed in water.   Lev. 6:28; 11:32-33

15:3–12 Preventing the Spread of Disease

Not only in their religious service, but in all the affairs of daily life was observed the distinction between clean and unclean. All who came in contact with contagious or contaminating diseases were isolated from the encampment, and they were not permitted to return without thorough cleansing of both the person and the clothing. *MH 277*

---

13 And when he that hath an issue is cleansed of his issue; then he shall number to himself seven days for his cleansing, and wash his clothes, and bathe his flesh in running water, and shall be clean.   Lev. 8:33

14 And on the eighth day he shall take to him two turtledoves, or two young pigeons, and come before the LORD unto the door of the tabernacle of the congregation, and give them unto the priest: Lev. 12:8

15 And the priest shall offer them, the one *for* a sin offering, and the other *for* a burnt offering; and the priest shall make an atonement for him before the LORD for his issue.   Lev. 4:26

16 And if any man's seed of copulation go out from him, then he shall wash all his flesh in water, and be unclean until the even.   Lev. 15:5; 22:4; Deut. 23:10-11

17 And every garment, and every skin, whereon is the seed of copulation, shall be washed with water, and be unclean until the even.

18 The woman also with whom man shall lie *with* seed of copulation, they shall *both* bathe *themselves* in water, and be unclean until the even.

19 And if a woman have an issue, *and* her issue in her flesh be blood, she shall be put apart seven days: and whosoever toucheth her shall be unclean until the even.   Lev. 12:2

20 And every thing that she lieth upon in her separation shall be unclean: every thing also that she sitteth upon shall be unclean.

21 And whosoever toucheth her bed shall wash his clothes, and bathe *himself* in water, and be unclean until the even.

22 And whosoever toucheth any thing that she sat upon shall wash his clothes, and bathe *himself* in water, and be unclean until the even.

23 And if it *be* on *her* bed, or on any thing whereon she sitteth, when he toucheth it, he shall be unclean until the even.

24 And if any man lie with her at all, and her flowers be upon him, he shall be unclean seven days; and all the bed whereon he lieth shall be unclean.   Lev. 18:19; 20:18; Ezek. 18:6

25 And if a woman have an issue of her blood many days out of the time of her separation, or if it run beyond the time of her separation; all the days of the issue of her uncleanness shall be as the days of her separation: she *shall be* unclean.   Matt. 9:20; Mark 5:25; Luke 8:43

26 Every bed whereon she lieth all the days of her issue shall be unto her as the bed of her separation: and whatsoever she sitteth upon shall be unclean, as the uncleanness of her separation.

27 And whosoever toucheth those things shall be unclean, and shall wash his clothes, and bathe *himself* in water, and be unclean until the even.

28 But if she be cleansed of her issue, then she shall number to herself seven days, and after that she shall be clean.   Lev. 15:13-15

29 And on the eighth day she shall take unto her two turtles, or two young pigeons, and bring them unto the priest, to the door of the tabernacle of the congregation.

15:19–33 Training in Health Principles

In the teaching that God gave to Israel, the preservation of health received careful attention. The people who had come from slavery with the uncleanly and unhealthful habits which it engenders, were subjected to the strictest training in the wilderness before entering Canaan. Health principles were taught and sanitary laws enforced. *MH 277*

---

30 And the priest shall offer the one *for* a sin offering, and the other *for* a burnt offering; and the priest shall make an atonement for her before the LORD for the issue of her uncleanness.

31 Thus shall ye separate the children of Israel from their uncleanness; that they die not in their uncleanness, when they defile my tabernacle that *is* among them.   Num. 5:3; 19:13

32 This *is* the law of him that hath an issue, and *of him* whose seed goeth from him, and is defiled therewith;

33 And of her that is sick of her flowers, and of him that hath an issue, of the man, and of the woman, and of him that lieth with her that is unclean.

How the High Priest Must Enter into the Holy Place

16 And the LORD spake unto Moses after the death of the two sons of Aaron, when they offered before the LORD, and died; Lev. 10:1-2

2 And the LORD said unto Moses, Speak unto Aaron thy brother, that he come not at all times into the holy *place* within the vail before the mercy seat, which *is* upon the ark; that he die not: for I will appear in the cloud upon the mercy seat. Ex. 40:34-35; 1 Kin. 8:10-12

3 Thus shall Aaron come into the holy *place*: with a young ᵀbullock for a sin offering, and a ram for a burnt offering. Lev. 4:3 ◆ *bull*

4 He shall put on the holy linen coat, and he shall have the linen ᵀbreeches upon his flesh, and shall be girded with a linen ᵀgirdle, and with the linen ᵀmitre shall he be attired: these *are* holy garments; therefore shall he wash his flesh in water, and *so* put them on. Ex. 30:20 ◆ *trousers* ◆ *belt* ◆ *turban*

5 And he shall take of the congregation of the children of Israel two kids of the goats for a sin offering, and one ram for a burnt offering. 2 Chr. 29:21

6 And Aaron shall offer his bullock of the sin offering, which *is* for himself, and make an atonement for himself, and for his house.

7 And he shall take the two goats, and present them before the LORD *at* the door of the tabernacle of the congregation.

8 And Aaron shall cast lots upon the two goats; one lot for the LORD, and the other lot for the scapegoat.

9 And Aaron shall bring the goat upon which the LORD's lot fell, and offer him *for* a sin offering.

10 But the goat, on which the lot fell to be the scapegoat, shall be presented alive before the LORD, to make an atonement with him, *and* to let him go for a scapegoat into the wilderness. 1 John 2:2

11 And Aaron shall bring the bullock of the sin offering, which *is* for himself, and shall make an atonement for himself, and for his house, and shall kill the bullock of the sin offering which *is* for himself: Lev. 16:6

12 And he shall take a ᵀcenser full of burning coals of fire from off the altar before the LORD, and his hands full of sweet incense beaten small, and bring *it* within the vail: Ex. 30:34-38; Num. 16:18 ◆ *holder for burning incense*

13 And he shall put the incense upon the fire before the LORD, that the cloud of the incense may cover the mercy seat that *is* upon the testimony, that he die not: Ex. 25:21

14 And he shall take of the blood of the bullock, and sprinkle *it* with his finger upon the mercy seat eastward; and before the mercy seat shall he sprinkle of the blood with his finger seven times. Lev. 4:5-6; Heb. 9:13, 25

The Sin Offering for the People

15 Then shall he kill the goat of the sin offering, that *is* for the people, and bring his blood within the ᵀvail, and do with that blood as he did with the blood of the bullock, and sprinkle it upon the mercy seat, and before the mercy seat: Heb. 9:3, 7, 12 ◆ *veil*

16 And he shall make an atonement for the holy *place*, because of the uncleanness of the children of Israel, and because of their transgressions in all their sins: and so shall he do for the tabernacle of the congregation, that remaineth among them in the midst of their uncleanness. Ex. 29:36-37

17 And there shall be no man in the tabernacle of the congregation when he goeth in to make an atonement in the holy *place*, until he come out, and have made an atonement for himself, and for his household, and for all the congregation of Israel. Luke 1:10

18 And he shall go out unto the altar that *is* before the LORD, and make an atonement for it; and shall take of the blood of the bullock,

---

Symbolism of Sacrifices

Leviticus 16

Important truths concerning the atonement are taught by the typical [symbolic] service. A substitute was accepted in the sinner's stead; but the sin was not canceled by the blood of the victim. A means was thus provided by which it was transferred to the sanctuary. By the offering of blood the sinner acknowledged the authority of the law, confessed his guilt in transgression, and expressed his desire for pardon through faith in a Redeemer to come; but he was not yet entirely released from the condemnation of the law. On the Day of Atonement the high priest, having taken an offering from the congregation, went into the most holy place with the blood of this offering, and sprinkled it upon the mercy seat, directly over the law, to make satisfaction for its claims. Then, in his character of mediator, he took the sins upon himself and bore them from the sanctuary. Placing his hands upon the head of the scapegoat, he confessed over him all these sins, thus in figure transferring them from himself to the goat. The goat then bore them away, and they were regarded as forever separated from the people.

Such was the service performed "unto the example and shadow of heavenly things." *GC 420*

and of the blood of the goat, and put *it* upon the horns of the altar round about.   Lev. 4:7
19 And he shall sprinkle of the blood upon it with his finger seven times, and cleanse it, and ᵀhallow it from the uncleanness of the children of Israel.   *render it as sacred*
20 And when he hath made an end of reconciling the holy *place*, and the tabernacle of the congregation, and the altar, he shall bring the live goat: Lev. 16:16
21 And Aaron shall lay both his hands upon the head of the live goat, and confess over him all the iniquities of the children of Israel, and all their ᵀtransgressions in all their sins, putting them upon the head of the goat, and shall send *him* away by the hand of a fit man into the wilderness: Is. 53:6 ◆ *violations of a law*
22 And the goat shall bear upon him all their iniquities unto a land not inhabited: and he shall let go the goat in the wilderness.   Is. 53:11-12

16:7–22 Atonement's Closing Work

In the typical [symbolic] system, which was a shadow of the sacrifice and priesthood of Christ, the cleansing of the sanctuary was the last service performed by the high priest in the yearly round of ministration. It was the closing work of the atonement—a removal or putting away of sin from Israel. It prefigured the closing work in the ministration of our High Priest in heaven, in the removal or blotting out of the sins of His people, which are registered in the heavenly records. *GC 352*

23 And Aaron shall come into the tabernacle of the congregation, and shall put off the linen garments, which he put on when he went into the holy *place*, and shall leave them there: Ezek. 42:14
24 And he shall wash his flesh with water in the holy place, and put on his garments, and come forth, and offer his burnt offering, and the burnt offering of the people, and make an atonement for himself, and for the people.   Lev. 16:3-5
25 And the fat of the sin offering shall he burn upon the altar.   Ex. 29:13
26 And he that let go the goat for the scapegoat shall wash his clothes, and bathe his flesh in water, and afterward come into the camp.   Lev. 16:10
27 And the bullock *for* the sin offering, and the goat *for* the sin offering, whose blood was brought in to make atonement in the holy *place*, shall *one* carry forth without the camp; and they shall burn in the fire their skins, and their flesh, and their dung.   Lev. 4:21
28 And he that burneth them shall wash his clothes, and bathe his flesh in water, and afterward he shall come into the camp.

The Annual Feast of Atonement
29 And *this* shall be a statute for ever unto you: *that* in the seventh month, on the tenth *day* of the month, ye shall afflict your souls, and do no work at all, *whether it be* one of your own country, or a stranger that sojourneth among you: Ex. 20:10; Num. 29:7; Is. 58:3
30 For on that day shall *the priest* make an atonement for you, to cleanse you, *that* ye may be clean from all your sins before the Lord.   Ps. 51:2; Jer. 33:8; Eph. 5:26
31 It *shall be* a sabbath of rest unto you, and ye shall afflict your souls, by a statute for ever.   Lev. 23:32

16:29–31 Observance of Atonement

Every man was required to afflict his soul while this work of atonement was going forward. All business was to be laid aside, and the whole congregation of Israel were to spend the day in solemn humiliation before God, with prayer, fasting, and deep searching of heart. *GC 419, 420*

32 And the priest, whom he shall anoint, and whom he shall ᵀconsecrate to minister in the priest's office in his father's stead, shall make the atonement, and shall put on the linen clothes, *even* the holy garments: Ex. 29:29-30 ◆ *set apart*
33 And he shall make an atonement for the holy sanctuary, and he shall make an atonement for the tabernacle of the congregation, and for the altar, and he shall make an atonement for the priests, and for all the people of the congregation.   Lev. 16:16
34 And this shall be an everlasting statute unto you, to make an atonement for the children of Israel for all their sins once a year. And he did as the Lord commanded Moses.   Ex. 30:10; Heb. 9:7, 25

Offering the Blood of Slain Beasts at the Door of the Tabernacle

17 And the Lord spake unto Moses, saying,
2 Speak unto Aaron, and unto his sons, and unto all the children of Israel, and say unto them; This *is* the thing which the Lord hath commanded, saying,
3 What man soever *there be* of the house of Israel, that killeth an ox, or lamb, or goat, in the camp, or that killeth *it* out of the camp,
4 And bringeth it not unto the door of the tabernacle of the congregation, to offer an offering unto the Lord before the tabernacle of the Lord; blood shall be imputed unto that man; he hath shed blood; and that man shall be cut off from among his people: Gen. 17:14
5 To the end that the children of Israel may bring their sacrifices, which they offer in the

open field, even that they may bring them unto the LORD, unto the door of the tabernacle of the congregation, unto the priest, and offer them *for* peace offerings unto the LORD.

6 And the priest shall sprinkle the blood upon the altar of the LORD *at* the door of the tabernacle of the congregation, and burn the fat for a sweet savour unto the LORD.

7 And they shall no more offer their sacrifices unto devils, after whom they have gone ᵀa whoring. This shall be a statute for ever unto them throughout their generations.   Ex. 34:15; 2 Chr. 11:15 ◆ *giving sex as a prostitute*

8 And thou shalt say unto them, Whatsoever man *there be* of the house of Israel, or of the strangers which sojourn among you, that offereth a burnt offering or sacrifice, Lev. 1:2-3

9 And bringeth it not unto the door of the tabernacle of the congregation, to offer it unto the LORD; even that man shall be cut off from among his people.   Lev. 17:4

All Eating of Blood Is Forbidden

10 And whatsoever man *there be* of the house of Israel, or of the strangers that sojourn among you, that eateth any manner of blood; I will even set my face against that soul that eateth blood, and will cut him off from among his people.   Gen. 9:4; Lev. 3:17; Deut. 12:16

11 For the life of the flesh *is* in the blood: and I have given it to you upon the altar to make an atonement for your souls: for it *is* the blood *that* maketh an atonement for the soul.   Matt. 26:28; Heb. 9:22; 1 John 1:7

> **17:11 Life of the Flesh Is in the Blood**
>
> Day by day the repentant sinner brought his offering to the door of the tabernacle and, placing his hand upon the victim's head, confessed his sins, thus in figure transferring them from himself to the innocent sacrifice. The animal was then slain. "Without shedding of blood," says the apostle, there is no remission of sin. "The life of the flesh is in the blood" (Leviticus 17:11). *GC 418*

12 Therefore I said unto the children of Israel, No soul of you shall eat blood, neither shall any stranger that sojourneth among you eat blood.

13 And whatsoever man *there be* of the children of Israel, or of the strangers that sojourn among you, which hunteth and catcheth any beast or fowl that may be eaten; he shall even pour out the blood thereof, and cover it with dust.   Lev. 7:26; Deut. 12:16, 24

14 For *it is* the life of all flesh; the blood of it *is* for the life thereof: therefore I said unto the children of Israel, Ye shall eat the blood of no manner of flesh: for the life of all flesh

is the blood thereof: whosoever eateth it shall be cut off.   Gen. 9:4

15 And every soul that eateth that which died *of itself*, or that which was torn *with beasts, whether it be* one of your own country, or a stranger, he shall both wash his clothes, and bathe *himself* in water, and be unclean until the even: then shall he be clean. Ex. 22:31

16 But if he wash *them* not, nor bathe his flesh; then he shall bear his iniquity.   Lev. 5:1

Unlawful Marriages and Unlawful Lusts

18 And the LORD spake unto Moses, saying,

2 Speak unto the children of Israel, and say unto them, I am the LORD your God.   Ex. 6:7

> **18 (chapter) Principles of Prosperity**
>
> The teaching of the Bible has a vital bearing upon man's prosperity in all the relations of this life. It unfolds the principles that are the cornerstone of a nation's prosperity—principles with which is bound up the well-being of society, and which are the safeguard of the family—principles without which no man can attain usefulness, happiness, and honor in this life, or can hope to secure the future, immortal life. *PP 599*

3 After the doings of the land of Egypt, wherein ye dwelt, shall ye not do: and after the doings of the land of Canaan, whither I bring you, shall ye not do: neither shall ye walk in their ordinances.   Ex. 23:24

4 Ye shall do my judgments, and keep mine ordinances, to walk therein: I *am* the LORD your God.   Lev. 18:2

5 Ye shall therefore keep my statutes, and my judgments: which if a man do, he shall live in them: I *am* the LORD.   Ezek. 20:11; Rom. 10:5

6 None of you shall approach to any that is near of kin to him, to uncover *their* nakedness: I *am* the LORD.   Lev. 18:7-19

7 The nakedness of thy father, or the nakedness of thy mother, shalt thou not uncover: she *is* thy mother; thou shalt not uncover her nakedness.   Lev. 20:11; Ezek. 22:10

8 The nakedness of thy father's wife shalt thou not uncover: it *is* thy father's nakedness.   Lev. 20:11; Deut. 22:30; 1 Cor. 5:1

9 The nakedness of thy sister, the daughter of thy father, or daughter of thy mother, *whether she be* born at home, or born abroad, *even* their nakedness thou shalt not uncover.   Lev. 20:17

10 The nakedness of thy son's daughter, or of thy daughter's daughter, *even* their nakedness thou shalt not uncover: for theirs *is* thine own nakedness.

11 The nakedness of thy father's wife's daughter, ᵀbegotten of thy father, she *is* thy

sister, thou shalt not uncover her nakedness.   *brought forth*
12 Thou shalt not uncover the nakedness of
thy father's sister: she *is* thy father's near
kinswoman.   Lev. 20:19
13 Thou shalt not uncover the nakedness of
thy mother's sister: for she *is* thy mother's
near kinswoman.
14 Thou shalt not uncover the nakedness of
thy father's brother, thou shalt not approach
to his wife: she *is* thine aunt.   Lev. 20:20
15 Thou shalt not uncover the nakedness of
thy daughter in law: she *is* thy son's wife; thou
shalt not uncover her nakedness.   Lev. 20:12
16 Thou shalt not uncover the nakedness of
thy brother's wife: it *is* thy brother's nakedness.   Lev. 20:21
17 Thou shalt not uncover the nakedness
of a woman and her daughter, neither shalt
thou take her son's daughter, or her daughter's daughter, to uncover her nakedness; *for*
they *are* her near kinswomen: it *is* wickedness.   Lev. 20:14
18 Neither shalt thou take a wife to her sister, to ᵀvex *her*, to uncover her nakedness,
beside the other in her life *time*.   *trouble*
19 Also thou shalt not approach unto a
woman to uncover her nakedness, as long as
she is put apart for her uncleanness.Lev. 20:18
20 Moreover thou shalt not lie carnally with
thy neighbour's wife, to defile thyself with
her.   Ex. 20:14; Lev. 20:10; Matt. 5:27-28
21 And thou shalt not let any of thy seed
pass through *the fire* to Molech, neither shalt
thou profane the name of thy God: I *am* the
LORD.   Lev. 19:12; 20:2-5; 21:6
22 Thou shalt not lie with mankind, as with
womankind: it *is* abomination.   Lev. 20:13
23 Neither shalt thou lie with any beast to
defile thyself therewith: neither shall any
woman stand before a beast to lie down
thereto: it *is* confusion. Ex. 22:19; Lev. 20:12, 15-16
24 Defile not ye yourselves in any of these
things: for in all these the nations are defiled
which I cast out before you: Lev. 18:30; Deut. 18:12
25 And the land is defiled: therefore I do
visit the iniquity thereof upon it, and the
land itself vomiteth out her inhabitants.
26 Ye shall therefore keep my statutes and
my judgments, and shall not commit *any* of
these abominations; *neither* any of your own
nation, nor any stranger that sojourneth
among you: Lev. 18:5
27 (For all these abominations have the men
of the land done, which *were* before you, and
the land is defiled;)
28 That the land spue not you out also,
when ye defile it, as it spued out the nations
that *were* before you.
29 For whosoever shall commit any of these
abominations, even the souls that commit
them shall be cut off from among their people.
30 Therefore shall ye keep mine ordinance,

that *ye* commit not *any one* of these abominable customs, which were committed before you, and that ye defile not yourselves
therein: I *am* the LORD your God.   Lev. 20:23

A Repetition of Various Laws

19 And the LORD spake unto Moses, saying,
2 Speak unto all the congregation of the
children of Israel, and say unto them, Ye
shall be holy: for I the LORD your God *am*
holy.   Ex. 19:6
3 Ye shall fear every man his mother, and his
father, and keep my sabbaths: I *am* the LORD
your God.   Ex. 16:29; 20:8, 12
4 Turn ye not unto idols, nor make to yourselves molten gods: I *am* the LORD your God.
5 And if ye offer a sacrifice of peace offerings
unto the LORD, ye shall offer it at your own
will.   Lev. 1:3
6 It shall be eaten the same day ye offer it,
and on the morrow: and if ought remain until
the third day, it shall be burnt in the fire.
7 And if it be eaten at all on the third day, it
is abominable; it shall not be accepted.
8 Therefore *every one* that eateth it shall bear
his iniquity, because he hath profaned the
hallowed thing of the LORD: and that soul
shall be cut off from among his people.
9 And when ye reap the harvest of your
land, thou shalt not wholly reap the corners
of thy field, neither shalt thou gather the
gleanings of thy harvest.   Lev. 23:22
10 And thou shalt not glean thy vineyard,
neither shalt thou gather *every* grape of thy
vineyard; thou shalt leave them for the poor
and stranger: I *am* the LORD your God.
11 Ye shall not steal, neither deal falsely,
neither lie one to another.   Ex. 20:15; Eph. 4:25
12 And ye shall not swear by my name
falsely, neither shalt thou profane the name
of thy God: I *am* the LORD. Ex. 20:7; Lev. 6:3; 18:21
13 Thou shalt not defraud thy neighbour,
neither rob *him*: the wages of him that is
hired shall not abide with thee all night until
the morning.   Deut. 24:14-15; Mal. 3:5; James 5:4

19:13–15, 35, 36 Taking Advantage of Others

He who would take advantage of another's
misfortunes in order to benefit himself, or
who seeks to profit himself through another's weakness or incompetence, is a transgressor both of the principles and of the precepts of the word of God. *MH 187*

14 Thou shalt not curse the deaf, nor put a
stumblingblock before the blind, but shalt
fear thy God: I *am* the LORD.   Lev. 19:32; 25:17
15 Ye shall do no unrighteousness in judgment: thou shalt not respect the person
of the poor, nor honour the person of the

mighty: *but* in righteousness shalt thou judge thy neighbour.   Ex. 23:2-3; Deut. 1:17; 16:19

16 Thou shalt not go up and down *as* a tale-bearer among thy people: neither shalt thou stand against the blood of thy neighbour: I *am* the LORD.   Ex. 23:1, 7; Ps. 15:3

17 Thou shalt not hate thy brother in thine heart: thou shalt in any wise rebuke thy neighbour, and not suffer sin upon him.

18 Thou shalt not avenge, nor bear any grudge against the children of thy people, but thou shalt love thy neighbour as thyself: I *am* the LORD.   Rom. 12:19; 13:9; Gal. 5:14

> **19:17, 18 Truths Obscured**
>
> Through Moses the Lord had said, "Thou shalt not hate . . . love thy neighbor as thyself." The truths which Christ presented were the same that had been taught by the prophets, but they had become obscured through hardness of heart and love of sin. *MB 55*

19 Ye shall keep my statutes. Thou shalt not let thy cattle ᵀgender with a diverse kind: thou shalt not sow thy field with mingled seed: neither shall a garment mingled of linen and woollen come upon thee.   Deut. 22:9-11 ◆ *breed*

20 And whosoever lieth carnally with a woman, that *is* a bondmaid, ᵀbetrothed to an husband, and not at all redeemed, nor freedom given her; she shall be ᵀscourged; they shall not be put to death, because she was not free.   Deut. 22:23-24 ◆ *engaged* ◆ *whipped*

21 And he shall bring his ᵀtrespass offering unto the LORD, unto the door of the tabernacle of the congregation, *even* a ram for a trespass offering.   *sin*

22 And the priest shall make an atonement for him with the ram of the trespass offering before the LORD for his sin which he hath done: and the sin which he hath done shall be forgiven him.

23 And when ye shall come into the land, and shall have planted all manner of trees for food, then ye shall count the fruit thereof as uncircumcised: three years shall it be as uncircumcised unto you: it shall not be eaten of.   Lev. 12:3

24 But in the fourth year all the fruit thereof shall be holy to praise the LORD *withal*.

25 And in the fifth year shall ye eat of the fruit thereof, that it may yield unto you the increase thereof: I *am* the LORD your God.

26 Ye shall not eat *any thing* with the blood: neither shall ye use enchantment, nor observe times.   Deut. 12:23

27 Ye shall not round the corners of your heads, neither shalt thou mar the corners of thy beard.   Lev. 21:5; Is. 15:2; Jer. 48:37

28 Ye shall not make any cuttings in your flesh for the dead, nor print any marks upon you: I *am* the LORD.   Deut. 14:1

29 Do not prostitute thy daughter, to cause her to be a ᵀwhore; lest the land fall to ᵀwhoredom, and the land become full of wickedness.   *prostitute* ◆ *prostitution*

30 Ye shall keep my sabbaths, and reverence my sanctuary: I *am* the LORD. Lev. 16:2; 19:3; 26:2

31 Regard not them that have familiar spirits, neither seek after wizards, to be defiled by them: I *am* the LORD your God.   Is. 8:19

32 Thou shalt rise up before the ᵀhoary head, and honour the face of the old man, and fear thy God: I *am* the LORD.   Lev. 19:14 ◆ *white colored*

33 And if a stranger sojourn with thee in your land, ye shall not ᵀvex him.   Ex. 22:21 ◆ *trouble*

34 *But* the stranger that dwelleth with you shall be unto you as one born among you, and thou shalt love him as thyself; for ye were strangers in the land of Egypt: I *am* the LORD your God.   Lev. 19:18

> **19:33, 34 The Law Amplified**
>
> These directions relating to the duty of the people to God, to one another, and to the stranger were only the principles of the Ten Commandments amplified and given in a specific manner, that none need err. *PP 364*

35 Ye shall do no unrighteousness in judgment, in ᵀmeteyard, in weight, or in measure.   Deut. 25:13 ◆ *measure of length*

36 Just balances, just weights, a just ephah, and a just hin, shall ye have: I *am* the LORD your God, which brought you out of the land of Egypt.   Ex. 20:2

37 Therefore shall ye observe all my statutes, and all my judgments, and do them: I *am* the LORD.   Lev. 18:4-5

Punishment for Sacrificing Children to Molech

20 And the LORD spake unto Moses, saying,

2 Again, thou shalt say to the children of Israel, Whosoever *he be* of the children of Israel, or of the strangers that sojourn in Israel, that giveth *any* of his seed unto Molech; he shall surely be put to death: the people of the land shall stone him with stones.

3 And I will set my face against that man, and will cut him off from among his people; because he hath given of his seed unto Molech, to defile my sanctuary, and to profane my holy name.   Lev. 17:10; 18:21; Ezek. 5:11

4 And if the people of the land do any ways hide their eyes from the man, when he giveth of his seed unto Molech, and kill him not:

5 Then I will set my face against that man, and against his family, and will cut him off, and all that go a whoring after him,

to commit ^Twhoredom with Molech, from among their people.   *prostitution*

6 And the soul that turneth after such as have familiar spirits, and after wizards, to go ^Ta whoring after them, I will even set my face against that soul, and will cut him off from among his people. Lev. 19:31 ◆ *giving sex as a prostitute*

> **20:6, 7 Wizards—or God**
>
> Shall those who have a holy God, infinite in wisdom and power, go unto wizards, whose knowledge comes from intimacy with the enemy of our Lord? God Himself is the light of His people; He bids them fix their eyes by faith upon the glories that are veiled from human sight. *PP 687, 688*

7 Sanctify yourselves therefore, and be ye holy: for I *am* the LORD your God.   Eph. 1:4

> **20:7 Work of Reconciliation**
>
> It is the work of conversion and sanctification to reconcile men to God by bringing them into accord with the principles of His law. *GC 467*

8 And ye shall keep my statutes, and do them: I *am* the LORD which sanctify you.

9 For every one that curseth his father or his mother shall be surely put to death: he hath cursed his father or his mother; his blood *shall be* upon him. Ex. 21:17; Deut. 27:16; 2 Sam. 1:16

Punishment for Adultery

10 And the man that committeth adultery with *another* man's wife, *even he* that committeth adultery with his neighbour's wife, the adulterer and the adulteress shall surely be put to death.   Ex. 20:14

11 And the man that lieth with his father's wife hath uncovered his father's nakedness: both of them shall surely be put to death; their blood *shall be* upon them.   Deut. 27:20

12 And if a man lie with his daughter in law, both of them shall surely be put to death: they have ^Twrought confusion; their blood *shall be* upon them.   Lev. 18:15, 23 ◆ *made*

13 If a man also lie with mankind, as he lieth with a woman, both of them have committed an abomination: they shall surely be put to death; their blood *shall be* upon them.   Lev. 18:22; Deut. 23:17; 1 Cor. 6:9

14 And if a man take a wife and her mother, it *is* wickedness: they shall be burnt with fire, both he and they; that there be no wickedness among you.   Lev. 18:17; Deut. 27:23

15 And if a man lie with a beast, he shall surely be put to death: and ye shall slay the beast.   Ex. 22:19; Lev. 18:23; Deut. 27:21

16 And if a woman approach unto any beast, and lie down thereto, thou shalt kill the woman, and the beast: they shall surely be put to death; their blood *shall be* upon them.

17 And if a man shall take his sister, his father's daughter, or his mother's daughter, and see her nakedness, and she see his nakedness; it *is* a wicked thing; and they shall be cut off in the sight of their people: he hath uncovered his sister's nakedness; he shall bear his iniquity.   Lev. 18:9; Deut. 27:22

18 And if a man shall lie with a woman having her sickness, and shall uncover her nakedness; he hath discovered her fountain, and she hath uncovered the fountain of her blood: and both of them shall be cut off from among their people.   Lev. 15:24; 18:19

19 And thou shalt not uncover the nakedness of thy mother's sister, nor of thy father's sister: for he uncovereth his near kin: they shall bear their iniquity.   Lev. 18:6

20 And if a man shall lie with his uncle's wife, he hath uncovered his uncle's nakedness: they shall bear their sin; they shall die childless.   Lev. 18:14

21 And if a man shall take his brother's

Deceptions of Spiritualism

Leviticus 20:6, 27

In the days of the Hebrews there was a class of people who claimed, as do the spiritualists of today, to hold communication with the dead. But the "familiar spirits," as these visitants from other worlds were called, are declared by the Bible to be "the spirits of devils." (Compare Numbers 25:1–3; Psalm 106:28; 1 Corinthians 10:20; Revelation 16:14.) The work of dealing with familiar spirits was pronounced an abomination to the Lord, and was solemnly forbidden under penalty of death (Leviticus 19:31; 20:27). The very name of witchcraft is now held in contempt. The claim that men can hold intercourse [communication] with evil spirits is regarded as a fable of the Dark Ages. But spiritualism, which numbers its converts by hundreds of thousands, yea, by millions, which has made its way into scientific circles, which has invaded churches, and has found favor in legislative bodies, and even in the courts of kings—this mammoth deception is but a revival, in a new disguise, of the witchcraft condemned and prohibited of old.

If there were no other evidence of the real character of spiritualism, it should be enough for the Christian that the spirits make no difference between righteousness and sin, between the noblest and purest of the apostles of Christ and the most corrupt of the servants of Satan. *GC 556, 557*

wife, it *is* an unclean thing: he hath uncovered his brother's nakedness; they shall be childless.　　　　Lev. 18:16

Obedience Is Required with Holiness

22 Ye shall therefore keep all my statutes, and all my judgments, and do them: that the land, whither I bring you to dwell therein, spue you not out.　　　　Lev. 18:25-28

23 And ye shall not walk in the manners of the nation, which I cast out before you: for they committed all these things, and therefore I ᵀabhorred them.　Lev. 18:3, 24, 30 ◆ *despised*

24 But I have said unto you, Ye shall inherit their land, and I will give it unto you to possess it, a land that floweth with milk and honey: I *am* the LORD your God, which have separated you from *other* people.　　1 Kin. 8:53

25 Ye shall therefore put difference between clean beasts and unclean, and between unclean fowls and clean: and ye shall not make your souls abominable by beast, or by fowl, or by any manner of living thing that creepeth on the ground, which I have separated from you as unclean.　　　　Lev. 11

26 And ye shall be holy unto me: for I the LORD *am* holy, and have severed you from *other* people, that ye should be mine. Lev. 19:2

27 A man also or woman that hath a familiar spirit, or that is a wizard, shall surely be put to death: they shall stone them with stones: their blood *shall be* upon them.　Lev. 19:31; 20:6

Rules for the Priests

21 And the LORD said unto Moses, Speak unto the priests the sons of Aaron, and say unto them, There shall none be defiled for the dead among his people: Lev. 21:11

2 But for his kin, that is near unto him, *that is,* for his mother, and for his father, and for his son, and for his daughter, and for his brother,

3 And for his sister a virgin, that is nigh unto him, which hath had no husband; for her may he be defiled.

4 *But* he shall not defile himself, *being* a chief man among his people, to profane himself.

5 They shall not make baldness upon their head, neither shall they shave off the corner of their beard, nor make any cuttings in their flesh.　　Lev. 19:27-28; Deut. 14:1; Ezek. 44:20

6 They shall be holy unto their God, and not profane the name of their God: for the offerings of the LORD made by fire, *and* the bread of their God, they do offer: therefore they shall be holy.　　　　Lev. 3:11; 18:21

7 They shall not take a wife *that is* a whore, or profane; neither shall they take a woman put away from her husband: for he *is* holy unto his God.　　　　Lev. 21:13-14

8 Thou shalt sanctify him therefore; for he offereth the bread of thy God: he shall be holy unto thee: for I the LORD, which sanctify you, *am* holy.　　　　Lev. 21:6

9 And the daughter of any priest, if she profane herself by playing the ᵀwhore, she profaneth her father: she shall be burnt with fire.　　　　Gen. 38:24 ◆ *prostitute*

10 And *he that is* the high priest among his brethren, upon whose head the anointing oil was poured, and that is ᵀconsecrated to put on the garments, shall not uncover his head, nor ᵀrend his clothes;　　set apart ◆ *tear apart*

11 Neither shall he go in to any dead body, nor defile himself for his father, or for his mother;　　Lev. 19:28; 21:1-2; Num. 19:14

12 Neither shall he go out of the sanctuary, nor profane the sanctuary of his God; for the crown of the anointing oil of his God *is* upon him: I *am* the LORD.　Ex. 29:6-7; Lev. 8:30; 10:7

Nothing But Perfection

Leviticus 21:10

A high priest was not to rend his garments. By the Levitical law, this was prohibited under sentence of death. Under no circumstances, on no occasion, was the priest to rend his robe. It was the custom among the Jews for the garments to be rent at the death of friends, but this custom the priests were not to observe. Express command had been given by Christ to Moses concerning this. Leviticus 10:6.

Everything worn by the priest was to be whole and without blemish. By those beautiful official garments was represented the character of the great antitype, Jesus Christ. Nothing but perfection, in dress and attitude, in word and spirit, could be acceptable to God. He is holy, and His glory and perfection must be represented by the earthly service. Nothing but perfection could properly represent the sacredness of the heavenly service. Finite man might rend his own heart by showing a contrite and humble spirit. This God would discern. But no rent must be made in the priestly robes, for this would mar the representation of heavenly things. The high priest who dared to appear in holy office, and engage in the service of the sanctuary, with a rent robe, was looked upon as having severed himself from God. By rending his garment he cut himself off from being a representative character. He was no longer accepted by God as an officiating priest. This course of action, as exhibited by Caiaphas, showed human passion, human imperfection. *DA 708, 709*

13 And he shall take a wife in her virginity.
14 A widow, or a divorced woman, or profane, *or* an harlot, these shall he not take: but he shall take a virgin of his own people to wife. Lev. 21:7
15 Neither shall he profane his seed among his people: for I the LORD do sanctify him.

Priests with Imperfections Are Not Allowed to Minister

16 And the LORD spake unto Moses, saying,
17 Speak unto Aaron, saying, Whosoever *he be* of thy seed in their generations that hath *any* blemish, let him not approach to offer the bread of his God. Lev. 10:3
18 For whatsoever man *he be* that hath a blemish, he shall not approach: a blind man, or a lame, or he that hath a flat nose, or any thing ᵀsuperfluous, Lev. 22:19-25 ◆ *more than needed*
19 Or a man that is brokenfooted, or brokenhanded,
20 Or crookbackt, or a dwarf, or that hath a blemish in his eye, or be scurvy, or scabbed, or hath his stones broken; Deut. 23:1
21 No man that hath a blemish of the seed of Aaron the priest shall come nigh to offer the offerings of the LORD made by fire: he hath a blemish; he shall not come nigh to offer the bread of his God. Lev. 21:6
22 He shall eat the bread of his God, *both* of the most holy, and of the holy. Lev. 2:3
23 Only he shall not go in unto the ᵀvail, nor come nigh unto the altar, because he hath a blemish; that he profane not my sanctuaries: for I the LORD do sanctify them. Lev. 21:12 ◆ *veil*
24 And Moses told *it* unto Aaron, and to his sons, and unto all the children of Israel.

The Priests in Their Uncleanness Must Abstain from the Holy Things

22 And the LORD spake unto Moses, saying,
2 Speak unto Aaron and to his sons, that they separate themselves from the holy things of the children of Israel, and that they profane not my holy name *in those things* which they ᵀhallow unto me: I *am* the LORD. Lev. 18:21 ◆ *render as sacred*
3 Say unto them, Whosoever *he be* of all your seed among your generations, that goeth unto the holy things, which the children of Israel hallow unto the LORD, having his uncleanness upon him, that soul shall be cut off from my presence: I *am* the LORD. Lev. 7:20-21
4 What man soever of the seed of Aaron *is* a leper, or hath a running issue; he shall not eat of the holy things, until he be clean. And whoso toucheth any thing *that is* unclean *by* the dead, or a man whose seed goeth from him; Lev. 11:39
5 Or whosoever toucheth any creeping

thing, whereby he may be made unclean, or a man of whom he may take uncleanness, whatsoever uncleanness he hath; Lev. 15:7
6 The soul which hath touched any such shall be unclean until even, and shall not eat of the holy things, unless he wash his flesh with water. Lev. 15:5
7 And when the sun is down, he shall be clean, and shall afterward eat of the holy things; because it *is* his food. Lev. 21:22
8 That which dieth of itself, or is torn *with beasts*, he shall not eat to defile himself therewith: I *am* the LORD. Lev. 17:15
9 They shall therefore keep mine ordinance, lest they bear sin for it, and die therefore, if they profane it: I the LORD do ᵀsanctify them. Ex. 28:43; Num. 18:22 ◆ *make them holy*

Who of the Priest's House May Eat of the Holy Things

10 There shall no stranger eat *of* the holy thing: a sojourner of the priest, or an hired servant, shall not eat *of* the holy thing.
11 But if the priest buy *any* soul with his money, he shall eat of it, and he that is born in his house: they shall eat of his meat.
12 If the priest's daughter also be *married* unto a stranger, she may not eat of an offering of the holy things.
13 But if the priest's daughter be a widow, or divorced, and have no child, and is returned unto her father's house, as in her youth, she shall eat of her father's meat: but there shall no stranger eat thereof. Gen. 38:11
14 And if a man eat *of* the holy thing unwittingly, then he shall put the fifth *part* thereof unto it, and shall give *it* unto the priest with the holy thing. Lev. 27:13
15 And they shall not profane the holy things of the children of Israel, which they offer unto the LORD; Lev. 19:8; Num. 18:32
16 Or suffer them to bear the iniquity of ᵀtrespass, when they eat their holy things: for I the LORD do sanctify them. Lev. 22:9 ◆ *sin*

The Sacrifices Must Be without Blemish

17 And the LORD spake unto Moses, saying,
18 Speak unto Aaron, and to his sons, and unto all the children of Israel, and say unto them, Whatsoever *he be* of the house of Israel, or of the strangers in Israel, that will offer his ᵀoblation for all his vows, and for all his freewill offerings, which they will offer unto the LORD for a burnt offering; Lev. 1:2 ◆ *offering*
19 *Ye shall offer* at your own will a male without blemish, of the ᵀbeeves, of the sheep, or of the goats. Lev. 1:3 ◆ *plowing cattle*
20 *But* whatsoever hath a blemish, *that* shall ye not offer: for it shall not be acceptable for you. Deut. 15:21; 17:1; Mal. 1:8
21 And whosoever offereth a sacrifice of

peace offerings unto the LORD to accomplish *his* vow, or a freewill offering in beeves or sheep, it shall be perfect to be accepted; there shall be no blemish therein. Lev. 3:6; Num. 15:3, 8

22 Blind, or broken, or maimed, or having a ^Twen, or scurvy, or scabbed, ye shall not offer these unto the LORD, nor make an offering by fire of them upon the altar unto the LORD.   Lev. 22:20 ◆ *oozing sore*

22:20–22 Spotless Sacrifice

In that ancient ritual which is the gospel in symbol, no blemished offering could be brought to God's altar. The sacrifice that was to represent Christ must be spotless. The word of God points to this as an illustration of what His children are to be—"a living sacrifice," "holy and without blemish" (Romans 12:1; Ephesians 5:27). *PK 489*

---

23 Either a bullock or a lamb that hath any thing superfluous or lacking in his parts, that mayest thou offer *for* a freewill offering; but for a vow it shall not be accepted.   Lev. 21:18

24 Ye shall not offer unto the LORD that which is bruised, or crushed, or broken, or cut; neither shall ye make *any offering thereof* in your land.   Lev. 22:20

25 Neither from a stranger's hand shall ye offer the bread of your God of any of these; because their corruption *is* in them, *and* blemishes *be* in them: they shall not be accepted for you.   Lev. 21:6

26 And the LORD spake unto Moses, saying,

27 When a ^Tbullock, or a sheep, or a goat, is brought forth, then it shall be seven days under the ^Tdam; and from the eighth day and thenceforth it shall be accepted for an offering made by fire unto the LORD.   *bull ◆ mother*

28 And *whether it be* cow or ewe, ye shall not kill it and her young both in one day.

29 And when ye will offer a sacrifice of thanksgiving unto the LORD, offer *it* at your own will.   Ps. 107:22

30 On the same day it shall be eaten up; ye shall leave none of it until the morrow: I *am* the LORD.

31 Therefore shall ye keep my commandments, and do them: I *am* the LORD. Lev. 19:37

32 Neither shall ye profane my holy name; but I will be hallowed among the children of Israel: I *am* the LORD which hallow you,

33 That brought you out of the land of Egypt, to be your God: I *am* the LORD.   Lev. 11:45

The Feasts of the Lord

23 And the LORD spake unto Moses, saying,

2 Speak unto the children of Israel, and say unto them, *Concerning* the feasts of the LORD, which ye shall proclaim *to be* holy convocations, *even* these *are* my feasts.   Ex. 23:14-17

3 Six days shall work be done: but the seventh day *is* the sabbath of rest, an holy convocation; ye shall do no work *therein*: it *is* the sabbath of the LORD in all your dwellings.   Ex. 20:8-11; 23:12; Lev. 19:3

The Passover

4 These *are* the feasts of the LORD, *even* holy convocations, which ye shall proclaim in their seasons.   Lev. 23:2

5 In the fourteenth *day* of the first month at even *is* the LORD's passover.   Deut. 16:1-8

6 And on the fifteenth day of the same month *is* the feast of unleavened bread unto the LORD: seven days ye must eat unleavened bread.   Ex. 12:15-16

Symbols and Reality

Leviticus 23

Says Paul: "Christ our Passover is sacrificed for us" (1 Corinthians 5:7). The sheaf of first fruits, which at the time of the Passover was waved before the Lord, was typical [symbolic] of the resurrection of Christ. Paul says, in speaking of the resurrection of the Lord and of all His people: "Christ the first fruits; afterward they that are Christ's at His coming" (1 Corinthians 15:23). Like the wave sheaf, which was the first ripe grain gathered before the harvest, Christ is the first fruits of that immortal harvest of redeemed ones that at the future resurrection shall be gathered into the garner of God.

These types [symbols] were fulfilled, not only as to the event, but as to the time. On the fourteenth day of the first Jewish month, the very day and month on which for fifteen long centuries the Passover lamb had been slain, Christ, having eaten the Passover with His disciples, instituted that feast which was to commemorate His own death as "the Lamb of God, which taketh away the sin of the world." That same night He was taken by wicked hands to be crucified and slain. And as the antitype [reality toward which the symbols pointed] of the wave sheaf our Lord was raised from the dead on the third day, "the first fruits of them that slept," a sample of all the resurrection just, whose "vile body" shall be changed, and "fashioned like unto His glorious body" (verse 20; Philippians 3:21).

In like manner the types [symbols] which relate to the second advent must be fulfilled at the time pointed out in the symbolic service. *GC 399, 400*

7 In the first day ye shall have an holy convocation: ye shall do no servile work therein.   Lev. 23:8

8 But ye shall offer an offering made by fire unto the LORD seven days: in the seventh day *is* an holy convocation: ye shall do no servile work *therein*.

9 And the LORD spake unto Moses, saying,

10 Speak unto the children of Israel, and say unto them, When ye be come into the land which I give unto you, and shall reap the harvest thereof, then ye shall bring a sheaf of the firstfruits of your harvest unto the priest: Ex. 23:19; 34:26; Num. 28:26

11 And he shall wave the sheaf before the LORD, to be accepted for you: on the morrow after the sabbath the priest shall wave it.

23:5–11 Symbols of Christ

All the ceremonies of the feast were types [symbols] of the work of Christ. The deliverance of Israel from Egypt was an object lesson of redemption, which the Passover was intended to keep in memory. The slain lamb, the unleavened bread, the sheaf of first fruits, represented the Saviour. *DA 77*

---

12 And ye shall offer that day when ye wave the sheaf an he lamb without blemish of the first year for a burnt offering unto the LORD.   Lev. 1:10

13 And the meat offering thereof *shall be* two tenth deals of fine flour mingled with oil, an offering made by fire unto the LORD *for* a sweet savour: and the drink offering thereof *shall be* of wine, the fourth *part* of an hin.   Lev. 2:14-16

14 And ye shall eat neither bread, nor parched corn, nor green ears, until the selfsame day that ye have brought an offering unto your God: *it shall be* a statute for ever throughout your generations in all your dwellings.   Ex. 34:26

The Feast of Pentecost

15 And ye shall count unto you from the morrow after the sabbath, from the day that ye brought the sheaf of the wave offering; seven sabbaths shall be complete: Ex. 34:22

16 Even unto the morrow after the seventh sabbath shall ye number fifty days; and ye shall offer a new meat offering unto the LORD.   Acts 2:1

17 Ye shall bring out of your habitations two wave loaves of two tenth deals: they shall be of fine flour; they shall be baken with leaven; *they are* the firstfruits unto the LORD. Lev. 23:10

18 And ye shall offer with the bread seven lambs without blemish of the first year, and one young [T]bullock, and two rams: they shall be *for* a burnt offering unto the LORD,

with their meat offering, and their drink offerings, *even* an offering made by fire, of sweet savour unto the LORD.   bull

19 Then ye shall sacrifice one kid of the goats for a sin offering, and two lambs of the first year for a sacrifice of peace offerings.   Num. 28:30

20 And the priest shall wave them with the bread of the firstfruits *for* a wave offering before the LORD, with the two lambs: they shall be holy to the LORD for the priest.   Deut. 18:4

21 And ye shall proclaim on the selfsame day, *that* it may be an holy convocation unto you: ye shall do no servile work *therein: it shall be* a statute for ever in all your dwellings throughout your generations.   Lev. 23:2

22 And when ye reap the harvest of your land, thou shalt not make clean riddance of the corners of thy field when thou reapest, neither shalt thou gather any [T]gleaning of thy harvest: thou shalt leave them unto the poor, and to the stranger: I *am* the LORD your God.   Deut. 24:19-21 ✦ *leftovers from a field*

The Feast of Trumpets

23 And the LORD spake unto Moses, saying,

24 Speak unto the children of Israel, saying, In the seventh month, in the first *day* of the month, shall ye have a sabbath, a memorial of blowing of trumpets, an holy convocation.   Lev. 25:9; Num. 10:9-10; 1 Cor. 15:52

25 Ye shall do no servile work *therein*: but ye shall offer an offering made by fire unto the LORD.   Lev. 23:21

26 And the LORD spake unto Moses, saying,

27 Also on the tenth *day* of this seventh month *there shall be* a day of atonement: it shall be an holy convocation unto you; and ye shall afflict your souls, and offer an offering made by fire unto the LORD.   Lev. 25:9

28 And ye shall do no work in that same day: for it *is* a day of atonement, to make an atonement for you before the LORD your God.   Lev. 16:34

29 For whatsoever soul *it be* that shall not be afflicted in that same day, he shall be cut off from among his people.   Gen. 17:14

30 And whatsoever soul *it be* that doeth any work in that same day, the same soul will I destroy from among his people.   Lev. 20:3

31 Ye shall do no manner of work: *it shall be* a statute for ever throughout your generations in all your dwellings.

32 It *shall be* unto you a sabbath of rest, and ye shall afflict your souls: in the ninth *day* of the month at even, from even unto even, shall ye celebrate your sabbath.

The Sabbath   See John 19:31.

The Feast of Tabernacles

33 And the LORD spake unto Moses, saying,
34 Speak unto the children of Israel, saying, The fifteenth day of this seventh month *shall be* the feast of tabernacles *for* seven days unto the LORD.   Ezra 3:4; Neh. 8:14; John 7:2
35 On the first day *shall be* an holy convocation: ye shall do no servile work *therein.*
36 Seven days ye shall offer an offering made by fire unto the LORD: on the eighth day shall be an holy convocation unto you; and ye shall offer an offering made by fire unto the LORD: it *is* a solemn assembly; *and* ye shall do no servile work *therein.*   Neh. 8:18; John 7:37
37 These *are* the feasts of the LORD, which ye shall proclaim *to be* holy convocations, to offer an offering made by fire unto the LORD, a burnt offering, and a meat offering, a sacrifice, and drink offerings, every thing upon his day: Lev. 23:2, 4
38 Beside the sabbaths of the LORD, and beside your gifts, and beside all your vows, and beside all your freewill offerings, which ye give unto the LORD.   Num. 29:39
39 Also in the fifteenth day of the seventh month, when ye have gathered in the fruit of the land, ye shall keep a feast unto the LORD seven days: on the first day *shall be* a sabbath, and on the eighth day *shall be* a sabbath.

23:34, 39 Pointing Back—and Ahead

The Feast of Tabernacles was not only commemorative but typical [symbolic]. It not only pointed back to the wilderness sojourn, but, as the feast of harvest, it celebrated the ingathering of the fruits of the earth, and pointed forward to the great day of final ingathering. *PP 541*

40 And ye shall take you on the first day the boughs of goodly trees, branches of palm trees, and the boughs of thick trees, and willows of the brook; and ye shall rejoice before the LORD your God seven days.   Deut. 16:14-15
41 And ye shall keep it a feast unto the LORD seven days in the year. *It shall be* a statute for ever in your generations: ye shall celebrate it in the seventh month.   Num. 29:12
42 Ye shall dwell in booths seven days; all that are Israelites born shall dwell in booths: Neh. 8:14-17
43 That your generations may know that I made the children of Israel to dwell in booths, when I brought them out of the land of Egypt: I *am* the LORD your God.   Deut. 31:10-13
44 And Moses declared unto the children of Israel the feasts of the LORD.

The Oil for the Lamps That They May Burn Continually

24 And the LORD spake unto Moses, saying,
2 Command the children of Israel, that they bring unto thee pure oil olive beaten for the light, to cause the lamps to burn continually.   Ex. 27:20-21
3 Without the [T]vail of the testimony, in the tabernacle of the congregation, shall Aaron order it from the evening unto the morning before the LORD continually: *it shall be* a statute for ever in your generations.   *veil*
4 He shall order the lamps upon the pure candlestick before the LORD continually.
5 And thou shalt take fine flour, and bake twelve cakes thereof: two tenth deals shall be in one cake.   Ex. 25:30; 40:23
6 And thou shalt set them in two rows, six on a row, upon the pure table before the LORD.   Ex. 25:23-24; 1 Kin. 7:48; 2 Chr. 4:19
7 And thou shalt put pure frankincense upon each row, that it may be on the bread for a memorial, *even* an offering made by fire unto the LORD.   Lev. 2:2
8 Every sabbath he shall set it in order before the LORD continually, *being taken* from the children of Israel by an everlasting covenant.   Num. 4:7; 1 Chr. 9:32; 2 Chr. 2:4
9 And it shall be Aaron's and his sons'; and they shall eat it in the holy place: for it *is* most holy unto him of the offerings of the LORD made by fire by a perpetual statute.   Lev. 8:31; Matt. 12:4; Mark 2:26

24:5–9 The Living Bread

Both the manna and the showbread pointed to Christ, the living Bread, who is ever in the presence of God for us. He Himself said, "I am the living Bread which came down from heaven" (John 6:48–51). Frankincense was placed upon the loaves. When the bread was removed every Sabbath, to be replaced by fresh loaves, the frankincense was burned upon the altar as a memorial before God. *PP 354*

Shelomith's Son Blasphemes

10 And the son of an Israelitish woman, whose father *was* an Egyptian, went out among the children of Israel: and this son of the Israelitish *woman* and a man of Israel strove together in the camp;
11 And the Israelitish woman's son blasphemed the name *of the* LORD, and cursed. And they brought him unto Moses: (and his mother's name *was* Shelomith, the daughter of Dibri, of the tribe of Dan:)   Ex. 3:15
12 And they put him in ward, that the mind of the LORD might be shewed them.
13 And the LORD spake unto Moses, saying,
14 Bring forth him that hath cursed without the camp; and let all that heard *him* lay their hands upon his head, and let all the congregation stone him.   Lev. 20:27; Deut. 17:7; 21:21
15 And thou shalt speak unto the children

of Israel, saying, Whosoever curseth his God shall bear his sin.   Lev. 5:1

16 And he that blasphemeth the name of the Lord, he shall surely be put to death, *and* all the congregation shall certainly stone him: as well the stranger, as he that is born in the land, when he blasphemeth the name *of the* Lord, shall be put to death.   Matt. 12:31

17 And he that killeth any man shall surely be put to death.   Gen. 9:5-6

18 And he that killeth a beast shall make it good; beast for beast.   Lev. 24:21

19 And if a man cause a blemish in his neighbour; as he hath done, so shall it be done to him;   Deut. 19:21

20 Breach for breach, eye for eye, tooth for tooth: as he hath caused a blemish in a man, so shall it be done to him *again*.   Deut. 19:21

21 And he that killeth a beast, he shall restore it: and he that killeth a man, he shall be put to death.   Lev. 24:17-18

22 Ye shall have one manner of law, as well for the stranger, as for one of your own country: for I *am* the Lord your God.   Ex. 12:49

23 And Moses spake to the children of Israel, that they should bring forth him that had cursed out of the camp, and stone him with stones. And the children of Israel did as the Lord commanded Moses.

The Sabbath of the Seventh Year and the Jubilee in the Fiftieth Year

25 And the Lord spake unto Moses in mount Sinai, saying,

2 Speak unto the children of Israel, and say unto them, When ye come into the land which I give you, then shall the land keep a sabbath unto the Lord.   Ex. 23:10

3 Six years thou shalt sow thy field, and six years thou shalt prune thy vineyard, and gather in the fruit thereof;

4 But in the seventh year shall be a sabbath of rest unto the land, a sabbath for the Lord: thou shalt neither sow thy field, nor prune thy vineyard.

5 That which groweth of its own accord of thy harvest thou shalt not reap, neither gather the grapes of thy vine undressed: *for* it is a year of rest unto the land.   2 Kin. 19:29

6 And the sabbath of the land shall be meat for you; for thee, and for thy servant, and for thy maid, and for thy hired servant, and for thy stranger that sojourneth with thee,

7 And for thy cattle, and for the beast that *are* in thy land, shall all the increase thereof be meat.

8 And thou shalt number seven sabbaths of years unto thee, seven times seven years; and the space of the seven sabbaths of years shall be unto thee forty and nine years.   Lev. 23:15

9 Then shalt thou cause the trumpet of the jubile to sound on the tenth *day* of the seventh month, in the day of atonement shall ye make the trumpet sound throughout all your land.   Lev. 23:24, 27

10 And ye shall ᵀhallow the fiftieth year, and proclaim liberty throughout *all* the land unto all the inhabitants thereof: it shall be a jubile unto you; and ye shall return every man unto his possession, and ye shall return every man unto his family.   Ex. 20:2; Jer. 34:8 ◆ *render as sacred*

11 A jubile shall that fiftieth year be unto you: ye shall not sow, neither reap that which groweth of itself in it, nor gather *the* grapes in it of thy vine undressed.

12 For it *is* the jubile; it shall be holy unto you: ye shall eat the increase thereof out of the field.   Lev. 25:6-7

On Social Equality

Leviticus 25

The Lord would place a check upon the inordinate love of property and power. Great evils would result from the continued accumulation of wealth by one class, and the poverty and degradation of another. Without some restraint the power of the wealthy would become a monopoly, and the poor, though in every respect fully as worthy in God's sight, would be regarded and treated as inferior to their more prosperous brethren. The sense of this oppression would arouse the passions of the poorer class. There would be a feeling of despair and desperation which would tend to demoralize society and open the door to crimes of every description. The regulations that God established were designed to promote social equality. The provisions of the sabbatical year and the jubilee would, in a great measure, set right that which during the interval had gone wrong in the social and political economy of the nation.

These regulations were designed to bless the rich no less than the poor. They would restrain avarice and a disposition for self-exaltation, and would cultivate a noble spirit of benevolence; and by fostering good will and confidence between all classes, they would promote social order, the stability of government. We are all woven together in the great web of humanity, and whatever we can do to benefit and uplift others will reflect in blessing upon ourselves. The law of mutual dependence runs through all classes of society. *PP 534, 535*

13 In the year of this jubile ye shall return every man unto his possession.   Lev. 25:10

14 And if thou sell ought unto thy neighbour, or buyest *ought* of thy neighbour's hand, ye shall not oppress one another: Lev. 19:13

15 According to the number of years after the jubile thou shalt buy of thy neighbour, *and* according unto the number of years of the fruits he shall sell unto thee:

16 According to the multitude of years thou shalt increase the price thereof, and according to the fewness of years thou shalt diminish the price of it: for *according* to the number *of the years* of the fruits doth he sell unto thee.

17 Ye shall not therefore oppress one another; but thou shalt fear thy God: for I *am* the LORD your God.   Lev. 19:14, 32; 25:43

25:14, 17 Considering Others

God's word sanctions no policy that will enrich one class by the oppression and suffering of another. In all our business transactions it teaches us to put ourselves in the place of those with whom we are dealing, to look not only on our own things, but also on the things of others. *MH 187*

---

18 Wherefore ye shall do my statutes, and keep my judgments, and do them; and ye shall dwell in the land in safety. Ps. 4:8; Jer. 23:6

19 And the land shall yield her fruit, and ye shall eat your fill, and dwell therein in safety.   Lev. 26:5

20 And if ye shall say, What shall we eat the seventh year? behold, we shall not sow, nor gather in our increase: Lev. 25:4

21 Then I will command my blessing upon you in the sixth year, and it shall bring forth fruit for three years.   Deut. 28:8

22 And ye shall sow the eighth year, and eat *yet* of old fruit until the ninth year; until her fruits come in ye shall eat *of* the old store.   Lev. 26:10

The Redemption of Land

23 The land shall not be sold for ever: for the land *is* mine; for ye *are* strangers and sojourners with me.   1 Chr. 29:15

24 And in all the land of your possession ye shall grant a redemption for the land.

25 If thy brother be waxen poor, and hath sold away *some* of his possession, and if any of his kin come to redeem it, then shall he redeem that which his brother sold. Ruth 2:20

26 And if the man have none to redeem it, and himself be able to redeem it;

27 Then let him count the years of the sale thereof, and restore the overplus unto the man to whom he sold it; that he may return unto his possession.

28 But if he be not able to restore *it* to him, then that which is sold shall remain in the hand of him that hath bought it until the year of jubile: and in the jubile it shall go out, and he shall return unto his possession.

29 And if a man sell a dwelling house in a walled city, then he may redeem it within a whole year after it is sold; *within* a full year may he redeem it.

30 And if it be not redeemed within the space of a full year, then the house that *is* in the walled city shall be established for ever to him that bought it throughout his generations: it shall not go out in the jubile.

31 But the houses of the villages which have no wall round about them shall be counted as the fields of the country: they may be redeemed, and they shall go out in the jubile.

32 Notwithstanding the cities of the Levites, *and* the houses of the cities of their possession, may the Levites redeem at any time.

33 And if a man purchase of the Levites, then the house that was sold, and the city of his possession, shall go out in *the year of* jubile: for the houses of the cities of the Levites *are* their possession among the children of Israel.

34 But the field of the suburbs of their cities may not be sold; for it *is* their perpetual possession.   Lev. 25:23

35 And if thy brother ᵀbe waxen poor, and fallen in decay with thee; then thou shalt relieve him: *yea, though he be* a stranger, or a sojourner; that he may live with thee.   becomes

36 Take thou no usury of him, or increase: but fear thy God; that thy brother may live with thee.   Ex. 22:25; Lev. 25:17; Deut. 23:19-20

37 Thou shalt not give him thy money upon ᵀusury, nor lend him thy ᵀvictuals for increase.   interest charged ◆ food

38 I *am* the LORD your God, which brought you forth out of the land of Egypt, to give you the land of Canaan, *and* to be your God.

The Usage of Bondmen

39 And if thy brother *that dwelleth* by thee be waxen poor, and be sold unto thee; thou shalt not compel him to serve as a bondservant: Ex. 21:2; Lev. 25:46; 1 Kin. 9:22

40 *But* as an hired servant, *and* as a sojourner, he shall be with thee, *and* shall serve thee unto the year of jubile:

41 And *then* shall he depart from thee, *both* he and his children with him, and shall return unto his own family, and unto the possession of his fathers shall he return. Ex. 21:3; Lev. 25:28

42 For they *are* my servants, which I brought forth out of the land of Egypt: they shall not be sold as bondmen.   Lev. 25:55

43 Thou shalt not rule over him with rigour; but shalt fear thy God.   Ex. 1:13-14; Col. 4:1

44 Both thy bondmen, and thy bondmaids, which thou shalt have, *shall be* of the heathen that are round about you; of them shall ye buy bondmen and bondmaids.
45 Moreover of the children of the strangers that do sojourn among you, of them shall ye buy, and of their families that *are* with you, which they ᵀbegat in your land: and they shall be your possession.   **brought forth**
46 And ye shall take them as an inheritance for your children after you, to inherit *them for* a possession; they shall be your bondmen for ever: but over your brethren the children of Israel, ye shall not rule one over another with rigour.
47 And if a sojourner or stranger ᵀwax rich by thee, and thy brother *that dwelleth* by him wax poor, and sell himself unto the stranger *or* sojourner by thee, or to the stock of the stranger's family: **becomes**
48 After that he is sold he may be redeemed again; one of his brethren may redeem him:
49 Either his uncle, or his uncle's son, may redeem him, or *any* that is nigh of kin unto him of his family may redeem him; or if he be able, he may redeem himself.   Lev. 25:26
50 And he shall reckon with him that bought him from the year that he was sold to him unto the year of jubile: and the price of his sale shall be according unto the number of years, according to the time of an hired servant shall it be with him.   Is. 16:14
51 If *there be* yet many years *behind*, according unto them he shall give again the price of his redemption out of the money that he was bought for.
52 And if there remain but few years unto the year of jubile, then he shall count with him, *and* according unto his years shall he give him again the price of his redemption.
53 *And* as a yearly hired servant shall he be with him: *and the other* shall not rule with rigour over him in thy sight.
54 And if he be not redeemed in these *years*, then he shall go out in the year of jubile, *both* he, and his children with him.   Ex. 21:2-3
55 For unto me the children of Israel *are* servants; they *are* my servants whom I brought forth out of the land of Egypt: I *am* the LORD your God.   Lev. 25:42

Blessings for Obedience

26 Ye shall make you no idols nor ᵀgraven image, neither rear you up a standing image, neither shall ye set up *any* image of stone in your land, to bow down unto it: for I *am* the LORD your God. Lev. 19:4 ◆ *engraved or cut out*
2 Ye shall keep my sabbaths, and reverence my sanctuary: I *am* the LORD.   Lev. 19:30
3 If ye walk in my statutes, and keep my commandments, and do them;   Deut. 28:1-14

4 Then I will give you rain in due season, and the land shall yield her increase, and the trees of the field shall yield their fruit. Ps. 67:6
5 And your threshing shall reach unto the vintage, and the vintage shall reach unto the sowing time: and ye shall eat your bread to the full, and dwell in your land safely.
6 And I will give peace in the land, and ye shall lie down, and none shall make *you* afraid: and I will rid evil beasts out of the land, neither shall the sword go through your land.   Is. 35:9; Jer. 30:10; Zeph. 3:13
7 And ye shall chase your enemies, and they shall fall before you by the sword.
8 And five of you shall chase an hundred, and an hundred of you shall put ten thousand to flight: and your enemies shall fall before you by the sword. Deut. 32:30; Josh. 23:10
9 For I will have respect unto you, and make you fruitful, and multiply you, and establish my covenant with you.   Gen. 17:6-7
10 And ye shall eat old store, and bring forth the old because of the new.   Lev. 25:22
11 And I will set my tabernacle among you: and my soul shall not ᵀabhor you.   *despise*
12 And I will walk among you, and will be your God, and ye shall be my people. Gen. 3:8
13 I *am* the LORD your God, which brought you forth out of the land of Egypt, that ye should not be their bondmen; and I have broken the bands of your yoke, and made you go upright.   Ex. 20:2; Lev. 25:38; Ezek. 34:27

26:3–13 Stewards of God's Goods

Great blessings were promised to Israel on condition of obedience to the Lord's directions. . . .
A diversity of condition is one of the means by which God designs to prove and develop character. Yet He intends that those who have worldly possessions shall regard themselves merely as stewards of His goods, as entrusted with means to be employed for the benefit of the suffering and the needy. *PP 535*

Curses for Disobedience

14 But if ye will not hearken unto me, and will not do all these commandments; Mal. 2:2
15 And if ye shall despise my statutes, or if your soul abhor my judgments, so that ye will not do all my commandments, *but* that ye break my covenant: 2 Kin. 17:15
16 I also will do this unto you; I will even appoint over you terror, consumption, and the burning ᵀague, that shall consume the eyes, and cause sorrow of heart: and ye shall sow your seed in vain, for your enemies shall eat it.   Deut. 28:21-22; 1 Sam. 2:33; Job 31:8 ◆ *fever*
17 And I will set my face against you, and ye shall be slain before your enemies: they that

hate you shall reign over you; and ye shall flee when none pursueth you. Lev. 17:10; Ps. 53:5
18 And if ye will not yet for all this hearken unto me, then I will punish you seven times more for your sins. Lev. 26:21, 24, 28
19 And I will break the pride of your power; and I will make your heaven as iron, and your earth as brass: Deut. 28:23
20 And your strength shall be spent in vain: for your land shall not yield her increase, neither shall the trees of the land yield their fruits. Lev. 26:4; Ps. 127:1; Is. 49:4
21 And if ye walk contrary unto me, and will not hearken unto me; I will bring seven times more plagues upon you according to your sins.
22 I will also send wild beasts among you, which shall rob you of your children, and destroy your cattle, and make you few in number; and your *high* ways shall be desolate. Deut. 32:24

26:14–33 Dangers of Disobedience

By the mouth of His servants He predicts the dangers of disobedience. .... His people are kept in prosperity only by His mercy, through the vigilant watchcare of chosen instrumentalities. He cannot uphold and guard a people who reject His counsel and despise His reproofs. For a time He may withhold His retributive judgments; yet He cannot always stay His hand. *PK 426*

---

23 And if ye will not be reformed by me by these things, but will walk contrary unto me; Jer. 2:30; 5:3; Amos 4:6-12
24 Then will I also walk contrary unto you, and will punish you yet seven times for your sins. 2 Sam. 22:27
25 And I will bring a sword upon you, that shall avenge the quarrel of *my* covenant: and when ye are gathered together within your cities, I will send the pestilence among you; and ye shall be delivered into the hand of the enemy. Num. 14:12; Deut. 28:21; Ezek. 5:17
26 *And* when I have broken the staff of your bread, ten women shall bake your bread in one oven, and they shall deliver *you* your bread again by weight: and ye shall eat, and not be satisfied. Ps. 105:16; Is. 3:1; Mic. 6:14
27 And if ye will not for all this hearken unto me, but walk contrary unto me; Lev. 26:21
28 Then I will walk contrary unto you also in fury; and I, even I, will chastise you seven times for your sins. Is. 59:18
29 And ye shall eat the flesh of your sons, and the flesh of your daughters shall ye eat.
30 And I will destroy your high places, and cut down your images, and cast your carcases upon the carcases of your idols, and my soul shall abhor you. 2 Kin. 23:20

31 And I will make your cities waste, and bring your sanctuaries unto desolation, and I will not smell the savour of your sweet odours. Neh. 2:3
32 And I will bring the land into desolation: and your enemies which dwell therein shall be astonished at it. Jer. 9:11; 18:16; 19:8
33 And I will scatter you among the heathen, and will draw out a sword after you: and your land shall be desolate, and your cities waste. Deut. 4:27; Ezek. 20:23; Zech. 7:14
34 Then shall the land enjoy her sabbaths, as long as it lieth desolate, and *ye be* in your enemies' land; *even* then shall the land rest, and enjoy her sabbaths. 2 Chr. 36:21
35 As long as it lieth desolate it shall rest; because it did not rest in your sabbaths, when ye dwelt upon it.
36 And upon them that are left *alive* of you I will send a faintness into their hearts in the lands of their enemies; and the sound of a shaken leaf shall chase them; and they shall flee, as fleeing from a sword; and they shall fall when none pursueth. Is. 30:17; Ezek. 21:7
37 And they shall fall one upon another, as it were before a sword, when none pursueth: and ye shall have no power to stand before your enemies. Josh. 7:12-13
38 And ye shall perish among the heathen, and the land of your enemies shall eat you up.
39 And they that are left of you shall pine away in their iniquity in your enemies' lands; and also in the iniquities of their fathers shall they pine away with them. Deut. 28:65

God Promises to Remember Those Who Repent

40 If they shall confess their iniquity, and the iniquity of their fathers, with their ᵀtrespass which they ᵀtrespassed against me, and that also they have walked contrary unto me; 1 Kin. 8:33-36 ♦ *sin* ♦ *sinned*
41 And *that* I also have walked contrary unto them, and have brought them into the land of their enemies; if then their uncircumcised hearts be humbled, and they then accept of the punishment of their iniquity: Ezek. 44:7
42 Then will I remember my covenant with Jacob, and also my covenant with Isaac, and also my covenant with Abraham will I remember; and I will remember the land. Ex. 2:24
43 The land also shall be left of them, and shall enjoy her sabbaths, while she lieth desolate without them: and they shall accept of the punishment of their iniquity: because, even because they despised my judgments, and because their soul ᵀabhorred my statutes. Lev. 26:15 ♦ *despised*
44 And yet for all that, when they be in the land of their enemies, I will not cast them

away, neither will I abhor them, to destroy them utterly, and to break my covenant with them: for I *am* the LORD their God.   Rom. 11:2

45 But I will for their sakes remember the covenant of their ancestors, whom I brought forth out of the land of Egypt in the sight of the heathen, that I might be their God: I *am* the LORD.   Lev. 22:33

46 These *are* the statutes and judgments and laws, which the LORD made between him and the children of Israel in mount Sinai by the hand of Moses.   Lev. 25:1; 27:34; Deut. 6:1

Gifts Pledged to the Lord

27 And the LORD spake unto Moses, saying,

2 Speak unto the children of Israel, and say unto them, When a man shall make a singular vow, the persons *shall be* for the LORD by thy estimation.   Num. 6:2

> **27:2–29 Full Consecration**
>
> He does not expect from all the same kind of service. . . . God accepts the offering of each. It is the consecration of the life and all its interests, that is necessary. Those who make this consecration will hear and obey the call of Heaven. *PK 221*

3 And thy estimation shall be of the male from twenty years old even unto sixty years old, even thy estimation shall be fifty shekels of silver, after the shekel of the sanctuary.   Ex. 30:13; Lev. 27:25; Num. 18:16

4 And if it *be* a female, then thy estimation shall be thirty shekels.

5 And if *it be* from five years old even unto twenty years old, then thy estimation shall be of the male twenty shekels, and for the female ten shekels.

6 And if *it be* from a month old even unto five years old, then thy estimation shall be of the male five shekels of silver, and for the female thy estimation *shall be* three shekels of silver.

7 And if *it be* from sixty years old and above; if *it be* a male, then thy estimation shall be fifteen shekels, and for the female ten shekels.

8 But if he be poorer than thy estimation, then he shall present himself before the priest, and the priest shall value him; according to his ability that vowed shall the priest value him.   Lev. 14:21-22

9 And if *it be* a beast, whereof men bring an offering unto the LORD, all that *any man* giveth of such unto the LORD shall be holy.

10 He shall not alter it, nor change it, a good for a bad, or a bad for a good: and if he shall at all change beast for beast, then it and the exchange thereof shall be holy.

11 And if *it be* any unclean beast, of which they do not offer a sacrifice unto the LORD, then he shall present the beast before the priest:

12 And the priest shall value it, whether it be good or bad: as thou valuest it, *who art* the priest, so shall it be.

13 But if he will at all redeem it, then he shall add a fifth *part* thereof unto thy estimation.   Lev. 27:15

Rules for Gifts Pledged to God

14 And when a man shall ᵀsanctify his house *to be* holy unto the LORD, then the priest shall estimate it, whether it be good or bad: as the priest shall estimate it, so shall it stand.   *make his house holy*

15 And if he that sanctified it will redeem his house, then he shall add the fifth *part* of the money of thy estimation unto it, and it shall be his.   Lev. 27:13

16 And if a man shall sanctify unto the LORD *some part* of a field of his possession, then thy estimation shall be according to the seed thereof: an homer of barley seed *shall be* valued at fifty shekels of silver.

17 If he sanctify his field from the year of jubile, according to thy estimation it shall stand.

18 But if he sanctify his field after the jubile, then the priest shall reckon unto him the money according to the years that remain, even unto the year of the jubile, and it shall be ᵀabated from thy estimation.   *diminished*

19 And if he that ᵀsanctified the field will in any wise redeem it, then he shall add the fifth *part* of the money of thy estimation unto it, and it shall be assured to him.   *made the field holy*

20 And if he will not redeem the field, or if he have sold the field to another man, it shall not be redeemed any more.

21 But the field, when it goeth out in the jubile, shall be holy unto the LORD, as a field devoted; the possession thereof shall be the priest's.   Lev. 25:10; Num. 18:14; Ezek. 44:29

22 And if *a man* sanctify unto the LORD a field which he hath bought, which *is* not of the fields of his possession;   Lev. 25:10

23 Then the priest shall reckon unto him the worth of thy estimation, *even* unto the year of the jubile: and he shall give thine estimation in that day, *as* a holy thing unto the LORD.   Lev. 27:18

24 In the year of the jubile the field shall return unto him of whom it was bought, *even* to him to whom the possession of the land *did belong*.   Lev. 25:28

25 And all thy estimations shall be according

to the shekel of the sanctuary: twenty gerahs shall be the shekel. Ex. 30:13; Num. 3:47

26 Only the ᵀfirstling of the beasts, which should be the LORD's firstling, no man shall sanctify it; whether *it be* ox, or sheep: it *is* the LORD's. Ex. 13:2, 12-13; 22:30 ◆ *firstborn*

27 And if *it be* of an unclean beast, then he shall redeem *it* according to thine estimation, and shall add a fifth *part* of it thereto: or if it be not redeemed, then it shall be sold according to thy estimation.

28 Notwithstanding no devoted thing, that a man shall devote unto the LORD of all that he hath, *both* of man and beast, and of the field of his possession, shall be sold or redeemed: every devoted thing *is* most holy unto the LORD. Ex. 22:20; Lev. 27:21; Josh. 6:17-19

29 None devoted, which shall be devoted of men, shall be redeemed; *but* shall surely be put to death.

30 And all the tithe of the land, *whether* of the seed of the land, *or* of the fruit of the tree, *is* the LORD's: *it is* holy unto the LORD.

31 And if a man will at all redeem *ought* of his tithes, he shall add thereto the fifth *part* thereof.

32 And concerning the ᵀtithe of the herd, or of the flock, *even* of whatsoever passeth under the rod, the tenth shall be holy unto the LORD. Jer. 33:13; Ezek. 20:37 ◆ *one-tenth*

Managing God's Gifts See Malachi 3:7, 8.

33 He shall not search whether it be good or bad, neither shall he change it: and if he change it at all, then both it and the change thereof shall be holy; it shall not be redeemed. Lev. 27:10

34 These *are* the commandments, which the LORD commanded Moses for the children of Israel in mount Sinai. Lev. 26:46

27:30-32

THE FOURTH BOOK OF MOSES CALLED

NUMBERS

The Book of Numbers describes the taking of two censuses (or numberings) of Israel's population. The first occurs at the beginning of the book, while the people are still at Mount Sinai, to assess the number of fighting men aged twenty and older in preparation for taking the Promised Land. Israel's population count at this time is estimated to be about two-and-one-half million. The second census is taken at the end of the book, over four decades later, on the Plains of Moab, as the people once again prepare to take the land. In between the two censuses is a story of unfaithfulness, defeat, and wandering—yet of God's great love and mercy through it all.

On the edge of the Promised Land, the people's faith dissipates, their fear overwhelms them, and they forget the great power of their God who had brought them out of Egypt. The report from the fact-finding mission of the spies about giants in the land causes a rebellion. Because of the people's lack of faith, God refuses to allow them to enter and sends them to wander. The journey from Mount Sinai to the Promised Land takes only eleven days, but that eleven-day journey turns into forty years—enough time for the faithless people to die and the new generation to receive the land and achieve the original goal.

Dates

Roughly thirty-nine years pass in Numbers (1444–1405 B.C.). The catalogue of Israel's journey begins from their last days at Mount Sinai (where they were camped at the end of the Book of Exodus), to the Promised Land the first time, wandering through Kadesh, and finally ends back at the Plains of Moab (chapter 33) and the people's second approach to the Promised Land.

Author

Moses' authorship has been championed based on external and internal evidence. Passages found in the New Testament, namely John 3:14, Acts 7, 1 Corinthians 10, Hebrews 3—4 (external evidence). Over eighty instances of God speaking directly to Moses can be found, along with statements of Moses' writing: "And the LORD spake unto Moses" (Numbers 1:1); "And Moses wrote their goings out according to their journeys by the commandment of the LORD" (33:2) (internal evidence).

Meaning of the Name

As with Leviticus, the title of Numbers in Hebrew is the first phrase in the book: *Wayyedabber,* which means "And He Said." In Jewish writings, however, it is referred to as *Bemidbar,* which means "In the Wilderness." *Bemidbar* is the fifth word in 1:1. The title, Numbers, was translated from the Greek word *Arithmoi.* In the Vulgate, the Latin *Liberi Numeri,* or "Book of Numbers," corresponds with the Greek title.

Christ in Numbers

Moses' lifting of a brass serpent foreshadows the lifting of Christ on the cross. Those bitten by snakes who look at the brass serpent are healed (21:4–9). Jesus refers to this incident in John 3:14: "And as Moses lifted up the serpent in the wilderness, even so must the Son of man be lifted up." Jesus also says, "And I, if I be lifted up from the earth, will draw all men unto me" (John 12:32).

Several items in the Book of Numbers symbolize the coming Messiah. The manna given daily (Exodus 16; Numbers 11) is known as the bread from heaven. Jesus calls Himself the "Bread of Life" (John 6:26–40). In that passage Jesus says, "Moses gave you not that bread from heaven; but my Father giveth you the true bread from heaven" (John 6:32). In 1 Corinthians 10, Paul compares Jesus to the rock God used to quench the thirst of the Israelites (Numbers 20): "And did all drink the same spiritual drink: for they drank of that spiritual Rock that followed them: and that Rock was Christ" (1 Corinthians 10:4). Also, the red heifer "without spot" (Numbers 19:2) used as a sacrifice symbolizes the sinless Savior who later would be sacrificed.

Balaam, the chosen instrument of King Balak of Moab to curse the Israelites, speaks a true prophecy that refers to the coming of Christ: "I shall see him, but not now: I shall behold him, but not nigh: there shall come a Star out of Jacob, and a Sceptre shall rise out of Israel, and shall smite the corners of Moab, and destroy all the children of Sheth" (24:17).

Overview

The nation of Israel goes from being a nation poised to enter a land to a nation wandering away from that land. Numbers has three major divisions:

(1) *Numbers 1—12, Mount Sinai to Kadesh:* In chapters 1—9, the people of Israel are numbered in preparation for entering and possessing the land of Canaan. But a series of poor decisions derail that journey. Constant complaints rouse God's anger, yet in His mercy He always provides (see, for example, 11:1–15). Even Miriam and Aaron are not above complaining (chapter 12).

(2) *Numbers 13:1—22:1, Delay at Kadesh:* A most regrettable situation occurs when the spies return from exploring the land of Canaan (chapters 13—14). While they present the bounty of the land, they also describe walled cities and gigantic people. The people rebel, saying that they should just return to Egypt. Israel's unwillingness to believe in God's ability to aid them in possessing the land ushers in a new era: that of aimless wandering.

(3) *Numbers 22:2—36:13, At Moab:* God begins to prepare a new generation to enter the land.

Unlocking Numbers

KEY PEOPLE:
Moses, Aaron, Miriam, Joshua, Caleb, Korah, Dathan, Abiram, Balaam, Og, Bashan, Balak, the daughters of Zelophehad

KEY EVENTS:
The census of Israel's fighting men and the positioning of the tribes for travel and for encampment; sending spies to Canaan and Israel's subsequent rebellion; the rebellion of some of Israel's leaders; Moses barred from entering the Promised Land; Moses lifts a brass serpent on a pole; Balaam's oracles; the inheritance request of the daughters of Zelophehad

KEY WORD:
Wanderings. Israel's rebellion leads to forty years of wandering in the wilderness.

KEY VERSES:
"Because all those men which have seen my glory, and my miracles, which I did in Egypt and in the wilderness, and have tempted me now these ten times, and have not hearkened to my voice; Surely they shall not see the land which I sware unto their fathers, neither shall any of them that provoked me see it: But my servant Caleb, because he had another spirit with him, and hath followed me fully, him will I bring into the land whereinto he went; and his seed shall possess it" (Numbers 14:22–24).

KEY CHAPTER:
Numbers 14 is the most pivotal moment in Israel's history as the people reject the counsel of Moses, Aaron, Joshua, and Caleb and turn their back on God's wishes for them. As a result, God promises them that only Joshua, Caleb, and their children will enter Canaan.

God Commands Moses to Number the People

1 And the LORD spake unto Moses in the wilderness of Sinai, in the tabernacle of the congregation, on the first *day* of the second month, in the second year after they were come out of the land of Egypt, saying,   Ex. 19:1

2 Take ye the sum of all the congregation of the children of Israel, after their families, by the house of their fathers, with the number of *their* names, every male by their polls;   Ex. 30:12

3 From twenty years old and upward, all that are able to go forth to war in Israel: thou and Aaron shall number them by their armies.   Ex. 30:14; Num. 14:29

4 And with you there shall be a man of every tribe; every one head of the house of his fathers.   Num. 1:16

5 And these *are* the names of the men that shall stand with you: of *the tribe of* Reuben; Elizur the son of Shedeur.   Num. 7:30

6 Of Simeon; Shelumiel the son of Zurishaddai.   Num. 7:36

7 Of Judah; Nahshon the son of Amminadab.   Luke 3:32

8 Of Issachar; Nethaneel the son of Zuar.

9 Of Zebulun; Eliab the son of Helon.

10 Of the children of Joseph: of Ephraim; Elishama the son of Ammihud: of Manasseh; Gamaliel the son of Pedahzur. Num. 7:48

11 Of Benjamin; Abidan the son of Gideoni.

12 Of Dan; Ahiezer the son of Ammishaddai.   Num. 7:66

13 Of Asher; Pagiel the son of Ocran. Num. 7:72

14 Of Gad; Eliasaph the son of Deuel.

15 Of Naphtali; Ahira the son of Enan.

16 These *were* the renowned of the congregation, princes of the tribes of their fathers, heads of thousands in Israel.   Ex. 18:21, 25

17 And Moses and Aaron took these men which are expressed by *their* names:

18 And they assembled all the congregation together on the first *day* of the second month, and they declared their pedigrees after their families, by the house of their fathers, according to the number of the names, from twenty years old and upward, by their polls.   Ezra 2:59

19 As the LORD commanded Moses, so he numbered them in the wilderness of Sinai.

20 And the children of Reuben, Israel's eldest son, by their generations, after their families, by the house of their fathers, according to the number of the names, by their polls, every male from twenty years old and upward, all that were able to go forth to war;   Num. 26:5-7

21 Those that were numbered of them, *even* of the tribe of Reuben, *were* forty and six thousand and five hundred.   Num. 26:7

22 Of the children of Simeon, by their generations, after their families, by the house of their fathers, those that were numbered of them, according to the number of the names, by their polls, every male from twenty years old and upward, all that were able to go forth to war;   Num. 26:12-14

23 Those that were numbered of them, *even* of the tribe of Simeon, *were* fifty and nine thousand and three hundred.   Num. 26:14

24 Of the children of Gad, by their generations, after their families, by the house of their fathers, according to the number of the names, from twenty years old and upward, all that were able to go forth to war; Num. 26:15-18

25 Those that were numbered of them, *even* of the tribe of Gad, *were* forty and five thousand six hundred and fifty.   Num. 26:18

26 Of the children of Judah, by their generations, after their families, by the house of their fathers, according to the number of the names, from twenty years old and upward, all that were able to go forth to war;   Gen. 29:35

27 Those that were numbered of them, *even* of the tribe of Judah, *were* [T]threescore and fourteen thousand and six hundred.   *sixty*

28 Of the children of Issachar, by their generations, after their families, by the house of their fathers, according to the number of the names, from twenty years old and upward, all that were able to go forth to war;

29 Those that were numbered of them, *even* of the tribe of Issachar, *were* fifty and four thousand and four hundred.   Num. 26:25

30 Of the children of Zebulun, by their generations, after their families, by the house of their fathers, according to the number of the names, from twenty years old and upward, all that were able to go forth to war; Num. 26:26-27

31 Those that were numbered of them, *even* of the tribe of Zebulun, *were* fifty and seven thousand and four hundred.   Num. 26:27

32 Of the children of Joseph, *namely*, of the children of Ephraim, by their generations, after their families, by the house of their fathers, according to the number of the names, from twenty years old and upward, all that were able to go forth to war;   Num. 26:35-37

33 Those that were numbered of them, *even* of the tribe of Ephraim, *were* forty thousand and five hundred.   Num. 26:37

34 Of the children of Manasseh, by their generations, after their families, by the house of their fathers, according to the number of the names, from twenty years old and upward, all that were able to go forth to war;

35 Those that were numbered of them, *even* of the tribe of Manasseh, *were* thirty and two thousand and two hundred.   Num. 26:34

36 Of the children of Benjamin, by their generations, after their families, by the house of their fathers, according to the number of the names, from twenty years old and upward, all that were able to go forth to war; Gen. 49:27
37 Those that were numbered of them, *even* of the tribe of Benjamin, *were* thirty and five thousand and four hundred. Num. 26:41
38 Of the children of Dan, by their generations, after their families, by the house of their fathers, according to the number of the names, from twenty years old and upward, all that were able to go forth to war; Gen. 46:23
39 Those that were numbered of them, *even* of the tribe of Dan, *were* threescore and two thousand and seven hundred. Num. 26:43
40 Of the children of Asher, by their generations, after their families, by the house of their fathers, according to the number of the names, from twenty years old and upward, all that were able to go forth to war;
41 Those that were numbered of them, *even* of the tribe of Asher, *were* forty and one thousand and five hundred. Num. 26:47
42 Of the children of Naphtali, throughout their generations, after their families, by the house of their fathers, according to the number of the names, from twenty years old and upward, all that were able to go forth to war;
43 Those that were numbered of them, *even* of the tribe of Naphtali, *were* fifty and three thousand and four hundred. Num. 26:50
44 These *are* those that were numbered, which Moses and Aaron numbered, and the princes of Israel, *being* twelve men: each one was for the house of his fathers. Num. 26:64
45 So were all those that were numbered of the children of Israel, by the house of their fathers, from twenty years old and upward, all that were able to go forth to war in Israel;
46 Even all they that were numbered were six hundred thousand and three thousand and five hundred and fifty. Ex. 12:37; Num. 26:51

The Levites Are Exempted for the Service of the Lord

47 But the Levites after the tribe of their fathers were not numbered among them.

> **1:47–54 An Honored Tribe**
>
> By divine direction the tribe of Levi was set apart for the service of the sanctuary. . . . Now, instead of the first-born of all Israel, the Lord accepted the tribe of Levi for the work of the sanctuary. By this signal honor He manifested His approval of their fidelity, both in adhering to His service and in executing His judgments when Israel apostatized in the worship of the golden calf. *PP 350*

48 For the LORD had spoken unto Moses, saying,
49 Only thou shalt not number the tribe of Levi, neither take the sum of them among the children of Israel: Num. 26:62
50 But thou shalt appoint the Levites over the tabernacle of testimony, and over all the vessels thereof, and over all things that *belong* to it: they shall bear the tabernacle, and all the vessels thereof; and they shall minister unto it, and shall encamp round about the tabernacle. Ex. 31:18; 38:21; Num. 4:15
51 And when the tabernacle setteth forward, the Levites shall take it down: and when the tabernacle is to be pitched, the Levites shall set it up: and the stranger that cometh nigh shall be put to death. Num. 3:10, 38; 18:22
52 And the children of Israel shall pitch their tents, every man by his own camp, and every man by his own ᵀstandard, throughout their hosts. Num. 2:2, 34 ♦ *flag*
53 But the Levites shall pitch round about the tabernacle of testimony, that there be no wrath upon the congregation of the children of Israel: and the Levites shall keep the charge of the tabernacle of testimony. Lev. 10:6; Num. 16:46
54 And the children of Israel did according to all that the LORD commanded Moses, so did they.

The Order of the Tribes in Their Tents

2 And the LORD spake unto Moses and unto Aaron, saying,
2 Every man of the children of Israel shall pitch by his own standard, with the ᵀensign of their father's house: far off about the tabernacle of the congregation shall they pitch. *banner*

> **2:2 Arrangement of Israel's Camp**
>
> The Hebrew camp was arranged in exact order. It was separated into three great divisions, each having its appointed position in the encampment. In the center was the tabernacle, the abiding place of the invisible King. Around it were stationed the priests and Levites. Beyond these were encamped all the other tribes. *PP 374, 375*

3 And on the east side toward the rising of the sun shall they of the standard of the camp of Judah pitch throughout their armies: and Nahshon the son of Amminadab *shall be* captain of the children of Judah. Ruth 4:20
4 And his host, and those that were numbered of them, *were* ᵀthreescore and fourteen thousand and six hundred. *sixty*
5 And those that do pitch next unto him *shall be* the tribe of Issachar: and Nethaneel the son of Zuar *shall be* captain of the children of Issachar. Num. 1:8

6 And his host, and those that were numbered thereof, *were* fifty and four thousand and four hundred.

7 *Then* the tribe of Zebulun: and Eliab the son of Helon *shall be* captain of the children of Zebulun.   Num. 1:9

8 And his host, and those that were numbered thereof, *were* fifty and seven thousand and four hundred.

9 All that were numbered in the camp of Judah *were* an hundred thousand and ^Tfourscore thousand and six thousand and four hundred, throughout their armies. These shall first set forth.   Num. 10:14 ◆ *eighty*

10 On the south side *shall be* the ^Tstandard of the camp of Reuben according to their armies: and the captain of the children of Reuben *shall be* Elizur the son of Shedeur.   *flag*

11 And his host, and those that were numbered thereof, *were* forty and six thousand and five hundred.

12 And those which pitch by him *shall be* the tribe of Simeon: and the captain of the children of Simeon *shall be* Shelumiel the son of Zurishaddai.   Num. 1:6

13 And his host, and those that were numbered of them, *were* fifty and nine thousand and three hundred.

14 Then the tribe of Gad: and the captain of the sons of Gad *shall be* Eliasaph the son of Reuel.   Num. 1:14

15 And his host, and those that were numbered of them, *were* forty and five thousand and six hundred and fifty.

16 All that were numbered in the camp of Reuben *were* an hundred thousand and fifty and one thousand and four hundred and fifty, throughout their armies. And they shall set forth in the second rank.   Num. 10:18

17 Then the tabernacle of the congregation shall set forward with the camp of the Levites in the midst of the camp: as they encamp, so shall they set forward, every man in his place by their standards.   Num. 10:21

18 On the west side *shall be* the standard of the camp of Ephraim according to their armies: and the captain of the sons of Ephraim *shall be* Elishama the son of Ammihud.   Num. 1:10

19 And his host, and those that were numbered of them, *were* forty thousand and five hundred.

20 And by him *shall be* the tribe of Manasseh: and the captain of the children of Manasseh *shall be* Gamaliel the son of Pedahzur.   Num. 1:10

21 And his host, and those that were numbered of them, *were* thirty and two thousand and two hundred.

22 Then the tribe of Benjamin: and the captain of the sons of Benjamin *shall be* Abidan the son of Gideoni.   Num. 1:11

23 And his host, and those that were numbered of them, *were* thirty and five thousand and four hundred.

24 All that were numbered of the camp of Ephraim *were* an hundred thousand and eight thousand and an hundred, throughout their armies. And they shall go forward in the third rank.   Num. 10:22

25 The standard of the camp of Dan *shall be* on the north side by their armies: and the captain of the children of Dan *shall be* Ahiezer the son of Ammishaddai.   Num. 1:12

26 And his host, and those that were numbered of them, *were* threescore and two thousand and seven hundred.

27 And those that encamp by him *shall be* the tribe of Asher: and the captain of the children of Asher *shall be* Pagiel the son of Ocran.   Num. 1:13

28 And his host, and those that were numbered of them, *were* forty and one thousand and five hundred.

29 Then the tribe of Naphtali: and the captain of the children of Naphtali *shall be* Ahira the son of Enan.   Num. 1:15

30 And his host, and those that were numbered of them, *were* fifty and three thousand and four hundred.

31 All they that were numbered in the camp of Dan *were* an hundred thousand and fifty and seven thousand and six hundred. They shall go hindmost with their standards.   Num. 10:25

32 These *are* those which were numbered of the children of Israel by the house of their fathers: all those that were numbered of the camps throughout their hosts *were* six hundred thousand and three thousand and five hundred and fifty.   Ex. 38:26; Num. 1:46

33 But the Levites were not numbered among the children of Israel; as the LORD commanded Moses.

34 And the children of Israel did according to all that the LORD commanded Moses: so they pitched by their standards, and so they set forward, every one after their families, according to the house of their fathers.   Num. 24:2

The Sons of Aaron

3 These also *are* the generations of Aaron and Moses in the day *that* the LORD spake with Moses in mount Sinai.   Ex. 6:20

2 And these *are* the names of the sons of Aaron; Nadab the firstborn, and Abihu, Eleazar, and Ithamar.   Ex. 6:23; Num. 26:60

3 These *are* the names of the sons of Aaron, the priests which were anointed, whom

he [T]consecrated to minister in the priest's office.   Ex. 28:41; Lev. 8:1-9, 12 ◆ *set apart*
4 And Nadab and Abihu died before the LORD, when they offered strange fire before the LORD, in the wilderness of Sinai, and they had no children: and Eleazar and Ithamar ministered in the priest's office in the sight of Aaron their father.   Lev. 10:1-2; Num. 26:61

3:4 Neglected Discipline

Nadab and Abihu had not in their youth been trained to habits of self-control. The father's yielding disposition, his lack of firmness for right, had led him to neglect the discipline of his children. . . . Habits of self-indulgence, long cherished, obtained a hold upon them which even the responsibility of the most sacred office had not power to break. They had not been taught to respect the authority of their father, and they did not realize the necessity of exact obedience to the requirements of God. *PP 360*

5 And the LORD spake unto Moses, saying,
6 Bring the tribe of Levi near, and present them before Aaron the priest, that they may minister unto him.
7 And they shall keep his charge, and the charge of the whole congregation before the tabernacle of the congregation, to do the service of the tabernacle.   Num. 1:50
8 And they shall keep all the instruments of the tabernacle of the congregation, and the charge of the children of Israel, to do the service of the tabernacle.
9 And thou shalt give the Levites unto Aaron and to his sons: they *are* wholly given unto him out of the children of Israel.
10 And thou shalt appoint Aaron and his sons, and they shall wait on their priest's office: and the stranger that cometh nigh shall be put to death.   Num. 1:51; 3:38; 18:7
11 And the LORD spake unto Moses, saying,
12 And I, behold, I have taken the Levites from among the children of Israel instead of all the firstborn that openeth the [T]matrix among the children of Israel: therefore the Levites shall be mine;   Num. 3:41 ◆ *womb*
13 Because all the firstborn *are* mine; *for* on the day that I smote all the firstborn in the land of Egypt I hallowed unto me all the firstborn in Israel, both man and beast: mine shall they be: I *am* the LORD.   Ex. 13:2

3:13 Importance of the First-Born

The dedication of the first-born had its origin in the earliest times. God had promised to give the First-born of heaven to save the sinner. This gift was to be acknowledged in every household by the consecration of the first-born son. He was to be devoted to the priesthood, as a representative of Christ among men. *DA 51*

The Levites Are Numbered by Their Families

14 And the LORD spake unto Moses in the wilderness of Sinai, saying,
15 Number the children of Levi after the house of their fathers, by their families: every male from a month old and upward shalt thou number them.   Num. 26:62
16 And Moses numbered them according to the word of the LORD, as he was commanded.
17 And these were the sons of Levi by their names; Gershon, and Kohath, and Merari.
18 And these *are* the names of the sons of Gershon by their families; Libni, and Shimei.
19 And the sons of Kohath by their families; Amram, and Izehar, Hebron, and Uzziel.
20 And the sons of Merari by their families; Mahli, and Mushi. These *are* the families of the Levites according to the house of their fathers.   Ex. 6:19
21 Of Gershon *was* the family of the Libnites, and the family of the Shimites: these *are* the families of the Gershonites.
22 Those that were numbered of them, according to the number of all the males, from a month old and upward, *even* those that were numbered of them *were* seven thousand and five hundred.
23 The families of the Gershonites shall pitch behind the tabernacle westward.   Num. 1:53
24 And the chief of the house of the father of the Gershonites *shall be* Eliasaph the son of Lael.
25 And the charge of the sons of Gershon in the tabernacle of the congregation *shall be* the tabernacle, and the tent, the covering thereof, and the hanging for the door of the tabernacle of the congregation,   Ex. 25:9
26 And the hangings of the court, and the curtain for the door of the court, which *is* by the tabernacle, and by the altar round about, and the cords of it for all the service thereof.   Ex. 35:18
27 And of Kohath *was* the family of the Amramites, and the family of the Izeharites, and the family of the Hebronites, and the family of the Uzzielites: these *are* the families of the Kohathites.   1 Chr. 26:23
28 In the number of all the males, from a month old and upward, *were* eight thousand and six hundred, keeping the charge of the sanctuary.
29 The families of the sons of Kohath shall pitch on the side of the tabernacle southward.   Num. 1:53
30 And the chief of the house of the father of the families of the Kohathites *shall be* Elizaphan the son of Uzziel.
31 And their charge *shall be* the ark, and the table, and the candlestick, and the altars,

and the vessels of the sanctuary wherewith they minister, and the hanging, and all the service thereof.

32 And Eleazar the son of Aaron the priest *shall be* chief over the chief of the Levites, *and have* the oversight of them that keep the charge of the sanctuary.

33 Of Merari *was* the family of the Mahlites, and the family of the Mushites: these *are* the families of Merari.

34 And those that were numbered of them, according to the number of all the males, from a month old and upward, *were* six thousand and two hundred.

35 And the chief of the house of the father of the families of Merari *was* Zuriel the son of Abihail: *these* shall pitch on the side of the tabernacle northward.　　　　　Num. 1:53

36 And *under* the custody and charge of the sons of Merari *shall be* the boards of the tabernacle, and the bars thereof, and the pillars thereof, and the sockets thereof, and all the vessels thereof, and all that serveth thereto,　　　　　　　　　Ex. 26:32

37 And the pillars of the court round about, and their sockets, and their pins, and their cords.

38 But those that encamp before the tabernacle toward the east, *even* before the tabernacle of the congregation eastward, *shall be* Moses, and Aaron and his sons, keeping the charge of the sanctuary for the charge of the children of Israel; and the stranger that cometh nigh shall be put to death.　　Num. 1:53; 2:3; 3:10

39 All that were numbered of the Levites, which Moses and Aaron numbered at the commandment of the LORD, throughout their families, all the males from a month old and upward, *were* twenty and two thousand.　　　　　　　　　Num. 26:62

The Firstborn Are Freed by the Levites

40 And the LORD said unto Moses, Number all the firstborn of the males of the children of Israel from a month old and upward, and take the number of their names.　　Num. 3:15

41 And thou shalt take the Levites for me (I *am* the LORD) instead of all the firstborn among the children of Israel; and the cattle of the Levites instead of all the firstlings among the cattle of the children of Israel. Num. 3:12, 45

42 And Moses numbered, as the LORD commanded him, all the firstborn among the children of Israel.

43 And all the firstborn males by the number of names, from a month old and upward, of those that were numbered of them, were twenty and two thousand two hundred and ᵀthreescore and thirteen.　　　　*sixty*

44 And the LORD spake unto Moses, saying,

45 Take the Levites instead of all the firstborn among the children of Israel, and the cattle of the Levites instead of their cattle; and the Levites shall be mine: I *am* the LORD.　　　　　　　Num. 3:12

46 And for those that are to be redeemed of the two hundred and threescore and thirteen of the firstborn of the children of Israel, which are more than the Levites;　Ex. 13:13

47 Thou shalt even take five shekels apiece by the ᵀpoll, after the shekel of the sanctuary shalt thou take *them*: (the shekel *is* twenty gerahs:)　　Ex. 30:13; Lev. 27:6, 25 ◆ *head*

48 And thou shalt give the money, wherewith the ᵀodd number of them is to be redeemed, unto Aaron and to his sons.　*excess*

49 And Moses took the redemption money of them that were over and above them that were redeemed by the Levites:

50 Of the firstborn of the children of Israel took he the money; a thousand three hundred and threescore and five *shekels*, after the shekel of the sanctuary:　　Num. 3:46-47

51 And Moses gave the money of them that were redeemed unto Aaron and to his sons, according to the word of the LORD, as the LORD commanded Moses.　　　Num. 3:48

The Age and Time of the Levites' Service

4 And the LORD spake unto Moses and unto Aaron, saying,

2 Take the sum of the sons of Kohath from among the sons of Levi, after their families, by the house of their fathers,

3 From thirty years old and upward even until fifty years old, all that enter into the host, to do the work in the tabernacle of the congregation.　　　　　　　Num. 4:23

4 This *shall be* the service of the sons of Kohath in the tabernacle of the congregation, *about* the most holy things:　　Num. 4:19

5 And when the camp setteth forward, Aaron shall come, and his sons, and they shall take down the covering ᵀvail, and cover the ark of testimony with it:　Matt. 27:51 ◆ *veil*

6 And shall put thereon the covering of badgers' skins, and shall spread over *it* a cloth wholly of blue, and shall put in the staves thereof.　　　　　　　Ex. 25:13-15

7 And upon the table of shewbread they shall spread a cloth of blue, and put thereon the dishes, and the spoons, and the bowls, and covers to cover ᵀwithal: and the continual bread shall be thereon:　Lev. 24:5-8 ◆ *with*

8 And they shall spread upon them a cloth of scarlet, and cover the same with a covering of badgers' skins, and shall put in the ᵀstaves thereof.　　　　*clubs or rods*

9 And they shall take a cloth of blue, and cover the candlestick of the light, and his lamps, and his tongs, and his snuffdishes,

and all the oil vessels thereof, wherewith they minister unto it: Ex. 25:31-39

10 And they shall put it and all the vessels thereof within a covering of badgers' skins, and shall put *it* upon a bar.

11 And upon the golden altar they shall spread a cloth of blue, and cover it with a covering of badgers' skins, and shall put to the staves thereof:

12 And they shall take all the instruments of ministry, wherewith they minister in the sanctuary, and put *them* in a cloth of blue, and cover them with a covering of badgers' skins, and shall put *them* on a bar: 1 Chr. 9:29

13 And they shall take away the ashes from the altar, and spread a purple cloth thereon:

14 And they shall put upon it all the vessels thereof, wherewith they minister about it, *even* the ᵀcensers, the fleshhooks, and the shovels, and the basons, all the vessels of the altar; and they shall spread upon it a covering of badgers' skins, and put to the staves of it.   *holders for burning incense*

15 And when Aaron and his sons have made an end of covering the sanctuary, and all the vessels of the sanctuary, as the camp is to set forward; after that, the sons of Kohath shall come to bear *it*: but they shall not touch *any* holy thing, lest they die. These *things are* the burden of the sons of Kohath in the tabernacle of the congregation.   Num. 7:9; 10:21; 2 Sam. 6:6-7

16 And to the office of Eleazar the son of Aaron the priest *pertaineth* the oil for the light, and the sweet incense, and the daily meat offering, and the anointing oil, *and* the oversight of all the tabernacle, and of all that therein *is*, in the sanctuary, and in the vessels thereof.   Ex. 25:6; 30:23-38; Lev. 24:2

4:5–16 Order Brings Success

God is a God of order. Everything connected with heaven is in perfect order; subjection and thorough discipline mark the movements of the angelic host. Success can only attend order and harmonious action. God requires order and system in His work now no less than in the days of Israel. All who are working for Him are to labor intelligently, not in a careless, haphazard manner. He would have His work done with faith and exactness, that He may place the seal of His approval upon it. *PP 376*

---

17 And the LORD spake unto Moses and unto Aaron, saying,

18 Cut ye not off the tribe of the families of the Kohathites from among the Levites:

19 But thus do unto them, that they may live, and not die, when they approach unto the most holy things: Aaron and his sons shall go in, and appoint them every one to his service and to his burden:

20 But they shall not go in to see when the holy things are covered, lest they die. Ex. 19:21

The Number of the Gershonites

21 And the LORD spake unto Moses, saying,

22 Take also the sum of the sons of Gershon, throughout the houses of their fathers, by their families;

23 From thirty years old and upward until fifty years old shalt thou number them; all that enter in to perform the service, to do the work in the tabernacle of the congregation.   Num. 4:3

24 This *is* the service of the families of the Gershonites, to serve, and for burdens:

25 And they shall bear the curtains of the tabernacle, and the tabernacle of the congregation, his covering, and the covering of the badgers' skins that *is* above upon it, and the hanging for the door of the tabernacle of the congregation,   Ex. 26:14

26 And the hangings of the court, and the hanging for the door of the gate of the court, which *is* by the tabernacle and by the altar round about, and their cords, and all the instruments of their service, and all that is made for them: so shall they serve.

27 At the appointment of Aaron and his sons shall be all the service of the sons of the Gershonites, in all their burdens, and in all their service: and ye shall appoint unto them in charge all their burdens.

28 This *is* the service of the families of the sons of Gershon in the tabernacle of the congregation: and their charge *shall be* under the hand of Ithamar the son of Aaron the priest.   Num. 4:33

29 As for the sons of Merari, thou shalt number them after their families, by the house of their fathers;

30 From thirty years old and upward even unto fifty years old shalt thou number them, every one that entereth into the service, to do the work of the tabernacle of the congregation.   Num. 4:3

31 And this *is* the charge of their burden, according to all their service in the tabernacle of the congregation; the boards of the tabernacle, and the bars thereof, and the pillars thereof, and sockets thereof,   Num. 3:36-37

32 And the pillars of the court round about, and their sockets, and their pins, and their cords, with all their instruments, and with all their service: and by name ye shall reckon the instruments of the charge of their burden.   Ex. 38:21

33 This *is* the service of the families of the sons of Merari, according to all their service, in the tabernacle of the congregation, under

the hand of Ithamar the son of Aaron the priest.   Num. 4:28

The Number of the Kohathites

34 And Moses and Aaron and the chief of the congregation numbered the sons of the Kohathites after their families, and after the house of their fathers,

35 From thirty years old and upward even unto fifty years old, every one that entereth into the service, for the work in the tabernacle of the congregation: Num. 4:23

36 And those that were numbered of them by their families were two thousand seven hundred and fifty.

37 These *were* they that were numbered of the families of the Kohathites, all that might do service in the tabernacle of the congregation, which Moses and Aaron did number according to the commandment of the Lord by the hand of Moses.

38 And those that were numbered of the sons of Gershon, throughout their families, and by the house of their fathers,

39 From thirty years old and upward even unto fifty years old, every one that entereth into the service, for the work in the tabernacle of the congregation,

40 Even those that were numbered of them, throughout their families, by the house of their fathers, were two thousand and six hundred and thirty.

41 These *are* they that were numbered of the families of the sons of Gershon, of all that might do service in the tabernacle of the congregation, whom Moses and Aaron did number according to the commandment of the Lord.

42 And those that were numbered of the families of the sons of Merari, throughout their families, by the house of their fathers,

43 From thirty years old and upward even unto fifty years old, every one that entereth into the service, for the work in the tabernacle of the congregation,

44 Even those that were numbered of them after their families, were three thousand and two hundred.

45 These *be* those that were numbered of the families of the sons of Merari, whom Moses and Aaron numbered according to the word of the Lord by the hand of Moses.

46 All those that were numbered of the Levites, whom Moses and Aaron and the chief of Israel numbered, after their families, and after the house of their fathers,

47 From thirty years old and upward even unto fifty years old, every one that came to do the service of the ministry, and the service of the burden in the tabernacle of the congregation,   Num. 4:3

48 Even those that were numbered of them, were eight thousand and five hundred and ᵀfourscore.   Num. 3:39 ◆ *eighty*

49 According to the commandment of the Lord they were numbered by the hand of Moses, every one according to his service, and according to his burden: thus were they numbered of him, as the Lord commanded Moses.   Num. 4:15

The Unclean Are Removed out of the Camp

5 And the Lord spake unto Moses, saying,

2 Command the children of Israel, that they put out of the camp every leper, and every one that hath an issue, and whosoever is defiled by the dead: Lev. 13:46; 21:1; Num. 9:6-10

3 Both male and female shall ye put out, without the camp shall ye put them; that

---

Most-Dreaded Disease

Numbers 5:2

Of all diseases known in the East the leprosy was most dreaded. Its incurable and contagious character, and its horrible effect upon its victims, filled the bravest with fear. Among the Jews it was regarded as a judgment on account of sin, and hence was called "the stroke," "the finger of God." Deep-rooted, ineradicable, deadly, it was looked upon as a symbol of sin. By the ritual law, the leper was pronounced unclean. Like one already dead, he was shut out from the habitations of men. Whatever he touched was unclean. The air was polluted by his breath. One who was suspected of having the disease must present himself to the priests, who were to examine and decide his case. If pronounced a leper, he was isolated from his family, cut off from the congregation of Israel, and was doomed to associate with those only who were similarly afflicted. The law was inflexible in its requirement. Even kings and rulers were not exempt. A monarch who was attacked by this terrible disease must yield up the scepter, and flee from society.

Away from his friends and his kindred, the leper must bear the curse of his malady. He was obliged to publish his own calamity, to rend his garments, and sound the alarm, warning all to flee from his contaminating presence. The cry, "Unclean! unclean!" coming in mournful tones from the lonely exile, was a signal heard with fear and abhorrence. *DA 262*

they defile not their camps, in the midst whereof I dwell.   Lev. 26:11-12

4 And the children of Israel did so, and put them out without the camp: as the LORD spake unto Moses, so did the children of Israel.

5 And the LORD spake unto Moses, saying,

6 Speak unto the children of Israel, When a man or woman shall commit any sin that men commit, to do a ᵀtrespass against the LORD, and that person be guilty;   *sin*

7 Then they shall confess their sin which they have done: and he shall ᵀrecompense his trespass with the principal thereof, and add unto it the fifth *part* thereof, and give *it* unto *him* against whom he hath ᵀtrespassed.   Lev. 5:5; 26:40; Josh. 7:19 ◆ *repay* ◆ *sinned*

8 But if the man have no kinsman to recompense the trespass unto, let the trespass be recompensed unto the LORD, *even* to the priest; beside the ram of the atonement, whereby an atonement shall be made for him.

9 And every offering of all the holy things of the children of Israel, which they bring unto the priest, shall be his.   Ex. 29:28

10 And every man's hallowed things shall be his: whatsoever any man giveth the priest, it shall be his.

The Trial of Unfaithfulness

11 And the LORD spake unto Moses, saying,

12 Speak unto the children of Israel, and say unto them, If any man's wife go aside, and commit a trespass against him,   Num. 5:19-20

13 And a man lie with her carnally, and it be hid from the eyes of her husband, and be kept close, and she be defiled, and *there be* no witness against her, neither she be taken *with the manner*;   Lev. 18:20; 20:10

14 And the spirit of jealousy come upon him, and he be jealous of his wife, and she be defiled: or if the spirit of jealousy come upon him, and he be jealous of his wife, and she be not defiled: Prov. 6:34

15 Then shall the man bring his wife unto the priest, and he shall bring her offering for her, the tenth *part* of an ephah of barley meal; he shall pour no oil upon it, nor put frankincense thereon; for it *is* an offering of jealousy, an offering of memorial, bringing iniquity to remembrance.   Lev. 5:11; Ezek. 29:16

16 And the priest shall bring her near, and set her before the LORD:

17 And the priest shall take holy water in an earthen vessel; and of the dust that is in the floor of the tabernacle the priest shall take, and put *it* into the water:

18 And the priest shall set the woman before the LORD, and uncover the woman's head, and put the offering of memorial in her hands, which *is* the jealousy offering: and the priest shall have in his hand the bitter water that causeth the curse:

19 And the priest shall charge her by an oath, and say unto the woman, If no man have lain with thee, and if thou hast not gone aside to uncleanness *with another* instead of thy husband, be thou free from this bitter water that causeth the curse:

20 But if thou hast gone aside *to another* instead of thy husband, and if thou be defiled, and some man have lain with thee beside thine husband:

21 Then the priest shall charge the woman with an oath of cursing, and the priest shall say unto the woman, The LORD make thee a curse and an oath among thy people, when the LORD doth make thy thigh to rot, and thy belly to swell;   Josh. 6:26

22 And this water that causeth the curse shall go into thy bowels, to make *thy* belly to swell, and *thy* thigh to rot: And the woman shall say, Amen, amen.   Ps. 109:18

23 And the priest shall write these curses in a book, and he shall blot *them* out with the bitter water:

24 And he shall cause the woman to drink the bitter water that causeth the curse: and the water that causeth the curse shall enter into her, *and become* bitter.

25 Then the priest shall take the jealousy offering out of the woman's hand, and shall wave the offering before the LORD, and offer it upon the altar: Lev. 8:27

26 And the priest shall take an handful of the offering, *even* the memorial thereof, and burn *it* upon the altar, and afterward shall cause the woman to drink the water. Lev. 2:2

27 And when he hath made her to drink the water, then it shall come to pass, *that*, if she be defiled, and have done trespass against her husband, that the water that causeth the curse shall enter into her, *and become* bitter, and her belly shall swell, and her thigh shall rot: and the woman shall be a curse among her people.   Jer. 29:18; 42:18; Zech. 8:13

28 And if the woman be not defiled, but be clean; then she shall be free, and shall conceive seed.

29 This *is* the law of jealousies, when a wife goeth aside *to another* instead of her husband, and is defiled;   Num. 5:19

30 Or when the spirit of jealousy cometh upon him, and he be jealous over his wife, and shall set the woman before the LORD, and the priest shall execute upon her all this law.

31 Then shall the man be guiltless from iniquity, and this woman shall bear her iniquity.

The Law of the Nazarites

6 And the LORD spake unto Moses, saying,

2 Speak unto the children of Israel, and say unto them, When either man or woman

shall separate *themselves* to vow a vow of a Nazarite, to separate *themselves* unto the LORD: Judg. 13:5; Amos 2:11-12; Rom. 1:1

3 He shall separate *himself* from wine and strong drink, and shall drink no vinegar of wine, or vinegar of strong drink, neither shall he drink any liquor of grapes, nor eat moist grapes, or dried.   Lev. 10:9; Judg. 13:14; Luke 1:15

4 All the days of his separation shall he eat nothing that is made of the vine tree, from the kernels even to the husk.   Num. 6:5

5 All the days of the vow of his separation there shall no razor come upon his head: until the days be fulfilled, in the which he separateth *himself* unto the LORD, he shall be holy, *and* shall let the locks of the hair of his head grow.   Judg. 13:5; 16:17; 1 Sam. 1:11

6 All the days that he separateth *himself* unto the LORD he shall come at no dead body.

> **6:2–6 Trained From Infancy**
>
> God directed that the future judge and deliverer of Israel should be trained to strict temperance from infancy. He was to be a Nazarite from his birth, thus being placed under a perpetual prohibition against the use of wine or strong drink. The lessons of temperance, self-denial, and self-control are to be taught to children even from babyhood. *PP 562*

7 He shall not make himself unclean for his father, or for his mother, for his brother, or for his sister, when they die: because the consecration of his God *is* upon his head.   Num. 9:6

8 All the days of his separation he *is* holy unto the LORD.

9 And if any man die very suddenly by him, and he hath defiled the head of his consecration; then he shall shave his head in the day of his cleansing, on the seventh day shall he shave it.   Num. 6:18

10 And on the eighth day he shall bring two turtles, or two young pigeons, to the priest, to the door of the tabernacle of the congregation: Lev. 15:14

11 And the priest shall offer the one for a sin offering, and the other for a burnt offering, and make an atonement for him, for that he sinned by the dead, and shall ᵀhallow his head that same day.   *render as sacred*

12 And he shall ᵀconsecrate unto the LORD the days of his separation, and shall bring a lamb of the first year for a trespass offering: but the days that were before shall be lost, because his separation was defiled.   *set apart*

13 And this *is* the law of the Nazarite, when the days of his separation are fulfilled: he shall be brought unto the door of the tabernacle of the congregation: Acts 21:26

14 And he shall offer his offering unto the LORD, one he lamb of the first year without blemish for a burnt offering, and one ewe lamb of the first year without blemish for a sin offering, and one ram without blemish for peace offerings,   Lev. 3:6

15 And a basket of unleavened bread, cakes of fine flour mingled with oil, and wafers of unleavened bread anointed with oil, and their meat offering, and their drink offerings.   Ex. 29:2; Lev. 2:4; Num. 15:10

16 And the priest shall bring *them* before the LORD, and shall offer his sin offering, and his burnt offering:

17 And he shall offer the ram *for* a sacrifice of peace offerings unto the LORD, with the basket of unleavened bread: the priest shall offer also his meat offering, and his drink offering.

18 And the Nazarite shall shave the head of his separation *at* the door of the tabernacle of the congregation, and shall take the hair of the head of his separation, and put *it* in the fire which *is* under the sacrifice of the peace offerings.   Num. 6:9; Acts 18:18; 21:24

19 And the priest shall take the sodden shoulder of the ram, and one unleavened cake out of the basket, and one unleavened wafer, and shall put *them* upon the hands of the Nazarite, after *the hair of* his separation is shaven: Lev. 7:30

20 And the priest shall wave them *for* a wave offering before the LORD: this *is* holy for the priest, with the wave breast and heave shoulder: and after that the Nazarite may drink wine.   Eccl. 9:7

21 This *is* the law of the Nazarite who hath vowed, *and of* his offering unto the LORD for his separation, beside *that* that his hand shall get: according to the vow which he vowed, so he must do after the law of his separation.

The Form of Blessing the People

22 And the LORD spake unto Moses, saying,

23 Speak unto Aaron and unto his sons, saying, On this wise ye shall bless the children of Israel, saying unto them,   Deut. 21:5; 1 Chr. 23:13

24 The LORD bless thee, and keep thee:

25 The LORD make his face shine upon thee, and be gracious unto thee: Ps. 31:16

26 The LORD lift up his ᵀcountenance upon thee, and give thee peace.   John 14:27 ♦ *face*

27 And they shall put my name upon the children of Israel; and I will bless them.

The Princes' Offering at the Dedication of the Tabernacle

7 And it came to pass on the day that Moses had fully set up the tabernacle, and had anointed it, and ᵀsanctified it, and all the instruments thereof, both the altar and all the vessels thereof, and had anointed them, and sanctified them;   Lev. 8:10-11 ♦ *made holy*

2 That the princes of Israel, heads of the house of their fathers, who *were* the princes of the tribes, and were over them that were numbered, offered: Num. 1:4-16
3 And they brought their offering before the LORD, six covered wagons, and twelve oxen; a wagon for two of the princes, and for each one an ox: and they brought them before the tabernacle.
4 And the LORD spake unto Moses, saying,
5 Take *it* of them, that they may be to do the service of the tabernacle of the congregation; and thou shalt give them unto the Levites, to every man according to his service.
6 And Moses took the wagons and the oxen, and gave them unto the Levites.
7 Two wagons and four oxen he gave unto the sons of Gershon, according to their service:
8 And four wagons and eight oxen he gave unto the sons of Merari, according unto their service, under the hand of Ithamar the son of Aaron the priest.
9 But unto the sons of Kohath he gave none: because the service of the sanctuary belonging unto them *was that* they should bear upon their shoulders. Num. 3:31

The Princes' Offerings at the Dedication of the Altar

10 And the princes offered for dedicating of the altar in the day that it was anointed, even the princes offered their offering before the altar. Deut. 20:5; 1 Kin. 8:63; 2 Chr. 7:9
11 And the LORD said unto Moses, They shall offer their offering, each prince on his day, for the dedicating of the altar.
12 And he that offered his offering the first day was Nahshon the son of Amminadab, of the tribe of Judah:
13 And his offering *was* one silver charger, the weight thereof *was* an hundred and thirty *shekels*, one silver bowl of seventy shekels, after the shekel of the sanctuary; both of them *were* full of fine flour mingled with oil for a meat offering: Ex. 30:13
14 One spoon of ten *shekels* of gold, full of incense:

15 One young ᵀbullock, one ram, one lamb of the first year, for a burnt offering: *bull*
16 One kid of the goats for a sin offering:
17 And for a sacrifice of peace offerings, two oxen, five rams, five he goats, five lambs of the first year: this *was* the offering of Nahshon the son of Amminadab.
18 On the second day Nethaneel the son of Zuar, prince of Issachar, did offer: Num. 1:8
19 He offered *for* his offering one silver ᵀcharger, the weight whereof *was* an hundred and thirty *shekels*, one silver bowl of seventy shekels, after the shekel of the sanctuary; both of them full of fine flour mingled with oil for a meat offering: *bowl*
20 One spoon of gold of ten *shekels*, full of incense:
21 One young bullock, one ram, one lamb of the first year, for a burnt offering:
22 One kid of the goats for a sin offering:
23 And for a sacrifice of peace offerings, two oxen, five rams, five he goats, five lambs of the first year: this *was* the offering of Nethaneel the son of Zuar. Lev. 7:11-13
24 On the third day Eliab the son of Helon, prince of the children of Zebulun, *did offer*:
25 His offering *was* one silver charger, the weight whereof *was* an hundred and thirty *shekels*, one silver bowl of seventy shekels, after the shekel of the sanctuary; both of them full of fine flour mingled with oil for a meat offering:
26 One golden spoon of ten *shekels*, full of incense:
27 One young bullock, one ram, one lamb of the first year, for a burnt offering:
28 One kid of the goats for a sin offering:
29 And for a sacrifice of peace offerings, two oxen, five rams, five he goats, five lambs of the first year: this *was* the offering of Eliab the son of Helon.
30 On the fourth day Elizur the son of Shedeur, prince of the children of Reuben, *did offer*: Num. 1:5
31 His offering *was* one silver charger of the weight of an hundred and thirty *shekels*, one silver bowl of seventy shekels, after

---

Instructions for the Ark

Numbers 7:9

Through Moses the Lord had given special instruction concerning the transportation of the ark. None but the priests, the descendants of Aaron, were to touch it, or even to look upon it uncovered. The divine direction was, "The sons of Kohath shall come to bear it: but they shall not touch any holy thing, lest they die" (Numbers 4:15). The priests were to cover the ark, and then the Kohathites must lift it by the staves, which were placed in rings upon each side of the ark and were never removed. To the Gershonites and Merarites, who had in charge the curtains and boards and pillars of the tabernacle, Moses gave carts and oxen for the transportation of that which was committed to them. "But unto the sons of Kohath he gave none: because the service of the sanctuary belonging unto them was that they should bear *upon their shoulders*." PP 705

the shekel of the sanctuary; both of them full of fine flour mingled with oil for a meat offering:

32 One golden spoon of ten *shekels*, full of incense:

33 One young bullock, one ram, one lamb of the first year, for a burnt offering:

34 One kid of the goats for a sin offering:

35 And for a sacrifice of peace offerings, two oxen, five rams, five he goats, five lambs of the first year: this *was* the offering of Elizur the son of Shedeur.

36 On the fifth day Shelumiel the son of Zurishaddai, prince of the children of Simeon, *did offer*:   Num. 1:6

37 His offering *was* one silver charger, the weight whereof *was* an hundred and thirty *shekels*, one silver bowl of seventy shekels, after the shekel of the sanctuary; both of them full of fine flour mingled with oil for a meat offering:

38 One golden spoon of ten *shekels*, full of incense:

39 One young bullock, one ram, one lamb of the first year, for a burnt offering:

40 One kid of the goats for a sin offering:

41 And for a sacrifice of peace offerings, two oxen, five rams, five he goats, five lambs of the first year: this *was* the offering of Shelumiel the son of Zurishaddai.

42 On the sixth day Eliasaph the son of Deuel, prince of the children of Gad, *offered*:

43 His offering *was* one silver charger of the weight of an hundred and thirty *shekels*, a silver bowl of seventy shekels, after the shekel of the sanctuary; both of them full of fine flour mingled with oil for a meat offering: Lev. 2:5

44 One golden spoon of ten *shekels*, full of incense:

45 One young bullock, one ram, one lamb of the first year, for a burnt offering:

46 One kid of the goats for a sin offering:

47 And for a sacrifice of peace offerings, two oxen, five rams, five he goats, five lambs of the first year: this *was* the offering of Eliasaph the son of Deuel.

48 On the seventh day Elishama the son of Ammihud, prince of the children of Ephraim, *offered*:   Num. 1:10; 2:18

49 His offering *was* one silver charger, the weight whereof *was* an hundred and thirty *shekels*, one silver bowl of seventy shekels, after the shekel of the sanctuary; both of them full of fine flour mingled with oil for a meat offering:

50 One golden spoon of ten *shekels*, full of incense:

51 One young bullock, one ram, one lamb of the first year, for a burnt offering:

52 One kid of the goats for a sin offering:

53 And for a sacrifice of peace offerings, two oxen, five rams, five he goats, five lambs of the first year: this *was* the offering of Elishama the son of Ammihud.

54 On the eighth day *offered* Gamaliel the son of Pedahzur, prince of the children of Manasseh: Num. 1:10

55 His offering *was* one silver charger of the weight of an hundred and thirty *shekels*, one silver bowl of seventy shekels, after the shekel of the sanctuary; both of them full of fine flour mingled with oil for a meat offering:

56 One golden spoon of ten *shekels*, full of incense:

57 One young bullock, one ram, one lamb of the first year, for a burnt offering:

58 One kid of the goats for a sin offering:

59 And for a sacrifice of peace offerings, two oxen, five rams, five he goats, five lambs of the first year: this *was* the offering of Gamaliel the son of Pedahzur.

60 On the ninth day Abidan the son of Gideoni, prince of the children of Benjamin, *offered*:   Num. 1:11; 2:22

61 His offering *was* one silver charger, the weight whereof *was* an hundred and thirty *shekels*, one silver bowl of seventy shekels, after the shekel of the sanctuary; both of them full of fine flour mingled with oil for a meat offering:

62 One golden spoon of ten *shekels*, full of incense:

63 One young bullock, one ram, one lamb of the first year, for a burnt offering:

64 One kid of the goats for a sin offering:

65 And for a sacrifice of peace offerings, two oxen, five rams, five he goats, five lambs of the first year: this *was* the offering of Abidan the son of Gideoni.

66 On the tenth day Ahiezer the son of Ammishaddai, prince of the children of Dan, *offered*:   Num. 1:12; 2:25

67 His offering *was* one silver charger, the weight whereof *was* an hundred and thirty *shekels*, one silver bowl of seventy shekels, after the shekel of the sanctuary; both of them full of fine flour mingled with oil for a meat offering:

68 One golden spoon of ten *shekels*, full of incense:

69 One young bullock, one ram, one lamb of the first year, for a burnt offering:

70 One kid of the goats for a sin offering:

71 And for a sacrifice of peace offerings, two oxen, five rams, five he goats, five lambs of the first year: this *was* the offering of Ahiezer the son of Ammishaddai.

72 On the eleventh day Pagiel the son of Ocran, prince of the children of Asher, *offered*:   Num. 1:13; 2:27

73 His offering *was* one silver charger, the weight whereof *was* an hundred and thirty *shekels*, one silver bowl of seventy shekels, after the shekel of the sanctuary; both of them full of fine flour mingled with oil for a meat offering:

74 One golden spoon of ten *shekels*, full of incense:

75 One young bullock, one ram, one lamb of the first year, for a burnt offering:

76 One kid of the goats for a sin offering:

77 And for a sacrifice of peace offerings, two oxen, five rams, five he goats, five lambs of the first year: this *was* the offering of Pagiel the son of Ocran.

78 On the twelfth day Ahira the son of Enan, prince of the children of Naphtali, *offered*: Num. 1:15; 2:29

79 His offering *was* one silver charger, the weight whereof *was* an hundred and thirty *shekels*, one silver bowl of seventy shekels, after the shekel of the sanctuary; both of them full of fine flour mingled with oil for a meat offering:

80 One golden spoon of ten *shekels*, full of incense:

81 One young bullock, one ram, one lamb of the first year, for a burnt offering:

82 One kid of the goats for a sin offering:

83 And for a sacrifice of peace offerings, two oxen, five rams, five he goats, five lambs of the first year: this *was* the offering of Ahira the son of Enan.

84 This *was* the dedication of the altar, in the day when it was anointed, by the princes of Israel: twelve chargers of silver, twelve silver bowls, twelve spoons of gold: Num. 7:10

85 Each charger of silver *weighing* an hundred and thirty *shekels*, each bowl seventy: all the silver vessels *weighed* two thousand and four hundred *shekels*, after the shekel of the sanctuary:

86 The golden spoons *were* twelve, full of incense, *weighing* ten *shekels* apiece, after the shekel of the sanctuary: all the gold of the spoons *was* an hundred and twenty *shekels*.

87 All the oxen for the burnt offering *were* twelve bullocks, the rams twelve, the lambs of the first year twelve, with their meat offering: and the kids of the goats for sin offering twelve.

88 And all the oxen for the sacrifice of the peace offerings *were* twenty and four bullocks, the rams sixty, the he goats sixty, the lambs of the first year sixty. This *was* the dedication of the altar, after that it was anointed. Num. 7:1, 10

89 And when Moses was gone into the tabernacle of the congregation to speak with him, then he heard the voice of one speaking unto him from off the mercy seat that *was* upon the ark of testimony, from between the two cherubims: and he spake unto him. Ps. 80:1

How the Seven Lamps Are to Be Lighted

8 And the LORD spake unto Moses, saying,

2 Speak unto Aaron, and say unto him, When thou lightest the lamps, the seven lamps shall give light over against the candlestick. Ex. 25:37

3 And Aaron did so; he lighted the lamps thereof over against the candlestick, as the LORD commanded Moses.

4 And this work of the candlestick *was of* beaten gold, unto the shaft thereof, unto the flowers thereof, *was* beaten work: according unto the pattern which the LORD had shewed Moses, so he made the candlestick. Ex. 25:9

The Consecration of the Levites

5 And the LORD spake unto Moses, saying,

6 Take the Levites from among the children of Israel, and cleanse them.

7 And thus shalt thou do unto them, to cleanse them: Sprinkle water of purifying upon them, and let them shave all their flesh, and let them wash their clothes, and *so* make themselves clean. Lev. 8:6

8 Then let them take a young ᵀbullock with his meat offering, *even* fine flour mingled with oil, and another young bullock shalt thou take for a sin offering. Lev. 2:1 ✦ *bull*

9 And thou shalt bring the Levites before the tabernacle of the congregation: and thou shalt gather the whole assembly of the children of Israel together: Ex. 40:12; Lev. 8:3

10 And thou shalt bring the Levites before the LORD: and the children of Israel shall put their hands upon the Levites: Lev. 1:4

11 And Aaron shall offer the Levites before the LORD *for* an offering of the children of Israel, that they may execute the service of the LORD. Lev. 7:30

12 And the Levites shall lay their hands upon the heads of the bullocks: and thou shalt offer the one *for* a sin offering, and the other *for* a burnt offering, unto the LORD, to make an atonement for the Levites. Ex. 29:10; Lev. 1:4

13 And thou shalt set the Levites before Aaron, and before his sons, and offer them *for* an offering unto the LORD. Num. 8:11

14 Thus shalt thou separate the Levites from among the children of Israel: and the Levites shall be mine. Num. 3:45

15 And after that shall the Levites go in to do the service of the tabernacle of the congregation: and thou shalt cleanse them, and offer them *for* an offering. Num. 8:11

16 For they *are* wholly given unto me from

among the children of Israel; instead of such as open every womb, *even instead of* the first-born of all the children of Israel, have I taken them unto me.   Num. 3:12, 45

17 For all the firstborn of the children of Israel *are* mine, *both* man and beast: on the day that I smote every firstborn in the land of Egypt I ᵀsanctified them for myself.   *made holy*

18 And I have taken the Levites for all the firstborn of the children of Israel.

19 And I have given the Levites *as* a gift to Aaron and to his sons from among the children of Israel, to do the service of the children of Israel in the tabernacle of the congregation, and to make an atonement for the children of Israel: that there be no plague among the children of Israel, when the children of Israel come nigh unto the sanctuary.   Num. 1:53; 16:46

20 And Moses, and Aaron, and all the congregation of the children of Israel, did to the Levites according unto all that the LORD commanded Moses concerning the Levites, so did the children of Israel unto them.

21 And the Levites were purified, and they washed their clothes; and Aaron offered them *as* an offering before the LORD; and Aaron made an atonement for them to cleanse them.   Num. 8:7, 11-13, 15

22 And after that went the Levites in to do their service in the tabernacle of the congregation before Aaron, and before his sons: as the LORD had commanded Moses concerning the Levites, so did they unto them.

23 And the LORD spake unto Moses, saying,

24 This *is it* that *belongeth* unto the Levites: from twenty and five years old and upward they shall go in to wait upon the service of the tabernacle of the congregation: Num. 4:3

25 And from the age of fifty years they shall cease waiting upon the service *thereof*, and shall serve no more:

26 But shall minister with their brethren in the tabernacle of the congregation, to keep the charge, and shall do no service. Thus shalt thou do unto the Levites touching their charge.   Num. 1:53

The Passover Is Commanded Again

9 And the LORD spake unto Moses in the wilderness of Sinai, in the first month of the second year after they were come out of the land of Egypt, saying,   Ex. 40:2; Num. 1:1

2 Let the children of Israel also keep the passover at his appointed season.   Lev. 23:5

3 In the fourteenth day of this month, at even, ye shall keep it in his appointed season: according to all the rites of it, and according to all the ceremonies thereof, shall ye keep it.   Ex. 12:6-11

4 And Moses spake unto the children of Israel, that they should keep the passover.

5 And they kept the passover on the fourteenth day of the first month at even in the wilderness of Sinai: according to all that the LORD commanded Moses, so did the children of Israel.   Josh. 5:10

6 And there were certain men, who were defiled by the dead body of a man, that they could not keep the passover on that day: and they came before Moses and before Aaron on that day: Ex. 18:15; Num. 5:2; 27:2

7 And those men said unto him, We *are* defiled by the dead body of a man: wherefore are we kept back, that we may not offer an offering of the LORD in his appointed season among the children of Israel?

8 And Moses said unto them, Stand still, and I will hear what the LORD will command concerning you.   Num. 27:5

9 And the LORD spake unto Moses, saying,

10 Speak unto the children of Israel, saying, If any man of you or of your posterity shall be unclean by reason of a dead body, or *be* in a journey afar off, yet he shall keep the passover unto the LORD.

11 The fourteenth day of the second month at even they shall keep it, *and* eat it with unleavened bread and bitter *herbs*.   2 Chr. 30:2-15

12 They shall leave none of it unto the morning, nor break any bone of it: according to all the ordinances of the passover they shall keep it.   Ex. 12:10, 43, 46

9:12 A Perfect Sacrifice

The lamb was to be prepared whole, not a bone of it being broken; so not a bone was to be broken of the Lamb of God, who was to die for us (John 19:36). Thus was also represented the completeness of Christ's sacrifice. *PP 277*

13 But the man that *is* clean, and is not in a journey, and ᵀforbeareth to keep the passover, even the same soul shall be cut off from among his people: because he brought not the offering of the LORD in his appointed season, that man shall bear his sin.   *refuses*

14 And if a stranger shall sojourn among you, and will keep the passover unto the LORD; according to the ordinance of the passover, and according to the manner thereof, so shall he do: ye shall have one ordinance, both for the stranger, and for him that was born in the land.   Ex. 12:48-49; Lev. 24:22

The Cloud Guides the Movements of the Camp

15 And on the day that the tabernacle was reared up the cloud covered the tabernacle, *namely*, the tent of the testimony: and

at even there was upon the tabernacle as it were the appearance of fire, until the morning. Ex. 13:21; 40:2, 34

16 So it was alway: the cloud covered it *by day*, and the appearance of fire by night.

17 And when the cloud was taken up from the tabernacle, then after that the children of Israel journeyed: and in the place where the cloud abode, there the children of Israel pitched their tents. Ex. 40:36-38

18 At the commandment of the LORD the children of Israel journeyed, and at the commandment of the LORD they pitched: as long as the cloud abode upon the tabernacle they rested in their tents. 1 Cor. 10:1

19 And when the cloud tarried long upon the tabernacle many days, then the children of Israel kept the charge of the LORD, and journeyed not.

20 And *so* it was, when the cloud was a few days upon the tabernacle; according to the commandment of the LORD they abode in their tents, and according to the commandment of the LORD they journeyed.

21 And *so* it was, when the cloud abode from even unto the morning, and *that* the cloud was taken up in the morning, then they journeyed: whether *it was* by day or by night that the cloud was taken up, they journeyed.

22 Or *whether it were* two days, or a month, or a year, that the cloud tarried upon the tabernacle, remaining thereon, the children of Israel abode in their tents, and journeyed not: but when it was taken up, they journeyed. Ex. 40:36-37

23 At the commandment of the LORD they rested in the tents, and at the commandment of the LORD they journeyed: they kept the charge of the LORD, at the commandment of the LORD by the hand of Moses.

The Use of the Silver Trumpets

10 And the LORD spake unto Moses, saying,

2 Make thee two trumpets of silver; of a whole piece shalt thou make them: that thou mayest use them for the calling of the assembly, and for the journeying of the camps. Is. 1:13

3 And when they shall blow with them, all the assembly shall assemble themselves to thee at the door of the tabernacle of the congregation. Jer. 4:5

4 And if they blow *but* with one *trumpet*, then the princes, *which are* heads of the thousands of Israel, shall gather themselves unto thee. Ex. 18:21; Num. 7:2

5 When ye blow an alarm, then the camps that lie on the east parts shall go forward.

6 When ye blow an alarm the second time, then the camps that lie on the south side

shall take their journey: they shall blow an alarm for their journeys. Num. 2:10-16

7 But when the congregation is to be gathered together, ye shall blow, but ye shall not sound an alarm. Joel 2:1

8 And the sons of Aaron, the priests, shall blow with the trumpets; and they shall be to you for an ordinance for ever throughout your generations. Num. 31:6

9 And if ye go to war in your land against the enemy that oppresseth you, then ye shall blow an alarm with the trumpets; and ye shall be remembered before the LORD your God, and ye shall be saved from your enemies. Gen. 8:1; Judg. 2:18; 1 Sam. 10:18

10 Also in the day of your gladness, and in your solemn days, and in the beginnings of your months, ye shall blow with the trumpets over your burnt offerings, and over the sacrifices of your peace offerings; that they may be to you for a memorial before your God: I *am* the LORD your God. Lev. 23:24; Num. 10:9

The Israelites Travel from Sinai to Paran

11 And it came to pass on the twentieth *day* of the second month, in the second year, that the cloud was taken up from off the tabernacle of the testimony.

12 And the children of Israel took their journeys out of the wilderness of Sinai; and the cloud rested in the wilderness of Paran.

13 And they first took their journey according to the commandment of the LORD by the hand of Moses.

10:11–13 Following the Cloud

At the signal from the trumpeters, however, the entire camp set forward, the tabernacle borne in the midst, and each tribe in its appointed position, under its own standard. All eyes were turned anxiously to see in what direction the cloud would lead. As it moved toward the east, where were only mountain masses huddled together, black and desolate, a feeling of sadness and doubt arose in many hearts. PP 377

14 In the first *place* went the standard of the camp of the children of Judah according to their armies: and over his host *was* Nahshon the son of Amminadab. Num. 1:7; 2:3-9

15 And over the host of the tribe of the children of Issachar *was* Nethaneel the son of Zuar.

16 And over the host of the tribe of the children of Zebulun *was* Eliab the son of Helon.

17 And the tabernacle was taken down; and the sons of Gershon and the sons of Merari set forward, bearing the tabernacle. Num. 1:51

18 And the standard of the camp of Reuben

set forward according to their armies: and over his host *was* Elizur the son of Shedeur.
19 And over the host of the tribe of the children of Simeon *was* Shelumiel the son of Zurishaddai.   Num. 1:6
20 And over the host of the tribe of the children of Gad *was* Eliasaph the son of Deuel.
21 And the Kohathites set forward, bearing the sanctuary: and *the other* did set up the tabernacle against they came.   Num. 4:4-16; 7:9
22 And the ᵀstandard of the camp of the children of Ephraim set forward according to their armies: and over his host *was* Elishama the son of Ammihud.   Num. 2:18-24 ◆ *flag*
23 And over the host of the tribe of the children of Manasseh *was* Gamaliel the son of Pedahzur.
24 And over the host of the tribe of the children of Benjamin *was* Abidan the son of Gideoni.   Num. 1:11
25 And the standard of the camp of the children of Dan set forward, *which was* the ᵀrereward of all the camps throughout their hosts: and over his host *was* Ahiezer the son of Ammishaddai.   Num. 1:12; Josh. 6:9 ◆ *rear guard*
26 And over the host of the tribe of the children of Asher *was* Pagiel the son of Ocran.
27 And over the host of the tribe of the children of Naphtali *was* Ahira the son of Enan.
28 Thus *were* the journeyings of the children of Israel according to their armies, when they set forward.   Num. 2:34

Hobab Is Entreated by Moses Not to Leave Them

29 And Moses said unto Hobab, the son of Raguel the Midianite, Moses' father in law, We are journeying unto the place of which the LORD said, I will give it you: come thou with us, and we will do thee good: for the LORD hath spoken good concerning Israel.   Gen. 12:7

> **10:29–32 Mercy Remembered**
>
> While inflicting judgment, God remembered mercy. The Amalekites were to be destroyed, but the Kenites, who dwelt among them, were spared. This people, though not wholly free from idolatry, were worshipers of God and were friendly to Israel. Of this tribe was the brother-in-law of Moses, Hobab, who had accompanied the Israelites in their travels through the wilderness, and by his knowledge of the country had rendered them valuable assistance. *PP 628*

30 And he said unto him, I will not go; but I will depart to mine own land, and to my kindred.
31 And he said, Leave us not, I pray thee; ᵀforasmuch as thou knowest how we are to encamp in the wilderness, and thou mayest be to us instead of eyes.   Job 29:15 ◆ *since*
32 And it shall be, if thou go with us, yea, it shall be, that what goodness the LORD shall do unto us, the same will we do unto thee.   Judg. 1:16
33 And they departed from the mount of the LORD three days' journey: and the ark of the covenant of the LORD went before them in the three days' journey, to search out a resting place for them.   Deut. 1:33
34 And the cloud of the LORD *was* upon them by day, when they went out of the camp.
35 And it came to pass, when the ark set forward, that Moses said, Rise up, LORD, and let thine enemies be scattered; and let them that hate thee flee before thee.   Ps. 68:1-2
36 And when it rested, he said, Return, O LORD, unto the many thousands of Israel.

Moses' Prayer Stops the Burning at Taberah

11 And *when* the people complained, it displeased the LORD: and the LORD heard *it*; and his anger was kindled; and the fire of the LORD burnt among them, and consumed *them that were* in the uttermost parts of the camp.   Lev. 10:2

> **11:1 Contagious Complaining**
>
> After three days' journey open complaints were heard. These originated with the mixed multitude, many of whom were not fully united with Israel, and were continually watching for some cause of censure. The complainers were not pleased with the direction of the march, and they were continually finding fault with the way in which *Moses* was leading them, though they well knew that he, as well as they, was following the guiding cloud. Dissatisfaction is contagious, and it soon spread in the encampment. *PP 377*

2 And the people cried unto Moses; and when Moses prayed unto the LORD, the fire was quenched.   Num. 16:45-48; 21:7; James 5:16
3 And he called the name of the place Taberah: because the fire of the LORD burnt among them.   Deut. 9:22

The People Lust for Meat and Loathe Manna

4 And the mixt multitude that *was* among them fell a lusting: and the children of Israel also wept again, and said, Who shall give us flesh to eat?   Ex. 12:38; Ps. 106:14; 1 Cor. 10:6
5 We remember the fish, which we did eat in Egypt freely; the cucumbers, and the melons, and the leeks, and the onions, and the garlick: Ex. 16:3

6 But now our soul *is* dried away: *there is* nothing at all, beside this manna, *before* our eyes. Num. 21:5

7 And the manna *was* as coriander seed, and the colour thereof as the colour of bdellium. Gen. 2:12; Ex. 16:31

8 *And* the people went about, and gathered *it*, and ground *it* in mills, or beat *it* in a mortar, and baked *it* in pans, and made cakes of it: and the taste of it was as the taste of fresh oil. Ex. 16:16-18

11:8 Bread From God

The people called it "manna." Moses said, "This is the bread which the Lord hath given you to eat." The people gathered the manna, and found that there was an abundant supply for all. . . . Some attempted to keep a supply until the next day, but it was then found to be unfit for food. The provision for the day must be gathered in the morning; for all that remained upon the ground was melted by the sun. *PP 295*

---

9 And when the dew fell upon the camp in the night, the manna fell upon it. Ex. 16:13-14

10 Then Moses heard the people weep throughout their families, every man in the door of his tent: and the anger of the LORD was kindled greatly; Moses also was displeased.

11 And Moses said unto the LORD, Wherefore hast thou afflicted thy servant? and wherefore have I not found favour in thy sight, that thou layest the burden of all this people upon me? Deut. 1:12

12 Have I conceived all this people? have I ᵀbegotten them, that thou shouldest say unto me, Carry them in thy bosom, as a nursing father beareth the sucking child, unto the land which thou swarest unto their fathers? Ex. 13:5; Is. 40:11; 49:23 ◆ *brought forth*

13 Whence should I have flesh to give unto all this people? for they weep unto me, saying, Give us flesh, that we may eat. Matt. 15:33

14 I am not able to bear all this people alone, because *it is* too heavy for me. Ex. 18:18

15 And if thou deal thus with me, kill me, I pray thee, out of hand, if I have found favour in thy sight; and let me not see my wretchedness. 1 Kin. 19:4

God Divides Moses' Burden among Seventy Elders

16 And the LORD said unto Moses, Gather unto me seventy men of the elders of Israel, whom thou knowest to be the elders of the people, and officers over them; and bring them unto the tabernacle of the congregation, that they may stand there with thee. Ex. 24:1

17 And I will come down and talk with thee there: and I will take of the spirit which *is* upon thee, and will put *it* upon them; and they shall bear the burden of the people with thee, that thou bear *it* not thyself alone. Num. 11:25; 1 Sam. 10:6; 2 Kin. 2:9

11:11-17 Moses Complains

The Lord permitted Moses to choose for himself the most faithful and efficient men to share the responsibility with him. . . . yet serious evils would eventually result from their promotion. They would never have been chosen had Moses manifested faith corresponding to the evidences he had witnessed of God's power and goodness. . . . He was not excusable in indulging, in the slightest degree. . . . Had he relied fully upon God, the Lord would have guided him continually and would have given him strength for every emergency. *PP 380*

---

18 And say thou unto the people, Sanctify yourselves against to morrow, and ye shall eat flesh: for ye have wept in the ears of the LORD, saying, Who shall give us flesh to eat? for *it was* well with us in Egypt: therefore the LORD will give you flesh, and ye shall eat. Ex. 19:10; Num. 11:1; Acts 7:39

19 Ye shall not eat one day, nor two days, nor five days, neither ten days, nor twenty days;

20 *But* even a whole month, until it come out at your nostrils, and it be loathsome unto you: because that ye have despised the LORD which *is* among you, and have wept before him, saying, Why came we forth out of Egypt? Ps. 106:15

21 And Moses said, The people, among whom I *am, are* six hundred thousand footmen; and thou hast said, I will give them flesh, that they may eat a whole month. Ex. 12:37

22 Shall the flocks and the herds be slain for them, to suffice them? or shall all the fish of the sea be gathered together for them, to suffice them? Matt. 15:33

23 And the LORD said unto Moses, Is the LORD's hand ᵀwaxed short? thou shalt see now whether my word shall come to pass unto thee or not. Is. 50:2; 59:1; Ezek. 12:25 ◆ *become*

24 And Moses went out, and told the people the words of the LORD, and gathered the seventy men of the elders of the people, and set them round about the tabernacle. Num. 11:16

25 And the LORD came down in a cloud, and spake unto him, and took of the spirit that *was* upon him, and gave *it* unto the seventy elders: and it came to pass, *that*, when the spirit rested upon them, they prophesied, and did not cease. Num. 11:17; 12:5; 1 Sam. 10:10

26 But there remained two *of the* men in the camp, the name of the one *was* Eldad, and

the name of the other Medad: and the spirit rested upon them; and they *were* of them that were written, but went not out unto the tabernacle: and they prophesied in the camp.

27 And there ran a young man, and told Moses, and said, Eldad and Medad do prophesy in the camp.

28 And Joshua the son of Nun, the servant of Moses, *one* of his young men, answered and said, My lord Moses, forbid them.

29 And Moses said unto him, Enviest thou for my sake? would God that all the LORD's people were prophets, *and* that the LORD would put his spirit upon them!   1 Cor. 14:5

30 And Moses gat him into the camp, he and the elders of Israel.

God Sends Quail

31 And there went forth a wind from the LORD, and brought quails from the sea, and let *them* fall by the camp, as it were a day's journey on this side, and as it were a day's journey on the other side, round about the camp, and as it were two cubits *high* upon the face of the earth.   Ex. 16:13; Ps. 105:40

32 And the people stood up all that day, and all *that* night, and all the next day, and they gathered the quails: he that gathered least gathered ten homers: and they spread *them* all abroad for themselves round about the camp.   Ezek. 45:11

33 And while the flesh *was* yet between their teeth, ᵀere it was chewed, the wrath of the LORD was kindled against the people, and the LORD smote the people with a very great plague.   Ps. 78:30-31 ◆ *before*

34 And he called the name of that place Kibroth-hattaavah: because there they buried the people that lusted.   Deut. 9:22

35 *And* the people journeyed from Kibroth-hattaavah unto Hazeroth; and abode at Hazeroth.   Num. 12:16; 33:17

God Rebukes Aaron and Miriam

12 And Miriam and Aaron spake against Moses because of the Ethiopian woman whom he had married: for he had married an Ethiopian woman.   Ex. 2:21

2 And they said, Hath the LORD indeed spoken only by Moses? hath he not spoken also by us? And the LORD heard *it*.   Num. 11:1

3 (Now the man Moses *was* very meek, above all the men which *were* upon the face of the earth.)   Matt. 11:29

12:3 Meekest Man on Earth

Patience and gentleness under wrong were not characteristics prized by the heathen or by the Jews. The statement made by Moses under the inspiration of the Holy Spirit, that he was the meekest man upon the earth, would not have been regarded by the people of his time as a commendation; it would rather have excited pity or contempt. But Jesus places meekness among the first qualifications for His kingdom. *MB 14*

---

4 And the LORD spake suddenly unto Moses, and unto Aaron, and unto Miriam, Come out ye three unto the tabernacle of the congregation. And they three came out.

5 And the LORD came down in the pillar of the cloud, and stood *in* the door of the tabernacle, and called Aaron and Miriam: and they both came forth.   Num. 11:25

6 And he said, Hear now my words: If there be a prophet among you, *I* the LORD will make myself known unto him in a vision, *and* will speak unto him in a dream.   Gen. 31:10-11

12:6

Gift of Prophecy   See 2 Peter 1:19-21.

---

7 My servant Moses *is* not so, who *is* faithful in all mine house.   Ps. 105:26

8 With him will I speak mouth to mouth, even apparently, and not in dark speeches; and the ᵀsimilitude of the LORD shall he

---

Rebellious Desires Gratified

Numbers 11

A strong wind blowing from the sea now brought flocks of quails, "about a day's journey on this side, and a day's journey on the other side, round about the camp, and about two cubits above the face of the earth" (Numbers 11:31, R.V.). All that day and night, and the following day, the people labored in gathering the food miraculously provided. Immense quantities were secured. "He that gathered least gathered ten homers." All that was not needed for present use was preserved by drying, so that the supply, as promised, was sufficient for a whole month.

God gave the people that which was not for their highest good, because they persisted in desiring it; they would not be satisfied with those things that would prove a benefit to them. Their rebellious desires were gratified, but they were left to suffer the result. They feasted without restraint, and their excesses were speedily punished. "The Lord smote the people with a very great plague." Large numbers were cut down by burning fevers, while the most guilty among them were smitten as soon as they tasted the food for which they had lusted. *PP 382*

behold: wherefore then were ye not afraid to speak against my servant Moses?   *image*

9 And the anger of the LORD was kindled against them; and he departed.

God Gives Miriam Leprosy, She Is Sent Outside the Camp

10 And the cloud departed from off the tabernacle; and, behold, Miriam *became* leprous, *white* as snow: and Aaron looked upon Miriam, and, behold, *she was* leprous.   Deut. 24:9

12:1–15 Sad Results of Envy

This manifestation of the Lord's displeasure was designed to be a warning to all Israel, to check the growing spirit of discontent and insubordination. If Miriam's envy and dissatisfaction had not been signally rebuked, it would have resulted in great evil. Envy is one of the most satanic traits that can exist in the human heart, and it is one of the most baleful in its effects. PP 385

---

11 And Aaron said unto Moses, Alas, my lord, I beseech thee, lay not the sin upon us, wherein we have done foolishly, and wherein we have sinned.   2 Sam. 19:19; 24:10; Prov. 30:32

12 Let her not be as one dead, of whom the flesh is half consumed when he cometh out of his mother's womb.

13 And Moses cried unto the LORD, saying, Heal her now, O God, I ᵀbeseech thee.   beg

14 And the LORD said unto Moses, If her father had but spit in her face, should she not be ashamed seven days? let her be shut out from the camp seven days, and after that let her be received in *again*.   Num. 5:2-3; Deut. 25:9; Job 30:10

15 And Miriam was shut out from the camp

seven days: and the people journeyed not till Miriam was brought in *again*.

16 And afterward the people removed from Hazeroth, and pitched in the wilderness of Paran.   Num. 11:35

Those Sent into Canaan

13 And the LORD spake unto Moses, saying,

2 Send thou men, that they may search the land of Canaan, which I give unto the children of Israel: of every tribe of their fathers shall ye send a man, every one a ruler among them.   Num. 32:8

3 And Moses by the commandment of the LORD sent them from the wilderness of Paran: all those men *were* heads of the children of Israel.   Num. 12:16

4 And these *were* their names: of the tribe of Reuben, Shammua the son of Zaccur.

5 Of the tribe of Simeon, Shaphat the son of Hori.

6 Of the tribe of Judah, Caleb the son of Jephunneh.   Num. 13:30; 14:6, 30

7 Of the tribe of Issachar, Igal the son of Joseph.

8 Of the tribe of Ephraim, Oshea the son of Nun.   Ex. 24:13

9 Of the tribe of Benjamin, Palti the son of Raphu.

10 Of the tribe of Zebulun, Gaddiel the son of Sodi.

11 Of the tribe of Joseph, *namely*, of the tribe of Manasseh, Gaddi the son of Susi.

12 Of the tribe of Dan, Ammiel the son of Gemalli.

13 Of the tribe of Asher, Sethur the son of Michael.

Blinded by Jealousy

Numbers 12

In the organization of the council of elders they felt that their position and authority had been ignored. Miriam and Aaron had never known the weight of care and responsibility which had rested upon Moses; yet because they had been chosen to aid him they regarded themselves as sharing equally with him the burden of leadership, and they regarded the appointment of further assistants as uncalled for.

Moses felt the importance of the great work committed to him as no other man had ever felt it. He realized his own weakness, and he made God his counselor. Aaron esteemed himself more highly, and trusted less in God. He had failed when entrusted with responsibility, giving evidence of the weakness of his character by his base compliance in the matter of the idolatrous worship at Sinai. But Miriam and Aaron, blinded by jealousy and ambition, lost sight of this. Aaron had been highly honored by God in the appointment of his family to the sacred office of the priesthood; yet even this now added to the desire for self-exaltation. "And they said, Hath the Lord indeed spoken only by Moses? hath He not spoken also by us?" Regarding themselves as equally favored by God, they felt that they were entitled to the same position and authority.

Yielding to the spirit of dissatisfaction, Miriam found cause of complaint in events that God had especially overruled. The marriage of Moses had been displeasing to her. That he should choose a woman of another nation, instead of taking a wife from among the Hebrews, was an offense to her family and national pride. Zipporah was treated with ill-disguised contempt. PP 383

14 Of the tribe of Naphtali, Nahbi the son of Vophsi.

15 Of the tribe of Gad, Geuel the son of Machi.

16 These *are* the names of the men which Moses sent to spy out the land. And Moses called Oshea the son of Nun Jehoshua.

17 And Moses sent them to spy out the land of Canaan, and said unto them, Get you up this *way* southward, and go up into the mountain: Gen. 12:9

18 And see the land, what it *is*; and the people that dwelleth therein, whether they *be* strong or weak, few or many;

19 And what the land *is* that they dwell in, whether it *be* good or bad; and what cities *they be* that they dwell in, whether in tents, or in strong holds;

20 And what the land *is*, whether it *be* fat or lean, whether there be wood therein, or not. And be ye of good courage, and bring of the fruit of the land. Now the time *was* the time of the firstripe grapes.   Deut. 31:23

The Activities of the Spies

21 So they went up, and searched the land from the wilderness of Zin unto Rehob, as men come to Hamath.   Num. 20:1; 27:14; 33:36

22 And they ascended by the south, and came unto Hebron; where Ahiman, Sheshai, and Talmai, the children of Anak, *were*. (Now Hebron was built seven years before Zoan in Egypt.)   Ps. 78:12, 43; Is. 19:11

23 And they came unto the brook of Eshcol, and cut down from thence a branch with one cluster of grapes, and they bare it between two upon a staff; and *they brought* of the pomegranates, and of the figs.   Num. 32:9

24 The place was called the brook Eshcol, because of the cluster of grapes which the children of Israel cut down from thence.

25 And they returned from searching of the land after forty days.

The Spies Give an Unfavorable Report

26 And they went and came to Moses, and to Aaron, and to all the congregation of the children of Israel, unto the wilderness of Paran, to Kadesh; and brought back word unto them, and unto all the congregation, and shewed them the fruit of the land.   Num. 20:1, 16; 32:8

27 And they told him, and said, We came unto the land whither thou sentest us, and surely it floweth with milk and honey; and this *is* the fruit of it.   Ex. 3:8, 17; 13:5

28 Nevertheless the people *be* strong that dwell in the land, and the cities *are* walled, *and* very great: and moreover we saw the children of Anak there.   Num. 13:33; Deut. 1:28

29 The Amalekites dwell in the land of the south: and the Hittites, and the Jebusites, and the Amorites, dwell in the mountains: and the Canaanites dwell by the sea, and by the coast of Jordan.   Num. 14:43

30 And Caleb stilled the people before Moses, and said, Let us go up at once, and possess it; for we are well able to overcome it.   Num. 14:24

31 But the men that went up with him said, We be not able to go up against the people; for they *are* stronger than we.   Josh. 14:8

32 And they brought up an evil report of the land which they had searched unto the children of Israel, saying, The land, through which we have gone to search it, *is* a land that eateth up the inhabitants thereof; and all the people that we saw in it *are* men of a great stature.   Num. 14:36-37; Amos 2:9

> **13:31, 32 Resolve to Discourage**
>
> [Israel's spies], having entered upon a wrong course, stubbornly set themselves against Caleb and Joshua, against Moses, and against God. Every advance step rendered them the more determined. They were resolved to discourage all effort to gain possession of Canaan. They distorted the truth in order to sustain their baleful influence. It "is a land that eateth up the inhabitants thereof," they said. This was not only an evil report, but it was also a lying one. It was inconsistent with itself. *PP 389*

33 And there we saw the giants, the sons of Anak, *which come* of the giants: and we were in our own sight as grasshoppers, and so we were in their sight.   Gen. 6:4

The People Murmur at the News

14 And all the congregation lifted up their voice, and cried; and the people wept that night.

2 And all the children of Israel murmured against Moses and against Aaron: and the whole congregation said unto them, Would God that we had died in the land of Egypt! or would God we had died in this wilderness!   Ex. 15:24

3 And wherefore hath the Lᴏʀᴅ brought us unto this land, to fall by the sword, that our wives and our children should be a prey? were it not better for us to return into Egypt?

> **14:1–3 Unbelief Limits God's Power**
>
> In their unbelief they limited the power of God and distrusted the hand that had hitherto safely guided them. And they repeated their former error of murmuring against Moses and Aaron. "This, then, is the end of our high hopes," they said. "This is the land we have traveled all the way from Egypt to possess." They accused their leaders of deceiving the people and bringing trouble upon Israel. *PP 388*

4 And they said one to another, Let us make a captain, and let us return into Egypt.

5 Then Moses and Aaron fell on their faces before all the assembly of the congregation of the children of Israel. 　Num. 16:4, 22, 45
6 And Joshua the son of Nun, and Caleb the son of Jephunneh, *which were* of them that searched the land, ᵀrent their clothes: *tore apart*
7 And they spake unto all the company of the children of Israel, saying, The land, which we passed through to search it, *is* an exceeding good land. 　Num. 13:27; Deut. 1:25
8 If the LORD delight in us, then he will bring us into this land, and give it us; a land which floweth with milk and honey. 　2 Sam. 22:20
9 Only rebel not ye against the LORD, neither fear ye the people of the land; for they *are* bread for us: their defence is departed from them, and the LORD *is* with us: fear them not. 　Deut. 7:18
10 But all the congregation bade stone them with stones. And the glory of the LORD appeared in the tabernacle of the congregation before all the children of Israel. Ex. 16:10; 17:4

> **14:10 Under Satan's Control**
>
> It is hardly possible for men to offer greater insult to God than to despise and reject the instrumentalities He would use for their salvation. The Israelites had not only done this, but had purposed to put both Moses and Aaron to death. .... That night of probation was not passed in repentance and confession, but in devising some way to resist the evidences which showed them to be the greatest of sinners. They still cherished hatred of the men of God's appointment, and braced themselves to resist their authority. *PP 402*

11 And the LORD said unto Moses, How long will this people provoke me? and how long will it be ᵀere they believe me, for all the signs which I have shewed among them? 　Num. 14:23; Ps. 78:22; 106:24 ◆ *before*
12 I will ᵀsmite them with the pestilence, and disinherit them, and will make of thee a greater nation and mightier than they. *strike*
13 And Moses said unto the LORD, Then the Egyptians shall hear *it*, (for thou broughtest up this people in thy might from among them;) 　Deut. 32:27; Ps. 106:23; Ezek. 20:9
14 And they will tell *it* to the inhabitants of this land: *for* they have heard that thou LORD *art* among this people, that thou LORD art seen face to face, and *that* thy cloud standeth over them, and *that* thou goest before them, by day time in a pillar of a cloud, and in a pillar of fire by night. 　Ex. 15:14
15 Now *if* thou shalt kill *all* this people as one man, then the nations which have heard the fame of thee will speak, saying,
16 Because the LORD was not able to bring this people into the land which he sware

unto them, therefore he hath slain them in the wilderness. 　Deut. 9:28
17 And now, I ᵀbeseech thee, let the power of my Lord be great, according as thou hast spoken, saying, 　*beg*
18 The LORD *is* longsuffering, and of great mercy, forgiving iniquity and ᵀtransgression, and by no means clearing *the guilty*, visiting the iniquity of the fathers upon the children unto the third and fourth *generation*. 　Ex. 20:5; 34:6-7; Ps. 145:8 ◆ *violation of a law*
19 Pardon, I beseech thee, the iniquity of this people according unto the greatness of thy mercy, and as thou hast forgiven this people, from Egypt even until now. 　Ex. 34:9; Ps. 78:38
20 And the LORD said, I have pardoned according to thy word:
21 But *as* truly *as* I live, all the earth shall be filled with the glory of the LORD. 　Deut. 32:40
22 Because all those men which have seen my glory, and my miracles, which I did in Egypt and in the wilderness, and have tempted me now these ten times, and have not hearkened to my voice; 　Gen. 31:7
23 Surely they shall not see the land which I sware unto their fathers, neither shall any of them that provoked me see it: Num. 26:64; 32:11
24 But my servant Caleb, because he had another spirit with him, and hath followed me fully, him will I bring into the land whereinto he went; and his seed shall possess it. 　Num. 14:6-9
25 (Now the Amalekites and the Canaanites dwelt in the valley.) To morrow turn you, and get you into the wilderness by the way of the Red sea. 　Num. 13:29
26 And the LORD spake unto Moses and unto Aaron, saying,
27 How long *shall I bear with* this evil congregation, which murmur against me? I have heard the murmurings of the children of Israel, which they murmur against me. Ex. 16:12
28 Say unto them, *As truly as* I live, saith the LORD, as ye have spoken in mine ears, so will I do to you: 　Num. 14:21, 23
29 Your carcases shall fall in this wilderness; and all that were numbered of you, according to your whole number, from twenty years old and upward, which have murmured against me, 　Num. 1:45; 26:64; Heb. 3:17
30 Doubtless ye shall not come into the land, *concerning* which I sware to make you dwell therein, save Caleb the son of Jephunneh, and Joshua the son of Nun.
31 But your little ones, which ye said should be a prey, them will I bring in, and they shall know the land which ye have despised.
32 But *as for* you, your carcases, they shall fall in this wilderness. 　1 Cor. 10:5
33 And your children shall wander in the wilderness forty years, and bear your ᵀwhore-

doms, until your carcases be wasted in the wilderness. Num. 32:13 ◆ *acts of prostitution*
34 After the number of the days in which ye searched the land, *even* forty days, each day for a year, shall ye bear your iniquities, *even* forty years, and ye shall know my breach of promise. Num. 13:25; Ezek. 4:6; Dan. 9:24
35 I the LORD have said, I will surely do it unto all this evil congregation, that are gathered together against me: in this wilderness they shall be consumed, and there they shall die. Num. 23:19

The Men Who Brought the Unfavorable Report Die by a Plague
36 And the men, which Moses sent to search the land, who returned, and made all the congregation to murmur against him, by bringing up a slander upon the land,
37 Even those men that did bring up the evil report upon the land, died by the plague before the LORD. Num. 16:49; 1 Cor. 10:10; Heb. 3:17
38 But Joshua the son of Nun, and Caleb the son of Jephunneh, *which were* of the men that went to search the land, lived *still*. Num. 26:65
39 And Moses told these sayings unto all the children of Israel: and the people mourned greatly. Ex. 33:4

14:40 Ignoring God's Command

Regardless of the divine sentence, the Israelites prepared to undertake the conquest of Canaan. Equipped with armor and weapons of war, they were, in their own estimation, fully prepared for conflict; but they were sadly deficient in the sight of God and His sorrowful servants. . . . But now, contrary to the command of God and the solemn prohibition of their leaders, without the ark, and without Moses, they went out to meet the armies of the enemy. *PP 393*

---

40 And they rose up early in the morning, and gat them up into the top of the mountain, saying, Lo, we *be here*, and will go up unto the place which the LORD hath promised: for we have sinned. Deut. 1:41
41 And Moses said, Wherefore now do ye ᵀtransgress the commandment of the LORD? but it shall not prosper. 2 Chr. 24:20 ◆ *violate*
42 Go not up, for the LORD *is* not among you; that ye be not smitten before your enemies. Deut. 1:42
43 For the Amalekites and the Canaanites *are* there before you, and ye shall fall by the sword: because ye are turned away from the LORD, therefore the LORD will not be with you. Num. 13:29
44 But they presumed to go up unto the hill top: nevertheless the ark of the covenant of the LORD, and Moses, departed not out of the camp. Deut. 1:43

45 Then the Amalekites came down, and the Canaanites which dwelt in that hill, and smote them, and discomfited them, *even* unto Hormah. Num. 21:3; Deut. 1:44; Judg. 1:17

The Law of the Meal Offering and the Drink Offering
15 And the LORD spake unto Moses, saying,
2 Speak unto the children of Israel, and say unto them, When ye be come into the land of your habitations, which I give unto you,
3 And will make an offering by fire unto the LORD, a burnt offering, or a sacrifice in performing a vow, or in a freewill offering, or in your solemn feasts, to make a sweet savour unto the LORD, of the herd, or of the flock: Gen. 8:21; Ex. 29:18; Num. 28:27
4 Then shall he that offereth his offering unto the LORD bring a meat offering of a tenth deal of flour mingled with the fourth *part* of an hin of oil. Ex. 29:40; Lev. 2:1; 23:13
5 And the fourth *part* of an hin of wine for a drink offering shalt thou prepare with the burnt offering or sacrifice, for one lamb. Num. 28:7
6 Or for a ram, thou shalt prepare *for* a meat offering two tenth deals of flour mingled with the third *part* of an hin of oil.
7 And for a drink offering thou shalt offer the third *part* of an hin of wine, *for* a sweet savour unto the LORD.
8 And when thou preparest a bullock *for* a burnt offering, or *for* a sacrifice in performing a vow, or peace offerings unto the LORD: Lev. 3:1
9 Then shall he bring with a bullock a meat offering of three tenth deals of flour mingled with half an hin of oil. Lev. 6:14
10 And thou shalt bring for a drink offering half an hin of wine, *for* an offering made by fire, of a sweet savour unto the LORD.
11 Thus shall it be done for one ᵀbullock, or for one ram, or for a lamb, or a kid. *bull*
12 According to the number that ye shall prepare, so shall ye do to every one according to their number.
13 All that are born of the country shall do these things after this manner, in offering an offering made by fire, of a sweet savour unto the LORD.
14 And if a stranger sojourn with you, or whosoever *be* among you in your generations, and will offer an offering made by fire, of a sweet savour unto the LORD; as ye do, so he shall do.
15 One ordinance *shall be both* for you of the congregation, and also for the stranger that sojourneth *with you*, an ordinance for ever in your generations: as ye *are*, so shall the stranger be before the LORD. Ex. 12:49; Num. 9:14

16 One law and one manner shall be for you, and for the stranger that sojourneth with you.
17 And the LORD spake unto Moses, saying,
18 Speak unto the children of Israel, and say unto them, When ye come into the land whither I bring you, Num. 15:2
19 Then it shall be, that, when ye eat of the bread of the land, ye shall offer up an heave offering unto the LORD. Josh. 5:11-12
20 Ye shall offer up a cake of the first of your dough *for* an heave offering: as *ye do* the heave offering of the threshingfloor, so shall ye heave it. Lev. 2:14
21 Of the first of your dough ye shall give unto the LORD an heave offering in your generations.

The Sacrifice for the Sin of Ignorance

22 And if ye have erred, and not observed all these commandments, which the LORD hath spoken unto Moses, Lev. 4:2
23 *Even* all that the LORD hath commanded you by the hand of Moses, from the day that the LORD commanded *Moses*, and henceforward among your generations;
24 Then it shall be, if *ought* be committed by ignorance without the knowledge of the congregation, that all the congregation shall offer one young bullock for a burnt offering, for a sweet savour unto the LORD, with his meat offering, and his drink offering, according to the manner, and one kid of the goats for a sin offering. Lev. 4:23
25 And the priest shall make an atonement for all the congregation of the children of Israel, and it shall be forgiven them; for it *is* ignorance: and they shall bring their offering, a sacrifice made by fire unto the LORD, and their sin offering before the LORD, for their ignorance: Lev. 4:20; Rom. 3:25
26 And it shall be forgiven all the congregation of the children of Israel, and the stranger that sojourneth among them; seeing all the people *were* in ignorance.
27 And if any soul sin through ignorance, then he shall bring a she goat of the first year for a sin offering. Lev. 4:27-28
28 And the priest shall make an atonement for the soul that sinneth ignorantly, when he sinneth by ignorance before the LORD, to make an atonement for him; and it shall be forgiven him. Lev. 4:35
29 Ye shall have one law for him that sinneth through ignorance, *both for* him that is born among the children of Israel, and for the stranger that sojourneth among them.

The Punishment of the Presumptuous Person

30 But the soul that doeth *ought* presumptuously, *whether he be* born in the land, or a stranger, the same reproacheth the LORD; and that soul shall be cut off from among his people. Deut. 1:43
31 Because he hath despised the word of the LORD, and hath broken his commandment, that soul shall utterly be cut off; his iniquity *shall be* upon him. 2 Sam. 12:9; Prov. 13:13; Ezek. 18:20

15:31 A Severe Punishment

There are those who will question God's love and His justice in visiting so severe punishment for words spoken in the heat of passion. But both love and justice require it to be shown that utterances prompted by malice against God are a great sin. . . . But had this man's sin been permitted to pass unpunished, others would have been demoralized; and as the result many lives must eventually have been sacrificed. *PP 408*

32 And while the children of Israel were in the wilderness, they found a man that gathered sticks upon the sabbath day. Ex. 35:2-3
33 And they that found him gathering sticks brought him unto Moses and Aaron, and unto all the congregation.
34 And they put him in ᵀward, because it was not declared what should be done to him. Lev. 24:12 ◆ *prison or guard*
35 And the LORD said unto Moses, The man shall be surely put to death: all the congregation shall stone him with stones without the camp. Ex. 31:14-15
36 And all the congregation brought him without the camp, and stoned him with stones, and he died; as the LORD commanded Moses.

The Law of Wearing Fringes as a Remembrance

37 And the LORD spake unto Moses, saying,
38 Speak unto the children of Israel, and bid them that they make them fringes in the borders of their garments throughout their generations, and that they put upon the fringe of the borders a ribband of blue: Deut. 22:12
39 And it shall be unto you for a fringe, that ye may look upon it, and remember all the commandments of the LORD, and do them; and that ye seek not after your own heart and your own eyes, after which ye use to go ᵀa whoring: Ps. 73:27 ◆ *giving sex as a prostitute*
40 That ye may remember, and do all my commandments, and be holy unto your God. Lev. 11:44-45
41 I *am* the LORD your God, which brought you out of the land of Egypt, to be your God: I *am* the LORD your God. Lev. 22:33

The Rebellion of Korah, Dathan, and Abiram

16 Now Korah, the son of Izhar, the son of Kohath, the son of Levi, and Dathan and Abiram, the sons of Eliab, and

On, the son of Peleth, sons of Reuben, took men: Ex. 6:18, 21; Jude 11

16:1–3 A Conspiracy of Rebellion

The judgments visited upon the Israelites served for a time to restrain their murmuring and insubordination, but the spirit of rebellion was still in the heart and eventually brought forth the bitterest fruits. The former rebellions had been mere popular tumults, arising from the sudden impulse of the excited multitude; but now a deep-laid conspiracy was formed, the result of a determined purpose to overthrow the authority of the leaders appointed by God Himself. *PP 395*

2 And they rose up before Moses, with certain of the children of Israel, two hundred and fifty princes of the assembly, famous in the congregation, men of renown: Num. 26:9
3 And they gathered themselves together against Moses and against Aaron, and said unto them, *Ye take* too much upon you, seeing all the congregation *are* holy, every one of them, and the LORD *is* among them: wherefore then lift ye up yourselves above the congregation of the LORD? Ex. 19:6; Ps. 106:16

16:3 A Spirit of Jealousy

Korah, the leading spirit in this movement, was a Levite, of the family of Kohath, and a cousin of Moses; he was a man of ability and influence. Though appointed to the service of the tabernacle, he had become dissatisfied with his position and aspired to the dignity of the priesthood. The bestowal upon Aaron and his house of the priestly office, which had formerly devolved upon the first-born son of every family, had given rise to jealousy and dissatisfaction. *PP 395*

4 And when Moses heard *it*, he fell upon his face: Num. 14:5; 20:6
5 And he spake unto Korah and unto all his company, saying, Even to morrow the LORD will shew who *are* his, and *who is* holy; and will cause *him* to come near unto him: even *him* whom he hath chosen will he cause to come near unto him. Lev. 10:3; Num. 17:5; Ps. 65:4
6 This do; Take you censers, Korah, and all his company; Lev. 10:1
7 And put fire therein, and put incense in them before the LORD to morrow: and it shall be *that* the man whom the LORD doth choose, he *shall be* holy: *ye take* too much upon you, ye sons of Levi. Num. 16:3
8 And Moses said unto Korah, Hear, I pray you, ye sons of Levi:
9 *Seemeth it but* a small thing unto you, that the God of Israel hath separated you from the congregation of Israel, to bring you near to himself to do the service of the tabernacle of the LORD, and to stand before the congregation to minister unto them? Deut. 10:8; Is. 7:13

10 And he hath brought thee near *to him*, and all thy brethren the sons of Levi with thee: and seek ye the priesthood also?
11 For which cause *both* thou and all thy company *are* gathered together against the LORD: and what *is* Aaron, that ye murmur against him? Ex. 16:7-8
12 And Moses sent to call Dathan and Abiram, the sons of Eliab: which said, We will not come up:

16:12 A Scheme Widens

Close to the tents of Korah and the Kohathites, on the south side of the tabernacle, was the encampment of the tribe of Reuben, the tents of Dathan and Abiram, two princes of this tribe, being near that of Korah. These princes readily joined in his ambitious schemes. Being descendants from the eldest son of Jacob, they claimed that the civil authority belonged to them, and they determined to divide with Korah the honors of the priesthood. *PP 395*

13 *Is it* a small thing that thou hast brought us up out of a land that floweth with milk and honey, to kill us in the wilderness, except thou make thyself altogether a prince over us? Acts 7:35
14 Moreover thou hast not brought us into a land that floweth with milk and honey, or given us inheritance of fields and vineyards: wilt thou put out the eyes of these men? we will not come up. Lev. 20:24
15 And Moses was very ᵀwroth, and said unto the LORD, Respect not thou their offering: I have not taken one ass from them, neither have I hurt one of them. Gen. 4:4-5 ♦ *angry*
16 And Moses said unto Korah, Be thou and all thy company before the LORD, thou, and they, and Aaron, to morrow: 1 Sam. 12:3
17 And take every man his censer, and put incense in them, and bring ye before the LORD every man his censer, two hundred and fifty ᵀcensers; thou also, and Aaron, each *of you* his censer. *holders for burning incense*
18 And they took every man his censer, and put fire in them, and laid incense thereon, and stood in the door of the tabernacle of the congregation with Moses and Aaron.
19 And Korah gathered all the congregation against them unto the door of the tabernacle of the congregation: and the glory of the LORD appeared unto all the congregation. Num. 14:10
20 And the LORD spake unto Moses and unto Aaron, saying,
21 Separate yourselves from among this congregation, that I may consume them in a moment. Ex. 32:10
22 And they fell upon their faces, and said, O

God, the God of the spirits of all flesh, shall one man sin, and wilt thou be wroth with all the congregation?   Gen. 18:23-25; Num. 14:5; 27:16

The Rebels and Their Families Are Swallowed by the Earth

23 And the LORD spake unto Moses, saying,
24 Speak unto the congregation, saying, Get you up from about the tabernacle of Korah, Dathan, and Abiram.
25 And Moses rose up and went unto Dathan and Abiram; and the elders of Israel followed him.
26 And he spake unto the congregation, saying, Depart, I pray you, from the tents of these wicked men, and touch nothing of theirs, lest ye be consumed in all their sins.   Is. 52:11; 2 Cor. 6:17; Rev. 18:4
27 So they gat up from the tabernacle of Korah, Dathan, and Abiram, on every side: and Dathan and Abiram came out, and stood in the door of their tents, and their wives, and their sons, and their little children.
28 And Moses said, Hereby ye shall know that the LORD hath sent me to do all these works; for I have not done them of mine own mind.   Ex. 3:12
29 If these men die the common death of all men, or if they be visited after the visitation of all men; then the LORD hath not sent me.   1 Kin. 22:28
30 But if the LORD make a new thing, and the earth open her mouth, and swallow them up, with all that ᵀappertain unto them, and they go down ᵀquick into the pit; then ye shall understand that these men have provoked the LORD.   Num. 16:33; Job 31:3; Ps. 55:15 ◆ belong ◆ living
31 And it came to pass, as he had made an end of speaking all these words, that the ground ᵀclave ᵀasunder that was under them: Num. 27:3 ◆ split ◆ apart
32 And the earth opened her mouth, and swallowed them up, and their houses, and all the men that appertained unto Korah, and all their goods.   Num. 26:11; 1 Chr. 6:22
33 They, and all that ᵀappertained to them, went down alive into the pit, and the earth closed upon them: and they perished from among the congregation.   Jude 11 ◆ beloned
34 And all Israel that were round about them fled at the cry of them: for they said, Lest the earth swallow us up also.
35 And there came out a fire from the LORD, and consumed the two hundred and fifty men that offered incense.   Lev. 10:2
36 And the LORD spake unto Moses, saying,
37 Speak unto Eleazar the son of Aaron the priest, that he take up the censers out of the burning, and scatter thou the fire yonder; for they are hallowed.
38 The censers of these sinners against their own souls, let them make them broad plates for a covering of the altar: for they offered them before the LORD, therefore they are hallowed: and they shall be a sign unto the children of Israel.   Num. 26:10
39 And Eleazar the priest took the brasen censers, wherewith they that were burnt had offered; and they were made broad plates for a covering of the altar:
40 To be a memorial unto the children of Israel, that no stranger, which is not of the seed of Aaron, come near to offer incense before the LORD; that he be not as Korah, and as his company: as the LORD said to him by the hand of Moses.   Num. 3:10

Many Are Slain for Murmuring against Moses and Aaron

41 But on the morrow all the congregation of the children of Israel murmured against Moses and against Aaron, saying, Ye have killed the people of the LORD.   Num. 14:2
42 And it came to pass, when the congregation was gathered against Moses and against Aaron, that they looked toward the tabernacle of the congregation: and, behold, the cloud covered it, and the glory of the LORD appeared.   Lev. 9:23; Num. 16:19; 20:6
43 And Moses and Aaron came before the tabernacle of the congregation.
44 And the LORD spake unto Moses, saying,
45 Get you up from among this congregation, that I may consume them as in a moment. And they fell upon their faces.   Num. 16:24
46 And Moses said unto Aaron, Take a censer, and put fire therein from off the altar, and put on incense, and go quickly unto the congregation, and make an atonement for them: for there is wrath gone out from the LORD; the plague is begun.   Lev. 10:6
47 And Aaron took as Moses commanded, and ran into the midst of the congregation; and, behold, the plague was begun among the people: and he put on incense, and made an atonement for the people.
48 And he stood between the dead and the living; and the plague was stayed. 2 Sam. 24:25
49 Now they that died in the plague were fourteen thousand and seven hundred, beside them that died about the matter of Korah.   Num. 25:9

16:49 Cutting Oneself Off From God

God works by the manifestation of His Spirit to reprove and convict the sinner; and if the Spirit's work is finally rejected, there is no more that God can do for the soul. The last resource of divine mercy has been employed. The transgressor has cut himself off from God, and sin has no remedy to cure itself. There is no reserved power by which God can work to convict and convert the sinner. "Let him alone" (Hosea 4:17) is the divine command. PP 405

50 And Aaron returned unto Moses unto the door of the tabernacle of the congregation: and the plague was ᵀstayed.   *held back*

Aaron's Rod Blossoms

17 And the LORD spake unto Moses, saying,

2 Speak unto the children of Israel, and take of every one of them a rod according to the house of *their* fathers, of all their princes according to the house of their fathers twelve rods: write thou every man's name upon his rod.

3 And thou shalt write Aaron's name upon the rod of Levi: for one rod *shall be* for the head of the house of their fathers.

4 And thou shalt lay them up in the tabernacle of the congregation before the testimony, where I will meet with you.

5 And it shall come to pass, *that* the man's rod, whom I shall choose, shall blossom: and I will make to cease from me the murmurings of the children of Israel, whereby they murmur against you.   Num. 16:5, 11

6 And Moses spake unto the children of Israel, and every one of their princes gave him a rod apiece, for each prince one, according to their fathers' houses, *even* twelve rods: and the rod of Aaron *was* among their rods.

7 And Moses laid up the rods before the LORD in the tabernacle of witness.   Ex. 38:21

8 And it came to pass, that on the morrow Moses went into the tabernacle of witness; and, behold, the rod of Aaron for the house of Levi was budded, and brought forth buds, and bloomed blossoms, and yielded almonds.   Ezek. 17:24

9 And Moses brought out all the rods from before the LORD unto all the children of Israel: and they looked, and took every man his rod.

10 And the LORD said unto Moses, Bring Aaron's rod again before the testimony, to be kept for a token against the rebels; and thou shalt quite take away their murmurings from me, that they die not.   Num. 16:38

17:10 Rebellion Repeated

In the rebellion of Korah is seen the working out, upon a narrower stage, of the same spirit that led to the rebellion of Satan in heaven. It was pride and ambition that prompted Lucifer to complain of the government of God, and to seek the overthrow of the order which had been established in heaven. Since his fall it has been his object to infuse the same spirit of envy and discontent, the same ambition for position and honor, into the minds of men. *PP 403*

11 And Moses did *so*: as the LORD commanded him, so did he.

12 And the children of Israel spake unto Moses, saying, Behold, we die, we perish, we all perish.

13 Whosoever cometh any thing near unto the tabernacle of the LORD shall die: shall we be consumed with dying?

God's Charge to the Priests and Levites

18 And the LORD said unto Aaron, Thou and thy sons and thy father's house with thee shall bear the iniquity of the sanctuary: and thou and thy sons with thee shall bear the iniquity of your priesthood. Ex. 28:38

18:1 A One-Family Priesthood

In the earliest times every man was the priest of his own household. In the days of Abraham the priesthood was regarded as the birthright of the eldest son. Now, instead of the first-born of all Israel, the Lord accepted the tribe of Levi for the work of the sanctuary. . . . The priesthood, however, was restricted to the family of Aaron. *PP 350*

2 And thy brethren also of the tribe of Levi, the tribe of thy father, bring thou with thee, that they may be joined unto thee, and minister unto thee: but thou and thy sons with thee *shall minister* before the tabernacle of witness.   Gen. 29:34

3 And they shall keep thy charge, and the charge of all the tabernacle: only they shall not come nigh the vessels of the sanctuary and the altar, that neither they, nor ye also, die.   Num. 3:25, 31; 4:15

4 And they shall be joined unto thee, and keep the charge of the tabernacle of the congregation, for all the service of the tabernacle: and a stranger shall not come nigh unto you.

5 And ye shall keep the charge of the sanctuary, and the charge of the altar: that there be no wrath any more upon the children of Israel.   Ex. 27:21; Lev. 24:3; Num. 16:46

6 And I, behold, I have taken your brethren the Levites from among the children of Israel: to you *they are* given *as* a gift for the LORD, to do the service of the tabernacle of the congregation.   Num. 3:9, 12, 45

7 Therefore thou and thy sons with thee shall keep your priest's office for every thing of the altar, and within the ᵀvail; and ye shall serve: I have given your priest's office *unto you* as a service of gift: and the stranger that cometh nigh shall be put to death.   Num. 3:10 ◆ *veil*

8 And the LORD spake unto Aaron, Behold, I also have given thee the charge of mine heave offerings of all the hallowed things of the children of Israel; unto thee have I given them by reason of the anointing, and to thy sons, by an ordinance for ever.   Lev. 6:16

9 This shall be thine of the most holy things, *reserved* from the fire: every ᵀoblation of theirs, every meat offering of theirs, and every sin offering of theirs, and every ᵀtrespass offering of theirs, which they shall render unto me, *shall be* most holy for thee and for thy sons.   Lev. 7:7 ◆ *offering* ◆ *sin*

10 In the most holy *place* shalt thou eat it; every male shall eat it: it shall be holy unto thee.   Lev. 6:29

11 And this *is* thine; the heave offering of their gift, with all the wave offerings of the children of Israel: I have given them unto thee, and to thy sons and to thy daughters with thee, by a statute for ever: every one that is clean in thy house shall eat of it.   Deut. 18:3

12 All the best of the oil, and all the best of the wine, and of the wheat, the firstfruits of them which they shall offer unto the LORD, them have I given thee.   Ex. 23:19

13 *And* whatsoever is first ripe in the land, which they shall bring unto the LORD, shall be thine; every one that is clean in thine house shall eat *of* it.   Ex. 22:29

14 Every thing devoted in Israel shall be thine.   Lev. 27:28

15 Every thing that openeth the ᵀmatrix in all flesh, which they bring unto the LORD, *whether it be* of men or beasts, shall be thine: nevertheless the firstborn of man shalt thou surely redeem, and the firstling of unclean beasts shalt thou redeem.   Ex. 13:2, 12-13 ◆ *womb*

16 And those that are to be redeemed from a month old shalt thou redeem, according to thine estimation, for the money of five shekels, after the shekel of the sanctuary, which *is* twenty gerahs.   Ex. 30:13

17 But the ᵀfirstling of a cow, or the firstling of a sheep, or the firstling of a goat, thou shalt not redeem; they *are* holy: thou shalt sprinkle their blood upon the altar, and shalt burn their fat *for* an offering made by fire, for a sweet savour unto the LORD.   *firstborn*

18 And the flesh of them shall be thine, as the wave breast and as the right shoulder are thine.

19 All the heave offerings of the holy things, which the children of Israel offer unto the LORD, have I given thee, and thy sons and thy daughters with thee, by a statute for ever: it *is* a covenant of salt for ever before the LORD unto thee and to thy seed with thee.   Lev. 2:13; Num. 18:11; 2 Chr. 13:5

20 And the LORD spake unto Aaron, Thou shalt have no inheritance in their land, neither shalt thou have any part among them: I *am* thy part and thine inheritance among the children of Israel.   Deut. 10:9; 12:12; 14:27

18:21 Tithes—and Offerings Too

The tithe was to be exclusively devoted to the use of the Levites, the tribe that had been set apart for the service of the sanctuary. But this was by no means the limit of the contributions for religious purposes. The tabernacle, as afterward the temple, was erected wholly by freewill offerings; and to provide for necessary repairs and other expenses. . . . From time to time sin offerings and thank offerings were brought to God. *PP 526*

21 And, behold, I have given the children of Levi all the tenth in Israel for an inheritance, for their service which they serve, *even* the service of the tabernacle of the congregation.   Deut. 14:22-29

Managing God's Gifts See 1 Corinthians 9:13, 14.

22 Neither must the children of Israel ᵀthenceforth come nigh the tabernacle of the congregation, lest they bear sin, and die.   Lev. 22:9 ◆ *from this time forward*

23 But the Levites shall do the service of the tabernacle of the congregation, and they shall bear their iniquity: *it shall be* a statute for ever throughout your generations, that among the children of Israel they have no inheritance.   Num. 3:7

24 But the tithes of the children of Israel, which they offer *as* an heave offering unto the LORD, I have given to the Levites to inherit: therefore I have said unto them, Among the children of Israel they shall have no inheritance.   Num. 18:26

25 And the LORD spake unto Moses, saying, 26 Thus speak unto the Levites, and say unto them, When ye take of the children of Israel the tithes which I have given you from them for your inheritance, then ye shall offer up an heave offering of it for the LORD, *even* a tenth *part* of the ᵀtithe.   Neh. 10:38 ◆ *one-tenth*

27 And *this* your heave offering shall be reckoned unto you, as though *it were* the corn of the threshingfloor, and as the fulness of the winepress.   Num. 18:30

28 Thus ye also shall offer an heave offering unto the LORD of all your tithes, which ye receive of the children of Israel; and ye shall give thereof the LORD's heave offering to Aaron the priest.

29 Out of all your gifts ye shall offer every heave offering of the LORD, of all the best thereof, *even* the hallowed part thereof out of it.

30 Therefore thou shalt say unto them, When ye have heaved the best thereof from it, then it shall be counted unto the Levites as the increase of the threshingfloor, and as the increase of the winepress.

31 And ye shall eat it in every place, ye and

your households: for it *is* your reward for your service in the tabernacle of the congregation.   Matt. 10:10
32 And ye shall bear no sin by reason of it, when ye have heaved from it the best of it: neither shall ye pollute the holy things of the children of Israel, lest ye die.   Lev. 19:8

The Water of Separation Made with the Ashes of a Red Heifer

19 And the LORD spake unto Moses and unto Aaron, saying,
2 This *is* the ordinance of the law which the LORD hath commanded, saying, Speak unto the children of Israel, that they bring thee a red heifer without spot, wherein *is* no blemish, *and* upon which never came yoke:
3 And ye shall give her unto Eleazar the priest, that he may bring her forth without the camp, and *one* shall slay her before his face: Lev. 4:12, 21
4 And Eleazar the priest shall take of her blood with his finger, and sprinkle of her blood directly before the tabernacle of the congregation seven times: Lev. 4:6, 17; 16:14
5 And *one* shall burn the heifer in his sight; her skin, and her flesh, and her blood, with her dung, shall he burn: Ex. 29:14; Lev. 4:11-12
6 And the priest shall take cedar wood, and hyssop, and scarlet, and cast *it* into the midst of the burning of the heifer.   Lev. 14:4, 6, 49
7 Then the priest shall wash his clothes, and he shall bathe his flesh in water, and afterward he shall come into the camp, and the priest shall be unclean until the even. Lev. 11:25
8 And he that burneth her shall wash his clothes in water, and bathe his flesh in water, and shall be unclean until the even.
9 And a man *that is* clean shall gather up the ashes of the heifer, and lay *them* up without the camp in a clean place, and it shall be kept for the congregation of the children of Israel for a water of separation: it *is* a purification for sin.   Num. 19:13
10 And he that gathereth the ashes of the heifer shall wash his clothes, and be unclean until the even: and it shall be unto the children of Israel, and unto the stranger that sojourneth among them, for a statute for ever.

The Law for the Use of the Water in Purification of the Unclean

11 He that toucheth the dead body of any man shall be unclean seven days.   Lev. 21:1
12 He shall purify himself with it on the third day, and on the seventh day he shall be clean: but if he purify not himself the third day, then the seventh day he shall not be clean.   Num. 31:19
13 Whosoever toucheth the dead body of any man that is dead, and purifieth not himself, defileth the tabernacle of the LORD; and

that soul shall be cut off from Israel: because the water of separation was not sprinkled upon him, he shall be unclean; his uncleanness *is* yet upon him.   Lev. 7:20; 15:31; 22:3
14 This *is* the law, when a man dieth in a tent: all that come into the tent, and all that *is* in the tent, shall be unclean seven days.
15 And every open vessel, which hath no covering bound upon it, *is* unclean. Lev. 11:32
16 And whosoever toucheth one that is slain with a sword in the open fields, or a dead body, or a bone of a man, or a grave, shall be unclean seven days.   Num. 31:19
17 And for an unclean *person* they shall take of the ashes of the burnt heifer of purification for sin, and running water shall be put thereto in a vessel:
18 And a clean person shall take hyssop, and dip *it* in the water, and sprinkle *it* upon the tent, and upon all the vessels, and upon the persons that were there, and upon him that touched a bone, or one slain, or one dead, or a grave: *bitter herb*
19 And the clean *person* shall sprinkle upon the unclean on the third day, and on the seventh day: and on the seventh day he shall purify himself, and wash his clothes, and bathe himself in water, and shall be clean at even.
20 But the man that shall be unclean, and shall not purify himself, that soul shall be cut off from among the congregation, because he hath defiled the sanctuary of the LORD: the water of separation hath not been sprinkled upon him; he *is* unclean. Num. 19:13
21 And it shall be a perpetual statute unto them, that he that sprinkleth the water of separation shall wash his clothes; and he that toucheth the water of separation shall be unclean until even.
22 And whatsoever the unclean *person* toucheth shall be unclean; and the soul that toucheth *it* shall be unclean until even.

The Israelites Come to Zin, Where Miriam Dies

20 Then came the children of Israel, *even* the whole congregation, into the desert of Zin in the first month: and the people abode in Kadesh; and Miriam died there, and was buried there. Ex. 15:20; Num. 13:21; 33:36

20:1 Sin-Dashed Hopes

Here Miriam died and was buried. From that scene of rejoicing on the shores of the Red Sea, when Israel went forth with song and dance to celebrate Jehovah's triumph, to the wilderness grave which ended a lifelong wandering—such had been the fate of millions who with high hopes had come forth from Egypt. Sin had dashed from their lips the cup of blessing. Would the next generation learn the lesson? *PP 410*

2 And there was no water for the congregation: and they gathered themselves together
against Moses and against Aaron.   Num. 16:19
3 And the people chode with Moses, and
spake, saying, Would God that we had died
when our brethren died before the LORD!
4 And why have ye brought up the congregation of the LORD into this wilderness, that
we and our cattle should die there?   Ex. 17:3
5 And wherefore have ye made us to come
up out of Egypt, to bring us in unto this evil
place? it *is* no place of seed, or of figs, or of
vines, or of pomegranates; neither *is* there
any water to drink.   Num. 16:14
6 And Moses and Aaron went from the presence of the assembly unto the door of the
tabernacle of the congregation, and they fell
upon their faces: and the glory of the LORD
appeared unto them.   Num. 14:5; 16:4, 19
7 And the LORD spake unto Moses, saying,
8 Take the rod, and gather thou the assembly together, thou, and Aaron thy brother,
and speak ye unto the rock before their eyes;
and it shall give forth his water, and thou
shalt bring forth to them water out of the
rock: so thou shalt give the congregation
and their beasts drink.   Ex. 4:17
9 And Moses took the rod from before the
LORD, as he commanded him.   Num. 17:10
10 And Moses and Aaron gathered the congregation together before the rock, and he
said unto them, Hear now, ye rebels; must we
fetch you water out of this rock?   Ps. 106:32-33
11 And Moses lifted up his hand, and with his
rod he smote the rock twice: and the water
came out abundantly, and the congregation
drank, and their beasts *also*.   1 Cor. 10:4

20:10, 11 A Rash Act   A Ruined Lesson

By his rash act Moses took away the force
of the lesson that God purposed to teach. The
rock, being a symbol of Christ, had been once
smitten, as Christ was to be once offered. The
second time it was needful only to speak to
the rock, as we have only to ask for blessings
in the name of Jesus. By the second smiting
of the rock the significance of this beautiful
figure of Christ was destroyed. *PP 418*

12 And the LORD spake unto Moses and
Aaron, Because ye believed me not, to
ᵀsanctify me in the eyes of the children of
Israel, therefore ye shall not bring this congregation into the land which I have given
them.   Num. 20:24; 27:14; Deut. 1:37 ◆ *make holy*
13 This *is* the water of Meribah; because the
children of Israel strove with the LORD, and
he was ᵀsanctified in them.   Ex. 17:7 ◆ *made holy*

Edom Denies Moses' Request for Passage

14 And Moses sent messengers from Kadesh unto the king of Edom, Thus saith thy
brother Israel, Thou knowest all the travail
that hath befallen us: Judg. 11:16-17
15 How our fathers went down into Egypt,
and we have dwelt in Egypt a long time; and
the Egyptians vexed us, and our fathers:
16 And when we cried unto the LORD, he
heard our voice, and sent an angel, and hath
brought us forth out of Egypt: and, behold,
we *are* in Kadesh, a city in the uttermost of
thy border: Ex. 14:19; 23:20; 33:2
17 Let us pass, I pray thee, through thy
country: we will not pass through the fields,
or through the vineyards, neither will we
drink *of* the water of the wells: we will go
by the king's *high* way, we will not turn to

God's Warning to Future Generations

Numbers 20:10–12

The history of Israel was to be placed on record for the instruction and warning of coming generations. Men of all future time must see the God of heaven as an impartial ruler, in no case justifying
sin. But few realize the exceeding sinfulness of sin. Men flatter themselves that God is too good to
punish the transgressor. But in the light of Bible history it is evident that God's goodness and His
love engage Him to deal with sin as an evil fatal to the peace and happiness of the universe.

Not even the integrity and faithfulness of Moses could avert the retribution of his fault. God had
forgiven the people greater transgressions, but He could not deal with sin in the leaders as in those
who were led. He had honored Moses above every other man upon the earth. . . . Past faithfulness
will not atone for one wrong act. The greater the light and privileges granted to man, the greater is
his responsibility, the more aggravated his failure, and the heavier his punishment. . . .

All who profess godliness are under the most sacred obligation to guard the spirit, and to exercise self-control under the greatest provocation. . . . God has made ample provision for His people;
and if they rely upon His strength, they will never become the sport of circumstances. The strongest
temptation cannot excuse sin. However great the pressure brought to bear upon the soul, transgression is our own act. It is not in the power of earth or hell to compel anyone to do evil. Satan attacks
us at our weak points, but we need not be overcome. However severe or unexpected the assault,
God has provided help for us, and in His strength we may conquer. *PP 420, 421*

the right hand nor to the left, until we have passed thy borders.   Deut. 2:27
18 And Edom said unto him, Thou shalt not pass by me, lest I come out against thee with the sword.
19 And the children of Israel said unto him, We will go by the high way: and if I and my cattle drink of thy water, then I will pay for it: I will only, without *doing* any thing *else*, go through on my feet.   Deut. 2:6, 28
20 And he said, Thou shalt not go through. And Edom came out against him with much people, and with a strong hand.   Judg. 11:17
21 Thus Edom refused to give Israel passage through his border: wherefore Israel turned away from him.   Judg. 11:18

20:21 No Delay

Had the people, when brought into trial, trusted in God, the Captain of the Lord's host would have led them through Edom. . . .

It is important to believe God's word and act upon it promptly, while His angels are waiting to work for us. Evil angels are ready to contest every step of advance. . . . God's servants should be minutemen, ever ready to move as fast as His providence opens the way. And delay on their part gives time for Satan to work to defeat them. *PP 422, 423*

Before He Dies, Aaron Gives His Role as High Priest to Eleazar

22 And the children of Israel, *even* the whole congregation, journeyed from Kadesh, and came unto mount Hor.   Num. 20:1
23 And the LORD spake unto Moses and Aaron in mount Hor, by the coast of the land of Edom, saying,
24 Aaron shall be gathered unto his people: for he shall not enter into the land which I have given unto the children of Israel, because ye rebelled against my word at the water of Meribah. Gen. 25:8; Num. 27:13; Deut. 32:50
25 Take Aaron and Eleazar his son, and bring them up unto mount Hor:
26 And strip Aaron of his garments, and put them upon Eleazar his son: and Aaron shall be gathered *unto his people*, and shall die there.   Num. 20:24
27 And Moses did as the LORD commanded: and they went up into mount Hor in the sight of all the congregation.
28 And Moses stripped Aaron of his garments, and put them upon Eleazar his son; and Aaron died there in the top of the mount: and Moses and Eleazar came down from the mount.   Ex. 29:29-30; Deut. 10:6
29 And when all the congregation saw that Aaron was dead, they mourned for Aaron thirty days, *even* all the house of Israel.

The King of Arad Attacks

21 And *when* king Arad the Canaanite, which dwelt in the south, heard tell that Israel came by the way of the spies; then he fought against Israel, and took *some* of them prisoners.   Num. 33:40; Josh. 12:14; Judg. 1:16
2 And Israel vowed a vow unto the LORD, and said, If thou wilt indeed deliver this people into my hand, then I will utterly destroy their cities.   Gen. 28:20
3 And the LORD hearkened to the voice of Israel, and delivered up the Canaanites; and they utterly destroyed them and their cities: and he called the name of the place Hormah.   Num. 14:45

The Brass Serpent on a Pole Saves the People from Snake Bites

4 And they journeyed from mount Hor by the way of the Red sea, to ᵀcompass the land of Edom: and the soul of the people was much discouraged because of the way. Ex. 6:9 ♦ *surround*
5 And the people spake against God, and against Moses, Wherefore have ye brought us up out of Egypt to die in the wilderness? for *there is* no bread, neither *is there any* water; and our soul loatheth this light bread. Ps. 78:19

21:5 The Spirit of Discontent

As the Israelites indulged the spirit of discontent, they were disposed to find fault even with their blessings. "And the people spake against God, and against Moses, Wherefore have ye brought us up out of Egypt to die in the wilderness? for there is no bread, neither is there any water; and our soul loatheth this light bread."

Moses faithfully set before the people their great sin. It was God's power alone that had preserved them. . . . *PP 428*

---

6 And the LORD sent fiery serpents among the people, and they bit the people; and much people of Israel died.   Deut. 8:15; Jer. 8:17
7 Therefore the people came to Moses, and said, We have sinned, for we have spoken against the LORD, and against thee; pray unto the LORD, that he take away the serpents from us. And Moses prayed for the people.   Ex. 8:8; Num. 11:2; Ps. 78:34

21:6 Protection Withdrawn

Because they had been shielded by divine power they had not realized the countless dangers by which they were continually surrounded. In their ingratitude and unbelief they had anticipated death, and now the Lord permitted death to come upon them. . . . As the protecting hand of God was removed from Israel, great numbers of the people were attacked by these venomous creatures. *PP 429*

8 And the LORD said unto Moses, Make thee a fiery serpent, and set it upon a pole: and it shall come to pass, that every one that is bitten, when he looketh upon it, shall live.
9 And Moses made a serpent of brass, and put it upon a pole, and it came to pass, that if a serpent had bitten any man, when he beheld the serpent of brass, he lived.   2 Kin. 18:4

21:9 Salvation in a Look

The people well knew that there was no power in the serpent of brass to cause such a change in those who looked upon it. The healing virtue was from God alone. In His wisdom He chose this way of displaying His power. By this simple means the people were made to realize that this affliction had been brought upon them by their sins. They were also assured that while obeying God they had no reason to fear, for He would preserve them. *PP 430*

Various Journeys of the Israelites
10 And the children of Israel set forward, and pitched in Oboth.
11 And they journeyed from Oboth, and pitched at Ijeabarim, in the wilderness which is before Moab, toward the sunrising.
12 From thence they removed, and pitched in the valley of Zared.   Deut. 2:13-14
13 From thence they removed, and pitched on the other side of Arnon, which is in the wilderness that cometh out of the coasts of the Amorites: for Arnon is the border of Moab, between Moab and the Amorites.   Judg. 11:18
14 Wherefore it is said in the book of the wars of the LORD, What he did in the Red sea, and in the brooks of Arnon,
15 And at the stream of the brooks that goeth down to the dwelling of Ar, and lieth upon the border of Moab.   Num. 21:28; Deut. 2:9, 18
16 And from thence they went to Beer: that is the well whereof the LORD spake unto Moses, Gather the people together, and I will give them water.   Ex. 17:6
17 Then Israel sang this song, Spring up, O well; sing ye unto it: Ps. 105:2
18 The princes digged the well, the nobles of the people digged it, by the direction of the lawgiver, with their ᵀstaves. And from the wilderness they went to Mattanah: clubs or rods
19 And from Mattanah to Nahaliel: and from Nahaliel to Bamoth:
20 And from Bamoth in the valley, that is in the country of Moab, to the top of Pisgah, which looketh toward Jeshimon.   Num. 23:28

The Amorite King Sihon Is Overcome
21 And Israel sent messengers unto Sihon king of the Amorites, saying,   Deut. 2:26-28
22 Let me pass through thy land: we will not turn into the fields, or into the vineyards; we will not drink of the waters of the well: but we will go along by the king's high way, until we be past thy borders.   Num. 20:17
23 And Sihon would not suffer Israel to pass through his border: but Sihon gathered all his people together, and went out against Israel into the wilderness: and he came to Jahaz, and fought against Israel.   Judg. 11:20
24 And Israel smote him with the edge of the sword, and possessed his land from Arnon unto Jabbok, even unto the children of Ammon: for the border of the children of Ammon was strong. Gen. 32:22; Josh. 24:8; Amos 2:9
25 And Israel took all these cities: and Israel dwelt in all the cities of the Amorites, in Heshbon, and in all the villages thereof.

The Brazen Serpent an Important Lesson

Numbers 21:5–9

The lifting up of the brazen serpent was to teach Israel an important lesson. They could not save themselves from the fatal effect of the poison in their wounds. God alone was able to heal them. Yet they were required to show their faith in the provision which He had made. They must look in order to live. It was their faith that was acceptable with God, and by looking upon the serpent their faith was shown. They knew that there was no virtue in the serpent itself, but it was a symbol of Christ; and the necessity of faith in His merits was thus presented to their minds. . . . The Lord would now teach them that their sacrifices, in themselves, had no more power or virtue than the serpent of brass, but were, like that, to lead their minds to Christ, the great sin offering.

"As Moses lifted up the serpent in the wilderness," even so was the Son of man "lifted up: that whosoever believeth in Him should not perish, but have eternal life" (John 3:14, 15). . . . The Israelites saved their lives by looking upon the uplifted serpent. That look implied faith. They lived because they believed God's word, and trusted in the means provided for their recovery. . . .

While the sinner cannot save himself, he still has something to do to secure salvation. "Him that cometh to Me," says Christ, "I will in no wise cast out" (John 6:37). But we must come to Him; and when we repent of our sins, we must believe that He accepts and pardons us. Faith is the gift of God, but the power to exercise it is ours. Faith is the hand by which the soul takes hold upon the divine offers of grace and mercy. *PP 430, 431*

26 For Heshbon *was* the city of Sihon the king of the Amorites, who had fought against the former king of Moab, and taken all his land out of his hand, even unto Arnon.

27 Wherefore they that speak in proverbs say, Come into Heshbon, let the city of Sihon be built and prepared:

28 For there is a fire gone out of Heshbon, a flame from the city of Sihon: it hath consumed Ar of Moab, *and* the lords of the high places of Arnon.   Num. 21:15; Jer. 48:45-46

29 Woe to thee, Moab! thou art undone, O people of Chemosh: he hath given his sons that escaped, and his daughters, into captivity unto Sihon king of the Amorites.   Judg. 11:24

30 We have shot at them; Heshbon is perished even unto Dibon, and we have laid them waste even unto Nophah, which *reacheth* unto Medeba.   Is. 15:2; Jer. 48:18, 22

31 Thus Israel dwelt in the land of the Amorites.

32 And Moses sent to spy out Jaazer, and they took the villages thereof, and drove out the Amorites that *were* there. Num. 32:1, 35; Jer. 48:32

33 And they turned and went up by the way of Bashan: and Og the king of Bashan went out against them, he, and all his people, to the battle at Edrei.   Deut. 1:4; 29:7; Josh. 13:12

34 And the LORD said unto Moses, Fear him not: for I have delivered him into thy hand, and all his people, and his land; and thou shalt do to him as thou didst unto Sihon king of the Amorites, which dwelt at Heshbon.

35 So they smote him, and his sons, and all his people, until there was none left him alive: and they possessed his land.

Balak's First Message for Balaam Is Refused

22 And the children of Israel set forward, and pitched in the plains of Moab on this side Jordan *by* Jericho.   Num. 33:48-50

2 And Balak the son of Zippor saw all that Israel had done to the Amorites.   Judg. 11:25

3 And Moab was sore afraid of the people, because they *were* many: and Moab was distressed because of the children of Israel.

4 And Moab said unto the elders of Midian, Now shall this company lick up all *that are* round about us, as the ox licketh up the grass of the field. And Balak the son of Zippor *was* king of the Moabites at that time. Num. 25:15-18

5 He sent messengers therefore unto Balaam the son of Beor to Pethor, which *is* by the river of the land of the children of his people, to call him, saying, Behold, there is a people come out from Egypt: behold, they cover the face of the earth, and they abide over against me: Deut. 23:4; Josh. 24:9; Mic. 6:5

6 Come now therefore, I pray thee, curse me this people; for they *are* too mighty for me: peradventure I shall prevail, *that* we may ᵀsmite them, and *that* I may drive them out of the land: for I ᵀwot that he whom thou blessest *is* blessed, and he whom thou cursest is cursed.   Num. 23:7-8 ◆ *strike* ◆ *know*

7 And the elders of Moab and the elders of Midian departed with the rewards of ᵀdivination in their hand; and they came unto Balaam, and spake unto him the words of Balak.   1 Sam. 9:7-8 ◆ *false magic*

8 And he said unto them, Lodge here this night, and I will bring you word again, as the LORD shall speak unto me: and the princes of Moab abode with Balaam.

9 And God came unto Balaam, and said, What men *are* these with thee?   Gen. 20:3; Num. 22:20

10 And Balaam said unto God, Balak the son of Zippor, king of Moab, hath sent unto me, *saying,*

11 Behold, *there is* a people come out of Egypt, which covereth the face of the earth: come now, curse me them; ᵀperadventure I shall be able to overcome them, and drive them out.   *maybe*

12 And God said unto Balaam, Thou shalt not go with them; thou shalt not curse the people: for they *are* blessed.   Gen. 12:2

22:5–12 Dallying With Temptation

Balaam was once a good man and a prophet of God; but he had apostatized, and had given himself up to covetousness; yet he still professed to be a servant of the Most High. He was not ignorant of God's work in behalf of Israel; and when the messengers announced their errand, he well knew that it was his duty to refuse the rewards of Balak and to dismiss the ambassadors. But he ventured to dally with temptation. *PP 439*

---

13 And Balaam rose up in the morning, and said unto the princes of Balak, Get you into your land: for the LORD refuseth to give me leave to go with you.

14 And the princes of Moab rose up, and they went unto Balak, and said, Balaam refuseth to come with us.

Balaam Goes with the Messengers

15 And Balak sent yet again princes, more, and more honourable than they.

16 And they came to Balaam, and said to him, Thus saith Balak the son of Zippor, Let nothing, I pray thee, hinder thee from coming unto me:

17 For I will promote thee unto very great honour, and I will do whatsoever thou sayest unto me: come therefore, I pray thee, curse me this people.   Num. 24:11

18 And Balaam answered and said unto the servants of Balak, If Balak would give me his house full of silver and gold, I cannot go beyond the word of the LORD my God, to do less or more.   Num. 24:13; 1 Kin. 22:14; 2 Chr. 18:13
19 Now therefore, I pray you, tarry ye also here this night, that I may know what the LORD will say unto me more.
20 And God came unto Balaam at night, and said unto him, If the men come to call thee, rise up, *and* go with them; but yet the word which I shall say unto thee, that shalt thou do.   Num. 22:35; 23:12, 26
21 And Balaam rose up in the morning, and saddled his ass, and went with the princes of Moab.

22:19–21 God Will Not Be Trifled With

There are thousands at the present day who are pursuing a similar course. They would have no difficulty in understanding their duty if it were in harmony with their inclinations. It is plainly set before them in the Bible or is clearly indicated by circumstances and reason. But because these evidences are contrary to their desires and inclinations they frequently set them aside and presume to go to God to learn their duty. . . . But God will not be trifled with. *PP 440, 441*

Balaam's Donkey Speaks

22 And God's anger was kindled because he went: and the angel of the LORD stood in the way for an adversary against him. Now he was riding upon his ass, and his two servants *were* with him.   Ex. 4:24
23 And the ass saw the angel of the LORD standing in the way, and his sword drawn in his hand: and the ass turned aside out of the way, and went into the field: and Balaam smote the ass, to turn her into the way.
24 But the angel of the LORD stood in a path of the vineyards, a wall *being* on this side, and a wall on that side.
25 And when the ass saw the angel of the LORD, she thrust herself unto the wall, and crushed Balaam's foot against the wall: and he smote her again.
26 And the angel of the LORD went further, and stood in a narrow place, where *was* no way to turn either to the right hand or to the left.
27 And when the ass saw the angel of the LORD, she fell down under Balaam: and Balaam's anger was kindled, and he smote the ass with a staff.
28 And the LORD opened the mouth of the ass, and she said unto Balaam, What have I done unto thee, that thou hast smitten me these three times?   2 Pet. 2:16

22:28 What Balaam Could Not See

The animal saw the divine messenger, who was unperceived by the man, and turned aside from the highway into a field. With cruel blows Balaam brought the beast back into the path; but again, in a narrow place shut in by walls, the angel appeared, and the animal, trying to avoid the menacing figure, crushed her master's foot against the wall. . . . The man became exasperated, and beating the ass unmercifully, forced it to proceed. *PP 441, 442*

29 And Balaam said unto the ass, Because thou hast mocked me: I would there were a sword in mine hand, for now would I kill thee.   Prov. 12:10
30 And the ass said unto Balaam, *Am* not I thine ass, upon which thou hast ridden ever since *I was* thine unto this day? was I ever ᵀwont to do so unto thee? And he said, Nay.   *accustomed*
31 Then the LORD opened the eyes of Balaam, and he saw the angel of the LORD standing in the way, and his sword drawn in his hand: and he bowed down his head, and fell flat on his face.   Gen. 21:19
32 And the angel of the LORD said unto him, Wherefore hast thou smitten thine ass these three times? behold, I went out to withstand thee, because *thy* way is perverse before me: Num. 22:22
33 And the ass saw me, and turned from me these three times: unless she had turned from me, surely now also I had slain thee, and saved her alive.
34 And Balaam said unto the angel of the LORD, I have sinned; for I knew not that thou stoodest in the way against me: now therefore, if it displease thee, I will get me back again.   1 Sam. 15:24; 2 Sam. 12:13; Job 34:31-32
35 And the angel of the LORD said unto Balaam, Go with the men: but only the word that I shall speak unto thee, that thou shalt speak. So Balaam went with the princes of Balak.

Balak Entertains Balaam

36 And when Balak heard that Balaam was come, he went out to meet him unto a city of Moab, which *is* in the border of Arnon, which *is* in the utmost coast.
37 And Balak said unto Balaam, Did I not earnestly send unto thee to call thee? wherefore camest thou not unto me? am I not able indeed to promote thee to honour? Num. 24:11
38 And Balaam said unto Balak, Lo, I am come unto thee: have I now any power at all to say any thing? the word that God putteth in my mouth, that shall I speak.   Num. 22:18
39 And Balaam went with Balak, and they came unto Kirjath-huzoth.

40 And Balak offered oxen and sheep, and sent to Balaam, and to the princes that *were* with him.   Num. 23:14

41 And it came to pass on the morrow, that Balak took Balaam, and brought him up into the high places of Baal, that thence he might see the utmost *part* of the people. Num. 23:13

Balak's Sacrifice

23 And Balaam said unto Balak, Build me here seven altars, and prepare me here seven oxen and seven rams. Num. 23:29

23:1 Wisdom Becomes Foolishness

Balaam had some knowledge of the sacrificial offerings of the Hebrews, and he hoped that by surpassing them in costly gifts he might secure the blessing of God and ensure the accomplishment of his sinful projects. Thus the sentiments of the idolatrous Moabites were gaining control of his mind. His wisdom had become foolishness; his spiritual vision was beclouded; he had brought blindness upon himself by yielding to the power of Satan. *PP 444*

2 And Balak did as Balaam had spoken; and Balak and Balaam offered on *every* altar a bullock and a ram.   Num. 23:14

3 And Balaam said unto Balak, Stand by thy burnt offering, and I will go: peradventure the LORD will come to meet me: and whatsoever he sheweth me I will tell thee. And he went to an high place.   Num. 23:15

4 And God met Balaam: and he said unto him, I have prepared seven altars, and I have offered upon *every* altar a bullock and a ram.   Num. 23:16

5 And the LORD put a word in Balaam's mouth, and said, Return unto Balak, and thus thou shalt speak.   Num. 23:16; Deut. 18:18; Jer. 1:9

6 And he returned unto him, and, lo, he stood by his burnt sacrifice, he, and all the princes of Moab.

7 And he took up his parable, and said, Balak the king of Moab hath brought me from Aram, out of the mountains of the east, *saying*, Come, curse me Jacob, and come, defy Israel.   Num. 22:5-6; 23:18; 24:3

8 How shall I curse, whom God hath not cursed? or how shall I defy, *whom* the LORD hath not defied?

9 For from the top of the rocks I see him, and from the hills I behold him: lo, the people shall dwell alone, and shall not be reckoned among the nations.   Ex. 33:16

10 Who can count the dust of Jacob, and the number of the fourth *part* of Israel? Let me die the death of the righteous, and let my last end be like his!   Gen. 13:16; Ps. 37:37; 116:15

23:10 Divine Protection

The great magician had tried his power of enchantment, in accordance with the desire of the Moabites. . . . While they were under the divine protection, no people or nation, though aided by all the power of Satan, should be able to prevail against them. . . . And the favor of God at this time manifested toward Israel was to be an assurance of His protecting care for His obedient, faithful children in all ages. *PP 449*

11 And Balak said unto Balaam, What hast thou done unto me? I took thee to curse mine enemies, and, behold, thou hast blessed *them* altogether.   Num. 24:10

12 And he answered and said, Must I not take heed to speak that which the LORD hath put in my mouth?   Num. 22:38

13 And Balak said unto him, Come, I pray thee, with me unto another place, from whence thou mayest see them: thou shalt see but the utmost part of them, and shalt not see them all: and curse me them from thence.

14 And he brought him into the field of Zophim, to the top of Pisgah, and built seven altars, and offered a bullock and a ram on *every* altar.   Num. 23:1-2

15 And he said unto Balak, Stand here by thy burnt offering, while I meet *the* LORD yonder.   Num. 23:3

16 And the LORD met Balaam, and put a word in his mouth, and said, Go again unto Balak, and say thus.   Num. 23:5

17 And when he came to him, behold, he stood by his burnt offering, and the princes of Moab with him. And Balak said unto him, What hath the LORD spoken?

18 And he took up his parable, and said, Rise up, Balak, and hear; hearken unto me, thou son of Zippor:

19 God *is* not a man, that he should lie; neither the son of man, that he should repent: hath he said, and shall he not do *it*? or hath he spoken, and shall he not make it good?   1 Sam. 15:29; Mal. 3:6; James 1:17

20 Behold, I have received *commandment* to bless: and he hath blessed; and I cannot reverse it.   Gen. 12:2; 22:17; Num. 22:12

21 He hath not beheld iniquity in Jacob, neither hath he seen perverseness in Israel: the LORD his God *is* with him, and the shout of a king *is* among them.   Ex. 29:45-46; Jer. 50:20

22 God brought them out of Egypt; he hath as it were the strength of an ᵀunicorn.   *wild ox*

23 Surely *there is* no enchantment against Jacob, neither *is there* any ᵀdivination against Israel: according to this time it shall be said of Jacob and of Israel, What hath God ᵀwrought!   Num. 24:1 ◆ *false magic* ◆ *made*

24 Behold, the people shall rise up as a great lion, and lift up himself as a young lion: he shall not lie down until he eat *of* the prey, and drink the blood of the slain.   Gen. 49:9, 27

25 And Balak said unto Balaam, Neither curse them at all, nor bless them at all.

26 But Balaam answered and said unto Balak, Told not I thee, saying, All that the LORD speaketh, that I must do?   Num. 22:18

27 And Balak said unto Balaam, Come, I pray thee, I will bring thee unto another place; ᵀperadventure it will please God that thou mayest curse me them from thence.   *maybe*

28 And Balak brought Balaam unto the top of Peor, that looketh toward Jeshimon.

29 And Balaam said unto Balak, Build me here seven altars, and prepare me here seven bullocks and seven rams.

30 And Balak did as Balaam had said, and offered a ᵀbullock and a ram on *every* altar.   *bull*

Balaam, Leaving Divination, Prophesies the Happiness of Israel

24 And when Balaam saw that it pleased the LORD to bless Israel, he went not, as at other times, to seek for ᵀenchantments, but he set his face toward the wilderness.   Num. 23:23 ♦ *secret arts*

2 And Balaam lifted up his eyes, and he saw Israel abiding *in his tents* according to their tribes; and the spirit of God came upon him.   1 Sam. 10:10; 19:20; 2 Chr. 15:1

3 And he took up his parable, and said, Balaam the son of Beor hath said, and the man whose eyes are open hath said: Num. 23:7

4 He hath said, which heard the words of God, which saw the vision of the Almighty, falling *into a trance*, but having his eyes open:

5 How goodly are thy tents, O Jacob, *and* thy tabernacles, O Israel!

6 As the valleys are they spread forth, as gardens by the river's side, as the trees of lign aloes which the LORD hath planted, *and* as cedar trees beside the waters. Ps. 1:3; 104:16

7 He shall pour the water out of his buckets, and his seed *shall be* in many waters, and his king shall be higher than Agag, and his kingdom shall be exalted.   2 Sam. 5:12

24:7 Israel's True and Mighty King

Balaam prophesied that Israel's King would be greater and more powerful than Agag. This was the name given to the kings of the Amalekites, who were at this time a very powerful nation; but Israel, if true to God, would subdue all her enemies. The King of Israel was the Son of God; and His throne was one day to be established in the earth, and His power to be exalted above all earthly kingdoms. *PP 450*

---

8 God brought him forth out of Egypt; he hath as it were the strength of an ᵀunicorn: he shall eat up the nations his enemies, and shall break their bones, and pierce *them* through with his arrows. Num. 23:22, 24 ♦ *wild ox*

9 He couched, he lay down as a lion, and as a great lion: who shall stir him up? Blessed *is* he that blesseth thee, and cursed *is* he that curseth thee.   Gen. 12:3; 49:9; Num. 23:24

Balak Angrily Dismisses Balaam

10 And Balak's anger was kindled against Balaam, and he smote his hands together: and Balak said unto Balaam, I called thee to curse mine enemies, and, behold, thou hast altogether blessed *them* these three times.

11 Therefore now flee thou to thy place: I thought to promote thee unto great honour; but, lo, the LORD hath kept thee back from honour.   Num. 22:17

12 And Balaam said unto Balak, Spake I not also to thy messengers which thou sentest unto me, saying,   Num. 22:18

13 If Balak would give me his house full of silver and gold, I cannot go beyond the commandment of the LORD, to do *either* good or bad of mine own mind; *but* what the LORD saith, that will I speak?

14 And now, behold, I go unto my people: come *therefore, and* I will ᵀadvertise thee what this people shall do to thy people in the latter days.   Gen. 49:1 ♦ *counsel*

Balaam Prophesies the Star of Jacob and the Destruction of Nations

15 And he took up his parable, and said, Balaam the son of Beor hath said, and the man whose eyes are open hath said: Num. 23:7

16 He hath said, which heard the words of God, and knew the knowledge of the most High, *which* saw the vision of the Almighty, falling *into a trance*, but having his eyes open: Num. 24:4

17 I shall see him, but not now: I shall behold him, but not nigh: there shall come a Star out of Jacob, and a Sceptre shall rise out of Israel, and shall ᵀsmite the corners of Moab, and destroy all the children of Sheth.   Gen. 49:10; 2 Sam. 8:2; Ps. 45:6 ♦ *strike*

18 And Edom shall be a possession, Seir also shall be a possession for his enemies; and Israel shall do valiantly.   Gen. 27:29; Amos 9:12

19 Out of Jacob shall come he that shall have dominion, and shall destroy him that remaineth of the city.   Gen. 49:10

20 And when he looked on Amalek, he took up his parable, and said, Amalek *was* the first of the nations; but his latter end *shall be* that he perish for ever.   Ex. 17:14

21 And he looked on the Kenites, and took up his parable, and said, Strong is thy

dwellingplace, and thou puttest thy nest in a rock.   Gen. 15:19
22 Nevertheless the Kenite shall be wasted, until Asshur shall carry thee away captive.
23 And he took up his parable, and said, Alas, who shall live when God doeth this!
24 And ships *shall come* from the coast of Chittim, and shall afflict Asshur, and shall afflict Eber, and he also shall perish for ever.   Gen. 10:4; Num. 24:20; Dan. 11:30
25 And Balaam rose up, and went and returned to his place: and Balak also went his way.   Num. 31:8

The Israelites Commit Idolatry at Shittim

25 And Israel abode in Shittim, and the people began to commit ᵀwhoredom with the daughters of Moab.   *prostitution*
2 And they called the people unto the sacrifices of their gods: and the people did eat, and bowed down to their gods.   Ex. 20:5; 34:15-16

> **25:2 Evil Public Worship**
>
> Amid these attractive surroundings [the Israelites] were to encounter an evil more deadly than mighty hosts of armed men or the wild beasts of the wilderness. . . . In the public worship of Baal, the leading deity, the most degrading and iniquitous scenes were constantly enacted. On every side were places noted for idolatry and licentiousness, the very names being suggestive of the vileness and corruption of the people. *PP 453*

3 And Israel joined himself unto Baal-peor: and the anger of the LORD was kindled against Israel.   Josh. 22:17

> **25:1–3 Traitors on the Inside**
>
> It was when the Israelites were in a condition of outward ease and security that they were led into sin. They failed to keep God ever before them, they neglected prayer and cherished a spirit of self-confidence. Ease and self-indulgence left the citadel of the soul unguarded, and debasing thoughts found entrance. It was the traitors within the walls that overthrew the strongholds of principle and betrayed Israel into the power of Satan. *PP 459*

4 And the LORD said unto Moses, Take all the heads of the people, and hang them up before the LORD against the sun, that the fierce anger of the LORD may be turned away from Israel.   Num. 25:11; Deut. 4:3; 13:17
5 And Moses said unto the judges of Israel, Slay ye every one his men that were joined unto Baal-peor.   Ex. 18:21

Phinehas Kills Zimri and Cozbi

6 And, behold, one of the children of Israel came and brought unto his brethren a Midianitish woman in the sight of Moses, and in the sight of all the congregation of the children of Israel, who *were* weeping *before* the door of the tabernacle of the congregation.   Joel 2:17
7 And when Phinehas, the son of Eleazar, the son of Aaron the priest, saw *it*, he rose up from among the congregation, and took a javelin in his hand;   Ex. 6:25
8 And he went after the man of Israel into the tent, and thrust both of them through, the man of Israel, and the woman through

> ## Venturing Upon Forbidden Ground
>
> ### Numbers 25:1–3
>
> At first there was little intercourse [association] between the Israelites and their heathen neighbors, but after a time Midianitish women began to steal into the camp. Their appearance excited no alarm, and so quietly were their plans conducted that the attention of Moses was not called to the matter. It was the object of these women, in their association with the Hebrews, to seduce them into transgression of the law of God, to draw their attention to heathen rites and customs, and lead them into idolatry. These motives were studiously concealed under the garb of friendship, so that they were not suspected, even by the guardians of the people.
>
> At Balaam's suggestion, a grand festival in honor of their gods was appointed by the king of Moab, and it was secretly arranged that Balaam should induce the Israelites to attend. . . . Great numbers of the people joined him in witnessing the festivities. They ventured upon the forbidden ground, and were entangled in the snare of Satan. Beguiled with music and dancing, and allured by the beauty of heathen vestals, they cast off their fealty to Jehovah. As they united in mirth and feasting, indulgence in wine beclouded their senses and broke down the barriers of self-control. . . . They offered sacrifice upon heathen altars and participated in the most degrading rites.
>
> It was not long before the poison had spread, like a deadly infection, through the camp of Israel. Those who would have conquered their enemies in battle were overcome by the wiles of heathen women. The people seemed to be infatuated. The rulers and the leading men were among the first to transgress, and so many of the people were guilty that the apostasy became national. "Israel joined himself unto Baalpeor." *PP 454*

her belly. So the plague was ᵀstayed from the children of Israel.   Num. 16:46-48 ◆ *held back*

9 And those that died in the plague were twenty and four thousand.   Num. 16:49-50

10 And the LORD spake unto Moses, saying,

11 Phinehas, the son of Eleazar, the son of Aaron the priest, hath turned my wrath away from the children of Israel, while he was zealous for my sake among them, that I consumed not the children of Israel in my jealousy.   Deut. 32:16

12 Wherefore say, Behold, I give unto him my covenant of peace: Mal. 2:4-5

13 And he shall have it, and his seed after him, *even* the covenant of an everlasting priesthood; because he was zealous for his God, and made an atonement for the children of Israel.   Ex. 40:15

14 Now the name of the Israelite that was slain, *even* that was slain with the Midianitish woman, *was* Zimri, the son of Salu, a prince of a chief house among the Simeonites.

15 And the name of the Midianitish woman that was slain *was* Cozbi, the daughter of Zur; he *was* head over a people, *and* of a chief house in Midian.   Num. 31:8; Josh. 13:21

The Midianites Are to Be Killed

16 And the LORD spake unto Moses, saying,

17 Vex the Midianites, and ᵀsmite them: *strike*

18 For they ᵀvex you with their wiles, wherewith they have ᵀbeguiled you in the matter of Peor, and in the matter of Cozbi, the daughter of a prince of Midian, their sister, which was slain in the day of the plague for Peor's sake.   Rev. 2:14 ◆ *trouble* ◆ *deceived*

A Second Census of Israel

26 And it came to pass after the plague, that the LORD spake unto Moses and unto Eleazar the son of Aaron the priest, saying,   Num. 25:9

2 Take the sum of all the congregation of the children of Israel, from twenty years old and upward, throughout their fathers' house, all that are able to go to war in Israel.   Ex. 38:25-26; Num. 1:2-3

3 And Moses and Eleazar the priest spake with them in the plains of Moab by Jordan *near* Jericho, saying,   Num. 22:1; 26:63; 33:48

4 *Take the sum of the people*, from twenty years old and upward; as the LORD commanded Moses and the children of Israel, which went forth out of the land of Egypt.   Num. 1:1

5 Reuben, the eldest son of Israel: the children of Reuben; Hanoch, *of whom cometh* the family of the Hanochites: of Pallu, the family of the Palluites: 1 Chr. 5:3

6 Of Hezron, the family of the Hezronites: of Carmi, the family of the Carmites.

7 These *are* the families of the Reubenites: and they that were numbered of them were forty and three thousand and seven hundred and thirty.

8 And the sons of Pallu; Eliab.

9 And the sons of Eliab; Nemuel, and Dathan, and Abiram. This *is that* Dathan and Abiram, *which were* famous in the congregation, who strove against Moses and against Aaron in the company of Korah, when they strove against the LORD: Num. 1:16

10 And the earth opened her mouth, and swallowed them up together with Korah, when that company died, what time the fire devoured two hundred and fifty men: and they became a sign.   Num. 16:31-35, 38; 2 Pet. 2:6

11 Notwithstanding the children of Korah died not.   Ex. 6:24

12 The sons of Simeon after their families: of Nemuel, the family of the Nemuelites: of Jamin, the family of the Jaminites: of Jachin, the family of the Jachinites: 1 Chr. 4:24

13 Of Zerah, the family of the Zarhites: of Shaul, the family of the Shaulites.   Gen. 46:10

14 These *are* the families of the Simeonites, twenty and two thousand and two hundred.

15 The children of Gad after their families: of Zephon, the family of the Zephonites: of Haggi, the family of the Haggites: of Shuni, the family of the Shunites: Gen. 46:16

16 Of Ozni, the family of the Oznites: of Eri, the family of the Erites:

17 Of Arod, the family of the Arodites: of Areli, the family of the Arelites.

18 These *are* the families of the children of Gad according to those that were numbered of them, forty thousand and five hundred.

19 The sons of Judah *were* Er and Onan: and Er and Onan died in the land of Canaan.

20 And the sons of Judah after their families were; of Shelah, the family of the Shelanites: of Pharez, the family of the Pharzites: of Zerah, the family of the Zarhites.   Gen. 46:12

21 And the sons of Pharez were; of Hezron, the family of the Hezronites: of Hamul, the family of the Hamulites.

22 These *are* the families of Judah according to those that were numbered of them, ᵀthreescore and sixteen thousand and five hundred.   *sixty*

23 *Of* the sons of Issachar after their families: *of* Tola, the family of the Tolaites: of Pua, the family of the Punites: Gen. 46:13; 1 Chr. 7:1

24 Of Jashub, the family of the Jashubites: of Shimron, the family of the Shimronites.

25 These *are* the families of Issachar according to those that were numbered of them, threescore and four thousand and three hundred.

26 *Of* the sons of Zebulun after their families: of Sered, the family of the Sardites: of

Elon, the family of the Elonites: of Jahleel, the family of the Jahleelites.   Gen. 46:14
27 These *are* the families of the Zebulunites according to those that were numbered of them, threescore thousand and five hundred.
28 The sons of Joseph after their families *were* Manasseh and Ephraim.   Gen. 46:20
29 Of the sons of Manasseh: of Machir, the family of the Machirites: and Machir begat Gilead: of Gilead *come* the family of the Gileadites.   Num. 36:1; Josh. 17:1; 1 Chr. 7:14-19
30 These *are* the sons of Gilead: *of* Jeezer, the family of the Jeezerites: of Helek, the family of the Helekites:
31 And *of* Asriel, the family of the Asrielites: and *of* Shechem, the family of the Shechemites:
32 And *of* Shemida, the family of the Shemidaites: and *of* Hepher, the family of the Hepherites.
33 And Zelophehad the son of Hepher had no sons, but daughters: and the names of the daughters of Zelophehad *were* Mahlah, and Noah, Hoglah, Milcah, and Tirzah.   Num. 27:1
34 These *are* the families of Manasseh, and those that were numbered of them, fifty and two thousand and seven hundred.
35 These *are* the sons of Ephraim after their families: of Shuthelah, the family of the Shuthalhites: of Becher, the family of the Bachrites: of Tahan, the family of the Tahanites.
36 And these *are* the sons of Shuthelah: of Eran, the family of the Eranites.
37 These *are* the families of the sons of Ephraim according to those that were numbered of them, thirty and two thousand and five hundred. These *are* the sons of Joseph after their families.
38 The sons of Benjamin after their families: of Bela, the family of the Belaites: of Ashbel, the family of the Ashbelites: of Ahiram, the family of the Ahiramites: 1 Chr. 8:1
39 Of Shupham, the family of the Shuphamites: of Hupham, the family of the Huphamites.
40 And the sons of Bela were Ard and Naaman: *of Ard*, the family of the Ardites: *and* of Naaman, the family of the Naamites. 1 Chr. 8:3
41 These *are* the sons of Benjamin after their families: and they that were numbered of them *were* forty and five thousand and six hundred.
42 These *are* the sons of Dan after their families: of Shuham, the family of the Shuhamites. These *are* the families of Dan after their families.   Gen. 46:23
43 All the families of the Shuhamites, according to those that were numbered of

them, *were* threescore and four thousand and four hundred.
44 *Of* the children of Asher after their families: of Jimna, the family of the Jimnites: of Jesui, the family of the Jesuites: of Beriah, the family of the Beriites.   Gen. 46:17
45 Of the sons of Beriah: of Heber, the family of the Heberites: of Malchiel, the family of the Malchielites.
46 And the name of the daughter of Asher *was* Sarah.
47 These *are* the families of the sons of Asher according to those that were numbered of them; *who were* fifty and three thousand and four hundred.
48 *Of* the sons of Naphtali after their families: of Jahzeel, the family of the Jahzeelites: of Guni, the family of the Gunites: Gen. 46:24
49 Of Jezer, the family of the Jezerites: of Shillem, the family of the Shillemites.
50 These *are* the families of Naphtali according to their families: and they that were numbered of them *were* forty and five thousand and four hundred.
51 These *were* the numbered of the children of Israel, six hundred thousand and a thousand seven hundred and thirty.   Num. 1:46

God's Rules for Dividing the Land among the Tribes of Israel

52 And the LORD spake unto Moses, saying,
53 Unto these the land shall be divided for an inheritance according to the number of names.   Josh. 11:23
54 To many thou shalt give the more inheritance, and to few thou shalt give the less inheritance: to every one shall his inheritance be given according to those that were numbered of him.   Num. 33:54
55 Notwithstanding the land shall be divided by lot: according to the names of the tribes of their fathers they shall inherit.   Num. 33:54
56 According to the lot shall the possession thereof be divided between many and few.

The Families and Number of the Levites

57 And these *are* they that were numbered of the Levites after their families: of Gershon, the family of the Gershonites: of Kohath, the family of the Kohathites: of Merari, the family of the Merarites.   Gen. 46:11; Ex. 6:16-19; 1 Chr. 6:1
58 These *are* the families of the Levites: the family of the Libnites, the family of the Hebronites, the family of the Mahlites, the family of the Mushites, the family of the Korathites. And Kohath [T]begat Amram. *brought forth*
59 And the name of Amram's wife *was* Jochebed, the daughter of Levi, whom *her mother* bare to Levi in Egypt: and she bare unto Amram Aaron and Moses, and Miriam their sister.   Ex. 2:1-2; 6:20

60 And unto Aaron was born Nadab, and Abihu, Eleazar, and Ithamar.   Num. 3:2
61 And Nadab and Abihu died, when they offered strange fire before the LORD. Num. 3:4
62 And those that were numbered of them were twenty and three thousand, all males from a month old and upward: for they were not numbered among the children of Israel, because there was no inheritance given them among the children of Israel.   Num. 1:49; 3:39

Caleb and Joshua Live to See the Land
63 These *are* they that were numbered by Moses and Eleazar the priest, who numbered the children of Israel in the plains of Moab by Jordan *near* Jericho.
64 But among these there was not a man of them whom Moses and Aaron the priest numbered, when they numbered the children of Israel in the wilderness of Sinai. Deut. 2:14-15
65 For the LORD had said of them, They shall surely die in the wilderness. And there was not left a man of them, save Caleb the son of Jephunneh, and Joshua the son of Nun.   Num. 14:28-30

The Daughters of Zelophehad Ask to Inherit Land
27 Then came the daughters of Zelophehad, the son of Hepher, the son of Gilead, the son of Machir, the son of Manasseh, of the families of Manasseh the son of Joseph: and these *are* the names of his daughters; Mahlah, Noah, and Hoglah, and Milcah, and Tirzah.   Num. 26:33
2 And they stood before Moses, and before Eleazar the priest, and before the princes and all the congregation, *by* the door of the tabernacle of the congregation, saying,
3 Our father died in the wilderness, and he was not in the company of them that gathered themselves together against the LORD in the company of Korah; but died in his own sin, and had no sons.   Num. 26:64-65
4 Why should the name of our father be done away from among his family, because he hath no son? Give unto us *therefore* a possession among the brethren of our father.   Josh. 17:4
5 And Moses brought their cause before the LORD.
6 And the LORD spake unto Moses, saying,
7 The daughters of Zelophehad speak right: thou shalt surely give them a possession of an inheritance among their father's brethren; and thou shalt cause the inheritance of their father to pass unto them.
8 And thou shalt speak unto the children of Israel, saying, If a man die, and have no son, then ye shall cause his inheritance to pass unto his daughter.

9 And if he have no daughter, then ye shall give his inheritance unto his brethren.
10 And if he have no brethren, then ye shall give his inheritance unto his father's brethren.
11 And if his father have no brethren, then ye shall give his inheritance unto his kinsman that is next to him of his family, and he shall possess it: and it shall be unto the children of Israel a statute of judgment, as the LORD commanded Moses. Num. 35:29; Ruth 4:3-6; Jer. 32:8

Moses Is Told of His Death
12 And the LORD said unto Moses, Get thee up into this mount Abarim, and see the land which I have given unto the children of Israel.   Num. 33:47-48

> **27:12 Gazing on the Land of Promise**
>
> The Lord announced to Moses that the appointed time for the possession of Canaan was at hand; and as the aged prophet stood upon the heights overlooking the river Jordan and the Promised Land, he gazed with deep interest upon the inheritance of his people. Would it be possible that the sentence pronounced against him for his sin at Kadesh might be revoked? *PP 462*

13 And when thou hast seen it, thou also shalt be gathered unto thy people, as Aaron thy brother was gathered.   Num. 31:2
14 For ye rebelled against my commandment in the desert of Zin, in the strife of the congregation, to ᵀsanctify me at the water before their eyes: that *is* the water of Meribah in Kadesh in the wilderness of Zin. Ex. 17:7 ♦ *make holy*

Moses Asks God to Appoint His Successor
15 And Moses spake unto the LORD, saying,
16 Let the LORD, the God of the spirits of all flesh, set a man over the congregation,
17 Which may go out before them, and which may go in before them, and which may lead them out, and which may bring them in; that the congregation of the LORD be not as sheep which have no shepherd.   Deut. 31:2; 1 Kin. 22:17
18 And the LORD said unto Moses, Take thee Joshua the son of Nun, a man in whom *is* the spirit, and lay thine hand upon him; Gen. 41:38

> **27:18 A New Leader for Israel**
>
> Joshua had long attended Moses; and being a man of wisdom, ability, and faith, he was chosen to succeed him.
> Through the laying on of hands by Moses, accompanied by a most impressive charge, Joshua was solemnly set apart as the leader of Israel. He was also admitted to a present share in the government. *PP 462, 463*

19 And set him before Eleazar the priest, and before all the congregation; and give him a charge in their sight.   Deut. 3:28

20 And thou shalt put *some* of thine honour upon him, that all the congregation of the children of Israel may be obedient. Josh. 1:16-18

21 And he shall stand before Eleazar the priest, who shall ask *counsel* for him after the judgment of Urim before the LORD: at his word shall they go out, and at his word they shall come in, *both* he, and all the children of Israel with him, even all the congregation.   Ex. 28:30; Josh. 9:14; 1 Sam. 28:6

22 And Moses did as the LORD commanded him: and he took Joshua, and set him before Eleazar the priest, and before all the congregation:

23 And he laid his hands upon him, and gave him a charge, as the LORD commanded by the hand of Moses.   Num. 27:19

Offerings Are to Be Observed

28 And the LORD spake unto Moses, saying,

2 Command the children of Israel, and say unto them, My offering, *and* my bread for my sacrifices made by fire, *for* a sweet savour unto me, shall ye observe to offer unto me in their due season.   Gen. 8:21; Lev. 3:11

3 And thou shalt say unto them, This *is* the offering made by fire which ye shall offer unto the LORD; two lambs of the first year without spot day by day, *for* a continual burnt offering.   Lev. 6:9

4 The one lamb shalt thou offer in the morning, and the other lamb shalt thou offer at even;

5 And a tenth *part* of an ephah of flour for a meat offering, mingled with the fourth *part* of an hin of beaten oil.   Ex. 16:36; Lev. 2:1

6 *It is* a continual burnt offering, which was ordained in mount Sinai for a sweet savour, a sacrifice made by fire unto the LORD. Amos 5:25

7 And the drink offering thereof *shall be* the fourth *part* of an hin for the one lamb: in the holy *place* shalt thou cause the strong wine to be poured unto the LORD *for* a drink offering.   Ex. 29:42

8 And the other lamb shalt thou offer at even: as the meat offering of the morning, and as the drink offering thereof, thou shalt offer *it*, a sacrifice made by fire, of a sweet savour unto the LORD.

Various Offerings

9 And on the sabbath day two lambs of the first year without spot, and two tenth deals of flour *for* a meat offering, mingled with oil, and the drink offering thereof:

10 *This is* the burnt offering of every sabbath, beside the continual burnt offering, and his drink offering.   Ezek. 46:4-5

11 And in the beginnings of your months ye shall offer a burnt offering unto the LORD; two young bullocks, and one ram, seven lambs of the first year without spot; Num. 10:10; Ezek. 46:6

12 And three tenth deals of flour *for* a meat offering, mingled with oil, for one bullock; and two tenth deals of flour *for* a meat offering, mingled with oil, for one ram; Num. 15:4-12

13 And a several tenth deal of flour mingled with oil *for* a meat offering unto one lamb; *for* a burnt offering of a sweet savour, a sacrifice made by fire unto the LORD.

14 And their drink offerings shall be half an hin of wine unto a bullock, and the third *part* of an hin unto a ram, and a fourth *part* of an hin unto a lamb: this *is* the burnt offering of every month throughout the months of the year.

Christ Manifested in Sacrifice

Numbers 28:1–4

The word of God includes the Scriptures of the Old Testament as well as of the New. One is not complete without the other. Christ declared that the truths of the Old Testament are as valuable as those of the New. Christ was as much man's Redeemer in the beginning of the world as He is today. . . . The rites of the Jewish economy were instituted by Christ Himself. He was the foundation of their system of sacrificial offerings, the great antitype of all their religious service. The blood shed as the sacrifices were offered pointed to the sacrifice of the Lamb of God. All the typical offerings were fulfilled in Him.

Christ as manifested to the patriarchs, as symbolized in the sacrificial service, as portrayed in the law, and as revealed by the prophets, is the riches of the Old Testament. Christ in His life, His death, and His resurrection, Christ as He is manifested by the Holy Spirit, is the treasure of the New Testament. Our Saviour, the outshining of the Father's glory, is both the Old and the New.

Of Christ's life and death and intercession, which prophets had foretold, the apostles were to go forth as witnesses. Christ in His humiliation, in His purity and holiness, in His matchless love, was to be their theme. And in order to preach the gospel in its fullness, they must present the Saviour not only as revealed in His life and teachings, but as foretold by the prophets of the Old Testament and as symbolized by the sacrificial service. *COL 126, 127*

15 And one kid of the goats for a sin offering unto the LORD shall be offered, beside the continual burnt offering, and his drink offering.   Num. 28:3

Observing Passover and Pentecost

16 And in the fourteenth day of the first month *is* the passover of the LORD.   Ex. 12:18
17 And in the fifteenth day of this month *is* the feast: seven days shall unleavened bread be eaten.   Lev. 23:6
18 In the first day *shall be* an holy convocation; ye shall do no manner of servile work *therein*:   Ex. 12:16
19 But ye shall offer a sacrifice made by fire *for* a burnt offering unto the LORD; two young bullocks, and one ram, and seven lambs of the first year: they shall be unto you without blemish: Deut. 15:21
20 And their meat offering *shall be of* flour mingled with oil: three tenth deals shall ye offer for a ᵀbullock, and two tenth deals for a ram;   *bull*
21 A several tenth deal shalt thou offer for every lamb, throughout the seven lambs:
22 And one goat *for* a sin offering, to make an atonement for you.
23 Ye shall offer these beside the burnt offering in the morning, which *is* for a continual burnt offering.   Num. 28:3
24 After this manner ye shall offer daily, throughout the seven days, the meat of the sacrifice made by fire, of a sweet savour unto the LORD: it shall be offered beside the continual burnt offering, and his drink offering.
25 And on the seventh day ye shall have an holy convocation; ye shall do no servile work.   Ex. 12:16; 13:6; Lev. 23:8
26 Also in the day of the firstfruits, when ye bring a new meat offering unto the LORD, after your weeks *be out*, ye shall have an holy convocation; ye shall do no servile work: Ex. 23:16; 34:22; Lev. 23:10
27 But ye shall offer the burnt offering for a sweet savour unto the LORD; two young bullocks, one ram, seven lambs of the first year;   Lev. 23:18-19
28 And their meat offering of flour mingled with oil, three tenth deals unto one bullock, two tenth deals unto one ram,
29 A several tenth deal unto one lamb, throughout the seven lambs;
30 *And* one kid of the goats, to make an atonement for you.   Num. 28:15
31 Ye shall offer *them* beside the continual burnt offering, and his meat offering, (they shall be unto you without blemish) and their drink offerings.   Num. 28:19

Observing Other Feasts

29 And in the seventh month, on the first *day* of the month, ye shall have an holy convocation; ye shall do no servile work: it is a day of blowing the trumpets unto you.   Lev. 23:24-25
2 And ye shall offer a burnt offering for a sweet savour unto the LORD; one young ᵀbullock, one ram, *and* seven lambs of the first year without blemish: *bull*
3 And their meat offering *shall be of* flour mingled with oil, three tenth deals for a bullock, *and* two tenth deals for a ram,
4 And one tenth deal for one lamb, throughout the seven lambs:
5 And one kid of the goats *for* a sin offering, to make an atonement for you: Num. 28:15
6 Beside the burnt offering of the month, and his meat offering, and the daily burnt offering, and his meat offering, and their drink offerings, according unto their manner, for a sweet savour, a sacrifice made by fire unto the LORD.   Num. 28:3-8
7 And ye shall have on the tenth *day* of this seventh month an holy convocation; and ye shall afflict your souls: ye shall not do any work *therein*:   Lev. 16:29-31

The Day of Atonement

Numbers 29

Important truths concerning the atonement are taught by the typical service. A substitute was accepted in the sinner's stead; but the sin was not canceled by the blood of the victim. A means was thus provided by which it was transferred to the sanctuary. By the offering of blood the sinner acknowledged the authority of the law, confessed his guilt in transgression, and expressed his desire for pardon through faith in a Redeemer to come; but he was not yet entirely released from the condemnation of the law. On the Day of Atonement the high priest, having taken an offering from the congregation, went into the most holy place with the blood of this offering, and sprinkled it upon the mercy seat, directly over the law, to make satisfaction for its claims. Then, in his character of mediator, he took the sins upon himself and bore them from the sanctuary. Placing his hands upon the head of the scapegoat, he confessed over him all these sins, thus in figure transferring them from himself to the goat. The goat then bore them away, and they were regarded as forever separated from the people. *GC 420*

29:7 Sin's Pollution

The whole ceremony was designed to impress the Israelites with the holiness of God and His abhorrence of sin; and, further, to show them that they could not come in contact with sin without becoming polluted. Every man was required to afflict his soul while this work of atonement was going forward. All business was to be laid aside, and the whole congregation of Israel were to spend the day in solemn humiliation before God, with prayer, fasting, and deep searching of heart. GC 419, 420

8 But ye shall offer a burnt offering unto the LORD *for* a sweet savour; one young bullock, one ram, *and* seven lambs of the first year; they shall be unto you without blemish:　　　　Num. 28:19

9 And their meat offering *shall be of* flour mingled with oil, three tenth deals to a bullock, *and* two tenth deals to one ram,

10 A several tenth deal for one lamb, throughout the seven lambs:

11 One kid of the goats *for* a sin offering; beside the sin offering of atonement, and the continual burnt offering, and the meat offering of it, and their drink offerings.　Lev. 16:3, 5

12 And on the fifteenth day of the seventh month ye shall have an holy convocation; ye shall do no servile work, and ye shall keep a feast unto the LORD seven days: Deut. 16:13-14

13 And ye shall offer a burnt offering, a sacrifice made by fire, of a sweet savour unto the LORD; thirteen young bullocks, two rams, *and* fourteen lambs of the first year; they shall be without blemish:　　　Num. 28:11

14 And their meat offering *shall be of* flour mingled with oil, three tenth deals unto every bullock of the thirteen bullocks, two tenth deals to each ram of the two rams,

15 And a several tenth deal to each lamb of the fourteen lambs:

16 And one kid of the goats *for* a sin offering; beside the continual burnt offering, his meat offering, and his drink offering.

17 And on the second day *ye shall offer* twelve young bullocks, two rams, fourteen lambs of the first year without spot:

18 And their meat offering and their drink offerings for the bullocks, for the rams, and for the lambs, *shall be* according to their number, after the manner:　　Num. 28:7

19 And one kid of the goats *for* a sin offering; beside the continual burnt offering, and the meat offering thereof, and their drink offerings.

20 And on the third day eleven bullocks, two rams, fourteen lambs of the first year without blemish;

21 And their meat offering and their drink offerings for the bullocks, for the rams, and

for the lambs, *shall be* according to their number, after the manner:

22 And one goat *for* a sin offering; beside the continual burnt offering, and his meat offering, and his drink offering.

23 And on the fourth day ten bullocks, two rams, *and* fourteen lambs of the first year without blemish:

24 Their meat offering and their drink offerings for the bullocks, for the rams, and for the lambs, *shall be* according to their number, after the manner:

25 And one kid of the goats *for* a sin offering; beside the continual burnt offering, his meat offering, and his drink offering.

26 And on the fifth day nine bullocks, two rams, *and* fourteen lambs of the first year without spot:

27 And their meat offering and their drink offerings for the bullocks, for the rams, and for the lambs, *shall be* according to their number, after the manner:

28 And one goat *for* a sin offering; beside the continual burnt offering, and his meat offering, and his drink offering.

29 And on the sixth day eight bullocks, two rams, *and* fourteen lambs of the first year without blemish:

30 And their meat offering and their drink offerings for the bullocks, for the rams, and for the lambs, *shall be* according to their number, after the manner:

31 And one goat *for* a sin offering; beside the continual burnt offering, his meat offering, and his drink offering.

32 And on the seventh day seven bullocks, two rams, *and* fourteen lambs of the first year without blemish:

33 And their meat offering and their drink offerings for the bullocks, for the rams, and for the lambs, *shall be* according to their number, after the manner:

34 And one goat *for* a sin offering; beside the continual burnt offering, his meat offering, and his drink offering.

35 On the eighth day ye shall have a solemn assembly: ye shall do no servile work *therein*:

36 But ye shall offer a burnt offering, a sacrifice made by fire, of a sweet savour unto the LORD: one bullock, one ram, seven lambs of the first year without blemish:

37 Their meat offering and their drink offerings for the bullock, for the ram, and for the lambs, *shall be* according to their number, after the manner:

38 And one goat *for* a sin offering; beside the continual burnt offering, and his meat offering, and his drink offering.

39 These *things* ye shall do unto the LORD in your set feasts, beside your vows, and your freewill offerings, for your burnt offerings, and for your meat offerings, and for your

drink offerings, and for your peace offerings. *Lev. 23:2; 1 Chr. 23:31; 2 Chr. 31:3*
40 And Moses told the children of Israel according to all that the LORD commanded Moses.

Vows Are Not to Be Broken

30 And Moses spake unto the heads of the tribes concerning the children of Israel, saying, This *is* the thing which the LORD hath commanded. *Num. 7:2*
2 If a man vow a vow unto the LORD, or swear an oath to bind his soul with a bond; he shall not break his word, he shall do according to all that proceedeth out of his mouth. *Job 22:27*

> **30:2 A Danger Signal**
>
> Not to the early church only, but to all future generations, this example of God's hatred of covetousness, fraud, and hypocrisy, was given as a danger-signal. It was covetousness that Ananias and Sapphira had first cherished. The desire to retain for themselves a part of that which they had promised to the Lord, led them into fraud and hypocrisy. *AA 74*

The Exception of a Young Woman's Vow

3 If a woman also vow a vow unto the LORD, and bind herself by a bond, *being* in her father's house in her youth;
4 And her father hear her vow, and her bond wherewith she hath bound her soul, and her father shall hold his peace at her: then all her vows shall stand, and every bond wherewith she hath bound her soul shall stand.
5 But if her father disallow her in the day that he heareth; not any of her vows, or of her bonds wherewith she hath bound her soul, shall stand: and the LORD shall forgive her, because her father ᵀdisallowed her.   *rejected*
6 And if she had at all an husband, when she vowed, or uttered ought out of her lips, wherewith she bound her soul; *Ps. 56:12*
7 And her husband heard *it*, and held his peace at her in the day that he heard *it*: then her vows shall stand, and her bonds wherewith she bound her soul shall stand.
8 But if her husband disallowed her on the day that he heard *it*; then he shall make her vow which she vowed, and that which she uttered with her lips, wherewith she bound her soul, of none effect: and the LORD shall forgive her. *Gen. 3:16*
9 But every vow of a widow, and of her that is divorced, wherewith they have bound their souls, shall stand against her.
10 And if she vowed in her husband's house, or bound her soul by a bond with an oath;
11 And her husband heard *it*, and held his

peace at her, *and* disallowed her not: then all her vows shall stand, and every bond wherewith she bound her soul shall stand.
12 But if her husband hath utterly made them void on the day he heard *them*; *then* whatsoever proceeded out of her lips concerning her vows, or concerning the bond of her soul, shall not stand: her husband hath made them void; and the LORD shall forgive her.
13 Every vow, and every binding oath to afflict the soul, her husband may establish it, or her husband may make it void.
14 But if her husband altogether hold his peace at her from day to day; then he establisheth all her vows, or all her bonds, which *are* upon her: he confirmeth them, because he held his peace at her in the day that he heard *them*.
15 But if he shall any ways make them void after that he hath heard *them*; then he shall bear her iniquity. *Lev. 5:1*
16 These *are* the statutes, which the LORD commanded Moses, between a man and his wife, between the father and his daughter, *being yet* in her youth in her father's house.

The Israelites Defeat the Midianites and Kill Balaam

31 And the LORD spake unto Moses, saying, 2 Avenge the children of Israel of the Midianites: afterward shalt thou be gathered unto thy people. *Num. 27:13*
3 And Moses spake unto the people, saying, Arm some of yourselves unto the war, and let them go against the Midianites, and avenge the LORD of Midian. *Lev. 26:25*
4 Of every tribe a thousand, throughout all the tribes of Israel, shall ye send to the war.
5 So there were delivered out of the thousands of Israel, a thousand of *every* tribe, twelve thousand armed for war.
6 And Moses sent them to the war, a thousand of *every* tribe, them and Phinehas the son of Eleazar the priest, to the war, with the holy instruments, and the trumpets to blow in his hand. *Num. 14:44*
7 And they warred against the Midianites, as the LORD commanded Moses; and they slew all the males. *1 Sam. 27:9; 1 Kin. 11:15-16*
8 And they slew the kings of Midian, beside the rest of them that were slain; *namely*, Evi, and Rekem, and Zur, and Hur, and Reba, five kings of Midian: Balaam also the son of Beor they slew with the sword. *Josh. 13:21-22*

> **31:8 Balaam Dies**
>
> Balaam was slain. He had felt a presentiment that his own end was near when he exclaimed, "Let me die the death of the righteous, and let my last end be like his!" (Numbers 23:10). But he had not chosen to live the life of the righteous, and his destiny was fixed with the enemies of God. *PP 451, 452*

9 And the children of Israel took *all* the women of Midian captives, and their little ones, and took the ᵀspoil of all their cattle, and all their flocks, and all their goods. *plunder*

10 And they burnt all their cities wherein they dwelt, and all their goodly castles, with fire.

11 And they took all the spoil, and all the prey, *both* of men and of beasts.   Deut. 20:14

12 And they brought the captives, and the prey, and the spoil, unto Moses, and Eleazar the priest, and unto the congregation of the children of Israel, unto the camp at the plains of Moab, which *are* by Jordan *near* Jericho.   Num. 22:1

Moses Is Angry with the Officers

13 And Moses, and Eleazar the priest, and all the princes of the congregation, went forth to meet them without the camp.

14 And Moses was ᵀwroth with the officers of the host, *with* the captains over thousands, and captains over hundreds, which came from the battle.   *angry*

15 And Moses said unto them, Have ye saved all the women alive?   1 Sam. 15:3

16 Behold, these caused the children of Israel, through the counsel of Balaam, to commit ᵀtrespass against the LORD in the matter of Peor, and there was a plague among the congregation of the LORD.   2 Pet. 2:15 ◆ *sin*

17 Now therefore kill every male among the little ones, and kill every woman that hath known man by lying with him.   Judg. 21:11-12

18 But all the women children, that have not known a man by lying with him, keep alive for yourselves.   Deut. 21:10-14

19 And do ye abide without the camp seven days: whosoever hath killed any person, and whosoever hath touched any slain, purify *both* yourselves and your captives on the third day, and on the seventh day.   Num. 5:2

20 And purify all *your* ᵀraiment, and all that is made of skins, and all work of goats' *hair*, and all things made of wood.   *clothing*

21 And Eleazar the priest said unto the men of war which went to the battle, This *is* the ordinance of the law which the LORD commanded Moses;

22 Only the gold, and the silver, the brass, the iron, the tin, and the lead,

23 Every thing that may abide the fire, ye shall make *it* go through the fire, and it shall be clean: nevertheless it shall be purified with the water of separation: and all that abideth not the fire ye shall make go through the water.   Num. 19:9, 17; 1 Cor. 3:13

24 And ye shall wash your clothes on the seventh day, and ye shall be clean, and afterward ye shall come into the camp.   Lev. 11:25

Proportions for Dividing the Spoils

25 And the LORD spake unto Moses, saying,

26 Take the sum of the prey that was taken, *both* of man and of beast, thou, and Eleazar the priest, and the chief fathers of the congregation:

27 And divide the prey into two parts; between them that took the war upon them, who went out to battle, and between all the congregation: Josh. 22:8

What One Cherished Sin Will Do

Numbers 31:8

Balaam witnessed the success of his diabolical scheme. He saw the curse of God visited upon His people, and thousands falling under His judgments; but the divine justice that punished sin in Israel did not permit the tempters to escape. In the war of Israel against the Midianites, Balaam was slain. He had felt a presentiment that his own end was near when he exclaimed, "Let me die the death of the righteous, and let my last end be like his!" But he had not chosen to live the life of the righteous, and his destiny was fixed with the enemies of God.

The fate of Balaam was similar to that of Judas, and their characters bear a marked resemblance to each other. Both these men tried to unite the service of God and mammon, and met with signal failure. Balaam acknowledged the true God, and professed to serve Him; Judas believed in Jesus as the Messiah, and united with His followers. But Balaam hoped to make the service of Jehovah the steppingstone to the acquirement of riches and worldly honor; and failing in this he stumbled and fell and was broken. Judas expected by his connection with Christ to secure wealth and promotion in that worldly kingdom which, as he believed, the Messiah was about to set up. The failure of his hopes drove him to apostasy and ruin. Both Balaam and Judas had received great light and enjoyed special privileges, but a single cherished sin poisoned the entire character and caused their destruction.

It is a perilous thing to allow an unchristian trait to live in the heart. One cherished sin will, little by little, debase the character, bringing all its nobler powers into subjection to the evil desire. The removal of one safeguard from the conscience, the indulgence of one evil habit, one neglect of the high claims of duty, breaks down the defenses of the soul and opens the way for Satan to come in and lead us astray. The only safe course is to let our prayers go forth daily from a sincere heart, as did David, "Hold up my goings in Thy paths, that my footsteps slip not" (Psalm 17:5). *PP 451, 452*

28 And levy a tribute unto the LORD of the men of war which went out to battle: one soul of five hundred, *both* of the persons, and of the beeves, and of the asses, and of the sheep: Num. 18:26

29 Take *it* of their half, and give it unto Eleazar the priest, *for* an heave offering of the LORD.

30 And of the children of Israel's half, thou shalt take one portion of fifty, of the persons, of the beeves, of the asses, and of the flocks, of all manner of beasts, and give them unto the Levites, which keep the charge of the tabernacle of the LORD.   Num. 3:7-8

31 And Moses and Eleazar the priest did as the LORD commanded Moses.

32 And the ᵀbooty, *being* the rest of the prey which the men of war had caught, was six hundred thousand and seventy thousand and five thousand sheep,   plunder

33 And threescore and twelve thousand ᵀbeeves,   plowing cattle

34 And threescore and one thousand asses,

35 And thirty and two thousand persons in all, of women that had not known man by lying with him.

36 And the half, *which was* the portion of them that went out to war, was in number three hundred thousand and seven and thirty thousand and five hundred sheep:

37 And the LORD's tribute of the sheep was six hundred and threescore and fifteen.

38 And the beeves *were* thirty and six thousand; of which the LORD's tribute *was* threescore and twelve.

39 And the asses *were* thirty thousand and five hundred; of which the LORD's tribute *was* threescore and one.

40 And the persons *were* sixteen thousand; of which the LORD's tribute *was* thirty and two persons.

41 And Moses gave the tribute, *which was* the LORD's heave offering, unto Eleazar the priest, as the LORD commanded Moses.

42 And of the children of Israel's half, which Moses divided from the men that warred,

43 (Now the half *that pertained unto* the congregation was three hundred thousand and thirty thousand *and* seven thousand and five hundred sheep,

44 And thirty and six thousand beeves,

45 And thirty thousand asses and five hundred,

46 And sixteen thousand persons;)

47 Even of the children of Israel's half, Moses took one portion of fifty, *both* of man and of beast, and gave them unto the Levites, which kept the charge of the tabernacle of the LORD; as the LORD commanded Moses.   Num. 31:30

The Voluntary Offering

48 And the officers which *were* over thousands of the host, the captains of thousands, and captains of hundreds, came near unto Moses:

49 And they said unto Moses, Thy servants have taken the sum of the men of war which *are* under our charge, and there lacketh not one man of us.

50 We have therefore brought an ᵀoblation for the LORD, what every man hath gotten, of jewels of gold, chains, and bracelets, rings, earrings, and tablets, to make an atonement for our souls before the LORD. Ex. 30:12 ♦ *offering*

51 And Moses and Eleazar the priest took the gold of them, *even* all wrought jewels.

52 And all the gold of the offering that they offered up to the LORD, of the captains of thousands, and of the captains of hundreds, was sixteen thousand seven hundred and fifty shekels.

53 (*For* the men of war had taken spoil, every man for himself.)   Deut. 20:14

54 And Moses and Eleazar the priest took the gold of the captains of thousands and of hundreds, and brought it into the tabernacle of the congregation, *for* a memorial for the children of Israel before the LORD.   Ex. 30:16

The Tribes of Reuben and Gad Request Land East of the Jordan

32 Now the children of Reuben and the children of Gad had a very great multitude of cattle: and when they saw the land of Jazer, and the land of Gilead, that, behold, the place *was* a place for cattle; Num. 21:32; 32:3

2 The children of Gad and the children of Reuben came and spake unto Moses, and to Eleazar the priest, and unto the princes of the congregation, saying,

3 Ataroth, and Dibon, and Jazer, and Nimrah, and Heshbon, and Elealeh, and Shebam, and Nebo, and Beon,   Num. 32:34-38

4 *Even* the country which the LORD smote before the congregation of Israel, *is* a land for cattle, and thy servants have cattle: Num. 21:24

5 Wherefore, said they, if we have found grace in thy sight, let this land be given unto thy servants for a possession, *and* bring us not over Jordan.

6 And Moses said unto the children of Gad and to the children of Reuben, Shall your brethren go to war, and shall ye sit here?

7 And wherefore discourage ye the heart of the children of Israel from going over into the land which the LORD hath given them?

8 Thus did your fathers, when I sent them from Kadesh-barnea to see the land.

9 For when they went up unto the valley of Eshcol, and saw the land, they discouraged the heart of the children of Israel, that they

should not go into the land which the LORD had given them.

10 And the LORD's anger was kindled the same time, and he sware, saying,   Num. 14:11

11 Surely none of the men that came up out of Egypt, from twenty years old and upward, shall see the land which I sware unto Abraham, unto Isaac, and unto Jacob; because they have not wholly followed me: Num. 14:28-30

12 Save Caleb the son of Jephunneh the Kenezite, and Joshua the son of Nun: for they have wholly followed the LORD.   Num. 14:24, 30

13 And the LORD's anger was kindled against Israel, and he made them wander in the wilderness forty years, until all the generation, that had done evil in the sight of the LORD, was consumed.   Num. 14:33-35

14 And, behold, ye are risen up in your fathers' stead, an increase of sinful men, to augment yet the fierce anger of the LORD toward Israel.

15 For if ye turn away from after him, he will yet again leave them in the wilderness; and ye shall destroy all this people.   2 Chr. 15:2

The Tribes Offer Conditions that Are Satisfactory to Moses

16 And they came near unto him, and said, We will build sheepfolds here for our cattle, and cities for our little ones:

17 But we ourselves will go ready armed before the children of Israel, until we have brought them unto their place: and our little ones shall dwell in the fenced cities because of the inhabitants of the land.   Josh. 4:12-13

18 We will not return unto our houses, until the children of Israel have inherited every man his inheritance.

19 For we will not inherit with them on yonder side Jordan, or forward; because our inheritance is fallen to us on this side Jordan eastward.   Josh. 13:8

20 And Moses said unto them, If ye will do this thing, if ye will go armed before the LORD to war,   Josh. 4:12-13

21 And will go all of you armed over Jordan before the LORD, until he hath driven out his enemies from before him,

22 And the land be subdued before the LORD: then afterward ye shall return, and be guiltless before the LORD, and before Israel; and this land shall be your possession before the LORD.   Deut. 3:20; Josh. 22:4, 9

23 But if ye will not do so, behold, ye have sinned against the LORD: and be sure your sin will find you out.   Gen. 4:7; 44:16; Is. 59:12

24 Build you cities for your little ones, and folds for your sheep; and do that which hath proceeded out of your mouth.   Num. 32:16

25 And the children of Gad and the children

of Reuben spake unto Moses, saying, Thy servants will do as my lord commandeth.

26 Our little ones, our wives, our flocks, and all our cattle, shall be there in the cities of Gilead: Josh. 1:14

27 But thy servants will pass over, every man armed for war, before the LORD to battle, as my lord saith.   Josh. 4:12

28 So concerning them Moses commanded Eleazar the priest, and Joshua the son of Nun, and the chief fathers of the tribes of the children of Israel: Josh. 1:13

29 And Moses said unto them, If the children of Gad and the children of Reuben will pass with you over Jordan, every man armed to battle, before the LORD, and the land shall be subdued before you; then ye shall give them the land of Gilead for a possession:

30 But if they will not pass over with you armed, they shall have possessions among you in the land of Canaan.

31 And the children of Gad and the children of Reuben answered, saying, As the LORD hath said unto thy servants, so will we do.

32 We will pass over armed before the LORD into the land of Canaan, that the possession of our inheritance on this side Jordan *may be* ours.

33 And Moses gave unto them, *even* to the children of Gad, and to the children of Reuben, and unto half the tribe of Manasseh the son of Joseph, the kingdom of Sihon king of the Amorites, and the kingdom of Og king of Bashan, the land, with the cities thereof in the coasts, *even* the cities of the country round about.   Deut. 3:12-17; 29:8; Josh. 12:6

34 And the children of Gad built Dibon, and Ataroth, and Aroer,   Num. 32:3; Deut. 2:36

35 And Atroth, Shophan, and Jaazer, and Jogbehah,   Num. 32:1

36 And Beth-nimrah, and Beth-haran, fenced cities: and folds for sheep.   Num. 32:3

37 And the children of Reuben built Heshbon, and Elealeh, and Kirjathaim,   Num. 21:27

38 And Nebo, and Baal-meon, (their names being changed,) and Shibmah: and gave other names unto the cities which they builded.   Ex. 23:13; Num. 32:3; Is. 46:1

39 And the children of Machir the son of Manasseh went to Gilead, and took it, and dispossessed the Amorite which *was* in it.

40 And Moses gave Gilead unto Machir the son of Manasseh; and he dwelt therein.

41 And Jair the son of Manasseh went and took the small towns thereof, and called them Havoth-jair.   Deut. 3:14; Josh. 13:30; Judg. 10:4

42 And Nobah went and took Kenath, and the villages thereof, and called it Nobah, after his own name.

Forty-two Journeys of the Israelites

33 These *are* the journeys of the children of Israel, which went forth out of the land of Egypt with their armies under the hand of Moses and Aaron.   Ps. 77:20

2 And Moses wrote their goings out according to their journeys by the commandment of the LORD: and these *are* their journeys according to their goings out.   Num. 9:17-23

3 And they departed from Rameses in the first month, on the fifteenth day of the first month; on the morrow after the passover the children of Israel went out with an high hand in the sight of all the Egyptians. Ex. 12:37; 13:4

4 For the Egyptians buried all *their* firstborn, which the LORD had smitten among them: upon their gods also the LORD executed judgments.   Ex. 12:12; Is. 19:1

5 And the children of Israel removed from Rameses, and pitched in Succoth.   Ex. 12:37

6 And they departed from Succoth, and pitched in Etham, which *is* in the edge of the wilderness.   Ex. 13:20

7 And they removed from Etham, and turned again unto Pi-hahiroth, which *is* before Baal-zephon: and they pitched before Migdol.   Ex. 14:2, 9

8 And they departed from before Pi-hahiroth, and passed through the midst of the sea into the wilderness, and went three days' journey in the wilderness of Etham, and pitched in Marah.

9 And they removed from Marah, and came unto Elim: and in Elim *were* twelve fountains of water, and [T]threescore and ten palm trees; and they pitched there.   Ex. 15:27 ◆ *sixty*

10 And they removed from Elim, and encamped by the Red sea.

11 And they removed from the Red sea, and encamped in the wilderness of Sin.   Ex. 16:1

12 And they took their journey out of the wilderness of Sin, and encamped in Dophkah.

13 And they departed from Dophkah, and encamped in Alush.

14 And they removed from Alush, and encamped at Rephidim, where was no water for the people to drink.

15 And they departed from Rephidim, and pitched in the wilderness of Sinai.   Ex. 19:1-2

16 And they removed from the desert of Sinai, and pitched at Kibroth-hattaavah.

17 And they departed from Kibroth-hattaavah, and encamped at Hazeroth.   Num. 11:35

18 And they departed from Hazeroth, and pitched in Rithmah.   Num. 12:16

19 And they departed from Rithmah, and pitched at Rimmon-parez.

20 And they departed from Rimmon-parez, and pitched in Libnah.

21 And they removed from Libnah, and pitched at Rissah.

22 And they journeyed from Rissah, and pitched in Kehelathah.

23 And they went from Kehelathah, and pitched in mount Shapher.

24 And they removed from mount Shapher, and encamped in Haradah.

25 And they removed from Haradah, and pitched in Makheloth.

26 And they removed from Makheloth, and encamped at Tahath.

27 And they departed from Tahath, and pitched at Tarah.

28 And they removed from Tarah, and pitched in Mithcah.

29 And they went from Mithcah, and pitched in Hashmonah.

30 And they departed from Hashmonah, and encamped at Moseroth.

31 And they departed from Moseroth, and pitched in Bene-jaakan.   Deut. 10:6

An Honored but Imperfect Leader

Numbers 33:38, 39

Aaron's work for Israel was done. Forty years before, at the age of eighty-three, God had called him to unite with Moses in his great and important mission. He had co-operated with his brother in leading the children of Israel from Egypt. He had held up the great leader's hands when the Hebrew hosts gave battle to Amalek. He had been permitted to ascend Mount Sinai, to approach into the presence of God, and to behold the divine glory. The Lord had conferred upon the family of Aaron the office of the priesthood, and had honored him with the sacred consecration of high priest. He had sustained him in the holy office by the terrible manifestations of divine judgment in the destruction of Korah and his company. It was through Aaron's intercession that the plague was stayed. When his two sons were slain for disregarding God's express command, he did not rebel or even murmur. Yet the record of his noble life had been marred. Aaron committed a grievous sin when he yielded to the clamors of the people and made the golden calf at Sinai; and again, when he united with Miriam in envy and murmuring against Moses. And he, with Moses, offended the Lord at Kadesh by disobeying the command to speak to the rock that it might give forth its water.
PP 425, 426

32 And they removed from Bene-jaakan, and encamped at Hor-hagidgad. Deut. 10:7
33 And they went from Hor-hagidgad, and pitched in Jotbathah. Deut. 10:7
34 And they removed from Jotbathah, and encamped at Ebronah.
35 And they departed from Ebronah, and encamped at Ezion-gaber. Deut. 2:8; 1 Kin. 9:26; 22:48
36 And they removed from Ezion-gaber, and pitched in the wilderness of Zin, which is Kadesh. Num. 20:1; 27:14
37 And they removed from Kadesh, and pitched in mount Hor, in the edge of the land of Edom. Num. 21:4
38 And Aaron the priest went up into mount Hor at the commandment of the LORD, and died there, in the fortieth year after the children of Israel were come out of the land of Egypt, in the first day of the fifth month. Deut. 10:6; 32:50
39 And Aaron was an hundred and twenty and three years old when he died in mount Hor.
40 And king Arad the Canaanite, which dwelt in the south in the land of Canaan, heard of the coming of the children of Israel.
41 And they departed from mount Hor, and pitched in Zalmonah.
42 And they departed from Zalmonah, and pitched in Punon.
43 And they departed from Punon, and pitched in Oboth. Num. 21:10
44 And they departed from Oboth, and pitched in Ijeabarim, in the border of Moab.
45 And they departed from Iim, and pitched in Dibon-gad.
46 And they removed from Dibon-gad, and encamped in Almon-diblathaim.
47 And they removed from Almon-diblathaim, and pitched in the mountains of Abarim, before Nebo. Deut. 32:49
48 And they departed from the mountains of Abarim, and pitched in the plains of Moab by Jordan near Jericho. Num. 22:1
49 And they pitched by Jordan, from Bethjesimoth even unto Abel-shittim in the plains of Moab.

The Canaanites Are to Be Destroyed

50 And the LORD spake unto Moses in the plains of Moab by Jordan near Jericho, saying,
51 Speak unto the children of Israel, and say unto them, When ye are passed over Jordan into the land of Canaan; Deut. 9:1; Josh. 3:17
52 Then ye shall drive out all the inhabitants of the land from before you, and destroy all their pictures, and destroy all their molten images, and quite pluck down all their high places: Ex. 23:24; Lev. 26:1
53 And ye shall dispossess the inhabitants of

the land, and dwell therein: for I have given you the land to possess it.
54 And ye shall divide the land by lot for an inheritance among your families: and to the more ye shall give the more inheritance, and to the fewer ye shall give the less inheritance: every man's inheritance shall be in the place where his lot falleth; according to the tribes of your fathers ye shall inherit. Num. 26:53-56
55 But if ye will not drive out the inhabitants of the land from before you; then it shall come to pass, that those which ye let remain of them shall be pricks in your eyes, and thorns in your sides, and shall ᵀvex you in the land wherein ye dwell. Judg. 2:3 ◆ trouble

---

33:55 Thorns in the Side

If faithful to Him, God intended that Israel should go on conquering and to conquer. .....
But regardless of their high destiny, they chose the course of ease and self-indulgence; they let slip their opportunities for completing the conquest of the land; and for many generations they were afflicted by the remnant of these idolatrous peoples, that were, as the prophet had foretold, as "pricks" [irritants] in their eyes, and as "thorns" in their sides. PP 544

---

56 Moreover it shall come to pass, that I shall do unto you, as I thought to do unto them. Deut. 28:63

The Borders of the Land

34 And the LORD spake unto Moses, saying,
2 Command the children of Israel, and say unto them, When ye come into the land of Canaan; (this is the land that shall fall unto you for an inheritance, even the land of Canaan with the coasts thereof:) Gen. 17:8; Deut. 1:7-8
3 Then your south quarter shall be from the wilderness of Zin along by the coast of Edom, and your south border shall be the outmost coast of the salt sea eastward: Gen. 14:3
4 And your border shall turn from the south to the ascent of Akrabbim, and pass on to Zin: and the going forth thereof shall be from the south to Kadesh-barnea, and shall go on to Hazar-addar, and pass on to Azmon: Num. 32:8
5 And the border shall fetch a ᵀcompass from Azmon unto the river of Egypt, and the goings out of it shall be at the sea. range
6 And as for the western border, ye shall even have the great sea for a border: this shall be your west border.
7 And this shall be your north border: from the great sea ye shall point out for you mount Hor: Num. 33:37

8 From mount Hor ye shall point out *your border* unto the entrance of Hamath; and the goings forth of the border shall be to Zedad: Num. 13:21
9 And the border shall go on to Ziphron, and the goings out of it shall be at Hazar-enan: this shall be your north border.   Ezek. 47:17
10 And ye shall point out your east border from Hazar-enan to Shepham:
11 And the coast shall go down from Shepham to Riblah, on the east side of Ain; and the border shall descend, and shall reach unto the side of the sea of Chinnereth eastward: Deut. 3:17; Josh. 11:2; 2 Kin. 23:33
12 And the border shall go down to Jordan, and the goings out of it shall be at the salt sea: this shall be your land with the coasts thereof round about.   Num. 34:3
13 And Moses commanded the children of Israel, saying, This *is* the land which ye shall inherit by lot, which the LORD commanded to give unto the nine tribes, and to the half tribe:
14 For the tribe of the children of Reuben according to the house of their fathers, and the tribe of the children of Gad according to the house of their fathers, have received *their inheritance*; and half the tribe of Manasseh have received their inheritance: Num. 32:33
15 The two tribes and the half tribe have received their inheritance on this side Jordan *near* Jericho eastward, toward the sunrising.

The Names of the Men Who Will Divide the Land

16 And the LORD spake unto Moses, saying,
17 These *are* the names of the men which shall divide the land unto you: Eleazar the priest, and Joshua the son of Nun.   Josh. 14:1
18 And ye shall take one prince of every tribe, to divide the land by inheritance.
19 And the names of the men *are* these: Of the tribe of Judah, Caleb the son of Jephunneh.   Num. 26:65
20 And of the tribe of the children of Simeon, Shemuel the son of Ammihud.
21 Of the tribe of Benjamin, Elidad the son of Chislon.
22 And the prince of the tribe of the children of Dan, Bukki the son of Jogli.
23 The prince of the children of Joseph, for the tribe of the children of Manasseh, Hanniel the son of Ephod.
24 And the prince of the tribe of the children of Ephraim, Kemuel the son of Shiphtan.
25 And the prince of the tribe of the children of Zebulun, Elizaphan the son of Parnach.
26 And the prince of the tribe of the children of Issachar, Paltiel the son of Azzan.
27 And the prince of the tribe of the children of Asher, Ahihud the son of Shelomi.
28 And the prince of the tribe of the children of Naphtali, Pedahel the son of Ammihud.
29 These *are they* whom the LORD commanded to divide the inheritance unto the children of Israel in the land of Canaan.

Forty-eight Levitical Cities

35 And the LORD spake unto Moses in the plains of Moab by Jordan *near* Jericho, saying,   Num. 22:1
2 Command the children of Israel, that they give unto the Levites of the inheritance of their possession cities to dwell in; and ye

---

Cities of Refuge

Numbers 35

The cities of refuge were so distributed as to be within a half day's journey of every part of the land. The roads leading to them were always to be kept in good repair; all along the way signposts were to be erected bearing the word "Refuge" in plain, bold characters, that the fleeing one might not be delayed for a moment. Any person—Hebrew, stranger, or sojourner—might avail himself of this provision. But while the guiltless were not to be rashly slain, neither were the guilty to escape punishment. . . . The guilty were given up to the avenger. And those who were entitled to protection could receive it only on condition of remaining within the appointed refuge. Should one wander away beyond the prescribed limits, and be found by the avenger of blood, his life would pay the penalty of his disregard of the Lord's provision. At the death of the high priest, however, all who had sought shelter in the cities of refuge were at liberty to return to their possessions.

In a trial for murder the accused was not to be condemned on the testimony of one witness, even though circumstantial evidence might be strong against him. . . . It was Christ who gave to Moses these directions for Israel. . . .

The cities of refuge appointed for God's ancient people were a symbol of the refuge provided in Christ. The same merciful Saviour who appointed those temporal cities of refuge has by the shedding of His own blood provided for the transgressors of God's law a sure retreat, into which they may flee for safety from the second death. No power can take out of His hands the souls that go to Him for pardon. *PP 515, 516*

shall give *also* unto the Levites suburbs for the cities round about them.   Josh. 14:3-4
3 And the cities shall they have to dwell in; and the suburbs of them shall be for their cattle, and for their goods, and for all their beasts.
4 And the suburbs of the cities, which ye shall give unto the Levites, *shall reach* from the wall of the city and outward a thousand cubits round about.
5 And ye shall measure from without the city on the east side two thousand cubits, and on the south side two thousand cubits, and on the west side two thousand cubits, and on the north side two thousand cubits; and the city *shall be* in the midst: this shall be to them the suburbs of the cities.
6 And among the cities which ye shall give unto the Levites *there shall be* six cities for refuge, which ye shall appoint for the manslayer, that he may flee thither: and to them ye shall add forty and two cities.   Josh. 21:3
7 *So* all the cities which ye shall give to the Levites *shall be* forty and eight cities: them *shall ye give* with their suburbs.
8 And the cities which ye shall give *shall be* of the possession of the children of Israel: from *them that have* many ye shall give many; but from *them that have* few ye shall give few: every one shall give of his cities unto the Levites according to his inheritance which he inheriteth.   Num. 26:54; 33:54

Law of Murder and Cities of Refuge
9 And the LORD spake unto Moses, saying,
10 Speak unto the children of Israel, and say unto them, When ye be come over Jordan into the land of Canaan;
11 Then ye shall appoint you cities to be cities of refuge for you; that the slayer may flee thither, which killeth any person at unawares.   Ex. 21:13; Josh. 20:2
12 And they shall be unto you cities for refuge from the avenger; that the manslayer die not, until he stand before the congregation in judgment.   Deut. 19:6
13 And of these cities which ye shall give six cities shall ye have for refuge.
14 Ye shall give three cities on this side Jordan, and three cities shall ye give in the land of Canaan, *which* shall be cities of refuge.
15 These six cities shall be a refuge, *both* for the children of Israel, and for the stranger, and for the sojourner among them: that every one that killeth any person unawares may flee thither.   Num. 15:16
16 And if he smite him with an instrument of iron, so that he die, he *is* a murderer: the murderer shall surely be put to death.   Lev. 24:17
17 And if he ᵀsmite him with throwing a stone, wherewith he may die, and he die, he

is a murderer: the murderer shall surely be put to death.   strike
18 Or *if* he smite him with an hand weapon of wood, wherewith he may die, and he die, he *is* a murderer: the murderer shall surely be put to death.
19 The revenger of blood himself shall slay the murderer: when he meeteth him, he shall slay him.   Num. 35:21
20 But if he thrust him of hatred, or hurl at him by laying of wait, that he die;   Gen. 4:8
21 Or in ᵀenmity smite him with his hand, that he die: he that smote *him* shall surely be put to death; *for* he *is* a murderer: the revenger of blood shall slay the murderer, when he meeteth him.   hostility
22 But if he thrust him suddenly without enmity, or have cast upon him any thing without laying of wait,   Ex. 21:13
23 Or with any stone, wherewith a man may die, seeing *him* not, and cast *it* upon him, that he die, and *was* not his enemy, neither sought his harm:
24 Then the congregation shall judge between the slayer and the revenger of blood according to these judgments: Num. 35:12
25 And the congregation shall deliver the slayer out of the hand of the revenger of blood, and the congregation shall restore him to the city of his refuge, whither he was fled: and he shall abide in it unto the death of the high priest, which was anointed with the holy oil.   Ex. 29:7
26 But if the slayer shall at any time come without the border of the city of his refuge, whither he was fled;
27 And the revenger of blood find him without the borders of the city of his refuge, and the revenger of blood kill the slayer; he shall not be guilty of blood:
28 Because he should have remained in the city of his refuge until the death of the high priest: but after the death of the high priest the slayer shall return into the land of his possession.
29 So these *things* shall be for a statute of judgment unto you throughout your generations in all your dwellings.   Num. 27:11
30 Whoso killeth any person, the murderer shall be put to death by the mouth of witnesses: but one witness shall not testify against any person *to cause him* to die. Deut. 19:15
31 Moreover ye shall take no satisfaction for the life of a murderer, which *is* guilty of death: but he shall be surely put to death.
32 And ye shall take no satisfaction for him that is fled to the city of his refuge, that he should come again to dwell in the land, until the death of the priest.
33 So ye shall not pollute the land wherein ye *are*: for blood it defileth the land: and the

land cannot be cleansed of the blood that is shed therein, but by the blood of him that shed it.   Mic. 4:11

34 Defile not therefore the land which ye shall inhabit, wherein I dwell: for I the LORD dwell among the children of Israel.   Num. 5:3

Expressions of Concern about Daughters Receiving Lands of Inheritance

36 And the chief fathers of the families of the children of Gilead, the son of Machir, the son of Manasseh, of the families of the sons of Joseph, came near, and spake before Moses, and before the princes, the chief fathers of the children of Israel: Num. 27:1

2 And they said, The LORD commanded my lord to give the land for an inheritance by lot to the children of Israel: and my lord was commanded by the LORD to give the inheritance of Zelophehad our brother unto his daughters.   Num. 33:54

3 And if they be married to any of the sons of the *other* tribes of the children of Israel, then shall their inheritance be taken from the inheritance of our fathers, and shall be put to the inheritance of the tribe whereunto they are received: so shall it be taken from the lot of our inheritance.

4 And when the jubile of the children of Israel shall be, then shall their inheritance be put unto the inheritance of the tribe whereunto they are received: so shall their inheritance be taken away from the inheritance of the tribe of our fathers.

Concern is Answered by Requiring that Daughters Marry in Their Own Tribes

5 And Moses commanded the children of Israel according to the word of the LORD, saying, The tribe of the sons of Joseph hath said well.   Num. 27:7

6 This *is* the thing which the LORD doth command concerning the daughters of Zelophehad, saying, Let them marry to whom they think best; only to the family of the tribe of their father shall they marry.   Num. 36:12

7 So shall not the inheritance of the children of Israel remove from tribe to tribe: for every one of the children of Israel shall keep himself to the inheritance of the tribe of his fathers.   1 Kin. 21:3

8 And every daughter, that possesseth an inheritance in any tribe of the children of Israel, shall be wife unto one of the family of the tribe of her father, that the children of Israel may enjoy every man the inheritance of his fathers.   1 Chr. 23:22

9 Neither shall the inheritance remove from *one* tribe to another tribe; but every one of the tribes of the children of Israel shall keep himself to his own inheritance.

10 Even as the LORD commanded Moses, so did the daughters of Zelophehad:

11 For Mahlah, Tirzah, and Hoglah, and Milcah, and Noah, the daughters of Zelophehad, were married unto their father's brothers' sons: Num. 27:1

12 *And* they were married into the families of the sons of Manasseh the son of Joseph, and their inheritance remained in the tribe of the family of their father.

13 These *are* the commandments and the judgments, which the LORD commanded by the hand of Moses unto the children of Israel in the plains of Moab by Jordan *near* Jericho.   Lev. 27:34

THE FIFTH BOOK OF MOSES CALLED

DEUTERONOMY

Jesus' Sermon on the Mount is probably the most well-known sermon in the New Testament. In the Old Testament, Deuteronomy is Moses' "Sermon on the Plains." Moses delivers a series of sermons—his final words to his people who are now on the brink of conquering the Promised Land. This is a new audience. The previous generation who had stood in this very spot had rebelled in fear against God, refusing to trust that He would help them take the land. Their punishment was to wander in the wilderness until all of the rebellious people died. They would never see the Promised Land—but their children would. Those children are now ready to do what their parents would not.

At 120 years old, Moses is still blessed with vigor. Yet God reveals that his time to die has come (32:48–52). Although prevented from entering Canaan because of a sinful act during the wilderness wanderings (see Numbers 20:12), Moses wants to remind his people to be faithful to their covenant with God and continue to obey God's law. Blessings will come as a result of obedience, while curses come with disobedience.

Dates

Deuteronomy was probably written in 1405 B.C. at the end of the forty years of wandering. As in Leviticus, about one month passes in Deuteronomy (see 1:3; 34:8; Joshua 1:1, 2; 5:6–12).

Author

While some might argue that Moses did not author the Book of Deuteronomy, evidence proves otherwise. Deuteronomy is referenced about eighty times in the New Testament. These references from both the old and new testaments cite Moses as the author (Joshua 1:7, 8; Judges 3:4; Malachi 4:4; Acts 3:22; Romans 10:19). Jesus also refers to Moses when quoting from Deuteronomy (Matthew 19:8, 9; Mark 7:10).

Within Deuteronomy, Moses is cited as the author (1:1–5; 4:44–46; 29:1; 31:9, 24–26). Moses' obituary, (chapter 34), however, is believed to have been written by Joshua.

Meaning of the Name

In the Hebrew, the name of this book is *Haddebharim*—"The Words." This phrase is in Deuteronomy 1:1. Deuteronomy also has been known as *Mishneh Hattorah,* or "repetition of the Law," because it repeats many of the laws mentioned in other books of the Pentateuch. In the Greek, *Mishneh Hattorah* becomes *To Deuteronomion Touto* or "This Second Law." This title was probably due to Deuteronomy 17:18, which mentions "a copy of this law."

Christ in Deuteronomy

Moses' prophecy in Deuteronomy 18:15 foretells the coming of Christ: "The LORD thy God will raise up unto thee a Prophet from the midst of thee, of thy brethren, like unto me; unto him ye shall hearken." Moses later appears during Jesus' Transfiguration (Matthew 17:3) as a confirmation of the prophecy. Some of the events of Moses' life also parallel those of Jesus: his ministry as a priest, prophet, and unofficial king; the death threats against him as a child.

Overview

Moses, the advocate between God and His people, advises the people of Israel of their duties under the law. Deuteronomy divides into four sections based on Moses' messages:

(1) *Deuteronomy 1:1—4:43, The First Message:* Moses' first message recounts the Exodus to the present.

(2) *Deuteronomy 4:44—29:1, The Second Message:* Here, Moses explains the covenant, including the laws the people had agreed to obey at Mount Sinai, and other reminders of Israel's status: the Ten Commandments (chapter 5); the confession of faith (the Shema—chapter 6); Israel's position as God's chosen people (7:1–11); the blessings of obedience (7:12—8:20; 11:1–32; 28:1–14); the consequences of disobedience (9:1–29; 28:15–68); worship and other daily ordinances (chapters 12—26). The solemn wording of chapter 27 makes the agreement legally binding.

The pluses and minuses of choosing a king (17:14–20) will later be reflected in the lives of Israel's kings. The blessings of obedience and curses that result from disobedience (chapter 28) can be clearly seen during Israel's later history.

(3) *Deuteronomy 29:2—30:20, The Third Message:* In this address, Moses provides the agreement to renew the covenant.

(4) *Deuteronomy 31:1—34:12, The Fourth Message:* In this last message, a transition in leadership is made.

Unlocking Deuteronomy

KEY PEOPLE:
Moses, Joshua, Caleb

KEY EVENTS:
Moses recounts some of the key events of Israel's history since the rebellion, including: the Ten Commandments; making another pair of tablets to replace the broken ones; establishment of cities of refuge; blessings of obedience and curses of disobedience; Joshua becoming the new leader. Moses' death and burial in an unknown location was added as a postscript, probably by Joshua.

KEY WORD:
Covenant. The book of Deuteronomy is a reminder to Israel to keep the covenant made with God on Mount Sinai: to be His holy and obedient people because of His great love for them. God's love is mentioned many times in Deuteronomy, in association with His covenant.

KEY VERSES:
"And now, Israel, what doth the LORD thy God require of thee, but to fear the LORD thy God, to walk in all his ways, and to love him, and to serve the LORD thy God with all thy heart and with all thy soul, to keep the commandments of the LORD, and his statutes, which I command thee this day for thy good?" (Deuteronomy 10:12, 13).

KEY CHAPTER:
Deuteronomy 27, where the people of Israel ratify the covenant made with God, newly inscribed on stone tablets.

Moses Speaks to the People

1 These *be* the words which Moses spake unto all Israel on this side Jordan in the wilderness, in the plain over against the Red *sea*, between Paran, and Tophel, and Laban, and Hazeroth, and Dizahab. 　　1 Sam. 25:1

1:1 The History of Deliverance

Before relinquishing his position as the visible leader of Israel, Moses was directed to rehearse to them the history of their deliverance from Egypt and their journeyings in the wilderness, and also to recapitulate the law spoken from Sinai. When the law was given, but few of the present congregation were old enough to comprehend the awful solemnity of the occasion. *PP 463*

2 (*There are* eleven days' *journey* from Horeb by the way of mount Seir unto Kadesh-bar-nea.) 　　Num. 13:26; 32:8; Deut. 9:23

3 And it came to pass in the fortieth year, in the eleventh month, on the first *day* of the month, *that* Moses spake unto the children of Israel, according unto all that the Lord had given him in commandment unto them; 　　Num. 33:38

4 After he had slain Sihon the king of the Amorites, which dwelt in Heshbon, and Og the king of Bashan, which dwelt at Astaroth in Edrei: 　　Num. 21:21-35

5 On this side Jordan, in the land of Moab, began Moses to declare this law, saying,

6 The Lord our God spake unto us in Horeb, saying, Ye have dwelt long enough in this mount: 　　Ex. 3:1

7 Turn you, and take your journey, and go to the mount of the Amorites, and unto all *the places* nigh thereunto, in the plain, in the hills, and in the ᵀvale, and in the south, and by the sea side, to the land of the Canaanites, and unto Lebanon, unto the great river, the river Euphrates. 　　Deut. 11:24 ◆ *valley*

8 Behold, I have set the land before you: go in and possess the land which the Lord sware unto your fathers, Abraham, Isaac, and Jacob, to give unto them and to their seed after them. 　　Gen. 12:7; 15:18; 17:7-8

9 And I spake unto you at that time, saying, I am not able to bear you myself alone: Ex. 18:18

10 The Lord your God hath multiplied you, and, behold, ye *are* this day as the stars of heaven for multitude. Gen. 15:5; Deut. 10:22; 28:62

11 (The Lord God of your fathers make you a thousand times so many more as ye *are*, and bless you, as he hath promised you!) 　　Gen. 22:17

12 How can I myself alone bear your cumbrance, and your burden, and your strife?

13 Take you wise men, and understanding, and known among your tribes, and I will make them rulers over you. 　　Ex. 18:21; Num. 11:16-17

14 And ye answered me, and said, The thing which thou hast spoken *is* good *for us* to do.

15 So I took the chief of your tribes, wise men, and known, and made them heads over you, captains over thousands, and captains over hundreds, and captains over fifties, and captains over tens, and officers among your tribes.

16 And I charged your judges at that time, saying, Hear *the causes* between your brethren, and judge righteously between *every* man and his brother, and the stranger *that is* with him. 　　Lev. 24:22; John 7:24

17 Ye shall not respect persons in judgment; *but* ye shall hear the small as well as the great; ye shall not be afraid of the face of man; for the judgment *is* God's: and the cause that is too hard for you, bring *it* unto me, and I will hear it. 　　Ex. 18:26; Lev. 19:15; Deut. 16:19

18 And I commanded you at that time all the things which ye should do.

Moses Tells of Sending the Spies and the People's Rebellion

19 And when we departed from Horeb, we went through all that great and terrible wilderness, which ye saw by the way of the mountain of the Amorites, as the Lord our God commanded us; and we came to Kadesh-barnea. 　　Deut. 1:2; 8:15; Jer. 2:6

20 And I said unto you, Ye are come unto the mountain of the Amorites, which the Lord our God doth give unto us.

21 Behold, the Lord thy God hath set the land before thee: go up *and* possess *it*, as the Lord God of thy fathers hath said unto thee; fear not, neither be discouraged. 　　Josh. 1:9

22 And ye came near unto me every one of you, and said, We will send men before us, and they shall search us out the land, and bring us word again by what way we must go up, and into what cities we shall come.

23 And the saying pleased me well: and I took twelve men of you, one of a tribe:

24 And they turned and went up into the mountain, and came unto the valley of Eshcol, and searched it out. 　　Num. 13:21-27

25 And they took of the fruit of the land in their hands, and brought *it* down unto us, and brought us word again, and said, *It is* a good land which the Lord our God doth give us.

26 Notwithstanding ye would not go up, but rebelled against the commandment of the Lord your God: 　　Num. 14:1-4

27 And ye murmured in your tents, and said, Because the Lord hated us, he hath brought us forth out of the land of Egypt, to

deliver us into the hand of the Amorites, to destroy us. Num. 14:3; Deut. 9:28; Ps. 106:25

28 Whither shall we go up? our brethren have discouraged our heart, saying, The people *is* greater and taller than we; the cities *are* great and walled up to heaven; and moreover we have seen the sons of the Anakims there. Deut. 9:1-2

29 Then I said unto you, Dread not, neither be afraid of them.

30 The LORD your God which goeth before you, he shall fight for you, according to all that he did for you in Egypt before your eyes; Ex. 14:14, 25; Neh. 4:20

31 And in the wilderness, where thou hast seen how that the LORD thy God bare thee, as a man doth bear his son, in all the way that ye went, until ye came into this place.

32 Yet in this thing ye did not believe the LORD your God, Ps. 106:24; Jude 5

33 Who went in the way before you, to search you out a place to pitch your tents *in*, in fire by night, to shew you by what way ye should go, and in a cloud by day. Num. 9:15-22; Ps. 78:14

34 And the LORD heard the voice of your words, and was wroth, and sware, saying,

35 Surely there shall not one of these men of this evil generation see that good land, which I sware to give unto your fathers,

36 Save Caleb the son of Jephunneh; he shall see it, and to him will I give the land that he hath ᵀtrodden upon, and to his children, because he hath wholly followed the LORD. Num. 14:24 ◆ *walked*

37 Also the LORD was angry with me for your sakes, saying, Thou also shalt not go in thither. Num. 20:12; 27:13-14; Deut. 4:21

38 *But* Joshua the son of Nun, which standeth before thee, he shall go in thither: encourage him: for he shall cause Israel to inherit it. Num. 14:30

39 Moreover your little ones, which ye said should be a prey, and your children, which in that day had no knowledge between good and evil, they shall go in thither, and unto them will I give it, and they shall possess it. Num. 14:3, 31; Is. 7:15-16

40 But *as for* you, turn you, and take your journey into the wilderness by the way of the Red sea. Num. 14:25

41 Then ye answered and said unto me, We have sinned against the LORD, we will go up and fight, according to all that the LORD our God commanded us. And when ye had girded on every man his weapons of war, ye were ready to go up into the hill.

42 And the LORD said unto me, Say unto them, Go not up, neither fight; for I *am* not among you; lest ye be smitten before your enemies.

43 So I spake unto you; and ye would not hear, but rebelled against the commandment of the LORD, and went presumptuously up into the hill. Num. 14:44

44 And the Amorites, which dwelt in that mountain, came out against you, and chased you, as bees do, and destroyed you in Seir, *even* unto Hormah. Num. 14:45; 21:3; Ps. 118:12

45 And ye returned and wept before the LORD; but the LORD would not hearken to your voice, nor give ear unto you.

1:40-45 Unbelief and Cowardice

The Lord promised to spare Israel from immediate destruction; but because of their unbelief and cowardice He could not manifest His power to subdue their enemies. Therefore in His mercy He bade them, as the only safe course, to turn back toward the Red Sea. PP 391

46 So ye abode in Kadesh many days, according unto the days that ye abode there. Num. 20:1

The Story of the Wilderness Wanderings

2 Then we turned, and took our journey into the wilderness by the way of the Red sea, as the LORD spake unto me: and we ᵀcompassed mount Seir many days. *surrounded*

2 And the LORD spake unto me, saying,

3 Ye have compassed this mountain long enough: turn you northward. Deut. 1:6

2:3 A Welcome Change

After passing to the south of Edom, the Israelites turned northward, and again set their faces toward the Promised Land. Their route now lay over a vast, elevated plain, swept by cool, fresh breezes from the hills. It was a welcome change from the parched valley through which they had been traveling, and they pressed forward, buoyant and hopeful. PP 433

4 And command thou the people, saying, Ye *are* to pass through the coast of your brethren the children of Esau, which dwell in Seir; and they shall be afraid of you: take ye good heed unto yourselves therefore: Num. 20:14-21

5 Meddle not with them; for I will not give you of their land, no, not so much as a foot breadth; because I have given mount Seir unto Esau *for* a possession. Gen. 36:8

6 Ye shall buy meat of them for money, that ye may eat; and ye shall also buy water of them for money, that ye may drink.

7 For the LORD thy God hath blessed thee in all the works of thy hand: he knoweth thy walking through this great wilderness: these forty years the LORD thy God *hath been* with thee; thou hast lacked nothing. Deut. 8:2-4

8 And when we passed by from our brethren the children of Esau, which dwelt in

Seir, through the way of the plain from Elath, and from Ezion-gaber, we turned and passed by the way of the wilderness of Moab.   Judg. 11:18; 1 Kin. 9:26; 2 Kin. 14:22

9 And the LORD said unto me, Distress not the Moabites, neither contend with them in battle: for I will not give thee of their land *for* a possession; because I have given Ar unto the children of Lot *for* a possession.   Gen. 19:36-37; Num. 21:15, 28

10 The Emims dwelt therein in times past, a people great, and many, and tall, as the Anakims;   Gen. 14:5

11 Which also were accounted giants, as the Anakims; but the Moabites call them Emims.

12 The Horims also dwelt in Seir beforetime; but the children of Esau succeeded them, when they had destroyed them from before them, and dwelt in their stead; as Israel did unto the land of his possession, which the LORD gave unto them.   Gen. 14:6; Deut. 2:22

13 Now rise up, *said I*, and get you over the brook Zered. And we went over the brook Zered.   Num. 21:12

14 And the space in which we came from Kadesh-barnea, until we were come over the brook Zered, *was* thirty and eight years; until all the generation of the men of war were wasted out from among the host, as the LORD sware unto them.   Deut. 1:34-35

15 For indeed the hand of the LORD was against them, to destroy them from among the host, until they were consumed.   Ps. 106:26

16 So it came to pass, when all the men of war were consumed and dead from among the people,

17 That the LORD spake unto me, saying,

18 Thou art to pass over through Ar, the coast of Moab, this day:

19 And *when* thou comest nigh over against the children of Ammon, distress them not, nor meddle with them: for I will not give thee of the land of the children of Ammon *any* possession; because I have given it unto the children of Lot *for* a possession.   Deut. 2:9

20 (That also was accounted a land of giants: giants dwelt therein in old time; and the Ammonites call them Zamzummims;   Gen. 14:5

21 A people great, and many, and tall, as the Anakims; but the LORD destroyed them before them; and they succeeded them, and dwelt in their stead:

22 As he did to the children of Esau, which dwelt in Seir, when he destroyed the Horims from before them; and they succeeded them, and dwelt in their stead even unto this day: Gen. 36:8

23 And the Avims which dwelt in Hazerim, *even* unto Azzah, the Caphtorims, which came

forth out of Caphtor, destroyed them, and dwelt in their stead.)   Gen. 10:14; Josh. 13:3; Amos 9:7

The Story of the Conquest of Sihon the Amorite, King of Heshbon

24 Rise ye up, take your journey, and pass over the river Arnon: behold, I have given into thine hand Sihon the Amorite, king of Heshbon, and his land: begin to possess *it*, and contend with him in battle.

25 This day will I begin to put the dread of thee and the fear of thee upon the nations *that are* under the whole heaven, who shall hear report of thee, and shall tremble, and be in anguish because of thee.   Ex. 15:14-16; Deut. 11:25

2:24, 25 The Pillar of Cloud

So far as skill in warfare was concerned, [the Israelites'] enemies had the advantage. To all human appearance, a speedy end would be made of [them].

But Moses kept his gaze fixed upon the cloudy pillar, and encouraged the people with the thought that the token of God's presence was still with them. At the same time he directed them to do all that human power could do in preparing for war. *PP 433, 434*

---

26 And I sent messengers out of the wilderness of Kedemoth unto Sihon king of Heshbon with words of peace, saying,   Josh. 13:18

27 Let me pass through thy land: I will go along by the high way, I will neither turn unto the right hand nor to the left. Judg. 11:19

28 Thou shalt sell me meat for money, that I may eat; and give me water for money, that I may drink: only I will pass through on my feet;   Num. 20:19

29 (As the children of Esau which dwell in Seir, and the Moabites which dwell in Ar, did unto me;) until I shall pass over Jordan into the land which the LORD our God giveth us.   Num. 20:18

30 But Sihon king of Heshbon would not let us pass by him: for the LORD thy God hardened his spirit, and made his heart obstinate, that he might deliver him into thy hand, as *appeareth* this day. Ex. 4:21; Num. 21:23

31 And the LORD said unto me, Behold, I have begun to give Sihon and his land before thee: begin to possess, that thou mayest inherit his land.   Deut. 1:8

32 Then Sihon came out against us, he and all his people, to fight at Jahaz.   Num. 21:23-30

33 And the LORD our God delivered him before us; and we smote him, and his sons, and all his people.   Deut. 7:2

34 And we took all his cities at that time, and utterly destroyed the men, and the women, and the little ones, of every city, we left none to remain: Deut. 7:2

35 Only the cattle we took for a prey unto ourselves, and the ᵀspoil of the cities which we took.   *plunder*
36 From Aroer, which *is* by the brink of the river of Arnon, and *from* the city that *is* by the river, even unto Gilead, there was not one city too strong for us: the LORD our God delivered all unto us: Deut. 3:12; 4:48; Josh. 13:9
37 Only unto the land of the children of Ammon thou camest not, *nor* unto any place of the river Jabbok, nor unto the cities in the mountains, nor unto whatsoever the LORD our God forbad us. Gen. 32:22; Num. 21:24; Deut. 3:16

The Story of the Conquest of Og, King of Bashan

3 Then we turned, and went up the way to Bashan: and Og the king of Bashan came out against us, he and all his people, to battle at Edrei.   Num. 21:33-35
2 And the LORD said unto me, Fear him not: for I will deliver him, and all his people, and his land, into thy hand; and thou shalt do unto him as thou didst unto Sihon king of the Amorites, which dwelt at Heshbon.   Num. 21:23-25
3 So the LORD our God delivered into our hands Og also, the king of Bashan, and all his people: and we smote him until none was left to him remaining.   Num. 21:35
4 And we took all his cities at that time, there was not a city which we took not from them, ᵀthreescore cities, all the region of Argob, the kingdom of Og in Bashan.   1 Kin. 4:13 ◆ *sixty*
5 All these cities *were* fenced with high walls, gates, and bars; beside unwalled towns a great many.
6 And we utterly destroyed them, as we did unto Sihon king of Heshbon, utterly destroying the men, women, and children, of every city.   Deut. 2:24, 34; Ps. 135:10-12
7 But all the cattle, and the ᵀspoil of the cities, we took for a prey to ourselves.   *plunder*
8 And we took at that time out of the hand of the two kings of the Amorites the land that *was* on this side Jordan, from the river of Arnon unto mount Hermon;   Josh. 12:2-6

3:8 Captain of the Lord's Host

The Israelites crossed the river Arnon and advanced upon the foe. An engagement took place, in which the armies of Israel were victorious; and, following up the advantage gained, they were soon in possession of the country of the Amorites. It was the Captain of the Lord's host who vanquished the enemies of His people; and He would have done the same thirty-eight years before had Israel trusted in Him. *PP 435*

---

9 (*Which* Hermon the Sidonians call Sirion; and the Amorites call it Shenir;)   1 Chr. 5:23
10 All the cities of the plain, and all Gilead, and all Bashan, unto Salchah and Edrei, cities of the kingdom of Og in Bashan.
11 For only Og king of Bashan remained of the remnant of giants; behold, his ᵀbedstead *was* a bedstead of iron; *is* it not in Rabbath of the children of Ammon? nine cubits *was* the length thereof, and four cubits the breadth of it, after the cubit of a man.   Gen. 14:5; Jer. 49:2 ◆ *couch or bed*

The Distribution of Land to the Tribes East of the Jordan

12 And this land, *which* we possessed at that time, from Aroer, which *is* by the river Arnon, and half mount Gilead, and the cities thereof, gave I unto the Reubenites and to the Gadites.   Num. 32:32-38; Deut. 2:36
13 And the rest of Gilead, and all Bashan, *being* the kingdom of Og, gave I unto the half tribe of Manasseh; all the region of Argob, with all Bashan, which was called the land of giants.   Num. 32:39-42
14 Jair the son of Manasseh took all the country of Argob unto the coasts of Geshuri and Maachathi; and called them after his own name, Bashan-havoth-jair, unto this day.   Num. 32:41; Josh. 13:13; 2 Sam. 3:3
15 And I gave Gilead unto Machir. Num. 32:39-40
16 And unto the Reubenites and unto the Gadites I gave from Gilead even unto the river Arnon half the valley, and the border even unto the river Jabbok, *which is* the border of the children of Ammon;   Num. 21:24; Deut. 2:37
17 The plain also, and Jordan, and the coast *thereof*, from Chinnereth even unto the sea of the plain, *even* the salt sea, under Ashdoth-pisgah eastward.   Gen. 14:3; Josh. 3:16; 12:3
18 And I commanded you at that time, saying, The LORD your God hath given you this land to possess it: ye shall pass over armed before your brethren the children of Israel, all *that are* meet for the war.   Josh. 4:12-13
19 But your wives, and your little ones, and your cattle, (*for* I know that ye have much cattle,) shall abide in your cities which I have given you;
20 Until the LORD have given rest unto your brethren, as well as unto you, and *until* they also possess the land which the LORD your God hath given them beyond Jordan: and *then* shall ye return every man unto his possession, which I have given you.   Josh. 22:4
21 And I commanded Joshua at that time, saying, Thine eyes have seen all that the LORD your God hath done unto these two kings: so shall the LORD do unto all the kingdoms whither thou passest.

22 Ye shall not fear them: for the LORD your God he shall fight for you. Ex. 14:14; Deut. 1:30
23 And I ^Tbesought the LORD at that time, saying,

begged

24 O Lord GOD, thou hast begun to shew thy servant thy greatness, and thy mighty hand: for what God *is there* in heaven or in earth, that can do according to thy works, and according to thy might? Ex. 15:11; Deut. 11:2; 2 Sam. 7:22
25 I pray thee, let me go over, and see the good land that *is* beyond Jordan, that goodly mountain, and Lebanon. Ex. 3:8
26 But the LORD was ^Twroth with me for your sakes, and would not hear me: and the LORD said unto me, Let it suffice thee; speak no more unto me of this matter. Deut. 1:37 ◆ *angry*
27 Get thee up into the top of Pisgah, and lift up thine eyes westward, and northward, and southward, and eastward, and behold *it* with thine eyes: for thou shalt not go over this Jordan. Num. 27:12

3:23–27 A Lesson for All Time

God shut Moses out of Canaan, to teach a lesson which should never be forgotten— that He requires exact obedience, and that men are to beware of taking to themselves the glory which is due to their Maker. He could not grant the prayer of Moses that he might share the inheritance of Israel, but He did not forget or forsake His servant. . . . On the top of Pisgah, God called Moses to an inheritance infinitely more glorious than the earthly Canaan. *PP 479*

28 But charge Joshua, and encourage him, and strengthen him: for he shall go over before this people, and he shall cause them to inherit the land which thou shalt see. Deut. 1:38
29 So we abode in the valley over against Beth-peor. Num. 25:3; Deut. 4:46; 34:6

An Exhortation to Obedience

4 Now therefore hearken, O Israel, unto the statutes and unto the judgments, which I teach you, for to do *them*, that ye may live, and go in and possess the land which the LORD God of your fathers giveth you. Deut. 8:1; Ezek. 20:11; Rom. 10:5
2 Ye shall not add unto the word which I command you, neither shall ye diminish *ought* from it, that ye may keep the commandments of the LORD your God which I command you. Deut. 12:32; Josh. 1:7; Prov. 30:6
3 Your eyes have seen what the LORD did because of Baal-peor: for all the men that followed Baal-peor, the LORD thy God hath destroyed them from among you. Num. 25:1-9
4 But ye that did cleave unto the LORD your God *are* alive every one of you this day.
5 Behold, I have taught you statutes and judgments, even as the LORD my God commanded me, that ye should do so in the land whither ye go to possess it.
6 Keep therefore and do *them*; for this *is* your wisdom and your understanding in the sight of the nations, which shall hear all these statutes, and say, Surely this great nation *is* a wise and understanding people. Job 28:28; Ps. 19:7

4:6 Self-Willed Israel

But the Israelites fixed their hopes upon worldly greatness. From the time of their entrance to the land of Canaan, they departed from the commandments of God, and followed the ways of the heathen. It was in vain that God sent them warning by His prophets. In vain they suffered the chastisement of heathen oppression. Every reformation was followed by deeper apostasy. *DA 28*

7 For what nation *is there* so great, who *hath* God *so* nigh unto them, as the LORD our God *is* in all *things that* we call upon him *for*?
8 And what nation *is there* so great, that hath statutes and judgments *so* righteous as all this law, which I set before you this day?
9 Only take heed to thyself, and keep thy soul diligently, lest thou forget the things which thine eyes have seen, and lest they depart from thy heart all the days of thy life: but teach them thy sons, and thy sons' sons; Gen. 18:19; Deut. 4:23; 6:7
10 *Specially* the day that thou stoodest before the LORD thy God in Horeb, when the LORD said unto me, Gather me the people together, and I will make them hear my words, that they may learn to fear me all the days that they shall live upon the earth, and *that* they may teach their children. Ex. 19:9
11 And ye came near and stood under the mountain; and the mountain burned with fire unto the midst of heaven, with darkness, clouds, and thick darkness. Deut. 5:23
12 And the LORD spake unto you out of the midst of the fire: ye heard the voice of the words, but saw no ^Tsimilitude; only *ye heard* a voice. Ex. 20:22 ◆ *image*
13 And he declared unto you his covenant, which he commanded you to perform, *even* ten commandments; and he wrote them upon two tables of stone. Ex. 24:12; 31:18; 34:28
14 And the LORD commanded me at that time to teach you statutes and judgments, that ye might do them in the land whither ye go over to possess it.
15 Take ye therefore good heed unto yourselves; for ye saw no manner of similitude on the day *that* the LORD spake unto you in Horeb out of the midst of the fire: Is. 40:18
16 Lest ye corrupt *yourselves*, and make you

a graven image, the similitude of any figure, the likeness of male or female,   Ex. 20:4-5

17 The likeness of any beast that *is* on the earth, the likeness of any winged fowl that flieth in the air,   Rom. 1:23

18 The likeness of any thing that creepeth on the ground, the likeness of any fish that *is* in the waters beneath the earth:

19 And lest thou lift up thine eyes unto heaven, and when thou seest the sun, and the moon, and the stars, *even* all the host of heaven, shouldest be driven to worship them, and serve them, which the LORD thy God hath divided unto all nations under the whole heaven.   Deut. 17:3; 2 Kin. 17:16; 21:3

20 But the LORD hath taken you, and brought you forth out of the iron furnace, *even* out of Egypt, to be unto him a people of inheritance, as *ye are* this day.   Deut. 9:29; 1 Kin. 8:51

21 Furthermore the LORD was angry with me for your sakes, and sware that I should not go over Jordan, and that I should not go in unto that good land, which the LORD thy God giveth thee *for* an inheritance: Num. 20:12

22 But I must die in this land, I must not go over Jordan: but ye shall go over, and possess that good land.   Deut. 3:25, 27

23 Take heed unto yourselves, lest ye forget the covenant of the LORD your God, which he made with you, and make you a ᵀgraven image, *or* the likeness of any *thing*, which the LORD thy God hath forbidden thee.   Deut. 4:9 ◆ *engraved* or *cut out*

24 For the LORD thy God *is* a consuming fire, *even* a jealous God. Ex. 24:17; Deut. 9:3; Heb. 12:29

4:24 A Consuming Fire

So it will be in the great final day, when judgment shall fall upon the rejecters of God's grace. Christ, their rock of offense, will then appear to them as an avenging mountain. The glory of His countenance, which to the righteous is life, will be to the wicked a consuming fire. Because of love rejected, grace despised, the sinner will be destroyed. DA 600

---

25 When thou shalt ᵀbeget children, and children's children, and ye shall have remained long in the land, and shall corrupt *yourselves*, and make a graven image, *or* the likeness of any *thing*, and shall do evil in the sight of the LORD thy God, to provoke him to anger: Deut. 4:16 ◆ *bring forth*

26 I call heaven and earth to witness against you this day, that ye shall soon utterly perish from off the land whereunto ye go over Jordan to possess it; ye shall not prolong *your* days upon it, but shall utterly be destroyed.   Deut. 30:18-19; Is. 1:2; Mic. 6:2

27 And the LORD shall scatter you among the nations, and ye shall be left *few* in number among the heathen, whither the LORD shall lead you.   Lev. 26:33

28 And there ye shall serve gods, the work of men's hands, wood and stone, which neither see, nor hear, nor eat, nor smell. Deut. 28:36, 64

29 But if from thence thou shalt seek the LORD thy God, thou shalt find *him*, if thou seek him with all thy heart and with all thy soul.   Deut. 30:1-3, 10; 2 Chr. 15:4

30 When thou art in tribulation, and all these things are come upon thee, *even* in the latter days, if thou turn to the LORD thy God, and shalt be obedient unto his voice;   Deut. 31:29

31 (For the LORD thy God *is* a merciful God;) he will not forsake thee, neither destroy thee, nor forget the covenant of thy fathers which he sware unto them. 2 Chr. 30:9; Neh. 9:31; Jon. 4:2

32 For ask now of the days that are past, which were before thee, since the day that God created man upon the earth, and *ask* from the one side of heaven unto the other, whether there hath been *any such thing* as this great thing *is*, or hath been heard like it?   Job 8:8; Matt. 24:31

33 Did *ever* people hear the voice of God speaking out of the midst of the fire, as thou hast heard, and live?   Ex. 24:11

34 Or hath God ᵀassayed to go *and* take him a nation from the midst of *another* nation, by temptations, by signs, and by wonders, and by war, and by a mighty hand, and by a stretched out arm, and by great terrors, according to all that the LORD your God did for you in Egypt before your eyes? Ex. 6:6; 7:3; Deut. 26:8 ◆ *attempted*

35 Unto thee it was shewed, that thou mightest know that the LORD he *is* God; *there is* none else beside him.   1 Sam. 2:2; Is. 45:5, 18

36 Out of heaven he made thee to hear his voice, that he might instruct thee: and upon earth he shewed thee his great fire; and thou heardest his words out of the midst of the fire.   Ex. 19:9, 19; Deut. 4:33

37 And because he loved thy fathers, therefore he chose their seed after them, and brought thee out in his sight with his mighty power out of Egypt;   Ex. 13:3, 9; Deut. 10:15

38 To drive out nations from before thee greater and mightier than thou *art*, to bring thee in, to give thee their land *for* an inheritance, as *it is* this day.   Deut. 7:1

39 Know therefore this day, and consider *it* in thine heart, that the LORD he *is* God in heaven above, and upon the earth beneath: *there is* none else. Deut. 4:35; Josh. 2:11; 2 Chr. 20:6

40 Thou shalt keep therefore his statutes, and his commandments, which I command thee this day, that it may go well with thee, and with thy children after thee, and that thou mayest prolong *thy* days upon the

earth, which the LORD thy God giveth thee, for ever.   Lev. 22:31; Deut. 5:16; 6:3

Moses Appoints the Three Cities of Refuge beyond Jordan

41 Then Moses severed three cities on this side Jordan toward the sunrising;   Num. 35:6
42 That the slayer might flee thither, which should kill his neighbour unawares, and hated him not in times past; and that fleeing unto one of these cities he might live:
43 *Namely*, Bezer in the wilderness, in the plain country, of the Reubenites; and Ramoth in Gilead, of the Gadites; and Golan in Bashan, of the Manassites.   Josh. 20:8
44 And this *is* the law which Moses set before the children of Israel:
45 These *are* the testimonies, and the statutes, and the judgments, which Moses spake unto the children of Israel, after they came forth out of Egypt,
46 On this side Jordan, in the valley over against Beth-peor, in the land of Sihon king of the Amorites, who dwelt at Heshbon, whom Moses and the children of Israel smote, after they were come forth out of Egypt: Deut. 3:29
47 And they possessed his land, and the land of Og king of Bashan, two kings of the Amorites, which *were* on this side Jordan toward the sunrising;
48 From Aroer, which *is* by the bank of the river Arnon, even unto mount Sion, which *is* Hermon,   Deut. 2:36; 3:9, 12
49 And all the plain on this side Jordan eastward, even unto the sea of the plain, under the springs of Pisgah.   Deut. 3:17

The Covenant Made at Mount Horeb

5 And Moses called all Israel, and said unto them, Hear, O Israel, the statutes and judgments which I speak in your ears this day, that ye may learn them, and keep, and do them.
2 The LORD our God made a covenant with us in Horeb.   Deut. 4:23

5:1, 2 The Law for All Mankind

God honored them by making them the guardians and keepers of His law, but it was to be held as a sacred trust for the whole world. The precepts of the Decalogue are adapted to all mankind, and they were given for the instruction and government of all. Ten precepts, brief, comprehensive, and authoritative, cover the duty of man to God and to his fellow man; and all based upon the great fundamental principle of love. *PP 305*

---

3 The LORD made not this covenant with our fathers, but with us, *even* us, who *are* all of us here alive this day.

4 The LORD talked with you face to face in the mount out of the midst of the fire,   Deut. 4:33
5 (I stood between the LORD and you at that time, to shew you the word of the LORD: for ye were afraid by reason of the fire, and went not up into the mount;) saying,   Gal. 3:19

The Ten Commandments

6 I *am* the LORD thy God, which brought thee out of the land of Egypt, from the house of bondage.   Ex. 20:2-17
7 Thou shalt have none other gods before me.   Ex. 20:3

5:7 God Deserves First Place

Jehovah, the eternal, self-existent, uncreated One, Himself the Source and Sustainer of all, is alone entitled to supreme reverence and worship. Man is forbidden to give to any other object the first place in his affections or his service. Whatever we cherish that tends to lessen our love for God or to interfere with the service due Him, of that do we make a god. *PP 305*

---

8 Thou shalt not make thee *any* ᵀgraven image, *or* any likeness *of any thing* that *is* in heaven above, or that *is* in the earth beneath, or that *is* in the waters beneath the earth: Ex. 20:4 ◆ *engraved or cut out*
9 Thou shalt not bow down thyself unto them, nor serve them: for I the LORD thy God *am* a jealous God, visiting the iniquity of the fathers upon the children unto the third and fourth *generation* of them that hate me,   Ex. 34:7, 14
10 And shewing mercy unto thousands of them that love me and keep my commandments.   Jer. 32:18
11 Thou shalt not take the name of the LORD thy God in vain: for the LORD will not hold *him* guiltless that taketh his name in vain.   Lev. 19:12
12 Keep the sabbath day to sanctify it, as the LORD thy God hath commanded thee.
13 Six days thou shalt labour, and do all thy work:
14 But the seventh day *is* the sabbath of the LORD thy God: *in it* thou shalt not do any work, thou, nor thy son, nor thy daughter, nor thy manservant, nor thy maidservant, nor thine ox, nor thine ass, nor any of thy cattle, nor thy stranger that *is* within thy gates; that thy manservant and thy maidservant may rest as well as thou.   Gen. 2:2; Ex. 16:29-30; Heb. 4:4
15 And remember that thou wast a servant in the land of Egypt, and *that* the LORD thy God brought thee out thence through a mighty hand and by a stretched out arm: therefore the LORD thy God commanded thee to keep the sabbath day.   Deut. 15:15

16 Honour thy father and thy mother, as the LORD thy God hath commanded thee; that thy days may be prolonged, and that it may go well with thee, in the land which the LORD thy God giveth thee. Ex. 20:12; Lev. 19:3; Deut. 4:40

17 Thou shalt not kill. Ex. 20:13

18 Neither shalt thou commit adultery.

19 Neither shalt thou steal. Ex. 20:15

20 Neither shalt thou bear false witness against thy neighbour. Ex. 20:16

21 Neither shalt thou desire thy neighbour's wife, neither shalt thou ᵀcovet thy neighbour's house, his field, or his manservant, or his maidservant, his ox, or his ass, or any *thing* that *is* thy neighbour's. Rom. 13:9 ◆ *desire*

22 These words the LORD spake unto all your assembly in the mount out of the midst of the fire, of the cloud, and of the thick darkness, with a great voice: and he added no more. And he wrote them in two tables of stone, and delivered them unto me. Ex. 24:12; 31:18

23 And it came to pass, when ye heard the voice out of the midst of the darkness, (for the mountain did burn with fire,) that ye came near unto me, *even* all the heads of your tribes, and your elders;

24 And ye said, Behold, the LORD our God hath shewed us his glory and his greatness, and we have heard his voice out of the midst of the fire: we have seen this day that God doth talk with man, and he liveth. Ex. 19:19

25 Now therefore why should we die? for this great fire will consume us: if we hear the voice of the LORD our God any more, then we shall die. Deut. 18:16

26 For who *is there of* all flesh, that hath heard the voice of the living God speaking out of the midst of the fire, as we *have*, and lived? Deut. 4:33

27 Go thou near, and hear all that the LORD our God shall say: and speak thou unto us all that the LORD our God shall speak unto thee; and we will hear *it*, and do *it*. Ex. 20:19

28 And the LORD heard the voice of your words, when ye spake unto me; and the LORD said unto me, I have heard the voice of the words of this people, which they have spoken unto thee: they have well said all that they have spoken. Deut. 18:17

29 O that there were such an heart in them, that they would fear me, and keep all my commandments always, that it might be well with them, and with their children for ever! Deut. 4:40; 11:1; Is. 48:18

30 Go say to them, Get you into your tents again.

31 But as for thee, stand thou here by me, and I will speak unto thee all the commandments, and the statutes, and the judgments, which thou shalt teach them, that they may do *them* in the land which I give them to possess it. Gal. 3:19

32 Ye shall observe to do therefore as the LORD your God hath commanded you: ye shall not turn aside to the right hand or to the left. Deut. 17:20; 28:14; Josh. 1:7

33 Ye shall walk in all the ways which the LORD your God hath commanded you, that ye may live, and *that it may be* well with you, and *that* ye may prolong *your* days in the land which ye shall possess. Deut. 4:40; 10:12; Jer. 7:23

The Purpose of the Law and an Exhortation to Obey It

6 Now these *are* the commandments, the statutes, and the judgments, which the LORD your God commanded to teach you, that ye might do *them* in the land whither ye go to possess it: Deut. 4:1

2 That thou mightest fear the LORD thy God, to keep all his statutes and his commandments, which I command thee, thou, and thy son, and thy son's son, all the days of thy life; and that thy days may be prolonged. Ex. 20:20

3 Hear therefore, O Israel, and observe to do

The Sabbath a Safeguard From Idolatry

Deuteronomy 5:12–15

Before entering the Promised Land, the Israelites were admonished by Moses to "keep the Sabbath day to sanctify it" (Deuteronomy 5:12). The Lord designed that by a faithful observance of the Sabbath command, Israel should continually be reminded of their accountability to Him as their Creator and their Redeemer. While they should keep the Sabbath in the proper spirit, idolatry could not exist; but should the claims of this precept of the Decalogue be set aside as no longer binding, the Creator would be forgotten and men would worship other gods. "I gave them My Sabbaths," God declared, "to be a sign between Me and them, that they might know that I am the Lord that sanctify them." Yet "they despised My judgments, and walked not in My statutes, but polluted My Sabbaths: for their heart went after their idols." And in His appeal to them to return to Him, He called their attention anew to the importance of keeping the Sabbath holy. "I am the Lord your God," He said; "walk in My statutes, and keep My judgments, and do them; and hallow My Sabbaths; and they shall be a sign between Me and you, that ye may know that I am the Lord your God" (Ezekiel 20:12, 16, 19, 20). *PK 181, 182*

it; that it may be well with thee, and that ye may increase mightily, as the Lord God of thy fathers hath promised thee, in the land that floweth with milk and honey.   Ex. 3:8

6:3 God Reveals Himself

Despite the efforts of Satan to thwart God's purpose for Israel, nevertheless even in some of the darkest hours of their history, when it seemed as if the forces of evil were about to gain the victory, the Lord graciously revealed Himself. He spread before Israel the things that were for the welfare of the nation. *PK 296*

---

4 Hear, O Israel: The Lord our God *is* one Lord: John 17:3
5 And thou shalt love the Lord thy God with all thine heart, and with all thy soul, and with all thy might.   Matt. 22:37; Mark 12:30; Luke 10:27
6 And these words, which I command thee this day, shall be in thine heart: Deut. 11:18; 32:46
7 And thou shalt teach them diligently unto thy children, and shalt talk of them when thou sittest in thine house, and when thou walkest by the way, and when thou liest down, and when thou risest up.   Deut. 11:19

6:6, 7 To Give We Must Have

As a preparation for teaching His precepts, God commands that they be hidden in the hearts of the parents. . . . In order to interest our children in the Bible, we ourselves must be interested in it. To awaken in them a love for its study, we must love it. Our instruction to them will have only the weight of influence given it by our own example and spirit. *Ed 187*

---

8 And thou shalt bind them for a sign upon thine hand, and they shall be as ᵀfrontlets between thine eyes.   Ex. 13:9, 16 ◆ *cases*
9 And thou shalt write them upon the posts of thy house, and on thy gates.   Deut. 11:20

Marriage   See Proverbs 22:6.

10 And it shall be, when the Lord thy God shall have brought thee into the land which he sware unto thy fathers, to Abraham, to Isaac, and to Jacob, to give thee great and goodly cities, which thou buildedst not,   Josh. 24:13; Neh. 9:25; Ps. 105:44
11 And houses full of all good *things*, which thou filledst not, and wells digged, which thou diggedst not, vineyards and olive trees, which thou plantedst not; when thou shalt have eaten and be full;
12 *Then* beware lest thou forget the Lord, which brought thee forth out of the land of Egypt, from the house of bondage.
13 Thou shalt fear the Lord thy God, and serve him, and shalt swear by his name.

14 Ye shall not go after other gods, of the gods of the people which *are* round about you;   Jer. 25:6
15 (For the Lord thy God *is* a jealous God among you) lest the anger of the Lord thy God be kindled against thee, and destroy thee from off the face of the earth. Ex. 20:5; Deut. 4:24
16 Ye shall not tempt the Lord your God, as ye tempted *him* in Massah.   Matt. 4:7; Luke 4:12
17 Ye shall diligently keep the commandments of the Lord your God, and his testimonies, and his statutes, which he hath commanded thee.   Deut. 11:22; Ps. 119:4
18 And thou shalt do *that which is* right and good in the sight of the Lord: that it may be well with thee, and that thou mayest go in and possess the good land which the Lord sware unto thy fathers,   Deut. 4:40
19 To cast out all thine enemies from before thee, as the Lord hath spoken.   Ex. 23:28-30
20 *And* when thy son asketh thee in time to come, saying, What *mean* the testimonies, and the statutes, and the judgments, which the Lord our God hath commanded you?   Ex. 12:26; 13:14
21 Then thou shalt say unto thy son, We were Pharaoh's bondmen in Egypt; and the Lord brought us out of Egypt with a mighty hand: Ex. 20:2
22 And the Lord shewed signs and wonders, great and sore, upon Egypt, upon Pharaoh, and upon all his household, before our eyes: Deut. 4:34
23 And he brought us out from thence, that he might bring us in, to give us the land which he sware unto our fathers.
24 And the Lord commanded us to do all these statutes, to fear the Lord our God, for our good always, that he might preserve us alive, as *it is* at this day. Deut. 4:1; Ps. 41:2; Jer. 32:39
25 And it shall be our righteousness, if we observe to do all these commandments before the Lord our God, as he hath commanded us.   Deut. 24:13; Rom. 10:3

God Commands Israel to Destroy the Canaanites and Their Idols

7 When the Lord thy God shall bring thee into the land whither thou goest to possess it, and hath cast out many nations before thee, the Hittites, and the Girgashites, and the Amorites, and the Canaanites, and the Perizzites, and the Hivites, and the Jebusites, seven nations greater and mightier than thou;   Deut. 4:38; 9:1; 31:3
2 And when the Lord thy God shall deliver them before thee; thou shalt ᵀsmite them, *and* utterly destroy them; thou shalt make no covenant with them, nor shew mercy unto them: Deut. 23:14 ◆ *strike*
3 Neither shalt thou make marriages with

them; thy daughter thou shalt not give unto his son, nor his daughter shalt thou take unto thy son.   Ex. 34:15-16

4 For they will turn away thy son from following me, that they may serve other gods: so will the anger of the LORD be kindled against you, and destroy thee suddenly.   Deut. 6:15

5 But thus shall ye deal with them; ye shall destroy their altars, and break down their images, and cut down their ᵀgroves, and burn their graven images with fire.   Ex. 23:24 ◆ idols

---

7:1–5 No Compromise

The principles set forth in Deuteronomy for the instruction of Israel are to be followed by God's people to the end of time. True prosperity is dependent on the continuance of our covenant relationship with God. Never can we afford to compromise principle by entering into alliance with those who do not fear Him. *PK 570*

---

6 For thou *art* an holy people unto the LORD thy God: the LORD thy God hath chosen thee to be a special people unto himself, above all people that *are* upon the face of the earth.   Ex. 19:5-6; Deut. 14:2; Jer. 2:3

7 The LORD did not set his love upon you, nor choose you, because ye were more in number than any people; for ye *were* the fewest of all people: Deut. 10:22

8 But because the LORD loved you, and because he would keep the oath which he had sworn unto your fathers, hath the LORD brought you out with a mighty hand, and redeemed you out of the house of bondmen, from the hand of Pharaoh king of Egypt.   Ex. 13:3; 32:13; Deut. 10:15

9 Know therefore that the LORD thy God, he *is* God, the faithful God, which keepeth covenant and mercy with them that love him and keep his commandments to a thousand generations;   Dan. 9:4; 1 Cor. 1:9; 2 Tim. 2:13

10 And repayeth them that hate him to their face, to destroy them: he will not be slack to him that hateth him, he will repay him to his face.   Is. 59:18

11 Thou shalt therefore keep the commandments, and the statutes, and the judgments, which I command thee this day, to do them.

12 Wherefore it shall come to pass, if ye hearken to these judgments, and keep, and do them, that the LORD thy God shall keep unto thee the covenant and the mercy which he sware unto thy fathers: Lev. 26:3-13

13 And he will love thee, and bless thee, and multiply thee: he will also bless the fruit of thy womb, and the fruit of thy land, thy corn, and thy wine, and thine oil, the increase of thy ᵀkine, and the flocks of thy sheep, in the land which he sware unto thy fathers to give thee.   John 14:21 ◆ cattle

14 Thou shalt be blessed above all people: there shall not be male or female barren among you, or among your cattle.   Ps. 127:3

15 And the LORD will take away from thee all sickness, and will put none of the evil diseases of Egypt, which thou knowest, upon thee; but will lay them upon all *them* that hate thee.   Ex. 15:26; Deut. 28:27, 60

7:6–15 God's Desire for Israel

God desired to make of His people Israel a praise and a glory. Every spiritual advantage was given them. God withheld from them nothing favorable to the formation of character that would make them representatives of Himself.

Their obedience to the law of God would make them marvels of prosperity before the nations of the world. *COL 288*

---

16 And thou shalt consume all the people which the LORD thy God shall deliver thee; thine eye shall have no pity upon them: neither shalt thou serve their gods; for that *will be* a snare unto thee.   Ex. 23:33; Deut. 7:2; Judg. 8:27

17 If thou shalt say in thine heart, These nations *are* more than I; how can I dispossess them?   Num. 33:53

18 Thou shalt not be afraid of them: *but* shalt well remember what the LORD thy God did unto Pharaoh, and unto all Egypt;   Deut. 1:29

19 The great temptations which thine eyes saw, and the signs, and the wonders, and the mighty hand, and the stretched out arm, whereby the LORD thy God brought thee out: so shall the LORD thy God do unto all the people of whom thou art afraid.   Deut. 4:34

20 Moreover the LORD thy God will send the hornet among them, until they that are left, and hide themselves from thee, be destroyed.   Josh. 24:12

21 Thou shalt not be ᵀaffrighted at them: for the LORD thy God *is* among you, a mighty God and terrible.   Deut. 10:17; Josh. 3:10; Neh. 9:32 ◆ scared

22 And the LORD thy God will put out those nations before thee by little and little: thou mayest not consume them at once, lest the beasts of the field increase upon thee.

23 But the LORD thy God shall deliver them unto thee, and shall destroy them with a mighty destruction, until they be destroyed.

24 And he shall deliver their kings into thine hand, and thou shalt destroy their name from under heaven: there shall no man be able to stand before thee, until thou have destroyed them.   Deut. 11:25; Josh. 1:5; 23:9

25 The graven images of their gods shall ye burn with fire: thou shalt not desire the silver or gold *that is* on them, nor take *it* unto thee,

lest thou be snared therein: for it *is* an abomination to the LORD thy God. Ex. 32:20; Deut. 17:1

26 Neither shalt thou bring an abomination into thine house, lest thou be a cursed thing like it: *but* thou shalt utterly detest it, and thou shalt utterly ᵀabhor it; for it *is* a cursed thing.   Deut. 13:17 ◆ *despise*

An Exhortation to Obedience and Remembrance

8 All the commandments which I command thee this day shall ye observe to do, that ye may live, and multiply, and go in and possess the land which the LORD sware unto your fathers.   Deut. 4:1; 5:32–6:3

2 And thou shalt remember all the way which the LORD thy God led thee these forty years in the wilderness, to humble thee, *and* to prove thee, to know what *was* in thine heart, whether thou wouldest keep his commandments, or no. Ex. 15:25; Deut. 8:16; Amos 2:10

3 And he humbled thee, and suffered thee to hunger, and fed thee with manna, which thou knewest not, neither did thy fathers know; that he might make thee know that man doth not live by bread only, but by every *word* that proceedeth out of the mouth of the LORD doth man live. Ex. 16:2–3; Matt. 4:4; Luke 4:4

8:3 Holiness Defined

Holiness is not rapture: it is an entire surrender of the will to God; it is living by every word that proceeds from the mouth of God; it is doing the will of our heavenly Father; it is trusting God in trial, in darkness as well as in the light; it is walking by faith and not by sight; it is relying on God with unquestioning confidence, and resting in His love. *AA 51*

---

4 Thy ᵀraiment ᵀwaxed not old upon thee, neither did thy foot swell, these forty years.   Deut. 29:5; Neh. 9:21 ◆ *clothing* ◆ *became*

5 Thou shalt also consider in thine heart, that, as a man ᵀchasteneth his son, *so* the LORD thy God chasteneth thee.   *disciplines*

6 Therefore thou shalt keep the commandments of the LORD thy God, to walk in his ways, and to fear him.   Deut. 5:33

7 For the LORD thy God bringeth thee into a good land, a land of brooks of water, of fountains and depths that spring out of valleys and hills;

8 A land of wheat, and barley, and vines, and fig trees, and pomegranates; a land of oil olive, and honey;

9 A land wherein thou shalt eat bread without scarceness, thou shalt not lack any *thing* in it; a land whose stones *are* iron, and out of whose hills thou mayest dig brass.

10 When thou hast eaten and art full, then thou shalt bless the LORD thy God for the good land which he hath given thee. Ps. 103:2

11 Beware that thou forget not the LORD thy God, in not keeping his commandments, and his judgments, and his statutes, which I command thee this day: 8:11-18

12 Lest *when* thou hast eaten and art full, and hast built goodly houses, and dwelt *therein;*   Prov. 30:9

13 And *when* thy herds and thy flocks multiply, and thy silver and thy gold is multiplied, and all that thou hast is multiplied;

14 Then thine heart be lifted up, and thou forget the LORD thy God, which brought thee forth out of the land of Egypt, from the house of bondage;   Deut. 8:11; Ps. 106:21

15 Who led thee through that great and terrible wilderness, *wherein were* fiery serpents, and scorpions, and drought, where *there was* no water; who brought thee forth water out of the rock of flint;   Num. 20:11; 21:6; Ps. 114:8

16 Who fed thee in the wilderness with manna, which thy fathers knew not, that he might humble thee, and that he might prove thee, to do thee good at thy latter end; Deut. 8:3

17 And thou say in thine heart, My power and the might of *mine* hand hath gotten me this wealth.   Deut. 9:4

18 But thou shalt remember the LORD thy God: for *it is* he that giveth thee power to get wealth, that he may establish his covenant which he sware unto thy fathers, as *it is* this day.   Deut. 7:8; Prov. 10:22; Hos. 2:8

Managing God's Gifts   See Leviticus 27:30-32.

---

19 And it shall be, if thou do at all forget the LORD thy God, and walk after other gods, and serve them, and worship them, I testify against you this day that ye shall surely perish.   Deut. 4:26

8:19 Cut Off From the Life of God

The Lord had through Moses set before His people the result of unfaithfulness. By refusing to keep His covenant, they would cut themselves off from the life of God, and His blessing could not come upon them. *COL 291*

---

20 As the nations which the LORD destroyeth before your face, so shall ye perish; because ye would not be obedient unto the voice of the LORD your God.   Dan. 9:11-12

Moses Reminds the People of their Many Rebellions

9 Hear, O Israel: Thou *art* to pass over Jordan this day, to go in to possess nations greater and mightier than thyself, cities great and fenced up to heaven,   Deut. 1:28; 4:38; 11:23

2 A people great and tall, the children of the

Anakims, whom thou knowest, and *of whom* thou hast heard *say*, Who can stand before the children of Anak!   Num. 13:22

3 Understand therefore this day, that the LORD thy God *is* he which goeth over before thee; *as* a consuming fire he shall destroy them, and he shall bring them down before thy face: so shalt thou drive them out, and destroy them quickly, as the LORD hath said unto thee.   Deut. 4:24; Josh. 3:11; Heb. 12:29

4 Speak not thou in thine heart, after that the LORD thy God hath cast them out from before thee, saying, For my righteousness the LORD hath brought me in to possess this land: but for the wickedness of these nations the LORD doth drive them out from before thee.   Deut. 8:17; 12:31

5 Not for thy righteousness, or for the uprightness of thine heart, dost thou go to possess their land: but for the wickedness of these nations the LORD thy God doth drive them out from before thee, and that he may perform the word which the LORD sware unto thy fathers, Abraham, Isaac, and Jacob.   Gen. 12:7; 13:15; Titus 3:5

6 Understand therefore, that the LORD thy God giveth thee not this good land to possess it for thy righteousness; for thou *art* a stiffnecked people.   Deut. 9:13

7 Remember, *and* forget not, how thou provokedst the LORD thy God to wrath in the wilderness: from the day that thou didst depart out of the land of Egypt, until ye came unto this place, ye have been rebellious against the LORD.   Ex. 14:11

9:7 Wilderness Discipline

The wilderness wandering was not only ordained as a judgment upon the rebels and murmurers, but it was to serve as a discipline for the rising generation, preparatory to their entrance into the Promised Land. *PP 407*

8 Also in Horeb ye provoked the LORD to wrath, so that the LORD was angry with you to have destroyed you.

9 When I was gone up into the mount to receive the tables of stone, *even* the tables of the covenant which the LORD made with you, then I abode in the mount forty days and forty nights, I neither did eat bread nor drink water: Ex. 24:12, 18; 34:28

10 And the LORD delivered unto me two tables of stone written with the finger of God; and on them *was written* according to all the words, which the LORD spake with you in the mount out of the midst of the fire in the day of the assembly.   Ex. 31:18

11 And it came to pass at the end of forty days and forty nights, *that* the LORD gave me the two tables of stone, *even* the tables of the covenant.   Deut. 9:9

12 And the LORD said unto me, Arise, get thee down quickly from hence; for thy people which thou hast brought forth out of Egypt have corrupted *themselves*; they are quickly turned aside out of the way which I commanded them; they have made them a molten image.   Ex. 32:7-8; Deut. 31:29; Judg. 2:17

13 Furthermore the LORD spake unto me, saying, I have seen this people, and, behold, it *is* a stiffnecked people: Deut. 9:6

14 Let me alone, that I may destroy them, and blot out their name from under heaven: and I will make of thee a nation mightier and greater than they.   Deut. 29:20

15 So I turned and came down from the mount, and the mount burned with fire: and the two tables of the covenant *were* in my two hands.   Ex. 19:18

16 And I looked, and, behold, ye had sinned against the LORD your God, *and* had made you a molten calf: ye had turned aside quickly out of the way which the LORD had commanded you.   Ex. 32:19

9:16 Pliant Aarons

How often, in our own day, is the love of pleasure disguised by a "form of godliness"! A religion that permits men, while observing the rites of worship, to devote themselves to selfish or sensual gratification, is as pleasing to the multitudes now as in the days of Israel. And there are still pliant Aarons, who, while holding positions of authority in the church, will yield to the desires of the unconsecrated, and thus encourage them in sin. *PP 317*

17 And I took the two tables, and cast them out of my two hands, and brake them before your eyes.

18 And I fell down before the LORD, as at the first, forty days and forty nights: I did neither eat bread, nor drink water, because of all your sins which ye sinned, in doing wickedly in the sight of the LORD, to provoke him to anger.   Ex. 34:28; Deut. 9:9; Ps. 106:23

19 For I was afraid of the anger and hot displeasure, wherewith the LORD was ᵀwroth against you to destroy you. But the LORD hearkened unto me at that time also.   angered

9:19 Moses Alone Before God

To the transgressor it is a fearful thing to fall into the hands of the living God; but Moses stood alone in the presence of the Eternal One, and he was not afraid; for his soul was in harmony with the will of his Maker. *PP 329*

20 And the LORD was very angry with Aaron to have destroyed him: and I prayed for Aaron also the same time.

21 And I took your sin, the calf which ye had made, and burnt it with fire, and stamped it, *and* ground *it* very small, *even* until it was as small as dust: and I cast the dust thereof into the brook that descended out of the mount. Ex. 32:20

22 And at Taberah, and at Massah, and at Kibroth-hattaavah, ye provoked the LORD to wrath. Ex. 17:7; Num. 11:34

23 Likewise when the LORD sent you from Kadesh-barnea, saying, Go up and possess the land which I have given you; then ye rebelled against the commandment of the LORD your God, and ye believed him not, nor hearkened to his voice. Ps. 106:24-25

24 Ye have been rebellious against the LORD from the day that I knew you. Deut. 31:27

25 Thus I fell down before the LORD forty days and forty nights, as I fell down *at the first*; because the LORD had said he would destroy you. Deut. 9:18

26 I prayed therefore unto the LORD, and said, O Lord GOD, destroy not thy people and thine inheritance, which thou hast redeemed through thy greatness, which thou hast brought forth out of Egypt with a mighty hand. Ex. 32:11-13

27 Remember thy servants, Abraham, Isaac, and Jacob; look not unto the stubbornness of this people, nor to their wickedness, nor to their sin:

28 Lest the land whence thou broughtest us out say, Because the LORD was not able to bring them into the land which he promised them, and because he hated them, he hath brought them out to slay them in the wilderness. Num. 14:16

29 Yet they *are* thy people and thine inheritance, which thou broughtest out by thy mighty power and by thy stretched out arm. Deut. 4:20, 34; Neh. 1:10

God's Mercy in Restoring the Two Tablets of the Ten Commandments

10 At that time the LORD said unto me, Hew thee two tables of stone like unto the first, and come up unto me into the mount, and make thee an ark of wood.

2 And I will write on the tables the words that were in the first tables which thou brakest, and thou shalt put them in the ark.

3 And I made an ark *of* shittim wood, and ᵀhewed two tables of stone like unto the first, and went up into the mount, having the two tables in mine hand. Ex. 25:5, 10; 34:4 ◆ cut

4 And he wrote on the tables, according to the first writing, the ten commandments, which the LORD spake unto you in the mount out of the midst of the fire in the day of the assembly: and the LORD gave them unto me. Ex. 34:28; Deut. 9:10; 18:16

5 And I turned myself and came down from the mount, and put the tables in the ark which I had made; and there they be, as the LORD commanded me. Ex. 34:29; 40:20

6 And the children of Israel took their journey from Beeroth of the children of Jaakan to Mosera: there Aaron died, and there he was buried; and Eleazar his son ministered in the priest's office in his stead. Num. 33:38

7 From thence they journeyed unto Gudgodah; and from Gudgodah to Jotbath, a land of rivers of waters.

8 At that time the LORD separated the tribe of Levi, to bear the ark of the covenant of the LORD, to stand before the LORD to minister unto him, and to bless in his name, unto this day. Lev. 9:22; Deut. 18:5; 21:5

10:8 Levi's Cruel Character

Of the sons of Jacob, Levi was one of the most cruel and vindictive, one of the two most guilty in the treacherous murder of the Shechemites. Levi's characteristics, reflected in his descendants, incurred for them the decree from God. . . . But repentance wrought reformation; and by their faithfulness to God amidst the apostasy of the other tribes, the curse was transformed into a token of highest honor. *Ed 148*

9 Wherefore Levi hath no part nor inheritance with his brethren; the LORD *is* his inheritance, according as the LORD thy God promised him. Deut. 18:1-2

10 And I stayed in the mount, according to the first time, forty days and forty nights; and the LORD hearkened unto me at that time also, *and* the LORD would not destroy thee. Ex. 34:28

11 And the LORD said unto me, Arise, take *thy* journey before the people, that they may go in and possess the land, which I sware unto their fathers to give unto them. Ex. 32:34

12 And now, Israel, what doth the LORD thy God require of thee, but to fear the LORD thy God, to walk in all his ways, and to love him, and to serve the LORD thy God with all thy heart and with all thy soul, Deut. 5:33; 6:5; Mic. 6:8

13 To keep the commandments of the LORD, and his statutes, which I command thee this day for thy good? Deut. 6:24

14 Behold, the heaven and the heaven of heavens *is* the LORD's thy God, the earth *also*, with all that therein *is*. Ex. 19:5; 1 Kin. 8:27; Neh. 9:6

15 Only the LORD had a delight in thy fathers to love them, and he chose their seed after them, *even* you above all people, as *it is* this day. Deut. 4:37

16 Circumcise therefore the foreskin of your heart, and be no more stiffnecked. Deut. 9:6; 30:6

17 For the LORD your God *is* God of gods,

and Lord of lords, a great God, a mighty, and a terrible, which regardeth not persons, nor taketh reward: Josh. 22:22; Dan. 2:47; Acts 10:34

18 He doth execute the judgment of the fatherless and widow, and loveth the stranger, in giving him food and raiment.   Ps. 68:5; 146:9

19 Love ye therefore the stranger: for ye were strangers in the land of Egypt. Ex. 22:21

20 Thou shalt fear the LORD thy God; him shalt thou serve, and to him shalt thou cleave, and swear by his name.   Deut. 6:13; 11:22; 13:4

21 He *is* thy praise, and he *is* thy God, that hath done for thee these great and terrible things, which thine eyes have seen.   Ex. 15:2

22 Thy fathers went down into Egypt with ᵀthreescore and ten persons; and now the LORD thy God hath made thee as the stars of heaven for multitude.   Gen. 15:5; Deut. 1:10 ◆ *sixty*

An Exhortation to Obey the Commandments

11 Therefore thou shalt love the LORD thy God, and keep his charge, and his statutes, and his judgments, and his commandments, alway.   Deut. 6:5

> **11:1 God's Perfect Law**
>
> Today the challenge to Israel might be repeated. The laws which God gave His ancient people were wiser, better, and more humane than those of the most civilized nations of the earth. The laws of the nations bear marks of the infirmities and passions of the unrenewed heart; but God's law bears the stamp of the divine. *PP 465*

2 And know ye this day: for *I speak* not with your children which have not known, and which have not seen the chastisement of the LORD your God, his greatness, his mighty hand, and his stretched out arm,   Deut. 5:24

3 And his miracles, and his acts, which he did in the midst of Egypt unto Pharaoh the king of Egypt, and unto all his land;   Deut. 7:19

4 And what he did unto the army of Egypt, unto their horses, and to their chariots; how he made the water of the Red sea to overflow them as they pursued after you, and *how* the LORD hath destroyed them unto this day;   Ex. 15:9-10

5 And what he did unto you in the wilderness, until ye came into this place;

6 And what he did unto Dathan and Abiram, the sons of Eliab, the son of Reuben: how the earth opened her mouth, and swallowed them up, and their households, and their tents, and all the substance that *was* in their possession, in the midst of all Israel: Ps. 106:17

7 But your eyes have seen all the great acts of the LORD which he did.

The Promise of God's Great Blessings

8 Therefore shall ye keep all the commandments which I command you this day, that ye may be strong, and go in and possess the land, whither ye go to possess it;   Josh. 1:6-7

9 And that ye may prolong *your* days in the land, which the LORD sware unto your fathers to give unto them and to their seed, a land that floweth with milk and honey.   Ex. 3:8

10 For the land, whither thou goest in to possess it, *is* not as the land of Egypt, from whence ye came out, where thou sowedst thy seed, and wateredst *it* with thy foot, as a garden of herbs:

11 But the land, whither ye go to possess it, *is* a land of hills and valleys, *and* drinketh water of the rain of heaven:

12 A land which the LORD thy God careth for: the eyes of the LORD thy God *are* always upon it, from the beginning of the year even unto the end of the year.   1 Kin. 9:3; Jer. 24:6

The Law in the Ark

Deuteronomy 10

"The temple of God was opened in heaven, and there was seen in His temple the ark of His testament" (Revelation 11:19). The ark of God's testament is in the holy of holies, the second apartment of the sanctuary. In the ministration of the earthly tabernacle, which served "unto the example and shadow of heavenly things," this apartment was opened only upon the great Day of Atonement for the cleansing of the sanctuary. . . .

The ark in the tabernacle on earth contained the two tables of stone, upon which were inscribed the precepts of the law of God. The ark was merely a receptacle for the tables of the law, and the presence of these divine precepts gave to it its value and sacredness. When the temple of God was opened in heaven, the ark of His testament was seen. Within the holy of holies, in the sanctuary in heaven, the divine law is sacredly enshrined—the law that was spoken by God Himself amid the thunders of Sinai and written with His own finger on the tables of stone.

The law of God in the sanctuary in heaven is the great original, of which the precepts inscribed upon the tables of stone and recorded by Moses in the Pentateuch were an unerring transcript. Those who arrived at an understanding of this important point were thus led to see the sacred, unchanging character of the divine law. *GC 433, 434*

13 And it shall come to pass, if ye shall hearken diligently unto my commandments which I command you this day, to love the LORD your God, and to serve him with all your heart and with all your soul,   Deut. 4:29
14 That I will give *you* the rain of your land in his due season, the first rain and the latter rain, that thou mayest gather in thy corn, and thy wine, and thine oil.   Lev. 26:4; James 5:7

15 And I will send grass in thy fields for thy cattle, that thou mayest eat and be full.
16 Take heed to yourselves, that your heart be not deceived, and ye turn aside, and serve other gods, and worship them; Deut. 8:19; 29:18
17 And *then* the LORD's wrath be kindled against you, and he shut up the heaven, that there be no rain, and that the land yield not her fruit; and *lest* ye perish quickly from off the good land which the LORD giveth you.   Deut. 4:26; 6:15; 1 Kin. 8:35

A Careful Study of God's Words Is Required
18 Therefore shall ye lay up these my words in your heart and in your soul, and bind them for a sign upon your hand, that they may be as frontlets between your eyes.   Ex. 13:9
19 And ye shall teach them your children, speaking of them when thou sittest in thine house, and when thou walkest by the way, when thou liest down, and when thou risest up.   Deut. 4:9-10
20 And thou shalt write them upon the door posts of thine house, and upon thy gates: Deut. 6:9
21 That your days may be multiplied, and the days of your children, in the land which the LORD sware unto your fathers to give them, as the days of heaven upon the earth.   Ps. 72:5
22 For if ye shall diligently keep all these commandments which I command you, to do them, to love the LORD your God, to walk in all his ways, and to cleave unto him;   Deut. 6:17; 10:20; 11:13
23 Then will the LORD drive out all these nations from before you, and ye shall possess greater nations and mightier than yourselves.   Deut. 4:38; 9:1

24 Every place whereon the soles of your feet shall tread shall be yours: from the wilderness and Lebanon, from the river, the river Euphrates, even unto the uttermost sea shall your coast be.   Ex. 23:31; Josh. 14:9
25 There shall no man be able to stand before you: *for* the LORD your God shall lay the fear of you and the dread of you upon all the land that ye shall tread upon, as he hath said unto you.   Ex. 23:27; Deut. 2:25; 7:24

A Blessing and a Curse Are Set before the People
26 Behold, I set before you this day a blessing and a curse;   Deut. 30:1
27 A blessing, if ye obey the commandments of the LORD your God, which I command you this day: Deut. 28:1-14
28 And a curse, if ye will not obey the commandments of the LORD your God, but turn aside out of the way which I command you this day, to go after other gods, which ye have not known.   Deut. 28:15-68
29 And it shall come to pass, when the LORD thy God hath brought thee in unto the land whither thou goest to possess it, that thou shalt put the blessing upon mount Gerizim, and the curse upon mount Ebal.
30 *Are* they not on the other side Jordan, by the way where the sun goeth down, in the land of the Canaanites, which dwell in the ᵀchampaign over against Gilgal, beside the plains of Moreh?   Gen. 12:6 ◆ *level country*
31 For ye shall pass over Jordan to go in to possess the land which the LORD your God giveth you, and ye shall possess it, and dwell therein.   Deut. 9:1
32 And ye shall observe to do all the statutes and judgments which I set before you this day.   Deut. 12:32

Monuments of Idolatry Are to Be Destroyed
12 These *are* the statutes and judgments, which ye shall observe to do in the land, which the LORD God of thy fathers giveth thee to possess it, all the days that ye live upon the earth.   1 Kin. 8:40
2 Ye shall utterly destroy all the places, wherein the nations which ye shall possess served their gods, upon the high mountains, and upon the hills, and under every green tree: Deut. 7:5, 25-26; 2 Kin. 16:4
3 And ye shall overthrow their altars, and break their pillars, and burn their ᵀgroves with fire; and ye shall ᵀhew down the graven images of their gods, and destroy the names of them out of that place.   Num. 33:52 ◆ *idols* ◆ *cut*
4 Ye shall not do so unto the LORD your God.

The Proper Place to Worship
5 But unto the place which the LORD your God shall choose out of all your tribes to

put his name there, *even* unto his habitation shall ye seek, and thither thou shalt come: Deut. 12:11; 16:2; 2 Chr. 7:12

6 And thither ye shall bring your burnt offerings, and your sacrifices, and your tithes, and heave offerings of your hand, and your vows, and your freewill offerings, and the firstlings of your herds and of your flocks: Deut. 15:19-20

7 And there ye shall eat before the LORD your God, and ye shall rejoice in all that ye put your hand unto, ye and your households, wherein the LORD thy God hath blessed thee.   Lev. 23:40; Deut. 12:18; 14:26

8 Ye shall not do after all *the things* that we do here this day, every man whatsoever *is* right in his own eyes.   Judg. 17:6

12:8 God's Will Not Mine

God has given men no liberty to depart from His requirements. . . . In deciding upon any course of action we are not to ask whether we can see that harm will result from it, but whether it is in keeping with the will of God. "There is a way which seemeth right unto a man; but the end thereof are the ways of death" (Proverbs 14:12). *PP 634*

9 For ye are not as yet come to the rest and to the inheritance, which the LORD your God giveth you.   Deut. 25:19

10 But *when* ye go over Jordan, and dwell in the land which the LORD your God giveth you to inherit, and *when* he giveth you rest from all your enemies round about, so that ye dwell in safety;   Deut. 11:31

11 Then there shall be a place which the LORD your God shall choose to cause his name to dwell there; thither shall ye bring all that I command you; your burnt offerings, and your sacrifices, your tithes, and the heave offering of your hand, and all your choice vows which ye vow unto the LORD: Deut. 12:5; 15:20; 17:8

12 And ye shall rejoice before the LORD your God, ye, and your sons, and your daughters, and your menservants, and your maidservants, and the Levite that *is* within your gates; ᵀforasmuch as he hath no part nor inheritance with you.   Deut. 10:9; 12:7; 14:29 ◆ *since*

13 Take heed to thyself that thou offer not thy burnt offerings in every place that thou seest:

14 But in the place which the LORD shall choose in one of thy tribes, there thou shalt offer thy burnt offerings, and there thou shalt do all that I command thee.   Deut. 12:5

15 Notwithstanding thou mayest kill and eat flesh in all thy gates, whatsoever thy soul lusteth after, according to the blessing of the LORD thy God which he hath given thee: the

unclean and the clean may eat thereof, as of the roebuck, and as of the hart.   Deut. 14:5

16 Only ye shall not eat the blood; ye shall pour it upon the earth as water.   Gen. 9:4

17 Thou mayest not eat within thy gates the ᵀtithe of thy corn, or of thy wine, or of thy oil, or the firstlings of thy herds or of thy flock, nor any of thy vows which thou vowest, nor thy freewill offerings, or heave offering of thine hand: Deut. 12:6 ◆ *one-tenth*

18 But thou must eat them before the LORD thy God in the place which the LORD thy God shall choose, thou, and thy son, and thy daughter, and thy manservant, and thy maidservant, and the Levite that *is* within thy gates: and thou shalt rejoice before the LORD thy God in all that thou puttest thine hands unto.   Deut. 12:5, 7; 14:23

19 Take heed to thyself that thou forsake not the Levite as long as thou livest upon the earth.

20 When the LORD thy God shall enlarge thy border, as he hath promised thee, and thou shalt say, I will eat flesh, because thy soul longeth to eat flesh; thou mayest eat flesh, whatsoever thy soul lusteth after.   Gen. 28:14

21 If the place which the LORD thy God hath chosen to put his name there be too far from thee, then thou shalt kill of thy herd and of thy flock, which the LORD hath given thee, as I have commanded thee, and thou shalt eat in thy gates whatsoever thy soul lusteth after.   Deut. 12:5

22 Even as the roebuck and the ᵀhart is eaten, so thou shalt eat them: the unclean and the clean shall eat *of* them alike.   *deer*

23 Only be sure that thou eat not the blood: for the blood *is* the life; and thou mayest not eat the life with the flesh.   Gen. 9:4; Lev. 17:11

24 Thou shalt not eat it; thou shalt pour it upon the earth as water.

25 Thou shalt not eat it; that it may go well with thee, and with thy children after thee, when thou shalt do *that which is* right in the sight of the LORD.   Ex. 15:26; Deut. 4:40; 1 Kin. 11:38

26 Only thy holy things which thou hast, and thy vows, thou shalt take, and go unto the place which the LORD shall choose: Num. 5:9-10

27 And thou shalt offer thy burnt offerings, the flesh and the blood, upon the altar of the LORD thy God: and the blood of thy sacrifices shall be poured out upon the altar of the LORD thy God, and thou shalt eat the flesh.   Lev. 1:9, 13; 17:11

28 Observe and hear all these words which I command thee, that it may go well with thee, and with thy children after thee for ever, when thou doest *that which is* good and right in the sight of the LORD thy God.

29 When the LORD thy God shall cut off the nations from before thee, whither thou goest

to possess them, and thou succeedest them, and dwellest in their land;   Deut. 19:1; Josh. 23:4

> **12:28 God Our Best Friend**
>
> Our God is a tender, merciful Father. . . . It should be a pleasure to worship the Lord and to take part in His work. God would not have His children, for whom so great salvation has been provided, act as if He were a hard, exacting taskmaster. He is their best friend; and when they worship Him, He expects to be with them, to bless and comfort them, filling their hearts with joy and love. *SC 103*

30 Take heed to thyself that thou be not snared by following them, after that they be destroyed from before thee; and that thou enquire not after their gods, saying, How did these nations serve their gods? even so will I do likewise.   Deut. 7:16
31 Thou shalt not do so unto the LORD thy God: for every abomination to the LORD, which he hateth, have they done unto their gods; for even their sons and their daughters they have burnt in the fire to their gods.   Jer. 32:35
32 What thing soever I command you, observe to do it: thou shalt not add thereto, nor diminish from it. Deut. 4:2; Josh. 1:7; Prov. 30:6

Dealing with False Prophets

13 If there arise among you a prophet, or a dreamer of dreams, and giveth thee a sign or a wonder,   Jer. 27:9
2 And the sign or the wonder come to pass, whereof he spake unto thee, saying, Let us go after other gods, which thou hast not known, and let us serve them;   Deut. 18:22
3 Thou shalt not hearken unto the words of that prophet, or that dreamer of dreams: for the LORD your God proveth you, to know whether ye love the LORD your God with all your heart and with all your soul. Deut. 6:5; 8:2
4 Ye shall walk after the LORD your God, and fear him, and keep his commandments, and obey his voice, and ye shall serve him, and cleave unto him. Deut. 10:20; 2 Kin. 23:3; 2 Chr. 34:31
5 And that prophet, or that dreamer of dreams, shall be put to death; because he hath spoken to turn *you* away from the LORD your God, which brought you out of the land of Egypt, and redeemed you out of the house of bondage, to thrust thee out of the way which the LORD thy God commanded thee to walk in. So shalt thou put the evil away from the midst of thee.   Deut. 13:10; 17:7; 1 Cor. 5:13

Dealing with a Family Member's Idolatry

6 If thy brother, the son of thy mother, or thy son, or thy daughter, or the wife of thy

bosom, or thy friend, which *is* as thine own soul, entice thee secretly, saying, Let us go and serve other gods, which thou hast not known, thou, nor thy fathers;   Deut. 28:54
7 *Namely*, of the gods of the people which *are* round about you, nigh unto thee, or far off from thee, from the *one* end of the earth even unto the *other* end of the earth;
8 Thou shalt not consent unto him, nor hearken unto him; neither shall thine eye pity him, neither shalt thou spare, neither shalt thou conceal him: Deut. 7:16; Prov. 1:10
9 But thou shalt surely kill him; thine hand shall be first upon him to put him to death, and afterwards the hand of all the people.
10 And thou shalt stone him with stones, that he die; because he hath sought to thrust thee away from the LORD thy God, which brought thee out of the land of Egypt, from the house of bondage.   Josh. 7:25
11 And all Israel shall hear, and fear, and shall do no more any such wickedness as this is among you.   Deut. 17:13; 19:20

Dealing with Idolatrous Cities

12 If thou shalt hear *say* in one of thy cities, which the LORD thy God hath given thee to dwell there, saying,
13 *Certain* men, the children of Belial, are gone out from among you, and have withdrawn the inhabitants of their city, saying, Let us go and serve other gods, which ye have not known;   Deut. 13:2
14 Then shalt thou enquire, and make search, and ask diligently; and, behold, *if it be* truth, *and* the thing certain, *that* such abomination is ᵀwrought among you;   Deut. 17:4 ◆ *made*
15 Thou shalt surely ᵀsmite the inhabitants of that city with the edge of the sword, destroying it utterly, and all that *is* therein, and the cattle thereof, with the edge of the sword.   Ex. 22:20 ◆ *strike*
16 And thou shalt gather all the ᵀspoil of it into the midst of the street thereof, and shalt burn with fire the city, and all the spoil thereof every ᵀwhit, for the LORD thy God: and it shall be an heap for ever; it shall not be built again. Josh. 6:24; 8:28; Jer. 49:2 ◆ *plunder* ◆ *bit*
17 And there shall cleave ᵀnought of the cursed thing to thine hand: that the LORD may turn from the fierceness of his anger, and shew thee mercy, and have compassion upon thee, and multiply thee, as he hath sworn unto thy fathers;   Gen. 26:4 ◆ *nothing*
18 When thou shalt hearken to the voice of the LORD thy God, to keep all his commandments which I command thee this day, to do *that which is* right in the eyes of the LORD thy God.   Deut. 12:25

God's Children Are Not to Disfigure Themselves in Mourning

14 Ye *are* the children of the LORD your God: ye shall not cut yourselves, nor make any baldness between your eyes for the dead.   Lev. 21:5; Rom. 9:8; Gal. 3:26

> **14:1 Our Bodies Are God's**
>
> Our bodies are Christ's purchased possession, and we are not at liberty to do with them as we please. All who understand the laws of health should realize their obligation to obey these laws which God has established in their being. . . . We must individually answer to God for our habits and practices. Therefore the question with us is not, "What is the world's practice?" but, "How shall I as an individual treat the habitation that God has given me?" *MH 310*

2 For thou *art* an holy people unto the LORD thy God, and the LORD hath chosen thee to be a ᵀpeculiar people unto himself, above all the nations that *are* upon the earth.   Lev. 20:26; Deut. 7:6; 26:18-19 ◆ *special*

3 Thou shalt not eat any abominable thing.

4 These *are* the beasts which ye shall eat: the ox, the sheep, and the goat,

5 The ᵀhart, and the roebuck, and the fallow deer, and the wild goat, and the pygarg, and the wild ox, and the ᵀchamois.   *deer* ◆ *wild sheep*

6 And every beast that parteth the hoof, and cleaveth the ᵀcleft into two claws, *and* cheweth the cud among the beasts, that ye shall eat.   *split* or *opening*

7 Nevertheless these ye shall not eat of them that chew the cud, or of them that divide the ᵀcloven hoof; *as* the camel, and the hare, and the coney: for they chew the cud, but divide not the hoof; *therefore* they *are* unclean unto you.   *divided*

8 And the swine, because it divideth the hoof, yet cheweth not the cud, it *is* unclean unto you: ye shall not eat of their flesh, nor touch their dead carcase.   Lev. 11:26-27

9 These ye shall eat of all that *are* in the waters: all that have fins and scales shall ye eat:

10 And whatsoever hath not fins and scales ye may not eat; it *is* unclean unto you.

11 *Of* all clean birds ye shall eat.

12 But these *are they* of which ye shall not eat: the eagle, and the ossifrage, and the ospray,

13 And the glede, and the kite, and the vulture after his kind,

14 And every raven after his kind,

15 And the owl, and the night hawk, and the cuckow, and the hawk after his kind,

16 The little owl, and the great owl, and the swan,

17 And the pelican, and the gierᵉ eagle, and the cormorant,

18 And the stork, and the heron after her kind, and the lapwing, and the bat.

19 And every creeping thing that flieth *is* unclean unto you: they shall not be eaten.

20 *But of* all clean fowls ye may eat.

21 Ye shall not eat *of* any thing that dieth of itself: thou shalt give it unto the stranger that *is* in thy gates, that he may eat it; or thou mayest sell it unto an alien: for thou *art* an holy people unto the LORD thy God. Thou shalt not ᵀseethe a kid in his mother's milk.   Ex. 23:19; 34:26; Lev. 17:15 ◆ *boil*

Giving God One-tenth of Everything

22 Thou shalt truly tithe all the increase of thy seed, that the field bringeth forth year by year.   Deut. 12:6, 17; Neh. 10:37

23 And thou shalt eat before the LORD thy God, in the place which he shall choose to place his name there, the ᵀtithe of thy corn, of thy wine, and of thine oil, and the firstlings of thy herds and of thy flocks; that thou mayest learn to fear the LORD thy God always.   Deut. 4:10 ◆ *one-tenth*

24 And if the way be too long for thee, so that thou art not able to carry it; *or* if the place be too far from thee, which the LORD thy God shall choose to set his name there, when the LORD thy God hath blessed thee: Deut. 12:21

25 Then shalt thou turn *it* into money, and bind up the money in thine hand, and shalt go unto the place which the LORD thy God shall choose:

26 And thou shalt ᵀbestow that money for whatsoever thy soul lusteth after, for oxen, or for sheep, or for wine, or for strong drink, or for whatsoever thy soul desireth: and thou shalt eat there before the LORD thy God, and thou shalt rejoice, thou, and thine household,   Deut. 12:7 ◆ *give*

27 And the Levite that *is* within thy gates; thou shalt not forsake him; for he hath no part nor inheritance with thee.   Num. 18:20

> **14:28, 29 Purpose of the Tithe**
>
> The consecration to God of a tithe of all increase, whether of the orchard and harvest field, the flocks and herds, or the labor of brain or hand, . . . tended to keep fresh before the people the truth of God's ownership of all, and of their opportunity to be channels of His blessings. It was a training adapted to kill out all narrowing selfishness, and to cultivate breadth and nobility of character. *Ed 44*

28 At the end of three years thou shalt bring forth all the tithe of thine increase the same year, and shalt lay *it* up within thy gates: Deut. 14:22

29 And the Levite, (because he hath no part nor inheritance with thee,) and the stranger, and the fatherless, and the widow, which *are* within thy gates, shall come, and shall eat and be satisfied; that the LORD thy God may bless thee in all the work of thine hand which thou doest.   Deut. 14:27; 15:10; 16:11

Canceling Debts Every Seven Years

15 At the end of *every* seven years thou shalt make a release. Lev. 25:2-4; Deut. 31:10

2 And this *is* the manner of the release: Every creditor that lendeth *ought* unto his neighbour shall release *it*; he shall not exact *it* of his neighbour, or of his brother; because it is called the LORD's release.
3 Of a foreigner thou mayest exact *it again*: but *that* which is thine with thy brother thine hand shall release;   Deut. 23:20
4 Save when there shall be no poor among you; for the LORD shall greatly bless thee in the land which the LORD thy God giveth thee *for* an inheritance to possess it:
5 Only if thou carefully hearken unto the voice of the LORD thy God, to observe to do all these commandments which I command thee this day.

6 For the LORD thy God blesseth thee, as he promised thee: and thou shalt lend unto many nations, but thou shalt not borrow; and thou shalt reign over many nations, but they shall not reign over thee. Deut. 28:12-13; 1 Kin. 4:21

7 If there be among you a poor man of one of thy brethren within any of thy gates in thy land which the LORD thy God giveth thee, thou shalt not harden thine heart, nor shut thine hand from thy poor brother: Deut. 15:9
8 But thou shalt open thine hand wide unto him, and shalt surely lend him sufficient for his need, *in that* which he wanteth. Matt. 5:42
9 Beware that there be not a thought in thy wicked heart, saying, The seventh year, the year of release, is at hand; and thine eye be evil against thy poor brother, and thou givest him Tnought; and he cry unto the LORD against thee, and it be sin unto thee.   Ex. 22:23; Deut. 24:15; Matt. 20:15 ◆ *nothing*
10 Thou shalt surely give him, and thine heart shall not be grieved when thou givest unto him: because that for this thing the LORD thy God shall bless thee in all thy works, and in all that thou puttest thine hand unto.   Deut. 14:29; 24:19; Prov. 22:9
11 For the poor shall never cease out of the land: therefore I command thee, saying, Thou shalt open thine hand wide unto thy brother, to thy poor, and to thy needy, in thy land.   Matt. 26:11; Mark 14:7; John 12:8

Laws Regarding Hebrew Slaves

12 *And* if thy brother, an Hebrew man, or an Hebrew woman, be sold unto thee, and serve

thee six years; then in the seventh year thou shalt let him go free from thee.   Ex. 21:2-6

13 And when thou sendest him out free from thee, thou shalt not let him go away empty:

14 Thou shalt furnish him liberally out of thy flock, and out of thy floor, and out of thy winepress: *of that* wherewith the LORD thy God hath blessed thee thou shalt give unto him.

15 And thou shalt remember that thou wast a bondman in the land of Egypt, and the LORD thy God redeemed thee: therefore I command thee this thing to day.   Deut. 16:12

16 And it shall be, if he say unto thee, I will not go away from thee; because he loveth thee and thine house, because he is well with thee;   Ex. 21:5-6

17 Then thou shalt take an aul, and thrust *it* through his ear unto the door, and he shall be thy servant for ever. And also unto thy maidservant thou shalt do likewise.

18 It shall not seem hard unto thee, when thou sendest him away free from thee; for he hath been worth a double hired servant *to thee*, in serving thee six years: and the LORD thy God shall bless thee in all that thou doest.

19 All the ᵀfirstling males that come of thy herd and of thy flock thou shalt sanctify unto the LORD thy God: thou shalt do no work with the firstling of thy ᵀbullock, nor shear the firstling of thy sheep.   Ex. 13:2, 12 ◆ *firstborn* ◆ *bull*

20 Thou shalt eat *it* before the LORD thy God year by year in the place which the LORD shall choose, thou and thy household.

21 And if there be *any* blemish therein, *as if it be* lame, or blind, *or have* any ill blemish, thou shalt not sacrifice it unto the LORD thy God.   Deut. 17:1

22 Thou shalt eat it within thy gates: the unclean and the clean *person shall eat it* alike, as the roebuck, and as the ᵀhart.   *deer*

23 Only thou shalt not eat the blood thereof; thou shalt pour it upon the ground as water.   Deut. 12:16

The Three Major Festivals

16 Observe the month of Abib, and keep the passover unto the LORD thy God: for in the month of Abib the LORD thy God brought thee forth out of Egypt by night.   Ex. 12:2-20; 13:4; 34:18

2 Thou shalt therefore sacrifice the passover unto the LORD thy God, of the flock and the herd, in the place which the LORD shall choose to place his name there.   Deut. 12:5

3 Thou shalt eat no leavened bread with it; seven days shalt thou eat unleavened bread therewith, *even* the bread of affliction; for thou camest forth out of the land of Egypt in haste: that thou mayest remember the day when thou camest forth out of the land of Egypt all the days of thy life.   Ex. 12:8, 39; 34:18

4 And there shall be no leavened bread seen with thee in all thy coast seven days; neither shall there be *any thing* of the flesh, which thou sacrificedst the first day at even, remain all night until the morning.   Ex. 12:10; 13:7; 34:25

5 Thou mayest not sacrifice the passover within any of thy gates, which the LORD thy God giveth thee:

6 But at the place which the LORD thy God shall choose to place his name in, there thou shalt sacrifice the passover at even, at the going down of the sun, at the season that thou camest forth out of Egypt.

7 And thou shalt roast and eat *it* in the place which the LORD thy God shall choose: and thou shalt turn in the morning, and go unto thy tents.   2 Chr. 35:13

8 Six days thou shalt eat unleavened bread: and on the seventh day *shall be* a solemn assembly to the LORD thy God: thou shalt do no work *therein*.   Lev. 23:36

16:1-8 An Object Lesson

All the ceremonies of the feast were types of the work of Christ. The deliverance of Israel from Egypt was an object lesson of redemption, which the Passover was intended to keep in memory. The slain lamb, the unleavened bread, the sheaf of first fruits, represented the Saviour. *DA 77*

9 Seven weeks shalt thou number unto thee: begin to number the seven weeks from *such time as* thou beginnest *to put* the sickle to the corn.   Ex. 23:16; 34:22; Acts 2:1

10 And thou shalt keep the feast of weeks unto the LORD thy God with a tribute of a freewill offering of thine hand, which thou shalt give *unto the LORD thy God*, according as the LORD thy God hath blessed thee: 1 Cor. 16:2

11 And thou shalt rejoice before the LORD thy God, thou, and thy son, and thy daughter, and thy manservant, and thy maidservant, and the Levite that *is* within thy gates, and the stranger, and the fatherless, and the widow, that *are* among you, in the place which the LORD thy God hath chosen to place his name there.   Deut. 12:7, 12, 18

12 And thou shalt remember that thou wast a bondman in Egypt: and thou shalt observe and do these statutes.   Deut. 15:15

13 Thou shalt observe the feast of tabernacles seven days, after that thou hast gathered in thy corn and thy wine: Ex. 23:16

14 And thou shalt rejoice in thy feast, thou, and thy son, and thy daughter, and thy manservant, and thy maidservant, and the Le-

vite, the stranger, and the fatherless, and the widow, that *are* within thy gates. Deut. 16:11
15 Seven days shalt thou keep a solemn feast unto the LORD thy God in the place which the LORD shall choose: because the LORD thy God shall bless thee in all thine increase, and in all the works of thine hands, therefore thou shalt surely rejoice.
16 Three times in a year shall all thy males appear before the LORD thy God in the place which he shall choose; in the feast of unleavened bread, and in the feast of weeks, and in the feast of tabernacles: and they shall not appear before the LORD empty: Ex. 23:14-17
17 Every man *shall give* as he is able, according to the blessing of the LORD thy God which he hath given thee. Deut. 16:10

16:17 No Dry Theory

Not as a dry theory were these things to be taught. Those who would impart truth must themselves practice its principles. Only by reflecting the character of God in the uprightness, nobility, and unselfishness of their own lives can they impress others. *Ed 41*

Laws about Administering Justice

18 Judges and officers shalt thou make thee in all thy gates, which the LORD thy God giveth thee, throughout thy tribes: and they shall judge the people with just judgment. 1 Chr. 23:4
19 Thou shalt not ᵀwrest judgment; thou shalt not respect persons, neither take a gift: for a gift doth blind the eyes of the wise, and pervert the words of the righteous. Ex. 23:2; Lev. 19:15; Eccl. 7:7 ◆ *twist*
20 That which is altogether just shalt thou follow, that thou mayest live, and inherit the land which the LORD thy God giveth thee. Deut. 4:1
21 Thou shalt not plant thee a grove of any trees near unto the altar of the LORD thy God, which thou shalt make thee. Ex. 34:13
22 Neither shalt thou set thee up *any* image; which the LORD thy God hateth. Ex. 20:4

Laws about the Sacrifices

17 Thou shalt not sacrifice unto the LORD thy God *any* ᵀbullock, or sheep, wherein is blemish, *or* any ᵀevilfavouredness: for that *is* an abomination unto the LORD thy God. Deut. 15:21 ◆ *bull* ◆ *flaw*
2 If there be found among you, within any of thy gates which the LORD thy God giveth thee, man or woman, that hath wrought wickedness in the sight of the LORD thy God, in ᵀtransgressing his covenant, *violating a law*

3 And hath gone and served other gods, and worshipped them, either the sun, or moon, or any of the host of heaven, which I have not commanded; Deut. 4:19
4 And it be told thee, and thou hast heard *of it*, and enquired diligently, and, behold, *it be* true, *and* the thing certain, *that* such abomination is ᵀwrought in Israel: Deut. 13:12-14 ◆ *made*
5 Then shalt thou bring forth that man or that woman, which have committed that wicked thing, unto thy gates, *even* that man or that woman, and shalt stone them with stones, till they die. Lev. 24:14, 16; Josh. 7:25
6 At the mouth of two witnesses, or three witnesses, shall he that is worthy of death be put to death; *but* at the mouth of one witness he shall not be put to death. Matt. 18:16
7 The hands of the witnesses shall be first upon him to put him to death, and afterward the hands of all the people. So thou shalt put the evil away from among you. Deut. 13:5, 9; 17:12

Hard Controversies Ruled Upon by the Priests and Judges

8 If there arise a matter too hard for thee in judgment, between blood and blood, between plea and plea, and between stroke and stroke, *being* matters of controversy within thy gates: then shalt thou arise, and get thee up into the place which the LORD thy God shall choose; Deut. 12:5; Hag. 2:11
9 And thou shalt come unto the priests the Levites, and unto the judge that shall be in those days, and enquire; and they shall shew thee the sentence of judgment: Ezek. 44:24
10 And thou shalt do according to the sentence, which they of that place which the LORD shall choose shall shew thee; and thou shalt observe to do according to all that they inform thee:
11 According to the sentence of the law which they shall teach thee, and according to the judgment which they shall tell thee, thou shalt do: thou shalt not decline from the sentence which they shall shew thee, *to* the right hand, nor *to* the left. Josh. 1:7
12 And the man that will do presumptuously, and will not hearken unto the priest that standeth to minister there before the LORD thy God, or unto the judge, even that man shall die: and thou shalt put away the evil from Israel. Num. 15:30
13 And all the people shall hear, and fear, and do no more presumptuously. Deut. 13:11

The Duties of a King

14 When thou art come unto the land which the LORD thy God giveth thee, and shalt

possess it, and shalt dwell therein, and shalt say, I will set a king over me, like as all the nations that *are* about me;   1 Sam. 8:19-20

15 Thou shalt in any wise set *him* king over thee, whom the LORD thy God shall choose: *one* from among thy brethren shalt thou set king over thee: thou mayest not set a stranger over thee, which *is* not thy brother.   1 Sam. 10:24; 1 Chr. 22:10; Jer. 30:21

17:14, 15 Losing Sight of the Honor

When the Israelites first settled in Canaan they acknowledged the principles of the theocracy, and the nation prospered under the rule of Joshua. But increase of population and intercourse [association] with other nations brought a change. The people adopted many of the customs of their heathen neighbors and thus sacrificed to a great degree their own peculiar, holy character. Gradually they lost their reverence for God and ceased to prize the honor of being His chosen people. *PP 603*

---

16 But he shall not multiply horses to himself, nor cause the people to return to Egypt, to the end that he should multiply horses: ᵀforasmuch as the LORD hath said unto you, Ye shall ᵀhenceforth return no more that way. Ex. 13:17; Ezek. 17:15 ◆ *since* ◆ *from this time forward*

17 Neither shall he multiply wives to himself, that his heart turn not away: neither shall he greatly multiply to himself silver and gold.   Neh. 13:26

18 And it shall be, when he sitteth upon the throne of his kingdom, that he shall write him a copy of this law in a book out of *that which is* before the priests the Levites: Deut. 31:9

19 And it shall be with him, and he shall read therein all the days of his life: that he may learn to fear the LORD his God, to keep all the words of this law and these statutes, to do them: Josh. 1:8

20 That his heart be not lifted up above his brethren, and that he turn not aside from the commandment, *to* the right hand, or *to* the left: to the end that he may prolong *his* days in his kingdom, he, and his children, in the midst of Israel.   Deut. 32; 1 Kin. 15:5

Laws about the Rightful Dues for the Priests and the Levites

18 The priests the Levites, *and* all the tribe of Levi, shall have no part nor inheritance with Israel: they shall eat the offerings of the LORD made by fire, and his inheritance.   Deut. 10:9

2 Therefore shall they have no inheritance among their brethren: the LORD *is* their inheritance, as he hath said unto them.

3 And this shall be the priest's due from the people, from them that offer a sacrifice, whether *it be* ox or sheep; and they shall give unto the priest the shoulder, and the two cheeks, and the ᵀmaw.   Lev. 7:30-34 ◆ *stomach*

4 The firstfruit *also* of thy corn, of thy wine, and of thine oil, and the first of the fleece of thy sheep, shalt thou give him.   Ex. 22:29

5 For the LORD thy God hath chosen him out of all thy tribes, to stand to minister in the name of the LORD, him and his sons for ever.   Deut. 10:8

6 And if a Levite come from any of thy gates out of all Israel, where he sojourned, and come with all the desire of his mind unto the place which the LORD shall choose; Num. 35:2-3

7 Then he shall minister in the name of the LORD his God, as all his brethren the Levites *do*, which stand there before the LORD.

8 They shall have like portions to eat, beside that which cometh of the sale of his patrimony.   2 Chr. 31:4; Neh. 12:44, 47

Laws about the Abominations of the Nations in the Land

9 When thou art come into the land which the LORD thy God giveth thee, thou shalt not learn to do after the abominations of those nations.   Deut. 12:29-31

God Expressly Forbids Spiritualism

Deuteronomy 18:9–14

God has given the world sufficient light to enable them to discover the snare. As already shown, the theory which forms the very foundation of spiritualism is at war with the plainest statements of Scripture. The Bible declares that the dead know not anything, that their thoughts have perished; they have no part in anything that is done under the sun; they know nothing of the joys or sorrows of those who were dearest to them on earth.

Furthermore, God has expressly forbidden all pretended communication with departed spirits. In the days of the Hebrews there was a class of people who claimed, as do the spiritualists of today, to hold communication with the dead. But the "familiar spirits," as these visitants from other worlds were called, are declared by the Bible to be "the spirits of devils" (compare Numbers 25:1–3; Psalm 106:28; 1 Corinthians 10:20; Revelation 16:14). The work of dealing with familiar spirits was pronounced an abomination to the Lord, and was solemnly forbidden under penalty of death (Leviticus 19:31; 20:27). *GC 556*

10 There shall not be found among you *any one* that maketh his son or his daughter to pass through the fire, or that useth ᵀdivination, *or* an observer of times, or an enchanter, or a witch,   Ex. 22:18; Lev. 19:26, 31 ◆ *false magic*
11 Or a charmer, or a consulter with familiar spirits, or a wizard, or a necromancer.
12 For all that do these things *are* an abomination unto the LORD: and because of these abominations the LORD thy God doth drive them out from before thee.   Lev. 18:24
13 Thou shalt be perfect with the LORD thy God.   Gen. 6:9
14 For these nations, which thou shalt possess, hearkened unto observers of times, and unto ᵀdiviners: but as for thee, the LORD thy God hath not suffered thee so *to do.*   *false prophets or magicians*

18:9–14 The Deception of Spiritualism

Spiritualism, which numbers its converts by hundreds of thousands, yea, by millions, which has made its way into scientific circles, which has invaded churches, and has found favor in legislative bodies, and even in the courts of kings—this mammoth deception is but a revival, in a new disguise, of the witchcraft condemned and prohibited of old. *GC 556*

The Lord Will Raise up a Prophet
15 The LORD thy God will raise up unto thee a Prophet from the midst of thee, of thy brethren, like unto me; unto him ye shall hearken;   Deut. 18:18-19; John 1:21; Acts 7:37
16 According to all that thou desiredst of the LORD thy God in Horeb in the day of the assembly, saying, Let me not hear again the voice of the LORD my God, neither let me see this great fire any more, that I die not.   Ex. 20:19; Deut. 9:10
17 And the LORD said unto me, They have well *spoken that* which they have spoken.
18 I will raise them up a Prophet from among their brethren, like unto thee, and will put my words in his mouth; and he shall speak unto them all that I shall command him.   John 4:25; 8:28; 12:49-50
19 And it shall come to pass, *that* whosoever will not hearken unto my words which he shall speak in my name, I will require *it* of him.   Acts 3:22-23
20 But the prophet, which shall presume to speak a word in my name, which I have not commanded him to speak, or that shall speak in the name of other gods, even that prophet shall die.   Deut. 13:1-5
21 And if thou say in thine heart, How shall we know the word which the LORD hath not spoken?

22 When a prophet speaketh in the name of the LORD, if the thing follow not, nor come to pass, that *is* the thing which the LORD hath not spoken, *but* the prophet hath spoken it presumptuously: thou shalt not be afraid of him.   Deut. 18:20

Laws about the Cities of Refuge
19 When the LORD thy God hath cut off the nations, whose land the LORD thy God giveth thee, and thou succeedest them, and dwellest in their cities, and in their houses;   Deut. 6:10; 12:29
2 Thou shalt separate three cities for thee in the midst of thy land, which the LORD thy God giveth thee to possess it.   Ex. 21:13

19:2 Refuge in Christ

The cities of refuge appointed for God's ancient people were a symbol of the refuge provided in Christ. The same merciful Saviour who appointed those temporal cities of refuge has by the shedding of His own blood provided for the transgressors of God's law a sure retreat, into which they may flee for safety from the second death. No power can take out of His hands the souls that go to Him for pardon. *PP 516*

3 Thou shalt prepare thee a way, and divide the coasts of thy land, which the LORD thy God giveth thee to inherit, into three parts, that every slayer may flee thither.
4 And this *is* the case of the slayer, which shall flee thither, that he may live: Whoso killeth his neighbour ignorantly, whom he hated not in time past;   Num. 35:15-24
5 As when a man goeth into the wood with his neighbour to ᵀhew wood, and his hand fetcheth a stroke with the axe to cut down the tree, and the head slippeth from the ᵀhelve, and lighteth upon his neighbour, that he die; he shall flee unto one of those cities, and live: *cut* ◆ *handle*
6 Lest the avenger of the blood pursue the slayer, while his heart is hot, and overtake him, because the way is long, and slay him; whereas he *was* not worthy of death, inasmuch as he hated him not in time past.

19:6 The Race to Safety

He who fled to the city of refuge could make no delay. Family and employment were left behind. There was no time to say farewell to loved ones. His life was at stake, and every other interest must be sacrificed to the one purpose—to reach the place of safety. Weariness was forgotten, difficulties were unheeded. The fugitive dared not for one moment slacken his pace until he was within the wall of the city. *PP 517*

7 Wherefore I command thee, saying, Thou shalt separate three cities for thee.

8 And if the LORD thy God enlarge thy coast, as he hath sworn unto thy fathers, and give thee all the land which he promised to give unto thy fathers; Gen. 15:18-21

9 If thou shalt keep all these commandments to do them, which I command thee this day, to love the LORD thy God, and to walk ever in his ways; then shalt thou add three cities more for thee, beside these three: Josh. 20:7-8

10 That innocent blood be not shed in thy land, which the LORD thy God giveth thee *for* an inheritance, and *so* blood be upon thee.

11 But if any man hate his neighbour, and lie in wait for him, and rise up against him, and ᵀsmite him mortally that he die, and fleeth into one of these cities: Num. 35:16-21 ◆ *strike*

12 Then the elders of his city shall send and fetch him thence, and deliver him into the hand of the avenger of blood, that he may die.

13 Thine eye shall not pity him, but thou shalt put away *the guilt of* innocent blood from Israel, that it may go well with thee. Deut. 7:2

Laws about Land Boundaries and Witnesses at Trial

14 Thou shalt not remove thy neighbour's landmark, which they of old time have set in thine inheritance, which thou shalt inherit in the land that the LORD thy God giveth thee to possess it. Deut. 27:17; Prov. 22:28; Hos. 5:10

15 One witness shall not rise up against a man for any iniquity, or for any sin, in any sin that he sinneth: at the mouth of two witnesses, or at the mouth of three witnesses, shall the matter be established. Num. 35:30

16 If a false witness rise up against any man to testify against him *that which is* wrong; Ps. 27:12

17 Then both the men, between whom the controversy *is*, shall stand before the LORD, before the priests and the judges, which shall be in those days; Deut. 17:9; 21:5

18 And the judges shall make diligent inquisition: and, behold, *if* the witness *be* a false witness, *and* hath testified falsely against his brother; Deut. 13:14

19 Then shall ye do unto him, as he had thought to have done unto his brother: so shalt thou put the evil away from among you. Deut. 22:24; Prov. 19:5, 9

20 And those which remain shall hear, and fear, and shall ᵀhenceforth commit no more any such evil among you. *from this time forward*

21 And thine eye shall not pity; *but* life *shall* go for life, eye for eye, tooth for tooth, hand for hand, foot for foot. Deut. 19:13

Laws about Warfare and the Soldiers Sent into Battle

20 When thou goest out to battle against thine enemies, and seest horses, and chariots, *and* a people more than thou, be not afraid of them: for the LORD thy God *is* with thee, which brought thee up out of the land of Egypt. Deut. 31:6, 8; Ps. 20:7

2 And it shall be, when ye are come nigh unto the battle, that the priest shall approach and speak unto the people, Num. 10:8-9

3 And shall say unto them, Hear, O Israel, ye approach this day unto battle against your enemies: let not your hearts faint, fear not, and do not tremble, neither be ye terrified because of them;

4 For the LORD your God *is* he that goeth with you, to fight for you against your enemies, to save you. Deut. 1:30; 3:22; Josh. 23:10

5 And the officers shall speak unto the people, saying, What man *is there* that hath built a new house, and hath not dedicated

---

Avenger of Blood

Deuteronomy 19:1–13

The appointment of these cities [of refuge] had been commanded by Moses, "that the slayer may flee thither, which killeth any person at unawares. And they shall be unto you cities for refuge," he said, "that the manslayer die not, until he stand before the congregation in judgment" (Numbers 35:11, 12). This merciful provision was rendered necessary by the ancient custom of private vengeance, by which the punishment of the murderer devolved on the nearest relative or the next heir of the deceased. In cases where guilt was clearly evident it was not necessary to wait for a trial by the magistrates. The avenger might pursue the criminal anywhere and put him to death wherever he should be found. The Lord did not see fit to abolish this custom at that time, but He made provision to ensure the safety of those who should take life unintentionally. . . .

But while the guiltless were not to be rashly slain, neither were the guilty to escape punishment. The case of the fugitive was to be fairly tried by the proper authorities, and only when found innocent of intentional murder was he to be protected in the city of refuge. The guilty were given up to the avenger. . . .

The safety and purity of the nation demanded that the sin of murder be severely punished. Human life, which God alone could give, must be sacredly guarded. *PP 515, 516*

it? let him go and return to his house, lest he die in the battle, and another man dedicate it.   Neh. 12:27

6 And what man *is he* that hath planted a vineyard, and hath not *yet* eaten of it? let him *also* go and return unto his house, lest he die in the battle, and another man eat of it.   Lev. 19:23-25

7 And what man *is there* that hath ᵀbetrothed a wife, and hath not taken her? let him go and return unto his house, lest he die in the battle, and another man take her.   *engaged*

8 And the officers shall speak further unto the people, and they shall say, What man *is there that is* fearful and fainthearted? let him go and return unto his house, lest his brethren's heart faint as well as his heart. Deut. 1:28; Judg. 7:3

9 And it shall be, when the officers have made an end of speaking unto the people, that they shall make captains of the armies to lead the people.

What to Do to the Cities That Accept or Refuse the Proclamation of Peace

10 When thou comest nigh unto a city to fight against it, then proclaim peace unto it.

11 And it shall be, if it make thee answer of peace, and open unto thee, then it shall be, *that* all the people *that is* found therein shall be tributaries unto thee, and they shall serve thee.

12 And if it will make no peace with thee, but will make war against thee, then thou shalt besiege it:

13 And when the LORD thy God hath delivered it into thine hands, thou shalt ᵀsmite every male thereof with the edge of the sword: *strike*

20:13 Dictates of Infinite Goodness

To many these commands seem to be contrary to the spirit of love and mercy enjoined in other portions of the Bible, but they were in truth the dictates of infinite wisdom and goodness. God was about to establish Israel in Canaan, to develop among them a nation and government that should be a manifestation of His kingdom upon the earth. *PP 492*

14 But the women, and the little ones, and the cattle, and all that is in the city, *even* all the ᵀspoil thereof, shalt thou take unto thyself; and thou shalt eat the spoil of thine enemies, which the LORD thy God hath given thee.   Num. 31:9; Josh. 8:2; 22:8 ◆ *plunder*

15 Thus shalt thou do unto all the cities *which are* very far off from thee, which *are* not of the cities of these nations.

16 But of the cities of these people, which the LORD thy God doth give thee *for* an inheritance, thou shalt save alive nothing that breatheth: Num. 21:2-3; 33:52; Josh. 11:14

17 But thou shalt utterly destroy them; *namely*, the Hittites, and the Amorites, the Canaanites, and the Perizzites, the Hivites, and the Jebusites; as the LORD thy God hath commanded thee:

18 That they teach you not to do after all their abominations, which they have done unto their gods; so should ye sin against the LORD your God.   Ex. 23:33; Deut. 12:30-31; Ps. 106:34-40

20:17, 18 Clearing the Land

[The Israelites] were not only to be inheritors of the true religion, but to disseminate its principles throughout the world. The Canaanites had abandoned themselves to the foulest and most debasing heathenism, and it was necessary that the land should be cleared of what would so surely prevent the fulfillment of God's gracious purposes. *PP 492*

19 When thou shalt besiege a city a long time, in making war against it to take it, thou shalt not destroy the trees thereof by forcing an axe against them: for thou mayest eat of them, and thou shalt not cut them down (for the tree of the field *is* man's *life*) to employ *them* in the siege:

20 Only the trees which thou knowest that they *be* not trees for meat, thou shalt destroy and cut them down; and thou shalt build ᵀbulwarks against the city that maketh war with thee, until it be subdued. *structures for defense*

The Expiation of an Uncertain Murder

21 If *one* be found slain in the land which the LORD thy God giveth thee to possess it, lying in the field, *and* it be not known who hath slain him:

2 Then thy elders and thy judges shall come forth, and they shall measure unto the cities which *are* round about him that is slain:

3 And it shall be, *that* the city *which is* next unto the slain man, even the elders of that city shall take an heifer, which hath not been ᵀwrought with, *and* which hath not drawn in the yoke;   Num. 19:2 ◆ *worked*

4 And the elders of that city shall bring down the heifer unto a rough valley, which is neither ᵀeared nor sown, and shall strike off the heifer's neck there in the valley: *plowed*

5 And the priests the sons of Levi shall come near; for them the LORD thy God hath chosen to minister unto him, and to bless in the name of the LORD; and by their word shall every controversy and every stroke be tried: 1 Chr. 23:13

6 And all the elders of that city, *that are* next unto the slain *man*, shall wash their

hands over the heifer that is beheaded in the valley: Ps. 26:6

7 And they shall answer and say, Our hands have not shed this blood, neither have our eyes seen *it*.

8 Be merciful, O LORD, unto thy people Israel, whom thou hast redeemed, and lay not innocent blood unto thy people of Israel's charge. And the blood shall be forgiven them.   Jon. 1:14

9 So shalt thou put away the *guilt of* innocent blood from among you, when thou shalt do *that which is* right in the sight of the LORD.

The Treatment of a Captive Taken for a Wife

10 When thou goest forth to war against thine enemies, and the LORD thy God hath delivered them into thine hands, and thou hast taken them captive,

11 And seest among the captives a beautiful woman, and hast a desire unto her, that thou wouldest have her to thy wife;

12 Then thou shalt bring her home to thine house; and she shall shave her head, and pare her nails;

13 And she shall put the ᵀraiment of her captivity from off her, and shall remain in thine house, and ᵀbewail her father and her mother a full month: and after that thou shalt go in unto her, and be her husband, and she shall be thy wife.   *clothing* ◆ *lament*

14 And it shall be, if thou have no delight in her, then thou shalt let her go whither she will; but thou shalt not sell her at all for money, thou shalt not make merchandise of her, because thou hast humbled her. Gen. 34:2

The Firstborn Is Not to Be Disinherited on Private Preference

15 If a man have two wives, one beloved, and another hated, and they have born him children, *both* the beloved and the hated; and *if* the firstborn son be hers that was hated: Gen. 29:33; 1 Sam. 1:4-5

16 Then it shall be, when he maketh his sons to inherit *that* which he hath, *that* he may not make the son of the beloved firstborn before the son of the hated, *which is* indeed the firstborn: 1 Chr. 26:10

17 But he shall acknowledge the son of the hated *for* the firstborn, by giving him a double portion of all that he hath: for he *is* the beginning of his strength; the right of the firstborn *is* his.   Gen. 25:31-34; 49:3

A Stubborn Son Shall Be Stoned to Death

18 If a man have a stubborn and rebellious son, which will not obey the voice of his father, or the voice of his mother, and *that*,

when they have ᵀchastened him, will not hearken unto them: Ex. 20:12 ◆ *disciplined*

19 Then shall his father and his mother lay hold on him, and bring him out unto the elders of his city, and unto the gate of his place;

20 And they shall say unto the elders of his city, This our son *is* stubborn and rebellious, he will not obey our voice; *he is* a glutton, and a drunkard.   Prov. 20:1

21 And all the men of his city shall stone him with stones, that he die: so shalt thou put evil away from among you; and all Israel shall hear, and fear.   Lev. 24:16

22 And if a man have committed a sin worthy of death, and he be to be put to death, and thou hang him on a tree: Matt. 26:66; Acts 23:29

23 His body shall not remain all night upon the tree, but thou shalt in any wise bury him that day; (for he that is hanged *is* accursed of God;) that thy land be not defiled, which the LORD thy God giveth thee *for* an inheritance.   Lev. 18:25; Deut. 7:26; Gal. 3:13

Laws about Personal Property

22 Thou shalt not see thy brother's ox or his sheep go astray, and hide thyself from them: thou shalt in any case bring them again unto thy brother.   Ex. 23:4-5

2 And if thy brother *be* not nigh unto thee, or if thou know him not, then thou shalt bring it unto thine own house, and it shall be with thee until thy brother seek after it, and thou shalt restore it to him again.

3 In like manner shalt thou do with his ass; and so shalt thou do with his ᵀraiment; and with all lost thing of thy brother's, which he hath lost, and thou hast found, shalt thou do likewise: thou mayest not hide thyself.   *clothing*

4 Thou shalt not see thy brother's ass or his ox fall down by the way, and hide thyself from them: thou shalt surely help him to lift *them* up again.

Varied Laws

5 The woman shall not wear that which pertaineth unto a man, neither shall a man put on a woman's garment: for all that do so *are* abomination unto the LORD thy God.

6 If a bird's nest chance to be before thee in the way in any tree, or on the ground, *whether they be* young ones, or eggs, and the ᵀdam sitting upon the young, or upon the eggs, thou shalt not take the dam with the young: Lev. 22:28 ◆ *mother*

7 *But* thou shalt in any wise let the dam go, and take the young to thee; that it may be well with thee, and *that* thou mayest prolong *thy* days.   Deut. 4:40

8 When thou buildest a new house, then

thou shalt make a ^Tbattlement for thy roof, that thou bring not blood upon thine house, if any man fall from thence.   Ex. 22:6 ◆ *wall*

9 Thou shalt not sow thy vineyard with ^Tdivers seeds: lest the fruit of thy seed which thou hast sown, and the fruit of thy vineyard, be defiled.   Lev. 19:19 ◆ *various*

10 Thou shalt not plow with an ox and an ass together.   2 Cor. 6:14-16

11 Thou shalt not wear a garment of divers sorts, *as* of woollen and linen together.

12 Thou shalt make thee fringes upon the four quarters of thy ^Tvesture, wherewith thou coverest *thyself*.   Matt. 23:5 ◆ *clothing*

Laws about Sex and Marriage

13 If any man take a wife, and go in unto her, and hate her,   Gen. 29:21

14 And give occasions of speech against her, and bring up an evil name upon her, and say, I took this woman, and when I came to her, I found her not a maid:

15 Then shall the father of the damsel, and her mother, take and bring forth *the tokens of* the damsel's virginity unto the elders of the city in the gate:

16 And the damsel's father shall say unto the elders, I gave my daughter unto this man to wife, and he hateth her;

17 And, lo, he hath given occasions of speech *against her*, saying, I found not thy daughter a maid; and yet these *are the tokens of* my daughter's virginity. And they shall spread the cloth before the elders of the city.

18 And the elders of that city shall take that man and chastise him;

19 And they shall ^Tamerce him in an hundred *shekels* of silver, and give *them* unto the father of the damsel, because he hath brought up an evil name upon a virgin of Israel: and she shall be his wife; he may not put her away all his days.   Deut. 22:29 ◆ *impose a fine*

20 But if this thing be true, *and the tokens of* virginity be not found for the damsel:

21 Then they shall bring out the damsel to the door of her father's house, and the men of her city shall stone her with stones that she die: because she hath ^Twrought folly in Israel, to play the ^Twhore in her father's house: so shalt thou put evil away from among you.   Gen. 34:7; Deut. 13:5; Judg. 20:6 ◆ *made* ◆ *prostitute*

22 If a man be found lying with a woman married to an husband, then they shall both of them die, *both* the man that lay with the woman, and the woman: so shalt thou put away evil from Israel.   Lev. 20:10; Heb. 13:4

23 If a damsel *that is* a virgin be betrothed unto an husband, and a man find her in the city, and lie with her;   Matt. 1:18-19

24 Then ye shall bring them both out unto the gate of that city, and ye shall stone them with stones that they die; the damsel, because she cried not, *being* in the city; and the man, because he hath humbled his neighbour's wife: so thou shalt put away evil from among you.   Deut. 21:14

25 But if a man find a ^Tbetrothed damsel in the field, and the man force her, and lie with her: then the man only that lay with her shall die: *engaged*

26 But unto the damsel thou shalt do nothing; *there is* in the damsel no sin *worthy* of death: for as when a man riseth against his neighbour, and slayeth him, even so *is* this matter: Deut. 21:22

27 For he found her in the field, *and* the betrothed damsel cried, and *there was* none to save her.

28 If a man find a damsel *that is* a virgin, which is not betrothed, and lay hold on her, and lie with her, and they be found; Ex. 22:16-17

29 Then the man that lay with her shall give unto the damsel's father fifty *shekels* of silver, and she shall be his wife; because he hath humbled her, he may not put her away all his days.   Deut. 21:14

30 A man shall not take his father's wife, nor discover his father's skirt.   Lev. 18:8; 20:11

Who May or May Not Enter into the Congregation

23 He that is wounded in the stones, or hath his privy member cut off, shall not enter into the congregation of the LORD.

2 A bastard shall not enter into the congregation of the LORD; even to his tenth generation shall he not enter into the congregation of the LORD.   Zech. 9:6

3 An Ammonite or Moabite shall not enter into the congregation of the LORD; even to their tenth generation shall they not enter into the congregation of the LORD for ever:

4 Because they met you not with bread and with water in the way, when ye came forth out of Egypt; and because they hired against thee Balaam the son of Beor of Pethor of Mesopotamia, to curse thee.   Neh. 13:2

5 Nevertheless the LORD thy God would not hearken unto Balaam; but the LORD thy God turned the curse into a blessing unto thee, because the LORD thy God loved thee.

6 Thou shalt not seek their peace nor their prosperity all thy days for ever.   Ezra 9:12

7 Thou shalt not ^Tabhor an Edomite; for he *is* thy brother: thou shalt not abhor an Egyptian; because thou wast a stranger in his land.   Ex. 22:21; 23:9; Deut. 10:19 ◆ *despise*

8 The children that are ^Tbegotten of them shall enter into the congregation of the LORD in their third generation.   *brought forth*

Uncleanness to Be Avoided in the Army

9 When the host goeth forth against thine enemies, then keep thee from every wicked thing.

10 If there be among you any man, that is not clean by reason of uncleanness that chanceth him by night, then shall he go abroad out of the camp, he shall not come within the camp: Lev. 15:16

11 But it shall be, when evening cometh on, he shall wash *himself* with water: and when the sun is down, he shall come into the camp *again*.   Lev. 14:9

12 Thou shalt have a place also without the camp, whither thou shalt go forth abroad:

13 And thou shalt have a paddle upon thy weapon; and it shall be, when thou wilt ease thyself abroad, thou shalt dig therewith, and shalt turn back and cover that which cometh from thee:

14 For the LORD thy God walketh in the midst of thy camp, to deliver thee, and to give up thine enemies before thee; therefore shall thy camp be holy: that he see no unclean thing in thee, and turn away from thee.   Lev. 26:12

23:14 Cleanliness and Godliness

Thorough-going sanitary regulations were enforced. These were enjoined on the people, not only as necessary to health, but as the condition of retaining among them the presence of the Holy One. *Ed 38*

Varied Laws

15 Thou shalt not deliver unto his master the servant which is escaped from his master unto thee: 1 Sam. 30:15

16 He shall dwell with thee, *even* among you, in that place which he shall choose in one of thy gates, where it liketh him best: thou shalt not oppress him.   Ex. 22:21

17 There shall be no whore of the daughters of Israel, nor a sodomite of the sons of Israel.   Lev. 19:29; Deut. 22:21; 2 Kin. 23:7

18 Thou shalt not bring the hire of a ᵀwhore, or the price of a dog, into the house of the LORD thy God for any vow: for even both these *are* abomination unto the LORD thy God.   Deut. 23:21 ♦ *prostitute*

19 Thou shalt not lend upon usury to thy brother; usury of money, usury of victuals, usury of any thing that is lent upon usury:

20 Unto a stranger thou mayest lend upon ᵀusury; but unto thy brother thou shalt not lend upon usury: that the LORD thy God may bless thee in all that thou settest thine hand to in the land whither thou goest to possess it.   Deut. 14:21; 15:3, 10 ♦ *interest charged*

21 When thou shalt vow a vow unto the LORD thy God, thou shalt not slack to pay it: for the LORD thy God will surely require it of thee; and it would be sin in thee.   Eccl. 5:4-5

22 But if thou shalt ᵀforbear to vow, it shall be no sin in thee.   *refuse*

23 That which is gone out of thy lips thou shalt keep and perform; *even* a freewill offering, according as thou hast vowed unto the LORD thy God, which thou hast promised with thy mouth.

24 When thou comest into thy neighbour's vineyard, then thou mayest eat grapes thy fill at thine own pleasure; but thou shalt not put *any* in thy vessel.

25 When thou comest into the standing corn of thy neighbour, then thou mayest pluck the ears with thine hand; but thou shalt not move a sickle unto thy neighbour's standing corn.   Mark 2:23

23:24, 25 God's Generous Law

The law of God gave the poor a right to a certain portion of the produce of the soil. When hungry, a man was at liberty to go to his neighbor's field or orchard or vineyard, and eat of the grain or fruit to satisfy his hunger. It was in accordance with this permission that the disciples of Jesus plucked and ate of the standing grain as they passed through a field upon the Sabbath day. *PP 531*

Laws about Divorce

24 When a man hath taken a wife, and married her, and it come to pass that she find no favour in his eyes, because he hath found some uncleanness in her: then let him write her a bill of divorcement, and give *it* in her hand, and send her out of his house.   Deut. 22:13, 19; Matt. 19:7-9

2 And when she is departed out of his house, she may go and be another man's *wife*.

3 And *if* the latter husband hate her, and write her a bill of divorcement, and giveth *it* in her hand, and sendeth her out of his house; or if the latter husband die, which took her *to be* his wife;

4 Her former husband, which sent her away, may not take her again to be his wife, after that she is defiled; for that *is* abomination before the LORD: and thou shalt not cause the land to sin, which the LORD thy God giveth thee *for* an inheritance.   Jer. 3:1

Varied Laws

5 When a man hath taken a new wife, he shall not go out to war, neither shall he be ᵀcharged with any business: *but* he shall be free at home one year, and shall cheer up his wife which he hath taken.   Deut. 20:7; Prov. 5:18 ♦ *burdened*

6 No man shall take the ᵀnether or the upper millstone to pledge: for he taketh *a man's* life to pledge.   Deut. 20:19 ◆ *lower*

7 If a man be found stealing any of his brethren of the children of Israel, and maketh merchandise of him, or selleth him; then that thief shall die; and thou shalt put evil away from among you. Ex. 21:16; 1 Tim. 1:10

8 Take heed in the plague of leprosy, that thou observe diligently, and do according to all that the priests the Levites shall teach you: as I commanded them, *so* ye shall observe to do.   Lev. 14:2

9 Remember what the LORD thy God did unto Miriam by the way, after that ye were come forth out of Egypt.   Num. 12:10-15

10 When thou dost lend thy brother any thing, thou shalt not go into his house to fetch his pledge.   Deut. 15:8

11 Thou shalt stand abroad, and the man to whom thou dost lend shall bring out the pledge abroad unto thee.

12 And if the man *be* poor, thou shalt not sleep with his pledge: Deut. 24:17

13 In any case thou shalt deliver him the pledge again when the sun goeth down, that he may sleep in his own raiment, and bless thee: and it shall be righteousness unto thee before the LORD thy God.   Deut. 6:25; Dan. 4:27

Varied Laws, Including Caring for the Poor, Widows, and Orphans

14 Thou shalt not oppress an hired servant *that is* poor and needy, *whether he be* of thy brethren, or of thy strangers that *are* in thy land within thy gates: Prov. 14:31

15 At his day thou shalt give *him* his hire, neither shall the sun go down upon it; for he *is* poor, and setteth his heart upon it: lest he cry against thee unto the LORD, and it be sin unto thee.   Lev. 19:13; Deut. 15:9; James 5:4

16 The fathers shall not be put to death for the children, neither shall the children be put to death for the fathers: every man shall be put to death for his own sin.   2 Chr. 25:4

17 Thou shalt not pervert the judgment of the stranger, *nor* of the fatherless; nor take a widow's ᵀraiment to pledge: Deut. 16:19 ◆ *clothing*

> **24:17 Unselfish Empathy**
>
> God's word sanctions no policy that will enrich one class by the oppression and suffering of another. In all our business transactions it teaches us to put ourselves in the place of those with whom we are dealing, to look not only on our own things, but also on the things of others. *MH 187*

18 But thou shalt remember that thou wast a bondman in Egypt, and the LORD thy God

redeemed thee thence: therefore I command thee to do this thing.   Deut. 5:15

19 When thou cuttest down thine harvest in thy field, and hast forgot a ᵀsheaf in the field, thou shalt not go again to fetch it: it shall be for the stranger, for the fatherless, and for the widow: that the LORD thy God may bless thee in all the work of thine hands. Lev. 19:9-10; 23:22; Deut. 14:29 ◆ *bundle of cut grain*

20 When thou beatest thine olive tree, thou shalt not go over the boughs again: it shall be for the stranger, for the fatherless, and for the widow.

21 When thou gatherest the grapes of thy vineyard, thou shalt not ᵀglean *it* afterward: it shall be for the stranger, for the fatherless, and for the widow.   *gather leftovers*

22 And thou shalt remember that thou wast a bondman in the land of Egypt: therefore I command thee to do this thing.   Deut. 24:18

A Condemned Man Must Not Be Beaten with More Than Forty Stripes

25 If there be a controversy between men, and they come unto judgment, that *the judges* may judge them; then they shall justify the righteous, and condemn the wicked.   Deut. 17:8-9

2 And it shall be, if the wicked man *be* worthy to be beaten, that the judge shall cause him to lie down, and to be beaten before his face, according to his fault, by a certain number.   Luke 12:47-48

3 Forty stripes he may give him, *and* not exceed: lest, *if* he should exceed, and beat him above these with many stripes, then thy brother should seem vile unto thee.   Job 18:3

4 Thou shalt not muzzle the ox when he treadeth out *the corn*.   Prov. 12:10

Laws about Keeping Family Lines

5 If brethren dwell together, and one of them die, and have no child, the wife of the dead shall not marry without unto a stranger: her husband's brother shall go in unto her, and take her to him to wife, and perform the duty of an husband's brother unto her.   Matt. 22:24; Mark 12:19; Luke 20:28

6 And it shall be, *that* the firstborn which she beareth shall succeed in the name of his brother *which is* dead, that his name be not put out of Israel.

7 And if the man like not to take his brother's wife, then let his brother's wife go up to the gate unto the elders, and say, My husband's brother refuseth to raise up unto his brother a name in Israel, he will not perform the duty of my husband's brother.

8 Then the elders of his city shall call him, and speak unto him: and *if* he stand *to it*, and say, I like not to take her;   Ruth 4:6

9 Then shall his brother's wife come unto him in the presence of the elders, and loose his shoe from off his foot, and spit in his face, and shall answer and say, So shall it be done unto that man that will not build up his brother's house.   Num. 12:14

10 And his name shall be called in Israel, The house of him that hath his shoe loosed.

11 When men strive together one with another, and the wife of the one draweth near for to deliver her husband out of the hand of him that ᵀsmiteth him, and putteth forth her hand, and taketh him by the secrets: *strikes*

12 Then thou shalt cut off her hand, thine eye shall not pity *her*.   Deut. 19:13

Varied Laws

13 Thou shalt not have in thy bag divers weights, a great and a small.   Prov. 11:1

14 Thou shalt not have in thine house ᵀdivers measures, a great and a small.   *various*

15 *But* thou shalt have a perfect and just weight, a perfect and just measure shalt thou have: that thy days may be lengthened in the land which the Lᴏʀᴅ thy God giveth thee.   Ex. 20:12

16 For all that do such things, *and* all that do unrighteously, *are* an abomination unto the Lᴏʀᴅ thy God.   Deut. 18:12; 22:5; Prov. 11:1

17 Remember what Amalek did unto thee by the way, when ye were come forth out of Egypt;   Ex. 17:8-16

18 How he met thee by the way, and smote the hindmost of thee, *even* all *that were* feeble behind thee, when thou *wast* faint and weary; and he feared not God.   Ps. 36:1

19 Therefore it shall be, when the Lᴏʀᴅ thy God hath given thee rest from all thine enemies round about, in the land which the Lᴏʀᴅ thy God giveth thee *for* an inheritance to possess it, *that* thou shalt blot out the remembrance of Amalek from under heaven; thou shalt not forget *it*.   Ex. 17:14

25:18, 19 Amalek Seals Its Doom

[The Amalekite] assault was wholly unprovoked. It was to manifest their hatred and defiance of God that they sought to destroy His people. The Amalekites had long been high-handed sinners, and their crimes had cried to God for vengeance, yet His mercy had still called them to repentance; but when the men of Amalek fell upon the wearied and defenseless ranks of Israel, they sealed their nation's doom. *PP 300*

Bringing the Firstfruits of the Land Before the Lord in Thankfulness

26 And it shall be, when thou *art* come in unto the land which the Lᴏʀᴅ thy God giveth thee *for* an inheritance, and possessest it, and dwellest therein;

2 That thou shalt take of the first of all the fruit of the earth, which thou shalt bring of thy land that the Lᴏʀᴅ thy God giveth thee, and shalt put *it* in a basket, and shalt go unto the place which the Lᴏʀᴅ thy God shall choose to place his name there.   Ex. 23:16, 19

3 And thou shalt go unto the priest that shall be in those days, and say unto him, I profess this day unto the Lᴏʀᴅ thy God, that I am come unto the country which the Lᴏʀᴅ sware unto our fathers for to give us.

4 And the priest shall take the basket out of thine hand, and set it down before the altar of the Lᴏʀᴅ thy God.

5 And thou shalt speak and say before the Lᴏʀᴅ thy God, A Syrian ready to perish *was* my father, and he went down into Egypt, and sojourned there with a few, and became there a nation, great, mighty, and populous: Gen. 43:1-2; 46:27; Deut. 10:22

6 And the Egyptians evil entreated us, and afflicted us, and laid upon us hard bondage: Ex. 1:11, 14

7 And when we cried unto the Lᴏʀᴅ God of our fathers, the Lᴏʀᴅ heard our voice, and looked on our affliction, and our labour, and our oppression: Ex. 3:9

8 And the Lᴏʀᴅ brought us forth out of Egypt with a mighty hand, and with an outstretched arm, and with great terribleness, and with signs, and with wonders: Ex. 12:37, 51; Deut. 4:34

9 And he hath brought us into this place, and hath given us this land, *even* a land that floweth with milk and honey.   Ex. 3:8

10 And now, behold, I have brought the firstfruits of the land, which thou, O Lᴏʀᴅ, hast given me. And thou shalt set it before the Lᴏʀᴅ thy God, and worship before the Lᴏʀᴅ thy God:

11 And thou shalt rejoice in every good *thing* which the Lᴏʀᴅ thy God hath given unto thee, and unto thine house, thou, and the Levite, and the stranger that *is* among you.

The Prayer of Him That Gives His Third Year Tithes

12 When thou hast made an end of tithing all the tithes of thine increase the third year, *which is* the year of tithing, and hast given *it* unto the Levite, the stranger, the fatherless, and the widow, that they may eat within thy gates, and be filled;   Lev. 27:30; Num. 18:24

13 Then thou shalt say before the Lᴏʀᴅ thy God, I have brought away the hallowed things out of *mine* house, and also have given them unto the Levite, and unto the stranger, to the fatherless, and to the widow, according to all thy commandments which thou hast commanded me: I have not ᵀtransgressed thy commandments, neither have I forgotten *them*:   Ps. 119:141, 153, 176 ◆ *violated*

14 I have not eaten thereof in my mourning, neither have I taken away *ought* thereof for *any* unclean *use*, nor given *ought* thereof for the dead: *but* I have hearkened to the voice of the LORD my God, *and* have done according to all that thou hast commanded me.   Lev. 7:20; 21:1, 11

15 Look down from thy holy habitation, from heaven, and bless thy people Israel, and the land which thou hast given us, as thou swarest unto our fathers, a land that floweth with milk and honey.   Is. 63:15; Zech. 2:13

The Covenant between God and the People

16 This day the LORD thy God hath commanded thee to do these statutes and judgments: thou shalt therefore keep and do them with all thine heart, and with all thy soul.

> **26:16 A Hedge of Protection**
>
> To this people were committed the oracles of God. They were hedged about by the precepts of His law, the everlasting principles of truth, justice, and purity. Obedience to these principles was to be their protection, for it would save them from destroying themselves by sinful practices. *PK 18*

17 Thou hast avouched the LORD this day to be thy God, and to walk in his ways, and to keep his statutes, and his commandments, and his judgments, and to hearken unto his voice: Ex. 24:7

18 And the LORD hath avouched thee this day to be his ᵀpeculiar people, as he hath promised thee, and that *thou* shouldest keep all his commandments;   Ex. 6:7; Deut. 7:6; 14:2 ◆ *special*

19 And to make thee high above all nations which he hath made, in praise, and in name, and in honour; and that thou mayest be an holy people unto the LORD thy God, as he hath spoken.   Ex. 19:6; Deut. 7:6; 28:1

> **26:19 God's Purpose for Israel**
>
> But it was God's purpose that by the revelation of His character through Israel men should be drawn unto Him. To all the world the gospel invitation was to be given. Through the teaching of the sacrificial service, Christ was to be uplifted before the nations, and all who would look unto Him should live. *PK 19*

The People Are Commanded to Write the Law upon Stones

27 And Moses with the elders of Israel commanded the people, saying, Keep all the commandments which I command you this day.

2 And it shall be on the day when ye shall pass over Jordan unto the land which the LORD thy God giveth thee, that thou shalt set thee up great stones, and plaister them with plaister: Josh. 4:1

3 And thou shalt write upon them all the words of this law, when thou art passed over, that thou mayest go in unto the land which the LORD thy God giveth thee, a land that floweth with milk and honey; as the LORD God of thy fathers hath promised thee.   Deut. 26:9

4 Therefore it shall be when ye be gone over Jordan, *that* ye shall set up these stones, which I command you this day, in mount Ebal, and thou shalt plaister them with plaister.

5 And there shalt thou build an altar unto the LORD thy God, an altar of stones: thou shalt not lift up *any* iron *tool* upon them.   Ex. 20:25

6 Thou shalt build the altar of the LORD thy God of whole stones: and thou shalt offer burnt offerings thereon unto the LORD thy God:

7 And thou shalt offer peace offerings, and shalt eat there, and rejoice before the LORD thy God.   Deut. 12:7

8 And thou shalt write upon the stones all the words of this law very plainly.   Hab. 2:2

> **27:1–8 Renewing the Covenant**
>
> Before taking possession of their inheritance, they must renew their covenant of loyalty to God. *PP 499*

9 And Moses and the priests the Levites spake unto all Israel, saying, Take heed, and hearken, O Israel; this day thou art become the people of the LORD thy God.

10 Thou shalt therefore obey the voice of the LORD thy God, and do his commandments and his statutes, which I command thee this day.

Reciting the Curses for Disobedience

11 And Moses charged the people the same day, saying,

12 These shall stand upon mount Gerizim to bless the people, when ye are come over Jordan; Simeon, and Levi, and Judah, and Issachar, and Joseph, and Benjamin: Judg. 9:7

13 And these shall stand upon mount Ebal to curse; Reuben, Gad, and Asher, and Zebulun, Dan, and Naphtali.

14 And the Levites shall speak, and say unto all the men of Israel with a loud voice,

15 Cursed *be* the man that maketh *any* ᵀgraven or molten image, an abomination unto the LORD, the work of the hands of the craftsman, and putteth *it* in *a* secret *place*. And all the people shall answer and say, Amen.   Ex. 20:4; 34:17; Lev. 19:4 ◆ *engraved* or *cut out*

16 Cursed *be* he that setteth light by his

father or his mother. And all the people shall say, Amen.   Ex. 20:12; 21:17; Lev. 19:3

17 Cursed *be* he that removeth his neighbour's landmark. And all the people shall say, Amen.   Deut. 19:14; Prov. 22:28

18 Cursed *be* he that maketh the blind to wander out of the way. And all the people shall say, Amen.   Lev. 19:14

19 Cursed *be* he that perverteth the judgment of the stranger, fatherless, and widow. And all the people shall say, Amen.   Deut. 10:18

20 Cursed *be* he that lieth with his father's wife; because he uncovereth his father's skirt. And all the people shall say, Amen.   Lev. 18:8

21 Cursed *be* he that lieth with any manner of beast. And all the people shall say, Amen.   Ex. 22:19; Lev. 18:23; 20:15

22 Cursed *be* he that lieth with his sister, the daughter of his father, or the daughter of his mother. And all the people shall say, Amen.   Lev. 18:9; 20:17; Ezek. 22:11

23 Cursed *be* he that lieth with his mother in law. And all the people shall say, Amen.

24 Cursed *be* he that 'smiteth his neighbour secretly. And all the people shall say, Amen.   Lev. 24:17 ◆ *strikes*

25 Cursed *be* he that taketh reward to slay an innocent person. And all the people shall say, Amen.   Ex. 23:7-8

26 Cursed *be* he that confirmeth not *all* the words of this law to do them. And all the people shall say, Amen.   Ps. 119:21; Gal. 3:10

27:26 The Law in Our Hearts

The same law that was engraved upon the tables of stone is written by the Holy Spirit upon the tables of the heart. Instead of going about to establish our own righteousness we accept the righteousness of Christ. His blood atones for our sins. His obedience is accepted for us. Then the heart renewed by the Holy Spirit will bring forth "the fruits of the Spirit." Through the grace of Christ we shall live in obedience to the law of God written upon our hearts. *PP 372*

Reciting the Blessings for Obedience

28 And it shall come to pass, if thou shalt hearken diligently unto the voice of the LORD thy God, to observe *and* to do all his commandments which I command thee this day, that the LORD thy God will set thee on high above all nations of the earth:

28:1, 2

2 And all these blessings shall come on thee, and overtake thee, if thou shalt hearken unto the voice of the LORD thy God.   Zech. 1:6

God's Law   See Psalm 19:7–11.

3 Blessed *shalt* thou *be* in the city, and blessed *shalt* thou *be* in the field.   Gen. 39:5

4 Blessed *shall be* the fruit of thy body, and the fruit of thy ground, and the fruit of thy cattle, the increase of thy ʳkine, and the flocks of thy sheep.   Gen. 49:25 ◆ *cows*

5 Blessed *shall be* thy basket and thy store.

6 Blessed *shalt* thou *be* when thou comest in, and blessed *shalt* thou *be* when thou goest out.   Ps. 121:8

7 The LORD shall cause thine enemies that rise up against thee to be smitten before thy face: they shall come out against thee one way, and flee before thee seven ways. Lev. 26:7-8

8 The LORD shall command the blessing upon thee in thy storehouses, and in all that thou settest thine hand unto; and he shall bless thee in the land which the LORD thy God giveth thee.   Lev. 25:21

9 The LORD shall establish thee an holy people unto himself, as he hath sworn unto thee, if thou shalt keep the commandments of the LORD thy God, and walk in his ways.   Ex. 19:5-6; Deut. 7:6; 13:17

10 And all people of the earth shall see that thou art called by the name of the LORD; and they shall be afraid of thee.   2 Chr. 7:14

11 And the LORD shall make thee plenteous in goods, in the fruit of thy body, and in the fruit of thy cattle, and in the fruit of thy ground, in the land which the LORD sware unto thy fathers to give thee.   Deut. 28:4

12 The LORD shall open unto thee his good treasure, the heaven to give the rain unto thy land in his season, and to bless all the work of thine hand: and thou shalt lend unto many nations, and thou shalt not borrow.   Lev. 26:4

13 And the LORD shall make thee the head, and not the tail; and thou shalt be above only, and thou shalt not be beneath; if that thou hearken unto the commandments of the LORD thy God, which I command thee this day, to observe and to do *them:* Deut. 28:1

14 And thou shalt not go aside from any of the words which I command thee this day, *to* the right hand, or *to* the left, to go after other gods to serve them.   Deut. 5:32

28:1–14 Blessings and Curses

Still the great leader was filled with fear that the people would depart from God. In a most sublime and thrilling address he set before them the blessings that would be theirs on condition of obedience, and the curses that would follow upon transgression. *PP 466*

Curses from the Lord

15 But it shall come to pass, if thou wilt not hearken unto the voice of the LORD thy God, to observe to do all his commandments and his statutes which I command thee this day;

that all these curses shall come upon thee, and overtake thee: Mal. 2:2

16 Cursed *shalt* thou *be* in the city, and cursed *shalt* thou *be* in the field.

17 Cursed *shall be* thy basket and thy store.

18 Cursed *shall be* the fruit of thy body, and the fruit of thy land, the increase of thy kine, and the flocks of thy sheep.   Deut. 28:4

19 Cursed *shalt* thou *be* when thou comest in, and cursed *shalt* thou *be* when thou goest out.   Deut. 28:6

20 The LORD shall send upon thee cursing, vexation, and rebuke, in all that thou settest thine hand unto for to do, until thou be destroyed, and until thou perish quickly; because of the wickedness of thy doings, whereby thou hast forsaken me. Is. 51:20; 66:15

21 The LORD shall make the pestilence cleave unto thee, until he have consumed thee from off the land, whither thou goest to possess it.   Lev. 26:25; Num. 14:12; Jer. 24:10

22 The LORD shall smite thee with a consumption, and with a fever, and with an inflammation, and with an extreme burning, and with the sword, and with blasting, and with mildew; and they shall pursue thee until thou perish.   Lev. 26:16; 1 Kin. 8:37; Amos 4:9

23 And thy heaven that *is* over thy head shall be brass, and the earth that is under thee *shall be* iron.   Lev. 26:19

24 The LORD shall make the rain of thy land powder and dust: from heaven shall it come down upon thee, until thou be destroyed.   Deut. 28:12

25 The LORD shall cause thee to be smitten before thine enemies: thou shalt go out one way against them, and flee seven ways before them: and shalt be removed into all the kingdoms of the earth.   Deut. 28:7; Is. 30:17; Ezek. 23:46

26 And thy carcase shall be meat unto all fowls of the air, and unto the beasts of the earth, and no man shall fray *them* away.

27 The LORD will smite thee with the botch of Egypt, and with the ᵀemerods, and with the scab, and with the itch, whereof thou canst not be healed.   1 Sam. 5:6 ◆ *tumors*

28 The LORD shall ᵀsmite thee with madness, and blindness, and astonishment of heart: *strike*

29 And thou shalt grope at noonday, as the blind gropeth in darkness, and thou shalt not prosper in thy ways: and thou shalt be only oppressed and spoiled evermore, and no man shall save *thee*.   Job 5:14

30 Thou shalt betroth a wife, and another man shall lie with her: thou shalt build an house, and thou shalt not dwell therein: thou shalt plant a vineyard, and shalt not gather the grapes thereof.   Job 31:10; Jer. 8:10; Amos 5:11

31 Thine ox *shall be* slain before thine eyes, and thou shalt not eat thereof: thine ass *shall* be violently taken away from before thy face, and shall not be restored to thee: thy sheep *shall be* given unto thine enemies, and thou shalt have none to rescue *them*.

32 Thy sons and thy daughters *shall be* given unto another people, and thine eyes shall look, and fail *with longing* for them all the day long: and *there shall be* no might in thine hand.   Deut. 28:41

33 The fruit of thy land, and all thy labours, shall a nation which thou knowest not eat up; and thou shalt be only oppressed and crushed alway: Jer. 5:17

34 So that thou shalt be mad for the sight of thine eyes which thou shalt see.

35 The LORD shall smite thee in the knees, and in the legs, with a sore ᵀbotch that cannot be healed, from the sole of thy foot unto the top of thy head.   Deut. 28:27 ◆ *ulcer*

36 The LORD shall bring thee, and thy king which thou shalt set over thee, unto a nation which neither thou nor thy fathers have known; and there shalt thou serve other gods, wood and stone.   Deut. 4:28; 2 Kin. 25:11; Jer. 16:13

37 And thou shalt become an astonishment, a proverb, and a byword, among all nations whither the LORD shall lead thee.   1 Kin. 9:7-8

38 Thou shalt carry much seed out into the field, and shalt gather *but* little in; for the locust shall consume it.   Joel 1:4; Mic. 6:15; Hag. 1:6

39 Thou shalt plant vineyards, and dress *them*, but shalt neither drink *of* the wine, nor gather *the grapes*; for the worms shall eat them.

40 Thou shalt have olive trees throughout all thy coasts, but thou shalt not anoint *thyself* with the oil; for thine olive shall cast *his* fruit.   Mic. 6:15

41 Thou shalt ᵀbeget sons and daughters, but thou shalt not enjoy them; for they shall go into captivity.   Deut. 28:32 ◆ *bring forth*

42 All thy trees and fruit of thy land shall the locust consume.

43 The stranger that *is* within thee shall get up above thee very high; and thou shalt come down very low.   Deut. 28:13

44 He shall lend to thee, and thou shalt not lend to him: he shall be the head, and thou shalt be the tail.   Deut. 28:12-13

45 Moreover all these curses shall come upon thee, and shall pursue thee, and overtake thee, till thou be destroyed; because thou hearkenedst not unto the voice of the LORD thy God, to keep his commandments and his statutes which he commanded thee: Deut. 28:15

46 And they shall be upon thee for a sign and for a wonder, and upon thy seed for ever.   Is. 8:18; Ezek. 14:8

47 Because thou servedst not the LORD thy

God with joyfulness, and with gladness of heart, for the abundance of all *things*;

48 Therefore shalt thou serve thine enemies which the LORD shall send against thee, in hunger, and in thirst, and in nakedness, and in want of all *things*: and he shall put a yoke of iron upon thy neck, until he have destroyed thee.   Jer. 28:13-14

49 The LORD shall bring a nation against thee from far, from the end of the earth, *as swift* as the eagle flieth; a nation whose tongue thou shalt not understand; Is. 5:26-30; Lam. 4:19; Hos. 8:1

50 A nation of fierce ᵀcountenance, which shall not regard the person of the old, nor shew favour to the young: Is. 47:6 ◆ *appearance*

51 And he shall eat the fruit of thy cattle, and the fruit of thy land, until thou be destroyed: which *also* shall not leave thee *either* corn, wine, or oil, *or* the increase of thy kine, or flocks of thy sheep, until he have destroyed thee.   Deut. 28:33

52 And he shall besiege thee in all thy gates, until thy high and fenced walls come down, wherein thou trustedst, throughout all thy land: and he shall besiege thee in all thy gates throughout all thy land, which the LORD thy God hath given thee.

53 And thou shalt eat the fruit of thine own body, the flesh of thy sons and of thy daughters, which the LORD thy God hath given thee, in the siege, and in the straitness, wherewith thine enemies shall distress thee: Lev. 26:29; 2 Kin. 6:28-29; Lam. 2:20

54 *So that* the man *that is* tender among you, and very delicate, his eye shall be evil toward his brother, and toward the wife of his bosom, and toward the remnant of his children which he shall leave: Deut. 13:6

55 So that he will not give to any of them of the flesh of his children whom he shall eat: because he hath nothing left him in the siege, and in the straitness, wherewith thine enemies shall distress thee in all thy gates.

56 The tender and delicate woman among you, which would not adventure to set the sole of her foot upon the ground for delicateness and tenderness, her eye shall be evil toward the husband of her bosom, and toward her son, and toward her daughter,

57 And toward her young one that cometh out from between her feet, and toward her children which she shall bear: for she shall eat them for want of all *things* secretly in the siege and straitness, wherewith thine enemy shall distress thee in thy gates.

58 If thou wilt not observe to do all the words of this law that are written in this book, that thou mayest fear this glorious and fearful name, THE LORD THY GOD;

59 Then the LORD will make thy plagues wonderful, and the plagues of thy seed, *even*

great plagues, and of long continuance, and sore sicknesses, and of long continuance.

60 Moreover he will bring upon thee all the diseases of Egypt, which thou wast afraid of; and they shall cleave unto thee.   Deut. 7:15

61 Also every sickness, and every plague, which *is* not written in the book of this law, them will the LORD bring upon thee, until thou be destroyed.

62 And ye shall be left few in number, whereas ye were as the stars of heaven for multitude; because thou wouldest not obey the voice of the LORD thy God.   Deut. 4:27

63 And it shall come to pass, *that* as the LORD rejoiced over you to do you good, and to multiply you; so the LORD will rejoice over you to destroy you, and to bring you to ᵀnought; and ye shall be plucked from off the land whither thou goest to possess it.   Deut. 30:9; Prov. 1:26; Jer. 32:41 ◆ *nothing*

64 And the LORD shall scatter thee among all people, from the one end of the earth even unto the other; and there thou shalt serve other gods, which neither thou nor thy fathers have known, *even* wood and stone.   Lev. 26:33; Deut. 4:27-28; Neh. 1:8

65 And among these nations shalt thou find no ease, neither shall the sole of thy foot have rest: but the LORD shall give thee there a trembling heart, and failing of eyes, and sorrow of mind: Lev. 26:16, 36; Amos 9:4

66 And thy life shall hang in doubt before thee; and thou shalt fear day and night, and shalt have none assurance of thy life:

67 In the morning thou shalt say, Would God it were even! and at even thou shalt say, Would God it were morning! for the fear of thine heart wherewith thou shalt fear, and for the sight of thine eyes which thou shalt see.   Deut. 28:34

68 And the LORD shall bring thee into Egypt again with ships, by the way whereof I spake unto thee, Thou shalt see it no more again: and there ye shall be sold unto your enemies for bondmen and bondwomen, and no man shall buy *you*.   Deut. 17:16

Israel's Past, Present, and Future

29 These *are* the words of the covenant, which the LORD commanded Moses to make with the children of Israel in the land of Moab, beside the covenant which he made with them in Horeb.   Deut. 5:2-3

2 And Moses called unto all Israel, and said unto them, Ye have seen all that the LORD did before your eyes in the land of Egypt unto Pharaoh, and unto all his servants, and unto all his land;   Ex. 19:4

3 The great temptations which thine eyes have seen, the signs, and those great miracles:

4 Yet the LORD hath not given you an heart to perceive, and eyes to see, and ears to hear, unto this day.   Is. 6:9-10; 63:17; Acts 28:26-27

5 And I have led you forty years in the wilderness: your clothes are not ᵀwaxen old upon you, and thy shoe is not waxen old upon thy foot.   Deut. 1:3; 8:2, 4 ◆ *becoming*

6 Ye have not eaten bread, neither have ye drunk wine or strong drink: that ye might know that I *am* the LORD your God.   Eph. 5:18

7 And when ye came unto this place, Sihon the king of Heshbon, and Og the king of Bashan, came out against us unto battle, and we smote them:

8 And we took their land, and gave it for an inheritance unto the Reubenites, and to the Gadites, and to the half tribe of Manasseh.   Num. 32:33; Deut. 3:12-13

9 Keep therefore the words of this covenant, and do them, that ye may prosper in all that ye do.   Deut. 4:6; Josh. 1:7; 1 Kin. 2:3

All Are Presented before the Lord to Enter into His Covenant

10 Ye stand this day all of you before the LORD your God; your captains of your tribes, your elders, and your officers, *with* all the men of Israel,

11 Your little ones, your wives, and thy stranger that *is* in thy camp, from the ᵀhewer of thy wood unto the drawer of thy water: Ex. 12:38 ◆ *woodcutter*

12 That thou shouldest enter into covenant with the LORD thy God, and into his oath, which the LORD thy God maketh with thee this day: 2 Chr. 15:12-15

13 That he may establish thee to day for a people unto himself, and *that* he may be unto thee a God, as he hath said unto thee, and as he hath sworn unto thy fathers, to Abraham, to Isaac, and to Jacob.   Gen. 17:7; Ex. 6:7; Deut. 28:9

14 Neither with you only do I make this covenant and this oath;

15 But with *him* that standeth here with us this day before the LORD our God, and also with *him* that *is* not here with us this day:

16 (For ye know how we have dwelt in the land of Egypt; and how we came through the nations which ye passed by;

17 And ye have seen their abominations, and their idols, wood and stone, silver and gold, which *were* among them:)

18 Lest there should be among you man, or woman, or family, or tribe, whose heart turneth away this day from the LORD our God, to go *and* serve the gods of these nations; lest there should be among you a root that beareth gall and wormwood;   Heb. 12:15

19 And it come to pass, when he heareth the words of this curse, that he bless himself in his heart, saying, I shall have peace, though I walk in the imagination of mine heart, to add drunkenness to thirst: Num. 15:30

20 The LORD will not spare him, but then the anger of the LORD and his jealousy shall smoke against that man, and all the curses that are written in this book shall lie upon him, and the LORD shall blot out his name from under heaven.   Deut. 9:14; Ps. 74:1; 79:5

21 And the LORD shall separate him unto evil out of all the tribes of Israel, according to all the curses of the covenant that are written in this book of the law:

22 So that the generation to come of your children that shall rise up after you, and the stranger that shall come from a far land, shall say, when they see the plagues of that land, and the sicknesses which the LORD hath laid upon it;

23 *And that* the whole land thereof *is* ᵀbrimstone, and salt, *and* burning, *that* it is not sown, nor beareth, nor any grass groweth therein, like the overthrow of Sodom, and Gomorrah, Admah, and Zeboim, which the LORD overthrew in his anger, and in his wrath: Gen. 19:24-25; Jer. 17:6; Zeph. 2:9 ◆ *sulphur*

24 Even all nations shall say, Wherefore hath the LORD done thus unto this land? what *meaneth* the heat of this great anger?   Jer. 22:8-9

25 Then men shall say, Because they have forsaken the covenant of the LORD God of their fathers, which he made with them when he brought them forth out of the land of Egypt:

26 For they went and served other gods, and worshipped them, gods whom they knew not, and *whom* he had not given unto them:

27 And the anger of the LORD was kindled against this land, to bring upon it all the curses that are written in this book:

28 And the LORD rooted them out of their land in anger, and in wrath, and in great indignation, and cast them into another land, as *it is* this day.   1 Kin. 14:15; 2 Chr. 7:20; Ps. 52:5

29 The secret *things belong* unto the LORD our God: but those *things which are* revealed *belong* unto us and to our children for ever, that *we* may do all the words of this law.   Acts 1:7

29:29 Blessing of Bible Study

The idea that certain portions of the Bible cannot be understood has led to neglect of some of its most important truths. The fact needs to be emphasized, and often repeated, that the mysteries of the Bible are not such because God has sought to conceal truth, but because our own weakness or ignorance makes us incapable of comprehending or appropriating truth. The limitation is not in His purpose, but in our capacity. *Ed 171*

Great Mercies Promised to the Repentant

30 And it shall come to pass, when all these things are come upon thee, the blessing and the curse, which I have set before thee, and thou shalt call *them* to mind among all the nations, whither the LORD thy God hath driven thee,　　Deut. 30:15

2 And shalt return unto the LORD thy God, and shalt obey his voice according to all that I command thee this day, thou and thy children, with all thine heart, and with all thy soul;　　Neh. 1:9; Lam. 3:40; Joel 2:12-13

3 That then the LORD thy God will turn thy captivity, and have compassion upon thee, and will return and gather thee from all the nations, whither the LORD thy God hath scattered thee.　　Ps. 147:2

4 If *any* of thine be driven out unto the outmost *parts* of heaven, from thence will the LORD thy God gather thee, and from thence will he fetch thee:　　Deut. 28:64; Neh. 1:9

5 And the LORD thy God will bring thee into the land which thy fathers possessed, and thou shalt possess it; and he will do thee good, and multiply thee above thy fathers.

6 And the LORD thy God will circumcise thine heart, and the heart of thy seed, to love the LORD thy God with all thine heart, and with all thy soul, that thou mayest live.　　Deut. 6:5; 10:16; Jer. 32:39

7 And the LORD thy God will put all these curses upon thine enemies, and on them that hate thee, which persecuted thee.

8 And thou shalt return and obey the voice of the LORD, and do all his commandments which I command thee this day.

9 And the LORD thy God will make thee plenteous in every work of thine hand, in the fruit of thy body, and in the fruit of thy cattle, and in the fruit of thy land, for good: for the LORD will again rejoice over thee for good, as he rejoiced over thy fathers:　　Jer. 32:41

10 If thou shalt hearken unto the voice of the LORD thy God, to keep his commandments and his statutes which are written in this book of the law, *and* if thou turn unto the LORD thy God with all thine heart, and with all thy soul.

The Commandment Is Not Hard

11 For this commandment which I command thee this day, it *is* not hidden from thee, neither *is* it far off.　　Is. 45:19

12 It *is* not in heaven, that thou shouldest say, Who shall go up for us to heaven, and bring it unto us, that we may hear it, and do it?

13 Neither *is* it beyond the sea, that thou shouldest say, Who shall go over the sea for us, and bring it unto us, that we may hear it, and do it?

14 But the word *is* very nigh unto thee, in thy mouth, and in thy heart, that thou mayest do it.

The Choice Between Death and Life

15 See, I have set before thee this day life and good, and death and evil;　　Deut. 11:26; 30:19

> **30:15 Life and Death**
>
> While life is the inheritance of the righteous, death is the portion of the wicked. *GC 544*

16 In that I command thee this day to love the LORD thy God, to walk in his ways, and to keep his commandments and his statutes and his judgments, that thou mayest live and multiply: and the LORD thy God shall bless thee in the land whither thou goest to possess it.　　Deut. 30:6

17 But if thine heart turn away, so that thou

Love and Justice

Deuteronomy 30

Satan deceives many with the plausible theory that God's love for His people is so great that He will excuse sin in them; he represents that while the threatenings of God's word are to serve a certain purpose in His moral government, they are never to be literally fulfilled. But in all His dealings with His creatures God has maintained the principles of righteousness by revealing sin in its true character—by demonstrating that its sure result is misery and death. The unconditional pardon of sin never has been, and never will be. Such pardon would show the abandonment of the principles of righteousness, which are the very foundation of the government of God. It would fill the unfallen universe with consternation. God has faithfully pointed out the results of sin, and if these warnings were not true, how could we be sure that His promises would be fulfilled? That so-called benevolence which would set aside justice is not benevolence but weakness.

God is the life-giver. From the beginning all His laws were ordained to life. But sin broke in upon the order that God had established, and discord followed. So long as sin exists, suffering and death are inevitable. It is only because the Redeemer has borne the curse of sin in our behalf that man can hope to escape, in his own person, its dire results. *PP 522*

wilt not hear, but shalt be drawn away, and worship other gods, and serve them;

18 I denounce unto you this day, that ye shall surely perish, *and that* ye shall not prolong *your* days upon the land, whither thou passest over Jordan to go to possess it.

19 I call heaven and earth to record this day against you, *that* I have set before you life and death, blessing and cursing: therefore choose life, that both thou and thy seed may live: Deut. 4:26

20 That thou mayest love the LORD thy God, *and* that thou mayest obey his voice, and that thou mayest cleave unto him: for he *is* thy life, and the length of thy days: that thou mayest dwell in the land which the LORD sware unto thy fathers, to Abraham, to Isaac, and to Jacob, to give them.   Deut. 10:20; Ps. 27:1; 66:9

30:20 The Head of All Nations

As He had wrought in their deliverance from Egyptian bondage, so would He work mightily in establishing them in the Land of Promise and in placing them at the head of the nations of earth. *PK 393*

Joshua Will Lead the People

31 And Moses went and spake these words unto all Israel.

2 And he said unto them, I *am* an hundred and twenty years old this day; I can no more go out and come in: also the LORD hath said unto me, Thou shalt not go over this Jordan.   Num. 27:17; Deut. 34:7; 1 Kin. 3:7

3 The LORD thy God, he will go over before thee, *and* he will destroy these nations from before thee, and thou shalt possess them: *and* Joshua, he shall go over before thee, as the LORD hath said.   Deut. 3:28; 9:3

31:1–3 Moses' Unfailing Care

The great Ruler of nations had declared that Moses was not to lead the congregation of Israel into the goodly land, and the earnest pleading of God's servant could not secure a reversing of His sentence. He knew that he must die. Yet he had not for a moment faltered in his care for Israel. He had faithfully sought to prepare the congregation to enter upon the promised inheritance. *PP 469*

---

4 And the LORD shall do unto them as he did to Sihon and to Og, kings of the Amorites, and unto the land of them, whom he destroyed.   Deut. 2:33

5 And the LORD shall give them up before your face, that ye may do unto them according unto all the commandments which I have commanded you.   Deut. 7:2

6 Be strong and of a good courage, fear not, nor be afraid of them: for the LORD thy God,

he *it is* that doth go with thee; he will not fail thee, nor forsake thee.   Josh. 10:25; 1 Chr. 22:13

7 And Moses called unto Joshua, and said unto him in the sight of all Israel, Be strong and of a good courage: for thou must go with this people unto the land which the LORD hath sworn unto their fathers to give them; and thou shalt cause them to inherit it.   Deut. 1:38; 3:28; 31:6

8 And the LORD, he *it is* that doth go before thee; he will be with thee, he will not fail thee, neither forsake thee: fear not, neither be dismayed.   Ex. 33:14

Moses Encourages Reading God's Law

9 And Moses wrote this law, and delivered it unto the priests the sons of Levi, which bare the ark of the covenant of the LORD, and unto all the elders of Israel.   Num. 4:15; Josh. 3:3

10 And Moses commanded them, saying, At the end of *every* seven years, in the solemnity of the year of release, in the feast of tabernacles,   Deut. 15:1-2

11 When all Israel is come to appear before the LORD thy God in the place which he shall choose, thou shalt read this law before all Israel in their hearing.   Josh. 8:34-35; 2 Kin. 23:2

12 Gather the people together, men, and women, and children, and thy stranger that *is* within thy gates, that they may hear, and that they may learn, and fear the LORD your God, and observe to do all the words of this law: Deut. 4:10

13 And *that* their children, which have not known *any thing*, may hear, and learn to fear the LORD your God, as long as ye live in the land whither ye go over Jordan to possess it.   Deut. 11:2

God Gives a Charge to Joshua

14 And the LORD said unto Moses, Behold, thy days approach that thou must die: call Joshua, and present yourselves in the tabernacle of the congregation, that I may give him a charge. And Moses and Joshua went, and presented themselves in the tabernacle of the congregation. Num. 27:13; Deut. 31:23; 34:5

15 And the LORD appeared in the tabernacle in a pillar of a cloud: and the pillar of the cloud stood over the door of the tabernacle.

16 And the LORD said unto Moses, Behold, thou shalt sleep with thy fathers; and this people will rise up, and go a whoring after the gods of the strangers of the land, whither they go *to be* among them, and will forsake me, and break my covenant which I have made with them.   Ex. 34:15; Judg. 2:12; 10:6

17 Then my anger shall be kindled against them in that day, and I will forsake them, and I will hide my face from them, and they shall be devoured, and many evils and troubles shall

befall them; so that they will say in that day,
Are not these evils come upon us, because our
God *is* not among us?   Num. 14:42; Judg. 6:13
18 And I will surely hide my face in that
day for all the evils which they shall have
Twrought, in that they are turned unto other
gods.   *done*
19 Now therefore write ye this song for you,
and teach it the children of Israel: put it in
their mouths, that this song may be a witness
for me against the children of Israel. Deut. 6:7
20 For when I shall have brought them into
the land which I sware unto their fathers, that
floweth with milk and honey; and they shall
have eaten and filled themselves, and Twaxen
fat; then will they turn unto other gods, and
serve them, and provoke me, and break my
covenant. Ex. 3:8; Deut. 6:10-12; Neh. 9:25-26 ◆ *become*
21 And it shall come to pass, when many
evils and troubles are befallen them, that
this song shall testify against them as a
witness; for it shall not be forgotten out of
the mouths of their seed: for I know their
imagination which they go about, even now,
before I have brought them into the land
which I sware.   Hos. 5:3
22 Moses therefore wrote this song the
same day, and taught it the children of Israel.   Deut. 31:19
23 And he gave Joshua the son of Nun a
charge, and said, Be strong and of a good
courage: for thou shalt bring the children
of Israel into the land which I sware unto
them: and I will be with thee. Deut. 31:7-8
24 And it came to pass, when Moses had
made an end of writing the words of this law
in a book, until they were finished, Deut. 31:9
25 That Moses commanded the Levites,
which bare the ark of the covenant of the
LORD, saying,
26 Take this book of the law, and put it in
the side of the ark of the covenant of the
LORD your God, that it may be there for a
witness against thee.   Deut. 31:19
27 For I know thy rebellion, and thy stiff
neck: behold, while I am yet alive with you
this day, ye have been rebellious against
the LORD; and how much more after my
death?   Deut. 9:24
28 Gather unto me all the elders of your
tribes, and your officers, that I may speak
these words in their ears, and call heaven and
earth to record against them. Deut. 4:26; 30:19
29 For I know that after my death ye will utterly corrupt *yourselves*, and turn aside from
the way which I have commanded you; and
evil will befall you in the latter days; because
ye will do evil in the sight of the LORD, to
provoke him to anger through the work of
your hands.   Gen. 49:1; Deut. 32:5; Judg. 2:19
30 And Moses spake in the ears of all the
congregation of Israel the words of this
song, until they were ended.

Moses' Song Which Sets Forth God's Mercy and Vengeance

32 Give ear, O ye heavens, and I will
speak; and hear, O earth, the words
of my mouth.   Deut. 4:26
2 My doctrine shall drop as the rain, my
speech shall distil as the dew, as the small
rain upon the tender herb, and as the showers
upon the grass: Job 29:22-23; Ps. 72:6; Is. 55:10-11
3 Because I will publish the name of the
LORD: ascribe ye greatness unto our God.
4 *He is* the Rock, his work *is* perfect: for all his
ways *are* judgment: a God of truth and without iniquity, just and right *is* he.   Ps. 92:15
5 They have corrupted themselves, their
spot *is* not *the spot* of his children: *they are* a
perverse and crooked generation. Deut. 31:29
6 Do ye thus Trequite the LORD, O foolish
people and unwise? *is* not he thy father *that*
hath bought thee? hath he not made thee, and
established thee? Deut. 32:15; Ps. 74:2; Is. 63:16 ◆ *repay*
7 Remember the days of old, consider the
years of many generations: ask thy father,
and he will shew thee; thy elders, and they
will tell thee.   Ex. 13:14; Ps. 44:1; Is. 63:11
8 When the most High divided to the na-
tions their inheritance, when he separated
the sons of Adam, he set the bounds of the
people according to the number of the children of Israel.   Acts 17:26
9 For the LORD's portion *is* his people; Jacob
is the lot of his inheritance.   Jer. 10:16
10 He found him in a desert land, and in the
waste howling wilderness; he led him about,
he instructed him, he kept him as the Tapple
of his eye.   Ps. 17:8; Prov. 7:2; Zech. 2:8 ◆ *pupil*
11 As an eagle stirreth up her nest, fluttereth
over her young, spreadeth abroad her wings,
taketh them, beareth them on her wings:
12 *So* the LORD alone did lead him, and *there*
was no strange god with him.   Ps. 78:52-53
13 He made him ride on the high places of
the earth, that he might eat the increase of
the fields; and he made him to suck honey
out of the rock, and oil out of the flinty
rock;   Job 29:6; Ps. 81:16; Is. 58:14
14 Butter of Tkine, and milk of sheep,
with fat of lambs, and rams of the breed of
Bashan, and goats, with the fat of kidneys of
wheat; and thou didst drink the pure blood
of the grape.   Gen. 49:11; Ps. 81:16; 147:14 ◆ *cows*
15 But Jeshurun Twaxed fat, and kicked: thou
art Twaxen fat, thou art grown thick, thou
art covered *with fatness*; then he forsook God
which made him, and lightly esteemed the
Rock of his salvation.   Ps. 89:26 ◆ *became* ◆ *become*
16 They provoked him to jealousy with
strange *gods*, with abominations provoked
they him to anger.   Ps. 78:58
17 They sacrificed unto devils, not to God;
to gods whom they knew not, to new *gods*
that came newly up, whom your fathers
feared not.   Lev. 17:7; Deut. 28:64; Judg. 5:8

18 Of the Rock that ᵀbegat thee thou art unmindful, and hast forgotten God that formed thee.   Deut. 32:4; Ps. 106:21; Is. 17:10 ◆ brought forth
19 And when the LORD saw it, he ᵀabhorred them, because of the provoking of his sons, and of his daughters.   Ps. 106:40 ◆ despised
20 And he said, I will hide my face from them, I will see what their end shall be: for they are a very ᵀfroward generation, children in whom is no faith.   Deut. 32:5 ◆ false, perverse
21 They have moved me to jealousy with that which is not God; they have provoked me to anger with their vanities: and I will move them to jealousy with those which are not a people; I will provoke them to anger with a foolish nation.   1 Kin. 16:13, 26; Rom. 10:19
22 For a fire is kindled in mine anger, and shall burn unto the lowest hell, and shall consume the earth with her increase, and set on fire the foundations of the mountains.   Num. 16:35; Jer. 15:14; Lam. 4:11
23 I will heap mischiefs upon them; I will spend mine arrows upon them.   Ezek. 5:16
24 They shall be burnt with hunger, and devoured with burning heat, and with bitter destruction: I will also send the teeth of beasts upon them, with the poison of serpents of the dust.   Lev. 26:22; Ezek. 5:17
25 The sword without, and terror within, shall destroy both the young man and the virgin, the suckling also with the man of gray hairs.   Lam. 1:20; Ezek. 7:15
26 I said, I would scatter them into corners, I would make the remembrance of them to cease from among men: Deut. 28:64
27 Were it not that I feared the wrath of the enemy, lest their adversaries should behave themselves strangely, and lest they should say, Our hand is high, and the LORD hath not done all this.   Ps. 140:8
28 For they are a nation void of counsel, neither is there any understanding in them.
29 O that they were wise, that they understood this, that they would consider their latter end!   Deut. 5:29; Ps. 81:13; Is. 47:7
30 How should one chase a thousand, and two put ten thousand to flight, except their Rock had sold them, and the LORD had shut them up?   Lev. 26:8; Judg. 2:14; Ps. 44:12
31 For their rock is not as our Rock, even our enemies themselves being judges.Ex.14:25
32 For their vine is of the vine of Sodom, and of the fields of Gomorrah: their grapes are grapes of gall, their clusters are bitter:
33 Their wine is the poison of dragons, and the cruel venom of asps.   Ps. 58:4
34 Is not this laid up in store with me, and sealed up among my treasures?   Job 14:17
35 To me belongeth vengeance, and recompence; their foot shall slide in due time: for the day of their calamity is at hand, and the things that shall come upon them make haste.
36 For the LORD shall judge his people, and

repent himself for his servants, when he seeth that their power is gone, and there is none shut up, or left.   Judg. 2:18; 1 Kin. 14:10; Ps. 135:14
37 And he shall say, Where are their gods, their rock in whom they trusted,   Jer. 2:28
38 Which did eat the fat of their sacrifices, and drank the wine of their drink offerings? let them rise up and help you, and be your protection.
39 See now that I, even I, am he, and there is no god with me: I kill, and I make alive; I wound, and I heal: neither is there any that can deliver out of my hand.   1 Sam. 2:6; Is. 41:4; 45:5
40 For I lift up my hand to heaven, and say, I live for ever.   Gen. 14:22
41 If I ᵀwhet my glittering sword, and mine hand take hold on judgment; I will render vengeance to mine enemies, and will reward them that hate me.   Is. 66:16 ◆ sharpen
42 I will make mine arrows drunk with blood, and my sword shall devour flesh; and that with the blood of the slain and of the captives, from the beginning of revenges upon the enemy.   Deut. 32:23
43 Rejoice, O ye nations, with his people: for he will avenge the blood of his servants, and will render vengeance to his adversaries, and will be merciful unto his land, and to his people.   Ps. 85:1; Rev. 6:10; 19:2
44 And Moses came and spake all the words of this song in the ears of the people, he, and Hoshea the son of Nun.   Num. 13:8, 16
45 And Moses made an end of speaking all these words to all Israel:
46 And he said unto them, Set your hearts unto all the words which I testify among you this day, which ye shall command your children to observe to do, all the words of this law.   Ezek. 40:4
47 For it is not a vain thing for you; because it is your life: and through this thing ye shall prolong your days in the land, whither ye go over Jordan to possess it.   Lev. 18:5
48 And the LORD spake unto Moses that selfsame day, saying,
49 Get thee up into this mountain Abarim, unto mount Nebo, which is in the land of Moab, that is over against Jericho; and behold the land of Canaan, which I give unto the children of Israel for a possession: Num. 27:12
50 And die in the mount whither thou goest up, and be gathered unto thy people; as Aaron thy brother died in mount Hor, and was gathered unto his people: Gen. 25:8
51 Because ye ᵀtrespassed against me among the children of Israel at the waters of Meribah-Kadesh, in the wilderness of Zin; because ye ᵀsanctified me not in the midst of the children of Israel.   Num. 27:14 ◆ sinned ◆ made me holy
52 Yet thou shalt see the land before thee; but thou shalt not go thither unto the land which I give the children of Israel.   Deut. 34:1-4

32:48–52 Lost in a Single Moment

Had these servants of God, when they stood before the rock at Kadesh, borne unmurmuringly the test there brought upon them, how different would have been their future! A wrong act can never be undone. It may be that the work of a lifetime will not recover what has been lost in a single moment of temptation or even thoughtlessness. *PP 426*

The Blessings of the Twelve Tribes

33 And this *is* the blessing, wherewith Moses the man of God blessed the children of Israel before his death.   Josh. 14:6
2 And he said, The LORD came from Sinai, and rose up from Seir unto them; he shined forth from mount Paran, and he came with ten thousands of saints: from his right hand *went* a fiery law for them.   Hab. 3:3; Acts 7:53
3 Yea, he loved the people; all his saints *are* in thy hand: and they sat down at thy feet; *every one* shall receive of thy words. Hos. 11:1; Luke 10:39
4 Moses commanded us a law, *even* the inheritance of the congregation of Jacob. Ps. 119:111
5 And he was king in Jeshurun, when the heads of the people *and* the tribes of Israel were gathered together.   Deut. 32:15
6 Let Reuben live, and not die; and let *not* his men be few.   Gen. 49:3-4
7 And this *is the blessing* of Judah: and he said, Hear, LORD, the voice of Judah, and bring him unto his people: let his hands be sufficient for him; and be thou an help *to him* from his enemies.   Gen. 49:8-12
8 And of Levi he said, *Let* thy Thummim and thy Urim *be* with thy holy one, whom thou didst prove at Massah, *and with* whom thou didst strive at the waters of Meribah; Ex. 17:7
9 Who said unto his father and to his mother, I have not seen him; neither did he acknowledge his brethren, nor knew his own children: for they have observed thy word, and kept thy covenant.
10 They shall teach Jacob thy judgments, and Israel thy law: they shall put incense before thee, and whole burnt sacrifice upon thine altar.   Ex. 30:7-8; Lev. 10:11; Ps. 51:19
11 Bless, LORD, his substance, and accept the work of his hands: ᵀsmite through the ᵀloins of them that rise against him, and of them that hate him, that they rise not again.   2 Sam. 24:23 ◆ *strike* ◆ *waist*
12 *And* of Benjamin he said, The beloved of the LORD shall dwell in safety by him; *and the LORD* shall cover him all the day long, and he shall dwell between his shoulders.
13 And of Joseph he said, Blessed of the LORD *be* his land, for the precious things of heaven, for the dew, and for the deep that coucheth beneath,   Gen. 49:22-26
14 And for the precious fruits *brought forth*

by the sun, and for the precious things put forth by the moon,
15 And for the chief things of the ancient mountains, and for the precious things of the lasting hills,   Gen. 49:26; Hab. 3:6
16 And for the precious things of the earth and fulness thereof, and *for the* good will of him that dwelt in the bush: let *the blessing* come upon the head of Joseph, and upon the top of the head of him *that was* separated from his brethren.   Ex. 3:2-4
17 His glory *is like* the ᵀfirstling of his ᵀbullock, and his horns *are like* the horns of unicorns: with them he shall push the people together to the ends of the earth: and they *are* the ten thousands of Ephraim, and they *are* the thousands of Manasseh.   Ps. 44:5 ◆ *firstborn* ◆ *bull*
18 And of Zebulun he said, Rejoice, Zebulun, in thy going out; and, Issachar, in thy tents.   Gen. 49:13-15
19 They shall call the people unto the mountain; there they shall offer sacrifices of righteousness: for they shall suck *of the* abundance of the seas, and *of* treasures hid in the sand.   Ps. 4:5; Is. 2:3; 60:5
20 And of Gad he said, Blessed *be* he that enlargeth Gad: he dwelleth as a lion, and teareth the arm with the crown of the head. Gen. 49:19
21 And he provided the first part for himself, because there, *in* a portion of the lawgiver, *was he* seated; and he came with the heads of the people, he executed the justice of the LORD, and his judgments with Israel. Josh. 1:14
22 And of Dan he said, Dan *is* a lion's whelp: he shall leap from Bashan.   Josh. 19:47
23 And of Naphtali he said, O Naphtali, satisfied with favour, and full with the blessing of the LORD: possess thou the west and the south.   Gen. 49:21
24 And of Asher he said, *Let* Asher *be* blessed with children; let him be acceptable to his brethren, and let him dip his foot in oil.   Gen. 49:20; Job 29:6
25 Thy shoes *shall be* iron and brass; and as thy days, *so shall* thy strength *be*.

The Everlasting Arms of the Eternal God

26 *There is* none like unto the God of Jeshurun, *who* rideth upon the heaven in thy help, and in his excellency on the sky.   Ex. 15:11
27 The eternal God *is thy* refuge, and underneath *are* the everlasting arms: and he shall thrust out the enemy from before thee; and shall say, Destroy *them*.   Gen. 49:24
28 Israel then shall dwell in safety alone: the fountain of Jacob *shall be* upon a land of corn and wine; also his heavens shall drop down dew.   Gen. 27:28; Num. 23:9; Jer. 23:6
29 Happy *art* thou, O Israel: who *is* like unto thee, O people saved by the LORD, the shield of thy help, and who *is* the sword of thy excellency! and thine enemies shall be found

liars unto thee; and thou shalt tread upon their high places. Gen. 15:1; 2 Sam. 7:23; Ps. 115:9-11

33:26–29 Blessing and Benediction

For the last time Moses stood in the assembly of his people. Again the Spirit of God rested upon him, and in the most sublime and touching language he pronounced a blessing upon each of the tribes, closing with a benediction upon them all. *PP 471*

Moses Views the Land from Mount Nebo

34 And Moses went up from the plains of Moab unto the mountain of Nebo, to the top of Pisgah, that *is* over against Jericho. And the LORD shewed him all the land of Gilead, unto Dan,   Deut. 32:49
2 And all Naphtali, and the land of Ephraim, and Manasseh, and all the land of Judah, unto the utmost sea,   Deut. 11:24
3 And the south, and the plain of the valley of Jericho, the city of palm trees, unto Zoar.
4 And the LORD said unto him, This *is* the land which I sware unto Abraham, unto Isaac, and unto Jacob, saying, I will give it unto thy seed: I have caused thee to see *it* with thine eyes, but thou shalt not go over thither.   Gen. 12:7; 26:3; 28:13

Moses Dies in the Land of Moab

5 So Moses the servant of the LORD died there in the land of Moab, according to the word of the LORD.   Deut. 32:50
6 And he buried him in a valley in the land of Moab, over against Beth-peor: but no man knoweth of his sepulchre unto this day. Jude 9

7 And Moses *was* an hundred and twenty years old when he died: his eye was not dim, nor his natural force ᵀabated. Gen. 27:1 ♦ *diminished*
8 And the children of Israel wept for Moses in the plains of Moab thirty days: so the days of weeping *and* mourning for Moses were ended.   Gen. 50:3

Joshua Succeeds Moses

9 And Joshua the son of Nun was full of the spirit of wisdom; for Moses had laid his hands upon him: and the children of Israel hearkened unto him, and did as the LORD commanded Moses.   Is. 11:2; Dan. 6:3
10 And there arose not a prophet since in Israel like unto Moses, whom the LORD knew face to face,   Ex. 33:11

34:10 The Desert Education

Such was the experience that Moses gained by his forty years of training in the desert. To impart such an experience, Infinite Wisdom counted not the period too long or the price too great. The results of that training, of the lessons there taught, are bound up, not only with the history of Israel, but with all which from that day to this has told for the world's progress. *Ed 64*

11 In all the signs and the wonders, which the LORD sent him to do in the land of Egypt to Pharaoh, and to all his servants, and to all his land,   Deut. 4:34
12 And in all that mighty hand, and in all the great terror which Moses shewed in the sight of all Israel.

A Wise Decision

Deuteronomy 34

In solitude Moses reviewed his life of vicissitudes and hardships since he turned from courtly honors and from a prospective kingdom in Egypt, to cast in his lot with God's chosen people. He called to mind those long years in the desert with the flocks of Jethro, the appearance of the Angel in the burning bush, and his own call to deliver Israel. Again he beheld the mighty miracles of God's power displayed in behalf of the chosen people, and His long-suffering mercy during the years of their wandering and rebellion.

Notwithstanding all that God had wrought for them, notwithstanding his own prayers and labors, only two of all the adults in the vast army that left Egypt had been found so faithful that they could enter the Promised Land. As Moses reviewed the result of his labors, his life of trial and sacrifice seemed to have been almost in vain.

Yet he did not regret the burdens he had borne. He knew that his mission and work were of God's own appointing. When first called to become the leader of Israel from bondage, he shrank from the responsibility; but since he had taken up the work he had not cast aside the burden. Even when the Lord had proposed to release him, and destroy rebellious Israel, Moses could not consent. Though his trials had been great, he had enjoyed special tokens of God's favor; he had obtained a rich experience during the sojourn in the wilderness, in witnessing the manifestations of God's power and glory, and in the communion of His love; he felt that he had made a wise decision in choosing to suffer affliction with the people of God, rather than to enjoy the pleasures of sin for a season. *PP 471, 472*

THE BOOK OF

JOSHUA

"Be strong and of a good courage." This command from the Lord is repeated several times in the Book of Joshua and serves as a banner of victory regarding things to come for the nation of Israel. They are about to face many challenges that only God can help them to overcome.

The Book of Joshua is about courage and faith. The people needed courage to move into the Promised Land. The previous generation's lack of courage had sent the nation wandering in the wilderness for forty years. Would they have the faith to follow through this time? Would they have the courage against the challenges that lay ahead?

Joshua is also about people. We read of Joshua, Rahab, Achan, and Caleb, and how their faith—or lack of it—played a key role in significant events. Through their experiences we learn to trust God's Word and obey His commands and that disobedience leads to consequences.

In the library of Scripture, Joshua serves as a connection between the books of the Pentateuch and the historical books. Joshua begins to tell the story of the history of Israel—from the death of Moses to the Book of Ruth.

Dates

The dates of Joshua run from roughly early 1405 B.C. through the death of Joshua in 1380 B.C. Using this as a general guideline, the dates are approximately as follows:
(1) *Joshua 1—5: March through April, 1405 B.C.*
(2) *Joshua 6—13: April 1405–1398 B.C.*
(3) *Joshua 13—21: 1398/7–1380 B.C.*
(4) *Joshua 22—24: 1380 B.C.* Joshua's death being noted in 1380 B.C.

Author

Jewish tradition holds that Joshua was the author of the book named after him. The book's style and structure give the impression that it was written by one author, with the exception of a few short sections that were most likely added after Joshua's death:
(1) The capture of Kirjath-sepher by Othniel, nephew of Caleb (15:13–19)
(2) The tribe of Dan's move north (19:47)
(3) Joshua's death and burial (24:29–33).

Since Joshua is the main character in the book, he is best positioned to write an account of what took place during his lifetime and the early history of Israel. Joshua 24:26 provides added evidence for his authorship: "And Joshua wrote these words in the book of the law of God."

Joshua had been born in Egypt and was part of the great Exodus under Moses. He became an assistant to Moses and was one of the twelve spies who entered Canaan (but only he and Caleb returned with faithful encouragement to enter the land, Numbers 14:5–9). He then suffered along with the rest of the nation in the wilderness wanderings but, because of his faith, did not die in the wilderness. Instead, as noted at the end of the Book of Deuteronomy, God instructed Moses to pass on to Joshua the leadership of the nation (Deuteronomy 31:14).

The lessons Joshua learned are apt both for Israel and also for every growing believer: obey God, follow His Word, and face life's battles courageously, even when the odds are against you.

Meaning of the Name

The name Joshua, for which the book is titled, means "Jehovah-saved" or "Yahweh is salvation." The Hebrew form of Joshua is *Yehoshua*. In the Greek, it is *Ieosous* or Jesus.

Christ in Joshua

While there are no messianic prophecies in Joshua, the book is filled with reminders of Christ. Joshua had the kind of leadership that Christ later modeled. Perhaps the most telling example is how Joshua leads Israel to take full possession of the land to which they

were promised (chapters 3—4). This is indeed similar to how Christ leads His followers into the Promised Land of eternal life for those who call upon His name for forgiveness and salvation (John 3:16).

The Book of Joshua also includes an appearance by a pre-incarnate Christ, the "captain of the host of the LORD," in Joshua 5:13–15 just before the battle of Jericho. Also, the scarlet line that Rahab hangs out her window as a sign of protection from the invaders (2:21) is seen as a symbol of the atoning blood of Christ. In addition, Rahab appears in the ancestral line of Jesus Christ (Matthew 1:5).

Overview

The book of Joshua can easily be divided into four parts:

(1) *Joshua 1—5, Entering the Promised Land:* The first five chapters show Israel's transition: the death of Moses, the new leadership of Joshua, crossing the Jordan River, and the preparation for battle against the enemies of Israel. Joshua sends out spies to Jericho and gains an ally in Rahab (chapter 2).

(2) *Joshua 6—12, Conquering the Promised Land:* God leads Israel from one decisive victory to the next in Canaan. But Israel stumbles at Ai because of the sin of Achan (chapter 7). After Joshua discovers the culprit and deals with the matter through execution, the victories continue.

(3) *Joshua 13—21, Distribution of the Promised Land:* This long process is completed through the use of lots. The division included six cities of refuge and forty-eight cities for the Levites.

(4) *Joshua 22—24, Epilogue, Ending an Era:* Chapters 22 through 24 highlight Joshua's role as leader of the people and culminates in his farewell address to them, where he exhorts them to serve the Lord and put off all other gods. The book ends with Joshua's death at 110 years of age.

Unlocking Joshua

KEY PEOPLE:
Joshua, Achan, Rahab, Caleb, Othniel

KEY EVENTS:
Crossing the Jordan River; alliance with Rahab; conquering Jericho; the sin of Achan; defeating many peoples/nations; the sun standing still; the death of Joshua

KEY WORD:
Conquest, in the Book of Joshua, is central to the book's message. Israel, under the leadership of Joshua, conquered many cities in Canaan. The book ends with the ultimate conquest of attaining and settling into the Promised Land.

KEY VERSES:
"This book of the law shall not depart out of thy mouth; but thou shalt meditate therein day and night, that thou mayest observe to do according to all that is written therein: for then thou shalt make thy way prosperous, and then thou shalt have good success. Have not I commanded thee? Be strong and of a good courage; be not afraid, neither be thou dismayed: for the LORD thy God is with thee whithersoever thou goest" (Joshua 1:8, 9).

"So Joshua took the whole land, according to all that the LORD said unto Moses; and Joshua gave it for an inheritance unto Israel according to their divisions by their tribes. And the land rested from war" (Joshua 11:23).

KEY CHAPTER:
Joshua 24, where Joshua gathers all the people of Israel for his farewell address. Joshua gives a brief history of Israel and encourages the people to trust the Lord and put away the false gods that their ancestors worshiped.

The Lord Appoints Joshua to Succeed Moses

1 Now after the death of Moses the servant of the LORD it came to pass, that the LORD spake unto Joshua the son of Nun, Moses' minister, saying,   Ex. 24:13
2 Moses my servant is dead; now therefore arise, go over this Jordan, thou, and all this people, unto the land which I do give to them, *even* to the children of Israel.
3 Every place that the sole of your foot shall tread upon, that have I given unto you, as I said unto Moses.   Deut. 11:24; Josh. 14:9

1:2, 3 A Leader of Strong Character

Courageous, resolute, and persevering, prompt, incorruptible, unmindful of selfish interests in his care for those committed to his charge, and, above all, inspired by a living faith in God—such was the character of the man divinely chosen to conduct the armies of Israel . . . by his quiet, unpretending fidelity, his steadfastness when others wavered, his firmness to maintain the truth in the midst of danger, [Joshua] had given evidence of his fitness to succeed Moses. . . . *PP 481, 482*

4 From the wilderness and this Lebanon even unto the great river, the river Euphrates, all the land of the Hittites, and unto the great sea toward the going down of the sun, shall be your coast.   Ex. 23:31
5 There shall not any man be able to stand before thee all the days of thy life: as I was with Moses, *so* I will be with thee: I will not fail thee, nor forsake thee.   Deut. 7:24; Josh. 1:17
6 Be strong and of a good courage: for unto this people shalt thou divide for an inheritance the land, which I sware unto their fathers to give them.   Josh. 1:7
7 Only be thou strong and very courageous, that thou mayest observe to do according to all the law, which Moses my servant commanded thee: turn not from it *to* the right hand or *to* the left, that thou mayest prosper whithersoever thou goest.   Deut. 5:32; 28:14

1:8 Remembering the Law

In the days of the wilderness wandering the Lord had made abundant provision for His children to keep in remembrance the words of His law. After the settlement in Canaan the divine precepts were to be repeated daily in every home; they were to be written plainly upon the doorposts and gates, and spread upon memorial tablets. They were to be set to music and chanted by young and old. *PK 464, 465*

8 This book of the law shall not depart out of thy mouth; but thou shalt meditate therein day and night, that thou mayest observe to do according to all that is written therein: for then thou shalt make thy way prosperous, and then thou shalt have good success.   Ps. 19:14
9 Have not I commanded thee? Be strong and of a good courage; be not afraid, neither be thou dismayed: for the LORD thy God *is* with thee whithersoever thou goest.   Gen. 28:15

Joshua Prepares the People to Pass over Jordan

10 Then Joshua commanded the officers of the people, saying,
11 Pass through the host, and command the people, saying, Prepare you victuals; for within three days ye shall pass over this Jordan, to go in to possess the land, which the LORD your God giveth you to possess it.   Josh. 3:2 ◆ food
12 And to the Reubenites, and to the Gadites, and to half the tribe of Manasseh, spake Joshua, saying,
13 Remember the word which Moses the servant of the LORD commanded you, saying, The LORD your God hath given you rest, and hath given you this land.   Num. 32:20-28
14 Your wives, your little ones, and your cattle, shall remain in the land which Moses gave you on this side Jordan; but ye shall pass before your brethren armed, all the mighty men of valour, and help them;
15 Until the LORD have given your brethren rest, as *he hath given* you, and they also have possessed the land which the LORD your God giveth them: then ye shall return unto the land of your possession, and enjoy it, which Moses the LORD's servant gave you on this side Jordan toward the sunrising.

The People Pledge Allegiance to Joshua

16 And they answered Joshua, saying, All that thou commandest us we will do, and whithersoever thou sendest us, we will go.
17 According as we hearkened unto Moses in all things, so will we hearken unto thee: only the LORD thy God be with thee, as he was with Moses.   Josh. 1:5
18 Whosoever *he be* that doth rebel against thy commandment, and will not hearken unto thy words in all that thou commandest him, he shall be put to death: only be strong and of a good courage.   Josh. 1:6-7

Two Spies Are Sent from Shittim and Rahab Aids Them

2 And Joshua the son of Nun sent out of Shittim two men to spy secretly, saying, Go view the land, even Jericho. And they went, and came into an harlot's house, named Rahab, and lodged there.   Heb. 11:31; James 2:25
2 And it was told the king of Jericho, saying,

Behold, there came men in ᵀThither to night of the children of Israel to search out the country. here

3 And the king of Jericho sent unto Rahab, saying, Bring forth the men that are come to thee, which are entered into thine house: for they be come to search out all the country.

4 And the woman took the two men, and hid them, and said thus, There came men unto me, but I ᵀwist not whence they were: 2 Sam. 17:19-20 ♦ knew

5 And it came to pass about the time of shutting of the gate, when it was dark, that the men went out: whither the men went I ᵀwot not: pursue after them quickly; for ye shall overtake them. know

6 But she had brought them up to the roof of the house, and hid them with the stalks of flax, which she had laid in order upon the roof. 2 Sam. 17:19

7 And the men pursued after them the way to Jordan unto the fords: and as soon as they which pursued after them were gone out, they shut the gate. Judg. 3:28

The Spies Make a Promise to Rahab

8 And before they were laid down, she came up unto them upon the roof;

9 And she said unto the men, I know that the LORD hath given you the land, and that your terror is fallen upon us, and that all the inhabitants of the land faint because of you. Gen. 35:5; Ex. 23:27; Deut. 2:25

10 For we have heard how the LORD dried up the water of the Red sea for you, when ye came out of Egypt; and what ye did unto the two kings of the Amorites, that were on the other side Jordan, Sihon and Og, whom ye utterly destroyed. Num. 21:21-35

11 And as soon as we had heard these things, our hearts did melt, neither did there remain any more courage in any man, because of you: for the LORD your God, he is God in heaven above, and in earth beneath. Deut. 4:39; Josh. 5:1; 7:5

> **2:10, 11 Intimidating the Nations**
> This exercise of divine power in behalf of Israel was designed also to increase the fear with which they were regarded by the surrounding nations, and thus prepare the way for their easier and complete triumph. When the tidings that God had stayed the waters of Jordan before the children of Israel, reached the kings of the Amorites and of the Canaanites, their hearts melted with fear. *PP 485*

12 Now therefore, I pray you, swear unto me by the LORD, since I have shewed you kindness, that ye will also shew kindness unto my father's house, and give me a true token: Josh. 2:18

13 And that ye will save alive my father, and my mother, and my brethren, and my sisters, and all that they have, and deliver our lives from death.

14 And the men answered her, Our life for yours, if ye utter not this our business. And it shall be, when the LORD hath given us the land, that we will deal kindly and truly with thee. Gen. 24:49

15 Then she let them down by a cord through the window: for her house was upon the town wall, and she dwelt upon the wall. Acts 9:25

16 And she said unto them, Get you to the mountain, lest the pursuers meet you; and hide yourselves there three days, until the pursuers be returned: and afterward may ye go your way.

17 And the men said unto her, We will be blameless of this thine oath which thou hast made us swear.

18 Behold, when we come into the land, thou shalt bind this line of scarlet thread in the window which thou didst let us down by: and thou shalt bring thy father, and thy mother, and thy brethren, and all thy father's household, home unto thee. Josh. 6:23

19 And it shall be, that whosoever shall go out of the doors of thy house into the street, his blood shall be upon his head, and we will be guiltless: and whosoever shall be with thee in the house, his blood shall be on our head, if any hand be upon him.

20 And if thou utter this our business, then we will be ᵀquit of thine oath which thou hast made us to swear. free

21 And she said, According unto your words, so be it. And she sent them away, and they departed: and she bound the scarlet line in the window.

22 And they went, and came unto the mountain, and abode there three days, until the pursuers were returned: and the pursuers sought them throughout all the way, but found them not.

23 So the two men returned, and descended from the mountain, and passed over, and came to Joshua the son of Nun, and told him all things that befell them:

24 And they said unto Joshua, Truly the LORD hath delivered into our hands all the land; for even all the inhabitants of the country do faint because of us. Ex. 23:31

Crossing the Jordan River

3 And Joshua rose early in the morning; and they removed from Shittim, and came to Jordan, he and all the children of

Israel, and lodged there before they passed over. Josh. 2:1

2 And it came to pass after three days, that the officers went through the host; Josh. 1:10-11

3 And they commanded the people, saying, When ye see the ark of the covenant of the LORD your God, and the priests the Levites bearing it, then ye shall remove from your place, and go after it. Num. 10:33; Deut. 31:9, 25

4 Yet there shall be a space between you and it, about two thousand cubits by measure: come not near unto it, that ye may know the way by which ye must go: for ye have not passed *this* way Theretofore. Ex. 19:12 ◆ *before*

5 And Joshua said unto the people, Sanctify yourselves: for to morrow the LORD will do wonders among you. Lev. 20:7; Josh. 7:13; 1 Sam. 16:5

6 And Joshua spake unto the priests, saying, Take up the ark of the covenant, and pass over before the people. And they took up the ark of the covenant, and went before the people.

The Lord Encourages Joshua

7 And the LORD said unto Joshua, This day will I begin to magnify thee in the sight of all Israel, that they may know that, as I was with Moses, *so* I will be with thee. Josh. 1:5; 1 Chr. 29:25

8 And thou shalt command the priests that bear the ark of the covenant, saying, When ye are come to the brink of the water of Jordan, ye shall stand still in Jordan. Josh. 3:3

9 And Joshua said unto the children of Israel, Come Thither, and hear the words of the LORD your God. *here*

10 And Joshua said, Hereby ye shall know that the living God *is* among you, and *that* he will without fail drive out from before you the Canaanites, and the Hittites, and the Hivites, and the Perizzites, and the Girgashites, and the Amorites, and the Jebusites. Ex. 33:2; Deut. 5:26; 7:1

11 Behold, the ark of the covenant of the Lord of all the earth passeth over before you into Jordan. Josh. 3:13; Ps. 24:1; Zech. 6:5

12 Now therefore take you twelve men out of the tribes of Israel, out of every tribe a man. Josh. 4:2

3:13 God Tests His People's Faith

In the upbuilding of His work the Lord does not always make everything plain before His servants. He sometimes tries the confidence of His people by bringing about circumstances which compel them to move forward in faith. Often He brings them into strait and trying places, and bids them advance when their feet seem to be touching the waters of Jordan. *AA 357*

13 And it shall come to pass, as soon as the soles of the feet of the priests that bear the ark of the LORD, the Lord of all the earth, shall rest in the waters of Jordan, *that* the waters of Jordan shall be cut off *from* the waters that come down from above; and they shall stand upon an heap. Ex. 15:8; Josh. 3:15-16; Ps. 78:13

The Jordan River Is Divided

14 And it came to pass, when the people removed from their tents, to pass over Jordan, and the priests bearing the ark of the covenant before the people; Acts 7:44-45

15 And as they that bare the ark were come unto Jordan, and the feet of the priests that bare the ark were dipped in the brim of the water, (for Jordan overfloweth all his banks all the time of harvest,) Josh. 4:18; 1 Chr. 12:15; Jer. 12:5

16 That the waters which came down from above stood *and* rose up upon an heap very far from the city Adam, that *is* beside Zaretan: and those that came down toward the sea of the plain, *even* the salt sea, failed, *and* were cut off: and the people passed over right against Jericho. Gen. 14:3

17 And the priests that bare the ark of the covenant of the LORD stood firm on dry ground in the midst of Jordan, and all the Israelites passed over on dry ground, until all the people were passed clean over Jordan. Ex. 14:22, 29

Twelve Stones Are Taken from the Jordan River for a Memorial

4 And it came to pass, when all the people were clean passed over Jordan, that the LORD spake unto Joshua, saying, Deut. 27:2

2 Take you twelve men out of the people, out of every tribe a man, Josh. 3:12

3 And command ye them, saying, Take you hence out of the midst of Jordan, out of the place where the priests' feet stood firm, twelve stones, and ye shall carry them over with you, and leave them in the lodging place, where ye shall lodge this night. Josh. 4:19-20

4:3 Monument to a Miracle

Coming generations were not to be without a witness to this great miracle. While the priests bearing the ark were still in the midst of Jordan, twelve men previously chosen, one from each tribe, took up each a stone from the river bed where the priests were standing, and carried it over to the western side. These stones were to be set up as a monument in the first camping place beyond the river. *PP 484*

4 Then Joshua called the twelve men, whom he had prepared of the children of Israel, out of every tribe a man:

5 And Joshua said unto them, Pass over

before the ark of the Lord your God into the midst of Jordan, and take ye up every man of you a stone upon his shoulder, according unto the number of the tribes of the children of Israel:

6 That this may be a sign among you, *that* when your children ask *their fathers* in time to come, saying, What *mean* ye by these stones? Ex. 13:14; Josh. 4:21

7 Then ye shall answer them, That the waters of Jordan were cut off before the ark of the covenant of the Lord; when it passed over Jordan, the waters of Jordan were cut off: and these stones shall be for a memorial unto the children of Israel for ever. Ex. 12:14

8 And the children of Israel did so as Joshua commanded, and took up twelve stones out of the midst of Jordan, as the Lord spake unto Joshua, according to the number of the tribes of the children of Israel, and carried them over with them unto the place where they lodged, and laid them down there.

9 And Joshua set up twelve stones in the midst of Jordan, in the place where the feet of the priests which bare the ark of the covenant stood: and they are there unto this day.

The Jordan River's Water Returns

10 For the priests which bare the ark stood in the midst of Jordan, until every thing was finished that the Lord commanded Joshua to speak unto the people, according to all that Moses commanded Joshua: and the people hasted and passed over.

11 And it came to pass, when all the people were clean passed over, that the ark of the Lord passed over, and the priests, in the presence of the people.

12 And the children of Reuben, and the children of Gad, and half the tribe of Manasseh, passed over armed before the children of Israel, as Moses spake unto them:

13 About forty thousand prepared for war passed over before the Lord unto battle, to the plains of Jericho.

14 On that day the Lord magnified Joshua in the sight of all Israel; and they feared him, as they feared Moses, all the days of his life. Josh. 3:7

15 And the Lord spake unto Joshua, saying,

16 Command the priests that bear the ark of the testimony, that they come up out of Jordan.

17 Joshua therefore commanded the priests, saying, Come ye up out of Jordan.

18 And it came to pass, when the priests that bare the ark of the covenant of the Lord were come up out of the midst of Jordan, *and* the soles of the priests' feet were lifted up unto the dry land, that the waters of Jordan

returned unto their place, and flowed over all his banks, as *they did* before. Josh. 3:15

19 And the people came up out of Jordan on the tenth *day* of the first month, and encamped in Gilgal, in the east border of Jericho. Josh. 5:9

The Twelve Stones Are Set up in Gilgal

20 And those twelve stones, which they took out of Jordan, did Joshua pitch in Gilgal. Josh. 4:3, 8

21 And he spake unto the children of Israel, saying, When your children shall ask their fathers in time to come, saying, What *mean* these stones? Josh. 4:6

22 Then ye shall let your children know, saying, Israel came over this Jordan on dry land. Josh. 3:17

23 For the Lord your God dried up the waters of Jordan from before you, until ye were passed over, as the Lord your God did to the Red sea, which he dried up from before us, until we were gone over: Ex. 14:21

24 That all the people of the earth might know the hand of the Lord, that it *is* mighty: that ye might fear the Lord your God for ever. Ex. 14:31; 15:16; Ps. 89:13

Preparations for the Passover

5 And it came to pass, when all the kings of the Amorites, which *were* on the side of Jordan westward, and all the kings of the Canaanites, which *were* by the sea, heard that the Lord had dried up the waters of Jordan from before the children of Israel, until we were passed over, that their heart melted, neither was there spirit in them any more, because of the children of Israel. Num. 13:29; Josh. 2:9-11; 1 Kin. 10:5

> **5:1 Evidence of God's Presence**
>
> To the Canaanites, to all Israel, and to Joshua himself, unmistakable evidence had been given that the living God, the King of heaven and earth, was among His people, and that He would not fail them nor forsake them. *PP 485*

2 At that time the Lord said unto Joshua, Make thee sharp knives, and circumcise again the children of Israel the second time. Ex. 4:25

3 And Joshua made him sharp knives, and circumcised the children of Israel at the hill of the foreskins.

4 And this *is* the cause why Joshua did circumcise: All the people that came out of Egypt, *that were* males, *even* all the men of war, died in the wilderness by the way, after they came out of Egypt. Num. 26:64-65

5 Now all the people that came out were

circumcised: but all the people *that were* born in the wilderness by the way as they came forth out of Egypt, *them* they had not circumcised.

6 For the children of Israel walked forty years in the wilderness, till all the people *that were* men of war, which came out of Egypt, were consumed, because they obeyed not the voice of the LORD: unto whom the LORD sware that he would not shew them the land, which the LORD sware unto their fathers that he would give us, a land that floweth with milk and honey.   Ex. 3:8; Deut. 2:7, 14

7 And their children, *whom* he raised up in their stead, them Joshua circumcised: for they were uncircumcised, because they had not circumcised them by the way. Num. 14:31

5:2–7 Reminders of Rejection

During these years the people were constantly reminded that they were under the divine rebuke. In the rebellion at Kadesh they had rejected God, and God had for the time rejected them. Since they had proved unfaithful to His covenant, they were not to receive the sign of the covenant, the rite of circumcision. *PP 406*

---

8 And it came to pass, when they had done circumcising all the people, that they abode in their places in the camp, till they were whole.   Gen. 34:25

9 And the LORD said unto Joshua, This day have I rolled away the reproach of Egypt from off you. Wherefore the name of the place is called Gilgal unto this day. Gen. 34:14

The Passover Is Kept at Gilgal

10 And the children of Israel encamped in Gilgal, and kept the passover on the fourteenth day of the month at even in the plains of Jericho.

11 And they did eat of the old corn of the land on the morrow after the passover, unleavened cakes, and parched *corn* in the selfsame day.   Lev. 23:14

12 And the manna ceased on the morrow after they had eaten of the old corn of the land; neither had the children of Israel manna any more; but they did eat of the fruit of the land of Canaan that year. Ex. 16:35

5:13 Assurance of Divine Guidance

To reduce Jericho was seen by Joshua to be the first step in the conquest of Canaan. But first of all he sought an assurance of divine guidance, and it was granted him. Withdrawing from the encampment to meditate and to pray that the God of Israel would go before His people, he beheld an armed warrior, of lofty stature and commanding presence. *PP 487*

---

13 And it came to pass, when Joshua was by Jericho, that he lifted up his eyes and looked, and, behold, there stood a man over against him with his sword drawn in his hand: and Joshua went unto him, and said unto him, Art thou for us, or for our adversaries?   Gen. 18:2; Num. 22:23; Dan. 10:5

14 And he said, Nay; but *as* captain of the host of the LORD am I now come. And Joshua fell on his face to the earth, and did worship, and said unto him, What saith my lord unto his servant?   Gen. 17:3

15 And the captain of the LORD's host said unto Joshua, Loose thy shoe from off thy foot; for the place whereon thou standest *is* holy. And Joshua did so.   Ex. 3:5

Jericho Is Destroyed

6 Now Jericho was ᵀstraitly shut up because of the children of Israel: none went out, and none came in.   strictly

2 And the LORD said unto Joshua, See, I have given into thine hand Jericho, and the king thereof, *and* the mighty men of valour.   Deut. 7:24; Josh. 2:9, 24

3 And ye shall ᵀcompass the city, all *ye* men of war, *and* go round about the city once. Thus shalt thou do six days.   surround

4 And seven priests shall bear before the ark seven trumpets of rams' horns: and the seventh day ye shall compass the city seven times, and the priests shall blow with the trumpets.

5 And it shall come to pass, that when they make a long *blast* with the ram's horn, *and* when ye hear the sound of the trumpet, all the people shall shout with a great shout; and the wall of the city shall fall down flat, and the people shall ascend up every man straight before him.   Josh. 6:20

6:3–5 Victory Without Attack

In obedience to the divine command Joshua marshaled the armies of Israel. No assault was to be made. They were simply to make the circuit of the city, bearing the ark of God and blowing upon trumpets. *PP 488*

---

6 And Joshua the son of Nun called the priests, and said unto them, Take up the ark of the covenant, and let seven priests bear seven trumpets of rams' horns before the ark of the LORD.

7 And he said unto the people, Pass on, and compass the city, and let him that is armed pass on before the ark of the LORD. Josh. 4:13

8 And it came to pass, when Joshua had spoken unto the people, that the seven priests bearing the seven trumpets of rams' horns passed on before the LORD, and blew with

the trumpets: and the ark of the covenant of the LORD followed them.

9 And the armed men went before the priests that blew with the trumpets, and the rereward came after the ark, *the priests* going on, and blowing with the trumpets.   Num. 10:25; Is. 58:8

10 And Joshua had commanded the people, saying, Ye shall not shout, nor make any noise with your voice, neither shall *any* word proceed out of your mouth, until the day I bid you shout; then shall ye shout.

11 So the ark of the LORD ᵀcompassed the city, going about *it* once: and they came into the camp, and lodged in the camp.   *circled*

12 And Joshua rose early in the morning, and the priests took up the ark of the LORD.

13 And seven priests bearing seven trumpets of rams' horns before the ark of the LORD went on continually, and blew with the trumpets: and the armed men went before them; but the ᵀrereward came after the ark of the LORD, *the priests* going on, and blowing with the trumpets.   *rear guard*

14 And the second day they compassed the city once, and returned into the camp: so they did six days.

15 And it came to pass on the seventh day, that they rose early about the dawning of the day, and compassed the city after the same manner seven times: only on that day they compassed the city seven times.

16 And it came to pass at the seventh time, when the priests blew with the trumpets, Joshua said unto the people, Shout; for the LORD hath given you the city.

6:16 God's Use of Simple Methods

The simple act of blowing a blast upon the trumpet by the army of Joshua around Jericho, and by Gideon's little band about the hosts of Midian, was made effectual, through the power of God, to overthrow the might of His enemies. The most complete system that men have ever devised, apart from the power and wisdom of God, will prove a failure, while the most unpromising methods will succeed when divinely appointed and entered upon with humility and faith. *PP 554*

Jericho Must Be Destroyed, Except for Rahab

17 And the city shall be accursed, *even* it, and all that *are* therein, to the LORD: only Rahab the harlot shall live, she and all that *are* with her in the house, because she hid the messengers that we sent.   Deut. 20:17

18 And ye, in any wise keep *yourselves* from the accursed thing, lest ye make *yourselves* accursed, when ye take of the accursed

thing, and make the camp of Israel a curse, and trouble it.   Josh. 7:1

19 But all the silver, and gold, and vessels of brass and iron, *are* ᵀconsecrated unto the LORD: they shall come into the treasury of the LORD.   1 Chr. 26:20 ◆ *set apart*

20 So the people shouted when *the priests* blew with the trumpets: and it came to pass, when the people heard the sound of the trumpet, and the people shouted with a great shout, that the wall fell down flat, so that the people went up into the city, every man straight before him, and they took the city.   Josh. 6:5; Heb. 11:30

21 And they utterly destroyed all that *was* in the city, both man and woman, young and old, and ox, and sheep, and ass, with the edge of the sword.

22 But Joshua had said unto the two men that had spied out the country, Go into the harlot's house, and bring out thence the woman, and all that she hath, as ye sware unto her.   Heb. 11:31

23 And the young men that were spies went in, and brought out Rahab, and her father, and her mother, and her brethren, and all that she had; and they brought out all her kindred, and left them without the camp of Israel.

24 And they burnt the city with fire, and all that *was* therein: only the silver, and the gold, and the vessels of brass and of iron, they put into the treasury of the house of the LORD.

25 And Joshua saved Rahab the harlot alive, and her father's household, and all that she had; and she dwelleth in Israel *even* unto this day; because she hid the messengers, which Joshua sent to spy out Jericho.   Heb. 11:31

26 And Joshua ᵀadjured *them* at that time, saying, Cursed *be* the man before the LORD, that riseth up and buildeth this city Jericho: he shall lay the foundation thereof in his firstborn, and in his youngest *son* shall he set up the gates of it.   1 Kin. 16:34 ◆ *charged*

6:26 Rebuilding of Jericho

Five centuries passed. The spot lay desolate, accursed of God. Even the springs that had made residence in this portion of the valley so desirable suffered the blighting effects of the curse. But in the days of Ahab's apostasy, when through Jezebel's influence the worship of Ashtoreth was revived, Jericho, the ancient seat of this worship, was rebuilt, though at a fearful cost to the builder. *PK 230*

---

27 So the LORD was with Joshua; and his fame was *noised* throughout all the country.   Josh. 1:5

The Israelites Are Defeated at Ai

7 But the children of Israel committed a ᵀtrespass in the accursed thing: for Achan, the son of Carmi, the son of Zabdi, the son of Zerah, of the tribe of Judah, took of the accursed thing: and the anger of the LORD was kindled against the children of Israel.   Josh. 22:20 ◆ sin

2 And Joshua sent men from Jericho to Ai, which is beside Beth-aven, on the east side of Beth-el, and spake unto them, saying, Go up and view the country. And the men went up and viewed Ai.   Josh. 18:12; 1 Sam. 13:5; 14:23

3 And they returned to Joshua, and said unto him, Let not all the people go up; but let about two or three thousand men go up and ᵀsmite Ai; and make not all the people to labour thither; for they are but few.   strike

4 So there went up thither of the people about three thousand men: and they fled before the men of Ai.   Lev. 26:17; Deut. 28:25

5 And the men of Ai smote of them about thirty and six men: for they chased them from before the gate even unto Shebarim, and smote them in the going down: wherefore the hearts of the people melted, and became as water.   Lev. 26:36; Josh. 2:9, 11

Joshua's Complaint

6 And Joshua ᵀrent his clothes, and fell to the earth upon his face before the ark of the LORD until the ᵀeventide, he and the elders of Israel, and put dust upon their heads.   Gen. 37:29 ◆ tore ◆ evening

7 And Joshua said, Alas, O Lord GOD, wherefore hast thou at all brought this people over Jordan, to deliver us into the hand of the Amorites, to destroy us? would to God we had been content, and dwelt on the other side Jordan!   2 Kin. 3:10

8 O Lord, what shall I say, when Israel turneth their backs before their enemies!

9 For the Canaanites and all the inhabitants of the land shall hear of it, and shall ᵀenviron us round, and cut off our name from the earth: and what wilt thou do unto thy great name?   Ex. 32:12 ◆ surround

Joshua Must Deal with Sin in the Camp

10 And the LORD said unto Joshua, Get thee up; wherefore liest thou thus upon thy face?

11 Israel hath sinned, and they have also ᵀtransgressed my covenant which I commanded them: for they have even taken of the accursed thing, and have also stolen, and dissembled also, and they have put it even among their own stuff.   Josh. 6:17-19 ◆ violated

12 Therefore the children of Israel could not stand before their enemies, but turned their backs before their enemies, because they were accursed: neither will I be with you any more, except ye destroy the accursed from among you.   Num. 14:45; Josh. 6:18; Judg. 2:14

13 Up, ᵀsanctify the people, and say, Sanctify yourselves against to morrow: for thus saith the LORD God of Israel, There is an accursed thing in the midst of thee, O Israel: thou canst not stand before thine enemies, until ye take away the accursed thing from among you.   Josh. 3:5 ◆ make holy

14 In the morning therefore ye shall be brought according to your tribes: and it shall be, that the tribe which the LORD taketh shall come according to the families thereof; and the family which the LORD shall take shall come by households; and the household which the LORD shall take shall come man by man.   Prov. 16:33

15 And it shall be, that he that is taken with the accursed thing shall be burnt with fire, he and all that he hath: because he hath transgressed the covenant of the LORD, and because he hath ᵀwrought folly in Israel. Gen. 34:7; Judg. 20:6; 1 Sam. 14:38-39 ◆ done

Achan's Sin Destroys Him and His Family

16 So Joshua rose up early in the morning, and brought Israel by their tribes; and the tribe of Judah was taken:

17 And he brought the family of Judah; and he took the family of the Zarhites: and he brought the family of the Zarhites man by man; and Zabdi was taken: Num. 26:20

18 And he brought his household man by man; and Achan, the son of Carmi, the son

---

Sin's Infection Communicable

Joshua 7:12

Achan's sin brought disaster upon the whole nation. For one man's sin the displeasure of God will rest upon His church till the transgression is searched out and put away. The influence most to be feared by the church is not that of open opposers, infidels, and blasphemers, but of inconsistent professors of Christ. These are the ones that keep back the blessing of the God of Israel and bring weakness upon His people.

When the church is in difficulty, when coldness and spiritual declension exist, giving occasion for the enemies of God to triumph, then, instead of folding their hands and lamenting their unhappy state, let its members inquire if there is not an Achan in the camp. With humiliation and searching of heart, let each seek to discover the hidden sins that shut out God's presence. PP 497

of Zabdi, the son of Zerah, of the tribe of Judah, was taken.　　　　*Num. 32:23*

19 And Joshua said unto Achan, My son, give, I pray thee, glory to the LORD God of Israel, and make confession unto him; and tell me now what thou hast done; hide *it* not from me.　　*1 Sam. 6:5; Jer. 13:16; John 9:24*

20 And Achan answered Joshua, and said, Indeed I have sinned against the LORD God of Israel, and thus and thus have I done:

21 When I saw among the spoils a goodly Babylonish garment, and two hundred shekels of silver, and a wedge of gold of fifty shekels weight, then I ᵀcoveted them, and took them; and, behold, they *are* hid in the earth in the midst of my tent, and the silver under it.　　*Deut. 7:25* ◆ *desired*

7:20, 21 A Deadly Sin

The deadly sin that led to Achan's ruin had its root in covetousness, of all sins one of the most common and the most lightly regarded. While other offenses meet with detection and punishment, how rarely does the violation of the tenth commandment so much as call forth censure. The enormity of this sin, and its terrible results, are the lessons of Achan's history. *PP 496*

---

22 So Joshua sent messengers, and they ran unto the tent; and, behold, *it was* hid in his tent, and the silver under it.

23 And they took them out of the midst of the tent, and brought them unto Joshua, and unto all the children of Israel, and laid them out before the LORD.

24 And Joshua, and all Israel with him, took Achan the son of Zerah, and the silver, and the garment, and the wedge of gold, and his sons, and his daughters, and his oxen, and his asses, and his sheep, and his tent, and all that he had: and they brought them unto the valley of Achor.　　*Josh. 7:26; 15:7; Is. 65:10*

25 And Joshua said, Why hast thou troubled us? the LORD shall trouble thee this day. And all Israel stoned him with stones, and burned them with fire, after they had stoned them with stones.　　*Lev. 20:2; 24:14; Josh. 6:18*

26 And they raised over him a great heap of stones unto this day. So the LORD turned from the fierceness of his anger. Wherefore the name of that place was called, The valley of Achor, unto this day.　　*Deut. 13:17*

God Encourages Joshua

8 And the LORD said unto Joshua, Fear not, neither be thou dismayed: take all the people of war with thee, and arise, go up to Ai: see, I have given into thy hand the king of Ai, and his people, and his city, and his land:　　*Deut. 1:21; Josh. 1:9; 6:2*

2 And thou shalt do to Ai and her king as thou didst unto Jericho and her king: only the spoil thereof, and the cattle thereof, shall ye take for a prey unto yourselves: lay thee an ambush for the city behind it.　　*Deut. 20:14*

Israel's Victory at Ai

3 So Joshua arose, and all the people of war, to go up against Ai: and Joshua chose out thirty thousand mighty men of valour, and sent them away by night.

4 And he commanded them, saying, Behold, ye shall lie in wait against the city, *even* behind the city: go not very far from the city, but be ye all ready:　　*Judg. 20:29*

5 And I, and all the people that *are* with me, will approach unto the city: and it shall come to pass, when they come out against us, as at the first, that we will flee before them,　　*Josh. 7:5*

6 (For they will come out after us) till we have drawn them from the city; for they will say, They flee before us, as at the first: therefore we will flee before them.

7 Then ye shall rise up from the ambush, and seize upon the city: for the LORD your God will deliver it into your hand.

8 And it shall be, when ye have taken the city, *that* ye shall set the city on fire: according to the commandment of the LORD shall ye do. See, I have commanded you.　　*2 Sam. 13:28*

9 Joshua therefore sent them forth: and they went to lie in ambush, and abode between Beth-el and Ai, on the west side of Ai: but Joshua lodged that night among the people.

10 And Joshua rose up early in the morning, and numbered the people, and went up, he and the elders of Israel, before the people to Ai.

11 And all the people, *even the people* of war that *were* with him, went up, and drew nigh, and came before the city, and pitched on the north side of Ai: now *there was* a valley between them and Ai.

12 And he took about five thousand men, and set them to lie in ambush between Beth-el and Ai, on the west side of the city.

13 And when they had set the people, *even* all the host that *was* on the north of the city, and their liers in wait on the west of the city, Joshua went that night into the midst of the valley.

14 And it came to pass, when the king of Ai saw *it*, that they hasted and rose up early, and the men of the city went out against Israel to battle, he and all his people, at a time appointed, before the plain; but he ᵀwist not that *there were* liers in ambush against him behind the city.　　*knew*

15 And Joshua and all Israel made as if they

were beaten before them, and fled by the way of the wilderness. *Josh. 18:12*

16 And all the people that *were* in Ai were called together to pursue after them: and they pursued after Joshua, and were drawn away from the city. *Judg. 20:31*

17 And there was not a man left in Ai or Beth-el, that went not out after Israel: and they left the city open, and pursued after Israel.

18 And the LORD said unto Joshua, Stretch out the spear that *is* in thy hand toward Ai; for I will give it into thine hand. And Joshua stretched out the spear that *he had* in his hand toward the city. *Josh. 8:26*

19 And the ambush arose quickly out of their place, and they ran as soon as he had stretched out his hand: and they entered into the city, and took it, and hasted and set the city on fire.

20 And when the men of Ai looked behind them, they saw, and, behold, the smoke of the city ascended up to heaven, and they had no power to flee this way or that way: and the people that fled to the wilderness turned back upon the pursuers.

21 And when Joshua and all Israel saw that the ambush had taken the city, and that the smoke of the city ascended, then they turned again, and slew the men of Ai.

22 And the other issued out of the city against them; so they were in the midst of Israel, some on this side, and some on that side: and they smote them, so that they let none of them remain or escape. *Deut. 7:2*

23 And the king of Ai they took alive, and brought him to Joshua. *1 Sam. 15:8*

24 And it came to pass, when Israel had made an end of slaying all the inhabitants of Ai in the field, in the wilderness wherein they chased them, and when they were all fallen on the edge of the sword, until they were consumed, that all the Israelites returned unto Ai, and smote it with the edge of the sword.

25 And *so* it was, *that* all that fell that day, both of men and women, *were* twelve thousand, *even* all the men of Ai.

26 For Joshua drew not his hand back, wherewith he stretched out the spear, until he had utterly destroyed all the inhabitants of Ai. *Ex. 17:11-12*

27 Only the cattle and the ᵀspoil of that city Israel took for a prey unto themselves, according unto the word of the LORD which he commanded Joshua. *Josh. 8:2 ◆ plunder*

28 And Joshua burnt Ai, and made it an heap for ever, *even* a desolation unto this day. *Deut. 13:16*

29 And the king of Ai he hanged on a tree until ᵀeventide: and as soon as the sun was down, Joshua commanded that they should take his carcase down from the tree, and cast it at the entering of the gate of the city, and raise thereon a great heap of stones, *that re-maineth* unto this day. *Deut. 21:22-23 ◆ evening*

The Lord Renews His Promise

30 Then Joshua built an altar unto the LORD God of Israel in mount Ebal,

8:30 The Solemn Service

The place appointed for this solemn service was one already sacred from its association with the history of their fathers. It was here that Abraham raised his first altar to Jehovah in the land of Canaan. Here both Abraham and Jacob had pitched their tents. Here the latter bought the field in which the tribes were to bury the body of Joseph. Here also was the well that Jacob had dug, and the oak under which he had buried the idolatrous images of his household. *PP 499, 500*

31 As Moses the servant of the LORD commanded the children of Israel, as it is written in the book of the law of Moses, an altar of whole stones, over which no man hath lift up *any* iron: and they offered thereon burnt offerings unto the LORD, and sacrificed peace offerings.

32 And he wrote there upon the stones a copy of the law of Moses, which he wrote in the presence of the children of Israel. *Deut. 27:2-3*

33 And all Israel, and their elders, and officers, and their judges, stood on this side the ark and on that side before the priests the Levites, which bare the ark of the covenant of the LORD, as well the stranger, as he that was born among them; half of them over against mount Gerizim, and half of them over against mount Ebal; as Moses the servant of the LORD had commanded before, that they should bless the people of Israel. *Deut. 11:29; 31:9, 12*

34 And afterward he read all the words of the law, the blessings and cursings, according to all that is written in the book of the law. *Neh. 8:2-3*

8:35 A Presentation Every Seven Years

The writings of Moses were taught by Joshua to all Israel. . . . This was in harmony with the express command of Jehovah providing for a public rehearsal of the words of the book of the law every seven years, during the Feast of Tabernacles. . . .

Had this counsel been heeded through the centuries that followed, how different would have been Israel's history! *PK 465*

35 There was not a word of all that Moses commanded, which Joshua read not before all

the congregation of Israel, with the women, and the little ones, and the strangers that were conversant among them.   Deut. 31:12

The Kings Combine against Israel

9 And it came to pass, when all the kings which *were* on this side Jordan, in the hills, and in the valleys, and in all the coasts of the great sea over against Lebanon, the Hittite, and the Amorite, the Canaanite, the Perizzite, the Hivite, and the Jebusite, heard *thereof*;   Ex. 3:17; 23:23; Num. 34:6

2 That they gathered themselves together, to fight with Joshua and with Israel, with one accord.

The Gibeonites Obtain a Treaty through Deception

3 And when the inhabitants of Gibeon heard what Joshua had done unto Jericho and to Ai,   Josh. 9:17; 10:2; 2 Sam. 21:1-2

4 They did work wilily, and went and made as if they had been ambassadors, and took old sacks upon their asses, and wine bottles, old, and rent, and bound up;

5 And old shoes and clouted upon their feet, and old garments upon them; and all the bread of their provision was dry *and* mouldy.

6 And they went to Joshua unto the camp at Gilgal, and said unto him, and to the men of Israel, We be come from a far country: now therefore make ye a league with us. Josh. 5:10

7 And the men of Israel said unto the Hivites, Peradventure ye dwell among us; and how shall we make a league with you?   Judg. 2:2

8 And they said unto Joshua, We *are* thy servants. And Joshua said unto them, Who *are* ye? and from whence come ye?   Deut. 20:11

9 And they said unto him, From a very far country thy servants are come because of the name of the LORD thy God: for we have heard the fame of him, and all that he did in Egypt,   Deut. 20:15

10 And all that he did to the two kings of the Amorites, that *were* beyond Jordan, to Sihon king of Heshbon, and to Og king of Bashan, which *was* at Ashtaroth.   Num. 21:24-35

11 Wherefore our elders and all the inhabitants of our country spake to us, saying, Take ᵀvictuals with you for the journey, and go to meet them, and say unto them, We *are* your servants: therefore now make ye a league with us.   *food*

12 This our bread we took hot *for* our provision out of our houses on the day we came forth to go unto you; but now, behold, it is dry, and it is mouldy:

13 And these bottles of wine, which we filled, *were* new; and, behold, they be ᵀrent: and these our garments and our shoes

are become old by reason of the very long journey.   *torn apart*

14 And the men took of their victuals, and asked not *counsel* at the mouth of the LORD.

15 And Joshua made peace with them, and made a league with them, to let them live: and the princes of the congregation sware unto them.   Josh. 11:19; 2 Sam. 21:2

> **9:15 Providences Convinced the Heathen**
>
> The marvelous providences connected with Israel's deliverance from Egyptian bondage and with their occupancy of the Promised Land led many of the heathen to recognize the God of Israel as the Supreme Ruler. *PK 369*

16 And it came to pass at the end of three days after they had made a league with them, that they heard that they *were* their neighbours, and *that* they dwelt among them.

17 And the children of Israel journeyed, and came unto their cities on the third day. Now their cities *were* Gibeon, and Chephirah, and Beeroth, and Kirjath-jearim.   Josh. 18:25-28

18 And the children of Israel smote them not, because the princes of the congregation had sworn unto them by the LORD God of Israel. And all the congregation murmured against the princes.   Ps. 15:4

19 But all the princes said unto all the congregation, We have sworn unto them by the LORD God of Israel: now therefore we may not touch them.

20 This we will do to them; we will even let them live, lest wrath be upon us, because of the oath which we sware unto them.

21 And the princes said unto them, Let them live; but let them be hewers of wood and drawers of water unto all the congregation; as the princes had promised them.   Deut. 29:11

The Gibeonites Are Condemned to Perpetual Bondage

22 And Joshua called for them, and he spake unto them, saying, Wherefore have ye ᵀbeguiled us, saying, We *are* very far from you; when ye dwell among us?   Josh. 9:6 ◆ *deceived*

23 Now therefore ye *are* cursed, and there shall none of you be freed from being bondmen, and hewers of wood and drawers of water for the house of my God.   Josh. 9:21

24 And they answered Joshua, and said, Because it was certainly told thy servants, how that the LORD thy God commanded his servant Moses to give you all the land, and to destroy all the inhabitants of the land from before you, therefore we were sore afraid of our lives because of you, and have done this thing.   Deut. 7:1-2

25 And now, behold, we *are* in thine hand:

as it seemeth good and right unto thee to do unto us, do.   *Gen. 16:6*

26 And so did he unto them, and delivered them out of the hand of the children of Israel, that they slew them not.

27 And Joshua made them that day hewers of wood and drawers of water for the congregation, and for the altar of the Lord, even unto this day, in the place which he should choose.   *Deut. 12:5*

Five Kings War against Gibeon

10 Now it came to pass, when Adoni-zedek king of Jerusalem had heard how Joshua had taken Ai, and had utterly destroyed it; as he had done to Jericho and her king, so he had done to Ai and her king; and how the inhabitants of Gibeon had made peace with Israel, and were among them;   *Josh. 6:21*

2 That they feared greatly, because Gibeon *was* a great city, as one of the royal cities, and because it *was* greater than Ai, and all the men thereof *were* mighty.   *Ex. 15:14-16*

3 Wherefore Adoni-zedek king of Jerusalem sent unto Hoham king of Hebron, and unto Piram king of Jarmuth, and unto Japhia king of Lachish, and unto Debir king of Eglon, saying,   *2 Chr. 11:9*

4 Come up unto me, and help me, that we may smite Gibeon: for it hath made peace with Joshua and with the children of Israel.

5 Therefore the five kings of the Amorites, the king of Jerusalem, the king of Hebron, the king of Jarmuth, the king of Lachish, the king of Eglon, gathered themselves together, and went up, they and all their hosts, and encamped before Gibeon, and made war against it.

6 And the men of Gibeon sent unto Joshua to the camp to Gilgal, saying, Slack not thy hand from thy servants; come up to us quickly, and save us, and help us: for all the kings of the Amorites that dwell in the mountains are gathered together against us.   *Josh. 5:10*

7 So Joshua ascended from Gilgal, he, and all the people of war with him, and all the mighty men of valour.   *Josh. 8:1*

8 And the Lord said unto Joshua, Fear not: for I have delivered them into thine hand; there shall not a man of them stand before thee.   *Deut. 3:2*

9 Joshua therefore came unto them suddenly, *and* went up from Gilgal all night.

10 And the Lord discomfited them before Israel, and slew them with a great slaughter at Gibeon, and chased them along the way that goeth up to Beth-horon, and smote them to Azekah, and unto Makkedah.   *Josh. 16:3*

11 And it came to pass, as they fled from before Israel, *and* were in the going down to Beth-horon, that the Lord cast down great stones from heaven upon them unto Azekah, and they died: *they were* more which died with hailstones than *they* whom the children of Israel slew with the sword.   *Is. 28:2*

12 Then spake Joshua to the Lord in the day when the Lord delivered up the Amorites before the children of Israel, and he said in the sight of Israel, Sun, stand thou still upon Gibeon; and thou, Moon, in the valley of Ajalon.   *Hab. 3:11*

13 And the sun stood still, and the moon ᵀstayed, until the people had avenged themselves upon their enemies. *Is* not this written in the book of Jasher? So the sun stood still

The Lesson of the Sun Standing Still

Joshua 10:12–14

Before the evening fell, God's promise to Joshua had been fulfilled. The entire host of the enemy had been given into his hand. Long were the events of that day to remain in the memory of Israel. "There was no day like that before it or after it, that Jehovah hearkened unto the voice of a man: for the Lord fought for Israel." . . .

The Spirit of God inspired Joshua's prayer, that evidence might again be given of the power of Israel's God. Hence the request did not show presumption on the part of the great leader. Joshua had received the promise that God would surely overthrow these enemies of Israel, yet he put forth as earnest effort as though success depended upon the armies of Israel alone. He did all that human energy could do, and then he cried in faith for divine aid. The secret of success is the union of divine power with human effort. Those who achieve the greatest results are those who rely most implicitly upon the Almighty Arm. The man who commanded, "Sun, stand thou still upon Gibeon; and thou, Moon, in the valley of Ajalon," is the man who for hours lay prostrate upon the earth in prayer in the camp of Gilgal. The men of prayer are the men of power.

This mighty miracle testifies that the creation is under the control of the Creator. Satan seeks to conceal from men the divine agency in the physical world—to keep out of sight the unwearied working of the first great cause. In this miracle all who exalt nature above the God of nature stand rebuked. *PP 508, 509*

in the midst of heaven, and hasted not to go down about a whole day. *2 Sam. 1:18 ♦ held back*

14 And there was no day like that before it or after it, that the LORD hearkened unto the voice of a man: for the LORD fought for Israel. *Deut. 1:30; Josh. 10:42; 23:3*

Joshua Defeats the Five Kings

15 And Joshua returned, and all Israel with him, unto the camp to Gilgal. *Josh. 10:43*
16 But these five kings fled, and hid themselves in a cave at Makkedah.
17 And it was told Joshua, saying, The five kings are found hid in a cave at Makkedah.
18 And Joshua said, Roll great stones upon the mouth of the cave, and set men by it for to keep them:
19 And stay ye not, *but* pursue after your enemies, and ᵀsmite the hindmost of them; suffer them not to enter into their cities: for the LORD your God hath delivered them into your hand. *strike*
20 And it came to pass, when Joshua and the children of Israel had made an end of slaying them with a very great slaughter, till they were consumed, that the rest *which* remained of them entered into fenced cities. *Josh. 8:24*
21 And all the people returned to the camp to Joshua at Makkedah in peace: none moved his tongue against any of the children of Israel. *Ex. 11:7*
22 Then said Joshua, Open the mouth of the cave, and bring out those five kings unto me out of the cave.
23 And they did so, and brought forth those five kings unto him out of the cave, the king of Jerusalem, the king of Hebron, the king of Jarmuth, the king of Lachish, *and* the king of Eglon.
24 And it came to pass, when they brought out those kings unto Joshua, that Joshua called for all the men of Israel, and said unto the captains of the men of war which went with him, Come near, put your feet upon the necks of these kings. And they came near, and put their feet upon the necks of them. *Mal. 4:3*
25 And Joshua said unto them, Fear not, nor be dismayed, be strong and of good cour-

age: for thus shall the LORD do to all your enemies against whom ye fight. *Deut. 7:19*
26 And afterward Joshua smote them, and slew them, and hanged them on five trees: and they were hanging upon the trees until the evening. *Josh. 8:29*
27 And it came to pass at the time of the going down of the sun, *that* Joshua commanded, and they took them down off the trees, and cast them into the cave wherein they had been hid, and laid great stones in the cave's mouth, *which remain* until this very day. *Josh. 8:29*

Joshua Defeats the Southern Kings

28 And that day Joshua took Makkedah, and smote it with the edge of the sword, and the king thereof he utterly destroyed, them, and all the souls that *were* therein; he let none remain: and he did to the king of Makkedah as he did unto the king of Jericho. *Josh. 6:21*
29 Then Joshua passed from Makkedah, and all Israel with him, unto Libnah, and fought against Libnah: *Josh. 21:13*
30 And the LORD delivered it also, and the king thereof, into the hand of Israel; and he smote it with the edge of the sword, and all the souls that *were* therein; he let none remain in it; but did unto the king thereof as he did unto the king of Jericho.
31 And Joshua passed from Libnah, and all Israel with him, unto Lachish, and encamped against it, and fought against it: *Josh. 10:3*
32 And the LORD delivered Lachish into the hand of Israel, which took it on the second day, and smote it with the edge of the sword, and all the souls that *were* therein, according to all that he had done to Libnah.
33 Then Horam king of Gezer came up to help Lachish; and Joshua smote him and his people, until he had left him none remaining. *Josh. 16:3, 10; Judg. 1:29*
34 And from Lachish Joshua passed unto Eglon, and all Israel with him; and they encamped against it, and fought against it:
35 And they took it on that day, and smote it with the edge of the sword, and all the souls that *were* therein he utterly destroyed that day, according to all that he had done to Lachish.
36 And Joshua went up from Eglon, and all Israel with him, unto Hebron; and they fought against it: *Num. 13:22; Josh. 15:13; Judg. 1:10*
37 And they took it, and smote it with the edge of the sword, and the king thereof, and all the cities thereof, and all the souls that *were* therein; he left none remaining, according to all that he had done to Eglon; but destroyed it utterly, and all the souls that *were* therein.

38 And Joshua returned, and all Israel with him, to Debir; and fought against it: Josh. 15:15
39 And he took it, and the king thereof, and all the cities thereof; and they smote them with the edge of the sword, and utterly destroyed all the souls that *were* therein; he left none remaining: as he had done to Hebron, so he did to Debir, and to the king thereof; as he had done also to Libnah, and to her king.
40 So Joshua smote all the country of the hills, and of the south, and of the ᵀvale, and of the springs, and all their kings: he left none remaining, but utterly destroyed all that breathed, as the LORD God of Israel commanded.　　　　　*valley*
41 And Joshua smote them from Kadesh-barnea even unto Gaza, and all the country of Goshen, even unto Gibeon.　　Josh. 11:16; 15:51
42 And all these kings and their land did Joshua take at one time, because the LORD God of Israel fought for Israel.　Josh. 10:14
43 And Joshua returned, and all Israel with him, unto the camp to Gilgal.　Josh. 10:15

Joshua Defeats the Northern Kings at the Waters of Merom

11 And it came to pass, when Jabin king of Hazor had heard *those things*, that he sent to Jobab king of Madon, and to the king of Shimron, and to the king of Achshaph,　　　　　　　Josh. 11:10
2 And to the kings that *were* on the north of the mountains, and of the plains south of Chinneroth, and in the valley, and in the borders of Dor on the west, Num. 34:11; Josh. 17:11
3 *And to* the Canaanite on the east and on the west, and *to* the Amorite, and the Hittite, and the Perizzite, and the Jebusite in the mountains, and *to* the Hivite under Hermon in the land of Mizpeh.　Gen. 31:49; Josh. 18:26; Judg. 3:3
4 And they went out, they and all their hosts with them, much people, even as the sand that *is* upon the sea shore in multitude, with horses and chariots very many.　Gen. 22:17; Judg. 7:12
5 And when all these kings were met together, they came and pitched together at the waters of Merom, to fight against Israel.
6 And the LORD said unto Joshua, Be not afraid because of them: for to morrow about this time will I deliver them up all slain before Israel: thou shalt ᵀthough their horses, and burn their chariots with fire.　　　2 Sam. 8:4 ♦ *disable*
7 So Joshua came, and all the people of war with him, against them by the waters of Merom suddenly; and they fell upon them.　　　　　　　Josh. 10:9
8 And the LORD delivered them into the hand of Israel, who smote them, and chased them unto great Zidon, and unto

Misrephoth-maim, and unto the valley of Mizpeh eastward; and they smote them, until they left them none remaining. Josh. 13:6; 19:28
9 And Joshua did unto them as the LORD bade him: he ᵀhoughed their horses, and burnt their chariots with fire. Josh. 11:6 ♦ *disabled*

Joshua Captures the Whole Land

10 And Joshua at that time turned back, and took Hazor, and smote the king thereof with the sword: for Hazor beforetime was the head of all those kingdoms.　Josh. 11:1
11 And they smote all the souls that *were* therein with the edge of the sword, utterly destroying *them*: there was not any left to breathe: and he burnt Hazor with fire.
12 And all the cities of those kings, and all the kings of them, did Joshua take, and smote them with the edge of the sword, *and* he utterly destroyed them, as Moses the servant of the LORD commanded.　Deut. 7:2
13 But *as for* the cities that stood still in their strength, Israel burned none of them, save Hazor only; *that* did Joshua burn.
14 And all the ᵀspoil of these cities, and the cattle, the children of Israel took for a prey unto themselves; but every man they smote with the edge of the sword, until they had destroyed them, neither left they any to breathe.　　　　　　　*plunder*
15 As the LORD commanded Moses his servant, so did Moses command Joshua, and so did Joshua; he left nothing undone of all that the LORD commanded Moses.　Josh. 1:7
16 So Joshua took all that land, the hills, and all the south country, and all the land of Goshen, and the valley, and the plain, and the mountain of Israel, and the valley of the same;　　　　Josh. 10:41; 11:21; 12:8
17 *Even* from the mount Halak, that goeth up to Seir, even unto Baal-gad in the valley of Lebanon under mount Hermon: and all their kings he took, and smote them, and slew them.　　　Deut. 7:24; Josh. 11:3; 13:5
18 Joshua made war a long time with all those kings.
19 There was not a city that made peace with the children of Israel, save the Hivites the inhabitants of Gibeon: all other they took in battle.
20 For it was of the LORD to harden their hearts, that they should come against Israel in battle, that he might destroy them utterly, *and* that they might have no favour, but that he might destroy them, as the LORD commanded Moses.　　　　Ex. 4:21
21 And at that time came Joshua, and cut off the Anakims from the mountains, from Hebron, from Debir, from Anab, and from all the mountains of Judah, and from all the

mountains of Israel: Joshua destroyed them utterly with their cities.   Deut. 9:2

22 There was none of the Anakims left in the land of the children of Israel: only in Gaza, in Gath, and in Ashdod, there remained.   Josh. 15:46; 1 Sam. 17:4

23 So Joshua took the whole land, according to all that the LORD said unto Moses; and Joshua gave it for an inheritance unto Israel according to their divisions by their tribes. And the land rested from war.   Num. 26:52-55

11:23 Apportionment of the Land

Joshua was not, however, to continue the war. There was another work for the great leader to perform before he should relinquish the command of Israel. The whole land, both the parts already conquered and that which was yet unsubdued, was to be apportioned among the tribes. And it was the duty of each tribe to fully subdue its own inheritance. *PP 511*

The Kings on the East and West of the Jordan River

12 Now these *are* the kings of the land, which the children of Israel smote, and possessed their land on the other side Jordan toward the rising of the sun, from the river Arnon unto mount Hermon, and all the plain on the east: Deut. 3:8-9

2 Sihon king of the Amorites, who dwelt in Heshbon, *and* ruled from Aroer, which *is* upon the bank of the river Arnon, and from the middle of the river, and from half Gilead, even unto the river Jabbok, *which is* the border of the children of Ammon;   Gen. 32:22

3 And from the plain to the sea of Chinneroth on the east, and unto the sea of the plain, *even* the salt sea on the east, the way to Beth-jeshimoth; and from the south, under Ashdoth-pisgah: Deut. 3:17; Josh. 11:2; 13:20

4 And the coast of Og king of Bashan, *which was* of the remnant of the giants, that dwelt at Ashtaroth and at Edrei,   Num. 21:33-35; Deut. 1:4

5 And reigned in mount Hermon, and in Salcah, and in all Bashan, unto the border of the Geshurites and the Maachathites, and half Gilead, the border of Sihon king of Heshbon.   Deut. 3:14; Josh. 13:11; 1 Sam. 27:8

6 Them did Moses the servant of the LORD and the children of Israel ᵀsmite: and Moses the servant of the LORD gave it *for* a possession unto the Reubenites, and the Gadites, and the half tribe of Manasseh. Num. 32:33 ◆ *strike*

7 And these *are* the kings of the country which Joshua and the children of Israel smote on this side Jordan on the west, from Baal-gad in the valley of Lebanon even unto the mount Halak, that goeth up

to Seir; which Joshua gave unto the tribes of Israel *for* a possession according to their divisions;   Josh. 11:17

8 In the mountains, and in the valleys, and in the plains, and in the springs, and in the wilderness, and in the south country; the Hittites, the Amorites, and the Canaanites, the Perizzites, the Hivites, and the Jebusites: Josh. 9:1; 10:40; 11:16

9 The king of Jericho, one; the king of Ai, which *is* beside Beth-el, one;

10 The king of Jerusalem, one; the king of Hebron, one;   Josh. 10:23

11 The king of Jarmuth, one; the king of Lachish, one;

12 The king of Eglon, one; the king of Gezer, one;   Josh. 10:33

13 The king of Debir, one; the king of Geder, one;   Josh. 10:38

14 The king of Hormah, one; the king of Arad, one;   Num. 21:1

15 The king of Libnah, one; the king of Adullam, one;

16 The king of Makkedah, one; the king of Beth-el, one;   Josh. 8:17

17 The king of Tappuah, one; the king of Hepher, one;   1 Kin. 4:10

18 The king of Aphek, one; the king of Lasharon, one;

19 The king of Madon, one; the king of Hazor, one;   Josh. 11:1

20 The king of Shimron-meron, one; the king of Achshaph, one;   Josh. 11:1

21 The king of Taanach, one; the king of Megiddo, one;   Josh. 17:11

22 The king of Kedesh, one; the king of Jokneam of Carmel, one;   Josh. 19:37

23 The king of Dor in the coast of Dor, one; the king of the nations of Gilgal, one; Josh. 11:2

24 The king of Tirzah, one: all the kings thirty and one.

The Land Yet to Be Conquered and the Tribes East of the Jordan

13 Now Joshua was old *and* stricken in years; and the LORD said unto him, Thou art old *and* stricken in years, and there remaineth yet very much land to be possessed.   Deut. 31:3; Josh. 14:10

2 This *is* the land that yet remaineth: all the borders of the Philistines, and all Geshuri,   Josh. 13:11

3 From Sihor, which *is* before Egypt, even unto the borders of Ekron northward, *which* is counted to the Canaanite: five lords of the Philistines; the Gazathites, and the Ashdothites, the Eshkalonites, the Gittites, and the Ekronites; also the Avites: Deut. 2:23

4 From the south, all the land of the Canaanites, and Mearah that *is* beside the Sidonians, unto Aphek, to the borders of the Amorites: Josh. 19:30

5 And the land of the Giblites, and all Lebanon, toward the sunrising, from Baal-gad under mount Hermon unto the entering into Hamath.   Josh. 12:7; 1 Kin. 5:6; Ps. 83:7

6 All the inhabitants of the hill country from Lebanon unto Misrephoth-maim, *and* all the Sidonians, them will I drive out from before the children of Israel: only divide thou it by lot unto the Israelites for an inheritance, as I have commanded thee.   Josh. 11:8; 23:13; Judg. 2:21-23

7 Now therefore divide this land for an inheritance unto the nine tribes, and the half tribe of Manasseh,

8 With whom the Reubenites and the Gadites have received their inheritance, which Moses gave them, beyond Jordan eastward, *even* as Moses the servant of the LORD gave them;   Josh. 12:6

9 From Aroer, that *is* upon the bank of the river Arnon, and the city that *is* in the midst of the river, and all the plain of Medeba unto Dibon;   Num. 21:30

10 And all the cities of Sihon king of the Amorites, which reigned in Heshbon, unto the border of the children of Ammon;

11 And Gilead, and the border of the Geshurites and Maachathites, and all mount Hermon, and all Bashan unto Salcah;

12 All the kingdom of Og in Bashan, which reigned in Ashtaroth and in Edrei, who remained of the remnant of the giants: for these did Moses ^Tsmite, and cast them out.   Josh. 12:4 ◆ *strike*

13 Nevertheless the children of Israel expelled not the Geshurites, nor the Maachathites: but the Geshurites and the Maachathites dwell among the Israelites until this day.   Josh. 13:11

14 Only unto the tribe of Levi he gave none inheritance; the sacrifices of the LORD God of Israel made by fire *are* their inheritance, as he said unto them.   Num. 18:20-24

15 And Moses gave unto the tribe of the children of Reuben *inheritance* according to their families.

16 And their coast was from Aroer, that *is* on the bank of the river Arnon, and the city that *is* in the midst of the river, and all the plain by Medeba;   Josh. 12:2; 13:9

13:16 A Needlessly Delayed Victory

The Israelites crossed the river Arnon and advanced upon the foe. An engagement took place, in which the armies of Israel were victorious; and, following up the advantage gained, they were soon in possession of the country of the Amorites. It was the Captain of the Lord's host who vanquished the enemies of His people; and He would have done the same thirty-eight years before had Israel trusted in Him. *PP 435*

17 Heshbon, and all her cities that *are* in the plain; Dibon, and Bamoth-baal, and Beth-baal-meon,

18 And Jahazah, and Kedemoth, and Mephaath,   Num. 21:23

19 And Kirjathaim, and Sibmah, and Zareth-shahar in the mount of the valley, Num. 32:37-38

20 And Beth-peor, and Ashdoth-pisgah, and Beth-jeshimoth,   Deut. 4:46

21 And all the cities of the plain, and all the kingdom of Sihon king of the Amorites, which reigned in Heshbon, whom Moses smote with the princes of Midian, Evi, and Rekem, and Zur, and Hur, and Reba, *which were* dukes of Sihon, dwelling in the country.   Num. 31:8; Deut. 3:10

22 Balaam also the son of Beor, the ^Tsoothsayer, did the children of Israel slay with the sword among them that were slain by them.   Num. 31:8 ◆ *one who tells the future by astrology*

23 And the border of the children of Reuben was Jordan, and the border *thereof*. This *was* the inheritance of the children of Reuben after their families, the cities and the villages thereof.

24 And Moses gave *inheritance* unto the tribe of Gad, *even* unto the children of Gad according to their families.

25 And their coast was Jazer, and all the cities of Gilead, and half the land of the children of Ammon, unto Aroer that *is* before Rabbah;   Num. 32:35

26 And from Heshbon unto Ramath-mizpeh, and Betonim; and from Mahanaim unto the border of Debir;   2 Sam. 17:27

27 And in the valley, Beth-aram, and Beth-nimrah, and Succoth, and Zaphon, the rest of the kingdom of Sihon king of Heshbon, Jordan and *his* border, *even* unto the edge of the sea of Chinnereth on the other side Jordan eastward.   Gen. 33:17

28 This *is* the inheritance of the children of Gad after their families, the cities, and their villages.

29 And Moses gave *inheritance* unto the half tribe of Manasseh: and *this* was *the possession* of the half tribe of the children of Manasseh by their families.

30 And their coast was from Mahanaim, all Bashan, all the kingdom of Og king of Bashan, and all the towns of Jair, which *are* in Bashan, ^Tthreescore cities: Josh. 13:26 ◆ *sixty*

31 And half Gilead, and Ashtaroth, and Edrei, cities of the kingdom of Og in Bashan, *were pertaining* unto the children of Machir the son of Manasseh, *even* to the one half of the children of Machir by their families. Josh. 12:4

32 These *are the countries* which Moses did distribute for inheritance in the plains of Moab, on the other side Jordan, by Jericho, eastward.

33 But unto the tribe of Levi Moses gave not *any* inheritance: the LORD God of Israel *was* their inheritance, as he said unto them.   Josh. 18:7

The Tribes West of the Jordan Receive Their Land by Lot

14 And these *are the* countries which the children of Israel inherited in the land of Canaan, which Eleazar the priest, and Joshua the son of Nun, and the heads of the fathers of the tribes of the children of Israel, distributed for inheritance to them.   Num. 34:17-29
2 By lot *was* their inheritance, as the LORD commanded by the hand of Moses, for the nine tribes, and *for* the half tribe.   Num. 33:54
3 For Moses had given the inheritance of two tribes and an half tribe on the other side Jordan: but unto the Levites he gave none inheritance among them.   Josh. 13:14
4 For the children of Joseph were two tribes, Manasseh and Ephraim: therefore they gave no part unto the Levites in the land, save cities to dwell *in*, with their suburbs for their cattle and for their substance.   Gen. 48:5; 1 Chr. 5:1-2
5 As the LORD commanded Moses, so the children of Israel did, and they divided the land.   Josh. 21:2

14:2–5 A Peaceful Solution

Were the principles of God's laws regarding the distribution of property carried out in the world today, how different would be the condition of the people! An observance of these principles would prevent the terrible evils that in all ages have resulted from the oppression of the poor by the rich and the hatred of the rich by the poor. . . . It would aid in bringing a peaceful solution of problems that now threaten to fill the world with anarchy and bloodshed. *Ed 44*

Caleb Obtains Hebron

6 Then the children of Judah came unto Joshua in Gilgal: and Caleb the son of Jephunneh the Kenezite said unto him, Thou knowest the thing that the LORD said unto Moses the man of God concerning me and thee in Kadesh-barnea.   Num. 13:6; 14:24, 30
7 Forty years old *was* I when Moses the servant of the LORD sent me from Kadesh-barnea to ᵀespy out the land; and I brought him word again as *it was* in mine heart.   Num. 13:6 ◆ *see*
8 Nevertheless my brethren that went up with me made the heart of the people melt: but I wholly followed the LORD my God.   Num. 14:24
9 And Moses sware on that day, saying, Surely the land whereon thy feet have ᵀtrodden shall be thine inheritance, and thy children's for ever, because thou hast wholly followed the LORD my God. Deut. 1:36 ◆ *trampled*
10 And now, behold, the LORD hath kept me alive, as he said, these forty and five years, even since the LORD spake this word unto Moses, while *the children of* Israel wandered in the wilderness: and now, lo, I *am* this day ᵀfourscore and five years old.   *eighty*

14:11, 12 Claim of a Faithful Leader

Caleb now reminded Joshua of the promise then made, as the reward of his faithfulness [Joshua 14:9]. . . . Hebron was the seat of the dreaded Anakim, whose formidable appearance had so terrified the spies, and through them destroyed the courage of all Israel. This, above all others, was the place which Caleb, trusting in the strength of God, chose for his inheritance. *PP 511, 512*

---

11 As yet I *am as* strong this day as *I was* in the day that Moses sent me: as my strength *was* then, even so *is* my strength now, for war, both to go out, and to come in.   Deut. 31:2; 34:7
12 Now therefore give me this mountain,

God's Laws Regarding Distribution

Joshua 14

In apportioning the inheritance of His people, it was God's purpose to teach them, and through them the people of after generations, correct principles concerning the ownership of the land. The land of Canaan was divided among the whole people, the Levites only, as ministers of the sanctuary, being excepted. Though one might for a season dispose of his possession, he could not barter away the inheritance of his children. When able to do so, he was at liberty at any time to redeem it; debts were remitted every seventh year, and in the fiftieth, or year of jubilee, all landed property reverted to the original owner. Thus every family was secured in its possession, and a safeguard was afforded against the extremes either of wealth or of poverty.

By the distribution of the land among the people, God provided for them, as for the dwellers in Eden, the occupation most favorable to development—the care of plants and animals. A further provision for education was the suspension of agricultural labor every seventh year, the land lying fallow, and its spontaneous products being left to the poor. Thus was given opportunity for more extended study, for social intercourse [association] and worship, and for the exercise of benevolence, so often crowded out by life's cares and labors. *Ed 43*

whereof the LORD spake in that day; for thou heardest in that day how the Anakims *were* there, and *that* the cities *were* great *and* fenced: if so be the LORD *will be* with me, then I shall be able to drive them out, as the LORD said.   Num. 13:28, 33

13 And Joshua blessed him, and gave unto Caleb the son of Jephunneh Hebron for an inheritance.   Josh. 22:6; Judg. 1:20; 1 Chr. 6:55-56

14 Hebron therefore became the inheritance of Caleb the son of Jephunneh the Kenezite unto this day, because that he wholly followed the LORD God of Israel.   Josh. 14:8-9

15 And the name of Hebron before *was* Kirjath-arba; *which Arba was* a great man among the Anakims. And the land had rest from war.   Gen. 23:2; Josh. 11:23; 15:13

Land for the Tribe of Judah

15 *This* then was the lot of the tribe of the children of Judah by their families; *even* to the border of Edom the wilderness of Zin southward *was* the uttermost part of the south coast.

2 And their south border was from the shore of the salt sea, from the bay that looketh southward:

3 And it went out to the south side to Maaleh-acrabbim, and passed along to Zin, and ascended up on the south side unto Kadesh-barnea, and passed along to Hezron, and went up to Adar, and ᵀfetched a compass to Karkaa: Num. 34:4; Judg. 1:36 ◆ *went around*

4 *From thence* it passed toward Azmon, and went out unto the river of Egypt; and the goings out of that coast were at the sea: this shall be your south coast.   Num. 34:5

5 And the east border *was* the salt sea, *even* unto the end of Jordan. And *their* border in the north quarter *was* from the bay of the sea at the uttermost part of Jordan: Num. 34:12

6 And the border went up to Beth-hogla, and passed along by the north of Beth-arabah; and the border went up to the stone of Bohan the son of Reuben: Josh. 18:17

7 And the border went up toward Debir from the valley of Achor, and so northward, looking toward Gilgal, that *is* before the going up to Adummim, which *is* on the south side of the river: and the border passed toward the waters of Enshemesh, and the goings out thereof were at Enrogel: 2 Sam. 17:17

8 And the border went up by the valley of the son of Hinnom unto the south side of the Jebusite; the same *is* Jerusalem: and the border went up to the top of the mountain that *lieth* before the valley of Hinnom westward, which *is* at the end of the valley of the giants northward: Josh. 15:63; 18:16, 28

9 And the border was drawn from the top of the hill unto the fountain of the water of Nephtoah, and went out to the cities of mount Ephron; and the border was drawn to Baalah, which *is* Kirjath-jearim: Judg. 18:12; 1 Chr. 13:6

10 And the border ᵀcompassed from Baalah westward unto mount Seir, and passed along unto the side of mount Jearim, which *is* Chesalon, on the north side, and went down to Beth-shemesh, and passed on to Timnah: Judg. 14:1 ◆ *ranged*

11 And the border went out unto the side of Ekron northward: and the border was drawn to Shicron, and passed along to mount Baalah, and went out unto Jabneel; and the goings out of the border were at the sea.

12 And the west border *was* to the great sea, and the coast *thereof*. This *is* the coast of the children of Judah round about according to their families.   Num. 34:6-7

13 And unto Caleb the son of Jephunneh he gave a part among the children of Judah, according to the commandment of the LORD to Joshua, *even* the city of Arba the father of Anak, which *city is* Hebron.

14 And Caleb drove thence the three sons of Anak, Sheshai, and Ahiman, and Talmai, the children of Anak.   Judg. 1:10

15 And he went up thence to the inhabitants of Debir: and the name of Debir before *was* Kirjath-sepher.   Josh. 10:38

16 And Caleb said, He that ᵀsmiteth Kirjath-sepher, and taketh it, to him will I give Achsah my daughter to wife.   *strikes*

17 And Othniel the son of Kenaz, the brother of Caleb, took it: and he gave him Achsah his daughter to wife.   Judg. 1:13

18 And it came to pass, as she came *unto him*, that she moved him to ask of her father a field: and she lighted off *her* ass; and Caleb said unto her, What wouldest thou?

19 Who answered, Give me a blessing; for thou hast given me a south land; give me also springs of water. And he gave her the upper springs, and the ᵀnether springs.   *lower*

The Cities of Judah

20 This *is* the inheritance of the tribe of the children of Judah according to their families.

21 And the uttermost cities of the tribe of the children of Judah toward the coast of Edom southward were Kabzeel, and Eder, and Jagur,   Gen. 35:21

22 And Kinah, and Dimonah, and Adadah,

23 And Kedesh, and Hazor, and Ithnan,

24 Ziph, and Telem, and Bealoth,   1 Sam. 23:14

25 And Hazor, Hadattah, and Kerioth, *and* Hezron, which *is* Hazor,

26 Amam, and Shema, and Moladah,   1 Chr. 4:28

27 And Hazar-gaddah, and Heshmon, and Beth-palet,

28 And Hazar-shual, and Beer-sheba, and Bizjothjah,   Gen. 26:33
29 Baalah, and Iim, and Azem,
30 And Eltolad, and Chesil, and Hormah,
31 And Ziklag, and Madmannah, and San-sannah,   1 Sam. 27:6; 30:1
32 And Lebaoth, and Shilhim, and Ain, and Rimmon: all the cities *are* twenty and nine, with their villages:
33 *And* in the valley, Eshtaol, and Zoreah, and Ashnah,   Judg. 13:25
34 And Zanoah, and En-gannim, Tappuah, and Enam,
35 Jarmuth, and Adullam, Socoh, and Azekah,   Josh. 10:3; 1 Sam. 17:1; 22:1
36 And Sharaim, and Adithaim, and Gede-rah, and Gederothaim; fourteen cities with their villages:
37 Zenan, and Hadashah, and Migdal-gad,
38 And Dilean, and Mizpeh, and Joktheel,
39 Lachish, and Bozkath, and Eglon, 2 Kin. 22:1
40 And Cabbon, and Lahmam, and Kithlish,
41 And Gederoth, Beth-dagon, and Naamah, and Makkedah; sixteen cities with their villages: Josh. 10:21
42 Libnah, and Ether, and Ashan, Josh. 10:29
43 And Jiphtah, and Ashnah, and Nezib,
44 And Keilah, and Achzib, and Mareshah; nine cities with their villages:
45 Ekron, with her towns and her villages:
46 From Ekron even unto the sea, all that *lay* near Ashdod, with their villages:
47 Ashdod with her towns and her villages, Gaza with her towns and her villages, unto the river of Egypt, and the great sea, and the border *thereof*:   Josh. 15:4
48 And in the mountains, Shamir, and Jattir, and Socoh,
49 And Dannah, and Kirjath-sannah, which *is* Debir,   Josh. 15:15
50 And Anab, and Eshtemoh, and Anim,
51 And Goshen, and Holon, and Giloh; eleven cities with their villages: Josh. 10:41
52 Arab, and Dumah, and Eshean,
53 And Janum, and Beth-tappuah, and Aphekah,
54 And Humtah, and Kirjath-arba, which *is* Hebron, and Zior; nine cities with their villages: Josh. 15:13
55 Maon, Carmel, and Ziph, and Juttah,
56 And Jezreel, and Jokdeam, and Zanoah,
57 Cain, Gibeah, and Timnah; ten cities with their villages: Josh. 15:10
58 Halhul, Beth-zur, and Gedor,
59 And Maarath, and Beth-anoth, and Elte-kon; six cities with their villages:
60 Kirjath-baal, which *is* Kirjath-jearim, and Rabbah; two cities with their villages: Josh. 18:14
61 In the wilderness, Beth-arabah, Middin, and Secacah,   Josh. 15:6

62 And Nibshan, and the city of Salt, and Engedi; six cities with their villages. 1 Sam. 23:29
63 As for the Jebusites the inhabitants of Jerusalem, the children of Judah could not drive them out: but the Jebusites dwell with the children of Judah at Jerusalem unto this day.   Judg. 1:8, 21

The Borders of the Land for the Sons of Joseph

16 And the lot of the children of Joseph fell from Jordan by Jericho, unto the water of Jericho on the east, to the wilderness that goeth up from Jericho throughout mount Beth-el,   Josh. 8:15; 18:12
2 And goeth out from Beth-el to Luz, and passeth along unto the borders of Archi to Ataroth,   Gen. 28:19; Josh. 18:13
3 And goeth down westward to the coast of Japhleti, unto the coast of Beth-horon the ᵀnether, and to Gezer: and the goings out thereof are at the sea.   Josh. 10:33 ◆ *lower*
4 So the children of Joseph, Manasseh and Ephraim, took their inheritance.   Josh. 17:14

The Border of the Land for the Tribe of Ephraim

5 And the border of the children of Ephraim according to their families was *thus*: even the border of their inheritance on the east side was Ataroth-addar, unto Beth-horon the upper;   Josh. 18:13
6 And the border went out toward the sea to Michmethah on the north side; and the border went about eastward unto Taanath-shiloh, and passed by it on the east to Janohah;   Josh. 17:7
7 And it went down from Janohah to Ata-roth, and to Naarath, and came to Jericho, and went out at Jordan.   1 Chr. 7:28
8 The border went out from Tappuah west-ward unto the river Kanah; and the goings out thereof were at the sea. This *is* the inheritance of the tribe of the children of Ephraim by their families.   Josh. 17:8-9
9 And the separate cities for the children of Ephraim *were* among the inheritance of the children of Manasseh, all the cities with their villages.
10 And they ᵀdrave not out the Canaanites that dwelt in Gezer: but the Canaanites dwell among the Ephraimites unto this day, and serve under tribute.   Judg. 1:29; 1 Kin. 9:16 ◆ *drove*

Land for the Tribe of Manasseh

17 There was also a lot for the tribe of Manasseh; for he *was* the firstborn of Joseph; ᵀ*to wit*, for Machir the firstborn of Manasseh, the father of Gilead: because he was a man of war, therefore he had Gilead and Bashan.   Gen. 41:51; 46:20; Num. 26:29 ◆ *namely*

2 There was also *a lot* for the rest of the children of Manasseh by their families; for the children of Abiezer, and for the children of Helek, and for the children of Asriel, and for the children of Shechem, and for the children of Hepher, and for the children of Shemida: these *were* the male children of Manasseh the son of Joseph by their families.   Num. 26:29-32

3 But Zelophehad, the son of Hepher, the son of Gilead, the son of Machir, the son of Manasseh, had no sons, but daughters: and these *are* the names of his daughters, Mahlah, and Noah, Hoglah, Milcah, and Tirzah.

4 And they came near before Eleazar the priest, and before Joshua the son of Nun, and before the princes, saying, The LORD commanded Moses to give us an inheritance among our brethren. Therefore according to the commandment of the LORD he gave them an inheritance among the brethren of their father.   Josh. 14:1

5 And there fell ten portions to Manasseh, beside the land of Gilead and Bashan, which *were* on the other side Jordan;

6 Because the daughters of Manasseh had an inheritance among his sons: and the rest of Manasseh's sons had the land of Gilead.

Manasseh's Boundaries

7 And the coast of Manasseh was from Asher to Michmethah, that *lieth* before Shechem; and the border went along on the right hand unto the inhabitants of En-tappuah.   Josh. 21:21

8 *Now* Manasseh had the land of Tappuah: but Tappuah on the border of Manasseh be*longed* to the children of Ephraim;   Josh. 16:8

9 And the coast descended unto the river Kanah, southward of the river: these cities of Ephraim *are* among the cities of Manasseh: the coast of Manasseh also *was* on the north side of the river, and the ᵀoutgoings of it were at the sea: *boundaries*

10 Southward *it was* Ephraim's, and northward *it was* Manasseh's, and the sea is his border; and they met together in Asher on the north, and in Issachar on the east.

11 And Manasseh had in Issachar and in Asher Beth-shean and her towns, and Ibleam and her towns, and the inhabitants of Dor and her towns, and the inhabitants of En-dor and her towns, and the inhabitants of Taanach and her towns, and the inhabitants of Megiddo and her towns, *even* three countries.   Josh. 12:23; Judg. 1:27; 1 Chr. 7:29

12 Yet the children of Manasseh could not drive out *the inhabitants of* those cities; but the Canaanites would dwell in that land.

13 Yet it came to pass, when the children of Israel were ᵀwaxen strong, that they put

the Canaanites to tribute; but did not utterly drive them out.   Josh. 16:10 ♦ *become*

The Children of Joseph Obtain Another Portion

14 And the children of Joseph spake unto Joshua, saying, Why hast thou given me *but* one lot and one portion to inherit, seeing I *am* a great people, ᵀforasmuch as the LORD hath blessed me ᵀhitherto? Gen. 48:19 ♦ *since* ♦ *up to now*

15 And Joshua answered them, If thou *be* a great people, *then* get thee up to the wood *country*, and cut down for thyself there in the land of the Perizzites and of the giants, if mount Ephraim be too narrow for thee.   Gen. 15:20

16 And the children of Joseph said, The hill is not enough for us: and all the Canaanites that dwell in the land of the valley have chariots of iron, *both they* who *are* of Beth-shean and her towns, and *they* who *are* of the valley of Jezreel.   Judg. 1:19

17:16 A Tribe Lacking Courage

[The Ephraimites'] reply showed the real cause of complaint. They lacked faith and courage to drive out the Canaanites. . . .

The power of the God of Israel had been pledged to His people, and had the Ephraimites possessed the courage and faith of Caleb, no enemy could have stood before them. Their evident desire to shun hardship and danger was firmly met by Joshua. *PP 514*

---

17 And Joshua spake unto the house of Joseph, *even* to Ephraim and to Manasseh, saying, Thou *art* a great people, and hast great power: thou shalt not have one lot *only*:

18 But the mountain shall be thine; for it *is* a wood, and thou shalt cut it down: and the outgoings of it shall be thine: for thou shalt drive out the Canaanites, though they have iron chariots, *and* though they *be* strong.

The Tabernacle Is Set up at Shiloh

18 And the whole congregation of the children of Israel assembled together at Shiloh, and set up the tabernacle of the congregation there. And the land was subdued before them.   Josh. 19:51; 21:2; Jer. 26:6

18:1 Permanent Tabernacle Location

Heretofore Gilgal had been the headquarters of the nation and the seat of the tabernacle. But now the tabernacle was to be removed to the place chosen for its permanent location. This was Shiloh, a little town in the lot of Ephraim. It was near the center of the land, and was easy of access to all the tribes. Here a portion of country had been thoroughly subdued, so that the worshipers would not be molested. *PP 514*

The Remainder of the Land Is Described and Divided

2 And there remained among the children of Israel seven tribes, which had not yet received their inheritance.

3 And Joshua said unto the children of Israel, How long *are* ye slack to go to possess the land, which the LORD God of your fathers hath given you?   Judg. 18:9

4 Give out from among you three men for *each* tribe: and I will send them, and they shall rise, and go through the land, and describe it according to the inheritance of them; and they shall come *again* to me.

5 And they shall divide it into seven parts: Judah shall abide in their coast on the south, and the house of Joseph shall abide in their coasts on the north.

6 Ye shall therefore describe the land *into* seven parts, and bring *the description* ᵀhither to me, that I may cast lots for you here before the LORD our God.   Josh. 14:2; 18:10 ◆ *here*

7 But the Levites have no part among you; for the priesthood of the LORD *is* their inheritance: and Gad, and Reuben, and half the tribe of Manasseh, have received their inheritance beyond Jordan on the east, which Moses the servant of the LORD gave them.   Num. 18:20; Josh. 13:33

8 And the men arose, and went away: and Joshua charged them that went to describe the land, saying, Go and walk through the land, and describe it, and come again to me, that I may here cast lots for you before the LORD in Shiloh.

9 And the men went and passed through the land, and described it by cities into seven parts in a book, and came *again* to Joshua to the host at Shiloh.

10 And Joshua cast lots for them in Shiloh before the LORD: and there Joshua divided the land unto the children of Israel according to their divisions.   Josh. 18:6

Land for the Tribe of Benjamin

11 And the lot of the tribe of the children of Benjamin came up according to their families: and the coast of their lot came forth between the children of Judah and the children of Joseph.

12 And their border on the north side was from Jordan; and the border went up to the side of Jericho on the north side, and went up through the mountains westward; and the goings out thereof were at the wilderness of Beth-aven.   Josh. 7:2; 16:1

13 And the border went over from thence toward Luz, to the side of Luz, which *is* Beth-el, southward; and the border descended to Ataroth-adar, near the hill that *lieth* on the south side of the ᵀnether Beth-horon. Gen. 28:19 ◆ *lower*

14 And the border was drawn *thence*, and ᵀcompassed the corner of the sea southward, from the hill that *lieth* before Beth-horon southward; and the goings out thereof were at Kirjath-baal, which *is* Kirjath-jearim, a city of the children of Judah: this *was* the west quarter.   Josh. 15:9 ◆ *extended around*

15 And the south quarter *was* from the end of Kirjath-jearim, and the border went out on the west, and went out to the well of waters of Nephtoah: Josh. 15:9

16 And the border came down to the end of the mountain that *lieth* before the valley of the son of Hinnom, *and* which *is* in the valley of the giants on the north, and descended to the valley of Hinnom, to the side of Jebusi on the south, and descended to En-rogel,   Josh. 15:7-8; 2 Kin. 23:10; Is. 30:33

17 And was drawn from the north, and went forth to En-shemesh, and went forth toward Geliloth, which *is* over against the going up of Adummim, and descended to the stone of Bohan the son of Reuben,   Josh. 15:6

18 And passed along toward the side over against Arabah northward, and went down unto Arabah: Josh. 15:6

19 And the border passed along to the side of Beth-hoglah northward: and the ᵀoutgoings of the border were at the north bay of the salt sea at the south end of Jordan: this *was* the south coast.   Gen. 14:3 ◆ *boundaries*

20 And Jordan was the border of it on the east side. This *was* the inheritance of the children of Benjamin, by the coasts thereof round about, according to their families.

21 Now the cities of the tribe of the children of Benjamin according to their families were Jericho, and Beth-hoglah, and the valley of Keziz,   Josh. 18:12

22 And Beth-arabah, and Zemaraim, and Beth-el,

23 And Avim, and Parah, and Ophrah,

24 And Chephar-haammonai, and Ophni, and Gaba; twelve cities with their villages:

25 Gibeon, and Ramah, and Beeroth, Josh. 9:17

26 And Mizpeh, and Chephirah, and Mozah,

27 And Rekem, and Irpeel, and Taralah,

28 And Zelah, Eleph, and Jebusi, which *is* Jerusalem, Gibeath, *and* Kirjath; fourteen cities with their villages. This *is* the inheritance of the children of Benjamin according to their families.   Josh. 15:8

18:28 Jebus Becomes Jerusalem

For centuries Jebus had been looked upon as impregnable; but it was besieged and taken by the Hebrews under the command of Joab, who, as the reward of his valor, was made commander-in-chief of the armies of Israel. Jebus now became the national capital, and its heathen name was changed to Jerusalem. *PP 703*

Land for the Tribe of Simeon

19 And the second lot came forth to Simeon, *even* for the tribe of the children of Simeon according to their families: and their inheritance was within the inheritance of the children of Judah.   Josh. 19:9

2 And they had in their inheritance Beer-sheba, or Sheba, and Moladah,   1 Chr. 4:28-30

3 And Hazar-shual, and Balah, and Azem,

4 And Eltolad, and Bethul, and Hormah,

5 And Ziklag, and Beth-marcaboth, and Hazar-susah,

6 And Beth-lebaoth, and Sharuhen; thirteen cities and their villages:

7 Ain, Remmon, and Ether, and Ashan; four cities and their villages: Josh. 15:42

8 And all the villages that *were* round about these cities to Baalath-beer, Ramath of the south. This *is* the inheritance of the tribe of the children of Simeon according to their families.

9 Out of the portion of the children of Judah *was* the inheritance of the children of Simeon: for the part of the children of Judah was too much for them: therefore the children of Simeon had their inheritance within the inheritance of them.

Land for the Tribe of Zebulun

10 And the third lot came up for the children of Zebulun according to their families: and the border of their inheritance was unto Sarid:

11 And their border went up toward the sea, and Maralah, and reached to Dabbasheth, and reached to the river that *is* before Jokneam;   Josh. 12:22

12 And turned from Sarid eastward toward the sunrising unto the border of Chisloth-tabor, and then goeth out to Daberath, and goeth up to Japhia,

13 And from thence passeth on along on the east to Gittah-hepher, to Ittah-kazin, and goeth out to Remmon-methoar to Neah;

14 And the border compasseth it on the north side to Hannathon: and the outgoings thereof are in the valley of Jiphthah-el:

15 And Kattath, and Nahallal, and Shimron, and Idalah, and Beth-lehem: twelve cities with their villages.   Josh. 11:1

16 This *is* the inheritance of the children of Zebulun according to their families, these cities with their villages.

Land for the Tribe of Issachar

17 *And* the fourth lot came out to Issachar, for the children of Issachar according to their families.

18 And their border was toward Jezreel, and Chesulloth, and Shunem,   1 Sam. 28:4; 2 Kin. 4:8

19 And Hapharaim, and Shion, and Anaharath,

20 And Rabbith, and Kishion, and Abez,

21 And Remeth, and En-gannim, and En-haddah, and Beth-pazzez;

22 And the coast reacheth to Tabor, and Shahazimah, and Beth-shemesh; and the outgoings of their border were at Jordan: sixteen cities with their villages.   Judg. 4:6 ◆ *boundaries*

23 This *is* the inheritance of the tribe of the children of Issachar according to their families, the cities and their villages.

Land for the Tribe of Asher

24 And the fifth lot came out for the tribe of the children of Asher according to their families.

25 And their border was Helkath, and Hali, and Beten, and Achshaph,

26 And Alammelech, and Amad, and Misheal; and reacheth to Carmel westward, and to Shihor-libnath;   1 Kin. 18:20

27 And turneth toward the sunrising to Beth-dagon, and reacheth to Zebulun, and to the valley of Jiphthah-el toward the north side of Beth-emek, and Neiel, and goeth out to Cabul on the left hand,   1 Kin. 9:13

28 And Hebron, and Rehob, and Hammon, and Kanah, *even* unto great Zidon;   Judg. 1:31

29 And *then* the coast turneth to Ramah, and to the strong city Tyre; and the coast turneth to Hosah; and the outgoings thereof are at the sea from the coast to Achzib: Judg. 1:31

30 Ummah also, and Aphek, and Rehob: twenty and two cities with their villages.

31 This *is* the inheritance of the tribe of the children of Asher according to their families, these cities with their villages.

Land for the Tribe of Naphtali

32 The sixth lot came out to the children of Naphtali, *even* for the children of Naphtali according to their families.

33 And their coast was from Heleph, from Allon to Zaanannim, and Adami, Nekeb, and Jabneel, unto Lakum; and the outgoings thereof were at Jordan: Judg. 4:11

34 And *then* the coast turneth westward to Aznoth-tabor, and goeth out from thence to Hukkok, and reacheth to Zebulun on the south side, and reacheth to Asher on the west side, and to Judah upon Jordan toward the sunrising.   Deut. 33:23

35 And the fenced cities *are* Ziddim, Zer, and Hammath, Rakkath, and Chinnereth, Josh. 11:2

36 And Adamah, and Ramah, and Hazor,

37 And Kedesh, and Edrei, and En-hazor,

38 And Iron, and Migdalel, Horem, and Beth-anath, and Beth-shemesh; nineteen cities with their villages.

39 This *is* the inheritance of the tribe of the

children of Naphtali according to their families, the cities and their villages.

Land for the Tribe of Dan, and for Joshua

40 *And* the seventh lot came out for the tribe of the children of Dan according to their families.

41 And the coast of their inheritance was Zorah, and Eshtaol, and Ir-shemesh,

42 And Shaalabbin, and Ajalon, and Jethlah,

43 And Elon, and Thimnathah, and Ekron,

44 And Eltekeh, and Gibbethon, and Baalath,

45 And Jehud, and Beneberak, and Gath-rimmon,   Josh. 21:24

46 And Me-jarkon, and Rakkon, with the border before Japho.   Jon. 1:3

47 And the coast of the children of Dan went out *too little* for them: therefore the children of Dan went up to fight against Leshem, and took it, and smote it with the edge of the sword, and possessed it, and dwelt therein, and called Leshem, Dan, after the name of Dan their father.   Judg. 1:34-35

48 This *is* the inheritance of the tribe of the children of Dan according to their families, these cities with their villages.

49 When they had made an end of dividing the land for inheritance by their coasts, the children of Israel gave an inheritance to Joshua the son of Nun among them:

50 According to the word of the LORD they gave him the city which he asked, *even* Timnath-serah in mount Ephraim: and he built the city, and dwelt therein.   Josh. 24:30; Judg. 2:9

19:49, 50 A Leader's Unselfish Claim

To [Joshua], as to Caleb, a special promise of inheritance had been given; yet he asked for no extensive province, but only a single city. . . . The name given to the city was Timnathserah, "the portion that remains"—a standing testimony to the noble character and unselfish spirit of the conqueror, who, instead of being the first to appropriate the spoils of conquest, deferred his claim until the humblest of his people had been served. *PP 515*

---

51 These *are* the inheritances, which Eleazar the priest, and Joshua the son of Nun, and the heads of the fathers of the tribes of the children of Israel, divided for an inheritance by lot in Shiloh before the LORD, at the door of the tabernacle of the congregation. So they made an end of dividing the country. Josh. 14:1

God Commands Cities of Refuge

20 The LORD also spake unto Joshua, saying,

2 Speak to the children of Israel, saying, Ap-point out for you cities of refuge, whereof I spake unto you by the hand of Moses: Num. 35:6

3 That the slayer that killeth *any* person un-awares *and* unwittingly may flee thither: and they shall be your refuge from the avenger of blood.

4 And when he that doth flee unto one of those cities shall stand at the entering of the gate of the city, and shall declare his cause in the ears of the elders of that city, they shall take him into the city unto them, and give him a place, that he may dwell among them.   Jer. 38:7

5 And if the avenger of blood pursue after him, then they shall not deliver the slayer up into his hand; because he smote his neighbour unwittingly, and hated him not before-time.   Num. 35:12

6 And he shall dwell in that city, until he stand before the congregation for judgment, *and* until the death of the high priest that shall be in those days: then shall the slayer return, and come unto his own city, and unto his own house, unto the city from whence he fled.   Num. 35:12, 24-25

The People Appoint the Six Cities of Refuge as God Commanded

7 And they appointed Kedesh in Galilee in mount Naphtali, and Shechem in mount Ephraim, and Kirjath-arba, which *is* Hebron, in the mountain of Judah.   Josh. 21:11; 1 Chr. 6:76

8 And on the other side Jordan by Jericho eastward, they assigned Bezer in the wilderness upon the plain out of the tribe of Reuben, and Ramoth in Gilead out of the tribe of Gad, and Golan in Bashan out of the tribe of Manasseh.   Josh. 21:36

9 These were the cities appointed for all the children of Israel, and for the stranger that sojourneth among them, that whosoever killeth *any* person at unawares might flee thither, and not die by the hand of the avenger of blood, until he stood before the congregation.   Num. 35:15

The Tribes Set Aside Forty-eight Cities for the Levites

21 Then came near the heads of the fathers of the Levites unto Eleazar the priest, and unto Joshua the son of Nun, and unto the heads of the fathers of the tribes of the children of Israel;   Josh. 14:1

2 And they spake unto them at Shiloh in the land of Canaan, saying, The LORD commanded by the hand of Moses to give us cities to dwell in, with the suburbs thereof for our cattle.   Josh. 18:1

3 And the children of Israel gave unto the Levites out of their inheritance, at the

commandment of the LORD, these cities and their suburbs.

4 And the lot came out for the families of the Kohathites: and the children of Aaron the priest, *which were* of the Levites, had by lot out of the tribe of Judah, and out of the tribe of Simeon, and out of the tribe of Benjamin, thirteen cities.

5 And the rest of the children of Kohath *had* by lot out of the families of the tribe of Ephraim, and out of the tribe of Dan, and out of the half tribe of Manasseh, ten cities.   Josh. 21:20-26

6 And the children of Gershon *had* by lot out of the families of the tribe of Issachar, and out of the tribe of Asher, and out of the tribe of Naphtali, and out of the half tribe of Manasseh in Bashan, thirteen cities.   Josh. 21:27-33

7 The children of Merari by their families *had* out of the tribe of Reuben, and out of the tribe of Gad, and out of the tribe of Zebulun, twelve cities.   Josh. 21:34-40

8 And the children of Israel gave by lot unto the Levites these cities with their suburbs, as the LORD commanded by the hand of Moses.   Josh. 21:3

9 And they gave out of the tribe of the children of Judah, and out of the tribe of the children of Simeon, these cities which are *here* mentioned by name,

10 Which the children of Aaron, *being* of the families of the Kohathites, *who were* of the children of Levi, had: for theirs was the first lot.   Josh. 21:4

11 And they gave them the city of Arba the father of Anak, which *city is* Hebron, in the hill *country* of Judah, with the suburbs thereof round about it.   1 Chr. 6:55; Luke 1:39

21:11 Judah's Chief City

Hebron was twenty miles north from Beersheba, and about midway between that city and the future site of Jerusalem. It was originally called Kirjath-arba, the city of Arba, the father of Anak. Later it was called Mamre, and here was the burial place of the patriarchs, "the cave of Machpelah." Hebron had been the possession of Caleb and was now the chief city of Judah. *PP 697*

---

12 But the fields of the city, and the villages thereof, gave they to Caleb the son of Jephunneh for his possession.

13 Thus they gave to the children of Aaron the priest Hebron with her suburbs, *to be* a city of refuge for the slayer; and Libnah with her suburbs,   Josh. 15:42

14 And Jattir with her suburbs, and Eshtemoa with her suburbs,   Josh. 15:48

15 And Holon with her suburbs, and Debir with her suburbs,   Josh. 15:49

16 And Ain with her suburbs, and Juttah with her suburbs, *and* Beth-shemesh with her suburbs; nine cities out of those two tribes.   Josh. 15:10

17 And out of the tribe of Benjamin, Gibeon with her suburbs, Geba with her suburbs,   Josh. 9:3

18 Anathoth with her suburbs, and Almon with her suburbs; four cities.

19 All the cities of the children of Aaron, the priests, *were* thirteen cities with their suburbs.

20 And the families of the children of Kohath, the Levites which remained of the children of Kohath, even they had the cities of their lot out of the tribe of Ephraim. 1 Chr. 6:66

21 For they gave them Shechem with her suburbs in mount Ephraim, *to be* a city of refuge for the slayer; and Gezer with her suburbs,   Josh. 20:7

22 And Kibzaim with her suburbs, and Beth-horon with her suburbs; four cities.

23 And out of the tribe of Dan, Eltekeh with her suburbs, Gibbethon with her suburbs,

24 Aijalon with her suburbs, Gath-rimmon with her suburbs; four cities.

25 And out of the half tribe of Manasseh, Tanach with her suburbs, and Gath-rimmon with her suburbs; two cities.

26 All the cities *were* ten with their suburbs for the families of the children of Kohath that remained.

27 And unto the children of Gershon, of the families of the Levites, out of the *other* half tribe of Manasseh *they gave* Golan in Bashan with her suburbs, *to be* a city of refuge for the slayer; and Beeshterah with her suburbs; two cities.   1 Chr. 6:71

28 And out of the tribe of Issachar, Kishon with her suburbs, Dabareh with her suburbs,

29 Jarmuth with her suburbs, En-gannim with her suburbs; four cities.

30 And out of the tribe of Asher, Mishal with her suburbs, Abdon with her suburbs,

31 Helkath with her suburbs, and Rehob with her suburbs; four cities.

32 And out of the tribe of Naphtali, Kedesh in Galilee with her suburbs, *to be* a city of refuge for the slayer; and Hammoth-dor with her suburbs, and Kartan with her suburbs; three cities.   Josh. 20:7

33 All the cities of the Gershonites according to their families *were* thirteen cities with their suburbs.

34 And unto the families of the children of Merari, the rest of the Levites, out of the tribe of Zebulun, Jokneam with her suburbs, and Kartah with her suburbs,   1 Chr. 6:77

35 Dimnah with her suburbs, Nahalal with her suburbs; four cities.

36 And out of the tribe of Reuben, Bezer with her suburbs, and Jahazah with her suburbs,   Deut. 4:43; Josh. 20:8
37 Kedemoth with her suburbs, and Mephaath with her suburbs; four cities.
38 And out of the tribe of Gad, Ramoth in Gilead with her suburbs, to be a city of refuge for the slayer; and Mahanaim with her suburbs,   Gen. 32:2
39 Heshbon with her suburbs, Jazer with her suburbs; four cities in all.
40 So all the cities for the children of Merari by their families, which were remaining of the families of the Levites, were by their lot twelve cities.
41 All the cities of the Levites within the possession of the children of Israel were forty and eight cities with their suburbs.
42 These cities were every one with their suburbs round about them: thus were all these cities.

God Gives the Land to the Israelites, Fulfilling His Promise

43 And the LORD gave unto Israel all the land which he sware to give unto their fathers; and they possessed it, and dwelt therein.   Gen. 13:15
44 And the LORD gave them rest round about, according to all that he sware unto their fathers: and there stood not a man of all their enemies before them; the LORD delivered all their enemies into their hand.   Josh. 11:23
45 There failed not ought of any good thing which the LORD had spoken unto the house of Israel; all came to pass.   Josh. 23:14-15

Joshua Sends Home the Tribes East of the Jordan

22 Then Joshua called the Reubenites, and the Gadites, and the half tribe of Manasseh,
2 And said unto them, Ye have kept all that Moses the servant of the LORD commanded you, and have obeyed my voice in all that I commanded you: Josh. 1:12-18
3 Ye have not left your brethren these many days unto this day, but have kept the charge of the commandment of the LORD your God.
4 And now the LORD your God hath given rest unto your brethren, as he promised them: therefore now return ye, and get you unto your tents, and unto the land of your possession, which Moses the servant of the LORD gave you on the other side Jordan.   Josh. 13:8
5 But take diligent heed to do the commandment and the law, which Moses the servant of the LORD charged you, to love the LORD your God, and to walk in all his ways, and to keep his commandments, and to cleave unto him, and to serve him with all your heart and with all your soul.   Deut. 6:17
6 So Joshua blessed them, and sent them away: and they went unto their tents.
7 Now to the one half of the tribe of Manasseh Moses had given possession in Bashan: but unto the other half thereof gave Joshua among their brethren on this side Jordan westward. And when Joshua sent them away also unto their tents, then he blessed them,   Josh. 17:1-12
8 And he spake unto them, saying, Return with much riches unto your tents, and with very much cattle, with silver, and with gold, and with brass, and with iron, and with very much raiment: divide the spoil of your enemies with your brethren.   Num. 31:27; 1 Sam. 30:24
9 And the children of Reuben and the children of Gad and the half tribe of Manasseh returned, and departed from the children of Israel out of Shiloh, which is in the land of Canaan, to go unto the country of Gilead, to the land of their possession, whereof they were possessed, according to the word of the LORD by the hand of Moses.   Num. 32:1, 26, 29

The Eastern Tribes Build an Altar for the Lord

10 And when they came unto the borders of Jordan, that are in the land of Canaan, the children of Reuben and the children of Gad and the half tribe of Manasseh built there an altar by Jordan, a great altar to see to.
11 And the children of Israel heard say, Behold, the children of Reuben and the children of Gad and the half tribe of Manasseh have built an altar over against the land of Canaan, in the borders of Jordan, at the passage of the children of Israel.   Deut. 13:12-14
12 And when the children of Israel heard of it, the whole congregation of the children of Israel gathered themselves together at Shiloh, to go up to war against them.

22:11, 12 Unsettling News

Beside the Jordan, near the place of Israel's miraculous passage of the river, the two and a half tribes had erected a great altar, similar to the altar of burnt offering at Shiloh. The law of God prohibited, on pain of death, the establishment of another worship than that at the sanctuary. If such was the object of this altar, it would, if permitted to remain, lead the people away from the true faith. *PP 518*

---

13 And the children of Israel sent unto the children of Reuben, and to the children of Gad, and to the half tribe of Manasseh, into the land of Gilead, Phinehas the son of Eleazar the priest,   Ex. 6:25; Num. 25:7; Judg. 20:28
14 And with him ten princes, of each chief

house a prince throughout all the tribes of Israel; and each one *was* an head of the house of their fathers among the thousands of Israel.   Num. 1:4

15 And they came unto the children of Reuben, and to the children of Gad, and to the half tribe of Manasseh, unto the land of Gilead, and they spake with them, saying,

16 Thus saith the whole congregation of the LORD, What ᵀtrespass *is* this that ye have committed against the God of Israel, to turn away this day from following the LORD, in that ye have builded you an altar, that ye might rebel this day against the LORD?   *sin*

17 *Is* the iniquity of Peor too little for us, from which we are not cleansed until this day, although there was a plague in the congregation of the LORD,

18 But that ye must turn away this day from following the LORD? and it will be, *seeing* ye rebel to day against the LORD, that to morrow he will be ᵀwroth with the whole congregation of Israel.   Num. 16:22; Josh. 22:16 ◆ *angry*

19 Notwithstanding, if the land of your possession *be* unclean, *then* pass ye over unto the land of the possession of the LORD, wherein the LORD's tabernacle dwelleth, and take possession among us: but rebel not against the LORD, nor rebel against us, in building you an altar beside the altar of the LORD our God.   Josh. 18:1

20 Did not Achan the son of Zerah commit a trespass in the accursed thing, and wrath fell on all the congregation of Israel? and that man perished not alone in his iniquity. Josh. 7:1, 5, 18

The Altar Is Explained Satisfactorily

21 Then the children of Reuben and the children of Gad and the half tribe of Manasseh answered, and said unto the heads of the thousands of Israel,

22 The LORD God of gods, the LORD God of gods, he knoweth, and Israel he shall know; if *it be* in rebellion, or if in ᵀtransgression against the LORD, (save us not this day,)   1 Kin. 8:39; Job 10:7 ◆ *violation of a law*

23 That we have built us an altar to turn from following the LORD, or if to offer thereon burnt offering or meat offering, or if to offer peace offerings thereon, let the LORD himself require *it*;   Deut. 18:19

24 And if we have not *rather* done it for fear of *this* thing, saying, In time to come your children might speak unto our children, saying, What have ye to do with the LORD God of Israel?   Josh. 4:6

25 For the LORD hath made Jordan a border between us and you, ye children of Reuben and children of Gad; ye have no part in the LORD: so shall your children make our children cease from fearing the LORD.

26 Therefore we said, Let us now prepare to build us an altar, not for burnt offering, nor for sacrifice:

27 But *that* it *may be* a witness between us, and you, and our generations after us, that we might do the service of the LORD before him with our burnt offerings, and with our sacrifices, and with our peace offerings; that your children may not say to our children in time to come, Ye have no part in the LORD.   Gen. 31:48; Deut. 12:5-6; Josh. 24:27

> **22:27 Questions Put to Rest**
>
> In reply the accused explained that their altar was not intended for sacrifice, but simply as a witness that, although separated by the river, they were of the same faith as their brethren in Canaan. They had feared that in future years their children might be excluded from the tabernacle, as having no part in Israel. Then this altar, erected after the pattern of the altar of the Lord at Shiloh, would be a witness that its builders were also worshipers of the living God. *PP 519*

28 Therefore said we, that it shall be, when they should *so* say to us or to our generations in time to come, that we may say *again*, Behold the pattern of the altar of the LORD, which our fathers made, not for burnt offerings, nor for sacrifices; but it *is* a witness between us and you.

29 God forbid that we should rebel against the LORD, and turn this day from following the LORD, to build an altar for burnt offerings, for meat offerings, or for sacrifices, beside the altar of the LORD our God that *is* before his tabernacle.   Deut. 12:13-14

30 And when Phinehas the priest, and the princes of the congregation and heads of the thousands of Israel which *were* with him, heard the words that the children of Reuben and the children of Gad and the children of Manasseh spake, it pleased them.   Josh. 22:33

31 And Phinehas the son of Eleazar the priest said unto the children of Reuben, and to the children of Gad, and to the children of Manasseh, This day we perceive that the LORD *is* among us, because ye have not committed this trespass against the LORD: now ye have delivered the children of Israel out of the hand of the LORD.   Lev. 26:11-12

32 And Phinehas the son of Eleazar the priest, and the princes, returned from the children of Reuben, and from the children of Gad, out of the land of Gilead, unto the land of Canaan, to the children of Israel, and brought them word again.

33 And the thing pleased the children of Israel; and the children of Israel blessed God, and did not intend to go up against them in battle, to destroy the land wherein the children of Reuben and Gad dwelt.   Dan. 2:19; Luke 2:28

22:33 Misjudged, Yet Without Resentment

The wisdom displayed by the Reubenites and their companions is worthy of imitation. While honestly seeking to promote the cause of true religion, they were misjudged and severely censured; yet they manifested no resentment. They listened with courtesy and patience to the charges of their brethren before attempting to make their defense, and then fully explained their motives and showed their innocence. Thus the difficulty which had threatened such serious consequences was amicably settled. *PP 520*

34 And the children of Reuben and the children of Gad called the altar *Ed*: for it *shall be* a witness between us that the LORD *is* God. *Josh. 22:27*

Joshua's Exhortation before His Death

23 And it came to pass a long time after that the LORD had given rest unto Israel from all their enemies round about, that Joshua ᵀwaxed old *and* stricken in age. *Josh. 13:1 ◆ became*
2 And Joshua called for all Israel, *and* for their elders, and for their heads, and for their judges, and for their officers, and said unto them, I am old *and* stricken in age: *1 Chr. 28:1*

23:1, 2 Joshua's Concern for the People

Some years had passed since the people had settled in their possessions, and already could be seen cropping out the same evils that had heretofore brought judgments upon Israel. As Joshua felt the infirmities of age stealing upon him, and realized that his work must soon close, he was filled with anxiety for the future of his people. *PP 521*

3 And ye have seen all that the LORD your God hath done unto all these nations because of you; for the LORD your God *is* he that hath fought for you. *Ex. 14:14*
4 Behold, I have divided unto you by lot these nations that remain, to be an inheritance for your tribes, from Jordan, with all the nations that I have cut off, even unto the great sea westward. *Josh. 13:2*
5 And the LORD your God, he shall expel them from before you, and drive them from out of your sight; and ye shall possess their land, as the LORD your God hath promised unto you. *Ex. 33:2*
6 Be ye therefore very courageous to keep and to do all that is written in the book of the law of Moses, that ye turn not aside therefrom *to* the right hand or *to* the left; *Deut. 5:32*
7 That ye come not among these nations, these that remain among you; neither make mention of the name of their gods, nor cause

to swear *by them*, neither serve them, nor bow yourselves unto them: *Ex. 23:13; Ps. 16:4; Jer. 5:7*

23:6 The Work Remaining

The Lord had faithfully fulfilled, on His part, the promises made to Israel; Joshua had broken the power of the Canaanites, and had distributed the land to the tribes. It only remained for them, trusting in the assurance of divine aid, to complete the work of dispossessing the inhabitants of the land. *PP 543*

8 But cleave unto the LORD your God, as ye have done unto this day. *Deut. 10:20*
9 For the LORD hath driven out from before you great nations and strong: but *as for* you, no man hath been able to stand before you unto this day. *Deut. 11:23*
10 One man of you shall chase a thousand: for the LORD your God, he *it is* that fighteth for you, as he hath promised you. *Ex. 14:14; Lev. 26:8*

Warnings against Forsaking God

11 Take good heed therefore unto yourselves, that ye love the LORD your God. *Josh. 22:5*
12 Else if ye do in any wise go back, and cleave unto the remnant of these nations, *even* these that remain among you, and shall make marriages with them, and go in unto them, and they to you: *Deut. 7:3*
13 Know for a certainty that the LORD your God will no more drive out *any of* these nations from before you; but they shall be snares and traps unto you, and ᵀscourges in your sides, and thorns in your eyes, until ye perish from off this good land which the LORD your God hath given you. *Ex. 23:33; Num. 33:55; Deut. 7:16 ◆ afflictions*
14 And, behold, this day I *am* going the way of all the earth: and ye know in all your hearts and in all your souls, that not one thing hath failed of all the good things which the LORD your God spake concerning you; all are come to pass unto you, *and* not one thing hath failed thereof. *1 Kin. 2:2*
15 Therefore it shall come to pass, *that* as all good things are come upon you, which the LORD your God promised you; so shall the LORD bring upon you all evil things, until he have destroyed you from off this good land which the LORD your God hath given you. *Deut. 28:15-68*
16 When ye have ᵀtransgressed the covenant of the LORD your God, which he commanded you, and have gone and served other gods, and bowed yourselves to them; then shall the anger of the LORD be kindled against you, and ye shall perish quickly from off the good land which he hath given unto you. *violated*

Joshua Assembles the Tribes at Shechem

24 And Joshua gathered all the tribes of Israel to Shechem, and called for the elders of Israel, and for their heads, and for their judges, and for their officers; and they presented themselves before God. 1 Sam. 10:19

2 And Joshua said unto all the people, Thus saith the LORD God of Israel, Your fathers dwelt on the other side of the flood in old time, *even* Terah, the father of Abraham, and the father of Nachor: and they served other gods. Gen. 31:53

3 And I took your father Abraham from the other side of the flood, and led him throughout all the land of Canaan, and multiplied his seed, and gave him Isaac. Gen. 12:1-4

4 And I gave unto Isaac Jacob and Esau: and I gave unto Esau mount Seir, to possess it; but Jacob and his children went down into Egypt. Gen. 25:24-26; 36:8; Deut. 2:5

5 I sent Moses also and Aaron, and I plagued Egypt, according to that which I did among them: and afterward I brought you out. Ex. 3:10

6 And I brought your fathers out of Egypt: and ye came unto the sea; and the Egyptians pursued after your fathers with chariots and horsemen unto the Red sea.

7 And when they cried unto the LORD, he put darkness between you and the Egyptians, and brought the sea upon them, and covered them; and your eyes have seen what I have done in Egypt: and ye dwelt in the wilderness a long season. Ex. 14:20

8 And I brought you into the land of the Amorites, which dwelt on the other side Jordan; and they fought with you: and I gave them into your hand, that ye might possess their land; and I destroyed them from before you. Num. 21:21-35

9 Then Balak the son of Zippor, king of Moab, arose and warred against Israel, and sent and called Balaam the son of Beor to curse you: Judg. 11:25

10 But I would not hearken unto Balaam; therefore he blessed you still: so I delivered you out of his hand.

11 And ye went over Jordan, and came unto Jericho: and the men of Jericho fought against you, the Amorites, and the Perizzites, and the Canaanites, and the Hittites, and the Girgashites, the Hivites, and the Jebusites; and I delivered them into your hand. Josh. 3:14-17

12 And I sent the hornet before you, which drave them out from before you, *even* the two kings of the Amorites; *but* not with thy sword, nor with thy bow. Ex. 23:28; Deut. 7:20

13 And I have given you a land for which ye did not labour, and cities which ye built not, and ye dwell in them; of the vineyards and oliveyards which ye planted not do ye eat. Josh. 11:13

14 Now therefore fear the LORD, and serve him in sincerity and in truth: and put away the gods which your fathers served on the other side of the flood, and in Egypt; and serve ye the LORD. Deut. 10:12; 1 Sam. 12:24

15 And if it seem evil unto you to serve the LORD, choose you this day whom ye will serve; whether the gods which your fathers served that *were* on the other side of the flood, or the gods of the Amorites, in whose land ye dwell: but as for me and my house, we will serve the LORD. Gen. 18:19; Judg. 6:10; 1 Kin. 18:21

24:15 To Choose the Right

The will is the governing power in the nature of man, the power of decision, or choice. Every human being possessed of reason has power to choose the right. In every experience of life, God's word to us is, "Choose you this day whom ye will serve." Everyone may place his will on the side of the will of God, may choose to obey Him, and by thus linking himself with divine agencies, he may stand where nothing can force him to do evil. *Ed 289*

16 And the people answered and said, God forbid that we should forsake the LORD, to serve other gods;

17 For the LORD our God, he *it is* that brought us up and our fathers out of the land of Egypt, from the house of bondage, and which did those great signs in our sight, and preserved us in all the way wherein we went, and among all the people through whom we passed:

18 And the LORD ᵀdrave out from before us all the people, even the Amorites which dwelt in the land: *therefore* will we also serve the LORD; for he *is* our God. drove

19 And Joshua said unto the people, Ye cannot serve the LORD: for he *is* an holy God; he *is* a jealous God; he will not forgive your transgressions nor your sins. Ex. 20:5; 23:21; Lev. 19:2

20 If ye forsake the LORD, and serve strange gods, then he will turn and do you hurt, and consume you, after that he hath done you good. 1 Chr. 28:9

24:19, 20 No Unconditional Pardon

Satan deceives many with the plausible theory that God's love for His people is so great that He will excuse sin in them. . . . But in all His dealings with His creatures God has maintained the principles of righteousness by revealing sin in its true character—by demonstrating that its sure result is misery and death. The unconditional pardon of sin never has been, and never will be. *PP 522*

21 And the people said unto Joshua, Nay; but we will serve the Lord.

22 And Joshua said unto the people, Ye *are* witnesses against yourselves that ye have chosen you the Lord, to serve him. And they said, *We are* witnesses.   Ps. 119:173

> **24:22 Joshua Reviews God's Faithfulness**
>
> Joshua appealed to the people themselves as witnesses that, so far as they had complied with the conditions, God had faithfully fulfilled His promises to them. *PP 522*

23 Now therefore put away, *said he,* the strange gods which *are* among you, and incline your heart unto the Lord God of Israel.   Josh. 24:14

24 And the people said unto Joshua, The Lord our God will we serve, and his voice will we obey.

25 So Joshua made a covenant with the people that day, and set them a statute and an ordinance in Shechem.   Ex. 15:25

26 And Joshua wrote these words in the book of the law of God, and took a great stone, and set it up there under an oak, that *was* by the sanctuary of the Lord.   Gen. 35:4; Judg. 9:6

27 And Joshua said unto all the people, Behold, this stone shall be a witness unto us; for it hath heard all the words of the Lord which he spake unto us: it shall be therefore a witness unto you, lest ye deny your God.   Josh. 22:34

28 So Joshua let the people depart, every man unto his inheritance.   Judg. 2:6

Joshua's Age, Death and Burial

29 And it came to pass after these things, that Joshua the son of Nun, the servant of the Lord, died, *being* an hundred and ten years old.   Judg. 2:8

> **24:29 A Great Leader's Work Closes**
>
> Joshua's work for Israel was done. He had "wholly followed the Lord;" and in the book of God he is written, "The servant of Jehovah." The noblest testimony to his character as a public leader is the history of the generation that had enjoyed his labors. *PP 524*

30 And they buried him in the border of his inheritance in Timnath-serah, which *is* in mount Ephraim, on the north side of the hill of Gaash.   Josh. 19:50

31 And Israel served the Lord all the days of Joshua, and all the days of the elders that overlived Joshua, and which had known all the works of the Lord, that he had done for Israel.   Judg. 2:7

32 And the bones of Joseph, which the children of Israel brought up out of Egypt, buried they in Shechem, in a parcel of ground which Jacob bought of the sons of Hamor the father of Shechem for an hundred pieces of silver: and it became the inheritance of the children of Joseph.   Gen. 33:19; 50:25; Ex. 13:19

33 And Eleazar the son of Aaron died; and they buried him in a hill *that pertained to* Phinehas his son, which was given him in mount Ephraim.   Ex. 6:25

THE BOOK OF

JUDGES

After Joshua's death, the next three centuries reveal a dark time for the nation. The Book of Judges reveals sin, rebellion, and restoration. A constant refrain cited in Judges is, "And the children of Israel did evil in the sight of the LORD" (2:11). This phrase, more than any other, encapsulates the entire book.

Judges serves as a sharp contrast to the Book of Joshua. In the Book of Joshua, we read about a leader and a people committed to following God's commands. In Judges, soon after Joshua dies, the people enter a period of apostasy where they lose sight of God. Consequently, God allows them to experience the sad consequences of disobedience. Enemy nations plague them. Each time, however, the people cry out for deliverance. God then raises up a judge or deliverer.

The Book of Judges showcases God's unique relationship with the people of Israel and their unwillingness to abide by their covenant with God. The book also teaches us of the patience and long-suffering nature of God, who remains faithful to Israel despite their unfaithfulness to Him.

It's a great lesson for us today—God is true to His promises, no matter how His people respond.

Dates

The events covered by the Book of Judges cover about 330 years—from 1380 B.C. to 1050 B.C. The author of the book, wrote Judges roughly between 1050 B.C. (the beginning of Saul's reign) and 1011 B.C. (David's capture of Jerusalem). Since Judges makes reference to the Jebusites still controlling Jerusalem, the book must have been written before David's capture of the city, which was roughly around 1011 B.C.

Author

While there is no clear indication who authored the book of Judges, Jewish tradition attributes the book to Samuel. Several events chronicled in the book suggest it was written during the time of Samuel, and thus adds evidence to the claim that he was the author. Judges 18:31 and 20:27 suggest the book was written after the ark was removed from Shiloh. The phrase, "In those days there was no king in Israel" (17:6; 18:1; 19:1; 21:25) indicates that Judges was written after the start of Saul's reign. Finally, Judges 1:21 says the Jebusites were dwelling in Jerusalem "unto this day," meaning the book was written before David evicted the Jebusites from the city at the beginning of his reign in approximately 1011 B.C. (2 Samuel 5:6–9).

While this evidence doesn't completely rule out authorship by someone other than Samuel—and since the book makes no definitive reference to its author—it does give credence to the view that Samuel was the author of Judges.

Meaning of the Name

The title of the book in Hebrew is *Shophetim* or "judges," "rulers," "deliverers," or "saviors." As the book title implies, Judges refers to those who "judged Israel."

Christ in Judges

There are no direct references to Christ in the Book of Judges. However, each judge mentioned in the book signifies an attribute of Christ: savior, ruler, and spiritual and political deliverer.

The judge, as an example of Christ, can deliver the people from their oppression only if they agree to abide by the commands God has given. The judge is also a ruler, giving the people God-ordained instructions as to how to walk with Him. Finally, the judge is a deliverer—both spiritually and politically. He or she was appointed to rescue the people from under the boot of oppression in order to live in freedom.

Overview

Judges can be divided into three main parts, which relate to Israel's willingness to abide by God's commands.

(1) *Judges 1—3, The Prologue:* This is the first example of Israel's disobedience to God,

where they did not purge the land as the Lord commanded them. Israel also "served Baalim" (2:11) and their idolatry results in servitude.

(2) *Judges 4—16, Disobedience and Deliverance:* This section serves as the heart of Judges, and it is where we read of the cycles of disobedience and deliverance. God sends Deborah, Gideon, Jephthah, Tola, Othniel, Gideon, Samson and others to deliver His people from their enemies.

(3) *Judges 17—21, Epilogue:* This last section of Judges is marked by Israel's continued unwillingness to obey God completely and follow His commands. The results—a terrible crime avenged by war—nearly results in the annihilation of one tribe—Benjamin.

Unlocking Judges

KEY PEOPLE:
Joshua, Deborah, Barak, Othniel, Abimelech, Gideon, Jephthah, Samson, Delilah, and Micah

KEY EVENTS:
Capture of Jerusalem; Joshua's death (mentioned in the Book of Joshua also); Deborah and Barak go to war against Sisera; Gideon's victory; rise and fall of Abimelech; Samson's fall at the hands of Delilah and his battles against the Philistines; and the civil war

KEY WORD:
Cycles, gives the reader of Judges a chance to see how sin and restoration are played out in the history of Israel. One of the main underlying themes of Judges is the constant disobedience of the people and God's restoration. The same cycle is repeated throughout the book—sometimes with surprising results.

KEY VERSES:
"And the anger of the LORD was hot against Israel; and he said, Because that this people hath transgressed my covenant which I commanded their fathers, and have not hearkened unto my voice; I also will not henceforth drive out any from before them of the nations which Joshua left when he died" (Judges 2:20, 21).

"In those days there was no king in Israel: every man did that which was right in his own eyes" (Judges 21:25).

KEY CHAPTER:
Judges 2, which sets the groundwork for the rest of the book. Here we read about Israel's disobedience and the Lord's decision to raise up judges to deliver the people from those who oppressed them.

Israel's Battles in Canaan

1 Now after the death of Joshua it came to pass, that the children of Israel asked the LORD, saying, Who shall go up for us against the Canaanites first, to fight against them?   Num. 27:21; Judg. 20:18

2 And the LORD said, Judah shall go up: behold, I have delivered the land into his hand.

3 And Judah said unto Simeon his brother, Come up with me into my lot, that we may fight against the Canaanites; and I likewise will go with thee into thy lot. So Simeon went with him.   Judg. 1:17

4 And Judah went up; and the LORD delivered the Canaanites and the Perizzites into their hand: and they slew of them in Bezek ten thousand men.   1 Sam. 11:8

5 And they found Adonibezek in Bezek: and they fought against him, and they slew the Canaanites and the Perizzites.

6 But Adonibezek fled; and they pursued after him, and caught him, and cut off his thumbs and his great toes.

7 And Adonibezek said, Threescore and ten kings, having their thumbs and their great toes cut off, gathered *their meat* under my table: as I have done, so God hath requited me. And they brought him to Jerusalem, and there he died.   1 Sam. 15:33

8 Now the children of Judah had fought against Jerusalem, and had taken it, and smitten it with the edge of the sword, and set the city on fire.   Josh. 15:63; Judg. 1:21

9 And afterward the children of Judah went down to fight against the Canaanites, that dwelt in the mountain, and in the south, and in the valley.

10 And Judah went against the Canaanites that dwelt in Hebron: (now the name of Hebron before *was* Kirjatharba:) and they slew Sheshai, and Ahiman, and Talmai.   Num. 13:22

11 And from thence he went against the inhabitants of Debir: and the name of Debir before *was* Kirjathsepher: Josh. 15:15

12 And Caleb said, He that ᵀsmiteth Kirjathsepher, and taketh it, to him will I give Achsah my daughter to wife.   *strikes*

13 And Othniel the son of Kenaz, Caleb's younger brother, took it: and he gave him Achsah his daughter to wife.   Judg. 3:9

14 And it came to pass, when she came *to him*, that she moved him to ask of her father a field: and she lighted from off *her* ass; and Caleb said unto her, What wilt thou?

15 And she said unto him, Give me a blessing: for thou hast given me a south land; give me also springs of water. And Caleb gave her the upper springs and the ᵀnether springs.   *lower*

16 And the children of the Kenite, Moses' father in law, went up out of the city of palm trees with the children of Judah into the wilderness of Judah, which *lieth* in the south of Arad; and they went and dwelt among the people.   Num. 10:29-32; 21:1; Deut. 34:3

17 And Judah went with Simeon his brother, and they slew the Canaanites that inhabited Zephath, and utterly destroyed it. And the name of the city was called Hormah.   Num. 21:3

18 Also Judah took Gaza with the coast thereof, and Askelon with the coast thereof, and Ekron with the coast thereof.   Josh. 11:22

19 And the LORD was with Judah; and he ᵀdrave out *the inhabitants of* the mountain; but could not drive out the inhabitants of the valley, because they had chariots of iron.   Judg. 1:2 ◆ *drove*

20 And they gave Hebron unto Caleb, as Moses said: and he expelled thence the three sons of Anak.   Num. 14:24; Josh. 15:13-14; Judg. 1:10

Israel Fails to Conquer Canaan

21 And the children of Benjamin did not drive out the Jebusites that inhabited Jerusalem; but the Jebusites dwell with the children of Benjamin in Jerusalem unto this day.   Josh. 15:63

22 And the house of Joseph, they also went up against Bethel: and the LORD *was* with them.   Judg. 1:19

23 And the house of Joseph sent to ᵀdescry Bethel. (Now the name of the city before *was* Luz.)   Gen. 28:19; 35:6; 48:3 ◆ *spy out*

24 And the spies saw a man come forth out of the city, and they said unto him, Shew us, we pray thee, the entrance into the city, and we will shew thee mercy.

25 And when he shewed them the entrance into the city, they smote the city with the edge of the sword; but they let go the man and all his family.

26 And the man went into the land of the Hittites, and built a city, and called the name thereof Luz: which *is* the name thereof unto this day.

27 Neither did Manasseh drive out *the inhabitants of* Beth-shean and her towns, nor Taanach and her towns, nor the inhabitants of Dor and her towns, nor the inhabitants of Ibleam and her towns, nor the inhabitants of Megiddo and her towns: but the Canaanites would dwell in that land.   Josh. 17:11-13

1:28 Resting on Laurels

The Lord had faithfully fulfilled, on His part, the promises made to Israel; Joshua had broken the power of the Canaanites, and had distributed the land to the tribes. . . . By entering into league with the Canaanites they directly transgressed the command of God, and thus failed to fulfill the condition on which He had promised to place them in possession of Canaan. *PP 543*

28 And it came to pass, when Israel was strong, that they put the Canaanites to tribute, and did not utterly drive them out.

29 Neither did Ephraim drive out the Canaanites that dwelt in Gezer; but the Canaanites dwelt in Gezer among them.   1 Kin. 9:16

30 Neither did Zebulun drive out the inhabitants of Kitron, nor the inhabitants of Nahalol; but the Canaanites dwelt among them, and became tributaries.   Josh. 19:15-16

31 Neither did Asher drive out the inhabitants of Accho, nor the inhabitants of Zidon, nor of Ahlab, nor of Achzib, nor of Helbah, nor of Aphik, nor of Rehob: Josh. 19:24-30

32 But the Asherites dwelt among the Canaanites, the inhabitants of the land: for they did not drive them out.

33 Neither did Naphtali drive out the inhabitants of Beth-shemesh, nor the inhabitants of Beth-anath; but he dwelt among the Canaanites, the inhabitants of the land: nevertheless the inhabitants of Beth-shemesh and of Beth-anath became tributaries unto them.   Josh. 19:32-38

34 And the Amorites forced the children of Dan into the mountain: for they would not suffer them to come down to the valley: Josh. 19:47

35 But the Amorites would dwell in mount Heres in Aijalon, and in Shaalbim: yet the hand of the house of Joseph prevailed, so that they became tributaries.   Josh. 19:42

36 And the coast of the Amorites *was* from the going up to Akrabbim, from the rock, and upward.   Num. 34:4

An Angel Rebukes the People

2 And an angel of the LORD came up from Gilgal to Bochim, and said, I made you to go up out of Egypt, and have brought you unto the land which I sware unto your fathers; and I said, I will never break my covenant with you.   Gen. 17:7-8

2 And ye shall make no league with the inhabitants of this land; ye shall throw down their altars: but ye have not obeyed my voice: why have ye done this?   Deut. 7:2-4

3 Wherefore I also said, I will not drive them out from before you; but they shall be *as thorns* in your sides, and their gods shall be a snare unto you. Num. 33:55; Deut. 7:16; Josh. 23:13

2:1–3 A Decline in Health

The simple habits of the Hebrews had secured them physical health; but association with the heathen led to the indulgence of appetite and passion, which gradually lessened physical strength and enfeebled the mental and moral powers. By their sins the Israelites were separated from God; His strength was removed from them, and they could no longer prevail against their enemies. *PP 545*

---

4 And it came to pass, when the angel of the LORD spake these words unto all the children of Israel, that the people lifted up their voice, and wept.

5 And they called the name of that place Bochim: and they sacrificed there unto the LORD.

The Wickedness of the New Generation after Joshua

6 And when Joshua had let the people go, the children of Israel went every man unto his inheritance to possess the land.   Josh. 24:28-31

7 And the people served the LORD all the days of Joshua, and all the days of the elders that outlived Joshua, who had seen all the great works of the LORD, that he did for Israel.   Josh. 24:31

8 And Joshua the son of Nun, the servant of the LORD, died, *being* an hundred and ten years old.

9 And they buried him in the border of his inheritance in Timnath-heres, in the mount of Ephraim, on the north side of the hill Gaash.   Josh. 19:50

10 And also all that generation were gathered unto their fathers: and there arose another generation after them, which knew not the LORD, nor yet the works which he had done for Israel.   Ex. 5:2

11 And the children of Israel did evil in the sight of the LORD, and served Baalim: Judg. 6:1

12 And they forsook the LORD God of their fathers, which brought them out of the land of Egypt, and followed other gods, of the gods of the people that *were* round about them, and bowed themselves unto them, and provoked the LORD to anger.   Ex. 20:5

13 And they forsook the LORD, and served Baal and Ashtaroth.   Judg. 3:7; 10:6; Ps. 106:36

14 And the anger of the LORD was hot against Israel, and he delivered them into the hands of spoilers that spoiled them, and he sold them into the hands of their enemies round about, so that they could not any longer stand before their enemies.   Lev. 26:37; Deut. 32:30

15 Whithersoever they went out, the hand of the LORD was against them for evil, as the LORD had said, and as the LORD had sworn unto them: and they were greatly distressed.   Deut. 28:15-68

2:11–15 Always a Faithful Remnant

Yet He did not utterly forsake His people. There was ever a remnant who were true to Jehovah; and from time to time the Lord raised up faithful and valiant men to put down idolatry and to deliver the Israelites from their enemies. *PP 545*

---

16 Nevertheless the LORD raised up judges, which delivered them out of the hand of those that spoiled them.   Acts 13:20

17 And yet they would not hearken unto their judges, but they went ᵀa whoring after other gods, and bowed themselves unto them: they turned quickly out of the way which their fathers walked in, obeying the commandments of the LORD; *but* they did not so.   Judg. 2:7 ◆ *giving sex as a prostitute*

18 And when the LORD raised them up judges, then the LORD was with the judge, and delivered them out of the hand of their enemies all the days of the judge: for it repented the LORD because of their groanings by reason of them that oppressed them and vexed them.   Gen. 6:6; Deut. 32:36; Josh. 1:5

19 And it came to pass, when the judge was dead, *that* they returned, and corrupted *themselves* more than their fathers, in following other gods to serve them, and to bow down unto them; they ceased not from their own doings, nor from their stubborn way.   Judg. 4:1

20 And the anger of the LORD was hot against Israel; and he said, Because that this people hath ᵀtransgressed my covenant which I commanded their fathers, and have not hearkened unto my voice;   Josh. 23:16 ◆ *violated*

21 I also will not ᵀhenceforth drive out any from before them of the nations which Joshua left when he died: Josh. 23:13 ◆ *from this time forward*

22 That through them I may prove Israel, whether they will keep the way of the LORD to walk therein, as their fathers did keep *it*, or not.   Deut. 8:2, 16; 13:3

23 Therefore the LORD left those nations, without driving them out hastily; neither delivered he them into the hand of Joshua.

The Nations Which Were Left to Test Israel

3 Now these *are* the nations which the LORD left, to prove Israel by them, *even* as many *of Israel* as had not known all the wars of Canaan;   Judg. 2:21-22

2 Only that the generations of the children of Israel might know, to teach them war, at the least such as before knew nothing thereof;

3 *Namely*, five lords of the Philistines, and all the Canaanites, and the Sidonians, and the Hivites that dwelt in mount Lebanon, from mount Baal-hermon unto the entering in of Hamath.   Josh. 13:3

4 And they were to prove Israel by them, to know whether they would hearken unto the commandments of the LORD, which he commanded their fathers by the hand of Moses.   Judg. 2:22

5 And the children of Israel dwelt among the Canaanites, Hittites, and Amorites, and Perizzites, and Hivites, and Jebusites: Ex. 3:8

6 And they took their daughters to be their wives, and gave their daughters to their sons, and served their gods.   Ex. 34:16; Deut. 7:3-4

7 And the children of Israel did evil in the sight of the LORD, and forgat the LORD their God, and served Baalim and the ᵀgroves.   Ex. 34:13 ◆ *idols*

Othniel Delivers Israel from Chushan-rishathaim

8 Therefore the anger of the LORD was hot against Israel, and he sold them into the hand of Chushan-rishathaim king of Mesopotamia: and the children of Israel served Chushan-rishathaim eight years.   Judg. 2:14; Hab. 3:7

> **3:7, 8 Sin Brought Weakness**
>
> By their sins the Israelites were separated from God; His strength was removed from them, and they could no longer prevail against their enemies. Thus they were brought into subjection to the very nations that through God they might have subdued. *PP 545*

9 And when the children of Israel cried unto the LORD, the LORD raised up a deliverer to the children of Israel, who delivered them, *even* Othniel the son of Kenaz, Caleb's younger brother.   Judg. 1:13; 3:15; 6:7

10 And the Spirit of the LORD came upon him, and he judged Israel, and went out to war: and the LORD delivered Chushan-rishathaim king of Mesopotamia into his hand; and his hand prevailed against Chushan-rishathaim.   Judg. 6:34

11 And the land had rest forty years. And Othniel the son of Kenaz died.   Josh. 11:23

Ehud Frees Israel from Moab

12 And the children of Israel did evil again in the sight of the LORD: and the LORD strengthened Eglon the king of Moab against Israel, because they had done evil in the sight of the LORD.   1 Sam. 12:9

13 And he gathered unto him the children of Ammon and Amalek, and went and smote Israel, and possessed the city of palm trees.   Deut. 34:3; Judg. 1:16

14 So the children of Israel served Eglon the king of Moab eighteen years.

15 But when the children of Israel cried unto the LORD, the LORD raised them up a deliverer, Ehud the son of Gera, a Benjamite, a man lefthanded: and by him the children of Israel sent a present unto Eglon the king of Moab.   Judg. 3:9

16 But Ehud made him a dagger which had two edges, of a cubit length; and he did ᵀgird it under his ᵀraiment upon his right thigh.   *fasten* ◆ *clothing*

17 And he brought the present unto Eglon king of Moab: and Eglon *was* a very fat man.

18 And when he had made an end to offer the present, he sent away the people that bare the present.

19 But he himself turned again from the quarries that *were* by Gilgal, and said, I have a secret errand unto thee, O king: who said, Keep silence. And all that stood by him went out from him.   Josh. 4:20

20 And Ehud came unto him; and he was sitting in a summer parlour, which he had for himself alone. And Ehud said, I have a message from God unto thee. And he arose out of *his* seat.   Amos 3:15

21 And Ehud put forth his left hand, and took the dagger from his right thigh, and thrust it into his belly:

22 And the ᵀhaft also went in after the blade; and the fat closed upon the blade, so that he could not draw the dagger out of his belly; and the dirt came out.   *handle*

23 Then Ehud went forth through the porch, and shut the doors of the parlour upon him, and locked them.

24 When he was gone out, his servants came; and when they saw that, behold, the doors of the parlour *were* locked, they said, Surely he covereth his feet in his summer chamber.   1 Sam. 24:3

25 And they tarried till they were ashamed: and, behold, he opened not the doors of the parlour; therefore they took a key, and opened *them*: and, behold, their lord *was* fallen down dead on the earth.

26 And Ehud escaped while they tarried, and passed beyond the quarries, and escaped unto Seirath.

27 And it came to pass, when he was come, that he blew a trumpet in the mountain of Ephraim, and the children of Israel went down with him from the mount, and he before them.   Judg. 6:34; 1 Sam. 13:3

28 And he said unto them, Follow after me: for the LORD hath delivered your enemies the Moabites into your hand. And they went down after him, and took the fords of Jordan toward Moab, and suffered not a man to pass over.   Josh. 2:7; Judg. 7:9; 12:5

29 And they slew of Moab at that time about ten thousand men, all lusty, and all men of valour; and there escaped not a man.

30 So Moab was subdued that day under the hand of Israel. And the land had rest ᵀfourscore years.   Judg. 3:11 ◆ *eighty*

Shamgar Delivers Israel from the Philistines

31 And after him was Shamgar the son of Anath, which slew of the Philistines six hundred men with an ox ᵀgoad: and he also delivered Israel.   Judg. 2:16; 5:6, 8 ◆ *pointed stick*

Deborah and Barak Save Israel from Jabin and Sisera

4 And the children of Israel again did evil in the sight of the LORD, when Ehud was dead.

2 And the LORD sold them into the hand of Jabin king of Canaan, that reigned in Hazor; the captain of whose host *was* Sisera, which dwelt in Harosheth of the Gentiles.   Josh. 11:1; Judg. 4:13, 16

3 And the children of Israel cried unto the LORD: for he had nine hundred chariots of iron; and twenty years he mightily oppressed the children of Israel.   Judg. 1:19; 3:9; Ps. 106:42

4 And Deborah, a prophetess, the wife of Lapidoth, she judged Israel at that time.

5 And she dwelt under the palm tree of Deborah between Ramah and Bethel in mount Ephraim: and the children of Israel came up to her for judgment.   Gen. 35:8

6 And she sent and called Barak the son of Abinoam out of Kedesh-naphtali, and said unto him, Hath not the LORD God of Israel commanded, *saying*, Go and draw toward mount Tabor, and take with thee ten thousand men of the children of Naphtali and of the children of Zebulun?   Josh. 19:37; Heb. 11:32

7 And I will draw unto thee to the river Kishon Sisera, the captain of Jabin's army, with his chariots and his multitude; and I will deliver him into thine hand.   Judg. 5:21

8 And Barak said unto her, If thou wilt go with me, then I will go: but if thou wilt not go with me, *then* I will not go.

9 And she said, I will surely go with thee: notwithstanding the journey that thou takest shall not be for thine honour; for the LORD shall sell Sisera into the hand of a woman. And Deborah arose, and went with Barak to Kedesh.   Judg. 2:14

10 And Barak called Zebulun and Naphtali to Kedesh; and he went up with ten thousand men at his feet: and Deborah went up with him.   Judg. 5:15, 18

11 Now Heber the Kenite, *which was* of the children of Hobab the father in law of Moses, had severed himself from the Kenites, and pitched his tent unto the plain of Zaanaim, which *is* by Kedesh.   Num. 10:29; Josh. 19:33

12 And they shewed Sisera that Barak the son of Abinoam was gone up to mount Tabor.

13 And Sisera gathered together all his chariots, *even* nine hundred chariots of iron, and all the people that *were* with him, from Harosheth of the Gentiles unto the river of Kishon.   Judg. 4:2-3

14 And Deborah said unto Barak, Up; for this *is* the day in which the LORD hath delivered Sisera into thine hand: is not the LORD

gone out before thee? So Barak went down from mount Tabor, and ten thousand men after him.   Deut. 9:3; 2 Sam. 5:24; Is. 52:12

15 And the LORD discomfited Sisera, and all *his* chariots, and all *his* host, with the edge of the sword before Barak; so that Sisera lighted down off *his* chariot, and fled away on his feet.   Josh. 10:10; Ps. 83:9-10

16 But Barak pursued after the chariots, and after the host, unto Harosheth of the Gentiles: and all the host of Sisera fell upon the edge of the sword; *and* there was not a man left.

17 Howbeit Sisera fled away on his feet to the tent of Jael the wife of Heber the Kenite: for *there was* peace between Jabin the king of Hazor and the house of Heber the Kenite.

18 And Jael went out to meet Sisera, and said unto him, Turn in, my lord, turn in to me; fear not. And when he had turned in unto her into the tent, she covered him with a ᵀmantle.   *large outside garment*

19 And he said unto her, Give me, I pray thee, a little water to drink; for I am thirsty. And she opened a bottle of milk, and gave him drink, and covered him.   Judg. 5:25-26

20 Again he said unto her, Stand in the door of the tent, and it shall be, when any man doth come and enquire of thee, and say, Is there any man here? that thou shalt say, No.

21 Then Jael Heber's wife took a nail of the tent, and took an hammer in her hand, and went softly unto him, and smote the nail into his temples, and fastened it into the ground: for he was fast asleep and weary. So he died.

22 And, behold, as Barak pursued Sisera, Jael came out to meet him, and said unto him, Come, and I will shew thee the man whom thou seekest. And when he came into her *tent*, behold, Sisera lay dead, and the nail *was* in his temples.

23 So God subdued on that day Jabin the king of Canaan before the children of Israel.   Neh. 9:24

24 And the hand of the children of Israel prospered, and prevailed against Jabin the king of Canaan, until they had destroyed Jabin king of Canaan.

The Song of Deborah and Barak

5 Then sang Deborah and Barak the son of Abinoam on that day, saying,   Ex. 15:1

2 Praise ye the LORD for the avenging of Israel, when the people willingly offered themselves.   Judg. 5:9; 2 Chr. 17:16; Ps. 110:3

3 Hear, O ye kings; give ear, O ye princes; I, *even* I, will sing unto the LORD; I will sing *praise* to the LORD God of Israel.

4 LORD, when thou wentest out of Seir, when thou marchedst out of the field of Edom, the earth trembled, and the heavens dropped, the clouds also dropped water.   2 Sam. 22:8; Ps. 68:7-8

5 The mountains melted from before the LORD, *even* that Sinai from before the LORD God of Israel.   Ex. 19:18; Ps. 97:5

6 In the days of Shamgar the son of Anath, in the days of Jael, the highways were unoccupied, and the travellers walked through byways.   Lev. 26:22; Judg. 3:31; Is. 33:8

7 *The inhabitants of* the villages ceased, they ceased in Israel, until that I Deborah arose, that I arose a mother in Israel.

8 They chose new gods; then *was* war in the gates: was there a shield or spear seen among forty thousand in Israel?   Deut. 32:16-17

9 My heart *is* toward the governors of Israel, that offered themselves willingly among the people. Bless ye the LORD.   Judg. 5:2

10 Speak, ye that ride on white asses, ye that sit in judgment, and walk by the way. Judg. 12:14

11 *They that are delivered* from the noise of archers in the places of drawing water, there shall they rehearse the righteous acts of the LORD, *even* the righteous acts *toward the inhabitants* of his villages in Israel: then shall the people of the LORD go down to the gates.   1 Sam. 12:7

12 Awake, awake, Deborah: awake, awake, utter a song: arise, Barak, and lead thy captivity captive, thou son of Abinoam. Ps. 57:8; Eph. 4:8

13 Then he made him that remaineth have dominion over the nobles among the people: the LORD made me have dominion over the mighty.

14 Out of Ephraim *was there* a root of them against Amalek; after thee, Benjamin, among thy people; out of Machir came down governors, and out of Zebulun they that handle the pen of the writer.   Num. 32:39-40

15 And the princes of Issachar *were* with Deborah; even Issachar, and also Barak: he was sent on foot into the valley. For the divisions of Reuben *there were* great thoughts of heart.   Judg. 4:14

16 Why abodest thou among the sheepfolds, to hear the bleatings of the flocks? For the divisions of Reuben *there were* great searchings of heart.   Num. 32:24

17 Gilead abode beyond Jordan: and why did Dan remain in ships? Asher continued on the sea shore, and abode in his breaches. Josh. 13:25

18 Zebulun and Naphtali *were* a people *that* jeoparded their lives unto the death in the high places of the field.   Judg. 4:6, 10

19 The kings came *and* fought, then fought the kings of Canaan in Taanach by the waters of Megiddo; they took no gain of money.   Judg. 1:27; 5:30; 1 Kin. 4:12

20 They fought from heaven; the stars in their courses fought against Sisera. Josh. 10:11

21 The river of Kishon swept them away, that

ancient river, the river Kishon. O my soul, thou hast trodden down strength.   Judg. 4:7

22 Then were the horsehoofs broken by the means of the prancings, the prancings of their mighty ones.

23 Curse ye Meroz, said the angel of the Lord, curse ye bitterly the inhabitants thereof; because they came not to the help of the Lord, to the help of the Lord against the mighty.   Judg. 21:9-10

24 Blessed above women shall Jael the wife of Heber the Kenite be, blessed shall she be above women in the tent.   Judg. 4:17

25 He asked water, *and* she gave *him* milk; she brought forth butter in a lordly dish.

26 She put her hand to the nail, and her right hand to the workmen's hammer; and with the hammer she smote Sisera, she smote off his head, when she had pierced and stricken through his temples.

27 At her feet he bowed, he fell, he lay down: at her feet he bowed, he fell: where he bowed, there he fell down dead.

28 The mother of Sisera looked out at a window, and cried through the lattice, Why is his chariot *so* long in coming? why tarry the wheels of his chariots?

29 Her wise ladies answered her, yea, she returned answer to herself,

30 Have they not sped? have they *not* divided the prey; to every man a damsel *or* two; to Sisera a prey of ᵀdivers colours, a prey of divers colours of needlework, of divers colours of needlework on both sides, *meet* for the necks of *them that take the* ᵀspoil?   Ex. 15:9 ♦ *various* ♦ *plunder*

31 So let all thine enemies perish, O Lord: but *let* them that love him *be* as the sun when he goeth forth in his might. And the land had rest forty years.   Judg. 3:11

The Israelites Are Oppressed by Midian

6 And the children of Israel did evil in the sight of the Lord: and the Lord delivered them into the hand of Midian seven years.   Gen. 25:2

2 And the hand of Midian prevailed against Israel: *and* because of the Midianites the children of Israel made them the dens which *are* in the mountains, and caves, and strong holds.   1 Sam. 13:6; Heb. 11:38

3 And *so* it was, when Israel had sown, that the Midianites came up, and the Amalekites, and the children of the east, even they came up against them;   Judg. 3:13

4 And they encamped against them, and destroyed the increase of the earth, till thou come unto Gaza, and left no sustenance for Israel, neither sheep, nor ox, nor ass.   Lev. 26:16; Deut. 28:33, 51

5 For they came up with their cattle and their tents, and they came as grasshoppers for multitude; *for* both they and their camels were without number: and they entered into the land to destroy it.   Judg. 7:12; 8:10

6 And Israel was greatly impoverished because of the Midianites; and the children of Israel cried unto the Lord.   Judg. 3:9

7 And it came to pass, when the children of Israel cried unto the Lord because of the Midianites,

---

6:1-7 Oppression Broken by Confession

Thus the Israelites dwelling in the open country were forced to abandon their homes, and to congregate in walled towns, to seek refuge in fortresses, or even to find shelter in caves and rocky fastnesses among the mountains. For seven years this oppression continued, and then, as the people in their distress gave heed to the Lord's reproof, and confessed their sins, God again raised up a helper for them. *PP 546*

---

8 That the Lord sent a prophet unto the children of Israel, which said unto them, Thus saith the Lord God of Israel, I brought you up from Egypt, and brought you forth out of the house of bondage;

9 And I delivered you out of the hand of the Egyptians, and out of the hand of all that oppressed you, and ᵀdrave them out from before you, and gave you their land;   Ps. 44:2-3 ♦ *drove*

10 And I said unto you, I *am* the Lord your God; fear not the gods of the Amorites, in whose land ye dwell: but ye have not obeyed my voice.   Jer. 10:2

Gideon Is Chosen to Deliver Israel from Midian

11 And there came an angel of the Lord, and sat under an oak which *was* in Ophrah, that *pertained* unto Joash the Abiezrite: and his son Gideon threshed wheat by the winepress, to hide *it* from the Midianites.   Josh. 17:2; Heb. 11:32

6:11 A Tribe of Courage and Honesty

Gideon was the son of Joash, of the tribe of Manasseh. The division to which this family belonged held no leading position, but the household of Joash was distinguished for courage and integrity. *PP 546*

---

12 And the angel of the Lord appeared unto him, and said unto him, The Lord *is* with thee, thou mighty man of valour.   Luke 1:28

13 And Gideon said unto him, Oh my Lord, if the Lord be with us, why then is all this befallen us? and where *be* all his miracles which our fathers told us of, saying, Did not the Lord bring us up from Egypt? but now the Lord hath forsaken us, and delivered us into the hands of the Midianites.   Ps. 44:1

14 And the Lord looked upon him, and said, Go in this thy might, and thou shalt save Israel from the hand of the Midianites: have not I sent thee?   Heb. 11:34

15 And he said unto him, Oh my Lord, wherewith shall I save Israel? behold, my family *is* poor in Manasseh, and I *am* the least in my father's house. Ex. 3:11; 1 Sam. 9:21

16 And the Lord said unto him, Surely I will be with thee, and thou shalt ᵀsmite the Midianites as one man.   Ex. 3:12; Josh. 1:5 ◆ *strike*

17 And he said unto him, If now I have found grace in thy sight, then shew me a sign that thou talkest with me.   Ex. 33:13

18 Depart not hence, I pray thee, until I come unto thee, and bring forth my present, and set *it* before thee. And he said, I will tarry until thou come again.   Gen. 18:3

19 And Gideon went in, and made ready a kid, and unleavened cakes of an ephah of flour: the flesh he put in a basket, and he put the broth in a pot, and brought *it* out unto him under the oak, and presented *it*.Gen. 18:6-8

20 And the angel of God said unto him, Take the flesh and the unleavened cakes, and lay *them* upon this rock, and pour out the broth. And he did so.   Judg. 13:19

21 Then the angel of the Lord put forth the end of the staff that *was* in his hand, and touched the flesh and the unleavened cakes; and there rose up fire out of the rock, and consumed the flesh and the unleavened cakes. Then the angel of the Lord departed out of his sight.   Lev. 9:24; 1 Kin. 18:38; 2 Chr. 7:1

22 And when Gideon perceived that he *was* an angel of the Lord, Gideon said, Alas, O Lord God! for because I have seen an angel of the Lord face to face.   Gen. 32:30; Ex. 33:20

6:22 Angels Sometimes in Human Form

In all ages, God has wrought through holy angels for the succor and deliverance of His people. Celestial beings have taken an active part in the affairs of men. They have appeared clothed in garments that shone as the lightning; they have come as men in the garb of wayfarers. Angels have appeared in human form to men of God. *GC 631*

23 And the Lord said unto him, Peace *be* unto thee; fear not: thou shalt not die.   Dan. 10:19

24 Then Gideon built an altar there unto the Lord, and called it Jehovah-shalom: unto this day it *is* yet in Ophrah of the Abiezrites.   Gen. 22:14; Ex. 17:15; Judg. 8:32

25 And it came to pass the same night, that the Lord said unto him, Take thy father's young bullock, even the second bullock of seven years old, and throw down the altar of Baal that thy father hath, and cut down the grove that *is* by it: Ex. 34:13

26 And build an altar unto the Lord thy God upon the top of this rock, in the ordered place, and take the second ᵀbullock, and offer a burnt sacrifice with the wood of the grove which thou shalt cut down.   *bull*

27 Then Gideon took ten men of his servants, and did as the Lord had said unto him: and *so* it was, because he feared his father's household, and the men of the city, that he could not do *it* by day, that he did *it* by night.

28 And when the men of the city arose early in the morning, behold, the altar of Baal was cast down, and the ᵀgrove was cut down that *was* by it, and the second bullock was offered upon the altar *that was* built.   *idol*

29 And they said one to another, Who hath done this thing? And when they enquired and asked, they said, Gideon the son of Joash hath done this thing.

30 Then the men of the city said unto Joash, Bring out thy son, that he may die: because he hath cast down the altar of Baal, and because he hath cut down the grove that *was* by it.

31 And Joash said unto all that stood against him, Will ye plead for Baal? will ye save him? he that will plead for him, let him be put to death whilst *it is yet* morning: if he *be* a god, let him plead for himself, because *one* hath cast down his altar.

32 Therefore on that day he called him Jerubbaal, saying, Let Baal plead against him, because he hath thrown down his altar.

Gideon's Army

33 Then all the Midianites and the Amalekites and the children of the east were gathered together, and went over, and pitched in the valley of Jezreel.   Josh. 17:16; Judg. 6:3

34 But the Spirit of the Lord came upon Gideon, and he blew a trumpet; and Abiezer was gathered after him. Judg. 3:10, 27; 1 Chr. 12:18

35 And he sent messengers throughout all Manasseh; who also was gathered after him: and he sent messengers unto Asher, and unto Zebulun, and unto Naphtali; and they came up to meet them.

36 And Gideon said unto God, If thou wilt save Israel by mine hand, as thou hast said,   Judg. 6:14

37 Behold, I will put a fleece of wool in the floor; *and* if the dew be on the fleece only, and *it* be dry upon all the earth *beside*, then shall I know that thou wilt save Israel by mine hand, as thou hast said.

38 And it was so: for he rose up early on the morrow, and thrust the fleece together, and wringed the dew out of the fleece, a bowl full of water.

39 And Gideon said unto God, Let not thine anger be hot against me, and I will speak but this once: let me prove, I pray thee, but this once with the fleece; let it now be dry only upon the fleece, and upon all the ground let there be dew. *Gen. 18:32*
40 And God did so that night: for it was dry upon the fleece only, and there was dew on all the ground.

God Reduces Gideon's Army to Three Hundred Men

7 Then Jerubbaal, who *is* Gideon, and all the people that *were* with him, rose up early, and pitched beside the well of Harod: so that the host of the Midianites were on the north side of them, by the hill of Moreh, in the valley. *Gen. 12:6; Judg. 6:32*
2 And the LORD said unto Gideon, The people that *are* with thee *are* too many for me to give the Midianites into their hands, lest Israel vaunt themselves against me, saying, Mine own hand hath saved me. *Is. 10:13; 2 Cor. 4:7*
3 Now therefore go to, proclaim in the ears of the people, saying, Whosoever *is* fearful and afraid, let him return and depart early from mount Gilead. And there returned of the people twenty and two thousand; and there remained ten thousand. *Deut. 20:8*
4 And the LORD said unto Gideon, The people *are* yet *too* many; bring them down unto the water, and I will try them for thee there: and it shall be, *that* of whom I say unto thee, This shall go with thee, the same shall go with thee; and of whomsoever I say unto thee, This shall not go with thee, the same shall not go.

7:4 No Half-Hearted Warriors

Those who were unwilling to face danger and hardships, or whose worldly interests would draw their hearts from the work of God, would add no strength to the armies of Israel. Their presence would prove only a cause of weakness. *PP 548*

5 So he brought down the people unto the water: and the LORD said unto Gideon, Every one that lappeth of the water with his tongue, as a dog lappeth, him shalt thou set by himself; likewise every one that boweth down upon his knees to drink.
6 And the number of them that lapped, *putting* their hand to their mouth, were three hundred men: but all the rest of the people bowed down upon their knees to drink water.
7 And the LORD said unto Gideon, By the three hundred men that lapped will I save you, and deliver the Midianites into thine hand: and let all the *other* people go every man unto his place. *1 Sam. 14:6*
8 So the people took ᵀvictuals in their hand, and their trumpets: and he sent all *the rest of* Israel every man unto his tent, and retained those three hundred men: and the host of Midian was beneath him in the valley. *food*

The Lord Calls Upon Gideon to Attack the Midianites

9 And it came to pass the same night, that the LORD said unto him, Arise, get thee down unto the host; for I have delivered it into thine hand. *Gen. 46:2-3*
10 But if thou fear to go down, go thou with Phurah thy servant down to the host:

7:6–9 Quality Versus Quantity

Success does not depend upon numbers. God can deliver by few as well as by many. He is honored not so much by the great numbers as by the character of those who serve Him. *PP 550*

11 And thou shalt hear what they say; and afterward shall thine hands be strengthened to go down unto the host. Then went he down with Phurah his servant unto the outside of the armed men that *were* in the host. *Judg. 7:13-15*
12 And the Midianites and the Amalekites and all the children of the east lay along in the valley like grasshoppers for multitude; and their camels *were* without number, as the sand by the sea side for multitude. *Judg. 6:5*
13 And when Gideon was come, behold,

How Character Is Often Tested

Judges 7

By the simplest means character is often tested. Those who in time of peril were intent upon supplying their own wants were not the men to be trusted in an emergency. The Lord has no place in His work for the indolent and self-indulgent. The men of His choice were the few who would not permit their own wants to delay them in the discharge of duty. The three hundred chosen men not only possessed courage and self-control, but they were men of faith. They had not defiled themselves with idolatry. God could direct them, and through them He could work deliverance for Israel. Success does not depend upon numbers. God can deliver by few as well as by many. He is honored not so much by the great numbers as by the character of those who serve Him. *PP 549, 550*

there was a man that told a dream unto his fellow, and said, Behold, I dreamed a dream, and, lo, a cake of barley bread tumbled into the host of Midian, and came unto a tent, and smote it that it fell, and overturned it, that the tent lay along.

14 And his fellow answered and said, This *is* nothing else save the sword of Gideon the son of Joash, a man of Israel: *for* into his hand hath God delivered Midian, and all the host. Josh. 2:9

15 And it was *so*, when Gideon heard the telling of the dream, and the interpretation thereof, that he worshipped, and returned into the host of Israel, and said, Arise; for the Lord hath delivered into your hand the host of Midian.

Gideon's Unusual Battle Plan Delivers Israel from the Midianites

16 And he divided the three hundred men *into* three companies, and he put a trumpet in every man's hand, with empty pitchers, and lamps within the pitchers.

17 And he said unto them, Look on me, and do likewise: and, behold, when I come to the outside of the camp, it shall be *that*, as I do, so shall ye do.

18 When I blow with a trumpet, I and all that *are* with me, then blow ye the trumpets also on every side of all the camp, and say, *The sword* of the Lord, and of Gideon.

19 So Gideon, and the hundred men that *were* with him, came unto the outside of the camp in the beginning of the middle watch; and they had but newly set the watch: and they blew the trumpets, and brake the pitchers that *were* in their hands.

20 And the three companies blew the trumpets, and brake the pitchers, and held the lamps in their left hands, and the trumpets in their right hands to blow ^T*withal*: and they cried, The sword of the Lord, and of Gideon. with

21 And they stood every man in his place round about the camp: and all the host ran, and cried, and fled.

22 And the three hundred blew the trumpets, and the Lord set every man's sword against his fellow, even throughout all the host: and the host fled to Beth-shittah in Zererath, *and* to the border of Abelmeholah, unto Tabbath. Josh. 6:20; 1 Kin. 4:12; 19:16

23 And the men of Israel gathered themselves together out of Naphtali, and out of Asher, and out of all Manasseh, and pursued after the Midianites. Judg. 6:35

24 And Gideon sent messengers throughout all mount Ephraim, saying, Come down against the Midianites, and take before them the waters unto Beth-barah and Jordan.

Then all the men of Ephraim gathered themselves together, and took the waters unto Beth-barah and Jordan.

25 And they took two princes of the Midianites, Oreb and Zeeb; and they slew Oreb upon the rock Oreb, and Zeeb they slew at the winepress of Zeeb, and pursued Midian, and brought the heads of Oreb and Zeeb to Gideon on the other side Jordan. Is. 10:26

Gideon Pacifies the Ephraimites

8 And the men of Ephraim said unto him, Why hast thou served us thus, that thou calledst us not, when thou wentest to fight with the Midianites? And they did chide with him sharply.

2 And he said unto them, What have I done now in comparison of you? *Is* not the ^Tgleaning of the grapes of Ephraim better than the vintage of Abiezer? *gathering of leftovers*

3 God hath delivered into your hands the princes of Midian, Oreb and Zeeb: and what was I able to do in comparison of you? Then their anger was ^Tabated toward him, when he had said that. Prov. 15:1 ◆ *diminished*

> **8:2, 3 The Spirit of Courtesy**
>
> The spirit of jealousy might easily have been fanned into a quarrel that would have caused strife and bloodshed; but Gideon's modest answer soothed the anger of the men of Ephraim, and they returned in peace to their homes. Firm and uncompromising where principle was concerned, and in war a "mighty man of valor," Gideon displayed also a spirit of courtesy that is rarely witnessed. *PP 555*

4 And Gideon came to Jordan, *and* passed over, he, and the three hundred men that *were* with him, faint, yet pursuing *them*.

5 And he said unto the men of Succoth, Give, I pray you, loaves of bread unto the people that follow me; for they *be* faint, and I am pursuing after Zebah and Zalmunna, kings of Midian. Gen. 33:17; Ps. 60:6

6 And the princes of Succoth said, *Are* the hands of Zebah and Zalmunna now in thine hand, that we should give bread unto thine army? 1 Kin. 20:11

7 And Gideon said, Therefore when the Lord hath delivered Zebah and Zalmunna into mine hand, then I will tear your flesh with the thorns of the wilderness and with briers.

8 And he went up thence to Penuel, and spake unto them likewise: and the men of Penuel answered him as the men of Succoth had answered *him*. Gen. 32:30-31

9 And he spake also unto the men of Penuel,

saying, When I come again in peace, I will break down this tower. Judg. 8:17

10 Now Zebah and Zalmunna *were* in Karkor, and their hosts with them, about fifteen thousand *men*, all that were left of all the hosts of the children of the east: for there fell an hundred and twenty thousand men that drew sword. Judg. 7:12

11 And Gideon went up by the way of them that dwelt in tents on the east of Nobah and Jogbehah, and smote the host: for the host was secure. Num. 32:35

12 And when Zebah and Zalmunna fled, he pursued after them, and took the two kings of Midian, Zebah and Zalmunna, and discomfited all the host. Ps. 83:11

13 And Gideon the son of Joash returned from battle before the sun *was up,*

14 And caught a young man of the men of Succoth, and enquired of him: and he described unto him the princes of Succoth, and the elders thereof, *even* ᵀthreescore and seventeen men. sixty

15 And he came unto the men of Succoth, and said, Behold Zebah and Zalmunna, with whom ye did ᵀupbraid me, saying, *Are* the hands of Zebah and Zalmunna now in thine hand, that we should give bread unto thy men *that are* weary? scold

16 And he took the elders of the city, and thorns of the wilderness and briers, and with them he taught the men of Succoth. Judg. 8:7

17 And he beat down the tower of Penuel, and slew the men of the city. Judg. 8:9

Gideon Avenges His Brothers' Deaths by Killing Two Midianite Kings

18 Then said he unto Zebah and Zalmunna, What manner of men *were they* whom ye slew at Tabor? And they answered, As thou *art,* so *were* they; each one resembled the children of a king. Judg. 4:6

19 And he said, They *were* my brethren, *even* the sons of my mother: *as* the LORD liveth, if ye had saved them alive, I would not slay you.

20 And he said unto Jether his firstborn, Up, *and* slay them. But the youth drew not his sword: for he feared, because he *was* yet a youth.

21 Then Zebah and Zalmunna said, Rise thou, and fall upon us: for as the man *is,* *so is* his strength. And Gideon arose, and slew Zebah and Zalmunna, and took away the ornaments that *were* on their camels' necks. Judg. 8:26

Gideon Makes a Gold Idol

22 Then the men of Israel said unto Gideon, Rule thou over us, both thou, and thy

son, and thy son's son also: for thou hast delivered us from the hand of Midian.

23 And Gideon said unto them, I will not rule over you, neither shall my son rule over you: the LORD shall rule over you. 1 Sam. 10:19; 12:12

24 And Gideon said unto them, I would desire a request of you, that ye would give me every man the earrings of his prey. (For they had golden earrings, because they *were* Ishmaelites.) Gen. 25:13

25 And they answered, We will willingly give *them.* And they spread a garment, and did cast therein every man the earrings of his prey.

26 And the weight of the golden earrings that he requested was a thousand and seven hundred *shekels* of gold; beside ornaments, and collars, and purple ᵀraiment that *was* on the kings of Midian, and beside the chains that *were* about their camels' necks. *clothing*

27 And Gideon made an ᵀephod thereof, and put it in his city, *even* in Ophrah: and all Israel went thither a whoring after it: which thing became a snare unto Gideon, and to his house. Deut. 7:16; Judg. 17:5; 18:14 ◆ *priestly garment*

28 Thus was Midian subdued before the children of Israel, so that they lifted up their heads no more. And the country was in quietness forty years in the days of Gideon. Judg. 5:31

Israel Returns to Idolatry

29 And Jerubbaal the son of Joash went and dwelt in his own house. Judg. 6:32

30 And Gideon had threescore and ten sons of his body ᵀbegotten: for he had many wives. Judg. 9:2, 5 ◆ *brought forth*

31 And his ᵀconcubine that *was* in Shechem, she also bare him a son, whose name he called Abimelech. *less important wife*

32 And Gideon the son of Joash died in a good old age, and was buried in the sepulchre of Joash his father, in Ophrah of the Abiezrites. Gen. 25:8

8:33–35 Influence of Words and Acts

There are few who realize how far-reaching is the influence of their words and acts. How often the errors of parents produce the most disastrous effects upon their children and children's children, long after the actors themselves have been laid in the grave. Everyone is exerting an influence upon others, and will be held accountable for the result of that influence. Words and actions have a telling power, and the long hereafter will show the effect of our life here. *PP 556*

---

33 And it came to pass, as soon as Gideon was dead, that the children of Israel turned again, and went a whoring after Baalim, and made Baal-berith their god. Judg. 2:17; 9:4, 46

34 And the children of Israel remembered not the LORD their God, who had delivered them out of the hands of all their enemies on every side: Ps. 78:11

35 Neither shewed they kindness to the house of Jerubbaal, *namely*, Gideon, according to all the goodness which he had shewed unto Israel.

Abimelech Kills His Brothers and Becomes King

9 And Abimelech the son of Jerubbaal went to Shechem unto his mother's brethren, and communed with them, and with all the family of the house of his mother's father, saying,   Judg. 8:31

2 Speak, I pray you, in the ears of all the men of Shechem, Whether *is* better for you, either that all the sons of Jerubbaal, *which are* threescore and ten persons, reign over you, or that one reign over you? remember also that I *am* your bone and your flesh.   Gen. 29:14; Judg. 8:30

3 And his mother's brethren spake of him in the ears of all the men of Shechem all these words: and their hearts inclined to follow Abimelech; for they said, He *is* our brother.   Gen. 29:15

4 And they gave him threescore and ten *pieces* of silver out of the house of Baal-berith, wherewith Abimelech hired vain and light persons, which followed him.   Judg. 8:33; 11:3; 2 Chr. 13:7

5 And he went unto his father's house at Ophrah, and slew his brethren the sons of Jerubbaal, *being* threescore and ten persons, upon one stone: notwithstanding yet Jotham the youngest son of Jerubbaal was left; for he hid himself.   2 Kin. 11:1-2

6 And all the men of Shechem gathered together, and all the house of Millo, and went, and made Abimelech king, by the plain of the pillar that *was* in Shechem.   2 Sam. 5:9

> **9:1-6 Results of Turning From God**
>
> Forgetful of all that they owed to Gideon, their judge and deliverer, the people of Israel accepted his baseborn son Abimelech as their king, who, to sustain his power, murdered all but one of Gideon's lawful children. When men cast off the fear of God they are not long in departing from honor and integrity. *PP 556, 557*

Jotham Rebukes the Citizens of Shechem for Crowning Abimelech

7 And when they told *it* to Jotham, he went and stood in the top of mount Gerizim, and lifted up his voice, and cried, and said unto them, Hearken unto me, ye men of Shechem, that God may hearken unto you.   Deut. 11:29; 27:12; John 4:20

8 The trees went forth *on a time* to anoint a king over them; and they said unto the olive tree, Reign thou over us.   Judg. 8:22-23

9 But the olive tree said unto them, Should I leave my fatness, wherewith by me they honour God and man, and go to be promoted over the trees?

10 And the trees said to the fig tree, Come thou, *and* reign over us.

11 But the fig tree said unto them, Should I forsake my sweetness, and my good fruit, and go to be promoted over the trees?

12 Then said the trees unto the vine, Come thou, *and* reign over us.

13 And the vine said unto them, Should I leave my wine, which cheereth God and man, and go to be promoted over the trees?   Ps. 104:15

14 Then said all the trees unto the ᵀbramble, Come thou, *and* reign over us.   thorny shrub

15 And the bramble said unto the trees, If in truth ye anoint me king over you, *then* come *and* put your trust in my shadow: and if not, let fire come out of the bramble, and devour the cedars of Lebanon.   Judg. 9:20

16 Now therefore, if ye have done truly and sincerely, in that ye have made Abimelech king, and if ye have dealt well with Jerubbaal and his house, and have done unto him according to the deserving of his hands;   Judg. 8:35

17 (For my father fought for you, and adventured his life far, and delivered you out of the hand of Midian:

18 And ye are risen up against my father's house this day, and have slain his sons, ᵀthreescore and ten persons, upon one stone, and have made Abimelech, the son of his maidservant, king over the men of Shechem, because he *is* your brother;)   Judg. 9:5-6 ◆ sixty

19 If ye then have dealt truly and sincerely with Jerubbaal and with his house this day, *then* rejoice ye in Abimelech, and let him also rejoice in you: Is. 8:6

20 But if not, let fire come out from Abimelech, and devour the men of Shechem, and the house of Millo; and let fire come out from the men of Shechem, and from the house of Millo, and devour Abimelech.   Judg. 9:15

21 And Jotham ran away, and fled, and went to Beer, and dwelt there, for fear of Abimelech his brother.   Num. 21:16

Gaal Conspires with the Shechemites against Abimelech

22 When Abimelech had reigned three years over Israel,

23 Then God sent an evil spirit between Abimelech and the men of Shechem; and the men of Shechem dealt treacherously with Abimelech: Is. 19:2, 14; 33:1

24 That the cruelty *done* to the threescore and ten sons of Jerubbaal might come, and their blood be laid upon Abimelech their brother, which slew them; and upon the men of Shechem, which aided him in the killing of his brethren.   1 Kin. 2:32

25 And the men of Shechem set liers in wait for him in the top of the mountains, and they robbed all that came along that way by them: and it was told Abimelech.

26 And Gaal the son of Ebed came with his brethren, and went over to Shechem: and the men of Shechem put their confidence in him.

27 And they went out into the fields, and gathered their vineyards, and ^Ttrode *the grapes*, and made merry, and went into the house of their god, and did eat and drink, and cursed Abimelech.   Judg. 9:4 ◆ *trampled*

28 And Gaal the son of Ebed said, Who *is* Abimelech, and who *is* Shechem, that we should serve him? *is* not *he* the son of Jerubbaal? and Zebul his officer? serve the men of Hamor the father of Shechem: for why should we serve him?   Gen. 34:2, 6; 1 Sam. 25:10

29 And would to God this people were under my hand! then would I remove Abimelech. And he said to Abimelech, Increase thine army, and come out.   2 Sam. 15:4

30 And when Zebul the ruler of the city heard the words of Gaal the son of Ebed, his anger was kindled.

31 And he sent messengers unto Abimelech ^Tprivily, saying, Behold, Gaal the son of Ebed and his brethren be come to Shechem; and, behold, they fortify the city against thee.   *in secret*

32 Now therefore up by night, thou and the people that *is* with thee, and lie in wait in the field:

33 And it shall be, *that* in the morning, as soon as the sun is up, thou shalt rise early, and set upon the city: and, behold, *when* he and the people that *is* with him come out against thee, then mayest thou do to them as thou shalt find occasion.   1 Sam. 10:7

34 And Abimelech rose up, and all the people that *were* with him, by night, and they laid wait against Shechem in four companies.

35 And Gaal the son of Ebed went out, and stood in the entering of the gate of the city: and Abimelech rose up, and the people that *were* with him, from lying in wait.

36 And when Gaal saw the people, he said to Zebul, Behold, there come people down from the top of the mountains. And Zebul said unto him, Thou seest the shadow of the mountains as *if they were* men.

37 And Gaal spake again and said, See there come people down by the middle of the land, and another company come along by the plain of Meonenim.

38 Then said Zebul unto him, Where *is* now thy mouth, wherewith thou saidst, Who *is* Abimelech, that we should serve him? *is* not this the people that thou hast despised? go out, I pray now, and fight with them.   Judg. 9:28-29

39 And Gaal went out before the men of Shechem, and fought with Abimelech.

40 And Abimelech chased him, and he fled before him, and many were overthrown *and* wounded, *even* unto the entering of the gate.

41 And Abimelech dwelt at Arumah: and Zebul thrust out Gaal and his brethren, that they should not dwell in Shechem.

42 And it came to pass on the morrow, that the people went out into the field; and they told Abimelech.

43 And he took the people, and divided them into three companies, and laid wait in the field, and looked, and, behold, the people *were* come forth out of the city; and he rose up against them, and smote them.

44 And Abimelech, and the company that *was* with him, rushed forward, and stood in the entering of the gate of the city: and the two *other* companies ran upon all *the people* that *were* in the fields, and slew them.

45 And Abimelech fought against the city all that day; and he took the city, and slew the people that *was* therein, and beat down the city, and sowed it with salt. Deut. 29:23; 2 Kin. 3:25

46 And when all the men of the tower of Shechem heard *that*, they entered into an hold of the house of the god Berith.   Judg. 8:33; 9:4

47 And it was told Abimelech, that all the men of the tower of Shechem were gathered together.

48 And Abimelech gat him up to mount Zalmon, he and all the people that *were* with him; and Abimelech took an axe in his hand, and cut down a bough from the trees, and took it, and laid *it* on his shoulder, and said unto the people that *were* with him, What ye have seen me do, make haste, *and* do as I have done.   Ps. 68:14

49 And all the people likewise cut down every man his bough, and followed Abimelech, and put *them* to the hold, and set the hold on fire upon them; so that all the men of the tower of Shechem died also, about a thousand men and women.

Abimelech Is Killed by a Millstone Dropped from the City Wall

50 Then went Abimelech to Thebez, and encamped against Thebez, and took it.

51 But there was a strong tower within the city, and thither fled all the men and women,

and all they of the city, and shut *it* to them, and gat them up to the top of the tower.

52 And Abimelech came unto the tower, and fought against it, and went hard unto the door of the tower to burn it with fire.

53 And a certain woman cast a piece of a millstone upon Abimelech's head, and all to brake his skull.   2 Sam. 11:21

54 Then he called hastily unto the young man his armourbearer, and said unto him, Draw thy sword, and slay me, that men say not of me, A woman slew him. And his young man thrust him through, and he died.

55 And when the men of Israel saw that Abimelech was dead, they departed every man unto his place.

56 Thus God rendered the wickedness of Abimelech, which he did unto his father, in slaying his seventy brethren: Ps. 94:23

57 And all the evil of the men of Shechem did God render upon their heads: and upon them came the curse of Jotham the son of Jerubbaal.   Judg. 9:20

Tola and Jair Serve as Judges

10 And after Abimelech there arose to defend Israel Tola the son of Puah, the son of Dodo, a man of Issachar; and he dwelt in Shamir in mount Ephraim. Judg. 2:16

2 And he judged Israel twenty and three years, and died, and was buried in Shamir.

3 And after him arose Jair, a Gileadite, and judged Israel twenty and two years.

4 And he had thirty sons that rode on thirty ass colts, and they had thirty cities, which are called Havothjair unto this day, which *are* in the land of Gilead.   Num. 32:41

5 And Jair died, and was buried in Camon.

The Philistines and Ammonites Oppress Israel

6 And the children of Israel did evil again in the sight of the LORD, and served Baalim, and Ashtaroth, and the gods of Syria, and the gods of Zidon, and the gods of Moab, and the gods of the children of Ammon, and the gods of the Philistines, and forsook the LORD, and served not him.   1 Kin. 11:5

7 And the anger of the LORD was hot against Israel, and he sold them into the hands of the Philistines, and into the hands of the children of Ammon.   Judg. 2:14

8 And that year they vexed and oppressed the children of Israel: eighteen years, all the children of Israel that *were* on the other side Jordan in the land of the Amorites, which *is* in Gilead.

9 Moreover the children of Ammon passed over Jordan to fight also against Judah, and against Benjamin, and against the house of Ephraim; so that Israel was sore distressed.

God Chides the People for Their Trust in Idols

10 And the children of Israel cried unto the LORD, saying, We have sinned against thee, both because we have forsaken our God, and also served Baalim.   1 Sam. 12:10

10:10 True and False Repentance

Again the people sought help from Him whom they had so forsaken and insulted. . . . But sorrow had not worked true repentance. The people mourned because their sins had brought suffering upon themselves, but not because they had dishonored God by transgression of His holy law. True repentance is more than sorrow for sin. It is a resolute turning away from evil. *PP 557*

11 And the LORD said unto the children of Israel, *Did* not *I deliver you* from the Egyptians, and from the Amorites, from the children of Ammon, and from the Philistines?   Ex. 14:30

12 The Zidonians also, and the Amalekites, and the Maonites, did oppress you; and ye cried to me, and I delivered you out of their hand.   Judg. 6:3

13 Yet ye have forsaken me, and served other gods: wherefore I will deliver you no more.   Jer. 2:13

14 Go and cry unto the gods which ye have chosen; let them deliver you in the time of your tribulation.   Deut. 32:37-38

15 And the children of Israel said unto the LORD, We have sinned: do thou unto us whatsoever seemeth good unto thee; deliver us only, we pray thee, this day.   1 Sam. 3:18

16 And they put away the strange gods from among them, and served the LORD: and his soul was grieved for the misery of Israel.   Is. 63:9

10:16 God Grieved Over Israel

Every departure from the right, every deed of cruelty, every failure of humanity to reach His ideal, brings grief to Him. When there came upon Israel the calamities that were the sure result of separation from God—subjugation by their enemies, cruelty, and death—it is said that "His soul was grieved for the misery of Israel." *Ed 263*

17 Then the children of Ammon were gathered together, and encamped in Gilead. And the children of Israel assembled themselves together, and encamped in Mizpeh.   Gen. 31:49; Judg. 11:11, 29

18 And the people *and* princes of Gilead said one to another, What man *is he* that will begin to fight against the children of Ammon? he shall be head over all the inhabitants of Gilead.   Judg. 11:11

The Covenant between Jephthah and Gilead

11 Now Jephthah the Gileadite was a mighty man of valour, and he *was* the son of an harlot: and Gilead ᵀbegat Jephthah. Judg. 6:12; 2 Kin. 5:1; Heb. 11:32 ◆ *brought forth*
2 And Gilead's wife bare him sons; and his wife's sons grew up, and they thrust out Jephthah, and said unto him, Thou shalt not inherit in our father's house; for thou *art* the son of a strange woman.
3 Then Jephthah fled from his brethren, and dwelt in the land of Tob: and there were gathered vain men to Jephthah, and went out with him. Judg. 9:4
4 And it came to pass in process of time, that the children of Ammon made war against Israel.
5 And it was so, that when the children of Ammon made war against Israel, the elders of Gilead went to fetch Jephthah out of the land of Tob:
6 And they said unto Jephthah, Come, and be our captain, that we may fight with the children of Ammon.
7 And Jephthah said unto the elders of Gilead, Did not ye hate me, and expel me out of my father's house? and why are ye come unto me now when ye are in distress? Gen. 26:27
8 And the elders of Gilead said unto Jephthah, Therefore we turn again to thee now, that thou mayest go with us, and fight against the children of Ammon, and be our head over all the inhabitants of Gilead. Judg. 10:18
9 And Jephthah said unto the elders of Gilead, If ye bring me home again to fight against the children of Ammon, and the LORD deliver them before me, shall I be your head?
10 And the elders of Gilead said unto Jephthah, The LORD be witness between us, if we do not so according to thy words. Jer. 29:23
11 Then Jephthah went with the elders of Gilead, and the people made him head and captain over them: and Jephthah uttered all his words before the LORD in Mizpeh. 1 Sam. 10:17

The Ammonites Reject Jephthah's Plea for Peace

12 And Jephthah sent messengers unto the king of the children of Ammon, saying, What hast thou to do with me, that thou art come against me to fight in my land?
13 And the king of the children of Ammon answered unto the messengers of Jephthah, Because Israel took away my land, when they came up out of Egypt, from Arnon even unto Jabbok, and unto Jordan: now therefore restore those lands again peaceably. Gen. 32:22; Num. 21:24-26
14 And Jephthah sent messengers again unto the king of the children of Ammon:
15 And said unto him, Thus saith Jephthah, Israel took not away the land of Moab, nor the land of the children of Ammon: Deut. 2:9
16 But when Israel came up from Egypt, and walked through the wilderness unto the Red sea, and came to Kadesh; Num. 14:25; Deut. 1:40
17 Then Israel sent messengers unto the king of Edom, saying, Let me, I pray thee, pass through thy land: but the king of Edom would not hearken *thereto*. And in like manner they sent unto the king of Moab: but he would not *consent*: and Israel abode in Kadesh. Num. 20:1
18 Then they went along through the wilderness, and ᵀcompassed the land of Edom, and the land of Moab, and came by the east side of the land of Moab, and pitched on the other side of Arnon, but came not within the border of Moab: for Arnon *was* the border of Moab. Num. 22:36 ◆ *bypassed*
19 And Israel sent messengers unto Sihon king of the Amorites, the king of Heshbon; and Israel said unto him, Let us pass, we pray thee, through thy land into my place.
20 But Sihon trusted not Israel to pass through his coast: but Sihon gathered all his people together, and pitched in Jahaz, and fought against Israel.
21 And the LORD God of Israel delivered Sihon and all his people into the hand of Israel, and they smote them: so Israel possessed all the land of the Amorites, the inhabitants of that country.
22 And they possessed all the coasts of the Amorites, from Arnon even unto Jabbok, and from the wilderness even unto Jordan.
23 So now the LORD God of Israel hath dispossessed the Amorites from before his people Israel, and shouldest thou possess it?
24 Wilt not thou possess that which Chemosh thy god giveth thee to possess? So whomsoever the LORD our God shall drive out from before us, them will we possess. Num. 21:29; Josh. 3:10; 1 Kin. 11:7
25 And now *art* thou any thing better than Balak the son of Zippor, king of Moab? did he ever strive against Israel, or did he ever fight against them, Mic. 6:5
26 While Israel dwelt in Heshbon and her towns, and in Aroer and her towns, and in all the cities that *be* along by the coasts of Arnon, three hundred years? why therefore did ye not recover *them* within that time? Deut. 2:36
27 Wherefore I have not sinned against thee, but thou doest me wrong to war against me: the LORD the Judge be judge this day between the children of Israel and the children of Ammon. Gen. 16:5; 18:25; 31:53

28 Howbeit the king of the children of Ammon hearkened not unto the words of Jephthah which he sent him.

Jephthah's Vow and His Conquest of the Ammonites

29 Then the Spirit of the Lord came upon Jephthah, and he passed over Gilead, and Manasseh, and passed over Mizpeh of Gilead, and from Mizpeh of Gilead he passed over *unto* the children of Ammon.   Num. 11:25

11:29 Israel's Recurring Lesson

A deliverer was raised up in the person of Jephthah, a Gileadite, who made war upon the Ammonites and effectually destroyed their power. For eighteen years at this time Israel had suffered under the oppression of her foes, yet again the lesson taught by suffering was forgotten.

As His people returned to their evil ways, the Lord permitted them to be still oppressed by their powerful enemies, the Philistines. *PP 558*

---

30 And Jephthah vowed a vow unto the Lord, and said, If thou shalt without fail deliver the children of Ammon into mine hands,   Gen. 28:20
31 Then it shall be, that whatsoever cometh forth of the doors of my house to meet me, when I return in peace from the children of Ammon, shall surely be the Lord's, and I will offer it up for a burnt offering.   1 Sam. 1:28
32 So Jephthah passed over unto the children of Ammon to fight against them; and the Lord delivered them into his hands.
33 And he smote them from Aroer, even till thou come to Minnith, *even* twenty cities, and unto the plain of the vineyards, with a very great slaughter. Thus the children of Ammon were subdued before the children of Israel.   Ezek. 27:17
34 And Jephthah came to Mizpeh unto his house, and, behold, his daughter came out to meet him with timbrels and with dances: and she *was his* only child; beside her he had neither son nor daughter.   Ex. 15:20; Jer. 31:4
35 And it came to pass, when he saw her, that he ᵀrent his clothes, and said, Alas, my daughter! thou hast brought me very low, and thou art one of them that trouble me: for I have opened my mouth unto the Lord, and I cannot go back.   tore
36 And she said unto him, My father, *if* thou hast opened thy mouth unto the Lord, do to me according to that which hath proceeded out of thy mouth; ᵀforasmuch as the Lord hath taken vengeance for

thee of thine enemies, *even* of the children of Ammon.   2 Sam. 18:19 ◆ *since*
37 And she said unto her father, Let this thing be done for me: let me alone two months, that I may go up and down upon the mountains, and ᵀbewail my virginity, I and my fellows.   Luke 1:25 ◆ *lament*
38 And he said, Go. And he sent her away *for* two months: and she went with her companions, and bewailed her virginity upon the mountains.
39 And it came to pass at the end of two months, that she returned unto her father, who did with her *according* to his vow which he had vowed: and she knew no man. And it was a custom in Israel,   Judg. 11:31
40 *That* the daughters of Israel went yearly to lament the daughter of Jephthah the Gileadite four days in a year.

The Ephraimites, Quarreling with Jephthah, Are Slain by the Gileadites

12 And the men of Ephraim gathered themselves together, and went northward, and said unto Jephthah, Wherefore passedst thou over to fight against the children of Ammon, and didst not call us to go with thee? we will burn thine house upon thee with fire.   Judg. 8:1
2 And Jephthah said unto them, I and my people were at great strife with the children of Ammon; and when I called you, ye delivered me not out of their hands.
3 And when I saw that ye delivered *me* not, I put my life in my hands, and passed over against the children of Ammon, and the Lord delivered them into my hand: wherefore then are ye come up unto me this day, to fight against me?   1 Sam. 19:5; 28:21; Job 13:14
4 Then Jephthah gathered together all the men of Gilead, and fought with Ephraim: and the men of Gilead smote Ephraim, because they said, Ye Gileadites *are* fugitives of Ephraim among the Ephraimites, *and* among the Manassites.   1 Sam. 25:10
5 And the Gileadites took the passages of Jordan before the Ephraimites: and it was *so*, that when those Ephraimites which were escaped said, Let me go over; that the men of Gilead said unto him, *Art* thou an Ephraimite? If he said, Nay;   Josh. 22:11; Judg. 3:28
6 Then said they unto him, Say now Shibboleth: and he said Sibboleth: for he could not frame to pronounce *it* right. Then they took him, and slew him at the passages of Jordan: and there fell at that time of the Ephraimites forty and two thousand.
7 And Jephthah judged Israel six years. Then died Jephthah the Gileadite, and was buried in *one of* the cities of Gilead.

Ibzan, Elon, and Abdon Serve as Judges

8 And after him Ibzan of Beth-lehem judged Israel.
9 And he had thirty sons, and thirty daughters, *whom* he sent abroad, and took in thirty daughters from abroad for his sons. And he judged Israel seven years.
10 Then died Ibzan, and was buried at Beth-lehem.
11 And after him Elon, a Zebulonite, judged Israel; and he judged Israel ten years.
12 And Elon the Zebulonite died, and was buried in Aijalon in the country of Zebulun.
13 And after him Abdon the son of Hillel, a Pirathonite, judged Israel.
14 And he had forty sons and thirty nephews, that rode on ᵀthreescore and ten ass colts: and he judged Israel eight years. Judg. 5:10 ◆ *sixty*
15 And Abdon the son of Hillel the Pirathonite died, and was buried in Pirathon in the land of Ephraim, in the mount of the Amalekites.   Judg. 5:14

Israel Conquered by the Philistines

13 And the children of Israel did evil again in the sight of the LORD; and the LORD delivered them into the hand of the Philistines forty years. Judg. 2:11; 1 Sam. 12:9
2 And there was a certain man of Zorah, of the family of the Danites, whose name *was* Manoah; and his wife *was* barren, and bare not.   Josh. 15:33; 19:41; Luke 1:7
3 And the angel of the LORD appeared unto the woman, and said unto her, Behold now, thou *art* barren, and bearest not: but thou shalt conceive, and bear a son.   Luke 1:11, 13

13:3 God Heard the Pleas of the Faithful

Amid the widespread apostasy the faithful worshipers of God continued to plead with Him for the deliverance of Israel. Though there was apparently no response, though year after year the power of the oppressor continued to rest more heavily upon the land, God's providence was preparing help for them. Even in the early years of the Philistine oppression a child was born through whom God designed to humble the power of these mighty foes. PP 560

---

4 Now therefore beware, I pray thee, and drink not wine nor strong drink, and eat not any unclean *thing*: Num. 6:2-3; Judg. 13:14; Luke 1:15

Health   See Proverbs 20:1.

5 For, lo, thou shalt conceive, and bear a son; and no razor shall come on his head: for the child shall be a Nazarite unto God from the womb: and he shall begin to deliver Israel out of the hand of the Philistines.   Num. 6:5; 1 Sam. 1:11; 7:13
6 Then the woman came and told her husband, saying, A man of God came unto me,

and his ᵀcountenance *was* like the countenance of an angel of God, very terrible: but I asked him not whence he *was*, neither told he me his name: Judg. 13:17-18 ◆ *appearance*
7 But he said unto me, Behold, thou shalt conceive, and bear a son; and now drink no wine nor strong drink, neither eat any unclean *thing*: for the child shall be a Nazarite to God from the womb to the day of his death.

13:7 Christ Enjoined Abstinence

It was Christ who directed that John the Baptist should drink neither wine nor strong drink. It was He who enjoined similar abstinence upon the wife of Manoah. Christ did not contradict His own teaching. MH 333

---

8 Then Manoah ᵀintreated the LORD, and said, O my Lord, let the man of God which thou didst send come again unto us, and teach us what we shall do unto the child that shall be born.   *pled with*
9 And God hearkened to the voice of Manoah; and the angel of God came again unto the woman as she sat in the field: but Manoah her husband *was* not with her.
10 And the woman made haste, and ran, and shewed her husband, and said unto him, Behold, the man hath appeared unto me, that came unto me the *other* day.
11 And Manoah arose, and went after his wife, and came to the man, and said unto him, *Art* thou the man that spakest unto the woman? And he said, I *am*.
12 And Manoah said, Now let thy words come to pass. How shall we order the child, and *how* shall we do unto him?
13 And the angel of the LORD said unto Manoah, Of all that I said unto the woman let her beware.
14 She may not eat of any *thing* that cometh of the vine, neither let her drink wine or strong drink, nor eat any unclean *thing*: all that I commanded her let her observe.   Judg. 13:4

Manoah's Sacrifice Identifies the Angel

15 And Manoah said unto the angel of the LORD, I pray thee, let us detain thee, until we shall have made ready a kid for thee.
16 And the angel of the LORD said unto Manoah, Though thou detain me, I will not eat of thy bread: and if thou wilt offer a burnt offering, thou must offer it unto the LORD. For Manoah knew not that he *was* an angel of the LORD.
17 And Manoah said unto the angel of the LORD, What *is* thy name, that when thy sayings come to pass we may do thee honour?
18 And the angel of the LORD said unto him,

13:4

Why askest thou thus after my name, seeing it *is* secret?   Gen. 32:29
19 So Manoah took a kid with a meat offering, and offered *it* upon a rock unto the LORD: and *the angel* did wondrously; and Manoah and his wife looked on.   Judg. 6:19-21
20 For it came to pass, when the flame went up toward heaven from off the altar, that the angel of the LORD ascended in the flame of the altar. And Manoah and his wife looked on *it*, and fell on their faces to the ground.   Lev. 9:24; 1 Chr. 21:16; Ezek. 1:28
21 But the angel of the LORD did no more appear to Manoah and to his wife. Then Manoah knew that he *was* an angel of the LORD.   Judg. 6:22
22 And Manoah said unto his wife, We shall surely die, because we have seen God.
23 But his wife said unto him, If the LORD were pleased to kill us, he would not have received a burnt offering and a meat offering at our hands, neither would he have shewed us all these *things*, nor would as at this time have told us *such things* as these.   Ps. 25:14

Samson Is Born

24 And the woman bare a son, and called his name Samson: and the child grew, and the LORD blessed him. 1 Sam. 3:19; Luke 1:80; 2:52
25 And the Spirit of the LORD began to move him at times in the camp of Dan between Zorah and Eshtaol.   Josh. 15:33; Judg. 3:10

Samson Desires a Wife of the Philistines

14 And Samson went down to Timnath, and saw a woman in Timnath of the daughters of the Philistines.   Gen. 38:12-13
2 And he came up, and told his father and his mother, and said, I have seen a woman in Timnath of the daughters of the Philistines: now therefore get her for me to wife. Gen. 34:4
3 Then his father and his mother said unto him, *Is there* never a woman among the daughters of thy brethren, or among all my people, that thou goest to take a wife of the uncircumcised Philistines? And Samson said unto his father, Get her for me; for she pleaseth me well.   Judg. 15:18

14:3 On Choosing a Marriage Partner

How many are pursuing the same course as did Samson! How often marriages are formed between the godly and the ungodly, because inclination governs in the selection of husband or wife! The parties do not ask counsel of God, nor have His glory in view. Christianity ought to have a controlling influence upon the marriage relation, but it is too often the case that the motives which lead to this union are not in keeping with Christian principles. *PP 563*

---

4 But his father and his mother knew not that it *was* of the LORD, that he sought an occasion against the Philistines: for at that time the Philistines had dominion over Israel.   Josh. 11:20; Judg. 13:1; 15:11
5 Then went Samson down, and his father and his mother, to Timnath, and came to the vineyards of Timnath: and, behold, a young lion roared against him.
6 And the Spirit of the LORD came mightily upon him, and he rent him as he would have rent a kid, and *he had* nothing in his hand: but he told not his father or his mother what he had done. Judg. 3:10; 13:25; 1 Sam. 11:6 ◆ *torn apart*
7 And he went down, and talked with the woman; and she pleased Samson well.
8 And after a time he returned to take her, and he turned aside to see the carcase of the

---

The Mother's Role for Her Children

Judges 13:7–14

The carefulness with which the mother should guard her habits of life is taught in the Scriptures. When the Lord would raise up Samson as a deliverer for Israel, "the angel of Jehovah" appeared to the mother, with special instruction concerning her habits, and also for the treatment of her child. "Beware," he said, "and now drink no wine nor strong drink, neither eat any unclean thing" (Judges 13:13, 7).

The effect of prenatal influences is by many parents looked upon as a matter of little moment; but heaven does not so regard it. The message sent by an angel of God, and twice given in the most solemn manner, shows it to be deserving of our most careful thought.

In the words spoken to the Hebrew mother, God speaks to all mothers in every age. "Let her beware," the angel said; "all that I commanded her let her observe." The well-being of the child will be affected by the habits of the mother. Her appetites and passions are to be controlled by principle. There is something for her to shun, something for her to work against, if she fulfills God's purpose for her in giving her a child. If before the birth of her child she is self-indulgent, if she is selfish, impatient, and exacting, these traits will be reflected in the disposition of the child. Thus many children have received as a birthright almost unconquerable tendencies to evil. *MH 372, 373*

lion: and, behold, *there was* a swarm of bees and honey in the carcase of the lion.

9 And he took thereof in his hands, and went on eating, and came to his father and mother, and he gave them, and they did eat: but he told not them that he had taken the honey out of the carcase of the lion.

Samson's Marriage Feast

10 So his father went down unto the woman: and Samson made there a feast; for so used the young men to do.

11 And it came to pass, when they saw him, that they brought thirty companions to be with him.

12 And Samson said unto them, I will now put forth a riddle unto you: if ye can certainly declare it me within the seven days of the feast, and find *it* out, then I will give you thirty sheets and thirty change of garments: Gen. 45:22; 1 Kin. 10:1; Ezek. 17:2

13 But if ye cannot declare *it* me, then shall ye give me thirty sheets and thirty change of garments. And they said unto him, Put forth thy riddle, that we may hear it.

14 And he said unto them, Out of the eater came forth meat, and out of the strong came forth sweetness. And they could not in three days ᵀexpound the riddle.   *explain*

15 And it came to pass on the seventh day, that they said unto Samson's wife, Entice thy husband, that he may declare unto us the riddle, lest we burn thee and thy father's house with fire: have ye called us to take that we have? *is it* not *so?*   Judg. 15:6; 16:5

16 And Samson's wife wept before him, and said, Thou dost but hate me, and lovest me not: thou hast put forth a riddle unto the children of my people, and hast not told *it* me. And he said unto her, Behold, I have not told *it* my father nor my mother, and shall I tell *it* thee?   Judg. 16:15

17 And she wept before him the seven days, while their feast lasted: and it came to pass on the seventh day, that he told her, because she lay sore upon him: and she told the riddle to the children of her people.   Judg. 16:16

18 And the men of the city said unto him on the seventh day before the sun went down, What *is* sweeter than honey? and what *is* stronger than a lion? And he said unto them, If ye had not plowed with my heifer, ye had not found out my riddle.

19 And the Spirit of the LORD came upon him, and he went down to Ashkelon, and slew thirty men of them, and took their ᵀspoil, and gave change of garments unto them which expounded the riddle. And his anger was kindled, and he went up to his father's house.   Judg. 3:10 ◆ *plunder*

20 But Samson's wife was *given* to his companion, whom he had used as his friend.

Samson Serves as a Judge

15 But it came to pass within a while after, in the time of wheat harvest, that Samson visited his wife with a kid; and he said, I will go in to my wife into the chamber. But her father would not suffer him to go in.   Gen. 38:17

2 And her father said, I ᵀverily thought that thou hadst utterly hated her; therefore I gave her to thy companion: *is* not her younger sister fairer than she? take her, I pray thee, instead of her.   Judg. 14:20 ◆ *truly*

3 And Samson said concerning them, Now shall I be more blameless than the Philistines, though I do them a displeasure.

4 And Samson went and caught three hundred foxes, and took firebrands, and turned tail to tail, and put a firebrand in the midst between two tails.

5 And when he had set the brands on fire, he let *them* go into the standing corn of the Philistines, and burnt up both the shocks, and also the standing corn, with the vineyards *and* olives.

6 Then the Philistines said, Who hath done this? And they answered, Samson, the son in law of the Timnite, because he had taken his wife, and given her to his companion. And the Philistines came up, and burnt her and her father with fire.   Judg. 14:15

7 And Samson said unto them, Though ye have done this, yet will I be avenged of you, and after that I will cease.

8 And he smote them hip and thigh with a great slaughter: and he went down and dwelt in the top of the rock Etam.

Samson Kills a Thousand Philistines with a Donkey's Jawbone

9 Then the Philistines went up, and pitched in Judah, and spread themselves in Lehi.   Judg. 15:17

10 And the men of Judah said, Why are ye come up against us? And they answered, To bind Samson are we come up, to do to him as he hath done to us.

11 Then three thousand men of Judah went to the top of the rock Etam, and said to Samson, Knowest thou not that the Philistines *are* rulers over us? what *is* this *that* thou hast done unto us? And he said unto them, As they did unto me, so have I done unto them.   Judg. 13:1; 14:4

12 And they said unto him, We are come down to bind thee, that we may deliver thee into the hand of the Philistines. And Samson said unto them, Swear unto me, that ye will not fall upon me yourselves.

13 And they spake unto him, saying, No; but we will bind thee fast, and deliver thee into their hand: but surely we will not kill thee. And they bound him with two new cords, and brought him up from the rock.

14 *And* when he came unto Lehi, the Philistines shouted against him: and the Spirit of the LORD came mightily upon him, and the cords that *were* upon his arms became as flax that was burnt with fire, and his bands loosed from off his hands. Judg. 3:10; 14:6, 19

15 And he found a new jawbone of an ass, and put forth his hand, and took it, and slew a thousand men therewith. Lev. 26:8; Josh. 23:10

16 And Samson said, With the jawbone of an ass, heaps upon heaps, with the jaw of an ass have I slain a thousand men.

17 And it came to pass, when he had made an end of speaking, that he cast away the jawbone out of his hand, and called that place Ramath-lehi.

15:11–17 A Lost Opportunity for Freedom

Had the Israelites been ready to unite with Samson and follow up the victory, they might at this time have freed themselves from the power of their oppressors. But they had become dispirited and cowardly. They had neglected the work which God commanded them to perform, in dispossessing the heathen, and had united with them in their degrading practices, tolerating their cruelty, and, so long as it was not directed against themselves, even countenancing their injustice. *PP 564*

God Provides a Fountain for Samson to Quench His Thirst

18 And he was sore athirst, and called on the LORD, and said, Thou hast given this great deliverance into the hand of thy servant: and now shall I die for thirst, and fall into the hand of the uncircumcised?

19 But God ᵀclave an ᵀhollow place that *was* in the jaw, and there came water thereout; and when he had drunk, his spirit came again, and he revived: wherefore he called the name thereof En-hakkore, which *is* in Lehi unto this day. Gen. 45:27 ◆ split ◆ recessed place

20 And he judged Israel in the days of the Philistines twenty years. Judg. 13:1; 16:31

Samson Escapes from Gaza and Carries Away the City Gates

16 Then went Samson to Gaza, and saw there an harlot, and went in unto her. Josh. 15:47

2 *And it was told* the Gazites, saying, Samson is come ᵀthither. And they compassed *him* in, and laid wait for him all night in the gate of the city, and were quiet all the night, saying, In the morning, when it is day, we shall kill him. 1 Sam. 23:26; Ps. 118:10-12; Acts 9:24 ◆ here

3 And Samson lay till midnight, and arose at midnight, and took the doors of the gate of the city, and the two posts, and went away with them, bar and all, and put *them* upon his shoulders, and carried them up to the top of an hill that *is* before Hebron.

Delilah Entices Samson to Tell Her the Secret of His Strength

4 And it came to pass afterward, that he loved a woman in the valley of Sorek, whose name *was* Delilah.

16:4 Wrecks of Character

All along through the ages there are strewn wrecks of character that have been stranded upon the rocks of sensual indulgence. As we approach the close of time, as the people of God stand upon the borders of the heavenly Canaan, Satan will, as of old, redouble his efforts to prevent them from entering the goodly land. *PP 457*

---

5 And the lords of the Philistines came up unto her, and said unto her, Entice him, and see wherein his great strength *lieth*, and by what *means* we may prevail against him, that we may bind him to afflict him: and we will give thee every one of us eleven hundred *pieces* of silver. Josh. 13:3; Judg. 14:15

6 And Delilah said to Samson, Tell me, I pray thee, wherein thy great strength *lieth*, and wherewith thou mightest be bound to afflict thee.

7 And Samson said unto her, If they bind me with seven green ᵀwiths that were never dried, then shall I be weak, and be as another man. ropes or cords

8 Then the lords of the Philistines brought up to her seven green withs which had not been dried, and she bound him with them.

9 Now *there were* men lying in wait, abiding with her in the chamber. And she said unto him, The Philistines *be* upon thee, Samson. And he brake the withs, as a thread of ᵀtow is broken when it toucheth the fire. So his strength was not known. flax fibers

10 And Delilah said unto Samson, Behold, thou hast mocked me, and told me lies: now tell me, I pray thee, wherewith thou mightest be bound.

11 And he said unto her, If they bind me fast with new ropes that never were occupied, then shall I be weak, and be as another man. Judg. 16:13

12 Delilah therefore took new ropes, and bound him therewith, and said unto him,

The Philistines *be* upon thee, Samson. And *there were* liers in wait abiding in the chamber. And he brake them from off his arms like a thread.

13 And Delilah said unto Samson, Hitherto thou hast mocked me, and told me lies: tell me wherewith thou mightest be bound. And he said unto her, If thou weavest the seven locks of my head with the web.

14 And she fastened *it* with the pin, and said unto him, The Philistines *be* upon thee, Samson. And he awaked out of his sleep, and went away with the pin of the beam, and with the web.

15 And she said unto him, How canst thou say, I love thee, when thine heart *is* not with me? thou hast mocked me these three times, and hast not told me wherein thy great strength *lieth*.   Judg. 14:16

16 And it came to pass, when she pressed him daily with her words, and urged him, *so* that his soul was vexed unto death;

17 That he told her all his heart, and said unto her, There hath not come a razor upon mine head; for I *have been* a Nazarite unto God from my mother's womb: if I be shaven, then my strength will go from me, and I shall become weak, and be like any *other* man.   Num. 6:5; Judg. 13:5; Mic. 7:5

18 And when Delilah saw that he had told her all his heart, she sent and called for the lords of the Philistines, saying, Come up this once, for he hath shewed me all his heart. Then the lords of the Philistines came up unto her, and brought money in their hand.   Judg. 16:5

19 And she made him sleep upon her knees; and she called for a man, and she caused him to shave off the seven locks of his head; and she began to afflict him, and his strength went from him.   Prov. 7:26-27

20 And she said, The Philistines *be* upon thee, Samson. And he awoke out of his sleep, and said, I will go out as at other times before, and shake myself. And he ^Twist not that the LORD was departed from him.   Josh. 7:12 ◆ *knew*

21 But the Philistines took him, and put out his eyes, and brought him down to Gaza, and bound him with ^Tfetters of brass; and he did grind in the prison house. Ex. 11:5 ◆ *chains*

Samson's Final Act Kills Many Philistines

22 Howbeit the hair of his head began to grow again after he was shaven.

23 Then the lords of the Philistines gathered them together for to offer a great sacrifice unto Dagon their god, and to rejoice: for they said, Our god hath delivered Samson our enemy into our hand.   1 Sam. 5:2-5

24 And when the people saw him, they praised their god: for they said, Our god hath delivered into our hands our enemy, and the destroyer of our country, which slew many of us.   Dan. 5:4

25 And it came to pass, when their hearts were merry, that they said, Call for Samson, that he may make us sport. And they called for Samson out of the prison house; and he made them sport: and they set him between the pillars.   Judg. 9:27

26 And Samson said unto the lad that held him by the hand, Suffer me that I may feel

---

Wrecks of Character

Judges 16:4

The Israelites, who could not be overcome by the arms or by the enchantments of Midian, fell a prey to her harlots. Such is the power that woman, enlisted in the service of Satan, has exerted to entrap and destroy souls. "She hath cast down many wounded: yea, many strong men have been slain by her" (Proverbs 7:26). It was thus that the children of Seth were seduced from their integrity, and the holy seed became corrupt. It was thus that Joseph was tempted. Thus Samson betrayed his strength, the defense of Israel, into the hands of the Philistines. Here David stumbled. And Solomon, the wisest of kings, who had thrice been called the beloved of his God, became a slave of passion, and sacrificed his integrity to the same bewitching power.

"Now all these things happened unto them for ensamples: and they are written for our admonition, upon whom the ends of the world are come. Wherefore let him that thinketh he standeth take heed lest he fall" (1 Corinthians 10:11, 12). Satan well knows the material with which he has to deal in the human heart. He knows—for he has studied with fiendish intensity for thousands of years—the points most easily assailed in every character; and through successive generations he has wrought to overthrow the strongest men, princes in Israel, by the same temptations that were so successful at Baalpeor. All along through the ages there are strewn wrecks of character that have been stranded upon the rocks of sensual indulgence. As we approach the close of time, as the people of God stand upon the borders of the heavenly Canaan, Satan will, as of old, redouble his efforts to prevent them from entering the goodly land. *PP 457*

the pillars whereupon the house standeth, that I may lean upon them.
27 Now the house was full of men and women; and all the lords of the Philistines *were* there; and *there were* upon the roof about three thousand men and women, that beheld while Samson made sport.   Deut. 22:8
28 And Samson called unto the LORD, and said, O Lord GOD, remember me, I pray thee, and strengthen me, I pray thee, only this once, O God, that I may be at once avenged of the Philistines for my two eyes.   Jer. 15:15
29 And Samson took hold of the two middle pillars upon which the house stood, and on which it was borne up, of the one with his right hand, and of the other with his left.
30 And Samson said, Let me die with the Philistines. And he bowed himself with *all his* might; and the house fell upon the lords, and upon all the people that *were* therein. So the dead which he slew at his death were more than *they* which he slew in his life.
31 Then his brethren and all the house of his father came down, and took him, and brought *him* up, and buried him between Zorah and Eshtaol in the buryingplace of Manoah his father. And he judged Israel twenty years.   Judg. 15:20

Micah Builds an Idol and a Shrine for Worship

17 And there was a man of mount Ephraim, whose name *was* Micah.
2 And he said unto his mother, The eleven hundred *shekels* of silver that were taken from thee, about which thou cursedst, and spakest of also in mine ears, behold, the silver *is* with me; I took it. And his mother said, Blessed *be thou* of the LORD, my son.   Neh. 13:25
3 And when he had restored the eleven hundred *shekels* of silver to his mother, his mother said, I had wholly dedicated the silver unto the LORD from my hand for my son, to make a graven image and a molten image: now therefore I will restore it unto thee.   Ex. 20:4, 23; Lev. 19:4
4 Yet he restored the money unto his mother; and his mother took two hundred *shekels* of silver, and gave them to the founder, who made thereof a Tgraven image and a molten image: and they were in the house of Micah.   *engraved or cut out*
5 And the man Micah had an house of gods, and made an Tephod, and Tteraphim, and consecrated one of his sons, who became his priest.   Gen. 31:19; Judg. 8:27 ◆ *priestly garment* ◆ *idols*
6 In those days *there was* no king in Israel, *but* every man did *that which was* right in his own eyes.   Deut. 12:8; Judg. 18:1; 19:1

Micah Hires a Levite to Be Priest

7 And there was a young man out of Beth-lehem-judah of the family of Judah, who *was* a Levite, and he sojourned there.   Matt. 2:1
8 And the man departed out of the city from Beth-lehem-judah to sojourn where he could find *a place*: and he came to mount Ephraim to the house of Micah, as he journeyed.
9 And Micah said unto him, Whence comest thou? And he said unto him, I *am* a Levite of Beth-lehem-judah, and I go to sojourn where I may find *a place*.
10 And Micah said unto him, Dwell with me, and be unto me a father and a priest, and I will give thee ten *shekels* of silver by the year, and a suit of apparel, and thy Tvictuals. So the Levite went in.   *food*
11 And the Levite was content to dwell with the man; and the young man was unto him as one of his sons.
12 And Micah Tconsecrated the Levite; and the young man became his priest, and was in the house of Micah.   Judg. 18:30 ◆ *set apart*
13 Then said Micah, Now know I that the LORD will do me good, seeing I have a Levite to *my* priest.

The Tribe of Dan Looks for Land to Conquer

18 In those days *there was* no king in Israel: and in those days the tribe of the Danites sought them an inheritance to dwell in; for unto that day *all their* inheritance had not fallen unto them among the tribes of Israel.   Josh. 19:40-48; Judg. 17:6; 19:1
2 And the children of Dan sent of their family five men from their coasts, men of valour, from Zorah, and from Eshtaol, to spy out the land, and to search it; and they said unto them, Go, search the land: who when they came to mount Ephraim, to the house of Micah, they lodged there.   Num. 13:17; Josh. 2:1
3 When they *were* by the house of Micah, they knew the voice of the young man the Levite: and they turned in thither, and said unto him, Who brought thee Thither? and what makest thou in this *place*? and what hast thou here?   *here*
4 And he said unto them, Thus and thus dealeth Micah with me, and hath hired me, and I am his priest.   Judg. 17:10
5 And they said unto him, Ask counsel, we pray thee, of God, that we may know whether our way which we go shall be prosperous.   1 Kin. 22:5
6 And the priest said unto them, Go in peace: before the LORD *is* your way wherein ye go.   1 Kin. 22:6

The Tribe of Dan Decides to Attack the City of Laish

7 Then the five men departed, and came to Laish, and saw the people that were therein, how they dwelt careless, after the manner of the Zidonians, quiet and secure; and there was no magistrate in the land, that might put them to shame in any thing; and they were far from the Zidonians, and had no business with any man.   Josh. 19:47; Judg. 18:27-28

8 And they came unto their brethren to Zorah and Eshtaol: and their brethren said unto them, What say ye?   Judg. 18:2

9 And they said, Arise, that we may go up against them: for we have seen the land, and, behold, it is very good: and are ye still? be not slothful to go, and to enter to possess the land.   Num. 13:30

10 When ye go, ye shall come unto a people secure, and to a large land: for God hath given it into your hands; a place where there is no want of any thing that is in the earth.   Judg. 18:7

11 And there went from thence of the family of the Danites, out of Zorah and out of Eshtaol, six hundred men appointed with weapons of war.

12 And they went up, and pitched in Kirjath-jearim, in Judah: wherefore they called that place Mahaneh-dan unto this day: behold, it is behind Kirjath-jearim.   Josh. 15:60; Judg. 13:25

13 And they passed thence unto mount Ephraim, and came unto the house of Micah.

The People of Dan Steal Micah's Idols and His Priest

14 Then answered the five men that went to spy out the country of Laish, and said unto their brethren, Do ye know that there is in these houses an ephod, and teraphim, and a graven image, and a molten image? now therefore consider what ye have to do.

15 And they turned thitherward, and came to the house of the young man the Levite, even unto the house of Micah, and saluted him.   Gen. 43:27

16 And the six hundred men appointed with their weapons of war, which were of the children of Dan, stood by the entering of the gate.

17 And the five men that went to spy out the land went up, and came in thither, and took the graven image, and the ephod, and the teraphim, and the molten image: and the priest stood in the entering of the gate with the six hundred men that were appointed with weapons of war.   Judg. 18:14

18 And these went into Micah's house, and fetched the carved image, the ᵀephod, and the

teraphim, and the molten image. Then said the priest unto them, What do ye? priestly garment

19 And they said unto him, Hold thy peace, lay thine hand upon thy mouth, and go with us, and be to us a father and a priest: is it better for thee to be a priest unto the house of one man, or that thou be a priest unto a tribe and a family in Israel?   Judg. 17:10; Job 21:5; 29:9

20 And the priest's heart was glad, and he took the ephod, and the ᵀteraphim, and the graven image, and went in the midst of the people.   idols

21 So they turned and departed, and put the little ones and the cattle and the carriage before them.

22 And when they were a good way from the house of Micah, the men that were in the houses near to Micah's house were gathered together, and overtook the children of Dan.

23 And they cried unto the children of Dan. And they turned their faces, and said unto Micah, What aileth thee, that thou comest with such a company?

24 And he said, Ye have taken away my gods which I made, and the priest, and ye are gone away: and what have I more? and what is this that ye say unto me, What aileth thee?

25 And the children of Dan said unto him, Let not thy voice be heard among us, lest angry fellows run upon thee, and thou lose thy life, with the lives of thy household.

26 And the children of Dan went their way: and when Micah saw that they were too strong for him, he turned and went back unto his house.

Laish Is Destroyed and Renamed Dan

27 And they took the things which Micah had made, and the priest which he had, and came unto Laish, unto a people that were at quiet and secure: and they smote them with the edge of the sword, and burnt the city with fire.   Josh. 19:47; Judg. 18:7, 10

28 And there was no deliverer, because it was far from Zidon, and they had no business with any man; and it was in the valley that lieth by Beth-rehob. And they built a city, and dwelt therein.   Num. 13:21; Judg. 18:7; 2 Sam. 10:6

29 And they called the name of the city Dan, after the name of Dan their father, who was born unto Israel: ᵀhowbeit the name of the city was Laish at the first.   Gen. 14:14 ◆ however

30 And the children of Dan set up the ᵀgraven image: and Jonathan, the son of Gershom, the son of Manasseh, he and his sons were priests to the tribe of Dan until the day of the captivity of the land.   Ex. 2:22 ◆ engraved or cut out

31 And they set them up Micah's graven image, which he made, all the time that the house of God was in Shiloh. Josh. 18:1; 1 Sam. 1:3

A Levite Persuades His Unfaithful Wife to Return to Him

19 And it came to pass in those days, when *there was* no king in Israel, that there was a certain Levite sojourning on the side of mount Ephraim, who took to him a concubine out of Beth-lehem-judah.   Josh. 24:33; Judg. 17:8; 18:1

2 And his concubine played the ᵀwhore against him, and went away from him unto her father's house to Beth-lehem-judah, and was there four whole months.   *prostitute*

3 And her husband arose, and went after her, to speak friendly unto her, *and* to bring her again, having his servant with him, and a couple of asses: and she brought him into her father's house: and when the father of the damsel saw him, he rejoiced to meet him.   Gen. 34:3

4 And his father in law, the damsel's father, retained him; and he abode with him three days: so they did eat and drink, and lodged there.

5 And it came to pass on the fourth day, when they arose early in the morning, that he rose up to depart: and the damsel's father said unto his son in law, Comfort thine heart with a morsel of bread, and afterward go your way.   Gen. 18:5; Judg. 19:8

6 And they sat down, and did eat and drink both of them together: for the damsel's father had said unto the man, Be content, I pray thee, and tarry all night, and let thine heart be merry.   Judg. 16:25; 19:9; Ruth 3:7

7 And when the man rose up to depart, his father in law urged him: therefore he lodged there again.

8 And he arose early in the morning on the fifth day to depart: and the damsel's father said, Comfort thine heart, I pray thee. And they tarried until afternoon, and they did eat both of them.

9 And when the man rose up to depart, he, and his ᵀconcubine, and his servant, his father in law, the damsel's father, said unto him, Behold, now the day draweth toward evening, I pray you tarry all night: behold, the day groweth to an end, lodge here, that thine heart may be merry; and to morrow get you early on your way, that thou mayest go home.   *less important wife*

10 But the man would not tarry that night, but he rose up and departed, and came over against Jebus, which *is* Jerusalem; and *there were* with him two asses saddled, his concubine also *was* with him.   Josh. 15:8

11 *And* when they *were* by Jebus, the day was far spent; and the servant said unto his master, Come, I pray thee, and let us turn in into this city of the Jebusites, and lodge in it.

12 And his master said unto him, We will not turn aside ᵀhither into the city of a stranger, that *is* not of the children of Israel; we will pass over to Gibeah.   *here*

13 And he said unto his servant, Come, and let us draw near to one of these places to lodge all night, in Gibeah, or in Ramah.

14 And they passed on and went their way; and the sun went down upon them *when they were* by Gibeah, which *belongeth* to Benjamin.

15 And they turned aside thither, to go in *and* to lodge in Gibeah: and when he went in, he sat him down in a street of the city: for *there was* no man that took them into his house to lodging.   Judg. 19:18

An Old Man Shows Hospitality

16 And, behold, there came an old man from his work out of the field at even, which *was* also of mount Ephraim; and he sojourned in Gibeah: but the men of the place *were* Benjamites.   Judg. 19:1

17 And when he had lifted up his eyes, he saw a wayfaring man in the street of the city: and the old man said, Whither goest thou? and whence comest thou?

18 And he said unto him, We *are* passing from Beth-lehem-judah toward the side of mount Ephraim; from thence *am* I: and I went to Beth-lehem-judah, but I *am now* going to the house of the LORD; and there *is* no man that receiveth me to house. Judg. 18:31

19 Yet there is both straw and ᵀprovender for our asses; and there is bread and wine also for me, and for thy handmaid, and for the young man *which is* with thy servants: *there is* no want of any thing.   *food for livestock*

20 And the old man said, Peace *be* with thee; howsoever *let* all thy wants *lie* upon me; only lodge not in the street.   Judg. 6:23

21 So he brought him into his house, and gave provender unto the asses: and they washed their feet, and did eat and drink.   Gen. 18:4

The Immoral Men of Gibeah Kill the Levite's Wife

22 *Now* as they were making their hearts merry, behold, the men of the city, certain sons of Belial, beset the house round about, *and* beat at the door, and spake to the master of the house, the old man, saying, Bring forth the man that came into thine house, that we may know him.   Gen. 19:4-5

23 And the man, the master of the house, went out unto them, and said unto them, Nay, my brethren, *nay*, I pray you, do not *so* wickedly; seeing that this man is come into mine house, do not this folly.   Judg. 20:6; 2 Sam. 13:12

24 Behold, *here is* my daughter a maiden, and his concubine; them I will bring out now, and humble ye them, and do with them what

seemeth good unto you: but unto this man do not so vile a thing. Gen. 19:8; 34:2; Deut. 21:14

25 But the men would not hearken to him: so the man took his concubine, and brought her forth unto them; and they knew her, and abused her all the night until the morning: and when the day began to spring, they let her go.

26 Then came the woman in the dawning of the day, and fell down at the door of the man's house where her lord was, till it was light.

27 And her lord rose up in the morning, and opened the doors of the house, and went out to go his way: and, behold, the woman his concubine was fallen down at the door of the house, and her hands were upon the threshold.

28 And he said unto her, Up, and let us be going. But none answered. Then the man took her up upon an ass, and the man rose up, and gat him unto his place.   Judg. 20:5

29 And when he was come into his house, he took a knife, and laid hold on his concubine, and divided her, together with her bones, into twelve pieces, and sent her into all the coasts of Israel.   1 Sam. 11:7

30 And it was so, that all that saw it said, There was no such deed done nor seen from the day that the children of Israel came up out of the land of Egypt unto this day: consider of it, take advice, and speak your minds.   Judg. 20:7; Prov. 13:10

The Levite Explains His Desire for Revenge

20 Then all the children of Israel went out, and the congregation was gathered together as one man, from Dan even to Beer-sheba, with the land of Gilead, unto the LORD in Mizpeh.   Judg. 11:11

2 And the chief of all the people, even of all the tribes of Israel, presented themselves in the assembly of the people of God, four hundred thousand footmen that drew sword.   Judg. 8:10; 20:15, 17

3 (Now the children of Benjamin heard that the children of Israel were gone up to Mizpeh.) Then said the children of Israel, Tell us, how was this wickedness?

4 And the Levite, the husband of the woman that was slain, answered and said, I came into Gibeah that belongeth to Benjamin, I and my ᵀconcubine, to lodge.   less important wife

5 And the men of Gibeah rose against me, and beset the house round about upon me by night, and thought to have slain me: and my concubine have they forced, that she is dead.   Judg. 19:22, 25-26

6 And I took my concubine, and cut her in pieces, and sent her throughout all the

country of the inheritance of Israel: for they have committed lewdness and folly in Israel.   Josh. 7:15; Judg. 19:23, 29

7 Behold, ye are all children of Israel; give here your advice and counsel.   Judg. 19:30

8 And all the people arose as one man, saying, We will not any of us go to his tent, neither will we any of us turn into his house.

9 But now this shall be the thing which we will do to Gibeah; we will go up by lot against it;

10 And we will take ten men of an hundred throughout all the tribes of Israel, and an hundred of a thousand, and a thousand out of ten thousand, to fetch victual for the people, that they may do, when they come to Gibeah of Benjamin, according to all the folly that they have ᵀwrought in Israel.   done

11 So all the men of Israel were gathered against the city, knit together as one man.

12 And the tribes of Israel sent men through all the tribe of Benjamin, saying, What wickedness is this that is done among you?   Deut. 13:14

13 Now therefore deliver us the men, the children of Belial, which are in Gibeah, that we may put them to death, and put away evil from Israel. But the children of Benjamin would not hearken to the voice of their brethren the children of Israel: Deut. 13:13

14 But the children of Benjamin gathered themselves together out of the cities unto Gibeah, to go out to battle against the children of Israel.

15 And the children of Benjamin were numbered at that time out of the cities twenty and six thousand men that drew sword, beside the inhabitants of Gibeah, which were numbered seven hundred chosen men.   Num. 26:41

16 Among all this people there were seven hundred chosen men lefthanded; every one could sling stones at an hair breadth, and not miss.   Judg. 3:15; 1 Chr. 12:2

17 And the men of Israel, beside Benjamin, were numbered four hundred thousand men that drew sword: all these were men of war.

The Tribe of Benjamin Defends Itself against Two Attacks

18 And the children of Israel arose, and went up to the house of God, and asked counsel of God, and said, Which of us shall go up first to the battle against the children of Benjamin? And the LORD said, Judah shall go up first.   Num. 27:21

19 And the children of Israel rose up in the morning, and encamped against Gibeah.

20 And the men of Israel went out to battle against Benjamin; and the men of Israel put themselves in array to fight against them at Gibeah.

21 And the children of Benjamin came forth out of Gibeah, and destroyed down to the ground of the Israelites that day twenty and two thousand men. Judg. 20:25

22 And the people the men of Israel encouraged themselves, and set their battle again in array in the place where they put themselves in array the first day.

23 (And the children of Israel went up and wept before the LORD until even, and asked counsel of the LORD, saying, Shall I go up again to battle against the children of Benjamin my brother? And the LORD said, Go up against him.) Judg. 20:26-27

24 And the children of Israel came near against the children of Benjamin the second day.

25 And Benjamin went forth against them out of Gibeah the second day, and destroyed down to the ground of the children of Israel again eighteen thousand men; all these drew the sword. Judg. 20:21

The Tribe of Benjamin Is Finally Destroyed

26 Then all the children of Israel, and all the people, went up, and came unto the house of God, and wept, and sat there before the LORD, and fasted that day until even, and offered burnt offerings and peace offerings before the LORD. Judg. 20:23

27 And the children of Israel enquired of the LORD, (for the ark of the covenant of God was there in those days, Josh. 18:1

28 And Phinehas, the son of Eleazar, the son of Aaron, stood before it in those days,) saying, Shall I yet again go out to battle against the children of Benjamin my brother, or shall I cease? And the LORD said, Go up; for to morrow I will deliver them into thine hand. Deut. 18:5

29 And Israel set liers in wait round about Gibeah. Josh. 8:4

30 And the children of Israel went up against the children of Benjamin on the third day, and put themselves in array against Gibeah, as at other times.

31 And the children of Benjamin went out against the people, and were drawn away from the city; and they began to ᵀsmite of the people, and kill, as at other times, in the highways, of which one goeth up to the house of God, and the other to Gibeah in the field, about thirty men of Israel. strike

32 And the children of Benjamin said, They are smitten down before us, as at the first. But the children of Israel said, Let us flee, and draw them from the city unto the highways.

33 And all the men of Israel rose up out of their place, and put themselves in array at Baal-tamar: and the liers in wait of Israel came forth out of their places, even out of the meadows of Gibeah.

34 And there came against Gibeah ten thousand chosen men out of all Israel, and the battle was sore: but they knew not that evil was near them. Josh. 8:14

35 And the LORD smote Benjamin before Israel: and the children of Israel destroyed of the Benjamites that day twenty and five thousand and an hundred men: all these drew the sword.

36 So the children of Benjamin saw that they were smitten: for the men of Israel gave place to the Benjamites, because they trusted unto the liers in wait which they had set beside Gibeah.

37 And the liers in wait hasted, and rushed upon Gibeah; and the liers in wait drew themselves along, and smote all the city with the edge of the sword. Josh. 8:19

38 Now there was an appointed sign between the men of Israel and the liers in wait, that they should make a great flame with smoke rise up out of the city.

39 And when the men of Israel retired in the battle, Benjamin began to smite and kill of the men of Israel about thirty persons: for they said, Surely they are smitten down before us, as in the first battle. Judg. 20:32

40 But when the flame began to arise up out of the city with a pillar of smoke, the Benjamites looked behind them, and, behold, the flame of the city ascended up to heaven. Josh. 8:20

41 And when the men of Israel turned again, the men of Benjamin were amazed: for they saw that evil was come upon them.

42 Therefore they turned their backs before the men of Israel unto the way of the wilderness; but the battle overtook them; and them which came out of the cities they destroyed in the midst of them.

43 Thus they inclosed the Benjamites round about, and chased them, and ᵀtrode them down with ease over against Gibeah toward the sunrising. trampled

44 And there fell of Benjamin eighteen thousand men; all these were men of valour.

45 And they turned and fled toward the wilderness unto the rock of Rimmon: and they gleaned of them in the highways five thousand men; and pursued hard after them unto Gidom, and slew two thousand men of them. Josh. 15:32

46 So that all which fell that day of Benjamin were twenty and five thousand men that drew the sword; all these were men of valour.

47 But six hundred men turned and fled to

the wilderness unto the rock Rimmon, and abode in the rock Rimmon four months.

48 And the men of Israel turned again upon the children of Benjamin, and smote them with the edge of the sword, as well the men of *every* city, as the beast, and all that came to hand: also they set on fire all the cities that they came to.

The People Bewail the Desolation of Benjamin

21 Now the men of Israel had sworn in Mizpeh, saying, There shall not any of us give his daughter unto Benjamin to wife.   Judg. 20:1

2 And the people came to the house of God, and abode there till even before God, and lifted up their voices, and wept sore; Judg. 20:26

3 And said, O LORD God of Israel, why is this come to pass in Israel, that there should be to day one tribe lacking in Israel?

4 And it came to pass on the morrow, that the people rose early, and built there an altar, and offered burnt offerings and peace offerings.   2 Sam. 24:25

5 And the children of Israel said, Who *is there* among all the tribes of Israel that came not up with the congregation unto the LORD? For they had made a great oath concerning him that came not up to the LORD to Mizpeh, saying, He shall surely be put to death.   Judg. 5:23

6 And the children of Israel repented them for Benjamin their brother, and said, There is one tribe cut off from Israel this day.   Judg. 21:15

7 How shall we do for wives for them that remain, seeing we have sworn by the LORD that we will not give them of our daughters to wives?   Judg. 21:1

8 And they said, What one *is there* of the tribes of Israel that came not up to Mizpeh to the LORD? And, behold, there came none to the camp from Jabesh-gilead to the assembly.   1 Sam. 31:11-13

9 For the people were numbered, and, behold, *there were* none of the inhabitants of Jabesh-gilead there.

10 And the congregation sent thither twelve thousand men of the valiantest, and commanded them, saying, Go and ᵀsmite the inhabitants of Jabesh-gilead with the edge of the sword, with the women and the children.   Judg. 5:23 ◆ *strike*

11 And this *is* the thing that ye shall do, Ye shall utterly destroy every male, and every woman that hath lain by man.   Num. 31:17-18

12 And they found among the inhabitants of Jabesh-gilead four hundred young virgins, that had known no man by lying with any male: and they brought them unto

the camp to Shiloh, which *is* in the land of Canaan.   Josh. 18:1

13 And the whole congregation sent *some* to speak to the children of Benjamin that *were* in the rock Rimmon, and to call peaceably unto them.   Deut. 20:10; Judg. 20:47

14 And Benjamin came again at that time; and they gave them wives which they had saved alive of the women of Jabesh-gilead: and yet so they sufficed them not.

15 And the people repented them for Benjamin, because that the LORD had made a breach in the tribes of Israel.   Judg. 21:6

Israel Provides Wives for the Surviving Men of Benjamin

16 Then the elders of the congregation said, How shall we do for wives for them that remain, seeing the women are destroyed out of Benjamin?

17 And they said, *There must be* an inheritance for them that be escaped of Benjamin, that a tribe be not destroyed out of Israel.

18 Howbeit we may not give them wives of our daughters: for the children of Israel have sworn, saying, Cursed *be* he that giveth a wife to Benjamin.   Judg. 21:1

19 Then they said, Behold, *there is* a feast of the LORD in Shiloh yearly *in a place* which *is* on the north side of Beth-el, on the east side of the highway that goeth up from Beth-el to Shechem, and on the south of Lebonah.

20 Therefore they commanded the children of Benjamin, saying, Go and lie in wait in the vineyards;

21 And see, and, behold, if the daughters of Shiloh come out to dance in dances, then come ye out of the vineyards, and catch you every man his wife of the daughters of Shiloh, and go to the land of Benjamin.   Ex. 15:20

22 And it shall be, when their fathers or their brethren come unto us to complain, that we will say unto them, Be favourable unto them for our sakes: because we reserved not to each man his wife in the war: for ye did not give unto them at this time, *that* ye should be guilty.   Judg. 21:1

23 And the children of Benjamin did so, and took *them* wives, according to their number, of them that danced, whom they caught: and they went and returned unto their inheritance, and repaired the cities, and dwelt in them.   Judg. 20:48

24 And the children of Israel departed thence at that time, every man to his tribe and to his family, and they went out from thence every man to his inheritance.

25 In those days *there was* no king in Israel: every man did *that which was* right in his own eyes.   Judg. 17:6; 18:1; 19:1

THE BOOK OF

RUTH

The Book of Ruth, which takes place during the time of the judges in Israel, is a beautiful story of love, redemption, fidelity, and sacrifice. For a book so short and seemingly devoid of conventional theology, it perhaps serves as one of the most significant teaching books of the entire Bible.

During the time of the judges, in the midst of a severe drought, we read of a woman named Naomi who, with her family, flees her country to survive. In a foreign land she loses her husband and two sons. Her heart grieves, but during her loss, however, she has gained a committed and devoted young woman: Ruth, who was married to one of Naomi's sons.

The two women, both struggling through their losses, form a strong bond and return to Israel—the land of Naomi—hoping to make a new start.

The Book of Ruth, at its core, is about the importance of devotion and redemption—devotion of one person to another and a chance for a fresh, clean start. Ruth is devoted to her mother-in-law and even follows Naomi back to her ancestral land, despite the fact that Naomi's ancestral land is not the home of Ruth's heritage. In fact, Ruth comes from a pagan background.

Ruth is also a story about the power of love. In a sense, it's a love story between Ruth and her new husband Boaz. But it also serves as a much larger love story demonstrating the redemptive love Christ has for us all. Despite our circumstances and what has happened in our lives, Christ's love for us can be described as devoted, committed, and powerful—a step beyond that demonstrated by Ruth, Naomi, and Boaz.

Dates

Since the purpose of the Book of Ruth was to tell a compelling and beautiful story, the historical setting and date are difficult to determine. However, we do know that the events described in the book take place during the time of the judges of Israel, corresponding well to the time of the high priest Eli. He served as a judge between the approximate years of 1139–1099 B.C.

Author

The author of Ruth is unknown, as the book gives no clear indication as to who the author was. However, Jewish tradition points to Samuel as the author. This is unlikely, though, since Ruth mentions David (4:17, 22), and he did not ascend to the throne before Samuel's death. Nevertheless, the fact that we do not know for certain the author of Ruth should not detract from the book's important and compelling message.

Meaning of the Name

The word *Ruth* is the Hebrew title of the book. Since Ruth was a Moabite, her name is not Hebrew, and the meaning of her name is uncertain. There is some thought, however, that it is related to the Hebrew word *reuit*, which means "friendship" or "association."

Christ in Ruth

While there are no specific references to Christ in the Book of Ruth, it is filled with allegories and examples of Christ and His work. The concept of "kinsman" or "kinsman-redeemer" signifies a Christlike person. For example, we learn from Scripture the criteria of a "kinsman-redeemer":

(1) He has to be a blood relative of those he redeems (Deuteronomy 25:5, 7–10; John 1:14; Romans 1:3; Philippians 2:5–8; Hebrews 2:14, 15).

(2) He must also be able to pay the cost of redemption (Ruth 2:1; 1 Peter 1:18, 19).

(3) He must be willing to redeem (Ruth 3:11; Matthew 20:28; John 10:15, 18; Hebrews 10:7).

(4) He must be free himself (Ruth 4:1–6).

The fact that the word "kinsman" or "kinsman-redeemer" is used so often in this short book gives a clear indication of the importance of what it portrays and how it relates to Christ.

In addition, Ruth and Boaz appear in the ancestral line of Jesus Christ (Matthew 1:5).

The Book of Ruth can be divided into four main parts and places.

(1) *Ruth 1:1–18, The Land of Moab:* This first section of the book sets the groundwork for the remaining chapters and scenes. We read about Naomi, her widowhood, and the deaths of her two sons, leaving two additional widows: Ruth and Orpah. Naomi and Ruth ultimately return to the land of Judah.

(2) *Ruth 1:19—2:23, The Fields of Boaz:* After returning to Beth-lehem, Ruth begins to work in the fields of Boaz, a kinsman of Naomi's husband. Boaz shows great kindness toward Ruth and Naomi.

(3) *Ruth 3:1–18, The Threshing Floor:* Naomi encourages Ruth to present herself as a bride to Boaz, appealing to his duty as a kinsman-redeemer. Boaz goes beyond what the law requires of him and arranges to marry Ruth.

(4) *Ruth 4:1–22, The Marriage of Ruth:* The last chapter chronicles the marriage of Ruth to Boaz. The couple gives birth to a child—Obed—who will be the father of Jesse, the father of Israel's great king, David.

Unlocking Ruth

KEY PEOPLE:
Naomi, Ruth, Boaz, Elimelech, Mahlon, and Chilion

KEY EVENTS:
Ruth not being willing to leave her mother-in-law; Naomi and Ruth leaving the land where their husbands died and moving to Beth-lehem; Ruth working in the fields of Boaz; the kindness Boaz showed to Ruth and Naomi; and the marriage of Boaz and Ruth

KEY WORD:
Kinsman-redeemer gives us a clear idea of what Christ's redeeming power and love look like. Boaz bought back the land of Naomi, married Ruth, and fathered a son. His actions are an example of a redeemer.

KEY VERSES:
"And Ruth said, Intreat me not to leave thee, or to return from following after thee: for whither thou goest, I will go; and where thou lodgest, I will lodge: thy people shall be my people, and thy God my God" (Ruth 1:16).

"And now, my daughter, fear not; I will do to thee all that thou requirest: for all the city of my people doth know that thou art a virtuous woman" (Ruth 3:11).

KEY CHAPTER:
Ruth 4, which encapsulates the entire story of Ruth. Boaz decided to marry Ruth, thus completing the redemption process that ultimately includes a son born to Boaz and Ruth who is in the family line of David and Jesus Christ.

The Move to Moab and Tragedy

1 Now it came to pass in the days when the judges ruled, that there was a famine in the land. And a certain man of Bethlehem-judah went to sojourn in the country of Moab, he, and his wife, and his two sons. *Gen. 12:10; 26:1; 43:1*

2 And the name of the man *was* Elimelech, and the name of his wife Naomi, and the name of his two sons Mahlon and Chilion, Ephrathites of Beth-lehem-judah. And they came into the country of Moab, and continued there. *Gen. 35:19*

3 And Elimelech Naomi's husband died; and she was left, and her two sons.

4 And they took them wives of the women of Moab; the name of the one *was* Orpah, and the name of the other Ruth: and they dwelled there about ten years. *Matt. 1:5*

5 And Mahlon and Chilion died also both of them; and the woman was left of her two sons and her husband.

Naomi's Appeal to Her Daughters-in-Law

6 Then she arose with her daughters in law, that she might return from the country of Moab: for she had heard in the country of Moab how that the LORD had visited his people in giving them bread. *Ex. 4:31; Ps. 132:15*

7 Wherefore she went forth out of the place where she was, and her two daughters in law with her; and they went on the way to return unto the land of Judah.

8 And Naomi said unto her two daughters in law, Go, return each to her mother's house: the LORD deal kindly with you, as ye have dealt with the dead, and with me. *Ruth 1:5*

9 The LORD grant you that ye may find rest, each *of you* in the house of her husband. Then she kissed them; and they lifted up their voice, and wept. *Ruth 3:1*

10 And they said unto her, Surely we will return with thee unto thy people.

11 And Naomi said, Turn again, my daughters: why will ye go with me? *are* there yet *any more* sons in my womb, that they may be your husbands? *Gen. 38:11; Deut. 25:5*

12 Turn again, my daughters, go *your way*; for I am too old to have an husband. If I should say, I have hope, *if* I should have an husband also to night, and should also bear sons;

13 Would ye tarry for them till they were grown? would ye stay for them from having husbands? nay, my daughters; for it grieveth me much for your sakes that the hand of the LORD is gone out against me. *Job 19:21; Ps. 32:4*

14 And they lifted up their voice, and wept again: and Orpah kissed her mother in law; but Ruth ᵀclave unto her. *Prov. 17:17* ◆ *clung*

15 And she said, Behold, thy sister in law is gone back unto her people, and unto her gods: return thou after thy sister in law.

16 And Ruth said, Intreat me not to leave thee, *or* to return from following after thee: for whither thou goest, I will go; and where thou lodgest, I will lodge: thy people *shall be* my people, and thy God my God: *Ruth 2:11-12*

> **1:16 From Idolatry to the True God**
>
> Through the teaching of the sacrificial service Christ was to be uplifted before the nations, and all who would look unto Him should live. All who, like Rahab the Canaanite, and Ruth the Moabitess, turned from idolatry to the worship of the true God, were to unite themselves with His chosen people. As the numbers of Israel increased they were to enlarge their borders, until their kingdom should embrace the world. *COL 290*

17 Where thou diest, will I die, and there will I be buried: the LORD do so to me, and more also, *if ought* but death part thee and me. *1 Sam. 3:17; 25:22; 2 Sam. 19:13*

18 When she saw that she was stedfastly minded to go with her, then she left speaking unto her. *Acts 21:14*

Naomi and Ruth Return Home, Where They Are Gladly Received

19 So they two went until they came to Beth-lehem. And it came to pass, when they were come to Beth-lehem, that all the city was moved about them, and they said, *Is* this Naomi? *Matt. 21:10*

20 And she said unto them, Call me not Naomi, call me Mara: for the Almighty hath dealt very bitterly with me. *Job 6:4*

21 I went out full, and the LORD hath brought me home again empty: why *then* call ye me Naomi, seeing the LORD hath testified against me, and the Almighty hath afflicted me? *Job 1:21*

22 So Naomi returned, and Ruth the Moabitess, her daughter in law, with her, which returned out of the country of Moab: and they came to Beth-lehem in the beginning of barley harvest. *Ruth 2:23*

Ruth Gleans in the Fields of Boaz

2 And Naomi had a ᵀkinsman of her husband's, a mighty man of wealth, of the family of Elimelech; and his name *was* Boaz. *Ruth 3:2* ◆ *nearest male blood relative*

2 And Ruth the Moabitess said unto Naomi, Let me now go to the field, and glean ears of corn after *him* in whose sight I shall find grace. And she said unto her, Go, my daughter. *Lev. 19:9*

3 And she went, and came, and gleaned in the field after the reapers: and her ᵀhap was to

light on a part of the field *belonging* unto Boaz, who *was* of the kindred of Elimelech.   *good fortune*

2:2 God's Law Provided for the Poor

The law of God gave the poor a right to a certain portion of the produce of the soil. When hungry, a man was at liberty to go to his neighbor's field or orchard or vineyard, and eat of the grain or fruit to satisfy his hunger. *PP 531*

Boaz Speaks with Ruth and Shows Her Great Favor

4 And, behold, Boaz came from Beth-lehem, and said unto the reapers, The LORD *be* with you. And they answered him, The LORD bless thee.   Ps. 129:7-8

5 Then said Boaz unto his servant that was set over the reapers, Whose damsel *is* this?

6 And the servant that was set over the reapers answered and said, It *is* the Moabitish damsel that came back with Naomi out of the country of Moab: Ruth 1:22

7 And she said, I pray you, let me ᵀglean and gather after the reapers among the sheaves: so she came, and hath continued even from the morning until now, that she tarried a little in the house.   *gather leftovers from a field*

8 Then said Boaz unto Ruth, Hearest thou not, my daughter? Go not to glean in another field, neither go from hence, but abide here fast by my maidens:

9 *Let* thine eyes *be* on the field that they do reap, and go thou after them: have I not charged the young men that they shall not touch thee? and when thou art athirst, go unto the vessels, and drink of *that* which the young men have drawn.

10 Then she fell on her face, and bowed herself to the ground, and said unto him, Why have I found grace in thine eyes, that thou shouldest take knowledge of me, seeing I *am* a stranger?   1 Sam. 25:23

11 And Boaz answered and said unto her, It hath fully been shewed me, all that thou hast done unto thy mother in law since the death of thine husband: and *how* thou hast left thy father and thy mother, and the land of thy nativity, and art come unto a people which thou knewest not ᵀheretofore.   *before*

12 The LORD ᵀrecompense thy work, and a full reward be given thee of the LORD God of Israel, under whose wings thou art come to trust.   Ruth 1:16; 1 Sam. 24:19; Ps. 17:8 ◆ *repay*

13 Then she said, Let me find favour in thy sight, my lord; for that thou hast comforted me, and for that thou hast spoken friendly unto thine handmaid, though I be not like unto one of thine handmaidens.   Gen. 33:15

14 And Boaz said unto her, At mealtime come thou ᵀhither, and eat of the bread, and dip thy morsel in the vinegar. And she sat beside the reapers: and he reached her parched *corn*, and she did eat, and was sufficed, and left.   Ruth 2:18 ◆ *here*

15 And when she was risen up to glean, Boaz commanded his young men, saying, Let her glean even among the sheaves, and reproach her not:

16 And let fall also *some* of the handfuls of purpose for her, and leave *them*, that she may glean *them*, and rebuke her not.

17 So she gleaned in the field until even, and beat out that she had gleaned: and it was about an ephah of barley.

18 And she took *it* up, and went into the city: and her mother in law saw what she had ᵀgleaned: and she brought forth, and gave to her that she had reserved after she was sufficed.   Ruth 2:14 ◆ *gathered leftovers from a field*

19 And her mother in law said unto her, Where hast thou gleaned to day? and where wroughtest thou? blessed be he that did take knowledge of thee. And she shewed her mother in law with whom she had ᵀwrought, and said, The man's name with whom I wrought to day *is* Boaz.   Ruth 2:10 ◆ *worked*

20 And Naomi said unto her daughter in law, Blessed *be* he of the LORD, who hath not left off his kindness to the living and to the dead. And Naomi said unto her, The man *is* near of kin unto us, one of our next kinsmen.   Ruth 3:9-10; 2 Sam. 2:5; Prov. 17:17

Nearest Kinsman a Redeemer

Ruth 2:20

Of Christ's relation to His people, there is a beautiful illustration in the laws given to Israel. When through poverty a Hebrew had been forced to part with his patrimony, and to sell himself as a bondservant, the duty of redeeming him and his inheritance fell to the one who was nearest of kin. See Leviticus 25:25, 47–49; Ruth 2:20. So the work of redeeming us and our inheritance, lost through sin, fell upon Him who is "near of kin" unto us. It was to redeem us that He became our kinsman. Closer than father, mother, brother, friend, or lover is the Lord our Saviour. "Fear not," He says, "for I have redeemed thee, I have called thee by thy name; thou art Mine." "Since thou wast precious in My sight, thou hast been honorable, and I have loved thee: therefore will I give men for thee, and people for thy life" (Isaiah 43:1, 4). *DA 327*

21 And Ruth the Moabitess said, He said unto me also, Thou shalt keep fast by my young men, until they have ended all my harvest.

22 And Naomi said unto Ruth her daughter in law, It is good, my daughter, that thou go out with his maidens, that they meet thee not in any other field.

23 So she kept fast by the maidens of Boaz to glean unto the end of barley harvest and of wheat harvest; and dwelt with her mother in law.

Naomi's Plan for Ruth's Marriage

3 Then Naomi her mother in law said unto her, My daughter, shall I not seek rest for thee, that it may be well with thee?   Ruth 1:9

2 And now is not Boaz of our kindred, with whose maidens thou wast? Behold, he winnoweth barley to night in the threshing-floor.   Ruth 2:8

3 Wash thyself therefore, and anoint thee, and put thy ᵀraiment upon thee, and get thee down to the floor: but make not thyself known unto the man, until he shall have done eating and drinking.   2 Sam. 14:2 ◆ clothing

4 And it shall be, when he lieth down, that thou shalt mark the place where he shall lie, and thou shalt go in, and uncover his feet, and lay thee down; and he will tell thee what thou shalt do.

5 And she said unto her, All that thou sayest unto me I will do.

6 And she went down unto the floor, and did according to all that her mother in law bade her.

7 And when Boaz had eaten and drunk, and his heart was merry, he went to lie down at the end of the heap of corn: and she came softly, and uncovered his feet, and laid her down.   Judg. 19:6, 9; 2 Sam. 13:28

8 And it came to pass at midnight, that the man was afraid, and turned himself: and, behold, a woman lay at his feet.

9 And he said, Who art thou? And she answered, I am Ruth thine handmaid: spread therefore thy skirt over thine handmaid; for thou art a near ᵀkinsman.   nearest male blood relative

10 And he said, Blessed be thou of the LORD, my daughter: for thou hast shewed more kindness in the latter end than at the beginning, inasmuch as thou followedst not young men, whether poor or rich.   Ruth 2:20

11 And now, my daughter, fear not; I will do to thee all that thou requirest: for all the city of my people doth know that thou art a virtuous woman.   Prov. 12:4; 31:10

12 And now it is true that I am thy near kinsman: ᵀhowbeit there is a kinsman nearer than I.   Ruth 4:1 ◆ however

13 Tarry this night, and it shall be in the morning, that if he will perform unto thee the part of a kinsman, well; let him do the kinsman's part: but if he will not do the part of a kinsman to thee, then will I do the part of a kinsman to thee, as the LORD liveth: lie down until the morning. Judg. 8:19; Ruth 4:5; Jer. 4:2

Boaz Sends Ruth Home with a Gift of Barley

14 And she lay at his feet until the morning: and she rose up before one could know another. And he said, Let it not be known that a woman came into the floor.   Rom. 14:16

15 Also he said, Bring the ᵀvail that thou hast upon thee, and hold it. And when she held it, he measured six measures of barley, and laid it on her: and she went into the city.   veil

16 And when she came to her mother in law, she said, Who art thou, my daughter? And she told her all that the man had done to her.

17 And she said, These six measures of barley gave he me; for he said to me, Go not empty unto thy mother in law.

18 Then said she, Sit still, my daughter, until thou know how the matter will fall: for the man will not be in rest, until he have finished the thing this day.   Ps. 37:3-5

Boaz Calls into Judgment the Next Kinsman

4 Then went Boaz up to the gate, and sat him down there: and, behold, the kinsman of whom Boaz spake came by; unto whom he said, Ho, such a one! turn aside, sit down here. And he turned aside, and sat down.   Ruth 3:12

2 And he took ten men of the elders of the city, and said, Sit ye down here. And they sat down.   1 Kin. 21:8; Prov. 31:23

3 And he said unto the ᵀkinsman, Naomi, that is come again out of the country of Moab, selleth a parcel of land, which was our brother Elimelech's: nearest male blood relative

4 And I thought to ᵀadvertise thee, saying, Buy it before the inhabitants, and before the elders of my people. If thou wilt redeem it, redeem it: but if thou wilt not redeem it, then tell me, that I may know: for there is none to redeem it beside thee; and I am after thee. And he said, I will redeem it.   counsel

5 Then said Boaz, What day thou buyest the field of the hand of Naomi, thou must buy it also of Ruth the Moabitess, the wife of the dead, to raise up the name of the dead upon his inheritance.   Gen. 38:8

6 And the kinsman said, I cannot redeem it for myself, lest I mar mine own inheritance: redeem thou my right to thyself; for I cannot redeem it.

7 Now this was the manner in former time in Israel concerning redeeming and

concerning changing, for to confirm all things; a man plucked off his shoe, and gave *it* to his neighbour: and this *was* a testimony in Israel.   Deut. 25:7-10

8 Therefore the kinsman said unto Boaz, Buy *it* for thee. So he drew off his shoe.

Boaz Buys the Inheritance and Marries Ruth

9 And Boaz said unto the elders, and *unto* all the people, Ye *are* witnesses this day, that I have bought all that *was* Elimelech's, and all that *was* Chilion's and Mahlon's, of the hand of Naomi.

10 Moreover Ruth the Moabitess, the wife of Mahlon, have I purchased to be my wife, to raise up the name of the dead upon his inheritance, that the name of the dead be not cut off from among his brethren, and from the gate of his place: ye *are* witnesses this day.   Deut. 25:6

11 And all the people that *were* in the gate, and the elders, said, *We are* witnesses. The LORD make the woman that is come into thine house like Rachel and like Leah, which two did build the house of Israel: and do thou worthily in Ephratah, and be famous in Beth-lehem: Deut. 25:9

12 And let thy house be like the house of Pharez, whom Tamar bare unto Judah, of the seed which the LORD shall give thee of this young woman.   Gen. 38:29; 46:12; 1 Sam. 2:20

Ruth Bears Obed, the Grandfather of David

13 So Boaz took Ruth, and she was his wife: and when he went in unto her, the LORD gave her conception, and she bare a son.   Gen. 29:31; 33:5; Ruth 3:11

14 And the women said unto Naomi, Blessed *be* the LORD, which hath not left thee this day without a kinsman, that his name may be famous in Israel.   Luke 1:58

15 And he shall be unto thee a restorer of *thy* life, and a nourisher of thine old age: for thy daughter in law, which loveth thee, which is better to thee than seven sons, hath born him.   1 Sam. 1:8

16 And Naomi took the child, and laid it in her bosom, and became nurse unto it.

17 And the women her neighbours gave it a name, saying, There is a son born to Naomi; and they called his name Obed: he *is* the father of Jesse, the father of David.

18 Now these *are* the generations of Pharez: Pharez begat Hezron,   1 Chr. 2:4-8

19 And Hezron Tbegat Ram, and Ram begat Amminadab,   *brought forth*

20 And Amminadab begat Nahshon, and Nahshon begat Salmon,   Num. 1:7

21 And Salmon begat Boaz, and Boaz begat Obed,   Matt. 1:5

22 And Obed begat Jesse, and Jesse begat David.

THE FIRST BOOK OF

SAMUEL

Samuel, the prophet and judge, ruled over Israel in a time of transition. The Israelites were unhappy with judges as rulers and wanted a king like the neighboring kingdoms. Samuel anointed Saul as the first king of Israel, but this choice proved even worse for Israel. Saul's disobedience led to his demise, but God brought forth a faithful man named David who proved to be one of the mightiest kings Israel ever knew.

Dates

The first book of Samuel encompasses the birth of Samuel the prophet until the death of Saul, first king of Israel. This was a transitional period for the nation, shifting from the judges' leadership to a monarchy. The date range is nearly a century from approximately 1100–1011 B.C.

Author

Samuel is believed to have authored most of 1 Samuel. He was the appointed leader over a company of prophets (1 Samuel 10:5; 19:20) and governor/judge over Israel (7:15), so he was in a unique position to write the account. Further, we know that Samuel did write a book (10:25) and the records were available. The prophets Gad and Nathan are believed to have written the events that follow Samuel's death (25:1), as they are mentioned as chronicling the life of David as well (1 Chronicles 29:29). Given the smooth transitions of both books of Samuel, it is likely that one person—possibly a member of one of the prophetic schools—compiled the information from all three writers. The books of 1 and 2 Samuel were originally one book in the Hebrew Bible.

Meaning of the Name

The name Samuel can be translated as "Asked of God," "His Name is God," "Heard of God," and "The Name of God." The Greek Septuagint refers to the books of Samuel as the "Books of Kingdoms," while the Latin Vulgate designates them *Libri Regum*, "Books of the Kings." This title was later changed to *Libri 1 Samuelis* or the First Book of Samuel.

Christ in 1 Samuel

David, who is described by Samuel as "a man after [God's] own heart" (13:14), is a foreshadowing of Jesus. Jesus' family lineage is traced to David (Matthew 1:6, 17). Both were born in Beth-lehem, both escaped death by tyrannical rulers. The psalms of David have thematical parallels to the suffering of Jesus (see, for example, Psalm 22). David and Jesus were the Lord's anointed ones (1 Samuel 16:13; Luke 4:18). Jesus is called "the son of David" (Matthew 1:1; 15:22; 22:42), "the seed of David" (Romans 1:3) and "the Root of David" (Revelation 5:5). Jesus will sit upon the throne of David (Luke 1:32) when He returns to earth to reign for all time.

Samuel is also a type of Jesus, in that he is a prophet, priest, and judge or ruler. Samuel brought the people into a new era of peace. Jesus brings us into the era of eternal peace.

Overview

The Book of 1 Samuel is a tale of three men: Samuel, Saul, and David. The chapters can be divided as follows:

(1) *1 Samuel 1—7, Samuel:* Samuel, a son born to a barren woman (Hannah, chapters 1—2) becomes God's chosen prophet and the last judge of Israel. At this point, the Israelites have lost their way by worshiping pagan gods, abandoning God's protection, and making themselves vulnerable to their enemies. Even Eli, the high priest, contributes to the problems by not disciplining his sinning sons (chapters 2—3). The Philistines, sworn enemies of the Israelites, defeat them in battle and make off with the holy ark of the testimony (also called ark of the covenant, chapter 4). God punishes the Philistines until they return the ark, but Israel is still in peril (chapters 5—6). When the Israelites call upon Samuel to lead them, he instructs them to put off their pagan worship and calls out to God with a sacrifice. God hears Samuel, sees the repentance of His people, and defeats the Philistines. Israel is saved (chapter 7).

(2) *1 Samuel 8—15, Saul:* As Samuel ages, he appoints his sons as leaders over the Israelites; ironically, they are as corrupt as Eli's sons. The people cry out for a king to rule them instead. God warns them through Samuel of the price they will pay, but the people are adamant; therefore, at God's direction, Samuel anoints Saul as the first king of Israel (chapters 8—9). While Saul starts off on the right foot (chapters 11—12), he later disobeys the direct commands of God, thus moving God to choose another man as king (chapters 13—15).

(3) *1 Samuel 16—31, David:* The anointing of David as the next king of Israel (chapter 16) and the slaying of Goliath (chapter 17) ushers in to David's life a period of running and hiding from an envious Saul seeking to kill his rival. The courage, faithfulness, and humility of David provide a sharp contrast to the anxious, power-clutching Saul, who realizes that the Spirit of the Lord has abandoned him in favor of David (18:12, 28; 28:6, 15). Another contrast to Saul's behavior comes from his own family: his own son Jonathan remains faithful to his friend David (chapters 19—20).

First Samuel ends on a sad note as Saul consults a witch for help in contacting the dead Samuel, and finally commits suicide after a defeat by the Philistines. Saul's sons are also killed, including David's dear friend Jonathan (chapter 31).

Unlocking 1 Samuel

KEY PEOPLE:
Samuel, Eli, Saul, David, Jonathan, Goliath, Michal

KEY EVENTS:
The birth of Samuel; anointing Saul king of Israel; David defeats Goliath; Saul pursues David; the death of Samuel; the death of Saul

KEY WORD:
Transition. First Samuel chronicles how Israel became a monarchy, leaving behind the tradition of ruling judges. The transition began with the replacement of Eli by Samuel as judge, Samuel by Saul as king, and Saul by David as king.

KEY VERSES:
"But now thy kingdom shall not continue: the LORD hath sought him a man after his own heart, and the LORD hath commanded him to be captain over his people, because thou hast not kept that which the LORD commanded thee" (1 Samuel 13:14).

"This day will the LORD deliver thee into mine hand; and I will smite thee, and take thine head from thee; and I will give the carcases of the host of the Philistines this day unto the fowls of the air, and to the wild beasts of the earth; that all the earth may know that there is a God in Israel" (1 Samuel 17:46).

KEY CHAPTER:
1 Samuel 15, where God regrets that He named Saul to be king over Israel, and commands Samuel to tell Saul his reign will end. Saul did not heed the words of God and sinned against Him, as did the other rulers in 1 Samuel who had God's blessing removed from them.

Elkanah and His Wives Go to Shiloh Every Year to Worship

1 Now there was a certain man of Ramathaim-zophim, of mount Ephraim, and his name *was* Elkanah, the son of Jeroham, the son of Elihu, the son of Tohu, the son of Zuph, an Ephrathite: 1 Sam. 1:19

2 And he had two wives; the name of the one *was* Hannah, and the name of the other Peninnah: and Peninnah had children, but Hannah had no children.

1:2 A Lack of Faith

The blessing so earnestly sought by every Hebrew was denied this godly pair [Elkanah and Hannah]; their home was not gladdened by the voice of childhood; and the desire to perpetuate his name led the husband—as it had led many others—to contract a second marriage. But this step, prompted by a lack of faith in God, did not bring happiness. *PP 569*

3 And this man went up out of his city yearly to worship and to sacrifice unto the LORD of hosts in Shiloh. And the two sons of Eli, Hophni and Phinehas, the priests of the LORD, *were* there.   Ex. 23:14; Deut. 12:5-7; Josh. 18:1

4 And when the time was that Elkanah offered, he gave to Peninnah his wife, and to all her sons and her daughters, portions: Deut. 12:17-18

5 But unto Hannah he gave a worthy portion; for he loved Hannah: but the LORD had shut up her womb.   Gen. 30:2

6 And her adversary also provoked her sore, for to make her ᵀfret, because the LORD had shut up her womb.   worry

7 And *as* he did so year by year, when she went up to the house of the LORD, so she provoked her; therefore she wept, and did not eat.

8 Then said Elkanah her husband to her, Hannah, why weepest thou? and why eatest thou not? and why is thy heart grieved? *am* not I better to thee than ten sons?   Ruth 4:15

Hannah Prays for a Child

9 So Hannah rose up after they had eaten in Shiloh, and after they had drunk. Now Eli the priest sat upon a seat by a post of the temple of the LORD.   1 Sam. 3:3

10 And she *was* in bitterness of soul, and prayed unto the LORD, and wept sore.   Job 7:11

11 And she vowed a vow, and said, O LORD of hosts, if thou wilt indeed look on the affliction of thine handmaid, and remember me, and not forget thine handmaid, but wilt give unto thine handmaid a man child, then I will give him unto the LORD all the days of his life, and there shall no razor come upon his head.   Gen. 29:32; Num. 6:5; Judg. 13:5

12 And it came to pass, as she continued praying before the LORD, that Eli marked her mouth.

13 Now Hannah, she spake in her heart; only her lips moved, but her voice was not heard: therefore Eli thought she had been drunken.   Gen. 24:42-45

14 And Eli said unto her, How long wilt thou be drunken? put away thy wine from thee.

15 And Hannah answered and said, No, my lord, I *am* a woman of a sorrowful spirit: I have drunk neither wine nor strong drink, but have poured out my soul before the LORD.   Ps. 42:4; 62:8; Lam. 2:19

16 Count not thine handmaid for a daughter of Belial: for out of the abundance of my complaint and grief have I spoken ᵀhitherto.   1 Sam. 2:12 ♦ *up to now*

17 Then Eli answered and said, Go in peace: and the God of Israel grant *thee* thy petition that thou hast asked of him. 2 Kin. 5:19; Mark 5:34

18 And she said, Let thine handmaid find grace in thy sight. So the woman went her way, and did eat, and her ᵀcountenance was no more *sad*. Gen. 33:15; Ruth 2:13; Eccl. 9:7 ♦ *appearance*

Hannah, Having Given Birth to Samuel, Stays at Home till He Is Weaned

19 And they rose up in the morning early, and worshipped before the LORD, and returned, and came to their house to Ramah: and Elkanah knew Hannah his wife; and the LORD remembered her.   Gen. 30:22

20 Wherefore it came to pass, when the time was come about after Hannah had conceived, that she bare a son, and called his name Samuel, *saying*, Because I have asked him of the LORD.   Gen. 41:51-52

21 And the man Elkanah, and all his house, went up to offer unto the LORD the yearly sacrifice, and his vow.   1 Sam. 1:3

22 But Hannah went not up; for she said unto her husband, *I will not go up* until the child be weaned, and *then* I will bring him, that he may appear before the LORD, and there abide for ever.   1 Sam. 1:11, 28; Luke 2:22

End of Sin/Hell See Malachi 4:1.

23 And Elkanah her husband said unto her, Do what seemeth thee good; tarry until thou have weaned him; only the LORD establish his word. So the woman abode, and gave her son suck until she weaned him.   2 Sam. 7:25

24 And when she had weaned him, she took him up with her, with three bullocks, and one ephah of flour, and a bottle of wine, and brought him unto the house of the LORD in Shiloh: and the child *was* young.   Num. 15:9-10; Deut. 12:5-6; Josh. 18:1

25 And they slew a ᵀbullock, and brought the child to Eli.   Luke 2:22 ◆ *bull*
26 And she said, Oh my lord, *as* thy soul liveth, my lord, I *am* the woman that stood by thee here, praying unto the LORD. 2 Kin. 2:2
27 For this child I prayed; and the LORD hath given me my petition which I asked of him: 1 Sam. 1:11-13
28 Therefore also I have lent him to the LORD; as long as he liveth he shall be lent to the LORD. And he worshipped the LORD there.   Gen. 24:26, 52

1:28 A Mother's Vow

As [Hannah] looked upon the child, she called him Samuel—"asked of God." As soon as the little one was old enough to be separated from his mother, she fulfilled her vow [to dedicate him in service to God]. She loved her child with all the devotion of a mother's heart. . . . He was her only son, the special gift of Heaven; but she had received him as a treasure consecrated to God, and she would not withhold from the Giver His own. *PP 570, 571*

Hannah's Song of Thankfulness

2 And Hannah prayed, and said, My heart rejoiceth in the LORD, mine horn is exalted in the LORD: my mouth is enlarged over mine enemies; because I rejoice in thy salvation.   Ps. 9:14; 13:5; 89:17
2 *There is* none holy as the LORD: for *there is* none beside thee: neither *is there* any rock like our God.   Ex. 15:11; 2 Sam. 22:32; Ps. 86:8
3 Talk no more so exceeding proudly; let *not* arrogancy come out of your mouth: for the LORD *is* a God of knowledge, and by him actions are weighed.   1 Kin. 8:39
4 The bows of the mighty men *are* broken, and they that stumbled are girded with strength.   Ps. 37:15; 46:9; 76:3
5 *They that were* full have hired out themselves for bread; and *they that were* hungry ceased: so that the barren hath born seven; and she that hath many children is ᵀwaxed feeble.   Ps. 113:9; Is. 54:1; Jer. 15:9 ◆ *become*
6 The LORD killeth, and maketh alive: he bringeth down to the grave, and bringeth up.   Deut. 32:39; 2 Kin. 5:7; Is. 26:19
7 The LORD maketh poor, and maketh rich: he bringeth low, and lifteth up. Job 5:11; Ps. 75:7
8 He raiseth up the poor out of the dust, *and* lifteth up the beggar from the dunghill, to set *them* among princes, and to make them inherit the throne of glory: for the pillars of the earth *are* the LORD's, and he hath set the world upon them.   Job 38:4-6; Ps. 104:5; 113:7-8
9 He will keep the feet of his saints, and the wicked shall be silent in darkness; for by strength shall no man prevail.   Ps. 33:16-17

10 The adversaries of the LORD shall be broken to pieces; out of heaven shall he thunder upon them: the LORD shall judge the ends of the earth; and he shall give strength unto his king, and exalt the horn of his anointed.   Ps. 2:9; 89:24; 96:13
11 And Elkanah went to Ramah to his house. And the child did minister unto the LORD before Eli the priest. 1 Sam. 1:28; 2:18; 3:1
12 Now the sons of Eli *were* sons of Belial; they knew not the LORD.   Jer. 2:8

2:12 An Indulgent Father

[Eli] held the highest and most responsible positions among the people of God. As a man divinely chosen for the sacred duties of the priesthood, and set over the land as the highest judicial authority, he was looked up to as an example, and he wielded a great influence over the tribes of Israel. But although he had been appointed to govern the people, he did not rule his own household. Eli was an indulgent father. *PP 575*

13 And the priests' custom with the people *was, that,* when any man offered sacrifice, the priest's servant came, while the flesh was ᵀin seething, with a ᵀfleshhook of three teeth in his hand;   *boiling* ◆ *large fork-type instrument*
14 And he struck *it* into the pan, or kettle, or caldron, or pot; all that the fleshhook brought up the priest took for himself. So they did in Shiloh unto all the Israelites that came thither.
15 Also before they burnt the fat, the priest's servant came, and said to the man that sacrificed, Give flesh to roast for the priest; for he will not have sodden flesh of thee, but raw.   Lev. 3:16
16 And *if* any man said unto him, Let them not fail to burn the fat presently, and *then* take *as much* as thy soul desireth; then he would answer him, *Nay;* but thou shalt give *it me* now: and if not, I will take *it* by force.

2:17, 18 Young Samuel's Commitment

Though Samuel's youth was passed at the tabernacle devoted to the worship of God, he was not free from evil influences or sinful example. The sons of Eli feared not God, nor honored their father; but Samuel did not seek their company nor follow their evil ways. It was his constant endeavor to become what God would have him. This is the privilege of every youth. God is pleased when even little children give themselves to His service. *PP 573*

17 Wherefore the sin of the young men was very great before the LORD: for men ᵀabhorred the offering of the LORD.   Gen. 6:11 ◆ *despised*
18 But Samuel ministered before the

LORD, *being* a child, girded with a linen ephod.   1 Sam. 2:11; 3:1; 2 Sam. 6:14
19 Moreover his mother made him a little coat, and brought *it* to him from year to year, when she came up with her husband to offer the yearly sacrifice.   1 Sam. 1:3, 21
20 And Eli blessed Elkanah and his wife, and said, The LORD give thee seed of this woman for the loan which is lent to the LORD. And they went unto their own home. 1 Sam. 1:27-28
21 And the LORD visited Hannah, so that she conceived, and bare three sons and two daughters. And the child Samuel grew before the LORD.   Gen. 21:1; Judg. 13:24; 1 Sam. 2:26
22 Now Eli was very old, and heard all that his sons did unto all Israel; and how they lay with the women that assembled *at* the door of the tabernacle of the congregation.   Ex. 38:8
23 And he said unto them, Why do ye such things? for I hear of your evil dealings by all this people.
24 Nay, my sons; for *it is* no good report that I hear: ye make the LORD's people to ᵀtransgress.   *violate a law*
25 If one man sin against another, the judge shall judge him: but if a man sin against the LORD, who shall ᵀintreat for him? Notwithstanding they hearkened not unto the voice of their father, because the LORD would slay them.   Num. 15:30; Josh. 11:20; 1 Sam. 3:14 ♦ *plead*
26 And the child Samuel grew on, and was in favour both with the LORD, and also with men.   Luke 2:52
27 And there came a man of God unto Eli, and said unto him, Thus saith the LORD, Did I plainly appear unto the house of thy father, when they were in Egypt in Pharaoh's house?   1 Kin. 13:1
28 And did I choose him out of all the tribes of Israel *to be* my priest, to offer upon mine altar, to burn incense, to wear an ᵀephod before me? and did I give unto the house of thy father all the offerings made by fire of the children of Israel?   Ex. 28:1, 4; Lev. 8:7-8 ♦ *priestly garment*
29 Wherefore kick ye at my sacrifice and at mine offering, which I have commanded *in my* habitation; and honourest thy sons above me, to make yourselves fat with the chiefest of all the offerings of Israel my people?   1 Sam. 2:13-17
30 Wherefore the LORD God of Israel saith, I said indeed *that* thy house, and the house of thy father, should walk before me for ever: but now the LORD saith, Be it far from me; for them that honour me I will honour, and they that despise me shall be lightly esteemed.   Ex. 29:9; Ps. 50:23; Jer. 18:9-10
31 Behold, the days come, that I will cut off thine arm, and the arm of thy father's house,

that there shall not be an old man in thine house.   1 Sam. 22:17-20
32 And thou shalt see an enemy *in my* habitation, in all *the wealth* which *God* shall give Israel: and there shall not be an old man in thine house for ever.   Ps. 78:59-64; Zech. 8:4
33 And the man of thine, *whom* I shall not cut off from mine altar, *shall be* to consume thine eyes, and to grieve thine heart: and all the increase of thine house shall die in the flower of their age.
34 And this *shall be* a sign unto thee, that shall come upon thy two sons, on Hophni and Phinehas; in one day they shall die both of them.   1 Sam. 4:11, 17; 1 Kin. 13:3
35 And I will raise me up a faithful priest, *that* shall do according to *that* which *is* in mine heart and in my mind: and I will build him a sure house; and he shall walk before mine anointed for ever. 2 Sam. 7:11, 27; 1 Kin. 11:38
36 And it shall come to pass, *that* every one that is left in thine house shall come *and* crouch to him for a piece of silver and a morsel of bread, and shall say, Put me, I pray thee, into one of the priests' offices, that I may eat a piece of bread.   1 Kin. 2:27

How the Word of the Lord Was First Revealed to Samuel

3 And the child Samuel ministered unto the LORD before Eli. And the word of the LORD was precious in those days; *there was* no open vision.   1 Sam. 2:11, 18; Ps. 74:9

3:1 A Cloud of Sin

God could not communicate with the high priest and his sons; their sins, like a thick cloud, had shut out the presence of His Holy Spirit. *PP 581*

2 And it came to pass at that time, when Eli *was* laid down in his place, and his eyes began to ᵀwax dim, *that* he could not see;   *become*
3 And ᵀere the lamp of God went out in the temple of the LORD, where the ark of God *was*, and Samuel was laid down *to sleep*;   Ex. 27:20-21 ♦ *before*
4 That the LORD called Samuel: and he answered, Here *am* I.
5 And he ran unto Eli, and said, Here *am* I; for thou calledst me. And he said, I called not; lie down again. And he went and lay down.
6 And the LORD called yet again, Samuel. And Samuel arose and went to Eli, and said, Here *am* I; for thou didst call me. And he answered, I called not, my son; lie down again.
7 Now Samuel did not yet know the LORD, neither was the word of the LORD yet revealed unto him.   Acts 19:2
8 And the LORD called Samuel again the

third time. And he arose and went to Eli, and said, Here *am* I; for thou didst call me. And Eli perceived that the LORD had called the child.

9 Therefore Eli said unto Samuel, Go, lie down: and it shall be, if he call thee, that thou shalt say, Speak, LORD; for thy servant heareth. So Samuel went and lay down in his place.

10 And the LORD came, and stood, and called as at other times, Samuel, Samuel. Then Samuel answered, Speak; for thy servant heareth.

11 And the LORD said to Samuel, Behold, I will do a thing in Israel, at which both the ears of every one that heareth it shall tingle. 2 Kin. 21:12; Jer. 19:3

12 In that day I will perform against Eli all *things* which I have spoken concerning his house: when I begin, I will also make an end. 1 Sam. 2:27-36

13 For I have told him that I will judge his house for ever for the iniquity which he knoweth; because his sons made themselves vile, and he restrained them not. 1 Sam. 2:12, 17

14 And therefore I have sworn unto the house of Eli, that the iniquity of Eli's house shall not be purged with sacrifice nor offering for ever. 1 Sam. 2:25; Is. 22:14

15 And Samuel lay until the morning, and opened the doors of the house of the LORD. And Samuel feared to shew Eli the vision.

16 Then Eli called Samuel, and said, Samuel, my son. And he answered, Here *am* I.

17 And he said, What *is* the thing that *the* LORD hath said unto thee? I pray thee hide *it* not from me: God do so to thee, and more also, if thou hide *any* thing from me of all the things that he said unto thee. Ruth 1:17

18 And Samuel told him every whit, and hid nothing from him. And he said, It *is* the LORD: let him do what seemeth him good.

3:18 Eli's Faulty Repentance

Yet Eli did not manifest the fruits of true repentance. He confessed his guilt, but failed to renounce the sin. Year after year the Lord delayed His threatened judgments. Much might have been done in those years to redeem the failures of the past, but the aged priest took no effective measures to correct the evils that were polluting the sanctuary of the Lord and leading thousands in Israel to ruin. *PP 582*

Samuel Grows in Favor

19 And Samuel grew, and the LORD was with him, and did let none of his words fall to the ground. Gen. 39:2; 1 Sam. 2:21; 9:6

20 And all Israel from Dan even to Beer-sheba knew that Samuel *was* established *to be* a prophet of the LORD. Judg. 20:1

21 And the LORD appeared again in Shiloh: for the LORD revealed himself to Samuel in Shiloh by the word of the LORD. Gen. 12:7

The Israelites Are Overcome by the Philistines

4 And the word of Samuel came to all Israel. Now Israel went out against the Philistines to battle, and pitched beside Eben-ezer: and the Philistines pitched in Aphek. Josh. 12:18; 1 Sam. 7:12; 29:1

2 And the Philistines put themselves in array against Israel: and when they joined battle, Israel was smitten before the Philistines: and they slew of the army in the field about four thousand men.

Reproving Sin God's Way

1 Samuel 3:13

God charged Eli with honoring his sons above the Lord. Eli had permitted the offering appointed by God as a blessing to Israel to be made a thing of abhorrence, rather than bring his sons to shame for their impious and abominable practices. Those who follow their own inclination, in blind affection for their children, indulging them in the gratification of their selfish desires, and do not bring to bear the authority of God to rebuke sin and correct evil, make it manifest that they are honoring their wicked children more than they honor God. They are more anxious to shield their reputation than to glorify God; more desirous to please their children than to please the Lord and to keep His service from every appearance of evil.

God held Eli, as a priest and judge of Israel, accountable for the moral and religious standing of his people, and in a special sense for the character of his sons. He should first have attempted to restrain evil by mild measures; but if these did not avail, he should have subdued the wrong by the severest means. He incurred the Lord's displeasure by not reproving sin and executing justice upon the sinner. He could not be depended upon to keep Israel pure. Those who have too little courage to reprove wrong, or who through indolence or lack of interest make no earnest effort to purify the family or the church of God, are held accountable for the evil that may result from their neglect of duty. We are just as responsible for evils that we might have checked in others by exercise of parental or pastoral authority as if the acts had been our own. *PP 578*

3 And when the people were come into the camp, the elders of Israel said, Wherefore hath the LORD smitten us to day before the Philistines? Let us fetch the ark of the covenant of the LORD out of Shiloh unto us, that, when it cometh among us, it may save us out of the hand of our enemies.

4 So the people sent to Shiloh, that they might bring from thence the ark of the covenant of the LORD of hosts, which dwelleth *between* the cherubims: and the two sons of Eli, Hophni and Phinehas, *were* there with the ark of the covenant of God.　　Num. 7:89; Ps. 80:1

5 And when the ark of the covenant of the LORD came into the camp, all Israel shouted with a great shout, so that the earth rang again.　　Josh. 6:5

6 And when the Philistines heard the noise of the shout, they said, What *meaneth* the noise of this great shout in the camp of the Hebrews? And they understood that the ark of the LORD was come into the camp.

7 And the Philistines were afraid, for they said, God is come into the camp. And they said, Woe unto us! for there hath not been such a thing ᵀheretofore.　　*before*

8 Woe unto us! who shall deliver us out of the hand of these mighty Gods? these *are* the Gods that smote the Egyptians with all the plagues in the wilderness.

9 Be strong, and ᵀquit yourselves like men, O ye Philistines, that ye be not servants unto the Hebrews, as they have been to you: quit yourselves like men, and fight.　　Judg. 13:1; 2 Sam. 10:12; 1 Cor. 16:13 ◆ *conduct*

Israel Is Defeated, the Ark Taken, Hophni and Phinehas Killed

10 And the Philistines fought, and Israel was smitten, and they fled every man into his tent: and there was a very great slaughter; for there fell of Israel thirty thousand footmen.　　Deut. 28:25; 1 Sam. 4:2; 2 Kin. 14:12

11 And the ark of God was taken; and the two sons of Eli, Hophni and Phinehas, were slain.　　1 Sam. 2:32, 34; Ps. 78:64

Eli Falls Backward and Breaks His Neck

12 And there ran a man of Benjamin out of the army, and came to Shiloh the same day with his clothes ᵀrent, and with earth upon his head.　　Josh. 7:6; 2 Sam. 1:2; 15:32 ◆ *torn apart*

13 And when he came, lo, Eli sat upon a seat by the wayside watching: for his heart trembled for the ark of God. And when the man came into the city, and told *it*, all the city cried out.　　1 Sam. 1:9; 4:18

14 And when Eli heard the noise of the crying, he said, What *meaneth* the noise of this tumult? And the man came in hastily, and told Eli.

15 Now Eli was ninety and eight years old; and his eyes were dim, that he could not see.　　1 Sam. 3:2

16 And the man said unto Eli, I *am* he that came out of the army, and I fled to day out of the army. And he said, What is there done, my son?　　2 Sam. 1:4

17 And the messenger answered and said, Israel is fled before the Philistines, and there hath been also a great slaughter among the people, and thy two sons also, Hophni and Phinehas, are dead, and the ark of God is taken.

18 And it came to pass, when he made mention of the ark of God, that he fell from off the seat backward by the side of the gate, and his neck brake, and he died: for he was an old man, and heavy. And he had judged Israel forty years.　　1 Sam. 4:13

Phinehas' Wife, Weakened by the News, Dies Giving Birth

19 And his daughter in law, Phinehas' wife, was with child, *near* to be delivered: and when she heard the tidings that the ark of God was taken, and that her father in law and her husband were dead, she bowed herself and travailed; for her pains came upon her.

20 And about the time of her death the women that stood by her said unto her, Fear not; for thou hast born a son. But she answered not, neither did she regard *it*.　　Gen. 35:17-18

21 And she named the child Ichabod, saying, The glory is departed from Israel: because the ark of God was taken, and because of her father in law and her husband.　　Ps. 26:8; Jer. 2:11

4:21 The Glory Is Gone

It was not enough that the ark and the sanctuary were in the midst of Israel. It was not enough that the priests offered sacrifices, and that the people were called the children of God. The Lord does not regard the request of those who cherish iniquity in the heart; it is written that "he that turneth away his ear from hearing the law, even his prayer shall be abomination" (Proverbs 28:9). PP 584

---

22 And she said, The glory is departed from Israel: for the ark of God is taken.

The Philistines Place the Ark in the Temple of Dagon

5 And the Philistines took the ark of God, and brought it from Eben-ezer unto Ashdod.　　Josh. 13:3; 1 Sam. 4:1; 7:12

2 When the Philistines took the ark of God, they brought it into the house of Dagon, and set it by Dagon.   Judg. 16:23; 1 Chr. 10:10
3 And when they of Ashdod arose early on the morrow, behold, Dagon *was* fallen upon his face to the earth before the ark of the LORD. And they took Dagon, and set him in his place again.   Is. 19:1; 46:1-2, 7
4 And when they arose early on the morrow morning, behold, Dagon *was* fallen upon his face to the ground before the ark of the LORD; and the head of Dagon and both the palms of his hands *were* cut off upon the threshold; only *the stump of* Dagon was left to him.   Jer. 50:2; Mic. 1:7
5 Therefore neither the priests of Dagon, nor any that come into Dagon's house, tread on the threshold of Dagon in Ashdod unto this day.   Zeph. 1:9
6 But the hand of the LORD was heavy upon them of Ashdod, and he destroyed them, and smote them with emerods, *even* Ashdod and the coasts thereof.   Ex. 9:3; 1 Sam. 5:11; Ps. 32:4

5:6 The Invisible Presence

But the Lord had not wholly cast aside His people, nor would He long suffer the exultation of the heathen. He had used the Philistines as the instrument to punish Israel, and He employed the ark to punish the Philistines. In time past the divine Presence had attended it, to be the strength and glory of His obedient people. That invisible Presence would still attend it, to bring terror and destruction to the transgressors of His holy law. *PP 585*

---

7 And when the men of Ashdod saw that *it was* so, they said, The ark of the God of Israel shall not abide with us: for his hand is sore upon us, and upon Dagon our god.
8 They sent therefore and gathered all the lords of the Philistines unto them, and said, What shall we do with the ark of the God of Israel? And they answered, Let the ark of the God of Israel be carried about unto Gath. And they carried the ark of the God of Israel about *thither*.
9 And it was *so*, that, after they had carried it about, the hand of the LORD was against the city with a very great destruction: and he smote the men of the city, both small and great, and they had emerods in their secret parts.   Deut. 2:15; 1 Sam. 5:6; 7:13
10 Therefore they sent the ark of God to Ekron. And it came to pass, as the ark of God came to Ekron, that the Ekronites cried out, saying, They have brought about the ark of the God of Israel to us, to slay us and our people.
11 So they sent and gathered together all the lords of the Philistines, and said, Send away the ark of the God of Israel, and let it go again to his own place, that it slay us not, and our people: for there was a deadly destruction throughout all the city; the hand of God was very heavy there.   1 Sam. 5:6, 8-9

5:10, 11 From Strength to a Curse

For seven months the ark remained in Philistia, and during all this time the Israelites made no effort for its recovery. But the Philistines were now as anxious to free themselves from its presence as they had been to obtain it. Instead of being a source of strength to them, it was a great burden and a heavy curse. Yet they knew not what course to pursue; for wherever it went the judgments of God followed. *PP 586, 587*

---

12 And the men that died not were smitten with the ᵀemerods: and the cry of the city went up to heaven.   Ex. 12:30 ♦ *tumors*

God's Amazing Long-suffering

1 Samuel 5

These wise men acknowledged a mysterious power accompanying the ark—a power which they had no wisdom to meet. Yet they did not counsel the people to turn from their idolatry to serve the Lord. They still hated the God of Israel, though compelled by overwhelming judgments to submit to His authority. Thus sinners may be convinced by the judgments of God that it is in vain to contend against Him. They may be compelled to submit to His power, while at heart they rebel against His control. Such submission cannot save the sinner. The heart must be yielded to God—must be subdued by divine grace—before man's repentance can be accepted.

How great is the long-suffering of God toward the wicked! The idolatrous Philistines and backsliding Israel had alike enjoyed the gifts of His providence. Ten thousand unnoticed mercies were silently falling in the pathway of ungrateful, rebellious men. Every blessing spoke to them of the Giver, but they were indifferent to His love. The forbearance of God was very great toward the children of men; but when they stubbornly persisted in their impenitence, He removed from them His protecting hand. They refused to listen to the voice of God in His created works, and in the warnings, counsels, and reproofs of His word, and thus He was forced to speak to them through judgments. *PP 587, 588*

The Philistines Take Counsel on How to Return the Ark to Israel

6 And the ark of the LORD was in the country of the Philistines seven months.
2 And the Philistines called for the priests and the diviners, saying, What shall we do to the ark of the LORD? tell us wherewith we shall send it to his place.   Gen. 41:8; Dan. 2:2
3 And they said, If ye send away the ark of the God of Israel, send it not empty; but in any wise return him a trespass offering: then ye shall be healed, and it shall be known to you why his hand is not removed from you.
4 Then said they, What *shall be* the trespass offering which we shall return to him? They answered, Five golden emerods, and five golden mice, *according to* the number of the lords of the Philistines: for one plague *was* on you all, and on your lords.   Josh. 13:3; Judg. 3:3

6:4 A Heathen Custom

To ward off or to remove a plague, it was anciently the custom among the heathen to make an image in gold, silver, or other material, of that which caused the destruction, or of the object or part of the body specially affected. This was set up on a pillar or in some conspicuous place, and was supposed to be an effectual protection against the evils thus represented. *PP 587*

---

5 Wherefore ye shall make images of your emerods, and images of your mice that mar the land; and ye shall give glory unto the God of Israel: peradventure he will lighten his hand from off you, and from off your gods, and from off your land.   Josh. 7:19; 1 Sam. 5:6-7, 11
6 Wherefore then do ye harden your hearts, as the Egyptians and Pharaoh hardened their hearts? when he had ᵀwrought wonderfully among them, did they not let the people go, and they departed?   Ex. 7:13; 8:15; 14:17 ◆ *done*
7 Now therefore make a new cart, and take two milch kine, on which there hath come no yoke, and tie the kine to the cart, and bring their calves home from them: Num. 19:2
8 And take the ark of the LORD, and lay it upon the cart; and put the jewels of gold, which ye return him *for* a ᵀtrespass offering, in a coffer by the side thereof; and send it away, that it may go.   *sin*
9 And see, if it goeth up by the way of his own coast to Beth-shemesh, *then* he hath done us this great evil: but if not, then we shall know that *it is* not his hand *that* smote us: it *was* a chance *that* happened to us.   Josh. 15:10; 21:16

The Philistines Return the Ark to Israel on a New Cart

10 And the men did so; and took two ᵀmilch kine, and tied them to the cart, and shut up their calves at home: *milk cows*

11 And they laid the ark of the LORD upon the cart, and the coffer with the mice of gold and the images of their ᵀemerods.   *tumors*
12 And the kine took the straight way to the way of Beth-shemesh, *and* went along the highway, ᵀlowing as they went, and turned not aside *to* the right hand or *to* the left; and the lords of the Philistines went after them unto the border of Beth-shemesh.   *mooing*
13 And *they of* Beth-shemesh *were* reaping their wheat harvest in the valley: and they lifted up their eyes, and saw the ark, and rejoiced to see *it*.
14 And the cart came into the field of Joshua, a Beth-shemite, and stood there, where *there was* a great stone: and they ᵀclave the wood of the cart, and offered the kine a burnt offering unto the LORD.   2 Sam. 24:22 ◆ *split*
15 And the Levites took down the ark of the LORD, and the coffer that *was* with it, wherein the jewels of gold *were*, and put *them* on the great stone: and the men of Beth-shemesh offered burnt offerings and sacrificed sacrifices the same day unto the LORD.
16 And when the five lords of the Philistines had seen *it*, they returned to Ekron the same day.   Josh. 13:3
17 And these *are* the golden emerods which the Philistines returned *for* a trespass offering unto the LORD; for Ashdod one, for Gaza one, for Askelon one, for Gath one, for Ekron one;
18 And the golden mice, *according to* the number of all the cities of the Philistines *belonging* to the five lords, *both* of fenced cities, and of country villages, even unto the great *stone of* Abel, whereon they set down the ark of the LORD: *which stone remaineth* unto this day in the field of Joshua, the Beth-shemite.

The People Are Killed for Looking into the Ark

19 And he smote the men of Beth-shemesh, because they had looked into the ark of the LORD, even he smote of the people fifty thousand and ᵀthreescore and ten men: and the people lamented, because the LORD had smitten *many* of the people with a great slaughter.   Ex. 19:21; Num. 4:15, 20 ◆ *sixty*

6:19 Irreverence for the Holy

All Israel had been taught to regard the ark with awe and reverence. When required to remove it from place to place the Levites were not so much as to look upon it. Only once a year was the high priest permitted to behold the ark of God. Even the heathen Philistines had not dared to remove its coverings. Angels of heaven, unseen, ever attended it in all its journeyings. The irreverent daring of the people at Beth-shemesh was speedily punished. *PP 589*

20 And the men of Beth-shemesh said, Who is able to stand before this holy LORD God? and to whom shall he go up from us?   Mal. 3:2

21 And they sent messengers to the inhabitants of Kirjath-jearim, saying, The Philistines have brought again the ark of the LORD; come ye down, *and* fetch it up to you.   Josh. 9:17; 18:14; 1 Chr. 13:5-6

The People of Kirjath-jearim Bring the Ark into the House of Abinadab

7 And the men of Kirjath-jearim came, and fetched up the ark of the LORD, and brought it into the house of Abinadab in the hill, and ᵀsanctified Eleazar his son to keep the ark of the LORD.   *made holy*

2 And it came to pass, while the ark abode in Kirjath-jearim, that the time was long; for it was twenty years: and all the house of Israel lamented after the LORD.

Through Samuel's Exhortation, the Israelites Repent of Their Sins

3 And Samuel spake unto all the house of Israel, saying, If ye do return unto the LORD with all your hearts, *then* put away the strange gods and Ashtaroth from among you, and prepare your hearts unto the LORD, and serve him only: and he will deliver you out of the hand of the Philistines.   Gen. 35:2; Deut. 6:13; Josh. 24:14

7:3 Samuel's Pleadings

The Israelites as a nation still continued in a state of irreligion and idolatry, and as a punishment they remained in subjection to the Philistines. During this time Samuel visited the cities and villages throughout the land, seeking to turn the hearts of the people to the God of their fathers; and his efforts were not without good results. *PP 590*

4 Then the children of Israel did put away Baalim and Ashtaroth, and served the LORD only.

5 And Samuel said, Gather all Israel to Mizpeh, and I will pray for you unto the LORD.   Judg. 20:1

6 And they gathered together to Mizpeh, and drew water, and poured *it* out before the LORD, and fasted on that day, and said there, We have sinned against the LORD. And Samuel judged the children of Israel in Mizpeh.   Judg. 10:10; 1 Sam. 1:15; Ps. 106:6

While Samuel Prays and Sacrifices, the Lord Discomfits the Philistines

7 And when the Philistines heard that the children of Israel were gathered together to Mizpeh, the lords of the Philistines went up against Israel. And when the children of Israel heard *it*, they were afraid of the Philistines.   1 Sam. 17:11

8 And the children of Israel said to Samuel, Cease not to cry unto the LORD our God for us, that he will save us out of the hand of the Philistines.   Is. 37:4

9 And Samuel took a sucking lamb, and offered *it for* a burnt offering wholly unto the LORD: and Samuel cried unto the LORD for Israel; and the LORD heard him. Ps. 99:6; Jer. 15:1

10 And as Samuel was offering up the burnt offering, the Philistines drew near to battle against Israel: but the LORD thundered with a great thunder on that day upon the Philistines, and discomfited them; and they were smitten before Israel.   Josh. 10:10; Judg. 5:20; 1 Sam. 2:10

11 And the men of Israel went out of Mizpeh, and pursued the Philistines, and smote them, until *they came* under Beth-car.

12 Then Samuel took a stone, and set *it* between Mizpeh and Shen, and called the name of it Eben-ezer, saying, Hitherto hath the LORD helped us.   Gen. 35:14; Josh. 4:9

7:12 Memories Refreshed

Let us look to the monumental pillars, reminders of what the Lord has done to comfort us and to save us from the hand of the destroyer. Let us keep fresh in our memory all the tender mercies that God has shown us—the tears He has wiped away, the pains He has soothed, the anxieties removed, the fears dispelled, the wants supplied, the blessings bestowed—thus strengthening ourselves for all that is before us through the remainder of our pilgrimage. *SC 125*

The Philistines Are Subdued

13 So the Philistines were subdued, and they came no more into the coast of Israel: and the hand of the LORD was against the Philistines all the days of Samuel.   Judg. 13:1

14 And the cities which the Philistines had taken from Israel were restored to Israel, from Ekron even unto Gath; and the coasts thereof did Israel deliver out of the hands of the Philistines. And there was peace between Israel and the Amorites.

15 And Samuel judged Israel all the days of his life.   Judg. 2:16; 1 Sam. 7:6

16 And he went from year to year in circuit to Beth-el, and Gilgal, and Mizpeh, and judged Israel in all those places.

17 And his return *was* to Ramah; for there *was* his house; and there he judged Israel; and there he built an altar unto the LORD.

Samuel's Sons Are Evil Leaders, So Israel Asks for a King

8 And it came to pass, when Samuel was old, that he made his sons judges over Israel.   Deut. 16:18-19

2 Now the name of his firstborn was Joel; and the name of his second, Abiah: *they were* judges in Beer-sheba.

3 And his sons walked not in his ways, but turned aside after lucre, and took bribes, and perverted judgment.   Ex. 18:21; Deut. 16:19; Ps. 15:5

4 Then all the elders of Israel gathered themselves together, and came to Samuel unto Ramah,   1 Sam. 7:17

5 And said unto him, Behold, thou art old, and thy sons walk not in thy ways: now make us a king to judge us like all the nations.   Deut. 17:14-15

> **8:5 God's Unchanging Purpose**
>
> As a nation the children of Israel failed of receiving the benefits that God desired to give them. They did not appreciate His purpose or co-operate in its execution. But though individuals and peoples may thus separate themselves from Him, His purpose for those who trust Him is unchanged. *Ed 50*

6 But the thing displeased Samuel, when they said, Give us a king to judge us. And Samuel prayed unto the LORD.   1 Sam. 15:11

7 And the LORD said unto Samuel, Hearken unto the voice of the people in all that they say unto thee: for they have not rejected thee, but they have rejected me, that I should not reign over them.   Ex. 16:8; 1 Sam. 10:19

8 According to all the works which they have done since the day that I brought them up out of Egypt even unto this day, wherewith they have forsaken me, and served other gods, so do they also unto thee.

9 Now therefore hearken unto their voice: howbeit yet protest solemnly unto them, and shew them the manner of the king that shall reign over them.   1 Sam. 8:11-18; 10:25

10 And Samuel told all the words of the LORD unto the people that asked of him a king.

11 And he said, This will be the manner of the king that shall reign over you: He will take your sons, and appoint *them* for himself, for his chariots, and *to be* his horsemen; and *some* shall run before his chariots.   1 Sam. 10:25; 14:52; 2 Sam. 15:1

12 And he will appoint him captains over thousands, and captains over fifties; and *will set them* to ear his ground, and to reap his harvest, and to make his instruments of war, and instruments of his chariots.

13 And he will take your daughters *to be* confectionaries, and *to be* cooks, and *to be* bakers.   *ointment makers*

14 And he will take your fields, and your vineyards, and your oliveyards, *even* the best *of them*, and give *them* to his servants.

15 And he will take the tenth of your seed, and of your vineyards, and give to his officers, and to his servants.

16 And he will take your menservants, and your maidservants, and your goodliest young men, and your asses, and put *them* to his work.

17 He will take the tenth of your sheep: and ye shall be his servants.

18 And ye shall cry out in that day because of your king which ye shall have chosen you; and the LORD will not hear you in that day.   Prov. 1:25-28; Is. 1:15; Mic. 3:4

19 Nevertheless the people refused to obey the voice of Samuel; and they said, Nay; but we will have a king over us;   Jer. 44:16

20 That we also may be like all the nations; and that our king may judge us, and go out before us, and fight our battles.   1 Sam. 8:5

21 And Samuel heard all the words of the people, and he rehearsed them in the ears of the LORD.   Judg. 11:11

22 And the LORD said to Samuel, Hearken unto their voice, and make them a king. And Samuel said unto the men of Israel, Go ye every man unto his city.   1 Sam. 8:7; Hos. 13:11

Saul Searches the Land for His Father's Donkeys

9 Now there was a man of Benjamin, whose name *was* Kish, the son of Abiel, the son of Zeror, the son of Bechorath, the son of Aphiah, a Benjamite, a mighty man of power.   1 Sam. 14:51; 1 Chr. 9:36-39

2 And he had a son, whose name *was* Saul, a choice young man, and a goodly: and *there was* not among the children of Israel a goodlier person than he: from his shoulders and upward *he was* higher than any of the people.

3 And the asses of Kish Saul's father were lost. And Kish said to Saul his son, Take now one of the servants with thee, and arise, go seek the asses.

4 And he passed through mount Ephraim, and passed through the land of Shalisha, but they found *them* not: then they passed through the land of Shalim, and *there they were* not: and he passed through the land of the Benjamites, but they found *them* not.

5 *And* when they were come to the land of Zuph, Saul said to his servant that *was* with him, Come, and let us return; lest my father leave *caring* for the asses, and take thought for us.   1 Sam. 1:1; 10:2

6 And he said unto him, Behold now, *there is* in this city a man of God, and *he is* an

honourable man; all that he saith cometh surely to pass: now let us go thither; ᵀperadventure he can shew us our way that we should go.   Deut. 33:1; 1 Kin. 13:1 ◆ *maybe*

7 Then said Saul to his servant, But, behold, *if* we go, what shall we bring the man? for the bread is spent in our vessels, and *there is* not a present to bring to the man of God: what have we?   1 Kin. 14:3; 2 Kin. 4:42; 8:8

8 And the servant answered Saul again, and said, Behold, I have here at hand the fourth part of a shekel of silver: *that* will I give to the man of God, to tell us our way.

9 (Beforetime in Israel, when a man went to enquire of God, thus he spake, Come, and let us go to the seer: for *he that is* now *called* a Prophet was beforetime called a Seer.)   2 Sam. 24:11

10 Then said Saul to his servant, Well said; come, let us go. So they went unto the city where the man of God *was*.

Saul Seeks Samuel

11 *And* as they went up the hill to the city, they found young maidens going out to draw water, and said unto them, Is the seer here?   Gen. 24:11; Ex. 2:16

12 And they answered them, and said, He is; behold, *he is* before you: make haste now, for he came to day to the city; for *there is* a sacrifice of the people to day in the high place: Gen. 31:54; 1 Sam. 10:5; 16:2

13 As soon as ye be come into the city, ye shall ᵀstraightway find him, before he go up to the high place to eat: for the people will not eat until he come, because he doth bless the sacrifice; *and* afterwards they eat that be bidden. Now therefore get you up; for about this time ye shall find him. John 6:11 ◆ *right away*

14 And they went up into the city: *and* when they were come into the city, behold, Samuel came out against them, for to go up to the high place.

15 Now the LORD had told Samuel in his ear a day before Saul came, saying,   1 Sam. 15:1

16 To morrow about this time I will send thee a man out of the land of Benjamin, and thou shalt anoint him *to be* captain over my people Israel, that he may save my people out of the hand of the Philistines: for I have looked upon my people, because their cry is come unto me.   Ex. 3:7-9; 1 Sam. 10:1

17 And when Samuel saw Saul, the LORD said unto him, Behold the man whom I spake to thee of! this same shall reign over my people.

Samuel Talks to Saul

18 Then Saul drew near to Samuel in the gate, and said, Tell me, I pray thee, where the seer's house *is*.

9:17 God Tries to Reach Saul

Under the rule of this king [Saul, Israel] would obtain the experience necessary in order that they might see their error, and return to their allegiance to God.

Yet the Lord, having placed on Saul the responsibility of the kingdom, did not leave him to himself. He caused the Holy Spirit to rest upon Saul to reveal to him his own weakness and his need of divine grace; and had Saul relied upon God, God would have been with him. *PP 636*

---

19 And Samuel answered Saul, and said, I *am* the seer: go up before me unto the high place; for ye shall eat with me to day, and to morrow I will let thee go, and will tell thee all that *is* in thine heart.

20 And as for thine asses that were lost three days ago, set not thy mind on them; for they are found. And on whom *is* all the desire of Israel? *Is it* not on thee, and on all thy father's house?

21 And Saul answered and said, *Am* not I a Benjamite, of the smallest of the tribes of Israel? and my family the least of all the families of the tribe of Benjamin? wherefore then speakest thou so to me?   Judg. 20:46-48; Ps. 68:27

22 And Samuel took Saul and his servant, and brought them into the parlour, and made them sit in the chiefest place among them that were bidden, which *were* about thirty persons.

23 And Samuel said unto the cook, Bring the portion which I gave thee, of which I said unto thee, Set it by thee.

24 And the cook took up the shoulder, and *that* which *was* upon it, and set *it* before Saul. And *Samuel* said, Behold that which is left! set *it* before thee, *and* eat: for unto this time hath it been kept for thee since I said, I have invited the people. So Saul did eat with Samuel that day.   Lev. 7:32-33; Ezek. 24:4

25 And when they were come down from the high place into the city, *Samuel* communed with Saul upon the top of the house.   Deut. 22:8; 2 Sam. 11:2; Acts 10:9

26 And they arose early: and it came to pass about the spring of the day, that Samuel called Saul to the top of the house, saying, Up, that I may send thee away. And Saul arose, and they went out both of them, he and Samuel, abroad.

27 *And* as they were going down to the end of the city, Samuel said to Saul, Bid the servant pass on before us, (and he passed on,) but stand thou still a while, that I may shew thee the word of God.

Samuel Anoints Saul

10 Then Samuel took a ᵀvial of oil, and poured *it* upon his head, and kissed him, and said, *Is it* not because the LORD hath anointed thee *to be* captain over his inheritance?   Deut. 32:9; 1 Sam. 16:13; Ps. 2:12

2 When thou art departed from me to day, then thou shalt find two men by Rachel's sepulchre in the border of Benjamin at Zelzah; and they will say unto thee, The asses which thou wentest to seek are found: and, lo, thy father hath left the care of the asses, and sorroweth for you, saying, What shall I do for my son?   1 Sam. 9:3-5

3 Then shalt thou go on forward from thence, and thou shalt come to the plain of Tabor, and there shall meet thee three men going up to God to Beth-el, one carrying three kids, and another carrying three loaves of bread, and another carrying a bottle of wine:

4 And they will salute thee, and give thee two *loaves* of bread; which thou shalt receive of their hands.

5 After that thou shalt come to the hill of God, where *is* the garrison of the Philistines: and it shall come to pass, when thou art come thither to the city, that thou shalt meet a company of prophets coming down from the high place with a psaltery, and a ᵀtabret, and a pipe, and a harp, before them; and they shall prophesy: 1 Sam. 13:3; 19:20; 2 Kin. 3:15 ◆ *tambourine*

6 And the Spirit of the LORD will come upon thee, and thou shalt prophesy with them, and shalt be turned into another man.   Num. 11:25; 1 Sam. 10:10; 19:23-24

7 And let it be, when these signs are come unto thee, *that* thou do as occasion serve thee; for God *is* with thee.   Ex. 4:8; Josh. 1:5; Judg. 6:12

8 And thou shalt go down before me to Gilgal; and, behold, I will come down unto thee, to offer burnt offerings, *and* to sacrifice sacrifices of peace offerings: seven days shalt thou tarry, till I come to thee, and shew thee what thou shalt do.   1 Sam. 11:14-15; 13:4

Saul's Heart Is Changed, and He Prophesies

9 And it was *so*, that when he had turned his back to go from Samuel, God gave him another heart: and all those signs came to pass that day.

10 And when they came thither to the hill, behold, a company of prophets met him; and the Spirit of God came upon him, and he prophesied among them.   1 Sam. 10:5-6

11 And it came to pass, when all that knew him beforetime saw that, behold, he prophesied among the prophets, then the people said one to another, What *is* this *that* is come

unto the son of Kish? *Is* Saul also among the prophets?   1 Sam. 19:24; Matt. 13:54-55; John 7:15

12 And one of the same place answered and said, But who *is* their father? Therefore it became a proverb, *Is* Saul also among the prophets?   Is. 54:13

10:10-12 Under Angelic Control

But an angel of God met [Saul] on the way and controlled him. The Spirit of God held him in Its power, and he went forward uttering prayers to God, interspersed with predictions and sacred melodies. He prophesied of the coming Messiah as the world's Redeemer. *PP 654*

13 And when he had made an end of prophesying, he came to the high place.

14 And Saul's uncle said unto him and to his servant, Whither went ye? And he said, To seek the asses: and when we saw that *they were* no where, we came to Samuel.   1 Sam. 14:50

15 And Saul's uncle said, Tell me, I pray thee, what Samuel said unto you.

16 And Saul said unto his uncle, He told us plainly that the asses were found. But of the matter of the kingdom, whereof Samuel spake, he told him not.   1 Sam. 9:20

The Lord Confirms His Choice of Saul

17 And Samuel called the people together unto the LORD to Mizpeh;   Judg. 20:1

18 And said unto the children of Israel, Thus saith the LORD God of Israel, I brought up Israel out of Egypt, and delivered you out of the hand of the Egyptians, and out of the hand of all kingdoms, *and* of them that oppressed you: Judg. 6:8-9

19 And ye have this day rejected your God, who himself saved you out of all your adversities and your tribulations; and ye have said unto him, Nay, but set a king over us. Now therefore present yourselves before the LORD by your tribes, and by your thousands.   Josh. 24:1; 1 Sam. 8:19; 12:12

20 And when Samuel had caused all the tribes of Israel to come near, the tribe of Benjamin was taken.

21 When he had caused the tribe of Benjamin to come near by their families, the family of Matri was taken, and Saul the son of Kish was taken: and when they sought him, he could not be found.

22 Therefore they enquired of the LORD further, if the man should yet come thither. And the LORD answered, Behold, he hath hid himself among the stuff.

23 And they ran and fetched him thence: and when he stood among the people, he was higher than any of the people from his shoulders and upward.   1 Sam. 9:2

24 And Samuel said to all the people, See ye him whom the LORD hath chosen, that *there is* none like him among all the people? And all the people shouted, and said, God save the king.   2 Sam. 21:6; 1 Kin. 1:25, 39
25 Then Samuel told the people the manner of the kingdom, and wrote *it* in a book, and laid *it* up before the LORD. And Samuel sent all the people away, every man to his house.   Deut. 17:14-20; 1 Sam. 8:11-18
26 And Saul also went home to Gibeah; and there went with him a band of men, whose hearts God had touched.   1 Sam. 11:4; 15:34
27 But the children of Belial said, How shall this man save us? And they despised him, and brought him no presents. But he held his peace.   Deut. 13:13; 1 Kin. 10:25; 2 Chr. 17:5

Saul Defeats King Nahash of Ammon

11 Then Nahash the Ammonite came up, and encamped against Jabesh-gilead: and all the men of Jabesh said unto Nahash, Make a covenant with us, and we will serve thee.   Judg. 21:8; 1 Sam. 12:12; 1 Kin. 20:34
2 And Nahash the Ammonite answered them, On this *condition* will I make *a covenant* with you, that I may thrust out all your right eyes, and lay it *for* a reproach upon all Israel. Gen. 34:14; Num. 16:14; 1 Sam. 17:26
3 And the elders of Jabesh said unto him, Give us seven days' respite, that we may send messengers unto all the coasts of Israel: and then, if *there be* no man to save us, we will come out to thee.
4 Then came the messengers to Gibeah of Saul, and told the tidings in the ears of the people: and all the people lifted up their voices, and wept.   Judg. 2:4; 21:2; 1 Sam. 10:26
5 And, behold, Saul came after the herd out of the field; and Saul said, What *aileth* the people that they weep? And they told him the tidings of the men of Jabesh.   1 Kin. 19:19

6 And the Spirit of God came upon Saul when he heard those tidings, and his anger was kindled greatly.   Judg. 3:10; 6:34; 1 Sam. 10:10
7 And he took a yoke of oxen, and ᵀhewed them in pieces, and sent *them* throughout all the coasts of Israel by the hands of messengers, saying, Whosoever cometh not forth after Saul and after Samuel, so shall it be done unto his oxen. And the fear of the LORD fell on the people, and they came out with one consent.   Judg. 19:29; 20:1 ◆ *cut*
8 And when he numbered them in Bezek, the children of Israel were three hundred thousand, and the men of Judah thirty thousand.   Judg. 1:4-5
9 And they said unto the messengers that came, Thus shall ye say unto the men of Jabesh-gilead, To morrow, by *that time* the sun be hot, ye shall have help. And the messengers came and shewed *it* to the men of Jabesh; and they were glad.
10 Therefore the men of Jabesh said, To morrow we will come out unto you, and ye shall do with us all that seemeth good unto you.
11 And it was *so* on the morrow, that Saul put the people in three companies; and they came into the midst of the host in the morning watch, and slew the Ammonites until the heat of the day: and it came to pass, that they which remained were scattered, so that two of them were not left together.   Judg. 7:16

Saul Is Confirmed in His Kingdom

12 And the people said unto Samuel, Who *is* he that said, Shall Saul reign over us? bring the men, that we may put them to death.   1 Sam. 10:27; Luke 19:27
13 And Saul said, There shall not a man be put to death this day: for to day the LORD hath wrought salvation in Israel.   Ex. 14:13

Long Live the King

1 Samuel 10:24

In Saul, God had given to Israel a king after their own heart, as Samuel said when the kingdom was confirmed to Saul at Gilgal, "Behold the king *whom ye have chosen, and whom ye have desired*" (1 Samuel 12:13). Comely in person, of noble stature and princely bearing, his appearance accorded with their conceptions of royal dignity; and his personal valor and his ability in the conduct of armies were the qualities which they regarded as best calculated to secure respect and honor from other nations. They felt little solicitude that their king should possess those higher qualities which alone could fit him to rule with justice and equity. They did not ask for one who had true nobility of character, who possessed the love and fear of God. They had not sought counsel from God as to the qualities a ruler should possess, in order to preserve their distinctive, holy character as His chosen people. They were not seeking God's way, but their own way. Therefore God gave them such a king as they desired—one whose character was a reflection of their own. Their hearts were not in submission to God, and their king also was unsubdued by divine grace. Under the rule of this king they would obtain the experience necessary in order that they might see their error, and return to their allegiance to God. *PP 636*

14 Then said Samuel to the people, Come, and let us go to Gilgal, and renew the kingdom there. 1 Sam. 10:8

15 And all the people went to Gilgal; and there they made Saul king before the LORD in Gilgal; and there they sacrificed sacrifices of peace offerings before the LORD; and there Saul and all the men of Israel rejoiced greatly. 1 Sam. 10:8, 17

Samuel Testifies to His Integrity

12 And Samuel said unto all Israel, Behold, I have hearkened unto your voice in all that ye said unto me, and have made a king over you. 1 Sam. 10:24; 11:14-15

2 And now, behold, the king walketh before you: and I am old and grayheaded; and, behold, my sons *are* with you: and I have walked before you from my childhood unto this day. 1 Sam. 8:1, 5, 20

3 Behold, here I *am*: witness against me before the LORD, and before his anointed: whose ox have I taken? or whose ass have I taken? or whom have I defrauded? whom have I oppressed? or of whose hand have I received *any* bribe to blind mine eyes therewith? and I will restore it you. Num. 16:15; 1 Sam. 10:1; 24:6

4 And they said, Thou hast not defrauded us, nor oppressed us, neither hast thou taken ought of any man's hand.

5 And he said unto them, The LORD *is* witness against you, and his anointed *is* witness this day, that ye have not found ought in my hand. And they answered, *He is* witness. Ex. 22:4; Acts 23:9; 24:20

Samuel Reproves the People for Their Ingratitude

6 And Samuel said unto the people, *It is* the LORD that advanced Moses and Aaron, and that brought your fathers up out of the land of Egypt. Ex. 6:26; Mic. 6:4

7 Now therefore stand still, that I may reason with you before the LORD of all the righteous acts of the LORD, which he did to you and to your fathers. Is. 1:18

8 When Jacob was come into Egypt, and your fathers cried unto the LORD, then the LORD sent Moses and Aaron, which brought forth your fathers out of Egypt, and made them dwell in this place. Ex. 4:14-16

9 And when they forgat the LORD their God, he sold them into the hand of Sisera, captain of the host of Hazor, and into the hand of the Philistines, and into the hand of the king of Moab, and they fought against them. Judg. 3:12; 4:2; 10:7

10 And they cried unto the LORD, and said, We have sinned, because we have forsaken the LORD, and have served Baalim and Ashtaroth: but now deliver us out of the hand of our enemies, and we will serve thee. Judg. 2:13; 3:7; 10:10

11 And the LORD sent Jerubbaal, and Bedan, and Jephthah, and Samuel, and delivered you out of the hand of your enemies on every side, and ye dwelled safe. Judg. 4:6; 6:14, 32

12 And when ye saw that Nahash the king of the children of Ammon came against you, ye said unto me, Nay; but a king shall reign over us: when the LORD your God *was* your king. Judg. 8:23; 1 Sam. 8:5-7; 10:19

13 Now therefore behold the king whom ye have chosen, *and* whom ye have desired! and, behold, the LORD hath set a king over you. 1 Sam. 8:5; 10:24; Hos. 13:11

12:13 Appearance, Not Character

Comely in person, of noble stature and princely bearing, his appearance accorded with [Israel's] conceptions of royal dignity; and his personal valor and his ability in the conduct of armies were the qualities which they regarded as best calculated to secure respect and honor from other nations. . . . They did not ask for one who had true nobility of character, who possessed the love and fear of God. *PP 636*

14 If ye will fear the LORD, and serve him, and obey his voice, and not rebel against the commandment of the LORD, then shall both ye and also the king that reigneth over you continue following the LORD your God: Josh. 24:14

15 But if ye will not obey the voice of the LORD, but rebel against the commandment of the LORD, then shall the hand of the LORD be against you, as *it was* against your fathers. Josh. 24:20; 1 Sam. 12:9; Is. 1:20

Samuel Warns the People about Their Sin in Asking for a King

16 Now therefore stand and see this great thing, which the LORD will do before your eyes. Ex. 14:13, 31

17 *Is it* not wheat harvest to day? I will call unto the LORD, and he shall send thunder and rain; that ye may perceive and see that your wickedness *is* great, which ye have done in the sight of the LORD, in asking you a king. 1 Sam. 7:9-10; 8:7; Prov. 26:1

18 So Samuel called unto the LORD; and the LORD sent thunder and rain that day: and all the people greatly feared the LORD and Samuel. Ex. 14:31; Ezra 10:9

19 And all the people said unto Samuel, Pray for thy servants unto the LORD thy God, that we die not: for we have added unto all our sins *this* evil, to ask us a king. Ex. 9:28; 1 John 5:16

20 And Samuel said unto the people, Fear not: ye have done all this wickedness: yet

turn not aside from following the Lord, but serve the Lord with all your heart; Deut. 11:16

12:19 The Consequences of Sin

In the days of Samuel the Israelites wandered from God. They were suffering the consequences of sin; for they had lost their faith in God, lost their discernment of His power and wisdom to rule the nation, lost their confidence in His ability to defend and vindicate His cause. They turned from the great Ruler of the universe and desired to be governed as were the nations around them. *SC 38, 39*

---

21 And turn ye not aside: for *then should ye go* after vain *things*, which cannot profit nor deliver; for they *are* vain.   Jer. 10:15; 16:19; Hab. 2:18
22 For the Lord will not forsake his people for his great name's sake: because it hath pleased the Lord to make you his people.   Josh. 7:9; 1 Kin. 6:13; Ps. 106:8
23 Moreover as for me, God forbid that I should sin against the Lord in ceasing to pray for you: but I will teach you the good and the right way: 1 Kin. 8:36; Ps. 34:11; Prov. 4:11
24 Only fear the Lord, and serve him in truth with all your heart: for consider how great *things* he hath done for you.   Ps. 126:2-3
25 But if ye shall still do wickedly, ye shall be consumed, both ye and your king.   Deut. 28:36

Saul's Select Band of Three Thousand Warriors

13 Saul reigned one year; and when he had reigned two years over Israel,
2 Saul chose him three thousand *men* of Israel; *whereof* two thousand were with Saul in Michmash and in mount Beth-el, and a thousand were with Jonathan in Gibeah of Benjamin: and the rest of the people he sent every man to his tent.   1 Sam. 10:26; 13:5; 14:31
3 And Jonathan smote the garrison of the Philistines that *was* in Geba, and the Philistines heard *of it*. And Saul blew the trumpet throughout all the land, saying, Let the Hebrews hear.   Judg. 3:27; 6:34; 1 Sam. 10:5

13:2, 3 Missed Opportunity

Here was a serious error. [Saul's] army was filled with hope and courage by the recent victory; and had he proceeded at once against other enemies of Israel, a telling blow might have been struck for the liberties of the nation.

Meanwhile their warlike neighbors, the Philistines, were active. After the defeat at Ebenezer they had still retained possession of some hill fortresses in the land of Israel, and now they established themselves in the very heart of the country. *PP 616*

---

4 And all Israel heard say *that* Saul had smitten a garrison of the Philistines, and *that*

Israel also was had in abomination with the Philistines. And the people were called together after Saul to Gilgal.   Gen. 34:30
5 And the Philistines gathered themselves together to fight with Israel, thirty thousand chariots, and six thousand horsemen, and people as the sand which *is* on the sea shore in multitude: and they came up, and pitched in Michmash, eastward from Beth-aven.   Josh. 11:4; 18:12; 1 Sam. 14:23
6 When the men of Israel saw that they were in ᵀa strait, (for the people were distressed,) then the people did hide themselves in caves, and in thickets, and in rocks, and in high places, and in pits.   Judg. 6:2; Heb. 11:38 ◆ *danger*
7 And *some of* the Hebrews went over Jordan to the land of Gad and Gilead. As for Saul, he *was* yet in Gilgal, and all the people followed him trembling.

Saul, Weary of Waiting for Samuel, Offers Sacrifice

8 And he tarried seven days, according to the set time that Samuel *had appointed*: but Samuel came not to Gilgal; and the people were scattered from him.   1 Sam. 10:8
9 And Saul said, Bring ᵀhither a burnt offering to me, and peace offerings. And he offered the burnt offering.   1 Kin. 3:4 ◆ *here*

13:9; 14:44 A Stubborn King

Saul had presumed to officiate as priest, contrary to the command of God. When reproved by Samuel, he had stubbornly justified himself [13:9, 11]. Now, when his own command was disobeyed—though the command was unreasonable and had been violated through ignorance—the king and father sentenced his son to death [14:44]. *PP 625*

---

10 And it came to pass, that as soon as he had made an end of offering the burnt offering, behold, Samuel came; and Saul went out to meet him, that he might salute him.   1 Sam. 15:13
11 And Samuel said, What hast thou done? And Saul said, Because I saw that the people were scattered from me, and *that* thou camest not within the days appointed, and *that* the Philistines gathered themselves together at Michmash;   1 Sam. 13:2
12 Therefore said I, The Philistines will come down now upon me to Gilgal, and I have not made supplication unto the Lord: I forced myself therefore, and offered a burnt offering.
13 And Samuel said to Saul, Thou hast done foolishly: thou hast not kept the commandment of the Lord thy God, which he commanded thee: for now would the Lord have

established thy kingdom upon Israel for ever. *1 Sam. 15:11, 22; 2 Chr. 16:9*

14 But now thy kingdom shall not continue: the LORD hath sought him a man after his own heart, and the LORD hath commanded him *to be* captain over his people, because thou hast not kept *that* which the LORD commanded thee. *1 Sam. 15:28; Acts 13:22*

15 And Samuel arose, and gat him up from Gilgal unto Gibeah of Benjamin. And Saul numbered the people *that were* present with him, about six hundred men. *1 Sam. 13:2, 6-7; 14:2*

16 And Saul, and Jonathan his son, and the people *that were* present with them, abode in Gibeah of Benjamin: but the Philistines encamped in Michmash.

17 And the spoilers came out of the camp of the Philistines in three companies: one company turned unto the way *that leadeth to* Ophrah, unto the land of Shual: *Josh. 18:23*

18 And another company turned the way *to* Beth-horon: and another company turned *to* the way of the border that looketh to the valley of Zeboim toward the wilderness. *Josh. 16:3; 18:13-14; Neh. 11:34*

19 Now there was no smith found throughout all the land of Israel: for the Philistines said, Lest the Hebrews make *them* swords or spears: *Judg. 5:8; 2 Kin. 24:14; Jer. 24:1*

20 But all the Israelites went down to the Philistines, to sharpen every man his share, and his ᵀcoulter, and his axe, and his ᵀmattock. *iron tool for farming ◆ farming tool*

21 Yet they had a file for the mattocks, and for the coulters, and for the forks, and for the axes, and to sharpen the ᵀgoads. *pointed sticks*

22 So it came to pass in the day of battle, that there was neither sword nor spear found in the hand of any of the people that *were* with Saul and Jonathan: but with Saul and with Jonathan his son was there found. *Judg. 5:8*

23 And the garrison of the Philistines went out to the passage of Michmash. *Is. 10:28*

Unknown to Saul, Jonathan Defeats the Philistines

14 Now it came to pass upon a day, that Jonathan the son of Saul said unto the young man that bare his armour, Come, and let us go over to the Philistines' garrison, that *is* on the other side. But he told not his father.

2 And Saul tarried in the uttermost part of Gibeah under a pomegranate tree which *is* in Migron: and the people that *were* with him *were* about six hundred men; *1 Sam. 13:15-16*

3 And Ahiah, the son of Ahitub, Ichabod's brother, the son of Phinehas, the son of Eli, the LORD's priest in Shiloh, wearing an ᵀephod.

And the people knew not that Jonathan was gone. *1 Sam. 2:28; 4:21; 22:20 ◆ priestly garment*

4 And between the passages, by which Jonathan sought to go over unto the Philistines' garrison, *there was* a sharp rock on the one side, and a sharp rock on the other side: and the name of the one *was* Bozez, and the name of the other Seneh. *1 Sam. 13:23*

5 The forefront of the one *was* situate northward over against Michmash, and the other southward over against Gibeah.

6 And Jonathan said to the young man that bare his armour, Come, and let us go over unto the garrison of these uncircumcised: it may be that the LORD will work for us: for *there is* no restraint to the LORD to save by many or by few. *1 Sam. 17:26*

7 And his armourbearer said unto him, Do all that *is* in thine heart: turn thee; behold, I *am* with thee according to thy heart.

8 Then said Jonathan, Behold, we will pass over unto *these* men, and we will discover ourselves unto them. *Judg. 7:9-14*

9 If they say thus unto us, Tarry until we come to you; then we will stand still in our place, and will not go up unto them.

10 But if they say thus, Come up unto us; then we will go up: for the LORD hath delivered them into our hand: and this *shall be* a sign unto us. *Gen. 24:14*

11 And both of them discovered themselves unto the garrison of the Philistines: and the Philistines said, Behold, the Hebrews come forth out of the holes where they had hid themselves. *1 Sam. 13:6; 14:22*

12 And the men of the garrison answered Jonathan and his armourbearer, and said, Come up to us, and we will shew you a thing. And Jonathan said unto his armourbearer, Come up after me: for the LORD hath delivered them into the hand of Israel. *1 Sam. 17:43-44*

13 And Jonathan climbed up upon his hands and upon his feet, and his armourbearer after him: and they fell before Jonathan; and his armourbearer slew after him.

14:6-13 God Chooses Another

Because of Saul's sin in his presumptuous offering, the Lord would not give him the honor of vanquishing the Philistines. Jonathan, the king's son, a man who feared the Lord, was chosen as the instrument to deliver Israel. Moved by a divine impulse, he proposed to his armor-bearer that they should make a secret attack upon the enemy's camp. *PP 623*

14 And that first slaughter, which Jonathan and his armourbearer made, was about twenty men, within as it were an half acre of land, *which* a yoke *of oxen might plow.*

15 And there was trembling in the host, in the field, and among all the people: the garrison, and the spoilers, they also trembled, and the earth quaked: so it was a very great trembling.   Gen. 35:5; 1 Sam. 13:17; 2 Kin. 7:6-7

16 And the watchmen of Saul in Gibeah of Benjamin looked; and, behold, the multitude melted away, and they went on beating down *one another*.

17 Then said Saul unto the people that *were* with him, Number now, and see who is gone from us. And when they had numbered, behold, Jonathan and his armourbearer *were* not *there*.

18 And Saul said unto Ahiah, Bring ᵀthither the ark of God. For the ark of God was at that time with the children of Israel.   *here*

19 And it came to pass, while Saul talked unto the priest, that the noise that *was* in the host of the Philistines went on and increased: and Saul said unto the priest, Withdraw thine hand.   Num. 27:21

20 And Saul and all the people that *were* with him assembled themselves, and they came to the battle: and, behold, every man's sword was against his fellow, *and there was* a very great discomfiture.   Judg. 7:22; 2 Chr. 20:23

21 Moreover the Hebrews *that* were with the Philistines before that time, which went up with them into the camp *from the country* round about, even they also *turned* to be with the Israelites that *were* with Saul and Jonathan.   1 Sam. 29:4

22 Likewise all the men of Israel which had hid themselves in mount Ephraim, *when* they heard that the Philistines fled, even they also followed hard after them in the battle.   1 Sam. 13:6

23 So the LORD saved Israel that day: and the battle passed over unto Beth-aven.   Ex. 14:30

Saul's Unadvised Command Hinders the Victory

24 And the men of Israel were distressed that day: for Saul had ᵀadjured the people, saying, Cursed *be* the man that eateth *any* food until evening, that I may be avenged on mine enemies. So none of the people tasted *any* food.   Josh. 6:26 ◆ *appealed to*

25 And all *they of* the land came to a wood; and there was honey upon the ground.

26 And when the people were come into the wood, behold, the honey dropped; but no man put his hand to his mouth: for the people feared the oath.

27 But Jonathan heard not when his father charged the people with the oath: wherefore he put forth the end of the rod that *was* in his hand, and dipped it in an honeycomb, and put his hand to his mouth; and his eyes were enlightened.   1 Sam. 30:12

28 Then answered one of the people, and said, Thy father ᵀstraitly charged the people with an oath, saying, Cursed *be* the man that eateth *any* food this day. And the people were faint.   *strictly*

29 Then said Jonathan, My father hath troubled the land: see, I pray you, how mine eyes have been enlightened, because I tasted a little of this honey.   1 Kin. 18:18

30 How much more, if ᵀhaply the people had eaten freely to day of the spoil of their enemies which they found? for had there not been now a much greater slaughter among the Philistines?   *maybe*

31 And they smote the Philistines that day from Michmash to Aijalon: and the people were very faint.   Josh. 10:12

32 And the people flew upon the spoil, and took sheep, and oxen, and calves, and slew *them* on the ground: and the people did eat *them* with the blood.   Gen. 9:4; Lev. 3:17; 1 Sam. 15:19

33 Then they told Saul, saying, Behold, the people sin against the LORD, in that they eat with the blood. And he said, Ye have ᵀtransgressed: roll a great stone unto me this day.   *violated a law*

34 And Saul said, Disperse yourselves among the people, and say unto them, Bring me hither every man his ox, and every man his sheep, and slay *them* here, and eat; and sin not against the LORD in eating with the blood. And all the people brought every man his ox with him that night, and slew *them* there.

35 And Saul built an altar unto the LORD: the same was the first altar that he built unto the LORD.   1 Sam. 7:17

Jonathan, Taken by Lot, Is Saved by the People

36 And Saul said, Let us go down after the Philistines by night, and ᵀspoil them until the morning light, and let us not leave a man of them. And they said, Do whatsoever seemeth good unto thee. Then said the priest, Let us draw near hither unto God.   *plunder*

37 And Saul asked counsel of God, Shall I go down after the Philistines? wilt thou deliver them into the hand of Israel? But he answered him not that day.   1 Sam. 28:6

38 And Saul said, Draw ye near hither, all the chief of the people: and know and see wherein this sin hath been this day.   1 Sam. 10:19-20

39 For, *as* the LORD liveth, which saveth Israel, though it be in Jonathan my son, he shall surely die. But *there was* not a man among all the people *that* answered him.   1 Sam. 14:44

40 Then said he unto all Israel, Be ye on one side, and I and Jonathan my son will be on the other side. And the people said unto Saul, Do what seemeth good unto thee.

41 Therefore Saul said unto the LORD God

of Israel, Give a perfect *lot*. And Saul and Jonathan were taken: but the people escaped.   Josh. 7:16-18; 1 Sam. 10:20-21; Acts 1:24

42 And Saul said, Cast *lots* between me and Jonathan my son. And Jonathan was taken.

43 Then Saul said to Jonathan, Tell me what thou hast done. And Jonathan told him, and said, I did but taste a little honey with the end of the rod that *was* in mine hand, *and*, lo, I must die.   Josh. 7:19; 1 Sam. 14:27

44 And Saul answered, God do so and more also: for thou shalt surely die, Jonathan.   Ruth 1:17; 1 Sam. 14:39; 25:22

45 And the people said unto Saul, Shall Jonathan die, who hath ᵀwrought this great salvation in Israel? God forbid: *as* the LORD liveth, there shall not one hair of his head fall to the ground; for he hath wrought with God this day. So the people rescued Jonathan, that he died not.   2 Sam. 14:11; 1 Kin. 1:52; Luke 21:18 ◆ *made*

46 Then Saul went up from following the Philistines: and the Philistines went to their own place.

Saul's Strength and Family

47 So Saul took the kingdom over Israel, and fought against all his enemies on every side, against Moab, and against the children of Ammon, and against Edom, and against the kings of Zobah, and against the Philistines: and whithersoever he turned himself, he vexed *them*.   2 Sam. 10:6

48 And he gathered an host, and smote the Amalekites, and delivered Israel out of the hands of them that spoiled them.

49 Now the sons of Saul were Jonathan, and Ishui, and Melchishua: and the names of his two daughters *were these*; the name of the firstborn Merab, and the name of the younger Michal: 1 Sam. 31:2; 2 Sam. 6:20-23; 1 Chr. 8:33

50 And the name of Saul's wife *was* Ahinoam, the daughter of Ahimaaz: and the name of the captain of his host *was* Abner, the son of Ner, Saul's uncle.   2 Sam. 2:8

51 And Kish *was* the father of Saul; and Ner the father of Abner *was* the son of Abiel.   1 Sam. 9:1, 21

52 And there was sore war against the Philistines all the days of Saul: and when Saul saw any strong man, or any valiant man, he took him unto him.   1 Sam. 8:11

Samuel Sends Saul to Destroy Amalek

15 Samuel also said unto Saul, The LORD sent me to anoint thee *to be* king over his people, over Israel: now therefore hearken thou unto the voice of the words of the LORD.   1 Sam. 9:16; 10:1

2 Thus saith the LORD of hosts, I remember *that* which Amalek did to Israel, how he laid *wait* for him in the way, when he came up from Egypt.   Ex. 17:8-16; Num. 24:20; Deut. 25:17-19

3 Now go and ᵀsmite Amalek, and utterly destroy all that they have, and spare them not; but slay both man and woman, infant and suckling, ox and sheep, camel and ass.   *strike*

4 And Saul gathered the people together, and numbered them in Telaim, two hundred thousand footmen, and ten thousand men of Judah.   Josh. 15:24

5 And Saul came to a city of Amalek, and laid wait in the valley.

6 And Saul said unto the Kenites, Go, depart, get you down from among the Amalekites, lest I destroy you with them: for ye shewed kindness to all the children of

---

Where Saul Went Wrong

1 Samuel 15

When called to the throne, Saul had a humble opinion of his own capabilities, and was willing to be instructed. He was deficient in knowledge and experience and had serious defects of character. But the Lord granted him the Holy Spirit as a guide and helper, and placed him in a position where he could develop the qualities requisite for a ruler of Israel. Had he remained humble, seeking constantly to be guided by divine wisdom, he would have been enabled to discharge the duties of his high position with success and honor. Under the influence of divine grace every good quality would have been gaining strength, while evil tendencies would have lost their power. This is the work which the Lord proposes to do for all who consecrate themselves to Him. There are many whom He has called to positions in His work because they have a humble and teachable spirit. In His providence He places them where they may learn of Him. He will reveal to them their defects of character, and to all who seek His aid He will give strength to correct their errors.

But Saul presumed upon his exaltation, and dishonored God by unbelief and disobedience. . . . He lost sight of his dependence upon God, and in heart departed from the Lord. Thus the way was prepared for his sin of presumption and sacrilege at Gilgal. The same blind self-confidence led him to reject Samuel's reproof. Saul acknowledged Samuel to be a prophet sent from God; hence he should have accepted the reproof, though he could not himself see that he had sinned. Had he been willing to see and confess his error, this bitter experience would have proved a safeguard for the future. *PP 632, 633*

Israel, when they came up out of Egypt. So the Kenites departed from among the Amalekites. Ex. 18:19; Num. 10:29-32; Judg. 1:16
7 And Saul smote the Amalekites from Havilah *until* thou comest to Shur, that *is* over against Egypt. Gen. 16:7; 25:18; 1 Sam. 14:48
8 And he took Agag the king of the Amalekites alive, and utterly destroyed all the people with the edge of the sword. Num. 24:7; Esth. 3:1
9 But Saul and the people spared Agag, and the best of the sheep, and of the oxen, and of the fatlings, and the lambs, and all *that was* good, and would not utterly destroy them: but every thing *that was* vile and refuse, that they destroyed utterly. 1 Sam. 15:3, 15, 19

God Rejects Saul for His Disobedience
10 Then came the word of the Lord unto Samuel, saying,
11 It repenteth me that I have set up Saul *to be* king: for he is turned back from following me, and hath not performed my commandments. And it grieved Samuel; and he cried unto the Lord all night. Gen. 6:6; Josh. 22:16; 1 Sam. 13:13
12 And when Samuel rose early to meet Saul in the morning, it was told Samuel, saying, Saul came to Carmel, and, behold, he set him up a place, and is gone about, and passed on, and gone down to Gilgal. Josh. 15:55; 1 Sam. 25:2
13 And Samuel came to Saul: and Saul said unto him, Blessed *be* thou of the Lord: I have performed the commandment of the Lord. Gen. 14:19
14 And Samuel said, What *meaneth* then this bleating of the sheep in mine ears, and the ᵀlowing of the oxen which I hear? *mooing*
15 And Saul said, They have brought them from the Amalekites: for the people spared the best of the sheep and of the oxen, to sacrifice unto the Lord thy God; and the rest we have utterly destroyed. 1 Sam. 15:9
16 Then Samuel said unto Saul, Stay, and I will tell thee what the Lord hath said to me this night. And he said unto him, Say on.
17 And Samuel said, When thou *wast* little in thine own sight, *wast* thou not made the head of the tribes of Israel, and the Lord anointed thee king over Israel? 1 Sam. 9:21; 10:22
18 And the Lord sent thee on a journey, and said, Go and utterly destroy the sinners the Amalekites, and fight against them until they be consumed.
19 Wherefore then didst thou not obey the voice of the Lord, but didst fly upon the ᵀspoil, and didst evil in the sight of the Lord? 1 Sam. 14:32 ◆ *plunder*
20 And Saul said unto Samuel, Yea, I have obeyed the voice of the Lord, and have gone the way which the Lord sent me, and have brought Agag the king of Amalek, and have utterly destroyed the Amalekites. 1 Sam. 15:13

21 But the people took of the spoil, sheep and oxen, the chief of the things which should have been utterly destroyed, to sacrifice unto the Lord thy God in Gilgal. 1 Sam. 15:15
22 And Samuel said, Hath the Lord *as great* delight in burnt offerings and sacrifices, as in obeying the voice of the Lord? Behold, to obey *is* better than sacrifice, *and* to hearken than the fat of rams. Jer. 7:22-23; Hos. 6:6; Mic. 6:6-8
23 For rebellion *is as* the sin of witchcraft, and stubbornness *is as* iniquity and idolatry. Because thou hast rejected the word of the Lord, he hath also rejected thee from *being* king. 1 Sam. 13:14

Saul's Humiliation
24 And Saul said unto Samuel, I have sinned: for I have transgressed the commandment of the Lord, and thy words: because I feared the people, and obeyed their voice. 2 Sam. 12:13; Prov. 29:25; Is. 51:12-13
25 Now therefore, I pray thee, pardon my sin, and turn again with me, that I may worship the Lord. Ex. 10:17

> **15:24, 25 Saul Adds Sin to Sin**
> It was not sorrow for sin, but fear of its penalty, that actuated the king of Israel as he entreated Samuel, "I pray thee, pardon my sin, and turn again with me, that I may worship the Lord." If Saul had had true repentance, he would have made public confession of his sin; but it was his chief anxiety to maintain his authority and retain the allegiance of the people. He desired the honor of Samuel's presence in order to strengthen his own influence with the nation. *PP 631*

26 And Samuel said unto Saul, I will not return with thee: for thou hast rejected the word of the Lord, and the Lord hath rejected thee from being king over Israel. 1 Sam. 13:14
27 And as Samuel turned about to go away, he laid hold upon the skirt of his ᵀmantle, and it rent. *large outside garment*
28 And Samuel said unto him, The Lord hath rent the kingdom of Israel from thee this day, and hath given it to a neighbour of thine, *that is* better than thou. 1 Sam. 28:17-18
29 And also the Strength of Israel will not lie nor repent: for he *is* not a man, that he should repent. Num. 23:19; Ezek. 24:14; Titus 1:2
30 Then he said, I have sinned: *yet* honour me now, I pray thee, before the elders of my people, and before Israel, and turn again with me, that I may worship the Lord thy God. Is. 29:13; John 5:44; 12:43
31 So Samuel turned again after Saul; and Saul worshipped the Lord.

Samuel Kills Agag

32 Then said Samuel, Bring ye ᵀhither to me Agag the king of the Amalekites. And Agag came unto him delicately. And Agag said, Surely the bitterness of death is past.   *here*
33 And Samuel said, As thy sword hath made women childless, so shall thy mother be childless among women. And Samuel ᵀhewed Agag in pieces before the LORD in Gilgal.   Gen. 9:6; Judg. 1:7; Matt. 7:2 ◆ *cut*

15:33 Samuel Rebukes Saul

An act of justice, stern and terrible, was yet to be performed. Samuel must publicly vindicate the honor of God and rebuke the course of Saul. He commanded that the king of the Amalekites be brought before him. Above all who had fallen by the sword of Israel, Agag was the most guilty and merciless; one who had hated and sought to destroy the people of God, and whose influence had been strongest to promote idolatry. *PP 632*

---

34 Then Samuel went to Ramah; and Saul went up to his house to Gibeah of Saul.
35 And Samuel came no more to see Saul until the day of his death: nevertheless Samuel mourned for Saul: and the LORD repented that he had made Saul king over Israel.   1 Sam. 15:11; 16:1; 19:24

Samuel Is Sent by God to Beth-lehem

16 And the LORD said unto Samuel, How long wilt thou mourn for Saul, seeing I have rejected him from reigning over Israel? fill thine horn with oil, and go, I will send thee to Jesse the Beth-lehemite: for I have provided me a king among his sons.   1 Sam. 9:16; 15:23, 35

16:1 Just One Cherished Sin

Even one wrong trait of character, one sinful desire, persistently cherished, will eventually neutralize all the power of the gospel. Every sinful indulgence strengthens the soul's aversion to God. The man who manifests an infidel hardihood, or a stolid indifference to divine truth, is but reaping the harvest of that which he has himself sown. *SC 34*

---

2 And Samuel said, How can I go? if Saul hear *it*, he will kill me. And the LORD said, Take an heifer with thee, and say, I am come to sacrifice to the LORD.   1 Sam. 9:12; 20:29
3 And call Jesse to the sacrifice, and I will shew thee what thou shalt do: and thou shalt anoint unto me *him* whom I name unto thee.   Ex. 4:15; 1 Sam. 9:16; Acts 9:6
4 And Samuel did that which the LORD spake, and came to Beth-lehem. And the elders of the town trembled at his coming, and said, Comest thou peaceably?   1 Kin. 2:13; 2 Kin. 9:22

5 And he said, Peaceably: I am come to sacrifice unto the LORD: ᵀsanctify yourselves, and come with me to the sacrifice. And he sanctified Jesse and his sons, and called them to the sacrifice.   Ex. 19:10 ◆ *make yourselves holy*

David Is Chosen to Be King

6 And it came to pass, when they were come, that he looked on Eliab, and said, Surely the LORD's anointed *is* before him.   1 Sam. 17:13
7 But the LORD said unto Samuel, Look not on his countenance, or on the height of his stature; because I have refused him: for *the* LORD *seeth* not as man seeth; *for* man looketh on the outward appearance, but the LORD looketh on the heart.   1 Chr. 28:9; Ps. 7:9
8 Then Jesse called Abinadab, and made him pass before Samuel. And he said, Neither hath the LORD chosen this.   1 Sam. 17:13
9 Then Jesse made Shammah to pass by. And he said, Neither hath the LORD chosen this.   1 Sam. 17:13
10 Again, Jesse made seven of his sons to pass before Samuel. And Samuel said unto Jesse, The LORD hath not chosen these.
11 And Samuel said unto Jesse, Are here all *thy* children? And he said, There remaineth yet the youngest, and, behold, he keepeth the sheep. And Samuel said unto Jesse, Send and fetch him: for we will not sit down till he come ᵀthither.   2 Sam. 7:8 ◆ *here*
12 And he sent, and brought him in. Now he *was* ruddy, *and* ᵀwithal of a beautiful countenance, and goodly to look to. And the LORD said, Arise, anoint him: for this *is* he.   1 Sam. 9:17; 17:42; Acts 7:20 ◆ *with*
13 Then Samuel took the horn of oil, and anointed him in the midst of his brethren: and the Spirit of the LORD came upon David from that day forward. So Samuel rose up, and went to Ramah.   Num. 27:18; 1 Sam. 10:1, 6

16:12, 13 The Lord Chooses David

The simple shepherd boy sang the songs of his own composing, and the music of his harp made a sweet accompaniment to the melody of his fresh young voice. The Lord had chosen David, and was preparing him, in his solitary life with his flocks, for the work He designed to commit to his trust in after years. *PP 637*

---

14 But the Spirit of the LORD departed from Saul, and an evil spirit from the LORD troubled him.   Judg. 9:23; 1 Sam. 18:10, 12
15 And Saul's servants said unto him, Behold now, an evil spirit from God troubleth thee.
16 Let our lord now command thy servants, *which are* before thee, to seek out a man, *who is* a cunning player on an harp: and it shall

come to pass, when the evil spirit from God is upon thee, that he shall play with his hand, and thou shalt be well. 1 Sam. 16:21-23; 2 Kin. 3:15
17 And Saul said unto his servants, Provide me now a man that can play well, and bring *him* to me.
18 Then answered one of the servants, and said, Behold, I have seen a son of Jesse the Beth-lehemite, *that is* cunning in playing, and a mighty valiant man, and a man of war, and prudent in matters, and a ᵀcomely person, and the LORD *is* with him. 1 Sam. 3:19 ◆ *handsome*
19 Wherefore Saul sent messengers unto Jesse, and said, Send me David thy son, which *is* with the sheep. 1 Sam. 16:11

> **16:18, 19 Lessons of Trust**
>
> God was teaching David lessons of trust. As Moses was trained for his work, so the Lord was fitting the son of Jesse to become the guide of His chosen people. In his watchcare for his flocks, he was gaining an appreciation of the care that the Great Shepherd has for the sheep of His pasture. *PP 644*

20 And Jesse took an ass ᵀladen with bread, and a bottle of wine, and a kid, and sent *them* by David his son unto Saul. 1 Sam. 10:27 ◆ *loaded*
21 And David came to Saul, and stood before him: and he loved him greatly; and he became his armourbearer. Gen. 41:46
22 And Saul sent to Jesse, saying, Let David, I pray thee, stand before me; for he hath found favour in my sight.
23 And it came to pass, when the *evil* spirit from God was upon Saul, that David took an harp, and played with his hand: so Saul was refreshed, and was well, and the evil spirit departed from him.

The Armies of the Israelites and Philistines Prepare to Fight

17 Now the Philistines gathered together their armies to battle, and were gathered together at Shochoh, which *belongeth* to Judah, and pitched between Shochoh and Azekah, in Ephes-dammim. 1 Chr. 11:13
2 And Saul and the men of Israel were gathered together, and pitched by the valley of Elah, and set the battle in array against the Philistines. 1 Sam. 17:19; 21:9
3 And the Philistines stood on a mountain on the one side, and Israel stood on a mountain on the other side: and *there was* a valley between them.
4 And there went out a champion out of the camp of the Philistines, named Goliath, of Gath, whose height *was* six cubits and a span. Josh. 11:22
5 And *he had* an helmet of brass upon his head, and he *was* armed with a coat of mail;

and the weight of the coat *was* five thousand shekels of brass.
6 And *he had* ᵀgreaves of brass upon his legs, and a target of brass between his shoulders. 1 Sam. 17:45 ◆ *shin armor*
7 And the staff of his spear *was* like a weaver's beam; and his spear's head *weighed* six hundred shekels of iron: and one bearing a shield went before him. 2 Sam. 21:19
8 And he stood and cried unto the armies of Israel, and said unto them, Why are ye come out to set *your* battle in array? *am* not I a Philistine, and ye servants to Saul? choose you a man for you, and let him come down to me. 1 Sam. 8:17
9 If he be able to fight with me, and to kill me, then will we be your servants: but if I prevail against him, and kill him, then shall ye be our servants, and serve us. 1 Sam. 11:1
10 And the Philistine said, I defy the armies of Israel this day; give me a man, that we may fight together. 1 Sam. 17:36, 45; 2 Sam. 21:21
11 When Saul and all Israel heard those words of the Philistine, they were dismayed, and greatly afraid.

David Defeats Goliath
12 Now David *was* the son of that Ephrathite of Beth-lehem-judah, whose name *was* Jesse; and he had eight sons: and the man went among men *for* an old man in the days of Saul. Gen. 35:19; Ruth 4:22; 1 Sam. 16:18
13 And the three eldest sons of Jesse went *and* followed Saul to the battle: and the names of his three sons that went to the battle *were* Eliab the firstborn, and next unto him Abinadab, and the third Shammah. 1 Chr. 2:13
14 And David *was* the youngest: and the three eldest followed Saul. 1 Sam. 16:11
15 But David went and returned from Saul to feed his father's sheep at Beth-lehem.

> **17:15 The Low Value of Human Glory**
>
> David in his youth was intimately associated with Saul, and his stay at court and his connection with the king's household gave him an insight into the cares and sorrows and perplexities concealed by the glitter and pomp of royalty. He saw of how little worth is human glory to bring peace to the soul. And it was with relief and gladness that he returned from the king's court to the sheepfolds and the flocks. *Ed 152*

16 And the Philistine drew near morning and evening, and presented himself forty days.
17 And Jesse said unto David his son, Take now for thy brethren an ephah of this parched *corn*, and these ten loaves, and run to the camp to thy brethren; 1 Sam. 25:18
18 And carry these ten cheeses unto the

captain of *their* thousand, and look how thy brethren fare, and take their pledge. Gen. 37:14
19 Now Saul, and they, and all the men of Israel, *were* in the valley of Elah, fighting with the Philistines.
20 And David rose up early in the morning, and left the sheep with a keeper, and took, and went, as Jesse had commanded him; and he came to the trench, as the host was going forth to the fight, and shouted for the battle.   1 Sam. 26:5
21 For Israel and the Philistines had put the battle in array, army against army.
22 And David left his carriage in the hand of the keeper of the carriage, and ran into the army, and came and saluted his brethren.
23 And as he talked with them, behold, there came up the champion, the Philistine of Gath, Goliath by name, out of the armies of the Philistines, and spake according to the same words: and David heard *them*.
24 And all the men of Israel, when they saw the man, fled from him, and were sore afraid.
25 And the men of Israel said, Have ye seen this man that is come up? surely to defy Israel is he come up: and it shall be, *that* the man who killeth him, the king will enrich him with great riches, and will give him his daughter, and make his father's house free in Israel.   Josh. 15:16
26 And David spake to the men that stood by him, saying, What shall be done to the man that killeth this Philistine, and taketh away the reproach from Israel? for who *is* this uncircumcised Philistine, that he should defy the armies of the living God?   Deut. 5:26
27 And the people answered him after this manner, saying, So shall it be done to the man that killeth him.
28 And Eliab his eldest brother heard when he spake unto the men; and Eliab's anger was kindled against David, and he said, Why camest thou down ᵀhither? and with whom hast thou left those few sheep in the wilderness? I know thy pride, and the naughtiness of thine heart; for thou art come down that thou mightest see the battle.   Gen. 37:4 ◆ *here*

17:28 Feelings of Jealousy

Eliab, David's eldest brother, when he heard these words, knew well the feelings that were stirring the young man's soul. Even as a shepherd, David had manifested daring, courage, and strength but rarely witnessed. . . . [The soldiers] looked upon him as merely a stripling shepherd, and now the question which he asked was regarded by Eliab as a censure upon his own cowardice in making no attempt to silence the giant of the Philistines. *PP 645*

---

29 And David said, What have I now done? *Is there* not a cause?
30 And he turned from him toward another, and spake after the same manner: and the people answered him again after the former manner.   1 Sam. 17:26-27
31 And when the words were heard which David spake, they rehearsed *them* before Saul: and he sent for him.
32 And David said to Saul, Let no man's heart fail because of him; thy servant will go and fight with this Philistine. Deut. 20:1-3; 1 Sam. 16:18
33 And Saul said to David, Thou art not able to go against this Philistine to fight with him: for thou *art but* a youth, and he a man of war from his youth.   Num. 13:31
34 And David said unto Saul, Thy servant kept his father's sheep, and there came a lion, and a bear, and took a lamb out of the flock:
35 And I went out after him, and smote him, and delivered *it* out of his mouth: and when he arose against me, I caught *him* by his beard, and smote him, and slew him.   Amos 3:12
36 Thy servant slew both the lion and the bear: and this uncircumcised Philistine shall be as one of them, seeing he hath defied the armies of the living God.   1 Sam. 17:10
37 David said moreover, The LORD that delivered me out of the paw of the lion, and out of the paw of the bear, he will deliver me out of the hand of this Philistine. And Saul said unto David, Go, and the LORD be with thee.   1 Sam. 20:13; 1 Chr. 22:11, 16
38 And Saul armed David with his armour, and he put an helmet of brass upon his head; also he armed him with a coat of mail.
39 And David girded his sword upon his armour, and he ᵀassayed to go; for he had not proved *it*. And David said unto Saul, I cannot go with these; for I have not proved *them*. And David put them off him.   *attempted*
40 And he took his staff in his hand, and chose him five smooth stones out of the brook, and put them in a shepherd's bag which he had, even in a ᵀscrip; and his sling *was* in his hand: and he drew near to the Philistine.   Judg. 20:16 ◆ *sack*
41 And the Philistine came on and drew near unto David; and the man that bare the shield *went* before him.
42 And when the Philistine looked about, and saw David, he disdained him: for he was *but* a youth, and ruddy, and of a fair ᵀcountenance.   1 Sam. 16:12; Ps. 123:3-4 ◆ *appearance*
43 And the Philistine said unto David, *Am* I a dog, that thou comest to me with ᵀstaves? And the Philistine cursed David by his gods.   2 Sam. 3:8; 2 Kin. 8:13 ◆ *clubs or rods*
44 And the Philistine said to David, Come to me, and I will give thy flesh unto the

fowls of the air, and to the beasts of the field. 1 Kin. 20:10-11

45 Then said David to the Philistine, Thou comest to me with a sword, and with a spear, and with a shield: but I come to thee in the name of the LORD of hosts, the God of the armies of Israel, whom thou hast defied. 2 Chr. 32:8

46 This day will the LORD deliver thee into mine hand; and I will ᵀsmite thee, and take thine head from thee; and I will give the carcases of the host of the Philistines this day unto the fowls of the air, and to the wild beasts of the earth; that all the earth may know that there is a God in Israel. Deut. 28:26; Josh. 4:24; 1 Kin. 8:43 ◆ strike

47 And all this assembly shall know that the LORD saveth not with sword and spear: for the battle is the LORD's, and he will give you into our hands. 1 Sam. 14:6; Hos. 1:7; Zech. 4:6

48 And it came to pass, when the Philistine arose, and came and drew nigh to meet David, that David hasted, and ran toward the army to meet the Philistine.

49 And David put his hand in his bag, and took thence a stone, and slang it, and smote the Philistine in his forehead, that the stone sunk into his forehead; and he fell upon his face to the earth.

50 So David prevailed over the Philistine with a sling and with a stone, and smote the Philistine, and slew him; but there was no sword in the hand of David.

51 Therefore David ran, and stood upon the Philistine, and took his sword, and drew it out of the ᵀsheath thereof, and slew him, and cut off his head therewith. And when the Philistines saw their champion was dead, they fled. 1 Sam. 21:9; 2 Sam. 23:21; Heb. 11:34 ◆ case for a sword

17:51 Heroic Young David

Amazement spread along the lines of the two armies. They had been confident that David would be slain; but when the stone went whizzing through the air, straight to the mark, they saw the mighty warrior tremble, and reach forth his hands, as if he were struck with sudden blindness. . . . David did not wait an instant. He sprang upon the prostrate form of the Philistine, and with both hands laid hold of Goliath's heavy sword. *PP 648*

52 And the men of Israel and of Judah arose, and shouted, and pursued the Philistines, until thou come to the valley, and to the gates of Ekron. And the wounded of the Philistines fell down by the way to Shaaraim, even unto Gath, and unto Ekron. Josh. 15:11

53 And the children of Israel returned from chasing after the Philistines, and they spoiled their tents.

54 And David took the head of the Philistine, and brought it to Jerusalem; but he put his armour in his tent.

55 And when Saul saw David go forth against the Philistine, he said unto Abner, the captain of the host, Abner, whose son is this youth? And Abner said, As thy soul liveth, O king, I cannot tell. 1 Sam. 16:21-22

56 And the king said, Enquire thou whose son the stripling is.

57 And as David returned from the slaughter of the Philistine, Abner took him, and brought him before Saul with the head of the Philistine in his hand.

58 And Saul said to him, Whose son art thou, thou young man? And David answered, I am the son of thy servant Jesse the Bethlehemite. 1 Sam. 17:12

The Friendship of Jonathan and David

18 And it came to pass, when he had made an end of speaking unto Saul, that the soul of Jonathan was knit with the soul of David, and Jonathan loved him as his own soul. Gen. 44:30; Deut. 13:6; 2 Sam. 1:26

18:1 A Name Treasured in Heaven

Jonathan, by birth heir to the throne, yet knowing himself set aside by the divine decree; to his rival the most tender and faithful of friends, shielding David's life at the peril of his own; steadfast at his father's side through the dark days of his declining power, and at his side falling at the last—the name of Jonathan is treasured in heaven, and it stands on earth a witness to the existence and the power of unselfish love. *Ed 157*

2 And Saul took him that day, and would let him go no more home to his father's house. 1 Sam. 17:15

3 Then Jonathan and David made a covenant, because he loved him as his own soul. 1 Sam. 20:8-17

4 And Jonathan stripped himself of the robe that was upon him, and gave it to David, and his garments, even to his sword, and to his bow, and to his ᵀgirdle. Gen. 41:42 ◆ belt

5 And David went out whithersoever Saul sent him, and behaved himself wisely: and Saul set him over the men of war, and he was accepted in the sight of all the people, and also in the sight of Saul's servants. 1 Sam. 18:14

6 And it came to pass as they came, when David was returned from the slaughter of the Philistine, that the women came out of all cities of Israel, singing and dancing, to meet king Saul, with tabrets, with joy, and with instruments of musick. Ex. 15:20; Judg. 11:34; Ps. 68:25

7 And the women answered *one another* as they played, and said, Saul hath slain his thousands, and David his ten thousands.

8 And Saul was very wroth, and the saying displeased him; and he said, They have ascribed unto David ten thousands, and to me they have ascribed *but* thousands: and *what* can he have more but the kingdom? 1 Sam. 15:28

9 And Saul eyed David from that day and forward.

10 And it came to pass on the morrow, that the evil spirit from God came upon Saul, and he prophesied in the midst of the house: and David played with his hand, as at other times: and *there was* a javelin in Saul's hand. 1 Sam. 19:9

11 And Saul cast the javelin; for he said, I will ᵀsmite David even to the wall *with it*. And David avoided out of his presence twice. 1 Sam. 20:33; Is. 54:17 ◆ strike

Saul's Jealousy of David

12 And Saul was afraid of David, because the LORD was with him, and was departed from Saul. 1 Sam. 18:15, 29; 28:15

13 Therefore Saul removed him from him, and made him his captain over a thousand; and he went out and came in before the people. 2 Sam. 5:2

14 And David behaved himself wisely in all his ways; and the LORD *was* with him.

15 Wherefore when Saul saw that he behaved himself very wisely, he was afraid of him.

16 But all Israel and Judah loved David, because he went out and came in before them. 1 Sam. 18:5

17 And Saul said to David, Behold my elder daughter Merab, her will I give thee to wife: only be thou valiant for me, and fight the LORD's battles. For Saul said, Let not mine hand be upon him, but let the hand of the Philistines be upon him. 1 Sam. 17:25; 18:25; 25:28

18:14 David and Saul

It was the providence of God that had connected David with Saul. David's position at court would give him a knowledge of affairs, in preparation for his future greatness. It would enable him to gain the confidence of the nation. The vicissitudes and hardships which befell him, through the enmity of Saul, would lead him to feel his dependence upon God, and to put his whole trust in Him. *PP 649*

---

18 And David said unto Saul, Who *am* I? and what *is* my life, *or* my father's family in Israel, that I should be son in law to the king? 1 Sam. 9:21; 18:23; 2 Sam. 7:18

19 But it came to pass at the time when Merab Saul's daughter should have been given to David, that she was given unto Adriel the Meholathite to wife. Judg. 7:22; 2 Sam. 21:8

20 And Michal Saul's daughter loved David: and they told Saul, and the thing pleased him. 1 Sam. 18:28

21 And Saul said, I will give him her, that she may be a snare to him, and that the hand of the Philistines may be against him. Wherefore Saul said to David, Thou shalt this day be my son in law in *the one of* the ᵀtwain. Ex. 10:7; 1 Sam. 18:17, 26 ◆ two

22 And Saul commanded his servants, *saying*, Commune with David secretly, and say, Behold, the king hath delight in thee, and all

---

Saul's Soul Was Poisoned

1 Samuel 18:6–9

The demon of jealousy entered the heart of the king. He was angry because David was exalted above himself in the song of the women of Israel. . . .

One great defect in the character of Saul was his love of approbation. This trait had had a controlling influence over his actions and thoughts; everything was marked by his desire for praise and self-exaltation. His standard of right and wrong was the low standard of popular applause. No man is safe who lives that he may please men, and does not seek first for the approbation of God. It was the ambition of Saul to be first in the estimation of men; and when this song of praise was sung, a settled conviction entered the mind of the king that David would obtain the hearts of the people and reign in his stead.

Saul opened his heart to the spirit of jealousy by which his soul was poisoned. Notwithstanding the lessons which he had received from the prophet Samuel, instructing him that God would accomplish whatsoever He chose, and that no one could hinder it, the king made it evident that he had no true knowledge of the plans or power of God. The monarch of Israel was opposing his will to the will of the Infinite One. Saul had not learned, while ruling the kingdom of Israel, that he should rule his own spirit. He allowed his impulses to control his judgment, until he was plunged into a fury of passion. He had paroxysms of rage, when he was ready to take the life of any who dared oppose his will. From this frenzy he would pass into a state of despondency and self-contempt, and remorse would take possession of his soul. *PP 650*

his servants love thee: now therefore be the king's son in law.

23 And Saul's servants spake those words in the ears of David. And David said, Seemeth it to you *a* light *thing* to be a king's son in law, seeing that I *am* a poor man, and lightly esteemed?

24 And the servants of Saul told him, saying, On this manner spake David.

25 And Saul said, Thus shall ye say to David, The king desireth not any †dowry, but an hundred foreskins of the Philistines, to be avenged of the king's enemies. But Saul thought to make David fall by the hand of the Philistines.   Gen. 34:12 ◆ *price paid for a wife*

26 And when his servants told David these words, it pleased David well to be the king's son in law: and the days were not expired.

27 Wherefore David arose and went, he and his men, and slew of the Philistines two hundred men; and David brought their foreskins, and they gave them in full †tale to the king, that he might be the king's son in law. And Saul gave him Michal his daughter to wife.   2 Sam. 3:14 ◆ *counted number*

28 And Saul saw and knew that the LORD *was* with David, and *that* Michal Saul's daughter loved him.

29 And Saul was yet the more afraid of David; and Saul became David's enemy continually.

30 Then the princes of the Philistines went forth: and it came to pass, after they went forth, *that* David behaved himself more wisely than all the servants of Saul; so that his name was much set by.   1 Sam. 18:5; 2 Sam. 11:1

Saul Plans to Kill David, but Jonathan Intervenes

19 And Saul spake to Jonathan his son, and to all his servants, that they should kill David.   1 Sam. 18:1

2 But Jonathan Saul's son delighted much in David: and Jonathan told David, saying, Saul my father seeketh to kill thee: now therefore, I pray thee, take heed to thyself until the morning, and abide in a secret *place*, and hide thyself:

3 And I will go out and stand beside my father in the field where thou *art*, and I will commune with my father of thee; and what I see, that I will tell thee.   1 Sam. 20:9

4 And Jonathan spake good of David unto Saul his father, and said unto him, Let not the king sin against his servant, against David; because he hath not sinned against thee, and because his works *have been* to thee-ward very good: Gen. 42:22; 1 Sam. 20:32; Jer. 18:20

5 For he did put his life in his hand, and slew the Philistine, and the LORD †wrought a great

salvation for all Israel: thou sawest *it*, and didst rejoice: wherefore then wilt thou sin against innocent blood, to slay David without a cause?   1 Sam. 11:13; 1 Chr. 11:14; Matt. 27:4 ◆ *worked*

6 And Saul hearkened unto the voice of Jonathan: and Saul sware, As the LORD liveth, he shall not be slain.

7 And Jonathan called David, and Jonathan shewed him all those things. And Jonathan brought David to Saul, and he was in his presence, as in times past. 1 Sam. 16:21; 18:2, 13

Saul Tries to Kill David, but Michal Intervenes

8 And there was war again: and David went out, and fought with the Philistines, and slew them with a great slaughter; and they fled from him.

9 And the evil spirit from the LORD was upon Saul, as he sat in his house with his javelin in his hand: and David played with *his* hand.   1 Sam. 16:14; 18:10-11

10 And Saul sought to †smite David even to the wall with the javelin; but he slipped away out of Saul's presence, and he smote the javelin into the wall: and David fled, and escaped that night.   1 Sam. 20:33 ◆ *strike*

11 Saul also sent messengers unto David's house, to watch him, and to slay him in the morning: and Michal David's wife told him, saying, If thou save not thy life to night, to morrow thou shalt be slain.   Judg. 16:2

12 So Michal let David down through a window: and he went, and fled, and escaped.   Josh. 2:15; Acts 9:24-25

13 And Michal took an image, and laid *it* in the bed, and put a pillow of goats' *hair* for his bolster, and covered *it* with a cloth. Gen. 31:19

14 And when Saul sent messengers to take David, she said, He *is* sick.   Josh. 2:5

15 And Saul sent the messengers *again* to see David, saying, Bring him up to me in the bed, that I may slay him.

16 And when the messengers were come in, behold, *there was* an image in the bed, with a pillow of goats' *hair* for his †bolster.   *pillow*

17 And Saul said unto Michal, Why hast thou deceived me so, and sent away mine enemy, that he is escaped? And Michal answered Saul, He said unto me, Let me go; why should I kill thee?   2 Sam. 2:22

David Escapes to Samuel

18 So David fled, and escaped, and came to Samuel to Ramah, and told him all that Saul had done to him. And he and Samuel went and dwelt in Naioth.   1 Sam. 7:17

19 And it was told Saul, saying, Behold, David *is* at Naioth in Ramah.

20 And Saul sent messengers to take David: and when they saw the company of the

prophets prophesying, and Samuel standing *as* appointed over them, the Spirit of God was upon the messengers of Saul, and they also prophesied.   1 Sam. 10:10; Joel 2:28; John 7:32

19:18 David at Samuel's Home

The home of Samuel was a peaceful place in contrast with the royal palace. It was here, amid the hills, that the honored servant of the Lord continued his work. A company of seers was with him, and they studied closely the will of God and listened reverently to the words of instruction that fell from the lips of Samuel. Precious were the lessons that David learned from the teacher of Israel. *PP 653*

21 And when it was told Saul, he sent other messengers, and they prophesied likewise. And Saul sent messengers again the third time, and they prophesied also.
22 Then went he also to Ramah, and came to a great well that *is* in Sechu: and he asked and said, Where *are* Samuel and David? And *one* said, Behold, *they be* at Naioth in Ramah.
23 And he went thither to Naioth in Ramah: and the Spirit of God was upon him also, and he went on, and prophesied, until he came to Naioth in Ramah.   1 Sam. 10:10
24 And he stripped off his clothes also, and prophesied before Samuel in like manner, and lay down naked all that day and all that night. Wherefore they say, *Is* Saul also among the prophets? 2 Sam. 6:20; Is. 20:2; Mic. 1:8

David Makes a Promise to Jonathan

20 And David fled from Naioth in Ramah, and came and said before Jonathan, What have I done? what *is* mine iniquity? and what *is* my sin before thy father, that he seeketh my life?
2 And he said unto him, God forbid; thou shalt not die: behold, my father will do nothing either great or small, but that he will shew it me: and why should my father hide this thing from me? it *is* not *so*.
3 And David sware moreover, and said, Thy father certainly knoweth that I have found grace in thine eyes; and he saith, Let not Jonathan know this, lest he be grieved: but truly *as* the LORD liveth, and *as* thy soul liveth, *there is* but a step between me and death.   Deut. 6:13
4 Then said Jonathan unto David, Whatsoever thy soul desireth, I will even do *it* for thee.
5 And David said unto Jonathan, Behold, to morrow *is* the new moon, and I should not fail to sit with the king at meat: but let me go, that I may hide myself in the field unto the third *day* at even. Num. 10:10; 28:11; 1 Sam. 19:2
6 If thy father at all miss me, then say, David earnestly asked *leave* of me that he might run to Beth-lehem his city: for *there is* a yearly sacrifice there for all the family.   1 Sam. 9:12
7 If he say thus, *It is* well; thy servant shall have peace: but if he be very wroth, *then* be sure that evil is determined by him. Esth. 7:7
8 Therefore thou shalt deal kindly with thy servant; for thou hast brought thy servant into a covenant of the LORD with thee: notwithstanding, if there be in me iniquity, slay me thyself; for why shouldest thou bring me to thy father?   1 Sam. 18:3; 23:18; 2 Sam. 14:32
9 And Jonathan said, Far be it from thee: for if I knew certainly that evil were determined by my father to come upon thee, then would not I tell it thee?

The World's True Nobility

1 Samuel 20

How often those who trusted the word of God, though in themselves utterly helpless, have withstood the power of the whole world—Enoch, pure in heart, holy in life, holding fast his faith in the triumph of righteousness against a corrupt and scoffing generation; Noah and his household against the men of his time, men of the greatest physical and mental strength and the most debased in morals; the children of Israel at the Red Sea, a helpless, terrified multitude of slaves, against the mightiest army of the mightiest nation on the globe; David, a shepherd lad, having God's promise of the throne, against Saul, the established monarch, bent on holding fast his power; Shadrach and his companions in the fire, and Nebuchadnezzar on the throne; Daniel among the lions, his enemies in the high places of the kingdom; Jesus on the cross, and the Jewish priests and rulers forcing even the Roman governor to work their will; Paul in chains led to a criminal's death, Nero the despot of a world empire.

Such examples are not found in the Bible only. They abound in every record of human progress. The Vaudois and the Huguenots, Wycliffe and Huss, Jerome and Luther, Tyndale and Knox, Zinzendorf and Wesley, with multitudes of others, have witnessed to the power of God's word against human power and policy in support of evil. These are the world's true nobility. This is its royal line. In this line the youth of today are called to take their places.

Faith is needed in the smaller no less than in the greater affairs of life. In all our daily interests and occupations the sustaining strength of God becomes real to us through an abiding trust. *Ed 254, 255*

10 Then said David to Jonathan, Who shall tell me? or what *if* thy father answer thee roughly?

11 And Jonathan said unto David, Come, and let us go out into the field. And they went out both of them into the field.

12 And Jonathan said unto David, O LORD God of Israel, when I have sounded my father about to morrow any time, *or* the third *day*, and, behold, *if there be* good toward David, and I then send not unto thee, and shew it thee;

13 The LORD do so and much more to Jonathan: but if it please my father *to do* thee evil, then I will shew it thee, and send thee away, that thou mayest go in peace: and the LORD be with thee, as he hath been with my father.   Josh. 1:5; Ruth 1:17; 1 Sam. 17:37

14 And thou shalt not only while yet I live shew me the kindness of the LORD, that I die not:

15 But *also* thou shalt not cut off thy kindness from my house for ever: no, not when the LORD hath cut off the enemies of David every one from the face of the earth.   2 Sam. 21:7

16 So Jonathan made *a covenant* with the house of David, *saying*, Let the LORD even require *it* at the hand of David's enemies.

17 And Jonathan caused David to swear again, because he loved him: for he loved him as he loved his own soul.   1 Sam. 18:1

18 Then Jonathan said to David, To morrow *is* the new moon: and thou shalt be missed, because thy seat will be empty.   1 Sam. 20:5

19 And *when* thou hast ᵀstayed three days, *then* thou shalt go down quickly, and come to the place where thou didst hide thyself when the business was *in hand*, and shalt remain by the stone Ezel.   1 Sam. 19:2 ◆ *held back*

20 And I will shoot three arrows on the side *thereof*, as though I shot at a mark.

21 And, behold, I will send a lad, *saying*, Go, find out the arrows. If I expressly say unto the lad, Behold, the arrows *are* on this side of thee, take them; then come thou: for *there is* peace to thee, and no hurt; *as* the LORD liveth.

22 But if I say thus unto the young man, Behold, the arrows *are* beyond thee; go thy way: for the LORD hath sent thee away. 1 Sam. 20:37

23 And *as touching* the matter which thou and I have spoken of, behold, the LORD *be* between thee and me for ever.   Gen. 31:50

Saul Seeks to Kill Jonathan out of Anger at David

24 So David hid himself in the field: and when the new moon was come, the king sat him down to eat meat.

25 And the king sat upon his seat, as at other times, *even* upon a seat by the wall: and Jonathan arose, and Abner sat by Saul's side, and David's place was empty.1 Sam. 20:18

26 Nevertheless Saul spake not any thing that day: for he thought, Something hath befallen him, he *is* not clean; surely he *is* not clean.   Lev. 15:5

27 And it came to pass on the morrow, *which was* the second *day* of the month, that David's place was empty: and Saul said unto Jonathan his son, Wherefore cometh not the son of Jesse to meat, neither yesterday, nor to day?

28 And Jonathan answered Saul, David earnestly asked *leave* of me *to go* to Bethlehem: 1 Sam. 20:6

29 And he said, Let me go, I pray thee; for our family hath a sacrifice in the city; and my brother, he hath commanded me *to be there*: and now, if I have found favour in thine eyes, let me get away, I pray thee, and see my brethren. Therefore he cometh not unto the king's table.

30 Then Saul's anger was kindled against Jonathan, and he said unto him, Thou son of the perverse rebellious *woman*, do not I know that thou hast chosen the son of Jesse to thine own confusion, and unto the confusion of thy mother's nakedness? Prov. 21:24

31 For as long as the son of Jesse liveth upon the ground, thou shalt not be established, nor thy kingdom. Wherefore now send and fetch him unto me, for he shall surely die.

32 And Jonathan answered Saul his father, and said unto him, Wherefore shall he be slain? what hath he done?   1 Sam. 19:5

33 And Saul cast a javelin at him to smite him: whereby Jonathan knew that it was determined of his father to slay David.   1 Sam. 18:11

34 So Jonathan arose from the table in fierce anger, and did eat no meat the second day of the month: for he was grieved for David, because his father had done him shame.

Jonathan and David Tearfully Part Ways

35 And it came to pass in the morning, that Jonathan went out into the field at the time appointed with David, and a little lad with him.

36 And he said unto his lad, Run, find out now the arrows which I shoot. *And* as the lad ran, he shot an arrow beyond him.

37 And when the lad was come to the place of the arrow which Jonathan had shot, Jonathan cried after the lad, and said, *Is* not the arrow beyond thee?   1 Sam. 20:22

38 And Jonathan cried after the lad, Make speed, haste, stay not. And Jonathan's lad gathered up the arrows, and came to his master.

39 But the lad knew not any thing: only Jonathan and David knew the matter.

40 And Jonathan gave his artillery unto his lad, and said unto him, Go, carry *them* to the city.

41 *And* as soon as the lad was gone, David arose out of *a place* toward the south, and fell on his face to the ground, and bowed himself three times: and they kissed one another, and wept one with another, until David exceeded.   1 Sam. 18:3

42 And Jonathan said to David, Go in peace, ^Tforasmuch as we have sworn both of us in the name of the LORD, saying, The LORD be between me and thee, and between my seed and thy seed for ever. And he arose and departed: and Jonathan went into the city.   1 Sam. 1:17 ◆ *since*

David at Nob Requisitions the Hallowed Bread

21 Then came David to Nob to Ahimelech the priest: and Ahimelech was afraid at the meeting of David, and said unto him, Why *art* thou alone, and no man with thee?   1 Sam. 16:4; Neh. 11:32; Is. 10:32

2 And David said unto Ahimelech the priest, The king hath commanded me a business, and hath said unto me, Let no man know any thing of the business whereabout I send thee, and what I have commanded thee: and I have appointed *my* servants to such and such a place.

> **21:1, 2 God Always Requires Truthfulness**
>
> Here [David] manifested a want of faith in God, and his sin resulted in causing the death of the high priest. Had the facts been plainly stated, Ahimelech would have known what course to pursue to preserve his life. God requires that truthfulness shall mark His people, even in the greatest peril. *PP 656*

3 Now therefore what is under thine hand? give *me* five *loaves of* bread in mine hand, or what there is present.

4 And the priest answered David, and said, *There is* no common bread under mine hand, but there is hallowed bread; if the young men have kept themselves at least from women.   Ex. 19:15; 25:30; Lev. 24:5-9

5 And David answered the priest, and said unto him, Of a truth women *have been* kept from us about these three days, since I came out, and the vessels of the young men are holy, and *the bread is* in a manner common, yea, though it were ^Tsanctified this day in the vessel.   *made holy*

6 So the priest gave him hallowed *bread:* for there was no bread there but the shewbread, that was taken from before the LORD,

to put hot bread in the day when it was taken away.   Matt. 12:3-4

7 Now a certain man of the servants of Saul *was* there that day, detained before the LORD; and his name *was* Doeg, an Edomite, the chiefest of the herdmen that *belonged* to Saul.   1 Sam. 22:9; 1 Chr. 27:29; Ps. 52

8 And David said unto Ahimelech, And is there not here under thine hand spear or sword? for I have neither brought my sword nor my weapons with me, because the king's business required haste.

9 And the priest said, The sword of Goliath the Philistine, whom thou slewest in the valley of Elah, behold, it *is here* wrapped in a cloth behind the ^Tephod: if thou wilt take that, take *it:* for *there is* no other save that here. And David said, *There is* none like that; give it me.   1 Sam. 17:2 ◆ *priestly garment*

David at Gath Pretends to Be Mad

10 And David arose, and fled that day for fear of Saul, and went to Achish the king of Gath.

> **21:10 The Spirit's Sweet Influence**
>
> [T]his experience was serving to teach David wisdom; for it led him to realize his weakness and the necessity of constant dependence upon God. Oh, how precious is the sweet influence of the Spirit of God as it comes to depressed or despairing souls, encouraging the fainthearted, strengthening the feeble, and imparting courage and help to the tried servants of the Lord! *PP 657*

11 And the servants of Achish said unto him, *Is* not this David the king of the land? did they not sing one to another of him in dances, saying, Saul hath slain his thousands, and David his ten thousands?   1 Sam. 29:5

12 And David laid up these words in his heart, and was sore afraid of Achish the king of Gath.   Luke 2:19

13 And he changed his behaviour before them, and feigned himself mad in their hands, and ^Tscrabbled on the doors of the gate, and let his ^Tspittle fall down upon his beard.   *scratched* ◆ *spit*

14 Then said Achish unto his servants, Lo, ye see the man is mad: wherefore *then* have ye brought him to me?

15 Have I need of mad men, that ye have brought this *fellow* to play the mad man in my presence? shall this *fellow* come into my house?

Many Gather around David as Their Commander

22 David therefore departed thence, and escaped to the cave Adullam: and when his brethren and all his father's

house heard *it*, they went down thither to him.   Josh. 12:15

22:1 God's Appointed Witnesses

In the cave of Adullam the family were united in sympathy and affection. The son of Jesse could make melody with voice and harp as he sang, "Behold, how good and how pleasant it is for brethren to dwell together in unity!" (Psalm 133:1). He had tasted the bitterness of distrust on the part of his own brothers; and the harmony that had taken the place of discord brought joy to the exile's heart. It was here that David composed the fifty-seventh psalm. *PP 658*

---

2 And every one *that was* in distress, and every one that *was* in debt, and every one *that was* discontented, gathered themselves unto him; and he became a captain over them: and there were with him about four hundred men.   Judg. 11:3

3 And David went thence to Mizpeh of Moab: and he said unto the king of Moab, Let my father and my mother, I pray thee, come forth, *and be* with you, till I know what God will do for me.

4 And he brought them before the king of Moab: and they dwelt with him all the while that David was in the hold.

5 And the prophet Gad said unto David, Abide not in the hold; depart, and get thee into the land of Judah. Then David departed, and came into the forest of Hareth. 2 Sam. 24:11

Saul Massacres the Priests at Nob

6 When Saul heard that David was discovered, and the men that *were* with him, (now Saul abode in Gibeah under a tree in Ramah, having his spear in his hand, and all his servants *were* standing about him;)

7 Then Saul said unto his servants that stood about him, Hear now, ye Benjamites; will the son of Jesse give every one of you fields and vineyards, *and* make you all captains of thousands, and captains of hundreds;

8 That all of you have conspired against me, and *there is* none that sheweth me that my son hath made a league with the son of Jesse, and *there is* none of you that is sorry for me, or sheweth unto me that my son hath stirred up my servant against me, to lie in wait, as at this day?   1 Sam. 18:3; 23:21

9 Then answered Doeg the Edomite, which was set over the servants of Saul, and said, I saw the son of Jesse coming to Nob, to Ahimelech the son of Ahitub.   Ps. 52

10 And he enquired of the LORD for him, and gave him Tvictuals, and gave him the sword of Goliath the Philistine.   Num. 27:21 ◆ *food*

11 Then the king sent to call Ahimelech the priest, the son of Ahitub, and all his father's house, the priests that *were* in Nob: and they came all of them to the king.

12 And Saul said, Hear now, thou son of Ahitub. And he answered, Here I *am*, my lord.

13 And Saul said unto him, Why have ye conspired against me, thou and the son of Jesse, in that thou hast given him bread, and a sword, and hast enquired of God for him, that he should rise against me, to lie in wait, as at this day?   1 Sam. 22:8

14 Then Ahimelech answered the king, and said, And who *is so* faithful among all thy servants as David, which is the king's son in law, and goeth at thy bidding, and is honourable in thine house?   1 Sam. 19:4-5

15 Did I then begin to enquire of God for him? be it far from me: let not the king Timpute *any* thing unto his servant, *nor* to all the house of my father: for thy servant knew nothing of all this, less or more.   1 Sam. 25:36 ◆ *count*

16 And the king said, Thou shalt surely die, Ahimelech, thou, and all thy father's house.

22:12–16 David's Lack of Faith

The first error of David was his distrust of God at Nob, and his second mistake was his deception before Achish. David had displayed noble traits of character, and his moral worth had won him favor with the people. . . . But as he had been hunted and persecuted, perplexity and distress had nearly hidden his heavenly Father from his sight. . . .

Every failure on the part of the children of God is due to their lack of faith. *PP 656, 657*

---

17 And the king said unto the footmen that stood about him, Turn, and slay the priests of the LORD; because their hand also *is* with David, and because they knew when he fled, and did not shew it to me. But the servants of the king would not put forth their hand to fall upon the priests of the LORD. Ex. 1:17

18 And the king said to Doeg, Turn thou, and fall upon the priests. And Doeg the Edomite turned, and he fell upon the priests, and slew on that day Tfourscore and five persons that did wear a linen Tephod.   *eighty* ◆ *priestly garment*

22:18, 19 Refusing God's Guidance

This is what Saul could do under the control of Satan. When God had said that the iniquity of the Amalekites was full, and had commanded him to destroy them utterly, he thought himself too compassionate to execute the divine sentence, . . . but now, without a command from God, under the guidance of Satan, he could slay the priests of the Lord. . . . Such is the perversity of the human heart that has refused the guidance of God. *PP 659*

19 And Nob, the city of the priests, smote he with the edge of the sword, both men and women, children and sucklings, and oxen, and asses, and sheep, with the edge of the sword.   1 Sam. 15:3

Abiathar Escapes and Brings News to David

20 And one of the sons of Ahimelech the son of Ahitub, named Abiathar, escaped, and fled after David. 1 Sam. 23:6; 30:7; 1 Kin. 2:26-27

21 And Abiathar shewed David that Saul had slain the LORD's priests.

22 And David said unto Abiathar, I knew *it* that day, when Doeg the Edomite *was* there, that he would surely tell Saul: I have occasioned *the death* of all the persons of thy father's house.

23 Abide thou with me, fear not: for he that seeketh my life seeketh thy life: but with me thou *shalt be* in safeguard.   1 Kin. 2:26

David, at the Word of the Lord, Rescues Keilah

23 Then they told David, saying, Behold, the Philistines fight against Keilah, and they rob the threshingfloors.   Neh. 3:17-18

2 Therefore David enquired of the LORD, saying, Shall I go and smite these Philistines? And the LORD said unto David, Go, and smite the Philistines, and save Keilah.   1 Sam. 23:4

3 And David's men said unto him, Behold, we be afraid here in Judah: how much more then if we come to Keilah against the armies of the Philistines?

4 Then David enquired of the LORD yet again. And the LORD answered him and said, Arise, go down to Keilah; for I will deliver the Philistines into thine hand.   Josh. 8:7; Judg. 7:7

5 So David and his men went to Keilah, and fought with the Philistines, and brought away their cattle, and smote them with a great slaughter. So David saved the inhabitants of Keilah.

6 And it came to pass, when Abiathar the son of Ahimelech fled to David to Keilah, *that* he came down *with* an ᵀephod in his hand.   1 Sam. 22:20 ♦ *priestly garment*

God Helps David Escape Saul at Keilah

7 And it was told Saul that David was come to Keilah. And Saul said, God hath delivered him into mine hand; for he is shut in, by entering into a town that hath gates and bars.

8 And Saul called all the people together to war, to go down to Keilah, to besiege David and his men.

9 And David knew that Saul secretly practised mischief against him; and he said

to Abiathar the priest, Bring ᵀhither the ephod.   Num. 27:21; 1 Sam. 23:6; 30:7 ♦ *here*

10 Then said David, O LORD God of Israel, thy servant hath certainly heard that Saul seeketh to come to Keilah, to destroy the city for my sake.

11 Will the men of Keilah deliver me up into his hand? will Saul come down, as thy servant hath heard? O LORD God of Israel, I ᵀbeseech thee, tell thy servant. And the LORD said, He will come down.   *beg*

12 Then said David, Will the men of Keilah deliver me and my men into the hand of Saul? And the LORD said, They will deliver thee up.   1 Sam. 23:20

13 Then David and his men, *which were* about six hundred, arose and departed out of Keilah, and went whithersoever they could go. And it was told Saul that David was escaped from Keilah; and he forbare to go forth.   1 Sam. 22:2; 25:13; 30:9-10

Jonathan Comforts David in the Wilderness

14 And David abode in the wilderness in strong holds, and remained in a mountain in the wilderness of Ziph. And Saul sought him every day, but God delivered him not into his hand.   Josh. 15:24, 55; Ps. 54:3-4

15 And David saw that Saul was come out to seek his life: and David *was* in the wilderness of Ziph in a wood.

16 And Jonathan Saul's son arose, and went to David into the wood, and strengthened his hand in God.   Neh. 2:18

17 And he said unto him, Fear not: for the hand of Saul my father shall not find thee; and thou shalt be king over Israel, and I shall be next unto thee; and that also Saul my father knoweth.   1 Sam. 20:31; 24:20; Is. 54:17

18 And they two made a covenant before the LORD: and David abode in the wood, and Jonathan went to his house.   1 Sam. 18:3; 2 Sam. 21:7

David in the Wilderness of Maon

19 Then came up the Ziphites to Saul to Gibeah, saying, Doth not David hide himself with us in strong holds in the wood, in the hill of Hachilah, which *is* on the south of Jeshimon?   1 Sam. 26:1, 3; Ps. 54

20 Now therefore, O king, come down according to all the desire of thy soul to come down; and our part *shall be* to deliver him into the king's hand.   1 Sam. 23:12

21 And Saul said, Blessed *be* ye of the LORD; for ye have compassion on me.   1 Sam. 22:8

22 Go, I pray you, prepare yet, and know and see his place where his ᵀhaunt is, *and* who hath seen him there: for it is told me *that* he dealeth very subtilly.   *hideout*

23 See therefore, and take knowledge of all

the lurking places where he hideth himself, and come ye again to me with the certainty, and I will go with you: and it shall come to pass, if he be in the land, that I will search him out throughout all the thousands of Judah.

24 And they arose, and went to Ziph before Saul: but David and his men *were* in the wilderness of Maon, in the plain on the south of Jeshimon.   Josh. 15:55; 1 Sam. 25:2

25 Saul also and his men went to seek *him*. And they told David: wherefore he came down into a rock, and abode in the wilderness of Maon. And when Saul heard *that*, he pursued after David in the wilderness of Maon.

26 And Saul went on this side of the mountain, and David and his men on that side of the mountain: and David made haste to get away for fear of Saul; for Saul and his men ᵀcompassed David and his men round about to take them.   Ps. 17:9 ♦ *surrounded*

27 But there came a messenger unto Saul, saying, Haste thee, and come; for the Philistines have invaded the land.   2 Kin. 19:9

28 Wherefore Saul returned from pursuing after David, and went against the Philistines: therefore they called that place Sela-hammahlekoth.

29 And David went up from thence, and dwelt in strong holds at En-gedi.   2 Chr. 20:2; Song 1:14

David Has a Chance to Kill Saul, but Spares Him

24 And it came to pass, when Saul was returned from following the Philistines, that it was told him, saying, Behold, David *is* in the wilderness of En-gedi.   1 Sam. 23:19, 28-29

2 Then Saul took three thousand chosen men out of all Israel, and went to seek David and his men upon the rocks of the wild goats.   1 Sam. 26:2

3 And he came to the sheepcotes by the way, where *was* a cave; and Saul went in to cover his feet: and David and his men remained in the sides of the cave.   Judg. 3:24; Ps. 57; 142

4 And the men of David said unto him, Behold the day of which the LORD said unto thee, Behold, I will deliver thine enemy into thine hand, that thou mayest do to him as it shall seem good unto thee. Then David arose, and cut off the skirt of Saul's robe ᵀprivily.   *in secret*

5 And it came to pass afterward, that David's heart smote him, because he had cut off Saul's skirt.   2 Sam. 24:10

6 And he said unto his men, The LORD forbid that I should do this thing unto my master, the LORD's anointed, to stretch forth

mine hand against him, seeing he *is* the anointed of the LORD.

7 So David ᵀstayed his servants with these words, and suffered them not to rise against Saul. But Saul rose up out of the cave, and went on *his* way.   Ps. 7:4 ♦ *held back*

8 David also arose afterward, and went out of the cave, and cried after Saul, saying, My lord the king. And when Saul looked behind him, David stooped with his face to the earth, and bowed himself.   1 Sam. 25:23-24

9 And David said to Saul, Wherefore hearest thou men's words, saying, Behold, David seeketh thy hurt?

10 Behold, this day thine eyes have seen how that the LORD had delivered thee to day into mine hand in the cave: and *some* bade *me* kill thee: but *mine eye* spared thee; and I said, I will not put forth mine hand against my lord; for he *is* the LORD's anointed.   1 Sam. 24:4

11 Moreover, my father, see, yea, see the skirt of thy robe in my hand: for in that I cut off the skirt of thy robe, and killed thee not, know thou and see that *there is* neither evil nor ᵀtransgression in mine hand, and I have not sinned against thee; yet thou huntest my soul to take it.   1 Sam. 23:14, 23; 26:20 ♦ *violation of a law*

12 The LORD judge between me and thee, and the LORD avenge me of thee: but mine hand shall not be upon thee.   Gen. 16:5; Judg. 11:27

13 As saith the proverb of the ancients, Wickedness proceedeth from the wicked: but mine hand shall not be upon thee.   Matt. 7:16-18

14 After whom is the king of Israel come out? after whom dost thou pursue? after a dead dog, after a flea.   1 Sam. 17:43; 26:20; 2 Sam. 9:8

15 The LORD therefore be judge, and judge between me and thee, and see, and plead my cause, and deliver me out of thine hand.   1 Sam. 24:12; Ps. 35:1; 43:1

Saul Expresses Sorrow to David and Returns Home

16 And it came to pass, when David had made an end of speaking these words unto Saul, that Saul said, *Is* this thy voice, my son David? And Saul lifted up his voice, and wept.   1 Sam. 26:17

17 And he said to David, Thou *art* more righteous than I: for thou hast rewarded me good, whereas I have rewarded thee evil.   Gen. 38:26; 1 Sam. 26:21; Matt. 5:44

18 And thou hast shewed this day how that thou hast dealt well with me: ᵀforasmuch as when the LORD had delivered me into thine hand, thou killedst me not.   1 Sam. 26:23 ♦ *since*

19 For if a man find his enemy, will he let him go well away? wherefore the LORD reward thee good for that thou hast done unto me this day.

20 And now, behold, I know well that thou

shalt surely be king, and that the kingdom of Israel shall be established in thine hand. *1 Sam. 23:17*

21 Swear now therefore unto me by the LORD, that thou wilt not cut off my seed after me, and that thou wilt not destroy my name out of my father's house. *Gen. 21:23; 2 Sam. 21:6-8*

22 And David sware unto Saul. And Saul went home; but David and his men gat them up unto the hold. *1 Sam. 23:29*

24:22 Assurances Not to Be Trusted

Knowing what he did of Saul's past course, David could put no confidence in the assurances of the king, nor hope that his penitent condition would long continue. So when Saul returned to his home David remained in the strongholds of the mountains. *PP 662*

Samuel Dies

25 And Samuel died; and all the Israelites were gathered together, and lamented him, and buried him in his house at Ramah. And David arose, and went down to the wilderness of Paran. *Num. 20:29; Deut. 34:8; 1 Sam. 28:3*

25:1 A Mistake Realized

As the people contrasted the course of Saul with that of Samuel, they saw what a mistake they had made in desiring a king that they might not be different from the nations around them. Many looked with alarm at the condition of society, fast becoming leavened with irreligion and godlessness. The example of their ruler was exerting a widespread influence, and well might Israel mourn that Samuel, the prophet of the Lord, was dead. *PP 663*

David, Nabal, and Abigail

2 And *there was* a man in Maon, whose possessions *were* in Carmel; and the man *was* very great, and he had three thousand sheep, and a thousand goats: and he was shearing his sheep in Carmel. *Gen. 38:13; Josh. 15:55; 1 Sam. 23:24*

3 Now the name of the man *was* Nabal; and the name of his wife Abigail: and *she was* a woman of good understanding, and of a beautiful ᵀcountenance: but the man *was* ᵀchurlish and evil in his doings; and he *was* of the house of Caleb. *appearance ◆ rude*

4 And David heard in the wilderness that Nabal did shear his sheep.

5 And David sent out ten young men, and David said unto the young men, Get you up to Carmel, and go to Nabal, and greet him in my name:

6 And thus shall ye say to him that liveth *in prosperity*, Peace *be* both to thee, and peace *be* to thine house, and peace *be* unto all that thou hast. *1 Chr. 12:18; Ps. 122:7; Luke 10:5*

7 And now I have heard that thou hast shearers: now thy shepherds which were with us, we hurt them not, neither was there ought missing unto them, all the while they were in Carmel. *1 Sam. 25:21*

8 Ask thy young men, and they will shew thee. Wherefore let the young men find favour in thine eyes: for we come in a good day: give, I pray thee, whatsoever cometh to thine hand unto thy servants, and to thy son David. *Esth. 9:19*

9 And when David's young men came, they spake to Nabal according to all those words in the name of David, and ceased.

10 And Nabal answered David's servants, and said, Who *is* David? and who *is* the son of Jesse? there be many servants now a days that break away every man from his master. *Judg. 9:28*

11 Shall I then take my bread, and my water, and my flesh that I have killed for my shearers, and give *it* unto men, whom I know not whence they *be*? *Judg. 8:6*

12 So David's young men turned their way, and went again, and came and told him all those sayings.

Conviction of Wrongdoing

1 Samuel 24:20

The enmity that is cherished toward the servants of God by those who have yielded to the power of Satan changes at times to a feeling of reconciliation and favor, but the change does not always prove to be lasting. After evil-minded men have engaged in doing and saying wicked things against the Lord's servants, the conviction that they have been in the wrong sometimes takes deep hold upon their minds. The Spirit of the Lord strives with them, and they humble their hearts before God, and before those whose influence they have sought to destroy, and they may change their course toward them. But as they again open the door to the suggestions of the evil one, the old doubts are revived, the old enmity is awakened, and they return to engage in the same work which they repented of, and for a time abandoned. Again they speak evil, accusing and condemning in the bitterest manner the very ones to whom they made most humble confession. Satan can use such souls with far greater power after such a course has been pursued than he could before, because they have sinned against greater light. *PP 662, 663*

13 And David said unto his men, Gird ye on every man his sword. And they girded on every man his sword; and David also girded on his sword: and there went up after David about four hundred men; and two hundred abode by the stuff.   1 Sam. 23:13

14 But one of the young men told Abigail, Nabal's wife, saying, Behold, David sent messengers out of the wilderness to salute our master; and he railed on them.

15 But the men *were* very good unto us, and we were not hurt, neither missed we any thing, as long as we were conversant with them, when we were in the fields: 1 Sam. 25:7, 21

16 They were a wall unto us both by night and day, all the while we were with them keeping the sheep.   Ex. 14:22; Job 1:10

17 Now therefore know and consider what thou wilt do; for evil is determined against our master, and against all his household: for he *is* such a son of Belial, that *a man* cannot speak to him.   1 Sam. 20:7

18 Then Abigail made haste, and took two hundred loaves, and two bottles of wine, and five sheep ready dressed, and five measures of parched *corn*, and an hundred clusters of raisins, and two hundred cakes of figs, and laid *them* on asses.   2 Sam. 16:1

19 And she said unto her servants, Go on before me; behold, I come after you. But she told not her husband Nabal.   Gen. 32:20

20 And it was *so, as* she rode on the ass, that she came down by the ᵀcovert of the hill, and, behold, David and his men came down against her; and she met them.   *hiding place*

21 Now David had said, Surely in vain have I kept all that this *fellow* hath in the wilderness, so that nothing was missed of all that *pertained* unto him: and he hath requited me evil for good.   Prov. 17:13

22 So and more also do God unto the enemies of David, if I leave of all that *pertain* to him by the morning light any that pisseth against the wall.   1 Sam. 3:17

23 And when Abigail saw David, she hasted, and lighted off the ass, and fell before David on her face, and bowed herself to the ground,   1 Sam. 20:41

24 And fell at his feet, and said, Upon me, my lord, *upon* me *let this* iniquity *be*: and let thine handmaid, I pray thee, speak in thine audience, and hear the words of thine handmaid.   2 Sam. 14:9

25 Let not my lord, I pray thee, regard this man of Belial, *even* Nabal: for as his name *is*, so *is* he; Nabal *is* his name, and folly *is* with him: but I thine handmaid saw not the young men of my lord, whom thou didst send.   1 Sam. 25:17

26 Now therefore, my lord, *as* the LORD liveth, and *as* thy soul liveth, seeing the LORD hath withholden thee from coming to *shed* blood, and from avenging thyself with thine own hand, now let thine enemies, and they that seek evil to my lord, be as Nabal.   Gen. 20:6; 2 Sam. 18:32; Heb. 10:30

27 And now this blessing which thine handmaid hath brought unto my lord, let it even be given unto the young men that follow my lord.   Gen. 33:11; 1 Sam. 30:26; 2 Kin. 5:15

28 I pray thee, forgive the ᵀtrespass of thine handmaid: for the LORD will certainly make my lord a sure house; because my lord fighteth the battles of the LORD, and evil hath not been found in thee *all* thy days.   2 Sam. 7:11 ◆ *sin*

29 Yet a man is risen to pursue thee, and to seek thy soul: but the soul of my lord shall be bound in the bundle of life with the LORD thy God; and the souls of thine enemies, them shall he sling out, *as out* of the middle of a sling.   Jer. 10:18

30 And it shall come to pass, when the LORD shall have done to my lord according to all the good that he hath spoken concerning thee, and shall have appointed thee ruler over Israel;   1 Sam. 13:14

31 That this shall be no grief unto thee, nor offence of heart unto my lord, either that thou hast shed blood causeless, or that my lord hath avenged himself: but when the LORD shall have dealt well with my lord, then remember thine handmaid.   Gen. 40:14

25:24–31 Abigail's Piety

These words could have come only from the lips of one who had partaken of the wisdom from above. . . . The Spirit of the Son of God was abiding in her soul. Her speech, seasoned with grace, and full of kindness and peace, shed a heavenly influence. Better impulses came to David, and he trembled as he thought what might have been the consequences of his rash purpose. *PP 667*

Abigail Pacifies David

32 And David said to Abigail, Blessed *be* the LORD God of Israel, which sent thee this day to meet me: Gen. 24:27; Ex. 18:10; Luke 1:68

33 And blessed *be* thy advice, and blessed *be* thou, which hast kept me this day from coming to *shed* blood, and from avenging myself with mine own hand.   1 Sam. 25:26

34 For in very deed, *as* the LORD God of Israel liveth, which hath kept me back from hurting thee, except thou hadst hasted and come to meet me, surely there had not been left unto Nabal by the morning light any that pisseth against the wall.

35 So David received of her hand *that* which she had brought him, and said unto her, Go up in peace to thine house; see, I have

hearkened to thy voice, and have accepted thy person.   Gen. 19:21

Nabal Dies, and David Marries Abigail

36 And Abigail came to Nabal; and, behold, he held a feast in his house, like the feast of a king; and Nabal's heart *was* merry within him, for he *was* very drunken: wherefore she told him nothing, less or more, until the morning light.   1 Sam. 25:19

37 But it came to pass in the morning, when the wine was gone out of Nabal, and his wife had told him these things, that his heart died within him, and he became *as* a stone.

38 And it came to pass about ten days *after*, that the LORD smote Nabal, that he died.   1 Sam. 26:10

39 And when David heard that Nabal was dead, he said, Blessed *be* the LORD, that hath pleaded the cause of my reproach from the hand of Nabal, and hath kept his servant from evil: for the LORD hath returned the wickedness of Nabal upon his own head. And David sent and communed with Abigail, to take her to him to wife.   1 Sam. 25:26

40 And when the servants of David were come to Abigail to Carmel, they spake unto her, saying, David sent us unto thee, to take thee to him to wife.

41 And she arose, and bowed herself on *her* face to the earth, and said, Behold, *let* thine handmaid *be* a servant to wash the feet of the servants of my lord.   Ruth 2:10

42 And Abigail hasted, and arose, and rode upon an ass, with five damsels of hers that went after her; and she went after the messengers of David, and became his wife.   Gen. 24:61-67

43 David also took Ahinoam of Jezreel; and they were also both of them his wives.   Josh. 15:56; 1 Sam. 27:3; 30:5

44 But Saul had given Michal his daughter, David's wife, to Phalti the son of Laish, which *was* of Gallim.   1 Sam. 18:27

Saul's Final Pursuit of David

26 And the Ziphites came unto Saul to Gibeah, saying, Doth not David hide himself in the hill of Hachilah, *which is* before Jeshimon?   1 Sam. 23:19; Ps. 54

2 Then Saul arose, and went down to the wilderness of Ziph, having three thousand chosen men of Israel with him, to seek David in the wilderness of Ziph.   1 Sam. 24:2

3 And Saul pitched in the hill of Hachilah, which *is* before Jeshimon, by the way. But David abode in the wilderness, and he saw that Saul came after him into the wilderness.

4 David therefore sent out spies, and understood that Saul was come in very deed.

5 And David arose, and came to the place where Saul had pitched: and David beheld the place where Saul lay, and Abner the son of Ner, the captain of his host: and Saul lay in the trench, and the people pitched round about him.   1 Sam. 14:50-51; 17:20, 55

6 Then answered David and said to Ahimelech the Hittite, and to Abishai the son of Zeruiah, brother to Joab, saying, Who will go down with me to Saul to the camp? And Abishai said, I will go down with thee.   Judg. 7:10-11

7 So David and Abishai came to the people by night: and, behold, Saul lay sleeping within the trench, and his spear stuck in the ground at his Tbolster: but Abner and the people lay round about him.   pillow

8 Then said Abishai to David, God hath delivered thine enemy into thine hand this day: now therefore let me Tsmite him, I pray thee, with the spear even to the earth at once, and I will not *smite* him the second time.   1 Sam. 24:4 ◆ strike

9 And David said to Abishai, Destroy him not: for who can stretch forth his hand against the LORD's anointed, and be guiltless?   2 Sam. 1:14

10 David said furthermore, *As* the LORD liveth, the LORD shall smite him; or his day shall come to die; or he shall descend into battle, and perish.   Gen. 47:29; Deut. 31:14; 1 Sam. 25:38

11 The LORD forbid that I should stretch forth mine hand against the LORD's anointed: but, I pray thee, take thou now the spear that *is* at his bolster, and the Tcruse of water, and let us go.   1 Sam. 24:6 ◆ pot

12 So David took the spear and the cruse of water from Saul's bolster; and they gat them away, and no man saw *it*, nor knew *it*, neither awaked: for they *were* all asleep; because a deep sleep from the LORD was fallen upon them.   Gen. 2:21; 15:12; Is. 29:10

David Reproves Abner and Pleads with Saul

13 Then David went over to the other side, and stood on the top of an hill afar off; a great space *being* between them:

14 And David cried to the people, and to Abner the son of Ner, saying, Answerest thou not, Abner? Then Abner answered and said, Who *art* thou *that* criest to the king?

15 And David said to Abner, *Art* not thou a *valiant* man? and who *is* like to thee in Israel? wherefore then hast thou not kept thy lord the king? for there came one of the people in to destroy the king thy lord.

16 This thing *is* not good that thou hast done. *As* the LORD liveth, ye *are* worthy to die, because ye have not kept your master, the LORD's anointed. And now see where the king's spear *is*, and the cruse of water that *was* at his bolster.   1 Sam. 20:31

17 And Saul knew David's voice, and said, *Is* this thy voice, my son David? And David said, *It is* my voice, my lord, O king.   1 Sam. 24:16

18 And he said, Wherefore doth my lord thus pursue after his servant? for what have I done? or what evil *is* in mine hand? 1 Sam. 24:9

19 Now therefore, I pray thee, let my lord the king hear the words of his servant. If the LORD have stirred thee up against me, let him accept an offering: but if *they be* the children of men, cursed *be* they before the LORD; for they have driven me out this day from abiding in the inheritance of the LORD, saying, Go, serve other gods.   2 Sam. 14:16

20 Now therefore, let not my blood fall to the earth before the face of the LORD: for the king of Israel is come out to seek a flea, as when one doth hunt a partridge in the mountains.   1 Sam. 24:14

Saul Acknowledges His Sin

21 Then said Saul, I have sinned: return, my son David: for I will no more do thee harm, because my soul was precious in thine eyes this day: behold, I have played the fool, and have erred exceedingly.   Ex. 9:27; 1 Sam. 15:24

26:21 Astonishing Kindness

This second instance of David's respect for his sovereign's life made a still deeper impression upon the mind of Saul and brought from him a more humble acknowledgment of his fault. He was astonished and subdued at the manifestation of such kindness. *PP 671, 672*

---

22 And David answered and said, Behold the king's spear! and let one of the young men come over and fetch it.

23 The LORD render to every man his righteousness and his faithfulness: for the LORD delivered thee into *my* hand to day, but I would not stretch forth mine hand against the LORD's anointed.

24 And, behold, as thy life was much set by this day in mine eyes, so let my life be much set by in the eyes of the LORD, and let him deliver me out of all tribulation.

25 Then Saul said to David, Blessed *be* thou, my son David: thou shalt both do great *things*, and also shalt still prevail. So David went on his way, and Saul returned to his place.   Gen. 32:28

David Escapes into Philistine Territory to Avoid Saul

27 And David said in his heart, I shall now perish one day by the hand of Saul: *there is* nothing better for me than that I should speedily escape into the land of the Philistines; and Saul shall despair of me, to seek me any more in any coast of Israel: so shall I escape out of his hand.

27:1 God's Plans Not Always Clear

Even while Saul was plotting and seeking to accomplish his destruction, the Lord was working to secure David the kingdom. God works out His plans, though to human eyes they are veiled in mystery. Men cannot understand the ways of God; and, looking at appearances, they interpret the trials and tests and provings that God permits to come upon them as things that are against them, and that will only work their ruin. Thus David looked on appearances, and not at the promises of God. *PP 672*

---

2 And David arose, and he passed over with the six hundred men that *were* with him unto Achish, the son of Maoch, king of Gath.   1 Sam. 21:10; 25:13

3 And David dwelt with Achish at Gath, he and his men, every man with his household,

---

David's Unbelief Dishonors God

1 Samuel 27

The Lord did not send David for protection to the Philistines, the most bitter foes of Israel. . . . God had appointed him to set up his standard in the land of Judah, and it was want of faith that led him to forsake his post of duty without a command from the Lord.

God was dishonored by David's unbelief. The Philistines had feared David more than they had feared Saul and his armies; and by placing himself under the protection of the Philistines, David discovered to them the weakness of his own people. Thus he encouraged these relentless foes to oppress Israel. David had been anointed to stand in defense of the people of God; and the Lord would not have His servants give encouragement to the wicked by disclosing the weakness of His people or by an appearance of indifference to their welfare. Furthermore, the impression was received by his brethren that he had gone to the heathen to serve their gods. By this act he gave occasion for misconstruing his motives, and many were led to hold prejudice against him. The very thing that Satan desired to have him do he was led to do; for, in seeking refuge among the Philistines, David caused great exultation to the enemies of God and His people. David did not renounce his worship of God nor cease his devotion to His cause; but he sacrificed his trust in Him to his personal safety, and thus tarnished the upright and faithful character that God requires His servants to possess. *PP 672, 673*

even David with his two wives, Ahinoam the Jezreelitess, and Abigail the Carmelitess, Nabal's wife. 1 Sam. 25:42-43

4 And it was told Saul that David was fled to Gath: and he sought no more again for him.

5 And David said unto Achish, If I have now found grace in thine eyes, let them give me a place in some town in the country, that I may dwell there: for why should thy servant dwell in the royal city with thee?

6 Then Achish gave him Ziklag that day: wherefore Ziklag pertaineth unto the kings of Judah unto this day. Neh. 11:28

7 And the time that David dwelt in the country of the Philistines was a full year and four months. 1 Sam. 29:3

David Pretends to Serve King Achish of the Philistines

8 And David and his men went up, and invaded the Geshurites, and the Gezrites, and the Amalekites: for those *nations were* of old the inhabitants of the land, as thou goest to Shur, even unto the land of Egypt. Josh. 13:2, 13; 1 Sam. 15:7-8

9 And David smote the land, and left neither man nor woman alive, and took away the sheep, and the oxen, and the asses, and the camels, and the apparel, and returned, and came to Achish. 1 Sam. 15:3

10 And Achish said, Whither have ye made a ᵀroad to day? And David said, Against the south of Judah, and against the south of the Jerahmeelites, and against the south of the Kenites. Judg. 1:16; 1 Chr. 2:9, 25 ◆ *raid*

11 And David saved neither man nor woman alive, to bring *tidings* to Gath, saying, Lest they should tell on us, saying, So did David, and so *will be* his manner all the while he dwelleth in the country of the Philistines.

12 And Achish believed David, saying, He hath made his people Israel utterly to ᵀabhor him; therefore he shall be my servant for ever. *despise*

Achish Puts Confidence in David

28 And it came to pass in those days, that the Philistines gathered their armies together for warfare, to fight with Israel. And Achish said unto David, Know thou assuredly, that thou shalt go out with me to battle, thou and thy men.

2 And David said to Achish, Surely thou shalt know what thy servant can do. And Achish said to David, Therefore will I make thee keeper of mine head for ever.

3 Now Samuel was dead, and all Israel had lamented him, and buried him in Ramah, even in his own city. And Saul had put away those that had familiar spirits, and the wizards, out of the land. Lev. 19:31; 20:27; 1 Sam. 25:1

28:3 Sorcery in Secret

Sorcery had been prohibited by the Mosaic law, on pain of death, yet from time to time it had been secretly practiced by apostate Jews. *AA 287*

---

4 And the Philistines gathered themselves together, and came and pitched in Shunem: and Saul gathered all Israel together, and they pitched in Gilboa. Josh. 19:18; 1 Sam. 31:1; 2 Kin. 4:8

5 And when Saul saw the host of the Philistines, he was afraid, and his heart greatly trembled.

6 And when Saul enquired of the LORD, the LORD answered him not, neither by dreams, nor by Urim, nor by prophets. Num. 12:6; 27:21

Saul Seeks for a Witch to Help Him

7 Then said Saul unto his servants, Seek me a woman that hath a familiar spirit, that I may go to her, and enquire of her. And his servants said to him, Behold, *there is* a woman that hath a familiar spirit at En-dor. Josh. 17:11; Ps. 83:10; Acts 16:16

28:7 Evil Angels Still at Work

The magicians of heathen times have their counterpart in the spiritualistic mediums, the clairvoyants, and the fortune-tellers of today. The mystic voices that spoke at Endor and at Ephesus are still by their lying words misleading the children of men. Could the veil be lifted from before our eyes, we should see evil angels employing all their arts to deceive and to destroy. Wherever an influence is exerted to cause men to forget God, there Satan is exercising his bewitching power. *AA 290*

---

8 And Saul disguised himself, and put on other raiment, and he went, and two men with him, and they came to the woman by night: and he said, I pray thee, divine unto me by the familiar spirit, and bring me *him* up, whom I shall name unto thee. 1 Chr. 10:13

9 And the woman said unto him, Behold, thou knowest what Saul hath done, how he hath cut off those that have familiar spirits, and the wizards, out of the land: wherefore then layest thou a snare for my life, to cause me to die? 1 Sam. 28:3

10 And Saul sware to her by the LORD, saying, *As* the LORD liveth, there shall no punishment happen to thee for this thing.

11 Then said the woman, Whom shall I bring up unto thee? And he said, Bring me up Samuel.

12 And when the woman saw Samuel, she cried with a loud voice: and the woman spake to Saul, saying, Why hast thou deceived me? for thou *art* Saul.

13 And the king said unto her, Be not afraid:

for what sawest thou? And the woman said unto Saul, I saw gods ascending out of the earth.

14 And he said unto her, What form *is* he of? And she said, An old man cometh up; and he *is* covered with a ᵀmantle. And Saul perceived that it *was* Samuel, and he stooped with *his* face to the ground, and bowed himself.   1 Sam. 15:27 ◆ *large outside garment*

28:13, 14 An Alliance Against God

Those who set themselves against the government of God have entered into an alliance with the arch-apostate, and he will exercise his power and cunning to captivate the senses and mislead the understanding. He will cause everything to appear in a false light. *PP 635*

Saul Is Told His Fate

15 And Samuel said to Saul, Why hast thou disquieted me, to bring me up? And Saul answered, I am sore distressed; for the Philistines make war against me, and God is departed from me, and answereth me no more, neither by prophets, nor by dreams: therefore I have called thee, that thou mayest make known unto me what I shall do.   1 Sam. 18:12; 28:6

16 Then said Samuel, Wherefore then dost thou ask of me, seeing the LORD is departed from thee, and is become thine enemy?

17 And the LORD hath done to him, as he spake by me: for the LORD hath ᵀrent the kingdom out of thine hand, and given it to thy neighbour, *even* to David: *torn*

18 Because thou obeyedst not the voice of the LORD, nor executedst his fierce wrath upon Amalek, therefore hath the LORD done this thing unto thee this day.   1 Kin. 20:42

19 Moreover the LORD will also deliver Israel with thee into the hand of the Philistines: and to morrow *shalt* thou and thy sons *be* with me: the LORD also shall deliver the host of Israel into the hand of the Philistines.

20 Then Saul fell ᵀstraightway all along on the earth, and was sore afraid, because of the words of Samuel: and there was no strength in him; for he had eaten no bread all the day, nor all the night.   *right away*

21 And the woman came unto Saul, and saw that he was sore troubled, and said unto him, Behold, thine handmaid hath obeyed thy voice, and I have put my life in my hand, and have hearkened unto thy words which thou spakest unto me.   Judg. 12:3; 1 Sam. 19:5; Job 13:14

22 Now therefore, I pray thee, hearken thou also unto the voice of thine handmaid, and

let me set a morsel of bread before thee; and eat, that thou mayest have strength, when thou goest on thy way.

23 But he refused, and said, I will not eat. But his servants, together with the woman, compelled him; and he hearkened unto their voice. So he arose from the earth, and sat upon the bed.   1 Kin. 21:4

24 And the woman had a fat calf in the house; and she hasted, and killed it, and took flour, and kneaded *it*, and did bake unleavened bread thereof: Luke 15:23

25 And she brought *it* before Saul, and before his servants; and they did eat. Then they rose up, and went away that night.

David Marches with the Philistines, but Is Rejected by Their Princes

29 Now the Philistines gathered together all their armies to Aphek: and the Israelites pitched by a fountain which *is* in Jezreel.   Josh. 12:18; 19:30; 1 Sam. 4:1

29:1 David in Perplexity

As the two armies prepared to join battle the son of Jesse found himself in a situation of great perplexity. It was expected that he would fight for the Philistines. . . . Yet he could not for a moment consent to fight against Israel. *PP 690*

2 And the lords of the Philistines passed on by hundreds, and by thousands: but David and his men passed on in the ᵀrereward with Achish.   1 Sam. 28:1-2 ◆ *rear guard*

3 Then said the princes of the Philistines, What *do* these Hebrews *here*? And Achish said unto the princes of the Philistines, *Is* not this David, the servant of Saul the king of Israel, which hath been with me these days, or these years, and I have found no fault in him since he fell *unto me* unto this day?   1 Sam. 27:7; Dan. 6:5

4 And the princes of the Philistines were ᵀwroth with him; and the princes of the Philistines said unto him, Make this fellow return, that he may go again to his place which thou hast appointed him, and let him not go down with us to battle, lest in the battle he be an adversary to us: for wherewith should he reconcile himself unto his master? *should it* not *be* with the heads of these men?   1 Sam. 14:21; 1 Chr. 12:19 ◆ *angered*

5 *Is* not this David, of whom they sang one to another in dances, saying, Saul slew his thousands, and David his ten thousands?

Achish Dismisses David, with Commendations

6 Then Achish called David, and said unto him, Surely, *as* the LORD liveth, thou hast

been upright, and thy going out and thy coming in with me in the host *is* good in my sight: for I have not found evil in thee since the day of thy coming unto me unto this day: nevertheless the lords favour thee not.   2 Sam. 3:25
7 Wherefore now return, and go in peace, that thou displease not the lords of the Philistines.

29:7 David's Misstep

David was caused to feel that he had missed his path. Far better would it have been for him to find refuge in God's strong fortresses of the mountains than with the avowed enemies of Jehovah and His people. But the Lord in His great mercy did not punish this error of His servant . . . for though David, losing his grasp on divine power, had faltered and turned aside from the path of strict integrity, it was still the purpose of his heart to be true to God. *PP 690*

8 And David said unto Achish, But what have I done? and what hast thou found in thy servant so long as I have been with thee unto this day, that I may not go fight against the enemies of my lord the king?
9 And Achish answered and said to David, I know that thou *art* good in my sight, as an angel of God: notwithstanding the princes of the Philistines have said, He shall not go up with us to the battle.   2 Sam. 14:17, 20; 19:27
10 Wherefore now rise up early in the morning with thy master's servants that are come with thee: and as soon as ye be up early in the morning, and have light, depart.   1 Chr. 12:19
11 So David and his men rose up early to depart in the morning, to return into the land of the Philistines. And the Philistines went up to Jezreel.

David Defeats the Amalekites

30 And it came to pass, when David and his men were come to Ziklag on the third day, that the Amalekites had invaded the south, and Ziklag, and smitten Ziklag, and burned it with fire; 1 Sam. 15:7; 27:8-10; 29:11
2 And had taken the women captives, that *were* therein: they slew not any, either great or small, but carried *them* away, and went on their way.   1 Sam. 27:11
3 So David and his men came to the city, and, behold, *it was* burned with fire; and their wives, and their sons, and their daughters, were taken captives.
4 Then David and the people that *were* with him lifted up their voice and wept, until they had no more power to weep.   Num. 14:1
5 And David's two wives were taken captives, Ahinoam the Jezreelitess, and Abigail the wife of Nabal the Carmelite. 1 Sam. 25:42-43

6 And David was greatly distressed; for the people spake of stoning him, because the soul of all the people was grieved, every man for his sons and for his daughters: but David encouraged himself in the LORD his God.   Ex. 17:4; Num. 14:10; Ps. 56:3-4

30:6 David Seeks God's Help

David seemed to be cut off from every human support. . . . Saul had driven him from his country; the Philistines had driven him from the camp; the Amalekites had plundered his city; his wives and children had been made prisoners; and his own familiar friends had banded against him, and threatened him even with death. In this hour of utmost extremity David, instead of permitting his mind to dwell upon these painful circumstances, looked earnestly to God for help. *PP 692*

7 And David said to Abiathar the priest, Ahimelech's son, I pray thee, bring me ᵀhither the ᵀephod. And Abiathar brought thither the ephod to David. 1 Sam. 22:20-21 ◆ here ◆ priestly garment
8 And David enquired at the LORD, saying, Shall I pursue after this troop? shall I overtake them? And he answered him, Pursue: for thou shalt surely overtake *them,* and without fail recover *all.*   1 Sam. 23:2
9 So David went, he and the six hundred men that *were* with him, and came to the brook Besor, where those that were left behind stayed.
10 But David pursued, he and four hundred men: for two hundred abode behind, which were so faint that they could not go over the brook Besor.   1 Sam. 30:21
11 And they found an Egyptian in the field, and brought him to David, and gave him bread, and he did eat; and they made him drink water;
12 And they gave him a piece of a cake of figs, and two clusters of raisins: and when he had eaten, his spirit came again to him: for he had eaten no bread, nor drunk *any* water, three days and three nights.   Judg. 15:19; 1 Sam. 14:27
13 And David said unto him, To whom *belongest* thou? and whence *art* thou? And he said, I *am* a young man of Egypt, servant to an Amalekite; and my master left me, because three days ᵀagone I fell sick.   past
14 We made an invasion *upon* the south of the Cherethites, and upon *the coast* which *belongeth* to Judah, and upon the south of Caleb; and we burned Ziklag with fire.   1 Kin. 1:38, 44
15 And David said to him, Canst thou bring me down to this company? And he said, Swear unto me by God, that thou wilt neither kill me, nor deliver me into the hands of my master, and I will bring thee down to this company.

16 And when he had brought him down, behold, *they were* spread abroad upon all the earth, eating and drinking, and dancing, because of all the great ᵀspoil that they had taken out of the land of the Philistines, and out of the land of Judah.   *plunder*
17 And David smote them from the twilight even unto the evening of the next day: and there escaped not a man of them, save four hundred young men, which rode upon camels, and fled.   1 Sam. 11:11
18 And David recovered all that the Amalekites had carried away: and David rescued his two wives.
19 And there was nothing lacking to them, neither small nor great, neither sons nor daughters, neither spoil, nor any *thing* that they had taken to them: David recovered all.   1 Sam. 30:8

> ### 30:18, 19 God's Ever-Active Power
> God's power is constantly exercised to counteract the agencies of evil; He is ever at work among men, not for their destruction, but for their correction and preservation. *PP 694*

20 And David took all the flocks and the herds, *which* they ᵀdrave before those *other* cattle, and said, This *is* David's spoil. ◆ *drove*
21 And David came to the two hundred men, which were so faint that they could not follow David, whom they had made also to abide at the brook Besor: and they went forth to meet David, and to meet the people that *were* with him: and when David came near to the people, he saluted them.   1 Sam. 30:10
22 Then answered all the wicked men and *men* of Belial, of those that went with David, and said, Because they went not with us, we will not give them *ought* of the spoil that we have recovered, save to every man his wife and his children, that they may lead *them* away, and depart.

23 Then said David, Ye shall not do so, my brethren, with that which the Lᴏʀᴅ hath given us, who hath preserved us, and delivered the company that came against us into our hand.
24 For who will hearken unto you in this matter? but as his part *is* that goeth down to the battle, so *shall* his part *be* that tarrieth by the stuff: they shall part alike.   Num. 31:27; Josh. 22:8
25 And it was *so* from that day forward, that he made it a statute and an ordinance for Israel unto this day.
26 And when David came to Ziklag, he sent of the spoil unto the elders of Judah, *even* to his friends, saying, Behold a present for you of the spoil of the enemies of the Lᴏʀᴅ;   1 Sam. 25:27
27 To *them* which *were* in Beth-el, and to *them* which *were* in south Ramoth, and to *them* which *were* in Jattir,   Gen. 28:19; Josh. 15:48; 19:8
28 And to *them* which *were* in Aroer, and to *them* which *were* in Siphmoth, and to *them* which *were* in Eshtemoa,   Josh. 13:16; 15:50
29 And to *them* which *were* in Rachal, and to *them* which *were* in the cities of the Jerahmeelites, and to *them* which *were* in the cities of the Kenites,   Judg. 1:16; 1 Sam. 27:10
30 And to *them* which *were* in Hormah, and to *them* which *were* in Chorashan, and to *them* which *were* in Athach,   Josh. 19:4; Judg. 1:17
31 And to *them* which *were* in Hebron, and to all the places where David himself and his men were wont to ᵀhaunt.   2 Sam. 2:1 ◆ *inhabit*

The Deaths of Saul and Jonathan

31 Now the Philistines fought against Israel: and the men of Israel fled from before the Philistines, and fell down slain in mount Gilboa. 1 Sam. 28:4; 2 Sam. 1:21; 1 Chr. 10:1-12
2 And the Philistines followed hard upon Saul and upon his sons; and the Philis-

> ## Greatest Battle Ever Fought
>
> ### 1 Samuel 31
>
> God desires to heal us, to set us free. But since this requires an entire transformation, a renewing of our whole nature, we must yield ourselves wholly to Him.
>
> The warfare against self is the greatest battle that was ever fought. The yielding of self, surrendering all to the will of God, requires a struggle; but the soul must submit to God before it can be renewed in holiness.
>
> The government of God is not, as Satan would make it appear, founded upon a blind submission, an unreasoning control. It appeals to the intellect and the conscience. . . . God does not force the will of His creatures. He cannot accept an homage that is not willingly and intelligently given. A mere forced submission would prevent all real development of mind or character; it would make man a mere automaton. Such is not the purpose of the Creator. He desires that man, the crowning work of His creative power, shall reach the highest possible development. He sets before us the height of blessing to which He desires to bring us through His grace. He invites us to give ourselves to Him, that He may work His will in us. It remains for us to choose whether we will be set free from the bondage of sin, to share the glorious liberty of the sons of God. *SC 43, 44*

tines slew Jonathan, and Abinadab, and Mal-
chishua, Saul's sons.   1 Chr. 8:33

3 And the battle went sore against Saul,
and the archers hit him; and he was sore
wounded of the archers.   2 Sam. 1:6

4 Then said Saul unto his armourbearer,
Draw thy sword, and thrust me through
therewith; lest these uncircumcised come
and thrust me through, and abuse me. But
his armourbearer would not; for he was sore
afraid. Therefore Saul took a sword, and fell
upon it.   Judg. 9:54; 1 Sam. 14:6; 17:26

31:4 A Failed Life

Thus the first king of Israel perished, with
the guilt of self-murder upon his soul. His
life had been a failure, and he went down in
dishonor and despair, because he had set up
his own perverse will against the will of God.
PP 682

5 And when his armourbearer saw that Saul
was dead, he fell likewise upon his sword,
and died with him.

6 So Saul died, and his three sons, and his
armourbearer, and all his men, that same
day together.

7 And when the men of Israel that *were* on
the other side of the valley, and *they* that
were on the other side Jordan, saw that the
men of Israel fled, and that Saul and his
sons were dead, they forsook the cities, and
fled; and the Philistines came and dwelt in
them.

The Philistines Triumph over Israel

8 And it came to pass on the morrow, when
the Philistines came to strip the slain, that
they found Saul and his three sons fallen in
mount Gilboa.

9 And they cut off his head, and stripped
off his armour, and sent into the land of
the Philistines round about, to publish *it*
in the house of their idols, and among the
people.   Judg. 16:23-24; 2 Sam. 1:20

10 And they put his armour in the house of
Ashtaroth: and they fastened his body to the
wall of Beth-shan. Josh. 17:11; Judg. 2:13; 1 Sam. 21:9

11 And when the inhabitants of Jabesh-
gilead heard of that which the Philistines
had done to Saul;

12 All the valiant men arose, and went all
night, and took the body of Saul and the
bodies of his sons from the wall of Beth-
shan, and came to Jabesh, and burnt them
there.   2 Sam. 2:4-7; 2 Chr. 16:14; Jer. 34:5

13 And they took their bones, and buried
them under a tree at Jabesh, and fasted seven
days.   Gen. 50:10

31:13 Legacy of a Noble Deed

[T]he noble deed performed forty years before, secured for Saul and his sons burial by
tender and pitying hands in that dark hour of
defeat and dishonor. *PP 682*

THE SECOND BOOK OF

SAMUEL

Second Samuel continues the story where 1 Samuel ended, and this book begins on a note of transition. King Saul and David's friend Jonathan are dead, and David weeps for them. David becomes king of Judah first, then of both Judah and Israel. But the young man who defeated Goliath soon realizes there is more to ruling a kingdom than simply sitting on a throne. Temptation leads David into sinful deeds, and he pays for it dearly.

Still, David remains a man after God's own heart and repents of his sins. The greatness he might have had would not be fully manifest until his son Solomon takes the throne. Through it all, David is faithful to God and is the model for all kings that follow him.

Dates

Second Samuel begins with David's reign in Hebron over the territory of Judah (1011 B.C. to 1004 B.C.) and extends to the end of his reign over both Judah and Israel (1004 B.C. to 971 B.C.).

Author

Samuel was dead before the chronicling of 2 Samuel (1 Samuel 25:1). Jewish tradition maintains that the author was likely a composite of the prophets Gad and Nathan, (1 Chronicles 29:29), who completed 1 Samuel as well as the ensuing 2 Samuel. In all Hebrew manuscripts before A.D. 1517, 1 and 2 Samuel existed as one book. Upon its division, Samuel was applied to both sections even though his name does not appear in the second book.

Meaning of the Name

As noted in the introduction for 1 Samuel, Samuel can be translated as "Asked of God," "His Name is God," "Heard of God," and "The Name of God." The Hebrew title for both books is simply Samuel. In the Greek, the title is *Basileion Beta* or "Second Kingdoms."

Christ in 2 Samuel

David is the most prominent Christ figure in the Old Testament. Not only was he a member of Jesus' family line (Matthew 1:1), he was a shepherd, king, and a man after God's heart (1 Samuel 13:14). Jesus was all three as well. When David becomes king of Israel, he sits on the throne of Melchizedek, the priest-king (see Genesis 14:18) in Jerusalem. Jesus is a priest after the order of Melchizedek (Psalm 110:4) and will sit on the throne of David in Jerusalem (Isaiah 9:7; Luke 1:32).

God promises David a kingdom that will last forever (2 Samuel 7:4–17), the same promise made about Jesus (Luke 1:32, 33). Jesus is called the "seed of David" (Romans 1:3); it is clear God's promises to David were fulfilled with Jesus.

Overview

David's story began in 1 Samuel 16 and ends in 1 Kings 2. The Book of 2 Samuel records the story of most of David's forty-year reign in three thematic phases:

2 Samuel 1—10, The triumphs of David: With God's help, David defeats the Philistines and transports the ark of the testimony to Jerusalem. David also conquers the fortress of Jerusalem (5:6–9). The promise of the anointing (1 Samuel 16) is finally fulfilled as David takes the throne, first of Judah, then all of Israel (2 Samuel 2; 5). David deals justly with all people, even going so far as to bring Saul's last grandson into his house and treat him as one of his own sons (chapter 9).

2 Samuel 11—12, The transgressions of David: A turning point in David's life occurs with his connection to Bath-sheba, the wife of Uriah the Hittite. David takes her for his own, then commands that Uriah be sent into battle at the front, where he is sure to die. When Uriah falls, David takes the pregnant Bath-sheba for his wife. God is displeased with David's sinful acts and sends the prophet Nathan to confront David (chapter 12). The child that Bath-sheba bears dies, much to David's sorrow.

2 Samuel 13—24, The troubles of David: As the prophet Nathan predicts, the sword never departs from David's house (see 12:10). David's family becomes more and more contentious, doing sinful deeds (chapter 13), until his son Absalom gains the loyalty of Israel and forces David and his followers to flee Jerusalem (chapter 15). Absalom comes against his father's forces in battle and dies, increasing David's sorrow even more (chapter 18). The kingdoms of Israel and Judah split in their loyalties, with only Judah choosing David to remain their king. The rebellion, however, is squelched (chapters 19—20). In the last few chapters—the latter years of David's life—David praises God, counts his army, and, to end a regretful census, builds an altar on the threshing floor of Araunah. Solomon will succeed David and build God's temple.

Unlocking 2 Samuel

KEY PEOPLE:
David, Joab, Bath-sheba, Uriah the Hittite, Absalom

KEY EVENTS:
David becomes king of Judah; David's conquests of his enemies; David becomes king of Israel; David and Bath-sheba's sin; David's repentance; Absalom's rebellion and death; the census that ends in the deaths of 70,000 people

KEY WORD:
David is the star of 2 Samuel. David loved God, but was not perfect. As with Saul and so many before and after him, David's disobedience brought him punishment, but his repentance and sorrow over his sin made him a man after God's own heart.

KEY VERSES:
"And when thy days be fulfilled, and thou shalt sleep with thy fathers, I will set up thy seed after thee, which shall proceed out of thy bowels, and I will establish his kingdom. He shall build an house for my name, and I will stablish the throne of his kingdom for ever" (2 Samuel 7:12, 13).

KEY CHAPTER:
2 Samuel 11 is the major turning point of the book. Up to this point, David was victorious. But a false step with Bath-sheba caused David to fall. Although David was forgiven (chapter 12), the consequences of his sin lasted throughout his life.

News of Saul's Overthrow Is Brought to David

1 Now it came to pass after the death of Saul, when David was returned from the slaughter of the Amalekites, and David had abode two days in Ziklag;

2 It came even to pass on the third day, that, behold, a man came out of the camp from Saul with his clothes rent, and earth upon his head: and so it was, when he came to David, that he fell to the earth, and did ᵀobeisance.   Josh. 7:6; 1 Sam. 4:12 ♦ homage

3 And David said unto him, From whence comest thou? And he said unto him, Out of the camp of Israel am I escaped.

4 And David said unto him, How went the matter? I pray thee, tell me. And he answered, That the people are fled from the battle, and many of the people also are fallen and dead; and Saul and Jonathan his son are dead also.   1 Sam. 4:16

5 And David said unto the young man that told him, How knowest thou that Saul and Jonathan his son be dead?

6 And the young man that told him said, As I happened by chance upon mount Gilboa, behold, Saul leaned upon his spear; and, lo, the chariots and horsemen followed hard after him.   1 Sam. 28:4

7 And when he looked behind him, he saw me, and called unto me. And I answered, Here am I.

8 And he said unto me, Who art thou? And I answered him, I am an Amalekite. 1 Sam. 30:13

9 He said unto me again, Stand, I pray thee, upon me, and slay me: for anguish is come upon me, because my life is yet whole in me.

10 So I stood upon him, and slew him, because I was sure that he could not live after that he was fallen: and I took the crown that was upon his head, and the bracelet that was on his arm, and have brought them ᵀhither unto my lord.   Judg. 9:54 ♦ here

11 Then David took hold on his clothes, and ᵀrent them; and likewise all the men that were with him: Gen. 37:29 ♦ tore

12 And they mourned, and wept, and fasted until even, for Saul, and for Jonathan his son, and for the people of the LORD, and for the house of Israel; because they were fallen by the sword.

1:11, 12 A Generous and Noble Spirit

David's grief at the death of Saul was sincere and deep, evincing the generosity of a noble nature. He did not exult in the fall of his enemy. The obstacle that had barred his access to the throne of Israel was removed, but at this he did not rejoice. Death had obliterated the remembrance of Saul's distrust and cruelty, and now nothing in his history was thought of but that which was noble and kingly. PP 695, 696

---

13 And David said unto the young man that told him, Whence art thou? And he answered, I am the son of a stranger, an Amalekite.

14 And David said unto him, How wast thou not afraid to stretch forth thine hand to destroy the LORD's anointed? 1 Sam. 24:6; 26:9; 31:4

15 And David called one of the young men, and said, Go near, and fall upon him. And he smote him that he died.

16 And David said unto him, Thy blood be upon thy head; for thy mouth hath testified against thee, saying, I have slain the LORD's anointed.   Matt. 27:25

David Laments Saul and Jonathan with a Song

17 And David lamented with this lamentation over Saul and over Jonathan his son:

18 (Also he bade them teach the children of Judah the use of the bow: behold, it is written in the book of Jasher.)   Josh. 10:13

1:17, 18 A Treasured Song

The song in which David gave utterance to the feelings of his heart became a treasure to his nation, and to the people of God in all subsequent ages. PP 696

---

19 The beauty of Israel is slain upon thy high places: how are the mighty fallen! 2 Sam. 1:25, 27

20 Tell it not in Gath, publish it not in the streets of Askelon; lest the daughters of the Philistines rejoice, lest the daughters of the uncircumcised triumph.   Ex. 15:20-21; Mic. 1:10

21 Ye mountains of Gilboa, let there be no dew, neither let there be rain, upon you, nor fields of offerings: for there the shield of the mighty is vilely cast away, the shield of Saul, as though he had not been anointed with oil.   1 Sam. 10:1; 31:1; Is. 21:5

22 From the blood of the slain, from the fat of the mighty, the bow of Jonathan turned not back, and the sword of Saul returned not empty.   1 Sam. 18:4; Is. 34:6-7

23 Saul and Jonathan were lovely and pleasant in their lives, and in their death they were not divided: they were swifter than eagles, they were stronger than lions.   Deut. 28:49; Jer. 4:13

24 Ye daughters of Israel, weep over Saul, who clothed you in scarlet, with other delights, who put on ornaments of gold upon your apparel.

25 How are the mighty fallen in the midst of the battle! O Jonathan, thou wast slain in thine high places.   2 Sam. 1:19

26 I am distressed for thee, my brother Jonathan: very pleasant hast thou been unto me: thy love to me was wonderful, passing the love of women.   1 Sam. 18:1-4

27 How are the mighty fallen, and the weapons of war perished!   2 Sam. 1:19, 25

David Goes to Hebron, Where He Is Made King of Judah

2 And it came to pass after this, that David enquired of the LORD, saying, Shall I go up into any of the cities of Judah? And the LORD said unto him, Go up. And David said, Whither shall I go up? And he said, Unto Hebron.   1 Sam. 23:2

2 So David went up thither, and his two wives also, Ahinoam the Jezreelitess, and Abigail Nabal's wife the Carmelite.   1 Sam. 25:42-43; 30:5

3 And his men that *were* with him did David bring up, every man with his household: and they dwelt in the cities of Hebron. 1 Sam. 27:2-3

4 And the men of Judah came, and there they anointed David king over the house of Judah. And they told David, saying, *That* the men of Jabesh-gilead *were they* that buried Saul.   1 Sam. 31:11-13; 2 Sam. 5:3, 5

5 And David sent messengers unto the men of Jabesh-gilead, and said unto them, Blessed *be* ye of the LORD, that ye have shewed this kindness unto your lord, *even* unto Saul, and have buried him.   1 Sam. 23:21

2:5–7 Brave Deeds Honored

Upon learning of the brave deed of the men of Jabesh-gilead in rescuing the bodies of the fallen leaders and giving them honorable burial, David sent an embassy to Jabesh with the message [of 2 Samuel 2:5, 6]. And he announced his own accession to the throne of Judah and invited the allegiance of those who had proved themselves so true-hearted. *PP 697, 698*

6 And now the LORD shew kindness and truth unto you: and I also will ᵀrequite you this kindness, because ye have done this thing.   *repay*

7 Therefore now let your hands be strengthened, and be ye valiant: for your master Saul is dead, and also the house of Judah have anointed me king over them.

Abner Makes Ish-bosheth King of Israel

8 But Abner the son of Ner, captain of Saul's host, took Ish-bosheth the son of Saul, and brought him over to Mahanaim;   Gen. 32:2

2:8 Selfish Plans and Purposes

[Abner] employed the representative of departed royalty to advance his own selfish ambitions and purposes. He knew that the people loved Jonathan. His memory was cherished, and Saul's first successful campaigns had not been forgotten by the army. With determination worthy of a better cause, this rebellious leader went forward to carry out his plans. *PP 699*

9 And made him king over Gilead, and over the Ashurites, and over Jezreel, and over Ephraim, and over Benjamin, and over all Israel.

10 Ish-bosheth Saul's son *was* forty years old when he began to reign over Israel, and reigned two years. But the house of Judah followed David.

11 And the time that David was king in Hebron over the house of Judah was seven years and six months.   1 Kin. 2:11

12 And Abner the son of Ner, and the servants of Ish-bosheth the son of Saul, went out from Mahanaim to Gibeon.   Josh. 18:25

13 And Joab the son of Zeruiah, and the servants of David, went out, and met together by the pool of Gibeon: and they sat down, the one on the one side of the pool, and the other on the other side of the pool. 2 Sam. 8:16

14 And Abner said to Joab, Let the young men now arise, and play before us. And Joab said, Let them arise.   2 Sam. 2:17

15 Then there arose and went over by number twelve of Benjamin, which *pertained* to Ish-bosheth the son of Saul, and twelve of the servants of David.

Disunity in the Kingdom

2 Samuel 2

But David's reign was not to be free from trouble. With his coronation began the dark record of conspiracy and rebellion. David did not sit upon a traitor's throne; God had chosen him to be king of Israel, and there had been no occasion for distrust or opposition. Yet hardly had his authority been acknowledged by the men of Judah, when through the influence of Abner, Ish-bosheth, the son of Saul, was proclaimed king, and set upon a rival throne in Israel.

Ish-bosheth was but a weak and incompetent representative of the house of Saul, while David was pre-eminently qualified to bear the responsibilities of the kingdom. Abner, the chief agent in raising Ish-bosheth to kingly power, had been commander-in-chief of Saul's army, and was the most distinguished man in Israel. Abner knew that David had been appointed by the Lord to the throne of Israel, but having so long hunted and pursued him, he was not now willing that the son of Jesse should succeed to the kingdom over which Saul had reigned. *PP 698*

16 And they caught every one his fellow by the head, and *thrust* his sword in his fellow's side; so they fell down together: wherefore that place was called Helkath-hazzurim, which *is* in Gibeon.

17 And there was a very sore battle that day; and Abner was beaten, and the men of Israel, before the servants of David.   2 Sam. 3:1

Conflicts between Abner and Joab

18 And there were three sons of Zeruiah there, Joab, and Abishai, and Asahel: and Asahel *was as* light of foot as a wild roe. Hab. 3:19

19 And Asahel pursued after Abner; and in going he turned not to the right hand nor to the left from following Abner.

20 Then Abner looked behind him, and said, *Art* thou Asahel? And he answered, I *am.*

21 And Abner said to him, Turn thee aside to thy right hand or to thy left, and lay thee hold on one of the young men, and take thee his armour. But Asahel would not turn aside from following of him.

22 And Abner said again to Asahel, Turn thee aside from following me: wherefore should I ᵀsmite thee to the ground? how then should I hold up my face to Joab thy brother?   2 Sam. 3:27 ♦ *strike*

23 Howbeit he refused to turn aside: wherefore Abner with the hinder end of the spear smote him under the fifth *rib*, that the spear came out behind him; and he fell down there, and died in the same place: and it came to pass, *that* as many as came to the place where Asahel fell down and died stood still.   2 Sam. 3:27

24 Joab also and Abishai pursued after Abner: and the sun went down when they were come to the hill of Ammah, that *lieth* before Giah by the way of the wilderness of Gibeon.

Abner Entreats Joab to End the Slaughter

25 And the children of Benjamin gathered themselves together after Abner, and became one troop, and stood on the top of an hill.

26 Then Abner called to Joab, and said, Shall the sword devour for ever? knowest thou not that it will be bitterness in the latter end? how long shall it be then, ᵀere thou bid the people return from following their brethren?   Jer. 46:10 ♦ *before*

27 And Joab said, *As* God liveth, unless thou hadst spoken, surely then in the morning the people had gone up every one from following his brother.   2 Sam. 2:14

28 So Joab blew a trumpet, and all the people stood still, and pursued after Israel no more, neither fought they any more.

29 And Abner and his men walked all that night through the plain, and passed over Jordan, and went through all Bithron, and they came to Mahanaim.   2 Sam. 2:8

30 And Joab returned from following Abner: and when he had gathered all the people together, there lacked of David's servants nineteen men and Asahel.

31 But the servants of David had smitten of Benjamin, and of Abner's men, *so that* three hundred and ᵀthreescore men died.   *sixty*

32 And they took up Asahel, and buried him in the sepulchre of his father, which *was in* Beth-lehem. And Joab and his men went all night, and they came to Hebron at break of day.

During the War David Still Waxes Stronger

3 Now there was long war between the house of Saul and the house of David: but David ᵀwaxed stronger and stronger, and the house of Saul waxed weaker and weaker.   1 Kin. 14:30 ♦ *became*

2 And unto David were sons born in Hebron: and his firstborn was Amnon, of Ahinoam the Jezreelitess;   1 Chr. 3:1-4

3 And his second, Chileab, of Abigail the wife of Nabal the Carmelite; and the third, Absalom the son of Maacah the daughter of Talmai king of Geshur;   1 Sam. 25:42; 27:8; 2 Sam. 13:37-38

4 And the fourth, Adonijah the son of Haggith; and the fifth, Shephatiah the son of Abital;

5 And the sixth, Ithream, by Eglah David's wife. These were born to David in Hebron.

6 And it came to pass, while there was war between the house of Saul and the house of David, that Abner made himself strong for the house of Saul.   2 Sam. 2:8-9

7 And Saul had a concubine, whose name *was* Rizpah, the daughter of Aiah: and *Ish-bosheth* said to Abner, Wherefore hast thou gone in unto my father's concubine?   2 Sam. 21:8-11

8 Then was Abner very ᵀwroth for the words of Ish-bosheth, and said, *Am* I a dog's head, which against Judah do shew kindness this day unto the house of Saul thy father, to his brethren, and to his friends, and have not delivered thee into the hand of David, that thou chargest me to day with a fault concerning this woman?   2 Sam. 9:8 ♦ *angry*

9 So do God to Abner, and more also, except, as the LORD hath sworn to David, even so I do to him;   Ruth 1:17; 1 Kin. 19:2

10 To translate the kingdom from the house of Saul, and to set up the throne of David over Israel and over Judah, from Dan even to Beer-sheba.   Judg. 20:1; 1 Sam. 15:28

11 And he could not answer Abner a word again, because he feared him.

12 And Abner sent messengers to David on his behalf, saying, Whose *is* the land? saying *also*, Make thy league with me, and, behold, my hand *shall be* with thee, to bring about all Israel unto thee.

13 And he said, Well; I will make a league with thee: but one thing I require of thee, that is, Thou shalt not see my face, except thou first bring Michal Saul's daughter, when thou comest to see my face.   Gen. 43:3

3:12, 13 A Rival Throne Overthrown

At last treachery overthrew the throne that malice and ambition had established. Abner, becoming incensed against the weak and incompetent Ish-bosheth, deserted to David, with the offer to bring over to him all the tribes of Israel. His proposals were accepted by the king, and he was dismissed with honor to accomplish his purpose. *PP 699*

14 And David sent messengers to Ish-bosheth Saul's son, saying, Deliver *me* my wife Michal, which I espoused to me for an hundred foreskins of the Philistines.   1 Sam. 18:25, 27

15 And Ish-bosheth sent, and took her from *her* husband, *even* from Phaltiel the son of Laish.   1 Sam. 25:44

16 And her husband went with her along weeping behind her to Bahurim. Then said Abner unto him, Go, return. And he returned.   2 Sam. 16:5; 17:18; 19:16

17 And Abner had communication with the elders of Israel, saying, Ye sought for David in times past *to be* king over you:

18 Now then do *it*: for the LORD hath spoken of David, saying, By the hand of my servant David I will save my people Israel out of the hand of the Philistines, and out of the hand of all their enemies.   1 Sam. 15:28

19 And Abner also spake in the ears of Benjamin: and Abner went also to speak in the ears of David in Hebron all that seemed good to Israel, and that seemed good to the whole house of Benjamin.   1 Sam. 10:20-21; 1 Chr. 12:29

20 So Abner came to David to Hebron, and twenty men with him. And David made Abner and the men that *were* with him a feast.

21 And Abner said unto David, I will arise and go, and will gather all Israel unto my lord the king, that they may make a league with thee, and that thou mayest reign over all that thine heart desireth. And David sent Abner away; and he went in peace.   1 Kin. 11:37

Joab Is Displeased with David and Kills Abner Himself

22 And, behold, the servants of David and Joab came from *pursuing* a troop, and brought in a great ᵀspoil with them: but Abner *was* not with David in Hebron; for he had sent him away, and he was gone in peace.   *plunder*

23 When Joab and all the host that *was* with him were come, they told Joab, saying, Abner the son of Ner came to the king, and he hath sent him away, and he is gone in peace.

24 Then Joab came to the king, and said, What hast thou done? behold, Abner came unto thee; why *is* it *that* thou hast sent him away, and he is quite gone?

25 Thou knowest Abner the son of Ner, that he came to deceive thee, and to know thy going out and thy coming in, and to know all that thou doest.   Deut. 28:6

26 And when Joab was come out from David, he sent messengers after Abner, which brought him again from the well of Sirah: but David knew *it* not.

27 And when Abner was returned to Hebron, Joab took him aside in the gate to speak with him quietly, and smote him there under the fifth *rib*, that he died, for the blood of Asahel his brother. 2 Sam. 20:9-10; 1 Kin. 2:5, 32

28 And afterward when David heard *it*, he said, I and my kingdom *are* guiltless before the LORD for ever from the blood of Abner the son of Ner:

29 Let it rest on the head of Joab, and on all his father's house; and let there not fail from the house of Joab one that hath an issue, or that is a leper, or that leaneth on a staff, or that falleth on the sword, or that lacketh bread.   2 Sam. 1:16

30 So Joab and Abishai his brother slew Abner, because he had slain their brother Asahel at Gibeon in the battle.

31 And David said to Joab, and to all the people that *were* with him, Rend your clothes, and ᵀgird you with sackcloth, and mourn before Abner. And king David *himself* followed the bier.   Gen. 37:34; Josh. 7:6; Judg. 11:35 ◆ *clothe*

32 And they buried Abner in Hebron: and the king lifted up his voice, and wept at the grave of Abner; and all the people wept.   Prov. 24:17

33 And the king lamented over Abner, and said, Died Abner as a fool dieth?   2 Sam. 1:17

34 Thy hands *were* not bound, nor thy feet put into ᵀfetters: as a man falleth before wicked men, *so* fellest thou. And all the people wept again over him.   *chains*

35 And when all the people came to cause David to eat meat while it was yet day, David sware, saying, So do God to me, and more also, if I taste bread, or ought else, till the sun be down.   Ruth 1:17; 2 Sam. 1:12; 12:17

36 And all the people took notice *of it*, and it pleased them: as whatsoever the king did pleased all the people.

37 For all the people and all Israel under-

stood that day that it was not of the king to slay Abner the son of Ner.

38 And the king said unto his servants, Know ye not that there is a prince and a great man fallen this day in Israel?

39 And I *am* this day weak, though anointed king; and these men the sons of Zeruiah *be* too hard for me: the LORD shall reward the doer of evil according to his wickedness.   1 Kin. 2:33-34

> **3:33–39 The King Trusts God's Justice**
>
> David's magnanimous recognition of one who had been his bitter enemy won the confidence and admiration of all Israel [see 2 Samuel 3:36, 37]. In the private circle of his trusted counselors and attendants the king spoke of the crime, and recognizing his own inability to punish the murderers as he desired, he left them to the justice of God. *PP 700*

Ish-bosheth Is Murdered and His Head Is Brought to David

4 And when Saul's son heard that Abner was dead in Hebron, his hands were feeble, and all the Israelites were troubled.   Ezra 4:4; Is. 13:7; Jer. 6:24

2 And Saul's son had two men *that were* captains of bands: the name of the one *was* Baanah, and the name of the other Rechab, the sons of Rimmon a Beerothite, of the children of Benjamin: (for Beeroth also was reckoned to Benjamin: Josh. 9:17; 18:25

3 And the Beerothites fled to Gittaim, and were sojourners there until this day.)

4 And Jonathan, Saul's son, had a son *that was* lame of *his* feet. He was five years old when the tidings came of Saul and Jonathan out of Jezreel, and his nurse took him up, and fled: and it came to pass, as she made haste to flee, that he fell, and became lame. And his name *was* Mephibosheth.   2 Sam. 9:3; 1 Chr. 8:34; 9:40

5 And the sons of Rimmon the Beerothite, Rechab and Baanah, went, and came about the heat of the day to the house of Ish-bosheth, who lay on a bed at noon.

6 And they came thither into the midst of the house, *as though* they would have fetched wheat; and they smote him under the fifth *rib*: and Rechab and Baanah his brother escaped.   2 Sam. 2:23

7 For when they came into the house, he lay on his bed in his bedchamber, and they smote him, and slew him, and beheaded him, and took his head, and gat them away through the plain all night.

8 And they brought the head of Ish-bosheth unto David to Hebron, and said to the king, Behold the head of Ish-bosheth the son of Saul thine enemy, which sought thy life; and the LORD hath avenged my lord the king this day of Saul, and of his seed.   1 Sam. 25:29

David Puts to Death the Men Who Murdered Ish-bosheth

9 And David answered Rechab and Baanah his brother, the sons of Rimmon the Beerothite, and said unto them, *As* the LORD liveth, who hath redeemed my soul out of all adversity,   Gen. 48:16; 1 Kin. 1:29

10 When one told me, saying, Behold, Saul is dead, thinking to have brought good tidings, I took hold of him, and slew him in Ziklag, who *thought* that I would have given him a reward for his tidings: 2 Sam. 1:2-16

11 How much more, when wicked men have slain a righteous person in his own house upon his bed? shall I not therefore now require his blood of your hand, and take you away from the earth?   Ps. 9:12

12 And David commanded his young men, and they slew them, and cut off their hands and their feet, and hanged *them* up over the pool in Hebron. But they took the head of Ish-bosheth, and buried *it* in the sepulchre of Abner in Hebron.   2 Sam. 1:15

The Tribes Come to Hebron to Anoint David King over Israel

5 Then came all the tribes of Israel to David unto Hebron, and spake, saying, Behold, we *are* thy bone and thy flesh.   1 Chr. 11:1-3

2 Also in time past, when Saul was king over us, thou wast he that leddest out and broughtest in Israel: and the LORD said to thee, Thou shalt feed my people Israel, and thou shalt be a captain over Israel.   1 Sam. 18:13, 16; 2 Sam. 7:7

3 So all the elders of Israel came to the king to Hebron; and king David made a league with them in Hebron before the LORD: and they anointed David king over Israel. 2 Sam. 2:4

> **5:1–3 King of a United Israel**
>
> After the death of Ish-bosheth there was a general desire among the leading men of Israel that David should become king of all the tribes. . . . Thus through the providence of God the way had been opened for him to come to the throne. He had no personal ambition to gratify, for he had not sought the honor to which he had been brought. *PP 701*

4 David *was* thirty years old when he began to reign, *and* he reigned forty years. 1 Chr. 26:31

5 In Hebron he reigned over Judah seven years and six months: and in Jerusalem he reigned thirty and three years over all Israel and Judah.   2 Sam. 2:11; 1 Chr. 3:4

David Captures Jerusalem and Names It the City of David

6 And the king and his men went to Jerusalem unto the Jebusites, the inhabitants of the land: which spake unto David, saying, Except

thou take away the blind and the lame, thou shalt not come in ᵀhither: thinking, David cannot come in hither.   Josh. 15:63; Judg. 1:8, 21 ◆ *here*

7 Nevertheless David took the strong hold of Zion: the same *is* the city of David.   1 Kin. 2:10

5:7 A Place Rich With History

Before Joshua had led the armies of Israel over Jordan it had been called Salem. Near this place Abraham had proved his loyalty to God. Eight hundred years before the coronation of David it had been the home of Melchizedek, the priest of the most high God. It held a central and elevated position in the country and was protected by an environment of hills. *PP 703*

8 And David said on that day, Whosoever getteth up to the gutter, and smiteth the Jebusites, and the lame and the blind, *that are* hated of David's soul, *he shall be chief and captain*. Wherefore they said, The blind and the lame shall not come into the house.

9 So David dwelt in the fort, and called it the city of David. And David built round about from Millo and inward. 2 Sam. 5:7; 1 Kin. 9:15, 24

10 And David went on, and grew great, and the LORD God of hosts *was* with him. 2 Sam. 3:1

David's Palace, Wives, and Children

11 And Hiram king of Tyre sent messengers to David, and cedar trees, and carpenters, and masons: and they built David an house.   1 Kin. 5:1-2, 18; 1 Chr. 14:1

12 And David perceived that the LORD had established him king over Israel, and that he had exalted his kingdom for his people Israel's sake.

13 And David took *him* more concubines and wives out of Jerusalem, after he was come from Hebron: and there were yet sons and daughters born to David.   Deut. 17:17; 1 Chr. 3:9

14 And these *be* the names of those that were born unto him in Jerusalem; Shammua, and Shobab, and Nathan, and Solomon,

15 Ibhar also, and Elishua, and Nepheg, and Japhia,

16 And Elishama, and Eliada, and Eliphalet.

The Philistines Attack David, but He Defeats Them

17 But when the Philistines heard that they had anointed David king over Israel, all the Philistines came up to seek David; and David heard *of it*, and went down to the hold.   2 Sam. 23:14; 1 Chr. 11:16

18 The Philistines also came and spread themselves in the valley of Rephaim. Gen. 14:5

19 And David enquired of the LORD, saying, Shall I go up to the Philistines? wilt thou deliver them into mine hand? And the LORD said unto David, Go up: for I will doubtless deliver the Philistines into thine hand.   1 Sam. 23:2; 2 Sam. 2:1

20 And David came to Baal-perazim, and David smote them there, and said, The LORD hath broken forth upon mine enemies before me, as the breach of waters. Therefore he called the name of that place Baal-perazim.   Is. 28:21

21 And there they left their images, and David and his men burned them.   Deut. 7:5

22 And the Philistines came up yet again, and spread themselves in the valley of Rephaim.

23 And when David enquired of the LORD, he said, Thou shalt not go up; *but* ᵀfetch a compass behind them, and come upon them over against the mulberry trees.   *go around*

24 And let it be, when thou hearest the sound of a going in the tops of the mulberry trees, that then thou shalt ᵀbestir thyself: for then shall the LORD go out

David's Coronation

2 Samuel 5:1–5

The change in the sentiments of the people was marked and decisive. The revolution was quiet and dignified, befitting the great work they were doing. Nearly half a million souls, the former subjects of Saul, thronged Hebron and its environs. The very hills and valleys were alive with the multitudes. The hour for the coronation was appointed; the man who had been expelled from the court of Saul, who had fled to the mountains and hills and to the caves of the earth to preserve his life, was about to receive the highest honor that can be conferred upon man by his fellow man. Priests and elders, clothed in the garments of their sacred office, officers and soldiers with glittering spear and helmet, and strangers from long distances, stood to witness the coronation of the chosen king. David was arrayed in the royal robe. The sacred oil was put upon his brow by the high priest, for the anointing by Samuel had been prophetic of what would take place at the inauguration of the king. The time had come, and David, by solemn rite, was consecrated to his office as God's vicegerent. The scepter was placed in his hands. The covenant of his righteous sovereignty was written, and the people gave their pledges of loyalty. The diadem was placed upon his brow, and the coronation ceremony was over. Israel had a king by divine appointment. He who had waited patiently for the Lord, beheld the promise of God fulfilled [see 2 Samuel 5:10]. *PP 701, 702*

before thee, to ^Tsmite the host of the Philistines.   Judg. 4:14; 2 Kin. 7:6 ◆ *stir to action* ◆ *strike*
25 And David did so, as the LORD had commanded him; and smote the Philistines from Geba until thou come to Gazer.   1 Chr. 14:16

David Brings the Ark to Jerusalem on a New Cart

6 Again, David gathered together all *the* chosen *men* of Israel, thirty thousand.
2 And David arose, and went with all the people that *were* with him from Baale of Judah, to bring up from thence the ark of God, whose name is called by the name of the LORD of hosts that dwelleth *between* the cherubims.   1 Sam. 4:4
3 And they set the ark of God upon a new cart, and brought it out of the house of Abinadab that *was* in Gibeah: and Uzzah and Ahio, the sons of Abinadab, ^Tdrave the new cart.   1 Sam. 6:7 ◆ *drove*
4 And they brought it out of the house of Abinadab which *was* at Gibeah, accompanying the ark of God: and Ahio went before the ark.   1 Chr. 13:7
5 And David and all the house of Israel played before the LORD on all manner of *instruments made of* fir wood, even on harps, and on ^Tpsalteries, and on timbrels, and on cornets, and on cymbals.   1 Chr. 13:8 ◆ *stringed instruments*

Uzzah Is Killed for Touching the Ark

6 And when they came to Nachon's threshingfloor, Uzzah put forth *his hand* to the ark of God, and took hold of it; for the oxen shook *it*.   Num. 4:15, 19-20; 1 Chr. 13:9
7 And the anger of the LORD was kindled against Uzzah; and God smote him there for *his* error; and there he died by the ark of God.   1 Sam. 6:19; 1 Chr. 15:13

> **6:7 Great Sin of Presumption**
>
> Upon Uzzah rested the greater guilt of presumption. Transgression of God's law had lessened his sense of its sacredness, and with unconfessed sins upon him he had, in face of the divine prohibition, presumed to touch the symbol of God's presence. God can accept no partial obedience, no lax way of treating His commandments. By the judgment upon Uzzah He designed to impress upon all Israel the importance of giving strict heed to His requirements. *PP 706*

8 And David was displeased, because the LORD had made a breach upon Uzzah: and he called the name of the place Perez-uzzah to this day.
9 And David was afraid of the LORD that day, and said, How shall the ark of the LORD come to me?   Ps. 119:120

10 So David would not remove the ark of the LORD unto him into the city of David: but David carried it aside into the house of Obed-edom the Gittite.   1 Chr. 26:4-8
11 And the ark of the LORD continued in the house of Obed-edom the Gittite three months: and the LORD blessed Obed-edom, and all his household.   Gen. 30:27

David Dances to Celebrate the Return of the Ark

12 And it was told king David, saying, The LORD hath blessed the house of Obededom, and all that *pertaineth* unto him, because of the ark of God. So David went and brought up the ark of God from the house of Obed-edom into the city of David with gladness.   1 Kin. 8:1
13 And it was *so*, that when they that bare the ark of the LORD had gone six paces, he sacrificed oxen and fatlings.   Num. 4:15; Josh. 3:3
14 And David danced before the LORD with all *his* might; and David *was* girded with a linen ^Tephod.   Ex. 15:20; Ps. 150:4 ◆ *priestly garment*

> **6:14 All Equal Before God**
>
> The king had laid aside his royal robes and had attired himself in a plain linen ephod, such as was worn by the priests. He did not by this act signify that he assumed priestly functions. . . . But in this holy service he would take his place as, before God, on an equality with his subjects. Upon that day Jehovah was to be adored. He was to be the sole object of reverence. *PP 706, 707*

15 So David and all the house of Israel brought up the ark of the LORD with shouting, and with the sound of the trumpet.
16 And as the ark of the LORD came into the city of David, Michal Saul's daughter looked through a window, and saw king David leaping and dancing before the LORD; and she despised him in her heart.   1 Chr. 15:29
17 And they brought in the ark of the LORD, and set it in his place, in the midst of the tabernacle that David had pitched for it: and David offered burnt offerings and peace offerings before the LORD.   1 Kin. 8:5; 1 Chr. 15:1
18 And as soon as David had made an end of offering burnt offerings and peace offerings, he blessed the people in the name of the LORD of hosts.   1 Kin. 8:55
19 And he dealt among all the people, *even* among the whole multitude of Israel, as well to the women as men, to every one a cake of bread, and a good piece *of flesh*, and a flagon *of wine*. So all the people departed every one to his house.   Neh. 8:10

Michal Despises David's Joy and Is Made Childless

20 Then David returned to bless his household. And Michal the daughter of Saul came out to meet David, and said, How glorious was the king of Israel to day, who uncovered himself to day in the eyes of the handmaids of his servants, as one of the vain fellows shamelessly uncovereth himself!　　Judg. 9:4; 2 Sam. 6:14

6:20 A Bitter Woman

But there was one who had witnessed the scene of rejoicing with a spirit widely different from that which moved the heart of David. . . . In the bitterness of her passion [Michal] could not await David's return to the palace, but went out to meet him, and to his kindly greeting poured forth a torrent of bitter words. Keen and cutting was the irony of her speech. *PP 708*

21 And David said unto Michal, *It was* before the LORD, which chose me before thy father, and before all his house, to appoint me ruler over the people of the LORD, over Israel: therefore will I play before the LORD.　　1 Sam. 13:14; 15:28
22 And I will yet be more vile than thus, and will be ᵀbase in mine own sight: and of the maidservants which thou hast spoken of, of them shall I be had in honour.　　*meek*
23 Therefore Michal the daughter of Saul had no child unto the day of her death.　　Matt. 1:25

David Desires to Build a Temple for God but Is Forbidden

7 And it came to pass, when the king sat in his house, and the LORD had given him rest round about from all his enemies;
2 That the king said unto Nathan the prophet, See now, I dwell in an house of cedar, but the ark of God dwelleth within curtains.　　2 Sam. 5:11; 12:1; 1 Chr. 29:29
3 And Nathan said to the king, Go, do all that *is* in thine heart; for the LORD *is* with thee.　　1 Kin. 8:17-18

7:1, 2 David Plans a Great Temple

It was David's purpose to make Jerusalem the religious center of the nation. He had erected a palace for himself, and he felt that it was not fitting for the ark of God to rest within a tent. He determined to build for it a temple of such magnificence as should express Israel's appreciation of the honor granted the nation in the abiding presence of Jehovah their King. *PP 711*

4 And it came to pass that night, that the word of the LORD came unto Nathan, saying,
5 Go and tell my servant David, Thus saith the LORD, Shalt thou build me an house for me to dwell in?
6 Whereas I have not dwelt in *any* house since the time that I brought up the children of Israel out of Egypt, even to this day, but have walked in a tent and in a tabernacle.　　Ex. 40:18-19; Josh. 18:1; 1 Kin. 8:16
7 In all *the places* wherein I have walked with all the children of Israel spake I a word with any of the tribes of Israel, whom I commanded to feed my people Israel, saying, Why build ye not me an house of cedar?　　Lev. 26:11-12; 2 Sam. 5:2; 1 Chr. 17:6
8 Now therefore so shalt thou say unto my servant David, Thus saith the LORD of hosts, I took thee from the sheepcote, from following the sheep, to be ruler over my people, over Israel:　　2 Sam. 6:21
9 And I was with thee whithersoever thou wentest, and have cut off all thine enemies out of thy sight, and have made thee a great name, like unto the name of the great *men* that *are* in the earth.　　2 Sam. 5:10
10 Moreover I will appoint a place for my people Israel, and will plant them, that they may dwell in a place of their own, and move no more; neither shall the children of wickedness afflict them any more, as beforetime,　　Ps. 89:22-23
11 And as since the time that I commanded judges *to be* over my people Israel, and have

David Dances Before the Lord

2 Samuel 6:14

David's dancing in reverent joy before God has been cited by pleasure lovers in justification of the fashionable modern dance, but there is no ground for such an argument. In our day dancing is associated with folly and midnight reveling. Health and morals are sacrificed to pleasure. By the frequenters of the ballroom God is not an object of thought and reverence; prayer or the song of praise would be felt to be out of place in their assemblies. This test should be decisive. Amusements that have a tendency to weaken the love for sacred things and lessen our joy in the service of God are not to be sought by Christians. The music and dancing in joyful praise to God at the removal of the ark had not the faintest resemblance to the dissipation of modern dancing. The one tended to the remembrance of God and exalted His holy name. The other is a device of Satan to cause men to forget God and to dishonor Him. *PP 707*

caused thee to rest from all thine enemies. Also the LORD telleth thee that he will make thee an house.   1 Sam. 12:9-11; 2 Sam. 7:1, 27

12 And when thy days be fulfilled, and thou shalt sleep with thy fathers, I will set up thy seed after thee, which shall proceed out of thy bowels, and I will establish his kingdom.   Deut. 31:16; 1 Kin. 2:1; 8:20

13 He shall build an house for my name, and I will stablish the throne of his kingdom for ever.   1 Kin. 5:5; 6:12; 8:19

14 I will be his father, and he shall be my son. If he commit iniquity, I will ᵀchasten him with the rod of men, and with the stripes of the children of men: 1 Chr. 17:13; Heb. 1:5 ◆ *discipline*

15 But my mercy shall not depart away from him, as I took *it* from Saul, whom I put away before thee.   1 Sam. 15:23, 28; 16:14

16 And thine house and thy kingdom shall be established for ever before thee: thy throne shall be established for ever. Gen. 49:10; Ps. 89:36

17 According to all these words, and according to all this vision, so did Nathan speak unto David.

David's Prayer and Thanksgiving

18 Then went king David in, and sat before the LORD, and he said, Who *am* I, O Lord GOD? and what *is* my house, that thou hast brought me ᵀhitherto?   Ex. 3:11 ◆ *here*

7:18 Submitting to God's Will

David knew that it would be an honor to his name and would bring glory to his government to perform the work that he had purposed in his heart to do, but he was ready to submit his will to the will of God. The grateful resignation thus manifested is rarely seen, even among Christians. *PP 712*

---

19 And this was yet a small thing in thy sight, O Lord GOD; but thou hast spoken also of thy servant's house for a great while to come. And *is* this the manner of man, O Lord GOD?   1 Chr. 17:17

20 And what can David say more unto thee? for thou, Lord GOD, knowest thy servant.   1 Sam. 16:7

21 For thy word's sake, and according to thine own heart, hast thou done all these great things, to make thy servant know *them.*

22 Wherefore thou art great, O LORD God: for *there is* none like thee, neither *is there any* God beside thee, according to all that we have heard with our ears.   Ex. 15:11; Deut. 3:24; Ps. 48:1

23 And what one nation in the earth *is* like thy people, *even* like Israel, whom God went to redeem for a people to himself, and to make him a name, and to do for you

great things and terrible, for thy land, before thy people, which thou redeemedst to thee from Egypt, *from* the nations and their gods?   Deut. 9:26; 10:21; 15:15

24 For thou hast confirmed to thyself thy people Israel *to be* a people unto thee for ever: and thou, LORD, art become their God.   Deut. 26:18

25 And now, O LORD God, the word that thou hast spoken concerning thy servant, and concerning his house, establish *it* for ever, and do as thou hast said.

26 And let thy name be magnified for ever, saying, The LORD of hosts *is* the God over Israel: and let the house of thy servant David be established before thee.   1 Chr. 17:23-24

27 For thou, O LORD of hosts, God of Israel, hast revealed to thy servant, saying, I will build thee an house: therefore hath thy servant found in his heart to pray this prayer unto thee.

28 And now, O Lord GOD, thou *art* that God, and thy words be true, and thou hast promised this goodness unto thy servant: John 17:17

29 Therefore now let it please thee to bless the house of thy servant, that it may continue for ever before thee: for thou, O Lord GOD, hast spoken *it*: and with thy blessing let the house of thy servant be blessed for ever.   Num. 6:24-26

David's Successes Over Various Kings and Nations

8 And after this it came to pass, that David smote the Philistines, and subdued them: and David took Metheg-ammah out of the hand of the Philistines.   1 Chr. 18

2 And he smote Moab, and measured them with a line, casting them down to the ground; even with two lines measured he to put to death, and with one full line to keep alive. And *so* the Moabites became David's servants, *and* brought gifts. Num. 24:17; 1 Sam. 10:27

3 David smote also Hadadezer, the son of Rehob, king of Zobah, as he went to recover his border at the river Euphrates.   1 Sam. 14:47

4 And David took from him a thousand *chariots,* and seven hundred horsemen, and twenty thousand footmen: and David ᵀhoughed all the chariot *horses,* but reserved of them *for* an hundred chariots.   Josh. 11:6 ◆ *disabled*

5 And when the Syrians of Damascus came to ᵀsuccour Hadadezer king of Zobah, David slew of the Syrians two and twenty thousand men.   1 Kin. 11:23-25 ◆ *help*

6 Then David put garrisons in Syria of Damascus: and the Syrians became servants to David, *and* brought gifts. And the LORD preserved David whithersoever he went. 2 Sam. 7:9

7 And David took the shields of gold that were on the servants of Hadadezer, and brought them to Jerusalem.

8 And from Betah, and from Berothai, cities of Hadadezer, king David took exceeding much brass.   1 Chr. 18:8

Toi Sends Joram with Presents to Bless David

9 When Toi king of Hamath heard that David had smitten all the host of Hadadezer,   1 Kin. 8:65

10 Then Toi sent Joram his son unto king David, to salute him, and to bless him, because he had fought against Hadadezer, and smitten him: for Hadadezer had wars with Toi. And *Joram* brought with him vessels of silver, and vessels of gold, and vessels of brass:

11 Which also king David did dedicate unto the LORD, with the silver and gold that he had dedicated of all nations which he subdued;   1 Kin. 7:51

12 Of Syria, and of Moab, and of the children of Ammon, and of the Philistines, and of Amalek, and of the ᵀspoil of Hadadezer, son of Rehob, king of Zobah.   2 Sam. 8:2; 10:14 ◆ *plunder*

13 And David gat *him* a name when he returned from smiting of the Syrians in the valley of salt, *being* eighteen thousand *men*.   2 Sam. 7:9; 2 Kin. 14:7; 1 Chr. 18:12

14 And he put garrisons in Edom; throughout all Edom put he garrisons, and all they of Edom became David's servants. And the LORD preserved David whithersoever he went.   Gen. 27:29

15 And David reigned over all Israel; and David executed judgment and justice unto all his people.

16 And Joab the son of Zeruiah *was* over the host; and Jehoshaphat the son of Ahilud *was* recorder;   2 Sam. 19:13; 1 Kin. 4:3; 1 Chr. 11:6

17 And Zadok the son of Ahitub, and Ahimelech the son of Abiathar, *were* the priests; and Seraiah *was* the scribe;   1 Chr. 6:8

18 And Benaiah the son of Jehoiada *was over* both the Cherethites and the Pelethites; and David's sons were chief rulers.   1 Sam. 30:14

David Keeps His Promise to Jonathan

9 And David said, Is there yet any that is left of the house of Saul, that I may shew him kindness for Jonathan's sake?   1 Sam. 20:14-17

2 And *there was* of the house of Saul a servant whose name *was* Ziba. And when they had called him unto David, the king said unto him, Art thou Ziba? And he said, Thy servant *is* he.   2 Sam. 16:1-4; 19:17

3 And the king said, *Is* there not yet any of the house of Saul, that I may shew the kindness of God unto him? And Ziba said unto

the king, Jonathan hath yet ᵃ son, *which is* lame on *his* feet.   2 Sam. 4:4

4 And the king said unto him, Where *is* he? And Ziba said unto the king, Behold, he *is* in the house of Machir, the son of Ammiel, in Lo-debar.   2 Sam. 17:27-29

5 Then king David sent, and fetched him out of the house of Machir, the son of Ammiel, from Lo-debar.

6 Now when Mephibosheth, the son of Jonathan, the son of Saul, was come unto David, he fell on his face, and did reverence. And David said, Mephibosheth. And he answered, Behold thy servant!   1 Sam. 25:23

7 And David said unto him, Fear not: for I will surely shew thee kindness for Jonathan thy father's sake, and will restore thee all the land of Saul thy father; and thou shalt eat bread at my table continually.   2 Sam. 9:1; 19:28; 1 Kin. 2:7

9:6, 7 A Heart Won Over

Through reports from the enemies of David, Mephibosheth had been led to cherish a strong prejudice against him as a usurper; but the monarch's generous and courteous reception of him and his continued kindness won the heart of the young man; he became strongly attached to David, and, like his father Jonathan, he felt that his interest was one with that of the king whom God had chosen. *PP 713*

---

8 And he bowed himself, and said, What *is* thy servant, that thou shouldest look upon such a dead dog as I *am?*   2 Sam. 16:9

David Cares for Ziba, Saul's Servant

9 Then the king called to Ziba, Saul's servant, and said unto him, I have given unto thy master's son all that pertained to Saul and to all his house.   2 Sam. 16:4

10 Thou therefore, and thy sons, and thy servants, shall till the land for him, and thou shalt bring in *the fruits,* that thy master's son may have food to eat: but Mephibosheth thy master's son shall eat bread alway at my table. Now Ziba had fifteen sons and twenty servants.   2 Sam. 9:7; 19:28

11 Then said Ziba unto the king, According to all that my lord the king hath commanded his servant, so shall thy servant do. As for Mephibosheth, *said the king,* he shall eat at my table, as one of the king's sons.   2 Sam. 16:1-4

12 And Mephibosheth had a young son, whose name *was* Micha. And all that dwelt in the house of Ziba *were* servants unto Mephibosheth.

13 So Mephibosheth dwelt in Jerusalem: for he did eat continually at the king's table; and was lame on both his feet.   2 Sam. 9:7

David's Messengers Are Treated Shamefully

10 And it came to pass after this, that the king of the children of Ammon died, and Hanun his son reigned in his stead.

2 Then said David, I will shew kindness unto Hanun the son of Nahash, as his father shewed kindness unto me. And David sent to comfort him by the hand of his servants for his father. And David's servants came into the land of the children of Ammon.   1 Sam. 11:1

3 And the princes of the children of Ammon said unto Hanun their lord, Thinkest thou that David doth honour thy father, that he hath sent comforters unto thee? hath not David *rather* sent his servants unto thee, to search the city, and to spy it out, and to overthrow it?   Gen. 42:9

4 Wherefore Hanun took David's servants, and shaved off the one half of their beards, and cut off their garments in the middle, *even* to their buttocks, and sent them away.   Lev. 19:27; Is. 15:2; 20:4

5 When they told *it* unto David, he sent to meet them, because the men were greatly ashamed: and the king said, Tarry at Jericho until your beards be grown, and *then* return.

The Ammonites Are Overcome by Joab and Abishai

6 And when the children of Ammon saw that they stank before David, the children of Ammon sent and hired the Syrians of Beth-rehob, and the Syrians of Zoba, twenty thousand footmen, and of king Maacah a thousand men, and of Ish-tob twelve thousand men.   Gen. 34:30; 2 Sam. 8:3, 5

7 And when David heard of *it*, he sent Joab, and all the host of the mighty men.

8 And the children of Ammon came out, and put the battle in array at the entering in of the gate: and the Syrians of Zoba, and of Rehob, and Ish-tob, and Maacah, *were* by themselves in the field.   2 Sam. 10:6

9 When Joab saw that the front of the battle was against him before and behind, he chose of all the choice *men* of Israel, and put *them* in ᵀarray against the Syrians: *battle formation*

10 And the rest of the people he delivered into the hand of Abishai his brother, that he might put *them* in array against the children of Ammon.

11 And he said, If the Syrians be too strong for me, then thou shalt help me: but if the children of Ammon be too strong for thee, then I will come and help thee.

12 Be of good courage, and let us play the men for our people, and for the cities of our God: and the LORD do that which seemeth him good.   Deut. 31:6; 1 Sam. 3:18; 1 Cor. 16:13

13 And Joab drew nigh, and the people that *were* with him, unto the battle against the Syrians: and they fled before him. 1 Kin. 20:13-21

14 And when the children of Ammon saw that the Syrians were fled, then fled they also before Abishai, and entered into the city. So Joab returned from the children of Ammon, and came to Jerusalem.

David Joins the Battle and Defeats the Syrians

15 And when the Syrians saw that they were smitten before Israel, they gathered themselves together.

16 And Hadarezer sent, and brought out the Syrians that *were* beyond the river: and they came to Helam; and Shobach the captain of the host of Hadarezer *went* before them.   1 Chr. 19:16

17 And when it was told David, he gathered all Israel together, and passed over Jordan, and came to Helam. And the Syrians set themselves in array against David, and fought with him.

10:1–17 A Hostile but Fruitless Alliance

Then there was formed against the kingdom of David a vast coalition of the surrounding nations, out of which grew the greatest wars and victories of his reign and the most extensive accessions to his power. This hostile alliance, which really sprang from jealousy of David's increasing power, had been unprovoked by him. *PP 713, 714*

---

18 And the Syrians fled before Israel; and David slew *the men of* seven hundred chariots of the Syrians, and forty thousand horsemen, and smote Shobach the captain of their host, who died there.   1 Chr. 19:18

19 And when all the kings *that were* servants to Hadarezer saw that they were smitten before Israel, they made peace with Israel, and served them. So the Syrians feared to help the children of Ammon any more.   2 Sam. 8:6

10:19 Years of Fulfilled Promise

The kingdom of Israel had now reached in extent the fulfillment of the promise given to Abraham, and afterward repeated to Moses [see Genesis 15:18]. Israel had become a mighty nation, respected and feared by surrounding peoples. In his own realm David's power had become very great. He commanded, as few sovereigns in any age have been able to command. . . . He had honored God, and God was now honoring him. *PP 716*

David Commits Adultery with Bath-sheba

11 And it came to pass, after the year was expired, at the time when kings go forth *to battle*, that David sent Joab, and his servants with him, and all Israel; and they destroyed the children of Ammon, and besieged Rabbah. But David tarried still at Jerusalem.   1 Kin. 20:22, 26; 1 Chr. 20:1

2 And it came to pass in an ᵀeveningtide, that David arose from off his bed, and walked upon the roof of the king's house: and from the roof he saw a woman washing herself; and the woman *was* very beautiful to look upon.   Deut. 22:8 ✦ *evening*

11:1, 2 David Lets Slip His Hold on God

It was now, while [David] was at ease and unguarded, that the tempter seized the opportunity to occupy his mind. The fact that God had taken David into so close connection with Himself and had manifested so great favor toward him, should have been to him the strongest of incentives to preserve his character unblemished. But when in ease and self-security he let go his hold upon God, David yielded to Satan and brought upon his soul the stain of guilt. PP 718

---

3 And David sent and enquired after the woman. And *one* said, *Is* not this Bath-sheba, the daughter of Eliam, the wife of Uriah the Hittite?   2 Sam. 23:39; 1 Chr. 3:5

4 And David sent messengers, and took her; and she came in unto him, and he lay with her; for she was purified from her uncleanness: and she returned unto her house.   Lev. 12:2-5; 18:19; James 1:14-15

5 And the woman conceived, and sent and told David, and said, I *am* with child.

David Brings Uriah Home to Conceal His Adultery

6 And David sent to Joab, *saying*, Send me Uriah the Hittite. And Joab sent Uriah to David.

7 And when Uriah was come unto him, David demanded *of him* how Joab did, and how the people did, and how the war prospered.   Gen. 37:14

8 And David said to Uriah, Go down to thy house, and wash thy feet. And Uriah departed out of the king's house, and there followed him a ᵀmess *of meat* from the king.   Gen. 18:4 ✦ *portion of food for a guest*

9 But Uriah slept at the door of the king's house with all the servants of his lord, and went not down to his house.

10 And when they had told David, saying, Uriah went not down unto his house, David said unto Uriah, Camest thou not from *thy* journey? why *then* didst thou not go down unto thine house?

11 And Uriah said unto David, The ark, and Israel, and Judah, abide in tents; and my lord Joab, and the servants of my lord, are encamped in the open fields; shall I then go into mine house, to eat and to drink, and to lie with my wife? *as* thou livest, and *as* thy soul liveth, I will not do this thing.   2 Sam. 7:2, 6; 20:6

12 And David said to Uriah, Tarry here to day also, and to morrow I will let thee depart. So Uriah abode in Jerusalem that day, and the morrow.

13 And when David had called him, he did eat and drink before him; and he made him drunk: and at even he went out to lie on his bed with the servants of his lord, but went not down to his house.

David Orders Joab to Let Uriah Die in Battle

14 And it came to pass in the morning, that David wrote a letter to Joab, and sent *it* by the hand of Uriah.   1 Kin. 21:8-10

15 And he wrote in the letter, saying, Set ye Uriah in the forefront of the hottest battle, and retire ye from him, that he may be smitten, and die.   2 Sam. 12:9

16 And it came to pass, when Joab observed the city, that he assigned Uriah unto a place where he knew that valiant men *were*.

11:15, 16 Taking Others Down

But as [David] departed from God and yielded himself to the wicked one, he became for the time the agent of Satan; yet he still held the position and authority that God had given him, and because of this, claimed obedience that would imperil the soul of him who should yield it. And Joab, whose allegiance had been given to the king rather than to God, transgressed God's law because the king commanded it. PP 719

---

17 And the men of the city went out, and fought with Joab: and there fell *some* of the people of the servants of David; and Uriah the Hittite died also.

18 Then Joab sent and told David all the things concerning the war;

19 And charged the messenger, saying, When thou hast made an end of telling the matters of the war unto the king,

20 And if so be that the king's wrath arise, and he say unto thee, Wherefore approached ye so nigh unto the city when ye did fight? knew ye not that they would shoot from the wall?

21 Who smote Abimelech the son of Jerubbesheth? did not a woman cast a piece of a millstone upon him from the wall, that he

died in Thebez? why went ye nigh the wall? then say thou, Thy servant Uriah the Hittite is dead also.

22 So the messenger went, and came and shewed David all that Joab had sent him for. 23 And the messenger said unto David, Surely the men prevailed against us, and came out unto us into the field, and we were upon them even unto the entering of the gate. 24 And the shooters shot from off the wall upon thy servants; and *some* of the king's servants be dead, and thy servant Uriah the Hittite is dead also. 25 Then David said unto the messenger, Thus shalt thou say unto Joab, Let not this thing displease thee, for the sword devoureth one as well as another: make thy battle more strong against the city, and overthrow it: and encourage thou him. 26 And when the wife of Uriah heard that Uriah her husband was dead, she mourned for her husband. 27 And when the mourning was past, David sent and fetched her to his house, and she became his wife, and bare him a son. But the thing that David had done displeased the LORD.   2 Sam. 12:9; Ps. 51:4-5

Nathan Reveals David's Sin with a Parable

12 And the LORD sent Nathan unto David. And he came unto him, and said unto him, There were two men in one city; the one rich, and the other poor.   1 Kin. 20:35-41 2 The rich *man* had exceeding many flocks and herds: 3 But the poor *man* had nothing, save one little ewe lamb, which he had bought and nourished up: and it grew up together with him, and with his children; it did eat of his own meat, and drank of his own cup, and lay in his bosom, and was unto him as a daughter.   2 Sam. 11:3

4 And there came a traveller unto the rich man, and he spared to take of his own flock and of his own herd, to dress for the wayfaring man that was come unto him; but took the poor man's lamb, and dressed it for the man that was come to him. 5 And David's anger was greatly kindled against the man; and he said to Nathan, *As* the LORD liveth, the man that hath done this *thing* shall surely die: 1 Sam. 26:16 6 And he shall restore the lamb fourfold, because he did this thing, and because he had no pity.   Ex. 22:1; Luke 19:8 7 And Nathan said to David, Thou *art* the man. Thus saith the LORD God of Israel, I anointed thee king over Israel, and I delivered thee out of the hand of Saul; 1 Sam. 16:13 8 And I gave thee thy master's house, and thy master's wives into thy bosom, and gave thee the house of Israel and of Judah; and if *that had been* too little, I would moreover have given unto thee such and such things. 9 Wherefore hast thou despised the commandment of the LORD, to do evil in his sight? thou hast killed Uriah the Hittite with the sword, and hast taken his wife *to be* thy wife, and hast slain him with the sword of the children of Ammon.   1 Sam. 15:19 10 Now therefore the sword shall never depart from thine house; because thou hast despised me, and hast taken the wife of Uriah the Hittite to be thy wife.   2 Sam. 18:14-15 11 Thus saith the LORD, Behold, I will raise up evil against thee out of thine own house, and I will take thy wives before thine eyes, and give *them* unto thy neighbour, and he shall lie with thy wives in the sight of this sun.   Deut. 28:30 12 For thou didst *it* secretly: but I will do this thing before all Israel, and before the sun.   2 Sam. 16:22 13 And David said unto Nathan, I have sinned against the LORD. And Nathan said

---

Self-Focus Brings a Fall

2 Samuel 12

The Bible has little to say in praise of men. Little space is given to recounting the virtues of even the best men who have ever lived. This silence is not without purpose; it is not without a lesson. All the good qualities that men possess are the gift of God; their good deeds are performed by the grace of God through Christ. Since they owe all to God the glory of whatever they are or do belongs to Him alone; they are but instruments in His hands. More than this—as all the lessons of Bible history teach—it is a perilous thing to praise or exalt men; for if one comes to lose sight of his entire dependence on God, and to trust to his own strength, he is sure to fall. Man is contending with foes who are stronger than he. [See Ephesians 6:12.] It is impossible for us in our own strength to maintain the conflict; and whatever diverts the mind from God, whatever leads to self-exaltation or to self-dependence, is surely preparing the way for our overthrow. The tenor of the Bible is to inculcate distrust of human power and to encourage trust in divine power.

It was the spirit of self-confidence and self-exaltation that prepared the way for David's fall. PP 717

unto David, The LORD also hath put away thy sin; thou shalt not die.   Lev. 20:10; Prov. 28:13

12:13 A Soul-Deep Confession

The prophet's rebuke touched the heart of David; conscience was aroused; his guilt appeared in all its enormity. His soul was bowed in penitence before God. With trembling lips he said, "I have sinned against the Lord." All wrong done to others reaches back from the injured one to God. David had committed a grievous sin, toward both Uriah and Bathsheba, and he keenly felt this. But infinitely greater was his sin against God. *PP 722*

---

14 Howbeit, because by this deed thou hast given great occasion to the enemies of the LORD to blaspheme, the child also *that is* born unto thee shall surely die.   Is. 52:5; Rom. 2:24

David Mourns and Prays for the Child

15 And Nathan departed unto his house. And the LORD struck the child that Uriah's wife bare unto David, and it was very sick.
16 David therefore ᵀbesought God for the child; and David fasted, and went in, and lay all night upon the earth.   2 Sam. 13:31 ✦ *begged*
17 And the elders of his house arose, *and went* to him, to raise him up from the earth: but he would not, neither did he eat bread with them.   2 Sam. 3:35
18 And it came to pass on the seventh day, that the child died. And the servants of David feared to tell him that the child was dead: for they said, Behold, while the child was yet alive, we spake unto him, and he would not hearken unto our voice: how will he then ᵀvex himself, if we tell him that the child is dead?   *trouble*
19 But when David saw that his servants whispered, David perceived that the child was dead: therefore David said unto his servants, Is the child dead? And they said, He is dead.

12:15–20 David's Interceding

Often when judgments had been pronounced upon persons or cities, humiliation and repentance had turned aside the blow, and the Ever-Merciful, swift to pardon, had sent messengers of peace. Encouraged by this thought, David persevered in his supplication so long as the child was spared. Upon learning that it was dead, he quietly submitted to the decree of God. *PP 722*

---

20 Then David arose from the earth, and washed, and anointed *himself*, and changed his apparel, and came into the house of the LORD, and worshipped: then he came to his own house; and when he required, they set bread before him, and he did eat.   Job 1:20

21 Then said his servants unto him, What thing *is* this that thou hast done? thou didst fast and weep for the child, *while it was* alive; but when the child was dead, thou didst rise and eat bread.
22 And he said, While the child was yet alive, I fasted and wept: for I said, Who can tell *whether* GOD will be gracious to me, that the child may live?   Is. 38:1-3
23 But now he is dead, wherefore should I fast? can I bring him back again? I shall go to him, but he shall not return to me.   Gen. 37:35
24 And David comforted Bath-sheba his wife, and went in unto her, and lay with her: and she bare a son, and he called his name Solomon: and the LORD loved him.   Matt. 1:6
25 And he sent by the hand of Nathan the prophet; and he called his name Jedidiah, because of the LORD.   Neh. 13:26

David Defeats the Ammonites and Plunders Their Cities

26 And Joab fought against Rabbah of the children of Ammon, and took the royal city.   Deut. 3:11
27 And Joab sent messengers to David, and said, I have fought against Rabbah, and have taken the city of waters.
28 Now therefore gather the rest of the people together, and encamp against the city, and take it: lest I take the city, and it be called after my name.
29 And David gathered all the people together, and went to Rabbah, and fought against it, and took it.
30 And he took their king's crown from off his head, the weight whereof *was* a talent of gold with the precious stones: and it was *set* on David's head. And he brought forth the spoil of the city in great abundance.   1 Chr. 20:2
31 And he brought forth the people that *were* therein, and put *them* under saws, and under harrows of iron, and under axes of iron, and made them pass through the brick-kiln: and thus did he unto all the cities of the children of Ammon. So David and all the people returned unto Jerusalem.   1 Chr. 20:3

Amnon Defiles Tamar

13 And it came to pass after this, that Absalom the son of David had a fair sister, whose name *was* Tamar; and Amnon the son of David loved her.   2 Sam. 3:2-3; 1 Chr. 3:2, 9
2 And Amnon was so vexed, that he fell sick for his sister Tamar; for she *was* a virgin; and Amnon thought it hard for him to do any thing to her.
3 But Amnon had a friend, whose name *was* Jonadab, the son of Shimeah David's brother: and Jonadab *was* a very subtil man.   1 Sam. 16:9

4 And he said unto him, Why *art* thou, *being* the king's son, lean from day to day? wilt thou not tell me? And Amnon said unto him, I love Tamar, my brother Absalom's sister.

5 And Jonadab said unto him, Lay thee down on thy bed, and make thyself sick: and when thy father cometh to see thee, say unto him, I pray thee, let my sister Tamar come, and give me meat, and dress the meat in my sight, that I may see *it,* and eat *it* at her hand.

6 So Amnon lay down, and made himself sick: and when the king was come to see him, Amnon said unto the king, I pray thee, let Tamar my sister come, and make me a couple of cakes in my sight, that I may eat at her hand.   Gen. 18:6

7 Then David sent home to Tamar, saying, Go now to thy brother Amnon's house, and dress him meat.

8 So Tamar went to her brother Amnon's house; and he was laid down. And she took flour, and kneaded *it,* and made cakes in his sight, and did bake the cakes.

9 And she took a pan, and poured *them* out before him; but he refused to eat. And Amnon said, Have out all men from me. And they went out every man from him.   Gen. 45:1

10 And Amnon said unto Tamar, Bring the meat into the chamber, that I may eat of thine hand. And Tamar took the cakes which she had made, and brought *them* into the chamber to Amnon her brother.

11 And when she had brought *them* unto him to eat, he took hold of her, and said unto her, Come lie with me, my sister.

12 And she answered him, Nay, my brother, do not force me; for no such thing ought to be done in Israel: do not thou this folly.   Lev. 20:17; Judg. 19:23; 20:6

13 And I, whither shall I cause my shame to go? and as for thee, thou shalt be as one of the fools in Israel. Now therefore, I pray thee, speak unto the king; for he will not withhold me from thee.

14 Howbeit he would not hearken unto her voice: but, being stronger than she, forced her, and lay with her.   2 Sam. 12:11

15 Then Amnon hated her exceedingly; so that the hatred wherewith he hated her *was* greater than the love wherewith he had loved her. And Amnon said unto her, Arise, be gone.

16 And she said unto him, *There is* no cause: this evil in sending me away *is* greater than the other that thou didst unto me. But he would not hearken unto her.

17 Then he called his servant that ministered unto him, and said, Put now this

woman out from me, and bolt the door after her.

18 And *she had* a garment of ᵀdivers colours upon her: for with such robes were the king's daughters *that were* virgins apparelled. Then his servant brought her out, and bolted the door after her.   Gen. 37:3 ♦ *various*

19 And Tamar put ashes on her head, and ᵀrent her garment of divers colours that *was* on her, and laid her hand on her head, and went on crying.   Josh. 7:6 ♦ *tore*

13:1–19 A Sin Unpunished

The shameful crime of Amnon, the first-born, was permitted by David to pass unpunished and unrebuked. The law pronounced death upon the adulterer, and the unnatural crime of Amnon made him doubly guilty. But David, self-condemned for his own sin, failed to bring the offender to justice. *PP 727*

---

20 And Absalom her brother said unto her, Hath Amnon thy brother been with thee? but hold now thy peace, my sister: he *is* thy brother; regard not this thing. So Tamar remained desolate in her brother Absalom's house.

21 But when king David heard of all these things, he was very ᵀwroth.   Gen. 34:7 ♦ *angry*

22 And Absalom spake unto his brother Amnon neither good nor bad: for Absalom hated Amnon, because he had forced his sister Tamar.   Gen. 24:50; 31:24; Lev. 19:17-18

23 And it came to pass after two full years, that Absalom had sheepshearers in Baal-hazor, which *is* beside Ephraim: and Absalom invited all the king's sons.   Gen. 38:12-13

13:23–29 Opportunities Squandered

Like other sons of David, Amnon had been left to selfish indulgence. He had sought to gratify every thought of his heart, regardless of the requirements of God. Notwithstanding his great sin, God had borne long with him. For two years he had been granted opportunity for repentance; but he continued in sin, and with his guilt upon him, he was cut down by death, to await the awful tribunal of the judgment. *PP 727*

---

24 And Absalom came to the king, and said, Behold now, thy servant hath sheepshearers; let the king, I ᵀbeseech thee, and his servants go with thy servant.   *beg*

25 And the king said to Absalom, Nay, my son, let us not all now go, lest we be chargeable unto thee. And he pressed him: ᵀhowbeit he would not go, but blessed him.   *however*

26 Then said Absalom, If not, I pray thee, let my brother Amnon go with us. And the king said unto him, Why should he go with thee?   2 Sam. 3:27

27 But Absalom pressed him, that he let Amnon and all the king's sons go with him. 28 Now Absalom had commanded his servants, saying, Mark ye now when Amnon's heart is merry with wine, and when I say unto you, Smite Amnon; then kill him, fear not: have not I commanded you? be courageous, and be valiant.   Judg. 19:6, 9, 22
29 And the servants of Absalom did unto Amnon as Absalom had commanded. Then all the king's sons arose, and every man gat him up upon his mule, and fled.   2 Sam. 18:9

David Grieves that Absalom Has Killed Amnon

30 And it came to pass, while they were in the way, that tidings came to David, saying, Absalom hath slain all the king's sons, and there is not one of them left.
31 Then the king arose, and tare his garments, and lay on the earth; and all his servants stood by with their clothes rent.   2 Sam. 1:11; 12:16
32 And Jonadab, the son of Shimeah David's brother, answered and said, Let not my lord suppose *that* they have slain all the young men the king's sons; for Amnon only is dead: for by the appointment of Absalom this hath been determined from the day that he forced his sister Tamar.
33 Now therefore let not my lord the king take the thing to his heart, to think that all the king's sons are dead: for Amnon only is dead.   2 Sam. 19:19

13:30–33 A Fateful Train of Circumstances

David had neglected the duty of punishing the crime of Amnon, and because of the unfaithfulness of the king and father and the impenitence of the son, the Lord permitted events to take their natural course, and did not restrain Absalom. When parents or rulers neglect the duty of punishing iniquity, God Himself will take the case in hand. His restraining power will be in a measure removed from the agencies of evil, so that a train of circumstances will arise which will punish sin with sin. *PP 728*

---

34 But Absalom fled. And the young man that kept the watch lifted up his eyes, and looked, and, behold, there came much people by the way of the hill side behind him.
35 And Jonadab said unto the king, Behold, the king's sons come: as thy servant said, so it is.
36 And it came to pass, as soon as he had made an end of speaking, that, behold, the king's sons came, and lifted up their voice and wept: and the king also and all his servants wept very sore.
37 But Absalom fled, and went to Talmai, the son of Ammihud, king of Geshur. And *David* mourned for his son every day.   2 Sam. 3:3; 13:34
38 So Absalom fled, and went to Geshur, and was there three years.
39 And *the soul of* king David longed to go forth unto Absalom: for he was comforted concerning Amnon, seeing he was dead.   Gen. 24:67

David Allows Absalom to Return to Jerusalem

14 Now Joab the son of Zeruiah perceived that the king's heart *was* toward Absalom.   2 Sam. 13:39
2 And Joab sent to Tekoah, and fetched thence a wise woman, and said unto her, I pray thee, feign thyself to be a mourner, and put on now mourning apparel, and anoint not thyself with oil, but be as a woman that had a long time mourned for the dead: Ruth 3:3; 2 Chr. 11:6; Amos 1:1
3 And come to the king, and speak on this manner unto him. So Joab put the words in her mouth.   Ex. 4:15; 2 Sam. 14:19
4 And when the woman of Tekoah spake to the king, she fell on her face to the ground, and did obeisance, and said, Help, O king.
5 And the king said unto her, What aileth thee? And she answered, I *am* indeed a widow woman, and mine husband is dead.
6 And thy handmaid had two sons, and they two strove together in the field, and *there was* none to part them, but the one smote the other, and slew him.
7 And, behold, the whole family is risen against thine handmaid, and they said, Deliver him that smote his brother, that we may kill him, for the life of his brother whom he slew; and we will destroy the heir also: and so they shall quench my coal which is left, and shall not leave to my husband *neither* name nor remainder upon the earth.   Num. 35:19
8 And the king said unto the woman, Go to thine house, and I will give charge concerning thee.
9 And the woman of Tekoah said unto the king, My lord, O king, the iniquity *be* on me, and on my father's house: and the king and his throne *be* guiltless.   1 Kin. 2:33; Matt. 27:25
10 And the king said, Whosoever saith *ought* unto thee, bring him to me, and he shall not touch thee any more.
11 Then said she, I pray thee, let the king remember the LORD thy God, that thou wouldest not suffer the revengers of blood to destroy any more, lest they destroy my son. And he said, *As* the LORD liveth, there shall not one hair of thy son fall to the earth.   Num. 35:19; 1 Sam. 14:45; Matt. 10:30
12 Then the woman said, Let thine hand-

maid, I pray thee, speak one word unto my lord the king. And he said, Say on.

13 And the woman said, Wherefore then hast thou thought such a thing against the people of God? for the king doth speak this thing as one which is faulty, in that the king doth not fetch home again his banished.

14 For we must needs die, and are as water spilt on the ground, which cannot be gathered up again; neither doth God respect any person: yet doth he devise means, that his banished be not expelled from him. Num. 35:15

14:13, 14 An Appeal Not Resisted

This tender and touching portrayal of the love of God toward the sinner—coming as it did from Joab, the rude soldier—is a striking evidence of the familiarity of the Israelites with the great truths of redemption. The king, feeling his own need of God's mercy, could not resist this appeal. *PP 728, 729*

---

15 Now therefore that I am come to speak of this thing unto my lord the king, it is because the people have made me afraid: and thy handmaid said, I will now speak unto the king; it may be that the king will perform the request of his handmaid.

16 For the king will hear, to deliver his handmaid out of the hand of the man that would destroy me and my son together out of the inheritance of God.   1 Sam. 26:19

17 Then thine handmaid said, The word of my lord the king shall now be comfortable: for as an angel of God, so is my lord the king to discern good and bad: therefore the LORD thy God will be with thee.   1 Sam. 29:9; 2 Sam. 19:27

18 Then the king answered and said unto the woman, Hide not from me, I pray thee, the thing that I shall ask thee. And the woman said, Let my lord the king now speak.

19 And the king said, Is not the hand of Joab with thee in all this? And the woman answered and said, As thy soul liveth, my lord the king, none can turn to the right hand or to the left from ought that my lord the king hath spoken: for thy servant Joab, he bade me, and he put all these words in the mouth of thine handmaid: 1 Sam. 1:26; 2 Sam. 14:3

20 To fetch about this form of speech hath thy servant Joab done this thing: and my lord is wise, according to the wisdom of an angel of God, to know all things that are in the earth.   2 Sam. 14:17; 19:27

21 And the king said unto Joab, Behold now, I have done this thing: go therefore, bring the young man Absalom again.   2 Sam. 14:11

22 And Joab fell to the ground on his face, and bowed himself, and thanked the king: and Joab said, To day thy servant knoweth that I have found grace in thy sight, my lord,

O king, in that the king hath fulfilled the request of his servant.

23 So Joab arose and went to Geshur, and brought Absalom to Jerusalem.

24 And the king said, Let him turn to his own house, and let him not see my face. So Absalom returned to his own house, and saw not the king's face.

25 But in all Israel there was none to be so much praised as Absalom for his beauty: from the sole of his foot even to the crown of his head there was no blemish in him.   Deut. 28:35

26 And when he polled his head, (for it was at every year's end that he polled it: because the hair was heavy on him, therefore he polled it:) he weighed the hair of his head at two hundred shekels after the king's weight.   2 Sam. 18:9

27 And unto Absalom there were born three sons, and one daughter, whose name was Tamar: she was a woman of a fair ᵀcountenance.   2 Sam. 13:1; 18:18 ♦ appearance

Joab Brings Absalom into the King's Presence

28 So Absalom dwelt two full years in Jerusalem, and saw not the king's face.

29 Therefore Absalom sent for Joab, to have sent him to the king; but he would not come to him: and when he sent again the second time, he would not come.

30 Therefore he said unto his servants, See, Joab's field is near mine, and he hath barley there; go and set it on fire. And Absalom's servants set the field on fire.   Judg. 15:4-5

31 Then Joab arose, and came to Absalom unto his house, and said unto him, Wherefore have thy servants set my field on fire?

32 And Absalom answered Joab, Behold, I sent unto thee, saying, Come ᵀhither, that I may send thee to the king, to say, Wherefore am I come from Geshur? it had been good for me to have been there still: now therefore let me see the king's face; and if there be any iniquity in me, let him kill me.   1 Sam. 20:8 ♦ here

33 So Joab came to the king, and told him: and when he had called for Absalom, he came to the king, and bowed himself on his face to the ground before the king: and the king kissed Absalom.   Gen. 33:4

Absalom Wins the Affection of Israel

15 And it came to pass after this, that Absalom prepared him chariots and horses, and fifty men to run before him.

2 And Absalom rose up early, and stood beside the way of the gate: and it was so, that when any man that had a controversy came to the king for judgment, then Absalom called unto him, and said, Of what city art

thou? And he said, Thy servant *is* of one of the tribes of Israel.

15:1 An Ambitious Schemer

Through the influence of Joab, Absalom was again admitted to his father's presence; but though there was an outward reconciliation, he continued his ambitious scheming. He now assumed an almost royal state, having chariots and horses, and fifty men to run before him. And while the king was more and more inclined to desire retirement and solitude, Absalom sedulously courted the popular favor. *PP 729*

---

3 And Absalom said unto him, See, thy matters *are* good and right; but *there is* no man ᵀ*deputed* of the king to hear thee.   appointed
4 Absalom said moreover, Oh that I were made judge in the land, that every man which hath any suit or cause might come unto me, and I would do him justice!   Judg. 9:29
5 And it was *so*, that when any man came nigh *to him* to do him ᵀobeisance, he put forth his hand, and took him, and kissed him.   2 Sam. 14:33 ◆ homage
6 And on this manner did Absalom to all Israel that came to the king for judgment: so Absalom stole the hearts of the men of Israel.   Rom. 16:18

15:2–6 A Plotter and Pretender

The influence of David's listlessness and irresolution extended to his subordinates; negligence and delay characterized the administration of justice. Absalom artfully turned every cause of dissatisfaction to his own advantage. . . . Absalom mingled with them and listened to their grievances, expressing sympathy with their sufferings and regret at the inefficiency of the government. *PP 729, 730*

Absalom Instigates a Conspiracy to Overthrow His Father

7 And it came to pass after forty years, that Absalom said unto the king, I pray thee, let me go and pay my vow, which I have vowed unto the LORD, in Hebron.
8 For thy servant vowed a vow while I abode at Geshur in Syria, saying, If the LORD shall bring me again indeed to Jerusalem, then I will serve the LORD.   Gen. 28:20-21
9 And the king said unto him, Go in peace. So he arose, and went to Hebron.
10 But Absalom sent spies throughout all the tribes of Israel, saying, As soon as ye hear the sound of the trumpet, then ye shall say, Absalom reigneth in Hebron.
11 And with Absalom went two hundred

men out of Jerusalem, *that were* called; and they went in their simplicity, and they knew not any thing.   1 Sam. 9:13
12 And Absalom sent for Ahithophel the Gilonite, David's counsellor, from his city, *even* from Giloh, while he offered sacrifices. And the conspiracy was strong; for the people increased continually with Absalom.   Josh. 15:51; 2 Sam. 15:31; Ps. 41:9

David Flees from Jerusalem

13 And there came a messenger to David, saying, The hearts of the men of Israel are after Absalom.   Judg. 9:3
14 And David said unto all his servants that *were* with him at Jerusalem, Arise, and let us flee; for we shall not *else* escape from Absalom: make speed to depart, lest he overtake us suddenly, and bring evil upon us, and ᵀsmite the city with the edge of the sword.   2 Sam. 19:9 ◆ strike
15 And the king's servants said unto the king, Behold, thy servants *are ready to do* whatsoever my lord the king shall appoint.
16 And the king went forth, and all his household after him. And the king left ten women, *which were* concubines, to keep the house.   2 Sam. 16:21-22; 20:3
17 And the king went forth, and all the people after him, and tarried in a place that was far off.
18 And all his servants passed on beside him; and all the Cherethites, and all the Pelethites, and all the Gittites, six hundred men which came after him from Gath, passed on before the king.   1 Sam. 30:14; 2 Sam. 8:18; 20:7
19 Then said the king to Ittai the Gittite, Wherefore goest thou also with us? return to thy place, and abide with the king: for thou *art* a stranger, and also an exile.   2 Sam. 18:2
20 Whereas thou camest *but* yesterday, should I this day make thee go up and down with us? seeing I go whither I may, return thou, and take back thy brethren: mercy and truth *be* with thee.   1 Sam. 23:13; 2 Sam. 2:6
21 And Ittai answered the king, and said, *As* the LORD liveth, and *as* my lord the king liveth, surely in what place my lord the king shall be, whether in death or life, even there also will thy servant be.   Ruth 1:16-17; Prov. 17:17
22 And David said to Ittai, Go and pass over. And Ittai the Gittite passed over, and all his men, and all the little ones that *were* with him.
23 And all the country wept with a loud voice, and all the people passed over: the king also himself passed over the brook Kidron, and all the people passed over, toward the way of the wilderness.   2 Sam. 16:2

Zadok and Abiathar Are Sent Back with the Ark

24 And lo Zadok also, and all the Levites *were* with him, bearing the ark of the covenant of God: and they set down the ark of God; and Abiathar went up, until all the people had done passing out of the city.   Num. 4:15

25 And the king said unto Zadok, Carry back the ark of God into the city: if I shall find favour in the eyes of the Lord, he will bring me again, and shew me *both* it, and his habitation: Ex. 15:13

26 But if he thus say, I have no delight in thee; behold, *here am* I, let him do to me as seemeth good unto him. 1 Sam. 3:18; 2 Sam. 22:20; 1 Kin. 10:9

27 The king said also unto Zadok the priest, *Art not* thou a seer? return into the city in peace, and your two sons with you, Ahimaaz thy son, and Jonathan the son of Abiathar.   1 Sam. 9:9; 2 Sam. 17:17

28 See, I will tarry in the plain of the wilderness, until there come word from you to certify me.   2 Sam. 15:23; 17:16

29 Zadok therefore and Abiathar carried the ark of God again to Jerusalem: and they tarried there.

30 And David went up by the ascent of *mount* Olivet, and wept as he went up, and had his head covered, and he went barefoot: and all the people that *was* with him covered every man his head, and they went up, weeping as they went up.   Esth. 6:12; Is. 20:2-4

David Prays against Ahithophel

31 And *one* told David, saying, Ahithophel *is* among the conspirators with Absalom. And David said, O Lord, I pray thee, turn the counsel of Ahithophel into foolishness.   2 Sam. 16:23; 17:14, 23

32 And it came to pass, that *when* David was come to the top *of the mount*, where he worshipped God, behold, Hushai the Archite came to meet him with his coat ᵀrent, and earth upon his head: Josh. 16:2; 2 Sam. 1:2 ◆ *torn apart*

33 Unto whom David said, If thou passest on with me, then thou shalt be a burden unto me: 2 Sam. 19:35

34 But if thou return to the city, and say unto Absalom, I will be thy servant, O king; *as* I *have been* thy father's servant ᵀhitherto, so *will* I now also *be* thy servant: then mayest thou for me defeat the counsel of Ahithophel.   *up to now*

35 And *hast thou* not there with thee Zadok and Abiathar the priests? therefore it shall be, *that* what thing soever thou shalt hear out of the king's house, thou shalt tell *it* to Zadok and Abiathar the priests.   2 Sam. 17:15-16

36 Behold, *they have* there with them their two sons, Ahimaaz Zadok's *son*, and Jonathan

Abiathar's *son*; and by them ye shall send unto me every thing that ye can hear.   2 Sam. 17:17

37 So Hushai David's friend came into the city, and Absalom came into Jerusalem.

Ziba Brings Presents to David and Secures His Master's Inheritance

16 And when David was a little past the top *of the hill*, behold, Ziba the servant of Mephibosheth met him, with a couple of asses saddled, and upon them two hundred *loaves* of bread, and an hundred bunches of raisins, and an hundred of summer fruits, and a bottle of wine.   1 Sam. 25:18; 2 Sam. 9:2-13

2 And the king said unto Ziba, What meanest thou by these? And Ziba said, The asses *be* for the king's household to ride on; and the bread and summer fruit for the young men to eat; and the wine, that such as be faint in the wilderness may drink. Judg. 5:10; 10:4; 2 Sam. 17:29

3 And the king said, And where *is* thy master's son? And Ziba said unto the king, Behold, he abideth at Jerusalem: for he said, To day shall the house of Israel restore me the kingdom of my father.   2 Sam. 9:9-10

4 Then said the king to Ziba, Behold, thine *are* all that *pertained* unto Mephibosheth. And Ziba said, I humbly ᵀbeseech thee *that* I may find grace in thy sight, my lord, O king.   *beg*

Shimei Curses David

5 And when king David came to Bahurim, behold, thence came out a man of the family of the house of Saul, whose name *was* Shimei, the son of Gera: he came forth, and cursed still as he came. Ex. 22:28; 2 Sam. 3:16; 1 Kin. 2:8-9

6 And he cast stones at David, and at all the servants of king David: and all the people and all the mighty men *were* on his right hand and on his left.

7 And thus said Shimei when he cursed, Come out, come out, thou bloody man, and thou man of Belial: 2 Sam. 12:9

8 The Lord hath returned upon thee all the blood of the house of Saul, in whose stead thou hast reigned; and the Lord hath delivered the kingdom into the hand of Absalom thy son: and, behold, thou *art taken* in thy mischief, because thou *art* a bloody man.   2 Sam. 1:16

9 Then said Abishai the son of Zeruiah unto the king, Why should this dead dog curse my lord the king? let me go over, I pray thee, and take off his head. Ex. 22:28; 1 Sam. 24:14; 2 Sam. 9:8

10 And the king said, What have I to do with you, ye sons of Zeruiah? so let him curse, because the Lord hath said unto him, Curse David. Who shall then say, Wherefore hast thou done so?   2 Sam. 3:39; 19:22; Rom. 9:20

11 And David said to Abishai, and to all his

servants, Behold, my son, which came forth of my bowels, seeketh my life: how much more now *may this* Benjamite *do it?* let him alone, and let him curse; for the LORD hath bidden him.

12 It may be that the LORD will look on mine affliction, and that the LORD will ᵀrequite me good for his cursing this day.   Deut. 23:5 ♦ *repay*

16:12 Highest While Lowest

And the Lord did not forsake David. This chapter in his experience, when, under cruelest wrong and insult, he shows himself to be humble, unselfish, generous, and submissive, is one of the noblest in his whole experience. Never was the ruler of Israel more truly great in the sight of heaven than at this hour of his deepest outward humiliation. *PP 738*

---

13 And as David and his men went by the way, Shimei went along on the hill's side over against him, and cursed as he went, and threw stones at him, and cast dust.

14 And the king, and all the people that *were* with him, came weary, and refreshed themselves there.

Hushai Insinuates Himself into Absalom's Counsel

15 And Absalom, and all the people the men of Israel, came to Jerusalem, and Ahithophel with him.   2 Sam. 15:37

16 And it came to pass, when Hushai the Archite, David's friend, was come unto Absalom, that Hushai said unto Absalom, God save the king, God save the king. 1 Sam. 10:24

17 And Absalom said to Hushai, *Is* this thy kindness to thy friend? why wentest thou not with thy friend?   2 Sam. 19:25

18 And Hushai said unto Absalom, Nay; but whom the LORD, and this people, and all the men of Israel, choose, his will I be, and with him will I abide.

19 And again, whom should I serve? *should I not serve* in the presence of his son? as I have served in thy father's presence, so will I be in thy presence.   2 Sam. 15:34

20 Then said Absalom to Ahithophel, Give counsel among you what we shall do.

16:20–22 Prophetic Words Fulfilled

Thus was fulfilled the word of God to David by the prophet [see 2 Samuel 12:11, 12]. Not that God prompted these acts of wickedness, but because of David's sin He did not exercise His power to prevent them. *PP 739*

---

21 And Ahithophel said unto Absalom, Go in unto thy father's concubines, which he hath left to keep the house; and all Israel shall hear that thou art ᵀabhorred of thy father: then shall the hands of all that *are* with thee be strong.   2 Sam. 15:16 ♦ *despised*

22 So they spread Absalom a tent upon the top of the house; and Absalom went in unto his father's concubines in the sight of all Israel.   2 Sam. 12:11-12; 15:16; 20:3

23 And the counsel of Ahithophel, which he counselled in those days, *was* as if a man had enquired at the oracle of God: so *was* all the counsel of Ahithophel both with David and with Absalom.   2 Sam. 15:12; 17:14, 23

Ahithophel's Counsel Is Overthrown by Hushai's

17 Moreover Ahithophel said unto Absalom, Let me now choose out twelve thousand men, and I will arise and pursue after David this night:

2 And I will come upon him while he *is* weary and weak handed, and will make him afraid: and all the people that *are* with him shall flee; and I will ᵀsmite the king only: Deut. 25:18; 2 Sam. 16:14; 1 Kin. 22:31 ♦ *strike*

3 And I will bring back all the people unto thee: the man whom thou seekest *is* as if all returned: *so* all the people shall be in peace.

4 And the saying pleased Absalom well, and all the elders of Israel.

17:1–4 God Directly Interposes

This plan was approved by the king's counselors. Had it been followed, David would surely have been slain, unless the Lord had directly interposed to save him. But a wisdom higher than that of the renowned Ahithophel was directing events [see 2 Samuel 17:14]. *PP 740*

---

5 Then said Absalom, Call now Hushai the Archite also, and let us hear likewise what he saith.

6 And when Hushai was come to Absalom, Absalom spake unto him, saying, Ahithophel hath spoken after this manner: shall we do *after* his saying? if not; speak thou.

7 And Hushai said unto Absalom, The counsel that Ahithophel hath given *is* not good at this time.

8 For, said Hushai, thou knowest thy father and his men, that they *be* mighty men, and they *be* chafed in their minds, as a bear robbed of her whelps in the field: and thy father *is* a man of war, and will not lodge with the people.   1 Sam. 16:18; Prov. 17:12; Hos. 13:8

9 Behold, he is hid now in some pit, or in some *other* place: and it will come to pass, when some of them be overthrown at the first, that whosoever heareth it will say, There is a slaughter among the people that follow Absalom.

10 And he also *that is* valiant, whose heart *is*

as the heart of a lion, shall utterly melt: for all Israel knoweth that thy father *is* a mighty man, and *they* which *be* with him *are* valiant men.   Josh. 2:9-11

11 Therefore I counsel that all Israel be generally gathered unto thee, from Dan even to Beer-sheba, as the sand that *is* by the sea for multitude; and that thou go to battle in thine own person.   Gen. 22:17; Josh. 11:4; Judg. 20:1

12 So shall we come upon him in some place where he shall be found, and we will light upon him as the dew falleth on the ground: and of him and of all the men that *are* with him there shall not be left so much as one.

13 Moreover, if he be gotten into a city, then shall all Israel bring ropes to that city, and we will draw it into the river, until there be not one small stone found there.

14 And Absalom and all the men of Israel said, The counsel of Hushai the Archite *is* better than the counsel of Ahithophel. For the Lord had appointed to defeat the good counsel of Ahithophel, to the intent that the Lord might bring evil upon Absalom.   2 Sam. 15:31, 34; 16:23

David Receives Secret Intelligence

15 Then said Hushai unto Zadok and to Abiathar the priests, Thus and thus did Ahithophel counsel Absalom and the elders of Israel; and thus and thus have I counselled.

16 Now therefore send quickly, and tell David, saying, Lodge not this night in the plains of the wilderness, but speedily pass over; lest the king be swallowed up, and all the people that *are* with him.   2 Sam. 15:28

17 Now Jonathan and Ahimaaz stayed by En-rogel; for they might not be seen to come into the city: and a wench went and told them; and they went and told king David.   Josh. 15:7; 18:16; 2 Sam. 15:27

18 Nevertheless a lad saw them, and told Absalom: but they went both of them away quickly, and came to a man's house in Bahurim, which had a well in his court; whither they went down.   2 Sam. 3:16; 16:5

19 And the woman took and spread a covering over the well's mouth, and spread ground corn thereon; and the thing was not known.

20 And when Absalom's servants came to the woman to the house, they said, Where *is* Ahimaaz and Jonathan? And the woman said unto them, They be gone over the brook of water. And when they had sought and could not find *them*, they returned to Jerusalem.

21 And it came to pass, after they were departed, that they came up out of the well, and went and told king David, and said unto David, Arise, and pass quickly over the water: for thus hath Ahithophel counselled against you.   2 Sam. 17:15-16

22 Then David arose, and all the people that *were* with him, and they passed over Jordan: by the morning light there lacked not one of them that was not gone over Jordan.

23 And when Ahithophel saw that his counsel was not followed, he saddled *his* ass, and arose, and gat him home to his house, to his city, and put his household in order, and hanged himself, and died, and was buried in the sepulchre of his father.   2 Kin. 20:1; Matt. 27:5

17:23 Deadly Promises

Such was the result of the wisdom of one, who, with all his high endowments, did not make God his counselor. Satan allures men with flattering promises, but in the end it will be found by every soul, that the "wages of sin is death" (Romans 6:23). *PP 741*

---

24 Then David came to Mahanaim. And Absalom passed over Jordan, he and all the men of Israel with him.   Gen. 32:2

25 And Absalom made Amasa captain of the host instead of Joab: which Amasa *was* a man's son, whose name *was* Ithra an Israelite, that went in to Abigail the daughter of Nahash, sister to Zeruiah Joab's mother.   2 Sam. 19:13; 20:9-12; 1 Chr. 2:16

26 So Israel and Absalom pitched in the land of Gilead.

27 And it came to pass, when David was come to Mahanaim, that Shobi the son of Nahash of Rabbah of the children of Ammon, and Machir the son of Ammiel of Lo-debar, and Barzillai the Gileadite of Rogelim,   2 Sam. 9:4; 10:1-2; 1 Kin. 2:7

28 Brought beds, and basons, and earthen vessels, and wheat, and barley, and flour, and parched *corn*, and beans, and lentiles, and parched ᵀ*pulse*,   *seeds used for food*

29 And honey, and butter, and sheep, and cheese of ᵀkine, for David, and for the people that *were* with him, to eat: for they said, The people *is* hungry, and weary, and thirsty, in the wilderness.   2 Sam. 16:2, 14 ◆ *cattle*

David Sets Out to Defeat Absalom, but Charges His Army to be Kind

18 And David numbered the people that *were* with him, and set captains of thousands and captains of hundreds over them.

2 And David sent forth a third part of the people under the hand of Joab, and a third part under the hand of Abishai the son of Zeruiah, Joab's brother, and a third part under the hand of Ittai the Gittite. And the king said unto the people, I will surely go forth with you myself also.   Judg. 7:16

3 But the people answered, Thou shalt not go forth: for if we flee away, they will not care for us; neither if half of us die, will they care for us: but now *thou art* worth ten thousand of us: therefore now *it is* better that thou ᵀsuccour us out of the city. 2 Sam. 21:17 ◆ *help*

4 And the king said unto them, What seemeth you best I will do. And the king stood by the gate side, and all the people came out by hundreds and by thousands. 2 Sam. 18:24

5 And the king commanded Joab and Abishai and Ittai, saying, *Deal* gently for my sake with the young man, *even* with Absalom. And all the people heard when the king gave all the captains charge concerning Absalom.

6 So the people went out into the field against Israel: and the battle was in the wood of Ephraim; Josh. 17:15, 18

7 Where the people of Israel were slain before the servants of David, and there was there a great slaughter that day of twenty thousand *men*.

8 For the battle was there scattered over the face of all the country: and the wood devoured more people that day than the sword devoured.

Caught by His Hair in a Tree, Absalom Is Slain by Joab

9 And Absalom met the servants of David. And Absalom rode upon a mule, and the mule went under the thick boughs of a great oak, and his head caught hold of the oak, and he was taken up between the heaven and the earth; and the mule that *was* under him went away. 2 Sam. 14:26

10 And a certain man saw *it*, and told Joab, and said, Behold, I saw Absalom hanged in an oak.

11 And Joab said unto the man that told him, And, behold, thou sawest *him*, and why didst thou not ᵀsmite him there to the ground? and I would have given thee ten *shekels* of silver, and a ᵀgirdle. *strike* ◆ *belt*

12 And the man said unto Joab, Though I should receive a thousand *shekels* of silver in mine hand, *yet* would I not put forth mine hand against the king's son: for in our hearing the king charged thee and Abishai and Ittai, saying, Beware that none *touch* the young man Absalom.

13 Otherwise I should have ᵀwrought falsehood against mine own life: for there is no matter hid from the king, and thou thyself wouldest have set thyself against me. 2 Sam. 14:19-20 ◆ *brought*

14 Then said Joab, I may not tarry thus with thee. And he took three darts in his hand, and thrust them through the heart of Absa-

lom, while he *was* yet alive in the midst of the oak.

15 And ten young men that bare Joab's armour ᵀcompassed about and smote Absalom, and slew him. *surrounded*

16 And Joab blew the trumpet, and the people returned from pursuing after Israel: for Joab held back the people. 2 Sam. 2:28

17 And they took Absalom, and cast him into a great pit in the wood, and laid a very great heap of stones upon him: and all Israel fled every one to his tent. Josh. 7:26; 8:29

18 Now Absalom in his lifetime had taken and reared up for himself a pillar, which *is* in the king's dale: for he said, I have no son to keep my name in remembrance: and he called the pillar after his own name: and it is called unto this day, Absalom's place. Gen. 14:17; 1 Sam. 15:12; 2 Sam. 14:27

David Receives News of Absalom's Death

19 Then said Ahimaaz the son of Zadok, Let me now run, and bear the king tidings, how that the LORD hath avenged him of his enemies. 2 Sam. 15:36; 18:31

20 And Joab said unto him, Thou shalt not bear tidings this day, but thou shalt bear tidings another day: but this day thou shalt bear no tidings, because the king's son is dead.

21 Then said Joab to Cushi, Go tell the king what thou hast seen. And Cushi bowed himself unto Joab, and ran.

22 Then said Ahimaaz the son of Zadok yet again to Joab, But howsoever, let me, I pray thee, also run after Cushi. And Joab said, Wherefore wilt thou run, my son, seeing that thou hast no tidings ready?

23 But howsoever, *said he*, let me run. And he said unto him, Run. Then Ahimaaz ran by the way of the plain, and overran Cushi.

24 And David sat between the two gates: and the watchman went up to the roof over the gate unto the wall, and lifted up his eyes, and looked, and behold a man running alone. 2 Sam. 19:8

25 And the watchman cried, and told the king. And the king said, If he *be* alone, *there* is tidings in his mouth. And he came ᵀapace, and drew near. *quickly*

26 And the watchman saw another man running: and the watchman called unto the ᵀporter, and said, Behold *another* man running alone. And the king said, He also bringeth tidings. *doorkeeper*

27 And the watchman said, Me thinketh the running of the foremost is like the running of Ahimaaz the son of Zadok. And the king said, He *is* a good man, and cometh with good tidings. 1 Kin. 1:42; 2 Kin. 9:20

28 And Ahimaaz called, and said unto the king, All is well. And he fell down to the earth upon his face before the king, and said, Blessed be the LORD thy God, which hath delivered up the men that lifted up their hand against my lord the king.   Gen. 14:20

29 And the king said, Is the young man Absalom safe? And Ahimaaz answered, When Joab sent the king's servant, and me thy servant, I saw a great tumult, but I knew not what it was.   2 Sam. 18:22

30 And the king said unto him, Turn aside, and stand here. And he turned aside, and stood still.

31 And, behold, Cushi came; and Cushi said, Tidings, my lord the king: for the LORD hath avenged thee this day of all them that rose up against thee.   2 Sam. 18:19

32 And the king said unto Cushi, Is the young man Absalom safe? And Cushi answered, The enemies of my lord the king, and all that rise against thee to do thee hurt, be as that young man is.   Judg. 5:31

33 And the king was much moved, and went up to the chamber over the gate, and wept: and as he went, thus he said, O my son Absalom, my son, my son Absalom! would God I had died for thee, O Absalom, my son, my son!   2 Sam. 19:4

Joab Causes the King to Cease His Mourning

19 And it was told Joab, Behold, the king weepeth and mourneth for Absalom.   2 Sam. 18:5

2 And the victory that day was turned into mourning unto all the people: for the people heard say that day how the king was grieved for his son.

3 And the people gat them by stealth that day into the city, as people being ashamed steal away when they flee in battle.

4 But the king covered his face, and the king cried with a loud voice, O my son Absalom, O Absalom, my son, my son!   2 Sam. 15:30

5 And Joab came into the house to the king, and said, Thou hast shamed this day the faces of all thy servants, which this day have saved thy life, and the lives of thy sons and of thy daughters, and the lives of thy wives, and the lives of thy concubines;

6 In that thou lovest thine enemies, and hatest thy friends. For thou hast declared this day, that thou regardest neither princes nor servants: for this day I perceive, that if Absalom had lived, and all we had died this day, then it had pleased thee well.

7 Now therefore arise, go forth, and speak comfortably unto thy servants: for I swear by the LORD, if thou go not forth, there will not tarry one with thee this night: and

that will be worse unto thee than all the evil that befell thee from thy youth until now.   Prov. 14:28

19:1–7 Victory, Yet Mourning

Joab was filled with indignation. God had given them reason for triumph and gladness; the greatest rebellion that had ever been known in Israel had been crushed; and yet this great victory was turned to mourning for him whose crime had cost the blood of thousands of brave men. The rude, blunt captain pushed his way into the presence of the king, and boldly [voiced his displeasure with David; see verses 5–7]. PP 745

8 Then the king arose, and sat in the gate. And they told unto all the people, saying, Behold, the king doth sit in the gate. And all the people came before the king: for Israel had fled every man to his tent.   2 Sam. 18:24

The Israelites Desire to Bring King David Back to Jerusalem

9 And all the people were at strife throughout all the tribes of Israel, saying, The king saved us out of the hand of our enemies, and he delivered us out of the hand of the Philistines; and now he is fled out of the land for Absalom.   2 Sam. 8:1-14; 15:14

10 And Absalom, whom we anointed over us, is dead in battle. Now therefore why speak ye not a word of bringing the king back?

11 And king David sent to Zadok and to Abiathar the priests, saying, Speak unto the elders of Judah, saying, Why are ye the last to bring the king back to his house? seeing the speech of all Israel is come to the king, even to his house.   2 Sam. 15:29

12 Ye are my brethren, ye are my bones and my flesh: wherefore then are ye the last to bring back the king?   2 Sam. 5:1

13 And say ye to Amasa, Art thou not of my bone, and of my flesh? God do so to me, and more also, if thou be not captain of the host before me continually in the room of Joab.   Ruth 1:17; 2 Sam. 8:16; 17:25

14 And he bowed the heart of all the men of Judah, even as the heart of one man; so that they sent this word unto the king, Return thou, and all thy servants.   Judg. 20:1

15 So the king returned, and came to Jordan. And Judah came to Gilgal, to go to meet the king, to conduct the king over Jordan.   Josh. 5:9

16 And Shimei the son of Gera, a Benjamite, which was of Bahurim, hasted and came down with the men of Judah to meet king David.   2 Sam. 16:5-13; 1 Kin. 2:8

17 And there were a thousand men of

Benjamin with him, and Ziba the servant of the house of Saul, and his fifteen sons and his twenty servants with him; and they went over Jordan before the king.   2 Sam. 9:2

18 And there went over a ferry boat to carry over the king's household, and to do what he thought good. And Shimei the son of Gera fell down before the king, as he was come over Jordan;

19 And said unto the king, Let not my lord ᵀimpute iniquity unto me, neither do thou remember that which thy servant did perversely the day that my lord the king went out of Jerusalem, that the king should take it to his heart.   1 Sam. 22:15 ◆ count

20 For thy servant doth know that I have sinned: therefore, behold, I am come the first this day of all the house of Joseph to go down to meet my lord the king.   2 Sam. 16:5

21 But Abishai the son of Zeruiah answered and said, Shall not Shimei be put to death for this, because he cursed the LORD's anointed?   Ex. 22:28; 1 Sam. 26:9

22 And David said, What have I to do with you, ye sons of Zeruiah, that ye should this day be adversaries unto me? shall there any man be put to death this day in Israel? for do not I know that I *am* this day king over Israel?   1 Sam. 11:13; 2 Sam. 3:39; 16:10

23 Therefore the king said unto Shimei, Thou shalt not die. And the king sware unto him.   1 Kin. 2:8-9

Mephibosheth Excused

24 And Mephibosheth the son of Saul came down to meet the king, and had neither dressed his feet, nor trimmed his beard, nor washed his clothes, from the day the king departed until the day he came *again* in peace.

25 And it came to pass, when he was come to Jerusalem to meet the king, that the king said unto him, Wherefore wentest not thou with me, Mephibosheth?   2 Sam. 16:17

26 And he answered, My lord, O king, my servant deceived me: for thy servant said, I will saddle me an ass, that I may ride thereon, and go to the king; because thy servant *is* lame.

27 And he hath slandered thy servant unto my lord the king; but my lord the king *is* as an angel of God: do therefore *what is* good in thine eyes.   1 Sam. 29:9; 2 Sam. 14:17, 20

28 For all *of* my father's house were but dead men before my lord the king: yet didst thou set thy servant among them that did eat at thine own table. What right therefore have I yet to cry any more unto the king? 2 Sam. 9:10

29 And the king said unto him, Why speakest thou any more of thy matters? I have said, Thou and Ziba divide the land.

30 And Mephibosheth said unto the king, Yea, let him take all, ᵀforasmuch as my lord the king is come again in peace unto his own house.   *since*

31 And Barzillai the Gileadite came down from Rogelim, and went over Jordan with the king, to conduct him over Jordan. 1 Kin. 2:7

32 Now Barzillai was a very aged man, *even* ᵀfourscore years old: and he had provided the king of sustenance while he lay at Mahanaim; for he *was* a very great man.   1 Sam. 25:2 ◆ eighty

33 And the king said unto Barzillai, Come thou over with me, and I will feed thee with me in Jerusalem.

34 And Barzillai said unto the king, How long have I to live, that I should go up with the king unto Jerusalem?

35 I *am* this day fourscore years old: *and* can I discern between good and evil? can thy servant taste what I eat or what I drink? can I hear any more the voice of singing men and singing women? wherefore then should thy servant be yet a burden unto my lord the king?   2 Sam. 15:33; Ezra 2:65; Ps. 90:10

36 Thy servant will go a little way over Jordan with the king: and why should the king ᵀrecompense it me with such a reward? *repay*

37 Let thy servant, I pray thee, turn back again, that I may die in mine own city, *and be buried* by the grave of my father and of my mother. But behold thy servant Chimham; let him go over with my lord the king; and do to him what shall seem good unto thee.   2 Sam. 19:40; 1 Kin. 2:7; Jer. 41:17

38 And the king answered, Chimham shall go over with me, and I will do to him that which shall seem good unto thee: and whatsoever thou shalt require of me, *that* will I do for thee.

39 And all the people went over Jordan. And when the king was come over, the king kissed Barzillai, and blessed him; and he returned unto his own place.   Gen. 31:55; 47:7; Ruth 1:14

40 Then the king went on to Gilgal, and Chimham went on with him: and all the people of Judah conducted the king, and also half the people of Israel.

41 And, behold, all the men of Israel came to the king, and said unto the king, Why have our brethren the men of Judah stolen thee away, and have brought the king, and his household, and all David's men with him, over Jordan?   Judg. 8:1

42 And all the men of Judah answered the men of Israel, Because the king *is* near of kin to us: wherefore then be ye angry for this matter? have we eaten at all of the king's *cost*? or hath he given us any gift? 2 Sam. 19:12

43 And the men of Israel answered the men of Judah, and said, We have ten parts in the king, and we have also more *right* in David

than ye: why then did ye despise us, that our advice should not be first had in bringing back our king? And the words of the men of Judah were fiercer than the words of the men of Israel.   2 Sam. 5:1

Sheba Incites a Rebellion against King David

20 And there happened to be there a man of Belial, whose name *was* Sheba, the son of Bichri, a Benjamite: and he blew a trumpet, and said, We have no part in David, neither have we inheritance in the son of Jesse: every man to his tents, O Israel.   Deut. 13:13; 1 Kin. 12:16; 2 Chr. 10:16

2 So every man of Israel went up from after David, *and* followed Sheba the son of Bichri: but the men of Judah ᵀclave unto their king, from Jordan even to Jerusalem.   *clung*

3 And David came to his house at Jerusalem; and the king took the ten women *his* concubines, whom he had left to keep the house, and put them in ᵀward, and fed them, but went not in unto them. So they were shut up unto the day of their death, living in widowhood.   2 Sam. 15:16; 16:21-22 ◆ *prison* or *guard*

Amasa, Made Captain over Judah, Is Slain by Joab

4 Then said the king to Amasa, Assemble me the men of Judah within three days, and be thou here present.   2 Sam. 17:25; 19:13

5 So Amasa went to assemble *the men of* Judah: but he tarried longer than the set time which he had appointed him. 1 Sam. 13:8

6 And David said to Abishai, Now shall Sheba the son of Bichri do us more harm than *did* Absalom: take thou thy lord's servants, and pursue after him, lest he get him fenced cities, and escape us.   2 Sam. 11:11

7 And there went out after him Joab's men, and the Cherethites, and the Pelethites, and all the mighty men: and they went out of Jerusalem, to pursue after Sheba the son of Bichri.   2 Sam. 8:18; 15:18; 1 Kin. 1:38

8 When they *were* at the great stone which *is* in Gibeon, Amasa went before them. And Joab's garment that he had put on was girded unto him, and upon it a ᵀgirdle *with* a sword fastened upon his ᵀloins in the ᵀsheath thereof; and as he went forth it fell out.   2 Sam. 2:13 ◆ *belt* ◆ *waist* ◆ *case for a sword*

9 And Joab said to Amasa, *Art* thou in health, my brother? And Joab took Amasa by the beard with the right hand to kiss him.

10 But Amasa took no heed to the sword that *was* in Joab's hand: so he smote him therewith in the fifth *rib*, and shed out his bowels to the ground, and struck him not again; and he died. So Joab and Abishai

his brother pursued after Sheba the son of Bichri.   Judg. 3:21; 2 Sam. 2:23; 3:27

11 And one of Joab's men stood by him, and said, He that favoureth Joab, and he that *is* for David, *let him go* after Joab.   2 Sam. 20:13

12 And Amasa ᵀwallowed in blood in the midst of the highway. And when the man saw that all the people stood still, he removed Amasa out of the highway into the field, and cast a cloth upon him, when he saw that every one that came by him stood still.   *rolled*

13 When he was removed out of the highway, all the people went on after Joab, to pursue after Sheba the son of Bichri.

Joab Pursues Sheba, Who Is Killed by the Citizens of Abel

14 And he went through all the tribes of Israel unto Abel, and to Beth-maachah, and all the Berites: and they were gathered together, and went also after him.   2 Kin. 15:29

15 And they came and besieged him in Abel of Beth-maachah, and they cast up a bank against the city, and it stood in the trench: and all the people that *were* with Joab battered the wall, to throw it down.   2 Kin. 19:32; Jer. 32:24

16 Then cried a wise woman out of the city, Hear, hear; say, I pray you, unto Joab, Come near ᵀhither, that I may speak with thee.   2 Sam. 14:2 ◆ *here*

17 And when he was come near unto her, the woman said, *Art* thou Joab? And he answered, I *am he*. Then she said unto him, Hear the words of thine handmaid. And he answered, I do hear.

18 Then she spake, saying, They were ᵀwont to speak in old time, saying, They shall surely ask *counsel* at Abel: and so they ended *the matter*.   *accustomed*

19 I *am* one of them that are peaceable *and* faithful in Israel: thou seekest to destroy a city and a mother in Israel: why wilt thou swallow up the inheritance of the LORD?   1 Sam. 26:19

20 And Joab answered and said, Far be it, far be it from me, that I should swallow up or destroy.

21 The matter *is* not so: but a man of mount Ephraim, Sheba the son of Bichri by name, hath lifted up his hand against the king, *even* against David: deliver him only, and I will depart from the city. And the woman said unto Joab, Behold, his head shall be thrown to thee over the wall.

22 Then the woman went unto all the people in her wisdom. And they cut off the head of Sheba the son of Bichri, and cast *it* out to Joab. And he blew a trumpet, and they retired from the city, every man to his tent. And Joab returned to Jerusalem unto the king.   2 Sam. 20:1

David's Officers

23 Now Joab *was* over all the host of Israel: and Benaiah the son of Jehoiada *was* over the Cherethites and over the Pelethites: 2 Sam. 8:16
24 And Adoram *was* over the tribute: and Jehoshaphat the son of Ahilud *was* recorder: 1 Kin. 4:3
25 And Sheva *was* scribe: and Zadok and Abiathar *were* the priests: 2 Sam. 8:17
26 And Ira also the Jairite was a chief ruler about David.   2 Sam. 23:38

God Calls David to Avenge the People of Gibeon

21 Then there was a famine in the days of David three years, year after year; and David enquired of the LORD. And the LORD answered, *It is* for Saul, and for *his* bloody house, because he slew the Gibeonites.   Gen. 12:10
2 And the king called the Gibeonites, and said unto them; (now the Gibeonites *were* not of the children of Israel, but of the remnant of the Amorites; and the children of Israel had sworn unto them: and Saul sought to slay them in his zeal to the children of Israel and Judah.)
3 Wherefore David said unto the Gibeonites, What shall I do for you? and wherewith shall I make the atonement, that ye may bless the inheritance of the LORD?   2 Sam. 20:19
4 And the Gibeonites said unto him, We will have no silver nor gold of Saul, nor of his house; neither for us shalt thou kill any man in Israel. And he said, What ye shall say, *that* will I do for you.
5 And they answered the king, The man that consumed us, and that devised against us *that* we should be destroyed from remaining in any of the coasts of Israel,   2 Sam. 21:1
6 Let seven men of his sons be delivered unto us, and we will hang them up unto the LORD in Gibeah of Saul, *whom* the LORD did choose. And the king said, I will give *them*.   1 Sam. 10:24, 26; 11:4
7 But the king spared Mephibosheth, the son of Jonathan the son of Saul, because of the LORD's oath that *was* between them, between David and Jonathan the son of Saul.   1 Sam. 18:3
8 But the king took the two sons of Rizpah the daughter of Aiah, whom she bare unto Saul, Armoni and Mephibosheth; and the five sons of Michal the daughter of Saul, whom she brought up for Adriel the son of Barzillai the Meholathite: 1 Sam. 18:19; 2 Sam. 3:7
9 And he delivered them into the hands of the Gibeonites, and they hanged them in the hill before the LORD: and they fell *all* seven together, and were put to death in the days

of harvest, in the first *days,* in the beginning of barley harvest.   Ruth 1:22

Rizpah's Kindness to the Dead

10 And Rizpah the daughter of Aiah took sackcloth, and spread it for her upon the rock, from the beginning of harvest until water dropped upon them out of heaven, and suffered neither the birds of the air to rest on them by day, nor the beasts of the field by night.   Deut. 21:23
11 And it was told David what Rizpah the daughter of Aiah, the ᵀconcubine of Saul, had done.   *less important wife*
12 And David went and took the bones of Saul and the bones of Jonathan his son from the men of Jabesh-gilead, which had stolen them from the street of Beth-shan, where the Philistines had hanged them, when the Philistines had slain Saul in Gilboa: Josh. 17:11
13 And he brought up from thence the bones of Saul and the bones of Jonathan his son; and they gathered the bones of them that were hanged.
14 And the bones of Saul and Jonathan his son buried they in the country of Benjamin in Zelah, in the sepulchre of Kish his father: and they performed all that the king commanded. And after that God was ᵀintreated for the land. Josh. 7:26; 18:28; 2 Sam. 24:25 ♦ *pled with*

David Slays Four Giant Philistine Warriors

15 Moreover the Philistines had yet war again with Israel; and David went down, and his servants with him, and fought against the Philistines: and David waxed faint.   2 Sam. 5:17
16 And Ishbi-benob, which *was* of the sons of the giant, the weight of whose spear *weighed* three hundred *shekels* of brass in weight, he being girded with a new *sword,* thought to have slain David.   2 Sam. 21:18
17 But Abishai the son of Zeruiah ᵀsuccoured him, and smote the Philistine, and killed him. Then the men of David sware unto him, saying, Thou shalt go no more out with us to battle, that thou quench not the light of Israel.   2 Sam. 18:3; 20:6-10; 1 Kin. 11:36 ♦ *helped*
18 And it came to pass after this, that there was again a battle with the Philistines at Gob: then Sibbechai the Hushathite slew Saph, which *was* of the sons of the giant. 1 Chr. 11:29
19 And there was again a battle in Gob with the Philistines, where Elhanan the son of Jaareoregim, a Beth-lehemite, slew *the brother of* Goliath the Gittite, the staff of whose spear *was* like a weaver's beam.   1 Chr. 20:5
20 And there was yet a battle in Gath, where was a man of *great* stature, that had on every hand six fingers, and on every foot six toes,

four and twenty in number; and he also was born to the giant.   2 Sam. 21:16

21 And when he defied Israel, Jonathan the son of Shimea the brother of David slew him.   1 Sam. 16:9

22 These four were born to the giant in Gath, and fell by the hand of David, and by the hand of his servants.   1 Chr. 20:8

A Psalm of Thanksgiving

22 And David spake unto the LORD the words of this song in the day *that* the LORD had delivered him out of the hand of all his enemies, and out of the hand of Saul: Ex. 15:1; Judg. 5:1

2 And he said, The LORD *is* my rock, and my fortress, and my deliverer;   Deut. 32:4; Ps. 31:3

3 The God of my rock; in him will I trust: *he is* my shield, and the horn of my salvation, my high tower, and my refuge, my saviour; thou savest me from violence.   Ps. 9:9; Luke 1:69

4 I will call on the LORD, *who is* worthy to be praised: so shall I be saved from mine enemies.   Ps. 48:1

5 When the waves of death compassed me, the floods of ungodly men made me afraid;

6 The sorrows of hell compassed me about; the snares of death prevented me;   Ps. 116:3

7 In my distress I called upon the LORD, and cried to my God: and he did hear my voice out of his temple, and my cry *did enter* into his ears.   Ps. 18:6; 116:4; 120:1

8 Then the earth shook and trembled; the foundations of heaven moved and shook, because he was wroth.   Judg. 5:4; Job 26:11; Ps. 97:4

9 There went up a smoke out of his nostrils, and fire out of his mouth devoured: coals were kindled by it.   Heb. 12:29

10 He bowed the heavens also, and came down; and darkness *was* under his feet. Ps. 97:2

11 And he rode upon a cherub, and did fly: and he was seen upon the wings of the wind.   Ps. 104:3

12 And he made darkness pavilions round about him, dark waters, *and* thick clouds of the skies.   2 Sam. 22:10

13 Through the brightness before him were coals of fire kindled.   2 Sam. 22:9

14 The LORD thundered from heaven, and the most High uttered his voice.   1 Sam. 2:10

15 And he sent out arrows, and scattered them; lightning, and discomfited them.

16 And the channels of the sea appeared, the foundations of the world were discovered, at the rebuking of the LORD, at the blast of the breath of his nostrils.   Nah. 1:4

17 He sent from above, he took me; he drew me out of many waters;   Ps. 144:7

18 He delivered me from my strong enemy, *and* from them that hated me: for they were too strong for me.

19 They prevented me in the day of my calamity: but the LORD was my stay.

20 He brought me forth also into a large place: he delivered me, because he delighted in me.   2 Sam. 15:26; Ps. 31:8; 118:5

21 The LORD rewarded me according to my righteousness: according to the cleanness of my hands hath he recompensed me.   Ps. 24:4

22 For I have kept the ways of the LORD, and have not wickedly departed from my God.   Gen. 18:19; Ps. 128:1; Prov. 8:32

23 For all his judgments *were* before me: and *as for* his statutes, I did not depart from them.   Ps. 119:30, 102

24 I was also upright before him, and have kept myself from mine iniquity.   Gen. 6:9; Job 1:1

25 Therefore the LORD hath recompensed me according to my righteousness; according to my cleanness in his eye sight.   2 Sam. 22:21

26 With the merciful thou wilt shew thyself merciful, *and* with the upright man thou wilt shew thyself upright.   Matt. 5:7

27 With the pure thou wilt shew thyself pure; and with the ᵀfroward thou wilt shew thyself unsavoury.   Matt. 5:8 ◆ *false, perverse*

28 And the afflicted people thou wilt save: but thine eyes *are* upon the haughty, *that* thou mayest bring *them* down.   Ps. 72:12; Is. 5:15

29 For thou *art* my lamp, O LORD: and the LORD will lighten my darkness.   Job 29:3

30 For by thee I have run through a troop: by my God have I leaped over a wall.

31 *As for* God, his way *is* perfect; the word of the LORD *is* tried: he *is* a buckler to all them that trust in him.   Deut. 32:4; Prov. 30:5; Matt. 5:48

32 For who *is* God, save the LORD? and who *is* a rock, save our God?   1 Sam. 2:2

33 God *is* my strength *and* power: and he maketh my way perfect.

34 He maketh my feet like hinds' *feet*: and setteth me upon my high places.   Hab. 3:19

35 He teacheth my hands to war; so that a bow of steel is broken by mine arms. Ps. 144:1

36 Thou hast also given me the shield of thy salvation: and thy gentleness hath made me great.   Eph. 6:16

37 Thou hast enlarged my steps under me; so that my feet did not slip.   Prov. 4:12

38 I have pursued mine enemies, and destroyed them; and turned not again until I had consumed them.

39 And I have consumed them, and wounded them, that they could not arise: yea, they are fallen under my feet.   Mal. 4:3

40 For thou hast girded me with strength to battle: them that rose up against me hast thou subdued under me.   Ps. 44:5

41 Thou hast also given me the necks of mine enemies, that I might destroy them that hate me.   Ex. 23:27; Josh. 10:24

42 They looked, but *there was* none to save; *even* unto the LORD, but he answered them not.   1 Sam. 28:6; Prov. 1:28; Is. 1:15

43 Then did I beat them as small as the dust of the earth, I did stamp them as the ᵀmire of the street, *and* did spread them abroad.   2 Kin. 13:7; Is. 10:6; Mic. 7:10 ◆ *mud*

44 Thou also hast delivered me from the strivings of my people, thou hast kept me *to be* head of the heathen: a people *which* I knew not shall serve me.   2 Sam. 3:1; 8:1-14; Is. 55:5

45 Strangers shall submit themselves unto me: as soon as they hear, they shall be obedient unto me.   Ps. 66:3

46 Strangers shall fade away, and they shall be afraid out of their close places.   Mic. 7:17

47 The LORD liveth; and blessed *be* my rock; and exalted be the God of the rock of my salvation.   Ps. 89:26

48 It *is* God that avengeth me, and that bringeth down the people under me,   Ps. 94:1; 144:2

49 And that bringeth me forth from mine enemies: thou also hast lifted me up on high above them that rose up against me: thou hast delivered me from the violent man.   Ps. 140:1

50 Therefore I will give thanks unto thee, O LORD, among the heathen, and I will sing praises unto thy name.   Rom. 15:9

51 *He is* the tower of salvation for his king: and sheweth mercy to his anointed, unto David, and to his seed for evermore. 2 Sam. 7:12

David Professes His Faith in God's Promises

23 Now these *be* the last words of David. David the son of Jesse said, and the man *who was* raised up on high, the anointed of the God of Jacob, and the sweet psalmist of Israel, said,   1 Sam. 16:12-13; 2 Sam. 7:8-9; Ps. 89:20

2 The Spirit of the LORD spake by me, and his word *was* in my tongue.   Matt. 22:43; 2 Pet. 1:21

3 The God of Israel said, the Rock of Israel spake to me, He that ruleth over men *must be* just, ruling in the fear of God.   Ex. 18:21

4 And *he shall be* as the light of the morning, *when* the sun riseth, *even* a morning without clouds; *as* the tender grass *springing* out of the earth by clear shining after rain.   Ps. 72:6; 89:36

5 Although my house *be* not so with God; yet he hath made with me an everlasting covenant, ordered in all *things*, and sure: for *this is* all my salvation, and all *my* desire, although he make *it* not to grow.   Is. 9:6-7; 55:3

6 But *the sons* of Belial *shall be* all of them as thorns thrust away, because they cannot be taken with hands:

7 But the man *that* shall touch them must be fenced with iron and the staff of a spear; and they shall be utterly burned with fire in the *same* place.   Heb. 6:8

A Catalogue of David's Mighty Men

8 These *be* the names of the mighty men whom David had: The Tachmonite that sat in the seat, chief among the captains; the same *was* Adino the Eznite: *he lift up his spear* against eight hundred, whom he slew at one time.

9 And after him *was* Eleazar the son of Dodo the Ahohite, *one* of the three mighty men with David, when they defied the Philistines *that* were there gathered together to battle, and the men of Israel were gone away: 1 Chr. 27:4

10 He arose, and smote the Philistines until his hand was weary, and his hand ᵀclave unto the sword: and the LORD wrought a great victory that day; and the people returned after him only to ᵀspoil.   1 Sam. 11:13 ◆ *clung* ◆ *plunder*

11 And after him *was* Shammah the son of Agee the Hararite. And the Philistines were gathered together into a troop, where was a piece of ground full of lentiles: and the people fled from the Philistines.

12 But he stood in the midst of the ground, and defended it, and slew the Philistines: and the LORD ᵀwrought a great victory. 2 Sam. 23:10

13 And three of the thirty chief went down, and came to David in the harvest time unto the cave of Adullam: and the troop of the Philistines pitched in the valley of Rephaim.   1 Sam. 22:1; 2 Sam. 5:18

14 And David *was* then in an hold, and the garrison of the Philistines *was* then *in* Bethlehem.   1 Sam. 22:4-5

15 And David longed, and said, Oh that one would give me drink of the water of the well of Beth-lehem, which *is* by the gate! John 4:14

16 And the three mighty men brake through the host of the Philistines, and drew water out of the well of Beth-lehem, that *was* by the gate, and took *it*, and brought *it* to David: nevertheless he would not drink thereof, but poured it out unto the LORD.

17 And he said, Be it far from me, O LORD, that I should do this: *is not this* the blood of the men that went in jeopardy of their lives? therefore he would not drink it. These things did these three mighty men. Lev. 17:10

18 And Abishai, the brother of Joab, the son of Zeruiah, was chief among three. And he lifted up his spear against three hundred, *and* slew *them*, and had the name among three.   2 Sam. 10:10

19 Was he not most honourable of three? therefore he was their captain: ᵀhowbeit he attained not unto the *first* three.   *however*

20 And Benaiah the son of Jehoiada, the son of a valiant man, of Kabzeel, who

had done many acts, he slew two lion-like men of Moab: he went down also and slew a lion in the midst of a pit in time of snow: Josh. 15:21; 2 Sam. 8:18; 20:23

21 And he slew an Egyptian, a goodly man: and the Egyptian had a spear in his hand; but he went down to him with a staff, and plucked the spear out of the Egyptian's hand, and slew him with his own spear.

22 These *things* did Benaiah the son of Jehoiada, and had the name among three mighty men.

23 He was more honourable than the thirty, but he attained not to the *first* three. And David set him over his guard.

24 Asahel the brother of Joab *was* one of the thirty; Elhanan the son of Dodo of Bethlehem, 2 Sam. 2:18; 1 Chr. 27:7

25 Shammah the Harodite, Elika the Harodite,

26 Helez the Paltite, Ira the son of Ikkesh the Tekoite, 2 Sam. 14:2

27 Abiezer the Anethothite, Mebunnai the Hushathite, Josh. 21:18

28 Zalmon the Ahohite, Maharai the Netophathite, 2 Kin. 25:23

29 Heleb the son of Baanah, a Netophathite, Ittai the son of Ribai out of Gibeah of the children of Benjamin,

30 Benaiah the Pirathonite, Hiddai of the brooks of Gaash, Judg. 12:15

31 Abialbon the Arbathite, Azmaveth the Barhumite, 2 Sam. 3:16

32 Eliahba the Shaalbonite, of the sons of Jashen, Jonathan,

33 Shammah the Hararite, Ahiam the son of Sharar the Hararite,

34 Eliphelet the son of Ahasbai, the son of the Maachathite, Eliam the son of Ahithophel the Gilonite, 2 Sam. 11:3; 15:12

35 Hezrai the Carmelite, Paarai the Arbite,

36 Igal the son of Nathan of Zobah, Bani the Gadite,

37 Zelek the Ammonite, Naharai the Beerothite, armourbearer to Joab the son of Zeruiah,

38 Ira an Ithrite, Gareb an Ithrite, 1 Chr. 2:53

39 Uriah the Hittite: thirty and seven in all.

David Forces Joab to Number the People

24 And again the anger of the LORD was kindled against Israel, and he moved David against them to say, Go, number Israel and Judah. 1 Chr. 27:23-24

2 For the king said to Joab the captain of the host, which *was* with him, Go now through all the tribes of Israel, from Dan even to Beersheba, and number ye the people, that I may know the number of the people. Judg. 20:1

3 And Joab said unto the king, Now the LORD thy God add unto the people, how many soever they be, an hundredfold, and that the eyes of my lord the king may see *it*: but why doth my lord the king delight in this thing? Deut. 1:11

24:3 An Unprincipled Endeavor

The proposed enrollment caused much dissatisfaction; consequently it was thought necessary to employ the military officers in place of the priests and magistrates, who had formerly taken the census. The object of the undertaking was directly contrary to the principles of a theocracy. Even Joab remonstrated, unscrupulous as he had heretofore shown himself. *PP 747*

4 Notwithstanding the king's word prevailed against Joab, and against the captains of the host. And Joab and the captains of the host went out from the presence of the king, to number the people of Israel.

5 And they passed over Jordan, and pitched

Driven by Pride

2 Samuel 24

Intercourse [association] with heathen peoples led to a desire to follow their national customs and kindled ambition for worldly greatness. As the people of Jehovah, Israel was to be honored; but as pride and self-confidence increased, the Israelites were not content with this pre-eminence. They cared rather for their standing among other nations. This spirit could not fail to invite temptation. With a view to extending his conquests among foreign nations, David determined to increase his army by requiring military service from all who were of proper age. To effect this, it became necessary to take a census of the population. It was pride and ambition that prompted this action of the king. The numbering of the people would show the contrast between the weakness of the kingdom when David ascended the throne and its strength and prosperity under his rule. This would tend still further to foster the already too great self-confidence of both king and people. [See 1 Chronicles 21:1.] The prosperity of Israel under David had been due to the blessing of God rather than to the ability of her king or the strength of her armies. But the increasing of the military resources of the kingdom would give the impression to surrounding nations that Israel's trust was in her armies, and not in the power of Jehovah. *PP 746, 747*

in Aroer, on the right side of the city that *lieth* in the midst of the river of Gad, and toward Jazer: Deut. 2:36; Josh. 13:9, 16

6 Then they came to Gilead, and to the land of Tahtim-hodshi; and they came to Dan-jaan, and about to Zidon, Josh. 19:28

7 And came to the strong hold of Tyre, and to all the cities of the Hivites, and of the Canaanites: and they went out to the south of Judah, *even* to Beer-sheba. Josh. 19:29

8 So when they had gone through all the land, they came to Jerusalem at the end of nine months and twenty days.

9 And Joab gave up the sum of the number of the people unto the king: and there were in Israel eight hundred thousand valiant men that drew the sword; and the men of Judah *were* five hundred thousand men.

Consequences of David's Sin

10 And David's heart smote him after that he had numbered the people. And David said unto the LORD, I have sinned greatly in that I have done: and now, I ᵀbeseech thee, O LORD, take away the iniquity of thy servant; for I have done very foolishly. 1 Sam. 13:13; 24:5; ◆ beg

11 For when David was up in the morning, the word of the LORD came unto the prophet Gad, David's seer, saying, 1 Sam. 9:9; 1 Chr. 29:29

12 Go and say unto David, Thus saith the LORD, I offer thee three *things*; choose thee one of them, that I may *do it* unto thee.

13 So Gad came to David, and told him, and said unto him, Shall seven years of famine come unto thee in thy land? or wilt thou flee three months before thine enemies, while they pursue thee? or that there be three days' pestilence in thy land? now advise, and see what answer I shall return to him that sent me. Lev. 26:25; 1 Chr. 21:12

14 And David said unto Gad, I am in a great ᵀstrait: let us fall now into the hand of the LORD; for his mercies *are* great: and let me not fall into the hand of man. Ps. 51:1 ◆ distress

15 So the LORD sent a pestilence upon Israel from the morning even to the time appointed: and there died of the people from Dan even to Beer-sheba seventy thousand men. 1 Chr. 21:14

16 And when the angel stretched out his hand upon Jerusalem to destroy it, the LORD repented him of the evil, and said to the angel that destroyed the people, It is enough: stay now thine hand. And the angel of the LORD

was by the threshingplace of Araunah the Jebusite. Gen. 6:6; Ex. 12:23; 1 Sam. 15:11

17 And David spake unto the LORD when he saw the angel that smote the people, and said, Lo, I have sinned, and I have done wickedly: but these sheep, what have they done? let thine hand, I pray thee, be against me, and against my father's house. Ps. 74:1

David Purchases Araunah's Threshing Floor, Where the Plague Ends

18 And Gad came that day to David, and said unto him, Go up, rear an altar unto the LORD in the threshingfloor of Araunah the Jebusite.

19 And David, according to the saying of Gad, went up as the LORD commanded.

20 And Araunah looked, and saw the king and his servants coming on toward him: and Araunah went out, and bowed himself before the king on his face upon the ground.

21 And Araunah said, Wherefore is my lord the king come to his servant? And David said, To buy the threshingfloor of thee, to build an altar unto the LORD, that the plague may be ᵀstayed from the people. held back

22 And Araunah said unto David, Let my lord the king take and offer up what *seemeth* good unto him: behold, *here be* oxen for burnt sacrifice, and threshing instruments and *other* instruments of the oxen for wood. 1 Sam. 6:14; 1 Kin. 19:21

23 All these *things* did Araunah, *as* a king, give unto the king. And Araunah said unto the king, The LORD thy God accept thee.

24 And the king said unto Araunah, Nay; but I will surely buy *it* of thee at a price: neither will I offer burnt offerings unto the LORD my God of that which doth cost me nothing. So David bought the threshingfloor and the oxen for fifty shekels of silver. 1 Chr. 21:24-25

25 And David built there an altar unto the LORD, and offered burnt offerings and peace offerings. So the LORD was ᵀintreated for the land, and the plague was stayed from Israel. 1 Sam. 7:17; 2 Sam. 21:14 ◆ pled with

> **24:25 A Holy Site**
>
> This spot [on Mount Moriah], memorable as the place where Abraham had built the altar to offer up his son, and now hallowed by this great deliverance, was afterward chosen as the site of the temple erected by Solomon. *PP 749*

THE FIRST BOOK OF THE

KINGS

What is the key to success? Any person wanting to make a difference needs to know the steps to take to get ahead. While the fundamentals for successful pursuits are the same, specifics will vary for the athlete, businessperson, musician, leader, or politician. As it related to the kings ruling Israel, the key to success was simple: live in strict allegiance to God's law. Obey God and your kingdom will flourish. Fail to do that and the curses described in the law (Deuteronomy 28:15–68) will come to pass.

The Book of 1 Kings includes the stories of those who followed God's law and those who did not. We read about Solomon's accomplishments as Israel rises to power under his leadership: his building of the temple, his building of his palace, his great wisdom bringing him worldwide respect. Yet in his later years, his pagan wives turn his heart away from God, resulting in a divided kingdom.

First Kings traces the downward spiral of these two nations as they move further from allegiance to God's truth. Based around the lives of the kings of the nations, the focus is on how the kings lead their nations spiritually, with each description including a statement as to whether or not the king did what was right in the eyes of the Lord. This book is a reminder that success comes as we stand with God, but disobedience reaps painful and serious punishment.

Dates

First Kings encompasses the 130 years from the beginning of Solomon's reign (971 B.C.) and ending with Ahaziah's reign (841 B.C.). In 931 B.C., the kingdom divides with ten of the original twelve tribes forming the northern kingdom of Israel, with its capital at Samaria, and the two remaining tribes of Judah and Benjamin forming the southern kingdom of Judah, with its capital at Jerusalem.

Author

The material in both 1 and 2 Kings has been prized in historical and archeological circles because the accuracy of the historical accounts is above reproach. Many of the details have been taken from official court or temple records. Other narratives are likely taken from records gathered at the schools of the prophets. The specifics are portrayed with such clarity and precision that they are without parallel, even from the historical records of Assyria, Egypt, or Babylon.

A compilation of selected materials assembled by an editor more aptly describes both books of Kings. Despite the assortment of material, the harmony and balance is striking. While the author of 1 Kings is unknown, Talmudic evidence traditionally supports the prophet Jeremiah as the author.

Meaning of the Name

The title Kings or *Melechim* comes from the first word in Hebrew text—*Vehamelech*—meaning "Now King." Originally 1 and 2 Kings were one book in the Hebrew Scripture, as were the books of Samuel. The Samuel books were called the "First and Second Kingdoms" while 1 and 2 Kings were titled the "Third and Fourth Kingdoms." Later, in the Septuagint, the Samuel books, the books of the Kings, and the Chronicles were divided into two books each.

Christ in 1 Kings

Besides the fact that King Solomon can be found in the family line of Jesus (Matthew 1:6, 7), Solomon characterizes Christ in a number of ways: His wisdom points to "Christ Jesus, who of God is made unto us wisdom" (1 Corinthians 1:30); his fame, glory, and honor foreshadow the Christ who embodies all of those characteristics; and his reign brought peace and worship, which can be likened to the reign of Christ in believer's hearts. Jesus even referred to Solomon's glory in the Sermon on the Mount, saying, "And why take ye thought for raiment? Consider the lilies of the field, how they grow; they toil not, neither do they spin: And yet I say unto you, That even Solomon in all his glory was not arrayed like one of these" (Matthew 6:28, 29).

Also, the prophet Elijah, while more typical of John the Baptist, points to Jesus because of his prophetic role and his miraculous works—including raising the dead (1 Kings 17:22, 23).

Overview

First Kings can be divided into two sections:

(1) *1 Kings 1—11, The United Kingdom:* Solomon amasses great wealth and displays awesome wisdom. He constructs the temple and his palace and leads Israel to the height of its size and glory. But his faith wavers as his many pagan wives turn him away from God. Consequently, God promises to tear the kingdom away from Solomon. Because of His covenant with David, however (2 Samuel 7:12–17), He will allow Judah to remain under the rule of Solomon's family.

(2) *1 Kings 12—22, The Divided Kingdom:* Following Solomon's death, Rehoboam, the son and successor of Solomon, becomes king. Because he accepts the poor advice of his friends, the kingdom is torn into two kingdoms—Israel (the northern kingdom) and Judah (the southern kingdom)—by civil strife. The various scenarios of the book revert back and forth between the two kingdoms, recording the lives of their kings and how they obey or disobey God. Elijah, the great prophet, confronts the great wickedness of King Ahab and Queen Jezebel of Israel. His contest with the prophets of Baal on Mount Carmel proves to the people that their God alone is the true God.

Unlocking 1 Kings

KEY PEOPLE:
David, Solomon, Queen of Sheba, Rehoboam, Jeroboam, Elijah, Elisha, Ahab, Jezebel, Jehoshaphat

KEY EVENTS:
Solomon asks for wisdom; the temple is built; Solomon's apostasy causes the kingdom to divide during Rehoboam's reign; Ahab's evil leads to a drought; Elijah's ministry; Elijah's contest with the prophets of Baal on Mount Carmel; the drought's end; Elisha commissioned

KEY WORD:
Division is a sad reality in 1 Kings. Instead of remaining unified, Israel divides due to sin. The poor examples of kings like Ahab causes further division between God and His people.

KEY VERSE:
"And if thou wilt walk before me, as David thy father walked, in integrity of heart, and in uprightness, to do according to all that I have commanded thee, and wilt keep my statutes and my judgments: Then I will establish the throne of thy kingdom upon Israel for ever, as I promised to David thy father, saying, There shall not fail thee a man upon the throne of Israel" (1 Kings 9:4, 5).

KEY CHAPTER:
1 Kings 12, which reveals the critical turning point when Solomon dies, and his son Rehoboam becomes king. Rehoboam's poor leadership leads the nation into a civil war. The nation is forever changed.

Abishag Ministers to David

1 Now king David was old *and* stricken in years; and they covered him with clothes, but he gat no heat.

2 Wherefore his servants said unto him, Let there be sought for my lord the king a young virgin: and let her stand before the king, and let her cherish him, and let her lie in thy bosom, that my lord the king may get heat.

3 So they sought for a fair damsel throughout all the coasts of Israel, and found Abishag a Shunammite, and brought her to the king.   Josh. 19:18; 1 Sam. 28:4

4 And the damsel *was* very fair, and cherished the king, and ministered to him: but the king knew her not.

Adonijah, David's Favored Son, Usurps the Kingdom

5 Then Adonijah the son of Haggith exalted himself, saying, I will be king: and he prepared him chariots and horsemen, and fifty men to run before him.   2 Sam. 3:4; 15:1

6 And his father had not displeased him at any time in saying, Why hast thou done so? and he also *was a* very goodly *man;* and *his mother* bare him after Absalom.   2 Sam. 3:3-4

7 And he conferred with Joab the son of Zeruiah, and with Abiathar the priest: and they following Adonijah helped *him.*   2 Sam. 20:25

8 But Zadok the priest, and Benaiah the son of Jehoiada, and Nathan the prophet, and Shimei, and Rei, and the mighty men which *belonged* to David, were not with Adonijah.   2 Sam. 20:25; 23:8-39; 1 Kin. 4:18

9 And Adonijah slew sheep and oxen and fat cattle by the stone of Zoheleth, which *is* by En-rogel, and called all his brethren the king's sons, and all the men of Judah the king's servants: 2 Sam. 17:17

10 But Nathan the prophet, and Benaiah, and the mighty men, and Solomon his brother, he called not.   2 Sam. 12:24

Nathan and Bath-sheba Tell David about Adonijah

11 Wherefore Nathan spake unto Bathsheba the mother of Solomon, saying, Hast thou not heard that Adonijah the son of Haggith doth reign, and David our lord knoweth *it* not?   2 Sam. 3:4

12 Now therefore come, let me, I pray thee, give thee counsel, that thou mayest save thine own life, and the life of thy son Solomon.

13 Go and get thee in unto king David, and say unto him, Didst not thou, my lord, O king, swear unto thine handmaid, saying, Assuredly Solomon thy son shall reign after me, and he shall sit upon my throne? why then doth Adonijah reign?   1 Kin. 1:17, 30

14 Behold, while thou yet talkest there with the king, I also will come in after thee, and confirm thy words.

15 And Bath-sheba went in unto the king into the chamber: and the king was very old; and Abishag the Shunammite ministered unto the king.

16 And Bath-sheba bowed, and did ᵀobeisance unto the king. And the king said, What wouldest thou?   homage

17 And she said unto him, My lord, thou swarest by the LORD thy God unto thine handmaid, *saying,* Assuredly Solomon thy son shall reign after me, and he shall sit upon my throne.   1 Kin. 1:13, 30

Thwarting a Conspiracy

1 Kings 1:1

Still another shadow was to gather over the last years of David. He had reached the age of threescore and ten. The hardships and exposures of his early wanderings, his many wars, the cares and afflictions of his later years, had sapped the fountain of life. Though his mind retained its clearness and strength, feebleness and age, with their desire for seclusion, prevented a quick apprehension of what was passing in the kingdom, and again rebellion sprang up in the very shadow of the throne. Again the fruit of David's parental indulgence was manifest. The one who now aspired to the throne was Adonijah, "a very goodly man" in person and bearing, but unprincipled and reckless. In his youth he had been subjected to but little restraint; for "his father had not displeased him at any time in saying, Why hast thou done so?" He now rebelled against the authority of God, who had appointed Solomon to the throne. . . . Although the choice of God had been clearly indicated, Adonijah did not fail to find sympathizers. Joab, though guilty of many crimes, had heretofore been loyal to the throne; but he now joined the conspiracy against Solomon, as did also Abiathar the priest.

The rebellion was ripe; the conspirators had assembled at a great feast just without the city to proclaim Adonijah king, when their plans were thwarted by the prompt action of a few faithful persons, chief among whom were Zadok the priest, Nathan the prophet, and Bathsheba the mother of Solomon. They represented the state of affairs to the king, reminding him of the divine direction that Solomon should succeed to the throne. David at once abdicated in favor of Solomon, who was immediately anointed and proclaimed king. The conspiracy was crushed. *PP 749*

18 And now, behold, Adonijah reigneth; and now, my lord the king, thou knowest *it* not: 1 Kin. 1:24

19 And he hath slain oxen and fat cattle and sheep in abundance, and hath called all the sons of the king, and Abiathar the priest, and Joab the captain of the host: but Solomon thy servant hath he not called.

20 And thou, my lord, O king, the eyes of all Israel *are* upon thee, that thou shouldest tell them who shall sit on the throne of my lord the king after him.

21 Otherwise it shall come to pass, when my lord the king shall sleep with his fathers, that I and my son Solomon shall be counted offenders.   Deut. 31:16; 1 Kin. 2:10

22 And, lo, while she yet talked with the king, Nathan the prophet also came in.

23 And they told the king, saying, Behold Nathan the prophet. And when he was come in before the king, he bowed himself before the king with his face to the ground.

24 And Nathan said, My lord, O king, hast thou said, Adonijah shall reign after me, and he shall sit upon my throne?

25 For he is gone down this day, and hath slain oxen and fat cattle and sheep in abundance, and hath called all the king's sons, and the captains of the host, and Abiathar the priest; and, behold, they eat and drink before him, and say, God save king Adonijah.   1 Sam. 10:24

26 But me, *even* me thy servant, and Zadok the priest, and Benaiah the son of Jehoiada, and thy servant Solomon, hath he not called.   1 Kin. 1:8, 10

27 Is this thing done by my lord the king, and thou hast not shewed *it* unto thy servant, who should sit on the throne of my lord the king after him?

28 Then king David answered and said, Call me Bath-sheba. And she came into the king's presence, and stood before the king.

29 And the king sware, and said, *As* the LORD liveth, that hath redeemed my soul out of all distress,   2 Sam. 4:9

30 Even as I sware unto thee by the LORD God of Israel, saying, Assuredly Solomon thy son shall reign after me, and he shall sit upon my throne in my stead; even so will I certainly do this day.   1 Kin. 1:13, 17

31 Then Bath-sheba bowed with *her* face to the earth, and did reverence to the king, and said, Let my lord king David live for ever.   Dan. 2:4

Solomon Is Anointed King at David's Command

32 And king David said, Call me Zadok the priest, and Nathan the prophet, and Benaiah the son of Jehoiada. And they came before the king.   1 Kin. 1:8

33 The king also said unto them, Take with you the servants of your lord, and cause Solomon my son to ride upon mine own mule, and bring him down to Gihon: 2 Chr. 32:30; 33:14

34 And let Zadok the priest and Nathan the prophet anoint him there king over Israel: and blow ye with the trumpet, and say, God save king Solomon.   1 Sam. 10:1; 2 Sam. 15:10; 1 Kin. 1:25

35 Then ye shall come up after him, that he may come and sit upon my throne; for he shall be king in my stead: and I have appointed him to be ruler over Israel and over Judah.

36 And Benaiah the son of Jehoiada answered the king, and said, Amen: the LORD God of my lord the king say so *too*.

37 As the LORD hath been with my lord the king, even so be he with Solomon, and make his throne greater than the throne of my lord king David.   Josh. 1:5; 1 Sam. 20:13; 1 Kin. 1:47

38 So Zadok the priest, and Nathan the prophet, and Benaiah the son of Jehoiada, and the Cherethites, and the Pelethites, went down, and caused Solomon to ride upon king David's mule, and brought him to Gihon.   2 Sam. 8:18; 1 Kin. 1:8

39 And Zadok the priest took an horn of oil out of the tabernacle, and anointed Solomon. And they blew the trumpet; and all the people said, God save king Solomon.   Ps. 89:20

1:39 God's Purpose for the New King

Solomon was anointed and proclaimed king in the closing years of his father David, who abdicated in his favor. His early life was bright with promise, and it was God's purpose that he should go on from strength to strength, from glory to glory, ever approaching nearer the similitude of the character of God, and thus inspiring His people to fulfill their sacred trust as the depositaries of divine truth. *PK 25*

40 And all the people came up after him, and the people piped with pipes, and rejoiced with great joy, so that the earth ᵀrent with the sound of them.   *was torn apart*

Adonijah Pleads for Mercy from Solomon

41 And Adonijah and all the guests that *were* with him heard *it* as they had made an end of eating. And when Joab heard the sound of the trumpet, he said, Wherefore *is this* noise of the city being in an uproar?

42 And while he yet spake, behold, Jonathan the son of Abiathar the priest came: and Adonijah said unto him, Come in; for thou *art* a valiant man, and bringest good tidings.   2 Sam. 15:36; 17:17; 18:27

43 And Jonathan answered and said to

Adonijah, Verily our lord king David hath made Solomon king.

44 And the king hath sent with him Zadok the priest, and Nathan the prophet, and Benaiah the son of Jehoiada, and the Cherethites, and the Pelethites, and they have caused him to ride upon the king's mule:

45 And Zadok the priest and Nathan the prophet have anointed him king in Gihon: and they are come up from thence rejoicing, so that the city rang again. This *is* the noise that ye have heard.   1 Kin. 1:40

46 And also Solomon sitteth on the throne of the kingdom.   1 Chr. 29:23

47 And moreover the king's servants came to bless our lord king David, saying, God make the name of Solomon better than thy name, and make his throne greater than thy throne. And the king bowed himself upon the bed.   Gen. 47:31; 1 Kin. 1:37

48 And also thus said the king, Blessed *be* the LORD God of Israel, which hath given *one* to sit on my throne this day, mine eyes even seeing *it*.   1 Kin. 3:6; Ps. 132:11-12

49 And all the guests that *were* with Adonijah were afraid, and rose up, and went every man his way.

50 And Adonijah feared because of Solomon, and arose, and went, and caught hold on the horns of the altar.   1 Kin. 2:28

51 And it was told Solomon, saying, Behold, Adonijah feareth king Solomon: for, lo, he hath caught hold on the horns of the altar, saying, Let king Solomon swear unto me to day that he will not slay his servant with the sword.

52 And Solomon said, If he will shew himself a worthy man, there shall not an hair of him fall to the earth: but if wickedness shall be found in him, he shall die.   Acts 27:34

53 So king Solomon sent, and they brought him down from the altar. And he came and bowed himself to king Solomon: and Solomon said unto him, Go to thine house.

2:1–4 David's Charge to His Son

David knew that God's high purpose for Israel could be met only as rulers and people should seek with unceasing vigilance to attain to the standard placed before them. He knew that in order for his son Solomon to fulfill the trust with which God was pleased to honor him, the youthful ruler must be not merely a warrior, a statesman, and a sovereign, but a strong, good man, a teacher of righteousness, an example of fidelity. *PK 26*

David Gives a Charge to Solomon

2 Now the days of David drew nigh that he should die; and he charged Solomon his son, saying,   Gen. 47:29; Deut. 31:14

2 I go the way of all the earth: be thou strong therefore, and shew thyself a man; Josh. 1:6-7

2:2 God-given Manhood

The last words of David to Solomon, then a young man, and soon to receive the crown of Israel, were, "Be . . . strong, . . . and show thyself a man" (1 Kings 2:2). To every child of humanity, the candidate for an immortal crown, are these words of inspiration spoken, "Be . . . strong, . . . and show thyself a man."

The self-indulgent must be led to see and feel that great moral renovation is necessary if they would be men. God calls upon them to arouse and in the strength of Christ win back the God-given manhood that has been sacrificed through sinful indulgence. *MH 174*

---

3 And keep the charge of the LORD thy God, to walk in his ways, to keep his statutes, and his commandments, and his judgments, and his testimonies, as it is written in the law of Moses, that thou mayest prosper in all that thou doest, and whithersoever thou turnest thyself: Deut. 17:18-20; 29:9; 1 Chr. 22:12-13

4 That the LORD may continue his word which he spake concerning me, saying, If thy children take heed to their way, to walk before me in truth with all their heart and with all their soul, there shall not fail thee (said he) a man on the throne of Israel. 1 Kin. 8:25; 2 Kin. 20:3

5 Moreover thou knowest also what Joab the son of Zeruiah did to me, *and* what he did to the two captains of the hosts of Israel, unto Abner the son of Ner, and unto Amasa the son of Jether, whom he slew, and shed the blood of war in peace, and put the blood of war upon his ᵀgirdle that *was* about his ᵀloins, and in his shoes that *were* on his feet.   2 Sam. 3:27; 18:5; 20:10 ♦ *belt* ♦ *waist*

6 Do therefore according to thy wisdom, and let not his hoar head go down to the grave in peace.   1 Kin. 2:9

7 But shew kindness unto the sons of Barzillai the Gileadite, and let them be of those that eat at thy table: for so they came to me when I fled because of Absalom thy brother.   2 Sam. 9:7, 10; 17:27-29

8 And, behold, *thou hast* with thee Shimei the son of Gera, a Benjamite of Bahurim, which cursed me with a grievous curse in the day when I went to Mahanaim: but he came down to meet me at Jordan, and I sware to him by the LORD, saying, I will not put thee to death with the sword. 2 Sam. 16:5-8

9 Now therefore hold him not guiltless: for thou *art* a wise man, and knowest what thou oughtest to do unto him; but his hoar head bring thou down to the grave with blood.   Gen. 42:38; 44:31; 1 Kin. 2:6

10 So David slept with his fathers, and was buried in the city of David. 2 Sam. 5:7; Acts 2:29

11 And the days that David reigned over Israel *were* forty years: seven years reigned he in Hebron, and thirty and three years reigned he in Jerusalem.   2 Sam. 5:4-5

Solomon Succeeds David as King

12 Then sat Solomon upon the throne of David his father; and his kingdom was established greatly.   2 Chr. 1:1

13 And Adonijah the son of Haggith came to Bath-sheba the mother of Solomon. And she said, Comest thou peaceably? And he said, Peaceably.

14 He said moreover, I have somewhat to say unto thee. And she said, Say on.

15 And he said, Thou knowest that the kingdom was mine, and *that* all Israel set their faces on me, that I should reign: howbeit the kingdom is turned about, and is become my brother's: for it was his from the LORD.   1 Kin. 1:5 ◆ *however*

16 And now I ask one petition of thee, deny me not. And she said unto him, Say on.

17 And he said, Speak, I pray thee, unto Solomon the king, (for he will not say thee nay,) that he give me Abishag the Shunammite to wife.

18 And Bath-sheba said, Well; I will speak for thee unto the king.

19 Bath-sheba therefore went unto king Solomon, to speak unto him for Adonijah. And the king rose up to meet her, and bowed himself unto her, and sat down on his throne, and caused a seat to be set for the king's mother; and she sat on his right hand.   Ps. 45:9

20 Then she said, I desire one small petition of thee; *I pray thee*, say me not nay. And the king said unto her, Ask on, my mother: for I will not say thee nay.

21 And she said, Let Abishag the Shunammite be given to Adonijah thy brother to wife.

22 And king Solomon answered and said unto his mother, And why dost thou ask Abishag the Shunammite for Adonijah? ask for him the kingdom also; for he *is* mine elder brother; even for him, and for Abiathar the priest, and for Joab the son of Zeruiah.   1 Chr. 3:2

23 Then king Solomon sware by the LORD, saying, God do so to me, and more also, if Adonijah have not spoken this word against his own life.   Ruth 1:17

24 Now therefore, *as* the LORD liveth, which hath established me, and set me on the throne of David my father, and who hath made me an house, as he promised, Adonijah shall be put to death this day. 1 Chr. 22:10

25 And king Solomon sent by the hand of Benaiah the son of Jehoiada; and he fell upon him that he died.   2 Sam. 8:18

Abiathar's Life Is Spared, but He Is Removed from the Priesthood

26 And unto Abiathar the priest said the king, Get thee to Anathoth, unto thine own fields; for thou *art* worthy of death: but I will not at this time put thee to death, because thou barest the ark of the Lord GOD before David my father, and because thou hast been afflicted in all wherein my father was afflicted.   Josh. 21:18; 1 Sam. 22:20-23; 26:16

27 So Solomon thrust out Abiathar from being priest unto the LORD; that he might fulfil the word of the LORD, which he spake concerning the house of Eli in Shiloh.

28 Then tidings came to Joab: for Joab had turned after Adonijah, though he turned not after Absalom. And Joab fled unto the tabernacle of the LORD, and caught hold on the horns of the altar.   2 Sam. 18:2; 1 Kin. 1:7, 50

29 And it was told king Solomon that Joab was fled unto the tabernacle of the LORD; and, behold, *he is* by the altar. Then Solomon sent Benaiah the son of Jehoiada, saying, Go, fall upon him.   1 Kin. 2:25

30 And Benaiah came to the tabernacle of the LORD, and said unto him, Thus saith the king, Come forth. And he said, Nay; but I will die here. And Benaiah brought the king word again, saying, Thus said Joab, and thus he answered me.

31 And the king said unto him, Do as he hath said, and fall upon him, and bury him; that thou mayest take away the innocent blood, which Joab shed, from me, and from the house of my father.   Num. 35:33; Deut. 21:8-9

32 And the LORD shall return his blood upon his own head, who fell upon two men more righteous and better than he, and slew them with the sword, my father David not knowing *thereof*, to wit, Abner the son of Ner, captain of the host of Israel, and Amasa the son of Jether, captain of the host of Judah.   Judg. 9:24, 57; 2 Chr. 21:13 ◆ *namely*

33 Their blood shall therefore return upon the head of Joab, and upon the head of his seed for ever: but upon David, and upon his seed, and upon his house, and upon his throne, shall there be peace for ever from the LORD.   1 Kin. 2:32

34 So Benaiah the son of Jehoiada went up, and fell upon him, and slew him: and he was buried in his own house in the wilderness.   Josh. 15:61

35 And the king put Benaiah the son of Jehoiada in his room over the host: and Zadok the priest did the king put in the room of Abiathar.   1 Kin. 2:27; 4:4; 1 Chr. 24:3

36 And the king sent and called for Shimei,

and said unto him, Build thee an house in Jerusalem, and dwell there, and go not forth thence any whither.

37 For it shall be, *that* on the day thou goest out, and passest over the brook Kidron, thou shalt know for certain that thou shalt surely die: thy blood shall be upon thine own head.   Josh. 2:19; 2 Sam. 1:16; 15:23

38 And Shimei said unto the king, The saying *is* good: as my lord the king hath said, so will thy servant do. And Shimei dwelt in Jerusalem many days.

39 And it came to pass at the end of three years, that two of the servants of Shimei ran away unto Achish son of Maachah king of Gath. And they told Shimei, saying, Behold, thy servants *be* in Gath.

40 And Shimei arose, and saddled his ass, and went to Gath to Achish to seek his servants: and Shimei went, and brought his servants from Gath.

41 And it was told Solomon that Shimei had gone from Jerusalem to Gath, and was come again.

42 And the king sent and called for Shimei, and said unto him, Did I not make thee to swear by the LORD, and protested unto thee, saying, Know for a certain, on the day thou goest out, and walkest abroad any whither, that thou shalt surely die? and thou saidst unto me, The word *that* I have heard *is* good.

43 Why then hast thou not kept the oath of the LORD, and the commandment that I have Tcharged thee with?   *burdened*

44 The king said moreover to Shimei, Thou knowest all the wickedness which thine heart is privy to, that thou didst to David my father: therefore the LORD shall return thy wickedness upon thine own head;   1 Sam. 25:39; Ps. 7:16

45 And king Solomon *shall be* blessed, and the throne of David shall be established before the LORD for ever.   Prov. 25:5

46 So the king commanded Benaiah the son of Jehoiada; which went out, and fell upon him, that he died. And the kingdom was established in the hand of Solomon.   2 Chr. 1:1

Solomon Marries Pharaoh's Daughter

3 And Solomon made affinity with Pharaoh king of Egypt, and took Pharaoh's daughter, and brought her into the city of David, until he had made an end of building his own house, and the house of the LORD, and the wall of Jerusalem round about.   2 Sam. 5:7; 1 Kin. 9:24

2 Only the people sacrificed in high places, because there was no house built unto the name of the LORD, until those days. Deut. 12:2-5

3 And Solomon loved the LORD, walking in the statutes of David his father: only he sacrificed and burnt incense in high places. Deut. 6:5

4 And the king went to Gibeon to sacrifice there; for that *was* the great high place: a thousand burnt offerings did Solomon offer upon that altar.   1 Chr. 16:39; 21:29; 2 Chr. 1:3

God Gives Solomon Wisdom, Riches, and Honor

5 In Gibeon the LORD appeared to Solomon in a dream by night: and God said, Ask what I shall give thee.   Num. 12:6; 1 Kin. 9:2; Matt. 1:20

6 And Solomon said, Thou hast shewed unto thy servant David my father great mercy, according as he walked before thee in truth, and in righteousness, and in uprightness of heart with thee; and thou hast kept for him this great kindness, that thou hast given him a son to sit on his throne, as *it is* this day.   1 Kin. 1:48; 2:4; 9:4

7 And now, O LORD my God, thou hast made thy servant king instead of David my father: and I *am but* a little child: I know not *how* to go out or come in.   Num. 27:17; 1 Chr. 29:1; Jer. 1:6

8 And thy servant *is* in the midst of thy people which thou hast chosen, a great people, that cannot be numbered nor counted for multitude.   Gen. 13:16; 15:5; 22:17

3:5-15 Solomon Seeks the Highest Good

Those who today occupy positions of trust should seek to learn the lesson taught by Solomon's prayer. The higher the position a man occupies, the greater the responsibility that he has to bear, the wider will be the influence that he exerts and the greater his need of dependence on God. . . . He is to stand before God in the attitude of a learner. Position does not give holiness of character. It is by honoring God and obeying His commands that a man is made truly great. *PK 30, 31*

9 Give therefore thy servant an understanding heart to judge thy people, that I may discern between good and bad: for who is able to judge this thy so great a people?   2 Sam. 14:17; Ps. 72:1-2; Heb. 5:14

10 And the speech pleased the Lord, that Solomon had asked this thing.

11 And God said unto him, Because thou hast asked this thing, and hast not asked for thyself long life; neither hast asked riches for thyself, nor hast asked the life of thine enemies; but hast asked for thyself understanding to discern judgment;

12 Behold, I have done according to thy words: lo, I have given thee a wise and an understanding heart; so that there was none like thee before thee, neither after thee shall any arise like unto thee.   Eccl. 1:16; 1 John 5:14-15

13 And I have also given thee that which thou hast not asked, both riches, and honour: so

that there shall not be any among the kings like unto thee all thy days.   Prov. 3:16; Matt. 6:33

14 And if thou wilt walk in my ways, to keep my statutes and my commandments, as thy father David did walk, then I will lengthen thy days.   1 Kin. 3:6; Ps. 91:16; Prov. 3:2

15 And Solomon awoke; and, behold, *it was* a dream. And he came to Jerusalem, and stood before the ark of the covenant of the LORD, and offered up burnt offerings, and offered peace offerings, and made a feast to all his servants.   Gen. 41:7; 1 Kin. 8:65; Esth. 1:3

Solomon's Wise Judgment

16 Then came there two women, *that were* harlots, unto the king, and stood before him.   Num. 27:2

17 And the one woman said, O my lord, I and this woman dwell in one house; and I was delivered of a child with her in the house.

18 And it came to pass the third day after that I was delivered, that this woman was delivered also: and we *were* together; *there was* no stranger with us in the house, save we two in the house.

19 And this woman's child died in the night; because she overlaid it.

20 And she arose at midnight, and took my son from beside me, while thine handmaid slept, and laid it in her bosom, and laid her dead child in my bosom.

21 And when I rose in the morning to give my child suck, behold, it was dead: but when I had considered it in the morning, behold, it was not my son, which I did bear.

22 And the other woman said, Nay; but the living *is* my son, and the dead *is* thy son. And this said, No; but the dead *is* thy son, and the living *is* my son. Thus they spake before the king.

23 Then said the king, The one saith, This *is* my son that liveth, and thy son *is* the dead: and the other saith, Nay; but thy son *is* the dead, and my son *is* the living.

24 And the king said, Bring me a sword. And they brought a sword before the king.

25 And the king said, Divide the living child in two, and give half to the one, and half to the other.

26 Then spake the woman whose the living child *was* unto the king, for her bowels yearned upon her son, and she said, O my lord, give her the living child, and in no wise slay it. But the other said, Let it be neither mine nor thine, *but* divide *it*.   Gen. 43:30; Is. 49:15

27 Then the king answered and said, Give her the living child, and in no wise slay it: she *is* the mother thereof.

28 And all Israel heard of the judgment which the king had judged; and they feared the king: for they saw that the wisdom of God *was* in him, to do judgment.   Col. 2:3

Solomon's Princes and Officers

4 So king Solomon was king over all Is-rael.

2 And these *were* the princes which he had; Azariah the son of Zadok the priest,

3 Elihoreph and Ahiah, the sons of Shisha, scribes; Jehoshaphat the son of Ahilud, the recorder.   2 Sam. 8:16

4 And Benaiah the son of Jehoiada *was* over the host: and Zadok and Abiathar *were* the priests: 1 Kin. 2:35

5 And Azariah the son of Nathan *was* over the officers: and Zabud the son of Nathan *was* principal officer, *and* the king's friend:

6 And Ahishar *was* over the household: and Adoniram the son of Abda *was* over the tribute.   2 Sam. 20:24

7 And Solomon had twelve officers over all Israel, which provided ᵀvictuals for the king and his household: each man his month in a year made provision.   *food*

8 And these *are* their names: The son of Hur, in mount Ephraim: Josh. 24:33

9 The son of Dekar, in Makaz, and in Sha-albim, and Beth-shemesh, and Elon-beth-hanan:

10 The son of Hesed, in Aruboth; to him *pertained* Sochoh, and all the land of Hepher: Josh. 12:17

11 The son of Abinadab, in all the region of Dor; which had Taphath the daughter of Solomon to wife: Josh. 11:2

12 Baana the son of Ahilud; *to him pertained* Taanach and Megiddo, and all Beth-shean, which *is* by Zartanah beneath Jezreel, from Beth-shean to Abel-meholah, *even* unto *the place that is* beyond Jokneam: Josh. 3:16; 17:11

13 The son of Geber, in Ramoth-gilead; to him *pertained* the towns of Jair the son of Manasseh, which *are* in Gilead; to him *also pertained* the region of Argob, which *is* in Bashan, threescore great cities with walls and brasen bars: Num. 32:41; Deut. 3:4; 1 Kin. 22:3

14 Ahinadab the son of Iddo *had* Mahanaim:

15 Ahimaaz *was* in Naphtali; he also took Basmath the daughter of Solomon to wife:

16 Baanah the son of Hushai *was* in Asher and in Aloth:

17 Jehoshaphat the son of Paruah, in Issa-char:

18 Shimei the son of Elah, in Benjamin:

19 Geber the son of Uri *was* in the country of Gilead, *in* the country of Sihon king of the Amorites, and of Og king of Bashan; and *he was* the only officer which *was* in the land.

The Peace of Solomon's Kingdom

20 Judah and Israel *were* many, as the sand which *is* by the sea in multitude, eating and drinking, and making merry. Gen. 22:17; 1 Kin. 3:8
21 And Solomon reigned over all kingdoms from the river unto the land of the Philistines, and unto the border of Egypt: they brought presents, and served Solomon all the days of his life. Gen. 15:18; Josh. 1:4; Ps. 68:29
22 And Solomon's provision for one day was thirty measures of fine flour, and ᵀthreescore measures of meal,   *sixty*
23 Ten fat oxen, and twenty oxen out of the pastures, and an hundred sheep, beside harts, and roebucks, and fallowdeer, and fatted fowl.
24 For he had dominion over all *the region* on this side the river, from Tiphsah even to Azzah, over all the kings on this side the river: and he had peace on all sides round about him.   Gen. 10:19; 1 Chr. 22:9; Ps. 72:11
25 And Judah and Israel dwelt safely, every man under his vine and under his fig tree, from Dan even to Beer-sheba, all the days of Solomon.   Judg. 20:1; Mic. 4:4; Zech. 3:10

> **4:24, 25 Solomon's Early Reign**
>
> While Solomon exalted the law of heaven, God was with him, and wisdom was given him to rule over Israel with impartiality and mercy. At first, as wealth and worldly honor came to him, he remained humble, and great was the extent of his influence. *PK 51*

26 And Solomon had forty thousand stalls of horses for his chariots, and twelve thousand horsemen.   2 Sam. 8:4; 2 Chr. 1:14; 9:25
27 And those officers provided victual for king Solomon, and for all that came unto king Solomon's table, every man in his month: they lacked nothing.
28 Barley also and straw for the horses and dromedaries brought they unto the place where *the officers* were, every man according to his charge.   Esth. 8:10

Solomon's Wisdom

29 And God gave Solomon wisdom and understanding exceeding much, and largeness of heart, even as the sand that *is* on the sea shore.   1 Kin. 3:12; 4:20
30 And Solomon's wisdom excelled the wisdom of all the children of the east country, and all the wisdom of Egypt. Gen. 25:6; Acts 7:22
31 For he was wiser than all men; than Ethan the Ezrahite, and Heman, and Chalcol, and Darda, the sons of Mahol: and his fame was in all nations round about.   1 Kin. 3:12
32 And he spake three thousand proverbs: and his songs were a thousand and five.
33 And he spake of trees, from the cedar tree that *is* in Lebanon even unto the ᵀhyssop that springeth out of the wall: he spake also of beasts, and of fowl, and of creeping things, and of fishes.   *bitter herb*

> **4:29-31 Solomon's Wealth and Wisdom**
>
> The wisdom that Solomon desired above riches, honor, or long life, God gave him. His petition for a quick mind, a large heart, and a tender spirit was granted. . . .
>
> His wealth and wisdom, the magnificent buildings and public works that he constructed during the early years of his reign, the energy, piety, justice, and magnanimity that he revealed in word and deed, won the loyalty of his subjects and the admiration and homage of the rulers of many lands. *PK 31, 32*

34 And there came of all people to hear the wisdom of Solomon, from all kings of the earth, which had heard of his wisdom.

King Hiram of Tyre Supplies Timber for the Temple

5 And Hiram king of Tyre sent his servants unto Solomon; for he had heard that they had anointed him king in the room of his father: for Hiram was ever a lover of David.   2 Sam. 5:11; 1 Chr. 14:1; 2 Chr. 2:3
2 And Solomon sent to Hiram, saying,
3 Thou knowest how that David my father could not build an house unto the name of the LORD his God for the wars which were about him on every side, until the LORD put them under the soles of his feet. 1 Chr. 22:8; 28:3
4 But now the LORD my God hath given me rest on every side, *so that there is* neither adversary nor evil occurrent. 1 Kin. 4:24; 1 Chr. 22:9
5 And, behold, I purpose to build an house unto the name of the LORD my God, as the LORD spake unto David my father, saying, Thy son, whom I will set upon thy throne in thy room, he shall build an house unto my name.   1 Chr. 17:12; 22:10; 28:6
6 Now therefore command thou that they ᵀhew me cedar trees out of Lebanon; and my servants shall be with thy servants: and unto thee will I give hire for thy servants according to all that thou shalt appoint: for thou knowest that *there is* not among us any that can skill to hew timber like unto the Sidonians.   2 Chr. 2:8 ♦ *cut*
7 And it came to pass, when Hiram heard the words of Solomon, that he rejoiced greatly, and said, Blessed *be* the LORD this day, which hath given unto David a wise son over this great people.
8 And Hiram sent to Solomon, saying, I have considered the things which thou sentest to me for: *and* I will do all thy desire concerning timber of cedar, and concerning timber of fir.

9 My servants shall bring *them* down from Lebanon unto the sea: and I will convey them by sea in floats unto the place that thou shalt appoint me, and will cause them to be discharged there, and thou shalt receive *them*: and thou shalt accomplish my desire, in giving food for my household. Ezek. 27:17; Acts 12:20

10 So Hiram gave Solomon cedar trees and fir trees *according to* all his desire.

11 And Solomon gave Hiram twenty thousand measures of wheat *for* food to his household, and twenty measures of pure oil: thus gave Solomon to Hiram year by year. 2 Chr. 2:10

12 And the LORD gave Solomon wisdom, as he promised him: and there was peace between Hiram and Solomon; and they two made a league together.   1 Kin. 3:12; Amos 1:9

13 And king Solomon raised a levy out of all Israel; and the levy was thirty thousand men.   1 Kin. 4:6; 9:15

14 And he sent them to Lebanon, ten thousand a month by courses: a month they were in Lebanon, *and* two months at home: and Adoniram *was* over the levy.

15 And Solomon had threescore and ten thousand that bare burdens, and fourscore thousand hewers in the mountains;   1 Kin. 9:20-22

16 Beside the chief of Solomon's officers which *were* over the work, three thousand and three hundred, which ruled over the people that wrought in the work.   2 Chr. 2:2

17 And the king commanded, and they brought great stones, costly stones, *and* ᵀhewed stones, to lay the foundation of the house.   1 Kin. 6:7; 1 Chr. 22:2 ♦ *cut*

18 And Solomon's builders and Hiram's builders did hew *them*, and the stonesquarers: so they prepared timber and stones to build the house.   Josh. 13:5; Ezek. 27:9

The Building of Solomon's Temple

6 And it came to pass in the four hundred and eightieth year after the children of Israel were come out of the land of Egypt, in the fourth year of Solomon's reign over Israel, in the month Zif, which *is* the second month, that he began to build the house of the LORD.   2 Chr. 3:1-2

2 And the house which king Solomon built for the LORD, the length thereof *was* ᵀthreescore cubits, and the breadth thereof twenty *cubits*, and the height thereof thirty cubits.   Ezek. 40:1-41 ♦ *sixty*

> **6:1, 2 Temple Replaced the Desert Tabernacle**
>
> After the settlement of the Hebrews in Canaan, the tabernacle was replaced by the temple of Solomon, which, though a permanent structure and upon a larger scale, observed the same proportions, and was similarly furnished. *GC 412*

3 And the porch before the temple of the house, twenty cubits *was* the length thereof, according to the breadth of the house; *and* ten cubits *was* the breadth thereof before the house.

4 And for the house he made windows of narrow lights.   Ezek. 40:16; 41:16, 26

5 And against the wall of the house he built chambers round about, *against* the walls of the house round about, *both* of the temple and of the oracle: and he made chambers round about: 1 Kin. 6:16, 19-21, 31

6 The ᵀnethermost chamber *was* five cubits broad, and the middle *was* six cubits broad, and the third *was* seven cubits broad: for without *in the wall* of the house he made narrowed rests round about, that *the beams* should not be fastened in the walls of the house.   *lowest*

7 And the house, when it was in building, was built of stone made ready before it was brought thither: so that there was neither hammer nor axe *nor* any tool of iron heard in the house, while it was in building. Deut. 27:5-6

8 The door for the middle chamber *was* in the right side of the house: and they went up with winding stairs into the middle *chamber*, and out of the middle into the third.

9 So he built the house, and finished it; and covered the house with beams and boards of cedar.   1 Kin. 6:14, 38

10 And *then* he built chambers against all

Mount Moriah a Consecrated Place

1 Kings 6

The spot on which the temple was built had long been regarded as a consecrated place. It was here that Abraham, the father of the faithful, had revealed his willingness to sacrifice his only son in obedience to the command of Jehovah. Here God had renewed with Abraham the covenant of blessing, which included the glorious Messianic promise to the human race of deliverance through the sacrifice of the Son of the Most High. See Genesis 22:9, 16–18. Here it was that when David offered burnt offerings and peace offerings to stay the avenging sword of the destroying angel, God had answered him by fire from heaven. See 1 Chronicles 21. And now once more the worshipers of Jehovah were here to meet their God and renew their vows of allegiance to Him. *PK 37*

the house, five cubits high: and they rested on the house with timber of cedar.

God's Promise Concerning the Temple

11 And the word of the LORD came to Solomon, saying,

12 *Concerning* this house which thou art in building, if thou wilt walk in my statutes, and execute my judgments, and keep all my commandments to walk in them; then will I perform my word with thee, which I spake unto David thy father: 1 Chr. 22:10

13 And I will dwell among the children of Israel, and will not forsake my people Israel.   Ex. 25:8; Lev. 26:11; Deut. 31:6

14 So Solomon built the house, and finished it.   1 Kin. 6:9, 38

Details about the Temple's Interior Adornment

15 And he built the walls of the house within with boards of cedar, both the floor of the house, and the walls of the cieling: *and* he covered *them* on the inside with wood, and covered the floor of the house with planks of fir.   1 Kin. 7:7

16 And he built twenty cubits on the sides of the house, both the floor and the walls with boards of cedar: he even built *them* for it within, *even* for the oracle, *even* for the most holy *place*.   Lev. 16:2; 1 Kin. 8:6; 2 Chr. 3:8

17 And the house, that *is*, the temple before it, was forty cubits *long*.

18 And the cedar of the house within *was* carved with ᵀknops and open flowers: all *was* cedar; there was no stone seen.   1 Kin. 7:24

19 And the oracle he prepared in the house within, to set there the ark of the covenant of the LORD.

20 And the oracle in the forepart *was* twenty cubits in length, and twenty cubits in breadth, and twenty cubits in the height thereof: and he overlaid it with pure gold; and *so* covered the altar *which was of* cedar.

21 So Solomon overlaid the house within with pure gold: and he made a partition by the chains of gold before the oracle; and he overlaid it with gold.

22 And the whole house he overlaid with gold, until he had finished all the house: also the whole altar that *was* by the oracle he overlaid with gold.   Ex. 30:1

23 And within the oracle he made two cherubims *of* olive tree, *each* ten cubits high.

24 And five cubits *was* the one wing of the cherub, and five cubits the other wing of the cherub: from the uttermost part of the one wing unto the uttermost part of the other *were* ten cubits.

25 And the other cherub *was* ten cubits:

both the cherubims *were* of one measure and one size.

26 The height of the one cherub *was* ten cubits, and so *was it* of the other cherub.

27 And he set the cherubims within the inner house: and they stretched forth the wings of the cherubims, so that the wing of the one touched the *one* wall, and the wing of the other cherub touched the other wall; and their wings touched one another in the midst of the house.   Ex. 25:20; 37:9; 2 Chr. 5:8

28 And he overlaid the cherubims with gold.

29 And he carved all the walls of the house round about with carved figures of cherubims and palm trees and open flowers, within and without.   1 Kin. 6:32

30 And the floor of the house he overlaid with gold, within and without.

31 And for the entering of the oracle he made doors *of* olive tree: the ᵀlintel *and* side posts *were* a fifth part *of the wall*. *top of door frame*

32 The two doors also *were of* olive tree; and he carved upon them carvings of cherubims and palm trees and open flowers, and overlaid *them* with gold, and spread gold upon the cherubims, and upon the palm trees.

33 So also made he for the door of the temple posts *of* olive tree, a fourth part *of the wall*.

34 And the two doors *were of* fir tree: the two leaves of the one door *were* folding, and the two leaves of the other door *were* folding.   Ezek. 41:23-25

35 And he carved *thereon* cherubims and palm trees and open flowers: and covered *them* with gold fitted upon the carved work.

36 And he built the inner court with three rows of ᵀhewed stone, and a row of cedar beams.   1 Kin. 7:12 ◆ *cut*

37 In the fourth year was the foundation of the house of the LORD laid, in the month Zif: 1 Kin. 6:1

38 And in the eleventh year, in the month Bul, which *is* the eighth month, was the house finished throughout all the parts thereof, and according to all the fashion of it. So was he seven years in building it.

The Building of Solomon's House

7 But Solomon was building his own house thirteen years, and he finished all his house.   1 Kin. 9:10; 2 Chr. 8:1

2 He built also the house of the forest of Lebanon; the length thereof *was* an hundred cubits, and the breadth thereof fifty cubits, and the height thereof thirty cubits, upon four rows of cedar pillars, with cedar beams upon the pillars.   1 Kin. 10:17; 2 Chr. 9:16

3 And *it was* covered with cedar above upon the beams, that *lay* on forty five pillars, fifteen *in* a row.

4 And *there were* windows *in* three rows, and light *was* against light *in* three ranks.

5 And all the doors and posts *were* square, with the windows: and light *was* against light *in* three ranks.

6 And he made a porch of pillars; the length thereof *was* fifty cubits, and the breadth thereof thirty cubits: and the porch *was* before them: and the *other* pillars and the thick beam *were* before them.

7 Then he made a porch for the throne where he might judge, *even* the porch of judgment: and *it was* covered with cedar from one side of the floor to the other.   Ps. 122:5

8 And his house where he dwelt *had* another court within the porch, *which* was of the like work. Solomon made also an house for Pharaoh's daughter, whom he had taken *to wife*, like unto this porch.   1 Kin. 3:1; 9:24; 2 Chr. 8:11

9 All these *were of* costly stones, according to the measures of ᵀhewed stones, sawed with saws, within and without, even from the foundation unto the coping, and *so* on the outside toward the great court.   cut

10 And the foundation *was of* costly stones, even great stones, stones of ten cubits, and stones of eight cubits.

11 And above *were* costly stones, after the measures of hewed stones, and cedars.

12 And the great court round about *was* with three rows of hewed stones, and a row of cedar beams, both for the inner court of the house of the LORD, and for the porch of the house.   1 Kin. 6:36

Solomon Sends for Hiram to Do the Brass Work

13 And king Solomon sent and fetched Hiram out of Tyre.   2 Chr. 4:11

14 He *was* a widow's son of the tribe of Naphtali, and his father *was* a man of Tyre, a worker in brass: and he was filled with wisdom, and understanding, and cunning to work all works in brass. And he came to king Solomon, and wrought all his work. 2 Chr. 2:14

15 For he cast two pillars of brass, of eighteen cubits high apiece: and a line of twelve cubits did compass either of them about.   Jer. 52:21

16 And he made two chapiters *of* molten brass, to set upon the tops of the pillars: the height of the one ᵀchapiter *was* five cubits, and the height of the other chapiter *was* five cubits: *capital at the top of the column*

17 *And* nets of checker work, and wreaths of chain work, for the ᵀchapiters which *were* upon the top of the pillars; seven for the one chapiter, and seven for the other chapiter.   *capitals*

18 And he made the pillars, and two rows round about upon the one network, to cover

the chapiters that *were* upon the top, with pomegranates: and so did he for the other chapiter.

19 And the chapiters that *were* upon the top of the pillars *were* of lily work in the porch, four cubits.

20 And the chapiters upon the two pillars *had* pomegranates also above, over against the belly which *was* by the network: and the pomegranates *were* two hundred in rows round about upon the other chapiter.   2 Chr. 3:16; 4:13

21 And he set up the pillars in the porch of the temple: and he set up the right pillar, and called the name thereof Jachin: and he set up the left pillar, and called the name thereof Boaz.   1 Kin. 6:3; 2 Chr. 3:17

22 And upon the top of the pillars *was* lily work: so was the work of the pillars finished.

23 And he made a molten sea, ten cubits from the one brim to the other: *it was* round all about, and his height *was* five cubits: and a line of thirty cubits did compass it round about.   2 Kin. 25:13; 2 Chr. 4:2; Jer. 52:17

24 And under the brim of it round about *there were* ᵀknops ᵀcompassing it, ten in a cubit, compassing the sea round about: the knops *were* cast in two rows, when it was cast.   1 Kin. 6:18 ◆ *architectural ornaments* ◆ *surrounding*

25 It stood upon twelve oxen, three looking toward the north, and three looking toward the west, and three looking toward the south, and three looking toward the east: and the sea *was set* above upon them, and all their hinder parts *were* inward.   2 Chr. 4:4-5; Jer. 52:20

26 And it *was* an hand breadth thick, and the brim thereof *was* ᵀwrought like the brim of a cup, with flowers of lilies: it contained two thousand baths.   2 Chr. 4:5 ◆ *made*

27 And he made ten bases of brass; four cubits *was* the length of one base, and four cubits the breadth thereof, and three cubits the height of it.   2 Kin. 25:13; 2 Chr. 4:14; Jer. 52:17

28 And the work of the bases *was* on this *manner*: they had borders, and the borders *were* between the ledges:

29 And on the borders that *were* between the ledges *were* lions, oxen, and cherubims: and upon the ledges *there was* a base above: and beneath the lions and oxen *were* certain additions made of thin work.

30 And every base had four brasen wheels, and plates of brass: and the four corners thereof had undersetters: under the ᵀlaver *were* undersetters molten, at the side of every addition.   *basin for washing*

31 And the mouth of it within the chapiter and above *was* a cubit: but the mouth thereof *was* round *after* the work of the base, a cubit and an half: and also upon the mouth of it *were* gravings with their borders, foursquare, not round.

32 And under the borders *were* four wheels; and the axletrees of the wheels *were joined* to the base: and the height of a wheel *was* a cubit and half a cubit.

33 And the work of the wheels *was* like the work of a chariot wheel: their axletrees, and their ᵀnaves, and their felloes, and their spokes, *were* all molten.   hubs

34 And *there were* four undersetters to the four corners of one base: *and* the undersetters *were* of the very base itself.

35 And in the top of the base *was there* a round compass of half a cubit high: and on the top of the base the ledges thereof and the borders thereof *were* of the same.

36 For on the plates of the ledges thereof, and on the borders thereof, he graved cherubims, lions, and palm trees, according to the proportion of every one, and additions round about.

37 After this *manner* he made the ten bases: all of them had one casting, one measure, *and* one size.

38 Then made he ten lavers of brass: one laver contained forty baths: *and* every laver was four cubits: *and* upon every one of the ten bases one laver.

39 And he put five bases on the right side of the house, and five on the left side of the house: and he set the sea on the right side of the house eastward over against the south.

40 And Hiram made the lavers, and the shovels, and the basons. So Hiram made an end of doing all the work that he made king Solomon for the house of the LORD: 2 Chr. 4:11-16

41 The two pillars, and the *two* bowls of the chapiters that *were* on the top of the two pillars; and the two networks, to cover the two bowls of the chapiters which *were* upon the top of the pillars;

42 And four hundred pomegranates for the two networks, *even* two rows of pomegranates for one network, to cover the two bowls of the chapiters that *were* upon the pillars;   1 Kin. 7:20

43 And the ten bases, and ten lavers on the bases;

44 And one sea, and twelve oxen under the sea;

45 And the pots, and the shovels, and the basons: and all these vessels, which Hiram made to king Solomon for the house of the LORD, *were of* bright brass. Ex. 27:3; 38:3; 2 Chr. 4:16

46 In the plain of Jordan did the king cast them, in the clay ground between Succoth and Zarthan.   Gen. 33:17; Josh. 3:16; 2 Chr. 4:17

47 And Solomon left all the vessels *unweighed*, because they were exceeding many: neither was the weight of the brass found out.   1 Chr. 22:14

48 And Solomon made all the vessels that

pertained unto the house of the LORD: the altar of gold, and the table of gold, whereupon the shewbread *was*,   Ex. 37:10-16

49 And the candlesticks of pure gold, five on the right *side*, and five on the left, before the oracle, with the flowers, and the lamps, and the tongs *of* gold,   2 Chr. 4:7

50 And the bowls, and the snuffers, and the basons, and the spoons, and the ᵀcensers *of* pure gold; and the hinges *of* gold, *both* for the doors of the inner house, the most holy *place, and* for the doors of the house, ᵀ*to wit*, of the temple.   holders for burning incense ◆ namely

51 So was ended all the work that king Solomon made for the house of the LORD. And Solomon brought in the things which David his father had dedicated; *even* the silver, and the gold, and the vessels, did he put among the treasures of the house of the LORD.   2 Chr. 5:1

> **7:15–51 Magnificence of the Temple**
>
> Of surpassing beauty and unrivaled splendor was the palatial building which Solomon and his associates erected for God and His worship. Garnished with precious stones, surrounded by spacious courts with magnificent approaches, and lined with carved cedar and burnished gold, the temple structure, with its broidered hangings and rich furnishings, was a fit emblem of the living church of God on earth, which through the ages has been building in accordance with the divine pattern. . . . *PK 36*

The Feast of the Dedication of the Temple

8 Then Solomon assembled the elders of Israel, and all the heads of the tribes, the chief of the fathers of the children of Israel, unto king Solomon in Jerusalem, that they might bring up the ark of the covenant of the LORD out of the city of David, which *is* Zion.   2 Chr. 5:2-10

2 And all the men of Israel assembled themselves unto king Solomon at the feast in the month Ethanim, which *is* the seventh month.   Lev. 23:34; 2 Chr. 7:8-10

3 And all the elders of Israel came, and the priests took up the ark.   Deut. 31:9

4 And they brought up the ark of the LORD, and the tabernacle of the congregation, and all the holy vessels that *were* in the tabernacle, even those did the priests and the Levites bring up.   1 Kin. 3:4; 2 Chr. 1:3

5 And king Solomon, and all the congregation of Israel, that were assembled unto him, *were* with him before the ark, sacrificing sheep and oxen, that could not be told nor numbered for multitude.   2 Sam. 6:13

6 And the priests brought in the ark of the covenant of the LORD unto his place, into the oracle of the house, to the most holy *place, even* under the wings of the cherubims.   2 Sam. 6:17
7 For the cherubims spread forth *their* two wings over the place of the ark, and the cherubims covered the ark and the ᵀstaves thereof above.   *poles or rods*
8 And they drew out the staves, that the ends of the staves were seen out in the holy *place* before the oracle, and they were not seen without: and there they are unto this day.   Ex. 25:13-15
9 *There was* nothing in the ark save the two tables of stone, which Moses put there at Horeb, when the LORD made *a covenant* with the children of Israel, when they came out of the land of Egypt.   Ex. 25:21; 40:20; Heb. 9:4

8:9 The Law in the Ark

The ark was merely a receptacle for the tables of the law, and the presence of these divine precepts gave to [the ark] its value and sacredness. When the temple of God was opened in heaven, the ark of His testament was seen. Within the holy of holies, in the sanctuary in heaven, the divine law is sacredly enshrined—the law that was spoken by God Himself amid the thunders of Sinai and written with His own finger on the tables of stone. *GC 433, 434*

10 And it came to pass, when the priests were come out of the holy *place*, that the cloud filled the house of the LORD, Ex. 40:34-35
11 So that the priests could not stand to minister because of the cloud: for the glory of the LORD had filled the house of the LORD.

Solomon Blesses the Congregation of Israel

12 Then spake Solomon, The LORD said that he would dwell in the thick darkness. Lev. 16:2
13 I have surely built thee an house to dwell in, a settled place for thee to abide in for ever.   Ex. 15:17; 2 Sam. 7:13; Ps. 132:13-14
14 And the king turned his face about, and blessed all the congregation of Israel: (and all the congregation of Israel stood;)   2 Sam. 6:18
15 And he said, Blessed *be* the LORD God of Israel, which spake with his mouth unto David my father, and hath with his hand fulfilled *it*, saying,   1 Chr. 29:10, 20; Luke 1:68
16 Since the day that I brought forth my people Israel out of Egypt, I chose no city out of all the tribes of Israel to build an house, that my name might be therein; but I chose David to be over my people Israel. Deut. 12:11; 1 Sam. 16:1
17 And it was in the heart of David my

father to build an house for the name of the LORD God of Israel.   2 Sam. 7:2-3
18 And the LORD said unto David my father, Whereas it was in thine heart to build an house unto my name, thou didst well that it was in thine heart.
19 Nevertheless thou shalt not build the house; but thy son that shall come forth out of thy loins, he shall build the house unto my name.   2 Sam. 7:5, 12-13; 1 Chr. 17:11-12
20 And the LORD hath performed his word that he spake, and I am risen up in the room of David my father, and sit on the throne of Israel, as the LORD promised, and have built an house for the name of the LORD God of Israel.   1 Chr. 28:5-6
21 And I have set there a place for the ark, wherein *is* the covenant of the LORD, which he made with our fathers, when he brought them out of the land of Egypt.   Deut. 31:26

Solomon's Prayer of Dedication and Thanksgiving for the Temple

22 And Solomon stood before the altar of the LORD in the presence of all the congregation of Israel, and spread forth his hands toward heaven: Ex. 9:33; 1 Kin. 8:54; Ezra 9:5
23 And he said, LORD God of Israel, *there is* no God like thee, in heaven above, or on earth beneath, who keepest covenant and mercy with thy servants that walk before thee with all their heart: Deut. 7:9; 1 Sam. 2:2; 2 Sam. 7:22
24 Who hast kept with thy servant David my father that thou promisedst him: thou spakest also with thy mouth, and hast fulfilled *it* with thine hand, as *it is* this day.   1 Kin. 8:15
25 Therefore now, LORD God of Israel, keep with thy servant David my father that thou promisedst him, saying, There shall not fail thee a man in my sight to sit on the throne of Israel; so that thy children take heed to their way, that they walk before me as thou hast walked before me.   1 Kin. 2:4
26 And now, O God of Israel, let thy word, I pray thee, be verified, which thou spakest unto thy servant David my father.
27 But will God indeed dwell on the earth? behold, the heaven and heaven of heavens cannot contain thee; how much less this house that I have builded?   Is. 66:1; Jer. 23:24
28 Yet have thou respect unto the prayer of thy servant, and to his supplication, O LORD my God, to hearken unto the cry and to the prayer, which thy servant prayeth before thee to day:
29 That thine eyes may be open toward this house night and day, *even* toward the place of which thou hast said, My name shall be there: that thou mayest hearken unto the

prayer which thy servant shall make toward this place. Deut. 12:11; 2 Chr. 6:20; Neh. 1:6

30 And hearken thou to the supplication of thy servant, and of thy people Israel, when they shall pray toward this place: and hear thou in heaven thy dwelling place: and when thou hearest, forgive. 1 Kin. 8:34

31 If any man ᵀtrespass against his neighbour, and an oath be laid upon him to cause him to swear, and the oath come before thine altar in this house: Ex. 22:8-11 ♦ sin

32 Then hear thou in heaven, and do, and judge thy servants, condemning the wicked, to bring his way upon his head; and justifying the righteous, to give him according to his righteousness. Deut. 25:1

33 When thy people Israel be smitten down before the enemy, because they have sinned against thee, and shall turn again to thee, and confess thy name, and pray, and make supplication unto thee in this house: Lev. 26:17, 25

34 Then hear thou in heaven, and forgive the sin of thy people Israel, and bring them again unto the land which thou gavest unto their fathers.

35 When heaven is shut up, and there is no rain, because they have sinned against thee; if they pray toward this place, and confess thy name, and turn from their sin, when thou afflictest them: Lev. 26:19

36 Then hear thou in heaven, and forgive the sin of thy servants, and of thy people Israel, that thou teach them the good way wherein they should walk, and give rain upon thy land, which thou hast given to thy people for an inheritance. 1 Sam. 12:23; Ps. 27:11; Jer. 6:16

37 If there be in the land famine, if there be pestilence, blasting, mildew, locust, or if there be caterpiller; if their enemy besiege them in the land of their cities; whatsoever plague, whatsoever sickness there be; Lev. 26:16

38 What prayer and supplication soever be made by any man, or by all thy people Israel, which shall know every man the plague of his own heart, and spread forth his hands toward this house:

39 Then hear thou in heaven thy dwelling place, and forgive, and do, and give to every man according to his ways, whose heart thou knowest; (for thou, even thou only, knowest the hearts of all the children of men;) 1 Sam. 16:7; 1 Chr. 28:9; Jer. 17:10

40 That they may fear thee all the days that they live in the land which thou gavest unto our fathers. Ps. 130:4

41 Moreover concerning a stranger, that is not of thy people Israel, but cometh out of a far country for thy name's sake; 1 Kin. 10:1-2

42 (For they shall hear of thy great name, and of thy strong hand, and of thy stretched

out arm;) when he shall come and pray toward this house; Deut. 3:24

43 Hear thou in heaven thy dwelling place, and do according to all that the stranger calleth to thee for: that all people of the earth may know thy name, to fear thee, as do thy people Israel; and that they may know that this house, which I have builded, is called by thy name. 1 Sam. 17:46

8:41–43 Solomon Prays for Temple Visitors

One of the most touching portions of Solomon's dedicatory prayer was his plea to God for the strangers that should come from countries afar to learn more of Him whose fame had been spread abroad among the nations. *PK 66*

44 If thy people go out to battle against their enemy, whithersoever thou shalt send them, and shall pray unto the LORD toward the city which thou hast chosen, and toward the house that I have built for thy name:

45 Then hear thou in heaven their prayer and their supplication, and maintain their cause.

46 If they sin against thee, (for there is no man that sinneth not,) and thou be angry with them, and deliver them to the enemy, so that they carry them away captives unto the land of the enemy, far or near; Lev. 26:34-39; Prov. 20:9

47 Yet if they shall ᵀbethink themselves in the land whither they were carried captives, and repent, and make supplication unto thee in the land of them that carried them captives, saying, We have sinned, and have done perversely, we have committed wickedness; Ezra 9:6-7; Ps. 106:6 ♦ remember

48 And so return unto thee with all their heart, and with all their soul, in the land of their enemies, which led them away captive, and pray unto thee toward their land, which thou gavest unto their fathers, the city which thou hast chosen, and the house which I have built for thy name: Deut. 4:29; Jer. 29:12-14; Dan. 6:10

49 Then hear thou their prayer and their supplication in heaven thy dwelling place, and maintain their cause,

50 And forgive thy people that have sinned against thee, and all their ᵀtransgressions wherein they have transgressed against thee, and give them compassion before them who carried them captive, that they may have compassion on them: Ps. 106:46; Acts 7:10 ♦ violations of a law

51 For they be thy people, and thine inheritance, which thou broughtest forth out of Egypt, from the midst of the furnace of iron: Deut. 4:20; Neh. 1:10; Jer. 11:4

52 That thine eyes may be open unto the supplication of thy servant, and unto the supplication of thy people Israel, to

hearken unto them in all that they call for unto thee.   1 Kin. 8:29

53 For thou didst separate them from among all the people of the earth, *to be* thine inheritance, as thou spakest by the hand of Moses thy servant, when thou broughtest our fathers out of Egypt, O Lord GOD.   Ex. 19:5-6

Solomon's Blessing

54 And it was *so*, that when Solomon had made an end of praying all this prayer and supplication unto the LORD, he arose from before the altar of the LORD, from kneeling on his knees with his hands spread up to heaven.   Luke 22:45

55 And he stood, and blessed all the congregation of Israel with a loud voice, saying,   Num. 6:23-26; 2 Sam. 6:18; 1 Kin. 8:14

56 Blessed *be* the LORD, that hath given rest unto his people Israel, according to all that he promised: there hath not failed one word of all his good promise, which he promised by the hand of Moses his servant. Deut. 12:10

57 The LORD our God be with us, as he was with our fathers: let him not leave us, nor forsake us: Deut. 31:6; Josh. 1:5; Heb. 13:5

58 That he may incline our hearts unto him, to walk in all his ways, and to keep his commandments, and his statutes, and his judgments, which he commanded our fathers.   Ps. 119:36; Jer. 31:33

59 And let these my words, wherewith I have made supplication before the LORD, be nigh unto the LORD our God day and night, that he maintain the cause of his servant, and the cause of his people Israel at all times, as the matter shall require:

60 That all the people of the earth may know that the LORD *is* God, *and that there is* none else.   Deut. 4:35; Josh. 4:24; 1 Kin. 18:39

61 Let your heart therefore be perfect with the LORD our God, to walk in his statutes, and to keep his commandments, as at this day.   1 Kin. 11:4; 15:3; 2 Kin. 20:3

Solomon Sacrifices Peace Offerings

62 And the king, and all Israel with him, offered sacrifice before the LORD. 2 Sam. 6:17-19

63 And Solomon offered a sacrifice of peace offerings, which he offered unto the LORD, two and twenty thousand oxen, and an hundred and twenty thousand sheep. So the king and all the children of Israel dedicated the house of the LORD.   Ezra 6:16-17; Neh. 12:27

64 The same day did the king hallow the middle of the court that *was* before the house of the LORD: for there he offered burnt offerings, and meat offerings, and the fat of the peace offerings: because the brasen altar that *was* before the LORD *was* too little to receive the burnt offerings, and meat offerings, and the fat of the peace offerings. 2 Chr. 4:1 ◆ *render as sacred*

65 And at that time Solomon held a feast, and all Israel with him, a great congregation, from the entering in of Hamath unto the river of Egypt, before the LORD our God, seven days and seven days, *even* fourteen days.   Num. 34:5, 8; 1 Kin. 8:2

66 On the eighth day he sent the people away: and they blessed the king, and went unto their tents joyful and glad of heart for all the goodness that the LORD had done for David his servant, and for Israel his people.

God's Covenant, in a Vision, with Solomon

9 And it came to pass, when Solomon had finished the building of the house of the LORD, and the king's house, and all Solomon's desire which he was pleased to do,   1 Kin. 9:19

2 That the LORD appeared to Solomon the second time, as he had appeared unto him at Gibeon.   1 Kin. 3:5; 11:9; 2 Chr. 7:12

3 And the LORD said unto him, I have heard thy prayer and thy supplication, that thou hast made before me: I have hallowed this house, which thou hast built, to put my name there for ever; and mine eyes and mine heart shall be there perpetually. Deut. 11:12; 1 Kin. 8:29

4 And if thou wilt walk before me, as David thy father walked, in integrity of heart, and in uprightness, to do according to all that I have commanded thee, *and* wilt keep my statutes and my judgments: Gen. 17:1

5 Then I will establish the throne of thy kingdom upon Israel for ever, as I promised to David thy father, saying, There shall not fail thee a man upon the throne of Israel.

6 *But* if ye shall at all turn from following me, ye or your children, and will not keep my commandments *and* my statutes which I have set before you, but go and serve other gods, and worship them: 2 Sam. 7:14-16

7 Then will I cut off Israel out of the land which I have given them; and this house, which I have hallowed for my name, will I cast out of my sight; and Israel shall be a proverb and a byword among all people: Deut. 28:37

8 And at this house, *which* is high, every one that passeth by it shall be astonished, and shall hiss; and they shall say, Why hath the LORD done thus unto this land, and to this house? Deut. 29:24-26; 2 Chr. 7:21; Jer. 22:8-9 ◆ *whistle*

9 And they shall answer, Because they forsook the LORD their God, who brought forth their fathers out of the land of Egypt, and have taken hold upon other gods, and have worshipped them, and served them: therefore hath the LORD brought upon them all this evil.   Deut. 29:25-28

Solomon and Hiram Give Each Other Gifts

10 And it came to pass at the end of twenty years, when Solomon had built the two houses, the house of the LORD, and the king's house, 1 Kin. 6:37–7:1
11 (Now Hiram the king of Tyre had furnished Solomon with cedar trees and fir trees, and with gold, according to all his desire,) that then king Solomon gave Hiram twenty cities in the land of Galilee. 2 Chr. 8:2
12 And Hiram came out from Tyre to see the cities which Solomon had given him; and they pleased him not.
13 And he said, What cities are these which thou hast given me, my brother? And he called them the land of Cabul unto this day. Josh. 19:27
14 And Hiram sent to the king sixscore talents of gold. 1 Kin. 9:11

Solomon's Workers

15 And this is the reason of the levy which king Solomon raised; for to build the house of the LORD, and his own house, and Millo, and the wall of Jerusalem, and Hazor, and Megiddo, and Gezer. Josh. 17:11; 2 Sam. 5:9; 1 Kin. 5:13
16 For Pharaoh king of Egypt had gone up, and taken Gezer, and burnt it with fire, and slain the Canaanites that dwelt in the city, and given it for a present unto his daughter, Solomon's wife. 1 Kin. 3:1
17 And Solomon built Gezer, and Beth-horon the ᵀnether, Josh. 16:3 ◆ lower
18 And Baalath, and Tadmor in the wilderness, in the land, Josh. 19:44
19 And all the cities of store that Solomon had, and cities for his chariots, and cities for his horsemen, and that which Solomon desired to build in Jerusalem, and in Lebanon, and in all the land of his dominion. 1 Kin. 9:1
20 And all the people that were left of the Amorites, Hittites, Perizzites, Hivites, and Jebusites, which were not of the children of Israel,
21 Their children that were left after them in the land, whom the children of Israel also were not able utterly to destroy, upon those did Solomon levy a tribute of bondservice unto this day. Josh. 15:63; 17:12; Judg. 1:21
22 But of the children of Israel did Solomon make no bondmen: but they were men of war, and his servants, and his princes, and his captains, and rulers of his chariots, and his horsemen. Lev. 25:39
23 These were the chief of the officers that were over Solomon's work, five hundred and fifty, which bare rule over the people that wrought in the work. 1 Kin. 5:16; 2 Chr. 8:10
24 But Pharaoh's daughter came up out of the city of David unto her house which

Solomon had built for her: then did he build Millo. 2 Sam. 5:9; 1 Kin. 7:8; 11:27
25 And three times in a year did Solomon offer burnt offerings and peace offerings upon the altar which he built unto the LORD, and he burnt incense upon the altar that was before the LORD. So he finished the house. Ex. 23:14-17
26 And king Solomon made a navy of ships in Ezion-geber, which is beside Eloth, on the shore of the Red sea, in the land of Edom. Num. 33:35; Deut. 2:8; 1 Kin. 22:48
27 And Hiram sent in the navy his servants, shipmen that had knowledge of the sea, with the servants of Solomon. 1 Kin. 5:6
28 And they came to Ophir, and fetched from thence gold, four hundred and twenty talents, and brought it to king Solomon. 1 Chr. 29:4

The Queen of Sheba Admires Solomon's Wisdom

10 And when the queen of Sheba heard of the fame of Solomon concerning the name of the LORD, she came to prove him with hard questions. Matt. 12:42; Luke 11:31
2 And she came to Jerusalem with a very great train, with camels that bare spices, and very much gold, and precious stones: and when she was come to Solomon, she communed with him of all that was in her heart.
3 And Solomon told her all her questions: there was not any thing hid from the king, which he told her not.
4 And when the queen of Sheba had seen all Solomon's wisdom, and the house that he had built,
5 And the meat of his table, and the sitting of his servants, and the attendance of his ministers, and their apparel, and his cupbearers, and his ascent by which he went up unto the house of the LORD; there was no more spirit in her. 1 Chr. 26:16
6 And she said to the king, It was a true report that I heard in mine own land of thy acts and of thy wisdom.
7 Howbeit I believed not the words, until I came, and mine eyes had seen it: and, behold, the half was not told me: thy wisdom and prosperity exceedeth the fame which I heard.
8 Happy are thy men, happy are these thy servants, which stand continually before thee, and that hear thy wisdom. Prov. 8:34
9 Blessed be the LORD thy God, which delighted in thee, to set thee on the throne of Israel: because the LORD loved Israel for ever, therefore made he thee king, to do judgment and justice. 2 Sam. 8:15; 1 Kin. 5:7; Ps. 72:2
10 And she gave the king an hundred and twenty talents of gold, and of spices very great store, and precious stones: there came

no more such abundance of spices as these which the queen of Sheba gave to king Solomon. 1 Kin. 10:2

11 And the navy also of Hiram, that brought gold from Ophir, brought in from Ophir great plenty of almug trees, and precious stones. 1 Kin. 9:27-28

12 And the king made of the almug trees pillars for the house of the LORD, and for the king's house, harps also and Tpsalteries for singers: there came no such almug trees, nor were seen unto this day. *stringed instruments*

13 And king Solomon gave unto the queen of Sheba all her desire, whatsoever she asked, beside *that* which Solomon gave her of his royal bounty. So she turned and went to her own country, she and her servants.

Solomon's Gold

14 Now the weight of gold that came to Solomon in one year was six hundred Tthree-score and six talents of gold, 1 Kin. 9:28 ◆ *sixty*

15 Beside *that he had* of the merchantmen, and of the Ttraffick of the spice merchants, and of all the kings of Arabia, and of the governors of the country. *trade*

16 And king Solomon made two hundred targets *of* beaten gold: six hundred *shekels* of gold went to one target. 1 Kin. 14:26-28

17 And *he made* three hundred shields *of* beaten gold; three pound of gold went to one shield: and the king put them in the house of the forest of Lebanon. 1 Kin. 7:2

18 Moreover the king made a great throne of ivory, and overlaid it with the best gold.

19 The throne had six steps, and the top of the throne *was* round behind: and *there were* stays on either side on the place of the seat, and two lions stood beside the stays.

20 And twelve lions stood there on the one side and on the other upon the six steps: there was not the like made in any kingdom.

21 And all king Solomon's drinking vessels *were of* gold, and all the vessels of the house of the forest of Lebanon *were of* pure gold; none *were of* silver: it was nothing accounted of in the days of Solomon. 1 Kin. 10:17

22 For the king had at sea a navy of Tharshish with the navy of Hiram: once in three years came the navy of Tharshish, bringing gold, and silver, ivory, and apes, and peacocks. 1 Kin. 22:48

23 So king Solomon exceeded all the kings of the earth for riches and for wisdom.

24 And all the earth sought to Solomon, to hear his wisdom, which God had put in his heart. 1 Kin. 3:9

> **10:23, 24 Solomon's Renowned Wisdom**
>
> In the early life of Solomon also are seen the results of God's method of education. Solomon in his youth made David's choice his own. Above every earthly good he asked of God a wise and understanding heart. And the Lord gave him not only that which he sought, but that also for which he had not sought—both riches and honor. The power of his understanding, the extent of his knowledge, the glory of his reign, became the wonder of the world. *Ed 48*

25 And they brought every man his present, vessels of silver, and vessels of gold, and garments, and armour, and spices, horses, and mules, a rate year by year.

26 And Solomon gathered together chariots and horsemen: and he had a thousand and four hundred chariots, and twelve thousand horsemen, whom he bestowed in the cities for chariots, and with the king at Jerusalem. Deut. 17:16; 1 Kin. 4:26; 2 Chr. 9:25

A Queen Visits Solomon

1 Kings 10:1–13

Hearing of his wisdom and of the magnificent temple he had built, [the queen of Sheba] determined "to prove him with hard questions" and to see for herself his famous works. Attended by a retinue of servants, and with camels bearing "spices, and gold in abundance, and precious stones," she made the long journey to Jerusalem. "And when she was come to Solomon, she communed with him of all that was in her heart." She talked with him of the mysteries of nature; and Solomon taught her of the God of nature, the great Creator, who dwells in the highest heaven and rules over all. "Solomon told her all her questions: there was not any thing hid from the king, which he told her not" (1 Kings 10:1–3; 2 Chronicles 9:1, 2). . . .

By the time of the close of her visit the queen had been so fully taught by Solomon as to the source of his wisdom and prosperity that she was constrained, not to extol the human agent, but to exclaim, "Blessed be the Lord thy God, which delighted in thee, to set thee on the throne of Israel: because the Lord loved Israel forever, therefore made He thee king, to do judgment and justice" (1 Kings 10:9). This is the impression that God designed should be made upon all peoples. And when "all the kings of the earth sought the presence of Solomon, to hear his wisdom, that God had put in his heart" (2 Chronicles 9:23), Solomon for a time honored God by reverently pointing them to the Creator of the heavens and the earth, the Ruler of the universe, the All-wise. *PK 66–68*

27 And the king made silver *to be* in Jerusalem as stones, and cedars made he *to be* as the sycomore trees that *are* in the ᵀvale, for abundance.   *valley*
28 And Solomon had horses brought out of Egypt, and linen yarn: the king's merchants received the linen yarn at a price.   Deut. 17:16
29 And a chariot came up and went out of Egypt for six hundred *shekels* of silver, and an horse for an hundred and fifty: and so for all the kings of the Hittites, and for the kings of Syria, did they bring *them* out by their means.

Solomon's Wives and Concubines Draw Him into Idolatry

11 But king Solomon loved many strange women, together with the daughter of Pharaoh, women of the Moabites, Ammonites, Edomites, Zidonians, *and* Hittites;
2 Of the nations *concerning* which the LORD said unto the children of Israel, Ye shall not go in to them, neither shall they come in unto you: *for* surely they will turn away your heart after their gods: Solomon ᵀclave unto these in love. Ex. 23:32-33; 34:16; Deut. 7:3-4 ◆ *clung*
3 And he had seven hundred wives, princesses, and three hundred concubines: and his wives turned away his heart. 2 Sam. 5:13-16
4 For it came to pass, when Solomon was old, *that* his wives turned away his heart after other gods: and his heart was not perfect with the LORD his God, as *was* the heart of David his father.   1 Kin. 8:61; 9:4
5 For Solomon went after Ashtoreth the goddess of the Zidonians, and after Milcom the abomination of the Ammonites.   Judg. 2:13
6 And Solomon did evil in the sight of the LORD, and went not fully after the LORD, as *did* David his father.

7 Then did Solomon build an high place for Chemosh, the abomination of Moab, in the hill that *is* before Jerusalem, and for Molech, the abomination of the children of Ammon.   Num. 21:29; Judg. 11:24; Acts 7:43
8 And likewise did he for all his strange wives, which burnt incense and sacrificed unto their gods.
9 And the LORD was angry with Solomon, because his heart was turned from the LORD God of Israel, which had appeared unto him twice,   1 Kin. 3:5; 9:2
10 And had commanded him concerning this thing, that he should not go after other gods: but he kept not that which the LORD commanded.
11 Wherefore the LORD said unto Solomon, Forasmuch as this is done of thee, and thou hast not kept my covenant and my statutes, which I have commanded thee, I will surely rend the kingdom from thee, and will give it to thy servant.   1 Kin. 11:31; 12:15-16, 20
12 Notwithstanding in thy days I will not do it for David thy father's sake: *but* I will ᵀrend it out of the hand of thy son.   *tear*
13 Howbeit I will not rend away all the kingdom; *but* will give one tribe to thy son for David my servant's sake, and for Jerusalem's sake which I have chosen.   Deut. 12:11

Solomon's Adversaries: Hadad of Edom and Rezon of Syria

14 And the LORD stirred up an adversary unto Solomon, Hadad the Edomite: he *was* of the king's seed in Edom.
15 For it came to pass, when David was in Edom, and Joab the captain of the host was gone up to bury the slain, after he had smitten every male in Edom; Deut. 20:13; 2 Sam. 8:14

Solomon's Tragic Fall

1 Kings 11:1–8

So gradual was Solomon's apostasy that before he was aware of it, he had wandered far from God. Almost imperceptibly he began to trust less and less in divine guidance and blessing, and to put confidence in his own strength. Little by little he withheld from God that unswerving obedience which was to make Israel a peculiar people, and he conformed more and more closely to the customs of the surrounding nations. Yielding to the temptations incident to his success and his honored position, he forgot the Source of his prosperity. An ambition to excel all other nations in power and grandeur led him to pervert for selfish purposes the heavenly gifts hitherto employed for the glory of God. The money which should have been held in sacred trust for the benefit of the worthy poor and for the extension of principles of holy living throughout the world, was selfishly absorbed in ambitious projects.

Engrossed in an overmastering desire to surpass other nations in outward display, the king overlooked the need of acquiring beauty and perfection of character. In seeking to glorify himself before the world, he sold his honor and integrity. The enormous revenues acquired through commerce with many lands were supplemented by heavy taxes. Thus pride, ambition, prodigality, and indulgence bore fruit in cruelty and exaction. The conscientious, considerate spirit that had marked his dealings with the people during the early part of his reign, was now changed. From the wisest and most merciful of rulers, he degenerated into a tyrant. Once the compassionate, God-fearing guardian of the people, he became oppressive and despotic. *PK 55, 56*

16 (For six months did Joab remain there with all Israel, until he had cut off every male in Edom:)
17 That Hadad fled, he and certain Edomites of his father's servants with him, to go into Egypt; Hadad *being* yet a little child.
18 And they arose out of Midian, and came to Paran: and they took men with them out of Paran, and they came to Egypt, unto Pharaoh king of Egypt; which gave him an house, and appointed him ᵀvictuals, and gave him land.   Num. 10:12; Deut. 1:1; 33:2 ◆ *food*
19 And Hadad found great favour in the sight of Pharaoh, so that he gave him to wife the sister of his own wife, the sister of Tahpenes the queen.
20 And the sister of Tahpenes bare him Genubath his son, whom Tahpenes weaned in Pharaoh's house: and Genubath was in Pharaoh's household among the sons of Pharaoh.
21 And when Hadad heard in Egypt that David slept with his fathers, and that Joab the captain of the host was dead, Hadad said to Pharaoh, Let me depart, that I may go to mine own country.   1 Kin. 2:10
22 Then Pharaoh said unto him, But what hast thou lacked with me, that, behold, thou seekest to go to thine own country? And he answered, Nothing: ᵀhowbeit let me go in any wise.   *however*

11:14–26 God Sends a Wake-up Call

By his own bitter experience, Solomon learned the emptiness of a life that seeks in earthly things its highest good. . . . For him there was no longer any joy of life or peace of mind, and the future was dark with despair.

Yet the Lord forsook him not. By messages of reproof and by severe judgments, He sought to arouse the king to a realization of the sinfulness of his course. He removed His protecting care and permitted adversaries to harass and weaken the kingdom. *PK 76, 77*

---

23 And God stirred him up *another* adversary, Rezon the son of Eliadah, which fled from his lord Hadadezer king of Zobah: 2 Sam. 8:3
24 And he gathered men unto him, and became captain over a band, when David slew them *of Zobah*: and they went to Damascus, and dwelt therein, and reigned in Damascus.   2 Sam. 10:8
25 And he was an adversary to Israel all the days of Solomon, beside the mischief that Hadad *did*: and he ᵀabhorred Israel, and reigned over Syria.   *despised*

Solomon's Adversary: Jeroboam, One of His Officials

26 And Jeroboam the son of Nebat, an Ephrathite of Zereda, Solomon's servant, whose mother's name *was* Zeruah, a widow woman, even he lifted up *his* hand against the king.   1 Sam. 1:1; 1 Kin. 12:2; 2 Chr. 13:6
27 And this *was* the cause that he lifted up *his* hand against the king: Solomon built Millo, *and* repaired the breaches of the city of David his father.   1 Kin. 9:15, 24
28 And the man Jeroboam *was* a mighty man of valour: and Solomon seeing the young man that he was industrious, he made him ruler over all the charge of the house of Joseph.   Prov. 22:29
29 And it came to pass at that time when Jeroboam went out of Jerusalem, that the prophet Ahijah the Shilonite found him in the way; and he had clad himself with a new garment; and they two *were* alone in the field: 1 Kin. 12:15; 14:2; 2 Chr. 9:29
30 And Ahijah caught the new garment that *was* on him, and rent it *in* twelve pieces:
31 And he said to Jeroboam, Take thee ten pieces: for thus saith the LORD, the God of Israel, Behold, I will rend the kingdom out of the hand of Solomon, and will give ten tribes to thee: 1 Kin. 11:11-12
32 (But he shall have one tribe for my servant David's sake, and for Jerusalem's sake, the city which I have chosen out of all the tribes of Israel:)   1 Kin. 11:13
33 Because that they have forsaken me, and have worshipped Ashtoreth the goddess of the Zidonians, Chemosh the god of the Moabites, and Milcom the god of the children of Ammon, and have not walked in my ways, to do *that which is* right in mine eyes, and *to* keep my statutes and my judgments, as *did* David his father.
34 Howbeit I will not take the whole kingdom out of his hand: but I will make him prince all the days of his life for David my servant's sake, whom I chose, because he kept my commandments and my statutes:
35 But I will take the kingdom out of his son's hand, and will give it unto thee, *even* ten tribes.
36 And unto his son will I give one tribe, that David my servant may have a light alway before me in Jerusalem, the city which I have chosen me to put my name there.   1 Kin. 11:13
37 And I will take thee, and thou shalt reign according to all that thy soul desireth, and shalt be king over Israel.   2 Sam. 3:21
38 And it shall be, if thou wilt hearken unto all that I command thee, and wilt walk in my ways, and do *that is* right in my sight, to keep my statutes and my commandments, as David my servant did; that I will be with thee, and build thee a sure house, as I built for David, and will give Israel unto thee. Deut. 31:8; Josh. 1:5
39 And I will for this afflict the seed of David, but not for ever.

40 Solomon sought therefore to kill Jeroboam. And Jeroboam arose, and fled into Egypt, unto Shishak king of Egypt, and was in Egypt until the death of Solomon.

Solomon Is Succeeded by Rehoboam after a Forty-Year Reign

41 And the rest of the acts of Solomon, and all that he did, and his wisdom, *are* they not written in the book of the acts of Solomon?   2 Chr. 9:29-31

42 And the time that Solomon reigned in Jerusalem over all Israel *was* forty years.

43 And Solomon slept with his fathers, and was buried in the city of David his father: and Rehoboam his son reigned in his stead.   1 Kin. 2:10

The Israelites Ask Rehoboam to Lighten Their Burdens

12 And Rehoboam went to Shechem: for all Israel were come to Shechem to make him king.   2 Chr. 10

12:1 When Early Training Is Neglected

Although Solomon had longed to prepare the mind of Rehoboam, his chosen successor, to meet with wisdom the crisis foretold by the prophet of God, he had never been able to exert a strong molding influence for good over the mind of his son, whose early training had been so grossly neglected. Rehoboam had received from his mother, an Ammonitess, the stamp of a vacillating character. . . . In the mistakes of Rehoboam's life and in his final apostasy is revealed the fearful result of Solomon's union with idolatrous women. *PK 88*

2 And it came to pass, when Jeroboam the son of Nebat, who was yet in Egypt, heard *of it*, (for he was fled from the presence of king Solomon, and Jeroboam dwelt in Egypt;)

3 That they sent and called him. And Jeroboam and all the congregation of Israel came, and spake unto Rehoboam, saying,

4 Thy father made our yoke grievous: now therefore make thou the grievous service of thy father, and his heavy yoke which he put upon us, lighter, and we will serve thee.   1 Sam. 8:11-18; 1 Kin. 4:7; 9:15

5 And he said unto them, Depart yet *for* three days, then come again to me. And the people departed.

6 And king Rehoboam consulted with the old men, that stood before Solomon his father while he yet lived, and said, How do ye advise that I may answer this people?   Job 12:12

7 And they spake unto him, saying, If thou wilt be a servant unto this people this day, and wilt serve them, and answer them, and speak good words to them, then they will be thy servants for ever.   Prov. 15:1

8 But he forsook the counsel of the old men, which they had given him, and consulted with the young men that were grown up with him, *and* which stood before him:

9 And he said unto them, What counsel give ye that we may answer this people, who have spoken to me, saying, Make the yoke which thy father did put upon us lighter?

10 And the young men that were grown up with him spake unto him, saying, Thus shalt thou speak unto this people that spake unto thee, saying, Thy father made our yoke heavy, but make thou *it* lighter unto us; thus shalt thou say unto them, My little *finger* shall be thicker than my father's ᵀloins. waist

11 And now whereas my father did ᵀlade you with a heavy yoke, I will add to your yoke: my father hath chastised you with whips, but I will chastise you with scorpions. load

12 So Jeroboam and all the people came to Rehoboam the third day, as the king had appointed, saying, Come to me again the third day.   1 Kin. 12:5

13 And the king answered the people roughly, and forsook the old men's counsel that they gave him;

14 And spake to them after the counsel of the young men, saying, My father made your yoke heavy, and I will add to your yoke: my father *also* chastised you with whips, but I will chastise you with scorpions.

15 Wherefore the king hearkened not unto the people; for the cause was from the LORD, that he might perform his saying, which the LORD spake by Ahijah the Shilonite unto Jeroboam the son of Nebat.   Deut. 2:30; Judg. 14:4

Ten Tribes Revolt against Rehoboam and Make Jeroboam Their King

16 So when all Israel saw that the king hearkened not unto them, the people answered the king, saying, What portion have we in David? neither *have we* inheritance in the son of Jesse: to your tents, O Israel: now see to thine own house, David. So Israel departed unto their tents.   2 Sam. 20:1

17 But *as for* the children of Israel which dwelt in the cities of Judah, Rehoboam reigned over them.   1 Kin. 11:13, 36

18 Then king Rehoboam sent Adoram, who *was* over the tribute; and all Israel stoned him with stones, that he died. Therefore king Rehoboam made speed to get him up to his chariot, to flee to Jerusalem.   1 Kin. 4:6; 5:14

19 So Israel rebelled against the house of David unto this day.   2 Kin. 17:21

20 And it came to pass, when all Israel heard that Jeroboam was come again, that they sent and called him unto the congregation,

and made him king over all Israel: there was none that followed the house of David, but the tribe of Judah only.   1 Kin. 11:13, 32

21 And when Rehoboam was come to Jerusalem, he assembled all the house of Judah, with the tribe of Benjamin, an hundred and ^Tfourscore thousand chosen men, which were warriors, to fight against the house of Israel, to bring the kingdom again to Rehoboam the son of Solomon.   2 Chr. 11:1-3 ◆ eighty

22 But the word of God came unto Shemaiah the man of God, saying,   2 Chr. 11:2

23 Speak unto Rehoboam, the son of Solomon, king of Judah, and unto all the house of Judah and Benjamin, and to the remnant of the people, saying,

24 Thus saith the LORD, Ye shall not go up, nor fight against your brethren the children of Israel: return every man to his house; for this thing is from me. They hearkened therefore to the word of the LORD, and returned to depart, according to the word of the LORD.   1 Kin. 12:15

Jeroboam Sets Up Idol Worship in Israel at Beth-el and Dan

25 Then Jeroboam built Shechem in mount Ephraim, and dwelt therein; and went out from thence, and built Penuel.   Gen. 32:30-31

26 And Jeroboam said in his heart, Now shall the kingdom return to the house of David:

27 If this people go up to do sacrifice in the house of the LORD at Jerusalem, then shall the heart of this people turn again unto their lord, even unto Rehoboam king of Judah, and they shall kill me, and go again to Rehoboam king of Judah.   Deut. 12:5-7

28 Whereupon the king took counsel, and made two calves of gold, and said unto them, It is too much for you to go up to Jerusalem: behold thy gods, O Israel, which brought thee up out of the land of Egypt. Ex. 32:4, 8; 2 Kin. 10:29

29 And he set the one in Beth-el, and the other put he in Dan.   Gen. 28:19

30 And this thing became a sin: for the people went to worship before the one, even unto Dan.   1 Kin. 13:34; 2 Kin. 17:21

31 And he made an house of high places, and made priests of the lowest of the people, which were not of the sons of Levi.

32 And Jeroboam ordained a feast in the eighth month, on the fifteenth day of the month, like unto the feast that is in Judah, and he offered upon the altar. So did he in Beth-el, sacrificing unto the calves that he had made: and he placed in Beth-el the priests of the high places which he had made.   1 Kin. 8:2

33 So he offered upon the altar which he had made in Beth-el the fifteenth day of the eighth month, even in the month which he had devised of his own heart; and ordained a feast unto the children of Israel: and he offered upon the altar, and burnt incense.   Num. 15:39

Jeroboam's Hand Withers and His Altar Splits Apart

13 And, behold, there came a man of God out of Judah by the word of the LORD unto Beth-el: and Jeroboam stood by the altar to burn incense.   1 Kin. 12:22, 32-33; 2 Kin. 23:17

2 And he cried against the altar in the word of the LORD, and said, O altar, altar, thus saith the LORD; Behold, a child shall be born unto the house of David, Josiah by name; and upon thee shall he offer the priests of the high places that burn incense upon thee, and men's bones shall be burnt upon thee.

3 And he gave a sign the same day, saying, This is the sign which the LORD hath spoken; Behold, the altar shall be rent, and the ashes that are upon it shall be poured out. 1 Cor. 1:22

4 And it came to pass, when king Jeroboam heard the saying of the man of God, which had cried against the altar in Beth-el, that he put forth his hand from the altar, saying, Lay hold on him. And his hand, which he put forth against him, dried up, so that he could not pull it in again to him.

5 The altar also was ^Trent, and the ashes poured out from the altar, according to the sign which the man of God had given by the word of the LORD.   torn apart

6 And the king answered and said unto the man of God, Intreat now the face of the LORD thy God, and pray for me, that my hand may be restored me again. And the man of God ^Tbesought the LORD, and the king's hand was restored him again, and became as it was before. Ex. 8:8; 9:28; 10:17 ◆ begged

13:1–6 Lord's Messengers Never to Fear Man

How firmly the man of God rebuked the king! And this firmness was essential; in no other way could the existing evils have been rebuked. . . . The messengers of the Lord are never to fear the face of man, but are to stand unflinchingly for the right. So long as they put their trust in God, they need not fear; for He who gives them their commission gives them also the assurance of His protecting care. PK 105

7 And the king said unto the man of God, Come home with me, and refresh thyself, and I will give thee a reward.   1 Sam. 9:7-8; 2 Kin. 5:15

8 And the man of God said unto the king, If thou wilt give me half thine house, I will not go in with thee, neither will I eat bread nor drink water in this place: Num. 22:18; 24:13

9 For so was it charged me by the word of

the LORD, saying, Eat no bread, nor drink water, nor turn again by the same way that thou camest.

10 So he went another way, and returned not by the way that he came to Beth-el.

The Man of God from Judah Is Enticed and Disobeys God

11 Now there dwelt an old prophet in Bethel; and his sons came and told him all the works that the man of God had done that day in Beth-el: the words which he had spoken unto the king, them they told also to their father.   2 Kin. 23:18

12 And their father said unto them, What way went he? For his sons had seen what way the man of God went, which came from Judah.

13 And he said unto his sons, Saddle me the ass. So they saddled him the ass: and he rode thereon,

14 And went after the man of God, and found him sitting under an oak: and he said unto him, *Art* thou the man of God that camest from Judah? And he said, I *am.*

15 Then he said unto him, Come home with me, and eat bread.

16 And he said, I may not return with thee, nor go in with thee: neither will I eat bread nor drink water with thee in this place:

17 For it was said to me by the word of the LORD, Thou shalt eat no bread nor drink water there, nor turn again to go by the way that thou camest.   1 Kin. 20:35

18 He said unto him, I *am* a prophet also as thou *art*; and an angel spake unto me by the word of the LORD, saying, Bring him back with thee into thine house, that he may eat bread and drink water. *But* he lied unto him.   Matt. 7:15

19 So he went back with him, and did eat bread in his house, and drank water.

20 And it came to pass, as they sat at the table, that the word of the LORD came unto the prophet that brought him back:

21 And he cried unto the man of God that came from Judah, saying, Thus saith the LORD, Forasmuch as thou hast disobeyed the mouth of the LORD, and hast not kept the commandment which the LORD thy God commanded thee,

22 But camest back, and hast eaten bread and drunk water in the place, of the which *the* LORD did say to thee, Eat no bread, and drink no water; thy carcase shall not come unto the sepulchre of thy fathers.

The Man of God Is Slain by a Lion

23 And it came to pass, after he had eaten bread, and after he had drunk, that he sad-

dled for him the ass, ᵀ*to wit,* for the prophet whom he had brought back.   namely

24 And when he was gone, a lion met him by the way, and slew him: and his carcase was cast in the way, and the ass stood by it, the lion also stood by the carcase. 1 Kin. 20:36

25 And, behold, men passed by, and saw the carcase cast in the way, and the lion standing by the carcase: and they came and told *it* in the city where the old prophet dwelt.

26 And when the prophet that brought him back from the way heard *thereof,* he said, It *is* the man of God, who was disobedient unto the word of the LORD: therefore the LORD hath delivered him unto the lion, which hath torn him, and slain him, according to the word of the LORD, which he spake unto him.

27 And he spake to his sons, saying, Saddle me the ass. And they saddled *him.*

28 And he went and found his carcase cast in the way, and the ass and the lion standing by the carcase: the lion had not eaten the carcase, nor torn the ass.

29 And the prophet took up the carcase of the man of God, and laid it upon the ass, and brought it back: and the old prophet came to the city, to mourn and to bury him.

30 And he laid his carcase in his own grave; and they mourned over him, *saying,* Alas, my brother!   Jer. 22:18

31 And it came to pass, after he had buried him, that he spake to his sons, saying, When I am dead, then bury me in the sepulchre wherein the man of God *is* buried; lay my bones beside his bones:

32 For the saying which he cried by the word of the LORD against the altar in Bethel, and against all the houses of the high places which *are* in the cities of Samaria, shall surely come to pass.   Lev. 26:30; 1 Kin. 13:2; 16:24

33 After this thing Jeroboam returned not from his evil way, but made again of the lowest of the people priests of the high places: whosoever would, he ᵀconsecrated him, and he became *one* of the priests of the high places.   2 Chr. 11:15 ◆ *set him apart*

34 And this thing became sin unto the house of Jeroboam, even to cut *it* off, and to destroy *it* from off the face of the earth. 1 Kin. 12:30; 14:10

Jeroboam Sends His Wife, Disguised, to the Prophet Ahijah

14 At that time Abijah the son of Jeroboam fell sick.

2 And Jeroboam said to his wife, Arise, I pray thee, and disguise thyself, that thou be not known to be the wife of Jeroboam; and get thee to Shiloh: behold, there *is* Ahijah the prophet, which told me that *I should be* king over this people.   1 Sam. 28:8

3 And take with thee ten loaves, and crack-nels, and a ᵀcruse of honey, and go to him: he shall tell thee what shall become of the child.   1 Sam. 9:7-8 ◆ pot

4 And Jeroboam's wife did so, and arose, and went to Shiloh, and came to the house of Ahijah. But Ahijah could not see; for his eyes were set by reason of his age. 1 Kin. 11:29

5 And the LORD said unto Ahijah, Behold, the wife of Jeroboam cometh to ask a thing of thee for her son; for he is sick: thus and thus shalt thou say unto her: for it shall be, when she cometh in, that she shall feign herself to be another woman.

6 And it was so, when Ahijah heard the sound of her feet, as she came in at the door, that he said, Come in, thou wife of Jeroboam; why feignest thou thyself to be another? for I am sent to thee with heavy tidings.

7 Go, tell Jeroboam, Thus saith the LORD God of Israel, Forasmuch as I exalted thee from among the people, and made thee prince over my people Israel,   2 Sam. 12:7-8; 1 Kin. 16:2

8 And ᵀrent the kingdom away from the house of David, and gave it thee: and yet thou hast not been as my servant David, who kept my commandments, and who followed me with all his heart, to do that only which was right in mine eyes;   1 Kin. 15:5 ◆ tore

9 But hast done evil above all that were before thee: for thou hast gone and made thee other gods, and molten images, to provoke me to anger, and hast cast me behind thy back: 1 Kin. 12:28; 2 Chr. 11:15; Neh. 9:26

10 Therefore, behold, I will bring evil upon the house of Jeroboam, and will cut off from Jeroboam him that pisseth against the wall, and him that is shut up and left in Israel, and will take away the remnant of the house of Jeroboam, as a man taketh away dung, till it be all gone.   Deut. 32:36; 1 Kin. 21:21; 2 Kin. 14:26

11 Him that dieth of Jeroboam in the city shall the dogs eat; and him that dieth in the field shall the fowls of the air eat: for the LORD hath spoken it.   1 Kin. 16:4

12 Arise thou therefore, get thee to thine own house: and when thy feet enter into the city, the child shall die.

13 And all Israel shall mourn for him, and bury him: for he only of Jeroboam shall come to the grave, because in him there is found some good thing toward the LORD God of Israel in the house of Jeroboam. 2 Chr. 12:12; 19:3

14 Moreover the LORD shall raise him up a king over Israel, who shall cut off the house of Jeroboam that day: but what? even now.   1 Kin. 15:27-29

15 For the LORD shall ᵀsmite Israel, as a reed is shaken in the water, and he shall root up Israel out of this good land, which

he gave to their fathers, and shall scatter them beyond the river, because they have made their ᵀgroves, provoking the LORD to anger.   Josh. 23:15-16; 2 Kin. 15:29 ◆ strike ◆ idols

16 And he shall give Israel up because of the sins of Jeroboam, who did sin, and who made Israel to sin.   1 Kin. 12:30

14:15, 16 God's Efforts to Reach His People

The apostasy introduced during Jeroboam's reign became more and more marked, until finally it resulted in the utter ruin of the kingdom of Israel. *PK 107*

17 And Jeroboam's wife arose, and departed, and came to Tirzah: and when she came to the threshold of the door, the child died;

18 And they buried him; and all Israel mourned for him, according to the word of the LORD, which he spake by the hand of his servant Ahijah the prophet.

19 And the rest of the acts of Jeroboam, how he warred, and how he reigned, behold, they are written in the book of the chronicles of the kings of Israel.   2 Chr. 13:2-20

20 And the days which Jeroboam reigned were two and twenty years: and he slept with his fathers, and Nadab his son reigned in his stead.

Rehoboam's Evil Reign over the Southern Kingdom of Judah

21 And Rehoboam the son of Solomon reigned in Judah. Rehoboam was forty and one years old when he began to reign, and he reigned seventeen years in Jerusalem, the city which the LORD did choose out of all the tribes of Israel, to put his name there. And his mother's name was Naamah an Ammon-itess.   1 Kin. 11:36; 14:31; 2 Chr. 12:13

22 And Judah did evil in the sight of the LORD, and they provoked him to jealousy with their sins which they had committed, above all that their fathers had done.   2 Chr. 12:1; Ps. 78:58

23 For they also built them high places, and images, and groves, on every high hill, and under every green tree. Deut. 12:2; 2 Kin. 17:9-10

24 And there were also sodomites in the land: and they did according to all the abominations of the nations which the LORD cast out before the children of Israel.   Deut. 23:17; 1 Kin. 15:12

25 And it came to pass in the fifth year of king Rehoboam, that Shishak king of Egypt came up against Jerusalem: 1 Kin. 11:40

26 And he took away the treasures of the house of the LORD, and the treasures of the king's house; he even took away all: and he took away all the shields of gold which Solomon had made.   1 Kin. 15:18; 2 Chr. 9:15-16

27 And king Rehoboam made in their stead brasen shields, and committed them unto

the hands of the chief of the guard, which kept the door of the king's house. 1 Sam. 8:11

14:25, 26 Relapsing Into Apostasy

The people had not yet gone to such lengths in apostasy that they despised the judgments of God. In the losses sustained by the invasion of Shishak, they recognized the hand of God and for a time humbled themselves. . . .

But as the hand of affliction was removed, and the nation prospered once more, many forgot their fears and turned again to idolatry. Among these was King Rehoboam himself. *PK 95*

---

28 And it was *so*, when the king went into the house of the LORD, that the guard bare them, and brought them back into the guard chamber.
29 Now the rest of the acts of Rehoboam, and all that he did, *are* they not written in the book of the chronicles of the kings of Judah?
30 And there was war between Rehoboam and Jeroboam all *their* days.   1 Kin. 12:21
31 And Rehoboam slept with his fathers, and was buried with his fathers in the city of David. And his mother's name *was* Naamah an Ammonitess. And Abijam his son reigned in his stead.   2 Chr. 12:16; Matt. 1:7

Abijam's Evil Reign over Judah

15 Now in the eighteenth year of king Jeroboam the son of Nebat reigned Abijam over Judah.
2 Three years reigned he in Jerusalem. And his mother's name *was* Maachah, the daughter of Abishalom.   2 Chr. 13:2
3 And he walked in all the sins of his father, which he had done before him: and his heart was not perfect with the LORD his God, as the heart of David his father.   1 Kin. 11:4; Ps. 119:80
4 Nevertheless for David's sake did the LORD his God give him a lamp in Jerusalem, to set up his son after him, and to establish Jerusalem: 1 Kin. 11:36; 2 Chr. 21:7
5 Because David did *that which was* right in the eyes of the LORD, and turned not aside from any *thing* that he commanded him all the days of his life, save only in the matter of Uriah the Hittite. 2 Sam. 11:15-17; 12:9-10; 1 Kin. 14:8
6 And there was war between Rehoboam and Jeroboam all the days of his life.   1 Kin. 14:30
7 Now the rest of the acts of Abijam, and all that he did, *are* they not written in the book of the chronicles of the kings of Judah? And there was war between Abijam and Jeroboam.   2 Chr. 13:2-22
8 And Abijam slept with his fathers; and they buried him in the city of David: and Asa his son reigned in his stead.   2 Chr. 14:1

Asa's Good Reign over Judah

9 And in the twentieth year of Jeroboam king of Israel reigned Asa over Judah.
10 And forty and one years reigned he in Jerusalem. And his mother's name *was* Maachah, the daughter of Abishalom.   1 Kin. 15:2
11 And Asa did *that which was* right in the eyes of the LORD, as *did* David his father. 2 Chr. 14:2
12 And he took away the sodomites out of the land, and removed all the idols that his fathers had made.   1 Kin. 22:46
13 And also Maachah his mother, even her he removed from *being* queen, because she had made an idol in a grove; and Asa destroyed her idol, and burnt *it* by the brook Kidron.   Ex. 32:20
14 But the high places were not removed: nevertheless Asa's heart was perfect with the LORD all his days.   1 Kin. 8:61; 15:3; 22:43
15 And he brought in the things which his father had dedicated, and the things which himself had dedicated, into the house of the LORD, silver, and gold, and vessels. 1 Kin. 7:51
16 And there was war between Asa and Baasha king of Israel all their days.   1 Kin. 15:32
17 And Baasha king of Israel went up against Judah, and built Ramah, that he might not suffer any to go out or come in to Asa king of Judah.   Josh. 18:25; 1 Kin. 12:27; 2 Chr. 16:1-6
18 Then Asa took all the silver and the gold *that were* left in the treasures of the house of the LORD, and the treasures of the king's house, and delivered them into the hand of his servants: and king Asa sent them to Benhadad, the son of Tabrimon, the son of Hezion, king of Syria, that dwelt at Damascus, saying,   1 Kin. 11:23-24; 14:26; 2 Kin. 12:18
19 *There is* a league between me and thee, *and* between my father and thy father: behold, I have sent unto thee a present of silver and gold; come and break thy league with Baasha king of Israel, that he may depart from me.
20 So Ben-hadad hearkened unto king Asa, and sent the captains of the hosts which he had against the cities of Israel, and smote Ijon, and Dan, and Abel-beth-maachah, and all Cinneroth, with all the land of Naphtali.   Josh. 11:2; Judg. 18:29; 2 Kin. 15:29
21 And it came to pass, when Baasha heard *thereof*, that he left off building of Ramah, and dwelt in Tirzah.   1 Kin. 14:17
22 Then king Asa made a proclamation throughout all Judah; none *was* exempted: and they took away the stones of Ramah, and the timber thereof, wherewith Baasha had builded; and king Asa built with them Geba of Benjamin, and Mizpah.   Josh. 18:24, 26; 21:17
23 The rest of all the acts of Asa, and all his might, and all that he did, and the cities which he built, *are* they not written in the

book of the chronicles of the kings of Judah? Nevertheless in the time of his old age he was diseased in his feet.

24 And Asa slept with his fathers, and was buried with his fathers in the city of David his father: and Jehoshaphat his son reigned in his stead.   1 Kin. 22:41-43; Matt. 1:8

Nadab's Evil Reign over the Northern Kingdom of Israel

25 And Nadab the son of Jeroboam began to reign over Israel in the second year of Asa king of Judah, and reigned over Israel two years.   1 Kin. 14:20

26 And he did evil in the sight of the LORD, and walked in the way of his father, and in his sin wherewith he made Israel to sin.

27 And Baasha the son of Ahijah, of the house of Issachar, conspired against him; and Baasha smote him at Gibbethon, which *belonged* to the Philistines; for Nadab and all Israel laid siege to Gibbethon.   Josh. 19:44; 21:23

28 Even in the third year of Asa king of Judah did Baasha slay him, and reigned in his stead.

29 And it came to pass, when he reigned, *that* he smote all the house of Jeroboam; he left not to Jeroboam any that breathed, until he had destroyed him, according unto the saying of the LORD, which he spake by his servant Ahijah the Shilonite: 1 Kin. 14:9-16

30 Because of the sins of Jeroboam which he sinned, and which he made Israel sin, by his provocation wherewith he provoked the LORD God of Israel to anger.   1 Kin. 15:26

31 Now the rest of the acts of Nadab, and all that he did, *are* they not written in the book of the chronicles of the kings of Israel?   1 Kin. 14:19

32 And there was war between Asa and Baasha king of Israel all their days.   1 Kin. 15:16

33 In the third year of Asa king of Judah began Baasha the son of Ahijah to reign over all Israel in Tirzah, twenty and four years.

34 And he did evil in the sight of the LORD, and walked in the way of Jeroboam, and in his sin wherewith he made Israel to sin. 1 Kin. 14:16

The Evil Reigns of Baasha and Elah over Israel

16 Then the word of the LORD came to Jehu the son of Hanani against Baasha, saying,   1 Kin. 16:7; 2 Chr. 19:2; 20:34

2 Forasmuch as I exalted thee out of the dust, and made thee prince over my people Israel; and thou hast walked in the way of Jeroboam, and hast made my people Israel to sin, to provoke me to anger with their sins;   1 Sam. 2:8; 1 Kin. 14:7; 15:34

3 Behold, I will take away the posterity of Baasha, and the posterity of his house; and

will make thy house like the house of Jeroboam the son of Nebat.   1 Kin. 14:10

4 Him that dieth of Baasha in the city shall the dogs eat; and him that dieth of his in the fields shall the fowls of the air eat. 1 Kin. 14:11

5 Now the rest of the acts of Baasha, and what he did, and his might, *are* they not written in the book of the chronicles of the kings of Israel?   1 Kin. 14:19

6 So Baasha slept with his fathers, and was buried in Tirzah: and Elah his son reigned in his stead.   1 Kin. 14:17; 15:21

7 And also by the hand of the prophet Jehu the son of Hanani came the word of the LORD against Baasha, and against his house, even for all the evil that he did in the sight of the LORD, in provoking him to anger with the work of his hands, in being like the house of Jeroboam; and because he killed him.   1 Kin. 14:14

8 In the twenty and sixth year of Asa king of Judah began Elah the son of Baasha to reign over Israel in Tirzah, two years.

9 And his servant Zimri, captain of half *his* chariots, conspired against him, as he was in Tirzah, drinking himself drunk in the house of Arza steward of *his* house in Tirzah. Gen. 24:2

10 And Zimri went in and smote him, and killed him, in the twenty and seventh year of Asa king of Judah, and reigned in his stead.

11 And it came to pass, when he began to reign, as soon as he sat on his throne, *that* he slew all the house of Baasha: he left him not one that pisseth against a wall, neither of his kinsfolks, nor of his friends. 1 Sam. 25:22

12 Thus did Zimri destroy all the house of Baasha, according to the word of the LORD, which he spake against Baasha by Jehu the prophet,   1 Kin. 16:1

13 For all the sins of Baasha, and the sins of Elah his son, by which they sinned, and by which they made Israel to sin, in provoking the LORD God of Israel to anger with their vanities.   Deut. 32:21; 1 Sam. 12:21; 1 Kin. 15:30

14 Now the rest of the acts of Elah, and all that he did, *are* they not written in the book of the chronicles of the kings of Israel?

The Evil Reigns of Zimri and Omri over Israel

15 In the twenty and seventh year of Asa king of Judah did Zimri reign seven days in Tirzah. And the people *were* encamped against Gibbethon, which *belonged* to the Philistines.   Josh. 19:44; 1 Kin. 15:27

16 And the people *that were* encamped heard say, Zimri hath conspired, and hath also slain the king: wherefore all Israel made Omri, the captain of the host, king over Israel that day in the camp.

17 And Omri went up from Gibbethon, and

all Israel with him, and they besieged Tirzah.
18 And it came to pass, when Zimri saw that
the city was taken, that he went into the palace of the king's house, and burnt the king's
house over him with fire, and died, 2 Sam. 17:23
19 For his sins which he sinned in doing evil
in the sight of the LORD, in walking in the
way of Jeroboam, and in his sin which he
did, to make Israel to sin.   1 Kin. 15:26
20 Now the rest of the acts of Zimri, and
his treason that he ᵀwrought, are they not
written in the book of the chronicles of the
kings of Israel?   1 Kin. 16:5 ♦ committed
21 Then were the people of Israel divided
into two parts: half of the people followed
Tibni the son of Ginath, to make him king;
and half followed Omri.
22 But the people that followed Omri prevailed against the people that followed Tibni
the son of Ginath: so Tibni died, and Omri
reigned.
23 In the thirty and first year of Asa king
of Judah began Omri to reign over Israel,
twelve years: six years reigned he in Tirzah.
24 And he bought the hill Samaria of Shemer for two talents of silver, and built on the
hill, and called the name of the city which
he built, after the name of Shemer, owner of
the hill, Samaria.   1 Kin. 13:32
25 But Omri wrought evil in the eyes of the
LORD, and did worse than all that were before him.   1 Kin. 14:9; 16:30-31; Mic. 6:16
26 For he walked in all the way of Jeroboam
the son of Nebat, and in his sin wherewith
he made Israel to sin, to provoke the LORD
God of Israel to anger with their vanities.

27 Now the rest of the acts of Omri which
he did, and his might that he shewed, are
they not written in the book of the chronicles of the kings of Israel?
28 So Omri slept with his fathers, and was
buried in Samaria: and Ahab his son reigned
in his stead.

Ahab's Most Wicked Reign over Israel

29 And in the thirty and eighth year of Asa
king of Judah began Ahab the son of Omri to
reign over Israel: and Ahab the son of Omri
reigned over Israel in Samaria twenty and
two years.
30 And Ahab the son of Omri did evil in the
sight of the LORD above all that were before
him.   1 Kin. 14:9; 16:25; 21:25
31 And it came to pass, as if it had been a
light thing for him to walk in the sins of Jeroboam the son of Nebat, that he took to wife
Jezebel the daughter of Ethbaal king of the
Zidonians, and went and served Baal, and
worshipped him.   Judg. 18:7; 2 Kin. 10:18; 17:16
32 And he reared up an altar for Baal in the
house of Baal, which he had built in Samaria.   2 Kin. 10:21, 26-27
33 And Ahab made a ᵀgrove; and Ahab did
more to provoke the LORD God of Israel to
anger than all the kings of Israel that were
before him.   Ex. 34:13; 1 Kin. 21:25; 2 Kin. 13:6 ♦ idol
34 In his days did Hiel the Bethelite build
Jericho: he laid the foundation thereof in
Abiram his firstborn, and set up the gates
thereof in his youngest son Segub, according
to the word of the LORD, which he spake by
Joshua the son of Nun.   Josh. 6:26

Ahab's Terrible Apostasy

1 Kings 16:29–33

Taking to wife Jezebel, "the daughter of Ethbaal king of the Zidonians" and high priest of Baal,
Ahab "served Baal, and worshiped him. And he reared up an altar for Baal in the house of Baal,
which he had built in Samaria" (verses 31, 32).

Not only did Ahab introduce Baal worship at the capital city, but under the leadership of Jezebel
he erected heathen altars in many "high places," where in the shelter of surrounding groves the
priests and others connected with this seductive form of idolatry exerted their baleful influence,
until well-nigh all Israel were following after Baal. . . .

Ahab was weak in moral power. His union by marriage with an idolatrous woman of decided
character and positive temperament resulted disastrously both to himself and to the nation. Unprincipled, and with no high standard of rightdoing, his character was easily molded by the determined spirit of Jezebel. His selfish nature was incapable of appreciating the mercies of God to Israel
and his own obligations as the guardian and leader of the chosen people. . . .

For many years they had been losing their sense of reverence and godly fear; and now it seemed
as if there were none who dared expose their lives by openly standing forth in opposition to the
prevailing blasphemy. The dark shadow of apostasy covered the whole land. Images of Baalim and
Ashtoreth were everywhere to be seen. Idolatrous temples and consecrated groves, wherein were
worshiped the works of men's hands, were multiplied. The air was polluted with the smoke of the
sacrifices offered to false gods. Hill and vale resounded with the drunken cries of a heathen priesthood who sacrificed to the sun, moon, and stars. *PK 114, 115*

The Prophet Elijah Is Fed by Ravens

17 And Elijah the Tishbite, *who was* of the inhabitants of Gilead, said unto Ahab, *As* the LORD God of Israel liveth, before whom I stand, there shall not be dew nor rain these years, but according to my word. Deut. 10:8; 2 Kin. 3:14; James 5:17

> **17:1 Elijah's Message to Ahab**
>
> To Elijah was entrusted the mission of delivering to Ahab Heaven's message of judgment. He did not seek to be the Lord's messenger; the word of the Lord came to him. And jealous for the honor of God's cause, he did not hesitate to obey the divine summons, though to obey seemed to invite swift destruction at the hand of the wicked king. *PK 120, 121*

2 And the word of the LORD came unto him, saying,
3 Get thee hence, and turn thee eastward, and hide thyself by the brook Cherith, that *is* before Jordan.
4 And it shall be, *that* thou shalt drink of the brook; and I have commanded the ravens to feed thee there. 1 Kin. 17:9
5 So he went and did according unto the word of the LORD: for he went and dwelt by the brook Cherith, that *is* before Jordan.
6 And the ravens brought him bread and flesh in the morning, and bread and flesh in the evening; and he drank of the brook.
7 And it came to pass after a while, that the brook dried up, because there had been no rain in the land.

Elijah Is Sent to the Widow of Zarephath

8 And the word of the LORD came unto him, saying,
9 Arise, get thee to Zarephath, which *belongeth* to Zidon, and dwell there: behold, I have commanded a widow woman there to sustain thee. 1 Kin. 17:4; Obad. 20; Luke 4:26
10 So he arose and went to Zarephath. And when he came to the gate of the city, behold, the widow woman *was* there gathering of sticks: and he called to her, and said, Fetch me, I pray thee, a little water in a vessel, that I may drink. Gen. 24:17
11 And as she was going to fetch *it*, he called to her, and said, Bring me, I pray thee, a morsel of bread in thine hand.
12 And she said, *As* the LORD thy God liveth, I have not a cake, but an handful of meal in a barrel, and a little oil in a cruse: and, behold, I *am* gathering two sticks, that I may go in and dress it for me and my son, that we may eat it, and die. Gen. 21:16; 1 Kin. 17:1; 2 Kin. 4:2-7
13 And Elijah said unto her, Fear not; go *and* do as thou hast said: but make me thereof a little cake first, and bring *it* unto me, and after make for thee and for thy son.
14 For thus saith the LORD God of Israel, The barrel of meal shall not waste, neither shall the ᵀcruse of oil fail, until the day *that* the LORD sendeth rain upon the earth. pot
15 And she went and did according to the saying of Elijah: and she, and he, and her house, did eat *many* days.
16 *And* the barrel of meal wasted not, neither did the cruse of oil fail, according to the word of the LORD, which he spake by Elijah.

Elijah Raises the Widow's Son from the Dead

17 And it came to pass after these things, *that* the son of the woman, the mistress of the house, fell sick; and his sickness was so sore, that there was no breath left in him.
18 And she said unto Elijah, What have I to do with thee, O thou man of God? art thou come unto me to call my sin to remembrance, and to slay my son? 2 Kin. 3:13

Elijah the Tishbite

1 Kings 17

Among the mountains of Gilead, east of the Jordan, there dwelt in the days of Ahab a man of faith and prayer whose fearless ministry was destined to check the rapid spread of apostasy in Israel. Far removed from any city of renown, and occupying no high station in life, Elijah the Tishbite nevertheless entered upon his mission confident in God's purpose to prepare the way before him and to give him abundant success. The word of faith and power was upon his lips, and his whole life was devoted to the work of reform. His was the voice of one crying in the wilderness to rebuke sin and press back the tide of evil. And while he came to the people as a reprover of sin, his message offered the balm of Gilead to the sin-sick souls of all who desired to be healed.

As Elijah saw Israel going deeper and deeper into idolatry, his soul was distressed and his indignation aroused. . . . Viewing this apostasy from his mountain retreat, Elijah was overwhelmed with sorrow. In anguish of soul he besought God to arrest the once-favored people in their wicked course, to visit them with judgments, if need be, that they might be led to see in its true light their departure from Heaven. He longed to see them brought to repentance before they should go to such lengths in evil-doing as to provoke the Lord to destroy them utterly. *PK 119, 120*

19 And he said unto her, Give me thy son. And he took him out of her bosom, and carried him up into a loft, where he abode, and laid him upon his own bed.

20 And he cried unto the LORD, and said, O LORD my God, hast thou also brought evil upon the widow with whom I sojourn, by slaying her son?

21 And he stretched himself upon the child three times, and cried unto the LORD, and said, O LORD my God, I pray thee, let this child's soul come into him again.   Acts 20:10

22 And the LORD heard the voice of Elijah; and the soul of the child came into him again, and he revived.

23 And Elijah took the child, and brought him down out of the chamber into the house, and delivered him unto his mother: and Elijah said, See, thy son liveth.

24 And the woman said to Elijah, Now by this I know that thou *art* a man of God, *and* that the word of the LORD in thy mouth *is* truth.   John 2:11; 3:2; 16:30

17:10–24 Blessings in Disguise

The widow of Zarephath shared her morsel with Elijah, and in return her life and that of her son were preserved. And to all who, in time of trial and want, give sympathy and assistance to others more needy, God has promised great blessing. He has not changed. . . .

Our heavenly Father still continues to place in the pathway of His children opportunities that are blessings in disguise; and those who improve these opportunities find great joy. *PK 131, 132*

The Lord's Faithful Servant Obadiah Meets Elijah

18 And it came to pass *after* many days, that the word of the LORD came to Elijah in the third year, saying, Go, shew thyself unto Ahab; and I will send rain upon the earth.   1 Kin. 17:1; Luke 4:25; James 5:17

2 And Elijah went to shew himself unto Ahab. And *there was* a sore famine in Samaria.

3 And Ahab called Obadiah, which *was* the governor of *his* house. (Now Obadiah feared the LORD greatly: Neh. 7:2

4 For it was *so*, when Jezebel cut off the prophets of the LORD, that Obadiah took an hundred prophets, and hid them by fifty in a cave, and fed them with bread and water.)   1 Kin. 18:13; Matt. 10:40-42

5 And Ahab said unto Obadiah, Go into the land, unto all fountains of water, and unto all brooks: ᵀperadventure we may find grass to save the horses and mules alive, that we lose not all the beasts.   *maybe*

6 So they divided the land between them to pass throughout it: Ahab went one way by himself, and Obadiah went another way by himself.

7 And as Obadiah was in the way, behold, Elijah met him: and he knew him, and fell on his face, and said, *Art* thou that my lord Elijah?   2 Kin. 1:6-8

8 And he answered him, I *am*: go, tell thy lord, Behold, Elijah *is here*.

9 And he said, What have I sinned, that thou wouldest deliver thy servant into the hand of Ahab, to slay me?

10 *As* the LORD thy God liveth, there is no nation or kingdom, whither my lord hath not sent to seek thee: and when they said, *He is* not *there*; he took an oath of the kingdom and nation, that they found thee not.   1 Kin. 17:1

11 And now thou sayest, Go, tell thy lord, Behold, Elijah *is here*.

12 And it shall come to pass, *as soon as* I am gone from thee, that the Spirit of the LORD shall carry thee whither I know not; and *so* when I come and tell Ahab, and he cannot find thee, he shall slay me: but I thy servant fear the LORD from my youth. Ezek. 8:3; Acts 8:39

13 Was it not told my lord what I did when Jezebel slew the prophets of the LORD, how I hid an hundred men of the LORD's prophets by fifty in a cave, and fed them with bread and water?   1 Kin. 18:4

14 And now thou sayest, Go, tell thy lord, Behold, Elijah *is here*: and he shall slay me.

15 And Elijah said, *As* the LORD of hosts liveth, before whom I stand, I will surely shew myself unto him to day.   1 Kin. 17:1

16 So Obadiah went to meet Ahab, and told him: and Ahab went to meet Elijah.

Elijah Calls Down Fire from Heaven

17 And it came to pass, when Ahab saw Elijah, that Ahab said unto him, *Art* thou he that troubleth Israel?   Josh. 7:25; 1 Kin. 21:20; Acts 16:20

18 And he answered, I have not troubled Israel; but thou, and thy father's house, in that ye have forsaken the commandments of the LORD, and thou hast followed Baalim.   1 Kin. 9:9; 16:31; 2 Chr. 15:2

18:18 The Fearless Prophet

Elijah makes no attempt to excuse himself or to flatter the king. Nor does he seek to evade the king's wrath by the good news that the drought is almost over. He has no apology to offer. Indignant, and jealous for the honor of God, he casts back the imputation of Ahab, fearlessly declaring to the king that it is *his* sins, and the sins of *his* fathers, that have brought upon Israel this terrible calamity. *PK 140*

19 Now therefore send, *and* gather to me all Israel unto mount Carmel, and the prophets of Baal four hundred and fifty, and the prophets of the ᵀgroves four hundred, which eat at Jezebel's table.   Josh. 19:26; 2 Kin. 2:25 ◆ *idols*

20 So Ahab sent unto all the children of Israel, and gathered the prophets together unto mount Carmel.

21 And Elijah came unto all the people, and said, How long halt ye between two opinions? if the LORD *be* God, follow him: but if Baal, *then* follow him. And the people answered him not a word.   Josh. 24:15; Matt. 6:24

18:21 Indifference and Disloyalty

The people answer [Elijah] not a word. Not one in that vast assembly dare reveal loyalty to Jehovah. . . . Each departure from rightdoing, each refusal to repent, had deepened their guilt and driven them farther from Heaven. And now, in this crisis, they persisted in refusing to take their stand for God.

The Lord abhors indifference and disloyalty in a time of crisis in His work. *PK 147, 148*

22 Then said Elijah unto the people, I, *even* I only, remain a prophet of the LORD; but Baal's prophets *are* four hundred and fifty men.   1 Kin. 19:10, 14

23 Let them therefore give us two bullocks; and let them choose one ᵀbullock for themselves, and cut it in pieces, and lay *it* on wood, and put no fire *under*: and I will dress the other bullock, and lay *it* on wood, and put no fire *under*:   *bull*

24 And call ye on the name of your gods, and I will call on the name of the LORD: and the God that answereth by fire, let him be God. And all the people answered and said, It is well spoken.   1 Kin. 18:38; 1 Chr. 21:26

25 And Elijah said unto the prophets of Baal, Choose you one bullock for yourselves, and dress *it* first; for ye *are* many; and call on the name of your gods, but put no fire *under*.

26 And they took the bullock which was given them, and they dressed *it*, and called on the name of Baal from morning even until noon, saying, O Baal, hear us. But *there was* no voice, nor any that answered. And they leaped upon the altar which was made.   Jer. 10:5

27 And it came to pass at noon, that Elijah mocked them, and said, Cry aloud: for he *is* a god; either he is talking, or he is pursuing, or he is in a journey, *or* peradventure he sleepeth, and must be awaked.

28 And they cried aloud, and cut themselves after their manner with knives and lancets, till the blood gushed out upon them.   Lev. 19:28

29 And it came to pass, when midday was past, and they prophesied until the *time* of the offering of the *evening* sacrifice, that *there was* neither voice, nor any to answer, nor any that regarded.   Ex. 29:41

30 And Elijah said unto all the people, Come near unto me. And all the people came near unto him. And he repaired the altar of the LORD *that was* broken down.   1 Kin. 19:10, 14

31 And Elijah took twelve stones, according to the number of the tribes of the sons of Jacob, unto whom the word of the LORD came, saying, Israel shall be thy name: Gen. 32:28; 35:10

The Voice of Stern Rebuke

1 Kings 18:18

Today there is need of the voice of stern rebuke; for grievous sins have separated the people from God. Infidelity is fast becoming fashionable. . . . The smooth sermons so often preached make no lasting impression; the trumpet does not give a certain sound. Men are not cut to the heart by the plain, sharp truths of God's word. . . .

So men who should be standing as faithful guardians of God's law have argued, till policy has taken the place of faithfulness, and sin is allowed to go unreproved. When will the voice of faithful rebuke be heard once more in the church? . . .

Those ministers who are men pleasers, who cry, Peace, peace, when God has not spoken peace, might well humble their hearts before God, asking pardon for their insincerity and their lack of moral courage. . . .

Would that every minister might realize the sacredness of his office and the holiness of his work, and show the courage that Elijah showed! As divinely appointed messengers, ministers are in a position of awful responsibility. They are to "reprove, rebuke, exhort with all long-suffering" (2 Timothy 4:2). In Christ's stead they are to labor as stewards of the mysteries of heaven, encouraging the obedient and warning the disobedient. With them worldly policy is to have no weight. Never are they to swerve from the path in which Jesus has bidden them walk. . . . Their message is to be, "Thus saith the Lord." God calls for men like Elijah, Nathan, and John the Baptist—men who will bear His message with faithfulness, regardless of the consequences; men who will speak the truth bravely, though it call for the sacrifice of all they have.

God cannot use men who, in time of peril, when the strength, courage, and influence of all are needed, are afraid to take a firm stand for the right. *PK 140–142*

32 And with the stones he built an altar in the name of the LORD: and he made a trench about the altar, as great as would contain two measures of seed.   Col. 3:17

33 And he put the wood in order, and cut the bullock in pieces, and laid *him* on the wood, and said, Fill four barrels with water, and pour *it* on the burnt sacrifice, and on the wood.   Gen. 22:9; Lev. 1:6-8; Judg. 6:20

34 And he said, Do *it* the second time. And they did *it* the second time. And he said, Do *it* the third time. And they did *it* the third time.

35 And the water ran round about the altar; and he filled the trench also with water.

36 And it came to pass at *the time of* the offering of the *evening* sacrifice, that Elijah the prophet came near, and said, LORD God of Abraham, Isaac, and of Israel, let it be known this day that thou *art* God in Israel, and *that* I *am* thy servant, and *that* I have done all these things at thy word.   Ex. 3:6; 1 Kin. 8:43; 18:29

37 Hear me, O LORD, hear me, that this people may know that thou *art* the LORD God, and *that* thou hast turned their heart back again.

38 Then the fire of the LORD fell, and consumed the burnt sacrifice, and the wood, and the stones, and the dust, and licked up the water that *was* in the trench. Lev. 9:24; Judg. 6:21

39 And when all the people saw *it*, they fell on their faces: and they said, The LORD, he *is* the God; the LORD, he *is* the God. 1 Kin. 18:21, 24

40 And Elijah said unto them, Take the prophets of Baal; let not one of them escape. And they took them: and Elijah brought them down to the brook Kishon, and slew them there.   Deut. 13:5

Elijah Prays for Rain

41 And Elijah said unto Ahab, Get thee up, eat and drink; for *there is* a sound of abundance of rain.

42 So Ahab went up to eat and to drink. And Elijah went up to the top of Carmel; and he cast himself down upon the earth, and put his face between his knees,

43 And said to his servant, Go up now, look toward the sea. And he went up, and looked, and said, *There is* nothing. And he said, Go again seven times.

44 And it came to pass at the seventh time, that he said, Behold, there ariseth a little cloud out of the sea, like a man's hand. And he said, Go up, say unto Ahab, Prepare *thy chariot*, and get thee down, that the rain stop thee not.   Luke 12:54

45 And it came to pass in the mean while, that the heaven was black with clouds and wind, and there was a great rain. And Ahab rode, and went to Jezreel.

46 And the hand of the LORD was on Elijah; and he girded up his loins, and ran before Ahab to the entrance of Jezreel. 2 Kin. 3:15; 4:29

Threatened by Jezebel, Elijah Flees to Beer-sheba, then to Mount Horeb

19 And Ahab told Jezebel all that Elijah had done, and ᵀwithal how he had slain all the prophets with the sword.   *also*

2 Then Jezebel sent a messenger unto Elijah, saying, So let the gods do *to me*, and more also, if I make not thy life as the life of one of them by to morrow about this time.   Ruth 1:17; 1 Kin. 20:10; 2 Kin. 6:31

3 And when he saw *that*, he arose, and went for his life, and came to Beer-sheba, which *belongeth* to Judah, and left his servant there.   Gen. 21:31

19:3 Elijah Makes a Wrong Choice

Elijah should not have fled from his post of duty. He should have met the threat of Jezebel with an appeal for protection to the One who had commissioned him to vindicate the honor of Jehovah. . . . Had he remained where he was, had he made God his refuge and strength, standing steadfast for the truth, he would have been shielded from harm. *PK 160*

---

4 But he himself went a day's journey into the wilderness, and came and sat down under a juniper tree: and he requested for himself that he might die; and said, It is enough; now, O LORD, take away my life; for I *am* not better than my fathers.   Num. 11:15; Jon. 4:3, 8

5 And as he lay and slept under a juniper tree, behold, then an angel touched him, and said unto him, Arise *and* eat.

6 And he looked, and, behold, *there was* a cake baken on the coals, and a ᵀcruse of water at his head. And he did eat and drink, and laid him down again.   Matt. 4:11 ◆ *pot*

7 And the angel of the LORD came again the second time, and touched him, and said, Arise *and* eat; because the journey *is* too great for thee.

8 And he arose, and did eat and drink, and went in the strength of that meat forty days and forty nights unto Horeb the mount of God.   Ex. 3:1; 24:18; 34:28

19:4-8 Angels Seeking to Help Us

Into the experience of all there come times of keen disappointment and utter discouragement—days when sorrow is the portion . . . ; days when troubles harass the soul, till death seems preferable to life. . . . Could we at such times discern with spiritual insight the meaning of God's providences we should see angels seeking to save us from ourselves, striving to plant our feet upon a foundation more firm than the everlasting hills. *PK 162*

God Sends Elijah to Anoint Hazael, Jehu, and Elisha

9 And he came thither unto a cave, and lodged there; and, behold, the word of the LORD *came* to him, and he said unto him, What doest thou here, Elijah? Ex. 33:21-22
10 And he said, I have been very jealous for the LORD God of hosts: for the children of Israel have forsaken thy covenant, thrown down thine altars, and slain thy prophets with the sword; and I, *even* I only, am left; and they seek my life, to take it away. Num. 25:13; 1 Kin. 18:4, 22
11 And he said, Go forth, and stand upon the mount before the LORD. And, behold, the LORD passed by, and a great and strong wind ᵀrent the mountains, and brake in pieces the rocks before the LORD; *but* the LORD *was* not in the wind: and after the wind an earthquake; *but* the LORD *was* not in the earthquake: Ex. 24:12; Ezek. 1:4; 37:7 ◆ *tore apart*
12 And after the earthquake a fire; *but* the LORD *was* not in the fire: and after the fire a still small voice. Job 4:16

19:12 A Still Small Voice

Not in mighty manifestations of divine power, but by "a still small voice," did God choose to reveal Himself to His servant. He desired to teach Elijah that it is not always the work that makes the greatest demonstration that is most successful in accomplishing His purpose. . . .

Not by eloquence or logic are men's hearts reached, but by the sweet influences of the Holy Spirit, which operate quietly yet surely in transforming and developing character. *PK 168, 169*

13 And it was *so*, when Elijah heard *it*, that he wrapped his face in his ᵀmantle, and went out, and stood in the entering in of the cave. And, behold, *there came* a voice unto him, and said, What doest thou here, Elijah? 1 Kin. 19:9 ◆ *large outside garment*
14 And he said, I have been very jealous for the LORD God of hosts: because the children of Israel have forsaken thy covenant, thrown down thine altars, and slain thy prophets with the sword; and I, *even* I only, am left; and they seek my life, to take it away.
15 And the LORD said unto him, Go, return on thy way to the wilderness of Damascus: and when thou comest, anoint Hazael *to be* king over Syria: 2 Kin. 8:7-15
16 And Jehu the son of Nimshi shalt thou anoint *to be* king over Israel: and Elisha the son of Shaphat of Abel-meholah shalt thou anoint *to be* prophet in thy room. 1 Kin. 19:19-21
17 And it shall come to pass, *that* him that escapeth the sword of Hazael shall Jehu slay: and him that escapeth from the sword of Jehu shall Elisha slay. 2 Kin. 8:12; 13:3, 22
18 Yet I have left *me* seven thousand in Israel, all the knees which have not bowed unto Baal, and every mouth which hath not kissed him. Hos. 13:2

Elisha Follows Elijah

19 So he departed thence, and found Elisha the son of Shaphat, who *was* plowing *with* twelve yoke *of oxen* before him, and he with the twelfth: and Elijah passed by him, and cast his mantle upon him. 1 Sam. 28:14; 2 Kin. 2:8
20 And he left the oxen, and ran after Elijah, and said, Let me, I pray thee, kiss my father and my mother, and *then* I will follow thee. And he said unto him, Go back again: for what have I done to thee? Matt. 8:21-22; Acts 20:37
21 And he returned back from him, and took a yoke of oxen, and slew them, and boiled their flesh with the instruments of the oxen, and gave unto the people, and they did eat.

The Fiercest Temptations

1 Kings 19

It is at the time of greatest weakness that Satan assails the soul with the fiercest temptations. It was thus that he hoped to prevail over the Son of God; for by this policy he had gained many victories over man. . . . So with Elijah. He who had maintained his trust in Jehovah during the years of drought and famine, he who had stood undaunted before Ahab, he who throughout that trying day on Carmel had stood before the whole nation of Israel the sole witness to the true God, in a moment of weariness allowed the fear of death to overcome his faith in God.

And so it is today. When we are encompassed with doubt, perplexed by circumstances, or afflicted by poverty or distress, Satan seeks to shake our confidence in Jehovah. It is then that he arrays before us our mistakes and tempts us to distrust God, to question His love. He hopes to discourage the soul and break our hold on God. . . .

Despondency may shake the most heroic faith and weaken the most steadfast will. But God understands, and He still pities and loves. He reads the motives and the purposes of the heart. To wait patiently, to trust when everything looks dark, is the lesson that the leaders in God's work need to learn. Heaven will not fail them in their day of adversity. Nothing is apparently more helpless, yet really more invincible, than the soul that feels its nothingness and relies wholly on God. *PK 174, 175*

Then he arose, and went after Elijah, and ministered unto him.   2 Sam. 24:22

Ben-hadad of Syria Besieges Samaria, but Is Defeated by Ahab

20 And Ben-hadad the king of Syria gathered all his host together: and *there were* thirty and two kings with him, and horses, and chariots: and he went up and besieged Samaria, and warred against it.   1 Kin. 15:18, 20; 22:31

2 And he sent messengers to Ahab king of Israel into the city, and said unto him, Thus saith Ben-hadad,

3 Thy silver and thy gold *is* mine; thy wives also and thy children, *even* the goodliest, *are* mine.

4 And the king of Israel answered and said, My lord, O king, according to thy saying, I *am* thine, and all that I have.

5 And the messengers came again, and said, Thus speaketh Ben-hadad, saying, Although I have sent unto thee, saying, Thou shalt deliver me thy silver, and thy gold, and thy wives, and thy children;

6 Yet I will send my servants unto thee to morrow about this time, and they shall search thine house, and the houses of thy servants; and it shall be, *that* whatsoever is pleasant in thine eyes, they shall put *it* in their hand, and take *it* away.

7 Then the king of Israel called all the elders of the land, and said, Mark, I pray you, and see how this *man* seeketh mischief: for he sent unto me for my wives, and for my children, and for my silver, and for my gold; and I denied him not.   2 Kin. 5:7

8 And all the elders and all the people said unto him, Hearken not *unto him*, nor consent.

9 Wherefore he said unto the messengers of Ben-hadad, Tell my lord the king, All that thou didst send for to thy servant at the first I will do: but this thing I may not do. And the messengers departed, and brought him word again.

10 And Ben-hadad sent unto him, and said, The gods do so unto me, and more also, if the dust of Samaria shall suffice for handfuls for all the people that follow me. Ex. 11:8; 1 Kin. 19:2

11 And the king of Israel answered and said, Tell *him*, Let not him that girdeth on *his harness* boast himself as he that putteth it off.   Prov. 27:1

12 And it came to pass, when *Ben-hadad* heard this message, as he *was* drinking, he and the kings in the pavilions, that he said unto his servants, Set *yourselves in array*. And they set *themselves in array* against the city.   1 Kin. 16:9; 20:16; Prov. 31:4-5

13 And, behold, there came a prophet unto Ahab king of Israel, saying, Thus saith the LORD, Hast thou seen all this great multitude? behold, I will deliver it into thine hand this day; and thou shalt know that I *am* the LORD.   1 Kin. 20:28

14 And Ahab said, By whom? And he said, Thus saith the LORD, *Even* by the young men of the princes of the provinces. Then he said, Who shall order the battle? And he answered, Thou.

15 Then he numbered the young men of the princes of the provinces, and they were two hundred and thirty two: and after them he numbered all the people, *even* all the children of Israel, *being* seven thousand.

16 And they went out at noon. But Ben-hadad *was* drinking himself drunk in the pavilions, he and the kings, the thirty and two kings that helped him.

17 And the young men of the princes of the provinces went out first; and Ben-hadad sent out, and they told him, saying, There are men come out of Samaria.

18 And he said, Whether they be come out for peace, take them alive; or whether they be come out for war, take them alive. 2 Kin. 14:8-12

19 So these young men of the princes of the provinces came out of the city, and the army which followed them.

20 And they slew every one his man: and the Syrians fled; and Israel pursued them: and Ben-hadad the king of Syria escaped on an horse with the horsemen.

21 And the king of Israel went out, and smote the horses and chariots, and slew the Syrians with a great slaughter.

As Ahab Was Forewarned, the Syrians Attack Again at Aphek

22 And the prophet came to the king of Israel, and said unto him, Go, strengthen thyself, and mark, and see what thou doest: for at the return of the year the king of Syria will come up against thee. 2 Sam. 11:1; 1 Kin. 20:13, 26

23 And the servants of the king of Syria said unto him, Their gods *are* gods of the hills; therefore they were stronger than we; but let us fight against them in the plain, and surely we shall be stronger than they.   1 Kin. 14:23

24 And do this thing, Take the kings away, every man out of his place, and put captains in their rooms:

25 And number thee an army, like the army that thou hast lost, horse for horse, and chariot for chariot: and we will fight against them in the plain, *and* surely we shall be stronger than they. And he hearkened unto their voice, and did so.

26 And it came to pass at the return of the year, that Ben-hadad numbered the Syrians,

and went up to Aphek, to fight against Israel. 1 Kin. 20:22; 2 Kin. 13:17
27 And the children of Israel were numbered, and were all present, and went against them: and the children of Israel pitched before them like two little flocks of kids; but the Syrians filled the country. Judg. 6:5
28 And there came a man of God, and spake unto the king of Israel, and said, Thus saith the LORD, Because the Syrians have said, The LORD *is* God of the hills, but he *is* not God of the valleys, therefore will I deliver all this great multitude into thine hand, and ye shall know that I *am* the LORD. 1 Kin. 17:18; 20:13
29 And they pitched one over against the other seven days. And *so* it was, that in the seventh day the battle was joined: and the children of Israel slew of the Syrians an hundred thousand footmen in one day.
30 But the rest fled to Aphek, into the city; and *there* a wall fell upon twenty and seven thousand of the men *that were* left. And Ben-hadad fled, and came into the city, into an inner chamber. 1 Kin. 20:26; 22:25; 2 Chr. 18:24

A Prophet Condemns Ahab for Making a Covenant with Ben-hadad

31 And his servants said unto him, Behold now, we have heard that the kings of the house of Israel *are* merciful kings: let us, I pray thee, put sackcloth on our loins, and ropes upon our heads, and go out to the king of Israel: [T]peradventure he will save thy life. Gen. 37:34 ◆ *maybe*
32 So they girded sackcloth on their [T]loins, and *put* ropes on their heads, and came to the king of Israel, and said, Thy servant Ben-hadad saith, I pray thee, let me live. And he said, *Is* he yet alive? he *is* my brother. *waists*
33 Now the men did diligently observe whether *any thing would come* from him, and did hastily catch *it*: and they said, Thy brother Ben-hadad. Then he said, Go ye, bring him. Then Ben-hadad came forth to him; and he caused him to come up into the chariot.
34 And *Ben-hadad* said unto him, The cities, which my father took from thy father, I will restore; and thou shalt make streets for thee in Damascus, as my father made in Samaria. Then *said Ahab*, I will send thee away with this covenant. So he made a covenant with him, and sent him away. 1 Kin. 15:20
35 And a certain man of the sons of the prophets said unto his neighbour in the word of the LORD, Smite me, I pray thee. And the man refused to [T]smite him. 1 Kin. 13:17-18 ◆ *strike*
36 Then said he unto him, Because thou hast not obeyed the voice of the LORD, behold, as soon as thou art departed from me, a lion shall slay thee. And as soon as he was

departed from him, a lion found him, and slew him.
37 Then he found another man, and said, Smite me, I pray thee. And the man smote him, so that in smiting he wounded *him*.
38 So the prophet departed, and waited for the king by the way, and disguised himself with ashes upon his face. 1 Kin. 14:2
39 And as the king passed by, he cried unto the king: and he said, Thy servant went out into the midst of the battle; and, behold, a man turned aside, and brought a man unto me, and said, Keep this man: if by any means he be missing, then shall thy life be for his life, or else thou shalt pay a [T]talent of silver. 2 Kin. 10:24 ◆ *weight or sum*
40 And as thy servant was busy here and there, he was gone. And the king of Israel said unto him, So *shall* thy judgment *be*; thyself hast decided *it*.
41 And he hasted, and took the ashes away from his face; and the king of Israel discerned him that he *was* of the prophets.
42 And he said unto him, Thus saith the LORD, Because thou hast let go out of *thy* hand a man whom I appointed to utter destruction, therefore thy life shall go for his life, and thy people for his people. 1 Kin. 20:39; 22:31-37
43 And the king of Israel went to his house heavy and displeased, and came to Samaria.

Ahab Is Denied Naboth's Vineyard

21 And it came to pass after these things, *that* Naboth the Jezreelite had a vineyard, which *was* in Jezreel, hard by the palace of Ahab king of Samaria. Judg. 6:33
2 And Ahab spake unto Naboth, saying, Give me thy vineyard, that I may have it for a garden of herbs, because it *is* near unto my house: and I will give thee for it a better vineyard than it; *or*, if it seem good to thee, I will give thee the worth of it in money. 1 Sam. 8:14
3 And Naboth said to Ahab, The LORD forbid it me, that I should give the inheritance of my fathers unto thee. Lev. 25:23; Num. 36:7

21:2–4 Fully Controlled by Selfishness

Naturally of a covetous disposition, Ahab, strengthened and sustained in wrongdoing by Jezebel, had followed the dictates of his evil heart until he was fully controlled by the spirit of selfishness. He could brook no refusal of his wishes; the things he desired he felt should by right be his. *PK 204*

---

4 And Ahab came into his house heavy and displeased because of the word which Naboth the Jezreelite had spoken to him: for he had said, I will not give thee the inheritance of my fathers. And he laid him down upon his bed, and turned away his face, and would eat no bread. 1 Kin. 20:43

Jezebel Has Naboth Killed, and Elijah Condemns both Ahab and Jezebel

5 But Jezebel his wife came to him, and said unto him, Why is thy spirit so sad, that thou eatest no bread?

6 And he said unto her, Because I spake unto Naboth the Jezreelite, and said unto him, Give me thy vineyard for money; or else, if it please thee, I will give thee *another* vineyard for it: and he answered, I will not give thee my vineyard.

7 And Jezebel his wife said unto him, Dost thou now govern the kingdom of Israel? arise, *and* eat bread, and let thine heart be merry: I will give thee the vineyard of Naboth the Jezreelite.

8 So she wrote letters in Ahab's name, and sealed *them* with his seal, and sent the letters unto the elders and to the nobles that *were* in his city, dwelling with Naboth.

9 And she wrote in the letters, saying, Proclaim a fast, and set Naboth on high among the people:

10 And set two men, sons of Belial, before him, to bear witness against him, saying, Thou didst blaspheme God and the king. And *then* carry him out, and stone him, that he may die.   Ex. 22:28; Lev. 24:15-16; Acts 6:11

11 And the men of his city, *even* the elders and the nobles who were the inhabitants in his city, did as Jezebel had sent unto them, *and* as it *was* written in the letters which she had sent unto them.

12 They proclaimed a fast, and set Naboth on high among the people.   Is. 58:4

13 And there came in two men, children of Belial, and sat before him: and the men of Belial witnessed against him, *even* against Naboth, in the presence of the people, saying, Naboth did blaspheme God and the king. Then they carried him forth out of the city, and stoned him with stones, that he died.   2 Kin. 9:26

14 Then they sent to Jezebel, saying, Naboth is stoned, and is dead.

15 And it came to pass, when Jezebel heard that Naboth was stoned, and was dead, that Jezebel said to Ahab, Arise, take possession of the vineyard of Naboth the Jezreelite, which he refused to give thee for money: for Naboth is not alive, but dead.

16 And it came to pass, when Ahab heard that Naboth was dead, that Ahab rose up to go down to the vineyard of Naboth the Jezreelite, to take possession of it.

17 And the word of the LORD came to Elijah the Tishbite, saying,

18 Arise, go down to meet Ahab king of Israel, which *is* in Samaria: behold, *he is* in the vineyard of Naboth, whither he is gone down to possess it.

19 And thou shalt speak unto him, saying, Thus saith the LORD, Hast thou killed, and also taken possession? And thou shalt speak unto him, saying, Thus saith the LORD, In the place where dogs licked the blood of Naboth shall dogs lick thy blood, even thine.   2 Sam. 12:9; 1 Kin. 22:38

20 And Ahab said to Elijah, Hast thou found me, O mine enemy? And he answered, I have found *thee*: because thou hast sold thyself to work evil in the sight of the LORD.   1 Kin. 18:17; 21:25; 2 Kin. 17:17

21 Behold, I will bring evil upon thee, and will take away thy posterity, and will cut off from Ahab him that pisseth against the wall, and him that is shut up and left in Israel,   1 Kin. 14:10

22 And will make thine house like the house of Jeroboam the son of Nebat, and like the house of Baasha the son of Ahijah, for the provocation wherewith thou hast provoked *me* to anger, and made Israel to sin. 1 Kin. 14:16

23 And of Jezebel also spake the LORD, saying, The dogs shall eat Jezebel by the wall of Jezreel.   2 Kin. 9:10

24 Him that dieth of Ahab in the city the dogs shall eat; and him that dieth in the field shall the fowls of the air eat.   1 Kin. 14:11; 16:4

25 But there was none like unto Ahab, which did sell himself to work wickedness in the sight of the LORD, whom Jezebel his wife stirred up.   1 Kin. 16:30-33; 21:20

26 And he did very abominably in following idols, according to all *things* as did the Amorites, whom the LORD cast out before the children of Israel.   Gen. 15:16; Lev. 18:25-30; 2 Kin. 21:11

> **21:25, 26 Jezebel's Evil Influence**
>
> The evil influence that Jezebel had exercised from the first over Ahab continued during the later years of his life and bore fruit in deeds of shame and violence such as have seldom been equaled in sacred history. *PK 204*

27 And it came to pass, when Ahab heard those words, that he ᵀrent his clothes, and put sackcloth upon his flesh, and fasted, and lay in sackcloth, and went softly.   tore

28 And the word of the LORD came to Elijah the Tishbite, saying,

29 Seest thou how Ahab humbleth himself before me? because he humbleth himself before me, I will not bring the evil in his days: *but* in his son's days will I bring the evil upon his house.   2 Kin. 9:25-26

Micaiah Prophesies That Ahab Will Be Slain at Ramoth-gilead

22 And they continued three years without war between Syria and Israel.

2 And it came to pass in the third year, that

Jehoshaphat the king of Judah came down to the king of Israel. 1 Kin. 15:24

3 And the king of Israel said unto his servants, Know ye that Ramoth in Gilead *is* ours, and we *be* still, *and* take it not out of the hand of the king of Syria? Deut. 4:43; Josh. 21:38; 1 Kin. 4:13

4 And he said unto Jehoshaphat, Wilt thou go with me to battle to Ramoth-gilead? And Jehoshaphat said to the king of Israel, I *am* as thou *art*, my people as thy people, my horses as thy horses. 2 Kin. 3:7

5 And Jehoshaphat said unto the king of Israel, Enquire, I pray thee, at the word of the LORD to day. 2 Kin. 3:11

6 Then the king of Israel gathered the prophets together, about four hundred men, and said unto them, Shall I go against Ramoth-gilead to battle, or shall I forbear? And they said, Go up; for the Lord shall deliver *it* into the hand of the king. 1 Kin. 18:19

7 And Jehoshaphat said, *Is there* not here a prophet of the LORD besides, that we might enquire of him?

8 And the king of Israel said unto Jehoshaphat, *There is* yet one man, Micaiah the son of Imlah, by whom we may enquire of the LORD: but I hate him; for he doth not prophesy good concerning me, but evil. And Jehoshaphat said, Let not the king say so. Amos 5:10

9 Then the king of Israel called an officer, and said, Hasten ^Thither Micaiah the son of Imlah. *here*

10 And the king of Israel and Jehoshaphat the king of Judah sat each on his throne, having put on their robes, in a void place in the entrance of the gate of Samaria; and all the prophets prophesied before them.

11 And Zedekiah the son of Chenaanah made him horns of iron: and he said, Thus saith the LORD, With these shalt thou push the Syrians, until thou have consumed them. Zech. 1:18-21

12 And all the prophets prophesied so, saying, Go up to Ramoth-gilead, and prosper: for the LORD shall deliver *it* into the king's hand.

13 And the messenger that was gone to call Micaiah spake unto him, saying, Behold now, the words of the prophets *declare* good unto the king with one mouth: let thy word, I pray thee, be like the word of one of them, and speak *that which is* good.

14 And Micaiah said, *As* the LORD liveth, what the LORD saith unto me, that will I speak. Num. 22:18; 24:13

15 So he came to the king. And the king said unto him, Micaiah, shall we go against Ramoth-gilead to battle, or shall we ^Tforbear? And he answered him, Go, and prosper: for

the LORD shall deliver *it* into the hand of the king. *refuse to act*

16 And the king said unto him, How many times shall I ^Tadjure thee that thou tell me nothing but *that which is* true in the name of the LORD? *appeal to*

17 And he said, I saw all Israel scattered upon the hills, as sheep that have not a shepherd: and the LORD said, These have no master: let them return every man to his house in peace. Num. 27:17; 1 Kin. 22:34-36; Matt. 9:36

18 And the king of Israel said unto Jehoshaphat, Did I not tell thee that he would prophesy no good concerning me, but evil? 1 Kin. 22:8

19 And he said, Hear thou therefore the word of the LORD: I saw the LORD sitting on his throne, and all the host of heaven standing by him on his right hand and on his left. Job 1:6; 2:1; Dan. 7:9-10

20 And the LORD said, Who shall persuade Ahab, that he may go up and fall at Ramoth-gilead? And one said on this manner, and another said on that manner.

21 And there came forth a spirit, and stood before the LORD, and said, I will persuade him.

22 And the LORD said unto him, Wherewith? And he said, I will go forth, and I will be a lying spirit in the mouth of all his prophets. And he said, Thou shalt persuade *him*, and prevail also: go forth, and do so. Judg. 9:23; Ezek. 14:9

23 Now therefore, behold, the LORD hath put a lying spirit in the mouth of all these thy prophets, and the LORD hath spoken evil concerning thee. Ezek. 14:9

24 But Zedekiah the son of Chenaanah went near, and smote Micaiah on the cheek, and said, Which way went the Spirit of the LORD from me to speak unto thee? Lam. 3:30; Mic. 5:1

25 And Micaiah said, Behold, thou shalt see in that day, when thou shalt go into an inner chamber to hide thyself. 1 Kin. 20:30

26 And the king of Israel said, Take Micaiah, and carry him back unto Amon the governor of the city, and to Joash the king's son;

27 And say, Thus saith the king, Put this *fellow* in the prison, and feed him with bread of affliction and with water of affliction, until I come in peace. 2 Chr. 16:10; 18:25-27

28 And Micaiah said, If thou return at all in peace, the LORD hath not spoken by me. And he said, Hearken, O people, every one of you. Mic. 1:2

29 So the king of Israel and Jehoshaphat the king of Judah went up to Ramoth-gilead.

30 And the king of Israel said unto Jehoshaphat, I will disguise myself, and enter into the battle; but put thou on thy robes. And the king of Israel disguised himself, and went into the battle. 2 Chr. 35:22

31 But the king of Syria commanded his thirty and two captains that had rule over his chariots, saying, Fight neither with small nor great, save only with the king of Israel.   1 Kin. 20:24

32 And it came to pass, when the captains of the chariots saw Jehoshaphat, that they said, Surely it is the king of Israel. And they turned aside to fight against him: and Jehoshaphat cried out.

33 And it came to pass, when the captains of the chariots perceived that it was not the king of Israel, that they turned back from pursuing him.

34 And a certain man drew a bow at a venture, and smote the king of Israel between the joints of the harness: wherefore he said unto the driver of his chariot, Turn thine hand, and carry me out of the host; for I am wounded.   2 Chr. 35:23

35 And the battle increased that day: and the king was ᵀstayed up in his chariot against the Syrians, and died at even: and the blood ran out of the wound into the midst of the chariot.   propped

36 And there went a proclamation throughout the host about the going down of the sun, saying, Every man to his city, and every man to his own country.   2 Kin. 14:12

37 So the king died, and was brought to Samaria; and they buried the king in Samaria.

38 And one washed the chariot in the pool of Samaria; and the dogs licked up his blood; and they washed his armour; according unto the word of the LORD which he spake.   1 Kin. 21:19

39 Now the rest of the acts of Ahab, and all that he did, and the ivory house which he made, and all the cities that he built, are they not written in the book of the chronicles of the kings of Israel?   Amos 3:15

40 So Ahab slept with his fathers; and Ahaziah his son reigned in his stead.

Jehoshaphat's Good Reign over Judah

41 And Jehoshaphat the son of Asa began to reign over Judah in the fourth year of Ahab king of Israel.   2 Chr. 20:31

42 Jehoshaphat was thirty and five years old when he began to reign; and he reigned twenty and five years in Jerusalem. And his mother's name was Azubah the daughter of Shilhi.

43 And he walked in all the ways of Asa his father; he turned not aside from it, doing that which was right in the eyes of the LORD: nevertheless the high places were not taken away; for the people offered and burnt incense yet in the high places.   1 Kin. 15:14; 2 Kin. 12:3

44 And Jehoshaphat made peace with the king of Israel.   1 Kin. 22:2

45 Now the rest of the acts of Jehoshaphat, and his might that he shewed, and how he warred, are they not written in the book of the chronicles of the kings of Judah?

46 And the remnant of the sodomites, which remained in the days of his father Asa, he took out of the land.   Deut. 23:17; 1 Kin. 14:24; 15:12

47 There was then no king in Edom: a deputy was king.   2 Sam. 8:14; 2 Kin. 3:9; 8:20

48 Jehoshaphat made ships of Tharshish to go to Ophir for gold: but they went not; for the ships were broken at Ezion-geber.

49 Then said Ahaziah the son of Ahab unto Jehoshaphat, Let my servants go with thy servants in the ships. But Jehoshaphat would not.

50 And Jehoshaphat slept with his fathers, and was buried with his fathers in the city of David his father: and Jehoram his son reigned in his stead.   2 Chr. 21:1

51 Ahaziah the son of Ahab began to reign over Israel in Samaria the seventeenth year of Jehoshaphat king of Judah, and reigned two years over Israel.

52 And he did evil in the sight of the LORD, and walked in the way of his father, and in the way of his mother, and in the way of Jeroboam the son of Nebat, who made Israel to sin: 1 Kin. 15:26; 21:25

53 For he served Baal, and worshipped him, and provoked to anger the LORD God of Israel, according to all that his father had done.   1 Kin. 16:30-32

THE SECOND BOOK OF THE

KINGS

A warning signifies impending danger. Warnings take many forms: signs, shouts, or the sound of a horn. To ignore a warning is to put one's life or that of another at risk.

God issues warnings, too. His warnings are not meant to hinder people's freedom, but to protect us physically, spiritually, and emotionally. When those warnings are consistently ignored, disasters follow.

The Book of 2 Kings continues the story of 1 Kings. God calls prophets like Isaiah, Jeremiah, and Nahum to speak to the kings and to warn His people about the dangers of apostasy and idolatry. If the kings and the people keep His laws and obey His ways, blessings and prosperity will follow. If they go their own way, living by their whims and desires, the disasters will occur such as famine, invasion, and drought.

Second Kings, written selectively and not exhaustively, shows how these disasters play out. Israel, the northern kingdom, is ruled by nineteen kings, all of them corrupt, which leads to their invasion by the empire of Assyria. Judah, the southern kingdom, experiences the occasional rule of godly kings and so remains in tack a bit longer until it too succumbs to invasion and exile by a new world power—Babylon.

Meanwhile, Elisha picks up the prophetic mantle of Elijah and ministers in Samaria. Other prophets with books that appear later in the Old Testament (Amos, Hosea, Obadiah, Joel, Isaiah, Micah, Nahum, Zephaniah, Jeremiah, and Habakkuk) also minister during these turbulent times.

Dates

The Book of 2 Kings tells the story of God's people from 853 B.C. to 560 B.C. Using the division noted above, the dates fall roughly as follows:

(1) *2 Kings 1—17, 853 to 722 B.C.*
This marks the time between King Ahaziah of Israel to the Assyrian captivity of Israel.
(2) *2 Kings 18—25, 729 to 560 B.C.*
Beginning with the reign of Hezekiah, this section concludes with the release of Jehoiachin in Babylon.

Author

One piece of evidence that suggests Jeremiah wrote Kings, as noted in 1 Kings, is that it includes a prophetic depiction of apostasy that just such an author would produce. Furthermore, the style of 1 and 2 Kings is similar to that found in the Book of Jeremiah. While the writer wanted the Israelites to learn their history, more importantly he desired to show that the success of kings or nations was dependent on their obedience to God and His law. God's righteous judgment on idolatry and immorality is emphasized in both books.

In addition, the author mentions several source documents, most likely used in compiling this history: "the book of the acts of Solomon" (11:41), "the book of the chronicles of the kings of Israel" (14:19; 15:31; 16:5, 14, 20, 27; 22:39), "the book of the chronicles of the kings of Judah" (14:29; 15:7, 23; 22:45).

Meaning of the Name

The title Kings or *Melechim* comes from the first word in Hebrew text—*Vehamelech*—meaning "Now King." In the Latin Vulgate, 1 and 2 Kings are known as *Liber Regum Tertius et Quartus* or "Third and Fourth Book of Kings."

Christ in 2 Kings

The house of David, from which Jesus was a direct descendant, was spared from annihilation when Queen Athaliah killed Ahaziah's children, except Joash (11:1–4). The covenant God made with David (2 Samuel 7:4–17) was kept intact.

The prophet Elisha, reminiscent of Jesus, lived among the people and preached a message of grace and hope, which Jesus proclaimed when He came to earth. He also performed several miracles very much like Jesus would later perform such as raising a child from the

dead (2 Kings 4:32–37), feeding many people with a few loaves of bread (4:42–44), and healing a man with leprosy (5:1–14).

Second Kings falls into two distinct sections:

(1) *2 Kings 1—17, The Kings of the Divided Kingdom:* The reigns of the various kings of Israel and Judah are chronicled. The ministry of the prophet Elisha is highlighted, including his aid to a widow (4:1–7), the raising of the Shunammite's son (4:8–37), miraculous meals (4:38–44), the healing of Naaman's leprosy (5:1–27), and the story of the floating axe head (6:1–7). During this period, Amos and Hosea prophesy in Israel, and Jonah goes to Assyria. At the end of chapter 17, the northern kingdom of Israel is attacked and conquered by the Assyrian Empire. The people are taken into exile.

(2) *2 Kings 18—25, The Kingdom of Judah:* With Judah miraculously saved from the Assyrian attack and destruction of their neighbor to the north (chapter 18), the southern kingdom of Judah continues. The rest of the book records the reigns of the remaining kings. Of special note are the revivals under Hezekiah (chapter 19) and Josiah (chapter 23). Unfortunately, the book ends when Judah is attacked and conquered by the Babylonian army. Jerusalem, its wall and its beautiful temple, are destroyed. Many of the best and brightest people are taken into captivity to serve in Babylon (as recorded in the Book of Daniel).

Isaiah, Jeremiah, Joel, Obadiah, Micah, Nahum, Habakkuk, and Zephaniah prophesy to the people of Judah. Yet despite their warnings, the people continue to dabble in idolatry, immorality, and disunity. Judgment comes in the form of invasion and exile. Judah's captivity occurrs 136 years after Israel's because of the influence of eight godly rulers.

Unlocking 2 Kings

✦ **KEY PEOPLE:**
Elijah, Elisha, Shunammite woman, Naaman, Jezebel, Jehu, Joash, Hezekiah, Sennacherib, Isaiah, Manasseh, Josiah, Jehoiakim, Zedekiah, Nebuchadnezzar

✦ **KEY EVENTS:**
Elisha, the protégé of Elijah, asked for twice the prophetic power of his mentor; Elijah is taken to heaven in a chariot of fire; Elisha's miraculous ministry was portrayed by the flowing olive oil; the healing of a Shunammite woman's son; the healing of Naaman's leprosy and the floating axe head; spiritual reforms and revivals during the reigns of Hezekiah and Josiah; Israel destroyed and Judah taken captive by Babylon

✦ **KEY WORD:**
Captivity. Failing to heed the warnings of God through the prophets, Israel was invaded and destroyed by the Assyrians, while Judah was led away to captivity by the Babylonians.

✦ **KEY VERSES:**
"For the children of Israel walked in all the sins of Jeroboam which he did; they departed not from them; until the LORD removed Israel out of his sight, as he had said by all his servants the prophets. So was Israel carried away out of their own land to Assyria, unto this day" (2 Kings 17:22, 23).

✦ **KEY CHAPTERS:**
2 Kings 17, recording the end of the northern kingdom of Israel; *2 Kings 25,* recording the utter destruction of the southern kingdom of Judah, along with Jerusalem and the glorious temple

Elijah Pronounces God's Judgment on Evil King Ahaziah of Israel

1 Then Moab rebelled against Israel after the death of Ahab.   2 Sam. 8:2
2 And Ahaziah fell down through a lattice in his upper chamber that *was* in Samaria, and was sick: and he sent messengers, and said unto them, Go, enquire of Baal-zebub the god of Ekron whether I shall recover of this disease.   2 Kin. 1:16; Matt. 10:25; Mark 3:22
3 But the angel of the LORD said to Elijah the Tishbite, Arise, go up to meet the messengers of the king of Samaria, and say unto them, *Is it* not because *there is* not a God in Israel, *that* ye go to enquire of Baal-zebub the god of Ekron?   1 Kin. 17:1
4 Now therefore thus saith the LORD, Thou shalt not come down from that bed on which thou art gone up, but shalt surely die. And Elijah departed.   2 Kin. 1:6

> **1:2–4 On Dangerous Ground**
>
> Through spiritualism many of the sick, the bereaved, the curious, are communicating with evil spirits. All who venture to do this are on dangerous ground. The word of truth declares how God regards them. In ancient times He pronounced a stern judgment on a king who had sent for counsel to a heathen oracle: ... "Now therefore thus saith the Lord, Thou shalt not come down from that bed on which thou art gone up, but shalt surely die" (2 Kings 1:3, 4). *AA 290*

5 And when the messengers turned back unto him, he said unto them, Why are ye now turned back?
6 And they said unto him, There came a man up to meet us, and said unto us, Go, turn again unto the king that sent you, and say unto him, Thus saith the LORD, *Is it* not because *there is* not a God in Israel, *that* thou sendest to enquire of Baal-zebub the god of Ekron? therefore thou shalt not come down from that bed on which thou art gone up, but shalt surely die.
7 And he said unto them, What manner of man *was he* which came up to meet you, and told you these words?
8 And they answered him, *He was* an hairy man, and ᵀgirt with a ᵀgirdle of leather about his loins. And he said, It *is* Elijah the Tishbite.   Zech. 13:4; Matt. 3:4; Mark 1:6 ◆ *wrapped* ◆ *belt*
9 Then the king sent unto him a captain of fifty with his fifty. And he went up to him: and, behold, he sat on the top of an hill. And he spake unto him, Thou man of God, the king hath said, Come down.   2 Kin. 6:13-14
10 And Elijah answered and said to the captain of fifty, If I *be* a man of God, then let fire come down from heaven, and consume

thee and thy fifty. And there came down fire from heaven, and consumed him and his fifty.   1 Kin. 18:36-38; Job 1:16; Luke 9:54
11 Again also he sent unto him another captain of fifty with his fifty. And he answered and said unto him, O man of God, thus hath the king said, Come down quickly.
12 And Elijah answered and said unto them, If I *be* a man of God, let fire come down from heaven, and consume thee and thy fifty. And the fire of God came down from heaven, and consumed him and his fifty.
13 And he sent again a captain of the third fifty with his fifty. And the third captain of fifty went up, and came and fell on his knees before Elijah, and ᵀbesought him, and said unto him, O man of God, I pray thee, let my life, and the life of these fifty thy servants, be precious in thy sight.   Is. 1:5 ◆ *begged*
14 Behold, there came fire down from heaven, and burnt up the two captains of the former fifties with their fifties: therefore let my life now be precious in thy sight.
15 And the angel of the LORD said unto Elijah, Go down with him: be not afraid of him. And he arose, and went down with him unto the king.   Is. 51:12
16 And he said unto him, Thus saith the LORD, Forasmuch as thou hast sent messengers to enquire of Baal-zebub the god of Ekron, *is it* not because *there is* no God in Israel to enquire of his word? therefore thou shalt not come down off that bed on which thou art gone up, but shalt surely die.
17 So he died according to the word of the LORD which Elijah had spoken. And Jehoram reigned in his stead in the second year of Jehoram the son of Jehoshaphat king of Judah; because he had no son.   2 Kin. 3:1
18 Now the rest of the acts of Ahaziah which he did, *are* they not written in the book of the chronicles of the kings of Israel?

Elisha Knows That Elijah Will Be Taken from Him

2 And it came to pass, when the LORD would take up Elijah into heaven by a whirlwind, that Elijah went with Elisha from Gilgal.   Gen. 5:24; Josh. 4:19; Heb. 11:5
2 And Elijah said unto Elisha, Tarry here, I pray thee; for the LORD hath sent me to Bethel. And Elisha said *unto him,* As the LORD liveth, and *as* thy soul liveth, I will not leave thee. So they went down to Bethel. 1 Sam. 1:26
3 And the sons of the prophets that *were* at Bethel came forth to Elisha, and said unto him, Knowest thou that the LORD will take away thy master from thy head to day? And he said, Yea, I know *it;* hold ye your peace.   1 Kin. 20:35; 2 Kin. 4:1, 38
4 And Elijah said unto him, Elisha, tarry here,

I pray thee; for the LORD hath sent me to Jericho. And he said, *As* the LORD liveth, and *as* thy soul liveth, I will not leave thee. So they came to Jericho.   Josh. 6:26; 1 Kin. 16:34; 2 Kin. 2:2

5 And the sons of the prophets that *were* at Jericho came to Elisha, and said unto him, Knowest thou that the LORD will take away thy master from thy head to day? And he answered, Yea, I know *it*; hold ye your peace.   2 Kin. 2:3

6 And Elijah said unto him, Tarry, I pray thee, here; for the LORD hath sent me to Jordan. And he said, *As* the LORD liveth, and *as* thy soul liveth, I will not leave thee. And they two went on.   2 Kin. 2:2

2:1–6 Refusing to Be Diverted

In his early labor of guiding the plow, Elisha had learned not to fail or to become discouraged; and now that he had set his hand to the plow in another line of duty, he would not be diverted from his purpose. As often as the invitation to turn back was given, his answer was, "As the Lord liveth, and as thy soul liveth, I will not leave thee" (2 Kings 2:2). *Ed 59*

7 And fifty men of the sons of the prophets went, and stood to view afar off: and they two stood by Jordan.

8 And Elijah took his mantle, and wrapped *it* together, and smote the waters, and they were divided hither and thither, so that they two went over on dry ground.   Ex. 14:21-22

Elijah Is Taken to Heaven in a Chariot of Fire

9 And it came to pass, when they were gone over, that Elijah said unto Elisha, Ask what I shall do for thee, before I be taken away from thee. And Elisha said, I pray thee, let a double portion of thy spirit be upon me.   Num. 11:17

10 And he said, Thou hast asked a hard thing: *nevertheless,* if thou see me *when I am* taken from thee, it shall be so unto thee; but if not, it shall not be *so.*

11 And it came to pass, as they still went on, and talked, that, behold, *there appeared* a chariot of fire, and horses of fire, and parted them both ᵀasunder; and Elijah went up by a whirlwind into heaven.   Ps. 68:17; 104:3-4 ◆ *apart*

2:11 Elijah Was a Type

Elijah was a type of the saints who will be living on the earth at the time of the second advent of Christ and who will be "changed, in a moment, in the twinkling of an eye, at the last trump," without tasting of death (1 Corinthians 15:51, 52). *PK 227*

12 And Elisha saw *it,* and he cried, My father, my father, the chariot of Israel, and the horsemen thereof. And he saw him no more: and he took hold of his own clothes, and ᵀrent them in two pieces.   2 Kin. 13:14 ◆ *tore*

13 He took up also the ᵀmantle of Elijah that fell from him, and went back, and stood by the bank of Jordan;   *large outside garment*

14 And he took the mantle of Elijah that fell from him, and smote the waters, and said, Where *is* the LORD God of Elijah? and when he also had smitten the waters, they parted ᵀhither and thither: and Elisha went over.   *here*

15 And when the sons of the prophets which *were* to view at Jericho saw him, they said, The spirit of Elijah doth rest on Elisha. And they came to meet him, and bowed themselves to the ground before him.

16 And they said unto him, Behold now, there be with thy servants fifty strong men; let them go, we pray thee, and seek thy master: lest ᵀperadventure the Spirit of the LORD hath taken him up, and cast him upon some mountain, or into some valley. And he said, Ye shall not send.   1 Kin. 18:12; Acts 8:39 ◆ *maybe*

17 And when they urged him till he was ashamed, he said, Send. They sent therefore fifty men; and they sought three days, but found him not.   2 Kin. 8:11

18 And when they came again to him, (for he tarried at Jericho,) he said unto them, Did I not say unto you, Go not?

Elisha Heals the Water, Is Jeered by Some Youths

19 And the men of the city said unto Elisha, Behold, I pray thee, the situation of this city *is* pleasant, as my lord seeth: but the water *is* ᵀnaught, and the ground barren.   *bad*

20 And he said, Bring me a new ᵀcruse, and put salt therein. And they brought *it* to him.   *pot*

21 And he went forth unto the spring of the waters, and cast the salt in there, and said, Thus saith the LORD, I have healed these waters; there shall not be from thence any more death or barren *land.*   Ex. 15:25-26; 2 Kin. 4:41; 6:6

22 So the waters were healed unto this day, according to the saying of Elisha which he spake.

23 And he went up from thence unto Beth-el: and as he was going up by the way, there came forth little children out of the city, and mocked him, and said unto him, Go up, thou bald head; go up, thou bald head.   2 Chr. 36:16

24 And he turned back, and looked on them, and cursed them in the name of the LORD. And there came forth two she bears out of the wood, and tare forty and two children of them.

25 And he went from thence to mount

Carmel, and from thence he returned to Samaria. 2 Kin. 4:25

Jehoram's Evil Reign over Israel

3 Now Jehoram the son of Ahab began to reign over Israel in Samaria the eighteenth year of Jehoshaphat king of Judah, and reigned twelve years. 2 Kin. 1:17
2 And he ᵀwrought evil in the sight of the LORD; but not like his father, and like his mother: for he put away the image of Baal that his father had made. 1 Kin. 21:25 ✦ did
3 Nevertheless he cleaved unto the sins of Jeroboam the son of Nebat, which made Israel to sin; he departed not therefrom.
4 And Mesha king of Moab was a sheepmaster, and rendered unto the king of Israel an hundred thousand lambs, and an hundred thousand rams, with the wool. 2 Sam. 8:2
5 But it came to pass, when Ahab was dead, that the king of Moab rebelled against the king of Israel. 2 Kin. 1:1

Jehoram of Israel and Jehoshaphat of Judah Defeat the Moabites

6 And king Jehoram went out of Samaria the same time, and numbered all Israel.
7 And he went and sent to Jehoshaphat the king of Judah, saying, The king of Moab hath rebelled against me: wilt thou go with me against Moab to battle? And he said, I will go up: I am as thou art, my people as thy people, and my horses as thy horses. 1 Kin. 22:4
8 And he said, Which way shall we go up? And he answered, The way through the wilderness of Edom.
9 So the king of Israel went, and the king of Judah, and the king of Edom: and they ᵀfetched a compass of seven days' journey: and there was no water for the host, and for the cattle that followed them. 1 Kin. 22:47 ✦ wandered
10 And the king of Israel said, Alas! that the LORD hath called these three kings together, to deliver them into the hand of Moab!
11 But Jehoshaphat said, Is there not here a prophet of the LORD, that we may enquire of the LORD by him? And one of the king of Israel's servants answered and said, Here is Elisha the son of Shaphat, which poured water on the hands of Elijah. 1 Kin. 19:21; 22:7; John 13:4-5
12 And Jehoshaphat said, The word of the LORD is with him. So the king of Israel and Jehoshaphat and the king of Edom went down to him.
13 And Elisha said unto the king of Israel, What have I to do with thee? get thee to the prophets of thy father, and to the prophets of thy mother. And the king of Israel said unto him, Nay: for the LORD hath called these three kings together, to deliver them into the hand of Moab. 1 Kin. 18:19
14 And Elisha said, As the LORD of hosts liveth, before whom I stand, surely, were it not that I regard the presence of Jehoshaphat the king of Judah, I would not look toward thee, nor see thee. 1 Kin. 17:1
15 But now bring me a minstrel. And it came to pass, when the minstrel played, that the hand of the LORD came upon him. 1 Sam. 16:23
16 And he said, Thus saith the LORD, Make this valley full of ditches.
17 For thus saith the LORD, Ye shall not see wind, neither shall ye see rain; yet that valley shall be filled with water, that ye may drink, both ye, and your cattle, and your beasts. Ps. 107:35
18 And this is but a light thing in the sight of the LORD: he will deliver the Moabites also into your hand. Jer. 32:17
19 And ye shall ᵀsmite every fenced city, and every choice city, and shall fell every good tree, and stop all wells of water, and mar every good piece of land with stones. strike
20 And it came to pass in the morning, when

Mocking God's Prophets

2 Kings 2:23, 24

Had Elisha allowed the mockery to pass unnoticed, he would have continued to be ridiculed and reviled by the rabble, and his mission to instruct and save in a time of grave national peril might have been defeated. This one instance of terrible severity was sufficient to command respect throughout his life. For fifty years he went in and out of the gate of Bethel, and to and fro in the land, from city to city, passing through crowds of idle, rude, dissolute youth; but none mocked him or made light of his qualifications as the prophet of the Most High.

Even kindness should have its limits. Authority must be maintained by a firm severity, or it will be received by many with mockery and contempt. The so-called tenderness, the coaxing and indulgence, used toward youth by parents and guardians, is one of the worst evils which can come upon them. In every family, firmness, decision, positive requirements, are essential.

Reverence, in which the youth who mocked Elisha were so lacking, is a grace that should be carefully cherished. Every child should be taught to show true reverence for God. Never should His name be spoken lightly or thoughtlessly. Angels, as they speak it, veil their faces. With what reverence should we, who are fallen and sinful, take it upon our lips! PK 236

the meat offering was offered, that, behold, there came water by the way of Edom, and the country was filled with water. Ex. 29:39-40
21 And when all the Moabites heard that the kings were come up to fight against them, they gathered all that were able to put on armour, and upward, and stood in the border.
22 And they rose up early in the morning, and the sun shone upon the water, and the Moabites saw the water on the other side *as* red as blood:
23 And they said, This *is* blood: the kings are surely slain, and they have smitten one another: now therefore, Moab, to the ᵀspoil.   plunder
24 And when they came to the camp of Israel, the Israelites rose up and smote the Moabites, so that they fled before them: but they went forward smiting the Moabites, even in *their* country.
25 And they beat down the cities, and on every good piece of land cast every man his stone, and filled it; and they stopped all the wells of water, and felled all the good trees: only in Kir-haraseth left they the stones thereof; ᵀhowbeit the slingers went about *it*, and smote it. 2 Kin. 3:19; Is. 16:7; Jer. 48:31 ♦ *however*
26 And when the king of Moab saw that the battle was too sore for him, he took with him seven hundred men that drew swords, to break through *even* unto the king of Edom: but they could not.
27 Then he took his eldest son that should have reigned in his stead, and offered him *for* a burnt offering upon the wall. And there was great ᵀindignation against Israel: and they departed from him, and returned to *their* own land.   Deut. 12:31; Judg. 11:31; Mic. 6:7 ♦ *anger*

Elisha Multiplies the Widow's Oil

4 Now there cried a certain woman of the wives of the sons of the prophets unto Elisha, saying, Thy servant my husband is dead; and thou knowest that thy servant did fear the LORD: and the creditor is come to take unto him my two sons to be bond-men.   Lev. 25:39-41, 48; 2 Kin. 2:3
2 And Elisha said unto her, What shall I do for thee? tell me, what hast thou in the house? And she said, Thine handmaid hath not any thing in the house, save a pot of oil.   1 Kin. 17:12
3 Then he said, Go, borrow thee vessels abroad of all thy neighbours, *even* empty vessels; borrow not a few.
4 And when thou art come in, thou shalt shut the door upon thee and upon thy sons, and shalt pour out into all those vessels, and thou shalt set aside that which is full.
5 So she went from him, and shut the door

upon her and upon her sons, who brought *the vessels* to her; and she poured out.
6 And it came to pass, when the vessels were full, that she said unto her son, Bring me yet a vessel. And he said unto her, *There is* not a vessel more. And the oil ᵀstayed.   ceased
7 Then she came and told the man of God. And he said, Go, sell the oil, and pay thy debt, and live thou and thy children of the rest.

Elisha Promises a Son to a Shunammite Woman

8 And it fell on a day, that Elisha passed to Shunem, where *was* a great woman; and she ᵀconstrained him to eat bread. And *so* it was, *that* as ᵀoft as he passed by, he turned in thither to eat bread.   Josh. 19:18 ♦ *compelled* ♦ *often*
9 And she said unto her husband, Behold now, I perceive that this *is* an holy man of God, which passeth by us continually.
10 Let us make a little chamber, I pray thee, on the wall; and let us set for him there a bed, and a table, and a stool, and a candle-stick: and it shall be, when he cometh to us, that he shall turn in thither.   Rom. 12:13
11 And it fell on a day, that he came thither, and he turned into the chamber, and lay there.
12 And he said to Gehazi his servant, Call this Shunammite. And when he had called her, she stood before him.   2 Kin. 8:4-5
13 And he said unto him, Say now unto her, Behold, thou hast been careful for us with all this care; what *is* to be done for thee? would-est thou be spoken for to the king, or to the captain of the host? And she answered, I dwell among mine own people.   2 Sam. 19:13
14 And he said, What then *is* to be done for her? And Gehazi answered, Verily she hath no child, and her husband is old.
15 And he said, Call her. And when he had called her, she stood in the door.
16 And he said, About this season, according to the time of life, thou shalt embrace a son. And she said, Nay, my lord, *thou* man of God, do not lie unto thine handmaid.   2 Kin. 4:28
17 And the woman conceived, and bare a son at that season that Elisha had said unto her, according to the time of life.

Elisha Raises the Woman's Son from the Dead

18 And when the child was grown, it fell on a day, that he went out to his father to the reapers.
19 And he said unto his father, My head, my head. And he said to a lad, Carry him to his mother.
20 And when he had taken him, and brought him to his mother, he sat on her knees till noon, and *then* died.
21 And she went up, and laid him on the

bed of the man of God, and shut *the door* upon him, and went out. 　　2 Kin. 4:32

22 And she called unto her husband, and said, Send me, I pray thee, one of the young men, and one of the asses, that I may run to the man of God, and come again.

23 And he said, Wherefore wilt thou go to him to day? *it is* neither new moon, nor sabbath. And she said, *It shall be* well. Num. 10:10

24 Then she saddled an ass, and said to her servant, Drive, and go forward; slack not *thy* riding for me, except I bid thee.

25 So she went and came unto the man of God to mount Carmel. And it came to pass, when the man of God saw her afar off, that he said to Gehazi his servant, Behold, *yonder is* that Shunammite: 　　2 Kin. 2:25

26 Run now, I pray thee, to meet her, and say unto her, Is it well with thee? is it well with thy husband? is it well with the child? And she answered, It is well.

27 And when she came to the man of God to the hill, she caught him by the feet: but Gehazi came near to thrust her away. And the man of God said, Let her alone; for her soul *is* vexed within her: and the LORD hath hid *it* from me, and hath not told me.

28 Then she said, Did I desire a son of my lord? did I not say, Do not deceive me?

29 Then he said to Gehazi, Gird up thy loins, and take my staff in thine hand, and go thy way: if thou meet any man, salute him not; and if any salute thee, answer him not again: and lay my staff upon the face of the child. Ex. 14:16; 1 Kin. 18:46; 2 Kin. 2:14

30 And the mother of the child said, As the LORD liveth, and *as* thy soul liveth, I will not leave thee. And he arose, and followed her.

31 And Gehazi passed on before them, and laid the staff upon the face of the child; but *there was* neither voice, nor hearing. Wherefore he went again to meet him, and told him, saying, The child is not awaked. 　　John 11:11

32 And when Elisha was come into the house, behold, the child was dead, *and* laid upon his bed.

33 He went in therefore, and shut the door upon them Ttwain, and prayed unto the LORD. 　　2 Kin. 4:4; Matt. 6:6 ◆ both

34 And he went up, and lay upon the child, and put his mouth upon his mouth, and his eyes upon his eyes, and his hands upon his hands: and he stretched himself upon the child; and the flesh of the child Twaxed warm. 　　1 Kin. 17:21; Acts 20:10 ◆ became

35 Then he returned, and walked in the house to and fro; and went up, and stretched himself upon him: and the child sneezed seven times, and the child opened his eyes. 　　2 Kin. 8:5

36 And he called Gehazi, and said, Call this Shunammite. So he called her. And when she was come in unto him, he said, Take up thy son. 　　Heb. 11:35

37 Then she went in, and fell at his feet, and bowed herself to the ground, and took up her son, and went out.

Elisha Heals Poisoned Stew and Multiplies Bread

38 And Elisha came again to Gilgal: and *there was* a Tdearth in the land; and the sons of the prophets *were* sitting before him: and he said unto his servant, Set on the great pot, and Tseethe pottage for the sons of the prophets. 　　2 Kin. 2:1, 3; 8:1 ◆ scarcity ◆ boil

39 And one went out into the field to gather herbs, and found a wild vine, and gathered thereof wild gourds his lap full, and came and shred *them* into the pot of Tpottage: for they knew *them* not. 　　stew

40 So they poured out for the men to eat. And it came to pass, as they were eating of the pottage, that they cried out, and said, O thou man of God, *there is* death in the pot. And they could not eat *thereof*. 　　Ex. 10:17

41 But he said, Then bring meal. And he cast *it* into the pot; and he said, Pour out for the people, that they may eat. And there was no harm in the pot. 　　Ex. 15:25; 2 Kin. 2:21

42 And there came a man from Baal-shalisha, and brought the man of God bread of the firstfruits, twenty loaves of barley, and full ears of corn in the husk thereof. And he said, Give unto the people, that they may eat. 　　1 Sam. 9:4, 7; John 6:9

43 And his servitor said, What, should I set this before an hundred men? He said again,

Give the people, that they may eat: for thus saith the LORD, They shall eat, and shall leave thereof.   Luke 9:13
44 So he set *it* before them, and they did eat, and left *thereof*, according to the word of the LORD.

Naaman Goes to Samaria to Be Cured of His Leprosy

5 Now Naaman, captain of the host of the king of Syria, was a great man with his master, and honourable, because by him the LORD had given deliverance unto Syria: he was also a mighty man in valour, *but he was* a leper.   Luke 4:27
2 And the Syrians had gone out by companies, and had brought away captive out of the land of Israel a little maid; and she waited on Naaman's wife.   2 Kin. 6:23; 13:20
3 And she said unto her mistress, Would God my lord *were* with the prophet that *is* in Samaria! for he would recover him of his leprosy.

5:2, 3 No Higher Trust

The conduct of the captive maid, the way that she bore herself in that heathen home, is a strong witness to the power of early home training. There is no higher trust than that committed to fathers and mothers in the care and training of their children. Parents have to do with the very foundations of habit and character. By their example and teaching the future of their children is largely decided. *PK 245*

---

4 And *one* went in, and told his lord, saying, Thus and thus said the maid that *is* of the land of Israel.
5 And the king of Syria said, Go to, go, and I will send a letter unto the king of Israel. And he departed, and took with him ten talents of silver, and six thousand *pieces* of gold, and ten changes of ᵀraiment. Judg. 14:12; 2 Kin. 8:8-9 ◆ *clothing*

6 And he brought the letter to the king of Israel, saying, Now when this letter is come unto thee, behold, I have *therewith* sent Naaman my servant to thee, that thou mayest recover him of his leprosy.
7 And it came to pass, when the king of Israel had read the letter, that he rent his clothes, and said, *Am* I God, to kill and to make alive, that this man doth send unto me to recover a man of his leprosy? wherefore consider, I pray you, and see how he seeketh a quarrel against me.   Gen. 30:2; 1 Sam. 2:6; 1 Kin. 20:7
8 And it was *so*, when Elisha the man of God had heard that the king of Israel had ᵀrent his clothes, that he sent to the king, saying, Wherefore hast thou rent thy clothes? let him come now to me, and he shall know that there is a prophet in Israel.   *torn apart*
9 So Naaman came with his horses and with his chariot, and stood at the door of the house of Elisha.
10 And Elisha sent a messenger unto him, saying, Go and wash in Jordan seven times, and thy flesh shall come again to thee, and thou shalt be clean.   Lev. 14:7; John 9:7
11 But Naaman was ᵀwroth, and went away, and said, Behold, I thought, He will surely come out to me, and stand, and call on the name of the LORD his God, and strike his hand over the place, and recover the leper.   *angered*
12 *Are* not Abana and Pharpar, rivers of Damascus, better than all the waters of Israel? may I not wash in them, and be clean? So he turned and went away in a rage.
13 And his servants came near, and spake unto him, and said, My father, *if* the prophet had bid thee *do some* great thing, wouldest thou not have done *it*? how much rather then, when he saith to thee, Wash, and be clean?   2 Kin. 2:12; 6:21; 13:14
14 Then went he down, and dipped himself seven times in Jordan, according to the

---

Early Home Training

2 Kings 5:2–4

Happy are the parents whose lives are a true reflection of the divine, so that the promises and commands of God awaken in the child gratitude and reverence; the parents whose tenderness and justice and long-suffering interpret to the child the love and justice and long-suffering of God, and who by teaching the child to love and trust and obey them, are teaching him to love and trust and obey his Father in heaven. Parents who impart to the child such a gift have endowed him with a treasure more precious than the wealth of all the ages, a treasure as enduring as eternity.

We know not in what line our children may be called to serve. They may spend their lives within the circle of the home; they may engage in life's common vocations, or go as teachers of the gospel to heathen lands; but all are alike called to be missionaries for God, ministers of mercy to the world. They are to obtain an education that will help them to stand by the side of Christ in unselfish service.

The parents of that Hebrew maid, as they taught her of God, did not know the destiny that would be hers. But they were faithful to their trust; and in the home of the captain of the Syrian host, their child bore witness to the God whom she had learned to honor. *PK 245, 246*

saying of the man of God: and his flesh came again like unto the flesh of a little child, and he was clean.   2 Kin. 5:10; Job 33:25; Luke 4:27

5:10–14 Struggling With Pride

The faith of Naaman was being tested, while pride struggled for the mastery. But faith conquered, and the haughty Syrian yielded his pride of heart and bowed in submission to the revealed will of Jehovah. *PK 249*

Elisha Declines Naaman's Gifts

15 And he returned to the man of God, he and all his company, and came, and stood before him: and he said, Behold, now I know that *there is* no God in all the earth, but in Israel: now therefore, I pray thee, take a blessing of thy servant.   1 Sam. 25:27
16 But he said, *As* the LORD liveth, before whom I stand, I will receive none. And he urged him to take *it*; but he refused.2 Kin. 3:14
17 And Naaman said, Shall there not then, I pray thee, be given to thy servant two mules' burden of earth? for thy servant will ᵀhenceforth offer neither burnt offering nor sacrifice unto other gods, but unto the LORD.   *from this time forward*
18 In this thing the LORD pardon thy servant, *that* when my master goeth into the house of Rimmon to worship there, and he leaneth on my hand, and I bow myself in the house of Rimmon: when I bow down myself in the house of Rimmon, the LORD pardon thy servant in this thing.   2 Kin. 7:2, 17
19 And he said unto him, Go in peace. So he departed from him a little way.   Ex. 4:18

Gehazi, Lying to Naaman in Elisha's Name, Is Smitten with Leprosy

20 But Gehazi, the servant of Elisha the man of God, said, Behold, my master hath spared Naaman this Syrian, in not receiving at his hands that which he brought: but, *as* the LORD liveth, I will run after him, and take somewhat of him.   Ex. 20:7
21 So Gehazi followed after Naaman. And when Naaman saw *him* running after him, he lighted down from the chariot to meet him, and said, *Is* all well?
22 And he said, All *is* well. My master hath sent me, saying, Behold, even now there be come to me from mount Ephraim two young men of the sons of the prophets: give them, I pray thee, a ᵀtalent of silver, and two changes of garments.   2 Kin. 5:5 ♦ *weight or sum*
23 And Naaman said, Be content, take two talents. And he urged him, and bound two talents of silver in two bags, with two changes of garments, and laid *them* upon two of his servants; and they bare *them* before him.
24 And when he came to the tower, he took *them* from their hand, and bestowed *them* in the house: and he let the men go, and they departed.   Josh. 7:1
25 But he went in, and stood before his master. And Elisha said unto him, Whence *comest thou*, Gehazi? And he said, Thy servant went no whither.   2 Kin. 5:22
26 And he said unto him, Went not mine heart *with thee*, when the man turned again from his chariot to meet thee? *Is it* a time to receive money, and to receive garments, and oliveyards, and vineyards, and sheep, and oxen, and menservants, and maidservants?   2 Kin. 5:16
27 The leprosy therefore of Naaman shall cleave unto thee, and unto thy seed for ever. And he went out from his presence a leper *as white* as snow.   Ex. 4:6; Num. 12:10; 2 Kin. 15:5

Elisha Makes an Axe Head Float

6 And the sons of the prophets said unto Elisha, Behold now, the place where we dwell with thee is too ᵀstrait for us.   *small*
2 Let us go, we pray thee, unto Jordan, and

True to Convictions

2 Kings 5

Centuries after Naaman returned to his Syrian home, healed in body and converted in spirit, his wonderful faith was referred to and commended by the Saviour as an object lesson for all who claim to serve God. "Many lepers were in Israel in the time of [Elisha] the prophet," the Saviour declared; "and none of them was cleansed, saving Naaman the Syrian" (Luke 4:27). God passed over the many lepers in Israel because their unbelief closed the door of good to them. A heathen nobleman who had been true to his convictions of right, and who felt his need of help, was in the sight of God more worthy of His blessing than were the afflicted in Israel, who had slighted and despised their God-given privileges. God works for those who appreciate His favors and respond to the light given them from heaven.

Today in every land there are those who are honest in heart, and upon these the light of heaven is shining. If they continue faithful in following that which they understand to be duty, they will be given increased light, until, like Naaman of old, they will be constrained to acknowledge that "there is no God in all the earth," save the living God, the Creator. *PK 252, 253*

take thence every man a beam, and let us make us a place there, where we may dwell. And he answered, Go ye.

3 And one said, Be content, I pray thee, and go with thy servants. And he answered, I will go.

4 So he went with them. And when they came to Jordan, they cut down wood.

5 But as one was felling a beam, the axe head fell into the water: and he cried, and said, Alas, master! for it was borrowed.

6 And the man of God said, Where fell it? And he shewed him the place. And he cut down a stick, and cast *it* in thither; and the iron did swim.   Ex. 15:25; 2 Kin. 2:21; 4:41

7 Therefore said he, Take *it* up to thee. And he put out his hand, and took it.

Elisha Discloses Syria's Plans to the King of Israel

8 Then the king of Syria warred against Israel, and took counsel with his servants, saying, In such and such a place *shall be* my camp.

9 And the man of God sent unto the king of Israel, saying, Beware that thou pass not such a place; for thither the Syrians are come down.

10 And the king of Israel sent to the place which the man of God told him and warned him of, and saved himself there, not once nor twice.

11 Therefore the heart of the king of Syria was sore troubled for this thing; and he called his servants, and said unto them, Will ye not shew me which of us *is* for the king of Israel?

12 And one of his servants said, None, my lord, O king: but Elisha, the prophet that *is* in Israel, telleth the king of Israel the words that thou speakest in thy bedchamber.

The Syrian Army Goes to Dothan to Seize Elisha, but Is Blinded

13 And he said, Go and spy where he *is*, that I may send and fetch him. And it was told him, saying, Behold, *he is* in Dothan. Gen. 37:17

14 Therefore sent he thither horses, and chariots, and a great host: and they came by night, and ᵀcompassed the city about.   *surrounded*

15 And when the servant of the man of God was risen early, and gone forth, behold, an host compassed the city both with horses and chariots. And his servant said unto him, Alas, my master! how shall we do?

16 And he answered, Fear not: for they that *be* with us *are* more than they that *be* with them.   Ex. 14:13; Ps. 55:18; Rom. 8:31

17 And Elisha prayed, and said, LORD, I pray thee, open his eyes, that he may see.

And the LORD opened the eyes of the young man; and he saw: and, behold, the mountain *was* full of horses and chariots of fire round about Elisha.   2 Kin. 2:11; Ps. 68:17; Zech. 6:1-7

6:17 To See as God Sees

God's faithful, praying ones are, as it were, shut in with Him. They themselves know not how securely they are shielded. Urged on by Satan, the rulers of this world are seeking to destroy them; but could the eyes of God's children be opened, as were the eyes of Elisha's servant at Dothan, they would see angels of God encamped about them, holding in check the hosts of darkness. *PK 590, 591*

---

18 And when they came down to him, Elisha prayed unto the LORD, and said, Smite this people, I pray thee, with blindness. And he smote them with blindness according to the word of Elisha.   Gen. 19:11

19 And Elisha said unto them, This *is* not the way, neither *is* this the city: follow me, and I will bring you to the man whom ye seek. But he led them to Samaria.

20 And it came to pass, when they were come into Samaria, that Elisha said, LORD, open the eyes of these *men*, that they may see. And the LORD opened their eyes, and they saw; and, behold, *they were* in the midst of Samaria.   2 Kin. 6:17

21 And the king of Israel said unto Elisha, when he saw them, My father, shall I smite *them*? shall I smite *them*?   2 Kin. 2:12; 5:13; 8:9

22 And he answered, Thou shalt not ᵀsmite *them*: wouldest thou smite those whom thou hast taken captive with thy sword and with thy bow? set bread and water before them, that they may eat and drink, and go to their master.   Gen. 48:22 ◆ *strike*

23 And he prepared great provision for them: and when they had eaten and drunk, he sent them away, and they went to their master. So the bands of Syria came no more into the land of Israel.   2 Kin. 5:2; 6:8-9; 24:2

The Severity of the Famine in Besieged Samaria

24 And it came to pass after this, that Benhadad king of Syria gathered all his host, and went up, and besieged Samaria.   Deut. 28:52

25 And there was a great famine in Samaria: and, behold, they besieged it, until an ass's head was *sold* for ᵀfourscore *pieces* of silver, and the fourth part of a cab of dove's dung for five *pieces* of silver.   *eighty*

26 And as the king of Israel was passing by upon the wall, there cried a woman unto him, saying, Help, my lord, O king.

27 And he said, If the LORD do not help

thee, whence shall I help thee? out of the barnfloor, or out of the winepress?

28 And the king said unto her, What aileth thee? And she answered, This woman said unto me, Give thy son, that we may eat him to day, and we will eat my son to morrow.   Judg. 18:23

29 So we boiled my son, and did eat him: and I said unto her on the next day, Give thy son, that we may eat him: and she hath hid her son.   Lev. 26:29

30 And it came to pass, when the king heard the words of the woman, that he ᵀrent his clothes; and he passed by upon the wall, and the people looked, and, behold, *he had* sackcloth within upon his flesh.   1 Kin. 21:27 ✦ *tore*

31 Then he said, God do so and more also to me, if the head of Elisha the son of Shaphat shall stand on him this day.   Ruth 1:17

32 But Elisha sat in his house, and the elders sat with him; and *the king* sent a man from before him: but ᵀere the messenger came to him, he said to the elders, See ye how this son of a murderer hath sent to take away mine head? look, when the messenger cometh, shut the door, and hold him fast at the door: *is* not the sound of his master's feet behind him? 1 Kin. 18:4; Ezek. 8:1; 14:1 ✦ *before*

33 And while he yet talked with them, behold, the messenger came down unto him: and he said, Behold, this evil *is* of the LORD; what should I wait for the LORD any longer?   Job 2:9

Elisha Prophesies the End of the Famine in Samaria

7 Then Elisha said, Hear ye the word of the LORD; Thus saith the LORD, To morrow about this time *shall* a measure of fine flour *be sold* for a shekel, and two measures of barley for a shekel, in the gate of Samaria.

2 Then a lord on whose hand the king leaned answered the man of God, and said, Behold, *if* the LORD would make windows in heaven, might this thing be? And he said, Behold, thou shalt see *it* with thine eyes, but shalt not eat thereof.   Gen. 7:11; 2 Kin. 5:18; Mal. 3:10

7:1, 2 Prisoners of Hope

God calls upon His faithful ones, who believe in Him, to talk courage to those who are unbelieving and hopeless. Turn to the Lord, ye prisoners of hope. Seek strength from God, the living God. Show an unwavering, humble faith in His power and His willingness to save. When in faith we take hold of His strength, He will change, wonderfully change, the most hopeless, discouraging outlook. He will do this for the glory of His name. *PK 260*

Four Lepers Discover That the Syrian Army Has Fled

3 And there were four leprous men at the entering in of the gate: and they said one to another, Why sit we here until we die? Num. 5:2-4

4 If we say, We will enter into the city, then the famine *is* in the city, and we shall die there: and if we sit still here, we die also. Now therefore come, and let us fall unto the host of the Syrians: if they save us alive, we shall live; and if they kill us, we shall but die.

5 And they rose up in the twilight, to go unto the camp of the Syrians: and when they were come to the uttermost part of the camp of Syria, behold, *there was* no man there.

6 For the Lord had made the host of the Syrians to hear a noise of chariots, and a noise of horses, *even* the noise of a great host: and they said one to another, Lo, the king of Israel hath hired against us the kings of the Hittites, and the kings of the Egyptians, to come upon us. 2 Sam. 5:24; 1 Kin. 10:29; 2 Chr. 12:2-3

7 Wherefore they arose and fled in the twilight, and left their tents, and their horses, and their asses, even the camp as it *was*, and fled for their life.   Ps. 48:4-6; Prov. 28:1

8 And when these lepers came to the uttermost part of the camp, they went into one tent, and did eat and drink, and carried thence silver, and gold, and ᵀraiment, and went and hid *it*; and came again, and entered into another tent, and carried thence *also*, and went and hid *it*.   Josh. 7:21 ✦ *clothing*

9 Then they said one to another, We do not well: this day *is* a day of good tidings, and we hold our peace: if we tarry till the morning light, some mischief will come upon us: now therefore come, that we may go and tell the king's household.

10 So they came and called unto the ᵀporter of the city: and they told them, saying, We came to the camp of the Syrians, and, behold, *there was* no man there, neither voice of man, but horses tied, and asses tied, and the tents as they *were*.   *doorkeeper*

11 And he called the porters; and they told *it* to the king's house within.

The King and the People Collect the Plunder

12 And the king arose in the night, and said unto his servants, I will now shew you what the Syrians have done to us. They know that we *be* hungry; therefore are they gone out of the camp to hide themselves in the field, saying, When they come out of the city, we shall catch them alive, and get into the city.

13 And one of his servants answered and said, Let *some* take, I pray thee, five of the horses that remain, which are left in the city, (behold, they *are* as all the multitude

of Israel that are left in it: behold, I say, they are even as all the multitude of the Israelites that are consumed:) and let us send and see.
14 They took therefore two chariot horses; and the king sent after the host of the Syrians, saying, Go and see.
15 And they went after them unto Jordan: and, lo, all the way was full of garments and vessels, which the Syrians had cast away in their haste. And the messengers returned, and told the king.
16 And the people went out, and spoiled the tents of the Syrians. So a measure of fine flour was sold for a shekel, and two measures of barley for a shekel, according to the word of the LORD.   2 Kin. 7:1; Is. 33:4, 23
17 And the king appointed the lord on whose hand he leaned to have the charge of the gate: and the people trode upon him in the gate, and he died, as the man of God had said, who spake when the king came down to him.   2 Kin. 6:32
18 And it came to pass as the man of God had spoken to the king, saying, Two measures of barley for a shekel, and a measure of fine flour for a shekel, shall be to morrow about this time in the gate of Samaria:
19 And that lord answered the man of God, and said, Now, behold, if the LORD should make windows in heaven, might such a thing be? And he said, Behold, thou shalt see it with thine eyes, but shalt not eat thereof.   2 Kin. 7:2
20 And so it fell out unto him: for the people ᵀtrode upon him in the gate, and he died.   trampled

The King Restores the Shunammite's Land

8 Then spake Elisha unto the woman, whose son he had restored to life, saying, Arise, and go thou and thine household, and sojourn wheresoever thou canst sojourn: for the LORD hath called for a famine; and it shall also come upon the land seven years.   2 Kin. 4:18; Ps. 105:16; Hag. 1:11
2 And the woman arose, and did after the saying of the man of God: and she went with her household, and sojourned in the land of the Philistines seven years.
3 And it came to pass at the seven years' end, that the woman returned out of the land of the Philistines: and she went forth to cry unto the king for her house and for her land.
4 And the king talked with Gehazi the servant of the man of God, saying, Tell me, I pray thee, all the great things that Elisha hath done.   2 Kin. 5:20-27
5 And it came to pass, as he was telling the king how he had restored a dead body to

life, that, behold, the woman, whose son he had restored to life, cried to the king for her house and for her land. And Gehazi said, My lord, O king, this is the woman, and this is her son, whom Elisha restored to life.   2 Kin. 4:35
6 And when the king asked the woman, she told him. So the king appointed unto her a certain officer, saying, Restore all that was hers, and all the fruits of the field since the day that she left the land, even until now.

Hazael Murders Ben-hadad and Becomes King of Syria

7 And Elisha came to Damascus; and Ben-hadad the king of Syria was sick; and it was told him, saying, The man of God is come ᵀhither.   1 Kin. 11:24; 20:1; 2 Kin. 6:24 ♦ here
8 And the king said unto Hazael, Take a present in thine hand, and go, meet the man of God, and enquire of the LORD by him, saying, Shall I recover of this disease?   1 Sam. 9:7
9 So Hazael went to meet him, and took a present with him, even of every good thing of Damascus, forty camels' burden, and came and stood before him, and said, Thy son Ben-hadad king of Syria hath sent me to thee, saying, Shall I recover of this disease?
10 And Elisha said unto him, Go, say unto him, Thou mayest certainly recover: ᵀhowbeit the LORD hath shewed me that he shall surely die.   however
11 And he settled his ᵀcountenance stedfastly, until he was ashamed: and the man of God wept.   Luke 19:41 ♦ appearance
12 And Hazael said, Why weepeth my lord? And he answered, Because I know the evil that thou wilt do unto the children of Israel: their strong holds wilt thou set on fire, and their young men wilt thou slay with the sword, and wilt ᵀdash their children, and rip up their women with child.   2 Kin. 12:17; 13:3, 7 ♦ beat
13 And Hazael said, But what, is thy servant a dog, that he should do this great thing? And Elisha answered, The LORD hath shewed me that thou shalt be king over Syria.   1 Sam. 17:43; 2 Sam. 9:8; 1 Kin. 19:15
14 So he departed from Elisha, and came to his master; who said to him, What said Elisha to thee? And he answered, He told me that thou shouldest surely recover.   2 Kin. 8:10
15 And it came to pass on the morrow, that he took a thick cloth, and dipped it in water, and spread it on his face, so that he died: and Hazael reigned in his stead.   2 Kin. 8:13

Jehoram's Evil Reign in Judah

16 And in the fifth year of Joram the son of Ahab king of Israel, Jehoshaphat being then king of Judah, Jehoram the son of Jehoshaphat king of Judah began to reign. 2 Kin. 1:17; 3:1
17 Thirty and two years old was he when he

began to reign; and he reigned eight years in Jerusalem.

18 And he walked in the way of the kings of Israel, as did the house of Ahab: for the daughter of Ahab was his wife: and he did evil in the sight of the LORD.   2 Kin. 8:26

19 Yet the LORD would not destroy Judah for David his servant's sake, as he promised him to give him alway a light, *and* to his children.   2 Sam. 7:12-13, 15; 1 Kin. 11:36

20 In his days Edom revolted from under the hand of Judah, and made a king over themselves.   1 Kin. 22:47; 2 Kin. 3:9, 27

21 So Joram went over to Zair, and all the chariots with him: and he rose by night, and smote the Edomites which ᵀcompassed him about, and the captains of the chariots: and the people fled into their tents.   *surrounded*

22 Yet Edom revolted from under the hand of Judah unto this day. Then Libnah revolted at the same time.   Josh. 21:13

23 And the rest of the acts of Joram, and all that he did, *are* they not written in the book of the chronicles of the kings of Judah?

24 And Joram slept with his fathers, and was buried with his fathers in the city of David: and Ahaziah his son reigned in his stead.   2 Chr. 21:1

Ahaziah's Evil Reign in Judah

25 In the twelfth year of Joram the son of Ahab king of Israel did Ahaziah the son of Jehoram king of Judah begin to reign.   2 Kin. 9:29

26 Two and twenty years old *was* Ahaziah when he began to reign; and he reigned one year in Jerusalem. And his mother's name *was* Athaliah, the daughter of Omri king of Israel.   2 Chr. 22:2

27 And he walked in the way of the house of Ahab, and did evil in the sight of the LORD, as *did* the house of Ahab: for he *was* the son in law of the house of Ahab.

28 And he went with Joram the son of Ahab to the war against Hazael king of Syria in Ramoth-gilead; and the Syrians wounded Joram.

29 And king Joram went back to be healed in Jezreel of the wounds which the Syrians had given him at Ramah, when he fought against Hazael king of Syria. And Ahaziah the son of Jehoram king of Judah went down to see Joram the son of Ahab in Jezreel, because he was sick.   2 Kin. 9:15-16

Elisha Sends a Prophet to Anoint Jehu King of Israel

9 And Elisha the prophet called one of the children of the prophets, and said unto him, Gird up thy loins, and take this box of oil in thine hand, and go to Ramoth-gilead: 1 Sam. 10:1; 16:1; 2 Kin. 4:29

2 And when thou comest thither, look out there Jehu the son of Jehoshaphat the son of Nimshi, and go in, and make him arise up from among his brethren, and carry him to an inner chamber;   2 Kin. 9:5

3 Then take the box of oil, and pour *it* on his head, and say, Thus saith the LORD, I have anointed thee king over Israel. Then open the door, and flee, and tarry not.   1 Kin. 19:16

4 So the young man, *even* the young man the prophet, went to Ramoth-gilead.

5 And when he came, behold, the captains of the host *were* sitting; and he said, I have an errand to thee, O captain. And Jehu said, Unto which of all us? And he said, To thee, O captain.

6 And he arose, and went into the house; and he poured the oil on his head, and said unto him, Thus saith the LORD God of Israel, I have anointed thee king over the people of the LORD, *even* over Israel.   1 Kin. 19:16

7 And thou shalt ᵀsmite the house of Ahab thy master, that I may avenge the blood of my servants the prophets, and the blood of all the servants of the LORD, at the hand of Jezebel.   Deut. 32:43; 1 Kin. 18:4; 21:15 ♦ *strike*

8 For the whole house of Ahab shall perish: and I will cut off from Ahab him that pisseth against the wall, and him that is shut up and left in Israel: Deut. 32:36; 1 Sam. 25:22; 2 Kin. 14:26

9 And I will make the house of Ahab like the house of Jeroboam the son of Nebat, and like the house of Baasha the son of Ahijah:

10 And the dogs shall eat Jezebel in the portion of Jezreel, and *there shall be* none to bury *her*. And he opened the door, and fled.

Jehu Kills Joram (Jehoram) of Israel and Ahaziah of Judah

11 Then Jehu came forth to the servants of his lord: and *one* said unto him, *Is* all well? wherefore came this mad *fellow* to thee? And he said unto them, Ye know the man, and his communication.   Jer. 29:26; Hos. 9:7; John 10:20

12 And they said, *It is* false; tell us now. And he said, Thus and thus spake he to me, saying, Thus saith the LORD, I have anointed thee king over Israel.

13 Then they hasted, and took every man his garment, and put *it* under him on the top of the stairs, and blew with trumpets, saying, Jehu is king.   2 Sam. 15:10; 1 Kin. 1:34, 39

14 So Jehu the son of Jehoshaphat the son of Nimshi conspired against Joram. (Now Joram had kept Ramoth-gilead, he and all Israel, because of Hazael king of Syria.   1 Kin. 22:3

15 But king Joram was returned to be healed in Jezreel of the wounds which the Syrians had given him, when he fought with Hazael king of Syria.) And Jehu said, If it be your

minds, *then* let none go forth *nor* escape out
of the city to go to tell *it* in Jezreel. 2 Kin. 8:29
16 So Jehu rode in a chariot, and went to
Jezreel; for Joram lay there. And Ahaziah
king of Judah was come down to see Joram.
17 And there stood a watchman on the
tower in Jezreel, and he spied the company
of Jehu as he came, and said, I see a company. And Joram said, Take an horseman,
and send to meet them, and let him say, *Is it*
peace?   1 Sam. 16:4
18 So there went one on horseback to meet
him, and said, Thus saith the king, *Is it*
peace? And Jehu said, What hast thou to do
with peace? turn thee behind me. And the
watchman told, saying, The messenger came
to them, but he cometh not again. 2 Kin. 9:19
19 Then he sent out a second on horseback,
which came to them, and said, Thus saith
the king, *Is it* peace? And Jehu answered,
What hast thou to do with peace? turn thee
behind me.
20 And the watchman told, saying, He came
even unto them, and cometh not again: and
the driving *is* like the driving of Jehu the son
of Nimshi; for he driveth furiously. 2 Sam. 18:27
21 And Joram said, Make ready. And his
chariot was made ready. And Joram king
of Israel and Ahaziah king of Judah went
out, each in his chariot, and they went out
against Jehu, and met him in the portion of
Naboth the Jezreelite.   1 Kin. 21:1-7
22 And it came to pass, when Joram saw
Jehu, that he said, *Is it* peace, Jehu? And he
answered, What peace, so long as the ᵀwhoredoms of thy mother Jezebel and her witch-
crafts *are so* many? 1 Kin. 16:30-33 ◆ *acts of prostitution*
23 And Joram turned his hands, and fled,
and said to Ahaziah, *There is* treachery, O
Ahaziah.   2 Kin. 11:14
24 And Jehu drew a bow with his full
strength, and smote Jehoram between his
arms, and the arrow went out at his heart,
and he sunk down in his chariot. 1 Kin. 22:34
25 Then said *Jehu* to Bidkar his captain, Take
up, *and* cast him in the portion of the field
of Naboth the Jezreelite: for remember how
that, when I and thou rode together after
Ahab his father, the LORD laid this burden
upon him;   1 Kin. 21:19, 24-29; Is. 13:1
26 Surely I have seen yesterday the blood of
Naboth, and the blood of his sons, saith the
LORD; and I will ᵀrequite thee in this plat,
saith the LORD. Now therefore take *and* cast
him into the plat *of ground*, according to the
word of the LORD.   *repay*
27 But when Ahaziah the king of Judah
saw *this*, he fled by the way of the garden
house. And Jehu followed after him, and
said, Smite him also in the chariot. *And they
did so* at the going up to Gur, which *is* by

Ibleam. And he fled to Megiddo, and died
there.   Josh. 17:11; Judg. 1:27
28 And his servants carried him in a chariot
to Jerusalem, and buried him in his sepulchre
with his fathers in the city of David. 2 Kin. 23:30
29 And in the eleventh year of Joram the
son of Ahab began Ahaziah to reign over
Judah.

Jezebel Dies Just as Elijah Had Predicted

30 And when Jehu was come to Jezreel, Jezebel heard *of it*; and she painted her face,
and tired her head, and looked out at a window.   Jer. 4:30; Ezek. 23:40
31 And as Jehu entered in at the gate, she
said, *Had* Zimri peace, who slew his master?   1 Kin. 16:9-20
32 And he lifted up his face to the window,
and said, Who *is* on my side? who? And
there looked out to him two *or* three ᵀeunuchs.   *castrated male servants*
33 And he said, Throw her down. So they
threw her down: and *some* of her blood was
sprinkled on the wall, and on the horses:
and he ᵀtrode her under foot.   *trampled*
34 And when he was come in, he did eat
and drink, and said, Go, see now this cursed
woman, and bury her: for she *is* a king's
daughter.   1 Kin. 16:31; 21:25
35 And they went to bury her: but they
found no more of her than the skull, and the
feet, and the palms of *her* hands.
36 Wherefore they came again, and told
him. And he said, This *is* the word of the
LORD, which he spake by his servant Elijah
the Tishbite, saying, In the portion of Jezreel
shall dogs eat the flesh of Jezebel: 1 Kin. 21:23
37 And the carcase of Jezebel shall be as
dung upon the face of the field in the portion of Jezreel; *so* that they shall not say, This
is Jezebel.   Ps. 83:10; Jer. 8:2; 16:4

Jehu Destroys Ahab's Family

10 And Ahab had seventy sons in Samaria. And Jehu wrote letters, and
sent to Samaria, unto the rulers of Jezreel,
to the elders, and to them that brought up
Ahab's *children*, saying,   Judg. 8:30
2 Now as soon as this letter cometh to you,
seeing your master's sons *are* with you, and
there are with you chariots and horses, a
fenced city also, and armour;   2 Kin. 5:6
3 Look even out the best and meetest of
your master's sons, and set *him* on his father's throne, and fight for your master's
house.
4 But they were exceedingly afraid, and said,
Behold, two kings stood not before him:
how then shall we stand?   2 Kin. 9:24
5 And he that *was* over the house, and he

that *was* over the city, the elders also, and the bringers up *of the children*, sent to Jehu, saying, We *are* thy servants, and will do all that thou shalt bid us; we will not make any king: do thou *that which is* good in thine eyes.   Josh. 9:11

6 Then he wrote a letter the second time to them, saying, If ye *be* mine, and *if* ye will hearken unto my voice, take ye the heads of the men your master's sons, and come to me to Jezreel by to morrow this time. Now the king's sons, *being* seventy persons, *were* with the great men of the city, which brought them up.

7 And it came to pass, when the letter came to them, that they took the king's sons, and slew seventy persons, and put their heads in baskets, and sent him *them* to Jezreel.   1 Kin. 21:21

8 And there came a messenger, and told him, saying, They have brought the heads of the king's sons. And he said, Lay ye them in two heaps at the entering in of the gate until the morning.

9 And it came to pass in the morning, that he went out, and stood, and said to all the people, Ye *be* righteous: behold, I conspired against my master, and slew him: but who slew all these?   2 Kin. 9:14-24

10 Know now that there shall fall unto the earth nothing of the word of the LORD, which the LORD spake concerning the house of Ahab: for the LORD hath done *that* which he spake by his servant Elijah.   1 Kin. 21:19, 29

11 So Jehu slew all that remained of the house of Ahab in Jezreel, and all his great men, and his kinsfolks, and his priests, until he left him none remaining.   Job 18:19

12 And he arose and departed, and came to Samaria. *And* as he *was* at the shearing house in the way,

13 Jehu met with the brethren of Ahaziah king of Judah, and said, Who *are* ye? And they answered, We *are* the brethren of Ahaziah; and we go down to salute the children of the king and the children of the queen.   2 Kin. 8:24, 29; 2 Chr. 21:17

14 And he said, Take them alive. And they took them alive, and slew them at the pit of the shearing house, *even* two and forty men; neither left he any of them.

Jehu Destroys the Worshippers of Baal

15 And when he was departed thence, he lighted on Jehonadab the son of Rechab *coming* to meet him: and he saluted him, and said to him, Is thine heart right, as my heart *is* with thy heart? And Jehonadab answered, It is. If it be, give *me* thine hand. And he gave *him* his hand; and he took him up to him into the chariot.   1 Chr. 2:55; Ezra 10:19; Ezek. 17:18

16 And he said, Come with me, and see my zeal for the LORD. So they made him ride in his chariot.   1 Kin. 19:10

17 And when he came to Samaria, he slew all that remained unto Ahab in Samaria, till he had destroyed him, according to the saying of the LORD, which he spake to Elijah.   2 Kin. 9:8; 2 Chr. 22:8

18 And Jehu gathered all the people together, and said unto them, Ahab served Baal a little; *but* Jehu shall serve him much.

19 Now therefore call unto me all the prophets of Baal, all his servants, and all his priests; let none be wanting: for I have a great sacrifice *to do* to Baal; whosoever shall be wanting, he shall not live. But Jehu did *it* in subtilty, to the intent that he might destroy the worshippers of Baal. 1 Kin. 18:19; 22:6

20 And Jehu said, Proclaim a solemn assembly for Baal. And they proclaimed *it*. Joel 1:14

21 And Jehu sent through all Israel: and all the worshippers of Baal came, so that there was not a man left that came not. And they came into the house of Baal; and the house of Baal was full from one end to another.

22 And he said unto him that *was* over the ᵀvestry, Bring forth ᵀvestments for all the worshippers of Baal. And he brought them forth vestments.   *wardrobe* ✦ *clothing*

23 And Jehu went, and Jehonadab the son of Rechab, into the house of Baal, and said unto the worshippers of Baal, Search, and look that there be here with you none of the servants of the LORD, but the worshippers of Baal only.

24 And when they went in to offer sacrifices and burnt offerings, Jehu appointed ᵀfourscore men without, and said, *If* any of the men whom I have brought into your hands escape, *he that letteth him go*, his life *shall be* for the life of him. 1 Kin. 20:30-42 ✦ *eighty*

25 And it came to pass, as soon as he had made an end of offering the burnt offering, that Jehu said to the guard and to the captains, Go in, *and* slay them; let none come forth. And they smote them with the edge of the sword; and the guard and the captains cast *them* out, and went to the city of the house of Baal.   1 Kin. 18:40

26 And they brought forth the images out of the house of Baal, and burned them.

27 And they brake down the image of Baal, and brake down the house of Baal, and made it a draught house unto this day.   Ezra 6:11

28 Thus Jehu destroyed Baal out of Israel.

Jehu Reigns in Israel, but Follows in Jeroboam's Sinful Path

29 Howbeit *from* the sins of Jeroboam the son of Nebat, who made Israel to sin, Jehu departed not from after them, ᵀ*to wit*, the

golden calves that *were* in Bethel, and that *were* in Dan. 1 Kin. 12:28-30; 13:33-34; 14:16 ✦ *namely*
30 And the LORD said unto Jehu, Because thou hast done well in executing *that which is* right in mine eyes, *and* hast done unto the house of Ahab according to all that *was* in mine heart, thy children of the fourth *generation* shall sit on the throne of Israel. 2 Kin. 10:35
31 But Jehu took no heed to walk in the law of the LORD God of Israel with all his heart: for he departed not from the sins of Jeroboam, which made Israel to sin.   2 Kin. 10:29
32 In those days the LORD began to cut Israel short: and Hazael smote them in all the coasts of Israel;   1 Kin. 19:17; 2 Kin. 8:12; 13:22
33 From Jordan eastward, all the land of Gilead, the Gadites, and the Reubenites, and the Manassites, from Aroer, which *is* by the river Arnon, even Gilead and Bashan.   Amos 1:3-4
34 Now the rest of the acts of Jehu, and all that he did, and all his might, *are* they not written in the book of the chronicles of the kings of Israel?
35 And Jehu slept with his fathers: and they buried him in Samaria. And Jehoahaz his son reigned in his stead.
36 And the time that Jehu reigned over Israel in Samaria *was* twenty and eight years.

In Judah, Young Joash Is Saved from Queen Athaliah's Murderous Rage

11 And when Athaliah the mother of Ahaziah saw that her son was dead, she arose and destroyed all the seed royal.
2 But Jehosheba, the daughter of king Joram, sister of Ahaziah, took Joash the son of Ahaziah, and stole him from among the king's sons *which were* slain; and they hid him, *even* him and his nurse, in the bedchamber from Athaliah, so that he was not slain.
3 And he was with her hid in the house of the LORD six years. And Athaliah did reign over the land.

Jehoiada Anoints Young Joash King over Judah

4 And the seventh year Jehoiada sent and fetched the rulers over hundreds, with the captains and the guard, and brought them to him into the house of the LORD, and made a covenant with them, and took an oath of them in the house of the LORD, and shewed them the king's son.   2 Kin. 11:9
5 And he commanded them, saying, This *is* the thing that ye shall do; A third part of you that enter in on the sabbath shall even be keepers of the watch of the king's house;   1 Chr. 9:25
6 And a third part *shall be* at the gate of Sur; and a third part at the gate behind the guard:

so shall ye keep the watch of the house, that it be not broken down.
7 And two parts of all you that go forth on the sabbath, even they shall keep the watch of the house of the LORD about the king.
8 And ye shall ᵀcompass the king round about, every man with his weapons in his hand: and he that cometh within the ranges, let him be slain: and be ye with the king as he goeth out and as he cometh in.   *surround*
9 And the captains over the hundreds did according to all *things* that Jehoiada the priest commanded: and they took every man his men that were to come in on the sabbath, with them that should go out on the sabbath, and came to Jehoiada the priest.   2 Chr. 23:8
10 And to the captains over hundreds did the priest give king David's spears and shields, that *were* in the temple of the LORD.   2 Sam. 8:7; 1 Chr. 18:7
11 And the guard stood, every man with his weapons in his hand, round about the king, from the right corner of the temple to the left corner of the temple, *along* by the altar and the temple.
12 And he brought forth the king's son, and put the crown upon him, and *gave him* the testimony; and they made him king, and anointed him; and they clapped their hands, and said, God save the king.   Ex. 25:16; 31:18

Athaliah Is Slain

13 And when Athaliah heard the noise of the guard *and* of the people, she came to the people into the temple of the LORD.
14 And when she looked, behold, the king stood by a pillar, as the manner *was*, and the princes and the trumpeters by the king, and all the people of the land rejoiced, and blew with trumpets: and Athaliah rent her clothes, and cried, Treason, Treason.   2 Kin. 9:23
15 But Jehoiada the priest commanded the captains of the hundreds, the officers of the host, and said unto them, Have her forth without the ranges: and him that followeth her kill with the sword. For the priest had said, Let her not be slain in the house of the LORD.
16 And they laid hands on her; and she went by the way by the which the horses came into the king's house: and there was she slain.   Gen. 9:6

Jehoiada Restores the Worship of God

17 And Jehoiada made a covenant between the LORD and the king and the people, that they should be the LORD's people; between the king also and the people.   Josh. 24:25
18 And all the people of the land went into the house of Baal, and brake it down; his

altars and his images brake they in pieces thoroughly, and slew Mattan the priest of Baal before the altars. And the priest appointed officers over the house of the LORD.   Deut. 12:3; 1 Kin. 18:40; 2 Kin. 10:26

19 And he took the rulers over hundreds, and the captains, and the guard, and all the people of the land; and they brought down the king from the house of the LORD, and came by the way of the gate of the guard to the king's house. And he sat on the throne of the kings.

20 And all the people of the land rejoiced, and the city was in quiet: and they slew Athaliah with the sword *beside* the king's house.   Prov. 11:10

21 Seven years old *was* Jehoash when he began to reign.   2 Chr. 24:1-14

Jehoash (Joash) Gives Orders to Repair the Temple

12 In the seventh year of Jehu Jehoash began to reign; and forty years reigned he in Jerusalem. And his mother's name *was* Zibiah of Beer-sheba.

2 And Jehoash did *that which was* right in the sight of the LORD all his days wherein Jehoiada the priest instructed him.

3 But the high places were not taken away: the people still sacrificed and burnt incense in the high places.   1 Kin. 15:14; 22:43; 2 Kin. 14:4

4 And Jehoash said to the priests, All the money of the dedicated things that is brought into the house of the LORD, *even* the money of every one that passeth *the account*, the money that every man is set at, *and* all the money that cometh into any man's heart to bring into the house of the LORD,   Ex. 35:5, 29; 2 Kin. 22:4

5 Let the priests take *it* to them, every man of his acquaintance: and let them repair the breaches of the house, wheresoever any breach shall be found.

6 But it was *so, that* in the three and twentieth year of king Jehoash the priests had not repaired the breaches of the house.

7 Then king Jehoash called for Jehoiada the priest, and the *other* priests, and said unto them, Why repair ye not the breaches of the house? now therefore receive no *more* money of your acquaintance, but deliver it for the breaches of the house.

8 And the priests consented to receive no *more* money of the people, neither to repair the breaches of the house.

9 But Jehoiada the priest took a chest, and bored a hole in the lid of it, and set it beside the altar, on the right side as one cometh into the house of the LORD: and the priests that kept the door put therein all the money *that was* brought into the house of the LORD.   Jer. 35:4; Mark 12:41; Luke 21:1

10 And it was *so*, when they saw that *there was* much money in the chest, that the king's scribe and the high priest came up, and they put up in bags, and told the money that was found in the house of the LORD.   2 Sam. 8:17

11 And they gave the money, being told, into the hands of them that did the work, that had the oversight of the house of the LORD: and they laid it out to the carpenters and builders, that ᵀwrought upon the house of the LORD,   worked

12 And to masons, and ᵀhewers of stone, and to buy timber and ᵀhewed stone to repair the breaches of the house of the LORD, and for all that was laid out for the house to repair *it*.   2 Kin. 22:5-6 ♦ cutters ♦ cut

13 Howbeit there were not made for the house of the LORD bowls of silver, snuffers, basons, trumpets, any vessels of gold, or vessels of silver, of the money *that was* brought into the house of the LORD: 2 Chr. 24:14

14 But they gave that to the workmen, and repaired therewith the house of the LORD.

15 Moreover they reckoned not with the men, into whose hand they delivered the money to be bestowed on workmen: for they dealt faithfully.   2 Kin. 22:7

16 The trespass money and sin money was not brought into the house of the LORD: it was the priests'.   Lev. 4:24; 5:15-18; 7:7

Hazael Is Diverted from Attacking Jerusalem by Gifts

17 Then Hazael king of Syria went up, and fought against Gath, and took it: and Hazael set his face to go up to Jerusalem. 2 Chr. 24:23-24

18 And Jehoash king of Judah took all the hallowed things that Jehoshaphat, and Jehoram, and Ahaziah, his fathers, kings of Judah, had dedicated, and his own hallowed things, and all the gold *that was* found in the treasures of the house of the LORD, and in the king's house, and sent *it* to Hazael king of Syria: and he went away from Jerusalem.   1 Kin. 15:18; 2 Kin. 18:15-16

19 And the rest of the acts of Joash, and all that he did, *are* they not written in the book of the chronicles of the kings of Judah?

20 And his servants arose, and made a conspiracy, and slew Joash in the house of Millo, which goeth down to Silla.   Judg. 9:6; 2 Sam. 5:9

21 For Jozachar the son of Shimeath, and Jehozabad the son of Shomer, his servants, smote him, and he died; and they buried him with his fathers in the city of David: and Amaziah his son reigned in his stead.

Jehoahaz's Evil Reign over Israel

13 In the three and twentieth year of Joash the son of Ahaziah king of Judah Jehoahaz the son of Jehu began to reign over Israel in Samaria, *and reigned* seventeen years.

2 And he did *that which was* evil in the sight of the LORD, and followed the sins of Jeroboam the son of Nebat, which made Israel to sin; he departed not therefrom.   1 Kin. 12:26-33

3 And the anger of the LORD was kindled against Israel, and he delivered them into the hand of Hazael king of Syria, and into the hand of Ben-hadad the son of Hazael, all *their* days.   Judg. 2:14; 1 Kin. 19:17; 2 Kin. 13:24-25

4 And Jehoahaz ᵀbesought the LORD, and the LORD hearkened unto him: for he saw the oppression of Israel, because the king of Syria oppressed them.   Ex. 3:7, 9; 2 Kin. 14:26 ◆ *begged*

5 (And the LORD gave Israel a saviour, so that they went out from under the hand of the Syrians: and the children of Israel dwelt in their tents, as beforetime.   2 Kin. 13:25

6 Nevertheless they departed not from the sins of the house of Jeroboam, who made Israel sin, *but* walked therein: and there remained the ᵀgrove also in Samaria.)   *idol*

7 Neither did he leave of the people to Jehoahaz but fifty horsemen, and ten chariots, and ten thousand footmen; for the king of Syria had destroyed them, and had made them like the dust by threshing.   Amos 1:3

8 Now the rest of the acts of Jehoahaz, and all that he did, and his might, *are* they not written in the book of the chronicles of the kings of Israel?

9 And Jehoahaz slept with his fathers; and they buried him in Samaria: and Joash his son reigned in his stead.

Jehoash's Evil Reign over Israel

10 In the thirty and seventh year of Joash king of Judah began Jehoash the son of Jehoahaz to reign over Israel in Samaria, *and reigned* sixteen years.

11 And he did *that which was* evil in the sight of the LORD; he departed not from all the sins of Jeroboam the son of Nebat, who made Israel sin: *but* he walked therein.   2 Kin. 13:2

12 And the rest of the acts of Joash, and all that he did, and his might wherewith he fought against Amaziah king of Judah, *are* they not written in the book of the chronicles of the kings of Israel?

13 And Joash slept with his fathers; and Jeroboam sat upon his throne: and Joash was buried in Samaria with the kings of Israel.

14 Now Elisha was fallen sick of his sickness whereof he died. And Joash the king of Israel came down unto him, and wept over his face, and said, O my father, my father, the chariot of Israel, and the horsemen thereof.   2 Kin. 2:12

15 And Elisha said unto him, Take bow and arrows. And he took unto him bow and arrows.

13:15–19 God Calls Men of Devotion

In proportion to the enthusiasm and perseverance with which the work is carried forward will be the success given. God can work miracles for His people only as they act their part with untiring energy. He calls for men of devotion to His work, men of moral courage, with ardent love for souls, and with a zeal that never flags. Such workers will find no task too arduous, no prospect too hopeless; they will labor on, undaunted, until apparent defeat is turned into glorious victory. *PK 263*

---

16 And he said to the king of Israel, Put thine hand upon the bow. And he put his hand *upon it*: and Elisha put his hands upon the king's hands.

17 And he said, Open the window eastward. And he opened *it*. Then Elisha said, Shoot. And he shot. And he said, The arrow of the

---

We Must Do Our Part

2 Kings 13:15–19

And now the prophet tested the faith of the king. Bidding Joash take up the arrows, [Elisha] said, "Smite upon the ground." Thrice the king smote the ground, and then he stayed his hand. "Thou shouldest have smitten five or six times," Elisha exclaimed in dismay; "then hadst thou smitten Syria till thou hadst consumed it: whereas now thou shalt smite Syria but thrice."

The lesson is for all in positions of trust. When God opens the way for the accomplishment of a certain work and gives assurance of success, the chosen instrumentality must do all in his power to bring about the promised result. In proportion to the enthusiasm and perseverance with which the work is carried forward will be the success given. God can work miracles for His people only as they act their part with untiring energy. He calls for men of devotion to His work, men of moral courage, with ardent love for souls, and with a zeal that never flags. Such workers will find no task too arduous, no prospect too hopeless; they will labor on, undaunted, until apparent defeat is turned into glorious victory. Not even prison walls nor the martyr's stake beyond, will cause them to swerve from their purpose of laboring together with God for the upbuilding of His kingdom. *PK 262, 263*

LORD's deliverance, and the arrow of deliverance from Syria: for thou shalt ᵀsmite the Syrians in Aphek, till thou have consumed *them.* 1 Kin. 20:26 ♦ *strike*

18 And he said, Take the arrows. And he took *them.* And he said unto the king of Israel, Smite upon the ground. And he smote ᵀthrice, and ᵀstayed. *three times* ♦ *stopped*

19 And the man of God was ᵀwroth with him, and said, Thou shouldest have smitten five or six times; then hadst thou smitten Syria till thou hadst consumed *it:* whereas now thou shalt smite Syria *but* thrice. 2 Kin. 13:25 ♦ *angry*

Elisha's Bones Raise a Dead Man

20 And Elisha died, and they buried him. And the bands of the Moabites invaded the land at the coming in of the year. 2 Kin. 3:7; 24:2

21 And it came to pass, as they were burying a man, that, behold, they spied a band *of men*; and they cast the man into the sepulchre of Elisha: and when the man was let down, and touched the bones of Elisha, he revived, and stood up on his feet.

22 But Hazael king of Syria oppressed Israel all the days of Jehoahaz. 2 Kin. 8:12

23 And the LORD was gracious unto them, and had compassion on them, and had respect unto them, because of his covenant with Abraham, Isaac, and Jacob, and would not destroy them, neither cast he them from his presence as yet. Gen. 13:16-17; 17:2-5; 2 Kin. 14:27

24 So Hazael king of Syria died; and Benhadad his son reigned in his stead.

25 And Jehoash the son of Jehoahaz took again out of the hand of Ben-hadad the son of Hazael the cities, which he had taken out of the hand of Jehoahaz his father by war. Three times did Joash beat him, and recovered the cities of Israel. 2 Kin. 10:32; 13:18-19

Amaziah's Good Reign over Judah

14 In the second year of Joash son of Jehoahaz king of Israel reigned Amaziah the son of Joash king of Judah. 2 Kin. 13:10

2 He was twenty and five years old when he began to reign, and reigned twenty and nine years in Jerusalem. And his mother's name *was* Jehoaddan of Jerusalem.

3 And he did *that which was* right in the sight of the LORD, yet not like David his father: he did according to all things as Joash his father did.

4 Howbeit the high places were not taken away: as yet the people did sacrifice and burnt incense on the high places. 2 Kin. 12:3; 16:4

5 And it came to pass, as soon as the kingdom was confirmed in his hand, that he slew his servants which had slain the king his father.

6 But the children of the murderers he slew not: according unto that which is written in the book of the law of Moses, wherein the LORD commanded, saying, The fathers shall not be put to death for the children, nor the children be put to death for the fathers; but every man shall be put to death for his own sin. Deut. 24:16; Ezek. 18:4, 20

7 He slew of Edom in the valley of salt ten thousand, and took Selah by war, and called the name of it Joktheel unto this day. Josh. 15:38

Jehoash of Israel Attacks Amaziah and Spoils Jerusalem

8 Then Amaziah sent messengers to Jehoash, the son of Jehoahaz son of Jehu, king of Israel, saying, Come, let us look one another in the face. 2 Chr. 25:17-24

9 And Jehoash the king of Israel sent to Amaziah king of Judah, saying, The thistle that *was* in Lebanon sent to the cedar that *was* in Lebanon, saying, Give thy daughter to my son to wife: and there passed by a wild beast that *was* in Lebanon, and ᵀtrode down the thistle. Judg. 9:8-15 ♦ *trampled*

10 Thou hast indeed smitten Edom, and thine heart hath lifted thee up: glory *of this*, and tarry at home: for why shouldest thou meddle to *thy* hurt, that thou shouldest fall, *even* thou, and Judah with thee? Deut. 8:14; 2 Chr. 26:16; 32:25

11 But Amaziah would not hear. Therefore Jehoash king of Israel went up; and he and Amaziah king of Judah looked one another in the face at Beth-shemesh, which *belongeth* to Judah. Josh. 19:38

12 And Judah was put to the worse before Israel; and they fled every man to their tents. 2 Sam. 18:17

13 And Jehoash king of Israel took Amaziah king of Judah, the son of Jehoash the son of Ahaziah, at Beth-shemesh, and came to Jerusalem, and brake down the wall of Jerusalem from the gate of Ephraim unto the corner gate, four hundred cubits. Neh. 8:16; 12:39

14 And he took all the gold and silver, and all the vessels that were found in the house of the LORD, and in the treasures of the king's house, and hostages, and returned to Samaria. 1 Kin. 7:51

Jeroboam II Succeeds Jehoash in Israel

15 Now the rest of the acts of Jehoash which he did, and his might, and how he fought with Amaziah king of Judah, *are* they not written in the book of the chronicles of the kings of Israel?

16 And Jehoash slept with his fathers, and was buried in Samaria with the kings of Israel; and Jeroboam his son reigned in his stead.

17 And Amaziah the son of Joash king of

Judah lived after the death of Jehoash son of Jehoahaz king of Israel fifteen years.

18 And the rest of the acts of Amaziah, *are* they not written in the book of the chronicles of the kings of Judah?

19 Now they made a conspiracy against him in Jerusalem: and he fled to Lachish; but they sent after him to Lachish, and slew him there.   Josh. 10:31

20 And they brought him on horses: and he was buried at Jerusalem with his fathers in the city of David.   2 Kin. 9:28

21 And all the people of Judah took Azariah, which *was* sixteen years old, and made him king instead of his father Amaziah.

22 He built Elath, and restored it to Judah, after that the king slept with his fathers.

Jeroboam's Evil Reign in Israel

23 In the fifteenth year of Amaziah the son of Joash king of Judah Jeroboam the son of Joash king of Israel began to reign in Samaria, *and reigned* forty and one years.

24 And he did *that which was* evil in the sight of the LORD: he departed not from all the sins of Jeroboam the son of Nebat, who made Israel to sin.

25 He restored the coast of Israel from the entering of Hamath unto the sea of the plain, according to the word of the LORD God of Israel, which he spake by the hand of his servant Jonah, the son of Amittai, the prophet, which *was* of Gath-hepher. Deut. 3:17; Josh. 19:13

26 For the LORD saw the affliction of Israel, *that it was* very bitter: for *there was* not any shut up, nor any left, nor any helper for Israel.   Ex. 3:7; Deut. 32:36; 2 Kin. 13:4

27 And the LORD said not that he would blot out the name of Israel from under heaven: but he saved them by the hand of Jeroboam the son of Joash.   2 Kin. 13:5, 23

28 Now the rest of the acts of Jeroboam, and all that he did, and his might, how he warred, and how he recovered Damascus, and Hamath, *which belonged* to Judah, for Israel, are they not written in the book of the chronicles of the kings of Israel?   2 Sam. 8:6; 1 Chr. 18:5-6

29 And Jeroboam slept with his fathers, *even* with the kings of Israel; and Zachariah his son reigned in his stead.

Azariah's (Uzziah's) Good Reign over Judah

15 In the twenty and seventh year of Jeroboam king of Israel began Azariah son of Amaziah king of Judah to reign. 2 Kin. 14:21

2 Sixteen years old was he when he began to reign, and he reigned two and fifty years in Jerusalem. And his mother's name *was* Jecholiah of Jerusalem.

3 And he did *that which was* right in the sight of the LORD, according to all that his father Amaziah had done;

4 Save that the high places were not removed: the people sacrificed and burnt incense still on the high places.

5 And the LORD smote the king, so that he was a leper unto the day of his death, and dwelt in a several house. And Jotham the king's son *was* over the house, judging the people of the land.   Lev. 13:46; Num. 12:14

6 And the rest of the acts of Azariah, and all that he did, *are* they not written in the book of the chronicles of the kings of Judah?

7 So Azariah slept with his fathers; and they buried him with his fathers in the city of David: and Jotham his son reigned in his stead.   2 Chr. 26:23

Zachariah, Shallum, and Others Reign Evilly over Israel

8 In the thirty and eighth year of Azariah king of Judah did Zachariah the son of Jeroboam reign over Israel in Samaria six months.

9 And he did *that which was* evil in the sight of the LORD, as his fathers had done: he departed not from the sins of Jeroboam the son of Nebat, who made Israel to sin.

10 And Shallum the son of Jabesh conspired against him, and smote him before the people, and slew him, and reigned in his stead.

11 And the rest of the acts of Zachariah, behold, they *are* written in the book of the chronicles of the kings of Israel.

12 This *was* the word of the LORD which he spake unto Jehu, saying, Thy sons shall sit on the throne of Israel unto the fourth *generation*. And so it came to pass.   2 Kin. 10:30

13 Shallum the son of Jabesh began to reign in the nine and thirtieth year of Uzziah king of Judah; and he reigned a full month in Samaria.   2 Kin. 15:1

14 For Menahem the son of Gadi went up from Tirzah, and came to Samaria, and smote Shallum the son of Jabesh in Samaria, and slew him, and reigned in his stead. 1 Kin. 14:17

15 And the rest of the acts of Shallum, and his conspiracy which he made, behold, they *are* written in the book of the chronicles of the kings of Israel.

16 Then Menahem smote Tiphsah, and all that *were* therein, and the coasts thereof from Tirzah: because they opened not *to him*, therefore he smote *it; and* all the women therein that were with child he ripped up.   Hos. 13:16

17 In the nine and thirtieth year of Azariah king of Judah began Menahem the son of Gadi to reign over Israel, *and reigned* ten years in Samaria.

18 And he did *that which was* evil in the sight

of the LORD: he departed not all his days from the sins of Jeroboam the son of Nebat, who made Israel to sin.

19 *And* Pul the king of Assyria came against the land: and Menahem gave Pul a thousand talents of silver, that his hand might be with him to confirm the kingdom in his hand. 2 Kin. 14:5

20 And Menahem exacted the money of Israel, *even* of all the mighty men of wealth, of each man fifty shekels of silver, to give to the king of Assyria. So the king of Assyria turned back, and stayed not there in the land.

21 And the rest of the acts of Menahem, and all that he did, *are* they not written in the book of the chronicles of the kings of Israel?

22 And Menahem slept with his fathers; and Pekahiah his son reigned in his stead.

23 In the fiftieth year of Azariah king of Judah Pekahiah the son of Menahem began to reign over Israel in Samaria, *and reigned* two years.

24 And he did *that which was* evil in the sight of the LORD: he departed not from the sins of Jeroboam the son of Nebat, who made Israel to sin. 2 Kin. 15:9

25 But Pekah the son of Remaliah, a captain of his, conspired against him, and smote him in Samaria, in the palace of the king's house, with Argob and Arieh, and with him fifty men of the Gileadites: and he killed him, and reigned in his room. 2 Chr. 28:6

26 And the rest of the acts of Pekahiah, and all that he did, behold, they *are* written in the book of the chronicles of the kings of Israel.

27 In the two and fiftieth year of Azariah king of Judah Pekah the son of Remaliah began to reign over Israel in Samaria, *and reigned* twenty years. Is. 7:1

28 And he did *that which was* evil in the sight of the LORD: he departed not from the sins of Jeroboam the son of Nebat, who made Israel to sin.

29 In the days of Pekah king of Israel came Tiglath-pileser king of Assyria, and took Ijon, and Abel-beth-maachah, and Janoah, and Kedesh, and Hazor, and Gilead, and Galilee, all the land of Naphtali, and carried them captive to Assyria. Josh. 20:7

30 And Hoshea the son of Elah made a conspiracy against Pekah the son of Remaliah, and smote him, and slew him, and reigned in his stead, in the twentieth year of Jotham the son of Uzziah. 2 Kin. 17:1

31 And the rest of the acts of Pekah, and all that he did, behold, they *are* written in the book of the chronicles of the kings of Israel.

Jotham's Good Reign over Judah

32 In the second year of Pekah the son of Remaliah king of Israel began Jotham the son of Uzziah king of Judah to reign. 2 Kin. 15:7

33 Five and twenty years old was he when he began to reign, and he reigned sixteen years in Jerusalem. And his mother's name *was* Jerusha, the daughter of Zadok. 2 Chr. 27:1

34 And he did *that which was* right in the sight of the LORD: he did according to all that his father Uzziah had done. 2 Chr. 26:4-5

35 Howbeit the high places were not removed: the people sacrificed and burned incense still in the high places. He built the higher gate of the house of the LORD. 2 Kin. 12:3

36 Now the rest of the acts of Jotham, and all that he did, *are* they not written in the book of the chronicles of the kings of Judah?

37 In those days the LORD began to send against Judah Rezin the king of Syria, and Pekah the son of Remaliah. 2 Kin. 16:5; Is. 7:1

38 And Jotham slept with his fathers, and was buried with his fathers in the city of David his father: and Ahaz his son reigned in his stead.

Ahaz's Evil Reign over Judah

16 In the seventeenth year of Pekah the son of Remaliah Ahaz the son of Jotham king of Judah began to reign. Is. 1:1

2 Twenty years old *was* Ahaz when he began to reign, and reigned sixteen years in Jerusalem, and did not *that which was* right in the sight of the LORD his God, like David his father.

3 But he walked in the way of the kings of Israel, yea, and made his son to pass through the fire, according to the abominations of the heathen, whom the LORD cast out from before the children of Israel. Lev. 18:21; Deut. 12:31

4 And he sacrificed and burnt incense in the high places, and on the hills, and under every green tree. Deut. 12:2; 1 Kin. 14:23

Ahaz, Attacked by Rezin and Pekah, Hires Tiglath-pileser to Fight

5 Then Rezin king of Syria and Pekah son of Remaliah king of Israel came up to Jerusalem to war: and they besieged Ahaz, but could not overcome *him*. 2 Kin. 15:37

6 At that time Rezin king of Syria recovered Elath to Syria, and ᵀdrave the Jews from Elath: and the Syrians came to Elath, and dwelt there unto this day. 2 Chr. 26:2 ◆ drove

7 So Ahaz sent messengers to Tiglath-pileser king of Assyria, saying, I *am* thy servant and thy son: come up, and save me out of the hand of the king of Syria, and out of the hand of the king of Israel, which rise up against me. 2 Kin. 15:29

16:5–7 Sin Brought Fear and Dread

Had Ahaz and the chief men of his realm been true servants of the Most High, they would have had no fear of so unnatural an alliance as had been formed against them. But repeated transgression had shorn them of strength. . . .

Well would it have been for the kingdom of Judah had Ahaz received this message as from heaven. But choosing to lean on the arm of flesh, he sought help from the heathen. *PK 328, 329*

8 And Ahaz took the silver and gold that was found in the house of the LORD, and in the treasures of the king's house, and sent *it for* a present to the king of Assyria.   2 Kin. 12:17-18
9 And the king of Assyria hearkened unto him: for the king of Assyria went up against Damascus, and took it, and carried *the people of* it captive to Kir, and slew Rezin.   Is. 22:6

Ahaz Sends the Pattern of an Altar in Damascus to Urijah

10 And king Ahaz went to Damascus to meet Tiglath-pileser king of Assyria, and saw an altar that *was* at Damascus: and king Ahaz sent to Urijah the priest the fashion of the altar, and the pattern of it, according to all the workmanship thereof.   Is. 8:2
11 And Urijah the priest built an altar according to all that king Ahaz had sent from Damascus: so Urijah the priest made *it* against king Ahaz came from Damascus.
12 And when the king was come from Damascus, the king saw the altar: and the king approached to the altar, and offered thereon.   2 Chr. 26:16-19
13 And he burnt his burnt offering and his meat offering, and poured his drink offering, and sprinkled the blood of his peace offerings, upon the altar.
14 And he brought also the brasen altar, which *was* before the LORD, from the forefront of the house, from between the altar and the house of the LORD, and put it on the north side of the altar.   Ex. 40:6, 29; 2 Chr. 4:1
15 And king Ahaz commanded Urijah the priest, saying, Upon the great altar burn the morning burnt offering, and the evening meat offering, and the king's burnt sacrifice, and his meat offering, with the burnt offering of all the people of the land, and their meat offering, and their drink offerings; and sprinkle upon it all the blood of the burnt offering, and all the blood of the sacrifice: and the brasen altar shall be for me to enquire by.   Ex. 29:39-41
16 Thus did Urijah the priest, according to all that king Ahaz commanded.

Ahaz Spoils the Temple

17 And king Ahaz cut off the borders of the bases, and removed the ᵀlaver from off them; and took down the sea from off the brasen oxen that *were* under it, and put it upon a pavement of stones.   *basin for washing*
18 And the ᵀcovert for the sabbath that they had built in the house, and the king's entry without, turned he from the house of the LORD for the king of Assyria.   *cover*
19 Now the rest of the acts of Ahaz which he did, *are* they not written in the book of the chronicles of the kings of Judah?
20 And Ahaz slept with his fathers, and was buried with his fathers in the city of David: and Hezekiah his son reigned in his stead.

During Hoshea's Evil Reign, Israel Is Conquered and Exiled

17 In the twelfth year of Ahaz king of Judah began Hoshea the son of Elah to reign in Samaria over Israel nine years.
2 And he did *that which was* evil in the sight of the LORD, but not as the kings of Israel that were before him.
3 Against him came up Shalmaneser king of Assyria; and Hoshea became his servant, and gave him presents.   Hos. 10:14
4 And the king of Assyria found conspiracy in Hoshea: for he had sent messengers to So king of Egypt, and brought no present to the king of Assyria, as *he had done* year by year: therefore the king of Assyria shut him up, and bound him in prison.
5 Then the king of Assyria came up throughout all the land, and went up to Samaria, and besieged it three years.
6 In the ninth year of Hoshea the king of Assyria took Samaria, and carried Israel away into Assyria, and placed them in Halah and in Habor *by* the river of Gozan, and in the cities of the Medes.   Deut. 28:64; 1 Chr. 5:26; Hos. 13:16
7 For *so* it was, that the children of Israel sinned against the LORD their God, which had brought them up out of the land of Egypt, from under the hand of Pharaoh king of Egypt, and had feared other gods,   Josh. 23:16
8 And walked in the statutes of the heathen, whom the LORD cast out from before the children of Israel, and of the kings of Israel, which they had made.   Lev. 18:3; Deut. 18:9; 2 Kin. 16:3
9 And the children of Israel did secretly *those* things that *were* not right against the LORD their God, and they built them high places in all their cities, from the tower of the watchmen to the fenced city.   2 Kin. 18:8
10 And they set them up images and ᵀgroves in every high hill, and under every green tree: Ex. 34:13; 1 Kin. 14:23; 2 Kin. 16:4 ◆ *idols*

11 And there they burnt incense in all the high places, as *did* the heathen whom the LORD carried away before them; and ᵀwrought wicked things to provoke the LORD to anger: *did*

12 For they served idols, whereof the LORD had said unto them, Ye shall not do this thing.

13 Yet the LORD testified against Israel, and against Judah, by all the prophets, *and by* all the seers, saying, Turn ye from your evil ways, and keep my commandments *and* my statutes, according to all the law which I commanded your fathers, and which I sent to you by my servants the prophets.   1 Sam. 9:9; Jer. 18:11; 35:15

14 Notwithstanding they would not hear, but hardened their necks, like to the neck of their fathers, that did not believe in the LORD their God.   Deut. 31:27

15 And they rejected his statutes, and his covenant that he made with their fathers, and his testimonies which he testified against them; and they followed vanity, and became vain, and went after the heathen that *were* round about them, *concerning* whom the LORD had charged them, that they should not do like them.   Deut. 12:30-31; 32:21; Jer. 2:5

16 And they left all the commandments of the LORD their God, and made them molten images, *even* two calves, and made a ᵀgrove, and worshipped all the host of heaven, and served Baal.   1 Kin. 12:28; 14:15, 23 ✦ *idol*

17 And they caused their sons and their daughters to pass through the fire, and used ᵀdivination and enchantments, and sold themselves to do evil in the sight of the LORD, to provoke him to anger. 2 Kin. 16:3; 21:6 ✦ *false magic*

18 Therefore the LORD was very angry with Israel, and removed them out of his sight: there was none left but the tribe of Judah only.   1 Kin. 11:13

19 Also Judah kept not the commandments of the LORD their God, but walked in the statutes of Israel which they made.   1 Kin. 14:22-23

20 And the LORD rejected all the seed of Israel, and afflicted them, and delivered them into the hand of spoilers, until he had cast them out of his sight.   2 Kin. 13:3; 15:29

21 For he ᵀrent Israel from the house of David; and they made Jeroboam the son of Nebat king: and Jeroboam ᵀdrave Israel from following the LORD, and made them sin a great sin.   1 Kin. 11:11, 31; 12:28-30 ✦ *tore* ✦ *drove*

22 For the children of Israel walked in all the sins of Jeroboam which he did; they departed not from them;

23 Until the LORD removed Israel out of his sight, as he had said by all his servants the prophets. So was Israel carried away out of their own land to Assyria unto this day.

The Foreign Nations, Transplanted in Samaria, Make a Mixture of Religions

24 And the king of Assyria brought *men* from Babylon, and from Cuthah, and from Ava, and from Hamath, and from Sepharvaim, and placed *them* in the cities of Samaria instead of the children of Israel: and they possessed Samaria, and dwelt in the cities thereof.   2 Kin. 18:34

25 And *so* it was at the beginning of their dwelling there, *that* they feared not the LORD: therefore the LORD sent lions among them, which slew *some* of them.   2 Kin. 17:32

26 Wherefore they spake to the king of Assyria, saying, The nations which thou hast removed, and placed in the cities of Samaria, know not the manner of the God of the land: therefore he hath sent lions among them, and, behold, they slay them, because they know not the manner of the God of the land.

27 Then the king of Assyria commanded, saying, Carry thither one of the priests whom ye brought from thence; and let them go and dwell there, and let him teach them the manner of the God of the land.

28 Then one of the priests whom they had carried away from Samaria came and dwelt in Bethel, and taught them how they should fear the LORD.

29 Howbeit every nation made gods of their own, and put *them* in the houses of the high places which the Samaritans had made, every nation in their cities wherein they dwelt.   1 Kin. 12:31

30 And the men of Babylon made Succothbenoth, and the men of Cuth made Nergal, and the men of Hamath made Ashima,

31 And the Avites made Nibhaz and Tartak, and the Sepharvites burnt their children in fire to Adrammelech and Anammelech, the gods of Sepharvaim.   2 Kin. 17:17, 24; 19:37

32 So they feared the LORD, and made unto themselves of the lowest of them priests of the high places, which sacrificed for them in the houses of the high places.   1 Kin. 12:31

33 They feared the LORD, and served their own gods, after the manner of the nations whom they carried away from thence.

34 Unto this day they do after the former manners: they fear not the LORD, neither do they after their statutes, or after their ordinances, or after the law and commandment which the LORD commanded the children of Jacob, whom he named Israel; Gen. 32:28; 35:10

35 With whom the LORD had made a covenant, and charged them, saying, Ye shall not fear other gods, nor bow yourselves to them, nor serve them, nor sacrifice to them: Judg. 6:10

36 But the LORD, who brought you up out of the land of Egypt with great power and

a stretched out arm, him shall ye fear, and him shall ye worship, and to him shall ye do sacrifice.   Ex. 6:6; 9:15; Deut. 6:13
37 And the statutes, and the ordinances, and the law, and the commandment, which he wrote for you, ye shall observe to do for evermore; and ye shall not fear other gods.
38 And the covenant that I have made with you ye shall not forget; neither shall ye fear other gods.   Deut. 4:23; 6:12
39 But the LORD your God ye shall fear; and he shall deliver you out of the hand of all your enemies.   2 Kin. 17:36
40 Howbeit they did not hearken, but they did after their former manner.
41 So these nations feared the LORD, and served their ᵀgraven images, both their children, and their children's children: as did their fathers, so do they unto this day. Zeph. 1:5

Hezekiah's Good Reign over Judah

18 Now it came to pass in the third year of Hoshea son of Elah king of Israel, *that* Hezekiah the son of Ahaz king of Judah began to reign.

18:1–3 No Halfway Measures

In sharp contrast with the reckless rule of Ahaz was the reformation wrought during the prosperous reign of his son. Hezekiah came to the throne determined to do all in his power to save Judah from the fate that was overtaking the northern kingdom. The messages of the prophets offered no encouragement to halfway measures. Only by most decided reformation could the threatened judgments be averted. *PK 331*

2 Twenty and five years old was he when he began to reign; and he reigned twenty and nine years in Jerusalem. His mother's name also *was* Abi, the daughter of Zachariah.
3 And he did *that which was* right in the sight of the LORD, according to all that David his father did.   2 Kin. 20:3
4 He removed the high places, and brake the images, and cut down the ᵀgroves, and brake in pieces the brasen serpent that Moses had made: for unto those days the children of Israel did burn incense to it: and he called it Nehushtan.   Num. 21:8-9; 2 Chr. 31:1 ◆ idols

18:3, 4 Man of Opportunity

In the crisis, Hezekiah proved to be a man of opportunity. No sooner had he ascended the throne than he began to plan and to execute. He first turned his attention to the restoration of the temple services, so long neglected; and in this work he earnestly solicited the co-operation of a band of priests and Levites who had remained true to their sacred calling. *PK 331*

5 He trusted in the LORD God of Israel; so that after him was none like him among all the kings of Judah, nor *any* that were before him.   2 Kin. 19:10; 23:25
6 For he ᵀclave to the LORD, *and* departed not from following him, but kept his commandments, which the LORD commanded Moses.   Deut. 10:20; Josh. 23:8; John 14:15 ◆ clung
7 And the LORD was with him; *and* he prospered whithersoever he went forth: and he rebelled against the king of Assyria, and served him not. Gen. 39:2-3; 1 Sam. 18:14; 2 Kin. 16:7
8 He smote the Philistines, *even* unto Gaza, and the borders thereof, from the tower of the watchmen to the fenced city.   Is. 14:29

Assyria Destroys Israel and Later Attacks Judah

9 And it came to pass in the fourth year of king Hezekiah, which *was* the seventh year of Hoshea son of Elah king of Israel, *that* Shalmaneser king of Assyria came up against Samaria, and besieged it.
10 And at the end of three years they took it: *even* in the sixth year of Hezekiah, that *is* the ninth year of Hoshea king of Israel, Samaria was taken.
11 And the king of Assyria did carry away Israel unto Assyria, and put them in Halah and in Habor *by* the river of Gozan, and in the cities of the Medes: 1 Chr. 5:26
12 Because they obeyed not the voice of the LORD their God, but ᵀtransgressed his covenant, *and* all that Moses the servant of the LORD commanded, and would not hear *them*, nor do *them*.   violated
13 Now in the fourteenth year of king Hezekiah did Sennacherib king of Assyria come up against all the fenced cities of Judah, and took them.   Is. 36
14 And Hezekiah king of Judah sent to the king of Assyria to Lachish, saying, I have offended; return from me: that which thou puttest on me will I bear. And the king of Assyria appointed unto Hezekiah king of Judah three hundred talents of silver and thirty talents of gold.   2 Kin. 18:7
15 And Hezekiah gave *him* all the silver that was found in the house of the LORD, and in the treasures of the king's house. 2 Kin. 12:18
16 At that time did Hezekiah cut off *the gold from* the doors of the temple of the LORD, and *from* the pillars which Hezekiah king of Judah had overlaid, and gave it to the king of Assyria.

Sennacherib Threatens to Destroy Jerusalem

17 And the king of Assyria sent Tartan and Rab-saris and Rab-shakeh from Lachish to king Hezekiah with a great host against

Jerusalem. And they went up and came to Jerusalem. And when they were come up, they came and stood by the conduit of the upper pool, which *is* in the highway of the ᵀfuller's field.   2 Kin. 20:20; Is. 7:3; 20:1 ♦ *one who washes clothes*

18 And when they had called to the king, there came out to them Eliakim the son of Hilkiah, which *was* over the household, and Shebna the scribe, and Joah the son of Asaph the recorder.   2 Kin. 19:2

19 And Rab-shakeh said unto them, Speak ye now to Hezekiah, Thus saith the great king, the king of Assyria, What confidence *is* this wherein thou trustest?   Is. 36:4

20 Thou sayest, (but *they are but* vain words,) *I have* counsel and strength for the war. Now on whom dost thou trust, that thou rebellest against me?

21 Now, behold, thou trustest upon the staff of this bruised reed, *even* upon Egypt, on which if a man lean, it will go into his hand, and pierce it: so *is* Pharaoh king of Egypt unto all that trust on him.   Is. 30:7; Ezek. 29:6-7

22 But if ye say unto me, We trust in the LORD our God: *is* not that he, whose high places and whose altars Hezekiah hath taken away, and hath said to Judah and Jerusalem, Ye shall worship before this altar in Jerusalem?   2 Chr. 31:1

23 Now therefore, I pray thee, give pledges to my lord the king of Assyria, and I will deliver thee two thousand horses, if thou be able on thy part to set riders upon them.

24 How then wilt thou turn away the face of one captain of the least of my master's servants, and put thy trust on Egypt for chariots and for horsemen?   Is. 10:8

25 Am I now come up without the LORD against this place to destroy it? The LORD said to me, Go up against this land, and destroy it.   2 Kin. 19:6

26 Then said Eliakim the son of Hilkiah, and Shebna, and Joah, unto Rab-shakeh, Speak, I pray thee, to thy servants in the Syrian language; for we understand *it:* and talk not with us in the Jews' language in the ears of the people that *are* on the wall.   Ezra 4:7; Dan. 2:4

27 But Rab-shakeh said unto them, Hath my master sent me to thy master, and to thee, to speak these words? *hath he* not *sent me* to the men which sit on the wall, that they may eat their own dung, and drink their own piss with you?

28 Then Rab-shakeh stood and cried with a loud voice in the Jews' language, and spake, saying, Hear the word of the great king, the king of Assyria:

29 Thus saith the king, Let not Hezekiah deceive you: for he shall not be able to deliver you out of his hand: 2 Chr. 32:15

30 Neither let Hezekiah make you trust in the LORD, saying, The LORD will surely deliver us, and this city shall not be delivered into the hand of the king of Assyria.

31 Hearken not to Hezekiah: for thus saith the king of Assyria, Make an agreement with me by a present, and come out to me, and then eat ye every man of his own vine, and every one of his fig tree, and drink ye every one the waters of his ᵀcistern: 1 Kin. 4:20, 25 ♦ *well*

32 Until I come and take you away to a land like your own land, a land of corn and wine, a land of bread and vineyards, a land of oil olive and of honey, that ye may live, and not die: and hearken not unto Hezekiah, when he persuadeth you, saying, The LORD will deliver us.   Deut. 8:7-9

33 Hath any of the gods of the nations delivered at all his land out of the hand of the king of Assyria?   Is. 10:10-11

34 Where *are* the gods of Hamath, and of Arpad? where *are* the gods of Sepharvaim, Hena, and Ivah? have they delivered Samaria out of mine hand?   Is. 10:9

35 Who *are* they among all the gods of the countries, that have delivered their country out of mine hand, that the LORD should deliver Jerusalem out of mine hand?   Dan. 3:15

36 But the people held their peace, and answered him not a word: for the king's commandment was, saying, Answer him not.

37 Then came Eliakim the son of Hilkiah, which *was* over the household, and Shebna the scribe, and Joah the son of Asaph the recorder, to Hezekiah with *their* clothes rent, and told him the words of Rab-shakeh.

Isaiah Prophesies Jerusalem's Deliverance from Sennacherib

19 And it came to pass, when king Hezekiah heard *it,* that he ᵀrent his clothes, and covered himself with sackcloth, and went into the house of the LORD.   1 Kin. 21:27 ♦ *tore*

2 And he sent Eliakim, which *was* over the household, and Shebna the scribe, and the elders of the priests, covered with sackcloth, to Isaiah the prophet the son of Amoz.   Is. 1:1

3 And they said unto him, Thus saith Hezekiah, This day *is* a day of trouble, and of rebuke, and blasphemy: for the children are come to the birth, and *there is* not strength to bring forth.

4 It may be the LORD thy God will hear all the words of Rab-shakeh, whom the king of Assyria his master hath sent to reproach the living God; and will reprove the words which the LORD thy God hath heard: wherefore lift up *thy* prayer for the remnant that are left.   Josh. 14:12; 2 Sam. 16:12

5 So the servants of king Hezekiah came to Isaiah.

6 And Isaiah said unto them, Thus shall ye say to your master, Thus saith the LORD, Be not afraid of the words which thou hast heard, with which the servants of the king of Assyria have blasphemed me.   2 Kin. 18:17
7 Behold, I will send a blast upon him, and he shall hear a rumour, and shall return to his own land; and I will cause him to fall by the sword in his own land.   2 Kin. 7:6

Sennacherib Sends a Blasphemous Letter to Hezekiah

8 So Rab-shakeh returned, and found the king of Assyria warring against Libnah: for he had heard that he was departed from Lachish.   Josh. 10:29; 2 Kin. 18:14
9 And when he heard say of Tirhakah king of Ethiopia, Behold, he is come out to fight against thee: he sent messengers again unto Hezekiah, saying,   1 Sam. 23:27
10 Thus shall ye speak to Hezekiah king of Judah, saying, Let not thy God in whom thou trustest deceive thee, saying, Jerusalem shall not be delivered into the hand of the king of Assyria.   2 Kin. 18:5, 29-30
11 Behold, thou hast heard what the kings of Assyria have done to all lands, by destroying them utterly: and shalt thou be delivered?
12 Have the gods of the nations delivered them which my fathers have destroyed; as Gozan, and Haran, and Rezeph, and the children of Eden which were in Thelasar? Gen. 11:31
13 Where is the king of Hamath, and the king of Arpad, and the king of the city of Sepharvaim, of Hena, and Ivah?   2 Kin. 18:34
14 And Hezekiah received the letter of the hand of the messengers, and read it: and Hezekiah went up into the house of the LORD, and spread it before the LORD. Is. 37:14
15 And Hezekiah prayed before the LORD, and said, O LORD God of Israel, which dwellest between the cherubims, thou art the God, even thou alone, of all the kingdoms of the earth; thou hast made heaven and earth.   Ex. 25:22; 1 Kin. 18:39; 2 Kin. 5:15
16 LORD, bow down thine ear, and hear: open, LORD, thine eyes, and see: and hear the words of Sennacherib, which hath sent him to reproach the living God.   2 Chr. 6:40; Ps. 31:2
17 Of a truth, LORD, the kings of Assyria have destroyed the nations and their lands,
18 And have cast their gods into the fire: for they were no gods, but the work of men's hands, wood and stone: therefore they have destroyed them.   Acts 17:29
19 Now therefore, O LORD our God, I ᵀbeseech thee, save thou us out of his hand, that all the kingdoms of the earth may know that thou art the LORD God, even thou only.   1 Kin. 8:43 ◆ beg

Isaiah Prophesies the Destruction of Sennacherib

20 Then Isaiah the son of Amoz sent to Hezekiah, saying, Thus saith the LORD God of Israel, That which thou hast prayed to me against Sennacherib king of Assyria I have heard.   2 Kin. 20:5

19:20 The Exercise of Faith

Nothing more quickly inspires faith than the exercise of faith. The king of Judah had prepared for the coming storm; and now, confident that the prophecy against the Assyrians would be fulfilled, he stayed his soul upon God. PK 351

21 This is the word that the LORD hath spoken concerning him; The virgin the daughter of Zion hath despised thee, and laughed thee to scorn; the daughter of Jerusalem hath shaken her head at thee.   Jer. 14:17; Lam. 2:13
22 Whom hast thou reproached and blasphemed? and against whom hast thou exalted thy voice, and lifted up thine eyes on high? even against the Holy One of Israel.   Ps. 71:22
23 By thy messengers thou hast reproached the Lord, and hast said, With the multitude of my chariots I am come up to the height of the mountains, to the sides of Lebanon, and will cut down the tall cedar trees thereof, and the choice fir trees thereof: and I will enter into the lodgings of his borders, and into the forest of his Carmel.   2 Kin. 18:17
24 I have digged and drunk strange waters, and with the sole of my feet have I dried up all the rivers of besieged places.
25 Hast thou not heard long ago how I have done it, and of ancient times that I have formed it? now have I brought it to pass, that thou shouldest be to lay waste fenced cities into ruinous heaps.   Is. 45:7
26 Therefore their inhabitants were of small power, they were dismayed and confounded; they were as the grass of the field, and as the green herb, as the grass on the housetops, and as corn blasted before it be grown up.
27 But I know thy abode, and thy going out, and thy coming in, and thy rage against me.
28 Because thy rage against me and thy tumult is come up into mine ears, therefore I will put my hook in thy nose, and my bridle in thy lips, and I will turn thee back by the way by which thou camest.   Job 41:2; Ezek. 29:4
29 And this shall be a sign unto thee, Ye shall eat this year such things as grow of themselves, and in the second year that which springeth of the same; and in the third year sow ye, and reap, and plant vineyards, and eat the fruits thereof. Ex. 3:12; 1 Sam. 2:34; 2 Kin. 20:8-9
30 And the remnant that is escaped of the

house of Judah shall yet again take root downward, and bear fruit upward.   *2 Chr. 32:22-23*

31 For out of Jerusalem shall go forth a remnant, and they that escape out of mount Zion: the zeal of the LORD *of hosts* shall do this.   *Is. 9:7*

32 Therefore thus saith the LORD concerning the king of Assyria, He shall not come into this city, nor shoot an arrow there, nor come before it with shield, nor cast a bank against it.   *2 Sam. 20:15*

33 By the way that he came, by the same shall he return, and shall not come into this city, saith the LORD.   *2 Kin. 19:28*

34 For I will defend this city, to save it, for mine own sake, and for my servant David's sake.   *1 Kin. 11:12-13; 2 Kin. 20:6; Is. 31:5*

The Angel of the Lord Slays the Assyrians

35 And it came to pass that night, that the angel of the LORD went out, and smote in the camp of the Assyrians an hundred ᵀfourscore and five thousand: and when they arose early in the morning, behold, they *were* all dead corpses.   *Ex. 12:29-30 ◆ eighty*

36 So Sennacherib king of Assyria departed, and went and returned, and dwelt at Nineveh.   *2 Kin. 19:7, 28; Jon. 1:2*

37 And it came to pass, as he was worshipping in the house of Nisroch his god, that Adrammelech and Sharezer his sons smote him with the sword: and they escaped into the land of Armenia. And Esar-haddon his son reigned in his stead.   *Gen. 8:4*

Hezekiah Is Warned of His Death, but His Life Is Lengthened

20 In those days was Hezekiah sick unto death. And the prophet Isaiah the son of Amoz came to him, and said unto him,

Thus saith the LORD, Set thine house in order; for thou shalt die, and not live.

2 Then he turned his face to the wall, and prayed unto the LORD, saying,

3 I ᵀbeseech thee, O LORD, remember now how I have walked before thee in truth and with a perfect heart, and have done *that which is* good in thy sight. And Hezekiah wept sore.   *2 Kin. 18:3-6; Neh. 5:19; 13:22 ◆ beg*

4 And it came to pass, afore Isaiah was gone out into the middle court, that the word of the LORD came to him, saying,

5 Turn again, and tell Hezekiah the captain of my people, Thus saith the LORD, the God of David thy father, I have heard thy prayer, I have seen thy tears: behold, I will heal thee: on the third day thou shalt go up unto the house of the LORD.   *1 Sam. 9:16; 2 Kin. 19:20; Ps. 39:12*

6 And I will add unto thy days fifteen years; and I will deliver thee and this city out of the hand of the king of Assyria; and I will defend this city for mine own sake, and for my servant David's sake.   *2 Kin. 19:34*

7 And Isaiah said, Take a lump of figs. And they took and laid *it* on the boil, and he recovered.   *Is. 38:21*

8 And Hezekiah said unto Isaiah, What *shall be* the sign that the LORD will heal me, and that I shall go up into the house of the LORD the third day?

9 And Isaiah said, This sign shalt thou have of the LORD, that the LORD will do the thing that he hath spoken: shall the shadow go forward ten degrees, or go back ten degrees?

10 And Hezekiah answered, It is a light thing for the shadow to go down ten degrees: nay, but let the shadow return backward ten degrees.

11 And Isaiah the prophet cried unto the LORD: and he brought the shadow ten

---

Natural Health Remedies

2 Kings 20:1–7

Those who seek healing by prayer should not neglect to make use of the remedial agencies within their reach. It is not a denial of faith to use such remedies as God has provided to alleviate pain and to aid nature in her work of restoration. It is no denial of faith to co-operate with God, and to place themselves in the condition most favorable to recovery. God has put it in our power to obtain a knowledge of the laws of life. This knowledge has been placed within our reach for use. We should employ every facility for the restoration of health, taking every advantage possible, working in harmony with natural laws. When we have prayed for the recovery of the sick, we can work with all the more energy, thanking God that we have the privilege of co-operating with Him, and asking His blessing on the means which He Himself has provided.

We have the sanction of the word of God for the use of remedial agencies. Hezekiah, king of Israel, was sick, and a prophet of God brought him the message that he should die. He cried unto the Lord, and the Lord heard His servant and sent him a message that fifteen years should be added to his life. Now, one word from God would have healed Hezekiah instantly; but special directions were given, "Let them take a lump of figs, and lay it for a plaster upon the boil, and he shall recover" (Isaiah 38:21). *MH 231, 232*

degrees backward, by which it had gone down in the dial of Ahaz.   Josh. 10:12-14

Berodach-baladan Sends Visitors to Hezekiah

12 At that time Berodach-baladan, the son of Baladan, king of Babylon, sent letters and a present unto Hezekiah: for he had heard that Hezekiah had been sick.   2 Chr. 32:31

13 And Hezekiah hearkened unto them, and shewed them all the house of his precious things, the silver, and the gold, and the spices, and the precious ointment, and *all* the house of his armour, and all that was found in his treasures: there was nothing in his house, nor in all his dominion, that Hezekiah shewed them not.

20:13 One Reckless Movement

The story of Hezekiah's failure to prove true to his trust at the time of the visit of the ambassadors is fraught with an important lesson for all. . . .

How great the need that we set a watch upon our lips and guard carefully our steps! One reckless movement, one imprudent step, and the surging waves of some strong temptation may sweep a soul into the downward path. We cannot gather up the thoughts we have planted in human minds. *PK 347, 348*

---

14 Then came Isaiah the prophet unto king Hezekiah, and said unto him, What said these men? and from whence came they unto thee? And Hezekiah said, They are come from a far country, *even* from Babylon. **15** And he said, What have they seen in thine house? And Hezekiah answered, All *the things* that *are* in mine house have they seen: there is nothing among my treasures that I have not shewed them.

16 And Isaiah said unto Hezekiah, Hear the word of the LORD.

17 Behold, the days come, that all that *is* in thine house, and that which thy fathers have laid up in store unto this day, shall be carried into Babylon: nothing shall be left, saith the LORD.   2 Kin. 24:13; 2 Chr. 36:10; Jer. 52:17-19

18 And of thy sons that shall issue from thee, which thou shalt ᵀbeget, shall they take away; and they shall be eunuchs in the palace of the king of Babylon.   2 Chr. 33:11; Dan. 1:3 ◆ *bring forth*

19 Then said Hezekiah unto Isaiah, Good *is* the word of the LORD which thou hast spoken. And he said, *Is it* not *good*, if peace and truth be in my days?   1 Sam. 3:18

20 And the rest of the acts of Hezekiah, and all his might, and how he made a pool, and a conduit, and brought water into the city, *are* they not written in the book of the chronicles of the kings of Judah?   2 Chr. 32:30, 32; Neh. 3:16

21 And Hezekiah slept with his fathers: and Manasseh his son reigned in his stead.

Manasseh's Evil Reign over Judah

21 Manasseh *was* twelve years old when he began to reign, and reigned fifty and five years in Jerusalem. And his mother's name *was* Hephzi-bah.   Is. 62:4

2 And he did *that which was* evil in the sight of the LORD, after the abominations of the heathen, whom the LORD cast out before the children of Israel.

3 For he built up again the high places which Hezekiah his father had destroyed; and he reared up altars for Baal, and made a ᵀgrove, as did Ahab king of Israel; and

---

Hezekiah's Failure Has Lessons for Us

2 Kings 20:12–19

The story of Hezekiah's failure to prove true to his trust at the time of the visit of the ambassadors is fraught with an important lesson for all. . . .

Those with whom we associate day by day need our help, our guidance. They may be in such a condition of mind that a word spoken in season will be as a nail in a sure place. Tomorrow some of these souls may be where we can never reach them again. What is our influence over these fellow travelers?

Every day of life is freighted with responsibilities which we must bear. Every day, our words and acts are making impressions upon those with whom we associate. How great the need that we set a watch upon our lips and guard carefully our steps! One reckless movement, one imprudent step, and the surging waves of some strong temptation may sweep a soul into the downward path. We cannot gather up the thoughts we have planted in human minds. If they have been evil, we may have set in motion a train of circumstances, a tide of evil, which we are powerless to stay.

On the other hand, if by our example we aid others in the development of good principles, we give them power to do good. In their turn they exert the same beneficial influence over others. Thus hundreds and thousands are helped by our unconscious influence. The true follower of Christ strengthens the good purposes of all with whom he comes in contact. Before an unbelieving, sin-loving world he reveals the power of God's grace and the perfection of His character. *PK 347, 348*

worshipped all the host of heaven, and served them.   Deut. 17:3; 2 Kin. 17:16; 18:4 ◆ idol

4 And he built altars in the house of the LORD, of which the LORD said, In Jerusalem will I put my name. 2 Sam. 7:13; 1 Kin. 8:29; Jer. 32:34

5 And he built altars for all the host of heaven in the two courts of the house of the LORD.   1 Kin. 6:36; 7:12; 2 Kin. 23:4

6 And he made his son pass through the fire, and observed times, and used ᵀenchantments, and dealt with familiar spirits and wizards: he ᵀwrought much wickedness in the sight of the LORD, to provoke *him* to anger.   Lev. 18:21; 19:31; 2 Kin. 17:17 ◆ secret arts ◆ did

7 And he set a ᵀgraven image of the grove that he had made in the house, of which the LORD said to David, and to Solomon his son, In this house, and in Jerusalem, which I have chosen out of all tribes of Israel, will I put my name for ever: 1 Kin. 8:29 ◆ engraved or cut out

8 Neither will I make the feet of Israel move any more out of the land which I gave their fathers; only if they will observe to do according to all that I have commanded them, and according to all the law that my servant Moses commanded them.   2 Sam. 7:10

9 But they hearkened not: and Manasseh seduced them to do more evil than did the nations whom the LORD destroyed before the children of Israel.   Prov. 29:12

Manasseh's Wickedness Causes Prophecies against Judah

10 And the LORD spake by his servants the prophets, saying,

11 Because Manasseh king of Judah hath done these abominations, *and* hath done wickedly above all that the Amorites did, which *were* before him, and hath made Judah also to sin with his idols: 2 Kin. 21:9; 24:3-4

12 Therefore thus saith the LORD God of Israel, Behold, I *am* bringing *such* evil upon Jerusalem and Judah, that whosoever heareth of it, both his ears shall tingle.   1 Sam. 3:11; Jer. 19:3

13 And I will stretch over Jerusalem the line of Samaria, and the plummet of the house of Ahab: and I will wipe Jerusalem as *a man* wipeth a dish, wiping *it*, and turning *it* upside down.   Is. 34:11; Lam. 2:8; Amos 7:7-8

14 And I will forsake the remnant of mine inheritance, and deliver them into the hand of their enemies; and they shall become a prey and a ᵀspoil to all their enemies;   plunder

15 Because they have done *that which was* evil in my sight, and have provoked me to anger, since the day their fathers came forth out of Egypt, even unto this day.

16 Moreover Manasseh shed innocent blood very much, till he had filled Jerusalem from one end to another; beside his sin wherewith

he made Judah to sin, in doing *that which was* evil in the sight of the LORD.   2 Kin. 21:11

17 Now the rest of the acts of Manasseh, and all that he did, and his sin that he sinned, *are* they not written in the book of the chronicles of the kings of Judah?

18 And Manasseh slept with his fathers, and was buried in the garden of his own house, in the garden of Uzza: and Amon his son reigned in his stead.   2 Chr. 33:20

Amon's Evil Reign over Judah

19 Amon *was* twenty and two years old when he began to reign, and he reigned two years in Jerusalem. And his mother's name *was* Meshullemeth, the daughter of Haruz of Jotbah.   2 Chr. 33:21-23

20 And he did *that which was* evil in the sight of the LORD, as his father Manasseh did.

21 And he walked in all the way that his father walked in, and served the idols that his father served, and worshipped them:

22 And he forsook the LORD God of his fathers, and walked not in the way of the LORD.   1 Kin. 11:33

23 And the servants of Amon conspired against him, and slew the king in his own house.   2 Kin. 12:20

24 And the people of the land slew all them that had conspired against king Amon; and the people of the land made Josiah his son king in his stead.   2 Kin. 14:5

25 Now the rest of the acts of Amon which he did, *are* they not written in the book of the chronicles of the kings of Judah?

26 And he was buried in his sepulchre in the garden of Uzza: and Josiah his son reigned in his stead.   2 Kin. 21:18

During Josiah's Good Reign over Judah, the Book of the Law Is Found

22 Josiah *was* eight years old when he began to reign, and he reigned thirty and one years in Jerusalem. And his mother's name *was* Jedidah, the daughter of Adaiah of Boscath.   Josh. 15:39

2 And he did *that which was* right in the sight of the LORD, and walked in all the way of David his father, and turned not aside to the right hand or to the left.   Deut. 5:32; Josh. 1:7

3 And it came to pass in the eighteenth year of king Josiah, *that* the king sent Shaphan the son of Azaliah, the son of Meshullam, the scribe, to the house of the LORD, saying,

4 Go up to Hilkiah the high priest, that he may sum the silver which is brought into the house of the LORD, which the keepers of the door have gathered of the people: 2 Kin. 12:4

5 And let them deliver it into the hand of the doers of the work, that have the oversight of

the house of the LORD: and let them give it to the doers of the work which *is* in the house of the LORD, to repair the breaches of the house,   *2 Kin. 12:11-14*

6 Unto carpenters, and builders, and masons, and to buy timber and ᵀhewn stone to repair the house.   *cut*

7 Howbeit there was no reckoning made with them of the money that was delivered into their hand, because they dealt faithfully.   *2 Kin. 12:15; 1 Cor. 4:2*

8 And Hilkiah the high priest said unto Shaphan the scribe, I have found the book of the law in the house of the LORD. And Hilkiah gave the book to Shaphan, and he read it.   *Deut. 31:24-26*

9 And Shaphan the scribe came to the king, and brought the king word again, and said, Thy servants have gathered the money that was found in the house, and have delivered it into the hand of them that do the work, that have the oversight of the house of the LORD.

10 And Shaphan the scribe shewed the king, saying, Hilkiah the priest hath delivered me a book. And Shaphan read it before the king.   *Jer. 36:21*

11 And it came to pass, when the king had heard the words of the book of the law, that he ᵀrent his clothes.   *tore*

12 And the king commanded Hilkiah the priest, and Ahikam the son of Shaphan, and Achbor the son of Michaiah, and Shaphan the scribe, and Asahiah a servant of the king's, saying,   *2 Kin. 25:22; Jer. 26:24*

13 Go ye, enquire of the LORD for me, and for the people, and for all Judah, concerning the words of this book that is found: for great *is* the wrath of the LORD that is kindled against us, because our fathers have not hearkened unto the words of this book, to do according unto all that which is written concerning us.   *Deut. 29:23-28*

14 So Hilkiah the priest, and Ahikam, and Achbor, and Shaphan, and Asahiah, went unto Huldah the prophetess, the wife of Shallum the son of Tikvah, the son of Harhas, keeper of the wardrobe; (now she dwelt in Jerusalem in the college;) and they communed with her.   *2 Chr. 34:22*

15 And she said unto them, Thus saith the LORD God of Israel, Tell the man that sent you to me,

16 Thus saith the LORD, Behold, I will bring evil upon this place, and upon the inhabitants thereof, *even* all the words of the book which the king of Judah hath read: *Josh. 23:15*

17 Because they have forsaken me, and have burned incense unto other gods, that they might provoke me to anger with all the works of their hands; therefore my wrath shall be kindled against this place, and shall not be quenched.

> **22:15–17 Time Runs Out**
>
> Through Huldah the Lord sent Josiah word that Jerusalem's ruin could not be averted. Even should the people now humble themselves before God, they could not escape their punishment. So long had their senses been deadened by wrongdoing that, if judgment should not come upon them, they would soon return to the same sinful course. *PK 399*

18 But to the king of Judah which sent you to enquire of the LORD, thus shall ye say to him, Thus saith the LORD God of Israel, *As touching* the words which thou hast heard;

19 Because thine heart was tender, and thou hast humbled thyself before the LORD, when thou heardest what I spake against this place, and against the inhabitants thereof, that they should become a desolation and a curse, and hast rent thy clothes, and wept before me; I also have heard *thee*, saith the LORD.   *1 Kin. 21:29; Ps. 51:17; Jer. 26:6*

20 Behold therefore, I will gather thee unto thy fathers, and thou shalt be gathered into thy grave in peace; and thine eyes shall not see all the evil which I will bring upon this place. And they brought the king word again.   *Ps. 37:37*

Josiah Reads the Book of the Law in a Solemn Assembly

23 And the king sent, and they gathered unto him all the elders of Judah and of Jerusalem.

2 And the king went up into the house of the LORD, and all the men of Judah and all the inhabitants of Jerusalem with him, and the priests, and the prophets, and all the people, both small and great: and he read in their ears all the words of the book of the covenant which was found in the house of the LORD.   *Deut. 31:10-13; 2 Kin. 22:8*

3 And the king stood by a pillar, and made a covenant before the LORD, to walk after the LORD, and to keep his commandments and his testimonies and his statutes with all *their* heart and all *their* soul, to perform the words of this covenant that were written in this book. And all the people stood to the covenant.   *Deut. 13:4; 2 Kin. 11:14, 17*

Josiah Destroys Idolatry

4 And the king commanded Hilkiah the high priest, and the priests of the second order, and the keepers of the door, to bring forth out of the temple of the LORD all the vessels that were made for Baal, and for the

^Tgrove, and for all the host of heaven: and he burned them without Jerusalem in the fields of Kidron, and carried the ashes of them unto Bethel. 2 Kin. 21:3 ◆ *idol*

5 And he put down the idolatrous priests, whom the kings of Judah had ordained to burn incense in the high places in the cities of Judah, and in the places round about Jerusalem; them also that burned incense unto Baal, to the sun, and to the moon, and to the planets, and to all the host of heaven.

6 And he brought out the grove from the house of the LORD, without Jerusalem, unto the brook Kidron, and burned it at the brook Kidron, and stamped *it* small to powder, and cast the powder thereof upon the graves of the children of the people. 2 Chr. 34:4

7 And he brake down the houses of the sodomites, that *were* by the house of the LORD, where the women wove hangings for the grove. 1 Kin. 14:24; 15:12; Ezek. 16:16

8 And he brought all the priests out of the cities of Judah, and defiled the high places where the priests had burned incense, from Geba to Beer-sheba, and brake down the high places of the gates that *were* in the entering in of the gate of Joshua the governor of the city, which *were* on a man's left hand at the gate of the city. Josh. 21:17; 1 Kin. 15:22

9 Nevertheless the priests of the high places came not up to the altar of the LORD in Jerusalem, but they did eat of the unleavened bread among their brethren. Ezek. 44:10-14

10 And he defiled Topheth, which *is* in the valley of the children of Hinnom, that no man might make his son or his daughter to pass through the fire to Molech. Lev. 18:21

11 And he took away the horses that the kings of Judah had given to the sun, at the entering in of the house of the LORD, by the chamber of Nathan-melech the ^Tchamberlain, which *was* in the suburbs, and burned the chariots of the sun with fire. Ezek. 8:16 ◆ *chief servant*

12 And the altars that *were* on the top of the upper chamber of Ahaz, which the kings of Judah had made, and the altars which Manasseh had made in the two courts of the house of the LORD, did the king beat down, and brake *them* down from thence, and cast the dust of them into the brook Kidron. Jer. 19:13

13 And the high places that *were* before Jerusalem, which *were* on the right hand of the mount of corruption, which Solomon the king of Israel had builded for Ashtoreth the abomination of the Zidonians, and for Chemosh the abomination of the Moabites, and for Milcom the abomination of the children of Ammon, did the king defile. Num. 21:29; 1 Kin. 11:5, 7

14 And he brake in pieces the images, and cut down the ^Tgroves, and filled their places with the bones of men. Ex. 23:24 ◆ *idols*

15 Moreover the altar that *was* at Bethel, *and* the high place which Jeroboam the son of Nebat, who made Israel to sin, had made, both that altar and the high place he brake down, and burned the high place, *and* stamped *it* small to powder, and burned the grove. 1 Kin. 14:16

16 And as Josiah turned himself, he spied the sepulchres that *were* there in the mount, and sent, and took the bones out of the sepulchres, and burned *them* upon the altar, and polluted it, according to the word of the LORD which the man of God proclaimed, who proclaimed these words.

17 Then he said, What title *is* that that I see? And the men of the city told him, *It is* the sepulchre of the man of God, which came from Judah, and proclaimed these things that thou hast done against the altar of Bethel. 1 Kin. 13:1

18 And he said, Let him alone; let no man move his bones. So they let his bones alone, with the bones of the prophet that came out of Samaria. 1 Kin. 13:31

19 And all the houses also of the high places that *were* in the cities of Samaria, which the kings of Israel had made to provoke *the* LORD to anger, Josiah took away, and did to them according to all the acts that he had done in Bethel. 2 Chr. 34:6-7

20 And he slew all the priests of the high places that *were* there upon the altars, and burned men's bones upon them, and returned to Jerusalem. Ex. 22:20; 2 Kin. 10:25; 11:18

21 And the king commanded all the people, saying, Keep the passover unto the LORD your God, as *it is* written in the book of this covenant. Deut. 16:1-8

22 Surely there was not ^Tholden such a passover from the days of the judges that judged Israel, nor in all the days of the kings of Israel, nor of the kings of Judah; *held*

23 But in the eighteenth year of king Josiah, *wherein* this passover was holden to the LORD in Jerusalem.

24 Moreover the *workers with* familiar spirits, and the wizards, and the images, and the idols, and all the abominations that were spied in the land of Judah and in Jerusalem, did Josiah put away, that he might perform the words of the law which were written in the book that Hilkiah the priest found in the house of the LORD. Gen. 31:19; Lev. 19:31; 2 Kin. 21:6

25 And like unto him was there no king before him, that turned to the LORD with all his heart, and with all his soul, and with all his might, according to all the law of Moses; neither after him arose there *any* like him. 2 Kin. 18:5

26 Notwithstanding the LORD turned not from the fierceness of his great wrath, where-

with his anger was kindled against Judah, because of all the provocations that Manasseh had provoked him ᵀwithal.   *with*

23:25, 26 Stubborn, Idolatrous Hearts

But the zeal of Josiah, acceptable though it was to God, could not atone for the sins of past generations; nor could the piety displayed by the king's followers effect a change of heart in many who stubbornly refused to turn from idolatry to the worship of the true God. *PK 405*

27 And the LORD said, I will remove Judah also out of my sight, as I have removed Israel, and will cast off this city Jerusalem which I have chosen, and the house of which I said, My name shall be there. 2 Kin. 17:18; 18:11; 21:13

23:27 Learning Lessons the Hard Way

The time was rapidly approaching when Jerusalem was to be utterly destroyed and the inhabitants of the land carried captive to Babylon, there to learn the lessons they had refused to learn under circumstances more favorable. *PK 406*

28 Now the rest of the acts of Josiah, and all that he did, *are* they not written in the book of the chronicles of the kings of Judah?
29 In his days Pharaoh-nechoh king of Egypt went up against the king of Assyria to the river Euphrates: and king Josiah went against him; and he slew him at Megiddo, when he had seen him.   Judg. 5:19; 2 Chr. 35:20-24; Jer. 46:2
30 And his servants carried him in a chariot dead from Megiddo, and brought him to Jerusalem, and buried him in his own sepulchre. And the people of the land took Jehoahaz the son of Josiah, and anointed him, and made him king in his father's stead.   2 Kin. 9:28; 2 Chr. 36:1-4

The Evil Reigns of Jehoahaz and Jehoiakim over Judah

31 Jehoahaz *was* twenty and three years old when he began to reign; and he reigned three months in Jerusalem. And his mother's name *was* Hamutal, the daughter of Jeremiah of Libnah. 2 Kin. 24:18; 1 Chr. 3:15; Jer. 22:11
32 And he did *that which was* evil in the sight of the LORD, according to all that his fathers had done.   2 Kin. 21:2-7
33 And Pharaoh-nechoh put him in bands at Riblah in the land of Hamath, that he might not reign in Jerusalem; and put the land to a tribute of an hundred talents of silver, and a ᵀtalent of gold. 1 Kin. 8:65; Jer. 39:5-6 ◆ *weight* or *sum*
34 And Pharaoh-nechoh made Eliakim the son of Josiah king in the room of Josiah his father, and turned his name to Jehoiakim, and

took Jehoahaz away: and he came to Egypt, and died there. 2 Kin. 24:17; 1 Chr. 3:15; Ezek. 19:3-4
35 And Jehoiakim gave the silver and the gold to Pharaoh; but he taxed the land to give the money according to the commandment of Pharaoh: he exacted the silver and the gold of the people of the land, of every one according to his taxation, to give *it* unto Pharaoh-nechoh.   2 Kin. 23:33
36 Jehoiakim *was* twenty and five years old when he began to reign; and he reigned eleven years in Jerusalem. And his mother's name *was* Zebudah, the daughter of Pedaiah of Rumah.   2 Chr. 36:5
37 And he did *that which was* evil in the sight of the LORD, according to all that his fathers had done.

Jehoiakim Is Subdued by Nebuchadnezzar of Babylon

24 In his days Nebuchadnezzar king of Babylon came up, and Jehoiakim became his servant three years: then he turned and rebelled against him.   Jer. 25:1, 9; Dan. 1:1
2 And the LORD sent against him bands of the Chaldees, and bands of the Syrians, and bands of the Moabites, and bands of the children of Ammon, and sent them against Judah to destroy it, according to the word of the LORD, which he spake by his servants the prophets.   2 Kin. 6:23; 23:27; Jer. 35:11
3 Surely at the commandment of the LORD came *this* upon Judah, to remove *them* out of his sight, for the sins of Manasseh, according to all that he did;   2 Kin. 18:25
4 And also for the innocent blood that he shed: for he filled Jerusalem with innocent blood; which the LORD would not pardon.
5 Now the rest of the acts of Jehoiakim, and all that he did, *are* they not written in the book of the chronicles of the kings of Judah?   2 Chr. 36:8
6 So Jehoiakim slept with his fathers: and Jehoiachin his son reigned in his stead.
7 And the king of Egypt came not again any more out of his land: for the king of Babylon had taken from the river of Egypt unto the river Euphrates all that pertained to the king of Egypt.   Gen. 15:18; Jer. 37:5-7; 46:2

During Jehoiachin's Evil Reign over Judah, Babylon Invades a Second Time

8 Jehoiachin *was* eighteen years old when he began to reign, and he reigned in Jerusalem three months. And his mother's name *was* Nehushta, the daughter of Elnathan of Jerusalem.   1 Chr. 3:16; 2 Chr. 36:9; Jer. 22:24
9 And he did *that which was* evil in the sight of the LORD, according to all that his father had done.

10 At that time the servants of Nebuchadnezzar king of Babylon came up against Jerusalem, and the city was besieged.

11 And Nebuchadnezzar king of Babylon came against the city, and his servants did besiege it.

12 And Jehoiachin the king of Judah went out to the king of Babylon, he, and his mother, and his servants, and his princes, and his officers: and the king of Babylon took him in the eighth year of his reign. *Jer. 24:1; 52:28*

13 And he carried out thence all the treasures of the house of the LORD, and the treasures of the king's house, and cut in pieces all the vessels of gold which Solomon king of Israel had made in the temple of the LORD, as the LORD had said. *1 Kin. 7:48-50; 2 Kin. 20:17; Is. 39:6*

14 And he carried away all Jerusalem, and all the princes, and all the mighty men of valour, *even* ten thousand captives, and all the craftsmen and smiths: none remained, save the poorest sort of the people of the land. *2 Kin. 25:12; Jer. 40:7; 52:28*

15 And he carried away Jehoiachin to Babylon, and the king's mother, and the king's wives, and his officers, and the mighty of the land, *those* carried he into captivity from Jerusalem to Babylon. *2 Chr. 36:10*

16 And all the men of might, *even* seven thousand, and craftsmen and smiths a thousand, all *that were* strong *and* apt for war, even them the king of Babylon brought captive to Babylon. *Jer. 52:28*

17 And the king of Babylon made Mattaniah his father's brother king in his stead, and changed his name to Zedekiah. *2 Chr. 36:4; Jer. 37:1*

18 Zedekiah *was* twenty and one years old when he began to reign, and he reigned eleven years in Jerusalem. And his mother's name *was* Hamutal, the daughter of Jeremiah of Libnah. *2 Kin. 23:31; Jer. 52:1-11*

19 And he did *that which was* evil in the sight of the LORD, according to all that Jehoiakim had done. *2 Kin. 23:37*

20 For through the anger of the LORD it came to pass in Jerusalem and Judah, until he had cast them out from his presence, that Zedekiah rebelled against the king of Babylon. *2 Chr. 36:13*

Nebuchadnezzar Attacks Jerusalem the Third and Final Time

25 And it came to pass in the ninth year of his reign, in the tenth month, in the tenth *day* of the month, *that* Nebuchadnezzar king of Babylon came, he, and all his host, against Jerusalem, and pitched against it; and they built forts against it round about. *Jer. 34:1-6*

2 And the city was besieged unto the eleventh year of king Zedekiah.

3 And on the ninth *day* of the *fourth* month the famine prevailed in the city, and there was no bread for the people of the land.

4 And the city was broken up, and all the men of war *fled* by night by the way of the gate between two walls, which *is* by the king's garden: (now the Chaldees *were* against the city round about:) and *the king* went the way toward the plain. *Ezek. 33:21*

5 And the army of the Chaldees pursued after the king, and overtook him in the plains of Jericho: and all his army were scattered from him.

6 So they took the king, and brought him up to the king of Babylon to Riblah; and they gave judgment upon him. *2 Kin. 23:33; Jer. 34:21-22*

7 And they slew the sons of Zedekiah before his eyes, and put out the eyes of Zedekiah, and bound him with ᵀfetters of brass, and carried him to Babylon. *Jer. 32:4-5 ♦ chains*

The Babylonians Destroy Jerusalem and Take a Final Wave of Captives

8 And in the fifth month, on the seventh *day* of the month, which *is* the nineteenth year of king Nebuchadnezzar king of Babylon, came Nebuzar-adan, captain of the guard, a servant of the king of Babylon, unto Jerusalem: *Jer. 52:12-16*

9 And he burnt the house of the LORD, and the king's house, and all the houses of Jerusalem, and every great *man's* house burnt he with fire. *2 Chr. 36:19; Ps. 74:3-7; Amos 2:5*

10 And all the army of the Chaldees, that *were with* the captain of the guard, brake down the walls of Jerusalem round about.

11 Now the rest of the people *that were* left in the city, and the fugitives that fell away to the king of Babylon, with the remnant of the multitude, did Nebuzar-adan the captain of the guard carry away.

12 But the captain of the guard left of the poor of the land *to be* vinedressers and ᵀhusbandmen. *2 Kin. 24:14; Jer. 40:7 ♦ farmers*

13 And the pillars of brass that *were* in the house of the LORD, and the bases, and the brasen sea that *was* in the house of the LORD, did the Chaldees break in pieces, and carried the brass of them to Babylon. *1 Kin. 7:15*

14 And the pots, and the shovels, and the snuffers, and the spoons, and all the vessels of brass wherewith they ministered, took they away. *Ex. 27:3; 1 Kin. 7:47-50*

15 And the firepans, and the bowls, *and* such things as *were* of gold, *in* gold, and of silver, *in* silver, the captain of the guard took away.

16 The two pillars, one sea, and the bases which Solomon had made for the house of the LORD; the brass of all these vessels was without weight. *1 Kin. 7:47*

17 The height of the one pillar *was* eighteen

cubits, and the ^Tchapiter upon it *was* brass: and the height of the chapiter three cubits; and the wreathen work, and pomegranates upon the chapiter round about, all of brass: and like unto these had the second pillar with wreathen work. *capital*

18 And the captain of the guard took Seraiah the chief priest, and Zephaniah the second priest, and the three keepers of the door:

19 And out of the city he took an officer that was set over the men of war, and five men of them that were in the king's presence, which were found in the city, and the principal scribe of the host, which mustered the people of the land, and ^Tthreescore men of the people of the land *that were* found in the city: Esth. 1:14 ◆ *sixty*

20 And Nebuzar-adan captain of the guard took these, and brought them to the king of Babylon to Riblah:

21 And the king of Babylon smote them, and slew them at Riblah in the land of Hamath. So Judah was carried away out of their land. Deut. 28:64; 2 Kin. 23:27

Gedaliah Is Slain, and the Rest of Those Left Behind Flee to Egypt

22 And *as for* the people that remained in the land of Judah, whom Nebuchadnezzar king of Babylon had left, even over them he made Gedaliah the son of Ahikam, the son of Shaphan, ruler. 2 Kin. 22:12; Jer. 39:14

23 And when all the captains of the armies, they and their men, heard that the king of Babylon had made Gedaliah governor, there came to Gedaliah to Mizpah, even Ishmael the son of Nethaniah, and Johanan the son of Careah, and Seraiah the son of Tanhumeth the Netophathite, and Jaazaniah the son of a Maachathite, they and their men. Jer. 40:7-9

24 And Gedaliah sware to them, and to their men, and said unto them, Fear not to be the servants of the Chaldees: dwell in the land, and serve the king of Babylon; and it shall be well with you.

25 But it came to pass in the seventh month, that Ishmael the son of Nethaniah, the son of Elishama, of the seed royal, came, and ten men with him, and smote Gedaliah, that he died, and the Jews and the Chaldees that were with him at Mizpah.

26 And all the people, both small and great, and the captains of the armies, arose, and came to Egypt: for they were afraid of the Chaldees. Jer. 43:4-7

27 And it came to pass in the seven and thirtieth year of the captivity of Jehoiachin king of Judah, in the twelfth month, on the seven and twentieth *day* of the month, *that* Evil-merodach king of Babylon in the year that he began to reign did lift up the head of Jehoiachin king of Judah out of prison; Gen. 40:13, 20; Jer. 52:31-34

28 And he spake kindly to him, and set his throne above the throne of the kings that *were* with him in Babylon; Dan. 2:37

29 And changed his prison garments: and he did eat bread continually before him all the days of his life. 2 Sam. 9:7

30 And his allowance *was* a continual allowance given him of the king, a daily rate for every day, all the days of his life. Neh. 11:23

THE FIRST BOOK OF THE

CHRONICLES

The northern kingdom of Israel had been conquered and dispersed into the Assyrian Empire. A little over a century later, the southern kingdom of Judah succumbed to the power of the Babylonians and many people were taken into exile. The Books of Ezra and Nehemiah will describe the people's return to their homeland.

After losing everything to the Assyrians and Babylonians, however, the remnant that returned to Jerusalem had little hope. They needed a divine perspective on the events of their recent past. The books of 1 and 2 Chronicles present a divine editorial on the history of God's people. While the Books of Samuel and Kings cover the political history of both Israel and Judah, the Books of 1 and 2 Chronicles focus on the religious history of the people. They highlight the southern kingdom of Judah (with little about the northern kingdom), with much emphasis on the temple.

The Book of 1 Chronicles concisely follows the family line of David from Adam to the time this book was written. The first eight chapters are a lengthy genealogy, followed by the history of David's royal line and its spiritual significance.

Dates

Using the division noted above, the dates fall roughly as follows:
   (1) *1 Chronicles 1—9, 4000 to 538 B.C.*
   The genealogies begin with Adam and extend to about 500 B.C., mentioning Zerubbabel, the grandson of King Jeconiah, who led the first return of the Jews from exile in 538 B.C.
   (2) *1 Chronicles 10—29, 1011 to 971 B.C.*
   The focus is on the reign of David.

Author

While 1 Chronicles does not mention an author by name, tradition indicates that Ezra, a priest and scribe authored it. Some reasons for this supposition:
   (1) The text emphasizes the temple, the priesthood, and the theocratic line of David.
   (2) The writing style is similar to both the Books of Ezra and Nehemiah. Case in point, the last verses of 2 Chronicles (36:22, 23) and the opening verses of Ezra (1:1–3) are nearly identical. Some scholars attest that Chronicles and Ezra were consecutive books of history, like Luke and Acts in the New Testament.

Ezra's contemporaries are Nehemiah, the political leader; and Malachi, the moral leader. Ezra led some exiles out of Babylonian captivity, to return to Jerusalem in 457 B.C., and serves as a spiritual leader to the people rebuilding their nation and their lives in Jerusalem. He wants to remind the people of their spiritual heritage and identity, and give them a divine perspective on the events of their recent past. He focuses on the reigns of David and Solomon, for those represented the pinnacle of the nation's history.

Meaning of the Name

Since 1 and 2 Chronicles were considered one book, the title in Hebrew was *Dibere Hayyamim*, which meant "Events of the Days." In the Septuagint, however, Chronicles was divided into two books and called *Paraleipomenon* or "Of Things Omitted." The "things omitted" were accounts omitted from 1 and 2 Samuel and 1 and 2 Kings. First Chronicles, in the Greek, is *Paraleipomenon Primus* or "The First Book of Things Omitted."

The title Chronicles comes from *Chronicorum Liber*, the title used in the Latin Vulgate Bible translated by Jerome (A.D. 385–405). In a sense, Jerome meant "The Chronicles of the Whole of Sacred History."

Christ in 1 Chronicles

David is a type of Christ. The promise of the supremacy of David's throne, a covenant made by God (17:2–15; see also 2 Samuel 7:4–17), points to the long-promised Messiah. Judah is listed first in the national genealogy, since the monarchy, temple, and the Messiah come through this tribe. Furthermore, the genealogies in chapters 1—9 are a preamble to the genealogy of Christ in Matthew's Gospel. (The books of the Chronicles are the last books of the Hebrew Bible; Matthew is the first book of the New Testament.)

First Chronicles falls into two main divisions:

(1) *1 Chronicles 1—9, David's Family Line:* The genealogies cover the time from Adam to David.

(2) *1 Chronicles 10—29, David's Reign:* These chapters highlight the reign of David over the united kingdoms of Israel and Judah. The author concentrates on the reigns of David and Solomon because they lead Israel to its pinnacle of power. The spiritual significance of David's righteous reign is revealed. Missing, however, are the accounts of David's sin with Bathsheba (2 Samuel 11–12) and David's problems with Absalom (2 Samuel 14—18).

Unlocking 1 Chronicles

KEY PEOPLE:
Jacob and his sons, Saul, David, Solomon

KEY EVENTS:
The death of Saul; the succession of David; the transfer of the ark of the covenant from the tabernacle to the temple; the establishment of David's rule; the arrival and installation of the ark; God's covenant with David; census of Judah and Israel; the preparation for succession from David to Solomon

KEY WORD:
Covenant, for God's promissory covenant with David is the source of David's dynasty and Solomon's temple.

KEY VERSES:
"And it shall come to pass, when thy days be expired that thou must go to be with thy fathers, that I will raise up thy seed after thee, which shall be of thy sons; and I will establish his kingdom. He shall build me an house, and I will stablish his throne for ever. I will be his father, and he shall be my son: and I will not take my mercy away from him, as I took it from him that was before thee: But I will settle him in mine house and in my kingdom for ever: and his throne shall be established for evermore" (1 Chronicles 17:11–14).

KEY CHAPTER:
1 Chronicles 17, which repeats God's covenant with David (see also 2 Samuel 7). David's house, kingdom, and throne will be established forever through Jesus Christ.

The Genealogy of Adam's Descendants

1 Adam, Sheth, Enosh,   Luke 3:38
  2 Kenan, Mahalaleel, Jered,   Luke 3:37
3 Henoch, Methuselah, Lamech,   Jude 14
4 Noah, Shem, Ham, and Japheth.   Gen. 5:32
5 The sons of Japheth; Gomer, and Magog, and Madai, and Javan, and Tubal, and Meshech, and Tiras.
6 And the sons of Gomer; Ashchenaz, and Riphath, and Togarmah.
7 And the sons of Javan; Elishah, and Tarshish, Kittim, and Dodanim.
8 The sons of Ham; Cush, and Mizraim, Put, and Canaan.   Gen. 10:6-7
9 And the sons of Cush; Seba, and Havilah, and Sabta, and Raamah, and Sabtecha. And the sons of Raamah; Sheba, and Dedan.
10 And Cush ᵀbegat Nimrod: he began to be mighty upon the earth.   *brought forth*
11 And Mizraim begat Ludim, and Anamim, and Lehabim, and Naphtuhim,
12 And Pathrusim, and Casluhim, (of whom came the Philistines,) and Caphthorim.
13 And Canaan begat Zidon his firstborn, and Heth,
14 The Jebusite also, and the Amorite, and the Girgashite,   Gen. 15:21
15 And the Hivite, and the Arkite, and the Sinite,
16 And the Arvadite, and the Zemarite, and the Hamathite.
17 The sons of Shem; Elam, and Asshur, and Arphaxad, and Lud, and Aram, and Uz, and Hul, and Gether, and Meshech.
18 And Arphaxad begat Shelah, and Shelah begat Eber.
19 And unto Eber were born two sons: the name of the one *was* Peleg; because in his days the earth was divided: and his brother's name *was* Joktan.
20 And Joktan begat Almodad, and Sheleph, and Hazar-maveth, and Jerah,
21 Hadoram also, and Uzal, and Diklah,
22 And Ebal, and Abimael, and Sheba,
23 And Ophir, and Havilah, and Jobab. All these *were* the sons of Joktan.
24 Shem, Arphaxad, Shelah,   Gen. 11:10-26
25 Eber, Peleg, Reu,   Luke 3:35
26 Serug, Nahor, Terah,
27 Abram; the same *is* Abraham.
28 The sons of Abraham; Isaac, and Ishmael.
29 These *are* their generations: The firstborn of Ishmael, Nebaioth; then Kedar, and Adbeel, and Mibsam,
30 Mishma, and Dumah, Massa, Hadad, and Tema,
31 Jetur, Naphish, and Kedemah. These are the sons of Ishmael.
32 Now the sons of Keturah, Abraham's ᵀconcubine: she bare Zimran, and Jokshan, and Medan, and Midian, and Ishbak, and

Shuah. And the sons of Jokshan; Sheba, and Dedan.   Gen. 25:1-4 *◆ less important wife*
33 And the sons of Midian; Ephah, and Epher, and Henoch, and Abida, and Eldaah. All these *are* the sons of Keturah.
34 And Abraham begat Isaac. The sons of Isaac; Esau and Israel.   Gen. 32:28
35 The sons of Esau; Eliphaz, Reuel, and Jeush, and Jaalam, and Korah.   Gen. 36:4-5
36 The sons of Eliphaz; Teman, and Omar, Zephi, and Gatam, Kenaz, and Timna, and Amalek.
37 The sons of Reuel; Nahath, Zerah, Shammah, and Mizzah.
38 And the sons of Seir; Lotan, and Shobal, and Zibeon, and Anah, and Dishon, and Ezer, and Dishan.
39 And the sons of Lotan; Hori, and Homam: and Timna *was* Lotan's sister.
40 The sons of Shobal; Alian, and Manahath, and Ebal, Shephi, and Onam. And the sons of Zibeon; Aiah, and Anah.
41 The sons of Anah; Dishon. And the sons of Dishon; Amram, and Eshban, and Ithran, and Cheran.
42 The sons of Ezer; Bilhan, and Zavan, *and* Jakan. The sons of Dishan; Uz, and Aran.
43 Now these *are* the kings that reigned in the land of Edom before *any* king reigned over the children of Israel; Bela the son of Beor: and the name of his city *was* Dinhabah.
44 And when Bela was dead, Jobab the son of Zerah of Bozrah reigned in his stead. Is. 34:6
45 And when Jobab was dead, Husham of the land of the Temanites reigned in his stead.
46 And when Husham was dead, Hadad the son of Bedad, which smote Midian in the field of Moab, reigned in his stead: and the name of his city *was* Avith.
47 And when Hadad was dead, Samlah of Masrekah reigned in his stead.
48 And when Samlah was dead, Shaul of Rehoboth by the river reigned in his stead.
49 And when Shaul was dead, Baal-hanan the son of Achbor reigned in his stead.
50 And when Baal-hanan was dead, Hadad reigned in his stead: and the name of his city *was* Pai; and his wife's name *was* Mehetabel, the daughter of Matred, the daughter of Mezahab.   Gen. 36:39
51 Hadad died also. And the dukes of Edom were; ᵀduke Timnah, duke Aliah, duke Jetheth,   *chief*
52 Duke Aholibamah, duke Elah, duke Pinon,
53 Duke Kenaz, duke Teman, duke Mibzar,
54 Duke Magdiel, duke Iram. These *are* the dukes of Edom.

Israel's Sons and Judah's Descendants

2 These *are* the sons of Israel; Reuben, Simeon, Levi, and Judah, Issachar, and Zebulun,   Gen. 29:32-35
2 Dan, Joseph, and Benjamin, Naphtali, Gad, and Asher.
3 The sons of Judah; Er, and Onan, and Shelah: *which* three were born unto him of the daughter of Shua the Canaanitess. And Er, the firstborn of Judah, was evil in the sight of the LORD; and he slew him.   Gen. 38:2-10
4 And Tamar his daughter in law bare him Pharez and Zerah. All the sons of Judah *were* five.   Gen. 38:13-30; Ruth 4:12; Matt. 1:3
5 The sons of Pharez; Hezron, and Hamul.
6 And the sons of Zerah; Zimri, and Ethan, and Heman, and Calcol, and Dara: five of them in all.
7 And the sons of Carmi; Achar, the troubler of Israel, who ᵀtransgressed in the thing accursed.   Josh. 6:18 ◆ *violated a law*
8 And the sons of Ethan; Azariah.
9 The sons also of Hezron, that were born unto him; Jerahmeel, and Ram, and Chelubai.   Ruth 4:19
10 And Ram begat Amminadab; and Amminadab begat Nahshon, prince of the children of Judah;   Num. 1:7; 2:3; Matt. 1:4
11 And Nahshon begat Salma, and Salma begat Boaz,   Ruth 4:21
12 And Boaz ᵀbegat Obed, and Obed begat Jesse,   *brought forth*
13 And Jesse begat his firstborn Eliab, and Abinadab the second, and Shimma the third,   1 Sam. 17:13
14 Nethaneel the fourth, Raddai the fifth,
15 Ozem the sixth, David the seventh:
16 Whose sisters *were* Zeruiah, and Abigail. And the sons of Zeruiah; Abishai, and Joab, and Asahel, three.   1 Sam. 26:6
17 And Abigail bare Amasa: and the father of Amasa *was* Jether the Ishmeelite.   2 Sam. 17:25

Caleb's Descendants

18 And Caleb the son of Hezron begat *children* of Azubah *his* wife, and of Jerioth: her sons *are* these; Jesher, and Shobab, and Ardon.
19 And when Azubah was dead, Caleb took unto him Ephrath, which bare him Hur.
20 And Hur begat Uri, and Uri begat Bezaleel.   Ex. 31:2
21 And afterward Hezron went in to the daughter of Machir the father of Gilead, whom he married when he *was* threescore years old; and she bare him Segub. Num. 27:1
22 And Segub begat Jair, who had three and twenty cities in the land of Gilead.
23 And he took Geshur, and Aram, with the towns of Jair, from them, with Kenath, and the towns thereof, *even* ᵀthreescore cities.

All these *belonged to* the sons of Machir the father of Gilead.   *sixty*
24 And after that Hezron was dead in Caleb-ephratah, then Abiah Hezron's wife bare him Ashur the father of Tekoa.   1 Chr. 4:5
25 And the sons of Jerahmeel the firstborn of Hezron were, Ram the firstborn, and Bunah, and Oren, and Ozem, *and* Ahijah.
26 Jerahmeel had also another wife, whose name *was* Atarah; she *was* the mother of Onam.
27 And the sons of Ram the firstborn of Jerahmeel were, Maaz, and Jamin, and Eker.
28 And the sons of Onam were, Shammai, and Jada. And the sons of Shammai; Nadab, and Abishur.
29 And the name of the wife of Abishur *was* Abihail, and she bare him Ahban, and Molid.
30 And the sons of Nadab; Seled, and Appaim: but Seled died without children.
31 And the sons of Appaim; Ishi. And the sons of Ishi; Sheshan. And the children of Sheshan; Ahlai.   1 Chr. 2:34-35
32 And the sons of Jada the brother of Shammai; Jether, and Jonathan: and Jether died without children.
33 And the sons of Jonathan; Peleth, and Zaza. These were the sons of Jerahmeel.
34 Now Sheshan had no sons, but daughters. And Sheshan had a servant, an Egyptian, whose name *was* Jarha.
35 And Sheshan gave his daughter to Jarha his servant to wife; and she bare him Attai.
36 And Attai begat Nathan, and Nathan begat Zabad,   1 Chr. 11:41
37 And Zabad begat Ephlal, and Ephlal begat Obed,
38 And Obed begat Jehu, and Jehu begat Azariah,
39 And Azariah begat Helez, and Helez begat Eleasah,
40 And Eleasah begat Sisamai, and Sisamai begat Shallum,
41 And Shallum begat Jekamiah, and Jekamiah begat Elishama.
42 Now the sons of Caleb the brother of Jerahmeel *were*, Mesha his firstborn, which was the father of Ziph; and the sons of Mareshah the father of Hebron.
43 And the sons of Hebron; Korah, and Tappuah, and Rekem, and Shema.
44 And Shema begat Raham, the father of Jorkoam: and Rekem begat Shammai.
45 And the son of Shammai *was* Maon: and Maon *was* the father of Beth-zur.   Josh. 15:58
46 And Ephah, Caleb's ᵀconcubine, bare Haran, and Moza, and Gazez: and Haran begat Gazez.   *less important wife*
47 And the sons of Jahdai; Regem, and Jotham, and Geshan, and Pelet, and Ephah, and Shaaph.

48 Maachah, Caleb's concubine, bare She-ber, and Tirhanah.

49 She bare also Shaaph the father of Madmannah, Sheva the father of Machbenah, and the father of Gibea: and the daughter of Caleb was Achsah.   Josh. 15:31

50 These were the sons of Caleb the son of Hur, the firstborn of Ephratah; Shobal the father of Kirjath-jearim,

51 Salma the father of Beth-lehem, Hareph the father of Beth-gader.   1 Chr. 4:4

52 And Shobal the father of Kirjath-jearim had sons; Haroeh, and half of the Manahethites.   1 Chr. 4:2

53 And the families of Kirjath-jearim; the Ithrites, and the Puhites, and the Shumathites, and the Mishraites; of them came the Zareathites, and the Eshtaulites.   2 Sam. 23:38

54 The sons of Salma; Beth-lehem, and the Netophathites, Ataroth, the house of Joab, and half of the Manahethites, the Zorites.

55 And the families of the scribes which dwelt at Jabez; the Tirathites, the Shimeathites, and Suchathites. These are the Kenites that came of Hemath, the father of the house of Rechab.   Judg. 1:16

The Sons of David

3 Now these were the sons of David, which were born unto him in Hebron; the firstborn Amnon, of Ahinoam the Jezreelitess; the second Daniel, of Abigail the Carmelitess: 2 Sam. 3:2-5

2 The third, Absalom the son of Maachah the daughter of Talmai king of Geshur: the fourth, Adonijah the son of Haggith:

3 The fifth, Shephatiah of Abital: the sixth, Ithream by Eglah his wife.

4 These six were born unto him in Hebron; and there he reigned seven years and six months: and in Jerusalem he reigned thirty and three years.   2 Sam. 2:11; 5:4-5; 1 Kin. 2:11

5 And these were born unto him in Jerusalem; Shimea, and Shobab, and Nathan, and Solomon, four, of Bath-shua the daughter of Ammiel: 2 Sam. 11:3; 12:24-25

6 Ibhar also, and Elishama, and Eliphelet,

7 And Nogah, and Nepheg, and Japhia,

8 And Elishama, and Eliada, and Eliphelet, nine.   1 Chr. 14:7

9 These were all the sons of David, beside the sons of the concubines, and Tamar their sister.

David's Descendants

10 And Solomon's son was Rehoboam, Abia his son, Asa his son, Jehoshaphat his son,

11 Joram his son, Ahaziah his son, Joash his son,   2 Kin. 8:24

12 Amaziah his son, Azariah his son, Jotham his son,   2 Kin. 14:1

13 Ahaz his son, Hezekiah his son, Manasseh his son,   2 Kin. 16:1

14 Amon his son, Josiah his son.   2 Kin. 23:30

15 And the sons of Josiah were, the firstborn Johanan, the second Jehoiakim, the third Zedekiah, the fourth Shallum.

16 And the sons of Jehoiakim: Jeconiah his son, Zedekiah his son.   2 Kin. 24:6

17 And the sons of Jeconiah; Assir, Salathiel his son,   Ezra 3:2

18 Malchiram also, and Pedaiah, and Shenazar, Jecamiah, Hoshama, and Nedabiah.

19 And the sons of Pedaiah were, Zerubbabel, and Shimei: and the sons of Zerubbabel; Meshullam, and Hananiah, and Shelomith their sister: Ezra 2:2

20 And Hashubah, and Ohel, and Berechiah, and Hasadiah, Jushab-hesed, five.

21 And the sons of Hananiah; Pelatiah, and Jesaiah: the sons of Rephaiah, the sons of Arnan, the sons of Obadiah, the sons of Shechaniah.

22 And the sons of Shechaniah; Shemaiah: and the sons of Shemaiah; Hattush, and Igeal, and Bariah, and Neariah, and Shaphat, six.   Ezra 8:2

23 And the sons of Neariah; Elioenai, and Hezekiah, and Azrikam, three.

24 And the sons of Elioenai were, Hodaiah, and Eliashib, and Pelaiah, and Akkub, and Johanan, and Dalaiah, and Anani, seven.

More of Judah's Descendants

4 The sons of Judah; Pharez, Hezron, and Carmi, and Hur, and Shobal.   Gen. 46:12

2 And Reaiah the son of Shobal begat Jahath; and Jahath begat Ahumai, and Lahad. These are the families of the Zorathites.

3 And these were of the father of Etam; Jezreel, and Ishma, and Idbash: and the name of their sister was Hazelelponi:

4 And Penuel the father of Gedor, and Ezer the father of Hushah. These are the sons of Hur, the firstborn of Ephratah, the father of Beth-lehem.   1 Chr. 2:50

5 And Ashur the father of Tekoa had two wives, Helah and Naarah.   1 Chr. 2:24

6 And Naarah bare him Ahuzam, and Hepher, and Temeni, and Haahashtari. These were the sons of Naarah.

7 And the sons of Helah were, Zereth, and Jezoar, and Ethnan.

8 And Coz begat Anub, and Zobebah, and the families of Aharhel the son of Harum.

9 And Jabez was more honourable than his brethren: and his mother called his name Jabez, saying, Because I bare him with sorrow.   Gen. 34:19

10 And Jabez called on the God of Israel, saying, Oh that thou wouldest bless me indeed, and enlarge my coast, and that thine

hand might be with me, and that thou wouldest keep me from evil, that it may not grieve me! And God granted him that which he requested.

11 And Chelub the brother of Shuah begat Mehir, which was the father of Eshton.

12 And Eshton begat Beth-rapha, and Paseah, and Tehinnah the father of Ir-nahash. These are the men of Rechah.

13 And the sons of Kenaz; Othniel, and Seraiah: and the sons of Othniel; Hathath.

14 And Meonothai begat Ophrah: and Seraiah begat Joab, the father of the valley of Charashim; for they were craftsmen.

15 And the sons of Caleb the son of Jephunneh; Iru, Elah, and Naam: and the sons of Elah, even Kenaz.   Num. 13:6

16 And the sons of Jehaleleel; Ziph, and Ziphah, Tiria, and Asareel.

17 And the sons of Ezra were, Jether, and Mered, and Epher, and Jalon: and she bare Miriam, and Shammai, and Ishbah the father of Eshtemoa.

18 And his wife Jehudijah bare Jered the father of Gedor, and Heber the father of Socho, and Jekuthiel the father of Zanoah. And these are the sons of Bithiah the daughter of Pharaoh, which Mered took.   1 Chr. 4:4

19 And the sons of his wife Hodiah the sister of Naham, the father of Keilah the Garmite, and Eshtemoa the Maachathite.   Josh. 15:44

20 And the sons of Shimon were, Amnon, and Rinnah, Ben-hanan, and Tilon. And the sons of Ishi were, Zoheth, and Ben-zoheth.

21 The sons of Shelah the son of Judah were, Er the father of Lecah, and Laadah the father of Mareshah, and the families of the house of them that ᵀwrought fine linen, of the house of Ashbea.   Gen. 38:5 ◆ made

22 And Jokim, and the men of Chozeba, and Joash, and Saraph, who had the dominion in Moab, and Jashubi-lehem. And these are ancient things.

23 These were the potters, and those that dwelt among plants and hedges: there they dwelt with the king for his work.

Simeon's Descendants

24 The sons of Simeon were, Nemuel, and Jamin, Jarib, Zerah, and Shaul: Gen. 46:10

25 Shallum his son, Mibsam his son, Mishma his son.

26 And the sons of Mishma; Hamuel his son, Zacchur his son, Shimei his son.

27 And Shimei had sixteen sons and six daughters; but his brethren had not many children, neither did all their family multiply, like to the children of Judah.   Num. 2:4

28 And they dwelt at Beer-sheba, and Moladah, and Hazar-shual,   Josh. 19:2-3

29 And at Bilhah, and at Ezem, and at Tolad,

30 And at Bethuel, and at Hormah, and at Ziklag,

31 And at Beth-marcaboth, and Hazar-susim, and at Beth-birei, and at Shaaraim. These were their cities unto the reign of David.   Josh. 19:5-6

32 And their villages were, Etam, and Ain, Rimmon, and Tochen, and Ashan, five cities:

33 And all their villages that were round about the same cities, unto Baal. These were their habitations, and their genealogy.   Josh. 19:8

34 And Meshobab, and Jamlech, and Joshah the son of Amaziah,

35 And Joel, and Jehu the son of Josibiah, the son of Seraiah, the son of Asiel,

36 And Elioenai, and Jaakobah, and Jeshohaiah, and Asaiah, and Adiel, and Jesimiel, and Benaiah,

37 And Ziza the son of Shiphi, the son of Allon, the son of Jedaiah, the son of Shimri, the son of Shemaiah;

38 These mentioned by their names were princes in their families: and the house of their fathers increased greatly.

39 And they went to the entrance of Gedor, even unto the east side of the valley, to seek pasture for their flocks.   Josh. 15:58

40 And they found fat pasture and good, and the land was wide, and quiet, and peaceable; for they of Ham had dwelt there of old.   Judg. 18:7-10

41 And these written by name came in the days of Hezekiah king of Judah, and smote their tents, and the habitations that were found there, and destroyed them utterly unto this day, and dwelt in their rooms: because there was pasture there for their flocks.

42 And some of them, even of the sons of Simeon, five hundred men, went to mount Seir, having for their captains Pelatiah, and Neariah, and Rephaiah, and Uzziel, the sons of Ishi.   Gen. 36:8-9

43 And they smote the rest of the Amalekites that were escaped, and dwelt there unto this day.   1 Sam. 15:7-8; 30:17; 2 Sam. 8:12

Reuben's Descendants

5 Now the sons of Reuben the firstborn of Israel, (for he was the firstborn; but, ᵀforasmuch as he defiled his father's bed, his birthright was given unto the sons of Joseph the son of Israel: and the genealogy is not to be reckoned after the birthright.   Gen. 29:32; 35:22; 48:15-22 ◆ since

2 For Judah prevailed above his brethren, and of him came the chief ruler; but the birthright was Joseph's:) Gen. 49:8-10; Mic. 5:2; Matt. 2:6

3 The sons, I say, of Reuben the firstborn of Israel were, Hanoch, and Pallu, Hezron, and Carmi.   Gen. 46:9; Ex. 6:14; Num. 26:5-9

4 The sons of Joel; Shemaiah his son, Gog his son, Shimei his son,

5 Micah his son, Reaia his son, Baal his son,

6 Beerah his son, whom Tilgath-pilneser king of Assyria carried away *captive*: he *was* prince of the Reubenites.   1 Chr. 5:26

7 And his brethren by their families, when the genealogy of their generations was reckoned, *were* the chief, Jeiel, and Zechariah,

8 And Bela the son of Azaz, the son of Shema, the son of Joel, who dwelt in Aroer, even unto Nebo and Baal-meon: Num. 32:34

9 And eastward he inhabited unto the entering in of the wilderness from the river Euphrates: because their cattle were multiplied in the land of Gilead.   Josh. 22:8-9

10 And in the days of Saul they made war with the Hagarites, who fell by their hand: and they dwelt in their tents throughout all the east *land* of Gilead.

Gad's Descendants

11 And the children of Gad dwelt over against them, in the land of Bashan unto Salchah: Josh. 13:11, 24-28

12 Joel the chief, and Shapham the next, and Jaanai, and Shaphat in Bashan.

13 And their brethren of the house of their fathers *were*, Michael, and Meshullam, and Sheba, and Jorai, and Jachan, and Zia, and Heber, seven.

14 These *are* the children of Abihail the son of Huri, the son of Jaroah, the son of Gilead, the son of Michael, the son of Jeshishai, the son of Jahdo, the son of Buz;

15 Ahi the son of Abdiel, the son of Guni, chief of the house of their fathers.

16 And they dwelt in Gilead in Bashan, and in her towns, and in all the suburbs of Sharon, upon their borders.   1 Chr. 27:29

17 All these were reckoned by genealogies in the days of Jotham king of Judah, and in the days of Jeroboam king of Israel. 2 Kin. 14:16, 28

The Census and Conquests of Reuben, Gad, and the Half Tribe of Manasseh

18 The sons of Reuben, and the Gadites, and half the tribe of Manasseh, of valiant men, men able to bear [T]buckler and sword, and to shoot with bow, and skilful in war, *were* four and forty thousand seven hundred and [T]threescore, that went out to the war.   Num. 1:3 ◆ *shield* ◆ *sixty*

19 And they made war with the Hagarites, with Jetur, and Nephish, and Nodab. Gen. 25:15

20 And they were helped against them, and the Hagarites were delivered into their hand, and all that *were* with them: for they cried to God in the battle, and he was [T]intreated of them; because they put their trust in him.   2 Chr. 18:31; Ps. 20:7-8; 22:4-5 ◆ *pled with*

21 And they took away their *cattle*; of their camels fifty thousand, and of sheep two hundred and fifty thousand, and of asses two thousand, and of men an hundred thousand.

22 For there fell down many slain, because the war *was* of God. And they dwelt in their steads until the captivity.   2 Kin. 15:29; 17:6

23 And the children of the half tribe of Manasseh dwelt in the land: they increased from Bashan unto Baal-hermon and Senir, and unto mount Hermon.   Deut. 3:8-9

24 And these *were* the heads of the house of their fathers, even Epher, and Ishi, and Eliel, and Azriel, and Jeremiah, and Hodaviah, and Jahdiel, mighty men of valour, famous men, *and* heads of the house of their fathers.

25 And they [T]transgressed against the God of their fathers, and went a whoring after the gods of the people of the land, whom God destroyed before them.   Ex. 34:15 ◆ *violated a law*

26 And the God of Israel stirred up the spirit of Pul king of Assyria, and the spirit of Tilgath-pilneser king of Assyria, and he carried them away, even the Reubenites, and the Gadites, and the half tribe of Manasseh, and brought them unto Halah, and Habor, and Hara, and to the river Gozan, unto this day.   2 Kin. 15:19, 29; 17:6

5:26 God Still Remembers Mercy

From [the] terrible blow [of being "carried away" by Assyria,] the northern kingdom never recovered. The feeble remnant continued the forms of government, though no longer possessed of power. Only one more ruler, Hoshea, was to follow Pekah. Soon the kingdom was to be swept away forever. But in that time of sorrow and distress God still remembered mercy, and gave the people another opportunity to turn from idolatry. *PK 287, 288*

Levi's Descendants

6 The sons of Levi; Gershon, Kohath, and Merari.   Gen. 46:11; Ex. 6:16; Num. 26:57

2 And the sons of Kohath; Amram, Izhar, and Hebron, and Uzziel.   Ex. 6:18

3 And the children of Amram; Aaron, and Moses, and Miriam. The sons also of Aaron; Nadab, and Abihu, Eleazar, and Ithamar.

4 Eleazar begat Phinehas, Phinehas begat Abishua,   Ex. 6:25

5 And Abishua [T]begat Bukki, and Bukki begat Uzzi,   *brought forth*

6 And Uzzi begat Zerahiah, and Zerahiah begat Meraioth,

7 Meraioth begat Amariah, and Amariah begat Ahitub,

8 And Ahitub begat Zadok, and Zadok begat Ahimaaz,   2 Sam. 8:17; 15:27

9 And Ahimaaz begat Azariah, and Azariah begat Johanan,

10 And Johanan begat Azariah, (he *it is* that executed the priest's office in the temple that Solomon built in Jerusalem:)   1 Kin. 6:1-7

11 And Azariah begat Amariah, and Amariah begat Ahitub,   Ezra 7:3

12 And Ahitub begat Zadok, and Zadok begat Shallum,   Neh. 11:11

13 And Shallum begat Hilkiah, and Hilkiah begat Azariah,   2 Kin. 22:12-14

14 And Azariah begat Seraiah, and Seraiah begat Jehozadak,   2 Kin. 25:18

15 And Jehozadak went *into captivity,* when the LORD carried away Judah and Jerusalem by the hand of Nebuchadnezzar.   2 Kin. 25:18

16 The sons of Levi; Gershom, Kohath, and Merari.   Ex. 6:16

17 And these *be* the names of the sons of Gershom; Libni, and Shimei.   1 Chr. 23:7

18 And the sons of Kohath *were,* Amram, and Izhar, and Hebron, and Uzziel.1 Chr. 23:12

19 The sons of Merari; Mahli, and Mushi. And these *are* the families of the Levites according to their fathers.   1 Chr. 23:21; 24:26

20 Of Gershom; Libni his son, Jahath his son, Zimmah his son,

21 Joah his son, Iddo his son, Zerah his son, Jeaterai his son.

22 The sons of Kohath; Amminadab his son, Korah his son, Assir his son,   Ex. 6:24

23 Elkanah his son, and Ebiasaph his son, and Assir his son,

24 Tahath his son, Uriel his son, Uzziah his son, and Shaul his son.

25 And the sons of Elkanah; Amasai, and Ahimoth.

26 *As for* Elkanah: the sons of Elkanah; Zophai his son, and Nahath his son,   1 Sam. 1:1

27 Eliab his son, Jeroham his son, Elkanah his son.   1 Sam. 1:1

28 And the sons of Samuel; the firstborn Vashni, and Abiah.   1 Sam. 8:2

29 The sons of Merari; Mahli, Libni his son, Shimei his son, Uzza his son,   1 Chr. 6:19

30 Shimea his son, Haggiah his son, Asaiah his son.

31 And these *are they* whom David set over the service of song in the house of the LORD, after that the ark had rest.   2 Sam. 6:17

32 And they ministered before the dwelling place of the tabernacle of the congregation with singing, until Solomon had built the house of the LORD in Jerusalem: and *then* they waited on their office according to their order.

33 And these *are* they that waited with their children. Of the sons of the Kohathites: Heman a singer, the son of Joel, the son of Shemuel,

34 The son of Elkanah, the son of Jeroham, the son of Eliel, the son of Toah,

35 The son of Zuph, the son of Elkanah, the son of Mahath, the son of Amasai,

36 The son of Elkanah, the son of Joel, the son of Azariah, the son of Zephaniah,

37 The son of Tahath, the son of Assir, the son of Ebiasaph, the son of Korah,

38 The son of Izhar, the son of Kohath, the son of Levi, the son of Israel.

39 And his brother Asaph, who stood on his right hand, *even* Asaph the son of Berachiah, the son of Shimea,   2 Chr. 5:12

40 The son of Michael, the son of Baaseiah, the son of Malchiah,

41 The son of Ethni, the son of Zerah, the son of Adaiah,

42 The son of Ethan, the son of Zimmah, the son of Shimei,

43 The son of Jahath, the son of Gershom, the son of Levi.

44 And their brethren the sons of Merari *stood* on the left hand: Ethan the son of Kishi, the son of Abdi, the son of Malluch,

45 The son of Hashabiah, the son of Amaziah, the son of Hilkiah,

46 The son of Amzi, the son of Bani, the son of Shamer,

47 The son of Mahli, the son of Mushi, the son of Merari, the son of Levi.

48 Their brethren also the Levites *were* appointed unto all manner of service of the tabernacle of the house of God.

49 But Aaron and his sons offered upon the altar of the burnt offering, and on the altar of incense, *and were appointed* for all the work of the *place* most holy, and to make an atonement for Israel, according to all that Moses the servant of God had commanded. Ex. 27:1-8

50 And these *are* the sons of Aaron; Eleazar his son, Phinehas his son, Abishua his son,

51 Bukki his son, Uzzi his son, Zerahiah his son,

52 Meraioth his son, Amariah his son, Ahitub his son,

53 Zadok his son, Ahimaaz his son. 2 Sam. 8:17

The Cities of the Priests and Levites

54 Now these *are* their dwelling places throughout their castles in their coasts, of the sons of Aaron, of the families of the Kohathites: for theirs was the lot.   Gen. 25:16

55 And they gave them Hebron in the land of Judah, and the suburbs thereof round about it.   Josh. 14:13

56 But the fields of the city, and the villages thereof, they gave to Caleb the son of Jephunneh.   Josh. 15:13

57 And to the sons of Aaron they gave the cities of Judah, *namely,* Hebron, *the city* of refuge,

and Libnah with her suburbs, and Jattir, and Eshtemoa, with their suburbs,   Josh. 15:48
58 And Hilen with her suburbs, Debir with her suburbs,   Josh. 10:3
59 And Ashan with her suburbs, and Beth-shemesh with her suburbs: Josh. 21:16
60 And out of the tribe of Benjamin; Geba with her suburbs, and Alemeth with her suburbs, and Anathoth with her suburbs. All their cities throughout their families *were* thirteen cities.   Jer. 1:1
61 And unto the sons of Kohath, *which were* left of the family of that tribe, *were cities given* out of the half tribe, *namely, out of* the half *tribe* of Manasseh, by lot, ten cities.
62 And to the sons of Gershom throughout their families out of the tribe of Issachar, and out of the tribe of Asher, and out of the tribe of Naphtali, and out of the tribe of Manasseh in Bashan, thirteen cities.
63 Unto the sons of Merari *were given* by lot, throughout their families, out of the tribe of Reuben, and out of the tribe of Gad, and out of the tribe of Zebulun, twelve cities. Josh. 21:7
64 And the children of Israel gave to the Levites *these* cities with their suburbs.
65 And they gave by lot out of the tribe of the children of Judah, and out of the tribe of the children of Simeon, and out of the tribe of the children of Benjamin, these cities, which are called by *their* names.
66 And *the residue* of the families of the sons of Kohath had cities of their coasts out of the tribe of Ephraim.
67 And they gave unto them, *of* the cities of refuge, Shechem in mount Ephraim with her suburbs; *they gave* also Gezer with her suburbs,   Josh. 21:21
68 And Jokmeam with her suburbs, and Beth-horon with her suburbs,
69 And Aijalon with her suburbs, and Gath-rimmon with her suburbs: Josh. 10:12
70 And out of the half tribe of Manasseh; Aner with her suburbs, and Bileam with her suburbs, for the family of the remnant of the sons of Kohath.
71 Unto the sons of Gershom *were given* out of the family of the half tribe of Manasseh, Golan in Bashan with her suburbs, and Ashtaroth with her suburbs: Josh. 9:10; 20:8; 21:27
72 And out of the tribe of Issachar; Kedesh with her suburbs, Daberath with her suburbs,
73 And Ramoth with her suburbs, and Anem with her suburbs:
74 And out of the tribe of Asher; Mashal with her suburbs, and Abdon with her suburbs,
75 And Hukok with her suburbs, and Rehob with her suburbs:
76 And out of the tribe of Naphtali; Kedesh

in Galilee with her suburbs, and Hammon with her suburbs, and Kirjathaim with her suburbs.   Josh. 21:32
77 Unto the rest of the children of Merari *were given* out of the tribe of Zebulun, Rimmon with her suburbs, Tabor with her suburbs: Josh. 21:34-35
78 And on the other side Jordan by Jericho, on the east side of Jordan, *were given them* out of the tribe of Reuben, Bezer in the wilderness with her suburbs, and Jahzah with her suburbs,   Josh. 20:8
79 Kedemoth also with her suburbs, and Mephaath with her suburbs:
80 And out of the tribe of Gad; Ramoth in Gilead with her suburbs, and Mahanaim with her suburbs,   Gen. 32:2
81 And Heshbon with her suburbs, and Jazer with her suburbs.   Josh. 21:39

Issachar's Descendants

7 Now the sons of Issachar *were*, Tola, and Puah, Jashub, and Shimron, four. Gen. 46:13
2 And the sons of Tola; Uzzi, and Rephaiah, and Jeriel, and Jahmai, and Jibsam, and Shemuel, heads of their father's house, ᵀ*to wit*, of Tola: *they were* valiant men of might in their generations; whose number *was* in the days of David two and twenty thousand and six hundred.   2 Sam. 24:1-9 ◆ *namely*
3 And the sons of Uzzi; Izrahiah: and the sons of Izrahiah; Michael, and Obadiah, and Joel, Ishiah, five: all of them chief men.
4 And with them, by their generations, after the house of their fathers, *were* bands of soldiers for war, six and thirty thousand *men*: for they had many wives and sons.
5 And their brethren among all the families of Issachar *were* valiant men of might, reckoned in all by their genealogies ᵀfourscore and seven thousand.   *eighty*

Benjamin's Descendants

6 *The sons* of Benjamin; Bela, and Becher, and Jediael, three.   Gen. 46:21
7 And the sons of Bela; Ezbon, and Uzzi, and Uzziel, and Jerimoth, and Iri, five; heads of the house of *their* fathers, mighty men of valour; and were reckoned by their genealogies twenty and two thousand and thirty and four.
8 And the sons of Becher; Zemira, and Joash, and Eliezer, and Elioenai, and Omri, and Jerimoth, and Abiah, and Anathoth, and Alameth. All these *are* the sons of Becher.
9 And the number of them, after their genealogy by their generations, heads of the house of their fathers, mighty men of valour, *was* twenty thousand and two hundred.
10 The sons also of Jediael; Bilhan: and the sons of Bilhan; Jeush, and Benjamin, and

Ehud, and Chenaanah, and Zethan, and Tharshish, and Ahishahar.

11 All these the sons of Jediael, by the heads of their fathers, mighty men of valour, *were* seventeen thousand and two hundred *soldiers*, fit to go out for war *and* battle.

12 Shuppim also, and Huppim, the children of Ir, *and* Hushim, the sons of Aher.

Naphtali's Descendants

13 The sons of Naphtali; Jahziel, and Guni, and Jezer, and Shallum, the sons of Bilhah.

Manasseh's Descendants Who Lived West of the Jordan

14 The sons of Manasseh; Ashriel, whom she bare: (*but* his ᵀconcubine the Aramitess bare Machir the father of Gilead:*less important wife*

15 And Machir took to wife *the sister* of Huppim and Shuppim, whose sister's name *was* Maachah;) and the name of the second *was* Zelophehad: and Zelophehad had daughters. Num. 26:33

16 And Maachah the wife of Machir bare a son, and she called his name Peresh; and the name of his brother *was* Sheresh; and his sons *were* Ulam and Rakem.

17 And the sons of Ulam; Bedan. These *were* the sons of Gilead, the son of Machir, the son of Manasseh. 1 Sam. 12:11

18 And his sister Hammoleketh bare Ishod, and Abi-ezer, and Mahalah.

19 And the sons of Shemida were, Ahian, and Shechem, and Likhi, and Aniam.

Ephraim's Descendants

20 And the sons of Ephraim; Shuthelah, and Bered his son, and Tahath his son, and Eladah his son, and Tahath his son, Num. 26:35-36

21 And Zabad his son, and Shuthelah his son, and Ezer, and Elead, whom the men of Gath *that were* born in *that* land slew, because they came down to take away their cattle.

22 And Ephraim their father mourned many days, and his brethren came to comfort him. Gen. 37:34

23 And when he went in to his wife, she conceived, and bare a son, and he called his name Beriah, because it went evil with his house.

24 (And his daughter *was* Sherah, who built Beth-horon the ᵀnether, and the upper, and Uzzen-sherah.) Josh. 16:3 ◆ *lower*

25 And Rephah *was* his son, also Resheph, and Telah his son, and Tahan his son,

26 Laadan his son, Ammihud his son, Elishama his son,

27 Non his son, Jehoshua his son. Ex. 17:9-14

28 And their possessions and habitations *were*, Beth-el and the towns thereof, and eastward Naaran, and westward Gezer, with the towns thereof; Shechem also and the towns thereof, unto Gaza and the towns thereof:

29 And by the borders of the children of Manasseh, Beth-shean and her towns, Taanach and her towns, Megiddo and her towns, Dor and her towns. In these dwelt the children of Joseph the son of Israel. Judg. 1:22-29

Asher's Descendants

30 The sons of Asher; Imnah, and Isuah, and Ishuai, and Beriah, and Serah their sister. Gen. 46:17; Num. 26:44-46

31 And the sons of Beriah; Heber, and Malchiel, who *is* the father of Birzavith.

32 And Heber ᵀbegat Japhlet, and Shomer, and Hotham, and Shua their sister. *brought forth*

33 And the sons of Japhlet; Pasach, and Bimhal, and Ashvath. These *are* the children of Japhlet.

34 And the sons of Shamer; Ahi, and Rohgah, Jehubbah, and Aram.

35 And the sons of his brother Helem; Zophah, and Imna, and Shelesh, and Amal.

36 The sons of Zophah; Suah, and Harnepher, and Shual, and Beri, and Imrah,

37 Bezer, and Hod, and Shamma, and Shilshah, and Ithran, and Beera.

38 And the sons of Jether; Jephunneh, and Pispah, and Ara.

39 And the sons of Ulla; Arah, and Haniel, and Rezia.

40 All these *were* the children of Asher, heads of *their* father's house, choice *and* mighty men of valour, chief of the princes. And the number throughout the genealogy of them that were apt to the war *and* to battle *was* twenty and six thousand men.

More on Benjamin's Descendants

8 Now Benjamin begat Bela his firstborn, Ashbel the second, and Aharah the third, Gen. 46:21; Num. 26:38; 1 Chr. 7:6-12

2 Nohah the fourth, and Rapha the fifth.

3 And the sons of Bela were, Addar, and Gera, and Abihud, Gen. 46:21

4 And Abishua, and Naaman, and Ahoah,

5 And Gera, and Shephuphan, and Huram.

6 And these *are* the sons of Ehud: these are the heads of the fathers of the inhabitants of Geba, and they removed them to Manahath: Judg. 3:20-30

7 And Naaman, and Ahiah, and Gera, he removed them, and ᵀbegat Uzza, and Ahihud. *brought forth*

8 And Shaharaim begat *children* in the country of Moab, after he had sent them away; Hushim and Baara *were* his wives.

9 And he begat of Hodesh his wife, Jobab, and Zibia, and Mesha, and Malcham,

10 And Jeuz, and Shachia, and Mirma. These *were* his sons, heads of the fathers.

11 And of Hushim he begat Abitub, and El-paal.

12 The sons of Elpaal; Eber, and Misham, and Shamed, who built Ono, and Lod, with the towns thereof: Ezra 2:33

13 Beriah also, and Shema, who *were* heads of the fathers of the inhabitants of Aijalon, who drove away the inhabitants of Gath:

14 And Ahio, Shashak, and Jeremoth,

15 And Zebadiah, and Arad, and Ader,

16 And Michael, and Ispah, and Joha, the sons of Beriah;

17 And Zebadiah, and Meshullam, and Hez-eki, and Heber,

18 Ishmerai also, and Jezliah, and Jobab, the sons of Elpaal;

19 And Jakim, and Zichri, and Zabdi,

20 And Elienai, and Zilthai, and Eliel,

21 And Adaiah, and Beraiah, and Shimrath, the sons of Shimhi;

22 And Ishpan, and Heber, and Eliel,

23 And Abdon, and Zichri, and Hanan,

24 And Hananiah, and Elam, and Antothi-jah,

25 And Iphedeiah, and Penuel, the sons of Shashak;

26 And Shamsherai, and Shehariah, and Athaliah,

27 And Jaresiah, and Eliah, and Zichri, the sons of Jeroham.

28 These *were* heads of the fathers, by their generations, chief *men.* These dwelt in Jerusalem.

29 And at Gibeon dwelt the father of Gibeon; whose wife's name *was* Maachah:

30 And his firstborn son Abdon, and Zur, and Kish, and Baal, and Nadab,

31 And Gedor, and Ahio, and Zacher.

32 And Mikloth begat Shimeah. And these also dwelt with their brethren in Jerusalem, over against them.

33 And Ner begat Kish, and Kish begat Saul, and Saul begat Jonathan, and Malchi-shua, and Abinadab, and Esh-baal.   1 Sam. 9:1; 31:2

34 And the son of Jonathan *was* Merib-baal; and Merib-baal begat Micah.   2 Sam. 9:12

35 And the sons of Micah *were,* Pithon, and Melech, and Tarea, and Ahaz.

36 And Ahaz begat Jehoadah; and Jehoadah begat Alemeth, and Azmaveth, and Zimri; and Zimri begat Moza,

37 And Moza begat Binea: Rapha *was* his son, Eleasah his son, Azel his son:

38 And Azel had six sons, whose names *are* these, Azrikam, Bocheru, and Ishmael, and Sheariah, and Obadiah, and Hanan. All these *were* the sons of Azel.

39 And the sons of Eshek his brother *were,* Ulam his firstborn, Jehush the second, and Eliphelet the third.

40 And the sons of Ulam were mighty men of valour, archers, and had many sons, and sons' sons, an hundred and fifty. All these *are* of the sons of Benjamin.

The People Who Lived in Jerusalem

9 So all Israel were reckoned by genealogies; and, behold, they were written in the book of the kings of Israel and Judah, who were carried away to Babylon for their ᵀtransgression.   *violation of a law*

2 Now the first inhabitants that *dwelt* in their possessions in their cities *were,* the Israelites, the priests, Levites, and the Nethinims.   Ezra 2:43, 58; Neh. 7:73

3 And in Jerusalem dwelt of the children of Judah, and of the children of Benjamin, and of the children of Ephraim, and Manasseh;   Neh. 11:1

4 Uthai the son of Ammihud, the son of Omri, the son of Imri, the son of Bani, of the children of Pharez the son of Judah. Gen. 46:12

5 And of the Shilonites; Asaiah the firstborn, and his sons.

6 And of the sons of Zerah; Jeuel, and their brethren, six hundred and ninety.

7 And of the sons of Benjamin; Sallu the son of Meshullam, the son of Hodaviah, the son of Hasenuah,

8 And Ibneiah the son of Jeroham, and Elah the son of Uzzi, the son of Michri, and Meshullam the son of Shephathiah, the son of Reuel, the son of Ibnijah;

9 And their brethren, according to their generations, nine hundred and fifty and six. All these men *were* chief of the fathers in the house of their fathers.

10 And of the priests; Jedaiah, and Jehoiarib, and Jachin,

11 And Azariah the son of Hilkiah, the son of Meshullam, the son of Zadok, the son of Meraioth, the son of Ahitub, the ruler of the house of God;   Neh. 11:11

12 And Adaiah the son of Jeroham, the son of Pashur, the son of Malchijah, and Maasiai the son of Adiel, the son of Jahzerah, the son of Meshullam, the son of Meshillemith, the son of Immer;

13 And their brethren, heads of the house of their fathers, a thousand and seven hundred and ᵀthreescore; very able men for the work of the service of the house of God.   *sixty*

14 And of the Levites; Shemaiah the son of Hasshub, the son of Azrikam, the son of Hashabiah, of the sons of Merari;

15 And Bakbakkar, Heresh, and Galal, and Mattaniah the son of Micah, the son of Zichri, the son of Asaph;   Neh. 11:22

16 And Obadiah the son of Shemaiah, the son of Galal, the son of Jeduthun, and Berechiah the son of Asa, the son of Elkanah, that dwelt in the villages of the Netophathites.

17 And the porters were, Shallum, and Akkub, and Talmon, and Ahiman, and their brethren: Shallum was the chief;
18 Who ᵀhitherto waited in the king's gate eastward: they were porters in the companies of the children of Levi.　Ezek. 46:1-2 ◆ up to now
19 And Shallum the son of Kore, the son of Ebiasaph, the son of Korah, and his brethren, of the house of his father, the Korahites, were over the work of the service, keepers of the gates of the tabernacle: and their fathers, being over the host of the LORD, were keepers of the entry.
20 And Phinehas the son of Eleazar was the ruler over them in time past, and the LORD was with him.
21 And Zechariah the son of Meshelemiah was ᵀporter of the door of the tabernacle of the congregation.　1 Chr. 26:14 ◆ doorkeeper
22 All these which were chosen to be porters in the gates were two hundred and twelve. These were reckoned by their genealogy in their villages, whom David and Samuel the seer did ordain in their set office.　1 Sam. 9:9
23 So they and their children had the oversight of the gates of the house of the LORD, namely, the house of the tabernacle, by wards.
24 In four quarters were the porters, toward the east, west, north, and south.
25 And their brethren, which were in their villages, were to come after seven days from time to time with them. 2 Kin. 11:5, 7; 2 Chr. 23:8
26 For these Levites, the four chief porters, were in their set office, and were over the chambers and treasuries of the house of God.
27 And they lodged round about the house of God, because the charge was upon them, and the opening thereof every morning pertained to them.
28 And certain of them had the charge of the ministering vessels, that they should bring them in and out by ᵀtale.　counted number
29 Some of them also were appointed to oversee the vessels, and all the instruments of the sanctuary, and the fine flour, and the wine, and the oil, and the frankincense, and the spices.　1 Chr. 23:29
30 And some of the sons of the priests made the ointment of the spices.　Ex. 30:23-25
31 And Mattithiah, one of the Levites, who was the firstborn of Shallum the Korahite, had the set office over the things that were made in the pans.　1 Chr. 9:19
32 And other of their brethren, of the sons of the Kohathites, were over the shewbread, to prepare it every sabbath.　Lev. 24:5-8
33 And these are the singers, chief of the fathers of the Levites, who remaining in the

chambers were free: for they were employed in that work day and night.　1 Chr. 6:31-33
34 These chief fathers of the Levites were chief throughout their generations; these dwelt at Jerusalem.

Saul's Descendants

35 And in Gibeon dwelt the father of Gibeon, Jehiel, whose wife's name was Maachah:
36 And his firstborn son Abdon, then Zur, and Kish, and Baal, and Ner, and Nadab,
37 And Gedor, and Ahio, and Zechariah, and Mikloth.
38 And Mikloth ᵀbegat Shimeam. And they also dwelt with their brethren at Jerusalem, over against their brethren.　brought forth
39 And Ner begat Kish; and Kish begat Saul; and Saul begat Jonathan, and Malchi-shua, and Abinadab, and Esh-baal.　1 Sam. 13:22
40 And the son of Jonathan was Merib-baal: and Merib-baal begat Micah.
41 And the sons of Micah were, Pithon, and Melech, and Tahrea, and Ahaz.　1 Chr. 8:35
42 And Ahaz begat Jarah; and Jarah begat Alemeth, and Azmaveth, and Zimri; and Zimri begat Moza;　1 Chr. 8:36
43 And Moza begat Binea; and Rephaiah his son, Eleasah his son, Azel his son. 1 Chr. 8:37
44 And Azel had six sons, whose names are these, Azrikam, Bocheru, and Ishmael, and Sheariah, and Obadiah, and Hanan: these were the sons of Azel.

Saul's Overthrow and Death

10 Now the Philistines fought against Israel; and the men of Israel fled from before the Philistines, and fell down slain in mount Gilboa.　1 Sam. 31
2 And the Philistines followed hard after Saul, and after his sons; and the Philistines slew Jonathan, and Abinadab, and Malchi-shua, the sons of Saul.
3 And the battle went sore against Saul, and the archers hit him, and he was wounded of the archers.
4 Then said Saul to his armourbearer, Draw thy sword, and thrust me through therewith; lest these uncircumcised come and abuse me. But his armourbearer would not; for he was sore afraid. So Saul took a sword, and fell upon it.　1 Sam. 31:4
5 And when his armourbearer saw that Saul was dead, he fell likewise on the sword, and died.
6 So Saul died, and his three sons, and all his house died together.
7 And when all the men of Israel that were in the valley saw that they fled, and that Saul and his sons were dead, then they forsook their cities, and fled: and the Philistines came and dwelt in them.

8 And it came to pass on the morrow, when the Philistines came to strip the slain, that they found Saul and his sons fallen in mount Gilboa.

9 And when they had stripped him, they took his head, and his armour, and sent into the land of the Philistines round about, to carry tidings unto their idols, and to the people.

10 And they put his armour in the house of their gods, and fastened his head in the temple of Dagon.

11 And when all Jabesh-gilead heard all that the Philistines had done to Saul,

12 They arose, all the valiant men, and took away the body of Saul, and the bodies of his sons, and brought them to Jabesh, and buried their bones under the oak in Jabesh, and fasted seven days.

13 So Saul died for his transgression which he committed against the LORD, *even* against the word of the LORD, which he kept not, and also for asking *counsel* of *one that had* a familiar spirit, to enquire *of it*; Lev. 19:31; 20:6; 1 Sam. 15:23

14 And enquired not of the LORD: therefore he slew him, and turned the kingdom unto David the son of Jesse.   1 Sam. 13:14; 15:28; 28:6

10:13, 14 Satan, Not Samuel

The act of Saul in consulting a sorceress is cited in Scripture as one reason why he was rejected by God and abandoned to destruction. . . . Here it is distinctly stated that Saul inquired of the familiar spirit, not of the Lord. He did not communicate with Samuel, the prophet of God; but through the sorceress he held intercourse [conversation] with Satan. Satan could not present the real Samuel, but he did present a counterfeit, that served his purpose of deception. *PP 683*

David Is Anointed King of Israel and Captures Jerusalem

11 Then all Israel gathered themselves to David unto Hebron, saying, Behold, we *are* thy bone and thy flesh.

2 And moreover in time past, even when Saul was king, thou *wast* he that leddest out and broughtest in Israel: and the LORD thy God said unto thee, Thou shalt feed my people Israel, and thou shalt be ruler over my people Israel.   2 Sam. 5:2

11:1–3 An Unsought Honor

Thus through the providence of God the way had been opened for [David] to come to the throne. He had no personal ambition to gratify, for he had not sought the honor to which he had been brought. *PP 701*

---

3 Therefore came all the elders of Israel

to the king to Hebron; and David made a covenant with them in Hebron before the LORD; and they anointed David king over Israel, according to the word of the LORD by Samuel.   1 Sam. 16:1, 3, 12-13

4 And David and all Israel went to Jerusalem, which *is* Jebus; where the Jebusites *were*, the inhabitants of the land. Gen. 10:16; 15:21; Judg. 1:21

5 And the inhabitants of Jebus said to David, Thou shalt not come hither. Nevertheless David took the castle of Zion, which *is* the city of David.   *here*

6 And David said, Whosoever ᵀsmiteth the Jebusites first shall be chief and captain. So Joab the son of Zeruiah went first up, and was chief.   2 Sam. 8:16 ◆ *strikes*

7 And David dwelt in the castle; therefore they called it the city of David.

8 And he built the city round about, even from Millo round about: and Joab repaired the rest of the city.

9 So David ᵀwaxed greater and greater: for the LORD of hosts *was* with him.   2 Sam. 3:1 ◆ *became*

David's Mighty Men

10 These also *are* the chief of the mighty men whom David had, who strengthened themselves with him in his kingdom, *and* with all Israel, to make him king, according to the word of the LORD concerning Israel.   1 Chr. 11:3

11 And this *is* the number of the mighty men whom David had; Jashobeam, an Hachmonite, the chief of the captains: he lifted up his spear against three hundred slain *by him* at one time.   2 Sam. 23:8

12 And after him *was* Eleazar the son of Dodo, the Ahohite, who *was one* of the three mighties.   1 Chr. 27:4

13 He was with David at Pas-dammim, and there the Philistines were gathered together to battle, where was a parcel of ground full of barley; and the people fled from before the Philistines.

14 And they set themselves in the midst of *that* parcel, and delivered it, and slew the Philistines; and the LORD saved *them* by a great deliverance.

15 Now three of the thirty captains went down to the rock to David, into the cave of Adullam; and the host of the Philistines encamped in the valley of Rephaim.   1 Chr. 14:9

16 And David *was* then in the hold, and the Philistines' garrison *was* then at Beth-lehem.

17 And David longed, and said, Oh that one would give me drink of the water of the well of Beth-lehem, that *is* at the gate!

18 And the three brake through the host of the Philistines, and drew water out of the well of Beth-lehem, that *was* by the gate, and took *it*, and brought *it* to David: but David

would not drink *of* it, but poured it out to the LORD,

19 And said, My God forbid it me, that I should do this thing: shall I drink the blood of these men that have put their lives in jeopardy? for with *the jeopardy of* their lives they brought it. Therefore he would not drink it. These things did these three mightiest.

11:17–19 David's Regard for Life

Of David's sacred regard for human life, striking evidence had been given, even while he himself was hunted like a beast of prey. . . . David had been a man of war, much of his life had been spent amid scenes of violence; but of all who have passed through such an ordeal, few indeed have been so little affected by its hardening, demoralizing influence as was David. *PP 736, 737*

---

20 And Abishai the brother of Joab, he was chief of the three: for lifting up his spear against three hundred, he slew *them*, and had a name among the three.   1 Sam. 26:6

21 Of the three, he was more honourable than the two; for he was their captain: howbeit he attained not to the *first* three.   however

22 Benaiah the son of Jehoiada, the son of a valiant man of Kabzeel, who had done many acts; he slew two lionlike men of Moab: also he went down and slew a lion in a pit in a snowy day.   Josh. 15:21

23 And he slew an Egyptian, a man of *great* stature, five cubits high; and in the Egyptian's hand *was* a spear like a weaver's beam; and he went down to him with a staff, and plucked the spear out of the Egyptian's hand, and slew him with his own spear.   1 Sam. 17:7

24 These *things* did Benaiah the son of Jehoiada, and had the name among the three mighties.

25 Behold, he was honourable among the thirty, but attained not to the *first* three: and David set him over his guard.

26 Also the valiant men of the armies *were*, Asahel the brother of Joab, Elhanan the son of Dodo of Beth-lehem,   1 Chr. 27:7

27 Shammoth the Harorite, Helez the Pelonite,

28 Ira the son of Ikkesh the Tekoite, Abiezer the Antothite,   1 Chr. 27:12

29 Sibbecai the Hushathite, Ilai the Ahohite,

30 Maharai the Netophathite, Heled the son of Baanah the Netophathite,

31 Ithai the son of Ribai of Gibeah, *that pertained* to the children of Benjamin, Benaiah the Pirathonite,

32 Hurai of the brooks of Gaash, Abiel the Arbathite,

33 Azmaveth the Baharumite, Eliahba the Shaalbonite,

34 The sons of Hashem the Gizonite, Jonathan the son of Shage the Hararite,

35 Ahiam the son of Sacar the Hararite, Eliphal the son of Ur,

36 Hepher the Mecherathite, Ahijah the Pelonite,

37 Hezro the Carmelite, Naarai the son of Ezbai,

38 Joel the brother of Nathan, Mibhar the son of Haggeri,

39 Zelek the Ammonite, Naharai the Berothite, the armourbearer of Joab the son of Zeruiah,

40 Ira the Ithrite, Gareb the Ithrite,

41 Uriah the Hittite, Zabad the son of Ahlai,

42 Adina the son of Shiza the Reubenite, a captain of the Reubenites, and thirty with him,

43 Hanan the son of Maachah, and Joshaphat the Mithnite,

44 Uzzia the Ashterathite, Shama and Jehiel the sons of Hothan the Aroerite,

45 Jediael the son of Shimri, and Joha his brother, the Tizite,

46 Eliel the Mahavite, and Jeribai, and Joshaviah, the sons of Elnaam, and Ithmah the Moabite,

47 Eliel, and Obed, and Jasiel the Mesobaite.

The Men Who Helped David Become King

12 Now these *are* they that came to David to Ziklag, while he yet kept himself close because of Saul the son of Kish: and they *were* among the mighty men, helpers of the war.   1 Sam. 27:2-6

2 *They were* armed with bows, and could use both the right hand and the left in *hurling* stones and *shooting* arrows out of a bow, *even* of Saul's brethren of Benjamin. Judg. 3:15; 20:16

3 The chief *was* Ahiezer, then Joash, the sons of Shemaah the Gibeathite; and Jeziel, and Pelet, the sons of Azmaveth; and Berachah, and Jehu the Antothite,   1 Chr. 11:28

4 And Ismaiah the Gibeonite, a mighty man among the thirty, and over the thirty; and Jeremiah, and Jahaziel, and Johanan, and Josabad the Gederathite,   Josh. 9:3

5 Eluzai, and Jerimoth, and Bealiah, and Shemariah, and Shephatiah the Haruphite,

6 Elkanah, and Jesiah, and Azareel, and Joezer, and Jashobeam, the Korhites,

7 And Joelah, and Zebadiah, the sons of Jeroham of Gedor.   Josh. 15:58

8 And of the Gadites there separated themselves unto David into the hold to the wilderness men of might, *and* men of war *fit* for the battle, that could handle shield and buckler, whose faces *were like* the faces of lions, and *were* as swift as the roes upon the mountains;   2 Sam. 2:18; 17:10

9 Ezer the first, Obadiah the second, Eliab the third,

10 Mishmannah the fourth, Jeremiah the fifth,

11 Attai the sixth, Eliel the seventh,

12 Johanan the eighth, Elzabad the ninth,

13 Jeremiah the tenth, Machbanai the eleventh.

14 These *were* of the sons of Gad, captains of the host: one of the least *was* over an hundred, and the greatest over a thousand.　　Lev. 26:8

15 These *are* they that went over Jordan in the first month, when it had overflown all his banks; and they put to flight all *them* of the valleys, *both* toward the east, and toward the west.　　Josh. 3:15; 4:18

16 And there came of the children of Benjamin and Judah to the hold unto David.

17 And David went out to meet them, and answered and said unto them, If ye be come peaceably unto me to help me, mine heart shall be knit unto you: but if *ye be come* to betray me to mine enemies, seeing *there is* no wrong in mine hands, the God of our fathers look *thereon*, and rebuke *it*.

18 Then the spirit came upon Amasai, *who was* chief of the captains, *and he said*, Thine *are* we, David, and on thy side, thou son of Jesse: peace, peace *be* unto thee, and peace *be* to thine helpers; for thy God helpeth thee. Then David received them, and made them captains of the band.　　Judg. 6:34

19 And there fell *some* of Manasseh to David, when he came with the Philistines against Saul to battle: but they helped them not: for the lords of the Philistines upon ᵀadvisement sent him away, saying, He will fall to his master Saul to *the jeopardy of* our heads.　　1 Sam. 29:2-9 ✦ *counsel*

20 As he went to Ziklag, there fell to him of Manasseh, Adnah, and Jozabad, and Jediael, and Michael, and Jozabad, and Elihu, and Zilthai, captains of the thousands that *were* of Manasseh.

21 And they helped David against the band *of the rovers*: for they *were* all mighty men of valour, and were captains in the host.

22 For at *that* time day by day there came to David to help him, until *it was* a great host, like the host of God.　　Gen. 32:2

23 And these *are* the numbers of the bands *that were* ready armed to the war, *and* came to David to Hebron, to turn the kingdom of Saul to him, according to the word of the LORD.　　1 Sam. 16:1; 2 Sam. 2:3-4; 1 Chr. 11:10

24 The children of Judah that bare shield and spear *were* six thousand and eight hundred, ready armed to the war.

25 Of the children of Simeon, mighty men of valour for the war, seven thousand and one hundred.

26 Of the children of Levi four thousand and six hundred.

27 And Jehoiada *was* the leader of the Aaronites, and with him *were* three thousand and seven hundred;

28 And Zadok, a young man mighty of valour, and of his father's house twenty and two captains.　　2 Sam. 8:17; 1 Chr. 6:8, 53

29 And of the children of Benjamin, the kindred of Saul, three thousand: for hitherto the greatest part of them had kept the ward of the house of Saul.　　2 Sam. 2:8-9; 1 Chr. 12:2

30 And of the children of Ephraim twenty thousand and eight hundred, mighty men of valour, famous throughout the house of their fathers.

31 And of the half tribe of Manasseh eighteen thousand, which were expressed by name, to come and make David king.

32 And of the children of Issachar, *which were men* that had understanding of the times, to know what Israel ought to do; the heads of them *were* two hundred; and all their brethren *were* at their commandment.　　Esth. 1:13

33 Of Zebulun, such as went forth to battle, expert in war, with all instruments of war, fifty thousand, which could keep rank: *they were* not of double heart.　　Ps. 12:2

34 And of Naphtali a thousand captains, and with them with shield and spear thirty and seven thousand.

35 And of the Danites expert in war twenty and eight thousand and six hundred.

36 And of Asher, such as went forth to battle, expert in war, forty thousand. 1 Chr. 12:33

37 And on the other side of Jordan, of the Reubenites, and the Gadites, and of the half tribe of Manasseh, with all manner of instruments of war for the battle, an hundred and twenty thousand.

38 All these men of war, that could keep rank, came with a perfect heart to Hebron, to make David king over all Israel: and all the rest also of Israel *were* of one heart to make David king.　　1 Kin. 8:61

39 And there they were with David three days, eating and drinking: for their brethren had prepared for them.

40 Moreover they that were nigh them, *even* unto Issachar and Zebulun and Naphtali, brought bread on asses, and on camels, and on mules, and on oxen, *and* meat, meal, cakes of figs, and bunches of raisins, and wine, and oil, and oxen, and sheep abundantly: for *there was* joy in Israel.　　1 Sam. 25:18; 2 Sam. 16:1

David Brings the Ark from Kirjath-jearim

13 And David consulted with the captains of thousands and hundreds, *and* with every leader.

2 And David said unto all the congregation of Israel, If *it seem* good unto you, and *that it be* of the LORD our God, let us send abroad unto our brethren every where, *that are* left in all the land of Israel, and with them *also* to the priests and Levites *which are* in their cities *and* suburbs, that they may gather themselves unto us: 1 Sam. 31:1

3 And let us bring again the ark of our God to us: for we enquired not at it in the days of Saul. 1 Sam. 7:1-2

> **13:1–3 The Ark to Return to Jerusalem**
>
> Now that David was firmly established upon the throne and free from the invasions of foreign foes, he turned to the accomplishment of a cherished purpose—to bring up the ark of God to Jerusalem. For many years the ark had remained at Kirjath-jearim, nine miles distant; but it was fitting that the capital of the nation should be honored with the token of the divine Presence. *PP 704*

4 And all the congregation said that they would do so: for the thing was right in the eyes of all the people.

5 So David gathered all Israel together, from Shihor of Egypt even unto the entering of Hemath, to bring the ark of God from Kirjath-jearim. 1 Sam. 6:21–7:1; 2 Sam. 6:1; 1 Kin. 8:65

6 And David went up, and all Israel, to Baalah, *that is*, to Kirjath-jearim, which *belonged* to Judah, to bring up thence the ark of God the LORD, that dwelleth *between* the cherubims, whose name is called *on it*. Ex. 25:22

7 And they carried the ark of God in a new cart out of the house of Abinadab: and Uzza and Ahio ᵀdrave the cart. Num. 4:15 ◆ drove

8 And David and all Israel played before God with all *their* might, and with singing, and with harps, and with ᵀpsalteries, and with timbrels, and with cymbals, and with trumpets. stringed instruments

Uzza Is Killed and the Ark Left at the House of Obed-edom

9 And when they came unto the threshing-floor of Chidon, Uzza put forth his hand to hold the ark; for the oxen stumbled. 2 Sam. 6:6

10 And the anger of the LORD was kindled against Uzza, and he smote him, because he put his hand to the ark: and there he died before God. Num. 4:15; 1 Chr. 15:13, 15

11 And David was displeased, because the LORD had made a breach upon Uzza: wherefore that place is called Perez-uzza to this day.

12 And David was afraid of God that day, saying, How shall I bring the ark of God *home* to me?

13 So David brought not the ark *home* to himself to the city of David, but carried it aside into the house of Obed-edom the Gittite. 1 Chr. 15:18

14 And the ark of God remained with the family of Obed-edom in his house three months. And the LORD blessed the house of Obed-edom, and all that he had. 1 Chr. 26:4-5

> **13:9–14 David Questions God**
>
> A sudden terror fell upon the rejoicing throng. David was astonished and greatly alarmed, and in his heart he questioned the justice of God. He had been seeking to honor the ark as the symbol of the divine Presence. Why, then, had that fearful judgment been sent to turn the season of gladness into an occasion of grief and mourning? Feeling that it would be unsafe to have the ark near him, David determined to let it remain where it was. *PP 705*

Hiram's Kindness to David

14 Now Hiram king of Tyre sent messengers to David, and timber of cedars, with masons and carpenters, to build him an house. 2 Sam. 5:11-16

2 And David perceived that the LORD had

> ### The Sin of Presumption
>
> #### 1 Chronicles 13:9–14
>
> David and his people had assembled to perform a sacred work, and they had engaged in it with glad and willing hearts; but the Lord could not accept the service, because it was not performed in accordance with His directions. The Philistines, who had not a knowledge of God's law, had placed the ark upon a cart when they returned it to Israel, and the Lord accepted the effort which they made. But the Israelites had in their hands a plain statement of the will of God in all these matters, and their neglect of these instructions was dishonoring to God. Upon Uzzah rested the greater guilt of presumption. Transgression of God's law had lessened his sense of its sacredness, and with unconfessed sins upon him he had, in face of the divine prohibition, presumed to touch the symbol of God's presence. God can accept no partial obedience, no lax way of treating His commandments. By the judgment upon Uzzah He designed to impress upon all Israel the importance of giving strict heed to His requirements. Thus the death of that one man, by leading the people to repentance, might prevent the necessity of inflicting judgments upon thousands. *PP 705, 706*

confirmed him king over Israel, for his kingdom was lifted up on high, because of his people Israel.   Num. 24:7

3 And David took more wives at Jerusalem: and David ᵀbegat more sons and daughters.   *brought forth*

4 Now these *are* the names of *his* children which he had in Jerusalem; Shammua, and Shobab, Nathan, and Solomon,   1 Chr. 3:5-9

5 And Ibhar, and Elishua, and Elpalet,

6 And Nogah, and Nepheg, and Japhia,

7 And Elishama, and Beeliada, and Eliphalet.   2 Sam. 5:16

David Defeats the Philistines

8 And when the Philistines heard that David was anointed king over all Israel, all the Philistines went up to seek David. And David heard *of it,* and went out against them.

9 And the Philistines came and spread themselves in the valley of Rephaim.   1 Chr. 11:15

10 And David enquired of God, saying, Shall I go up against the Philistines? and wilt thou deliver them into mine hand? And the LORD said unto him, Go up; for I will deliver them into thine hand.

11 So they came up to Baal-perazim; and David smote them there. Then David said, God hath broken in upon mine enemies by mine hand like the breaking forth of waters: therefore they called the name of that place Baal-perazim.   Is. 28:21

12 And when they had left their gods there, David gave a commandment, and they were burned with fire.   Ex. 32:20

13 And the Philistines yet again spread themselves abroad in the valley.   1 Chr. 14:9

14 Therefore David enquired again of God; and God said unto him, Go not up after them; turn away from them, and come upon them over against the mulberry trees.

15 And it shall be, when thou shalt hear a sound of going in the tops of the mulberry trees, *that* then thou shalt go out to battle: for God is gone forth before thee to ᵀsmite the host of the Philistines.   *strike*

14:16, 17 The Vital Difference

If David, like Saul, had chosen his own way, success would not have attended him. But he did as the Lord had commanded. . . . *PP 704*

---

16 David therefore did as God commanded him: and they smote the host of the Philistines from Gibeon even to Gazer.

17 And the fame of David went out into all lands; and the LORD brought the fear of him upon all nations. Ex. 15:14-16; Deut. 2:25; Josh. 6:27

David Joyfully Brings the Ark to Jerusalem

15 And *David* made him houses in the city of David, and prepared a place for the ark of God, and pitched for it a tent.

15:1 David Tries Again

At the end of three months [David] resolved to make another attempt to remove the ark, and he now gave earnest heed to carry out in every particular the directions of the Lord. *PP 706*

---

2 Then David said, None ought to carry the ark of God but the Levites: for them hath the LORD chosen to carry the ark of God, and to minister unto him for ever.   Deut. 10:8

3 And David gathered all Israel together to Jerusalem, to bring up the ark of the LORD unto his place, which he had prepared for it.   1 Kin. 8:1; 1 Chr. 13:5; 15:1

4 And David assembled the children of Aaron, and the Levites:

5 Of the sons of Kohath; Uriel the chief, and his brethren an hundred and twenty:

6 Of the sons of Merari; Asaiah the chief, and his brethren two hundred and twenty:

7 Of the sons of Gershom; Joel the chief, and his brethren an hundred and thirty:

8 Of the sons of Elizaphan; Shemaiah the chief, and his brethren two hundred: Ex. 6:22

9 Of the sons of Hebron; Eliel the chief, and his brethren ᵀfourscore: Ex. 6:18 ◆ *eighty*

10 Of the sons of Uzziel; Amminadab the chief, and his brethren an hundred and twelve.

11 And David called for Zadok and Abiathar the priests, and for the Levites, for Uriel, Asaiah, and Joel, Shemaiah, and Eliel, and Amminadab,   1 Chr. 12:28

12 And said unto them, Ye *are* the chief of the fathers of the Levites: ᵀsanctify yourselves, *both* ye and your brethren, that ye may bring up the ark of the LORD God of Israel unto *the place that* I have prepared for it.   Ex. 19:14-15; 2 Chr. 35:6 ◆ *make holy*

13 For because ye *did it* not at the first, the LORD our God made a breach upon us, for that we sought him not after the due order.

14 So the priests and the Levites ᵀsanctified themselves to bring up the ark of the LORD God of Israel.   *made themselves holy*

15 And the children of the Levites bare the ark of God upon their shoulders with the staves thereon, as Moses commanded according to the word of the LORD.   Num. 4:15

16 And David spake to the chief of the Levites to appoint their brethren *to be* the singers with instruments of musick, psalteries and harps and cymbals, sounding, by lifting up the voice with joy.   1 Chr. 13:8; 16:42; 23:5

17 So the Levites appointed Heman the son of Joel; and of his brethren, Asaph the son of Berechiah; and of the sons of Merari their brethren, Ethan the son of Kushaiah; 1 Chr. 6:33
18 And with them their brethren of the second *degree*, Zechariah, Ben, and Jaaziel, and Shemiramoth, and Jehiel, and Unni, Eliab, and Benaiah, and Maaseiah, and Mattithiah, and Eliopheleh, and Mikneiah, and Obededom, and Jeiel, the porters. 1 Chr. 26:4
19 So the singers, Heman, Asaph, and Ethan, *were appointed* to sound with cymbals of brass; 1 Chr. 25:6
20 And Zechariah, and Aziel, and Shemiramoth, and Jehiel, and Unni, and Eliab, and Maaseiah, and Benaiah, with ᵀpsalteries on Alamoth; *stringed instruments*
21 And Mattithiah, and Elipheleh, and Mikneiah, and Obed-edom, and Jeiel, and Azaziah, with harps on the Sheminith to excel.
22 And Chenaniah, chief of the Levites, *was* for song: he instructed about the song, because he *was* skilful.
23 And Berechiah and Elkanah *were* doorkeepers for the ark.
24 And Shebaniah, and Jehoshaphat, and Nethaneel, and Amasai, and Zechariah, and Benaiah, and Eliezer, the priests, did blow with the trumpets before the ark of God: and Obed-edom and Jehiah *were* doorkeepers for the ark. Num. 10:8; 1 Chr. 15:28; 16:6
25 So David, and the elders of Israel, and the captains over thousands, went to bring up the ark of the covenant of the LORD out of the house of Obed-edom with joy.
26 And it came to pass, when God helped the Levites that bare the ark of the covenant of the LORD, that they offered seven bullocks and seven rams. Num. 23:29
27 And David *was* clothed with a robe of fine linen, and all the Levites that bare the ark, and the singers, and Chenaniah the master of the song with the singers: David also *had* upon him an ᵀephod of linen. 2 Sam. 6:14 ◆ *priestly garment*

15:27 The King Humbles Himself

[King David] had laid aside his royal robes and had attired himself in a plain linen ephod, such as was worn by the priests. He did not by this act signify that he assumed priestly functions, for the ephod was sometimes worn by others besides the priests. But in this holy service he would take his place as, before God, on an equality with his subjects. Upon that day Jehovah was to be adored. He was to be the sole object of reverence. *PP 706, 707*

---

28 Thus all Israel brought up the ark of the covenant of the LORD with shouting, and with sound of the cornet, and with trumpets, and with cymbals, making a noise with psalteries and harps. 1 Chr. 13:8
29 And it came to pass, *as* the ark of the covenant of the LORD came to the city of David, that Michal the daughter of Saul looking out at a window saw king David dancing and playing: and she despised him in her heart. 2 Sam. 6:16

David's Festival Sacrifice

16 So they brought the ark of God, and set it in the midst of the tent that David had pitched for it: and they offered burnt sacrifices and peace offerings before God. 1 Chr. 15:1

16:1 The Ark Returns Home

The gates were opened wide, the procession entered, and with reverent awe the ark was deposited in the tent that had been prepared for its reception. Before the sacred enclosure altars for sacrifice were erected; the smoke of peace offerings and burnt offerings, and the clouds of incense, with the praises and supplications of Israel, ascended to heaven. The service ended, the king himself pronounced a benediction upon his people. *PP 708*

---

2 And when David had made an end of offering the burnt offerings and the peace offerings, he blessed the people in the name of the LORD.
3 And he dealt to every one of Israel, both man and woman, to every one a loaf of bread, and a good piece of flesh, and a flagon *of wine*.
4 And he appointed *certain* of the Levites to minister before the ark of the LORD, and to record, and to thank and praise the LORD God of Israel:
5 Asaph the chief, and next to him Zechariah, Jeiel, and Shemiramoth, and Jehiel, and Mattithiah, and Eliab, and Benaiah, and Obed-edom: and Jeiel with ᵀpsalteries and with harps; but Asaph made a sound with cymbals; 1 Chr. 6:39 ◆ *stringed instruments*
6 Benaiah also and Jahaziel the priests with trumpets continually before the ark of the covenant of God.

The Psalm of Thanksgiving

7 Then on that day David delivered first *this psalm* to thank the LORD into the hand of Asaph and his brethren. 2 Sam. 22:1
8 Give thanks unto the LORD, call upon his name, make known his deeds among the people. 2 Kin. 19:19
9 Sing unto him, sing psalms unto him, talk ye of all his wondrous works.

10 Glory ye in his holy name: let the heart of them rejoice that seek the LORD.

11 Seek the LORD and his strength, seek his face continually.   Ps. 24:6

12 Remember his marvellous works that he hath done, his wonders, and the judgments of his mouth;   Ps. 78:43

13 O ye seed of Israel his servant, ye children of Jacob, his chosen ones.

14 He *is* the LORD our God; his judgments *are* in all the earth.

15 Be ye mindful always of his covenant; the word *which* he commanded to a thousand generations;

16 *Even of the covenant* which he made with Abraham, and of his oath unto Isaac; Gen. 17:2

17 And hath confirmed the same to Jacob for a law, *and* to Israel *for* an everlasting covenant,   Gen. 35:11-12

18 Saying, Unto thee will I give the land of Canaan, the lot of your inheritance; Gen. 13:15

19 When ye were but few, even a few, and strangers in it.   Gen. 34:30

20 And *when* they went from nation to nation, and from *one* kingdom to another people;

21 He suffered no man to do them wrong: yea, he reproved kings for their sakes, Gen. 20:3

22 *Saying,* Touch not mine anointed, and do my prophets no harm.   Gen. 20:7

23 Sing unto the LORD, all the earth; shew forth from day to day his salvation.   Ps. 96

24 Declare his glory among the heathen; his marvellous works among all nations.

25 For great *is* the LORD, and greatly to be praised: he also *is* to be feared above all gods.   Ps. 89:7

16:24, 25 The Power of Praise

If more praising of God were engaged in now, hope and courage and faith would steadily increase. And would not this strengthen the hands of the valiant soldiers who today are standing in defense of truth? *PK 202*

---

26 For all the gods of the people *are* idols: but the LORD made the heavens.   Lev. 19:4

27 Glory and honour *are* in his presence; strength and gladness *are* in his place.

28 Give unto the LORD, ye kindreds of the people, give unto the LORD glory and strength.   Ps. 29:1-2

29 Give unto the LORD the glory *due* unto his name: bring an offering, and come before him: worship the LORD in the beauty of holiness.   Ps. 29:2

30 Fear before him, all the earth: the world also shall be stable, that it be not moved.

31 Let the heavens be glad, and let the earth rejoice: and let *men* say among the nations, The LORD reigneth.   Ps. 96:10

32 Let the sea roar, and the fulness thereof: let the fields rejoice, and all that *is* therein.

33 Then shall the trees of the wood sing out at the presence of the LORD, because he cometh to judge the earth.   Ps. 98:9

34 O give thanks unto the LORD; for *he is* good; for his mercy *endureth* for ever. 2 Chr. 5:13

35 And say ye, Save us, O God of our salvation, and gather us together, and deliver us from the heathen, that we may give thanks to thy holy name, *and* glory in thy praise.

36 Blessed *be* the LORD God of Israel for ever and ever. And all the people said, Amen, and praised the LORD.   1 Kin. 8:15, 56; Neh. 8:6

David Appoints Many to Serve Continually before the Ark

37 So he left there before the ark of the covenant of the LORD Asaph and his brethren, to minister before the ark continually, as every day's work required: 2 Chr. 8:14

38 And Obed-edom with their brethren, threescore and eight; Obed-edom also the son of Jeduthun and Hosah *to be* porters: sixty

39 And Zadok the priest, and his brethren the priests, before the tabernacle of the LORD in the high place that *was* at Gibeon,

40 To offer burnt offerings unto the LORD upon the altar of the burnt offering continually morning and evening, and *to do* according to all that is written in the law of the LORD, which he commanded Israel;   Num. 28:3-8

41 And with them Heman and Jeduthun, and the rest that were chosen, who were expressed by name, to give thanks to the LORD, because his mercy *endureth* for ever; Num. 1:17

42 And with them Heman and Jeduthun with trumpets and cymbals for those that should make a sound, and with musical instruments of God. And the sons of Jeduthun *were* porters.

43 And all the people departed every man to his house: and David returned to bless his house.   2 Sam. 6:19-20

Though David Desires to Build God's House, God Says No

17 Now it came to pass, as David sat in his house, that David said to Nathan the prophet, Lo, I dwell in an house of cedars, but the ark of the covenant of the LORD *remaineth* under curtains.   1 Chr. 15:1

2 Then Nathan said unto David, Do all that *is* in thine heart; for God *is* with thee.

3 And it came to pass the same night, that the word of God came to Nathan, saying,

4 Go and tell David my servant, Thus saith the LORD, Thou shalt not build me an house to dwell in: 1 Chr. 28:2-3

5 For I have not dwelt in an house since the day that I brought up Israel unto this day; but have gone from tent to tent, and from *one* tabernacle *to another.*   2 Sam. 7:6

6 Wheresoever I have walked with all Israel, spake I a word to any of the judges of Israel, whom I commanded to feed my people, saying, Why have ye not built me an house of cedars?   2 Sam. 7:7

7 Now therefore thus shalt thou say unto my servant David, Thus saith the LORD of hosts, I took thee from the sheepcote, *even* from following the sheep, that thou shouldest be ruler over my people Israel: 2 Sam. 6:21

8 And I have been with thee whithersoever thou hast walked, and have cut off all thine enemies from before thee, and have made thee a name like the name of the great men that *are* in the earth.

9 Also I will ordain a place for my people Israel, and will plant them, and they shall dwell in their place, and shall be moved no more; neither shall the children of wickedness waste them any more, as at the beginning,

10 And since the time that I commanded judges *to be* over my people Israel. Moreover I will subdue all thine enemies. Furthermore I tell thee that the LORD will build thee an house.   2 Sam. 7:11

11 And it shall come to pass, when thy days be expired that thou must go *to be* with thy fathers, that I will raise up thy seed after thee, which shall be of thy sons; and I will establish his kingdom.   Ps. 132:11

12 He shall build me an house, and I will stablish his throne for ever.   1 Kin. 5:5

13 I will be his father, and he shall be my son: and I will not take my mercy away from him, as I took *it* from *him* that was before thee: 1 Sam. 15:28; 1 Chr. 10:14; Heb. 1:5

14 But I will ᵀsettle him in mine house and in my kingdom for ever: and his throne shall be established for evermore.   *lodge*

15 According to all these words, and according to all this vision, so did Nathan speak unto David.

David's Prayer and Thanksgiving

16 And David the king came and sat before the LORD, and said, Who *am* I, O LORD God, and what *is* mine house, that thou hast brought me ᵀhitherto?   2 Sam. 7:18 ◆ *up to now*

17 And *yet* this was a small thing in thine eyes, O God; for thou hast *also* spoken of thy servant's house for a great while to come, and hast regarded me according to the estate of a man of high degree, O LORD God.

18 What can David *speak* more to thee for the honour of thy servant? for thou knowest thy servant.

19 O LORD, for thy servant's sake, and according to thine own heart, hast thou done all this greatness, in making known all *these* great things.   Is. 37:35

20 O LORD, *there is* none like thee, neither *is there any* God beside thee, according to all that we have heard with our ears.   Ex. 15:11

21 And what one nation in the earth *is* like thy people Israel, whom God went to redeem *to be* his own people, to make thee a name of greatness and terribleness, by driving out nations from before thy people, whom thou hast redeemed out of Egypt?

22 For thy people Israel didst thou make thine own people for ever; and thou, LORD, becamest their God.   Ex. 19:5-6

23 Therefore now, LORD, let the thing that thou hast spoken concerning thy servant and concerning his house be established for ever, and do as thou hast said.

24 Let it even be established, that thy name may be magnified for ever, saying, The LORD of hosts *is* the God of Israel, *even* a God to Israel: and *let* the house of David thy servant *be* established before thee.

25 For thou, O my God, hast told thy servant that thou wilt build him an house: therefore thy servant hath found *in his heart* to pray before thee.

Letting God Choose Our Work

1 Chronicles 17:1–19

Though the cherished purpose of his heart had been denied, David received the message [from Nathan the prophet] with gratitude . . . and he then renewed his covenant with God.

David knew that it would be an honor to his name and would bring glory to his government to perform the work that he had purposed in his heart to do, but he was ready to submit his will to the will of God. The grateful resignation thus manifested is rarely seen, even among Christians. How often do those who have passed the strength of manhood cling to the hope of accomplishing some great work upon which their hearts are set, but which they are unfitted to perform! God's providence may speak to them, as did His prophet to David, declaring that the work which they so much desire is not committed to them. It is theirs to prepare the way for another to accomplish it. But instead of gratefully submitting to the divine direction, many fall back as if slighted and rejected, feeling that if they cannot do the one thing which they desire to do, they will do nothing. Many cling with desperate energy to responsibilities which they are incapable of bearing, and vainly endeavor to accomplish a work for which they are insufficient, while that which they might do, lies neglected. *PP 712, 713*

26 And now, LORD, thou art God, and hast promised this goodness unto thy servant:
27 Now therefore let it please thee to bless the house of thy servant, that it may be before thee for ever: for thou blessest, O LORD, and *it shall be* blessed for ever.

David Subdues the Philistines and the Moabites

18 Now after this it came to pass, that David smote the Philistines, and subdued them, and took Gath and her towns out of the hand of the Philistines.   2 Sam. 8
2 And he smote Moab; and the Moabites became David's servants, *and* brought gifts.
3 And David smote Hadarezer king of Zobah unto Hamath, as he went to stablish his dominion by the river Euphrates.   2 Sam. 8:3

> **18:1–3 War—and Peace**
>
> After David's establishment upon the throne of Israel the nation enjoyed a long interval of peace. The surrounding peoples, seeing the strength and unity of the kingdom, soon thought it prudent to desist from open hostilities; and David, occupied with the organization and upbuilding of his kingdom, refrained from aggressive war. At last, however, he made war upon Israel's old enemies, the Philistines, and upon the Moabites, and succeeded in overcoming both and making them tributary. *PP 713*

4 And David took from him a thousand chariots, and seven thousand horsemen, and twenty thousand footmen: David also Thoughed all the chariot *horses,* but reserved of them an hundred chariots. 2 Sam. 8:4 ◆ *disabled*
5 And when the Syrians of Damascus came to help Hadarezer king of Zobah, David slew of the Syrians two and twenty thousand men.   1 Chr. 19:6
6 Then David put *garrisons* in Syria-damascus; and the Syrians became David's servants, *and* brought gifts. Thus the LORD preserved David whithersoever he went.
7 And David took the shields of gold that were on the servants of Hadarezer, and brought them to Jerusalem.
8 Likewise from Tibhath, and from Chun, cities of Hadarezer, brought David very much brass, wherewith Solomon made the brasen sea, and the pillars, and the vessels of brass.   2 Sam. 8:8

Tou Sends Hadoram with Presents to Congratulate David

9 Now when Tou king of Hamath heard how David had smitten all the host of Hadarezer king of Zobah;   2 Sam. 8:9
10 He sent Hadoram his son to king David, to enquire of his welfare, and to congratulate him, because he had fought against Hadarezer, and smitten him; (for Hadarezer had war with Tou;) and *with him* all manner of vessels of gold and silver and brass. 2 Sam. 8:10
11 Them also king David dedicated unto the LORD, with the silver and the gold that he brought from all *these* nations; from Edom, and from Moab, and from the children of Ammon, and from the Philistines, and from Amalek.
12 Moreover Abishai the son of Zeruiah slew of the Edomites in the valley of salt eighteen thousand.   1 Sam. 26:6
13 And he put garrisons in Edom; and all the Edomites became David's servants. Thus the LORD preserved David whithersoever he went.   1 Chr. 18:6
14 So David reigned over all Israel, and executed judgment and justice among all his people.
15 And Joab the son of Zeruiah *was* over the host; and Jehoshaphat the son of Ahilud, recorder.   1 Chr. 11:6
16 And Zadok the son of Ahitub, and Abimelech the son of Abiathar, *were* the priests; and Shavsha was scribe;   2 Sam. 8:17; 20:25; 1 Kin. 4:3
17 And Benaiah the son of Jehoiada *was* over the Cherethites and the Pelethites; and the sons of David *were* chief about the king.

David's Messengers Are Treated Shamefully

19 Now it came to pass after this, that Nahash the king of the children of Ammon died, and his son reigned in his stead.
2 And David said, I will shew kindness unto Hanun the son of Nahash, because his father shewed kindness to me. And David sent messengers to comfort him concerning his father. So the servants of David came into the land of the children of Ammon to Hanun, to comfort him.
3 But the princes of the children of Ammon said to Hanun, Thinkest thou that David doth honour thy father, that he hath sent comforters unto thee? are not his servants come unto thee for to search, and to overthrow, and to spy out the land?
4 Wherefore Hanun took David's servants, and shaved them, and cut off their garments in the midst hard by their buttocks, and sent them away.
5 Then there went *certain,* and told David how the men were served. And he sent to meet them: for the men were greatly ashamed. And the king said, Tarry at Jericho until your beards be grown, and *then* return.

David Defeats Ammon and Syria

6 And when the children of Ammon saw that they had made themselves Todious to David, Hanun and the children of Ammon sent a thousand talents of silver to hire them chariots and horsemen out of Mesopotamia, and out of Syria-maachah, and out of Zobah.   Gen. 34:30 ◆ *hateful*

7 So they hired thirty and two thousand chariots, and the king of Maachah and his people; who came and pitched before Medeba. And the children of Ammon gathered themselves together from their cities, and came to battle.   Num. 21:30; Josh. 13:9, 16

19:1–7 No League With Evil

The Ammonites had been permitted to carry out the evil purposes of their hearts without restraint, that their real character might be revealed to David. It was not God's will that Israel should enter into a league with this treacherous heathen people. *PP 714*

8 And when David heard *of it*, he sent Joab, and all the host of the mighty men.

9 And the children of Ammon came out, and put the battle in array before the gate of the city: and the kings that were come *were* by themselves in the field.

10 Now when Joab saw that the battle was set against him before and behind, he chose out of all the choice of Israel, and put *them* in array against the Syrians.

11 And the rest of the people he delivered unto the hand of Abishai his brother, and they set *themselves* in array against the children of Ammon.   1 Chr. 18:12

12 And he said, If the Syrians be too strong for me, then thou shalt help me: but if the children of Ammon be too strong for thee, then I will help thee.

13 Be of good courage, and let us behave ourselves valiantly for our people, and for the cities of our God: and let the LORD do *that which is* good in his sight.

19:8–13 Conflict Imminent

The Hebrews did not wait for the invasion of their country. Their forces, under Joab, crossed the Jordan and advanced toward the Ammonite capital. As the Hebrew captain led his army to the field he sought to inspire them for the conflict. . . . *PP 715*

14 So Joab and the people that *were* with him drew nigh before the Syrians unto the battle; and they fled before him.

15 And when the children of Ammon saw that the Syrians were fled, they likewise fled before Abishai his brother, and entered into the city. Then Joab came to Jerusalem.

16 And when the Syrians saw that they were put to the worse before Israel, they sent messengers, and drew forth the Syrians that *were* beyond the river: and Shophach the captain of the host of Hadarezer *went* before them.   2 Sam. 10:16

17 And it was told David; and he gathered all Israel, and passed over Jordan, and came upon them, and set *the battle* in array against them. So when David had put the battle in array against the Syrians, they fought with him.

18 But the Syrians fled before Israel; and David slew of the Syrians seven thousand *men which fought in* chariots, and forty thousand footmen, and killed Shophach the captain of the host.   2 Sam. 10:18

19 And when the servants of Hadarezer saw that they were put to the worse before Israel, they made peace with David, and became his servants: neither would the Syrians help the children of Ammon any more.

19:16–19 Defeat and Surrender

David, realizing how much was dependent upon the result of this contest, took the field in person, and by the blessing of God inflicted upon the allies a defeat so disastrous that the Syrians, from Lebanon to the Euphrates, not only gave up the war, but became tributary to Israel. *PP 715*

David Defeats Rabbah

20 And it came to pass, that after the year was expired, at the time that kings go out *to battle*, Joab led forth the power of the army, and wasted the country of the children of Ammon, and came and besieged Rabbah. But David tarried at Jerusalem. And Joab smote Rabbah, and destroyed it.   2 Sam. 11:1

2 And David took the crown of their king from off his head, and found it to weigh a talent of gold, and *there were* precious stones in it; and it was set upon David's head: and he brought also exceeding much Tspoil out of the city.

plunder

3 And he brought out the people that *were* in it, and cut *them* with saws, and with harrows of iron, and with axes. Even so dealt David with all the cities of the children of Ammon. And David and all the people returned to Jerusalem.

20:1–3 Out of Danger, Greatness

The dangers which had threatened the nation with utter destruction proved, through the providence of God, to be the very means by which it rose to unprecedented greatness. *PP 715*

David's Victories over the Philistines

4 And it came to pass after this, that there arose war at Gezer with the Philistines; at which time Sibbechai the Hushathite slew Sippai, *that was* of the children of the giant: and they were subdued.   2 Sam. 21:18-22

5 And there was war again with the Philistines; and Elhanan the son of Jair slew Lahmi the brother of Goliath the Gittite, whose spear staff *was* like a weaver's beam.   2 Sam. 21:19

6 And yet again there was war at Gath, where was a man of *great* stature, whose fingers and toes *were* four and twenty, six *on each hand*, and six *on each foot*: and he also was the son of the giant.

7 But when he defied Israel, Jonathan the son of Shimea David's brother slew him. 1 Sam. 16:9

8 These were born unto the giant in Gath; and they fell by the hand of David, and by the hand of his servants.

David, Tempted by Satan, Takes a Census

21 And Satan stood up against Israel, and provoked David to number Israel.   Job 1:6-12

2 And David said to Joab and to the rulers of the people, Go, number Israel from Beersheba even to Dan; and bring the number of them to me, that I may know *it*. 1 Chr. 27:23-24

3 And Joab answered, The LORD make his people an hundred times so many more as they *be*: but, my lord the king, *are* they not all my lord's servants? why then doth my lord require this thing? why will he be a cause of ᵀtrespass to Israel?   *sin*

4 Nevertheless the king's word prevailed against Joab. Wherefore Joab departed, and went throughout all Israel, and came to Jerusalem.

> **21:1–4 Pride**
>
> It was pride and ambition that prompted this action of the king. . . . This would tend still further to foster the already too great self-confidence of both king and people. . . . The prosperity of Israel under David had been due to the blessing of God rather than to the ability of her king or the strength of her armies. *PP 747*

5 And Joab gave the sum of the number of the people unto David. And all *they of* Israel were a thousand thousand and an hundred thousand men that drew sword: and Judah *was* four hundred ᵀthreescore and ten thousand men that drew sword.   2 Sam. 24:9 ◆ *sixty*

6 But Levi and Benjamin counted he not among them: for the king's word was abominable to Joab.

7 And God was displeased with this thing; therefore he smote Israel.

8 And David said unto God, I have sinned greatly, because I have done this thing: but now, I ᵀbeseech thee, do away the iniquity of thy servant; for I have done very foolishly.   2 Sam. 12:13 ◆ *beg*

9 And the LORD spake unto Gad, David's seer, saying,   1 Sam. 9:9; 2 Sam. 24:11; 1 Chr. 29:29

10 Go and tell David, saying, Thus saith the LORD, I offer thee three *things*: choose thee one of them, that I may do *it* unto thee.

11 So Gad came to David, and said unto him, Thus saith the LORD, Choose thee

12 Either three years' famine; or three months to be destroyed before thy foes, while that the sword of thine enemies overtaketh *thee*; or else three days the sword of the LORD, even the pestilence, in the land, and the angel of the LORD destroying throughout all the coasts of Israel. Now therefore advise thyself what word I shall bring again to him that sent me.

13 And David said unto Gad, I am in a great ᵀstrait: let me fall now into the hand of the LORD; for very great *are* his mercies: but let me not fall into the hand of man.   *difficulty*

14 So the LORD sent pestilence upon Israel: and there fell of Israel seventy thousand men.

15 And God sent an angel unto Jerusalem to destroy it: and as he was destroying, the LORD beheld, and he repented him of the evil, and said to the angel that destroyed, It is enough, stay now thine hand. And the angel of the LORD stood by the threshingfloor of Ornan the Jebusite.   Gen. 6:6

16 And David lifted up his eyes, and saw the angel of the LORD stand between the earth and the heaven, having a drawn sword in his hand stretched out over Jerusalem. Then David and the elders *of Israel,* who *were* clothed in sackcloth, fell upon their faces.   Num. 14:5

17 And David said unto God, *Is it* not I *that* commanded the people to be numbered? even I it is that have sinned and done evil indeed; but *as for* these sheep, what have they done? let thine hand, I pray thee, O LORD my God, be on me, and on my father's house; but not on thy people, that they should be plagued.

David Purchases Ornan's Threshingfloor

18 Then the angel of the LORD commanded Gad to say to David, that David should go up, and set up an altar unto the LORD in the threshingfloor of Ornan the Jebusite. 2 Chr. 3:1

19 And David went up at the saying of Gad, which he spake in the name of the LORD.

20 And Ornan turned back, and saw the angel; and his four sons with him hid themselves. Now Ornan was threshing wheat.   Judg. 6:11

21 And as David came to Ornan, Ornan looked and saw David, and went out of the threshingfloor, and bowed himself to David with *his* face to the ground.

22 Then David said to Ornan, Grant me the place of *this* threshingfloor, that I may build an altar therein unto the LORD: thou shalt grant it me for the full price: that the plague may be ᵀstayed from the people.   *held back*

23 And Ornan said unto David, Take *it* to thee, and let my lord the king do *that which is* good in his eyes: lo, I give *thee* the oxen *also* for burnt offerings, and the threshing instruments for wood, and the wheat for the meat offering; I give it all.

24 And king David said to Ornan, Nay; but I will ᵀverily buy it for the full price: for I will not take *that* which *is* thine for the LORD, nor offer burnt offerings without cost.   *surely*

25 So David gave to Ornan for the place six hundred shekels of gold by weight.

26 And David built there an altar unto the LORD, and offered burnt offerings and peace offerings, and called upon the LORD; and he answered him from heaven by fire upon the altar of burnt offering.   Lev. 9:24; Judg. 6:21

27 And the LORD commanded the angel; and he put up his sword again into the ᵀsheath thereof.   *case for a sword*

28 At that time when David saw that the LORD had answered him in the threshingfloor of Ornan the Jebusite, then he sacrificed there.

29 For the tabernacle of the LORD, which Moses made in the wilderness, and the altar of the burnt offering, *were* at that season in the high place at Gibeon.   1 Chr. 16:39; 2 Chr. 1:3

30 But David could not go before it to enquire of God: for he was afraid because of the sword of the angel of the LORD.

David Helps Solomon Prepare for Building the Temple

22 Then David said, This *is* the house of the LORD God, and this *is* the altar of the burnt offering for Israel.   Gen. 28:17; 2 Chr. 3:1

2 And David commanded to gather together the strangers that *were* in the land of Israel; and he set masons to ᵀhew ᵀwrought stones to build the house of God.   *cut* ◆ *carved*

3 And David prepared iron in abundance for the nails for the doors of the gates, and for the joinings; and brass in abundance without weight;   1 Kin. 7:47; 1 Chr. 22:14; 29:2

4 Also cedar trees in abundance: for the Zidonians and they of Tyre brought much cedar wood to David.   1 Kin. 5:6-10

5 And David said, Solomon my son *is* young and tender, and the house *that is* to be builded for the LORD *must be* exceeding magnifical, of fame and of glory throughout all countries: I will *therefore* now make preparation for it. So David prepared abundantly before his death.   1 Kin. 3:7; 1 Chr. 29:1

David Instructs Solomon about Building God's Temple

6 Then he called for Solomon his son, and charged him to build an house for the LORD God of Israel.

7 And David said to Solomon, My son, as for me, it was in my mind to build an house unto the name of the LORD my God: Deut. 12:5

8 But the word of the LORD came to me, saying, Thou hast shed blood abundantly, and hast made great wars: thou shalt not build an house unto my name, because thou hast shed much blood upon the earth in my sight.   1 Kin. 5:3; 1 Chr. 28:3

God's Plans the Best

1 Chronicles 22:6-10

Our plans are not always God's plans. He may see that it is best for us and for His cause to refuse our very best intentions, as He did in the case of David. But of one thing we may be assured, He will bless and use in the advancement of His cause those who sincerely devote themselves and all they have to His glory. If He sees it best not to grant their desires He will counterbalance the refusal by giving them tokens of His love and entrusting to them another service.

In His loving care and interest for us, often He who understands us better than we understand ourselves refuses to permit us selfishly to seek the gratification of our own ambition. He does not permit us to pass by the homely but sacred duties that lie next us. Often these duties afford the very training essential to prepare us for a higher work. Often our plans fail that God's plans for us may succeed.

We are never called upon to make a real sacrifice for God. Many things He asks us to yield to Him, but in doing this we are but giving up that which hinders us in the heavenward way. Even when called upon to surrender those things which in themselves are good, we may be sure that God is thus working out for us some higher good. *MH 473, 474*

9 Behold, a son shall be born to thee, who shall be a man of rest; and I will give him rest from all his enemies round about: for his name shall be Solomon, and I will give peace and quietness unto Israel in his days.   1 Kin. 4:20
10 He shall build an house for my name; and he shall be my son, and I *will be* his father; and I will establish the throne of his kingdom over Israel for ever.   2 Sam. 7:13-14
11 Now, my son, the LORD be with thee; and prosper thou, and build the house of the LORD thy God, as he hath said of thee.
12 Only the LORD give thee wisdom and understanding, and give thee charge concerning Israel, that thou mayest keep the law of the LORD thy God.   1 Kin. 3:9-12
13 Then shalt thou prosper, if thou takest heed to fulfil the statutes and judgments which the LORD charged Moses with concerning Israel: be strong, and of good courage; dread not, nor be dismayed.   Josh. 1:6-9
14 Now, behold, in my trouble I have prepared for the house of the LORD an hundred thousand talents of gold, and a thousand thousand talents of silver; and of brass and iron without weight; for it is in abundance: timber also and stone have I prepared; and thou mayest add thereto.   1 Chr. 22:3
15 Moreover *there are* workmen with thee in abundance, ᵀhewers and workers of stone and timber, and all manner of cunning men for every manner of work.   *woodcutters*
16 Of the gold, the silver, and the brass, and the iron, *there is* no number. Arise *therefore*, and be doing, and the LORD be with thee.

David Commands the Princes to Assist His Son

17 David also commanded all the princes of Israel to help Solomon his son, *saying*,
18 *Is* not the LORD your God with you? and hath he *not* given you rest on every side? for he hath given the inhabitants of the land into mine hand; and the land is subdued before the LORD, and before his people.   2 Sam. 7:1; 1 Chr. 22:9; 23:25
19 Now set your heart and your soul to seek the LORD your God; arise therefore, and build ye the sanctuary of the LORD God, to bring the ark of the covenant of the LORD, and the holy vessels of God, into the house that is to be built to the name of the LORD.   1 Kin. 8:6; 1 Chr. 22:7; 2 Chr. 5:7

David Organizes the Levites to Serve in the Temple

23 So when David was old and full of days, he made Solomon his son king over Israel.   1 Kin. 1:33-39; 1 Chr. 28:5; 29:28

2 And he gathered together all the princes of Israel, with the priests and the Levites.
3 Now the Levites were numbered from the age of thirty years and upward: and their number by their polls, man by man, was thirty and eight thousand.   1 Chr. 23:24
4 Of which, twenty and four thousand *were* to set forward the work of the house of the LORD; and six thousand *were* officers and judges: 2 Chr. 19:8
5 Moreover four thousand *were* porters; and four thousand praised the LORD with the instruments which I made, *said David*, to praise *therewith*.   2 Chr. 29:25-26
6 And David divided them into courses among the sons of Levi, *namely*, Gershon, Kohath, and Merari.   1 Chr. 6:1
7 Of the Gershonites *were*, Laadan, and Shimei.   1 Chr. 26:21
8 The sons of Laadan; the chief *was* Jehiel, and Zetham, and Joel, three.
9 The sons of Shimei; Shelomith, and Haziel, and Haran, three. These *were* the chief of the fathers of Laadan.
10 And the sons of Shimei *were*, Jahath, Zina, and Jeush, and Beriah. These four *were* the sons of Shimei.
11 And Jahath was the chief, and Zizah the second: but Jeush and Beriah had not many sons; therefore they were in one reckoning, according to *their* father's house.
12 The sons of Kohath; Amram, Izhar, Hebron, and Uzziel, four.   Ex. 6:18
13 The sons of Amram; Aaron and Moses: and Aaron was separated, that he should ᵀsanctify the most holy things, he and his sons for ever, to burn incense before the LORD, to minister unto him, and to bless in his name for ever.   Ex. 6:20; 30:6-10; Deut. 21:5 ♦ *make holy*
14 Now *concerning* Moses the man of God, his sons were named of the tribe of Levi.
15 The sons of Moses *were*, Gershom, and Eliezer.   Ex. 2:22
16 Of the sons of Gershom, Shebuel *was* the chief.   1 Chr. 26:24
17 And the sons of Eliezer *were*, Rehabiah the chief. And Eliezer had none other sons; but the sons of Rehabiah were very many.
18 Of the sons of Izhar; Shelomith the chief.
19 Of the sons of Hebron; Jeriah the first, Amariah the second, Jahaziel the third, and Jekameam the fourth.   1 Chr. 24:23
20 Of the sons of Uzziel; Michah the first, and Jesiah the second.
21 The sons of Merari; Mahli, and Mushi. The sons of Mahli; Eleazar, and Kish. Ex. 6:19
22 And Eleazar died, and had no sons, but daughters: and their brethren the sons of Kish took them.   1 Chr. 24:28
23 The sons of Mushi; Mahli, and Eder, and Jeremoth, three.   1 Chr. 24:30

24 These *were* the sons of Levi after the house of their fathers; *even the* chief of the fathers, as they were counted by number of names by their polls, that did the work for the service of the house of the LORD, from the age of twenty years and upward.   Num. 10:17, 21; 1 Chr. 23:3

25 For David said, The LORD God of Israel hath given rest unto his people, that they may dwell in Jerusalem for ever: 1 Chr. 22:18

26 And also unto the Levites; they shall no *more* carry the tabernacle, nor any vessels of it for the service thereof.   Num. 4:5, 15; 7:9

27 For by the last words of David the Levites *were* numbered from twenty years old and above: 1 Chr. 23:24

28 Because their office *was* to wait on the sons of Aaron for the service of the house of the LORD, in the courts, and in the chambers, and in the purifying of all holy things, and the work of the service of the house of God;   Neh. 13:9

29 Both for the shewbread, and for the fine flour for meat offering, and for the unleavened cakes, and for *that which is baked in* the pan, and for that is fried, and for all manner of measure and size;   Lev. 19:35-36

30 And to stand every morning to thank and praise the LORD, and likewise at even;

31 And to offer all burnt sacrifices unto the LORD in the sabbaths, in the new moons, and on the set feasts, by number, according to the order commanded unto them, continually before the LORD: Is. 1:13-14

32 And that they should keep the charge of the tabernacle of the congregation, and the charge of the holy *place*, and the charge of the sons of Aaron their brethren, in the service of the house of the LORD.   Num. 1:53; 3:6-9, 38

The Organization of the Priests

24 Now *these are* the divisions of the sons of Aaron. The sons of Aaron; Nadab, and Abihu, Eleazar, and Ithamar.   Ex. 6:23

2 But Nadab and Abihu died before their father, and had no children: therefore Eleazar and Ithamar executed the priest's office.   Lev. 10:2; Num. 3:4; 26:61

3 And David distributed them, both Zadok of the sons of Eleazar, and Ahimelech of the sons of Ithamar, according to their offices in their service.   2 Sam. 8:17

4 And there were more chief men found of the sons of Eleazar than of the sons of Ithamar; and *thus* were they divided. Among the sons of Eleazar *there were* sixteen chief men of the house of *their* fathers, and eight among the sons of Ithamar according to the house of their fathers.

5 Thus were they divided by lot, one sort with another; for the governors of the sanctuary, and governors *of the house* of God, were

of the sons of Eleazar, and of the sons of Ithamar.   1 Chr. 24:31

6 And Shemaiah the son of Nethaneel the scribe, *one* of the Levites, wrote them before the king, and the princes, and Zadok the priest, and Ahimelech the son of Abiathar, and *before* the chief of the fathers of the priests and Levites: one principal household being taken for Eleazar, and *one* taken for Ithamar.   1 Chr. 18:16

7 Now the first lot came forth to Jehoiarib, the second to Jedaiah,   Ezra 2:36

8 The third to Harim, the fourth to Seorim,

9 The fifth to Malchijah, the sixth to Mijamin,

10 The seventh to Hakkoz, the eighth to Abijah,   Neh. 12:4, 17; Luke 1:5

11 The ninth to Jeshua, the tenth to Shecaniah,

12 The eleventh to Eliashib, the twelfth to Jakim,

13 The thirteenth to Huppah, the fourteenth to Jeshebeab,

14 The fifteenth to Bilgah, the sixteenth to Immer,

15 The seventeenth to Hezir, the eighteenth to Aphses,

16 The nineteenth to Pethahiah, the twentieth to Jehezekel,

17 The one and twentieth to Jachin, the two and twentieth to Gamul,

18 The three and twentieth to Delaiah, the four and twentieth to Maaziah.

19 These *were* the orderings of them in their service to come into the house of the LORD, according to their manner, under Aaron their father, as the LORD God of Israel had commanded him.   1 Chr. 9:25

The Organization of the Levites

20 And the rest of the sons of Levi *were these*: Of the sons of Amram; Shubael: of the sons of Shubael; Jehdeiah.

21 Concerning Rehabiah: of the sons of Rehabiah, the first *was* Isshiah.   1 Chr. 23:17

22 Of the Izharites; Shelomoth: of the sons of Shelomoth; Jahath.   1 Chr. 23:18

23 And the sons *of Hebron*; Jeriah *the first*, Amariah the second, Jahaziel the third, Jekameam the fourth.   1 Chr. 23:19

24 *Of* the sons of Uzziel; Michah: of the sons of Michah; Shamir.   1 Chr. 23:20

25 The brother of Michah *was* Isshiah: of the sons of Isshiah; Zechariah.

26 The sons of Merari *were* Mahli and Mushi: the sons of Jaaziah; Beno.

27 The sons of Merari by Jaaziah; Beno, and Shoham, and Zaccur, and Ibri.

28 Of Mahli *came* Eleazar, who had no sons.

29 Concerning Kish: the son of Kish *was* Jerahmeel.

30 The sons also of Mushi; Mahli, and Eder, and Jerimoth. These *were* the sons of the Levites after the house of their fathers.

31 These likewise cast lots over against their brethren the sons of Aaron in the presence of David the king, and Zadok, and Ahimelech, and the chief of the fathers of the priests and Levites, even the principal fathers over against their younger brethren.   1 Chr. 24:5-6; 25:8; 26:13

David Appoints Musicians for the Temple

25 Moreover David and the captains of the host separated to the service of the sons of Asaph, and of Heman, and of Jeduthun, who should prophesy with harps, with psalteries, and with cymbals: and the number of the workmen according to their service was: 2 Kin. 3:15; 1 Chr. 6:33, 39

2 Of the sons of Asaph; Zaccur, and Joseph, and Nethaniah, and Asarelah, the sons of Asaph under the hands of Asaph, which prophesied according to the order of the king.   1 Chr. 25:6

3 Of Jeduthun: the sons of Jeduthun; Gedaliah, and Zeri, and Jeshaiah, Hashabiah, and Mattithiah, six, under the hands of their father Jeduthun, who prophesied with a harp, to give thanks and to praise the LORD.   1 Chr. 16:41-42

4 Of Heman: the sons of Heman; Bukkiah, Mattaniah, Uzziel, Shebuel, and Jerimoth, Hananiah, Hanani, Eliathah, Giddalti, and Romamti-ezer, Joshbekashah, Mallothi, Hothir, *and* Mahazioth:

5 All these *were* the sons of Heman the king's seer in the words of God, to lift up the horn. And God gave to Heman fourteen sons and three daughters.   1 Chr. 21:9

6 All these *were* under the hands of their father for song *in* the house of the LORD, with cymbals, [T]psalteries, and harps, for the service of the house of God, according to the king's order to Asaph, Jeduthun, and Heman.   1 Chr. 25:1-3 ♦ *stringed instruments*

7 So the number of them, with their brethren that were instructed in the songs of the LORD, *even* all that were cunning, was two hundred [T]fourscore and eight.   *eighty*

8 And they cast lots, [T]ward against *ward*, as well the small as the great, the teacher as the scholar.   1 Chr. 26:13 ♦ *guard* or *duty*

9 Now the first lot came forth for Asaph to Joseph: the second to Gedaliah, who with his brethren and sons *were* twelve:

10 The third to Zaccur, *he*, his sons, and his brethren, *were* twelve:

11 The fourth to Izri, *he*, his sons, and his brethren, *were* twelve:

12 The fifth to Nethaniah, *he*, his sons, and his brethren, *were* twelve:

13 The sixth to Bukkiah, *he*, his sons, and his brethren, *were* twelve:

14 The seventh to Jesharelah, *he*, his sons, and his brethren, *were* twelve:

15 The eighth to Jeshaiah, *he*, his sons, and his brethren, *were* twelve:

16 The ninth to Mattaniah, *he*, his sons, and his brethren, *were* twelve:

17 The tenth to Shimei, *he*, his sons, and his brethren, *were* twelve:

18 The eleventh to Azareel, *he*, his sons, and his brethren, *were* twelve:

19 The twelfth to Hashabiah, *he*, his sons, and his brethren, *were* twelve:

20 The thirteenth to Shubael, *he*, his sons, and his brethren, *were* twelve:

21 The fourteenth to Mattithiah, *he*, his sons, and his brethren, *were* twelve:

22 The fifteenth to Jeremoth, *he*, his sons, and his brethren, *were* twelve:

23 The sixteenth to Hananiah, *he*, his sons, and his brethren, *were* twelve:

24 The seventeenth to Joshbekashah, *he*, his sons, and his brethren, *were* twelve:

25 The eighteenth to Hanani, *he*, his sons, and his brethren, *were* twelve:

26 The nineteenth to Mallothi, *he*, his sons, and his brethren, *were* twelve:

27 The twentieth to Eliathah, *he*, his sons, and his brethren, *were* twelve:

28 The one and twentieth to Hothir, *he*, his sons, and his brethren, *were* twelve:

29 The two and twentieth to Giddalti, *he*, his sons, and his brethren, *were* twelve:

30 The three and twentieth to Mahazioth, *he*, his sons, and his brethren, *were* twelve:

31 The four and twentieth to Romamti-ezer, *he*, his sons, and his brethren, *were* twelve.

David Appoints Porters for the Temple

26 Concerning the divisions of the porters: Of the Korhites *was* Meshelemiah the son of Kore, of the sons of Asaph.

2 And the sons of Meshelemiah *were*, Zechariah the firstborn, Jediael the second, Zebadiah the third, Jathniel the fourth,

3 Elam the fifth, Jehohanan the sixth, Elioenai the seventh.

4 Moreover the sons of Obed-edom *were*, Shemaiah the firstborn, Jehozabad the second, Joah the third, and Sacar the fourth, and Nethaneel the fifth,   1 Chr. 15:18

5 Ammiel the sixth, Issachar the seventh, Peulthai the eighth: for God blessed him.

6 Also unto Shemaiah his son were sons born, that ruled throughout the house of their father: for they *were* mighty men of valour.

7 The sons of Shemaiah; Othni, and Rephael, and Obed, Elzabad, whose brethren *were* strong men, Elihu, and Semachiah.

8 All these of the sons of Obed-edom: they and their sons and their brethren, able men for strength for the service, *were* ᵀthreescore and two of Obed-edom.   *sixty*

9 And Meshelemiah had sons and brethren, strong men, eighteen.

10 Also Hosah, of the children of Merari, had sons; Simri the chief, (for *though* he was not the firstborn, yet his father made him the chief;)   1 Chr. 16:38

11 Hilkiah the second, Tebaliah the third, Zechariah the fourth: all the sons and brethren of Hosah *were* thirteen.

12 Among these *were* the divisions of the porters, *even* among the chief men, *having* wards one against another, to minister in the house of the LORD.

13 And they cast lots, as well the small as the great, according to the house of their fathers, for every gate.   1 Chr. 24:31; 25:8

14 And the lot eastward fell to Shelemiah. Then for Zechariah his son, a wise counsellor, they cast lots; and his lot came out northward.

15 To Obed-edom southward; and to his sons the house of Asuppim.   2 Chr. 25:24

16 To Shuppim and Hosah *the lot came forth* westward, with the gate Shallecheth, by the causeway of the going up, ᵀward against ward.   *guard* or *duty*

17 Eastward *were* six Levites, northward four a day, southward four a day, and toward Asuppim two *and* two.

18 At Parbar westward, four at the causeway, *and* two at Parbar.

19 These *are* the divisions of the porters among the sons of Kore, and among the sons of Merari.

David Appoints Treasurers for the Temple

20 And of the Levites, Ahijah *was* over the treasures of the house of God, and over the treasures of the dedicated things. 1 Chr. 26:22

21 *As concerning* the sons of Laadan; the sons of the Gershonite Laadan, chief fathers, *even* of Laadan the Gershonite, *were* Jehieli.

22 The sons of Jehieli; Zetham, and Joel his brother, *which were* over the treasures of the house of the LORD.   1 Chr. 23:8

23 Of the Amramites, *and* the Izharites, the Hebronites, *and* the Uzzielites: Num. 3:27

24 And Shebuel the son of Gershom, the son of Moses, *was* ruler of the treasures. 1 Chr. 24:20

25 And his brethren by Eliezer; Rehabiah his son, and Jeshaiah his son, and Joram his son, and Zichri his son, and Shelomith his son.   1 Chr. 23:17-18

26 Which Shelomith and his brethren *were* over all the treasures of the dedicated things, which David the king, and the chief fathers, the captains over thousands and hundreds, and the captains of the host, had dedicated.   2 Sam. 8:11

27 Out of the spoils won in battles did they dedicate to maintain the house of the LORD.

28 And all that Samuel the seer, and Saul the son of Kish, and Abner the son of Ner, and Joab the son of Zeruiah, had dedicated; *and* whosoever had dedicated *any thing, it was* under the hand of Shelomith, and of his brethren.   1 Sam. 9:9

David Appoints Levites to Oversee Israel's Worship

29 Of the Izharites, Chenaniah and his sons *were* for the outward business over Israel, for officers and judges.   1 Chr. 23:4; Neh. 11:16

30 *And* of the Hebronites, Hashabiah and his brethren, men of valour, a thousand and seven hundred, *were* officers among them of Israel on this side Jordan westward in all the business of the LORD, and in the service of the king.   1 Chr. 27:17

31 Among the Hebronites *was* Jerijah the chief, *even* among the Hebronites, according to the generations of his fathers. In the fortieth year of the reign of David they were sought for, and there were found among them mighty men of valour at Jazer of Gilead.   Josh. 21:39; 1 Chr. 23:19

32 And his brethren, men of valour, *were* two thousand and seven hundred chief fathers, whom king David made rulers over the Reubenites, the Gadites, and the half tribe of Manasseh, for every matter pertaining to God, and affairs of the king.   2 Chr. 19:11

The Twelve Captains, One for Each Month

27 Now the children of Israel after their number, ᵀ*to wit*, the chief fathers and captains of thousands and hundreds, and their officers that served the king in any matter of the courses, which came in and went out month by month throughout all the months of the year, of every course *were* twenty and four thousand.   *namely*

2 Over the first course for the first month *was* Jashobeam the son of Zabdiel: and in his course *were* twenty and four thousand.

3 Of the children of Perez *was* the chief of all the captains of the host for the first month.   Num. 26:20

4 And over the course of the second month *was* Dodai an Ahohite, and of his course *was* Mikloth also the ruler: in his course likewise *were* twenty and four thousand.   2 Sam. 23:9

5 The third captain of the host for the third

month *was* Benaiah the son of Jehoiada, a chief priest: and in his course *were* twenty and four thousand.

6 This *is that* Benaiah, *who was* mighty *among* the thirty, and above the thirty: and in his course *was* Ammizabad his son. 2 Sam. 23:20-23

7 The fourth *captain* for the fourth month *was* Asahel the brother of Joab, and Zebadiah his son after him: and in his course *were* twenty and four thousand.   1 Chr. 11:26

8 The fifth captain for the fifth month *was* Shamhuth the Izrahite: and in his course *were* twenty and four thousand.   1 Chr. 11:27

9 The sixth *captain* for the sixth month *was* Ira the son of Ikkesh the Tekoite: and in his course *were* twenty and four thousand.

10 The seventh *captain* for the seventh month *was* Helez the Pelonite, of the children of Ephraim: and in his course *were* twenty and four thousand.   1 Chr. 11:27

11 The eighth *captain* for the eighth month *was* Sibbecai the Hushathite, of the Zarhites: and in his course *were* twenty and four thousand.   2 Sam. 21:18

12 The ninth *captain* for the ninth month *was* Abi-ezer the Anetothite, of the Benjamites: and in his course *were* twenty and four thousand.   1 Chr. 11:28

13 The tenth *captain* for the tenth month *was* Maharai the Netophathite, of the Zarhites: and in his course *were* twenty and four thousand.   1 Chr. 11:30

14 The eleventh *captain* for the eleventh month *was* Benaiah the Pirathonite, of the children of Ephraim: and in his course *were* twenty and four thousand.   1 Chr. 11:31

15 The twelfth *captain* for the twelfth month *was* Heldai the Netophathite, of Othniel: and in his course *were* twenty and four thousand.   2 Sam. 23:29

The Princes of the Twelve Tribes

16 Furthermore over the tribes of Israel: the ruler of the Reubenites *was* Eliezer the son of Zichri: of the Simeonites, Shephatiah the son of Maachah:

17 Of the Levites, Hashabiah the son of Kemuel: of the Aaronites, Zadok: 1 Chr. 26:30

18 Of Judah, Elihu, *one* of the brethren of David: of Issachar, Omri the son of Michael:

19 Of Zebulun, Ishmaiah the son of Obadiah: of Naphtali, Jerimoth the son of Azriel:

20 Of the children of Ephraim, Hoshea the son of Azaziah: of the half tribe of Manasseh, Joel the son of Pedaiah:

21 Of the half *tribe* of Manasseh in Gilead, Iddo the son of Zechariah: of Benjamin, Jaasiel the son of Abner:

22 Of Dan, Azareel the son of Jeroham. These *were* the princes of the tribes of Israel.

23 But David took not the number of them from twenty years old and under: because the LORD had said he would increase Israel like to the stars of the heavens. Gen. 15:5

24 Joab the son of Zeruiah began to number, but he finished not, because there fell wrath for it against Israel; neither was the number put in the account of the chronicles of king David.

25 And over the king's treasures *was* Azmaveth the son of Adiel: and over the storehouses in the fields, in the cities, and in the villages, and in the castles, *was* Jehonathan the son of Uzziah:

26 And over them that did the work of the field for ᵀtillage of the ground *was* Ezri the son of Chelub: *plowing*

27 And over the vineyards *was* Shimei the Ramathite: over the increase of the vineyards for the wine cellars *was* Zabdi the Shiphmite:

28 And over the olive trees and the sycomore trees that *were* in the low plains *was* Baal-hanan the Gederite: and over the cellars of oil *was* Joash: 1 Kin. 10:27

29 And over the herds that fed in Sharon *was* Shitrai the Sharonite: and over the herds *that were* in the valleys *was* Shaphat the son of Adlai: 1 Chr. 5:16

30 Over the camels also *was* Obil the Ishmaelite: and over the asses *was* Jehdeiah the Meronothite:

31 And over the flocks *was* Jaziz the Hagerite. All these *were* the rulers of the substance which *was* king David's.

32 Also Jonathan David's uncle was a counsellor, a wise man, and a scribe: and Jehiel the son of Hachmoni *was* with the king's sons:

33 And Ahithophel *was* the king's counsellor: and Hushai the Archite *was* the king's companion: 2 Sam. 15:12, 32, 37

34 And after Ahithophel *was* Jehoiada the son of Benaiah, and Abiathar: and the general of the king's army *was* Joab. 1 Kin. 1:7; 1 Chr. 11:6

David Exhorts the People to Fear God

28 And David assembled all the princes of Israel, the princes of the tribes, and the captains of the companies that ministered to the king by course, and the captains over the thousands, and captains over the hundreds, and the stewards over all the substance and possession of the king, and of his sons, with the officers, and with the mighty men, and with all the valiant men, unto Jerusalem.   1 Chr. 11:10-47

2 Then David the king stood up upon his feet, and said, Hear me, my brethren, and my people: *As for me,* I *had* in mine heart to build an house of rest for the ark of the covenant of the LORD, and for the footstool

of our God, and had made ready for the building: Ps. 99:5

3 But God said unto me, Thou shalt not build an house for my name, because thou *hast been* a man of war, and hast shed blood. 1 Chr. 22:8

4 Howbeit the LORD God of Israel chose me before all the house of my father to be king over Israel for ever: for he hath chosen Judah *to be* the ruler; and of the house of Judah, the house of my father; and among the sons of my father he liked me to make *me* king over all Israel: 1 Sam. 16:1, 6-13; 1 Chr. 5:2

5 And of all my sons, (for the LORD hath given me many sons,) he hath chosen Solomon my son to sit upon the throne of the kingdom of the LORD over Israel.   1 Chr. 3:1-9

6 And he said unto me, Solomon thy son, he shall build my house and my courts: for I have chosen him *to be* my son, and I will be his father.   2 Sam. 7:13-14

7 Moreover I will establish his kingdom for ever, if he be constant to do my commandments and my judgments, as at this day.

8 Now therefore in the sight of all Israel the congregation of the LORD, and in the audience of our God, keep and seek for all the commandments of the LORD your God: that ye may possess this good land, and leave *it* for an inheritance for your children after you for ever.   Deut. 4:1

9 And thou, Solomon my son, know thou the God of thy father, and serve him with a perfect heart and with a willing mind: for the LORD searcheth all hearts, and understandeth all the imaginations of the thoughts: if thou seek him, he will be found of thee; but if thou forsake him, he will cast thee off for ever.   1 Sam. 16:7; 1 Kin. 8:61; 2 Chr. 15:2

10 Take heed now; for the LORD hath chosen thee to build an house for the sanctuary: be strong, and do *it*.

David Gives Solomon Plans for the Temple and Its Vessels

11 Then David gave to Solomon his son the pattern of the porch, and of the houses thereof, and of the treasuries thereof, and of the upper chambers thereof, and of the inner parlours thereof, and of the place of the mercy seat,   Ex. 25:40

12 And the pattern of all that he had by the spirit, of the courts of the house of the LORD, and of all the chambers round about, of the treasuries of the house of God, and of the treasuries of the dedicated things: 1 Chr. 26:20

13 Also for the courses of the priests and the Levites, and for all the work of the service of the house of the LORD, and for all the vessels of service in the house of the LORD.

14 *He gave* of gold by weight for *things* of gold, for all instruments of all manner of service; *silver also* for all instruments of silver

by weight, for all instruments of every kind of service:

15 Even the weight for the candlesticks of gold, and for their lamps of gold, by weight for every candlestick, and for the lamps thereof: and for the candlesticks of silver by weight, *both* for the candlestick, and *also* for the lamps thereof, according to the use of every candlestick.   Ex. 25:31-39

16 And by weight *he gave* gold for the tables of shewbread, for every table; and *likewise* silver for the tables of silver:

17 Also pure gold for the fleshhooks, and the bowls, and the cups: and for the golden basons *he gave gold* by weight for every bason; and *likewise silver* by weight for every bason of silver:

18 And for the altar of incense refined gold by weight; and gold for the pattern of the chariot of the cherubims, that spread out *their wings*, and covered the ark of the covenant of the LORD.   Ex. 25:18-22; 30:1-10

19 All *this, said David*, the LORD made me understand in writing by *his* hand upon me, *even* all the works of this pattern.   1 Chr. 28:11-12

20 And David said to Solomon his son, Be strong and of good courage, and do *it*: fear not, nor be dismayed: for the LORD God, *even* my God, *will be* with thee; he will not fail thee, nor forsake thee, until thou hast finished all the work for the service of the house of the LORD.   1 Chr. 22:13; Heb. 13:5

21 And, behold, the courses of the priests and the Levites, *even they shall be with thee* for all the service of the house of God: and *there shall be* with thee for all manner of workmanship every willing skilful man, for any manner of service: also the princes and all the people *will be* wholly at thy commandment.   1 Chr. 24:1-26

David Gives to the Temple and Urges the People to Follow His Example

29 Furthermore David the king said unto all the congregation, Solomon my son, whom alone God hath chosen, *is yet* young and tender, and the work *is* great: for the palace *is* not for man, but for the LORD God.   1 Kin. 3:7; 1 Chr. 22:5; 2 Chr. 13:7

2 Now I have prepared with all my might for the house of my God the gold for *things to be made* of gold, and the silver for *things* of silver, and the brass for *things* of brass, the iron for *things* of iron, and wood for *things* of wood; onyx stones, and *stones* to be set, ᵀglistering stones, and of ᵀdivers colours, and all manner of precious stones, and marble stones in abundance.   1 Chr. 22:3-5 ◆ *glistening* ◆ *various*

3 Moreover, because I have set my affection to the house of my God, I have of mine own proper good, of gold and silver, *which* I have given to the house of my God, over

and above all that I have prepared for the holy house,

4 *Even* three thousand talents of gold, of the gold of Ophir, and seven thousand talents of refined silver, to overlay the walls of the houses ^Twithal: 1 Kin. 9:28 ◆ *with*

5 The gold for *things* of gold, and the silver for *things* of silver, and for all manner of work *to be made* by the hands of artificers. And who *then* is willing to ^Tconsecrate his service this day unto the Lᴏʀᴅ?   *set apart*

6 Then the chief of the fathers and princes of the tribes of Israel, and the captains of thousands and of hundreds, with the rulers of the king's work, offered willingly,

7 And gave for the service of the house of God of gold five thousand talents and ten thousand drams, and of silver ten thousand talents, and of brass eighteen thousand talents, and one hundred thousand talents of iron.

8 And they with whom *precious* stones were found gave *them* to the treasure of the house of the Lᴏʀᴅ, by the hand of Jehiel the Gershonite.

9 Then the people rejoiced, for that they offered willingly, because with perfect heart they offered willingly to the Lᴏʀᴅ: and David the king also rejoiced with great joy.   1 Kin. 8:61

29:2–9 Willing to Give

David had felt deeply his own unworthiness in gathering the material for the house of God, and the expression of loyalty in the ready response of the nobles of his kingdom, as with willing hearts they dedicated their treasures to Jehovah and devoted themselves to His service, filled him with joy. . . . It was all of the Lord; if His love had not moved upon the hearts of the people, the king's efforts would have been vain, and the temple would never have been erected. *PP 753*

David's Thanksgiving and Prayer

10 Wherefore David blessed the Lᴏʀᴅ before all the congregation: and David said, Blessed *be* thou, Lᴏʀᴅ God of Israel our father, for ever and ever.

11 Thine, O Lᴏʀᴅ, *is* the greatness, and the power, and the glory, and the victory, and the majesty: for all *that is* in the heaven and in the earth *is thine*; thine *is* the kingdom, O Lᴏʀᴅ, and thou art exalted as head above all.   Dan. 4:34-35

29:12

12 Both riches and honour *come* of thee, and thou reignest over all; and in thine hand *is* power and might; and in thine hand *it is* to make great, and to give strength unto all.   2 Chr. 1:12

Managing God's Gifts See Deuteronomy 8:11–18.

13 Now therefore, our God, we thank thee, and praise thy glorious name.

14 But who *am* I, and what *is* my people, that we should be able to offer so willingly after this sort? for all things *come* of thee, and of thine own have we given thee.

15 For we *are* strangers before thee, and sojourners, as *were* all our fathers: our days on the earth *are* as a shadow, and *there is* none abiding.   Job 14:2; Ps. 39:12; 102:11

16 O Lᴏʀᴅ our God, all this store that we have prepared to build thee an house for thine holy name *cometh* of thine hand, and *is* all thine own.

17 I know also, my God, that thou triest the heart, and hast pleasure in uprightness. As for me, in the uprightness of mine heart I have willingly offered all these things: and now have I seen with joy thy people, which are present here, to offer willingly unto thee.   1 Sam. 16:7; 1 Chr. 28:9; Prov. 11:20

18 O Lᴏʀᴅ God of Abraham, Isaac, and of Israel, our fathers, keep this for ever in the imagination of the thoughts of the heart of thy people, and prepare their heart unto thee:

19 And give unto Solomon my son a perfect heart, to keep thy commandments, thy testimonies, and thy statutes, and to do all *these things*, and to build the palace, *for* the which I have made provision.   1 Chr. 22:14; 28:9; Ps. 72:1

20 And David said to all the congregation, Now bless the Lᴏʀᴅ your God. And all the congregation blessed the Lᴏʀᴅ God of their fathers, and bowed down their heads, and worshipped the Lᴏʀᴅ, and the king.   Ex. 4:31

21 And they sacrificed sacrifices unto the Lᴏʀᴅ, and offered burnt offerings unto the Lᴏʀᴅ, on the morrow after that day, *even* a thousand bullocks, a thousand rams, *and* a thousand lambs, with their drink offerings, and sacrifices in abundance for all Israel:

22 And did eat and drink before the Lᴏʀᴅ on that day with great gladness. And they made Solomon the son of David king the second time, and anointed *him* unto the Lᴏʀᴅ *to be* the chief governor, and Zadok *to be* priest.   1 Chr. 23:1

Solomon Takes the Throne

23 Then Solomon sat on the throne of the Lᴏʀᴅ as king instead of David his father, and prospered; and all Israel obeyed him.   1 Kin. 2:12

24 And all the princes, and the mighty men, and all the sons likewise of king David, submitted themselves unto Solomon the king.

25 And the Lᴏʀᴅ magnified Solomon exceedingly in the sight of all Israel, and bestowed upon him *such* royal majesty as had not been on any king before him in Israel.   1 Kin. 3:13

26 Thus David the son of Jesse reigned over all Israel. _{1 Chr. 18:14}
27 And the time that he reigned over Israel *was* forty years; seven years reigned he in Hebron, and thirty and three *years* reigned he in Jerusalem. _{2 Sam. 5:4-5; 1 Kin. 2:11; 1 Chr. 3:4}
28 And he died in a good old age, full of days, riches, and honour: and Solomon his son reigned in his stead. _{Gen. 15:15; 1 Chr. 23:1; Job 5:26}

29 Now the acts of David the king, first and last, behold, they *are* written in the book of Samuel the seer, and in the book of Nathan the prophet, and in the book of Gad the seer, _{1 Sam. 9:9; 22:5; 2 Sam. 7:2-4}
30 With all his reign and his might, and the times that went over him, and over Israel, and over all the kingdoms of the countries. _{Dan. 4:23}

THE SECOND BOOK OF THE

CHRONICLES

From the very beginning of time, God's people have made attending worship a priority. Taking time out for worship communicates God's precedence in our lives. Through a song, a prayer, the reading of Scripture, the message of the pastor, or the counsel of a friend, God connects with us. Our spiritual survival depends on it.

The centrality of temple worship is a special emphasis of 2 Chronicles. The temple symbolizes God's presence and reminds the exiles—who had returned from captivity to rebuild their lives and their nation—of their high calling as God's special people.

Second Chronicles repeatedly teaches that whenever God's people forsake Him, He withdraws His blessings. Faithfulness to the Lord, however, brings victory.

Dates

Using the divisions noted above, the dates fall roughly as follows:
(1) *2 Chronicles 1—9, 971 to 931 B.C.*
(2) *2 Chronicles 10—36, 931 to 538 B.C.*

Author

Early Jewish writers attribute the authorship of Chronicles to Ezra. His intent is to encourage the people to accept the new temple raised in the site of the old. He reminds them of their true calling to be God's people and that God's faithfulness remains despite deplorable circumstances. He compiles his information, both for 1 and 2 Chronicles, from a variety of sources:
(1) The Book of the Kings of Israel and Judah (or Judah and Israel) (16:11; 20:34; 25:26; 27:7; 28:26; 32:32; 33:18; 35:27; 36:8; see also 1 Chronicles 9:1)
(2) A Commentary on and Annotations of the Book of the Kings (2 Chronicles 24:27)
(3) The Book of Samuel the Seer (1 Chronicles 29:29)
(4) The Book of Nathan the Prophet (2 Chronicles 9:29; see also 1 Chronicles 29:29)
(5) The Book of Gad the Seer (1 Chronicles 29:29)
(6) The Prophecy of Ahijah the Shilonite (2 Chronicles 9:29)
(7) The Visions and Annotations of Iddo the Seer (9:29; 12:15; 13:22)
(8) Records of Shemaiah the Prophet (12:15)
(9) Records of Iddo the Prophet on Genealogies (12:15)
(10) The Annals of Jehu the Son of Hanani (20:34)
(11) The Acts of Uzziah by Isaiah the Prophet (26:22)
(12) The Vision of Isaiah the Prophet (32:32)
(13) The Account of the Chronicles of King David (1 Chronicles 27:24)
(14) The Writing of David and His Son Solomon (2 Chronicles 35:4).
Also, the author/compiler had access to genealogical lists and documents such as the message and letters of Sennacherib (32:10–17).

Meaning of the Name

As mentioned in the introduction to 1 Chronicles, the name Chronicles comes from *Chronicorum Liber* or "The Chronicles of the Whole of Sacred History," which was used in the Latin Vulgate Bible translated by Jerome (A.D. 385–405). Originally, 1 and 2 Chronicles were one book called *Dibere Hayyamim*, which meant "Events of the Days."

Christ in 2 Chronicles

The fulfillment of Christ can be seen in the genealogies that connect the Chronicles with the genealogies of Matthew and Luke. The temple anticipates Christ. Jesus said, "In this place is one greater than the temple" (Matthew 12:6). He also likened His body to the temple: "Destroy this temple, and in three days I will raise it up" (John 2:19). Someday, Jesus will replace the temple in heaven: "I saw no temple therein: for the Lord God Almighty and the Lamb are the temple of it" (Revelation 21:22).

Overview

The temple in Jerusalem is the major unifying theme of 2 Chronicles. This book can be divided into two sections:

    (1) *2 Chronicles 1—9, The Construction and Consecration of the Temple:* While Solomon's glory and wisdom are carefully noted, the crowning achievement of his reign is the construction of the temple. Six of the nine chapters detail the building and dedication of the temple. Solomon's idolatry (1 Kings 11) is omitted, however.

    (2) *2 Chronicles 10—36, Judah's Decline and Exile:* The kings of Israel (the northern kingdom) are omitted because they have no ties with the temple and because of their false worship. The reigns of Asa, Jehoshaphat, Joash, Hezekiah, and Josiah are given prominence because they restore the temple. Judah's greatness is tied to its covenant mission to bring others to God. Only what is done according to God's will has lasting value.

    The book ends on a hopeful note with Cyrus's edict to rebuild the temple (36:22, 23).

Unlocking 2 Chronicles

❀ KEY PEOPLE:
Solomon, the queen of Sheba, Rehoboam, Asa, Jehoshaphat, Jehoram, Ahab, Joash, Uzziah, Ahaz, Hezekiah, Manasseh, Josiah

❀ KEY EVENTS:
Solomon's request for wisdom; the building and dedication of the first temple; the queen of Sheba's visit; Asa's reign; Ahab's death; Joash's repair of the temple; Hezekiah celebrates the Passover; Sennacherib's threat and defeat; the finding of the Book of the Law

❀ KEY PHRASE:
Priestly View of Judah, for 2 Chronicles is written from a priestly point of view, with an emphasis on priests, Levites, the temple, and other elements of Judah's worship life.

❀ KEY VERSE:
"If my people, which are called by my name, shall humble themselves, and pray, and seek my face, and turn from their wicked ways; then will I hear from heaven, and will forgive their sin, and will heal their land" (2 Chronicles 7:14).

❀ KEY CHAPTER:
2 Chronicles 34, which details the dramatic revival under King Josiah when the Book of the Law was rediscovered.

God Appears to Solomon

1 And Solomon the son of David was strengthened in his kingdom, and the LORD his God *was* with him, and magnified him exceedingly.   1 Kin. 2:12, 46; 1 Chr. 29:25

2 Then Solomon spake unto all Israel, to the captains of thousands and of hundreds, and to the judges, and to every governor in all Israel, the chief of the fathers.   1 Chr. 28:1

3 So Solomon, and all the congregation with him, went to the high place that *was* at Gibeon; for there was the tabernacle of the congregation of God, which Moses the servant of the LORD had made in the wilderness.   1 Chr. 16:39

1:2, 3 Guidance for Leadership

Comprehending something of the magnitude of the duties connected with the kingly office, Solomon knew that those bearing heavy burdens must seek the Source of Wisdom for guidance, if they would fulfill their responsibilities acceptably. This led him to encourage his counselors to unite with him heartily in making sure of their acceptance with God. *PK 27, 28*

---

4 But the ark of God had David brought up from Kirjath-jearim to *the place which* David had prepared for it: for he had pitched a tent for it at Jerusalem.   2 Sam. 6:2

5 Moreover the brasen altar, that Bezaleel the son of Uri, the son of Hur, had made, he put before the tabernacle of the LORD: and Solomon and the congregation sought unto it.   Ex. 31:2

6 And Solomon went up thither to the brasen altar before the LORD, which *was* at the tabernacle of the congregation, and offered a thousand burnt offerings upon it.   1 Kin. 3:4

7 In that night did God appear unto Solomon, and said unto him, Ask what I shall give thee.

8 And Solomon said unto God, Thou hast shewed great mercy unto David my father, and hast made me to reign in his stead.

9 Now, O LORD God, let thy promise unto David my father be established: for thou hast made me king over a people like the dust of the earth in multitude.   Gen. 13:16

10 Give me now wisdom and knowledge, that I may go out and come in before this people: for who can judge this thy people, *that is so* great?   Num. 27:17; Deut. 31:2; 2 Sam. 5:2

11 And God said to Solomon, Because this was in thine heart, and thou hast not asked riches, wealth, or honour, nor the life of thine enemies, neither yet hast asked long life; but hast asked wisdom and knowledge for thyself, that thou mayest judge my people, over whom I have made thee king:

12 Wisdom and knowledge *is* granted unto thee; and I will give thee riches, and wealth, and honour, such as none of the kings have had that *have been* before thee, neither shall there any after thee have the like.   1 Chr. 29:25; 2 Chr. 9:22

Solomon's Strength and Wealth

13 Then Solomon came *from his journey* to the high place that *was* at Gibeon to Jerusalem, from before the tabernacle of the congregation, and reigned over Israel.

14 And Solomon gathered chariots and horsemen: and he had a thousand and four hundred chariots, and twelve thousand horsemen, which he placed in the chariot cities, and with the king at Jerusalem.   1 Kin. 4:26; 9:19

15 And the king made silver and gold at Jerusalem *as plenteous* as stones, and cedar trees made he as the sycomore trees that *are* in the ᵀvale for abundance.   2 Chr. 9:27 ◆ valley

16 And Solomon had horses brought out of Egypt, and linen yarn: the king's merchants received the linen yarn at a price.

17 And they fetched up, and brought forth out of Egypt a chariot for six hundred *shekels* of silver, and an horse for an hundred and

---

Solomon's Early Reign

2 Chronicles 1:1

For many years Solomon's life was marked with devotion to God, with uprightness and firm principle, and with strict obedience to God's commands. He directed in every important enterprise and managed wisely the business matters connected with the kingdom. His wealth and wisdom, the magnificent buildings and public works that he constructed during the early years of his reign, the energy, piety, justice, and magnanimity that he revealed in word and deed, won the loyalty of his subjects and the admiration and homage of the rulers of many lands.

The name of Jehovah was greatly honored during the first part of Solomon's reign. The wisdom and righteousness revealed by the king bore witness to all nations of the excellency of the attributes of the God whom he served. For a time Israel was as the light of the world, showing forth the greatness of Jehovah. Not in the surpassing wisdom, the fabulous riches, the far-reaching power and fame that were his, lay the real glory of Solomon's early reign; but in the honor that he brought to the name of the God of Israel through a wise use of the gifts of Heaven. *PK 32, 33*

fifty: and so brought they out *horses* for all the kings of the Hittites, and for the kings of Syria, by their means.

Solomon's Laborers for the Building of the Temple

2 And Solomon determined to build an house for the name of the LORD, and an house for his kingdom.　　　　　1 Kin. 5:5
2 And Solomon told out threescore and ten thousand men to bear burdens, and ᵀfourscore thousand to ᵀhew in the mountain, and three thousand and six hundred to oversee them.　　1 Kin. 5:15-16; 2 Chr. 2:18 ♦ *eighty* ♦ *cut stone*
3 And Solomon sent to Huram the king of Tyre, saying, As thou didst deal with David my father, and didst send him cedars to build him an house to dwell therein, *even so deal with me.*　　　　2 Sam. 5:11; 1 Chr. 14:1
4 Behold, I build an house to the name of the LORD my God, to dedicate *it* to him, *and* to burn before him sweet incense, and for the continual shewbread, and for the burnt offerings morning and evening, on the sabbaths, and on the new moons, and on the solemn feasts of the LORD our God. This *is an ordinance* for ever to Israel.　　Ex. 25:30; 29:38-42; 30:7
5 And the house which I build *is* great: for great *is* our God above all gods. Ex. 15:11; Ps. 135:5
6 But who is able to build him an house, seeing the heaven and heaven of heavens cannot contain him? who *am* I then, that I should build him an house, save only to burn sacrifice before him?　　Ex. 3:11; 1 Kin. 8:27; 2 Chr. 6:18
7 Send me now therefore a man cunning to work in gold, and in silver, and in brass, and in iron, and in purple, and crimson, and blue, and that can skill to grave with

the cunning men that *are* with me in Judah and in Jerusalem, whom David my father did provide.　　　　　　　　　　Ex. 31:3-5

> ### 2:7 Solomon's Faith Falters
>
> Minute specifications, in writing, regarding every portion of the sacred structure, had been entrusted to the king [Solomon]; and he could have looked to God in faith for consecrated helpers, to whom would have been granted special skill for doing with exactness the work required. But Solomon lost sight of this opportunity to exercise faith in God. He sent to the king of Tyre for a man. . . . *PK 63*

8 Send me also cedar trees, fir trees, and algum trees, out of Lebanon: for I know that thy servants can skill to cut timber in Lebanon; and, behold, my servants *shall be* with thy servants,　　　　　　　　　1 Kin. 5:6
9 Even to prepare me timber in abundance: for the house which I am about to build *shall be* wonderful great.

> ### 2:9 The Magnificent Temple
>
> Of surpassing beauty and unrivaled splendor was the palatial building which Solomon and his associates erected for God and His worship. Garnished with precious stones, surrounded by spacious courts with magnificent approaches, and lined with carved cedar and burnished gold, the temple structure, with its broidered hangings and rich furnishings, was a fit emblem of the living church of God on earth. *PK 36*

10 And, behold, I will give to thy servants, the ᵀhewers that cut timber, twenty thousand measures of beaten wheat, and twenty thousand measures of barley, and twenty

---

The Difference Between a Calling and a Job

2 Chronicles 2

Thus at the head of Solomon's company of workmen there was placed a man [Huram] whose efforts were not prompted by an unselfish desire to render service to God. He served the god of this world, mammon. The very fibers of his being were inwrought with the principles of selfishness.

Because of his unusual skill, Huram demanded large wages. Gradually the wrong principles that he cherished came to be accepted by his associates. As they labored with him day after day, they yielded to the inclination to compare his wages with their own, and they began to lose sight of the holy character of their work. The spirit of self-denial left them, and in its place came the spirit of covetousness. The result was a demand for higher wages, which was granted. . . .

The sharp contrast between the spirit and motives of the people building the wilderness tabernacle, and of those engaged in erecting Solomon's temple, has a lesson of deep significance. The self-seeking that characterized the workers on the temple finds its counterpart today in the selfishness that rules in the world. The spirit of covetousness, of seeking for the highest position and the highest wage, is rife. . . . Our divine Master has given an example of how His disciples are to work. To those whom He bade, "Follow Me, and I will make you fishers of men" (Matthew 4:19), He offered no stated sum as a reward for their services. They were to share with Him in self-denial and sacrifice.

Not for the wages we receive are we to labor. The motive that prompts us to work for God should have in it nothing akin to self-serving. Unselfish devotion and a spirit of sacrifice have always been and always will be the first requisite of acceptable service. *PK 63-65*

thousand baths of wine, and twenty thousand baths of oil.   1 Kin. 5:11 ♦ *woodcutters*

11 Then Huram the king of Tyre answered in writing, which he sent to Solomon, Because the LORD hath loved his people, he hath made thee king over them.   1 Kin. 10:9; 2 Chr. 9:8

12 Huram said moreover, Blessed *be* the LORD God of Israel, that made heaven and earth, who hath given to David the king a wise son, endued with prudence and understanding, that might build an house for the LORD, and an house for his kingdom.   Ps. 33:6

13 And now I have sent a cunning man, ᵀendued with understanding, of Huram my father's,   *supplied*

14 The son of a woman of the daughters of Dan, and his father *was* a man of Tyre, skilful to work in gold, and in silver, in brass, in iron, in stone, and in timber, in purple, in blue, and in fine linen, and in crimson; also to grave any manner of graving, and to find out every device which shall be put to him, with thy cunning men, and with the cunning men of my lord David thy father.   2 Chr. 2:7

15 Now therefore the wheat, and the barley, the oil, and the wine, which my lord hath spoken of, let him send unto his servants:

16 And we will cut wood out of Lebanon, as much as thou shalt need: and we will bring it to thee in floats by sea to Joppa; and thou shalt carry it up to Jerusalem.   Josh. 19:46

17 And Solomon numbered all the strangers that *were* in the land of Israel, after the numbering wherewith David his father had numbered them; and they were found an hundred and fifty thousand and three thousand and six hundred.   1 Chr. 22:2

18 And he set ᵀthreescore and ten thousand of them *to be* bearers of burdens, and fourscore thousand *to be* hewers in the mountain, and three thousand and six hundred overseers to set the people a work.   2 Chr. 2:2 ♦ *sixty*

The Temple Is Built

3 Then Solomon began to build the house of the LORD at Jerusalem in mount Moriah, where *the* LORD appeared unto David his father, in the place that David had prepared in the threshingfloor of Ornan the Jebusite.   Gen. 22:2, 14; 1 Chr. 21:18

2 And he began to build in the second *day* of the second month, in the fourth year of his reign.

3 Now these *are the things wherein* Solomon was instructed for the building of the house of God. The length by cubits after the first measure *was* ᵀthreescore cubits, and the breadth twenty cubits.   1 Kin. 6:2-3 ♦ *sixty*

4 And the porch that *was* in the front *of the house*, the length *of it was* according to the breadth of the house, twenty cubits, and the height *was* an hundred and twenty: and he overlaid it within with pure gold.

5 And the greater house he cieled with fir tree, which he overlaid with fine gold, and set thereon palm trees and chains.

6 And he garnished the house with precious stones for beauty: and the gold *was* gold of Parvaim.

7 He overlaid also the house, the beams, the posts, and the walls thereof, and the doors thereof, with gold; and graved cherubims on the walls.   1 Kin. 6:20-22

8 And he made the most holy house, the length whereof *was* according to the breadth of the house, twenty cubits, and the breadth thereof twenty cubits: and he overlaid it with fine gold, *amounting* to six hundred talents.   Ex. 26:33

9 And the weight of the nails *was* fifty shekels of gold. And he overlaid the upper chambers with gold.

10 And in the most holy house he made two cherubims of image work, and overlaid them with gold.   1 Kin. 6:23-28

11 And the wings of the cherubims *were* twenty cubits long: one wing *of the one cherub was* five cubits, reaching to the wall of the house: and the other wing *was likewise* five cubits, reaching to the wing of the other cherub.

12 And *one* wing of the other cherub *was* five cubits, reaching to the wall of the house: and the other wing *was* five cubits *also*, joining to the wing of the other cherub.

13 The wings of these cherubims spread themselves forth twenty cubits: and they stood on their feet, and their faces *were* inward.

14 And he made the ᵀvail *of* blue, and purple, and crimson, and fine linen, and ᵀwrought cherubims thereon.   Heb. 9:3 ♦ *veil* ♦ *wove*

15 Also he made before the house two pillars of thirty and five cubits high, and the ᵀchapiter that *was* on the top of each of them *was* five cubits.   *top of a column*

16 And he made chains, *as* in the oracle, and put *them* on the heads of the pillars; and made an hundred pomegranates, and put *them* on the chains.   1 Kin. 7:20

17 And he reared up the pillars before the temple, one on the right hand, and the other on the left; and called the name of that on the right hand Jachin, and the name of that on the left Boaz.   1 Kin. 7:21

The Furnishings for the Temple

4 Moreover he made an altar of brass, twenty cubits the length thereof, and twenty cubits the breadth thereof, and ten cubits the height thereof.   1 Kin. 8:64

2 Also he made a molten sea of ten cubits

from brim to brim, round in compass, and five cubits the height thereof; and a line of thirty cubits did compass it round about.

3 And under it *was* the ᵀsimilitude of oxen, which did compass it round about: ten in a cubit, ᵀcompassing the sea round about. Two rows of oxen *were* cast, when it was cast. *image ◆ surrounding*

4 It stood upon twelve oxen, three looking toward the north, and three looking toward the west, and three looking toward the south, and three looking toward the east: and the sea *was set* above upon them, and all their hinder parts *were* inward.

5 And the thickness of it *was* ᵀan handbreadth, and the brim of it like the work of the brim of a cup, with flowers of lilies; *and* it received and held three thousand baths. *about four inches*

6 He made also ten lavers, and put five on the right hand, and five on the left, to wash in them: such things as they offered for the burnt offering they washed in them; but the sea *was* for the priests to wash in. *1 Kin. 7:38*

7 And he made ten candlesticks of gold according to their form, and set *them* in the temple, five on the right hand, and five on the left. *Ex. 25:31-40*

8 He made also ten tables, and placed *them* in the temple, five on the right side, and five on the left. And he made an hundred basons of gold. *1 Kin. 7:48*

9 Furthermore he made the court of the priests, and the great court, and doors for the court, and overlaid the doors of them with brass. *1 Kin. 6:36; 2 Kin. 21:5*

10 And he set the sea on the right side of the east end, over against the south. *1 Kin. 7:39*

11 And Huram made the pots, and the shovels, and the basons. And Huram finished the work that he was to make for king Solomon for the house of God;

12 ᵀ*To wit*, the two pillars, and the pommels, and the ᵀchapiters *which were* on the top of the two pillars, and the two wreaths to cover the two pommels of the chapiters which *were* on the top of the pillars; *namely ◆ capitals*

13 And four hundred pomegranates on the two wreaths; two rows of pomegranates on each wreath, to cover the two pommels of the chapiters which *were* upon the pillars.

14 He made also bases, and lavers made he upon the bases; *1 Kin. 7:27-43*

15 One sea, and twelve oxen under it.

16 The pots also, and the shovels, and the fleshhooks, and all their instruments, did Huram his father make to king Solomon for the house of the LORD of bright brass. *2 Chr. 2:13*

17 In the plain of Jordan did the king cast them, in the clay ground between Succoth and Zeredathah.

18 Thus Solomon made all these vessels in great abundance: for the weight of the brass could not be found out. *1 Kin. 7:47*

19 And Solomon made all the vessels that *were for* the house of God, the golden altar also, and the tables whereon the shewbread *was set*;

20 Moreover the candlesticks with their lamps, that they should burn after the manner before the oracle, of pure gold; *Ex. 25:31-37*

21 And the flowers, and the lamps, and the tongs, *made he of* gold, *and* that perfect gold;

22 And the snuffers, and the basons, and the spoons, and the ᵀcensers, *of* pure gold: and the entry of the house, the inner doors thereof for the most holy *place*, and the doors of the house of the temple, *were of* gold. *holders for burning incense*

The Lord's Glory Fills the Temple

5 Thus all the work that Solomon made for the house of the LORD was finished: and Solomon brought in *all* the things that David his father had dedicated; and the silver, and the gold, and all the instruments, put he among the treasures of the house of God. *1 Kin. 7:51*

2 Then Solomon assembled the elders of Israel, and all the heads of the tribes, the chief of the fathers of the children of Israel, unto Jerusalem, to bring up the ark of the covenant of the LORD out of the city of David, which *is* Zion. *2 Sam. 6:12; 2 Chr. 1:4*

3 Wherefore all the men of Israel assembled themselves unto the king in the feast which *was* in the seventh month. *1 Kin. 8:2; 2 Chr. 7:8-10*

4 And all the elders of Israel came; and the Levites took up the ark. *Josh. 3:6*

5 And they brought up the ark, and the tabernacle of the congregation, and all the holy vessels that *were* in the tabernacle, these did the priests *and* the Levites bring up.

6 Also king Solomon, and all the congregation of Israel that were assembled unto him before the ark, sacrificed sheep and oxen, which could not be told nor numbered for multitude.

7 And the priests brought in the ark of the covenant of the LORD unto his place, to the oracle of the house, into the most holy *place*, *even* under the wings of the cherubims:

5:7 The Ark Travels to the Temple

In bringing to the temple the sacred ark containing the two tables of stone on which were written by the finger of God the precepts of the Decalogue, Solomon had followed the example of his father David. Every six paces he sacrificed. With singing and with music and with great ceremony. . . . *PK 38*

8 For the cherubims spread forth *their* wings over the place of the ark, and the cherubims

covered the ark and the ᵀstaves thereof above. *poles or rods*

9 And they drew out the staves *of the ark*, that the ends of the staves were seen from the ark before the oracle; but they were not seen without. And there it is unto this day.

10 *There was* nothing in the ark save the two tables which Moses put *therein* at Horeb, when the LORD made *a covenant* with the children of Israel, when they came out of Egypt. *Heb. 9:4*

5:10 Source of the Ark's Value

The ark in the tabernacle on earth contained the two tables of stone, upon which were inscribed the precepts of the law of God. The ark was merely a receptacle for the tables of the law, and the presence of these divine precepts gave to it its value and sacredness. *GC 433*

11 And it came to pass, when the priests were come out of the holy *place*: (for all the priests *that were* present were ᵀsanctified, *and* did not *then* wait by course: *made holy*

12 Also the Levites *which were* the singers, all of them of Asaph, of Heman, of Jeduthun, with their sons and their brethren, *being* ᵀarrayed in white linen, having cymbals and ᵀpsalteries and harps, stood at the east end of the altar, and with them an hundred and twenty priests sounding with trumpets:) 1 Chr. 6:33, 39 ◆ *clothed* ◆ *stringed instruments*

13 It came even to pass, as the trumpeters and singers *were* as one, to make one sound to be heard in praising and thanking the LORD; and when they lifted up *their* voice with the trumpets and cymbals and instruments of musick, and praised the LORD, *saying*, For *he is* good; for his mercy *endureth* for ever: that *then* the house was filled with a cloud, *even* the house of the LORD; *2 Chr. 7:3*

14 So that the priests could not stand to minister by reason of the cloud: for the glory of the LORD had filled the house of God. *Ex. 40:35; 2 Chr. 7:2; Ezek. 10:4*

Solomon Blesses the People and Praises God

6 Then said Solomon, The LORD hath said that he would dwell in the thick darkness. *Ex. 20:21*

2 But I have built an house of habitation for thee, and a place for thy dwelling for ever.

3 And the king turned his face, and blessed the whole congregation of Israel: and all the congregation of Israel stood. *1 Kin. 8:14*

4 And he said, Blessed *be* the LORD God of Israel, who hath with his hands fulfilled *that* which he spake with his mouth to my father David, saying,

5 Since the day that I brought forth my people out of the land of Egypt I chose no city among all the tribes of Israel to build an house in, that my name might be there; neither chose I any man to be a ruler over my people Israel:

6 But I have chosen Jerusalem, that my name might be there; and have chosen David to be over my people Israel. *1 Chr. 28:4; 2 Chr. 12:13*

7 Now it was in the heart of David my father to build an house for the name of the LORD God of Israel. *1 Kin. 5:3*

8 But the LORD said to David my father, Forasmuch as it was in thine heart to build an house for my name, thou didst well in that it was in thine heart:

9 Notwithstanding thou shalt not build the house; but thy son which shall come forth out of thy ᵀloins, he shall build the house for my name. *body*

10 The LORD therefore hath performed his word that he hath spoken: for I am risen up in the room of David my father, and am set on the throne of Israel, as the LORD promised, and have built the house for the name of the LORD God of Israel.

11 And in it have I put the ark, wherein *is* the covenant of the LORD, that he made with the children of Israel. *2 Chr. 5:7, 10*

6:3-11 Living Sacrifice of Self

Our Lord and Master designs that not one thread of selfishness shall be woven into His work. Into our efforts we are to bring the tact and skill, the exactitude and wisdom, that the God of perfection required of the builders of the earthly tabernacle; yet in all our labors we are to remember that the greatest talents or the most splendid services are acceptable only when self is laid upon the altar, a living, consuming sacrifice. *PK 65*

Solomon's Prayer at the Dedication of the Temple

12 And he stood before the altar of the LORD in the presence of all the congregation of Israel, and spread forth his hands:

13 For Solomon had made a brasen scaffold, of five cubits long, and five cubits broad, and three cubits high, and had set it in the midst of the court: and upon it he stood, and kneeled down upon his knees before all the congregation of Israel, and spread forth his hands toward heaven, *1 Kin. 8:54*

14 And said, O LORD God of Israel, *there is* no God like thee in the heaven, nor in the earth; which keepest covenant, and *shewest* mercy unto thy servants, that walk before thee with all their hearts: *Ex. 15:11; Deut. 7:9*

15 Thou which hast kept with thy servant David my father that which thou hast promised him; and spakest with thy mouth, and

hast fulfilled *it* with thine hand, as *it is* this day.   1 Chr. 22:9-10

16 Now therefore, O LORD God of Israel, keep with thy servant David my father that which thou hast promised him, saying, There shall not fail thee a man in my sight to sit upon the throne of Israel; yet so that thy children take heed to their way to walk in my law, as thou hast walked before me.   1 Kin. 2:4; Ps. 132:12

17 Now then, O LORD God of Israel, let thy word be verified, which thou hast spoken unto thy servant David.

18 But will God in very deed dwell with men on the earth? behold, heaven and the heaven of heavens cannot contain thee; how much less this house which I have built!   Is. 66:1

19 Have respect therefore to the prayer of thy servant, and to his supplication, O LORD my God, to hearken unto the cry and the prayer which thy servant prayeth before thee:

20 That thine eyes may be open upon this house day and night, upon the place whereof thou hast said that thou wouldest put thy name there; to hearken unto the prayer which thy servant prayeth toward this place. Ps. 34:15

21 Hearken therefore unto the supplications of thy servant, and of thy people Israel, which they shall make toward this place: hear thou from thy dwelling place, *even* from heaven; and when thou hearest, forgive.   Is. 43:25

22 If a man sin against his neighbour, and an oath be laid upon him to make him swear, and the oath come before thine altar in this house;   Ex. 22:11

23 Then hear thou from heaven, and do, and judge thy servants, by requiting the wicked, by [T]recompensing his way upon his own head; and by justifying the righteous, by giving him according to his righteousness. *repaying*

24 And if thy people Israel be put to the worse before the enemy, because they have sinned against thee; and shall return and confess thy name, and pray and make supplication before thee in this house; Lev. 26:17

25 Then hear thou from the heavens, and forgive the sin of thy people Israel, and bring them again unto the land which thou gavest to them and to their fathers.

26 When the heaven is shut up, and there is no rain, because they have sinned against thee; *yet* if they pray toward this place, and confess thy name, and turn from their sin, when thou dost afflict them;   Lev. 26:19

27 Then hear thou from heaven, and forgive the sin of thy servants, and of thy people Israel, when thou hast taught them the good way, wherein they should walk; and send rain upon thy land, which thou hast given unto thy people for an inheritance.   Ps. 94:12

28 If there be [T]dearth in the land, if there be pestilence, if there be blasting, or mildew, locusts, or caterpillers; if their enemies besiege them in the cities of their land; whatsoever sore or whatsoever sickness *there be*:   *scarcity*

29 *Then* what prayer *or* what supplication soever shall be made of any man, or of all thy people Israel, when every one shall know his own sore and his own grief, and shall spread forth his hands in this house:

30 Then hear thou from heaven thy dwelling place, and forgive, and render unto every man according unto all his ways, whose heart thou knowest; (for thou only knowest the hearts of the children of men:) 1 Chr. 28:9

31 That they may fear thee, to walk in thy ways, so long as they live in the land which thou gavest unto our fathers.

32 Moreover concerning the stranger, which is not of thy people Israel, but is come from a far country for thy great name's sake, and thy mighty hand, and thy stretched out arm; if they come and pray in this house; Ex. 3:19-20

33 Then hear thou from the heavens, *even* from thy dwelling place, and do according to

---

"Solomon's Temple"

2 Chronicles 6:33

Had Solomon continued in humility of mind to turn the attention of men from himself to the One who had given him wisdom and riches and honor, what a history might have been his! But while the pen of inspiration records his virtues, it also bears faithful witness to his downfall. Raised to a pinnacle of greatness and surrounded with the gifts of fortune, Solomon became dizzy, lost his balance, and fell. Constantly extolled by men of the world, he was at length unable to withstand the flattery offered him. The wisdom entrusted to him that he might glorify the Giver, filled him with pride. He finally permitted men to speak of him as the one most worthy of praise for the matchless splendor of the building planned and erected for the honor of "the name of the Lord God of Israel."

Thus it was that the temple of Jehovah came to be known throughout the nations as "Solomon's temple." The human agent had taken to himself the glory that belonged to the One "higher than the highest" (Ecclesiastes 5:8). Even to this day the temple of which Solomon declared, "This house which I have built is called by Thy name" (2 Chronicles 6:33), is oftenest spoken of, not as the temple of Jehovah, but as "Solomon's temple." PK 68

all that the stranger calleth to thee for; that all people of the earth may know thy name, and fear thee, as *doth* thy people Israel, and may know that this house which I have built is called by thy name.　　2 Chr. 7:14

34 If thy people go out to war against their enemies by the way that thou shalt send them, and they pray unto thee toward this city which thou hast chosen, and the house which I have built for thy name;

35 Then hear thou from the heavens their prayer and their supplication, and maintain their cause.

36 If they sin against thee, (for *there is* no man which sinneth not,) and thou be angry with them, and deliver them over before *their* enemies, and they carry them away captives unto a land far off or near;　　Eccl. 7:20

37 Yet *if* they ᵀbethink themselves in the land whither they are carried captive, and turn and pray unto thee in the land of their captivity, saying, We have sinned, we have done amiss, and have dealt wickedly; *consider*

38 If they return to thee with all their heart and with all their soul in the land of their captivity, whither they have carried them captives, and pray toward their land, which thou gavest unto their fathers, and *toward* the city which thou hast chosen, and toward the house which I have built for thy name:

39 Then hear thou from the heavens, *even* from thy dwelling place, their prayer and their supplications, and maintain their cause, and forgive thy people which have sinned against thee.

40 Now, my God, let, I ᵀbeseech thee, thine eyes be open, and *let* thine ears *be* attent unto the prayer *that is made* in this place.　*beg*

41 Now therefore arise, O LORD God, into thy resting place, thou, and the ark of thy strength: let thy priests, O LORD God, be clothed with salvation, and let thy saints rejoice in goodness.　　1 Chr. 28:2

42 O LORD God, turn not away the face of thine anointed: remember the mercies of David thy servant.　　Is. 55:3

6:12–42 A God Unlike Those of the Heathen

In that which was said during the dedicatory services, Solomon had sought to remove from the minds of those present the superstitions in regard to the Creator, that had beclouded the minds of the heathen. The God of heaven is not, like the gods of the heathen, confined to temples made with hands; yet He would meet with His people by His Spirit when they should assemble at the house dedicated to His worship. *PK 49*

God Recognizes Solomon's Prayer by Fire from Heaven

7 Now when Solomon had made an end of praying, the fire came down from heaven, and consumed the burnt offering and the sacrifices; and the glory of the LORD filled the house.　　Lev. 9:23-24; 1 Kin. 18:24, 38

2 And the priests could not enter into the house of the LORD, because the glory of the LORD had filled the LORD's house.　2 Chr. 5:14

3 And when all the children of Israel saw how the fire came down, and the glory of the LORD upon the house, they bowed themselves with their faces to the ground upon the pavement, and worshipped, and praised the LORD, *saying,* For *he is* good; for his mercy *endureth* for ever.　　2 Chr. 5:13; 20:21

4 Then the king and all the people offered sacrifices before the LORD.

5 And king Solomon offered a sacrifice of twenty and two thousand oxen, and an hundred and twenty thousand sheep: so the king and all the people dedicated the house of God.

6 And the priests waited on their offices: the Levites also with instruments of musick of the LORD, which David the king had made to praise the LORD, because his mercy *endureth* for ever, when David praised by their ministry; and the priests sounded trumpets before them, and all Israel stood.　　1 Chr. 15:16-21

7 Moreover Solomon hallowed the middle of the court that *was* before the house of the LORD: for there he offered burnt offerings, and the fat of the peace offerings, because the brasen altar which Solomon had made was not able to receive the burnt offerings, and the meat offerings, and the fat.

8 Also at the same time Solomon kept the feast seven days, and all Israel with him, a very great congregation, from the entering in of Hamath unto the river of Egypt.　Gen. 15:18

9 And in the eighth day they made a solemn assembly: for they kept the dedication of the altar seven days, and the feast seven days.　　Lev. 23:36

10 And on the three and twentieth day of the seventh month he sent the people away into their tents, glad and merry in heart for the goodness that the LORD had shewed unto David, and to Solomon, and to Israel his people.

11 Thus Solomon finished the house of the LORD, and the king's house: and all that came into Solomon's heart to make in the house of the LORD, and in his own house, he prosperously effected.　　1 Kin. 9:1-9

God Answers Solomon's Prayer

12 And the LORD appeared to Solomon by night, and said unto him, I have heard thy

prayer, and have chosen this place to myself for an house of sacrifice.   Deut. 12:11

13 If I shut up heaven that there be no rain, or if I command the locusts to devour the land, or if I send pestilence among my people;   2 Chr. 6:26-28

14 If my people, which are called by my name, shall humble themselves, and pray, and seek my face, and turn from their wicked ways; then will I hear from heaven, and will forgive their sin, and will heal their land.   2 Chr. 6:27

15 Now mine eyes shall be open, and mine ears attent unto the prayer *that is made* in this place.   2 Chr. 6:20, 40

16 For now have I chosen and ᵀsanctified this house, that my name may be there for ever: and mine eyes and mine heart shall be there perpetually.   2 Chr. 7:12 ◆ *made holy*

17 And as for thee, if thou wilt walk before me, as David thy father walked, and do according to all that I have commanded thee, and shalt observe my statutes and my judgments;

18 Then will I stablish the throne of thy kingdom, according as I have covenanted with David thy father, saying, There shall not fail thee a man *to be* ruler in Israel.   2 Chr. 6:16

19 But if ye turn away, and forsake my statutes and my commandments, which I have set before you, and shall go and serve other gods, and worship them;   Lev. 26:14; Deut. 28:15

20 Then will I pluck them up by the roots out of my land which I have given them; and this house, which I have sanctified for my name, will I cast out of my sight, and will make it *to be* a proverb and a byword among all nations.   Deut. 28:37; 29:28

21 And this house, which is high, shall be an astonishment to every one that passeth by it; so that he shall say, Why hath the LORD done thus unto this land, and unto this house?   Jer. 22:8-9

22 And it shall be answered, Because they forsook the LORD God of their fathers, which brought them forth out of the land of Egypt, and laid hold on other gods, and worshipped them, and served them: therefore hath he brought all this evil upon them.

7:20–22 Warnings Against Apostasy

Had Solomon continued to serve the Lord in humility, his entire reign would have exerted a powerful influence for good over the surrounding nations, nations that had been so favorably impressed by the reign of David his father and by the wise words and the magnificent works of the earlier years of his own reign. Foreseeing the terrible temptations that attend prosperity and worldly honor, God warned Solomon against the evil of apostasy and foretold the awful results of sin. *PK 47*

Solomon's Construction Projects

8 And it came to pass at the end of twenty years, wherein Solomon had built the house of the LORD, and his own house,

2 That the cities which Huram had restored to Solomon, Solomon built them, and caused the children of Israel to dwell there.

3 And Solomon went to Hamath-zobah, and prevailed against it.

4 And he built Tadmor in the wilderness, and all the store cities, which he built in Hamath.

5 Also he built Beth-horon the upper, and Beth-horon the ᵀnether, fenced cities, with walls, gates, and bars;   1 Chr. 7:24 ◆ *lower*

6 And Baalath, and all the store cities that Solomon had, and all the chariot cities, and the cities of the horsemen, and all that Solomon desired to build in Jerusalem, and in Lebanon, and throughout all the land of his dominion.

8:2–6 The Spirit of Commercialism

The missionary spirit that God had implanted in the heart of Solomon and in the hearts of all true Israelites was supplanted by a spirit of commercialism. The opportunities afforded by contact with many nations were used for personal aggrandizement. Solomon sought to strengthen his position politically by building fortified cities at the gateways of commerce. *PK 71*

7 *As for* all the people *that were* left of the Hittites, and the Amorites, and the Perizzites, and the Hivites, and the Jebusites, which *were* not of Israel,

8 *But* of their children, who were left after them in the land, whom the children of Israel consumed not, them did Solomon make to pay tribute until this day.   Josh. 16:10

9 But of the children of Israel did Solomon make no servants for his work; but they *were* men of war, and chief of his captains, and captains of his chariots and horsemen.

10 And these *were* the chief of king Solomon's officers, *even* two hundred and fifty, that bare rule over the people.

11 And Solomon brought up the daughter of Pharaoh out of the city of David unto the house that he had built for her: for he said, My wife shall not dwell in the house of David king of Israel, because *the places are* holy, whereunto the ark of the LORD hath come.   1 Kin. 3:1; 7:8; 9:24

Solomon's Sacrifices

12 Then Solomon offered burnt offerings unto the LORD on the altar of the LORD, which he had built before the porch,   2 Chr. 4:1

13 Even after a certain rate every day, offering

according to the commandment of Moses, on the sabbaths, and on the new moons, and on the solemn feasts, three times in the year, *even* in the feast of unleavened bread, and in the feast of weeks, and in the feast of tabernacles. Ex. 23:14-17; 29:38-42; Deut. 16:16

14 And he appointed, according to the order of David his father, the courses of the priests to their service, and the Levites to their charges, to praise and minister before the priests, as the duty of every day required: the porters also by their courses at every gate: for so had David the man of God commanded. 1 Chr. 9:17

15 And they departed not from the commandment of the king unto the priests and Levites concerning any matter, or concerning the treasures.

16 Now all the work of Solomon was prepared unto the day of the foundation of the house of the LORD, and until it was finished. *So* the house of the LORD was perfected.

17 Then went Solomon to Ezion-geber, and to Eloth, at the sea side in the land of Edom. 2 Kin. 14:22

18 And Huram sent him by the hands of his servants ships, and servants that had knowledge of the sea; and they went with the servants of Solomon to Ophir, and took thence four hundred and fifty talents of gold, and brought *them* to king Solomon. 2 Chr. 9:10

8:18 The Cost of Shortsightedness

The revenue of the king and of many of his subjects was greatly increased, but at what a cost! Through the cupidity and shortsightedness of those to whom had been entrusted the oracles of God, the countless multitudes who thronged the highways of travel were allowed to remain in ignorance of Jehovah. *PK 72, 73*

The Queen of Sheba Admires Solomon's Wisdom

9 And when the queen of Sheba heard of the fame of Solomon, she came to prove Solomon with hard questions at Jerusalem, with a very great company, and camels that bare spices, and gold in abundance, and precious stones: and when she was come to Solomon, she communed with him of all that was in her heart. Matt. 12:42; Luke 11:31

2 And Solomon told her all her questions: and there was nothing hid from Solomon which he told her not.

3 And when the queen of Sheba had seen the wisdom of Solomon, and the house that he had built,

4 And the meat of his table, and the sitting of his servants, and the attendance of his ministers, and their apparel; his cupbearers

also, and their apparel; and his ascent by which he went up into the house of the LORD; there was no more spirit in her.

5 And she said to the king, It *was* a true report which I heard in mine own land of thine acts, and of thy wisdom:

6 Howbeit I believed not their words, until I came, and mine eyes had seen *it*: and, behold, the one half of the greatness of thy wisdom was not told me: *for* thou exceedest the fame that I heard.

7 Happy *are* thy men, and happy *are* these thy servants, which stand continually before thee, and hear thy wisdom.

8 Blessed be the LORD thy God, which delighted in thee to set thee on his throne, *to be* king for the LORD thy God: because thy God loved Israel, to establish them for ever, therefore made he thee king over them, to do judgment and justice. Deut. 7:8; 1 Chr. 29:23; 2 Chr. 2:11

9 And she gave the king an hundred and twenty talents of gold, and of spices great abundance, and precious stones: neither was there any such spice as the queen of Sheba gave king Solomon.

10 And the servants also of Huram, and the servants of Solomon, which brought gold from Ophir, brought algum trees and precious stones. 1 Kin. 10:11; 2 Chr. 8:18

11 And the king made *of* the algum trees terraces to the house of the LORD, and to the king's palace, and harps and ᵀpsalteries for singers: and there were none such seen before in the land of Judah. *stringed instruments*

12 And king Solomon gave to the queen of Sheba all her desire, whatsoever she asked, beside *that* which she had brought unto the king. So she turned, and went away to her own land, she and her servants. 1 Kin. 10:13

Solomon's Wealth

13 Now the weight of gold that came to Solomon in one year was six hundred and ᵀthreescore and six talents of gold; *sixty*

14 Beside *that which* ᵀchapmen and merchants brought. And all the kings of Arabia and governors of the country brought gold and silver to Solomon. *traders*

15 And king Solomon made two hundred targets *of* beaten gold: six hundred *shekels* of beaten gold went to one target.

16 And three hundred shields *made he of* beaten gold: three hundred *shekels* of gold went to one shield. And the king put them in the house of the forest of Lebanon. 1 Kin. 7:2

17 Moreover the king made a great throne of ivory, and overlaid it with pure gold.

18 And *there were* six steps to the throne, with a footstool of gold, *which were* fastened to the throne, and stays on each side of the

sitting place, and two lions standing by the stays:

19 And twelve lions stood there on the one side and on the other upon the six steps. There was not the like made in any kingdom.

20 And all the drinking vessels of king Solomon *were of* gold, and all the vessels of the house of the forest of Lebanon *were of* pure gold: none *were of* silver; it was *not* any thing accounted of in the days of Solomon.

21 For the king's ships went to Tarshish with the servants of Huram: every three years once came the ships of Tarshish bringing gold, and silver, ivory, and apes, and peacocks.

22 And king Solomon passed all the kings of the earth in riches and wisdom.   2 Chr. 1:12

23 And all the kings of the earth sought the presence of Solomon, to hear his wisdom, that God had put in his heart.   1 Kin. 4:34

24 And they brought every man his present, vessels of silver, and vessels of gold, and ᵀraiment, harness, and spices, horses, and mules, a rate year by year.   *clothing*

25 And Solomon had four thousand stalls for horses and chariots, and twelve thousand horsemen; whom he bestowed in the chariot cities, and with the king at Jerusalem.   1 Kin. 4:26; 10:26; 2 Chr. 1:14

26 And he reigned over all the kings from the river even unto the land of the Philistines, and to the border of Egypt.   Gen. 15:18

27 And the king made silver in Jerusalem as stones, and cedar trees made he as the sycomore trees that *are* in the low plains in abundance.   2 Chr. 1:15-17

28 And they brought unto Solomon horses out of Egypt, and out of all lands.   2 Chr. 1:16

Solomon's Death

29 Now the rest of the acts of Solomon, first and last, *are* they not written in the book of Nathan the prophet, and in the prophecy of Ahijah the Shilonite, and in the visions of Iddo the seer against Jeroboam the son of Nebat?   1 Kin. 11:29, 41-43; 1 Chr. 29:29

9:26 A Golden Opportunity

Through [Israel's] territory ran many natural highways of the world's commerce, and caravans from distant lands were constantly passing to and fro. Thus there was given to Solomon and his people opportunity to reveal to men of all nations the character of the King of kings, and to teach them to reverence and obey Him. To all the world this knowledge was to be given. Through the teaching of the sacrificial offerings, Christ was to be uplifted before the nations, that all who would might live. *PK 70, 71*

---

30 And Solomon reigned in Jerusalem over all Israel forty years.   1 Kin. 11:42-43

31 And Solomon slept with his fathers, and he was buried in the city of David his father: and Rehoboam his son reigned in his stead.   1 Kin. 2:10

Rehoboam Foolishly Rejects the People's Request

10 And Rehoboam went to Shechem: for to Shechem were all Israel come to make him king.

10:1 Apostasy Repeated

At times [Rehoboam] endeavored to serve God and was granted a measure of prosperity; but he was not steadfast, and at last he yielded to the influences for evil that had surrounded him from infancy. In the mistakes of Rehoboam's life and in his final apostasy is revealed the fearful result of Solomon's union with idolatrous women. *PK 88*

---

2 And it came to pass, when Jeroboam the son of Nebat, who *was* in Egypt, whither he had fled from the presence of Solomon the

---

Solomon's Tragic Fall

2 Chronicles 9:21, 22

The silver of Tarshish and the gold of Ophir were procured by the sacrifice of integrity, the betrayal of sacred trusts. Association with idolaters, marriage with heathen wives, corrupted [Solomon's] faith. The barriers that God had erected for the safety of His people were thus broken down, and Solomon gave himself up to the worship of false gods. On the summit of the Mount of Olives, confronting the temple of Jehovah, were erected gigantic images and altars for the service of heathen deities. As he cast off his allegiance to God, Solomon lost the mastery of himself. His fine sensibilities became blunted. The conscientious, considerate spirit of his early reign was changed. Pride, ambition, prodigality, and indulgence bore fruit in cruelty and exaction. He who had been a just, compassionate, and God-fearing ruler, became tyrannical and oppressive. He who at the dedication of the temple had prayed for his people that their hearts might be undividedly given to the Lord, became their seducer. Solomon dishonored himself, dishonored Israel, and dishonored God.

The nation, of which he had been the pride, followed his leading. Though he afterward repented, his repentance did not prevent the fruition of the evil he had sown. *Ed 49*

king, heard *it*, that Jeroboam returned out of Egypt.   1 Kin. 11:40

3 And they sent and called him. So Jeroboam and all Israel came and spake to Rehoboam, saying,

4 Thy father made our yoke grievous: now therefore ease thou somewhat the grievous servitude of thy father, and his heavy yoke that he put upon us, and we will serve thee.

5 And he said unto them, Come again unto me after three days. And the people departed.

6 And king Rehoboam took counsel with the old men that had stood before Solomon his father while he yet lived, saying, What counsel give ye *me* to return answer to this people?   Job 32:7

7 And they spake unto him, saying, If thou be kind to this people, and please them, and speak good words to them, they will be thy servants for ever.   Prov. 15:1

8 But he forsook the counsel which the old men gave him, and took counsel with the young men that were brought up with him, that stood before him.   2 Sam. 17:14

9 And he said unto them, What advice give ye that we may return answer to this people, which have spoken to me, saying, Ease somewhat the yoke that thy father did put upon us?

10 And the young men that were brought up with him spake unto him, saying, Thus shalt thou answer the people that spake unto thee, saying, Thy father made our yoke heavy, but make thou *it* somewhat lighter for us; thus shalt thou say unto them, My little *finger* shall be thicker than my father's ᵀloins.   *waist*

11 For whereas my father put a heavy yoke upon you, I will put more to your yoke: my father chastised you with whips, but I *will chastise you* with scorpions.

12 So Jeroboam and all the people came to Rehoboam on the third day, as the king bade, saying, Come again to me on the third day.

13 And the king answered them roughly; and king Rehoboam forsook the counsel of the old men,

14 And answered them after the advice of the young men, saying, My father made your yoke heavy, but I will add thereto: my father chastised you with whips, but I *will chastise you* with scorpions.

15 So the king hearkened not unto the people: for the cause was of God, that the Lord might perform his word, which he spake by the hand of Ahijah the Shilonite to Jeroboam the son of Nebat.   1 Kin. 11:29-39

16 And when all Israel *saw* that the king would not hearken unto them, the people answered the king, saying, What portion have we in David? and *we have* none inheritance in the son of Jesse: every man to your tents, O Israel: *and* now, David, see to thine own house. So all Israel went to their tents.   2 Sam. 20:1

10:15, 16 Rebellion Arises

The Lord did not allow Rehoboam to carry out the policy he had outlined. Among the tribes were many thousands who had become thoroughly aroused over the oppressive measures of Solomon's reign, and these now felt that they could not do otherwise than rebel against the house of David. *PK 90*

17 But *as for* the children of Israel that dwelt in the cities of Judah, Rehoboam reigned over them.

18 Then king Rehoboam sent Hadoram that *was* over the tribute; and the children of Israel stoned him with stones, that he died. But king Rehoboam made speed to get him up to *his* chariot, to flee to Jerusalem.   1 Kin. 4:6; 5:14

19 And Israel rebelled against the house of David unto this day.

Rehoboam Raises an Army to Subdue the Rebellion

11 And when Rehoboam was come to Jerusalem, he gathered of the house of Judah and Benjamin an hundred and ᵀfourscore thousand chosen *men*, which were warriors, to fight against Israel, that he might bring the kingdom again to Rehoboam.   *eighty*

2 But the word of the Lord came to Shemaiah the man of God, saying,   2 Chr. 12:15

3 Speak unto Rehoboam the son of Solomon, king of Judah, and to all Israel in Judah and Benjamin, saying,

4 Thus saith the Lord, Ye shall not go up, nor fight against your brethren: return every man to his house: for this thing is done of me. And they obeyed the words of the Lord, and returned from going against Jeroboam.

5 And Rehoboam dwelt in Jerusalem, and built cities for defence in Judah.   2 Chr. 8:2-6

6 He built even Beth-lehem, and Etam, and Tekoa,

7 And Beth-zur, and Shoco, and Adullam,

8 And Gath, and Mareshah, and Ziph,

9 And Adoraim, and Lachish, and Azekah,

10 And Zorah, and Aijalon, and Hebron, which *are* in Judah and in Benjamin fenced cities.

11 And he fortified the strong holds, and put captains in them, and store of victual, and of oil and wine.

12 And in every several city *he put* shields and spears, and made them exceeding

strong, having Judah and Benjamin on his side.

The Priests and Levites Come to Judah

13 And the priests and the Levites that *were* in all Israel resorted to him out of all their coasts.

14 For the Levites left their suburbs and their possession, and came to Judah and Jerusalem: for Jeroboam and his sons had cast them off from executing the priest's office unto the LORD: Num. 35:2-5; 1 Kin. 12:28-33; 2 Chr. 13:9

15 And he ordained him priests for the high places, and for the devils, and for the calves which he had made.   1 Kin. 12:28

16 And after them out of all the tribes of Israel such as set their hearts to seek the LORD God of Israel came to Jerusalem, to sacrifice unto the LORD God of their fathers. 2 Chr. 15:9

17 So they strengthened the kingdom of Judah, and made Rehoboam the son of Solomon strong, three years: for three years they walked in the way of David and Solomon.   2 Chr. 12:1

Rehoboam's Family

18 And Rehoboam took him Mahalath the daughter of Jerimoth the son of David to wife, *and* Abihail the daughter of Eliab the son of Jesse;   1 Sam. 16:6

19 Which bare him children; Jeush, and Shamariah, and Zaham.

20 And after her he took Maachah the daughter of Absalom; which bare him Abijah, and Attai, and Ziza, and Shelomith.   2 Chr. 13:2

21 And Rehoboam loved Maachah the daughter of Absalom above all his wives and his concubines: (for he took eighteen wives, and ᵀthreescore concubines; and ᵀbegat twenty and eight sons, and threescore daughters.) Deut. 17:17 ◆ *sixty* ◆ *brought forth*

22 And Rehoboam made Abijah the son of Maachah the chief, *to be* ruler among his brethren: for *he thought* to make him king.

23 And he dealt wisely, and dispersed of all his children throughout all the countries of Judah and Benjamin, unto every fenced city: and he gave them victual in abundance. And he desired many wives.

Shishak Takes the Temple Treasures

12 And it came to pass, when Rehoboam had established the kingdom, and had strengthened himself, he forsook the law of the LORD, and all Israel with him. 2 Chr. 11:17

2 And it came to pass, *that* in the fifth year of king Rehoboam Shishak king of Egypt came up against Jerusalem, because they had ᵀtransgressed against the LORD,   *sinned*

3 With twelve hundred chariots, and ᵀthreescore thousand horsemen: and the people *were* without number that came with him out of Egypt; the Lubims, the Sukkiims, and the Ethiopians.   2 Chr. 16:8; Dan. 11:43; Nah. 3:9 ◆ *sixty*

4 And he took the fenced cities which *pertained* to Judah, and came to Jerusalem.

5 Then came Shemaiah the prophet to Rehoboam, and *to* the princes of Judah, that were gathered together to Jerusalem because of Shishak, and said unto them, Thus saith the LORD, Ye have forsaken me, and therefore have I also left you in the hand of Shishak.   1 Kin. 12:22; 2 Chr. 11:2; 15:2

6 Whereupon the princes of Israel and the king humbled themselves; and they said, The LORD *is* righteous.   Ex. 9:27; Dan. 9:14

7 And when the LORD saw that they humbled themselves, the word of the LORD came to Shemaiah, saying, They have humbled themselves; *therefore* I will not destroy them, but I will grant them some deliverance; and

---

The Influence of a Wrong Example

2 Chronicles 12:1

Naturally headstrong, confident, self-willed, and inclined to idolatry, nevertheless, had [Rehoboam] placed his trust wholly in God, he would have developed strength of character, steadfast faith, and submission to the divine requirements. But as time passed, the king put his trust in the power of position and in the strongholds he had fortified. Little by little he gave way to inherited weakness, until he threw his influence wholly on the side of idolatry. . . .

How sad, how filled with significance, the words, "And all Israel with him"! The people whom God had chosen to stand as a light to the surrounding nations were turning from their Source of strength and seeking to become like the nations about them. As with Solomon, so with Rehoboam—the influence of wrong example led many astray. And as with them, so to a greater or less degree is it today with everyone who gives himself up to work evil—the influence of wrongdoing is not confined to the doer. No man liveth unto himself. None perish alone in their iniquity. Every life is a light that brightens and cheers the pathway of others, or a dark and desolating influence that tends toward despair and ruin. We lead others either upward to happiness and immortal life, or downward to sorrow and eternal death. And if by our deeds we strengthen or force into activity the evil powers of those around us, we share their sin. *PK 93, 94*

my wrath shall not be poured out upon Jerusalem by the hand of Shishak. 2 Chr. 34:25

8 Nevertheless they shall be his servants; that they may know my service, and the service of the kingdoms of the countries.

9 So Shishak king of Egypt came up against Jerusalem, and took away the treasures of the house of the LORD, and the treasures of the king's house; he took all: he carried away also the shields of gold which Solomon had made. 1 Kin. 10:16-17

10 Instead of which king Rehoboam made shields of brass, and committed *them* to the hands of the chief of the guard, that kept the entrance of the king's house.

11 And when the king entered into the house of the LORD, the guard came and fetched them, and brought them again into the guard chamber.

12 And when he humbled himself, the wrath of the LORD turned from him, that he would not destroy *him* altogether: and also in Judah things went well. 1 Kin. 14:13; 2 Chr. 12:6-7; 19:3

Rehoboam's Death

13 So king Rehoboam strengthened himself in Jerusalem, and reigned: for Rehoboam *was* one and forty years old when he began to reign, and he reigned seventeen years in Jerusalem, the city which the LORD had chosen out of all the tribes of Israel, to put his name there. And his mother's name *was* Naamah an Ammonitess. 1 Kin. 14:21

14 And he did evil, because he prepared not his heart to seek the LORD. 2 Chr. 19:3

15 Now the acts of Rehoboam, first and last, *are* they not written in the book of Shemaiah the prophet, and of Iddo the seer concerning genealogies? And *there were* wars between Rehoboam and Jeroboam continually. 1 Kin. 12:22

16 And Rehoboam slept with his fathers, and was buried in the city of David: and Abijah his son reigned in his stead.

Abijah Becomes King of Judah

13 Now in the eighteenth year of king Jeroboam began Abijah to reign over Judah. 2 Chr. 12:16

2 He reigned three years in Jerusalem. His mother's name also *was* Michaiah the daughter of Uriel of Gibeah. And there was war between Abijah and Jeroboam. 2 Chr. 11:20

3 And Abijah set the battle in array with an army of valiant men of war, *even* four hundred thousand chosen men: Jeroboam also set the battle in array against him with eight hundred thousand chosen men, *being* mighty men of valour.

4 And Abijah stood up upon mount Zemaraim, which *is* in mount Ephraim, and said, Hear me, thou Jeroboam, and all Israel;

5 Ought ye not to know that the LORD God of Israel gave the kingdom over Israel to David for ever, *even* to him and to his sons by a covenant of salt? Lev. 2:13; Num. 18:19

6 Yet Jeroboam the son of Nebat, the servant of Solomon the son of David, is risen up, and hath rebelled against his lord. 1 Kin. 11:26; 12:20

7 And there are gathered unto him vain men, the children of Belial, and have strengthened themselves against Rehoboam the son of Solomon, when Rehoboam was young and tenderhearted, and could not withstand them. Judg. 9:4

8 And now ye think to withstand the kingdom of the LORD in the hand of the sons of David; and ye *be* a great multitude, and *there are* with you golden calves, which Jeroboam made you for gods. 1 Kin. 12:28; 2 Chr. 11:15

9 Have ye not cast out the priests of the LORD, the sons of Aaron, and the Levites, and have made you priests after the manner of the nations of *other* lands? so that whosoever cometh to ᵀconsecrate himself with a young ᵀbullock and seven rams, *the same* may be a priest of *them that are* no gods. Ex. 29:35; Jer. 2:11 ✦ set apart ✦ bull

10 But as for us, the LORD *is* our God, and we have not forsaken him; and the priests, which minister unto the LORD, *are* the sons of Aaron, and the Levites *wait* upon *their* business:

11 And they burn unto the LORD every morning and every evening burnt sacrifices and sweet incense: the shewbread also *set they in order* upon the pure table; and the candlestick of gold with the lamps thereof, to burn every evening: for we keep the charge of the LORD our God; but ye have forsaken him. Ex. 25:30-39; 27:20-21; 2 Chr. 2:4

12 And, behold, God himself *is* with us for *our* captain, and his priests with sounding trumpets to cry alarm against you. O children of Israel, fight ye not against the LORD God of your fathers; for ye shall not prosper. Num. 10:8-9

Trusting in God, Abijah Overcomes Jeroboam of Israel

13 But Jeroboam caused an ambushment to come about behind them: so they were before Judah, and the ambushment *was* behind them. Josh. 8:4

14 And when Judah looked back, behold, the battle *was* before and behind: and they cried unto the LORD, and the priests sounded with the trumpets. 2 Chr. 14:11

15 Then the men of Judah gave a shout: and as the men of Judah shouted, it came to pass, that God smote Jeroboam and all Israel before Abijah and Judah. 2 Chr. 14:12

16 And the children of Israel fled before

Judah: and God delivered them into their hand.   2 Chr. 16:8

17 And Abijah and his people slew them with a great slaughter: so there fell down slain of Israel five hundred thousand chosen men.

18 Thus the children of Israel were brought under at that time, and the children of Judah prevailed, because they relied upon the LORD God of their fathers.   1 Chr. 5:20

19 And Abijah pursued after Jeroboam, and took cities from him, Beth-el with the towns thereof, and Jeshanah with the towns thereof, and Ephrain with the towns thereof.   Josh. 15:9

20 Neither did Jeroboam recover strength again in the days of Abijah: and the LORD struck him, and he died.   1 Sam. 25:38

21 But Abijah ᵀwaxed mighty, and married fourteen wives, and ᵀbegat twenty and two sons, and sixteen daughters. *became* ◆ *brought forth*

22 And the rest of the acts of Abijah, and his ways, and his sayings, *are* written in the story of the prophet Iddo.   2 Chr. 9:29

Asa Becomes King of Judah

14 So Abijah slept with his fathers, and they buried him in the city of David: and Asa his son reigned in his stead. In his days the land was quiet ten years.

2 And Asa did *that which was* good and right in the eyes of the LORD his God:

3 For he took away the altars of the strange *gods*, and the high places, and brake down the images, and cut down the ᵀgroves: *idols*

4 And commanded Judah to seek the LORD God of their fathers, and to do the law and the commandment.

5 Also he took away out of all the cities of Judah the high places and the images: and the kingdom was quiet before him.   2 Chr. 34:4, 7

6 And he built fenced cities in Judah: for the land had rest, and he had no war in those years; because the LORD had given him rest.   1 Chr. 22:9; 2 Chr. 15:15

7 Therefore he said unto Judah, Let us build these cities, and make about *them* walls, and towers, gates, and bars, *while* the land *is* yet before us; because we have sought the LORD our God, we have sought *him*, and he hath given us rest on every side. So they built and prospered.   2 Chr. 14:6

8 And Asa had an army *of men* that bare targets and spears, out of Judah three hundred thousand; and out of Benjamin, that bare shields and drew bows, two hundred and ᵀfourscore thousand: all these *were* mighty men of valour.   2 Chr. 13:3 ◆ *eighty*

Asa Overthrows Zerah and Plunders the Ethiopians

9 And there came out against them Zerah the Ethiopian with an host of a thousand thousand, and three hundred chariots; and came unto Mareshah.   Josh. 15:44; 2 Chr. 11:8; 16:8

10 Then Asa went out against him, and they set the battle in array in the valley of Zephathah at Mareshah.

11 And Asa cried unto the LORD his God, and said, LORD, *it is* nothing with thee to help, whether with many, or with them that have no power: help us, O LORD our God; for we rest on thee, and in thy name we go against this multitude. O LORD, thou *art* our God; let not man prevail against thee.   Ex. 14:10; 2 Chr. 13:14, 18

12 So the LORD smote the Ethiopians before Asa, and before Judah; and the Ethiopians fled.   2 Chr. 13:15

13 And Asa and the people that *were* with him pursued them unto Gerar: and the Ethiopians were overthrown, that they could not recover themselves; for they were destroyed before the LORD, and before his

---

Asa's Prayer

2 Chronicles 14:11

From every human viewpoint the vast host from Egypt would sweep everything before it. But in time of peace Asa had not been giving himself to amusement and pleasure; he had been preparing for any emergency. He had an army trained for conflict; he had endeavored to lead his people to make their peace with God. And now, although his forces were fewer in number than the enemy, his faith in the One whom he had made his trust did not weaken.

Having sought the Lord in the days of prosperity, the king could now rely upon Him in the day of adversity. His petitions showed that he was not a stranger to God's wonderful power. . . .

The prayer of Asa is one that every Christian believer may fittingly offer. We fight in a warfare, not against flesh and blood, but against principalities and powers, and against spiritual wickedness in high places. See Ephesians 6:12. In life's conflict we must meet evil agencies that have arrayed themselves against the right. Our hope is not in man, but in the living God. With full assurance of faith we may expect that He will unite His omnipotence with the efforts of human instrumentalities, for the glory of His name. Clad with the armor of His righteousness, we may gain the victory over every foe. *PK 110, 111*

host; and they carried away very much ^Tspoil.   Gen. 10:19; 20:1; 26:1 ♦ *plunder*
14 And they smote all the cities round about Gerar; for the fear of the LORD came upon them: and they spoiled all the cities; for there was exceeding much spoil in them.   Gen. 35:5; 2 Chr. 17:10; 20:29
15 They smote also the tents of cattle, and carried away sheep and camels in abundance, and returned to Jerusalem.

Asa, Judah, and Many of Israel Make a Covenant with God

15 And the Spirit of God came upon Azariah the son of Oded: 2 Chr. 20:14; 24:20
2 And he went out to meet Asa, and said unto him, Hear ye me, Asa, and all Judah and Benjamin; The LORD *is* with you, while ye be with him; and if ye seek him, he will be found of you; but if ye forsake him, he will forsake you.   1 Chr. 28:9
3 Now for a long season Israel *hath been* without the true God, and without a teaching priest, and without law.   Lev. 10:11
4 But when they in their trouble did turn unto the LORD God of Israel, and sought him, he was found of them.   Deut. 4:29-30
5 And in those times *there was* no peace to him that went out, nor to him that came in, but great vexations *were* upon all the inhabitants of the countries.   Judg. 5:6
6 And nation was destroyed of nation, and city of city: for God did ^Tvex them with all adversity.   *trouble*
7 Be ye strong therefore, and let not your hands be weak: for your work shall be rewarded.   Josh. 1:7, 9; Ps. 58:11
8 And when Asa heard these words, and the prophecy of Oded the prophet, he took courage, and put away the abominable idols out of all the land of Judah and Benjamin, and out of the cities which he had taken from mount Ephraim, and renewed the altar of the LORD, that *was* before the porch of the LORD.   2 Chr. 4:1; 8:12; 13:19
9 And he gathered all Judah and Benjamin, and the strangers with them out of Ephraim and Manasseh, and out of Simeon: for they fell to him out of Israel in abundance, when they saw that the LORD his God *was* with him.   2 Chr. 11:16
10 So they gathered themselves together at Jerusalem in the third month, in the fifteenth year of the reign of Asa.
11 And they offered unto the LORD the same time, of the ^Tspoil *which* they had brought, seven hundred oxen and seven thousand sheep.   2 Chr. 14:13-15 ♦ *plunder*
12 And they entered into a covenant to seek the LORD God of their fathers with all their heart and with all their soul;   2 Chr. 23:16

13 That whosoever would not seek the LORD God of Israel should be put to death, whether small or great, whether man or woman.   Ex. 22:20
14 And they sware unto the LORD with a loud voice, and with shouting, and with trumpets, and with cornets.
15 And all Judah rejoiced at the oath: for they had sworn with all their heart, and sought him with their whole desire; and he was found of them: and the LORD gave them rest round about.   2 Chr. 14:7
16 And also *concerning* Maachah the mother of Asa the king, he removed her from *being* queen, because she had made an idol in a grove: and Asa cut down her idol, and stamped *it*, and burnt *it* at the brook Kidron.
17 But the high places were not taken away out of Israel: nevertheless the heart of Asa was perfect all his days.
18 And he brought into the house of God the things that his father had dedicated, and that he himself had dedicated, silver, and gold, and vessels.
19 And there was no *more* war unto the five and thirtieth year of the reign of Asa.

Asa's War with Baasha of Israel

16 In the six and thirtieth year of the reign of Asa Baasha king of Israel came up against Judah, and built Ramah, to the intent that he might let none go out or come in to Asa king of Judah.   2 Chr. 15:9
2 Then Asa brought out silver and gold out of the treasures of the house of the LORD and of the king's house, and sent to Ben-hadad king of Syria, that dwelt at Damascus, saying,
3 *There is* a league between me and thee, as *there was* between my father and thy father: behold, I have sent thee silver and gold; go, break thy league with Baasha king of Israel, that he may depart from me.
4 And Ben-hadad hearkened unto king Asa, and sent the captains of his armies against the cities of Israel; and they smote Ijon, and Dan, and Abel-maim, and all the store cities of Naphtali.
5 And it came to pass, when Baasha heard *it*, that he left off building of Ramah, and let his work cease.
6 Then Asa the king took all Judah; and they carried away the stones of Ramah, and the timber thereof, wherewith Baasha was building; and he built therewith Geba and Mizpah.

Asa Is Reprimanded for Trusting in Syria and Not in the Lord

7 And at that time Hanani the seer came to Asa king of Judah, and said unto him, Because thou hast relied on the king of Syria, and not relied on the LORD thy God, therefore

is the host of the king of Syria escaped out of thine hand. 1 Kin. 16:1; 2 Chr. 19:2; 32:7-8

8 Were not the Ethiopians and the Lubims a huge host, with very many chariots and horsemen? yet, because thou didst rely on the LORD, he delivered them into thine hand. 2 Chr. 12:3; 13:16

9 For the eyes of the LORD run to and fro throughout the whole earth, to shew himself strong in the behalf of *them* whose heart *is* perfect toward him. Herein thou hast done foolishly: therefore from henceforth thou shalt have wars. 1 Sam. 13:13; Prov. 15:3; Zech. 4:10

10 Then Asa was ᵀwroth with the seer, and put him in a prison house; for *he was* in a rage with him because of this *thing*. And Asa oppressed *some* of the people the same time. 2 Chr. 18:26 ♦ *angry*

11 And, behold, the acts of Asa, first and last, lo, they *are* written in the book of the kings of Judah and Israel.

12 And Asa in the thirty and ninth year of his reign was diseased in his feet, until his disease *was* exceeding *great*: yet in his disease he sought not to the LORD, but to the physicians. Jer. 17:5

13 And Asa slept with his fathers, and died in the one and fortieth year of his reign.

14 And they buried him in his own sepulchres, which he had made for himself in the city of David, and laid him in the bed which was filled with sweet odours and ᵀdivers kinds *of spices* prepared by the apothecaries' art: and they made a very great burning for him. Gen. 50:2; 2 Chr. 21:19; Jer. 34:5 ♦ *various*

Jehoshaphat Becomes King of Judah

17 And Jehoshaphat his son reigned in his stead, and strengthened himself against Israel. 1 Kin. 15:24

2 And he placed forces in all the fenced cities of Judah, and set garrisons in the land of Judah, and in the cities of Ephraim, which Asa his father had taken. 2 Chr. 15:8

3 And the LORD was with Jehoshaphat, because he walked in the first ways of his father David, and sought not unto Baalim;

4 But sought to the LORD God of his father, and walked in his commandments, and not after the doings of Israel. 1 Kin. 12:28

5 Therefore the LORD stablished the kingdom in his hand; and all Judah brought to Jehoshaphat presents; and he had riches and honour in abundance. 1 Sam. 10:27; 2 Chr. 18:1; 32:23

6 And his heart was lifted up in the ways of the LORD: moreover he took away the high places and ᵀgroves out of Judah. *idols*

7 Also in the third year of his reign he sent to his princes, *even* to Ben-hail, and to Obadiah, and to Zechariah, and to Nethaneel, and to Michaiah, to teach in the cities of Judah. 2 Chr. 15:3; 35:3

8 And with them *he sent* Levites, *even* Shemaiah, and Nethaniah, and Zebadiah, and Asahel, and Shemiramoth, and Jehonathan, and Adonijah, and Tobijah, and Tob-adonijah, Levites; and with them Elishama and Jehoram, priests. 2 Chr. 19:8

9 And they taught in Judah, and *had* the book of the law of the LORD with them, and went about throughout all the cities of Judah, and taught the people.

Some of Judah's Enemies, Being Afraid of God, Bring Presents and Tribute

10 And the fear of the LORD fell upon all the kingdoms of the lands that *were* round about Judah, so that they made no war against Jehoshaphat. Gen. 35:5; 2 Chr. 14:14

11 Also *some* of the Philistines brought

Great Gain in Obeying God

2 Chronicles 17:7–9

Throughout the kingdom the people were in need of instruction in the law of God. In an understanding of this law lay their safety; by conforming their lives to its requirements they would become loyal both to God and to man. Knowing this, Jehoshaphat took steps to ensure to his people thorough instruction in the Holy Scriptures. The princes in charge of the different portions of his realm were directed to arrange for the faithful ministry of teaching priests. By royal appointment these instructors, working under the direct supervision of the princes, "went about throughout all the cities of Judah, and taught the people" (2 Chronicles 17:7–9). And as many endeavored to understand God's requirements and to put away sin, a revival was effected.

To this wise provision for the spiritual needs of his subjects, Jehoshaphat owed much of his prosperity as a ruler. In obedience to God's law there is great gain. In conformity to the divine requirements there is a transforming power that brings peace and good will among men. If the teachings of God's word were made the controlling influence in the life of every man and woman, if mind and heart were brought under its restraining power, the evils that now exist in national and in social life would find no place. From every home would go forth an influence that would make men and women strong in spiritual insight and in moral power, and thus nations and individuals would be placed on vantage ground. *PK 191, 192*

Jehoshaphat presents, and tribute silver; and the Arabians brought him flocks, seven thousand and seven hundred rams, and seven thousand and seven hundred he goats.　　　　2 Sam. 8:2; 2 Chr. 9:14; 26:8

12 And Jehoshaphat ᵀwaxed great exceedingly; and he built in Judah castles, and cities of store.　　　　became

13 And he had much business in the cities of Judah: and the men of war, mighty men of valour, were in Jerusalem.

14 And these are the numbers of them according to the house of their fathers: Of Judah, the captains of thousands; Adnah the chief, and with him mighty men of valour three hundred thousand.

15 And next to him was Jehohanan the captain, and with him two hundred and ᵀfourscore thousand.　　　　eighty

16 And next him was Amasiah the son of Zichri, who willingly offered himself unto the LORD; and with him two hundred thousand mighty men of valour.　　　　Judg. 5:2, 9; 1 Chr. 29:9

17 And of Benjamin; Eliada a mighty man of valour, and with him armed men with bow and shield two hundred thousand.

18 And next him was Jehozabad, and with him an hundred and fourscore thousand ready prepared for the war.

19 These waited on the king, beside those whom the king put in the fenced cities throughout all Judah.　　　　2 Chr. 17:2

Jehoshaphat Makes an Alliance with Ahab

18 Now Jehoshaphat had riches and honour in abundance, and joined affinity with Ahab.　　　　2 Kin. 8:18; 2 Chr. 17:5; 21:6

2 And after certain years he went down to Ahab to Samaria. And Ahab killed sheep and oxen for him in abundance, and for the people that he had with him, and persuaded him to go up with him to Ramoth-gilead.

3 And Ahab king of Israel said unto Jehoshaphat king of Judah, Wilt thou go with me to Ramoth-gilead? And he answered him, I am as thou art, and my people as thy people; and we will be with thee in the war.

Ahab Is Slain, according to the Word of Micaiah

4 And Jehoshaphat said unto the king of Israel, Enquire, I pray thee, at the word of the LORD to day.

5 Therefore the king of Israel gathered together of prophets four hundred men, and said unto them, Shall we go to Ramoth-gilead to battle, or shall I ᵀforbear? And they said, Go up; for God will deliver it into the king's hand.　　　　refuse to act

6 But Jehoshaphat said, Is there not here a prophet of the LORD besides, that we might enquire of him?

7 And the king of Israel said unto Jehoshaphat, There is yet one man, by whom we may enquire of the LORD: but I hate him; for he never prophesied good unto me, but always evil: the same is Micaiah the son of Imla. And Jehoshaphat said, Let not the king say so.　　　　Luke 6:22

8 And the king of Israel called for one of his officers, and said, Fetch quickly Micaiah the son of Imla.

9 And the king of Israel and Jehoshaphat king of Judah sat either of them on his throne, clothed in their robes, and they sat in a void place at the entering in of the gate of Samaria; and all the prophets prophesied before them.

10 And Zedekiah the son of Chenaanah had made him horns of iron, and said, Thus saith the LORD, With these thou shalt push Syria until they be consumed.

11 And all the prophets prophesied so, saying, Go up to Ramoth-gilead, and prosper: for the LORD shall deliver it into the hand of the king.

12 And the messenger that went to call Micaiah spake to him, saying, Behold, the words of the prophets declare good to the king with one ᵀassent; let thy word therefore, I pray thee, be like one of theirs, and speak thou good.　　　　accord

13 And Micaiah said, As the LORD liveth, even what my God saith, that will I speak.

14 And when he was come to the king, the king said unto him, Micaiah, shall we go to Ramoth-gilead to battle, or shall I forbear? And he said, Go ye up, and prosper, and they shall be delivered into your hand.

15 And the king said to him, How many times shall I ᵀadjure thee that thou say nothing but the truth to me in the name of the LORD?　　　　appeal to

16 Then he said, I did see all Israel scattered upon the mountains, as sheep that have no shepherd: and the LORD said, These have no master; let them return therefore every man to his house in peace.　　　　Matt. 9:36

18:3–16 Warnings Ignored

The words of the prophet should have been enough to show the kings that their project was not favored by Heaven, but neither ruler felt inclined to heed the warning. Ahab had marked out his course, and he was determined to follow it. Jehoshaphat had given his word of honor . . . and after making such a promise, he was reluctant to withdraw his forces. *PK 196*

17 And the king of Israel said to Jehosha-phat, Did I not tell thee *that* he would not prophesy good unto me, but evil?

18 Again he said, Therefore hear the word of the LORD; I saw the LORD sitting upon his throne, and all the host of heaven standing on his right hand and *on* his left.   Dan. 7:9

19 And the LORD said, Who shall entice Ahab king of Israel, that he may go up and fall at Ramoth-gilead? And one spake saying after this manner, and another saying after that manner.

20 Then there came out a spirit, and stood before the LORD, and said, I will entice him. And the LORD said unto him, Where-with?   Job 1:6

21 And he said, I will go out, and be a lying spirit in the mouth of all his prophets. And *the LORD* said, Thou shalt entice *him*, and thou shalt also prevail: go out, and do *even* so.   John 8:44

22 Now therefore, behold, the LORD hath put a lying spirit in the mouth of these thy prophets, and the LORD hath spoken evil against thee.   Is. 19:14

23 Then Zedekiah the son of Chenaanah came near, and smote Micaiah upon the cheek, and said, Which way went the Spirit of the LORD from me to speak unto thee?   Jer. 20:2

24 And Micaiah said, Behold, thou shalt see on that day when thou shalt go into an inner chamber to hide thyself.

25 Then the king of Israel said, Take ye Mi-caiah, and carry him back to Amon the gov-ernor of the city, and to Joash the king's son;   2 Chr. 18:8

26 And say, Thus saith the king, Put this *fel-low* in the prison, and feed him with bread of affliction and with water of affliction, until I return in peace.   2 Chr. 16:10

27 And Micaiah said, If thou certainly return in peace, *then* hath not the LORD spoken by me. And he said, Hearken, all ye people.

28 So the king of Israel and Jehoshaphat the king of Judah went up to Ramoth-gilead.

29 And the king of Israel said unto Je-hoshaphat, I will disguise myself, and will go to the battle; but put thou on thy robes. So the king of Israel disguised himself; and they went to the battle.   1 Sam. 28:8

30 Now the king of Syria had commanded the captains of the chariots that *were* with him, saying, Fight ye not with small or great, save only with the king of Israel.

31 And it came to pass, when the captains of the chariots saw Jehoshaphat, that they said, It *is* the king of Israel. Therefore they ᵀcompassed about him to fight: but Je-hoshaphat cried out, and the LORD helped him; and God moved them *to depart* from him.   2 Chr. 13:14 ♦ *circled*

32 For it came to pass, that, when the cap-tains of the chariots perceived that it was not the king of Israel, they turned back again from pursuing him.

33 And a *certain* man drew a bow at a ven-ture, and smote the king of Israel between the joints of the harness: therefore he said to his chariot man, Turn thine hand, that thou mayest carry me out of the host; for I am wounded.

34 And the battle increased that day: ᵀhow-beit the king of Israel ᵀstayed *himself* up in *his* chariot against the Syrians until the even: and about the time of the sun going down he died.   *however* ♦ *propped*

Jehoshaphat's Religious Reforms

19 And Jehoshaphat the king of Judah returned to his house in peace to Je-rusalem.

2 And Jehu the son of Hanani the seer went out to meet him, and said to king Jehoshaphat, Shouldest thou help the un-godly, and love them that hate the LORD? therefore *is* wrath upon thee from before the LORD.   1 Kin. 16:1; 2 Chr. 16:7; 20:34

3 Nevertheless there are good things found in thee, in that thou hast taken away the ᵀgroves out of the land, and hast prepared thine heart to seek God. 1 Kin. 14:13; 2 Chr. 12:12; Ezra 7:10 ♦ *idols*

4 And Jehoshaphat dwelt at Jerusalem: and he went out again through the people from Beer-sheba to mount Ephraim, and brought them back unto the LORD God of their fa-thers.   2 Chr. 15:8-13

Jehoshaphat's Instructions to the Judges

5 And he set judges in the land throughout all the fenced cities of Judah, city by city,

6 And said to the judges, Take heed what ye do: for ye judge not for man, but for the LORD, who *is* with you in the judgment.   Deut. 1:17

7 Wherefore now let the fear of the LORD be upon you; take heed and do *it*: for *there is* no iniquity with the LORD our God, nor respect of persons, nor taking of gifts.   Gen. 18:25

8 Moreover in Jerusalem did Jehoshaphat set of the Levites, and *of* the priests, and of the chief of the fathers of Israel, for the judgment of the LORD, and for controversies, when they returned to Jerusalem. 2 Chr. 17:8-9

9 And he charged them, saying, Thus shall ye do in the fear of the LORD, faithfully, and with a perfect heart.   2 Sam. 23:3

10 And what cause soever shall come to you of your brethren that dwell in their cities, between blood and blood, between law and commandment, statutes and judgments, ye shall even warn them that they ᵀtrespass not against the LORD, and *so* wrath come upon

you, and upon your brethren: this do, and ye shall not trespass. Deut. 17:8-13 ◆ *sin*
11 And, behold, Amariah the chief priest *is* over you in all matters of the LORD; and Zebadiah the son of Ishmael, the ruler of the house of Judah, for all the king's matters: also the Levites *shall be* officers before you. Deal courageously, and the LORD shall be with the good. 1 Chr. 26:30

Jehoshaphat Proclaims a Fast

20 It came to pass after this also, *that* the children of Moab, and the children of Ammon, and with them *other* beside the Ammonites, came against Jehoshaphat to battle.
2 Then there came some that told Jehoshaphat, saying, There cometh a great multitude against thee from beyond the sea on this side Syria; and, behold, they *be* in Hazazon-tamar, which *is* Engedi. Gen. 14:7
3 And Jehoshaphat feared, and set himself to seek the LORD, and proclaimed a fast throughout all Judah. 1 Sam. 7:6; 2 Chr. 19:3; Jer. 36:9

> **20:1-3 Victory Through Faith**
> Jehoshaphat was a man of courage and valor. For years he had been strengthening his armies and his fortified cities. He was well prepared to meet almost any foe; yet in this crisis he put not his trust in the arm of flesh. Not by disciplined armies and fenced cities, but by a living faith in the God of Israel, could he hope to gain the victory. *PK 198*

4 And Judah gathered themselves together, to ask *help* of the LORD: even out of all the cities of Judah they came to seek the LORD.
5 And Jehoshaphat stood in the congregation of Judah and Jerusalem, in the house of the LORD, before the new court,
6 And said, O LORD God of our fathers, *art* not thou God in heaven? and rulest *not* thou over all the kingdoms of the heathen? and in thine hand *is there not* power and might, so that none is able to withstand thee? Deut. 4:39
7 *Art* not thou our God, *who* didst drive out the inhabitants of this land before thy people Israel, and gavest it to the seed of Abraham thy friend for ever? Ps. 44:2; Is. 41:8; James 2:23
8 And they dwelt therein, and have built thee a sanctuary therein for thy name, saying,
9 If, *when* evil cometh upon us, *as* the sword, judgment, or pestilence, or famine, we stand before this house, and in thy presence, (for thy name *is* in this house,) and cry unto thee in our affliction, then thou wilt hear and help. 2 Chr. 6:20
10 And now, behold, the children of Ammon and Moab and mount Seir, whom

thou wouldest not let Israel invade, when they came out of the land of Egypt, but they turned from them, and destroyed them not; Num. 20:17-21
11 Behold, *I say, how* they reward us, to come to cast us out of thy possession, which thou hast given us to inherit. Ps. 83:3-12
12 O our God, wilt thou not judge them? for we have no might against this great company that cometh against us; neither know we what to do: but our eyes *are* upon thee. Judg. 11:27; Ps. 25:15; 121:1-2

> **20:12 Jehoshaphat Not Alone**
> With confidence Jehoshaphat could say to the Lord, "Our eyes are upon Thee." For years he had taught the people to trust in the One who in past ages had so often interposed to save His chosen ones from utter destruction; and now, when the kingdom was in peril, Jehoshaphat did not stand alone. . . . Unitedly they fasted and prayed; unitedly they besought the Lord to put their enemies to confusion, that the name of Jehovah might be glorified. *PK 200*

13 And all Judah stood before the LORD, with their little ones, their wives, and their children.

The Prophecy of Jahaziel

14 Then upon Jahaziel the son of Zechariah, the son of Benaiah, the son of Jeiel, the son of Mattaniah, a Levite of the sons of Asaph, came the Spirit of the LORD in the midst of the congregation; 2 Chr. 15:1; 24:20
15 And he said, Hearken ye, all Judah, and ye inhabitants of Jerusalem, and thou king Jehoshaphat, Thus saith the LORD unto you, Be not afraid nor dismayed by reason of this great multitude; for the battle *is* not yours, but God's. Ex. 14:13-14; 1 Sam. 17:47; 2 Chr. 32:7-8
16 To morrow go ye down against them: behold, they come up by the cliff of Ziz; and ye shall find them at the end of the brook, before the wilderness of Jeruel.
17 Ye shall not *need* to fight in this *battle*: set yourselves, stand ye *still*, and see the salvation of the LORD with you, O Judah and Jerusalem: fear not, nor be dismayed; to morrow go out against them: for the LORD *will be* with you. Ex. 14:13-14; Num. 14:9; 2 Chr. 15:2
18 And Jehoshaphat bowed his head with *his* face to the ground: and all Judah and the inhabitants of Jerusalem fell before the LORD, worshipping the LORD. Ex. 4:31
19 And the Levites, of the children of the Kohathites, and of the children of the Korhites, stood up to praise the LORD God of Israel with a loud voice on high.

Jehoshaphat Defeats Judah's Enemies

20:20

20 And they rose early in the morning, and went forth into the wilderness of Tekoa: and as they went forth, Jehoshaphat stood and said, Hear me, O Judah, and ye inhabitants of Jerusalem; Believe in the LORD your God, so shall ye be established; believe his prophets, so shall ye prosper.   2 Sam. 14:2; Is. 7:9

> **Gift of Prophecy** See Acts 3:23.

21 And when he had consulted with the people, he appointed singers unto the LORD, and that should praise the beauty of holiness, as they went out before the army, and to say, Praise the LORD; for his mercy *endureth* for ever.   1 Chr. 16:29, 34; Ps. 29:2

> **20:21 To Battle With Singing**
>
> It was a singular way of going to battle against the enemy's army—praising the Lord with singing, and exalting the God of Israel. This was their battle song. They possessed the beauty of holiness. If more praising of God were engaged in now, hope and courage and faith would steadily increase. And would not this strengthen the hands of the valiant soldiers who today are standing in defense of truth? *PK 202*

22 And when they began to sing and to praise, the LORD set ambushments against the children of Ammon, Moab, and mount Seir, which were come against Judah; and they were smitten.   Judg. 7:22
23 For the children of Ammon and Moab stood up against the inhabitants of mount Seir, utterly to slay and destroy *them*: and when they had made an end of the inhabitants of Seir, every one helped to destroy another.   Judg. 7:22
24 And when Judah came toward the watch tower in the wilderness, they looked unto the multitude, and, behold, they *were* dead bodies fallen to the earth, and none escaped.
25 And when Jehoshaphat and his people came to take away the ᵀspoil of them, they found among them in abundance both riches with the dead bodies, and precious jewels, which they stripped off for themselves, more than they could carry away: and they were three days in gathering of the spoil, it was so much.   *plunder*
26 And on the fourth day they assembled themselves in the valley of Berachah; for there they blessed the LORD: therefore the name of the same place was called, The valley of Berachah, unto this day.
27 Then they returned, every man of Judah and Jerusalem, and Jehoshaphat in the forefront of them, to go again to Jerusalem with joy; for the LORD had made them to rejoice over their enemies.   Neh. 12:43
28 And they came to Jerusalem with ᵀpsalteries and harps and trumpets unto the house of the LORD.   *stringed instruments*
29 And the fear of God was on all the kingdoms of *those* countries, when they had heard that the LORD fought against the enemies of Israel.   Gen. 35:5; 2 Chr. 14:14; 17:10
30 So the realm of Jehoshaphat was quiet: for his God gave him rest round about.

Jehoshaphat's Reign

31 And Jehoshaphat reigned over Judah: *he was* thirty and five years old when he began to reign, and he reigned twenty and five years in Jerusalem. And his mother's name *was* Azubah the daughter of Shilhi.
32 And he walked in the way of Asa his father, and departed not from it, doing *that which was* right in the sight of the LORD.
33 Howbeit the high places were not taken away: for as yet the people had not prepared their hearts unto the God of their fathers.   2 Chr. 12:14; 17:6; 19:3
34 Now the rest of the acts of Jehoshaphat, first and last, behold, they *are* written in the book of Jehu the son of Hanani, who *is* mentioned in the book of the kings of Israel.   1 Kin. 16:1
35 And after this did Jehoshaphat king of Judah join himself with Ahaziah king of Israel, who did very wickedly: 1 Kin. 22:48-49
36 And he joined himself with him to make ships to go to Tarshish: and they made the ships in Ezion-geber.
37 Then Eliezer the son of Dodavah of Mareshah prophesied against Jehoshaphat, saying, Because thou hast joined thyself with Ahaziah, the LORD hath broken thy works. And the ships were broken, that they were not able to go to Tarshish.   Prov. 13:20

Jehoram Becomes King of Judah

21 Now Jehoshaphat slept with his fathers, and was buried with his fathers in the city of David. And Jehoram his son reigned in his stead.   1 Kin. 22:50
2 And he had brethren the sons of Jehoshaphat, Azariah, and Jehiel, and Zechariah, and Azariah, and Michael, and Shephatiah: all these *were* the sons of Jehoshaphat king of Israel.   2 Chr. 12:6
3 And their father gave them great gifts of silver, and of gold, and of precious things, with fenced cities in Judah: but the kingdom gave he to Jehoram; because he *was* the firstborn.   2 Chr. 11:23
4 Now when Jehoram was risen up to the kingdom of his father, he strengthened himself, and slew all his brethren with the

sword, and ᵀ*divers* also of the princes of Israel. Judg. 9:5 ◆ *various*

5 Jehoram *was* thirty and two years old when he began to reign, and he reigned eight years in Jerusalem.

6 And he walked in the way of the kings of Israel, like as did the house of Ahab: for he had the daughter of Ahab to wife: and he ᵀwrought *that which was* evil in the eyes of the LORD. 1 Kin. 12:28-30; 2 Kin. 8:18; 2 Chr. 18:1 ◆ *did*

21:5, 6 A Disastrous Alliance

Some years after coming to the throne, Jehoshaphat, now in the height of his prosperity, consented to the marriage of his son, Jehoram, to Athaliah, daughter of Ahab and Jezebel. By this union there was formed between the kingdoms of Judah and Israel an alliance which was not in the order of God and which in a time of crisis brought disaster to the king and to many of his subjects. *PK 192, 195*

---

7 Howbeit the LORD would not destroy the house of David, because of the covenant that he had made with David, and as he promised to give a light to him and to his sons for ever. 2 Sam. 7:12-17; 1 Kin. 11:13, 36

8 In his days the Edomites revolted from under the dominion of Judah, and made themselves a king.

9 Then Jehoram went forth with his princes, and all his chariots with him: and he rose up by night, and smote the Edomites which ᵀcompassed him in, and the captains of the chariots. *closed*

10 So the Edomites revolted from under the hand of Judah unto this day. The same time *also* did Libnah revolt from under his hand; because he had forsaken the LORD God of his fathers.

11 Moreover he made high places in the mountains of Judah, and caused the inhabitants of Jerusalem to commit fornication, and compelled Judah *thereto*. Lev. 20:5

Elijah Prophesies against Jehoram

12 And there came a writing to him from Elijah the prophet, saying, Thus saith the LORD God of David thy father, Because thou hast not walked in the ways of Jehoshaphat thy father, nor in the ways of Asa king of Judah, 2 Chr. 14:2-5

13 But hast walked in the way of the kings of Israel, and hast made Judah and the inhabitants of Jerusalem to go ᵀa whoring, like to the whoredoms of the house of Ahab, and also hast slain thy brethren of thy father's house, *which were* better than thyself: 2 Chr. 21:4, 11 ◆ *giving sex as a prostitute*

14 Behold, with a great plague will the LORD ᵀsmite thy people, and thy children, and thy wives, and all thy goods: *strike*

15 And thou *shalt have* great sickness by disease of thy bowels, until thy bowels fall out by reason of the sickness day by day.

16 Moreover the LORD stirred up against Jehoram the spirit of the Philistines, and of the Arabians, that *were* near the Ethiopians: 1 Kin. 11:14, 23; 2 Chr. 17:11

17 And they came up into Judah, and brake into it, and carried away all the substance that was found in the king's house, and his sons also, and his wives; so that there was never a son left him, save Jehoahaz, the youngest of his sons. 2 Chr. 22:1, 6; 25:23

18 And after all this the LORD smote him in his bowels with an incurable disease.

19 And it came to pass, that in process of time, after the end of two years, his bowels fell out by reason of his sickness: so he died of sore diseases. And his people made no burning for him, like the burning of his fathers. 2 Chr. 16:14

21:11–19 Apostasy Reproved

The king of Judah was not permitted to continue his terrible apostasy unreproved. The prophet Elijah had not yet been translated, and he could not remain silent while the kingdom of Judah was pursuing the same course that had brought the northern kingdom to the verge of ruin. The prophet sent to Jehoram of Judah a written communication, in which the wicked king read the awful words. . . . *PK 213*

---

20 Thirty and two years old was he when he began to reign, and he reigned in Jerusalem eight years, and departed without being desired. Howbeit they buried him in the city of David, but not in the sepulchres of the kings. 2 Chr. 24:25; Jer. 22:18, 28

Ahaziah Becomes King of Judah

22 And the inhabitants of Jerusalem made Ahaziah his youngest son king in his stead: for the band of men that came with the Arabians to the camp had slain all the eldest. So Ahaziah the son of Jehoram king of Judah reigned. 2 Kin. 8:24-29; 2 Chr. 21:16-17; 23:3

2 Forty and two years old *was* Ahaziah when he began to reign, and he reigned one year in Jerusalem. His mother's name also *was* Athaliah the daughter of Omri. 2 Kin. 8:26

3 He also walked in the ways of the house of Ahab: for his mother was his counsellor to do wickedly.

4 Wherefore he did evil in the sight of the LORD like the house of Ahab: for they were his counsellors after the death of his father to his destruction. Prov. 13:20

5 He walked also after their counsel, and went with Jehoram the son of Ahab king of Israel to war against Hazael king of Syria at Ramoth-gilead: and the Syrians smote Joram.

6 And he returned to be healed in Jezreel because of the wounds which were given him at Ramah, when he fought with Hazael king of Syria. And Azariah the son of Jehoram king of Judah went down to see Jehoram the son of Ahab at Jezreel, because he was sick.   2 Kin. 9:15

7 And the destruction of Ahaziah was of God by coming to Joram: for when he was come, he went out with Jehoram against Jehu the son of Nimshi, whom the LORD had anointed to cut off the house of Ahab.   2 Kin. 9:21

8 And it came to pass, that, when Jehu was executing judgment upon the house of Ahab, and found the princes of Judah, and the sons of the brethren of Ahaziah, that ministered to Ahaziah, he slew them.

9 And he sought Ahaziah: and they caught him, (for he was hid in Samaria,) and brought him to Jehu: and when they had slain him, they buried him: Because, said they, he is the son of Jehoshaphat, who sought the LORD with all his heart. So the house of Ahaziah had no power to keep still the kingdom.

Athaliah Usurps the Throne of Judah

10 But when Athaliah the mother of Ahaziah saw that her son was dead, she arose and destroyed all the seed royal of the house of Judah.

11 But Jehoshabeath, the daughter of the king, took Joash the son of Ahaziah, and stole him from among the king's sons that were slain, and put him and his nurse in a bedchamber. So Jehoshabeath, the daughter of king Jehoram, the wife of Jehoiada the priest, (for she was the sister of Ahaziah,) hid him from Athaliah, so that she slew him not.

12 And he was with them hid in the house of God six years: and Athaliah reigned over the land.

Jehoiada Makes Joash King of Judah

23 And in the seventh year Jehoiada strengthened himself, and took the captains of hundreds, Azariah the son of Jeroham, and Ishmael the son of Jehohanan, and Azariah the son of Obed, and Maaseiah the son of Adaiah, and Elishaphat the son of Zichri, into covenant with him.

2 And they went about in Judah, and gathered the Levites out of all the cities of Judah, and the chief of the fathers of Israel, and they came to Jerusalem.   2 Chr. 11:13-17

3 And all the congregation made a covenant with the king in the house of God. And he said unto them, Behold, the king's son shall reign, as the LORD hath said of the sons of David.   2 Sam. 7:12

4 This is the thing that ye shall do; A third part of you entering on the sabbath, of the priests and of the Levites, shall be porters of the doors;

5 And a third part shall be at the king's house; and a third part at the gate of the foundation: and all the people shall be in the courts of the house of the LORD.

6 But let none come into the house of the LORD, save the priests, and they that minister of the Levites; they shall go in, for they are holy: but all the people shall keep the watch of the LORD.   1 Chr. 23:28-32

7 And the Levites shall Tcompass the king round about, every man with his weapons in his hand; and whosoever else cometh into the house, he shall be put to death: but be ye with the king when he cometh in, and when he goeth out.   *surround*

8 So the Levites and all Judah did according to all things that Jehoiada the priest had commanded, and took every man his men that were to come in on the sabbath, with them that were to go out on the sabbath: for Jehoiada the priest dismissed not the courses.   2 Kin. 11:9

9 Moreover Jehoiada the priest delivered to the captains of hundreds spears, and bucklers, and shields, that had been king David's, which were in the house of God.

10 And he set all the people, every man having his weapon in his hand, from the right side of the temple to the left side of the temple, along by the altar and the temple, by the king round about.

11 Then they brought out the king's son, and put upon him the crown, and gave him the testimony, and made him king. And Jehoiada and his sons anointed him, and said, God save the king.   Ex. 25:16; 1 Sam. 10:24

Athaliah Is Slain

12 Now when Athaliah heard the noise of the people running and praising the king, she came to the people into the house of the LORD:

13 And she looked, and, behold, the king stood at his pillar at the entering in, and the princes and the trumpets by the king: and all the people of the land rejoiced, and sounded with trumpets, also the singers with instruments of musick, and such as taught to sing praise. Then Athaliah Trent her clothes, and said, Treason, Treason.   *tore apart*

14 Then Jehoiada the priest brought out the captains of hundreds that were set over the host, and said unto them, Have her forth of the ranges: and whoso followeth her, let him

be slain with the sword. For the priest said, Slay her not in the house of the LORD.

15 So they laid hands on her; and when she was come to the entering of the horse gate by the king's house, they slew her there.

23:12–15 An Evil Alliance

Thus perished the last member of the house of Ahab. The terrible evil that had been wrought through [Ahab's] alliance with Jezebel, continued till the last of his descendants was destroyed. Even in the land of Judah, where the worship of the true God had never been formally set aside, Athaliah had succeeded in seducing many. *PK 216*

---

16 And Jehoiada made a covenant between him, and between all the people, and between the king, that they should be the LORD's people.   2 Kin. 11:17

17 Then all the people went to the house of Baal, and brake it down, and brake his altars and his images in pieces, and slew Mattan the priest of Baal before the altars. 1 Kin. 18:40

18 Also Jehoiada appointed the offices of the house of the LORD by the hand of the priests the Levites, whom David had distributed in the house of the LORD, to offer the burnt offerings of the LORD, as *it is* written in the law of Moses, with rejoicing and with singing, *as it was ordained* by David.   2 Chr. 5:5

19 And he set the porters at the gates of the house of the LORD, that none *which was* unclean in any thing should enter in.

20 And he took the captains of hundreds, and the nobles, and the governors of the people, and all the people of the land, and brought down the king from the house of the LORD: and they came through the high gate into the king's house, and set the king upon the throne of the kingdom.   2 Kin. 11:19

21 And all the people of the land rejoiced: and the city was quiet, after that they had slain Athaliah with the sword.   2 Kin. 11:20

23:16–21 A Reformation After Rebellion

A reformation followed. Those who took part in acclaiming Joash king, had solemnly covenanted "that they should be the Lord's people." And now that the evil influence of the daughter of Jezebel had been removed from the kingdom of Judah, and the priests of Baal had been slain and their temple destroyed, "all the people of the land rejoiced: and the city was quiet" (2 Chronicles 23:16, 21). *PK 216*

Joash's Reign over Judah

24 Joash *was* seven years old when he began to reign, and he reigned forty years in Jerusalem. His mother's name also *was* Zibiah of Beer-sheba.

2 And Joash did *that which was* right in the sight of the LORD all the days of Jehoiada the priest.   2 Chr. 25:2

3 And Jehoiada took for him two wives; and he ᵀbegat sons and daughters.   *brought forth*

4 And it came to pass after this, *that* Joash was minded to repair the house of the LORD.

5 And he gathered together the priests and the Levites, and said to them, Go out unto the cities of Judah, and gather of all Israel money to repair the house of your God from year to year, and see that ye hasten the matter. Howbeit the Levites hastened *it* not.

6 And the king called for Jehoiada the chief, and said unto him, Why hast thou not required of the Levites to bring in out of Judah and out of Jerusalem the collection, *according to the commandment* of Moses the servant of the LORD, and of the congregation of Israel, for the tabernacle of witness? Ex. 30:12-16; Num. 1:50

7 For the sons of Athaliah, that wicked woman, had broken up the house of God; and also all the dedicated things of the house of the LORD did they bestow upon Baalim.   2 Chr. 21:17

8 And at the king's commandment they made a chest, and set it without at the gate of the house of the LORD.

9 And they made a proclamation through Judah and Jerusalem, to bring in to the LORD the collection *that* Moses the servant of God laid upon Israel in the wilderness.   2 Chr. 24:6

10 And all the princes and all the people rejoiced, and brought in, and cast into the chest, until they had made an end. 1 Chr. 29:9

11 Now it came to pass, that at what time the chest was brought unto the king's office by the hand of the Levites, and when they saw that *there was* much money, the king's scribe and the high priest's officer came and emptied the chest, and took it, and carried it to his place again. Thus they did day by day, and gathered money in abundance.

12 And the king and Jehoiada gave it to such as did the work of the service of the house of the LORD, and hired masons and carpenters to repair the house of the LORD, and also such as ᵀwrought iron and brass to mend the house of the LORD.   *worked in*

13 So the workmen wrought, and the work was perfected by them, and they set the house of God in his state, and strengthened it.

14 And when they had finished *it*, they brought the rest of the money before the king and Jehoiada, whereof were made vessels for the house of the LORD, *even* vessels to minister, and to offer ᵀwithal, and spoons, and vessels of gold and silver. And they offered burnt offerings in the house

of the LORD continually all the days of Jehoiada.   *with*

Joash's Sin Leads to His Assassination

15 But Jehoiada ᵀwaxed old, and was full of days when he died; an hundred and thirty years old *was he* when he died.   *became*
16 And they buried him in the city of David among the kings, because he had done good in Israel, both toward God, and toward his house.
17 Now after the death of Jehoiada came the princes of Judah, and made ᵀobeisance to the king. Then the king hearkened unto them.   *homage*
18 And they left the house of the LORD God of their fathers, and served groves and idols: and wrath came upon Judah and Jerusalem for this their ᵀtrespass.   Josh. 22:20 ◆ *sin*
19 Yet he sent prophets to them, to bring them again unto the LORD; and they testified against them: but they would not give ear.
20 And the Spirit of God came upon Zechariah the son of Jehoiada the priest, which stood above the people, and said unto them, Thus saith God, Why ᵀtransgress ye the commandments of the LORD, that ye cannot prosper? because ye have forsaken the LORD, he hath also forsaken you.   Num. 14:41 ◆ *violate*
21 And they conspired against him, and stoned him with stones at the commandment of the king in the court of the house of the LORD.   Neh. 9:26
22 Thus Joash the king remembered not the kindness which Jehoiada his father had done to him, but slew his son. And when he died, he said, The LORD look upon *it*, and require *it*.   Gen. 9:5

24:20–22 A Stain Not to Be Erased

While the words of warning from God were upon [Zechariah's] lips, a satanic fury seized the apostate king, and at his command the prophet was put to death. His blood had imprinted itself upon the very stones of the temple court, and could not be erased; it remained to bear testimony against apostate Israel. As long as the temple should stand, there would be the stain of that righteous blood, crying to God to be avenged. *DA 619*

---

23 And it came to pass at the end of the year, *that* the host of Syria came up against him: and they came to Judah and Jerusalem, and destroyed all the princes of the people from among the people, and sent all the ᵀspoil of them unto the king of Damascus.   *plunder*
24 For the army of the Syrians came with a small company of men, and the LORD delivered a very great host into their hand, because they had forsaken the LORD God

of their fathers. So they executed judgment against Joash.   Lev. 26:8
25 And when they were departed from him, (for they left him in great diseases,) his own servants conspired against him for the blood of the sons of Jehoiada the priest, and slew him on his bed, and he died: and they buried him in the city of David, but they buried him not in the sepulchres of the kings. 2 Chr. 24:21-22
26 And these are they that conspired against him; Zabad the son of Shimeath an Ammonitess, and Jehozabad the son of Shimrith a Moabitess.   2 Kin. 12:21
27 Now *concerning* his sons, and the greatness of the burdens *laid* upon him, and the repairing of the house of God, behold, they *are* written in the story of the book of the kings. And Amaziah his son reigned in his stead.

Amaziah Becomes King of Judah

25 Amaziah *was* twenty and five years old *when* he began to reign, and he reigned twenty and nine years in Jerusalem. And his mother's name *was* Jehoaddan of Jerusalem.
2 And he did *that which was* right in the sight of the LORD, but not with a perfect heart.
3 Now it came to pass, when the kingdom was established to him, that he slew his servants that had killed the king his father.
4 But he slew not their children, but *did* as *it is* written in the law in the book of Moses, where the LORD commanded, saying, The fathers shall not die for the children, neither shall the children die for the fathers, but every man shall die for his own sin.   Ezek. 18:20
5 Moreover Amaziah gathered Judah together, and made them captains over thousands, and captains over hundreds, according to the houses of *their* fathers, throughout all Judah and Benjamin: and he numbered them from twenty years old and above, and found them three hundred thousand choice *men, able* to go forth to war, that could handle spear and shield.   Num. 1:3; 2 Chr. 11:1; 17:14-18
6 He hired also an hundred thousand mighty men of valour out of Israel for an hundred talents of silver.
7 But there came a man of God to him, saying, O king, let not the army of Israel go with thee; for the LORD *is* not with Israel, *to wit,* with all the children of Ephraim.   2 Chr. 19:2
8 But if thou wilt go, do *it*, be strong for the battle: God shall make thee fall before the enemy: for God hath power to help, and to cast down.   2 Chr. 14:11; 20:6
9 And Amaziah said to the man of God, But what shall we do for the hundred talents which I have given to the army of Israel?

And the man of God answered, The LORD is able to give thee much more than this.

10 Then Amaziah separated them, ᵀto wit, the army that was come to him out of Ephraim, to go home again: wherefore their anger was greatly kindled against Judah, and they returned home in great anger.   *namely*

11 And Amaziah strengthened himself, and led forth his people, and went to the valley of salt, and smote of the children of Seir ten thousand.   2 Kin. 14:7

12 And *other* ten thousand *left* alive did the children of Judah carry away captive, and brought them unto the top of the rock, and cast them down from the top of the rock, that they all were broken in pieces.

13 But the soldiers of the army which Amaziah sent back, that they should not go with him to battle, fell upon the cities of Judah, from Samaria even unto Beth-horon, and smote three thousand of them, and took much ᵀspoil.   *plunder*

Amaziah Serves the Gods of Edom

14 Now it came to pass, after that Amaziah was come from the slaughter of the Edomites, that he brought the gods of the children of Seir, and set them up *to be* his gods, and bowed down himself before them, and burned incense unto them.   2 Chr. 28:23

15 Wherefore the anger of the LORD was kindled against Amaziah, and he sent unto him a prophet, which said unto him, Why hast thou sought after the gods of the people, which could not deliver their own people out of thine hand?   2 Chr. 25:11-12

16 And it came to pass, as he talked with him, that *the king* said unto him, Art thou made of the king's counsel? ᵀforbear; why shouldest thou be smitten? Then the prophet forbare, and said, I know that God hath determined to destroy thee, because thou hast done this, and hast not hearkened unto my counsel.   *cease*

Amaziah's Sin Leads to His Defeat

17 Then Amaziah king of Judah took advice, and sent to Joash, the son of Jehoahaz, the son of Jehu, king of Israel, saying, Come, let us see one another in the face.   2 Kin. 14:8-14

18 And Joash king of Israel sent to Amaziah king of Judah, saying, The thistle that *was* in Lebanon sent to the cedar that *was* in Lebanon, saying, Give thy daughter to my son to wife: and there passed by a wild beast that *was* in Lebanon, and ᵀtrode down the thistle.   Judg. 9:8-15 ♦ *trampled*

19 Thou sayest, Lo, thou hast smitten the Edomites; and thine heart lifteth thee up to boast: abide now at home; why shouldest thou meddle to *thine* hurt, that thou

shouldest fall, *even* thou, and Judah with thee?   2 Chr. 26:16

20 But Amaziah would not hear; for it *came* of God, that he might deliver them into the hand *of their enemies*, because they sought after the gods of Edom.   1 Kin. 12:15

21 So Joash the king of Israel went up; and they saw one another in the face, *both* he and Amaziah king of Judah, at Beth-shemesh, which *belongeth* to Judah.

22 And Judah was put to the worse before Israel, and they fled every man to his tent.

23 And Joash the king of Israel took Amaziah king of Judah, the son of Joash, the son of Jehoahaz, at Beth-shemesh, and brought him to Jerusalem, and brake down the wall of Jerusalem from the gate of Ephraim to the corner gate, four hundred cubits.   2 Chr. 21:17

24 And *he took* all the gold and the silver, and all the vessels that were found in the house of God with Obededom, and the treasures of the king's house, the hostages also, and returned to Samaria.   1 Chr. 26:15

25 And Amaziah the son of Joash king of Judah lived after the death of Joash son of Jehoahaz king of Israel fifteen years. 2 Kin. 14:17-22

26 Now the rest of the acts of Amaziah, first and last, behold, *are* they not written in the book of the kings of Judah and Israel?

27 Now after the time that Amaziah did turn away from following the LORD they made a conspiracy against him in Jerusalem; and he fled to Lachish: but they sent to Lachish after him, and slew him there.

28 And they brought him upon horses, and buried him with his fathers in the city of Judah.

Uzziah Becomes King of Judah

26 Then all the people of Judah took Uzziah, who *was* sixteen years old, and made him king in the room of his father Amaziah.   2 Chr. 22:1

2 He built Eloth, and restored it to Judah, after that the king slept with his fathers.

3 Sixteen years old *was* Uzziah when he began to reign, and he reigned fifty and two years in Jerusalem. His mother's name also *was* Jecoliah of Jerusalem.   2 Kin. 15:2-3

4 And he did *that which was* right in the sight of the LORD, according to all that his father Amaziah did.

5 And he sought God in the days of Zechariah, who had understanding in the visions of God: and as long as he sought the LORD, God made him to prosper.   2 Chr. 15:2; 24:2; Dan. 1:17

6 And he went forth and warred against the Philistines, and brake down the wall of Gath, and the wall of Jabneh, and the wall of Ashdod, and built cities about Ashdod, and among the Philistines.   Is. 14:29

7 And God helped him against the Philistines, and against the Arabians that dwelt in Gur-baal, and the Mehunims.   2 Chr. 21:16
8 And the Ammonites gave gifts to Uzziah: and his name spread abroad *even* to the entering in of Egypt; for he strengthened *himself* exceedingly.   Gen. 19:38
9 Moreover Uzziah built towers in Jerusalem at the corner gate, and at the valley gate, and at the turning *of the wall*, and fortified them.   2 Kin. 14:13; 2 Chr. 25:23; Neh. 3:13
10 Also he built towers in the desert, and digged many wells: for he had much cattle, both in the low country, and in the plains: ᵀhusbandmen *also*, and vine dressers in the mountains, and in Carmel: for he loved ᵀhusbandry.   Gen. 26:18-21 ◆ *farmers* ◆ *farming*
11 Moreover Uzziah had an host of fighting men, that went out to war by bands, according to the number of their account by the hand of Jeiel the scribe and Maaseiah the ruler, under the hand of Hananiah, *one* of the king's captains.
12 The whole number of the chief of the fathers of the mighty men of valour *were* two thousand and six hundred.
13 And under their hand *was* an army, three hundred thousand and seven thousand and five hundred, that made war with mighty power, to help the king against the enemy.
14 And Uzziah prepared for them throughout all the host shields, and spears, and helmets, and habergeons, and bows, and slings *to cast* stones.
15 And he made in Jerusalem engines, invented by cunning men, to be on the towers and upon the ᵀbulwarks, to shoot arrows and great stones ᵀwithal. And his name spread far abroad; for he was marvellously helped, till he was strong.   *structures for defense* ◆ *with*

Uzziah Is Smitten with Leprosy

16 But when he was strong, his heart was lifted up to *his* destruction: for he transgressed against the LORD his God, and went into the temple of the LORD to burn incense upon the altar of incense.   Deut. 8:14; 2 Chr. 25:19
17 And Azariah the priest went in after him, and with him ᵀfourscore priests of the LORD, *that were* valiant men: 1 Chr. 6:10 ◆ *eighty*
18 And they withstood Uzziah the king, and said unto him, It ᵀappertaineth not unto thee, Uzziah, to burn incense unto the LORD, but to the priests the sons of Aaron, that are ᵀconsecrated to burn incense: go out of the sanctuary; for thou hast ᵀtrespassed; neither *shall it be* for thine honour from the LORD God.   Ex. 30:7-8 ◆ *belongs* ◆ *set apart* ◆ *sinned*
19 Then Uzziah was ᵀwroth, and *had* a ᵀcenser in his hand to burn incense: and while he was wroth with the priests, the leprosy even rose up in his forehead before the priests in the house of the LORD, from beside the incense altar. Num. 12:10 ◆ *angered* ◆ *holder for burning incense*
20 And Azariah the chief priest, and all the priests, looked upon him, and, behold, he *was* leprous in his forehead, and they thrust him out from thence; yea, himself hasted also to go out, because the LORD had smitten him.

26:16–21 Judgment on Rebellion

Unto the day of his death, some years later, Uzziah remained a leper—a living example of the folly of departing from a plain "Thus saith the Lord." Neither his exalted position nor his long life of service could be pleaded as an excuse for the presumptuous sin by which he marred the closing years of his reign, and brought upon himself the judgment of Heaven.

God is no respecter of persons. *PK 304*

The Sin of Presumption

2 Chronicles 26:1–18

The long reign of Uzziah [also known as Azariah] in the land of Judah and Benjamin was characterized by a prosperity greater than that of any other ruler since the death of Solomon, nearly two centuries before. For many years the king ruled with discretion. Under the blessing of Heaven his armies regained some of the territory that had been lost in former years. Cities were rebuilt and fortified, and the position of the nation among the surrounding peoples was greatly strengthened. Commerce revived, and the riches of the nations flowed into Jerusalem. . . .

This outward prosperity, however, was not accompanied by a corresponding revival of spiritual power. The temple services were continued as in former years, and multitudes assembled to worship the living God; but pride and formality gradually took the place of humility and sincerity. Of Uzziah himself it is written: "When he was strong, his heart was lifted up to his destruction; for he transgressed against the Lord his God" (2 Chronicles 26:16).

The sin that resulted so disastrously to Uzziah was one of presumption. In violation of a plain command of Jehovah, that none but the descendants of Aaron should officiate as priests, the king entered the sanctuary "to burn incense upon the altar." Azariah the high priest and his associates remonstrated, and pleaded with him to turn from his purpose. "Thou hast trespassed," they urged; "neither shall it be for thine honor" (2 Chronicles 26:16, 18). *PK 303, 304*

21 And Uzziah the king was a leper unto the day of his death, and dwelt in a several house, *being* a leper; for he was cut off from the house of the LORD: and Jotham his son *was* over the king's house, judging the people of the land.   Lev. 13:46

22 Now the rest of the acts of Uzziah, first and last, did Isaiah the prophet, the son of Amoz, write.   Is. 1:1; 6:1

23 So Uzziah slept with his fathers, and they buried him with his fathers in the field of the burial which *belonged* to the kings; for they said, He *is* a leper: and Jotham his son reigned in his stead.   2 Chr. 21:20

Jotham Becomes King of Judah

27 Jotham *was* twenty and five years old when he began to reign, and he reigned sixteen years in Jerusalem. His mother's name also *was* Jerushah, the daughter of Zadok.   1 Chr. 3:12

2 And he did *that which was* right in the sight of the LORD, according to all that his father Uzziah did: ᵀhowbeit he entered not into the temple of the LORD. And the people did yet corruptly.   *however*

3 He built the high gate of the house of the LORD, and on the wall of Ophel he built much.   2 Chr. 33:14; Neh. 3:26-27

4 Moreover he built cities in the mountains of Judah, and in the forests he built castles and towers.

5 He fought also with the king of the Ammonites, and prevailed against them. And the children of Ammon gave him the same year an hundred talents of silver, and ten thousand measures of wheat, and ten thousand of barley. So much did the children of Ammon pay unto him, both the second year, and the third.

6 So Jotham became mighty, because he prepared his ways before the LORD his God.

7 Now the rest of the acts of Jotham, and all his wars, and his ways, lo, they *are* written in the book of the kings of Israel and Judah.

8 He was five and twenty years old when he began to reign, and reigned sixteen years in Jerusalem.

9 And Jotham slept with his fathers, and they buried him in the city of David: and Ahaz his son reigned in his stead.

Ahaz Becomes King of Judah

28 Ahaz *was* twenty years old when he began to reign, and he reigned sixteen years in Jerusalem: but he did not *that which was* right in the sight of the LORD, like David his father: 1 Chr. 3:13

2 For he walked in the ways of the kings of Israel, and made also molten images for Baalim.   Ex. 34:17; Judg. 2:11

3 Moreover he burnt incense in the valley of the son of Hinnom, and burnt his children in the fire, after the abominations of the heathen whom the LORD had cast out before the children of Israel.   Lev. 18:21; 2 Chr. 33:2, 6

4 He sacrificed also and burnt incense in the high places, and on the hills, and under every green tree.

28:2-4 Great Peril; Dark Prospects

This was indeed a time of great peril for the chosen nation. Only a few short years, and the ten tribes of the kingdom of Israel were to be scattered among the nations of heathendom. And in the kingdom of Judah also the outlook was dark. The forces for good were rapidly diminishing, the forces for evil multiplying. *PK 324*

5 Wherefore the LORD his God delivered him into the hand of the king of Syria; and they smote him, and carried away a great multitude of them captives, and brought *them* to Damascus. And he was also delivered into the hand of the king of Israel, who smote him with a great slaughter.   2 Kin. 16:5-6; 2 Chr. 24:24

Oded the Prophet Brings about Release of the Children of Judah

6 For Pekah the son of Remaliah slew in Judah an hundred and twenty thousand in one day, *which were* all valiant men; because they had forsaken the LORD God of their fathers.   2 Kin. 15:27

7 And Zichri, a mighty man of Ephraim, slew Maaseiah the king's son, and Azrikam the governor of the house, and Elkanah *that was* next to the king.

8 And the children of Israel carried away captive of their brethren two hundred thousand, women, sons, and daughters, and took also away much spoil from them, and brought the spoil to Samaria.   Deut. 28:25, 41; 2 Chr. 11:4

9 But a prophet of the LORD was there, whose name *was* Oded: and he went out before the host that came to Samaria, and said unto them, Behold, because the LORD God of your fathers was ᵀwroth with Judah, he hath delivered them into your hand, and ye have slain them in a rage *that* reacheth up unto heaven.   Ezra 9:6; Is. 47:6; Rev. 18:5 ◆ *angry*

10 And now ye purpose to keep under the children of Judah and Jerusalem for bondmen and bondwomen unto you: *but are there* not with you, even with you, sins against the LORD your God?   Lev. 25:39-46

11 Now hear me therefore, and deliver the captives again, which ye have taken captive of your brethren: for the fierce wrath of the LORD *is* upon you.   James 2:13

12 Then certain of the heads of the children

of Ephraim, Azariah the son of Johanan, Berechiah the son of Meshillemoth, and Jehizkiah the son of Shallum, and Amasa the son of Hadlai, stood up against them that came from the war,

13 And said unto them, Ye shall not bring in the captives ᵀhither: for whereas we have offended against the LORD *already*, ye intend to add *more* to our sins and to our trespass: for our trespass is great, and *there is* fierce wrath against Israel.   *here*

14 So the armed men left the captives and the ᵀspoil before the princes and all the congregation.   *plunder*

15 And the men which were expressed by name rose up, and took the captives, and with the spoil clothed all that were naked among them, and ᵀarrayed them, and shod them, and gave them to eat and to drink, and anointed them, and carried all the feeble of them upon asses, and brought them to Jericho, the city of palm trees, to their brethren: then they returned to Samaria.   Deut. 34:3; 2 Kin. 6:22 ◆ *clothed*

Ahaz Sends to Assyria for Aid but to No Avail

16 At that time did king Ahaz send unto the kings of Assyria to help him.

17 For again the Edomites had come and smitten Judah, and carried away captives.

18 The Philistines also had invaded the cities of the low country, and of the south of Judah, and had taken Beth-shemesh, and Ajalon, and Gederoth, and Shocho with the villages thereof, and Timnah with the villages thereof, Gimzo also and the villages thereof: and they dwelt there. Ezek. 16:27, 57

19 For the LORD brought Judah low because of Ahaz king of Israel; for he made Judah naked, and ᵀtransgressed sore against the LORD.   *sinned*

20 And Tilgath-pilneser king of Assyria came unto him, and distressed him, but strengthened him not.   2 Kin. 15:29

21 For Ahaz took away a portion *out* of the house of the LORD, and *out* of the house of the king, and of the princes, and gave *it* unto the king of Assyria: but he helped him not.

22 And in the time of his distress did he ᵀtrespass yet more against the LORD: this *is* *that* king Ahaz.   Is. 1:5 ◆ *sin*

23 For he sacrificed unto the gods of Damascus, which smote him: and he said, Because the gods of the kings of Syria help them, *therefore* will I sacrifice to them, that they may help me. But they were the ruin of him, and of all Israel.   2 Chr. 25:14

24 And Ahaz gathered together the vessels of the house of God, and cut in pieces the vessels of the house of God, and shut up the doors

of the house of the LORD, and he made him altars in every corner of Jerusalem.   2 Chr. 29:7

28:24 Loyalty in the Midst of Darkness

As the apostate king neared the end of his reign, he caused the doors of the temple to be closed. . . . Deserting the courts of the house of God and locking fast its doors, the inhabitants of the godless city boldly set up altars for the worship of heathen deities on the street corners throughout Jerusalem. Heathenism had seemingly triumphed; the powers of darkness had well-nigh prevailed.

But in Judah there dwelt some who maintained their allegiance to Jehovah, steadfastly refusing to be led into idolatry. *PK 330*

---

25 And in every several city of Judah he made high places to burn incense unto other gods, and provoked to anger the LORD God of his fathers.   2 Chr. 28:3

26 Now the rest of his acts and of all his ways, first and last, behold, they *are* written in the book of the kings of Judah and Israel.   2 Kin. 16:19-20

27 And Ahaz slept with his fathers, and they buried him in the city, *even* in Jerusalem: but they brought him not into the sepulchres of the kings of Israel: and Hezekiah his son reigned in his stead.   2 Chr. 21:20

Hezekiah Becomes King of Judah

29 Hezekiah began to reign *when he was* five and twenty years old, and he reigned nine and twenty years in Jerusalem. And his mother's name *was* Abijah, the daughter of Zechariah.   2 Kin. 18:1-3

2 And he did *that which was* right in the sight of the LORD, according to all that David his father had done.

3 He in the first year of his reign, in the first month, opened the doors of the house of the LORD, and repaired them.   2 Chr. 28:24; 29:7

4 And he brought in the priests and the Levites, and gathered them together into the east street,

5 And said unto them, Hear me, ye Levites, sanctify now yourselves, and sanctify the house of the LORD God of your fathers, and carry forth the filthiness out of the holy *place*.   1 Chr. 15:12; 2 Chr. 35:6

6 For our fathers have ᵀtrespassed, and done *that which was* evil in the eyes of the LORD our God, and have forsaken him, and have turned away their faces from the habitation of the LORD, and turned *their* backs.   Jer. 2:27 ◆ *sinned*

7 Also they have shut up the doors of the porch, and put out the lamps, and have not burned incense nor offered burnt offerings in the holy *place* unto the God of Israel. 2 Chr. 28:24

8 Wherefore the wrath of the LORD was upon

Judah and Jerusalem, and he hath delivered them to trouble, to astonishment, and to ᵀhissing, as ye see with your eyes.   *jeering*
9 For, lo, our fathers have fallen by the sword, and our sons and our daughters and our wives *are* in captivity for this.   2 Chr. 28:5-8, 17
10 Now *it is* in mine heart to make a covenant with the LORD God of Israel, that his fierce wrath may turn away from us.   2 Chr. 23:16
11 My sons, be not now negligent: for the LORD hath chosen you to stand before him, to serve him, and that ye should minister unto him, and burn incense.

Priests and Levites Sanctify Themselves and Cleanse the Temple

12 Then the Levites arose, Mahath the son of Amasai, and Joel the son of Azariah, of the sons of the Kohathites: and of the sons of Merari, Kish the son of Abdi, and Azariah the son of Jehalelel: and of the Gershonites; Joah the son of Zimmah, and Eden the son of Joah:
13 And of the sons of Elizaphan; Shimri, and Jeiel: and of the sons of Asaph; Zechariah, and Mattaniah: 1 Chr. 6:39
14 And of the sons of Heman; Jehiel, and Shimei: and of the sons of Jeduthun; Shemaiah, and Uzziel.   1 Chr. 6:33
15 And they gathered their brethren, and sanctified themselves, and came, according to the commandment of the king, by the words of the LORD, to cleanse the house of the LORD.   1 Chr. 23:28; 2 Chr. 29:5; 30:12
16 And the priests went into the inner part of the house of the LORD, to cleanse *it*, and brought out all the uncleanness that they found in the temple of the LORD into the court of the house of the LORD. And the Levites took *it*, to carry *it* out abroad into the brook Kidron.   2 Chr. 15:16
17 Now they began on the first *day* of the first month to sanctify, and on the eighth day of the month came they to the porch of the LORD: so they ᵀsanctified the house of the LORD in eight days; and in the sixteenth day of the first month they made an end.   *made holy*
18 Then they went in to Hezekiah the king, and said, We have cleansed all the house of the LORD, and the altar of burnt offering, with all the vessels thereof, and the shewbread table, with all the vessels thereof.
19 Moreover all the vessels, which king Ahaz in his reign did cast away in his ᵀtransgression, have we prepared and sanctified, and, behold, they *are* before the altar of the LORD.   2 Chr. 28:24 ♦ *violation of a law*

Hezekiah Rededicates the Temple

20 Then Hezekiah the king rose early, and gathered the rulers of the city, and went up to the house of the LORD.
21 And they brought seven bullocks, and seven rams, and seven lambs, and seven he goats, for a sin offering for the kingdom, and for the sanctuary, and for Judah. And he commanded the priests the sons of Aaron to offer *them* on the altar of the LORD.   Lev. 4:3-14
22 So they killed the bullocks, and the priests received the blood, and sprinkled *it* on the altar: likewise, when they had killed the rams, they sprinkled the blood upon the altar: they killed also the lambs, and they sprinkled the blood upon the altar.   Lev. 4:18
23 And they brought forth the he goats *for* the sin offering before the king and the congregation; and they laid their hands upon them: Lev. 4:15
24 And the priests killed them, and they made reconciliation with their blood upon the altar, to make an atonement for all Israel: for the king commanded *that* the burnt offering and the sin offering *should be made* for all Israel.
25 And he set the Levites in the house of the LORD with cymbals, with ᵀpsalteries, and with harps, according to the commandment of David, and of Gad the king's seer, and Nathan the prophet: for *so was* the commandment of the LORD by his prophets.   2 Sam. 24:11; 1 Chr. 23:5 ♦ *stringed instruments*
26 And the Levites stood with the instruments of David, and the priests with the trumpets.   1 Chr. 15:24; 23:5; Amos 6:5
27 And Hezekiah commanded to offer the burnt offering upon the altar. And when the burnt offering began, the song of the LORD began *also* with the trumpets, and with the instruments *ordained* by David king of Israel.   2 Chr. 23:18
28 And all the congregation worshipped, and the singers sang, and the trumpeters sounded: *and* all *this continued* until the burnt offering was finished.

29 And when they had made an end of offering, the king and all that were present with him bowed themselves, and worshipped.

30 Moreover Hezekiah the king and the princes commanded the Levites to sing praise unto the LORD with the words of David, and of Asaph the seer. And they sang praises with gladness, and they bowed their heads and worshipped.

31 Then Hezekiah answered and said, Now ye have consecrated yourselves unto the LORD, come near and bring sacrifices and thank offerings into the house of the LORD. And the congregation brought in sacrifices and thank offerings; and as many as were of a free heart burnt offerings.   2 Chr. 13:9

32 And the number of the burnt offerings, which the congregation brought, was ᵀthreescore and ten bullocks, an hundred rams, *and* two hundred lambs: all these *were* for a burnt offering to the LORD.   *sixty*

33 And the ᵀconsecrated things *were* six hundred oxen and three thousand sheep. *set apart*

34 But the priests were too few, so that they could not flay all the burnt offerings: wherefore their brethren the Levites did help them, till the work was ended, and until the *other* priests had sanctified themselves: for the Levites *were* more upright in heart to sanctify themselves than the priests.   2 Chr. 30:3; 35:11

35 And also the burnt offerings *were* in abundance, with the fat of the peace offerings, and the drink offerings for *every* burnt offering. So the service of the house of the LORD was set in order.   Num. 15:5-10

36 And Hezekiah rejoiced, and all the people, that God had prepared the people: for the thing was *done* suddenly.

Hezekiah Celebrates Passover

30 And Hezekiah sent to all Israel and Judah, and wrote letters also to Ephraim and Manasseh, that they should come to the house of the LORD at Jerusalem, to keep the passover unto the LORD God of Israel.

2 For the king had taken counsel, and his princes, and all the congregation in Jerusalem, to keep the passover in the second month.   Num. 9:10-11

3 For they could not keep it at that time, because the priests had not sanctified themselves sufficiently, neither had the people gathered themselves together to Jerusalem.   Ex. 12:6, 18; 2 Chr. 29:34

4 And the thing pleased the king and all the congregation.

5 So they established a decree to make proclamation throughout all Israel, from Beersheba even to Dan, that they should come to keep the passover unto the LORD

God of Israel at Jerusalem: for they had not done *it* of a long *time in such sort* as it was written.   Judg. 20:1

6 So the posts went with the letters from the king and his princes throughout all Israel and Judah, and according to the commandment of the king, saying, Ye children of Israel, turn again unto the LORD God of Abraham, Isaac, and Israel, and he will return to the remnant of you, that are escaped out of the hand of the kings of Assyria.   Esth. 8:14

7 And be not ye like your fathers, and like your brethren, which ᵀtrespassed against the LORD God of their fathers, *who* therefore gave them up to desolation, as ye see.   *sinned*

8 Now be ye not stiffnecked, as your fathers *were, but* yield yourselves unto the LORD, and enter into his sanctuary, which he hath sanctified for ever: and serve the LORD your God, that the fierceness of his wrath may turn away from you.   Ex. 32:9; Deut. 10:16; 2 Chr. 29:10

9 For if ye turn again unto the LORD, your brethren and your children *shall find* compassion before them that lead them captive, so that they shall come again into this land: for the LORD your God *is* gracious and merciful, and will not turn away *his* face from you, if ye return unto him.   Ex. 34:6-7

10 So the posts passed from city to city through the country of Ephraim and Manasseh even unto Zebulun: but they laughed them to scorn, and mocked them.   2 Chr. 30:6

11 Nevertheless ᵀdivers of Asher and Manasseh and of Zebulun humbled themselves, and came to Jerusalem.   2 Chr. 30:18 ◆ *various*

30:1–11 Reform and Celebration

In the third year of Hoshea's reign, good King Hezekiah began to rule in Judah and as speedily as possible instituted important reforms in the temple service at Jerusalem. A Passover celebration was arranged for, and to this feast were invited not only the tribes of Judah and Benjamin, over which Hezekiah had been anointed king, but all the northern tribes as well. *PK 288*

12 Also in Judah the hand of God was to give them one heart to do the commandment of the king and of the princes, by the word of the LORD.   Phil. 2:13

The People Celebrate the Feast of Unleavened Bread

13 And there assembled at Jerusalem much people to keep the feast of unleavened bread in the second month, a very great congregation.

14 And they arose and took away the altars that *were* in Jerusalem, and all the altars for

incense took they away, and cast *them* into the brook Kidron. 2 Sam. 15:23; 2 Chr. 15:16; 28:24

15 Then they killed the passover on the fourteenth *day* of the second month: and the priests and the Levites were ashamed, and ᵀsanctified themselves, and brought in the burnt offerings into the house of the LORD.   2 Chr. 29:34 ◆ *made themselves holy*

16 And they stood in their place after their manner, according to the law of Moses the man of God: the priests sprinkled the blood, *which they received* of the hand of the Levites.   Deut. 33:1

17 For *there were* many in the congregation that were not sanctified: therefore the Levites had the charge of the killing of the passovers for every one *that was* not clean, to ᵀsanctify *them* unto the LORD. 2 Chr. 29:34 ◆ *make them holy*

18 For a multitude of the people, *even* many of Ephraim, and Manasseh, Issachar, and Zebulun, had not cleansed themselves, yet did they eat the passover otherwise than it was written. But Hezekiah prayed for them, saying, The good LORD pardon every one

19 *That* prepareth his heart to seek God, the LORD God of his fathers, though *he be* not *cleansed* according to the purification of the sanctuary.   2 Chr. 19:3

20 And the LORD hearkened to Hezekiah, and healed the people.

21 And the children of Israel that were present at Jerusalem kept the feast of unleavened bread seven days with great gladness: and the Levites and the priests praised the LORD day by day, *singing* with loud instruments unto the LORD.   Ex. 12:15; 13:6

22 And Hezekiah spake comfortably unto all the Levites that taught the good knowledge of the LORD: and they did eat throughout the feast seven days, offering peace offerings, and making confession to the LORD God of their fathers.   2 Chr. 32:6

30:22–26 A Feast Extended

The seven days usually allotted to the Passover feast passed all too quickly, and the worshipers determined to spend another seven days in learning more fully the way of the Lord. . . . As the great meeting drew to a close, it was evident that God had wrought marvelously in the conversion of backsliding Judah and in stemming the tide of idolatry which threatened to sweep all before it. The solemn warnings of the prophets had not been uttered in vain. *PK 337, 338*

---

23 And the whole assembly took counsel to keep other seven days: and they kept *other* seven days with gladness. 1 Kin. 8:65; 2 Chr. 7:9

24 For Hezekiah king of Judah did give to the congregation a thousand bullocks and seven thousand sheep; and the princes gave to the congregation a thousand bullocks and ten thousand sheep: and a great number of priests sanctified themselves. 2 Chr. 29:34; 35:7-8

25 And all the congregation of Judah, with the priests and the Levites, and all the congregation that came out of Israel, and the strangers that came out of the land of Israel, and that dwelt in Judah, rejoiced. 2 Chr. 30:11, 18

26 So there was great joy in Jerusalem: for since the time of Solomon the son of David king of Israel *there was* not the like in Jerusalem.   2 Chr. 7:8-10

27 Then the priests the Levites arose and blessed the people: and their voice was heard, and their prayer came *up* to his holy dwelling place, *even* unto heaven. Num. 6:23-26; Deut. 26:15

Hezekiah Reforms Judah's Worship

31 Now when all this was finished, all Israel that were present went out to the cities of Judah, and brake the images in pieces, and cut down the ᵀgroves, and threw down the high places and the altars out of all Judah and Benjamin, in Ephraim also and Manasseh, until they had utterly destroyed them all. Then all the children of Israel returned, every man to his possession, into their own cities. 2 Kin. 18:4; 2 Chr. 32:12 ◆ *idols*

2 And Hezekiah appointed the courses of the priests and the Levites after their courses, every man according to his service, the priests and Levites for burnt offerings and for peace offerings, to minister, and to give thanks, and to praise in the gates of the tents of the LORD.   1 Chr. 24:1

3 *He appointed* also the king's portion of his substance for the burnt offerings, *to wit*, for the morning and evening burnt offerings, and the burnt offerings for the sabbaths, and for the new moons, and for the set feasts, as *it is* written in the law of the LORD.   2 Chr. 35:7

4 Moreover he commanded the people that dwelt in Jerusalem to give the portion of the priests and the Levites, that they might be encouraged in the law of the LORD. Mal. 2:7

5 And as soon as the commandment came abroad, the children of Israel brought in abundance the firstfruits of corn, wine, and oil, and honey, and of all the increase of the field; and the tithe of all *things* brought they in abundantly. Num. 18:12; Neh. 13:12

6 And *concerning* the children of Israel and Judah, that dwelt in the cities of Judah, they also brought in the ᵀtithe of oxen and sheep, and the tithe of holy things which were ᵀconsecrated unto the LORD their God, and laid *them* by heaps. Lev. 27:30 ◆ *one-tenth* ◆ *set apart*

7 In the third month they began to lay the foundation of the heaps, and finished *them* in the seventh month.

8 And when Hezekiah and the princes came and saw the heaps, they blessed the LORD, and his people Israel.

9 Then Hezekiah questioned with the priests and the Levites concerning the heaps.

10 And Azariah the chief priest of the house of Zadok answered him, and said, Since *the people* began to bring the offerings into the house of the LORD, we have had enough to eat, and have left plenty: for the LORD hath blessed his people; and that which is left *is* this great store.   1 Chr. 6:8; Mal. 3:10

11 Then Hezekiah commanded to prepare chambers in the house of the LORD; and they prepared *them*,

12 And brought in the offerings and the tithes and the dedicated *things* faithfully: over which Cononiah the Levite *was* ruler, and Shimei his brother *was* the next.   2 Chr. 35:9

13 And Jehiel, and Azaziah, and Nahath, and Asahel, and Jerimoth, and Jozabad, and Eliel, and Ismachiah, and Mahath, and Benaiah, *were* overseers under the hand of Cononiah and Shimei his brother, at the commandment of Hezekiah the king, and Azariah the ruler of the house of God.

14 And Kore the son of Imnah the Levite, the ᵀporter toward the east, *was* over the freewill offerings of God, to distribute the oblations of the LORD, and the most holy things.   doorkeeper

15 And next him *were* Eden, and Miniamin, and Jeshua, and Shemaiah, Amariah, and Shecaniah, in the cities of the priests, in *their* set office, to give to their brethren by courses, as well to the great as to the small: Josh. 21:9-19

16 Beside their genealogy of males, from three years old and upward, *even* unto every one that entereth into the house of the LORD, his daily portion for their service in their charges according to their courses;   Ezra 3:4

17 Both to the genealogy of the priests by the house of their fathers, and the Levites from twenty years old and upward, in their charges by their courses;   1 Chr. 23:24

18 And to the genealogy of all their little ones, their wives, and their sons, and their daughters, through all the congregation: for in their set office they ᵀsanctified themselves in holiness: made themselves holy

19 Also of the sons of Aaron the priests, *which were* in the fields of the suburbs of their cities, in every several city, the men that were expressed by name, to give portions to all the males among the priests, and to all that were reckoned by genealogies among the Levites.   Lev. 25:34; Num. 35:2-5; 2 Chr. 31:12-15

20 And thus did Hezekiah throughout all Judah, and ᵀwrought *that which was* good and right and truth before the LORD his God.   did

21 And in every work that he began in the service of the house of God, and in the law, and in the commandments, to seek his God, he did *it* with all his heart, and prospered.

God Saves Judah from the Assyrians

32 After these things, and the establishment thereof, Sennacherib king of Assyria came, and entered into Judah, and encamped against the fenced cities, and thought to win them for himself.   2 Kin. 18:13-37

2 And when Hezekiah saw that Sennacherib was come, and that he was purposed to fight against Jerusalem,

3 He took counsel with his princes and his mighty men to stop the waters of the fountains which *were* without the city: and they did help him.

4 So there was gathered much people together, who stopped all the fountains, and the brook that ran through the midst of the land, saying, Why should the kings of Assyria come, and find much water?   2 Chr. 32:30

5 Also he strengthened himself, and built up all the wall that was broken, and raised *it* up to the towers, and another wall without, and repaired Millo *in* the city of David, and made darts and shields in abundance.   2 Sam. 5:9

6 And he set captains of war over the people, and gathered them together to him in the street of the gate of the city, and spake comfortably to them, saying,   2 Chr. 30:22

7 Be strong and courageous, be not afraid nor dismayed for the king of Assyria, nor for all the multitude that *is* with him: for *there be* more with us than with him: 2 Kin. 6:16

8 With him *is* an arm of flesh; but with us *is* the LORD our God to help us, and to fight our battles. And the people rested themselves upon the words of Hezekiah king of Judah.   2 Chr. 13:12; 20:17; Jer. 17:5

32:8 Faith Inspires More Faith

Nothing more quickly inspires faith than the exercise of faith. The king of Judah had prepared for the coming storm; and now, confident that the prophecy against the Assyrians would be fulfilled, he stayed his soul upon God. *PK 351*

Sennacherib's Blasphemous Messages

9 After this did Sennacherib king of Assyria send his servants to Jerusalem, (but he *himself laid siege* against Lachish, and all his power with him,) unto Hezekiah king of Judah, and unto all Judah that *were* at Jerusalem, saying,   Josh. 10:31

10 Thus saith Sennacherib king of Assyria, Whereon do ye trust, that ye abide in the siege in Jerusalem?

11 Doth not Hezekiah persuade you to

give over yourselves to die by famine and by thirst, saying, The LORD our God shall deliver us out of the hand of the king of Assyria?

12 Hath not the same Hezekiah taken away his high places and his altars, and commanded Judah and Jerusalem, saying, Ye shall worship before one altar, and burn incense upon it?   2 Chr. 31:1

13 Know ye not what I and my fathers have done unto all the people of *other* lands? were the gods of the nations of those lands any ways able to deliver their lands out of mine hand?   2 Kin. 18:33-35

14 Who *was there* among all the gods of those nations that my fathers utterly destroyed, that could deliver his people out of mine hand, that your God should be able to deliver you out of mine hand?

15 Now therefore let not Hezekiah deceive you, nor persuade you on this manner, neither yet believe him: for no god of any nation or kingdom was able to deliver his people out of mine hand, and out of the hand of my fathers: how much less shall your God deliver you out of mine hand?   Ex. 5:2

16 And his servants spake yet *more* against the LORD God, and against his servant Hezekiah.

17 He wrote also letters to rail on the LORD God of Israel, and to speak against him, saying, As the gods of the nations of *other* lands have not delivered their people out of mine hand, so shall not the God of Hezekiah deliver his people out of mine hand. 2 Kin. 19:12

18 Then they cried with a loud voice in the Jews' speech unto the people of Jerusalem that *were* on the wall, to ᵀaffright them, and to trouble them; that they might take the city.   scare

19 And they spake against the God of Jerusalem, as against the gods of the people of the earth, *which were* the work of the hands of man.   2 Kin. 19:18

20 And for this *cause* Hezekiah the king, and the prophet Isaiah the son of Amoz, prayed and cried to heaven.

32:21 God's Honor Vindicated

The God of the Hebrews had prevailed over the proud Assyrian. The honor of Jehovah was vindicated in the eyes of the surrounding nations. In Jerusalem the hearts of the people were filled with holy joy. Their earnest entreaties for deliverance had been mingled with confession of sin and with many tears. In their great need they had trusted wholly in the power of God to save, and He had not failed them. *PK 361, 362*

21 And the LORD sent an angel, which cut off all the mighty men of valour, and the leaders and captains in the camp of the king of Assyria. So he returned with shame of face to his own land. And when he was come into the house of his god, they that came forth of his own bowels slew him there with the sword.

22 Thus the LORD saved Hezekiah and the inhabitants of Jerusalem from the hand of Sennacherib the king of Assyria, and from the hand of all *other*, and guided them on every side.

23 And many brought gifts unto the LORD to Jerusalem, and presents to Hezekiah king of Judah: so that he was magnified in the sight of all nations from thenceforth.   2 Chr. 17:5

Other Events in Hezekiah's Life

24 In those days Hezekiah was sick to the death, and prayed unto the LORD: and he spake unto him, and he gave him a sign.

25 But Hezekiah rendered not again according to the benefit *done* unto him; for his heart was lifted up: therefore there was wrath upon him, and upon Judah and Jerusalem.   2 Kin. 14:10; 2 Chr. 24:18; 26:16

26 Notwithstanding Hezekiah humbled himself for the pride of his heart, *both* he and the inhabitants of Jerusalem, so that the wrath of the LORD came not upon them in the days of Hezekiah.   2 Chr. 33:12; 34:27-28; Jer. 26:18-19

27 And Hezekiah had exceeding much riches and honour: and he made himself treasuries for silver, and for gold, and for precious stones, and for spices, and for shields, and for all manner of pleasant jewels;

28 Storehouses also for the increase of corn, and wine, and oil; and stalls for all manner of beasts, and ᵀcotes for flocks.   pens

29 Moreover he provided him cities, and possessions of flocks and herds in abundance: for God had given him substance very much.   1 Chr. 29:12

30 This same Hezekiah also stopped the upper watercourse of Gihon, and brought it straight down to the west side of the city of David. And Hezekiah prospered in all his works.   1 Kin. 1:33

31 Howbeit in *the business of* the ambassadors of the princes of Babylon, who sent unto him to enquire of the wonder that was *done* in the land, God left him, to try him, that he might know all *that was* in his heart.   Gen. 22:1; Deut. 8:2, 16

32 Now the rest of the acts of Hezekiah, and his goodness, behold, they *are* written in the vision of Isaiah the prophet, the son of Amoz, *and* in the book of the kings of Judah and Israel.   2 Kin. 18:1-20

33 And Hezekiah slept with his fathers, and they buried him in the chiefest of the sepulchres of the sons of David: and all Judah and

the inhabitants of Jerusalem did him honour at his death. And Manasseh his son reigned in his stead.					Prov. 10:7

Manasseh Becomes King of Judah

33 Manasseh *was* twelve years old when he began to reign, and he reigned fifty and five years in Jerusalem:					1 Chr. 3:13
2 But did *that which was* evil in the sight of the LORD, like unto the abominations of the heathen, whom the LORD had cast out before the children of Israel. Deut. 18:9; 2 Chr. 28:3
3 For he built again the high places which Hezekiah his father had broken down, and he reared up altars for Baalim, and made groves, and worshipped all the host of heaven, and served them.					Deut. 16:21; 17:3; 2 Chr. 31:1
4 Also he built altars in the house of the LORD, whereof the LORD had said, In Jerusalem shall my name be for ever.					2 Chr. 7:16
5 And he built altars for all the host of heaven in the two courts of the house of the LORD.					2 Chr. 4:9
6 And he caused his children to pass through the fire in the valley of the son of Hinnom: also he observed times, and used Tenchantments, and used witchcraft, and dealt with a familiar spirit, and with wizards: he Twrought much evil in the sight of the LORD, to provoke him to anger.	Lev. 18:21; 2 Kin. 21:6 ♦ *secret arts* ♦ *did*
7 And he set a carved image, the idol which he had made, in the house of God, of which God had said to David and to Solomon his son, In this house, and in Jerusalem, which I have chosen before all the tribes of Israel, will I put my name for ever:					2 Chr. 33:4
8 Neither will I any more remove the foot of Israel from out of the land which I have appointed for your fathers; so that they will take heed to do all that I have commanded them, according to the whole law and the statutes and the ordinances by the hand of Moses.					2 Sam. 7:10
9 So Manasseh made Judah and the inhabitants of Jerusalem to Terr, *and* to do worse than the heathen, whom the LORD had destroyed before the children of Israel.					*stray*
10 And the LORD spake to Manasseh, and to his people: but they would not hearken.

Manasseh Is Taken Captive to Babylon

11 Wherefore the LORD brought upon them the captains of the host of the king of Assyria, which took Manasseh among the thorns, and bound him with Tfetters, and carried him to Babylon.					Deut. 28:36 ♦ *chains*
12 And when he was in affliction, he Tbesought the LORD his God, and humbled himself greatly before the God of his fathers,					2 Chr. 32:26 ♦ *begged*
13 And prayed unto him: and he was

Tintreated of him, and heard his supplication, and brought him again to Jerusalem into his kingdom. Then Manasseh knew that the LORD he *was* God.					1 Chr. 5:20 ♦ *pled with*
14 Now after this he built a wall without the city of David, on the west side of Gihon, in the valley, even to the entering in at the fish gate, and Tcompassed about Ophel, and raised it up a very great height, and put captains of war in all the fenced cities of Judah.					1 Kin. 1:33; Neh. 3:3 ♦ *surrounded*
15 And he took away the strange gods, and the idol out of the house of the LORD, and all the altars that he had built in the mount of the house of the LORD, and in Jerusalem, and cast *them* out of the city.					2 Chr. 33:3-7
16 And he repaired the altar of the LORD, and sacrificed thereon peace offerings and thank offerings, and commanded Judah to serve the LORD God of Israel.
17 Nevertheless the people did sacrifice still in the high places, *yet* unto the LORD their God only.					2 Chr. 32:12
18 Now the rest of the acts of Manasseh, and his prayer unto his God, and the words of the seers that spake to him in the name of the LORD God of Israel, behold, they *are written* in the book of the kings of Israel.					1 Sam. 9:9
19 His prayer also, and *how God* was intreated of him, and all his sin, and his Ttrespass, and the places wherein he built high places, and set up Tgroves and Tgraven images, before he was humbled: behold, they *are* written among the sayings of the seers.					*sin* ♦ *idols* ♦ *engraved* or *cut out*
20 So Manasseh slept with his fathers, and they buried him in his own house: and Amon his son reigned in his stead.

Amon Becomes King of Judah

21 Amon *was* two and twenty years old when he began to reign, and reigned two years in Jerusalem.
22 But he did *that which was* evil in the sight of the LORD, as did Manasseh his father: for Amon sacrificed unto all the carved images which Manasseh his father had made, and served them;
23 And humbled not himself before the LORD, as Manasseh his father had humbled himself; but Amon Ttrespassed more and more.					2 Chr. 33:12, 19 ♦ *sinned*
24 And his servants conspired against him, and slew him in his own house.
25 But the people of the land slew all them that had conspired against king Amon; and the people of the land made Josiah his son king in his stead.

Josiah Becomes King of Judah

34 Josiah *was* eight years old when he began to reign, and he reigned in Jerusalem one and thirty years.   Jer. 1:2

2 And he did *that which was* right in the sight of the LORD, and walked in the ways of David his father, and declined *neither* to the right hand, nor to the left.   2 Chr. 29:2

3 For in the eighth year of his reign, while he was yet young, he began to seek after the God of David his father: and in the twelfth year he began to purge Judah and Jerusalem from the high places, and the ᵀgroves, and the carved images, and the molten images.   2 Chr. 15:2 ◆ *idols*

4 And they brake down the altars of Baalim in his presence; and the images, that *were* on high above them, he cut down; and the groves, and the carved images, and the molten images, he brake in pieces, and made dust *of them*, and ᵀstrowed *it* upon the graves of them that had sacrificed unto them.   Ex. 32:20 ◆ *scattered*

5 And he burnt the bones of the priests upon their altars, and cleansed Judah and Jerusalem.   1 Kin. 13:2

6 And *so did he* in the cities of Manasseh, and Ephraim, and Simeon, even unto Naphtali, with their mattocks round about.

7 And when he had broken down the altars and the groves, and had beaten the ᵀgraven images into powder, and cut down all the idols throughout all the land of Israel, he returned to Jerusalem. 2 Chr. 31:1 ◆ *engraved or cut out*

Josiah Repairs the Temple

8 Now in the eighteenth year of his reign, when he had purged the land, and the house, he sent Shaphan the son of Azaliah, and Maaseiah the governor of the city, and Joah the son of Joahaz the recorder, to repair the house of the LORD his God.   2 Sam. 8:16

9 And when they came to Hilkiah the high priest, they delivered the money that was brought into the house of God, which the Levites that kept the doors had gathered of the hand of Manasseh and Ephraim, and of all the remnant of Israel, and of all Judah and Benjamin; and they returned to Jerusalem.   2 Chr. 30:10

10 And they put *it* in the hand of the workmen that had the oversight of the house of the LORD, and they gave it to the workmen that ᵀwrought in the house of the LORD, to repair and amend the house: *worked*

11 Even to the artificers and builders gave they *it*, to buy ᵀhewn stone, and timber for couplings, and to floor the houses which the kings of Judah had destroyed. 2 Chr. 33:4-7 ◆ *cut*

12 And the men did the work faithfully: and the overseers of them *were* Jahath and Obadiah, the Levites, of the sons of Merari; and Zechariah and Meshullam, of the sons of the Kohathites, to set *it* forward; and *other of* the Levites, all that could skill of instruments of musick.   2 Kin. 12:15

13 Also *they were* over the bearers of burdens, and *were* overseers of all that wrought the work in any manner of service: and of the Levites *there were* scribes, and officers, and porters.   Neh. 4:10

14 And when they brought out the money that was brought into the house of the LORD, Hilkiah the priest found a book of the law of the LORD *given* by Moses.

15 And Hilkiah answered and said to Shaphan the scribe, I have found the book of the law in the house of the LORD. And Hilkiah delivered the book to Shaphan.

16 And Shaphan carried the book to the king, and brought the king word back again, saying, All that was committed to thy servants, they do *it*.

17 And they have gathered together the

Josiah's Great Burden

2 Chronicles 34:18–28

Thus Josiah, from his earliest manhood, had endeavored to take advantage of his position as king to exalt the principles of God's holy law. And now, while Shaphan the scribe was reading to him out of the book of the law, the king discerned in this volume a treasure of knowledge, a powerful ally, in the work of reform he so much desired to see wrought in the land. He resolved to walk in the light of its counsels, and also to do all in his power to acquaint his people with its teachings and to lead them, if possible, to cultivate reverence and love for the law of heaven.

But was it possible to bring about the needed reform? Israel had almost reached the limit of divine forbearance; soon God would arise to punish those who had brought dishonor upon His name. Already the anger of the Lord was kindled against the people. Overwhelmed with sorrow and dismay, Josiah rent his garments and bowed before God in agony of spirit, seeking pardon for the sins of an impenitent nation.

At that time the prophetess Huldah was living in Jerusalem, near the temple. The mind of the king, filled with anxious foreboding, reverted to her, and he determined to inquire of the Lord through this chosen messenger to learn, if possible, whether by any means within his power he might save erring Judah, now on the verge of ruin. *PK 398*

money that was found in the house of the LORD, and have delivered it into the hand of the overseers, and to the hand of the workmen.

18 Then Shaphan the scribe told the king, saying, Hilkiah the priest hath given me a book. And Shaphan read it before the king.

19 And it came to pass, when the king had heard the words of the law, that he ᵀrent his clothes.   Josh. 7:6 ◆ tore apart

20 And the king commanded Hilkiah, and Ahikam the son of Shaphan, and Abdon the son of Micah, and Shaphan the scribe, and Asaiah a servant of the king's, saying,

21 Go, enquire of the LORD for me, and for them that are left in Israel and in Judah, concerning the words of the book that is found: for great is the wrath of the LORD that is poured out upon us, because our fathers have not kept the word of the LORD, to do after all that is written in this book.

22 And Hilkiah, and they that the king had appointed, went to Huldah the prophetess, the wife of Shallum the son of Tikvath, the son of Hasrah, keeper of the wardrobe; (now she dwelt in Jerusalem in the college:) and they spake to her to that effect.   Ex. 15:20

23 And she answered them, Thus saith the LORD God of Israel, Tell ye the man that sent you to me,

24 Thus saith the LORD, Behold, I will bring evil upon this place, and upon the inhabitants thereof, even all the curses that are written in the book which they have read before the king of Judah: 2 Chr. 36:14-20

25 Because they have forsaken me, and have burned incense unto other gods, that they might provoke me to anger with all the works of their hands; therefore my wrath shall be poured out upon this place, and shall not be quenched.   Jer. 7:20

34:22–25 Judgment Inevitable

Through Huldah the Lord sent Josiah word that Jerusalem's ruin could not be averted. Even should the people now humble themselves before God, they could not escape their punishment. So long had their senses been deadened by wrongdoing that, if judgment should not come upon them, they would soon return to the same sinful course. PK 399

---

26 And as for the king of Judah, who sent you to enquire of the LORD, so shall ye say unto him, Thus saith the LORD God of Israel concerning the words which thou hast heard;

27 Because thine heart was tender, and thou didst humble thyself before God, when thou heardest his words against this place, and against the inhabitants thereof, and humbledst thyself before me, and

didst ᵀrend thy clothes, and weep before me; I have even heard thee also, saith the LORD.   2 Chr. 32:26 ◆ tear

28 Behold, I will gather thee to thy fathers, and thou shalt be gathered to thy grave in peace, neither shall thine eyes see all the evil that I will bring upon this place, and upon the inhabitants of the same. So they brought the king word again.   2 Chr. 35:24

The Book of the Covenant Is Read in a Solemn Assembly

29 Then the king sent and gathered together all the elders of Judah and Jerusalem.

30 And the king went up into the house of the LORD, and all the men of Judah, and the inhabitants of Jerusalem, and the priests, and the Levites, and all the people, great and small: and he read in their ears all the words of the book of the covenant that was found in the house of the LORD.   2 Kin. 23:2

31 And the king stood in his place, and made a covenant before the LORD, to walk after the LORD, and to keep his commandments, and his testimonies, and his statutes, with all his heart, and with all his soul, to perform the words of the covenant which are written in this book.   2 Chr. 23:16

32 And he caused all that were present in Jerusalem and Benjamin to stand to it. And the inhabitants of Jerusalem did according to the covenant of God, the God of their fathers.

33 And Josiah took away all the abominations out of all the countries that pertained to the children of Israel, and made all that were present in Israel to serve, even to serve the LORD their God. And all his days they departed not from following the LORD, the God of their fathers.   2 Chr. 34:3-7

Josiah Celebrates Passover

35 Moreover Josiah kept a passover unto the LORD in Jerusalem: and they killed the passover on the fourteenth day of the first month.   Ex. 12:6; Num. 9:3; 2 Kin. 23:21-23

2 And he set the priests in their charges, and encouraged them to the service of the house of the LORD,   2 Chr. 31:2

3 And said unto the Levites that taught all Israel, which were holy unto the LORD, Put the holy ark in the house which Solomon the son of David king of Israel did build; it shall not be a burden upon your shoulders: serve now the LORD your God, and his people Israel,   Deut. 33:10

4 And prepare yourselves by the houses of your fathers, after your courses, according to the writing of David king of Israel, and according to the writing of Solomon his son.   1 Chr. 23:1-26; 2 Chr. 8:14

5 And stand in the holy *place* according to the divisions of the families of the fathers of your brethren the people, and *after* the division of the families of the Levites.   Ps. 134:1

6 So kill the passover, and sanctify yourselves, and prepare your brethren, that *they* may do according to the word of the LORD by the hand of Moses.   2 Chr. 29:5, 15

7 And Josiah gave to the people, of the flock, lambs and kids, all for the passover offerings, for all that were present, to the number of thirty thousand, and three thousand bullocks: these *were* of the king's substance.   1 Kin. 8:63

8 And his princes gave willingly unto the people, to the priests, and to the Levites: Hilkiah and Zechariah and Jehiel, rulers of the house of God, gave unto the priests for the passover offerings two thousand and six hundred *small cattle*, and three hundred oxen.   2 Chr. 29:31-33

9 Conaniah also, and Shemaiah and Nethaneel, his brethren, and Hashabiah and Jeiel and Jozabad, chief of the Levites, gave unto the Levites for passover offerings five thousand *small cattle*, and five hundred oxen.

10 So the service was prepared, and the priests stood in their place, and the Levites in their courses, according to the king's commandment.   2 Chr. 30:16

11 And they killed the passover, and the priests sprinkled *the blood* from their hands, and the Levites flayed *them*.   2 Chr. 29:34

12 And they removed the burnt offerings, that they might give according to the divisions of the families of the people, to offer unto the LORD, as *it is* written in the book of Moses. And so *did they* with the oxen.

13 And they roasted the passover with fire according to the ordinance: but the *other* holy *offerings* ᵀsod they in pots, and in caldrons, and in pans, and divided *them* speedily among all the people.   Ex. 12:8-9; Lev. 6:28 ♦ *cooked*

14 And afterward they made ready for themselves, and for the priests: because the priests the sons of Aaron *were busied* in offering of burnt offerings and the fat until night; therefore the Levites prepared for themselves, and for the priests the sons of Aaron.

15 And the singers the sons of Asaph *were* in their place, according to the commandment of David, and Asaph, and Heman, and Jeduthun the king's seer; and the porters *waited* at every gate; they might not depart from their service; for their brethren the Levites prepared for them.   1 Chr. 9:17-19

16 So all the service of the LORD was prepared the same day, to keep the passover, and to offer burnt offerings upon the altar of the LORD, according to the commandment of king Josiah.

17 And the children of Israel that were present kept the passover at that time, and the feast of unleavened bread seven days.

18 And there was no passover like to that kept in Israel from the days of Samuel the prophet; neither did all the kings of Israel keep such a passover as Josiah kept, and the priests, and the Levites, and all Judah and Israel that were present, and the inhabitants of Jerusalem.   2 Kin. 23:21-23

19 In the eighteenth year of the reign of Josiah was this passover kept.

35:1-19 The Limits of Josiah's Zeal

But the zeal of Josiah, acceptable though it was to God, could not atone for the sins of past generations; nor could the piety displayed by the king's followers effect a change of heart in many who stubbornly refused to turn from idolatry to the worship of the true God. *PK 405*

Josiah's Sin Leads to His Death

20 After all this, when Josiah had prepared the temple, Necho king of Egypt came up to fight against Carchemish by Euphrates: and Josiah went out against him.   2 Kin. 23:29-30

21 But he sent ambassadors to him, saying, What have I to do with thee, thou king of Judah? *I come* not against thee this day, but against the house wherewith I have war: for God commanded me to make haste: ᵀforbear thee from *meddling with* God, who *is* with me, that he destroy thee not.   2 Kin. 18:25 ♦ *refrain*

22 Nevertheless Josiah would not turn his face from him, but disguised himself, that he might fight with him, and hearkened not unto the words of Necho from the mouth of God, and came to fight in the valley of Megiddo.   Judg. 5:19; 1 Kin. 22:30; 2 Chr. 18:29

23 And the archers shot at king Josiah; and the king said to his servants, Have me away; for I am sore wounded.   1 Kin. 22:34

24 His servants therefore took him out of that chariot, and put him in the second chariot that he had; and they brought him to Jerusalem, and he died, and was buried in *one of* the sepulchres of his fathers. And all Judah and Jerusalem mourned for Josiah. Zech. 12:11

25 And Jeremiah lamented for Josiah: and all the singing men and the singing women spake of Josiah in their lamentations to this day, and made them an ordinance in Israel: and, behold, they *are* written in the lamentations.   Jer. 22:10

26 Now the rest of the acts of Josiah, and his goodness, according to *that which was* written in the law of the LORD,

27 And his deeds, first and last, behold, they

are written in the book of the kings of Israel and Judah.

Jehoahaz Becomes King of Judah

36 Then the people of the land took Jehoahaz the son of Josiah, and made him king in his father's stead in Jerusalem.

2 Jehoahaz *was* twenty and three years old when he began to reign, and he reigned three months in Jerusalem.

3 And the king of Egypt put him down at Jerusalem, and condemned the land in an hundred talents of silver and a talent of gold.

4 And the king of Egypt made Eliakim his brother king over Judah and Jerusalem, and turned his name to Jehoiakim. And Necho took Jehoahaz his brother, and carried him to Egypt.   Jer. 22:10-12

Jehoiakim Becomes King of Judah

5 Jehoiakim *was* twenty and five years old when he began to reign, and he reigned eleven years in Jerusalem: and he did *that which was* evil in the sight of the LORD his God.

6 Against him came up Nebuchadnezzar king of Babylon, and bound him in ᵀfetters, to carry him to Babylon.   2 Chr. 33:11 ◆ *chains*

7 Nebuchadnezzar also carried of the vessels of the house of the LORD to Babylon, and put them in his temple at Babylon.   2 Kin. 24:13

36:5–7 Approaching Doom

The first years of Jehoiakim's reign were filled with warnings of approaching doom. The word of the Lord spoken by the prophets was about to be fulfilled. . . .

Within a few short years the king of Babylon was to be used as the instrument of God's wrath upon impenitent Judah. Again and again Jerusalem was to be invested and entered by the besieging armies of Nebuchadnezzar. *PK 422*

---

8 Now the rest of the acts of Jehoiakim, and his abominations which he did, and that which was found in him, behold, they *are* written in the book of the kings of Israel and Judah: and Jehoiachin his son reigned in his stead.   2 Kin. 24:5-6

Jehoiachin Becomes King of Judah

9 Jehoiachin *was* eight years old when he began to reign, and he reigned three months and ten days in Jerusalem: and he did *that which was* evil in the sight of the LORD.

10 And when the year was expired, king Nebuchadnezzar sent, and brought him to Babylon, with the goodly vessels of the house of the LORD, and made Zedekiah his brother king over Judah and Jerusalem. 2 Chr. 36:7; Jer. 37:1

Zedekiah Becomes King of Judah

11 Zedekiah *was* one and twenty years old when he began to reign, and reigned eleven years in Jerusalem.   2 Kin. 24:18-20

12 And he did *that which was* evil in the sight of the LORD his God, *and* humbled not himself before Jeremiah the prophet *speaking* from the mouth of the LORD.   2 Chr. 33:23

13 And he also rebelled against king Nebuchadnezzar, who had made him swear by God: but he stiffened his neck, and hardened his heart from turning unto the LORD God of Israel.   2 Chr. 30:8

14 Moreover all the chief of the priests, and the people, ᵀtransgressed very much after all the abominations of the heathen; and polluted the house of the LORD which he had hallowed in Jerusalem.   *sinned*

15 And the LORD God of their fathers sent to them by his messengers, rising up ᵀbetimes, and sending; because he had compassion on his people, and on his dwelling place: *early*

36:14–17 ‡

36:12–15 End of a Disastrous Reign

Scorning the unusual privileges granted him, Judah's king willfully followed a way of his own choosing. . . . Within a few years [Zedekiah] closed his disastrous reign in ignominy, rejected of Heaven, unloved by his people, and despised by the rulers of Babylon whose confidence he had betrayed—and all as the result of his fatal mistake in turning from the purpose of God as revealed through His appointed messenger. *PK 438*

---

16 But they mocked the messengers of God, and despised his words, and misused his prophets, until the wrath of the LORD arose against his people, till *there was* no remedy.   2 Chr. 30:10

17 Therefore he brought upon them the king of the Chaldees, who slew their young men with the sword in the house of their sanctuary, and had no compassion upon young man or maiden, old man, or him that stooped for age: he gave *them* all into his hand.   Ps. 74:20

Gift of Prophecy

18 And all the vessels of the house of God, great and small, and the treasures of the house of the LORD, and the treasures of the king, and of his princes; all *these* he brought to Babylon.   2 Chr. 36:7, 10

19 And they burnt the house of God, and brake down the wall of Jerusalem, and burnt all the palaces thereof with fire, and destroyed all the goodly vessels thereof. Ps. 79:1

20 And them that had escaped from the sword carried he away to Babylon; where

they were servants to him and his sons until the reign of the kingdom of Persia: Jer. 27:7
21 To fulfil the word of the LORD by the mouth of Jeremiah, until the land had enjoyed her sabbaths: *for* as long as she lay desolate she kept sabbath, to fulfil ᵀthreescore and ten years. Jer. 29:10 ◆ *sixty*

Cyrus of Persia Allows the Jews to Return to Their Land

22 Now in the first year of Cyrus king of Persia, that the word of the LORD *spoken* by the mouth of Jeremiah might be accomplished, the LORD stirred up the spirit of Cyrus king of Persia, that he made a proclamation throughout all his kingdom, and *put it* also in writing, saying, Ezra 1:1-3; Jer. 25:12; 29:10
23 Thus saith Cyrus king of Persia, All the kingdoms of the earth hath the LORD God of heaven given me; and he hath charged me to build him an house in Jerusalem, which *is* in Judah. Who *is there* among you of all his people? The LORD his God *be* with him, and let him go up.

THE BOOK OF

EZRA

God's promise to return His people to their land after their exile begins to be fulfilled in the Book of Ezra. The book continues where 2 Chronicles ends, and events therein take place after the horror of the fall of Jerusalem and the deportation of the people of Judah to Babylon (2 Kings 25; 2 Chronicles 36:15–21). The book also triumphantly shows how God's promise through His prophet Jeremiah would be fulfilled: "For thus saith the LORD, That after seventy years be accomplished at Babylon I will visit you, and perform my good word toward you, in causing you to return to this place" (Jeremiah 29:10).

The Babylonians conquered the southern kingdom of Judah, only to be defeated by the Medo-Persians (as recorded in Daniel 5:30). It is under the proclamation of Cyrus, king of Persia, that the exiles are given the first opportunity to return to their homeland and rebuild. This, too, had been prophesied, for Isaiah named Cyrus as God's servant who would return His people to their land, saying "That saith of Cyrus, He is my shepherd, and shall perform all my pleasure: even saying to Jerusalem, Thou shalt be built; and to the temple, Thy foundation shall be laid" (Isaiah 44:28).

Ezra, a priest and scribe from the line of Aaron, makes his appearance well after the halfway point of the book (Ezra 7), having returned to Jerusalem under the authority of King Artaxerxes of Persia. With the temple renovation already completed, Ezra returns with silver, gold, and other items for use in the temple, as well as priests to offer sacrifices.

Ezra is a man who has "prepared his heart to seek the law of the LORD, and to do it, and to teach in Israel statutes and judgments" (7:10). Having learned that many priests and Levites married women of other nations in the area, Ezra's work is arduous.

Dates

The Book of Ezra was probably written between 457 B.C. and 444 B.C. Cyrus had overthrown the Babylonians in 539 B.C. He allowed the Jews to return in 538 B.C., and Zerubbabel led a return of about fifty thousand exiles to Jerusalem at that time. In 536 B.C., the temple was rebuilt in Jerusalem. The prophets Haggai and Zechariah served the exiles during this time as well. Ezra returned with a group of exiles in 457 B.C., followed by Nehemiah who arrived in Jerusalem in 444 B.C. Using the divisions noted above, the dates fall roughly as follows:

(1) *Ezra 1—6, 538 to 515 B.C.*
(2) *Ezra 7—10, 457 to 444 B.C.*

The intervening decades between chapters 6 and 7 are when the events in the Book of Esther took place.

Author

Like the Chronicles, Ezra and Nehemiah were believed to be one document. The Talmud indicates Ezra as the primary author and Nehemiah as the one who completes the work.

Ezra was a priest and direct descendant of Aaron, Israel's first high priest (7:1–5). Ezra was also a scribe. In that role as scribe, he gathered his information using various official public documents such as decrees (Ezra 1:2–4; 6:6–12), letters (4:11–16; 5:7–17), lists 2:1–67, and other source material. In doing so, he preserved an authentic description of the awe-inspiring events of his time.

Meaning of the Name

With Aramaic being the official language of Persia, *Ezra* is the Aramaic equivalent of *ezer*, a Hebrew word meaning "help." It could also mean "Yahweh helps."

Christ in Ezra

This book confirms the promise God made through His prophets to restore the city of Jerusalem, rebuild His temple, and bring His people back from captivity. Three decrees by three Medo-Persian kings turn God's promise to reality.

The first decree, by Cyrus, is recorded in Ezra 1:1–4 and allowed the Jews still in exile to return to their homeland and rebuild their temple. The second decree, by Darius, is recorded in 6:3–12 and allowed the Jews to continue to rebuild (after their adversaries seek

to stop their work of restoration), and that the gold and silver articles Nebuchadnezzar had taken when he destroyed the temple should be returned. Finally, a third decree, by Artaxerxes I and recorded in 7:11–26, is carried by Ezra to Jerusalem. It instructs the people returning with Ezra to carry the articles taken by Nebuchadnezzar, as well as telling Ezra to offer sacrifices to God on His altar upon their return, and to teach the people the laws of God. Ezra 7:7 explains that this decree was given in "the seventh year of Artaxerxes the king," making the date of this decree 457 B.C. The date of this third decree sets the beginning of the seventy prophetic "weeks" as recorded by Daniel 9:24–27 and also clearly confirms Jesus Christ as the promised Messiah.

According to Numbers 14:34 and Ezekiel 4:6, the terminology of "day" represents a "year" in Bible prophecy. Thus, the "seventy weeks" translates into 70 x 7 days (years), equaling 490 years. This time span is divided into two segments. The *first segment* is 69 weeks (or 483 years). This spans the time from Artaxerxes' decree to the appearance of "Messiah the Prince" as recorded in Daniel 9:25. With the date of Artaxerxes' decree set at 457 B.C., the appearance of the Messiah would come 483 years later, making the date A.D. 27, which coincides exactly with the year that Jesus began His public ministry.

Jesus began His ministry at age thirty. The Bible clearly says that Jesus' baptism occurred "in the fifteenth year of the reign of Tiberius Caesar" (Luke 3:1). Tiberius Caesar began his rule in A.D. 12 as co-regent with Caesar Augustus (who is mentioned in Luke 2:1). Scholars agree that Jesus was born about the year 4 B.C. and, without counting the zero year between B.C. and A.D., Jesus would have been thirty years old in A.D. 27.

The *second segment* of time, the final one week (seven years), begins at A.D. 27 and is also divided into two segments. Daniel 9:27 predicts that "in the midst of the week" (meaning three-and-a-half years into those final seven years), Christ "shall cause the sacrifice and the oblation to cease." In A.D. 31, three-and-a-half years after Jesus began His ministry, He was crucified, effectively ending the Jewish sacrificial system (Matthew 27:50–53). The second three-and-a-half years of the seventieth week is completed in A.D. 34, the year when Stephen was stoned (Acts 7:54–60). At this point, the gospel message, having been rejected by the Jews, is taken to the Gentiles.

Therefore, the date of this decree by an ancient Persian king provides the starting point of Daniel's prophecy, which undoubtedly points to the baptism and crucifixion of Jesus Christ. This timeline plainly demonstrates Him as the promised Messiah.

Overview

Ezra, along with Nehemiah, documents the history that reveals how God puts into motion His plan to restore the Jewish nation. In reviving this people, God provides for them another opportunity to espouse His leading to prove their right to be His chosen people. In validating the prophecies of Daniel 8 and 9, Ezra also shows the fulfillment of Isaiah's and Jeremiah's prophecies; thereby, he firmly anchors the truth of the Bible in world history.

In a sequence of instructive examples, Ezra demonstrates how just a few people can accomplish much when they listen to the leading of God through His sincere, unselfish, and determined servants. Both the books of Ezra and Nehemiah edify and strengthen faith in the unfailing leadership of God.

The Book of Ezra divides into two sections, each with a theme of renovation:

(1) *Ezra 1—6, The Temple Is Restored:* The exiles led by Zerubbabel return to Jerusalem and begin the work of rebuilding the temple. Zerubbabel, the governor, and Jeshua (Joshua in Haggai 1), the high priest, experienced opposition to the cause. Work on the temple ceased by order of King Artaxerxes (chapter 4), but continued under the urging of the prophets Haggai and Zechariah (chapter 5). Later Tattenai, a Persian leader in charge of the province west of the Euphrates (including Palestine), and others sent a letter to King Darius to call a halt to the work on the temple. Finally, Darius issues a decree to allow the work to continue (chapter 6).

(2) *Ezra 7—10, The People Reform:* Ezra leads a return to Jerusalem with another group of exiles. This signals needed change in Jerusalem, and Ezra will work to rebuild the people's spiritual condition. Grieving over the Jews intermarrying with those of heathen lands, Ezra intercedes on behalf of his erring people and begs for pardon as though he was the guilty party.

KEY PEOPLE:
Ezra, Cyrus, Artaxerxes, Zerubbabel, Jeshua, Darius, Haggai, Zechariah, Tattenai

KEY EVENTS:
The decree of Cyrus, king of Persia, prompts a group of exiles to return to Jerusalem (chapter 1); worship is reinstated in Jerusalem; the temple is rebuilt, despite opposition (chapters 4—6); Darius makes a decree to finish restoring and rebuilding Jerusalem, so Ezra returns to Jerusalem (chapter 7); Ezra intercedes in regard to the intermarriages (chapter 9); the people publicly repent (chapter 10)

KEY WORD:
Temple. Since the temple was the central place of worship, the events of Ezra cluster around the renovation of the temple and the restoration of worship there. Worship could not be fully restored unless the people repented.

KEY VERSES:
"Now for a little space grace hath been shewed from the LORD our God, to leave us a remnant to escape, and to give us a nail in his holy place, that our God may lighten our eyes, and give us a little reviving in our bondage. For we were bondmen; yet our God hath not forsaken us in our bondage, but hath extended mercy unto us in the sight of the kings of Persia, to give us a reviving, to set up the house of our God, and to repair the desolations thereof, and to give us a wall in Judah and in Jerusalem" (Ezra 9:8, 9).

KEY CHAPTER:
Ezra 7 contains the decree of Artaxerxes to restore and rebuild the temple in Jerusalem. Although the returning exiles endured much opposition and discouragement, this decree enabled them to finish the process. The decree is also the starting point of the seventy-week prophecy of Daniel 9:24, 25.

Cyrus Allows the Jews to Return from Babylon

1 Now in the first year of Cyrus king of Persia, that the word of the LORD by the mouth of Jeremiah might be fulfilled, the LORD stirred up the spirit of Cyrus king of Persia, that he made a proclamation throughout all his kingdom, and *put it* also in writing, saying,   2 Chr. 36:22-23; Jer. 29:10

2 Thus saith Cyrus king of Persia, The LORD God of heaven hath given me all the kingdoms of the earth; and he hath charged me to build him an house at Jerusalem, which *is* in Judah.   Is. 45:12-13

3 Who *is there* among you of all his people? his God be with him, and let him go up to Jerusalem, which *is* in Judah, and build the house of the LORD God of Israel, (he *is* the God,) which *is* in Jerusalem.   Dan. 6:26

4 And whosoever remaineth in any place where he sojourneth, let the men of his place help him with silver, and with gold, and with goods, and with beasts, beside the freewill offering for the house of God that *is* in Jerusalem.

The People Provide for the Rebuilding of the Temple

5 Then rose up the chief of the fathers of Judah and Benjamin, and the priests, and the Levites, with all *them* whose spirit God had raised, to go up to build the house of the LORD which *is* in Jerusalem.   Ezra 1:1; Phil. 2:13

6 And all they that *were* about them strengthened their hands with vessels of silver, with gold, with goods, and with beasts, and with precious things, beside all *that* was willingly offered.

7 Also Cyrus the king brought forth the vessels of the house of the LORD, which Nebuchadnezzar had brought forth out of Jerusalem, and had put them in the house of his gods;   2 Kin. 24:13; 2 Chr. 36:7; Ezra 5:14

8 Even those did Cyrus king of Persia bring forth by the hand of Mithredath the treasurer, and numbered them unto Sheshbazzar, the prince of Judah.   Ezra 5:14

9 And this *is* the number of them: thirty chargers of gold, a thousand chargers of silver, nine and twenty knives,

10 Thirty basons of gold, silver basons of a second *sort* four hundred and ten, *and* other vessels a thousand.

11 All the vessels of gold and of silver *were* five thousand and four hundred. All *these* did Sheshbazzar bring up with *them of* the captivity that were brought up from Babylon unto Jerusalem.

1:5-11 Answered Prayers

Tidings of [Cyrus's] decree reached the farthermost provinces of the king's realm, and everywhere among the children of the dispersion there was great rejoicing. Many, like Daniel, had been studying the prophecies, and had been seeking God for His promised intervention in behalf of Zion. And now their prayers were being answered. *PK 559*

The Numbers of People Who Return with Zerubbabel

2 Now these *are* the children of the province that went up out of the captivity, of those which had been carried away, whom Nebuchadnezzar the king of Babylon had carried away unto Babylon, and came again unto Jerusalem and Judah, every one unto his city;   2 Kin. 24:14-16

2 Which came with Zerubbabel: Jeshua, Nehemiah, Seraiah, Reelaiah, Mordecai,

Daniel and Cyrus

Ezra 1

The deliverance of Daniel from the den of lions had been used of God to create a favorable impression upon the mind of Cyrus the Great. The sterling qualities of the man of God as a statesman of farseeing ability led the Persian ruler to show him marked respect and to honor his judgment. And now, just at the time God had said He would cause His temple at Jerusalem to be rebuilt, He moved upon Cyrus as His agent to discern the prophecies concerning himself, with which Daniel was so familiar, and to grant the Jewish people their liberty.

As the king saw the words foretelling, more than a hundred years before his birth, the manner in which Babylon should be taken; as he read the message addressed to him by the Ruler of the universe, "I girded thee, though thou hast not known Me: that they may know from the rising of the sun, and from the west, that there is none beside Me;" as he saw before his eyes the declaration of the eternal God, "For Jacob My servant's sake, and Israel Mine elect, I have even called thee by thy name: I have surnamed thee, though thou hast not known Me;" as he traced the inspired record, "I have raised him up in righteousness, and I will direct all his ways: he shall build My city, and he shall let go My captives, not for price nor reward," his heart was profoundly moved, and he determined to fulfill his divinely appointed mission (Isaiah 45:5, 6, 4, 13). He would let the Judean captives go free; he would help them restore the temple of Jehovah. *PK 557, 558*

Bilshan, Mispar, Bigvai, Rehum, Baanah. The number of the men of the people of Israel: Neh. 7:7

3 The children of Parosh, two thousand an hundred seventy and two.   Ezra 8:3

4 The children of Shephatiah, three hundred seventy and two.

5 The children of Arah, seven hundred seventy and five.   Neh. 7:10

6 The children of Pahath-moab, of the children of Jeshua *and* Joab, two thousand eight hundred and twelve.   Neh. 7:11

7 The children of Elam, a thousand two hundred fifty and four.

8 The children of Zattu, nine hundred forty and five.   Neh. 7:13

9 The children of Zaccai, seven hundred and ᵀthreescore.   *sixty*

10 The children of Bani, six hundred forty and two.

11 The children of Bebai, six hundred twenty and three.

12 The children of Azgad, a thousand two hundred twenty and two.   Neh. 7:17

13 The children of Adonikam, six hundred sixty and six.   Ezra 8:13

14 The children of Bigvai, two thousand fifty and six.

15 The children of Adin, four hundred fifty and four.   Neh. 7:20

16 The children of Ater of Hezekiah, ninety and eight.

17 The children of Bezai, three hundred twenty and three.

18 The children of Jorah, an hundred and twelve.

19 The children of Hashum, two hundred twenty and three.   Neh. 7:22

20 The children of Gibbar, ninety and five.

21 The children of Beth-lehem, an hundred twenty and three.

22 The men of Netophah, fifty and six.

23 The men of Anathoth, an hundred twenty and eight.

24 The children of Azmaveth, forty and two.

25 The children of Kirjath-arim, Chephirah, and Beeroth, seven hundred and forty and three.

26 The children of Ramah and Gaba, six hundred twenty and one.

27 The men of Michmas, an hundred twenty and two.

28 The men of Bethel and Ai, two hundred twenty and three.   Gen. 12:8

29 The children of Nebo, fifty and two.

30 The children of Magbish, an hundred fifty and six.

31 The children of the other Elam, a thousand two hundred fifty and four.   Ezra 2:7

32 The children of Harim, three hundred and twenty.

33 The children of Lod, Hadid, and Ono, seven hundred twenty and five.

34 The children of Jericho, three hundred forty and five.   1 Kin. 16:34

35 The children of Senaah, three thousand and six hundred and thirty.

The Numbers of Priests, Levites, and Others Who Return with Zerubbabel

36 The priests: the children of Jedaiah, of the house of Jeshua, nine hundred seventy and three.

37 The children of Immer, a thousand fifty and two.   1 Chr. 24:14

38 The children of Pashur, a thousand two hundred forty and seven.   1 Chr. 9:12

39 The children of Harim, a thousand and seventeen.   1 Chr. 24:8

40 The Levites: the children of Jeshua and Kadmiel, of the children of Hodaviah, seventy and four.   Ezra 3:9

41 The singers: the children of Asaph, an hundred twenty and eight.   1 Chr. 6:39

42 The children of the porters: the children of Shallum, the children of Ater, the children of Talmon, the children of Akkub, the children of Hatita, the children of Shobai, *in* all an hundred thirty and nine.

43 The Nethinims: the children of Ziha, the children of Hasupha, the children of Tabbaoth,   1 Chr. 9:2

44 The children of Keros, the children of Siaha, the children of Padon,

45 The children of Lebanah, the children of Hagabah, the children of Akkub,

46 The children of Hagab, the children of Shalmai, the children of Hanan,

47 The children of Giddel, the children of Gahar, the children of Reaiah,

48 The children of Rezin, the children of Nekoda, the children of Gazzam,

49 The children of Uzza, the children of Paseah, the children of Besai,

50 The children of Asnah, the children of Mehunim, the children of Nephusim,

51 The children of Bakbuk, the children of Hakupha, the children of Harhur,

52 The children of Bazluth, the children of Mehida, the children of Harsha,

53 The children of Barkos, the children of Sisera, the children of Thamah,

54 The children of Neziah, the children of Hatipha.

55 The children of Solomon's servants: the children of Sotai, the children of Sophereth, the children of Peruda,   1 Kin. 9:21

56 The children of Jaalah, the children of Darkon, the children of Giddel,

57 The children of Shephatiah, the children of Hattil, the children of Pochereth of Zebaim, the children of Ami.   Neh. 7:59

58 All the Nethinims, and the children of Solomon's servants, *were* three hundred ninety and two.   1 Kin. 9:21

59 And these *were* they which went up from Tel-melah, Tel-harsa, Cherub, Addan, *and* Immer: but they could not shew their father's house, and their seed, whether they *were* of Israel:

60 The children of Delaiah, the children of Tobiah, the children of Nekoda, six hundred fifty and two.

61 And of the children of the priests: the children of Habaiah, the children of Koz, the children of Barzillai; which took a wife of the daughters of Barzillai the Gileadite, and was called after their name: 2 Sam. 17:27; 1 Kin. 2:7

62 These sought their register *among* those that were reckoned by genealogy, but they were not found: therefore were they, as polluted, put from the priesthood.   Num. 3:10

63 And the Tirshatha said unto them, that they should not eat of the most holy things, till there stood up a priest with Urim and with Thummim.   Ex. 28:30; Lev. 2:3, 10

The Total Number of the People and Animals Returning from Exile

64 The whole congregation together *was* forty and two thousand three hundred *and* threescore,

65 Beside their servants and their maids, of whom *there were* seven thousand three hundred thirty and seven: and *there were* among them two hundred singing men and singing women.   2 Sam. 19:35

2:64, 65 Return of Only a Remnant

Nearly fifty thousand of the children of the captivity had taken advantage of the decree permitting their return. These, however, in comparison with the hundreds of thousands scattered throughout the provinces of Medo-Persia, were but a mere remnant. The great majority of the Israelites had chosen to remain in the land of their exile rather than undergo the hardships of the return journey and the re-establishment of their desolated cities and homes. *PK 598*

---

66 Their horses *were* seven hundred thirty and six; their mules, two hundred forty and five;

67 Their camels, four hundred thirty and five; *their* asses, six thousand seven hundred and twenty.

68 And *some* of the chief of the fathers, when they came to the house of the LORD which *is* at Jerusalem, offered freely for the house of God to set it up in his place:

69 They gave after their ability unto the treasure of the work threescore and one thousand drams of gold, and five thousand pound of silver, and one hundred priests' garments.   Ezra 8:25-34

70 So the priests, and the Levites, and *some* of the people, and the singers, and the porters, and the Nethinims, dwelt in their cities, and all Israel in their cities.   Neh. 7:73

Worship at the Temple Site Begins Again

3 And when the seventh month was come, and the children of Israel *were* in the cities, the people gathered themselves together as one man to Jerusalem.   Lev. 23:24

2 Then stood up Jeshua the son of Jozadak, and his brethren the priests, and Zerubbabel the son of Shealtiel, and his brethren, and builded the altar of the God of Israel, to offer burnt offerings thereon, as *it is* written in the law of Moses the man of God.   1 Chr. 3:17; Ezra 2:2; Hag. 1:1

3 And they set the altar upon his bases; for fear *was* upon them because of the people of those countries: and they offered burnt offerings thereon unto the LORD, *even* burnt offerings morning and evening.   Num. 28:2-8

4 They kept also the feast of tabernacles, as *it is* written, and *offered* the daily burnt offerings by number, according to the custom, as the duty of every day required;   Ex. 23:16; Num. 29:12-38

5 And afterward *offered* the continual burnt offering, both of the new moons, and of all the set feasts of the LORD that were ᵀconsecrated, and of every one that willingly offered a freewill offering unto the LORD.   Num. 29:39 ♦ *set apart*

The Faithful Remnant

Ezra 3:1–6

The setting up of the altar of daily burnt offerings greatly cheered the faithful remnant. Heartily they entered into the preparations necessary for the rebuilding of the temple, gathering courage as these preparations advanced from month to month. They had for many years been deprived of the visible tokens of God's presence. And now, surrounded as they were by many sad reminders of the apostasy of their fathers, they longed for some abiding token of divine forgiveness and favor. Above the regaining of personal property and ancient privileges, they valued the approval of God. Wonderfully had He wrought in their behalf, and they felt the assurance of His presence with them; yet they desired greater blessings still. With joyous anticipation they looked forward to the time when, with temple rebuilt, they might behold the shining forth of His glory from within. *PK 560–563*

6 From the first day of the seventh month began they to offer burnt offerings unto the LORD. But the foundation of the temple of the LORD was not *yet* laid.

7 They gave money also unto the masons, and to the carpenters; and meat, and drink, and oil, unto them of Zidon, and to them of Tyre, to bring cedar trees from Lebanon to the sea of Joppa, according to the grant that they had of Cyrus king of Persia.   1 Kin. 5:6

The Foundations of the Temple Are Laid, with Both Joy and Mourning

8 Now in the second year of their coming unto the house of God at Jerusalem, in the second month, began Zerubbabel the son of Shealtiel, and Jeshua the son of Jozadak, and the remnant of their brethren the priests and the Levites, and all they that were come out of the captivity unto Jerusalem; and appointed the Levites, from twenty years old and upward, to set forward the work of the house of the LORD.

9 Then stood Jeshua *with* his sons and his brethren, Kadmiel and his sons, the sons of Judah, together, to set forward the workmen in the house of God: the sons of Henadad, *with* their sons and their brethren the Levites.   Ezra 2:40

10 And when the builders laid the foundation of the temple of the LORD, they set the priests in their apparel with trumpets, and the Levites the sons of Asaph with cymbals, to praise the LORD, after the ordinance of David king of Israel.   Zech. 4:10

11 And they sang together by course in praising and giving thanks unto the LORD; because *he is* good, for his mercy *endureth* for ever toward Israel. And all the people shouted with a great shout, when they praised the LORD, because the foundation of the house of the LORD was laid.   1 Chr. 16:34, 41; 2 Chr. 7:3

3:12, 13 The Weight of Words

Could those who failed to rejoice at the laying of the foundation stone of the temple have foreseen the results of their lack of faith on that day, they would have been appalled. Little did they realize the weight of their words of disapproval and disappointment; little did they know how much their expressed dissatisfaction would delay the completion of the Lord's house. *PK 565*

---

12 But many of the priests and Levites and chief of the fathers, *who were* ancient men, that had seen the first house, when the foundation of this house was laid before their eyes, wept with a loud voice; and many shouted aloud for joy: Hag. 2:3

13 So that the people could not discern the noise of the shout of joy from the noise of the weeping of the people: for the people shouted with a loud shout, and the noise was heard afar off.

The People's Enemies Try to Hinder the Work

4 Now when the adversaries of Judah and Benjamin heard that the children of the captivity builded the temple unto the LORD God of Israel;   Ezra 1:11

2 Then they came to Zerubbabel, and to the chief of the fathers, and said unto them, Let us build with you: for we seek your God, as ye *do*; and we do sacrifice unto him since the days of Esar-haddon king of Assur, which brought us up ᵀhither. 2 Kin. 17:24, 41; 19:37 ◆ *here*

3 But Zerubbabel, and Jeshua, and the rest of the chief of the fathers of Israel, said unto them, Ye have nothing to do with us to build an house unto our God; but we ourselves together will build unto the LORD God of Israel, as king Cyrus the king of Persia hath commanded us.   Neh. 2:20

4 Then the people of the land weakened the hands of the people of Judah, and troubled them in building,   Ezra 3:3

5 And hired counsellors against them, to frustrate their purpose, all the days of Cyrus king of Persia, even until the reign of Darius king of Persia.

4:1–5 Be on the Alert

Those who, like the adversaries of Judah and Benjamin, come with smooth words and fair speeches, apparently seeking for friendly alliance with God's children, have greater power to deceive. Against such every soul should be on the alert, lest some carefully concealed and masterly snare take him unaware. . . . But though the conflict is a ceaseless one, none are left to struggle alone. Angels help and protect those who walk humbly before God. *PK 571*

---

6 And in the reign of Ahasuerus, in the beginning of his reign, wrote they *unto him* an accusation against the inhabitants of Judah and Jerusalem.   Esth. 1:1

7 And in the days of Artaxerxes wrote Bishlam, Mithredath, Tabeel, and the rest of their companions, unto Artaxerxes king of Persia; and the writing of the letter *was* written in the Syrian tongue, and interpreted in the Syrian tongue.   2 Kin. 18:26; Is. 36:11; Dan. 2:4

8 Rehum the chancellor and Shimshai the scribe wrote a letter against Jerusalem to Artaxerxes the king in this sort:

9 Then *wrote* Rehum the chancellor, and Shimshai the scribe, and the rest of their companions; the Dinaites, the Apharsathchites, the

Tarpelites, the Apharsites, the Archevites, the Babylonians, the Susanchites, the Dehavites, *and* the Elamites,   2 Kin. 17:24; Ezra 5:6; 6:6

10 And the rest of the nations whom the great and noble Asnappar brought over, and set in the cities of Samaria, and the rest *that are* on this side the river, and at such a time.   Ezra 4:17

11 This *is* the copy of the letter that they sent unto him, *even* unto Artaxerxes the king; Thy servants the men on this side the river, and at such a time.

12 Be it known unto the king, that the Jews which came up from thee to us are come unto Jerusalem, building the rebellious and the bad city, and have set up the walls *thereof*, and joined the foundations.   2 Chr. 36:13

13 Be it known now unto the king, that, if this city be builded, and the walls set up *again, then* will they not pay toll, tribute, and custom, and *so* thou shalt ᵀendamage the revenue of the kings. Ezra 7:24; Neh. 5:4 ♦ *diminish*

14 Now because we have maintenance from *the king's* palace, and it was not meet for us to see the king's dishonour, therefore have we sent and certified the king;

15 That search may be made in the book of the records of thy fathers: so shalt thou find in the book of the records, and know that this city *is* a rebellious city, and hurtful unto kings and provinces, and that they have moved sedition within the same of old time: for which cause was this city destroyed.

16 We certify the king that, if this city be builded *again*, and the walls thereof set up, by this means thou shalt have no portion on this side the river.

The Decree of Artaxerxes Stops Work on the Temple

17 *Then* sent the king an answer unto Rehum the chancellor, and *to* Shimshai the scribe, and *to* the rest of their companions that dwell in Samaria, and *unto* the rest beyond the river, Peace, and at such a time.

18 The letter which ye sent unto us hath been plainly read before me.

19 And I commanded, and search hath been made, and it is found that this city of old time hath made insurrection against kings, and *that* rebellion and sedition have been made therein.   2 Kin. 18:7

20 There have been mighty kings also over Jerusalem, which have ruled over all *countries* beyond the river; and toll, tribute, and custom, was paid unto them. Gen. 15:18; 1 Kin. 4:21

21 Give ye now commandment to cause these men to cease, and that this city be not builded, until *another* commandment shall be given from me.

22 Take heed now that ye fail not to do this: why should damage grow to the hurt of the kings?

23 Now when the copy of king Artaxerxes' letter *was* read before Rehum, and Shimshai the scribe, and their companions, they went up in haste to Jerusalem unto the Jews, and made them to cease by force and power.

24 Then ceased the work of the house of God which *is* at Jerusalem. So it ceased unto the second year of the reign of Darius king of Persia.   Hag. 1:15

Israel's Leaders and Prophets Continue Rebuilding of the Temple

5 Then the prophets, Haggai the prophet, and Zechariah the son of Iddo, prophesied unto the Jews that *were* in Judah and Jerusalem in the name of the God of Israel, *even* unto them.

2 Then rose up Zerubbabel the son of Shealtiel, and Jeshua the son of Jozadak, and began to build the house of God which *is* at Jerusalem: and with them *were* the prophets of God helping them.   Ezra 3:2; 6:14

5:1, 2 The Cause of Troubles

The prophets Haggai and Zechariah were raised up to meet the crisis. In stirring testimonies these appointed messengers revealed to the people the cause of their troubles. The lack of temporal prosperity was the result of a neglect to put God's interests first, the prophets declared. Had the Israelites honored God, had they shown Him due respect and courtesy, by making the building of His house their first work, they would have invited His presence and blessing. *PK 573, 574*

Permission for Rebuilding Is Requested from Darius

3 At the same time came to them Tatnai, governor on this side the river, and Shethar-boznai, and their companions, and said thus unto them, Who hath commanded you to build this house, and to make up this wall?   Ezra 1:3; 5:9; 6:6

4 Then said we unto them after this manner, What are the names of the men that make this building?

5 But the eye of their God was upon the elders of the Jews, that they could not cause them to cease, till the matter came to Darius: and then they returned answer by letter concerning this *matter*. Ezra 7:6, 28; Ps. 33:18

6 The copy of the letter that Tatnai, governor on this side the river, and Shethar-boznai, and his companions the Apharsachites, which *were* on this side the river, sent unto Darius the king: Ezra 4:9

7 They sent a letter unto him, wherein

was written thus; Unto Darius the king, all peace.

8 Be it known unto the king, that we went into the province of Judea, to the house of the great God, which is builded with great stones, and timber is laid in the walls, and this work goeth fast on, and prospereth in their hands.

9 Then asked we those elders, *and* said unto them thus, Who commanded you to build this house, and to make up these walls?

10 We asked their names also, to certify thee, that we might write the names of the men that *were* the chief of them.

11 And thus they returned us answer, saying, We are the servants of the God of heaven and earth, and build the house that was builded these many years ago, which a great king of Israel builded and set up.

12 But after that our fathers had provoked the God of heaven unto wrath, he gave them into the hand of Nebuchadnezzar the king of Babylon, the Chaldean, who destroyed this house, and carried the people away into Babylon.   2 Chr. 36:16-17

13 But in the first year of Cyrus the king of Babylon *the same* king Cyrus made a decree to build this house of God.

14 And the vessels also of gold and silver of the house of God, which Nebuchadnezzar took out of the temple that *was* in Jerusalem, and brought them into the temple of Babylon, those did Cyrus the king take out of the temple of Babylon, and they were delivered unto *one*, whose name *was* Sheshbazzar, whom he had made governor;   Ezra 5:16; 6:5

15 And said unto him, Take these vessels, go, carry them into the temple that *is* in Jerusalem, and let the house of God be builded in his place.

16 Then came the same Sheshbazzar, *and* laid the foundation of the house of God which *is* in Jerusalem: and since that time even until now hath it been in building, and *yet* it is not finished.   Ezra 3:8, 10; 6:15

17 Now therefore, if *it seem* good to the king, let there be search made in the king's treasure house, which *is* there at Babylon, whether it be *so*, that a decree was made of Cyrus the king to build this house of God at Jerusalem, and let the king send his pleasure to us concerning this matter.   Ezra 4:15

Darius Decrees that the Building Can Continue

6 Then Darius the king made a decree, and search was made in the house of the rolls, where the treasures were laid up in Babylon.   Ezra 4:15; 5:17

2 And there was found at Achmetha, in the palace that *is* in the province of the Medes, a roll, and therein *was* a record thus written:

3 In the first year of Cyrus the king *the same* Cyrus the king made a decree *concerning* the house of God at Jerusalem, Let the house be builded, the place where they offered sacrifices, and let the foundations thereof be strongly laid; the height thereof [T]threescore cubits, *and* the breadth thereof threescore cubits;   *sixty*

4 *With* three rows of great stones, and a row of new timber: and let the expenses be given out of the king's house: 1 Kin. 6:36

5 And also let the golden and silver vessels of the house of God, which Nebuchadnezzar took forth out of the temple which *is* at Jerusalem, and brought unto Babylon, be restored, and brought again unto the temple which *is* at Jerusalem, *every one* to his place, and place *them* in the house of God.   Ezra 1:7-8

6 Now *therefore*, Tatnai, governor beyond the river, Shethar-boznai, and your companions the Apharsachites, which *are* beyond the river, be ye far from thence: Ezra 5:3, 6

7 Let the work of this house of God alone; let the governor of the Jews and the elders of the Jews build this house of God in his place.

8 Moreover I make a decree what ye shall do to the elders of these Jews for the building of this house of God: that of the king's goods, *even* of the tribute beyond the river, [T]forthwith expenses be given unto these men, that they be not hindered.   Ezra 6:4 ◆ *immediately*

6:6–8 God's Purpose for Trials

God has a purpose in sending trial to His children. He never leads them otherwise than they would choose to be led if they could see the end from the beginning, and discern the glory of the purpose that they are fulfilling. All that He brings upon them in test and trial comes that they may be strong to do and to suffer for Him. *PK 578*

---

9 And that which they have need of, both young bullocks, and rams, and lambs, for the burnt offerings of the God of heaven, wheat, salt, wine, and oil, according to the appointment of the priests which *are* at Jerusalem, let it be given them day by day without fail: Lev. 1:10

10 That they may offer sacrifices of sweet savours unto the God of heaven, and pray for the life of the king, and of his sons.   Ezra 7:23

11 Also I have made a decree, that whosoever shall alter this word, let timber be pulled down from his house, and being set up, let him be hanged thereon; and let his house be made a dunghill for this.   Ezra 7:26; Dan. 2:5; 3:29

12 And the God that hath caused his name

to dwell there destroy all kings and people, that shall put to their hand to alter *and* to destroy this house of God which *is* at Jerusalem. I Darius have made a decree; let it be done with speed.   Ex. 20:24; Deut. 12:5; 1 Kin. 9:3

The Temple Is Finished and Passover Is Celebrated

13 Then Tatnai, governor on this side the river, Shethar-boznai, and their companions, according to that which Darius the king had sent, so they did speedily.   Ezra 4:9

14 And the elders of the Jews builded, and they prospered through the prophesying of Haggai the prophet and Zechariah the son of Iddo. And they builded, and finished *it*, according to the commandment of the God of Israel, and according to the commandment of Cyrus, and Darius, and Artaxerxes king of Persia.   Ezra 4:24–5:2; 5:13; 7:1

15 And this house was finished on the third day of the month Adar, which was in the sixth year of the reign of Darius the king.   Esth. 3:7

16 And the children of Israel, the priests, and the Levites, and the rest of the children of the captivity, kept the dedication of this house of God with joy,   1 Kin. 8:63; 2 Chr. 7:5

17 And offered at the dedication of this house of God an hundred bullocks, two hundred rams, four hundred lambs; and for a sin offering for all Israel, twelve he goats, according to the number of the tribes of Israel.   Ezra 8:35

18 And they set the priests in their divisions, and the Levites in their courses, for the service of God, which *is* at Jerusalem; as it is written in the book of Moses.   Num. 3:6

19 And the children of the captivity kept the passover upon the fourteenth *day* of the first month.

20 For the priests and the Levites were purified together, all of them *were* pure, and killed the passover for all the children of the captivity, and for their brethren the priests, and for themselves.   2 Chr. 29:34; 35:11

21 And the children of Israel, which were come again out of captivity, and all such as had separated themselves unto them from the filthiness of the heathen of the land, to seek the LORD God of Israel, did eat,   Ezra 9:11; Neh. 9:2

22 And kept the feast of unleavened bread seven days with joy: for the LORD had made them joyful, and turned the heart of the king of Assyria unto them, to strengthen their hands in the work of the house of God, the God of Israel.   Ezra 1:1

Ezra Travels to Jerusalem from Babylon

7 Now after these things, in the reign of Artaxerxes king of Persia, Ezra the son of Seraiah, the son of Azariah, the son of Hilkiah,   2 Kin. 22:4; 1 Chr. 6:4-14; Neh. 2:1

2 The son of Shallum, the son of Zadok, the son of Ahitub,

3 The son of Amariah, the son of Azariah, the son of Meraioth,

4 The son of Zerahiah, the son of Uzzi, the son of Bukki,

5 The son of Abishua, the son of Phinehas, the son of Eleazar, the son of Aaron the chief priest:

6 This Ezra went up from Babylon; and he *was* a ready scribe in the law of Moses, which the LORD God of Israel had given: and the king granted him all his request, according to the hand of the LORD his God upon him.   Ezra 7:9

7 And there went up *some* of the children of Israel, and of the priests, and the Levites, and the singers, and the porters, and the Nethinims, unto Jerusalem, in the seventh year of Artaxerxes the king.   Ezra 8:1-20

8 And he came to Jerusalem in the fifth month, which *was* in the seventh year of the king.

9 For upon the first *day* of the first month began he to go up from Babylon, and on the first *day* of the fifth month came he to Jerusalem, according to the good hand of his God upon him.   Ezra 7:6; Neh. 2:8

10 For Ezra had prepared his heart to seek the law of the LORD, and to do *it*, and to teach in Israel statutes and judgments.   Deut. 33:10; Mal. 2:7

7:10 Ezra Longing to Be in Full Harmony

But [Ezra] was not satisfied with his spiritual condition. He longed to be in full harmony with God; he longed for wisdom to carry out the divine will. And so he "prepared his heart to seek the law of the Lord, and to do it" (Ezra 7:10). . . . He searched the historical and poetical books of the Bible to learn why the Lord had permitted Jerusalem to be destroyed and His people carried captive into a heathen land. *PK 608*

The Gracious Commission of Artaxerxes to Ezra

11 Now this *is* the copy of the letter that the king Artaxerxes gave unto Ezra the priest, the scribe, *even* a scribe of the words of the commandments of the LORD, and of his statutes to Israel.

12 Artaxerxes, king of kings, unto Ezra the priest, a scribe of the law of the God of heaven, perfect *peace*, and at such a time.   Ezek. 26:7

13 I make a decree, that all they of the people of Israel, and *of* his priests and Levites, in my realm, which are minded of their

own freewill to go up to Jerusalem, go with thee.   Ezra 6:1

14 Forasmuch as thou art sent of the king, and of his seven counsellors, to enquire concerning Judah and Jerusalem, according to the law of thy God which *is* in thine hand;   Esth. 1:14

15 And to carry the silver and gold, which the king and his counsellors have freely offered unto the God of Israel, whose habitation *is* in Jerusalem, 2 Chr. 6:2; Ezra 6:12; Ps. 135:21

16 And all the silver and gold that thou canst find in all the province of Babylon, with the freewill offering of the people, and of the priests, offering willingly for the house of their God which *is* in Jerusalem: 1 Chr. 29:6

17 That thou mayest buy speedily with this money bullocks, rams, lambs, with their meat offerings and their drink offerings, and offer them upon the altar of the house of your God which *is* in Jerusalem.   Deut. 12:5-11

18 And whatsoever shall seem good to thee, and to thy brethren, to do with the rest of the silver and the gold, to do after the will of your God.

19 The vessels also that are given thee for the service of the house of thy God, *those* deliver thou before the God of Jerusalem.

20 And whatsoever more shall be needful for the house of thy God, which thou shalt have occasion to ᵀbestow, bestow *it* out of the king's treasure house.   Ezra 6:4 ◆ *provide*

21 And I, *even* I Artaxerxes the king, do make a decree to all the treasurers which *are* beyond the river, that whatsoever Ezra the priest, the scribe of the law of the God of heaven, shall require of you, it be done speedily,   Ezra 7:6

22 Unto an hundred talents of silver, and to an hundred measures of wheat, and to an hundred baths of wine, and to an hundred baths of oil, and salt without prescribing *how much*.

23 Whatsoever is commanded by the God of heaven, let it be diligently done for the house of the God of heaven: for why should there be wrath against the realm of the king and his sons?

24 Also we certify you, that touching any of the priests and Levites, singers, porters, Nethinims, or ministers of this house of God, it shall not be lawful to impose toll, tribute, or custom, upon them.   Ezra 4:13

25 And thou, Ezra, after the wisdom of thy God, that *is* in thine hand, set magistrates and judges, which may judge all the people that *are* beyond the river, all such as know the laws of thy God; and teach ye them that know *them* not.   Deut. 16:18; Ezra 7:10; Mal. 2:7

26 And whosoever will not do the law of thy God, and the law of the king, let judgment be executed speedily upon him, whether *it be* unto death, or to banishment, or to confiscation of goods, or to imprisonment.   Ezra 6:11

Ezra Praises God for His Favor

27 Blessed *be* the LORD God of our fathers, which hath put *such a thing* as this in the king's heart, to beautify the house of the LORD which *is* in Jerusalem: Ezra 6:22

28 And hath extended mercy unto me before the king, and his counsellors, and before all the king's mighty princes. And I was strengthened as the hand of the LORD my God *was* upon me, and I gathered together out of Israel chief men to go up with me.   Ezra 5:5; 9:9

The Time Is Fulfilled

Ezra 7:12–26

    The burden of Christ's preaching was, "The time is fulfilled, and the kingdom of God is at hand; repent ye, and believe the gospel." Thus the gospel message, as given by the Saviour Himself, was based on the prophecies. The "time" which He declared to be fulfilled was the period made known by the angel Gabriel to Daniel. "Seventy weeks," said the angel, "are determined upon thy people and upon thy holy city, to finish the transgression, and to make an end of sins, and to make reconciliation for iniquity, and to bring in everlasting righteousness, and to seal up the vision and prophecy, and to anoint the most holy" (Daniel 9:24). A day in prophecy stands for a year. See Numbers 14:34; Ezekiel 4:6. The seventy weeks, or four hundred and ninety days, represent four hundred and ninety years. A starting point for this period is given: "Know therefore and understand, that from the going forth of the commandment to restore and to build Jerusalem unto the Messiah the Prince shall be seven weeks, and threescore and two weeks," sixty-nine weeks, or four hundred and eighty-three years (Daniel 9:25). The commandment to restore and build Jerusalem, as completed by the decree of Artaxerxes Longimanus (see Ezra 6:14; 7:1, 9, margin), went into effect in the autumn of B.C. 457. From this time four hundred and eighty-three years extend to the autumn of A.D. 27. According to the prophecy, this period was to reach to the Messiah, the Anointed One. In A.D. 27, Jesus at His baptism received the anointing of the Holy Spirit, and soon afterward began His ministry. Then the message was proclaimed, "The time is fulfilled." DA 233

The Numbers of People Who Returned from Babylon with Ezra

8 These *are* now the chief of their fathers, and *this is* the genealogy of them that went up with me from Babylon, in the reign of Artaxerxes the king.   *Ezra 7:7*

2 Of the sons of Phinehas; Gershom: of the sons of Ithamar; Daniel: of the sons of David; Hattush.   *1 Chr. 3:22*

3 Of the sons of Shechaniah, of the sons of Pharosh; Zechariah: and with him were reckoned by genealogy of the males an hundred and fifty.   *Ezra 2:3*

4 Of the sons of Pahath-moab; Elihoenai the son of Zerahiah, and with him two hundred males.   *Ezra 2:6*

5 Of the sons of Shechaniah; the son of Jahaziel, and with him three hundred males.

6 Of the sons also of Adin; Ebed the son of Jonathan, and with him fifty males.   *Ezra 2:15*

7 And of the sons of Elam; Jeshaiah the son of Athaliah, and with him seventy males.

8 And of the sons of Shephatiah; Zebadiah the son of Michael, and with him ᵀfourscore males.   *eighty*

9 Of the sons of Joab; Obadiah the son of Jehiel, and with him two hundred and eighteen males.

10 And of the sons of Shelomith; the son of Josiphiah, and with him an hundred and ᵀthreescore males.   *sixty*

11 And of the sons of Bebai; Zechariah the son of Bebai, and with him twenty and eight males.   *Ezra 10:28*

12 And of the sons of Azgad; Johanan the son of Hakkatan, and with him an hundred and ten males.

13 And of the last sons of Adonikam, whose names *are* these, Eliphelet, Jeiel, and Shemaiah, and with them threescore males. *Ezra 2:13*

14 Of the sons also of Bigvai; Uthai, and Zabbud, and with them seventy males.

15 And I gathered them together to the river that runneth to Ahava; and there abode we in tents three days: and I viewed the people, and the priests, and found there none of the sons of Levi.   *Ezra 7:7; 8:21, 31*

8:15 Ezra Is Very Disappointed

Ezra had expected that a large number would return to Jerusalem, but the number who responded to the call was disappointingly small. Many who had acquired houses and lands had no desire to sacrifice these possessions. They loved ease and comfort and were well satisfied to remain. Their example proved a hindrance to others who otherwise might have chosen to cast in their lot with those who were advancing by faith. *PK 612*

---

16 Then sent I for Eliezer, for Ariel, for Shemaiah, and for Elnathan, and for Jarib, and for Elnathan, and for Nathan, and for Zechariah, and for Meshullam, chief men; also for Joiarib, and for Elnathan, men of understanding.

17 And I sent them with commandment unto Iddo the chief at the place Casiphia, and I told them what they should say unto Iddo, *and* to his brethren the Nethinims, at the place Casiphia, that they should bring unto us ministers for the house of our God.   *Ezra 2:43*

18 And by the good hand of our God upon us they brought us a man of understanding, of the sons of Mahli, the son of Levi, the son of Israel; and Sherebiah, with his sons and his brethren, eighteen;   *1 Chr. 6:19*

19 And Hashabiah, and with him Jeshaiah of the sons of Merari, his brethren and their sons, twenty;   *1 Chr. 6:1*

20 Also of the Nethinims, whom David and the princes had appointed for the service of the Levites, two hundred and twenty Nethinims: all of them were expressed by name.

21 Then I proclaimed a fast there, at the river of Ahava, that we might afflict our-

---

Strength Through God's Favor

Ezra 8:21-23

All were now ready to set forth. Before them was a journey that would occupy several months. The men were taking with them their wives and children, and their substance, besides large treasure for the temple and its service. Ezra was aware that enemies lay in wait by the way, ready to plunder and destroy him and his company; yet he had asked from the king no armed force for protection. . . .

In this matter, Ezra and his companions saw an opportunity to magnify the name of God before the heathen. Faith in the power of the living God would be strengthened if the Israelites themselves should now reveal implicit faith in their divine Leader. They therefore determined to put their trust wholly in Him. They would ask for no guard of soldiers. They would give the heathen no occasion to ascribe to the strength of man the glory that belongs to God alone. They could not afford to arouse in the minds of their heathen friends one doubt as to the sincerity of their dependence on God as His people. Strength would be gained, not through wealth, not through the power and influence of idolatrous men, but through the favor of God. Only by keeping the law of the Lord before them, and striving to obey it, would they be protected. *PK 615, 616*

selves before our God, to seek of him a right way for us, and for our little ones, and for all our substance.   Lev. 16:29; 2 Chr. 20:3; Ps. 5:8

22 For I was ashamed to require of the king a band of soldiers and horsemen to help us against the enemy in the way: because we had spoken unto the king, saying, The hand of our God *is* upon all them for good that seek him; but his power and his wrath *is* against all them that forsake him.   2 Chr. 15:2; Ezra 7:6, 9

23 So we fasted and ᵀbesought our God for this: and he was ᵀintreated of us. *begged* ◆ *pled with*

Ezra Commits the Treasury to the Custody of the Priests

24 Then I separated twelve of the chief of the priests, Sherebiah, Hashabiah, and ten of their brethren with them,   Ezra 8:18-19

25 And weighed unto them the silver, and the gold, and the vessels, *even* the offering of the house of our God, which the king, and his counsellors, and his lords, and all Israel *there* present, had offered: Ezra 8:33

26 I even weighed unto their hand six hundred and fifty talents of silver, and silver vessels an hundred talents, *and* of gold an hundred talents;

27 Also twenty basons of gold, of a thousand drams; and two vessels of fine copper, precious as gold.

28 And I said unto them, Ye *are* holy unto the LORD; the vessels *are* holy also; and the silver and the gold *are* a freewill offering unto the LORD God of your fathers.   Lev. 21:6-8; 22:2-3

29 Watch ye, and keep *them*, until ye weigh *them* before the chief of the priests and the Levites, and chief of the fathers of Israel, at Jerusalem, in the chambers of the house of the LORD.   Ezra 8:33-34

30 So took the priests and the Levites the weight of the silver, and the gold, and the vessels, to bring *them* to Jerusalem unto the house of our God.

The People Leave Ahava and Arrive in Jerusalem

31 Then we departed from the river of Ahava on the twelfth *day* of the first month, to go unto Jerusalem: and the hand of our God was upon us, and he delivered us from the hand of the enemy, and of such as lay in wait by the way.   Ezra 7:9

32 And we came to Jerusalem, and abode there three days.   Neh. 2:11

33 Now on the fourth day was the silver and the gold and the vessels weighed in the house of our God by the hand of Meremoth the son of Uriah the priest; and with him *was* Eleazar the son of Phinehas; and with them *was* Jozabad the son of Jeshua, and Noadiah the son of Binnui, Levites;   Ezra 8:30; Neh. 3:4, 21

34 By number *and* by weight of every one: and all the weight was written at that time.

35 *Also* the children of those that had been carried away, which were come out of the captivity, offered burnt offerings unto the God of Israel, twelve bullocks for all Israel, ninety and six rams, seventy and seven lambs, twelve he goats *for* a sin offering: all *this was* a burnt offering unto the LORD.   Ezra 6:17

36 And they delivered the king's commissions unto the king's lieutenants, and to the governors on this side the river: and they furthered the people, and the house of God.   Ezra 7:21-24

Ezra Mourns because of Israel's Apostasy

9 Now when these things were done, the princes came to me, saying, The people of Israel, and the priests, and the Levites, have not separated themselves from the people of the lands, *doing* according to their abominations, *even* of the Canaanites, the Hittites, the Perizzites, the Jebusites, the Ammonites, the Moabites, the Egyptians, and the Amorites.   Lev. 18:24-30; Deut. 12:30-31; Neh. 9:2

> **9:1-4 Israel's Apostasy**
>
> Ezra had learned that Israel's apostasy was largely traceable to their mingling with heathen nations. He had seen that if they had obeyed God's command to keep separate from the nations surrounding them, they would have been spared many sad and humiliating experiences. Now when he learned that . . . men of prominence had dared transgress the laws given as a safeguard against apostasy, his heart was stirred within him. *PK 620*

2 For they have taken of their daughters for themselves, and for their sons: so that the holy seed have mingled themselves with the people of *those* lands: yea, the hand of the princes and rulers hath been chief in this ᵀtrespass.   Ex. 22:31 ◆ *sin*

3 And when I heard this thing, I rent my garment and my ᵀmantle, and plucked off the hair of my head and of my beard, and sat down ᵀastonied.   Neh. 1:4 ◆ *large outside garment* ◆ *surprised*

4 Then were assembled unto me every one that trembled at the words of the God of Israel, because of the transgression of those that had been carried away; and I sat astonied until the evening sacrifice.   Ex. 29:39; Ezra 10:3

Ezra Prays

5 And at the evening sacrifice I arose up from my heaviness; and having ᵀrent my garment and my mantle, I fell upon my knees, and spread out my hands unto the LORD my God,   Ex. 9:29 ◆ *torn*

6 And said, O my God, I am ashamed and blush to lift up my face to thee, my God: for our iniquities are increased over *our* head, and our trespass is grown up unto the heavens.   2 Chr. 28:9; Ps. 38:4; Rev. 18:5

7 Since the days of our fathers *have* we *been* in a great trespass unto this day; and for our iniquities have we, our kings, *and* our priests, been delivered into the hand of the kings of the lands, to the sword, to captivity, and to a ᵀspoil, and to confusion of face, as *it is* this day.   2 Chr. 29:6 ◆ *plunder*

8 And now for a little space grace hath been *shewed* from the LORD our God, to leave us a remnant to escape, and to give us a nail in his holy place, that our God may lighten our eyes, and give us a little reviving in our bondage.   Ps. 13:3; Eccl. 12:11

9 For we *were* bondmen; yet our God hath not forsaken us in our bondage, but hath extended mercy unto us in the sight of the kings of Persia, to give us a reviving, to set up the house of our God, and to repair the desolations thereof, and to give us a wall in Judah and in Jerusalem.

10 And now, O our God, what shall we say after this? for we have forsaken thy commandments,

11 Which thou hast commanded by thy servants the prophets, saying, The land, unto which ye go to possess it, is an unclean land with the filthiness of the people of the lands, with their abominations, which have filled it from one end to another with their uncleanness.   Ezra 6:21

12 Now therefore give not your daughters unto their sons, neither take their daughters unto your sons, nor seek their peace or their wealth for ever: that ye may be strong, and eat the good of the land, and leave *it* for an inheritance to your children for ever. Deut. 7:3

13 And after all that is come upon us for our evil deeds, and for our great trespass, seeing that thou our God hast punished us less than our iniquities *deserve*, and hast given us *such* deliverance as this;   Ps. 103:10

14 Should we again break thy commandments, and join in affinity with the people of these abominations? wouldest not thou be angry with us till thou hadst consumed

us, so that *there should be* no remnant nor escaping?   Deut. 9:8, 14; Ezra 9:2

15 O LORD God of Israel, thou *art* righteous: for we remain yet escaped, as *it is* this day: behold, we *are* before thee in our ᵀtrespasses: for we cannot stand before thee because of this.   Ps. 130:3; Dan. 9:14 ◆ *sins*

Shechaniah Encourages Ezra to Reform the Foreign Marriages

10 Now when Ezra had prayed, and when he had confessed, weeping and casting himself down before the house of God, there assembled unto him out of Israel a very great congregation of men and women and children: for the people wept very sore.   2 Chr. 20:9; Dan. 9:20

2 And Shechaniah the son of Jehiel, *one* of the sons of Elam, answered and said unto Ezra, We have ᵀtrespassed against our God, and have taken strange wives of the people of the land: yet now there is hope in Israel concerning this thing.   Neh. 13:27 ◆ *sinned*

3 Now therefore let us make a covenant with our God to put away all the wives, and such as are born of them, according to the counsel of my lord, and of those that tremble at the commandment of our God; and let it be done according to the law.   Deut. 7:2-3; Ezra 9:4

4 Arise; for *this* matter *belongeth* unto thee: we also *will be* with thee: be of good courage, and do *it*.   1 Chr. 28:10

5 Then arose Ezra, and made the chief priests, the Levites, and all Israel, to swear that they should do according to this word. And they sware.   Neh. 5:12; 13:25

Ezra, Mourning, Assembles the People

6 Then Ezra rose up from before the house of God, and went into the chamber of Johanan the son of Eliashib: and *when* he came thither, he did eat no bread, nor drink water: for he mourned because of the ᵀtransgression of them that had been carried away.   Deut. 9:18; Neh. 3:1; 12:22 ◆ *disobedience*

7 And they made proclamation throughout Judah and Jerusalem unto all the children of the captivity, that they should gather themselves together unto Jerusalem;

8 And that whosoever would not come within three days, according to the counsel

of the princes and the elders, all his substance should be forfeited, and himself separated from the congregation of those that had been carried away.

9 Then all the men of Judah and Benjamin gathered themselves together unto Jerusalem within three days. It *was* the ninth month, on the twentieth *day* of the month; and all the people sat in the street of the house of God, trembling because of *this* matter, and for the great rain.

10 And Ezra the priest stood up, and said unto them, Ye have transgressed, and have taken strange wives, to increase the ᵀtrespass of Israel.   sin

11 Now therefore make confession unto the LORD God of your fathers, and do his pleasure: and separate yourselves from the people of the land, and from the strange wives.   Josh. 7:19

12 Then all the congregation answered and said with a loud voice, As thou hast said, so must we do.

13 But the people *are* many, and *it is* a time of much rain, and we are not able to stand without, neither *is this* a work of one day or two: for we are many that have ᵀtransgressed in this thing.   sinned

14 Let now our rulers of all the congregation stand, and let all them which have taken strange wives in our cities come at appointed times, and with them the elders of every city, and the judges thereof, until the fierce wrath of our God for this matter be turned from us.   Num. 25:4; 2 Chr. 29:10; 30:8

10:1–17 Blessings of Obedience

With infinite patience and tact, and with a careful consideration for the rights and welfare of every individual concerned, Ezra and his associates strove to lead the penitent of Israel into the right way. Above all else, Ezra was a teacher of the law; and as he gave personal attention to the examination of every case, he sought to impress the people with the holiness of this law and the blessings to be gained through obedience. *PK 622*

Those Who Were Guilty of Marrying Foreign Women

15 Only Jonathan the son of Asahel and Jahaziah the son of Tikvah were employed about this *matter*: and Meshullam and Shabbethai the Levite helped them.   Neh. 11:16

16 And the children of the captivity did so. And Ezra the priest, *with* certain chief of the fathers, after the house of their fathers, and all of them by *their* names, were separated, and sat down in the first day of the tenth month to examine the matter.

17 And they made an end with all the men that had taken strange wives by the first day of the first month.

18 And among the sons of the priests there were found that had taken strange wives: *namely*, of the sons of Jeshua the son of Jozadak, and his brethren; Maaseiah, and Eliezer, and Jarib, and Gedaliah.   Ezra 2:2

19 And they gave their hands that they would put away their wives; and *being* guilty, *they offered* a ram of the flock for their trespass.   Lev. 6:6; 2 Kin. 10:15

20 And of the sons of Immer; Hanani, and Zebadiah.   1 Chr. 24:14

21 And of the sons of Harim; Maaseiah, and Elijah, and Shemaiah, and Jehiel, and Uzziah.   1 Chr. 24:8

22 And of the sons of Pashur; Elioenai, Maaseiah, Ishmael, Nethaneel, Jozabad, and Elasah.   1 Chr. 9:12

23 Also of the Levites; Jozabad, and Shimei, and Kelaiah, (the same *is* Kelita,) Pethahiah, Judah, and Eliezer.

24 Of the singers also; Eliashib: and of the porters; Shallum, and Telem, and Uri.

25 Moreover of Israel: of the sons of Parosh; Ramiah, and Jeziah, and Malchiah, and Miamin, and Eleazar, and Malchijah, and Benaiah.   Ezra 2:3

26 And of the sons of Elam; Mattaniah, Zechariah, and Jehiel, and Abdi, and Jeremoth, and Eliah.   Ezra 10:2

27 And of the sons of Zattu; Elioenai, Eliashib, Mattaniah, and Jeremoth, and Zabad, and Aziza.   Ezra 2:8

28 Of the sons also of Bebai; Jehohanan, Hananiah, Zabbai, *and* Athlai.

29 And of the sons of Bani; Meshullam, Malluch, and Adaiah, Jashub, and Sheal, and Ramoth.

30 And of the sons of Pahath-moab; Adna, and Chelal, Benaiah, Maaseiah, Mattaniah, Bezaleel, and Binnui, and Manasseh.

31 And *of* the sons of Harim; Eliezer, Ishijah, Malchiah, Shemaiah, Shimeon,   Neh. 3:11

32 Benjamin, Malluch, *and* Shemariah.

33 Of the sons of Hashum; Mattenai, Mattathah, Zabad, Eliphelet, Jeremai, Manasseh, *and* Shimei.

34 Of the sons of Bani; Maadai, Amram, and Uel,

35 Benaiah, Bedeiah, Chelluh,

36 Vaniah, Meremoth, Eliashib,

37 Mattaniah, Mattenai, and Jaasau,

38 And Bani, and Binnui, Shimei,

39 And Shelemiah, and Nathan, and Adaiah,

40 Machnadebai, Shashai, Sharai,

41 Azareel, and Shelemiah, Shemariah,

42 Shallum, Amariah, *and* Joseph.

43 Of the sons of Nebo; Jeiel, Mattithiah, Zabad, Zebina, Jadau, and Joel, Benaiah.

44 All these had taken strange wives: and *some* of them had wives by whom they had children.

THE BOOK OF

NEHEMIAH

Like the Book of Ezra, the Book of Nehemiah tells the story of a man of integrity who is faced with a crisis. Having learned of the plight of his unprotected people in the city of Jerusalem—a plight due to the broken city walls—Nehemiah decided to act. But as a cup-bearer to King Artaxerxes, the stepson of Queen Esther, Nehemiah refused to overstep his authority and act on his own. His first action was prayer. Having first sought the authority of God, the next link in the chain was to seek the permission of the king.

That granted, Nehemiah heads to Jerusalem, surveys the broken-down walls, and lays out a plan of action. As in Ezra's day, opposition to the building project arose from the people surrounding the city who were not anxious to see Jerusalem return to any manner of power. However, under Nehemiah's leadership, the former exiles learned to work with one hand and keep a weapon in the other. Despite the plans of their enemies, the work on the wall was completed in just fifty-two days. But the work of renovating the hearts of the people of Israel had just begun. Both Ezra and Nehemiah provide histories of divine diligence in restoring God's chosen people. The Jews are given yet another opportunity to work according to the will of the eternal God and confirm their right to exist as a na-tion. Most importantly the book of Nehemiah, along with Ezra, demonstrates how a small number of people can accomplish marvelous things for God when led by humble, but determined, leaders.

Dates

As Ezra the priest leads a spiritual revival among the exiles, Nehemiah leads the people politically and morally. The Book of Nehemiah was probably written between 464 B.C. and 423 B.C., roughly within the timeframe of the reign of the Persian king Artaxerxes I. While Ezra journeyed to Jerusalem in the seventh year of Artaxerxes' reign, Nehemiah arrives in Jerusalem in the king's twentieth year, around 444 B.C., and serves as governor from 444 to 432 B.C. (5:14; 8:9; 10:1; 13:6). He then returns to Persia in Artaxerxes' thirty-second year (432 B.C.), and leaves again for Jerusalem, possibly around 425 B.C. The prophet Malachi also lives and ministers during Nehemiah's time. The end of the book of Nehemiah is at the end of Old Testament history, closing at about four hundred years before the birth of Christ.

Author

In the Septuagint, Ezra and Nehemiah were known under the collective term of *Esdras Deuteron* or "Second Esdras," the first being the apocryphal book of Esdras. In the Vulgate, Nehemiah was first called *Liber Secundus Esdrae* or the "Second Book of Ezra" (2 Ezra). It then became known as *Liber Nehemiae* or the "Book of Nehemiah."

Jewish custom holds that Ezra, probably due to the fact that he was a scribe, was the primary author of both Ezra and Nehemiah, which was one book in the early manuscripts. Tradition also indicates Nehemiah completed Ezra's work. These books both produce a historical and scholarly continuum with 1 and 2 Chronicles. An examination of the writing style shows that both books, in large part, had the same author.

Meaning of the Name

Nehemiah in the Hebrew is *Nehemyah*, which means "Comfort of Yahweh."

Christ in Nehemiah

Nehemiah can be seen as a type of Christ. Like Christ, the high priest, Nehemiah inter-cedes on behalf of his people. He comes to Jerusalem to rebuild the walls of a nation in peril—a specific mission. Christ came to fulfill a specific mission as well—to build the wall of a new city, on the foundation of the apostles and prophets, with people who would be-come a holy priesthood: "Ye also, as lively stones, are built up a spiritual house, an holy priesthood, to offer up spiritual sacrifices, acceptable to God by Jesus Christ" (1 Peter 2:5).

Nehemiah has a similar structure to Ezra. Its two sections include:

(1) *Nehemiah 1—7, The Walls Are Rebuilt:* Like Ezra, Nehemiah also is given a letter of authority from the king, granting him safe passage to Jerusalem. With every work of God comes opposition, this time it is initiated by Sanballat and Tobiah the Ammonite. Yet neither of them could halt the renovation.

(2) *Nehemiah 8—13, The People Are Rebuilt:* The rebuilt walls are only half the story. After Ezra reads from the Book of the Law, the people's hearts are pierced. Repentance and a new covenant are the results (chapters 8—10). But after the dedication of the newly rebuilt wall (12:27–43), other reforms are needed upon the discovery Tobiah the Ammonite is living in the temple.

Unlocking Nehemiah

✤ **KEY PEOPLE:**
Nehemiah, Artaxerxes, Ezra, Sanballat, Tobiah, Noadiah

✤ **KEY EVENTS:**
Sanballat and Tobiah oppose rebuilding the wall (4:1—6:14); the walls are completed in fifty-two days (6:15–19); Ezra reads the Book of the Law (chapter 8); the people confess sins (chapter 9)

✤ **KEY WORD:**
Wall. As with the Book of Ezra, a building project is the major event in Nehemiah, with the work on the wall around Jerusalem taking center stage. But "wall" is also a metaphor for the renovation work needed in the hearts of the people. A wall of complacency had been erected around their hearts. The reading of the Book of the Law broke through that wall.

✤ **KEY VERSES:**
"So the wall was finished in the twenty and fifth day of the moth Elul, in fifty and two days. And it came to pass, that when all our enemies heard thereof, and all the heathen that were about us saw these things, they were much cast down in their own eyes: for they perceived that this work was wrought of our God" (Nehemiah 6:15–16).

"So they read in the book in the law of God distinctly, and gave the sense, and caused them to understand the reading" (Nehemiah 8:8).

✤ **KEY CHAPTER:**
Nehemiah 9, with its emphasis on a renewal of the covenant between God and His people, is reminiscent of Deuteronomy 27. After Ezra reads the Book of the Law to the people (chapter 8), they confess their sins and agree to adhere to the covenant.

Nehemiah Learns the Distressing News That Jerusalem's Wall Is Broken Down

1 The words of Nehemiah the son of Hachaliah. And it came to pass in the month Chisleu, in the twentieth year, as I was in Shushan the palace, Neh. 10:1; Esth. 1:2; Zech. 7:1
2 That Hanani, one of my brethren, came, he and *certain* men of Judah; and I asked them concerning the Jews that had escaped, which were left of the captivity, and concerning Jerusalem. Neh. 7:2
3 And they said unto me, The remnant that are left of the captivity there in the province *are* in great affliction and reproach: the wall of Jerusalem also *is* broken down, and the gates thereof are burned with fire. 2 Kin. 25:10
4 And it came to pass, when I heard these words, that I sat down and wept, and mourned *certain* days, and fasted, and prayed before the God of heaven, Neh. 2:4

1:1–4 A Position of Influence

Nehemiah, one of the Hebrew exiles, occupied a position of influence and honor in the Persian court. As cupbearer to the king he was admitted freely to the royal presence. By virtue of his position, and because of his abilities and fidelity, he had become the monarch's friend and counselor. The recipient of royal favor, however, though surrounded by pomp and splendor, did not forget his God nor his people. *PK 628*

Nehemiah's Prayer

5 And said, I ᵀbeseech thee, O LORD God of heaven, the great and terrible God, that keepeth covenant and mercy for them that love him and observe his commandments: beg
6 Let thine ear now be attentive, and thine eyes open, that thou mayest hear the prayer of thy servant, which I pray before thee now, day and night, for the children of Israel thy servants, and confess the sins of the children of Israel, which we have sinned against thee: both I and my father's house have sinned. Dan. 9:20
7 We have dealt very corruptly against thee,

and have not kept the commandments, nor the statutes, nor the judgments, which thou commandedst thy servant Moses. Ps. 106:6
8 Remember, I beseech thee, the word that thou commandedst thy servant Moses, saying, *If* ye ᵀtransgress, I will scatter you abroad among the nations: Deut. 4:25-27 ◆ *violate a law*
9 But *if* ye turn unto me, and keep my commandments, and do them; though there were of you cast out unto the uttermost part of the heaven, *yet* will I gather them from thence, and will bring them unto the place that I have chosen to set my name there. Deut. 12:5
10 Now these *are* thy servants and thy people, whom thou hast redeemed by thy great power, and by thy strong hand. Ex. 32:11
11 O Lord, I beseech thee, let now thine ear be attentive to the prayer of thy servant, and to the prayer of thy servants, who desire to fear thy name: and prosper, I pray thee, thy servant this day, and grant him mercy in the sight of this man. For I was the king's cupbearer. Gen. 40:21; Neh. 1:6; 2:1

1:4–11 A Holy Purpose Formed

Nehemiah had often poured out his soul in behalf of his people. But now as he prayed a holy purpose formed in his mind. He resolved that if he could obtain the consent of the king, and the necessary aid in procuring implements and material, he would himself undertake the task of rebuilding the walls of Jerusalem and restoring Israel's national strength. And he asked the Lord to grant him favor in the sight of the king, that this plan might be carried out. *PK 629, 630*

Artaxerxes Allows Nehemiah to Return to Jerusalem

2 And it came to pass in the month Nisan, in the twentieth year of Artaxerxes the king, *that* wine *was* before him: and I took up the wine, and gave *it* unto the king. Now I had not been *beforetime* sad in his presence. Ezra 7:1; Neh. 1:1, 11

Prayer: A Resource in the Hour of Need

Nehemiah 2:4

To pray as Nehemiah prayed in his hour of need is a resource at the command of the Christian under circumstances when other forms of prayer may be impossible. Toilers in the busy walks of life, crowded and almost overwhelmed with perplexity, can send up a petition to God for divine guidance. Travelers by sea and land, when threatened with some great danger, can thus commit themselves to Heaven's protection. In times of sudden difficulty or peril the heart may send up its cry for help to One who has pledged Himself to come to the aid of His faithful, believing ones whenever they call upon Him. In every circumstance, under every condition, the soul weighed down with grief and care, or fiercely assailed by temptation, may find assurance, support, and succor in the unfailing love and power of a covenant-keeping God. *PK 631, 632*

2 Wherefore the king said unto me, Why *is* thy ^Tcountenance sad, seeing thou *art* not sick? this *is* nothing *else* but sorrow of heart. Then I was very sore afraid, Prov. 15:13 ◆ *appearance*

3 And said unto the king, Let the king live for ever: why should not my countenance be sad, when the city, the place of my fathers' sepulchres, *lieth* waste, and the gates thereof are consumed with fire?   1 Kin. 1:31; Neh. 1:3; Dan. 2:4

4 Then the king said unto me, For what dost thou make request? So I prayed to the God of heaven.   Neh. 1:4

5 And I said unto the king, If it please the king, and if thy servant have found favour in thy sight, that thou wouldest send me unto Judah, unto the city of my fathers' sepulchres, that I may build it.

6 And the king said unto me, (the queen also sitting by him,) For how long shall thy journey be? and when wilt thou return? So it pleased the king to send me; and I set him a time.   Neh. 5:14; 13:6

2:3-6 Importance of Careful Planning

Nehemiah did not regard his duty done when he had wept and prayed before the Lord. . . . Careful consideration and well-matured plans are as essential to the carrying forward of sacred enterprises today as in the time of the rebuilding of Jerusalem's walls. *PK 634*

---

7 Moreover I said unto the king, If it please the king, let letters be given me to the governors beyond the river, that they may convey me over till I come into Judah;   Ezra 7:21

8 And a letter unto Asaph the keeper of the king's forest, that he may give me timber to make beams for the gates of the palace which ^Tappertained to the house, and for the wall of the city, and for the house that I shall enter into. And the king granted me, according to the good hand of my God upon me.   Ezra 5:5; 7:6; Neh. 7:2 ◆ *belonged*

2:7, 8 Donors to God's Cause

Nehemiah did not depend upon uncertainty. The means that he lacked he solicited from those who were able to bestow. And the Lord is still willing to move upon the hearts of those in possession of His goods, in behalf of the cause of truth. . . . The donors may have no faith in Christ, no acquaintance with His word; but their gifts are not on this account to be refused. *PK 634*

Nehemiah Arrives in Jerusalem and Surveys the Damage to the Walls

9 Then I came to the governors beyond the river, and gave them the king's letters. Now the king had sent captains of the army and horsemen with me.   Ezra 8:22

10 When Sanballat the Horonite, and Tobiah the servant, the Ammonite, heard *of it*, it grieved them exceedingly that there was come a man to seek the welfare of the children of Israel.   Neh. 2:19; 4:7; 6:1

11 So I came to Jerusalem, and was there three days.   Ezra 8:32

12 And I arose in the night, I and some few men with me; neither told I *any* man what my God had put in my heart to do at Jerusalem: neither *was there any* beast with me, save the beast that I rode upon.

13 And I went out by night by the gate of the valley, even before the dragon well, and to the dung port, and viewed the walls of Jerusalem, which were broken down, and the gates thereof were consumed with fire.   2 Chr. 26:9

14 Then I went on to the gate of the fountain, and to the king's pool: but *there was* no place for the beast *that was* under me to pass.   2 Kin. 18:17; 20:20; Neh. 3:15

15 Then went I up in the night by the brook, and viewed the wall, and turned back, and entered by the gate of the valley, and *so* returned.   2 Sam. 15:23

16 And the rulers knew not whither I went, or what I did; neither had I as yet told *it* to the Jews, nor to the priests, nor to the nobles, nor to the rulers, nor to the rest that did the work.

17 Then said I unto them, Ye see the distress that we *are* in, how Jerusalem *lieth* waste, and the gates thereof are burned with fire: come, and let us build up the wall of Jerusalem, that we be no more a reproach.   Neh. 1:3; Ps. 44:13

18 Then I told them of the hand of my God which was good upon me; as also the king's words that he had spoken unto me. And they said, Let us rise up and build. So they strengthened their hands for *this* good work.   2 Sam. 2:7

2:17, 18 Wholehearted Commitment

Nehemiah's whole soul was in the enterprise he had undertaken. His hope, his energy, his enthusiasm, his determination, were contagious, inspiring others with the same high courage and lofty purpose. Each man became a Nehemiah in his turn and helped to make stronger the heart and hand of his neighbor. *PK 638*

---

19 But when Sanballat the Horonite, and Tobiah the servant, the Ammonite, and Geshem the Arabian, heard *it*, they laughed us to scorn, and despised us, and said, What *is* this thing that ye do? will ye rebel against the king?   Neh. 6:1-2, 6; Ps. 44:13-14

20 Then answered I them, and said unto

them, The God of heaven, he will prosper us; therefore we his servants will arise and build: but ye have no portion, nor right, nor memorial, in Jerusalem.   Ezra 4:3

A List of the People Rebuilding Jerusalem's Walls

3 Then Eliashib the high priest rose up with his brethren the priests, and they builded the sheep gate; they ᵀsanctified it, and set up the doors of it; even unto the tower of Meah they sanctified it, unto the tower of Hananeel.   Neh. 12:39; 13:28; Jer. 31:38 ◆ *made it holy*

3:1 Cooperation of Priests

Among the first to catch Nehemiah's spirit of zeal and earnestness were the priests. Because of their influential position, these men could do much to advance or hinder the work; and their ready co-operation, at the very outset, contributed not a little to its success. *PK 638*

2 And next unto him builded the men of Jericho. And next to them builded Zaccur the son of Imri.   Neh. 7:36
3 But the fish gate did the sons of Hassenaah build, who *also* laid the beams thereof, and set up the doors thereof, the locks thereof, and the bars thereof.   2 Chr. 33:14; Neh. 2:8; 12:39
4 And next unto them repaired Meremoth the son of Urijah, the son of Koz. And next unto them repaired Meshullam the son of Berechiah, the son of Meshezabeel. And next unto them repaired Zadok the son of Baana.   Ezra 8:33
5 And next unto them the Tekoites repaired; but their nobles put not their necks to the work of their Lord.   2 Sam. 14:2

3:5 Aloofness in God's Cause

In every religious movement there are some who, while they cannot deny that the cause is God's, still hold themselves aloof, refusing to make any effort to help. It were well for such ones to remember the record kept on high—that book in which there are no omissions, no mistakes, and out of which they will be judged. *PK 639*

6 Moreover the old gate repaired Jehoiada the son of Paseah, and Meshullam the son of Besodeiah; they laid the beams thereof, and set up the doors thereof, and the locks thereof, and the bars thereof.   Neh. 12:39
7 And next unto them repaired Melatiah the Gibeonite, and Jadon the Meronothite, the men of Gibeon, and of Mizpah, unto the throne of the governor on this side the river.
8 Next unto him repaired Uzziel the son of Harhaiah, of the goldsmiths. Next unto him

also repaired Hananiah the son of *one of* the apothecaries, and they fortified Jerusalem unto the broad wall.   Neh. 3:31-32; 12:38
9 And next unto them repaired Rephaiah the son of Hur, the ruler of the half part of Jerusalem.   Neh. 3:12
10 And next unto them repaired Jedaiah the son of Harumaph, even over against his house. And next unto him repaired Hattush the son of Hashabniah.
11 Malchijah the son of Harim, and Hashub the son of Pahath-moab, repaired the other piece, and the tower of the furnaces. Neh. 12:38
12 And next unto him repaired Shallum the son of Halohesh, the ruler of the half part of Jerusalem, he and his daughters.   Neh. 3:9
13 The valley gate repaired Hanun, and the inhabitants of Zanoah; they built it, and set up the doors thereof, the locks thereof, and the bars thereof, and a thousand cubits on the wall unto the dung gate. Josh. 15:34; Neh. 2:13
14 But the dung gate repaired Malchiah the son of Rechab, the ruler of part of Beth-haccerem; he built it, and set up the doors thereof, the locks thereof, and the bars thereof.   Neh. 2:13; Jer. 6:1
15 But the gate of the fountain repaired Shallun the son of Colhozeh, the ruler of part of Mizpah; he built it, and covered it, and set up the doors thereof, the locks thereof, and the bars thereof, and the wall of the pool of Siloah by the king's garden, and unto the stairs that go down from the city of David.   Neh. 12:37
16 After him repaired Nehemiah the son of Azbuk, the ruler of the half part of Beth-zur, unto *the place* over against the sepulchres of David, and to the pool that was made, and unto the house of the mighty.   2 Kin. 20:20
17 After him repaired the Levites, Rehum the son of Bani. Next unto him repaired Hashabiah, the ruler of the half part of Keilah, in his part.   Josh. 15:44
18 After him repaired their brethren, Bavai the son of Henadad, the ruler of the half part of Keilah.
19 And next to him repaired Ezer the son of Jeshua, the ruler of Mizpah, another piece over against the going up to the armoury at the turning *of the wall.*   2 Chr. 26:9
20 After him Baruch the son of Zabbai earnestly repaired the other piece, from the turning *of the wall* unto the door of the house of Eliashib the high priest.   Neh. 3:1
21 After him repaired Meremoth the son of Urijah the son of Koz another piece, from the door of the house of Eliashib even to the end of the house of Eliashib.
22 And after him repaired the priests, the men of the plain.   Neh. 12:28

23 After him repaired Benjamin and Hashub over against their house. After him repaired Azariah the son of Maaseiah the son of Ananiah by his house.

24 After him repaired Binnui the son of Henadad another piece, from the house of Azariah unto the turning *of the wall,* even unto the corner.   Neh. 3:19

3:1–32 Nehemiah's Influence

With tireless vigilance [Nehemiah] superintended the building, directing the workmen, noting the hindrances, and providing for emergencies. Along the whole extent of that three miles of wall his influence was constantly felt. With timely words he encouraged the fearful, aroused the laggard, and approved the diligent. And ever he watched the movements of their enemies, who . . . attempted to divert their attention. *PK 639, 640*

25 Palal the son of Uzai, over against the turning *of the wall,* and the tower which lieth out from the king's high house, that *was* by the court of the prison. After him Pedaiah the son of Parosh.   Ezra 2:3; Jer. 32:2; 37:21

26 Moreover the Nethinims dwelt in Ophel, unto *the place* over against the water gate toward the east, and the tower that lieth out.   Neh. 8:1, 3; 11:21

27 After them the Tekoites repaired another piece, over against the great tower that lieth out, even unto the wall of Ophel.   Neh. 3:5

28 From above the horse gate repaired the priests, every one over against his house.

29 After them repaired Zadok the son of Immer over against his house. After him repaired also Shemaiah the son of Shechaniah, the keeper of the east gate.

30 After him repaired Hananiah the son of Shelemiah, and Hanun the sixth son of Zalaph, another piece. After him repaired Meshullam the son of Berechiah over against his chamber.

31 After him repaired Malchiah the goldsmith's son unto the place of the Nethinims, and of the merchants, over against the gate Miphkad, and to the going up of the corner.   Neh. 3:8

32 And between the going up of the corner unto the sheep gate repaired the goldsmiths and the merchants.   Neh. 3:1; 12:39; John 5:2

While the Enemies Scoff, Nehemiah Prays and Continues the Work

4 But it came to pass, that when Sanballat heard that we builded the wall, he was wroth, and took great ᵀindignation, and mocked the Jews.   Neh. 2:10, 19 ♦ *anger*

2 And he spake before his brethren and the army of Samaria, and said, What do these feeble Jews? will they fortify themselves? will they sacrifice? will they make an end in a day? will they revive the stones out of the heaps of the rubbish which are burned?   Ezra 4:9-10

3 Now Tobiah the Ammonite *was* by him, and he said, Even that which they build, if a fox go up, he shall even break down their stone wall.   Neh. 2:10

4 Hear, O our God; for we are despised: and turn their reproach upon their own head, and give them for a prey in the land of captivity: Ps. 79:12; 123:3-4

5 And cover not their iniquity, and let not their sin be blotted out from before thee: for they have provoked *thee* to anger before the builders.   Ps. 51:1; 109:14; Jer. 18:23

6 So built we the wall; and all the wall was joined together unto the half thereof: for the people had a mind to work.

Go Steadily Forward

Nehemiah 4

The opposition and discouragement that the builders in Nehemiah's day met from open enemies and pretended friends is typical of the experience that those today will have who work for God. Christians are tried, not only by the anger, contempt, and cruelty of enemies, but by the indolence, inconsistency, lukewarmness, and treachery of avowed friends and helpers. Derision and reproach are hurled at them. And the same enemy that leads to contempt, at a favorable opportunity uses more cruel and violent measures.

Satan takes advantage of every unconsecrated element for the accomplishment of his purposes. Among those who profess to be the supporters of God's cause there are those who unite with His enemies and thus lay His cause open to the attacks of His bitterest foes. Even some who desire the work of God to prosper will yet weaken the hands of His servants by hearing, reporting, and half believing the slanders, boasts, and menaces of His adversaries. Satan works with marvelous success through his agents, and all who yield to their influence are subject to a bewitching power that destroys the wisdom of the wise and the understanding of the prudent. But, like Nehemiah, God's people are neither to fear nor to despise their enemies. Putting their trust in God, they are to go steadily forward, doing His work with unselfishness, and committing to His providence the cause for which they stand. *PK 644, 645*

Nehemiah Overcomes Opposition from Sanballat

7 But it came to pass, *that* when Sanballat, and Tobiah, and the Arabians, and the Ammonites, and the Ashdodites, heard that the walls of Jerusalem were made up, *and* that the breaches began to be stopped, then they were very ᵀwroth,   Neh. 2:10 ◆ *angry*

8 And conspired all of them together to come *and* to fight against Jerusalem, and to hinder it.   Ps. 83:3-11

9 Nevertheless we made our prayer unto our God, and set a watch against them day and night, because of them.   Neh. 4:11

10 And Judah said, The strength of the bearers of burdens is decayed, and *there is* much rubbish; so that we are not able to build the wall.

11 And our adversaries said, They shall not know, neither see, till we come in the midst among them, and slay them, and cause the work to cease.

12 And it came to pass, that when the Jews which dwelt by them came, they said unto us ten times, From all places whence ye shall return unto us *they will be upon you.*

13 Therefore set I in the lower places behind the wall, *and* on the higher places, I even set the people after their families with their swords, their spears, and their bows.

14 And I looked, and rose up, and said unto the nobles, and to the rulers, and to the rest of the people, Be not ye afraid of them: remember the Lord, *which is* great and terrible, and fight for your brethren, your sons, and your daughters, your wives, and your houses.   Num. 14:9; Deut. 1:29-30; 2 Sam. 10:12

15 And it came to pass, when our enemies heard that it was known unto us, and God had brought their counsel to ᵀnought, that we returned all of us to the wall, every one unto his work.   2 Sam. 17:14 ◆ *nothing*

4:15 The Response of Faith

However craftily the plots of Satan and his agents may be laid, God can detect them, and bring to nought all their counsels. The response of faith today will be the response made by Nehemiah, "Our God shall fight for us;" for God is in the work, and no man can prevent its ultimate success. *PK 645*

16 And it came to pass from that time forth, *that* the half of my servants ᵀwrought in the work, and the other half of them held both the spears, the shields, and the bows, and the habergeons; and the rulers *were* behind all the house of Judah.   *labored*

17 They which builded on the wall, and they that bare burdens, with those that ᵀladed, *every one* with one of his hands wrought in the work, and with the other *hand* held a weapon.   *loaded*

18 For the builders, every one had his sword girded by his side, and *so* builded. And he that sounded the trumpet *was* by me.

19 And I said unto the nobles, and to the rulers, and to the rest of the people, The work *is* great and large, and we are separated upon the wall, one far from another.

20 In what place *therefore* ye hear the sound of the trumpet, resort ye thither unto us: our God shall fight for us.   Ex. 14:14; Deut. 1:30; 20:4

21 So we laboured in the work: and half of them held the spears from the rising of the morning till the stars appeared.

22 Likewise at the same time said I unto the people, Let every one with his servant lodge within Jerusalem, that in the night they may be a guard to us, and labour on the day.

23 So neither I, nor my brethren, nor my servants, nor the men of the guard which followed me, none of us put off our clothes, *saving that* every one put them off for washing.

The Poor Complain about Their Rich Relatives

5 And there was a great cry of the people and of their wives against their brethren the Jews.   Is. 5:7

5:1-7 Corrupting Faith; Destroying Spirituality

Even among those who profess to be walking in the fear of the Lord, there are some who are acting over again the course pursued by the nobles of Israel. . . . Extravagance, overreaching, extortion, are corrupting the faith of many and destroying their spirituality. *PK 651*

2 For there were that said, We, our sons, and our daughters, *are* many: therefore we take up corn *for them*, that we may eat, and live.

3 *Some* also there were that said, We have mortgaged our lands, vineyards, and houses, that we might buy corn, because of the ᵀdearth.   *famine*

4 There were also that said, We have borrowed money for the king's tribute, *and that* upon our lands and vineyards.   Ezra 4:13, 20

5 Yet now our flesh *is* as the flesh of our brethren, our children as their children: and, lo, we bring into bondage our sons and our daughters to be servants, and *some* of our daughters are brought unto bondage *already*: neither *is it* in our power *to redeem* them; for other men have our lands and vineyards.   Gen. 37:27; Lev. 25:39-43; 2 Kin. 4:1

Nehemiah Stops the Rich from Taking Advantage of the Poor

6 And I was very angry when I heard their cry and these words.   Ex. 11:8

7 Then I consulted with myself, and I rebuked the nobles, and the rulers, and said unto them, Ye exact usury, every one of his brother. And I set a great assembly against them.   Ex. 22:25; Lev. 25:36; Deut. 23:19-20

8 And I said unto them, We after our ability have redeemed our brethren the Jews, which were sold unto the heathen; and will ye even sell your brethren? or shall they be sold unto us? Then held they their peace, and found nothing *to answer*.   Lev. 25:47-49

9 Also I said, It *is* not good that ye do: ought ye not to walk in the fear of our God because of the reproach of the heathen our enemies?   Lev. 25:36

10 I likewise, *and* my brethren, and my servants, might exact of them money and corn: I pray you, let us leave off this usury.

11 Restore, I pray you, to them, even this day, their lands, their vineyards, their oliveyards, and their houses, also the hundredth *part* of the money, and of the corn, the wine, and the oil, that ye exact of them.   Is. 58:6

5:8–11 Injustice Against the Golden Rule

Every unjust act toward a fellow being is a violation of the golden rule. Every wrong done to the children of God is done to Christ Himself in the person of His saints. Every attempt to take advantage of the ignorance, weakness, or misfortune of another is registered as fraud in the ledger of heaven. *PK 652*

---

12 Then said they, We will restore *them*, and will require nothing of them; so will we do as thou sayest. Then I called the priests, and took an oath of them, that they should do according to this promise.   Ezra 10:5

13 Also I shook my lap, and said, So God shake out every man from his house, and from his labour, that performeth not this promise, even thus be he shaken out, and emptied. And all the congregation said, Amen, and praised the Lord. And the people did according to this promise.   1 Chr. 16:36; Matt. 10:14; Acts 18:6

Nehemiah Never Takes What Is Rightfully His as Governor

14 Moreover from the time that I was appointed to be their governor in the land of Judah, from the twentieth year even unto the two and thirtieth year of Artaxerxes the king, *that is*, twelve years, I and my brethren have not eaten the bread of the governor.   Neh. 2:1; 13:6

15 But the former governors that *had been* before me were chargeable unto the people, and had taken of them bread and wine, beside forty shekels of silver; yea, even their servants bare rule over the people: but so did not I, because of the fear of God. Neh. 5:9

16 Yea, also I continued in the work of this wall, neither bought we any land: and all my servants *were* gathered thither unto the work.

17 Moreover *there were* at my table an hundred and fifty of the Jews and rulers, beside those that came unto us from among the heathen that *are* about us.   1 Kin. 18:19

18 Now *that* which was prepared *for me* daily *was* one ox *and* six choice sheep; also fowls were prepared for me, and once in ten days store of all sorts of wine: yet for all this required not I the bread of the governor, because the bondage was heavy upon this people.   1 Kin. 4:22-23

19 Think upon me, my God, for good, *according* to all that I have done for this people.   Neh. 13:14, 22, 31

5:14–19 Nehemiah's Liberality

Nehemiah showed them that he himself, being invested with authority from the Persian king, might have demanded large contributions for his personal benefit. But instead of this he had not taken even that which justly belonged to him, but had given liberally to relieve the poor in their need. *PK 650*

Sanballat Tries to Harm Nehemiah

6 Now it came to pass, when Sanballat, and Tobiah, and Geshem the Arabian, and the rest of our enemies, heard that I had builded the wall, and *that* there was no breach left therein; (though at that time I had not set up the doors upon the gates;)   Neh. 2:10

2 That Sanballat and Geshem sent unto me, saying, Come, let us meet together in *some one of* the villages in the plain of Ono. But they thought to do me mischief.   Ps. 37:12

3 And I sent messengers unto them, saying, I *am* doing a great work, so that I cannot come down: why should the work cease, whilst I leave it, and come down to you?

6:3 Refusing to Depart From Duty

Every device that the prince of darkness can suggest will be employed to induce God's servants to form a confederacy with the agents of Satan. Repeated solicitations will come to call them from duty; but, like Nehemiah, they should steadfastly reply, "I am doing a great work, so that I cannot come down." *PK 659*

---

4 Yet they sent unto me four times after this sort; and I answered them after the same manner.

5 Then sent Sanballat his servant unto me in like manner the fifth time with an open letter in his hand;

6 Wherein *was* written, It is reported among the heathen, and Gashmu saith *it, that* thou and the Jews think to rebel: for which cause thou buildest the wall, that thou mayest be their king, according to these words. Neh. 2:19

7 And thou hast also appointed prophets to preach of thee at Jerusalem, saying, *There is* a king in Judah: and now shall it be reported to the king according to these words. Come now therefore, and let us take counsel together.

8 Then I sent unto him, saying, There are no such things done as thou sayest, but thou feignest them out of thine own heart. Job 13:4

9 For they all made us afraid, saying, Their hands shall be weakened from the work, that it be not done. Now therefore, *O God,* strengthen my hands. Ps. 138:3

10 Afterward I came unto the house of Shemaiah the son of Delaiah the son of Mehetabeel, who *was* shut up; and he said, Let us meet together in the house of God, within the temple, and let us shut the doors of the temple: for they will come to slay thee; yea, in the night will they come to slay thee. Jer. 36:5

6:10 Ignoring Bad Counsel

Had Nehemiah followed this treacherous counsel, he would have sacrificed his faith in God, and in the eyes of the people he would have appeared cowardly and contemptible. . . . That one unwise move on the part of Nehemiah would have been a virtual surrender of all that had been gained. *PK 655*

11 And I said, Should such a man as I flee? and who *is there,* that, *being* as I *am,* would go into the temple to save his life? I will not go in. Prov. 28:1

12 And, lo, I perceived that God had not sent him; but that he pronounced this prophecy against me: for Tobiah and Sanballat had hired him. Ezek. 13:22

13 Therefore *was* he hired, that I should be afraid, and do so, and sin, and *that* they might have *matter* for an evil report, that they might reproach me. Neh. 6:6

14 My God, think thou upon Tobiah and Sanballat according to these their works, and on the prophetess Noadiah, and the rest of the prophets, that would have put me in fear. Neh. 13:29

The Wall Is Rebuilt, in Spite of Opposition

15 So the wall was finished in the twenty and fifth *day* of *the month* Elul, in fifty and two days. Neh. 4:1-2

16 And it came to pass, that when all our enemies heard *thereof,* and all the heathen that *were* about us saw *these things,* they were much cast down in their own eyes: for they perceived that this work was ᵀwrought of our God. Neh. 2:10 ◆ *made*

17 Moreover in those days the nobles of Judah sent many letters unto Tobiah, and *the letters* of Tobiah came unto them.

6:17–19 Secret Enemies

Open opposition may be fierce and cruel, but it is fraught with far less peril to God's cause than is the secret enmity of those who, while professing to serve God, are at heart the servants of Satan. These have it in their power to place every advantage in the hands of those who will use their knowledge to hinder the work of God and injure His servants. *PK 658*

18 For *there were* many in Judah sworn unto him, because he *was* the son in law of Shechaniah the son of Arah; and his son Johanan had taken the daughter of Meshullam the son of Berechiah. Ezra 2:5

19 Also they reported his good deeds before

Divine Assistance for All Emergencies

Nehemiah 6

In Nehemiah's firm devotion to the work of God, and his equally firm reliance on God, lay the reason of the failure of his enemies to draw him into their power. The soul that is indolent falls an easy prey to temptation; but in the life that has a noble aim, an absorbing purpose, evil finds little foothold. The faith of him who is constantly advancing does not weaken; for above, beneath, beyond, he recognizes Infinite Love, working out all things to accomplish His good purpose. God's true servants work with a determination that will not fail because the throne of grace is their constant dependence.

God has provided divine assistance for all the emergencies to which our human resources are unequal. He gives the Holy Spirit to help in every strait, to strengthen our hope and assurance, to illuminate our minds and purify our hearts. He provides opportunities and opens channels of working. If His people are watching the indications of His providence, and are ready to co-operate with Him, they will see mighty results. *PK 660*

me, and uttered my words to him. *And* Tobiah sent letters to put me in fear.

Nehemiah Places Hanani and Hananiah in Charge of Guarding the City Gates

7 Now it came to pass, when the wall was built, and I had set up the doors, and the porters and the singers and the Levites were appointed,   Neh. 6:1, 15

2 That I gave my brother Hanani, and Hananiah the ruler of the palace, charge over Jerusalem: for he *was* a faithful man, and feared God above many.   Neh. 1:2; 2:8; 10:23

3 And I said unto them, Let not the gates of Jerusalem be opened until the sun be hot; and while they stand by, let them shut the doors, and bar *them*: and appoint ᵀwatches of the inhabitants of Jerusalem, every one in his watch, and every one *to be* over against his house.   *guards between sunset and sunrise*

4 Now the city *was* large and great: but the people *were* few therein, and the houses *were* not builded.

A Register of the Jewish Exiles Who First Returned to Jerusalem

5 And my God put into mine heart to gather together the nobles, and the rulers, and the people, that they might be reckoned by genealogy. And I found a register of the genealogy of them which came up at the first, and found written therein,

6 These *are* the children of the province, that went up out of the captivity, of those that had been carried away, whom Nebuchadnezzar the king of Babylon had carried away, and came again to Jerusalem and to Judah, every one unto his city;   Ezra 2

7 Who came with Zerubbabel, Jeshua, Nehemiah, Azariah, Raamiah, Nahamani, Mordecai, Bilshan, Mispereth, Bigvai, Nehum, Baanah. The number, *I say*, of the men of the people of Israel *was this*;   Ezra 2:2

8 The children of Parosh, two thousand an hundred seventy and two.

9 The children of Shephatiah, three hundred seventy and two.

10 The children of Arah, six hundred fifty and two.   Ezra 2:5

11 The children of Pahath-moab, of the children of Jeshua and Joab, two thousand and eight hundred *and* eighteen.   Ezra 2:6

12 The children of Elam, a thousand two hundred fifty and four.

13 The children of Zattu, eight hundred forty and five.   Ezra 2:8

14 The children of Zaccai, seven hundred and ᵀthreescore.   *sixty*

15 The children of Binnui, six hundred forty and eight.   Ezra 2:10

16 The children of Bebai, six hundred twenty and eight.

17 The children of Azgad, two thousand three hundred twenty and two.   Ezra 2:12

18 The children of Adonikam, six hundred threescore and seven.

19 The children of Bigvai, two thousand threescore and seven.

20 The children of Adin, six hundred fifty and five.   Ezra 2:15

21 The children of Ater of Hezekiah, ninety and eight.

22 The children of Hashum, three hundred twenty and eight.   Ezra 2:19

23 The children of Bezai, three hundred twenty and four.   Ezra 2:17

24 The children of Hariph, an hundred and twelve.

25 The children of Gibeon, ninety and five.

26 The men of Beth-lehem and Netophah, an hundred ᵀfourscore and eight.   *eighty*

27 The men of Anathoth, an hundred twenty and eight.

28 The men of Beth-azmaveth, forty and two.

29 The men of Kirjath-jearim, Chephirah, and Beeroth, seven hundred forty and three.   Josh. 18:25

30 The men of Ramah and Geba, six hundred twenty and one.

31 The men of Michmas, an hundred and twenty and two.

32 The men of Beth-el and Ai, an hundred twenty and three.   Ezra 2:28

33 The men of the other Nebo, fifty and two.

34 The children of the other Elam, a thousand two hundred fifty and four.   Neh. 7:12

35 The children of Harim, three hundred and twenty.

36 The children of Jericho, three hundred forty and five.

37 The children of Lod, Hadid, and Ono, seven hundred twenty and one.   1 Chr. 8:12

38 The children of Senaah, three thousand nine hundred and thirty.

39 The priests: the children of Jedaiah, of the house of Jeshua, nine hundred seventy and three.

40 The children of Immer, a thousand fifty and two.   1 Chr. 24:14

41 The children of Pashur, a thousand two hundred forty and seven.   1 Chr. 9:12

42 The children of Harim, a thousand and seventeen.   1 Chr. 24:8

43 The Levites: the children of Jeshua, of Kadmiel, *and* of the children of Hodevah, seventy and four.   Ezra 2:40

44 The singers: the children of Asaph, an hundred forty and eight.

45 The porters: the children of Shallum, the children of Ater, the children of Talmon, the children of Akkub, the children of Hatita,

the children of Shobai, an hundred thirty and eight.

46 The Nethinims: the children of Ziha, the children of Hashupha, the children of Tabbaoth,

47 The children of Keros, the children of Sia, the children of Padon,   Ezra 2:44

48 The children of Lebana, the children of Hagaba, the children of Shalmai,

49 The children of Hanan, the children of Giddel, the children of Gahar,

50 The children of Reaiah, the children of Rezin, the children of Nekoda,

51 The children of Gazzam, the children of Uzza, the children of Phaseah,

52 The children of Besai, the children of Meunim, the children of Nephishesim, Ezra 2:50

53 The children of Bakbuk, the children of Hakupha, the children of Harhur,

54 The children of Bazlith, the children of Mehida, the children of Harsha,   Ezra 2:52

55 The children of Barkos, the children of Sisera, the children of Tamah,

56 The children of Neziah, the children of Hatipha.

57 The children of Solomon's servants: the children of Sotai, the children of Sophereth, the children of Perida,   Ezra 2:55

58 The children of Jaala, the children of Darkon, the children of Giddel,

59 The children of Shephatiah, the children of Hattil, the children of Pochereth of Zebaim, the children of Amon.   Ezra 2:57

60 All the Nethinims, and the children of Solomon's servants, *were* three hundred ninety and two.

61 And these *were* they which went up *also* from Tel-melah, Tel-haresha, Cherub, Addon, and Immer: but they could not shew their father's house, nor their seed, whether they *were* of Israel.   Ezra 2:59

62 The children of Delaiah, the children of Tobiah, the children of Nekoda, six hundred forty and two.

63 And of the priests: the children of Habaiah, the children of Koz, the children of Barzillai, which took *one* of the daughters of Barzillai the Gileadite to wife, and was called after their name.

64 These sought their register *among* those that were reckoned by genealogy, but it was not found: therefore were they, as polluted, put from the priesthood.

65 And the Tirshatha said unto them, that they should not eat of the most holy things, till there stood *up* a priest with Urim and Thummim.   Ex. 28:30; Neh. 8:9; 10:1

66 The whole congregation together *was* forty and two thousand three hundred and threescore,   Ezra 2:64

67 Beside their manservants and their maidservants, of whom *there were* seven thousand three hundred thirty and seven: and they had two hundred forty and five singing men and singing women.

68 Their horses, seven hundred thirty and six: their mules, two hundred forty and five:

69 *Their* camels, four hundred thirty and five: six thousand seven hundred and twenty asses.

70 And some of the chief of the fathers gave unto the work. The Tirshatha gave to the treasure a thousand drams of gold, fifty basons, five hundred and thirty priests' garments.   Neh. 8:9

71 And *some* of the chief of the fathers gave to the treasure of the work twenty thousand drams of gold, and two thousand and two hundred pound of silver.

72 And *that* which the rest of the people gave *was* twenty thousand drams of gold, and two thousand pound of silver, and threescore and seven priests' garments.

73 So the priests, and the Levites, and the porters, and the singers, and *some* of the people, and the Nethinims, and all Israel, dwelt in their cities; and when the seventh month came, the children of Israel *were* in their cities.

The Public Reading of Moses' Law and Teachings

8 And all the people gathered themselves together as one man into the street that *was* before the water gate; and they spake unto Ezra the scribe to bring the book of the law of Moses, which the LORD had commanded to Israel.   2 Chr. 34:15; Ezra 7:6; Neh. 3:26

2 And Ezra the priest brought the law before the congregation both of men and women, and all that could hear with understanding, upon the first day of the seventh month.   Lev. 23:24; Num. 29:1

3 And he read therein before the street that *was* before the water gate from the morning until midday, before the men and the women, and those that could understand; and the ears of all the people *were* attentive unto the book of the law.

4 And Ezra the scribe stood upon a pulpit of wood, which they had made for the purpose; and beside him stood Mattithiah, and Shema, and Anaiah, and Urijah, and Hilkiah, and Maaseiah, on his right hand; and on his left hand, Pedaiah, and Mishael, and Malchiah, and Hashum, and Hashbadana, Zechariah, *and* Meshullam.

5 And Ezra opened the book in the sight of all the people; (for he was above all the people;) and when he opened it, all the people stood up: Judg. 3:20

6 And Ezra blessed the LORD, the great God.

And all the people answered, Amen, Amen, with lifting up their hands: and they bowed their heads, and worshipped the LORD with *their* faces to the ground.   Ex. 4:31
7 Also Jeshua, and Bani, and Sherebiah, Jamin, Akkub, Shabbethai, Hodijah, Maaseiah, Kelita, Azariah, Jozabad, Hanan, Pelaiah, and the Levites, caused the people to understand the law: and the people *stood* in their place.   Ezra 10:22-23; Neh. 3:23; 9:4
8 So they read in the book in the law of God distinctly, and gave the sense, and caused *them* to understand the reading.

Nehemiah, Ezra, and the Levites Comfort the People
9 And Nehemiah, which *is* the Tirshatha, and Ezra the priest the scribe, and the Levites that taught the people, said unto all the people, This day *is* holy unto the LORD your God; mourn not, nor weep. For all the people wept, when they heard the words of the law.   Deut. 12:7; Neh. 7:65, 70
10 Then he said unto them, Go your way, eat the fat, and drink the sweet, and send portions unto them for whom nothing is prepared: for *this* day *is* holy unto our Lord: neither be ye sorry; for the joy of the LORD is your strength.   Deut. 26:11-13

8:9, 10 The Keynote of Life
Gratitude, rejoicing, benevolence, trust in God's love and care—these are health's greatest safeguard. To the Israelites they were to be the very keynote of life. . . .
So, in later years, when the law of God was read in Jerusalem to the captives returned from Babylon, and the people wept because of their transgressions, . . . gracious words were spoken. . . . *MH 281*

11 So the Levites stilled all the people, saying, Hold your peace, for the day *is* holy; neither be ye grieved.
12 And all the people went their way to eat, and to drink, and to send portions, and to make great ᵀmirth, because they had understood the words that were declared unto them.   Neh. 8:7-8 ♦ *gladness*

The People Observe the Festival of Booths (Tabernacles)
13 And on the second day were gathered together the chief of the fathers of all the people, the priests, and the Levites, unto Ezra the scribe, even to understand the words of the law.
14 And they found written in the law which the LORD had commanded by Moses, that the children of Israel should dwell in booths in the feast of the seventh month: Lev. 23:34

15 And that they should publish and proclaim in all their cities, and in Jerusalem, saying, Go forth unto the mount, and fetch olive branches, and pine branches, and myrtle branches, and palm branches, and branches of thick trees, to make booths, as *it is* written.   Lev. 23:4
16 So the people went forth, and brought *them*, and made themselves booths, every one upon the roof of his house, and in their courts, and in the courts of the house of God, and in the street of the water gate, and in the street of the gate of Ephraim.   2 Kin. 14:13; Neh. 12:37, 39
17 And all the congregation of them that were come again out of the captivity made booths, and sat under the booths: for since the days of Jeshua the son of Nun unto that day had not the children of Israel done so. And there was very great gladness.   2 Chr. 7:8-10; 8:13; Ezra 3:4
18 Also day by day, from the first day unto the last day, he read in the book of the law of God. And they kept the feast seven days; and on the eighth day *was* a solemn assembly, according unto the manner.   Lev. 23:36; Num. 29:35

A Day of Fasting and Confession
9 Now in the twenty and fourth day of this month the children of Israel were assembled with fasting, and with sackclothes, and earth upon them.   Josh. 7:6
2 And the seed of Israel separated themselves from all strangers, and stood and confessed their sins, and the iniquities of their fathers.   Ezra 10:11; Neh. 13:3, 30
3 And they stood up in their place, and read in the book of the law of the LORD their God *one* fourth part of the day; and *another* fourth part they confessed, and worshipped the LORD their God.   Neh. 8:7-8

A Day of Prayer
4 Then stood up upon the stairs, of the Levites, Jeshua, and Bani, Kadmiel, Shebaniah, Bunni, Sherebiah, Bani, *and* Chenani, and cried with a loud voice unto the LORD their God.   Neh. 8:7
5 Then the Levites, Jeshua, and Kadmiel, Bani, Hashabniah, Sherebiah, Hodijah, Shebaniah, *and* Pethahiah, said, Stand up *and* bless the LORD your God for ever and ever: and blessed be thy glorious name, which is exalted above all blessing and praise. 1 Chr. 29:13
6 Thou, *even* thou, *art* LORD alone; thou hast made heaven, the heaven of heavens, with all their host, the earth, and all *things* that *are* therein, the seas, and all that *is* therein, and thou preservest them all; and the host of heaven worshippeth thee. Gen. 1:1; 2:1; 2 Kin. 19:15
7 Thou *art* the LORD the God, who didst choose Abram, and broughtest him forth

out of Ur of the Chaldees, and gavest him
the name of Abraham;   Gen. 11:31; 17:5

9:6 Our Immediate Dependence on God for Life

The power of God is still exercised in upholding the objects of His creation. It is not
because the mechanism once set in motion
continues to act by its own inherent energy that the pulse beats, and breath follows
breath. Every breath, every pulsation of the
heart, is an evidence of the care of Him in
whom we live and move and have our being.
From the smallest insect to man, every living
creature is daily dependent upon His providence. *Ed 131*

---

8 And foundest his heart faithful before
thee, and madest a covenant with him to give
the land of the Canaanites, the Hittites, the
Amorites, and the Perizzites, and the Jebusites, and the Girgashites, to give *it, I say*, to
his seed, and hast performed thy words; for
thou *art* righteous: Gen. 12:7; 15:6, 18-21
9 And didst see the affliction of our fathers
in Egypt, and heardest their cry by the Red
sea;
10 And shewedst signs and wonders upon
Pharaoh, and on all his servants, and on all
the people of his land: for thou knewest that
they dealt proudly against them. So didst
thou get thee a name, as *it is* this day. Jer. 32:20
11 And thou didst divide the sea before
them, so that they went through the midst
of the sea on the dry land; and their persecutors thou threwest into the deeps, as a stone
into the mighty waters.   Ps. 78:13
12 Moreover thou leddest them in the day
by a cloudy pillar; and in the night by a pillar
of fire, to give them light in the way wherein
they should go.   Ex. 13:21-22
13 Thou camest down also upon mount
Sinai, and spakest with them from heaven,
and gavest them right judgments, and true
laws, good statutes and commandments:
14 And madest known unto them thy holy
sabbath, and commandedst them precepts,
statutes, and laws, by the hand of Moses thy
servant: Gen. 2:3
15 And gavest them bread from heaven for
their hunger, and broughtest forth water for
them out of the rock for their thirst, and
promisedst them that they should go in to
possess the land which thou hadst sworn to
give them.   Ex. 16:4; 17:6; Deut. 1:8
16 But they and our fathers dealt proudly,
and hardened their necks, and hearkened
not to thy commandments,   Deut. 31:27
17 And refused to obey, neither were mindful of thy wonders that thou didst among
them; but hardened their necks, and in their
rebellion appointed a captain to return to

their bondage: but thou *art* a God ready
to pardon, gracious and merciful, slow to
anger, and of great kindness, and forsookest
them not.   Ps. 78:11; 86:5, 15
18 Yea, when they had made them a molten
calf, and said, This *is* thy God that brought
thee up out of Egypt, and had ᵀwrought
great provocations;   Ex. 32:4-8 ♦ made
19 Yet thou in thy manifold mercies forsookest them not in the wilderness: the pillar of
the cloud departed not from them by day,
to lead them in the way; neither the pillar
of fire by night, to shew them light, and the
way wherein they should go.   Neh. 9:12
20 Thou gavest also thy good spirit to instruct them, and withheldest not thy manna
from their mouth, and gavest them water for
their thirst.   Ex. 16:15, 35; Num. 11:17
21 Yea, forty years didst thou sustain them
in the wilderness, *so that* they lacked nothing; their clothes ᵀwaxed not old, and their
feet swelled not.   Deut. 2:7; 8:4 ♦ became
22 Moreover thou gavest them kingdoms
and nations, and didst divide them into corners: so they possessed the land of Sihon,
and the land of the king of Heshbon, and the
land of Og king of Bashan.   Num. 21:21-35
23 Their children also multipliedst thou as
the stars of heaven, and broughtest them
into the land, concerning which thou hadst
promised to their fathers, that they should
go in to possess *it*.   Gen. 15:5
24 So the children went in and possessed
the land, and thou subduedst before them
the inhabitants of the land, the Canaanites,
and gavest them into their hands, with their
kings, and the people of the land, that they
might do with them as they would. Josh. 11:23
25 And they took strong cities, and a fat land,
and possessed houses full of all goods, wells
digged, vineyards, and oliveyards, and fruit
trees in abundance: so they did eat, and were
filled, and became fat, and delighted themselves in thy great goodness.   Deut. 3:5; 32:15
26 Nevertheless they were disobedient,
and rebelled against thee, and cast thy law
behind their backs, and slew thy prophets
which testified against them to turn them
to thee, and they wrought great provocations.   Judg. 2:11-12; 1 Kin. 14:9; Neh. 9:18
27 Therefore thou deliveredst them into the
hand of their enemies, who vexed them: and
in the time of their trouble, when they cried
unto thee, thou heardest *them* from heaven;
and according to thy manifold mercies thou
gavest them saviours, who saved them out
of the hand of their enemies.
28 But after they had rest, they did evil
again before thee: therefore leftest thou
them in the hand of their enemies, so that
they had the dominion over them: yet

when they returned, and cried unto thee, thou heardest *them* from heaven; and many times didst thou deliver them according to thy mercies;   Judg. 3:11-12

29 And testifiedst against them, that thou mightest bring them again unto thy law: yet they dealt proudly, and hearkened not unto thy commandments, but sinned against thy judgments, (which if a man do, he shall live in them;) and withdrew the shoulder, and hardened their neck, and would not hear.   Lev. 18:5; Neh. 9:10, 16

30 Yet many years didst thou ᵀforbear them, and testifiedst against them by thy spirit in thy prophets: yet would they not give ear: therefore gavest thou them into the hand of the people of the lands.   Neh. 9:20 ◆ *endure*

31 Nevertheless for thy great mercies' sake thou didst not utterly consume them, nor forsake them; for thou *art* a gracious and merciful God.   Neh. 9:17; Jer. 4:27; 5:10

32 Now therefore, our God, the great, the mighty, and the terrible God, who keepest covenant and mercy, let not all the trouble seem little before thee, that hath come upon us, on our kings, on our princes, and on our priests, and on our prophets, and on our fathers, and on all thy people, since the time of the kings of Assyria unto this day.   2 Kin. 17:3

33 Howbeit thou *art* just in all that is brought upon us; for thou hast done right, but we have done wickedly: Gen. 18:25

34 Neither have our kings, our princes, our priests, nor our fathers, kept thy law, nor hearkened unto thy commandments and thy testimonies, wherewith thou didst testify against them.

35 For they have not served thee in their kingdom, and in thy great goodness that thou gavest them, and in the large and fat land which thou gavest before them, neither turned they from their wicked works.   Deut. 28:47

36 Behold, we *are* servants this day, and *for* the land that thou gavest unto our fathers to eat the fruit thereof and the good thereof, behold, we *are* servants in it: Deut. 28:48

37 And it yieldeth much increase unto the kings whom thou hast set over us because of our sins: also they have dominion over our bodies, and over our cattle, at their pleasure, and we *are* in great distress.   Deut. 28:33, 51

38 And because of all this we make a sure *covenant*, and write *it*; and our princes, Levites, *and* priests, seal *unto it*.   2 Kin. 23:3; Neh. 10:1, 29

The Names of Those Who Sealed the Covenant

10 Now those that sealed *were*, Nehemiah, the Tirshatha, the son of Hachaliah, and Zidkijah,   Neh. 9:38

2 Seraiah, Azariah, Jeremiah,

3 Pashur, Amariah, Malchijah,

4 Hattush, Shebaniah, Malluch,

5 Harim, Meremoth, Obadiah,

6 Daniel, Ginnethon, Baruch,

7 Meshullam, Abijah, Mijamin,

8 Maaziah, Bilgai, Shemaiah: these *were* the priests.

9 And the Levites: both Jeshua the son of Azaniah, Binnui of the sons of Henadad, Kadmiel;

10 And their brethren, Shebaniah, Hodijah, Kelita, Pelaiah, Hanan,

11 Micha, Rehob, Hashabiah,

12 Zaccur, Sherebiah, Shebaniah,

13 Hodijah, Bani, Beninu.

14 The chief of the people; Parosh, Pahathmoab, Elam, Zatthu, Bani,   Neh. 7:8

15 Bunni, Azgad, Bebai,

16 Adonijah, Bigvai, Adin,

17 Ater, Hizkijah, Azzur,

18 Hodijah, Hashum, Bezai,

19 Hariph, Anathoth, Nebai,

20 Magpiash, Meshullam, Hezir,

21 Meshezabeel, Zadok, Jaddua,

22 Pelatiah, Hanan, Anaiah,

23 Hoshea, Hananiah, Hashub,

24 Hallohesh, Pileha, Shobek,

25 Rehum, Hashabnah, Maaseiah,

26 And Ahijah, Hanan, Anan,

27 Malluch, Harim, Baanah.

28 And the rest of the people, the priests, the Levites, the porters, the singers, the Nethinims, and all they that had separated themselves from the people of the lands unto the law of God, their wives, their sons, and their daughters, every one having knowledge, and having understanding;   Neh. 9:2

29 They ᵀclave to their brethren, their nobles, and entered into a curse, and into an oath, to walk in God's law, which was given by Moses the servant of God, and to observe and do all the commandments of the Lᴏʀᴅ our Lord, and his judgments and his statutes;   Ps. 119:106 ◆ *clung*

> **10:28, 29 Israel's Confession and Repentance**
>
> Israel had returned to God with deep sorrow for backsliding. They had made confession with mourning and lamentation. They had acknowledged the righteousness of God's dealings with them, and had covenanted to obey His law. Now they must manifest faith in His promises. God had accepted their repentance; they were now to rejoice in the assurance of sins forgiven and their restoration to divine favor. *PK 667, 668*

30 And that we would not give our daughters unto the people of the land, nor take their daughters for our sons: Ex. 34:16; Deut. 7:3

31 And *if* the people of the land bring ware

or any ᵀvictuals on the sabbath day to sell, *that* we would not buy it of them on the sabbath, or on the holy day: and *that* we would leave the seventh year, and the exaction of every debt.   Ex. 23:10-11 ◆ *food*

32 Also we made ordinances for us, to charge ourselves yearly with the third part of a shekel for the service of the house of our God;   Ex. 30:11-16

33 For the shewbread, and for the continual meat offering, and for the continual burnt offering, of the sabbaths, of the new moons, for the set feasts, and for the holy *things*, and for the sin offerings to make an atonement for Israel, and *for* all the work of the house of our God.   2 Chr. 2:4

34 And we cast the lots among the priests, the Levites, and the people, for the wood offering, to bring *it* into the house of our God, after the houses of our fathers, at times appointed year by year, to burn upon the altar of the LORD our God, as *it is* written in the law: Neh. 13:31; Is. 40:16

35 And to bring the firstfruits of our ground, and the firstfruits of all fruit of all trees, year by year, unto the house of the LORD: Ex. 23:19

36 Also the firstborn of our sons, and of our cattle, as *it is* written in the law, and the firstlings of our herds and of our flocks, to bring to the house of our God, unto the priests that minister in the house of our God: Ex. 13:2

37 And *that* we should bring the firstfruits of our dough, and our offerings, and the fruit of all manner of trees, of wine and of oil, unto the priests, to the chambers of the house of our God; and the tithes of our ground unto the Levites, that the same Levites might have the tithes in all the cities of our ᵀtillage.   Lev. 23:17; Num. 18:21; Deut. 18:4 ◆ *plowed land*

38 And the priest the son of Aaron shall be with the Levites, when the Levites take tithes: and the Levites shall bring up the ᵀtithe of the tithes unto the house of our God, to the chambers, into the treasure house.   Neh. 13:12-13 ◆ *one-tenth*

39 For the children of Israel and the children of Levi shall bring the offering of the corn, of the new wine, and the oil, unto the chambers, where *are* the vessels of the sanctuary, and the priests that minister, and the porters, and the singers: and we will not forsake the house of our God.   2 Chr. 31:12

> **10:28-39 Promised Blessings Follow Obedience**
>
> Nehemiah's efforts to restore the worship of the true God had been crowned with success. As long as the people were true to the oath they had taken, as long as they were obedient to God's word, so long would the Lord fulfill His promise by pouring rich blessings upon them. *PK 668*

New Residents for Jerusalem

11 And the rulers of the people dwelt at Jerusalem: the rest of the people also cast lots, to bring one of ten to dwell in Jerusalem the holy city, and nine parts *to dwell* in *other* cities.   Neh. 10:34; 11:18; Is. 48:2

2 And the people blessed all the men, that willingly offered themselves to dwell at Jerusalem.   Judg. 5:9

3 Now these *are* the chief of the province that dwelt in Jerusalem: but in the cities of Judah dwelt every one in his possession in their cities, ᵀto wit, Israel, the priests, and the Levites, and the Nethinims, and the children of Solomon's servants.   Ezra 2:43 ◆ *namely*

4 And at Jerusalem dwelt *certain* of the children of Judah, and of the children of Benjamin. Of the children of Judah; Athaiah the son of Uzziah, the son of Zechariah, the son of Amariah, the son of Shephatiah, the son of Mahalaleel, of the children of Perez; Gen. 38:29

5 And Maaseiah the son of Baruch, the son of Col-hozeh, the son of Hazaiah, the son of Adaiah, the son of Joiarib, the son of Zechariah, the son of Shiloni.

6 All the sons of Perez that dwelt at Jerusa-

Rejoicing for Sins Forgiven

Nehemiah 10

For those who are convicted of sin and weighed down with a sense of their unworthiness, there are lessons of faith and encouragement in this record. The Bible faithfully presents the result of Israel's apostasy; but it portrays also the deep humiliation and repentance, the earnest devotion and generous sacrifice, that marked their seasons of return to the Lord.

Every true turning to the Lord brings abiding joy into the life. When a sinner yields to the influence of the Holy Spirit, he sees his own guilt and defilement in contrast with the holiness of the great Searcher of hearts. He sees himself condemned as a transgressor. But he is not, because of this, to give way to despair; for his pardon has already been secured. He may rejoice in the sense of sins forgiven, in the love of a pardoning heavenly Father. It is God's glory to encircle sinful, repentant human beings in the arms of His love, to bind up their wounds, to cleanse them from sin, and to clothe them with the garments of salvation. *PK 668*

lem *were* four hundred ᵀthreescore and eight valiant men.   *sixty*

7 And these *are* the sons of Benjamin; Sallu the son of Meshullam, the son of Joed, the son of Pedaiah, the son of Kolaiah, the son of Maaseiah, the son of Ithiel, the son of Jesaiah.

8 And after him Gabbai, Sallai, nine hundred twenty and eight.

9 And Joel the son of Zichri *was* their overseer: and Judah the son of Senuah *was* second over the city.

10 Of the priests: Jedaiah the son of Joiarib, Jachin.

11 Seraiah the son of Hilkiah, the son of Meshullam, the son of Zadok, the son of Meraioth, the son of Ahitub, *was* the ruler of the house of God.

12 And their brethren that did the work of the house *were* eight hundred twenty and two: and Adaiah the son of Jeroham, the son of Pelaliah, the son of Amzi, the son of Zechariah, the son of Pashur, the son of Malchiah,

13 And his brethren, chief of the fathers, two hundred forty and two: and Amashai the son of Azareel, the son of Ahasai, the son of Meshillemoth, the son of Immer,

14 And their brethren, mighty men of valour, an hundred twenty and eight: and their overseer *was* Zabdiel, the son of *one of* the great men.

15 Also of the Levites: Shemaiah the son of Hashub, the son of Azrikam, the son of Hashabiah, the son of Bunni;

16 And Shabbethai and Jozabad, of the chief of the Levites, *had* the oversight of the outward business of the house of God.

17 And Mattaniah the son of Micha, the son of Zabdi, the son of Asaph, *was* the principal to begin the thanksgiving in prayer: and Bakbukiah the second among his brethren, and Abda the son of Shammua, the son of Galal, the son of Jeduthun.   1 Chr. 9:15

18 All the Levites in the holy city *were* two hundred ᵀfourscore and four. Neh. 11:1 ♦ *eighty*

19 Moreover the porters, Akkub, Talmon, and their brethren that kept the gates, *were* an hundred seventy and two.

The Remainder Dwell in Other Cities

20 And the residue of Israel, of the priests, *and* the Levites, *were* in all the cities of Judah, every one in his inheritance.

21 But the Nethinims dwelt in Ophel: and Ziha and Gispa *were* over the Nethinims.

22 The overseer also of the Levites at Jerusalem *was* Uzzi the son of Bani, the son of Hashabiah, the son of Mattaniah, the son of Micha. Of the sons of Asaph, the singers *were* over the business of the house of God.   Neh. 12:42

23 For *it was* the king's commandment concerning them, that a certain portion should be for the singers, due for every day. Ezra 6:8-9

24 And Pethahiah the son of Meshezabeel, of the children of Zerah the son of Judah, *was* at the king's hand in all matters concerning the people.   Gen. 38:30

25 And for the villages, with their fields, *some* of the children of Judah dwelt at Kirjath-arba, and *in* the villages thereof, and at Dibon, and *in* the villages thereof, and at Jekabzeel, and *in* the villages thereof, Josh. 14:15

26 And at Jeshua, and at Moladah, and at Beth-phelet,

27 And at Hazar-shual, and at Beer-sheba, and *in* the villages thereof,

28 And at Ziklag, and at Mekonah, and in the villages thereof,   1 Sam. 27:6

29 And at En-rimmon, and at Zareah, and at Jarmuth,

30 Zanoah, Adullam, and *in* their villages, at Lachish, and the fields thereof, at Azekah, and *in* the villages thereof. And they dwelt from Beer-sheba unto the valley of Hinnom.   Josh. 10:3

31 The children also of Benjamin from Geba *dwelt* at Michmash, and Aija, and Beth-el, and *in* their villages,

32 *And* at Anathoth, Nob, Ananiah, Josh. 21:18

33 Hazor, Ramah, Gittaim,   2 Sam. 4:3

34 Hadid, Zeboim, Neballat,   1 Sam. 13:18

35 Lod, and Ono, the valley of craftsmen.

36 And of the Levites *were* divisions *in* Judah, *and* in Benjamin.

The Priests

12 Now these *are* the priests and the Levites that went up with Zerubbabel the son of Shealtiel, and Jeshua: Seraiah, Jeremiah, Ezra,   Ezra 2:1-2

2 Amariah, Malluch, Hattush,

3 Shechaniah, Rehum, Meremoth,

4 Iddo, Ginnetho, Abijah,   Luke 1:5

5 Miamin, Maadiah, Bilgah,

6 Shemaiah, and Joiarib, Jedaiah,

7 Sallu, Amok, Hilkiah, Jedaiah. These *were* the chief of the priests and of their brethren in the days of Jeshua.

8 Moreover the Levites: Jeshua, Binnui, Kadmiel, Sherebiah, Judah, *and* Mattaniah, *which was* over the thanksgiving, he and his brethren.   Neh. 11:17

9 Also Bakbukiah and Unni, their brethren, *were* over against them in the watches.

10 And Jeshua begat Joiakim, Joiakim also begat Eliashib, and Eliashib begat Joiada,

11 And Joiada begat Jonathan, and Jonathan begat Jaddua.

12 And in the days of Joiakim were priests, the chief of the fathers: of Seraiah, Meraiah; of Jeremiah, Hananiah;

13 Of Ezra, Meshullam; of Amariah, Jehohanan;

14 Of Melicu, Jonathan; of Shebaniah, Joseph;

15 Of Harim, Adna; of Meraioth, Helkai;

16 Of Iddo, Zechariah; of Ginnethon, Meshullam;

17 Of Abijah, Zichri; of Miniamin, of Moadiah, Piltai;

18 Of Bilgah, Shammua; of Shemaiah, Jehonathan;

19 And of Joiarib, Mattenai; of Jedaiah, Uzzi;

20 Of Sallai, Kallai; of Amok, Eber;

21 Of Hilkiah, Hashabiah; of Jedaiah, Nethaneel.

22 The Levites in the days of Eliashib, Joiada, and Johanan, and Jaddua, *were* recorded chief of the fathers: also the priests, to the reign of Darius the Persian.

23 The sons of Levi, the chief of the fathers, *were* written in the book of the chronicles, even until the days of Johanan the son of Eliashib.

24 And the chief of the Levites: Hashabiah, Sherebiah, and Jeshua the son of Kadmiel, with their brethren over against them, to praise *and* to give thanks, according to the commandment of David the man of God, ward over against ward.   1 Chr. 25:1-26

25 Mattaniah, and Bakbukiah, Obadiah, Meshullam, Talmon, Akkub, *were* porters keeping the ^Tward at the thresholds of the gates.   watch

26 These *were* in the days of Joiakim the son of Jeshua, the son of Jozadak, and in the days of Nehemiah the governor, and of Ezra the priest, the scribe.   Neh. 8:9

Jerusalem's Walls Are Dedicated to God

27 And at the dedication of the wall of Jerusalem they sought the Levites out of all their places, to bring them to Jerusalem, to keep the dedication with gladness, both with thanksgivings, and with singing, *with* cymbals, psalteries, and with harps. 1 Chr. 15:16, 28

28 And the sons of the singers gathered themselves together, both out of the plain country round about Jerusalem, and from the villages of Netophathi;   1 Chr. 9:16

29 Also from the house of Gilgal, and out of the fields of Geba and Azmaveth: for the singers had builded them villages round about Jerusalem.

30 And the priests and the Levites purified themselves, and purified the people, and the gates, and the wall.   Ex. 19:10

31 Then I brought up the princes of Judah upon the wall, and appointed two great *companies of them that gave* thanks, *whereof one* went on the right hand upon the wall toward the dung gate: Neh. 2:13; 12:38

32 And after them went Hoshaiah, and half of the princes of Judah,

33 And Azariah, Ezra, and Meshullam,

34 Judah, and Benjamin, and Shemaiah, and Jeremiah,

35 And *certain* of the priests' sons with trumpets; *namely*, Zechariah the son of Jonathan, the son of Shemaiah, the son of Mattaniah, the son of Michaiah, the son of Zaccur, the son of Asaph:

36 And his brethren, Shemaiah, and Azarael, Milalai, Gilalai, Maai, Nethaneel, and Judah, Hanani, with the musical instruments of David the man of God, and Ezra the scribe before them.   Neh. 12:24

37 And at the fountain gate, which was over against them, they went up by the stairs of the city of David, at the going up of the wall, above the house of David, even unto the water gate eastward.   Neh. 2:14; 3:26; 8:1

38 And the other *company of them that gave* thanks went over against *them*, and I after them, and the half of the people upon the wall, from beyond the tower of the furnaces even unto the broad wall;   Neh. 3:8, 11

39 And from above the gate of Ephraim, and above the old gate, and above the fish gate, and the tower of Hananeel, and the tower of Meah, even unto the sheep gate: and they stood still in the prison gate.   Neh. 3:1, 3, 6

40 So stood the two *companies of them that gave* thanks in the house of God, and I, and the half of the rulers with me:

41 And the priests; Eliakim, Maaseiah, Miniamin, Michaiah, Elioenai, Zechariah, *and* Hananiah, with trumpets;

42 And Maaseiah, and Shemaiah, and Eleazar, and Uzzi, and Jehohanan, and Malchijah, and Elam, and Ezer. And the singers sang loud, with Jezrahiah *their* overseer.

43 Also that day they offered great sacrifices, and rejoiced: for God had made them rejoice with great joy: the wives also and the children rejoiced: so that the joy of Jerusalem was heard even afar off.   Ps. 92:4

The Duties of the Priests and Levites Appointed to Temple Service

44 And at that time were some appointed over the chambers for the treasures, for the offerings, for the firstfruits, and for the tithes, to gather into them out of the fields of the cities the portions of the law for the priests and Levites: for Judah rejoiced for the priests and for the Levites that waited.   Neh. 13:12-13

45 And both the singers and the porters kept the ward of their God, and the ward of the purification, according to the commandment of David, *and* of Solomon his son.   1 Chr. 25:1-26

46 For in the days of David and Asaph of old

there were chief of the singers, and songs of praise and thanksgiving unto God. 2 Chr. 29:30
47 And all Israel in the days of Zerubbabel, and in the days of Nehemiah, gave the portions of the singers and the porters, every day his portion: and they sanctified *holy things* unto the Levites; and the Levites sanctified *them* unto the children of Aaron.

The Israelites Are Separated from the Mixed Multitude

13 On that day they read in the book of Moses in the audience of the people; and therein was found written, that the Ammonite and the Moabite should not come into the congregation of God for ever; Deut. 23:3-5
2 Because they met not the children of Israel with bread and with water, but hired Balaam against them, that he should curse them: ᵀhowbeit our God turned the curse into a blessing. Deut. 23:5 ♦ *however*
3 Now it came to pass, when they had heard the law, that they separated from Israel all the mixed multitude. Ex. 12:38; Num. 11:4; Neh. 9:2
4 And before this, Eliashib the priest, having the oversight of the chamber of the house of our God, *was* allied unto Tobiah: Neh. 2:10; 12:44
5 And he had prepared for him a great chamber, where ᵀaforetime they laid the meat offerings, the frankincense, and the vessels, and the tithes of the corn, the new wine, and the oil, which was commanded *to be given* to the Levites, and the singers, and the porters; and the offerings of the priests. *before*
6 But in all this *time* was not I at Jerusalem: for in the two and thirtieth year of Artaxerxes king of Babylon came I unto the king, and after certain days obtained I leave of the king: Neh. 5:14

7 And I came to Jerusalem, and understood of the evil that Eliashib did for Tobiah, in preparing him a chamber in the courts of the house of God. Neh. 13:5
8 And it grieved me sore: therefore I cast forth all the household stuff of Tobiah out of the chamber.
9 Then I commanded, and they cleansed the chambers: and thither brought I again the vessels of the house of God, with the meat offering and the frankincense. 2 Chr. 29:5

Nehemiah Ensures that the Levites Receive Their Portion

10 And I perceived that the portions of the Levites had not been given *them*: for the Levites and the singers, that did the work, were fled every one to his field. Neh. 10:37
11 Then contended I with the rulers, and said, Why is the house of God forsaken? And I gathered them together, and set them in their place. Neh. 10:39; 13:17, 25
12 Then brought all Judah the ᵀtithe of the corn and the new wine and the oil unto the treasuries. Neh. 10:37-39 ♦ *tenth*

> ### 13:8–13 Prompt and Decisive Action
>
> Prompt and decisive action at the right time will gain glorious triumphs, while delay and neglect result in failure and dishonor to God. If the leaders in the cause of truth show no zeal, if they are indifferent and purposeless, the church will be careless, indolent, and pleasure-loving; but if they are filled with a holy purpose to serve God and Him alone, the people will be united, hopeful, eager. *PK 676*

13 And I made treasurers over the treasuries, Shelemiah the priest, and Zadok the scribe, and of the Levites, Pedaiah: and next to them *was* Hanan the son of Zaccur, the son of Mattaniah: for they were counted

The Success of Nehemiah

Nehemiah 13

In their work, Ezra and Nehemiah humbled themselves before God, confessing their sins and the sins of their people, and entreating pardon as if they themselves were the offenders. Patiently they toiled and prayed and suffered. That which made their work most difficult was not the open hostility of the heathen, but the secret opposition of pretended friends, who, by lending their influence to the service of evil, increased tenfold the burden of God's servants. These traitors furnished the Lord's enemies with material to use in their warfare upon His people. Their evil passions and rebellious wills were ever at war with the plain requirements of God.

The success attending Nehemiah's efforts shows what prayer, faith, and wise, energetic action will accomplish. Nehemiah was not a priest; he was not a prophet; he made no pretension to high title. He was a reformer raised up for an important time. It was his aim to set his people right with God. Inspired with a great purpose, he bent every energy of his being to its accomplishment. High, unbending integrity marked his efforts. As he came into contact with evil and opposition to right he took so determined a stand that the people were roused to labor with fresh zeal and courage. They could not but recognize his loyalty, his patriotism, and his deep love for God; and, seeing this, they were willing to follow where he led. *PK 675, 676*

faithful, and their office *was* to distribute unto their brethren.   Neh. 7:2

14 Remember me, O my God, concerning this, and wipe not out my good deeds that I have done for the house of my God, and for the offices thereof.   Neh. 5:19

Nehemiah Ensures That No Work is Done on the Sabbath

15 In those days saw I in Judah *some* treading wine presses on the sabbath, and bringing in sheaves, and ᵀlading asses; as also wine, grapes, and figs, and all *manner of* burdens, which they brought into Jerusalem on the sabbath day: and I testified *against them* in the day wherein they sold ᵀvictuals. Ex. 34:21; Neh. 10:31; 13:21 ♦ *loading* ♦ *food*

16 There dwelt men of Tyre also therein, which brought fish, and all manner of ware, and sold on the sabbath unto the children of Judah, and in Jerusalem.

17 Then I contended with the nobles of Judah, and said unto them, What evil thing *is* this that ye do, and profane the sabbath day?   Neh. 13:11

18 Did not your fathers thus, and did not our God bring all this evil upon us, and upon this city? yet ye bring more wrath upon Israel by profaning the sabbath.   Jer. 17:21-23

19 And it came to pass, that when the gates of Jerusalem began to be dark before the sabbath, I commanded that the gates should be shut, and charged that they should not be opened till after the sabbath: and *some* of my servants set I at the gates, *that* there should no burden be brought in on the sabbath day.   Lev. 23:32

20 So the merchants and sellers of all kind of ware lodged without Jerusalem once or twice.

21 Then I testified against them, and said unto them, Why lodge ye about the wall? if ye do *so* again, I will lay hands on you. From that time forth came they no *more* on the sabbath.

22 And I commanded the Levites that they should cleanse themselves, and *that* they should come *and* keep the gates, to sanctify the sabbath day. Remember me, O my God, *concerning* this also, and spare me according to the greatness of thy mercy.   Neh. 12:30; 13:14, 31

Nehemiah Dissolves Marriages to Foreigners

23 In those days also saw I Jews *that* had married wives of Ashdod, of Ammon, *and* of Moab: Neh. 10:30

24 And their children spake half in the speech of Ashdod, and could not speak in the Jews' language, but according to the language of each people.

25 And I contended with them, and cursed them, and smote certain of them, and plucked off their hair, and made them swear by God, *saying*, Ye shall not give your daughters unto their sons, nor take their daughters unto your sons, or for yourselves.   Ezra 10:5

26 Did not Solomon king of Israel sin by these things? yet among many nations was there no king like him, who was beloved of his God, and God made him king over all Israel: nevertheless even him did outlandish women cause to sin.   2 Sam. 12:24-25; 1 Kin. 3:13; 2 Chr. 1:12

27 Shall we then hearken unto you to do all this great evil, to ᵀtransgress against our God in marrying strange wives?   Ezra 10:2 ♦ *sin*

28 And *one* of the sons of Joiada, the son of Eliashib the high priest, *was* son in law to Sanballat the Horonite: therefore I chased him from me.   Neh. 2:19

13:23-28 Speaking Out Against Wrong

Those upon whom rests the burden of this work will not hold their peace when wrong is done, neither will they cover evil with a cloak of false charity. They will remember that God is no respecter of persons, and that severity to a few may prove mercy to many. They will remember also that in the one who rebukes evil the spirit of Christ should ever be revealed. *PK 675*

---

29 Remember them, O my God, because they have defiled the priesthood, and the covenant of the priesthood, and of the Levites.   Neh. 6:14

30 Thus cleansed I them from all strangers, and appointed the wards of the priests and the Levites, every one in his business;   Neh. 10:30

31 And for the wood offering, at times appointed, and for the firstfruits. Remember me, O my God, for good.   Neh. 10:34; 13:14, 22

THE BOOK OF

ESTHER

The story of Esther is an enduringly popular story for children's Bible study. Yet, the spiritual lessons to be gained are great. Esther, a beautiful young Jewish woman, becomes the wife of a powerful king.

While many of her fellow Jews had returned to their homeland in Jerusalem under the earlier edict by Cyrus, others still remained in their land of exile. Living in Persia, Esther is taken into the king's harem where she gains favor with the eunuch in charge of all the young ladies. In due course she becomes the queen of this worldwide empire. This story's adversary Haman, one of the king's advisors, threatens the lives of all of the Jews living in the kingdom. They need a miracle to prevent this people from being massacred. In the Book of Esther, divine power and human effort come together to save an entire nation from genocide. Although God is not named in the book, His presence can be seen in the unfolding of events.

The deliverance of the Jews is presented in the book as the result of living faith—particularly the faith of Mordecai and Esther. While it seems that Haman has the upper hand, his earthly power cannot compete against God's power, for He takes great delight in humbling the proud and exalting his humble and faithful servants.

Every year, Jewish people still celebrate the Festival of Purim, where the story of Esther is read aloud to commemorate this amazing delivery of God's people.

Dates

The Book of Esther was written during the reign of the Persian king Khshayarsh (or its Hebrew form, *Ahasuerus*). Ahasuerus (or Xerxes in the Greek) reigned from 486–465 B.C. The Book of Esther was probably written between 465 and 435 B.C. after Purim had been observed for some years.

The story of Esther occurs between the events described in chapters 6 and 7 of the Book of Ezra. The campaigns of King Ahasuerus help to date this book. The great feast took place in his third year (1:3), in approximately 483 B.C., when he was planning a military attack on Greece. According to the Greek historian Herodotus, Ahasuerus suffered a defeat by the Greeks at Salamis in 479 B.C. After this defeat, he returned home and at that time sought to replace the queen he had deposed.

Persian kings ruled during the following dates:

Cyrus (553–530 B.C.); Cambyses (530–522 B.C.); Smerdis (522 B.C.);
Darius I (521–486 B.C.); Ahasuerus (486–465 B.C.); Artaxerxes I (465–423 B.C.);
Darius II (423–404 B.C.)

Author

The author of Esther is neither mentioned in the biblical text nor has archeological documents revealed its authorship. Based on the information given on Jewish customs, the records of Mordecai, and the Book of the Chronicles of the Kings of Media and Persia, the author is believed to be a Jewish individual living in Shushan (Susa). Ezra, Nehemiah, and Mordecai have been suggested as possible authors.

Meaning of the Name

The book was named after Esther, whose Hebrew name is Hadassah. *Hadassah* means "myrtle." Esther is the Greek version of *Ester,* which comes from *stara*—the Persian word for star.

Christ in Esther

Esther's risking of her life to save her people points to the work of Christ. Like Christ, she becomes an advocate for the lives of her people, when an enemy tries to destroy them. While Esther's life was spared, Jesus gave His life.

Overview

The hand of God is evident throughout the book of Esther, though He remains unnamed within the narrative. The story of Esther shows the power of God to protect His people by placing just the right person in the right place "for such a time as this" (4:14). Within its pages, the book of Esther reveals an emergency for God's people in that the danger of

extermination is imminent. Even though she is queen, Esther is still willing to die for her people. In her dedication to God, she exhibits the necessary traits that God has given her for this occasion: clear thinking, self-restraint, and surrender of self.

When the king responds by holding out his scepter to her, she does not reveal the wicked offender—Haman—lest other court personnel leak the information to him. Through a series of remarkable events, he is executed by the same means that he intended for Mordecai.

In this whole scenario, God's love for His chosen people is exposed mightily, using humble and willing souls. Our lesson is that God uses human effort, but deliverance comes only from Him.

Like Ezra and Nehemiah, Esther has two sections:

(1) *Esther 1—4, A Threat Exposed:* Having felt shamed by the refusal of Queen Vashti to appear before him at a feast, Ahasuerus is goaded by his advisors into replacing Vashti as queen (chapter 1). Hadassah (Esther), an orphan raised by her cousin Mordecai, is chosen as Vashti's successor (chapter 2). During the course of chapter 2, Mordecai learns of a conspiracy to murder the king and reports it. Having recently been promoted, the stage is set for Haman's plot against the Jews to be revealed—a plot sparked by anger over Mordecai's refusal to pay homage to him (chapter 3). This plot is more than just one proud man's resentment over a perceived insult. Haman was an Amalekite. Centuries of enmity between the Amalekites and Israelites likely fueled his ire. At Haman's instigation Ahasuerus issues a decree allowing the genocide of the Jews, so Mordecai seeks the new queen's help to save their people (chapter 4). This suggestion is risky, because Esther has not revealed her heritage nor has she been summoned before the king. In the latter instance, death could result for anyone appearing before the king without being summoned. However, she appears before him believing that God has preceded her and prepared the king to receive her.

(2) *Esther 5—10, A Threat Defused:* Esther becomes the instrument of God's deliverance of the Jews. A series of banquets given by Esther allow her to reveal Haman's plot to the king. The once proud Haman is humbled and later executed on the device meant for Mordecai (chapters 5—8). A new decree is issued (chapter 8), so on the day that the Jews are to be exterminated, they instead destroy their tormentors (chapter 9). In celebration of the salvation of the Jews, the Festival of Purim is established to commemorate God's deliverance of His people (chapter 9). Purim comes from the word *pur,* which means "lot," so named because Haman had cast lots while plotting against the Jews. At the close of the book of Esther, the king promotes Mordecai to second in command in the kingdom (chapter 10).

Unlocking Esther

KEY PEOPLE:
Esther, Mordecai, Ahasuerus, Vashti, Haman

KEY EVENTS:
Vashti is deposed as queen (chapters 1—2); Esther is selected as queen from among the king's harem; Haman plots against the Jews while Mordecai uncovers a plot against the king (chapter 3); Mordecai solicits Esther's help to save their people (chapter 4); after Esther appears before the king, and through a series of feasts, the king issues a decree allowing the Jews the power to defend themselves (chapters 5—8); Purim is established (chapter 9); Mordecai is promoted to prime minister (chapter 10)

KEY WORD:
Providence. God's providence is a prominent theme of Esther. Through God's providence, Esther becomes queen and, like Joseph (Genesis 41), is placed in a position of authority to plead on behalf of her people.

KEY VERSES:
"Then Mordecai commanded to answer Esther, Think not with thyself that thou shalt escape in the king's house, more than all the Jews. For if thou altogether holdest thy peace at this time, then shall there enlargement and deliverance arise to the Jews from another place; but thou and thy father's house shall be destroyed: and who knoweth whether thou art come to the kingdom for such a time as this?" (Esther 4:13–14).

KEY CHAPTER:
In *Esther 8,* Esther reveals Haman's plot to Ahasuerus. Because Persian law cannot be changed, the king issues a decree allowing the Jews the right to defend themselves against any attackers, thus quashing Haman's plot.

Ahasuerus Makes a Royal Feast

1 Now it came to pass in the days of Ahasuerus, (this *is* Ahasuerus which reigned, from India even unto Ethiopia, *over* an hundred and seven and twenty provinces:)
2 *That* in those days, when the king Ahasuerus sat on the throne of his kingdom, which *was* in Shushan the palace,   1 Kin. 1:46; Neh. 1:1
3 In the third year of his reign, he made a feast unto all his princes and his servants; the power of Persia and Media, the nobles and princes of the provinces, *being* before him: Gen. 40:20; 1 Kin. 3:15; Esth. 2:18
4 When he shewed the riches of his glorious kingdom and the honour of his excellent majesty many days, *even* an hundred and ᵀfourscore days.   *eighty*
5 And when these days were expired, the king made a feast unto all the people that were present in Shushan the palace, both unto great and small, seven days, in the court of the garden of the king's palace;   Esth. 7:7-8
6 *Where were* white, green, and blue, *hangings*, fastened with cords of fine linen and purple to silver rings and pillars of marble: the beds *were of* gold and silver, upon a pavement of red, and blue, and white, and black, marble.   Esth. 7:8; Ezek. 23:41; Amos 6:4
7 And they gave *them* drink in vessels of gold, (the vessels being diverse one from another,) and royal wine in abundance, according to the state of the king.
8 And the drinking *was* according to the law; none did compel: for so the king had appointed to all the officers of his house, that they should do according to every man's pleasure.
9 Also Vashti the queen made a feast for the women *in* the royal house which *belonged* to king Ahasuerus.

Vashti Disobeys the King's Command to Appear before Him

10 On the seventh day, when the heart of the king was merry with wine, he commanded Mehuman, Biztha, Harbona, Bigtha, and Abagtha, Zethar, and Carcas, the seven chamberlains that served in the presence of Ahasuerus the king,   Judg. 16:25
11 To bring Vashti the queen before the king with the crown royal, to shew the people and the princes her beauty: for she *was* fair to look on.
12 But the queen Vashti refused to come at the king's commandment by *his* chamberlains: therefore was the king very ᵀwroth, and his anger burned in him.   Prov. 19:12 ◆ *angry*
13 Then the king said to the wise men, which knew the times, (for so *was* the king's manner toward all that knew law and judgment: 1 Chr. 12:32; Jer. 10:7; Dan. 2:12

14 And the next unto him *was* Carshena, Shethar, Admatha, Tarshish, Meres, Marsena, *and* Memucan, the seven princes of Persia and Media, which saw the king's face, *and* which sat the first in the kingdom;)   2 Kin. 25:19; Ezra 7:14
15 What shall we do unto the queen Vashti according to law, because she hath not performed the commandment of the king Ahasuerus by the chamberlains?
16 And Memucan answered before the king and the princes, Vashti the queen hath not done wrong to the king only, but also to all the princes, and to all the people that *are* in all the provinces of the king Ahasuerus.
17 For *this* deed of the queen shall come abroad unto all women, so that they shall despise their husbands in their eyes, when it shall be reported, The king Ahasuerus commanded Vashti the queen to be brought in before him, but she came not.
18 *Likewise* shall the ladies of Persia and Media say this day unto all the king's princes, which have heard of the deed of the queen. Thus *shall there arise* too much contempt and wrath.
19 If it please the king, let there go a royal commandment from him, and let it be written among the laws of the Persians and the Medes, that it be not altered, That Vashti come no more before king Ahasuerus; and let the king give her royal estate unto another that is better than she.   Esth. 8:8
20 And when the king's decree which he shall make shall be published throughout all his empire, (for it is great,) all the wives shall give to their husbands honour, both to great and small.   Col. 3:18
21 And the saying pleased the king and the princes; and the king did according to the word of Memucan:
22 For he sent letters into all the king's provinces, into every province according to the writing thereof, and to every people after their language, that every man should bear rule in his own house, and that *it* should be published according to the language of every people.   Esth. 3:12; 8:9; Eph. 5:22-24

Esther Becomes Queen

2 After these things, when the wrath of king Ahasuerus was appeased, he remembered Vashti, and what she had done, and what was decreed against her.   Esth. 7:10
2 Then said the king's servants that ministered unto him, Let there be fair young virgins sought for the king: 1 Kin. 1:2
3 And let the king appoint officers in all the provinces of his kingdom, that they may gather together all the fair young virgins unto Shushan the palace, to the house of the women, unto the custody of Hege the

king's chamberlain, keeper of the women; and let their things for purification be given *them*: Esth. 1:1-2

4 And let the maiden which pleaseth the king be queen instead of Vashti. And the thing pleased the king; and he did so.

5 *Now* in Shushan the palace there was a certain Jew, whose name *was* Mordecai, the son of Jair, the son of Shimei, the son of Kish, a Benjamite; 1 Sam. 9:1

6 Who had been carried away from Jerusalem with the captivity which had been carried away with Jeconiah king of Judah, whom Nebuchadnezzar the king of Babylon had carried away. 2 Kin. 24:14-15

7 And he brought up Hadassah, that *is*, Esther, his uncle's daughter: for she had neither father nor mother, and the maid *was* fair and beautiful; whom Mordecai, when her father and mother were dead, took for his own daughter. Esth. 2:15

8 So it came to pass, when the king's commandment and his decree was heard, and when many maidens were gathered together unto Shushan the palace, to the custody of Hegai, that Esther was brought also unto the king's house, to the custody of Hegai, keeper of the women. Esth. 2:3

9 And the maiden pleased him, and she obtained kindness of him; and he speedily gave her her things for purification, with such things as belonged to her, and seven maidens, *which were* meet to be given her, out of the king's house: and he preferred her and her maids unto the best *place* of the house of the women. Gen. 39:21; Esth. 2:3, 12

10 Esther had not shewed her people nor her kindred: for Mordecai had [T]charged her that she should not shew *it*. Esth. 2:20 ◆ *burdened*

11 And Mordecai walked every day before the court of the women's house, to know how Esther did, and what should become of her.

12 Now when every maid's turn was come to go in to king Ahasuerus, after that she had been twelve months, according to the manner of the women, (for so were the days of their purifications accomplished, [T]*to wit*, six months with oil of myrrh, and six months with sweet odours, and with *other* things for the purifying of the women;) *namely*

13 Then thus came *every* maiden unto the king; whatsoever she desired was given her to go with her out of the house of the women unto the king's house.

14 In the evening she went, and on the morrow she returned into the second house of the women, to the custody of Shaashgaz, the king's [T]chamberlain, which kept the concubines: she came in unto the king no more,

except the king delighted in her, and that she were called by name. Esth. 4:11 ◆ *chief servant*

15 Now when the turn of Esther, the daughter of Abihail the uncle of Mordecai, who had taken her for his daughter, was come to go in unto the king, she required nothing but what Hegai the king's chamberlain, the keeper of the women, appointed. And Esther obtained favour in the sight of all them that looked upon her. Esth. 9:29

16 So Esther was taken unto king Ahasuerus into his house royal in the tenth month, which *is* the month Tebeth, in the seventh year of his reign.

17 And the king loved Esther above all the women, and she obtained grace and favour in his sight more than all the virgins; so that he set the royal crown upon her head, and made her queen instead of Vashti. Esth. 1:11

18 Then the king made a great feast unto all his princes and his servants, *even* Esther's feast; and he made a release to the provinces, and gave gifts, according to the state of the king.

19 And when the virgins were gathered together the second time, then Mordecai sat in the king's gate. Esth. 2:3-4, 21; 5:13

20 Esther had not *yet* shewed her kindred nor her people; as Mordecai had charged her: for Esther did the commandment of Mordecai, like as when she was brought up with him. Esth. 2:10

Mordecai's Loyalty Is Recorded in the Official Chronicles

21 In those days, while Mordecai sat in the king's gate, two of the king's chamberlains, Bigthan and Teresh, of those which kept the door, were [T]wroth, and sought to lay hand on the king Ahasuerus. Esth. 6:2 ◆ *angered*

22 And the thing was known to Mordecai, who told *it* unto Esther the queen; and Esther certified the king *thereof* in Mordecai's name.

23 And when inquisition was made of the matter, it was found out; therefore they were both hanged on a tree: and it was written in the book of the chronicles before the king. Gen. 40:19

Mordecai Refuses to Bow to Haman

3 After these things did king Ahasuerus promote Haman the son of Hammedatha the Agagite, and advanced him, and set his seat above all the princes that *were* with him. Num. 24:7; Esth. 3:10; 5:11

2 And all the king's servants, that *were* in the king's gate, bowed, and reverenced Haman: for the king had so commanded concerning him. But Mordecai bowed not, nor did *him* reverence. Esth. 2:19

3 Then the king's servants, which *were* in the king's gate, said unto Mordecai, Why [T]transgressest thou the king's commandment?   Esth. 3:2 ◆ *violate*

4 Now it came to pass, when they spake daily unto him, and he hearkened not unto them, that they told Haman, to see whether Mordecai's matters would stand: for he had told them that he *was* a Jew.   Gen. 39:10

5 And when Haman saw that Mordecai bowed not, nor did him reverence, then was Haman full of wrath.   Esth. 5:9

6 And he thought scorn to lay hands on Mordecai alone; for they had shewed him the people of Mordecai: wherefore Haman sought to destroy all the Jews that *were* throughout the whole kingdom of Ahasuerus, *even* the people of Mordecai.   Ps. 83:4

Haman's Plot against the Jews

7 In the first month, that *is,* the month Nisan, in the twelfth year of king Ahasuerus, they cast Pur, that *is,* the lot, before Haman from day to day, and from month to month, *to* the twelfth *month,* that *is,* the month Adar.   Ezra 6:15; Esth. 9:24-26

8 And Haman said unto king Ahasuerus, There is a certain people scattered abroad and dispersed among the people in all the provinces of thy kingdom; and their laws *are* diverse from all people; neither keep they the king's laws: therefore it *is* not for the king's profit to suffer them.   Ezra 4:12-15; Acts 16:20-21

9 If it please the king, let it be written that they may be destroyed: and I will pay ten thousand talents of silver to the hands of those that have the charge of the business, to bring *it* into the king's treasuries.

3:8, 9 Satan's Scheme

Misled by the false statements of Haman, Xerxes was induced to issue a decree providing for the massacre of all the Jews "scattered abroad and dispersed among the people in all the provinces" of the Medo-Persian kingdom (Esther 3:8). . . . Little did the king realize the far-reaching results that would have accompanied the complete carrying out of this decree. Satan himself, the hidden instigator of the scheme, was trying to rid the earth of those who preserved the knowledge of the true God. *PK 600, 601*

---

10 And the king took his ring from his hand, and gave it unto Haman the son of Hammedatha the Agagite, the Jews' enemy.

11 And the king said unto Haman, The silver *is* given to thee, the people also, to do with them as it seemeth good to thee.

12 Then were the king's scribes called on the thirteenth day of the first month, and there was written according to all that Haman had commanded unto the king's lieutenants, and to the governors that *were* over every province, and to the rulers of every people of every province according to the writing thereof, and *to* every people after their language; in the name of king Ahasuerus was it written, and sealed with the king's ring.   1 Kin. 21:8; Esth. 1:22

13 And the letters were sent by posts into all the king's provinces, to destroy, to kill, and to cause to perish, all Jews, both young and old, little children and women, in one day, *even* upon the thirteenth *day* of the twelfth month, which is the month Adar, and *to take* the [T]spoil of them for a prey.   2 Chr. 30:6 ◆ *plunder*

14 The copy of the writing for a commandment to be given in every province was published unto all people, that they should be ready against that day.   Esth. 8:13-14

15 The posts went out, being hastened by the king's commandment, and the decree was given in Shushan the palace. And the king and Haman sat down to drink; but the city Shushan was perplexed.   Esth. 8:15

The Great Mourning of Mordecai and the Jews

4 When Mordecai perceived all that was done, Mordecai [T]rent his clothes, and put on sackcloth with ashes, and went out into the midst of the city, and cried with a loud and a bitter cry;   2 Sam. 1:11 ◆ *tore*

2 And came even before the king's gate: for none *might* enter into the king's gate clothed with sackcloth.

3 And in every province, whithersoever the king's commandment and his decree came, *there was* great mourning among the Jews, and fasting, and weeping, and wailing; and many lay in sackcloth and ashes.   Is. 58:5

4 So Esther's maids and her chamberlains came and told *it* her. Then was the queen exceedingly grieved; and she sent [T]raiment to clothe Mordecai, and to take away his sackcloth from him: but he received *it* not. *clothing*

5 Then called Esther for Hatach, *one* of the king's chamberlains, whom he had appointed to attend upon her, and gave him a commandment to Mordecai, to know what it *was,* and why it *was.*

6 So Hatach went forth to Mordecai unto the street of the city, which *was* before the king's gate.

7 And Mordecai told him of all that had happened unto him, and of the sum of the money that Haman had promised to pay to the king's treasuries for the Jews, to destroy them.

8 Also he gave him the copy of the writing of the decree that was given at Shushan to

destroy them, to shew it unto Esther, and to declare it unto her, and to charge her that she should go in unto the king, to make supplication unto him, and to make request before him for her people.

9 And Hatach came and told Esther the words of Mordecai.

10 Again Esther spake unto Hatach, and gave him commandment unto Mordecai;

11 All the king's servants, and the people of the king's provinces, do know, that whosoever, whether man or woman, shall come unto the king into the inner court, who is not called, there is one law of his to put him to death, except such to whom the king shall hold out the golden sceptre, that he may live: but I have not been called to come in unto the king these thirty days. Esth. 5:1-2; 8:4; Dan. 2:9

12 And they told to Mordecai Esther's words.

13 Then Mordecai commanded to answer Esther, Think not with thyself that thou shalt escape in the king's house, more than all the Jews.

14 For if thou altogether holdest thy peace at this time, then shall there enlargement and deliverance arise to the Jews from another place; but thou and thy father's house shall be destroyed: and who knoweth whether thou art come to the kingdom for such a time as this?

15 Then Esther bade them return Mordecai this answer,

16 Go, gather together all the Jews that are present in Shushan, and fast ye for me, and neither eat nor drink three days, night or day: I also and my maidens will fast likewise; and so will I go in unto the king, which is not according to the law: and if I perish, I perish. Gen. 43:14

17 So Mordecai went his way, and did according to all that Esther had commanded him.

4:14-17 The Source of Esther's Strength

The crisis that Esther faced demanded quick, earnest action; but both she and Mordecai realized that unless God should work mightily in their behalf, their own efforts would be unavailing. So Esther took time for communion with God, the source of her strength. PK 601

Esther Risks the King's Disfavor to Bring Her Request to Him

5 Now it came to pass on the third day, that Esther put on her royal apparel, and stood in the inner court of the king's house, over against the king's house: and the king sat upon his royal throne in the royal house, over against the gate of the house. Esth. 4:11, 16; 6:4

2 And it was so, when the king saw Esther the queen standing in the court, that she obtained favour in his sight: and the king held out to Esther the golden sceptre that was in his hand. So Esther drew near, and touched the top of the sceptre. Esth. 4:11; 8:4; Prov. 21:1

3 Then said the king unto her, What wilt thou, queen Esther? and what is thy request? it shall be even given thee to the half of the kingdom. Esth. 7:2; Mark 6:23

4 And Esther answered, If it seem good unto the king, let the king and Haman come this day unto the banquet that I have prepared for him. Esth. 5:8

5 Then the king said, Cause Haman to make haste, that he may do as Esther hath said. So the king and Haman came to the banquet that Esther had prepared. Esth. 6:14

6 And the king said unto Esther at the banquet of wine, What is thy petition? and it shall be granted thee: and what is thy request? even to the half of the kingdom it shall be performed. Esth. 5:3; 7:2; 9:12

7 Then answered Esther, and said, My petition and my request is;

8 If I have found favour in the sight of the king, and if it please the king to grant my petition, and to perform my request, let the king and Haman come to the banquet that I shall prepare for them, and I will do to morrow as the king hath said. Esth. 7:3

Haman Is Disgraced because of Mordecai

9 Then went Haman forth that day joyful and with a glad heart: but when Haman saw Mordecai in the king's gate, that he stood not up, nor moved for him, he was full of ᵀindignation against Mordecai. Esth. 3:5 ◆ anger

10 Nevertheless Haman refrained himself: and when he came home, he sent and called for his friends, and Zeresh his wife. Esth. 6:13

11 And Haman told them of the glory of his riches, and the multitude of his children, and all the things wherein the king had promoted him, and how he had advanced him above the princes and servants of the king. Esth. 3:1; 9:7-10

12 Haman said moreover, Yea, Esther the queen did let no man come in with the king unto the banquet that she had prepared but myself; and to morrow am I invited unto her also with the king.

13 Yet all this availeth me nothing, so long as I see Mordecai the Jew sitting at the king's gate.

14 Then said Zeresh his wife and all his friends unto him, Let a gallows be made of fifty cubits high, and to morrow speak thou unto the king that Mordecai may be hanged thereon: then go thou in merrily with the

king unto the banquet. And the thing pleased Haman; and he caused the gallows to be made. 1 Kin. 21:7; Esth. 6:4; 7:9-10

Ahasuerus Reads of Mordecai's Good Service

6 On that night could not the king sleep, and he commanded to bring the book of records of the chronicles; and they were read before the king. Esth. 2:23; 10:2; Dan. 6:18

2 And it was found written, that Mordecai had told of Bigthana and Teresh, two of the king's chamberlains, the keepers of the door, who sought to lay hand on the king Ahasuerus.

3 And the king said, What honour and dignity hath been done to Mordecai for this? Then said the king's servants that ministered unto him, There is nothing done for him. Eccl. 9:15

Haman Unwittingly Gives Counsel on How to Honor Mordecai

4 And the king said, Who is in the court? Now Haman was come into the outward court of the king's house, to speak unto the king to hang Mordecai on the gallows that he had prepared for him. Esth. 4:11

5 And the king's servants said unto him, Behold, Haman standeth in the court. And the king said, Let him come in.

6 So Haman came in. And the king said unto him, What shall be done unto the man whom the king delighteth to honour? Now Haman thought in his heart, To whom would the king delight to do honour more than to myself?

7 And Haman answered the king, For the man whom the king delighteth to honour,

8 Let the royal apparel be brought which the king useth to wear, and the horse that the king rideth upon, and the crown royal which is set upon his head: 1 Kin. 1:33

9 And let this apparel and horse be delivered to the hand of one of the king's most noble princes, that they may Tarray the man Twithal whom the king delighteth to honour, and bring him on horseback through the street of the city, and proclaim before him, Thus shall it be done to the man whom the king delighteth to honour. Gen. 41:43 ◆ clothe ◆ with

10 Then the king said to Haman, Make haste, and take the apparel and the horse, as thou hast said, and do even so to Mordecai the Jew, that sitteth at the king's gate: let nothing fail of all that thou hast spoken.

11 Then took Haman the apparel and the horse, and Tarrayed Mordecai, and brought him on horseback through the street of the city, and proclaimed before him, Thus shall

it be done unto the man whom the king delighteth to honour. clothed

Haman Is Warned about Going against Mordecai

12 And Mordecai came again to the king's gate. But Haman hasted to his house mourning, and having his head covered. 2 Sam. 15:30

13 And Haman told Zeresh his wife and all his friends every thing that had befallen him. Then said his wise men and Zeresh his wife unto him, If Mordecai be of the seed of the Jews, before whom thou hast begun to fall, thou shalt not prevail against him, but shalt surely fall before him. Prov. 28:18

14 And while they were yet talking with him, came the king's chamberlains, and hasted to bring Haman unto the banquet that Esther had prepared. Esth. 5:8

Esther Pleads for Her Own Life and the Lives of Her People

7 So the king and Haman came to banquet with Esther the queen.

2 And the king said again unto Esther on the second day at the banquet of wine, What is thy petition, queen Esther? and it shall be granted thee: and what is thy request? and it shall be performed, even to the half of the kingdom. Esth. 5:6

3 Then Esther the queen answered and said, If I have found favour in thy sight, O king, and if it please the king, let my life be given me at my petition, and my people at my request:

4 For we are sold, I and my people, to be destroyed, to be slain, and to perish. But if we had been sold for bondmen and bondwomen, I had held my tongue, although the enemy could not Tcountervail the king's damage. Deut. 28:68; Esth. 3:9, 13 ◆ compensate for

5 Then the king Ahasuerus answered and said unto Esther the queen, Who is he, and where is he, that Tdurst presume in his heart to do so? dare

6 And Esther said, The adversary and enemy is this wicked Haman. Then Haman was afraid before the king and the queen.

Haman Is Hanged upon the Gallows He Built for Mordecai

7 And the king arising from the banquet of wine in his wrath went into the palace garden: and Haman stood up to make request for his life to Esther the queen; for he saw that there was evil determined against him by the king. Esth. 1:12

8 Then the king returned out of the palace garden into the place of the banquet of wine; and Haman was fallen upon the bed whereon Esther was. Then said the king, Will he force

the queen also before me in the house? As the word went out of the king's mouth, they covered Haman's face.   Esth. 1:6; 6:12

9 And Harbonah, one of the chamberlains, said before the king, Behold also, the gallows fifty cubits high, which Haman had made for Mordecai, who had spoken good for the king, standeth in the house of Haman. Then the king said, Hang him thereon.   Esth. 5:14

10 So they hanged Haman on the gallows that he had prepared for Mordecai. Then was the king's wrath pacified.

Mordecai Is Promoted

8 On that day did the king Ahasuerus give the house of Haman the Jews' enemy unto Esther the queen. And Mordecai came before the king; for Esther had told what he *was* unto her.   Esth. 2:7, 15; 7:6

2 And the king took off his ring, which he had taken from Haman, and gave it unto Mordecai. And Esther set Mordecai over the house of Haman.   Gen. 41:42; Esth. 3:10; Dan. 2:48

8:2–8 God's Intervention

God wrought marvelously for His penitent people; and a counter decree issued by the king, allowing them to fight for their lives, was rapidly communicated to every part of the realm by mounted couriers, who were "hastened and pressed on by the king's commandment" (Esther 8:14). *PK 602*

Esther Makes a Plea to Reverse Haman's Letters

3 And Esther spake yet again before the king, and fell down at his feet, and ᵀbesought him with tears to put away the mischief of Haman the Agagite, and his device that he had devised against the Jews.   begged

4 Then the king held out the golden sceptre toward Esther. So Esther arose, and stood before the king,   Esth. 4:11; 5:2

5 And said, If it please the king, and if I have found favour in his sight, and the thing *seem* right before the king, and I *be* pleasing in his eyes, let it be written to reverse the letters devised by Haman the son of Hammedatha the Agagite, which he wrote to destroy the Jews which *are* in all the king's provinces: Esth. 7:3

6 For how can I endure to see the evil that shall come unto my people? or how can I endure to see the destruction of my kindred?   Esth. 7:4

7 Then the king Ahasuerus said unto Esther the queen and to Mordecai the Jew, Behold, I have given Esther the house of Haman, and him they have hanged upon the gallows, because he laid his hand upon the Jews.

8 Write ye also for the Jews, as it liketh you, in the king's name, and seal *it* with the king's ring: for the writing which is written in the king's name, and sealed with the king's ring, may no man reverse.   Esth. 1:19; 3:12; Dan. 6:8

9 Then were the king's scribes called at that time in the third month, that *is*, the month Sivan, on the three and twentieth *day* thereof; and it was written according to all that Mordecai commanded unto the Jews, and to the lieutenants, and the deputies and rulers of the provinces which *are* from India unto Ethiopia, an hundred twenty and seven provinces, unto every province according to the writing thereof, and unto every people after their language, and to the Jews according to their writing, and according to their language.   Esth. 1:1, 22

10 And he wrote in the king Ahasuerus' name, and sealed *it* with the king's ring, and sent letters by posts on horseback, *and* riders on mules, camels, *and* young dromedaries:

11 Wherein the king granted the Jews which *were* in every city to gather themselves together, and to stand for their life, to destroy, to slay, and to cause to perish, all the power of the people and province that would assault them, *both* little ones and women, and *to take* the ᵀspoil of them for a prey, Esth. 3:13 ♦ *plunder*

12 Upon one day in all the provinces of king Ahasuerus, *namely*, upon the thirteenth *day* of the twelfth month, which *is* the month Adar.   Esth. 9:1

13 The copy of the writing for a commandment to be given in every province *was* published unto all people, and that the Jews should be ready against that day to avenge themselves on their enemies.   Esth. 3:14

14 *So* the posts that rode upon mules *and* camels went out, being hastened and pressed on by the king's commandment. And the decree was given at Shushan the palace.

Mordecai's Honor and the Joy of the Jews

15 And Mordecai went out from the presence of the king in royal apparel of blue and white, and with a great crown of gold, and with a garment of fine linen and purple: and the city of Shushan rejoiced and was glad.   Gen. 41:42; Esth. 1:6; 3:15

16 The Jews had light, and gladness, and joy, and honour.   Ps. 97:11

17 And in every province, and in every city, whithersoever the king's commandment and his decree came, the Jews had joy and gladness, a feast and a good day. And many of the people of the land became Jews; for the fear of the Jews fell upon them. Ex. 15:16; Deut. 11:25

The Jews Defend Themselves and Slay Their Enemies

9 Now in the twelfth month, that *is,* the month Adar, on the thirteenth day of the same, when the king's commandment and his decree drew near to be put in execution, in the day that the enemies of the Jews hoped to have power over them, (though it was turned to the contrary, that the Jews had rule over them that hated them;)   Esth. 3:13; 8:12

2 The Jews gathered themselves together in their cities throughout all the provinces of the king Ahasuerus, to lay hand on such as sought their hurt: and no man could withstand them; for the fear of them fell upon all people.   Esth. 8:11, 17; Ps. 71:13

3 And all the rulers of the provinces, and the lieutenants, and the deputies, and officers of the king, helped the Jews; because the fear of Mordecai fell upon them.   Ezra 8:36

4 For Mordecai *was* great in the king's house, and his fame went out throughout all the provinces: for this man Mordecai ᵀwaxed greater and greater. 2 Sam. 3:1; 1 Chr. 11:9 ◆ *became*

5 Thus the Jews smote all their enemies with the stroke of the sword, and slaughter, and destruction, and did what they would unto those that hated them.

6 And in Shushan the palace the Jews slew and destroyed five hundred men.

7 And Parshandatha, and Dalphon, and Aspatha,

8 And Poratha, and Adalia, and Aridatha,

9 And Parmashta, and Arisai, and Aridai, and Vajezatha,

10 The ten sons of Haman the son of Hammedatha, the enemy of the Jews, slew they; but on the ᵀspoil laid they not their hand.   Gen. 14:23; Esth. 5:11; 8:11 ◆ *plunder*

11 On that day the number of those that were slain in Shushan the palace was brought before the king.

12 And the king said unto Esther the queen, The Jews have slain and destroyed five hundred men in Shushan the palace, and the ten sons of Haman; what have they done in the rest of the king's provinces? now what

is thy petition? and it shall be granted thee: or what *is* thy request further? and it shall be done.   Esth. 5:6; 7:2

13 Then said Esther, If it please the king, let it be granted to the Jews which *are* in Shushan to do to morrow also according unto this day's decree, and let Haman's ten sons be hanged upon the gallows.   Esth. 8:11

14 And the king commanded it so to be done: and the decree was given at Shushan; and they hanged Haman's ten sons.

15 For the Jews that *were* in Shushan gathered themselves together on the fourteenth day also of the month Adar, and slew three hundred men at Shushan; but on the prey they laid not their hand.   Esth. 8:11

16 But the other Jews that *were* in the king's provinces gathered themselves together, and stood for their lives, and had rest from their enemies, and slew of their foes seventy and five thousand, but they laid not their hands on the prey,   Lev. 26:7-8; Esth. 8:11; 9:2

17 On the thirteenth day of the month Adar; and on the fourteenth day of the same rested they, and made it a day of feasting and gladness.   Esth. 9:1

18 But the Jews that *were* at Shushan assembled together on the thirteenth *day* thereof, and on the fourteenth thereof; and on the fifteenth *day* of the same they rested, and made it a day of feasting and gladness.

19 Therefore the Jews of the villages, that dwelt in the unwalled towns, made the fourteenth day of the month Adar *a day of* gladness and feasting, and a good day, and of sending portions one to another.   Esth. 9:22

Mordecai and Esther Institute the Festival of Purim

20 And Mordecai wrote these things, and sent letters unto all the Jews that *were* in all the provinces of the king Ahasuerus, *both* nigh and far,

21 To stablish *this* among them, that they should keep the fourteenth day of the month Adar, and the fifteenth day of the same, yearly,

22 As the days wherein the Jews rested from their enemies, and the month which was

---

Persecution Past and Future

Esther

The trying experiences that came to God's people in the days of Esther were not peculiar to that age alone. The revelator, looking down the ages to the close of time, has declared, "The dragon was wroth with the woman, and went to make war with the remnant of her seed, which keep the commandments of God, and have the testimony of Jesus Christ" (Revelation 12:17). Some who today are living on the earth will see these words fulfilled. The same spirit that in ages past led men to persecute the true church, will in the future lead to the pursuance of a similar course toward those who maintain their loyalty to God. Even now preparations are being made for this last great conflict. *PK 605*

turned unto them from sorrow to joy, and from mourning into a good day: that they should make them days of feasting and joy, and of sending portions one to another, and gifts to the poor. Ps. 30:11

23 And the Jews undertook to do as they had begun, and as Mordecai had written unto them;

24 Because Haman the son of Hammedatha, the Agagite, the enemy of all the Jews, had devised against the Jews to destroy them, and had cast Pur, that *is*, the lot, to consume them, and to destroy them;

25 But when *Esther* came before the king, he commanded by letters that his wicked device, which he devised against the Jews, should return upon his own head, and that he and his sons should be hanged on the gallows. Ps. 7:16

26 Wherefore they called these days Purim after the name of Pur. Therefore for all the words of this letter, and *of that* which they had seen concerning this matter, and which had come unto them, Esth. 9:20

27 The Jews ordained, and took upon them, and upon their seed, and upon all such as joined themselves unto them, so as it should not fail, that they would keep these two days according to their writing, and according to their *appointed* time every year; Esth. 8:17

28 And *that* these days *should be* remembered and kept throughout every generation, every family, every province, and every city; and *that* these days of Purim should not fail from among the Jews, nor the memorial of them perish from their seed.

29 Then Esther the queen, the daughter of Abihail, and Mordecai the Jew, wrote with all authority, to confirm this second letter of Purim. Esth. 9:20

30 And he sent the letters unto all the Jews, to the hundred twenty and seven provinces of the kingdom of Ahasuerus, *with* words of peace and truth, Esth. 1:1; 8:9

31 To confirm these days of Purim in their times *appointed*, according as Mordecai the Jew and Esther the queen had [T]enjoined them, and as they had decreed for themselves and for their seed, the matters of the fastings and their cry. Esth. 4:3, 16 ◆ commanded

32 And the decree of Esther confirmed these matters of Purim; and it was written in the book.

Mordecai's Greatness

10 And the king Ahasuerus laid a tribute upon the land, and *upon* the isles of the sea. Ps. 72:10; Is. 24:15

2 And all the acts of his power and of his might, and the declaration of the greatness of Mordecai, whereunto the king advanced him, *are* they not written in the book of the chronicles of the kings of Media and Persia? Esth. 2:23; 8:15; 9:4

10:3 God's Favor Manifest

Mordecai was given the position of honor formerly occupied by Haman. He "was next unto King Ahasuerus, and great among the Jews, and accepted of the multitude of his brethren" (Esther 10:3); and he sought to promote the welfare of Israel. Thus did God bring His chosen people once more into favor at the Medo-Persian court. . . . *PK 602*

---

3 For Mordecai the Jew *was* next unto king Ahasuerus, and great among the Jews, and accepted of the multitude of his brethren, seeking the wealth of his people, and speaking peace to all his seed. 2 Chr. 28:7; Neh. 2:10

THE BOOK OF

JOB

Job is the quintessential godly man—described in the text as "perfect and upright, and one that feared God, and eschewed evil" (1:1). His story, however, is the story of suffering, thanks to Satan's intervention in his life—intervention allowed by God. The book opens with the curtains pulled back for the reader to see the conversation in heaven between God and Satan. The readers, therefore, are privy to information about the cause of Job's suffering that Job and his friends are not. We understand that the trials are a test of Job's faithfulness; Job does not, but he passes the test. His faith questions but stays strong despite the incessant talk from his friends about his supposed sinfulness as cause for his suffering.

In the end, Job questions God's justness in allowing him to suffer and demands an answer. God does speak to Job, but reproves him for questioning His sovereignty. When Job repents of his demand to know why and simply accepts who God is, God blesses him. The friends, who encouraged Job to forsake God, are reprimanded and told to offer sacrifices and burnt offerings to atone for their sinful words to Job. And "the LORD blessed the latter end of Job more than his beginning" (42:12).

Dates

The dates of the events of Job are uncertain, but several clues anchor them to the times of the patriarchs (Abraham was born about 1950 B.C.; Jacob entered Egypt about 1660 B.C.; the Exodus began about 1445 B.C.):

(1) *Job's age:* Job lived about 200 years, similar to the age of Abraham (175 years—Genesis 25:7).

(2) *Job's wealth:* His wealth was counted in livestock (Job 1:3; 42:12) rather than in the later trade metals like gold or silver.

(3) *Job's position:* Job is the priest of his family, similar to Abraham, Isaac, and Jacob, and offers sacrifices.

(4) *Job's name for God:* Job referred to God as *Shaddai* ("the Almighty") and Yahweh ("The LORD"), both of which are rare and ancient names for God. No mention is made of the Exodus in the book of Job. Thus, Moses likely wrote it during his time in Midian, which would have been about 1485–1445 B.C.

Author

Many authors have been suggested for the Book of Job, including Moses, Elihu, Solomon, Isaiah, Hezekiah, Jeremiah, Baruch, Ezra, and even Job himself. Although not unanimously, early Jewish tradition gives credence to Moses as the author. When Moses dwelled in Midian for forty years, he was near Job's homeland, Uz (1:1). Moreover, Moses had the education of a prince of Egypt and would likely have been able to transcribe ancient texts left by Job or Elihu. Also, noticeable likenesses of writing style are exhibited between Job and the Pentateuch. For example, words and terms that are used in these books appear nowhere else in the Old Testament.

Meaning of the Name

Job is *Iyyôb*, a Hebrew word for "Persecuted One." In the Arabic, it means "repent" or "to Come Back." Both meanings have relevance to the story of Job, so both are acceptable.

Christ in Job

The message of Job is a strong one for every believer. Just as with Job, we are not to depend on our own righteousness or see ourselves as righteous outside of God. Jesus' sacrifice alone makes us righteous. We have no ability in ourselves to reach that state of being (Romans 10:9–10).

Job mentions his redeemer (Job 19:25–27), who would come in the person of Jesus. He also seeks a mediator (9:33). Jesus is also our Mediator with God (Hebrews 4:15). Also, when God speaks (Job 38—41), He clearly reveals His divineness, using the phenomenon of creation to make His point. God's progression in His speeches is the antithesis of the repetitive speeches of Job's friends.

The book of Job can be divided into three sections:

(1) *Job 1—2, Tragedy Strikes:* Here we see Job as a righteous man—the "greatest of all the men of the east" (1:3). He has wealth, a family, and a sterling reputation. He is also conscientious about his family's relationships with God. Job makes sacrifices for his sons "continually" (1:5) to keep them in good standing. But Job's life alters after Satan, the accuser, and God have two talks about Job. Satan assumes that Job will curse God if everything Job possesses is taken from him. Unbeknownst to Job, midway through chapter 1, God allows Satan to attack Job on three fronts: his wealth, his children, and his body. Job's wife tells him to curse God, but Job refuses and goes into deep mourning.

(2) *Job 3—37, Tragedy Debated:* Three friends of Job—Eliphaz, Bildad, and Zophar—come to console Job. Job asks his friends to correct him if he's done wrong (6:24), and they falsely accuse him of being wicked. Despite his friends' harsh words about God, Job still does not see God as an enemy, although he does feel like God is treating him as such. Job also has a sense of remoteness and inaccessibility to God. Job has no understanding as to why, so he has an intense desire to speak directly with God about his case (19:6-13; 23:3-5; 30:20; 31). Elihu then adds to the debate, first chiding Job's friends for falsely accusing Job, then chiding Job for questioning God's sovereignty (chapters 32—37).

(3) *Job 38—42, Tragedy Overturned:* God provides the final perspective on the situation (38—41), adding that Job has no right to instruct Him (40:2). Job repents and makes a sacrifice for himself and for his friends, which God receives (42:3-9). God blesses Job with more sons and daughters and doubles his wealth.

Unlocking Job

KEY PEOPLE:
God, Job, Satan, Elihu, Eliphaz, Bildad, Zophar

KEY EVENTS:
Job's sacrifices; Satan afflicts Job; Job's lament and argument with his friends; Elihu's chiding of Job; God's talk with Job; Job's repentance and restoration

KEY WORD:
Sovereignty. While Job debated the reason behind his suffering, the key issue was God's allowing of said suffering. Many besides Job have struggled with this issue. Is God still good if the righteous suffer? God's perspective on the matter (chapters 38—41) shows His sovereignty over the universe.

KEY VERSES:
"Though he slay me, yet will I trust in him: but I will maintain mine own ways before him. He also shall be my salvation: for an hypocrite shall not come before him" (Job 13:15, 16).

"Touching the Almighty, we cannot find him out: he is excellent in power, and in judgment, and in plenty of justice: he will not afflict. Men do therefore fear him: he respecteth not any that are wise of heart" (Job 37:23-24).

KEY CHAPTER:
Job 42. After a long struggle, Job's life has now come full circle. He finally admits to the error of questioning God's inerrant righteousness.

Job's Life, Family, and Faith

1 There was a man in the land of Uz, whose name *was* Job; and that man was perfect and upright, and one that feared God, and ᵀeschewed evil.   Gen. 6:9; 17:1; Jer. 25:20 ◆ *avoided*

2 And there were born unto him seven sons and three daughters.   Job 42:13

3 His substance also was seven thousand sheep, and three thousand camels, and five hundred yoke of oxen, and five hundred she asses, and a very great household; so that this man was the greatest of all the men of the east.   Job 29:25

4 And his sons went and feasted *in their* houses, every one his day; and sent and called for their three sisters to eat and to drink with them.

5 And it was so, when the days of *their* feasting were gone about, that Job sent and sanctified them, and rose up early in the morning, and offered burnt offerings *according* to the number of them all: for Job said, It may be that my sons have sinned, and cursed God in their hearts. Thus did Job continually.   Gen. 8:20; 1 Kin. 21:10; Job 42:8

Satan Asks to Test Job

6 Now there was a day when the sons of God came to present themselves before the LORD, and Satan came also among them.   1 Chr. 21:1

7 And the LORD said unto Satan, Whence comest thou? Then Satan answered the LORD, and said, From going to and fro in the earth, and from walking up and down in it.   Job 2:2; 1 Pet. 5:8

8 And the LORD said unto Satan, Hast thou considered my servant Job, that *there is* none like him in the earth, a perfect and an upright man, one that feareth God, and ᵀescheweth evil?   Job 1:1; 2:3 ◆ *avoids*

9 Then Satan answered the LORD, and said, Doth Job fear God for ᵀnought?   *nothing*

10 Hast not thou made an hedge about him, and about his house, and about all that he hath on every side? thou hast blessed the work of his hands, and his substance is increased in the land.   Job 31:25; Ps. 34:7

1:6–12 The Ministry of Sorrow

For those who love God, those who are "the called according to His purpose" (Romans 8:28), Bible biography has a yet higher lesson of the ministry of sorrow. "Ye are My witnesses, saith the Lord, that I am God" (Isaiah 43:12)—witnesses that He is good, and that goodness is supreme. "We are made a theater unto the world, both (R.V., margin) to angels, and to men" (1 Corinthians 4:9, margin). *Ed 154*

---

11 But put forth thine hand now, and touch all that he hath, and he will curse thee to thy face.   Job 1:5; 2:5; 19:21

12 And the LORD said unto Satan, Behold, all that he hath *is* in thy power; only upon himself put not forth thine hand. So Satan went forth from the presence of the LORD.

Job Holds Fast Under Great Stress

Job 1

Unselfishness, the principle of God's kingdom, is the principle that Satan hates; its very existence he denies. . . . To disprove Satan's claim is the work of Christ and of all who bear His name. . . .

To choose the right because it is right; to stand for truth at the cost of suffering and sacrifice—"this is the heritage of the servants of the Lord, and their righteousness is of Me, saith the Lord" (Isaiah 54:17).

Very early in the history of the world is given the life record of one over whom this controversy of Satan's was waged.

Of Job, the patriarch of Uz, the testimony of the Searcher of hearts was, "There is none like him . . ." (Job 1:8).

Against this man, Satan brought scornful charge: "Doth Job fear God for nought? . . ." (Job 1:9) "touch his bone and his flesh, and he will curse Thee to Thy face" (Job 2:5).

The Lord said unto Satan, "All that he hath is in thy power." "Behold, he is in thine hand; but save his life."

Thus permitted, Satan swept away all that Job possessed—flocks and herds, menservants and maidens, sons and daughters; and he "smote Job with sore boils from the sole of his foot unto his crown" (Job 1:8–12; 2:5–7).

Still another element of bitterness was added to [Job's] cup. His friends, seeing in adversity but the retribution of sin, pressed on his bruised and burdened spirit their accusations of wrongdoing.

Seemingly forsaken of heaven and earth, yet holding fast his faith in God and his consciousness of integrity, in anguish and perplexity he cried: "My soul is weary of my life" (Job 10:1). . . .

According to his faith, so was it unto Job. "When He hath tried me," he said, "I shall come forth as gold" (Job 23:10). So it came to pass. By his patient endurance he vindicated his own character, and thus the character of Him whose representative he was. *Ed 154–156*

Job Loses His Family and Wealth

13 And there was a day when his sons and his daughters *were* eating and drinking wine in their eldest brother's house:

14 And there came a messenger unto Job, and said, The oxen were plowing, and the asses feeding beside them:

15 And the Sabeans fell *upon them,* and took them away; yea, they have slain the servants with the edge of the sword; and I only am escaped alone to tell thee. Gen. 10:7

16 While he *was* yet speaking, there came also another, and said, The fire of God is fallen from heaven, and hath burned up the sheep, and the servants, and consumed them; and I only am escaped alone to tell thee. Gen. 19:24

17 While he *was* yet speaking, there came also another, and said, The Chaldeans made out three bands, and fell upon the camels, and have carried them away, yea, and slain the servants with the edge of the sword; and I only am escaped alone to tell thee. Gen. 11:28

18 While he *was* yet speaking, there came also another, and said, Thy sons and thy daughters *were* eating and drinking wine in their eldest brother's house: Job 1:4

19 And, behold, there came a great wind from the wilderness, and smote the four corners of the house, and it fell upon the young men, and they are dead; and I only am escaped alone to tell thee.

20 Then Job arose, and ᵀrent his mantle, and shaved his head, and fell down upon the ground, and worshipped, Gen. 37:29, 34 ◆ *tore*

21 And said, Naked came I out of my mother's womb, and naked shall I return thither: the LORD gave, and the LORD hath taken away; blessed be the name of the LORD. Eph. 5:20

22 In all this Job sinned not, nor charged God foolishly. Job 2:10

Satan Asks to Test Job Further

2 Again there was a day when the sons of God came to present themselves before the LORD, and Satan came also among them to present himself before the LORD. Heb. 1:14

2 And the LORD said unto Satan, From whence comest thou? And Satan answered the LORD, and said, From going to and fro in the earth, and from walking up and down in it.

3 And the LORD said unto Satan, Hast thou considered my servant Job, that *there is* none like him in the earth, a perfect and an upright man, one that feareth God, and ᵀescheweth evil? and still he holdeth fast his integrity, although thou movedst me against him, to destroy him without cause. Job 1:1 ◆ *avoids*

4 And Satan answered the LORD, and said,

Skin for skin, yea, all that a man hath will he give for his life.

5 But put forth thine hand now, and touch his bone and his flesh, and he will curse thee to thy face. Job 1:5, 11

6 And the LORD said unto Satan, Behold, he *is* in thine hand; but save his life. Job 1:12

Job Loses His Health

7 So went Satan forth from the presence of the LORD, and smote Job with sore boils from the sole of his foot unto his crown. Deut. 28:27

> **2:5, 7 Satan Destroys; God Restores**
>
> Sickness, suffering, and death are work of an antagonistic power. Satan is the destroyer; God is the restorer. *MH 113*

8 And he took him a potsherd to scrape himself ᵀwithal; and he sat down among the ashes. Job 42:6; Ezek. 27:30; Jon. 3:6 ◆ *with*

9 Then said his wife unto him, Dost thou still retain thine integrity? curse God, and die. Job 2:3

10 But he said unto her, Thou speakest as one of the foolish women speaketh. What? shall we receive good at the hand of God, and shall we not receive evil? In all this did not Job sin with his lips. Job 1:21-22; Ps. 39:1

> **2:9, 10 Job: Deprived, Afflicted, Abhorred**
>
> Job was deprived of his worldly possessions, and so afflicted in body that he was abhorred by his relatives and friends; yet he maintained his integrity. *AA 575*

Three Friends Mourn with Him in Silence

11 Now when Job's three friends heard of all this evil that was come upon him, they came every one from his own place; Eliphaz the Temanite, and Bildad the Shuhite, and Zophar the Naamathite: for they had made an appointment together to come to mourn with him and to comfort him. Gen. 25:2; Rom. 12:15

12 And when they lifted up their eyes afar off, and knew him not, they lifted up their voice, and wept; and they ᵀrent every one his mantle, and sprinkled dust upon their heads toward heaven. Neh. 9:1; Lam. 2:10 ◆ *tore*

13 So they sat down with him upon the ground seven days and seven nights, and none spake a word unto him: for they saw that *his* grief was very great. Gen. 50:10; Ezek. 3:15

Job Curses the Day He Was Born

3 After this opened Job his mouth, and cursed his day.

2 And Job spake, and said,

3 Let the day perish wherein I was born, and

the night *in which* it was said, There is a man child conceived. Job 10:18-19

4 Let that day be darkness; let not God regard it from above, neither let the light shine upon it.

5 Let darkness and the shadow of death stain it; let a cloud dwell upon it; let the blackness of the day terrify it. Job 10:21-22

6 *As for* that night, let darkness seize upon it; let it not be joined unto the days of the year, let it not come into the number of the months.

7 Lo, let that night be solitary, let no joyful voice come therein.

8 Let them curse it that curse the day, who are ready to raise up their mourning.

9 Let the stars of the twilight thereof be dark; let it look for light, but *have* none; neither let it see the dawning of the day: Job 41:18

10 Because it shut not up the doors of my *mother's* womb, nor hid sorrow from mine eyes.

11 Why died I not from the womb? *why* did I *not* give up the ghost when I came out of the belly?

12 Why did the knees ᵀprevent me? or why the breasts that I should suck? *receive*

13 For now should I have lain still and been quiet, I should have slept: then had I been at rest,

> **3:3, 11–13, 16 Great Trials Come to All**
>
> Into the experience of all there come times of keen disappointment and utter discouragement—days when sorrow is the portion, and it is hard to believe that God is still the kind benefactor of His earthborn children; days when troubles harass the soul, till death seems preferable to life. *PK 162*

14 With kings and counsellors of the earth, which built desolate places for themselves;

15 Or with princes that had gold, who filled their houses with silver:

16 Or as an hidden untimely birth I had not been; as infants *which* never saw light. Ps. 58:8

17 There the wicked cease *from* troubling; and there the weary be at rest. Job 17:16

18 *There* the prisoners rest together; they hear not the voice of the oppressor. Job 39:7

19 The small and great are there; and the servant *is* free from his master.

Job: Why Live a Life of Anguish?

20 Wherefore is light given to him that is in misery, and life unto the bitter *in* soul;

21 Which long for death, but it *cometh* not; and dig for it more than for hid treasures;

22 Which rejoice exceedingly, *and* are glad, when they can find the grave?

23 *Why is light given* to a man whose way is hid, and whom God hath hedged in? Job 19:8

24 For my sighing cometh before I eat, and my roarings are poured out like the waters.

25 For the thing which I greatly feared is come upon me, and that which I was afraid of is come unto me.

26 I was not in safety, neither had I rest, neither was I quiet; yet trouble came.

Eliphaz Tells Job to be Patient

4 Then Eliphaz the Temanite answered and said,

2 If we ᵀassay to commune with thee, wilt thou be grieved? but who can withhold himself from speaking? Job 32:18-20 ♦ *attempt*

3 Behold, thou hast instructed many, and thou hast strengthened the weak hands. Is. 35:3

4 Thy words have upholden him that was falling, and thou hast strengthened the feeble knees. Heb. 12:12

> **4:3, 4 Speak Encouraging Words**
>
> As followers of Christ we should make our words such as to be a help and an encouragement to one another in the Christian life. *COL 338*

5 But now it is come upon thee, and thou faintest; it toucheth thee, and thou art troubled. Job 19:21

6 *Is* not *this* thy fear, thy confidence, thy hope, and the uprightness of thy ways? Prov. 3:26

Eliphaz: Only Evil People Suffer

7 Remember, I pray thee, who *ever* perished, being innocent? or where were the righteous cut off? Ps. 37:25

8 Even as I have seen, they that plow iniquity, and sow wickedness, reap the same. Prov. 22:8

9 By the blast of God they perish, and by the breath of his nostrils are they consumed.

10 The roaring of the lion, and the voice of the fierce lion, and the teeth of the young lions, are broken. Job 29:17; Ps. 3:7; 58:6

11 The old lion perisheth for lack of prey, and the ᵀstout lion's whelps are scattered abroad. Ps. 34:10 ♦ *strong*

Eliphaz: Purity Before God Is Impossible

12 Now a thing was secretly brought to me, and mine ear received a little thereof. Job 26:14

13 In thoughts from the visions of the night, when deep sleep falleth on men, Gen. 2:21

14 Fear came upon me, and trembling, which made all my bones to shake. Hab. 3:16

15 Then a spirit passed before my face; the hair of my flesh stood up:

16 It stood still, but I could not discern the form thereof: an image *was* before mine

eyes, *there was* silence, and I heard a voice, saying,
1 Kin. 19:12

17 Shall mortal man be more just than God? shall a man be more pure than his maker?
Job 9:2; 25:4

After Death See Ezekiel 18:20.

18 Behold, he put no trust in his servants; and his angels he charged with folly:

19 How much less *in* them that dwell in houses of clay, whose foundation *is* in the dust, *which* are crushed before the moth?

20 They are destroyed from morning to evening: they perish for ever without any regarding *it*.
Job 20:7

21 Doth not their excellency *which is* in them go away? they die, even without wisdom.

Eliphaz: Seek God's Help

5 Call now, if there be any that will answer thee; and to which of the saints wilt thou turn?
Job 15:15

2 For wrath killeth the foolish man, and envy slayeth the silly one.

3 I have seen the foolish taking root: but suddenly I cursed his habitation. Ps. 37:35-36

4 His children are far from safety, and they are crushed in the gate, neither *is there* any to deliver *them*.
Ps. 119:155

5 Whose harvest the hungry eateth up, and taketh it even out of the thorns, and the robber swalloweth up their substance.

6 Although affliction cometh not forth of the dust, neither doth trouble spring out of the ground;

7 Yet man is born unto trouble, as the sparks fly upward.
Gen. 3:17-19; Job 14:1

8 I would seek unto God, and unto God would I commit my cause:
Ps. 50:15

9 Which doeth great things and unsearchable; marvellous things without number:

10 Who giveth rain upon the earth, and sendeth waters upon the fields: Ps. 147:8

11 To set up on high those that be low; that those which mourn may be exalted to safety.

12 He disappointeth the devices of the crafty, so that their hands cannot perform *their* enterprise.
Neh. 4:15

13 He taketh the wise in their own craftiness: and the counsel of the ᵀfroward is carried headlong.
Ps. 9:15-16 ◆ *false, perverse*

14 They meet with darkness in the daytime, and grope in the noonday as in the night.
Deut. 28:29; Job 12:25; Is. 59:10

15 But he saveth the poor from the sword, from their mouth, and from the hand of the mighty.
Ps. 35:10

16 So the poor hath hope, and iniquity stoppeth her mouth.
Ps. 63:11; 107:42

Eliphaz: The Blessing of God's Correction

17 Behold, happy *is* the man whom God correcteth: therefore despise not thou the chastening of the Almighty:
Ps. 94:12; Heb. 12:5-11

18 For he maketh sore, and bindeth up: he woundeth, and his hands make whole. Is. 30:26

19 He shall deliver thee in six troubles: yea, in seven there shall no evil touch thee. Ps. 34:19

20 In famine he shall redeem thee from death: and in war from the power of the sword.
Ps. 33:19

21 Thou shalt be hid from the ᵀscourge of the tongue: neither shalt thou be afraid of destruction when it cometh. Ps. 31:20 ◆ *whip*

22 At destruction and famine thou shalt laugh: neither shalt thou be afraid of the beasts of the earth.
Is. 35:9; 65:25; Ezek. 34:25

23 For thou shalt be in league with the stones of the field: and the beasts of the field shall be at peace with thee.

24 And thou shalt know that thy tabernacle *shall be* in peace; and thou shalt visit thy habitation, and shalt not sin.

25 Thou shalt know also that thy seed *shall*

Suffering Is From Satan, Not God

Job 5

It was generally believed by the Jews that sin is punished in this life. Every affliction was regarded as the penalty of some wrongdoing, either of the sufferer himself or of his parents. It is true that all suffering results from the transgression of God's law, but this truth had become perverted. Satan, the author of sin and all its results, had led men to look upon disease and death as proceeding from God—as punishment arbitrarily inflicted on account of sin. Hence one upon whom some great affliction or calamity had fallen had the additional burden of being regarded as a great sinner.

Thus the way was prepared for the Jews to reject Jesus. He who "hath borne our griefs, and carried our sorrows" was looked upon by the Jews as "stricken, smitten of God, and afflicted;" and they hid their faces from Him (Isaiah 53:4, 3).

God had given a lesson designed to prevent this. The history of Job had shown that suffering is inflicted by Satan, and is overruled by God for purposes of mercy. But Israel did not understand the lesson. The same error for which God had reproved the friends of Job was repeated by the Jews in their rejection of Christ. DA 471

be great, and thine offspring as the grass of the earth. Ps. 72:16; 112:2

26 Thou shalt come to *thy* grave in a full age, like as a shock of corn cometh in in his season. Gen. 15:15

27 Lo this, we have searched it, so it *is*; hear it, and know thou *it* for thy good. Ps. 111:2

Job: God Has Attacked Me without Cause

6 But Job answered and said,

2 Oh that my grief were throughly weighed, and my calamity laid in the balances together!

3 For now it would be heavier than the sand of the sea: therefore my words are swallowed up. Prov. 27:3

4 For the arrows of the Almighty *are* within me, the poison whereof drinketh up my spirit: the terrors of God do set themselves in array against me. Job 30:15; Ps. 38:2; 88:15-16

5 Doth the wild ass bray when he hath grass? or loweth the ox over his fodder?

6 Can that which is unsavoury be eaten without salt? or is there *any* taste in the white of an egg? Lev. 2:13

7 The things *that* my soul refused to touch *are* as my sorrowful meat.

Job: I Desire the Comfort of Death

8 Oh that I might have my request; and that God would grant *me* the thing that I long for!

9 Even that it would please God to destroy me; that he would let loose his hand, and cut me off! 1 Kin. 19:4

10 Then should I yet have comfort; yea, I would harden myself in sorrow: let him not spare; for I have not concealed the words of the Holy One. Lev. 19:2

11 What *is* my strength, that I should hope? and what *is* mine end, that I should prolong my life?

12 *Is* my strength the strength of stones? or *is* my flesh of brass?

13 *Is* not my help in me? and is wisdom driven quite from me?

> **6:14 Kindness: As Cold Water to the Thirsty**
>
> Kind words, looks of sympathy, expressions of appreciation, would be to many a struggling and lonely one as the cup of cold water to a thirsty soul. A word of sympathy, an act of kindness, would lift burdens that rest heavily upon weary shoulders. *MB 23*

Job: You Are Treating Me Unkindly

14 To him that is afflicted pity *should be* shewed from his friend; but he forsaketh the fear of the Almighty. Prov. 17:17

15 My brethren have dealt deceitfully as a brook, *and* as the stream of brooks they pass away; Ps. 38:11; 41:9; Jer. 15:18

16 Which are blackish by reason of the ice, *and* wherein the snow is hid:

17 What time they ᵀwax warm, they vanish: when it is hot, they are consumed out of their place. *become*

18 The paths of their way are turned aside; they go to nothing, and perish.

19 The troops of Tema looked, the companies of Sheba waited for them. Gen. 25:15; Is. 21:14

20 They were confounded because they had hoped; they came thither, and were ashamed.

21 For now ye are nothing; ye see *my* casting down, and are afraid. Ps. 38:11

22 Did I say, Bring unto me? or, Give a reward for me of your substance?

23 Or, Deliver me from the enemy's hand? or, Redeem me from the hand of the mighty?

24 Teach me, and I will hold my tongue: and cause me to understand wherein I have erred.

25 How forcible are right words! but what doth your arguing reprove?

26 Do ye imagine to reprove words, and the speeches of one that is desperate, *which are* as wind? Job 8:2

27 Yea, ye overwhelm the fatherless, and ye dig *a pit* for your friend. Job 22:9

> **6:15, 27 Tried by Both Enemies and Friends**
>
> Christians are tried, not only by the anger, contempt, and cruelty of enemies, but by the indolence, inconsistency, lukewarmness, and treachery of avowed friends and helpers. Derision and reproach are hurled at them. *PK 644, 645*

28 Now therefore be content, look upon me; for *it is* evident unto you if I lie.

29 Return, I pray you, let it not be iniquity; yea, return again, my righteousness *is* in it.

30 Is there iniquity in my tongue? cannot my taste discern perverse things? Job 12:11

Job: Human Existence Is Futile

7 *Is there* not an appointed time to man upon earth? *are not* his days also like the days of ᵀan hireling? Job 14:5-6 ◆ *a temporary laborer*

2 As a servant earnestly desireth the shadow, and as an hireling looketh for *the reward of* his work: Lev. 19:13

3 So am I made to possess months of vanity, and wearisome nights are appointed to me. Ps. 6:6

4 When I lie down, I say, When shall I arise, and the night be gone? and I am full of tossings to and fro unto the dawning of the day. Deut. 28:67; Job 7:13-14

5 My flesh is clothed with worms and clods

of dust; my skin is broken, and become loathsome. *Job 17:14*

6 My days are swifter than a weaver's shuttle, and are spent without hope. *Job 9:25; 17:11, 15*

Job: I Loathe My Life

7 O remember that my life *is* wind: mine eye shall no more see good. *Ps. 78:39; James 4:14*

8 The eye of him that hath seen me shall see me no *more*: thine eyes *are* upon me, and I *am* not. *Job 20:9; Ps. 37:36*

9 *As* the cloud is consumed and vanisheth away: so he that goeth down to the grave shall come up no *more*. *2 Sam. 12:23*

10 He shall return no more to his house, neither shall his place know him any more.

> **After Death** See Job 21:32.

11 Therefore I will not refrain my mouth; I will speak in the anguish of my spirit; I will complain in the bitterness of my soul. *Ps. 40:9*

12 *Am* I a sea, or a whale, that thou settest a watch over me?

13 When I say, My bed shall comfort me, my couch shall ease my complaint; *Ps. 6:6*

14 Then thou scarest me with dreams, and terrifiest me through visions:

15 So that my soul chooseth strangling, *and* death rather than my life.

16 I loathe *it*; I would not live alway: let me alone; for my days *are* vanity. *Job 6:9; 9:21; 10:1*

> **7:11, 15, 16 Hope for Weary Job**
>
> . . . But though weary of life, Job was not allowed to die. To him were pointed out the possibilities of the future, and there was given him the message of hope. *PK 163*

17 What *is* man, that thou shouldest magnify him? and that thou shouldest set thine heart upon him? *Ps. 8:4; 144:3; Heb. 2:6*

18 And *that* thou shouldest visit him every morning, *and* try him every moment?

19 How long wilt thou not depart from me, nor let me alone till I swallow down my spittle?

20 I have sinned; what shall I do unto thee, O thou preserver of men? why hast thou set me as a mark against thee, so that I am a burden to myself? *Ps. 36:6*

21 And why dost thou not pardon my ᵀtransgression, and take away mine iniquity? for now shall I sleep in the dust; and thou shalt seek me in the morning, but I *shall* not *be*. *Job 10:14 ♦ violation of a law*

Bildad: You Are Unjustly Accusing God

8 Then answered Bildad the Shuhite, and said, *Job 2:11*

2 How long wilt thou speak these *things*? and *how* long *shall* the words of thy mouth *be* like a strong wind? *Job 6:26*

3 Doth God pervert judgment? or doth the Almighty pervert justice? *Gen. 18:25; Deut. 32:4*

4 If thy children have sinned against him, and he have cast them away for their ᵀtransgression; *Job 1:5 ♦ violation of a law*

5 If thou wouldest seek unto God ᵀbetimes, and make thy supplication to the Almighty; *Job 11:13 ♦ early*

6 If thou *wert* pure and upright; surely now he would awake for thee, and make the habitation of thy righteousness prosperous. *Ps. 7:6*

7 Though thy beginning was small, yet thy latter end should greatly increase.

> **8:4–7 Spirit of Christ; Spirit of Pharisaism**
>
> The spirit of Pharisaism is the spirit of human nature; and as the Saviour showed the contrast between His own spirit and methods and those of the rabbis, His teaching is equally applicable to the people of all time.
>
> In the days of Christ the Pharisees were continually trying to earn the favor of Heaven in order to secure the worldly honor and prosperity which they regarded as the reward of virtue. *MB 79*

Bildad: God Does Not Punish the Innocent

8 For enquire, I pray thee, of the former age, and prepare thyself to the search of their fathers: *Deut. 4:32; 32:7; Job 15:18*

9 (For we *are but of* yesterday, and know nothing, because our days upon earth *are* a shadow:) *1 Chr. 29:15*

10 Shall not they teach thee, *and* tell thee, and utter words out of their heart?

11 Can the ᵀrush grow up without ᵀmire? can the flag grow without water? *reed ♦ mud*

12 Whilst it *is* yet in his greenness, *and* not cut down, it withereth before any *other* herb. *Jer. 17:6*

13 So *are* the paths of all that forget God; and the hypocrite's hope shall perish: *Job 13:16; 15:34*

14 Whose hope shall be cut off, and whose trust *shall be* a spider's web. *Is. 59:5-6*

15 He shall lean upon his house, but it shall not stand: he shall hold it fast, but it shall not endure. *Job 27:18*

16 He *is* green before the sun, and his branch shooteth forth in his garden. *Ps. 80:11*

17 His roots are wrapped about the heap, *and* seeth the place of stones.

18 If he destroy him from his place, then *it* shall deny him, *saying*, I have not seen thee. *Job 7:10*

19 Behold, this *is* the joy of his way, and out of the earth shall others grow. *Job 20:5*

20 Behold, God will not cast away a perfect *man*, neither will he help the evil doers: *Job 4:7*

7:9, 10

21 Till he fill thy mouth with laughing, and thy lips with rejoicing. Gen. 21:6; Ps. 126:2
22 They that hate thee shall be clothed with shame; and the dwelling place of the wicked shall come to nought. Ps. 35:26; 109:29; 132:18

Job: It Is Futile to Argue with God

9 Then Job answered and said,
2 I know *it is* so of a truth: but how should man be just with God? Job 4:17; 25:4; Ps. 143:2

> **9:2 Made Righteous Only Through Christ**
>
> How shall a man be just with God? How shall the sinner be made righteous? It is only through Christ that we can be brought into harmony with God, with holiness. *SC 23*

3 If he will contend with him, he cannot answer him one of a thousand. Job 10:2; 40:2
4 *He is* wise in heart, and mighty in strength: who hath hardened *himself* against him, and hath prospered? Job 36:5
5 Which removeth the mountains, and they know not: which overturneth them in his anger.
6 Which shaketh the earth out of her place, and the pillars thereof tremble. Job 26:11; Is. 2:21
7 Which commandeth the sun, and it riseth not; and sealeth up the stars. Is. 13:10
8 Which alone spreadeth out the heavens, and treadeth upon the waves of the sea.
9 Which maketh Arcturus, Orion, and Pleiades, and the chambers of the south. Gen. 1:16
10 Which doeth great things past finding out; yea, and wonders without number.

> **9:8–10 Unreachable Depths and Heights**
>
> He who studies most deeply into the mysteries of nature will realize most fully his own ignorance and weakness. He will realize that there are depths and heights which he cannot reach, secrets which he cannot penetrate, vast fields of truth lying before him unentered. *Ed 133*

11 Lo, he goeth by me, and I see *him* not: he passeth on also, but I perceive him not.
12 Behold, he taketh away, who can hinder him? who will say unto him, What doest thou? Job 11:10; 23:13; Is. 45:9
13 *If* God will not withdraw his anger, the proud helpers do stoop under him. Is. 30:7
14 How much less shall I answer him, *and* choose out my words *to reason* with him?
15 Whom, though I were righteous, *yet* would I not answer, *but* I would make supplication to my judge. Job 8:5; 10:15
16 If I had called, and he had answered me; *yet* would I not believe that he had hearkened unto my voice.

17 For he breaketh me with a ᵀtempest, and multiplieth my wounds without cause. Job 2:3
18 He will not suffer me to take my breath, but filleth me with bitterness. Job 7:19
19 If *I speak* of strength, lo, *he is* strong: and if of judgment, who shall set me a time *to* plead? Job 9:4
20 If I justify myself, mine own mouth shall condemn me: *if I say,* I *am* perfect, it shall also prove me perverse.
21 *Though* I *were* perfect, *yet* would I not know my soul: I would despise my life. Job 1:1
22 This *is* one *thing,* therefore I said *it,* He destroyeth the perfect and the wicked.
23 If the ᵀscourge slay suddenly, he will laugh at the trial of the innocent. whip
24 The earth is given into the hand of the wicked: he covereth the faces of the judges thereof; if not, where, *and* who *is* he? Job 10:3
25 Now my days are swifter than a post: they flee away, they see no good. Job 7:6-7
26 They are passed away as the swift ships: as the eagle *that* hasteth to the prey. Is. 18:2
27 If I say, I will forget my complaint, I will leave off my heaviness, and comfort *myself:* Job 7:13
28 I am afraid of all my sorrows, I know that thou wilt not hold me innocent. Ps. 119:120
29 *If* I be wicked, why then labour I in vain?
30 If I wash myself with snow water, and make my hands never so clean; Jer. 2:22
31 Yet shalt thou plunge me in the ditch, and mine own clothes shall ᵀabhor me. despise
32 For *he is* not a man, as I *am, that* I should answer him, *and* we should come together in judgment. Ps. 143:2; Eccl. 6:10; Rom. 9:20
33 Neither is there any daysman ᵀbetwixt us, *that* might lay his hand upon us both. between
34 Let him take his rod away from me, and let not his fear terrify me: Ps. 39:10
35 *Then* would I speak, and not fear him; but *it is* not so with me.

Job: My Soul Is Weary of My Life

10 My soul is weary of my life; I will leave my complaint upon myself; I will speak in the bitterness of my soul. Num. 11:15
2 I will say unto God, Do not condemn me; shew me wherefore thou contendest with me. Job 9:29

> **10:1, 2 God Hears Our Cries**
>
> Let all who are afflicted or unjustly used, cry to God. . . . Not one sincere prayer is lost. . . . God hears the cries of the weakest human being. *COL 174*

3 *Is it* good unto thee that thou shouldest oppress, that thou shouldest despise the work of thine hands, and shine upon the counsel of the wicked? Job 14:15; Ps. 138:8; Is. 64:8

4 Hast thou eyes of flesh? or seest thou as man seeth?   1 Sam. 16:7

5 *Are* thy days as the days of man? *are* thy years as man's days,   2 Pet. 3:8

6 That thou enquirest after mine iniquity, and searchest after my sin?   Job 14:16

7 Thou knowest that I am not wicked; and *there is* none that can deliver out of thine hand.   Deut. 32:39

8 Thine hands have made me and fashioned me together round about; yet thou dost destroy me.   Job 10:3; Ps. 119:73

9 Remember, I ᵀbeseech thee, that thou hast made me as the clay; and wilt thou bring me into dust again?   Gen. 2:7 ◆ *beg*

10 Hast thou not poured me out as milk, and curdled me like cheese?

11 Thou hast clothed me with skin and flesh, and hast fenced me with bones and sinews.

12 Thou hast granted me life and favour, and thy visitation hath preserved my spirit.

13 And these *things* hast thou hid in thine heart: I know that this *is* with thee.   Job 23:13

14 If I sin, then thou markest me, and thou wilt not acquit me from mine iniquity.   Job 7:21

15 If I be wicked, woe unto me; and *if* I be righteous, *yet* will I not lift up my head. *I am* full of confusion; therefore see thou mine affliction;   Job 9:15; 10:7; Is. 3:11

16 For it increaseth. Thou huntest me as a fierce lion: and again thou shewest thyself marvellous upon me.   Job 5:9; Is. 38:13; Lam. 3:10

17 Thou renewest thy witnesses against me, and increasest thine ᵀindignation upon me; changes and war *are* against me.   Ruth 1:21 ◆ *anger*

18 Wherefore then hast thou brought me forth out of the womb? Oh that I had given up the ghost, and no eye had seen me!

19 I should have been as though I had not been; I should have been carried from the womb to the grave.

20 *Are* not my days few? cease *then, and* let me alone, that I may take comfort a little,

21 Before I go *whence* I shall not return, *even* to the land of darkness and the shadow of death;   2 Sam. 12:23; Job 3:5; Ps. 23:4

22 A land of darkness, as darkness *itself; and* of the shadow of death, without any order, and *where* the light *is* as darkness.

Zophar: God Can Do As He Pleases

11 Then answered Zophar the Naamathite, and said,   Job 2:11

2 Should not the multitude of words be answered? and should a man full of talk be justified?   Job 18:2

3 Should thy lies make men hold their peace? and when thou mockest, shall no man make thee ashamed?   Job 17:2

4 For thou hast said, My doctrine *is* pure, and I am clean in thine eyes.   Job 6:10; 10:7

5 But oh that God would speak, and open his lips against thee;

6 And that he would shew thee the secrets of wisdom, that *they are* double to that which is! Know therefore that God exacteth of thee *less* than thine iniquity *deserveth.*   Ezra 9:13

7 Canst thou by searching find out God? canst thou find out the Almighty unto perfection?   Job 5:9; Eccl. 3:11; Rom. 11:33

8 *It is* as high as heaven; what canst thou do? deeper than hell; what canst thou know?

9 The measure thereof *is* longer than the earth, and broader than the sea.

> **11:7–9 God Beyond Our Comprehension**
>
> The mightiest intellects of earth cannot comprehend God. Men may be ever searching, ever learning, and still there is an infinity beyond. *PP 116*

10 If he cut off, and shut up, or gather together, then who can hinder him?   Job 9:12-13

11 For he knoweth vain men: he seeth wickedness also; will he not then consider *it?*

12 For vain man would be wise, though man be born *like* a wild ass's colt.   Job 39:5-8

Zophar: Confess Your Sin and Be Forgiven

13 If thou prepare thine heart, and stretch out thine hands toward him;   Ps. 78:8; 88:9

14 If iniquity *be* in thine hand, put it far away, and let not wickedness dwell in thy tabernacles.   Job 22:23

15 For then shalt thou lift up thy face without spot; yea, thou shalt be ᵀstedfast, and shalt not fear: Job 22:26 ◆ *steadfast*

16 Because thou shalt forget *thy* misery, *and* remember *it* as waters *that* pass away: Is. 65:16

17 And *thine* age shall be clearer than the noonday; thou shalt shine forth, thou shalt be as the morning.   Ps. 37:6

> **11:11–20 Those Who Accuse God's Servants**
>
> Accusers of the brethren are not few, and they are always active when God is at work and His servants are rendering Him true homage. They will put a false coloring upon the words and acts of those who love and obey the truth. They will represent the most earnest, zealous, self-denying servants of Christ as deceived or deceivers. *GC 519*

18 And thou shalt be secure, because there is hope; yea, thou shalt dig *about thee, and* thou shalt take thy rest in safety.   Lev. 26:5-6

19 Also thou shalt lie down, and none shall make *thee* afraid; yea, many shall make suit unto thee.   Ps. 45:12

20 But the eyes of the wicked shall fail, and they shall not escape, and their hope *shall be as* the giving up of the ghost.   Deut. 28:65

Job: You Have No Wisdom

12 And Job answered and said,
2 No doubt but ye *are* the people, and wisdom shall die with you.
3 But I have understanding as well as you; I *am* not inferior to you: yea, who knoweth not such things as these?
4 I am *as* one mocked of his neighbour, who calleth upon God, and he answereth him: the just upright *man is* laughed to scorn.   Job 17:6
5 He that is ready to slip with *his* feet *is as* a lamp despised in the thought of him that is at ease.
6 The tabernacles of robbers prosper, and they that provoke God are secure; into whose hand God bringeth *abundantly*.   Job 9:24
7 But ask now the beasts, and they shall teach thee; and the fowls of the air, and they shall tell thee:
8 Or speak to the earth, and it shall teach thee: and the fishes of the sea shall declare unto thee.
9 Who knoweth not in all these that the hand of the LORD hath ᵀwrought this? Is. 41:20 ◆ *done*
10 In whose hand *is* the soul of every living thing, and the breath of all mankind.   Job 27:3

> **12:7–10 Hymn of the Levites**
>
> In the hymn recorded by Nehemiah, the Levites sang, "Thou, even Thou, art Lord alone; Thou hast made heaven, the heaven of heavens, with all their host, the earth, and all things that are therein, the seas, and all that is therein, and Thou preservest them all" (Nehemiah 9:6). *Ed 130*

11 Doth not the ear try words? and the mouth taste his meat?   Job 34:3

Job: Wisdom Comes from God

12 With the ancient *is* wisdom; and in length of days understanding.   Job 15:10; 32:7
13 With him *is* wisdom and strength, he hath counsel and understanding. Job 9:4; 36:5
14 Behold, he breaketh down, and it cannot be built again: he shutteth up a man, and there can be no opening.   Job 11:10
15 Behold, he withholdeth the waters, and they dry up: also he sendeth them out, and they overturn the earth.   1 Kin. 17:1
16 With him *is* strength and wisdom: the deceived and the deceiver *are* his.
17 He leadeth counsellors away spoiled, and maketh the judges fools.   2 Sam. 17:23
18 He looseth the bond of kings, and girdeth their ᵀloins with a ᵀgirdle. Ps. 116:16 ◆ *waist* ◆ *belt*

19 He leadeth princes away spoiled, and overthroweth the mighty.
20 He removeth away the speech of the trusty, and taketh away the understanding of the aged.   Job 17:4; 32:9
21 He poureth contempt upon princes, and weakeneth the strength of the mighty.
22 He discovereth deep things out of darkness, and bringeth out to light the shadow of death.   Job 3:5; Dan. 2:22; 1 Cor. 4:5
23 He increaseth the nations, and destroyeth them: he enlargeth the nations, and ᵀstraiteneth them *again*. Ps. 107:38; Is. 9:3; 26:15 ◆ *lessens*
24 He taketh away the heart of the chief of the people of the earth, and causeth them to wander in a wilderness *where there is* no way.   Ps. 107:40
25 They grope in the dark without light, and he maketh them to stagger like *a* drunken *man*.   Job 5:14; Ps. 107:27; Is. 19:14

> **12:23–25 God at Work in Human History**
>
> In the annals of human history, the growth of nations, the rise and fall of empires, appear as if dependent on the will and prowess of man; the shaping of events seems, to a great degree, to be determined by his power, ambition, or caprice. But in the word of God the curtain is drawn aside, and we behold, above, behind, and through all the play and counterplay of human interest and power and passions, the agencies of the All-merciful One, silently, patiently working out the counsels of His own will. *PK 499, 500*

Job: Though God Slay Me, I Will Trust Him

13 Lo, mine eye hath seen all *this*, mine ear hath heard and understood it.
2 What ye know, *the same* do I know also: I *am* not inferior unto you.   Job 12:3
3 Surely I would speak to the Almighty, and I desire to reason with God.   Job 13:22
4 But ye *are* forgers of lies, ye *are* all physicians of no value.   Job 16:2; Ps. 119:69
5 O that ye would altogether hold your peace! and it should be your wisdom.   Prov. 17:28
6 Hear now my reasoning, and hearken to the pleadings of my lips.
7 Will ye speak wickedly for God? and talk deceitfully for him?   Job 36:4
8 Will ye accept his person? will ye contend for God?   Prov. 24:23
9 Is it good that he should search you out? or as one man mocketh another, do ye *so* mock him?
10 He will surely reprove you, if ye do secretly accept persons.
11 Shall not his excellency make you afraid? and his dread fall upon you?   Job 31:23

12 Your remembrances *are* like unto ashes, your bodies to bodies of clay.
13 Hold your peace, let me alone, that I may speak, and let come on me what *will*.　Job 13:5
14 Wherefore do I take my flesh in my teeth, and put my life in mine hand?　　Judg. 12:3
15 Though he slay me, yet will I trust in him: but I will maintain mine own ways before him.　　Job 27:5; Ps. 23:4; Prov. 14:32
16 He also *shall be* my salvation: for an hypocrite shall not come before him.

13:15, 16 Job's Triumphant Trust

From the depths of discouragement and despondency Job rose to the heights of implicit trust in the mercy and the saving power of God. Triumphantly he declared: "Though He slay me, yet will I trust in Him: . . . He also shall be my salvation" (Job 13:15, 16). *PK 163, 164*

Job: God, Please Hear Me

17 Hear diligently my speech, and my declaration with your ears.
18 Behold now, I have ordered *my* cause; I know that I shall be justified.　　Job 23:4

13:18 God Will Vindicate Us

God is acquainted with all that is misunderstood and misinterpreted by men, and we can safely leave our case in His hands. He will as surely vindicate the cause of those who put their trust in Him. . . . *PP 520*

19 Who *is* he *that* will plead with me? for now, if I hold my tongue, I shall give up the ghost.
20 Only do not two *things* unto me: then will I not hide myself from thee.
21 Withdraw thine hand far from me: and let not thy dread make me afraid.　　Job 9:34
22 Then call thou, and I will answer: or let me speak, and answer thou me.　　Job 14:15

23 How many *are* mine iniquities and sins? make me to know my ᵀtransgression and my sin.　　　　　　*violation of a law*
24 Wherefore hidest thou thy face, and holdest me for thine enemy?　Deut. 32:20; Lam. 2:5
25 Wilt thou break a leaf driven to and fro? and wilt thou pursue the dry stubble?
26 For thou writest bitter things against me, and makest me to possess the iniquities of my youth.　　　　　　Ps. 25:7
27 Thou puttest my feet also in the stocks, and lookest narrowly unto all my paths; thou settest a print upon the heels of my feet.　　　　　　Job 33:11
28 And he, as a rotten thing, consumeth, as a garment that is moth eaten.　　Job 4:19

Job: God, Consider My Frail Human Nature

14 Man *that is* born of a woman *is* of few days, and full of trouble.　Gen. 47:9
2 He cometh forth like a flower, and is cut down: he fleeth also as a shadow, and continueth not.　　Job 8:9; 1 Pet. 1:24
3 And dost thou open thine eyes upon such an one, and bringest me into judgment with thee?　　　Ps. 8:4; 143:2; 144:3
4 Who can bring a clean *thing* out of an unclean? not one.　Job 15:14; Ps. 51:5; John 3:6

14:4 We Cannot Change Our Hearts

It is impossible for us, of ourselves, to escape from the pit of sin in which we are sunken. Our hearts are evil, and we cannot change them. . . . Education, culture, the exercise of the will, human effort, all have their proper sphere, but here they are powerless. They may produce an outward correctness of behavior, but they cannot change the heart. *SC 18*

5 Seeing his days *are* determined, the number of his months *are* with thee, thou hast appointed his bounds that he cannot pass;　　　Job 7:1; 21:21; Ps. 39:4

God's Personal Love for Us

Job 13

Keep your wants, your joys, your sorrows, your cares, and your fears before God. You cannot burden Him; you cannot weary Him. He who numbers the hairs of your head is not indifferent to the wants of His children. "The Lord is very pitiful, and of tender mercy" (James 5:11). His heart of love is touched by our sorrows and even by our utterances of them. Take to Him everything that perplexes the mind. Nothing is too great for Him to bear, for He holds up worlds, He rules over all the affairs of the universe. Nothing that in any way concerns our peace is too small for Him to notice. There is no chapter in our experience too dark for Him to read; there is no perplexity too difficult for Him to unravel. No calamity can befall the least of His children, no anxiety harass the soul, no joy cheer, no sincere prayer escape the lips, of which our heavenly Father is unobservant, or in which He takes no immediate interest. "He healeth the broken in heart, and bindeth up their wounds" (Psalm 147:3). The relations between God and each soul are as distinct and full as though there were not another soul upon the earth to share His watchcare, not another soul for whom He gave His beloved Son. *SC 100*

6 Turn from him, that he may rest, till he shall accomplish, as an hireling, his day.

7 For there is hope of a tree, if it be cut down, that it will sprout again, and that the tender branch thereof will not cease.

8 Though the root thereof ᵀwax old in the earth, and the stock thereof die in the ground;   *become*

9 *Yet* through the scent of water it will bud, and bring forth boughs like a plant.

10 But man dieth, and wasteth away: yea, man giveth up the ghost, and where *is* he?

11 *As* the waters fail from the sea, and the flood decayeth and drieth up: Is. 19:5

12 So man lieth down, and riseth not: till the heavens *be* no more, they shall not awake, nor be raised out of their sleep.   Job 3:13

13 O that thou wouldest hide me in the grave, that thou wouldest keep me secret, until thy wrath be past, that thou wouldest appoint me a set time, and remember me!

14 If a man die, shall he live *again*? all the days of my appointed time will I wait, till my change come.   Job 7:1

15 Thou shalt call, and I will answer thee: thou wilt have a desire to the work of thine hands.   Job 10:3

16 For now thou numberest my steps: dost thou not watch over my sin? Job 10:6; 31:4; 34:21

17 My transgression *is* sealed up in a bag, and thou sewest up mine iniquity. Deut. 32:34

18 And surely the mountain falling cometh to ᵀnought, and the rock is removed out of his place.   Job 18:4 ♦ *nothing*

19 The waters wear the stones: thou washest away the things which grow *out* of the dust of the earth; and thou destroyest the hope of man.

20 Thou prevailest for ever against him, and he passeth: thou changest his ᵀcountenance, and sendest him away.   *appearance*

21 His sons come to honour, and he knoweth *it* not; and they are brought low, but he perceiveth *it* not of them.   Eccl. 9:5; Is. 63:16

14:10–12, 21 The Dead Know Nothing

The Bible clearly teaches that the dead do not go immediately to heaven. They are represented as sleeping until the resurrection (1 Thessalonians 4:14; Job 14:10–12). . . . . They that go down to the grave are in silence. They know no more of anything that is done under the sun (Job 14:21). *GC 550*

---

22 But his flesh upon him shall have pain, and his soul within him shall mourn.

Eliphaz: You Are Speaking Sinfully

15 Then answered Eliphaz the Temanite, and said,   Job 2:11

2 Should a wise man utter vain knowledge, and fill his belly with the east wind? Job 6:26

3 Should he reason with unprofitable talk? or with speeches wherewith he can do no good?

4 Yea, thou castest off fear, and restrainest prayer before God.

5 For thy mouth uttereth thine iniquity, and thou choosest the tongue of the crafty.

6 Thine own mouth condemneth thee, and not I: yea, thine own lips testify against thee.   Luke 19:22

15:2–6 We're Not Qualified to Judge Others

"Judge nothing before the time . . ." (1 Corinthians 4:5). We cannot read the heart. Ourselves faulty, we are not qualified to sit in judgment upon others. Finite men can judge only from outward appearance. To Him alone who knows the secret springs of action, and who deals tenderly and compassionately, is it given to decide the case of every soul. *MB 124*

---

7 *Art* thou the first man *that* was born? or wast thou made before the hills?   Ps. 90:2

8 Hast thou heard the secret of God? and dost thou restrain wisdom to thyself?   Rom. 11:34

9 What knowest thou, that we know not? *what* understandest thou, which *is* not in us?   Job 13:2

10 With us *are* both the grayheaded and very aged men, much elder than thy father. Job 32:6-7

11 *Are* the consolations of God small with thee? is there any secret thing with thee?

12 Why doth thine heart carry thee away? and what do thy eyes wink at,

13 That thou turnest thy spirit against God, and lettest *such* words go out of thy mouth?

14 What *is* man, that he should be clean? and *he which is* born of a woman, that he should be righteous? Job 14:4; Prov. 20:9; Eccl. 7:20

15 Behold, he putteth no trust in his saints; yea, the heavens are not clean in his sight.

16 How much more abominable and filthy *is* man, which drinketh iniquity like water?

Eliphaz: Wicked People Live Tortured Lives

17 I will shew thee, hear me; and that *which* I have seen I will declare;

18 Which wise men have told from their fathers, and have not hid *it*:   Job 8:8

19 Unto whom alone the earth was given, and no stranger passed among them. Joel 3:17

20 The wicked man travaileth with pain all *his* days, and the number of years is hidden to the oppressor.   Job 24:1

21 A dreadful sound *is* in his ears: in prosperity the destroyer shall come upon him.

22 He believeth not that he shall return out of darkness, and he is waited for of the sword.

23 He wandereth abroad for bread, *saying,*

Where *is it?* he knoweth that the day of darkness is ready at his hand. Ps. 59:15

24 Trouble and anguish shall make him afraid; they shall prevail against him, as a king ready to the battle.

25 For he stretcheth out his hand against God, and strengtheneth himself against the Almighty.

26 He runneth upon him, *even* on *his* neck, upon the thick bosses of his bucklers:

27 Because he covereth his face with his fatness, and maketh collops of fat on *his* flanks. Ps. 17:10

28 And he dwelleth in desolate cities, *and* in houses which no man inhabiteth, which are ready to become heaps. Job 3:14

29 He shall not be rich, neither shall his substance continue, neither shall he prolong the perfection thereof upon the earth. Job 27:16-17

30 He shall not depart out of darkness; the flame shall dry up his branches, and by the breath of his mouth shall he go away. Job 4:9

31 Let not him that is deceived trust in vanity: for vanity shall be his recompence. Is. 59:4

32 It shall be accomplished before his time, and his branch shall not be green. Job 22:16

33 He shall shake off his unripe grape as the vine, and shall cast off his flower as the olive.

34 For the congregation of hypocrites *shall be* desolate, and fire shall consume the tabernacles of bribery. Job 8:13

35 They conceive mischief, and bring forth vanity, and their belly prepareth deceit.

Job: You, My Friends, Lack Mercy

16 Then Job answered and said,

2 I have heard many such things: miserable comforters *are* ye all.

3 Shall vain words have an end? or what emboldeneth thee that thou answerest? Job 6:26

4 I also could speak as ye *do*: if your soul were in my soul's stead, I could heap up words against you, and shake mine head at you. Ps. 22:7; 109:25; Lam. 2:15

5 *But* I would strengthen you with my mouth, and the moving of my lips should ᵀassuage *your grief.* relieve

16:1–5 Friends Who Depress and Dishearten

Oh, how often those who think themselves the friends of a good man, and who are eager to show their fidelity to him, prove to be his most dangerous enemies! How often, instead of strengthening his faith, their words depress and dishearten! *DA 215*

6 Though I speak, my grief is not ᵀassuaged: and *though* I forbear, what am I eased? subsided

7 But now he hath made me weary: thou hast made desolate all my company. Job 7:3

8 And thou hast filled me with wrinkles, *which* is a witness *against me*: and my leanness rising up in me beareth witness to my face. Ruth 1:21; Job 10:17

Job: My Eyes Pour Out Tears to God

9 He teareth *me* in his wrath, who hateth me: he gnasheth upon me with his teeth; mine enemy sharpeneth his eyes upon me. Ps. 35:16

10 They have gaped upon me with their mouth; they have smitten me upon the cheek reproachfully; they have gathered themselves together against me. Ps. 22:13; 35:15; Is. 50:6

11 God hath delivered me to the ungodly, and turned me over into the hands of the wicked.

12 I was at ease, but he hath broken me ᵀasunder: he hath also taken *me* by my neck, and shaken me to pieces, and set me up for his mark. Job 7:20 ♦ apart

13 His archers ᵀcompass me round about, he ᵀcleaveth my ᵀreins asunder, and doth not spare; he poureth out my gall upon the ground. Job 20:25 ♦ surround ♦ splits ♦ desires

14 He breaketh me with breach upon breach, he runneth upon me like a giant.

15 I have sewed sackcloth upon my skin, and defiled my horn in the dust. Ps. 7:5

16 My face is foul with weeping, and on my eyelids *is* the shadow of death;

17 Not for *any* injustice in mine hands: also my prayer *is* pure.

18 O earth, cover not thou my blood, and let my cry have no place. Is. 26:21

19 Also now, behold, my witness *is* in heaven, and my record *is* on high. Rom. 1:9

20 My friends scorn me: *but* mine eye poureth out *tears* unto God.

21 O that one might plead for a man with God, as a man *pleadeth* for his neighbour!

22 When a few years are come, then I shall go the way *whence* I shall not return. Eccl. 12:5

16:19–22 Jesus Our Advocate

The books of record in heaven, in which the names and the deeds of men are registered, are to determine the decisions of the judgment. . . .

The righteous dead will not be raised until after the judgment at which they are accounted worthy of "the resurrection of life." Hence they will not be present in person at the tribunal when their records are examined and their cases decided.

Jesus will appear as their advocate, to plead in their behalf before God. *GC 480–482*

Job: You, My Friends, Have No Wisdom

17 My breath is corrupt, my days are extinct, the graves *are ready* for me.

2 *Are there* not mockers with me? and doth

not mine eye continue in their provocation? *1 Sam. 1:6-7*

3 Lay down now, put me in a surety with thee; who *is* he *that* will strike hands with me? *Prov. 11:15*

4 For thou hast hid their heart from understanding: therefore shalt thou not exalt *them.*

5 He that speaketh flattery to *his* friends, even the eyes of his children shall fail. *Job 11:20*

6 He hath made me also a byword of the people; and aforetime I was as a tabret. *Job 30:9*

7 Mine eye also is dim by reason of sorrow, and all my members *are* as a shadow. *Job 16:16*

8 Upright *men* shall be ᵀastonied at this, and the innocent shall stir up himself against the hypocrite.   *surprised*

9 The righteous also shall hold on his way, and he that hath clean hands shall be stronger and stronger. *Prov. 4:18*

10 But as for you all, do ye return, and come now: for I cannot find *one* wise *man* among you. *Job 6:29*

11 My days are past, my purposes are broken off, *even* the thoughts of my heart. *Job 7:6*

12 They change the night into day: the light *is* short because of darkness.

13 If I wait, the grave *is* mine house: I have made my bed in the darkness.

14 I have said to corruption, Thou *art* my father: to the worm, Thou *art* my mother, and my sister. *Ps. 16:10*

15 And where *is* now my hope? as for my hope, who shall see it?

16 They shall go down to the bars of the pit, when *our* rest together *is* in the dust. *Job 3:17-19*

17:1, 15, 16 Trusting When All Is Dark

When we are encompassed with doubt, perplexed by circumstances, or afflicted by poverty or distress, Satan seeks to shake our confidence in Jehovah. . . .

Despondency may shake the most heroic faith and weaken the most steadfast will. But God understands, and He still pities and loves. He reads the motives and the purposes of the heart. To wait patiently, to trust when everything looks dark, is the lesson that the leaders in God's work need to learn. Heaven will not fail them in their day of adversity. *PK 174*

Bildad; When Will You Stop Talking?

18 Then answered Bildad the Shuhite, and said, *Job 2:11*

2 How long *will it be* ᵀ*ere* ye make an end of words? mark, and afterwards we will speak.   *before*

3 Wherefore are we counted as beasts, *and* reputed vile in your sight? *Ps. 73:22*

4 He teareth himself in his anger: shall the earth be forsaken for thee? and shall the rock be removed out of his place? *Job 13:14*

Bildad: The Wicked Live in Terror

5 Yea, the light of the wicked shall be put out, and the spark of his fire shall not shine. *Prov. 13:9; 20:20; 24:20*

6 The light shall be dark in his tabernacle, and his candle shall be put out with him.

7 The steps of his strength shall be ᵀstraitened, and his own counsel shall cast him down. *Prov. 4:12* ◆ *hindered*

8 For he is cast into a net by his own feet, and he walketh upon a snare. *Job 22:10*

9 The ᵀgin shall take *him* by the heel, *and* the robber shall prevail against him. *trap*

10 The snare *is* laid for him in the ground, and a trap for him in the way.

11 Terrors shall make him afraid on every side, and shall drive him to his feet. *Jer. 6:25*

12 His strength shall be hungerbitten, and destruction *shall be* ready at his side.

13 It shall devour the strength of his skin: *even* the firstborn of death shall devour his strength. *Is. 14:30*

14 His confidence shall be rooted out of his tabernacle, and it shall bring him to the king of terrors.

15 It shall dwell in his tabernacle, because *it is* none of his: ᵀbrimstone shall be scattered upon his habitation. *Ps. 11:6* ◆ *sulphur*

16 His roots shall be dried up beneath, and above shall his branch be cut off. *Is. 5:24*

17 His remembrance shall perish from the earth, and he shall have no name in the street. *Ps. 34:16; 109:13; Prov. 10:7*

18 He shall be driven from light into darkness, and chased out of the world. *Job 10:22*

19 He shall neither have son nor nephew among his people, nor any remaining in his dwellings. *Jer. 22:30*

20 They that come after *him* shall be ᵀastonied at his day, as they that went before were affrighted. *Ps. 37:13; Jer. 50:27; Ezek. 21:25* ◆ *surprised*

21 Surely such *are* the dwellings of the wicked, and this *is* the place *of him that* knoweth not God. *Jer. 9:3*

18:4–21 Inhumanity of Man to Man

The inhumanity of man toward man is our greatest sin. Many think that they are representing the justice of God while they wholly fail of representing His tenderness and His great love. *MH 163*

Job: God Is Mistreating Me

19 Then Job answered and said, 2 How long will ye ᵀvex my soul, and break me in pieces with words? *trouble*

3 These ten times have ye reproached me:

ye are not ashamed *that* ye make yourselves strange to me. Gen. 31:7

4 And be it indeed *that* I have erred, mine error remaineth with myself.

5 If indeed ye will magnify *yourselves* against me, and plead against me my reproach:

6 Know now that God hath overthrown me, and hath compassed me with his net.

7 Behold, I cry out of wrong, but I am not heard: I cry aloud, but *there is* no judgment.

8 He hath fenced up my way that I cannot pass, and he hath set darkness in my paths.

9 He hath stripped me of my glory, and taken the crown *from* my head. Ps. 89:39, 44; Lam. 5:16

10 He hath destroyed me on every side, and I am gone: and mine hope hath he removed like a tree. Job 24:20

11 He hath also kindled his wrath against me, and he counteth me unto him as *one of* his enemies. Job 13:24; 16:9; 33:10

12 His troops come together, and raise up their way against me, and encamp round about my tabernacle. Job 30:12

13 He hath put my brethren far from me, and mine acquaintance are ᵀverily estranged from me. Ps. 69:8; 88:8, 18 ◆ *truly*

14 My kinsfolk have failed, and my familiar friends have forgotten me. Ps. 38:11

15 They that dwell in mine house, and my maids, count me for a stranger: I am an alien in their sight.

16 I called my servant, and he gave *me* no answer; I intreated him with my mouth.

17 My breath is strange to my wife, though I intreated for the children's *sake* of mine own body.

18 Yea, young children despised me; I arose, and they spake against me. 2 Kin. 2:23

19 All my inward friends abhorred me: and they whom I loved are turned against me.

20 My bone ᵀcleaveth to my skin and to my flesh, and I am escaped with the skin of my teeth. Ps. 102:5; Lam. 4:8 ◆ *clings*

21 Have pity upon me, have pity upon me, O ye my friends; for the hand of God hath touched me. Job 1:11

22 Why do ye persecute me as God, and are not satisfied with my flesh? Ps. 69:26

Job: I Maintain Confidence in My God

23 Oh that my words were now written! oh that they were printed in a book! Is. 30:8

24 That they were ᵀgraven with an iron pen and lead in the rock for ever! Jer. 17:1 ◆ *engraved*

25 For I know *that* my redeemer liveth, and *that* he shall stand at the latter *day* upon the earth: Ps. 19:14

26 And *though* after my skin *worms* destroy this *body*, yet in my flesh shall I see God:

27 Whom I shall see for myself, and mine eyes shall behold, and not another; *though* my ᵀreins be consumed within me. Ps. 73:26 ◆ *desires*

28 But ye should say, Why persecute we him, seeing the root of the matter is found in me? Job 19:22

29 Be ye afraid of the sword: for wrath *bringeth* the punishments of the sword, that ye may know *there is* a judgment.

Zophar: The Wicked Have Little Joy, Much Pain

20 Then answered Zophar the Naamathite, and said, Job 2:11

2 Therefore do my thoughts cause me to answer, and for *this* I make haste.

3 I have heard the ᵀcheck of my reproach, and the spirit of my understanding causeth me to answer. *rebuke*

4 Knowest thou *not* this of old, since man was placed upon earth,

---

Precious Hope of the Second Coming

Job 19:25–27

One of the most solemn and yet most glorious truths revealed in the Bible is that of Christ's second coming to complete the great work of redemption. To God's pilgrim people, so long left to sojourn in "the region and shadow of death," a precious, joy-inspiring hope is given in the promise of His appearing, who is "the resurrection and the life," to "bring home again His banished." The doctrine of the second advent is the very keynote of the Sacred Scriptures. From the day when the first pair turned their sorrowing steps from Eden, the children of faith have waited the coming of the Promised One to break the destroyer's power and bring them again to the lost Paradise. Holy men of old looked forward to the advent of the Messiah in glory, as the consummation of their hope. Enoch, only the seventh in descent from them that dwelt in Eden . . . was permitted to behold from afar the coming of the Deliverer. "Behold," he declared, "the Lord cometh with ten thousands of His saints, to execute judgment upon all" (Jude 14, 15). The patriarch Job in the night of his affliction exclaimed with unshaken trust: "I know that my Redeemer liveth, and that He shall stand at the latter day upon the earth: . . . in my flesh shall I see God: whom I shall see for myself, and mine eyes shall behold, and not another" (Job 19:25–27).

The coming of Christ to usher in the reign of righteousness has inspired the most sublime and impassioned utterances of the sacred writers. GC 299, 300

5 That the triumphing of the wicked *is* short, and the joy of the hypocrite *but* for a moment? Ps. 37:35-36

6 Though his excellency mount up to the heavens, and his head reach unto the clouds;

7 *Yet* he shall perish for ever like his own dung: they which have seen him shall say, Where *is* he? 1 Kin. 14:10

8 He shall fly away as a dream, and shall not be found: yea, he shall be chased away as a vision of the night. Ps. 73:20; 90:5; Is. 29:7-8

9 The eye also *which* saw him shall *see him* no more; neither shall his place any more behold him. Job 7:8, 10; 8:18

10 His children shall seek to please the poor, and his hands shall restore their goods.

11 His bones are full *of the sin* of his youth, which shall lie down with him in the dust.

12 Though wickedness be sweet in his mouth, *though* he hide it under his tongue; Job 15:16

13 *Though* he spare it, and forsake it not; but keep it still within his mouth:

14 *Yet* his meat in his bowels is turned, *it is* the ᵀgall of asps within him. *venom*

15 He hath swallowed down riches, and he shall vomit them up again: God shall cast them out of his belly.

16 He shall suck the poison of asps: the ᵀviper's tongue shall slay him. *snake's*

17 He shall not see the rivers, the floods, the brooks of honey and butter. Deut. 32:13-14

18 That which he laboured for shall he restore, and shall not swallow *it* down: according to *his* substance *shall* the restitution *be*, and he shall not rejoice *therein*. Job 20:10

19 Because he hath oppressed *and* hath forsaken the poor; *because* he hath violently taken away an house which he builded not; Job 35:9

20 Surely he shall not feel quietness in his belly, he shall not save of that which he desired. Eccl. 5:13-14

21 There shall none of his meat be left; therefore shall no man look for his goods.

22 In the fulness of his sufficiency he shall be in straits: every hand of the wicked shall come upon him.

20:23–26 God Is Redemptive, Not Condemning

[God] is not vindictive. He seeks not to punish, but to redeem. Even the severity which He manifests through His providences is manifested for the salvation of the wayward. He yearns with intense desire to relieve the woes of men and to apply His balsam to their wounds. It is true that God "will by no means clear the guilty" (Exodus 34:7), but He would take away the guilt. *MB 22*

---

23 *When* he is about to fill his belly, *God* shall cast the fury of his wrath upon him, and shall rain *it* upon him while he is eating. Num. 11:33

24 He shall flee from the iron weapon, *and* the bow of steel shall strike him through.

25 It is drawn, and cometh out of the body; yea, the glittering sword cometh out of his gall: terrors *are* upon him. Deut. 32:41; Job 16:13

26 All darkness *shall be* hid in his secret places: a fire not blown shall consume him; it shall go ill with him that is left in his tabernacle. Ps. 21:9

27 The heaven shall reveal his iniquity; and the earth shall rise up against him. Job 16:18

28 The increase of his house shall depart, *and his goods* shall flow away in the day of his wrath.

29 This *is* the portion of a wicked man from God, and the heritage appointed unto him by God. Job 18:21; 27:13; 31:2-3

Job: Please Listen and Hear Me, My Friends

21 But Job answered and said,
2 Hear diligently my speech, and let this be your consolations.

3 Suffer me that I may speak; and after that I have spoken, mock on. Job 16:10

4 As for me, *is* my complaint to man? and if *it were so*, why should not my spirit be troubled?

5 Mark me, and be astonished, and lay *your* hand upon *your* mouth. Judg. 18:19; Job 29:9; 40:4

6 Even when I remember I am afraid, and trembling taketh hold on my flesh.

Job: Sometimes the Wicked Do Prosper

7 Wherefore do the wicked live, become old, yea, are mighty in power? Job 12:6

21:7, 13–15, 30 God's Strange Act

[God's] long forbearance with the wicked emboldens men in transgression, but their punishment is nonetheless certain and terrible because it is long delayed. "The Lord shall rise up as in Mount Perazim, He shall be wroth as in the valley of Gibeon, that He may do His work, His strange work; and bring to pass His act, His strange act" (Isaiah 28:21). To our merciful God the act of punishment is a strange act. *GC 627*

---

8 Their seed is established in their sight with them, and their offspring before their eyes.

9 Their houses *are* safe from fear, neither *is* the rod of God upon them. Job 9:34

10 Their bull gendereth, and faileth not; their cow calveth, and casteth not her calf. Ex. 23:26

11 They send forth their little ones like a flock, and their children dance.

12 They take the ᵀtimbrel and harp, and rejoice at the sound of the organ. *tambourine*

13 They spend their days in wealth, and in a moment go down to the grave. Job 36:11
14 Therefore they say unto God, Depart from us; for we desire not the knowledge of thy ways. Job 22:17; Prov. 1:29
15 What *is* the Almighty, that we should serve him? and what profit should we have, if we pray unto him? Ex. 5:2; Job 34:9
16 Lo, their good *is* not in their hand: the counsel of the wicked is far from me. Job 22:18
17 How ᵀoft is the candle of the wicked put out! and *how oft* cometh their destruction upon them! *God* distributeth sorrows in his anger. Job 18:5-6 ◆ *often*
18 They are as stubble before the wind, and as chaff that the storm carrieth away. Ps. 1:4
19 God layeth up his iniquity for his children: he rewardeth him, and he shall know *it.* Ex. 20:5
20 His eyes shall see his destruction, and he shall drink of the wrath of the Almighty.
21 For what pleasure *hath* he in his house after him, when the number of his months is cut off in the midst? Job 14:5

Job: No One Understands God's Dealings
22 Shall *any* teach God knowledge? seeing he judgeth those that are high. Is. 40:13-14
23 One dieth in his full strength, being wholly at ease and quiet.
24 His breasts are full of milk, and his bones are moistened with marrow. Prov. 3:8
25 And another dieth in the bitterness of his soul, and never eateth with pleasure. Job 7:11
26 They shall lie down alike in the dust, and the worms shall cover them. Job 20:11; Eccl. 9:2
27 Behold, I know your thoughts, and the devices *which* ye wrongfully imagine against me.
28 For ye say, Where *is* the house of the prince? and where *are* the dwelling places of the wicked? Job 8:22
29 Have ye not asked them that go by the way? and do ye not know their tokens,
30 That the wicked is reserved to the day of destruction? they shall be brought forth to the day of wrath. Job 20:28; Prov. 16:4
31 Who shall declare his way to his face? and who shall repay him *what* he hath done? Deut. 7:10
32 Yet shall he be brought to the grave, and shall remain in the tomb.

After Death See John 5:28, 29.

33 The clods of the valley shall be sweet unto him, and every man shall draw after him, as *there are* innumerable before him. Job 30:23
34 How then comfort ye me in vain, seeing in your answers there remaineth falsehood? Job 16:2

21:32

Eliphaz: Man's Goodness Does Not Profit God
22 Then Eliphaz the Temanite answered and said,
2 Can a man be profitable unto God, as he that is wise may be profitable unto himself? Luke 17:10
3 *Is it* any pleasure to the Almighty, that thou art righteous? or *is it* gain *to him,* that thou makest thy ways perfect?
4 Will he reprove thee for fear of thee? will he enter with thee into judgment? Ps. 143:2

Eliphaz: Admit You Are Wicked
5 *Is* not thy wickedness great? and thine iniquities infinite?
6 For thou hast taken a pledge from thy brother for ᵀnought, and stripped the naked of their clothing. Ex. 22:26; Ezek. 18:16 ◆ *nothing*
7 Thou hast not given water to the weary to drink, and thou hast withholden bread from the hungry. Job 31:17; Is. 58:7; Ezek. 18:7
8 But *as for* the mighty man, he had the earth; and the honourable man dwelt in it. Is. 9:15
9 Thou hast sent widows away empty, and the arms of the fatherless have been broken. Job 24:3
10 Therefore snares *are* round about thee, and sudden fear troubleth thee; Job 18:8-10
11 Or darkness, *that* thou canst not see; and abundance of waters cover thee. Ps. 69:1-2
12 *Is* not God in the height of heaven? and behold the height of the stars, how high they are! Job 11:8
13 And thou sayest, How doth God know? can he judge through the dark cloud? Ps. 59:7
14 Thick clouds *are* a covering to him, that he seeth not; and he walketh in the circuit of heaven. Ps. 139:11-12
15 Hast thou marked the old way which wicked men have ᵀtrodden? *trampled*
16 Which were cut down out of time, whose foundation was overflown with a flood:
17 Which said unto God, Depart from us: and what can the Almighty do for them?
18 Yet he filled their houses with good *things:* but the counsel of the wicked is far from me. Job 12:6; 21:16
19 The righteous see *it,* and are glad: and the innocent laugh them to scorn. Ps. 52:6; 58:10
20 Whereas our substance is not cut down, but the remnant of them the fire consumeth. Job 1:16

Eliphaz: Repent and Make Peace with God
21 Acquaint now thyself with him, and be at peace: thereby good shall come unto thee.
22 Receive, I pray thee, the law from his mouth, and lay up his words in thine heart. Job 23:12

23 If thou return to the Almighty, thou shalt be built up, thou shalt put away iniquity far from thy tabernacles. Job 11:13-14

24 Then shalt thou lay up gold as dust, and the *gold* of Ophir as the stones of the brooks. 1 Kin. 9:28

25 Yea, the Almighty shall be thy defence, and thou shalt have plenty of silver. Is. 33:6

26 For then shalt thou have thy delight in the Almighty, and shalt lift up thy face unto God. Job 27:10; Ps. 37:4; Is. 58:14

27 Thou shalt make thy prayer unto him, and he shall hear thee, and thou shalt pay thy vows. Job 33:26; Ps. 50:14-15; Is. 58:9

28 Thou shalt also decree a thing, and it shall be established unto thee: and the light shall shine upon thy ways. Ps. 112:4

29 When *men* are cast down, then thou shalt say, *There is* lifting up; and he shall save the humble person. Ps. 138:6; James 4:6; 1 Pet. 5:5

30 He shall deliver the island of the innocent: and it is delivered by the pureness of thine hands.

Job: Where Can I Find God?

23 Then Job answered and said,
2 Even to day *is* my complaint bitter: my stroke is heavier than my groaning. Job 10:1

3 Oh that I knew where I might find him! *that* I might come *even* to his seat! Job 13:3

4 I would order *my* cause before him, and fill my mouth with arguments. Job 13:18

5 I would know the words *which* he would answer me, and understand what he would say unto me.

6 Will he plead against me with *his* great power? No; but he would put *strength* in me. Job 13:21

7 There the righteous might dispute with him; so should I be delivered for ever from my judge.

8 Behold, I go forward, but he *is* not *there*; and backward, but I cannot perceive him:

9 On the left hand, where he doth work, but I cannot behold *him*: he hideth himself on the right hand, that I cannot see *him*:

10 But he knoweth the way that I take: *when* he hath tried me, I shall come forth as gold. Ps. 66:10; 139:1-3; 1 Pet. 1:7

11 My foot hath held his steps, his way have I kept, and not declined. Ps. 17:5; 44:18; 125:5

12 Neither have I gone back from the commandment of his lips; I have esteemed the words of his mouth more than my necessary *food*. John 4:32

Job: God Will Not Change His Mind

13 But he *is* in one *mind*, and who can turn him? and *what* his soul desireth, even *that* he doeth. Ps. 115:3

14 For he performeth *the thing that is* appointed for me: and many such *things are* with him. 1 Thess. 3:3

15 Therefore am I troubled at his presence: when I consider, I am afraid of him.

16 For God maketh my heart soft, and the Almighty troubleth me: Job 27:2

17 Because I was not cut off before the darkness, *neither* hath he covered the darkness from my face. Job 19:8

Job: Wickedness Often Goes Unpunished

24 Why, seeing times are not hidden from the Almighty, do they that know him not see his days? Acts 1:7

2 *Some* remove the landmarks; they violently take away flocks, and feed *thereof*. Deut. 19:14

3 They drive away the ass of the fatherless, they take the widow's ox for a pledge. Deut. 24:6

4 They turn the needy out of the way: the poor of the earth hide themselves together. Job 24:14; Prov. 28:28; Amos 2:7

5 Behold, *as* wild asses in the desert, go they forth to their work; rising Tbetimes for a prey: the wilderness *yieldeth* food for them *and* for *their* children. Job 39:5-7 ◆ *early*

6 They reap *every one* his corn in the field: and they gather the vintage of the wicked.

7 They cause the naked to lodge without clothing, that *they have* no covering in the cold. Ex. 22:26-27

8 They are wet with the showers of the mountains, and embrace the rock for want of a shelter. Lam. 4:5

9 They pluck the fatherless from the breast, and take a pledge of the poor.

10 They cause *him* to go naked without clothing, and they take away the Tsheaf *from* the hungry; *bundle of cut grain*

11 *Which* make oil within their walls, *and* tread *their* winepresses, and suffer thirst.

12 Men groan from out of the city, and the soul of the wounded crieth out: yet God layeth not folly *to them*.

13 They are of those that rebel against the light; they know not the ways thereof, nor abide in the paths thereof.   John 3:19-20

14 The murderer rising with the light killeth the poor and needy, and in the night is as a thief.

15 The eye also of the adulterer waiteth for the twilight, saying, No eye shall see me: and disguiseth his face.   Ps. 10:11

16 In the dark they dig through houses, which they had marked for themselves in the daytime: they know not the light.   John 3:20

17 For the morning is to them even as the shadow of death: if one know them, they are in the terrors of the shadow of death.   Job 3:5

18 He is swift as the waters; their portion is cursed in the earth: he beholdeth not the way of the vineyards.

19 Drought and heat consume the snow waters: so doth the grave those which have sinned.   Job 21:13

20 The womb shall forget him; the worm shall feed sweetly on him; he shall be no more remembered; and wickedness shall be broken as a tree.   Job 18:16-17; Prov. 10:7; Dan. 4:14

21 He evil entreateth the barren that beareth not: and doeth not good to the widow.

22 He draweth also the mighty with his power: he riseth up, and no man is sure of life.

23 Though it be given him to be in safety, whereon he resteth; yet his eyes are upon their ways.   Prov. 15:3

24 They are exalted for a little while, but are gone and brought low; they are taken out of the way as all other, and cut off as the tops of the ears of corn.   Ps. 37:10

25 And if it be not so now, who will make me a liar, and make my speech nothing worth?   Job 9:24

Bildad: No One Is Justified before God

25 Then answered Bildad the Shuhite, and said,

2 Dominion and fear are with him, he maketh peace in his high places.

3 Is there any number of his armies? and upon whom doth not his light arise? James 1:17

4 How then can man be justified with God? or how can he be clean that is born of a woman?   Job 9:2

5 Behold even to the moon, and it shineth not; yea, the stars are not pure in his sight.

6 How much less man, that is a worm? and the son of man, which is a worm?   Ps. 22:6

25:6 Man's Insignificance

As we learn more and more of what God is, and of what we ourselves are in His sight, we shall fear and tremble before Him. MH 435

Job: Your Advice Is Useless

26 But Job answered and said,

2 How hast thou helped him that is without power? how savest thou the arm that hath no strength?

3 How hast thou counselled him that hath no wisdom? and how hast thou plentifully declared the thing as it is?

4 To whom hast thou uttered words? and whose spirit came from thee?

Job: God's Power Is Infinite and Unsearchable

5 Dead things are formed from under the waters, and the inhabitants thereof.   Gen. 6:4

6 Hell is naked before him, and destruction hath no covering.   Ps. 139:8

7 He stretcheth out the north over the empty place, and hangeth the earth upon nothing.   Gen. 1:1-2; Job 9:8; Is. 40:22

8 He bindeth up the waters in his thick clouds; and the cloud is not ᵀrent under them.   Prov. 30:4 ◆ torn apart

9 He holdeth back the face of his throne, and spreadeth his cloud upon it.   Ps. 97:2

10 He hath ᵀcompassed the waters with bounds, until the day and night come to an end.   Job 38:8-11; Ps. 33:7; Prov. 8:29 ◆ enclosed

11 The pillars of heaven tremble and are astonished at his reproof.

12 He divideth the sea with his power, and by his understanding he ᵀsmiteth through the proud.   Is. 51:15; Jer. 31:35 ◆ strikes

13 By his spirit he hath garnished the heavens; his hand hath formed the crooked serpent.   Gen. 1:2; Ps. 104:30; Is. 27:1

14 Lo, these are parts of his ways: but how little a portion is heard of him? but the thunder of his power who can understand?

26:7-14 Mysteries of Nature

The deepest students of science are constrained to recognize in nature the working of infinite power. But to man's unaided reason, nature's teaching cannot but be contradictory and disappointing. Only in the light of revelation can it be read aright. "Through faith we understand" (Hebrews 11:3). Ed 134

Job: I Am Innocent

27 Moreover Job continued his parable, and said,   Num. 23:7

2 As God liveth, who hath taken away my judgment; and the Almighty, who hath vexed my soul;   2 Kin. 4:27; Job 34:5

3 All the while my breath is in me, and the spirit of God is in my nostrils;   Gen. 2:7

4 My lips shall not speak wickedness, nor my tongue utter deceit.   Job 13:7

5 God forbid that I should justify you: till

I die I will not remove mine integrity from me.
Job 2:9

6 My righteousness I hold fast, and will not let it go: my heart shall not reproach *me* so long as I live.
Job 2:3; Acts 24:16

7 Let mine enemy be as the wicked, and he that riseth up against me as the unrighteous.

8 For what *is* the hope of the hypocrite, though he hath gained, when God taketh away his soul?
Job 11:20

9 Will God hear his cry when trouble cometh upon him?
Prov. 1:28; Is. 1:15; Jer. 14:12

10 Will he delight himself in the Almighty? will he always call upon God?
Job 22:26-27

Job: The Wicked Will Face Punishment

11 I will teach you by the hand of God: *that* which *is* with the Almighty will I not conceal.

12 Behold, all ye yourselves have seen *it*; why then are ye thus altogether vain?

13 This *is* the portion of a wicked man with God, and the heritage of oppressors, *which* they shall receive of the Almighty.

14 If his children be multiplied, *it is* for the sword: and his offspring shall not be satisfied with bread.
Deut. 28:41

15 Those that remain of him shall be buried in death: and his widows shall not weep.

16 Though he heap up silver as the dust, and prepare †raiment as the clay; *Zech. 9:3* ♦ *clothing*

17 He may prepare *it*, but the just shall put *it* on, and the innocent shall divide the silver.
Eccl. 2:26

18 He buildeth his house as a moth, and as a booth *that* the keeper maketh.
Job 8:14-15

19 The rich man shall lie down, but he shall not be gathered: he openeth his eyes, and he *is* not.
Job 24:24

20 Terrors take hold on him as waters, a †tempest stealeth him away in the night.
storm

21 The east wind carrieth him away, and he departeth: and as a storm hurleth him out of his place.

22 For *God* shall cast upon him, and not spare: he would †fain flee out of his hand.
desire to

23 *Men* shall clap their hands at him, and shall †hiss him out of his place.
Lam. 2:15 ♦ *mock*

Job: True Wisdom Is God's Alone

28 Surely there is a vein for the silver, and a place for gold *where* they fine *it*.

2 Iron is taken out of the earth, and brass *is* molten *out of* the stone.
Deut. 8:9

3 He setteth an end to darkness, and searcheth out all perfection: the stones of darkness, and the shadow of death.
Eccl. 1:13

4 The flood breaketh out from the inhabitant; *even the waters* forgotten of the foot: they are dried up, they are gone away from men.

5 *As for* the earth, out of it cometh bread: and under it is turned up as it were fire.

6 The stones of it *are* the place of sapphires: and it hath dust of gold.
Ex. 24:10

7 *There is* a path which no fowl knoweth, and which the vulture's eye hath not seen:

8 The lion's whelps have not †trodden it, nor the fierce lion passed by it.
trampled

9 He putteth forth his hand upon the rock; he overturneth the mountains by the roots.

10 He cutteth out rivers among the rocks; and his eye seeth every precious thing.

11 He bindeth the floods from overflowing; and *the thing that is* hid bringeth he forth to light.

12 But where shall wisdom be found? and where *is* the place of understanding? *Job 28:28*

13 Man knoweth not the price thereof; neither is it found in the land of the living.

14 The depth saith, It *is* not in me: and the sea saith, *It is* not with me.

15 It cannot be gotten for gold, neither shall silver be weighed *for* the price thereof.

16 It cannot be valued with the gold of Ophir, with the precious onyx, or the sapphire.
Ps. 45:9

17 The gold and the crystal cannot equal it: and the exchange of it *shall not be for* jewels of fine gold.

18 No mention shall be made of coral, or of pearls: for the price of wisdom *is* above rubies.
Prov. 3:15

19 The topaz of Ethiopia shall not equal it, neither shall it be valued with pure gold.

20 Whence then cometh wisdom? and where *is* the place of understanding?

21 Seeing it is hid from the eyes of all living, and kept close from the fowls of the air.

22 Destruction and death say, We have heard the fame thereof with our ears. *Job 26:6*

23 God understandeth the way thereof, and he knoweth the place thereof.
Prov. 8:22-31

24 For he looketh to the ends of the earth, *and* seeth under the whole heaven;
Prov. 15:3

25 To make the weight for the winds; and he weigheth the waters by measure.
Ps. 135:7

26 When he made a decree for the rain, and a way for the lightning of the thunder:

28:28 Character Development

He who lives in accordance with the Creator's will is securing to himself the truest and noblest development of character. . . .

There are few who realize the influence of the little things of life upon the development of character. Nothing with which we have to do is really small. The varied circumstances that we meet day by day are designed to test our faithfulness and to qualify us for greater trusts. *PP 222, 223*

27 Then did he see it, and declare it; he prepared it, yea, and searched it out.
28 And unto man he said, Behold, the fear of the Lord, that *is* wisdom; and to depart from evil *is* understanding. Deut. 4:6; Ps. 111:10; Prov. 1:7

Job: I Grieve for My Former Prosperity and Honor

29 Moreover Job continued his parable, and said, Job 27:1
2 Oh that I were as *in* months past, as *in* the days *when* God preserved me;
3 When his candle shined upon my head, *and when* by his light I walked *through* darkness; Job 18:6
4 As I was in the days of my youth, when the secret of God *was* upon my tabernacle;
5 When the Almighty *was* yet with me, *when* my children *were* about me; Ps. 128:3
6 When I washed my steps with butter, and the rock poured me out rivers of oil;
7 When I went out to the gate through the city, *when* I prepared my seat in the street!
8 The young men saw me, and hid themselves: and the aged arose, *and* stood up.
9 The princes refrained talking, and laid *their* hand on their mouth. Job 21:5
10 The nobles held their peace, and their tongue cleaved to the roof of their mouth.
11 When the ear heard *me*, then it blessed me; and when the eye saw *me*, it gave witness to me:
12 Because I delivered the poor that cried, and the fatherless, and *him that had* none to help him. Ps. 72:12; Prov. 21:13
13 The blessing of him that was ready to perish came upon me: and I caused the widow's heart to sing for joy. Is. 27:13
14 I put on righteousness, and it clothed me: my judgment *was* as a robe and a ᵀdiadem. Ps. 132:9; Is. 59:17; 61:10 ◆ *crown*
15 I was eyes to the blind, and feet *was* I to the lame. Num. 10:31
16 I *was* a father to the poor: and the cause *which* I knew not I searched out. Prov. 29:7
17 And I brake the jaws of the wicked, and plucked the spoil out of his teeth. Ps. 3:7
18 Then I said, I shall die in my nest, and I shall multiply *my* days as the sand.
19 My root *was* spread out by the waters, and the dew lay all night upon my branch. Job 18:16
20 My glory *was* fresh in me, and my bow was renewed in my hand. Gen. 49:24; Is. 40:31
21 Unto me *men* gave ear, and waited, and kept silence at my counsel.
22 After my words they spake not again; and my speech dropped upon them. Deut. 32:2
23 And they waited for me as for the rain; and they opened their mouth wide *as* for the latter rain. Zech. 10:1
24 *If* I laughed on them, they believed *it* not;

and the light of my ᵀcountenance they cast not down. *appearance*
25 I chose out their way, and sat chief, and dwelt as a king in the army, as one *that* comforteth the mourners.

Job: I Am an Object of Ridicule

30 But now *they that are* younger than I have me in derision, whose fathers I would have disdained to have set with the dogs of my flock. Job 12:4
2 Yea, whereto *might* the strength of their hands *profit* me, in whom old age was perished?
3 For want and famine *they were* solitary; fleeing into the wilderness in former time desolate and waste.
4 Who cut up mallows by the bushes, and juniper roots *for* their meat.
5 They were driven forth from among *men*, (they cried after them as *after* a thief;)
6 To dwell in the clifts of the valleys, *in* caves of the earth, and *in* the rocks.
7 Among the bushes they ᵀbrayed; under the nettles they were gathered together. *wailed*
8 *They were* children of fools, yea, children of base men: they were viler than the earth.
9 And now am I their song, yea, I am their byword. Job 17:6; Lam. 3:14, 63
10 They abhor me, they flee far from me, and spare not to spit in my face. Num. 12:14
11 Because he hath loosed my cord, and afflicted me, they have also let loose the bridle before me.
12 Upon *my* right *hand* rise the youth; they push away my feet, and they raise up against me the ways of their destruction. Job 19:12
13 They mar my path, they set forward my calamity, they have no helper.
14 They came *upon me* as a wide breaking in *of waters*: in the desolation they rolled themselves *upon me*.

Job: I Am Being Punished by God

15 Terrors are turned upon me: they pursue my soul as the wind: and my welfare passeth away as a cloud. Hos. 13:3
16 And now my soul is poured out upon me; the days of affliction have taken hold upon me. Ps. 22:14
17 My bones are pierced in me in the night season: and my sinews take no rest.
18 By the great force *of my disease* is my garment changed: it bindeth me about as the collar of my coat. Job 2:7
19 He hath cast me into the ᵀmire, and I am become like dust and ashes. Gen. 18:27 ◆ *mud*
20 I cry unto thee, and thou dost not hear me: I stand up, and thou regardest me *not*. Job 19:7
21 Thou art become cruel to me: with thy

strong hand thou opposest thyself against me.

22 Thou liftest me up to the wind; thou causest me to ride *upon it*, and dissolvest my substance.   Job 27:21

23 For I know *that* thou wilt bring me *to* death, and *to* the house appointed for all living.

24 Howbeit he will not stretch out *his* hand to the grave, though they cry in his destruction.

25 Did not I weep for him that was in trouble? was *not* my soul grieved for the poor?

26 When I looked for good, then evil came *unto me*: and when I waited for light, there came darkness.   Job 3:25-26; Jer. 8:15; 14:19

27 My bowels boiled, and rested not: the days of affliction prevented me.   Lam. 2:11

28 I went mourning without the sun: I stood up, *and* I cried in the congregation.   Ps. 38:6

29 I am a brother to dragons, and a companion to owls.   Ps. 102:6; Mic. 1:8

30 My skin is black upon me, and my bones are burned with heat.   Ps. 102:3; 119:83; Lam. 4:8

31 My harp also is *turned* to mourning, and my organ into the voice of them that weep.

Job: What Sin Have I Committed?

31 I made a covenant with mine eyes; why then should I think upon a maid?   1 John 2:16

2 For what portion of God *is there* from above? and *what* inheritance of the Almighty from on high?   Job 20:29

3 *Is* not destruction to the wicked? and a strange *punishment* to the workers of iniquity?   Job 21:30

4 Doth not he see my ways, and count all my steps?   2 Chr. 16:9; Job 14:16; Prov. 5:21

5 If I have walked with vanity, or if my foot hath hasted to deceit;

6 Let me be weighed in an even balance, that God may know mine integrity.   Dan. 5:27

7 If my step hath turned out of the way, and mine heart walked after mine eyes, and if any blot hath cleaved to mine hands;   Num. 15:39

8 *Then* let me sow, and let another eat; yea, let my offspring be rooted out.   Lev. 26:16

9 If mine heart have been deceived by a woman, or *if* I have laid wait at my neighbour's door;

10 *Then* let my wife grind unto another, and let others bow down upon her. Ex. 11:5; Is. 47:2

11 For this *is* an heinous crime; yea, it *is* an iniquity *to be punished by* the judges. Gen. 38:24

12 For it *is* a fire *that* consumeth to destruction, and would root out all mine increase.   Prov. 6:27

13 If I did despise the cause of my manservant or of my maidservant, when they contended with me;

14 What then shall I do when God riseth up? and when he visiteth, what shall I answer him?

15 Did not he that made me in the womb make him? and did not one fashion us in the womb?   Job 34:19

16 If I have withheld the poor from *their* desire, or have caused the eyes of the widow to fail;

17 Or have eaten my morsel myself alone, and the fatherless hath not eaten thereof;

18 (For from my youth he was brought up with me, as *with* a father, and I have guided her from my mother's womb;)

19 If I have seen any perish for want of clothing, or any poor without covering;   Job 22:6

20 If his ᵀloins have not blessed me, and *if* he were *not* warmed with the fleece of my sheep;   Deut. 24:13 ◆ *heart*

21 If I have lifted up my hand against the fatherless, when I saw my help in the gate:

22 *Then* let mine arm fall from my shoulder blade, and mine arm be broken from the bone.

23 For destruction *from* God *was* a terror to me, and by reason of his highness I could not endure.   Job 13:11

24 If I have made gold my hope, or have said to the fine gold, *Thou art* my confidence;

25 If I rejoiced because my wealth *was* great, and because mine hand had gotten much;   Ps. 62:10

26 If I beheld the sun when it shined, or the moon walking *in* brightness;   Deut. 4:19; 17:3

27 And my heart hath been secretly enticed, or my mouth hath kissed my hand:

28 This also *were* an iniquity *to be punished by* the judge: for I should have denied the God *that is* above.   Deut. 17:2-7

29 If I rejoiced at the destruction of him that hated me, or lifted up myself when evil found him: Prov. 17:5; 24:17-18

30 Neither have I suffered my mouth to sin by wishing a curse to his soul.   Rom. 12:14

31 If the men of my tabernacle said not, Oh that we had of his flesh! we cannot be satisfied.

32 The stranger did not lodge in the street: *but* I opened my doors to the traveller.   Gen. 19:2-3

33 If I covered my ᵀtransgressions as Adam, by hiding mine iniquity in my bosom: Prov. 28:13; Hos. 6:7 ◆ *violations of a law*

34 Did I fear a great multitude, or did the contempt of families terrify me, that I kept silence, *and* went not out of the door? Ex. 23:2

35 Oh that one would hear me! behold, my desire *is, that* the Almighty would answer me, and *that* mine adversary had written a book.

36 Surely I would take it upon my shoulder, *and* bind it *as* a crown to me.   Is. 22:22

37 I would declare unto him the number of my steps; as a prince would I go near unto him.

38 If my land cry against me, or that the furrows likewise thereof complain;

39 If I have eaten the fruits thereof without money, or have caused the owners thereof to lose their life: 1 Kin. 21:19; James 5:4

40 Let thistles grow instead of wheat, and ᵀcockle instead of barley. The words of Job are ended.   *weeds*

A Fourth Friend, Elihu, Decides to Speak

32 So these three men ceased to answer Job, because he *was* righteous in his own eyes.   Job 10:7

2 Then was kindled the wrath of Elihu the son of Barachel the Buzite, of the kindred of Ram: against Job was his wrath kindled, because he justified himself rather than God.   Gen. 22:21; Job 35:2; 40:8

3 Also against his three friends was his wrath kindled, because they had found no answer, and *yet* had condemned Job.   Job 8:6

4 Now Elihu had waited till Job had spoken, because they *were* elder than he.

5 When Elihu saw that *there was* no answer in the mouth of *these* three men, then his wrath was kindled.

Elihu: I Am Young, But Your Words Anger Me

6 And Elihu the son of Barachel the Buzite answered and said, I *am* young, and ye *are* very old; wherefore I was afraid, and ᵀdurst not shew you mine opinion.   Job 15:10 ◆ *dared*

7 I said, Days should speak, and multitude of years should teach wisdom.

8 But *there is* a spirit in man: and the inspiration of the Almighty giveth them understanding.   Job 33:4

9 Great men are not *always* wise: neither do the aged understand judgment.   Job 12:20

10 Therefore I said, Hearken to me; I also will shew mine opinion.

11 Behold, I waited for your words; I gave ear to your reasons, whilst ye searched out what to say.

12 Yea, I attended unto you, and, behold, *there was* none of you that convinced Job, *or* that answered his words:

13 Lest ye should say, We have found out wisdom: God thrusteth him down, not man.   Jer. 9:23

14 Now he hath not directed *his* words against me: neither will I answer him with your speeches.

15 They were amazed, they answered no more: they left off speaking.

16 When I had waited, (for they spake not, but stood still, *and* answered no more;)

17 *I said*, I will answer also my part, I also will shew mine opinion.

18 For I am full of matter, the spirit within me ᵀconstraineth me.   *compels*

19 Behold, my belly *is* as wine *which* hath no vent; it is ready to burst like new bottles.   Matt. 9:17

20 I will speak, that I may be refreshed: I will open my lips and answer.

21 Let me not, I pray you, accept any man's person, neither let me give flattering titles unto man.   Lev. 19:15; Job 13:8; 34:19

22 For I know not to give flattering titles; *in so doing* my maker would soon take me away.

Elihu: I Want to Reason with You

33 Wherefore, Job, I pray thee, hear my speeches, and hearken to all my words.   Job 13:6

2 Behold, now I have opened my mouth, my tongue hath spoken in my mouth.   Job 3:1

3 My words *shall be of* the uprightness of my heart: and my lips shall utter knowledge clearly.   Job 27:4

4 The Spirit of God hath made me, and the breath of the Almighty hath given me life.

5 If thou canst answer me, set *thy words* in order before me, stand up.

6 Behold, I *am* according to thy wish in God's stead: I also am formed out of the clay.   Job 4:19

7 Behold, my terror shall not make thee afraid, neither shall my hand be heavy upon thee.   Job 9:34; 13:21

Elihu: God Does Not Have to Answer You

8 Surely thou hast spoken in mine hearing, and I have heard the voice of *thy* words, *saying*,

9 I am clean without transgression, I *am* innocent; neither *is there* iniquity in me.   Job 10:7

10 Behold, he findeth occasions against me, he counteth me for his enemy,

11 He putteth my feet in the stocks, he marketh all my paths.   Job 13:27; 31:4

12 Behold, *in* this thou art not just: I will answer thee, that God is greater than man.

13 Why dost thou strive against him? for he giveth not account of any of his matters.   Job 40:2; Is. 45:9

Elihu: God Calls Man to Repentance in Many Ways

14 For God speaketh once, yea twice, *yet man* perceiveth it not.   Job 40:5; Ps. 62:11

15 In a dream, in a vision of the night, when deep sleep falleth upon men, in slumberings upon the bed;   Num. 12:6; Job 4:13

16 Then he openeth the ears of men, and sealeth their instruction, Job 36:10, 15; Ps. 40:6
17 That he may withdraw man *from his* purpose, and hide pride from man.
18 He keepeth back his soul from the pit, and his life from perishing by the sword.
19 He is ᵀchastened also with pain upon his bed, and the multitude of his bones with strong *pain:*　　Job 30:17 ◆ *disciplined*
20 So that his life ᵀabhorreth bread, and his soul dainty meat.　　　　　　　*despises*
21 His flesh is consumed away, that it cannot be seen; and his bones *that* were not seen stick out.　　　　　Job 19:20
22 Yea, his soul draweth near unto the grave, and his life to the destroyers.　2 Sam. 24:16
23 If there be a messenger with him, an interpreter, one among a thousand, to shew unto man his uprightness:　　Eccl. 7:28
24 Then he is gracious unto him, and saith, Deliver him from going down to the pit: I have found a ransom.　　　Job 33:18

33:24 God's Mercy and Justice

As the bow in the cloud results from the union of sunshine and shower, so the bow above God's throne represents the union of His mercy and His justice. To the sinful but repentant soul God says, Live thou; "I have found a ransom" (Job 33:24). *Ed 115*

25 His flesh shall be fresher than a child's: he shall return to the days of his youth:
26 He shall pray unto God, and he will be favourable unto him: and he shall see his face with joy: for he will render unto man his righteousness.　　　　Ps. 50:15
27 He looketh upon men, and *if any* say, I have sinned, and perverted *that which was* right, and it profited me not; 2 Sam. 12:13; Ps. 14:2
28 He will deliver his soul from going into the pit, and his life shall see the light. Job 3:9
29 Lo, all these *things* worketh God oftentimes with man,　　　　　Eph. 1:11
30 To bring back his soul from the pit, to be enlightened with the light of the living.
31 Mark well, O Job, hearken unto me: hold thy peace, and I will speak.
32 If thou hast any thing to say, answer me: speak, for I desire to justify thee.
33 If not, hearken unto me: hold thy peace, and I shall teach thee wisdom.　　Ps. 34:11

Elihu: Do Not Charge God with Injustice

34 Furthermore Elihu answered and said,
2 Hear my words, O ye wise *men;* and give ear unto me, ye that have knowledge.
3 For the ear trieth words, as the mouth tasteth meat.　　　　　　Job 12:11

4 Let us choose to us judgment: let us know among ourselves what *is* good.　1 Thess. 5:21
5 For Job hath said, I am righteous: and God hath taken away my judgment.　Job 27:2; 33:9
6 Should I lie against my right? my wound *is* incurable without transgression.　　Job 6:4
7 What man *is* like Job, *who* drinketh up scorning like water?　　　　Job 15:16
8 Which goeth in company with the workers of iniquity, and walketh with wicked men.　　　　　　　　　　Ps. 1:1
9 For he hath said, It profiteth a man nothing that he should delight himself with God.　　　　Job 9:22-23, 30-31; 35:3

Elihu: God Cannot Be Unjust

10 Therefore hearken unto me, ye men of understanding: far be it from God, *that he should do* wickedness; and *from* the Almighty, *that he should commit* iniquity.　Gen. 18:25; Deut. 32:4
11 For the work of a man shall he render unto him, and cause every man to find according to *his* ways. Ps. 62:12; Jer. 32:19; Matt. 16:27
12 Yea, surely God will not do wickedly, neither will the Almighty pervert judgment.
13 Who hath given him a charge over the earth? or who hath disposed the whole world?
14 If he set his heart upon man, *if* he gather unto himself his spirit and his breath;
15 All flesh shall perish together, and man shall turn again unto dust.　　Gen. 3:19
16 If now *thou hast* understanding, hear this: hearken to the voice of my words.
17 Shall even he that hateth right govern? and wilt thou condemn him that is most just?　　　　　　　　2 Sam. 23:3
18 *Is it fit* to say to a king, *Thou art* wicked? *and* to princes, *Ye are* ungodly?　Ex. 22:28
19 *How much less to him* that accepteth not the persons of princes, nor regardeth the rich more than the poor? for they all *are* the work of his hands.　　Deut. 10:17; 2 Chr. 19:7; Acts 10:34
20 In a moment shall they die, and the people shall be troubled at midnight, and pass away: and the mighty shall be taken away without hand.
21 For his eyes *are* upon the ways of man, and he seeth all his goings.　Job 31:4; Prov. 5:21
22 *There is* no darkness, nor shadow of death, where the workers of iniquity may hide themselves. Job 3:5; Ps. 139:11-12; Amos 9:2-3

34:22 We Cannot Hide From God

The accounts of every business, the details of every transaction, pass the scrutiny of unseen auditors, agents of Him who never compromises with injustice, never overlooks evil, never palliates wrong. *Ed 144*

23 For he will not lay upon man more *than right*; that he should enter into judgment with God.

24 He shall break in pieces mighty men without number, and set others in their stead. Ps. 2:9

25 Therefore he knoweth their works, and he overturneth *them* in the night, so that they are destroyed. Job 34:20

26 He striketh them as wicked men in the open sight of others;

27 Because they turned back from him, and would not consider any of his ways: Is. 5:12

28 So that they cause the cry of the poor to come unto him, and he heareth the cry of the afflicted. Ex. 3:7; Job 35:9; James 5:4

29 When he giveth quietness, who then can make trouble? and when he hideth *his* face, who then can behold him? whether *it be done* against a nation, or against a man only:

30 That the hypocrite reign not, lest the people be ensnared.

Elihu: Humble Yourself before God

31 Surely it is meet to be said unto God, I have borne *chastisement*, I will not offend *any more*:

32 *That which* I see not teach thou me: if I have done iniquity, I will do no more. Ps. 19:12

33 *Should it be* according to thy mind? he will ᵀrecompense it, whether thou refuse, or whether thou choose; and not I: therefore speak what thou knowest. Job 33:32 ◆ repay

34 Let men of understanding tell me, and let a wise man hearken unto me.

35 Job hath spoken without knowledge, and his words *were* without wisdom. Job 35:16; 38:2

36 My desire *is that* Job may be tried unto the end because of *his* answers for wicked men.

37 For he addeth rebellion unto his sin, he clappeth *his hands* among us, and multiplieth his words against God. Job 27:23

Elihu: Human Behavior Cannot Change God

35 Elihu spake moreover, and said,

2 Thinkest thou this to be right, *that* thou saidst, My righteousness *is* more than God's?

3 For thou saidst, What advantage will it be unto thee? *and*, What profit shall I have, *if I be cleansed* from my sin? Job 34:9

4 I will answer thee, and thy companions with thee. Job 34:8

5 Look unto the heavens, and see; and behold the clouds *which* are higher than thou.

6 If thou sinnest, what doest thou against him? or *if* thy transgressions be multiplied, what doest thou unto him? Prov. 8:36; Jer. 7:19

7 If thou be righteous, what givest thou him? or what receiveth he of thine hand? Job 22:2-3

8 Thy wickedness *may hurt* a man as thou *art*; and thy righteousness *may profit* the son of man.

9 By reason of the multitude of oppressions they make *the oppressed* to cry: they cry out by reason of the arm of the mighty. Ex. 2:23

10 But none saith, Where *is* God my maker, who giveth songs in the night; Ps. 42:8; 149:5

11 Who teacheth us more than the beasts of the earth, and maketh us wiser than the fowls of heaven? Ps. 94:12

12 There they cry, but none giveth answer, because of the pride of evil men. Prov. 1:28

13 Surely God will not hear vanity, neither will the Almighty regard it. Prov. 15:29

14 Although thou sayest thou shalt not see him, *yet* judgment *is* before him; therefore trust thou in him. Job 9:11

15 But now, because *it is* not *so*, he hath visited in his anger; yet he knoweth *it* not in great extremity: Ps. 89:32

16 Therefore doth Job open his mouth in vain; he multiplieth words without knowledge. Job 38:2

Elihu: God Is Just in All His Ways

36 Elihu also proceeded, and said,

2 Suffer me a little, and I will shew thee that *I have* yet to speak on God's behalf.

3 I will fetch my knowledge from afar, and will ascribe righteousness to my Maker.

4 For truly my words *shall* not *be* false: he that is perfect in knowledge *is* with thee.

5 Behold, God *is* mighty, and despiseth not *any: he is* mighty in strength *and* wisdom.

6 He preserveth not the life of the wicked: but giveth right to the poor.

7 He withdraweth not his eyes from the righteous: but with kings *are they* on the throne; yea, he doth establish them for ever, and they are exalted. Ps. 33:18; 34:15

8 And if *they be* bound in ᵀfetters, *and* be holden in cords of affliction; chains

9 Then he sheweth them their work, and their ᵀtransgressions that they have exceeded. Job 15:25 ◆ violations of a law

10 He openeth also their ear to discipline, and commandeth that they return from iniquity. Job 36:15

11 If they obey and serve *him*, they shall spend their days in prosperity, and their years in pleasures.

12 But if they obey not, they shall perish by the sword, and they shall die without knowledge. Job 4:21

13 But the hypocrites in heart heap up wrath: they cry not when he bindeth them. Job 36:8

14 They die in youth, and their life *is* among the unclean. Deut. 23:17

15 He delivereth the poor in his affliction, and openeth their ears in oppression.

16 Even so would he have removed thee out of the ᵀstrait *into* a broad place, where *there is* no straitness; and that which should be set on thy table *should be* full of fatness.   narrow

17 But thou hast fulfilled the judgment of the wicked: judgment and justice take hold *on thee*.

18 Because *there is* wrath, *beware* lest he take thee away with *his* stroke: then a great ransom cannot deliver thee.   Job 33:24

19 Will he esteem thy riches? *no*, not gold, nor all the forces of strength.   Prov. 11:4

20 Desire not the night, when people are cut off in their place.   Job 34:20

21 Take heed, regard not iniquity: for this hast thou chosen rather than affliction.   Ps. 66:18

22 Behold, God exalteth by his power: who teacheth like him?

23 Who hath enjoined him his way? or who can say, Thou hast ᵀwrought iniquity?   made

Elihu: Magnify God's Works

24 Remember that thou magnify his work, which men behold.   Luke 1:46

25 Every man may see it; man may behold *it* afar off.

26 Behold, God *is* great, and we know *him* not, neither can the number of his years be searched out.   Job 11:7-9; Ps. 90:2; Heb. 1:12

27 For he maketh small the drops of water: they pour down rain according to the vapour thereof: Ps. 147:8

28 Which the clouds do drop *and* distil upon man abundantly.   Prov. 3:20

29 Also can *any* understand the spreadings of the clouds, *or* the noise of his tabernacle?   Job 37:16

30 Behold, he spreadeth his light upon it, and covereth the bottom of the sea.

31 For by them judgeth he the people; he giveth meat in abundance.   Job 37:13; Ps. 136:25

32 With clouds he covereth the light; and commandeth it *not to shine* by *the cloud* that cometh ᵀbetwixt.   in between

33 The noise thereof sheweth concerning it, the cattle also concerning the vapour.   Job 37:2

Elihu: God Is to Be Feared

37 At this also my heart trembleth, and is moved out of his place.

2 Hear attentively the noise of his voice, and the sound *that* goeth out of his mouth.

3 He directeth it under the whole heaven, and his lightning unto the ends of the earth.

4 After it a voice roareth: he thundereth with the voice of his excellency; and he will not stay them when his voice is heard.   Ps. 29:3-9

5 God thundereth marvellously with his voice; great things doeth he, which we cannot comprehend.   Job 5:9; 26:14; 36:26

6 For he saith to the snow, Be thou *on* the earth; likewise to the small rain, and to the great rain of his strength.   Job 36:27

7 He sealeth up the hand of every man; that all men may know his work.   Ps. 109:27

8 Then the beasts go into dens, and remain in their places.   Job 38:40; Ps. 104:22

9 Out of the south cometh the whirlwind: and cold out of the north.   Job 9:9

10 By the breath of God frost is given: and the breadth of the waters is ᵀstraitened.   confined

11 Also by watering he wearieth the thick cloud: he scattereth his bright cloud:

12 And it is turned round about by his counsels: that they may do whatsoever he commandeth them upon the face of the world in the earth.   Ps. 148:8

13 He causeth it to come, whether for correction, or for his land, or for mercy.   1 Kin. 18:45

14 Hearken unto this, O Job: stand still, and consider the wondrous works of God.

15 Dost thou know when God disposed them, and caused the light of his cloud to shine?

16 Dost thou know the balancings of the clouds, the wondrous works of him which is perfect in knowledge?   Job 36:4

17 How thy garments *are* warm, when he quieteth the earth by the south *wind*?

18 Hast thou with him spread out the sky, *which is* strong, *and* as a molten looking ᵀglass?   Ex. 38:8; Ps. 104:2; Is. 44:24 ◆ mirror

19 Teach us what we shall say unto him; *for* we cannot order *our speech* by reason of darkness.

20 Shall it be told him that I speak? if a man speak, surely he shall be swallowed up.

21 And now *men* see not the bright light which *is* in the clouds: but the wind passeth, and cleanseth them.

22 Fair weather cometh out of the north: with God *is* terrible majesty.   Ps. 104:1

23 *Touching* the Almighty, we cannot find him out: *he is* excellent in power, and in judgment, and in plenty of justice: he will not afflict.   Job 9:4; 36:5; 1 Tim. 6:16

24 Men do therefore fear him: he respecteth not any *that are* wise of heart.   Job 5:13; Matt. 10:28

God: Who Is Able to Challenge Me?

38 Then the LORD answered Job out of the whirlwind, and said,   Job 40:6

2 Who *is* this that darkeneth counsel by words without knowledge?   Job 35:16; 42:3

3 Gird up now thy loins like a man; for I will demand of thee, and answer thou me.

God: Where Were You During Creation?

4 Where wast thou when I laid the foundations of the earth? declare, if thou hast understanding.   Ps. 104:5; Prov. 30:4

5 Who hath laid the measures thereof, if thou knowest? or who hath stretched the line upon it? Is. 40:12

6 Whereupon are the foundations thereof fastened? or who laid the corner stone thereof; Job 26:7

7 When the morning stars sang together, and all the sons of God shouted for joy?

8 Or *who* shut up the sea with doors, when it brake forth, *as if* it had issued out of the womb? Gen. 1:9; Ps. 33:7; Jer. 5:22

9 When I made the cloud the garment thereof, and thick darkness a swaddlingband for it,

10 And brake up for it my decreed *place*, and set bars and doors, Ps. 104:9

11 And said, Hitherto shalt thou come, but no further: and here shall thy proud waves be ᵀstayed? Ps. 89:9 ◆ held back

12 Hast thou commanded the morning since thy days; *and* caused the ᵀdayspring to know his place; Ps. 74:16 ◆ sunrise

13 That it might take hold of the ends of the earth, that the wicked might be shaken out of it? Job 37:3

14 It is turned as clay *to* the seal; and they stand as a garment.

15 And from the wicked their light is withholden, and the high arm shall be broken.

16 Hast thou entered into the springs of the sea? or hast thou walked in the search of the depth? Ps. 77:19

17 Have the gates of death been opened unto thee? or hast thou seen the doors of the shadow of death? Ps. 9:13

18 Hast thou perceived the breadth of the earth? declare if thou knowest it all.

19 Where *is* the way *where* light dwelleth? and *as for* darkness, where *is* the place thereof,

20 That thou shouldest take it to the bound thereof, and that thou shouldest know the paths *to* the house thereof?

21 Knowest thou *it*, because thou wast then born? or *because* the number of thy days *is* great? Job 15:7

22 Hast thou entered into the treasures of the snow? or hast thou seen the treasures of the hail, Job 37:6

23 Which I have reserved against the time of trouble, against the day of battle and war?

24 By what way is the light parted, *which* scattereth the east wind upon the earth?

25 Who hath divided a watercourse for the overflowing of waters, or a way for the lightning of thunder; Job 28:26

26 To cause it to rain on the earth, *where* no man *is; on* the wilderness, wherein *there is* no man; Ps. 107:35

27 To satisfy the desolate and waste *ground*; and to cause the bud of the tender herb to spring forth?

28 Hath the rain a father? or who hath begotten the drops of dew? Ps. 147:8; Jer. 14:22

29 Out of whose womb came the ice? and the ᵀhoary frost of heaven, who hath gendered it? Ps. 147:16-17 ◆ white colored

30 The waters are hid as *with* a stone, and the face of the deep is frozen. Job 37:10

31 Canst thou bind the sweet influences of Pleiades, or loose the bands of Orion? Job 9:9

32 Canst thou bring forth Mazzaroth in his season? or canst thou guide Arcturus with his sons?

33 Knowest thou the ordinances of heaven? canst thou set the dominion thereof in the earth? Jer. 31:35-36

34 Canst thou lift up thy voice to the clouds, that abundance of waters may cover thee? Job 22:11

35 Canst thou send lightnings, that they may go, and say unto thee, Here we *are*?

36 Who hath put wisdom in the inward parts? or who hath given understanding to the heart? Job 32:8; Ps. 51:6; Eccl. 2:26

37 Who can number the clouds in wisdom? or who can stay the bottles of heaven,

38 When the dust groweth into hardness, and the clods cleave fast together?

39 Wilt thou hunt the prey for the lion? or fill the appetite of the young lions, Ps. 104:21

40 When they ᵀcouch in *their* dens, *and* abide in the covert to lie in wait? Job 37:8 ◆ lie down

41 Who provideth for the raven his food? when his young ones cry unto God, they wander for lack of meat. Ps. 147:9; Matt. 6:26; Luke 12:24

God: Consider My Amazing Creation

39 Knowest thou the time when the wild goats of the rock bring forth? *or* canst thou mark when the ᵀhinds do calve? 1 Sam. 24:2 ◆ deer gives birth

2 Canst thou number the months *that* they fulfil? or knowest thou the time when they bring forth?

3 They bow themselves, they bring forth their young ones, they cast out their sorrows.

4 Their young ones are in good liking, they grow up with corn; they go forth, and return not unto them.

5 Who hath sent out the wild ass free? or who hath loosed the bands of the wild ass?

6 Whose house I have made the wilderness, and the barren land his dwellings. Ps. 107:34

7 He scorneth the multitude of the city, neither regardeth he the crying of the driver.

8 The range of the mountains *is* his pasture, and he searcheth after every green thing.

9 Will the ᵀunicorn be willing to serve thee, or abide by thy crib? Num. 23:22; Ps. 92:10 ◆ wild ox

10 Canst thou bind the unicorn with his band in the furrow? or will he ᵀharrow the valleys after thee?   *till the ground*

11 Wilt thou trust him, because his strength *is* great? or wilt thou leave thy labour to him?

12 Wilt thou believe him, that he will bring home thy seed, and gather *it into* thy barn?

13 *Gavest thou* the goodly wings unto the peacocks? or wings and feathers unto the ostrich?

14 Which leaveth her eggs in the earth, and warmeth them in dust,

15 And forgetteth that the foot may crush them, or that the wild beast may break them.

16 She is hardened against her young ones, as though *they were* not hers: her labour is in vain without fear;   Lam. 4:3

17 Because God hath deprived her of wisdom, neither hath he imparted to her understanding.   Job 35:11

18 What time she lifteth up herself on high, she scorneth the horse and his rider.

19 Hast thou given the horse strength? hast thou clothed his neck with thunder?

20 Canst thou make him afraid as a grasshopper? the glory of his nostrils *is* terrible.

21 He paweth in the valley, and rejoiceth in *his* strength: he goeth on to meet the armed men.   Jer. 8:6

22 He mocketh at fear, and is not affrighted; neither turneth he back from the sword.

23 The quiver rattleth against him, the glittering spear and the shield.

24 He swalloweth the ground with fierceness and rage: neither believeth he that *it is* the sound of the trumpet.

25 He saith among the trumpets, Ha, ha; and he smelleth the battle afar off, the thunder of the captains, and the shouting.

26 Doth the hawk fly by thy wisdom, *and* stretch her wings toward the south?

27 Doth the eagle mount up at thy command, and make her nest on high?   Jer. 49:16; Obad. 4

28 She dwelleth and abideth on the rock, upon the crag of the rock, and the strong place.

29 From thence she seeketh the prey, *and* her eyes behold afar off.   Job 9:26

30 Her young ones also suck up blood: and where the slain *are*, there *is* she.   Matt. 24:28

Job: God, I Humble Myself before You

40 Moreover the LORD answered Job, and said,   Job 38:1

2 Shall he that contendeth with the Almighty instruct *him*? he that reproveth God, let him answer it.   Job 33:13

3 Then Job answered the LORD, and said,

4 Behold, I am vile; what shall I answer thee? I will lay mine hand upon my mouth.   Job 21:5

5 Once have I spoken; but I will not answer: yea, twice; but I will proceed no further.

God: Can You Be Like Me?

6 Then answered the LORD unto Job out of the whirlwind, and said,   Job 38:1

7 Gird up thy loins now like a man: I will demand of thee, and declare thou unto me.

8 Wilt thou also ᵀdisannul my judgment? wilt thou condemn me, that thou mayest be righteous?   Job 10:3 ◆ *negate*

9 Hast thou an arm like God? or canst thou thunder with a voice like him?   Job 37:4-5

10 Deck thyself now *with* majesty and excellency; and ᵀarray thyself with glory and beauty.   Ps. 93:1 ◆ *clothe*

11 Cast abroad the rage of thy wrath: and behold every one *that is* proud, and ᵀabase him.   Is. 2:11-12, 17; Dan. 4:37 ◆ *bring him low*

12 Look on every one *that is* proud, *and* bring him low; and tread down the wicked in their place.   Job 36:20

13 Hide them in the dust together; *and* bind their faces in secret.   Is. 2:10

14 Then will I also confess unto thee that thine own right hand can save thee.

15 Behold now ᵀbehemoth, which I made with thee; he eateth grass as an ox. *huge animal*

16 Lo now, his strength *is* in his ᵀloins, and his force *is* in the navel of his belly.   *waist*

17 He moveth his tail like a cedar: the sinews of his stones are wrapped together.

18 His bones *are as* strong pieces of brass; his bones *are* like bars of iron.

19 He *is* the chief of the ways of God: he that made him can make his sword to approach *unto him*.

20 Surely the mountains bring him forth food, where all the beasts of the field play.   Ps. 104:14

21 He lieth under the shady trees, in the ᵀcovert of the reed, and fens.   *hiding place*

22 The shady trees cover him *with* their shadow; the willows of the brook ᵀcompass him about.   *surround*

23 Behold, he drinketh up a river, *and* hasteth not: he trusteth that he can draw up Jordan into his mouth.   Gen. 13:10

24 He taketh it with his eyes: *his* nose pierceth through snares.

God: Can You Conquer Leviathan?

41 Canst thou draw out leviathan with an hook? or his tongue with a cord *which* thou lettest down?   Job 3:8; Ps. 104:26; Is. 27:1

2 Canst thou put an hook into his nose? or bore his jaw through with a thorn?   Is. 37:29

3 Will he make many supplications unto thee? will he speak soft *words* unto thee?

4 Will he make a covenant with thee? wilt thou take him for a servant for ever?   Ex. 21:6

5 Wilt thou play with him as *with* a bird? or wilt thou bind him for thy maidens?

6 Shall the companions make a banquet of him? shall they part him among the merchants?

7 Canst thou fill his skin with barbed irons? or his head with fish spears?

8 Lay thine hand upon him, remember the battle, do no more.

9 Behold, the hope of him is in vain: shall not *one* be cast down even at the sight of him?

10 None *is so* fierce that dare stir him up: who then is able to stand before me?

11 Who hath prevented me, that I should repay *him? whatsoever is* under the whole heaven is mine.   Ex. 19:5; Ps. 24:1; Rom. 11:35

12 I will not conceal his parts, nor his power, nor his ᵀcomely proportion.   *appropriate*

13 Who can discover the face of his garment? *or* who can come *to him* with his double bridle?

14 Who can open the doors of his face? his teeth *are* terrible round about.

15 *His* scales *are his* pride, shut up together *as with* a close seal.

16 One is so near to another, that no air can come between them.

17 They are joined one to another, they stick together, that they cannot be sundered.

18 By his ᵀneesings a light doth shine, and his eyes *are* like the eyelids of the morning.   Job 3:9 ◆ *sneezings*

19 Out of his mouth go burning lamps, *and* sparks of fire leap out.

20 Out of his nostrils goeth smoke, as *out of* a ᵀseething pot or ᵀcaldron.   *boiling ◆ pot*

21 His breath kindleth coals, and a flame goeth out of his mouth.   Ps. 18:8

22 In his neck remaineth strength, and sorrow is turned into joy before him.

23 The flakes of his flesh are joined together: they are firm in themselves; they cannot be moved.

24 His heart is as firm as a stone; yea, as hard as a piece of the ᵀnether *millstone.*   *lower*

25 When he raiseth up himself, the mighty are afraid: by reason of breakings they purify themselves.

26 The sword of him that layeth at him cannot hold: the spear, the dart, nor the ᵀhabergeon.   *military garment*

27 He esteemeth iron as straw, *and* brass as rotten wood.

28 The arrow cannot make him flee: slingstones are turned with him into stubble.

29 Darts are counted as stubble: he laugheth at the shaking of a spear.

30 Sharp stones *are* under him: he spreadeth sharp pointed things upon the ᵀmire.   *mud*

31 He maketh the deep to boil like a pot: he maketh the sea like a pot of ointment.

32 He maketh a path to shine after him; *one* would think the deep *to be* ᵀhoary.   *white colored*

33 Upon earth there is not his like, who is made without fear.   Job 40:19

34 He beholdeth all high *things*: he *is* a king over all the children of pride.   Job 28:8

Job Submits Himself to God

42 Then Job answered the LORD, and said,

2 I know that thou canst do every *thing*, and *that* no thought can be withholden from thee.   Gen. 18:14; Matt. 19:26

3 Who *is* he that hideth counsel without knowledge? therefore have I uttered that I understood not; things too wonderful for me, which I knew not.   Job 38:2; Ps. 40:5; 131:1

4 Hear, I ᵀbeseech thee, and I will speak: I will demand of thee, and declare thou unto me.   Job 38:3; 40:7 ◆ *beg*

5 I have heard of thee by the hearing of the ear: but now mine eye seeth thee.   Rom. 10:17

The Fruit of Faith

Job 42:10–13

Hope and courage are essential to perfect service for God. These are the fruit of faith. Despondency is sinful and unreasonable. God is able and willing "more abundantly" (Hebrews 6:17) to bestow upon His servants the strength they need for test and trial. The plans of the enemies of His work may seem to be well laid and firmly established, but God can overthrow the strongest of these. And this He does in His own time and way, when He sees that the faith of His servants has been sufficiently tested.

For the disheartened there is a sure remedy—faith, prayer, work. Faith and activity will impart assurance and satisfaction that will increase day by day. Are you tempted to give way to feelings of anxious foreboding or utter despondency? In the darkest days, when appearances seem most forbidding, fear not. Have faith in God. He knows your need. He has all power. His infinite love and compassion never weary. Fear not that He will fail of fulfilling His promise. He is eternal truth. Never will He change the covenant He has made with those who love Him. And He will bestow upon His faithful servants the measure of efficiency that their need demands. *PK 164, 165*

6 Wherefore I ᵀabhor *myself*, and repent in dust and ashes.   Ezra 9:6 ◆ *despise*

God Disciplines Job's Friends

7 And it was *so*, that after the LORD had spoken these words unto Job, the LORD said to Eliphaz the Temanite, My wrath is kindled against thee, and against thy two friends: for ye have not spoken of me *the thing that is right*, as my servant Job *hath*.   Job 2:11

42:7 Suffering Is Inflicted by Satan

It was generally believed by the Jews that sin is punished in this life. Every affliction was regarded as the penalty of some wrongdoing, either of the sufferer himself or of his parents. . . .

Thus the way was prepared for the Jews to reject Jesus. . . .

The history of Job had shown that suffering is inflicted by Satan, and is overruled by God for purposes of mercy. . . . The same error for which God had reproved the friends of Job was repeated by the Jews in their rejection of Christ. *DA 471*

---

8 Therefore take unto you now seven bullocks and seven rams, and go to my servant Job, and offer up for yourselves a burnt offering; and my servant Job shall pray for you: for him will I accept: lest I deal with you *after your* folly, in that ye have not spoken of me *the thing which is* right, like my servant Job.   Gen. 20:17; Num. 23:1; Job 1:5

9 So Eliphaz the Temanite and Bildad the Shuhite *and* Zophar the Naamathite went, and did according as the LORD commanded them: the LORD also accepted Job.

God Restores and Blesses Job

10 And the LORD turned the captivity of Job, when he prayed for his friends: also the LORD gave Job twice as much as he had before.   Deut. 30:3; Ps. 14:7; 126:1

11 Then came there unto him all his brethren, and all his sisters, and all they that had been of his acquaintance before, and did eat bread with him in his house: and they bemoaned him, and comforted him over all the evil that the LORD had brought upon him: every man also gave him a piece of money, and every one an earring of gold.   Job 2:11

12 So the LORD blessed the latter end of Job more than his beginning: for he had fourteen thousand sheep, and six thousand camels, and a thousand yoke of oxen, and a thousand she asses.   Job 1:3

13 He had also seven sons and three daughters.   Job 1:2

14 And he called the name of the first, Jemima; and the name of the second, Kezia; and the name of the third, Keren-happuch.

15 And in all the land were no women found *so* fair as the daughters of Job: and their father gave them inheritance among their brethren.   Num. 27:7

16 After this lived Job an hundred and forty years, and saw his sons, and his sons' sons, *even* four generations.   Gen. 50:23

17 So Job died, *being* old and full of days.

THE BOOK OF

PSALMS

Three categories depict the Hebrew sacred writings, the Law, the prophets, and the writings. The three books—Psalms, Proverbs, Job—constitute the poetic portion of "the writings." Psalms, the Psalter or songbook, is the largest book of the Bible. It is easily the most emotion-filled book of the Bible and therefore, the most relatable. Many children memorize Psalm 23 at an early age or are urged to commit to memory other passages from the Psalms.

The breadth of subjects touched on in this book surpass an easy accounting, with songs concerning praise, lament, war, peace, jubilation, judgment, and prophecies of the Messiah.

Dates

The five books of Psalms were compiled over several centuries and span the time of Moses to the time of Ezra (c. 1410 B.C–430 B.C.).

Author

There are several authors of Psalms, including fifty that are anonymous and traditionally attributed to Ezra. The known authors include

(1) David: 3—9; 11—32; 34—41; 51—65; 68—70; 86; 95; 101; 103; 108—110; 122; 124; 131; 133; 138—145

(2) Asaph (a priest who headed the music service; see 1 Chronicles 15:19; Ezra 2:41): 50; 73—83

(3) The Sons of Korah (a guild of singers/composers; see Numbers 26:9–11): 42; 44—49; 84—85; 87

(4) Solomon: 72; 127

(5) Moses: 90

(6) Heman (a wise man; see 1 Kings 4:31; 1 Chronicles 15:19): 88

(7) Ethan (a wise man; see 1 Chronicles 15:19): 89

Meaning of the Name

The Book of Psalms is well named *Sepher Tehillim*, "Book of Praises," in Hebrew. Each psalm contains praise to God. In Greek, Psalms is *Psalmoi*, which refers to poems set to musical accompaniment.

Christ in Psalms

The book of Psalms includes five types of Messianic references:

(1) *Typical Messianic:* Provides some reference to the Messiah to come (34:20; 69:4, 9)

(2) *Typical Prophetic:* Describes events that will come to pass with Jesus (22)

(3) *Indirectly Messianic:* Awaits fulfillment in Jesus (2; 45; 72)

(4) *Purely Prophetic:* Refers to Jesus (110)

(5) *Enthronement:* Anticipates the coming Messianic Kingdom (96—99)

Some of the prophecies and their fulfillment:

Prophecy in the Psalms	New Testament Fulfillment
God's declaration of Him as His Son (2:7)	Matthew 3:17
All things under His feet (8:6)	Hebrews 2:8
Resurrected from the dead (16:10)	Mark 16:6–7
Forsaken by God (22:1)	Matthew 27:46
Mocked and scorned (22:7–8, 17)	Luke 23:35
Hands and feet pierced (22:16)	John 20:25, 27
Clothes gambled for (22:18)	Matthew 27:35–36
No bones broken (34:20)	John 19:32–33, 36
Accused by false witnesses (35:11)	Mark 14:57–59
Hated without a cause (35:19)	John 15:25
Here to do God's will (40:7–8)	Hebrews 10:7
Betrayed by a friend (41:9)	Luke 22:47; John 13:26–27

Eternal throne (45:6)	Hebrews 1:8
Ascension (68:18)	Mark 16:19; Acts 1:9
Consumed by zeal for God's house (69:9)	John 2:17
Given gall to drink (69:21)	Matthew 27:34
Prays for enemies (109:4)	Luke 23:34
Betrayer's position taken by someone else (109:8)	Acts 1:20
Enemies placed under his authority (110:1)	Matthew 22:44
Priest like Melchizedek (110:4)	Hebrews 5:6
Chief cornerstone (118:22)	Matthew 21:42; 1 Peter 2:7
Sent in the name of the Lord (118:26)	Matthew 21:9

Overview

There are different types of psalms:
(1) *Mizmor* or psalms, which are songs to be accompanied by a stringed instrument
(2) *Shir* or song
(3) *Maschil* or prayerful poems
(4) *Miktam* or epigram—a poem with an inscription
(5) *Tepillah*, a Hebrew word meaning "prayer"
(6) *Tehillah*, a Hebrew word meaning praise
(7) Creation psalms (8; 19)
(8) Exodus account (78)
(9) Penitence (6)
(10) Pilgrimage psalms (120—134)
(11) Messianic psalms

First Chronicles 16:4, however, lists three categories of psalms:
(1) Record (Commemorate)
(2) Thanksgiving
(3) Praise

The Book of Psalms is organized into five thematic "songbooks":
(1) *Psalms 1—41:* Many are David's songs, which speak of his own experiences and his relationship with God. "The LORD is my shepherd" (23:1) sums up his thoughts well.
(2) *Psalms 42—72:* This section can be termed "the Exodus book." Here we see the cries of the nation of Israel to God for deliverance. "Deliver me from mine enemies, O my God" (59:1).
(3) *Psalms 73—89:* Many of these psalms provide praise to the deliverer of Israel and solicit God's just treatment of the people of Israel. "Make a joyful noise unto the God of Jacob" (81:1).
(4) *Psalms 90—106:* Here God is praised as the unchanging Guide and Protector of the people of Israel. "I will say of the LORD, He is my refuge and my fortress" (91:2).
(5) *Psalms 107—150:* These are psalms of thanksgiving to God, praising Him as Deliverer. "Our help is in the name of the LORD, who made heaven and earth" (124:8).

Unlocking Psalms

KEY PEOPLE:
David, Asaph, the Sons of Korah, Solomon, Moses, Heman, Ethan

KEY EVENTS:
The deliverance of Israel; the coming Messiah; God's nature and goodness

KEY WORD:
Worship. God is praised in every way, for all the blessings He bestows.

KEY VERSE:
"Let the words of my mouth, and the meditation of my heart, be acceptable in thy sight, O LORD, my strength, and my redeemer" (Psalm 19:14).

KEY CHAPTER:
Psalm 100. This succinct psalm highlights the central themes of both worship and praise.

PSALM 1

The Godly and the Ungodly

Blessed *is* the man that walketh not in the counsel of the ungodly, nor standeth in the way of sinners, nor sitteth in the seat of the scornful.   Job 21:16; Ps. 26:4-5; Jer. 15:17

2 But his delight *is* in the law of the LORD; and in his law doth he meditate day and night.   Josh. 1:8; Ps. 119:11, 35

3 And he shall be like a tree planted by the rivers of water, that bringeth forth his fruit in his season; his leaf also shall not wither; and whatsoever he doeth shall prosper. Gen. 39:3, 23

1:3 A Tree Planted Near the Water

You are just as dependent upon Christ, in order to live a holy life, as is the branch upon the parent stock for growth and fruitfulness. Apart from Him you have no life. You have no power to resist temptation or to grow in grace and holiness. Abiding in Him, you may flourish. Drawing your life from Him, you will not wither nor be fruitless. You will be like a tree planted by the rivers of water. *SC 69*

---

4 The ungodly *are* not so: but *are* like the chaff which the wind driveth away.   Job 21:18

5 Therefore the ungodly shall not stand in the judgment, nor sinners in the congregation of the righteous.   Ps. 5:5; Luke 21:36

6 For the LORD knoweth the way of the righteous: but the way of the ungodly shall perish.   Nah. 1:7; John 10:14; 2 Tim. 2:19

PSALM 2

The Kingdom of Christ

Why do the heathen rage, and the people imagine a vain thing?   Ps. 46:6

2 The kings of the earth set themselves, and the rulers take counsel together, against the LORD, and against his anointed, *saying*, Ps. 45:7

3 Let us break their bands ᵀasunder, and cast away their cords from us.   Jer. 5:5 ◆ *apart*

4 He that sitteth in the heavens shall laugh: the Lord shall have them in derision. Ps. 37:13

5 Then shall he speak unto them in his wrath, and ᵀvex them in his sore displeasure.   *trouble*

6 Yet have I set my king upon my holy hill of Zion.   Ps. 45:6

7 I will declare the decree: the LORD hath said unto me, Thou *art* my Son; this day have I ᵀbegotten thee. Acts 13:33; Heb. 5:5 ◆ *brought thee forth*

8 Ask of me, and I shall give *thee* the heathen *for* thine inheritance, and the uttermost parts of the earth *for* thy possession. Ps. 22:27

9 Thou shalt break them with a rod of iron; thou shalt ᵀdash them in pieces like a potter's vessel.   Ps. 89:23; 110:5-6; Rev. 12:5 ◆ *beat*

10 Be wise now therefore, O ye kings: be instructed, ye judges of the earth.

11 Serve the LORD with fear, and rejoice with trembling.   Phil. 2:12

12 Kiss the Son, lest he be angry, and ye perish *from* the way, when his wrath is kindled but a little. Blessed *are* all they that put their trust in him.   John 5:23

2:12 Trusting in Christ's Strength

All are exposed to temptation, and are liable to error. Upon no finite being can we depend for guidance. The Rock of faith is the living presence of Christ in the church. Upon this the weakest may depend, and those who think themselves the strongest will prove to be the weakest, unless they make Christ their efficiency. "Cursed be the man that trusteth in man, and maketh flesh his arm" (Jeremiah 17:5). *DA 414*

PSALM 3

The Security of God's Protection

A Psalm of David, when he fled
from Absalom his son.

LORD, how are they increased that trouble me! many *are* they that rise up against me.

2 Many *there be* which say of my soul, *There is* no help for him in God. Selah. Ps. 22:7; 71:11

3 But thou, O LORD, *art* a shield for me; my glory, and the lifter up of mine head. Gen. 15:1

4 I cried unto the LORD with my voice, and he heard me out of his holy hill. Selah. Ps. 2:6

5 I laid me down and slept; I awaked; for the LORD sustained me.   Lev. 26:6; Ps. 4:8; Prov. 3:24

6 I will not be afraid of ten thousands of people, that have set *themselves* against me round about.   Ps. 118:10-12

3:1–8 In Dark Trial, the King Turns to God

"A mighty valiant man," a man of war, a king, whose word was law, betrayed by his son whom he had loved and indulged and unwisely trusted, wronged and deserted by subjects bound to him by the strongest ties of honor and fealty—in what words did David pour out the feelings of his soul? In the hour of his darkest trial David's heart was stayed upon God, and he sang: "Lord, how are they increased that trouble me! . . . Many there be which say of my soul, There is no help for him in God. But Thou, O Lord, art a shield for me . . ." (Psalm 3:1–8). *PP 741, 742*

---

7 Arise, O LORD; save me, O my God: for thou hast smitten all mine enemies *upon* the cheek bone; thou hast broken the teeth of the ungodly.   Job 16:10; 29:17; Ps. 58:6

8 Salvation *belongeth* unto the Lord: thy blessing *is* upon thy people. Selah.   Is. 43:11

PSALM 4

David Prays for God to Hear Him

To the chief Musician on Neginoth, A Psalm of David.

Hear me when I call, O God of my righ-
teousness: thou hast enlarged me *when I was* in distress; have mercy upon me, and hear my prayer.   Job 36:16

2 O ye sons of men, how long *will ye turn* my glory into shame? *how long* will ye love van-ity, *and* seek after ᵀleasing? Selah. Ps. 3:3 ◆ *deceit*

3 But know that the Lord hath set apart him that is godly for himself: the Lord will hear when I call unto him.

4 Stand in awe, and sin not: commune with your own heart upon your bed, and be still. Selah.   Ps. 77:6; Eph. 4:26

5 Offer the sacrifices of righteousness, and put your trust in the Lord.   Deut. 33:19; Ps. 37:3

6 *There be* many that say, Who will shew us *any* good? Lord, lift thou up the light of thy ᵀcountenance upon us.   Num. 6:26 ◆ *appearance*

7 Thou hast put gladness in my heart, more than in the time *that* their corn and their wine increased.   Is. 9:3

8 I will both lay me down in peace, and sleep: for thou, Lord, only makest me dwell in safety.   Lev. 25:18-19; 26:5; Ps. 3:5

PSALM 5

David Prays That God Will Defend and Guide Him

To the chief Musician upon Ne-
hiloth, A Psalm of David.

Give ear to my words, O Lord, consider my meditation.   Ps. 54:2

2 Hearken unto the voice of my cry, my King, and my God: for unto thee will I pray.   Ps. 3:4

3 My voice shalt thou hear in the morning, O Lord; in the morning will I direct *my prayer* unto thee, and will look up.   Ps. 88:13; 119:147

5:3 The Morning Is Most Important

In arousing and strengthening a love for Bible study, much depends on the use of the hour of worship. The hours of morning and evening worship should be the sweetest and most helpful of the day. Let it be understood that into these hours no troubled, unkind thoughts are to intrude; that parents and children assemble to meet with Jesus, and to invite into the home the presence of holy an-gels. *Ed 186*

---

4 For thou *art* not a God that hath pleasure in wickedness: neither shall evil dwell with thee.

5 The foolish shall not stand in thy sight: thou hatest all workers of iniquity. Ps. 1:5; 11:5

6 Thou shalt destroy them that speak ᵀleas-ing: the Lord will abhor the bloody and de-ceitful man.   Ps. 4:2; 55:23; Rev. 21:8 ◆ *deceit*

7 But as for me, I will come *into* thy house in the multitude of thy mercy: *and* in thy fear will I worship toward thy holy temple.

8 Lead me, O Lord, in thy righteousness because of mine enemies; make thy way straight before my face.   Ps. 25:4-5; 27:11

9 For *there is* no faithfulness in their mouth; their inward part *is* very wickedness; their throat *is* an open sepulchre; they flatter with their tongue.   Ps. 52:2; 62:4; Rom. 3:13

10 Destroy thou them, O God; let them fall by their own counsels; cast them out in the mul-titude of their ᵀtransgressions; for they have rebelled against thee. 2 Sam. 15:31 ◆ *violations of a law*

11 But let all those that put their trust in thee rejoice: let them ever shout for joy, be-cause thou defendest them: let them also that love thy name be joyful in thee.   Ps. 2:12

12 For thou, Lord, wilt bless the righteous; with favour wilt thou ᵀcompass him as *with* a shield.   Ps. 29:11 ◆ *surround*

PSALM 6

David Prays for Deliverance

To the chief Musician on Neginoth
upon Sheminith, A Psalm of David.

O Lord, rebuke me not in thine anger, neither ᵀchasten me in thy hot displea-sure.   1 Chr. 15:21; Ps. 38:1; Jer. 46:28 ◆ *discipline*

2 Have mercy upon me, O Lord; for I *am* weak: O Lord, heal me; for my bones are vexed.   Hos. 6:1

3 My soul is also sore vexed: but thou, O Lord, how long?   Ps. 90:13; John 12:27

4 Return, O Lord, deliver my soul: oh save me for thy mercies' sake.   Ps. 17:13

6:5 The Bible Versus Popular Theology

Popular theology represents the righteous dead as in heaven, entered into bliss and praising God with an immortal tongue; but Hezekiah could see no such glorious pros-pect in death. With his words agrees the tes-timony of the psalmist: "In death there is no remembrance of Thee: in the grave who shall give Thee thanks?" "The dead praise not the Lord, neither any that go down into silence" (Psalms 6:5; 115:17). *GC 546*

---

5 For in death *there is* no remembrance of thee: in the grave who shall give thee thanks?   Ps. 30:9; 88:10-12; 115:17

After Death See Psalm 115:17.

6 I am weary with my groaning; all the night

make I my bed to swim; I water my ^Tcouch with my tears. Ps. 38:9; 42:3; 69:3 ✦ bed

7 Mine eye is consumed because of grief; it waxeth old because of all mine enemies.

8 Depart from me, all ye workers of iniquity; for the LORD hath heard the voice of my weeping. Ps. 119:115; Matt. 7:23; Luke 13:27

9 The LORD hath heard my supplication; the LORD will receive my prayer. Ps. 66:19-20

10 Let all mine enemies be ashamed and sore vexed: let them return and be ashamed suddenly. Ps. 71:13

PSALM 7

David Prays for Justice

Shiggaion of David, which he sang
unto the LORD, concerning the
words of Cush the Benjamite.

O LORD my God, in thee do I put my trust: save me from all them that persecute me, and deliver me: Ps. 11:1; 31:15; Hab. 3:1

2 Lest he tear my soul like a lion, rending it in pieces, while there is none to deliver. Ps. 50:22

3 O LORD my God, if I have done this; if there be iniquity in my hands; 1 Sam. 24:11; 2 Sam. 16:7-8

4 If I have rewarded evil unto him that was at peace with me; (yea, I have delivered him that without cause is mine enemy:) 1 Sam. 24:7

5 Let the enemy persecute my soul, and take it; yea, let him tread down my life upon the earth, and lay mine honour in the dust. Selah.

6 Arise, O LORD, in thine anger, lift up thyself because of the rage of mine enemies: and awake for me to the judgment that thou hast commanded. Ps. 3:7; 35:23; 44:23

7 So shall the congregation of the people ^Tcompass thee about: for their sakes therefore return thou on high. surround

8 The LORD shall judge the people: judge me, O LORD, according to my righteousness, and according to mine integrity that is in me. Ps. 26:1

9 Oh let the wickedness of the wicked come to an end; but establish the just: for the righteous God trieth the hearts and ^Treins. 1 Chr. 28:9; Jer. 11:20; Rev. 2:23 ✦ desires

10 My defence is of God, which saveth the upright in heart. Ps. 125:4

11 God judgeth the righteous, and God is angry with the wicked every day.

12 If he turn not, he will ^Twhet his sword; he hath bent his bow, and made it ready. sharpen

13 He hath also prepared for him the instruments of death; he ordaineth his arrows against the persecutors. Ps. 45:5

14 Behold, he travaileth with iniquity, and hath conceived mischief, and brought forth falsehood. Job 15:35; Is. 33:11; James 1:15

15 He made a pit, and digged it, and is fallen into the ditch which he made. Job 4:8

16 His mischief shall return upon his own head, and his violent dealing shall come down upon his own ^Tpate. Esth. 9:25 ✦ forehead

17 I will praise the LORD according to his righteousness: and will sing praise to the name of the LORD most high. Ps. 9:2; 71:15-16

PSALM 8

Man Is God's Marvelous Creation

To the chief Musician upon Gittith,
A Psalm of David.

O LORD our Lord, how excellent is thy name in all the earth! who hast set thy glory above the heavens. Ps. 81:1; 148:13

2 Out of the mouth of babes and sucklings hast thou ordained strength because of thine enemies, that thou mightest still the enemy and the avenger. Ps. 44:16; Matt. 21:16; 1 Cor. 1:27

3 When I consider thy heavens, the work of thy fingers, the moon and the stars, which thou hast ordained; Ps. 111:2

4 What is man, that thou art mindful of him? and the son of man, that thou visitest him? Gen. 21:1; Job 7:17; Ps. 144:3

5 For thou hast made him a little lower than the angels, and hast crowned him with glory and honour. Gen. 1:26-27; 2:7; Heb. 2:9

6 Thou madest him to have dominion over the works of thy hands; thou hast put all things under his feet: Gen. 1:26, 28; Matt. 28:18

7 All sheep and oxen, yea, and the beasts of the field;

8 The fowl of the air, and the fish of the sea, and whatsoever passeth through the paths of the seas.

9 O LORD our Lord, how excellent is thy name in all the earth! Ps. 8:1

> **8:4-9 A Little Lower Than Angels**
>
> Next to the angelic beings, the human family, formed in the image of God, are the noblest of His created works. God desires them to become all that He has made it possible for them to be, and to do their very best with the powers He has given them. . . .
>
> We are here for a purpose. God has given us His plan for our life, and He desires us to reach the highest standard of development. MH 397

PSALM 9

David Praises God for Victory

To the chief Musician upon Muthlab-
ben, A Psalm of David.

I will praise thee, O LORD, with my whole heart; I will shew forth all thy marvellous works. Ps. 86:12

2 I will be glad and rejoice in thee: I will sing praise to thy name, O thou most High.
3 When mine enemies are turned back, they shall fall and perish at thy presence.
4 For thou hast maintained my right and my cause; thou satest in the throne judging right.   Ps. 140:12; 1 Pet. 2:23
5 Thou hast rebuked the heathen, thou hast destroyed the wicked, thou hast put out their name for ever and ever.   Deut. 9:14; Prov. 10:7
6 O thou enemy, destructions are come to a perpetual end: and thou hast destroyed cities; their memorial is perished with them.

9:5, 6 God Will Make an End to Sin

Since it is impossible for God, consistently with His justice and mercy, to save the sinner in his sins, He deprives him of the existence which his transgressions have forfeited and of which he has proved himself unworthy. Says an inspired writer: "Yet a little while, and the wicked shall not be: yea, thou shalt diligently consider his place, and it shall not be." And another declares: "They shall be as though they had not been" (Psalm 37:10; Obadiah 16). . . .

Thus will be made an end of sin, with all the woe and ruin which have resulted from it. GC 544, 545

7 But the LORD shall endure for ever: he hath prepared his throne for judgment.
8 And he shall judge the world in righteousness, he shall minister judgment to the people in uprightness.   Ps. 96:13; 98:9
9 The LORD also will be a refuge for the oppressed, a refuge in times of trouble. Ps. 32:7
10 And they that know thy name will put their trust in thee: for thou, LORD, hast not forsaken them that seek thee.   Ps. 91:14
11 Sing praises to the LORD, which dwelleth in Zion: declare among the people his doings.   Ps. 76:2; 107:22
12 When he maketh inquisition for blood, he remembereth them: he forgetteth not the cry of the humble.   Gen. 9:5
13 Have mercy upon me, O LORD; consider my trouble which I suffer of them that hate me, thou that liftest me up from the gates of death: Ps. 30:3
14 That I may shew forth all thy praise in the gates of the daughter of Zion: I will rejoice in thy salvation.   Ps. 13:5; 20:5; 35:9
15 The heathen are sunk down in the pit that they made: in the net which they hid is their own foot taken.   Ps. 7:15-16
16 The LORD is known by the judgment which he executeth: the wicked is snared in the work of his own hands. Higgaion. Selah.   Ex. 7:5
17 The wicked shall be turned into hell, and all the nations that forget God. Job 8:13; Rev. 20:15
18 For the needy shall not alway be forgotten: the expectation of the poor shall not perish for ever.   Ps. 9:12; 12:5; Prov. 23:18
19 Arise, O LORD; let not man prevail: let the heathen be judged in thy sight.   Ps. 3:7
20 Put them in fear, O LORD: that the nations may know themselves to be but men. Selah.   Is. 31:3

PSALM 10

David Complains to God about the Wicked

Why standest thou afar off, O LORD? why hidest thou thyself in times of trouble?   Ps. 22:1
2 The wicked in his pride doth persecute the poor: let them be taken in the devices that they have imagined.   Ps. 7:16
3 For the wicked boasteth of his heart's desire, and blesseth the Tcovetous, whom the LORD Tabhorreth. Ps. 49:6; 94:4 ♦ desirous ♦ despises
4 The wicked, through the pride of his Tcountenance, will not seek after God: God is not in all his thoughts.   Ps. 53:1 ♦ appearance
5 His ways are always grievous; thy judgments are far above out of his sight: as for all his enemies, he puffeth at them.   Ps. 12:5
6 He hath said in his heart, I shall not be moved: for I shall never be in adversity.
7 His mouth is full of cursing and deceit and fraud: under his tongue is mischief and vanity.   Job 20:12; Ps. 7:14; 36:3
8 He sitteth in the lurking places of the villages: in the secret places doth he murder the innocent: his eyes are Tprivily set against the poor.   Hab. 3:14 ♦ secretly
9 He lieth in wait secretly as a lion in his den: he lieth in wait to catch the poor: he doth catch the poor, when he draweth him into his net.   Ps. 17:12; 59:3; Mic. 7:2
10 He croucheth, and humbleth himself, that the poor may fall by his strong ones.
11 He hath said in his heart, God hath forgotten: he hideth his face; he will never see it.   Ps. 73:11
12 Arise, O LORD; O God, lift up thine hand: forget not the humble.   Ps. 3:7; 9:12; Mic. 5:9
13 Wherefore doth the wicked Tcontemn God? he hath said in his heart, Thou wilt not require it.   mock
14 Thou hast seen it; for thou beholdest mischief and spite, to requite it with thy hand: the poor committeth himself unto thee; thou art the helper of the fatherless. Ps. 68:5; 146:9
15 Break thou the arm of the wicked and the evil man: seek out his wickedness till thou find none.   Ps. 37:17
16 The LORD is King for ever and ever: the heathen are perished out of his land.
17 LORD, thou hast heard the desire of the

humble: thou wilt prepare their heart, thou wilt cause thine ear to hear: 1 Chr. 29:18; Ps. 9:18
18 To judge the fatherless and the oppressed, that the man of the earth may no more oppress.   Ps. 82:3

PSALM 11

David Takes Refuge in God

To the chief Musician, *A Psalm* of David.

In the LORD put I my trust: how say ye to my soul, Flee *as* a bird to your mountain?   1 Sam. 23:14
2 For, lo, the wicked bend *their* bow, they make ready their arrow upon the string, that they may ᵀprivily shoot at the upright in heart.   Ps. 7:10 ◆ *secretly*
3 If the foundations be destroyed, what can the righteous do?   Ps. 82:5
4 The LORD *is* in his holy temple, the LORD's throne *is* in heaven: his eyes behold, his eyelids try, the children of men.   Ps. 18:6; 103:19

11:4 God's Incomprehensible Greatness

The hand that sustains the worlds in space, the hand that holds in their orderly arrangement and tireless activity all things throughout the universe of God, is the hand that was nailed to the cross for us.

The greatness of God is to us incomprehensible. "The Lord's throne is in heaven" (Psalm 11:4); yet by His Spirit He is everywhere present. He has an intimate knowledge of, and a personal interest in, all the works of His hand. *Ed 132*

5 The LORD trieth the righteous: but the wicked and him that loveth violence his soul hateth.   Gen. 22:1; James 1:12
6 Upon the wicked he shall rain snares, fire and ᵀbrimstone, and an horrible tempest: *this shall be* the portion of their cup.   *sulphur*
7 For the righteous LORD loveth righteousness; his ᵀcountenance doth behold the upright.   Ps. 17:15 ◆ *appearance*

PSALM 12

David Craves God's Protection

To the chief Musician upon Sheminith, A Psalm of David.

Help, LORD; for the godly man ceaseth; for the faithful fail from among the children of men.   Is. 57:1
2 They speak vanity every one with his neighbour: *with* flattering lips *and* with a double heart do they speak.   Ps. 10:7; 41:6; Rom. 16:18
3 The LORD shall cut off all flattering lips, *and* the tongue that speaketh proud things:
4 Who have said, With our tongue will we prevail; our lips *are* our own: who *is* lord over us?

5 For the oppression of the poor, for the sighing of the needy, now will I arise, saith the LORD; I will set *him* in safety *from him that* puffeth at him.   Is. 33:10
6 The words of the LORD *are* pure words: *as* silver tried in a furnace of earth, purified seven times.   2 Sam. 22:31; Ps. 18:30; Prov. 30:5

12:6 Showing Reverence for God's Word

We should reverence God's word. For the printed volume we should show respect, never putting it to common uses, or handling it carelessly. And never should Scripture be quoted in a jest, or paraphrased to point a witty saying. *Ed 244*

7 Thou shalt keep them, O LORD, thou shalt preserve them from this generation for ever.   Ps. 37:28
8 The wicked walk on every side, when the ᵀvilest men are exalted.   *worst*

PSALM 13

David Prays for Intervening Grace

To the chief Musician, A Psalm of David.

How long wilt thou forget me, O LORD? for ever? how long wilt thou hide thy face from me?   Job 13:24; Ps. 10:12; 89:46
2 How long shall I take counsel in my soul, *having* sorrow in my heart daily? how long shall mine enemy be exalted over me?
3 Consider *and* hear me, O LORD my God: lighten mine eyes, lest I sleep the *sleep of* death;   1 Sam. 14:27; Ezra 9:8; Jer. 51:39

After Death See Daniel 12:2.

4 Lest mine enemy say, I have prevailed against him; *and* those that trouble me rejoice when I am moved.   Ps. 25:2
5 But I have trusted in thy mercy; my heart shall rejoice in thy salvation.   Ps. 9:14; 52:8
6 I will sing unto the LORD, because he hath dealt bountifully with me.   Ps. 116:7

PSALM 14

David Describes Foolish People

To the chief Musician, *A Psalm* of David.

The fool hath said in his heart, *There is* no God. They are corrupt, they have done abominable works, *there is* none that doeth good.   Gen. 6:5; Ps. 10:4; Rom. 3:10-12
2 The LORD looked down from heaven upon the children of men, to see if there were any that did understand, *and* seek God.   Gen. 6:12
3 They are all gone aside, they are *all* together become filthy: *there is* none that doeth good, no, not one.   Job 14:4
4 Have all the workers of iniquity no knowl-

edge? who eat up my people *as* they eat bread, and call not upon the LORD.   Ps. 79:6; Is. 64:7

5 There were they in great fear: for God *is* in the generation of the righteous.   Ps. 73:15

6 Ye have shamed the counsel of the poor, because the LORD *is* his refuge.   Ps. 9:9

7 Oh that the salvation of Israel *were come* out of Zion! when the LORD bringeth back the captivity of his people, Jacob shall rejoice, *and* Israel shall be glad.   Ps. 53:6

PSALM 15

David Describes the Citizens of Zion

A Psalm of David.

L ORD, who shall abide in thy tabernacle? who shall dwell in thy holy hill?   Ps. 61:4

2 He that walketh uprightly, and worketh righteousness, and speaketh the truth in his heart.   Prov. 28:18; Is. 33:15; Eph. 4:25

3 *He that* backbiteth not with his tongue, nor doeth evil to his neighbour, nor taketh up a reproach against his neighbour.   Lev. 19:16

4 In whose eyes a vile person is contemned; but he honoureth them that fear the LORD. *He that* sweareth to *his own* hurt, and changeth not.   Judg. 11:35; Esth. 3:2

5 *He that* putteth not out his money to ᵀusury, nor taketh reward against the innocent. He that doeth these *things* shall never be moved.

Deut. 16:19; Ezek. 18:8 ◆ *charge interest*

PSALM 16

David Flees to God for Safety

Michtam of David.

P reserve me, O God: for in thee do I put my trust.   Ps. 17:8

2 *O my soul*, thou hast said unto the LORD, Thou *art* my Lord: my goodness *extendeth* not to thee;   Ps. 73:25

3 *But* to the saints that *are* in the earth, and *to* the excellent, in whom *is* all my delight.   Ps. 119:63

4 Their sorrows shall be multiplied *that*

hasten *after* another *god*: their drink offerings of blood will I not offer, nor take up their names into my lips.   Ex. 23:13; Josh. 23:7; Ps. 32:10

5 The LORD *is* the portion of mine inheritance and of my cup: thou maintainest my lot.   Ps. 23:5; 73:26; 119:57

6 The lines are fallen unto me in pleasant *places*; yea, I have a goodly heritage.   Ps. 78:55

7 I will bless the LORD, who hath given me counsel: my ᵀreins also instruct me in the night seasons.   Ps. 73:24 ◆ *desires*

8 I have set the LORD always before me: because *he is* at my right hand, I shall not be moved.   Ps. 73:23

16:8 Following and Abiding in Jesus

Our growth in grace, our joy, our usefulness—all depend upon our union with Christ. It is by communion with Him, daily, hourly—by abiding in Him—that we are to grow in grace. He is not only the Author, but the Finisher of our faith. It is Christ first and last and always. He is to be with us, not only at the beginning and the end of our course, but at every step of the way. *SC 69*

---

9 Therefore my heart is glad, and my glory rejoiceth: my flesh also shall rest in hope.

10 For thou wilt not leave my soul in hell; neither wilt thou suffer thine Holy One to see corruption.   Ps. 49:15

11 Thou wilt shew me the path of life: in thy presence *is* fulness of joy; at thy right hand *there are* pleasures for evermore.   Matt. 7:14

PSALM 17

David Pleas for Justice against His Enemies

A Prayer of David.

H ear the right, O LORD, attend unto my cry, give ear unto my prayer, *that goeth* not out of feigned lips.   Ps. 61:1; 86:1; 142:6

2 Let my sentence come forth from thy pres-

Backbiters Are Haters of God

Psalm 15:2, 3

We think with horror of the cannibal who feasts on the still warm and trembling flesh of his victim; but are the results of even this practice more terrible than are the agony and ruin caused by misrepresenting motive, blackening reputation, dissecting character? Let the children, and the youth as well, learn what God says about these things:

"Death and life are in the power of the tongue" (Proverbs 18:21).

In Scripture, backbiters are classed with "haters of God," with "inventors of evil things," with those who are "without natural affection, implacable, unmerciful," "full of envy, murder, debate, deceit, malignity." It is "the judgment of God, that they which commit such things are worthy of death" (Romans 1:30, 31, 29, 32). He whom God accounts a citizen of Zion is he that "speaketh the truth in his heart;" "that backbiteth not with his tongue," "nor taketh up a reproach against his neighbor" (Psalm 15:2, 3). *Ed 235, 236*

ence; let thine eyes behold the things that are equal.

3 Thou hast proved mine heart; thou hast visited *me* in the night; thou hast tried me, *and* shalt find nothing; I am purposed *that* my mouth shall not transgress.   Job 23:10; Ps. 26:2

4 Concerning the works of men, by the word of thy lips I have kept *me from* the paths of the destroyer.

5 Hold up my goings in thy paths, *that* my footsteps slip not.   Ps. 18:36

17:5 Our Spiritual Defense

It is a perilous thing to allow an unchristian trait to live in the heart. One cherished sin will, little by little, debase the character, bringing all its nobler powers into subjection to the evil desire. The removal of one safeguard from the conscience, the indulgence of one evil habit, one neglect of the high claims of duty, breaks down the defenses of the soul and opens the way for Satan to come in and lead us astray. *PP 452*

---

6 I have called upon thee, for thou wilt hear me, O God: incline thine ear unto me, *and hear* my speech.   Ps. 86:7; 116:2

7 Shew thy marvellous lovingkindness, O thou that savest by thy right hand them which put their trust *in thee* from those that rise up *against them.*   Ps. 20:6; 31:21

8 Keep me as the ᵀapple of the eye, hide me under the shadow of thy wings,   Ps. 36:7 ◆ *pupil*

9 From the wicked that oppress me, *from* my deadly enemies, *who* compass me about.

10 They are inclosed in their own fat: with their mouth they speak proudly.   1 Sam. 2:3

11 They have now ᵀcompassed us in our steps: they have set their eyes bowing down to the earth;   *surrounded*

12 Like as a lion *that* is greedy of his prey,

and as it were a young lion lurking in secret places.   Ps. 7:2

13 Arise, O LORD, disappoint him, cast him down: deliver my soul from the wicked, *which is* thy sword: Ps. 3:7

14 From men *which are* thy hand, O LORD, from men of the world, *which have* their portion in *this* life, and whose belly thou fillest with thy hid *treasure:* they are full of children, and leave the rest of their *substance* to their babes.   Luke 16:8

15 As for me, I will behold thy face in righteousness: I shall be satisfied, when I awake, with thy likeness.   Job 19:26-27; Ps. 11:7; 16:11

PSALM 18

David Praises God for His Marvelous Blessings

To the chief Musician, *A Psalm* of David, the servant of the LORD, who spake unto the LORD the words of this song in the day *that* the LORD delivered him from the hand of all his enemies, and from the hand of Saul: And he said,

I will love thee, O LORD, my strength.   2 Sam. 22

2 The LORD *is* my rock, and my fortress, and my deliverer; my God, my strength, in whom I will trust; my ᵀbuckler, and the horn of my salvation, *and* my high tower.   *shield*

3 I will call upon the LORD, *who is worthy* to be praised: so shall I be saved from mine enemies.   Ps. 48:1

4 The sorrows of death compassed me, and the floods of ungodly men made me afraid.

5 The sorrows of hell ᵀcompassed me about: the snares of death prevented me.   *surrounded*

6 In my distress I called upon the LORD, and cried unto my God: he heard my voice out of his temple, and my cry came before him, *even* into his ears.   Ps. 11:4

When Tempted, Rely on God's Word

Psalm 17:4

"The prince of this world cometh," said Jesus, "and hath nothing in Me" (John 14:30). There was in Him nothing that responded to Satan's sophistry. He did not consent to sin. Not even by a thought did He yield to temptation. So it may be with us. Christ's humanity was united with divinity; He was fitted for the conflict by the indwelling of the Holy Spirit. And He came to make us partakers of the divine nature. So long as we are united to Him by faith, sin has no more dominion over us. God reaches for the hand of faith in us to direct it to lay fast hold upon the divinity of Christ, that we may attain to perfection of character.

And how this is accomplished, Christ has shown us. By what means did He overcome in the conflict with Satan? By the word of God. Only by the word could He resist temptation. "It is written," He said. And unto us are given "exceeding great and precious promises: that by these ye might be partakers of the divine nature, having escaped the corruption that is in the world through lust" (2 Peter 1:4). Every promise in God's word is ours. "By every word that proceedeth out of the mouth of God" are we to live. When assailed by temptation, look not to circumstances or to the weakness of self, but to the power of the word. All its strength is yours. "Thy word," says the psalmist, "have I hid in mine heart, that I might not sin against Thee." "By the word of Thy lips I have kept me from the paths of the destroyer" (Psalms 119:11; 17:4). *DA 123*

7 Then the earth shook and trembled; the foundations also of the hills moved and were shaken, because he was ᵀwroth. Judg. 5:4 ◆ *angry*

8 There went up a smoke out of his nostrils, and fire out of his mouth devoured: coals were kindled by it.   Ps. 21:9

9 He bowed the heavens also, and came down: and darkness *was* under his feet.

10 And he rode upon a cherub, and did fly: yea, he did fly upon the wings of the wind.

11 He made darkness his secret place; his pavilion round about him *were* dark waters *and* thick clouds of the skies. Deut. 4:11; Ps. 97:2

12 At the brightness *that was* before him his thick clouds passed, hail *stones* and coals of fire.   Josh. 10:11

13 The LORD also thundered in the heavens, and the Highest gave his voice; hail *stones* and coals of fire.   Ps. 104:7

14 Yea, he sent out his arrows, and scattered them; and he shot out lightnings, and discomfited them.   Deut. 32:23; Ps. 144:6; Hab. 3:11

15 Then the channels of waters were seen, and the foundations of the world were discovered at thy rebuke, O LORD, at the blast of the breath of thy nostrils.   Ex. 15:8; Ps. 106:9

16 He sent from above, he took me, he drew me out of many waters.   Ex. 2:10; Ps. 144:7

17 He delivered me from my strong enemy, and from them which hated me: for they were too strong for me.   Ps. 35:10

18 They prevented me in the day of my calamity: but the LORD was my stay.

19 He brought me forth also into a large place; he delivered me, because he delighted in me.   Ps. 31:8; 37:23; 118:5

20 The LORD rewarded me according to my righteousness; according to the cleanness of my hands hath he recompensed me.   Ps. 24:4

21 For I have kept the ways of the LORD, and have not wickedly departed from my God.

22 For all his judgments *were* before me, and I did not put away his statutes from me.

23 I was also upright before him, and I kept myself from mine iniquity.

24 Therefore hath the LORD ᵀrecompensed me according to my righteousness, according to the cleanness of my hands in his eyesight.   *repaid*

25 With the merciful thou wilt shew thyself merciful; with an upright man thou wilt shew thyself upright;   Matt. 5:7

26 With the pure thou wilt shew thyself pure; and with the ᵀfroward thou wilt shew thyself froward. Lev. 26:23-24, 27-28; Prov. 3:34 ◆ *false or perverse*

27 For thou wilt save the afflicted people; but wilt bring down high looks.   Ps. 101:5

28 For thou wilt light my candle: the LORD my God will enlighten my darkness.   1 Kin. 11:36

29 For by thee I have run through a troop; and by my God have I leaped over a wall.

30 *As for* God, his way *is* perfect: the word of the LORD is tried: he *is* a buckler to all those that trust in him.   Deut. 32:4; Ps. 12:6; 17:7

31 For who *is* God save the LORD? or who *is* a rock save our God?   Deut. 32:31, 39; Ps. 86:8

32 *It is* God that girdeth me with strength, and maketh my way perfect.   Is. 45:5

33 He maketh my feet like hinds' *feet*, and setteth me upon my high places.   Deut. 32:13

34 He teacheth my hands to war, so that a bow of steel is broken by mine arms. Ps. 144:1

35 Thou hast also given me the shield of thy salvation: and thy right hand hath ᵀholden me up, and thy gentleness hath made me great.   *held*

18:35 Christ's Gentle Pleading

The sincere, contrite soul is precious in the sight of God. He places His own signet upon men, not by their rank, not by their wealth, not by their intellectual greatness, but by their oneness with Christ. The Lord of glory is satisfied with those who are meek and lowly in heart. "Thou hast also given me," said David, "the shield of Thy salvation: . . . and Thy gentleness"—as an element in the human character—"hath made me great" (Psalm 18:35). *DA 437*

36 Thou hast enlarged my steps under me, that my feet did not slip.   Prov. 4:12

37 I have pursued mine enemies, and overtaken them: neither did I turn again till they were consumed.

38 I have wounded them that they were not able to rise: they are fallen under my feet.

39 For thou hast girded me with strength unto the battle: thou hast subdued under me those that rose up against me.   Ps. 18:32

40 Thou hast also given me the necks of mine enemies; that I might destroy them that hate me.   Ps. 21:12

41 They cried, but *there was* none to save *them: even* unto the LORD, but he answered them not.   Prov. 1:28

42 Then did I beat them small as the dust before the wind: I did cast them out as the dirt in the streets.   2 Kin. 13:7

43 Thou hast delivered me from the strivings of the people; *and* thou hast made me the head of the heathen: a people *whom* I have not known shall serve me. 2 Sam. 3:1; Is. 52:15; 55:5

44 As soon as they hear of me, they shall obey me: the strangers shall submit themselves unto me.   Deut. 33:29; Ps. 66:3; 81:15

45 The strangers shall fade away, and be afraid out of their close places.   Mic. 7:17

46 The LORD liveth; and blessed *be* my rock; and let the God of my salvation be exalted.   Ps. 18:2

47 *It is* God that avengeth me, and subdueth the people under me.   Ps. 47:3
48 He delivereth me from mine enemies: yea, thou liftest me up above those that rise up against me: thou hast delivered me from the violent man.   Ps. 140:1
49 Therefore will I give thanks unto thee, O LORD, among the heathen, and sing praises unto thy name.   Rom. 15:9
50 Great deliverance giveth he to his king; and sheweth mercy to his anointed, to David, and to his seed for evermore.   2 Sam. 7:13

PSALM 19

God's Creation and Word Show His Glory

To the chief Musician, A Psalm of David.

The heavens declare the glory of God; and the ᵀfirmament sheweth his handy-work.   Rom. 1:19-20 ◆ *sky*

19:1 The Mighty Creator's Care

From the stars that in their trackless cours-es through space follow from age to age their appointed path, down to the minutest atom, the things of nature obey the Creator's will. And God cares for everything and sustains everything that He has created. He who up-holds the unnumbered worlds throughout immensity, at the same time cares for the wants of the little brown sparrow that sings its humble song without fear. . . . No tears are shed that God does not notice. There is no smile that He does not mark. *SC 86*

2 Day unto day uttereth speech, and night unto night sheweth knowledge.   Ps. 74:16
3 *There is* no speech nor language, *where* their voice is not heard.
4 Their line is gone out through all the earth, and their words to the end of the world. In them hath he set a tabernacle for the sun,   Rom. 10:18
5 Which *is* as a bridegroom coming out of his chamber, *and* rejoiceth as a strong man to run a race.
6 His going forth *is* from the end of the heaven, and his circuit unto the ends of it: and there is nothing hid from the heat thereof.   Eccl. 1:5

19:7-11

7 The law of the LORD *is* perfect, converting the soul: the testimony of the LORD *is* sure, making wise the simple.   Ps. 23:3; 93:5; 111:7
8 The statutes of the LORD *are* right, rejoicing the heart: the commandment of the LORD *is* pure, enlightening the eyes. Ps. 12:6; 13:3; 119:128
9 The fear of the LORD *is* clean, enduring for ever: the judgments of the LORD *are* true *and* righteous altogether.   Ps. 119:142
10 More to be desired *are they* than gold,

yea, than much fine gold: sweeter also than honey and the honeycomb.   Ps. 119:72
11 Moreover by them is thy servant warned: *and* in keeping of them *there is* great reward.   Prov. 29:18

> God's Law See Jeremiah 31:31–33.

12 Who can understand *his* errors? cleanse thou me from secret *faults.*   Ps. 40:12; 90:8

19:7-11 The Law of the Lord Is Perfect

Without the law, men have no just concep-tion of the purity and holiness of God or of their own guilt and uncleanness. They have no true conviction of sin and feel no need of repentance. Not seeing their lost condition as violators of God's law, they do not real-ize their need of the atoning blood of Christ. The hope of salvation is accepted without a radical change of heart or reformation of life. Thus superficial conversions abound, and multitudes are joined to the church who have never been united to Christ. *GC 468*

13 Keep back thy servant also from pre-sumptuous *sins;* let them not have domin-ion over me: then shall I be upright, and I shall be innocent from the great ᵀtransgres-sion.   Ps. 119:133 ◆ *violation of the law*
14 Let the words of my mouth, and the meditation of my heart, be acceptable in thy sight, O LORD, my strength, and my re-deemer.   Is. 47:4

PSALM 20

David Prays for Victory in Battle

To the chief Musician, A Psalm of David.

The LORD hear thee in the day of trouble; the name of the God of Jacob defend thee;   Ps. 46:7
2 Send thee help from the sanctuary, and strengthen thee out of Zion;   Ps. 73:17
3 Remember all thy offerings, and accept thy burnt sacrifice; Selah.   Acts 10:4
4 Grant thee according to thine own heart, and fulfil all thy counsel.   Ps. 21:2; 145:19
5 We will rejoice in thy salvation, and in the name of our God we will set up *our* banners: the LORD fulfil all thy petitions.   Ps. 9:14; 60:4
6 Now know I that the LORD saveth his anointed; he will hear him from his holy heaven with the saving strength of his right hand.   Ps. 28:8
7 Some *trust* in chariots, and some in horses: but we will remember the name of the LORD our God.   2 Chr. 32:8; Prov. 21:31; Is. 31:1
8 They are brought down and fallen: but we are risen, and stand upright.
9 Save, LORD: let the king hear us when we call.

PSALM 21

David Thanks God for Victory

To the chief Musician, A Psalm of David.

The king shall joy in thy strength, O LORD; and in thy salvation how greatly shall he rejoice!   Ps. 28:7
2 Thou hast given him his heart's desire, and hast not withholden the request of his lips. Selah.   Ps. 20:4-5
3 For thou preventest him with the blessings of goodness: thou settest a crown of pure gold on his head.   2 Sam. 12:30; 1 Chr. 20:2
4 He asked life of thee, *and* thou gavest *it* him, *even* length of days for ever and ever.
5 His glory *is* great in thy salvation: honour and majesty hast thou laid upon him.
6 For thou hast made him most blessed for ever: thou hast made him exceeding glad with thy ᵀcountenance.   Ps. 16:11 ◆ *appearance*
7 For the king trusteth in the LORD, and through the mercy of the most High he shall not be moved.   Ps. 16:8
8 Thine hand shall find out all thine enemies: thy right hand shall find out those that hate thee.   Is. 10:10
9 Thou shalt make them as a fiery oven in the time of thine anger: the LORD shall swallow them up in his wrath, and the fire shall devour them.   Ps. 2:5; Lam. 2:2; Mal. 4:1
10 Their fruit shalt thou destroy from the earth, and their seed from among the children of men.   1 Kin. 13:34; Ps. 37:28; 109:13
11 For they intended evil against thee: they imagined a mischievous device, *which* they are not able *to perform.*   Ps. 2:1; 10:2
12 Therefore shalt thou make them turn their back, *when* thou shalt make ready *thine arrows* upon thy strings against the face of them.   Ps. 7:12-13
13 Be thou exalted, LORD, in thine own strength: *so* will we sing and praise thy power.

PSALM 22

In Great Suffering, David Prays

To the chief Musician upon Aijeleth Shahar, A Psalm of David.

My God, my God, why hast thou forsaken me? *why art thou so* far from helping me, *and from* the words of my roaring?   Job 3:24; Matt. 27:46; Mark 15:34
2 O my God, I cry in the daytime, but thou hearest not; and in the night season, and am not silent.   Ps. 42:3
3 But thou *art* holy, *O thou* that inhabitest the praises of Israel.   Deut. 10:21
4 Our fathers trusted in thee: they trusted, and thou didst deliver them.
5 They cried unto thee, and were delivered:

they trusted in thee, and were not confounded.   Ps. 31:1; 71:1; Is. 49:23
6 But I *am* a worm, and no man; a reproach of men, and despised of the people.   Job 25:6
7 All they that see me laugh me to scorn: they shoot out the lip, they shake the head, *saying,*   Ps. 44:14; 109:25; Mark 15:29
8 He trusted on the LORD *that* he would deliver him: let him deliver him, seeing he delighted in him.   Ps. 18:19; 37:5; 91:14

> **22:6-8 Christ's Sufferings Prophesied**
>
> Through the psalmist Christ had foretold the treatment that He should receive from men. . . .
> How unmistakably plain were Isaiah's prophecies of Christ's sufferings and death! *AA 225*

9 But thou *art* he that took me out of the womb: thou didst make me hope *when I was* upon my mother's breasts.   Ps. 71:6; Is. 9:6
10 I was cast upon thee from the womb: thou *art* my God from my mother's belly.   Is. 49:1
11 Be not far from me; for trouble *is* near; for *there is* none to help.   Ps. 72:12
12 Many bulls have ᵀcompassed me: strong *bulls* of Bashan have beset me round. *surrounded*
13 They gaped upon me *with* their mouths, *as* a ravening and a roaring lion.   Job 16:10
14 I am poured out like water, and all my bones are out of joint: my heart is like wax; it is melted in the midst of my bowels.   Dan. 5:6
15 My strength is dried up like a ᵀpotsherd; and my tongue ᵀcleaveth to my jaws; and thou hast brought me into the dust of death.   John 19:28 ◆ *broken piece of pottery* ◆ *stays close*
16 For dogs have compassed me: the assembly of the wicked have inclosed me: they pierced my hands and my feet.   Ps. 59:6; Zech. 12:10
17 I may tell all my bones: they look *and* stare upon me.   Is. 52:14; Luke 23:27, 35
18 They part my garments among them, and cast lots upon my ᵀvesture. Mark 15:24 ◆ *clothing*
19 But be not thou far from me, O LORD: O my strength, haste thee to help me.   Ps. 22:11
20 Deliver my soul from the sword; my ᵀdarling from the power of the dog.   *beloved*
21 Save me from the lion's mouth: for thou hast heard me from the horns of the unicorns.   Num. 23:22
22 I will declare thy name unto my brethren: in the midst of the congregation will I praise thee.   Ps. 40:9-10
23 Ye that fear the LORD, praise him; all ye the seed of Jacob, glorify him; and fear him, all ye the seed of Israel.   Ps. 50:23; 135:19-20
24 For he hath not despised nor abhorred the affliction of the afflicted; neither hath he hid his face from him; but when he cried unto him, he heard.   Heb. 5:7

25 My praise *shall be* of thee in the great congregation: I will pay my vows before them that fear him.   Ps. 35:18; 40:9-10; 66:13
26 The meek shall eat and be satisfied: they shall praise the LORD that seek him: your heart shall live for ever.   Ps. 69:32; Is. 25:6; 65:13
27 All the ends of the world shall remember and turn unto the LORD: and all the kindreds of the nations shall worship before thee.
28 For the kingdom *is* the LORD's: and he *is* the governor among the nations.   Ps. 47:7-8
29 All *they that be* fat upon earth shall eat and worship: all they that go down to the dust shall bow before him: and none can keep alive his own soul.   Ps. 45:12; Is. 26:19; Phil. 2:10
30 A seed shall serve him; it shall be accounted to the Lord for a generation.
31 They shall come, and shall declare his righteousness unto a people that shall be born, that he hath done *this*. Ps. 78:6; 86:9; 102:18

PSALM 23

David's Confidence in God as His Shepherd

A Psalm of David.

The LORD *is* my shepherd; I shall not want.   Is. 40:11; John 10:11; 1 Pet. 2:25
2 He maketh me to lie down in green pastures: he leadeth me beside the still waters.   Rev. 7:17
3 He restoreth my soul: he leadeth me in the paths of righteousness for his name's sake.   Ps. 5:8; 19:7; Prov. 8:20
4 Yea, though I walk through the valley of the shadow of death, I will fear no evil: for thou *art* with me; thy rod and thy staff they comfort me.   Job 10:21-22; Ps. 3:6; Mic. 7:14
5 Thou preparest a table before me in the presence of mine enemies: thou anointest my head with oil; my cup runneth over.   Ps. 16:5
6 Surely goodness and mercy shall follow me all the days of my life: and I will dwell in the house of the LORD for ever.   Ps. 21:4

PSALM 24

David Calls All to Worship

A Psalm of David.

The earth *is* the LORD's, and the fulness thereof; the world, and they that dwell therein.   Ex. 9:29; Ps. 89:11; 1 Cor. 10:26

24:1

> Managing God's Gifts See Acts 17:25.

2 For he hath founded it upon the seas, and established it upon the floods.   Ps. 136:6

24:1 God Owns All; We Are His Stewards

Under the Jewish system the people were taught to cherish a spirit of liberality both in sustaining the cause of God and in supplying the wants of the needy. . . .

Thus they were reminded that God was the proprietor of their fields, their flocks, and their herds; that it was He who sent them the sunshine and the rain that developed and ripened the harvest. Everything that they possessed was His; they were but the stewards of His goods. *AA 337*

3 Who shall ascend into the hill of the LORD? or who shall stand in his holy place?   Ps. 2:6; 15:1; 68:18
4 He that hath clean hands, and a pure heart; who hath not lifted up his soul unto vanity, nor sworn deceitfully.   Job 17:9; Ps. 73:1; Matt. 5:8
5 He shall receive the blessing from the LORD, and righteousness from the God of his salvation.   Ps. 88:1

Christ, the Good Shepherd

Psalm 23:1

"I am the Good Shepherd: the good shepherd giveth his life for the sheep." "I am the Good Shepherd, and know My sheep, and am known of Mine. As the Father knoweth Me, even so know I the Father: and I lay down My life for the sheep."

Again Jesus found access to the minds of His hearers by the pathway of their familiar associations. He had likened the Spirit's influence to the cool, refreshing water. He had represented Himself as the light, the source of life and gladness to nature and to man. Now in a beautiful pastoral picture He represents His relation to those that believe on Him. No picture was more familiar to His hearers than this, and Christ's words linked it forever with Himself. Never could the disciples look on the shepherds tending their flocks without recalling the Saviour's lesson. They would see Christ in each faithful shepherd. They would see themselves in each helpless and dependent flock. . . .

"He shall feed His flock like a shepherd: He shall gather the lambs with His arm, and carry them in His bosom" (Isaiah 40:9–11). David had sung, "The Lord is my shepherd; I shall not want" (Psalm 23:1). And the Holy Spirit through Ezekiel had declared: "I will set up one Shepherd over them, and He shall feed them" (Ezekiel 34:23). . . .

Christ applied these prophecies to Himself, and He showed the contrast between His own character and that of the leaders in Israel. *DA 476, 477*

6 This *is* the generation of them that seek him, that seek thy face, O Jacob. Selah. Ps. 27:8
7 Lift up your heads, O ye gates; and be ye lift up, ye everlasting doors; and the King of glory shall come in.   Ps. 97:6; Is. 26:2; 1 Cor. 2:8
8 Who *is* this King of glory? The LORD strong and mighty, the LORD mighty in battle.
9 Lift up your heads, O ye gates; even lift *them* up, ye everlasting doors; and the King of glory shall come in.
10 Who is this King of glory? The LORD of hosts, he *is* the King of glory. Selah.

PSALM 25

David's Confidence in Prayer

A Psalm of David.

U nto thee, O LORD, do I lift up my soul.
2 O my God, I trust in thee: let me not be ashamed, let not mine enemies triumph over me.   Ps. 31:1; 41:11; 71:1
3 Yea, let none that wait on thee be ashamed: let them be ashamed which ᵀtransgress without cause.   Is. 49:23 ◆ *violate a law*
4 Shew me thy ways, O LORD; teach me thy paths.   Ex. 33:13; Ps. 27:11; 86:11
5 Lead me in thy truth, and teach me: for thou *art* the God of my salvation; on thee do I wait all the day.   Ps. 88:1
6 Remember, O LORD, thy tender mercies and thy lovingkindnesses; for they *have been* ever of old.   Ps. 98:3; 103:17; Is. 63:15
7 Remember not the sins of my youth, nor my ᵀtransgressions: according to thy mercy remember thou me for thy goodness' sake, O LORD.   Job 13:26; 20:11; Ps. 51:1 ◆ *violations of a law*
8 Good and upright *is* the LORD: therefore will he teach sinners in the way.   Ps. 92:15
9 The meek will he guide in judgment: and the meek will he teach his way.   Ps. 23:3

25:9 The Meek Guided by God

The meek are guided by the Lord, because they are teachable, willing to be instructed. They have a sincere desire to know and to do the will of God. . . . But His promise is only to those who are willing to follow the Lord wholly. God does not force the will of any; hence He cannot lead those who are too proud to be taught, who are bent upon having their own way. *PP 384*

10 All the paths of the LORD *are* mercy and truth unto such as keep his covenant and his testimonies.   John 1:17
11 For thy name's sake, O LORD, pardon mine iniquity; for it *is* great.   Ps. 31:3
12 What man *is* he that feareth the LORD? him shall he teach in the way *that* he shall choose.   Ps. 37:23
13 His soul shall dwell at ease; and his seed shall inherit the earth.   Ps. 37:11

14 The secret of the LORD *is* with them that fear him; and he will shew them his covenant.   Prov. 3:32
15 Mine eyes *are* ever toward the LORD; for he shall pluck my feet out of the net. Ps. 31:4
16 Turn thee unto me, and have mercy upon me; for I *am* desolate and afflicted.   Ps. 86:16
17 The troubles of my heart are enlarged: *O* bring thou me out of my distresses.
18 Look upon mine affliction and my pain; and forgive all my sins.   2 Sam. 16:12
19 Consider mine enemies; for they are many; and they hate me with cruel hatred.
20 O keep my soul, and deliver me: let me not be ashamed; for I put my trust in thee.
21 Let integrity and uprightness preserve me; for I wait on thee.   Ps. 41:12
22 Redeem Israel, O God, out of all his troubles.   Ps. 130:8

PSALM 26

David Declares His Loyalty to God

A Psalm of David.

J udge me, O LORD; for I have walked in mine integrity: I have trusted also in the LORD; *therefore* I shall not slide.   2 Kin. 20:3
2 Examine me, O LORD, and prove me; try my ᵀreins and my heart.   Ps. 7:9; 17:3 ◆ *desires*
3 For thy lovingkindness *is* before mine eyes: and I have walked in thy truth.   2 Kin. 20:3
4 I have not sat with vain persons, neither will I go in with ᵀdissemblers. Ps. 1:1 ◆ *deceivers*
5 I have hated the congregation of evil doers; and will not sit with the wicked.   Ps. 31:6
6 I will wash mine hands in innocency: so will I ᵀcompass thine altar, O LORD: *surround*
7 That I may publish with the voice of thanksgiving, and tell of all thy wondrous works.   Ps. 9:1
8 LORD, I have loved the habitation of thy house, and the place where thine honour dwelleth.
9 Gather not my soul with sinners, nor my life with bloody men: Ps. 139:19
10 In whose hands *is* mischief, and their right hand is full of bribes.   Ex. 23:8
11 But as for me, I will walk in mine integrity: redeem me, and be merciful unto me.
12 My foot standeth in an even place: in the congregations will I bless the LORD. Ps. 27:11

PSALM 27

David Is Confident in God's Power

A Psalm of David.

T he LORD *is* my light and my salvation; whom shall I fear? the LORD *is* the strength of my life; of whom shall I be afraid?   Ex. 15:2; Ps. 18:28; 118:6

2 When the wicked, *even* mine enemies and my foes, came upon me to eat up my flesh, they stumbled and fell.   Ps. 14:4

3 Though an host should encamp against me, my heart shall not fear: though war should rise against me, in this *will* I *be* confident.   Ps. 3:6

4 One *thing* have I desired of the LORD, that will I seek after; that I may dwell in the house of the LORD all the days of my life, to behold the beauty of the LORD, and to enquire in his temple.   Ps. 23:6; 26:8; 90:17

5 For in the time of trouble he shall hide me in his pavilion: in the secret of his tabernacle shall he hide me; he shall set me up upon a rock.   Ps. 31:20; 40:2; 50:15

6 And now shall mine head be lifted up above mine enemies round about me: therefore will I offer in his tabernacle sacrifices of joy; I will sing, yea, I will sing praises unto the LORD.   Ps. 3:3; 107:22

7 Hear, O LORD, *when* I cry with my voice: have mercy also upon me, and answer me.

8 *When thou saidst*, Seek ye my face; my heart said unto thee, Thy face, LORD, will I seek.   Ps. 105:4

9 Hide not thy face *far* from me; put not thy servant away in anger: thou hast been my help; leave me not, neither forsake me, O God of my salvation.   Ps. 24:5; 69:17; 102:2

10 When my father and my mother forsake me, then the LORD will take me up.   Is. 40:11

11 Teach me thy way, O LORD, and lead me in a plain path, because of mine enemies.

12 Deliver me not over unto the will of mine enemies: for false witnesses are risen up against me, and such as breathe out cruelty.   Ps. 35:11; Matt. 26:59-60; Acts 9:1

13 *I had fainted*, unless I had believed to see the goodness of the LORD in the land of the living.   Ps. 52:5

14 Wait on the LORD: be of good courage, and he shall strengthen thine heart: wait, I say, on the LORD.   Ps. 25:3; 31:24; 62:5

PSALM 28

God Is David's Rock of Safety

A Psalm of David.

U nto thee will I cry, O LORD my rock; be not silent to me: lest, *if* thou be silent to me, I become like them that go down into the pit.   Ps. 18:2; 35:22; 83:1

2 Hear the voice of my supplications, when I cry unto thee, when I lift up my hands toward thy holy oracle.   Ps. 5:7; 134:2; 138:2

3 Draw me not away with the wicked, and with the workers of iniquity, which speak peace to their neighbours, but mischief *is* in their hearts.   Ps. 12:2; 26:9; 55:21

4 Give them according to their deeds, and according to the wickedness of their endeavours: give them after the work of their hands; render to them their desert.   Ps. 62:12; 2 Tim. 4:14

5 Because they regard not the works of the LORD, nor the operation of his hands, he shall destroy them, and not build them up.

6 Blessed *be* the LORD, because he hath heard the voice of my supplications.

7 The LORD *is* my strength and my shield; my heart trusted in him, and I am helped: therefore my heart greatly rejoiceth; and with my song will I praise him.   Ps. 13:5

8 The LORD *is* their strength, and he *is* the saving strength of his anointed.   Ps. 20:6

9 Save thy people, and bless thine inheritance: feed them also, and lift them up for ever.   Deut. 9:29; 1 Kin. 8:51; Is. 40:11

PSALM 29

David Ascribes All Glory to God

A Psalm of David.

G ive unto the LORD, O ye mighty, give unto the LORD glory and strength.

2 Give unto the LORD the glory due unto his name; worship the LORD in the beauty of holiness.   2 Chr. 20:21

3 The voice of the LORD *is* upon the waters: the God of glory thundereth: the LORD *is* upon many waters.

In the Time of Trouble God Will Hide You

Psalm 27:5

The eye of God, looking down the ages, was fixed upon the crisis which His people are to meet, when earthly powers shall be arrayed against them. Like the captive exile, they will be in fear of death by starvation or by violence. But the Holy One who divided the Red Sea before Israel, will manifest His mighty power and turn their captivity. . . . Says the psalmist: "In the time of trouble He shall hide me in His pavilion: in the secret of His tabernacle shall He hide me" (Psalm 27:5). Christ has spoken: "Come, My people, enter thou into thy chambers, and shut thy doors about thee: hide thyself as it were for a little moment, until the indignation be overpast. For, behold, the Lord cometh out of His place to punish the inhabitants of the earth for their iniquity" (Isaiah 26:20, 21). Glorious will be the deliverance of those who have patiently waited for His coming and whose names are written in the book of life. *GC 634*

4 The voice of the LORD *is* powerful; the voice of the LORD *is* full of majesty.   Ps. 68:33
5 The voice of the LORD breaketh the cedars; yea, the LORD breaketh the cedars of Lebanon.   Judg. 9:15
6 He maketh them also to skip like a calf; Lebanon and Sirion like a young unicorn.
7 The voice of the LORD divideth the flames of fire.
8 The voice of the LORD shaketh the wilderness; the LORD shaketh the wilderness of Kadesh.   Num. 13:26
9 The voice of the LORD maketh the ᵀhinds to calve, and discovereth the forests: and in his temple doth every one speak of *his* glory.   Job 39:1-3 ◆ *deer to give birth*
10 The LORD sitteth upon the flood; yea, the LORD sitteth King for ever.   Gen. 6:17; Ps. 10:16
11 The LORD will give strength unto his people; the LORD will bless his people with peace.   Ps. 68:35

PSALM 30

David Praises God for His Deliverance

A Psalm *and* Song *at* the dedication of the house of David.

I will ᵀextol thee, O LORD; for thou hast lifted me up, and hast not made my foes to rejoice over me.   2 Sam. 5:11; Ps. 25:2; 35:19 ◆ *praise*
2 O LORD my God, I cried unto thee, and thou hast healed me.   Ps. 6:2; 88:13
3 O LORD, thou hast brought up my soul from the grave: thou hast kept me alive, that I should not go down to the pit. Ps. 16:10; 28:1
4 Sing unto the LORD, O ye saints of his, and give thanks at the remembrance of his holiness.   1 Chr. 16:4; Ps. 97:12
5 For his anger *endureth but* a moment; in his favour *is* life: weeping may endure for a night, but joy *cometh* in the morning. Ps. 103:9
6 And in my prosperity I said, I shall never be moved.
7 LORD, by thy favour thou hast made my mountain to stand strong: thou didst hide thy face, *and* I was troubled.   Deut. 31:17
8 I cried to thee, O LORD; and unto the LORD I made supplication.
9 What profit *is there* in my blood, when I go down to the pit? Shall the dust praise thee? shall it declare thy truth?   Ps. 6:5
10 Hear, O LORD, and have mercy upon me: LORD, be thou my helper.   Ps. 54:4
11 Thou hast turned for me my mourning into dancing: thou hast put off my sackcloth, and girded me with gladness;   Ps. 149:3; 150:4
12 To the end that *my* glory may sing praise to thee, and not be silent. O LORD my God, I will give thanks unto thee for ever. Ps. 16:9; 57:8

PSALM 31

David Calls to God in Stress and Fear

To the chief Musician, A Psalm of David.

I n thee, O LORD, do I put my trust; let me never be ashamed: deliver me in thy righteousness.   Ps. 25:2
2 Bow down thine ear to me; deliver me speedily: be thou my strong rock, for an house of defence to save me.   Ps. 71:2-3
3 For thou *art* my rock and my fortress; therefore for thy name's sake lead me, and guide me.   Ps. 25:11
4 Pull me out of the net that they have laid privily for me: for thou *art* my strength.
5 Into thine hand I commit my spirit: thou hast redeemed me, O LORD God of truth.
6 I have hated them that regard lying vanities: but I trust in the LORD.   Ps. 26:5
7 I will be glad and rejoice in thy mercy: for thou hast considered my trouble; thou hast known my soul in adversities;   Ps. 1:6
8 And hast not shut me up into the hand of the enemy: thou hast set my feet in a large room.   Deut. 32:30; Job 36:16
9 Have mercy upon me, O LORD, for I am in trouble: mine eye is consumed with grief, *yea,* my soul and my belly.   Ps. 6:7
10 For my life is spent with grief, and my years with sighing: my strength faileth because of mine iniquity, and my bones are consumed.   Ps. 38:3
11 I was a reproach among all mine enemies, but especially among my neighbours, and a fear to mine acquaintance: they that did see me without fled from me. Job 19:13-14; Ps. 38:11
12 I am forgotten as a dead man out of mind: I am like a broken vessel.   Ps. 88:4-5
13 For I have heard the slander of many: fear *was* on every side: while they took counsel together against me, they devised to take away my life.   Jer. 20:10; Lam. 2:22; Matt. 27:1
14 But I trusted in thee, O LORD: I said, Thou *art* my God.   Ps. 22:1-2
15 My times *are* in thy hand: deliver me from the hand of mine enemies, and from them that persecute me.   2 Sam. 7:12; Job 24:1
16 Make thy face to shine upon thy servant: save me for thy mercies' sake. Ps. 4:6; 6:4; 80:3
17 Let me not be ashamed, O LORD; for I have called upon thee: let the wicked be ashamed, *and* let them be silent in the grave.   1 Sam. 2:9
18 Let the lying lips be put to silence; which speak grievous things proudly and contemptuously against the righteous.   Ps. 94:4
19 *Oh* how great *is* thy goodness, which thou hast laid up for them that fear thee; *which* thou hast ᵀwrought for them that trust in thee before the sons of men!   Is. 64:4 ◆ *made*
20 Thou shalt hide them in the secret of thy presence from the pride of man: thou shalt

keep them secretly in a pavilion from the strife of tongues. Job 5:21; Ps. 27:5; 32:7

21 Blessed *be* the LORD: for he hath shewed me his marvellous kindness in a strong city. Ps. 17:7

22 For I said in my haste, I am cut off from before thine eyes: nevertheless thou heardest the voice of my supplications when I cried unto thee. Ps. 116:11; Jon. 2:4

23 O love the LORD, all ye his saints: *for* the LORD preserveth the faithful, and plentifully rewardeth the proud doer. Ps. 30:4

24 Be of good courage, and he shall strengthen your heart, all ye that hope in the LORD. Ps. 27:14

PSALM 32

David Sings of the Blessings of Forgiveness

A Psalm of David, Maschil.

Blessed *is he whose* transgression *is* forgiven, *whose* sin *is* covered. Ps. 85:2; Rom. 4:6-8

2 Blessed *is* the man unto whom the LORD imputeth not iniquity, and in whose spirit *there is* no ᵀguile. John 1:47 ◆ *deceit*

3 When I kept silence, my bones ᵀwaxed old through my roaring all the day long. *became*

4 For day and night thy hand was heavy upon me: my moisture is turned into the drought of summer. Selah. Job 33:7

5 I acknowledged my sin unto thee, and mine iniquity have I not hid. I said, I will confess my ᵀtransgressions unto the LORD; and thou forgavest the iniquity of my sin. Selah. 2 Sam. 12:13; Prov. 28:13 ◆ *violations of a law*

6 For this shall every one that is godly pray unto thee in a time when thou mayest be found: surely in the floods of great waters they shall not come nigh unto him. Is. 43:2

7 Thou *art* my hiding place; thou shalt preserve me from trouble; thou shalt ᵀcompass me about with songs of deliverance. Selah. Judg. 5:1; Ps. 9:9; 31:20 ◆ *surround*

32:5–7 The Depths of David's Repentance

David's repentance was sincere and deep. There was no effort to palliate his crime. No desire to escape the judgments threatened, inspired his prayer. But he saw the enormity of his transgression against God; he saw the defilement of his soul; he loathed his sin. It was not for pardon only that he prayed, but for purity of heart. David did not in despair give over the struggle. In the promises of God to repentant sinners he saw the evidence of his pardon and acceptance. *PP 725*

---

8 I will instruct thee and teach thee in the way which thou shalt go: I will guide thee with mine eye. Ps. 33:18

9 Be ye not as the horse, *or* as the mule, *which* have no understanding: whose mouth must be held in with bit and bridle, lest they come near unto thee. Job 35:11; Prov. 26:3; James 3:3

10 Many sorrows *shall be* to the wicked: but he that trusteth in the LORD, mercy shall compass him about. Ps. 5:12; Prov. 13:21; 16:20

11 Be glad in the LORD, and rejoice, ye righteous: and shout for joy, all *ye that are* upright in heart. Ps. 64:10; 68:3; 97:12

PSALM 33

Praise God for His Goodness and Providence

Rejoice in the LORD, O ye righteous: *for* praise is comely for the upright. Ps. 32:11

2 Praise the LORD with harp: sing unto him with the ᵀpsaltery *and* an instrument of ten strings. Ps. 144:9 ◆ *stringed instrument*

3 Sing unto him a new song; play skilfully with a loud noise. Ps. 96:1; 98:1; Is. 42:10

4 For the word of the LORD *is* right; and all his works *are done* in truth. Ps. 19:8

5 He loveth righteousness and judgment: the earth is full of the goodness of the LORD. Ps. 11:7; 45:7; 119:64

6 By the word of the LORD were the heavens made; and all the host of them by the breath of his mouth. Gen. 2:1; Job 26:13; Heb. 11:3

7 He gathereth the waters of the sea together as an heap: he layeth up the depth in storehouses. Ex. 15:8

8 Let all the earth fear the LORD: let all the inhabitants of the world stand in awe of him.

9 For he spake, and it was *done*; he commanded, and it stood fast. Gen. 1:3; Ps. 148:5-6

10 The LORD bringeth the counsel of the heathen to ᵀnought: he maketh the devices of the people of none effect. Is. 19:3 ◆ *nothing*

11 The counsel of the LORD standeth for ever, the thoughts of his heart to all generations. Prov. 19:21

12 Blessed *is* the nation whose God *is* the LORD; *and* the people *whom* he hath chosen for his own inheritance. Deut. 33:29; Ps. 28:9; 144:15

13 The LORD looketh from heaven; he beholdeth all the sons of men. Job 28:24; Ps. 11:4

14 From the place of his habitation he looketh upon all the inhabitants of the earth.

15 He fashioneth their hearts alike; he considereth all their works. Jer. 32:19

16 There is no king saved by the multitude of an host: a mighty man is not delivered by much strength.

17 An horse *is* a vain thing for safety: neither shall he deliver *any* by his great strength. Ps. 20:7; 147:10; Prov. 21:31

18 Behold, the eye of the LORD *is* upon them that fear him, upon them that hope in his mercy; Job 36:7; Ps. 147:11; 1 Pet. 3:12

19 To deliver their soul from death, and to keep them alive in famine.   Ps. 37:19

20 Our soul waiteth for the LORD: he *is* our help and our shield.

21 For our heart shall rejoice in him, because we have trusted in his holy name.   Zech. 10:7

22 Let thy mercy, O LORD, be upon us, according as we hope in thee.

PSALM 34

David Praises God at All Times

A Psalm of David, when he changed
his behaviour before Abimelech; who
drove him away, and he departed.

I will bless the LORD at all times: his praise *shall* continually *be* in my mouth.   Eph. 5:20

2 My soul shall make her boast in the LORD: the humble shall hear *thereof,* and be glad.

3 O magnify the LORD with me, and let us exalt his name together. Ps. 35:27; 69:30; Luke 1:46

4 I sought the LORD, and he heard me, and delivered me from all my fears. Ps. 56:3; Matt. 7:7

5 They looked unto him, and were lightened: and their faces were not ashamed.

> **34:5 Changed by Beholding**
>
> As we make Christ our daily companion we shall feel that the powers of an unseen world are all around us; and by looking unto Jesus we shall become assimilated to His image. By beholding we become changed. The character is softened, refined, and ennobled for the heavenly kingdom. *MB 85*

6 This poor man cried, and the LORD heard *him,* and saved him out of all his troubles.

7 The angel of the LORD encampeth round about them that fear him, and delivereth them.   2 Kin. 6:17; Ps. 91:11; Dan. 6:22

> **34:7 Angels Will Protect Us**
>
> So, in all ages, angels have been near to Christ's faithful followers. The vast confederacy of evil is arrayed against all who would overcome; but Christ would have us look to the things which are not seen, to the armies of heaven encamped about all who love God, to deliver them. From what dangers, seen and unseen, we have been preserved through the interposition of the angels, we shall never know, until in the light of eternity we see the providences of God. *DA 240*

8 O taste and see that the LORD *is* good: blessed *is* the man *that* trusteth in him.

9 O fear the LORD, ye his saints: for *there is* no want to them that fear him.   Ps. 23:1

10 The young lions do lack, and suffer hunger: but they that seek the LORD shall not want any good *thing.*   Job 4:10-11; Ps. 84:11

> **34:8–10 The Evidence of Experience**
>
> God invites us to prove for ourselves the reality of His word, the truth of His promises. He bids us "taste and see that the Lord is good" (Psalm 34:8). Instead of depending upon the word of another, we are to taste for ourselves. *SC 111*

11 Come, ye children, hearken unto me: I will teach you the fear of the LORD.   Ps. 32:8

12 What man *is he that* desireth life, *and* loveth *many* days, that he may see good?

13 Keep thy tongue from evil, and thy lips from speaking ᵀguile. James 1:26; 1 Pet. 2:22 ◆ *deceit*

14 Depart from evil, and do good; seek peace, and pursue it.   Ps. 37:27; Is. 1:16-17; Heb. 12:14

15 The eyes of the LORD *are* upon the righteous, and his ears *are open* unto their cry.

16 The face of the LORD *is* against them that do evil, to cut off the remembrance of them from the earth.   Lev. 17:10; Prov. 10:7; Jer. 44:11

17 *The righteous* cry, and the LORD heareth, and delivereth them out of all their troubles.   Ps. 34:6

18 The LORD *is* nigh unto them that are of a broken heart; and saveth such as be of a ᵀcontrite spirit. Ps. 51:17; 145:18; Is. 57:15 ◆ *remorseful*

> **34:18 A Truly Contrite Heart**
>
> Real sorrow for sin is the result of the working of the Holy Spirit. The Spirit reveals the ingratitude of the heart that has slighted and grieved the Saviour, and brings us in contrition to the foot of the cross. By every sin Jesus is wounded afresh; and as we look upon Him whom we have pierced, we mourn for the sins that have brought anguish upon Him. Such mourning will lead to the renunciation of sin. *DA 300*

19 Many *are* the afflictions of the righteous: but the LORD delivereth him out of them all.   Ps. 34:6

20 He keepeth all his bones: not one of them is broken.   Ps. 91:12; John 19:36

21 Evil shall slay the wicked: and they that hate the righteous shall be desolate. Ps. 94:23

22 The LORD redeemeth the soul of his servants: and none of them that trust in him shall be desolate.   1 Kin. 1:29

PSALM 35

David Appeals to God for Justice

A Psalm of David.

Plead *my* cause, O LORD, with them that strive with me: fight against them that fight against me.   Ex. 14:25

2 Take hold of shield and ᵀbuckler, and stand up for mine help.   *small shield*

3 Draw out also the spear, and stop *the way* against them that persecute me: say unto my soul, I *am* thy salvation.

4 Let them be confounded and put to shame that seek after my soul: let them be turned back and brought to confusion that devise my hurt.   Ps. 129:5

5 Let them be as chaff before the wind: and let the angel of the LORD chase *them*. Job 21:18

6 Let their way be dark and slippery: and let the angel of the LORD persecute them. Ps. 73:18

7 For without cause have they hid for me their net *in* a pit, *which* without cause they have digged for my soul.   Job 18:8

8 Let destruction come upon him at unawares; and let his net that he hath hid catch himself: into that very destruction let him fall.   1 Thess. 5:3

9 And my soul shall be joyful in the LORD: it shall rejoice in his salvation.   Is. 61:10

10 All my bones shall say, LORD, who *is* like unto thee, which deliverest the poor from him that is too strong for him, yea, the poor and the needy from him that spoileth him?   Ex. 15:11; Ps. 18:17; 51:8

11 False witnesses did rise up; they laid to my charge *things* that I knew not.   Ps. 27:12

12 They rewarded me evil for good *to* the spoiling of my soul. Ps. 38:20; Jer. 18:20; John 10:32

13 But as for me, when they were sick, my clothing *was* sackcloth: I humbled my soul with fasting; and my prayer returned into mine own bosom. Job 30:25; Ps. 69:10-11; Matt. 10:13

14 I behaved myself as though *he had been* my friend *or* brother: I bowed down heavily, as one that mourneth *for his* mother.

15 But in mine adversity they rejoiced, and gathered themselves together: *yea*, the abjects gathered themselves together against me, and I knew *it* not; they did tear *me*, and ceased not: Ps. 7:2

16 With hypocritical mockers in feasts, they gnashed upon me with their teeth.   Job 16:9

17 Lord, how long wilt thou look on? rescue my soul from their destructions, my ᵀdarling from the lions.   Ps. 22:20-21; Hab. 1:13 ◆ *beloved*

18 I will give thee thanks in the great congregation: I will praise thee among much people.

19 Let not them that are mine enemies wrongfully rejoice over me: *neither* let them wink with the eye that hate me without a cause.   Ps. 13:4; 38:19; 69:4

20 For they speak not peace: but they devise deceitful matters against *them that are* quiet in the land.

21 Yea, they opened their mouth wide against me, *and* said, Aha, aha, our eye hath seen *it*.   Ps. 22:13; 40:15; 70:3

22 *This* thou hast seen, O LORD: keep not silence: O Lord, be not far from me. Ps. 10:1; 28:1

23 Stir up thyself, and awake to my judgment, *even* unto my cause, my God and my Lord.   Ps. 7:6; 44:23; 80:2

24 Judge me, O LORD my God, according to thy righteousness; and let them not rejoice over me.   Ps. 7:8

25 Let them not say in their hearts, Ah, so would we have it: let them not say, We have swallowed him up.   Lam. 2:16

26 Let them be ashamed and brought to confusion together that rejoice at mine hurt: let them be clothed with shame and dishonour that magnify *themselves* against me.   Job 19:5

27 Let them shout for joy, and be glad, that favour my righteous cause: yea, let them say continually, Let the LORD be magnified, which hath pleasure in the prosperity of his servant.   Ps. 40:16; 70:4; 149:4

28 And my tongue shall speak of thy righteousness *and* of thy praise all the day long.   Ps. 71:24

PSALM 36

David Proclaims God's Steadfast Love

To the chief Musician, *A Psalm* of David the servant of the LORD.

The ᵀtransgression of the wicked saith within my heart, *that there is* no fear of God before his eyes.   Rom. 3:18 ◆ *sins*

2 For he flattereth himself in his own eyes, until his iniquity be found to be hateful.

3 The words of his mouth *are* iniquity and deceit: he hath left off to be wise, *and* to do good.   Jer. 4:22

4 He deviseth mischief upon his bed; he setteth himself in a way *that is* not good; he ᵀabhorreth not evil.   Is. 65:2; Mic. 2:1 ◆ *despises*

5 Thy mercy, O LORD, *is* in the heavens; *and* thy faithfulness *reacheth* unto the clouds.

6 Thy righteousness *is* like the great mountains; thy judgments *are* a great deep: O LORD, thou preservest man and beast.   Ps. 71:19; 77:19

7 How excellent *is* thy lovingkindness, O God! therefore the children of men put their trust under the shadow of thy wings. Ruth 2:12

8 They shall be abundantly satisfied with the fatness of thy house; and thou shalt make them drink of the river of thy pleasures.   Job 20:17; Ps. 16:11; 65:4

9 For with thee *is* the fountain of life: in thy light shall we see light. Jer. 2:13; John 4:10; 1 Pet. 2:9

10 O continue thy lovingkindness unto them that know thee; and thy righteousness to the upright in heart.   Jer. 22:16

11 Let not the foot of pride come against me, and let not the hand of the wicked remove me.

12 There are the workers of iniquity fallen:

they are cast down, and shall not be able to rise.   Ps. 1:5

36:9 Glorious Things Revealed

In His light shall we see light, until mind and heart and soul are transformed into the image of His holiness.

For those who thus lay hold of the divine assurances of God's word, there are wonderful possibilities. Before them lie vast fields of truth, vast resources of power. Glorious things are to be revealed. Privileges and duties which they do not even suspect to be in the Bible will be made manifest. All who walk in the path of humble obedience, fulfilling His purpose, will know more and more of the oracles of God. *MH 465*

PSALM 37

David Contrasts the Godly and the Wicked

A Psalm of David.

F ret not thyself because of evildoers, neither be thou envious against the workers of iniquity.   Ps. 73:3; Prov. 23:17; 24:19
2 For they shall soon be cut down like the grass, and wither as the green herb. Ps. 90:5-6
3 Trust in the LORD, and do good; *so* shalt thou dwell in the land, and ᵀverily thou shalt be fed.

truly

4 Delight thyself also in the LORD; and he shall give thee the desires of thine heart.

37:5, 6 Commit Your Ways to God

We need to follow more closely God's plan of life. To do our best in the work that lies nearest, to commit our ways to God, and to watch for the indications of His providence— these are rules that ensure safe guidance in the choice of an occupation. *Ed 267*

5 Commit thy way unto the LORD; trust also in him; and he shall bring *it* to pass. Ps. 55:22
6 And he shall bring forth thy righteousness as the light, and thy judgment as the noonday.   Job 11:17
7 Rest in the LORD, and wait patiently for him: ᵀfret not thyself because of him who prospereth in his way, because of the man who bringeth wicked devices to pass.   Ps. 40:1 ◆ *worry*
8 Cease from anger, and forsake wrath: fret not thyself in any wise to do evil.   Prov. 14:29
9 For evildoers shall be cut off: but those that wait upon the LORD, they shall inherit the earth.   Ps. 25:13; Is. 57:13; 60:21
10 For yet a little while, and the wicked *shall* not *be*: yea, thou shalt diligently consider his place, and it *shall* not *be*.   Job 7:10; 24:24
11 But the meek shall inherit the earth; and shall delight themselves in the abundance of peace.   Ps. 72:7; 119:165; Matt. 5:5
12 The wicked plotteth against the just, and gnasheth upon him with his teeth.   Ps. 35:16
13 The Lord shall laugh at him: for he seeth that his day is coming.   1 Sam. 26:10; Ps. 2:4
14 The wicked have drawn out the sword, and have bent their bow, to cast down the poor and needy, *and* to slay such as be of upright ᵀconversation.   Ps. 11:2 ◆ *conduct*
15 Their sword shall enter into their own heart, and their bows shall be broken.Ps. 46:9
16 A little that a righteous man hath *is* better than the riches of many wicked.   Prov. 16:8
17 For the arms of the wicked shall be broken: but the LORD upholdeth the righteous.   Job 38:15; Ps. 10:15; 145:14
18 The LORD knoweth the days of the upright: and their inheritance shall be for ever.   Ps. 1:6
19 They shall not be ashamed in the evil time: and in the days of famine they shall be satisfied.   Ps. 33:19

Trust; Don't Fear

Psalm 37:3

The psalmist says, "Trust in the Lord, and do good; so shalt thou dwell in the land, and verily thou shalt be fed" (Psalm 37:3). "Trust in the Lord." Each day has its burdens, its cares and perplexities; and when we meet how ready we are to talk of our difficulties and trials. So many borrowed troubles intrude, so many fears are indulged, such a weight of anxiety is expressed, that one might suppose we had no pitying, loving Saviour ready to hear all our requests and to be to us a present help in every time of need.

Some are always fearing, and borrowing trouble. Every day they are surrounded with the tokens of God's love; every day they are enjoying the bounties of His providence; but they overlook these present blessings. Their minds are continually dwelling upon something disagreeable which they fear may come; or some difficulty may really exist which, though small, blinds their eyes to the many things that demand gratitude. The difficulties they encounter, instead of driving them to God, the only source of their help, separate them from Him because they awaken unrest and repining.

Do we well to be thus unbelieving? Why should we be ungrateful and distrustful? Jesus is our friend; all heaven is interested in our welfare. We should not allow the perplexities and worries of everyday life to fret the mind and cloud the brow. *SC 121, 122*

20 But the wicked shall perish, and the ene-mies of the LORD *shall be* as the fat of lambs: they shall consume; into smoke shall they consume away. Ps. 68:2; 102:3

21 The wicked borroweth, and payeth not again: but the righteous sheweth mercy, and giveth. Ps. 112:5

22 For *such as be* blessed of him shall inherit the earth; and *they that be* cursed of him shall be cut off. Prov. 3:33

23 The steps of a *good* man are ordered by the LORD: and he delighteth in his way. Ps. 40:2

24 Though he fall, he shall not be utterly cast down: for the LORD upholdeth *him with* his hand. Ps. 145:14; Prov. 24:16

25 I have been young, and *now* am old; yet have I not seen the righteous forsaken, nor his seed begging bread. Heb. 13:5

37:25

Managing God's Gifts See 2 Corinthians 9:6, 7.

26 *He is* ever merciful, and lendeth; and his seed *is* blessed. Ps. 37:21

27 Depart from evil, and do good; and dwell for evermore. Ps. 34:14

28 For the LORD loveth judgment, and for-saketh not his saints; they are preserved for ever: but the seed of the wicked shall be cut off. Ps. 11:7; 21:10; Prov. 2:22

29 The righteous shall inherit the land, and dwell therein for ever. Ps. 37:9

30 The mouth of the righteous speaketh wisdom, and his tongue talketh of judg-ment.

31 The law of his God *is* in his heart; none of his steps shall slide. Deut. 6:6

32 The wicked watcheth the righteous, and seeketh to slay him.

33 The LORD will not leave him in his hand, nor condemn him when he is judged. 2 Pet. 2:9

34 Wait on the LORD, and keep his way, and he shall exalt thee to inherit the land: when the wicked are cut off, thou shalt see *it*. Ps. 91:8

35 I have seen the wicked in great power, and spreading himself like a green ᵀbay tree. Job 5:3 ◆ brownish-red color

36 Yet he passed away, and, lo, he *was* not: yea, I sought him, but he could not be found. Ps. 37:10

37 Mark the perfect *man*, and behold the up-right: for the end of *that* man *is* peace.

38 But the ᵀtransgressors shall be destroyed together: the end of the wicked shall be cut off. Ps. 1:4-6 ◆ lawbreakers

39 But the salvation of the righteous *is* of the LORD: he *is* their strength in the time of trouble. Ps. 3:8; 9:9

40 And the LORD shall help them, and de-liver them: he shall deliver them from the wicked, and save them, because they trust in him. 1 Chr. 5:20; Is. 31:5; Dan. 3:17

PSALM 38

David Appeals to God for Mercy

A Psalm of David, to bring to remembrance.

O LORD, rebuke me not in thy wrath: nei-ther ᵀchasten me in thy hot displea-sure. Ps. 6:1; 70:1 ◆ discipline

2 For thine arrows stick fast in me, and thy hand presseth me sore. Job 6:4; Ps. 32:4

3 *There is* no soundness in my flesh because of thine anger; neither *is there any* rest in my bones because of my sin. Ps. 6:2

4 For mine iniquities are gone over mine head: as an heavy burden they are too heavy for me. Ezra 9:6; Ps. 40:12

5 My wounds stink *and* are corrupt because of my foolishness.

6 I am troubled; I am bowed down greatly; I go mourning all the day long. Job 30:28; Ps. 42:9

7 For my ᵀloins are filled with a loathsome *disease*: and *there is* no soundness in my flesh. waist is

8 I am feeble and sore broken: I have roared by reason of the disquietness of my heart. Job 3:24

9 Lord, all my desire *is* before thee; and my groaning is not hid from thee. Ps. 6:6

10 My heart panteth, my strength faileth me: as for the light of mine eyes, it also is gone from me. Ps. 6:7; 69:3; 88:9

11 My lovers and my friends stand aloof from my sore; and my kinsmen stand afar off. Job 19:13-17; Ps. 31:11; Luke 23:49

12 They also that seek after my life lay snares *for me*: and they that seek my hurt speak mischievous things, and imagine de-ceits all the day long. 2 Sam. 16:7-8; Ps. 35:20; 140:5

13 But I, as a deaf *man*, heard not; and *I was* as a ᵀdumb man *that* openeth not his mouth. Ps. 39:2 ◆ mute

14 Thus I was as a man that heareth not, and in whose mouth *are* no reproofs.

15 For in thee, O LORD, do I hope: thou wilt hear, O Lord my God. Ps. 39:7

16 For I said, *Hear me*, lest *otherwise* they should rejoice over me: when my foot slip-peth, they magnify *themselves* against me.

17 For I *am* ready to ᵀhalt, and my sorrow *is* continually before me. Ps. 35:15 ◆ become crippled

18 For I will declare mine iniquity; I will be sorry for my sin. Ps. 32:5; Prov. 28:13

19 But mine enemies *are* ᵀlively, *and* they are strong: and they that hate me wrongfully are multiplied. Ps. 35:19 ◆ alive

20 They also that render evil for good are mine adversaries; because I follow *the thing that* good *is*. Ps. 35:12; 1 John 3:12

21 Forsake me not, O LORD: O my God, be not far from me. Ps. 22:19

22 Make haste to help me, O Lord my salva-tion. Ps. 27:1; 40:13, 17

PSALM 39

David Places His Hope in God

To the chief Musician, *even* to Jeduthun, A Psalm of David.

I said, I will take heed to my ways, that I
sin not with my tongue: I will keep my
mouth with a bridle, while the wicked is before me.   1 Kin. 2:4; 2 Kin. 10:31; 1 Chr. 16:41
2 I was dumb with silence, I held my peace,
even from good; and my sorrow was stirred.
3 My heart was hot within me, while I was
musing the fire burned: *then* spake I with my
tongue,   Jer. 20:9
4 Lord, make me to know mine end, and
the measure of my days, what it *is*; *that* I may
know how frail I *am*.   Ps. 90:12; 119:84
5 Behold, thou hast made my days *as* an
handbreadth; and mine age *is* as nothing before thee: verily every man at his best state *is*
altogether vanity. Selah.   Ps. 62:9
6 Surely every man walketh in a vain shew:
surely they are disquieted in vain: he heapeth up *riches*, and knoweth not who shall
gather them.   Eccl. 2:26
7 And now, Lord, what wait I for? my hope
is in thee.   Ps. 38:15
8 Deliver me from all my transgressions:
make me not the reproach of the foolish.
9 I was dumb, I opened not my mouth; because thou didst *it*.   2 Sam. 16:10; Job 2:10
10 Remove thy stroke away from me: I am
consumed by the blow of thine hand. Job 9:34
11 When thou with rebukes dost correct
man for iniquity, thou makest his beauty to
consume away like a moth: surely every man
is vanity. Selah.   Job 13:28; Is. 50:9
12 Hear my prayer, O Lord, and give ear unto
my cry; hold not thy peace at my tears: for I
am a stranger with thee, *and* a sojourner, as all
my fathers *were*.   Gen. 47:9; Heb. 11:13; 1 Pet. 2:11
13 O spare me, that I may recover strength,
before I go hence, and be no more. Job 10:20-21

PSALM 40

David Waits Paitently on God

To the chief Musician, A Psalm of David.

I waited patiently for the Lord; and he inclined unto me, and heard my cry.   Ps. 37:7
2 He brought me up also out of an horrible
pit, out of the miry clay, and set my feet upon
a rock, *and* established my goings. Ps. 27:5; 37:23
3 And he hath put a new song in my mouth,
even praise unto our God: many shall see *it*,
and fear, and shall trust in the Lord.   Ps. 33:3
4 Blessed *is* that man that maketh the Lord
his trust, and respecteth not the proud, nor
such as turn aside to lies.   Ps. 34:8
5 Many, O Lord my God, *are* thy wonderful works *which* thou hast done, and thy

thoughts *which are* [T]to us-ward: they cannot
be reckoned up in order unto thee: *if* I would
declare and speak *of them*, they are more than
can be numbered.   Ps. 71:15 ◆ *toward us*
6 Sacrifice and offering thou didst not desire;
mine ears hast thou opened: burnt offering
and sin offering hast thou not required.
7 Then said I, Lo, I come: in the volume of
the book *it is* written of me,   Luke 24:44
8 I delight to do thy will, O my God: yea, thy
law *is* within my heart.   Ps. 119:16, 24; John 4:34

> **40:8 His Words Are Re-echoed**
>
> When Satan rebelled against the law of Je-
> hovah, the thought that there was a law came
> to the angels almost as an awakening to some-
> thing unthought of. In their ministry the an-
> gels are not as servants, but as sons. There is
> perfect unity between them and their Creator.
> Obedience is to them no drudgery. Love for
> God makes their service a joy. So in every soul
> wherein Christ, the hope of glory, dwells, His
> words [Psalm 40:8] are re-echoed. *MB 109*

9 I have preached righteousness in the great
congregation: lo, I have not refrained my lips,
O Lord, thou knowest.   Ps. 22:22, 25; 119:13
10 I have not hid thy righteousness within
my heart; I have declared thy faithfulness
and thy salvation: I have not concealed thy
lovingkindness and thy truth from the great
congregation.
11 Withhold not thou thy tender mercies
from me, O Lord: let thy lovingkindness and
thy truth continually preserve me.   Ps. 43:3
12 For innumerable evils have compassed me
about: mine iniquities have taken hold upon
me, so that I am not able to look up; they are
more than the hairs of mine head: therefore
my heart faileth me.   Ps. 38:4; 69:4; 73:26
13 Be pleased, O Lord, to deliver me: O
Lord, make haste to help me.   Ps. 38:22
14 Let them be ashamed and confounded
together that seek after my soul to destroy
it; let them be driven backward and put to
shame that wish me evil.   Ps. 35:4, 26; 71:13
15 Let them be desolate for a reward of their
shame that say unto me, Aha, aha.   Ps. 35:21
16 Let all those that seek thee rejoice and be
glad in thee: let such as love thy salvation say
continually, The Lord be magnified. Ps. 35:27
17 But I *am* poor and needy; *yet* the Lord
thinketh upon me: thou *art* my help and my
deliverer; make no tarrying, O my God.Ps. 70:5

PSALM 41

God's Care for the Poor

To the chief Musician, A Psalm of David.

B lessed *is* he that considereth the poor:
the Lord will deliver him in time of
trouble.   Ps. 37:19; Prov. 14:21

2 The LORD will preserve him, and keep him alive; *and* he shall be blessed upon the earth: and thou wilt not deliver him unto the will of his enemies.   Ps. 27:12

3 The LORD will strengthen him upon the bed of ᵀlanguishing: thou wilt make all his bed in his sickness.   *withering*

41:1–3 A Compassionate Spirit

There is sweet peace for the compassionate spirit, a blessed satisfaction in the life of self-forgetful service for the good of others. The Holy Spirit that abides in the soul and is manifest in the life will soften hard hearts and awaken sympathy and tenderness. You will reap that which you sow. *MB 23*

---

4 I said, LORD, be merciful unto me: heal my soul; for I have sinned against thee.   Ps. 103:3

5 Mine enemies speak evil of me, When shall he die, and his name perish?

6 And if he come to see me, he speaketh vanity: his heart gathereth iniquity to itself; *when* he goeth abroad, he telleth *it*.   Prov. 26:24-26

7 All that hate me whisper together against me: against me do they devise my hurt.

8 An evil disease, *say they*, ᵀcleaveth fast unto him: and *now* that he lieth he shall rise up no more.   Ps. 71:11 ◆ *clings*

9 Yea, mine own familiar friend, in whom I trusted, which did eat of my bread, hath lifted up *his* heel against me.   2 Sam. 15:12; John 13:18

10 But thou, O LORD, be merciful unto me, and raise me up, that I may requite them.

11 By this I know that thou favourest me, because mine enemy doth not triumph over me.

12 And as for me, thou upholdest me in mine integrity, and settest me before thy face for ever.   Job 36:7

13 Blessed *be* the LORD God of Israel from everlasting, and to everlasting. Amen, and Amen.   Ps. 72:18-19; 89:52; 106:48

PSALM 42

Souls That Thirst after God Shall Be Quenched

To the chief Musician, Maschil, for the sons of Korah.

As the ᵀhart panteth after the water brooks, so panteth my soul after thee, O God.   *deer*

2 My soul thirsteth for God, for the living God: when shall I come and appear before God?   Ps. 63:1; 84:2; Jer. 10:10

3 My tears have been my meat day and night, while they continually say unto me, Where *is* thy God?   Ps. 79:10; 80:5; 102:9

4 When I remember these *things*, I pour out my soul in me: for I had gone with the multitude, I went with them to the house of God, with the voice of joy and praise, with a multitude that kept holyday.   Ps. 122:1; Is. 30:29

5 Why art thou cast down, O my soul? and *why* art thou disquieted in me? hope thou in God: for I shall yet praise him *for* the help of his countenance.   Ps. 42:11

6 O my God, my soul is cast down within me: therefore will I remember thee from the land of Jordan, and of the Hermonites, from the hill Mizar.   2 Sam. 17:22

7 Deep calleth unto deep at the noise of thy waterspouts: all thy waves and thy billows are gone over me.   Ps. 88:7; Jon. 2:3

8 *Yet* the LORD will command his lovingkindness in the daytime, and in the night his song *shall be* with me, *and* my prayer unto the God of my life.   Job 35:10; Ps. 63:6; 149:5

9 I will say unto God my rock, Why hast thou forgotten me? why go I mourning because of the oppression of the enemy?   Ps. 18:2; 38:6; 43:2

10 *As* with a sword in my bones, mine enemies reproach me; while they say daily unto me, Where *is* thy God?   Ps. 42:3; Joel 2:17

11 Why art thou cast down, O my soul? and why art thou disquieted within me? hope thou in God: for I shall yet praise him, *who is* the health of my ᵀcountenance, and my God.   Ps. 42:5 ◆ *appearance*

42:11 Do Not Be Discouraged

There are those who have known the pardoning love of Christ and who really desire to be children of God, yet they realize that their character is imperfect, their life faulty, and they are ready to doubt whether their hearts have been renewed by the Holy Spirit. To such I would say, Do not draw back in despair. *SC 64*

PSALM 43

Downcast Souls Must Hope in God

Judge me, O God, and plead my cause against an ungodly nation: O deliver me from the deceitful and unjust man.   1 Sam. 24:15

2 For thou *art* the God of my strength: why dost thou cast me off? why go I mourning because of the oppression of the enemy?   Ps. 28:7

3 O send out thy light and thy truth: let them lead me; let them bring me unto thy holy hill, and to thy tabernacles.   Ps. 2:6

4 Then will I go unto the altar of God, unto God my exceeding joy: yea, upon the harp will I praise thee, O God my God.   Ps. 57:8

5 Why art thou cast down, O my soul? and why art thou disquieted within me? hope in God: for I shall yet praise him, *who is* the health of my countenance, and my God.

PSALM 44

A Reminder of Past Victories and a Plea for Help

To the chief Musician for the sons of Korah, Maschil.

We have heard with our ears, O God, our fathers have told us, *what* work thou didst in their days, in the times of old.   Ex. 13:14-15

2 *How* thou didst drive out the heathen with thy hand, and plantedst them; *how* thou didst afflict the people, and cast them out.   Ex. 15:17; Ps. 78:55; 135:10-12

3 For they got not the land in possession by their own sword, neither did their own arm save them: but thy right hand, and thine arm, and the light of thy ᵀcountenance, because thou hadst a favour unto them.   Deut. 7:7-8; 8:17-18; Josh. 24:12 ◆ *appearance*

4 Thou art my King, O God: command deliverances for Jacob.   Ps. 42:8; 74:12

5 Through thee will we push down our enemies: through thy name will we tread them under that rise up against us.   Deut. 33:17

6 For I will not trust in my bow, neither shall my sword save me.   Hos. 1:7

7 But thou hast saved us from our enemies, and hast put them to shame that hated us.

8 In God we boast all the day long, and praise thy name for ever. Selah.   Ps. 34:2

9 But thou hast cast off, and put us to shame; and goest not forth with our armies.   Ps. 60:1, 10; 74:1

10 Thou makest us to turn back from the enemy: and they which hate us ᵀspoil for themselves.   Lev. 26:17; Josh. 7:8, 12 ◆ *plunder*

11 Thou hast given us like sheep *appointed* for meat; and hast scattered us among the heathen.   Deut. 4:27

12 Thou sellest thy people for ᵀnought, and dost not increase *thy wealth* by their price.   Deut. 32:30; Is. 52:3-4; Jer. 15:13 ◆ *nothing*

13 Thou makest us a reproach to our neighbours, a scorn and a derision to them that are round about us.   Ps. 79:4; 80:6

14 Thou makest us a byword among the heathen, a shaking of the head among the people.   2 Kin. 19:21; Job 16:4; Jer. 24:9

15 My confusion *is* continually before me, and the shame of my face hath covered me,

16 For the voice of him that reproacheth and blasphemeth; by reason of the enemy and avenger.   Ps. 8:2

17 All this is come upon us; yet have we not forgotten thee, neither have we dealt falsely in thy covenant.   Dan. 9:13

18 Our heart is not turned back, neither have our steps declined from thy way;   Ps. 119:51

19 Though thou hast sore broken us in the place of dragons, and covered us with the shadow of death.   Job 3:5; Ps. 23:4; 51:8

20 If we have forgotten the name of our God, or stretched out our hands to a strange god;   Job 11:13

21 Shall not God search this out? for he knoweth the secrets of the heart.   Jer. 17:10

22 Yea, for thy sake are we killed all the day long; we are counted as sheep for the slaughter.   Rom. 8:36

23 Awake, why sleepest thou, O Lord? arise, cast *us* not off for ever.   Ps. 7:6

24 Wherefore hidest thou thy face, *and* forgettest our affliction and our oppression?

25 For our soul is bowed down to the dust: our belly cleaveth unto the earth.   Ps. 119:25

26 Arise for our help, and redeem us for thy mercies' sake.   Ps. 25:22

PSALM 45

The Majesty and Grace of Christ's Kingdom

To the chief Musician upon Shoshannim, for the sons of Korah, Maschil, A Song of loves.

My heart is ᵀinditing a good matter: I speak of the things which I have made touching the king: my tongue *is* the pen of a ready writer.   *overflowing with*

2 Thou art fairer than the children of men: grace is poured into thy lips: therefore God hath blessed thee for ever.   Is. 50:4; Luke 4:22

3 Gird thy sword upon *thy* thigh, O *most* mighty, with thy glory and thy majesty.

4 And in thy majesty ride prosperously because of truth and meekness *and* righteousness; and thy right hand shall teach thee terrible things.   Ps. 65:5

5 Thine arrows *are* sharp in the heart of the king's enemies; *whereby* the people fall under thee.

6 Thy throne, O God, *is* for ever and ever: the sceptre of thy kingdom *is* a right sceptre.   Ps. 93:2; Is. 9:6-7; Dan. 2:44

7 Thou lovest righteousness, and hatest wickedness: therefore God, thy God, hath anointed thee with the oil of gladness above thy fellows.   Ps. 21:6

8 All thy garments *smell* of myrrh, and aloes, *and* cassia, out of the ivory palaces, whereby they have made thee glad.   John 19:39

9 Kings' daughters *were* among thy honourable women: upon thy right hand did stand the queen in gold of Ophir.   1 Kin. 2:19

10 Hearken, O daughter, and consider, and incline thine ear; forget also thine own people, and thy father's house;   Deut. 21:13

11 So shall the king greatly desire thy beauty: for he *is* thy Lord; and worship thou him.   Ps. 95:6

12 And the daughter of Tyre *shall be there* with

a gift; *even* the rich among the people shall ^Tintreat thy favour.   Ps. 22:29; Is. 49:23 ◆ *plead*

13 The king's daughter *is* all glorious within: her clothing *is* of wrought gold.   Is. 61:10

14 She shall be brought unto the king in ^Traiment of needlework: the virgins her companions that follow her shall be brought unto thee.   Judg. 5:30 ◆ *clothing*

15 With gladness and rejoicing shall they be brought: they shall enter into the king's palace.

16 Instead of thy fathers shall be thy children, whom thou mayest make princes in all the earth.   1 Pet. 2:9

17 I will make thy name to be remembered in all generations: therefore shall the people praise thee for ever and ever.   Mal. 1:11

PSALM 46

God Is Our Refuge and Strength

To the chief Musician for the sons of
Korah, A Song upon Alamoth.

God *is* our refuge and strength, a very present help in trouble.   Deut. 4:7; Ps. 9:9

2 Therefore will not we fear, though the earth be removed, and though the mountains be carried into the midst of the sea;   Ps. 23:4

3 *Though* the waters thereof roar *and* be troubled, *though* the mountains shake with the swelling thereof. Selah.   Ps. 93:3-4

4 *There is* a river, the streams whereof shall make glad the city of God, the holy *place* of the tabernacles of the most High.   Ps. 48:1; 87:3

5 God *is* in the midst of her; she shall not be moved: God shall help her, *and that* right early.   Deut. 23:14; Is. 12:6; Ezek. 43:7

6 The heathen raged, the kingdoms were moved: he uttered his voice, the earth melted.   Amos 9:5

7 The LORD of hosts *is* with us; the God of Jacob *is* our refuge. Selah.   Num. 14:9; 2 Chr. 13:12

8 Come, behold the works of the LORD, what desolations he hath made in the earth.   Ps. 66:5

9 He maketh wars to cease unto the end of the earth; he breaketh the bow, and cutteth the spear in sunder; he burneth the chariot in the fire.   Is. 2:4

10 Be still, and know that I *am* God: I will be exalted among the heathen, I will be exalted in the earth.   Ps. 100:3; Is. 2:11, 17

46:10 Christ Speaks in Quietness

In all who are under the training of God is to be revealed a life that is not in harmony with the world, its customs, or its practices; and everyone needs to have a personal experience in obtaining a knowledge of the will of God. We must individually hear Him speaking to the heart. When every other voice is hushed, and in quietness we wait before Him, the silence of the soul makes more distinct the voice of God. *DA 363*

---

11 The LORD of hosts *is* with us; the God of Jacob *is* our refuge. Selah.

PSALM 47

God Is King over All the Earth

To the chief Musician, A Psalm
for the sons of Korah.

O clap your hands, all ye people; shout unto God with the voice of triumph.

2 For the LORD most high *is* terrible; *he is* a great King over all the earth.   Deut. 7:21

3 He shall subdue the people under us, and the nations under our feet.   Ps. 18:47

4 He shall choose our inheritance for us, the excellency of Jacob whom he loved. Selah.   Amos 6:8; 8:7; 1 Pet. 1:4

The Secret of Strength

Psalm 46:10

An intensity such as never before was seen is taking possession of the world. In amusement, in moneymaking, in the contest for power, in the very struggle for existence, there is a terrible force that engrosses body and mind and soul. In the midst of this maddening rush, God is speaking. He bids us come apart and commune with Him. "Be still, and know that I am God" (Psalm 46:10).

Many, even in their seasons of devotion, fail of receiving the blessing of real communion with God. They are in too great haste. With hurried steps they press through the circle of Christ's loving presence, pausing perhaps a moment within the sacred precincts, but not waiting for counsel. They have no time to remain with the divine Teacher. With their burdens they return to their work.

These workers can never attain the highest success until they learn the secret of strength. They must give themselves time to think, to pray, to wait upon God for a renewal of physical, mental, and spiritual power. They need the uplifting influence of His Spirit. Receiving this, they will be quickened by fresh life. The wearied frame and tired brain will be refreshed, the burdened heart will be lightened.

Not a pause for a moment in His presence, but personal contact with Christ, to sit down in companionship with Him—this is our need. *Ed 260, 261*

5 God is gone up with a shout, the LORD with the sound of a trumpet. 2 Sam. 6:15
6 Sing praises to God, sing praises: sing praises unto our King, sing praises.
7 For God *is* the King of all the earth: sing ye praises with understanding. Zech. 14:9; Col. 3:16
8 God reigneth over the heathen: God sitteth upon the throne of his holiness. 1 Chr. 16:31
9 The princes of the people are gathered together, *even* the people of the God of Abraham: for the shields of the earth *belong* unto God: he is greatly exalted. Ps. 72:11; 89:18

PSALM 48

Great Is the Lord and Greatly to Be Praised

A Song *and* Psalm for the sons of Korah.

G reat *is* the LORD, and greatly to be praised in the city of our God, *in* the mountain of his holiness. Ps. 46:4; Mic. 4:1; Zech. 8:3
2 Beautiful for situation, the joy of the whole earth, *is* mount Zion, *on* the sides of the north, the city of the great King. Ps. 50:2
3 God is known in her palaces for a refuge.
4 For, lo, the kings were assembled, they passed by together. 2 Sam. 10:6-19
5 They saw *it, and* so they marvelled; they were troubled, *and* hasted away.
6 Fear took hold upon them there, *and* pain, as of a woman in travail. Hos. 13:13
7 Thou breakest the ships of Tarshish with an east wind. 1 Kin. 22:48; Jer. 18:17; Ezek. 27:25-26
8 As we have heard, so have we seen in the city of the LORD of hosts, in the city of our God: God will establish it for ever. Selah.
9 We have thought of thy lovingkindness, O God, in the midst of thy temple. Ps. 26:3; 40:10
10 According to thy name, O God, so *is* thy praise unto the ends of the earth: thy right hand is full of righteousness. Deut. 28:58; Josh. 7:9
11 Let mount Zion rejoice, let the daughters of Judah be glad, because of thy judgments. Ps. 97:8
12 Walk about Zion, and go round about her: tell the towers thereof.
13 Mark ye well her ᵀbulwarks, consider her palaces; that ye may tell *it* to the generation following. Ps. 122:7 ♦ *structures for defense*
14 For this God *is* our God for ever and ever: he will be our guide *even* unto death. Ps. 73:24

PSALM 49

Earthly Riches Will Not Last

To the chief Musician, A Psalm for the sons of Korah.

H ear this, all *ye* people; give ear, all *ye* inhabitants of the world: Ps. 78:1; Is. 49:6
2 Both low and high, rich and poor, together. Ps. 62:9
3 My mouth shall speak of wisdom; and the meditation of my heart *shall be* of understanding.
4 I will incline mine ear to a parable: I will open my dark saying upon the harp. Num. 12:8
5 Wherefore should I fear in the days of evil, *when* the iniquity of my heels shall ᵀcompass me about? *surround*
6 They that trust in their wealth, and boast themselves in the multitude of their riches; Ps. 52:7
7 None *of them* can by any means redeem his brother, nor give to God a ransom for him: Matt. 16:26
8 (For the redemption of their soul *is* precious, and it ceaseth for ever:) Job 36:18-19
9 That he should still live for ever, *and* not see corruption. Ps. 16:10; 89:48
10 For he seeth *that* wise men die, likewise the fool and the ᵀbrutish person perish, and leave their wealth to others. Ps. 39:6 ♦ *dumb*
11 Their inward thought *is, that* their houses *shall continue* for ever, *and* their dwelling places to all generations; they call *their* lands after their own names. Gen. 4:17; Ps. 5:9; 64:6
12 Nevertheless man *being* in honour abideth not: he is like the beasts *that* perish.
13 This their way *is* their folly: yet their posterity approve their sayings. Selah. Luke 12:20
14 Like sheep they are laid in the grave; death shall feed on them; and the upright shall have dominion over them in the morning; and their beauty shall consume in the grave from their dwelling. Job 30:23; Mal. 4:3; 1 Cor. 6:2
15 But God will redeem my soul from the power of the grave: for he shall receive me. Selah. Ps. 56:13; 73:24; Hos. 13:14
16 Be not thou afraid when one is made rich, when the glory of his house is increased;
17 For when he dieth he shall carry nothing away: his glory shall not descend after him. Job 27:19; 1 Tim. 6:7
18 Though while he lived he blessed his soul: and *men* will praise thee, when thou doest well to thyself. Deut. 29:19; Luke 12:19
19 He shall go to the generation of his fathers; they shall never see light. Gen. 15:15; Job 33:30
20 Man *that is* in honour, and understandeth not, is like the beasts *that* perish. Ps. 49:12

PSALM 50

God Desires Obedience More than Sacrifices

A Psalm of Asaph.

T he mighty God, *even* the LORD, hath spoken, and called the earth from the rising of the sun unto the going down thereof. Josh. 22:22; Ps. 113:3
2 Out of Zion, the perfection of beauty, God hath shined. Deut. 33:2; Ps. 48:2; 80:1
3 Our God shall come, and shall not keep silence: a fire shall devour before him, and

it shall be very tempestuous round about him.   Lev. 10:2; Num. 16:35; Dan. 7:10

4 He shall call to the heavens from above, and to the earth, that he may judge his people.   Deut. 31:28; 32:1; Is. 1:2

5 Gather my saints together unto me; those that have made a covenant with me by sacrifice.

6 And the heavens shall declare his righteousness: for God *is* judge himself. Selah.

7 Hear, O my people, and I will speak; O Israel, and I will testify against thee: I *am* God, *even* thy God.   Ex. 20:2; Ps. 81:8

8 I will not reprove thee for thy sacrifices or thy burnt offerings, *to have been* continually before me.   Hos. 6:6

9 I will take no ᵀbullock out of thy house, *nor* he goats out of thy folds.   bull

10 For every beast of the forest *is* mine, *and* the cattle upon a thousand hills.

50:10†

| Managing God's Gifts See Haggai 2:8. |

11 I know all the fowls of the mountains: and the wild beasts of the field *are* mine.

12 If I were hungry, I would not tell thee: for the world *is* mine, and the fulness thereof.

13 Will I eat the flesh of bulls, or drink the blood of goats?

14 Offer unto God thanksgiving; and pay thy vows unto the most High: Deut. 23:21; Ps. 76:11

15 And call upon me in the day of trouble: I will deliver thee, and thou shalt glorify me.

50:15 Calling on God in Trouble

The Lord says, "Call upon Me in the day of trouble" (Psalm 50:15). He invites us to present to Him our perplexities and necessities, and our need of divine help. He bids us be instant in prayer. As soon as difficulties arise, we are to offer to Him our sincere, earnest petitions. By our importunate prayers we give evidence of our strong confidence in God. The sense of our need leads us to pray earnestly, and our heavenly Father is moved by our supplications. *COL 172*

16 But unto the wicked God saith, What hast thou to do to declare my statutes, or *that* thou shouldest take my covenant in thy mouth?

17 Seeing thou hatest instruction, and castest my words behind thee.   Neh. 9:26; Prov. 12:1

18 When thou sawest a thief, then thou consentedst with him, and hast been partaker with adulterers.   Rom. 1:32; 1 Tim. 5:22

19 Thou givest thy mouth to evil, and thy tongue frameth deceit.   Ps. 10:7

20 Thou sittest *and* speakest against thy brother; thou slanderest thine own mother's son.   Matt. 10:21

21 These *things* hast thou done, and I kept silence; thou thoughtest that I was alto-

gether *such an one* as thyself: *but* I will reprove thee, and set *them* in order before thine eyes.

22 Now consider this, ye that forget God, lest I tear *you* in pieces, and *there be* none to deliver.   Job 8:13; Ps. 7:2; 9:17

23 Whoso offereth praise glorifieth me: and to him that ordereth *his* ᵀconversation *aright* will I shew the salvation of God.   conduct

50:23 Praise and Thanksgiving

A congregation may be the poorest in the land. It may be without the attraction of any outward show; but if the members possess the principles of the character of Christ, they will have His joy in their souls. Angels will unite with them in their worship. The praise and thanksgiving from grateful hearts will ascend to God as a sweet oblation. *COL 298*

PSALM 51

David Confesses Sin and Prays for Forgiveness

To the chief Musician, A Psalm of David, when Nathan the prophet came unto him, after he had gone in to Bathsheba.

Have mercy upon me, O God, according to thy lovingkindness: according unto the multitude of thy tender mercies blot out my transgressions.   Is. 43:25; Acts 3:19; Col. 2:14

2 Wash me throughly from mine iniquity, and cleanse me from my sin.   Ps. 51:7; Rev. 1:5

3 For I acknowledge my ᵀtransgressions: and my sin *is* ever before me.   violations of a law

4 Against thee, thee only, have I sinned, and done *this* evil in thy sight: that thou mightest be justified when thou speakest, *and* be clear when thou judgest.   Gen. 20:6; Luke 15:21; Rom. 3:4

5 Behold, I was shapen in iniquity; and in sin did my mother conceive me.   Job 14:4; Ps. 58:3

6 Behold, thou desirest truth in the inward parts: and in the hidden *part* thou shalt make me to know wisdom.   Job 38:36

51:7 Come to Christ for Cleansing

Do not listen to the enemy's suggestion to stay away from Christ until you have made yourself better; until you are good enough to come to God. If you wait until then, you will never come. When Satan points to your filthy garments, repeat the promise of Jesus, "Him that cometh to Me I will in no wise cast out" (John 6:37). Tell the enemy that the blood of Jesus Christ cleanses from all sin. Make the prayer of David your own. . . . *COL 205, 206*

7 Purge me with ᵀhyssop, and I shall be clean: wash me, and I shall be whiter than snow.   Is. 1:18; Heb. 9:19 ♦ bitter herbs

8 Make me to hear joy and gladness; *that* the bones *which* thou hast broken may rejoice.

9 Hide thy face from my sins, and blot out all mine iniquities. _Jer. 16:17_
10 Create in me a clean heart, O God; and renew a right spirit within me. _Ps. 78:37; Matt. 5:8_

51:10 Earnestly Seek a Clean Heart

Many accept an intellectual religion, a form of godliness, when the heart is not cleansed. Let it be your prayer, "Create in me a clean heart, O God; and renew a right [steadfast] spirit within me" (Psalm 51:10). Deal truly with your own soul. Be as earnest, as persistent, as you would be if your mortal life were at stake. This is a matter to be settled between God and your own soul, settled for eternity. A supposed hope, and nothing more, will prove your ruin. _SC 35_

11 Cast me not away from thy presence; and take not thy holy spirit from me. _2 Kin. 13:23_
12 Restore unto me the joy of thy salvation; and uphold me _with thy_ free spirit. _Ps. 13:5_
13 _Then_ will I teach ᵀtransgressors thy ways; and sinners shall be converted unto thee. _Luke 22:32_ ♦ _those who violate the law_
14 Deliver me from bloodguiltiness, O God, thou God of my salvation: _and_ my tongue shall sing aloud of thy righteousness. _Ps. 26:9_
15 O Lord, open thou my lips; and my mouth shall shew forth thy praise.
16 For thou desirest not sacrifice; else would I give _it_: thou delightest not in burnt offering.
17 The sacrifices of God _are_ a broken spirit: a broken and a ᵀcontrite heart, O God, thou wilt not despise. _Ps. 34:18_ ♦ _remorseful_

51:17 Contrite and Emptied of Self

Man must be emptied of self before he can be, in the fullest sense, a believer in Jesus. When self is renounced, then the Lord can make man a new creature. New bottles can contain the new wine. The love of Christ will animate the believer with new life. In him who looks unto the Author and Finisher of our faith the character of Christ will be manifest. _DA 280_

18 Do good in thy good pleasure unto Zion: build thou the walls of Jerusalem. _Ps. 102:16_
19 Then shalt thou be pleased with the sacrifices of righteousness, with burnt offering and whole burnt offering: then shall they offer bullocks upon thine altar. _Ps. 4:5; Mal. 3:3_

PSALM 52

David Prays against Evildoers

To the chief Musician, Maschil, _A Psalm of David, when Doeg the Edomite came and told Saul, and said unto him, David is come to the house of Ahimelech._

WHY boastest thou thyself in mischief, O mighty man? the goodness of God _endureth_ continually. _1 Sam. 21:7_

2 Thy tongue deviseth mischiefs; like a sharp razor, working deceitfully. _Ps. 57:4_
3 Thou lovest evil more than good; _and_ lying rather than to speak righteousness. Selah.
4 Thou lovest all devouring words, O _thou_ deceitful tongue.
5 God shall likewise destroy thee for ever, he shall take thee away, and pluck thee out of _thy_ dwelling place, and root thee out of the land of the living. Selah. _Ps. 27:13; Prov. 2:22_
6 The righteous also shall see, and fear, and shall laugh at him: _Job 22:19; Ps. 37:34; 40:3_
7 Lo, _this is_ the man _that_ made not God his strength; but trusted in the abundance of his riches, _and_ strengthened himself in his wickedness.
8 But I _am_ like a green olive tree in the house of God: I trust in the mercy of God for ever and ever. _Ps. 1:3; 13:5; Jer. 11:16_
9 I will praise thee for ever, because thou hast done _it_: and I will wait on thy name; for _it is_ good before thy saints. _Ps. 54:6_

PSALM 53

David Describes Man's Sinfulness

To the chief Musician upon Maha-lath, Maschil, _A Psalm_ of David.

THE fool hath said in his heart, _There is_ no God. Corrupt are they, and have done abominable iniquity: _there is_ none that doeth good. _Ps. 10:4; 14; 88:1_
2 God looked down from heaven upon the children of men, to see if there were _any_ that did understand, that did seek God. _2 Chr. 15:2_
3 Every one of them is gone back: they are altogether become filthy; _there is_ none that doeth good, no, not one. _Rom. 3:12_
4 Have the workers of iniquity no knowledge? who eat up my people _as_ they eat bread: they have not called upon God. _Jer. 4:22_
5 There were they in great fear, _where_ no fear was: for God hath scattered the bones of him that encampeth _against_ thee: thou hast put _them_ to shame, because God hath despised them. _Lev. 26:17, 36; Ezek. 6:5_
6 Oh that the salvation of Israel _were_ come out of Zion! When God bringeth back the captivity of his people, Jacob shall rejoice, _and_ Israel shall be glad. _Ps. 14:7_

PSALM 54

David Trusts in God's Help

To the chief Musician on Neginoth, Maschil, _A Psalm_ of David, when the Ziphims came and said to Saul, Doth not David hide himself with us?

SAVE me, O God, by thy name, and judge me by thy strength. _Ps. 20:1_
2 Hear my prayer, O God; give ear to the words of my mouth.

3 For strangers are risen up against me, and oppressors seek after my soul: they have not set God before them. Selah.   Ps. 36:1; 86:14
4 Behold, God *is* mine helper: the Lord *is* with them that uphold my soul.   Is. 41:10
5 He shall reward evil unto mine enemies: cut them off in thy truth.   Ps. 89:49; 143:12
6 I will freely sacrifice unto thee: I will praise thy name, O LORD; for *it is* good.   Ps. 52:9
7 For he hath delivered me out of all trouble: and mine eye hath seen *his desire* upon mine enemies.   Ps. 59:10; 92:11; 112:8

PSALM 55

David Is Hurt by a Close Friend

To the chief Musician on Neginoth, Maschil, *A Psalm* of David.

Give ear to my prayer, O God; and hide not thyself from my supplication. Ps. 61:1
2 Attend unto me, and hear me: I mourn in my complaint, and make a noise;   Is. 38:14
3 Because of the voice of the enemy, because of the oppression of the wicked: for they cast iniquity upon me, and in wrath they hate me.
4 My heart is sore pained within me: and the terrors of death are fallen upon me. Ps. 18:4-5
5 Fearfulness and trembling are come upon me, and horror hath overwhelmed me.
6 And I said, Oh that I had wings like a dove! *for then* would I fly away, and be at rest.
7 Lo, *then* would I wander far off, *and* remain in the wilderness. Selah.   Jer. 9:2
8 I would hasten my escape from the windy storm *and* tempest.
9 Destroy, O Lord, *and* divide their tongues: for I have seen violence and strife in the city.
10 Day and night they go about it upon the walls thereof: mischief also and sorrow *are* in the midst of it.
11 Wickedness *is* in the midst thereof: deceit and guile depart not from her streets.
12 For *it was* not an enemy *that* reproached me; then I could have borne *it*: neither *was*

it he that hated me *that* did magnify *himself* against me; then I would have hid myself from him:
13 But *it was* thou, a man mine equal, my guide, and mine acquaintance. 2 Sam. 15:12; 16:23
14 We took sweet counsel together, *and* walked unto the house of God in company.
15 Let death seize upon them, *and* let them go down ᵀquick into hell: for wickedness *is* in their dwellings, *and* among them.   living
16 As for me, I will call upon God; and the LORD shall save me.
17 Evening, and morning, and at noon, will I pray, and cry aloud: and he shall hear my voice.
18 He hath delivered my soul in peace from the battle *that was* against me: for there were many with me.
19 God shall hear, and afflict them, even he that abideth of old. Selah. Because they have no changes, therefore they fear not God.
20 He hath put forth his hands against such as be at peace with him: he hath broken his covenant.   Ps. 7:4
21 *The words* of his mouth were smoother than butter, but war *was* in his heart: his words were softer than oil, yet *were* they drawn swords.   Ps. 28:3; 57:4; Prov. 5:3-4
22 Cast thy burden upon the LORD, and he shall sustain thee: he shall never suffer the righteous to be moved.   Ps. 37:5, 24; 1 Pet. 5:7
23 But thou, O God, shalt bring them down into the pit of destruction: bloody and deceitful men shall not live out half their days; but I will trust in thee.   Job 15:32; Ps. 5:6; Prov. 10:27

PSALM 56

David Fears His Enemies, but Trusts God

To the chief Musician upon Jonath-
elem-rechokim, Michtam of David, when
the Philistines took him in Gath.

Be merciful unto me, O God: for man would swallow me up; he fighting daily oppresseth me.   Ps. 16:1

Cast Your Burdens on Jesus

Psalm 55:22

Keep your wants, your joys, your sorrows, your cares, and your fears before God. You cannot burden Him; you cannot weary Him. He who numbers the hairs of your head is not indifferent to the wants of His children. "The Lord is very pitiful, and of tender mercy" (James 5:11). His heart of love is touched by our sorrows and even by our utterances of them. Take to Him everything that perplexes the mind. Nothing is too great for Him to bear, for He holds up worlds, He rules over all the affairs of the universe. Nothing that in any way concerns our peace is too small for Him to notice. There is no chapter in our experience too dark for Him to read; there is no perplexity too difficult for Him to unravel. No calamity can befall the least of His children, no anxiety harass the soul, no joy cheer, no sincere prayer escape the lips, of which our heavenly Father is unobservant, or in which He takes no immediate interest. "He healeth the broken in heart, and bindeth up their wounds" (Psalm 147:3). The relations between God and each soul are as distinct and full as though there were not another soul upon the earth to share His watchcare, not another soul for whom He gave His beloved Son. *SC 100*

2 Mine enemies would daily swallow *me* up: for *they be* many that fight against me, O thou most High.

3 What time I am afraid, I will trust in thee.

4 In God I will praise his word, in God I have put my trust; I will not fear what flesh can do unto me. Ps. 27:1; 118:6; Heb. 13:6

5 Every day they ᵀwrest my words: all their thoughts *are* against me for evil. 2 Pet. 3:16 ◆ *twist*

6 They gather themselves together, they hide themselves, they mark my steps, when they wait for my soul. Ps. 59:3; 71:10; 140:2

7 Shall they escape by iniquity? in *thine* anger cast down the people, O God. Ps. 55:23

8 Thou tellest my wanderings: put thou my tears into thy bottle: *are they* not in thy book? 2 Kin. 20:5; Ps. 39:12; Mal. 3:16

56:8 God's Book of Remembrance

In the book of God's remembrance every deed of righteousness is immortalized. There every temptation resisted, every evil overcome, every word of tender pity expressed, is faithfully chronicled. And every act of sacrifice, every suffering and sorrow endured for Christ's sake, is recorded. *GC 481*

---

9 When I cry *unto thee*, then shall mine enemies turn back: this I know; for God *is* for me. Ps. 102:2; Rom. 8:31

10 In God will I praise *his* word: in the LORD will I praise *his* word.

11 In God have I put my trust: I will not be afraid what man can do unto me.

12 Thy vows *are* upon me, O God: I will render praises unto thee. Ps. 50:14

13 For thou hast delivered my soul from death: *wilt* not *thou deliver* my feet from fall-

ing, that I may walk before God in the light of the living? Job 33:30

PSALM 57

In Time of Trial, David Exalts God

To the chief Musician, Al-taschith, Michtam of David, when he fled from Saul in the cave.

B e merciful unto me, O God, be merciful unto me: for my soul trusteth in thee: yea, in the shadow of thy wings will I make my refuge, until *these* calamities be overpast. Ruth 2:12; Ps. 91:4; Is. 26:20

57:1–11 David Composes This Psalm in a Cave

In the cave of Adullam the family were united in sympathy and affection. The son of Jesse could make melody with voice and harp as he sang, "Behold, how good and how pleasant it is for brethren to dwell together in unity!" (Psalm 133:1). He had tasted the bitterness of distrust on the part of his own brothers; and the harmony that had taken the place of discord brought joy to the exile's heart. It was here that David composed the fifty-seventh psalm. *PP 658*

---

2 I will cry unto God most high; unto God that performeth *all things* for me. Ps. 138:8

3 He shall send from heaven, and save me *from* the reproach of him that would swallow me up. Selah. God shall send forth his mercy and his truth. Ps. 40:11; 43:3; 56:1-2

4 My soul *is* among lions: *and* I lie *even among* them that are set on fire, *even* the sons of men, whose teeth *are* spears and arrows, and their tongue a sharp sword. Ps. 55:21; 58:6; Prov. 30:14

5 Be thou exalted, O God, above the heavens; *let* thy glory *be* above all the earth. Ps. 57:11

David's Hardships; God's Hidden Blessings

Psalm 57

Among the mountains of Judah, David sought refuge from the pursuit of Saul. He made good his escape to the cave of Adullam, a place that, with a small force, could be held against a large army. "And when his brethren and all his father's house heard it, they went down thither to him." The family of David could not feel secure, knowing that at any time the unreasonable suspicions of Saul might be directed against them on account of their relation to David. They had now learned—what was coming to be generally known in Israel—that God had chosen David as the future ruler of His people; and they believed that they would be safer with him, even though he was a fugitive in a lonely cave, than they could be while exposed to the insane madness of a jealous king. . . .

Here David had a little kingdom of his own, and in it order and discipline prevailed. But even in his retreat in the mountains he was far from feeling secure, for he received continual evidence that the king had not relinquished his murderous purpose. . . .

The experience through which David was passing was not unnecessary or fruitless. God was giving him a course of discipline to fit him to become a wise general as well as a just and merciful king. With his band of fugitives he was gaining a preparation to take up the work that Saul, because of his murderous passion and blind indiscretion, was becoming wholly unfitted to do. Men cannot depart from the counsel of God and still retain that calmness and wisdom which will enable them to act with justice and discretion. There is no insanity so dreadful, so hopeless, as that of following human wisdom, unguided by the wisdom of God. *PP 657,658*

6 They have prepared a net for my steps; my soul is bowed down: they have digged a pit before me, into the midst whereof they are fallen *themselves*. Selah.   Ps. 140:5
7 My heart is fixed, O God, my heart is fixed: I will sing and give praise.   Ps. 112:7
8 Awake up, my glory; awake, psaltery and harp: I *myself* will awake early. Judg. 5:12; Ps. 16:9

57:8 Your First Work

Consecrate yourself to God in the morning; make this your very first work. Let your prayer be, "Take me, O Lord, as wholly Thine. I lay all my plans at Thy feet. Use me today in Thy service. Abide with me, and let all my work be wrought in Thee." This is a daily matter. Each morning consecrate yourself to God for that day. *SC 70*

---

9 I will praise thee, O Lord, among the people: I will sing unto thee among the nations.
10 For thy mercy *is* great unto the heavens, and thy truth unto the clouds. Ps. 36:5; 103:11
11 Be thou exalted, O God, above the heavens: *let* thy glory *be* above all the earth. Ps. 57:5

PSALM 58

David Reproves Wicked Judges

To the chief Musician, Al-taschith, Michtam of David.

D o ye indeed speak righteousness, O congregation? do ye judge uprightly, O ye sons of men?   Ps. 57:1
2 Yea, in heart ye work wickedness; ye weigh the violence of your hands in the earth.
3 The wicked are estranged from the womb: they go astray as soon as they be born, speaking lies.   Ps. 51:5; Is. 48:8
4 Their poison *is* like the poison of a serpent: *they are* like the deaf ᵀadder *that* stoppeth her ear; Ps. 140:3; Eccl. 10:11 ◆ *venomous snake*
5 Which will not hearken to the voice of charmers, charming never so wisely.
6 Break their teeth, O God, in their mouth: break out the great teeth of the young lions, O Lᴏʀᴅ.   Job 29:17; Ps. 3:7
7 Let them melt away as waters *which* run continually: *when* he bendeth *his bow to shoot* his arrows, let them be as cut in pieces.
8 As a snail *which* melteth, let *every one of them* pass away: *like* the untimely birth of a woman, *that* they may not see the sun. Job 3:16; Eccl. 6:3
9 Before your pots can feel the thorns, he shall take them away as with a whirlwind, both living, and in *his* wrath. Ps. 118:12; Eccl. 7:6
10 The righteous shall rejoice when he seeth the vengeance: he shall wash his feet in the blood of the wicked.   Ps. 64:10; 68:23; 107:42
11 So that a man shall say, Verily *there is* a reward for the righteous: ᵀverily he is a God that judgeth in the earth.
                    Ps. 67:4 ◆ *surely*

PSALM 59

David Prays for Deliverance from Enemies

To the chief Musician, Al-taschith, Michtam of David; when Saul sent, and they watched the house to kill him.

D eliver me from mine enemies, O my God: defend me from them that rise up against me.   Ps. 18:48
2 Deliver me from the workers of iniquity, and save me from bloody men.   Ps. 139:19
3 For, lo, they lie in wait for my soul: the mighty are gathered against me; not *for* my transgression, nor *for* my sin, O Lᴏʀᴅ.
4 They run and prepare themselves without *my* fault: awake to help me, and behold.
5 Thou therefore, O Lᴏʀᴅ God of hosts, the God of Israel, awake to visit all the heathen: be not merciful to any wicked ᵀtransgressors. Selah.   *those who violate the law*
6 They return at evening: they make a noise like a dog, and go round about the city.
7 Behold, they belch out with their mouth: swords *are* in their lips: for who, *say they,* doth hear?   Ps. 10:11; 57:4; Prov. 15:2
8 But thou, O Lᴏʀᴅ, shalt laugh at them; thou shalt have all the heathen in derision.
9 *Because of* his strength will I wait upon thee: for God *is* my defence.   Ps. 9:9; 62:2
10 The God of my mercy shall ᵀprevent me: God shall let me see *my desire* upon mine enemies.   Ps. 54:7 ◆ *go before*
11 Slay them not, lest my people forget: scatter them by thy power; and bring them down, O Lord our shield.   Ps. 3:3
12 *For* the sin of their mouth *and* the words of their lips let them even be taken in their pride: and for cursing and lying *which* they speak.   Prov. 12:13
13 Consume *them* in wrath, consume *them*, that they *may* not *be*: and let them know that God ruleth in Jacob unto the ends of the earth. Selah.   Ps. 7:9; 83:18
14 And at evening let them return; *and* let them make a noise like a dog, and go round about the city.   Ps. 22:16
15 Let them wander up and down for meat, and grudge if they be not satisfied. Job 15:23
16 But I will sing of thy power; yea, I will sing aloud of thy mercy in the morning: for thou hast been my defence and refuge in the day of my trouble.   Ps. 21:13
17 Unto thee, O my strength, will I sing: for God *is* my defence, *and* the God of my mercy.   Ps. 59:9-10

PSALM 60

David Prays for Israel's Deliverance

To the chief Musician upon Shushan-eduth, Michtam of David, to teach; when he strove with Aram-naharaim and with Aram-zobah, when Joab returned, and smote of Edom in the valley of salt twelve thousand.

O God, thou hast cast us off, thou hast scattered us, thou hast been displeased; O turn thyself to us again. 2 Sam. 5:20; Ps. 44:9
2 Thou hast made the earth to tremble; thou hast broken it: heal the breaches thereof; for it shaketh. 2 Chr. 7:14; Is. 30:26
3 Thou hast shewed thy people hard things: thou hast made us to drink the wine of astonishment. Ps. 71:20; Is. 51:17, 22
4 Thou hast given a banner to them that fear thee, that it may be displayed because of the truth. Selah. Ps. 20:5
5 That thy beloved may be delivered; save *with* thy right hand, and hear me. Ps. 17:7
6 God hath spoken in his holiness; I will rejoice, I will divide Shechem, and mete out the valley of Succoth. Gen. 12:6; Josh. 13:27; Ps. 89:35
7 Gilead *is* mine, and Manasseh *is* mine; Ephraim also *is* the strength of mine head; Judah *is* my lawgiver; Gen. 49:10; Deut. 33:17
8 Moab *is* my washpot; over Edom will I cast out my shoe: Philistia, triumph thou because of me. 2 Sam. 8:1-2
9 Who will bring me *into* the strong city? who will lead me into Edom?
10 *Wilt* not thou, O God, *which* hadst cast us off? and *thou*, O God, *which* didst not go out with our armies? Josh. 7:12
11 Give us help from trouble: for vain *is* the help of man. Ps. 146:3
12 Through God we shall do valiantly: for he *it is that* shall tread down our enemies. Ps.44:5

PSALM 61

David Takes Refuge in God

To the chief Musician upon Neginah, A Psalm of David.

Hear my cry, O God; attend unto my prayer.
2 From the end of the earth will I cry unto thee, when my heart is overwhelmed: lead me to the rock *that* is higher than I.

61:2 Who Is the Rock?

The same beautiful and expressive figures are carried throughout the Bible. Centuries before the advent of Christ, Moses pointed to Him as the rock of Israel's salvation (Deuteronomy 32:15); the psalmist sang of Him as "my Redeemer," "the rock of my strength," "the rock that is higher than I," "a rock of habitation," "rock of my heart," "rock of my refuge" (Psalms 19:14; 62:7; 61:2; 71:3 [margin]; 73:26 [margin]; 94:22). *PP 413*

3 For thou hast been a shelter for me, *and* a strong tower from the enemy. Prov. 18:10
4 I will abide in thy tabernacle for ever: I will trust in the covert of thy wings. Selah. Ps. 17:8
5 For thou, O God, hast heard my vows: thou hast given *me* the heritage of those that fear thy name. Ps. 56:12
6 Thou wilt prolong the king's life: *and* his years as many generations. Ps. 21:4
7 He shall abide before God for ever: O prepare mercy and truth, *which* may preserve him. Ps. 40:11; 41:12
8 So will I sing praise unto thy name for ever, that I may daily perform my vows. Ps. 65:1

PSALM 62

David's Soul Rests in God

To the chief Musician, to Jeduthun, A Psalm of David.

Truly my soul waiteth upon God: from him *cometh* my salvation. Ps. 33:20; 37:7, 39
2 He only *is* my rock and my salvation; *he is* my defence; I shall not be greatly moved.
3 How long will ye imagine mischief against a man? ye shall be slain all of you: as a bowing wall *shall ye be, and as* a tottering fence.
4 They only consult to cast *him* down from his excellency: they delight in lies: they bless with their mouth, but they curse inwardly. Selah. Ps. 28:3; 55:21
5 My soul, wait thou only upon God; for my expectation *is* from him.
6 He only *is* my rock and my salvation: *he is* my defence; I shall not be moved. Ps. 62:2
7 In God *is* my salvation and my glory: the rock of my strength, *and* my refuge, *is* in God.

62:6, 7 Jesus the Rock of Strength

"Upon this rock," said Jesus, "I will build My church." In the presence of God, and all the heavenly intelligences, in the presence of the unseen army of hell, Christ founded His church upon the living Rock. That Rock is Himself—His own body, for us broken and bruised. Against the church built upon this foundation, the gates of hell shall not prevail. *DA 413*

8 Trust in him at all times; *ye* people, pour out your heart before him: God *is* a refuge for us. Selah. 1 Sam. 1:15; Ps. 42:4; Lam. 2:19
9 Surely men of low degree *are* vanity, *and* men of high degree *are* a lie: to be laid in the balance, they *are* altogether *lighter* than vanity. Ps. 39:5; Is. 40:15, 17
10 Trust not in oppression, and become not vain in robbery: if riches increase, set not your heart *upon them*. Ps. 52:7
11 God hath spoken once; twice have I heard this; that power *belongeth* unto God. Job 33:14

12 Also unto thee, O Lord, *belongeth* mercy: for thou renderest to every man according to his work.   Job 34:11; Ps. 103:8; Matt. 16:27

PSALM 63

David Thirsts for God

A Psalm of David, when he was
in the wilderness of Judah.

O God, thou *art* my God; early will I seek thee: my soul thirsteth for thee, my flesh longeth for thee in a dry and thirsty land, where no water is;   Ps. 78:34; 84:2; 143:6
2 To see thy power and thy glory, so *as* I have seen thee in the sanctuary.   Ps. 27:4; 78:61
3 Because thy lovingkindness *is* better than life, my lips shall praise thee.   Ps. 69:16
4 Thus will I bless thee while I live: I will lift up my hands in thy name. Ps. 28:2; 104:33; 134:2
5 My soul shall be satisfied as *with* marrow and fatness; and my mouth shall praise *thee* with joyful lips: Ps. 71:23
6 When I remember thee upon my bed, *and* meditate on thee in the *night* watches. Ps. 42:8
7 Because thou hast been my help, therefore in the shadow of thy wings will I rejoice.
8 My soul followeth hard after thee: thy right hand upholdeth me.   Ps. 18:35
9 But those *that* seek my soul, to destroy *it*, shall go into the lower parts of the earth.
10 They shall fall by the sword: they shall be a portion for foxes.   Jer. 18:21
11 But the king shall rejoice in God; every one that sweareth by him shall glory: but the mouth of them that speak lies shall be stopped.   Deut. 6:13; Ps. 21:1; Is. 45:23

PSALM 64

David Prays against a Conspiracy

To the chief Musician, A Psalm of David.

H ear my voice, O God, in my prayer: preserve my life from fear of the enemy.
2 Hide me from the secret counsel of the wicked; from the insurrection of the workers of iniquity: Ps. 56:6

3 Who ᵀwhet their tongue like ᵃ sword, *and* bend *their bows to shoot* their arrows, *even* bitter words: Ps. 58:7 ♦ *sharpen*
4 That they may shoot in secret at the perfect: suddenly do they shoot at him, and fear not.   Ps. 55:19
5 They encourage themselves *in* an evil matter: they commune of laying snares ᵀprivily; they say, Who shall see them? Ps. 10:11 ♦ *in secret*
6 They search out iniquities; they accomplish a diligent search: both the inward *thought* of every one *of them*, and the heart, is deep.
7 But God shall shoot at them *with* an arrow; suddenly shall they be wounded.   Ps. 7:12-13
8 So they shall make their own tongue to fall upon themselves: all that see them shall flee away.   Ps. 22:7; Prov. 12:13; 18:7

> **64:2–8 A Life and Death Warning**
>
> Closely connected with Christ's warning in regard to the sin against the Holy Spirit is a warning against idle and evil words. The words are an indication of that which is in the heart. . . . Jesus said, "Every idle word that men shall speak, they shall give account thereof in the day of judgment. For by thy words thou shalt be justified, and by thy words thou shalt be condemned" [Matthew 12:36, 37]. *DA 323*

9 And all men shall fear, and shall declare the work of God; for they shall wisely consider of his doing.   Ps. 40:3; Jer. 50:28; 51:10
10 The righteous shall be glad in the LORD, and shall trust in him; and all the upright in heart shall glory.

PSALM 65

David Praises God for His Provision

To the chief Musician, A Psalm
and Song of David.

P raise waiteth for thee, O God, in Sion: and unto thee shall the vow be performed.   Ps. 62:1

David Finds Christ Through the Sanctuary

Psalm 63:1, 2

Moses made the earthly sanctuary, "according to the fashion that he had seen." Paul declares that "the tabernacle, and all the vessels of the ministry," when completed, were "the patterns of things in the heavens" (Acts 7:44; Hebrews 9:21, 23). And John says that he saw the sanctuary in heaven. That sanctuary, in which Jesus ministers in our behalf, is the great original, of which the sanctuary built by Moses was a copy.

The heavenly temple, the abiding place of the King of kings, where "thousand thousands ministered unto Him, and ten thousand times ten thousand stood before Him" (Daniel 7:10), that temple filled with the glory of the eternal throne, where seraphim, its shining guardians, veil their faces in adoration—no earthly structure could represent its vastness and its glory. Yet important truths concerning the heavenly sanctuary and the great work there carried forward for man's redemption were to be taught by the earthly sanctuary and its services. *PP 357*

2 O thou that hearest prayer, unto thee shall all flesh come. Ps. 86:9

3 Iniquities prevail against me: *as for* our Ttransgressions, thou shalt purge them away. Ps. 38:4; 40:12; 79:9 ♦ *sins*

4 Blessed *is the man whom* thou choosest, and causest to approach *unto thee, that* he may dwell in thy courts: we shall be satisfied with the goodness of thy house, *even* of thy holy temple. Ps. 4:3; 33:12; 36:8

65:6–13 Love Revealed in Creation

In the beginning, God was revealed in all the works of creation. It was Christ that spread the heavens, and laid the foundations of the earth. It was His hand that hung the worlds in space, and fashioned the flowers of the field. . . . It was He that filled the earth with beauty, and the air with song. And upon all things in earth, and air, and sky, He wrote the message of the Father's love. *DA 20*

---

5 *By* terrible things in righteousness wilt thou answer us, O God of our salvation; *who art* the confidence of all the ends of the earth, and of them that are afar off *upon* the sea: Ps. 22:27

6 Which by his strength setteth fast the mountains; *being* girded with power: Ps. 93:1

7 Which stilleth the noise of the seas, the noise of their waves, and the tumult of the people. Ps. 89:9; 93:3-4; Is. 17:12-13

8 They also that dwell in the uttermost parts are afraid at thy tokens: thou makest the outgoings of the morning and evening to rejoice. Ps. 2:8

9 Thou visitest the earth, and waterest it: thou greatly enrichest it with the river of God, *which* is full of water: thou preparest them corn, when thou hast so provided for it. Ps. 46:4; 68:9-10; 104:13-15

10 Thou waterest the ridges thereof abundantly: thou settlest the furrows thereof: thou makest it soft with showers: thou blessest the springing thereof. Ps. 147:8

11 Thou crownest the year with thy goodness; and thy paths drop fatness.

12 They drop *upon* the pastures of the wilderness: and the little hills rejoice on every side. Job 38:26-27

13 The pastures are clothed with flocks; the valleys also are covered over with corn; they shout for joy, they also sing. Is. 55:12

PSALM 66

Come and See the Works of God

To the chief Musician, A Song *or* Psalm.

Make a joyful noise unto God, all ye lands: Ps. 81:1; 98:4; 100:1

2 Sing forth the honour of his name: make his praise glorious.

3 Say unto God, How terrible *art thou in* thy works! through the greatness of thy power shall thine enemies submit themselves unto thee. Ps. 18:44; 47:2; 65:5

4 All the earth shall worship thee, and shall sing unto thee; they shall sing *to* thy name. Selah. Ps. 22:27; 117:1

5 Come and see the works of God: *he is* terrible *in his* doing toward the children of men. Ps. 46:8

6 He turned the sea into dry *land*: they went through the flood on foot: there did we rejoice in him. Josh. 3:16

7 He ruleth by his power for ever; his eyes behold the nations: let not the rebellious exalt themselves. Selah. Ps. 11:4

8 O bless our God, ye people, and make the voice of his praise to be heard:

9 Which holdeth our soul in life, and suffereth not our feet to be moved. Ps. 121:3

10 For thou, O God, hast proved us: thou hast tried us, as silver is tried. Ps. 17:3

11 Thou broughtest us into the net; thou laidst affliction upon our Tloins. Lam. 1:13 ♦ *waist*

12 Thou hast caused men to ride over our heads; we went through fire and through water: but thou broughtest us out into a wealthy *place*. Is. 51:23

13 I will go into thy house with burnt offerings: I will pay thee my vows, Eccl. 5:4

14 Which my lips have uttered, and my mouth hath spoken, when I was in trouble.

15 I will offer unto thee burnt sacrifices of

God in Control of His Creation

Psalm 65:9–13

The material world is under God's control. The laws of nature are obeyed by nature. Everything speaks and acts the will of the Creator. Cloud and sunshine, dew and rain, wind and storm, all are under the supervision of God, and yield implicit obedience to His command. It is in obedience to the law of God that the spire of grain bursts through the ground, "first the blade, then the ear, after that the full corn in the ear" (Mark 4:28). These the Lord develops in their proper season because they do not resist His working. And can it be that man, made in the image of God, endowed with reason and speech, shall alone be unappreciative of His gifts and disobedient to His will? Shall rational beings alone cause confusion in our world? *COL 81, 82*

fatlings, with the incense of rams; I will offer bullocks with goats. Selah.

66:12 Jesus Will Never Fail Us

We are prone to look to our fellow men for sympathy and uplifting, instead of looking to Jesus. In His mercy and faithfulness God often permits those in whom we place confidence to fail us, in order that we may learn the folly of trusting in man and making flesh our arm. Let us trust fully, humbly, unselfishly in God. . . . When all things seem dark and unexplainable, remember the words of Christ, "What I do thou knowest not now; but thou shalt know hereafter" (John 13:7). *MH 486, 487*

16 Come *and* hear, all ye that fear God, and I will declare what he hath done for my soul.   Ps. 34:11
17 I cried unto him with my mouth, and he was extolled with my tongue.   Ps. 30:1
18 If I regard iniquity in my heart, the Lord will not hear *me*:   Prov. 28:9; Is. 1:15; James 4:3

66:18 When God Will Not Hear Prayer

If we regard iniquity in our hearts, if we cling to any known sin, the Lord will not hear us; but the prayer of the penitent, contrite soul is always accepted. When all known wrongs are righted, we may believe that God will answer our petitions. Our own merit will never commend us to the favor of God; it is the worthiness of Jesus that will save us, His blood that will cleanse us; yet we have a work to do in complying with the conditions of acceptance. *SC 95*

19 But [T]verily God hath heard *me*; he hath attended to the voice of my prayer.   surely
20 Blessed *be* God, which hath not turned away my prayer, nor his mercy from me.

PSALM 67

May God's Face Shine upon His People

To the chief Musician on Neginoth, A Psalm *or* Song.

God be merciful unto us, and bless us; *and* cause his face to shine upon us; Selah.   Ps. 4:1, 6; 31:16
2 That thy way may be known upon earth, thy saving health among all nations. Ps. 98:2-3
3 Let the people praise thee, O God; let all the people praise thee.
4 O let the nations be glad and sing for joy: for thou shalt judge the people righteously, and govern the nations upon earth. Selah.   Ps. 9:8
5 Let the people praise thee, O God; let all the people praise thee.   Ps. 67:3
6 *Then* shall the earth yield her increase; *and* God, *even* our own God, shall bless us. Lev. 26:4

67:5 The Privilege of Praise

Those who dwell upon God's great mercies, and are not unmindful of His lesser gifts, will put on the girdle of gladness and make melody in their hearts to the Lord. The daily blessings that we receive from the hand of God, and above all else the death of Jesus to bring happiness and heaven within our reach, should be a theme for constant gratitude. *PP 289*

7 God shall bless us; and all the ends of the earth shall fear him.   Ps. 22:27

PSALM 68

David Honors God as Defender and Provider

To the chief Musician, A Psalm *or* Song of David.

Let God arise, let his enemies be scattered: let them also that hate him flee before him.   Num. 10:35; Ps. 89:10; Is. 33:3
2 As smoke is driven away, *so* drive *them* away: as wax melteth before the fire, *so* let the wicked perish at the presence of God.
3 But let the righteous be glad; let them rejoice before God: yea, let them exceedingly rejoice.   Ps. 64:10
4 Sing unto God, sing praises to his name: [T]extol him that rideth upon the heavens by his name JAH, and rejoice before him.   praise
5 A father of the fatherless, and a judge of the widows, *is* God in his holy habitation.
6 God setteth the solitary in families: he bringeth out those which are bound with chains: but the rebellious dwell in a dry land.   Ps. 107:10, 14; 113:9
7 O God, when thou wentest forth before thy people, when thou didst march through the wilderness; Selah: Ex. 13:21; Judg. 4:14; 5:4
8 The earth shook, the heavens also dropped at the presence of God: *even* Sinai itself *was* moved at the presence of God, the God of Israel.   Ex. 19:16, 18; Judg. 5:4-5
9 Thou, O God, didst send a plentiful rain, whereby thou didst confirm thine inheritance, when it was weary.   Ezek. 34:26
10 Thy congregation hath dwelt therein: thou, O God, hast prepared of thy goodness for the poor.   Ps. 74:19
11 The Lord gave the word: great *was* the company of those that published *it*.
12 Kings of armies did flee [T]apace: and she that tarried at home divided the spoil.   swiftly
13 Though ye have lien among the pots, *yet* shall ye be as the wings of a dove covered with silver, and her feathers with yellow gold.
14 When the Almighty scattered kings in it, it was *white* as snow in Salmon.
15 The hill of God *is as* the hill of Bashan; an high hill *as* the hill of Bashan.

16 Why leap ye, ye high hills? *this is* the hill *which* God desireth to dwell in; yea, the LORD will dwell *in it* for ever.   Deut. 12:5; Ps. 132:13-14
17 The chariots of God *are* twenty thousand, *even* thousands of angels: the Lord *is* among them, *as in* Sinai, in the holy *place*.   Deut. 33:2
18 Thou hast ascended on high, thou hast led captivity captive: thou hast received gifts for men; yea, *for* the rebellious also, that the LORD God might dwell among them.   Judg. 5:12
19 Blessed *be* the Lord, *who* daily loadeth us *with benefits, even* the God of our salvation. Selah.
20 *He that is* our God *is* the God of salvation; and unto GOD the Lord *belong* the issues from death.   Deut. 32:39
21 But God shall wound the head of his enemies, *and* the hairy scalp of such an one as goeth on still in his ᵀtrespasses. Hab. 3:13 ◆ *sins*
22 The Lord said, I will bring again from Bashan, I will bring *my people* again from the depths of the sea: Num. 21:33
23 That thy foot may be dipped in the blood of *thine* enemies, *and* the tongue of thy dogs in the same.   1 Kin. 21:19; 22:38; Ps. 58:10
24 They have seen thy goings, O God; *even* the goings of my God, my King, in the sanctuary.
25 The singers went before, the players on instruments *followed* after; among *them were* the damsels playing with timbrels.   Ex. 15:20
26 Bless ye God in the congregations, *even* the Lord, from the fountain of Israel.   Is. 48:1
27 There *is* little Benjamin *with* their ruler, the princes of Judah *and* their council, the princes of Zebulun, *and* the princes of Naphtali.   1 Sam. 9:21
28 Thy God hath commanded thy strength: strengthen, O God, that which thou hast ᵀwrought for us.   Ps. 42:8 ◆ *made*
29 Because of thy temple at Jerusalem shall kings bring presents unto thee.   1 Kin. 10:10
30 Rebuke the company of spearmen, the multitude of the bulls, with the calves of the people, *till every one* submit himself with pieces of silver: scatter thou the people *that* delight in war.
31 Princes shall come out of Egypt; Ethiopia shall soon stretch out her hands unto God.   Ps. 44:20; Is. 45:14; Zeph. 3:10
32 Sing unto God, ye kingdoms of the earth; O sing praises unto the Lord; Selah:
33 To him that rideth upon the heavens of heavens, *which were* of old; lo, he doth send out his voice, *and that* a mighty voice. Ps. 18:10
34 Ascribe ye strength unto God: his excellency *is* over Israel, and his strength *is* in the clouds.
35 O God, *thou art* terrible out of thy holy places: the God of Israel *is* he that giveth

strength and power unto *his* people. Blessed *be* God.   Ps. 29:11; 65:5; 66:5

> ### 68:32–34 A Song of Welcoming Angels
>
> While the disciples were gazing upward to catch the last glimpse of their ascending Lord, He was received into the rejoicing ranks of heavenly angels. As these angels escorted Him to the courts above, they sang in triumph, "Sing unto God, ye kingdoms of the earth; O sing praises unto the Lord, to Him that rideth upon the heavens of heavens. . . . Ascribe ye strength unto God: His excellency is over Israel, and His strength is in the heavens" (Psalm 68:32–34, margin). *AA 32, 33*

PSALM 69

David Needs Rescue from His Enemies

To the chief Musician upon Shoshannim, *A Psalm* of David.

Save me, O God; for the waters are come in unto *my* soul.   Ps. 69:14-15
2 I sink in deep ᵀmire, where *there is* no standing: I am come into deep waters, where the floods overflow me.   Ps. 40:2 ◆ *mud*
3 I am weary of my crying: my throat is dried: mine eyes fail while I wait for my God.   Ps. 6:6; 119:82; Is. 38:14
4 They that hate me without a cause are more than the hairs of mine head: they that would destroy me, *being* mine enemies wrongfully, are mighty: then I restored *that* which I took not away.   Ps. 35:19; 40:12; John 15:25
5 O God, thou knowest my foolishness; and my sins are not hid from thee.
6 Let not them that wait on thee, O Lord GOD of hosts, be ashamed for my sake: let not those that seek thee be confounded for my sake, O God of Israel.
7 Because for thy sake I have borne reproach; shame hath covered my face.   Ps. 44:22; Is. 50:6
8 I am become a stranger unto my brethren, and an alien unto my mother's children.
9 For the zeal of thine house hath eaten me up; and the reproaches of them that reproached thee are fallen upon me. Ps. 89:50-51
10 When I wept, *and* ᵀchastened my soul with fasting, that was to my reproach.   *disciplined*
11 I made sackcloth also my garment; and I became a proverb to them.   1 Kin. 9:7
12 They that sit in the gate speak against me; and I *was* the song of the drunkards.
13 But as for me, my prayer *is* unto thee, O LORD, *in* an acceptable time: O God, in the multitude of thy mercy hear me, in the truth of thy salvation.   Is. 49:8; 2 Cor. 6:2
14 Deliver me out of the mire, and let me not sink: let me be delivered from them that hate me, and out of the deep waters. Ps. 144:7

15 Let not the waterflood overflow me, neither let the deep swallow me up, and let not the pit shut her mouth upon me.

16 Hear me, O LORD; for thy lovingkindness *is* good: turn unto me according to the multitude of thy tender mercies.   Ps. 25:16; 63:3

17 And hide not thy face from thy servant; for I am in trouble: hear me speedily.   Ps. 27:9

18 Draw nigh unto my soul, *and* redeem it: deliver me because of mine enemies.

19 Thou hast known my reproach, and my shame, and my dishonour: mine adversaries *are* all before thee.   Heb. 12:2

20 Reproach hath broken my heart; and I am full of heaviness: and I looked *for some* to take pity, but *there was* none; and for comforters, but I found none.   Job 16:2; Ps. 142:4; Is. 63:5

21 They gave me also ᵀgall for my meat; and in my thirst they gave me vinegar to drink.   Matt. 27:34, 48; Mark 15:23 ◆ *bitter substance*

69:20, 21 Christ's Strength in Suffering

To those who suffered death by the cross, it was permitted to give a stupefying potion, to deaden the sense of pain. This was offered to Jesus; but when He had tasted it, He refused it. He would receive nothing that could becloud His mind. His faith must keep fast hold upon God. This was His only strength. To becloud His senses would give Satan an advantage. *DA 746*

22 Let their table become a snare before them: and *that which should have been* for *their* welfare, *let it become* a trap.

23 Let their eyes be darkened, that they see not; and make their ᵀloins continually to shake.   Dan. 5:6 ◆ *waists*

24 Pour out thine ᵀindignation upon them, and let thy wrathful anger take hold of them.   Ps. 79:6 ◆ *anger*

25 Let their habitation be desolate; *and* let none dwell in their tents.   Matt. 23:38; Acts 1:20

26 For they persecute *him* whom thou hast smitten; and they talk to the grief of those whom thou hast wounded.   2 Chr. 28:9; Is. 53:4

27 Add iniquity unto their iniquity: and let them not come into thy righteousness.

28 Let them be blotted out of the book of the living, and not be written with the righteous.   Ezek. 13:9; Luke 10:20; Phil. 4:3

29 But I *am* poor and sorrowful: let thy salvation, O God, set me up on high.

30 I will praise the name of God with a song, and will magnify him with thanksgiving.

31 *This* also shall please the LORD better than an ox *or* ᵀbullock that hath horns and hoofs.   Ps. 50:13-14 ◆ *bull*

32 The humble shall see *this, and* be glad: and your heart shall live that seek God.   Ps. 22:26

33 For the LORD heareth the poor, and despiseth not his prisoners.   Ps. 68:6

34 Let the heaven and earth praise him, the seas, and every thing that moveth therein.   Ps. 96:11; Is. 49:13; 55:12

35 For God will save Zion, and will build the cities of Judah: that they may dwell there, and have it in possession.   Ps. 51:18; Is. 44:26

36 The seed also of his servants shall inherit it: and they that love his name shall dwell therein.   Ps. 37:29; 102:28

PSALM 70

David's Urgent Plea

To the chief Musician, *A Psalm* of David, to bring to remembrance.

Make haste, O God, to deliver me; make haste to help me, O LORD.   Ps. 40:13-17

2 Let them be ashamed and confounded that seek after my soul: let them be turned backward, and put to confusion, that desire my hurt.   Ps. 35:4

3 Let them be turned back for a reward of their shame that say, Aha, aha.   Ps. 40:15

4 Let all those that seek thee rejoice and be glad in thee: and let such as love thy salvation say continually, Let God be magnified.

5 But I *am* poor and needy: make haste unto me, O God: thou *art* my help and my deliverer; O LORD, make no tarrying. Ps. 40:17; 141:1

PSALM 71

God's Constant Presence and Help

In thee, O LORD, do I put my trust: let me never be put to confusion.   Ps. 25:2-3

2 Deliver me in thy righteousness, and cause me to escape: incline thine ear unto me, and save me.   Ps. 17:6

3 Be thou my strong habitation, whereunto I may continually resort: thou hast given commandment to save me; for thou *art* my rock and my fortress.   Ps. 18:2; 31:2-3; 44:4

4 Deliver me, O my God, out of the hand of the wicked, out of the hand of the unrighteous and cruel man.

5 For thou *art* my hope, O Lord GOD: *thou art* my trust from my youth.   Jer. 17:7

6 By thee have I been ᵀholden up from the womb: thou art he that took me out of my mother's bowels: my praise *shall be* continually of thee.   Ps. 22:9-10; 34:1; Jer. 1:5 ◆ *held*

7 I am as a wonder unto many; but thou *art* my strong refuge.   Is. 8:18; 1 Cor. 4:9

8 Let my mouth be filled *with* thy praise *and* with thy honour all the day.   Ps. 35:28

9 Cast me not off in the time of old age; forsake me not when my strength faileth.

10 For mine enemies speak against me; and

they that lay wait for my soul take counsel together,   Ps. 56:6

11 Saying, God hath forsaken him: persecute and take him; for *there is* none to deliver *him.*   Ps. 7:2

12 O God, be not far from me: O my God, make haste for my help.   Ps. 35:22

13 Let them be confounded *and* consumed that are adversaries to my soul; let them be covered *with* reproach and dishonour that seek my hurt.   Ps. 35:4

14 But I will hope continually, and will yet praise thee more and more.

15 My mouth shall shew forth thy righteousness *and* thy salvation all the day; for I know not the numbers *thereof.*   Ps. 35:28; 40:5

16 I will go in the strength of the Lord GOD: I will make mention of thy righteousness, *even* of thine only.   Ps. 51:14

17 O God, thou hast taught me from my youth: and ᵀhitherto have I declared thy wondrous works.   *up to now*

18 Now also when I am old and grayheaded, O God, forsake me not; until I have shewed thy strength unto *this* generation, *and* thy power to every one *that* is to come.   Ps. 71:9

19 Thy righteousness also, O God, *is* very high, who hast done great things: O God, who *is* like unto thee!   Ps. 35:10; 36:5-6; 57:10

20 *Thou,* which hast shewed me great and sore troubles, shalt ᵀquicken me again, and shalt bring me up again from the depths of the earth.   Ps. 60:3; 80:18; 138:7 ♦ *revive*

21 Thou shalt increase my greatness, and comfort me on every side.

22 I will also praise thee with the ᵀpsaltery, *even* thy truth, O my God: unto thee will I sing with the harp, O thou Holy One of Israel.   2 Kin. 19:22; Ps. 33:2; 89:18 ♦ *stringed instrument*

23 My lips shall greatly rejoice when I sing unto thee; and my soul, which thou hast redeemed.   Ps. 103:4

24 My tongue also shall talk of thy righteousness all the day long: for they are confounded, for they are brought unto shame, that seek my hurt.   Ps. 71:13

PSALM 72

A Prayer for Israel's King

A Psalm for Solomon.

Give the king thy judgments, O God, and thy righteousness unto the king's son.

2 He shall judge thy people with righteousness, and thy poor with judgment. Is. 9:7; 32:1

3 The mountains shall bring peace to the people, and the little hills, by righteousness.   Is. 52:7

4 He shall judge the poor of the people, he shall save the children of the needy, and shall break in pieces the oppressor.   Is. 11:4

5 They shall fear thee as long as the sun and moon endure, throughout all generations.

6 He shall come down like rain upon the mown grass: as showers *that* water the earth.   Deut. 32:2; 2 Sam. 23:4; Hos. 6:3

7 In his days shall the righteous flourish; and abundance of peace so long as the moon endureth.   Ps. 92:12; Is. 2:4

8 He shall have dominion also from sea to sea, and from the river unto the ends of the earth.   Ex. 23:31; Ps. 2:8; Zech. 9:10

9 They that dwell in the wilderness shall bow before him; and his enemies shall lick the dust.   Is. 49:23

10 The kings of Tarshish and of the isles shall bring presents: the kings of Sheba and Seba shall offer gifts.   1 Kin. 10:1

11 Yea, all kings shall fall down before him: all nations shall serve him.   Ps. 86:9

12 For he shall deliver the needy when he crieth; the poor also, and *him* that hath no helper.   Job 29:12

13 He shall spare the poor and needy, and shall save the souls of the needy.

14 He shall redeem their soul from deceit and violence: and precious shall their blood be in his sight.   Ps. 116:15

15 And he shall live, and to him shall be given of the gold of Sheba: prayer also shall be made for him continually; *and* daily shall he be praised.

16 There shall be an handful of corn in the earth upon the top of the mountains; the fruit thereof shall shake like Lebanon: and *they* of the city shall flourish like grass of the earth.

17 His name shall endure for ever: his name shall be continued as long as the sun: and *men* shall be blessed in him: all nations shall call him blessed.   Gen. 12:3; 22:18; Ps. 89:36

Psalm 72 Solomon's Great Opportunity

   With tender earnestness David entreated Solomon to be manly and noble, to show mercy and loving-kindness to his subjects, and in all his dealings with the nations of earth to honor and glorify the name of God and to make manifest the beauty of holiness. . . .

   Oh, what an opportunity was Solomon's! Should he follow the divinely inspired instruction of his father, his reign would be a reign of righteousness, like that described in the seventy-second psalm. *PK 26*

18 Blessed *be* the LORD God, the God of Israel, who only doeth wondrous things.

19 And blessed *be* his glorious name for ever: and let the whole earth be filled *with* his glory; Amen, and Amen. Num. 14:21; Neh. 9:5

20 The prayers of David the son of Jesse are ended.   2 Sam. 23:1

PSALM 73

Holy Living Will Bring Future Rewards

A Psalm of Asaph.

Truly God *is* good to Israel, *even* to such as are of a clean heart.   Matt. 5:8
2 But as for me, my feet were almost gone; my steps had well nigh slipped.   Ps. 94:18
3 For I was envious at the foolish, *when* I saw the prosperity of the wicked.   Job 21:7; Ps. 37:1
4 For *there are* no bands in their death: but their strength *is* firm.
5 They *are* not in trouble *as other* men; neither are they plagued like *other* men.   Ps. 73:12
6 Therefore pride ᵀcompasseth them about as a chain; violence covereth them *as a garment.*   Judg. 8:26; Ps. 109:18; Prov. 1:9 ◆ surrounds
7 Their eyes stand out with fatness: they have more than heart could wish.   Job 15:27
8 They are corrupt, and speak wickedly *concerning* oppression: they speak loftily.   Jude 16
9 They set their mouth against the heavens, and their tongue walketh through the earth.   Rev. 13:6
10 Therefore his people return ᵀhither: and waters of a full *cup* are wrung out to them.   here
11 And they say, How doth God know? and is there knowledge in the most High?

73:11 A Line That Can't Be Passed

Because of His long forbearance, men have trampled upon His authority. They have strengthened one another in oppression and cruelty toward His heritage, saying, "How doth God know? and is there knowledge in the Most High?" (Psalm 73:11). But there is a line beyond which they cannot pass. The time is near when they will have reached the prescribed limit. . . . The Lord will interpose to vindicate His own honor, to deliver His people, and to repress the swellings of unrighteousness. *COL 177, 178*

---

12 Behold, these *are* the ungodly, who prosper in the world; they increase *in* riches.
13 Verily I have cleansed my heart *in* vain, and washed my hands in innocency.   Job 21:15
14 For all the day long have I been plagued, and ᵀchastened every morning.   disciplined
15 If I say, I will speak thus; behold, I should offend *against* the generation of thy children.
16 When I thought to know this, it *was* too painful for me;   Eccl. 8:17
17 Until I went into the sanctuary of God; *then* understood I their end.   Ps. 77:13
18 Surely thou didst set them in slippery places: thou castedst them down into destruction.   Ps. 35:6
19 How are they *brought* into desolation, as in a moment! they are utterly consumed with terrors.
20 As a dream when *one* awaketh; *so*, O Lord, when thou awakest, thou shalt despise their image.   Job 20:8; Ps. 78:65
21 Thus my heart was grieved, and I was pricked in my ᵀreins.   desires
22 So foolish *was* I, and ignorant: I was *as* a beast before thee.   Ps. 92:6
23 Nevertheless I *am* continually with thee: thou hast ᵀholden *me* by my right hand.   held
24 Thou shalt guide me with thy counsel, and afterward receive me *to* glory.   Ps. 32:8
25 Whom have I in heaven *but thee?* and *there is* none upon earth *that* I desire beside thee.   Phil. 3:8
26 My flesh and my heart faileth: *but* God *is* the strength of my heart, and my portion for ever.   Ps. 18:2; 40:12; 84:2
27 For, lo, they that are far from thee shall perish: thou hast destroyed all them that go a whoring from thee.   Ex. 34:15; Num. 15:39; Ps. 119:155
28 But *it is* good for me to draw near to God: I have put my trust in the Lord GOD, that I may declare all thy works.   Ps. 65:4; 118:17; James 4:8

PSALM 74

A Prayer for a Devastated People

Maschil of Asaph.

O God, why hast thou cast *us* off for ever? *why* doth thine anger smoke against the sheep of thy pasture?   Deut. 29:20; Ps. 79:13; 95:7
2 Remember thy congregation, *which* thou hast purchased of old; the rod of thine inheritance, *which* thou hast redeemed; this mount Zion, wherein thou hast dwelt.   Ex. 15:16
3 Lift up thy feet unto the perpetual desolations; *even* all *that* the enemy hath done wickedly in the sanctuary.   Ps. 79:1
4 Thine enemies roar in the midst of thy congregations; they set up their ensigns *for* signs.   Num. 2:2; Lam. 2:7; Matt. 24:15
5 *A man* was famous according as he had lifted up axes upon the thick trees.
6 But now they break down the carved work thereof at once with axes and hammers.
7 They have cast fire into thy sanctuary, they have defiled *by casting down* the dwelling place of thy name to the ground.   2 Kin. 25:9
8 They said in their hearts, Let us destroy them together: they have burned up all the synagogues of God in the land.   Ps. 83:4
9 We see not our signs: *there is* no more any prophet: neither *is there* among us any that knoweth how long.   1 Sam. 3:1; Amos 8:11
10 O God, how long shall the adversary reproach? shall the enemy blaspheme thy name for ever?
11 Why withdrawest thou thy hand, even thy right hand? pluck *it* out of thy bosom.   Lam. 2:3

12 For God *is* my King of old, working salvation in the midst of the earth. Ps. 44:4

13 Thou didst divide the sea by thy strength: thou brakest the heads of the dragons in the waters. Ex. 14:21; Ps. 78:13; Ezek. 29:3

14 Thou brakest the heads of ᵀleviathan in pieces, *and* gavest him *to be* meat to the people inhabiting the wilderness. Is. 27:1 ◆ *crocodiles*

15 Thou didst cleave the fountain and the flood: thou driedst up mighty rivers. Ex. 17:5-6

16 The day *is* thine, the night also *is* thine: thou hast prepared the light and the sun.

17 Thou hast set all the borders of the earth: thou hast made summer and winter. Gen. 8:22

18 Remember this, *that* the enemy hath reproached, O Lᴏʀᴅ, and *that* the foolish people have blasphemed thy name. Deut. 32:6

19 O deliver not the soul of thy turtledove unto the multitude *of the wicked*: forget not the congregation of thy poor for ever. Song 2:14

20 Have respect unto the covenant: for the dark places of the earth are full of the habitations of cruelty. Gen. 17:7-8; Ps. 106:45

21 O let not the oppressed return ashamed: let the poor and needy praise thy name.

22 Arise, O God, plead thine own cause: remember how the foolish man reproacheth thee daily. Ps. 74:18

23 Forget not the voice of thine enemies: the tumult of those that rise up against thee increaseth continually. Ps. 65:7

PSALM 75

God Will Judge Uprightly

To the chief Musician, Al-taschith,
A Psalm *or* Song of Asaph.

Unto thee, O God, do we give thanks, *unto thee* do we give thanks: for *that* thy name is near thy wondrous works declare. Ps. 57:1

2 When I shall receive the congregation I will judge uprightly.

3 The earth and all the inhabitants thereof are dissolved: I bear up the pillars of it. Selah. 1 Sam. 2:8; Is. 24:19

4 I said unto the fools, Deal not foolishly: and to the wicked, Lift not up the horn:

5 Lift not up your horn on high: speak *not* with a stiff neck.

6 For promotion *cometh* neither from the east, nor from the west, nor from the south.

7 But God *is* the judge: he putteth down one, and setteth up another. Ps. 50:6

8 For in the hand of the Lᴏʀᴅ *there is* a cup, and the wine is red; it is full of mixture; and he poureth out of the same: but the dregs thereof, all the wicked of the earth shall wring *them* out, *and* drink *them*. Job 21:20; Prov. 23:30

75:6, 7 Every Man Has His Place

Let those who feel that their work is not appreciated, and who crave a position of greater responsibility, consider that "promotion cometh neither from the east, nor from the west, nor from the south. But God is the Judge: He putteth down one, and setteth up another" (Psalm 75:6, 7). Every man has his place in the eternal plan of heaven. Whether we fill that place depends upon our own faithfulness in co-operating with God. *MH 476*

---

9 But I will declare for ever; I will sing praises to the God of Jacob.

10 All the horns of the wicked also will I cut off; *but* the horns of the righteous shall be exalted. Ps. 89:17; 92:10; 148:14

PSALM 76

God Alone Is to Be Feared

To the chief Musician on
Neginoth, A Psalm *or* Song of Asaph.

In Judah *is* God known: his name *is* great in Israel. Ps. 4:1

2 In Salem also is his tabernacle, and his dwelling place in Zion. Gen. 14:18

3 There brake he the arrows of the bow, the shield, and the sword, and the battle. Selah. Ps. 46:9

4 Thou *art* more glorious *and* excellent than the mountains of prey.

5 The ᵀstouthearted are spoiled, they have slept their sleep: and none of the men of might have found their hands. Ps. 13:3 ◆ *courageous*

6 At thy rebuke, O God of Jacob, both the chariot and horse are cast into a dead sleep. Ex. 15:1, 21; Ps. 80:16

7 Thou, *even* thou, *art* to be feared: and who may stand in thy sight when once thou art angry? Nah. 1:6

8 Thou didst cause judgment to be heard from heaven; the earth feared, and was still, 2 Chr. 20:29-30; Hab. 2:20

9 When God arose to judgment, to save all the meek of the earth. Selah.

10 Surely the wrath of man shall praise thee: the remainder of wrath shalt thou restrain.

11 Vow, and pay unto the Lᴏʀᴅ your God: let all that be round about him bring presents unto him that ought to be feared. Gen. 31:42

12 He shall cut off the spirit of princes: *he is* terrible to the kings of the earth.

PSALM 77

Remember God's Help in the Past

To the chief Musician, to
Jeduthun, A Psalm of Asaph.

I cried unto God with my voice, *even* unto God with my voice; and he gave ear unto me. Ps. 3:4; 39:1; 50:1

2 In the day of my trouble I sought the Lord: my sore ran in the night, and ceased not: my soul refused to be comforted. Gen. 37:35; Is. 26:9

3 I remembered God, and was troubled: I complained, and my spirit was overwhelmed. Selah. Ps. 61:2

4 Thou holdest mine eyes waking: I am so troubled that I cannot speak.

5 I have considered the days of old, the years of ancient times. Deut. 32:7; Ps. 143:5; Is. 51:9

6 I call to remembrance my song in the night: I commune with mine own heart: and my spirit made diligent search. Ps. 4:4

7 Will the Lord cast off for ever? and will he be favourable no more? Ps. 85:1, 5

8 Is his mercy clean gone for ever? doth *his* promise fail for evermore? Rom. 9:6

9 Hath God forgotten to be gracious? hath he in anger shut up his tender mercies? Selah.

10 And I said, This *is* my infirmity: *but I will remember* the years of the right hand of the most High. Ps. 31:22

11 I will remember the works of the LORD: surely I will remember thy wonders of old.

12 I will meditate also of all thy work, and talk of thy doings.

13 Thy way, O God, *is* in the sanctuary: who *is so* great a God as *our* God? Ex. 15:11

14 Thou *art* the God that doest wonders: thou hast declared thy strength among the people. Ps. 72:18

77:13, 14 Worship in God's Sanctuary

Although God dwells not in temples made with hands, yet He honors with His presence the assemblies of His people. He has promised that when they come together to seek Him, to acknowledge their sins, and to pray for one another, He will meet with them by His Spirit. But those who assemble to worship Him should put away every evil thing. Unless they worship Him in spirit and truth and in the beauty of holiness, their coming together will be of no avail. *PK 50*

---

15 Thou hast with *thine* arm redeemed thy people, the sons of Jacob and Joseph. Selah. Ex. 6:6; Deut. 9:29

16 The waters saw thee, O God, the waters saw thee; they were afraid: the depths also were troubled. Ex. 14:21; Josh. 3:15-16

17 The clouds poured out water: the skies sent out a sound: thine arrows also went abroad. Ps. 18:14

18 The voice of thy thunder *was* in the heaven: the lightnings lightened the world: the earth trembled and shook. Ps. 97:4

19 Thy way *is* in the sea, and thy path in the great waters, and thy footsteps are not known. Hab. 3:15

20 Thou leddest thy people like a flock by the hand of Moses and Aaron. Ex. 13:21; 14:19; Ps. 78:52

77:20 The Divine Shepherd

However large the flock, the shepherd knows every sheep. Every one has its name, and responds to the name at the shepherd's call.

As an earthly shepherd knows his sheep, so does the divine Shepherd know His flock that are scattered throughout the world. *DA 479*

PSALM 78

Israel's Rich History

Maschil of Asaph.

Give ear, O my people, *to* my law: incline your ears to the words of my mouth.

2 I will open my mouth in a parable: I will utter dark sayings of old: Ps. 49:4; Prov. 1:6

3 Which we have heard and known, and our fathers have told us. Ps. 44:1

4 We will not hide *them* from their children, shewing to the generation to come the praises of the LORD, and his strength, and his wonderful works that he hath done. Deut. 6:7; 11:19; Joel 1:3

5 For he established a testimony in Jacob, and appointed a law in Israel, which he commanded our fathers, that they should make them known to their children: Deut. 6:7; Ps. 81:5

6 That the generation to come might know *them, even* the children *which* should be born; *who* should arise and declare *them* to their children: Ps. 102:18

7 That they might set their hope in God, and not forget the works of God, but keep his commandments: Deut. 5:29

8 And might not be as their fathers, a stubborn and rebellious generation; a generation *that* set not their heart aright, and whose spirit was not stedfast with God. Ex. 32:9

9 The children of Ephraim, *being* armed, *and* carrying bows, turned back in the day of battle.

10 They kept not the covenant of God, and refused to walk in his law;

11 And forgat his works, and his wonders that he had shewed them. Ps. 106:13

12 Marvellous things did he in the sight of their fathers, in the land of Egypt, *in* the field of Zoan. Num. 13:22; Is. 19:11; Ezek. 30:14

13 He divided the sea, and caused them to pass through; and he made the waters to stand as an heap. Ex. 14:21

14 In the daytime also he led them with a cloud, and all the night with a light of fire.

15 He clave the rocks in the wilderness, and gave *them* drink as *out of* the great depths.

16 He brought streams also out of the rock, and caused waters to run down like rivers.

17 And they sinned yet more against him by provoking the most High in the wilderness.   Is. 63:10
18 And they tempted God in their heart by asking meat for their lust.   Num. 11:4
19 Yea, they spake against God; they said, Can God furnish a table in the wilderness?
20 Behold, he smote the rock, that the waters gushed out, and the streams overflowed; can he give bread also? can he provide flesh for his people?   Num. 20:11
21 Therefore the LORD heard *this*, and was ᵀwroth: so a fire was kindled against Jacob, and anger also came up against Israel; *angered*
22 Because they believed not in God, and trusted not in his salvation: Heb. 3:18-19
23 Though he had commanded the clouds from above, and opened the doors of heaven,   Gen. 7:11; Mal. 3:10
24 And had rained down manna upon them to eat, and had given them of the corn of heaven.   Ex. 16:4; Ps. 105:40
25 Man did eat angels' food: he sent them meat to the full.   Ps. 103:20

78:24, 25 God's Unfailing Care

For forty years they were daily reminded by this miraculous provision, of God's unfailing care and tender love. In the words of the psalmist, God gave them "of the corn of heaven. Man did eat angels' food" (Psalm 78:24, 25)—that is, food provided for them by the angels. Sustained by "the corn of heaven," they were daily taught that, having God's promise, they were as secure from want as if surrounded by fields of waving grain on the fertile plains of Canaan. *PP 297*

---

26 He caused an east wind to blow in the heaven: and by his power he brought in the south wind.   Num. 11:31
27 He rained flesh also upon them as dust, and feathered fowls like as the sand of the sea:
28 And he let *it* fall in the midst of their camp, round about their habitations.
29 So they did eat, and were well filled: for he gave them their own desire;
30 They were not estranged from their lust. But while their meat *was* yet in their mouths,
31 The wrath of God came upon them, and slew the fattest of them, and smote down the chosen *men* of Israel.   Is. 10:16
32 For all this they sinned still, and believed not for his wondrous works.   Num. 14
33 Therefore their days did he consume in vanity, and their years in trouble.   Num. 14:29
34 When he slew them, then they sought him: and they returned and enquired early after God.   Num. 21:7; Hos. 5:15

35 And they remembered that God *was* their rock, and the high God their redeemer.
36 Nevertheless they did flatter him with their mouth, and they lied unto him with their tongues.   Is. 29:13; Ezek. 33:31
37 For their heart was not right with him, neither were they ᵀstedfast in his covenant.   Ps. 78:8 ◆ *steadfast* or *faithful*
38 But he, *being* full of compassion, forgave *their* iniquity, and destroyed *them* not: yea, many a time turned he his anger away, and did not stir up all his wrath.   Num. 14:18-20
39 For he remembered that they *were but* flesh; a wind that passeth away, and cometh not again.   Gen. 6:3; Job 7:7; James 4:14
40 How oft did they provoke him in the wilderness, *and* grieve him in the desert!
41 Yea, they turned back and tempted God, and limited the Holy One of Israel. Num. 14:22
42 They remembered not his hand, *nor* the day when he delivered them from the enemy.
43 How he had ᵀwrought his signs in Egypt, and his wonders in the field of Zoan: *made*
44 And had turned their rivers into blood; and their floods, that they could not drink.
45 He sent ᵀdivers sorts of flies among them, which devoured them; and frogs, which destroyed them.   Ex. 8:21-24 ◆ *various*
46 He gave also their increase unto the caterpiller, and their labour unto the locust.
47 He destroyed their vines with hail, and their sycomore trees with frost.
48 He gave up their cattle also to the hail, and their flocks to hot thunderbolts.
49 He cast upon them the fierceness of his anger, wrath, and ᵀindignation, and trouble, by sending evil angels *among them*.   *anger*
50 He made a way to his anger; he spared not their soul from death, but gave their life over to the pestilence;
51 And smote all the firstborn in Egypt; the chief of *their* strength in the tabernacles of Ham: Ps. 105:23; 106:22; 135:8
52 But made his own people to go forth like sheep, and guided them in the wilderness like a flock.   Ps. 77:20
53 And he led them on safely, so that they feared not: but the sea overwhelmed their enemies.   Ex. 14:19-20
54 And he brought them to the border of his sanctuary, *even to* this mountain, *which* his right hand had purchased.   Ex. 15:17; Ps. 44:3
55 He cast out the heathen also before them, and divided them an inheritance by line, and made the tribes of Israel to dwell in their tents.   Josh. 13:7; Ps. 44:2
56 Yet they tempted and provoked the most high God, and kept not his testimonies:
57 But turned back, and dealt unfaithfully like their fathers: they were turned aside like a deceitful bow.   Hos. 7:16

78:55–58 The Oft-Repeated Cycle

There was ever a remnant who were true to Jehovah; and from time to time the Lord raised up faithful and valiant men to put down idolatry and to deliver the Israelites from their enemies. But when the deliverer was dead, and the people were released from his authority, they would gradually return to their idols. And thus the story of backsliding and chastisement, of confession and deliverance, was repeated again and again. *PP 545*

58 For they provoked him to anger with their high places, and moved him to jealousy with their graven images.   Lev. 26:30; Deut. 12:2; 32:21
59 When God heard *this*, he was wroth, and greatly ᵀabhorred Israel: Ps. 106:40 ◆ *despised*
60 So that he forsook the tabernacle of Shiloh, the tent *which* he placed among men;
61 And delivered his strength into captivity, and his glory into the enemy's hand. Ps. 132:8
62 He gave his people over also unto the sword; and was wroth with his inheritance.
63 The fire consumed their young men; and their maidens were not given to marriage.   Jer. 7:34; 16:9
64 Their priests fell by the sword; and their widows made no lamentation.   1 Sam. 4:17
65 Then the Lord awaked as one out of sleep, *and* like a mighty man that shouteth by reason of wine.   Ps. 44:23
66 And he smote his enemies in the hinder parts: he put them to a perpetual reproach.
67 Moreover he refused the tabernacle of Joseph, and chose not the tribe of Ephraim:
68 But chose the tribe of Judah, the mount Zion which he loved.   Ps. 87:2
69 And he built his sanctuary like high *palaces*, like the earth which he hath established for ever.
70 He chose David also his servant, and took him from the sheepfolds: 1 Sam. 16:11-12
71 From following the ewes great with young he brought him to feed Jacob his people, and Israel his inheritance.   Gen. 33:13; 2 Sam. 5:2
72 So he fed them according to the integrity of his heart; and guided them by the skilfulness of his hands.   1 Kin. 9:4

PSALM 79

A Cry to God after the Desolation of Jerusalem

A Psalm of Asaph.

O God, the heathen are come into thine inheritance; thy holy temple have they defiled; they have laid Jerusalem on heaps.   2 Chr. 36:19
2 The dead bodies of thy servants have they given *to be* meat unto the fowls of the heaven,

the flesh of thy saints unto the beasts of the earth.   Jer. 7:33; 16:4; 34:20
3 Their blood have they shed like water round about Jerusalem; and *there was* none to bury *them*.   Jer. 14:16
4 We are become a reproach to our neighbours, a scorn and derision to them that are round about us.   Ps. 80:6
5 How long, LORD? wilt thou be angry for ever? shall thy jealousy burn like fire? Ps. 74:1
6 Pour out thy wrath upon the heathen that have not known thee, and upon the kingdoms that have not called upon thy name.   Ps. 14:4; Jer. 10:25; 2 Thess. 1:8
7 For they have devoured Jacob, and laid waste his dwelling place.
8 O remember not against us former iniquities: let thy tender mercies speedily prevent us: for we are brought very low. Ps. 116:6; 142:6
9 Help us, O God of our salvation, for the glory of thy name: and deliver us, and purge away our sins, for thy name's sake. 2 Chr. 14:11
10 Wherefore should the heathen say, Where *is* their God? let him be known among the heathen in our sight *by* the revenging of the blood of thy servants *which is* shed.   Ps. 42:10
11 Let the sighing of the prisoner come before thee; according to the greatness of thy power preserve thou those that are appointed to die;   Ps. 102:20
12 And render unto our neighbours sevenfold into their bosom their reproach, wherewith they have reproached thee, O Lord.
13 So we thy people and sheep of thy pasture will give thee thanks for ever: we will shew forth thy praise to all generations. Ps. 74:1; 95:7

PSALM 80

A Prayer for Restoration

To the chief Musician upon Shoshannim-Eduth, A Psalm of Asaph.

G ive ear, O Shepherd of Israel, thou that leadest Joseph like a flock; thou that dwellest *between* the cherubims, shine forth.   1 Sam. 4:4
2 Before Ephraim and Benjamin and Manasseh stir up thy strength, and come *and* save us.   Num. 2:18-24; Ps. 35:23
3 Turn us again, O God, and cause thy face to shine; and we shall be saved.   Ps. 4:6; 85:4
4 O LORD God of hosts, how long wilt thou be angry against the prayer of thy people?
5 Thou feedest them with the bread of tears; and givest them tears to drink in great measure.   Ps. 42:3; 102:9; Is. 30:20
6 Thou makest us a strife unto our neighbours: and our enemies laugh among themselves.   Ps. 79:4

7 Turn us again, O God of hosts, and cause thy face to shine; and we shall be saved.
8 Thou hast brought a vine out of Egypt: thou hast cast out the heathen, and planted it.   Ps. 44:2; Jer. 2:21; Ezek. 17:6
9 Thou preparedst *room* before it, and didst cause it to take deep root, and it filled the land.   Josh. 24:12
10 The hills were covered with the shadow of it, and the boughs thereof *were like* the goodly cedars.
11 She sent out her boughs unto the sea, and her branches unto the river.   Ps. 72:8
12 Why hast thou *then* broken down her hedges, so that all they which pass by the way do pluck her?   Is. 5:5
13 The boar out of the wood doth waste it, and the wild beast of the field doth devour it.   Jer. 5:6
14 Return, we ᵀbeseech thee, O God of hosts: look down from heaven, and behold, and visit this vine;   Ps. 90:13; Is. 63:15 ◆ *beg*
15 And the vineyard which thy right hand hath planted, and the branch *that* thou madest strong for thyself.   Ps. 80:8
16 *It is* burned with fire, *it is* cut down: they perish at the rebuke of thy countenance.
17 Let thy hand be upon the man of thy right hand, upon the son of man *whom* thou madest strong for thyself.   Ps. 89:21
18 So will not we go back from thee: ᵀquicken us, and we will call upon thy name.   *revive*
19 Turn us again, O LORD God of hosts, cause thy face to shine; and we shall be saved.   Ps. 80:3

PSALM 81

A Celebration of the Exodus from Egypt

To the chief Musician upon Gittith, *A Psalm* of Asaph.

S ing aloud unto God our strength: make a joyful noise unto the God of Jacob. Ps. 8:1
2 Take a psalm, and bring ᵀhither the ᵀtimbrel, the pleasant harp with the ᵀpsaltery.   Ps. 92:3 ◆ *here* ◆ *tambourine* ◆ *stringed instrument*
3 Blow up the trumpet in the new moon, in the time appointed, on our solemn feast day.
4 For this *was* a statute for Israel, *and* a law of the God of Jacob.
5 This he ordained in Joseph *for* a testimony, when he went out through the land of Egypt: *where* I heard a language *that* I understood not.   Deut. 28:49; Ps. 114:1; Jer. 5:15
6 I removed his shoulder from the burden: his hands were delivered from the pots. Is. 9:4
7 Thou calledst in trouble, and I delivered thee; I answered thee in the secret place of thunder: I proved thee at the waters of Meribah. Selah.   Ex. 2:23; 19:19; Ps. 50:15

8 Hear, O my people, and I will testify unto thee: O Israel, if thou wilt hearken unto me;   Ps. 50:7
9 There shall no strange god be in thee; neither shalt thou worship any strange god.
10 I *am* the LORD thy God, which brought thee out of the land of Egypt: open thy mouth wide, and I will fill it. Ex. 20:2; Ps. 37:3-4
11 But my people would not hearken to my voice; and Israel would none of me.   Ex. 32:1
12 So I gave them up unto their own hearts' lust: *and* they walked in their own counsels.   Jer. 7:24; Acts 7:42; Rom. 1:24

81:11, 12 Do Not Seek to Be Excused From Duty

There are thousands at the present day who are pursuing a similar course [to Balaam's (choosing his own way, not seeking the will of God; see Numbers 22—24)]. They would have no difficulty in understanding their duty if it were in harmony with their inclinations. . . . [God] often permits such persons to follow their own desires and to suffer the result. . . . When one clearly sees a duty, let him not presume to go to God with the prayer that he may be excused from performing it. He should rather, with a humble, submissive spirit, ask for divine strength and wisdom to meet its claims. PP 440, 441

---

13 Oh that my people had hearkened unto me, *and* Israel had walked in my ways!   Deut. 5:29
14 I should soon have subdued their enemies, and turned my hand against their adversaries.   Amos 1:8
15 The haters of the LORD should have submitted themselves unto him: but their time should have endured for ever.   Rom. 1:30
16 He should have fed them also with the finest of the wheat: and with honey out of the rock should I have satisfied thee. Deut. 32:13-14

PSALM 82

God Will Judge the Wicked

A Psalm of Asaph.

G od standeth in the congregation of the mighty; he judgeth among the gods.
2 How long will ye judge unjustly, and accept the persons of the wicked? Selah.
3 Defend the poor and fatherless: do justice to the afflicted and needy.   Ps. 10:18
4 Deliver the poor and needy: rid *them* out of the hand of the wicked.   Job 29:12
5 They know not, neither will they understand; they walk on in darkness: all the foundations of the earth are out of course. Ps. 11:3
6 I have said, Ye *are* gods; and all of you *are* children of the most High.   Ps. 82:1
7 But ye shall die like men, and fall like one of the princes.   Job 21:32; Ps. 49:12; Ezek. 31:14

8 Arise, O God, judge the earth: for thou shalt inherit all nations.   Ps. 2:8; 12:5; Rev. 11:15

PSALM 83

God Is Most High over All the Earth

A Song or Psalm of Asaph.

Keep not thou silence, O God: hold not thy peace, and be not still, O God. Ps. 28:1; 50:3
2 For, lo, thine enemies make a tumult: and they that hate thee have lifted up the head.   Ps. 81:15
3 They have taken crafty counsel against thy people, and consulted against thy hidden ones.   Ps. 27:5
4 They have said, Come, and let us cut them off from being a nation; that the name of Israel may be no more in remembrance.   Jer. 11:19
5 For they have consulted together with one consent: they are confederate against thee: Ps. 2:2
6 The tabernacles of Edom, and the Ishmaelites; of Moab, and the Hagarenes; 1 Chr. 5:10
7 Gebal, and Ammon, and Amalek; the Philistines with the inhabitants of Tyre; Josh. 13:5
8 Assur also is joined with them: they have Tholpen the children of Lot. Selah.   helped
9 Do unto them as unto the Midianites; as to Sisera, as to Jabin, at the brook of Kison:
10 Which perished at Endor: they became as dung for the earth.   Zeph. 1:17
11 Make their nobles like Oreb, and like Zeeb: yea, all their princes as Zebah, and as Zalmunna: Judg. 7:25; 8:12-21
12 Who said, Let us take to ourselves the houses of God in possession.   2 Chr. 20:11
13 O my God, make them like a wheel; as the stubble before the wind.   Job 21:18
14 As the fire burneth a wood, and as the flame setteth the mountains on fire;   Is. 9:18
15 So persecute them with thy Ttempest, and make them afraid with thy storm.   storm
16 Fill their faces with shame; that they may seek thy name, O LORD.
17 Let them be confounded and troubled for ever; yea, let them be put to shame, and perish: Ps. 35:4
18 That men may know that thou, whose name alone is JEHOVAH, art the most high over all the earth.   Ex. 6:3; Ps. 59:13

PSALM 84

The Joy of Fellowship in God's House

To the chief Musician upon Gittith,
A Psalm for the sons of Korah.

How Tamiable are thy tabernacles, O LORD of hosts!   Ps. 27:4 ◆ lovely
2 My soul longeth, yea, even fainteth for the courts of the LORD: my heart and my flesh crieth out for the living God.   Ps. 42:1-2; 73:26
3 Yea, the sparrow hath found an house, and the swallow a nest for herself, where she may lay her young, even thine altars, O LORD of hosts, my King, and my God.   Ps. 5:2
4 Blessed are they that dwell in thy house: they will be still praising thee. Selah. Ps. 65:4
5 Blessed is the man whose strength is in thee; in whose heart are the ways of them.
6 Who passing through the valley of Baca make it a well; the rain also filleth the pools.   Joel 2:23
7 They go from strength to strength, every one of them in Zion appeareth before God.
8 O LORD God of hosts, hear my prayer: give ear, O God of Jacob. Selah.
9 Behold, O God our shield, and look upon the face of thine anointed.   Ps. 2:2
10 For a day in thy courts is better than a thousand. I had rather be a doorkeeper in

---

How God Answers Our Prayers

Psalm 84:11, 12

Another element of prevailing prayer is faith. "He that cometh to God must believe that He is, and that He is a rewarder of them that diligently seek Him" (Hebrews 11:6). Jesus said to His disciples, "What things soever ye desire, when ye pray, believe that ye receive them, and ye shall have them" (Mark 11:24). Do we take Him at His word?

The assurance is broad and unlimited, and He is faithful who has promised. When we do not receive the very things we asked for, at the time we ask, we are still to believe that the Lord hears and that He will answer our prayers. We are so erring and short-sighted that we sometimes ask for things that would not be a blessing to us, and our heavenly Father in love answers our prayers by giving us that which will be for our highest good—that which we ourselves would desire if with vision divinely enlightened we could see all things as they really are. When our prayers seem not to be answered, we are to cling to the promise; for the time of answering will surely come, and we shall receive the blessing we need most. But to claim that prayer will always be answered in the very way and for the particular thing that we desire, is presumption. God is too wise to err, and too good to withhold any good thing from them that walk uprightly. Then do not fear to trust Him, even though you do not see the immediate answer to your prayers. Rely upon His sure promise, "Ask, and it shall be given you" [Matthew 7:7]. SC 96

the house of my God, than to dwell in the tents of wickedness. Ps. 27:4

11 For the LORD God *is* a sun and shield: the LORD will give grace and glory: no good *thing* will he withhold from them that walk uprightly. Gen. 15:1; Prov. 2:7; Rev. 21:23

12 O LORD of hosts, blessed *is* the man that trusteth in thee. Ps. 2:12

PSALM 85

A Prayer for Mercy and Salvation

To the chief Musician, A Psalm for the sons of Korah.

LORD, thou hast been favourable unto thy land: thou hast brought back the captivity of Jacob. Ps. 14:7; 77:7; Jer. 30:18

2 Thou hast forgiven the iniquity of thy people, thou hast covered all their sin. Selah.

3 Thou hast taken away all thy wrath: thou hast turned *thyself* from the fierceness of thine anger. Deut. 13:17; Ps. 78:38; 106:23

4 Turn us, O God of our salvation, and cause thine anger toward us to cease. Ps. 80:3, 7

5 Wilt thou be angry with us for ever? wilt thou draw out thine anger to all generations? Ps. 74:1; 79:5; 80:4

6 Wilt thou not revive us again: that thy people may rejoice in thee? Ps. 80:18

7 Shew us thy mercy, O LORD, and grant us thy salvation.

8 I will hear what God the LORD will speak: for he will speak peace unto his people, and to his saints: but let them not turn again to folly. Ps. 29:11; 50:5; Zech. 9:10

9 Surely his salvation *is* nigh them that fear him; that glory may dwell in our land. Is. 46:13

10 Mercy and truth are met together; righteousness and peace have kissed *each other*.

> **85:10 Justice Linked With Mercy**
>
> God's love has been expressed in His justice no less than in His mercy. Justice is the foundation of His throne, and the fruit of His love. It had been Satan's purpose to divorce mercy from truth and justice. He sought to prove that the righteousness of God's law is an enemy to peace. But Christ shows that in God's plan they are indissolubly joined together; the one cannot exist without the other. *DA 762*

11 Truth shall spring out of the earth; and righteousness shall look down from heaven. Is. 45:8

12 Yea, the LORD shall give *that which is* good; and our land shall yield her increase. Ps. 67:6

13 Righteousness shall go before him; and shall set *us* in the way of his steps. Ps. 89:14

PSALM 86

David's Faith Is Firmly Rooted

A Prayer of David.

BOW down thine ear, O LORD, hear me: for I *am* poor and needy. Ps. 31:2

2 Preserve my soul; for I *am* holy: O thou my God, save thy servant that trusteth in thee. Ps. 4:3

3 Be merciful unto me, O Lord: for I cry unto thee daily. Ps. 4:1; 57:1; 88:9

4 Rejoice the soul of thy servant: for unto thee, O Lord, do I lift up my soul. Ps. 25:1; 143:8

5 For thou, Lord, *art* good, and ready to forgive; and plenteous in mercy unto all them that call upon thee. Ex. 34:6; Ps. 103:8; Joel 2:13

6 Give ear, O LORD, unto my prayer; and attend to the voice of my supplications.

7 In the day of my trouble I will call upon thee: for thou wilt answer me. Ps. 50:15

8 Among the gods *there is* none like unto thee, O Lord; neither *are there any works* like unto thy works. Ex. 15:11; Deut. 3:24; Ps. 89:6

9 All nations whom thou hast made shall come and worship before thee, O Lord; and shall glorify thy name. Ps. 66:4; Is. 66:23; Rev. 15:4

10 For thou *art* great, and doest wondrous things: thou *art* God alone. Ps. 72:18; Is. 37:16

11 Teach me thy way, O LORD; I will walk in thy truth: unite my heart to fear thy name. Ps. 26:3

12 I will praise thee, O Lord my God, with all my heart: and I will glorify thy name for evermore.

13 For great *is* thy mercy toward me: and thou hast delivered my soul from the lowest hell. Ps. 88:6

14 O God, the proud are risen against me, and the assemblies of violent *men* have sought after my soul; and have not set thee before them. Ps. 54:3

15 But thou, O Lord, *art* a God full of compassion, and gracious, longsuffering, and plenteous in mercy and truth. Neh. 9:17

16 O turn unto me, and have mercy upon me; give thy strength unto thy servant, and save the son of thine handmaid. Ps. 25:16; 116:16

17 Shew me a token for good; that they which hate me may see *it*, and be ashamed: because thou, LORD, hast ᵀholpen me, and comforted me. *helped*

PSALM 87

The Glorious City of God

A Psalm *or* Song for the sons of Korah.

HIS foundation *is* in the holy mountains. 2 The LORD loveth the gates of Zion more than all the dwellings of Jacob.

3 Glorious things are spoken of thee, O city of God. Selah. Ps. 46:4

4 I will make mention of Rahab and Babylon to them that know me: behold Philistia, and Tyre, with Ethiopia; this *man* was born there.   Ps. 45:12
5 And of Zion it shall be said, This and that man was born in her: and the highest himself shall establish her.
6 The LORD shall count, when he writeth up the people, *that* this *man* was born there. Selah.   Is. 4:3
7 As well the singers as the players on instruments *shall be there*: all my springs *are* in thee.   Ps. 36:9

PSALM 88

A Prayer from Deep Misery

A Song *or* Psalm for the sons of Korah, to the chief Musician upon Mahalath Leannoth, Maschil of Heman the Ezrahite.

O LORD God of my salvation, I have cried day *and* night before thee: Ps. 22:2; 27:9
2 Let my prayer come before thee: incline thine ear unto my cry;
3 For my soul is full of troubles: and my life draweth nigh unto the grave.   Ps. 107:18
4 I am counted with them that go down into the pit: I am as a man *that hath* no strength: Ps. 28:1; 143:7
5 Free among the dead, like the slain that lie in the grave, whom thou rememberest no more: and they are cut off from thy hand.   Ps. 31:22; Is. 53:8
6 Thou hast laid me in the lowest pit, in darkness, in the deeps.   Ps. 69:15; 86:13; 143:3
7 Thy wrath lieth hard upon me, and thou hast afflicted *me* with all thy waves. Selah.
8 Thou hast put away mine acquaintance far from me; thou hast made me an abomination unto them: *I am* shut up, and I cannot come forth.   Ps. 31:11; Is. 49:7; Jer. 32:2
9 Mine eye mourneth by reason of affliction: LORD, I have called daily upon thee, I have stretched out my hands unto thee.   Job 11:13
10 Wilt thou shew wonders to the dead? shall the dead arise *and* praise thee? Selah.
11 Shall thy lovingkindness be declared in the grave? *or* thy faithfulness in destruction?
12 Shall thy wonders be known in the dark? and thy righteousness in the land of forgetfulness?   Eccl. 9:5
13 But unto thee have I cried, O LORD; and in the morning shall my prayer ᵀprevent thee.   Ps. 5:3; 30:2 ◆ *go before*
14 LORD, why castest thou off my soul? *why* hidest thou thy face from me? Job 13:24; Ps. 13:1
15 I *am* afflicted and ready to die from *my* youth up: *while* I suffer thy terrors I am distracted.   Job 6:4

16 Thy fierce wrath goeth over me; thy terrors have cut me off.
17 They came round about me daily like water; they compassed me about together.
18 Lover and friend hast thou put far from me, *and* mine acquaintance into darkness.

PSALM 89

Praise to God for His Covenant Promises

Maschil of Ethan the Ezrahite.

I will sing of the mercies of the LORD for ever: with my mouth will I make known thy faithfulness to all generations. Ps. 89:33, 49
2 For I have said, Mercy shall be built up for ever: thy faithfulness shalt thou establish in the very heavens.   Ps. 36:5; 103:17
3 I have made a covenant with my chosen, I have sworn unto David my servant, Ps. 132:11
4 Thy seed will I establish for ever, and build up thy throne to all generations. Selah.
5 And the heavens shall praise thy wonders, O LORD: thy faithfulness also in the congregation of the saints.   Ps. 19:1; 50:6; 97:6
6 For who in the heaven can be compared unto the LORD? *who* among the sons of the mighty can be likened unto the LORD?Ps. 29:1
7 God is greatly to be feared in the assembly of the saints, and to be had in reverence of all *them that are* about him.   Ps. 47:2

89:7 The Grace of True Reverence

Every child should be taught to show true reverence for God. Never should His name be spoken lightly or thoughtlessly. Angels, as they speak it, veil their faces. With what reverence should we, who are fallen and sinful, take it upon our lips!

Reverence should be shown for God's representatives—for ministers, teachers, and parents, who are called to speak and act in His stead. *PK 236, 237*

---

8 O LORD God of hosts, who *is* a strong LORD like unto thee? or to thy faithfulness round about thee?   Ps. 35:10
9 Thou rulest the raging of the sea: when the waves thereof arise, thou stillest them.
10 Thou hast broken Rahab in pieces, as one that is slain; thou hast scattered thine enemies with thy strong arm.   Ps. 144:6
11 The heavens *are* thine, the earth also *is* thine: *as for* the world and the fulness thereof, thou hast founded them.   Gen. 1:1; 1 Chr. 29:11
12 The north and the south thou hast created them: Tabor and Hermon shall rejoice in thy name.   Josh. 12:1
13 Thou hast a mighty arm: strong is thy hand, *and* high is thy right hand.
14 Justice and judgment *are* the habitation

of thy throne: mercy and truth shall go before thy face. Ps. 85:13; 97:2

89:14 The Foundation of God's Throne

Satan declared that mercy destroyed justice, that the death of Christ abrogated the
Father's law. Had it been possible for the law
to be changed or abrogated, then Christ need
not have died. But to abrogate the law would
be to immortalize transgression, and place
the world under Satan's control. . . . Yet the
very means by which Christ established the
law Satan represented as destroying it. Here
will come the last conflict of the great controversy between Christ and Satan. *DA 762,763*

15 Blessed *is* the people that know the joyful
sound: they shall walk, O Lord, in the light
of thy ᵀcountenance. Ps. 4:6 ◆ *appearance*
16 In thy name shall they rejoice all the day:
and in thy righteousness shall they be exalted.
17 For thou *art* the glory of their strength:
and in thy favour our horn shall be exalted. Ps. 75:10; 92:10; 148:14
18 For the Lord *is* our defence; and the Holy
One of Israel *is* our king. Ps. 47:9; 71:22
19 Then thou spakest in vision to thy holy
one, and saidst, I have laid help upon *one that
is* mighty; I have exalted *one* chosen out of
the people. 1 Kin. 11:34
20 I have found David my servant; with my
holy oil have I anointed him: 1 Sam. 16:1
21 With whom my hand shall be established: mine arm also shall strengthen him.
22 The enemy shall not exact upon him; nor
the son of wickedness afflict him. 2 Sam. 7:10
23 And I will beat down his foes before his
face, and plague them that hate him. 2 Sam. 7:9
24 But my faithfulness and my mercy *shall
be* with him: and in my name shall his horn
be exalted.
25 I will set his hand also in the sea, and his
right hand in the rivers.
26 He shall cry unto me, Thou *art* my father,
my God, and the rock of my salvation.

27 Also I will make him *my* firstborn, higher
than the kings of the earth. Num. 24:7; Col. 1:18
28 My mercy will I keep for him for evermore, and my covenant shall stand fast with
him. Is. 55:3
29 His seed also will I make *to endure* for ever,
and his throne as the days of heaven.
30 If his children forsake my law, and walk
not in my judgments; 2 Sam. 7:14
31 If they break my statutes, and keep not
my commandments;
32 Then will I visit their transgression with
the rod, and their iniquity with stripes.
33 Nevertheless my lovingkindness will
I not utterly take from him, nor suffer my
faithfulness to fail. 2 Sam. 7:15
34 My covenant will I not break, nor alter the
thing that is gone out of my lips. Num. 23:19
35 Once have I sworn by my holiness that I
will not lie unto David. Amos 4:2
36 His seed shall endure for ever, and his
throne as the sun before me. Ps. 72:5
37 It shall be established for ever as the
moon, and *as* a faithful witness in heaven.
Selah.
38 But thou hast cast off and abhorred, thou
hast been ᵀwroth with thine anointed. *angry*
39 Thou hast made void the covenant of thy
servant: thou hast profaned his crown *by
casting it* to the ground. Ps. 74:7
40 Thou hast broken down all his hedges;
thou hast brought his strong holds to ruin.
41 All that pass by the way ᵀspoil him: he is
a reproach to his neighbours. Ps. 79:4 ◆ *plunder*
42 Thou hast set up the right hand of his
adversaries; thou hast made all his enemies
to rejoice.
43 Thou hast also turned the edge of his
sword, and hast not made him to stand in
the battle.
44 Thou hast made his glory to cease, and
cast his throne down to the ground.
45 The days of his youth hast thou shortened: thou hast covered him with shame.
Selah. Ps. 44:15; 109:29

God Does Not Tolerate or Excuse Sin

Psalm 89:31–33

Had God permitted David to go on unrebuked in sin, and while transgressing the divine precepts,
to remain in peace and prosperity upon his throne, the skeptic and infidel might have had some
excuse for citing the history of David as a reproach to the religion of the Bible. But in the experience through which He caused David to pass, the Lord shows that He cannot tolerate or excuse sin.
And David's history enables us to see also the great ends which God has in view in His dealings
with sin; it enables us to trace, even through darkest judgments, the working out of His purposes
of mercy and beneficence. He caused David to pass under the rod, but He did not destroy him; the
furnace is to purify, but not to consume. The Lord says, "If they break My statutes, and keep not My
commandments; then will I visit their transgression with the rod, and their iniquity with stripes.
Nevertheless My loving-kindness will I not utterly take from him, nor suffer My faithfulness to fail"
(Psalm 89:31–33). *PP 738*

46 How long, LORD? wilt thou hide thyself for ever? shall thy wrath burn like fire?   Ps. 78:63
47 Remember how short my time is: wherefore hast thou made all men in vain?   Job 7:7
48 What man *is he that* liveth, and shall not see death? shall he deliver his soul from the hand of the grave? Selah.   Ps. 49:15
49 Lord, where *are* thy former lovingkindnesses, *which* thou swarest unto David in thy truth?   2 Sam. 7:15
50 Remember, Lord, the reproach of thy servants; *how* I do bear in my bosom *the reproach of* all the mighty people;   Ps. 74:18
51 Wherewith thine enemies have reproached, O LORD; wherewith they have reproached the footsteps of thine anointed.
52 Blessed *be* the LORD for evermore. Amen, and Amen.   Ps. 41:13

PSALM 90

Moses Prays for the Nation

A Prayer of Moses the man of God.

Lord, thou hast been our dwelling place in all generations.   Deut. 33:27
2 Before the mountains were brought forth, or ever thou hadst formed the earth and the world, even from everlasting to everlasting, thou *art* God.   Gen. 1:1
3 Thou turnest man to destruction; and sayest, Return, ye children of men.   Gen. 3:19
4 For a thousand years in thy sight *are but* as yesterday when it is past, and *as* a watch in the night.   2 Pet. 3:8
5 Thou carriest them away as with a flood; they are *as* a sleep: in the morning *they are* like grass *which* groweth up. Job 22:16; Ps. 73:20; Is. 40:6
6 In the morning it flourisheth, and groweth up; in the evening it is cut down, and withereth.   Job 14:2
7 For we are consumed by thine anger, and by thy wrath are we troubled.   Ps. 39:11
8 Thou hast set our iniquities before thee, our secret *sins* in the light of thy ᵀcountenance.   Ps. 19:12; 50:21; Jer. 16:17 ◆ *appearance*
9 For all our days are passed away in thy wrath: we spend our years as a tale *that is told*.   Ps. 78:33
10 The days of our years *are* ᵀthreescore years and ten; and if by reason of strength *they be* ᵀfourscore years, yet *is* their strength labour and sorrow; for it is soon cut off, and we fly away.   Ps. 78:39 ◆ *sixty* ◆ *eighty*
11 Who knoweth the power of thine anger? even according to thy fear, *so is* thy wrath.
12 So teach *us* to number our days, that we may apply *our* hearts unto wisdom. Deut. 32:29
13 Return, O LORD, how long? and let it repent thee concerning thy servants. Deut. 32:36
14 O satisfy us early with thy mercy; that we may rejoice and be glad all our days.   Ps. 65:4

15 Make us glad according to the days wherein thou hast afflicted us, *and* the years wherein we have seen evil.   Deut. 2:14-16
16 Let thy work appear unto thy servants, and thy glory unto their children.   Ps. 44:1; Hab. 3:2
17 And let the beauty of the LORD our God be upon us: and establish thou the work of our hands upon us; yea, the work of our hands establish thou it.   Ps. 27:4; Is. 26:12; 1 Cor. 3:7

> **90:17 Jesus Sees What We Might Be**
>
> In every human being [Jesus] discerned infinite possibilities. He saw men as they might be, transfigured by His grace—in "the beauty of the Lord our God" (Psalm 90:17). Looking upon them with hope, He inspired hope. Meeting them with confidence, He inspired trust. Revealing in Himself man's true ideal, He awakened, for its attainment, both desire and faith. . . . To many a despairing one there opened the possibility of a new life. *Ed 80*

PSALM 91

God Will Protect and Rescue

He that dwelleth in the secret place of the most High shall abide under the shadow of the Almighty.   Ps. 17:8
2 I will say of the LORD, *He is* my refuge and my fortress: my God; in him will I trust.
3 Surely he shall deliver thee from the snare of the ᵀfowler, *and* from the ᵀnoisome pestilence.   Ps. 91:6; 124:7 ◆ *one who captures birds* ◆ *harmful*
4 He shall cover thee with his feathers, and under his wings shalt thou trust: his truth *shall be thy* shield and ᵀbuckler. Ps. 17:8; 35:2 ◆ *shield*
5 Thou shalt not be afraid for the terror by night; *nor* for the arrow *that* flieth by day;
6 *Nor* for the pestilence *that* walketh in darkness; *nor* for the destruction *that* wasteth at noonday.   2 Kin. 19:35
7 A thousand shall fall at thy side, and ten thousand at thy right hand; *but* it shall not come nigh thee.   Gen. 7:23
8 Only with thine eyes shalt thou behold and see the reward of the wicked. Ps. 37:34; Mal. 1:5
9 Because thou hast made the LORD, *which is* my refuge, *even* the most High, thy habitation;   Ps. 71:3
10 There shall no evil befall thee, neither shall any plague come nigh thy dwelling. Prov. 12:21

> **91:11 Protection by the Angels**
>
> In the time of trouble just before the coming of Christ, the righteous will be preserved through the ministration of heavenly angels; but there will be no security for the transgressor of God's law. Angels cannot then protect those who are disregarding one of the divine precepts. *PP 256*

11 For he shall give his angels charge over thee, to keep thee in all thy ways. Ps. 34:7

12 They shall bear thee up in *their* hands, lest thou [T]dash thy foot against a stone. *strike*

13 Thou shalt tread upon the lion and [T]adder: the young lion and the dragon shalt thou trample under feet. Dan. 6:22 ◆ *venomous snake*

14 Because he hath set his love upon me, therefore will I deliver him: I will set him on high, because he hath known my name. Ps. 9:10

15 He shall call upon me, and I will answer him: I *will be* with him in trouble; I will deliver him, and honour him. 1 Sam. 2:30; Ps. 50:15

16 With long life will I satisfy him, and shew him my salvation. Ps. 21:4; 50:23; Prov. 3:2

PSALM 92

It Is a Good Thing to Praise God

A Psalm *or* Song for the sabbath day.

*I*t is a good *thing* to give thanks unto the LORD, and to sing praises unto thy name, O most High: Ps. 135:3; 147:1

2 To shew forth thy lovingkindness in the morning, and thy faithfulness every night,

3 Upon an instrument of ten strings, and upon the [T]psaltery; upon the harp with a solemn sound. 1 Sam. 10:5; Neh. 12:27 ◆ *stringed instrument*

4 For thou, LORD, hast made me glad through thy work: I will triumph in the works of thy hands. Ps. 8:6

5 O LORD, how great are thy works! *and* thy thoughts are very deep. Ps. 40:5; 139:17; Rev. 15:3

6 A [T]brutish man knoweth not; neither doth a fool understand this. Ps. 49:10; 73:22; 94:8 ◆ *dumb*

7 When the wicked spring as the grass, and when all the workers of iniquity do flourish; *it is* that they shall be destroyed for ever: Job 12:6; Ps. 37:38; 73:18-20

8 But thou, LORD, *art most* high for evermore. Ps. 83:18

9 For, lo, thine enemies, O LORD, for, lo, thine enemies shall perish; all the workers of iniquity shall be scattered. Ps. 89:10

10 But my horn shalt thou exalt like *the horn of* an [T]unicorn: I shall be anointed with fresh oil. Num. 23:22; Ps. 23:5; 89:17 ◆ *wild ox*

11 Mine eye also shall see *my desire* on mine enemies, *and* mine ears shall hear *my desire* of the wicked that rise up against me. Ps. 37:34

92:12 God's People Like the Palm Tree

The palm tree, beaten by the scorching sun and the fierce sandstorm, stands green and flourishing and fruitful in the midst of the desert. . . .

The tree of the desert is a symbol of what God means the life of His children in this world to be. They are to guide weary souls, full of unrest, and ready to perish in the desert of sin, to the living water. *Ed 116*

---

12 The righteous shall flourish like the palm tree: he shall grow like a cedar in Lebanon. Ps. 1:3; 52:8; Hos. 14:5-6

13 Those that be planted in the house of the LORD shall flourish in the courts of our God. Ps. 100:4; 135:2; Is. 60:21

14 They shall still bring forth fruit in old age; they shall be fat and flourishing;

15 To shew that the LORD *is* upright: *he is* my rock, and *there is* no unrighteousness in him. Ps. 18:2

PSALM 93

The Lord Reigns

*T*he LORD reigneth, he is clothed with majesty; the LORD is clothed with strength, *wherewith* he hath girded himself: the world also is stablished, that it cannot be moved. Ps. 65:6; 96:10; 97:1

2 Thy throne *is* established of old: thou *art* from everlasting. Ps. 45:6; 90:2

3 The floods have lifted up, O LORD, the floods have lifted up their voice; the floods lift up their waves. Ps. 96:11

4 The LORD on high *is* mightier than the noise of many waters, *yea, than* the mighty waves of the sea. Ps. 65:7; 89:6, 9

5 Thy testimonies are very sure: holiness becometh thine house, O LORD, for ever. Ps. 29:2

PSALM 94

The Lord Will Avenge His People

O LORD God, to whom vengeance belongeth; O God, to whom vengeance belongeth, shew thyself. Deut. 32:35; Is. 35:4; Nah. 1:2

2 Lift up thyself, thou judge of the earth: render a reward to the proud. Gen. 18:25

3 LORD, how long shall the wicked, how long shall the wicked triumph? Job 20:5

4 *How long* shall they utter *and* speak hard things? *and* all the workers of iniquity boast themselves? Ps. 31:18; 52:1

5 They break in pieces thy people, O LORD, and afflict thine heritage. Is. 3:15

6 They slay the widow and the stranger, and murder the fatherless. Is. 10:2

7 Yet they say, The LORD shall not see, neither shall the God of Jacob regard *it*.

8 Understand, ye brutish among the people: and *ye* fools, when will ye be wise? Ps. 49:10; 92:6

9 He that planted the ear, shall he not hear? he that formed the eye, shall he not see?

10 He that chastiseth the heathen, shall not he correct? he that teacheth man knowledge, *shall not he know*? Job 35:11; Ps. 44:2; Is. 28:26

11 The LORD knoweth the thoughts of man, that they *are* vanity. 1 Cor. 3:20

12 Blessed *is* the man whom thou [T]chastenest, O LORD, and teachest him out of thy law; Job 5:17; Ps. 119:71; 1 Cor. 11:32 ◆ *disciplines*

13 That thou mayest give him rest from the days of adversity, until the pit be digged for the wicked.   Ps. 9:15; 55:23; Hab. 3:16
14 For the LORD will not cast off his people, neither will he forsake his inheritance.
15 But judgment shall return unto righteousness: and all the upright in heart shall follow it.   Mic. 7:9
16 Who will rise up for me against the evildoers? or who will stand up for me against the workers of iniquity?
17 Unless the LORD had been my help, my soul had almost dwelt in silence.   Ps. 124:1-2
18 When I said, My foot slippeth; thy mercy, O LORD, held me up.   Ps. 38:16
19 In the multitude of my thoughts within me thy comforts delight my soul.
20 Shall the throne of iniquity have fellowship with thee, which frameth mischief by a law?   Ps. 58:2; Is. 10:1; Amos 6:3
21 They gather themselves together against the soul of the righteous, and condemn the innocent blood.   Prov. 17:15
22 But the LORD is my defence; and my God is the rock of my refuge.   Ps. 18:2; 59:9
23 And he shall bring upon them their own iniquity, and shall cut them off in their own wickedness; yea, the LORD our God shall cut them off.   Ps. 7:16; Prov. 2:22

PSALM 95

An Invitation to Praise God

O come, let us sing unto the LORD: let us make a joyful noise to the rock of our salvation.   Ps. 81:1
2 Let us come before his presence with thanksgiving, and make a joyful noise unto him with psalms.   Ps. 100:4
3 For the LORD is a great God, and a great King above all gods.   Ps. 96:4; 97:9; 135:5
4 In his hand are the deep places of the earth: the strength of the hills is his also.   Ps. 135:6
5 The sea is his, and he made it: and his hands formed the dry land.   Gen. 1:9-10
6 O come, let us worship and bow down: let us kneel before the LORD our maker. 2Chr. 6:13

95:6 Kneeling Before God

Both in public and in private worship it is our privilege to bow on our knees before God when we offer our petitions to Him. Jesus, our example, "kneeled down, and prayed" (Luke 22:41). Of his disciples it is recorded that they, too, "kneeled down, and prayed" (Acts 9:40)....

True reverence for God is inspired by a sense of His infinite greatness and a realization of His presence. PK 48

---

7 For he is our God; and we are the people of his pasture, and the sheep of his hand. To day if ye will hear his voice,   Heb. 3:15

8 Harden not your heart, as in the provocation, and as in the day of temptation in the wilderness: Ex. 17:7; Num. 20:13; Deut. 6:16
9 When your fathers tempted me, proved me, and saw my work. Num. 14:22; Ps. 78:56; 1 Cor. 10:9
10 Forty years long was I grieved with this generation, and said, It is a people that do Terr in their heart, and they have not known my ways: Acts 7:36; Heb. 3:17 ◆ stray
11 Unto whom I sware in my wrath that they should not enter into my rest.   Num. 14:23

PSALM 96

Sing to the Lord a New Song

O sing unto the LORD a new song: sing unto the LORD, all the earth. 1 Chr. 16:23-33
2 Sing unto the LORD, bless his name; shew forth his salvation from day to day.   Ps. 71:15
3 Declare his glory among the heathen, his wonders among all people.
4 For the LORD is great, and greatly to be praised: he is to be feared above all gods.
5 For all the gods of the nations are idols: but the LORD made the heavens. Ps. 115:15; Is. 42:5
6 Honour and majesty are before him: strength and beauty are in his sanctuary.   Ps. 104:1
7 Give unto the LORD, O ye kindreds of the people, give unto the LORD glory and strength.   Ps. 22:27; 29:1-2
8 Give unto the LORD the glory due unto his name: bring an offering, and come into his courts.   Ps. 45:12
9 O worship the LORD in the beauty of holiness: fear before him, all the earth.   Ps. 29:2
10 Say among the heathen that the LORD reigneth: the world also shall be established that it shall not be moved: he shall judge the people righteously.   Ps. 9:8; 67:4; 93:1
11 Let the heavens rejoice, and let the earth be glad; let the sea roar, and the fulness thereof.   Ps. 69:34
12 Let the field be joyful, and all that is therein: then shall all the trees of the wood rejoice   Is. 55:12-13
13 Before the LORD: for he cometh, for he cometh to judge the earth: he shall judge the world with righteousness, and the people with his truth.   Rev. 19:11

PSALM 97

The Majesty of God's Kingdom

The LORD reigneth; let the earth rejoice; let the multitude of isles be glad thereof.   Ps. 96:10-11
2 Clouds and darkness are round about him: righteousness and judgment are the habitation of his throne.   Ex. 19:9; Ps. 89:14
3 A fire goeth before him, and burneth up his enemies round about.   Ps. 18:8

97:2 God's Heavenly Throne

In the temple in heaven, the dwelling place of God, His throne is established in righteousness and judgment. In the most holy place is His law, the great rule of right by which all mankind are tested. The ark that enshrines the tables of the law is covered with the mercy seat, before which Christ pleads His blood in the sinner's behalf. Thus is represented the union of justice and mercy in the plan of human redemption. *GC 415*

4 His lightnings enlightened the world: the earth saw, and trembled. Ps. 77:18
5 The hills melted like wax at the presence of the Lord, at the presence of the Lord of the whole earth. Nah. 1:5
6 The heavens declare his righteousness, and all the people see his glory. Ps. 19:1; 50:6; Is. 6:3
7 Confounded be all they that serve graven images, that boast themselves of idols: worship him, all *ye* gods. Is. 42:17; Jer. 10:14; Heb. 1:6
8 Zion heard, and was glad; and the daughters of Judah rejoiced because of thy judgments, O Lord. Ps. 48:11
9 For thou, Lord, *art* high above all the earth: thou art exalted far above all gods. Ex. 18:11
10 Ye that love the Lord, hate evil: he preserveth the souls of his saints; he delivereth them out of the hand of the wicked. Ps. 34:14
11 Light is sown for the righteous, and gladness for the upright in heart. Job 22:28
12 Rejoice in the Lord, ye righteous; and give thanks at the remembrance of his holiness. Ps. 30:4

PSALM 98

Make a Joyful Noise unto the Lord

A Psalm.

O sing unto the Lord a new song; for he hath done marvellous things: his right hand, and his holy arm, hath gotten him the victory. Ex. 15:6; Ps. 33:3; Is. 52:10
2 The Lord hath made known his salvation: his righteousness hath he openly shewed in the sight of the heathen. Is. 49:6; 52:10; 62:2
3 He hath remembered his mercy and his truth toward the house of Israel: all the ends of the earth have seen the salvation of our God. Ps. 22:27
4 Make a joyful noise unto the Lord, all the earth: make a loud noise, and rejoice, and sing praise. Ps. 66:1; 100:1; Is. 44:23
5 Sing unto the Lord with the harp; with the harp, and the voice of a psalm. Is. 51:3
6 With trumpets and sound of cornet make a joyful noise before the Lord, the King.
7 Let the sea roar, and the fulness thereof; the world, and they that dwell therein. Ps. 24:1

8 Let the floods clap *their* hands: let the hills be joyful together Is. 55:12
9 Before the Lord; for he cometh to judge the earth: with righteousness shall he judge the world, and the people with equity. Ps. 96:10

PSALM 99

The Lord Is Great in Zion

THe Lord reigneth; let the people tremble: he sitteth *between* the cherubims; let the earth be moved. Ex. 25:22
2 The Lord *is* great in Zion; and he *is* high above all the people. Ps. 97:9
3 Let them praise thy great and terrible name; *for* it *is* holy. Deut. 28:58

99:1-3 Proof of God's Mercy

Man cannot by searching find out God. Let none seek with presumptuous hand to lift the veil that conceals His glory. "Unsearchable are His judgments, and His ways past finding out" (Romans 11:33). It is a proof of His mercy that there is the hiding of His power; for to lift the veil that conceals the divine presence is death. No mortal mind can penetrate the secrecy in which the Mighty One dwells and works. Only that which He sees fit to reveal can we comprehend of Him. *MH 438*

4 The king's strength also loveth judgment; thou dost establish ᵀequity, thou executest judgment and righteousness in Jacob. *fairness*
5 Exalt ye the Lord our God, and worship at his footstool; *for* he *is* holy. Ex. 15:2; 1 Chr. 28:2
6 Moses and Aaron among his priests, and Samuel among them that call upon his name; they called upon the Lord, and he answered them. Ex. 14:15; 24:6-8; Jer. 15:1
7 He spake unto them in the cloudy pillar: they kept his testimonies, and the ordinance *that* he gave them. Ex. 33:9; Num. 12:5
8 Thou answeredst them, O Lord our God: thou wast a God that forgavest them, though thou tookest vengeance of their inventions. Num. 20:12
9 Exalt the Lord our God, and worship at his holy hill; for the Lord our God *is* holy. Ps. 2:6

PSALM 100

An Invitation to Praise God Cheerfully

A Psalm of praise.

Make a joyful noise unto the Lord, all ye lands. Ps. 98:4
2 Serve the Lord with gladness: come before his presence with singing. Deut. 12:12; Ps. 95:2
3 Know ye that the Lord he *is* God: *it is* he *that* hath made us, and not we ourselves; *we are* his people, and the sheep of his pasture. Ps. 46:10; 95:6-7; Ezek. 34:30-31

100:2 Music a Form of Worship

Music forms a part of God's worship in the courts above, and we should endeavor, in our songs of praise, to approach as nearly as possible to the harmony of the heavenly choirs. The proper training of the voice is an important feature in education and should not be neglected. Singing, as a part of religious service, is as much an act of worship as is prayer. The heart must feel the spirit of the song to give it right expression. *PP 594*

4 Enter into his gates with thanksgiving, *and* into his courts with praise: be thankful unto him, *and* bless his name.　　　　　Ps. 96:2

100:4 What Inspires Our Reverence

True reverence for God is inspired by a sense of His infinite greatness and a realization of His presence. With this sense of the Unseen the heart of every child should be deeply impressed. The hour and place of prayer and the services of public worship the child should be taught to regard as sacred because God is there. And as reverence is manifested in attitude and demeanor, the feeling that inspires it will be deepened. *Ed 242, 243*

5 For the LORD *is* good; his mercy *is* everlasting; and his truth *endureth* to all generations.　　　　　Ezra 3:11; Ps. 106:1; Jer. 33:11

PSALM 101

David Prays to Live with Integrity

A Psalm of David.

I will sing of mercy and judgment: unto thee, O LORD, will I sing.　　Ps. 89:1
2 I will behave myself wisely in a perfect way. O when wilt thou come unto me? I will walk within my house with a perfect heart.　　　　　1 Kin. 9:4
3 I will set no wicked thing before mine eyes: I hate the work of them that turn aside; *it* shall not cleave to me. Deut. 15:9; Josh. 23:6; Ps. 40:4
4 A ᵀfroward heart shall depart from me: I will not know a wicked *person*.　　*false* or *perverse*
5 Whoso ᵀprivily slandereth his neighbour, him will I cut off: him that hath an high look and a proud heart will not I suffer.　　*secretly*
6 Mine eyes *shall be* upon the faithful of the land, that they may dwell with me: he that walketh in a perfect way, he shall serve me.
7 He that worketh deceit shall not dwell within my house: he that telleth lies shall not tarry in my sight.
8 I will early destroy all the wicked of the land; that I may cut off all wicked doers from the city of the LORD.　Ps. 48:8; 75:10; Jer. 21:12

PSALM 102

Comfort in the Mercy of God

A Prayer of the afflicted, when he is overwhelmed, and poureth out his complaint before the LORD.

Hear my prayer, O LORD, and let my cry come unto thee. Ex. 2:23; 1 Sam. 9:16; Ps. 18:6
2 Hide not thy face from me in the day *when* I am in trouble; incline thine ear unto me: in the day *when* I call answer me speedily.　　　　　Ps. 27:9; 69:17
3 For my days are consumed like smoke, and my bones are burned as an hearth.　Job 30:30
4 My heart is smitten, and withered like grass; so that I forget to eat my bread. Ezra 10:6; Is. 40:7
5 By reason of the voice of my groaning my bones cleave to my skin.　　　　Job 19:20
6 I am like a pelican of the wilderness: I am like an owl of the desert.　　　Zeph. 2:14
7 I watch, and am as a sparrow alone upon the house top.　　　　　Ps. 38:11; 77:4
8 Mine enemies reproach me all the day; *and* they that are mad against me are sworn against me.　　　　　Acts 26:11
9 For I have eaten ashes like bread, and mingled my drink with weeping,　　Ps. 42:3; 80:5
10 Because of thine ᵀindignation and thy wrath: for thou hast lifted me up, and cast me down.　　　Ps. 38:3 ◆ *anger*
11 My days *are* like a shadow that declineth; and I am withered like grass.　　Job 14:2
12 But thou, O LORD, shalt endure for ever; and thy remembrance unto all generations.　　　Ex. 3:15; Ps. 9:7; 135:13
13 Thou shalt arise, *and* have mercy upon Zion: for the time to favour her, yea, the set time, is come.　　　　　Ps. 44:26
14 For thy servants take pleasure in her stones, and favour the dust thereof.　Neh. 4:2
15 So the heathen shall fear the name of the LORD, and all the kings of the earth thy glory.　　　　1 Kin. 8:43; Ps. 138:4
16 When the LORD shall build up Zion, he shall appear in his glory.　Ps. 147:2; Is. 60:1-2
17 He will regard the prayer of the destitute, and not despise their prayer. Neh. 1:6; Ps. 22:24
18 This shall be written for the generation to come: and the people which shall be created shall praise the LORD.　Ps. 22:30-31; Is. 43:21
19 For he hath looked down from the height of his sanctuary; from heaven did the LORD behold the earth;　　　　Deut. 26:15
20 To hear the groaning of the prisoner; to loose those that are appointed to death;
21 To declare the name of the LORD in Zion, and his praise in Jerusalem;　　Ps. 22:22
22 When the people are gathered together, and the kingdoms, to serve the LORD.
23 He weakened my strength in the way; he shortened my days.

24 I said, O my God, take me not away in the midst of my days: thy years *are* throughout all generations.   Hab. 1:12

25 Of old hast thou laid the foundation of the earth: and the heavens *are* the work of thy hands.   Gen. 1:1; 2:1; Heb. 1:10-12

26 They shall perish, but thou shalt endure: yea, all of them shall wax old like a garment; as a ᵀvesture shalt thou change them, and they shall be changed: Is. 34:4; 51:6 ◆ *piece of clothing*

27 But thou *art* the same, and thy years shall have no end.   Mal. 3:6

28 The children of thy servants shall continue, and their seed shall be established before thee.

PSALM 103

David Praises God's Great Love

A Psalm of David.

Bless the LORD, O my soul: and all that is within me, *bless* his holy name.

2 Bless the LORD, O my soul, and forget not all his benefits:

3 Who forgiveth all thine iniquities; who healeth all thy diseases;   Ex. 15:26; Ps. 30:2; 130:8

4 Who redeemeth thy life from destruction; who crowneth thee with lovingkindness and tender mercies;   Ps. 56:13

5 Who satisfieth thy mouth with good *things; so that* thy youth is renewed like the eagle's.   Ps. 107:9; Is. 40:31

6 The LORD executeth righteousness and judgment for all that are oppressed. Ps. 146:7

7 He made known his ways unto Moses, his acts unto the children of Israel.   Ps. 147:19

8 The LORD *is* merciful and gracious, slow to anger, and plenteous in mercy.   Num. 14:18

9 He will not always chide: neither will he keep *his anger* for ever.   Ps. 30:5; Is. 57:16; Jer. 3:5

10 He hath not dealt with us after our sins; nor rewarded us according to our iniquities.   Ezra 9:13; Lam. 3:22

11 For as the heaven is high above the earth, *so* great is his mercy toward them that fear him.   Ps. 36:5

12 As far as the east is from the west, *so* far hath he removed our ᵀtransgressions from us.   Is. 43:25 ◆ *sins*

103:12 God's Transforming Forgiveness

God's forgiveness is not merely a judicial act by which He sets us free from condemnation. It is not only forgiveness for sin, but reclaiming from sin. It is the outflow of redeeming love that transforms the heart. *MB 114*

---

13 Like as a father pitieth *his* children, *so* the LORD pitieth them that fear him.

14 For he knoweth our frame; he remembereth that we *are* dust.   Gen. 3:19

15 *As for* man, his days *are* as grass: as a flower of the field, so he flourisheth.1 Pet. 1:24

16 For the wind passeth over it, and it is gone; and the place thereof shall know it no more.   Job 20:9; Is. 40:7

17 But the mercy of the LORD *is* from everlasting to everlasting upon them that fear him, and his righteousness unto children's children;   Ex. 20:6

18 To such as keep his covenant, and to those that remember his commandments to do them.   Deut. 7:9; Ps. 25:10

19 The LORD hath prepared his throne in the heavens; and his kingdom ruleth over all.   Ps. 11:4; 47:2; Dan. 4:25

20 Bless the LORD, ye his angels, that excel in strength, that do his commandments, hearkening unto the voice of his word.   Ps. 78:25

103:20 Angels That Excel in Strength

It would be well to consider that in all our work we have the co-operation and care of heavenly beings. Invisible armies of light and power attend the meek and lowly ones who believe and claim the promises of God. Cherubim and seraphim and angels that excel in strength—ten thousand times ten thousand and thousands of thousands—stand at His right hand, "all ministering spirits, sent forth to minister for them who shall be heirs of salvation" (Hebrews 1:14). *COL 176*

---

21 Bless ye the LORD, all *ye* his hosts; *ye* ministers of his, that do his pleasure.   Gen. 32:2

When Our Eyes Are Opened

Psalm 103:13, 14

In his restless youth the prodigal looked upon his father as stern and severe. How different his conception of him now! So those who are deceived by Satan look upon God as hard and exacting. They regard Him as watching to denounce and condemn, as unwilling to receive the sinner so long as there is a legal excuse for not helping him. His law they regard as a restriction upon men's happiness, a burdensome yoke from which they are glad to escape. But he whose eyes have been opened by the love of Christ will behold God as full of compassion. He does not appear as a tyrannical, relentless being, but as a father longing to embrace his repenting son. The sinner will exclaim with the Psalmist, "Like as a father pitieth his children, so the Lord pitieth them that fear him" (Psalm 103:13). *COL 204*

22 Bless the LORD, all his works in all places of his dominion: bless the LORD, O my soul. Ps. 145:10

PSALM 104

A Meditation upon God's Mighty Creative Power

Bless the LORD, O my soul. O LORD my God, thou art very great; thou art clothed with honour and majesty. Ps. 93:1; 103:1-2, 22

2 Who coverest *thyself* with light as *with* a garment: who stretchest out the heavens like a curtain: Is. 40:22; Dan. 7:9

3 Who layeth the beams of his chambers in the waters: who maketh the clouds his chariot: who walketh upon the wings of the wind: 2 Sam. 22:11; Is. 19:1; Amos 9:6

4 Who maketh his angels spirits; his ministers a flaming fire: 2 Kin. 2:11; 6:17; Heb. 1:7

5 *Who* laid the foundations of the earth, *that* it should not be removed for ever. Ps. 24:2; 136:6

6 Thou coveredst it with the deep as *with* a garment: the waters stood above the mountains. Gen. 7:19

7 At thy rebuke they fled; at the voice of thy thunder they hasted away. Gen. 8:1

8 They go up by the mountains; they go down by the valleys unto the place which thou hast founded for them.

9 Thou hast set a ᵀbound that they may not pass over; that they turn not again to cover the earth. Gen. 9:11-15 ◆ *landmark*

10 He sendeth the springs into the valleys, *which* run among the hills. Is. 41:18

11 They give drink to every beast of the field: the wild asses quench their thirst.

12 By them shall the fowls of the heaven have their habitation, *which* sing among the branches.

13 He watereth the hills from his chambers: the earth is satisfied with the fruit of thy works. Deut. 11:11; Ps. 147:8; Jer. 10:13

14 He causeth the grass to grow for the cattle, and herb for the service of man: that he may bring forth food out of the earth; Gen. 3:18

15 And wine *that* maketh glad the heart of man, *and* oil to make *his* face to shine, and bread *which* strengtheneth man's heart.

16 The trees of the LORD are full *of sap*; the cedars of Lebanon, which he hath planted;

17 Where the birds make their nests: as for the stork, the fir trees *are* her house. Ps. 104:12

18 The high hills *are* a refuge for the wild goats; *and* the rocks for the conies. Job 39:1

19 He appointed the moon for seasons: the sun knoweth his going down.

20 Thou makest darkness, and it is night: wherein all the beasts of the forest do creep forth. Ps. 74:16; Is. 45:7

104:19, 20 True Science Is in Harmony With God

God is the foundation of everything. All true science is in harmony with His works; all true education leads to obedience to His government. Science opens new wonders to our view; she soars high, and explores new depths; but she brings nothing from her research that conflicts with divine revelation. Ignorance may seek to support false views of God by appeals to science, but the book of nature and the written word shed light upon each other. *PP 115*

---

21 The young lions roar after their prey, and seek their meat from God. Job 38:39; Joel 1:20

22 The sun ariseth, they gather themselves together, and lay them down in their dens.

23 Man goeth forth unto his work and to his labour until the evening. Gen. 3:19

24 O LORD, how manifold are thy works! in wisdom hast thou made them all: the earth is full of thy riches. Ps. 40:5

25 *So is* this great and wide sea, wherein *are* things creeping innumerable, both small and great beasts. Ps. 69:34

26 There go the ships: *there is* that leviathan, *whom* thou hast made to play therein. Ps. 74:14

27 These wait all upon thee; that thou mayest give *them* their meat in due season. Ps. 136:25

28 *That* thou givest them they gather: thou openest thine hand, they are filled with good. Ps. 145:16

29 Thou hidest thy face, they are troubled: thou takest away their breath, they die, and return to their dust. Gen. 3:19

30 Thou sendest forth thy spirit, they are created: and thou renewest the face of the earth. Job 26:13; 33:4; Ezek. 37:9

31 The glory of the LORD shall endure for ever: the LORD shall rejoice in his works.

32 He looketh on the earth, and it trembleth: he toucheth the hills, and they smoke. Ex. 19:18; Ps. 144:5; Hab. 3:10

33 I will sing unto the LORD as long as I live: I will sing praise to my God while I have my being. Ps. 63:4; 146:2

34 My meditation of him shall be sweet: I will be glad in the LORD.

35 Let the sinners be consumed out of the earth, and let the wicked be no more. Bless thou the LORD, O my soul. Praise ye the LORD. Ps. 37:38

PSALM 105

David Recalls God's Miracles for Israel

O give thanks unto the LORD; call upon his name: make known his deeds among the people. 1 Chr. 16:34; Ps. 99:6; Is. 12:4

2 Sing unto him, sing psalms unto him: talk ye of all his wondrous works. Ps. 77:12

3 Glory ye in his holy name: let the heart of them rejoice that seek the LORD.
4 Seek the LORD, and his strength: seek his face evermore. Ps. 27:8; 78:61
5 Remember his marvellous works that he hath done; his wonders, and the judgments of his mouth; Ps. 77:11; 119:13
6 O ye seed of Abraham his servant, ye children of Jacob his chosen.
7 He *is* the LORD our God: his judgments *are* in all the earth. Is. 26:9
8 He hath remembered his covenant for ever, the word *which* he commanded to a thousand generations. Deut. 7:9
9 Which *covenant* he made with Abraham, and his oath unto Isaac; Gen. 17:2; 22:16-18; 26:3
10 And confirmed the same unto Jacob for a law, *and* to Israel *for* an everlasting covenant:
11 Saying, Unto thee will I give the land of Canaan, the lot of your inheritance: Gen. 13:15
12 When they were *but* a few men in number; yea, very few, and strangers in it. Gen. 34:30
13 When they went from one nation to another, from *one* kingdom to another people;
14 He suffered no man to do them wrong: yea, he reproved kings for their sakes; Gen. 35:5
15 *Saying*, Touch not mine anointed, and do my prophets no harm. Gen. 20:7; 26:11
16 Moreover he called for a famine upon the land: he brake the whole staff of bread.
17 He sent a man before them, *even* Joseph, *who* was sold for a servant: Gen. 37:36; 50:20
18 Whose feet they hurt with †fetters: he was laid in iron: Gen. 39:20 ◆ *chains*
19 Until the time that his word came: the word of the LORD tried him. Gen. 40:20-21
20 The king sent and loosed him; *even* the ruler of the people, and let him go free.

21 He made him lord of his house, and ruler of all his substance: Gen. 41:40-44
22 To bind his princes at his pleasure; and teach his senators wisdom.
23 Israel also came into Egypt; and Jacob sojourned in the land of Ham. Ps. 78:51
24 And he increased his people greatly; and made them stronger than their enemies. Deut. 26:5
25 He turned their heart to hate his people, to deal subtilly with his servants. Acts 7:19
26 He sent Moses his servant; *and* Aaron whom he had chosen. Ex. 3:10
27 They shewed his signs among them, and wonders in the land of Ham. Ps. 78:43-51
28 He sent darkness, and made it dark; and they rebelled not against his word. Ps. 99:7
29 He turned their waters into blood, and slew their fish. Ex. 7:20-21
30 Their land brought forth frogs in abundance, in the chambers of their kings.
31 He spake, and there came †divers sorts of flies, *and* lice in all their coasts. *various*
32 He gave them hail for rain, *and* flaming fire in their land.
33 He smote their vines also and their fig trees; and brake the trees of their coasts.
34 He spake, and the locusts came, and caterpillers, and that without number, Ex. 10:12-15
35 And did eat up all the herbs in their land, and devoured the fruit of their ground.
36 He smote also all the firstborn in their land, the chief of all their strength. Gen. 49:3
37 He brought them forth also with silver and gold: and *there was* not one feeble *person* among their tribes. Ex. 12:35-36
38 Egypt was glad when they departed: for the fear of them fell upon them. Ex. 12:33

Joseph's Pure, True Character a Great Witness

Psalm 105:17–22

From the dungeon Joseph was exalted to be ruler over all the land of Egypt. It was a position of high honor, yet it was beset with difficulty and peril. One cannot stand upon a lofty height without danger. As the tempest leaves unharmed the lowly flower of the valley, while it uproots the stately tree upon the mountaintop, so those who have maintained their integrity in humble life may be dragged down to the pit by the temptations that assail worldly success and honor. But Joseph's character bore the test alike of adversity and prosperity. The same fidelity to God was manifest when he stood in the palace of the Pharaohs as when in a prisoner's cell. . . . Through Joseph the attention of the king and great men of Egypt was directed to the true God; and though they adhered to their idolatry, they learned to respect the principles revealed in the life and character of the worshiper of Jehovah.

How was Joseph enabled to make such a record of firmness of character, uprightness, and wisdom?—In his early years he had consulted duty rather than inclination; and the integrity, the simple trust, the noble nature, of the youth bore fruit in the deeds of the man. A pure and simple life had favored the vigorous development of both physical and intellectual powers. Communion with God through His works and the contemplation of the grand truths entrusted to the inheritors of faith had elevated and ennobled his spiritual nature, broadening and strengthening the mind as no other study could do. Faithful attention to duty in every station, from the lowliest to the most exalted, had been training every power for its highest service. *PP 222*

105:37 Conditions for Enjoying Good Health

When [Israel] fulfilled the conditions, the promise was verified to them. "There was not one feeble person among their tribes" (Psalm 105:37). . . .

The Lord is not pleased with ignorance in regard to His laws, either natural or spiritual. We are to be workers together with God for the restoration of health to the body as well as to the soul. . . .

The very essence of the gospel is restoration, and the Saviour would have us bid the sick, the hopeless, and the afflicted take hold upon His strength. *DA 824, 825*

---

39 He spread a cloud for a covering; and fire to give light in the night.   Neh. 9:12
40 *The people* asked, and he brought quails, and satisfied them with the bread of heaven.   Ps. 78:18
41 He opened the rock, and the waters gushed out; they ran in the dry places *like a* river.   Ex. 17:6

105:41 Christ the Smitten Rock

That rock was a symbol of Him who by His death would cause living streams of salvation to flow to all who are athirst. Christ's words were the water of life. There in the presence of the assembled multitude He set Himself apart to be smitten, that the water of life might flow to the world. In smiting Christ, Satan thought to destroy the Prince of life; but from the smitten rock there flowed living water. *DA 454*

---

42 For he remembered his holy promise, *and* Abraham his servant.   Ex. 2:24
43 And he brought forth his people with joy, *and* his chosen with gladness:
44 And gave them the lands of the heathen: and they inherited the labour of the people;   Ps. 78:55
45 That they might observe his statutes, and keep his laws. Praise ye the LORD.   Deut. 4:40

PSALM 106

Israel Repents and Praises God

Praise ye the LORD. O give thanks unto the LORD; for *he is* good: for his mercy *endureth* for ever.   1 Chr. 16:34
2 Who can utter the mighty acts of the LORD? *who* can shew forth all his praise?
3 Blessed *are* they that keep judgment, *and* he that doeth righteousness at all times.   Ps. 15:2
4 Remember me, O LORD, with the favour *that thou bearest unto* thy people: O visit me with thy salvation;   Ps. 119:132
5 That I may see the good of thy chosen, that I may rejoice in the gladness of thy na-

tion, that I may glory with thine inheritance.   Ps. 105:6
6 We have sinned with our fathers, we have committed iniquity, we have done wickedly.   1 Kin. 8:47
7 Our fathers understood not thy wonders in Egypt; they remembered not the multitude of thy mercies; but provoked *him* at the sea, *even* at the Red sea.   Ex. 14:11-12
8 Nevertheless he saved them for his name's sake, that he might make his mighty power to be known.   Ex. 9:16; Ezek. 20:9, 14
9 He rebuked the Red sea also, and it was dried up: so he led them through the depths, as through the wilderness. Ps. 18:15; 78:13; Nah. 1:4
10 And he saved them from the hand of him that hated *them*, and redeemed them from the hand of the enemy.   Ex. 14:30; Ps. 107:2
11 And the waters covered their enemies: there was not one of them left. Ex. 14:27-28; 15:5
12 Then believed they his words; they sang his praise.   Ex. 14:31-15:21
13 They soon forgat his works; they waited not for his counsel: Ex. 15:24; 16:2; Ps. 78:11
14 But lusted exceedingly in the wilderness, and tempted God in the desert.   Ex. 17:2
15 And he gave them their request; but sent leanness into their soul.   Is. 10:16
16 They envied Moses also in the camp, *and* Aaron the saint of the LORD.
17 The earth opened and swallowed up Dathan, and covered the company of Abiram.   Deut. 11:6
18 And a fire was kindled in their company; the flame burned up the wicked.
19 They made a calf in Horeb, and worshipped the molten image.
20 Thus they changed their glory into the Tsimilitude of an ox that eateth grass.   *image*
21 They forgat God their saviour, which had done great things in Egypt;   Ps. 106:13
22 Wondrous works in the land of Ham, *and* terrible things by the Red sea.   Ps. 78:51
23 Therefore he said that he would destroy them, had not Moses his chosen stood before him in the breach, to turn away his wrath, lest he should destroy *them*. Deut. 9:25
24 Yea, they despised the pleasant land, they believed not his word: Num. 14:31
25 But murmured in their tents, *and* hearkened not unto the voice of the LORD.
26 Therefore he lifted up his hand against them, to overthrow them in the wilderness: Num. 14:28-35; Ps. 95:11; Ezek. 20:15
27 To overthrow their seed also among the nations, and to scatter them in the lands.
28 They joined themselves also unto Baalpeor, and ate the sacrifices of the dead.Deut.4:3
29 Thus they provoked *him* to anger with their inventions: and the plague brake in upon them.

30 Then stood up Phinehas, and executed judgment: and *so* the plague was stayed.
31 And that was counted unto him for righteousness unto all generations for evermore.   Num. 25:11-13
32 They angered *him* also at the waters of strife, so that it went ill with Moses for their sakes: Ps. 81:7
33 Because they provoked his spirit, so that he spake unadvisedly with his lips.
34 They did not destroy the nations, concerning whom the LORD commanded them:
35 But were mingled among the heathen, and learned their works.   Judg. 3:5-6
36 And they served their idols: which were a snare unto them.   Deut. 7:16
37 Yea, they sacrificed their sons and their daughters unto devils,   Deut. 32:17; 2 Kin. 16:3
38 And shed innocent blood, *even* the blood of their sons and of their daughters, whom they sacrificed unto the idols of Canaan: and the land was polluted with blood.   Num. 35:33
39 Thus were they defiled with their own works, and went a whoring with their own inventions.   Lev. 17:7; Num. 15:39; Ezek. 20:18
40 Therefore was the wrath of the LORD kindled against his people, insomuch that he abhorred his own inheritance.   Deut. 9:29; 32:19
41 And he gave them into the hand of the heathen; and they that hated them ruled over them.   Judg. 2:14
42 Their enemies also oppressed them, and they were brought into subjection under their hand.
43 Many times did he deliver them; but they provoked *him* with their counsel, and were brought low for their iniquity.   Judg. 2:16-18
44 Nevertheless he regarded their affliction, when he heard their cry: Judg. 3:9; 4:3
45 And he remembered for them his covenant, and repented according to the multitude of his mercies.   Judg. 2:18; Ps. 69:16; 105:8
46 He made them also to be pitied of all those that carried them captives.   1 Kin. 8:50; Ezra 9:9
47 Save us, O LORD our God, and gather us from among the heathen, to give thanks unto thy holy name, *and* to triumph in thy praise.
48 Blessed *be* the LORD God of Israel from everlasting to everlasting: and let all the people say, Amen. Praise ye the LORD.   Ps. 41:13

PSALM 107

A Celebration of the Return from Exile

O give thanks unto the LORD, for *he is* good: for his mercy *endureth* for ever.   1 Chr. 16:34
2 Let the redeemed of the LORD say *so,* whom he hath redeemed from the hand of the enemy;   Ps. 106:10; Is. 35:9; Gal. 3:13
3 And gathered them out of the lands, from the east, and from the west, from the north, and from the south.   Ps. 106:47; Is. 43:5-6; Jer. 29:14
4 They wandered in the wilderness in a solitary way; they found no city to dwell in.
5 Hungry and thirsty, their soul fainted in them.
6 Then they cried unto the LORD in their trouble, *and* he delivered them out of their distresses.   Ps. 50:15
7 And he led them forth by the right way, that they might go to a city of habitation.   Ps. 107:4
8 Oh that *men* would praise the LORD *for* his goodness, and *for* his wonderful works to the children of men!   Ps. 107:15

107:8 Do Not Spare in Giving Thanks

Our devotional exercises should not consist wholly in asking and receiving. Let us not be always thinking of our wants and never of the benefits we receive. We do not pray any too much, but we are too sparing of giving thanks. We are the constant recipients of God's mercies, and yet how little gratitude we express, how little we praise Him for what He has done for us. *SC 102, 103*

9 For he satisfieth the longing soul, and filleth the hungry soul with goodness. Ps. 34:10
10 Such as sit in darkness and in the shadow of death, *being* bound in affliction and iron;   Luke 1:79
11 Because they rebelled against the words of God, and contemned the counsel of the most High: Ps. 73:24
12 Therefore he brought down their heart with labour; they fell down, and *there was* none to help.   Ps. 22:11
13 Then they cried unto the LORD in their trouble, *and* he saved them out of their distresses.   Ps. 107:6
14 He brought them out of darkness and the shadow of death, and brake their bands in sunder.   Ps. 116:16
15 Oh that *men* would praise the LORD *for* his goodness, and *for* his wonderful works to the children of men!   Ps. 107:8
16 For he hath broken the gates of brass, and cut the bars of iron in sunder.   Is. 45:1-2
17 Fools because of their ᵀtransgression, and because of their iniquities, are afflicted.   Lam. 3:39 ♦ *violation of a law*
18 Their soul ᵀabhorreth all manner of meat; and they draw near unto the gates of death.   Ps. 9:13; 88:3 ♦ *despises*
19 Then they cry unto the LORD in their trouble, *and* he saveth them out of their distresses.
20 He sent his word, and healed them, and delivered *them* from their destructions.
21 Oh that *men* would praise the LORD *for*

his goodness, and *for* his wonderful works
to the children of men!   Ps. 107:8
22 And let them sacrifice the sacrifices of
thanksgiving, and declare his works with
rejoicing.   Ps. 9:11; 50:14; 118:17
23 They that go down to the sea in ships,
that do business in great waters;
24 These see the works of the LORD, and his
wonders in the deep.
25 For he commandeth, and raiseth the
stormy wind, which lifteth up the waves
thereof.   Ps. 93:3; 148:8; Jon. 1:4
26 They mount up to the heaven, they go
down again to the depths: their soul is
melted because of trouble.   Ps. 22:14; 119:28
27 They reel to and fro, and stagger like a
drunken man, and are at their wits' end.
28 Then they cry unto the LORD in their
trouble, and he bringeth them out of their
distresses.
29 He maketh the storm a calm, so that the
waves thereof are still.   Ps. 65:7
30 Then are they glad because they be quiet;
so he bringeth them unto their desired
haven.

107:29, 30 Jesus Can Calm Our Storms

How often the disciples' experience is
ours! . . . We trust to our own strength till
our hope is lost, and we are ready to perish. Then we remember Jesus, and if we call
upon Him to save us, we shall not cry in vain.
Though He sorrowfully reproves our unbelief
and self-confidence, He never fails to give us
the help we need. . . . Living faith in the Redeemer will smooth the sea of life, and will
deliver us from danger in the way that He
knows to be best. *DA 336*

---

31 Oh that *men* would praise the LORD *for*
his goodness, and *for* his wonderful works
to the children of men!   Ps. 107:8
32 Let them exalt him also in the congregation of the people, and praise him in the
assembly of the elders.   Ps. 22:22, 25; 99:5
33 He turneth rivers into a wilderness, and
the watersprings into dry ground;   Is. 42:15
34 A fruitful land into barrenness, for the
wickedness of them that dwell therein.
35 He turneth the wilderness into a standing water, and dry ground into watersprings.   Ps. 114:8; Is. 35:6-7
36 And there he maketh the hungry to
dwell, that they may prepare a city for habitation;   Ps. 107:7
37 And sow the fields, and plant vineyards,
which may yield fruits of increase.
38 He blesseth them also, so that they are
multiplied greatly; and suffereth not their
cattle to decrease.   Gen. 12:2; 17:20; Ex. 1:7
39 Again, they are ᵀminished and brought

low through oppression, affliction, and sorrow.   2 Kin. 10:32 ◆ *diminished*
40 He poureth contempt upon princes, and
causeth them to wander in the wilderness,
where there is no way.   Job 12:21, 24
41 Yet setteth he the poor on high from
affliction, and maketh *him* families like a
flock.   1 Sam. 2:8; Job 21:11; Ps. 78:52
42 The righteous shall see *it*, and rejoice: and
all iniquity shall stop her mouth.   Job 22:19
43 Whoso *is* wise, and will observe these
things, even they shall understand the lovingkindness of the LORD.   Ps. 64:9; Jer. 9:12; Hos. 14:9

PSALM 108

David Praises God's Faithfulness

A Song *or* Psalm of David.

O God, my heart is fixed; I will sing and
give praise, even with my glory. Ps. 57:7-11
2 Awake, ᵀpsaltery and harp: I *myself* will
awake early.   *lute*
3 I will praise thee, O LORD, among the people: and I will sing praises unto thee among
the nations.
4 For thy mercy *is* great above the heavens:
and thy truth *reacheth* unto the clouds. Ps. 36:5
5 Be thou exalted, O God, above the heavens: and thy glory above all the earth; Ps. 57:5
6 That thy beloved may be delivered: save
with thy right hand, and answer me. Ps. 60:5-12
7 God hath spoken in his holiness; I will rejoice, I will divide Shechem, and ᵀmete out
the valley of Succoth.   *measure out*
8 Gilead *is* mine; Manasseh *is* mine; Ephraim
also *is* the strength of mine head; Judah *is*
my lawgiver;   Gen. 49:10
9 Moab *is* my washpot; over Edom will I cast
out my shoe; over Philistia will I triumph.
10 Who will bring me into the strong city?
who will lead me into Edom?
11 *Wilt* not *thou*, O God, *who* hast cast us
off? and wilt not thou, O God, go forth with
our hosts?   Ps. 44:9
12 Give us help from trouble: for vain *is* the
help of man.
13 Through God we shall do valiantly: for he
it is that shall tread down our enemies. Is. 63:3

PSALM 109

David Prays against Slanderous
Enemies

To the chief Musician, A Psalm of David.

Hold not thy peace, O God of my praise;
2 For the mouth of the wicked and the
mouth of the deceitful are opened against
me: they have spoken against me with a
lying tongue.   Ps. 52:4
3 They ᵀcompassed me about also with

words of hatred; and fought against me without a cause.　　Ps. 35:7; 69:4 ♦ *surrounded*

4 For my love they are my adversaries: but I *give myself unto* prayer.　　Ps. 38:20

5 And they have rewarded me evil for good, and hatred for my love.

6 Set thou a wicked man over him: and let Satan stand at his right hand.　　Zech. 3:1

7 When he shall be judged, let him be condemned: and let his prayer become sin.

8 Let his days be few; *and* let another take his office.　　Ps. 55:23

9 Let his children be fatherless, and his wife a widow.　　Ex. 22:24; Jer. 18:21

10 Let his children be continually ᵀvaga-bonds, and beg: let them seek *their bread* also out of their desolate places. Ps. 37:25 ♦ *wanderers*

11 Let the extortioner catch all that he hath; and let the strangers ᵀspoil his labour. *plunder*

12 Let there be none to extend mercy unto him: neither let there be any to favour his fatherless children.

13 Let his posterity be cut off; *and* in the generation following let their name be blotted out.　　Job 18:19; Ps. 37:28; Prov. 10:7

14 Let the iniquity of his fathers be remembered with the LORD; and let not the sin of his mother be blotted out.　　Ex. 20:5; Neh. 4:5

15 Let them be before the LORD continually, that he may cut off the memory of them from the earth.　　Job 18:17; Ps. 34:16; 90:8

16 Because that he remembered not to shew mercy, but persecuted the poor and needy man, that he might even slay the broken in heart.　　Ps. 34:18

17 As he loved cursing, so let it come unto him: as he delighted not in blessing, so let it be far from him. Prov. 14:14; Ezek. 35:6; Matt. 7:2

18 As he clothed himself with cursing like as with his garment, so let it come into his bowels like water, and like oil into his bones.　　Num. 5:22; Ps. 73:6

19 Let it be unto him as the garment *which* covereth him, and for a ᵀgirdle wherewith he is girded continually.　　Ps. 109:29 ♦ *belt*

20 *Let* this *be* the reward of mine adversaries from the LORD, and of them that speak evil against my soul.

21 But do thou for me, O GOD the Lord, for thy name's sake: because thy mercy *is* good, deliver thou me.　　Ps. 25:11

22 For I *am* poor and needy, and my heart is wounded within me.　　Ps. 40:17

23 I am gone like the shadow when it declineth: I am tossed up and down as the locust.　　Ex. 10:19

24 My knees are weak through fasting; and my flesh faileth of fatness.　　Heb. 12:12

25 I became also a reproach unto them: *when* they looked upon me they shaked their heads.　　Ps. 22:6-7; 69:19-20

26 Help me, O LORD my God: O save me according to thy mercy:　　Ps. 119:86

27 That they may know that this *is* thy hand; *that* thou, LORD, hast done it.　　Job 37:7

28 Let them curse, but bless thou: when they arise, let them be ashamed; but let thy servant rejoice.

29 Let mine adversaries be clothed with shame, and let them cover themselves with their own confusion, as with a mantle.

30 I will greatly praise the LORD with my mouth; yea, I will praise him among the multitude.　　Ps. 35:18

31 For he shall stand at the right hand of the poor, to save *him* from those that condemn his soul.　　Ps. 16:8; 73:23; 121:5

PSALM 110

David Prophesies of the Coming Messiah

A Psalm of David.

Tʜᴇ LORD said unto my Lord, Sit thou at my right hand, until I make thine enemies thy footstool.　　1 Cor. 15:25; Heb. 1:3, 13

2 The LORD shall send the rod of thy strength out of Zion: rule thou in the midst of thine enemies.

3 Thy people *shall be* willing in the day of thy power, in the beauties of holiness from the womb of the morning: thou hast the dew of thy youth.　　Judg. 5:2; Ps. 96:9

4 The LORD hath sworn, and will not repent, Thou *art* a priest for ever after the order of Melchizedek.　　Num. 23:19; Heb. 5:6; 7:17

5 The Lord at thy right hand shall strike through kings in the day of his wrath. Ps. 16:8

6 He shall judge among the heathen, he shall fill *the places* with the dead bodies; he shall wound the heads over many countries.　　Ps. 68:21; Is. 2:4; Mic. 4:3

7 He shall drink of the brook in the way: therefore shall he lift up the head. Judg. 7:5-6

PSALM 111

The Works of the Lord Are Great

Pʀᴀɪsᴇ ye the LORD. I will praise the LORD with *my* whole heart, in the assembly of the upright, and *in* the congregation. Ps. 138:1

2 The works of the LORD *are* great, sought out of all them that have pleasure therein.

3 His work *is* honourable and glorious: and his righteousness endureth for ever. Ps. 119:142

4 He hath made his wonderful works to be remembered: the LORD *is* gracious and full of compassion.　　Ps. 103:8

5 He hath given meat unto them that fear him: he will ever be mindful of his covenant.　　Ps. 105:8

6 He hath shewed his people the power of

his works, that he may give them the heritage of the heathen.

7 The works of his hands *are* ᵀverity and judgment; all his commandments *are* sure.   truth

8 They stand fast for ever and ever, *and are* done in truth and uprightness. Ps. 19:9; Is. 40:8

111:7-9

111:7, 8 Principles of Education Do Not Change

The great principles of education are unchanged. "They stand fast for ever and ever" (Psalm 111:8); for they are the principles of the character of God. To aid the student in comprehending these principles, and in entering into that relation with Christ which will make them a controlling power in the life, should be the teacher's first effort and his constant aim. The teacher who accepts this aim is in truth a co-worker with Christ, a laborer together with God. *Ed 30*

9 He sent redemption unto his people: he hath commanded his covenant for ever: holy and reverend *is* his name. Ps. 99:3; Luke 1:49, 68

God's Law See Romans 5:12–14.

111:9 Holiness of God and His Name

We are never in any manner to treat lightly the titles or appellations of the Deity. In prayer we enter the audience chamber of the Most High; and we should come before Him with holy awe. The angels veil their faces in His presence. The cherubim and the bright and holy seraphim approach His throne with solemn reverence. How much more should we, finite, sinful beings, come in a reverent manner before the Lord, our Maker! *MB 106*

10 The fear of the LORD *is* the beginning of wisdom: a good understanding have all they that do *his commandments*: his praise endureth for ever.   Prov. 1:7; 3:4; 9:10

PSALM 112

The Blessings of Godliness

Praise ye the LORD. Blessed *is* the man *that* feareth the LORD, *that* delighteth greatly in his commandments.   Ps. 111:10; 119:16; 128:1

2 His seed shall be mighty upon earth: the generation of the upright shall be blessed.

3 Wealth and riches *shall be* in his house: and his righteousness endureth for ever. Prov. 3:16

4 Unto the upright there ariseth light in the darkness: *he is* gracious, and full of compassion, and righteous. Job 11:17; Ps. 97:11; John 12:46

5 A good man sheweth favour, and lendeth: he will guide his affairs with discretion.

6 Surely he shall not be moved for ever: the righteous shall be in everlasting remembrance.   Ps. 15:5; Prov. 10:7

7 He shall not be afraid of evil tidings: his heart is fixed, trusting in the LORD. Ps. 57:7; 64:10

112:6 Legacy of the Good Lasts Forever

As the glow of the descending sun lights up the mountain peaks long after the sun itself has sunk behind the hills, so the works of the pure, the holy, and the good shed light upon the world long after the actors themselves have passed away. Their works, their words, their example, will forever live. "The righteous shall be in everlasting remembrance" (Psalm 112:6). *PP 481*

8 His heart *is* established, he shall not be afraid, until he see *his desire* upon his enemies.   Ps. 59:10

9 He hath dispersed, he hath given to the poor; his righteousness endureth for ever; his horn shall be exalted with honour.

10 The wicked shall see *it*, and be grieved; he shall gnash with his teeth, and melt away: the desire of the wicked shall perish. Ps. 37:12

PSALM 113

Who Is Like the Lord?

Praise ye the LORD. Praise, O ye servants of the LORD, praise the name of the LORD.

2 Blessed be the name of the LORD from this time forth and for evermore.   Dan. 2:20

3 From the rising of the sun unto the going down of the same the LORD's name *is* to be praised.   Is. 59:19; Mal. 1:11

4 The LORD *is* high above all nations, *and* his glory above the heavens.   Ps. 8:1; 97:9; 99:2

5 Who *is* like unto the LORD our God, who dwelleth on high,   Ps. 89:6

6 Who humbleth *himself* to behold *the things that are* in heaven, and in the earth!   Ps. 11:4

7 He raiseth up the poor out of the dust, *and* lifteth the needy out of the dunghill; Ps. 107:41

8 That he may set *him* with princes, *even* with the princes of his people.   Job 36:7

9 He maketh the barren woman to keep house, *and to be* a joyful mother of children. Praise ye the LORD.   1 Sam. 2:5; Ps. 68:6; Is. 54:1

PSALM 114

Praise to God Who Delivered Israel out of Egypt

When Israel went out of Egypt, the house of Jacob from a people of strange language;   Ex. 13:3

2 Judah was his sanctuary, *and* Israel his dominion.   Ex. 25:8

3 The sea saw *it*, and fled: Jordan was driven back.   Ex. 14:21; Josh. 3:13-16; Ps. 77:16

4 The mountains skipped like rams, *and* the little hills like lambs.   Ex. 19:18

5 What *ailed* thee, O thou sea, that thou fleddest? thou Jordan, *that* thou wast driven back?   Hab. 3:8

6 Ye mountains, *that* ye skipped like rams; *and* ye little hills, like lambs?
7 Tremble, thou earth, at the presence of the Lord, at the presence of the God of Jacob;
8 Which turned the rock into a standing water, the flint into a fountain of waters. Ex. 17:6

PSALM 115

God Is Truly Glorious

N ot unto us, O Lord, not unto us, but unto thy name give glory, for thy mercy, *and* for thy truth's sake. Is. 48:11; Ezek. 36:32
2 Wherefore should the heathen say, Where *is* now their God? Ex. 32:12; Ps. 42:3; 79:10
3 But our God *is* in the heavens: he hath done whatsoever he hath pleased. Ps. 135:6
4 Their idols *are* silver and gold, the work of men's hands. Deut. 4:28; Jer. 10:3-5; Acts 19:26
5 They have mouths, but they speak not: eyes have they, but they see not:
6 They have ears, but they hear not: noses have they, but they smell not:
7 They have hands, but they handle not: feet have they, but they walk not: neither speak they through their throat.
8 They that make them are like unto them; *so is* every one that trusteth in them. Ps. 135:18

115:8 A Law of the Human Mind

It is a law of the human mind that by beholding we become changed. Man will rise no higher than his conceptions of truth, purity, and holiness. If the mind is never exalted above the level of humanity, if it is not uplifted by faith to contemplate infinite wisdom and love, the man will be constantly sinking lower and lower. *PP 91*

---

9 O Israel, trust thou in the Lord: he *is* their help and their shield. Ps. 62:8
10 O house of Aaron, trust in the Lord: he *is* their help and their shield.

11 Ye that fear the Lord, trust in the Lord: he *is* their help and their shield.
12 The Lord hath been mindful of us: he will bless *us*; he will bless the house of Israel; he will bless the house of Aaron.
13 He will bless them that fear the Lord, *both* small and great. Ps. 112:1
14 The Lord shall increase you more and more, you and your children. Deut. 1:11
15 Ye *are* blessed of the Lord which made heaven and earth. Gen. 1:1; 14:19; Ps. 96:5
16 The heaven, *even* the heavens, *are* the Lord's: but the earth hath he given to the children of men. Ps. 89:11

115:17 Dead Do Not Praise God

Popular theology represents the righteous dead as in heaven, entered into bliss and praising God with an immortal tongue; but Hezekiah could see no such glorious prospect in death. With his words agrees the testimony of the psalmist: "In death there is no remembrance of Thee: in the grave who shall give Thee thanks?" "The dead praise not the Lord, neither any that go down into silence" (Psalms 6:5; 115:17). *GC 546*

---

17 The dead praise not the Lord, neither any that go down into silence. Ps. 6:5; 31:17; 88:10-12

115:17

After Death See Psalm 146:3, 4.

18 But we will bless the Lord from this time forth and for evermore. Praise the Lord.

PSALM 116

Gracious Is the Lord

I love the Lord, because he hath heard my voice *and* my supplications.
2 Because he hath inclined his ear unto me, therefore will I call upon *him* as long as I live.
3 The sorrows of death ᵀcompassed me, and

Cause for Gratitude and Praise

Psalm 115:1

"Not unto us, O Lord, not unto us, but unto Thy name give glory, for Thy mercy, and for Thy truth's sake" (Psalm 115:1). Such was the spirit that pervaded Israel's song of deliverance, and it is the spirit that should dwell in the hearts of all who love and fear God. In freeing our souls from the bondage of sin, God has wrought for us a deliverance greater than that of the Hebrews at the Red Sea. Like the Hebrew host, we should praise the Lord with heart and soul and voice for His "wonderful works to the children of men" [Psalm 107:8, 15, 21, 31]. Those who dwell upon God's great mercies, and are not unmindful of His lesser gifts, will put on the girdle of gladness and make melody in their hearts to the Lord. The daily blessings that we receive from the hand of God, and above all else the death of Jesus to bring happiness and heaven within our reach, should be a theme for constant gratitude. What compassion, what matchless love, has God shown to us, lost sinners, in connecting us with Himself, to be to Him a peculiar treasure! What a sacrifice has been made by our Redeemer, that we may be called children of God! We should praise God for the blessed hope held out before us in the great plan of redemption, we should praise Him for the heavenly inheritance and for His rich promises; praise Him that Jesus lives to intercede for us. *PP 289*

the pains of hell gat hold upon me: I found trouble and sorrow.   *surrounded*

4 Then called I upon the name of the LORD; O LORD, I ᵀbeseech thee, deliver my soul. *beg*

5 Gracious *is* the LORD, and righteous; yea, our God *is* merciful.   Ezra 9:15; Neh. 9:8; Ps. 145:17

6 The LORD preserveth the simple: I was brought low, and he helped me.   Ps. 19:7; 79:8

7 Return unto thy rest, O my soul; for the LORD hath dealt bountifully with thee. Ps. 13:6

8 For thou hast delivered my soul from death, mine eyes from tears, *and* my feet from falling.   Ps. 56:13; 86:13

9 I will walk before the LORD in the land of the living.   Ps. 27:13

10 I believed, therefore have I spoken: I was greatly afflicted: 2 Cor. 4:13

11 I said in my haste, All men *are* liars.

12 What shall I render unto the LORD *for* all his benefits toward me?   Ps. 103:2

116:12 Remembering With Gratitude

The Christian should often review his past life and recall with gratitude the precious deliverances that God has wrought for him, supporting him in trial, opening ways before him when all seemed dark and forbidding, refreshing him when ready to faint. He should recognize all of them as evidences of the watchcare of heavenly angels. In view of these innumerable blessings he should often ask, with subdued and grateful heart, "What shall I render unto the Lord for all His benefits toward me?" (Psalm 116:12). *PP 187*

---

13 I will take the cup of salvation, and call upon the name of the LORD.   Ps. 105:1

14 I will pay my vows unto the LORD now in the presence of all his people.   Ps. 22:25

15 Precious *is* the sight of the LORD *is* the death of his saints.   Ps. 72:14

16 O LORD, truly I *am* thy servant; I *am* thy servant, *and* the son of thine handmaid: thou hast loosed my bonds.   Ps. 86:16; 119:125; 143:12

17 I will offer to thee the sacrifice of thanksgiving, and will call upon the name of the LORD.   Lev. 7:12; Ps. 50:14; 116:13

18 I will pay my vows unto the LORD now in the presence of all his people,   Ps. 116:14

19 In the courts of the LORD's house, in the midst of thee, O Jerusalem. Praise ye the LORD.   Ps. 96:8

PSALM 117

An Exhortation for All Nations to Praise the Lord

O praise the LORD, all ye nations: praise him, all ye people.   Rom. 15:11

2 For his merciful kindness is great toward us: and the truth of the LORD *endureth* for ever. Praise ye the LORD.

PSALM 118

God's Love Is Eternal

O give thanks unto the LORD; for *he is* good: because his mercy *endureth* for ever.   1 Chr. 16:8

2 Let Israel now say, that his mercy *endureth* for ever.   Ps. 115:9-11

3 Let the house of Aaron now say, that his mercy *endureth* for ever.

4 Let them now that fear the LORD say, that his mercy *endureth* for ever.

5 I called upon the LORD in distress: the LORD answered me, *and set me* in a large place.   Ps. 18:6, 19; 120:1

6 The LORD *is* on my side; I will not fear: what can man do unto me? Ps. 56:4, 9; Heb. 13:6

7 The LORD taketh my part with them that help me: therefore shall I see *my desire* upon them that hate me.   Ps. 54:4, 7; 59:10

8 *It is* better to trust in the LORD than to put confidence in man.   Ps. 40:4

9 *It is* better to trust in the LORD than to put confidence in princes.

10 All nations compassed me about: but in the name of the LORD will I destroy them.

11 They compassed me about; yea, they compassed me about: but in the name of the LORD I will destroy them.   Ps. 88:17

12 They compassed me about like bees; they are quenched as the fire of thorns: for in the name of the LORD I will destroy them.

13 Thou hast thrust sore at me that I might fall: but the LORD helped me.   Ps. 140:4

14 The LORD *is* my strength and song, and is become my salvation.   Is. 12:2

15 The voice of rejoicing and salvation *is* in the tabernacles of the righteous: the right hand of the LORD doeth valiantly.   Ps. 89:13

16 The right hand of the LORD is exalted: the right hand of the LORD doeth valiantly.

17 I shall not die, but live, and declare the works of the LORD.   Ps. 6:5; 73:28; 107:22

18 The LORD hath ᵀchastened me sore: but he hath not given me over unto death.   *disciplined*

19 Open to me the gates of righteousness: I will go into them, *and* I will praise the LORD: Is. 26:2

20 This gate of the LORD, into which the righteous shall enter.   Ps. 24:3-4

21 I will praise thee: for thou hast heard me, and art become my salvation. Ps. 116:1; 118:14

22 The stone *which* the builders refused is become the head *stone* of the corner.   Matt. 21:42

23 This is the LORD's doing; it *is* marvellous in our eyes.

24 This *is* the day *which* the LORD hath made; we will rejoice and be glad in it.   Ps. 84:10

25 Save now, I beseech thee, O LORD: O LORD, I beseech thee, send now prosperity.

26 Blessed *be* he that cometh in the name of the LORD: we have blessed you out of the house of the LORD.   Matt. 21:9; 23:39; Luke 19:38
27 God *is* the LORD, which hath shewed us light: bind the sacrifice with cords, *even* unto the horns of the altar. Ex. 27:2; Esth. 8:16; 1 Pet. 2:9
28 Thou *art* my God, and I will praise thee: *thou art* my God, I will exalt thee.   Ex. 15:2
29 O give thanks unto the LORD; for *he is* good: for his mercy *endureth* for ever. Ps. 118:1

PSALM 119

Praise for God's Wonderful Word

ALEPH

B lessed *are* the undefiled in the way, who walk in the law of the LORD.   Ps. 128:1
2 Blessed *are* they that keep his testimonies, *and that* seek him with the whole heart.
3 They also do no iniquity: they walk in his ways.   1 John 3:9; 5:18
4 Thou hast commanded *us* to keep thy precepts diligently.
5 O that my ways were directed to keep thy statutes!
6 Then shall I not be ashamed, when I have respect unto all thy commandments. Job 22:26
7 I will praise thee with uprightness of heart, when I shall have learned thy righteous judgments.
8 I will keep thy statutes: O forsake me not utterly.

BETH

9 Wherewithal shall a young man cleanse his way? by taking heed *thereto* according to thy word.   Ps. 25:7

The Bible See Hebrews 4:12.

10 With my whole heart have I sought thee: O let me not wander from thy commandments.   2 Chr. 15:15

119:11 Power and Strength of the Word

Every promise in God's word is ours. "By every word that proceedeth out of the mouth of God" [Matthew 4:4] are we to live. When assailed by temptation, look not to circumstances or to the weakness of self, but to the power of the word. All its strength is yours. *DA 123*

11 Thy word have I hid in mine heart, that I might not sin against thee.   Ps. 37:31

The Bible See Psalm 119:105.

12 Blessed *art* thou, O LORD: teach me thy statutes.   Ps. 119:64
13 With my lips have I declared all the judgments of thy mouth.
14 I have rejoiced in the way of thy testimonies, as *much as* in all riches.   Ps. 119:111

15 I will meditate in thy precepts, and have respect unto thy ways.   Ps. 1:2
16 I will delight myself in thy statutes: I will not forget thy word.   Ps. 119:24

GIMEL

17 Deal bountifully with thy servant, *that* I may live, and keep thy word.   Ps. 13:6
18 Open thou mine eyes, that I may behold wondrous things out of thy law.

119:18 The Word Our Defense

The Bible should never be studied without prayer. The Holy Spirit alone can cause us to feel the importance of those things easy to be understood, or prevent us from wresting truths difficult of comprehension. It is the office of heavenly angels to prepare the heart so to comprehend God's word that we shall be charmed with its beauty, admonished by its warnings, or animated and strengthened by its promises. We should make the psalmist's petition our own: "Open Thou mine eyes, that I may behold wondrous things out of Thy law" (Psalm 119:18). *GC 599, 600*

19 I *am* a stranger in the earth: hide not thy commandments from me.   1 Chr. 29:15
20 My soul breaketh for the longing *that it hath* unto thy judgments at all times. Ps. 63:1
21 Thou hast rebuked the proud *that are* cursed, which do ᵀerr from thy commandments.   Ps. 119:10 ◆ *stray*
22 Remove from me reproach and contempt; for I have kept thy testimonies.   Ps. 39:8
23 Princes also did sit *and* speak against me: *but* thy servant did meditate in thy statutes.
24 Thy testimonies also *are* my delight *and* my counsellors.   Ps. 119:16

DALETH

25 My soul ᵀcleaveth unto the dust: quicken thou me according to thy word.   *clings*
26 I have declared my ways, and thou heardest me: teach me thy statutes.   Ps. 25:4
27 Make me to understand the way of thy precepts: so shall I talk of thy wondrous works.   Ps. 105:2
28 My soul melteth for heaviness: strengthen thou me according unto thy word. Ps. 107:26
29 Remove from me the way of lying: and grant me thy law graciously.
30 I have chosen the way of truth: thy judgments have I laid *before me*.
31 I have stuck unto thy testimonies: O LORD, put me not to shame.
32 I will run the way of thy commandments, when thou shalt enlarge my heart. 1 Kin. 4:29

HE

33 Teach me, O LORD, the way of thy statutes; and I shall keep it *unto* the end. Ps. 119:12
34 Give me understanding, and I shall keep

thy law; yea, I shall observe it with *my* whole heart.   Ps. 119:69

35 Make me to go in the path of thy commandments; for therein do I delight. Ps. 119:16

36 Incline my heart unto thy testimonies, and not to covetousness.   1 Kin. 8:58; Luke 12:15

37 Turn away mine eyes from beholding vanity; *and* quicken thou me in thy way. Ps. 119:25

38 Stablish thy word unto thy servant, who *is devoted* to thy fear.

39 Turn away my reproach which I fear: for thy judgments *are* good.   Ps. 119:22

40 Behold, I have longed after thy precepts: quicken me in thy righteousness.   Ps. 119:20

VAU

41 Let thy mercies come also unto me, O LORD, *even* thy salvation, according to thy word.   Ps. 119:58

42 So shall I have wherewith to answer him that reproacheth me: for I trust in thy word.

43 And take not the word of truth utterly out of my mouth; for I have hoped in thy judgments.

44 So shall I keep thy law continually for ever and ever.

45 And I will walk at liberty: for I seek thy precepts.   Ps. 119:94

119:45 The Law Preserves Liberty

The youth have an inborn love of liberty; they desire freedom; and they need to understand that these inestimable blessings are to be enjoyed only in obedience to the law of God. This law is the preserver of true freedom and liberty. It points out and prohibits those things that degrade and enslave, and thus to the obedient it affords protection from the power of evil. *Ed 291*

---

46 I will speak of thy testimonies also before kings, and will not be ashamed.   Acts 26:1-2

47 And I will delight myself in thy commandments, which I have loved.   Ps. 119:16

48 My hands also will I lift up unto thy commandments, which I have loved; and I will meditate in thy statutes.   Ps. 119:15

ZAIN

49 Remember the word unto thy servant, upon which thou hast caused me to hope.

50 This *is* my comfort in my affliction: for thy word hath ᵀquickened me.   Rom. 15:4 ◆ *made alive*

51 The proud have had me greatly in derision: *yet* have I not declined from thy law.

52 I remembered thy judgments of old, O LORD; and have comforted myself.

53 Horror hath taken hold upon me because of the wicked that forsake thy law.   Ezra 9:3

54 Thy statutes have been my songs in the house of my pilgrimage.   Gen. 47:9

55 I have remembered thy name, O LORD, in the night, and have kept thy law.   Ps. 42:8

56 This I had, because I kept thy precepts.

CHETH

57 *Thou art* my portion, O LORD: I have said that I would keep thy words.   Ps. 16:5

58 I ᵀintreated thy favour with *my* whole heart: be merciful unto me according to thy word.   Ps. 119:41 ◆ *pled with*

59 I thought on my ways, and turned my feet unto thy testimonies.

60 I made haste, and delayed not to keep thy commandments.

61 The bands of the wicked have robbed me: *but* I have not forgotten thy law.   Ps. 119:176

62 At midnight I will rise to give thanks unto thee because of thy righteous judgments.   Ps. 119:7

63 I *am* a companion of all *them* that fear thee, and of them that keep thy precepts.

64 The earth, O LORD, is full of thy mercy: teach me thy statutes.   Ps. 33:5; 119:12

TETH

65 Thou hast dealt well with thy servant, O LORD, according unto thy word.

66 Teach me good judgment and knowledge: for I have believed thy commandments.

67 Before I was afflicted I went astray: but now have I kept thy word.   Ps. 119:71, 75

68 Thou *art* good, and doest good; teach me thy statutes.   Ps. 106:1; 107:1; 119:12

69 The proud have forged a lie against me: *but* I will keep thy precepts with *my* whole heart.   Job 13:4

70 Their heart is as fat as grease; *but* I delight in thy law.   Ps. 17:10

71 *It is* good for me that I have been afflicted; that I might learn thy statutes.   Ps. 119:67

72 The law of thy mouth *is* better unto me than thousands of gold and silver.   Ps. 19:10

119:72 More Valuable Than Money

Even in this age of passion for money getting, when competition is so sharp and methods are so unscrupulous, it is still widely acknowledged that, for a young man starting in life, integrity, diligence, temperance, purity, and thrift constitute a better capital than any amount of mere money. *Ed 137*

JOD

73 Thy hands have made me and fashioned me: give me understanding, that I may learn thy commandments.   Ps. 100:3

74 They that fear thee will be glad when they see me; because I have hoped in thy word.

75 I know, O LORD, that thy judgments *are* right, and *that* thou in faithfulness hast afflicted me.   Heb. 12:10-11

76 Let, I pray thee, thy merciful kindness be for my comfort, according to thy word unto thy servant.
77 Let thy tender mercies come unto me, that I may live: for thy law *is* my delight.   Ps. 119:41
78 Let the proud be ashamed; for they dealt perversely with me without a cause: *but* I will meditate in thy precepts.
79 Let those that fear thee turn unto me, and those that have known thy testimonies.
80 Let my heart be sound in thy statutes; that I be not ashamed.

CAPH

81 My soul fainteth for thy salvation: *but* I hope in thy word.   Ps. 84:2
82 Mine eyes fail for thy word, saying, When wilt thou comfort me?   Ps. 69:3
83 For I am become like a bottle in the smoke; *yet* do I not forget thy statutes.   Job 30:30
84 How many *are* the days of thy servant? when wilt thou execute judgment on them that persecute me?
85 The proud have digged pits for me, which *are* not after thy law.   Ps. 35:7
86 All thy commandments *are* faithful: they persecute me wrongfully; help thou me.
87 They had almost consumed me upon earth; but I forsook not thy precepts.
88 Quicken me after thy lovingkindness; so shall I keep the testimony of thy mouth.

LAMED

89 For ever, O LORD, thy word is settled in heaven.   Ps. 89:2; 119:160; 1 Pet. 1:25
90 Thy faithfulness *is* unto all generations: thou hast established the earth, and it abideth.   Ps. 36:5
91 They continue this day according to thine ordinances: for all *are* thy servants.   Jer. 33:25
92 Unless thy law *had been* my delights, I should then have perished in mine affliction.
93 I will never forget thy precepts: for with them thou hast quickened me.   Ps. 119:16
94 I *am* thine, save me; for I have sought thy precepts.
95 The wicked have waited for me to destroy me: *but* I will consider thy testimonies.
96 I have seen an end of all perfection: *but* thy commandment *is* exceeding broad.

MEM

97 O how love I thy law! it *is* my meditation all the day.   Ps. 1:2; 119:48, 127
98 Thou through thy commandments hast made me wiser than mine enemies: for they *are* ever with me.   Deut. 4:6
99 I have more understanding than all my teachers: for thy testimonies *are* my meditation.
100 I understand more than the ancients, because I keep thy precepts.
101 I have refrained my feet from every evil way, that I might keep thy word.   Prov. 1:15

102 I have not departed from thy judgments: for thou hast taught me.
103 How sweet are thy words unto my taste! *yea, sweeter* than honey to my mouth! Ps. 19:10
104 Through thy precepts I get understanding: therefore I hate every false way. Ps. 119:128

NUN

105 Thy word *is* a lamp unto my feet, and a light unto my path.   Prov. 6:23

The Bible See Psalm 119:9.

106 I have sworn, and I will perform *it*, that I will keep thy righteous judgments. Neh. 10:29
107 I am afflicted very much: quicken me, O LORD, according unto thy word.   Ps. 119:25
108 Accept, I ᵀbeseech thee, the freewill offerings of my mouth, O LORD, and teach me thy judgments. Ps. 119:12; Hos. 14:2; Heb. 13:15 ♦ *beg*
109 My soul *is* continually in my hand: yet do I not forget thy law.   Judg. 12:3
110 The wicked have laid a snare for me: yet I erred not from thy precepts.   Ps. 119:10
111 Thy testimonies have I taken as an heritage for ever: for they *are* the rejoicing of my heart.   Deut. 33:4
112 I have inclined mine heart to perform thy statutes alway, *even unto* the end. Ps. 119:33

119:104–112 God's Word David's Instructor

The principles taught in the schools of the prophets were the same that molded David's character and shaped his life. The word of God was his instructor. "Through Thy precepts," he said, "I get understanding. . . . I have inclined mine heart to perform Thy statutes" (Psalm 119:104–112). It was this that caused the Lord to pronounce David, when in his youth He called him to the throne, "a man after Mine own heart" (Acts 13:22). *Ed 48*

SAMECH

113 I hate *vain* thoughts: but thy law do I love.
114 Thou *art* my hiding place and my shield: I hope in thy word.   Ps. 32:7
115 Depart from me, ye evildoers: for I will keep the commandments of my God.   Ps. 6:8
116 Uphold me according unto thy word, that I may live: and let me not be ashamed of my hope.   Ps. 25:2
117 Hold thou me up, and I shall be safe: and I will have respect unto thy statutes continually.   Ps. 119:6
118 Thou hast ᵀtrodden down all them that err from thy statutes: for their deceit *is* falsehood.   Ps. 119:10 ♦ *trampled*
119 Thou puttest away all the wicked of the earth *like* ᵀdross: therefore I love thy testimonies.   Mal. 3:2-3 ♦ *waste from melting metal*
120 My flesh trembleth for fear of thee; and I am afraid of thy judgments.   Hab. 3:16

AIN

121 I have done judgment and justice: leave me not to mine oppressors.   2 Sam. 8:15
122 Be surety for thy servant for good: let not the proud oppress me.   Job 17:3
123 Mine eyes fail for thy salvation, and for the word of thy righteousness.
124 Deal with thy servant according unto thy mercy, and teach me thy statutes.   Ps. 119:12
125 I *am* thy servant; give me understanding, that I may know thy testimonies.   Ps. 116:16
126 *It is* time for *thee*, LORD, to work: *for* they have made void thy law.
127 Therefore I love thy commandments above gold; yea, above fine gold.   Ps. 19:10
128 Therefore I esteem all *thy* precepts *concerning* all *things to be* right; *and* I hate every false way.   Ps. 119:104

PE

129 Thy testimonies *are* wonderful: therefore doth my soul keep them.   Ps. 119:18
130 The entrance of thy words giveth light; it giveth understanding unto the simple.
131 I opened my mouth, and panted: for I longed for thy commandments. Ps. 42:1; 119:20
132 Look thou upon me, and be merciful unto me, as thou usest to do unto those that love thy name.   Ps. 106:4
133 Order my steps in thy word: and let not any iniquity have dominion over me. Ps. 17:5
134 Deliver me from the oppression of man: so will I keep thy precepts.
135 Make thy face to shine upon thy servant; and teach me thy statutes. Ps. 4:6; 80:3, 7
136 Rivers of waters run down mine eyes, because they keep not thy law.   Jer. 9:1

TZADDI

137 Righteous *art* thou, O LORD, and upright *are* thy judgments.   Ezra 9:15
138 Thy testimonies *that* thou hast commanded *are* righteous and very faithful.
139 My zeal hath consumed me, because mine enemies have forgotten thy words.
140 Thy word *is* very pure: therefore thy servant loveth it.   Ps. 12:6; 19:8
141 I *am* small and despised: *yet* do not I forget thy precepts.   Ps. 22:6
142 Thy righteousness *is* an everlasting righteousness, and thy law *is* the truth.   Ps. 19:9
143 Trouble and anguish have taken hold on me: *yet* thy commandments *are* my delights.
144 The righteousness of thy testimonies *is* everlasting: give me understanding, and I shall live.

KOPH

145 I cried with *my* whole heart; hear me, O LORD: I will keep thy statutes.   Ps. 119:10
146 I cried unto thee; save me, and I shall keep thy testimonies.

147 I prevented the dawning of the morning, and cried: I hoped in thy word.   Ps. 5:3
148 Mine eyes prevent the *night* watches, that I might meditate in thy word.   Ps. 63:6
149 Hear my voice according unto thy lovingkindness: O LORD, quicken me according to thy judgment.   Ps. 119:25
150 They draw nigh that follow after mischief: they are far from thy law.
151 Thou *art* near, O LORD; and all thy commandments *are* truth.   Ps. 119:142; 145:18
152 Concerning thy testimonies, I have known of old that thou hast founded them for ever.   Luke 21:33

119:151, 152 God's Unchanging Law

Not one command has been annulled, not a jot or tittle has been changed. Those principles that were made known to man in Paradise as the great law of life will exist unchanged in Paradise restored. When Eden shall bloom on earth again, God's law of love will be obeyed by all beneath the sun. *MB 50, 51*

RESH

153 Consider mine affliction, and deliver me: for I do not forget thy law.   Lam. 5:1
154 Plead my cause, and deliver me: quicken me according to thy word.   1 Sam. 24:15
155 Salvation *is* far from the wicked: for they seek not thy statutes.   Job 5:4
156 Great *are* thy tender mercies, O LORD: quicken me according to thy judgments.
157 Many *are* my persecutors and mine enemies; *yet* do I not decline from thy testimonies.   Ps. 119:51
158 I beheld the transgressors, and was grieved; because they kept not thy word.
159 Consider how I love thy precepts: quicken me, O LORD, according to thy lovingkindness.
160 Thy word *is* true *from* the beginning: and every one of thy righteous judgments *endureth* for ever.   Ps. 119:142

SCHIN

161 Princes have persecuted me without a cause: but my heart standeth in awe of thy word.   1 Sam. 26:18
162 I rejoice at thy word, as one that findeth great ᵀspoil.   1 Sam. 30:16 ◆ *plunder*
163 I hate and ᵀabhor lying: *but* thy law do I love.   Ps. 119:128 ◆ *despise*
164 Seven times a day do I praise thee because of thy righteous judgments.
165 Great peace have they which love thy law: and nothing shall offend them.   Is. 32:17
166 LORD, I have hoped for thy salvation, and done thy commandments.   Gen. 49:18

167 My soul hath kept thy testimonies; and I love them exceedingly.

168 I have kept thy precepts and thy testimonies: for all my ways *are* before thee.

TAU

169 Let my cry come near before thee, O LORD: give me understanding according to thy word.   Ps. 18:6

170 Let my supplication come before thee: deliver me according to thy word.

171 My lips shall utter praise, when thou hast taught me thy statutes.

172 My tongue shall speak of thy word: for all thy commandments *are* righteousness.

173 Let thine hand help me; for I have chosen thy precepts.   Josh. 24:22

174 I have longed for thy salvation, O LORD; and thy law *is* my delight.   Ps. 119:16

175 Let my soul live, and it shall praise thee; and let thy judgments help me.

176 I have gone astray like a lost sheep; seek thy servant; for I do not forget thy commandments.   Is. 53:6

PSALM 120

A Prayer When in Distress

A Song of degrees.

In my distress I cried unto the LORD, and he heard me.   Jon. 2:2

2 Deliver my soul, O LORD, from lying lips, *and* from a deceitful tongue.

3 What shall be given unto thee? or what shall be done unto thee, thou false tongue?

4 Sharp arrows of the mighty, with coals of juniper.   Ps. 45:5

5 Woe is me, that I sojourn in Mesech, *that* I dwell in the tents of Kedar!   Gen. 10:2; 25:13

6 My soul hath long dwelt with him that hateth peace.

7 I *am for* peace: but when I speak, they *are* for war.

PSALM 121

The Lord Will Preserve You from Evil

A Song of degrees.

I will lift up mine eyes unto the hills, from whence cometh my help.   Ps. 87:1

2 My help *cometh* from the LORD, which made heaven and earth.   Ps. 115:15; 124:8

3 He will not suffer thy foot to be moved: he that keepeth thee will not slumber. 1 Sam. 2:9

4 Behold, he that keepeth Israel shall neither slumber nor sleep.

5 The LORD *is* thy keeper: the LORD *is* thy shade upon thy right hand.   Ps. 16:8

6 The sun shall not ᵀsmite thee by day, nor the moon by night.   Is. 49:10; Rev. 7:16 ◆ *strike*

7 The LORD shall preserve thee from all evil: he shall preserve thy soul.   Ps. 41:2

8 The LORD shall preserve thy going out and thy coming in from this time forth, and even for evermore.   Deut. 28:6; Ps. 113:2; 115:18

PSALM 122

David Prays for Peace in Jerusalem

A Song of degrees of David.

I was glad when they said unto me, Let us go into the house of the LORD.   Is. 2:3

2 Our feet shall stand within thy gates, O Jerusalem.

3 Jerusalem is builded as a city that is compact together: 2 Sam. 5:9

4 Whither the tribes go up, the tribes of the LORD, unto the testimony of Israel, to give thanks unto the name of the LORD. Deut. 16:16

5 For there are set thrones of judgment, the thrones of the house of David.   Deut. 17:8

6 Pray for the peace of Jerusalem: they shall prosper that love thee.   Ps. 51:18

7 Peace be within thy walls, *and* prosperity within thy palaces.   Ps. 48:3

8 For my brethren and companions' sakes, I will now say, Peace *be* within thee.

9 Because of the house of the LORD our God I will seek thy good.   Neh. 2:10

PSALM 123

The Godly Profess Their Confidence in God

A Song of degrees.

Unto thee lift I up mine eyes, O thou that dwellest in the heavens. Ps. 2:4; 121:1; 141:8

2 Behold, as the eyes of servants *look* unto the hand of their masters, *and* as the eyes of a maiden unto the hand of her mistress; so

our eyes *wait* upon the LORD our God, until that he have mercy upon us.

3 Have mercy upon us, O LORD, have mercy upon us: for we are exceedingly filled with contempt.

4 Our soul is exceedingly filled with the scorning of those that are at ease, *and* with the contempt of the proud.   Job 12:5

PSALM 124

God Delivers Those Who Trust Him

A Song of degrees of David.

If *it had not been* the LORD who was on our side, now may Israel say;   Ps. 120:1; 129:1

2 If *it had not been* the LORD who was on our side, when men rose up against us:

3 Then they had swallowed us up quick, when their wrath was kindled against us:

4 Then the waters had overwhelmed us, the stream had gone over our soul:

5 Then the proud waters had gone over our soul.   Job 38:11

6 Blessed *be* the LORD, who hath not given us *as* a prey to their teeth.

7 Our soul is escaped as a bird out of the snare of the ᵀfowlers: the snare is broken, and we are escaped.   Ps. 91:3; Prov. 6:5 ◆ *those who capture birds*

8 Our help *is* in the name of the LORD, who made heaven and earth. Gen. 1:1; Ps. 121:2; 134:3

PSALM 125

The Safety of Those Who Trust God

A Song of degrees.

They that trust in the LORD *shall be* as mount Zion, *which* cannot be removed, *but* abideth for ever.   Ps. 25:2

2 As the mountains *are* round about Jerusalem, so the LORD *is* round about his people from henceforth even for ever.   Zech. 2:5

125:1, 2 Christ Stands by Our Side

Never is the tempest-tried soul more dearly loved by His Saviour than when he is suffering reproach for the truth's sake. . . . When for the truth's sake the believer stands at the bar of earthly tribunals, Christ stands by his side. When he is confined within prison walls, Christ manifests Himself to him and cheers his heart with His love. When he suffers death for Christ's sake, the Saviour says to him, They may kill the body, but they cannot hurt the soul. *AA 85*

3 For the rod of the wicked shall not rest upon the lot of the righteous; lest the righteous put forth their hands unto iniquity.   Prov. 22:8

4 Do good, O LORD, unto *those that be* good, and to *them that are* upright in their hearts.

5 As for such as turn aside unto their crooked ways, the LORD shall lead them

forth with the workers of iniquity: *but* peace *shall be* upon Israel.   Ps. 40:4; 128:6; Prov. 2:15

PSALM 126

The Lord Has Done Great Things

A Song of degrees.

When the LORD turned again the captivity of Zion, we were like them that dream.   Ps. 85:1

2 Then was our mouth filled with laughter, and our tongue with singing: then said they among the heathen, The LORD hath done great things for them.   Job 8:21; Ps. 71:19

3 The LORD hath done great things for us; *whereof* we are glad.

4 Turn again our captivity, O LORD, as the streams in the south.

5 They that sow in tears shall reap in joy.

6 He that goeth forth and weepeth, bearing precious seed, shall doubtless come again with rejoicing, bringing his sheaves *with him*.

PSALM 127

The Virtue of God's Blessing

A Song of degrees for Solomon.

Except the LORD build the house, they labour in vain that build it: except the LORD keep the city, the watchman waketh *but* in vain.

2 *It is* vain for you to rise up early, to sit up late, to eat the bread of sorrows: *for* so he giveth his beloved sleep.   Eccl. 5:12

3 Lo, children *are* an heritage of the LORD: *and* the fruit of the womb *is his* reward. Gen. 1:28; 33:5

127:3 Children Are From God

Let parents search their own hearts, examine their habits and practices. Children are the heritage of the Lord, and we are answerable to Him for our management of His property.

There are fathers and mothers who long to labor in some foreign mission field; there are many who are active in Christian work outside the home, while their own children are strangers to the Saviour and His love. *COL 195*

4 As arrows *are* in the hand of a mighty man; so *are* children of the youth.

5 Happy *is* the man that hath his quiver full of them: they shall not be ashamed, but they shall speak with the enemies in the gate.

PSALM 128

Blessings for Those Who Fear God

A Song of degrees.

Blessed *is* every one that feareth the LORD; that walketh in his ways.   Ps. 112:1; 119:1

2 For thou shalt eat the labour of thine

hands: happy *shalt* thou *be*, and *it shall be* well with thee.   Eccl. 8:12; Is. 3:10; Eph. 6:3

3 Thy wife *shall be* as a fruitful vine by the sides of thine house: thy children like olive plants round about thy table.   Ps. 52:8; 144:12; Ezek. 19:10

4 Behold, that thus shall the man be blessed that feareth the LORD.

5 The LORD shall bless thee out of Zion: and thou shalt see the good of Jerusalem all the days of thy life.   Ps. 20:2; 134:3

6 Yea, thou shalt see thy children's children, *and* peace upon Israel. Gen. 50:23; Job 42:16; Ps. 125:5

PSALM 129

Praise God for Deliverance from Affliction

A Song of degrees.

Many a time have they afflicted me from my youth, may Israel now say: Ps. 124:1

2 Many a time have they afflicted me from my youth: yet they have not prevailed against me.   Matt. 16:18

3 The plowers plowed upon my back: they made long their furrows.   Is. 51:23

4 The LORD *is* righteous: he hath cut [T]asunder the cords of the wicked.   *apart*

5 Let them all be confounded and turned back that hate Zion.

6 Let them be as the grass *upon* the housetops, which withereth afore it groweth up:

7 Wherewith the mower filleth not his hand; nor he that bindeth sheaves his bosom.

8 Neither do they which go by say, The blessing of the LORD *be* upon you: we bless you in the name of the LORD.   Ruth 2:4; Ps. 118:26

PSALM 130

God Offers Forgiveness

A Song of degrees.

Out of the depths have I cried unto thee, O LORD.   Ps. 42:7

2 Lord, hear my voice: let thine ears be attentive to the voice of my supplications. 2 Chr. 6:40

3 If thou, LORD, shouldest mark iniquities, O Lord, who shall stand? Job 10:14; Ps. 76:7; 143:2

4 But *there is* forgiveness with thee, that thou mayest be feared.   1 Kin. 8:39-40; Ps. 86:5; Is. 55:7

5 I wait for the LORD, my soul doth wait, and in his word do I hope.   Ps. 33:20; 119:81; Is. 8:17

6 My soul *waiteth* for the Lord more than they that watch for the morning: *I say, more than* they that watch for the morning. Ps. 63:6

7 Let Israel hope in the LORD: for with the LORD *there is* mercy, and with him *is* plenteous redemption.   Ps. 86:5; 131:3

8 And he shall redeem Israel from all his iniquities.   Titus 2:14

PSALM 131

David Professes Humility

A Song of degrees of David.

LORD, my heart is not haughty, nor mine eyes lofty: neither do I exercise myself in great matters, or in things too high for me.   Job 42:3; Jer. 45:5; Rom. 12:16

2 Surely I have behaved and quieted myself, as a child that is weaned of his mother: my soul *is* even as a weaned child.   Ps. 62:1; 1 Cor. 14:20

3 Let Israel hope in the LORD from [T]henceforth and for ever.   Ps. 130:7 ◆ *from this time forward*

PSALM 132

Praise for the Ark's Return to Jerusalem

A Song of degrees.

LORD, remember David, *and* all his afflictions: Ps. 120:1

2 How he sware unto the LORD, *and* vowed unto the mighty *God* of Jacob;   Gen. 49:24

3 Surely I will not come into the tabernacle of my house, nor go up into my bed;

4 I will not give sleep to mine eyes, *or* slumber to mine eyelids,   Prov. 6:4

5 Until I find out a place for the LORD, an habitation for the mighty *God* of Jacob.

6 Lo, we heard of it at Ephratah: we found it in the fields of the wood.   1 Sam. 7:1; 17:12

7 We will go into his tabernacles: we will worship at his footstool.   Ps. 5:7; 99:5

8 Arise, O LORD, into thy rest; thou, and the ark of thy strength.   Ps. 68:1

9 Let thy priests be clothed with righteousness; and let thy saints shout for joy. Job 29:14

10 For thy servant David's sake turn not away the face of thine anointed.

11 The LORD hath sworn *in* truth unto David; he will not turn from it; Of the fruit of thy body will I set upon thy throne.   2 Sam. 7:12

12 If thy children will keep my covenant and my testimony that I shall teach them, their children shall also sit upon thy throne for evermore.

13 For the LORD hath chosen Zion; he hath desired *it* for his habitation.   Ps. 68:16

14 This *is* my rest for ever: here will I dwell; for I have desired it.   Ps. 132:8

15 I will abundantly bless her provision: I will satisfy her poor with bread.   Ps. 147:14

16 I will also clothe her priests with salvation: and her saints shall shout aloud for joy.   2 Chr. 6:41; Ps. 132:9

17 There will I make the horn of David to bud: I have ordained a lamp for mine anointed.   1 Kin. 11:36; 2 Chr. 21:7; Ezek. 29:21

18 His enemies will I clothe with shame: but upon himself shall his crown flourish. Job 8:22

PSALM 133

Benefits from the Harmony of Believers

A Song of degrees of David.

Behold, how good and how pleasant *it is* for brethren to dwell together in unity!

133:1 Unity—The Evidence of Discipleship

It is the will of God that union and brotherly love should exist among His people. . . . While we are not to sacrifice one principle of truth, it should be our constant aim to reach this state of unity. This is the evidence of our discipleship. Said Jesus, "By this shall all men know that ye are My disciples, if ye have love one to another" (John 13:35). *PP 520*

---

2 *It is* like the precious ointment upon the head, that ran down upon the beard, *even* Aaron's beard: that went down to the skirts of his garments;   Lev. 8:12
3 As the dew of Hermon, *and as the dew* that descended upon the mountains of Zion: for there the LORD commanded the blessing, *even* life for evermore. Lev. 25:21; Deut. 4:48; 28:8

PSALM 134

An Exhortation to Bless God

A Song of degrees.

Behold, bless ye the LORD, all *ye* servants of the LORD, which by night stand in the house of the LORD. Lev. 8:35; 1 Chr. 9:33; Ps. 135:1-2
2 Lift up your hands *in* the sanctuary, and bless the LORD.   Ps. 28:2; 63:4; 1 Tim. 2:8
3 The LORD that made heaven and earth bless thee out of Zion.   Ps. 124:8; 128:5

PSALM 135

A Hymn of Praise

Praise ye the LORD. Praise ye the name of the LORD; praise *him*, O ye servants of the LORD.   Ps. 134:1
2 Ye that stand in the house of the LORD, in the courts of the house of our God, Ps. 92:13
3 Praise the LORD; for the LORD *is* good: sing praises unto his name; for *it is* pleasant.
4 For the LORD hath chosen Jacob unto himself, *and* Israel for his ᵀpeculiar treasure. special

---

135:4 A Chosen, Treasured People

From a race of slaves the Israelites had been exalted above all peoples to be the peculiar treasure of the King of kings. God had separated them from the world, that He might commit to them a sacred trust. He had made them the depositaries of His law, and He purposed, through them, to preserve among men the knowledge of Himself. . . . If the Israelites would be true to their trust, they would become a power in the world. *PP 314*

---

5 For I know that the LORD *is* great, and *that* our Lord *is* above all gods.   Ps. 48:1
6 Whatsoever the LORD pleased, *that* did he in heaven, and in earth, in the seas, and all deep places.   Ps. 115:3
7 He causeth the vapours to ascend from the ends of the earth; he maketh lightnings for the rain; he bringeth the wind out of his treasuries.   Jer. 10:13; 51:16; Zech. 10:1
8 Who smote the firstborn of Egypt, both of man and beast.   Ex. 12:12; Ps. 78:51; 105:36
9 *Who* sent tokens and wonders into the midst of thee, O Egypt, upon Pharaoh, and upon all his servants.   Ps. 136:15
10 Who smote great nations, and slew mighty kings;   Ps. 136:17-22
11 Sihon king of the Amorites, and Og king of Bashan, and all the kingdoms of Canaan: Josh. 12:7-24
12 And gave their land *for* an heritage, an heritage unto Israel his people. Ps. 78:55; 136:21-22
13 Thy name, O LORD, *endureth* for ever; *and* thy memorial, O LORD, throughout all generations.   Ex. 3:15; Ps. 102:12
14 For the LORD will judge his people, and he will repent himself concerning his servants.   Deut. 32:36; Ps. 50:4
15 The idols of the heathen *are* silver and gold, the work of men's hands.   Ps. 115:4-8
16 They have mouths, but they speak not; eyes have they, but they see not;
17 They have ears, but they hear not; neither is there *any* breath in their mouths.
18 They that make them are like unto them: *so is* every one that trusteth in them.
19 Bless the LORD, O house of Israel: bless the LORD, O house of Aaron:
20 Bless the LORD, O house of Levi: ye that fear the LORD, bless the LORD.
21 Blessed be the LORD out of Zion, which dwelleth at Jerusalem. Praise ye the LORD.

PSALM 136

God's Mercy Endures Forever

O give thanks unto the LORD; for *he is* good: for his mercy *endureth* for ever. 1 Chr. 16:34
2 O give thanks unto the God of gods: for his mercy *endureth* for ever.   Deut. 10:17
3 O give thanks to the Lord of lords: for his mercy *endureth* for ever.
4 To him who alone doeth great wonders: for his mercy *endureth* for ever.   Ps. 72:18
5 To him that by wisdom made the heavens: for his mercy *endureth* for ever. Gen. 1:1; Jer. 51:15
6 To him that stretched out the earth above the waters: for his mercy *endureth* for ever.   Gen. 1:9; Ps. 24:2; Is. 44:24
7 To him that made great lights: for his mercy *endureth* for ever:

8 The sun to rule by day: for his mercy *endureth* for ever:

9 The moon and stars to rule by night: for his mercy *endureth* for ever.

10 To him that smote Egypt in their first-born: for his mercy *endureth* for ever: Ex. 12:29

11 And brought out Israel from among them: for his mercy *endureth* for ever: Ex. 12:51; 13:3

12 With a strong hand, and with a stretched out arm: for his mercy *endureth* for ever. Ex. 6:6

13 To him which divided the Red sea into parts: for his mercy *endureth* for ever: Ps. 78:13

14 And made Israel to pass through the midst of it: for his mercy *endureth* for ever:

15 But overthrew Pharaoh and his host in the Red sea: for his mercy *endureth* for ever.

16 To him which led his people through the wilderness: for his mercy *endureth* for ever.

17 To him which smote great kings: for his mercy *endureth* for ever: Ps. 135:10-12

18 And slew famous kings: for his mercy *endureth* for ever:

19 Sihon king of the Amorites: for his mercy *endureth* for ever:

20 And Og the king of Bashan: for his mercy *endureth* for ever: Num. 21:33

21 And gave their land for an heritage: for his mercy *endureth* for ever:

22 *Even* an heritage unto Israel his servant: for his mercy *endureth* for ever.

23 Who remembered us in our low estate: for his mercy *endureth* for ever: Gen. 8:1

24 And hath redeemed us from our enemies: for his mercy *endureth* for ever.   Ps. 107:2

25 Who giveth food to all flesh: for his mercy *endureth* for ever.   Ps. 104:27; 145:15

26 O give thanks unto the God of heaven: for his mercy *endureth* for ever.

PSALM 137

The Bitterness of Exile

By the rivers of Babylon, there we sat down, yea, we wept, when we remembered Zion.   Ezek. 1:1

2 We hanged our harps upon the willows in the midst thereof.   Is. 24:8

3 For there they that carried us away captive required of us a song; and they that wasted us *required of us* ᵀmirth, *saying*, Sing us *one* of the songs of Zion.   *gladness*

4 How shall we sing the LORD's song in a strange land?

5 If I forget thee, O Jerusalem, let my right hand forget *her cunning*.

6 If I do not remember thee, let my tongue cleave to the roof of my mouth; if I prefer not Jerusalem above my chief joy. Ps. 22:15; Ezek. 3:26

7 Remember, O LORD, the children of Edom in the day of Jerusalem; who said, Rase *it*, rase *it, even* to the foundation thereof.   Jer. 49:7-22

8 O daughter of Babylon, who art to be destroyed; happy *shall he be*, that rewardeth thee as thou hast served us.   Is. 13; Rev. 18:6

9 Happy *shall he be*, that taketh and dasheth thy little ones against the stones.   2 Kin. 8:12

PSALM 138

David Praises God for Answered Prayer

A Psalm of David.

I will praise thee with my whole heart: before the gods will I sing praise unto thee.   Ps. 111:1

2 I will worship toward thy holy temple, and praise thy name for thy lovingkindness and for thy truth: for thou hast magnified thy word above all thy name.   Ps. 5:7; 28:2; Is. 42:21

3 In the day when I cried thou answeredst me, *and* strengthenedst me *with* strength in my soul.

4 All the kings of the earth shall praise thee, O LORD, when they hear the words of thy mouth.   Ps. 72:11; 102:15

5 Yea, they shall sing in the ways of the LORD: for great *is* the glory of the LORD.   Ps. 21:5

6 Though the LORD *be* high, yet hath he respect unto the lowly: but the proud he knoweth afar off.   Ps. 113:5-6; Prov. 3:34; James 4:6

> **138:6 How God Views the Humble**
>
> Not only the wise, the great, the beneficent, will gain a passport to the heavenly courts; not only the busy worker, full of zeal and restless activity. No; the poor in spirit, who crave the presence of an abiding Christ, the humble in heart, whose highest ambition is to do God's will—these will gain an abundant entrance. They will be among that number who have washed their robes and made them white in the blood of the Lamb. *DA 301, 302*

7 Though I walk in the midst of trouble, thou wilt revive me: thou shalt stretch forth thine hand against the wrath of mine enemies, and thy right hand shall save me.   Ps. 60:5

8 The LORD will perfect *that which* concerneth me: thy mercy, O LORD, *endureth* for ever: forsake not the works of thine own hands.   Job 10:3; Ps. 57:2; Phil. 1:6

PSALM 139

David Praises God for His All-seeing Providence

To the chief Musician, A Psalm of David.

O LORD, thou hast searched me, and known *me*.   Ps. 17:3; 44:21; Jer. 12:3

2 Thou knowest my downsitting and mine

uprising, thou understandest my thought afar off.   2 Kin. 19:27; Ps. 94:11; Matt. 9:4

3 Thou compassest my path and my lying down, and art acquainted *with* all my ways.

4 For *there is* not a word in my tongue, *but,* lo, O LORD, thou knowest it altogether.

5 Thou hast beset me behind and before, and laid thine hand upon me.

6 *Such* knowledge *is* too wonderful for me; it is high, I cannot *attain* unto it.   Job 42:3; Rom. 11:33

7 Whither shall I go from thy spirit? or whither shall I flee from thy presence? Jon. 1:3

8 If I ascend up into heaven, thou *art* there: if I make my bed in hell, behold, thou *art* there.   Job 26:6

9 *If* I take the wings of the morning, *and* dwell in the uttermost parts of the sea;

10 Even there shall thy hand lead me, and thy right hand shall hold me.   Ps. 23:3

11 If I say, Surely the darkness shall cover me; even the night shall be light about me.

12 Yea, the darkness hideth not from thee; but the night shineth as the day: the darkness and the light *are* both alike *to thee.*   Job 34:22

13 For thou hast possessed my ᵀreins: thou hast covered me in my mother's womb. *desires*

14 I will praise thee; for I am fearfully *and* wonderfully made: marvellous *are* thy works; and *that* my soul knoweth right well.   Gen. 1:26-27

139:14 Caring for the Body God Gave Us

Let pupils be impressed with the thought that the body is a temple in which God desires to dwell, that it must be kept pure, the abiding place of high and noble thoughts. As in the study of physiology they see that they are indeed "fearfully and wonderfully made" (Psalm 139:14), they will be inspired with reverence. . . . Thus they will come to regard obedience to the laws of health, not as a matter of sacrifice or self-denial, but as it really is, an inestimable privilege and blessing. *Ed 201*

---

15 My substance was not hid from thee, when I was made in secret, *and* curiously ᵀwrought in the lowest parts of the earth.   Ps. 63:9 ♦ *made*

16 Thine eyes did see my substance, yet being unperfect; and in thy book all *my members* were written, *which* in continuance were fashioned, when *as yet there was* none of them.   Ps. 56:8

17 How precious also are thy thoughts unto me, O God! how great is the sum of them!   Ps. 40:5

18 *If* I should count them, they are more in number than the sand: when I awake, I am still with thee.   Ps. 3:5

19 Surely thou wilt slay the wicked, O God: depart from me therefore, ye bloody men.

20 For they speak against thee wickedly, *and* thine enemies take *thy name* in vain.

21 Do not I hate them, O LORD, that hate thee? and am not I grieved with those that rise up against thee?   2 Chr. 19:2; Ps. 31:6; 119:158

22 I hate them with perfect hatred: I count them mine enemies.

23 Search me, O God, and know my heart: try me, and know my thoughts: Job 31:6; Ps. 26:2

24 And see if *there be any* wicked way in me, and lead me in the way everlasting.   Ps. 5:8

PSALM 140

David Prays for Deliverance from Evil Men

To the chief Musician, A Psalm of David.

Deliver me, O LORD, from the evil man: preserve me from the violent man;

2 Which imagine mischiefs in *their* heart; continually are they gathered together *for* war.   Ps. 36:4; 56:6

3 They have sharpened their tongues like a serpent; ᵀadders' poison *is* under their lips. Selah.   Ps. 57:4; 58:4 ♦ *venomous snakes*

4 Keep me, O LORD, from the hands of the wicked; preserve me from the violent

---

Search Me, O God

Psalm 139:23, 24

"Man looketh on the outward appearance, but the Lord looketh on the heart"—the human heart, with its conflicting emotions of joy and sorrow; the wandering, wayward heart, which is the abode of so much impurity and deceit (1 Samuel 16:7). He knows its motives, its very intents and purposes. Go to Him with your soul all stained as it is. Like the psalmist, throw its chambers open to the all-seeing eye, exclaiming, "Search me, O God, and know my heart: try me, and know my thoughts: and see if there be any wicked way in me, and lead me in the way everlasting" (Psalm 139:23, 24).

Many accept an intellectual religion, a form of godliness, when the heart is not cleansed. Let it be your prayer, "Create in me a clean heart, O God; and renew a right spirit within me" (Psalm 51:10). Deal truly with your own soul. Be as earnest, as persistent, as you would be if your mortal life were at stake. This is a matter to be settled between God and your own soul, settled for eternity. A supposed hope, and nothing more, will prove your ruin. *SC 34, 35*

man; who have purposed to overthrow my goings. Ps. 71:4

5 The proud have hid a snare for me, and cords; they have spread a net by the wayside; they have set gins for me. Selah. Ps. 35:7; 57:6

6 I said unto the LORD, Thou *art* my God: hear the voice of my supplications, O LORD. Ps. 16:2

7 O GOD the Lord, the strength of my salvation, thou hast covered my head in the day of battle. Ps. 144:10

8 Grant not, O LORD, the desires of the wicked: further not his wicked device; *lest* they exalt themselves. Selah.

9 *As for* the head of those that ᵀcompass me about, let the mischief of their own lips cover them. Ps. 7:16; Prov. 12:13; 18:7 ◆ surround

10 Let burning coals fall upon them: let them be cast into the fire; into deep pits, that they rise not up again. Ps. 11:6; 21:9

11 Let not an evil speaker be established in the earth: evil shall hunt the violent man to overthrow *him*. Ps. 34:21

12 I know that the LORD will maintain the cause of the afflicted, *and* the right of the poor. 1 Kin. 8:45, 49; Ps. 9:4

13 Surely the righteous shall give thanks unto thy name: the upright shall dwell in thy presence. Ps. 11:7

PSALM 141

David Prays That His Plea May Be Acceptable

A Psalm of David.

LORD, I cry unto thee: make haste unto me; give ear unto my voice, when I cry unto thee. Ps. 40:13; 70:5

2 Let my prayer be set forth before thee *as* incense; *and* the lifting up of my hands *as* the evening sacrifice. Ex. 29:39; 1 Tim. 2:8; Rev. 5:8

3 Set a watch, O LORD, before my mouth; keep the door of my lips. Mic. 7:5

4 Incline not my heart to *any* evil thing, to practise wicked works with men that work iniquity: and let me not eat of their dainties. Ps. 119:36

141:2 Altars of Prayer in the Home

If ever there was a time when every house should be a house of prayer, it is now. Fathers and mothers should often lift up their hearts to God in humble supplication for themselves and their children. Let the father, as priest of the household, lay upon the altar of God the morning and evening sacrifice, while the wife and children unite in prayer and praise. In such a household Jesus will love to tarry. *PP 144*

---

5 Let the righteous ᵀsmite me; *it shall be* a kindness: and let him reprove me; *it shall be* an excellent oil, *which* shall not break my head: for yet my prayer also *shall be* in their calamities. Prov. 19:25 ◆ strike

6 When their judges are overthrown in stony places, they shall hear my words; for they are sweet.

7 Our bones are scattered at the grave's mouth, as when one cutteth and ᵀcleaveth *wood* upon the earth. Ps. 53:5 ◆ splits

8 But mine eyes *are* unto thee, O GOD the Lord: in thee is my trust; leave not my soul destitute.

9 Keep me from the snares *which* they have laid for me, and the gins of the workers of iniquity. Ps. 140:5

10 Let the wicked fall into their own nets, whilst that I ᵀwithal escape. Ps. 35:8 ◆ together with

PSALM 142

David's Comfort in Prayer

Maschil of David; A Prayer when he was in the cave.

I cried unto the LORD with my voice; with my voice unto the LORD did I make my supplication. Ps. 30:8

Our Words Are Powerful

Psalm 141:3, 4

Every day of life is freighted with responsibilities which we must bear. Every day, our words and acts are making impressions upon those with whom we associate. How great the need that we set a watch upon our lips and guard carefully our steps! One reckless movement, one imprudent step, and the surging waves of some strong temptation may sweep a soul into the downward path. We cannot gather up the thoughts we have planted in human minds. If they have been evil, we may have set in motion a train of circumstances, a tide of evil, which we are powerless to stay.

On the other hand, if by our example we aid others in the development of good principles, we give them power to do good. In their turn they exert the same beneficial influence over others. Thus hundreds and thousands are helped by our unconscious influence. The true follower of Christ strengthens the good purposes of all with whom he comes in contact. Before an unbelieving, sin-loving world he reveals the power of God's grace and the perfection of His character. *PK 348*

2 I poured out my complaint before him; I shewed before him my trouble. Is. 26:16

3 When my spirit was overwhelmed within me, then thou knewest my path. In the way wherein I walked have they ᵀprivily laid a snare for me. Ps. 140:5; 143:4 ♦ *in secret*

4 I looked on *my* right hand, and beheld, but *there was* no man that would know me: refuge failed me; no man cared for my soul.

5 I cried unto thee, O Lᴏʀᴅ: I said, Thou *art* my refuge *and* my portion in the land of the living. Ps. 16:5; 27:13; 46:1

6 Attend unto my cry; for I am brought very low: deliver me from my persecutors; for they are stronger than I. Ps. 17:1; 79:8; 116:6

7 Bring my soul out of prison, that I may praise thy name: the righteous shall ᵀcompass me about; for thou shalt deal bountifully with me. Ps. 13:6; 143:11; 146:7 ♦ *surround*

PSALM 143

David Prays for Favor in Judgment

A Psalm of David.

H ear my prayer, O Lᴏʀᴅ, give ear to my supplications: in thy faithfulness answer me, *and* in thy righteousness. Ps. 71:2

2 And enter not into judgment with thy servant: for in thy sight shall no man living be justified. Job 14:3; 25:4; Eccl. 7:20

3 For the enemy hath persecuted my soul; he hath smitten my life down to the ground; he hath made me to dwell in darkness, as those that have been long dead. Ps. 88:4-6

4 Therefore is my spirit overwhelmed within me; my heart within me is desolate. Ps. 77:3

5 I remember the days of old; I meditate on all thy works; I muse on the work of thy hands. Ps. 77:5-6

6 I stretch forth my hands unto thee: my soul *thirsteth* after thee, as a thirsty land. Selah. Job 11:13; Ps. 63:1; 88:9

7 Hear me speedily, O Lᴏʀᴅ: my spirit faileth: hide not thy face from me, lest I be like unto them that go down into the pit. Ps. 27:9

8 Cause me to hear thy lovingkindness in the morning; for in thee do I trust: cause me to know the way wherein I should walk; for I lift up my soul unto thee. Ps. 27:11

9 Deliver me, O Lᴏʀᴅ, from mine enemies: I flee unto thee to hide me.

10 Teach me to do thy will; for thou *art* my God: thy spirit *is* good; lead me into the land of uprightness. Neh. 9:20; Ps. 25:4-5; 119:12

11 Quicken me, O Lᴏʀᴅ, for thy name's sake: for thy righteousness' sake bring my soul out of trouble. Ps. 31:1

12 And of thy mercy cut off mine enemies, and destroy all them that afflict my soul: for I *am* thy servant. Ps. 54:5; 116:16

PSALM 144

David Promises to Praise God

A Psalm of David.

B lessed *be* the Lᴏʀᴅ my strength, which teacheth my hands to war, *and* my fingers to fight: 2 Sam. 22:35; Ps. 18:2, 34

2 My goodness, and my fortress; my high tower, and my deliverer; my shield, and *he* in whom I trust; who subdueth my people under me. Ps. 18:2

3 Lᴏʀᴅ, what *is* man, that thou takest knowledge of him! *or* the son of man, that thou makest account of him! Job 7:17; Ps. 8:4; Heb. 2:6

4 Man is like to vanity: his days *are* as a shadow that passeth away. Job 8:9; Ps. 102:11; 109:23

5 Bow thy heavens, O Lᴏʀᴅ, and come down: touch the mountains, and they shall smoke. Ps. 18:9; 104:32

6 Cast forth lightning, and scatter them: shoot out thine arrows, and destroy them.

7 Send thine hand from above; rid me, and deliver me out of great waters, from the hand of strange children; Ps. 18:16

8 Whose mouth speaketh vanity, and their right hand *is* a right hand of falsehood. Ps. 12:2

9 I will sing a new song unto thee, O God: upon a psaltery *and* an instrument of ten strings will I sing praises unto thee. Ps. 33:2-3

10 *It is he* that giveth salvation unto kings: who delivereth David his servant from the hurtful sword. Ps. 18:50; 140:7

11 Rid me, and deliver me from the hand of strange children, whose mouth speaketh vanity, and their right hand *is* a right hand of falsehood:

12 That our sons *may be* as plants grown up in their youth; *that* our daughters *may be* as corner stones, polished *after* the ᵀsimilitude of a palace: Ps. 128:3 ♦ *image*

> **144:12 The Mother's Sacred Charge**
>
> In the children committed to her care, every mother has a sacred charge from God. "Take this son, this daughter," He says; "train it for Me; give it a character polished after the similitude of a palace, that it may shine in the courts of the Lord forever." *MH 376*

13 *That* our garners *may be* full, affording all manner of store: *that* our sheep may bring forth thousands and ten thousands in our streets:

14 *That* our oxen *may be* strong to labour; *that there be* no breaking in, nor going out; that *there be* no complaining in our streets.

15 Happy *is that* people, that is in such a case: *yea,* happy *is that* people, whose God *is* the Lᴏʀᴅ. Deut. 33:29; Ps. 33:12; 146:5

13 Let them praise the name of the LORD: for his name alone is excellent; his glory *is* above the earth and heaven.Ps. 8:1; 113:4; Is. 12:4

14 He also exalteth the horn of his people, the praise of all his saints; *even* of the children of Israel, a people near unto him. Praise ye the LORD.   1 Sam. 2:1

PSALM 149

Let All the Saints Praise the Lord

Praise ye the LORD. Sing unto the LORD a new song, *and* his praise in the congregation of saints.   Ps. 33:3

2 Let Israel rejoice in him that made him: let the children of Zion be joyful in their King.   Job 35:10; Ps. 95:6; Zech. 9:9

3 Let them praise his name in the dance: let them sing praises unto him with the ᵀtimbrel and harp.   Ex. 15:20 ◆ *tambourine*

149:4 The True Secret of Blessing

Far better would it be for us to suffer under false accusation than to inflict upon ourselves the torture of retaliation upon our enemies. The spirit of hatred and revenge originated with Satan, and can bring only evil to him who cherishes it. Lowliness of heart, that meekness which is the fruit of abiding in Christ, is the true secret of blessing. "He will beautify the meek with salvation" (Psalm 149:4). *MB 17*

---

4 For the LORD taketh pleasure in his people: he will beautify the meek with salvation.

5 Let the saints be joyful in glory: let them sing aloud upon their beds.   Job 35:10; Ps. 42:8

6 *Let* the high *praises* of God *be* in their mouth, and a twoedged sword in their hand;

7 To execute vengeance upon the heathen, *and* punishments upon the people;

8 To bind their kings with chains, and their nobles with ᵀfetters of iron;   *chains*

9 To execute upon them the judgment written: this honour have all his saints. Praise ye the LORD.   Ps. 148:14

PSALM 150

Praise the Lord

Praise ye the LORD. Praise God in his sanctuary: praise him in the ᵀfirmament of his power.   Ps. 134:2 ◆ *sky*

2 Praise him for his mighty acts: praise him according to his excellent greatness. Deut. 3:24

3 Praise him with the sound of the trumpet: praise him with the psaltery and harp.Ps.33:2

4 Praise him with the ᵀtimbrel and dance: praise him with stringed instruments and organs.   Ex. 15:20; Ps. 149:3; Is. 38:20 ◆ *tambourine*

5 Praise him upon the loud cymbals: praise him upon the high sounding cymbals.

6 Let every thing that hath breath praise the LORD. Praise ye the LORD.   Ps. 103:22

Praising Jesus; Talking of His Love

Psalm 150

If we would but think of God as often as we have evidence of His care for us we should keep Him ever in our thoughts and should delight to talk of Him and to praise Him. We talk of temporal things because we have an interest in them. We talk of our friends because we love them; our joys and our sorrows are bound up with them. Yet we have infinitely greater reason to love God than to love our earthly friends; it should be the most natural thing in the world to make Him first in all our thoughts, to talk of His goodness and tell of His power. The rich gifts He has bestowed upon us were not intended to absorb our thoughts and love so much that we should have nothing to give to God; they are constantly to remind us of Him and to bind us in bonds of love and gratitude to our heavenly Benefactor. We dwell too near the lowlands of earth. Let us raise our eyes to the open door of the sanctuary above, where the light of the glory of God shines in the face of Christ, who "is able also to save them to the uttermost that come unto God by Him" (Hebrews 7:25).

We need to praise God more "for His goodness, and for His wonderful works to the children of men" (Psalm 107:8). *SC 102*

THE BOOK OF

PROVERBS

Many self-help books and advice columns claim to offer wise advice from experts. Much of this advice is humanistic—not taking into account the truth of a loving Creator or human beings' need for a relationship with Him. But the wisdom books in the Bible (Job, some of the Psalms, Proverbs, and Ecclesiastes) offer advice from wise men who sought wisdom at its source: God.

Wisdom literature is a common feature of ancient cultures of the Near East. Written examples in Egypt date from 2700 B.C. However, the emphasis on God makes the wisdom literature of the Bible decidedly different from the wisdom literature of other cultures.

Through a combination of poetry, parables, questions, and maxims, Proverbs presents a guide for the affairs of everyday life. Topics in Proverbs range from raising children, being a faithful friend, honesty and integrity in all areas of life, and even how to deal with events on a national scale. The book serves as a generational legacy: to impart wisdom, knowledge, guidance, competence, prudence, understanding, discretion, correction, counsel, and truth.

Dates

Solomon's proverbs and those he collected were likely written during Solomon's reign (971–931 B.C.). They were certainly written before he descended into idolatry. The remainder of Solomon's proverbs in the Book of Proverbs was assembled by Hezekiah's scribes more than two centuries later, likely during Hezekiah's reign (c. 729–686 B.C.).

Author

Wise King Solomon is the author of Proverbs (1:1; 10:1; 25:1). He penned the book of Proverbs near the beginning of his reign (c. 971–931 B.C.) when he still had obedience in his heart for God. Under Solomon, Israel was at its spiritual, political, and economic summit. This collection represents only a fraction of the three thousand proverbs and more than one thousand songs for which he was known (1 Kings 4:32). His God-given acumen (see 1 Kings 3:5–9) helped bring prosperity and glory to Israel (compare 1 Kings 11:4).

Other compilers of Proverbs include:

(1) The scribes of King Hezekiah (Proverbs 25—29) put in writing some of Solomon's proverbs, which may have come from written or oral resources. The prophet Isaiah, the scribe Shebna, and the chronicler Joah may have assisted in this task.

(2) Agur (an oracle) (chapter 30) is considered by various Jewish historians to be a figurative name for Solomon.

(3) Lemuel (a king and oracle) (chapter 31) is like Agur in that there are those who deem Lemuel as another name for Solomon because, other than Proverbs 30, the writing style is much more similar to the other proverbs.

Meaning of the Name

The Hebrew title for Proverbs is *Mishle Shelomoh*, "Proverbs of Solomon," or *Sepher Hokhmah*, "Book of Wisdom." In the Greek, Proverbs is *Paroimiai Salomontos*, "Proverbs of Solomon," while the Latin version is *Liber Proverbiorum* "Book of Proverbs." The Latin terms *pro verba* (*proverb*) refers to the reduction of many thoughts into a few words.

Christ in Proverbs

Jesus is called the "wisdom of God" (1 Corinthians 1:24). Little wonder that when He spoke to the people He told them that "a greater than Solomon is here" (Luke 11:31). The eighth chapter of Proverbs gives us the nature of wisdom as the source of life (Proverbs 8:35), righteousness (8:8–9), and freely available to all (8:1–6, 32–35). This fits the nature of Jesus, who is our life and righteousness.

The words of Jesus are the words of wisdom and shall not pass away (Matthew 24:35). Just as we are admonished to receive the words of wisdom in Proverbs, Jesus admonishes us to receive His words, as an act of loving Him (John 14:23).

The Book of Proverbs is probably most known for its figurative language, repetition, and comparisons. It has six thematic parts:

(1) *Proverbs 1:1–7, The Purpose:* The theme of Proverbs is summed up here: "To know wisdom and instruction; to perceive the words of understanding; to receive the instruction of wisdom, justice, and judgment, and equity; to give subtilty to the simple, to the young man knowledge and discretion" (1:2–4).

(2) *Proverbs 1:8—9:18, Proverbs to the Youth:* A father offering wisdom to a beloved son is the pattern for these exhortations. Here, wisdom and folly are contrasted. Wisdom is the fence behind which the wise person remains. The wise person is obedient to parents, rejects wicked companions, and embraces the safety of wisdom. Much evil can be avoided (chapters 5—7) through wisdom, which is personified in chapters 8—9.

(3) *Proverbs 10:1—24:34, Proverbs of Solomon:* These chapters have varying themes, many of which are expressed through antithetic parallelism (two lines expressing the same idea but in opposite ways) or synonymous parallelism (two lines expressing the same idea, but with different wording. An example of antithetical parallelism: "A wise son maketh a glad father: but a foolish son is the heaviness of his mother" (10:1). An example of synonymous parallelism: "A wicked doer giveth heed to false lips; and a liar giveth ear to a naughty tongue" (17:4).

(4) *Proverbs 25:1—29:27, Proverbs of Solomon:* These proverbs were transcribed by "the men of Hezekiah" (25:1). Quite possibly they put to writing the oral tradition of Solomon's wisdom.

(5) *Proverbs 30, The Words of Agur:* This section has rhetorical questions similar to those found in Job 38.

(6) *Proverbs 31, The Words of King Lemuel:* The last part of this chapter (verses 10–31) is an acrostic on the characteristics of "a virtuous woman" (verse 10).

Unlocking Proverbs

KEY PEOPLE:
Solomon, Hezekiah, Agur, Lemuel

KEY EVENTS:
The teaching of moral discernment as well as mental clarity and perception

KEY WORD:
Wisdom. To be righteous before God requires knowledge and wisdom. Proverbs makes clear the need for both in chapters 1—9. The Book of Proverbs provides a guide for avoiding a sinful lifestyle and retaining holiness before God. The purpose statement in Proverbs states the book's intent for us the readers: wisdom (*hokhmah*) or "skill" and instruction (*musar*) or "discipline." Proverbs lays out the most fundamental skill: practical righteousness before God in all parts of life. This requires experience, knowledge, and a willingness to put God's words and principles first (see 3:5–7).

KEY VERSES:
"A wise man will hear, and will increase learning; and a man of understanding shall attain unto wise counsels: to understand a proverb, and the interpretation; the words of the wise, and their dark saying. The fear of the LORD is the beginning of knowledge: but fools despise wisdom and instruction" (Proverbs 1:5–7).

"Trust in the LORD with all thine heart; and lean not unto thine own understanding. In all thy ways acknowledge him, and he shall direct thy paths" (Proverbs 3:5–6).

KEY CHAPTER:
In *Proverbs 31*, the noble character of a wise woman is described. She is a marked contrast to the adulterous woman of chapter 7. The wise actions of this woman epitomize the benefits of wisdom.

The Reasons for the Proverbs

1 The proverbs of Solomon the son of David, king of Israel; Prov. 10:1; 25:1; Eccl. 12:9
2 To know wisdom and instruction; to perceive the words of understanding;
3 To receive the instruction of wisdom, justice, and judgment, and ᵀequity;   *uprightness*
4 To give subtilty to the simple, to the young man knowledge and discretion.   Prov. 8:5
5 A wise *man* will hear, and will increase learning; and a man of understanding shall attain unto wise counsels: Prov. 9:9
6 To understand a proverb, and the interpretation; the words of the wise, and their dark sayings.   Ps. 49:4; 78:2

Listen to Wisdom

7 The fear of the LORD *is* the beginning of knowledge: *but* fools despise wisdom and instruction.   Job 28:28; Prov. 9:10; Eccl. 12:13
8 My son, hear the instruction of thy father, and forsake not the law of thy mother:
9 For they *shall be* an ornament of grace unto thy head, and chains about thy neck. Prov. 4:9
10 My son, if sinners entice thee, consent thou not.   Eph. 5:11
11 If they say, Come with us, let us lay wait for blood, let us lurk privily for the innocent without cause: Prov. 1:18; 12:6; Jer. 5:26
12 Let us swallow them up alive as the grave; and whole, as those that go down into the pit: Ps. 28:1; 124:3
13 We shall find all precious substance, we shall fill our houses with ᵀspoil: *plunder*
14 Cast in thy lot among us; let us all have one purse:
15 My son, walk not thou in the way with them; refrain thy foot from their path: Ps. 1:1
16 For their feet run to evil, and make haste to shed blood.   Prov. 6:18; Is. 59:7
17 Surely in vain the net is spread in the sight of any bird.
18 And they lay wait for their *own* blood; they lurk ᵀprivily for their *own* lives.   *in secret*
19 So *are* the ways of every one that is greedy of gain; *which* taketh away the life of the owners thereof.

1:19

Christian Behavior See Proverbs 15:27.

---

20 Wisdom crieth without; she uttereth her voice in the streets: Prov. 9:3; John 7:37
21 She crieth in the chief place of concourse, in the openings of the gates: in the city she uttereth her words, *saying,*
22 How long, ye simple ones, will ye love simplicity? and the scorners delight in their scorning, and fools hate knowledge?   Ps. 1:1
23 Turn you at my reproof: behold, I will pour out my spirit unto you, I will make known my words unto you.   Joel 2:28
24 Because I have called, and ye refused; I

have stretched out my hand, and no man regarded;   Is. 65:12; 66:4; Jer. 7:13
25 But ye have set at ᵀnought all my counsel, and would none of my reproof: Ps. 107:11 ◆ *nothing*
26 I also will laugh at your calamity; I will mock when your fear cometh; Ps. 2:4; Prov. 10:24
27 When your fear cometh as desolation, and your destruction cometh as a whirlwind; when distress and anguish cometh upon you.
28 Then shall they call upon me, but I will not answer; they shall seek me early, but they shall not find me: Job 27:9; Is. 1:15; Jer. 11:11
29 For that they hated knowledge, and did not choose the fear of the LORD: Prov. 1:22
30 They would none of my counsel: they despised all my reproof.   Ps. 81:11; Prov. 1:25
31 Therefore shall they eat of the fruit of their own way, and be filled with their own devices.   Job 4:8; Prov. 14:14; Jer. 6:19
32 For the turning away of the simple shall slay them, and the prosperity of fools shall destroy them.   Jer. 2:19
33 But whoso hearkeneth unto me shall dwell safely, and shall be quiet from fear of evil.   Ps. 25:12-13

The Benefit of Wisdom

2 My son, if thou wilt receive my words, and hide my commandments with thee;
2 So that thou incline thine ear unto wisdom, *and* apply thine heart to understanding;
3 Yea, if thou criest after knowledge, *and* liftest up thy voice for understanding;
4 If thou seekest her as silver, and searchest for her as *for* hid treasures; Job 3:21; Matt. 13:44
5 Then shalt thou understand the fear of the LORD, and find the knowledge of God.

2:3–5 Reward of Searching

No one can search the Scriptures in the spirit of Christ without being rewarded. When man is willing to be instructed as a little child, when he submits wholly to God, he will find the truth in His word. If men would be obedient, they would understand the plan of God's government.... Human beings would be altogether different from what they now are, for by exploring the mines of truth men would be ennobled. *COL 114*

---

6 For the LORD giveth wisdom: out of his mouth *cometh* knowledge and understanding.

2:6 Wisdom Comes From God

In a knowledge of God all true knowledge and real development have their source. Wherever we turn, in the physical, the mental, or the spiritual realm; in whatever we behold, apart from the blight of sin, this knowledge is revealed. *Ed 14*

7 He layeth up sound wisdom for the righteous: *he is* a ᵀbuckler to them that walk uprightly.   Ps. 84:11; Prov. 30:5 ◆ *shield*
8 He keepeth the paths of judgment, and preserveth the way of his saints.   1 Sam. 2:9; Ps. 66:9
9 Then shalt thou understand righteousness, and judgment, and ᵀequity; *yea,* every good path.   *uprightness*
10 When wisdom entereth into thine heart, and knowledge is pleasant unto thy soul;
11 Discretion shall preserve thee, understanding shall keep thee: Prov. 4:6
12 To deliver thee from the way of the evil *man,* from the man that speaketh ᵀfroward things;   *false, perverse*
13 Who leave the paths of uprightness, to walk in the ways of darkness;   Prov. 4:19
14 Who rejoice to do evil, *and* delight in the frowardness of the wicked;   Prov. 10:23; Jer. 11:15
15 Whose ways *are* crooked, and *they* froward in their paths: Ps. 125:5; Prov. 21:8
16 To deliver thee from the strange woman, *even* from the stranger *which* flattereth with her words;   Prov. 6:24; 7:5-23; 23:27
17 Which forsaketh the guide of her youth, and forgetteth the covenant of her God. Jer. 3:4
18 For her house inclineth unto death, and her paths unto the dead.
19 None that go unto her return again, neither take they hold of the paths of life. Eccl. 7:26
20 That thou mayest walk in the way of good *men,* and keep the paths of the righteous.
21 For the upright shall dwell in the land, and the perfect shall remain in it.   Ps. 37:29
22 But the wicked shall be cut off from the earth, and the ᵀtransgressors shall be rooted out of it.   Ps. 52:5 ◆ *those who violate the law*

Using Wisdom

3 My son, forget not my law; but let thine heart keep my commandments: Prov. 4:5
2 For length of days, and long life, and peace, shall they add to thee.   Ps. 91:16; Prov. 4:10; 9:11

3 Let not mercy and truth forsake thee: bind them about thy neck; write them upon the table of thine heart: Prov. 6:21; 7:3; 2 Cor. 3:3
4 So shalt thou find favour and good understanding in the sight of God and man.
5 Trust in the Lᴏʀᴅ with all thine heart; and lean not unto thine own understanding.
6 In all thy ways acknowledge him, and he shall direct thy paths. 1 Chr. 28:9; Prov. 16:3; Jer. 10:23
7 Be not wise in thine own eyes: fear the Lᴏʀᴅ, and depart from evil.   Job 1:1; 28:28
8 It shall be health to thy navel, and marrow to thy bones.   Job 21:24; Prov. 4:22
9 Honour the Lᴏʀᴅ with thy substance, and with the firstfruits of all thine increase:
10 So shall thy barns be filled with plenty, and thy presses shall burst out with new wine.   Deut. 28:8

3:9, 10 Returning Means to God

Not until God ceases to bless His children will they cease to be under bonds to return to Him the portion that He claims. . . . With joyful hearts they should dedicate to the Creator the first fruits of their bounties—their choicest possessions, their best and holiest service. Thus they will gain rich blessings. *AA 339, 340*

---

11 My son, despise not the ᵀchastening of the Lᴏʀᴅ; neither be weary of his correction: Job 5:17 ◆ *disciplining*
12 For whom the Lᴏʀᴅ loveth he correcteth; even as a father the son *in whom* he delighteth.   Deut. 8:5
13 Happy *is* the man *that* findeth wisdom, and the man *that* getteth understanding.
14 For the merchandise of it *is* better than the merchandise of silver, and the gain thereof than fine gold.   Prov. 8:19; 16:16
15 She *is* more precious than rubies: and all the things thou canst desire are not to be compared unto her.   Job 28:18; Prov. 8:11

Plans for the Future

Proverbs 3:6

Many are unable to make definite plans for the future. Their life is unsettled. They cannot discern the outcome of affairs, and this often fills them with anxiety and unrest. Let us remember that the life of God's children in this world is a pilgrim life. We have not wisdom to plan our own lives. It is not for us to shape our future. "By faith Abraham, when he was called to go out into a place which he should after receive for an inheritance, obeyed; and he went out, not knowing whither he went" (Hebrews 11:8).

Christ in His life on earth made no plans for Himself. He accepted God's plans for Him, and day by day the Father unfolded His plans. So should we depend upon God, that our lives may be the simple outworking of His will. As we commit our ways to Him, He will direct our steps.

Too many, in planning for a brilliant future, make an utter failure. Let God plan for you. As a little child, trust to the guidance of Him who will "keep the feet of His saints" (1 Samuel 2:9). God never leads His children otherwise than they would choose to be led, if they could see the end from the beginning and discern the glory of the purpose which they are fulfilling as co-workers with Him. *MH 478, 479*

16 Length of days *is* in her right hand; *and* in her left hand riches and honour.   Prov. 3:2

17 Her ways *are* ways of pleasantness, and all her paths *are* peace.   Ps. 119:165

18 She *is* a tree of life to them that lay hold upon her: and happy *is every one* that retaineth her.   Gen. 2:9; Prov. 11:30; 13:12

19 The LORD by wisdom hath founded the earth; by understanding hath he established the heavens.   Ps. 104:24; 136:5; Prov. 8:27-29

20 By his knowledge the depths are broken up, and the clouds drop down the dew.

21 My son, let not them depart from thine eyes: keep sound wisdom and discretion:

22 So shall they be life unto thy soul, and grace to thy neck.   Prov. 1:9; 4:22

23 Then shalt thou walk in thy way safely, and thy foot shall not stumble.   Prov. 4:12; 10:9

24 When thou liest down, thou shalt not be afraid: yea, thou shalt lie down, and thy sleep shall be sweet.   Lev. 26:6; Ps. 3:5; Prov. 6:22

25 Be not afraid of sudden fear, neither of the desolation of the wicked, when it cometh.   Ps. 91:5

26 For the LORD shall be thy confidence, and shall keep thy foot from being taken.

27 Withhold not good from them to whom it is due, when it is in the power of thine hand to do *it*.   Gal. 6:10

28 Say not unto thy neighbour, Go, and come again, and to morrow I will give; when thou hast it by thee.   Lev. 19:13

29 Devise not evil against thy neighbour, seeing he dwelleth securely by thee.   Prov. 6:14

30 Strive not with a man without cause, if he have done thee no harm.

31 Envy thou not the oppressor, and choose none of his ways.   Ps. 37:1; Prov. 24:1

32 For the froward *is* abomination to the LORD: but his secret *is* with the righteous.

33 The curse of the LORD *is* in the house of the wicked: but he blesseth the habitation of the just.   Ps. 1:3; 37:22; Mal. 2:2

34 Surely he scorneth the scorners: but he giveth grace unto the lowly.   Ps. 138:6; James 4:6

35 The wise shall inherit glory: but shame shall be the promotion of fools.

Cherish Wisdom

4 Hear, ye children, the instruction of a father, and attend to know understanding.   Ps. 34:11; Prov. 1:8

2 For I give you good doctrine, forsake ye not my law.   Deut. 32:2

3 For I was my father's son, tender and only *beloved* in the sight of my mother.   1 Chr. 22:5

4 He taught me also, and said unto me, Let thine heart retain my words: keep my commandments, and live. 1 Chr. 28:9; Prov. 7:2; Eph. 6:4

5 Get wisdom, get understanding: forget *it*

not; neither decline from the words of my mouth.

6 Forsake her not, and she shall preserve thee: love her, and she shall keep thee.

7 Wisdom *is* the principal thing; *therefore* get wisdom: and with all thy getting get understanding.   Matt. 13:44-46

> **4:7 The Most Important Work**
>
> True education imparts this wisdom. It teaches the best use not only of one but of all our powers and acquirements. . . .
>
> Character building is the most important work ever entrusted to human beings; and never before was its diligent study so important as now. Never was any previous generation called to meet issues so momentous; never before were young men and young women confronted by perils so great as confront them today. *Ed 225*

8 Exalt her, and she shall promote thee: she shall bring thee to honour, when thou dost embrace her.   1 Sam. 2:30

9 She shall give to thine head an ornament of grace: a crown of glory shall she deliver to thee.   Prov. 1:9

10 Hear, O my son, and receive my sayings; and the years of thy life shall be many. Prov. 3:2

11 I have taught thee in the way of wisdom; I have led thee in right paths.

12 When thou goest, thy steps shall not be ᵀstraitened; and when thou runnest, thou shalt not stumble.   Ps. 18:36; Prov. 3:23 ◆ hindered

13 Take fast hold of instruction; let *her* not go: keep her; for she *is* thy life.   Prov. 3:18

Stay on the Path of Wisdom

14 Enter not into the path of the wicked, and go not in the way of evil *men*.   Ps. 1:1; Prov. 1:15

15 Avoid it, pass not by it, turn from it, and pass away.

16 For they sleep not, except they have done mischief; and their sleep is taken away, unless they cause *some* to fall.   Ps. 36:4; Mic. 2:1

17 For they eat the bread of wickedness, and drink the wine of violence.

18 But the path of the just *is* as the shining light, that shineth more and more unto the perfect day.   2 Sam. 23:4; Job 11:17; Matt. 5:14

19 The way of the wicked *is* as darkness: they know not at what they stumble.   Is. 59:9-10

Stay Focused on Wisdom

20 My son, attend to my words; incline thine ear unto my sayings.   Prov. 5:1

21 Let them not depart from thine eyes; keep them in the midst of thine heart. Prov. 2:1; 3:21

22 For they *are* life unto those that find them, and health to all their flesh.   Prov. 3:8

23 Keep thy heart with all diligence; for out of it *are* the issues of life.   Luke 6:45

4:23 Issues of Life

The restoration and uplifting of humanity begins in the home. The work of parents underlies every other. Society is composed of families, and is what the heads of families make it. Out of the heart are "the issues of life" (Proverbs 4:23); and the heart of the community, of the church, and of the nation is the household. The well-being of society, the success of the church, the prosperity of the nation, depend upon home influences. *MH 349*

---

24 Put away from thee a ᵀfroward mouth, and perverse lips put far from thee.   *false, perverse*
25 Let thine eyes look right on, and let thine eyelids look straight before thee.
26 Ponder the path of thy feet, and let all thy ways be established.   Prov. 5:6
27 Turn not to the right hand nor to the left: remove thy foot from evil.   Deut. 5:32; 28:14

Avoid Adultery

5 My son, attend unto my wisdom, *and* bow thine ear to my understanding: Prov. 2:1
2 That thou mayest regard discretion, and *that* thy lips may keep knowledge.
3 For the lips of a strange woman drop *as* an honeycomb, and her mouth *is* smoother than oil: Ps. 55:21; Prov. 2:16
4 But her end is bitter as wormwood, sharp as a twoedged sword. Ps. 55:21; Eccl. 7:26; Heb. 4:12
5 Her feet go down to death; her steps take hold on hell.   Prov. 7:27
6 Lest thou shouldest ponder the path of life, her ways are moveable, *that* thou canst not know *them*.   Prov. 4:26
7 Hear me now therefore, O ye children, and depart not from the words of my mouth.
8 Remove thy way far from her, and come not nigh the door of her house:
9 Lest thou give thine honour unto others, and thy years unto the cruel:

10 Lest strangers be filled with thy wealth; and thy labours *be* in the house of a stranger;
11 And thou mourn at the last, when thy flesh and thy body are consumed,
12 And say, How have I hated instruction, and my heart despised reproof;   Prov. 1:22, 25; 12:1
13 And have not obeyed the voice of my teachers, nor inclined mine ear to them that instructed me!
14 I was almost in all evil in the midst of the congregation and assembly.
15 Drink waters out of thine own ᵀcistern, and running waters out of thine own well. *well*
16 Let thy fountains be dispersed abroad, *and* rivers of waters in the streets.   Ps. 68:26
17 Let them be only thine own, and not strangers' with thee.
18 Let thy fountain be blessed: and rejoice with the wife of thy youth.   Eccl. 9:9
19 *Let her be as* the loving hind and pleasant roe; let her breasts satisfy thee at all times; and be thou ravished always with her love.
20 And why wilt thou, my son, be ravished with a strange woman, and embrace the bosom of a stranger?   Prov. 6:24
21 For the ways of man *are* before the eyes of the Lᴏʀᴅ, and he pondereth all his goings.   Job 31:4; Hos. 7:2; Heb. 4:13
22 His own iniquities shall take the wicked himself, and he shall be ᵀholden with the cords of his sins.   Ps. 7:15-16 ◆ *held*

5:22 Evil Habits

We should beware of treating sin as a light thing. Terrible is its power over the wrongdoer. "His own iniquities shall take the wicked himself, and he shall be holden with the cords of his sins" (Proverbs 5:22). The greatest wrong done to a child or youth is to allow him to become fastened in the bondage of evil habit. *Ed 291*

---

23 He shall die without instruction; and in the greatness of his folly he shall go astray.

Sins of Adultery

Proverbs 5:3–8

Israel's sin at Beth-peor brought the judgments of God upon the nation, and though the same sins may not now be punished as speedily, they will as surely meet retribution. "If any man defile the temple of God, him shall God destroy" (1 Corinthians 3:17). Nature has affixed terrible penalties to these crimes—penalties which, sooner or later, will be inflicted upon every transgressor. It is these sins more than any other that have caused the fearful degeneracy of our race, and the weight of disease and misery with which the world is cursed. Men may succeed in concealing their transgression from their fellow men, but they will no less surely reap the result, in suffering, disease, imbecility, or death. And beyond this life stands the tribunal of the judgment, with its award of eternal penalties. "They which do such things shall not inherit the kingdom of God," but with Satan and evil angels shall have their part in that "lake of fire" which "is the second death" (Galatians 5:21; Revelation 20:14). *PP 461*

Avoid Disaster

6 My son, if thou be surety for thy friend, *if* thou hast stricken thy hand with a stranger,   Prov. 11:15

2 Thou art snared with the words of thy mouth, thou art taken with the words of thy mouth.

3 Do this now, my son, and deliver thyself, when thou art come into the hand of thy friend; go, humble thyself, and make sure thy friend.

4 Give not sleep to thine eyes, nor slumber to thine eyelids.   Ps. 132:4

5 Deliver thyself as a roe from the hand *of the hunter*, and as a bird from the hand of the ᵀfowler.   Ps. 91:3 ◆ *one who captures birds*

6 Go to the ant, thou sluggard; consider her ways, and be wise: Prov. 10:26

6:6 Lessons Through Nature

The ants teach lessons of patient industry, of perseverance in surmounting obstacles, of providence for the future. And the birds are teachers of the sweet lesson of trust. Our heavenly Father provides for them; but they must gather the food, they must build their nests and rear their young. Every moment they are exposed to enemies that seek to destroy them. Yet how cheerily they go about their work! how full of joy are their little songs! *Ed 117, 118*

---

7 Which having no guide, overseer, or ruler,
8 Provideth her meat in the summer, *and* gathereth her food in the harvest.   Prov. 10:5
9 How long wilt thou sleep, O sluggard? when wilt thou arise out of thy sleep?   Prov. 24:33-34
10 *Yet* a little sleep, a little slumber, a little folding of the hands to sleep:

11 So shall thy poverty come as one that travelleth, and thy want as an armed man.

Christian Behavior See Proverbs 19:15.

12 A naughty person, a wicked man, walketh with a ᵀfroward mouth.   Prov. 4:24 ◆ *false, perverse*
13 He winketh with his eyes, he speaketh with his feet, he teacheth with his fingers;
14 Frowardness *is* in his heart, he deviseth mischief continually; he soweth discord.
15 Therefore shall his calamity come suddenly; suddenly shall he be broken without remedy.   2 Chr. 36:16; Prov. 29:1; Jer. 19:11
16 These six *things* doth the LORD hate: yea, seven *are* an abomination unto him:
17 A proud look, a lying tongue, and hands that shed innocent blood,   Ps. 101:5; Prov. 12:22
18 An heart that deviseth wicked imaginations, feet that be swift in running to mischief,   Gen. 6:5; Prov. 1:16; Is. 59:7
19 A false witness *that* speaketh lies, and he that soweth discord among brethren. Ps. 27:12

More Advice about Avoiding Adultery

20 My son, keep thy father's commandment, and forsake not the law of thy mother: Eph. 6:1
21 Bind them continually upon thine heart, *and* tie them about thy neck.   Prov. 3:3
22 When thou goest, it shall lead thee; when thou sleepest, it shall keep thee; and *when* thou awakest, it shall talk with thee. Prov. 2:11
23 For the commandment *is* a lamp; and the law *is* light; and reproofs of instruction *are* the way of life: Ps. 19:8; 119:105
24 To keep thee from the evil woman, from the flattery of the tongue of a strange woman.   Prov. 2:16

Freedom From Sin

Proverbs 5:22

Even one wrong trait of character, one sinful desire, persistently cherished, will eventually neutralize all the power of the gospel. Every sinful indulgence strengthens the soul's aversion to God. The man who manifests an infidel hardihood, or a stolid indifference to divine truth, is but reaping the harvest of that which he has himself sown. In all the Bible there is not a more fearful warning against trifling with evil than the words of the wise man that the sinner "shall be holden with the cords of his sins" (Proverbs 5:22).

Christ is ready to set us free from sin, but He does not force the will; and if by persistent transgression the will itself is wholly bent on evil, and we do not *desire* to be set free, if we *will* not accept His grace, what more can He do? We have destroyed ourselves by our determined rejection of His love. . . .

As you see the enormity of sin, as you see yourself as you really are, do not give up to despair. It was sinners that Christ came to save. We have not to reconcile God to us, but—O wondrous love!—God in Christ is "reconciling the world unto Himself" (2 Corinthians 5:19). He is wooing by His tender love the hearts of His erring children. No earthly parent could be as patient with the faults and mistakes of his children, as is God with those He seeks to save. No one could plead more tenderly with the transgressor. No human lips ever poured out more tender entreaties to the wanderer than does He. All His promises, His warnings, are but the breathing of unutterable love. *SC 34, 35*

6:6-11

25 Lust not after her beauty in thine heart; neither let her take thee with her eyelids.
26 For by means of a whorish woman *a man is brought* to a piece of bread: and the adulteress will hunt for the precious life.   1 Sam. 2:36
27 Can a man take fire in his bosom, and his clothes not be burned?
28 Can one go upon hot coals, and his feet not be burned?
29 So he that goeth in to his neighbour's wife; whosoever toucheth her shall not be innocent.
30 *Men* do not despise a thief, if he steal to satisfy his soul when he is hungry;
31 But *if* he be found, he shall restore sevenfold; he shall give all the substance of his house.
32 *But* whoso committeth adultery with a woman lacketh understanding: he *that* doeth it destroyeth his own soul.   Prov. 7:7
33 A wound and dishonour shall he get; and his reproach shall not be wiped away.
34 For jealousy *is* the rage of a man: therefore he will not spare in the day of vengeance.   Prov. 27:4
35 He will not regard any ransom; neither will he rest content, though thou givest many gifts.

Advice about Avoiding the Adulteress

7 My son, keep my words, and lay up my commandments with thee.   Prov. 1:8
2 Keep my commandments, and live; and my law as the ᵀapple of thine eye. Deut. 32:10 ◆ *pupil*
3 Bind them upon thy fingers, write them upon the table of thine heart.   Prov. 3:3; 6:21
4 Say unto wisdom, Thou *art* my sister; and call understanding *thy* kinswoman:
5 That they may keep thee from the strange woman, from the stranger *which* flattereth with her words.   Prov. 2:16
6 For at the window of my house I looked through my ᵀcasement,   *window*
7 And beheld among the simple ones, I discerned among the youths, a young man void of understanding,   Prov. 1:4, 22; 6:32
8 Passing through the street near her corner; and he went the way to her house,
9 In the twilight, in the evening, in the black and dark night:
10 And, behold, there met him a woman *with* the attire of an harlot, and subtil of heart.   Gen. 38:14-15
11 (She *is* loud and stubborn; her feet abide not in her house: Prov. 9:13; Titus 2:5
12 Now *is she* without, now in the streets, and lieth in wait at every corner.)   Prov. 9:14; 23:28
13 So she caught him, and kissed him, *and* with an ᵀimpudent face said unto him, *stubborn*
14 *I have* peace offerings with me; this day have I payed my vows.   Lev. 7:11

15 Therefore came I forth to meet thee, diligently to seek thy face, and I have found thee.
16 I have decked my bed with coverings of tapestry, with carved *works*, with fine linen of Egypt.   Is. 19:9
17 I have perfumed my bed with myrrh, aloes, and cinnamon.   Ps. 45:8
18 Come, let us take our fill of love until the morning: let us solace ourselves with loves.
19 For the ᵀgoodman *is* not at home, he is gone a long journey: *male leader of a household*
20 He hath taken a bag of money with him, *and* will come home at the day appointed.
21 With her much fair speech she caused him to yield, with the flattering of her lips she forced him.   Ps. 12:2; Prov. 5:3
22 He goeth after her ᵀstraightway, as an ox goeth to the slaughter, or as a fool to the correction of the stocks;   *right away*
23 Till a dart strike through his liver; as a bird hasteth to the snare, and knoweth not that it *is* for his life.   Eccl. 9:12
24 Hearken unto me now therefore, O ye children, and attend to the words of my mouth.   Prov. 5:7
25 Let not thine heart decline to her ways, go not astray in her paths.   Prov. 5:8
26 For she hath cast down many wounded: yea, many strong *men* have been slain by her.   Neh. 13:26

7:26 Seduced From Integrity

The Israelites, who could not be overcome by the arms or by the enchantments of Midian, fell a prey to her harlots. Such is the power that woman, enlisted in the service of Satan, has exerted to entrap and destroy souls. . . . It was thus that the children of Seth were seduced from their integrity. . . . It was thus that Joseph was tempted. Thus Samson betrayed his strength. . . . Here David stumbled. And Solomon . . . sacrificed his integrity to the same bewitching power. *PP 457*

27 Her house *is* the way to hell, going down to the chambers of death.   Prov. 5:5; 9:18

Wisdom's Announcement

8 Doth not wisdom cry? and understanding put forth her voice?   Prov. 1:20-21
2 She standeth in the top of high places, by the way in the places of the paths.
3 She crieth at the gates, at the entry of the city, at the coming in at the doors.   Job 29:7
4 Unto you, O men, I call; and my voice *is* to the sons of man.
5 O ye simple, understand wisdom: and, ye fools, be ye of an understanding heart.
6 Hear; for I will speak of excellent things;

and the opening of my lips *shall be* right things.

7 For my mouth shall speak truth; and wickedness *is* an abomination to my lips. John 8:14

8 All the words of my mouth *are* in righteousness; *there is* nothing ᵀfroward or perverse in them.   *false, perverse*

9 They *are* all plain to him that understandeth, and right to them that find knowledge.   Prov. 14:6

10 Receive my instruction, and not silver; and knowledge rather than choice gold.   Ps. 119:72

11 For wisdom *is* better than rubies; and all the things that may be desired are not to be compared to it.   Job 28:15-19

Wisdom's Authority

12 I wisdom dwell with prudence, and find out knowledge of witty inventions.   Prov. 1:4

13 The fear of the LORD *is* to hate evil: pride, and arrogancy, and the evil way, and the froward mouth, do I hate.   1 Sam. 2:3; Ps. 97:10

14 Counsel *is* mine, and sound wisdom: I *am* understanding; I have strength. Eccl. 7:19; Is. 9:6

15 By me kings reign, and princes decree justice.   Dan. 2:21; Matt. 28:18; Rom. 13:1

16 By me princes rule, and nobles, *even* all the judges of the earth.

17 I love them that love me; and those that seek me early shall find me. 1 Sam. 2:30; James 1:5

18 Riches and honour *are* with me; *yea*, durable riches and righteousness.   Prov. 3:16

19 My fruit *is* better than gold, yea, than fine gold; and my revenue than choice silver.

20 I lead in the way of righteousness, in the midst of the paths of judgment:

21 That I may cause those that love me to inherit substance; and I will fill their treasures.

Wisdom as Creator

22 The LORD possessed me in the beginning of his way, before his works of old.   Prov. 3:19

23 I was set up from everlasting, from the beginning, or ever the earth was.   Ps. 2:6

24 When *there were* no depths, I was brought forth; when *there were* no fountains abounding with water.

25 Before the mountains were settled, before the hills was I brought forth: Ps. 90:2

26 While as yet he had not made the earth, nor the fields, nor the highest part of the dust of the world.

27 When he prepared the heavens, I *was* there: when he set a ᵀcompass upon the face of the depth: Prov. 3:19 ◆ *surround*

28 When he established the clouds above: when he strengthened the fountains of the deep:

29 When he gave to the sea his decree, that the waters should not pass his command-

ment: when he appointed the foundations of the earth: Ps. 104:9

30 Then I was by him, *as one* brought up *with him*: and I was daily *his* delight, rejoicing always before him;   John 1:1-3

31 Rejoicing in the habitable part of his earth; and my delights *were* with the sons of men.   Ps. 16:3

Wisdom as Lifegiver

32 Now therefore hearken unto me, O ye children: for blessed *are they that* keep my ways.   Ps. 119:1-2; 128:1; Luke 11:28

33 Hear instruction, and be wise, and refuse it not.   Prov. 4:1

34 Blessed *is* the man that heareth me, watching daily at my gates, waiting at the posts of my doors.   Prov. 3:13

35 For whoso findeth me findeth life, and shall obtain favour of the LORD.   Prov. 3:13-18

36 But he that sinneth against me wrongeth his own soul: all they that hate me love death.   Prov. 1:31

8:36 Reap What You Sow

God is the fountain of life; and when one chooses the service of sin, he separates from God, and thus cuts himself off from life. . . . God gives [those who are cut off] existence for a time that they may develop their character and reveal their principles. This accomplished, they receive the results of their own choice. By a life of rebellion, Satan and all who unite with him place themselves so out of harmony with God that His very presence is to them a consuming fire. The glory of Him who is love will destroy them. *DA 764*

Wisdom Hosts a Banquet

9 Wisdom hath builded her house, she hath ᵀhewn out her seven pillars: Matt. 16:18 ◆ *cut*

2 She hath killed her beasts; she hath mingled her wine; she hath also furnished her table.   Prov. 23:30

3 She hath sent forth her maidens: she crieth upon the highest places of the city,   Prov. 8:1-3

4 Whoso *is* simple, let him turn in hither: *as for* him that wanteth understanding, she saith to him,   Prov. 6:32; 8:5; 9:16

5 Come, eat of my bread, and drink of the wine *which* I have mingled.   Song 5:1

6 Forsake the foolish, and live; and go in the way of understanding.

7 He that reproveth a scorner getteth to himself shame: and he that rebuketh a wicked *man getteth* himself a blot.

8 Reprove not a scorner, lest he hate thee: rebuke a wise man, and he will love thee.

9 Give *instruction* to a wise *man*, and he will

be yet wiser: teach a just *man,* and he will increase in learning.   Prov. 1:5

10 The fear of the LORD is the beginning of wisdom: and the knowledge of the holy *is* understanding.   Job 28:28; Ps. 111:10; Prov. 1:7

9:10 True Education

The great work of life is character building, and a knowledge of God is the foundation of all true education. To impart this knowledge and to mold the character in harmony with it should be the object of the teacher's work. The law of God is a reflection of His character. . . . God has revealed Himself to us in His word and in the works of creation. Through the volume of inspiration and the book of nature we are to obtain a knowledge of God. *PP 596*

---

11 For by me thy days shall be multiplied, and the years of thy life shall be increased.

12 If thou be wise, thou shalt be wise for thyself: but *if* thou scornest, thou alone shalt bear *it.*   Job 22:2-3

Stupidity Imitates Wisdom's Banquet

13 A foolish woman *is* clamorous: *she is* simple, and knoweth nothing.   Prov. 5:6; 7:11

14 For she sitteth at the door of her house, on a seat in the high places of the city,   Prov. 9:3

15 To call passengers who go right on their ways:

16 Whoso *is* simple, let him turn in ᵀhither: and *as for* him that wanteth understanding, she saith to him,   *here*

17 Stolen waters are sweet, and bread *eaten* in secret is pleasant.   Prov. 20:17; 30:20

18 But he knoweth not that the dead *are* there; *and that* her guests *are* in the depths of hell.   Prov. 7:27

A Wise Son Is Righteous

10 The proverbs of Solomon. A wise son maketh a glad father: but a foolish son *is* the heaviness of his mother.   Prov. 1:1; 15:20

2 Treasures of wickedness profit nothing: but righteousness delivereth from death.

3 The LORD will not suffer the soul of the righteous to famish: but he casteth away the substance of the wicked.   Ps. 34:9-10

4 He becometh poor that dealeth *with* a slack hand: but the hand of the diligent maketh rich.   Prov. 12:24; 13:4; 21:5

5 He that gathereth in summer *is* a wise son: *but* he that sleepeth in harvest *is* a son that causeth shame.   Prov. 6:8

Christian Behavior See Proverbs 14:23.

---

6 Blessings *are* upon the head of the just: but violence covereth the mouth of the wicked.

7 The memory of the just *is* blessed: but the name of the wicked shall rot.   Ps. 9:5-6; 109:13

Proverbs Concerning the Mouth

8 The wise in heart will receive commandments: but a ᵀprating fool shall fall.   *gabbing*

9 He that walketh uprightly walketh surely: but he that perverteth his ways shall be known.   Ps. 23:4; Prov. 28:18; Is. 33:15-16

10 He that winketh with the eye causeth sorrow: but a prating fool shall fall.   Ps. 35:19

11 The mouth of a righteous *man is* a well of life: but violence covereth the mouth of the wicked.   Prov. 10:6; 13:14; 18:4

12 Hatred stirreth up strifes: but love covereth all sins.   Prov. 17:9; James 5:20; 1 Pet. 4:8

13 In the lips of him that hath understanding wisdom is found: but a rod *is* for the back of him that is void of understanding.   Prov. 6:32

14 Wise *men* lay up knowledge: but the mouth of the foolish *is* near destruction.

15 The rich man's wealth *is* his strong city: the destruction of the poor *is* their poverty.

16 The labour of the righteous *tendeth* to life: the fruit of the wicked to sin.

17 He *is in* the way of life that keepeth instruction: but he that refuseth reproof erreth.   Prov. 6:23

18 He that hideth hatred *with* lying lips, and he that uttereth a slander, *is* a fool.

19 In the multitude of words there wanteth not sin: but he that refraineth his lips *is* wise.   Eccl. 5:3; James 1:19; 3:2

20 The tongue of the just *is as* choice silver: the heart of the wicked *is* little worth.

21 The lips of the righteous feed many: but fools die for want of wisdom. Prov. 5:23; Hos. 4:6

22 The blessing of the LORD, it maketh rich, and he addeth no sorrow with it.   Gen. 24:35

23 *It is* as sport to a fool to do mischief: but a man of understanding hath wisdom.

Contrast of Righteous and Wicked

24 The fear of the wicked, it shall come upon him: but the desire of the righteous shall be granted. Ps. 145:19; Matt. 5:6; 1 John 5:14-15

25 As the whirlwind passeth, so *is* the wicked no *more:* but the righteous *is* an everlasting foundation.   Ps. 15:5; 58:9; Prov. 12:3

26 As vinegar to the teeth, and as smoke to the eyes, so *is* the sluggard to them that send him.

27 The fear of the LORD prolongeth days: but the years of the wicked shall be shortened.   Job 15:32-33

28 The hope of the righteous *shall be* gladness: but the expectation of the wicked shall perish.   Job 8:13; 11:20; Prov. 11:7

29 The way of the LORD *is* strength to the upright: but destruction *shall be* to the workers of iniquity.   Prov. 21:15

30 The righteous shall never be removed: but the wicked shall not inhabit the earth. Ps. 37:22

31 The mouth of the just bringeth forth wisdom: but the ᵀfroward tongue shall be cut out. Ps. 37:30; Prov. 10:13 ✦ false, perverse
32 The lips of the righteous know what is acceptable: but the mouth of the wicked *speaketh* frowardness. Eccl. 12:10

The Value of Righteousness

11 A false balance *is* abomination to the LORD: but a just weight *is* his delight. Prov. 16:11; 20:10, 23
2 *When* pride cometh, then cometh shame: but with the lowly *is* wisdom. Prov. 29:23
3 The integrity of the upright shall guide them: but the perverseness of ᵀtransgressors shall destroy them. Prov. 13:6 ✦ those who violate the law
4 Riches profit not in the day of wrath: but righteousness delivereth from death. Gen. 7:1
5 The righteousness of the perfect shall direct his way: but the wicked shall fall by his own wickedness. Prov. 5:22
6 The righteousness of the upright shall deliver them: but transgressors shall be taken in *their own* naughtiness. Eccl. 10:8
7 When a wicked man dieth, *his* expectation shall perish: and the hope of unjust *men* perisheth. Job 8:13-14; Prov. 10:28
8 The righteous is delivered out of trouble, and the wicked cometh in his stead. Prov. 21:18
9 An hypocrite with *his* mouth destroyeth his neighbour: but through knowledge shall the just be delivered.
10 When it goeth well with the righteous, the city rejoiceth: and when the wicked perish, *there is* shouting. Prov. 28:12
11 By the blessing of the upright the city is exalted: but it is overthrown by the mouth of the wicked. Prov. 29:8
12 He that is void of wisdom despiseth his neighbour: but a man of understanding holdeth his peace.
13 A talebearer revealeth secrets: but he that is of a faithful spirit concealeth the matter. Lev. 19:16; Prov. 20:19
14 Where no counsel *is*, the people fall: but in the multitude of counsellors *there is* safety. Prov. 15:22; 20:18; 24:6
15 He that is surety for a stranger shall smart *for it*: and he that hateth suretiship is sure. Prov. 17:18
16 A gracious woman retaineth honour: and strong *men* retain riches. Prov. 31:30-31
17 The merciful man doeth good to his own soul: but *he that is* cruel troubleth his own flesh. Matt. 5:7
18 The wicked worketh a deceitful work: but to him that soweth righteousness *shall be* a sure reward. Gal. 6:8-9
19 As righteousness *tendeth* to life: so he that pursueth evil *pursueth it* to his own death. Prov. 10:16

20 They that are of a ᵀfroward heart *are* abomination to the LORD: but *such as are* upright in *their* way *are* his delight. 1 Chr. 29:17 ✦ false, perverse
21 *Though* hand *join* in hand, the wicked shall not be unpunished: but the seed of the righteous shall be delivered. Prov. 16:5
22 *As* a jewel of gold in a swine's snout, *so is* a fair woman which is without discretion.
23 The desire of the righteous *is* only good: *but* the expectation of the wicked *is* wrath.
24 There is that scattereth, and yet increaseth; and *there is* that withholdeth more than is meet, but *it tendeth* to poverty. Ps. 112:9

> **11:24 Blessings Increased**
>
> The sower multiplies his seed by casting it away. So it is with those who are faithful in distributing God's gifts. By imparting they increase their blessings. *AA 345*

25 The liberal soul shall be made fat: and he that watereth shall be watered also himself. Matt. 5:7
26 He that withholdeth corn, the people shall curse him: but blessing *shall be* upon the head of him that selleth *it*. Job 29:13
27 He that diligently seeketh good ᵀprocureth favour: but he that seeketh mischief, it shall come unto him. Esth. 7:10 ✦ finds
28 He that trusteth in his riches shall fall: but the righteous shall flourish as a branch. Ps. 1:3; Jer. 17:8; 1 Tim. 6:17
29 He that troubleth his own house shall inherit the wind: and the fool *shall be* servant to the wise of heart. Eccl. 5:16
30 The fruit of the righteous *is* a tree of life; and he that winneth souls *is* wise. Prov. 3:18
31 Behold, the righteous shall be ᵀrecompensed in the earth: much more the wicked and the sinner. Jer. 25:29 ✦ repaid

Varied Observations on Virtues and Vices

12 Whoso loveth instruction loveth knowledge: but he that hateth reproof *is* ᵀbrutish. Prov. 9:7-8 ✦ dumb
2 A good *man* obtaineth favour of the LORD: but a man of wicked devices will he condemn. Prov. 8:35
3 A man shall not be established by wickedness: but the root of the righteous shall not be moved. Prov. 10:25
4 A virtuous woman *is* a crown to her husband: but she that maketh ashamed *is* as rottenness in his bones. Prov. 14:30; Hab. 3:16
5 The thoughts of the righteous *are* right: *but* the counsels of the wicked *are* deceit.
6 The words of the wicked *are* to lie in wait for blood: but the mouth of the upright shall deliver them. Prov. 14:3

7 The wicked are overthrown, and *are* not: but the house of the righteous shall stand.

8 A man shall be commended according to his wisdom: but he that is of a perverse heart shall be despised.

9 *He that is* despised, and hath a servant, *is* better than he that honoureth himself, and lacketh bread.

10 A righteous *man* regardeth the life of his beast: but the tender mercies of the wicked *are* cruel.   Deut. 25:4

11 He that tilleth his land shall be satisfied with bread: but he that followeth vain *persons is* void of understanding.   Judg. 9:4; Prov. 28:19

12 The wicked desireth the net of evil *men:* but the root of the righteous yieldeth *fruit.*

13 The wicked is snared by the ᵀtransgression of *his* lips: but the just shall come out of trouble.   2 Pet. 2:9 ◆ *sin*

14 A man shall be satisfied with good by the fruit of *his* mouth: and the recompence of a man's hands shall be rendered unto him.   Prov. 13:2; Is. 3:10-11

15 The way of a fool *is* right in his own eyes: but he that hearkeneth unto counsel *is* wise.   Prov. 3:7; 16:2, 25

16 A fool's wrath is presently known: but a prudent *man* covereth shame.   Prov. 29:11

17 *He that* speaketh truth sheweth forth righteousness: but a false witness deceit. Prov. 14:5

18 There is that speaketh like the piercings of a sword: but the tongue of the wise *is* health.   Ps. 57:4; Prov. 16:24

12:18 Harsh Words

In one moment, by the hasty, passionate, careless tongue, may be wrought evil that a whole lifetime's repentance cannot undo. Oh, the hearts that are broken, the friends estranged, the lives wrecked, by the harsh, hasty words of those who might have brought help and healing! *Ed 236, 237*

19 The lip of truth shall be established for ever: but a lying tongue *is* but for a moment.   Prov. 19:9

20 Deceit *is* in the heart of them that imagine evil: but to the counsellors of peace *is* joy.

21 There shall no evil happen to the just: but the wicked shall be filled with mischief.   Ps. 91:10

22 Lying lips *are* abomination to the LORD: but they that deal truly *are* his delight.

12:22 Lying Lips

God would have us learn also how deep is His hatred and contempt for all hypocrisy and deception. . . . Lying lips are an abomination to Him. . . . Let truth telling be held with no loose hand or uncertain grasp. Let it become a part of the life. . . .

God has clearly manifested His abhorrence of this sin; and all who give themselves up to hypocrisy and covetousness may be sure that they are destroying their own souls. *AA 75, 76*

23 A prudent man concealeth knowledge: but the heart of fools proclaimeth foolishness.   Prov. 11:13; 13:16; 15:2

24 The hand of the diligent shall bear rule: but the slothful shall be under tribute.

25 Heaviness in the heart of man maketh it stoop: but a good word maketh it glad. Is. 50:4

26 The righteous *is* more excellent than his neighbour: but the way of the wicked seduceth them.

27 The slothful *man* roasteth not that which he took in hunting: but the substance of a diligent man *is* precious.   Prov. 13:4

28 In the way of righteousness *is* life; and *in* the pathway *thereof there is* no death. 3 John 11

A Wise Son Lives Righteously

13 A wise son *heareth* his father's instruction: but a scorner heareth not rebuke.   Prov. 10:1

Abusing Animals

Proverbs 12:10

Few realize as they should the sinfulness of abusing animals or leaving them to suffer from neglect. He who created man made the lower animals also, and "His tender mercies are over all His works" (Psalm 145:9). The animals were created to serve man, but he has no right to cause them pain by harsh treatment or cruel exaction.

It is because of man's sin that "the whole creation groaneth and travaileth in pain together" (Romans 8:22). Suffering and death were thus entailed, not only upon the human race, but upon the animals. Surely, then, it becomes man to seek to lighten, instead of increasing, the weight of suffering which his transgression has brought upon God's creatures. He who will abuse animals because he has them in his power is both a coward and a tyrant. A disposition to cause pain, whether to our fellow men or to the brute creation, is satanic. Many do not realize that their cruelty will ever be known, because the poor dumb animals cannot reveal it. But could the eyes of these men be opened, as were those of Balaam, they would see an angel of God standing as a witness, to testify against them in the courts above. A record goes up to heaven, and a day is coming when judgment will be pronounced against those who abuse God's creatures. *PP 443*

2 A man shall eat good by the fruit of *his* mouth: but the soul of the transgressors *shall eat* violence.   Prov. 1:31; 12:14

3 He that keepeth his mouth keepeth his life: *but* he that openeth wide his lips shall have destruction.   Prov. 12:13; 18:7; 21:23

4 The soul of the sluggard desireth, and *hath* nothing: but the soul of the diligent shall be made fat.   Prov. 10:4

5 A righteous *man* hateth lying: but a wicked *man* is loathsome, and cometh to shame.   Prov. 3:35

6 Righteousness keepeth *him that is* upright in the way: but wickedness overthroweth the sinner.   Prov. 11:3, 5-6

7 There is that maketh himself rich, yet *hath* nothing: *there is* that maketh himself poor, yet *hath* great riches.   2 Cor. 6:10

8 The ransom of a man's life *are* his riches: but the poor heareth not rebuke.

9 The light of the righteous rejoiceth: but the lamp of the wicked shall be put out.   Prov. 4:18

10 Only by pride cometh contention: but with the well advised *is* wisdom.

11 Wealth *gotten* by vanity shall be diminished: but he that gathereth by labour shall increase.   Prov. 10:2; 20:21

12 Hope deferred maketh the heart sick: but *when* the desire cometh, *it is* a tree of life.   Prov. 3:18

13 Whoso despiseth the word shall be destroyed: but he that feareth the commandment shall be rewarded.   Num. 15:31; 2 Chr. 36:16

14 The law of the wise *is* a fountain of life, to depart from the snares of death.   Prov. 10:11

15 Good understanding giveth favour: but the way of transgressors *is* hard.   Prov. 3:4

16 Every prudent *man* dealeth with knowledge: but a fool layeth open *his* folly.   Prov. 15:2

17 A wicked messenger falleth into mischief: but a faithful ambassador *is* health.   Prov. 25:13

18 Poverty and shame *shall be to* him that refuseth instruction: but he that regardeth reproof shall be honoured.   Prov. 15:5, 31-32

19 The desire accomplished is sweet to the soul: but *it is* abomination to fools to depart from evil.   Prov. 13:12

20 He that walketh with wise *men* shall be wise: but a companion of fools shall be destroyed.   1 Kin. 12:8

21 Evil pursueth sinners: but to the righteous good shall be repayed.   Ps. 32:10

22 A good *man* leaveth an inheritance to his children's children: and the wealth of the sinner *is* laid up for the just.   Job 27:16-17

23 Much food *is* in the ᵀtillage of the poor: but there is *that is* destroyed for want of judgment.   Prov. 12:11 ◆ *plowed land*

24 He that spareth his rod hateth his son: but he that loveth him ᵀchasteneth him ᵀbetimes.   Prov. 19:18; 22:15; 29:15 ◆ *disciplines* ◆ *early*

13:23 Helping Others Help Themselves

By instruction in practical lines we can often help the poor most effectively. As a rule, those who have not been trained to work do not have habits of industry, perseverance, economy, and self-denial. They do not know how to manage. Often through lack of carefulness and right judgment there is wasted that which would maintain their families in decency and comfort if it were carefully and economically used. *MH 194, 195*

25 The righteous eateth to the satisfying of his soul: but the belly of the wicked shall want.   Ps. 34:10

Wise People Live Righteously

14 Every wise woman buildeth her house: but the foolish plucketh it down with her hands.   Ruth 4:11

2 He that walketh in his uprightness feareth the LORD: but *he that is* perverse in his ways despiseth him.   Prov. 28:6

3 In the mouth of the foolish *is* a rod of pride: but the lips of the wise shall preserve them.

4 Where no oxen *are*, the crib *is* clean: but much increase *is* by the strength of the ox.

5 A faithful witness will not lie: but a false witness will utter lies.   Ex. 23:1; Prov. 6:19; 12:17

6 A scorner seeketh wisdom, and *findeth it* not: but knowledge *is* easy unto him that understandeth.   Prov. 8:9

7 Go from the presence of a foolish man, when thou perceivest not *in him* the lips of knowledge.

8 The wisdom of the prudent *is* to understand his way: but the folly of fools *is* deceit.

9 Fools make a mock at sin: but among the righteous *there is* favour.   Prov. 10:23

10 The heart knoweth his own bitterness; and a stranger doth not intermeddle with his joy.   1 Sam. 1:10

11 The house of the wicked shall be overthrown: but the tabernacle of the upright shall flourish.   Job 8:15

12 There is a way which seemeth right unto a man, but the end thereof *are* the ways of death.   Prov. 12:15; 16:25; Rom. 6:21

14:12 Deciding Right From Wrong

In deciding upon any course of action we are not to ask whether we can see that harm will result from it, but whether it is in keeping with the will of God. *PP 634*

13 Even in laughter the heart is sorrowful; and the end of that ᵀmirth *is* heaviness. *gladness*

14 The backslider in heart shall be filled with his own ways: and a good man *shall be satisfied* from himself.   Prov. 12:14

15 The simple believeth every word: but the prudent *man* looketh well to his going.

16 A wise *man* feareth, and departeth from evil: but the fool rageth, and is confident.
17 *He that is* soon angry dealeth foolishly: and a man of wicked devices is hated.   Prov. 14:29
18 The simple inherit folly: but the prudent are crowned with knowledge.
19 The evil bow before the good; and the wicked at the gates of the righteous. Gen. 42:6
20 The poor is hated even of his own neighbour: but the rich *hath* many friends. Prov. 19:4
21 He that despiseth his neighbour sinneth: but he that hath mercy on the poor, happy *is* he.   Prov. 11:12; 19:17
22 Do they not ᵀerr that devise evil? but mercy and truth *shall be* to them that devise good.   Prov. 12:2 ◆ *stray*
23 In all labour there is profit: but the talk of the lips *tendeth* only to ᵀpenury.   *poverty*

Christian Behavior See Proverbs 23:4, 5.

24 The crown of the wise *is* their riches: *but* the foolishness of fools *is* folly.
25 A true witness delivereth souls: but a deceitful *witness* speaketh lies.   Prov. 14:5
26 In the fear of the LORD *is* strong confidence: and his children shall have a place of refuge.   Prov. 18:10
27 The fear of the LORD *is* a fountain of life, to depart from the snares of death. Prov. 13:14
28 In the multitude of people *is* the king's honour: but in the want of people *is* the destruction of the prince.
29 *He that is* slow to wrath *is* of great understanding: but *he that is* hasty of spirit exalteth folly.   Prov. 16:32; Eccl. 7:9; James 1:19
30 A sound heart *is* the life of the flesh: but envy the rottenness of the bones.   Ps. 112:10
31 He that oppresseth the poor reproacheth his Maker: but he that honoureth him hath mercy on the poor.   Prov. 17:5; 19:17; 22:2
32 The wicked is driven away in his wickedness: but the righteous hath hope in his death.   Gen. 49:18; 2 Cor. 1:9; 2 Tim. 4:18
33 Wisdom resteth in the heart of him that hath understanding: but *that which is* in the midst of fools is made known.   Prov. 12:16
34 Righteousness exalteth a nation: but sin *is* a reproach to any people.

14:34 How True Strength Is Measured

In the word of God only is this clearly set forth. Here it is shown that the strength of nations, as of individuals, is not found in the opportunities or facilities that appear to make them invincible; it is not found in their boasted greatness. It is measured by the fidelity with which they fulfill God's purpose. *Ed 175*

35 The king's favour *is* toward a wise servant: but his wrath is *against* him that causeth shame.   Prov. 22:11

Wise Ways to Live

15 A soft answer turneth away wrath: but grievous words stir up anger. Judg. 8:1-3

15:1 Silence Can Be Golden

If impatient words are spoken to you, never reply in the same spirit. Remember that "a soft answer turneth away wrath" (Proverbs 15:1). And there is wonderful power in silence. Words spoken in reply to one who is angry sometimes serve only to exasperate. But anger met with silence, in a tender, forbearing spirit, quickly dies away. *MH 486*

2 The tongue of the wise useth knowledge aright: but the mouth of fools poureth out foolishness.   Prov. 12:23; 13:16; 15:28
3 The eyes of the LORD *are* in every place, beholding the evil and the good. Jer. 16:17; Heb. 4:13
4 A wholesome tongue *is* a tree of life: but perverseness therein *is* a breach in the spirit.   Prov. 3:18
5 A fool despiseth his father's instruction: but he that regardeth reproof is prudent.
6 In the house of the righteous *is* much treasure: but in the revenues of the wicked is trouble.   Prov. 8:21
7 The lips of the wise disperse knowledge: but the heart of the foolish *doeth* not so.
8 The sacrifice of the wicked *is* an abomination to the LORD: but the prayer of the upright *is* his delight.   Prov. 15:29; 21:27; Jer. 6:20
9 The way of the wicked *is* an abomination unto the LORD: but he loveth him that followeth after righteousness. Prov. 21:21; 1 Tim. 6:11
10 Correction *is* grievous unto him that forsaketh the way: *and* he that hateth reproof shall die.   Prov. 5:12
11 Hell and destruction *are* before the LORD: how much more then the hearts of the children of men?   2 Chr. 6:30; Job 26:6; Ps. 44:21
12 A scorner loveth not one that reproveth him: neither will he go unto the wise.
13 A merry heart maketh a cheerful ᵀcountenance: but by sorrow of the heart the spirit is broken.   Prov. 12:25; 17:22; 18:14 ◆ *appearance*
14 The heart of him that hath understanding seeketh knowledge: but the mouth of fools feedeth on foolishness.
15 All the days of the afflicted *are* evil: but he that is of a merry heart *hath* a continual feast.
16 Better *is* little with the fear of the LORD than great treasure and trouble therewith.
17 Better *is* a dinner of herbs where love is, than a stalled ox and hatred therewith.
18 A wrathful man stirreth up strife: but *he that is* slow to anger appeaseth strife.
19 The way of the slothful *man is* as an hedge of thorns: but the way of the righteous *is* made plain.   Prov. 22:5

14:23

20 A wise son maketh a glad father: but a foolish man despiseth his mother.   Prov. 10:1

21 Folly *is* joy to *him that is* destitute of wisdom: but a man of understanding walketh uprightly.   Prov. 10:23

22 Without counsel purposes are disappointed: but in the multitude of counsellors they are established.   Prov. 11:14

23 A man hath joy by the answer of his mouth: and a word *spoken* in due season, how good *is it!*   Prov. 12:14

24 The way of life *is* above to the wise, that he may depart from hell beneath.   Prov. 2:18

25 The LORD will destroy the house of the proud: but he will establish the border of the widow.   Ps. 146:9

26 The thoughts of the wicked *are* an abomination to the LORD: but *the words* of the pure *are* pleasant words.

27 He that is greedy of gain troubleth his own house; but he that hateth gifts shall live.   Ex. 23:8

Christian Behavior See Proverbs 21:5.

28 The heart of the righteous studieth to answer: but the mouth of the wicked poureth out evil things.   Prov. 15:2; 1 Pet. 3:15

29 The LORD *is* far from the wicked: but he heareth the prayer of the righteous.   Prov. 15:8

30 The light of the eyes rejoiceth the heart: *and* a good report maketh the bones fat.

31 The ear that heareth the reproof of life abideth among the wise.   Prov. 15:5

32 He that refuseth instruction despiseth his own soul: but he that heareth reproof getteth understanding.

33 The fear of the LORD *is* the instruction of wisdom; and before honour *is* humility.

15:33 Humility Is Essential

The Lord can work most effectually through those who are most sensible of their own insufficiency, and who will rely upon Him as their leader and source of strength. He will make them strong by uniting their weakness to His might, and wise by connecting their ignorance with His wisdom.

If they would cherish true humility, the Lord could do much more for His people. *PP 553*

Wisdom's Blessings Come from the Lord

16 The preparations of the heart in man, and the answer of the tongue, *is* from the LORD.   Prov. 19:21

2 All the ways of a man *are* clean in his own eyes; but the LORD weigheth the spirits.

3 Commit thy works unto the LORD, and thy thoughts shall be established.   Ps. 55:22

4 The LORD hath made all *things* for himself: yea, even the wicked for the day of evil.

5 Every one *that is* proud in heart *is* an abomination to the LORD: *though* hand *join* in hand, he shall not be unpunished.   Prov. 11:21

6 By mercy and truth iniquity is purged: and by the fear of the LORD *men* depart from evil.   Job 28:28; Prov. 14:16; Dan. 4:27

7 When a man's ways please the LORD, he maketh even his enemies to be at peace with him.   Gen. 33:4

8 Better *is* a little with righteousness than great revenues without right.   Ps. 37:16

9 A man's heart deviseth his way: but the LORD directeth his steps.   Ps. 37:23; Prov. 16:1

10 A [T]divine sentence *is* in the lips of the king: his mouth [T]transgresseth not in judgment.   *determine by false magic* ♦ *sins*

11 A just weight and balance *are* the LORD's: all the weights of the bag *are* his work.

12 *It is* an abomination to kings to commit wickedness: for the throne is established by righteousness.   Prov. 25:5; 29:14

13 Righteous lips *are* the delight of kings; and they love him that speaketh right.   Prov. 14:35

14 The wrath of a king *is as* messengers of death: but a wise man will pacify it. Prov. 19:12

15 In the light of the king's [T]countenance *is* life; and his favour *is* as a cloud of the latter rain.   Job 29:23-24 ♦ *appearance*

16 How much better *is it* to get wisdom than gold! and to get understanding rather to be chosen than silver!   Prov. 8:10-11, 19

17 The highway of the upright *is* to depart from evil: he that keepeth his way preserveth his soul.   Is. 35:8

18 Pride *goeth* before destruction, and an haughty spirit before a fall.   Prov. 11:2; 18:12

19 Better *it is to be* of an humble spirit with the lowly, than to divide the [T]spoil with the proud.   Ex. 15:9 ♦ *plunder*

20 He that handleth a matter wisely shall find good: and whoso trusteth in the LORD, happy *is* he.   Ps. 2:12; 34:8; Prov. 19:8

21 The wise in heart shall be called prudent: and the sweetness of the lips increaseth learning.

22 Understanding *is* a wellspring of life unto him that hath it: but the instruction of fools *is* folly.   Prov. 10:11

23 The heart of the wise teacheth his mouth, and addeth learning to his lips.   Prov. 15:28

24 Pleasant words *are as* an honeycomb, sweet to the soul, and health to the bones.

25 There is a way that seemeth right unto a man, but the end thereof *are* the ways of death.   Prov. 14:12

26 He that laboureth laboureth for himself; for his mouth craveth it of him.   Eccl. 6:7

27 An ungodly man diggeth up evil: and in his lips *there is* as a burning fire.   James 3:6

Ignorance is no excuse for error or sin, when there is every opportunity to know the will of God. A man is traveling and comes to a place where there are several roads and a guide-board indicating where each one leads. If he disregards the guideboard, and takes which-ever road seems to him to be right, he may be ever so sincere, but will in all probability find himself on the wrong road. *GC 597, 598*

28 A froward man soweth strife: and a whis-perer separateth chief friends.   Prov. 15:18
29 A violent man enticeth his neighbour, and leadeth him into the way *that is* not good.
30 He shutteth his eyes to devise froward things: moving his lips he bringeth evil to pass.
31 The hoary head *is* a crown of glory, *if* it be found in the way of righteousness.   Prov. 20:29

And God has especially enjoined tender re-spect toward the aged. He says, "The hoary head is a crown of glory, if it be found in the way of righteousness" (Proverbs 16:31). It tells of battles fought, and victories gained; of burdens borne, and temptations resisted. It tells of weary feet nearing their rest, of places soon to be vacant. Help the children to think of this, and they will smooth the path of the aged by their courtesy and respect. . . . *Ed 244*

32 *He that is* slow to anger *is* better than the mighty; and he that ruleth his spirit than he that taketh a city.   Prov. 14:29
33 The lot is cast into the lap; but the whole disposing thereof *is* of the LORD.   Prov. 29:26

The Consequences of Being a Fool

17 Better *is* a dry morsel, and quietness therewith, than an house full of sacri-fices *with* strife.   Prov. 15:17

2 A wise servant shall have rule over a son that causeth shame, and shall have part of the inheritance among the brethren. Prov. 10:5
3 The fining pot *is* for silver, and the furnace for gold: but the LORD trieth the hearts.
4 A wicked doer giveth heed to false lips; *and* a liar giveth ear to a naughty tongue.
5 Whoso mocketh the poor reproacheth his Maker: *and* he that is glad at calamities shall not be unpunished.   Job 31:29; Prov. 14:31; 16:5
6 Children's children *are* the crown of old men; and the glory of children *are* their fa-thers.
7 Excellent speech becometh not a fool: much less do lying lips a prince.
8 A gift *is as* a precious stone in the eyes of him that hath it: whithersoever it turneth, it prospereth.   Ex. 23:8
9 He that covereth a transgression seeketh love; but he that repeateth a matter separat-eth *very* friends.   Prov. 10:12; 16:28; 1 Pet. 4:8
10 A reproof entereth more into a wise man than an hundred stripes into a fool.
11 An evil *man* seeketh only rebellion: there-fore a cruel messenger shall be sent against him.
12 Let a bear robbed of her whelps meet a man, rather than a fool in his folly. 2 Sam. 17:8
13 Whoso rewardeth evil for good, evil shall not depart from his house.   Ps. 35:12
14 The beginning of strife *is as* when one letteth out water: therefore leave off conten-tion, before it be meddled with.   Prov. 20:3; 25:8
15 He that justifieth the wicked, and he that condemneth the just, even they both *are* abomination to the LORD.   Ex. 23:7; Is. 5:23
16 Wherefore *is there* a price in the hand of a fool to get wisdom, seeing *he hath* no heart *to it?*   Prov. 23:23
17 A friend loveth at all times, and a brother is born for adversity.   Ruth 1:16; Prov. 18:24
18 A man void of understanding striketh

Power of the Mind

Proverbs 17:22

The relation that exists between the mind and the body is very intimate. When one is affected, the other sympathizes. The condition of the mind affects the health to a far greater degree than many realize. Many of the diseases from which men suffer are the result of mental depression. Grief, anxiety, discontent, remorse, guilt, distrust, all tend to break down the life forces and to in-vite decay and death.

Disease is sometimes produced, and is often greatly aggravated, by the imagination. Many are lifelong invalids who might be well if they only thought so. Many imagine that every slight exposure will cause illness, and the evil effect is produced because it is expected. Many die from disease the cause of which is wholly imaginary.

Courage, hope, faith, sympathy, love, promote health and prolong life. A contented mind, a cheerful spirit, is health to the body and strength to the soul. "A merry [rejoicing] heart doeth good like a medicine" (Proverbs 17:22).

In the treatment of the sick the effect of mental influence should not be overlooked. Rightly used, this influence affords one of the most effective agencies for combating disease. *MH 241*

hands, *and* becometh surety in the presence of his friend. Prov. 6:1-5; 11:15

19 He loveth ᵀtransgression that loveth strife: *and* he that exalteth his gate seeketh destruction. Prov. 16:18 ♦ *sin*

20 He that hath a ᵀfroward heart findeth no good: and he that hath a perverse tongue falleth into mischief. *false, perverse*

21 He that begetteth a fool *doeth it* to his sorrow: and the father of a fool hath no joy.

22 A merry heart doeth good *like* a medicine: but a broken spirit drieth the bones. Ps. 22:15

17:22 Positive Attitude

Gratitude, rejoicing, benevolence, trust in God's love and care—these are health's greatest safeguard. To the Israelites they were to be the very keynote of life. *MH 281*

23 A wicked *man* taketh a gift out of the bosom to pervert the ways of judgment.

24 Wisdom *is* before him that hath understanding; but the eyes of a fool *are* in the ends of the earth. Prov. 14:6; 15:14; Eccl. 2:14

25 A foolish son *is* a grief to his father, and bitterness to her that bare him. Prov. 10:1; 19:13

26 Also to punish the just *is* not good, *nor* to strike princes for ᵀequity. Prov. 17:15 ♦ *uprightness*

27 He that hath knowledge spareth his words: *and* a man of understanding is of an excellent spirit. Prov. 10:19; James 1:19

28 Even a fool, when he holdeth his peace, is counted wise: *and* he that shutteth his lips *is esteemed* a man of understanding. Job 13:5

How Fools Live

18 Through desire a man, having separated himself, seeketh *and* intermeddleth with all wisdom. Jude 19

2 A fool hath no delight in understanding, but that his heart may discover itself.

3 When the wicked cometh, *then* cometh also contempt, and with ᵀignominy reproach. *shame*

4 The words of a man's mouth *are as* deep waters, *and* the wellspring of wisdom *as* a flowing brook. Prov. 20:5

5 *It is* not good to accept the person of the wicked, to overthrow the righteous in judgment. Lev. 19:15; Prov. 24:23; 28:21

6 A fool's lips enter into contention, and his mouth calleth for strokes.

7 A fool's mouth *is* his destruction, and his lips *are* the snare of his soul. Prov. 10:14; 12:13; 13:3

8 The words of a talebearer *are* as wounds, and they go down into the innermost parts of the belly. Prov. 16:28

9 He also that is slothful in his work is brother to him that is a great waster. Prov. 10:4; 28:24

10 The name of the LORD *is* a strong tower: the righteous runneth into it, and is safe.

18:10 The Lord Our Refuge

We cannot save ourselves from the tempter's power; he has conquered humanity, and when we try to stand in our own strength, we shall become a prey to his devices; but "the name of the Lord is a strong tower: the righteous runneth into it, and is safe" (Proverbs 18:10). Satan trembles and flees before the weakest soul who finds refuge in that mighty name. *DA 131*

11 The rich man's wealth *is* his strong city, and as an high wall in his own conceit.

12 Before destruction the heart of man is haughty, and before honour *is* humility.

13 He that answereth a matter before he heareth *it*, it *is* folly and shame unto him.

14 The spirit of a man will sustain his infirmity; but a wounded spirit who can bear?

15 The heart of the prudent getteth knowledge; and the ear of the wise seeketh knowledge. Prov. 15:14

16 A man's gift maketh room for him, and bringeth him before great men. Gen. 32:20

17 *He that is* first in his own cause *seemeth* just; but his neighbour cometh and searcheth him.

18 The lot causeth contentions to cease, and parteth between the mighty. Prov. 16:33

19 A brother offended *is harder to be won* than a strong city: and *their* contentions *are* like the bars of a castle.

20 A man's belly shall be satisfied with the fruit of his mouth; *and* with the increase of his lips shall he be filled.

21 Death and life *are* in the power of the tongue: and they that love it shall eat the fruit thereof.

18:21 The Terrible Tongue

We think with horror of the cannibal who feasts on the still warm and trembling flesh of his victim; but are the results of even this practice more terrible than are the agony and ruin caused by misrepresenting motive, blackening reputation, dissecting character? Let the children, and the youth as well, learn what God says about these things: "Death and life are in the power of the tongue" (Proverbs 18:21). *Ed 235*

22 *Whoso* findeth a wife findeth a good *thing*, and obtaineth favour of the LORD. Prov. 8:35

23 The poor useth ᵀintreaties; but the rich answereth roughly. James 2:3 ♦ *pleas*

24 A man *that hath* friends must shew himself friendly: and there is a friend *that* sticketh closer than a brother. Prov. 17:17

How to Avoid Fools and Foolishness

19 Better *is* the poor that walketh in his integrity, than *he that is* perverse in his lips, and is a fool. Prov. 28:6

18:22 Finding Your Life Partner

Let those who are contemplating marriage weigh every sentiment and watch every development of character in the one with whom they think to unite their life destiny. Let every step toward a marriage alliance be characterized by modesty, simplicity, sincerity, and an earnest purpose to please and honor God. Marriage affects the afterlife both in this world and in the world to come. A sincere Christian will make no plans that God cannot approve. *MH 359*

2 Also, *that* the soul *be* without knowledge, *it is* not good; and he that hasteth with *his* feet sinneth.   Prov. 21:5
3 The foolishness of man perverteth his way: and his heart ᵀfretteth against the LORD.   Ps. 37:7 ◆ *worries*
4 Wealth maketh many friends; but the poor is separated from his neighbour.   Prov. 14:20
5 A false witness shall not be unpunished, and *he that* speaketh lies shall not escape.

19:5 Nothing but the Truth

Truth is of God; deception in all its myriad forms is of Satan, and whoever in any way departs from the straight line of truth is betraying himself into the power of the wicked one. *PK 252*

6 Many will ᵀintreat the favour of the prince: and every man *is* a friend to him that giveth gifts.   Prov. 17:8 ◆ *plead with*
7 All the brethren of the poor do hate him: how much more do his friends go far from him? he pursueth *them with* words, *yet* they *are* wanting *to him*.   Ps. 38:11; Prov. 18:23; 19:4
8 He that getteth wisdom loveth his own soul: he that keepeth understanding shall find good.   Prov. 16:20
9 A false witness shall not be unpunished, and *he that* speaketh lies shall perish. Prov. 19:5
10 Delight is not seemly for a fool; much less for a servant to have rule over princes.
11 The discretion of a man deferreth his anger; and *it is* his glory to pass over a ᵀtransgression.   Prov. 14:29; 15:18; 16:32 ◆ *violation of a law*
12 The king's wrath *is* as the roaring of a lion; but his favour *is* as dew upon the grass.   Prov. 16:14-15
13 A foolish son *is* the calamity of his father: and the contentions of a wife *are* a continual dropping.   Prov. 10:1; 21:9; 27:15
14 House and riches *are* the inheritance of fathers: and a prudent wife *is* from the LORD.   Prov. 18:22; 2 Cor. 12:14
15 Slothfulness casteth into a deep sleep; and an idle soul shall suffer hunger.   Prov. 6:9-10

Christian Behavior See Proverbs 24:30–34.

16 He that keepeth the commandment keepeth his own soul; *but* he that despiseth his ways shall die.   Prov. 13:13; 16:17; Luke 10:28
17 He that hath pity upon the poor lendeth unto the LORD; and that which he hath given will he pay him again.   Prov. 28:27; Eccl. 11:1
18 Chasten thy son while there is hope, and let not thy soul spare for his crying. Prov. 13:24
19 A man of great wrath shall suffer punishment: for if thou deliver *him*, yet thou must do it again.
20 Hear counsel, and receive instruction, that thou mayest be wise in thy latter end.
21 *There are* many devices in a man's heart; nevertheless the counsel of the LORD, that shall stand.   Ps. 33:10-11
22 The desire of a man *is* his kindness: and a poor man *is* better than a liar.
23 The fear of the LORD *tendeth* to life: and *he that hath it* shall abide satisfied; he shall not be visited with evil.   Prov. 12:21
24 A slothful *man* hideth his hand in *his* bosom, and will not so much as bring it to his mouth again.   Prov. 15:19
25 Smite a scorner, and the simple will beware: and reprove one that hath understanding, *and* he will understand knowledge.
26 He that wasteth *his* father, *and* chaseth away *his* mother, *is* a son that causeth shame, and bringeth reproach.   Prov. 10:5
27 Cease, my son, to hear the instruction *that causeth* to err from the words of knowledge.
28 An ungodly witness scorneth judgment: and the mouth of the wicked devoureth iniquity.   Job 15:16; 20:12-13; 34:7
29 Judgments are prepared for scorners, and stripes for the back of fools. Prov. 9:12; 10:13; 26:3

20:1 Evils of Alcohol

Oh, how often has the life of the innocent been sacrificed through the intemperance of those who should have been guardians of justice! He who puts the intoxicating cup to his lips makes himself responsible for all the injustice he may commit under its besotting power. By benumbing his senses he makes it impossible for him to judge calmly or to have a clear perception of right and wrong. He opens the way for Satan to work through him in oppressing and destroying the innocent. *DA 222*

Foolproof Instructions

20 Wine *is* a mocker, strong drink *is* raging: and whosoever is deceived thereby is not wise.   Prov. 31:4; Is. 28:7; Hos. 4:11

Health See Proverbs 23:29–32.

2 The fear of a king *is* as the roaring of a lion: *whoso* provoketh him to anger sinneth *against* his own soul.   1 Kin. 2:23; Prov. 8:36; 19:12

3 *It is* an honour for a man to cease from strife: but every fool will be meddling.

4 The sluggard will not plow by reason of the cold; *therefore* shall he beg in harvest, and *have* nothing.   Prov. 10:4; 19:15, 24

5 Counsel in the heart of man *is like* deep water; but a man of understanding will draw it out.   Prov. 18:4

6 Most men will proclaim every one his own goodness: but a faithful man who can find?   Ps. 12:1; Prov. 25:14; Luke 18:8

7 The just *man* walketh in his integrity: his children *are* blessed after him.   Ps. 37:26; 112:2

8 A king that sitteth in the throne of judgment scattereth away all evil with his eyes.

9 Who can say, I have made my heart clean, I am pure from my sin?   1 Kin. 8:46; 2 Chr. 6:36

10 Divers weights, *and* ᵀdivers measures, both of them *are* alike abomination to the LORD.   Prov. 11:1; 20:23 ♦ *various*

11 Even a child is known by his doings, whether his work *be* pure, and whether *it be* right.   Matt. 7:16

12 The hearing ear, and the seeing eye, the LORD hath made even both of them.   Ex. 4:11

13 Love not sleep, lest thou come to poverty; open thine eyes, *and* thou shalt be satisfied with bread.   Prov. 6:9-11; 12:11; 19:15

14 *It is* ᵀnaught, *it is* naught, saith the buyer: but when he is gone his way, then he boasteth.   *nothing*

15 There is gold, and a multitude of rubies: but the lips of knowledge *are* a precious jewel.   Prov. 3:15

16 Take his garment that is surety *for* a stranger: and take a pledge of him for a strange woman.   Prov. 27:13

17 Bread of deceit *is* sweet to a man; but afterwards his mouth shall be filled with gravel.

18 *Every* purpose is established by counsel: and with good advice make war. Prov. 15:22; 24:6

19 He that goeth about *as* a talebearer revealeth secrets: therefore meddle not with him that flattereth with his lips.   Prov. 11:13

20 Whoso curseth his father or his mother, his lamp shall be put out in obscure darkness.   Ex. 21:17; Lev. 20:9; Prov. 30:11

21 An inheritance *may be* gotten hastily at the beginning; but the end thereof shall not be blessed.

22 Say not thou, I will ᵀrecompense evil; *but* wait on the LORD, and he shall save thee. *repay*

23 Divers weights *are* an abomination unto the LORD; and a false balance *is* not good.

24 Man's goings *are* of the LORD; how can a man then understand his own way? Prov. 16:9

25 *It is* a snare to the man *who* devoureth *that which is* holy, and after vows to make enquiry.

26 A wise king scattereth the wicked, and bringeth the wheel over them.   Prov. 20:8

27 The spirit of man *is* the candle of the LORD, searching all the inward parts of the belly.   1 Cor. 2:11

28 Mercy and truth preserve the king: and his throne is upholden by mercy.   Prov. 29:14

29 The glory of young men *is* their strength: and the beauty of old men *is* the gray head.   Prov. 16:31

30 The blueness of a wound cleanseth away evil: so *do* stripes the inward parts of the belly.   Prov. 22:15

The Lord Controls Wise and Foolish People

21 The king's heart *is* in the hand of the LORD, *as* the rivers of water: he turneth it whithersoever he will.

2 Every way of a man *is* right in his own eyes: but the LORD pondereth the hearts.   Prov. 16:2

3 To do justice and judgment *is* more acceptable to the LORD than sacrifice.   1 Sam. 15:22

4 An high look, and a proud heart, *and* the plowing of the wicked, *is* sin.   Prov. 6:17

5 The thoughts of the diligent *tend* only to plenteousness; but of every one *that is* hasty only to want.   Prov. 10:4; 13:4; 28:22

Christian Behavior

6 The getting of treasures by a lying tongue *is* a vanity tossed to and fro of them that seek death.   Prov. 8:36

7 The robbery of the wicked shall destroy them; because they refuse to do judgment.

8 The way of man *is* froward and strange: but *as for* the pure, his work *is* right.   Prov. 2:15

9 *It is* better to dwell in a corner of the housetop, than with a brawling woman in a wide house.   Prov. 21:19

10 The soul of the wicked desireth evil: his neighbour findeth no favour in his eyes.

11 When the scorner is punished, the simple is made wise: and when the wise is instructed, he receiveth knowledge. Prov. 19:25

12 The righteous *man* wisely considereth the house of the wicked: *but God* overthroweth the wicked for *their* wickedness.   Ps. 37:35-36

13 Whoso stoppeth his ears at the cry of the poor, he also shall cry himself, but shall not be heard.

14 A gift in secret pacifieth anger: and a reward in the bosom strong wrath. Prov. 17:8; 19:6

15 *It is* joy to the just to do judgment: but destruction *shall be* to the workers of iniquity.   Prov. 10:29

16 The man that wandereth out of the way of understanding shall remain in the congregation of the dead.   Ps. 49:14

17 He that loveth pleasure *shall be* a poor

man: he that loveth wine and oil shall not be rich. Prov. 23:21

18 The wicked *shall be* a ransom for the righteous, and the ᵀtransgressor for the upright. Prov. 11:8 ◆ one who violates the law

19 *It is* better to dwell in the wilderness, than with a ᵀcontentious and an angry woman. Prov. 21:9 ◆ enjoying quarrels

20 *There is* treasure to be desired and oil in the dwelling of the wise; but a foolish man spendeth it up. Ps. 112:3

21 He that followeth after righteousness and mercy findeth life, righteousness, and honour. Prov. 15:9; Matt. 5:6; 1 Cor. 15:58

22 A wise *man* scaleth the city of the mighty, and casteth down the strength of the confidence thereof. Eccl. 7:19

23 Whoso keepeth his mouth and his tongue keepeth his soul from troubles. Prov. 12:13; 13:3

24 Proud *and* haughty scorner *is* his name, who dealeth in proud wrath. Ps. 1:1

25 The desire of the slothful killeth him; for his hands refuse to labour. Prov. 13:4

26 He ᵀcoveteth greedily all the day long: but the righteous giveth and spareth not. desires

27 The sacrifice of the wicked *is* abomination: how much more, *when* he bringeth it with a wicked mind? Prov. 15:8; Is. 66:3; Jer. 6:20

21:27 Refusing God's Grace

It is not because He is unwilling to forgive that He turns from the transgressor; it is because the sinner refuses to make use of the abundant provisions of grace, that God is unable to deliver from sin. *PK 323*

28 A false witness shall perish: but the man that heareth speaketh constantly. Prov. 19:5, 9

29 A wicked man hardeneth his face: but *as for* the upright, he directeth his way. Prov. 11:5

30 *There is* no wisdom nor understanding nor counsel against the LORD. Jer. 9:23

31 The horse *is* prepared against the day of battle: but safety *is* of the LORD. Ps. 3:8; 20:7

Wisdom Regarding Work and Being a Neighbor

22 A *good* name *is* rather to be chosen than great riches, *and* loving favour rather than silver and gold. Eccl. 7:1

2 The rich and poor meet together: the LORD *is* the maker of them all. Job 31:15; Prov. 14:31

22:2 Equality With God

Caste is hateful to God. He ignores everything of this character. In His sight the souls of all men are of equal value. . . . Without distinction of age, or rank, or nationality, or religious privilege, all are invited to come unto Him and live. *DA 403*

3 A prudent *man* foreseeth the evil, and hideth himself: but the simple pass on, and are punished. Prov. 14:16; 27:12

4 By humility *and* the fear of the LORD *are* riches, and honour, and life. Prov. 21:21

5 Thorns *and* snares *are* in the way of the ᵀfroward: he that doth keep his soul shall be far from them. Prov. 15:19; 1 John 5:18 ◆ false, perverse

6 Train up a child in the way he should go: and when he is old, he will not depart from it. Eph. 6:4; 2 Tim. 3:15

22:6

Marriage See Ephesians 6:1–4.

7 The rich ruleth over the poor, and the borrower *is* servant to the lender. James 2:6

8 He that soweth iniquity shall reap vanity: and the rod of his anger shall fail. Job 4:8

9 He that hath a bountiful eye shall be blessed; for he giveth of his bread to the poor. Prov. 19:17; Heb. 13:16

10 Cast out the scorner, and contention shall go out; yea, strife and reproach shall cease. Gen. 21:9-10

11 He that loveth pureness of heart, *for* the grace of his lips the king *shall be* his friend. Ps. 101:6; Prov. 16:13; Matt. 5:8

22:11 Character Development

It is not by arbitrary law or rule that the graces of character are developed. It is by dwelling in the atmosphere of the pure, the noble, the true. And wherever there is purity of heart and nobleness of character, it will be revealed in purity and nobleness of action and of speech. *Ed 237*

12 The eyes of the LORD preserve knowledge, and he overthroweth the words of the ᵀtransgressor. one who violates the law

13 The slothful *man* saith, There is a lion without, I shall be slain in the streets.

14 The mouth of strange women *is* a deep pit: he that is ᵀabhorred of the LORD shall fall therein. Prov. 23:27; Eccl. 7:26 ◆ despised

15 Foolishness *is* bound in the heart of a child; *but* the rod of correction shall drive it far from him. Prov. 13:24; 19:18; 23:13-14

16 He that oppresseth the poor to increase his *riches, and* he that giveth to the rich, *shall* surely *come* to want. James 2:13

17 Bow down thine ear, and hear the words of the wise, and apply thine heart unto my knowledge. Prov. 23:12

18 For *it is* a pleasant thing if thou keep them within thee; they shall ᵀwithal be fitted in thy lips. Prov. 2:10 ◆ together with

19 That thy trust may be in the LORD, I have made known to thee this day, even to thee. Prov. 3:5

20 Have not I written to thee excellent things in counsels and knowledge, Prov. 8:6

21 That I might make thee know the certainty of the words of truth; that thou mightest answer the words of truth to them that send unto thee? Luke 1:3-4; 1 Pet. 3:15

22 Rob not the poor, because he *is* poor: neither oppress the afflicted in the gate: Ex. 23:6

23 For the LORD will plead their cause, and spoil the soul of those that spoiled them.

24 Make no friendship with an angry man; and with a furious man thou shalt not go:

25 Lest thou learn his ways, and get a snare to thy soul. 1 Cor. 15:33

26 Be not thou *one* of them that strike hands, *or* of them that are sureties for debts. Prov. 11:15

27 If thou hast nothing to pay, why should he take away thy bed from under thee? Prov. 20:16

28 Remove not the ancient landmark, which thy fathers have set. Deut. 19:14; 27:17; Prov. 23:10

29 Seest thou a man diligent in his business? he shall stand before kings; he shall not stand before mean *men*. Gen. 41:46

Live a Disciplined Life

23 When thou sittest to eat with a ruler, consider diligently what *is* before thee:

2 And put a knife to thy throat, if thou *be* a man given to appetite.

3 Be not desirous of his dainties: for they *are* deceitful meat. Ps. 141:4; Prov. 23:6; Dan. 1:8

4 Labour not to be rich: cease from thine own wisdom. Prov. 3:5; 26:12; 28:20

5 Wilt thou set thine eyes upon that which is not? for *riches* certainly make themselves wings; they fly away as an eagle toward heaven. Prov. 27:24; 1 Tim. 6:17

> Christian Behavior See 2 Corinthians 6:14.

6 Eat thou not the bread of *him that hath* an evil eye, neither desire thou his dainty meats: Deut. 15:9; Ps. 141:4; Prov. 23:3

7 For as he thinketh in his heart, so *is* he: Eat and drink, saith he to thee; but his heart *is* not with thee. Ps. 12:2

8 The morsel *which* thou hast eaten shalt thou vomit up, and lose thy sweet words.

9 Speak not in the ears of a fool: for he will despise the wisdom of thy words. Matt. 7:6

10 Remove not the old landmark; and enter not into the fields of the fatherless: Prov. 22:28

11 For their redeemer *is* mighty; he shall plead their cause with thee. Job 19:25; Prov. 22:23

12 Apply thine heart unto instruction, and thine ears to the words of knowledge.

13 Withhold not correction from the child: for *if* thou beatest him with the rod, he shall not die. Prov. 13:24; 19:18; 29:15

14 Thou shalt beat him with the rod, and shalt deliver his soul from hell. 1 Cor. 5:5

15 My son, if thine heart be wise, my heart shall rejoice, even mine. Prov. 29:3

16 Yea, my ᵀreins shall rejoice, when thy lips speak right things. Prov. 8:6 ◆ inmost being

17 Let not thine heart envy sinners: but *be thou* in the fear of the LORD all the day long. Prov. 24:1; 28:14

18 For surely there is an end; and thine expectation shall not be cut off. Ps. 9:18; Prov. 24:14

19 Hear thou, my son, and be wise, and guide thine heart in the way.

20 Be not among winebibbers; among riotous eaters of flesh: Is. 5:22; Rom. 13:13; Eph. 5:18

21 For the drunkard and the glutton shall come to poverty: and drowsiness shall clothe *a man* with rags. Prov. 21:17

22 Hearken unto thy father that ᵀbegat thee, and despise not thy mother when she is old. Prov. 1:8; 30:17; Eph. 6:1-2 ◆ brought forth

23 Buy the truth, and sell *it* not; *also* wisdom, and instruction, and understanding. Matt. 13:44

24 The father of the righteous shall greatly rejoice: and he that ᵀbegetteth a wise *child* shall have joy of him. Prov. 10:1 ◆ brings forth

25 Thy father and thy mother shall be glad, and she that bare thee shall rejoice. Prov. 17:25

26 My son, give me thine heart, and let thine eyes observe my ways.

27 For a ᵀwhore *is* a deep ditch; and a strange woman *is* a narrow pit. Prov. 22:14 ◆ prostitute

28 She also lieth in wait as *for* a prey, and increaseth the transgressors among men.

29 Who hath woe? who hath sorrow? who hath contentions? who hath babbling? who hath wounds without cause? who hath redness of eyes? Gen. 49:12

30 They that tarry long at the wine; they that go to seek mixed wine. Ps. 75:8; Is. 5:11; Eph. 5:18

31 Look not thou upon the wine when it is red, when it giveth his colour in the cup, *when* it moveth itself aright.

32 At the last it biteth like a serpent, and stingeth like an ᵀadder. venomous snake

> Health See 1 Corinthians 6:9, 10.

33 Thine eyes shall behold strange women, and thine heart shall utter perverse things.

34 Yea, thou shalt be as he that lieth down in the midst of the sea, or as he that lieth upon the top of a mast.

35 They have stricken me, *shalt thou say, and* I was not sick; they have beaten me, *and* I felt *it* not: when shall I awake? I will seek it yet again. Is. 56:12

23:29–35 The Curse of Alcohol

No argument is needed to show the evil effects of intoxicants on the drunkard. The bleared, besotted wrecks of humanity—souls for whom Christ died, and over whom angels weep—are everywhere. They are a blot on our boasted civilization. They are the shame and curse and peril of every land. *MH 331*

23:4, 5

23:29-32

Fear the Lord

24 Be not thou envious against evil men, neither desire to be with them. Ps. 37:1
2 For their heart studieth destruction, and their lips talk of mischief.   Job 15:35; Ps. 10:7
3 Through wisdom is an house builded; and by understanding it is established: Prov. 9:1; 14:1
4 And by knowledge shall the chambers be filled with all precious and pleasant riches.
5 A wise man *is* strong; yea, a man of knowledge increaseth strength.   Prov. 21:22
6 For by wise counsel thou shalt make thy war: and in multitude of counsellors *there is* safety.   Prov. 11:14; 20:18; Luke 14:31
7 Wisdom *is* too high for a fool: he openeth not his mouth in the gate.   Prov. 14:6
8 He that deviseth to do evil shall be called a mischievous person.   Rom. 1:30
9 The thought of foolishness *is* sin: and the scorner *is* an abomination to men.   Matt. 15:19
10 *If* thou faint in the day of adversity, thy strength *is* small.   Job 4:5
11 If thou ᵀforbear to deliver *them that are* drawn unto death, and *those that are* ready to be slain;   Ps. 82:4; Is. 58:6-7 ◆ *refuse to act*
12 If thou sayest, Behold, we knew it not; doth not he that pondereth the heart consider *it?* and he that keepeth thy soul, doth *not* he know *it?* and shall *not* he render to *every* man according to his works?   1 Sam. 16:7; Job 34:11

24:11, 12 Living for Self

In the great Judgment day, those who have not worked for Christ, who have drifted along thinking of themselves, caring for themselves, will be placed by the Judge of the whole earth with those who did evil. They receive the same condemnation. *DA 641*

13 My son, eat thou honey, because *it is* good; and the honeycomb, *which is* sweet to thy taste: Song 5:1
14 So *shall* the knowledge of wisdom *be* unto thy soul: when thou hast found *it*, then there shall be a reward, and thy expectation shall not be cut off.   Ps. 119:103; Prov. 2:10; 23:18
15 Lay not wait, O wicked *man*, against the dwelling of the righteous; ᵀspoil not his resting place: *plunder*
16 For a just *man* falleth seven times, and riseth up again: but the wicked shall fall into mischief.   Job 5:19; Ps. 34:19; 37:24
17 Rejoice not when thine enemy falleth, and let not thine heart be glad when he stumbleth: Job 31:29
18 Lest the Lord see *it*, and it displease him, and he turn away his wrath from him.
19 Fret not thyself because of evil *men*, neither be thou envious at the wicked;   Ps. 37:1
20 For there shall be no reward to the evil man; the candle of the wicked shall be put out.   Job 18:5-6; 21:17; Prov. 13:9

24:17, 18 Enemies Need the Bread of Life

The whole earthly life of Jesus was a manifestation of this principle. It was to bring the bread of life to His enemies that our Saviour left His home in heaven. Though calumny and persecution were heaped upon Him from the cradle to the grave, they called forth from Him only the expression of forgiving love. *MB 71*

21 My son, fear thou the Lord and the king: *and* meddle not with them that are given to change: Rom. 13:1-7
22 For their calamity shall rise suddenly; and who knoweth the ruin of them both?
23 These *things* also *belong* to the wise. *It is* not good to have respect of persons in judgment.   Prov. 18:5
24 He that saith unto the wicked, Thou *art* righteous; him shall the people curse, nations shall ᵀabhor him: Prov. 11:26; 17:15; Is. 5:23 ◆ *despise*
25 But to them that rebuke *him* shall be delight, and a good blessing shall come upon them.   Prov. 28:23
26 *Every man* shall kiss *his* lips that giveth a right answer.
27 Prepare thy work without, and make it fit for thyself in the field; and afterwards build thine house.
28 Be not a witness against thy neighbour without cause; and deceive *not* with thy lips.   Eph. 4:25
29 Say not, I will do so to him as he hath done to me: I will render to the man according to his work.   Prov. 20:22
30 I went by the field of the slothful, and by the vineyard of the man void of understanding;
31 And, lo, it was all grown over with thorns, *and* nettles had covered the face thereof, and the stone wall thereof was broken down.
32 Then I saw, *and* considered *it* well: I looked upon *it, and* received instruction.
33 *Yet* a little sleep, a little slumber, a little folding of the hands to sleep:
34 So shall thy poverty come *as* one that travelleth; and thy want as an armed man.

24:30-34

Christian Behavior See Proverbs 1:19.

Advice for Kings

25 These *are* also proverbs of Solomon, which the men of Hezekiah king of Judah copied out.   1 Kin. 4:32; Prov. 1:1
2 *It is* the glory of God to conceal a thing: but the honour of kings *is* to search out a matter.   Deut. 29:29
3 The heaven for height, and the earth for

depth, and the heart of kings *is* unsearchable.

4 Take away the dross from the silver, and there shall come forth a vessel for the finer.

5 Take away the wicked *from* before the king, and his throne shall be established in righteousness.   Prov. 16:12; 20:8; 29:14

6 Put not forth thyself in the presence of the king, and stand not in the place of great *men*:

7 For better *it is* that it be said unto thee, Come up ᵀhither; than that thou shouldest be put lower in the presence of the prince whom thine eyes have seen.   *here*

8 Go not forth hastily to strive, lest *thou know not* what to do in the end thereof, when thy neighbour hath put thee to shame. Prov. 17:14

9 Debate thy cause with thy neighbour *himself*; and discover not a secret to another: Prov. 11:13

10 Lest he that heareth *it* put thee to shame, and thine ᵀinfamy turn not away. *evil report about*

11 A word fitly spoken *is like* apples of gold in pictures of silver.   Prov. 15:23; Is. 50:4

12 *As* an earring of gold, and an ornament of fine gold, *so is* a wise reprover upon an obedient ear.   Ps. 141:5

13 As the cold of snow in the time of harvest, *so is* a faithful messenger to them that send him: for he refresheth the soul of his masters.   Prov. 13:17

14 Whoso boasteth himself of a false gift *is like* clouds and wind without rain. Prov. 20:6

15 By long forbearing is a prince persuaded, and a soft tongue breaketh the bone.Prov. 15:1

16 Hast thou found honey? eat so much as is sufficient for thee, lest thou be filled therewith, and vomit it.   Prov. 25:27

17 Withdraw thy foot from thy neighbour's house; lest he be weary of thee, and *so* hate thee.

18 A man that beareth false witness against his neighbour *is* a ᵀmaul, and a sword, and a sharp arrow.   Ps. 57:4; Prov. 12:18; Jer. 9:8 ◆ *mallet*

19 Confidence in an unfaithful man in time of trouble *is like* a broken tooth, and a foot out of joint.   Is. 36:6

20 *As* he that taketh away a garment in cold weather, *and as* vinegar upon nitre, so *is* he that singeth songs to an heavy heart. Rom. 12:15

21 If thine enemy be hungry, give him bread to eat; and if he be thirsty, give him water to drink: Ex. 23:4-5

22 For thou shalt heap coals of fire upon his head, and the LORD shall reward thee.

23 The north wind driveth away rain: so *doth* an angry ᵀcountenance a ᵀbackbiting tongue.   Ps. 101:5 ◆ *appearance* ◆ *slandering*

24 *It is* better to dwell in the corner of the housetop, than with a brawling woman and in a wide house.   Prov. 21:9

25 *As* cold waters to a thirsty soul, so *is* good news from a far country.   Prov. 15:30

26 A righteous man falling down before the wicked *is as* a troubled fountain, and a corrupt spring.

27 *It is* not good to eat much honey: so *for men* to search their own glory *is not* glory. Prov. 27:2

28 He that *hath* no rule over his own spirit *is like* a city *that is* broken down, *and* without walls.   Prov. 16:32

25:28 Lifetime Effect of One Moment

In one moment, by the hasty, passionate, careless tongue, may be wrought evil that a whole lifetime's repentance cannot undo. Oh, the hearts that are broken, the friends estranged, the lives wrecked, by the harsh, hasty words of those who might have brought help and healing! *Ed 236, 237*

Observations about Fools

26 As snow in summer, and as rain in harvest, so honour is not seemly for a fool.

2 As the bird by wandering, as the swallow by flying, so the curse causeless shall not come.   Num. 23:8; 2 Sam. 16:12

3 A whip for the horse, a bridle for the ass, and a rod for the fool's back.Ps. 32:9; Prov. 10:13

4 Answer not a fool according to his folly, lest thou also be like unto him.

5 Answer a fool according to his folly, lest he be wise in his own conceit.   Prov. 28:11

6 He that sendeth a message by the hand of a fool cutteth off the feet, *and* drinketh damage.   Prov. 10:26

7 The legs of the lame are not equal: so *is* a parable in the mouth of fools.   Prov. 26:9

8 As he that bindeth a stone in a sling, so *is* he that giveth honour to a fool.   Prov. 26:1

9 *As* a thorn goeth up into the hand of a drunkard, so *is* a parable in the mouth of fools.   Prov. 23:35

10 The great *God* that formed all *things* both rewardeth the fool, and rewardeth ᵀtransgressors.   *those who violate the law*

11 As a dog returneth to his vomit, *so* a fool returneth to his folly.   Ex. 8:15; 2 Pet. 2:22

12 Seest thou a man wise in his own conceit? *there is* more hope of a fool than of him.   Prov. 26:5; 29:20; Matt. 21:31

13 The slothful *man* saith, *There is* a lion in the way; a lion *is* in the streets.   Prov. 22:13

14 *As* the door turneth upon his hinges, so *doth* the slothful upon his bed.

15 The slothful hideth his hand in his bosom; it grieveth him to bring it again to his mouth.   Prov. 19:24

16 The sluggard *is* wiser in his own conceit than seven men that can render a reason.

17 He that passeth by, *and* meddleth with strife *belonging* not to him, *is like* one that taketh a dog by the ears.

18 As a mad *man* who casteth firebrands, arrows, and death,

19 So *is* the man *that* deceiveth his neighbour, and saith, Am not I in sport?   Eph. 5:4

26:18, 19 Evils of Sly Innuendo

Closely allied to gossip is the covert insinuation, the sly innuendo, by which the unclean in heart seek to insinuate the evil they dare not openly express. Every approach to these practices the youth should be taught to shun as they would shun the leprosy. *Ed 236*

20 Where no wood is, *there* the fire goeth out: so where *there is* no talebearer, the strife ceaseth.   Prov. 16:28; 22:10

21 *As* coals *are* to burning coals, and wood to fire; so *is* a ᵀcontentious man to kindle strife.   Prov. 15:18; 29:22 ◆ *enjoying quarrels*

22 The words of a talebearer *are* as wounds, and they go down into the innermost parts of the belly.   Prov. 18:8

23 Burning lips and a wicked heart *are like* a potsherd covered with silver dross.

24 He that hateth ᵀdissembleth with his lips, and layeth up deceit within him;   *deceives*

25 When he speaketh fair, believe him not: for *there are* seven abominations in his heart.

26 *Whose* hatred is covered by deceit, his wickedness shall be shewed before the *whole* congregation.

27 Whoso diggeth a pit shall fall therein: and he that rolleth a stone, it will return upon him.   Esth. 7:10; Prov. 28:10

28 A lying tongue hateth *those that are* afflicted by it; and a flattering mouth worketh ruin.

Observations about Life

27 Boast not thyself of to morrow; for thou knowest not what a day may bring forth.   Luke 12:19-20; James 4:13-16

2 Let another man praise thee, and not thine own mouth; a stranger, and not thine own lips.   Prov. 25:27; 2 Cor. 10:12, 18

3 A stone *is* heavy, and the sand weighty; but a fool's wrath *is* heavier than them both.   Prov. 17:12

4 Wrath *is* cruel, and anger *is* outrageous; but who *is* able to stand before envy?   Prov. 6:34

27:4 Harboring Envy/Jealousy

Envy [Jealousy] is one of the most satanic traits that can exist in the human heart, and it is one of the most baleful in its effects. Says the wise man, "Wrath is cruel, and anger is outrageous; but who is able to stand before envy?" (Proverbs 27:4). It was envy that first caused discord in heaven, and its indulgence has wrought untold evil among men. *PP 385*

5 Open rebuke *is* better than secret love.

6 Faithful *are* the wounds of a friend; but the kisses of an enemy *are* deceitful.   Ps. 141:5

7 The full soul loatheth an honeycomb; but to the hungry soul every bitter thing is sweet.

8 As a bird that wandereth from her nest, so *is* a man that wandereth from his place. Is. 16:2

9 Ointment and perfume rejoice the heart: so *doth* the sweetness of a man's friend by hearty counsel.

10 Thine own friend, and thy father's friend, forsake not; neither go into thy brother's house in the day of thy calamity: *for* better *is* a neighbour *that is* near than a brother far off.   1 Kin. 12:6-8

11 My son, be wise, and make my heart glad, that I may answer him that reproacheth me.   Ps. 119:42; Prov. 10:1; 23:15-16

12 A prudent *man* foreseeth the evil, *and* hideth himself; *but* the simple pass on, *and* are punished.   Prov. 22:3

13 Take his garment that is surety for a stranger, and take a pledge of him for a strange woman.   Prov. 20:16

14 He that blesseth his friend with a loud voice, rising early in the morning, it shall be counted a curse to him.

15 A continual dropping in a very rainy day and a contentious woman are alike. Prov. 19:13

16 Whosoever hideth her hideth the wind, and the ointment of his right hand, *which* bewrayeth *itself.*

17 Iron sharpeneth iron; so a man sharpeneth the ᵀcountenance of his friend. *appearance*

18 Whoso keepeth the fig tree shall eat the fruit thereof: so he that waiteth on his master shall be honoured.   Song 8:12; Luke 12:43-44

19 As in water face *answereth* to face, so the heart of man to man.

20 Hell and destruction are never full; so the eyes of man are never satisfied.   Prov. 30:15-16

21 *As* the fining pot for silver, and the furnace for gold; so *is* a man to his praise.   Prov. 17:3

22 Though thou shouldest ᵀbray a fool in a mortar among wheat with a pestle, *yet* will not his foolishness depart from him.   *crush*

23 Be thou diligent to know the state of thy flocks, *and* look well to thy herds.   1 Pet. 5:2

24 For riches *are* not for ever: and doth the crown *endure* to every generation?   Prov. 23:5

25 The hay appeareth, and the tender grass sheweth itself, and herbs of the mountains are gathered.

26 The lambs *are* for thy clothing, and the goats *are* the price of the field.

27 And *thou shalt have* goats' milk enough for thy food, for the food of thy household, and *for* the maintenance for thy maidens.

Observations on Impiety and Religious Integrity

28 The wicked flee when no man pursueth: but the righteous are bold as a lion. Lev. 26:17, 36; Ps. 53:5

2 For the ᵀtransgression of a land many *are* the princes thereof: but by a man of understanding *and* knowledge the state *thereof* shall be prolonged. *violation of a law*

3 A poor man that oppresseth the poor *is like* a sweeping rain which leaveth no food.

4 They that forsake the law praise the wicked: but such as keep the law contend with them. 1 Kin. 18:18

5 Evil men understand not judgment: but they that seek the LORD understand all *things*. Ps. 92:6

6 Better *is* the poor that walketh in his uprightness, than *he that is* perverse *in his* ways, though he *be* rich. Prov. 19:1; 28:18

7 Whoso keepeth the law *is* a wise son: but he that is a companion of riotous *men* shameth his father. Prov. 29:3

8 He that by ᵀusury and unjust gain increaseth his substance, he shall gather it for him that will pity the poor. Lev. 25:36 ♦ *interest charged*

9 He that turneth away his ear from hearing the law, even his prayer *shall be* abomination. Ps. 66:18; 109:7; Prov. 15:8

28:9 Insulting God

Those who bring their petitions to God, claiming His promise while they do not comply with the conditions, insult Jehovah. They bring the name of Christ as their authority for the fulfillment of the promise, but they do not those things that would show faith in Christ and love for Him. *COL 143*

---

10 Whoso causeth the righteous to go astray in an evil way, he shall fall himself into his own pit: but the upright shall have good *things* in possession. Prov. 26:27

11 The rich man *is* wise in his own conceit; but the poor that hath understanding searcheth him out. Prov. 26:16

12 When righteous *men* do rejoice, *there is* great glory: but when the wicked rise, a man is hidden. Prov. 11:10; 28:28; 29:2

13 He that covereth his sins shall not prosper: but whoso confesseth and forsaketh *them* shall have mercy. Job 31:33; Ps. 32:3-5; 1 John 1:8-10

14 Happy *is* the man that feareth alway: but he that hardeneth his heart shall fall into mischief. Prov. 23:17

15 *As* a roaring lion, and a ᵀranging bear; *so is* a wicked ruler over the poor people. *wandering*

16 The prince that wanteth understanding *is* also a great oppressor: *but* he that hateth ᵀcovetousness shall prolong *his* days. *strong desire*

17 A man that doeth violence to the blood of *any* person shall flee to the pit; let no man stay him. Gen. 9:6; Ex. 21:14

18 Whoso walketh uprightly shall be saved: but *he that is* perverse *in his* ways shall fall at once. Prov. 10:9

Observations on Wealth and Poverty

19 He that tilleth his land shall have plenty of bread: but he that followeth after vain *persons* shall have poverty enough. Prov. 12:11

20 A faithful man shall abound with blessings: but he that maketh haste to be rich shall not be innocent. Prov. 28:22

28:20 Getting Rich Quick

How many a man might have escaped financial failure and ruin by heeding the warnings, so often repeated and emphasized in the Scriptures:

"He that maketh haste to be rich shall not be innocent" (Proverbs 28:20). *Ed 136*

---

21 To have respect of persons *is* not good: for for a piece of bread *that* man will ᵀtransgress. Prov. 18:5; 24:23; Ezek. 13:19 ♦ *violate a law*

22 He that hasteth to be rich *hath* an evil eye, and considereth not that poverty shall come upon him. Prov. 23:6; 28:20; 1 Tim. 6:9

23 He that rebuketh a man afterwards shall find more favour than he that flattereth with the tongue. Prov. 27:5-6

Confessing Our Sins

Proverbs 28:13

If those who hide and excuse their faults could see how Satan exults over them, how he taunts Christ and holy angels with their course, they would make haste to confess their sins and to put them away. Through defects in the character, Satan works to gain control of the whole mind, and he knows that if these defects are cherished, he will succeed. Therefore he is constantly seeking to deceive the followers of Christ with his fatal sophistry that it is impossible for them to overcome. But Jesus pleads in their behalf His wounded hands, His bruised body; and He declares to all who would follow Him: "My grace is sufficient for thee" (2 Corinthians 12:9). "Take My yoke upon you, and learn of Me; for I am meek and lowly in heart: and ye shall find rest unto your souls. For My yoke is easy, and My burden is light" (Matthew 11:29, 30). Let none, then, regard their defects as incurable. God will give faith and grace to overcome them. *GC 489*

24 Whoso robbeth his father or his mother, and saith, *It is* no transgression; the same *is* the companion of a destroyer. Prov. 18:9; 19:26

25 He that is of a proud heart stirreth up strife: but he that putteth his trust in the LORD shall be made fat. Prov. 11:25

26 He that trusteth in his own heart is a fool: but whoso walketh wisely, he shall be delivered. Prov. 3:5

27 He that giveth unto the poor shall not lack: but he that hideth his eyes shall have many a curse. Deut. 15:7; Prov. 19:17; 22:9

28 When the wicked rise, men hide themselves: but when they perish, the righteous increase. Prov. 28:12

Observations on Living in Community

29 He, that being often reproved hardeneth *his* neck, shall suddenly be destroyed, and that without remedy. 1 Sam. 2:25

2 When the righteous are in authority, the people rejoice: but when the wicked beareth rule, the people mourn. Esth. 8:15; Prov. 11:10; 28:12

3 Whoso loveth wisdom rejoiceth his father: but he that keepeth company with harlots spendeth *his* substance. Prov. 6:26; 10:1; Luke 15:30

4 The king by judgment establisheth the land: but he that receiveth gifts overthroweth it. Prov. 29:14

5 A man that flattereth his neighbour spreadeth a net for his feet. Ps. 5:9

6 In the ᵀtransgression of an evil man *there is* a snare: but the righteous doth sing and rejoice. Eccl. 9:12 ◆ *sin*

7 The righteous considereth the cause of the poor: *but* the wicked regardeth not to know *it*. Job 29:16; Ps. 41:1

8 Scornful men bring a city into a snare: but wise *men* turn away wrath. Prov. 11:11

9 *If* a wise man contendeth with a foolish man, whether he rage or laugh, *there is* no rest.

10 The bloodthirsty hate the upright: but the just seek his soul. Gen. 4:5-8

11 A fool uttereth all his mind: but a wise *man* keepeth it in till afterwards. Prov. 12:16

12 If a ruler hearken to lies, all his servants *are* wicked.

13 The poor and the deceitful man meet together: the LORD lighteneth both their eyes. Ps. 13:3; Prov. 22:2; Matt. 5:45

14 The king that faithfully judgeth the poor, his throne shall be established for ever.

15 The rod and reproof give wisdom: but a child left *to himself* bringeth his mother to shame. Prov. 10:1; 17:25; 22:15

16 When the wicked are multiplied, transgression increaseth: but the righteous shall see their fall. Ps. 37:36; 58:10; 91:8

17 Correct thy son, and he shall give thee rest; yea, he shall give delight unto thy soul. Prov. 13:24

18 Where *there is* no vision, the people perish: but he that keepeth the law, happy *is* he. 1 Sam. 3:1; Ps. 119:2; John 13:17

19 A servant will not be corrected by words: for though he understand he will not answer.

20 Seest thou a man *that is* hasty in his words? *there is* more hope of a fool than of him. Prov. 26:12; James 1:19

> **29:20 Impatient Speech**
>
> In the use of language there is perhaps no error that old and young are more ready to pass over lightly in themselves than hasty, impatient speech. They think it a sufficient excuse to plead, "I was off my guard, and did not really mean what I said." But God's word does not treat it lightly. *Ed 236*

21 He that delicately bringeth up his servant from a child shall have him become *his* son at the length.

22 An angry man stirreth up strife, and a furious man aboundeth in transgression.

23 A man's pride shall bring him low: but honour shall uphold the humble in spirit.

24 Whoso is partner with a thief hateth his own soul: he heareth cursing, and bewrayeth *it* not. Lev. 5:1; Prov. 8:36

25 The fear of man bringeth a snare: but whoso putteth his trust in the LORD shall be safe. Gen. 20:2

26 Many seek the ruler's favour; but *every* man's judgment *cometh* from the LORD. Ps. 20:9

27 An unjust man *is* an abomination to the just: and *he that is* upright in the way *is* abomination to the wicked. Ps. 139:21

Agur's Confession of Faith

30 The words of Agur the son of Jakeh, *even* the prophecy: the man spake unto Ithiel, even unto Ithiel and Ucal,

2 Surely I *am* more ᵀbrutish than *any* man, and have not the understanding of a man. *dumb*

3 I neither learned wisdom, nor have the knowledge of the holy. Prov. 9:10

4 Who hath ascended up into heaven, or descended? who hath gathered the wind in his fists? who hath bound the waters in a garment? who hath established all the ends of the earth? what *is* his name, and what *is* his son's name, if thou canst tell? Job 26:8; Ps. 2:7

5 Every word of God *is* pure: he *is* a shield unto them that put their trust in him. Ps. 12:6

6 Add thou not unto his words, lest he reprove thee, and thou be found a liar. Deut. 4:2

7 Two *things* have I required of thee; deny me *them* not before I die:

8 Remove far from me vanity and lies: give

me neither poverty nor riches; feed me with food ᵀconvenient for me: Luke 11:3 ◆ *appropriate*

30:5 Respect and Reverence God's Word

We should reverence God's word. For the printed volume we should show respect, never putting it to common uses, or handling it carelessly. And never should Scripture be quoted in a jest, or paraphrased to point a witty saying. "Every word of God is pure;" "as silver tried in a furnace of earth, purified seven times" (Proverbs 30:5; Psalm 12:6). *Ed 244*

---

9 Lest I be full, and deny *thee*, and say, Who *is* the LORD? or lest I be poor, and steal, and take the name of my God *in vain*.   Ex. 20:7
10 Accuse not a servant unto his master, lest he curse thee, and thou be found guilty.
11 *There is* a generation *that* curseth their father, and doth not bless their mother.
12 *There is* a generation *that are* pure in their own eyes, and *yet* is not washed from their filthiness.   Prov. 16:2; Is. 65:5; Luke 18:11
13 *There is* a generation, O how lofty are their eyes! and their eyelids are lifted up.   Prov. 6:17
14 *There is* a generation, whose teeth *are as* swords, and their jaw teeth *as* knives, to devour the poor from off the earth, and the needy from *among* men.   Job 29:17; Ps. 14:4; 57:4
15 The horseleach hath two daughters, *crying*, Give, give. There are three *things that* are never satisfied, *yea*, four *things* say not, *It is* enough: Prov. 6:16
16 The grave; and the barren womb; the earth *that* is not filled with water; and the fire *that* saith not, *It is* enough.   Prov. 27:20; Hab. 2:5
17 The eye *that* mocketh at *his* father, and despiseth to obey *his* mother, the ravens of the valley shall pick it out, and the young eagles shall eat it.   Prov. 23:22
18 There be three *things which* are too wonderful for me, yea, four which I know not:
19 The way of an eagle in the air; the way of a serpent upon a rock; the way of a ship in the midst of the sea; and the way of a man with a maid.
20 Such *is* the way of an adulterous woman; she eateth, and wipeth her mouth, and saith, I have done no wickedness.
21 For three *things* the earth is disquieted, and for four *which* it cannot bear:
22 For a servant when he reigneth; and a fool when he is filled with meat; Prov. 19:10; Eccl. 10:7
23 For an ᵀodious *woman* when she is married; and an handmaid that is heir to her mistress.   *hateful*
24 There be four *things which are* little upon the earth, but they *are* exceeding wise:
25 The ants *are* a people not strong, yet they prepare their meat in the summer; Prov. 6:6-8

26 The conies *are but* a feeble folk, yet make they their houses in the rocks;   Lev. 11:5
27 The locusts have no king, yet go they forth all of them by bands;   Joel 2:25
28 The spider taketh hold with her hands, and is in kings' palaces.
29 There be three *things* which go well, yea, four are ᵀcomely in going: *stately*
30 A lion *which is* strongest among beasts, and turneth not away for any;   Judg. 14:18
31 A greyhound; an he goat also; and a king, against whom *there is* no rising up.
32 If thou hast done foolishly in lifting up thyself, or if thou hast thought evil, *lay* thine hand upon thy mouth.   Job 21:5; 40:4
33 Surely the churning of milk bringeth forth butter, and the wringing of the nose bringeth forth blood: so the forcing of wrath bringeth forth strife.   Prov. 29:22

Lemuel's Lesson

31 The words of king Lemuel, the prophecy that his mother taught him.
2 What, my son? and what, the son of my womb? and what, the son of my vows?
3 Give not thy strength unto women, nor thy ways to that which destroyeth kings.
4 *It is* not for kings, O Lemuel, *it is* not for kings to drink wine; nor for princes strong drink: Prov. 20:1; Eccl. 10:17; Is. 5:22
5 Lest they drink, and forget the law, and pervert the judgment of any of the afflicted.
6 Give strong drink unto him that is ready to perish, and wine unto those that be of heavy hearts.   1 Tim. 5:23
7 Let him drink, and forget his poverty, and remember his misery no more.
8 Open thy mouth for the ᵀdumb in the cause of all such as are appointed to destruction.   Ps. 82:3-4 ◆ *mute*
9 Open thy mouth, judge righteously, and plead the cause of the poor and needy.

Praise for a Good Wife

10 Who can find a virtuous woman? for her price *is* far above rubies. Ruth 3:11; Prov. 12:4; 19:14
11 The heart of her husband doth safely trust in her, so that he shall have no need of ᵀspoil.   *plunder*
12 She will do him good and not evil all the days of her life.
13 She seeketh wool, and flax, and worketh willingly with her hands.
14 She is like the merchants' ships; she bringeth her food from afar.
15 She riseth also while it is yet night, and giveth meat to her household, and a portion to her maidens.   Luke 12:42
16 She considereth a field, and buyeth it:

with the fruit of her hands she planteth a vineyard.

17 She girdeth her [T]loins with strength, and strengtheneth her arms. *1 Kin. 18:46 ◆ waist*

18 She perceiveth that her merchandise *is* good: her candle goeth not out by night.

19 She layeth her hands to the spindle, and her hands hold the [T]distaff. *tool for twisting threads*

20 She stretcheth out her hand to the poor; yea, she reacheth forth her hands to the needy. *Job 31:16-20; Prov. 22:9; Eph. 4:28*

21 She is not afraid of the snow for her household: for all her household *are* clothed with scarlet.

22 She maketh herself coverings of tapestry; her clothing *is* silk and purple. *Gen. 41:42*

23 Her husband is known in the gates, when he sitteth among the elders of the land.

24 She maketh fine linen, and selleth *it*; and delivereth girdles unto the merchant.

25 Strength and honour *are* her clothing; and she shall rejoice in time to come. *1 Tim. 2:10*

26 She openeth her mouth with wisdom; and in her tongue *is* the law of kindness.

27 She looketh well to the ways of her household, and eateth not the bread of idleness.

28 Her children arise up, and call her blessed; her husband *also*, and he praiseth her.

29 Many daughters have done virtuously, but thou excellest them all.

30 Favour *is* deceitful, and beauty *is* vain: *but* a woman *that* feareth the LORD, she shall be praised.

31 Give her of the fruit of her hands; and let her own works praise her in the gates.

A Foretaste of Heaven

Proverbs 31:10–31

Let a young woman accept as a life companion only one who possesses pure, manly traits of character, one who is diligent, aspiring, and honest, one who loves and fears God. Let a young man seek one to stand by his side who is fitted to bear her share of life's burdens, one whose influence will ennoble and refine him, and who will make him happy in her love. . . .

As life with its burden of perplexity and care meets the newly wedded pair, the romance with which imagination so often invests marriage disappears. Husband and wife learn each other's character as it was impossible to learn it in their previous association. This is a most critical period in their experience. The happiness and usefulness of their whole future life depend upon their taking a right course now. Often they discern in each other unsuspected weaknesses and defects; but the hearts that love has united will discern excellencies also heretofore unknown. Let all seek to discover the excellencies rather than the defects. Often it is our own attitude, the atmosphere that surrounds ourselves, which determines what will be revealed to us in another. . . . Love cannot long exist without expression. Let not the heart of one connected with you starve for the want of kindness and sympathy.

Though difficulties, perplexities, and discouragements may arise, let neither husband nor wife harbor the thought that their union is a mistake or a disappointment. Determine to be all that it is possible to be to each other. Continue the early attentions. In every way encourage each other in fighting the battles of life. Study to advance the happiness of each other. Let there be mutual love, mutual forbearance. Then marriage, instead of being the end of love, will be as it were the very beginning of love. The warmth of true friendship, the love that binds heart to heart, is a foretaste of the joys of heaven. *MH 359, 360*

THE BOOK OF
ECCLESIASTES

Empty. Empty trash cans. Empty glasses. Empty seats. Empty dreams. Empty bank accounts. Empty hearts. Emptiness is rampant, even when calendars are full. In the search for meaning too many people become unfulfilled as they learn that power, popularity, prestige, pleasure never completely satisfy.

Ecclesiastes is about emptiness—the void found in seeking fulfillment apart from God. The book analyzes life from a human perspective, viewing life on earth "under the sun" (1:9; 2:22; 3:16) and its "vanity" or emptiness. The writer chronicles his search for purpose, for meaning, and for satisfaction by pursuing pleasure, good works, popularity, and honor. But everything becomes to him "vanity of vanities," utterly worthless.

The book considers that everything has a time, its season under heaven, with the well-known section from chapter 3 that begins, "To every thing there is a season, and a time to every purpose under the heaven: A time to be born, and a time to die . . ." (3:1, 2).

Finally, the writer comes to the conclusion that the vacuum in the human heart can only be filled by God. All else is empty and meaningless. Once we have God in His rightful place, life takes on a new meaning and purpose.

Solomon, the king of Israel, knew about emptiness though he had every earthly thing possible—wisdom, wealth, accomplishment, possessions. Ecclesiastes serves as a warning sign to all those who seek to live life on their terms, disregarding God. If the wisest and richest man to ever live came up short in his pursuit for meaning without God, what makes us think we can do better?

Dates

Tradition asserts that Solomon wrote Song of Solomon in his early years, Proverbs in his middle years, and Ecclesiastes in his latter years. If this be so, Solomon's reign was fading (he died c. 931 B.C.), Israel was about to split into two kingdoms. Ecclesiastes, therefore, was probably written around 935 B.C.

Author

The Preacher, the author, is traditionally thought to be Solomon. The author is identified as "the son of David, king in Jerusalem" (1:1). Solomon was the wisest, richest, and most influential king in Israel's history. As chapter 2 details his pursuit of pleasures, his accomplishments, and his wealth, only King Solomon would have these kinds of resources. Further confirmation to Solomon's authorship is that the proverbs in Ecclesiastes are similar to those in the Book of Proverbs. Jewish Talmudic tradition attributes Solomon as the author, though Hezekiah's scribes may have edited the text.

Meaning of the Name

The title Ecclesiastes comes from the Greek word *ekklesia* ("assembly, congregation, church") and means "the speaker before an assembly or preacher." The Hebrew title *Qoheleth* means "one who addresses an assembly, a preacher."

Christ in Ecclesiastes

Life without a relationship with Christ leads to futility and emptiness. Only Christ can provide lasting satisfaction, unending joy, and insightful wisdom. The search for meaning is found in the "one shepherd" (12:11).

Solomon's conclusion, "Fear God, and keep his commandments: for this is the whole duty of man. For God shall bring every work into judgment, with every secret thing, whether it be good, or whether it be evil" (12:13, 14), points to the future judgment seat of Christ: "And I saw a great white throne, and him that sat on it, from whose face the earth and the heaven fled away; and there was found no place for them. And I saw the dead, small and great, stand before God; and the books were opened: and another book was opened, which is the book of life: and the dead were judged out of those things which were written in the books, according to their works" (Revelation 20:11, 12).

Ecclesiastes convincingly portrays the emptiness and perplexity of life apart from a relationship with God. The author, who is now an old man, once sought pleasure through his wealth, wives, idolatry, and position. He has come to the conclusion that God has placed in us a hunger to know who we are and where we fit in the universe. God has also a purpose for creating each one of us, including Solomon. By turning our backs on self, we can lead an enriched life in cooperating with our Creator. Ecclesiastes general set of divisions is as follows:

(1) *Ecclesiastes 1:1–11, "All Is Vanity"*: The Preacher's hypothesis—life seems meaningless and pointless—is revealed.

(2) *Ecclesiastes 1:12—6:12, No Fulfillment under the Sun*: Fulfillment in life is not found in pleasure, work, or success.

(3) *Ecclesiastes 7—12, Now to Enjoy Life*: When one realizes that life is a gift from God, life can be enjoyed to the fullest by accepting that gift and live according to His will. The wise person will live according to God's desires.

Unlocking Ecclesiastes

KEY PEOPLE:
Solomon

KEY EVENTS:
No references to historical events are presented, only the personal aspects of the author's life.

KEY WORD:
Vanity, appearing thirty-seven times, describes the diligent yet unsuccessful quest for meaning and satisfaction in human life. The author continually sees the emptiness and futility of power, prestige, and pleasure apart from God. The answer to true fulfillment in life—in the ability to enjoy pleasure and to use power and prestige wisely—is found in accepting all that comes in life as "from the hand of God" (2:24). The conclusion, as noted below, is to fear God and keep His commandments. Life itself is a gift from God, meant to be lived from beginning to end for Him.

KEY VERSES:
"Let us hear the conclusion of the whole matter: Fear God and keep his commandments: for this is the whole duty of man. For God shall bring every work into judgment, with every secret thing, whether it be good, or whether it be evil" (Ecclesiastes 12:13, 14).

KEY CHAPTER:
Ecclesiastes 12, which looks back on the author's life when he realizes that no amount of activities, possessions, or success can satisfy the emptiness of one's heart. Only when life is viewed from God's perspective does it take on meaning. Chapter 12 resolves the author's quest for the meaning of life with this conclusion: "Fear God and keep his commandments: for this is the whole duty of man" (12:13).

The Preacher Speaks of Vanity

1 The words of the Preacher, the son of David, king in Jerusalem.   Eccl. 1:12; 7:27

2 Vanity of vanities, saith the Preacher, vanity of vanities; all *is* vanity.   Ps. 39:5-6; Eccl. 12:8

3 What profit hath a man of all his labour which he taketh under the sun?   Eccl. 2:11; 3:9

Life Is an Endless Circle

4 *One* generation passeth away, and *another* generation cometh: but the earth abideth for ever.   Ps. 104:5

5 The sun also ariseth, and the sun goeth down, and hasteth to his place where he arose.   Ps. 19:4-6

6 The wind goeth toward the south, and turneth about unto the north; it whirleth about continually, and the wind returneth again according to his circuits.   John 3:8

7 All the rivers run into the sea; yet the sea *is* not full; unto the place from whence the rivers come, thither they return again.

8 All things *are* full of labour; man cannot utter *it*: the eye is not satisfied with seeing, nor the ear filled with hearing. Prov. 27:20; Eccl. 4:8

Nothing New Under the Sun

9 The thing that hath been, it *is that* which shall be; and that which is done *is* that which shall be done: and *there is* no new *thing* under the sun.   Eccl. 2:12; 3:15

10 Is there *any* thing whereof it may be said, See, this *is* new? it hath been already of old time, which was before us.

11 *There is* no remembrance of former *things*; neither shall there be *any* remembrance of *things* that are to come with *those* that shall come after.   Eccl. 2:16

The Preacher Undertakes His Study

12 I the Preacher was king over Israel in Jerusalem.   Eccl. 1:1

13 And I gave my heart to seek and search out by wisdom concerning all *things* that are done under heaven: this sore travail hath God given to the sons of man to be exercised therewith.   Gen. 3:19; Eccl. 1:17; 3:10

14 I have seen all the works that are done under the sun; and, behold, all *is* vanity and vexation of spirit.   Eccl. 2:11, 17, 26

15 *That which is* crooked cannot be made straight: and that which is wanting cannot be numbered.

16 I communed with mine own heart, saying, Lo, I am come to great estate, and have gotten more wisdom than all *they* that have been before me in Jerusalem: yea, my heart had great experience of wisdom and knowledge.   1 Kin. 3:12-13; 4:30; Eccl. 2:9

17 And I gave my heart to know wisdom, and to know madness and folly: I perceived that this also is vexation of spirit.   Eccl. 2:3

18 For in much wisdom *is* much grief: and he that increaseth knowledge increaseth sorrow.

The Vanity of Pleasure and Achievement

2 I said in mine heart, Go to now, I will prove thee with mirth, therefore enjoy pleasure: and, behold, this also *is* vanity.

2 I said of laughter, *It is* mad: and of mirth, What doeth it?   Prov. 14:13

3 I sought in mine heart to give myself unto wine, yet acquainting mine heart with wisdom; and to lay hold on folly, till I might see what *was* that good for the sons of men, which they should do under the heaven all the days of their life.   Prov. 20:1

4 I made me great works; I builded me houses; I planted me vineyards: 1 Kin. 7:1-12

5 I made me gardens and orchards, and I planted trees in them of all *kind of* fruits:

6 I made me pools of water, to water therewith the wood that bringeth forth trees:

7 I got *me* servants and maidens, and had servants born in my house; also I had great possessions of great and small cattle above all that were in Jerusalem before me:

8 I gathered me also silver and gold, and the ᵀpeculiar treasure of kings and of the provinces: I gat me men singers and women singers, and the delights of the sons of men, *as* musical instruments, and that of all sorts.   2 Sam. 19:35; 1 Kin. 9:28; 10:10 ◆ *special*

9 So I was great, and increased more than all that were before me in Jerusalem: also my wisdom remained with me. 1 Chr. 29:25; Eccl. 1:16

2:9 Pride and Pleasure

Noble in youth, noble in manhood, the beloved of his God, Solomon entered on a reign that gave high promise of prosperity and honor. Nations marveled at the knowledge and insight of the man to whom God had given wisdom. But the pride of prosperity brought separation from God. From the joy of divine communion Solomon turned to find satisfaction in the pleasures of sense. *Ed 152, 153*

---

10 And whatsoever mine eyes desired I kept not from them, I withheld not my heart from any joy; for my heart rejoiced in all my labour: and this was my portion of all my labour.   Eccl. 3:22

11 Then I looked on all the works that my hands had wrought, and on the labour that I had laboured to do: and, behold, all *was* vanity and vexation of spirit, and *there was* no profit under the sun.   Eccl. 1:3, 14

Without God Everything Is Pointless

12 And I turned myself to behold wisdom, and madness, and folly: for what *can* the man *do* that cometh after the king? *even* that which hath been already done.   Eccl. 1:17; 7:25
13 Then I saw that wisdom excelleth folly, as far as light excelleth darkness.   Eccl. 7:11-12
14 The wise man's eyes *are* in his head; but the fool walketh in darkness: and I myself perceived also that one event happeneth to them all.   Ps. 49:10; Prov. 17:24; Eccl. 3:19
15 Then said I in my heart, As it happeneth to the fool, so it happeneth even to me; and why was I then more wise? Then I said in my heart, that this also *is* vanity.   Eccl. 6:8
16 For *there is* no remembrance of the wise more than of the fool for ever; seeing that which now *is* in the days to come shall all be forgotten. And how dieth the wise *man?* as the fool.   Eccl. 1:11; 9:5
17 Therefore I hated life; because the work that is ᵀwrought under the sun *is* grievous unto me: for all *is* vanity and vexation of spirit.   Eccl. 2:11 ◆ *made*

2:17 Vain Promises
[Solomon] erected altars to heathen gods, only to learn how vain is their promise of rest to the spirit. Gloomy and soul-harassing thoughts troubled him night and day. For him there was no longer any joy of life or peace of mind, and the future was dark with despair. Yet the Lord forsook him not. *PK 76, 77*

18 Yea, I hated all my labour which I had taken under the sun: because I should leave it unto the man that shall be after me. Ps. 39:6
19 And who knoweth whether he shall be a wise *man* or a fool? yet shall he have rule over all my labour wherein I have laboured, and wherein I have shewed myself wise under the sun. This *is* also vanity.
20 Therefore I went about to cause my heart to despair of all the labour which I took under the sun.
21 For there is a man whose labour *is* in wisdom, and in knowledge, and in ᵀequity; yet to a man that hath not laboured therein shall he leave it *for* his portion. This also *is* vanity and a great evil.   *uprightness*
22 For what hath man of all his labour, and of the vexation of his heart, wherein he hath laboured under the sun?   Eccl. 1:3; 3:9
23 For all his days *are* sorrows, and his travail grief; yea, his heart taketh not rest in the night. This is also vanity. Job 5:7; 14:1; Ps. 127:2
24 *There is* nothing better for a man, *than* that he should eat and drink, and *that* he should make his soul enjoy good in his labour. This also I saw, that it *was* from the hand of God.   Eccl. 3:12-13, 22; 8:15

2:22, 23 Wasted Years
By his own bitter experience, Solomon learned the emptiness of a life that seeks in earthly things its highest good. . . .
In his later years, turning wearied and thirsting from earth's broken cisterns, Solomon returned to drink at the fountain of life. The history of his wasted years, with their lessons of warning, he by the Spirit of inspiration recorded for after generations. *Ed 153, 154*

25 For who can eat, or who else can hasten *hereunto*, more than I?
26 For *God* giveth to a man that *is* good in his sight wisdom, and knowledge, and joy: but to the sinner he giveth travail, to gather and to heap up, that he may give to *him that is* good before God. This also *is* vanity and vexation of spirit.   Job 27:16-17; Prov. 13:22

Everything in God's Own Time

3 To every *thing there is* a season, and a time to every purpose under the heaven: Eccl. 3:17
2 A time to be born, and a time to die; a time to plant, and a time to pluck up *that which is* planted;   Heb. 9:27
3 A time to kill, and a time to heal; a time to break down, and a time to build up; 1 Sam. 2:6
4 A time to weep, and a time to laugh; a time to mourn, and a time to dance; Ex. 15:20
5 A time to cast away stones, and a time to gather stones together; a time to embrace, and a time to refrain from embracing;   2 Kin. 3:25
6 A time to get, and a time to lose; a time to keep, and a time to cast away;
7 A time to rend, and a time to sew; a time to keep silence, and a time to speak;   Gen. 37:29

3:7 A Time for Everything
There was a time to be silent, and a time to speak. [Jesus] had not spoken until directly questioned [Matthew 26:57, 62–64]. He knew that to answer now would make His death certain. But the appeal was made by the highest acknowledged authority of the nation, and in the name of the Most High. Christ would not fail to show proper respect for the law. More than this, His own relation to the Father was called in question. He must plainly declare His character and mission. *DA 706*

8 A time to love, and a time to hate; a time of war, and a time of peace.   Luke 14:26
9 What profit hath he that worketh in that wherein he laboureth?   Eccl. 1:3; 2:11; 5:16
10 I have seen the travail, which God hath given to the sons of men to be exercised in it.   Gen. 3:19

The Excellency of God's Works

11 He hath made every *thing* beautiful in his time: also he hath set the world in their heart, so that no man can find out the work that God maketh from the beginning to the end. Gen. 1:31; Eccl. 8:17; Rom. 11:33

3:11 Do Not Lift the Veil

Man cannot by searching find out God. Let none seek with presumptuous hand to lift the veil that conceals His glory. . . . No mortal mind can penetrate the secrecy in which the Mighty One dwells and works. Only that which He sees fit to reveal can we comprehend of Him. Reason must acknowledge an authority superior to itself. Heart and intellect must bow to the great I AM. *MH 438*

12 I know that *there is* no good in them, but for *a man* to rejoice, and to do good in his life. Ps. 37:3
13 And also that every man should eat and drink, and enjoy the good of all his labour, it *is* the gift of God. Eccl. 2:24
14 I know that, whatsoever God doeth, it shall be for ever: nothing can be put to it, nor any thing taken from it: and God doeth *it*, that *men* should fear before him. James 1:17

3:14 God Never Changes

While there are different degrees of development and different manifestations of His power to meet the wants of men in the different ages, God's work in all time is the same. The Teacher is the same. God's character and His plan are the same. With Him "is no variableness, neither shadow of turning" (James 1:17). *Ed 50*

15 That which hath been is now; and that which is to be hath already been; and God requireth that which is past.

All Living Things Meet the Same End

16 And moreover I saw under the sun the place of judgment, *that* wickedness *was* there; and the place of righteousness, *that* iniquity *was* there. Eccl. 4:1; 5:8
17 I said in mine heart, God shall judge the righteous and the wicked: for *there is* a time there for every purpose and for every work. Gen. 18:25; Eccl. 3:1; Matt. 16:27
18 I said in mine heart concerning the estate of the sons of men, that God might ᵀmanifest them, and that they might see that they themselves are beasts. Ps. 73:22 ◆ *reveal*
19 For that which befalleth the sons of men befalleth beasts; even one thing befalleth them: as the one dieth, so dieth the other; yea, they have all one breath; so that a man hath no preeminence above a beast: for all *is* vanity. Ps. 49:12

20 All go unto one place; all are of the dust, and all turn to dust again. Gen. 3:19; Job 34:15
21 Who knoweth the spirit of man that goeth upward, and the spirit of the beast that goeth downward to the earth? Eccl. 12:7
22 Wherefore I perceive that *there is* nothing better, than that a man should rejoice in his own works; for that *is* his portion: for who shall bring him to see what shall be after him? Eccl. 2:24; 6:12; 8:7

Acts of Oppression

4 So I returned, and considered all the oppressions that are done under the sun: and behold the tears of *such as were* oppressed, and they had no comforter; and on the side of their oppressors *there was* power; but they had no comforter. Eccl. 3:16; 5:8; Is. 5:7
2 Wherefore I praised the dead which are already dead more than the living which are yet alive. Eccl. 2:17
3 Yea, better *is he* than both they, which hath not yet been, who hath not seen the evil work that is done under the sun. Luke 23:29

Hard Work versus Laziness

4 Again, I considered all travail, and every right work, that for this a man is envied of his neighbour. This *is* also vanity and vexation of spirit. Eccl. 1:14; 2:21
5 The fool foldeth his hands together, and eateth his own flesh. Is. 9:20
6 Better *is* an handful *with* quietness, than both the hands full *with* travail and vexation of spirit. Prov. 15:16-17

Two Are Better than One

7 Then I returned, and I saw vanity under the sun. Eccl. 4:1
8 There is one *alone*, and *there is* not a second; yea, he hath neither child nor brother: yet *is there* no end of all his labour; neither is his eye satisfied with riches; neither *saith he*, For whom do I labour, and bereave my soul of good? This *is* also vanity, yea, it *is* a sore travail. Prov. 27:20; Eccl. 1:8, 13
9 Two *are* better than one; because they have a good reward for their labour.
10 For if they fall, the one will lift up his fellow: but woe to him *that is* alone when he falleth; for *he hath* not another to help him up.
11 Again, if two lie together, then they have heat: but how can one be warm *alone*?
12 And if one prevail against him, two shall withstand him; and a threefold cord is not quickly broken.

Rulers and Fickle Citizens

13 Better *is* a poor and a wise child than an old and foolish king, who will no more be admonished. Eccl. 9:15-16

14 For out of prison he cometh to reign; whereas also *he that is* born in his kingdom becometh poor.   Gen. 41:14

15 I considered all the living which walk under the sun, with the second child that shall stand up in his stead.

16 *There is* no end of all the people, *even* of all that have been before them: they also that come after shall not rejoice in him. Surely this also *is* vanity and vexation of spirit.   Eccl. 1:14

Vanities in Worship

5 Keep thy foot when thou goest to the house of God, and be more ready to hear, than to give the sacrifice of fools: for they consider not that they do evil.   Ex. 3:5

2 Be not rash with thy mouth, and let not thine heart be hasty to utter *any* thing before God: for God *is* in heaven, and thou upon earth: therefore let thy words be few. Prov. 10:19

3 For a dream cometh through the multitude of business; and a fool's voice *is known* by multitude of words.   Prov. 10:19

4 When thou vowest a vow unto God, ᵀdefer not to pay it; for *he hath* no pleasure in fools: pay that which thou hast vowed.   *postpone*

5 Better *is it* that thou shouldest not vow, than that thou shouldest vow and not pay.   Acts 5:4

6 Suffer not thy mouth to cause thy flesh to sin; neither say thou before the angel, that it *was* an error: wherefore should God be angry at thy voice, and destroy the work of thine hands?   1 Cor. 11:10

7 For in the multitude of dreams and many words *there are* also ᵀ*divers* vanities: but fear thou God.   Eccl. 7:18; 8:12; 12:13 ◆ *various*

8 If thou seest the oppression of the poor, and violent perverting of judgment and justice in a province, marvel not at the matter: for *he that is* higher than the highest regardeth; and *there be* higher than they.   Ps. 12:5; 82:1; Eccl. 4:1

Vanities in Riches

9 Moreover the profit of the earth is for all: the king *himself* is served by the field.

10 He that loveth silver shall not be satisfied with silver; nor he that loveth abundance with increase: this *is* also vanity. Eccl. 2:11; 4:8

11 When goods increase, they are increased that eat them: and what good *is there* to the owners thereof, saving the beholding *of them* with their eyes?

12 The sleep of a labouring man *is* sweet, whether he eat little or much: but the abundance of the rich will not suffer him to sleep.   Prov. 3:24

13 There is a sore evil *which* I have seen under the sun, *namely*, riches kept for the owners thereof to their hurt.   Eccl. 6:1-2

14 But those riches perish by evil travail: and he ᵀbegetteth a son, and *there is* nothing in his hand.   *brings forth*

15 As he came forth of his mother's womb, naked shall he return to go as he came, and shall take nothing of his labour, which he may carry away in his hand. Job 1:21; Ps. 49:17; 1 Tim. 6:7

16 And this also *is* a sore evil, *that* in all points as he came, so shall he go: and what

profit hath he that hath laboured for the wind?   Prov. 11:29; Eccl. 1:3

17 All his days also he eateth in darkness, and *he hath* much sorrow and wrath with his sickness.   Ps. 127:2

God Alone Gives Contentment

18 Behold *that* which I have seen: *it is* good and ᵀcomely *for one* to eat and to drink, and to enjoy the good of all his labour that he taketh under the sun all the days of his life, which God giveth him: for it *is* his portion.   Eccl. 2:10, 24; 3:22 ◆ *appropriate*

19 Every man also to whom God hath given riches and wealth, and hath given him power to eat thereof, and to take his portion, and to rejoice in his labour; this *is* the gift of God.   Eccl. 3:13; 6:2

20 For he shall not much remember the days of his life; because God answereth *him* in the joy of his heart.

The Vanity of Riches without Use

6 There is an evil which I have seen under the sun, and it *is* common among men:

2 A man to whom God hath given riches, wealth, and honour, so that he wanteth nothing for his soul of all that he desireth, yet God giveth him not power to eat thereof, but a stranger eateth it: this *is* vanity, and it *is* an evil disease.   1 Kin. 3:13; Ps. 17:14; Eccl. 5:19

3 If a man ᵀbeget an hundred *children*, and live many years, so that the days of his years be many, and his soul be not filled with good, and also *that* he have no burial; I say, *that* an untimely birth *is* better than he.   Job 3:16; Eccl. 4:3; Jer. 22:19 ◆ *bring forth*

4 For he cometh in with vanity, and departeth in darkness, and his name shall be covered with darkness.

5 Moreover he hath not seen the sun, nor known *any thing*: this hath more rest than the other.

6 Yea, though he live a thousand years twice *told*, yet hath he seen no good: do not all go to one place?

7 All the labour of man *is* for his mouth, and yet the appetite is not filled.   Prov. 16:26

8 For what hath the wise more than the fool? what hath the poor, that knoweth to walk before the living?

9 Better *is* the sight of the eyes than the wandering of the desire: this *is* also vanity and vexation of spirit.   Eccl. 1:14

10 That which hath been is named already, and it is known that it *is* man: neither may he contend with him that is mightier than he.   Job 9:32

The Conclusion of Vanities

11 Seeing there be many things that increase vanity, what *is* man the better?

12 For who knoweth what *is* good for man in *this* life, all the days of his vain life which he spendeth as a shadow? for who can tell a man what shall be after him under the sun?   Job 14:2

Remedies against Vanity

7 A good name *is* better than precious ointment; and the day of death than the day of one's birth.   Prov. 22:1; Eccl. 4:2; Song 1:3

2 *It is* better to go to the house of mourning, than to go to the house of feasting: for that is the end of all men; and the living will lay it to his heart.   Ps. 90:12

3 Sorrow *is* better than laughter: for by the sadness of the ᵀcountenance the heart is made better.   *appearance*

4 The heart of the wise *is* in the house of mourning; but the heart of fools *is* in the house of ᵀmirth.   *gladness*

5 *It is* better to hear the rebuke of the wise, than for a man to hear the song of fools.

6 For as the crackling of thorns under a pot, so *is* the laughter of the fool: this also *is* vanity.   Ps. 58:9; 118:12; Eccl. 2:2

7 Surely oppression maketh a wise man mad; and a gift destroyeth the heart.   Deut. 16:19

8 Better *is* the end of a thing than the beginning thereof: *and* the patient in spirit *is* better than the proud in spirit.   Prov. 14:29; 16:32

9 Be not hasty in thy spirit to be angry: for anger resteth in the bosom of fools.   Prov. 14:17

10 Say not thou, What is *the cause* that the former days were better than these? for thou dost not enquire wisely concerning this.

11 Wisdom *is* good with an inheritance: and *by it there is* profit to them that see the sun.   Eccl. 11:7

12 For wisdom *is* a defence, *and* money *is* a defence: but the excellency of knowledge *is, that* wisdom giveth life to them that have it.   Prov. 3:18

7:12 Commands Are Promises

The creative energy that called the worlds into existence is in the word of God. This word imparts power; it begets life. Every command is a promise; accepted by the will, received into the soul, it brings with it the life of the Infinite One. It transforms the nature and re-creates the soul in the image of God. *Ed 126*

---

13 Consider the work of God: for who can make *that* straight, which he hath made crooked?   Job 12:14; Eccl. 1:15; Is. 14:27

14 In the day of prosperity be joyful, but in the day of adversity consider: God also

hath set the one over against the other, to the end that man should find nothing after him.   Eccl. 3:22

15 All *things* have I seen in the days of my vanity: there is a just *man* that perisheth in his righteousness, and there is a wicked *man* that prolongeth *his* life in his wickedness.   Eccl. 6:12; 8:12-14

16 Be not righteous over much; neither make thyself over wise: why shouldest thou destroy thyself?   Rom. 12:3

17 Be not over much wicked, neither be thou foolish: why shouldest thou die before thy time?   Ps. 55:23

18 *It is* good that thou shouldest take hold of this; yea, also from this withdraw not thine hand: for he that feareth God shall come forth of them all.   Eccl. 8:12

19 Wisdom strengtheneth the wise more than ten mighty *men* which are in the city.

20 For *there is* not a just man upon earth, that doeth good, and sinneth not. 1 Kin. 8:46

21 Also take no heed unto all words that are spoken; lest thou hear thy servant curse thee: Prov. 30:10

22 For oftentimes also thine own heart knoweth that thou thyself likewise hast cursed others.

The Advantages of Wisdom

23 All this have I proved by wisdom: I said, I will be wise; but it *was* far from me. Rom. 1:22

24 That which is far off, and exceeding deep, who can find it out?   Rom. 11:33

25 I applied mine heart to know, and to search, and to seek out wisdom, and the reason *of things*, and to know the wickedness of folly, even of foolishness *and* madness:

26 And I find more bitter than death the woman, whose heart *is* snares and nets, *and* her hands *as* bands: whoso pleaseth God shall escape from her; but the sinner shall be taken by her.   Prov. 2:18-19; 5:3-5; 22:14

27 Behold, this have I found, saith the preacher, *counting* one by one, to find out the account:

28 Which yet my soul seeketh, but I find not: one man among a thousand have I found; but a woman among all those have I not found.   Job 33:23

---

29 Lo, this only have I found, that God hath made man upright; but they have sought out many inventions.   Gen. 3:6-7

Enjoy Life

8 Who *is* as the wise *man*? and who knoweth the interpretation of a thing? a man's wisdom maketh his face to shine, and the boldness of his face shall be changed. Deut. 28:50

2 I *counsel thee* to keep the king's commandment, and *that* in regard of the oath of God.   1 Kin. 2:43

3 Be not hasty to go out of his sight: stand not in an evil thing; for he doeth whatsoever pleaseth him.   Eccl. 10:4

4 Where the word of a king *is, there is* power: and who may say unto him, What doest thou?   Job 9:12

5 Whoso keepeth the commandment shall feel no evil thing: and a wise man's heart discerneth both time and judgment.

6 Because to every purpose there is time and judgment, therefore the misery of man *is* great upon him.   Eccl. 3:1, 17

7 For he knoweth not that which shall be: for who can tell him when it shall be?   Eccl. 6:12

8 *There is* no man that hath power over the spirit to retain the spirit; neither *hath he* power in the day of death: and *there is* no discharge in *that* war; neither shall wickedness deliver those that are given to it.   Job 14:5

9 All this have I seen, and applied my heart unto every work that is done under the sun: *there is* a time wherein one man ruleth over another to his own hurt.   Eccl. 5:8

10 And so I saw the wicked buried, who had come and gone from the place of the holy, and they were forgotten in the city where they had so done: this *is* also vanity. Eccl. 9:5

11 Because sentence against an evil work is not executed speedily, therefore the heart of the sons of men is fully set in them to do evil.   Ps. 10:6

---

12 Though a sinner do evil an hundred times, and his *days* be prolonged, yet surely I know that it shall be well with them that fear God, which fear before him: Ps. 37:11, 18-19; Eccl. 7:15

13 But it shall not be well with the wicked, neither shall he prolong *his* days, *which are* as a shadow; because he feareth not before God. Job 14:2

14 There is a vanity which is done upon the earth; that there be just *men*, unto whom it happeneth according to the work of the wicked; again, there be wicked *men*, to whom it happeneth according to the work of the righteous: I said that this also *is* vanity. Job 21:7; Eccl. 7:15; Mal. 3:15

15 Then I commended ᵀmirth, because a man hath no better thing under the sun, than to eat, and to drink, and to be merry: for that shall abide with him of his labour the days of his life, which God giveth him under the sun. Eccl. 2:24; 3:12-13; 5:18 ◆ *gladness*

16 When I applied mine heart to know wisdom, and to see the business that is done upon the earth: (for also *there is that* neither day nor night seeth sleep with his eyes:)

17 Then I beheld all the work of God, that a man cannot find out the work that is done under the sun: because though a man labour to seek *it* out, yet he shall not find *it*; yea further; though a wise *man* think to know *it*, yet shall he not be able to find *it*. Ps. 73:16; Eccl. 3:11

Everything Is in God's Hands

9 For all this I considered in my heart even to declare all this, that the righteous, and the wise, and their works, *are* in the hand of God: no man knoweth either love or hatred *by* all *that is* before them. Deut. 33:3; Eccl. 8:14

2 All *things come* alike to all: *there is* one event to the righteous, and to the wicked; to the good and to the clean, and to the unclean; to him that sacrificeth, and to him that sacrificeth not: as *is* the good, so *is* the sinner; *and* he that sweareth, as *he* that feareth an oath.

3 This *is* an evil among all *things* that are done under the sun, that *there is* one event unto all: yea, also the heart of the sons of men is full of evil, and madness *is* in their heart while they live, and after that *they go* to the dead. Eccl. 1:17

4 For to him that is joined to all the living there is hope: for a living dog is better than a dead lion.

5 For the living know that they shall die: but the dead know not any thing, neither have they any more a reward; for the memory of them is forgotten. Job 14:21; Eccl. 2:16; Is. 26:14

6 Also their love, and their hatred, and their envy, is now perished; neither have they any more a portion for ever in any *thing* that is done under the sun.

After Death See Job 7:9, 10.

7 Go thy way, eat thy bread with joy, and drink thy wine with a merry heart; for God now accepteth thy works. Eccl. 8:15

8 Let thy garments be always white; and let thy head lack no ointment. Ps. 23:5

9 Live joyfully with the wife whom thou lovest all the days of the life of thy vanity, which he hath given thee under the sun, all the days of thy vanity: for that *is* thy portion in *this* life, and in thy labour which thou takest under the sun. Eccl. 2:10

10 Whatsoever thy hand findeth to do, do *it* with thy might; for *there is* no work, nor device, nor knowledge, nor wisdom, in the grave, whither thou goest. Ps. 6:5; Rom. 12:11

Christian Behavior See Matthew 6:14, 15.

11 I returned, and saw under the sun, that the race *is* not to the swift, nor the battle to the strong, neither yet bread to the wise, nor yet riches to men of understanding, nor yet favour to men of skill; but time and chance happeneth to them all. Jer. 9:23

12 For man also knoweth not his time: as the fishes that are taken in an evil net, and as the birds that are caught in the snare; so *are* the sons of men snared in an evil time, when it falleth suddenly upon them. Prov. 29:6; 1 Thess. 5:3

13 This wisdom have I seen also under the sun, and it *seemed* great unto me:

14 *There was* a little city, and few men within it; and there came a great king against it, and besieged it, and built great ᵀbulwarks against it: *structures for defense*

15 Now there was found in it a poor wise man, and he by his wisdom delivered the city; yet no man remembered that same poor man. Eccl. 4:13

16 Then said I, Wisdom *is* better than strength: nevertheless the poor man's wisdom *is* despised, and his words are not heard. Prov. 21:22; Eccl. 7:19; Mark 6:2-3

17 The words of wise *men are* heard in quiet more than the cry of him that ruleth among fools.

18 Wisdom *is* better than weapons of war: but one sinner destroyeth much good. Josh. 7:1

9:18 Legacy of the King's Sin

Though the king confessed his sin and wrote out for the benefit of after generations a record of his folly and repentance, he could never hope entirely to destroy the baleful influence of his wrong deeds. Emboldened by his apostasy, many continued to do evil, and evil only. And in the downward course of many of the rulers who followed him may be traced the sad influence of the prostitution of his God-given powers. *PK 85*

Observations of Wisdom and Folly

10 Dead flies cause the ointment of the ᵀapothecary to send forth a stinking savour: *so doth* a little folly him that is in reputation for wisdom *and* honour. *maker of perfumes*

2 A wise man's heart *is* at his right hand; but a fool's heart at his left.

3 Yea also, when he that is a fool walketh by the way, his wisdom faileth *him*, and he saith to every one *that* he *is* a fool.   Prov. 13:16; 18:2

4 If the spirit of the ruler rise up against thee, leave not thy place; for yielding pacifieth great offences.   Prov. 25:15; Eccl. 8:3

5 There is an evil *which* I have seen under the sun, as an error *which* proceedeth from the ruler:

6 Folly is set in great dignity, and the rich sit in low place.   Esth. 3:1

7 I have seen servants upon horses, and princes walking as servants upon the earth.

8 He that diggeth a pit shall fall into it; and whoso breaketh an hedge, a serpent shall bite him.   Prov. 26:27; Amos 5:19

9 Whoso removeth stones shall be hurt therewith; *and* he that ᵀcleaveth wood shall be endangered thereby.   *stays close to*

10 If the iron be blunt, and he do not ᵀwhet the edge, then must he put to more strength: but wisdom *is* profitable to direct.   *sharpen*

11 Surely the serpent will bite without enchantment; and a babbler is no better.   Jer. 8:17

12 The words of a wise man's mouth *are* gracious; but the lips of a fool will swallow up himself.   Luke 4:22

13 The beginning of the words of his mouth *is* foolishness: and the end of his talk *is* mischievous madness.

14 A fool also is full of words: a man cannot tell what shall be; and what shall be after him, who can tell him?   Prov. 15:2; Eccl. 3:22; 5:3

15 The labour of the foolish wearieth every one of them, because he knoweth not how to go to the city.

16 Woe to thee, O land, when thy king *is* a child, and thy princes eat in the morning!

17 Blessed *art* thou, O land, when thy king is the son of nobles, and thy princes eat in due season, for strength, and not for drunkenness!

10:17 Temperance and Self-Control

The observance of temperance and regularity in all things has a wonderful power. It will do more than circumstances or natural endowments in promoting that sweetness and serenity of disposition which count so much in smoothing life's pathway. At the same time the power of self-control thus acquired will be found one of the most valuable of equipments for grappling successfully with the stern duties and realities that await every human being. *Ed 206*

18 By much slothfulness the building decayeth; and through idleness of the hands the house droppeth through.   Prov. 20:4

19 A feast is made for laughter, and wine maketh merry: but money answereth all *things*.   Ps. 104:15

20 Curse not the king, no not in thy thought; and curse not the rich in thy bedchamber: for a bird of the air shall carry the voice, and that which hath wings shall tell the matter.   Ex. 22:28; Acts 23:5

Directions for Charity

11 Cast thy bread upon the waters: for thou shalt find it after many days.

2 Give a portion to seven, and also to eight; for thou knowest not what evil shall be upon the earth.   Ps. 112:9

3 If the clouds be full of rain, they empty *themselves* upon the earth: and if the tree fall toward the south, or toward the north, in the place where the tree falleth, there it shall be.

4 He that observeth the wind shall not sow; and he that regardeth the clouds shall not reap.

The Power of Our Influence

Ecclesiastes 10:1

Among the many lessons taught by Solomon's life, none is more strongly emphasized than the power of influence for good or for ill. However contracted may be our sphere, we still exert an influence for weal or woe. Beyond our knowledge or control, it tells upon others in blessing or cursing. It may be heavy with the gloom of discontent and selfishness, or poisonous with the deadly taint of some cherished sin; or it may be charged with the life-giving power of faith, courage, and hope, and sweet with the fragrance of love. But potent for good or for ill it will surely be.

That our influence should be a savor of death unto death is a fearful thought, yet it is possible. One soul misled, forfeiting eternal bliss—who can estimate the loss! And yet one rash act, one thoughtless word, on our part may exert so deep an influence on the life of another that it will prove the ruin of his soul. One blemish on the character may turn many away from Christ.

As the seed sown produces a harvest, and this in turn is sown, the harvest is multiplied. In our relation to others, this law holds true. Every act, every word, is a seed that will bear fruit. Every deed of thoughtful kindness, of obedience, of self-denial, will reproduce itself in others, and through them in still others. . . . Thus the sowing of good and evil goes on for time and for eternity. *PK 85, 86*

5 As thou knowest not what *is* the way of the spirit, *nor* how the bones *do grow* in the womb of her that is with child: even so thou knowest not the works of God who maketh all.   Eccl. 8:17; John 3:8

6 In the morning sow thy seed, and in the evening withhold not thine hand: for thou knowest not whether shall prosper, either this or that, or whether they both *shall be* alike good.   Eccl. 9:10

> **11:6 Work; Then Leave Results to God**
>
> The good seed may for a time lie unnoticed in a cold, selfish, worldly heart, giving no evidence that it has taken root; but afterward, as the Spirit of God breathes on the soul, the hidden seed springs up. . . . In our lifework we know not which shall prosper, this or that. This is not a question for us to settle. We are to do our work, and leave the results with God. *COL 65*

Enjoy Life

7 Truly the light *is* sweet, and a pleasant *thing it is* for the eyes to behold the sun: Eccl. 7:11

8 But if a man live many years, *and* rejoice in them all; yet let him remember the days of darkness; for they shall be many. All that cometh *is* vanity.

9 Rejoice, O young man, in thy youth; and let thy heart cheer thee in the days of thy youth, and walk in the ways of thine heart, and in the sight of thine eyes: but know thou, that for all these *things* God will bring thee into judgment.   Job 31:7; Eccl. 2:10; 12:14

10 Therefore remove sorrow from thy heart, and put away evil from thy flesh: for childhood and youth *are* vanity.   2 Cor. 7:1

> **11:7-10 The Folly of Self-Trust**
>
> In the battle with inward sin and outward temptation, even the wise and powerful Solomon was vanquished. His failure teaches us that, whatever a man's intellectual qualities may be, and however faithfully he may have served God in the past, he can never with safety trust in his own wisdom and integrity. *PK 82*

Remember Your Creator in Your Youth

12 Remember now thy Creator in the days of thy youth, while the evil days come not, nor the years draw nigh, when thou shalt say, I have no pleasure in them;   2 Sam. 19:35; Eccl. 11:8; Lam. 3:27

2 While the sun, or the light, or the moon, or the stars, be not darkened, nor the clouds return after the rain:

3 In the day when the keepers of the house shall tremble, and the strong men shall bow themselves, and the grinders cease because they are few, and those that look out of the windows be darkened,

4 And the doors shall be shut in the streets, when the sound of the grinding is low, and he shall rise up at the voice of the bird, and all the daughters of musick shall be brought low;   2 Sam. 19:35

5 Also *when* they shall be afraid of *that which is* high, and fears *shall be* in the way, and the almond tree shall flourish, and the grasshopper shall be a burden, and desire shall fail: because man goeth to his long home, and the mourners go about the streets: Job 17:13; 30:23

6 Or ever the silver cord be loosed, or the golden bowl be broken, or the pitcher be broken at the fountain, or the wheel broken at the ᵀcistern.   well

7 Then shall the dust return to the earth as it was: and the spirit shall return unto God who gave it.   Gen. 2:7; 3:19; Zech. 12:1

       After Death See John 11:11–14.

Fear God and Keep His Commands

8 Vanity of vanities, saith the preacher; all *is* vanity.   Eccl. 1:2

9 And moreover, because the preacher was wise, he still taught the people knowledge; yea, he gave good heed, and sought out, *and* set in order many proverbs.   1 Kin. 4:32

10 The preacher sought to find out acceptable words: and *that which was* written *was* upright, *even* words of truth.

11 The words of the wise *are* as ᵀgoads, and as nails fastened *by* the masters of assemblies, *which* are given from one shepherd.   pointed sticks

12 And further, by these, my son, be admonished: of making many books *there is* no end; and much study *is* a weariness of the flesh.   Eccl. 1:18

13 Let us hear the conclusion of the whole matter: Fear God, and keep his commandments: for this *is* the whole *duty* of man.

14 For God shall bring every work into judgment, with every secret thing, whether *it be* good, or whether *it be* evil.   Eccl. 11:9; Rom. 2:16

> **12:14 Heaven's Records**
>
> When the records of heaven shall be opened, the Judge will not in words declare to man his guilt, but will cast one penetrating, convicting glance, and every deed, every transaction of life, will be vividly impressed upon the memory of the wrongdoer. . . . His own lips will confess his shame. The sins hidden from the knowledge of men will then be proclaimed to the whole world. *PP 498*

THE
SONG OF SOLOMON

Love songs touch the heart, grip the soul, and move the emotions. Some of the most memorable convey the deep affection between a man and a woman. Many are recorded over and over by various artists or sung at weddings generation after generation.

The Song of Solomon is a biblical love song expressing the courtship and marriage of a couple. In dramatic imagery and moving metaphors, Solomon, the king of Israel, tells of his love for a beautiful Jewish shepherdess, the Shulamite woman. The song also celebrates the consummation of the marriage, the honeymoon, the deepening of the marriage, and the maturity of love.

Some believe that the book tells the love story between King Solomon and a poor but beautiful girl that never really happened. Others claim that it is purely allegorical to illustrate God's love for His people, Israel, or Christ's love for the church. But historically, scholars believe the story is true. The song offers proper perspectives on human love and sexuality. Beyond that, however, the book does serve as an allegory picturing the nation of Israel as God's bride (see also Hosea 2:19, 20) and the church as the bride of Christ (see also Revelation 21:9).

Solomon is credited with more than one thousand songs (1 Kings 4:32); this beautiful love song surpasses them all.

Dates

The Song of Solomon was probably written early in Solomon's reign, possibly c. 965 B.C. Since Solomon was known for his harem, the story of his courtship to one woman seems an anomaly. Since many of his marriages were political alliances, Solomon could be reflecting on the only romantic alliance he had early in his reign—perhaps his first love. But here we see a far different Solomon before he grew older and turned to the idols of his wives (see 1 Kings 11:4).

Author

Solomon is believed to be the author. He is specifically mentioned seven times (Song of Solomon 1:1, 5; 3:7, 9, 11; 8:11, 12). He is identified as the groom. The book speaks of royal luxury and rich imported goods (see 3:6–11) that could have only been obtained by a king like Solomon.

Another interesting side note is the species of plants and animals mentioned in the book, along with various geographical locations. This too gives credence to the opinion of Solomon's authorship because 1 Kings 4:33 refers to the king's knowledge of plant and animal life.

Meaning of the Name

The book is sometimes called Song of Songs or Song of Solomon, since each of those words are mentioned in the first verse: "The song of songs, which is Solomon's" (Song of Solomon 1:1). The Hebrew title *Shir Hashirim* means "the song of songs." In the Greek, the title is *Asma Asmaton*; in Latin it is *Canticum Canticorum* (meaning "Song of Songs").

Christ in Song of Solomon

In the Old Testament, Israel is regarded as the bride of Yahweh. In the New Testament, the church is depicted as the bride of Christ. The Song of Solomon illustrates the former and anticipates the latter. Human life finds completion in the love of man and woman; spiritual life finds fulfillment in Christ's love, evidenced by His sacrifice on the cross.

The book reads like a drama with three main characters: the bride (Shulamite woman), the king (Solomon), and a chorus (daughters of Jerusalem). A simple outline is as follows:

(1) *Song of Solomon 1:1—5:1, Love Begins:* The courtship of King Solomon and a hardworking shepherdess and vineyard worker is reminiscent of the story of Ruth. Having pledged their love for each other Solomon and his bride extol each other's virtues and anticipate the joys of the wedded union.

(2) *Song of Solomon 5:2—8:14, Love Grows:* The marriage between Solomon and his bride grows deeper as they deal with issues like jealousy and physical separation.

Scholars who believe this to be a true account have two main views about this book. Some believe it to be historical, telling the romantic story of King Solomon's love for a Shulamite woman. It is, therefore, an endorsement of sexuality in the context of marriage and, by extension, does have allegorical elements. Other scholars, however, view this book as possibly telling a love story, but far more importantly it provides an allegory to illustrate God's great love for His people Israel. Other Old Testament Scriptures use the picture of husband and wife to describe this relationship between God and His people, "For thy Maker is thine husband; the LORD of hosts is his name; and thy Redeemer the Holy One of Israel; the God of the whole earth shall he be called" (Isaiah 54:5; see also 62:5; Jeremiah 2:2; 3:14, 20; 31:32; Ezekiel 16:32, 38; Hosea 2:2, 7, 16). The Book of Revelation also uses the allegory to describe Christ and His church: "And I John saw the holy city, new Jerusalem, coming down from God out of heaven, prepared as a bride adorned for her husband" (Revelation 21:2; see also verse 9; 22:17).

KEY PEOPLE:
King Solomon, the Shulamite woman, the daughters of Jerusalem

KEY EVENTS:
No key events are recorded.

KEY WORD:
Love, for the Song of Solomon depicts the romance between a man and a woman, expressing that love in physical beauty and sexuality. While the poetry of the book is very sensual, the joy Solomon and his bride find in each other shows the right perspective of love and sexuality in the context of marriage. This is the oneness that God intended for man and woman (Genesis 2:24).

KEY VERSE:
"Many waters cannot quench love, neither can the floods drown it: if a man would give all the substance of his house for love, it would utterly be contemned" (Song of Solomon 8:7).

KEY CHAPTER:
Song of Solomon 8, While the entirety of the book is a continuous story woven together to depict the love of a married couple, chapter 8 offers characteristics of true love akin to 1 Corinthians 13.

Solomon and the Young Woman

1 The song of songs, which is Solomon's.
2 Let him kiss me with the kisses of his mouth: for thy love is better than wine.
3 Because of the savour of thy good ointments thy name is as ointment poured forth, therefore do the virgins love thee.
4 Draw me, we will run after thee: the king hath brought me into his chambers: we will be glad and rejoice in thee, we will remember thy love more than wine: the upright love thee.   Ps. 45:14-15
5 I am black, but ᵀcomely, O ye daughters of Jerusalem, as the tents of Kedar, as the curtains of Solomon.   Ps. 120:5 ◆ lovely
6 Look not upon me, because I am black, because the sun hath looked upon me: my mother's children were angry with me; they made me the keeper of the vineyards; but mine own vineyard have I not kept.   Ps. 69:8; Song 8:11-12
7 Tell me, O thou whom my soul loveth, where thou feedest, where thou makest thy flock to rest at noon: for why should I be as one that turneth aside by the flocks of thy companions?   Ps. 23:1-2; Song 3:1-4; Is. 13:20
8 If thou know not, O thou fairest among women, go thy way forth by the footsteps of the flock, and feed thy kids beside the shepherds' tents.   Song 5:9; 6:1

Solomon Desires the Young Woman's Love

9 I have compared thee, O my love, to a company of horses in Pharaoh's chariots. Song 2:2
10 Thy cheeks are comely with rows of jewels, thy neck with chains of gold.   Song 5:13
11 We will make thee borders of gold with studs of silver.
12 While the king sitteth at his table, my spikenard sendeth forth the smell thereof.   John 12:3
13 A bundle of myrrh is my wellbeloved unto me; he shall lie all night ᵀbetwixt my breasts.   Ps. 45:8 ◆ between
14 My beloved is unto me as a cluster of camphire in the vineyards of En-gedi.
15 Behold, thou art fair, my love; behold, thou art fair; thou hast doves' eyes.   Song 4:1, 7; 5:12
16 Behold, thou art fair, my beloved, yea, pleasant: also our bed is green.   Song 2:3
17 The beams of our house are cedar, and our rafters of fir.

Their Love Is Great

2 I am the rose of Sharon, and the lily of the valleys.   Song 5:13
2 As the lily among thorns, so is my love among the daughters.
3 As the apple tree among the trees of the wood, so is my beloved among the sons. I sat down under his shadow with great delight, and his fruit was sweet to my taste.
4 He brought me to the banqueting house, and his banner over me was love.   Song 1:4

2:3, 4 Take Time With Jesus

Not a pause for a moment in His presence, but personal contact with Christ, to sit down in companionship with Him—this is our need. Happy will it be for the children of our homes and the students of our schools when parents and teachers shall learn in their own lives the precious experience pictured in these words. Ed 261

---

5 Stay me with flagons, comfort me with apples: for I am sick of love.   2 Sam. 6:19; Song 5:8
6 His left hand is under my head, and his right hand doth embrace me.
7 I charge you, O ye daughters of Jerusalem, by the roes, and by the ᵀhinds of the field, that ye stir not up, nor awake my love, till he please.   Song 1:5; 3:5; 8:4 ◆ deer

Remembering One Spring Day

8 The voice of my beloved! behold, he cometh leaping upon the mountains, skipping upon the hills.
9 My beloved is like a roe or a young hart: behold, he standeth behind our wall, he looketh forth at the windows, shewing himself through the lattice.   Song 2:17; 8:14
10 My beloved spake, and said unto me, Rise up, my love, my fair one, and come away.   Song 2:13
11 For, lo, the winter is past, the rain is over and gone;
12 The flowers appear on the earth; the time of the singing of birds is come, and the voice of the ᵀturtle is heard in our land;   turtledove
13 The fig tree putteth forth her green figs, and the vines with the tender grape give a good smell. Arise, my love, my fair one, and come away.   Song 2:10
14 O my dove, that art in the clefts of the rock, in the secret places of the stairs, let me see thy ᵀcountenance, let me hear thy voice; for sweet is thy voice, and thy countenance is ᵀcomely.   Song 1:5; 5:2; 8:13 ◆ appearance ◆ lovely
15 Take us the foxes, the little foxes, that ᵀspoil the vines: for our vines have tender grapes.   Song 2:13 ◆ plunder
16 My beloved is mine, and I am his: he feedeth among the lilies.   Song 4:5; 6:3; 7:10
17 Until the day break, and the shadows flee away, turn, my beloved, and be thou like a roe or a young ᵀhart upon the mountains of Bether.   Song 4:6 ◆ deer

Searching for the Beloved

3 By night on my bed I sought him whom my soul loveth: I sought him, but I found him not.   Song 1:7; 5:6; Is. 26:9
2 I will rise now, and go about the city in the streets, and in the broad ways I will seek

him whom my soul loveth: I sought him, but I found him not.

3 The watchmen that go about the city found me: *to whom I said,* Saw ye him whom my soul loveth?   Song 5:7; Is. 21:6-8, 11-12

4 *It was* but a little that I passed from them, but I found him whom my soul loveth: I held him, and would not let him go, until I had brought him into my mother's house, and into the chamber of her that conceived me.   Prov. 4:13

5 I charge you, O ye daughters of Jerusalem, by the roes, and by the ᵀhinds of the field, that ye stir not up, nor awake *my* love, till he please.   Song 2:7; 8:4 ◆ *deer*

The Royal Procession

6 Who *is* this that cometh out of the wilderness like pillars of smoke, perfumed with myrrh and frankincense, with all powders of the merchant?   Song 1:13; 4:6; 8:5

7 Behold his bed, which *is* Solomon's; ᵀthreescore valiant men *are* about it, of the valiant of Israel.   *sixty*

8 They all hold swords, *being* expert in war: every man *hath* his sword upon his thigh because of fear in the night.   Ps. 45:3

9 King Solomon made himself a chariot of the wood of Lebanon.

10 He made the pillars thereof *of* silver, the bottom thereof *of* gold, the covering of it *of* purple, the midst thereof being paved *with* love, for the daughters of Jerusalem.

11 Go forth, O ye daughters of Zion, and behold king Solomon with the crown wherewith his mother crowned him in the day of his espousals, and in the day of the gladness of his heart.   Is. 4:4; 62:5

Solomon Is Charmed by His Beloved

4 Behold, thou *art* fair, my love; behold, thou *art* fair; thou *hast* doves' eyes within thy locks: thy hair *is* as a flock of goats, that appear from mount Gilead.   Song 1:15; 6:5, 7

2 Thy teeth *are* like a flock *of sheep that are even* shorn, which came up from the

washing; whereof every one bear twins, and none *is* barren among them.   Song 6:6

3 Thy lips *are* like a thread of scarlet, and thy speech *is* ᵀcomely: thy temples *are* like a piece of a pomegranate within thy locks.   *lovely*

4 Thy neck *is* like the tower of David builded for an armoury, whereon there hang a thousand ᵀbucklers, all shields of mighty men.   Neh. 3:19; Song 7:4 ◆ *small shields*

5 Thy two breasts *are* like two young roes that are twins, which feed among the lilies.   Song 2:16

6 Until the day break, and the shadows flee away, I will get me to the mountain of myrrh, and to the hill of frankincense.   Song 2:17; 4:14

7 Thou *art* all fair, my love; *there* is no spot in thee.   Song 1:15

4:7 The Symbolism of Marriage

Christ honored the marriage relation by making it also a symbol of the union between Him and His redeemed ones. He Himself is the Bridegroom; the bride is the church, of which, as His chosen one, He says, "Thou art all fair, My love; there is no spot in thee" (Song of Solomon 4:7). *MH 356*

8 Come with me from Lebanon, *my* spouse, with me from Lebanon: look from the top of Amana, from the top of Shenir and Hermon, from the lions' dens, from the mountains of the leopards.   Deut. 3:9; 1 Chr. 5:23; Ps. 45:10

9 Thou hast ravished my heart, my sister, *my* spouse; thou hast ravished my heart with one of thine eyes, with one chain of thy neck.   Song 5:1-2

10 How fair is thy love, my sister, *my* spouse! how much better is thy love than wine! and the smell of thine ointments than all spices!   Song 1:2-4

11 Thy lips, O *my* spouse, drop *as* the honeycomb: honey and milk *are* under thy tongue; and the smell of thy garments *is* like the smell of Lebanon.   Gen. 27:27

12 A garden inclosed *is* my sister, *my* spouse; a spring shut up, a fountain sealed.   Prov. 5:15-18

A Tender and Sacred Union

Song of Solomon 2:16; 4:7; 5:10

Like every other one of God's good gifts entrusted to the keeping of humanity, marriage has been perverted by sin; but it is the purpose of the gospel to restore its purity and beauty. In both the Old and the New Testament the marriage relation is employed to represent the tender and sacred union that exists between Christ and His people, the redeemed ones whom He has purchased at the cost of Calvary. "Fear not," He says; "thy Maker is thine husband; the Lord of hosts is His name; and thy Redeemer, the Holy One of Israel." "Turn, O backsliding children, saith the Lord; for I am married unto you" (Isaiah 54:4, 5; Jeremiah 3:14). In the "Song of Songs" we hear the bride's voice saying, "My Beloved is mine, and I am His." And He who is to her "the chiefest among ten thousand," speaks to His chosen one, "Thou art all fair, My love; there is no spot in thee" (Song of Solomon 2:16; 5:10; 4:7). *MB 64*

13 Thy plants *are* an orchard of pomegranates, with pleasant fruits; camphire, with spikenard,   Eccl. 2:5; Song 1:14; 6:11
14 Spikenard and saffron; calamus and cinnamon, with all trees of frankincense; myrrh and aloes, with all the chief spices: Ex. 30:23
15 A fountain of gardens, a well of living waters, and streams from Lebanon.   John 4:10

4:15 Deeper, Richer, More Abundant

"Give, and it shall be given unto you" (Luke 6:38); for the word of God is "a fountain of gardens, a well of living waters, and streams of Lebanon" (Song of Solomon 4:15). The heart that has once tasted the love of Christ, cries out continually for a deeper draft, and as you impart you will receive in richer and more abundant measure. Every revelation of God to the soul increases the capacity to know and to love. *MB 20*

---

16 Awake, O north wind; and come, thou south; blow upon my garden, *that* the spices thereof may flow out. Let my beloved come into his garden, and eat his pleasant fruits.   Song 5:1; 6:2

The Young Woman Dreams of Marriage

5 I am come into my garden, my sister, *my* spouse: I have gathered my myrrh with my spice; I have eaten my honeycomb with my honey; I have drunk my wine with my milk: eat, O friends; drink, yea, drink abundantly, O beloved.   Song 6:2
2 I sleep, but my heart waketh: *it is* the voice of my beloved that knocketh, *saying,* Open to me, my sister, my love, my dove, my undefiled: for my head is filled with dew, *and* my locks with the drops of the night.   Song 2:14; 6:9; Rev. 3:20
3 I have put off my coat; how shall I put it on? I have washed my feet; how shall I defile them?   Luke 11:7
4 My beloved put in his hand by the hole *of the door,* and my bowels were moved for him.

5 I rose up to open to my beloved; and my hands dropped *with* myrrh, and my fingers *with* sweet smelling myrrh, upon the handles of the lock.   Song 5:13
6 I opened to my beloved; but my beloved had withdrawn himself, *and* was gone: my soul failed when he spake: I sought him, but I could not find him; I called him, but he gave me no answer.   Song 5:2
7 The watchmen that went about the city found me, they smote me, they wounded me; the keepers of the walls took away my veil from me.   Song 3:3
8 I charge you, O daughters of Jerusalem, if ye find my beloved, that ye tell him, that I *am* sick of love.   Song 2:5, 7
9 What *is* thy beloved more than *another* beloved, O thou fairest among women? what *is* thy beloved more than *another* beloved, that thou dost so charge us?   Song 1:8; 6:1
10 My beloved *is* white and ruddy, the chiefest among ten thousand.   Ps. 45:2

5:10, 16 Sharing Jesus With Others

So it should be with us. Wherever we are, we should watch for opportunities of speaking to others of the Saviour. If we follow Christ's example in doing good, hearts will open to us as they did to Him. Not abruptly, but with tact born of divine love, we can tell them of Him who is the "Chiefest among ten thousand" and the One "altogether lovely" (Song of Solomon 5:10, 16). This is the very highest work in which we can employ the talent of speech. It was given to us that we might present Christ as the sin-pardoning Saviour. *COL 339*

---

11 His head *is as* the most fine gold, his locks *are* bushy, *and* black as a raven.
12 His eyes *are* as *the eyes* of doves by the rivers of waters, washed with milk, *and* fitly set.   Song 1:15; 4:1
13 His cheeks *are* as a bed of spices, *as* sweet flowers: his lips *like* lilies, dropping sweet smelling myrrh.   Song 1:10

The Beauty of Holiness

Song of Solomon 5:10–16

The great motive powers of the soul are faith, hope, and love; and it is to these that Bible study, rightly pursued, appeals. The outward beauty of the Bible, the beauty of imagery and expression, is but the setting, as it were, for its real treasure—the beauty of holiness. In its record of the men who walked with God, we may catch glimpses of His glory. In the One "altogether lovely" we behold Him, of whom all beauty of earth and heaven is but a dim reflection. "I, if I be lifted up," He said, "will draw all men unto Me" (John 12:32). As the student of the Bible beholds the Redeemer, there is awakened in the soul the mysterious power of faith, adoration, and love. Upon the vision of Christ the gaze is fixed, and the beholder grows into the likeness of that which he adores. The words of the apostle Paul become the language of the soul: "I count all things but loss for the excellency of the knowledge of Christ Jesus my Lord: . . . that I may know Him, and the power of His resurrection, and the fellowship of His sufferings" (Philippians 3:8–10). *Ed 192*

14 His hands *are as* gold rings set with the ᵀberyl: his belly *is as* bright ivory overlaid *with* sapphires.   Ex. 24:10 ◆ *precious stone*

15 His legs *are as* pillars of marble, set upon sockets of fine gold: his ᵀcountenance *is* as Lebanon, excellent as the cedars.   *appearance*

16 His mouth *is* most sweet: yea, he *is* altogether lovely. This *is* my beloved, and this *is* my friend, O daughters of Jerusalem. Ps. 45:2

Solomon Desires Her Love

6 Whither is thy beloved gone, O thou fairest among women? whither is thy beloved turned aside? that we may seek him with thee.   Song 1:8

2 My beloved is gone down into his garden, to the beds of spices, to feed in the gardens, and to gather lilies.   Song 5:13

3 I *am* my beloved's, and my beloved *is* mine: he feedeth among the lilies.   Song 2:16; 7:10

4 Thou *art* beautiful, O my love, as Tirzah, ᵀcomely as Jerusalem, terrible as *an army* with banners.   1 Kin. 14:17; Ps. 48:2; Song 6:10 ◆ *lovely*

5 Turn away thine eyes from me, for they have overcome me: thy hair *is* as a flock of goats that appear from Gilead.

6 Thy teeth *are* as a flock of sheep which go up from the washing, whereof every one beareth twins, and *there is* not one barren among them.   Song 4:2

7 As a piece of a pomegranate *are* thy temples within thy locks.   Song 4:3

8 There are ᵀthreescore queens, and ᵀfourscore concubines, and virgins without number.   Ps. 45:14 ◆ *sixty* ◆ *eighty*

9 My dove, my undefiled is *but* one; she *is* the *only* one of her mother, she *is* the choice *one* of her that bare her. The daughters saw her, and blessed her; *yea*, the queens and the concubines, and they praised her.   Song 2:14; 5:2

10 Who *is* she *that* looketh forth as the morning, fair as the moon, clear as the sun, *and* terrible as *an army* with banners? Song 6:4

6:10 The Conquering Church

Clad in the armor of Christ's righteousness, the church is to enter upon her final conflict. "Fair as the moon, clear as the sun, and terrible as an army with banners" (Song of Solomon 6:10) she is to go forth into all the world, conquering and to conquer. PK 725

---

11 I went down into the garden of nuts to see the fruits of the valley, *and* to see whether the vine flourished, *and* the pomegranates budded.   Song 7:12

12 Or ever I was aware, my soul made me *like* the chariots of Amminadib.

13 Return, return, O Shulamite; return, return, that we may look upon thee. What will ye see in the Shulamite? As it were the company of two armies.

The Bride's Beauty

7 How beautiful are thy feet with shoes, O prince's daughter! the joints of thy thighs *are* like jewels, the work of the hands of a cunning workman.   Ps. 45:13

2 Thy navel *is like* a round goblet, *which* wanteth not liquor: thy belly *is like* an heap of wheat set about with lilies.

3 Thy two breasts *are* like two young roes *that are* twins.   Song 4:5

4 Thy neck *is* as a tower of ivory; thine eyes *like* the fishpools in Heshbon, by the gate of Bath-rabbim: thy nose *is* as the tower of Lebanon which looketh toward Damascus.   Ps. 144:12; Song 4:4

5 Thine head upon thee *is* like Carmel, and the hair of thine head like purple; the king *is* held in the galleries.   Is. 35:2

6 How fair and how pleasant art thou, O love, for delights!   Song 1:15-16

7 This thy stature is like to a palm tree, and thy breasts to clusters *of grapes*.   Song 4:5

8 I said, I will go up to the palm tree, I will take hold of the boughs thereof: now also thy breasts shall be as clusters of the vine, and the smell of thy nose like apples;

9 And the roof of thy mouth like the best wine for my beloved, that goeth *down* sweetly, causing the lips of those that are asleep to speak.   Song 5:16

10 I *am* my beloved's, and his desire *is* toward me.   Ps. 45:11; Song 2:16; 6:3

11 Come, my beloved, let us go forth into the field; let us lodge in the villages. Song 4:8

12 Let us get up early to the vineyards; let us see if the vine flourish, *whether* the tender grape appear, *and* the pomegranates bud forth: there will I give thee my loves. Song 6:11

13 The mandrakes give a smell, and at our gates *are* all manner of pleasant *fruits*, new and old, *which* I have laid up for thee, O my beloved.   Gen. 30:14; Matt. 13:52

The Young Woman's Love

8 O that thou *wert* as my brother, that sucked the breasts of my mother! *when* I should find thee without, I would kiss thee; yea, I should not be despised.

2 I would lead thee, *and* bring thee into my mother's house, *who* would instruct me: I would cause thee to drink of spiced wine of the juice of my pomegranate. Prov. 9:2; Song 3:4

3 His left hand *should be* under my head, and his right hand should embrace me.   Song 2:6

4 I charge you, O daughters of Jerusalem, that ye stir not up, nor awake *my* love, until he please.   Song 2:7; 3:5

5 Who *is* this that cometh up from the

wilderness, leaning upon her beloved? I raised thee up under the apple tree: there thy mother brought thee forth: there she brought thee forth *that* bare thee.   Song 2:3; 3:4, 6

6 Set me as a seal upon thine heart, as a seal upon thine arm: for love *is* strong as death; jealousy *is* cruel as the grave: the coals thereof *are* coals of fire, *which hath a* most vehement flame.   Is. 49:16

7 Many waters cannot quench love, neither can the floods drown it: if *a* man would give all the substance of his house for love, it would utterly be contemned.   Prov. 6:35

8:7 Love a Principle, Not a Feeling

Love is a precious gift, which we receive from Jesus. Pure and holy affection is not a feeling, but a principle. Those who are actuated by true love are neither unreasonable nor blind. Taught by the Holy Spirit, they love God supremely, and their neighbor as themselves. *MH 358*

---

8 We have a little sister, and she hath no breasts: what shall we do for our sister in the day when she shall be spoken for?

9 If she *be* a wall, we will build upon her a palace of silver: and if she *be* a door, we will inclose her with boards of cedar.

10 I *am* a wall, and my breasts like towers: then was I in his eyes as one that found favour.   Song 4:5

11 Solomon had a vineyard at Baal-hamon; he let out the vineyard unto keepers; every one for the fruit thereof was to bring a thousand *pieces* of silver.   Eccl. 2:4; Is. 7:23

12 My vineyard, which *is* mine, *is* before me: thou, O Solomon, *must have* a thousand, and those that keep the fruit thereof two hundred.   Song 1:6

13 Thou that dwellest in the gardens, the companions hearken to thy voice: cause me to hear *it*.   Song 1:7

14 Make haste, my beloved, and be thou like to a roe or to a young [T]hart upon the mountains of spices.   Song 2:17 ♦ *deer*

THE BOOK OF

ISAIAH

If there is one book that sums up the prophetic words about the Messiah, it is Isaiah. The Book of Isaiah is a masterpiece in its literary and prophetic product, but it is for the veracity of his prophecies that readers today still value Isaiah's work. Many find hope in his words as they anticipate the Messiah's Second Advent.

The Book of Isaiah has been compared to a miniature Bible. The first thirty-nine chapters of Isaiah seem to reflect the theme of judgment found in the thirty-nine books of the Old Testament: Humanity is sinful and must be judged. The final twenty-seven chapters of Isaiah reflect the message of the twenty-seven books of the New Testament, proclaiming the message of hope through a Savior.

Isaiah's prophetic ministry covers forty years, during which the kingdoms of Israel and Judah declined increasingly toward God's judgment (10:1–19, 28–33). Like his contemporaries Hosea and Micah, Isaiah warns the people to turn back to God, knowing the consequences of disobedience: bitter defeat and exile.

Dates

Isaiah's ministry extended over the rule of five kings. He started around 745 B.C. near the end of Uzziah's reign (790–739 B.C.) and ended about 685 B.C. during the reign of Manasseh (686–642 B.C.), son of Hezekiah, when Manasseh likely had him executed (Hebrews 11:37 possibly refers to this event). Isaiah served under Jotham (739–731 B.C.), Ahaz (731–715 B.C.), and Hezekiah (715–686 B.C.).

Isaiah lived during the time of the divided kingdoms of Israel and Judah. Assyria threatened both Hebrew nations with its military might. Assyria takes all of Israel and part of Judah but not Jerusalem. Isaiah warned the kings of Judah to trust in Yahweh first and not in military alliances to save the kingdom. Judah was sinful, and Isaiah warned that if they did not turn from their wickedness, they would meet their downfall at the hands of the Babylonians (Chaldeans), rather than the Assyrians.

Author

Isaiah was known in the royal court, and like Moses had the benefits of a good education. He had a prophetess wife and at least two sons (Isaiah 7:3; 8:3). He was known for being sincere and compassionate, yet unwavering in serving as a court preacher in Jerusalem where he was quite influential.

Some circles challenge that there are two authors who wrote Isaiah, but the various quotes from Isaiah in the New Testament quickly debunk that notion (see Matthew 3:3; 12:17–21; Luke 3:4–6; 4:17–19; John 12:37–41; Acts 8:28, 32, 33; Romans 9:27, 29; 10:16–21). Isaiah is quoted in the New Testament more than any other Old Testament prophet. Following are some examples:

Reference in Isaiah	New Testament Citation
1:9	Romans 9:29
6:9,10	Matthew 13:14, 15
6:9,10	John 12:40, 41
6:9,10	Acts 28:25–27
9:1,2	Matthew 4:14–16
11:10	Romans 15:12
29:13	Matthew 15:7–9
29:13	Mark 7:6, 7
40:3	Matthew 3:3
40:3	Mark 1:3
40:3	John 1:23
40:3–5	Luke 3:4–6
42:1–4	Matthew 12:17–21
53:1	John 12:38
53:1	Romans 10:16

Reference in Isaiah	New Testament Citation
53:4	Matthew 8:17
53:7,8	Acts 8:32, 33
65:1,2	Romans 10:20, 21

Critics are quick to speak of the differences in tone between the first and second parts of Isaiah. Considering the subject matter—judgment versus salvation—the harsh tone Isaiah used early on was entirely appropriate, just as his gentler tone was correct in the latter chapters.

The comparison of Jesus as "King" in the early chapters and the notion of the "Suffering Servant" in the latter chapters also invite criticism. If critics looked more closely, they would see that both terms are used in both parts of Isaiah.

Finally, some critics challenge Isaiah's authorship by the presence of the prophecies that the book contains, essentially denying the supernatural inspiration of the Word. However, these critics cannot account for the many and specific Messianic prophecies and their later fulfillment by Jesus.

Meaning of the Name

The name Isaiah in the Hebrew is *yesha'yahu* or more briefly *yeshaiah*, which means "Yahweh is Salvation." In Latin Isaiah is *Isaias* while in Greek, it is *Hesaias*.

Christ in Isaiah

The prophetic portrayal of Jesus is presented most strongly in Isaiah. His prophecies are clear and detailed, leaving no doubt for those who observed the life of Jesus, for He fulfilled more than a hundred of them in His life and ministry on earth, His First Advent. Even a few of these prophecies coming true (much less all of them) in the life of one man is well beyond the limits of statistical chance.

Isaiah's tone is more like that of a New Testament writer when speaking of the coming Messiah. His words speak to the work and the Person of Jesus, often blending the descriptions of His First and Second Advents.

The following chart highlights Isaiah's prophecies of Christ's First Advent and their fulfillments, as well as the prophecies of His Second Advent (for a chart of more of the prophecies fulfilled by Christ, see "Prophecies of the Messiah Fulfilled in Jesus Christ" beginning on page 1417).

First Advent	New Testament Fulfillment
7:14	Matthew 1:22, 23; Luke 2:7
9:1, 2	Matthew 4:12–16
9:6	Luke 2:11; Ephesians 2:14–18
11:1, 10	Luke 3:23, 32; Acts 13:22, 23
11:2	Luke 3:22
28:16	1 Peter 2:4–6
40:3–5	Matthew 3:1–3
42:1–4	Matthew 12:15–21
42:6	Luke 2:29–32
50:6	Matthew 26:67; 27:26, 30
52:14	Philippians 2:7–11
53:3	Luke 23:18; John 1:11; 7:5
53:4, 5	Romans 5:6, 8
53:7	Matthew 27:12–14; John 1:29; 1 Peter 1:18, 19
53:9	Matthew 27:57–60
53:12	Mark 15:28
61:1, 2	Luke 4:17–19, 21

Second Advent
4:2; 11:2–6, 10; 32:1–8; 49:7; 52:13, 15; 59:20, 21; 60:1–3; 61:2, 3

Overview

The book of Isaiah has two major focuses and three thematic subdivisions:

(1) *Isaiah 1—35, Charges against Judah and Israel:* The first twelve chapters discuss the corruption of Judah and the judgment their actions reaped. Like Joel and other Old Testament prophets, Isaiah describes God's coming judgment as the "day of the Lord" (chapter 2). Within this section, however, Isaiah includes prophecies of the Messiah's First and Second Advents (7:14; 9:2, 6; 11—12) before moving on to God's judgment against other nations

(chapters 13—23). The Book of Isaiah includes apocalyptic writing (chapters 24—27), as a period of tribulation is followed by blessing. In chapters 28—33, Isaiah prophesies six woes against Israel and Judah. The section ends with encouragement as aspects of the Messiah's ministry are foretold (35:3–6).

(2) *Isaiah 36—39, A Historical Perspective:* Isaiah discusses the Assyrian invasion during the time of King Hezekiah (chapters 36—37; see also 2 Kings 18—19) and the coming invasion by Babylon (chapter 39).

(3) *Isaiah 40—66, The Messiah Is Coming:* This section aptly starts with "Comfort ye, comfort ye my people" (40:1) as the prophecies turn from condemnation to encouragement through the promise of a future restoration. Isaiah discusses the sovereign nature of God (chapters 40—48) and the Messiah's advent (chapters 49—57). The blessings of trusting in God are described (chapters 58—66).

Unlocking Isaiah

KEY PEOPLE:
The Messiah, Isaiah, Uzziah, Jotham, Ahaz, Hezekiah, Manasseh

KEY EVENTS:
Prophecies of the Messiah; warnings to Judah; warnings to the enemies of Israel; promises of future preservation to Israel

KEY WORD:
Salvation, which is proclaimed throughout Isaiah. The word *salvation* appears twenty-six times in the book, more than in any other Old Testament book. The first half of Isaiah presents the need for salvation, and the last half the prophecies of the Savior.

KEY VERSES:
"For unto us a child is born, unto us a son is given; and the government shall be upon his shoulder: and his name shall be called Wonderful, Counsellor, The mighty God, The everlasting Father, The Prince of Peace. Of the increase of his government and peace there shall be no end, upon the throne of David, and upon his kingdom, to order it, and to establish it with judgment and with justice from henceforth even for ever. The zeal of the LORD of hosts will perform this" (Isaiah 9:6, 7).

KEY CHAPTER:
Isaiah 53, which represents Jesus in microcosm. His perfect character (verses 1–3), His atonement for peace with God (verses 4–6), His eternal payment for sinners' transgressions (verses 7–9), and His death as the sacrifice for sin (verses 10–12).

Isaiah Describes Judah's Rebellion

1 The vision of Isaiah the son of Amoz, which he saw concerning Judah and Jerusalem in the days of Uzziah, Jotham, Ahaz, *and* Hezekiah, kings of Judah. Is. 2:1
2 Hear, O heavens, and give ear, O earth: for the Lord hath spoken, I have nourished and brought up children, and they have rebelled against me. Deut. 4:26; 32:1; Mic. 1:2
3 The ox knoweth his owner, and the ass his master's ᵀcrib: *but* Israel doth not know, my people doth not consider. Jer. 8:7 ◆ *feeding trough*
4 Ah sinful nation, a people ᵀladen with iniquity, a seed of evildoers, children that are corrupters: they have forsaken the Lord, they have provoked the Holy One of Israel unto anger, they are gone away backward. *loaded*
5 Why should ye be stricken any more? ye will revolt more and more: the whole head is sick, and the whole heart faint. Is. 9:13
6 From the sole of the foot even unto the head *there is* no soundness in it; *but* wounds, and bruises, and ᵀputrifying sores: they have not been closed, neither bound up, neither mollified with ointment. Jer. 6:14 ◆ *decaying*
7 Your country *is* desolate, your cities *are* burned with fire: your land, strangers devour it in your presence, and *it is* desolate, as overthrown by strangers. Lev. 26:34
8 And the daughter of Zion is left as a cottage in a vineyard, as a lodge in a garden of cucumbers, as a besieged city. Job 27:18; Is. 10:32; 37:22
9 Except the Lord of hosts had left unto us a very small remnant, we should have been as Sodom, *and* we should have been like unto Gomorrah. Gen. 19:24; Is. 37:4; Rom. 9:29

1:8, 9 The Discouraged Few

Iniquitous practices had become so prevalent among all classes that the few who remained true to God were often tempted to lose heart and to give way to discouragement and despair. It seemed as if God's purpose for Israel were about to fail and that the rebellious nation was to suffer a fate similar to that of Sodom and Gomorrah. *PK 306*

Israel's Corrupt Religion

10 Hear the word of the Lord, ye rulers of Sodom; give ear unto the law of our God, ye people of Gomorrah. Deut. 32:32; Is. 3:9; Rev. 11:8
11 To what purpose *is* the multitude of your sacrifices unto me? saith the Lord: I am full of the burnt offerings of rams, and the fat of fed beasts; and I delight not in the blood of bullocks, or of lambs, or of he goats. 1 Sam. 15:22; Ps. 50:8; Jer. 6:20
12 When ye come to appear before me, who hath required this at your hand, to tread my courts? Ex. 23:17; 34:23

13 Bring no more vain oblations; incense is an abomination unto me; the new moons and sabbaths, the calling of assemblies, I cannot away with; *it is* iniquity, even the solemn meeting. Is. 66:3
14 Your new moons and your appointed feasts my soul hateth: they are a trouble unto me; I am weary to bear *them*. Is. 43:24
15 And when ye spread forth your hands, I will hide mine eyes from you: yea, when ye make many prayers, I will not hear: your hands are full of blood. 1 Kin. 8:22; Is. 59:2-3; Mic. 3:4

Isaiah Exhorts Israel to Repentance

16 Wash you, make you clean; put away the evil of your doings from before mine eyes; cease to do evil; Ps. 26:6
17 Learn to do well; seek judgment, relieve the oppressed, judge the fatherless, plead for the widow. Jer. 22:3
18 Come now, and let us reason together, saith the Lord: though your sins be as scarlet, they shall be as white as snow; though they be red like crimson, they shall be as wool. Ps. 51:7; Mic. 6:2; Rev. 7:14

1:18 Yielding to Be Transformed

The whole heart must be yielded to God, or the change can never be wrought in us by which we are to be restored to His likeness. By nature we are alienated from God. . . . God desires to heal us, to set us free. But since this requires an entire transformation, a renewing of our whole nature, we must yield ourselves wholly to Him. *SC 43*

---

19 If ye be willing and obedient, ye shall eat the good of the land: Deut. 30:15-16
20 But if ye refuse and rebel, ye shall be devoured with the sword: for the mouth of the Lord hath spoken *it*. Num. 23:19; Is. 40:5; 58:14

Jerusalem's Future

21 How is the faithful city become an harlot! it was full of judgment; righteousness lodged in it; but now murderers.
22 Thy silver is become ᵀdross, thy wine mixed with water: *waste from melting metal*
23 Thy princes *are* rebellious, and companions of thieves: every one loveth gifts, and followeth after rewards: they judge not the fatherless, neither doth the cause of the widow come unto them. Ex. 23:8; Mic. 7:3; Zech. 7:10
24 Therefore saith the Lord, the Lord of hosts, the mighty One of Israel, Ah, I will ease me of mine adversaries, and avenge me of mine enemies: Deut. 28:63
25 And I will turn my hand upon thee, and purely purge away thy dross, and take away all thy tin: Mal. 3:3
26 And I will restore thy judges as at the

first, and thy counsellors as at the beginning: afterward thou shalt be called, The city of righteousness, the faithful city.　　Jer. 33:7

27 Zion shall be redeemed with judgment, and her converts with righteousness.

28 And the destruction of the ᵀtransgressors and of the sinners *shall be* together, and they that forsake the LORD shall be consumed.　　Job 31:3　◆ *lawbreakers*

29 For they shall be ashamed of the oaks which ye have desired, and ye shall be confounded for the gardens that ye have chosen.　　Is. 57:5; 65:3; 66:17

30 For ye shall be as an oak whose leaf fadeth, and as a garden that hath no water.

31 And the strong shall be as ᵀtow, and the maker of it as a spark, and they shall both burn together, and none shall quench *them*.　　*tinder*

Isaiah Prophesies the Coming of Christ's Kingdom

2 The word that Isaiah the son of Amoz saw concerning Judah and Jerusalem.　　Is. 1:1

2 And it shall come to pass in the last days, *that* the mountain of the LORD's house shall be established in the top of the mountains, and shall be exalted above the hills; and all nations shall flow unto it.　　Is. 27:13

3 And many people shall go and say, Come ye, and let us go up to the mountain of the LORD, to the house of the God of Jacob; and he will teach us of his ways, and we will walk in his paths: for out of Zion shall go forth the law, and the word of the LORD from Jerusalem.　　Is. 51:4-5; Zech. 8:20-23; Luke 24:47

4 And he shall judge among the nations, and shall rebuke many people: and they shall beat their swords into plowshares, and their spears into pruninghooks: nation shall not lift up sword against nation, neither shall they learn war any more.　　Hos. 2:18; Joel 3:10; Zech. 9:10

5 O house of Jacob, come ye, and let us walk in the light of the LORD.　　Eph. 5:8

The People's Sins

6 Therefore thou hast forsaken thy people the house of Jacob, because they be replenished from the east, and *are* soothsayers like the Philistines, and they please themselves in the children of strangers.　　2 Kin. 1:2

7 Their land also is full of silver and gold, neither *is there any* end of their treasures; their land is also full of horses, neither *is there any* end of their chariots:　　Is. 30:16

8 Their land also is full of idols; they worship the work of their own hands, that which their own fingers have made:　　Ps. 115:4-8

9 And the mean man boweth down, and the great man humbleth himself: therefore forgive them not.　　Ps. 49:2; Is. 5:15

Fear the Power of God's Majesty

10 Enter into the rock, and hide thee in the dust, for fear of the LORD, and for the glory of his majesty.　　Rev. 6:15-16

11 The lofty looks of man shall be humbled, and the haughtiness of men shall be bowed down, and the LORD alone shall be exalted in that day.　　Ps. 18:27

12 For the day of the LORD of hosts *shall be* upon every *one that is* proud and lofty, and upon every *one that is* lifted up; and he shall be brought low:　　Mal. 4:1

2:11, 12 Truth Will Triumph

But the Lord will not always suffer His law to be broken and despised with impunity. . . . Skepticism may treat the claims of God's law with jest, scoffing, and denial. The spirit of worldliness may contaminate the many and control the few, the cause of God may hold its ground only by great exertion and continual sacrifice, yet in the end the truth will triumph gloriously. *PK 186*

13 And upon all the cedars of Lebanon, *that are* high and lifted up, and upon all the oaks of Bashan,　　Is. 14:8

14 And upon all the high mountains, and upon all the hills *that are* lifted up,　　Is. 30:25

15 And upon every high tower, and upon every fenced wall,

16 And upon all the ships of Tarshish, and upon all pleasant pictures.　　1 Kin. 10:22; Is. 23:1

17 And the loftiness of man shall be bowed down, and the haughtiness of men shall be made low: and the LORD alone shall be exalted in that day.　　Is. 2:11

18 And the idols he shall utterly abolish.

19 And they shall go into the holes of the rocks, and into the caves of the earth, for fear of the LORD, and for the glory of his majesty, when he ariseth to shake terribly the earth.　　Is. 2:10, 21; Heb. 12:26

2:20, 21 Rebellion's Ruin

Then it will be seen that Satan's rebellion against God has resulted in ruin to himself and to all that chose to become his subjects. He has represented that great good would result from transgression; but it will be seen that "the wages of sin is death" [Romans 6:23]. *PP 341*

20 In that day a man shall cast his idols of silver, and his idols of gold, which they made *each one* for himself to worship, to the moles and to the bats;　　Is. 30:22

21 To go into the clefts of the rocks, and into the tops of the ragged rocks, for fear of the LORD, and for the glory of his majesty, when he ariseth to shake terribly the earth.　　Is. 2:19

22 Cease ye from man, whose breath *is*

in his nostrils: for wherein is he to be accounted of? Ps. 8:4; 146:3; Jer. 17:5

The Lord's Judgment on Sin

3 For, behold, the Lord, the LORD of hosts, doth take away from Jerusalem and from Judah the stay and the staff, the whole stay of bread, and the whole stay of water, Lev. 26:26; Is. 1:24
2 The mighty man, and the man of war, the judge, and the prophet, and the prudent, and the ancient, Ezek. 17:13
3 The captain of fifty, and the honourable man, and the counsellor, and the cunning ᵀartificer, and the eloquent orator. *craftsman*
4 And I will give children *to be* their princes, and babes shall rule over them. Eccl. 10:16

3:1–4 Childish Leadership

Solomon had written, "Woe to thee, O land, when thy king is a child!" (Ecclesiastes 10:16). Thus it was with the land of Judah. Through continued transgression her rulers had become as children. Isaiah called the attention of the people to the weakness of their position among the nations of earth, and he showed that this was the result of wickedness in high places. *PK 323*

---

5 And the people shall be oppressed, every one by another, and every one by his neighbour: the child shall behave himself proudly against the ancient, and the ᵀbase against the honourable. Jer. 9:3-8 ◆ *despised*
6 When a man shall take hold of his brother of the house of his father, *saying*, Thou hast clothing, be thou our ruler, and *let* this ruin *be* under thy hand: Is. 4:1
7 In that day shall he swear, saying, I will not be an healer; for in my house *is* neither bread nor clothing: make me not a ruler of the people. Hos. 5:13
8 For Jerusalem is ruined, and Judah is

fallen: because their tongue and their doings *are* against the LORD, to provoke the eyes of his glory.

The Impudence of the People

9 The shew of their ᵀcountenance doth witness against them; and they declare their sin as Sodom, they hide *it* not. Woe unto their soul! for they have rewarded evil unto themselves. Gen. 13:13; Rom. 6:23 ◆ *appearance*
10 Say ye to the righteous, that *it shall be* well *with him*: for they shall eat the fruit of their doings. Eccl. 8:12
11 Woe unto the wicked! *it shall be* ill *with him*: for the reward of his hands shall be given him. Deut. 28:15-68

3:10, 11 Who We Are; What We Do

No truth does the Bible more clearly teach than that what we do is the result of what we are. To a great degree the experiences of life are the fruition of our own thoughts and deeds. . . .

Terrible is this truth, and deeply should it be impressed. Every deed reacts upon the doer. Never a human being but may recognize, in the evils that curse his life, fruitage of his own sowing. *Ed 146*

---

12 *As for* my people, children *are* their oppressors, and women rule over them. O my people, they which lead thee cause *thee* to ᵀerr, and destroy the way of thy paths. Is. 3:4 ◆ *stray*
13 The LORD standeth up to plead, and standeth to judge the people. Mic. 6:2
14 The LORD will enter into judgment with the ancients of his people, and the princes thereof: for ye have eaten up the vineyard; the ᵀspoil of the poor *is* in your houses. *plunder*
15 What mean ye *that* ye beat my people to pieces, and grind the faces of the poor? saith the Lord GOD of hosts. Ps. 94:5

Condition of an Unrenewed Heart

Isaiah 2:19–21

In his sinless state, man held joyful communion with Him "in whom are hid all the treasures of wisdom and knowledge" (Colossians 2:3). But after his sin, he could no longer find joy in holiness, and he sought to hide from the presence of God. Such is still the condition of the unrenewed heart. It is not in harmony with God, and finds no joy in communion with Him. The sinner could not be happy in God's presence; he would shrink from the companionship of holy beings. Could he be permitted to enter heaven, it would have no joy for him. The spirit of unselfish love that reigns there—every heart responding to the heart of Infinite Love—would touch no answering chord in his soul. His thoughts, his interests, his motives, would be alien to those that actuate the sinless dwellers there. He would be a discordant note in the melody of heaven. Heaven would be to him a place of torture; he would long to be hidden from Him who is its light, and the center of its joy. It is no arbitrary decree on the part of God that excludes the wicked from heaven; they are shut out by their own unfitness for its companionship. The glory of God would be to them a consuming fire. They would welcome destruction, that they might be hidden from the face of Him who died to redeem them. *SC 17, 18*

3:16-24

Judgments for the Women's Pride

16 Moreover the LORD saith, Because the daughters of Zion are haughty, and walk with stretched forth necks and [T]wanton eyes, walking and mincing *as* they go, and making a tinkling with their feet: Is. 4:4 ♦ *seductive*

17 Therefore the Lord will smite with a scab the crown of the head of the daughters of Zion, and the LORD will discover their secret parts.

18 In that day the Lord will take away the [T]bravery of *their* tinkling ornaments *about their feet*, and *their* [T]cauls, and *their* round [T]tires like the moon,   Judg. 8:21 ♦ *beauty* ♦ *headpieces* ♦ *turbans*

19 The chains, and the bracelets, and the [T]mufflers,   *light veils*

20 The bonnets, and the ornaments of the legs, and the headbands, and the tablets, and the earrings,   Ex. 39:28

21 The rings, and nose jewels,   Gen. 24:47

22 The changeable suits of apparel, and the mantles, and the wimples, and the crisping pins,

23 The glasses, and the fine linen, and the hoods, and the [T]vails.   *veils*

24 And it shall come to pass, *that* instead of sweet smell there shall be stink; and instead of a [T]girdle a rent; and instead of well set hair baldness; and instead of a [T]stomacher a girding of sackcloth; *and* burning instead of beauty.   Is. 22:12; Lam. 2:10; Ezek. 27:31 ♦ *belt* ♦ *rich robe*

> Christian Behavior See 1 Timothy 2:9, 10.

25 Thy men shall fall by the sword, and thy mighty in the war.

26 And her gates shall lament and mourn; and she *being* desolate shall sit upon the ground.   Jer. 14:2; Lam. 1:4; 2:10

The Lord's New Glory for Jerusalem

4 And in that day seven women shall take hold of one man, saying, We will eat our own bread, and wear our own apparel: only let us be called by thy name, *to* take away our reproach.   Gen. 30:23; Is. 13:12

2 In that day shall the branch of the LORD be beautiful and glorious, and the fruit of the earth *shall be* excellent and comely for them that are escaped of Israel.   Jer. 23:5; Zech. 3:8; 6:12

3 And it shall come to pass, *that* he that is left in Zion, and *he that* remaineth in Jerusalem, shall be called holy, *even* every one that is written among the living in Jerusalem: Is. 52:1

4 When the Lord shall have washed away the filth of the daughters of Zion, and shall have purged the blood of Jerusalem from the midst thereof by the spirit of judgment, and by the spirit of burning.   Mal. 3:2-3

5 And the LORD will create upon every dwelling place of mount Zion, and upon her assemblies, a cloud and smoke by day, and the shining of a flaming fire by night: for upon all the glory *shall be* a defence.   Ex. 13:21-22

6 And there shall be a tabernacle for a shadow in the daytime from the heat, and for a place of refuge, and for a [T]covert from storm and from rain.   Ps. 27:5; Is. 25:4; 32:2 ♦ *hiding place*

4:5, 6 Symbols of God's Care

In one of the most beautiful and comforting passages of Isaiah's prophecy, reference is made to the pillar of cloud and of fire to represent God's care for His people in the great final struggle with the powers of evil: "The Lord will create upon every dwelling place of Mount Zion, and upon her assemblies, a cloud and smoke by day, and the shining of a flaming fire by night: for above all the glory shall be a covering" (Isaiah 4:5). *PP 283*

The Parable of the Vineyard

5 Now will I sing to my wellbeloved a song of my beloved touching his vineyard. My wellbeloved hath a vineyard in a very fruitful hill: Ps. 80:8; Matt. 21:33; Mark 12:1

The Lord's Vineyard

Isaiah 5:1–7

The husbandman chooses a piece of land from the wilderness; he fences, clears, and tills it, and plants it with choice vines, expecting a rich harvest. This plot of ground, in its superiority to the uncultivated waste, he expects to do him honor by showing the results of his care and toil in its cultivation. So God had chosen a people from the world to be trained and educated by Christ. The prophet says, "The vineyard of the Lord of hosts is the house of Israel, and the men of Judah His pleasant plant" (Isaiah 5:7). Upon this people God had bestowed great privileges, blessing them richly from His abundant goodness. He looked for them to honor Him by yielding fruit. They were to reveal the principles of His kingdom. In the midst of a fallen, wicked world they were to represent the character of God.

As the Lord's vineyard they were to produce fruit altogether different from that of the heathen nations. These idolatrous peoples had given themselves up to work wickedness. Violence and crime, greed, oppression, and the most corrupt practices, were indulged without restraint. Iniquity, degradation, and misery were the fruits of the corrupt tree. In marked contrast was to be the fruit borne on the vine of God's planting. *COL 285*

2 And he fenced it, and gathered out the stones thereof, and planted it with the choicest vine, and built a tower in the midst of it, and also made a winepress therein: and he looked that it should bring forth grapes, and it brought forth wild grapes. Jer. 2:21; Matt. 21:19
3 And now, O inhabitants of Jerusalem, and men of Judah, judge, I pray you, ᵀbetwixt me and my vineyard. *between*
4 What could have been done more to my vineyard, that I have not done in it? wherefore, when I looked that it should bring forth grapes, brought it forth wild grapes? Matt.23:37
5 And now go to; I will tell you what I will do to my vineyard: I will take away the hedge thereof, and it shall be eaten up; *and* break down the wall thereof, and it shall be ᵀtrodden down: Is. 28:18 ◆ *trampled*
6 And I will lay it waste: it shall not be pruned, nor digged; but there shall come up briers and thorns: I will also command the clouds that they rain no rain upon it. Is. 7:23-25
7 For the vineyard of the LORD of hosts *is* the house of Israel, and the men of Judah his pleasant plant: and he looked for judgment, but behold oppression; for righteousness, but behold a cry. Ps. 80:8-11

Six Sins Condemned

8 Woe unto them that join house to house, *that* lay field to field, till *there be* no place, that they may be placed alone in the midst of the earth! Jer. 22:13-17; Mic. 2:2; Hab. 2:9-12
9 In mine ears *said* the LORD of hosts, Of a truth many houses shall be desolate, *even* great and fair, without inhabitant. Matt. 23:38
10 Yea, ten acres of vineyard shall yield one bath, and the seed of an homer shall yield an ephah. Lev. 26:26
11 Woe unto them that rise up early in the morning, *that* they may follow strong drink; that continue until night, *till* wine inflame them! Prov. 23:29-30; Eccl. 10:16-17; Is. 5:22
12 And the harp, and the viol, the tabret, and pipe, and wine, are in their feasts: but they regard not the work of the LORD, neither consider the operation of his hands. Job 34:27
13 Therefore my people are gone into captivity, because *they have* no knowledge: and their honourable men *are* famished, and their multitude dried up with thirst. Is. 1:3; Hos. 4:6
14 Therefore hell hath enlarged herself, and opened her mouth without measure: and their glory, and their multitude, and their pomp, and he that rejoiceth, shall descend into it. Hab. 2:5
15 And the mean man shall be brought down, and the mighty man shall be humbled, and the eyes of the lofty shall be humbled: Is. 2:9
16 But the LORD of hosts shall be exalted in judgment, and God that is holy shall be ᵀsanctified in righteousness. Is. 29:23 ◆ *made holy*
17 Then shall the lambs feed after their manner, and the waste places of the fat ones shall strangers eat. Is. 7:25
18 Woe unto them that draw iniquity with cords of vanity, and sin as it were with a cart rope: Jer. 23:14
19 That say, Let him make speed, *and* hasten his work, that we may see *it*: and let the counsel of the Holy One of Israel draw nigh and come, that we may know *it*! Jer. 17:15; Ezek. 12:22
20 Woe unto them that call evil good, and good evil; that put darkness for light, and light for darkness; that put bitter for sweet, and sweet for bitter! Prov. 17:15

> **5:20 Behind Enemy Lines**
>
> Satan will work with all his deceptive power to influence the heart and becloud the understanding, to make evil appear good, and good evil. The stronger and purer the faith of God's people, and the firmer their determination to obey Him, the more fiercely will Satan strive to stir up against them the rage of those who, while claiming to be righteous, trample upon the law of God. It will require the firmest trust, the most heroic purpose, to hold fast the faith once delivered to the saints. *AA 431*

21 Woe unto *them that are* wise in their own eyes, and prudent in their own sight! Prov. 3:7
22 Woe unto *them that are* mighty to drink wine, and men of strength to mingle strong drink: Is. 5:11; 28:7; Hab. 2:15
23 Which justify the wicked for reward, and take away the righteousness of the righteous from him! Ps. 94:21

Another Nation Will Punish Israel

24 Therefore as the fire devoureth the stubble, and the flame consumeth the chaff, *so* their root shall be as rottenness, and their blossom shall go up as dust: because they have cast away the law of the LORD of hosts, and despised the word of the Holy One of Israel. Job 18:16; Is. 30:12; Joel 2:5
25 Therefore is the anger of the LORD kindled against his people, and he hath stretched forth his hand against them, and hath smitten them: and the hills did tremble, and their carcases *were* torn in the midst of the streets. For all this his anger is not turned away, but his hand *is* stretched out still. 2 Kin. 9:37; Is. 9:17, 21
26 And he will lift up an ensign to the nations from far, and will hiss unto them from the end of the earth: and, behold, they shall come with speed swiftly: Deut. 28:49; Is. 7:18; Zech. 10:8
27 None shall be weary nor stumble

among them; none shall slumber nor sleep; neither shall the ᵀgirdle of their ᵀloins be loosed, nor the ᵀlatchet of their shoes be broken: Job 12:18 ◆ *belt* ◆ *waist* ◆ *sandal strap*
28 Whose arrows *are* sharp, and all their bows bent, their horses' hoofs shall be counted like flint, and their wheels like a whirlwind: Ps. 45:5
29 Their roaring *shall be* like a lion, they shall roar like young lions: yea, they shall roar, and lay hold of the prey, and shall carry *it* away safe, and none shall deliver *it*.   Is. 42:22
30 And in that day they shall roar against them like the roaring of the sea: and if *one* look unto the land, behold darkness *and* sorrow, and the light is darkened in the heavens thereof.   Is. 8:22; Jer. 4:23-28; Joel 2:10

Isaiah's Vision of the Lord's Glory

6 In the year that king Uzziah died I saw also the Lord sitting upon a throne, high and lifted up, and his train filled the temple.   2 Kin. 15:7; John 12:41; Rev. 4:2
2 Above it stood the seraphims: each one had six wings; with ᵀtwain he covered his face, and with twain he covered his feet, and with twain he did fly. Ps. 103:20; Ezek. 1:11; Rev. 4:8 ◆ *two*
3 And one cried unto another, and said, Holy, holy, holy, *is* the LORD of hosts: the whole earth *is* full of his glory.   Num. 14:21; Ps. 72:19

> **6:3 In Contrast With Perfection**
>
> As Isaiah beheld this revelation of the glory and majesty of his Lord, he was overwhelmed with a sense of the purity and holiness of God. How sharp the contrast between the matchless perfection of his Creator, and the sinful course of those who, with himself, had long been numbered among the chosen people of Israel and Judah! *PK 307*

4 And the posts of the door moved at the voice of him that cried, and the house was filled with smoke.   Rev. 15:8
5 Then said I, Woe *is* me! for I am undone; because I *am* a man of unclean lips, and I dwell in the midst of a people of unclean lips: for mine eyes have seen the King, the LORD of hosts.

> **6:5 Walking in the Shadow of the Cross**
>
> There can be no self-exaltation, no boastful claim to freedom from sin, on the part of those who walk in the shadow of Calvary's cross. They feel that it was their sin which caused the agony that broke the heart of the Son of God, and this thought will lead them to self-abasement. Those who live nearest to Jesus discern most clearly the frailty and sinfulness of humanity, and their only hope is in the merit of a crucified and risen Saviour. *GC 471*

6 Then flew one of the seraphims unto me, having a live coal in his hand, *which* he had taken with the tongs from off the altar:

7 And he laid *it* upon my mouth, and said, Lo, this hath touched thy lips; and thine iniquity is taken away, and thy sin purged.
8 Also I heard the voice of the Lord, saying, Whom shall I send, and who will go for us? Then said I, Here *am* I; send me.   Gen. 1:26

> **6:8 We Each Have Our Work**
>
> To everyone who becomes a partaker of His grace the Lord appoints a work for others. Individually we are to stand in our lot and place, saying, "Here am I; send me" (Isaiah 6:8). Upon the minister of the word, the missionary nurse, the Christian physician, the individual Christian, whether he be merchant or farmer, professional man or mechanic— the responsibility rests upon all. *MH 148*

Isaiah's Message for Israel

9 And he said, Go, and tell this people, Hear ye indeed, but understand not; and see ye indeed, but perceive not.   Matt. 13:14-15; Mark 4:12
10 Make the heart of this people fat, and make their ears heavy, and shut their eyes; lest they see with their eyes, and hear with their ears, and understand with their heart, and convert, and be healed.   Deut. 32:15; Jer. 5:21; Matt. 13:15
11 Then said I, Lord, how long? And he answered, Until the cities be wasted without inhabitant, and the houses without man, and the land be utterly desolate,   Is. 1:7
12 And the LORD have removed men far away, and *there be* a great forsaking in the midst of the land.   Jer. 4:29
13 But yet in it *shall be* a tenth, and *it* shall return, and shall be eaten: as a teil tree, and as an oak, whose substance *is* in them, when they cast *their leaves: so* the holy seed *shall be* the substance thereof.   Ezra 9:2

The Virgin Will Have a Child

7 And it came to pass in the days of Ahaz the son of Jotham, the son of Uzziah, king of Judah, *that* Rezin the king of Syria, and Pekah the son of Remaliah, king of Israel, went up toward Jerusalem to war against it, but could not prevail against it. 2 Kin. 15:37; 16:1
2 And it was told the house of David, saying, Syria is confederate with Ephraim. And his heart was moved, and the heart of his people, as the trees of the wood are moved with the wind.   Is. 7:13
3 Then said the LORD unto Isaiah, Go forth now to meet Ahaz, thou, and Shear-jashub thy son, at the end of the conduit of the upper pool in the highway of the ᵀfuller's field;   2 Kin. 18:17; Is. 36:2 ◆ *one who washes clothes*
4 And say unto him, Take heed, and be quiet; fear not, neither be fainthearted for the two tails of these smoking firebrands,

for the fierce anger of Rezin with Syria, and of the son of Remaliah.   Deut. 20:3

5 Because Syria, Ephraim, and the son of Remaliah, have taken evil counsel against thee, saying,

6 Let us go up against Judah, and ᵀvex it, and let us make a breach therein for us, and set a king in the midst of it, *even* the son of Tabeal: *trouble*

7 Thus saith the Lord GOD, It shall not stand, neither shall it come to pass.   Is. 8:10

8 For the head of Syria *is* Damascus, and the head of Damascus *is* Rezin; and within ᵀthreescore and five years shall Ephraim be broken, that it be not a people. Is. 17:1-3 ◆ *sixty*

9 And the head of Ephraim *is* Samaria, and the head of Samaria *is* Remaliah's son. If ye will not believe, surely ye shall not be established.   2 Chr. 20:20

10 Moreover the LORD spake again unto Ahaz, saying,

11 Ask thee a sign of the LORD thy God; ask it either in the depth, or in the height above.   Is. 37:30

12 But Ahaz said, I will not ask, neither will I tempt the LORD.

13 And he said, Hear ye now, O house of David; *Is it* a small thing for you to weary men, but will ye weary my God also? Is. 43:24

14 Therefore the Lord himself shall give you a sign; Behold, a virgin shall conceive, and bear a son, and shall call his name Immanuel.   Is. 8:8; 9:6; Matt. 1:23

> **Jesus** See Isaiah 9:6, 7.

15 Butter and honey shall he eat, that he may know to refuse the evil, and choose the good.   Is. 7:22

7:15 Using Our Power to Reason

The power to discriminate between right and wrong we can possess only through individual dependence upon God. Each for himself is to learn from Him through His word. Our reasoning powers were given us for use, and God desires them to be exercised. "Come now, and let us reason together" (Isaiah 1:18), He invites us. In reliance upon Him we may have wisdom to "refuse the evil, and choose the good" (Isaiah 7:15; James 1:5). *Ed 231*

---

16 For before the child shall know to refuse the evil, and choose the good, the land that thou ᵀabhorrest shall be forsaken of both her kings.   Is. 8:4 ◆ *despise*

17 The LORD shall bring upon thee, and upon thy people, and upon thy father's house, days that have not come, from the day that Ephraim departed from Judah; *even* the king of Assyria.   Is. 8:7-8

18 And it shall come to pass in that day, *that*

the LORD shall hiss for the fly that *is* in the uttermost part of the rivers of Egypt, and for the bee that *is* in the land of Assyria.   Is. 5:26

19 And they shall come, and shall rest all of them in the desolate valleys, and in the holes of the rocks, and upon all thorns, and upon all bushes.   Is. 2:19; Jer. 16:16

20 In the same day shall the Lord shave with a razor that is hired, *namely*, by them beyond the river, by the king of Assyria, the head, and the hair of the feet: and it shall also consume the beard.   Is. 8:7

21 And it shall come to pass in that day, *that* a man shall nourish a young cow, and two sheep;   Is. 5:17

22 And it shall come to pass, for the abundance of milk *that* they shall give he shall eat butter: for butter and honey shall every one eat that is left in the land.   Is. 7:15

23 And it shall come to pass in that day, *that* every place shall be, where there were a thousand vines at a thousand ᵀsilverlings, it shall *even* be for briers and thorns.   Is. 5:6 ◆ *silver coins*

24 With arrows and with bows shall *men* come thither; because all the land shall become briers and thorns.

25 And *on* all hills that shall be digged with the ᵀmattock, there shall not come thither the fear of briers and thorns: but it shall be for the sending forth of oxen, and for the treading of lesser cattle.   *farming tool*

Isaiah's Child Is a Sign

8 Moreover the LORD said unto me, Take thee a great roll, and write in it with a man's pen concerning Maher-shalal-hash-baz.   Is. 30:8

2 And I took unto me faithful witnesses to record, Uriah the priest, and Zechariah the son of Jeberechiah.   2 Kin. 16:10-11

3 And I went unto the prophetess; and she conceived, and bare a son. Then said the LORD to me, Call his name Maher-shalal-hashbaz.

4 For before the child shall have knowledge to cry, My father, and my mother, the riches of Damascus and the ᵀspoil of Samaria shall be taken away before the king of Assyria.   *plunder*

Assyria Will Not Conquer Judah

5 The LORD spake also unto me again, saying,

6 Forasmuch as this people refuseth the waters of Shiloah that go softly, and rejoice in Rezin and Remaliah's son;   John 9:7

7 Now therefore, behold, the Lord bringeth up upon them the waters of the river, strong and many, *even* the king of Assyria, and all his glory: and he shall come up over all his channels, and go over all his banks: Is. 7:17, 20

8 And he shall pass through Judah; he shall

overflow and go over, he shall reach *even* to the neck; and the stretching out of his wings shall fill the breadth of thy land, O Immanuel.   Is. 7:14; 30:28

9 Associate yourselves, O ye people, and ye shall be broken in pieces; and give ear, all ye of far countries: ᵀgird yourselves, and ye shall be broken in pieces; gird yourselves, and ye shall be broken in pieces.   equip

10 Take counsel together, and it shall come to ᵀnought; speak the word, and it shall not stand: for God *is* with us. Job 5:12; Ps. 46:7 ◆ *nothing*

Some in Jerusalem Will Stumble

11 For the LORD spake thus to me with a strong hand, and instructed me that I should not walk in the way of this people, saying,   Ezek. 3:14

12 Say ye not, A confederacy, to all *them to* whom this people shall say, A confederacy; neither fear ye their fear, nor be afraid.

13 Sanctify the LORD of hosts himself; and *let* him *be* your fear, and *let* him *be* your dread.

14 And he shall be for a sanctuary; but for a stone of stumbling and for a rock of offence to both the houses of Israel, for a ᵀgin and for a snare to the inhabitants of Jerusalem.   Ezek. 11:16; Luke 2:34; 1 Pet. 2:8 ◆ *trap*

8:16 The Seal of the Law

The seal of God's law is found in the fourth commandment. This only, of all the ten, brings to view both the name and the title of the Lawgiver. It declares Him to be the Creator of the heavens and the earth, and thus shows His claim to reverence and worship above all others. Aside from this precept, there is nothing in the Decalogue to show by whose authority the law is given. *GC 452*

15 And many among them shall stumble, and fall, and be broken, and be snared, and be taken.   Is. 28:13

16 Bind up the testimony, seal the law among my disciples.   Dan. 12:4

17 And I will wait upon the LORD, that hideth his face from the house of Jacob, and I will look for him.   Ps. 27:14; Is. 54:8; Hab. 2:3

18 Behold, I and the children whom the LORD hath given me *are* for signs and for wonders in Israel from the LORD of hosts, which dwelleth in mount Zion.   Ps. 9:11

8:19, 20 Error of Consulting the Dead

If men had been willing to receive the truth so plainly stated in the Scriptures concerning the nature of man and the state of the dead, they would see in the claims and manifestations of spiritualism the working of Satan with power and signs and lying wonders. . . .

Many will be confronted by the spirits of devils personating beloved relatives or friends and declaring the most dangerous heresies. . . . We must be prepared to withstand them with the Bible truth that the dead know not anything and that they who thus appear are the spirits of devils. *GC 559, 560*

19 And when they shall say unto you, Seek unto them that have familiar spirits, and unto wizards that peep, and that mutter: should not a people seek unto their God? for the living to the dead?   Lev. 20:6; 1 Sam. 28:8; Is. 19:3

20 To the law and to the testimony: if they speak not according to this word, *it is* because *there is* no light in them.   Mic. 3:6

Gift of Prophecy See Jeremiah 23:16, 17.

21 And they shall pass through it, hardly bestead and hungry: and it shall come to

Prepared for a Final Delusion

Isaiah 8:20

The people of God are directed to the Scriptures as their safeguard against the influence of false teachers and the delusive power of spirits of darkness. Satan employs every possible device to prevent men from obtaining a knowledge of the Bible; for its plain utterances reveal his deceptions. At every revival of God's work the prince of evil is aroused to more intense activity; he is now putting forth his utmost efforts for a final struggle against Christ and His followers. The last great delusion is soon to open before us. Antichrist is to perform his marvelous works in our sight. So closely will the counterfeit resemble the true that it will be impossible to distinguish between them except by the Holy Scriptures. By their testimony every statement and every miracle must be tested.

Those who endeavor to obey all the commandments of God will be opposed and derided. They can stand only in God. In order to endure the trial before them, they must understand the will of God as revealed in His word; they can honor Him only as they have a right conception of His character, government, and purposes, and act in accordance with them. None but those who have fortified the mind with the truths of the Bible will stand through the last great conflict. To every soul will come the searching test: Shall I obey God rather than men? The decisive hour is even now at hand. Are our feet planted on the rock of God's immutable word? Are we prepared to stand firm in defense of the commandments of God and the faith of Jesus? *GC 593, 594*

pass, that when they shall be hungry, they shall ᵀfret themselves, and curse their king and their God, and look upward. Is. 9:20 ◆ *worry*

22 And they shall look unto the earth; and behold trouble and darkness, dimness of anguish; and *they shall be* driven to darkness. Is. 5:30; Jer. 13:16; Zeph. 1:14-15

The Coming Prince of Peace

9 Nevertheless the dimness *shall* not *be* such as *was* in her vexation, when at the first he lightly afflicted the land of Zebulun and the land of Naphtali, and afterward did more grievously afflict *her* by the way of the sea, beyond Jordan, in Galilee of the nations. 2 Kin. 15:29; 2 Chr. 16:4; Is. 8:22

2 The people that walked in darkness have seen a great light: they that dwell in the land of the shadow of death, upon them hath the light shined. Matt. 4:16; Luke 1:78-79; Eph. 5:8

> ### 9:2 Hope for an End to the Gloom
>
> For centuries preceding Christ's first advent, darkness covered the earth, and gross darkness the people. Satan was throwing his hellish shadow athwart the pathway of men, that he might prevent them from gaining a knowledge of God and of the future world. Multitudes were sitting in the shadow of death. Their only hope was for this gloom to be lifted, that God might be revealed. *PK 687, 688*

3 Thou hast multiplied the nation, *and* not increased the joy: they joy before thee according to the joy in harvest, *and* as *men* rejoice when they divide the ᵀspoil. 1 Sam. 30:16 ◆ *plunder*

4 For thou hast broken the yoke of his burden, and the staff of his shoulder, the rod of his oppressor, as in the day of Midian.

5 For every battle of the warrior *is* with confused noise, and garments rolled in blood; but *this* shall be with burning *and* fuel of fire.

6 For unto us a child is born, unto us a son is given: and the government shall be upon his shoulder: and his name shall be called Wonderful, Counsellor, The mighty God, The everlasting Father, The Prince of Peace. Is. 7:14; Matt. 28:18; Luke 2:11

> ### 9:6 Heaven's Best and Greatest
>
> In the Teacher sent from God, heaven gave to men its best and greatest. He who had stood in the councils of the Most High, who had dwelt in the innermost sanctuary of the Eternal, was the One chosen to reveal in person to humanity the knowledge of God. *Ed 73*

7 Of the increase of *his* government and peace *there shall be* no end, upon the throne of David, and upon his kingdom, to order it, and to establish it with judgment and with justice from ᵀhenceforth even for ever.

The zeal of the LORD of hosts will perform this. Dan. 2:44; Luke 1:32-33 ◆ *this time forward*

Jesus See Micah 5:2.

Judgments upon the People for Pride

8 The Lord sent a word into Jacob, and it hath lighted upon Israel.

9 And all the people shall know, *even* Ephraim and the inhabitant of Samaria, that say in the pride and ᵀstoutness of heart, Is. 46:12 ◆ *arrogance*

10 The bricks are fallen down, but we will build with ᵀhewn stones: the sycomores are cut down, but we will change *them into* cedars. Mal. 1:4 ◆ *cut*

11 Therefore the LORD shall set up the adversaries of Rezin against him, and join his enemies together;

12 The Syrians before, and the Philistines behind; and they shall devour Israel with open mouth. For all this his anger is not turned away, but his hand *is* stretched out still. 2 Kin. 16:6; 2 Chr. 28:18; Is. 5:25

13 For the people turneth not unto him that ᵀsmiteth them, neither do they seek the LORD of hosts. Is. 31:1; Jer. 5:3; Hos. 7:10 ◆ *strikes*

14 Therefore the LORD will cut off from Israel head and tail, branch and ᵀrush, in one day. Is. 19:15; Rev. 18:8 ◆ *reed*

15 The ancient and honourable, he *is* the head; and the prophet that teacheth lies, he *is* the tail. Is. 3:2-3

16 For the leaders of this people cause *them* to ᵀerr; and *they that are* led of them *are* destroyed. Is. 3:12 ◆ *stray*

17 Therefore the Lord shall have no joy in their young men, neither shall have mercy on their fatherless and widows: for every one *is* an hypocrite and an evildoer, and every mouth speaketh folly. For all this his anger is not turned away, but his hand *is* stretched out still. Is. 5:25; 10:6; 27:11

18 For wickedness burneth as the fire: it shall devour the briers and thorns, and shall kindle in the thickets of the forest, and they shall mount up *like* the lifting up of smoke. Mal. 4:1

19 Through the wrath of the LORD of hosts is the land darkened, and the people shall be as the fuel of the fire: no man shall spare his brother. Mic. 7:2, 6

20 And he shall snatch on the right hand, and be hungry; and he shall eat on the left hand, and they shall not be satisfied: they shall eat every man the flesh of his own arm: Is. 49:26

21 Manasseh, Ephraim; and Ephraim, Manasseh: *and* they together *shall be* against Judah. For all this his anger is not turned away, but his hand *is* stretched out still. Is. 5:25

Woe upon Tyrants

10 Woe unto them that decree unrighteous decrees, and that write grievousness *which* they have prescribed;   Ps. 58:2

2 To turn aside the needy from judgment, and to take away the right from the poor of my people, that widows may be their prey, and *that* they may rob the fatherless!   Is. 3:14

3 And what will ye do in the day of visitation, and in the desolation *which* shall come from far? to whom will ye flee for help? and where will ye leave your glory?   Job 31:14; Hos. 9:7

4 Without me they shall bow down under the prisoners, and they shall fall under the slain. For all this his anger is not turned away, but his hand *is* stretched out still.   Is. 5:25

Assyria Shall Be Broken

5 O Assyrian, the rod of mine anger, and the staff in their hand is mine ᵀindignation. *anger*

6 I will send him against an hypocritical nation, and against the people of my wrath will I give him a charge, to take the ᵀspoil, and to take the prey, and to tread them down like the ᵀmire of the streets.   Is. 9:17 ♦ *plunder* ♦ *mud*

7 Howbeit he meaneth not so, neither doth his heart think so; but *it is* in his heart to destroy and cut off nations not a few.   Gen. 50:20

8 For he saith, *Are* not my princes altogether kings?

9 *Is* not Calno as Carchemish? *is* not Hamath as Arpad? *is* not Samaria as Damascus?

10 As my hand hath found the kingdoms of the idols, and whose graven images did excel them of Jerusalem and of Samaria;

11 Shall I not, as I have done unto Samaria and her idols, so do to Jerusalem and her idols?

12 Wherefore it shall come to pass, *that* when the Lord hath performed his whole work upon mount Zion and on Jerusalem, I will punish the fruit of the ᵀstout heart of the king of Assyria, and the glory of his high looks.   2 Kin. 19:31 ♦ *arrogant*

13 For he saith, By the strength of my hand I have done *it*, and by my wisdom; for I am prudent: and I have removed the bounds of the people, and have robbed their treasures, and I have put down the inhabitants like a valiant *man*:   Dan. 4:30

14 And my hand hath found as a nest the riches of the people: and as one gathereth eggs *that are* left, have I gathered all the earth; and there was none that moved the wing, or opened the mouth, or peeped.   Job 31:25

15 Shall the axe boast itself against him that ᵀheweth therewith? *or* shall the saw magnify itself against him that shaketh it? as if the rod should shake *itself* against them that lift it up, *or* as if the staff should lift up *itself, as if it were* no wood.   Is. 10:5; 45:9; Rom. 9:20-21 ♦ *cuts*

16 Therefore shall the Lord, the Lord of hosts, send among his fat ones leanness; and under his glory he shall kindle a burning like the burning of a fire.   Ps. 106:15

17 And the light of Israel shall be for a fire, and his Holy One for a flame: and it shall burn and devour his thorns and his briers in one day;   Num. 11:1-3

18 And shall consume the glory of his forest, and of his fruitful field, both soul and body: and they shall be as when a standard-bearer fainteth.   2 Kin. 19:23

19 And the rest of the trees of his forest shall be few, that a child may write them.

A Remnant Shall Be Saved

20 And it shall come to pass in that day, *that* the remnant of Israel, and such as are escaped of the house of Jacob, shall no more again stay upon him that smote them; but

The Gift Is for All

Isaiah 10:20

At the time when Jerusalem was destroyed and the temple laid in ruins, many thousands of the Jews were sold to serve as bondmen in heathen lands. Like wrecks on a desert shore they were scattered among the nations. For eighteen hundred years the Jews have wandered from land to land throughout the world, and in no place have they been given the privilege of regaining their ancient prestige as a nation. Maligned, hated, persecuted, from century to century theirs has been a heritage of suffering.

Notwithstanding the awful doom pronounced upon the Jews as a nation at the time of their rejection of Jesus of Nazareth, there have lived from age to age many noble, God-fearing Jewish men and women who have suffered in silence. God has comforted their hearts in affliction and has beheld with pity their terrible situation. He has heard the agonizing prayers of those who have sought Him with all the heart for a right understanding of His word. Some have learned to see in the lowly Nazarene whom their forefathers rejected and crucified, the true Messiah of Israel. As their minds have grasped the significance of the familiar prophecies so long obscured by tradition and misinterpretation, their hearts have been filled with gratitude to God for the unspeakable gift He bestows upon every human being who chooses to accept Christ as a personal Saviour. *AA 379, 380*

shall stay upon the LORD, the Holy One of Israel, in truth.   2 Kin. 16:7

21 The remnant shall return, *even* the remnant of Jacob, unto the mighty God.   Is. 9:6
22 For though thy people Israel be as the sand of the sea, *yet* a remnant of them shall return: the consumption decreed shall overflow with righteousness.   Is. 6:13; Dan. 9:27; Rom. 9:27-28
23 For the Lord GOD of hosts shall make a consumption, even determined, in the midst of all the land.
24 Therefore thus saith the Lord GOD of hosts, O my people that dwellest in Zion, be not afraid of the Assyrian: he shall ᵀsmite thee with a rod, and shall lift up his staff against thee, after the manner of Egypt.   Is. 37:6 ◆ *strike*
25 For yet a very little while, and the indignation shall cease, and mine anger in their destruction.   Dan. 11:36
26 And the LORD of hosts shall stir up a ᵀscourge for him according to the slaughter of Midian at the rock of Oreb: and *as* his rod *was* upon the sea, so shall he lift it up after the manner of Egypt. Judg. 7:25; 2 Kin. 19:35; Is. 9:4 ◆ *whip*
27 And it shall come to pass in that day, *that* his burden shall be taken away from off thy shoulder, and his yoke from off thy neck, and the yoke shall be destroyed because of the anointing.   Is. 9:4; 14:25
28 He is come to Aiath, he is passed to Migron; at Michmash he hath laid up his carriages: 1 Sam. 13:2, 5; 14:2
29 They are gone over the passage: they have taken up their lodging at Geba; Ramah is afraid; Gibeah of Saul is fled.   1 Sam. 7:17
30 Lift up thy voice, O daughter of Gallim: cause it to be heard unto Laish, O poor Anathoth.   Josh. 21:18; 1 Sam. 25:44; Jer. 1:1
31 Madmenah is removed; the inhabitants of Gebim gather themselves to flee.
32 As yet shall he remain at Nob that day: he shall shake his hand *against* the mount of the daughter of Zion, the hill of Jerusalem.   1 Sam. 21:1; 22:19; Is. 19:16
33 Behold, the Lord, the LORD of hosts, shall lop the bough with terror: and the high

ones of stature *shall be* ᵀhewn down, and the haughty shall be humbled.   Amos 2:9 ◆ *cut*
34 And he shall cut down the thickets of the forest with iron, and Lebanon shall fall by a mighty one.   Is. 37:24

The Branch out of the Root of Jesse

11 And there shall come forth a rod out of the stem of Jesse, and a Branch shall grow out of his roots: Is. 4:2; 11:10; 53:2
2 And the spirit of the LORD shall rest upon him, the spirit of wisdom and understanding, the spirit of counsel and might, the spirit of knowledge and of the fear of the LORD;   Is. 42:1; 61:1; Matt. 3:16
3 And shall make him of quick understanding in the fear of the LORD: and he shall not judge after the sight of his eyes, neither reprove after the hearing of his ears: John 7:24
4 But with righteousness shall he judge the poor, and reprove with ᵀequity for the meek of the earth: and he shall ᵀsmite the earth with the rod of his mouth, and with the breath of his lips shall he slay the wicked.   Job 4:9; Ps. 2:9; Mal. 4:6 ◆ *uprightness* ◆ *strike*
5 And righteousness shall be the ᵀgirdle of his ᵀloins, and faithfulness the girdle of his ᵀreins.   Is. 25:1; Eph. 6:14 ◆ *belt* ◆ *waist* ◆ *desires*
6 The wolf also shall dwell with the lamb, and the leopard shall lie down with the kid; and the calf and the young lion and the fatling together; and a little child shall lead them.   Is. 65:25; Hos. 2:18
7 And the cow and the bear shall feed; their young ones shall lie down together: and the lion shall eat straw like the ox.
8 And the sucking child shall play on the hole of the ᵀasp, and the weaned child shall put his hand on the ᵀcockatrice' den.   *snake* ◆ *viper's*
9 They shall not hurt nor destroy in all my holy mountain: for the earth shall be full of the knowledge of the LORD, as the waters cover the sea.   Job 5:23; Ps. 98:2-3; Hab. 2:14

The Restoration of Israel

10 And in that day there shall be a root of Jesse, which shall stand for an ensign of the

people; to it shall the Gentiles seek: and his rest shall be glorious. Is. 11:1; 32:17-18; Luke 2:32

11 And it shall come to pass in that day, *that* the Lord shall set his hand again the second time to recover the remnant of his people, which shall be left, from Assyria, and from Egypt, and from Pathros, and from Cush, and from Elam, and from Shinar, and from Hamath, and from the islands of the sea. Gen. 10:22; Is. 42:4; Mic. 7:12

12 And he shall set up an ensign for the nations, and shall assemble the outcasts of Israel, and gather together the dispersed of Judah from the four corners of the earth.

13 The envy also of Ephraim shall depart, and the adversaries of Judah shall be cut off: Ephraim shall not envy Judah, and Judah shall not ᵀvex Ephraim. Jer. 3:18 ◆ *trouble*

14 But they shall fly upon the shoulders of the Philistines toward the west; they shall ᵀspoil them of the east together: they shall lay their hand upon Edom and Moab; and the children of Ammon shall obey them. *plunder*

15 And the Lord shall utterly destroy the tongue of the Egyptian sea; and with his mighty wind shall he shake his hand over the river, and shall smite it in the seven streams, and make *men* go over ᵀdryshod. *wearing shoes*

16 And there shall be an highway for the remnant of his people, which shall be left, from Assyria; like as it was to Israel in the day that he came up out of the land of Egypt. Ex. 14:26-29; Is. 11:11; 19:23

A Hymn of Joyful Thanksgiving

12 And in that day thou shalt say, O Lord, I will praise thee: though thou wast angry with me, thine anger is turned away, and thou comfortedst me. Is. 25:1

2 Behold, God *is* my salvation; I will trust, and not be afraid: for the Lord JEHOVAH *is* my strength and *my* song; he also is become my salvation. Ex. 15:2; Ps. 118:14; Is. 7:14

3 Therefore with joy shall ye draw water out of the wells of salvation. Jer. 2:13

4 And in that day shall ye say, Praise the Lord, call upon his name, declare his doings among the people, make mention that his name is exalted. Ps. 105:1; 145:4-6

5 Sing unto the Lord; for he hath done excellent things: this *is* known in all the earth. Ex. 15:1; Ps. 98:1

6 Cry out and shout, thou inhabitant of Zion: for great *is* the Holy One of Israel in the midst of thee. Zeph. 3:14-17

Babylon Will be Punished

13 The burden of Babylon, which Isaiah the son of Amoz did see. Is. 1:1

2 Lift ye up a banner upon the high mountain, exalt the voice unto them, shake the hand, that they may go into the gates of the nobles. Is. 5:26

3 I have commanded my ᵀsanctified ones, I have also called my mighty ones for mine anger, *even* them that rejoice in my highness. Joel 3:11 ◆ *chosen*

4 The noise of a multitude in the mountains, like as of a great people; a tumultuous noise of the kingdoms of nations gathered together: the Lord of hosts mustereth the host of the battle. Joel 3:14

5 They come from a far country, from the end of heaven, *even* the Lord, and the weapons of his ᵀindignation, to destroy the whole land. *anger*

6 Howl ye; for the day of the Lord *is* at hand; it shall come as a destruction from the Almighty. Is. 2:12; Joel 1:15; Zeph. 1:7

7 Therefore shall all hands be faint, and every man's heart shall melt: Ezek. 21:7

8 And they shall be afraid: pangs and sorrows shall take hold of them; they shall be in pain as a woman that travaileth: they shall be amazed one at another; their faces *shall be as* flames. Is. 26:17

9 Behold, the day of the Lord cometh, cruel both with wrath and fierce anger, to lay the land desolate: and he shall destroy the sinners thereof out of it. Ps. 104:35

10 For the stars of heaven and the constellations thereof shall not give their light: the sun shall be darkened in his going forth, and the moon shall not cause her light to shine. Is. 5:30; Matt. 24:29; Mark 13:24

11 And I will punish the world for *their* evil, and the wicked for their iniquity; and I will cause the arrogancy of the proud to cease, and will lay low the haughtiness of the terrible. Is. 2:17

12 I will make a man more precious than fine gold; even a man than the golden wedge of Ophir. Is. 4:1

13:12 Heavenly Treasure

God desires us to choose the heavenly in place of the earthly. He opens before us the possibilities of a heavenly investment. He would give encouragement to our loftiest aims, security to our choicest treasure. He declares "I will make a man more precious than fine gold; even a man than the golden wedge of Ophir" (Isaiah 13:12). When the riches that moth devours and rust corrupts shall be swept away, Christ's followers can rejoice in their heavenly treasure, the riches that are imperishable. *COL 374*

---

13 Therefore I will shake the heavens, and the earth shall remove out of her place, in the wrath of the Lord of hosts, and in the day of his fierce anger. Lam. 1:12

14 And it shall be as the chased roe, and as a sheep that no man taketh up: they shall every man turn to his own people, and flee every one into his own land.   1 Kin. 22:17

15 Every one that is found shall be thrust through; and every one that is joined *unto them* shall fall by the sword.

16 Their children also shall be dashed to pieces before their eyes; their houses shall be spoiled, and their wives ravished.   Nah. 3:10

17 Behold, I will stir up the Medes against them, which shall not regard silver; and *as for* gold, they shall not delight in it.   Prov. 6:34-35

18 *Their* bows also shall ᵀdash the young men to pieces; and they shall have no pity on the fruit of the womb; their eye shall not spare children.   2 Kin. 8:12 ◆ *beat*

The Desolation of Babylon

19 And Babylon, the glory of kingdoms, the beauty of the Chaldees' excellency, shall be as when God overthrew Sodom and Gomorrah.   Gen. 19:24; Deut. 29:23; Dan. 4:30

13:19–22 Rise and Fall of Nations

Every nation that has come upon the stage of action has been permitted to occupy its place on the earth, that the fact might be determined whether it would fulfill the purposes of the Watcher and the Holy One. Prophecy has traced the rise and progress of the world's great empires—Babylon, Medo-Persia, Greece, and Rome. With each of these, as with the nations of less power, history has repeated itself. Each has had its period of test; each has failed, its glory faded, its power departed. *PK 535*

---

20 It shall never be inhabited, neither shall it be dwelt in from generation to generation:

neither shall the Arabian pitch tent there; neither shall the shepherds make their fold there.   Is. 14:23

21 But wild beasts of the desert shall lie there; and their houses shall be full of ᵀdoleful creatures; and owls shall dwell there, and satyrs shall dance there.   Rev. 18:2 ◆ *howling*

22 And the wild beasts of the islands shall cry in their desolate houses, and dragons in *their* pleasant palaces: and her time *is* near to come, and her days shall not be prolonged.   Is. 25:2

God Will Rescue His People from Babylon

14 For the Lᴏʀᴅ will have mercy on Jacob, and will yet choose Israel, and set them in their own land: and the strangers shall be joined with them, and they shall cleave to the house of Jacob.   Ps. 102:13; Is. 54:7-8; Zech. 1:17

2 And the people shall take them, and bring them to their place: and the house of Israel shall possess them in the land of the Lᴏʀᴅ for servants and handmaids: and they shall take them captives, whose captives they were; and they shall rule over their oppressors.   Is. 60:14; 61:5; Dan. 7:18

3 And it shall come to pass in the day that the Lᴏʀᴅ shall give thee rest from thy sorrow, and from thy fear, and from the hard bondage wherein thou wast made to serve,   Ezra 9:8-9

4 That thou shalt take up this proverb against the king of Babylon, and say, How hath the oppressor ceased! the golden city ceased!   Is. 49:26

5 The Lᴏʀᴅ hath broken the staff of the wicked, *and* the sceptre of the rulers. Ps. 125:3

6 He who smote the people in wrath with a

A Preview of the Future

Isaiah 13:11

The forbearance of God has been very great—so great that when we consider the continuous insult to His holy commandments, we marvel. The Omnipotent One has been exerting a restraining power over His own attributes. But He will certainly arise to punish the wicked, who so boldly defy the just claims of the Decalogue.

God allows men a period of probation; but there is a point beyond which divine patience is exhausted, and the judgments of God are sure to follow. The Lord bears long with men, and with cities, mercifully giving warnings to save them from divine wrath; but a time will come when pleadings for mercy will no longer be heard, and the rebellious element that continues to reject the light of truth will be blotted out, in mercy to themselves and to those who would otherwise be influenced by their example.

The time is at hand when there will be sorrow in the world that no human balm can heal. The Spirit of God is being withdrawn. Disasters by sea and by land follow one another in quick succession. How frequently we hear of earthquakes and tornadoes, of destruction by fire and flood, with great loss of life and property! Apparently these calamities are capricious outbreaks of disorganized, unregulated forces of nature, wholly beyond the control of man; but in them all, God's purpose may be read. They are among the agencies by which He seeks to arouse men and women to a sense of their danger. *PK 276, 277*

continual stroke, he that ruled the nations in anger, is persecuted, *and* none hindereth. 7 The whole earth is at rest, *and* is quiet: they break forth into singing.   Ps. 126:1-3

8 Yea, the fir trees rejoice at thee, *and* the cedars of Lebanon, *saying,* Since thou art laid down, no feller is come up against us.

9 Hell from beneath is moved for thee to meet *thee* at thy coming: it stirreth up the dead for thee, *even* all the chief ones of the earth; it hath raised up from their thrones all the kings of the nations.

14:12* Sin Begins With Lucifer

Sin originated with him who, next to Christ, had been most honored of God and who stood highest in power and glory among the inhabitants of heaven. Before his fall, Lucifer was first of the covering cherubs, holy and undefiled. . . .

Lucifer might have remained in favor with God, beloved and honored by all the angelic host, exercising his noble powers to bless others and to glorify his Maker. . . . Instead of seeking to make God supreme in the affections and allegiance of His creatures, it was Lucifer's endeavor to win their service and homage to himself. *GC 493, 494*

10 All they shall speak and say unto thee, Art thou also become weak as we? art thou become like unto us?

11 Thy pomp is brought down to the grave, *and* the noise of thy viols: the worm is spread under thee, and the worms cover thee.

12 How art thou fallen from heaven, O Lucifer, son of the morning! *how* art thou cut down to the ground, which didst weaken the nations!   Luke 10:18; 2 Pet. 1:19; Rev. 2:28

13 For thou hast said in thine heart, I will ascend into heaven, I will exalt my throne above the stars of God: I will sit also upon the mount of the congregation, in the sides of the north: Ezek. 28:2

14 I will ascend above the heights of the clouds; I will be like the most High.   Is. 47:8

Salvation from Sin See Revelation 12:7–9.

15 Yet thou shalt be brought down to hell, to the sides of the pit.   Ezek. 32:23; Matt. 11:23

16 They that see thee shall narrowly look upon thee, *and* consider thee, *saying, Is* this the man that made the earth to tremble, that did shake kingdoms;   Jer. 50:23

17 *That* made the world as a wilderness, and destroyed the cities thereof; *that* opened not the house of his prisoners?   Joel 2:3

18 All the kings of the nations, *even* all of them, lie in glory, every one in his own house.

19 But thou art cast out of thy grave like an abominable branch, *and as* the raiment of those that are slain, thrust through with a sword, that go down to the stones of the pit; as a carcase trodden under feet.   Jer. 41:7

The Circle of Love Is Broken, Part One

Isaiah 14:12–14*

Pride in his own glory nourished the desire for supremacy. The high honors conferred upon Lucifer were not appreciated as the gift of God and called forth no gratitude to the Creator. He gloried in his brightness and exaltation, and aspired to be equal with God. He was beloved and reverenced by the heavenly host. Angels delighted to execute his commands, and he was clothed with wisdom and glory above them all. . . .

Working with mysterious secrecy, and for a time concealing his real purpose under an appearance of reverence for God, he endeavored to excite dissatisfaction concerning the laws that governed heavenly beings, intimating that they imposed an unnecessary restraint. Since their natures were holy, he urged that the angels should obey the dictates of their own will. He sought to create sympathy for himself by representing that God had dealt unjustly with him in bestowing supreme honor upon Christ. He claimed that in aspiring to greater power and honor he was not aiming at self-exaltation, but was seeking to secure liberty for all the inhabitants of heaven, that by this means they might attain to a higher state of existence.

God in His great mercy bore long with Lucifer. . . . Though he had forsaken his position as covering cherub, yet if he had been willing to return to God, acknowledging the Creator's wisdom, and satisfied to fill the place appointed him in God's great plan, he would have been reinstated in his office. But pride forbade him to submit. He persistently defended his own course, maintained that he had no need of repentance, and fully committed himself, in the great controversy, against his Maker.

All the powers of his master mind were now bent to the work of deception, to secure the sympathy of the angels that had been under his command. . . . All whom he could not subvert and bring fully to his side he accused of indifference to the interests of heavenly beings. The very work which he himself was doing he charged upon those who remained true to God. And to sustain his charge of God's injustice toward him, he resorted to misrepresentation of the words and acts of the Creator. *GC 495–497*

* For more information on how and why there is sin, see pages 1428–1435 of this Bible.

20 Thou shalt not be joined with them in burial, because thou hast destroyed thy land, *and* slain thy people: the seed of evildoers shall never be renowned. Job 18:16, 19; Ps. 21:10
21 Prepare slaughter for his children for the iniquity of their fathers; that they do not rise, nor possess the land, nor fill the face of the world with cities. Ex. 20:5; Lev. 26:39; Matt. 23:35
22 For I will rise up against them, saith the LORD of hosts, and cut off from Babylon the name, and remnant, and son, and nephew, saith the LORD. 1 Kin. 14:10
23 I will also make it a possession for the bittern, and pools of water: and I will sweep it with the besom of destruction, saith the LORD of hosts. 1 Kin. 14:10; Is. 34:11-15; Zeph. 2:14

Assyria Will be Punished
24 The LORD of hosts hath sworn, saying, Surely as I have thought, so shall it come to pass; and as I have purposed, *so* shall it stand: Acts 4:28
25 That I will break the Assyrian in my land, and upon my mountains tread him under foot: then shall his yoke depart from off them, and his burden depart from off their shoulders. Is. 9:4; Nah. 1:13
26 This *is* the purpose that is purposed upon the whole earth: and this *is* the hand that is stretched out upon all the nations.
27 For the LORD of hosts hath purposed, and who shall ᵀdisannul *it*? and his hand *is* stretched out, and who shall turn it back? ᵇʳᵉᵃᵏ

The Philistines Will be Punished
28 In the year that king Ahaz died was this burden. 2 Kin. 16:20; 2 Chr. 28:27; Is. 13:1
29 Rejoice not thou, whole Palestina, because the rod of him that smote thee is broken: for out of the serpent's root shall come forth a ᵀcockatrice, and his fruit *shall be* a fiery flying serpent. 2 Chr. 26:6 ♦ snake
30 And the firstborn of the poor shall feed, and the needy shall lie down in safety: and I will kill thy root with famine, and he shall slay thy remnant. Is. 7:21-22
31 Howl, O gate; cry, O city; thou, whole Palestina, *art* dissolved: for there shall come from the north a smoke, and none *shall be* alone in his appointed times. Jer. 1:14
32 What shall *one* then answer the messengers of the nation? That the LORD hath founded Zion, and the poor of his people shall trust in it. Ps. 87:1, 5; 102:16

Moab Will be Punished
15 The burden of Moab. Because in the night Ar of Moab is laid waste, *and* brought to silence; because in the night Kir of Moab is laid waste, *and* brought to silence; Num. 21:28
2 He is gone up to Bajith, and to Dibon, the high places, to weep: Moab shall howl

The Circle of Love Is Broken, Part Two

Isaiah 14:12–14*

God in His wisdom permitted Satan to carry forward his work, until the spirit of disaffection ripened into active revolt. It was necessary for his plans to be fully developed, that their true nature and tendency might be seen by all. . . .

Until fully developed, sin would not appear the evil thing it was. Heretofore it had had no place in the universe of God, and holy beings had no conception of its nature and malignity. They could not discern the terrible consequences that would result from setting aside the divine law. . . .

In His dealing with sin, God could employ only righteousness and truth. Satan could use what God could not—flattery and deceit. . . .Therefore it must be demonstrated before the inhabitants of heaven, as well as of all the worlds, that God's government was just, His law perfect. Satan had made it appear that he himself was seeking to promote the good of the universe. The true character of the usurper, and his real object, must be understood by all. He must have time to manifest himself by his wicked works. . . .

Had he been immediately blotted from existence, they would have served God from fear rather than from love. The influence of the deceiver would not have been fully destroyed, nor would the spirit of rebellion have been utterly eradicated. Evil must be permitted to come to maturity. For the good of the entire universe through ceaseless ages Satan must more fully develop his principles, that his charges against the divine government might be seen in their true light by all created beings, that the justice and mercy of God and the immutability of His law might forever be placed beyond all question.

Satan's rebellion was to be a lesson to the universe through all coming ages, a perpetual testimony to the nature and terrible results of sin. The working out of Satan's rule, its effects upon both men and angels, would show what must be the fruit of setting aside the divine authority.
GC 497–499

* *For more information on how and why there is sin, see pages 1428–1435 of this Bible.*

over Nebo, and over Medeba: on all their heads *shall be* baldness, *and* every beard cut off. Lev. 21:5

3 In their streets they shall ᵀgird themselves with sackcloth: on the tops of their houses, and in their streets, every one shall howl, weeping abundantly. Jon. 3:6-8 ◆ *equip*

4 And Heshbon shall cry, and Elealeh: their voice shall be heard *even* unto Jahaz: therefore the armed soldiers of Moab shall cry out; his life shall be grievous unto him. Jer. 48:34

5 My heart shall cry out for Moab; his fugitives *shall flee* unto Zoar, an heifer of three years old: for by the mounting up of Luhith with weeping shall they go it up; for in the way of Horonaim they shall raise up a cry of destruction. Jer. 4:20; 48:5

6 For the waters of Nimrim shall be desolate: for the hay is withered away, the grass faileth, there is no green thing. Num. 32:36

7 Therefore the abundance they have gotten, and that which they have laid up, shall they carry away to the brook of the willows. Jer. 48:36

8 For the cry is gone round about the borders of Moab; the howling thereof unto Eglaim, and the howling thereof unto Beerelim.

9 For the waters of Dimon shall be full of blood: for I will bring more upon Dimon, lions upon him that escapeth of Moab, and upon the remnant of the land. 2 Kin. 17:25

Judgment upon Moab

16 Send ye the lamb to the ruler of the land from Sela to the wilderness, unto the mount of the daughter of Zion. 2 Kin. 3:4

2 For it shall be, *that,* as a wandering bird cast out of the nest, *so* the daughters of Moab shall be at the fords of Arnon. Prov. 27:8

3 Take counsel, execute judgment; make thy shadow as the night in the midst of the noonday; hide the outcasts; ᵀbewray not him that wandereth. 1 Kin. 18:4 ◆ *betray*

4 Let mine outcasts dwell with thee, Moab; be thou a ᵀcovert to them from the face of the spoiler: for the extortioner is at an end, the spoiler ceaseth, the oppressors are consumed out of the land. Is. 14:4 ◆ *hiding place*

16:3, 4 Nature's Resources

The plan of life that God gave to Israel was intended as an object lesson for all mankind. If these principles were carried out today, what a different place this world would be! *MH 188*

---

5 And in mercy shall the throne be established: and he shall sit upon it in truth in the tabernacle of David, judging, and seeking judgment, and hasting righteousness. Is. 9:6-7

16:5 The Mystery of Mercy

This is the mystery of mercy into which angels desire to look—that God can be just while He justifies the repenting sinner and renews His intercourse [association] with the fallen race; that Christ could stoop to raise unnumbered multitudes from the abyss of ruin and clothe them with the spotless garments of His own righteousness to unite with angels who have never fallen and to dwell forever in the presence of God. *GC 415*

---

6 We have heard of the pride of Moab; *he is* very proud: *even* of his haughtiness, and his pride, and his wrath: *but* his lies *shall* not *be* so. Amos 2:1

7 Therefore shall Moab howl for Moab, every one shall howl: for the foundations of Kir-hareseth shall ye mourn; surely *they are* stricken. 2 Kin. 3:25; Jer. 48:20

8 For the fields of Heshbon ᵀlanguish, *and* the vine of Sibmah: the lords of the heathen have broken down the principal plants thereof, they are come *even* unto Jazer, they wandered *through* the wilderness: her branches are stretched out, they are gone over the sea. Num. 32:38 ◆ *weaken*

9 Therefore I will ᵀbewail with the weeping of Jazer the vine of Sibmah: I will water thee with my tears, O Heshbon, and Elealeh: for the shouting for thy summer fruits and for thy harvest is fallen. Jer. 40:12 ◆ *lament*

10 And gladness is taken away, and joy out of the plentiful field; and in the vineyards there shall be no singing, neither shall there be shouting: the treaders shall tread out no wine in *their* presses; I have made *their* vintage shouting to cease. Jer. 48:33

11 Wherefore my bowels shall sound like an harp for Moab, and mine inward parts for Kir-haresh. Is. 15:5; 63:15; Jer. 48:36

12 And it shall come to pass, when it is seen that Moab is weary on the high place, that he shall come to his sanctuary to pray; but he shall not prevail. Num. 23:14; Is. 15:2

13 This *is* the word that the LORD hath spoken concerning Moab since that time.

14 But now the LORD hath spoken, saying, Within three years, as the years of an ᵀhireling, and the glory of Moab shall be contemned, with all that great multitude; and the remnant *shall be* very small *and* feeble. Is. 21:16 ◆ *temporary laborer*

Syria and Israel Will be Punished

17 The burden of Damascus. Behold, Damascus is taken away from *being* a city, and it shall be a ruinous heap. Gen. 14:15; Is. 25:2

2 The cities of Aroer *are* forsaken: they shall be for flocks, which shall lie down, and none shall make *them* afraid. Ezek. 25:5

3 The fortress also shall cease from Ephraim, and the kingdom from Damascus, and the remnant of Syria: they shall be as the glory of the children of Israel, saith the LORD of hosts.   Is. 7:8, 16; 8:4
4 And in that day it shall come to pass, *that* the glory of Jacob shall be made thin, and the fatness of his flesh shall ᵀwax lean.   become
5 And it shall be as when the harvestman gathereth the corn, and reapeth the ears with his arm; and it shall be as he that gathereth ears in the valley of Rephaim.   2 Sam. 5:18
6 Yet gleaning grapes shall be left in it, as the shaking of an olive tree, two *or* three berries in the top of the uppermost bough, four *or* five in the outmost fruitful branches thereof, saith the LORD God of Israel.   Deut. 4:27; Is. 24:13
7 At that day shall a man look to his Maker, and his eyes shall have respect to the Holy One of Israel.   Mic. 7:7
8 And he shall not look to the altars, the work of his hands, neither shall respect *that* which his fingers have made, either the ᵀgroves, or the images.   Is. 27:9 ◆ idols

---

17:7, 8 A Prophet's Words Bear Fruit

The exhortations of the prophet to Judah to behold the living God, and to accept His gracious offers, were not in vain. There were some who gave earnest heed, and who turned from their idols to the worship of Jehovah. They learned to see in their Maker love and mercy and tender compassion. *PK 320*

---

9 In that day shall his strong cities be as a forsaken bough, and an uppermost branch, which they left because of the children of Israel: and there shall be desolation. Is. 27:10
10 Because thou hast forgotten the God of thy salvation, and hast not been mindful of the rock of thy strength, therefore shalt thou plant pleasant plants, and shalt set it with strange ᵀslips: Deut. 32:4 ◆ branches
11 In the day shalt thou make thy plant to grow, and in the morning shalt thou make thy seed to flourish: *but* the harvest *shall be* a heap in the day of grief and of desperate sorrow.   Job 4:8
12 Woe to the multitude of many people, *which* make a noise like the noise of the seas; and to the rushing of nations, *that* make a rushing like the rushing of mighty waters!   Ps. 18:4
13 The nations shall rush like the rushing of many waters: but *God* shall rebuke them, and they shall flee far off, and shall be chased as the chaff of the mountains before the wind, and like a rolling thing before the whirlwind.   Job 21:18; Ps. 1:4; 9:5
14 And behold at ᵀeveningtide trouble; *and* before the morning he *is* not. This *is* the

portion of them that ᵀspoil us, and the lot of them that rob us. 2 Kin. 19:35 ◆ evening ◆ plunder

Ethiopia Will be Punished

18 Woe to the land shadowing with wings, which *is* beyond the rivers of Ethiopia: 2 Kin. 19:9
2 That sendeth ambassadors by the sea, even in vessels of bulrushes upon the waters, *saying*, Go, ye swift messengers, to a nation scattered and peeled, to a people terrible from their beginning ᵀhitherto; a nation ᵀmeted out and trodden down, whose land the rivers have spoiled!   up to now ◆ measured out
3 All ye inhabitants of the world, and dwellers on the earth, see ye, when he lifteth up an ᵀensign on the mountains; and when he bloweth a trumpet, hear ye.   Is. 5:26 ◆ banner
4 For so the LORD said unto me, I will take my rest, and I will consider in my dwelling place like a clear heat upon herbs, *and* like a cloud of dew in the heat of harvest.   Is. 26:21
5 For afore the harvest, when the bud is perfect, and the sour grape is ripening in the flower, he shall both cut off the sprigs with pruning hooks, and take away *and* cut down the branches.   Ezek. 17:6-10
6 They shall be left together unto the fowls of the mountains, and to the beasts of the earth: and the fowls shall summer upon them, and all the beasts of the earth shall winter upon them.   Jer. 7:33
7 In that time shall the present be brought unto the LORD of hosts of a people scattered and peeled, and from a people terrible from their beginning hitherto; a nation meted out and ᵀtrodden under foot, whose land the rivers have spoiled, to the place of the name of the LORD of hosts, the mount Zion.   Is. 45:14 ◆ trampled

Egypt Will be Punished

19 The burden of Egypt. Behold, the LORD rideth upon a swift cloud, and shall come into Egypt: and the idols of Egypt shall be moved at his presence, and the heart of Egypt shall melt in the midst of it.   Ex. 12:12; Josh. 2:11; Joel 3:19
2 And I will set the Egyptians against the Egyptians: and they shall fight every one against his brother, and every one against his neighbour; city against city, *and* kingdom against kingdom.   Judg. 7:22; 1 Sam. 14:20
3 And the spirit of Egypt shall fail in the midst thereof; and I will destroy the counsel thereof: and they shall seek to the idols, and to the charmers, and to them that have familiar spirits, and to the wizards.   1 Chr. 10:13; Dan. 2:2
4 And the Egyptians will I give over into the hand of a cruel lord; and a fierce king shall

rule over them, saith the Lord, the LORD of hosts. _{Is. 20:4; Jer. 46:26; Ezek. 29:19}

5 And the waters shall fail from the sea, and the river shall be wasted and dried up. _{Jer. 51:36}

6 And they shall turn the rivers far away; *and* the brooks of defence shall be emptied and dried up: the reeds and flags shall wither.

7 The paper reeds by the brooks, by the mouth of the brooks, and every thing sown by the brooks, shall wither, be driven away, and be no *more*.

8 The fishers also shall mourn, and all they that cast ^Tangle into the brooks shall lament, and they that spread nets upon the waters shall ^Tlanguish. _{Ezek. 47:10 ◆ *fish hook* ◆ *weaken*}

9 Moreover they that work in fine flax, and they that weave networks, shall be confounded. _{Prov. 7:16; Ezek. 27:7}

10 And they shall be broken in the purposes thereof, all that make sluices *and* ponds for fish.

11 Surely the princes of Zoan *are* fools, the counsel of the wise counsellors of Pharaoh is become ^Tbrutish: how say ye unto Pharaoh, I *am* the son of the wise, the son of ancient kings? _{Num. 13:22; 1 Kin. 4:30; Ps. 78:43 ◆ *dumb*}

12 Where *are* they? where *are* thy wise *men*? and let them tell thee now, and let them know what the LORD of hosts hath purposed upon Egypt. _{1 Cor. 1:20}

13 The princes of Zoan are become fools, the princes of Noph are deceived; they have also seduced Egypt, *even they that are* the stay of the tribes thereof. _{Jer. 2:16; 46:14; Ezek. 30:13}

14 The LORD hath mingled a perverse spirit in the midst thereof: and they have caused Egypt to ^Terr in every work thereof, as a drunken *man* staggereth in his vomit. _{*stray*}

15 Neither shall there be *any* work for Egypt, which the head or tail, branch or ^Trush, may do. _{Is. 9:14-15 ◆ *reed*}

16 In that day shall Egypt be like unto women: and it shall be afraid and fear because of the shaking of the hand of the LORD of hosts, which he shaketh over it. _{Is. 11:15}

17 And the land of Judah shall be a terror unto Egypt, every one that maketh mention thereof shall be afraid in himself, because of the counsel of the LORD of hosts, which he hath determined against it. _{Is. 14:24}

18 In that day shall five cities in the land of Egypt speak the language of Canaan, and swear to the LORD of hosts; one shall be called, The city of destruction. _{Zeph. 3:9}

19 In that day shall there be an altar to the LORD in the midst of the land of Egypt, and a pillar at the border thereof to the LORD.

20 And it shall be for a sign and for a witness unto the LORD of hosts in the land of Egypt: for they shall cry unto the LORD because of the oppressors, and he shall send them a saviour, and a great one, and he shall deliver them.

21 And the LORD shall be known to Egypt, and the Egyptians shall know the LORD in that day, and shall do sacrifice and ^Toblation; yea, they shall vow a vow unto the LORD, and perform *it*. _{Is. 11:9 ◆ *offering*}

22 And the LORD shall ^Tsmite Egypt: he shall smite and heal *it*: and they shall return *even* to the LORD, and he shall be ^Tintreated of them, and shall heal them. _{*strike* ◆ *pled with*}

23 In that day shall there be a highway out of Egypt to Assyria, and the Assyrian shall come into Egypt, and the Egyptian into Assyria, and the Egyptians shall serve with the Assyrians. _{Is. 11:16}

24 In that day shall Israel be the third with Egypt and with Assyria, *even* a blessing in the midst of the land: _{Is. 65:8}

25 Whom the LORD of hosts shall bless, saying, Blessed *be* Egypt my people, and Assyria the work of my hands, and Israel mine inheritance. _{Ps. 100:3; Is. 29:23; Hos. 2:23}

The Shame of Those Allied with Egypt

20 In the year that Tartan came unto Ashdod, (when Sargon the king of Assyria sent him,) and fought against Ashdod, and took it; _{2 Kin. 18:17}

2 At the same time spake the LORD by Isaiah the son of Amoz, saying, Go and loose the sackcloth from off thy ^Tloins, and put off thy shoe from thy foot. And he did so, walking naked and barefoot. _{1 Sam. 19:24; Mic. 1:8 ◆ *waist*}

3 And the LORD said, Like as my servant Isaiah hath walked naked and barefoot three years *for* a sign and wonder upon Egypt and upon Ethiopia; _{Is. 8:18}

4 So shall the king of Assyria lead away the Egyptians prisoners, and the Ethiopians captives, young and old, naked and barefoot, even with *their* buttocks uncovered, to the shame of Egypt. _{Is. 19:4; Jer. 13:22, 26}

5 And they shall be afraid and ashamed of Ethiopia their expectation, and of Egypt their glory. _{Is. 30:3}

6 And the inhabitant of this isle shall say in that day, Behold, such *is* our expectation, whither we flee for help to be delivered from the king of Assyria: and how shall we escape? _{Matt. 23:33}

The Fall of Babylon

21 The burden of the desert of the sea. As whirlwinds in the south pass through; *so* it cometh from the desert, from a terrible land. _{Is. 13:1}

2 A grievous vision is declared unto me; the treacherous dealer dealeth treacherously, and the spoiler spoileth. Go up, O Elam: be-

siege, O Media; all the sighing thereof have I made to cease. Ps. 60:3; Is. 24:16; 33:1

3 Therefore are my ᵀloins filled with pain: pangs have taken hold upon me, as the pangs of a woman that travaileth: I was bowed down at the hearing of it; I was dismayed at the seeing of it. Ps. 48:6; Is. 13:8; 26:17 ◆ waist

4 My heart panted, fearfulness ᵀaffrighted me: the night of my pleasure hath he turned into fear unto me. scared

5 Prepare the table, watch in the watchtower, eat, drink: arise, ye princes, and anoint the shield. Jer. 51:39

6 For thus hath the Lord said unto me, Go, set a watchman, let him declare what he seeth. 2 Kin. 9:17-20

7 And he saw a chariot with a couple of horsemen, a chariot of asses, and a chariot of camels; and he hearkened diligently with much heed: Is. 21:9

8 And he cried, A lion: My lord, I stand continually upon the watchtower in the daytime, and I am set in my ᵀward whole nights: prison or guard

9 And, behold, here cometh a chariot of men, with a couple of horsemen. And he answered and said, Babylon is fallen, is fallen; and all the graven images of her gods he hath broken unto the ground. Jer. 51:8; Rev. 14:8; 18:2

10 O my threshing, and the corn of my floor: that which I have heard of the LORD of hosts, the God of Israel, have I declared unto you. Jer. 51:33; Mic. 4:13

Someone Calling from Seir

11 The burden of Dumah. He calleth to me out of Seir, Watchman, what of the night? Watchman, what of the night? Gen. 25:14

12 The watchman said, The morning cometh, and also the night: if ye will enquire, enquire ye: return, come.

Arabia Will be Punished

13 The burden upon Arabia. In the forest in Arabia shall ye lodge, O ye travelling companies of Dedanim. Jer. 25:23-24

14 The inhabitants of the land of Tema brought water to him that was thirsty, they prevented with their bread him that fled.

15 For they fled from the swords, from the drawn sword, and from the bent bow, and from the grievousness of war.

16 For thus hath the Lord said unto me, Within a year, according to the years of an ᵀhireling, and all the glory of Kedar shall fail: Ps. 120:5; Is. 16:14; 60:7 ◆ temporary laborer

17 And the residue of the number of archers, the mighty men of the children of Kedar, shall be diminished: for the LORD God of Israel hath spoken it. Num. 23:19

Judah Will be Punished

22 The burden of the valley of vision. What aileth thee now, that thou art wholly gone up to the housetops?

2 Thou that art full of stirs, a tumultuous city, a joyous city: thy slain men are not slain with the sword, nor dead in battle. Is. 23:7; 32:13

3 All thy rulers are fled together, they are bound by the archers: all that are found in thee are bound together, which have fled from far.

4 Therefore said I, Look away from me; I will weep bitterly, labour not to comfort me, because of the spoiling of the daughter of my people. Jer. 9:1; Mic. 1:8

5 For it is a day of trouble, and of treading down, and of perplexity by the Lord GOD of hosts in the valley of vision, breaking down the walls, and of crying to the mountains.

6 And Elam bare the quiver with chariots of men and horsemen, and Kir uncovered the shield. 2 Kin. 16:9; Is. 21:2; Amos 1:5

7 And it shall come to pass, that thy choicest valleys shall be full of chariots, and the horsemen shall set themselves in array at the gate.

8 And he discovered the covering of Judah, and thou didst look in that day to the armour of the house of the forest. 1 Kin. 7:2

9 Ye have seen also the breaches of the city of David, that they are many: and ye gathered together the waters of the lower pool.

10 And ye have numbered the houses of Jerusalem, and the houses have ye broken down to fortify the wall.

11 Ye made also a ditch between the two walls for the water of the old pool: but ye have not looked unto the maker thereof, neither had respect unto him that fashioned it long ago.

12 And in that day did the Lord GOD of hosts call to weeping, and to mourning, and to baldness, and to girding with sackcloth: Joel 1:13; 2:17; Mic. 1:16

13 And behold joy and gladness, slaying oxen, and killing sheep, eating flesh, and drinking wine: let us eat and drink; for to morrow we shall die. Is. 56:12; Luke 17:26-29; 1 Cor. 15:32

14 And it was revealed in mine ears by the LORD of hosts, Surely this iniquity shall not be purged from you till ye die, saith the Lord GOD of hosts. 1 Sam. 3:14

Shebna's Dismissal from His Position

15 Thus saith the Lord GOD of hosts, Go, get thee unto this treasurer, even unto Shebna, which is over the house, and say, 2 Kin. 18:18, 37

16 What hast thou here? and whom hast thou here, that thou hast ᵀhewed thee out a sepulchre here, as he that heweth him out a sepulchre on high, and that graveth an habitation for himself in a rock? 2 Sam. 18:18; Matt. 27:60 ◆ cut

17 Behold, the LORD will carry thee away with a mighty captivity, and will surely cover thee.

18 He will surely violently turn and toss thee *like* a ball into a large country: there shalt thou die, and there the chariots of thy glory *shall be* the shame of thy lord's house.   Is. 17:13

19 And I will drive thee from thy station, and from thy state shall he pull thee down.

20 And it shall come to pass in that day, that I will call my servant Eliakim the son of Hilkiah: 2 Kin. 18:18; Is. 36:3; 37:2

21 And I will clothe him with thy robe, and strengthen him with thy girdle, and I will commit thy government into his hand: and he shall be a father to the inhabitants of Jerusalem, and to the house of Judah.   Gen. 45:8

22 And the key of the house of David will I lay upon his shoulder; so he shall open, and none shall shut; and he shall shut, and none shall open.   Job 12:14; Rev. 3:7

23 And I will fasten him *as* a nail in a sure place; and he shall be for a glorious throne to his father's house.   1 Sam. 2:8

22:23 What Is Our Influence?

Those with whom we associate day by day need our help, our guidance. They may be in such a condition of mind that a word spoken in season will be as a nail in a sure place. Tomorrow some of these souls may be where we can never reach them again. What is our influence over these fellow travelers? *PK 348*

---

24 And they shall hang upon him all the glory of his father's house, the offspring and the issue, all vessels of small quantity, from the vessels of cups, even to all the vessels of flagons.

25 In that day, saith the LORD of hosts, shall the nail that is fastened in the sure place be removed, and be cut down, and fall; and the burden that *was* upon it shall be cut off: for the LORD hath spoken *it*.   Is. 46:11

Tyre Will be Punished

23 The burden of Tyre. Howl, ye ships of Tarshish; for it is laid waste, so that there is no house, no entering in: from the land of Chittim it is revealed to them.   Gen. 10:4

2 Be still, ye inhabitants of the isle; thou whom the merchants of Zidon, that pass over the sea, have replenished.   Is. 47:5

3 And by great waters the seed of Sihor, the harvest of the river, *is* her revenue; and she is a mart of nations.   1 Chr. 13:5

4 Be thou ashamed, O Zidon: for the sea hath spoken, *even* the strength of the sea, saying, I travail not, nor bring forth chil-

dren, neither do I nourish up young men, *nor* bring up virgins.

5 As at the report concerning Egypt, *so* shall they be sorely pained at the report of Tyre.   Ex. 15:14-16

6 Pass ye over to Tarshish; howl, ye inhabitants of the isle.   Is. 23:12

7 *Is* this your joyous *city*, whose antiquity *is* of ancient days? her own feet shall carry her afar off to sojourn.   Is. 22:2

8 Who hath taken this counsel against Tyre, the crowning *city*, whose merchants *are* princes, whose traffickers *are* the honourable of the earth?

9 The LORD of hosts hath purposed it, to stain the pride of all glory, *and* to bring into contempt all the honourable of the earth.

10 Pass through thy land as a river, O daughter of Tarshish: *there is* no more strength.

11 He stretched out his hand over the sea, he shook the kingdoms: the LORD hath given a commandment against the merchant *city*, to destroy the strong holds thereof.   Zech. 9:3-4

12 And he said, Thou shalt no more rejoice, O thou oppressed virgin, daughter of Zidon: arise, pass over to Chittim; there also shalt thou have no rest.   Rev. 18:22

13 Behold the land of the Chaldeans; this people was not, *till* the Assyrian founded it for them that dwell in the wilderness: they set up the towers thereof, they raised up the palaces thereof; *and* he brought it to ruin.

14 Howl, ye ships of Tarshish: for your strength is laid waste.   Is. 23:1

15 And it shall come to pass in that day, that Tyre shall be forgotten seventy years, according to the days of one king: after the end of seventy years shall Tyre sing as an harlot.   Jer. 25:22

16 Take an harp, go about the city, thou harlot that hast been forgotten; make sweet melody, sing many songs, that thou mayest be remembered.

17 And it shall come to pass after the end of seventy years, that the LORD will visit Tyre, and she shall turn to her hire, and shall commit fornication with all the kingdoms of the world upon the face of the earth.   Nah. 3:4

18 And her merchandise and her hire shall be holiness to the LORD: it shall not be treasured nor laid up; for her merchandise shall be for them that dwell before the LORD, to eat sufficiently, and for durable clothing.   Ps. 72:10

God's Judgments upon the Land

24 Behold, the LORD maketh the earth empty, and maketh it waste, and turneth it upside down, and scattereth abroad the inhabitants thereof.

2 And it shall be, as with the people, so with the priest; as with the servant, so with his

master; as with the maid, so with her mistress; as with the buyer, so with the seller; as with the lender, so with the borrower; as with the taker of ᵀusury, so with the giver of usury to him.   Hos. 4:9 ◆ *interest charged*

3 The land shall be utterly emptied, and utterly spoiled: for the LORD hath spoken this word.   Is. 6:11

4 The earth mourneth *and* fadeth away, the world languisheth *and* fadeth away, the haughty people of the earth do languish.

5 The earth also is defiled under the inhabitants thereof; because they have ᵀtransgressed the laws, changed the ordinance, broken the everlasting covenant.   *violated a law*

6 Therefore hath the curse devoured the earth, and they that dwell therein are desolate: therefore the inhabitants of the earth are burned, and few men left.   Zech. 5:3-4

24:1–6 An Empty Earth

At the coming of Christ the wicked are blotted from the face of the whole earth— consumed with the spirit of His mouth and destroyed by the brightness of His glory. Christ takes His people to the City of God, and the earth is emptied of its inhabitants. *GC 657*

---

7 The new wine mourneth, the vine languisheth, all the merryhearted do sigh.

8 The mirth of tabrets ceaseth, the noise of them that rejoice endeth, the joy of the harp ceaseth.   Jer. 7:34; Ezek. 26:13; Hos. 2:11

9 They shall not drink wine with a song; strong drink shall be bitter to them that drink it.   Eccl. 9:7

10 The city of confusion is broken down: every house is shut up, that no man may come in.

11 *There is* a crying for wine in the streets; all joy is darkened, the ᵀmirth of the land is gone.   *gladness*

12 In the city is left desolation, and the gate is smitten with destruction.

A Remnant Shall Joyfully Praise God

13 When thus it shall be in the midst of the land among the people, *there shall be* as the shaking of an olive tree, *and* as the gleaning grapes when the vintage is done.

14 They shall lift up their voice, they shall sing for the majesty of the LORD, they shall cry aloud from the sea.   Is. 54:1

24:14 Music in the Hereafter

There will be music there, and song, such music and song as, save in the visions of God, no mortal ear has heard or mind conceived. *Ed 307*

---

15 Wherefore glorify ye the LORD in the fires, *even* the name of the LORD God of Israel in the isles of the sea.   Mal. 1:11

God Will Advance His Kingdom

16 From the uttermost part of the earth have we heard songs, *even* glory to the righteous. But I said, My leanness, my leanness, woe unto me! the treacherous dealers have dealt treacherously; yea, the treacherous dealers have dealt very treacherously. Is. 21:2; 33:1; Jer. 5:11

17 Fear, and the pit, and the snare, *are* upon thee, O inhabitant of the earth.   Jer. 48:43-44

18 And it shall come to pass, *that* he who fleeth from the noise of the fear shall fall into the pit; and he that cometh up out of the midst of the pit shall be taken in the snare: for the windows from on high are

---

Winds of Strife

Isaiah 24:4, 5

Satan works through the elements also to garner his harvest of unprepared souls. He has studied the secrets of the laboratories of nature, and he uses all his power to control the elements as far as God allows. When he was suffered to afflict Job, how quickly flocks and herds, servants, houses, children, were swept away, one trouble succeeding another as in a moment. It is God that shields His creatures and hedges them in from the power of the destroyer. But the Christian world have shown contempt for the law of Jehovah; and the Lord will do just what He has declared that He would—He will withdraw His blessings from the earth and remove His protecting care from those who are rebelling against His law and teaching and forcing others to do the same. Satan has control of all whom God does not especially guard. He will favor and prosper some in order to further his own designs, and he will bring trouble upon others and lead men to believe that it is God who is afflicting them.

While appearing to the children of men as a great physician who can heal all their maladies, he will bring disease and disaster, until populous cities are reduced to ruin and desolation. Even now he is at work. In accidents and calamities by sea and by land, in great conflagrations, in fierce tornadoes and terrific hailstorms, in tempests, floods, cyclones, tidal waves, and earthquakes, in every place and in a thousand forms, Satan is exercising his power. He sweeps away the ripening harvest, and famine and distress follow. He imparts to the air a deadly taint, and thousands perish by the pestilence. These visitations are to become more and more frequent and disastrous. *GC 589, 590*

open, and the foundations of the earth do shake.   Gen. 7:11; Ps. 18:7

19 The earth is utterly broken down, the earth is clean dissolved, the earth is moved exceedingly.

20 The earth shall reel to and fro like a drunkard, and shall be removed like a cottage; and the ᵀtransgression thereof shall be heavy upon it; and it shall fall, and not rise again.   Is. 19:14; 29:9; Dan. 11:19 ♦ violation of a law

---

24:20 Earthquakes—and Christ

An earthquake marked the hour when Christ laid down His life, and another earthquake witnessed the moment when He took it up in triumph. He who had vanquished death and the grave came forth from the tomb with the tread of a conqueror, amid the reeling of the earth, the flashing of lightning, and the roaring of thunder. When He shall come to the earth again, He will shake "not the earth only, but also heaven" (Hebrews 12:26). *DA 780*

---

21 And it shall come to pass in that day, *that* the LORD shall punish the host of the high ones *that are* on high, and the kings of the earth upon the earth.   Ps. 76:12

22 And they shall be gathered together, *as* prisoners are gathered in the pit, and shall be shut up in the prison, and after many days shall they be visited.   Zech. 9:11

23 Then the moon shall be confounded, and the sun ashamed, when the LORD of hosts shall reign in mount Zion, and in Jerusalem, and before his ancients gloriously.   Is. 13:10

Isaiah Praises God for His Judgments

25 O LORD, thou *art* my God; I will exalt thee, I will praise thy name; for thou hast done wonderful *things; thy* counsels of old *are* faithfulness *and* truth.   Ex. 15:2

25:1 Access to the Father

Our Redeemer has opened the way, so that the most sinful, the most needy, the most oppressed and despised, may find access to the Father. *PK 702*

---

2 For thou hast made of a city an heap; *of* a defenced city a ruin: a palace of strangers to be no city; it shall never be built.   Is. 13:22; 17:1

3 Therefore shall the strong people glorify thee, the city of the terrible nations shall fear thee.

4 For thou hast been a strength to the poor, a strength to the needy in his distress, a refuge from the storm, a shadow from the heat, when the blast of the terrible ones *is* as a storm *against* the wall.   Is. 14:32

5 Thou shalt bring down the noise of strangers, as the heat in a dry place; *even* the heat

with the shadow of a cloud: the branch of the terrible ones shall be brought low.

Death Will be Swallowed Up

6 And in this mountain shall the LORD of hosts make unto all people a feast of fat things, a feast of wines on the ᵀlees, of fat things full of marrow, of wines on the lees well refined.   Is. 2:2-3 ♦ dregs

7 And he will destroy in this mountain the face of the covering cast over all people, and the ᵀvail that is spread over all nations.   veil

8 He will swallow up death in victory; and the Lord GOD will wipe away tears from off all faces; and the rebuke of his people shall he take away from off all the earth: for the LORD hath spoken *it.*   Hos. 13:14; 1 Cor. 15:54; Rev. 21:4

God's Victorious Salvation

9 And it shall be said in that day, Lo, this *is* our God; we have waited for him, and he will save us: this *is* the LORD; we have waited for him, we will be glad and rejoice in his salvation.   Ps. 20:5

25:8, 9 God Will Set Things Right

Christ will gather His children to Himself. On earth they have been destitute, afflicted, and tormented. Millions have gone down to the grave loaded with infamy because they refused to yield to the deceptive claims of Satan. By human tribunals the children of God have been adjudged the vilest criminals. But the day is near when "God is judge Himself" (Psalm 50:6). Then the decisions of earth shall be reversed. *COL 179*

---

10 For in this mountain shall the hand of the LORD rest, and Moab shall be ᵀtrodden down under him, even as straw is trodden down for the dunghill.   Is. 25:6 ♦ trampled

11 And he shall spread forth his hands in the midst of them, as he that swimmeth spreadeth forth *his hands* to swim: and he shall bring down their pride together with the spoils of their hands.   Is. 5:25

12 And the fortress of the high fort of thy walls shall he bring down, lay low, *and* bring to the ground, *even* to the dust.   Is. 26:5

A Song of Confidence in God

26 In that day shall this song be sung in the land of Judah; We have a strong city; salvation will *God* appoint *for* walls and ᵀbulwarks.   Is. 12:1; 60:18 ♦ structures for defense

2 Open ye the gates, that the righteous nation which keepeth the truth may enter in.   Ps. 118:20

3 Thou wilt keep *him* in perfect peace, *whose* mind *is* ᵀstayed *on thee*: because he trusteth in thee.   held back

26:3 Untangling Our Lives

Those who take Christ at His word, and surrender their souls to His keeping, their lives to His ordering, will find peace and quietude. Nothing of the world can make them sad when Jesus makes them glad by His presence. In perfect acquiescence there is perfect rest. . . . Our lives may seem a tangle; but as we commit ourselves to the wise Master Worker, He will bring out the pattern of life and character that will be to His own glory. *DA 331*

4 Trust ye in the LORD for ever: for in the LORD JEHOVAH *is* everlasting strength: Is. 12:2
5 For he bringeth down them that dwell on high; the lofty city, he layeth it low; he layeth it low, *even* to the ground; he bringeth it *even* to the dust. Job 40:11-13
6 The foot shall tread it down, *even* the feet of the poor, *and* the steps of the needy.
7 The way of the just *is* uprightness: thou, most upright, dost weigh the path of the just.
8 Yea, in the way of thy judgments, O LORD, have we waited for thee; the desire of *our* soul *is* to thy name, and to the remembrance of thee.
9 With my soul have I desired thee in the night; yea, with my spirit within me will I seek thee early: for when thy judgments *are* in the earth, the inhabitants of the world will learn righteousness. Ps. 63:1
10 Let favour be shewed to the wicked, *yet* will he not learn righteousness: in the land of uprightness will he deal unjustly, and will not behold the majesty of the LORD. Hos. 11:7
11 LORD, *when* thy hand is lifted up, they will not see: *but* they shall see, and be ashamed for *their* envy at the people; yea, the fire of thine enemies shall devour them. Is. 5:24

12 LORD, thou wilt ordain peace for us: for thou also hast ᵀwrought all our works in us.   *made*
13 O LORD our God, *other* lords beside thee have had dominion over us: *but* by thee only will we make mention of thy name. Is. 2:8
14 *They are* dead, they shall not live; *they are* deceased, they shall not rise: therefore hast thou visited and destroyed them, and made all their memory to perish. Is. 8:19
15 Thou hast increased the nation, O LORD, thou hast increased the nation: thou art glorified: thou hadst removed *it* far *unto* all the ends of the earth. Is. 9:3
16 LORD, in trouble have they visited thee, they poured out a prayer *when* thy ᵀchastening *was* upon them.   Hos. 5:15 ◆ *disciplining*
17 Like as a woman with child, *that* draweth near the time of her delivery, is in pain, *and* crieth out in her pangs; so have we been in thy sight, O LORD. Is. 13:8
18 We have been with child, we have been in pain, we have as it were brought forth wind; we have not wrought any deliverance in the earth; neither have the inhabitants of the world fallen. Ps. 17:14
19 Thy dead *men* shall live, *together with* my dead body shall they arise. Awake and sing, ye that dwell in dust: for thy dew *is as* the dew of herbs, and the earth shall cast out the dead. Is. 25:8; Dan. 12:2; Hos. 13:14

26:19 Christ Has Life in Himself

To the believer, Christ is the resurrection and the life. In our Saviour the life that was lost through sin is restored; for He has life in Himself to quicken whom He will. He is invested with the right to give immortality. The life that He laid down in humanity, He takes up again, and gives to humanity. *DA 786, 787*

The Lord Will Interpose

Isaiah 26:20, 21

The world has become bold in transgression of God's law. Because of His long forbearance, men have trampled upon His authority. They have strengthened one another in oppression and cruelty toward His heritage, saying, "How doth God know? and is there knowledge in the Most High?" (Psalm 73:11). But there is a line beyond which they cannot pass. The time is near when they will have reached the prescribed limit. Even now they have almost exceeded the bounds of the longsuffering of God, the limits of His grace, the limits of His mercy. The Lord will interpose to vindicate His own honor, to deliver His people, and to repress the swellings of unrighteousness. . . .

From age to age the Lord has made known the manner of His working. When a crisis has come, He has revealed Himself, and has interposed to hinder the working out of Satan's plans. With nations, with families, and with individuals, He has often permitted matters to come to a crisis, that His interference might become marked. Then He has made manifest that there is a God in Israel who will maintain His law and vindicate His people.

In this time of prevailing iniquity we may know that the last great crisis is at hand. When the defiance of God's law is almost universal, when His people are oppressed and afflicted by their fellow men, the Lord will interpose. *COL 177, 178*

20 Come, my people, enter thou into thy chambers, and shut thy doors about thee: hide thyself as it were for a little moment, until the ᵀindignation be overpast.   Ps. 30:5 ✦ anger
21 For, behold, the LORD cometh out of his place to punish the inhabitants of the earth for their iniquity: the earth also shall disclose her blood, and shall no more cover her slain.   Job 16:18

God's Care for His People

27 In that day the LORD with his sore and great and strong sword shall punish ᵀleviathan the piercing serpent, even leviathan that crooked serpent; and he shall slay the dragon that *is* in the sea. Ps. 104:26 ✦ crocodile
2 In that day sing ye unto her, A vineyard of red wine.   Jer. 2:21
3 I the LORD do keep it; I will water it every moment: lest *any* hurt it, I will keep it night and day.   Is. 58:11
4 Fury *is* not in me: who would set the briers *and* thorns against me in battle? I would go through them, I would burn them together.   Is. 10:17; Matt. 3:12; Heb. 6:8
5 Or let him take hold of my strength, *that* he may make peace with me; *and* he shall make peace with me.   Job 22:21
6 He shall cause them that come of Jacob to take root: Israel shall blossom and bud, and fill the face of the world with fruit. Hos. 14:5-6

27:6 Fulfilling Prophecy

In proclaiming the truths of the everlasting gospel to every nation, kindred, tongue, and people, God's church on earth today is fulfilling the ancient prophecy, "Israel shall blossom and bud, and fill the face of the world with fruit" (Isaiah 27:6). The followers of Jesus, in co-operation with heavenly intelligences, are rapidly occupying the waste places of the earth; and, as the result of their labors, an abundant fruitage of precious souls is developing. *PK 703*

---

7 Hath he smitten him, as he smote those that smote him? *or* is he slain according to the slaughter of them that are slain by him?   Is. 37:36-38
8 In measure, when it shooteth forth, thou wilt debate with it: he ᵀstayeth his rough wind in the day of the east wind.   Jer. 4:11 ✦ holds back
9 By this therefore shall the iniquity of Jacob be purged; and this *is* all the fruit to take away his sin; when he maketh all the stones of the altar as chalkstones that are beaten in sunder, the ᵀgroves and images shall not stand up.   Is. 17:8 ✦ idols
10 Yet the defenced city *shall be* desolate, *and* the habitation forsaken, and left like a wilderness: there shall the calf feed, and there

shall he lie down, and consume the branches thereof.   Is. 17:2
11 When the boughs thereof are withered, they shall be broken off: the women come, *and* set them on fire: for it *is* a people of no understanding: therefore he that made them will not have mercy on them, and he that formed them will shew them no favour.   Is. 1:3
12 And it shall come to pass in that day, *that* the LORD shall beat off from the channel of the river unto the stream of Egypt, and ye shall be gathered one by one, O ye children of Israel.   Gen. 15:18; Deut. 30:3-4; Neh. 1:9
13 And it shall come to pass in that day, *that* the great trumpet shall be blown, and they shall come which were ready to perish in the land of Assyria, and the outcasts in the land of Egypt, and shall worship the LORD in the holy mount at Jerusalem.   Lev. 25:9; 1 Chr. 15:24

Ephraim Will Fall

28 Woe to the crown of pride, to the drunkards of Ephraim, whose glorious beauty *is* a fading flower, which *are* on the head of the fat valleys of them that are overcome with wine!   Is. 28:3-4, 7; Hos. 7:5
2 Behold, the Lord hath a mighty and strong one, *which* as a ᵀtempest of hail *and* a destroying storm, as a flood of mighty waters overflowing, shall cast down to the earth with the hand.   Is. 30:30 ✦ storm
3 The crown of pride, the drunkards of Ephraim, shall be ᵀtrodden under feet: *trampled*
4 And the glorious beauty, which *is* on the head of the fat valley, shall be a fading flower, *and* as the hasty fruit before the summer; which *when* he that looketh upon it seeth, while it is yet in his hand he eateth it up.
5 In that day shall the LORD of hosts be for a crown of glory, and for a ᵀdiadem of beauty, unto the residue of his people, Is. 62:3 ✦ crown
6 And for a spirit of judgment to him that sitteth in judgment, and for strength to them that turn the battle to the gate.   1 Kin. 3:28
7 But they also have erred through wine, and through strong drink are out of the way; the priest and the prophet have erred through strong drink, they are swallowed up of wine, they are out of the way through strong drink; they ᵀerr in vision, they stumble *in* judgment.   Ps. 107:27 ✦ stray
8 For all tables are full of vomit *and* filthiness, *so that there is* no place *clean.*   Jer. 48:26
9 Whom shall he teach knowledge? and whom shall he make to understand doctrine? *them that are* weaned from the milk, *and* drawn from the breasts.   Ps. 131:2
10 For precept *must be* upon precept, precept upon precept; line upon line, line upon line; here a little, *and* there a little:

11 For with stammering lips and another tongue will he speak to this people. 1 Cor. 14:21
12 To whom he said, This *is* the rest *wherewith* ye may cause the weary to rest; and this *is* the refreshing: yet they would not hear. Is. 30:15; Jer. 6:16; Matt. 11:28-29
13 But the word of the LORD was unto them precept upon precept, precept upon precept; line upon line, line upon line; here a little, *and* there a little; that they might go, and fall backward, and be broken, and snared, and taken. Matt. 21:44

A Message to Jerusalem

14 Wherefore hear the word of the LORD, ye scornful men, that rule this people which *is* in Jerusalem. Is. 1:10
15 Because ye have said, We have made a covenant with death, and with hell are we at agreement; when the overflowing scourge shall pass through, it shall not come unto us: for we have made lies our refuge, and under falsehood have we hid ourselves: Is. 8:7-8
16 Therefore thus saith the Lord GOD, Behold, I lay in Zion for a foundation a stone, a tried stone, a precious corner *stone*, a sure foundation: he that believeth shall not make haste. Ps. 118:22; Matt. 21:42; Rom. 9:33

17 Judgment also will I lay to the line, and righteousness to the plummet: and the hail shall sweep away the refuge of lies, and the waters shall overflow the hiding place. Is. 28:2
18 And your covenant with death shall be disannulled, and your agreement with hell shall not stand; when the overflowing Tscourge shall pass through, then ye shall be trodden down by it. Is. 7:7 ♦ *whip*

19 From the time that it goeth forth it shall take you: for morning by morning shall it pass over, by day and by night: and it shall be a vexation only *to* understand the report.
20 For the bed is shorter than that *a man* can stretch himself *on it*: and the covering narrower than that he can wrap himself *in it*.
21 For the LORD shall rise up as *in* mount Perazim, he shall be Twroth as *in* the valley of Gibeon, that he may do his work, his strange work; and bring to pass his act, his strange act. Josh. 10:10, 12; 1 Chr. 14:11 ♦ *angered*
22 Now therefore be ye not mockers, lest your bands be made strong: for I have heard from the Lord GOD of hosts a consumption, even determined upon the whole earth. Is. 10:22-23
23 Give ye ear, and hear my voice; hearken, and hear my speech.
24 Doth the plowman plow all day to sow? doth he open and break the clods of his ground?
25 When he hath made plain the face thereof, doth he not cast abroad the fitches, and scatter the Tcummin, and cast in the principal wheat and the appointed barley and the Trie in their place? *aromatic seed plant* ♦ *rye*
26 For his God doth instruct him to discretion, *and* doth teach him.
27 For the Tfitches are not threshed with a threshing instrument, neither is a cart wheel turned about upon the cummin; but the fitches are beaten out with a staff, and the cummin with a rod. Amos 1:3 ♦ *black cummin*
28 Bread *corn* is bruised; because he will not ever be threshing it, nor break *it with* the wheel of his cart, nor bruise it *with* his horsemen.
29 This also cometh forth from the LORD of hosts, *which* is wonderful in counsel, *and* excellent in working. Is. 9:6; Jer. 32:19; Rom. 11:33

God's Heavy Judgment upon Jerusalem

29 Woe to Ariel, to Ariel, the city *where* David dwelt! add ye year to year; let them kill sacrifices. 2 Sam. 5:9
2 Yet I will distress Ariel, and there shall be heaviness and sorrow: and it shall be unto me as Ariel.
3 And I will camp against thee round about, and will lay siege against thee with a mount, and I will raise forts against thee. Luke 19:43-44
4 And thou shalt be brought down, *and* shalt speak out of the ground, and thy speech shall be low out of the dust, and thy voice shall be, as of one that hath a familiar spirit, out of the ground, and thy speech shall whisper out of the dust. Is. 8:19
5 Moreover the multitude of thy strangers shall be like small dust, and the multitude of the terrible ones *shall be* as chaff that

passeth away: yea, it shall be at an instant suddenly.   1 Thess. 5:3

6 Thou shalt be visited of the LORD of hosts with thunder, and with earthquake, and great noise, with storm and ᵀtempest, and the flame of devouring fire.   Matt. 24:7 ◆ storm

7 And the multitude of all the nations that fight against Ariel, even all that fight against her and her munition, and that distress her, shall be as a dream of a night vision.   Job 20:8; Ps. 73:20; Mic. 4:11-12

8 It shall even be as when an hungry man dreameth, and, behold, he eateth; but he awaketh, and his soul is empty: or as when a thirsty man dreameth, and, behold, he drinketh; but he awaketh, and, behold, he is faint, and his soul hath appetite: so shall the multitude of all the nations be, that fight against mount Zion.

9 Stay yourselves, and wonder; cry ye out, and cry: they are drunken, but not with wine; they stagger, but not with strong drink.   Is. 51:21-22

10 For the LORD hath poured out upon you the spirit of deep sleep, and hath closed your eyes: the prophets and your rulers, the seers hath he covered.   Ps. 69:23; Is. 6:9-10; Rom. 11:8

11 And the vision of all is become unto you as the words of a book that is sealed, which men deliver to one that is learned, saying, Read this, I pray thee: and he saith, I cannot; for it is sealed: Is. 8:16; Dan. 12:4; Matt. 13:11

12 And the book is delivered to him that is not learned, saying, Read this, I pray thee: and he saith, I am not learned.

13 Wherefore the Lord said, Forasmuch as this people draw near me with their mouth, and with their lips do honour me, but have removed their heart far from me, and their fear toward me is taught by the precept of men: Col. 2:22

14 Therefore, behold, I will proceed to do a marvellous work among this people, even a marvellous work and a wonder: for the wisdom of their wise men shall perish, and the understanding of their prudent men shall be hid.   Is. 6:9-10; Jer. 49:7; Hab. 1:5

15 Woe unto them that seek deep to hide their counsel from the LORD, and their works are in the dark, and they say, Who seeth us? and who knoweth us?   Is. 30:1

16 Surely your turning of things upside down shall be esteemed as the potter's clay: for shall the work say of him that made it, He made me not? or shall the thing framed say of him that framed it, He had no understanding?

17 Is it not yet a very little while, and Lebanon shall be turned into a fruitful field, and the fruitful field shall be esteemed as a forest?   Is. 32:15

18 And in that day shall the deaf hear the words of the book, and the eyes of the blind shall see out of obscurity, and out of darkness.   Is. 35:5; Matt. 11:5; Mark 7:37

19 The meek also shall increase their joy in the LORD, and the poor among men shall rejoice in the Holy One of Israel.   Is. 61:1; Matt. 5:5

20 For the terrible one is brought to ᵀnought, and the scorner is consumed, and all that watch for iniquity are cut off: Mic. 2:1 ◆ nothing

21 That make a man an offender for a word, and lay a snare for him that reproveth in the gate, and turn aside the just for a thing of nought.   Amos 5:10-12

22 Therefore thus saith the LORD, who redeemed Abraham, concerning the house of Jacob, Jacob shall not now be ashamed, neither shall his face now ᵀwax pale. Is. 51:2 ◆ become

23 But when he seeth his children, the work of mine hands, in the midst of him, they shall ᵀsanctify my name, and sanctify the Holy One of Jacob, and shall fear the God of Israel.   Is. 8:13 ◆ make holy

24 They also that erred in spirit shall come to understanding, and they that murmured shall learn doctrine.   Is. 28:7

Trust the Lord, Not Egypt

30 Woe to the rebellious children, saith the LORD, that take counsel, but not of me; and that cover with a covering, but not of my spirit, that they may add sin to sin: Is. 1:2; 29:15; 30:9

2 That walk to go down into Egypt, and have not asked at my mouth; to strengthen themselves in the strength of Pharaoh, and to trust in the shadow of Egypt!   Num. 27:21

3 Therefore shall the strength of Pharaoh be your shame, and the trust in the shadow of Egypt your confusion.   Is. 20:5

4 For his princes were at Zoan, and his ambassadors came to Hanes.   Is. 19:11; Jer. 43:7

5 They were all ashamed of a people that could not profit them, nor be an help nor profit, but a shame, and also a reproach.   Jer. 2:36

6 The burden of the beasts of the south: into the land of trouble and anguish, from whence come the young and old lion, the ᵀviper and fiery flying serpent, they will carry their riches upon the shoulders of young asses, and their treasures upon the bunches of camels, to a people that shall not profit them.   Deut. 8:15; Is. 46:1-2; Jer. 11:4 ◆ snake

7 For the Egyptians shall help in vain, and to no purpose: therefore have I cried concerning this, Their strength is to sit still.

8 Now go, write it before them in a table, and note it in a book, that it may be for the time to come for ever and ever: Is. 8:1

9 That this is a rebellious people, lying chil-

dren, children *that* will not hear the law of the LORD: Is. 30:1

10 Which say to the seers, See not; and to the prophets, Prophesy not unto us right things, speak unto us smooth things, prophesy deceits: Jer. 11:21; Amos 2:12; 7:13

11 Get you out of the way, turn aside out of the path, cause the Holy One of Israel to cease from before us.

30:11 Satan at the Head of a Nation

The Jews had accepted false testimony to condemn the innocent Son of God. Now false accusations made their own lives uncertain. By their actions they had long been saying: "Cause the Holy One of Israel to cease from before us" (Isaiah 30:11). Now their desire was granted. The fear of God no longer disturbed them. Satan was at the head of the nation, and the highest civil and religious authorities were under his sway. *GC 28, 29*

12 Wherefore thus saith the Holy One of Israel, Because ye despise this word, and trust in oppression and perverseness, and stay thereon: Is. 5:24

13 Therefore this iniquity shall be to you as a breach ready to fall, swelling out in a high wall, whose breaking cometh suddenly at an instant. 1 Kin. 20:30

14 And he shall break it as the breaking of the potters' vessel that is broken in pieces; he shall not spare: so that there shall not be found in the bursting of it a ᵀsherd to take fire from the hearth, or to take water *withal* out of the pit. Ps. 2:9; Jer. 19:10-11 ◆ *fragment*

15 For thus saith the Lord GOD, the Holy One of Israel; In returning and rest shall ye be saved; in quietness and in confidence shall be your strength: and ye would not. Is. 32:17

30:15 Christ Our Rest

This rest is not found in inactivity; for in the Saviour's invitation the promise of rest is united with the call to labor: "Take My yoke upon you: . . . and ye shall find rest" (Matthew 11:28, 29). The heart that rests most fully upon Christ will be most earnest and active in labor for Him. *SC 71*

16 But ye said, No; for we will flee upon horses; therefore shall ye flee: and, We will ride upon the swift; therefore shall they that pursue you be swift. Is. 31:1, 3

17 One thousand *shall flee* at the rebuke of one; at the rebuke of five shall ye flee: till ye be left as a beacon upon the top of a mountain, and as an ᵀensign on an hill. *banner*

The Lord Will Heal His People

18 And therefore will the LORD wait, that he may be gracious unto you, and therefore

will he be exalted, that he may have mercy upon you: for the LORD *is* a God of judgment: blessed *are* all they that wait for him. Is. 25:9

19 For the people shall dwell in Zion at Jerusalem: thou shalt weep no more: he will be very gracious unto thee at the voice of thy cry; when he shall hear it, he will answer thee. Ps. 50:15

20 And *though* the Lord give you the bread of adversity, and the water of affliction, yet shall not thy teachers be removed into a corner any more, but thine eyes shall see thy teachers: 1 Kin. 22:27; Ps. 74:9; 80:5

21 And thine ears shall hear a word behind thee, saying, This *is* the way, walk ye in it, when ye turn to the right hand, and when ye turn to the left. Ps. 25:8-9

30:21 Quiet: Do You Hear Something?

God speaks to us through His providential workings and through the influence of His Spirit upon the heart. In our circumstances and surroundings, in the changes daily taking place around us, we may find precious lessons if our hearts are but open to discern them. . . .

God speaks to us in His word. Here we have in clearer lines the revelation of His character, of His dealings with men, and the great work of redemption. *SC 87*

22 Ye shall defile also the covering of thy ᵀgraven images of silver, and the ornament of thy molten images of gold: thou shalt cast them away as a menstruous cloth; thou shalt say unto it, Get thee hence. *engraved or cut out*

23 Then shall he give the rain of thy seed, that thou shalt sow the ground ᵀwithal; and bread of the increase of the earth, and it shall be fat and plenteous: in that day shall thy cattle feed in large pastures. Is. 32:20 ◆ *together with*

24 The oxen likewise and the young asses that ear the ground shall eat clean ᵀprovender, which hath been winnowed with the shovel and with the ᵀfan. *food for livestock ◆ farm tool*

25 And there shall be upon every high mountain, and upon every high hill, rivers *and* streams of waters in the day of the great slaughter, when the towers fall. Is. 35:6-7

26 Moreover the light of the moon shall be as the light of the sun, and the light of the sun shall be sevenfold, as the light of seven days, in the day that the LORD bindeth up the breach of his people, and healeth the stroke of their wound. Deut. 32:39; Is. 24:23; 60:19-20

Joy over the Destruction of Assyria

27 Behold, the name of the LORD cometh from far, burning *with* his anger, and the burden *thereof is* heavy: his lips are full of

^Tindignation, and his tongue as a devouring fire; *anger*

28 And his breath, as an overflowing stream, shall reach to the midst of the neck, to sift the nations with the sieve of vanity: and *there shall be* a bridle in the jaws of the people, causing *them* to ^Terr.   Is. 8:8; 11:4; 37:29 ✦ *stray*

29 Ye shall have a song, as in the night *when* a holy solemnity is kept; and gladness of heart, as when one goeth with a pipe to come into the mountain of the Lord, to the mighty One of Israel.   Ps. 42:4; Is. 2:3; 26:4

30 And the Lord shall cause his glorious voice to be heard, and shall shew the lighting down of his arm, with the indignation of *his* anger, and *with* the flame of a devouring fire, *with* scattering, and ^Ttempest, and hailstones.   Ps. 18:13-14 ✦ *storm*

31 For through the voice of the Lord shall the Assyrian be beaten down, *which* smote with a rod.   Is. 9:4

32 And *in* every place where the grounded staff shall pass, which the Lord shall lay upon him, *it* shall be with tabrets and harps: and in battles of shaking will he fight with it.   Is. 11:15

33 For Tophet *is* ordained of old; yea, for the king it is prepared; he hath made *it* deep *and* large: the pile thereof *is* fire and much wood; the breath of the Lord, like a stream of ^Tbrimstone, doth kindle it.   2 Kin. 23:10; Jer. 19:6 ✦ *sulphur*

The Lord Will Protect His People

31 Woe to them that go down to Egypt for help; and stay on horses, and trust in chariots, because *they are* many; and in horsemen, because they are very strong; but they look not unto the Holy One of Israel, neither seek the Lord!   Deut. 17:16; Ps. 20:7; Is. 30:16

2 Yet he also *is* wise, and will bring evil, and will not call back his words: but will arise against the house of the evildoers, and against the help of them that work iniquity.   Num. 23:19; Is. 45:7

3 Now the Egyptians *are* men, and not God; and their horses flesh, and not spirit. When the Lord shall stretch out his hand, both he that helpeth shall fall, and he that is ^Tholpen shall fall down, and they all shall fail together.   Is. 9:17 ✦ *helped*

4 For thus hath the Lord spoken unto me, Like as the lion and the young lion roaring on his prey, when a multitude of shepherds is called forth against him, *he* will not be afraid of their voice, nor ^Tabase himself for the noise of them: so shall the Lord of hosts come down to fight for mount Zion, and for the hill thereof.   Is. 42:13; Hos. 11:10; Amos 3:8 ✦ *bring low*

5 As birds flying, so will the Lord of hosts defend Jerusalem; defending also he will deliver *it; and* passing over he will preserve it.   Deut. 32:11; Ps. 91:4

6 Turn ye unto *him from* whom the children of Israel have deeply revolted.   Is. 55:7

7 For in that day every man shall cast away his idols of silver, and his idols of gold, which your own hands have made unto you *for* a sin.   Is. 2:20; 30:22

8 Then shall the Assyrian fall with the sword, not of a mighty man; and the sword, not of a mean man, shall devour him: but he shall flee from the sword, and his young men shall be discomfited.   Is. 14:25

9 And he shall pass over to his strong hold for fear, and his princes shall be afraid of the ^Tensign, saith the Lord, whose fire *is* in Zion, and his furnace in Jerusalem.   Deut. 32:31 ✦ *banner*

The Lord Will Pour out His Spirit

32 Behold, a king shall reign in righteousness, and princes shall rule in judgment.   Is. 9:6-7

2 And a man shall be as an hiding place from the wind, and a covert from the tempest; as rivers of water in a dry place, as the shadow of a great rock in a weary land.   Is. 25:4

> **32:2 The Shadow of a Great Rock**
>
> When the darkness is deepest, the light of a godlike character will shine the brightest. When every other trust fails, then it will be seen who have an abiding trust in Jehovah. And while the enemies of truth are on every side, watching the Lord's servants for evil, God will watch over them for good. He will be to them as the shadow of a great rock in a weary land. *AA 432*

3 And the eyes of them that see shall not be dim, and the ears of them that hear shall hearken.   Is. 29:18

4 The heart also of the rash shall understand knowledge, and the tongue of the stammerers shall be ready to speak plainly.   Is. 29:24

5 The vile person shall be no more called liberal, nor the ^Tchurl said *to be* bountiful. *deceiver*

6 For the vile person will speak ^Tvillany, and his heart will work iniquity, to practise hypocrisy, and to utter error against the Lord, to make empty the soul of the hungry, and he will cause the drink of the thirsty to fail.   1 Sam. 24:13 ✦ *foolishness*

7 The instruments also of the churl *are* evil: he deviseth wicked devices to destroy the poor with lying words, even when the needy speaketh right.   Jer. 5:26-28

8 But the liberal deviseth liberal things; and by liberal things shall he stand.

Desolation Is Foretold

9 Rise up, ye women that are at ease; hear my voice, ye careless daughters; give ear unto my speech.   Is. 28:23

10 Many days and years shall ye be troubled, ye careless women: for the vintage shall fail, the gathering shall not come. Is. 7:23
11 Tremble, ye women that are at ease; be troubled, ye careless ones: strip you, and make you bare, and ᵀgird sackcloth upon *your* ᵀloins.
equip ◆ waist
12 They shall lament for the teats, for the pleasant fields, for the fruitful vine.
13 Upon the land of my people shall come up thorns *and* briers; yea, upon all the houses of joy *in* the joyous city: Is. 22:2
14 Because the palaces shall be forsaken; the multitude of the city shall be left; the forts and towers shall be for dens for ever, a joy of wild asses, a pasture of flocks; Is. 24:10
15 Until the spirit be poured upon us from on high, and the wilderness be a fruitful field, and the fruitful field be counted for a forest. Is. 29:17; 35:1-2; 44:3
16 Then judgment shall dwell in the wilderness, and righteousness remain in the fruitful field.
17 And the work of righteousness shall be peace; and the effect of righteousness quietness and assurance for ever. Ps. 72:2-3; 119:165

32:17 An Intense Longing

Your sins may be as mountains before you; but if you humble your heart and confess your sins, trusting in the merits of a crucified and risen Saviour, He will forgive and will cleanse you from all unrighteousness. . . . Desire the fullness of the grace of Christ. Let your heart be filled with an intense longing for His righteousness, the work of which God's word declares is peace, and its effect quietness and assurance forever. *AA 566*

18 And my people shall dwell in a peaceable habitation, and in sure dwellings, and in quiet resting places; Hos. 2:18-23
19 When it shall hail, coming down on the forest; and the city shall be low in a low place. Is. 26:5; 28:2, 17
20 Blessed *are* ye that sow beside all waters, that send forth *thither* the feet of the ox and the ass. Eccl. 11:1; Is. 30:23-24

32:20 Continual Giving

To sow beside all waters means a continual imparting of God's gifts. It means giving wherever the cause of God or the needs of humanity demand our aid. This will not tend to poverty. *COL 85, 86*

The Lord Will Rescue Jerusalem from Assyria

33 Woe to thee that spoilest, and thou *wast* not spoiled; and dealest treacherously, and they dealt not treacherously with thee! when thou shalt cease to spoil, thou shalt be spoiled; *and* when thou shalt make an end to deal treacherously, they shall deal treacherously with thee. Is. 10:12; 21:2; Matt. 7:2
2 O Lᴏʀᴅ, be gracious unto us; we have waited for thee: be thou their arm every morning, our salvation also in the time of trouble. Is. 25:9; 26:8; 30:18-19
3 At the noise of the tumult the people fled; at the lifting up of thyself the nations were scattered.
4 And your ᵀspoil shall be gathered *like* the gathering of the caterpiller: as the running to and fro of locusts shall he run upon them. *plunder*
5 The Lᴏʀᴅ is exalted; for he dwelleth on high: he hath filled Zion with judgment and righteousness. Is. 2:17
6 And wisdom and knowledge shall be the stability of thy times, *and* strength of salvation: the fear of the Lᴏʀᴅ *is* his treasure. Matt. 6:33

33:6 One Safe and Sure Rule

Here is the only safeguard for individual integrity, for the purity of the home, the well-being of society, or the stability of the nation. Amidst all life's perplexities and dangers and conflicting claims, the one safe and sure rule is to do what God says. *PK 83*

7 Behold, their valiant ones shall cry without: the ambassadors of peace shall weep bitterly. 2 Kin. 18:18
8 The highways lie waste, the wayfaring man ceaseth: he hath broken the covenant, he hath despised the cities, he regardeth no man. Judg. 5:6
9 The earth mourneth *and* ᵀlanguisheth: Lebanon is ashamed *and* ᵀhewn down: Sharon is like a wilderness; and Bashan and Carmel shake off *their fruits.* Is. 35:2 ◆ *weakens ◆ cut*
10 Now will I rise, saith the Lᴏʀᴅ; now will I be exalted; now will I lift up myself. Ps. 12:5
11 Ye shall conceive chaff, ye shall bring forth stubble: your breath, *as* fire, shall devour you. Ps. 7:14; Is. 59:4; James 1:15
12 And the people shall be *as* the burnings of lime: *as* thorns cut up shall they be burned in the fire. 2 Sam. 23:6-7

The Privileges of the Godly

13 Hear, ye *that are* far off, what I have done; and, ye *that are* near, acknowledge my might. Ps. 48:10
14 The sinners in Zion are afraid; fearfulness hath surprised the hypocrites. Who among us shall dwell with the devouring fire? who among us shall dwell with everlasting burnings? Is. 66:24; Matt. 18:8; Heb. 12:29
15 He that walketh righteously, and speaketh uprightly; he that despiseth the gain of

oppressions, that shaketh his hands from holding of bribes, that stoppeth his ears from hearing of blood, and shutteth his eyes from seeing evil; Ps. 119:37

16 He shall dwell on high: his place of defence *shall be* the munitions of rocks: bread shall be given him; his waters *shall be* sure.

17 Thine eyes shall see the king in his beauty: they shall behold the land that is very far off. Is. 6:5

18 Thine heart shall meditate terror. Where *is* the scribe? where *is* the receiver? where *is* he that counted the towers? 2 Kin. 18:14

19 Thou shalt not see a fierce people, a people of a deeper speech than thou canst perceive; of a stammering tongue, *that thou canst* not understand. Deut. 28:49-50; Is. 28:11; Jer. 5:15

20 Look upon Zion, the city of our solemnities: thine eyes shall see Jerusalem a quiet habitation, a tabernacle *that* shall not be taken down; not one of the stakes thereof shall ever be removed, neither shall any of the cords thereof be broken. Ps. 46:5

21 But there the glorious LORD *will be* unto us a place of broad rivers *and* streams; wherein shall go no galley with oars, neither shall gallant ship pass thereby. Ps. 46:4-5

22 For the LORD *is* our judge, the LORD *is* our lawgiver, the LORD *is* our king; he will save us. Ps. 89:18; Is. 25:9; James 4:12

23 Thy tacklings are loosed; they could not well strengthen their mast, they could not spread the sail: then is the prey of a great spoil divided; the lame take the prey. 2 Kin. 7:8

24 And the inhabitant shall not say, I am sick:

the people that dwell therein *shall be* forgiven *their* iniquity. Is. 44:22; Jer. 50:20; 1 John 1:7-9

Edom Will Fall

34 Come near, ye nations, to hear; and hearken, ye people: let the earth hear, and all that is therein; the world, and all things that come forth of it. Deut. 32:1

2 For the ᵀindignation of the LORD *is* upon all nations, and *his* fury upon all their armies: he hath utterly destroyed them, he hath delivered them to the slaughter. anger

3 Their slain also shall be cast out, and their stink shall come up out of their carcases, and the mountains shall be melted with their blood. Is. 34:7; Ezek. 39:4; Joel 2:20

4 And all the host of heaven shall be dissolved, and the heavens shall be rolled together as a scroll: and all their host shall fall down, as the leaf falleth off from the vine, and as a falling *fig* from the fig tree. Ezek. 32:7-8; Matt. 24:29; Rev. 6:13-14

5 For my sword shall be bathed in heaven: behold, it shall come down upon Idumea, and upon the people of my curse, to judgment. Is. 63:1; Jer. 46:10; Mal. 1:4

6 The sword of the LORD is filled with blood, it is made fat with fatness, *and* with the blood of lambs and goats, with the fat of the kidneys of rams: for the LORD hath a sacrifice in Bozrah, and a great slaughter in the land of Idumea. Is. 63:1; Jer. 49:13

7 And the unicorns shall come down with them, and the bullocks with the bulls; and their land shall be soaked with blood, and their dust made fat with fatness. Num. 23:22

8 For *it is* the day of the LORD's vengeance,

God Doesn't Forget His People

Isaiah 33:16

As the decree issued by the various rulers of Christendom against commandment keepers shall withdraw the protection of government and abandon them to those who desire their destruction, the people of God will flee from the cities and villages and associate together in companies, dwelling in the most desolate and solitary places. Many will find refuge in the strongholds of the mountains. Like the Christians of the Piedmont valleys, they will make the high places of the earth their sanctuaries and will thank God for "the munitions of rocks" (Isaiah 33:16). But many of all nations and of all classes, high and low, rich and poor, black and white, will be cast into the most unjust and cruel bondage. The beloved of God pass weary days, bound in chains, shut in by prison bars, sentenced to be slain, some apparently left to die of starvation in dark and loathsome dungeons. No human ear is open to hear their moans; no human hand is ready to lend them help.

Will the Lord forget His people in this trying hour? Did He forget faithful Noah when judgments were visited upon the antediluvian world? Did He forget Lot when the fire came down from heaven to consume the cities of the plain? Did He forget Joseph surrounded by idolaters in Egypt? Did He forget Elijah when the oath of Jezebel threatened him with the fate of the prophets of Baal? Did He forget Jeremiah in the dark and dismal pit of his prison house? Did He forget the three worthies in the fiery furnace? or Daniel in the den of lions?

"Zion said, The Lord hath forsaken me, and my Lord hath forgotten me. Can a woman forget her sucking child, that she should not have compassion on the son of her womb? yea, they may forget, yet will I not forget thee. Behold, I have graven thee upon the palms of My hands" (Isaiah 49:14-16). *GC 626*

and the year of recompences for the controversy of Zion.   Is. 35:4; 61:2; 63:4

9 And the streams thereof shall be turned into pitch, and the dust thereof into ᵀbrimstone, and the land thereof shall become burning pitch.   Deut. 29:23 ◆ *sulphur*

10 It shall not be quenched night nor day; the smoke thereof shall go up for ever: from generation to generation it shall lie waste; none shall pass through it for ever and ever.   Is. 13:20; 66:24; Rev. 19:3

11 But the ᵀcormorant and the bittern shall possess it; the owl also and the raven shall dwell in it: and he shall stretch out upon it the line of confusion, and the stones of emptiness.   2 Kin. 21:13; Lam. 2:8; Zeph. 2:14 ◆ *bird*

12 They shall call the nobles thereof to the kingdom, but none *shall be* there, and all her princes shall be nothing.

13 And thorns shall come up in her palaces, nettles and brambles in the fortresses thereof: and it shall be an habitation of dragons, *and* a court for owls.   Jer. 9:11

14 The wild beasts of the desert shall also meet with the wild beasts of the island, and the ᵀsatyr shall cry to his fellow; the screech owl also shall rest there, and find for herself a place of rest.   Is. 13:21-22 ◆ *male goat*

15 There shall the great owl make her nest, and lay, and hatch, and gather under her shadow: there shall the vultures also be gathered, every one with her mate.   Deut. 14:13

16 Seek ye out of the book of the LORD, and read: no one of these shall fail, none shall want her mate: for my mouth it hath commanded, and his spirit it hath gathered them.   Is. 30:8

17 And he hath cast the lot for them, and his

hand hath divided it unto them by line: they shall possess it for ever, from generation to generation shall they dwell therein.   Is. 34:10

The Lord's People Will Have Joy

35 The wilderness and the solitary place shall be glad for them; and the desert shall rejoice, and blossom as the rose. Is. 51:3

35:1 The Only Power to Create True Peace

Men cannot manufacture peace. Human plans for the purification and uplifting of individuals or of society will fail of producing peace, because they do not reach the heart. The only power that can create or perpetuate true peace is the grace of Christ. When this is implanted in the heart, it will cast out the evil passions that cause strife and dissension. . . . and life's desert "shall rejoice, and blossom as the rose" (Isaiah 35:1). *DA 305*

---

2 It shall blossom abundantly, and rejoice even with joy and singing: the glory of Lebanon shall be given unto it, the excellency of Carmel and Sharon, they shall see the glory of the LORD, *and* the excellency of our God.   Song 7:5; Is. 25:9; 60:13

3 Strengthen ye the weak hands, and confirm the feeble knees.   Job 4:3-4; Heb. 12:12

4 Say to them *that are* of a fearful heart, Be strong, fear not: behold, your God will come *with* vengeance, *even* God *with* a recompence; he will come and save you.   Is. 34:8

5 Then the eyes of the blind shall be opened, and the ears of the deaf shall be unstopped.

6 Then shall the lame *man* leap as an ᵀhart, and the tongue of the ᵀdumb sing: for in the wilderness shall waters break out, and streams in the desert.   Luke 11:14 ◆ *deer* ◆ *mute*

35:4-10

Bible Mysteries

Isaiah 35:8

We have no reason to doubt God's word because we cannot understand the mysteries of His providence. In the natural world we are constantly surrounded with wonders beyond our comprehension. Should we then be surprised to find in the spiritual world also mysteries that we cannot fathom? The difficulty lies solely in the weakness and narrowness of the human mind.

The mysteries of the Bible, so far from being an argument against it, are among the strongest evidences of its divine inspiration. If it contained no account of God but that which we could comprehend; if His greatness and majesty could be grasped by finite minds, then the Bible would not, as now, bear the unmistakable evidences of divinity. The greatness of its themes should inspire faith in it as the word of God.

The Bible unfolds truth with a simplicity and an adaptation to the needs and longings of the human heart that has astonished and charmed the most highly cultivated minds, while to the humble and uncultured it makes plain the way of life. "The wayfaring men, though fools, shall not err therein" (Isaiah 35:8). No child need mistake the path. Not one trembling seeker need fail of walking in pure and holy light. Yet the most simply stated truths lay hold upon themes elevated, far-reaching, infinitely beyond the power of human comprehension—mysteries that are the hiding of His glory, mysteries that overpower the mind in its research—while they inspire the sincere seeker for truth with reverence and faith. The more we search the Bible, the deeper is our conviction that it is the word of the living God, and human reason bows before the majesty of divine revelation. *Ed 170*

7 And the parched ground shall become a pool, and the thirsty land springs of water: in the habitation of dragons, where each lay, *shall be* grass with reeds and rushes.   Is. 13:22

35:6, 7 Streams in the Desert

So it is with the true child of God. The religion of Christ reveals itself as a vitalizing, pervading principle, a living, working, spiritual energy. When the heart is opened to the heavenly influence of truth and love, these principles will flow forth again like streams in the desert, causing fruitfulness to appear where now are barrenness and dearth. *PK 234*

---

8 And an highway shall be there, and a way, and it shall be called The way of holiness; the unclean shall not pass over it; but it *shall be* for those: the wayfaring men, though fools, shall not ᵀerr *therein*.   Is. 11:16; 19:23; 52:1 ◆ *stray*
9 No lion shall be there, nor *any* ravenous beast shall go up thereon, it shall not be found there; but the redeemed shall walk *there*:   Is. 62:12

35:10 The Gift of Music

The history of the songs of the Bible is full of suggestion as to the uses and benefits of music and song. Music is often perverted to serve purposes of evil, and it thus becomes one of the most alluring agencies of temptation. But, rightly employed, it is a precious gift of God, designed to uplift the thoughts to high and noble themes, to inspire and elevate the soul. *Ed 167*

---

10 And the ransomed of the LORD shall return, and come to Zion with songs and everlasting joy upon their heads: they shall obtain joy and gladness, and sorrow and sighing shall flee away.   Is. 25:8; 30:19; Rev. 21:4

The New Earth See Isaiah 65:17–25.

Sennacherib of Assyria Invades Judah

36 Now it came to pass in the fourteenth year of king Hezekiah, *that* Sennacherib king of Assyria came up against all the defenced cities of Judah, and took them.   2 Kin. 18:13, 17; 2 Chr. 32:1
2 And the king of Assyria sent Rabshakeh from Lachish to Jerusalem unto king Hezekiah with a great army. And he stood by the conduit of the upper pool in the highway of the fuller's field.   2 Kin. 18:17-37; 2 Chr. 32:9-23
3 Then came forth unto him Eliakim, Hilkiah's son, which was over the house, and Shebna the scribe, and Joah, Asaph's son, the recorder.
4 And Rabshakeh said unto them, Say ye now to Hezekiah, Thus saith the great king,

the king of Assyria, What confidence *is* this wherein thou trustest?
5 I say, *sayest thou*, (but *they* are but vain words) *I have* counsel and strength for war: now on whom dost thou trust, that thou rebellest against me?   2 Kin. 18:7
6 Lo, thou trustest in the staff of this broken reed, on Egypt; whereon if a man lean, it will go into his hand, and pierce it: so *is* Pharaoh king of Egypt to all that trust in him.
7 But if thou say to me, We trust in the LORD our God: *is it* not he, whose high places and whose altars Hezekiah hath taken away, and said to Judah and to Jerusalem, Ye shall worship before this altar?   2 Kin. 18:4-5
8 Now therefore give pledges, I pray thee, to my master the king of Assyria, and I will give thee two thousand horses, if thou be able on thy part to set riders upon them.
9 How then wilt thou turn away the face of one captain of the least of my master's servants, and put thy trust on Egypt for chariots and for horsemen?   Is. 10:8
10 And am I now come up without the LORD against this land to destroy it? the LORD said unto me, Go up against this land, and destroy it.   1 Kin. 13:18
11 Then said Eliakim and Shebna and Joah unto Rabshakeh, Speak, I pray thee, unto thy servants in the Syrian language; for we understand *it*: and speak not to us in the Jews' language, in the ears of the people that *are* on the wall.   Ezra 4:7; Dan. 2:4
12 But Rabshakeh said, Hath my master sent me to thy master and to thee to speak these words? *hath he* not *sent me* to the men that sit upon the wall, that they may eat their own dung, and drink their own piss with you?
13 Then Rabshakeh stood, and cried with a loud voice in the Jews' language, and said, Hear ye the words of the great king, the king of Assyria.   2 Chr. 32:18
14 Thus saith the king, Let not Hezekiah deceive you: for he shall not be able to deliver you.
15 Neither let Hezekiah make you trust in the LORD, saying, The LORD will surely deliver us: this city shall not be delivered into the hand of the king of Assyria.
16 Hearken not to Hezekiah: for thus saith the king of Assyria, Make *an* agreement with me *by* a present, and come out to me: and eat ye every one of his vine, and every one of his fig tree, and drink ye every one the waters of his own ᵀcistern;   1 Kin. 4:25 ◆ *well*
17 Until I come and take you away to a land like your own land, a land of corn and wine, a land of bread and vineyards.
18 *Beware* lest Hezekiah persuade you, saying, The LORD will deliver us. Hath any of

the gods of the nations delivered his land out of the hand of the king of Assyria? Is. 36:15
19 Where *are* the gods of Hamath and Arphad? where *are* the gods of Sepharvaim? and have they delivered Samaria out of my hand? Is. 10:9-11; Jer. 49:23
20 Who *are they* among all the gods of these lands, that have delivered their land out of my hand, that the LORD should deliver Jerusalem out of my hand? 2 Chr. 32:19
21 But they held their peace, and answered him not a word: for the king's commandment was, saying, Answer him not. Prov. 26:4
22 Then came Eliakim, the son of Hilkiah, that *was* over the household, and Shebna the scribe, and Joah, the son of Asaph, the recorder, to Hezekiah with *their* clothes rent, and told him the words of Rabshakeh. Is. 36:3

Hezekiah Asks Isaiah to Pray for the Nation

37 And it came to pass, when king Hezekiah heard *it*, that he ᵀrent his clothes, and covered himself with sackcloth, and went into the house of the LORD.   *tore apart*
2 And he sent Eliakim, who *was* over the household, and Shebna the scribe, and the elders of the priests covered with sackcloth, unto Isaiah the prophet the son of Amoz. Is. 1:1
3 And they said unto him, Thus saith Hezekiah, This day *is* a day of trouble, and of rebuke, and of blasphemy: for the children are come to the birth, and *there is* not strength to bring forth. Is. 26:17-18; 66:9; Hos. 13:13
4 It may be the LORD thy God will hear the words of Rabshakeh, whom the king of Assyria his master hath sent to reproach the living God, and will reprove the words which the LORD thy God hath heard: wherefore lift up *thy* prayer for the remnant that is left. Is. 1:9; 10:22; 36:20
5 So the servants of king Hezekiah came to Isaiah.
6 And Isaiah said unto them, Thus shall ye say unto your master, Thus saith the LORD, Be not afraid of the words that thou hast heard, wherewith the servants of the king of Assyria have blasphemed me. Is. 7:4
7 Behold, I will send a blast upon him, and he shall hear a rumour, and return to his own land; and I will cause him to fall by the sword in his own land. Is. 37:9

Sennacherib Sends a Blasphemous Letter to Hezekiah

8 So Rabshakeh returned, and found the king of Assyria warring against Libnah: for he had heard that he was departed from Lachish. Josh. 10:29

9 And he heard say concerning Tirhakah king of Ethiopia, He is come forth to make war with thee. And when he heard *it*, he sent messengers to Hezekiah, saying,
10 Thus shall ye speak to Hezekiah king of Judah, saying, Let not thy God, in whom thou trustest, deceive thee, saying, Jerusalem shall not be given into the hand of the king of Assyria. Is. 36:15
11 Behold, thou hast heard what the kings of Assyria have done to all lands by destroying them utterly; and shalt thou be delivered? Is. 36:18-20
12 Have the gods of the nations delivered them which my fathers have destroyed, *as* Gozan, and Haran, and Rezeph, and the children of Eden which *were* in Telassar? Gen. 11:31
13 Where *is* the king of Hamath, and the king of Arphad, and the king of the city of Sepharvaim, Hena, and Ivah?
14 And Hezekiah received the letter from the hand of the messengers, and read it: and Hezekiah went up unto the house of the LORD, and spread it before the LORD.
15 And Hezekiah prayed unto the LORD, saying,
16 O LORD of hosts, God of Israel, that dwellest *between* the cherubims, thou *art* the God, *even* thou alone, of all the kingdoms of the earth: thou hast made heaven and earth. Ex. 25:22
17 Incline thine ear, O LORD, and hear; open thine eyes, O LORD, and see: and hear all the words of Sennacherib, which hath sent to reproach the living God. 2 Chr. 6:40; Ps. 17:6; 74:22
18 Of a truth, LORD, the kings of Assyria have laid waste all the nations, and their countries, 2 Kin. 15:29
19 And have cast their gods into the fire: for they *were* no gods, but the work of men's hands, wood and stone: therefore they have destroyed them.
20 Now therefore, O LORD our God, save us from his hand, that all the kingdoms of the earth may know that thou *art* the LORD, *even* thou only. Ps. 46:10

Isaiah's Prophecy against Sennacherib

21 Then Isaiah the son of Amoz sent unto Hezekiah, saying, Thus saith the LORD God of Israel, Whereas thou hast prayed to me against Sennacherib king of Assyria:
22 This *is* the word which the LORD hath spoken concerning him; The virgin, the daughter of Zion, hath despised thee, *and* laughed thee to scorn; the daughter of Jerusalem hath shaken her head at thee. Job 16:4
23 Whom hast thou reproached and blasphemed? and against whom hast thou exalted *thy* voice, and lifted up thine eyes on high? *even* against the Holy One of Israel. Ezek. 39:7

24 By thy servants hast thou reproached the Lord, and hast said, By the multitude of my chariots am I come up to the height of the mountains, to the sides of Lebanon; and I will cut down the tall cedars thereof, *and* the choice fir trees thereof: and I will enter into the height of his border, *and* the forest of his Carmel.   Is. 10:18; 14:8

25 I have digged, and drunk water; and with the sole of my feet have I dried up all the rivers of the besieged places.   1 Kin. 20:10

26 Hast thou not heard long ago, *how* I have done it; *and* of ancient times, that I have formed it? now have I brought it to pass, that thou shouldest be to lay waste defenced cities *into* ruinous heaps.   Acts 2:23

27 Therefore their inhabitants *were* of small power, they were dismayed and confounded: they were *as* the grass of the field, and *as* the green herb, *as* the grass on the housetops, and *as* corn blasted before it be grown up.   Ps. 129:6

28 But I know thy abode, and thy going out, and thy coming in, and thy rage against me.

29 Because thy rage against me, and thy tumult, is come up into mine ears, therefore will I put my hook in thy nose, and my bridle in thy lips, and I will turn thee back by the way by which thou camest.   Is. 30:28

30 And this *shall be* a sign unto thee, Ye shall eat *this* year such as groweth of itself; and the second year that which springeth of the same: and in the third year sow ye, and reap, and plant vineyards, and eat the fruit thereof.

31 And the remnant that is escaped of the house of Judah shall again take root downward, and bear fruit upward: Is. 27:6

32 For out of Jerusalem shall go forth a remnant, and they that escape out of mount Zion: the zeal of the Lord of hosts shall do this.   2 Kin. 19:31; Is. 9:7; 59:17

33 Therefore thus saith the Lord concerning the king of Assyria, He shall not come into this city, nor shoot an arrow there, nor come before it with shields, nor cast a bank against it.

34 By the way that he came, by the same shall he return, and shall not come into this city, saith the Lord.   Is. 37:29

35 For I will defend this city to save it for mine own sake, and for my servant David's sake.   2 Kin. 20:6; Is. 31:5; 38:6

36 Then the angel of the Lord went forth, and smote in the camp of the Assyrians a hundred and Tfourscore and five thousand: and when they arose early in the morning, behold, they *were* all dead corpses.   Is. 10:12 ◆ *eighty*

37 So Sennacherib king of Assyria departed, and went and returned, and dwelt at Nineveh.   Jon. 1:2

38 And it came to pass, as he was worshipping in the house of Nisroch his god, that Adrammelech and Sharezer his sons smote him with the sword; and they escaped into the land of Armenia: and Esar-haddon his son reigned in his stead. Gen. 8:4; Ezra 4:2; Jer. 51:27

Hezekiah's Illness

38 In those days was Hezekiah sick unto death. And Isaiah the prophet the son of Amoz came unto him, and said unto him, Thus saith the Lord, Set thine house in order: for thou shalt die, and not live.   2 Sam. 17:23

2 Then Hezekiah turned his face toward the wall, and prayed unto the Lord,

3 And said, Remember now, O Lord, I Tbeseech thee, how I have walked before thee in truth and with a perfect heart, and have done *that which is* good in thy sight. And Hezekiah wept sore.   1 Chr. 29:19 ◆ *beg*

4 Then came the word of the Lord to Isaiah, saying,

5 Go, and say to Hezekiah, Thus saith the Lord, the God of David thy father, I have heard thy prayer, I have seen thy tears: behold, I will add unto thy days fifteen years. 2 Kin. 18:2

6 And I will deliver thee and this city out of the hand of the king of Assyria: and I will defend this city.   Is. 37:35

7 And this *shall be* a sign unto thee from the Lord, that the Lord will do this thing that he hath spoken;   Judg. 6:37-39

8 Behold, I will bring again the shadow of the degrees, which is gone down in the sun dial of Ahaz, ten degrees backward. So the sun returned ten degrees, by which degrees it was gone down.   Josh. 10:12-14

Hezekiah's Song of Thanksgiving

9 The writing of Hezekiah king of Judah, when he had been sick, and was recovered of his sickness:

10 I said in the cutting off of my days, I shall go to the gates of the grave: I am deprived of the residue of my years.   2 Cor. 1:9

11 I said, I shall not see the Lord, *even* the Lord, in the land of the living: I shall behold man no more with the inhabitants of the world.   Ps. 27:13

12 Mine age is departed, and is removed from me as a shepherd's tent: I have cut off like a weaver my life: he will cut me off with pining sickness: from day *even* to night wilt thou make an end of me.   Ps. 73:14

13 I reckoned till morning, *that*, as a lion, so will he break all my bones: from day *even* to night wilt thou make an end of me.   Ps. 51:8

14 Like a crane *or* a swallow, so did I chatter: I did mourn as a dove: mine eyes fail *with looking* upward: O Lord, I am oppressed; undertake for me.   Job 30:29; Ps. 69:3; Is. 59:11

15 What shall I say? he hath both spoken unto me, and himself hath done *it*: I shall go softly all my years in the bitterness of my soul.   1 Kin. 21:27; Job 7:11; 10:1

16 O Lord, by these *things* men live, and in all these *things is* the life of my spirit: so wilt thou recover me, and make me to live.   Deut. 8:3

17 Behold, for peace I had great bitterness: but thou hast in love to my soul *delivered it* from the pit of corruption: for thou hast cast all my sins behind thy back.   Ps. 30:3

18 For the grave cannot praise thee, death can *not* celebrate thee: they that go down into the pit cannot hope for thy truth.   Ps. 6:5; 30:9

19 The living, the living, he shall praise thee, as I *do* this day: the father to the children shall make known thy truth.   Deut. 4:9; 6:7; Ps. 78:3-6

20 The LORD *was ready* to save me: therefore we will sing my songs to the stringed instruments all the days of our life in the house of the LORD.

21 For Isaiah had said, Let them take a lump of figs, and lay *it* for a plaister upon the boil, and he shall recover.

22 Hezekiah also had said, What *is* the sign that I shall go up to the house of the LORD?

Hezekiah Shows the Babylonians His Treasures

39 At that time Merodach-baladan, the son of Baladan, king of Babylon, sent letters and a present to Hezekiah: for he had heard that he had been sick, and was recovered.   2 Kin. 20:12-19

2 And Hezekiah was glad of them, and shewed them the house of his precious things, the silver, and the gold, and the spices, and the precious ointment, and all the house of his armour, and all that was found in his treasures: there was nothing in his house, nor in all his dominion, that Hezekiah shewed them not.   2 Chr. 32:25

3 Then came Isaiah the prophet unto king Hezekiah, and said unto him, What said these men? and from whence came they unto thee? And Hezekiah said, They are come from a far country unto me, *even* from Babylon.   Deut. 28:49

4 Then said he, What have they seen in thine house? And Hezekiah answered, All that *is* in mine house have they seen: there is nothing among my treasures that I have not shewed them.

5 Then said Isaiah to Hezekiah, Hear the word of the LORD of hosts: 1 Sam. 13:13-14

6 Behold, the days come, that all that *is* in thine house, and *that* which thy fathers have laid up in store until this day, shall be carried to Babylon: nothing shall be left, saith the LORD.   2 Kin. 24:13; 25:13-15; Jer. 20:5

7 And of thy sons that shall issue from thee, which thou shalt ᵀbeget, shall they take away; and they shall be eunuchs in the palace of the king of Babylon.   2 Kin. 24:12 ◆ *bring forth*

8 Then said Hezekiah to Isaiah, Good *is* the word of the LORD which thou hast spoken. He said moreover, For there shall be peace and truth in my days.   2 Chr. 32:26

Comfort for the People

40 Comfort ye, comfort ye my people, saith your God.   Is. 51:3, 12; Zeph. 3:14-17

2 Speak ye comfortably to Jerusalem, and cry unto her, that her warfare is accomplished, that her iniquity is pardoned: for she hath received of the LORD's hand double for all her sins.   Is. 61:7; Jer. 16:18; Zech. 9:12

Prophecy of John the Baptist

3 The voice of him that crieth in the wilderness, Prepare ye the way of the LORD, make straight in the desert a highway for our God.   Mal. 3:1; 4:5-6; John 1:23

4 Every valley shall be exalted, and every mountain and hill shall be made low: and

---

God's Simple Healing Methods

Isaiah 38:21

Those who seek healing by prayer should not neglect to make use of the remedial agencies within their reach. It is not a denial of faith to use such remedies as God has provided to alleviate pain and to aid nature in her work of restoration. It is no denial of faith to co-operate with God, and to place themselves in the condition most favorable to recovery. God has put it in our power to obtain a knowledge of the laws of life. This knowledge has been placed within our reach for use. We should employ every facility for the restoration of health, taking every advantage possible, working in harmony with natural laws. . . .

We have the sanction of the word of God for the use of remedial agencies. Hezekiah, king of Israel, was sick, and a prophet of God brought him the message that he should die. He cried unto the Lord, and the Lord heard His servant and sent him a message that fifteen years should be added to his life. Now, one word from God would have healed Hezekiah instantly; but special directions were given, "Let them take a lump of figs, and lay it for a plaster upon the boil, and he shall recover" (Isaiah 38:21). *MH 231, 232*

the crooked shall be made straight, and the rough places plain:
Is. 45:2

5 And the glory of the LORD shall be revealed, and all flesh shall see *it* together: for the mouth of the LORD hath spoken *it*.
Is. 1:20

6 The voice said, Cry. And he said, What shall I cry? All flesh *is* grass, and all the goodliness thereof *is* as the flower of the field:
Job 14:2; Ps. 102:11

7 The grass withereth, the flower fadeth: because the spirit of the LORD bloweth upon it: surely the people *is* grass.

8 The grass withereth, the flower fadeth: but the word of our God shall stand for ever.
Matt. 5:18

40:8 The Word Is a Rock

Whatever is built upon the authority of man will be overthrown; but that which is founded upon the rock of God's immutable word shall stand forever. *GC 288*

9 O Zion, that bringest good tidings, get thee up into the high mountain; O Jerusalem, that bringest good tidings, lift up thy voice with strength; lift *it* up, be not afraid; say unto the cities of Judah, Behold your God!
Is. 25:9

10 Behold, the Lord GOD will come with strong *hand*, and his arm shall rule for him: behold, his reward *is* with him, and his work before him.
Is. 9:6-7; 62:11; Rev. 22:12

40:9, 10 Making Known God's Character

It is the darkness of misapprehension of God that is enshrouding the world. Men are losing their knowledge of His character. It has been misunderstood and misinterpreted. At this time a message from God is to be proclaimed, a message illuminating in its influence and saving in its power. His character is to be made known. . . .

Those who wait for the Bridegroom's coming are to say to the people, "Behold your God." The last rays of merciful light, the last message of mercy to be given to the world, is a revelation of His character of love. *COL 415*

11 He shall feed his flock like a shepherd: he shall gather the lambs with his arm, and carry *them* in his bosom, *and* shall gently lead those that are with young.
Is. 42:3; Ezek. 34:23

The Omnipotence of God

12 Who hath measured the waters in the ᵀhollow of his hand, and ᵀmeted out heaven with the span, and comprehended the dust of the earth in a measure, and weighed the mountains in scales, and the hills in a balance?
Prov. 30:4 ◆ *recessed place* ◆ *measured out*

13 Who hath directed the Spirit of the LORD, or *being* his counsellor hath taught him?

14 With whom took he counsel, and *who* instructed him, and taught him in the path of judgment, and taught him knowledge, and shewed to him the way of understanding?
Col. 2:3

15 Behold, the nations *are* as a drop of a bucket, and are counted as the small dust of the balance: behold, he taketh up the isles as a very little thing.
Jer. 10:10

16 And Lebanon *is* not sufficient to burn, nor the beasts thereof sufficient for a burnt offering.
Mic. 6:6-7

17 All nations before him *are* as nothing; and they are counted to him less than nothing, and vanity.
Ps. 62:9

18 To whom then will ye liken God? or what likeness will ye compare unto him?
Ex. 8:10

19 The workman melteth a graven image, and the goldsmith spreadeth it over with gold, and casteth silver chains.
Ps. 115:4-8

20 He that *is* so impoverished that he hath no ᵀoblation chooseth a tree *that* will not rot; he seeketh unto him a cunning workman to prepare a graven image, *that* shall not be moved.
1 Sam. 5:3-4 ◆ *offering*

21 Have ye not known? have ye not heard? hath it not been told you from the beginning? have ye not understood from the foundations of the earth?
Acts 14:17

22 *It is* he that sitteth upon the circle of the earth, and the inhabitants thereof *are* as grasshoppers; that stretcheth out the heavens as a curtain, and spreadeth them out as a tent to dwell in:
Num. 13:33; Job 9:8; Ps. 104:2

23 That bringeth the princes to nothing; he maketh the judges of the earth as vanity.
Job 12:21; Ps. 107:40; Jer. 25:18-27

24 Yea, they shall not be planted; yea, they shall not be sown: yea, their stock shall not take root in the earth: and he shall also blow upon them, and they shall wither, and the whirlwind shall take them away as stubble.
Is. 41:16

25 To whom then will ye liken me, or shall I be equal? saith the Holy One.
Is. 40:18

26 Lift up your eyes on high, and behold who hath created these *things*, that bringeth out their host by number: he calleth them all by names by the greatness of his might, for that *he is* strong in power; not one faileth.
Ps. 89:11-13

27 Why sayest thou, O Jacob, and speakest, O Israel, My way is hid from the LORD, and my judgment is passed over from my God?

28 Hast thou not known? hast thou not heard, *that* the everlasting God, the LORD, the Creator of the ends of the earth, fainteth not, neither is weary? *there is* no searching of his understanding.
Gen. 21:33; Ps. 147:5; Is. 57:15

29 He giveth power to the faint; and to *them that have* no might he increaseth strength.

30 Even the youths shall faint and be weary, and the young men shall utterly fall: Is. 9:17

31 But they that wait upon the LORD shall renew *their* strength; they shall mount up with wings as eagles; they shall run, and not be weary; *and* they shall walk, and not faint.   Ex. 19:4; Ps. 103:5; 2 Cor. 4:16

God Reasons with His People

41 Keep silence before me, O islands; and let the people renew *their* strength: let them come near; then let them speak: let us come near together to judgment.   Is. 1:18; Hab. 2:20; Zech. 2:13

2 Who raised up the righteous *man* from the east, called him to his foot, gave the nations before him, and made *him* rule over kings? he gave *them* as the dust to his sword, *and* as driven stubble to his bow.   2 Sam. 22:43; Is. 40:24

3 He pursued them, *and* passed safely; *even* by the way *that* he had not gone with his feet.

4 Who hath wrought and done *it,* calling the generations from the beginning? I the LORD, the first, and with the last; I *am* he.   Is. 41:26

5 The isles saw *it,* and feared; the ends of the earth were afraid, drew near, and came.

6 They helped every one his neighbour; and *every one* said to his brother, Be of good courage.

7 So the carpenter encouraged the goldsmith, *and* he that smootheth *with* the hammer him that smote the anvil, saying, It *is* ready for the sodering: and he fastened it with nails, *that* it should not be moved.   Is. 40:19-20

8 But thou, Israel, *art* my servant, Jacob whom I have chosen, the seed of Abraham my friend.   2 Chr. 20:7; Is. 44:1-2; James 2:23

9 *Thou* whom I have taken from the ends of the earth, and called thee from the chief men thereof, and said unto thee, Thou *art*

my servant; I have chosen thee, and not cast thee away.

God Is with His People

10 Fear thou not; for I *am* with thee: be not dismayed; for I *am* thy God: I will strengthen thee; yea, I will help thee; yea, I will uphold thee with the right hand of my righteousness.   Josh. 1:9; Is. 41:13-14; 43:5

11 Behold, all they that were incensed against thee shall be ashamed and confounded: they shall be as nothing; and they that strive with thee shall perish.   Ex. 23:22; Is. 45:24

12 Thou shalt seek them, and shalt not find them, *even* them that contended with thee: they that war against thee shall be as nothing, and as a thing of ᵀnought.   Ps. 37:35-36 ◆ *nothing*

13 For I the LORD thy God will hold thy right hand, saying unto thee, Fear not; I will help thee.   Is. 45:1

41:10–13 Strength for the Powerless

The heart of Infinite Love yearns after those who feel powerless to free themselves from the snares of Satan; and He graciously offers to strengthen them to live for Him. *PK 316*

---

14 Fear not, thou worm Jacob, *and* ye men of Israel; I will help thee, saith the LORD, and thy redeemer, the Holy One of Israel. Ps. 22:6

15 Behold, I will make thee a new sharp threshing instrument having teeth: thou shalt thresh the mountains, and beat *them* small, and shalt make the hills as chaff.   Mic. 4:13

16 Thou shalt ᵀfan them, and the wind shall carry them away, and the whirlwind shall scatter them: and thou shalt rejoice in the LORD, *and* shalt glory in the Holy One of Israel.   Jer. 51:2 ◆ *winnow*

17 *When* the poor and needy seek water, and *there is* none, *and* their tongue faileth for

---

He Gives Power to the Weak

Isaiah 40:26–29

From the stars that in their trackless courses through space follow from age to age their appointed path, down to the minutest atom, the things of nature obey the Creator's will. And God cares for everything and sustains everything that He has created. He who upholds the unnumbered worlds throughout immensity, at the same time cares for the wants of the little brown sparrow that sings its humble song without fear. When men go forth to their daily toil, as when they engage in prayer; when they lie down at night, and when they rise in the morning; when the rich man feasts in his palace, or when the poor man gathers his children about the scanty board, each is tenderly watched by the heavenly Father. No tears are shed that God does not notice. There is no smile that He does not mark.

If we would but fully believe this, all undue anxieties would be dismissed. Our lives would not be so filled with disappointment as now; for everything, whether great or small, would be left in the hands of God, who is not perplexed by the multiplicity of cares, or overwhelmed by their weight. We should then enjoy a rest of soul to which many have long been strangers. *SC 86*

thirst, I the LORD will hear them, *I* the God of Israel will not forsake them.   Is. 30:19

41:17 God's Care in Famine

That God who cared for Elijah will not pass by one of His self-sacrificing children. He who numbers the hairs of their head will care for them, and in time of famine they shall be satisfied. While the wicked are dying from hunger and pestilence, angels will shield the righteous and supply their wants. *GC 629*

---

18 I will open rivers in high places, and fountains in the midst of the valleys: I will make the wilderness a pool of water, and the dry land springs of water.   Ps. 107:35
19 I will plant in the wilderness the cedar, the shittah tree, and the myrtle, and the oil tree; I will set in the desert the fir tree, *and* the pine, and the box tree together: Is. 35:1; 55:13; 60:13
20 That they may see, and know, and consider, and understand together, that the hand of the LORD hath done this, and the Holy One of Israel hath created it.   Job 12:9

The Worthlessness of Idols

21 Produce your cause, saith the LORD; bring forth your strong *reasons*, saith the King of Jacob.
22 Let them bring *them* forth, and shew us what shall happen: let them shew the former things, what they *be,* that we may consider them, and know the latter end of them; or declare us things for to come.   Is. 45:21; 46:10
23 Shew the things that are to come hereafter, that we may know that ye *are* gods: yea, do good, or do evil, that we may be dismayed, and behold *it* together.   Is. 42:9
24 Behold, ye *are* of nothing, and your work of nought: an abomination *is he that* chooseth you.   Ps. 115:8; Is. 41:29; 1 Cor. 8:4
25 I have raised up *one* from the north, and he shall come: from the rising of the sun shall he call upon my name: and he shall come upon princes as *upon* morter, and as the potter treadeth clay.   2 Sam. 22:43; Is. 10:6; 41:2
26 Who hath declared from the beginning, that we may know? and beforetime, that we may say, *He is* righteous? yea, *there is* none that sheweth, yea, *there is* none that declareth, yea, *there is* none that heareth your words.   Is. 41:22
27 The first *shall say* to Zion, Behold, behold them: and I will give to Jerusalem one that bringeth good tidings.   Is. 40:9; 44:28; 52:7
28 For I beheld, and *there was* no man; even among them, and *there was* no counsellor, that, when I asked of them, could answer a word.   Is. 63:5
29 Behold, they *are* all vanity; their works *are*

nothing: their molten images *are* wind and confusion.   Is. 41:24

The Work of Christ, the Servant

42 Behold my servant, whom I uphold; mine elect, *in whom* my soul delighteth; I have put my spirit upon him: he shall bring forth judgment to the Gentiles.   Is. 43:10
2 He shall not cry, nor lift up, nor cause his voice to be heard in the street.   Zech. 9:9
3 A bruised reed shall he not break, and the smoking flax shall he not quench: he shall bring forth judgment unto truth.   Ps. 96:13

42:2, 3 Christ's Example

In His life no self-assertion was to be mingled. The homage which the world gives to position, to wealth, and to talent, was to be foreign to the Son of God. None of the means that men employ to win allegiance or to command homage, was the Messiah to use. *PK 692, 693*

---

4 He shall not fail nor be discouraged, till he have set judgment in the earth: and the isles shall wait for his law.   Gen. 49:10

God's Promise to Christ

5 Thus saith God the LORD, he that created the heavens, and stretched them out; he that spread forth the earth, and that which cometh out of it; he that giveth breath unto the people upon it, and spirit to them that walk therein: Job 12:10; 33:4; Acts 17:25
6 I the LORD have called thee in righteousness, and will hold thine hand, and will keep thee, and give thee for a covenant of the people, for a light of the Gentiles; Is. 49:6, 8; Luke 2:32
7 To open the blind eyes, to bring out the prisoners from the prison, *and* them that sit in darkness out of the prison house.   Is. 35:5
8 I *am* the LORD: that *is* my name: and my glory will I not give to another, neither my praise to graven images.   Ex. 20:3-5; Ps. 83:18
9 Behold, the former things are come to pass, and new things do I declare: before they spring forth I tell you of them.   Is. 43:19

A Song about the Lord

10 Sing unto the LORD a new song, *and* his praise from the end of the earth, ye that go down to the sea, and all that is therein; the isles, and the inhabitants thereof.   Ps. 33:3; 40:3
11 Let the wilderness and the cities thereof lift up *their voice,* the villages *that* Kedar doth inhabit: let the inhabitants of the rock sing, let them shout from the top of the mountains.   Is. 32:16
12 Let them give glory unto the LORD, and declare his praise in the islands.
13 The LORD shall go forth as a mighty man,

he shall stir up jealousy like a man of war: he shall cry, yea, roar; he shall prevail against his enemies.   Ps. 78:65

14 I have long time ᵀholden my peace; I have been still, *and* refrained myself: *now* will I cry like a travailing woman; I will destroy and devour at once.   held

15 I will make waste mountains and hills, and dry up all their herbs; and I will make the rivers islands, and I will dry up the pools.   Is. 2:12-16; 50:2; Nah. 1:4-6

16 And I will bring the blind by a way *that* they knew not; I will lead them in paths *that* they have not known: I will make darkness light before them, and crooked things straight. These things will I do unto them, and not forsake them.   Is. 29:18

17 They shall be turned back, they shall be greatly ashamed, that trust in ᵀgraven images, that say to the molten images, Ye *are* our gods.   Ps. 97:7; Is. 1:29; 44:11 ◆ *engraved or cut out*

The Lord Will Bring His People Home

18 Hear, ye deaf; and look, ye blind, that ye may see.   Is. 29:18

19 Who *is* blind, but my servant? or deaf, as my messenger *that* I sent? who *is* blind as *he that is* perfect, and blind as the LORD's servant?   Jer. 5:21

20 Seeing many things, but thou observest not; opening the ears, but he heareth not.

21 The LORD is well pleased for his righteousness' sake; he will magnify the law, and make *it* honourable.

42:21 God's Unchanging Law

In the precepts of His holy law, God has given a perfect rule of life; and He has declared that until the close of time this law, unchanged in a single jot or tittle, is to maintain its claim upon human beings. Christ came to magnify the law and make it honorable. He showed that it is based upon the broad foundation of love to God and love to man. . . . *AA 505*

---

22 But this *is* a people robbed and spoiled; *they are* all of them snared in holes, and they are hid in prison houses: they are for a prey, and none delivereth; for a spoil, and none saith, Restore.   Is. 14:17

23 Who among you will give ear to this? *who* will hearken and hear for the time to come?   Is. 48:18

24 Who gave Jacob for a ᵀspoil, and Israel to the robbers? did not the LORD, he against whom we have sinned? for they would not walk in his ways, neither were they obedient unto his law.   plunder

25 Therefore he hath poured upon him the fury of his anger, and the strength of battle: and it hath set him on fire round about, yet he knew not; and it burned him, yet he laid *it* not to heart.   2 Kin. 25:9; Is. 57:11; Hos. 7:9

The Lord Comforts with His Promises

43 But now thus saith the LORD that created thee, O Jacob, and he that formed thee, O Israel, Fear not: for I have redeemed thee, I have called *thee* by thy name; thou *art* mine.   Is. 43:7, 21; 44:2

2 When thou passest through the waters, I *will be* with thee; and through the rivers, they shall not overflow thee: when thou walkest through the fire, thou shalt not be burned; neither shall the flame kindle upon thee.   Ps. 66:12; Dan. 3:25-27

3 For I *am* the LORD thy God, the Holy One of Israel, thy Saviour: I gave Egypt *for* thy ransom, Ethiopia and Seba for thee.   Ex. 20:2

4 Since thou wast precious in my sight, thou hast been honourable, and I have loved thee: therefore will I give men for thee, and people for thy life.   Ex. 19:5-6

5 Fear not: for I *am* with thee: I will bring thy seed from the east, and gather thee from the west;   Is. 44:2; 49:12; Jer. 30:10-11

6 I will say to the north, Give up; and to the south, Keep not back: bring my sons from far, and my daughters from the ends of the earth;

An Illustration of Christ's Relation to Us

Isaiah 43:1–4

Those who accept Christ as their personal Saviour are not left as orphans, to bear the trials of life alone. He receives them as members of the heavenly family; He bids them call His Father their Father. They are His "little ones," dear to the heart of God, bound to Him by the most tender and abiding ties. He has toward them an exceeding tenderness, as far surpassing what our father or mother has felt toward us in our helplessness as the divine is above the human.

Of Christ's relation to His people, there is a beautiful illustration in the laws given to Israel. When through poverty a Hebrew had been forced to part with his patrimony, and to sell himself as a bondservant, the duty of redeeming him and his inheritance fell to the one who was nearest of kin. See Leviticus 25:25, 47–49; Ruth 2:20. So the work of redeeming us and our inheritance, lost through sin, fell upon Him who is "near of kin" unto us. It was to redeem us that He became our kinsman. Closer than father, mother, brother, friend, or lover is the Lord our Saviour. *DA 327*

7 *Even* every one that is called by my name: for I have created him for my glory, I have formed him; yea, I have made him.   Ps. 100:3

8 Bring forth the blind people that have eyes, and the deaf that have ears.   Is. 6:9

9 Let all the nations be gathered together, and let the people be assembled: who among them can declare this, and shew us former things? let them bring forth their witnesses, that they may be justified: or let them hear, and say, *It is* truth.   Is. 41:1

10 Ye *are* my witnesses, saith the LORD, and my servant whom I have chosen: that ye may know and believe me, and understand that I *am* he: before me there was no God formed, neither shall there be after me.   Is. 41:4

11 I, *even* I, *am* the LORD; and beside me *there is* no saviour.   Deut. 6:4; Is. 12:2; Hos. 13:4

12 I have declared, and have saved, and I have shewed, when *there was* no strange *god* among you: therefore ye *are* my witnesses, saith the LORD, that I *am* God.   Deut. 32:12

43:12 Power of Our Testimony

Our confession of His faithfulness is Heaven's chosen agency for revealing Christ to the world. We are to acknowledge His grace as made known through the holy men of old; but that which will be most effectual is the testimony of our own experience. We are witnesses for God as we reveal in ourselves the working of a power that is divine. *MH 100*

---

13 Yea, before the day *was* I *am* he; and *there is* none that can deliver out of my hand: I will work, and who shall let it?   Job 9:12; Ps. 90:2

The Destruction of Babylon

14 Thus saith the LORD, your redeemer, the Holy One of Israel; For your sake I have sent to Babylon, and have brought down all their nobles, and the Chaldeans, whose cry *is* in the ships.   Is. 23:13

15 I *am* the LORD, your Holy One, the creator of Israel, your King.   Is. 43:1

16 Thus saith the LORD, which maketh a way in the sea, and a path in the mighty waters;   Ps. 77:19; Is. 51:10

17 Which bringeth forth the chariot and horse, the army and the power; they shall lie down together, they shall not rise: they are extinct, they are quenched as tow.   Ex. 14:4-9; Ps. 76:5-6

The Lord Will Forgive

18 Remember ye not the former things, neither consider the things of old.   Is. 65:17

19 Behold, I will do a new thing; now it shall spring forth; shall ye not know it? I will even make a way in the wilderness, *and* rivers in the desert.   Ex. 17:6

20 The beast of the field shall honour me, the dragons and the owls: because I give waters in the wilderness, *and* rivers in the desert, to give drink to my people, my chosen.   Is. 48:21

21 This people have I formed for myself; they shall shew forth my praise.   Ps. 102:18; 1 Pet. 2:9

The Lord Reproves the People

22 But thou hast not called upon me, O Jacob; but thou hast been weary of me, O Israel.   Mic. 6:3

23 Thou hast not brought me the small cattle of thy burnt offerings; neither hast thou honoured me with thy sacrifices. I have not caused thee to serve with an offering, nor wearied thee with incense.   Amos 5:25; Zech. 7:5-6

24 Thou hast bought me no sweet cane with money, neither hast thou filled me with the fat of thy sacrifices: but thou hast made me to serve with thy sins, thou hast wearied me with thine iniquities.   Is. 1:14

25 I, *even* I, *am* he that blotteth out thy ᵀtransgressions for mine own sake, and will not remember thy sins.   Is. 37:35 ◆ *violations of a law*

43:25 Sins Blotted Out

All who have truly repented of sin, and by faith claimed the blood of Christ as their atoning sacrifice, have had pardon entered against their names in the books of heaven; as they have become partakers of the righteousness of Christ, and their characters are found to be in harmony with the law of God, their sins will be blotted out, and they themselves will be accounted worthy of eternal life. *GC 483*

---

26 Put me in remembrance: let us plead together: declare thou, that thou mayest be justified.   Is. 1:18; 43:9

27 Thy first father hath sinned, and thy teachers have transgressed against me.   Is. 28:7

28 Therefore I have profaned the princes of the sanctuary, and have given Jacob to the curse, and Israel to reproaches.   Ps. 79:4; Jer. 24:9

The Lord Will Help His People

44 Yet now hear, O Jacob my servant; and Israel, whom I have chosen: Is. 41:8

2 Thus saith the LORD that made thee, and formed thee from the womb, *which* will help thee; Fear not, O Jacob, my servant; and thou, Jesurun, whom I have chosen.   Is. 41:10; 43:1

3 For I will pour water upon him that is thirsty, and floods upon the dry ground: I will pour my spirit upon thy seed, and my blessing upon thine offspring: Is. 59:21; Joel 2:28; 3:18

4 And they shall spring up *as* among the grass, as willows by the water courses.   Ps. 1:3

5 One shall say, I *am* the LORD's; and another shall call *himself* by the name of Jacob;

and another shall subscribe *with* his hand unto the LORD, and surname *himself* by the name of Israel.

44:3 We Must Feel Our Need

There are certain conditions upon which we may expect that God will hear and answer our prayers. One of the first of these is that we feel our need of help from Him. He has promised, "I will pour water upon him that is thirsty, and floods upon the dry ground" (Isaiah 44:3). Those who hunger and thirst after righteousness, who long after God, may be sure that they will be filled. *SC 95*

6 Thus saith the LORD the King of Israel, and his redeemer the LORD of hosts; I *am* the first, and I *am* the last; and beside me *there is* no God.   Is. 41:4; 43:1; Rev. 1:8
7 And who, as I, shall call, and shall declare it, and set it in order for me, since I appointed the ancient people? and the things that are coming, and shall come, let them shew unto them.   Is. 41:22, 26
8 Fear ye not, neither be afraid: have not I told thee from that time, and have declared *it*? ye *are* even my witnesses. Is there a God beside me? yea, *there is* no God; I know not *any*.   Deut. 4:35; 1 Sam. 2:2; Is. 43:10
9 They that make a ᵀgraven image *are* all of them vanity; and their delectable things shall not profit; and they *are* their own witnesses; they see not, nor know; that they may be ashamed.   Is. 41:24 ◆ *engraved or cut out*
10 Who hath formed a god, or molten a graven image *that* is profitable for nothing?
11 Behold, all his fellows shall be ashamed: and the workmen, they *are* of men: let them all be gathered together, let them stand up; *yet* they shall fear, *and* they shall be ashamed together.   Ps. 97:7; Is. 42:17; 45:16
12 The smith with the tongs both worketh in the coals, and fashioneth it with hammers, and worketh it with the strength of his arms: yea, he is hungry, and his strength faileth: he drinketh no water, and is faint.   Is. 40:19
13 The carpenter stretcheth out *his* rule; he marketh it out with a line; he fitteth it with planes, and he marketh it out with the compass, and maketh it after the figure of a man, according to the beauty of a man; that it may remain in the house.   Judg. 17:4-5
14 He ᵀheweth him down cedars, and taketh the cypress and the oak, which he strengtheneth for himself among the trees of the forest: he planteth an ash, and the rain doth nourish *it*.   Is. 40:20 ◆ *cuts*
15 Then shall it be for a man to burn: for he will take thereof, and warm himself; yea, he kindleth *it*, and baketh bread; yea,

he maketh a god, and worshippeth *it*; he maketh it a graven image, and falleth down thereto.   2 Chr. 25:14
16 He burneth part thereof in the fire; with part thereof he eateth flesh; he roasteth roast, and is satisfied: yea, he warmeth *himself*, and saith, Aha, I am warm, I have seen the fire:
17 And the residue thereof he maketh a god, *even* his graven image: he falleth down unto it, and worshippeth *it*, and prayeth unto it, and saith, Deliver me; for thou *art* my god.   Is. 45:20
18 They have not known nor understood: for he hath shut their eyes, that they cannot see; *and* their hearts, that they cannot understand.   Ps. 81:12
19 And none considereth in his heart, neither *is there* knowledge nor understanding to say, I have burned part of it in the fire; yea, also I have baked bread upon the coals thereof; I have roasted flesh, and eaten *it*: and shall I make the residue thereof an abomination? shall I fall down to the stock of a tree?   Deut. 27:15; 1 Kin. 11:5, 7
20 He feedeth on ashes: a deceived heart hath turned him aside, that he cannot deliver his soul, nor say, *Is there* not a lie in my right hand?   Job 15:31

A Prophecy about Cyrus

21 Remember these, O Jacob and Israel; for thou *art* my servant: I have formed thee; thou *art* my servant: O Israel, thou shalt not be forgotten of me.   Is. 44:1-2
22 I have blotted out, as a thick cloud, thy transgressions, and, as a cloud, thy sins: return unto me; for I have redeemed thee.

44:22 New White Robes

None are so sinful that they cannot find strength, purity, and righteousness in Jesus, who died for them. He is waiting to strip them of their garments stained and polluted with sin, and to put upon them the white robes of righteousness; He bids them live and not die. *SC 53*

23 Sing, O ye heavens; for the LORD hath done *it*: shout, ye lower parts of the earth: break forth into singing, ye mountains, O forest, and every tree therein: for the LORD hath redeemed Jacob, and glorified himself in Israel.   Ps. 69:34
24 Thus saith the LORD, thy redeemer, and he that formed thee from the womb, I *am* the LORD that maketh all *things*; that stretcheth forth the heavens alone; that spreadeth abroad the earth by myself;   Is. 42:5; 43:14; 44:2
25 That frustrateth the tokens of the liars, and maketh ᵀdiviners mad; that turneth wise

men backward, and maketh their knowledge foolish;   2 Sam. 15:31 ◆ *false prophets or magicians*

26 That confirmeth the word of his servant, and performeth the counsel of his messengers; that saith to Jerusalem, Thou shalt be inhabited; and to the cities of Judah, Ye shall be built, and I will raise up the decayed places thereof: Zech. 1:6

27 That saith to the deep, Be dry, and I will dry up thy rivers: Is. 42:15

28 That saith of Cyrus, *He is* my shepherd, and shall perform all my pleasure: even saying to Jerusalem, Thou shalt be built; and to the temple, Thy foundation shall be laid.   2 Chr. 36:22–Ezra 1:3

God Calls Cyrus

45 Thus saith the LORD to his anointed, to Cyrus, whose right hand I have ^Tholden, to subdue nations before him; and I will loose the ^Tloins of kings, to open before him the two leaved gates; and the gates shall not be shut;   Ps. 73:23; Is. 41:13; 42:6 ◆ *held* ◆ *waist*

2 I will go before thee, and make the crooked places straight: I will break in pieces the gates of brass, and cut in sunder the bars of iron: Ps. 107:16; Is. 40:4

3 And I will give thee the treasures of darkness, and hidden riches of secret places, that thou mayest know that I, the LORD, which call *thee* by thy name, *am* the God of Israel.   Ex. 33:12; Is. 43:1; Jer. 50:37

4 For Jacob my servant's sake, and Israel mine elect, I have even called thee by thy name: I have surnamed thee, though thou hast not known me.   Is. 41:8-9

The Lord Alone Is God

5 I *am* the LORD, and *there is* none else, *there is* no God beside me: I girded thee, though thou hast not known me: Job 12:21; Ps. 18:39; Is. 44:8

6 That they may know from the rising of the sun, and from the west, that *there is* none beside me. I *am* the LORD, and *there is* none else.   Is. 37:20; Mal. 1:11

45:1–6 The Destiny of Cyrus

The deliverance of Daniel from the den of lions had been used of God to create a favorable impression upon the mind of Cyrus the Great. . . .

As the king saw the words foretelling, more than a hundred years before his birth, the manner in which Babylon should be taken; as he read the message addressed to him by the Ruler of the universe . . . his heart was profoundly moved, and he determined to fulfill his divinely appointed mission. *PK 557*

---

7 I form the light, and create darkness: I make peace, and create evil: I the LORD do all these *things.*   Amos 3:6

8 Drop down, ye heavens, from above, and let the skies pour down righteousness: let the earth open, and let them bring forth salvation, and let righteousness spring up together; I the LORD have created it.   Ps. 72:6; Is. 61:11; Hos. 10:12

9 Woe unto him that striveth with his Maker! Let the ^Tpotsherd *strive* with the potsherds of the earth. Shall the clay say to him that fashioneth it, What makest thou? or thy work, He hath no hands?   Is. 29:16 ◆ *broken piece of pottery*

10 Woe unto him that saith unto *his* father, What ^Tbegettest thou? or to the woman, What hast thou brought forth?   *bring forth*

11 Thus saith the LORD, the Holy One of Israel, and his Maker, Ask me of things to come concerning my sons, and concerning the work of my hands command ye me.   Is. 29:23

12 I have made the earth, and created man upon it: I, *even* my hands, have stretched out the heavens, and all their host have I commanded.   Gen. 2:1; Neh. 9:6; Is. 42:5

13 I have raised him up in righteousness, and I will direct all his ways: he shall build my city, and he shall let go my captives, not for price nor reward, saith the LORD of hosts.   2 Chr. 36:22-23; Is. 41:2; 49:25

14 Thus saith the LORD, The labour of Egypt, and merchandise of Ethiopia and of the Sabeans, men of stature, shall come over unto thee, and they shall be thine: they shall come after thee; in chains they shall come over, and they shall fall down unto thee, they shall make supplication unto thee, *saying,* Surely God *is* in thee; and *there is* none else, *there is* no God.   Is. 49:23; Jer. 16:19; Zech. 8:20-23

15 Verily thou *art* a God that hidest thyself, O God of Israel, the Saviour.   Ps. 44:24

16 They shall be ashamed, and also confounded, all of them: they shall go to confusion together *that are* makers of idols.   Is. 42:17

17 *But* Israel shall be saved in the LORD with an everlasting salvation: ye shall not be ashamed nor confounded world without end.   Is. 26:4

45:17 Soon the Victory

He who died for the sins of the world is opening wide the gates of Paradise to all who believe on Him. Soon the battle will have been fought, the victory won. Soon we shall see Him in whom our hopes of eternal life are centered. And in His presence the trials and sufferings of this life will seem as nothingness. *PK 731, 732*

---

18 For thus saith the LORD that created the heavens; God himself that formed the earth and made it; he hath established it, he created it not in vain, he formed it to be inhabited: I *am* the LORD; and *there is* none else.   Gen. 1:2; Ps. 115:16; Is. 42:5

19 I have not spoken in secret, in a dark place of the earth: I said not unto the seed of Jacob, Seek ye me in vain: I the LORD speak righteousness, I declare things that are right.   2 Chr. 15:2; Is. 48:16; 63:1

God Shows the Worthlessness of Idols

20 Assemble yourselves and come; draw near together, ye *that are* escaped of the nations: they have no knowledge that set up the wood of their ᵀgraven image, and pray unto a god *that* cannot save.   Is. 43:9 ◆ *engraved or cut out*
21 Tell ye, and bring *them* near; yea, let them take counsel together: who hath declared this from ancient time? *who* hath told it from that time? *have* not I the LORD? and *there is* no God else beside me; a just God and a Saviour; *there is* none beside me.   Is. 43:9
22 Look unto me, and be ye saved, all the ends of the earth: for I *am* God, and *there is* none else.   Num. 21:8-9
23 I have sworn by myself, the word is gone out of my mouth *in* righteousness, and shall not return, That unto me every knee shall bow, every tongue shall swear.   Ps. 63:11; Is. 55:11
24 Surely, shall *one* say, in the LORD have I righteousness and strength: *even* to him shall *men* come; and all that are incensed against him shall be ashamed.   Is. 41:11
25 In the LORD shall all the seed of Israel be justified, and shall glory.   Is. 41:16

Babylon's Idols Cannot Save Themselves

46 Bel boweth down, Nebo stoopeth, their idols were upon the beasts, and upon the cattle: your carriages *were* heavy loaden; *they are* a burden to the weary *beast*.   Is. 21:9; Jer. 50:2; 51:44
2 They stoop, they bow down together; they could not deliver the burden, but themselves are gone into captivity.   Judg. 18:17-18
3 Hearken unto me, O house of Jacob, and all the remnant of the house of Israel, which are borne *by me* from the belly, which are carried from the womb: Deut. 1:31
4 And *even* to *your* old age I *am* he; and *even* to hoar hairs will I carry *you*: I have made, and I will bear; even I will carry, and will deliver *you*.   Ps. 71:18; Is. 41:4; 43:13

Idols Are Powerless

5 To whom will ye liken me, and make *me* equal, and compare me, that we may be like?   Is. 40:18, 25
6 They lavish gold out of the bag, and weigh silver in the balance, *and* hire a goldsmith; and he maketh it a god: they fall down, yea, they worship.
7 They bear him upon the shoulder, they carry him, and set him in his place, and he

standeth; from his place shall he not remove: yea, *one* shall cry unto him, yet can he not answer, nor save him out of his trouble.   Is. 45:20; Jer. 10:5
8 Remember this, and shew yourselves men: bring *it* again to mind, O ye ᵀtransgressors.   *those who violate the law*
9 Remember the former things of old: for I *am* God, and *there is* none else; *I am* God, and *there is* none like me,   Deut. 32:7
10 Declaring the end from the beginning, and from ancient times *the things* that are not *yet* done, saying, My counsel shall stand, and I will do all my pleasure: Ps. 33:11; Prov. 19:21

> **46:9, 10 Unfolding Revelations**
>
> Even the prophets who were favored with the special illumination of the Spirit did not fully comprehend the import of the revelations committed to them. The meaning was to be unfolded from age to age, as the people of God should need the instruction therein contained. *GC 344*

11 Calling a ravenous bird from the east, the man that executeth my counsel from a far country: yea, I have spoken *it*, I will also bring it to pass; I have purposed *it*, I will also do it.   Num. 23:19
12 Hearken unto me, ye ᵀstouthearted, that *are* far from righteousness: Ps. 119:150 ◆ *courageous*
13 I bring near my righteousness; it shall not be far off, and my salvation shall not tarry: and I will place salvation in Zion for Israel my glory.   Is. 44:23; 51:5; 61:3

God's Judgment upon Babylon

47 Come down, and sit in the dust, O virgin daughter of Babylon, sit on the ground: *there is* no throne, O daughter of the Chaldeans: for thou shalt no more be called tender and delicate.   Ps. 137:8; Is. 3:26; Jer. 50:42
2 Take the millstones, and grind meal: uncover thy locks, make bare the leg, uncover the thigh, pass over the rivers.   Ex. 11:5
3 Thy nakedness shall be uncovered, yea, thy shame shall be seen: I will take vengeance, and I will not meet *thee as* a man.   Nah. 3:5
4 *As for* our redeemer, the LORD of hosts *is* his name, the Holy One of Israel.   Is. 41:14
5 Sit thou silent, and get thee into darkness, O daughter of the Chaldeans: for thou shalt no more be called, The lady of kingdoms.   Is. 47:7
6 I was ᵀwroth with my people, I have polluted mine inheritance, and given them into thine hand: thou didst shew them no mercy; upon the ancient hast thou very heavily laid thy yoke.   Deut. 28:50 ◆ *angered*
7 And thou saidst, I shall be a lady for ever: *so* that thou didst not lay these *things* to thy

heart, neither didst remember the latter end of it.   Deut. 32:29

8 Therefore hear now this, *thou that art* given to pleasures, that dwellest carelessly, that sayest in thine heart, I *am*, and none else beside me; I shall not sit *as* a widow, neither shall I know the loss of children: Is. 32:9; 45:6; Zeph. 2:15

9 But these two *things* shall come to thee in a moment in one day, the loss of children, and widowhood: they shall come upon thee in their perfection for the multitude of thy sorceries, *and* for the great abundance of thine enchantments.   Ps. 73:19; Nah. 3:4; 1 Thess. 5:3

10 For thou hast trusted in thy wickedness: thou hast said, None seeth me. Thy wisdom and thy knowledge, it hath perverted thee; and thou hast said in thine heart, I *am*, and none else beside me.   Ps. 52:7

11 Therefore shall evil come upon thee; thou shalt not know from whence it riseth: and mischief shall fall upon thee; thou shalt not be able to put it off: and desolation shall come upon thee suddenly, *which* thou shalt not know.   1 Thess. 5:3

12 Stand now with thine ᵀenchantments, and with the multitude of thy sorceries, wherein thou hast laboured from thy youth; if so be thou shalt be able to profit, if so be thou mayest prevail.   *secret arts*

13 Thou art wearied in the multitude of thy counsels. Let now the astrologers, the stargazers, the monthly prognosticators, stand up, and save thee from *these things* that shall come upon thee.   Is. 44:25; 57:10

14 Behold, they shall be as stubble; the fire shall burn them; they shall not deliver themselves from the power of the flame: *there shall* not *be* a coal to warm at, *nor* fire to sit before it.   Is. 10:17; Nah. 1:10; Mal. 4:1

15 Thus shall they be unto thee with whom thou hast laboured, *even* thy merchants, from thy youth: they shall wander every one to his quarter; none shall save thee.

The Lord Will Refine and Rescue

48 Hear ye this, O house of Jacob, which are called by the name of Israel, and are come forth out of the waters of Judah, which swear by the name of the LORD, and make mention of the God of Israel, *but* not in truth, nor in righteousness.   Ps. 68:26

2 For they call themselves of the holy city, and stay themselves upon the God of Israel; The LORD of hosts *is* his name.   Is. 10:20; 52:1

3 I have declared the former things from the beginning; and they went forth out of my mouth, and I shewed them; I did *them* suddenly, and they came to pass.   Is. 41:22

4 Because I knew that thou *art* obstinate, and thy neck *is* an iron sinew, and thy brow brass;   Ex. 32:9; Deut. 31:27; Acts 7:51

5 I have even from the beginning declared *it* to thee; before it came to pass I shewed *it* thee: lest thou shouldest say, Mine idol hath done them, and my graven image, and my molten image, hath commanded them. Is. 48:3

6 Thou hast heard, see all this; and will not ye declare *it*? I have shewed thee new things from this time, even hidden things, and thou didst not know them.   Is. 42:9

7 They are created now, and not from the beginning; even before the day when thou heardest them not; lest thou shouldest say, Behold, I knew them.

8 Yea, thou heardest not; yea, thou knewest not; yea, from that time *that* thine ear was not opened: for I knew that thou wouldest deal very treacherously, and wast called a transgressor from the womb.   Ps. 58:3

God Will Save His People for His Name's Sake

9 For my name's sake will I ᵀdefer mine anger, and for my praise will I refrain for thee, that I cut thee not off. Ps. 78:38 ◆ *postpone*

10 Behold, I have refined thee, but not with silver; I have chosen thee in the furnace of affliction.   Deut. 4:20

48:10 Embracing the Cross

The fact that we are called upon to endure trial shows that the Lord Jesus sees in us something precious which He desires to develop. *MH 471*

11 For mine own sake, *even* for mine own sake, will I do *it*: for how should *my name* be polluted? and I will not give my glory unto another.   Deut. 32:26-27; Is. 42:8; Ezek. 20:9

12 Hearken unto me, O Jacob and Israel, my called; I *am* he; I *am* the first, I also *am* the last.   Is. 41:4; 44:6; Rev. 22:13

13 Mine hand also hath laid the foundation of the earth, and my right hand hath spanned the heavens: *when* I call unto them, they stand up together.   Ex. 20:11; Ps. 102:25; Is. 40:26

14 All ye, assemble yourselves, and hear; which among them hath declared these *things*? The Lord hath loved him: he will do his pleasure on Babylon, and his arm *shall be* on the Chaldeans.   Is. 43:9

15 I, *even* I, have spoken; yea, I have called him: I have brought him, and he shall make his way prosperous.

God Calls His People to Listen

16 Come ye near unto me, hear ye this; I have not spoken in secret from the beginning; from the time that it was, there *am* I: and now the Lord God, and his Spirit, hath sent me.   Is. 45:19

17 Thus saith the Lord, thy Redeemer, the Holy One of Israel; I *am* the Lord thy God which teacheth thee to profit, which leadeth thee by the way *that* thou shouldest go. Ps. 32:8

18 O that thou hadst hearkened to my commandments! then had thy peace been as a river, and thy righteousness as the waves of the sea: Deut. 32:29; Ps. 119:165; Is. 66:12

19 Thy seed also had been as the sand, and the offspring of thy bowels like the gravel thereof; his name should not have been cut off nor destroyed from before me.   Gen. 22:17

20 Go ye forth of Babylon, flee ye from the Chaldeans, with a voice of singing declare ye, tell this, utter it *even* to the end of the earth; say ye, The Lord hath redeemed his servant Jacob.   Is. 52:9; Jer. 50:8; 51:6

21 And they thirsted not *when* he led them through the deserts: he caused the waters to flow out of the rock for them: he clave the rock also, and the waters gushed out. Ex. 17:6

22 *There is* no peace, saith the Lord, unto the wicked.   Is. 57:21

48:22 Benefits of Obedience

Atheists, infidels, and apostates oppose and denounce God's law; but the results of their influence prove that the well-being of man is bound up with his obedience of the divine statutes. Those who will not read the lesson from the book of God are bidden to read it in the history of nations. *GC 285*

The Lord's Servant Will Bring Salvation

49 Listen, O isles, unto me; and hearken, ye people, from far; The Lord hath called me from the womb; from the bowels of my mother hath he made mention of my name.   Jer. 1:5

2 And he hath made my mouth like a sharp sword; in the shadow of his hand hath he hid me, and made me a polished shaft; in his quiver hath he hid me;   Is. 11:4; 51:16; Rev. 1:16

3 And said unto me, Thou *art* my servant, O Israel, in whom I will be glorified.   Is. 42:1

4 Then I said, I have laboured in vain, I have spent my strength for ᵀnought, and in vain: *yet* surely my judgment *is* with the Lord, and my work with my God. Is. 53:10-12 ◆ *nothing*

5 And now, saith the Lord that formed me from the womb *to be* his servant, to bring Jacob again to him, Though Israel be not gathered, yet shall I be glorious in the eyes of the Lord, and my God shall be my strength.   Matt. 17:5

6 And he said, It is a light thing that thou shouldest be my servant to raise up the tribes of Jacob, and to restore the preserved of Israel: I will also give thee for a light to the Gentiles, that thou mayest be my salvation unto the end of the earth.   Is. 42:6; Luke 2:32; Acts 13:47

7 Thus saith the Lord, the Redeemer of Israel, *and* his Holy One, to him whom man despiseth, to him whom the nation ᵀabhorreth, to a servant of rulers, Kings shall see and arise, princes also shall worship, because of the Lord that is faithful, *and* the Holy One of Israel, and he shall choose thee.   Ps. 22:6-8; Is. 52:15; 53:3 ◆ *despises*

8 Thus saith the Lord, In an acceptable time

have I heard thee, and in a day of salvation have I helped thee: and I will preserve thee, and give thee for a covenant of the people, to establish the earth, to cause to inherit the desolate heritages;   Ps. 69:13; Is. 42:6; 2 Cor. 6:2

9 That thou mayest say to the prisoners, Go forth; to them that *are* in darkness, Shew yourselves. They shall feed in the ways, and their pastures *shall be* in all high places. Is. 41:18; 42:7

10 They shall not hunger nor thirst; neither shall the heat nor sun [T]smite them: for he that hath mercy on them shall lead them, even by the springs of water shall he guide them.   Rev. 7:16-17 ◆ *strike*

11 And I will make all my mountains a way, and my highways shall be exalted.   Is. 11:16

12 Behold, these shall come from far: and, lo, these from the north and from the west; and these from the land of Sinim.   Is. 43:5-6

The Lord Has Not Forgotten His People

13 Sing, O heavens; and be joyful, O earth; and break forth into singing, O mountains: for the Lord hath comforted his people, and will have mercy upon his afflicted. Is. 44:23; 51:3

14 But Zion said, The Lord hath forsaken me, and my Lord hath forgotten me. Is. 40:27

15 Can a woman forget her sucking child, that she should not have compassion on the son of her womb? yea, they may forget, yet will I not forget thee.   Is. 44:21

16 Behold, I have [T]graven thee upon the palms of *my* hands; thy walls *are* continually before me.   Song 8:6; Hag. 2:23 ◆ *engraved or cut out*

49:15, 16 Christ's Great Love

Circumstances may separate friends; the restless waters of the wide sea may roll between us and them. But no circumstances, no distance, can separate us from the Saviour. Wherever we may be, He is at our right hand, to support, maintain, uphold, and cheer. Greater than the love of a mother for her child is Christ's love for His redeemed. It is our privilege to rest in His love, to say, "I will trust Him; for He gave His life for me." *MH 72*

---

17 Thy children shall make haste; thy destroyers and they that made thee waste shall go forth of thee.

The Restoration of the Church

18 Lift up thine eyes round about, and behold: all these gather themselves together, *and* come to thee. *As* I live, saith the Lord, thou shalt surely clothe thee with them all, as with an ornament, and bind them *on thee*, as a bride *doeth*.   Is. 49:12

19 For thy waste and thy desolate places, and the land of thy destruction, shall even now be too narrow by reason of the inhabitants,

and they that swallowed thee up shall be far away.   Ps. 56:1-2; Is. 51:3; Zech. 10:10

20 The children which thou shalt have, after thou hast lost the other, shall say again in thine ears, The place *is* too [T]strait for me: give place to me that I may dwell.   *narrow*

21 Then shalt thou say in thine heart, Who hath [T]begotten me these, seeing I have lost my children, and am desolate, a captive, and removing to and fro? and who hath brought up these? Behold, I was left alone; these, where *had* they *been*?   *brought forth*

22 Thus saith the Lord God, Behold, I will lift up mine hand to the Gentiles, and set up my [T]standard to the people: and they shall bring thy sons in *their* arms, and thy daughters shall be carried upon *their* shoulders.   *flag*

23 And kings shall be thy nursing fathers, and their queens thy nursing mothers: they shall bow down to thee with *their* face toward the earth, and lick up the dust of thy feet; and thou shalt know that I *am* the Lord: for they shall not be ashamed that wait for me.   Is. 60:3, 16; Mic. 7:17

24 Shall the prey be taken from the mighty, or the lawful captive delivered?   Matt. 12:29

25 But thus saith the Lord, Even the captives of the mighty shall be taken away, and the prey of the terrible shall be delivered: for I will contend with him that contendeth with thee, and I will save thy children.   Jer. 50:33-34

49:24, 25 A Golden Chain of Mercy

The Lord God through Jesus Christ holds out His hand all the day long in invitation to the sinful and fallen. He will receive all. He welcomes all. It is His glory to pardon the chief of sinners. He will take the prey from the mighty, He will deliver the captive, He will pluck the brand from the burning. He will lower the golden chain of His mercy to the lowest depths of human wretchedness. *MH 161*

---

26 And I will feed them that oppress thee with their own flesh; and they shall be drunken with their own blood, as with sweet wine: and all flesh shall know that I the Lord *am* thy Saviour and thy Redeemer, the mighty One of Jacob.   Is. 9:20; Ezek. 39:7; Rev. 16:6

Punishment because of Sin

50 Thus saith the Lord, Where *is* the bill of your mother's divorcement, whom I have put away? or which of my creditors *is it* to whom I have sold you? Behold, for your iniquities have ye sold yourselves, and for your [T]transgressions is your mother put away.   Deut. 32:30; 2 Kin. 4:1; Jer. 3:8 ◆ *violations of a law*

2 Wherefore, when I came, *was there* no man? when I called, *was there* none to an-

swer? Is my hand shortened at all, that it cannot redeem? or have I no power to deliver? behold, at my rebuke I dry up the sea, I make the rivers a wilderness: their fish stinketh, because *there is* no water, and dieth for thirst.   Num. 11:23; Josh. 3:16; Is. 59:1

3 I clothe the heavens with blackness, and I make sackcloth their covering.   Rev. 6:12

The Lord's Servant Trust in the Lord's Help

4 The Lord God hath given me the tongue of the learned, that I should know how to speak a word in season to *him that is* weary: he wakeneth morning by morning, he wakeneth mine ear to hear as the learned.   Ex. 4:11-12

50:4 Kind Words

We should accustom ourselves to speak in pleasant tones, to use pure and correct language, and words that are kind and courteous. Sweet, kind words are as dew and gentle showers to the soul. The Scripture says of Christ that grace was poured into His lips that He might "know how to speak a word in season to him that is weary" (Psalm 45:2; Isaiah 50:4). *COL 336*

5 The Lord God hath opened mine ear, and I was not rebellious, neither turned away back.   Matt. 26:39; John 14:31; Heb. 5:8

6 I gave my back to the smiters, and my cheeks to them that plucked off the hair: I hid not my face from shame and spitting.

50:6 Jesus and His Enemies

It was to bring the bread of life to His enemies that our Saviour left His home in heaven. Though calumny and persecution were heaped upon Him from the cradle to the grave, they called forth from Him only the expression of forgiving love. *MB 71*

7 For the Lord God will help me; therefore shall I not be confounded: therefore have I set my face like a flint, and I know that I shall not be ashamed.   Is. 42:1; 49:8; Ezek. 3:8-9

8 *He is* near that justifieth me; who will contend with me? let us stand together: who *is* mine adversary? let him come near to me.

9 Behold, the Lord God will help me; who *is* he *that* shall condemn me? lo, they all shall ᵀwax old as a garment; the moth shall eat them up.   Job 13:28 ◆ *become*

10 Who *is* among you that feareth the Lord, that obeyeth the voice of his servant, that walketh *in* darkness, and hath no light? let him trust in the name of the Lord, and stay upon his God.   Is. 9:2

11 Behold, all ye that kindle a fire, that ᵀcompass *yourselves* about with sparks: walk in the light of your fire, and in the sparks *that* ye

have kindled. This shall ye have of mine hand; ye shall lie down in sorrow.   Is. 8:22 ◆ *surround*

The Lord Will Save His People

51 Hearken to me, ye that follow after righteousness, ye that seek the Lord: look unto the rock *whence* ye are ᵀhewn, and to the hole of the pit *whence* ye are digged.   Gen. 17:15-17; Ps. 94:15; Is. 51:7 ◆ *cut*

2 Look unto Abraham your father, and unto Sarah *that* bare you: for I called him alone, and blessed him, and increased him.   Ezek. 33:24

3 For the Lord shall comfort Zion: he will comfort all her waste places; and he will make her wilderness like Eden, and her desert like the garden of the Lord; joy and gladness shall be found therein, thanksgiving, and the voice of melody.   Gen. 13:10; Is. 52:9; Joel 2:3

Listen to the Word of the Lord

4 Hearken unto me, my people; and give ear unto me, O my nation: for a law shall proceed from me, and I will make my judgment to rest for a light of the people.   Is. 2:3

5 My righteousness *is* near; my salvation is gone forth, and mine arms shall judge the people; the isles shall wait upon me, and on mine arm shall they trust.   Is. 42:4; 46:13; 60:9

6 Lift up your eyes to the heavens, and look upon the earth beneath: for the heavens shall vanish away like smoke, and the earth shall wax old like a garment, and they that dwell therein shall die in like manner: but my salvation shall be for ever, and my righteousness shall not be abolished.   Is. 34:4; 40:26

7 Hearken unto me, ye that know righteousness, the people in whose heart *is* my law; fear ye not the reproach of men, neither be ye afraid of their revilings.   Ps. 37:31; Matt. 5:11

8 For the moth shall eat them up like a garment, and the worm shall eat them like wool: but my righteousness shall be for ever, and my salvation from generation to generation.   Is. 50:9; 51:6; 66:24

9 Awake, awake, put on strength, O arm of the Lord; awake, as in the ancient days, in the generations of old. *Art* thou not it that hath cut Rahab, *and* wounded the dragon?

10 *Art* thou not it which hath dried the sea, the waters of the great deep; that hath made the depths of the sea a way for the ransomed to pass over?   Ex. 14:21-22

51:11 Conflicts, Then Peace

The precious Saviour will send help just when we need it. The way to heaven is consecrated by His footprints. Every thorn that wounds our feet has wounded His. Every cross that we are called to bear He has borne before us. The Lord permits conflicts, to prepare the soul for peace. *GC 633*

11 Therefore the redeemed of the LORD shall return, and come with singing unto Zion; and everlasting joy *shall be* upon their head: they shall obtain gladness and joy; *and* sorrow and mourning shall flee away.   Is. 35:10

12 I, *even* I, *am* he that comforteth you: who *art* thou, that thou shouldest be afraid of a man *that* shall die, and of the son of man *which* shall be made *as* grass;   Ps. 118:6; Is. 2:22

13 And forgettest the LORD thy maker, that hath stretched forth the heavens, and laid the foundations of the earth; and hast feared continually every day because of the fury of the oppressor, as if he were ready to destroy? and where *is* the fury of the oppressor?   Ps. 104:2

14 The captive exile hasteneth that he may be loosed, and that he should not die in the pit, nor that his bread should fail.   Is. 48:20

15 But I *am* the LORD thy God, that divided the sea, whose waves roared: The LORD of hosts *is* his name.   Jer. 31:35

16 And I have put my words in thy mouth, and I have covered thee in the shadow of mine hand, that I may plant the heavens, and lay the foundations of the earth, and say unto Zion, Thou *art* my people.   Deut. 18:18; Is. 49:2

Awake, Jerusalem!

17 Awake, awake, stand up, O Jerusalem, which hast drunk at the hand of the LORD the cup of his fury; thou hast drunken the dregs of the cup of trembling, *and* wrung them out.   Job 21:20; Ps. 60:3; Is. 52:1

18 *There is* none to guide her among all the sons *whom* she hath brought forth; neither *is there any* that taketh her by the hand of all the sons *that* she hath brought up.   Ps. 88:18

19 These two *things* are come unto thee; who shall be sorry for thee? desolation, and destruction, and the famine, and the sword: by whom shall I comfort thee?   Is. 47:9

20 Thy sons have fainted, they lie at the head of all the streets, as a wild bull in a net: they are full of the fury of the LORD, the rebuke of thy God.   Lam. 2:11-12

21 Therefore hear now this, thou afflicted, and drunken, but not with wine:

22 Thus saith thy Lord the LORD, and thy God *that* pleadeth the cause of his people, Behold, I have taken out of thine hand the cup of trembling, *even* the ᵀdregs of the cup of my fury; thou shalt no more drink it again: Is. 49:25; 51:17; Jer. 50:34 ◆ *sediment at the bottom*

23 But I will put it into the hand of them that afflict thee; which have said to thy soul, Bow down, that we may go over: and thou hast laid thy body as the ground, and as the street, to them that went over.   Josh. 10:24

The Lord Will Comfort His People

52 Awake, awake; put on thy strength, O Zion; put on thy beautiful garments, O Jerusalem, the holy city: for henceforth there shall no more come into thee the uncircumcised and the unclean.   Neh. 11:1; Is. 51:17; Rev. 21:27

2 Shake thyself from the dust; arise, *and* sit down, O Jerusalem: loose thyself from the bands of thy neck, O captive daughter of Zion.   Is. 51:14

3 For thus saith the LORD, Ye have sold yourselves for nought; and ye shall be redeemed without money.   Ps. 44:12; Is. 45:13; 50:1

4 For thus saith the Lord GOD, My people went down ᵀaforetime into Egypt to sojourn there; and the Assyrian oppressed them without cause.   Gen. 46:6 ◆ *before*

5 Now therefore, what have I here, saith the LORD, that my people is taken away for ᵀnought? they that rule over them make them to howl, saith the LORD; and my name continually every day *is* blasphemed.   Rom. 2:24 ◆ *nothing*

6 Therefore my people shall know my name: therefore *they shall know* in that day that I *am* he that doth speak: behold, *it is* I.

7 How beautiful upon the mountains are the feet of him that bringeth good tidings, that publisheth peace; that bringeth good tidings of good, that publisheth salvation; that saith unto Zion, Thy God reigneth!   Ps. 93:1; Is. 40:9

8 Thy watchmen shall lift up the voice; with the voice together shall they sing: for they shall see eye to eye, when the LORD shall bring again Zion.   Is. 62:6; 1 Cor. 13:12

9 Break forth into joy, sing together, ye waste places of Jerusalem: for the LORD hath comforted his people, he hath redeemed Jerusalem.   Ps. 98:4; Is. 48:20; 51:3

10 The LORD hath made bare his holy arm in the eyes of all the nations; and all the ends of the earth shall see the salvation of our God.   Is. 51:9

11 Depart ye, depart ye, go ye out from thence, touch no unclean *thing*; go ye out of the midst of her; be ye clean, that bear the vessels of the LORD.   Is. 48:20; Jer. 50:8; 2 Cor. 6:17

12 For ye shall not go out with haste, nor go by flight: for the LORD will go before you; and the God of Israel *will be* your ᵀreward.   Ex. 12:33 ◆ *rear guard*

Christ's Kingdom Shall Be Exalted

13 Behold, my servant shall deal prudently, he shall be exalted and extolled, and be very high.   Is. 9:6-7; 42:1; 53:10-11

14 As many were astonied at thee; his visage was so marred more than any man, and his form more than the sons of men: Ps. 22:15

15 So shall he sprinkle many nations; the kings shall shut their mouths at him: for *that* which had not been told them shall they see;

and *that* which they had not heard shall they consider.   Is. 49:7

The Suffering Servant

53 Who hath believed our report? and to whom is the arm of the LORD revealed?   Is. 51:9; John 1:12; 12:38
2 For he shall grow up before him as a tender plant, and as a root out of a dry ground: he hath no form nor comeliness; and when we shall see him, *there is* no beauty that we should desire him.   Is. 11:1; 52:14; Jer. 23:5
3 He is despised and rejected of men; a man of sorrows, and acquainted with grief: and we hid as it were *our* faces from him; he was despised, and we esteemed him not. Is. 49:7; 53:10

> **53:3 Truly Seeing Jesus**
>
> When we see Jesus, a Man of Sorrows and acquainted with grief, working to save the lost, slighted, scorned, derided, driven from city to city till His mission was accomplished; when we behold Him in Gethsemane, sweating great drops of blood, and on the cross dying in agony—when we see this, self will no longer clamor to be recognized. *DA 439*

Christ's Passion Foretold

4 Surely he hath borne our griefs, and carried our sorrows: yet we did esteem him stricken, smitten of God, and afflicted. Is. 53:5-6; Matt. 8:17
5 But he *was* wounded for our transgressions, *he was* bruised for our iniquities: the chastisement of our peace *was* upon him; and with his stripes we are healed.   Gen. 3:15
6 All we like sheep have gone astray; we have turned every one to his own way; and the LORD hath laid on him the iniquity of us all.   Ps. 69:4
7 He was oppressed, and he was afflicted, yet he opened not his mouth: he is brought as a lamb to the slaughter, and as a sheep before her shearers is ᵀdumb, so he openeth not his mouth.   Matt. 26:63; Mark 14:61; John 19:9 ◆ *mute*
8 He was taken from prison and from judgment: and who shall declare his generation? for he was cut off out of the land of the living: for the ᵀtransgression of my people was he stricken.   Dan. 9:26 ◆ *violation of a law*
9 And he made his grave with the wicked, and with the rich in his death; because he had done no violence, neither *was any* deceit in his mouth.   Is. 42:1-3; Matt. 27:57-60; 1 Pet. 2:22

> *Jesus* See 1 John 3:16.

The Sacrifice of the Righteous Servant

10 Yet it pleased the LORD to bruise him; he hath put *him* to grief: when thou shalt make *his* soul an offering for sin, he shall see *his* seed, he shall prolong *his* days, and the pleasure of the LORD shall prosper in his hand.   Ps. 22:30
11 He shall see of the travail of his soul, *and* shall be satisfied: by his knowledge shall my righteous servant justify many; for he shall bear their iniquities.   Is. 42:1; 45:25; Rom. 5:18-19

> **53:11 Jesus Sustained in Sacrifice**
>
> What sustained the Son of God during His life of toil and sacrifice? He saw the results of the travail of His soul and was satisfied. Looking into eternity, He beheld the happiness of those who through His humiliation had received pardon and everlasting life. His ear caught the shout of the redeemed. He heard the ransomed ones singing the song of Moses and the Lamb. *AA 601*

12 Therefore will I divide him *a portion* with the great, and he shall divide the ᵀspoil with the strong; because he hath poured out his soul unto death: and he was numbered with

---

Love and Sacrifice

Isaiah 53:5

It was to redeem us that Jesus lived and suffered and died. He became "a Man of Sorrows," that we might be made partakers of everlasting joy. God permitted His beloved Son, full of grace and truth, to come from a world of indescribable glory, to a world marred and blighted with sin, darkened with the shadow of death and the curse. He permitted Him to leave the bosom of His love, the adoration of the angels, to suffer shame, insult, humiliation, hatred, and death. "The chastisement of our peace was upon Him; and with His stripes we are healed" (Isaiah 53:5). Behold Him in the wilderness, in Gethsemane, upon the cross! The spotless Son of God took upon Himself the burden of sin. He who had been one with God, felt in His soul the awful separation that sin makes between God and man. This wrung from His lips the anguished cry, "My God, My God, why hast Thou forsaken Me?" (Matthew 27:46). It was the burden of sin, the sense of its terrible enormity, of its separation of the soul from God—it was this that broke the heart of the Son of God.

But this great sacrifice was not made in order to create in the Father's heart a love for man, not to make Him willing to save. No, no! "God so loved the world, that He gave His only-begotten Son" (John 3:16). The Father loves us, not because of the great propitiation, but He provided the propitiation because He loves us. *SC 13*

the ᵀtransgressors; and he bare the sin of many, and made intercession for the transgressors. Mark 15:27 ◆ *plunder* ◆ *those who violate the law*

The Lord's Compassion for the Childless

54 Sing, O barren, thou *that* didst not bear; break forth into singing, and cry aloud, thou *that* didst not travail with child: for more *are* the children of the desolate than the children of the married wife, saith the LORD.   1 Sam. 2:5; Is. 62:4; Gal. 4:27
2 Enlarge the place of thy tent, and let them stretch forth the curtains of thine habitations: spare not, lengthen thy cords, and strengthen thy stakes;   Ex. 35:18; 39:40; Is. 49:19-20
3 For thou shalt break forth on the right hand and on the left; and thy seed shall inherit the Gentiles, and make the desolate cities to be inhabited.   Is. 43:5-6
4 Fear not; for thou shalt not be ashamed: neither be thou confounded; for thou shalt not be put to shame: for thou shalt forget the shame of thy youth, and shalt not remember the reproach of thy widowhood any more.   Jer. 31:19
5 For thy Maker *is* thine husband; the LORD of hosts *is* his name; and thy Redeemer the Holy One of Israel; The God of the whole earth shall he be called.   Jer. 3:14

54:4, 5 Gospel Restores Marriage

Like every other one of God's good gifts entrusted to the keeping of humanity, marriage has been perverted by sin; but it is the purpose of the gospel to restore its purity and beauty. In both the Old and the New Testament the marriage relation is employed to represent the tender and sacred union that exists between Christ and His people, the redeemed ones whom He has purchased at the cost of Calvary. *MB 64*

Certain Deliverance from Affliction

6 For the LORD hath called thee as a woman forsaken and grieved in spirit, and a wife of youth, when thou wast refused, saith thy God.   Is. 62:4
7 For a small moment have I forsaken thee; but with great mercies will I gather thee.
8 In a little wrath I hid my face from thee for a moment; but with everlasting kindness will I have mercy on thee, saith the LORD thy Redeemer.   Is. 54:5
9 For this *is as* the waters of Noah unto me: for *as* I have sworn that the waters of Noah should no more go over the earth; so have I sworn that I would not be ᵀwroth with thee, nor rebuke thee.   Gen. 8:21 ◆ *angered*
10 For the mountains shall depart, and the

hills be removed; but my kindness shall not depart from thee, neither shall the covenant of my peace be removed, saith the LORD that hath mercy on thee.   2 Sam. 23:5

God Will Restore

11 O thou afflicted, tossed with ᵀtempest, *and* not comforted, behold, I will lay thy stones with fair colours, and lay thy foundations with sapphires.   1 Chr. 29:2 ◆ *storm*
12 And I will make thy windows of agates, and thy gates of carbuncles, and all thy borders of pleasant stones.
13 And all thy children *shall be* taught of the LORD; and great *shall be* the peace of thy children.   Ps. 119:165; Is. 48:18; John 6:45
14 In righteousness shalt thou be established: thou shalt be far from oppression; for thou shalt not fear: and from terror; for it shall not come near thee.   Is. 1:26
15 Behold, they shall surely gather together, *but* not by me: whosoever shall gather together against thee shall fall for thy sake.
16 Behold, I have created the smith that bloweth the coals in the fire, and that bringeth forth an instrument for his work; and I have created the waster to destroy.
17 No weapon that is formed against thee shall prosper; and every tongue *that* shall rise against thee in judgment thou shalt condemn. This *is* the heritage of the servants of the LORD, and their righteousness *is* of me, saith the LORD.   Is. 50:8

Come to the Waters and Drink

55 Ho, every one that thirsteth, come ye to the waters, and he that hath no money; come ye, buy, and eat; yea, come, buy wine and milk without money and without price.   Song 5:1

55:1 Righteousness Is Free

Not by painful struggles or wearisome toil, not by gift or sacrifice, is righteousness obtained; but it is freely given to every soul who hungers and thirsts to receive it. *MB 18*

2 Wherefore do ye spend money for *that which is* not bread? and your labour for *that which* satisfieth not? hearken diligently unto me, and eat ye *that which is* good, and let your soul delight itself in fatness.   Ps. 22:26
3 Incline your ear, and come unto me: hear, and your soul shall live; and I will make an everlasting covenant with you, *even* the sure mercies of David.   Is. 54:8; 61:8; Acts 13:34
4 Behold, I have given him *for* a witness to the people, a leader and commander to the people.   Jer. 30:9; Dan. 9:25; Hos. 3:5
5 Behold, thou shalt call a nation *that* thou knowest not, and nations *that* knew not thee

shall run unto thee because of the LORD thy God, and for the Holy One of Israel; for he hath glorified thee.   Is. 60:9

Seek the Lord

6 Seek ye the LORD while he may be found, call ye upon him while he is near: Ps. 32:6
7 Let the wicked forsake his way, and the unrighteous man his thoughts: and let him return unto the LORD, and he will have mercy upon him; and to our God, for he will abundantly pardon.   Prov. 28:13; Is. 43:25; 44:22
8 For my thoughts are not your thoughts, neither are your ways my ways, saith the LORD.
9 For as the heavens are higher than the earth, so are my ways higher than your ways, and my thoughts than your thoughts.
10 For as the rain cometh down, and the snow from heaven, and returneth not thither, but watereth the earth, and maketh it bring forth and bud, that it may give seed to the sower, and bread to the eater: Is. 30:23

55:10 We Do Not Live for Self

The plant does not germinate, grow, or bring forth fruit for itself, but to "give seed to the sower, and bread to the eater" (Isaiah 55:10). So no man is to live unto himself. The Christian is in the world as a representative of Christ, for the salvation of other souls.

There can be no growth or fruitfulness in the life that is centered in self. *COL 67*

---

11 So shall my word be that goeth forth out of my mouth: it shall not return unto me void, but it shall accomplish that which I please, and it shall prosper in the thing whereto I sent it.   Is. 45:23
12 For ye shall go out with joy, and be led forth with peace: the mountains and the hills shall break forth before you into singing, and all the trees of the field shall clap their hands.   Is. 44:23

13 Instead of the thorn shall come up the fir tree, and instead of the brier shall come up the myrtle tree: and it shall be to the LORD for a name, for an everlasting sign that shall not be cut off.   Is. 41:19

Salvation for All People

56 Thus saith the LORD, Keep ye judgment, and do justice: for my salvation is near to come, and my righteousness to be revealed.   Ps. 85:9
2 Blessed is the man that doeth this, and the son of man that layeth hold on it; that keepeth the sabbath from polluting it, and keepeth his hand from doing any evil.   Ex. 31:13-16; Ps. 112:1
3 Neither let the son of the stranger, that hath joined himself to the LORD, speak, saying, The LORD hath utterly separated me from his people: neither let the ᵀeunuch say, Behold, I am a dry tree.   castrated male servant
4 For thus saith the LORD unto the ᵀeunuchs that keep my sabbaths, and choose the things that please me, and take hold of my covenant;   castrated male servants
5 Even unto them will I give in mine house and within my walls a place and a name better than of sons and of daughters: I will give them an everlasting name, that shall not be cut off.   Is. 55:13
6 Also the sons of the stranger, that join themselves to the LORD, to serve him, and to love the name of the LORD, to be his servants, every one that keepeth the sabbath from polluting it, and taketh hold of my covenant;
7 Even them will I bring to my holy mountain, and make them joyful in my house of prayer: their burnt offerings and their sacrifices shall be accepted upon mine altar; for mine house shall be called an house of prayer for all people.   Matt. 21:13; Mark 11:17; Luke 19:46
8 The Lord GOD which gathereth the

Do You Hear the Voice?

Isaiah 55:3

Have you, reader, chosen your own way? Have you wandered far from God? Have you sought to feast upon the fruits of transgression, only to find them turn to ashes upon your lips? And now, your life plans thwarted and your hopes dead, do you sit alone and desolate? That voice which has long been speaking to your heart, but to which you would not listen, comes to you distinct and clear, "Arise ye, and depart; for this is not your rest: because it is polluted, it shall destroy you, even with a sore destruction" (Micah 2:10). Return to your Father's house. He invites you, saying, "Return unto Me; for I have redeemed thee." "Come unto Me: hear, and your soul shall live; and I will make an everlasting covenant with you, even the sure mercies of David" (Isaiah 44:22; 55:3).

Do not listen to the enemy's suggestion to stay away from Christ until you have made yourself better, until you are good enough to come to God. If you wait until then you will never come. When Satan points to your filthy garments, repeat the promise of the Saviour, "Him that cometh to Me I will in no wise cast out" (John 6:37). Tell the enemy that the blood of Jesus Christ cleanses from all sin. Make the prayer of David your own: "Purge me with hyssop, and I shall be clean: wash me, and I shall be whiter than snow" (Psalm 51:7). *PK 319, 320*

outcasts of Israel saith, Yet will I gather *others* to him, beside those that are gathered unto him. Is. 60:3-11; 66:18-21; John 10:16

56:7 Reformation, Then Apostasy

Concerning the temple at Jerusalem, the Lord declared through Isaiah, "Mine house shall be called an house of prayer for all peoples" (Isaiah 56:7, R.V.).

But the Israelites fixed their hopes upon worldly greatness. From the time of their entrance to the land of Canaan, they departed from the commandments of God, and followed the ways of the heathen. . . . Every reformation was followed by deeper apostasy. *DA 27, 28*

God Denounces Blind Watchmen

9 All ye beasts of the field, come to devour, *yea,* all ye beasts in the forest. Jer. 12:9
10 His watchmen *are* blind: they are all ignorant, they *are* all ᵀdumb dogs, they cannot bark; sleeping, lying down, loving to slumber. Is. 29:10 ◆ *mute*
11 Yea, *they are* greedy dogs *which* can never have enough, and they *are* shepherds *that* cannot understand: they all look to their own way, every one for his gain, from his quarter. Ezek. 13:19
12 Come ye, *say they,* I will fetch wine, and we will fill ourselves with strong drink; and to morrow shall be as this day, *and* much more abundant. Ps. 10:6

The Blessed Death of the Righteous

57 The righteous perisheth, and no man layeth *it* to heart: and merciful men *are* taken away, none considering that the righteous is taken away from the evil *to* come. 2 Kin. 22:20
2 He shall enter into peace: they shall rest in their beds, *each one* walking *in* his uprightness. 2 Chr. 16:14

God Reproves the People's Idolatry

3 But draw near ᵀhither, ye sons of the sorceress, the seed of the adulterer and the ᵀwhore. Matt. 16:4 ◆ *here* ◆ *prostitute*
4 Against whom do ye sport yourselves? against whom make ye a wide mouth, *and* draw out the tongue? *are* ye not children of transgression, a seed of falsehood, Ps. 35:21
5 Enflaming yourselves with idols under every green tree, slaying the children in the valleys under the clifts of the rocks?
6 Among the smooth *stones* of the stream *is* thy portion; they, they *are* thy lot: even to them hast thou poured a drink offering, thou hast offered a meat offering. Should I receive comfort in these? Jer. 3:9
7 Upon a lofty and high mountain hast thou set thy bed: even thither wentest thou up to offer sacrifice. Ezek. 16:16; 23:41
8 Behind the doors also and the posts hast thou set up thy remembrance: for thou hast discovered *thyself to another* than me, and art gone up; thou hast enlarged thy bed, and made thee a *covenant* with them; thou lovedst their bed where thou sawest *it.*
9 And thou wentest to the king with ointment, and didst increase thy perfumes, and didst send thy messengers far off, and didst debase *thyself even* unto hell. Ezek. 23:16-17
10 Thou art wearied in the greatness of thy way; *yet* saidst thou not, There is no hope: thou hast found the life of thine hand; therefore thou wast not grieved. Jer. 2:25; 18:12
11 And of whom hast thou been afraid or feared, that thou hast lied, and hast not remembered me, nor laid *it* to thy heart? have not I held my peace even of old, and thou fearest me not? Ps. 50:21; Prov. 29:25; Is. 51:12-13
12 I will declare thy righteousness, and thy works; for they shall not profit thee. Mic. 3:2-4

The Absence of Christ Brings Sadness

Isaiah 57:15

The life in which the fear of the Lord is cherished will not be a life of sadness and gloom. It is the absence of Christ that makes the countenance sad, and the life a pilgrimage of sighs. Those who are filled with self-esteem and self-love do not feel the need of a living, personal union with Christ. The heart that has not fallen on the Rock is proud of its wholeness. Men want a dignified religion. They desire to walk in a path wide enough to take in their own attributes. Their self-love, their love of popularity and love of praise, exclude the Saviour from their hearts, and without Him there is gloom and sadness. But Christ dwelling in the soul is a wellspring of joy. For all who receive Him, the very keynote of the word of God is rejoicing. . . .

It was when Moses was hidden in the cleft of the rock that he beheld the glory of God. It is when we hide in the riven Rock that Christ will cover us with His own pierced hand, and we shall hear what the Lord saith unto His servants. To us as to Moses, God will reveal Himself as "merciful and gracious, long-suffering, and abundant in goodness and truth, keeping mercy for thousands, forgiving iniquity and transgression and sin" (Exodus 34:6, 7). *COL 162*

God Promises Forgiveness to the Penitent

13 When thou criest, let thy companies deliver thee; but the wind shall carry them all away; vanity shall take *them*: but he that putteth his trust in me shall possess the land, and shall inherit my holy mountain;   Ps. 37:3, 9
14 And shall say, Cast ye up, cast ye up, prepare the way, take up the stumblingblock out of the way of my people.   Is. 40:3; 62:10
15 For thus saith the high and lofty One that inhabiteth eternity, whose name *is* Holy; I dwell in the high and holy *place*, with him also *that is* of a contrite and humble spirit, to revive the spirit of the humble, and to revive the heart of the contrite ones.   Ps. 34:18
16 For I will not contend for ever, neither will I be always [T]wroth: for the spirit should fail before me, and the souls *which* I have made.   Ps. 85:5 ◆ *angered*
17 For the iniquity of his [T]covetousness was I wroth, and smote him: I hid me, and was wroth, and he went on frowardly in the way of his heart.   Is. 56:11; Jer. 6:13 ◆ *strong desire*
18 I have seen his ways, and will heal him: I will lead him also, and restore comforts unto him and to his mourners.   Jer. 3:22
19 I create the fruit of the lips; Peace, peace to *him that is* far off, and to *him that is* near, saith the LORD; and I will heal him.   Acts 2:39
20 But the wicked *are* like the troubled sea, when it cannot rest, whose waters cast up [T]mire and dirt.   Job 18:5-14 ◆ *mud*
21 *There is* no peace, saith my God, to the wicked.   Is. 48:22

Isaiah Reproves Hypocrisy

58 Cry aloud, spare not, lift up thy voice like a trumpet, and shew my people their [T]transgression, and the house of Jacob their sins.   *violation of a law*

58:1 Giving the Trumpet a Certain Sound

To the servant of God at this time is the command addressed: "Lift up thy voice like a trumpet, and show My people their transgression, and the house of Jacob their sins" [Isaiah 58:1].

So far as his opportunities extend, everyone who has received the light of truth is under the same solemn and fearful responsibility as was the prophet of Israel. . . . *GC 459*

---

2 Yet they seek me daily, and delight to know my ways, as a nation that did righteousness, and forsook not the ordinance of their God: they ask of me the ordinances of justice; they take delight in approaching to God.

True Fasting

3 Wherefore have we fasted, *say they*, and thou seest not? *wherefore* have we afflicted our soul, and thou takest no knowledge? Behold, in the day of your fast ye find pleasure, and exact all your labours.   Lev. 16:29; Neh. 5:7
4 Behold, ye fast for strife and debate, and to [T]smite with the fist of wickedness: ye shall not fast as *ye do this* day, to make your voice to be heard on high.   1 Kin. 21:9-13 ◆ *strike*
5 Is it such a fast that I have chosen? a day for a man to afflict his soul? *is it* to bow down his head as a bulrush, and to spread sackcloth and ashes *under him*? wilt thou call this a fast, and an acceptable day to the LORD?
6 *Is* not this the fast that I have chosen? to loose the bands of wickedness, to undo the heavy burdens, and to let the oppressed go free, and that ye break every yoke?   Neh. 5:10-12
7 *Is it* not to deal thy bread to the hungry, and that thou bring the poor that are cast out to thy house? when thou seest the naked, that thou cover him; and that thou hide not thyself from thine own flesh?   Is. 58:10; Ezek. 18:7, 16

The Rewards of Godliness

8 Then shall thy light break forth as the morning, and thine health shall spring forth speedily: and thy righteousness shall go before thee; the glory of the LORD shall be thy [T]rereward.   Ex. 14:19 ◆ *rear guard*
9 Then shalt thou call, and the LORD shall answer; thou shalt cry, and he shall say, Here I *am*. If thou take away from the midst of thee the yoke, the putting forth of the finger, and speaking vanity;   Ps. 12:2; 50:15; Prov. 6:13
10 And *if* thou draw out thy soul to the hungry, and satisfy the afflicted soul; then shall thy light rise in obscurity, and thy darkness *be* as the noonday: Job 11:17
11 And the LORD shall guide thee continually, and satisfy thy soul in drought, and make fat thy bones: and thou shalt be like a watered garden, and like a spring of water, whose waters fail not.   Song 4:15
12 And *they that shall be* of thee shall build the old waste places: thou shalt raise up the foundations of many generations; and thou shalt be called, The repairer of the breach, The restorer of paths to dwell in.   Is. 61:4

58:12 Repairers of the Breach

The prophet here describes a people who, in a time of general departure from truth and righteousness, are seeking to restore the principles that are the foundation of the kingdom of God. They are repairers of a breach that has been made in God's law—the wall that He has placed around His chosen ones for their protection, and obedience to whose precepts of justice, truth, and purity is to be their perpetual safeguard. *PK 677, 678*

Keep the Sabbath

13 If thou turn away thy foot from the sabbath, *from* doing thy pleasure on my holy day; and call the sabbath a delight, the holy of the Lord, honourable; and shalt honour him, not doing thine own ways, nor finding thine own pleasure, nor speaking *thine own* words:　　　　Ps. 84:2

14 Then shalt thou delight thyself in the Lord; and I will cause thee to ride upon the high places of the earth, and feed thee with the heritage of Jacob thy father: for the mouth of the Lord hath spoken *it*.　　Deut. 32:13; 33:29

> The Sabbath See Matthew 12:11–13.

Sin Separates from God

59 Behold, the Lord's hand is not shortened, that it cannot save; neither his ear heavy, that it cannot hear: Num. 11:23; Is. 50:2

> **59:1–21 Important Prophecies of Isaiah**
>
> The very words of prophecy were so perverted as to sanction error. Had the people in sincerity studied the word for themselves, they would not have been misled. The sixty-first chapter of Isaiah testifies that Christ was to do the very work He did. Chapter fifty-three sets forth His rejection and sufferings in the world, and chapter fifty-nine describes the character of the priests and rabbis. *DA 458*

2 But your iniquities have separated between you and your God, and your sins have hid *his* face from you, that he will not hear.　　　　Is. 50:1

3 For your hands are defiled with blood, and your fingers with iniquity; your lips have spoken lies, your tongue hath muttered perverseness.　　Is. 1:15, 21; Jer. 2:30

4 None calleth for justice, nor *any* pleadeth for truth: they trust in vanity, and speak lies; they conceive mischief, and bring forth iniquity.　　Job 15:35; Is. 30:12; Jer. 7:4

5 They hatch ᵀcockatrice' eggs, and weave the spider's web: he that eateth *of* their eggs dieth, and that which is crushed breaketh out into a viper.　　*snake*

6 Their webs shall not become garments, neither shall they cover themselves with their works: their works *are* works of iniquity, and the act of violence *is* in their hands.　　Is. 57:12

7 Their feet run to evil, and they make haste to shed innocent blood: their thoughts *are* thoughts of iniquity; wasting and destruction *are* in their paths.　　Prov. 1:16

8 The way of peace they know not; and *there is* no judgment in their goings: they have made them crooked paths: whosoever goeth therein shall not know peace.　　Luke 1:79

9 Therefore is judgment far from us, neither doth justice overtake us: we wait for light, but behold obscurity; for brightness, *but* we walk in darkness.　　Is. 5:30

10 We grope for the wall like the blind, and we grope as if *we had* no eyes: we stumble at noonday as in the night; *we are* in desolate places as dead *men*.　　Deut. 28:29; Job 5:14; Lam. 3:6

11 We roar all like bears, and mourn sore like doves: we look for judgment, but *there is* none; for salvation, *but* it is far off from us.　　Is. 38:14; Ezek. 7:16

12 For our ᵀtransgressions are multiplied before thee, and our sins testify against us: for our transgressions *are* with us; and *as for* our iniquities, we know them;　　*violations of a law*

13 In ᵀtransgressing and lying against the Lord, and departing away from our God, speaking oppression and revolt, conceiving and uttering from the heart words of falsehood.　　Mark 7:21-22 ◆ *violating a law*

14 And judgment is turned away backward, and justice standeth afar off: for truth is fallen in the street, and ᵀequity cannot enter.　　Hab. 1:4 ◆ *uprightness*

15 Yea, truth faileth; and he *that* departeth from evil maketh himself a prey: and the Lord saw *it*, and it displeased him that *there was* no judgment.

Keeping the Sabbath God's Way

Isaiah 58:13, 14

God has given men six days wherein to labor, and He requires that their own work be done in the six working days. Acts of necessity and mercy are permitted on the Sabbath, the sick and suffering are at all times to be cared for; but unnecessary labor is to be strictly avoided. "Turn away thy foot from the Sabbath, from doing thy pleasure on My holy day; and call the Sabbath a delight, the holy of the Lord, honorable; and . . . honor Him, not doing thine own ways, nor finding thine own pleasure." (Isaiah 58:13). Nor does the prohibition end here. "Nor speaking thine own words," says the prophet. Those who discuss business matters or lay plans on the Sabbath are regarded by God as though engaged in the actual transaction of business. To keep the Sabbath holy, we should not even allow our minds to dwell upon things of a worldly character. And the commandment includes all within our gates. The inmates of the house are to lay aside their worldly business during the sacred hours. All should unite to honor God by willing service upon His holy day. *PP 307, 308*

16 And he saw that *there was* no man, and wondered that *there was* no intercessor: therefore his arm brought salvation unto him; and his righteousness, it sustained him. 17 For he put on righteousness as a ᵀbreastplate, and an helmet of salvation upon his head; and he put on the garments of vengeance *for* clothing, and was clad with zeal as a ᵀcloke.   Is. 9:7; Eph. 6:14, 17 ◆ *piece of armor* ◆ *clothing* 18 According to *their* deeds, accordingly he will repay, fury to his adversaries, recompence to his enemies; to the islands he will repay recompence.   Job 34:11; Is. 63:6; Jer. 17:10 19 So shall they fear the name of the Lᴏʀᴅ from the west, and his glory from the rising of the sun. When the enemy shall come in like a flood, the Spirit of the Lᴏʀᴅ shall lift up a ᵀstandard against him.   Ps. 113:3; Is. 49:12 ◆ *flag*

20 And the Redeemer shall come to Zion, and unto them that turn from ᵀtransgression in Jacob, saith the Lᴏʀᴅ.   *violation of a law* 21 As for me, this *is* my covenant with them, saith the Lᴏʀᴅ; My spirit that *is* upon thee, and my words which I have put in thy mouth, shall not depart out of thy mouth, nor out of the mouth of thy seed, nor out of the mouth of thy seed's seed, saith the Lᴏʀᴅ, from ᵀhenceforth and for ever.   Is. 51:16 ◆ *from this time forward*

The Lord Will Be Jerusalem's Glory

60 Arise, shine; for thy light is come, and the glory of the Lᴏʀᴅ is risen upon thee.   Eph. 5:8

2 For, behold, the darkness shall cover the earth, and ᵀgross darkness the people: but the Lᴏʀᴅ shall arise upon thee, and his glory shall be seen upon thee.   *total* 3 And the Gentiles shall come to thy light, and kings to the brightness of thy rising. 4 Lift up thine eyes round about, and see: all they gather themselves together, they come to thee: thy sons shall come from far, and thy daughters shall be nursed at *thy* side. Is. 49:18 5 Then thou shalt see, and flow together, and thine heart shall fear, and be enlarged; because the abundance of the sea shall be converted unto thee, the forces of the Gentiles shall come unto thee.   Is. 61:6 6 The multitude of camels shall cover thee, the dromedaries of Midian and Ephah; all they from Sheba shall come: they shall bring gold and incense; and they shall shew forth the praises of the Lᴏʀᴅ.   Gen. 25:3-4; Ps. 72:10 7 All the flocks of Kedar shall be gathered together unto thee, the rams of Nebaioth shall minister unto thee: they shall come up with acceptance on mine altar, and I will glorify the house of my glory.   Gen. 25:13; Is. 56:7 8 Who *are* these *that* fly as a cloud, and as the doves to their windows? 9 Surely the isles shall wait for me, and the ships of Tarshish first, to bring thy sons from far, their silver and their gold with them, unto the name of the Lᴏʀᴅ thy God, and to the Holy One of Israel, because he hath glorified thee.   Is. 2:16; 51:5; 55:5 10 And the sons of strangers shall build up thy walls, and their kings shall minister unto thee: for in my wrath I smote thee, but in my favour have I had mercy on thee.   Is. 49:23 11 Therefore thy gates shall be open continually; they shall not be shut day nor night; that *men* may bring unto thee the forces of the Gentiles, and *that* their kings *may be* brought.   Is. 60:5 12 For the nation and kingdom that will not serve thee shall perish; yea, *those* nations shall be utterly wasted. 13 The glory of Lebanon shall come unto thee, the fir tree, the pine tree, and the box together, to beautify the place of my sanctuary; and I will make the place of my feet glorious. 14 The sons also of them that afflicted thee shall come bending unto thee; and all they that despised thee shall bow themselves down at the soles of thy feet; and they shall call thee, The city of the Lᴏʀᴅ, The Zion of the Holy One of Israel.   Is. 14:1-2; 49:23; Rev. 3:9 15 Whereas thou hast been forsaken and hated, so that no man went through *thee*, I will make thee an eternal excellency, a joy of many generations.   Is. 65:18 16 Thou shalt also suck the milk of the Gentiles, and shalt suck the breast of kings: and

thou shalt know that I the LORD *am* thy Saviour and thy Redeemer, the mighty One of Jacob.   Is. 49:23

17 For brass I will bring gold, and for iron I will bring silver, and for wood brass, and for stones iron: I will also make thy officers peace, and thine exactors righteousness.

18 Violence shall no more be heard in thy land, wasting nor destruction within thy borders; but thou shalt call thy walls Salvation, and thy gates Praise.   Is. 11:9; 26:1

19 The sun shall be no more thy light by day; neither for brightness shall the moon give light unto thee: but the LORD shall be unto thee an everlasting light, and thy God thy glory.   Zech. 2:5; Rev. 21:23; 22:5

20 Thy sun shall no more go down; neither shall thy moon withdraw itself: for the LORD shall be thine everlasting light, and the days of thy mourning shall be ended.   Rev. 21:4

21 Thy people also *shall be* all righteous: they shall inherit the land for ever, the branch of my planting, the work of my hands, that I may be glorified.   Ps. 37:11

22 A little one shall become a thousand, and a small one a strong nation: I the LORD will hasten it in his time.   Hab. 2:3

The Work of Christ

61 The Spirit of the Lord GOD *is* upon me; because the LORD hath anointed me to preach good tidings unto the meek;

he hath sent me to bind up the brokenhearted, to proclaim liberty to the captives, and the opening of the prison to *them that are* bound;   Ps. 45:7; Is. 42:7; Luke 7:22

2 To proclaim the acceptable year of the LORD, and the day of vengeance of our God; to comfort all that mourn;   Is. 34:8; 57:18; Matt. 5:4

3 To appoint unto them that mourn in Zion, to give unto them beauty for ashes, the oil of joy for mourning, the garment of praise for the spirit of heaviness; that they might be called trees of righteousness, the planting of the LORD, that he might be glorified.   Ps. 45:7

4 And they shall build the old wastes, they shall raise up the former desolations, and they shall repair the waste cities, the desolations of many generations.   Is. 58:12

5 And strangers shall stand and feed your flocks, and the sons of the alien *shall be* your plowmen and your vinedressers.   Is. 14:1-2

6 But ye shall be named the Priests of the LORD: *men* shall call you the Ministers of our God: ye shall eat the riches of the Gentiles, and in their glory shall ye boast yourselves.   Ex. 19:6

7 For your shame *ye shall have* double; and *for* confusion they shall rejoice in their portion: therefore in their land they shall possess the double: everlasting joy shall be unto them.   Ps. 16:11; Is. 40:2; Zech. 9:12

8 For I the LORD love judgment, I hate robbery for burnt offering; and I will direct their work in truth, and I will make an everlasting covenant with them.   Gen. 17:7; Ps. 11:7; Is. 55:3

9 And their seed shall be known among the Gentiles, and their offspring among the people: all that see them shall acknowledge them, that they *are* the seed which the LORD hath blessed.   Is. 44:3

10 I will greatly rejoice in the LORD, my soul shall be joyful in my God; for he hath clothed

me with the garments of salvation, he hath covered me with the robe of righteousness, as a bridegroom decketh *himself* with ornaments, and as a bride adorneth *herself* with her jewels.   Is. 49:18; 52:1; Rev. 21:2

11 For as the earth bringeth forth her bud, and as the garden causeth the things that are sown in it to spring forth; so the Lord GOD will cause righteousness and praise to spring forth before all the nations.   Ps. 85:11

61:11 Sowing Spiritual Seed

As in the natural, so in the spiritual sowing; the teacher of truth must seek to prepare the soil of the heart; he must sow the seed; but the power that alone can produce life is from God. There is a point beyond which human effort is in vain. While we are to preach the word, we can not impart the power that will quicken the soul, and cause righteousness and praise to spring forth. *COL 63, 64*

Jerusalem's Salvation Is Coming

62 For Zion's sake will I not hold my peace, and for Jerusalem's sake I will not rest, until the righteousness thereof go forth as brightness, and the salvation thereof as a lamp *that* burneth.   Prov. 4:18

2 And the Gentiles shall see thy righteousness, and all kings thy glory: and thou shalt be called by a new name, which the mouth of the LORD shall name.   Is. 62:4

3 Thou shalt also be a crown of glory in the hand of the LORD, and a royal ᵀdiadem in the hand of thy God.   Zech. 9:16; 1 Thess. 2:19 ♦ *crown*

4 Thou shalt no more be termed Forsaken; neither shall thy land any more be termed Desolate: but thou shalt be called Hephzi-bah, and thy land Beulah: for the LORD delighteth in thee, and thy land shall be married.   Jer. 32:41

5 For *as* a young man marrieth a virgin, *so* shall thy sons marry thee: and *as* the bridegroom rejoiceth over the bride, *so* shall thy God rejoice over thee.   Is. 65:19

6 I have set watchmen upon thy walls, O Jerusalem, *which* shall never hold their peace day nor night: ye that make mention of the LORD, keep not silence,   Ps. 74:2; Is. 52:8; 56:10

7 And give him no rest, till he establish, and till he make Jerusalem a praise in the earth.   Jer. 33:9

8 The LORD hath sworn by his right hand, and by the arm of his strength, Surely I will no more give thy corn *to be* meat for thine enemies; and the sons of the stranger shall not drink thy wine, for the which thou hast laboured: Deut. 28:31, 33; Jer. 5:17

9 But they that have gathered it shall eat it, and praise the LORD; and they that have

brought it together shall drink it in the courts of my holiness.   Deut. 12:12

The Savior Is Coming

10 Go through, go through the gates; prepare ye the way of the people; cast up, cast up the highway; gather out the stones; lift up a ᵀstandard for the people.   Is. 11:10; 49:22; 57:14 ♦ *flag*

11 Behold, the LORD hath proclaimed unto the end of the world, Say ye to the daughter of Zion, Behold, thy salvation cometh; behold, his reward *is* with him, and his work before him.   Zech. 9:9; Matt. 21:5; Rev. 22:12

12 And they shall call them, The holy people, The redeemed of the LORD: and thou shalt be called, Sought out, A city not forsaken.   Is. 35:9; 62:4; 1 Pet. 2:9

62:12 Worth It All

Whatever crosses they have been called to bear, whatever losses they have sustained, whatever persecution they have suffered, even to the loss of their temporal life, the children of God are amply recompensed. "They shall see His face; and His name shall be in their foreheads" (Revelation 22:4). *COL 180*

The Lord Will Be Victorious

63 Who *is* this that cometh from Edom, with dyed garments from Bozrah? this *that is* glorious in his apparel, travelling in the greatness of his strength? I that speak in righteousness, mighty to save.   Ps. 137:7

2 Wherefore *art thou* red in thine apparel, and thy garments like him that treadeth in the ᵀwinefat?   *trough beneath winepress*

3 I have trodden the winepress alone; and of the people *there was* none with me: for I will tread them in mine anger, and trample them in my fury; and their blood shall be sprinkled upon my garments, and I will stain all my ᵀraiment.   Mic. 7:10 ♦ *clothing*

63:3 Silence in Heaven

The Saviour trod the wine press alone, and of the people there was none with Him.
But God suffered with His Son. Angels beheld the Saviour's agony. They saw their Lord enclosed by legions of satanic forces, His nature weighed down with a shuddering, mysterious dread. There was silence in heaven. No harp was touched. *DA 693*

4 For the day of vengeance *is* in mine heart, and the year of my redeemed is come. Is. 34:8

5 And I looked, and *there was* none to help; and I wondered that *there was* none to uphold: therefore mine own arm brought salvation unto me; and my fury, it upheld me.   Ps. 44:3

6 And I will tread down the people in mine

anger, and make them drunk in my fury, and I will bring down their strength to the earth.   Is. 49:26

The Lord's People Pray

7 I will mention the lovingkindnesses of the LORD, *and* the praises of the LORD, according to all that the LORD hath bestowed on us, and the great goodness toward the house of Israel, which he hath bestowed on them according to his mercies, and according to the multitude of his lovingkindnesses.   Ps. 51:1

8 For he said, Surely they *are* my people, children *that* will not lie: so he was their Saviour.   Ex. 6:7

9 In all their affliction he was afflicted, and the angel of his presence saved them: in his love and in his pity he redeemed them; and he bare them, and carried them all the days of old.   Ex. 33:14; Deut. 1:31; 7:7-8

10 But they rebelled, and vexed his holy Spirit: therefore he was turned to be their enemy, *and* he fought against them. Ps. 78:40; Acts 7:51; Eph. 4:30

11 Then he remembered the days of old, Moses, *and* his people, *saying,* Where *is* he that brought them up out of the sea with the shepherd of his flock? where *is* he that put his holy Spirit within him?   Num. 11:17

12 That led *them* by the right hand of Moses with his glorious arm, dividing the water before them, to make himself an everlasting name?   Ex. 15:16

13 That led them through the deep, as an horse in the wilderness, *that* they should not stumble?

14 As a beast goeth down into the valley, the Spirit of the LORD caused him to rest: so didst thou lead thy people, to make thyself a glorious name.   Josh. 23:1

15 Look down from heaven, and behold from the habitation of thy holiness and of thy glory: where *is* thy zeal and thy strength, the sounding of thy bowels and of thy mercies toward me? are they restrained? Ps. 80:14; 123:1

16 Doubtless thou *art* our father, though Abraham be ignorant of us, and Israel acknowledge us not: thou, O LORD, *art* our father, our redeemer; thy name *is* from everlasting.   Deut. 32:6; Is. 41:14; 44:6

17 O LORD, why hast thou made us to ᵀerr from thy ways, *and* hardened our heart from thy fear? Return for thy servants' sake, the tribes of thine inheritance.   Num. 10:36 ♦ *stray*

18 The people of thy holiness have possessed *it* but a little while: our adversaries have ᵀtrodden down thy sanctuary. Ps. 74:3-7 ♦ *trampled*

19 We are *thine:* thou never barest rule over them; they were not called by thy name.

Prayer for a Sign of God's Power

64 Oh that thou wouldest ᵀrend the heavens, that thou wouldest come down, that the mountains might flow down at thy presence,   Mic. 1:3-4 ♦ *tear apart*

2 As *when* the melting fire burneth, the fire causeth the waters to boil, to make thy name known to thine adversaries, *that* the nations may tremble at thy presence!   Ps. 99:1

3 When thou didst terrible things *which* we looked not for, thou camest down, the mountains flowed down at thy presence.   Ps. 66:3

4 For since the beginning of the world *men* have not heard, nor perceived by the ear, neither hath the eye seen, O God, beside thee, *what* he hath prepared for him that waiteth for him.   Ps. 31:19; Is. 25:9

5 Thou meetest him that rejoiceth and worketh righteousness, *those that* remember

---

Are Your Clothes Made from Fig Leaves?

Isaiah 64:6

The white robe of innocence was worn by our first parents when they were placed by God in holy Eden. They lived in perfect conformity to the will of God. All the strength of their affections was given to their heavenly Father. A beautiful soft light, the light of God, enshrouded the holy pair. This robe of light was a symbol of their spiritual garments of heavenly innocence. Had they remained true to God it would ever have continued to enshroud them. But when sin entered, they severed their connection with God, and the light that had encircled them departed. Naked and ashamed, they tried to supply the place of the heavenly garments by sewing together fig leaves for a covering.

This is what the transgressors of God's law have done ever since the day of Adam and Eve's disobedience. They have sewed together fig leaves to cover the nakedness caused by transgression. They have worn the garments of their own devising, by works of their own they have tried to cover their sins, and make themselves acceptable with God.

But this they can never do. Nothing can man devise to supply the place of his lost robe of innocence. No fig-leaf garment, no worldly citizen dress, can be worn by those who sit down with Christ and angels at the marriage supper of the Lamb.

Only the covering which Christ Himself has provided can make us meet to appear in God's presence. This covering, the robe of His own righteousness, Christ will put upon every repenting, believing soul. *COL 310, 311*

thee in thy ways: behold, thou art ᵀwroth; for we have sinned: in those is continuance, and we shall be saved.   Ex. 20:24 ◆ *angered*
6 But we are all as an unclean *thing*, and all our righteousnesses *are* as filthy rags; and we all do fade as a leaf; and our iniquities, like the wind, have taken us away.   Ps. 90:5-6; Is. 6:5
7 And *there is* none that calleth upon thy name, that stirreth up himself to take hold of thee: for thou hast hid thy face from us, and hast consumed us, because of our iniquities.   Ezek. 22:30
8 But now, O LORD, thou *art* our father; we *are* the clay, and thou our potter; and we all *are* the work of thy hand.   Is. 29:16; 45:9; 63:16

64:8 Potter and Clay

The great Master Worker desires to mold and fashion us. And as the clay is in the hands of the potter, so are we to be in His hands. We are not to try to do the work of the potter. Our part is to yield ourselves to be molded by the Master Worker. *MH 472*

9 Be not wroth very sore, O LORD, neither remember iniquity for ever: behold, see, we ᵀbeseech thee, we *are* all thy people.   beg
10 Thy holy cities are a wilderness, Zion is a wilderness, Jerusalem a desolation.   Is. 1:7
11 Our holy and our beautiful house, where our fathers praised thee, is burned up with fire: and all our pleasant things are laid waste.   2 Kin. 25:9
12 Wilt thou refrain thyself for these *things*, O LORD? wilt thou hold thy peace, and afflict us very sore?   Ps. 74:10-11, 18-19; Is. 42:14

The Calling of the Gentiles

65 I am sought of *them that* asked not *for me*; I am found of *them that* sought me not: I said, Behold me, behold me, unto a nation *that* was not called by my name.   Hos. 1:10; Rom. 9:24-26; 10:20
2 I have spread out my hands all the day unto a rebellious people, which walketh in a way *that was* not good, after their own thoughts;   Is. 1:2; Rom. 10:21
3 A people that provoketh me to anger continually to my face; that sacrificeth in gardens, and burneth incense upon altars of brick;   Job 1:11; Is. 1:29; 66:17
4 Which remain among the graves, and lodge in the monuments, which eat swine's flesh, and broth of abominable *things is in* their vessels;   Lev. 11:7
5 Which say, Stand by thyself, come not near to me; for I am holier than thou. These *are* a smoke in my nose, a fire that burneth all the day.   Matt. 9:11
6 Behold, *it is* written before me: I will not keep silence, but will ᵀrecompense, even recompense into their bosom, Ps. 50:3; 79:12 ◆ *repay*

7 Your iniquities, and the iniquities of your fathers together, saith the LORD, which have burned incense upon the mountains, and blasphemed me upon the hills: therefore will I measure their former work into their bosom.   Ex. 20:5

65:6, 7 Books of Heaven

Every man's work passes in review before God and is registered for faithfulness or unfaithfulness. Opposite each name in the books of heaven is entered with terrible exactness every wrong word, every selfish act, every unfulfilled duty, and every secret sin, with every artful dissembling. Heaven-sent warnings or reproofs neglected, wasted moments, unimproved opportunities, the influence exerted for good or for evil, with its far-reaching results, all are chronicled by the recording angel. *GC 482*

A Remnant Shall Be Saved

8 Thus saith the LORD, As the new wine is found in the cluster, and *one* saith, Destroy it not; for a blessing *is* in it: so will I do for my servants' sakes, that I may not destroy them all.
9 And I will bring forth a seed out of Jacob, and out of Judah an inheritor of my mountains: and mine elect shall inherit it, and my servants shall dwell there.   Amos 9:11-15
10 And Sharon shall be a fold of flocks, and the valley of Achor a place for the herds to lie down in, for my people that have sought me.   Is. 33:9; 35:2; Hos. 2:15

Judgments of the Wicked, and Blessings on the Godly

11 But ye *are* they that forsake the LORD, that forget my holy mountain, that prepare a table for that troop, and that furnish the drink offering unto that number.   Is. 1:28
12 Therefore will I number you to the sword, and ye shall all bow down to the slaughter: because when I called, ye did not answer; when I spake, ye did not hear; but did evil before mine eyes, and did choose *that* wherein I delighted not.   2 Chr. 36:15-16; Is. 50:2; Jer. 7:13
13 Therefore thus saith the Lord GOD, Behold, my servants shall eat, but ye shall be hungry: behold, my servants shall drink, but ye shall be thirsty: behold, my servants shall rejoice, but ye shall be ashamed: Is. 61:7
14 Behold, my servants shall sing for joy of heart, but ye shall cry for sorrow of heart, and shall howl for vexation of spirit.   Matt. 8:12
15 And ye shall leave your name for a curse unto my chosen: for the Lord GOD shall slay thee, and call his servants by another name: Is. 62:2; 65:9; Zech. 8:13

16 That he who blesseth himself in the earth shall bless himself in the God of truth; and he that sweareth in the earth shall swear by the God of truth; because the former troubles are forgotten, and because they are hid from mine eyes. Ps. 31:5

New Heavens and a New Earth

17 For, behold, I create new heavens and a new earth: and the former shall not be remembered, nor come into mind. Is. 66:22

18 But be ye glad and rejoice for ever *in that* which I create: for, behold, I create Jerusalem a rejoicing, and her people a joy. Ps. 98

19 And I will rejoice in Jerusalem, and joy in my people: and the voice of weeping shall be no more heard in her, nor the voice of crying. Is. 25:8; 35:10; Rev. 7:17

20 There shall be no more thence an infant of days, nor an old man that hath not filled his days: for the child shall die an hundred years old; but the sinner *being* an hundred years old shall be accursed. Deut. 4:40

21 And they shall build houses, and inhabit *them*; and they shall plant vineyards, and eat the fruit of them. Amos 9:14

22 They shall not build, and another inhabit; they shall not plant, and another eat: for as the days of a tree *are* the days of my people, and mine elect shall long enjoy the work of their hands. Ps. 92:12-14

23 They shall not labour in vain, nor bring forth for trouble; for they *are* the seed of the blessed of the LORD, and their offspring with them. Deut. 28:3-12; Is. 61:9; Acts 2:39

24 And it shall come to pass, that before they call, I will answer; and while they are yet speaking, I will hear. Dan. 9:20-23

25 The wolf and the lamb shall feed together, and the lion shall eat straw like the ᵀbullock: and dust *shall be* the serpent's meat. They shall not hurt nor destroy in all my holy mountain, saith the LORD. Is. 65:11 ◆ bull

> The New Earth See Revelation 21:1–5.

God Will Be Served in Humble Sincerity

66 Thus saith the LORD, The heaven *is* my throne, and the earth *is* my footstool: where *is* the house that ye build unto me? and where *is* the place of my rest? 1 Kin. 8:27

2 For all those *things* hath mine hand made, and all those *things* have been, saith the LORD: but to this *man* will I look, *even* to *him that is* poor and of a ᵀcontrite spirit, and trembleth at my word. Ps. 34:18; Is. 40:26; 57:15 ◆ broken spirit

3 He that killeth an ox *is as if* he slew a man; he that sacrificeth a lamb, *as if* he cut off a dog's neck; he that offereth an ᵀoblation, *as if he offered* swine's blood; he that burneth incense, *as if* he blessed an idol. Yea, they have

chosen their own ways, and their soul delighteth in their abominations. Lev. 2:2 ◆ offering

> **66:2 Oneness With Christ**
>
> The sincere, contrite soul is precious in the sight of God. He places His own signet upon men, not by their rank, not by their wealth, not by their intellectual greatness, but by their oneness with Christ. The Lord of glory is satisfied with those who are meek and lowly in heart. *DA 437*

4 I also will choose their delusions, and will bring their fears upon them; because when I called, none did answer; when I spake, they did not hear: but they did evil before mine eyes, and chose *that* in which I delighted not. 2 Kin. 21:2, 6; Is. 65:12

God Comforts the Humble with Marvels

5 Hear the word of the LORD, ye that tremble at his word; Your brethren that hated you, that cast you out for my name's sake, said, Let the LORD be glorified: but he shall appear to your joy, and they shall be ashamed. Ps. 38:20

6 A voice of noise from the city, a voice from the temple, a voice of the LORD that rendereth recompence to his enemies. Is. 59:18

7 Before she travailed, she brought forth; before her pain came, she was delivered of a man child. Is. 54:1

8 Who hath heard such a thing? who hath seen such things? Shall the earth be made to bring forth in one day? *or* shall a nation be born at once? for as soon as Zion travailed, she brought forth her children. Is. 64:4

9 Shall I bring to the birth, and not cause to bring forth? saith the LORD: shall I cause to bring forth, and shut *the womb*? saith thy God. Is. 37:3

10 Rejoice ye with Jerusalem, and be glad with her, all ye that love her: rejoice for joy with her, all ye that mourn for her: Deut. 32:43

11 That ye may suck, and be satisfied with the breasts of her consolations; that ye may milk out, and be delighted with the abundance of her glory. Is. 60:16

12 For thus saith the LORD, Behold, I will extend peace to her like a river, and the glory of the Gentiles like a flowing stream: then shall ye suck, ye shall be borne upon *her* sides, and be dandled upon *her* knees. Is. 48:18; 60:16

13 As one whom his mother comforteth, so will I comfort you; and ye shall be comforted in Jerusalem. Is. 51:3

14 And when ye see *this*, your heart shall rejoice, and your bones shall flourish like an herb: and the hand of the LORD shall be known toward his servants, and *his* ᵀindignation toward his enemies. Ezra 8:31 ◆ anger

The New Creation

15 For, behold, the LORD will come with fire, and with his chariots like a whirlwind, to render his anger with fury, and his rebuke with flames of fire.   Ps. 68:17

16 For by fire and by his sword will the LORD plead with all flesh: and the slain of the LORD shall be many.   Is. 27:1

17 They that ᵀsanctify themselves, and purify themselves in the gardens behind one *tree* in the midst, eating swine's flesh, and the abomination, and the mouse, shall be consumed together, saith the LORD.   Is. 65:3-4 ◆ *make holy*

18 For I *know* their works and their thoughts: it shall come, that I will gather all nations and tongues; and they shall come, and see my glory.   Is. 2:2

19 And I will set a sign among them, and I will send those that escape of them unto the nations, *to* Tarshish, Pul, and Lud, that draw the bow, *to* Tubal, and Javan, *to* the isles afar off, that have not heard my fame, neither have seen my glory; and they shall declare my glory among the Gentiles.   Gen. 10:2; Is. 62:10; Ezek. 27:10

20 And they shall bring all your brethren *for* an offering unto the LORD out of all nations upon horses, and in chariots, and in litters, and upon mules, and upon swift beasts, to my holy mountain Jerusalem, saith the LORD, as the children of Israel bring an offering in a clean vessel into the house of the LORD.   Is. 11:9

21 And I will also take of them for priests *and* for Levites, saith the LORD.   Ex. 19:6; Is. 61:6

22 For as the new heavens and the new earth, which I will make, shall remain before me, saith the LORD, so shall your seed and your name remain.   Is. 65:17; John 10:27-29; Rev. 21:1

23 And it shall come to pass, *that* from one new moon to another, and from one sabbath to another, shall all flesh come to worship before me, saith the LORD.   Ezek. 46:1

> The Sabbath See Isaiah 58:13, 14.

24 And they shall go forth, and look upon the carcases of the men that have ᵀtransgressed against me: for their worm shall not die, neither shall their fire be quenched; and they shall be an ᵀabhorring unto all flesh.   Is. 14:11 ◆ *violated a law* ◆ *despising*

The Sabbath Is Forever

Isaiah 66:22, 23

   The Sabbath was embodied in the law given from Sinai; but it was not then first made known as a day of rest. The people of Israel had a knowledge of it before they came to Sinai. On the way thither the Sabbath was kept. When some profaned it, the Lord reproved them, saying, "How long refuse ye to keep My commandments and My laws?" (Exodus 16:28).

   The Sabbath was not for Israel merely, but for the world. It had been made known to man in Eden, and, like the other precepts of the Decalogue, it is of imperishable obligation. Of that law of which the fourth commandment forms a part, Christ declares, "Till heaven and earth pass, one jot or one tittle shall in nowise pass from the law." So long as the heavens and the earth endure, the Sabbath will continue as a sign of the Creator's power. And when Eden shall bloom on earth again, God's holy rest day will be honored by all beneath the sun. "From one Sabbath to another" the inhabitants of the glorified new earth shall go up "to worship before Me, saith the Lord" (Matthew 5:18; Isaiah 66:23). *DA 283*

THE BOOK OF
JEREMIAH

Before his birth, Jeremiah was anointed by God as a prophet to warn the people of Judah and Israel to turn from their wickedness. God instructed Jeremiah to speak to all of His mercy and willingness to forgive once they confessed their transgressions.

Jeremiah used every weapon in his arsenal in seeking to stop Judah's decline into wickedness. However, his godly counsel went unheeded. God's people continued to descend into the mire of their apostasy and refused to repent or even listen to Jeremiah's warnings. Jeremiah was beaten, imprisoned, and ostracized. His grief grew as he came to understand that there was no way to save his people from God's judgment. At times he wanted to resign from his office as prophet: "I said, I will not make mention of him, nor speak any more in his name. But his word was in mine heart as a burning fire shut up in my bones, and I was weary with forbearing, and I could not stay" (20:9). He continued to speak for God until Judah was conquered. Truly, he earned his title, "the weeping prophet."

Dates

Jeremiah's ministry began about the year 627 B.C. and lasted until around 580 B.C. He lived during the time of Daniel, Zephaniah, Habakkuk, and Ezekiel and prophesied during some of Judah's darkest days. When King Josiah's reign ended, four godless kings followed in his stead and hastened Judah's slide toward judgment.

He was friends with King Josiah (640–609 B.C.), and lamented his death at the hands of the Egyptian Pharaoh, Necho II. Other key events in Jeremiah include:

(1) *Jeremiah's prophetic warnings about Assyria and Egypt—627–605 B.C.*
(2) *Babylon defeats Egypt; Nebuchadnezzar takes Palestine—605 B.C.*
(3) *Jehoiakim's reign—609–598 B.C.*
(4) *Nebuchadnezzar captures Jerusalem—598 B.C.*
(5) *Nebuchadnezzar overthrows Jerusalem—586 B.C.*

Author

Jeremiah relates that he is the author of this book (1:1). He dictates his prophecies to his secretary, Baruch, who is suspected of adding chapter 52 to the book—a supplement that is nearly identical to 2 Kings 24:18—25:30. Prior to including chapter 52 as a historical addendum, the author clearly stipulates, "Thus far are the words of Jeremiah" (51:64).

Jeremiah came from a priestly family. Like the prophets Isaiah and Ezekiel, Jeremiah's life was sometimes used as an object lesson. He had to buy a linen belt and bury it (13:1–11), could not marry (16:2), and had to buy a field (32:1–15) in order to convey God's messages to Judah.

Daniel makes reference to Jeremiah's prophecies (Daniel 9:2), as do many of the New Testament books, including Matthew (Matthew 2:17, 18; 21:13), Mark (Mark 11:17), Luke (Luke 19:43), Romans (Romans 11:34), and Hebrews (Hebrews 8:8–13).

During his ministry, Jeremiah's life was in constant danger, similar to Paul's. Jeremiah received threats to his life at his home in Anathoth, near Jerusalem, and also stood trial for his life in Jerusalem. He was at different times placed in stocks, thrown into a cistern, and publicly humiliated.

Meaning of the Name

Jeremiah is *Yirmeyahu* or *Yirmeyah* in Hebrew, which means "Yahweh Throws." It can also mean "Yahweh establishes, appoints, or sends." In Greek, Jeremiah is *Ieremias*, while the Latin derivation is *Jeremias*.

Christ in Jeremiah

The beginning of Jeremiah 23 is a clear prophetic picture of the Messiah. Jesus is termed the "righteous Branch" and the coming King (23:5), as well as "THE LORD OUR RIGHTEOUSNESS" (23:6).

This prophecy places Jesus on a par with His Father, and indeed agrees with a statement that Jesus says, "I and my Father are one" (John 10:30).

Jeremiah prophesies that Jesus will bring the New Covenant (Jeremiah 31:31–34), ful-

filling the covenants with Abraham (Genesis 12:1–3; 17:1–8), Moses and the people (Deuteronomy 28—30), and David (2 Samuel 7:4–17).

During this time, God speaks of the evil of King Jehoiakim, son of King Josiah, who reigned for eleven years in Jerusalem (2 Chronicles 36:5). Jehoiakim did evil in the sight of God, so much so that his works were called "abominations" (2 Chronicles 36:8). God declared there would be no lamenting his death (Jeremiah 22:18, 19).

Overview

Various themes are depicted in the Book of Jeremiah. The sections break down as follows:

(1) *Jeremiah 1, The Call of Jeremiah:* Jeremiah's prophetic call is detailed. The people of Judah had turned from God and His teachings, worshiping idols and doing whatever sinful acts their desires craved. God was angry and filled His servant Jeremiah with His words of condemnation and warning.

(2) *Jeremiah 2—45, The Messages for Judah:* The message is plain: surrender to God's will or face the judgment to come. Jeremiah obeys God, though obedience makes him a depressed outcast at times. He details the cause of Judah's trouble, and implores them to listen and repent.

The people refuse to listen to Jeremiah and instead do as they please. When they are taken into captivity, God through Jeremiah promises the captives that they will return to Jerusalem. He also prophesies the eventual overthrow of Babylon.

Even in judgment, God is merciful. He delays His judgment as long as He can, giving all a chance to repent. The metaphor of the potter's house teaches that a potter can repair an earthen vessel when it is wet (18:1–4) but once dry, a damaged vessel is only good for the trash (19:10, 11).

(3) *Jeremiah 46—51, The Messages for Gentiles:* Jeremiah prophesies God's judgment against Egypt (chapter 46), Philistia (chapter 47), Moab (chapter 48), Ammon (49:1–6), Edom (49:7–22), Syria (symbolized by its capital, Damascus—49:23–27), the Arabian countries of Kedar and Hazor (49:28–33), Elam (49:34–39), and Babylon (chapters 50—51). Unlike Babylon, Philistia, and Arabia, Egypt, Ammon, Moab, and Elam have a chance at restoration.

(4) *Jeremiah 52, The Fall of Jerusalem:* This chapter is a record of events in 2 Kings 25 and Jeremiah 39.

Unlocking Jeremiah

KEY PEOPLE:
Jeremiah, Josiah, Jehoiachin, Hananiah, Zedekiah, Pashhur, Nebuchadnezzar

KEY EVENTS:
Jeremiah's call, ministry, and persecutions; the fall of Jerusalem

KEY WORD:
Judgment of Judah, because the repeated warnings of Jeremiah went unheeded. God allowed Babylon to conquer Judah and take her people captive.

KEY VERSES:
"But this thing commanded I them, saying, Obey my voice, and I will be your God, and ye shall be my people: and walk ye in all the ways that I have commanded you, that it may be well unto you. But they hearkened not, nor inclined their ear, but walked in the counsels and in the imagination of their evil heart, and went backward, and not forward" (Jeremiah 7:23, 24).

"For they have healed the hurt of the daughter of my people slightly, saying, Peace, peace; when there is no peace. Were they ashamed when they had committed abomination? nay, they were not at all ashamed, neither could they blush: therefore shall they fall among them that fall: in the time of their visitation they shall be cast down, saith the LORD" (Jeremiah 8:11, 12).

"And ye have done worse than your fathers; for, behold, ye walk every one after the imagination of his evil heart, that they may not hearken unto me: Therefore will I cast you out of this land into a land that ye know not, neither ye nor your fathers; and there shall ye serve other gods day and night; where I will not shew you favour" (Jeremiah 16:12, 13).

KEY CHAPTER:
Jeremiah 31, where we see the mercy of God. Despite Judah's unwillingness to turn to God, He would yet preserve them. In Jeremiah 31:33, God declares through Jeremiah that He will "put my law in their inward parts, and write it in their hearts; and will be their God, and they shall be my people." This promise was fulfilled in the life, death, and resurrection of Jesus (compare Matthew 26:26–29).

The Prophet Jeremiah

1 The words of Jeremiah the son of Hilkiah, of the priests that *were* in Anathoth in the land of Benjamin: 1 Chr. 6:60

2 To whom the word of the LORD came in the days of Josiah the son of Amon king of Judah, in the thirteenth year of his reign.

3 It came also in the days of Jehoiakim the son of Josiah king of Judah, unto the end of the eleventh year of Zedekiah the son of Josiah king of Judah, unto the carrying away of Jerusalem captive in the fifth month.   2 Kin. 23:34

The Calling of Jeremiah

4 Then the word of the LORD came unto me, saying,

5 Before I formed thee in the belly I knew thee; and before thou camest forth out of the womb I ᵀsanctified thee, *and* I ordained thee a prophet unto the nations.   Is. 49:1 ◆ *made holy*

6 Then said I, Ah, Lord GOD! behold, I cannot speak: for I *am* a child.   Ex. 6:12

7 But the LORD said unto me, Say not, I *am* a child: for thou shalt go to all that I shall send thee, and whatsoever I command thee thou shalt speak.   Num. 22:20

8 Be not afraid of their faces: for I *am* with thee to deliver thee, saith the LORD.   Ex. 3:12

9 Then the LORD put forth his hand, and touched my mouth. And the LORD said unto me, Behold, I have put my words in thy mouth.   Ex. 4:11-12

10 See, I have this day set thee over the nations and over the kingdoms, to root out, and to pull down, and to destroy, and to throw down, to build, and to plant. Is. 44:26-28; Jer. 24:6

Visions of an Almond Rod and a Boiling Pot

11 Moreover the word of the LORD came unto me, saying, Jeremiah, what seest thou? And I said, I see a rod of an almond tree.   Amos 7:8

12 Then said the LORD unto me, Thou hast well seen: for I will hasten my word to perform it.

13 And the word of the LORD came unto me the second time, saying, What seest thou? And I said, I see a ᵀseething pot; and the face thereof *is* toward the north. Ezek. 11:3 ◆ *boiling*

14 Then the LORD said unto me, Out of the north an evil shall break forth upon all the inhabitants of the land.   Is. 41:25

15 For, lo, I will call all the families of the kingdoms of the north, saith the LORD; and they shall come, and they shall set every one his throne at the entering of the gates of Jerusalem, and against all the walls thereof round about, and against all the cities of Judah.   Jer. 4:16

16 And I will utter my judgments against them touching all their wickedness, who have forsaken me, and have burned incense unto other gods, and worshipped the works of their own hands.   Deut. 28:20; Jer. 7:9; 19:4

17 Thou therefore ᵀgird up thy ᵀloins, and arise, and speak unto them all that I command thee: be not dismayed at their faces, lest I confound thee before them. 1 Kin. 18:46 ◆ *equip* ◆ *waist*

18 For, behold, I have made thee this day a defenced city, and an iron pillar, and brasen walls against the whole land, against the kings of Judah, against the princes thereof, against the priests thereof, and against the people of the land.   Is. 50:7

19 And they shall fight against thee; but they shall not prevail against thee; for I *am* with thee, saith the LORD, to deliver thee.   Jer. 1:8

God's People Continue to Reject Him

2 Moreover the word of the LORD came to me, saying,

2 Go and cry in the ears of Jerusalem, saying, Thus saith the LORD; I remember thee, the kindness of thy youth, the love of thine espousals, when thou wentest after

---

An Extraordinary and Faithful Prophet

Jeremiah 1

For forty years Jeremiah was to stand before the nation as a witness for truth and righteousness. In a time of unparalleled apostasy he was to exemplify in life and character the worship of the only true God. During the terrible sieges of Jerusalem he was to be the mouthpiece of Jehovah. He was to predict the downfall of the house of David and the destruction of the beautiful temple built by Solomon. And when imprisoned because of his fearless utterances, he was still to speak plainly against sin in high places. Despised, hated, rejected of men, he was finally to witness the literal fulfillment of his own prophecies of impending doom, and share in the sorrow and woe that should follow the destruction of the fated city.

Yet amid the general ruin into which the nation was rapidly passing, Jeremiah was often permitted to look beyond the distressing scenes of the present to the glorious prospects of the future, when God's people should be ransomed from the land of the enemy and planted again in Zion. He foresaw the time when the Lord would renew His covenant relationship with them. *PK 408*

me in the wilderness, in a land *that was* not sown.   Deut. 2:7; Ezek. 16:8, 60

3 Israel *was* holiness unto the LORD, *and* the firstfruits of his increase: all that devour him shall offend; evil shall come upon them, saith the LORD.   Ex. 19:5-6; Deut. 7:6; James 1:18

4 Hear ye the word of the LORD, O house of Jacob, and all the families of the house of Israel:

5 Thus saith the LORD, What iniquity have your fathers found in me, that they are gone far from me, and have walked after vanity, and are become vain?   2 Kin. 17:15; Jer. 2:31; 14:22

6 Neither said they, Where *is* the LORD that brought us up out of the land of Egypt, that led us through the wilderness, through a land of deserts and of pits, through a land of drought, and of the shadow of death, through a land that no man passed through, and where no man dwelt?   Deut. 32:10; Is. 63:11-13; Hos. 13:4

7 And I brought you into a plentiful country, to eat the fruit thereof and the goodness thereof; but when ye entered, ye defiled my land, and made mine heritage an abomination.   Num. 13:27; Deut. 8:7-9; Jer. 16:18

8 The priests said not, Where *is* the LORD? and they that handle the law knew me not: the pastors also transgressed against me, and the prophets prophesied by Baal, and walked after *things that* do not profit. Hab. 2:18

God's People Exchanged Him for Idols

9 Wherefore I will yet plead with you, saith the LORD, and with your children's children will I plead.   Ex. 20:5; Jer. 2:35; Ezek. 20:35-36

10 For pass over the isles of Chittim, and see; and send unto Kedar, and consider diligently, and see if there be such a thing.   Ps. 120:5

11 Hath a nation changed *their* gods, which *are* yet no gods? but my people have changed their glory for *that which* doth not profit.   Ps. 106:20; Is. 37:19; Jer. 16:20

12 Be astonished, O ye heavens, at this, and be horribly afraid, be ye very desolate, saith the LORD.   Is. 1:2

13 For my people have committed two evils; they have forsaken me the fountain of living waters, *and* ᵀhewed them out cisterns, broken cisterns, that can hold no water.   Ps. 36:9; Jer. 17:13; John 4:14 ◆ *cut*

How Bitter It Is to Abandon God

14 *Is* Israel a servant? *is* he a homeborn *slave*? why is he spoiled?   Ex. 4:22

15 The young lions roared upon him, *and* yelled, and they made his land waste: his cities are burned without inhabitant. Is. 1:7; Jer. 4:7

16 Also the children of Noph and Tahapanes have broken the crown of thy head.   Is. 19:13

17 Hast thou not procured this unto thy-

self, in that thou hast forsaken the LORD thy God, when he led thee by the way?   Jer. 4:18

18 And now what hast thou to do in the way of Egypt, to drink the waters of Sihor? or what hast thou to do in the way of Assyria, to drink the waters of the river?   Josh. 13:3

19 Thine own wickedness shall correct thee, and thy backslidings shall reprove thee: know therefore and see that *it is* an evil *thing* and bitter, that thou hast forsaken the LORD thy God, and that my fear *is* not in thee, saith the Lord GOD of hosts.   Ps. 36:1; Is. 3:9; Hos. 5:5

The Sins of Judah

20 For of old time I have broken thy yoke, *and* burst thy bands; and thou saidst, I will not transgress; when upon every high hill and under every green tree thou wanderest, playing the harlot.   Lev. 26:13; Deut. 12:2; Is. 1:21

21 Yet I had planted thee a noble vine, wholly a right seed: how then art thou turned into the ᵀdegenerate plant of a strange vine unto me?   Ex. 15:17; Ps. 80:8; Is. 5:4 ◆ *fallen*

2:21 God's Desire for All Human Beings

God desired to bring all peoples under His merciful rule. He desired that the earth should be filled with joy and peace. He created man for happiness, and He longs to fill human hearts with the peace of heaven. He desires that the families below shall be a symbol of the great family above.

But Israel did not fulfill God's purpose. *COL 290*

---

22 For though thou wash thee with nitre, and take thee much soap, *yet* thine iniquity is marked before me, saith the Lord GOD.

23 How canst thou say, I am not polluted, I have not gone after Baalim? see thy way in the valley, know what thou hast done: *thou art* a swift ᵀdromedary traversing her ways;   Prov. 30:12; Jer. 7:31 ◆ *camel*

24 A wild ass used to the wilderness, *that* snuffeth up the wind at her pleasure; in her occasion who can turn her away? all they that seek her will not weary themselves; in her month they shall find her.   Jer. 14:6

25 Withhold thy foot from being unshod, and thy throat from thirst: but thou saidst, There is no hope: no; for I have loved strangers, and after them will I go.   Deut. 32:16; Jer. 3:13

26 As the thief is ashamed when he is found, so is the house of Israel ashamed; they, their kings, their princes, and their priests, and their prophets,   Jer. 32:32

27 Saying to a stock, Thou *art* my father; and to a stone, Thou hast brought me forth: for they have turned *their* back unto me, and not *their* face: but in the time of their trouble they will say, Arise, and save us.   Is. 26:16

28 But where *are* thy gods that thou hast made thee? let them arise, if they can save thee in the time of thy trouble: for *according to* the number of thy cities are thy gods, O Judah.　　　Deut. 32:37; Is. 45:20; Jer. 11:13

29 Wherefore will ye plead with me? ye all have ᵀtransgressed against me, saith the LORD.　　　Jer. 5:1 ◆ *violated a law*

30 In vain have I smitten your children; they received no correction: your own sword hath devoured your prophets, like a destroying lion.　　　Neh. 9:26; Is. 1:5; 1 Thess. 2:15

31 O generation, see ye the word of the LORD. Have I been a wilderness unto Israel? a land of darkness? wherefore say my people, We are lords; we will come no more unto thee?　　　Deut. 32:15

32 Can a maid forget her ornaments, *or* a bride her attire? yet my people have forgotten me days without number.　　　Ps. 106:21

33 Why trimmest thou thy way to seek love? therefore hast thou also taught the wicked ones thy ways.

34 Also in thy skirts is found the blood of the souls of the poor innocents: I have not found it by secret search, but upon all these.　　　2 Kin. 21:16; 24:4; Jer. 19:4

35 Yet thou sayest, Because I am innocent, surely his anger shall turn from me. Behold, I will plead with thee, because thou sayest, I have not sinned.　　　Prov. 28:13

36 Why ᵀgaddest thou about so much to change thy way? thou also shalt be ashamed of Egypt, as thou wast ashamed of Assyria.　　　2 Chr. 28:16; Hos. 5:13 ◆ *do you go*

37 Yea, thou shalt go forth from him, and thine hands upon thine head: for the LORD hath rejected thy confidences, and thou shalt not prosper in them.　　　2 Sam. 13:19; Jer. 37:7-10

The People Act Shamelessly

3 They say, If a man put away his wife, and she go from him, and become another man's, shall he return unto her again? shall not that land be greatly polluted? but thou hast played the harlot with many lovers; yet return again to me, saith the LORD. Deut. 24:1-4

2 Lift up thine eyes unto the high places, and see where thou hast not been lien with. In the ways hast thou sat for them, as the Arabian in the wilderness; and thou hast polluted the land with thy ᵀwhoredoms and with thy wickedness. Gen. 38:14 ◆ *acts of prostitution*

3 Therefore the showers have been withholden, and there hath been no latter rain; and thou hadst a whore's forehead, thou refusedst to be ashamed.　　　Lev. 26:19; Jer. 5:3; 6:15

4 Wilt thou not from this time cry unto me, My father, thou *art* the guide of my youth?　　　Jer. 2:2

5 Will he reserve *his anger* for ever? will he keep *it* to the end? Behold, thou hast spoken and done evil things as thou couldest. Is. 57:16

Judah Is Worse Than Israel

6 The LORD said also unto me in the days of Josiah the king, Hast thou seen *that* which backsliding Israel hath done? she is gone up upon every high mountain and under every green tree, and there hath played the harlot.

7 And I said after she had done all these *things,* Turn thou unto me. But she returned not. And her treacherous sister Judah saw *it.*　　　Ezek. 16:46

8 And I saw, when for all the causes whereby backsliding Israel committed adultery I had put her away, and given her a bill of divorce; yet her treacherous sister Judah feared not, but went and played the harlot also. Deut. 24:1

9 And it came to pass through the lightness of her ᵀwhoredom, that she defiled the land, and committed adultery with stones and with stocks.　　　Is. 57:6; Jer. 2:27; 3:2 ◆ *prostitution*

10 And yet for all this her treacherous sister Judah hath not turned unto me with her whole heart, but feignedly, saith the LORD.　　　Hos. 7:14

11 And the LORD said unto me, The backsliding Israel hath justified herself more than treacherous Judah.　　　Ezek. 16:51-52

The Promises of God to the Penitent

12 Go and proclaim these words toward the north, and say, Return, thou backsliding Israel, saith the LORD; *and* I will not cause mine anger to fall upon you: for I *am* merciful, saith the LORD, *and* I will not keep *anger* for ever.　　　2 Kin. 17:6; Ps. 86:15; Ezek. 33:11

13 Only acknowledge thine iniquity, that thou hast ᵀtransgressed against the LORD thy God, and hast scattered thy ways to the strangers under every green tree, and ye have not obeyed my voice, saith the LORD.　　　Deut. 12:2 ◆ *violated a law*

3:12, 13 Real Repentance

We often sorrow because our evil deeds bring unpleasant consequences to ourselves; but this is not repentance. Real sorrow for sin is the result of the working of the Holy Spirit. The Spirit reveals the ingratitude of the heart that has slighted and grieved the Saviour, and brings us in contrition to the foot of the cross. By every sin Jesus is wounded afresh . . . we mourn for the sins that have brought anguish upon Him. Such mourning will lead to the renunciation of sin. *DA 300*

---

14 Turn, O backsliding children, saith the LORD; for I am married unto you: and I will take you one of a city, and two of a family, and I will bring you to Zion:　　　Is. 54:5

15 And I will give you pastors according to mine heart, which shall feed you with knowledge and understanding. Ezek. 34:23; Acts 20:28
16 And it shall come to pass, when ye be multiplied and increased in the land, in those days, saith the LORD, they shall say no more, The ark of the covenant of the LORD: neither shall it come to mind: neither shall they remember it; neither shall they visit *it*; neither shall *that* be done any more. Is. 65:17
17 At that time they shall call Jerusalem the throne of the LORD; and all the nations shall be gathered unto it, to the name of the LORD, to Jerusalem: neither shall they walk any more after the imagination of their evil heart. Jer. 11:8
18 In those days the house of Judah shall walk with the house of Israel, and they shall come together out of the land of the north to the land that I have given for an inheritance unto your fathers. Jer. 31:8; 50:4; Hos. 1:11
19 But I said, How shall I put thee among the children, and give thee a pleasant land, a goodly heritage of the hosts of nations? and I said, Thou shalt call me, My father; and shalt not turn away from me. Is. 63:16; Jer. 3:4
20 Surely *as* a wife treacherously departeth from her husband, so have ye dealt treacherously with me, O house of Israel, saith the LORD. Is. 48:8

3:20 The Parallel of the World

The unfaithfulness of the church to Christ in permitting her confidence and affection to be turned from Him, and allowing the love of worldly things to occupy the soul, is likened to the violation of the marriage vow. . . .
Says the apostle James: "Ye adulterers and adulteresses, know ye not that the friendship of the world is enmity with God? whosoever therefore will be a friend of the world is the enemy of God" [James 4:4]. *GC 381, 382*

21 A voice was heard upon the high places, weeping *and* supplications of the children of Israel: for they have perverted their way, *and* they have forgotten the LORD their God. Is. 15:2
22 Return, ye backsliding children, *and* I will heal your backslidings. Behold, we come unto thee; for thou *art* the LORD our God. Hos. 14:4
23 Truly in vain *is salvation hoped for* from the hills, *and from* the multitude of mountains: truly in the LORD our God *is* the salvation of Israel. Ps. 3:8; 121:1-2
24 For shame hath devoured the labour of our fathers from our youth; their flocks and their herds, their sons and their daughters. Hos. 9:10
25 We lie down in our shame, and our

confusion covereth us: for we have sinned against the LORD our God, we and our fathers, from our youth even unto this day, and have not obeyed the voice of the LORD our God. Jer. 22:21

God Calls Israel by His Promise

4 If thou wilt return, O Israel, saith the LORD, return unto me: and if thou wilt put away thine abominations out of my sight, then shalt thou not remove. Jer. 3:1, 22; Joel 2:12
2 And thou shalt swear, The LORD liveth, in truth, in judgment, and in righteousness; and the nations shall bless themselves in him, and in him shall they glory. Gen. 22:18; Is. 65:16

Destruction from the North

3 For thus saith the LORD to the men of Judah and Jerusalem, Break up your fallow ground, and sow not among thorns. Hos. 10:12; Matt. 13:7

4:3 Cooperate With the Heavenly Gardener

The garden of the heart must be cultivated. The soil must be broken up by deep repentance for sin. Poisonous, Satanic plants must be uprooted. The soil once overgrown by thorns can be reclaimed only by diligent labor. So the evil tendencies of the natural heart can be overcome only by earnest effort in the name and strength of Jesus. . . . This work He desires to accomplish for us, and He asks us to co-operate with Him. *COL 56*

4 Circumcise yourselves to the LORD, and take away the foreskins of your heart, ye men of Judah and inhabitants of Jerusalem: lest my fury come forth like fire, and burn that none can quench *it*, because of the evil of your doings. Deut. 10:16; Jer. 9:26; Rom. 2:28-29
5 Declare ye in Judah, and publish in Jerusalem; and say, Blow ye the trumpet in the land: cry, gather together, and say, Assemble yourselves, and let us go into the defenced cities. Josh. 10:20; Jer. 6:1; 8:14
6 Set up the standard toward Zion: retire, stay not: for I will bring evil from the north, and a great destruction. Jer. 1:13-15
7 The lion is come up from his thicket, and the destroyer of the Gentiles is on his way; he is gone forth from his place to make thy land desolate; *and* thy cities shall be laid waste, without an inhabitant. Is. 1:7; 6:11; Jer. 2:15
8 For this gird you with sackcloth, lament and howl: for the fierce anger of the LORD is not turned back from us. Is. 5:25; 22:12; Jer. 6:26
9 And it shall come to pass at that day, saith the LORD, *that* the heart of the king shall perish, and the heart of the princes; and the priests shall be astonished, and the prophets shall wonder. Is. 22:3-5
10 Then said I, Ah, Lord GOD! surely thou

hast greatly deceived this people and Jerusalem, saying, Ye shall have peace; whereas the sword reacheth unto the soul.   Jer. 5:12

11 At that time shall it be said to this people and to Jerusalem, A dry wind of the high places in the wilderness toward the daughter of my people, not to ^Tfan, nor to cleanse,   Ezek. 17:10 ◆ winnow

12 *Even* a full wind from those *places* shall come unto me: now also will I give sentence against them.   Jer. 1:16

13 Behold, he shall come up as clouds, and his chariots *shall be* as a whirlwind: his horses are swifter than eagles. Woe unto us! for we are spoiled.   Is. 5:28; 19:1; 66:15

14 O Jerusalem, wash thine heart from wickedness, that thou mayest be saved. How long shall thy vain thoughts lodge within thee?   Prov. 1:22; Jer. 13:27; James 4:8

4:14 Faithful Despite Discouragements

But by the great mass of the people the call to repentance and reformation was unheeded. . . . Jeremiah had little hope of saving his beloved land from destruction and the people from captivity. Yet he was not permitted to remain silent while utter ruin threatened the kingdom. Those who had remained loyal to God must be encouraged to persevere in rightdoing, and sinners must, if possible, be induced to turn from iniquity. *PK 412*

15 For a voice declareth from Dan, and publisheth affliction from mount Ephraim.

16 Make ye mention to the nations; behold, publish against Jerusalem, *that* watchers come from a far country, and give out their voice against the cities of Judah.   Jer. 5:15

17 As keepers of a field, are they against her round about; because she hath been rebellious against me, saith the LORD.   Jer. 5:23

18 Thy way and thy doings have ^Tprocured these *things* unto thee; this *is* thy wickedness, because it is bitter, because it reacheth unto thine heart. Ps. 107:17; Is. 50:1; Jer. 2:19 ◆ brought about

A Lament for the Miseries of Judah

19 My bowels, my bowels! I am pained at my very heart; my heart maketh a noise in me; I cannot hold my peace, because thou hast heard, O my soul, the sound of the trumpet, the alarm of war. Is. 16:11; 22:4; Jer. 9:1

20 Destruction upon destruction is cried; for the whole land is spoiled: suddenly are my tents spoiled, *and* my curtains in a moment.   Ps. 42:7

21 How long shall I see the ^Tstandard, *and* hear the sound of the trumpet?   flag

22 For my people *is* foolish, they have not known me; they *are* ^Tsottish children, and they have none understanding: they *are*

wise to do evil, but to do good they have no knowledge.   Is. 1:3; Rom. 16:19; 1 Cor. 14:20 ◆ foolish

23 I beheld the earth, and, lo, *it was* without form, and void; and the heavens, and they *had* no light.   Gen. 1:2; Is. 5:30

24 I beheld the mountains, and, lo, they trembled, and all the hills moved lightly.   Is. 5:25

25 I beheld, and, lo, *there was* no man, and all the birds of the heavens were fled.

26 I beheld, and, lo, the fruitful place *was* a wilderness, and all the cities thereof were broken down at the presence of the LORD, *and* by his fierce anger.   Ps. 107:34

27 For thus hath the LORD said, The whole land shall be desolate; yet will I not make a full end.   Jer. 5:10, 18; 30:11

28 For this shall the earth mourn, and the heavens above be black: because I have spoken *it*, I have purposed *it*, and will not repent, neither will I turn back from it.   Num. 23:19

29 The whole city shall flee for the noise of the horsemen and bowmen; they shall go into thickets, and climb up upon the rocks: every city *shall be* forsaken, and not a man dwell therein.   Is. 2:19-21

30 And *when* thou *art* spoiled, what wilt thou do? Though thou clothest thyself with crimson, though thou deckest thee with ornaments of gold, though thou rentest thy face with painting, in vain shalt thou make thyself fair; *thy* lovers will despise thee, they will seek thy life.   2 Kin. 9:30; Is. 10:3; Lam. 1:2

31 For I have heard a voice as of a woman in travail, *and* the anguish as of her that bringeth forth her first child, the voice of the daughter of Zion, *that* bewaileth herself, *that* spreadeth her hands, *saying*, Woe *is* me now! for my soul is wearied because of murderers.   Is. 1:15; 13:8; Lam. 1:17

Judah's Complete Rejection of the Lord

5 Run ye to and fro through the streets of Jerusalem, and see now, and know, and seek in the broad places thereof, if ye can find a man, if there be *any* that executeth judgment, that seeketh the truth; and I will pardon it.   Gen. 18:23-32; 2 Chr. 16:9; Ezek. 22:30

2 And though they say, The LORD liveth; surely they swear falsely.   Titus 1:16

3 O LORD, *are* not thine eyes upon the truth? thou hast stricken them, but they have not grieved; thou hast consumed them, *but* they have refused to receive correction: they have made their faces harder than a rock; they have refused to return. 2 Chr. 16:9; Is. 9:13; Jer. 2:30

4 Therefore I said, Surely these *are* poor; they are foolish: for they know not the way of the LORD, *nor* the judgment of their God.   Is. 27:11; Jer. 8:7; Hos. 4:6

5 I will get me unto the great men, and will speak unto them; for they have known the

way of the LORD, *and* the judgment of their God: but these have altogether broken the yoke, *and* burst the bonds.   Jer. 2:20

6 Wherefore a lion out of the forest shall slay them, *and* a wolf of the evenings shall ᵀspoil them, a leopard shall watch over their cities: every one that goeth out thence shall be torn in pieces: because their ᵀtransgressions are many, *and* their backslidings are increased.   Jer. 4:7 ◆ plunder ◆ violations of a law

7 How shall I pardon thee for this? thy children have forsaken me, and sworn by *them that are* no gods: when I had fed them to the full, they then committed adultery, and assembled themselves by troops in the harlots' houses.   Deut. 32:21; Josh. 23:7; Gal. 4:8

8 They were *as* fed horses in the morning: every one neighed after his neighbour's wife.   Jer. 13:27

9 Shall I not visit for these *things?* saith the LORD: and shall not my soul be avenged on such a nation as this?   Jer. 5:29; 9:9

10 Go ye up upon her walls, and destroy; but make not a full end: take away her battlements; for they *are* not the LORD's. Jer. 4:27

11 For the house of Israel and the house of Judah have dealt very treacherously against me, saith the LORD.   Jer. 3:20

12 They have ᵀbelied the LORD, and said, *It is* not he; neither shall evil come upon us; neither shall we see sword nor famine: lied about

13 And the prophets shall become wind, and the word *is* not in them: thus shall it be done unto them.   Jer. 14:15

14 Wherefore thus saith the LORD God of hosts, Because ye speak this word, behold, I will make my words in thy mouth fire,

and this people wood, and it shall devour them.   Jer. 1:9; 23:29; Hos. 6:5

15 Lo, I will bring a nation upon you from far, O house of Israel, saith the LORD: it *is* a mighty nation, it *is* an ancient nation, a nation whose language thou knowest not, neither understandest what they say.   Deut. 28:49

16 Their quiver *is* as an open sepulchre, they *are* all mighty men.   Ps. 5:9

17 And they shall eat up thine harvest, and thy bread, *which* thy sons and thy daughters should eat: they shall eat up thy flocks and thine herds: they shall eat up thy vines and thy fig trees: they shall impoverish thy fenced cities, wherein thou trustedst, with the sword.   Lev. 26:16; Deut. 28:33

18 Nevertheless in those days, saith the LORD, I will not make a full end with you.   Jer. 4:27

19 And it shall come to pass, when ye shall say, Wherefore doeth the LORD our God all these *things* unto us? then shalt thou answer them, Like as ye have forsaken me, and served strange gods in your land, so shall ye serve strangers in a land *that is* not yours.   1 Kin. 9:8-9

20 Declare this in the house of Jacob, and publish it in Judah, saying,

21 Hear now this, O foolish people, and without understanding; which have eyes, and see not; which have ears, and hear not: Is. 6:9-10

22 Fear ye not me? saith the LORD: will ye not tremble at my presence, which have placed the sand *for* the bound of the sea by a perpetual decree, that it cannot pass it: and though the waves thereof toss themselves, yet can they not prevail; though they roar, yet can they not pass over it?   Deut. 28:58; Job 38:10-11

We Are on Trial

Jeremiah 5:9

The professed followers of Christ are on trial before the heavenly universe; but the coldness of their zeal and the feebleness of their efforts in God's service mark them as unfaithful. If what they are doing were the best they could do, condemnation would not rest upon them; but were their hearts enlisted in the work, they could do much more. . . .

There are many whose names are on the church books, but who are not under Christ's rule. They are not heeding His instruction or doing His work. Therefore they are under the control of the enemy. They are doing no positive good; therefore they are doing incalculable harm. Because their influence is not a savor of life unto life, it is a savor of death unto death.

The Lord says, "Shall I not visit for these things?" (Jeremiah 5:9). Because they failed of fulfilling God's purpose, the children of Israel were set aside, and God's call was extended to other peoples. If these too prove unfaithful, will they not in like manner be rejected? . . .

In the Jewish nation it was the priests and teachers who, by misleading the people, had robbed God of the service which He claimed. It was they who turned the nation away from Christ. . . .

They would not give up their man-made commandments in order to obey the requirements of the word of God. They would not, for the truth's sake, sacrifice the pride of reason and the praise of men. . . . They would not accept His rebukes and warnings, and they set themselves to turn the people against Him and to compass His destruction.

For the rejection of Christ, with the results that followed, they were responsible. A nation's sin and a nation's ruin were due to the religious leaders. *COL 303–305*

23 But this people hath a revolting and a rebellious heart; they are revolted and gone.
24 Neither say they in their heart, Let us now fear the LORD our God, that giveth rain, both the former and the latter, in his season: he reserveth unto us the appointed weeks of the harvest.   Gen. 8:22; Ps. 147:8; Joel 2:23
25 Your iniquities have turned away these *things*, and your sins have withholden good *things* from you.   Jer. 3:3
26 For among my people are found wicked *men*: they lay wait, as he that setteth snares; they set a trap, they catch men.   Prov. 1:11
27 As a cage is full of birds, so *are* their houses full of deceit: therefore they are become great, and Twaxen rich.   *become*
28 They are waxen fat, they shine: yea, they overpass the deeds of the wicked: they judge not the cause, the cause of the fatherless, yet they prosper; and the right of the needy do they not judge.   Deut. 32:15; Is. 1:23; Zech. 7:10
29 Shall I not visit for these *things*? saith the LORD: shall not my soul be avenged on such a nation as this?   Jer. 5:9
30 A wonderful and horrible thing is committed in the land;   Jer. 23:14; Hos. 6:10
31 The prophets prophesy falsely, and the priests bear rule by their means; and my people love *to have it* so: and what will ye do in the end thereof? Jer. 14:14; Ezek. 13:6; Mic. 2:11

The Lord's Rejection of Judah

6 O ye children of Benjamin, gather yourselves to flee out of the midst of Jerusalem, and blow the trumpet in Tekoa, and set up a sign of fire in Beth-haccerem: for evil appeareth out of the north, and great destruction.   Judg. 1:21; 2 Sam. 14:2; Neh. 3:14
2 I have likened the daughter of Zion to a Tcomely and delicate *woman*.   Is. 1:8 ◆ *lovely*

6:2 Christ Loves His Church

Very close and sacred is the relation between Christ and His church—He the bridegroom, and the church the bride; He the head, and the church the body. Connection with Christ, then, involves connection with His church.

The church is organized for service; and in a life of service to Christ, connection with the church is one of the first steps. . . . This is an important part of one's training; and in a church imbued with the Master's life, it will lead directly to effort for the world without. *Ed 268, 269*

---

3 The shepherds with their flocks shall come unto her; they shall pitch *their* tents against her round about; they shall feed every one in his place.   Luke 19:43
4 Prepare ye war against her; arise, and let us go up at noon. Woe unto us! for the day goeth away, for the shadows of the evening are stretched out.   Jer. 15:8; Joel 3:9; Zeph. 2:4
5 Arise, and let us go by night, and let us destroy her palaces.   Is. 32:14
6 For thus hath the LORD of hosts said, Hew ye down trees, and cast a mount against Jerusalem: this *is* the city to be visited; she *is* wholly oppression in the midst of her.
7 As a fountain casteth out her waters, so she casteth out her wickedness: violence and spoil is heard in her; before me continually *is* grief and wounds. Jer. 20:8; Ezek. 7:11, 23
8 Be thou instructed, O Jerusalem, lest my soul depart from thee; lest I make thee desolate, a land not inhabited.   Jer. 17:23; Ezek. 23:18
9 Thus saith the LORD of hosts, They shall throughly Tglean the remnant of Israel as a vine: turn back thine hand as a grapegatherer into the baskets. Jer. 16:16 ◆ *gather leftovers from a field*
10 To whom shall I speak, and give warning, that they may hear? behold, their ear *is* uncircumcised, and they cannot hearken: behold, the word of the LORD is unto them a reproach; they have no delight in it.   Ex. 6:12
11 Therefore I am full of the fury of the LORD; I am weary with holding in: I will pour it out upon the children abroad, and upon the assembly of young men together: for even the husband with the wife shall be taken, the aged with *him that is* full of days.   Job 32:18-19; Jer. 9:21
12 And their houses shall be turned unto others, *with their* fields and wives together: for I will stretch out my hand upon the inhabitants of the land, saith the LORD.   Is. 5:25; Jer. 8:10
13 For from the least of them even unto the greatest of them every one *is* given to covetousness; and from the prophet even unto the priest every one dealeth falsely. Is. 57:17; Jer. 8:10
14 They have healed also the hurt *of the daughter* of my people slightly, saying, Peace, peace; when *there is* no peace.   Jer. 4:10; 14:13; Ezek. 13:10

6:14 People-Pleasing Pastors

Those ministers who are men pleasers, who cry, Peace, peace, when God has not spoken peace, might well humble their hearts before God, asking pardon for their insincerity and their lack of moral courage. It is not from love for their neighbor that they smooth down the message entrusted to them, but because they are self-indulgent and ease-loving. True love seeks first the honor of God and the salvation of souls. *PK 141*

---

15 Were they ashamed when they had committed abomination? nay, they were not at all ashamed, neither could they blush: therefore they shall fall among them that fall: at the time *that* I visit them they shall be cast down, saith the LORD.   Jer. 3:3; 8:12
16 Thus saith the LORD, Stand ye in the ways, and see, and ask for the old paths, where *is*

the good way, and walk therein, and ye shall find rest for your souls. But they said, We will not walk *therein*.   Is. 8:20; Jer. 18:15; Mal. 4:4

17 Also I set watchmen over you, *saying*, Hearken to the sound of the trumpet. But they said, We will not hearken.   Is. 21:11

18 Therefore hear, ye nations, and know, O congregation, what *is* among them.

19 Hear, O earth: behold, I will bring evil upon this people, *even* the fruit of their thoughts, because they have not hearkened unto my words, nor to my law, but rejected it.   Is. 1:2; Jer. 8:9; 22:29

20 To what purpose cometh there to me incense from Sheba, and the sweet cane from a far country? your burnt offerings *are* not acceptable, nor your sacrifices sweet unto me.   Ps. 40:6; Is. 1:11; 60:6

21 Therefore thus saith the LORD, Behold, I will lay stumblingblocks before this people, and the fathers and the sons together shall fall upon them; the neighbour and his friend shall perish.   Is. 8:14

22 Thus saith the LORD, Behold, a people cometh from the north country, and a great nation shall be raised from the sides of the earth.   Jer. 10:22

23 They shall lay hold on bow and spear; they *are* cruel, and have no mercy; their voice roareth like the sea; and they ride upon horses, set in array as men for war against thee, O daughter of Zion.   Is. 13:18; Jer. 50:42

24 We have heard the fame thereof: our hands ᵀwax feeble: anguish hath taken hold of us, *and* pain, as of a woman in travail.   become

25 Go not forth into the field, nor walk by the way; for the sword of the enemy *and* fear *is* on every side.   Jer. 49:29

26 O daughter of my people, ᵀgird *thee* with sackcloth, and ᵀwallow thyself in ashes: make thee mourning, *as for* an only son, most bitter lamentation: for the spoiler shall suddenly come upon us.   Jer. 4:8; Zech. 12:10 ◆ *equip* ◆ *roll*

27 I have set thee *for* a tower *and* a fortress among my people, that thou mayest know and try their way.   Jer. 1:18

28 They *are* all grievous revolters, walking with slanders: *they are* brass and iron; they *are* all corrupters.   Jer. 5:23; 9:4

29 The bellows are burned, the lead is consumed of the fire; the founder melteth in vain: for the wicked are not plucked away.

30 Reprobate silver shall *men* call them, because the LORD hath rejected them. Ps. 119:119

Judah Trusts the Wrong Things

7 The word that came to Jeremiah from the LORD, saying,

2 Stand in the gate of the LORD's house, and proclaim there this word, and say, Hear the word of the LORD, all *ye of* Judah, that enter in at these gates to worship the LORD. Jer. 26:2

7:2–7 Deferred Discipline

Though they had wandered long in idolatry and had slighted His warnings, yet He now declares His willingness to defer chastisement and grant yet another opportunity for repentance. . . . In vain would be the trust they might place in the temple and its services. Rites and ceremonies could not atone for sin. . . . Reformation of heart and of the life practice alone could save them from the inevitable result of continued transgression. *PK 413, 414*

---

3 Thus saith the LORD of hosts, the God of Israel, Amend your ways and your doings, and I will cause you to dwell in this place.   Jer. 18:11

4 Trust ye not in lying words, saying, The temple of the LORD, The temple of the LORD, The temple of the LORD, *are* these.   Mic. 3:11

5 For if ye throughly amend your ways and your doings; if ye throughly execute judgment between a man and his neighbour;   Is. 1:19

6 *If* ye oppress not the stranger, the fatherless, and the widow, and shed not innocent blood in this place, neither walk after other gods to your hurt: Deut. 8:19

7 Then will I cause you to dwell in this place, in the land that I gave to your fathers, for ever and ever.   Deut. 4:40; Jer. 3:18

8 Behold, ye trust in lying words, that cannot profit.   Jer. 7:4

9 Will ye steal, murder, and commit adultery, and swear falsely, and burn incense unto Baal, and walk after other gods whom ye know not;   Ex. 20:3

10 And come and stand before me in this house, which is called by my name, and say, We are delivered to do all these abominations?   Jer. 7:11; 32:34; Ezek. 23:39

11 Is this house, which is called by my name, become a den of robbers in your eyes? Behold, even I have seen *it*, saith the LORD.   Is. 56:7; Matt. 21:13; Mark 11:17

12 But go ye now unto my place which *was* in Shiloh, where I set my name at the first, and see what I did to it for the wickedness of my people Israel.   Josh. 18:1; Judg. 18:31; 1 Sam. 4:10-11

7:13–15 Hoarded Blessings

The warning was not heeded by the Jewish people. They forgot God, and lost sight of their high privilege as His representatives. The blessings they had received brought no blessing to the world. All their advantages were appropriated for their own glorification. They robbed God of the service He required of them, and they robbed their fellow men of religious guidance and a holy example. *COL 291, 292*

---

13 And now, because ye have done all these works, saith the LORD, and I spake unto

you, rising up early and speaking, but ye heard not; and I called you, but ye answered not;   Prov. 1:24; Is. 65:12; Jer. 7:25

14 Therefore will I do unto *this* house, which is called by my name, wherein ye trust, and unto the place which I gave to you and to your fathers, as I have done to Shiloh. Jer. 7:4

15 And I will cast you out of my sight, as I have cast out all your brethren, *even* the whole seed of Ephraim.   2 Kin. 17:23

16 Therefore pray not thou for this people, neither lift up cry nor prayer for them, neither make intercession to me: for I will not hear thee.   Ex. 32:10; Deut. 9:14; Jer. 11:14

17 Seest thou not what they do in the cities of Judah and in the streets of Jerusalem?

18 The children gather wood, and the fathers kindle the fire, and the women knead *their* dough, to make cakes to the queen of heaven, and to pour out drink offerings unto other gods, that they may provoke me to anger.   1 Kin. 14:9; Jer. 19:13; 44:17-19

19 Do they provoke me to anger? saith the LORD: *do they* not *provoke* themselves to the confusion of their own faces?   1 Cor. 10:22

20 Therefore thus saith the Lord GOD; Behold, mine anger and my fury shall be poured out upon this place, upon man, and upon beast, and upon the trees of the field, and upon the fruit of the ground; and it shall burn, and shall not be quenched.   Jer. 42:18; Lam. 2:3-5; 4:11

The Lord Rejects the Sacrifices of the Disobedient

21 Thus saith the LORD of hosts, the God of Israel; Put your burnt offerings unto your sacrifices, and eat flesh.   Jer. 6:20

22 For I spake not unto your fathers, nor commanded them in the day that I brought them out of the land of Egypt, concerning burnt offerings or sacrifices: 1 Sam. 15:22; Hos. 6:6

23 But this thing commanded I them, saying, Obey my voice, and I will be your God, and ye shall be my people: and walk ye in all the ways that I have commanded you, that it may be well unto you. Ex. 15:26; Deut. 5:33; 6:3

24 But they hearkened not, nor inclined their ear, but walked in the counsels *and* in the imagination of their evil heart, and went backward, and not forward.   Ps. 81:11-12

25 Since the day that your fathers came forth out of the land of Egypt unto this day I have even sent unto you all my servants the prophets, daily rising up early and sending *them*:   2 Chr. 36:15

26 Yet they hearkened not unto me, nor inclined their ear, but hardened their neck: they did worse than their fathers. 2 Chr. 30:8; Jer. 7:24

27 Therefore thou shalt speak all these words unto them; but they will not hearken

to thee: thou shalt also call unto them; but they will not answer thee.   Is. 50:2

28 But thou shalt say unto them, This *is* a nation that obeyeth not the voice of the LORD their God, nor receiveth correction: truth is perished, and is cut off from their mouth.

Jeremiah Tells the People to Mourn

29 Cut off thine hair, *O Jerusalem,* and cast *it* away, and take up a lamentation on high places; for the LORD hath rejected and forsaken the generation of his wrath.   Job 1:20

30 For the children of Judah have done evil in my sight, saith the LORD: they have set their abominations in the house which is called by my name, to pollute it.   2 Kin. 21:4; Jer. 32:34

31 And they have built the high places of Tophet, which *is* in the valley of the son of Hinnom, to burn their sons and their daughters in the fire; which I commanded *them* not, neither came it into my heart. Deut. 17:3

32 Therefore, behold, the days come, saith the LORD, that it shall no more be called Tophet, nor the valley of the son of Hinnom, but the valley of slaughter: for they shall bury in Tophet, till there be no place.   Jer. 19:6, 11

33 And the carcases of this people shall be meat for the fowls of the heaven, and for the beasts of the earth; and none shall ᵀfray *them* away.   Deut. 28:26; Jer. 12:9; 16:4 ♦ *scare*

34 Then will I cause to cease from the cities of Judah, and from the streets of Jerusalem, the voice of ᵀmirth, and the voice of gladness, the voice of the bridegroom, and the voice of the bride: for the land shall be desolate.   Lev. 26:33; Ezek. 26:13; Rev. 18:23 ♦ *gladness*

The Calamity Visited upon the People

8 At that time, saith the LORD, they shall bring out the bones of the kings of Judah, and the bones of his princes, and the bones of the priests, and the bones of the prophets, and the bones of the inhabitants of Jerusalem, out of their graves: Ezek. 6:5

2 And they shall spread them before the sun, and the moon, and all the host of heaven, whom they have loved, and whom they have served, and after whom they have walked, and whom they have sought, and whom they have worshipped: they shall not be gathered, nor be buried; they shall be for dung upon the face of the earth. 2 Kin. 23:5; Jer. 9:22; Acts 7:42

3 And death shall be chosen rather than life by all the residue of them that remain of this evil family, which remain in all the places whither I have driven them, saith the LORD of hosts.   Job 7:15-16; Jer. 23:3; Rev. 9:6

Judgment on False Religion

4 Moreover thou shalt say unto them, Thus saith the LORD; Shall they fall, and not arise? shall he turn away, and not return? Prov. 24:16

5 Why *then* is this people of Jerusalem slidden back by a perpetual backsliding? they hold fast deceit, they refuse to return.   Jer. 5:3; 9:6
6 I hearkened and heard, *but* they spake not aright: no man repented him of his wickedness, saying, What have I done? every one turned to his course, as the horse rusheth into the battle.   Ps. 14:2
7 Yea, the stork in the heaven knoweth her appointed times; and the ᵀturtle and the crane and the swallow observe the time of their coming; but my people know not the judgment of the LORD.   Song 2:12; Is. 1:3; Jer. 5:4-5 ◆ *dove*
8 How do ye say, We *are* wise, and the law of the LORD *is* with us? Lo, certainly in vain made he *it*; the pen of the scribes *is* in vain.
9 The wise *men* are ashamed, they are dismayed and taken: lo, they have rejected the word of the LORD; and what wisdom *is* in them?   Jer. 6:15
10 Therefore will I give their wives unto others, *and* their fields to them that shall inherit *them*: for every one from the least even unto the greatest is given to ᵀcovetousness, from the prophet even unto the priest every one dealeth falsely.   Jer. 6:12-13 ◆ *greed*
11 For they have healed the hurt of the daughter of my people slightly, saying, Peace, peace; when *there is* no peace.   Jer. 6:14
12 Were they ashamed when they had committed abomination? nay, they were not at all ashamed, neither could they blush: therefore shall they fall among them that fall: in the time of their visitation they shall be cast down, saith the LORD.   Ps. 52:7; Is. 3:9; Jer. 3:3
13 I will surely consume them, saith the LORD: *there shall be* no grapes on the vine, nor figs on the fig tree, and the leaf shall fade; and *the things that* I have given them shall pass away from them.   Joel 1:7; Matt. 21:19
14 Why do we sit still? assemble yourselves, and let us enter into the defenced cities, and let us be silent there: for the LORD our God

hath put us to silence, and given us water of ᵀgall to drink, because we have sinned against the LORD.   Jer. 9:15; 23:15; 35:11 ◆ *a bitter substance*
15 We looked for peace, but no good *came; and* for a time of health, and behold trouble!   Jer. 14:19
16 The snorting of his horses was heard from Dan: the whole land trembled at the sound of the neighing of his strong ones; for they are come, and have devoured the land, and all that is in it; the city, and those that dwell therein.   Judg. 5:22
17 For, behold, I will send serpents, ᵀcockatrices, among you, which *will* not *be* charmed, and they shall bite you, saith the LORD.   Deut. 32:24 ◆ *snakes*

Jeremiah's Grief over His People's Sin

18 *When* I would comfort myself against sorrow, my heart *is* faint in me.   Is. 22:4
19 Behold the voice of the cry of the daughter of my people because of them that dwell in a far country: *Is* not the LORD in Zion? *is* not her king in her? Why have they provoked me to anger with their ᵀgraven images, *and* with strange vanities?   Is. 39:3 ◆ *engraved* or *cut out*
20 The harvest is past, the summer is ended, and we are not saved.
21 For the hurt of the daughter of my people am I hurt; I am black; astonishment hath taken hold on me.   Jer. 14:17; Joel 2:6; Nah. 2:10
22 *Is there* no balm in Gilead; *is there* no physician there? why then is not the health of the daughter of my people recovered?   Gen. 37:25

Jeremiah Laments the Coming Judgment

9 Oh that my head were waters, and mine eyes a fountain of tears, that I might weep day and night for the slain of the daughter of my people!   Is. 22:4; Jer. 6:26; 13:17
2 Oh that I had in the wilderness a lodging place of wayfaring men; that I might leave

---

Share God's Love With the World

Jeremiah 8:22

All around us are heard the wails of a world's sorrow. On every hand are the needy and distressed. It is ours to aid in relieving and softening life's hardships and misery. The wants of the soul only the love of Christ can satisfy. If Christ is abiding in us, our hearts will be full of divine sympathy. The sealed fountains of earnest, Christlike love will be unsealed.

There are many from whom hope has departed. Bring back the sunshine to them. Many have lost their courage. Speak to them words of cheer. Pray for them. There are those who need the bread of life. Read to them from the word of God. Upon many is a soul sickness which no earthly balm can reach nor physician heal. Pray for these souls. Bring them to Jesus. Tell them that there is a balm in Gilead and a Physician there.

Light is a blessing, a universal blessing, pouring forth its treasures on a world unthankful, unholy, demoralized. So it is with the light of the Sun of Righteousness. The whole earth, wrapped as it is in the darkness of sin and sorrow and pain, is to be lighted with the knowledge of God's love. From no sect, rank, or class of people is the light shining from heaven's throne to be excluded. *PK 719*

my people, and go from them! for they *be* all adulterers, an assembly of treacherous men.   Jer. 5:7-8; 23:10; Hos. 4:2

3 And they bend their tongues *like* their bow *for* lies: but they are not valiant for the truth upon the earth; for they proceed from evil to evil, and they know not me, saith the LORD.   Judg. 2:10

4 Take ye heed every one of his neighbour, and trust ye not in any brother: for every brother will utterly ᵀsupplant, and every neighbour will walk with slanders.   Jer. 6:28 ◆ *deceive*

5 And they will deceive every one his neighbour, and will not speak the truth: they have taught their tongue to speak lies, *and* weary themselves to commit iniquity.   Mic. 6:12

6 Thine habitation *is* in the midst of deceit; through deceit they refuse to know me, saith the LORD.   Job 21:14-15

7 Therefore thus saith the LORD of hosts, Behold, I will melt them, and try them; for how shall I do for the daughter of my people?   Is. 1:25; Jer. 6:27; Mal. 3:3

8 Their tongue *is as* an arrow shot out; it speaketh deceit: *one* speaketh peaceably to his neighbour with his mouth, but in heart he layeth his wait.   Ps. 28:3

9 Shall I not visit them for these *things*? saith the LORD: shall not my soul be avenged on such a nation as this?   Is. 1:24; Jer. 5:9, 29

10 For the mountains will I take up a weeping and wailing, and for the habitations of the wilderness a lamentation, because they are burned up, so that none can pass through *them*; neither can *men* hear the voice of the cattle; both the fowl of the heavens and the beast are fled; they are gone. Jer. 7:29; 12:4; Hos. 4:3

11 And I will make Jerusalem heaps, *and* a den of dragons; and I will make the cities of Judah desolate, without an inhabitant.   Is. 25:2; 34:13

12 Who *is* the wise man, that may understand this? and *who is he* to whom the mouth of the LORD hath spoken, that he may declare it, for what the land perisheth *and* is burned up like a wilderness, that none passeth through?   Ps. 107:34, 43; Hos. 14:9

13 And the LORD saith, Because they have forsaken my law which I set before them, and have not obeyed my voice, neither walked therein;   2 Chr. 7:19

14 But have walked after the imagination of their own heart, and after Baalim, which their fathers taught them: Jer. 7:24

15 Therefore thus saith the LORD of hosts, the God of Israel; Behold, I will feed them, *even* this people, with wormwood, and give them water of gall to drink.   Ps. 80:5; Jer. 8:14; Lam. 3:15

16 I will scatter them also among the heathen, whom neither they nor their fathers have known: and I will send a sword after them, till I have consumed them. Lev. 26:33; Deut. 28:64

17 Thus saith the LORD of hosts, Consider ye, and call for the mourning women, that they may come; and send for cunning *women*, that they may come: 2 Chr. 35:25; Eccl. 12:5

18 And let them make haste, and take up a wailing for us, that our eyes may run down with tears, and our eyelids gush out with waters.   Is. 22:4; Jer. 9:1; 14:17

19 For a voice of wailing is heard out of Zion, How are we spoiled! we are greatly confounded, because we have forsaken the land, because our dwellings have cast *us* out.

20 Yet hear the word of the LORD, O ye women, and let your ear receive the word of his mouth, and teach your daughters wailing, and every one her neighbour lamentation.

21 For death is come up into our windows, *and* is entered into our palaces, to cut off the children from without, *and* the young men from the streets.   2 Chr. 36:17

22 Speak, Thus saith the LORD, Even the carcases of men shall fall as dung upon the open field, and as the handful after the harvestman, and none shall gather *them*.   Ps. 83:10

9:23, 24 Knowing God Is All-Important

Like our Saviour, we are in this world to do service for God. We are here to become like God in character, and by a life of service to reveal Him to the world. . . .

A knowledge of God is the foundation of all true education and of all true service. It is the only real safeguard against temptation. It is this alone that can make us like God in character. *MH 409*

The Lord Will Bring Justice

23 Thus saith the LORD, Let not the wise *man* glory in his wisdom, neither let the mighty *man* glory in his might, let not the rich *man* glory in his riches: 1 Kin. 20:10-11; Job 31:24-25

24 But let him that glorieth glory in this, that he understandeth and knoweth me, that I *am* the LORD which exercise lovingkindness, judgment, and righteousness, in the earth: for in these *things* I delight, saith the LORD.   Mic. 7:18; 1 Cor. 1:31; 2 Cor. 10:17

9:24 God Continues to Woo Us

The unwillingness of the Lord to chastise is here vividly shown. . . . He makes plain the fact that only by the most thorough heart reformation could the impending doom be averted. In vain would be the trust [the people] might place in the temple and its services. Rites and ceremonies could not atone for sin. Notwithstanding their claim to be the chosen people of God, reformation of heart and of the life practice alone could save them from the inevitable result of continued transgression. *PK 413, 414*

25 Behold, the days come, saith the LORD, that I will punish all *them which are* circumcised with the uncircumcised;   Rom. 2:8-9
26 Egypt, and Judah, and Edom, and the children of Ammon, and Moab, and all *that are* in the utmost corners, that dwell in the wilderness: for all *these* nations *are* uncircumcised, and all the house of Israel *are* uncircumcised in the heart.   Lev. 26:41; Jer. 4:4; Ezek. 44:7

The Lord Is the Only True God

10 Hear ye the word which the LORD speaketh unto you, O house of Israel:
2 Thus saith the LORD, Learn not the way of the heathen, and be not dismayed at the signs of heaven; for the heathen are dismayed at them.   Lev. 20:23
3 For the customs of the people *are* vain: for *one* cutteth a tree out of the forest, the work of the hands of the workman, with the axe.   Is. 44:9-20
4 They deck it with silver and with gold; they fasten it with nails and with hammers, that it move not.   Is. 40:19-20
5 They *are* upright as the palm tree, but speak not: they must needs be borne, because they cannot go. Be not afraid of them; for they cannot do evil, neither also *is it* in them to do good.   Is. 41:23-24; 46:7; 1 Cor. 12:2
6 Forasmuch as *there is* none like unto thee, O LORD; thou *art* great, and thy name *is* great in might.   Ex. 15:11
7 Who would not fear thee, O King of nations? for to thee doth it ᵀappertain: forasmuch as among all the wise *men* of the nations, and in all their kingdoms, *there is* none like unto thee.   Ps. 22:28; Jer. 5:22; Rev. 15:4 ◆ *belong*
8 But they are altogether brutish and foolish: the stock *is* a doctrine of vanities. Is. 41:29
9 Silver spread into plates is brought from Tarshish, and gold from Uphaz, the work of the workman, and of the hands of the founder: blue and purple *is* their clothing: they *are* all the work of cunning *men*.   1 Kin. 10:22; Ps. 115:4
10 But the LORD *is* the true God, he *is* the living God, and an everlasting king: at his wrath the earth shall tremble, and the nations shall not be able to abide his indignation.
11 Thus shall ye say unto them, The gods that have not made the heavens and the earth, *even* they shall perish from the earth, and from under these heavens.   Ps. 96:5; Is. 2:18; Jer. 10:15
12 He hath made the earth by his power, he hath established the world by his wisdom, and hath stretched out the heavens by his discretion.   Gen. 1:1; Job 9:8; Is. 40:22

10:10–12 Things Created Are Not the Creator

The mighty power that works through all nature and sustains all things is not, as some men of science represent, merely an all-pervading principle, an actuating energy. God is a Spirit; yet He is a personal Being; for so He has revealed Himself: "The Lord is the true God, He is the living God, and an everlasting King" (Jeremiah 10:10). . . .

So while nature is an expression of God's thought, it is not nature, but the God of nature, that is to be exalted. *MH 413*

---

13 When he uttereth his voice, *there is* a multitude of waters in the heavens, and he causeth the vapours to ascend from the ends of the earth; he maketh lightnings with rain, and bringeth forth the wind out of his treasures.   Job 38:22, 34-35; Ps. 135:7
14 Every man is brutish in *his* knowledge: every founder is confounded by the ᵀgraven image: for his molten image *is* falsehood, and *there is* no breath in them.   *engraved or cut out*
15 They *are* vanity, *and* the work of errors: in the time of their visitation they shall perish.   Is. 41:24

Science and the Word

Jeremiah 10:12, 13

God is the foundation of everything. All true science is in harmony with His works; all true education leads to obedience to His government. Science opens new wonders to our view; she soars high, and explores new depths; but she brings nothing from her research that conflicts with divine revelation. Ignorance may seek to support false views of God by appeals to science, but the book of nature and the written word shed light upon each other. We are thus led to adore the Creator and to have an intelligent trust in His word.

No finite mind can fully comprehend the existence, the power, the wisdom, or the works of the Infinite One. Says the sacred writer: "Canst thou by searching find out God? canst thou find out the Almighty unto perfection? It is as high as heaven; what canst thou do? deeper than hell; what canst thou know? The measure thereof is longer than the earth, and broader than the sea" (Job 11:7–9). The mightiest intellects of earth cannot comprehend God. Men may be ever searching, ever learning, and still there is an infinity beyond.

Yet the works of creation testify of God's power and greatness. "The heavens declare the glory of God; and the firmament showeth His handiwork" (Psalm 19:1). Those who take the written word as their counselor will find in science an aid to understand God. *PP 115, 116*

It is not by inherent power that year by year the earth yields its bounties and continues its march around the sun. The hand of the Infinite One is perpetually at work guiding this planet. It is God's power continually exercised that keeps the earth in position in its rotation. It is God who causes the sun to rise in the heavens. He opens the windows of heaven and gives rain. *MH 416*

16 The portion of Jacob *is* not like them: for he *is* the former of all *things*; and Israel *is* the rod of his inheritance: The LORD of hosts *is* his name.   Deut. 32:9; Jer. 31:35; 32:18
17 Gather up thy wares out of the land, O inhabitant of the fortress.   Ezek. 12:3-12
18 For thus saith the LORD, Behold, I will sling out the inhabitants of the land at this once, and will distress them, that they may find *it so*.   1 Sam. 25:29
19 Woe is me for my hurt! my wound is grievous: but I said, Truly this *is* a grief, and I must bear it.   Mic. 7:9
20 My tabernacle is spoiled, and all my cords are broken: my children are gone forth of me, and they *are* not: *there is* none to stretch forth my tent any more, and to set up my curtains.   Is. 54:2; Jer. 4:20; 31:15
21 For the pastors are become ᵀbrutish, and have not sought the LORD: therefore they shall not prosper, and all their flocks shall be scattered.   Jer. 2:8 ◆ senseless
22 Behold, the noise of the ᵀbruit is come, and a great commotion out of the north country, to make the cities of Judah desolate, *and* a den of dragons.   Jer. 9:11 ◆ news
23 O LORD, I know that the way of man *is* not in himself: *it is* not in man that walketh to direct his steps.   Prov. 16:1; 20:24
24 O LORD, correct me, but with judgment; not in thine anger, lest thou bring me to nothing.   Ps. 6:1; 38:1; Jer. 30:11
25 Pour out thy fury upon the heathen that know thee not, and upon the families that call not on thy name: for they have eaten up Jacob, and devoured him, and consumed him, and have made his habitation desolate.   Job 18:21; Ps. 79:6-7; Jer. 8:16

Judah Has Disobeyed God's Covenant

11 The word that came to Jeremiah from the LORD, saying,
2 Hear ye the words of this covenant, and speak unto the men of Judah, and to the inhabitants of Jerusalem;   Jer. 11:6
3 And say thou unto them, Thus saith the LORD God of Israel; Cursed *be* the man that obeyeth not the words of this covenant,
4 Which I commanded your fathers in the day *that* I brought them forth out of the land

of Egypt, from the iron furnace, saying, Obey my voice, and do them, according to all which I command you: so shall ye be my people, and I will be your God: Lev. 26:3, 12; Deut. 4:20

Only as a reverence for God's Holy Word was cherished in the hearts of the people, could they hope to fulfill the divine purpose. It was regard for the law of God that gave Israel strength during the reign of David and the earlier years of Solomon's rule; it was through faith in the living word that reformation was wrought in the days of Elijah and of Josiah. And it was to these same Scriptures of truth, Israel's richest heritage, that Jeremiah appealed in his efforts toward reform. *PK 465, 466*

5 That I may perform the oath which I have sworn unto your fathers, to give them a land flowing with milk and honey, as *it is* this day. Then answered I, and said, So be it, O LORD.   Deut. 7:12-13
6 Then the LORD said unto me, Proclaim all these words in the cities of Judah, and in the streets of Jerusalem, saying, Hear ye the words of this covenant, and do them.   Rom. 2:13
7 For I earnestly protested unto your fathers in the day *that* I brought them up out of the land of Egypt, *even* unto this day, rising early and protesting, saying, Obey my voice.   Ex. 15:26
8 Yet they obeyed not, nor inclined their ear, but walked every one in the imagination of their evil heart: therefore I will bring upon them all the words of this covenant, which I commanded *them* to do; but they did *them* not.   Jer. 3:17; 7:24, 26
9 And the LORD said unto me, A conspiracy is found among the men of Judah, and among the inhabitants of Jerusalem.   Hos. 6:9
10 They are turned back to the iniquities of their forefathers, which refused to hear my words; and they went after other gods to serve them: the house of Israel and the house of Judah have broken my covenant which I made with their fathers.   Deut. 31:16
11 Therefore thus saith the LORD, Behold, I will bring evil upon them, which they shall not be able to escape; and though they shall cry unto me, I will not hearken unto them.   Prov. 1:28; Is. 1:15; Ezek. 8:18
12 Then shall the cities of Judah and inhabitants of Jerusalem go, and cry unto the gods unto whom they offer incense: but they shall not save them at all in the time of their trouble.   Deut. 32:37
13 For *according to* the number of thy cities were thy gods, O Judah; and *according to* the number of the streets of Jerusalem have ye

set up altars to *that* shameful thing, *even* altars to burn incense unto Baal.   2 Kin. 23:13
14 Therefore pray not thou for this people, neither lift up a cry or prayer for them: for I will not hear *them* in the time that they cry unto me for their trouble. Ex. 32:10; Jer. 7:16; 11:11
15 What hath my beloved to do in mine house, *seeing* she hath ᵀwrought lewdness with many, and the holy flesh is passed from thee? when thou doest evil, then thou rejoicest.   Prov. 2:14 ◆ committed
16 The LORD called thy name, A green olive tree, fair, *and* of goodly fruit: with the noise of a great tumult he hath kindled fire upon it, and the branches of it are broken. Ps. 52:8
17 For the LORD of hosts, that planted thee, hath pronounced evil against thee, for the evil of the house of Israel and of the house of Judah, which they have done against themselves to provoke me to anger in offering incense unto Baal.   Is. 5:2; Jer. 2:21; 12:2

Jeremiah's Life Is Threatened

18 And the LORD hath given me knowledge *of it,* and I know *it:* then thou shewedst me their doings.   1 Sam. 23:11-12
19 But I *was* like a lamb *or* an ox *that* is brought to the slaughter; and I knew not that they had devised devices against me, *saying,* Let us destroy the tree with the fruit thereof, and let us cut him off from the land of the living, that his name may be no more remembered.   Job 28:13; Ps. 83:4; Jer. 18:18
20 But, O LORD of hosts, that judgest righteously, that triest the reins and the heart, let me see thy vengeance on them: for unto thee have I revealed my cause.   1 Sam. 16:7; Ps. 7:9
21 Therefore thus saith the LORD of the men of Anathoth, that seek thy life, saying, Prophesy not in the name of the LORD, that thou die not by our hand: Is. 30:10
22 Therefore thus saith the LORD of hosts, Behold, I will punish them: the young men shall die by the sword; their sons and their daughters shall die by famine: Jer. 18:21
23 And there shall be no remnant of them: for I will bring evil upon the men of Anathoth, *even* the year of their visitation. Jer. 23:12; Hos. 9:7

12:1 True Character of Wicked Revealed

God permits the wicked to prosper and to reveal their enmity against Him, that when they shall have filled up the measure of their iniquity all may see His justice and mercy in their utter destruction. The day of His vengeance hastens, when all who have transgressed His law and oppressed His people will meet the just recompense of their deeds; when every act of cruelty or injustice toward God's faithful ones will be punished as though done to Christ Himself. *GC 48*

Jeremiah's Question

12 Righteous *art* thou, O LORD, when I plead with thee: yet let me talk with thee of *thy* judgments: Wherefore doth the way of the wicked prosper? *wherefore* are all they happy that deal very treacherously?
2 Thou hast planted them, yea, they have taken root: they grow, yea, they bring forth fruit: thou *art* near in their mouth, and far from their ᵀreins. Is. 29:13; Jer. 11:17; Titus 1:16 ◆ hearts
3 But thou, O LORD, knowest me: thou hast seen me, and tried mine heart toward thee: pull them out like sheep for the slaughter, and prepare them for the day of slaughter. Jer. 17:18
4 How long shall the land mourn, and the herbs of every field wither, for the wickedness of them that dwell therein? the beasts are consumed, and the birds; because they said, He shall not see our last end. Jer. 4:25; 9:10

The Lord's Reply

5 If thou hast run with the footmen, and they have wearied thee, then how canst thou contend with horses? and *if* in the land of peace, *wherein* thou trustedst, *they wearied thee,* then how wilt thou do in the swelling of Jordan?   Josh. 3:15; Jer. 49:19; 50:44
6 For even thy brethren, and the house of thy father, even they have dealt treacherously with thee; yea, they have called a multitude after thee: believe them not, though they speak fair words unto thee.   Ps. 12:2; Prov. 26:25
7 I have forsaken mine house, I have left mine heritage; I have given the dearly beloved of my soul into the hand of her enemies.   Jer. 11:15
8 Mine heritage is unto me as a lion in the forest; it crieth out against me: therefore have I hated it.   Hos. 9:15
9 Mine heritage *is* unto me *as* a speckled bird, the birds round about *are* against her; come ye, assemble all the beasts of the field, come to devour.   2 Kin. 24:2; Is. 56:9; Jer. 7:33
10 Many pastors have destroyed my vineyard, they have ᵀtrodden my portion under foot, they have made my pleasant portion a desolate wilderness.   Is. 5:1-7 ◆ trampled
11 They have made it desolate, *and being* desolate it mourneth unto me; the whole land is made desolate, because no man layeth *it* to heart.   Is. 42:25; Jer. 14:2; 23:10
12 The spoilers are come upon all high places through the wilderness: for the sword of the LORD shall devour from the *one* end of the land even to the *other* end of the land: no flesh shall have peace.   Jer. 47:6
13 They have sown wheat, but shall reap thorns: they have put themselves to pain, *but* shall not profit: and they shall be ashamed of your revenues because of the fierce anger of the LORD.   Deut. 28:38; Mic. 6:15; Hag. 1:6

God Promises the Penitent They Will Return

14 Thus saith the LORD against all mine evil neighbours, that touch the inheritance which I have caused my people Israel to inherit; Behold, I will pluck them out of their land, and pluck out the house of Judah from among them.   Deut. 30:3; Ps. 106:47; Zech. 2:8
15 And it shall come to pass, after that I have plucked them out I will return, and have compassion on them, and will bring them again, every man to his heritage, and every man to his land.   Jer. 48:47; 49:6, 39
16 And it shall come to pass, if they will diligently learn the ways of my people, to swear by my name, The LORD liveth; as they taught my people to swear by Baal; then shall they be built in the midst of my people. Josh. 23:7; Jer. 4:2
17 But if they will not obey, I will utterly pluck up and destroy that nation, saith the LORD.   Ps. 2:8-12; Is. 60:12

Jeremiah's Linen Belt

13 Thus saith the LORD unto me, Go and get thee a linen girdle, and put it upon thy loins, and put it not in water.   Jer. 13:11
2 So I got a girdle according to the word of the LORD, and put it on my loins.   Is. 20:2
3 And the word of the LORD came unto me the second time, saying,
4 Take the girdle that thou hast got, which is upon thy Tloins, and arise, go to Euphrates, and hide it there in a hole of the rock.   waist
5 So I went, and hid it by Euphrates, as the LORD commanded me.   Ex. 40:16
6 And it came to pass after many days, that the LORD said unto me, Arise, go to Euphrates, and take the Tgirdle from thence, which I commanded thee to hide there.   belt
7 Then I went to Euphrates, and digged, and took the girdle from the place where I had hid it: and, behold, the girdle was marred, it was profitable for nothing.
8 Then the word of the LORD came unto me, saying,
9 Thus saith the LORD, After this manner will I mar the pride of Judah, and the great pride of Jerusalem.   Lev. 26:19; Is. 2:10-17; 23:9
10 This evil people, which refuse to hear my words, which walk in the imagination of their heart, and walk after other gods, to serve them, and to worship them, shall even be as this girdle, which is good for nothing.   Num. 14:11; Jer. 9:14; 16:12
11 For as the girdle Tcleaveth to the loins of a man, so have I caused to cleave unto me the whole house of Israel and the whole house of Judah, saith the LORD; that they might be unto me for a people, and for a name, and for a praise, and for a glory: but they would not hear.   Ex. 19:5-6; Ps. 81:11; Jer. 33:9 ◆ stays close to

12 Therefore thou shalt speak unto them this word; Thus saith the LORD God of Israel, Every bottle shall be filled with wine: and they shall say unto thee, Do we not certainly know that every bottle shall be filled with wine?
13 Then shalt thou say unto them, Thus saith the LORD, Behold, I will fill all the inhabitants of this land, even the kings that sit upon David's throne, and the priests, and the prophets, and all the inhabitants of Jerusalem, with drunkenness.   Ps. 60:3
14 And I will dash them one against another, even the fathers and the sons together, saith the LORD: I will not pity, nor spare, nor have mercy, but destroy them.   Deut. 29:20
15 Hear ye, and give ear; be not proud: for the LORD hath spoken.   Is. 28:14-22
16 Give glory to the LORD your God, before he cause darkness, and before your feet stumble upon the dark mountains, and, while ye look for light, he turn it into the shadow of death, and make it Tgross darkness.   Josh. 7:19; Is. 5:30; 59:9 ◆ thick
17 But if ye will not hear it, my soul shall weep in secret places for your pride; and mine eye shall weep sore, and run down with tears, because the LORD's flock is carried away captive.   Ps. 80:1; Jer. 9:1; 14:17
18 Say unto the king and to the queen, Humble yourselves, sit down: for your principalities shall come down, even the crown of your glory.   2 Kin. 24:12
19 The cities of the south shall be shut up, and none shall open them: Judah shall be carried away captive all of it, it shall be wholly carried away captive.   Jer. 52:27
20 Lift up your eyes, and behold them that come from the north: where is the flock that was given thee, thy beautiful flock?   Hab. 1:6

13:20 Shepherds of the Church

The church of Christ has been purchased with His blood, and every shepherd should realize that the sheep under his care cost an infinite sacrifice. He should regard them each as of priceless worth, and should be unwearied in his efforts to keep them in a healthy, flourishing condition. The shepherd who is imbued with the spirit of Christ will imitate His self-denying example, constantly laboring for the welfare of his charge; and the flock will prosper under his care. PP 192

21 What wilt thou say when he shall punish thee? for thou hast taught them to be captains, and as chief over thee: shall not sorrows take thee, as a woman in travail? Is. 13:8
22 And if thou say in thine heart, Wherefore come these things upon me? For the greatness

of thine iniquity are thy skirts discovered, *and* thy heels made bare.   Deut. 7:17; Nah. 3:5

23 Can the Ethiopian change his skin, or the leopard his spots? *then* may ye also do good, that are accustomed to do evil.   Prov. 27:22

24 Therefore will I scatter them as the stubble that passeth away by the wind of the wilderness.   Lev. 26:33

25 This *is* thy lot, the portion of thy measures from me, saith the LORD; because thou hast forgotten me, and trusted in falsehood.   Job 20:29; Ps. 11:6; Jer. 2:32

26 Therefore will I discover thy skirts upon thy face, that thy shame may appear.   Lam. 1:8

27 I have seen thine adulteries, and thy neighings, the lewdness of thy ᵀwhoredom, *and* thine abominations on the hills in the fields. Woe unto thee, O Jerusalem! wilt thou not be made clean? when *shall it* once *be?*   Ezek. 6:13 ◆ prostitution

The Grievous Famine

14 The word of the LORD that came to Jeremiah concerning the ᵀdearth.   famine

2 Judah mourneth, and the gates thereof ᵀlanguish; they are black unto the ground; and the cry of Jerusalem is gone up.   1 Sam. 5:12 ◆ weaken

3 And their nobles have sent their little ones to the waters: they came to the pits, *and* found no water; they returned with their vessels empty; they were ashamed and confounded, and covered their heads.   2 Sam. 15:30; 2 Kin. 18:31

4 Because the ground is chapt, for there was no rain in the earth, the plowmen were ashamed, they covered their heads.   Jer. 3:3

5 Yea, the hind also calved in the field, and forsook *it*, because there was no grass. Ps. 29:9

6 And the wild asses did stand in the high places, they snuffed up the wind like dragons; their eyes did fail, because *there was* no grass.   Job 39:5-6; Jer. 2:24; Joel 1:18

7 O LORD, though our iniquities testify against us, do thou *it* for thy name's sake: for our backslidings are many; we have sinned against thee.   Ps. 25:11

8 O the hope of Israel, the saviour thereof in time of trouble, why shouldest thou be as a stranger in the land, and as a wayfaring man *that* turneth aside to tarry for a night?   Ps. 9:9

14:9 Representing God to the World

God sends you into the world as His representative. In every act of life you are to make manifest the name of God. This petition calls upon you to possess His character. You cannot hallow His name, you cannot represent Him to the world, unless in life and character you represent the very life and character of God. This you can do only through the acceptance of the grace and righteousness of Christ. *MB 107*

---

9 Why shouldest thou be as a man ᵀastonied, as a mighty man *that* cannot save? yet thou, O LORD, *art* in the midst of us, and we are called by thy name; leave us not.   Is. 59:1 ◆ surprised

The Lord Refuses to Hear

10 Thus saith the LORD unto this people, Thus have they loved to wander, they have not refrained their feet, therefore the LORD doth not accept them; he will now remember their iniquity, and visit their sins.   Ps. 119:101

11 Then said the LORD unto me, Pray not for this people for *their* good.   Jer. 7:16

12 When they fast, I will not hear their cry; and when they offer burnt offering and an oblation, I will not accept them: but I will consume them by the sword, and by the famine, and by the pestilence.   Prov. 1:28; Jer. 6:20

13 Then said I, Ah, Lord GOD! behold, the prophets say unto them, Ye shall not see the sword, neither shall ye have famine; but I will give you assured peace in this place.   Jer. 6:14

14 Then the LORD said unto me, The prophets prophesy lies in my name: I sent them not, neither have I commanded them, neither spake unto them: they prophesy unto you a false vision and ᵀdivination, and a thing of ᵀnought, and the deceit of their heart.   Jer. 27:9-10 ◆ false magic ◆ no value

15 Therefore thus saith the LORD concerning the prophets that prophesy in my name, and I sent them not, yet they say, Sword and famine shall not be in this land; By sword and famine shall those prophets be consumed.   Jer. 5:12-13

16 And the people to whom they prophesy shall be cast out in the streets of Jerusalem because of the famine and the sword; and they shall have none to bury them, them, their wives, nor their sons, nor their daughters: for I will pour their wickedness upon them.   Prov. 1:31

Jeremiah Voices Their Complaint

17 Therefore thou shalt say this word unto them; Let mine eyes run down with tears night and day, and let them not cease: for the virgin daughter of my people is broken with a great breach, with a very grievous blow.   Jer. 8:21; 9:1; 13:17

18 If I go forth into the field, then behold the slain with the sword! and if I enter into the city, then behold them that are sick with famine! yea, both the prophet and the priest go about into a land that they know not.   Jer. 5:31; 6:13; Ezek. 7:15

19 Hast thou utterly rejected Judah? hath thy soul lothed Zion? why hast thou smitten us, and *there is* no healing for us? we looked for peace, and *there is* no good; and for the time of healing, and behold trouble!   Job 30:26; Jer. 8:15

20 We acknowledge, O LORD, our wickedness, *and* the iniquity of our fathers: for we have sinned against thee. Neh. 9:2

21 Do not abhor *us*, for thy name's sake, do not disgrace the throne of thy glory: remember, break not thy covenant with us. Ps. 106:45

22 Are there *any* among the vanities of the Gentiles that can cause rain? or can the heavens give showers? *art* not thou he, O LORD our God? therefore we will wait upon thee: for thou hast made all these *things*. Deut. 32:21; 1 Kin. 17:1; Is. 30:23

God's Rejection of His People

15 Then said the LORD unto me, Though Moses and Samuel stood before me, *yet* my mind *could* not *be* toward this people: cast *them* out of my sight, and let them go forth. 1 Sam. 7:9; Ps. 99:6; Ezek. 14:14

2 And it shall come to pass, if they say unto thee, Whither shall we go forth? then thou shalt tell them, Thus saith the LORD; Such as *are* for death, to death; and such as *are* for the sword, to the sword; and such as *are* for the famine, to the famine; and such as *are* for the captivity, to the captivity. Ezek. 5:12

15:1, 2 Intercession Almost Over With

The time had come for deep heart searching. . . . The sins of the nation were such that the time for intercession had all but passed by. . . .

A refusal to heed the invitation of mercy that God was now offering would bring upon the impenitent nation the judgments that had befallen the northern kingdom of Israel over a century before. *PK 415*

---

3 And I will appoint over them four kinds, saith the LORD: the sword to slay, and the dogs to tear, and the fowls of the heaven, and the beasts of the earth, to devour and destroy. Lev. 26:16, 22; Deut. 28:26

4 And I will cause them to be removed into all kingdoms of the earth, because of Manasseh the son of Hezekiah king of Judah, for *that* which he did in Jerusalem. Deut. 28:25; Jer. 24:9

5 For who shall have pity upon thee, O Jerusalem? or who shall bemoan thee? or who shall go aside to ask how thou doest? Is. 51:19

6 Thou hast forsaken me, saith the LORD, thou art gone backward: therefore will I stretch out my hand against thee, and destroy thee; I am weary with repenting. Is. 1:4; Jer. 7:24; Zeph. 1:4

7 And I will ᵀfan them with a fan in the gates of the land; I will bereave *them* of children, I will destroy my people, *since* they return not from their ways. Is. 9:13 ◆ *winnow*

8 Their widows are increased to me above the sand of the seas: I have brought upon them against the mother of the young men a spoiler at noonday: I have caused *him* to fall upon it suddenly, and terrors upon the city. Is. 3:25–4:1

9 She that hath borne seven ᵀlanguisheth: she hath given up the ghost; her sun is gone down while *it was* yet day: she hath been ashamed and confounded: and the residue of them will I deliver to the sword before their enemies, saith the LORD. 1 Sam. 2:5; Is. 47:9; Lam. 1:1 ◆ *weakens*

Jeremiah Complains Bitterly

10 Woe is me, my mother, that thou hast borne me a man of strife and a man of contention to the whole earth! I have neither lent on ᵀusury, nor men have lent to me on usury; *yet* every one of them doth curse me. Ex. 22:25 ◆ *interest charged*

11 The LORD said, Verily it shall be well with thy remnant; ᵀverily I will cause the enemy to ᵀentreat thee *well* in the time of evil and in the time of affliction. *truly* ◆ *treat*

12 Shall iron break the northern iron and the steel?

13 Thy substance and thy treasures will I give to the spoil without price, and *that* for all thy sins, even in all thy borders. Ps. 44:12; Is. 52:3

14 And I will make *thee* to pass with thine enemies into a land *which* thou knowest not: for a fire is kindled in mine anger, *which* shall burn upon you. Deut. 28:36; 32:22; Jer. 16:13

Jeremiah Prays

15 O LORD, thou knowest: remember me, and visit me, and revenge me of my persecutors; take me not away in thy longsuffering: know that for thy sake I have suffered rebuke. Ps. 69:7-9; Jer. 12:3; 17:16

16 Thy words were found, and I did eat them; and thy word was unto me the joy and rejoicing of mine heart: for I am called by thy name, O LORD God of hosts. Job 23:12; Ps. 119:72; Jer. 14:9

17 I sat not in the assembly of the mockers, nor rejoiced; I sat alone because of thy hand: for thou hast filled me with ᵀindignation. Ps. 1:1 ◆ *anger*

18 Why is my pain perpetual, and my wound incurable, *which* refuseth to be healed? wilt thou be altogether unto me as a liar, *and as* waters *that* fail? Job 34:6; Jer. 30:15; Mic. 1:9

19 Therefore thus saith the LORD, If thou return, then will I bring thee again, *and* thou shalt stand before me: and if thou take forth the precious from the vile, thou shalt be as my mouth: let them return unto thee; but return not thou unto them. Jer. 15:1

20 And I will make thee unto this people a fenced brasen wall: and they shall fight against thee, but they shall not prevail against thee: for I *am* with thee to save thee and to deliver thee, saith the LORD. Jer. 1:18-19

21 And I will deliver thee out of the hand of

the wicked, and I will redeem thee out of the hand of the terrible.   Gen. 48:16

Jeremiah Must Not Marry

16 The word of the LORD came also unto me, saying,

2 Thou shalt not take thee a wife, neither shalt thou have sons or daughters in this place.   1 Cor. 7:26-27

3 For thus saith the LORD concerning the sons and concerning the daughters that are born in this place, and concerning their mothers that bare them, and concerning their fathers that ᵀbegat them in this land;   *brought forth*

4 They shall die of grievous deaths; they shall not be lamented; neither shall they be buried; *but* they shall be as dung upon the face of the earth: and they shall be consumed by the sword, and by famine; and their carcases shall be meat for the fowls of heaven, and for the beasts of the earth.   Ps. 83:10; Jer. 9:22; 25:33

5 For thus saith the LORD, Enter not into the house of mourning, neither go to lament nor bemoan them: for I have taken away my peace from this people, saith the LORD, *even* lovingkindness and mercies.   Ezek. 24:16-23

6 Both the great and the small shall die in this land: they shall not be buried, neither shall *men* lament for them, nor cut themselves, nor make themselves bald for them: Lev. 19:28

7 Neither shall *men* tear *themselves* for them in mourning, to comfort them for the dead; neither shall *men* give them the cup of consolation to drink for their father or for their mother.   Deut. 26:14; Ezek. 24:17; Hos. 9:4

8 Thou shalt not also go into the house of feasting, to sit with them to eat and to drink.   Eccl. 7:2-4

9 For thus saith the LORD of hosts, the God of Israel; Behold, I will cause to cease out of this place in your eyes, and in your days, the voice of ᵀmirth, and the voice of gladness, the voice of the bridegroom, and the voice of the bride.   Jer. 7:34 ◆ *gladness*

Answers to Why

10 And it shall come to pass, when thou shalt shew this people all these words, and they shall say unto thee, Wherefore hath the LORD pronounced all this great evil against us? or what *is* our iniquity? or what *is* our sin that we have committed against the LORD our God?   Jer. 5:19; 13:22

11 Then shalt thou say unto them, Because your fathers have forsaken me, saith the LORD, and have walked after other gods, and have served them, and have worshipped them, and have forsaken me, and have not kept my law;   Ps. 106:35-41

12 And ye have done worse than your fathers; for, behold, ye walk every one after the imagination of his evil heart, that they may not hearken unto me: Eccl. 9:3; Jer. 7:26; 13:10

13 Therefore will I cast you out of this land into a land that ye know not, *neither* ye nor your fathers; and there shall ye serve other gods day and night; where I will not shew you favour.   Deut. 4:26-28; 28:36; Jer. 17:4

14 Therefore, behold, the days come, saith the LORD, that it shall no more be said, The LORD liveth, that brought up the children of Israel out of the land of Egypt;   Deut. 15:15

15 But, The LORD liveth, that brought up the children of Israel from the land of the north, and from all the lands whither he had driven them: and I will bring them again into their land that I gave unto their fathers.   Ps. 106:47

16 Behold, I will send for many fishers, saith the LORD, and they shall fish them; and after will I send for many hunters, and they shall hunt them from every mountain, and from every hill, and out of the holes of the rocks.   1 Sam. 26:20; Amos 4:2; Mic. 7:2

17 For mine eyes *are* upon all their ways: they are not hid from my face, neither is their iniquity hid from mine eyes.   2 Chr. 16:9; Ps. 90:8

18 And first I will ᵀrecompense their iniquity and their sin double; because they have defiled my land, they have filled mine inheritance with the carcases of their detestable and abominable things.   Is. 40:2 ◆ *repay*

19 O LORD, my strength, and my fortress, and my refuge in the day of affliction, the Gentiles shall come unto thee from the ends of the earth, and shall say, Surely our fathers have inherited lies, vanity, and *things* wherein *there is* no profit.   Is. 25:4

20 Shall a man make gods unto himself, and they *are* no gods?   Is. 37:19

21 Therefore, behold, I will this once cause them to know, I will cause them to know mine hand and my might; and they shall know that my name *is* The LORD.   Jer. 33:2

The Captivity of Judah

17 The sin of Judah *is* written with a pen of iron, *and* with the point of a diamond: *it is* graven upon the table of their heart, and upon the horns of your altars;   Prov. 3:3; 7:3

2 Whilst their children remember their altars and their ᵀgroves by the green trees upon the high hills.   2 Chr. 24:18 ◆ *idols*

3 O my mountain in the field, I will give thy substance *and* all thy treasures to the ᵀspoil, *and* thy high places for sin, throughout all thy borders.   2 Kin. 24:13; Jer. 15:13; 26:18 ◆ *plunder*

4 And thou, even thyself, shalt discontinue from thine heritage that I gave thee; and I will cause thee to serve thine enemies in the land which thou knowest not: for ye have kindled a fire in mine anger, *which* shall burn for ever.   Jer. 7:20; 15:14; 16:13

Do Not Trust in Humans

5 Thus saith the LORD; Cursed *be* the man that trusteth in man, and maketh flesh his arm, and whose heart departeth from the LORD.   2 Chr. 32:8

17:5 Look to Jesus, Not Other People

We are prone to look to our fellow men for sympathy and uplifting, instead of looking to Jesus. In His mercy and faithfulness God often permits those in whom we place confidence to fail us, in order that we may learn the folly of trusting in man and making flesh our arm. Let us trust fully, humbly, unselfishly in God. He knows the sorrows that we feel to the depths of our being, but which we cannot express. *MH 486, 487*

---

6 For he shall be like the heath in the desert, and shall not see when good cometh; but shall inhabit the parched places in the wilderness, *in* a salt land and not inhabited.   Deut. 29:23; Job 20:17; Jer. 48:6

7 Blessed *is* the man that trusteth in the LORD, and whose hope the LORD is.   Ps. 2:12; 34:8

8 For he shall be as a tree planted by the waters, and *that* spreadeth out her roots by the river, and shall not see when heat cometh, but her leaf shall be green; and shall not be careful in the year of drought, neither shall cease from yielding fruit.   Ps. 1:3; Ezek. 47:12

9 The heart *is* deceitful above all *things*, and desperately wicked: who can know it? Eccl. 9:3

10 I the LORD search the heart, *I* try the ᵀreins, even to give every man according to his ways, *and* according to the fruit of his doings.   1 Sam. 16:7; Ps. 62:12; Jer. 32:19 ♦ *desires*

11 *As* the partridge sitteth *on eggs*, and hatcheth *them* not; *so* he that getteth riches, and not by right, shall leave them in the midst of his days, and at his end shall be a fool.   Ps. 55:23

17:9 How to See Ourselves Accurately

No man can of himself understand his errors. . . . In one way only can a true knowledge of self be obtained. We must behold Christ. . . . When we contemplate His purity and excellence, we shall see our own weakness and poverty and defects as they really are. We shall see ourselves lost and hopeless. . . . We shall see that if we are ever saved, it will not be through our own goodness, but through God's infinite grace. *COL 159*

Hope and Salvation Are to Be Found in God

12 A glorious high throne from the beginning *is* the place of our sanctuary.   Jer. 3:17

13 O LORD, the hope of Israel, all that forsake thee shall be ashamed, *and* they that depart from me shall be written in the earth, because they have forsaken the LORD, the fountain of living waters.   Is. 1:28; Jer. 14:8; Luke 10:20

14 Heal me, O LORD, and I shall be healed; save me, and I shall be saved: for thou *art* my praise.   Deut. 10:21

15 Behold, they say unto me, Where *is* the word of the LORD? let it come now.   Is. 5:19

16 As for me, I have not hastened from *being* a pastor to follow thee: neither have I desired the woeful day; thou knowest: that which came out of my lips was *right* before thee.

17 Be not a terror unto me: thou *art* my hope in the day of evil.   Ps. 88:15-16; Jer. 16:19; Nah. 1:7

18 Let them be confounded that persecute me, but let not me be confounded: let them

---

The Heart Is Desperately Wicked; Who Can Know It?

Jeremiah 17:9

No man can of himself understand his errors. "The heart is deceitful above all things, and desperately wicked; who can know it?" (Jeremiah 17:9). The lips may express a poverty of soul that the heart does not acknowledge. While speaking to God of poverty of spirit, the heart may be swelling with the conceit of its own superior humility and exalted righteousness. In one way only can a true knowledge of self be obtained. We must behold Christ. It is ignorance of Him that makes men so uplifted in their own righteousness. When we contemplate His purity and excellence, we shall see our own weakness and poverty and defects as they really are. We shall see ourselves lost and hopeless, clad in garments of self-righteousness, like every other sinner. We shall see that if we are ever saved, it will not be through our own goodness, but through God's infinite grace.

The prayer of the publican was heard because it showed dependence reaching forth to lay hold upon Omnipotence. Self to the publican appeared nothing but shame. Thus it must be seen by all who seek God. By faith—faith that renounces all self-trust—the needy suppliant is to lay hold upon infinite power.

No outward observances can take the place of simple faith and entire renunciation of self. But no man can empty himself of self. We can only consent for Christ to accomplish the work. . . .

It is not only at the beginning of the Christian life that this renunciation of self is to be made. At every advance step heavenward it is to be renewed. All our good works are dependent on a power outside of ourselves. *COL 159, 160*

be dismayed, but let not me be dismayed: bring upon them the day of evil, and destroy them with double destruction. Ps. 35:4, 8; 40:14

Remember the Sabbath

19 Thus said the LORD unto me; Go and stand in the gate of the children of the people, whereby the kings of Judah come in, and by the which they go out, and in all the gates of Jerusalem;   Jer. 7:2
20 And say unto them, Hear ye the word of the LORD, ye kings of Judah, and all Judah, and all the inhabitants of Jerusalem, that enter in by these gates: Jer. 19:3
21 Thus saith the LORD; Take heed to yourselves, and bear no burden on the sabbath day, nor bring it in by the gates of Jerusalem;   Num. 15:32-36
22 Neither carry forth a burden out of your houses on the sabbath day, neither do ye any work, but hallow ye the sabbath day, as I commanded your fathers.   Ex. 20:8-10; Is. 56:2-6
23 But they obeyed not, neither inclined their ear, but made their neck stiff, that they might not hear, nor receive instruction.   Jer. 11:10
24 And it shall come to pass, if ye diligently hearken unto me, saith the LORD, to bring in no burden through the gates of this city on the sabbath day, but ᵀhallow the sabbath day, to do no work therein; Jer. 17:21-22 ◆ render as sacred
25 Then shall there enter into the gates of this city kings and princes sitting upon the throne of David, riding in chariots and on horses, they, and their princes, the men of Judah, and the inhabitants of Jerusalem: and this city shall remain for ever.   2 Sam. 7:16; Is. 9:7; Jer. 22:4
26 And they shall come from the cities of Judah, and from the places about Jerusalem, and from the land of Benjamin, and from the plain, and from the mountains, and from the south, bringing burnt offerings, and sacrifices, and meat offerings, and incense, and bringing sacrifices of praise, unto the house of the LORD.   Jer. 32:44; 33:13; Zech. 7:7
27 But if ye will not hearken unto me to hallow the sabbath day, and not to bear a burden, even entering in at the gates of Jerusalem on the sabbath day; then will I kindle a fire in the gates thereof, and it shall devour the palaces of Jerusalem, and it shall not be quenched.   2 Kin. 25:9; Jer. 7:20; Lam. 4:11

The Clay and the Potter

18 The word which came to Jeremiah from the LORD, saying,
2 Arise, and go down to the potter's house, and there I will cause thee to hear my words.   Jer. 19:1-2
3 Then I went down to the potter's house, and, behold, he ᵀwrought a work on the wheels.   made

4 And the vessel that he made of clay was marred in the hand of the potter: so he made it again another vessel, as seemed good to the potter to make it.
5 Then the word of the LORD came to me, saying,
6 O house of Israel, cannot I do with you as this potter? saith the LORD. Behold, as the clay is in the potter's hand, so are ye in mine hand, O house of Israel.   Is. 64:8

> **18:3–6 Clay in the Potter's Hands**
>
> The potter takes the clay and molds it according to his will. . . . Thus it becomes a vessel fit for use. So the great Master Worker desires to mold and fashion us. And as the clay is in the hands of the potter, so are we to be in His hands. We are not to try to do the work of the potter. Our part is to yield ourselves to be molded by the Master Worker. *MH 471, 472*

7 At what instant I shall speak concerning a nation, and concerning a kingdom, to pluck up, and to pull down, and to destroy it; Jer. 1:10
8 If that nation, against whom I have pronounced, turn from their evil, I will repent of the evil that I thought to do unto them. Jer. 26:3
9 And at what instant I shall speak concerning a nation, and concerning a kingdom, to build and to plant it;   Jer. 1:10
10 If it do evil in my sight, that it obey not my voice, then I will repent of the good, wherewith I said I would benefit them.   1 Sam. 2:30

Judgments Threatened to Judah

11 Now therefore go to, speak to the men of Judah, and to the inhabitants of Jerusalem, saying, Thus saith the LORD; Behold, I frame evil against you, and devise a device against you: return ye now every one from his evil way, and make your ways and your doings good.   2 Kin. 17:13; Is. 1:16-19; Jer. 7:3
12 And they said, There is no hope: but we will walk after our own devices, and we will every one do the imagination of his evil heart.   Deut. 29:19; Is. 57:10; Jer. 2:25
13 Therefore thus saith the LORD; Ask ye now among the heathen, who hath heard such things: the virgin of Israel hath done a very horrible thing.   Is. 66:8; Jer. 5:30; 14:17
14 Will a man leave the snow of Lebanon which cometh from the rock of the field? or shall the cold flowing waters that come from another place be forsaken?
15 Because my people hath forgotten me, they have burned incense to vanity, and they have caused them to stumble in their ways from the ancient paths, to walk in paths, in a way not cast up;   Is. 57:14; Jer. 6:16; 10:15
16 To make their land desolate, and a

perpetual hissing; every one that passeth thereby shall be astonished, and wag his head.   Ps. 22:7

17 I will scatter them as with an east wind before the enemy; I will shew them the back, and not the face, in the day of their calamity.   Job 27:21; Jer. 2:27; 13:24

Jeremiah Prays

18 Then said they, Come, and let us devise devices against Jeremiah; for the law shall not perish from the priest, nor counsel from the wise, nor the word from the prophet. Come, and let us ᵀsmite him with the tongue, and let us not give heed to any of his words.   Ps. 52:2; Jer. 11:19; Mal. 2:7 ♦ strike

19 Give heed to me, O LORD, and hearken to the voice of them that contend with me.

20 Shall evil be ᵀrecompensed for good? for they have digged a pit for my soul. Remember that I stood before thee to speak good for them, and to turn away thy wrath from them.   Ps. 35:7; 57:6; 106:23 ♦ repaid

21 Therefore deliver up their children to the famine, and pour out their blood by the force of the sword; and let their wives be bereaved of their children, and be widows; and let their men be put to death; let their young men be slain by the sword in battle.   Ps. 109:9-20

22 Let a cry be heard from their houses, when thou shalt bring a troop suddenly upon them: for they have digged a pit to take me, and hid snares for my feet. Ps. 140:5; Jer. 6:26

23 Yet, LORD, thou knowest all their counsel against me to slay me: forgive not their iniquity, neither blot out their sin from thy sight, but let them be overthrown before thee; deal thus with them in the time of thine anger.   Is. 2:9

Israel Will Be Destroyed

19 Thus saith the LORD, Go and get a potter's earthen bottle, and take of the ancients of the people, and of the ancients of the priests;   Num. 11:16

2 And go forth unto the valley of the son of Hinnom, which is by the entry of the east gate, and proclaim there the words that I shall tell thee,   Josh. 15:8; 2 Kin. 23:10; Jer. 7:31-32

3 And say, Hear ye the word of the LORD, O kings of Judah, and inhabitants of Jerusalem; Thus saith the LORD of hosts, the God of Israel; Behold, I will bring evil upon this place, the which whosoever heareth, his ears shall tingle.   1 Sam. 3:11; Jer. 17:20

4 Because they have forsaken me, and have estranged this place, and have burned incense in it unto other gods, whom neither they nor their fathers have known, nor the kings of Judah, and have filled this place with the blood of innocents; Deut. 28:20; 2 Kin. 21:16; Jer. 2:34

5 They have built also the high places of Baal, to burn their sons with fire for burnt offerings unto Baal, which I commanded not, nor spake it, neither came it into my mind: Lev. 18:21; Ps. 106:37-38; Jer. 32:35

6 Therefore, behold, the days come, saith the LORD, that this place shall no more be called Tophet, nor The valley of the son of Hinnom, but The valley of slaughter. Josh. 15:8

7 And I will make void the counsel of Judah and Jerusalem in this place; and I will cause them to fall by the sword before their enemies, and by the hands of them that seek their lives: and their carcases will I give to be meat for the fowls of the heaven, and for the beasts of the earth. Lev. 26:17; Ps. 33:10-11; Jer. 16:4

8 And I will make this city desolate, and an hissing; every one that passeth thereby shall be astonished and hiss because of all the plagues thereof.   1 Kin. 9:8; Jer. 18:16; 49:13

9 And I will cause them to eat the flesh of their sons and the flesh of their daughters, and they shall eat every one the flesh of his friend in the siege and straitness, wherewith their enemies, and they that seek their lives, shall straiten them.   Lev. 26:29; Is. 9:20; Lam. 4:10

10 Then shalt thou break the bottle in the sight of the men that go with thee,   Jer. 19:1

11 And shalt say unto them, Thus saith the LORD of hosts; Even so will I break this people and this city, as one breaketh a potter's vessel, that cannot be made whole again: and they shall bury them in Tophet, till there be no place to bury.   Ps. 2:9; Is. 30:14; Lam. 4:2

12 Thus will I do unto this place, saith the LORD, and to the inhabitants thereof, and even make this city as Tophet:

13 And the houses of Jerusalem, and the houses of the kings of Judah, shall be defiled as the place of Tophet, because of all the houses upon whose roofs they have burned incense unto all the host of heaven, and have poured out drink offerings unto other gods.   2 Kin. 23:12; Jer. 7:18; 32:29

14 Then came Jeremiah from Tophet, whither the LORD had sent him to prophesy; and he stood in the court of the LORD's house, and said to all the people,   2 Chr. 20:5; Jer. 19:2-3; 26:2

15 Thus saith the LORD of hosts, the God of Israel; Behold, I will bring upon this city and upon all her towns all the evil that I have pronounced against it, because they have hardened their necks, that they might not hear my words.   Neh. 9:17; Jer. 7:26; 17:23

Pashur Imprisons Jeremiah

20 Now Pashur the son of Immer the priest, who was also chief governor in the house of the LORD, heard that Jeremiah prophesied these things. 2 Kin. 25:18; 1 Chr. 24:14

2 Then Pashur smote Jeremiah the prophet,

and put him in the stocks that *were* in the high gate of Benjamin, which *was* by the house of the LORD.   Jer. 1:19; 37:13

3 And it came to pass on the morrow, that Pashur brought forth Jeremiah out of the stocks. Then said Jeremiah unto him, The LORD hath not called thy name Pashur, but Magor-missabib.   Jer. 20:10

4 For thus saith the LORD, Behold, I will make thee a terror to thyself, and to all thy friends: and they shall fall by the sword of their enemies, and thine eyes shall behold *it*: and I will give all Judah into the hand of the king of Babylon, and he shall carry them captive into Babylon, and shall slay them with the sword.   Jer. 29:21

5 Moreover I will deliver all the strength of this city, and all the labours thereof, and all the precious things thereof, and all the treasures of the kings of Judah will I give into the hand of their enemies, which shall ᵀspoil them, and take them, and carry them to Babylon.   2 Kin. 20:17-18 ♦ *plunder*

6 And thou, Pashur, and all that dwell in thine house shall go into captivity: and thou shalt come to Babylon, and there thou shalt die, and shalt be buried there, thou, and all thy friends, to whom thou hast prophesied lies.   Jer. 14:14-15

Jeremiah Prays to the Lord

7 O LORD, thou hast deceived me, and I was deceived: thou art stronger than I, and hast prevailed: I am in derision daily, every one mocketh me.   Lam. 3:14

8 For since I spake, I cried out, I cried violence and spoil; because the word of the LORD was made a reproach unto me, and a derision, daily.   2 Chr. 36:16; Jer. 6:10

9 Then I said, I will not make mention of him, nor speak any more in his name. But *his word* was in mine heart as a burning fire shut up in my bones, and I was weary with forbearing, and I could not *stay*.   Job 32:18-20; Ps. 39:3; Acts 4:20

10 For I heard the defaming of many, fear on every side. Report, *say they*, and we will report it. All my familiars watched for my halting, *saying*, Peradventure he will be enticed, and we shall prevail against him, and we shall take our revenge on him.   1 Kin. 19:2; Ps. 31:13; 41:9

11 But the LORD *is* with me as a mighty terrible one: therefore my persecutors shall stumble, and they shall not prevail: they shall be greatly ashamed; for they shall not prosper: *their* everlasting confusion shall never be forgotten.   Jer. 1:8; 15:20; 23:40

12 But, O LORD of hosts, that triest the righteous, *and* seest the ᵀreins and the heart, let me see thy vengeance on them: for unto thee have I opened my cause.   Ps. 54:7; 59:10 ♦ *desires*

13 Sing unto the LORD, praise ye the LORD: for he hath delivered the soul of the poor from the hand of evildoers.   Ps. 34:6

14 Cursed *be* the day wherein I was born: let not the day wherein my mother bare me be blessed.   Jer. 15:10

15 Cursed *be* the man who brought tidings to my father, saying, A man child is born unto thee; making him very glad.

16 And let that man be as the cities which

the LORD overthrew, and repented not: and let him hear the cry in the morning, and the shouting at noontide; Jer. 18:22

17 Because he slew me not from the womb; or that my mother might have been my grave, and her womb *to be* always great *with me*. Job 3:10-11

18 Wherefore came I forth out of the womb to see labour and sorrow, that my days should be consumed with shame? Job 3:20

Jerusalem Will Be Captured by the Babylonians

21 The word which came unto Jeremiah from the LORD, when king Zedekiah sent unto him Pashur the son of Melchiah, and Zephaniah the son of Maaseiah the priest, saying, Jer. 29:25; 37:3; 38:1

2 Enquire, I pray thee, of the LORD for us; for Nebuchadrezzar king of Babylon maketh war against us; if so be that the LORD will deal with us according to all his wondrous works, that he may go up from us. Jer. 37:3

3 Then said Jeremiah unto them, Thus shall ye say to Zedekiah:

4 Thus saith the LORD God of Israel; Behold, I will turn back the weapons of war that *are* in your hands, wherewith ye fight against the king of Babylon, and *against* the Chaldeans, which besiege you without the walls, and I will assemble them into the midst of this city. Is. 13:4; Jer. 32:5; 37:8-10

5 And I myself will fight against you with an outstretched hand and with a strong arm, even in anger, and in fury, and in great wrath. Ex. 6:6

6 And I will ᵀsmite the inhabitants of this city, both man and beast: they shall die of a great pestilence. Jer. 32:24 ◆ strike

7 And afterward, saith the LORD, I will deliver Zedekiah king of Judah, and his servants, and the people, and such as are left in this city from the pestilence, from the sword, and from the famine, into the hand of Nebuchadrezzar king of Babylon, and into the hand of their enemies, and into the hand of those that seek their life: and he shall smite them with the edge of the sword; he shall not spare them, neither have pity, nor have mercy. Deut. 28:50; Jer. 37:17; Ezek. 7:9

Jeremiah Counsels Surrender

8 And unto this people thou shalt say, Thus saith the LORD; Behold, I set before you the way of life, and the way of death. Deut. 30:15

9 He that abideth in this city shall die by the sword, and by the famine, and by the pestilence: but he that goeth out, and falleth to the Chaldeans that besiege you, he shall live, and his life shall be unto him for a prey. Jer. 38:2; 39:18; 45:5

10 For I have set my face against this city for evil, and not for good, saith the LORD: it shall be given into the hand of the king of Babylon, and he shall burn it with fire. Jer. 44:11; 52:13

11 And touching the house of the king of Judah, *say*, Hear ye the word of the LORD;

12 O house of David, thus saith the LORD; Execute judgment in the morning, and deliver *him that is* spoiled out of the hand of the oppressor, lest my fury go out like fire, and burn that none can quench *it*, because of the evil of your doings. Ps. 101:8; Is. 1:17, 31

13 Behold, I *am* against thee, O inhabitant of the valley, *and* rock of the plain, saith the LORD; which say, Who shall come down against us? or who shall enter into our habitations? Ps. 125:2

14 But I will punish you according to the fruit of your doings, saith the LORD: and I will kindle a fire in the forest thereof, and it shall devour all things round about it. 2 Chr. 36:19

Warnings to the Wicked Kings

22 Thus saith the LORD; Go down to the house of the king of Judah, and speak there this word,

2 And say, Hear the word of the LORD, O king of Judah, that sittest upon the throne of David, thou, and thy servants, and thy people that enter in by these gates: Luke 1:32

3 Thus saith the LORD; Execute ye judgment and righteousness, and deliver the spoiled out of the hand of the oppressor: and do no wrong, do no violence to the stranger, the fatherless, nor the widow, neither shed innocent blood in this place. Jer. 21:12; 22:17; Mic. 6:8

4 For if ye do this thing indeed, then shall there enter in by the gates of this house kings sitting upon the throne of David, riding in chariots and on horses, he, and his servants, and his people. Jer. 17:25

5 But if ye will not hear these words, I swear by myself, saith the LORD, that this house shall become a desolation. Gen. 22:16; Heb. 6:13

6 For thus saith the LORD unto the king's house of Judah; Thou *art* Gilead unto me, *and* the head of Lebanon: *yet* surely I will make thee a wilderness, *and* cities *which* are not inhabited. Gen. 37:25

7 And I will prepare destroyers against thee, every one with his weapons: and they shall cut down thy choice cedars, and cast *them* into the fire. Is. 37:24

8 And many nations shall pass by this city, and they shall say every man to his neighbour, Wherefore hath the LORD done thus unto this great city? 1 Kin. 9:8-9

9 Then they shall answer, Because they have forsaken the covenant of the LORD their God, and worshipped other gods, and served them. 2 Kin. 22:17

10 Weep ye not for the dead, neither ᵀbemoan him: *but* weep sore for him that goeth away: for he shall return no more, nor see his native country.   Eccl. 4:2 ◆ *lament*
11 For thus saith the Lᴏʀᴅ touching Shallum the son of Josiah king of Judah, which reigned instead of Josiah his father, which went forth out of this place; He shall not return thither any more: 1 Chr. 3:15
12 But he shall die in the place whither they have led him captive, and shall see this land no more.   2 Kin. 23:34
13 Woe unto him that buildeth his house by unrighteousness, and his chambers by wrong; *that* useth his neighbour's service without wages, and giveth him not for his work;   Lev. 19:13; Mic. 3:10; James 5:4
14 That saith, I will build me a wide house and large chambers, and cutteth him out windows; and *it is* cieled with cedar, and painted with ᵀvermilion.   2 Sam. 7:2 ◆ *red*
15 Shalt thou reign, because thou closest *thyself* in cedar? did not thy father eat and drink, and do judgment and justice, *and* then *it was* well with him? 2 Kin. 23:25; Is. 3:10; Jer. 21:12
16 He judged the cause of the poor and needy; then *it was* well *with him: was* not this to know me? saith the Lᴏʀᴅ.   Ps. 72:1-4
17 But thine eyes and thine heart *are* not but for thy ᵀcovetousness, and for to shed innocent blood, and for oppression, and for violence, to do *it*.   2 Kin. 24:4 ◆ *strong desire*
18 Therefore thus saith the Lᴏʀᴅ concerning Jehoiakim the son of Josiah king of Judah; They shall not lament for him, *saying*, Ah my brother! or, Ah sister! they shall not lament for him, *saying*, Ah lord! or, Ah his glory!   1 Kin. 13:30
19 He shall be buried with the burial of an ass, drawn and cast forth beyond the gates of Jerusalem.   1 Kin. 21:23-24; Jer. 36:30
20 Go up to Lebanon, and cry; and lift up thy voice in Bashan, and cry from the passages: for all thy lovers are destroyed.   Num. 27:12
21 I spake unto thee in thy prosperity; *but* thou saidst, I will not hear. This *hath been* thy manner from thy youth, that thou obeyedst not my voice.   Jer. 3:25; 32:30
22 The wind shall eat up all thy pastors, and thy lovers shall go into captivity: surely then shalt thou be ashamed and confounded for all thy wickedness.   Jer. 20:11
23 O inhabitant of Lebanon, that makest thy nest in the cedars, how gracious shalt thou be when pangs come upon thee, the pain as of a woman in travail!   Jer. 6:24
24 *As* I live, saith the Lᴏʀᴅ, though Coniah the son of Jehoiakim king of Judah were the ᵀsignet upon my right hand, yet would I pluck thee thence;   Song 8:6 ◆ *identifying seal*
25 And I will give thee into the hand of them that seek thy life, and into the hand *of them* whose face thou fearest, even into the hand of Nebuchadrezzar king of Babylon, and into the hand of the Chaldeans.   2 Kin. 24:15-16
26 And I will cast thee out, and thy mother that bare thee, into another country, where ye were not born; and there shall ye die.
27 But to the land whereunto they desire to return, thither shall they not return.
28 *Is* this man Coniah a despised broken idol? *is he* a vessel wherein *is* no pleasure? wherefore are they cast out, he and his seed, and are cast into a land which they know not?   Ps. 31:12; Jer. 48:38; Hos. 8:8
29 O earth, earth, earth, hear the word of the Lᴏʀᴅ.   Jer. 6:19
30 Thus saith the Lᴏʀᴅ, Write ye this man childless, a man *that* shall not prosper in his days: for no man of his seed shall prosper, sitting upon the throne of David, and ruling any more in Judah.   Ps. 94:20

The Righteous Branch

23 Woe be unto the pastors that destroy and scatter the sheep of my pasture! saith the Lᴏʀᴅ.   Is. 56:9-12; Jer. 2:8; 10:21
2 Therefore thus saith the Lᴏʀᴅ God of Israel against the pastors that feed my people; Ye have scattered my flock, and driven them away, and have not visited them: behold, I will visit upon you the evil of your doings, saith the Lᴏʀᴅ.   Ex. 32:34

> **23:1, 2 Woe to Unfaithful Shepherds**
>
> Unfaithful pastors have prophesied smooth things; they have led their hearers to make void the law of God and to persecute those who would keep it holy. Now, in their despair, these teachers confess before the world their work of deception. The multitudes are filled with fury. "We are lost!" they cry, "and you are the cause of our ruin;" and they turn upon the false shepherds. The very ones that once admired them most will pronounce the most dreadful curses upon them. The very hands that once crowned them with laurels will be raised for their destruction. *GC 655, 656*

3 And I will gather the remnant of my flock out of all countries whither I have driven them, and will bring them again to their folds; and they shall be fruitful and increase.
4 And I will set up shepherds over them which shall feed them: and they shall fear no more, nor be dismayed, neither shall they be lacking, saith the Lᴏʀᴅ.   1 Pet. 1:5
5 Behold, the days come, saith the Lᴏʀᴅ, that I will raise unto David a righteous Branch, and a King shall reign and prosper, and shall execute judgment and justice in the earth.   Is. 4:2; 9:7; 11:1-5

6 In his days Judah shall be saved, and Israel shall dwell safely: and this *is* his name whereby he shall be called, THE LORD OUR RIGHTEOUSNESS.   Is. 9:6; Jer. 33:16; 1 Cor. 1:30

7 Therefore, behold, the days come, saith the LORD, that they shall no more say, The LORD liveth, which brought up the children of Israel out of the land of Egypt;   Jer. 16:14-15

8 But, The LORD liveth, which brought up and which led the seed of the house of Israel out of the north country, and from all countries whither I had driven them; and they shall dwell in their own land.   Is. 43:5-6

Warnings to the False Prophets

9 Mine heart within me is broken because of the prophets; all my bones shake; I am like a drunken man, and like a man whom wine hath overcome, because of the LORD, and because of the words of his holiness.   Hab. 3:16

10 For the land is full of adulterers; for because of swearing the land mourneth; the pleasant places of the wilderness are dried up, and their course is evil, and their force *is* not right.   Ps. 107:34; Jer. 9:2, 10

11 For both prophet and priest are profane; yea, in my house have I found their wickedness, saith the LORD.   Jer. 6:13; 7:30; Zeph. 3:4

12 Wherefore their way shall be unto them as slippery *ways* in the darkness: they shall be driven on, and fall therein: for I will bring evil upon them, *even* the year of their visitation, saith the LORD.   Ps. 35:6; Jer. 11:23; 13:16

13 And I have seen folly in the prophets of Samaria; they prophesied in Baal, and caused my people Israel to err.   1 Kin. 18:18-21; Is. 9:16

14 I have seen also in the prophets of Jerusalem an horrible thing: they commit adultery, and walk in lies: they strengthen also the hands of evildoers, that none doth return from his wickedness: they are all of them unto me as Sodom, and the inhabitants thereof as Gomorrah.   Gen. 18:20; Is. 1:9-10; Jer. 29:23

15 Therefore thus saith the LORD of hosts concerning the prophets; Behold, I will feed them with ᵀwormwood, and make them drink the water of ᵀgall: for from the prophets of Jerusalem is profaneness gone forth into all the land.   Jer. 8:14; 9:15 ◆ *a bitter plant* ◆ *a bitter substance*

16 Thus saith the LORD of hosts, Hearken not unto the words of the prophets that prophesy unto you: they make you vain: they speak a vision of their own heart, *and* not out of the mouth of the LORD.   Jer. 14:14

17 They say still unto them that despise me, The LORD hath said, Ye shall have peace; and they say unto every one that walketh after the imagination of his own heart, No evil shall come upon you.   Jer. 8:11; 13:10; Mic. 3:11

23:16, 17

Gift of Prophecy   See Jeremiah 28:9.

18 For who hath stood in the counsel of the LORD, and hath perceived and heard his word? who hath marked his word, and heard *it*?   Jer. 23:22

19 Behold, a whirlwind of the LORD is gone forth in fury, even a grievous whirlwind: it shall fall grievously upon the head of the wicked.   Jer. 25:32; 30:23; Amos 1:14

20 The anger of the LORD shall not return, until he have executed, and till he have performed the thoughts of his heart: in the latter days ye shall consider it perfectly.   Gen. 49:1

21 I have not sent these prophets, yet they ran: I have not spoken to them, yet they prophesied.   Jer. 14:14; 23:32; 27:15

22 But if they had stood in my counsel, and had caused my people to hear my words, then they should have turned them from their evil way, and from the evil of their doings.   Jer. 23:18

23 *Am* I a God at hand, saith the LORD, and not a God afar off?   Ps. 139:1-10

24 Can any hide himself in secret places that I shall not see him? saith the LORD. Do not I fill heaven and earth? saith the LORD.   Is. 66:1

25 I have heard what the prophets said, that prophesy lies in my name, saying, I have dreamed, I have dreamed.   Jer. 23:28

26 How long shall *this* be in the heart of the prophets that prophesy lies? yea, *they are* prophets of the deceit of their own heart;

27 Which think to cause my people to forget my name by their dreams which they tell every man to his neighbour, as their fathers have forgotten my name for Baal.   Judg. 3:7

28 The prophet that hath a dream, let him tell a dream; and he that hath my word, let him speak my word faithfully. What *is* the chaff to the wheat? saith the LORD.   1 Cor. 3:12-13

23:28 The Word—Not Human Wisdom

Philosophical theories or literary essays, however brilliant, cannot satisfy the heart. The assertions and inventions of men are of no value. Let the word of God speak to the people. Let those who have heard only traditions and human theories and maxims hear the voice of Him whose word can renew the soul unto everlasting life. *COL 40*

29 *Is* not my word like as a fire? saith the LORD; and like a hammer *that* breaketh the rock in pieces?   Jer. 5:14

30 Therefore, behold, I *am* against the prophets, saith the LORD, that steal my words every one from his neighbour.   Deut. 18:20; Ps. 34:16

31 Behold, I *am* against the prophets, saith the LORD, that use their tongues, and say, He saith.   Jer. 23:17

32 Behold, I *am* against them that prophesy false dreams, saith the LORD, and do tell

them, and cause my people to ᵀerr by their lies, and by their lightness; yet I sent them not, nor commanded them: therefore they shall not profit this people at all, saith the LORD.   Jer. 7:8 ♦ *stray*

33 And when this people, or the prophet, or a priest, shall ask thee, saying, What *is* the burden of the LORD? thou shalt then say unto them, What burden? I will even forsake you, saith the LORD.   Mal. 1:1

34 And *as for* the prophet, and the priest, and the people, that shall say, The burden of the LORD, I will even punish that man and his house.

35 Thus shall ye say every one to his neighbour, and every one to his brother, What hath the LORD answered? and, What hath the LORD spoken?

36 And the burden of the LORD shall ye mention no more: for every man's word shall be his burden; for ye have perverted the words of the living God, of the LORD of hosts our God.   2 Pet. 3:16

37 Thus shalt thou say to the prophet, What hath the LORD answered thee? and, What hath the LORD spoken?

38 But since ye say, The burden of the LORD; therefore thus saith the LORD; Because ye say this word, The burden of the LORD, and I have sent unto you, saying, Ye shall not say, The burden of the LORD;

39 Therefore, behold, I, even I, will utterly forget you, and I will forsake you, and the city that I gave you and your fathers, *and cast you* out of my presence: Jer. 23:33

40 And I will bring an everlasting reproach upon you, and a perpetual shame, which shall not be forgotten.   Jer. 20:11; 42:18; Ezek. 5:14-15

Good and Bad Figs

24 The LORD shewed me, and, behold, two baskets of figs *were* set before the temple of the LORD, after that Nebuchadrezzar king of Babylon had carried away captive Jeconiah the son of Jehoiakim king of Judah, and the princes of Judah, with the carpenters and smiths, from Jerusalem, and had brought them to Babylon. 2 Kin. 24:12-16; 2 Chr. 36:10; Jer. 29:2

2 One basket *had* very good figs, *even* like the figs *that are* first ripe: and the other basket *had* very naughty figs, which could not be eaten, they were so bad.   Is. 5:4

3 Then said the LORD unto me, What seest thou, Jeremiah? And I said, Figs; the good figs, very good; and the evil, very evil, that cannot be eaten, they are so evil.   Amos 8:2

4 Again the word of the LORD came unto me, saying,

5 Thus saith the LORD, the God of Israel; Like these good figs, so will I acknowledge

them that are carried away captive of Judah, whom I have sent out of this place into the land of the Chaldeans for *their* good. Nah. 1:7

6 For I will set mine eyes upon them for good, and I will bring them again to this land: and I will build them, and not pull *them* down; and I will plant them, and not pluck *them* up.   Jer. 12:15; 29:10; 42:10

7 And I will give them an heart to know me, that I *am* the LORD: and they shall be my people, and I will be their God: for they shall return unto me with their whole heart. Jer. 30:22

8 And as the evil figs, which cannot be eaten, they are so evil; surely thus saith the LORD, So will I give Zedekiah the king of Judah, and his princes, and the residue of Jerusalem, that remain in this land, and them that dwell in the land of Egypt: Jer. 24:2

9 And I will deliver them to be removed into all the kingdoms of the earth for *their* hurt, *to be* a reproach and a proverb, a taunt and a curse, in all places whither I shall drive them.   Deut. 28:37; Jer. 15:4; 29:18

10 And I will send the sword, the famine, and the pestilence, among them, till they be consumed from off the land that I gave unto them and to their fathers.   Is. 51:19

Judgment on Judah and the Nations

25 The word that came to Jeremiah concerning all the people of Judah in the fourth year of Jehoiakim the son of Josiah king of Judah, that *was* the first year of Nebuchadrezzar king of Babylon; 2 Kin. 24:1-2; Jer. 36:1

2 The which Jeremiah the prophet spake unto all the people of Judah, and to all the inhabitants of Jerusalem, saying,   Jer. 18:11

3 From the thirteenth year of Josiah the son of Amon king of Judah, even unto this day, that *is* the three and twentieth year, the word of the LORD hath come unto me, and I have spoken unto you, rising early and speaking; but ye have not hearkened.   Jer. 1:2; 7:13; 11:7

4 And the LORD hath sent unto you all his servants the prophets, rising early and sending *them*; but ye have not hearkened, nor inclined your ear to hear.   Jer. 25:3

5 They said, Turn ye again now every one from his evil way, and from the evil of your doings, and dwell in the land that the LORD hath given unto you and to your fathers for ever and ever: Jer. 7:7

6 And go not after other gods to serve them, and to worship them, and provoke me not to anger with the works of your hands; and I will do you no hurt.   Deut. 8:19

7 Yet ye have not hearkened unto me, saith the LORD; that ye might provoke me to anger with the works of your hands to your own hurt.   2 Kin. 21:15

Jeremiah Foretells the Seventy Years' Captivity

8 Therefore thus saith the LORD of hosts; Because ye have not heard my words,

9 Behold, I will send and take all the families of the north, saith the LORD, and Nebuchadrezzar the king of Babylon, my servant, and will bring them against this land, and against the inhabitants thereof, and against all these nations round about, and will utterly destroy them, and make them an astonishment, and an hissing, and perpetual desolations. *Is. 13:3; Jer. 1:15; 18:16*

10 Moreover I will take from them the voice of ᵀmirth, and the voice of gladness, the voice of the bridegroom, and the voice of the bride, the sound of the millstones, and the light of the candle. *Jer. 7:34; Ezek. 26:13; Rev. 18:22-23 ♦ gladness*

11 And this whole land shall be a desolation, *and* an astonishment; and these nations shall serve the king of Babylon seventy years. *Dan. 9:2*

12 And it shall come to pass, when seventy years are accomplished, *that* I will punish the king of Babylon, and that nation, saith the LORD, for their iniquity, and the land of the Chaldeans, and will make it perpetual desolations. *Is. 13:19; 14:23; Jer. 29:10*

13 And I will bring upon that land all my words which I have pronounced against it, *even* all that is written in this book, which Jeremiah hath prophesied against all the nations. *Jer. 1:5*

14 For many nations and great kings shall serve themselves of them also: and I will ᵀrecompense them according to their deeds, and according to the works of their own hands. *Jer. 27:7; 50:9; 51:6 ♦ repay*

The Coming Destruction of the Nations

15 For thus saith the LORD God of Israel unto me; Take the wine cup of this fury at my hand, and cause all the nations, to whom I send thee, to drink it. *Job 21:20; Ps. 75:8; Is. 51:17*

16 And they shall drink, and be moved, and be mad, because of the sword that I will send among them. *Nah. 3:11*

17 Then took I the cup at the LORD's hand, and made all the nations to drink, unto whom the LORD had sent me: *Jer. 1:10*

18 ᵀ*To wit,* Jerusalem, and the cities of Judah, and the kings thereof, and the princes thereof, to make them a desolation, an astonishment, an ᵀhissing, and a curse; as *it is* this day; *Ps. 60:3 ♦ Namely ♦ whistling*

19 Pharaoh king of Egypt, and his servants, and his princes, and all his people; *Jer. 46:2*

20 And all the mingled people, and all the kings of the land of Uz, and all the kings of the land of the Philistines, and Ashkelon, and Azzah, and Ekron, and the remnant of Ashdod, *Job 1:1; Is. 20:1; Jer. 50:37*

21 Edom, and Moab, and the children of Ammon, *Jer. 48:1-49:22*

22 And all the kings of Tyrus, and all the kings of Zidon, and the kings of the isles which *are* beyond the sea, *Jer. 47:4*

23 Dedan, and Tema, and Buz, and all *that are* in the utmost corners, *Jer. 9:26; 49:8, 32*

24 And all the kings of Arabia, and all the kings of the mingled people that dwell in the desert, *2 Chr. 9:14; Jer. 25:20; 50:37*

25 And all the kings of Zimri, and all the kings of Elam, and all the kings of the Medes, *Gen. 10:22*

26 And all the kings of the north, far and near, one with another, and all the kingdoms of the world, which *are* upon the face of the earth: and the king of Sheshach shall drink after them. *Jer. 25:9; 51:41*

27 Therefore thou shalt say unto them, Thus saith the LORD of hosts, the God of Israel; Drink ye, and be drunken, and spue, and fall, and rise no more, because of the sword which I will send among you. *Jer. 25:16; Lam. 4:21; Hab. 2:16*

28 And it shall be, if they refuse to take the cup at thine hand to drink, then shalt thou say unto them, Thus saith the LORD of hosts; Ye shall certainly drink. *Job 34:33*

29 For, lo, I begin to bring evil on the city which is called by my name, and should ye be utterly unpunished? Ye shall not be unpunished: for I will call for a sword upon all the inhabitants of the earth, saith the LORD of hosts. *Prov. 11:31; Ezek. 38:21; 1 Pet. 4:17*

30 Therefore prophesy thou against them all these words, and say unto them, The LORD shall roar from on high, and utter his voice from his holy habitation; he shall mightily roar upon his habitation; he shall give a shout, as they that tread *the grapes,* against all the inhabitants of the earth. *Is. 42:13; Joel 3:16*

31 A noise shall come *even* to the ends of the earth; for the LORD hath a controversy with the nations, he will plead with all flesh; he will give them *that are* wicked to the sword, saith the LORD. *Is. 66:16; Hos. 4:1; Joel 3:2*

32 Thus saith the LORD of hosts, Behold, evil shall go forth from nation to nation, and a great whirlwind shall be raised up from the coasts of the earth. *2 Chr. 15:6; Is. 34:2; Jer. 23:19*

33 And the slain of the LORD shall be at that day from *one* end of the earth even unto the *other* end of the earth: they shall not be lamented, neither gathered, nor buried; they shall be dung upon the ground. *Ps. 79:3; Is. 5:25*

34 Howl, ye shepherds, and cry; and ᵀwallow yourselves *in the ashes,* ye principal of the flock: for the days of your slaughter and of your dispersions are accomplished; and ye shall fall like a pleasant vessel. *Jer. 6:26 ♦ roll*

35 And the shepherds shall have no way to flee, nor the principal of the flock to escape.   Job 11:20

36 A voice of the cry of the shepherds, and an howling of the principal of the flock, *shall be heard*: for the LORD hath spoiled their pasture.   Jer. 4:8

37 And the peaceable habitations are cut down because of the fierce anger of the LORD.   Is. 27:10-11

38 He hath forsaken his ᵀcovert, as the lion: for their land is desolate because of the fierceness of the oppressor, and because of his fierce anger.   Jer. 4:7 ◆ *hiding place*

Jeremiah Is Arrested

26 In the beginning of the reign of Jehoiakim the son of Josiah king of Judah came this word from the LORD, saying,

2 Thus saith the LORD; Stand in the court of the LORD's house, and speak unto all the cities of Judah, which come to worship in the LORD's house, all the words that I command thee to speak unto them; diminish not a word: Deut. 4:2; Jer. 19:14; Acts 20:27

3 If so be they will hearken, and turn every man from his evil way, that I may repent me of the evil, which I purpose to do unto them because of the evil of their doings. Jer. 18:7-10

26:2, 3 Jeremiah Leaves Nothing Undone

Jeremiah had little hope of saving his beloved land from destruction and the people from captivity. Yet he was not permitted to remain silent while utter ruin threatened the kingdom. Those who had remained loyal to God must be encouraged to persevere in rightdoing, and sinners must, if possible, be induced to turn from iniquity. *PK 412*

---

4 And thou shalt say unto them, Thus saith the LORD; If ye will not hearken to me, to walk in my law, which I have set before you,   1 Kin. 9:6

5 To hearken to the words of my servants the prophets, whom I sent unto you, both rising up early, and sending *them*, but ye have not hearkened;   Jer. 25:3-4

6 Then will I make this house like Shiloh, and will make this city a curse to all the nations of the earth.   2 Kin. 22:19

7 So the priests and the prophets and all the people heard Jeremiah speaking these words in the house of the LORD.   Jer. 5:31

8 Now it came to pass, when Jeremiah had made an end of speaking all that the LORD had commanded *him* to speak unto all the people, that the priests and the prophets and all the people took him, saying, Thou shalt surely die.   Lam. 4:13-14

9 Why hast thou prophesied in the name of the LORD, saying, This house shall be like Shiloh, and this city shall be desolate without an inhabitant? And all the people were gathered against Jeremiah in the house of the LORD.

10 When the princes of Judah heard these things, then they came up from the king's house unto the house of the LORD, and sat down in the entry of the new gate of the LORD's *house*.   Jer. 36:10

11 Then spake the priests and the prophets unto the princes and to all the people, saying, This man *is* worthy to die; for he hath prophesied against this city, as ye have heard with your ears.   Deut. 18:20; Jer. 38:4; Matt. 26:66

12 Then spake Jeremiah unto all the princes and to all the people, saying, The LORD sent me to prophesy against this house and against this city all the words that ye have heard.   Jer. 26:15

13 Therefore now amend your ways and your doings, and obey the voice of the LORD

A Nation Self-Deluded

Jeremiah 26:2–6

A refusal to heed the invitation of mercy that God was now offering would bring upon the impenitent nation [the southern kingdom of Judah] the judgments that had befallen the northern kingdom of Israel over a century before. . . .

Those who stood in the temple court listening to Jeremiah's discourse understood clearly this reference to Shiloh, and to the time in the days of Eli when the Philistines had overcome Israel and carried away the ark of the testament.

The sin of Eli had consisted in passing lightly over the iniquity of his sons in sacred office, and over the evils prevailing throughout the land. His neglect to correct these evils had brought upon Israel a fearful calamity. His sons had fallen in battle, Eli himself had lost his life, the ark of God had been taken from the land of Israel, thirty thousand of the people had been slain—and all because sin had been allowed to flourish unrebuked and unchecked. Israel had vainly thought that, notwithstanding their sinful practices, the presence of the ark would ensure them victory over the Philistines. In like manner, during the days of Jeremiah, the inhabitants of Judah were prone to believe that a strict observance of the divinely appointed services of the temple would preserve them from a just punishment for their wicked course. *PK 415, 416*

your God; and the LORD will repent him of the evil that he hath pronounced against you. Jer. 26:3

14 As for me, behold, I *am* in your hand: do with me as seemeth good and meet unto you. Jer. 38:5

15 But know ye for certain, that if ye put me to death, ye shall surely bring innocent blood upon yourselves, and upon this city, and upon the inhabitants thereof: for of a truth the LORD hath sent me unto you to speak all these words in your ears. Num. 35:33

Jeremiah Is Acquitted

16 Then said the princes and all the people unto the priests and to the prophets; This man *is* not worthy to die: for he hath spoken to us in the name of the LORD our God. Acts 5:34-39

17 Then rose up certain of the elders of the land, and spake to all the assembly of the people, saying, Acts 5:34

18 Micah the Morasthite prophesied in the days of Hezekiah king of Judah, and spake to all the people of Judah, saying, Thus saith the LORD of hosts; Zion shall be plowed *like* a field, and Jerusalem shall become heaps, and the mountain of the house as the high places of a forest. Neh. 4:2

19 Did Hezekiah king of Judah and all Judah put him at all to death? did he not fear the LORD, and ᵀbesought the LORD, and the LORD repented him of the evil which he had pronounced against them? Thus might we procure great evil against our souls. Ex. 32:14; 2 Sam. 24:16; Is. 37:15-20 ◆ *begged*

20 And there was also a man that prophesied in the name of the LORD, Urijah the son of Shemaiah of Kirjath-jearim, who prophesied against this city and against this land according to all the words of Jeremiah:

21 And when Jehoiakim the king, with all his mighty men, and all the princes, heard his words, the king sought to put him to death: but when Urijah heard it, he was afraid, and fled, and went into Egypt; Matt. 10:23

22 And Jehoiakim the king sent men into Egypt, *namely*, Elnathan the son of Achbor, and *certain* men with him into Egypt. 2 Kin. 22:12

23 And they fetched forth Urijah out of Egypt, and brought him unto Jehoiakim the king; who slew him with the sword, and cast his dead body into the graves of the common people. Jer. 2:30

24 Nevertheless the hand of Ahikam the son of Shaphan was with Jeremiah, that they should not give him into the hand of the people to put him to death. 1 Kin. 18:4

26:7–24 Jeremiah Not Intimidated

Had the prophet been intimidated by the threatening attitude of those high in authority, his message would have been without effect, and he would have lost his life; but the courage with which he delivered the solemn warning commanded the respect of the people and turned the princes of Israel in his favor. . . . Thus God raised up defenders for His servant. *PK 418*

The Yoke of Babylon

27 In the beginning of the reign of Jehoiakim the son of Josiah king of Judah came this word unto Jeremiah from the LORD, saying,

2 Thus saith the LORD to me; Make thee bonds and yokes, and put them upon thy neck,

3 And send them to the king of Edom, and to the king of Moab, and to the king of the Ammonites, and to the king of Tyrus, and to the king of Zidon, by the hand of the messengers which come to Jerusalem unto Zedekiah king of Judah;

4 And command them to say unto their masters, Thus saith the LORD of hosts, the God of Israel; Thus shall ye say unto your masters;

5 I have made the earth, the man and the beast that *are* upon the ground, by my great power and by my outstretched arm, and have given it unto whom it seemed meet unto me. Ps. 115:15-16

6 And now have I given all these lands into the hand of Nebuchadnezzar the king of Babylon, my servant; and the beasts of the field have I given him also to serve him. Ezek. 29:18-20

7 And all nations shall serve him, and his son, and his son's son, until the very time of his land come: and then many nations and great kings shall serve themselves of him. Is. 14:4-6

8 And it shall come to pass, *that* the nation and kingdom which will not serve the same Nebuchadnezzar the king of Babylon, and that will not put their neck under the yoke of the king of Babylon, that nation will I punish, saith the LORD, with the sword, and with the famine, and with the pestilence, until I have consumed them by his hand. Jer. 24:10

9 Therefore hearken not ye to your prophets, nor to your ᵀdiviners, nor to your dreamers, nor to your enchanters, nor to your sorcerers, which speak unto you, saying, Ye shall not serve the king of Babylon: *false prophets or magicians*

10 For they prophesy a lie unto you, to remove you far from your land; and that I should drive you out, and ye should perish.

11 But the nations that bring their neck under the yoke of the king of Babylon, and serve him, those will I let remain still in their own land, saith the LORD; and they shall till it, and dwell therein.   Jer. 21:9

27:6–11 The People Face a Choice

The lightest punishment that a merciful God could inflict upon so rebellious a people was submission to the rule of Babylon, but if they warred against this decree of servitude they were to feel the full vigor of His chastisement. *PK 444*

12 I spake also to Zedekiah king of Judah according to all these words, saying, Bring your necks under the yoke of the king of Babylon, and serve him and his people, and live.   Jer. 28:1
13 Why will ye die, thou and thy people, by the sword, by the famine, and by the pestilence, as the LORD hath spoken against the nation that will not serve the king of Babylon?   Prov. 8:36; Jer. 27:8; Ezek. 18:31
14 Therefore hearken not unto the words of the prophets that speak unto you, saying, Ye shall not serve the king of Babylon: for they prophesy a lie unto you. Jer. 14:14; 23:21; 27:9-10
15 For I have not sent them, saith the LORD, yet they prophesy a lie in my name; that I might drive you out, and that ye might perish, ye, and the prophets that prophesy unto you.   Jer. 27:10
16 Also I spake to the priests and to all this people, saying, Thus saith the LORD; Hearken not to the words of your prophets that prophesy unto you, saying, Behold, the vessels of the LORD's house shall now shortly be brought again from Babylon: for they prophesy a lie unto you.   2 Kin. 24:13; Jer. 27:10; 28:3
17 Hearken not unto them; serve the king of Babylon, and live: wherefore should this city be laid waste?
18 But if they be prophets, and if the word of the LORD be with them, let them now make intercession to the LORD of hosts, that the vessels which are left in the house of the LORD, and in the house of the king of Judah, and at Jerusalem, go not to Babylon. 1 Sam. 7:8
19 For thus saith the LORD of hosts concerning the pillars, and concerning the sea, and concerning the bases, and concerning the residue of the vessels that remain in this city,   2 Kin. 25:13, 17; Jer. 52:17-23
20 Which Nebuchadnezzar king of Babylon took not, when he carried away captive Jeconiah the son of Jehoiakim king of Judah from Jerusalem to Babylon, and all the nobles of Judah and Jerusalem; 2 Kin. 24:14-16; 2 Chr. 36:10
21 Yea, thus saith the LORD of hosts, the God of Israel, concerning the vessels that

remain in the house of the LORD, and in the house of the king of Judah and of Jerusalem;
22 They shall be carried to Babylon, and there shall they be until the day that I visit them, saith the LORD; then will I bring them up, and restore them to this place. Ezra 7:19; Jer. 29:10; 32:5

Hananiah Prophesies Falsely

28 And it came to pass the same year, in the beginning of the reign of Zedekiah king of Judah, in the fourth year, and in the fifth month, that Hananiah the son of Azur the prophet, which was of Gibeon, spake unto me in the house of the LORD, in the presence of the priests and of all the people, saying,   Jer. 27:1
2 Thus speaketh the LORD of hosts, the God of Israel, saying, I have broken the yoke of the king of Babylon.
3 Within two full years will I bring again into this place all the vessels of the LORD's house, that Nebuchadnezzar king of Babylon took away from this place, and carried them to Babylon: 2 Kin. 24:13
4 And I will bring again to this place Jeconiah the son of Jehoiakim king of Judah, with all the captives of Judah, that went into Babylon, saith the LORD: for I will break the yoke of the king of Babylon.   Jer. 22:24
5 Then the prophet Jeremiah said unto the prophet Hananiah in the presence of the priests, and in the presence of all the people that stood in the house of the LORD, Jer. 28:1
6 Even the prophet Jeremiah said, Amen: the LORD do so: the LORD perform thy words which thou hast prophesied, to bring again the vessels of the LORD's house, and all that is carried away captive, from Babylon into this place.   1 Kin. 1:36
7 Nevertheless hear thou now this word that I speak in thine ears, and in the ears of all the people;   1 Kin. 22:28
8 The prophets that have been before me and before thee of old prophesied both against many countries, and against great kingdoms, of war, and of evil, and of pestilence.   1 Kin. 17:1
9 The prophet which prophesieth of peace, when the word of the prophet shall come to pass, then shall the prophet be known, that the LORD hath truly sent him. Deut. 18:22; Jer. 6:14

28:9

Gift of Prophecy   See 1 Corinthians 14:3, 4.

Hananiah Breaks Jeremiah's Yoke
10 Then Hananiah the prophet took the yoke from off the prophet Jeremiah's neck, and brake it.   Jer. 27:2
11 And Hananiah spake in the presence of all the people, saying, Thus saith the LORD; Even so will I break the yoke of

Nebuchadnezzar king of Babylon from the neck of all nations within the space of two full years. And the prophet Jeremiah went his way.

12 Then the word of the LORD came unto Jeremiah *the prophet*, after that Hananiah the prophet had broken the yoke from off the neck of the prophet Jeremiah, saying, Jer. 1:2

13 Go and tell Hananiah, saying, Thus saith the LORD; Thou hast broken the yokes of wood; but thou shalt make for them yokes of iron.

14 For thus saith the LORD of hosts, the God of Israel; I have put a yoke of iron upon the neck of all these nations, that they may serve Nebuchadnezzar king of Babylon; and they shall serve him: and I have given him the beasts of the field also. Deut. 28:48; Jer. 27:6-7

15 Then said the prophet Jeremiah unto Hananiah the prophet, Hear now, Hananiah; The LORD hath not sent thee; but thou makest this people to trust in a lie. Lam. 2:14

28:15 False Representatives of God

To the end of time, men will arise to create confusion and rebellion among those who claim to be representatives of the true God. Those who prophesy lies will encourage men to look upon sin as a light thing. When the terrible results of their evil deeds are made manifest, they will seek, if possible, to make the one who has faithfully warned them, responsible for their difficulties, even as the Jews charged Jeremiah with their evil fortunes. *PK 442*

---

16 Therefore thus saith the LORD; Behold, I will cast thee from off the face of the earth: this year thou shalt die, because thou hast taught rebellion against the LORD. Gen. 7:4

17 So Hananiah the prophet died the same year in the seventh month.

Jeremiah Writes to the Captives in Babylon

29 Now these *are* the words of the letter that Jeremiah the prophet sent from Jerusalem unto the residue of the elders which were carried away captives, and to the priests, and to the prophets, and to all the people whom Nebuchadnezzar had carried away captive from Jerusalem to Babylon; Esth. 9:20

2 (After that Jeconiah the king, and the queen, and the ᵀeunuchs, the princes of Judah and Jerusalem, and the carpenters, and the smiths, were departed from Jerusalem;) Jer. 22:24-28 ◆ *castrated male servants*

3 By the hand of Elasah the son of Shaphan, and Gemariah the son of Hilkiah, (whom Zedekiah king of Judah sent unto Babylon to Nebuchadnezzar king of Babylon) saying,

4 Thus saith the LORD of hosts, the God of Israel, unto all that are carried away captives, whom I have caused to be carried away from Jerusalem unto Babylon; Jer. 24:5

5 Build ye houses, and dwell *in them*; and plant gardens, and eat the fruit of them;

6 Take ye wives, and ᵀbeget sons and daughters; and take wives for your sons, and give your daughters to husbands, that they may bear sons and daughters; that ye may be increased there, and not diminished. Jer. 16:2-4

7 And seek the peace of the city whither I have caused you to be carried away captives, and pray unto the LORD for it: for in the peace thereof shall ye have peace. Ezra 6:10; 7:23

8 For thus saith the LORD of hosts, the God of Israel; Let not your prophets and your

---

God Keeps His People Informed

Jeremiah 29

Through Jeremiah, Zedekiah and all Judah, including those taken to Babylon, were counseled to submit quietly to the temporary rule of their conquerors. . . . This, however, was contrary to the inclinations of the human heart; and Satan, taking advantage of the circumstances, caused false prophets to arise among the people, both in Jerusalem and in Babylon, who declared that the yoke of bondage would soon be broken and the former prestige of the nation restored. . . .

Lest an insurrection be incited and great suffering ensue, the Lord commanded Jeremiah to meet the crisis without delay, by warning the king of Judah of the sure consequence of rebellion. The captives also were admonished, by written communications, not to be deluded into believing their deliverance near. . . .

[God] knew that should they be persuaded by false prophets to look for a speedy deliverance, their position in Babylon would be made very difficult. Any demonstration or insurrection on their part would awaken the vigilance and severity of the Chaldean authorities and would lead to a further restriction of their liberties. Suffering and disaster would result. He desired them to submit quietly to their fate and make their servitude as pleasant as possible; and His counsel to them was: "Build ye houses, and dwell in them; and plant gardens, and eat the fruit of them; . . . and seek the peace of the city whither I have caused you to be carried away captives, and pray unto the Lord for it: for in the peace thereof shall ye have peace" (Jeremiah 29:5–7). *PK 440–442*

ᵀdiviners, that *be* in the midst of you, deceive you, neither hearken to your dreams which ye cause to be dreamed.   *false prophets or magicians*
9 For they prophesy falsely unto you in my name: I have not sent them, saith the LORD.   Jer. 27:15
10 For thus saith the LORD, That after seventy years be accomplished at Babylon I will visit you, and perform my good word toward you, in causing you to return to this place.   Jer. 25:12; 27:22; Dan. 9:2
11 For I know the thoughts that I think toward you, saith the LORD, thoughts of peace, and not of evil, to give you an expected end.   Ps. 40:5

29:11 The Blessings in Our Trials

God permits trials to assail His people, that by their constancy and obedience they themselves may be spiritually enriched, and that their example may be a source of strength to others. . . . The very trials that task our faith most severely and make it seem that God has forsaken us, are to lead us closer to Christ, that we may lay all our burdens at His feet and experience the peace which He will give us in exchange. *PP 129*

---

12 Then shall ye call upon me, and ye shall go and pray unto me, and I will hearken unto you.   Jer. 33:3
13 And ye shall seek me, and find *me*, when ye shall search for me with all your heart.
14 And I will be found of you, saith the LORD: and I will turn away your captivity, and I will gather you from all the nations, and from all the places whither I have driven you, saith the LORD; and I will bring you again into the place whence I caused you to be carried away captive. Ps. 32:6; Is. 55:6; Jer. 30:3
15 Because ye have said, The LORD hath raised us up prophets in Babylon;
16 *Know* that thus saith the LORD of the king that sitteth upon the throne of David, and of all the people that dwelleth in this city, *and* of your brethren that are not gone forth with you into captivity;   Jer. 38:2-3
17 Thus saith the LORD of hosts; Behold, I will send upon them the sword, the famine, and the pestilence, and will make them like vile figs, that cannot be eaten, they are so evil.   Jer. 24:8-10
18 And I will persecute them with the sword, with the famine, and with the pestilence, and will deliver them to be removed to all the kingdoms of the earth, to be a curse, and an astonishment, and an ᵀhissing, and a reproach, among all the nations whither I have driven them: 2 Chr. 29:8; Jer. 15:4; 42:18 ◆ *whistling*
19 Because they have not hearkened to my words, saith the LORD, which I sent unto

them by my servants the prophets, rising up early and sending *them*; but ye would not hear, saith the LORD.   Jer. 6:19
20 Hear ye therefore the word of the LORD, all ye of the captivity, whom I have sent from Jerusalem to Babylon: Jer. 24:5; Mic. 4:10
21 Thus saith the LORD of hosts, the God of Israel, of Ahab the son of Kolaiah, and of Zedekiah the son of Maaseiah, which prophesy a lie unto you in my name; Behold, I will deliver them into the hand of Nebuchadrezzar king of Babylon; and he shall slay them before your eyes;   Jer. 14:14-15
22 And of them shall be taken up a curse by all the captivity of Judah which *are* in Babylon, saying, The LORD make thee like Zedekiah and like Ahab, whom the king of Babylon roasted in the fire; Is. 65:15; Dan. 3:6, 21
23 Because they have committed ᵀvillany in Israel, and have committed adultery with their neighbours' wives, and have spoken lying words in my name, which I have not commanded them; even I know, and *am* a witness, saith the LORD.   Mal. 3:5; Heb. 4:13 ◆ *evil*

Shemaiah Writes a Letter against Jeremiah

24 *Thus* shalt thou also speak to Shemaiah the Nehelamite, saying,   Jer. 29:31-32
25 Thus speaketh the LORD of hosts, the God of Israel, saying, Because thou hast sent letters in thy name unto all the people that *are* at Jerusalem, and to Zephaniah the son of Maaseiah the priest, and to all the priests, saying,   Jer. 29:29
26 The LORD hath made thee priest in the stead of Jehoiada the priest, that ye should be officers in the house of the LORD, for every man *that is* mad, and maketh himself a prophet, that thou shouldest put him in prison, and in the stocks.   2 Kin. 9:11; Jer. 20:1-2; Hos. 9:7
27 Now therefore why hast thou not reproved Jeremiah of Anathoth, which maketh himself a prophet to you?
28 For therefore he sent unto us *in* Babylon, saying, This *captivity is* long: build ye houses, and dwell *in them*; and plant gardens, and eat the fruit of them.   Jer. 29:5
29 And Zephaniah the priest read this letter in the ears of Jeremiah the prophet.
30 Then came the word of the LORD unto Jeremiah, saying,
31 Send to all them of the captivity, saying, Thus saith the LORD concerning Shemaiah the Nehelamite; Because that Shemaiah hath prophesied unto you, and I sent him not, and he caused you to trust in a lie: Jer. 29:9
32 Therefore thus saith the LORD; Behold, I will punish Shemaiah the Nehelamite, and his seed: he shall not have a man to dwell among this people; neither shall he behold

the good that I will do for my people, saith the LORD; because he hath taught rebellion against the LORD.   1 Sam. 2:30-34; Jer. 17:6; 28:16

The Future Glorious Return of the Jews

30 The word that came to Jeremiah from the LORD, saying,

2 Thus speaketh the LORD God of Israel, saying, Write thee all the words that I have spoken unto thee in a book.   Is. 30:8

3 For, lo, the days come, saith the LORD, that I will bring again the captivity of my people Israel and Judah, saith the LORD: and I will cause them to return to the land that I gave to their fathers, and they shall possess it.   Jer. 16:15; 29:14; 30:18

4 And these are the words that the LORD spake concerning Israel and concerning Judah.

5 For thus saith the LORD; We have heard a voice of trembling, of fear, and not of peace.   Is. 5:30

6 Ask ye now, and see whether a man doth travail with child? wherefore do I see every man with his hands on his ᵀloins, as a woman in travail, and all faces are turned into paleness?   Jer. 4:31 ♦ waist

7 Alas! for that day is great, so that none is like it: it is even the time of Jacob's trouble; but he shall be saved out of it. Jer. 30:10; Dan. 12:1; Joel 2:11

30:5-7 Jacob's Experience Repeated

Jacob's night of anguish, when he wrestled in prayer for deliverance from the hand of Esau (Genesis 32:24-30), represents the experience of God's people in the time of trouble. . . . Jacob's company, unarmed and defenseless, seemed about to fall helpless victims of violence and slaughter. And to the burden of anxiety and fear was added the crushing weight of self-reproach, for it was his own sin that had brought this danger. His only hope was in the mercy of God; his only defense must be prayer. GC 616

8 For it shall come to pass in that day, saith the LORD of hosts, that I will break his yoke from off thy neck, and will burst thy bonds, and strangers shall no more serve themselves of him: Is. 9:4; Jer. 27:2; Ezek. 34:27

9 But they shall serve the LORD their God, and David their king, whom I will raise up unto them.   Is. 55:3-5; Hos. 3:5; Luke 1:69

10 Therefore fear thou not, O my servant Jacob, saith the LORD; neither be dismayed, O Israel: for, lo, I will save thee from afar, and thy seed from the land of their captivity; and Jacob shall return, and shall be in rest, and be quiet, and none shall make him afraid.   Is. 35:9; 43:5; Jer. 46:27-28

11 For I am with thee, saith the LORD, to save thee: though I make a full end of all nations whither I have scattered thee, yet will I not make a full end of thee: but I will correct thee in measure, and will not leave thee altogether unpunished.   Ps. 6:1; Jer. 4:27; 10:24

30:10, 11 Comfort in Dark Hours

Thus was the church of God comforted in one of the darkest hours of her long conflict with the forces of evil. Satan had seemingly triumphed in his efforts to destroy Israel; but the Lord was overruling the events of the present, and during the years that were to follow, His people were to have opportunity to redeem the past. PK 474

12 For thus saith the LORD, Thy bruise is incurable, and thy wound is grievous. 2 Chr. 36:16

13 There is none to plead thy cause, that thou mayest be bound up: thou hast no healing medicines.   Jer. 8:22

14 All thy lovers have forgotten thee; they seek thee not; for I have wounded thee with the wound of an enemy, with the chastisement of a cruel one, for the multitude of thine iniquity; because thy sins were increased.   Job 30:21; Jer. 5:6; Lam. 1:2

15 Why criest thou for thine affliction? thy sorrow is incurable for the multitude of thine iniquity: because thy sins were increased, I have done these things unto thee.   Jer. 30:12

16 Therefore all they that devour thee shall be devoured; and all thine adversaries, every one of them, shall go into captivity; and they that ᵀspoil thee shall be a spoil, and all that prey upon thee will I give for a prey.   Is. 14:2; 33:1; Jer. 10:25 ♦ plunder

17 For I will restore health unto thee, and I will heal thee of thy wounds, saith the LORD; because they called thee an Outcast, saying, This is Zion, whom no man seeketh after.   Ex. 15:26

18 Thus saith the LORD; Behold, I will bring again the captivity of Jacob's tents, and have mercy on his dwellingplaces; and the city shall be builded upon her own heap, and the palace shall remain after the manner thereof.   1 Chr. 29:1; Ps. 102:13; Jer. 30:3

19 And out of them shall proceed thanksgiving and the voice of them that make merry: and I will multiply them, and they shall not be few; I will also glorify them, and they shall not be small.   Ps. 126:1-2; Is. 35:10; 51:11

20 Their children also shall be as ᵀaforetime, and their congregation shall be established before me, and I will punish all that oppress them.   before

21 And their nobles shall be of themselves, and their governor shall proceed from the midst of them; and I will cause him to draw

near, and he shall approach unto me: for who *is* this that engaged his heart to approach unto me? saith the LORD.   Gen. 49:10; Num. 16:5

22 And ye shall be my people, and I will be your God.   Jer. 24:7

23 Behold, the whirlwind of the LORD goeth forth with fury, a continuing whirlwind: it shall fall with pain upon the head of the wicked.   Jer. 23:19-20

24 The fierce anger of the LORD shall not return, until he have done *it*, and until he have performed the intents of his heart: in the latter days ye shall consider it.   Jer. 23:20

The Restoration of Israel and Judah

31 At the same time, saith the LORD, will I be the God of all the families of Israel, and they shall be my people.   Gen. 17:7-8

2 Thus saith the LORD, The people *which were* left of the sword found grace in the wilderness; *even* Israel, when I went to cause him to rest.   Num. 10:33

3 The LORD hath appeared of old unto me, *saying*, Yea, I have loved thee with an everlasting love: therefore with lovingkindness have I drawn thee.   Hos. 11:4

31:3 The True Motive for Following Christ

It is not the fear of punishment, or the hope of everlasting reward, that leads the disciples of Christ to follow Him. They behold the Saviour's matchless love, revealed throughout His pilgrimage on earth, from the manger of Bethlehem to Calvary's cross, and the sight of Him attracts, it softens and subdues the soul. Love awakens in the heart of the beholders. They hear His voice, and they follow Him. *DA 480*

---

4 Again I will build thee, and thou shalt be built, O virgin of Israel: thou shalt again be adorned with thy tabrets, and shalt go forth in the dances of them that make merry.   Jer. 31:13

5 Thou shalt yet plant vines upon the mountains of Samaria: the planters shall plant, and shall eat *them* as common things.   Deut. 28:30

6 For there shall be a day, *that* the watchmen upon the mount Ephraim shall cry, Arise ye, and let us go up to Zion unto the LORD our God.   Jer. 50:4-5

7 For thus saith the LORD; Sing with gladness for Jacob, and shout among the chief of the nations: publish ye, praise ye, and say, O LORD, save thy people, the remnant of Israel.   Ps. 14:7

8 Behold, I will bring them from the north country, and gather them from the coasts of the earth, *and* with them the blind and the lame, the woman with child and her that tra-

vaileth with child together: a great company shall return thither.   Is. 42:16

9 They shall come with weeping, and with supplications will I lead them: I will cause them to walk by the rivers of waters in a straight way, wherein they shall not stumble: for I am a father to Israel, and Ephraim *is* my firstborn.   Ex. 4:22; Is. 63:13; Jer. 3:4

10 Hear the word of the LORD, O ye nations, and declare *it* in the isles afar off, and say, He that scattered Israel will gather him, and keep him, as a shepherd *doth* his flock.   Is. 40:11; 66:19; Ezek. 34:12

11 For the LORD hath redeemed Jacob, and ransomed him from the hand of *him that was* stronger than he.   Ps. 142:6; Is. 44:23; 48:20

12 Therefore they shall come and sing in the height of Zion, and shall flow together to the goodness of the LORD, for wheat, and for wine, and for oil, and for the young of the flock and of the herd: and their soul shall be as a watered garden; and they shall not sorrow any more at all.   Is. 35:10; 58:11; 65:19

13 Then shall the virgin rejoice in the dance, both young men and old together: for I will turn their mourning into joy, and will comfort them, and make them rejoice from their sorrow.   Ps. 30:11; Is. 51:11; 61:3

14 And I will satiate the soul of the priests with fatness, and my people shall be satisfied with my goodness, saith the LORD.   Jer. 31:25

15 Thus saith the LORD; A voice was heard in Ramah, lamentation, *and* bitter weeping; Rahel weeping for her children refused to be comforted for her children, because they *were* not.   Gen. 37:35; Josh. 18:25; Jer. 40:1

16 Thus saith the LORD; Refrain thy voice from weeping, and thine eyes from tears: for thy work shall be rewarded, saith the LORD; and they shall come again from the land of the enemy.   Ruth 2:12

17 And there is hope in thine end, saith the LORD, that thy children shall come again to their own border.

18 I have surely heard Ephraim bemoaning himself *thus*; Thou hast chastised me, and I was chastised, as a ᵀbullock unaccustomed *to the yoke*: turn thou me, and I shall be turned; for thou *art* the LORD my God.   Job 5:17; Ps. 80:3; Jer. 31:9 ◆ *bull*

19 Surely after that I was turned, I repented; and after that I was instructed, I smote upon *my* thigh: I was ashamed, yea, even confounded, because I did bear the reproach of my youth.   Jer. 3:25; Ezek. 21:12; 36:31

20 *Is* Ephraim my dear son? *is he* a pleasant child? for since I spake against him, I do earnestly remember him still: therefore my bowels are troubled for him; I will surely have mercy upon him, saith the LORD.   Is. 55:7

21 Set thee up waymarks, make thee high

heaps: set thine heart toward the highway, *even* the way *which* thou wentest: turn again, O virgin of Israel, turn again to these thy cities.   Is. 48:20; 57:14; Jer. 50:5

22 How long wilt thou go about, O thou backsliding daughter? for the LORD hath created a new thing in the earth, A woman shall ᵀcompass a man.   Jer. 2:23 ◆ *surround*

23 Thus saith the LORD of hosts, the God of Israel; As yet they shall use this speech in the land of Judah and in the cities thereof, when I shall bring again their captivity; The LORD bless thee, O habitation of justice, *and* mountain of holiness.   Is. 1:26; Jer. 50:7; Zech. 8:3

24 And there shall dwell in Judah itself, and in all the cities thereof together, ᵀhusbandmen, and they *that* go forth with flocks.   Zech. 8:4-8 ◆ *farmers*

25 For I have satiated the weary soul, and I have replenished every sorrowful soul. Jer. 31:14

26 Upon this I awaked, and beheld; and my sleep was sweet unto me.

27 Behold, the days come, saith the LORD, that I will sow the house of Israel and the house of Judah with the seed of man, and with the seed of beast.   Ezek. 36:9, 11; Hos. 2:23

28 And it shall come to pass, *that* like as I have watched over them, to pluck up, and to break down, and to throw down, and to destroy, and to afflict; so will I watch over them, to build, and to plant, saith the LORD.

29 In those days they shall say no more, The fathers have eaten a sour grape, and the children's teeth are set on edge.   Lam. 5:7; Ezek. 18:2-3

30 But every one shall die for his own iniquity: every man that eateth the sour grape, his teeth shall be set on edge.   Is. 3:11

The New Promise

31 Behold, the days come, saith the LORD, that I will make a new covenant with the house of Israel, and with the house of Judah:

32 Not according to the covenant that I made with their fathers in the day *that* I took them by the hand to bring them out of the land of Egypt; which my covenant they brake, although I was an husband unto them, saith the LORD: Deut. 1:31

31:31-33

31:33 The Law, Written on Our Hearts

The same law that was engraved upon the tables of stone is written by the Holy Spirit upon the tables of the heart. Instead of going about to establish our own righteousness we accept the righteousness of Christ. His blood atones for our sins. His obedience is accepted for us. Then the heart renewed by the Holy Spirit will bring forth "the fruits of the Spirit." Through the grace of Christ we shall live in obedience to the law of God written upon our hearts. *PP 372*

---

33 But this *shall be* the covenant that I will make with the house of Israel; After those days, saith the LORD, I will put my law in their inward parts, and write it in their hearts; and will be their God, and they shall be my people.   Jer. 24:7; 2 Cor. 3:3; Heb. 10:16

God's Law   See Matthew 22:36-40.

34 And they shall teach no more every man his neighbour, and every man his brother, saying, Know the LORD: for they shall all know me, from the least of them unto the greatest of them, saith the LORD: for I will forgive their iniquity, and I will remember their sin no more.   Is. 54:13; Jer. 33:8; 50:20

35 Thus saith the LORD, which giveth the sun for a light by day, *and* the ordinances of the moon and of the stars for a light by night, which divideth the sea when the waves thereof roar; The LORD of hosts *is* his name: Ps. 136:7-9; Is. 51:15; Jer. 10:16

36 If those ordinances depart from before me, saith the LORD, *then* the seed of Israel also shall cease from being a nation before me for ever.   Ps. 89:36-37; Is. 54:9-10; Jer. 33:20-26

37 Thus saith the LORD; If heaven above can be measured, and the foundations of the earth searched out beneath, I will also cast off all the seed of Israel for all that they have done, saith the LORD.   Jer. 33:22

38 Behold, the days come, saith the LORD, that the city shall be built to the LORD from the tower of Hananeel unto the gate of the corner.   2 Kin. 14:13; Jer. 30:18; Zech. 14:10

39 And the measuring line shall yet go forth over against it upon the hill Gareb, and shall compass about to Goath.   Zech. 2:1-2

40 And the whole valley of the dead bodies, and of the ashes, and all the fields unto the brook of Kidron, unto the corner of the horse gate toward the east, *shall be* holy unto the LORD; it shall not be plucked up, nor thrown down any more for ever.   2 Sam. 15:23; 2 Kin. 11:16

Jeremiah Buys a Field

32 The word that came to Jeremiah from the LORD in the tenth year of Zedekiah king of Judah, which *was* the eighteenth year of Nebuchadrezzar.   2 Kin. 25:1-2

2 For then the king of Babylon's army besieged Jerusalem: and Jeremiah the prophet was shut up in the court of the prison, which *was* in the king of Judah's house.   Neh. 3:25

3 For Zedekiah king of Judah had shut him up, saying, Wherefore dost thou prophesy, and say, Thus saith the LORD, Behold, I will give this city into the hand of the king of Babylon, and he shall take it; Jer. 21:4-7; 26:8-9; 34:2-3

4 And Zedekiah king of Judah shall not escape out of the hand of the Chaldeans, but shall surely be delivered into the hand of the

king of Babylon, and shall speak with him mouth to mouth, and his eyes shall behold his eyes;   Jer. 38:18

5 And he shall lead Zedekiah to Babylon, and there shall he be until I visit him, saith the LORD: though ye fight with the Chaldeans, ye shall not prosper.   Jer. 27:22

6 And Jeremiah said, The word of the LORD came unto me, saying,

7 Behold, Hanameel the son of Shallum thine uncle shall come unto thee, saying, Buy thee my field that *is* in Anathoth: for the right of redemption *is* thine to buy *it*.   Jer. 1:1

8 So Hanameel mine uncle's son came to me in the court of the prison according to the word of the LORD, and said unto me, Buy my field, I pray thee, that *is* in Anathoth, which *is* in the country of Benjamin: for the right of inheritance *is* thine, and the redemption *is* thine; buy *it* for thyself. Then I knew that this *was* the word of the LORD.   Jer. 32:2

9 And I bought the field of Hanameel my uncle's son, that *was* in Anathoth, and weighed him the money, *even* seventeen shekels of silver.

10 And I subscribed the evidence, and sealed *it*, and took witnesses, and weighed *him* the money in the balances. Deut. 32:34; Jer. 32:12, 44

11 So I took the evidence of the purchase, *both* that which was sealed *according* to the law and custom, and that which was open:

12 And I gave the evidence of the purchase unto Baruch the son of Neriah, the son of Maaseiah, in the sight of Hanameel mine uncle's *son*, and in the presence of the witnesses that subscribed the book of the purchase, before all the Jews that sat in the court of the prison.   Jer. 32:16

13 And I charged Baruch before them, saying,

14 Thus saith the LORD of hosts, the God of Israel; Take these evidences, this evidence of the purchase, both which is sealed, and this evidence which is open; and put them in an earthen vessel, that they may continue many days.

15 For thus saith the LORD of hosts, the God of Israel; Houses and fields and vineyards shall be possessed again in this land. Jer. 30:18

Jeremiah's Prayer

16 Now when I had delivered the evidence of the purchase unto Baruch the son of Neriah, I prayed unto the LORD, saying,   Gen. 32:9-12

32:16-25 A Distressed Prophet Goes to God

So discouraging was the outlook for Judah at the time of this extraordinary transaction that immediately after perfecting the details of the purchase and arranging for the preservation of the written records, the faith of Jeremiah, unshaken though it had been, was now sorely tried. Had he, in his endeavor to encourage Judah, acted presumptuously? . . .

Perplexed in spirit, bowed down with sorrow over the sufferings of those who had refused to repent of their sins, the prophet appealed to God for further enlightenment concerning the divine purpose for mankind. *PK 469, 470*

---

17 Ah Lord GOD! behold, thou hast made the heaven and the earth by thy great power and stretched out arm, *and* there is nothing too hard for thee: Gen. 18:14; 2 Kin. 19:15; Ps. 102:25

18 Thou shewest lovingkindness unto thousands, and ᵀrecompensest the iniquity of the fathers into the bosom of their children after

---

A Purchase to Inspire Hope

Jeremiah 32:8–15

   Laying fast hold on the promises of God, Jeremiah, by means of an acted parable, illustrated before the inhabitants of the fated city his strong faith in the ultimate fulfillment of God's purpose for His people. In the presence of witnesses, and with careful observance of all necessary legal forms, he purchased for seventeen shekels of silver an ancestral field situated in the neighboring village of Anathoth.

   From every human point of view this purchase of land in territory already under the control of the Babylonians, appeared to be an act of folly. The prophet himself had been foretelling the destruction of Jerusalem, the desolation of Judea, and the utter ruin of the kingdom. He had been prophesying a long period of captivity in faraway Babylon. Already advanced in years, he could never hope to receive personal benefit from the purchase he had made. However, his study of the prophecies that were recorded in the Scriptures had created within his heart a firm conviction that the Lord purposed to restore to the children of the captivity their ancient possession of the Land of Promise. With the eye of faith Jeremiah saw the exiles returning at the end of the years of affliction and reoccupying the land of their fathers. Through the purchase of the Anathoth estate he would do what he could to inspire others with the hope that brought so much comfort to his own heart. *PK 466–469*

them: the Great, the Mighty God, the LORD of hosts, *is* his name,   Ex. 34:7; Deut. 5:9-10 ◆ *repay*

19 Great in counsel, and mighty in work: for thine eyes *are* open upon all the ways of the sons of men: to give every one according to his ways, and according to the fruit of his doings: Is. 28:29; Jer. 16:17; 17:10

20 Which hast set signs and wonders in the land of Egypt, *even* unto this day, and in Israel, and among *other* men; and hast made thee a name, as at this day; Ex. 9:16; 2 Sam. 7:23; Neh. 9:10

21 And hast brought forth thy people Israel out of the land of Egypt with signs, and with wonders, and with a strong hand, and with a stretched out arm, and with great terror;   Ex. 6:6; Deut. 26:8; 1 Chr. 17:21

22 And hast given them this land, which thou didst swear to their fathers to give them, a land flowing with milk and honey; Ex. 3:8; 13:5

23 And they came in, and possessed it; but they obeyed not thy voice, neither walked in thy law; they have done nothing of all that thou commandedst them to do: therefore thou hast caused all this evil to come upon them: Ezra 9:7; Ps. 78:54-55; Dan. 9:10-14

24 Behold the mounts, they are come unto the city to take it; and the city is given into the hand of the Chaldeans, that fight against it, because of the sword, and of the famine, and of the pestilence: and what thou hast spoken is come to pass; and, behold, thou seest *it*.   Deut. 4:26

25 And thou hast said unto me, O Lord GOD, Buy thee the field for money, and take witnesses; for the city is given into the hand of the Chaldeans.   Jer. 32:24

Nothing Is Too Hard for the Lord

26 Then came the word of the LORD unto Jeremiah, saying,

27 Behold, I *am* the LORD, the God of all flesh: is there any thing too hard for me? Num. 16:22

32:26, 27 Jeremiah's Prayer Is Answered

The prayer of the prophet was graciously answered. "The word of the Lord unto Jeremiah" in that hour of distress, when the faith of the messenger of truth was being tried as by fire, was: "Behold, I am the Lord, the God of all flesh: is there anything too hard for Me?" (Jeremiah 32:26, 27) *PK 471*

---

28 Therefore thus saith the LORD; Behold, I will give this city into the hand of the Chaldeans, and into the hand of Nebuchadrezzar king of Babylon, and he shall take it: Jer. 19:7-12

29 And the Chaldeans, that fight against this city, shall come and set fire on this city, and burn it with the houses, upon whose roofs they have offered incense unto Baal, and

poured out drink offerings unto other gods, to provoke me to anger. 2 Chr. 36:19; Jer. 19:13; 21:10

30 For the children of Israel and the children of Judah have only done evil before me from their youth: for the children of Israel have only provoked me to anger with the work of their hands, saith the LORD.   Deut. 9:7-12

31 For this city hath been to me *as* a provocation of mine anger and of my fury from the day that they built it even unto this day; that I should remove it from before my face,   1 Kin. 11:7-8; 2 Kin. 21:4-7; 23:27

32 Because of all the evil of the children of Israel and of the children of Judah, which they have done to provoke me to anger, they, their kings, their princes, their priests, and their prophets, and the men of Judah, and the inhabitants of Jerusalem.   Is. 1:4-6

33 And they have turned unto me the back, and not the face: though I taught them, rising up early and teaching *them*, yet they have not hearkened to receive instruction. Jer. 2:27

34 But they set their abominations in the house, which is called by my name, to defile it.   2 Kin. 21:4-7; Jer. 7:30; 23:11

35 And they built the high places of Baal, which *are* in the valley of the son of Hinnom, to cause their sons and their daughters to pass through *the fire* unto Molech; which I commanded them not, neither came it into my mind, that they should do this abomination, to cause Judah to sin.   Lev. 18:21; 20:2-5

36 And now therefore thus saith the LORD, the God of Israel, concerning this city, whereof ye say, It shall be delivered into the hand of the king of Babylon by the sword, and by the famine, and by the pestilence; Jer. 32:24

37 Behold, I will gather them out of all countries, whither I have driven them in mine anger, and in my fury, and in great wrath; and I will bring them again unto this place, and I will cause them to dwell safely: Ps. 106:47

38 And they shall be my people, and I will be their God: Jer. 24:7

39 And I will give them one heart, and one way, that they may fear me for ever, for the good of them, and of their children after them: Deut. 11:18-21

40 And I will make an everlasting covenant with them, that I will not turn away from them, to do them good; but I will put my fear in their hearts, that they shall not depart from me.   Is. 55:3; Jer. 50:5; Ezek. 39:29

41 Yea, I will rejoice over them to do them good, and I will plant them in this land assuredly with my whole heart and with my whole soul.   Deut. 30:9; Jer. 24:6; 31:28

42 For thus saith the LORD; Like as I have brought all this great evil upon this people, so will I bring upon them all the good that I have promised them.   Jer. 31:28; Zech. 8:14-15

43 And fields shall be bought in this land, whereof ye say, *It is* desolate without man or beast; it is given into the hand of the Chaldeans.   Jer. 32:15
44 Men shall buy fields for money, and subscribe evidences, and seal *them*, and take witnesses in the land of Benjamin, and in the places about Jerusalem, and in the cities of Judah, and in the cities of the mountains, and in the cities of the valley, and in the cities of the south: for I will cause their captivity to return, saith the LORD.   Jer. 17:26; 33:7, 11

God Promises to End the Captivity

33 Moreover the word of the LORD came unto Jeremiah the second time, while he was yet shut up in the court of the prison, saying,   Jer. 37:21
2 Thus saith the LORD the maker thereof, the LORD that formed it, to establish it; the LORD *is* his name;   Ex. 6:3
3 Call unto me, and I will answer thee, and shew thee great and mighty things, which thou knowest not.   Ps. 91:15; Is. 48:6; Jer. 29:12
4 For thus saith the LORD, the God of Israel, concerning the houses of this city, and concerning the houses of the kings of Judah, which are thrown down by the mounts, and by the sword;   Jer. 32:24; Ezek. 4:2; Hab. 1:10
5 They come to fight with the Chaldeans, but *it is* to fill them with the dead bodies of men, whom I have slain in mine anger and in my fury, and for all whose wickedness I have hid my face from this city.   Is. 8:17
6 Behold, I will bring it health and cure, and I will cure them, and will reveal unto them the abundance of peace and truth.   Is. 30:26
7 And I will cause the captivity of Judah and the captivity of Israel to return, and will build them, as at the first. Is. 1:26; Jer. 30:3; 32:44
8 And I will cleanse them from all their iniquity, whereby they have sinned against me; and I will pardon all their iniquities, whereby they have sinned, and whereby they have ᵀtransgressed against me.   Ps. 51:2 ◆ *violated a law*

33:6–8 The Promise of Restoration

Satan had seemingly triumphed in his efforts to destroy Israel; but the Lord was overruling the events of the present, and during the years that were to follow, His people were to have opportunity to redeem the past. *PK 474*

---

9 And it shall be to me a name of joy, a praise and an honour before all the nations of the earth, which shall hear all the good that I do unto them: and they shall fear and tremble for all the goodness and for all the prosperity that I ᵀprocure unto it.   Is. 60:5; 62:7; Jer. 13:11 ◆ *provide*
10 Thus saith the LORD; Again there shall

be heard in this place, which ye say *shall be* desolate without man and without beast, *even* in the cities of Judah, and in the streets of Jerusalem, that are desolate, without man, and without inhabitant, and without beast,   Jer. 32:43
11 The voice of joy, and the voice of gladness, the voice of the bridegroom, and the voice of the bride, the voice of them that shall say, Praise the LORD of hosts: for the LORD *is* good; for his mercy *endureth* for ever: *and* of them that shall bring the sacrifice of praise into the house of the LORD. For I will cause to return the captivity of the land, as at the first, saith the LORD.   1 Chr. 16:8, 34; 2 Chr. 5:13
12 Thus saith the LORD of hosts; Again in this place, which is desolate without man and without beast, and in all the cities thereof, shall be an habitation of shepherds causing *their* flocks to lie down.   Is. 65:10; Jer. 31:24; 36:29
13 In the cities of the mountains, in the cities of the ᵀvale, and in the cities of the south, and in the land of Benjamin, and in the places about Jerusalem, and in the cities of Judah, shall the flocks pass again under the hands of him that telleth *them*, saith the LORD.   Lev. 27:32; Jer. 17:26; Luke 15:4 ◆ *valley*
14 Behold, the days come, saith the LORD, that I will perform that good thing which I have promised unto the house of Israel and to the house of Judah.   Is. 32:1-2; Jer. 23:5; 29:10
15 In those days, and at that time, will I cause the Branch of righteousness to grow up unto David; and he shall execute judgment and righteousness in the land. Ps. 72:1-5; Is. 4:2; 11:1-5
16 In those days shall Judah be saved, and Jerusalem shall dwell safely: and this *is the name* wherewith she shall be called, The LORD our righteousness.   Is. 45:17; Jer. 23:6; 1 Cor. 1:30
17 For thus saith the LORD; David shall never want a man to sit upon the throne of the house of Israel;   1 Kin. 2:4; 8:25; Ps. 89:29-37
18 Neither shall the priests the Levites want a man before me to offer burnt offerings, and to kindle meat offerings, and to do sacrifice continually.
19 And the word of the LORD came unto Jeremiah, saying,
20 Thus saith the LORD; If ye can break my covenant of the day, and my covenant of the night, and that there should not be day and night in their season;   Gen. 8:22
21 *Then* may also my covenant be broken with David my servant, that he should not have a son to reign upon his throne; and with the Levites the priests, my ministers.   2 Chr. 7:18
22 As the host of heaven cannot be numbered, neither the sand of the sea measured: so will I multiply the seed of David my servant, and the Levites that minister unto me.   Gen. 15:5

23 Moreover the word of the LORD came to Jeremiah, saying,
24 Considerest thou not what this people have spoken, saying, The two families which the LORD hath chosen, he hath even cast them off? thus they have despised my people, that they should be no more a nation before them.   Neh. 4:2-4
25 Thus saith the LORD; If my covenant be not with day and night, and if I have not appointed the ordinances of heaven and earth;   Gen. 8:22; Ps. 74:16-17; Jer. 31:35-36
26 Then will I cast away the seed of Jacob, and David my servant, so that I will not take any of his seed to be rulers over the seed of Abraham, Isaac, and Jacob: for I will cause their captivity to return, and have mercy on them.   Is. 14:1

Jeremiah Prophesies the Captivity of Zedekiah and the City

34 The word which came unto Jeremiah from the LORD, when Nebuchadnezzar king of Babylon, and all his army, and all the kingdoms of the earth of his dominion, and all the people, fought against Jerusalem, and against all the cities thereof, saying,   Jer. 1:15
2 Thus saith the LORD, the God of Israel; Go and speak to Zedekiah king of Judah, and tell him, Thus saith the LORD; Behold, I will give this city into the hand of the king of Babylon, and he shall burn it with fire: Jer. 21:10
3 And thou shalt not escape out of his hand, but shalt surely be taken, and delivered into his hand; and thine eyes shall behold the eyes of the king of Babylon, and he shall speak with thee mouth to mouth, and thou shalt go to Babylon.   2 Kin. 25:4-7; Jer. 21:7; 32:4
4 Yet hear the word of the LORD, O Zedekiah king of Judah; Thus saith the LORD of thee, Thou shalt not die by the sword:
5 But thou shalt die in peace: and with the burnings of thy fathers, the former kings which were before thee, so shall they burn odours for thee; and they will lament thee, saying, Ah lord! for I have pronounced the word, saith the LORD.   2 Chr. 16:14; Jer. 22:18
6 Then Jeremiah the prophet spake all these words unto Zedekiah king of Judah in Jerusalem,   1 Sam. 3:18
7 When the king of Babylon's army fought against Jerusalem, and against all the cities of Judah that were left, against Lachish, and against Azekah: for these defenced cities remained of the cities of Judah.   Josh. 10:3; 15:35
8 This is the word that came unto Jeremiah from the LORD, after that the king Zedekiah had made a covenant with all the people which were at Jerusalem, to proclaim liberty unto them;   Lev. 25:10; 2 Kin. 11:17; Jer. 34:17

9 That every man should let his manservant, and every man his maidservant, being an Hebrew or an Hebrewess, go free; that none should serve himself of them, [T]to wit, of a Jew his brother.   Gen. 14:13 ◆ namely
10 Now when all the princes, and all the people, which had entered into the covenant, heard that every one should let his manservant, and every one his maidservant, go free, that none should serve themselves of them any more, then they obeyed, and let them go.   Jer. 26:10
11 But afterward they turned, and caused the servants and the handmaids, whom they had let go free, to return, and brought them into subjection for servants and for handmaids.
12 Therefore the word of the LORD came to Jeremiah from the LORD, saying,
13 Thus saith the LORD, the God of Israel; I made a covenant with your fathers in the day that I brought them forth out of the land of Egypt, out of the house of bondmen, saying,   Josh. 24:17
14 At the end of seven years let ye go every man his brother an Hebrew, which hath been sold unto thee; and when he hath served thee six years, thou shalt let him go free from thee: but your fathers hearkened not unto me, neither inclined their ear.   Deut. 15:12; 1 Sam. 8:7-8; 1 Kin. 9:22
15 And ye were now turned, and had done right in my sight, in proclaiming liberty every man to his neighbour; and ye had made a covenant before me in the house which is called by my name: 2 Kin. 23:3; Neh. 10:29; Jer. 34:8
16 But ye turned and polluted my name, and caused every man his servant, and every man his handmaid, whom ye had set at liberty at their pleasure, to return, and brought them into subjection, to be unto you for servants and for handmaids.   Ex. 20:7; Lev. 19:12; Jer. 34:11
17 Therefore thus saith the LORD; Ye have not hearkened unto me, in proclaiming liberty, every one to his brother, and every man to his neighbour: behold, I proclaim a liberty for you, saith the LORD, to the sword, to the pestilence, and to the famine; and I will make you to be removed into all the kingdoms of the earth.   Deut. 28:25; Jer. 29:18; Matt. 7:2
18 And I will give the men that have [T]transgressed my covenant, which have not performed the words of the covenant which they had made before me, when they cut the calf in twain, and passed between the parts thereof,   Gen. 15:10; Deut. 17:2; Hos. 6:7 ◆ violated
19 The princes of Judah, and the princes of Jerusalem, the [T]eunuchs, and the priests, and all the people of the land, which passed between the parts of the calf;   castrated male servants
20 I will even give them into the hand of their

enemies, and into the hand of them that seek their life: and their dead bodies shall be for meat unto the fowls of the heaven, and to the beasts of the earth.   Jer. 7:33; 11:21; 19:7

21 And Zedekiah king of Judah and his princes will I give into the hand of their enemies, and into the hand of them that seek their life, and into the hand of the king of Babylon's army, which are gone up from you.   Jer. 39:6

22 Behold, I will command, saith the LORD, and cause them to return to this city; and they shall fight against it, and take it, and burn it with fire: and I will make the cities of Judah a desolation without an inhabitant.   Jer. 9:11

The Obedience of the Rechabites

35 The word which came unto Jeremiah from the LORD in the days of Jehoiakim the son of Josiah king of Judah, saying,   2 Kin. 23:35

35:1–16 Obedience and Rebellion in Contrast

God sought thus to bring into sharp contrast the obedience of the Rechabites with the disobedience and rebellion of His people. The Rechabites had obeyed the command of their father and now refused to be enticed into transgression. But the men of Judah had hearkened not to the words of the Lord, and were in consequence about to suffer His severest judgments. *PK 424*

---

2 Go unto the house of the Rechabites, and speak unto them, and bring them into the house of the LORD, into one of the chambers, and give them wine to drink.   1 Kin. 6:5-6

3 Then I took Jaazaniah the son of Jeremiah, the son of Habaziniah, and his brethren, and all his sons, and the whole house of the Rechabites;

4 And I brought them into the house of the LORD, into the chamber of the sons of Hanan, the son of Igdaliah, a man of God, which *was* by the chamber of the princes, which *was* above the chamber of Maaseiah the son of Shallum, the keeper of the door: Deut. 33:1

5 And I set before the sons of the house of the Rechabites pots full of wine, and cups, and I said unto them, Drink ye wine.   Amos 2:12

6 But they said, We will drink no wine: for Jonadab the son of Rechab our father commanded us, saying, Ye shall drink no wine, *neither ye,* nor your sons for ever: Lev. 10:9

7 Neither shall ye build house, nor sow seed, nor plant vineyard, nor have *any:* but all your days ye shall dwell in tents; that ye may live many days in the land where ye *be* strangers.   Gen. 25:27

8 Thus have we obeyed the voice of Jonadab the son of Rechab our father in all that he hath charged us, to drink no wine all our days, we, our wives, our sons, nor our daughters;   Col. 3:20

9 Nor to build houses for us to dwell in: neither have we vineyard, nor field, nor seed: 1 Tim. 6:6

10 But we have dwelt in tents, and have obeyed, and done according to all that Jonadab our father commanded us.

11 But it came to pass, when Nebuchadrezzar king of Babylon came up into the land, that we said, Come, and let us go to Jerusalem for fear of the army of the Chaldeans, and for fear of the army of the Syrians: so we dwell at Jerusalem.   Jer. 8:14

Jeremiah Condemns the Disobedience of the Jews

12 Then came the word of the LORD unto Jeremiah, saying,

13 Thus saith the LORD of hosts, the God of Israel; Go and tell the men of Judah and the inhabitants of Jerusalem, Will ye not receive instruction to hearken to my words? saith the LORD.   Jer. 5:3

14 The words of Jonadab the son of Rechab, that he commanded his sons not to drink wine, are performed; for unto this day they drink none, but obey their father's commandment: notwithstanding I have spoken unto you, rising early and speaking; but ye hearkened not unto me.   Is. 30:9

15 I have sent also unto you all my servants the prophets, rising up early and sending *them,* saying, Return ye now every man from his evil way, and amend your doings, and go not after other gods to serve them, and ye shall dwell in the land which I have given to you and to your fathers: but ye have not inclined your ear, nor hearkened unto me.   Jer. 18:11; 25:5-6; Ezek. 18:30-32

16 Because the sons of Jonadab the son of Rechab have performed the commandment of their father, which he commanded them; but this people hath not hearkened unto me: Mal. 1:6

17 Therefore thus saith the LORD God of hosts, the God of Israel; Behold, I will bring upon Judah and upon all the inhabitants of Jerusalem all the evil that I have pronounced against them: because I have spoken unto them, but they have not heard; and I have called unto them, but they have not answered.   Is. 65:12

18 And Jeremiah said unto the house of the Rechabites, Thus saith the LORD of hosts, the God of Israel; Because ye have obeyed the commandment of Jonadab your father, and kept all his precepts, and done according unto all that he hath commanded you: Ex. 20:12

19 Therefore thus saith the LORD of hosts, the God of Israel; Jonadab the son of Rechab shall not want a man to stand before me for ever. *Jer. 15:19*

35:18, 19 God Again Links Blessings and Obedience

Upon the house of the Rechabites was pronounced a continued blessing. . . . Thus God taught His people that faithfulness and obedience would be reflected back upon Judah in blessing, even as the Rechabites were blessed for obedience to their father's command. *PK 425*

The Prophecies Are Read and Burned

36 And it came to pass in the fourth year of Jehoiakim the son of Josiah king of Judah, *that* this word came unto Jeremiah from the LORD, saying, *Jer. 25:1*
2 Take thee a roll of a book, and write therein all the words that I have spoken unto thee against Israel, and against Judah, and against all the nations, from the day I spake unto thee, from the days of Josiah, even unto this day. *Ex. 17:14; Jer. 25:3; 30:2*
3 It may be that the house of Judah will hear all the evil which I purpose to do unto them; that they may return every man from his evil way; that I may forgive their iniquity and their sin. *Jer. 18:8; 26:3; Ezek. 12:3*

36:3 How God Tries to Reach the Erring

God pities men struggling in the blindness of perversity; He seeks to enlighten the darkened understanding by sending reproofs and threatenings designed to cause the most exalted to feel their ignorance and to deplore their errors. He endeavors to help the self-complacent to become dissatisfied with their vain attainments and to seek for spiritual blessing through a close connection with heaven. *PK 435*

4 Then Jeremiah called Baruch the son of Neriah: and Baruch wrote from the mouth of Jeremiah all the words of the LORD, which he had spoken unto him, upon a roll of a book. *Jer. 32:12; 36:32; Ezek. 2:9*
5 And Jeremiah commanded Baruch, saying, I *am* shut up; I cannot go into the house of the LORD: *Jer. 32:2*
6 Therefore go thou, and read in the roll, which thou hast written from my mouth, the words of the LORD in the ears of the people in the LORD's house upon the fasting day: and also thou shalt read them in the ears of all Judah that come out of their cities. *Jer. 36:8-9*
7 It may be they will present their supplication before the LORD, and will return every one from his evil way: for great *is* the anger and the fury that the LORD hath pronounced against this people. *2 Kin. 22:13, 17; Jer. 36:3*
8 And Baruch the son of Neriah did according to all that Jeremiah the prophet commanded him, reading in the book the words of the LORD in the LORD's house. *Jer. 1:17*
9 And it came to pass in the fifth year of Jehoiakim the son of Josiah king of Judah, in the ninth month, *that* they proclaimed a fast before the LORD to all the people in Jerusalem, and to all the people that came from the cities of Judah unto Jerusalem. *2 Chr. 20:3*
10 Then read Baruch in the book the words of Jeremiah in the house of the LORD, in the chamber of Gemariah the son of Shaphan the scribe, in the higher court, at the entry of the new gate of the LORD's house, in the ears of all the people. *Jer. 26:10; 36:11; 52:25*
11 When Michaiah the son of Gemariah, the son of Shaphan, had heard out of the book all the words of the LORD,
12 Then he went down into the king's house, into the scribe's chamber: and, lo, all the princes sat there, *even* Elishama the scribe,

---

Purpose of God's Judgments

Jeremiah 36

God's plan is not to send messengers who will please and flatter sinners; He delivers no messages of peace to lull the unsanctified into carnal security. Instead, He lays heavy burdens upon the conscience of the wrongdoer and pierces his soul with sharp arrows of conviction. Ministering angels present to him the fearful judgments of God, to deepen the sense of need and to prompt the agonizing cry, "What must I do to be saved?" (Acts 16:30). But the Hand that humbles to the dust, rebukes sin, and puts pride and ambition to shame, is the Hand that lifts up the penitent, stricken one. With deepest sympathy He who permits the chastisement to fall, inquires, "What wilt thou that I shall do unto thee?"

When man has sinned against a holy and merciful God, he can pursue no course so noble as to repent sincerely and confess his errors in tears and bitterness of soul. This God requires of him; He accepts nothing less than a broken heart and a contrite spirit. But King Jehoiakim and his lords, in their arrogance and pride, refused the invitation of God. They would not heed the warning, and repent. The gracious opportunity proffered them at the time of the burning of the sacred roll, was their last. *PK 435, 436*

and Delaiah the son of Shemaiah, and Elnathan the son of Achbor, and Gemariah the son
of Shaphan, and Zedekiah the son of Hana-
niah, and all the princes.   2 Kin. 22:12; Jer. 26:22
13 Then Michaiah declared unto them all the
words that he had heard, when Baruch read
the book in the ears of the people. 2 Kin. 22:10
14 Therefore all the princes sent Jehudi the
son of Nethaniah, the son of Shelemiah, the
son of Cushi, unto Baruch, saying, Take in
thine hand the roll wherein thou hast read
in the ears of the people, and come. So Baruch the son of Neriah took the roll in his
hand, and came unto them.   Jer. 36:2
15 And they said unto him, Sit down now,
and read it in our ears. So Baruch read *it* in
their ears.
16 Now it came to pass, when they had heard
all the words, they were afraid both one and
other, and said unto Baruch, We will surely
tell the king of all these words.   Jer. 13:18
17 And they asked Baruch, saying, Tell us
now, How didst thou write all these words
at his mouth?   John 9:15
18 Then Baruch answered them, He pronounced all these words unto me with his
mouth, and I wrote *them* with ink in the
book.   Jer. 36:4
19 Then said the princes unto Baruch, Go,
hide thee, thou and Jeremiah; and let no
man know where ye be.   1 Kin. 17:3
20 And they went in to the king into the
court, but they laid up the roll in the chamber of Elishama the scribe, and told all the
words in the ears of the king.   Jer. 36:12
21 So the king sent Jehudi to fetch the roll:
and he took it out of Elishama the scribe's
chamber. And Jehudi read it in the ears of
the king, and in the ears of all the princes
which stood beside the king.   2 Kin. 22:10
22 Now the king sat in the winterhouse in
the ninth month: and *there was a fire* on the
hearth burning before him.   Amos 3:15
23 And it came to pass, *that* when Jehudi had
read three or four leaves, he cut it with the
penknife, and cast *it* into the fire that *was* on
the hearth, until all the roll was consumed
in the fire that *was* on the hearth.   1 Kin. 22:8
24 Yet they were not afraid, nor ᵀrent their
garments, *neither* the king, nor any of his servants that heard all these words.   tore
25 Nevertheless Elnathan and Delaiah and
Gemariah had made intercession to the
king that he would not burn the roll: but he
would not hear them.   Gen. 37:22
26 But the king commanded Jerahmeel the
son of Hammelech, and Seraiah the son of
Azriel, and Shelemiah the son of Abdeel,
to take Baruch the scribe and Jeremiah the
prophet: but the LORD hid them.   1 Kin. 19:1-3
27 Then the word of the LORD came to

Jeremiah, after that the king had burned the
roll, and the words which Baruch wrote at
the mouth of Jeremiah, saying,
28 Take thee again another roll, and write in
it all the former words that were in the first
roll, which Jehoiakim the king of Judah hath
burned.   Zech. 1:5-6
29 And thou shalt say to Jehoiakim king
of Judah, Thus saith the LORD; Thou hast
burned this roll, saying, Why hast thou
written therein, saying, The king of Babylon
shall certainly come and destroy this land,
and shall cause to cease from thence man
and beast?   Is. 30:10
30 Therefore thus saith the LORD of Jehoiakim king of Judah; He shall have none to sit
upon the throne of David: and his dead body
shall be cast out in the day to the heat, and
in the night to the frost.   Jer. 22:30
31 And I will punish him and his seed and
his servants for their iniquity; and I will
bring upon them, and upon the inhabitants
of Jerusalem, and upon the men of Judah,
all the evil that I have pronounced against
them; but they hearkened not.   Prov. 29:1
32 Then took Jeremiah another roll, and
gave it to Baruch the scribe, the son of Neriah; who wrote therein from the mouth of
Jeremiah all the words of the book which
Jehoiakim king of Judah had burned in the
fire: and there were added besides unto
them many like words.   Ex. 4:15-16; Jer. 36:4, 18

Jeremiah Advises Zedekiah

37 And king Zedekiah the son of Josiah
reigned instead of Coniah the son of
Jehoiakim, whom Nebuchadrezzar king of
Babylon made king in the land of Judah.
2 But neither he, nor his servants, nor the
people of the land, did hearken unto the
words of the LORD, which he spake by the
prophet Jeremiah.   2 Kin. 24:19-20
3 And Zedekiah the king sent Jehucal the
son of Shelemiah and Zephaniah the son of
Maaseiah the priest to the prophet Jeremiah,
saying, Pray now unto the LORD our God for
us.   1 Kin. 13:6; Jer. 21:1-2; 29:25
4 Now Jeremiah came in and went out
among the people: for they had not put him
into prison.   Jer. 37:15
5 Then Pharaoh's army was come forth out
of Egypt: and when the Chaldeans that besieged Jerusalem heard tidings of them, they
departed from Jerusalem.   2 Kin. 24:7; Jer. 34:21
6 Then came the word of the LORD unto the
prophet Jeremiah, saying,
7 Thus saith the LORD, the God of Israel;
Thus shall ye say to the king of Judah, that
sent you unto me to enquire of me; Behold,
Pharaoh's army, which is come forth to help

you, shall return to Egypt into their own land. 2 Kin. 22:18; Jer. 21:2; Lam. 4:17
8 And the Chaldeans shall come again, and fight against this city, and take it, and burn it with fire. Jer. 38:23
9 Thus saith the LORD; Deceive not yourselves, saying, The Chaldeans shall surely depart from us: for they shall not depart. Obad. 3
10 For though ye had smitten the whole army of the Chaldeans that fight against you, and there remained *but* wounded men among them, *yet* should they rise up every man in his tent, and burn this city with fire. Lev. 26:36-38

Jeremiah Is Taken for a Traitor

11 And it came to pass, that when the army of the Chaldeans was broken up from Jerusalem for fear of Pharaoh's army,
12 Then Jeremiah went forth out of Jerusalem to go into the land of Benjamin, to separate himself thence in the midst of the people. Jer. 1:1
13 And when he was in the gate of Benjamin, a captain of the ᵀward *was* there, whose name *was* Irijah, the son of Shelemiah, the son of Hananiah; and he took Jeremiah the prophet, saying, Thou fallest away to the Chaldeans. Jer. 38:7 ◆ *prison or guard*
14 Then said Jeremiah, *It is* false; I fall not away to the Chaldeans. But he hearkened not to him: so Irijah took Jeremiah, and brought him to the princes. Ps. 27:12
15 Wherefore the princes were ᵀwroth with Jeremiah, and smote him, and put him in prison in the house of Jonathan the scribe: for they had made that the prison. Jer. 38:26 ◆ *angry*
16 When Jeremiah was entered into the dungeon, and into the ᵀcabins, and Jeremiah had remained there many days; Jer. 38:6 ◆ *prison cells*
17 Then Zedekiah the king sent, and took him out: and the king asked him secretly in his house, and said, Is there *any* word from the LORD? And Jeremiah said, There is: for, said he, thou shalt be delivered into the hand of the king of Babylon. 1 Kin. 14:1-4; 22:16; Jer. 21:7

37:17 A Weak and Willful King

The king dared not openly manifest any faith in Jeremiah. Though his fear drove him to seek information of him privately, yet he was too weak to brave the disapprobation of his princes and of the people by submitting to the will of God as declared by the prophet. *PK 455*

18 Moreover Jeremiah said unto king Zedekiah, What have I offended against thee, or against thy servants, or against this people, that ye have put me in prison? John 10:32
19 Where *are* now your prophets which prophesied unto you, saying, The king of Babylon shall not come against you, nor against this land? 2 Kin. 3:13
20 Therefore hear now, I pray thee, O my lord the king: let my supplication, I pray thee, be accepted before thee; that thou cause me not to return to the house of Jonathan the scribe, lest I die there. Jer. 36:7
21 Then Zedekiah the king commanded that they should commit Jeremiah into the court of the prison, and that they should give him daily a piece of bread out of the bakers' street, until all the bread in the city were spent. Thus Jeremiah remained in the court of the prison. Jer. 32:2; 38:13, 28

Jeremiah Is Thrown into a Dungeon

38 Then Shephatiah the son of Mattan, and Gedaliah the son of Pashur, and Jucal the son of Shelemiah, and Pashur the son of Malchiah, heard the words that Jeremiah had spoken unto all the people, saying,
2 Thus saith the LORD, He that remaineth in this city shall die by the sword, by the famine, and by the pestilence: but he that goeth forth to the Chaldeans shall live; for he shall have his life for a prey, and shall live. Jer. 34:17
3 Thus saith the LORD, This city shall surely be given into the hand of the king of Babylon's army, which shall take it. Jer. 21:10
4 Therefore the princes said unto the king, We beseech thee, let this man be put to death: for thus he weakeneth the hands of the men of war that remain in this city, and the hands of all the people, in speaking such words unto them: for this man seeketh not the welfare of this people, but the hurt. Ex. 5:4; 1 Kin. 18:17-18; Jer. 26:11
5 Then Zedekiah the king said, Behold, he *is* in your hand: for the king *is* not *he that* can do *any* thing against you. 2 Sam. 3:39

38:4, 5 The King Betrays the Prophet

The cowardly king knew that the charges were false; but in order to propitiate those who occupied high and influential positions in the nation, he feigned to believe their falsehoods and gave Jeremiah into their hands to do with him as they pleased. *PK 456*

6 Then took they Jeremiah, and cast him into the dungeon of Malchiah the son of Hammelech, that *was* in the court of the prison: and they let down Jeremiah with cords. And in the dungeon *there was* no water, but ᵀmire: so Jeremiah sunk in the mire. Jer. 37:16 ◆ *mud*
7 Now when Ebedmelech the Ethiopian, one of the ᵀeunuchs which was in the king's house, heard that they had put Jeremiah in

the dungeon; the king then sitting in the gate of Benjamin;   Jer. 29:2 ◆ *castrated male servants*

8 Ebedmelech went forth out of the king's house, and spake to the king, saying,

9 My lord the king, these men have done evil in all that they have done to Jeremiah the prophet, whom they have cast into the dungeon; and he is like to die for hunger in the place where he is: for *there is* no more bread in the city.   Jer. 52:6

10 Then the king commanded Ebed-melech the Ethiopian, saying, Take from hence thirty men with thee, and take up Jeremiah the prophet out of the dungeon, before he die.

11 So Ebed-melech took the men with him, and went into the house of the king under the treasury, and took thence old cast ᵀclouts and old rotten rags, and let them down by cords into the dungeon to Jeremiah.   *patches*

12 And Ebed-melech the Ethiopian said unto Jeremiah, Put now *these* old cast clouts and rotten rags under thine ᵀarmholes under the cords. And Jeremiah did so.   *armpits*

13 So they drew up Jeremiah with cords, and took him up out of the dungeon: and Jeremiah remained in the court of the prison.   Jer. 37:21

14 Then Zedekiah the king sent, and took Jeremiah the prophet unto him into the third entry that *is* in the house of the LORD: and the king said unto Jeremiah, I will ask thee a thing; hide nothing from me.   1 Sam. 3:17-18

15 Then Jeremiah said unto Zedekiah, If I declare *it* unto thee, wilt thou not surely put me to death? and if I give thee counsel, wilt thou not hearken unto me?   Luke 22:67-68

16 So Zedekiah the king sware secretly unto Jeremiah, saying, *As* the LORD liveth, that made us this soul, I will not put thee to death,

neither will I give thee into the hand of these men that seek thy life.

17 Then said Jeremiah unto Zedekiah, Thus saith the LORD, the God of hosts, the God of Israel; If thou wilt assuredly go forth unto the king of Babylon's princes, then thy soul shall live, and this city shall not be burned with fire; and thou shalt live, and thine house: Jer. 27:12

38:17–19 When Fear Controls

Had the king chosen to obey, the lives of the people might have been spared, and the city saved from conflagration; but he thought he had gone too far to retrace his steps. He was afraid of the Jews, afraid of ridicule, afraid for his life. After years of rebellion against God, Zedekiah thought it too humiliating to say to his people, I accept the word of the Lord, as spoken through the prophet Jeremiah. *PK 457*

---

18 But if thou wilt not go forth to the king of Babylon's princes, then shall this city be given into the hand of the Chaldeans, and they shall burn it with fire, and thou shalt not escape out of their hand.   Jer. 38:3

19 And Zedekiah the king said unto Jeremiah, I am afraid of the Jews that are fallen to the Chaldeans, lest they deliver me into their hand, and they mock me.   John 12:42

20 But Jeremiah said, They shall not deliver *thee.* Obey, I beseech thee, the voice of the LORD, which I speak unto thee: so it shall be well unto thee, and thy soul shall live.   Is. 55:3

21 But if thou refuse to go forth, this *is* the word that the LORD hath shewed me:

22 And, behold, all the women that are left in the king of Judah's house *shall be* brought forth to the king of Babylon's princes, and those *women* shall say, Thy friends have set thee on, and have prevailed against thee: thy

---

Choices—and Consequences

Jeremiah 38:19, 24

[Zedekiah] sacrificed the noble freedom of his manhood and became a cringing slave to public opinion. With no fixed purpose to do evil, he was also without resolution to stand boldly for the right. Convicted though he was of the value of the counsel given by Jeremiah, he had not the moral stamina to obey; and as a consequence he advanced steadily in the wrong direction.

The king was even too weak to be willing that his courtiers and people should know that he had held a conference with Jeremiah, so fully had the fear of man taken possession of his soul. If Zedekiah had stood up bravely and declared that he believed the words of the prophet, already half fulfilled, what desolation might have been averted! He should have said, I will obey the Lord, and save the city from utter ruin. I dare not disregard the commands of God because of the fear or favor of man. I love the truth, I hate sin, and I will follow the counsel of the Mighty One of Israel.

Then the people would have respected his courageous spirit, and those who were wavering between faith and unbelief would have taken a firm stand for the right. The very fearlessness and justice of this course would have inspired his subjects with admiration and loyalty. He would have had ample support, and Judah would have been spared the untold woe of carnage and famine and fire. *PK 458*

feet are sunk in the mire, *and* they are turned away back.   Jer. 20:10
23 So they shall bring out all thy wives and thy children to the Chaldeans: and thou shalt not escape out of their hand, but shalt be taken by the hand of the king of Babylon: and thou shalt cause this city to be burned with fire.   Jer. 38:18; 39:6; 41:10

Jeremiah and Zedekiah Make an Agreement

24 Then said Zedekiah unto Jeremiah, Let no man know of these words, and thou shalt not die.
25 But if the princes hear that I have talked with thee, and they come unto thee, and say unto thee, Declare unto us now what thou hast said unto the king, hide it not from us, and we will not put thee to death; also what the king said unto thee: Jer. 38:4-6
26 Then thou shalt say unto them, I presented my supplication before the king, that he would not cause me to return to Jonathan's house, to die there.   Jer. 37:20
27 Then came all the princes unto Jeremiah, and asked him: and he told them according to all these words that the king had commanded. So they left off speaking with him; for the matter was not perceived.
28 So Jeremiah abode in the court of the prison until the day that Jerusalem was taken: and he was *there* when Jerusalem was taken.   Jer. 37:21

Jerusalem Is Captured

39 In the ninth year of Zedekiah king of Judah, in the tenth month, came Nebuchadrezzar king of Babylon and all his army against Jerusalem, and they besieged it.   Jer. 52:4-7
2 *And* in the eleventh year of Zedekiah, in the fourth month, the ninth *day* of the month, the city was broken up.
3 And all the princes of the king of Babylon came in, and sat in the middle gate, *even* Nergal-sharezer, Samgar-nebo, Sarsechim, Rab-saris, Nergal-sharezer, Rab-mag, with all the residue of the princes of the king of Babylon.   Jer. 21:4
4 And it came to pass, *that* when Zedekiah the king of Judah saw them, and all the men of war, then they fled, and went forth out of the city by night, by the way of the king's garden, by the gate ᵀbetwixt the two walls: and he went out the way of the plain.   *in between*
5 But the Chaldeans' army pursued after them, and overtook Zedekiah in the plains of Jericho: and when they had taken him, they brought him up to Nebuchadnezzar king of Babylon to Riblah in the land of Hamath, where he gave judgment upon him. Josh. 4:13

6 Then the king of Babylon slew the sons of Zedekiah in Riblah before his eyes: also the king of Babylon slew all the nobles of Judah.   Jer. 52:10
7 Moreover he put out Zedekiah's eyes, and bound him with chains, to carry him to Babylon.   Judg. 16:21; 2 Kin. 25:7; Ezek. 12:13
8 And the Chaldeans burned the king's house, and the houses of the people, with fire, and brake down the walls of Jerusalem.   Neh. 1:3; Jer. 21:10; 38:18
9 Then Nebuzar-adan the captain of the guard carried away captive into Babylon the remnant of the people that remained in the city, and those that fell away, that fell to him, with the rest of the people that remained.   Gen. 37:36; 2 Kin. 25:11; Jer. 40:1
10 But Nebuzar-adan the captain of the guard left of the poor of the people, which had nothing, in the land of Judah, and gave them vineyards and fields at the same time.   2 Kin. 25:12; Jer. 40:7

Nebuchadrezzar Commands Good Treatment for Jeremiah

11 Now Nebuchadrezzar king of Babylon gave charge concerning Jeremiah to Nebuzar-adan the captain of the guard, saying, Jer. 15:21
12 Take him, and look well to him, and do him no harm; but do unto him even as he shall say unto thee.   Prov. 16:7
13 So Nebuzar-adan the captain of the guard sent, and Nebushasban, Rab-saris, and Nergal-sharezer, Rab-mag, and all the king of Babylon's princes;   Jer. 39:3
14 Even they sent, and took Jeremiah out of the court of the prison, and committed him unto Gedaliah the son of Ahikam the son of Shaphan, that he should carry him home: so he dwelt among the people. 2 Kin. 22:12; 25:22-25
15 Now the word of the LORD came unto Jeremiah, while he was shut up in the court of the prison, saying,
16 Go and speak to Ebedmelech the Ethiopian, saying, Thus saith the LORD of hosts, the God of Israel; Behold, I will bring my words upon this city for evil, and not for good; and they shall be *accomplished* in that day before thee.   Dan. 9:12; Zech. 1:6
17 But I will deliver thee in that day, saith the LORD: and thou shalt not be given into the hand of the men of whom thou *art* afraid.   Ps. 41:1-2
18 For I will surely deliver thee, and thou shalt not fall by the sword, but thy life shall be for a prey unto thee: because thou hast put thy trust in me, saith the LORD. Ps. 34:22; Jer. 21:9

Jeremiah Is Freed

40 The word that came to Jeremiah from the LORD, after that

Nebuzar-adan the captain of the guard had let him go from Ramah, when he had taken him being bound in chains among all that were carried away captive of Jerusalem and Judah, which were carried away captive unto Babylon.   Jer. 31:15

2 And the captain of the guard took Jeremiah, and said unto him, The LORD thy God hath pronounced this evil upon this place.   Deut. 29:24-28

3 Now the LORD hath brought *it*, and done according as he hath said: because ye have sinned against the LORD, and have not obeyed his voice, therefore this thing is come upon you.   Rom. 2:5

4 And now, behold, I loose thee this day from the chains which *were* upon thine hand. If it seem good unto thee to come with me into Babylon, come; and I will look well unto thee: but if it seem ill unto thee to come with me into Babylon, ᵀforbear: behold, all the land *is* before thee: whither it seemeth good and ᵀconvenient for thee to go, thither go.   *refuse to act ◆ appropriate*

5 Now while he was not yet gone back, *he said*, Go back also to Gedaliah the son of Ahikam the son of Shaphan, whom the king of Babylon hath made governor over the cities of Judah, and dwell with him among the people: or go wheresoever it seemeth convenient unto thee to go. So the captain of the guard gave him ᵀvictuals and a reward, and let him go.   2 Kin. 8:7-9; Jer. 39:14; 41:2 ◆ *food*

6 Then went Jeremiah unto Gedaliah the son of Ahikam to Mizpah; and dwelt with him among the people that were left in the land.   Judg. 20:1

The Dispersed Jews Rally around Gedaliah

7 Now when all the captains of the forces which *were* in the fields, *even* they and their men, heard that the king of Babylon had made Gedaliah the son of Ahikam governor in the land, and had committed unto him men, and women, and children, and of the poor of the land, of them that were not carried away captive to Babylon;   Jer. 39:10

8 Then they came to Gedaliah to Mizpah, even Ishmael the son of Nethaniah, and Johanan and Jonathan the sons of Kareah, and Seraiah the son of Tanhumeth, and the sons of Ephai the Netophathite, and Jezaniah the son of a Maachathite, they and their men.   Deut. 3:14; Josh. 12:5; Jer. 42:1

9 And Gedaliah the son of Ahikam the son of Shaphan sware unto them and to their men, saying, Fear not to serve the Chaldeans: dwell in the land, and serve the king of Babylon, and it shall be well with you.   Jer. 27:11

10 As for me, behold, I will dwell at Mizpah to serve the Chaldeans, which will come unto us: but ye, gather ye wine, and summer fruits, and oil, and put *them* in your vessels, and dwell in your cities that ye have taken.   Jer. 40:12

11 Likewise when all the Jews that *were* in Moab, and among the Ammonites, and in Edom, and that *were* in all the countries, heard that the king of Babylon had left a remnant of Judah, and that he had set over them Gedaliah the son of Ahikam the son of Shaphan;   Is. 16:4

12 Even all the Jews returned out of all places whither they were driven, and came to the land of Judah, to Gedaliah, unto Mizpah, and gathered wine and summer fruits very much.   Jer. 43:5

13 Moreover Johanan the son of Kareah, and all the captains of the forces that *were* in the fields, came to Gedaliah to Mizpah,

14 And said unto him, Dost thou certainly know that Baalis the king of the Ammonites hath sent Ishmael the son of Nethaniah to slay thee? But Gedaliah the son of Ahikam believed them not.   2 Sam. 10:1-6; Jer. 25:21; 41:10

15 Then Johanan the son of Kareah spake to Gedaliah in Mizpah secretly, saying, Let me go, I pray thee, and I will slay Ishmael the son of Nethaniah, and no man shall know *it*: wherefore should he slay thee, that all the Jews which are gathered unto thee should be scattered, and the remnant in Judah perish?   1 Sam. 26:8

16 But Gedaliah the son of Ahikam said unto Johanan the son of Kareah, Thou shalt not do this thing: for thou speakest falsely of Ishmael.

Ishamel Slays Gedaliah

41 Now it came to pass in the seventh month, *that* Ishmael the son of Nethaniah the son of Elishama, of the seed royal, and the princes of the king, even ten men with him, came unto Gedaliah the son of Ahikam to Mizpah; and there they did eat bread together in Mizpah.   Ps. 41:9; Jer. 40:6, 8

2 Then arose Ishmael the son of Nethaniah, and the ten men that were with him, and smote Gedaliah the son of Ahikam the son of Shaphan with the sword, and slew him, whom the king of Babylon had made governor over the land.   2 Kin. 25:25

3 Ishmael also slew all the Jews that were with him, *even* with Gedaliah, at Mizpah, and the Chaldeans that were found there, *and* the men of war.

4 And it came to pass the second day after he had slain Gedaliah, and no man knew *it*,

5 That there came certain from Shechem, from Shiloh, and from Samaria, *even* ᵀfourscore men, having their beards shaven, and

their clothes rent, and having cut themselves, with offerings and incense in their hand, to bring *them* to the house of the LORD.   Deut. 14:1; Josh. 18:1; 1 Kin. 16:24 ◆ *eighty*

6 And Ishmael the son of Nethaniah went forth from Mizpah to meet them, weeping all along as he went: and it came to pass, as he met them, he said unto them, Come to Gedaliah the son of Ahikam.   2 Sam. 3:16

7 And it was *so*, when they came into the midst of the city, that Ishmael the son of Nethaniah slew them, *and cast them* into the midst of the pit, he, and the men that *were* with him.   Ps. 55:23

8 But ten men were found among them that said unto Ishmael, Slay us not: for we have treasures in the field, of wheat, and of barley, and of oil, and of honey. So he forbare, and slew them not among their brethren.

9 Now the pit wherein Ishmael had cast all the dead bodies of the men, whom he had slain because of Gedaliah, *was* it which Asa the king had made for fear of Baasha king of Israel: *and* Ishmael the son of Nethaniah filled it with *them that were* slain.   Judg. 6:2

10 Then Ishmael carried away captive all the residue of the people that *were* in Mizpah, *even* the king's daughters, and all the people that remained in Mizpah, whom Nebuzaradan the captain of the guard had committed to Gedaliah the son of Ahikam: and Ishmael the son of Nethaniah carried them away captive, and departed to go over to the Ammonites.   Neh. 2:10; Jer. 40:7, 14

Plans to Flee into Egypt

11 But when Johanan the son of Kareah, and all the captains of the forces that *were* with him, heard of all the evil that Ishmael the son of Nethaniah had done,   Jer. 40:7-8

12 Then they took all the men, and went to fight with Ishmael the son of Nethaniah, and found him by the great waters that *are* in Gibeon.   Gen. 14:14-16; 1 Sam. 30:1-8; 2 Sam. 2:13

13 Now it came to pass, *that* when all the people which *were* with Ishmael saw Johanan the son of Kareah, and all the captains of the forces that *were* with him, then they were glad.

14 So all the people that Ishmael had carried away captive from Mizpah cast about and returned, and went unto Johanan the son of Kareah.

15 But Ishmael the son of Nethaniah escaped from Johanan with eight men, and went to the Ammonites.

16 Then took Johanan the son of Kareah, and all the captains of the forces that *were* with him, all the remnant of the people whom he had recovered from Ishmael the son of Nethaniah, from Mizpah, after *that* he had slain

Gedaliah the son of Ahikam, *even* mighty men of war, and the women, and the children, and the ᵀeunuchs, whom he had brought again from Gibeon: Jer. 42:8 ◆ *castrated male servants*

17 And they departed, and dwelt in the habitation of Chimham, which is by Bethlehem, to go to enter into Egypt,   2 Sam. 19:37-38

18 Because of the Chaldeans: for they were afraid of them, because Ishmael the son of Nethaniah had slain Gedaliah the son of Ahikam, whom the king of Babylon made governor in the land.   Jer. 40:5; 42:16; Luke 12:4-5

Jeremiah Warns the People Not to Go to Egypt

42 Then all the captains of the forces, and Johanan the son of Kareah, and Jezaniah the son of Hoshaiah, and all the people from the least even unto the greatest, came near,   Jer. 6:13; 40:13; 41:11

2 And said unto Jeremiah the prophet, Let, we ᵀbeseech thee, our supplication be accepted before thee, and pray for us unto the LORD thy God, *even* for all this remnant; (for we are left *but* a few of many, as thine eyes do behold us:)   Lev. 26:22; 1 Sam. 7:8; Jer. 36:7 ◆ *beg*

3 That the LORD thy God may shew us the way wherein we may walk, and the thing that we may do.   Ps. 86:11

4 Then Jeremiah the prophet said unto them, I have heard *you*; behold, I will pray unto the LORD your God according to your words; and it shall come to pass, *that* whatsoever thing the LORD shall answer you, I will declare *it* unto you; I will keep nothing back from you.   Ex. 8:29

5 Then they said to Jeremiah, The LORD be a true and faithful witness between us, if we do not even according to all things for the which the LORD thy God shall send thee to us.   Gen. 31:50; Judg. 11:10; Mic. 1:2

6 Whether *it be* good, or whether *it be* evil, we will obey the voice of the LORD our God, to whom we send thee; that it may be well with us, when we obey the voice of the LORD our God.   Deut. 5:29, 33; Jer. 7:23

7 And it came to pass after ten days, that the word of the LORD came unto Jeremiah.

8 Then called he Johanan the son of Kareah, and all the captains of the forces which *were* with him, and all the people from the least even to the greatest,   Jer. 42:1

9 And said unto them, Thus saith the LORD, the God of Israel, unto whom ye sent me to present your supplication before him; 2 Kin. 19:4

10 If ye will still abide in this land, then will I build you, and not pull *you* down, and I will plant you, and not pluck *you* up: for I repent me of the evil that I have done unto you.   Jer. 24:6; 31:28; Ezek. 36:36

11 Be not afraid of the king of Babylon, of

whom ye are afraid; be not afraid of him, saith the LORD: for I *am* with you to save you, and to deliver you from his hand.   Is. 43:5; Rom. 8:31

12 And I will shew mercies unto you, that he may have mercy upon you, and cause you to return to your own land.   Neh. 1:11

13 But if ye say, We will not dwell in this land, neither obey the voice of the LORD your God,   Ex. 5:2; Jer. 44:16

14 Saying, No; but we will go into the land of Egypt, where we shall see no war, nor hear the sound of the trumpet, nor have hunger of bread; and there will we dwell: Jer. 4:19

15 And now therefore hear the word of the LORD, ye remnant of Judah; Thus saith the LORD of hosts, the God of Israel; If ye wholly set your faces to enter into Egypt, and go to sojourn there;   Deut. 17:16

16 Then it shall come to pass, *that* the sword, which ye feared, shall overtake you there in the land of Egypt, and the famine, whereof ye were afraid, shall follow close after you there in Egypt; and there ye shall die.   Jer. 44:27; Ezek. 11:8; Amos 9:1-4

17 So shall it be with all the men that set their faces to go into Egypt to sojourn there; they shall die by the sword, by the famine, and by the pestilence: and none of them shall remain or escape from the evil that I will bring upon them.   Jer. 42:22

18 For thus saith the LORD of hosts, the God of Israel; As mine anger and my fury hath been poured forth upon the inhabitants of Jerusalem; so shall my fury be poured forth upon you, when ye shall enter into Egypt: and ye shall be an execration, and an astonishment, and a curse, and a reproach; and ye shall see this place no more. Jer. 7:20; 18:16; 29:18

19 The LORD hath said concerning you, O ye remnant of Judah; Go ye not into Egypt: know certainly that I have admonished you this day.   Deut. 17:16

20 For ye ᵀdissembled in your hearts, when ye sent me unto the LORD your God, saying, Pray for us unto the LORD our God; and according unto all that the LORD our God shall say, so declare unto us, and we will do *it*.   lied

21 And *now* I have this day declared *it* to you; but ye have not obeyed the voice of the LORD your God, nor any *thing* for the which he hath sent me unto you.   Ezek. 2:7

22 Now therefore know certainly that ye shall die by the sword, by the famine, and by the pestilence, in the place whither ye desire to go *and* to sojourn.   Jer. 42:17

Jeremiah Is Forced to Go to Egypt

43 And it came to pass, *that* when Jeremiah had made an end of speaking unto all the people all the words of the LORD their God, for which the LORD their God had sent him to them, *even* all these words,   Jer. 26:8

2 Then spake Azariah the son of Hoshaiah, and Johanan the son of Kareah, and all the proud men, saying unto Jeremiah, Thou speakest falsely: the LORD our God hath not sent thee to say, Go not into Egypt to sojourn there: 2 Chr. 36:13

3 But Baruch the son of Neriah setteth thee on against us, for to deliver us into the hand of the Chaldeans, that they might put us to death, and carry us away captives into Babylon.   Jer. 36:4

4 So Johanan the son of Kareah, and all the captains of the forces, and all the people, obeyed not the voice of the LORD, to dwell in the land of Judah.   Jer. 42:5-6

5 But Johanan the son of Kareah, and all the captains of the forces, took all the remnant of Judah, that were returned from all nations, whither they had been driven, to dwell in the land of Judah;   Jer. 40:11-12

6 *Even* men, and women, and children, and the king's daughters, and every person that Nebuzar-adan the captain of the guard had left with Gedaliah the son of Ahikam the son of Shaphan, and Jeremiah the prophet, and Baruch the son of Neriah.   Jer. 39:10

7 So they came into the land of Egypt: for they obeyed not the voice of the LORD: thus came they *even* to Tahpanhes.   Is. 30:4; Jer. 2:16; 44:1

Jeremiah Prophesies the Conquest of Egypt by Babylon

8 Then came the word of the LORD unto Jeremiah in Tahpanhes, saying,

9 Take great stones in thine hand, and hide them in the clay in the brickkiln, which *is* at the entry of Pharaoh's house in Tahpanhes, in the sight of the men of Judah;

10 And say unto them, Thus saith the LORD of hosts, the God of Israel; Behold, I will send and take Nebuchadrezzar the king of Babylon, my servant, and will set his throne upon these stones that I have hid; and he shall spread his royal pavilion over them.   Ps. 18:11

11 And when he cometh, he shall ᵀsmite the land of Egypt, *and deliver* such *as are* for death to death; and such *as are* for captivity to captivity; and such *as are* for the sword to the sword.   Jer. 15:2; 44:13; Ezek. 29:19-20 ✦ *strike*

12 And I will kindle a fire in the houses of the gods of Egypt; and he shall burn them, and carry them away captives: and he shall array himself with the land of Egypt, as a shepherd putteth on his garment; and he shall go forth from thence in peace.   Ex. 12:12; Jer. 46:25

13 He shall break also the images of Beth-shemesh, that *is* in the land of Egypt; and

the houses of the gods of the Egyptians shall he burn with fire.

Punishment for Idolatry

44 The word that came to Jeremiah concerning all the Jews which dwell in the land of Egypt, which dwell at Migdol, and at Tahpanhes, and at Noph, and in the country of Pathros, saying,   Ex. 14:2; Is. 11:11; Jer. 46:14

2 Thus saith the LORD of hosts, the God of Israel; Ye have seen all the evil that I have brought upon Jerusalem, and upon all the cities of Judah; and, behold, this day they *are* a desolation, and no man dwelleth therein,   Is. 6:11

3 Because of their wickedness which they have committed to provoke me to anger, in that they went to burn incense, *and* to serve other gods, whom they knew not, *neither* they, ye, nor your fathers.   Deut. 13:6

4 Howbeit I sent unto you all my servants the prophets, rising early and sending *them*, saying, Oh, do not this abominable thing that I hate.   Jer. 7:13

5 But they hearkened not, nor inclined their ear to turn from their wickedness, to burn no incense unto other gods.

6 Wherefore my fury and mine anger was poured forth, and was kindled in the cities of Judah and in the streets of Jerusalem; and they are wasted *and* desolate, as at this day.   Is. 51:17

7 Therefore now thus saith the LORD, the God of hosts, the God of Israel; Wherefore commit ye *this* great evil against your souls, to cut off from you man and woman, child and suckling, out of Judah, to leave you none to remain;   Num. 16:38

8 In that ye provoke me unto wrath with the works of your hands, burning incense unto other gods in the land of Egypt, whither ye be gone to dwell, that ye might cut yourselves off, and that ye might be a curse and a reproach among all the nations of the earth?   Jer. 25:6-7; 42:18; 44:3

9 Have ye forgotten the wickedness of your fathers, and the wickedness of the kings of Judah, and the wickedness of their wives, and your own wickedness, and the wickedness of your wives, which they have committed in the land of Judah, and in the streets of Jerusalem?   Jer. 7:17-18

10 They are not humbled *even* unto this day, neither have they feared, nor walked in my law, nor in my statutes, that I set before you and before your fathers.   Prov. 28:14

11 Therefore thus saith the LORD of hosts, the God of Israel; Behold, I will set my face against you for evil, and to cut off all Judah.   Lev. 17:10; Jer. 21:10; Amos 9:4

12 And I will take the remnant of Judah, that have set their faces to go into the land of Egypt to sojourn there, and they shall all be consumed, *and* fall in the land of Egypt; they shall *even* be consumed by the sword *and* by the famine: they shall die, from the least even unto the greatest, by the sword and by the famine: and they shall be an ᵀexecration, *and* an astonishment, and a curse, and a reproach.   Jer. 42:15-18 ◆ *curse*

13 For I will punish them that dwell in the land of Egypt, as I have punished Jerusalem, by the sword, by the famine, and by the pestilence: Jer. 11:22

14 So that none of the remnant of Judah, which are gone into the land of Egypt to sojourn there, shall escape or remain, that they should return into the land of Judah, to the which they have a desire to return to dwell there: for none shall return but such as shall escape.   Jer. 22:26-27

The Obstinacy of the Jews

15 Then all the men which knew that their wives had burned incense unto other gods, and all the women that stood by, a great multitude, even all the people that dwelt in the land of Egypt, in Pathros, answered Jeremiah, saying,

16 *As for* the word that thou hast spoken unto us in the name of the LORD, we will not hearken unto thee.

17 But we will certainly do whatsoever thing goeth forth out of our own mouth, to burn incense unto the queen of heaven, and to pour out drink offerings unto her, as we have done, we, and our fathers, our kings, and our princes, in the cities of Judah, and in the streets of Jerusalem: for *then* had we plenty of ᵀvictuals, and were well, and saw no evil.   Deut. 23:23; Neh. 9:34; Jer. 7:18 ◆ *food*

18 But since we left off to burn incense to the queen of heaven, and to pour out drink offerings unto her, we have wanted all *things*, and have been consumed by the sword and by the famine.   Mal. 3:13-15

19 And when we burned incense to the queen of heaven, and poured out drink offerings unto her, did we make her cakes to worship her, and pour out drink offerings unto her, without our men?   Jer. 7:18; 44:15

Jeremiah Threatens Destruction

20 Then Jeremiah said unto all the people, to the men, and to the women, and to all the people which had given him *that* answer, saying,

21 The incense that ye burned in the cities of Judah, and in the streets of Jerusalem, ye, and your fathers, your kings, and your princes, and the people of the land, did not

the LORD remember them, and came it *not* into his mind?   Ps. 79:8

22 So that the LORD could no longer bear, because of the evil of your doings, *and* because of the abominations which ye have committed; therefore is your land a desolation, and an astonishment, and a curse, without an inhabitant, as at this day. Jer. 25:18

23 Because ye have burned incense, and because ye have sinned against the LORD, and have not obeyed the voice of the LORD, nor walked in his law, nor in his statutes, nor in his testimonies; therefore this evil is happened unto you, as at this day.   1 Kin. 9:9

24 Moreover Jeremiah said unto all the people, and to all the women, Hear the word of the LORD, all Judah that *are* in the land of Egypt: Jer. 42:15; 43:7; 44:15-16

25 Thus saith the LORD of hosts, the God of Israel, saying; Ye and your wives have both spoken with your mouths, and fulfilled with your hand, saying, We will surely perform our vows that we have vowed, to burn incense to the queen of heaven, and to pour out drink offerings unto her: ye will surely accomplish your vows, and surely perform your vows.   Matt. 14:9

26 Therefore hear ye the word of the LORD, all Judah that dwell in the land of Egypt; Behold, I have sworn by my great name, saith the LORD, that my name shall no more be named in the mouth of any man of Judah in all the land of Egypt, saying, The Lord GOD liveth.   Gen. 22:16

27 Behold, I will watch over them for evil, and not for good: and all the men of Judah that *are* in the land of Egypt shall be consumed by the sword and by the famine, until there be an end of them.   2 Kin. 21:14; Jer. 1:10; 31:28

28 Yet a small number that escape the sword shall return out of the land of Egypt into the land of Judah, and all the remnant of Judah, that are gone into the land of Egypt to sojourn there, shall know whose words shall stand, mine, or theirs.   Is. 10:19; Jer. 44:14, 25-26

44:28 Mercy for the Loyal

The prophecies of doom pronounced by Jeremiah upon the remnant that had rebelled against Nebuchadnezzar by fleeing to Egypt were mingled with promises of pardon to those who should repent of their folly and stand ready to return. While the Lord would not spare those who turned from His counsel to the seductive influences of Egyptian idolatry, yet He would show mercy to those who should prove loyal and true. *PK 460, 461*

---

29 And this *shall be* a sign unto you, saith the LORD, that I will punish you in this place, that ye may know that my words shall surely stand against you for evil: Prov. 19:21; Is. 40:8; Jer. 44:30

30 Thus saith the LORD; Behold, I will give Pharaoh-hophra king of Egypt into the hand of his enemies, and into the hand of them that seek his life; as I gave Zedekiah king of Judah into the hand of Nebuchadrezzar king of Babylon, his enemy, and that sought his life.   2 Kin. 25:4-7

The Lord's Promise to Baruch

45 The word that Jeremiah the prophet spake unto Baruch the son of Neriah, when he had written these words in a book at the mouth of Jeremiah, in the fourth year of Jehoiakim the son of Josiah king of Judah, saying,   Jer. 32:12; 36:1, 4

2 Thus saith the LORD, the God of Israel, unto thee, O Baruch;

3 Thou didst say, Woe is me now! for the

For Those Who Feel Unappreciated

Jeremiah 45:5

Let those who feel that their work is not appreciated, and who crave a position of greater responsibility, consider that "promotion cometh neither from the east, nor from the west, nor from the south. But God is the Judge: He putteth down one, and setteth up another" (Psalm 75:6, 7). Every man has his place in the eternal plan of heaven. Whether we fill that place depends upon our own faithfulness in co-operating with God.

We need to beware of self-pity. Never indulge the feeling that you are not esteemed as you should be, that your efforts are not appreciated, that your work is too difficult. Let the memory of what Christ has endured for us silence every murmuring thought. We are treated better than was our Lord. "Seekest thou great things for thyself? seek them not" (Jeremiah 45:5). The Lord has no place in His work for those who have a greater desire to win the crown than to bear the cross. He wants men who are more intent upon doing their duty than upon receiving their reward—men who are more solicitous for principle than for promotion.

Those who are humble, and who do their work as unto God, may not make so great a show as do those who are full of bustle and self-importance; but their work counts for more. Often those who make a great parade call attention to self, interposing between the people and God, and their work proves a failure. *MH 476, 477*

LORD hath added grief to my sorrow; I fainted in my sighing, and I find no rest.   2 Cor. 4:1

4 Thus shalt thou say unto him, The LORD saith thus; Behold, *that* which I have built will I break down, and that which I have planted I will pluck up, even this whole land.   Jer. 18:7-10

5 And seekest thou great things for thyself? seek *them* not: for, behold, I will bring evil upon all flesh, saith the LORD: but thy life will I give unto thee for a prey in all places whither thou goest.   Jer. 21:9; 38:2; 39:18

45:5 God Says Quit Complaining

Never indulge the feeling that you are not esteemed as you should be, that your efforts are not appreciated, that your work is too difficult. Let the memory of what Christ has endured for us silence every murmuring thought. We are treated better than was our Lord. "Seekest thou great things for thyself? seek them not" (Jeremiah 45:5). The Lord has no place in His work for those who have a greater desire to win the crown than to bear the cross. *MH 476*

A Prophecy Against Egypt

46 The word of the LORD which came to Jeremiah the prophet against the Gentiles;   Jer. 1:10

2 Against Egypt, against the army of Pharaoh-necho king of Egypt, which was by the river Euphrates in Carchemish, which Nebuchadrezzar king of Babylon smote in the fourth year of Jehoiakim the son of Josiah king of Judah.   2 Kin. 23:29; Is. 10:9; Jer. 25:1

3 Order ye the ᵀbuckler and shield, and draw near to battle.   Is. 21:5 ◆ *small shield*

4 Harness the horses; and get up, ye horsemen, and stand forth with *your* helmets; ᵀfurbish the spears, *and* put on the ᵀbrigandines.   Ezek. 21:9-11 ◆ *polish* ◆ *coats of armor*

5 Wherefore have I seen them dismayed *and* turned away back? and their mighty ones are beaten down, and are fled ᵀapace, and look not back: *for* fear *was* round about, saith the LORD.   Jer. 6:25 ◆ *quickly*

6 Let not the swift flee away, nor the mighty man escape; they shall stumble, and fall toward the north by the river Euphrates. Jer. 46:12

7 Who *is* this *that* cometh up as a flood, whose waters are moved as the rivers? Is. 8:7-8; Jer. 47:2

8 Egypt riseth up like a flood, and *his* waters are moved like the rivers; and he saith, I will go up, *and* will cover the earth; I will destroy the city and the inhabitants thereof.

9 Come up, ye horses; and rage, ye chariots; and let the mighty men come forth; the Ethiopians and the Libyans, that handle

the shield; and the Lydians, that handle *and* bend the bow.   Is. 66:19; Ezek. 27:10; Nah. 3:9

10 For this *is* the day of the Lord GOD of hosts, a day of vengeance, that he may avenge him of his adversaries: and the sword shall devour, and it shall be satiate and made drunk with their blood: for the Lord GOD of hosts hath a sacrifice in the north country by the river Euphrates.   Deut. 32:42; Jer. 46:2; Joel 1:15

11 Go up into Gilead, and take ᵀbalm, O virgin, the daughter of Egypt: in vain shalt thou use many medicines; *for* thou shalt not be cured.   Is. 47:1; Jer. 8:22; Mic. 1:9 ◆ *medicine*

12 The nations have heard of thy shame, and thy cry hath filled the land: for the mighty man hath stumbled against the mighty, *and* they are fallen both together.   Nah. 3:8-10

13 The word that the LORD spake to Jeremiah the prophet, how Nebuchadrezzar king of Babylon should come *and* ᵀsmite the land of Egypt.   Jer. 43:10-13 ◆ *strike*

14 Declare ye in Egypt, and publish in Migdol, and publish in Noph and in Tahpanhes: say ye, Stand fast, and prepare thee; for the sword shall devour round about thee. Jer. 44:1

15 Why are thy valiant *men* swept away? they stood not, because the LORD did drive them.   Is. 66:15-16

16 He made many to fall, yea, one fell upon another: and they said, Arise, and let us go again to our own people, and to the land of our nativity, from the oppressing sword.

17 They did cry there, Pharaoh king of Egypt *is but* a noise; he hath passed the time appointed.   Is. 19:11-16

18 *As* I live, saith the King, whose name *is* the LORD of hosts, Surely as Tabor *is* among the mountains, and as Carmel by the sea, *so* shall he come.   Josh. 19:22; Judg. 4:6; Jer. 48:15

19 O thou daughter dwelling in Egypt, furnish thyself to go into captivity: for Noph shall be waste and desolate without an inhabitant.   Is. 20:4

20 Egypt *is like* a very fair heifer, *but* destruction cometh; it cometh out of the north.

21 Also her hired men *are* in the midst of her like fatted bullocks; for they also are turned back, *and* are fled away together: they did not stand, because the day of their calamity was come upon them, *and* the time of their visitation.   2 Kin. 7:6

22 The voice thereof shall go like a serpent; for they shall march with an army, and come against her with axes, as ᵀhewers of wood.   Is. 14:8 ◆ *woodcutters*

23 They shall cut down her forest, saith the LORD, though it cannot be searched; because they are more than the grasshoppers, and *are* innumerable.   Judg. 6:5; 7:12; Joel 2:25

24 The daughter of Egypt shall be con-

founded; she shall be delivered into the hand of the people of the north.   Jer. 1:15
25 The LORD of hosts, the God of Israel, saith; Behold, I will punish the multitude of No, and Pharaoh, and Egypt, with their gods, and their kings; even Pharaoh, and *all* them that trust in him: Ex. 12:12
26 And I will deliver them into the hand of those that seek their lives, and into the hand of Nebuchadrezzar king of Babylon, and into the hand of his servants: and afterward it shall be inhabited, as in the days of old, saith the LORD.   Jer. 44:30; Ezek. 29:8-14; 32:11
27 But fear not thou, O my servant Jacob, and be not dismayed, O Israel: for, behold, I will save thee from afar off, and thy seed from the land of their captivity; and Jacob shall return, and be in rest and at ease, and none shall make *him* afraid.   Is. 43:5
28 Fear thou not, O Jacob my servant, saith the LORD: for I *am* with thee; for I will make a full end of all the nations whither I have driven thee: but I will not make a full end of thee, but correct thee in measure; yet will I not leave thee wholly unpunished.   Jer. 4:27

A Prophecy Against Philistia

47 The word of the LORD that came to Jeremiah the prophet against the Philistines, before that Pharaoh smote Gaza.   Gen. 10:19; 1 Kin. 4:24; Jer. 25:20
2 Thus saith the LORD; Behold, waters rise up out of the north, and shall be an overflowing flood, and shall overflow the land, and all that is therein; the city, and them that dwell therein: then the men shall cry, and all the inhabitants of the land shall howl.   Is. 8:7-8
3 At the noise of the stamping of the hoofs of his strong *horses*, at the rushing of his chariots, *and at* the rumbling of his wheels, the fathers shall not look back to *their* children for feebleness of hands;   Judg. 5:22
4 Because of the day that cometh to spoil all the Philistines, *and* to cut off from Tyrus and Zidon every helper that remaineth: for the LORD will spoil the Philistines, the remnant of the country of Caphtor.   Deut. 2:23; Is. 20:6
5 Baldness is come upon Gaza; Ashkelon is cut off *with* the remnant of their valley: how long wilt thou cut thyself?   Jer. 25:20; 41:5; 48:37
6 O thou sword of the LORD, how long *will it be* ᵀere thou be quiet? put up thyself into thy scabbard, rest, and be still.   Jer. 12:12 ◆ *before*
7 How can it be quiet, seeing the LORD hath given it a charge against Ashkelon, and against the sea shore? there hath he appointed it.   Ezek. 14:17

A Prophecy Against Moab

48 Against Moab thus saith the LORD of hosts, the God of Israel; Woe unto Nebo! for it is spoiled: Kiriathaim is confounded *and* taken: Misgab is confounded and dismayed.   Num. 32:3
2 *There shall be* no more praise of Moab: in Heshbon they have devised evil against it; come, and let us cut it off from *being* a nation. Also thou shalt be cut down, O Madmen; the sword shall pursue thee.   Num. 32:37
3 A voice of crying *shall be* from Horonaim, spoiling and great destruction.   Is. 15:5; Jer. 48:5
4 Moab is destroyed; her little ones have caused a cry to be heard.
5 For in the going up of Luhith continual weeping shall go up; for in the going down of Horonaim the enemies have heard a cry of destruction.   Is. 15:5
6 Flee, save your lives, and be like the heath in the wilderness.   Jer. 17:6
7 For because thou hast trusted in thy works and in thy treasures, thou shalt also be taken: and Chemosh shall go forth into captivity *with* his priests and his princes together.   Num. 21:29; 1 Kin. 11:33; Jer. 49:3
8 And the spoiler shall come upon every city, and no city shall escape: the valley also shall perish, and the plain shall be destroyed, as the LORD hath spoken.   Jer. 6:26
9 Give wings unto Moab, that it may flee and get away: for the cities thereof shall be desolate, without any to dwell therein.   Ps. 11:1
10 Cursed *be* he that doeth the work of the LORD deceitfully, and cursed *be* he that keepeth back his sword from blood.   Judg. 5:23
11 Moab hath been at ease from his youth, and he hath settled on his ᵀlees, and hath not been emptied from vessel to vessel, neither hath he gone into captivity: therefore his taste remained in him, and his scent is not changed.   Nah. 2:2; Zeph. 1:12; Zech. 1:15 ◆ *dregs*
12 Therefore, behold, the days come, saith the LORD, that I will send unto him wanderers, that shall cause him to wander, and shall empty his vessels, and break their bottles.
13 And Moab shall be ashamed of Chemosh, as the house of Israel was ashamed of Bethel their confidence.   Judg. 11:24
14 How say ye, We *are* mighty and strong men for the war?   Ps. 33:16
15 Moab is spoiled, and gone up *out of* her cities, and his chosen young men are gone down to the slaughter, saith the King, whose name *is* the LORD of hosts.   Jer. 46:18; 50:27; 51:57
16 The calamity of Moab *is* near to come, and his affliction hasteth fast.   Is. 13:22
17 All ye that are about him, ᵀbemoan him; and all ye that know his name, say, How is the strong staff broken, *and* the beautiful rod!   Is. 9:4 ◆ *lament for*

18 Thou daughter that dost inhabit Dibon, come down from *thy* glory, and sit in thirst; for the spoiler of Moab shall come upon thee, *and* he shall destroy thy strong holds.   Is. 15:2

19 O inhabitant of Aroer, stand by the way, and espy; ask him that fleeth, and her that escapeth, *and* say, What is done?   Deut. 2:36

20 Moab is confounded; for it is broken down: howl and cry; tell ye it in Arnon, that Moab is spoiled;   Is. 16:2

21 And judgment is come upon the plain country; upon Holon, and upon Jahazah, and upon Mephaath,   Num. 21:23; Josh. 13:18; Is. 15:4

22 And upon Dibon, and upon Nebo, and upon Beth-diblathaim,   Num. 33:46

23 And upon Kiriathaim, and upon Beth-gamul, and upon Beth-meon,   Josh. 13:17

24 And upon Kerioth, and upon Bozrah, and upon all the cities of the land of Moab, far or near.   Jer. 48:41; Amos 2:2

25 The horn of Moab is cut off, and his arm is broken, saith the LORD.   Job 22:9; Ps. 10:15; 75:10

26 Make ye him drunken: for he magnified *himself* against the LORD: Moab also shall ᵀwallow in his vomit, and he also shall be in derision.   Is. 19:14 ◆ *roll*

27 For was not Israel a derision unto thee? was he found among thieves? for since thou spakest of him, thou skippedst for joy.   Jer. 2:26

28 O ye that dwell in Moab, leave the cities, and dwell in the rock, and be like the dove *that* maketh her nest in the sides of the hole's mouth.   Judg. 6:2

29 We have heard the pride of Moab, (he is exceeding proud) his loftiness, and his arrogancy, and his pride, and the haughtiness of his heart.   Ps. 138:6; Is. 16:6

30 I know his wrath, saith the LORD; but *it* shall not *be* so; his lies shall not so effect *it*.

31 Therefore will I howl for Moab, and I will cry out for all Moab; *mine heart* shall mourn for the men of Kir-heres.   2 Kin. 3:25; Is. 15:5; Jer. 48:36

32 O vine of Sibmah, I will weep for thee with the weeping of Jazer: thy plants are gone over the sea, they reach *even* to the sea of Jazer: the spoiler is fallen upon thy summer fruits and upon thy vintage.   Num. 21:32; Josh. 13:19; Is. 16:8-9

33 And joy and gladness is taken from the plentiful field, and from the land of Moab; and I have caused wine to fail from the winepresses: none shall tread with shouting; *their* shouting *shall be* no shouting.   Is. 5:10

34 From the cry of Heshbon *even* unto Elealeh, *and even* unto Jahaz, have they uttered their voice, from Zoar *even* unto Horonaim, *as* an heifer of three years old: for the waters also of Nimrim shall be desolate.   Is. 15:4-6

35 Moreover I will cause to cease in Moab, saith the LORD, him that offereth in the high places, and him that burneth incense to his gods.   Is. 15:2; 16:12

36 Therefore mine heart shall sound for Moab like pipes, and mine heart shall sound like pipes for the men of Kir-heres: because the riches *that* he hath gotten are perished.   Is. 15:5

37 For every head *shall be* bald, and every beard clipped: upon all the hands *shall be* cuttings, and upon the ᵀloins sackcloth.   *waist*

38 *There shall be* lamentation generally upon all the housetops of Moab, and in the streets thereof: for I have broken Moab like a vessel wherein *is* no pleasure, saith the LORD.   Is. 22:1; Jer. 22:28; 25:34

39 They shall howl, *saying*, How is it broken down! how hath Moab turned the back with shame! so shall Moab be a derision and a dismaying to all them about him.

40 For thus saith the LORD; Behold, he shall fly as an eagle, and shall spread his wings over Moab.   Deut. 28:49; Is. 8:8; Jer. 49:22

41 Kerioth is taken, and the strong holds are surprised, and the mighty men's hearts in Moab at that day shall be as the heart of a woman in her pangs.   Is. 13:8

42 And Moab shall be destroyed from *being* a people, because he hath magnified *himself* against the LORD.   Jer. 48:2

43 Fear, and the pit, and the snare, *shall be* upon thee, O inhabitant of Moab, saith the LORD.   Is. 24:17-18

44 He that fleeth from the fear shall fall into the pit; and he that getteth up out of the pit shall be taken in the snare: for I will bring upon it, *even* upon Moab, the year of their visitation, saith the LORD.   1 Kin. 19:17

45 They that fled stood under the shadow of Heshbon because of the force: but a fire shall come forth out of Heshbon, and a flame from the midst of Sihon, and shall devour the corner of Moab, and the crown of the head of the tumultuous ones.   Num. 21:28; 24:17

46 Woe be unto thee, O Moab! the people of Chemosh perisheth: for thy sons are taken captives, and thy daughters captives.   Num. 21:29

47 Yet will I bring again the captivity of Moab in the latter days, saith the LORD. Thus far *is* the judgment of Moab.   Jer. 49:6, 39

A Prophecy Against Ammon

49 Concerning the Ammonites, thus saith the LORD; Hath Israel no sons? hath he no heir? why *then* doth their king inherit Gad, and his people dwell in his cities?   Deut. 23:3

2 Therefore, behold, the days come, saith the LORD, that I will cause an alarm of war to be heard in Rabbah of the Ammonites; and it shall be a desolate heap, and her daughters shall be burned with fire: then shall Israel be heir unto them that were his heirs, saith the LORD.   Deut. 3:11; Jer. 4:19; Ezek. 21:20

3 Howl, O Heshbon, for Ai is spoiled: cry,

at her, spare no arrows: for she hath sinned against the LORD.   Jer. 50:7, 9, 29
15 Shout against her round about: she hath given her hand: her foundations are fallen, her walls are thrown down: for it *is* the vengeance of the LORD: take vengeance upon her; as she hath done, do unto her. Jer. 46:10; 51:6, 58
16 Cut off the sower from Babylon, and him that handleth the sickle in the time of harvest: for fear of the oppressing sword they shall turn every one to his people, and they shall flee every one to his own land.   Is. 13:14
17 Israel *is* a scattered sheep; the lions have driven *him* away: first the king of Assyria hath devoured him; and last this Nebuchadrezzar king of Babylon hath broken his bones.   2 Kin. 18:9-13; Jer. 2:15; 50:6
18 Therefore thus saith the LORD of hosts, the God of Israel; Behold, I will punish the king of Babylon and his land, as I have punished the king of Assyria.   Is. 10:12
19 And I will bring Israel again to his habitation, and he shall feed on Carmel and Bashan, and his soul shall be satisfied upon mount Ephraim and Gilead.   Jer. 31:6
20 In those days, and in that time, saith the LORD, the iniquity of Israel shall be sought for, and *there shall be* none; and the sins of Judah, and they shall not be found: for I will pardon them whom I reserve.   Is. 1:9; Mic. 7:19
21 Go up against the land of Merathaim, *even* against it, and against the inhabitants of Pekod: waste and utterly destroy after them, saith the LORD, and do according to all that I have commanded thee.   Ezek. 23:23
22 A sound of battle *is* in the land, and of great destruction.   Jer. 4:19-21
23 How is the hammer of the whole earth cut ᵀasunder and broken! how is Babylon become a desolation among the nations!   *apart*
24 I have laid a snare for thee, and thou art also taken, O Babylon, and thou wast not aware: thou art found, and also caught, because thou hast striven against the LORD.
25 The LORD hath opened his armoury, and hath brought forth the weapons of his ᵀindignation: for this *is* the work of the Lord GOD of hosts in the land of the Chaldeans.   Jer. 51:25 ◆ *anger*
26 Come against her from the utmost border, open her storehouses: cast her up as heaps, and destroy her utterly: let nothing of her be left.   Is. 14:23
27 Slay all her bullocks; let them go down to the slaughter: woe unto them! for their day is come, the time of their visitation.   Is. 34:7
28 The voice of them that flee and escape out of the land of Babylon, to declare in Zion the vengeance of the LORD our God, the vengeance of his temple.   Is. 48:20
29 Call together the archers against Babylon:

all ye that bend the bow, camp against it round about; let none thereof escape: ᵀrecompense her according to her work; according to all that she hath done, do unto her: for she hath been proud against the LORD, against the Holy One of Israel. Is. 47:10 ◆ *repay*
30 Therefore shall her young men fall in the streets, and all her men of war shall be cut off in that day, saith the LORD. Jer. 9:21; 18:21; 49:26
31 Behold, I *am* against thee, O *thou* most proud, saith the Lord GOD of hosts: for thy day is come, the time *that* I will visit thee.
32 And the most proud shall stumble and fall, and none shall raise him up: and I will kindle a fire in his cities, and it shall devour all round about him.   Jer. 21:14
33 Thus saith the LORD of hosts; The children of Israel and the children of Judah *were* oppressed together: and all that took them captives held them fast; they refused to let them go.   Is. 14:17; 58:6
34 Their Redeemer *is* strong; the LORD of hosts *is* his name: he shall throughly plead their cause, that he may give rest to the land, and ᵀdisquiet the inhabitants of Babylon.   Prov. 23:11; Is. 43:14; Jer. 51:36 ◆ *disturb*
35 A sword *is* upon the Chaldeans, saith the LORD, and upon the inhabitants of Babylon, and upon her princes, and upon her wise *men*.   Jer. 47:6
36 A sword *is* upon the liars; and they shall ᵀdote: a sword *is* upon her mighty men; and they shall be dismayed.   Jer. 49:22 ◆ *become foolish*
37 A sword *is* upon their horses, and upon their chariots, and upon all the mingled people that *are* in the midst of her; and they shall become as women: a sword *is* upon her treasures; and they shall be robbed. Jer. 25:20; 51:21
38 A drought *is* upon her waters; and they shall be dried up: for it *is* the land of graven images, and they are mad upon *their* idols.
39 Therefore the wild beasts of the desert with the wild beasts of the islands shall dwell *there*, and the owls shall dwell therein: and it shall be no more inhabited for ever; neither shall it be dwelt in from generation to generation.   Is. 13:20-22
40 As God overthrew Sodom and Gomorrah and the neighbour *cities* thereof, saith the LORD; *so* shall no man abide there, neither shall any son of man dwell therein. Gen. 19:24-25
41 Behold, a people shall come from the north, and a great nation, and many kings shall be raised up from the coasts of the earth.   Jer. 51:27-28
42 They shall hold the bow and the lance: they *are* cruel, and will not shew mercy: their voice shall roar like the sea, and they shall ride upon horses, *every one* put in array, like a man to the battle, against thee, O daughter of Babylon.   Is. 5:30

43 The king of Babylon hath heard the report of them, and his hands ᵀwaxed feeble: anguish took hold of him, *and* pangs as of a woman in travail.   Jer. 49:24 ✦ *became*

44 Behold, he shall come up like a lion from the swelling of Jordan unto the habitation of the strong: but I will make them suddenly run away from her: and who *is* a chosen *man, that* I may appoint over her? for who *is* like me? and who will appoint me the time? and who *is* that shepherd that will stand before me?   Jer. 49:19-21

45 Therefore hear ye the counsel of the LORD, that he hath taken against Babylon; and his purposes, that he hath purposed against the land of the Chaldeans: Surely the least of the flock shall draw them out: surely he shall make *their* habitation desolate with them.   Jer. 49:20

46 At the noise of the taking of Babylon the earth is moved, and the cry is heard among the nations.   Jer. 49:21

The Severe Judgment of God on Babylon

51 Thus saith the LORD; Behold, I will raise up against Babylon, and against them that dwell in the midst of them that rise up against me, a destroying wind;   Jer. 4:11-12

2 And will send unto Babylon fanners, that shall ᵀfan her, and shall empty her land: for in the day of trouble they shall be against her round about.   Is. 41:16; Jer. 15:7; Matt. 3:12 ✦ *winnow*

3 Against *him that* bendeth let the archer bend his bow, and against *him that* lifteth himself up in his ᵀbrigandine: and spare ye not her young men; destroy ye utterly all her host.   Jer. 46:4 ✦ *coat of armor*

4 Thus the slain shall fall in the land of the Chaldeans, and *they that are* thrust through in her streets.   Is. 13:15; Jer. 49:26; 50:30

5 For Israel *hath* not *been* forsaken, nor Judah of his God, of the LORD of hosts; though their land was filled with sin against the Holy One of Israel.   Hos. 4:1

6 Flee out of the midst of Babylon, and deliver every man his soul: be not cut off in her iniquity; for this *is* the time of the LORD's vengeance; he will render unto her a recompence.   Jer. 50:8, 15, 28

51:6 Fleeing Babylon—Then, and Now

As the captive exiles heeded the message, "Flee out of the midst of Babylon" (Jeremiah 51:6), and were restored to the Land of Promise, so those who fear God today are heeding the message to withdraw from spiritual Babylon, and soon they are to stand as trophies of divine grace in the earth made new, the heavenly Canaan. *PK 715*

7 Babylon *hath been* a golden cup in the LORD's hand, that made all the earth drunken: the nations have drunken of her wine; therefore the nations are mad.   Rev. 14:8; 17:2, 4

8 Babylon is suddenly fallen and destroyed: howl for her; take ᵀbalm for her pain, if so be she may be healed.   Is. 21:9; Rev. 14:8 ✦ *medicine*

9 We would have healed Babylon, but she is not healed: forsake her, and let us go every one into his own country: for her judgment reacheth unto heaven, and is lifted up *even* to the skies.   Is. 13:14; Jer. 50:16; Rev. 18:5

10 The LORD hath brought forth our righteousness: come, and let us declare in Zion the work of the LORD our God.   Ps. 37:6; Is. 40:2

11 Make bright the arrows; gather the shields: the LORD hath raised up the spirit of the kings of the Medes: for his device *is* against Babylon, to destroy it; because it *is* the vengeance of the LORD, the vengeance of his temple.   Jer. 46:4, 9; 50:45

12 Set up the ᵀstandard upon the walls of Babylon, make the watch strong, set up the watchmen, prepare the ambushes: for the LORD hath both devised and done that which he spake against the inhabitants of Babylon.   Is. 13:2 ✦ *flag*

13 O thou that dwellest upon many waters, abundant in treasures, thine end is come, *and* the measure of thy covetousness.   Is. 45:3

14 The LORD of hosts hath sworn by himself, *saying,* Surely I will fill thee with men, as with caterpillers; and they shall lift up a shout against thee.   Jer. 49:13

15 He hath made the earth by his power, he hath established the world by his wisdom, and hath stretched out the heaven by his understanding.   Job 9:8

16 When he uttereth *his* voice, *there is* a multitude of waters in the heavens; and he causeth the vapours to ascend from the ends of the earth: he maketh lightnings with rain, and bringeth forth the wind out of his treasures.   Ps. 18:13; 135:7; Jon. 1:4

17 Every man is ᵀbrutish by *his* knowledge; every founder is confounded by the graven image: for his molten image *is* falsehood, and *there is* no breath in them.   Is. 44:18-20 ✦ *dumb*

18 They *are* vanity, the work of errors: in the time of their visitation they shall perish.

19 The portion of Jacob *is* not like them; for he *is* the former of all things: and *Israel is* the rod of his inheritance: the LORD of hosts *is* his name.   Ps. 73:26; Jer. 10:16

20 Thou *art* my battle axe *and* weapons of war: for with thee will I break in pieces the nations, and with thee will I destroy kingdoms;   Is. 10:5

21 And with thee will I break in pieces the horse and his rider; and with thee will I break in pieces the chariot and his rider;   Ex. 15:1

22 With thee also will I break in pieces man and woman; and with thee will I break in pieces old and young; and with thee will I break in pieces the young man and the maid;   2 Chr. 36:17; Is. 13:18
23 I will also break in pieces with thee the shepherd and his flock; and with thee will I break in pieces the ᵀhusbandman and his yoke of oxen; and with thee will I break in pieces captains and rulers.   farmer
24 And I will render unto Babylon and to all the inhabitants of Chaldea all their evil that they have done in Zion in your sight, saith the LORD.   Jer. 50:15
25 Behold, I am against thee, O destroying mountain, saith the LORD, which destroyest all the earth: and I will stretch out mine hand upon thee, and roll thee down from the rocks, and will make thee a burnt mountain.   Is. 13:2; Zech. 4:7; Rev. 8:8
26 And they shall not take of thee a stone for a corner, nor a stone for foundations; but thou shalt be desolate for ever, saith the LORD.   Is. 13:19-22
27 Set ye up a standard in the land, blow the trumpet among the nations, prepare the nations against her, call together against her the kingdoms of Ararat, Minni, and Ashchenaz; appoint a captain against her; cause the horses to come up as the rough caterpillers.   Gen. 8:4; 10:3; Jer. 25:14
28 Prepare against her the nations with the kings of the Medes, the captains thereof, and all the rulers thereof, and all the land of his dominion.   Jer. 51:11
29 And the land shall tremble and sorrow: for every purpose of the LORD shall be performed against Babylon, to make the land of Babylon a desolation without an inhabitant.   Jer. 8:16
30 The mighty men of Babylon have forborn to fight, they have remained in their holds: their might hath failed; they became as women: they have burned her dwellingplaces; her bars are broken.   Is. 13:7-8; Lam. 2:9; Nah. 3:13
31 One post shall run to meet another, and one messenger to meet another, to shew the king of Babylon that his city is taken at one end,   2 Sam. 18:19-31
32 And that the passages are stopped, and the reeds they have burned with fire, and the men of war are ᵀaffrighted.   scared
33 For thus saith the LORD of hosts, the God of Israel; The daughter of Babylon is like a threshingfloor, it is time to thresh her: yet a little while, and the time of her harvest shall come.   Is. 21:10; Hos. 6:11; Joel 3:13
34 Nebuchadrezzar the king of Babylon hath devoured me, he hath crushed me, he hath made me an empty vessel, he hath swallowed me up like a dragon, he hath filled his belly with my delicates, he hath cast me out.   Job 20:15; Jer. 50:17; 51:44
35 The violence done to me and to my flesh be upon Babylon, shall the inhabitant of Zion say; and my blood upon the inhabitants of Chaldea, shall Jerusalem say.
36 Therefore thus saith the LORD; Behold, I will plead thy cause, and take vengeance for thee; and I will dry up her sea, and make her springs dry.   Ps. 140:12; Jer. 50:38; Rom. 12:19
37 And Babylon shall become heaps, a dwellingplace for dragons, an astonishment, and an ᵀhissing, without an inhabitant.   whistling
38 They shall roar together like lions: they shall yell as lions' whelps.   Jer. 2:15
39 In their heat I will make their feasts, and I will make them drunken, that they may rejoice, and sleep a perpetual sleep, and not wake, saith the LORD.   Jer. 25:27; 51:57
40 I will bring them down like lambs to the slaughter, like rams with he goats.   Jer. 50:27
41 How is Sheshach taken! and how is the praise of the whole earth surprised! how is Babylon become an astonishment among the nations!   Is. 13:19; Jer. 25:26; 49:25

51:41 Pride Threatens

It is not surprising that the successful monarch [Nebuchadnezzer], so ambitious and so proud-spirited, should be tempted to turn aside from the path of humility, which alone leads to true greatness. . . . The city of Babylon became . . . "the praise of the whole earth." . . . Success . . . ministered to his pride, until he was in grave danger of spoiling his record as a wise ruler whom God could continue to use as an instrument for the carrying out of the divine purpose. PK 515

42 The sea is come up upon Babylon: she is covered with the multitude of the waves thereof.   Is. 8:7-8
43 Her cities are a desolation, a dry land, and a wilderness, a land wherein no man dwelleth, neither doth any son of man pass thereby.   Is. 13:20
44 And I will punish Bel in Babylon, and I will bring forth out of his mouth that which he hath swallowed up: and the nations shall not flow together any more unto him: yea, the wall of Babylon shall fall.   Is. 2:2; Jer. 51:34, 58
45 My people, go ye out of the midst of her, and deliver ye every man his soul from the fierce anger of the LORD.   Is. 48:20; Jer. 50:8; 51:6
46 And lest your heart faint, and ye fear for the rumour that shall be heard in the land; a rumour shall both come one year, and after that in another year shall come a rumour, and violence in the land, ruler against ruler.
47 Therefore, behold, the days come, that I will do judgment upon the graven images of

Babylon: and her whole land shall be confounded, and all her slain shall fall in the midst of her. Is. 46:1-2; Jer. 50:2; 51:52

48 Then the heaven and the earth, and all that *is* therein, shall sing for Babylon: for the spoilers shall come unto her from the north, saith the LORD. Is. 44:23; Jer. 50:3; Rev. 18:20

49 As Babylon *hath caused* the slain of Israel to fall, so at Babylon shall fall the slain of all the earth. Jer. 50:29

50 Ye that have escaped the sword, go away, stand not still: remember the LORD afar off, and let Jerusalem come into your mind.

51 We are confounded, because we have heard reproach: shame hath covered our faces: for strangers are come into the sanctuaries of the LORD's house. Ps. 44:13-16; 74:3-7; Lam. 1:10

52 Wherefore, behold, the days come, saith the LORD, that I will do judgment upon her ᵀgraven images: and through all her land the wounded shall groan. Jer. 51:47 ♦ *engraved* or *cut out*

53 Though Babylon should mount up to heaven, and though she should fortify the height of her strength, *yet* from me shall spoilers come unto her, saith the LORD.

54 A sound of a cry *cometh* from Babylon, and great destruction from the land of the Chaldeans: Jer. 48:3-5; 50:22, 46

55 Because the LORD hath spoiled Babylon, and destroyed out of her the great voice; when her waves do roar like great waters, a noise of their voice is uttered:

56 Because the spoiler is come upon her, *even* upon Babylon, and her mighty men are taken, every one of their bows is broken: for the LORD God of recompences shall surely ᵀrequite. Ps. 46:9 ♦ *repay*

57 And I will make drunk her princes, and her wise *men*, her captains, and her rulers, and her mighty men: and they shall sleep a perpetual sleep, and not wake, saith the King, whose name *is* the LORD of hosts. Jer. 25:27; 46:18; 48:15

58 Thus saith the LORD of hosts; The broad walls of Babylon shall be utterly broken, and her high gates shall be burned with fire; and the people shall labour in vain, and the folk in the fire, and they shall be weary. Jer. 50:15; 51:64; Hab. 2:13

59 The word which Jeremiah the prophet commanded Seraiah the son of Neriah, the son of Maaseiah, when he went with Zedekiah the king of Judah into Babylon in the fourth year of his reign. And *this* Seraiah *was* a quiet prince. Jer. 32:12

60 So Jeremiah wrote in a book all the evil that should come upon Babylon, *even* all these words that are written against Babylon. Is. 30:8

61 And Jeremiah said to Seraiah, When thou comest to Babylon, and shalt see, and shalt read all these words;

62 Then shalt thou say, O LORD, thou hast spoken against this place, to cut it off, that none shall remain in it, neither man nor beast, but that it shall be desolate for ever.

63 And it shall be, when thou hast made an end of reading this book, *that* thou shalt bind a stone to it, and cast it into the midst of Euphrates: Jer. 19:10-11

64 And thou shalt say, Thus shall Babylon sink, and shall not rise from the evil that I will bring upon her: and they shall be weary. Thus far *are* the words of Jeremiah. Job 31:40

The Fall of Jerusalem

52 Zedekiah *was* one and twenty years old when he began to reign, and he reigned eleven years in Jerusalem. And his mother's name *was* Hamutal the daughter of Jeremiah of Libnah. Josh. 10:29; 2 Kin. 24:18; 2 Chr. 36:11

2 And he did *that which was* evil in the eyes of the LORD, according to all that Jehoiakim had done. 1 Kin. 14:22

3 For through the anger of the LORD it came to pass in Jerusalem and Judah, till he had cast them out from his presence, that Zedekiah rebelled against the king of Babylon. 2 Chr. 36:13

4 And it came to pass in the ninth year of his reign, in the tenth month, in the tenth *day* of the month, *that* Nebuchadrezzar king of Babylon came, he and all his army, against Jerusalem, and pitched against it, and built forts against it round about. Ezek. 24:1-2; Zech. 8:19

5 So the city was besieged unto the eleventh year of king Zedekiah.

6 And in the fourth month, in the ninth *day* of the month, the famine was sore in the city, so that there was no bread for the people of the land. Is. 3:1

7 Then the city was broken up, and all the men of war fled, and went forth out of the city by night by the way of the gate between the two walls, which *was* by the king's garden; (now the Chaldeans *were* by the city round about:) and they went by the way of the plain. 2 Kin. 25:4

8 But the army of the Chaldeans pursued after the king, and overtook Zedekiah in the plains of Jericho; and all his army was scattered from him. Jer. 21:7

9 Then they took the king, and carried him up unto the king of Babylon to Riblah in the land of Hamath; where he gave judgment upon him. Num. 13:21

10 And the king of Babylon slew the sons of Zedekiah before his eyes: he slew also all the princes of Judah in Riblah. Jer. 22:30

11 Then he put out the eyes of Zedekiah; and the king of Babylon bound him in chains, and carried him to Babylon, and put him in prison till the day of his death.

12 Now in the fifth month, in the tenth *day*

of the month, which was the nineteenth year of Nebuchadrezzar king of Babylon, came Nebuzar-adan, captain of the guard, which served the king of Babylon, into Jerusalem,   2 Kin. 25:8; Jer. 39:9; 52:29

13 And burned the house of the LORD, and the king's house; and all the houses of Jerusalem, and all the houses of the great men, burned he with fire: 2 Chr. 36:19

14 And all the army of the Chaldeans, that were with the captain of the guard, brake down all the walls of Jerusalem round about.   Neh. 1:3

15 Then Nebuzar-adan the captain of the guard carried away captive certain of the poor of the people, and the residue of the people that remained in the city, and those that fell away, that fell to the king of Babylon, and the rest of the multitude.

16 But Nebuzar-adan the captain of the guard left certain of the poor of the land for vinedressers and for ᵀhusbandmen.   farmers

17 Also the pillars of brass that were in the house of the LORD, and the bases, and the brasen sea that was in the house of the LORD, the Chaldeans brake, and carried all the brass of them to Babylon.   Jer. 27:19-22

18 The caldrons also, and the shovels, and the snuffers, and the bowls, and the spoons, and all the vessels of brass wherewith they ministered, took they away.   Ex. 27:3

19 And the basons, and the firepans, and the bowls, and the caldrons, and the candlesticks, and the spoons, and the cups; that which was of gold in gold, and that which was of silver in silver, took the captain of the guard away.   1 Kin. 7:49-50

20 The two pillars, one sea, and twelve brasen bulls that were under the bases, which king Solomon had made in the house of the LORD: the brass of all these vessels was without weight.   1 Kin. 7:47

21 And concerning the pillars, the height of one pillar was eighteen cubits; and a fillet of twelve cubits did ᵀcompass it; and the thickness thereof was four fingers: it was hollow.   2 Kin. 25:17 ◆ encircle

22 And a ᵀchapiter of brass was upon it; and the height of one chapiter was five cubits, with network and pomegranates upon the chapiters round about, all of brass. The second pillar also and the pomegranates were like unto these.   capital at the top of the column

23 And there were ninety and six pomegranates on a side; and all the pomegranates upon the network were an hundred round about.   1 Kin. 7:20

24 And the captain of the guard took Seraiah the chief priest, and Zephaniah the second priest, and the three keepers of the door: 2 Kin. 25:18; 1 Chr. 6:14; Jer. 21:1

25 He took also out of the city an ᵀeunuch, which had the charge of the men of war; and seven men of them that were near the king's person, which were found in the city; and the principal scribe of the host, who mustered the people of the land; and threescore men of the people of the land, that were found in the midst of the city.   Esth. 1:14 ◆ castrated male servant

26 So Nebuzar-adan the captain of the guard took them, and brought them to the king of Babylon to Riblah.

27 And the king of Babylon smote them, and put them to death in Riblah in the land of Hamath. Thus Judah was carried away captive out of his own land.   Is. 6:11-12

28 This is the people whom Nebuchadrezzar carried away captive: in the seventh year three thousand Jews and three and twenty: 2 Kin. 24:2-3

29 In the eighteenth year of Nebuchadrezzar he carried away captive from Jerusalem eight hundred thirty and two persons: Jer. 52:12

30 In the three and twentieth year of Nebuchadrezzar Nebuzar-adan the captain of the guard carried away captive of the Jews seven hundred forty and five persons: all the persons were four thousand and six hundred.

Jehoiachin Is Released from Prison

31 And it came to pass in the seven and thirtieth year of the captivity of Jehoiachin king of Judah, in the twelfth month, in the five and twentieth day of the month, that Evil-merodach king of Babylon in the first year of his reign lifted up the head of Jehoiachin king of Judah, and brought him forth out of prison,   Gen. 40:13

32 And spake kindly unto him, and set his throne above the throne of the kings that were with him in Babylon,

33 And changed his prison garments: and he did continually eat bread before him all the days of his life.   2 Sam. 9:7

34 And for his diet, there was a continual diet given him of the king of Babylon, every day a portion until the day of his death, all the days of his life.   2 Sam. 9:10

THE BOOK OF

LAMENTATIONS

Imagine that your favorite city in the world has just been devastated and all of its people are gone. You're left alone in the ruins to reflect on the tragedy. That's exactly the situation Jeremiah faces, standing in the middle of a desolate Jerusalem. The five chapters of Lamentations are a funeral rite for the city and for a people who would not listen.

We need only read the Book of Jeremiah to see that the people's punishment was not for lack of warning on Jeremiah's part. He had told the people over and over again—at times even with visual aids—of the city's impending destruction, but the people and the leaders only persecuted him. They burned up the hand-written scroll of warnings (and left Jeremiah and his scribe Baruch to simply start over), threw him into prison, then tossed him into a dungeon that was no more than a muddy cistern without water (see Jeremiah 36—38).

Yet through it all, Jeremiah never wavered in his message, and he always remembered God's goodness and faithfulness. So here, in his lament over the fallen city and captured people, he weeps and grieves, even as he trusts in God's ultimate faithfulness to His promises.

The first four chapters of this book are acrostic poems. Each chapter begins with the first letter of the Hebrew alphabet, *aleph*, and then each verse begins with a successive letter. Thus, each chapter has twenty-two verses; chapter 3 has sixty-six verses, for it is written with three verses for each letter of the Hebrew alphabet.

Dates

A long siege by Nebuchadnezzar's forces (588 B.C. to 586 B.C.) led to the fall of Jerusalem. Culminating with the burning of Jerusalem, it is likely Jeremiah wrote Lamentations soon after the burning, before his own countrymen took him captive to Egypt (Jeremiah 43:1–7).

Author

The Septuagint, Talmud, the Aramaic Targum of Jonathon, and early Christian writers such as Origen and Jerome all attribute the book of Lamentations to Jeremiah. Jeremiah was the logical person to write it, being left behind after the fall of Jerusalem (Jeremiah 39; 52). The laments in the books of Jeremiah and Lamentations also speak to a common writing style.

Meaning of the Name

As with many Hebrew books, the title for Lamentations was chosen from the first couple of words written, in this case "Ah, how!" The Hebrew word *Ginoth* (meaning "Elegies" or "Lamentations") is also used, as it better represents the book's theme. The Greeks term it *Threnoi* ("Dirges" or "Laments"), while the Latin texts use *Threni* ("Tears" or "Lamentations").

Christ in Lamentations

Jesus and Jeremiah both wept over Jerusalem. Perhaps Jesus remembered Jeremiah's words when He looked down upon the city and said, "O Jerusalem, Jerusalem, thou that killest the prophets, and stonest them which are sent unto thee, how often would I have gathered thy children together, even as a hen gathereth her chickens under her wings, and ye would not! Behold, your house is left unto you desolate" (Matthew 23:37, 38).

Jesus is also the ultimate deliverer of Israel. Jeremiah took solace in knowing his people would be delivered, as he wrote, "Great is thy faithfulness" (Lamentations 3:23). He also remembered the words of the Lord that had told him that the people would return (Jeremiah 16:15).

Overview

For forty years, Jeremiah warns and implores the Hebrews to return to God. In 586 B.C., King Nebuchadnezzar destroys Jerusalem and takes most of the people of Judah as captives to Babylon. Jeremiah is left behind, facing the bitter taste of failure.

Jeremiah is far from vengeful toward his wayward people, who are now gone. He feels the sorrow of seeing his dead city and the people that God loved taken away. His five chapters constitute five funeral dirges and contain the following themes:

(1) *Lamentations 1, A Grieving City.* Jeremiah grieves over the sins which led to the siege

and destruction of Jerusalem and the exile of its people. Like Jeremiah, the personified city grieves over its losses.

(2) *Lamentations 2, An Angry God.* Babylon is a tool in the hands of an angry God as the predicted Judgment Day comes and Jerusalem falls (Jeremiah 10; 39:16).

(3) *Lamentations 3, A Need for Mercy.* Even as he reflects on the devastation wrought by the forces of Babylon and the suffering of his people, Jeremiah recalls the mercy of God.

(4) *Lamentations 4, A City under Siege.* Jeremiah reflects on the siege of Jerusalem and the famine it caused.

(5) *Lamentations 5, A Prayer for Restoration.* Here, Jeremiah appeals to God, seeking His restoration of the people of Judah.

Unlocking Lamentations

KEY PEOPLE:
Jeremiah

KEY EVENTS:
The destruction of Jerusalem; the captivity of the people of Judah; Jeremiah's lamentations for Jerusalem and the people

KEY WORD:
Lamentations. Jeremiah weeps for what has happened, acknowledges that God was righteous in His judgment of the people, and expresses hope in God's promise to bring the people home in the future.

KEY VERSES:
"It is of the LORD's mercies that we are not consumed, because his compassions fail not. They are new every morning: great is thy faithfulness" (Lamentations 3:22, 23).

KEY CHAPTER:
Lamentations 3, the heart of Jeremiah's hope. With all the destruction and desolation around him, Jeremiah does not forget that God is good, and expresses his faith and hope that salvation and freedom will return to his people.

The Misery of Jerusalem because of Her Sin

1 How doth the city sit solitary, *that was* full of people! *how* is she become as a widow! she *that was* great among the nations, *and* princess among the provinces, *how* is she become tributary!   1 Kin. 4:21

2 She weepeth sore in the night, and her tears *are* on her cheeks: among all her lovers she hath none to comfort *her*: all her friends have dealt treacherously with her, they are become her enemies. Job 19:13-14; Ps. 6:6; Mic. 7:5

3 Judah is gone into captivity because of affliction, and because of great servitude: she dwelleth among the heathen, she findeth no rest: all her persecutors overtook her between the straits.   Deut. 28:64-67

4 The ways of Zion do mourn, because none come to the solemn feasts: all her gates are desolate: her priests sigh, her virgins are afflicted, and she *is* in bitterness.   Jer. 9:11

5 Her adversaries are the chief, her enemies prosper; for the LORD hath afflicted her for the multitude of her ᵀtransgressions: her children are gone into captivity before the enemy.   Ps. 90:7-8 ◆ *violations of a law*

1:1-5 The Folly of Human Wisdom

The sorrow of the prophet over the utter perversity of those who should have been the spiritual light of the world, his sorrow over the fate of Zion and of the people carried captive to Babylon, is revealed in the lamentations he has left on record as a memorial of the folly of turning from the counsels of Jehovah to human wisdom. *PK 461*

---

6 And from the daughter of Zion all her beauty is departed: her princes are become like harts *that* find no pasture, and they are gone without strength before the pursuer.

7 Jerusalem remembered in the days of her affliction and of her miseries all her pleasant things that she had in the days of old, when her people fell into the hand of the enemy, and none did help her: the adversaries saw her, *and* did mock at her sabbaths.   Ps. 42:4

8 Jerusalem hath grievously sinned; therefore she is removed: all that honoured her despise her, because they have seen her nakedness: yea, she sigheth, and turneth backward.   Is. 59:2-13

9 Her filthiness *is* in her skirts; she remembereth not her last end; therefore she came down wonderfully: she had no comforter. O LORD, behold my affliction: for the enemy hath magnified *himself*. Deut. 32:29; Ps. 25:18; Is. 47:7

10 The adversary hath spread out his hand upon all her pleasant things: for she hath seen *that* the heathen entered into her sanctuary, whom thou didst command *that* they should not enter into thy congregation.   Deut. 23:3; Neh. 13:1; Jer. 51:51

11 All her people sigh, they seek bread; they have given their pleasant things for meat to relieve the soul: see, O LORD, and consider; for I am become vile.   Jer. 38:9; 52:6; Lam. 2:12

Jerusalem Complains of Her Grief

12 *Is it* nothing to you, all ye that pass by? behold, and see if there be any sorrow like unto my sorrow, which is done unto me, wherewith the LORD hath afflicted *me* in the day of his fierce anger.   Dan. 9:12

13 From above hath he sent fire into my bones, and it prevaileth against them: he hath spread a net for my feet, he hath turned me back: he hath made me desolate *and* faint all the day.   Job 30:30

14 The yoke of my transgressions is bound by his hand: they are wreathed, *and* come up upon my neck: he hath made my strength to fall, the Lord hath delivered me into *their* hands, *from whom* I am not able to rise up.   Deut. 28:48

15 The Lord hath ᵀtrodden under foot all my mighty *men* in the midst of me: he hath called an assembly against me to crush my young men: the Lord hath trodden the virgin, the daughter of Judah, *as* in a winepress.   Is. 28:18 ◆ *trampled*

16 For these *things* I weep; mine eye, mine eye runneth down with water, because the comforter that should relieve my soul is far from me: my children are desolate, because the enemy prevailed.   Jer. 13:17; 14:17; Lam. 1:2

17 Zion spreadeth forth her hands, *and there is* none to comfort her: the LORD hath commanded concerning Jacob, *that* his adversaries *should be* round about him: Jerusalem is as a menstruous woman among them.   Is. 1:15; Jer. 4:31; Lam. 1:9

18 The LORD is righteous; for I have rebelled against his commandment: hear, I pray you, all people, and behold my sorrow: my virgins and my young men are gone into captivity.   1 Sam. 12:14-15

19 I called for my lovers, *but* they deceived me: my priests and mine elders gave up the ghost in the city, while they sought their meat to relieve their souls.   Lam. 1:2

20 Behold, O LORD; for I *am* in distress: my bowels are troubled; mine heart is turned within me; for I have grievously rebelled: abroad the sword bereaveth, at home *there is* as death.   Deut. 32:25; Is. 16:11; Lam. 2:11

21 They have heard that I sigh: *there is* none to comfort me: all mine enemies have heard of my trouble; they are glad that thou hast done *it*: thou wilt bring the day *that* thou hast called, and they shall be like unto me. Jer. 50:11

22 Let all their wickedness come before thee;

and do unto them, as thou hast done unto me for all my transgressions: for my sighs *are* many, and my heart *is* faint.   Neh. 4:4-5

Jeremiah Laments the Misery of Jerusalem

2 How hath the Lord covered the daughter of Zion with a cloud in his anger, *and* cast down from heaven unto the earth the beauty of Israel, and remembered not his footstool in the day of his anger!   Ps. 99:5
2 The Lord hath swallowed up all the habitations of Jacob, and hath not pitied: he hath thrown down in his wrath the strong holds of the daughter of Judah; he hath brought *them* down to the ground: he hath polluted the kingdom and the princes thereof.   Ps. 89:39-40; Lam. 2:17; 3:43
3 He hath cut off in *his* fierce anger all the horn of Israel: he hath drawn back his right hand from before the enemy, and he burned against Jacob like a flaming fire, *which* devoureth round about.   Ps. 74:11; 75:5, 10
4 He hath bent his bow like an enemy: he stood with his right hand as an adversary, and slew all *that were* pleasant to the eye in the tabernacle of the daughter of Zion: he poured out his fury like fire.   Is. 42:25
5 The Lord was as an enemy: he hath swallowed up Israel, he hath swallowed up all her palaces: he hath destroyed his strong holds, and hath increased in the daughter of Judah mourning and lamentation. 2 Kin. 25:9; Jer. 30:14
6 And he hath violently taken away his tabernacle, as *if it were of* a garden: he hath destroyed his places of the assembly: the LORD hath caused the solemn feasts and sabbaths to be forgotten in Zion, and hath despised in the indignation of his anger the king and the priest.   Lam. 1:4; 4:16; Zeph. 3:18
7 The Lord hath cast off his altar, he hath ᵀabhorred his sanctuary, he hath given up into the hand of the enemy the walls of her palaces; they have made a noise in the house of the LORD, as in the day of a solemn feast.   Ps. 74:3-8 ◆ *despised*
8 The LORD hath purposed to destroy the wall of the daughter of Zion: he hath stretched out a line, he hath not withdrawn his hand from destroying: therefore he made the ᵀrampart and the wall to lament; they ᵀlanguished together. 2 Kin. 21:13; Is. 3:26; 34:11 ◆ *fortification* ◆ *weakened*
9 Her gates are sunk into the ground; he hath destroyed and broken her bars: her king and her princes *are* among the Gentiles: the law *is* no *more*; her prophets also find no vision from the LORD.   Neh. 1:3
10 The elders of the daughter of Zion sit upon the ground, *and* keep silence: they have cast up dust upon their heads; they have girded themselves with sackcloth: the

virgins of Jerusalem hang down their heads to the ground.   Job 2:12-13; Is. 3:26; 15:3
11 Mine eyes do fail with tears, my bowels are troubled, my liver is poured upon the earth, for the destruction of the daughter of my people; because the children and the sucklings swoon in the streets of the city.   Job 16:13
12 They say to their mothers, Where *is* corn and wine? when they swooned as the wounded in the streets of the city, when their soul was poured out into their mothers' bosom.
13 What thing shall I take to witness for thee? what thing shall I liken to thee, O daughter of Jerusalem? what shall I equal to thee, that I may comfort thee, O virgin daughter of Zion? for thy breach *is* great like the sea: who can heal thee?   2 Sam. 5:20; Jer. 8:22; Lam. 1:12
14 Thy prophets have seen vain and foolish things for thee: and they have not discovered thine iniquity, to turn away thy captivity; but have seen for thee false burdens and causes of banishment.   Is. 58:1; Jer. 5:31; Ezek. 22:28
15 All that pass by clap *their* hands at thee; they ᵀhiss and wag their head at the daughter of Jerusalem, *saying, Is* this the city that *men* call The perfection of beauty, The joy of the whole earth? Ps. 48:2; 50:2; Jer. 18:16 ◆ *whistle*
16 All thine enemies have opened their mouth against thee: they hiss and gnash the teeth: they say, We have swallowed *her* up: certainly this *is* the day that we looked for; we have found, we have seen *it*. Job 16:9-10; Ps. 35:21
17 The LORD hath done *that* which he had devised; he hath fulfilled his word that he had commanded in the days of old: he hath thrown down, and hath not pitied: and he hath caused *thine* enemy to rejoice over thee, he hath set up the horn of thine adversaries.   Deut. 28:15-68; Ps. 89:42; Ezek. 5:11
18 Their heart cried unto the Lord, O wall of the daughter of Zion, let tears run down like a river day and night: give thyself no rest; let not the ᵀapple of thine eye cease.   *pupil*
19 Arise, cry out in the night: in the beginning of the watches pour out thine heart like water before the face of the Lord: lift up thy hands toward him for the life of thy young children, that faint for hunger in the top of every street.   1 Sam. 1:15; Ps. 62:8; Is. 26:9
20 Behold, O LORD, and consider to whom thou hast done this. Shall the women eat their fruit, *and* children of a span long? shall the priest and the prophet be slain in the sanctuary of the Lord? Ps. 78:64; Jer. 19:9; Lam. 4:10
21 The young and the old lie on the ground in the streets: my virgins and my young men are fallen by the sword; thou hast slain *them* in the day of thine anger; thou hast killed, *and* not pitied.   2 Chr. 36:17; Jer. 13:14; Lam. 3:43
22 Thou hast called as in a solemn day my

terrors round about, so that in the day of the LORD's anger none escaped nor remained: those that I have swaddled and brought up hath mine enemy consumed.   Ps. 31:13; Jer. 6:25

Jeremiah Despairs, Yet Hopes

3 I *am* the man *that* hath seen affliction by the rod of his wrath.   Ps. 88:7

2 He hath led me, and brought *me into* darkness, but not *into* light.   Job 30:26

3 Surely against me is he turned; he turneth his hand *against me* all the day.

4 My flesh and my skin hath he made old; he hath broken my bones. Ps. 51:8; Is. 38:13; Jer. 50:17

5 He hath builded against me, and compassed *me* with gall and travail.   Job 19:8; Jer. 23:15

6 He hath set me in dark places, as *they that be* dead of old.   Ps. 88:5-6

7 He hath hedged me about, that I cannot get out: he hath made my chain heavy.   Job 3:23

8 Also when I cry and shout, he shutteth out my prayer.   Job 19:7; 30:20; Ps. 22:2

9 He hath inclosed my ways with ᵀhewn stone, he hath made my paths crooked.   cut

10 He *was* unto me as *a* bear lying in wait, *and as* a lion in secret places.

11 He hath turned aside my ways, and pulled me in pieces: he hath made me desolate.   Hos. 6:1

12 He hath bent his bow, and set me as a mark for the arrow.   Job 7:20

13 He hath caused the arrows of his quiver to enter into my ᵀreins.   Job 6:4 ◆ heart

14 I was a derision to all my people; *and* their song all the day. Ps. 22:6-7; Jer. 20:7; Lam. 3:63

15 He hath filled me with bitterness, he hath made me drunken with wormwood.   Jer. 9:15

3:14 Loyal but Sensitive

Cruel were the mockings he was called upon to endure. His sensitive soul was pierced through and through by the arrows of derision hurled at him by those who despised his messages and made light of his burden for their conversion. "I was a derision to all my people," he declared, "and their song all the day" (Lamentations 3:14). *PK 420*

---

16 He hath also broken my teeth with gravel stones, he hath covered me with ashes. Ps. 3:7

17 And thou hast removed my soul far off from peace: I forgat prosperity.   Is. 59:11

18 And I said, My strength and my hope is perished from the LORD: Job 17:15

19 Remembering mine affliction and my misery, the wormwood and the gall.   Lam. 3:5

20 My soul hath *them* still in remembrance, and is humbled in me.   Ps. 42:5-6

21 This I recall to my mind, therefore have I hope.   Ps. 130:7

22 *It is of* the LORD's mercies that we are not consumed, because his compassions fail not.   Ps. 78:38; Mal. 3:6

3:18, 22–24 Recalling the Providences of God

When called to drink of the cup of tribulation and sorrow, and when tempted in his misery to say, "My strength and my hope is perished from the Lord," he recalled the providences of God in his behalf and triumphantly exclaimed, "It is of the Lord's mercies that we are not consumed, because His compassions fail not. They are new every morning: great is Thy faithfulness. The Lord is my portion, saith my soul; therefore will I hope in Him" (Lamentations 3:18, 22–24). *PK 421*

Being Faithful at Any Cost

Lamentations 3

Naturally of a timid and shrinking disposition, Jeremiah longed for the peace and quiet of a life of retirement, where he need not witness the continued impenitence of his beloved nation. His heart was wrung with anguish over the ruin wrought by sin. . . .

Cruel were the mockings he was called upon to endure. His sensitive soul was pierced through and through by the arrows of derision hurled at him by those who despised his messages and made light of his burden for their conversion. "I was a derision to all my people," he declared, "and their song all the day." "I am in derision daily, everyone mocketh me." "All my familiars watched for my halting, saying, Peradventure he will be enticed, and we shall prevail against him, and we shall take our revenge on him" (Lamentations 3:14; Jeremiah 20:7, 10).

But the faithful prophet was daily strengthened to endure. "The Lord is with me as a mighty terrible One," he declared in faith; "therefore my persecutors shall stumble, and they shall not prevail: they shall be greatly ashamed; for they shall not prosper: their everlasting confusion shall never be forgotten." "Sing unto the Lord, praise ye the Lord: for He hath delivered the soul of the poor from the hand of evildoers" (Jeremiah 20:11, 13).

The experiences through which Jeremiah passed in the days of his youth and also in the later years of his ministry, taught him the lesson that "the way of man is not in himself: it is not in man that walketh to direct his steps." He learned to pray, "O Lord, correct me, but with judgment; not in Thine anger, lest Thou bring me to nothing" (Jeremiah 10:23, 24). *PK 419–421*

23 *They are* new every morning: great *is* thy faithfulness. Zeph. 3:5

24 The LORD *is* my portion, saith my soul; therefore will I hope in him. Ps. 16:5; 33:18; 73:26

25 The LORD *is* good unto them that wait for him, to the soul *that* seeketh him. Is. 25:9

26 *It is* good that *a man* should both hope and quietly wait for the salvation of the LORD. Ps. 37:7

3:26 Trials Well Borne Develop Character

None who receive God's word are exempt from difficulty and trial; but when affliction comes, the true Christian does not become restless, distrustful, or despondent. . . . Remembering the tender mercies of the Lord, we should cast our care upon Him, and with patience wait for His salvation.

Through conflict the spiritual life is strengthened. Trials well borne will develop steadfastness of character and precious spiritual graces. The perfect fruit of faith, meekness, and love often matures best amid storm clouds and darkness. *COL 60, 61*

27 *It is* good for a man that he bear the yoke in his youth. Eccl. 12:1

28 He sitteth alone and keepeth silence, because he hath borne *it* upon him. Jer. 15:17

29 He putteth his mouth in the dust; if so be there may be hope. Job 40:4

30 He giveth *his* cheek to him that ᵀsmiteth him: he is filled full with reproach. strikes

31 For the Lord will not cast off for ever:

32 But though he cause grief, yet will he have compassion according to the multitude of his mercies. Ps. 78:38

33 For he doth not afflict willingly nor grieve the children of men. Ezek. 33:11

34 To crush under his feet all the prisoners of the earth,

35 To turn aside the right of a man before the face of the most High,

36 To subvert a man in his cause, the Lord approveth not. Hab. 1:13

37 Who *is* he *that* saith, and it cometh to pass, *when* the Lord commandeth *it* not? Ps. 33:9-11

38 Out of the mouth of the most High proceedeth not evil and good? Job 2:10; Is. 45:7

39 Wherefore doth a living man complain, a man for the punishment of his sins? Mic. 7:9

40 Let us search and try our ways, and turn again to the LORD. Ps. 119:59

41 Let us lift up our heart with *our* hands unto God in the heavens. Ps. 25:1; 28:2; 141:2

42 We have ᵀtransgressed and have rebelled: thou hast not pardoned. 2 Kin. 24:4 ◆ *violated a law*

43 Thou hast covered with anger, and persecuted us: thou hast slain, thou hast not pitied. Ps. 83:15; Lam. 2:17, 21

44 Thou hast covered thyself with a cloud, that *our* prayer should not pass through.

45 Thou hast made us *as* the ᵀoffscouring and refuse in the midst of the people. scum

46 All our enemies have opened their mouths against us. Ps. 22:6-8; Lam. 2:16

47 Fear and a snare is come upon us, desolation and destruction. Is. 24:17-18

48 Mine eye runneth down with rivers of water for the destruction of the daughter of my people. Lam. 2:11

49 Mine eye trickleth down, and ceaseth not, without any intermission, Jer. 14:17

50 Till the LORD look down, and behold from heaven. Is. 63:15; Lam. 5:1

51 Mine eye affecteth mine heart because of all the daughters of my city.

52 Mine enemies chased me sore, like a bird, without cause. Ps. 35:7

53 They have cut off my life in the dungeon, and cast a stone upon me. Jer. 38:6

54 Waters flowed over mine head; *then* I said, I am cut off. Jon. 2:3-5

55 I called upon thy name, O LORD, out of the low dungeon.

56 Thou hast heard my voice: hide not thine ear at my breathing, at my cry. Ps. 55:1

57 Thou drewest near in the day *that* I called upon thee: thou saidst, Fear not. Is. 41:10

58 O Lord, thou hast pleaded the causes of my soul; thou hast redeemed my life. Jer. 51:36

59 O LORD, thou hast seen my wrong: judge thou my cause. Ps. 26:1

60 Thou hast seen all their vengeance *and* all their imaginations against me. Jer. 11:19-20

61 Thou hast heard their reproach, O LORD, *and* all their imaginations against me; Lam. 5:1

62 The lips of those that rose up against me, and their device against me all the day.

63 Behold their sitting down, and their rising up; I *am* their musick. Ps. 139:2

64 Render unto them a recompence, O LORD, according to the work of their hands. Ps. 28:4

65 Give them sorrow of heart, thy curse unto them. Is. 6:10

66 Persecute and destroy them in anger from under the heavens of the LORD. Ps. 8:3

Zion Bewails Her Pitiful State

4 How is the gold become dim! *how* is the most fine gold changed! the stones of the sanctuary are poured out in the top of every street. Lam. 2:19

2 The precious sons of Zion, comparable to fine gold, how are they esteemed as earthen pitchers, the work of the hands of the potter! Jer. 19:11

3 Even the sea monsters draw out the breast, they give suck to their young ones: the daughter of my people *is become* cruel, like the ostriches in the wilderness. Is. 49:15

4 The tongue of the sucking child ᵀcleaveth to the roof of his mouth for thirst: the young

children ask bread, *and* no man breaketh *it* unto them.   Ps. 22:15; Lam. 2:11-12 ◆ *clings*

5 They that did feed delicately are desolate in the streets: they that were brought up in scarlet embrace dunghills.   Amos 6:3-7

6 For the punishment of the iniquity of the daughter of my people is greater than the punishment of the sin of Sodom, that was overthrown as in a moment, and no hands ᵀstayed on her.   Gen. 19:25; Luke 10:12 ◆ *helped*

7 Her Nazarites were purer than snow, they were whiter than milk, they were more ruddy in body than rubies, their polishing *was* of sapphire: Ps. 51:7

8 Their ᵀvisage is blacker than a coal; they are not known in the streets: their skin cleaveth to their bones; it is withered, it is become like a stick.   Job 30:30 ◆ *appearance*

9 *They that be* slain with the sword are better than *they that be* slain with hunger: for these pine away, stricken through for *want of* the fruits of the field.   Lev. 26:39

10 The hands of the pitiful women have sodden their own children: they were their meat in the destruction of the daughter of my people.   Lam. 2:20

4:10 Natural Affection Destroyed

Thousands perished from famine and pestilence. Natural affection seemed to have been destroyed. Husbands robbed their wives, and wives their husbands. Children would be seen snatching the food from the mouths of their aged parents. The question of the prophet, "Can a woman forget her sucking child?" received the answer within the walls of that doomed city: "The hands of the pitiful women have sodden their own children: they were their meat in the destruction of the daughter of my people" (Isaiah 49:15; Lamentations 4:10). *GC 32*

11 The LORD hath accomplished his fury; he hath poured out his fierce anger, and hath kindled a fire in Zion, and it hath devoured the foundations thereof.   Jer. 7:20

12 The kings of the earth, and all the inhabitants of the world, would not have believed that the adversary and the enemy should have entered into the gates of Jerusalem.

13 For the sins of her prophets, *and* the iniquities of her priests, that have shed the blood of the just in the midst of her,   Jer. 5:31; 6:13

14 They have wandered *as* blind *men* in the streets, they have polluted themselves with blood, so that men could not touch their garments.   Jer. 2:34

15 They cried unto them, Depart ye; *it is* unclean; depart, depart, touch not: when they fled away and wandered, they said among the heathen, They shall no more sojourn *there*.

16 The anger of the LORD hath divided them; he will no more regard them: they respected not the persons of the priests, they favoured not the elders.   Is. 9:14-16

17 As for us, our eyes as yet failed for our vain help: in our watching we have watched for a nation *that* could not save *us*.   Ezek. 29:16

18 They hunt our steps, that we cannot go in our streets: our end is near, our days are fulfilled; for our end is come.   Jer. 16:16; Ezek. 7:2-12

19 Our persecutors are swifter than the eagles of the heaven: they pursued us upon the mountains, they laid wait for us in the wilderness.   Is. 5:26-28

20 The breath of our nostrils, the anointed of the LORD, was taken in their pits, of whom we said, Under his shadow we shall live among the heathen.   Gen. 2:7

Edom's Impending Doom

21 Rejoice and be glad, O daughter of Edom, that dwellest in the land of Uz; the cup also shall pass through unto thee: thou shalt be drunken, and shalt make thyself naked. Job 1:1

22 The punishment of thine iniquity is accomplished, O daughter of Zion; he will no more carry thee away into captivity: he will visit thine iniquity, O daughter of Edom; he will discover thy sins.   Ps. 137:7; Is. 40:2

Jeremiah's Prayer

5 Remember, O LORD, what is come upon us: consider, and behold our reproach.   Ps. 44:13-16

2 Our inheritance is turned to strangers, our houses to aliens.   Zeph. 1:13

3 We are orphans and fatherless, our mothers *are* as widows.   Jer. 18:21

4 We have drunken our water for money; our wood is sold unto us.   Is. 3:1

5 Our necks *are* under persecution: we labour, *and* have no rest.   Neh. 9:36-37

6 We have given the hand *to* the Egyptians, *and to* the Assyrians, to be satisfied with bread.   Hos. 9:3

7 Our fathers have sinned, *and are* not; and we have borne their iniquities.   Jer. 16:12

8 Servants have ruled over us: *there is* none that doth deliver *us* out of their hand. Neh. 5:15

9 We gat our bread with *the peril of* our lives because of the sword of the wilderness.

10 Our skin was black like an oven because of the terrible famine.   Job 30:30; Lam. 4:8

11 They ravished the women in Zion, *and* the maids in the cities of Judah.   Zech. 14:2

12 Princes are hanged up by their hand: the faces of elders were not honoured.   Is. 47:6

13 They took the young men to grind, and the children fell under the wood.   Judg. 16:21

14 The elders have ceased from the gate, the young men from their musick.   Jer. 7:34

15 The joy of our heart is ceased; our dance is turned into mourning. *Amos 8:10*

16 The crown is fallen *from* our head: woe unto us, that we have sinned! *Job 19:9; Ps. 89:39*

17 For this our heart is faint; for these *things* our eyes are dim. *Job 17:7; Is. 1:5; Lam. 2:11*

18 Because of the mountain of Zion, which is desolate, the foxes walk upon it. *Mic. 3:12*

19 Thou, O LORD, remainest for ever; thy throne from generation to generation. *Ps. 45:6*

20 Wherefore dost thou forget us for ever, *and* forsake us so long time? *Ps. 13:1; 44:24*

21 Turn thou us unto thee, O LORD, and we shall be turned; renew our days as of old.

22 But thou hast utterly rejected us; thou art very ᵀwroth against us. *Ps. 60:1-2* ◆ *angered*

THE BOOK OF

EZEKIEL

Taken captive by the Babylonians prior to Jerusalem's destruction, the priest and prophet Ezekiel prophesied the destruction of Judah. He also prophesied against its future enemies, proclaiming that God would stand in the gap for His chosen people. As a result, all would know that "I am the LORD" (6:7).

Like Jeremiah, Ezekiel warned Judah of God's judgment. Like Isaiah, Ezekiel spoke of the future restoration of God's people, giving them hope. The same themes of condemnation and consolation we see in the books of the prophets before him are well represented in Ezekiel's messages.

Throughout the Book of Ezekiel, the prophet is guided by the Spirit of God (see 8:3) as he prophesies through the darkest days in the history of his people.

Dates

Ezekiel was born in 622 B.C., about the same time as Daniel. The central event of the time was the destruction of the southern kingdom of Judah, which came in three stages. In 605 B.C., Nebuchadnezzar overthrew King Jehoiakim and carried a small number of hostages off to Babylon including Daniel. In 597 B.C., Jehoiakim and his son Jehoiachin rebelled against their conqueror, compelling Nebuchadnezzar to return and force Jerusalem's surrender again. At this second stage, he took ten thousand hostages, including Ezekiel and King Jehoiakim's son, Jehoiachin. Finally, in 586 B.C., Nebuchadnezzar ended a long siege of Jerusalem, destroyed the city and scattered the remainder of the kingdom of Judah. This third stage of the destruction left Jerusalem desolate, a shell of a once-great city.

Ezekiel was about twenty-five when he was taken hostage and thirty when he received God's commission as prophet (1:1–3). From the beginning of his ministry, he argued that there was no hope of escape for the Hebrew people; however, they believed only when they heard the news of Jerusalem's fall. Ezekiel prophesied among the captives in Babylon from 592 B.C. and died about 570 B.C.

Author

Ezekiel is believed to be the author of this book. He was the son of Buzi (1:3), who came from a line of priests. Ezekiel's wife died as a sign to Judah of the coming judgment as Nebuchadnezzar prepared for his final assault on Jerusalem (24:16–24). Ezekiel was called by God as a prophet, in the line of Jeremiah, but with a more priestly view of matters. His words touch upon priesthood, the temple, sacrifices, and God's Shekinah glory.

Critics have brought a few objections to Ezekiel as the author, but they are few and largely unsubstantiated. The Book of Ezekiel uses the first person singular throughout, showing a consistency of style. Ezekiel proclaims himself as author twice (1:3; 24:24), and the phraseology of the book indicates a single writer. Phrases such as "Son of man"—the title by which Ezekiel was known—"the word of the LORD came unto me" point to Ezekiel and are repeated throughout the book's chapters (see 2:1; 3:1; 4:1; 5:1; 6:1; 7:1 and so forth).

Meaning of the Name

Ezekiel in Hebrew is Yeheze'l, or "God Strengthens" or "Strengthened by God." This name was particularly apt, since Ezekiel and the people of Judah needed strength to abide their time of captivity in Babylon. In Greek Ezekiel is Iezekiel, with Ezechiel in the Latin Vulgate.

Christ in Ezekiel

Ezekiel, like the other prophets of his time, makes several references to the coming Messiah. In various references, Jesus is called a tender twig that will become a "goodly cedar" (17:22, 23). This parallels the imagery of Jesus as a "righteous Branch" in other books (Isaiah 11:1; Jeremiah 23:5; 33:15; Zechariah 3:8; 6:12).

Jesus is portrayed as a lowly one that will be exalted and made King (Ezekiel 21:26, 27). Ezekiel also refers to Him as the Shepherd (34:11–31) who will tend the flock of the righteous, an image Jesus applied to Himself (John 10:11–14). Also, the fact that Ezekiel

is called "Son of man" points to Jesus, who later called Himself "Son of man" (Matthew 8:20; Luke 19:10). This shepherd metaphor is a special one for Israel. They were like wayward sheep who had broken down the fences of God's laws and wandered wherever their reckless hearts led them. Like all people, they needed a shepherd to guide them in the ways of truth. As David recognized, God is our Good Shepherd (Psalm 23:1).

Overview

Ezekiel was taken captive by the Babylonians a few years before Jerusalem's destruction. As the Book of Ezekiel opens, Ezekiel lives at Tel Abib, the principal colony of Jewish exiles along the River Chebar, Nebuchadnezzar's "Grand Canal" (1:1; 3:15, 23).

Ezekiel's prophetic message is similar to his predecessor Jeremiah's—a combination of God's judgment on Judah and the hope of future restoration. While Jeremiah prophesies to the Jews who were left in Judea, Ezekiel carries on a corresponding work to those in Babylonian captivity. His purpose is to remind the captive generation in Babylon of the cause of their captivity, to proclaim the coming judgment of the Gentile nations, and to trumpet the future restoration of Israel. The chief image of the message is the departure of God's glory from Israel and the promise of its return (43:2).

The chapters of Ezekiel can be divided into four thematic sections:

(1) *Ezekiel 1—3, Ezekiel's Call:* Like Isaiah, Ezekiel's prophetic call comes with a vision of God and cherubim (chapter 1) as well as a description of the call. Ezekiel is warned to speak the word regardless of the reactions he is sure to receive.

(2) *Ezekiel 4—24, Judah's Punishment:* Ezekiel's life becomes the stage through which God reveals His plan of judgment against Judah. Ezekiel acts out a siege against Jerusalem by lying on his side and baking bread meant to be defiled (chapter 4). He shaves his head and divides the hair according to God's instruction, burns some, strikes some with a sword, and scatters some to the wind as a further sign of what will occur to the people (chapter 5). He details the sins of Judah through visions of "abominations" in the temple and other sins, which culminate in the glory of God leaving the temple (chapters 8—11). Ezekiel uses parables and signs to describe the coming judgment (chapters 12—24). The idolatrous practices of many prophets and leaders are condemned.

(3) *Ezekiel 25—32, The Gentiles Are Judged:* God promises to judge the nations around Judah: Ammon, Moab, Edom, Philistia, Tyre, Sidon, and Egypt (chapters 25—32). The strong emphasis on Tyre (chapters 27—28) points also to Satan—the unseen "prince of Tyrus" (28:2, 11–19).

(4) *Ezekiel 33—48, Israel Will Be Restored:* Prior to the destruction of Jerusalem, the watchman, Ezekiel (chapter 33), prophesies a coming restoration. The false shepherds will be judged and replaced by a true shepherd—the Messiah (chapter 34). God will judge Edom (chapter 35), and other nations (chapter 36). The "dry bones" of Israel will live once more (chapter 37) even through an invasion (chapter 38). In chapters 40—48, the vision of the restored temple symbolizes the further restoration of Israel.

Unlocking Ezekiel

KEY PEOPLE:
Ezekiel, the people of Judah, the coming Messiah, the Ammonites, the prince of Tyrus (Tyre), the Pharaoh, the shepherds of Israel, Gog of Magog

KEY EVENTS:
The captivity of Ezekiel and Judah; judgments against Judah; prophetic judgments of the Gentiles; the promise of deliverance and the coming King

KEY WORD:
Restoration. Even in the pangs of captivity, Ezekiel reminds his people that they are not without God. They might have turned from Him, but He was not slack to remember His promises. They would be delivered, and they would be a nation again.

KEY VERSES:
"For I will take you from among the heathen, and gather you out of all countries, and will bring you into your own land. Then will I sprinkle clean water upon you, and ye shall be clean: from all your filthiness, and from all your idols, will I cleanse you. A new heart also will I give you, and a new spirit will I put within you: and I will take away the stony heart out of your flesh, and I will give you an heart of flesh" (Ezekiel 36:24–26).

"Thus saith the Lord GOD; In the day that I shall have cleansed you from all your iniquities I will also cause you to dwell in the cities, and the wastes shall be builded. And the desolate land shall be tilled, whereas it lay desolate in the sight of all that passed by. And they shall say, This land that was desolate is become like the garden of Eden; and the waste and desolate and ruined cities are become fenced, and are inhabited" (Ezekiel 36:33–35).

⚜ KEY CHAPTER:
Ezekiel 37, as the hope for the future of God's people.

The Time of Ezekiel's Prophecy at Chebar

1 Now it came to pass in the thirtieth year, in the fourth *month,* in the fifth *day* of the month, as I *was* among the captives by the river of Chebar, *that* the heavens were opened, and I saw visions of God.   Acts 7:56

2 In the fifth *day* of the month, which *was* the fifth year of king Jehoiachin's captivity,

3 The word of the LORD came expressly unto Ezekiel the priest, the son of Buzi, in the land of the Chaldeans by the river Chebar; and the hand of the LORD was there upon him.   1 Kin. 18:46; 2 Kin. 3:15; Ezek. 3:22

Ezekiel's Vision of Four Living Creatures

4 And I looked, and, behold, a whirlwind came out of the north, a great cloud, and a fire infolding itself, and a brightness *was* about it, and out of the midst thereof as the colour of amber, out of the midst of the fire.   Jer. 23:19; Ezek. 1:27; 8:2

5 Also out of the midst thereof *came* the likeness of four living creatures. And this *was* their appearance; they had the likeness of a man.

6 And every one had four faces, and every one had four wings.   Ezek. 10:14

7 And their feet *were* straight feet; and the sole of their feet *was* like the sole of a calf's foot: and they sparkled like the colour of burnished brass.   Dan. 10:6; Rev. 1:15

8 And *they had* the hands of a man under their wings on their four sides; and they four had their faces and their wings.   Ezek. 10:21

9 Their wings *were* joined one to another; they turned not when they went; they went every one straight forward.   Ezek. 10:22

10 As for the likeness of their faces, they four had the face of a man, and the face of a lion, on the right side: and they four had the face of an ox on the left side; they four also had the face of an eagle.   Ezek. 10:14; Rev. 4:7

11 Thus *were* their faces: and their wings *were* stretched upward; two *wings* of every one *were* joined one to another, and two covered their bodies.   Is. 6:2; Ezek. 1:23

12 And they went every one straight forward: whither the spirit was to go, they went; *and* they turned not when they went.   Ezek. 1:9

13 As for the likeness of the living creatures, their appearance *was* like burning coals of fire, *and* like the appearance of lamps: it went up and down among the living creatures; and the fire was bright, and out of the fire went forth lightning.   Ps. 104:4

14 And the living creatures ran and returned as the appearance of a flash of lightning.   Zech. 4:10

Ezekiel's Vision of Four Wheels

15 Now as I beheld the living creatures, behold one wheel upon the earth by the living creatures, with his four faces.   Ezek. 10:9

16 The appearance of the wheels and their work *was* like unto the colour of a ᵀberyl: and they four had one likeness: and their appearance and their work *was* as it were a wheel in the middle of a wheel.   Dan. 10:6 ◆ *precious stone*

17 When they went, they went upon their four sides: *and* they turned not when they went.   Ezek. 1:9, 12

18 As for their rings, they were so high that they were dreadful; and their rings *were* full of eyes round about them four.   Ezek. 10:12

1:15–18 Complex Wheels

The wheels were so complicated in arrangement that at first sight they appeared to be in confusion; yet they moved in perfect harmony. . . .

As the wheellike complications were under the guidance of the hand beneath the wings of the cherubim, so the complicated play of human events is under divine control. *PK 535, 536*

---

19 And when the living creatures went, the wheels went by them: and when the living creatures were lifted up from the earth, the wheels were lifted up.   Ezek. 10:16

20 Whithersoever the spirit was to go, they went, thither *was their* spirit to go; and the wheels were lifted up over against them: for the spirit of the living creature *was* in the wheels.   Ezek. 1:12

21 When those went, *these* went; and when those stood, *these* stood; and when those were lifted up from the earth, the wheels were lifted up over against them: for the spirit of the living creature *was* in the wheels.   Ezek. 10:17

22 And the likeness of the firmament upon the heads of the living creature *was* as the colour of the terrible crystal, stretched forth over their heads above.   Ezek. 1:26; 10:1; Rev. 4:6

23 And under the ᵀfirmament *were* their wings straight, the one toward the other: every one had two, which covered on this side, and every one had two, which covered on that side, their bodies.   *sky*

24 And when they went, I heard the noise of their wings, like the noise of great waters, as the voice of the Almighty, the voice of speech, as the noise of an host: when they stood, they let down their wings. Ezek. 43:2; Dan. 10:6; Rev. 1:15

25 And there was a voice from the firmament that *was* over their heads, when they stood, *and* had let down their wings.

Ezekiel Sees the Glory of God

26 And above the firmament that *was* over their heads *was* the likeness of a throne, as the appearance of a sapphire stone: and upon the likeness of the throne *was* the likeness as the appearance of a man above upon it.   Ex. 24:10; Ezek. 10:1; Rev. 1:13

27 And I saw as the colour of amber, as the appearance of fire round about within it, from the appearance of his ᵀloins even upward, and from the appearance of his loins even downward, I saw as it were the appearance of fire, and it had brightness round about.   Ezek. 1:4; 8:2 ◆ waist

28 As the appearance of the bow that is in the cloud in the day of rain, so *was* the appearance of the brightness round about. This *was* the appearance of the likeness of the glory of the LORD. And when I saw *it*, I fell upon my face, and I heard a voice of one that spake.   Ezek. 3:23; 8:4; Rev. 10:1

1:28 Rainbow of Promise and Assurance

The rainbow of promise encircling the throne on high is an everlasting testimony. . . . It testifies to the universe that God will never forsake His children in the struggle with evil. It is an assurance to us of strength and protection as long as the throne itself shall endure. *MH 94*

Ezekiel's Commission

2 And he said unto me, Son of man, stand upon thy feet, and I will speak unto thee.   Ezek. 3:1, 4; Dan. 10:11

2 And the spirit entered into me when he spake unto me, and set me upon my feet, that I heard him that spake unto me.   Dan. 8:18

3 And he said unto me, Son of man, I send thee to the children of Israel, to a rebellious nation that hath rebelled against me: they and their fathers have ᵀtransgressed against me, *even* unto this very day.   Jer. 3:25 ◆ sinned

2:1–3 Raised Up to Warn and Comfort

While Jeremiah continued to bear his testimony in the land of Judah, the prophet Ezekiel was raised up from among the captives in Babylon, to warn and to comfort the exiles, and also to confirm the word of the Lord that was being spoken through Jeremiah. . . . He was also instructed to foretell, by means of a variety of symbols and solemn messages, the siege and utter destruction of Jerusalem. *PK 448*

4 For *they are* ᵀimpudent children and stiffhearted. I do send thee unto them; and thou shalt say unto them, Thus saith the Lord GOD.   Ps. 95:8; Is. 48:4; Ezek. 3:7 ◆ stubborn

5 And they, whether they will hear, or whether they will forbear, (for they *are* a rebellious house,) yet shall know that there hath been a prophet among them.   Ezek. 2:7; 3:27; 33:33

6 And thou, son of man, be not afraid of them, neither be afraid of their words, though briers and thorns *be* with thee, and thou dost dwell among scorpions: be not afraid of their words, nor be dismayed at their looks, though they *be* a rebellious house.   Jer. 1:8, 17; Mic. 7:4

7 And thou shalt speak my words unto them, whether they will hear, or whether they will ᵀforbear: for they *are* most rebellious.   Jer. 1:7 ◆ refuse to act

2:7 Opposition to Truth

In view of this, what is the duty of the messenger of truth? Shall he conclude that the truth ought not to be presented, since often its only effect is to arouse men to evade or resist its claims? No; he has no more reason for withholding the testimony of God's word, because it excites opposition, than had earlier Reformers. *GC 459*

8 But thou, son of man, hear what I say unto thee; Be not thou rebellious like that rebellious house: open thy mouth, and eat that I give thee.   Is. 50:5; Jer. 15:16; Rev. 10:9

9 And when I looked, behold, an hand *was* sent unto me; and, lo, a roll of a book *was* therein;   Ezek. 3:1; 8:3; Dan. 10:10

10 And he spread it before me; and it *was* written within and without: and *there was* written therein lamentations, and mourning, and woe.   Rev. 8:13

Ezekiel's Vision of a Scroll

3 Moreover he said unto me, Son of man, eat that thou findest; eat this roll, and go speak unto the house of Israel.   Ezek. 2:8-9

2 So I opened my mouth, and he caused me to eat that roll.   Jer. 25:17

3 And he said unto me, Son of man, cause thy belly to eat, and fill thy bowels with this roll that I give thee. Then did I eat *it*; and it was in my mouth as honey for sweetness.   Ps. 19:10; 119:103; Jer. 15:16

4 And he said unto me, Son of man, go, get thee unto the house of Israel, and speak with my words unto them.

5 For thou *art* not sent to a people of a strange speech and of an hard language, *but* to the house of Israel;   Jon. 1:2

6 Not to many people of a strange speech and of an hard language, whose words thou canst not understand. Surely, had I sent thee to them, they would have hearkened unto thee.

7 But the house of Israel will not hearken unto thee; for they will not hearken unto

me: for all the house of Israel *are* ᵀimpudent and hardhearted. Ezek. 2:4 ✦ *stubborn*

8 Behold, I have made thy face strong against their faces, and thy forehead strong against their foreheads. Jer. 1:18

9 As an ᵀadamant harder than flint have I made thy forehead: fear them not, neither be dismayed at their looks, though they *be* a rebellious house. Is. 50:7 ✦ *hard substance*

10 Moreover he said unto me, Son of man, all my words that I shall speak unto thee receive in thine heart, and hear with thine ears. Job 22:22

11 And go, get thee to them of the captivity, unto the children of thy people, and speak unto them, and tell them, Thus saith the Lord GOD; whether they will hear, or whether they will ᵀforbear. Ezek. 2:7 ✦ *refuse to act*

12 Then the spirit took me up, and I heard behind me a voice of a great rushing, *saying*, Blessed *be* the glory of the LORD from his place. Ezek. 3:14; 8:3; Acts 8:39

13 *I heard* also the noise of the wings of the living creatures that touched one another, and the noise of the wheels over against them, and a noise of a great rushing. Ezek. 1:24

14 So the spirit lifted me up, and took me away, and I went in bitterness, in the heat of my spirit; but the hand of the LORD was strong upon me. 2 Kin. 3:15; Ezek. 1:3; 37:1

15 Then I came to them of the captivity at Telabib, that dwelt by the river of Chebar, and I sat where they sat, and remained there astonished among them seven days. Gen. 50:10

Ezekiel Is Appointed to be a Watchman

16 And it came to pass at the end of seven days, that the word of the LORD came unto me, saying, Jer. 42:7

17 Son of man, I have made thee a watchman unto the house of Israel: therefore hear the word at my mouth, and give them warning from me. 2 Chr. 19:10; Is. 52:8; Jer. 6:17

18 When I say unto the wicked, Thou shalt surely die; and thou givest him not warning, nor speakest to warn the wicked from his wicked way, to save his life; the same wicked *man* shall die in his iniquity; but his blood will I require at thine hand. Gen. 2:17; Ezek. 3:20; 33:6

19 Yet if thou warn the wicked, and he turn not from his wickedness, nor from his wicked way, he shall die in his iniquity; but thou hast delivered thy soul. Ezek. 14:14, 20; 33:9

20 Again, When a righteous *man* doth turn from his righteousness, and commit iniquity, and I lay a stumblingblock before him, he shall die: because thou hast not given him warning, he shall die in his sin, and his righteousness which he hath done shall not be remembered; but his blood will I require at thine hand. Ps. 125:5; Ezek. 3:18; 18:24

21 Nevertheless if thou warn the righteous *man*, that the righteous sin not, and he doth not sin, he shall surely live, because he is warned; also thou hast delivered thy soul. Acts 20:31

The Lord Instructs Ezekiel

22 And the hand of the LORD was there upon me; and he said unto me, Arise, go forth into the plain, and I will there talk with thee. Ezek. 1:3; 8:4; Acts 9:6

23 Then I arose, and went forth into the plain: and, behold, the glory of the LORD stood there, as the glory which I saw by the river of Chebar: and I fell on my face. Ezek. 1:28; Acts 7:55

24 Then the spirit entered into me, and set me upon my feet, and spake with me, and said unto me, Go, shut thyself within thine house. Ezek. 2:2

25 But thou, O son of man, behold, they shall put bands upon thee, and shall bind thee with them, and thou shalt not go out among them: Ezek. 4:8

26 And I will make thy tongue cleave to the roof of thy mouth, that thou shalt be ᵀdumb, and shalt not be to them a reprover: for they *are* a rebellious house. Ezek. 24:27 ✦ *mute*

27 But when I speak with thee, I will open thy mouth, and thou shalt say unto them,

---

Principle, Not Policy

Ezekiel 3:7

The great obstacle both to the acceptance and to the promulgation of truth is the fact that it involves inconvenience and reproach. This is the only argument against the truth which its advocates have never been able to refute. But this does not deter the true followers of Christ. These do not wait for truth to become popular. Being convinced of their duty, they deliberately accept the cross, with the apostle Paul counting that "our light affliction, which is but for a moment, worketh for us a far more exceeding and eternal weight of glory;" with one of old, "esteeming the reproach of Christ greater riches than the treasures in Egypt" (2 Corinthians 4:17; Hebrews 11:26).

Whatever may be their profession, it is only those who are world servers at heart that act from policy rather than principle in religious things. We should choose the right because it is right, and leave consequences with God. To men of principle, faith, and daring, the world is indebted for its great reforms. *GC 460*

Thus saith the Lord GOD; He that heareth, let him hear; and he that ᵀforbeareth, let him forbear: for they *are* a rebellious house.   Ezek. 3:11; 12:2-3; 24:27 ◆ *refuses*

Ezekiel Foretells the Siege of Jerusalem

4 Thou also, son of man, take thee a tile, and lay it before thee, and pourtray upon it the city, *even* Jerusalem:

2 And lay siege against it, and build a fort against it, and cast a mount against it; set the camp also against it, and set *battering* rams against it round about.   Ezek. 21:22

3 Moreover take thou unto thee an iron pan, and set it *for* a wall of iron between thee and the city: and set thy face against it, and it shall be besieged, and thou shalt lay siege against it. This *shall be* a sign to the house of Israel.   Is. 8:18; 20:3; Ezek. 12:6

4 Lie thou also upon thy left side, and lay the iniquity of the house of Israel upon it: *according* to the number of the days that thou shalt lie upon it thou shalt bear their iniquity.   Lev. 16:22

5 For I have laid upon thee the years of their iniquity, according to the number of the days, three hundred and ninety days: so shalt thou bear the iniquity of the house of Israel.

6 And when thou hast accomplished them, lie again on thy right side, and thou shalt bear the iniquity of the house of Judah forty days: I have appointed thee each day for a year.   Num. 14:34; Dan. 9:24-26; 12:11-12

7 Therefore thou shalt set thy face toward the siege of Jerusalem, and thine arm *shall be* uncovered, and thou shalt prophesy against it.   Is. 52:10

8 And, behold, I will lay bands upon thee, and thou shalt not turn thee from one side to another, till thou hast ended the days of thy siege.   Ezek. 3:25

9 Take thou also unto thee wheat, and barley, and beans, and lentiles, and millet, and ᵀfitches, and put them in one vessel, and make thee bread thereof, *according* to the number of the days that thou shalt lie upon thy side, three hundred and ninety days shalt thou eat thereof.   *spelt*

10 And thy meat which thou shalt eat *shall be* by weight, twenty shekels a day: from time to time shalt thou eat it.

11 Thou shalt drink also water by measure, the sixth part of an hin: from time to time shalt thou drink.

12 And thou shalt eat it *as* barley cakes, and thou shalt bake it with dung that cometh out of man, in their sight.

13 And the LORD said, Even thus shall the children of Israel eat their defiled bread among the Gentiles, whither I will drive them.   Dan. 1:8

14 Then said I, Ah Lord GOD! behold, my soul hath not been polluted: for from my youth up even till now have I not eaten of that which dieth of itself, or is torn in pieces; neither came there abominable flesh into my mouth.   Ezek. 9:8; 20:49; Acts 10:14

15 Then he said unto me, Lo, I have given thee cow's dung for man's dung, and thou shalt prepare thy bread therewith.

16 Moreover he said unto me, Son of man, behold, I will break the staff of bread in Jerusalem: and they shall eat bread by weight, and with care; and they shall drink water by measure, and with astonishment: Lev. 26:26

17 That they may want bread and water, and be astonied one with another, and consume away for their iniquity. Lev. 26:39; Ezek. 24:23; 33:10

The Coming Fall of Jerusalem

5 And thou, son of man, take thee a sharp knife, take thee a barber's razor, and cause *it* to pass upon thine head and upon thy beard: then take thee balances to weigh, and divide the *hair*.   Lev. 21:5; Is. 7:20; Ezek. 44:20

2 Thou shalt burn with fire a third part in the midst of the city, when the days of the siege are fulfilled: and thou shalt take a third part, *and* smite about it with a knife: and a third part thou shalt scatter in the wind; and I will draw out a sword after them.   Lev. 26:33; Jer. 9:16

3 Thou shalt also take thereof a few in number, and bind them in thy skirts.   Jer. 39:10

4 Then take of them again, and cast them into the midst of the fire, and burn them in the fire; *for* thereof shall a fire come forth into all the house of Israel.

5 Thus saith the Lord GOD; This *is* Jerusalem: I have set it in the midst of the nations and countries *that are* round about her.   Ezek. 4:1

6 And she hath changed my judgments into wickedness more than the nations, and my statutes more than the countries that *are* round about her: for they have refused my judgments and my statutes, they have not walked in them.   Jer. 11:10

7 Therefore thus saith the Lord GOD; Because ye multiplied more than the nations that *are* round about you, *and* have not walked in my statutes, neither have kept my judgments, neither have done according to the judgments of the nations that *are* round about you;   2 Chr. 33:9

8 Therefore thus saith the Lord GOD; Behold, I, even I, *am* against thee, and will execute judgments in the midst of thee in the sight of the nations.   Ezek. 15:7

9 And I will do in thee that which I have not done, and whereunto I will not do

any more the like, because of all thine abominations. Dan. 9:12; Amos 3:2; Matt. 24:21
10 Therefore the fathers shall eat the sons in the midst of thee, and the sons shall eat their fathers; and I will execute judgments in thee, and the whole remnant of thee will I scatter into all the winds. Deut. 28:64; Ezek. 12:14; Zech. 2:6
11 Wherefore, *as* I live, saith the Lord GOD; Surely, because thou hast defiled my sanctuary with all thy detestable things, and with all thine abominations, therefore will I also diminish *thee*; neither shall mine eye spare, neither will I have any pity. 2 Chr. 36:14; Ezek. 7:4
12 A third part of thee shall die with the pestilence, and with famine shall they be consumed in the midst of thee: and a third part shall fall by the sword round about thee; and I will scatter a third part into all the winds, and I will draw out a sword after them. Jer. 15:2; 21:9; Ezek. 5:2
13 Thus shall mine anger be accomplished, and I will cause my fury to rest upon them, and I will be comforted: and they shall know that I the LORD have spoken *it* in my zeal, when I have accomplished my fury in them. Is. 1:24
14 Moreover I will make thee waste, and a reproach among the nations that *are* round about thee, in the sight of all that pass by.
15 So it shall be a reproach and a taunt, an instruction and an astonishment unto the nations that *are* round about thee, when I shall execute judgments in thee in anger and in fury and in furious rebukes. I the LORD have spoken *it*. 1 Kin. 9:7; Jer. 22:8-9; Ezek. 25:17
16 When I shall send upon them the evil arrows of famine, which shall be for *their* destruction, *and* which I will send to destroy you: and I will increase the famine upon you, and will break your staff of bread: Deut. 32:23-24
17 So will I send upon you famine and evil beasts, and they shall bereave thee; and pestilence and blood shall pass through thee; and I will bring the sword upon thee. I the LORD have spoken *it*. Lev. 26:22; Deut. 32:24; Ezek. 38:22

The Judgment of Israel for Idolatry

6 And the word of the LORD came unto me, saying,
2 Son of man, set thy face toward the mountains of Israel, and prophesy against them, Ezek. 13:17
3 And say, Ye mountains of Israel, hear the word of the Lord GOD; Thus saith the Lord GOD to the mountains, and to the hills, to the rivers, and to the valleys; Behold, I, *even* I, will bring a sword upon you, and I will destroy your high places. Lev. 26:30
4 And your altars shall be desolate, and your images shall be broken: and I will cast down your slain *men* before your idols. Lev. 26:30

5 And I will lay the dead carcases of the children of Israel before their idols; and I will scatter your bones round about your altars.
6 In all your dwellingplaces the cities shall be laid waste, and the high places shall be desolate; that your altars may be laid waste and made desolate, and your idols may be broken and cease, and your images may be cut down, and your works may be abolished. Is. 6:11
7 And the slain shall fall in the midst of you, and ye shall know that I *am* the LORD.

A Remnant Shall Be Blessed

8 Yet will I leave a remnant, that ye may have *some* that shall escape the sword among the nations, when ye shall be scattered through the countries. Is. 6:13; Jer. 44:14; Ezek. 14:22
9 And they that escape of you shall remember me among the nations whither they shall be carried captives, because I am broken with their whorish heart, which hath departed from me, and with their eyes, which go a whoring after their idols: and they shall lothe themselves for the evils which they have committed in all their abominations. Ps. 78:40; Is. 7:13; Ezek. 20:43
10 And they shall know that I *am* the LORD, *and that* I have not said in vain that I would do this evil unto them.

The Faithful Are Exhorted to Lament

11 Thus saith the Lord GOD; Smite with thine hand, and stamp with thy foot, and say, Alas for all the evil abominations of the house of Israel! for they shall fall by the sword, by the famine, and by the pestilence. Ezek. 5:12; 9:4; 25:6
12 He that is far off shall die of the pestilence; and he that is near shall fall by the sword; and he that remaineth and is besieged shall die by the famine: thus will I accomplish my fury upon them. Ezek. 5:13
13 Then shall ye know that I *am* the LORD, when their slain *men* shall be among their idols round about their altars, upon every high hill, in all the tops of the mountains, and under every green tree, and under every thick oak, the place where they did offer sweet savour to all their idols. 1 Kin. 14:23; Ezek. 20:28
14 So will I stretch out my hand upon them, and make the land desolate, yea, more desolate than the wilderness toward Diblath, in all their habitations: and they shall know that I *am* the LORD. Is. 5:25; 9:12; Ezek. 20:33-34

The Final Desolation of Israel

7 Moreover the word of the LORD came unto me, saying,
2 Also, thou son of man, thus saith the Lord GOD unto the land of Israel; An end,

the end is come upon the four corners of the land. Amos 8:2

3 Now *is* the end *come* upon thee, and I will send mine anger upon thee, and will judge thee according to thy ways, and will recompense upon thee all thine abominations. Ezek. 18:30

4 And mine eye shall not spare thee, neither will I have pity: but I will ᵀrecompense thy ways upon thee, and thine abominations shall be in the midst of thee: and ye shall know that I *am* the LORD. Ezek. 5:11 ◆ *repay*

5 Thus saith the Lord GOD; An evil, an only evil, behold, is come. 2 Kin. 21:12-13

6 An end is come, the end is come: it watcheth for thee; behold, it is come. Zech. 13:7

7 The morning is come unto thee, O thou that dwellest in the land: the time is come, the day of trouble *is* near, and not the sounding again of the mountains. Is. 22:5

8 Now will I shortly pour out my fury upon thee, and accomplish mine anger upon thee: and I will judge thee according to thy ways, and will recompense thee for all thine abominations. Is. 42:25; Ezek. 9:8; 14:19

9 And mine eye shall not spare, neither will I have pity: I will recompense thee according to thy ways and thine abominations *that* are in the midst of thee; and ye shall know that I *am* the LORD that ᵀsmiteth. *strikes*

10 Behold the day, behold, it is come: the morning is gone forth; the rod hath blossomed, pride hath budded. Is. 10:5

11 Violence is risen up into a rod of wickedness: none of them *shall remain*, nor of their multitude, nor of any of theirs: neither *shall there be* wailing for them. Zeph. 1:18

12 The time is come, the day draweth near: let not the buyer rejoice, nor the seller mourn: for wrath *is* upon all the multitude thereof. Is. 5:13-14

13 For the seller shall not return to that which is sold, although they were yet alive: for the vision *is* touching the whole multitude thereof, *which* shall not return; neither shall any strengthen himself in the iniquity of his life. Lev. 25:24-28

14 They have blown the trumpet, even to make all ready; but none goeth to the battle: for my wrath *is* upon all the multitude thereof. Jer. 4:5

15 The sword *is* without, and the pestilence and the famine within: he that *is* in the field shall die with the sword; and he that *is* in the city, famine and pestilence shall devour him. Jer. 14:18; Lam. 1:20; Ezek. 5:12

The Repentance of Those Who Escape

16 But they that escape of them shall escape, and shall be on the mountains like doves of the valleys, all of them mourning, every one for his iniquity. Ezra 9:15

17 All hands shall be feeble, and all knees shall be weak *as* water. Jer. 6:24; Ezek. 21:7

18 They shall also ᵀgird *themselves* with sackcloth, and horror shall cover them; and shame *shall be* upon all faces, and baldness upon all their heads. Is. 15:2-3 ◆ *clothe*

19 They shall cast their silver in the streets, and their gold shall be removed: their silver and their gold shall not be able to deliver them in the day of the wrath of the LORD: they shall not satisfy their souls, neither fill their bowels: because it is the stumblingblock of their iniquity. Prov. 11:4; Is. 2:20; Zeph. 1:18

20 As for the beauty of his ornament, he set it in majesty: but they made the images of their abominations *and* of their detestable things therein: therefore have I set it far from them. Is. 64:11; Jer. 7:30; Ezek. 24:21

21 And I will give it into the hands of the strangers for a prey, and to the wicked of the earth for a ᵀspoil; and they shall pollute it. 2 Kin. 24:13 ◆ *plunder*

22 My face will I turn also from them, and they shall pollute my secret *place*: for the robbers shall enter into it, and defile it. Jer. 18:17

The Figure of a Chain

23 Make a chain: for the land is full of bloody crimes, and the city is full of violence. Jer. 27:2

24 Wherefore I will bring the worst of the heathen, and they shall possess their houses: I will also make the pomp of the strong to cease; and their holy places shall be defiled. Ezek. 28:7

25 Destruction cometh; and they shall seek peace, and *there shall be* none.

26 Mischief shall come upon mischief, and rumour shall be upon rumour; then shall they seek a vision of the prophet; but the law shall perish from the priest, and counsel from the ancients. Ps. 74:9; Jer. 4:20; Ezek. 14:1

27 The king shall mourn, and the prince shall be clothed with desolation, and the hands of the people of the land shall be troubled: I will do unto them after their way, and according to their deserts will I judge them; and they shall know that I *am* the LORD.

Idolatry in Jerusalem

8 And it came to pass in the sixth year, in the sixth *month*, in the fifth *day* of the month, *as* I sat in mine house, and the elders of Judah sat before me, that the hand of the Lord GOD fell there upon me. Ezek. 1:2-3; 14:1

2 Then I beheld, and lo a likeness as the appearance of fire: from the appearance of his ᵀloins even downward, fire; and from his loins even upward, as the appearance of brightness, as the colour of amber. Ezek. 1:4, 26-27 ◆ *waist*

3 And he put forth the form of an hand, and took me by a lock of mine head; and the spirit lifted me up between the earth and the heaven, and brought me in the visions of God to Jerusalem, to the door of the inner gate that looketh toward the north; where *was* the seat of the image of jealousy, which provoketh to jealousy.   Ex. 20:5; Deut. 32:16; Ezek. 11:1
4 And, behold, the glory of the God of Israel *was* there, according to the vision that I saw in the plain.   Ezek. 3:22-23
5 Then said he unto me, Son of man, lift up thine eyes now the way toward the north. So I lifted up mine eyes the way toward the north, and behold northward at the gate of the altar this image of jealousy in the entry.   Ezek. 8:3
6 He said furthermore unto me, Son of man, seest thou what they do? *even* the great abominations that the house of Israel committeth here, that I should go far off from my sanctuary? but turn thee yet again, *and* thou shalt see greater abominations.   Ezek. 5:11; 8:9; 10:19

The Chambers of Idolatry

7 And he brought me to the door of the court; and when I looked, behold a hole in the wall.
8 Then said he unto me, Son of man, dig now in the wall: and when I had digged in the wall, behold a door.   Is. 29:15
9 And he said unto me, Go in, and behold the wicked abominations that they do here.
10 So I went in and saw; and behold every form of creeping things, and abominable beasts, and all the idols of the house of Israel, pourtrayed upon the wall round about.   Ex. 20:4
11 And there stood before them seventy men of the ancients of the house of Israel, and in the midst of them stood Jaazaniah the son of Shaphan, with every man his ᵀcenser in his hand; and a thick cloud of incense went up.   Num. 11:16 ◆ *holder for burning incense*
12 Then said he unto me, Son of man, hast thou seen what the ancients of the house of Israel do in the dark, every man in the chambers of his imagery? for they say, The LORD seeth us not; the LORD hath forsaken the earth.   Ps. 10:11; Is. 29:15; Ezek. 9:9

The Mourners for Tammuz

13 He said also unto me, Turn thee yet again, *and* thou shalt see greater abominations that they do.   Ezek. 8:6
14 Then he brought me to the door of the gate of the LORD's house which *was* toward the north; and, behold, there sat women weeping for Tammuz.   Ezek. 44:4
15 Then said he unto me, Hast thou seen *this*, O son of man? turn thee yet again, *and*

thou shalt see greater abominations than these.
16 And he brought me into the inner court of the LORD's house, and, behold, at the door of the temple of the LORD, between the porch and the altar, *were* about five and twenty men, with their backs toward the temple of the LORD, and their faces toward the east; and they worshipped the sun toward the east.   Deut. 4:19; 17:3; Jer. 2:27
17 Then he said unto me, Hast thou seen *this*, O son of man? Is it a light thing to the house of Judah that they commit the abominations which they commit here? for they have filled the land with violence, and have returned to provoke me to anger: and, lo, they put the branch to their nose.   Ezek. 7:23
18 Therefore will I also deal in fury: mine eye shall not spare, neither will I have pity: and though they cry in mine ears with a loud voice, *yet* will I not hear them.   Is. 1:15; Jer. 11:11

The Coming Destruction of the Temple

9 He cried also in mine ears with a loud voice, saying, Cause them that have charge over the city to draw near, even every man *with* his destroying weapon in his hand.   Is. 6:8
2 And, behold, six men came from the way of the higher gate, which lieth toward the north, and every man a slaughter weapon in his hand; and one man among them *was* clothed with linen, with a writer's inkhorn by his side: and they went in, and stood beside the brasen altar.   Lev. 16:4
3 And the glory of the God of Israel was gone up from the cherub, whereupon he was, to the threshold of the house. And he called to the man clothed with linen, which *had* the writer's inkhorn by his side;   Ezek. 10:4; 11:22-23
4 And the LORD said unto him, Go through the midst of the city, through the midst of Jerusalem, and set a mark upon the foreheads of the men that sigh and that cry for all the abominations that be done in the midst thereof.   Ex. 12:7; Ps. 119:53, 136

9:4 Tearful Warnings

In the time of the end the people of God will sigh and cry for the abominations done in the land. With tears they will warn the wicked of their danger in trampling upon the divine law. . . . The wicked will mock their sorrow and ridicule their solemn appeals. . . . It is because they are drawing nearer to Christ, because their eyes are fixed on His perfect purity, that they discern so clearly the exceeding sinfulness of sin. *PK 590*

5 And to the others he said in mine hearing, Go ye after him through the city, and

ᵀsmite: let not your eye spare, neither have ye pity: Ezek. 5:11 ◆ *strike*

6 Slay utterly old *and* young, both maids, and little children, and women: but come not near any man upon whom *is* the mark; and begin at my sanctuary. Then they began at the ancient men which *were* before the house.   2 Chr. 36:17; Jer. 25:29; Rev. 9:4

> ### 9:6 The Professed Guardians Are Judged First
>
> The mark of deliverance has been set upon those "that sigh and that cry for all the abominations that be done" [Ezekiel 9:4]. . . . The work of destruction begins among those who have professed to be the spiritual guardians of the people. The false watchmen are the first to fall. There are none to pity or to spare. Men, women, maidens, and little children perish together. *GC 656*

7 And he said unto them, Defile the house, and fill the courts with the slain: go ye forth. And they went forth, and slew in the city.   2 Chr. 36:17

8 And it came to pass, while they were slaying them, and I was left, that I fell upon my face, and cried, and said, Ah Lord Gᴏᴅ! wilt thou destroy all the residue of Israel in thy pouring out of thy fury upon Jerusalem?   Num. 14:5; Josh. 7:6; Ezek. 11:13

9 Then said he unto me, The iniquity of the house of Israel and Judah *is* exceeding great, and the land is full of blood, and the city full of perverseness: for they say, The Lᴏʀᴅ hath forsaken the earth, and the Lᴏʀᴅ seeth not.   Job 22:13; Ezek. 7:23; 8:12

10 And as for me also, mine eye shall not spare, neither will I have pity, *but* I will ᵀrecompense their way upon their head.   *repay*

11 And, behold, the man clothed with linen, which *had* the inkhorn by his side, reported the matter, saying, I have done as thou hast commanded me.

The Lord's Glory Leaves the Temple

10 Then I looked, and, behold, in the ᵀfirmament that was above the head of the cherubims there appeared over them as it were a sapphire stone, as the appearance of the likeness of a throne.   Ex. 24:10 ◆ *sky*

2 And he spake unto the man clothed with linen, and said, Go in between the wheels, *even* under the cherub, and fill thine hand with coals of fire from between the cherubims, and scatter *them* over the city. And he went in in my sight.   Ps. 18:12-13; Ezek. 1:13; Rev. 8:5

3 Now the cherubims stood on the right side of the house, when the man went in; and the cloud filled the inner court.

4 Then the glory of the Lᴏʀᴅ went up from the cherub, *and stood* over the threshold of the house; and the house was filled with the cloud, and the court was full of the brightness of the Lᴏʀᴅ's glory.   Ex. 40:35; Ezek. 1:28; 9:3

5 And the sound of the cherubims' wings was heard *even* to the outer court, as the voice of the Almighty God when he speaketh.   Job 40:9; Ezek. 1:24

6 And it came to pass, *that* when he had commanded the man clothed with linen, saying, Take fire from between the wheels, from between the cherubims; then he went in, and stood beside the wheels.   Ezek. 10:2

7 And *one* cherub stretched forth his hand

Sighing and Crying for God's Church

Ezekiel 9:1–7

At times the Lord may seem to have forgotten the perils of His church and the injury done her by her enemies. But God has not forgotten. Nothing in this world is so dear to the heart of God as His church. It is not His will that worldly policy shall corrupt her record. He does not leave His people to be overcome by Satan's temptations. He will punish those who misrepresent Him, but He will be gracious to all who sincerely repent. . . .

In the time of the end the people of God will sigh and cry for the abominations done in the land. With tears they will warn the wicked of their danger in trampling upon the divine law, and with unutterable sorrow they will humble themselves before the Lord in penitence. The wicked will mock their sorrow and ridicule their solemn appeals. But the anguish and humiliation of God's people is unmistakable evidence that they are regaining the strength and nobility of character lost in consequence of sin. It is because they are drawing nearer to Christ, because their eyes are fixed on His perfect purity, that they discern so clearly the exceeding sinfulness of sin. Meekness and lowliness are the conditions of success and victory. . . .

As the people of God afflict their souls before Him, pleading for purity of heart, the command is given, "Take away the filthy garments," and the encouraging words are spoken, "Behold, I have caused thine iniquity to pass from thee, and I will clothe thee with change of raiment" (Zechariah 3:4). The spotless robe of Christ's righteousness is placed upon the tried, tempted, faithful children of God. . . . They have resisted the wiles of the deceiver; they have not been turned from their loyalty by the dragon's roar. Now they are eternally secure from the tempter's devices. *PK 590, 591*

from between the cherubims unto the fire that *was* between the cherubims, and took *thereof*, and put *it* into the hands of *him that was* clothed with linen: who took *it*, and went out.

8 And there appeared in the cherubims the form of a man's hand under their wings.

> **10:8 Success Through Divine Power**
>
> In the vision of the prophet Ezekiel there was the appearance of a hand beneath the wings of the cherubim. This is to teach God's servants that it is divine power that gives success. Those whom God employs as His messengers are not to feel that His work is dependent on them. Finite beings are not left to carry this burden of responsibility. He who slumbers not, who is continually at work for the accomplishment of His designs, will carry forward His work. *PK 176*

9 And when I looked, behold the four wheels by the cherubims, one wheel by one cherub, and another wheel by another cherub: and the appearance of the wheels *was* as the colour of a beryl stone.   Dan. 10:6

10 And *as for* their appearances, they four had one likeness, as if a wheel had been in the midst of a wheel.

11 When they went, they went upon their four sides; they turned not as they went, but to the place whither the head looked they followed it; they turned not as they went.   Ezek. 1:17

12 And their whole body, and their backs, and their hands, and their wings, and the wheels, *were* full of eyes round about, *even* the wheels that they four had.   Ezek. 1:18; Rev. 4:6, 8

13 As for the wheels, it was cried unto them in my hearing, O wheel.

14 And every one had four faces: the first face *was* the face of a cherub, and the second face *was* the face of a man, and the third the face of a lion, and the fourth the face of an eagle.   1 Kin. 7:36

15 And the cherubims were lifted up. This *is* the living creature that I saw by the river of Chebar.   Ezek. 1:5

16 And when the cherubims went, the wheels went by them: and when the cherubims lifted up their wings to mount up from the earth, the same wheels also turned not from beside them.

17 When they stood, *these* stood; and when they were lifted up, *these* lifted up themselves *also*: for the spirit of the living creature *was* in them.   Ezek. 1:20-21

18 Then the glory of the LORD departed from off the threshold of the house, and stood over the cherubims.   Ps. 18:10

19 And the cherubims lifted up their wings,

and mounted up from the earth in my sight: when they went out, the wheels also *were* beside them, and *every* one stood at the door of the east gate of the LORD's house; and the glory of the God of Israel *was* over them above.

20 This *is* the living creature that I saw under the God of Israel by the river of Chebar; and I knew that they *were* the cherubims.   Ezek. 1:1

21 Every one had four faces apiece, and every one four wings; and the likeness of the hands of a man *was* under their wings.   Ezek. 1:6

22 And the likeness of their faces *was* the same faces which I saw by the river of Chebar, their appearances and themselves: they went every one straight forward.   Ezek. 1:10

Judgment on Israel's Rulers

11 Moreover the spirit lifted me up, and brought me unto the east gate of the LORD's house, which looketh eastward: and behold at the door of the gate five and twenty men; among whom I saw Jaazaniah the son of Azur, and Pelatiah the son of Benaiah, princes of the people.   Ezek. 3:12

2 Then said he unto me, Son of man, these *are* the men that devise mischief, and give wicked counsel in this city: Ps. 2:1-2

3 Which say, *It is* not near; let us build houses: this *city is* the caldron, and we *be* the flesh.

4 Therefore prophesy against them, prophesy, O son of man.

5 And the Spirit of the LORD fell upon me, and said unto me, Speak; Thus saith the LORD; Thus have ye said, O house of Israel: for I know the things that come into your mind, *every one of* them.   Jer. 17:10

6 Ye have multiplied your slain in this city, and ye have filled the streets thereof with the slain.   Is. 1:15; Ezek. 7:23; 22:2-6

7 Therefore thus saith the Lord GOD; Your slain whom ye have laid in the midst of it, they *are* the flesh, and this *city is* the caldron: but I will bring you forth out of the midst of it.   Ezek. 24:3-13

8 Ye have feared the sword; and I will bring a sword upon you, saith the Lord GOD. Prov. 10:24

9 And I will bring you out of the midst thereof, and deliver you into the hands of strangers, and will execute judgments among you.   Deut. 28:36; Ps. 106:41; Ezek. 5:8

10 Ye shall fall by the sword; I will judge you in the border of Israel; and ye shall know that I *am* the LORD.

11 This *city* shall not be your ᵀcaldron, neither shall ye be the flesh in the midst thereof; *but* I will judge you in the border of Israel: Ezek. 11:3 ◆ *pot*

12 And ye shall know that I *am* the LORD: for

ye have not walked in my statutes, neither executed my judgments, but have done after the manners of the heathen that *are* round about you.   Ezek. 8:10, 14, 16

13 And it came to pass, when I prophesied, that Pelatiah the son of Benaiah died. Then fell I down upon my face, and cried with a loud voice, and said, Ah Lord GOD! wilt thou make a full end of the remnant of Israel?   Ezek. 9:8; 11:1; Acts 5:5

God Will Gather Israel

14 Again the word of the LORD came unto me, saying,

15 Son of man, thy brethren, *even* thy brethren, the men of thy kindred, and all the house of Israel wholly, *are* they unto whom the inhabitants of Jerusalem have said, Get you far from the LORD: unto us is this land given in possession.   Ezek. 33:24

16 Therefore say, Thus saith the Lord GOD; Although I have cast them far off among the heathen, and although I have scattered them among the countries, yet will I be to them as a little sanctuary in the countries where they shall come.   Ps. 31:20; 90:1; Is. 8:14

17 Therefore say, Thus saith the Lord GOD; I will even gather you from the people, and assemble you out of the countries where ye have been scattered, and I will give you the land of Israel.   Jer. 3:18; 24:5; Ezek. 28:25

18 And they shall come thither, and they shall take away all the detestable things thereof and all the abominations thereof from thence.   Ezek. 5:11; 7:20; 37:23

19 And I will give them one heart, and I will put a new spirit within you; and I will take the stony heart out of their flesh, and will give them an heart of flesh: Ezek. 18:31; 36:26-27

20 That they may walk in my statutes, and keep mine ordinances, and do them: and they shall be my people, and I will be their God.   Ps. 105:45; Jer. 30:22; Ezek. 14:11

21 But *as for them* whose heart walketh after the heart of their detestable things and their abominations, I will ᵀrecompense their way upon their own heads, saith the Lord GOD.   Ezek. 9:10 ◆ repay

The Lord's Glory Leaves Jerusalem

22 Then did the cherubims lift up their wings, and the wheels beside them; and the glory of the God of Israel *was* over them above.   Ezek. 10:19

23 And the glory of the LORD went up from the midst of the city, and stood upon the mountain which *is* on the east side of the city.   Ezek. 8:4; 10:4; Zech. 14:4

24 Afterwards the spirit took me up, and brought me in a vision by the Spirit of God into Chaldea, to them of the captivity. So

the vision that I had seen went up from me.   Ezek. 8:3

25 Then I spake unto them of the captivity all the things that the LORD had shewed me.   Ezek. 3:4

Ezekiel Foretells Israel's Exile

12 The word of the LORD also came unto me, saying,

2 Son of man, thou dwellest in the midst of a rebellious house, which have eyes to see, and see not; they have ears to hear, and hear not: for they *are* a rebellious house. Ps. 78:40

3 Therefore, thou son of man, prepare thee stuff for removing, and remove by day in their sight; and thou shalt remove from thy place to another place in their sight: it may be they will consider, though they *be* a rebellious house.   Jer. 26:3; 36:3; 2 Tim. 2:25

4 Then shalt thou bring forth thy stuff by day in their sight, as stuff for removing: and thou shalt go forth at even in their sight, as they that go forth into captivity.   2 Kin. 25:4; Jer. 39:4

5 Dig thou through the wall in their sight, and carry out thereby.

6 In their sight shalt thou bear *it* upon *thy* shoulders, *and* carry *it* forth in the twilight: thou shalt cover thy face, that thou see not the ground: for I have set thee *for* a sign unto the house of Israel.   Is. 8:18; Ezek. 4:3; 24:24

7 And I did so as I was commanded: I brought forth my stuff by day, as stuff for captivity, and in the even I digged through the wall with mine hand; I brought *it* forth in the twilight, *and* I bare *it* upon *my* shoulder in their sight.   Ezek. 24:18; 37:7, 10

8 And in the morning came the word of the LORD unto me, saying,

9 Son of man, hath not the house of Israel, the rebellious house, said unto thee, What doest thou?   Ezek. 17:12; 20:49; 24:19

10 Say thou unto them, Thus saith the Lord GOD; This burden *concerneth* the prince in Jerusalem, and all the house of Israel that *are* among them.   2 Kin. 9:25

11 Say, I *am* your sign: like as I have done, so shall it be done unto them: they shall remove *and* go into captivity.   Jer. 15:2

12 And the prince that *is* among them shall bear upon *his* shoulder in the twilight, and shall go forth: they shall dig through the wall to carry out thereby: he shall cover his face, that he see not the ground with *his* eyes.   2 Kin. 25:4

13 My net also will I spread upon him, and he shall be taken in my snare: and I will bring him to Babylon *to* the land of the Chaldeans; yet shall he not see it, though he shall die there.   Is. 24:17-18; Ezek. 17:20; Hos. 7:12

14 And I will scatter toward every wind all that *are* about him to help him, and all his

bands; and I will draw out the sword after them. _Ezek. 5:2_
15 And they shall know that I _am_ the LORD, when I shall scatter them among the nations, and disperse them in the countries. _Ezek. 6:7_
16 But I will leave a few men of them from the sword, from the famine, and from the pestilence; that they may declare all their abominations among the heathen whither they come; and they shall know that I _am_ the LORD. _Jer. 22:8-9_

12:15, 16 Imparting a Knowledge of God

Not only were they themselves to learn the lesson of obedience and trust; in their places of exile they were also to impart to others a knowledge of the living God. Many from among the sons of the strangers were to learn to love Him as their Creator and their Redeemer. _PK 372_

The Coming Desolation

17 Moreover the word of the LORD came to me, saying,
18 Son of man, eat thy bread with quaking, and drink thy water with trembling and with carefulness;
19 And say unto the people of the land, Thus saith the Lord GOD of the inhabitants of Jerusalem, _and_ of the land of Israel; They shall eat their bread with carefulness, and drink their water with astonishment, that her land may be desolate from all that is therein, because of the violence of all them that dwell therein. _Ezek. 6:6-7, 14; Zech. 7:14_
20 And the cities that are inhabited shall be laid waste, and the land shall be desolate; and ye shall know that I _am_ the LORD. _Is. 7:23-24_

Every Vision Will Come True

21 And the word of the LORD came unto me, saying,

12:21–28 Approaching Doom

The day of doom for the kingdom of Judah was fast approaching. No longer could the Lord set before them the hope of averting the severest of His judgments. "Should ye be utterly unpunished?" He inquired. "Ye shall not be unpunished" (Jeremiah 25:29).

Even these words were received with mocking derision. "The days are prolonged, and every vision faileth," declared the impenitent [Ezekiel 12:22]. But through Ezekiel this denial of the sure word of prophecy was sternly rebuked. _PK 450_

22 Son of man, what _is_ that proverb _that_ ye have in the land of Israel, saying, The days are prolonged, and every vision faileth? _Ezek. 11:3_
23 Tell them therefore, Thus saith the Lord GOD; I will make this proverb to cease, and they shall no more use it as a proverb in Israel; but say unto them, The days are at hand, and the effect of every vision. _Joel 2:1_
24 For there shall be no more any vain vision nor flattering ᵀdivination within the house of Israel. _Jer. 14:13-16; Ezek. 13:23; Zech. 13:2-4 ◆ false magic_
25 For I _am_ the LORD: I will speak, and the word that I shall speak shall come to pass; it shall be no more prolonged: for in your days, O rebellious house, will I say the word, and will perform it, saith the Lord GOD. _Is. 14:24_
26 Again the word of the LORD came to me, saying,
27 Son of man, behold, _they of_ the house of Israel say, The vision that he seeth _is_ for many days _to come_, and he prophesieth of the times _that are_ far off. _Ezek. 12:22; Dan. 10:14; 2 Pet. 3:4_
28 Therefore say unto them, Thus saith the Lord GOD; There shall none of my words be prolonged any more, but the word which I have spoken shall be done, saith the Lord GOD.

12:27, 28 God's Purpose, Through History

We need to study the working out of God's purpose in the history of nations and in the revelation of things to come, that we may estimate at their true value things seen and things unseen. . . . Thus, learning here the principles of His kingdom and becoming its subjects and citizens, we may be prepared at His coming to enter with Him into its possession. _Ed 184_

False Prophets Are Condemned

13 And the word of the LORD came unto me, saying,
2 Son of man, prophesy against the prophets of Israel that prophesy, and say thou unto them that prophesy out of their own hearts, Hear ye the word of the LORD; _Jer. 37:19_
3 Thus saith the Lord GOD; Woe unto the foolish prophets, that follow their own spirit, and have seen nothing! _Jer. 23:28-32_
4 O Israel, thy prophets are like the foxes in the deserts.
5 Ye have not gone up into the gaps, neither made up the hedge for the house of Israel to stand in the battle in the day of the LORD. _Ps. 106:23; Is. 58:12; Ezek. 22:30_
6 They have seen vanity and lying divination, saying, The LORD saith: and the LORD hath not sent them: and they have made _others_ to hope that they would confirm the word. _Jer. 14:14; 28:15; Ezek. 22:28_
7 Have ye not seen a vain vision, and have ye not spoken a lying ᵀdivination, whereas ye say, The LORD saith _it_; albeit I have not spoken? _false magic_

8 Therefore thus saith the Lord GOD; Because ye have spoken vanity, and seen lies, therefore, behold, I *am* against you, saith the Lord GOD.   Ezek. 5:8
9 And mine hand shall be upon the prophets that see vanity, and that [T]divine lies: they shall not be in the assembly of my people, neither shall they be written in the writing of the house of Israel, neither shall they enter into the land of Israel; and ye shall know that I *am* the Lord GOD. Ps. 69:28 ◆ *determine by false magic*
10 Because, even because they have seduced my people, saying, Peace; and *there was* no peace; and one built up a wall, and, lo, others daubed it with untempered *morter*:   Jer. 6:14
11 Say unto them which [T]daub *it* with untempered *morter*, that it shall fall: there shall be an overflowing shower; and ye, O great hailstones, shall fall; and a stormy wind shall [T]rend *it*. Is. 28:2; Ezek. 38:22 ◆ *cover* ◆ *tear apart*
12 Lo, when the wall is fallen, shall it not be said unto you, Where *is* the daubing wherewith ye have daubed *it?*
13 Therefore thus saith the Lord GOD; I will even rend *it* with a stormy wind in my fury; and there shall be an overflowing shower in mine anger, and great hailstones in *my* fury to consume *it*.   Ps. 148:8; Is. 30:30; Rev. 11:19
14 So will I break down the wall that ye have daubed with untempered *morter*, and bring it down to the ground, so that the foundation thereof shall be discovered, and it shall fall, and ye shall be consumed in the midst thereof: and ye shall know that I *am* the LORD.   Jer. 6:15
15 Thus will I accomplish my wrath upon the wall, and upon them that have daubed it with untempered *morter*, and will say unto you, The wall *is* no *more*, neither they that daubed it;
16 [T]*To wit*, the prophets of Israel which prophesy concerning Jerusalem, and which see visions of peace for her, and *there is* no peace, saith the Lord GOD. Jer. 6:14 ◆ *Namely*
17 Likewise, thou son of man, set thy face against the daughters of thy people, which prophesy out of their own heart; and prophesy thou against them,   Judg. 4:4; 2 Kin. 22:14
18 And say, Thus saith the Lord GOD; Woe to the *women* that sew pillows to all [T]armholes, and make kerchiefs upon the head of every stature to hunt souls! Will ye hunt the souls of my people, and will ye save the souls alive *that come* unto you?   Ezek. 13:20 ◆ *armpits*
19 And will ye pollute me among my people for handfuls of barley and for pieces of bread, to slay the souls that should not die, and to save the souls alive that should not live, by your lying to my people that hear *your* lies?   Prov. 28:21; Jer. 23:14; Mic. 3:5
20 Wherefore thus saith the Lord GOD;

Behold, I *am* against your pillows, wherewith ye there hunt the souls *to* make *them* fly, and I will tear them from your arms, and will let the souls go, *even* the souls that ye hunt to make *them* fly.
21 Your kerchiefs also will I tear, and deliver my people out of your hand, and they shall be no more in your hand to be hunted; and ye shall know that I *am* the LORD.
22 Because with lies ye have made the heart of the righteous sad, whom I have not made sad; and strengthened the hands of the wicked, that he should not return from his wicked way, by promising him life: Jer. 23:14
23 Therefore ye shall see no more vanity, nor divine [T]divinations: for I will deliver my people out of your hand: and ye shall know that I *am* the LORD. Ezek. 12:24; 13:21; Mic. 3:6 ◆ *false magic*

Idolaters Are Condemned

14 Then came certain of the elders of Israel unto me, and sat before me.
2 And the word of the LORD came unto me, saying,
3 Son of man, these men have set up their idols in their heart, and put the stumblingblock of their iniquity before their face: should I be enquired of at all by them? Is. 1:15; Ezek. 7:19
4 Therefore speak unto them, and say unto them, Thus saith the Lord GOD; Every man of the house of Israel that setteth up his idols in his heart, and putteth the stumblingblock of his iniquity before his face, and cometh to the prophet; I the LORD will answer him that cometh according to the multitude of his idols;   2 Kin. 1:16
5 That I may take the house of Israel in their own heart, because they are all estranged from me through their idols.   Is. 1:4
6 Therefore say unto the house of Israel, Thus saith the Lord GOD; Repent, and turn *yourselves* from your idols; and turn away your faces from all your abominations.   Is. 2:20
7 For every one of the house of Israel, or of the stranger that sojourneth in Israel, which separateth himself from me, and setteth up his idols in his heart, and putteth the stumblingblock of his iniquity before his face, and cometh to a prophet to enquire of him concerning me; I the LORD will answer him by myself: Ex. 12:48
8 And I will set my face against that man, and will make him a sign and a proverb, and I will cut him off from the midst of my people; and ye shall know that I *am* the LORD.   Jer. 44:11
9 And if the prophet be deceived when he hath spoken a thing, I the LORD have deceived that prophet, and I will stretch out my hand upon him, and will destroy him from the midst of my people Israel. Jer. 4:10
10 And they shall bear the punishment

of their iniquity: the punishment of the prophet shall be even as the punishment of him that seeketh *unto him*;

11 That the house of Israel may go no more astray from me, neither be polluted any more with all their transgressions; but that they may be my people, and I may be their God, saith the Lord God.   Ezek. 11:18-20; 37:23; 48:11

12 The word of the Lord came again to me, saying,

13 Son of man, when the land sinneth against me by ᵀtrespassing grievously, then will I stretch out mine hand upon it, and will break the staff of the bread thereof, and will send famine upon it, and will cut off man and beast from it: Lev. 26:26 ◆ *sinning*

14 Though these three men, Noah, Daniel, and Job, were in it, they should deliver *but* their own souls by their righteousness, saith the Lord God.   Jer. 15:1; Ezek. 14:20; 28:3

14:14 Unceasing Endeavor

The Christian life is a battle and a march. In this warfare there is no release; the effort must be continuous and persevering. It is by unceasing endeavor that we maintain the victory over the temptations of Satan. Christian integrity must be sought with resistless energy and maintained with a resolute fixedness of purpose. *MH 453*

---

15 If I cause noisome beasts to pass through the land, and they ᵀspoil it, so that it be desolate, that no man may pass through because of the beasts: Lev. 26:22; Ezek. 5:17 ◆ *plunder*

16 *Though* these three men *were* in it, *as* I live, saith the Lord God, they shall deliver neither sons nor daughters; they only shall be delivered, but the land shall be desolate.   Gen. 19:29

17 Or *if* I bring a sword upon that land, and say, Sword, go through the land; so that I cut off man and beast from it: Lev. 26:25; Ezek. 5:12

18 Though these three men *were* in it, *as* I live, saith the Lord God, they shall deliver neither sons nor daughters, but they only shall be delivered themselves.

19 Or *if* I send a pestilence into that land, and pour out my fury upon it in blood, to cut off from it man and beast: Ezek. 38:22

14:20 Character Not Transferable

The grace of God has been freely offered to every soul. The message of the gospel has been heralded, "Let him that is athirst come. And whosoever will, let him take the water of life freely" (Revelation 22:17). But character is not transferable. No man can believe for another. No man can receive the Spirit for another. No man can impart to another the character which is the fruit of the Spirit's working. *COL 412*

---

20 Though Noah, Daniel, and Job, *were* in it, *as* I live, saith the Lord God, they shall deliver neither son nor daughter; they shall *but* deliver their own souls by their righteousness.   Ezek. 14:14

21 For thus saith the Lord God; How much more when I send my four sore judgments upon Jerusalem, the sword, and the famine, and the noisome beast, and the pestilence, to cut off from it man and beast?   Ezek. 5:17; 14:13

22 Yet, behold, therein shall be left a remnant that shall be brought forth, *both* sons and daughters: behold, they shall come forth unto you, and ye shall see their way and their doings: and ye shall be comforted concerning the evil that I have brought upon Jerusalem, *even* concerning all that I have brought upon it.   Ezek. 20:43

23 And they shall comfort you, when ye see their ways and their doings: and ye shall know that I have not done without cause all that I have done in it, saith the Lord God.   Jer. 22:8-9

Jerusalem Is a Worthless Vine

15 And the word of the Lord came unto me, saying,

2 Son of man, What is the vine tree more than any tree, *or than* a branch which is among the trees of the forest?   Is. 5:1-7

3 Shall wood be taken thereof to do any work? or will *men* take a pin of it to hang any vessel thereon?

4 Behold, it is cast into the fire for fuel; the fire devoureth both the ends of it, and the midst of it is burned. Is it meet for *any* work?   John 15:6

5 Behold, when it was whole, it was meet for no work: how much less shall it be meet yet for *any* work, when the fire hath devoured it, and it is burned?

6 Therefore thus saith the Lord God; As the vine tree among the trees of the forest, which I have given to the fire for fuel, so will I give the inhabitants of Jerusalem.

7 And I will set my face against them; they shall go out from *one* fire, and *another* fire shall devour them; and ye shall know that I *am* the Lord, when I set my face against them.   Ps. 34:16; Is. 24:18; Ezek. 14:8

8 And I will make the land desolate, because they have committed a ᵀtrespass, saith the Lord God.   Ezek. 6:14 ◆ *sin*

A Description of Jerusalem's Sins

16 Again the word of the Lord came unto me, saying,

2 Son of man, cause Jerusalem to know her abominations,   Is. 58:1; Ezek. 20:4; 22:2

3 And say, Thus saith the Lord God unto Jerusalem; Thy birth and thy nativity *is* of the

land of Canaan; thy father *was* an Amorite, and thy mother an Hittite. Gen. 15:16; Ezek. 16:45
4 And *as for* thy nativity, in the day thou wast born thy navel was not cut, neither wast thou washed in water to ᵀsupple *thee*; thou wast not salted at all, nor swaddled at all. Hos. 2:3 ◆ *wash clean*
5 None eye pitied thee, to do any of these unto thee, to have compassion upon thee; but thou wast cast out in the open field, to the lothing of thy person, in the day that thou wast born.

God's Extraordinary Love

6 And when I passed by thee, and saw thee polluted in thine own blood, I said unto thee *when thou wast* in thy blood, Live; yea, I said unto thee *when thou wast* in thy blood, Live.
7 I have caused thee to multiply as the bud of the field, and thou hast increased and ᵀwaxen great, and thou art come to excellent ornaments: *thy* breasts are fashioned, and thine hair is grown, whereas thou *wast* naked and bare. Ex. 1:7; Deut. 1:10; Ezek. 16:22 ◆ *become*
8 Now when I passed by thee, and looked upon thee, behold, thy time *was* the time of love; and I spread my skirt over thee, and covered thy nakedness: yea, I sware unto thee, and entered into a covenant with thee, saith the Lord GOD, and thou becamest mine. Ruth 3:9; Jer. 2:2-3

16:8 Joined to Christ

In the Bible the sacred and enduring character of the relation that exists between Christ and His church is represented by the union of marriage. The Lord has joined His people to Himself by a solemn covenant, He promising to be their God, and they pledging themselves to be His and His alone. *GC 381*

---

9 Then washed I thee with water; yea, I throughly washed away thy blood from thee, and I anointed thee with oil. Ruth 3:3
10 I clothed thee also with broidered work, and shod thee with badgers' skin, and I girded thee about with fine linen, and I covered thee with silk. Ex. 26:36; Ezek. 16:13, 18
11 I decked thee also with ornaments, and I put bracelets upon thy hands, and a chain on thy neck. Gen. 24:22, 47; 41:42
12 And I put a jewel on thy forehead, and earrings in thine ears, and a beautiful crown upon thine head.
13 Thus wast thou decked with gold and silver; and thy ᵀraiment *was of* fine linen, and silk, and broidered work; thou didst eat fine flour, and honey, and oil: and thou wast exceeding beautiful, and thou didst prosper into a kingdom. Deut. 32:13-14 ◆ *clothing*
14 And thy renown went forth among the heathen for thy beauty: for it *was* perfect through my comeliness, which I had put upon thee, saith the Lord GOD. 1 Kin. 10:24; Lam. 2:15

Jerusalem's Lewdness

15 But thou didst trust in thine own beauty, and playedst the harlot because of thy renown, and pouredst out thy fornications on every one that passed by; his it was. Is. 57:8; Jer. 2:20; Ezek. 16:25
16 And of thy garments thou didst take, and deckedst thy high places with ᵀdivers colours, and playedst the harlot thereupon: *the like things* shall not come, neither shall it be *so*. 2 Kin. 23:7 ◆ *various*
17 Thou hast also taken thy fair jewels of my gold and of my silver, which I had given thee, and madest to thyself images of men, and didst commit ᵀwhoredom with them, *prostitution*
18 And tookest thy broidered garments, and coveredst them: and thou hast set mine oil and mine incense before them.
19 My meat also which I gave thee, fine flour, and oil, and honey, *wherewith* I fed thee, thou hast even set it before them for a sweet savour: and *thus* it was, saith the Lord GOD. Ezek. 16:13
20 Moreover thou hast taken thy sons and thy daughters, whom thou hast borne unto me, and these hast thou sacrificed unto them to be devoured. *Is this* of thy whoredoms a small matter, Ex. 13:2; Ps. 106:37-38; Ezek. 23:37
21 That thou hast slain my children, and delivered them to cause them to pass through *the fire* for them? 2 Kin. 17:17
22 And in all thine abominations and thy whoredoms thou hast not remembered the days of thy youth, when thou wast naked and bare, *and* wast polluted in thy blood. Jer. 2:2
23 And it came to pass after all thy wickedness, (woe, woe unto thee! saith the Lord GOD;)
24 *That* thou hast also built unto thee an eminent place, and hast made thee an high place in every street. Ps. 78:58
25 Thou hast built thy high place at every head of the way, and hast made thy beauty to be ᵀabhorred, and hast opened thy feet to every one that passed by, and multiplied thy whoredoms. Jer. 3:2 ◆ *despised*
26 Thou hast also committed fornication with the Egyptians thy neighbours, great of flesh; and hast increased thy whoredoms, to provoke me to anger. Ezek. 23:19-21
27 Behold, therefore I have stretched out my hand over thee, and have diminished thine ordinary *food*, and delivered thee unto the will of them that hate thee, the daughters of the Philistines, which are ashamed of thy lewd way. Is. 9:12; Ezek. 16:37, 57
28 Thou hast played the whore also with the

Assyrians, because thou wast unsatiable; yea, thou hast played the harlot with them, and yet couldest not be satisfied.   2 Kin. 16:7, 10-18

29 Thou hast moreover multiplied thy fornication in the land of Canaan unto Chaldea; and yet thou wast not satisfied herewith.

30 How weak is thine heart, saith the Lord God, seeing thou doest all these *things*, the work of an Timperious whorish woman;   bold

31 In that thou buildest thine Teminent place in the head of every way, and makest thine high place in every street; and hast not been as an harlot, in that thou scornest hire;   Is. 52:3 ◆ high

32 *But as* a wife that committeth adultery, *which* taketh strangers instead of her husband!

33 They give gifts to all Twhores: but thou givest thy gifts to all thy lovers, and hirest them, that they may come unto thee on every side for thy whoredom.   Is. 57:9 ◆ prostitutes

34 And the contrary is in thee from *other* women in thy Twhoredoms, whereas none followeth thee to commit whoredoms: and in that thou givest a reward, and no reward is given unto thee, therefore thou art contrary.   acts of prostitution

Jerusalem's Punishment

35 Wherefore, O harlot, hear the word of the Lord:

36 Thus saith the Lord God; Because thy filthiness was poured out, and thy nakedness discovered through thy whoredoms with thy lovers, and with all the idols of thy abominations, and by the blood of thy children, which thou didst give unto them;   Ezek. 23:10

37 Behold, therefore I will gather all thy lovers, with whom thou hast taken pleasure, and all *them* that thou hast loved, with all *them* that thou hast hated; I will even gather them round about against thee, and will discover thy nakedness unto them, that they may see all thy nakedness.   Jer. 13:22

38 And I will judge thee, as women that break wedlock and shed blood are judged; and I will give thee blood in fury and jealousy.   Lev. 20:10

39 And I will also give thee into their hand, and they shall throw down thine eminent place, and shall break down thy high places: they shall strip thee also of thy clothes, and shall take thy fair jewels, and leave thee naked and bare.   Ezek. 16:24-25; 23:26; Hos. 2:3

40 They shall also bring up a company against thee, and they shall stone thee with stones, and thrust thee through with their swords.   Ezek. 23:47

41 And they shall burn thine houses with fire, and execute judgments upon thee in the sight of many women: and I will cause thee to cease from playing the harlot, and thou also shalt give no hire any more.   2 Kin. 25:9; Jer. 39:8

42 So will I make my fury toward thee to rest, and my jealousy shall depart from thee, and I will be quiet, and will be no more angry.   Is. 40:1-2; Ezek. 5:13; 39:29

43 Because thou hast not remembered the days of thy youth, but hast Tfretted me in all these *things*; behold, therefore I also will Trecompense thy way upon *thine* head, saith the Lord God: and thou shalt not commit this lewdness above all thine abominations.   Ps. 78:42; Ezek. 11:21; 16:22 ◆ worried ◆ repay

44 Behold, every one that useth proverbs shall use *this* proverb against thee, saying, As *is* the mother, *so is* her daughter.   Ezek. 18:2-3

45 Thou *art* thy mother's daughter, that lotheth her husband and her children; and thou *art* the sister of thy sisters, which lothed their husbands and their children: your mother *was* an Hittite, and your father an Amorite.   Is. 1:4

46 And thine elder sister *is* Samaria, she and her daughters that dwell at thy left hand: and thy younger sister, that dwelleth at thy right hand, *is* Sodom and her daughters.   Jer. 3:8-11; Ezek. 16:48-49; 23:4

47 Yet hast thou not walked after their ways, nor done after their abominations: but, as *if that were* a very little *thing*, thou wast corrupted more than they in all thy ways.

48 *As* I live, saith the Lord God, Sodom thy sister hath not done, she nor her daughters, as thou hast done, thou and thy daughters.   Matt. 10:15

49 Behold, this was the iniquity of thy sister Sodom, pride, fulness of bread, and abundance of idleness was in her and in her daughters, neither did she strengthen the hand of the poor and needy.   Gen. 13:10

16:49 Physical Activity Is Vital

"Pride, fullness of bread, and abundance of idleness," are as deadly foes to human progress in this generation as when they led to the destruction of Sodom.

Teachers should understand these things, and should instruct their pupils in these lines. Teach the students that right living depends on right thinking, and that physical activity is essential to purity of thought. *Ed 209*

---

50 And they were haughty, and committed abomination before me: therefore I took them away as I saw *good*.   Gen. 13:13

51 Neither hath Samaria committed half of thy sins; but thou hast multiplied thine abominations more than they, and hast justified thy sisters in all thine abominations which thou hast done.   Jer. 3:8-11

52 Thou also, which hast judged thy sisters, bear thine own shame for thy sins that thou hast committed more abominable than they: they are more righteous than thou: yea, be thou confounded also, and bear thy shame, in that thou hast justified thy sisters.

53 When I shall bring again their captivity, the captivity of Sodom and her daughters, and the captivity of Samaria and her daughters, then *will I bring again* the captivity of thy captives in the midst of them: Is. 19:24-25

54 That thou mayest bear thine own shame, and mayest be confounded in all that thou hast done, in that thou art a comfort unto them.   Jer. 2:26

55 When thy sisters, Sodom and her daughters, shall return to their former estate, and Samaria and her daughters shall return to their former estate, then thou and thy daughters shall return to your former estate.   Ezek. 16:53

56 For thy sister Sodom was not mentioned by thy mouth in the day of thy pride,

57 Before thy wickedness was discovered, as at the time of *thy* reproach of the daughters of Syria, and all *that are* round about her, the daughters of the Philistines, which despise thee round about.   2 Kin. 16:5-7

58 Thou hast borne thy lewdness and thine abominations, saith the LORD.   Ezek. 23:49

59 For thus saith the Lord GOD; I will even deal with thee as thou hast done, which hast despised the oath in breaking the covenant.   Is. 24:5

60 Nevertheless I will remember my covenant with thee in the days of thy youth, and I will establish unto thee an everlasting covenant.   Lev. 26:42

61 Then thou shalt remember thy ways, and be ashamed, when thou shalt receive thy sisters, thine elder and thy younger: and I will give them unto thee for daughters, but not by thy covenant.   Jer. 50:4-5

62 And I will establish my covenant with thee; and thou shalt know that I *am* the LORD: Jer. 24:7

63 That thou mayest remember, and be confounded, and never open thy mouth any more because of thy shame, when I am pacified toward thee for all that thou hast done, saith the Lord GOD. Ps. 39:9; Dan. 9:7-8; Rom. 3:19

16:62, 63 Christ Alone Our Sufficiency

Then our lips will not be opened in self-glorification. We shall know that our sufficiency is in Christ alone. We shall make the apostle's confession our own. "I know that in me (that is, in my flesh) dwelleth no good thing" (Romans 7:18). "God forbid that I should glory, save in the cross of our Lord Jesus Christ, by whom the world is crucified unto me, and I unto the world" (Galatians 6:14). *COL 161*

Judah Is Compared to a Tree

17 And the word of the LORD came unto me, saying,

2 Son of man, put forth a riddle, and speak a parable unto the house of Israel; Ezek. 20:49

3 And say, Thus saith the Lord GOD; A great eagle with great wings, longwinged, full of feathers, which had ᵀdivers colours, came unto Lebanon, and took the highest branch of the cedar: Jer. 48:40 ❦ various

4 He cropped off the top of his young twigs, and carried it into a land of ᵀtraffick; he set it in a city of merchants.   trade

5 He took also of the seed of the land, and planted it in a fruitful field; he placed *it* by great waters, *and* set it *as* a willow tree.

6 And it grew, and became a spreading vine of low stature, whose branches turned toward him, and the roots thereof were under him: so it became a vine, and brought forth branches, and shot forth sprigs.   Ezek. 17:14

7 There was also another great eagle with

The Snare of Idleness

Ezekiel 16:49, 50

Idleness and riches make the heart hard that has never been oppressed by want or burdened by sorrow. The love of pleasure was fostered by wealth and leisure, and the people gave themselves up to sensual indulgence. "Behold," says the prophet, "this was the iniquity of thy sister Sodom, pride, fullness of bread, and abundance of idleness was in her and in her daughters, neither did she strengthen the hand of the poor and needy. And they were haughty, and committed abomination before Me: therefore I took them away as I saw good" (Ezekiel 16:49, 50). There is nothing more desired among men than riches and leisure, and yet these gave birth to the sins that brought destruction upon the cities of the plain. Their useless, idle life made them a prey to Satan's temptations, and they defaced the image of God, and became satanic rather than divine. Idleness is the greatest curse that can fall upon man, for vice and crime follow in its train. It enfeebles the mind, perverts the understanding, and debases the soul. Satan lies in ambush, ready to destroy those who are unguarded, whose leisure gives him opportunity to insinuate himself under some attractive disguise. He is never more successful than when he comes to men in their idle hours. *PP 156, 157*

great wings and many feathers: and, behold, this vine did bend her roots toward him, and shot forth her branches toward him, that he might water it by the furrows of her plantation.   Ezek. 17:15

8 It was planted in a good soil by great waters, that it might bring forth branches, and that it might bear fruit, that it might be a goodly vine.

9 Say thou, Thus saith the Lord GOD; Shall it prosper? shall he not pull up the roots thereof, and cut off the fruit thereof, that it wither? it shall wither in all the leaves of her spring, even without great power or many people to pluck it up by the roots thereof.

10 Yea, behold, *being* planted, shall it prosper? shall it not utterly wither, when the east wind toucheth it? it shall wither in the furrows where it grew.   Hos. 13:15

11 Moreover the word of the LORD came unto me, saying,

12 Say now to the rebellious house, Know ye not what these *things mean*? tell *them*, Behold, the king of Babylon is come to Jerusalem, and hath taken the king thereof, and the princes thereof, and led them with him to Babylon;   Ezek. 24:19

13 And hath taken of the king's seed, and made a covenant with him, and hath taken an oath of him: he hath also taken the mighty of the land: 2 Kin. 24:15-17; 2 Chr. 36:13; Ezek. 17:5

14 That the kingdom might be ᵀbase, that it might not lift itself up, *but* that by keeping of his covenant it might stand.   Ezek. 29:14 ◆ *meek*

17:15–18 The King a Rebel

Foremost among those who were rapidly leading the nation to ruin was Zedekiah their king. Forsaking utterly the counsels of the Lord . . . forgetting the debt of gratitude he owed Nebuchadnezzar, violating his solemn oath of allegiance taken in the name of the Lord God of Israel, Judah's king rebelled against the prophets, against his benefactor, and against his God. In the vanity of his own wisdom he turned for help to the ancient enemy of Israel's prosperity. *PK 450, 451*

---

15 But he rebelled against him in sending his ambassadors into Egypt, that they might give him horses and much people. Shall he prosper? shall he escape that doeth such *things*? or shall he break the covenant, and be delivered?   Deut. 17:16

16 *As* I live, saith the Lord GOD, surely in the place *where* the king *dwelleth* that made him king, whose oath he despised, and whose covenant he brake, *even* with him in the midst of Babylon he shall die.   Jer. 52:11; Ezek. 12:13; 16:59

17 Neither shall Pharaoh with *his* mighty army and great company make for him in the war, by casting up mounts, and building forts, to cut off many persons: Is. 36:6; Jer. 37:7; Ezek. 4:2

18 Seeing he despised the oath by breaking the covenant, when, lo, he had given his hand, and hath done all these *things*, he shall not escape.   1 Chr. 29:24

19 Therefore thus saith the Lord GOD; *As* I live, surely mine oath that he hath despised, and my covenant that he hath broken, even it will I ᵀrecompense upon his own head.   *repay*

20 And I will spread my net upon him, and he shall be taken in my snare, and I will bring him to Babylon, and will plead with him there for his ᵀtrespass that he hath ᵀtrespassed against me. Jer. 2:35; Ezek. 12:13; 20:35-36 ◆ *sin* ◆ *sinned*

21 And all his fugitives with all his bands shall fall by the sword, and they that remain shall be scattered toward all winds: and ye shall know that I the LORD have spoken *it*.   2 Kin. 25:5

God Promises to Plant the Cedar

22 Thus saith the Lord GOD; I will also take of the highest branch of the high cedar, and will set *it*; I will crop off from the top of his young twigs a tender one, and will plant *it* upon an high mountain and ᵀeminent: Ezek. 20:40 ◆ *prominent*

23 In the mountain of the height of Israel will I plant it: and it shall bring forth boughs, and bear fruit, and be a goodly cedar: and under it shall dwell all fowl of every wing; in the shadow of the branches thereof shall they dwell.   Ezek. 31:6

24 And all the trees of the field shall know that I the LORD have brought down the high tree, have exalted the low tree, have dried up the green tree, and have made the dry tree to flourish: I the LORD have spoken and have done *it*.   Ezek. 22:14

Everyone Will Suffer for His Own Sins

18 The word of the LORD came unto me again, saying,

2 What mean ye, that ye use this proverb concerning the land of Israel, saying, The fathers have eaten sour grapes, and the children's teeth are set on edge?   Is. 3:15

3 *As* I live, saith the Lord GOD, ye shall not have *occasion* any more to use this proverb in Israel.

4 Behold, all souls are mine; as the soul of the father, so also the soul of the son is mine: the soul that sinneth, it shall die.   Num. 16:22

5 But if a man be just, and do that which is lawful and right,

6 *And* hath not eaten upon the mountains, neither hath lifted up his eyes to the idols of the house of Israel, neither hath defiled his

neighbour's wife, neither hath come near to a menstruous woman, Deut. 4:19; Ezek. 6:13; 18:15

7 And hath not oppressed any, *but* hath restored to the debtor his pledge, hath spoiled none by violence, hath given his bread to the hungry, and hath covered the naked with a garment;   Ex. 22:26; Ezek. 18:12, 16

8 He *that* hath not given forth upon usury, neither hath taken any increase, *that* hath withdrawn his hand from iniquity, hath executed true judgment between man and man,   Ex. 22:25; Deut. 23:19-20; Zech. 8:16

9 Hath walked in my statutes, and hath kept my judgments, to deal truly; he *is* just, he shall surely live, saith the Lord GOD. Ezek. 18:17; 20:11

10 If he ᵀbeget a son *that is* a robber, a shedder of blood, and *that* doeth the like to *any* one of these *things*,   Ex. 21:12 ✦ *brings forth*

11 And that doeth not any of those *duties*, but even hath eaten upon the mountains, and defiled his neighbour's wife,

12 Hath oppressed the poor and needy, hath spoiled by violence, hath not restored the pledge, and hath lifted up his eyes to the idols, hath committed abomination,   2 Kin. 21:11

13 Hath given forth upon ᵀusury, and hath taken increase: shall he then live? he shall not live: he hath done all these abominations; he shall surely die; his blood shall be upon him.   Ex. 22:25 ✦ *interest charged*

14 Now, lo, *if* he beget a son, that seeth all his father's sins which he hath done, and considereth, and doeth not such like,   2 Chr. 34:21

15 *That* hath not eaten upon the mountains, neither hath lifted up his eyes to the idols of the house of Israel, hath not defiled his neighbour's wife,

16 Neither hath oppressed any, hath not withholden the pledge, neither hath spoiled by violence, *but* hath given his bread to the hungry, and hath covered the naked with a garment,   Ezek. 18:7

17 *That* hath taken off his hand from the poor, *that* hath not received usury nor increase, hath executed my judgments, hath walked in my statutes; he shall not die for the iniquity of his father, he shall surely live.   Ezek. 18:8-9

18 *As for* his father, because he cruelly oppressed, spoiled his brother by violence, and did *that* which *is* not good among his people, lo, even he shall die in his iniquity. Ezek. 3:18

19 Yet say ye, Why? doth not the son bear the iniquity of the father? When the son hath done that which is lawful and right, *and* hath kept all my statutes, and hath done them, he shall surely live.   Ex. 20:5; Jer. 15:4; Zech. 1:3-6

20 The soul that sinneth, it shall die. The son shall not bear the iniquity of the father, neither shall the father bear the iniquity of the son: the righteousness of the righteous

shall be upon him, and the wickedness of the wicked shall be upon him. Deut. 24:16; 2 Kin. 14:6

After Death   See 1 Timothy 6:15, 16.

21 But if the wicked will turn from all his sins that he hath committed, and keep all my statutes, and do that which is lawful and right, he shall surely live, he shall not die.   Prov. 28:13; Ezek. 18:27-28; 33:19

22 All his transgressions that he hath committed, they shall not be mentioned unto him: in his righteousness that he hath done he shall live.   Ps. 18:20-24

23 Have I any pleasure at all that the wicked should die? saith the Lord GOD: *and* not that he should return from his ways, and live?   Ps. 147:11; Ezek. 18:32; 33:11

24 But when the righteous turneth away from his righteousness, and committeth iniquity, *and* doeth according to all the abominations that the wicked *man* doeth, shall he live? All his righteousness that he hath done shall not be mentioned: in his ᵀtrespass that he hath trespassed, and in his sin that he hath sinned, in them shall he die.   1 Sam. 15:11 ✦ *sin*

25 Yet ye say, The way of the Lord is not equal. Hear now, O house of Israel; Is not my way equal? are not your ways unequal?

26 When a righteous *man* turneth away from his righteousness, and committeth iniquity, and dieth in them; for his iniquity that he hath done shall he die.

27 Again, when the wicked *man* turneth away from his wickedness that he hath committed, and doeth that which is lawful and right, he shall save his soul alive.   Is. 1:18

28 Because he considereth, and turneth away from all his ᵀtransgressions that he hath committed, he shall surely live, he shall not die.   *violations of a law*

29 Yet saith the house of Israel, The way of the Lord is not equal. O house of Israel, are not my ways equal? are not your ways unequal?

30 Therefore I will judge you, O house of Israel, every one according to his ways, saith the Lord GOD. Repent, and turn *yourselves* from all your transgressions; so iniquity shall not be your ruin.   Ezek. 7:3; 14:6; 18:21

31 Cast away from you all your transgressions, whereby ye have transgressed; and make you a new heart and a new spirit: for why will ye die, O house of Israel?   Ps. 51:10

18:32 Do Not Listen to the Tempter

Satan is ready to steal away the blessed assurances of God. He desires to take every glimmer of hope and every ray of light from the soul; but you must not permit him to do this. Do not give ear to the tempter, but say, "Jesus has died that I might live. He loves me, and wills not that I should perish." *SC 53*

32 For I have no pleasure in the death of him that dieth, saith the Lord GOD: wherefore turn *yourselves*, and live ye.   Ezek. 18:23

A Lamentation for Israel's Princes

19 Moreover take thou up a lamentation for the princes of Israel,   Jer 22:18

2 And say, What *is* thy mother? A lioness: she lay down among lions, she nourished her whelps among young lions.

3 And she brought up one of her whelps: it became a young lion, and it learned to catch the prey; it devoured men.

4 The nations also heard of him; he was taken in their pit, and they brought him with chains unto the land of Egypt.   2 Kin. 23:33-34

5 Now when she saw that she had waited, *and* her hope was lost, then she took another of her whelps, *and* made him a young lion.

6 And he went up and down among the lions, he became a young lion, and learned to catch the prey, *and* devoured men.

7 And he knew their desolate palaces, and he laid waste their cities; and the land was desolate, and the fulness thereof, by the noise of his roaring.   Ezek. 30:12

8 Then the nations set against him on every side from the provinces, and spread their net over him: he was taken in their pit.   Ezek. 12:13

9 And they put him in Tward in chains, and brought him to the king of Babylon: they brought him into holds, that his voice should no more be heard upon the mountains of Israel.   2 Chr. 36:6 ◆ *prison* or *guard*

A Lamentation for Jerusalem

10 Thy mother *is* like a vine in thy blood, planted by the waters: she was fruitful and full of branches by reason of many waters.

11 And she had strong rods for the sceptres of them that bare rule, and her stature was exalted among the thick branches, and she appeared in her height with the multitude of her branches.   Ezek. 31:3

12 But she was plucked up in fury, she was cast down to the ground, and the east wind dried up her fruit: her strong rods were broken and withered; the fire consumed them.   Is. 27:11; Ezek. 17:10; Hos. 13:15

13 And now she *is* planted in the wilderness, in a dry and thirsty ground. Ezek. 19:10; Hos. 2:3

14 And fire is gone out of a rod of her branches, *which* hath devoured her fruit, so that she hath no strong rod *to be* a sceptre to rule. This *is* a lamentation, and shall be for a lamentation.   2 Kin. 24:20

Israel's Past and Present Sins

20 And it came to pass in the seventh year, in the fifth *month*, the tenth *day* of the month, *that* certain of the elders of Israel came to enquire of the LORD, and sat before me.   Ezek. 1:2; 8:1; 24:1

2 Then came the word of the LORD unto me, saying,

3 Son of man, speak unto the elders of Israel, and say unto them, Thus saith the Lord GOD; Are ye come to enquire of me? *As* I live, saith the Lord GOD, I will not be enquired of by you.   Mic. 3:7

4 Wilt thou judge them, son of man, wilt thou judge *them*? cause them to know the abominations of their fathers: Ezek. 22:2; 23:36

Israel's Rebellions in Egypt

5 And say unto them, Thus saith the Lord GOD; In the day when I chose Israel, and lifted up mine hand unto the seed of the house of Jacob, and made myself known unto them in the land of Egypt, when I lifted up mine hand unto them, saying, I *am* the LORD your God;   Gen. 14:22

6 In the day *that* I lifted up mine hand unto them, to bring them forth of the land of Egypt into a land that I had espied for them, flowing with milk and honey, which *is* the glory of all lands: Ex. 3:8; Ps. 48:2; Ezek. 20:15

7 Then said I unto them, Cast ye away every man the abominations of his eyes, and defile not yourselves with the idols of Egypt: I *am* the LORD your God. Ex. 20:2; Lev. 18:3; Deut. 29:16-18

8 But they rebelled against me, and would not hearken unto me: they did not every man cast away the abominations of their eyes, neither did they forsake the idols of Egypt: then I said, I will pour out my fury upon them, to accomplish my anger against them in the midst of the land of Egypt.   Is. 63:10

9 But I wrought for my name's sake, that it should not be polluted before the heathen, among whom they *were*, in whose sight I made myself known unto them, in bringing them forth out of the land of Egypt. Ezek. 20:14

Israel's Rebellions in the Wilderness

10 Wherefore I caused them to go forth out of the land of Egypt, and brought them into the wilderness.

11 And I gave them my statutes, and shewed them my judgments, which *if* a man do, he shall even live in them. Lev. 18:5; Deut. 4:8; Rom. 10:5

12 Moreover also I gave them my sabbaths, to be a sign between me and them, that they might know that I *am* the LORD that Tsanctify them.   Ex. 20:8-11 ◆ *makes them holy*

The Sabbath   See Exodus 16:22, 23.

13 But the house of Israel rebelled against me in the wilderness: they walked not in my statutes, and they despised my judgments, which *if* a man do, he shall even live

in them; and my sabbaths they greatly polluted: then I said, I would pour out my fury upon them in the wilderness, to consume them.   Deut. 9:8; Ezek. 20:8, 21

14 But I ᵀwrought for my name's sake, that it should not be polluted before the heathen, in whose sight I brought them out. Ezek. 20:9 ◆ *acted*

15 Yet also I lifted up my hand unto them in the wilderness, that I would not bring them into the land which I had given *them*, flowing with milk and honey, which *is* the glory of all lands;   Ps. 95:11; 106:26

16 Because they despised my judgments, and walked not in my statutes, but polluted my sabbaths: for their heart went after their idols.   Num. 15:39

20:16 The Sabbath a Reminder

The Lord designed that by a faithful observance of the Sabbath command, Israel should continually be reminded of their accountability to Him as their Creator and their Redeemer. While they should keep the Sabbath in the proper spirit, idolatry could not exist; but should the claims of this precept of the Decalogue be set aside as no longer binding, the Creator would be forgotten and men would worship other gods. *PK 182*

---

17 Nevertheless mine eye spared them from destroying them, neither did I make an end of them in the wilderness.   Ezek. 11:13

18 But I said unto their children in the wilderness, Walk ye not in the statutes of your fathers, neither observe their judgments, nor defile yourselves with their idols: Deut. 4:3-6

19 I *am* the LORD your God; walk in my statutes, and keep my judgments, and do them;

20 And hallow my sabbaths; and they shall be a sign between me and you, that ye may know that I *am* the LORD your God. Jer. 17:22; Ezek. 20:12

21 Notwithstanding the children rebelled against me: they walked not in my statutes, neither kept my judgments to do them, which *if* a man do, he shall even live in them; they polluted my sabbaths: then I said, I would pour out my fury upon them, to accomplish my anger against them in the wilderness.   Num. 21:5; Ezek. 20:8, 13

22 Nevertheless I withdrew mine hand, and wrought for my name's sake, that it should not be polluted in the sight of the heathen, in whose sight I brought them forth.   Ps. 78:38

23 I lifted up mine hand unto them also in the wilderness, that I would scatter them among the heathen, and disperse them through the countries;   Lev. 26:33

24 Because they had not executed my judgments, but had despised my statutes, and had polluted my sabbaths, and their eyes were after their fathers' idols.   Ezek. 6:9

25 Wherefore I gave them also statutes *that were* not good, and judgments whereby they should not live;   Ps. 81:12; Is. 66:4; Ezek. 20:39

26 And I polluted them in their own gifts, in that they caused to pass through *the fire* all that openeth the womb, that I might make them desolate, to the end that they might know that I *am* the LORD.   Lev. 18:21

Israel's Rebellion in the Promised Land

27 Therefore, son of man, speak unto the house of Israel, and say unto them, Thus saith the Lord GOD; Yet in this your fathers have blasphemed me, in that they have committed a ᵀtrespass against me.   Rom. 2:24 ◆ *sin*

28 For when I had brought them into the land, *for* the which I lifted up mine hand to give it to them, then they saw every high hill, and all the thick trees, and they offered there their sacrifices, and there they presented the provocation of their offering: there also they made

---

A Sign and a Delight

Ezekiel 20:12

The institutions that God has established are for the benefit of mankind. . . .

Since He made all things, He made the Sabbath. By Him it was set apart as a memorial of the work of creation. It points to Him as both the Creator and the Sanctifier. It declares that He who created all things in heaven and in earth, and by whom all things hold together, is the head of the church, and that by His power we are reconciled to God. For, speaking of Israel, He said, "I gave them My Sabbaths, to be a sign between Me and them, that they might know that I am the Lord that sanctify them,"—make them holy (Ezekiel 20:12). Then the Sabbath is a sign of Christ's power to make us holy. And it is given to all whom Christ makes holy. As a sign of His sanctifying power, the Sabbath is given to all who through Christ become a part of the Israel of God.

And the Lord says, "If thou turn away thy foot from the Sabbath, from doing thy pleasure on My holy day; and call the Sabbath a delight, the holy of the Lord, honorable; . . . then shalt thou delight thyself in the Lord" (Isaiah 58:13, 14). To all who receive the Sabbath as a sign of Christ's creative and redeeming power, it will be a delight. Seeing Christ in it, they delight themselves in Him. The Sabbath points them to the works of creation as an evidence of His mighty power in redemption. *DA 288, 289*

their sweet savour, and poured out there their drink offerings.   Josh. 23:14; Neh. 9:22-26; Ezek. 6:13
29 Then I said unto them, What *is* the high place whereunto ye go? And the name thereof is called Bamah unto this day.
30 Wherefore say unto the house of Israel, Thus saith the Lord God; Are ye polluted after the manner of your fathers? and commit ye ᵀwhoredom after their abominations?   Jer. 16:12 ◆ *prostitution*
31 For when ye offer your gifts, when ye make your sons to pass through the fire, ye pollute yourselves with all your idols, even unto this day: and shall I be enquired of by you, O house of Israel? *As* I live, saith the Lord God, I will not be enquired of by you.   Ps. 106:37-39
32 And that which cometh into your mind shall not be at all, that ye say, We will be as the heathen, as the families of the countries, to serve wood and stone.   Jer. 44:17
33 *As* I live, saith the Lord God, surely with a mighty hand, and with a stretched out arm, and with fury poured out, will I rule over you: Jer. 21:5
34 And I will bring you out from the people, and will gather you out of the countries wherein ye are scattered, with a mighty hand, and with a stretched out arm, and with fury poured out.   Ezek. 20:38

Israel's Future

35 And I will bring you into the wilderness of the people, and there will I plead with you face to face.   Hos. 2:14
36 Like as I pleaded with your fathers in the wilderness of the land of Egypt, so will I plead with you, saith the Lord God.   Num. 11
37 And I will cause you to pass under the rod, and I will bring you into the bond of the covenant: Lev. 27:32; Jer. 33:13
38 And I will purge out from among you the rebels, and them that ᵀtransgress against me: I will bring them forth out of the country where they sojourn, and they shall not enter into the land of Israel: and ye shall know that I *am* the Lord.   Ps. 95:11; Ezek. 13:9; Amos 9:9-10 ◆ *sin*
39 As for you, O house of Israel, thus saith the Lord God; Go ye, serve ye every one his idols, and hereafter *also*, if ye will not hearken unto me: but pollute ye my holy name no more with your gifts, and with your idols.   Judg. 10:14
40 For in mine holy mountain, in the mountain of the height of Israel, saith the Lord God, there shall all the house of Israel, all of them in the land, serve me: there will I accept them, and there will I require your offerings, and the firstfruits of your oblations, with all your holy things.   Is. 56:7; 60:7; Mal. 3:4
41 I will accept you with your sweet savour, when I bring you out from the people, and

gather you out of the countries wherein ye have been scattered; and I will be sanctified in you before the heathen.   Is. 5:16; Ezek. 11:17
42 And ye shall know that I *am* the Lord, when I shall bring you into the land of Israel, into the country *for* the which I lifted up mine hand to give it to your fathers.   Ezek. 34:13
43 And there shall ye remember your ways, and all your doings, wherein ye have been defiled; and ye shall lothe yourselves in your own sight for all your evils that ye have committed.   Jer. 31:18; Ezek. 6:9; Hos. 5:15
44 And ye shall know that I *am* the Lord, when I have wrought with you for my name's sake, not according to your wicked ways, nor according to your corrupt doings, O ye house of Israel, saith the Lord God.   Ezek. 24:24

The Burning Forest

45 Moreover the word of the Lord came unto me, saying,
46 Son of man, set thy face toward the south, and drop *thy word* toward the south, and prophesy against the forest of the south field;   Jer. 13:19; Ezek. 21:2; Amos 7:16
47 And say to the forest of the south, Hear the word of the Lord; Thus saith the Lord God; Behold, I will kindle a fire in thee, and it shall devour every green tree in thee, and every dry tree: the flaming flame shall not be quenched, and all faces from the south to the north shall be burned therein.   Is. 9:18-19; Jer. 21:14; Ezek. 17:24
48 And all flesh shall see that I the Lord have kindled it: it shall not be quenched.
49 Then said I, Ah Lord God! they say of me, Doth he not speak parables?   John 16:25

The Sword of the Lord

21 And the word of the Lord came unto me, saying,
2 Son of man, set thy face toward Jerusalem, and drop *thy word* toward the holy places, and prophesy against the land of Israel,   Ezek. 4:7
3 And say to the land of Israel, Thus saith the Lord; Behold, I *am* against thee, and will draw forth my sword out of his ᵀsheath, and will cut off from thee the righteous and the wicked.   Job 9:22 ◆ *case*
4 Seeing then that I will cut off from thee the righteous and the wicked, therefore shall my sword go forth out of his sheath against all flesh from the south to the north: Ezek. 20:47
5 That all flesh may know that I the Lord have drawn forth my sword out of his sheath: it shall not return any more.   1 Sam. 3:12; Nah. 1:9
6 Sigh therefore, thou son of man, with the breaking of *thy* loins; and with bitterness sigh before their eyes.   Is. 22:4
7 And it shall be, when they say unto thee, Wherefore sighest thou? that thou shalt

answer, For the tidings; because it cometh: and every heart shall melt, and all hands shall be feeble, and every spirit shall faint, and all knees shall be weak *as* water: behold, it cometh, and shall be brought to pass, saith the Lord GOD.   Ezek. 7:17

8 Again the word of the LORD came unto me, saying,

9 Son of man, prophesy, and say, Thus saith the LORD; Say, A sword, a sword is sharpened, and also ᵀfurbished: Ezek. 21:3 ◆ *polished*

10 It is sharpened to make a sore slaughter; it is furbished that it may glitter: should we then make ᵀmirth? it contemneth the rod of my son, *as* every tree.   Ps. 110:5-6 ◆ *gladness*

11 And he hath given it to be furbished, that it may be handled: this sword is sharpened, and it is furbished, to give it into the hand of the slayer.   Ezek. 21:19

12 Cry and howl, son of man: for it shall be upon my people, it *shall be* upon all the princes of Israel: terrors by reason of the sword shall be upon my people: ᵀsmite therefore upon *thy* thigh.   Ezek. 21:6 ◆ *strike*

13 Because *it is* a trial, and what if *the sword* ᵀcontemn even the rod? it shall be no *more*, saith the Lord GOD.   Ezek. 21:10 ◆ *mock*

14 Thou therefore, son of man, prophesy, and smite *thine* hands together, and let the sword be doubled the third time, the sword of the slain: it *is* the sword of the great *men that are* slain, which entereth into their privy chambers.   Num. 24:10

15 I have set the point of the sword against all their gates, that *their* heart may faint, and *their* ruins be multiplied: ah! *it is* made bright, *it is* wrapped up for the slaughter.   Jer. 17:27

16 Go thee one way or other, *either* on the right hand, *or* on the left, whithersoever thy face *is* set.

17 I will also smite mine hands together, and I will cause my fury to rest: I the LORD have said *it*.   Ezek. 5:13; 21:14; 22:13

The Sword of Babylon's King

18 The word of the LORD came unto me again, saying,

19 Also, thou son of man, appoint thee two ways, that the sword of the king of Babylon may come: both ᵀtwain shall come forth out of one land: and choose thou a place, choose *it* at the head of the way to the city.   Jer. 1:10 ◆ *two*

20 Appoint a way, that the sword may come to Rabbath of the Ammonites, and to Judah in Jerusalem the defenced.   Deut. 3:11; Jer. 49:2

21 For the king of Babylon stood at the parting of the way, at the head of the two ways, to use divination: he made *his* arrows bright, he consulted with images, he looked in the liver.   Gen. 31:19

22 At his right hand was the divination for Jerusalem, to appoint captains, to open the mouth in the slaughter, to lift up the voice with shouting, to appoint *battering* rams against the gates, to cast a mount, *and* to build a fort.   Ezek. 4:2; 26:9

23 And it shall be unto them as a false ᵀdivination in their sight, to them that have sworn oaths: but he will call to remembrance the iniquity, that they may be taken.   *false magic*

24 Therefore thus saith the Lord GOD; Because ye have made your iniquity to be remembered, in that your ᵀtransgressions are discovered, so that in all your doings your sins do appear; because, *I say*, that ye are come to remembrance, ye shall be taken with the hand.   *violations of the law*

25 And thou, profane wicked prince of Israel, whose day is come, when iniquity *shall have* an end,   Ezek. 35:5

26 Thus saith the Lord GOD; Remove the ᵀdiadem, and take off the crown: this *shall* not *be* the same: exalt *him that is* low, and abase *him that is* high.   Ps. 75:7; Jer. 13:18; Ezek. 17:24 ◆ *headband*

27 I will overturn, overturn, overturn, it: and it shall be no *more*, until he come whose right it is; and I will give it *him*.   Gen. 49:10; Ps. 2:6

A Prophecy against the Ammonites

28 And thou, son of man, prophesy and say, Thus saith the Lord GOD concerning the Ammonites, and concerning their reproach; even say thou, The sword, the sword *is* drawn: for the slaughter *it is* furbished, to consume because of the glittering: Ezek. 21:9-10

29 Whiles they see vanity unto thee, whiles they divine a lie unto thee, to bring thee upon the necks of *them that are* slain, of the wicked, whose day is come, when their iniquity *shall have* an end.   Jer. 27:9; Ezek. 21:25; 22:28

30 Shall I cause *it* to return into his sheath? I will judge thee in the place where thou wast created, in the land of thy nativity.   Jer. 47:6-7

31 And I will pour out mine indignation upon thee, I will blow against thee in the fire of my wrath, and deliver thee into the hand of brutish men, *and* skilful to destroy.   Ps. 18:15

32 Thou shalt be for fuel to the fire; thy blood shall be in the midst of the land; thou shalt be no *more* remembered: for I the LORD have spoken *it*.   Ezek. 20:47-48; 25:10; Mal. 4:1

The Sins of Jerusalem

22 Moreover the word of the LORD came unto me, saying,

2 Now, thou son of man, wilt thou judge, wilt thou judge the bloody city? yea, thou shalt shew her all her abominations.   Ezek. 20:4

3 Then say thou, Thus saith the Lord GOD, The city sheddeth blood in the midst of it,

that her time may come, and maketh idols against herself to defile herself.   Ezek. 22:27

4 Thou art become guilty in thy blood that thou hast shed; and hast defiled thyself in thine idols which thou hast made; and thou hast caused thy days to draw near, and art come *even* unto thy years: therefore have I made thee a reproach unto the heathen, and a mocking to all countries.   2 Kin. 21:16

5 *Those that be* near, and *those that be* far from thee, shall mock thee, *which art* infamous *and* much vexed.

6 Behold, the princes of Israel, every one were in thee to their power to shed blood.   Is. 1:23

7 In thee have they set light by father and mother: in the midst of thee have they dealt by oppression with the stranger: in thee have they vexed the fatherless and the widow.   Ex. 22:21-22; Lev. 20:9; Deut. 27:16

8 Thou hast despised mine holy things, and hast profaned my sabbaths.   Ezek. 20:13

9 In thee are men that carry tales to shed blood: and in thee they eat upon the mountains: in the midst of thee they commit lewdness.   Lev. 19:16

10 In thee have they discovered their fathers' nakedness: in thee have they humbled her that was set apart for pollution. Lev. 18:19

11 And one hath committed abomination with his neighbour's wife; and another hath lewdly defiled his daughter in law; and another in thee hath humbled his sister, his father's daughter.   Lev. 18:9, 15; 20:17

12 In thee have they taken gifts to shed blood; thou hast taken ᵀusury and increase, and thou hast greedily gained of thy neighbours by extortion, and hast forgotten me, saith the Lord GOD.   Lev. 25:35-36; Deut. 27:25; Ezek. 23:35 ◆ *interest*

13 Behold, therefore I have smitten mine hand at thy dishonest gain which thou hast made, and at thy blood which hath been in the midst of thee.   Is. 33:15

14 Can thine heart endure, or can thine hands be strong, in the days that I shall deal with thee? I the LORD have spoken *it*, and will do *it*.   Ezek. 17:24; 21:7; 24:14

15 And I will scatter thee among the heathen, and disperse thee in the countries, and will consume thy filthiness out of thee.   Deut. 4:27

16 And thou shalt take thine inheritance in thyself in the sight of the heathen, and thou shalt know that I *am* the LORD.   Ezek. 6:7

17 And the word of the LORD came unto me, saying,

18 Son of man, the house of Israel is to me become dross: all they *are* brass, and tin, and iron, and lead, in the midst of the furnace; they are *even* the dross of silver.   Ps. 119:119

19 Therefore thus saith the Lord GOD; Because ye are all become ᵀdross, behold, therefore I will gather you into the midst of Jerusalem.   *waste from melting metal*

20 *As* they gather silver, and brass, and iron, and lead, and tin, into the midst of the furnace, to blow the fire upon it, to melt *it*; so will I gather *you* in mine anger and in my fury, and I will leave *you there*, and melt you.

21 Yea, I will gather you, and blow upon you in the fire of my wrath, and ye shall be melted in the midst thereof.

22 As silver is melted in the midst of the furnace, so shall ye be melted in the midst thereof; and ye shall know that I the LORD have poured out my fury upon you. Ezek. 20:8

The People's Corruption

23 And the word of the LORD came unto me, saying,

24 Son of man, say unto her, Thou *art* the land that is not cleansed, nor rained upon in the day of ᵀindignation.   Is. 9:13 ◆ *anger*

25 *There is* a conspiracy of her prophets in the midst thereof, like a roaring lion ᵀravening the prey; they have devoured souls;

The Sabbath Profaned and Perverted

Ezekiel 22:8, 31

In calling the attention of Judah to the sins that finally brought upon them the Babylonian Captivity, the Lord declared: "Thou hast . . . . profaned My Sabbaths." "Therefore have I poured out Mine indignation upon them; I have consumed them with the fire of My wrath: their own way have I recompensed upon their heads" (Ezekiel 22:8, 31).

At the restoration of Jerusalem, in the days of Nehemiah, Sabbathbreaking was met with the stern inquiry, "Did not your fathers thus, and did not our God bring all this evil upon us, and upon this city? yet ye bring more wrath upon Israel by profaning the Sabbath" (Nehemiah 13:18).

Christ, during His earthly ministry, emphasized the binding claims of the Sabbath; in all His teaching He showed reverence for the institution He Himself had given. In His days the Sabbath had become so perverted that its observance reflected the character of selfish and arbitrary men rather than the character of God. Christ set aside the false teaching by which those who claimed to know God had misrepresented Him. Although followed with merciless hostility by the rabbis, He did not even appear to conform to their requirements, but went straight forward keeping the Sabbath according to the law of God. *PK 182, 183*

they have taken the treasure and precious things; they have made her many widows in the midst thereof.   Hos. 6:9 ✦ *tearing*

26 Her priests have violated my law, and have profaned mine holy things: they have put no difference between the holy and profane, neither have they shewed *difference* between the unclean and the clean, and have hid their eyes from my sabbaths, and I am profaned among them.   Lev. 10:10; 1 Sam. 2:12-17; Jer. 2:8

27 Her princes in the midst thereof *are* like wolves ravening the prey, to shed blood, *and* to destroy souls, to get dishonest gain.

28 And her prophets have daubed them with untempered *morter*, seeing vanity, and divining lies unto them, saying, Thus saith the Lord GOD, when the LORD hath not spoken.   Jer. 23:25-32

29 The people of the land have used oppression, and exercised robbery, and have vexed the poor and needy: yea, they have oppressed the stranger wrongfully. Ex. 23:9; Is. 5:7; Ezek. 22:7

30 And I sought for a man among them, that should make up the hedge, and stand in the gap before me for the land, that I should not destroy it: but I found none.   Ps. 106:23; Jer. 5:1

31 Therefore have I poured out mine indignation upon them; I have consumed them with the fire of my wrath: their own way have I ᵀrecompensed upon their heads, saith the Lord GOD.   Ezek. 7:8-9 ✦ *repaid*

The Lewdness of Jerusalem and Samaria

23 The word of the LORD came again unto me, saying,

2 Son of man, there were two women, the daughters of one mother:

3 And they committed whoredoms in Egypt; they committed whoredoms in their youth: there were their breasts pressed, and there they bruised the teats of their virginity. Lev. 17:7

4 And the names of them *were* Aholah the elder, and Aholibah her sister: and they were mine, and they bare sons and daughters. Thus *were* their names; Samaria *is* Aholah, and Jerusalem Aholibah.   Ezek. 16:8

5 And Aholah played the harlot when she was mine; and she doted on her lovers, on the Assyrians *her* neighbours,   2 Kin. 15:19

6 *Which were* clothed with blue, captains and rulers, all of them desirable young men, horsemen riding upon horses.

7 Thus she committed her whoredoms with them, with all them *that were* the chosen men of Assyria, and with all on whom she doted: with all their idols she defiled herself. Hos. 5:3

8 Neither left she her whoredoms *brought* from Egypt: for in her youth they lay with her, and they bruised the breasts of her virginity, and poured their ᵀwhoredom upon her.   Ex. 32:4 ✦ *prostitution*

9 Wherefore I have delivered her into the hand of her lovers, into the hand of the Assyrians, upon whom she doted.   2 Kin. 15:29

10 These discovered her nakedness: they took her sons and her daughters, and slew her with the sword: and she became famous among women; for they had executed judgment upon her.   Ezek. 23:29

11 And when her sister Aholibah saw *this*, she was more corrupt in her ᵀinordinate love than she, and in her whoredoms more than her sister in *her* whoredoms.   Jer. 3:8-11 ✦ *unrestrained*

12 She doted upon the Assyrians *her* neighbours, captains and rulers clothed most gorgeously, horsemen riding upon horses, all of them desirable young men.   2 Kin. 16:7-15

13 Then I saw that she was defiled, *that* they *took* both one way,

14 And *that* she increased her whoredoms: for when she saw men pourtrayed upon the wall, the images of the Chaldeans pourtrayed with ᵀvermilion, Jer. 22:14; Ezek. 8:10 ✦ *red*

15 Girded with girdles upon their ᵀloins, exceeding in dyed attire upon their heads, all of them princes to look to, after the manner of the Babylonians of Chaldea, the land of their nativity: *waists*

16 And as soon as she saw them with her eyes, she doted upon them, and sent messengers unto them into Chaldea.   Ezek. 16:29

17 And the Babylonians came to her into the bed of love, and they defiled her with their whoredom, and she was polluted with them, and her mind was alienated from them.   Ezek. 23:22

18 So she discovered her whoredoms, and discovered her nakedness: then my mind was alienated from her, like as my mind was alienated from her sister.   Ps. 78:59

19 Yet she multiplied her whoredoms, in calling to remembrance the days of her youth, wherein she had played the harlot in the land of Egypt.   Ezek. 23:3

20 For she doted upon their paramours, whose flesh *is as* the flesh of asses, and whose issue *is like* the issue of horses.   Ezek. 16:26

21 Thus thou calledst to remembrance the lewdness of thy youth, in bruising thy teats by the Egyptians for the ᵀpaps of thy youth.   *breasts*

22 Therefore, O Aholibah, thus saith the Lord GOD; Behold, I will raise up thy lovers against thee, from whom thy mind is alienated, and I will bring them against thee on every side;   Ezek. 16:37

23 The Babylonians, and all the Chaldeans, Pekod, and Shoa, and Koa, *and* all the Assyrians with them: all of them desirable young men, captains and rulers, great lords

and renowned, all of them riding upon horses. 2 Kin. 20:14-17; 24:2; Jer. 50:21
24 And they shall come against thee with chariots, wagons, and wheels, and with an assembly of people, *which* shall set against thee ᵀbuckler and shield and helmet round about: and I will set judgment before them, and they shall judge thee according to their judgments. Jer. 39:5-6 ◆ *small shield*
25 And I will set my jealousy against thee, and they shall deal furiously with thee: they shall take away thy nose and thine ears; and thy remnant shall fall by the sword: they shall take thy sons and thy daughters; and thy residue shall be devoured by the fire. Ezek. 23:47
26 They shall also strip thee out of thy clothes, and take away thy fair jewels. Jer. 13:22
27 Thus will I make thy lewdness to cease from thee, and thy whoredom *brought* from the land of Egypt: so that thou shalt not lift up thine eyes unto them, nor remember Egypt any more. Ezek. 16:41; 23:3, 19
28 For thus saith the Lord GOD; Behold, I will deliver thee into the hand *of them* whom thou hatest, into the hand *of them* from whom thy mind is alienated: Jer. 34:20
29 And they shall deal with thee hatefully, and shall take away all thy labour, and shall leave thee naked and bare: and the nakedness of thy whoredoms shall be discovered, both thy lewdness and thy whoredoms. Ezek. 16:39
30 I will do these *things* unto thee, because thou hast gone ᵀa whoring after the heathen, *and* because thou art polluted with their idols. Ezek. 6:9 ◆ *giving sex as a prostitute*
31 Thou hast walked in the way of thy sister; therefore will I give her cup into thine hand. 2 Kin. 21:13
32 Thus saith the Lord GOD; Thou shalt drink of thy sister's cup deep and large: thou shalt be laughed to scorn and had in derision; it containeth much. Ps. 60:3
33 Thou shalt be filled with drunkenness and sorrow, with the cup of astonishment and desolation, with the cup of thy sister Samaria. Is. 51:17
34 Thou shalt even drink it and suck *it* out, and thou shalt break the sherds thereof, and pluck off thine own breasts: for I have spoken *it*, saith the Lord GOD. Ps. 75:8; Is. 51:17
35 Therefore thus saith the Lord GOD; Because thou hast forgotten me, and cast me behind thy back, therefore bear thou also thy lewdness and thy whoredoms. 1 Kin. 14:9
36 The LORD said moreover unto me; Son of man, wilt thou judge Aholah and Aholibah? yea, declare unto them their abominations; Is. 58:1; Ezek. 16:2; 22:2
37 That they have committed adultery, and blood *is* in their hands, and with their idols

have they committed adultery, and have also caused their sons, whom they bare unto me, to pass for them through *the fire*, to devour *them*. Ezek. 16:20-21, 36, 38
38 Moreover this they have done unto me: they have defiled my sanctuary in the same day, and have profaned my sabbaths. Ezek. 20:13
39 For when they had slain their children to their idols, then they came the same day into my sanctuary to profane it; and, lo, thus have they done in the midst of mine house. 2 Kin. 21:4
40 And furthermore, that ye have sent for men to come from far, unto whom a messenger *was* sent; and, lo, they came: for whom thou didst wash thyself, paintedst thy eyes, and deckedst thyself with ornaments, 2 Kin. 9:30; Jer. 4:30; Ezek. 16:13-16
41 And satest upon a stately bed, and a table prepared before it, whereupon thou hast set mine incense and mine oil. Esth. 1:6; Is. 65:11
42 And a voice of a multitude being at ease *was* with her: and with the men of the common sort *were* brought Sabeans from the wilderness, which put bracelets upon their hands, and beautiful crowns upon their heads. Ezek. 16:11-12
43 Then said I unto *her that was* old in adulteries, Will they now commit ᵀwhoredoms with her, and she *with them*? *acts of prostitution*
44 Yet they went in unto her, as they go in unto a woman that playeth the harlot: so went they in unto Aholah and unto Aholibah, the lewd women.
45 And the righteous men, they shall judge them after the manner of adulteresses, and after the manner of women that shed blood; because they *are* adulteresses, and blood *is* in their hands. Lev. 20:10
46 For thus saith the Lord GOD; I will bring up a company upon them, and will give them to be removed and spoiled. Ezek. 16:40
47 And the company shall stone them with stones, and dispatch them with their swords; they shall slay their sons and their daughters, and burn up their houses with fire. Jer. 39:8
48 Thus will I cause lewdness to cease out of the land, that all women may be taught not to do after your lewdness. Ezek. 16:41
49 And they shall ᵀrecompense your lewdness upon you, and ye shall bear the sins of your idols: and ye shall know that I *am* the Lord GOD. Ezek. 7:4 ◆ *repay*

Judah Is a Boiling Pot

24 Again in the ninth year, in the tenth month, in the tenth *day* of the month, the word of the LORD came unto me, saying, Ezek. 8:1
2 Son of man, write thee the name of the

day, *even* of this same day: the king of Babylon set himself against Jerusalem this same day.   2 Kin. 25:1

3 And utter a parable unto the rebellious house, and say unto them, Thus saith the Lord GOD; Set on a pot, set *it* on, and also pour water into it: Ezek. 11:3; 17:2; 20:49

4 Gather the pieces thereof into it, *even* every good piece, the thigh, and the shoulder; fill *it* with the choice bones.   Mic. 3:2-3

5 Take the choice of the flock, and burn also the bones under it, *and* make it boil well, and let them ᵀseethe the bones of it therein.   Jer. 52:10 ◆ *boil*

6 Wherefore thus saith the Lord GOD; Woe to the bloody city, to the pot whose scum *is* therein, and whose scum is not gone out of it! bring it out piece by piece; let no lot fall upon it.   2 Kin. 24:4; Ezek. 22:2; Nah. 3:1

7 For her blood is in the midst of her; she set it upon the top of a rock; she poured it not upon the ground, to cover it with dust;

8 That it might cause fury to come up to take vengeance; I have set her blood upon the top of a rock, that it should not be covered.

9 Therefore thus saith the Lord GOD; Woe to the bloody city! I will even make the pile for fire great.   Is. 30:33

10 Heap on wood, kindle the fire, consume the flesh, and spice it well, and let the bones be burned.

11 Then set it empty upon the coals thereof, that the brass of it may be hot, and may burn, and *that* the filthiness of it may be molten in it, *that* the scum of it may be consumed.   Jer. 21:10

12 She hath wearied *herself* with lies, and her great scum went not forth out of her: her scum *shall be* in the fire.   Jer. 9:5

13 In thy filthiness *is* lewdness: because I have purged thee, and thou wast not purged, thou shalt not be purged from thy filthiness any more, till I have caused my fury to rest upon thee.   Jer. 6:28-30

14 I the LORD have spoken *it*: it shall come to pass, and I will do *it*; I will not go back, neither will I spare, neither will I repent; according to thy ways, and according to thy doings, shall they judge thee, saith the Lord GOD.   Ezek. 18:30

Ezekiel Silently Mourns

15 Also the word of the LORD came unto me, saying,

16 Son of man, behold, I take away from thee the desire of thine eyes with a stroke: yet neither shalt thou mourn nor weep, neither shall thy tears run down.   Jer. 13:17

17 Forbear to cry, make no mourning for the dead, bind the ᵀtire of thine head upon

thee, and put on thy shoes upon thy feet, and cover not *thy* lips, and eat not the bread of men.   Hos. 9:4 ◆ *turban*

18 So I spake unto the people in the morning: and at even my wife died; and I did in the morning as I was commanded.

19 And the people said unto me, Wilt thou not tell us what these *things are* to us, that thou doest *so*?   Ezek. 12:9

20 Then I answered them, The word of the LORD came unto me, saying,

21 Speak unto the house of Israel, Thus saith the Lord GOD; Behold, I will profane my sanctuary, the excellency of your strength, the desire of your eyes, and that which your soul pitieth; and your sons and your daughters whom ye have left shall fall by the sword.   Ps. 27:4; Jer. 7:14; Ezek. 23:47

22 And ye shall do as I have done: ye shall not cover *your* lips, nor eat the bread of men.

23 And your ᵀtires *shall be* upon your heads, and your shoes upon your feet: ye shall not mourn nor weep; but ye shall pine away for your iniquities, and mourn one toward another.   Lev. 26:39 ◆ *turbans*

24 Thus Ezekiel is unto you a sign: according to all that he hath done shall ye do: and when this cometh, ye shall know that I *am* the Lord GOD.   Is. 20:3; Ezek. 4:3; 6:7

25 Also, thou son of man, *shall it* not *be* in the day when I take from them their strength, the joy of their glory, the desire of their eyes, and that whereupon they set their minds, their sons and their daughters,   Ezek. 24:21

26 *That* he that escapeth in that day shall come unto thee, to cause *thee* to hear *it* with *thine* ears?   Job 1:15-19

27 In that day shall thy mouth be opened to him which is escaped, and thou shalt speak, and be no more ᵀdumb: and thou shalt be a sign unto them; and they shall know that I *am* the LORD.   Ezek. 33:22 ◆ *mute*

Judgment on Ammon

25 The word of the LORD came again unto me, saying,

2 Son of man, set thy face against the Ammonites, and prophesy against them; Jer. 49:1-6

3 And say unto the Ammonites, Hear the word of the Lord GOD; Thus saith the Lord GOD; Because thou saidst, Aha, against my sanctuary, when it was profaned; and against the land of Israel, when it was desolate; and against the house of Judah, when they went into captivity;   Ps. 70:2-3; Prov. 17:5; Ezek. 36:2

4 Behold, therefore I will deliver thee to the men of the east for a possession, and they shall set their palaces in thee, and make their dwellings in thee: they shall eat thy fruit, and they shall drink thy milk.   Deut. 28:33

5 And I will make Rabbah a stable for

camels, and the Ammonites a couchingplace for flocks: and ye shall know that I *am* the LORD.   2 Sam. 12:26; Is. 17:2; Ezek. 21:20
6 For thus saith the Lord GOD; Because thou hast clapped *thine* hands, and stamped with the feet, and rejoiced in heart with all thy despite against the land of Israel; Obad. 12; Zeph. 2:8
7 Behold, therefore I will stretch out mine hand upon thee, and will deliver thee for a ᵀspoil to the heathen; and I will cut thee off from the people, and I will cause thee to perish out of the countries: I will destroy thee; and thou shalt know that I *am* the LORD.   Zeph. 1:4 ✦ plunder

Judgment on Moab

8 Thus saith the Lord GOD; Because that Moab and Seir do say, Behold, the house of Judah *is* like unto all the heathen;   Is. 15
9 Therefore, behold, I will open the side of Moab from the cities, from his cities *which are* on his frontiers, the glory of the country, Beth-jeshimoth, Baal-meon, and Kiria-thaim,   Josh. 13:17
10 Unto the men of the east with the Ammonites, and will give them in possession, that the Ammonites may not be remembered among the nations.   Ezek. 21:32
11 And I will execute judgments upon Moab; and they shall know that I *am* the LORD.

Judgment on Edom

12 Thus saith the Lord GOD; Because that Edom hath dealt against the house of Judah by taking vengeance, and hath greatly offended, and revenged himself upon them;   Ps. 137:7
13 Therefore thus saith the Lord GOD; I will also stretch out mine hand upon Edom, and will cut off man and beast from it; and I will make it desolate from Teman; and they of Dedan shall fall by the sword.   Jer. 25:23
14 And I will lay my vengeance upon Edom by the hand of my people Israel: and they shall do in Edom according to mine anger and according to my fury; and they shall know my vengeance, saith the Lord GOD.   Is. 11:14

Judgment on Philistia

15 Thus saith the Lord GOD; Because the Philistines have dealt by revenge, and have taken vengeance with a despiteful heart, to destroy *it* for the old hatred;   Is. 14:29-31
16 Therefore thus saith the Lord GOD; Behold, I will stretch out mine hand upon the Philistines, and I will cut off the Cherethims, and destroy the remnant of the sea coast.   1 Sam. 30:14; Ezek. 25:13
17 And I will execute great vengeance upon them with furious rebukes; and they shall know that I *am* the LORD, when I shall lay my vengeance upon them.   Ezek. 25:11

Judgment on Tyrus (Tyre)

26 And it came to pass in the eleventh year, in the first *day* of the month, *that* the word of the LORD came unto me, saying,   Ezek. 20:1
2 Son of man, because that Tyrus hath said against Jerusalem, Aha, she is broken *that was* the gates of the people: she is turned unto me: I shall be replenished, *now* she is laid waste: Is. 23
3 Therefore thus saith the Lord GOD; Behold, I *am* against thee, O Tyrus, and will cause many nations to come up against thee, as the sea causeth his waves to come up.   Is. 5:30
4 And they shall destroy the walls of Tyrus, and break down her towers: I will also scrape her dust from her, and make her like the top of a rock.   Is. 23:11
5 It shall be *a place for* the spreading of nets in the midst of the sea: for I have spoken *it*, saith the Lord GOD: and it shall become a spoil to the nations.   Ezek. 29:19
6 And her daughters which *are* in the field shall be slain by the sword; and they shall know that I *am* the LORD.   Ezek. 16:46
7 For thus saith the Lord GOD; Behold, I will bring upon Tyrus Nebuchadrezzar king of Babylon, a king of kings, from the north, with horses, and with chariots, and with horsemen, and companies, and much people.   Ezra 7:12; Ezek. 23:24; Dan. 2:37

26:7 God Used Nebuchadnezzar

An idolater by birth and training, and at the head of an idolatrous people, [Nebuchadnezzar] had nevertheless an innate sense of justice and right, and God was able to use him as an instrument for the punishment of the rebellious and for the fulfillment of the divine purpose. *PK 514, 515*

8 He shall slay with the sword thy daughters in the field: and he shall make a fort against thee, and cast a mount against thee, and lift up the ᵀbuckler against thee. Ezek. 21:22 ✦ shield
9 And he shall set engines of war against thy walls, and with his axes he shall break down thy towers.
10 By reason of the abundance of his horses their dust shall cover thee: thy walls shall shake at the noise of the horsemen, and of the wheels, and of the chariots, when he shall enter into thy gates, as men enter into a city wherein is made a breach.   Jer. 47:3
11 With the hoofs of his horses shall he tread down all thy streets: he shall slay thy people by the sword, and thy strong garrisons shall go down to the ground.   Is. 5:28
12 And they shall make a ᵀspoil of thy riches, and make a prey of thy merchandise: and they shall break down thy walls, and

destroy thy pleasant houses: and they shall lay thy stones and thy timber and thy dust in the midst of the water.   Is. 23:8 ◆ *plunder*

13 And I will cause the noise of thy songs to cease; and the sound of thy harps shall be no more heard.   Is. 23:16

14 And I will make thee like the top of a rock: thou shalt be *a place* to spread nets upon; thou shalt be built no more: for I the LORD have spoken *it*, saith the Lord GOD.   Job 12:14

The Coming Fall of Tyrus (Tyre)

15 Thus saith the Lord GOD to Tyrus; Shall not the isles shake at the sound of thy fall, when the wounded cry, when the slaughter is made in the midst of thee?   Jer. 49:21; Ezek. 26:18

16 Then all the princes of the sea shall come down from their thrones, and lay away their robes, and put off their broidered garments: they shall clothe themselves with trembling; they shall sit upon the ground, and shall tremble at *every* moment, and be astonished at thee.   Job 8:22; Ezek. 32:10; Hos. 11:10

17 And they shall take up a lamentation for thee, and say to thee, How art thou destroyed, *that wast* inhabited of seafaring men, the renowned city, which wast strong in the sea, she and her inhabitants, which cause their terror *to be* on all that haunt it!   Is. 14:12; 23:4; Ezek. 19:1

18 Now shall the isles tremble in the day of thy fall; yea, the isles that *are* in the sea shall be troubled at thy departure.   Is. 23:5-7

19 For thus saith the Lord GOD; When I shall make thee a desolate city, like the cities that are not inhabited; when I shall bring up the deep upon thee, and great waters shall cover thee;   Is. 8:7-8

20 When I shall bring thee down with them that descend into the pit, with the people of old time, and shall set thee in the low parts of the earth, in places desolate of old, with them that go down to the pit, that thou be not inhabited; and I shall set glory in the land of the living;   Ps. 27:13

21 I will make thee a terror, and thou *shalt be* no *more*: though thou be sought for, yet shalt thou never be found again, saith the Lord GOD.   Ezek. 27:36; 28:19; Rev. 18:21

A Funeral Song for Tyrus (Tyre)

27 The word of the LORD came again unto me, saying,

2 Now, thou son of man, take up a lamentation for Tyrus;   Jer. 9:10

3 And say unto Tyrus, O thou that art situate at the entry of the sea, *which art* a merchant of the people for many isles, Thus saith the Lord GOD; O Tyrus, thou hast said, I *am* of perfect beauty.   Ezek. 27:4

4 Thy borders *are* in the midst of the seas, thy builders have perfected thy beauty.

5 They have made all thy *ship* boards of fir trees of Senir: they have taken cedars from Lebanon to make masts for thee.   Deut. 3:9

6 *Of* the oaks of Bashan have they made thine oars; the company of the Ashurites have made thy benches *of* ivory, *brought* out of the isles of Chittim.   Gen. 10:4; Is. 2:13; Zech. 11:2

7 Fine linen with broidered work from Egypt was that which thou spreadest forth to be thy sail; blue and purple from the isles of Elishah was that which covered thee.   Ex. 25:4

8 The inhabitants of Zidon and Arvad were thy mariners: thy wise *men*, O Tyrus, *that* were in thee, were thy pilots.   Gen. 10:18; 1 Kin. 9:27

9 The ancients of Gebal and the wise *men* thereof were in thee thy calkers: all the ships of the sea with their mariners were in thee to occupy thy merchandise.   Josh. 13:5; 1 Kin. 5:18

10 They of Persia and of Lud and of Phut were in thine army, thy men of war: they hanged the shield and helmet in thee; they set forth thy comeliness. Song 4:4; Ezek. 30:5; 38:5

11 The men of Arvad with thine army *were* upon thy walls round about, and the Gammadims *were* in thy towers: they hanged their shields upon thy walls round about; they have made thy beauty perfect.

12 Tarshish *was* thy merchant by reason of the multitude of all *kind of* riches; with silver, iron, tin, and lead, they traded in thy ᵀfairs.   Gen. 10:4 ◆ *merchandise*

13 Javan, Tubal, and Meshech, they *were* thy merchants: they traded the persons of men and vessels of brass in thy market.   Gen. 10:2

14 They of the house of Togarmah traded in thy fairs with horses and horsemen and mules.   Gen. 10:3; Ezek. 38:6

15 The men of Dedan *were* thy merchants; many isles *were* the merchandise of thine hand: they brought thee *for* a present horns of ivory and ebony.   Gen. 10:7

16 Syria *was* thy merchant by reason of the multitude of the wares of thy making: they occupied in thy fairs with emeralds, purple, and broidered work, and fine linen, and coral, and agate.   Judg. 10:6

17 Judah, and the land of Israel, they *were* thy merchants: they traded in thy market wheat of Minnith, and Pannag, and honey, and oil, and ᵀbalm. Judg. 11:33; 1 Kin. 5:9 ◆ *medicine*

18 Damascus *was* thy merchant in the multitude of the wares of thy making, for the multitude of all riches; in the wine of Helbon, and white wool.   Is. 7:8

19 Dan also and Javan going to and fro occupied in thy fairs: bright iron, cassia, and calamus, were in thy market.   Ex. 30:23-24

20 Dedan *was* thy merchant in precious clothes for chariots.   Gen. 25:3

21 Arabia, and all the princes of Kedar, they

occupied with thee in lambs, and rams, and goats: in these *were they* thy merchants.

22 The merchants of Sheba and Raamah, they *were* thy merchants: they occupied in thy fairs with chief of all spices, and with all precious stones, and gold.   Gen. 10:7; Is. 60:6

23 Haran, and Canneh, and Eden, the merchants of Sheba, Asshur, *and* Chilmad, *were* thy merchants.   Gen. 10:22; 2 Kin. 19:12; Is. 37:12

24 These *were* thy merchants in all sorts *of things*, in blue clothes, and broidered work, and in chests of rich apparel, bound with cords, and made of cedar, among thy merchandise.

25 The ships of Tarshish did sing of thee in thy market: and thou wast replenished, and made very glorious in the midst of the seas.   Ps. 48:7; Is. 2:16; 23:14

26 Thy rowers have brought thee into great waters: the east wind hath broken thee in the midst of the seas.   Ps. 48:7

27 Thy riches, and thy fairs, thy merchandise, thy mariners, and thy pilots, thy ᵀcalkers, and the occupiers of thy merchandise, and all thy men of war, that *are* in thee, and in all thy company which *is* in the midst of thee, shall fall into the midst of the seas in the day of thy ruin.   Prov. 11:4 ♦ *repairers of seams in ships*

28 The suburbs shall shake at the sound of the cry of thy pilots.   Ezek. 26:10

29 And all that handle the oar, the mariners, *and* all the pilots of the sea, shall come down from their ships, they shall stand upon the land;

30 And shall cause their voice to be heard against thee, and shall cry bitterly, and shall cast up dust upon their heads, they shall wallow themselves in the ashes: 2 Sam. 1:2; Jer. 6:26

31 And they shall make themselves utterly bald for thee, and ᵀgird them with sackcloth, and they shall weep for thee with bitterness of heart *and* bitter wailing.   Is. 16:9 ♦ *clothe*

32 And in their wailing they shall take up a lamentation for thee, and lament over thee, *saying*, What *city is* like Tyrus, like the destroyed in the midst of the sea?   Ezek. 26:17

33 When thy wares went forth out of the seas, thou filledst many people; thou didst enrich the kings of the earth with the multitude of thy riches and of thy merchandise.   Rev. 18:19

34 In the time *when* thou shalt be broken by the seas in the depths of the waters thy merchandise and all thy company in the midst of thee shall fall.   Ezek. 27:26-27

35 All the inhabitants of the isles shall be astonished at thee, and their kings shall be sore afraid, they shall be troubled in *their* ᵀcountenance.   Is. 23:6 ♦ *appearance*

36 The merchants among the people shall hiss at thee; thou shalt be a terror, and never *shalt be* any more.   Ps. 37:10, 36; Jer. 18:16

God's Judgment on the Prince of Tyrus (Tyre)

28 The word of the LORD came again unto me, saying,

2 Son of man, say unto the prince of Tyrus, Thus saith the Lord GOD; Because thine heart *is* lifted up, and thou hast said, I *am* a God, I sit *in* the seat of God, in the midst of the seas; yet thou *art* a man, and not God, though thou set thine heart as the heart of God: Is. 31:3; Ezek. 28:9; 2 Thess. 2:4

3 Behold, thou *art* wiser than Daniel; there is no secret that they can hide from thee:

4 With thy wisdom and with thine understanding thou hast gotten thee riches, and hast gotten gold and silver into thy treasures:

5 By thy great wisdom *and* by thy traffick hast thou increased thy riches, and thine heart is lifted up because of thy riches: Ps. 52:7; 62:10

6 Therefore thus saith the Lord GOD; Because thou hast set thine heart as the heart of God;   Ezek. 28:2

7 Behold, therefore I will bring strangers upon thee, the terrible of the nations: and they shall draw their swords against the beauty of thy wisdom, and they shall defile thy brightness.   Ezek. 30:11; 31:12; 32:12

8 They shall bring thee down to the pit, and thou shalt die the deaths of *them that are* slain in the midst of the seas.   Ezek. 27:26-27

9 Wilt thou yet say before him that slayeth thee, I *am* God? but thou *shalt be* a man, and no God, in the hand of him that slayeth thee.   Ezek. 28:2

10 Thou shalt die the deaths of the uncircumcised by the hand of strangers: for I have spoken *it*, saith the Lord GOD.   1 Sam. 17:26

28:6–10 Choices and Consequences

God is the fountain of life; and when one chooses the service of sin, he separates from God, and thus cuts himself off from life. . . . God gives them existence for a time that they may develop their character and reveal their principles. . . . By a life of rebellion, Satan and all who unite with him place themselves so out of harmony with God that His very presence is to them a consuming fire. *DA 764*

A Lamentation for the King

11 Moreover the word of the LORD came unto me, saying,

12 Son of man, take up a lamentation upon the king of Tyrus, and say unto him, Thus saith the Lord GOD; Thou sealest up the sum, full of wisdom, and perfect in beauty.   Ezek. 19:1

28:12–19* Why Satan Was Spared

Satan is a deceiver. When he sinned in heaven, even the loyal angels did not fully discern his character. This was why God did not at once destroy Satan. Had He done so, the holy angels would not have perceived the justice and love of God. A doubt of God's goodness would have been as evil seed that would yield the bitter fruit of sin and woe. Therefore the author of evil was spared, fully to develop his character. *COL 72*

13 Thou hast been in Eden the garden of God; every precious stone *was* thy covering, the sardius, topaz, and the diamond, the ᵀberyl, the onyx, and the jasper, the sapphire, the emerald, and the carbuncle, and gold: the workmanship of thy tabrets and of thy pipes was prepared in thee in the day that thou wast created.   Gen. 2:8; Ezek. 27:16; 31:8-9 ◆ *precious stone*

14 Thou *art* the anointed cherub that covereth; and I have set thee *so*: thou wast upon the holy mountain of God; thou hast walked up and down in the midst of the stones of fire.   Ex. 25:17-20

15 Thou *wast* perfect in thy ways from the day that thou wast created, till iniquity was found in thee.   Ezek. 27:3-4

16 By the multitude of thy merchandise they have filled the midst of thee with violence, and thou hast sinned: therefore I will cast thee as profane out of the mountain of God: and I will destroy thee, O covering cherub, from the midst of the stones of fire. Hab. 2:17

17 Thine heart was lifted up because of thy beauty, thou hast corrupted thy wisdom by reason of thy brightness: I will cast thee to the ground, I will lay thee before kings, that they may behold thee.   Ezek. 28:2

18 Thou hast defiled thy sanctuaries by the multitude of thine iniquities, by the iniquity of thy ᵀtraffick; therefore will I bring forth a fire from the midst of thee, it shall devour thee, and I will bring thee to ashes upon the earth in the sight of all them that behold thee.   Mal. 4:3 ◆ *trade*

Salvation From Sin   See Isaiah 14:12–14.

19 All they that know thee among the people shall be astonished at thee: thou shalt be a terror, and never *shalt* thou *be* any more.

28:18, 19* Sin—Never Again

The whole universe will have become witnesses to the nature and results of sin. And its utter extermination, which in the beginning would have brought fear to angels and dishonor to God, will now vindicate His love and establish His honor before the universe of beings who delight to do His will, and in whose heart is His law. Never will evil again be manifest. Says the word of God: "Affliction shall not rise up the second time" (Nahum 1:9). *GC 504*

Judgment on Zidon (Sidon)

20 Again the word of the LORD came unto me, saying,

21 Son of man, set thy face against Zidon, and prophesy against it,   Gen. 10:15; Jer. 25:22; Ezek. 6:2

22 And say, Thus saith the Lord GOD; Behold, I *am* against thee, O Zidon; and I will be glorified in the midst of thee: and they shall know that I *am* the LORD, when I shall have executed judgments in her, and shall be sanctified in her.   Ezek. 39:13

23 For I will send into her pestilence, and blood into her streets; and the wounded

God's Principles—and Satan's

Ezekiel 28:12–15*

It was a being of wonderful power and glory that had set himself against God. Of Lucifer the Lord says, "Thou sealest up the sum, full of wisdom, and perfect in beauty" (Ezekiel 28:12). Lucifer had been the covering cherub. He had stood in the light of God's presence. He had been the highest of all created beings, and had been foremost in revealing God's purposes to the universe. After he had sinned, his power to deceive was the more deceptive, and the unveiling of his character was the more difficult, because of the exalted position he had held with the Father.

God could have destroyed Satan and his sympathizers as easily as one can cast a pebble to the earth; but He did not do this. Rebellion was not to be overcome by force. Compelling power is found only under Satan's government. The Lord's principles are not of this order. His authority rests upon goodness, mercy, and love; and the presentation of these principles is the means to be used. God's government is moral, and truth and love are to be the prevailing power.

It was God's purpose to place things on an eternal basis of security, and in the councils of heaven it was decided that time must be given for Satan to develop the principles which were the foundation of his system of government. He had claimed that these were superior to God's principles. Time was given for the working of Satan's principles, that they might be seen by the heavenly universe. *DA 758, 759*

---

* For more information on how and why there is sin, see pages 1428–1435 of this Bible.

shall be judged in the midst of her by the sword upon her on every side; and they shall know that I *am* the LORD. Ezek. 38:22

24 And there shall be no more a pricking brier unto the house of Israel, nor *any* grieving thorn of all *that are* round about them, that despised them; and they shall know that I *am* the Lord GOD. Num. 33:55; Josh. 23:13; Is. 55:13

25 Thus saith the Lord GOD; When I shall have gathered the house of Israel from the people among whom they are scattered, and shall be ᵀsanctified in them in the sight of the heathen, then shall they dwell in their land that I have given to my servant Jacob. Ps. 106:47 ◆ *made holy*

26 And they shall dwell safely therein, and shall build houses, and plant vineyards; yea, they shall dwell with confidence, when I have executed judgments upon all those that despise them round about them; and they shall know that I *am* the LORD their God. Jer. 32:15; Ezek. 28:22, 24

Judgment on Egypt

29 In the tenth year, in the tenth *month*, in the twelfth *day* of the month, the word of the LORD came unto me, saying, Ezek. 26:1

2 Son of man, set thy face against Pharaoh king of Egypt, and prophesy against him, and against all Egypt: Ezek. 6:2

3 Speak, and say, Thus saith the Lord GOD; Behold, I *am* against thee, Pharaoh king of Egypt, the great dragon that lieth in the midst of his rivers, which hath said, My river *is* mine own, and I have made *it* for myself. Ps. 74:13-14; Is. 27:1; Ezek. 32:2

4 But I will put hooks in thy jaws, and I will cause the fish of thy rivers to stick unto thy scales, and I will bring thee up out of the midst of thy rivers, and all the fish of thy rivers shall stick unto thy scales. 2 Kin. 19:28

5 And I will leave thee *thrown* into the wilderness, thee and all the fish of thy rivers: thou shalt fall upon the open fields; thou shalt not be brought together, nor gathered: I have given thee for meat to the beasts of the field and to the fowls of the heaven. Jer. 7:33

6 And all the inhabitants of Egypt shall know that I *am* the LORD, because they have been a staff of reed to the house of Israel.

7 When they took hold of thee by thy hand, thou didst break, and ᵀrend all their shoulder: and when they leaned upon thee, thou brakest, and madest all their loins to be at a stand. Ezek. 17:15-17 ◆ *tear apart*

The Desolation of Egypt

8 Therefore thus saith the Lord GOD; Behold, I will bring a sword upon thee, and cut off man and beast out of thee. Ezek. 14:17

9 And the land of Egypt shall be desolate and waste; and they shall know that I *am* the LORD: because he hath said, The river *is* mine, and I have made *it*. Ezek. 29:3

10 Behold, therefore I *am* against thee, and against thy rivers, and I will make the land of Egypt utterly waste *and* desolate, from the tower of Syene even unto the border of Ethiopia. Ezek. 30:12

11 No foot of man shall pass through it, nor foot of beast shall pass through it, neither shall it be inhabited forty years. Jer. 43:11-12

12 And I will make the land of Egypt desolate in the midst of the countries *that are* desolate, and her cities among the cities *that are* laid waste shall be desolate forty years:

Love Versus Lies

Ezekiel 28:12–19*

Sin originated in self-seeking. Lucifer, the covering cherub, desired to be first in heaven. He sought to gain control of heavenly beings, to draw them away from their Creator, and to win their homage to himself. Therefore he misrepresented God, attributing to Him the desire for self-exaltation. With his own evil characteristics he sought to invest the loving Creator. Thus he deceived angels. Thus he deceived men. He led them to doubt the word of God, and to distrust His goodness. Because God is a God of justice and terrible majesty, Satan caused them to look upon Him as severe and unforgiving. Thus he drew men to join him in rebellion against God, and the night of woe settled down upon the world.

The earth was dark through misapprehension of God. That the gloomy shadows might be lightened, that the world might be brought back to God, Satan's deceptive power was to be broken. This could not be done by force. The exercise of force is contrary to the principles of God's government; He desires only the service of love; and love cannot be commanded; it cannot be won by force or authority. Only by love is love awakened. To know God is to love Him; His character must be manifested in contrast to the character of Satan. This work only one Being in all the universe could do. Only He who knew the height and depth of the love of God could make it known. Upon the world's dark night the Sun of Righteousness must rise, "with healing in His wings" (Malachi 4:2). DA 21, 22

---

* *For more information on how and why there is sin, see pages 1428–1435 of this Bible.*

and I will scatter the Egyptians among the nations, and will disperse them through the countries. Jer. 46:19; Ezek. 30:7, 23

13 Yet thus saith the Lord GOD; At the end of forty years will I gather the Egyptians from the people whither they were scattered:

14 And I will bring again the captivity of Egypt, and will cause them to return *into* the land of Pathros, into the land of their habitation; and they shall be there a ᵀbase kingdom. Is. 11:11; Jer. 44:1; Ezek. 30:14 ◆ lowly

15 It shall be the basest of the kingdoms; neither shall it exalt itself any more above the nations: for I will diminish them, that they shall no more rule over the nations. Ezek. 30:13

16 And it shall be no more the confidence of the house of Israel, which bringeth *their* iniquity to remembrance, when they shall look after them: but they shall know that I *am* the Lord GOD. Hos. 8:13

Egypt to be Conquered by Babylon

17 And it came to pass in the seven and twentieth year, in the first *month*, in the first *day* of the month, the word of the LORD came unto me, saying, Ezek. 29:1

18 Son of man, Nebuchadrezzar king of Babylon caused his army to serve a great service against Tyrus: every head *was* made bald, and every shoulder *was* peeled: yet had he no wages, nor his army, for Tyrus, for the service that he had served against it: Jer. 27:6

19 Therefore thus saith the Lord GOD; Behold, I will give the land of Egypt unto Nebuchadrezzar king of Babylon; and he shall take her multitude, and take her ᵀspoil, and take her prey; and it shall be the wages for his army. Jer. 43:10-13 ◆ plunder

20 I have given him the land of Egypt *for* his labour wherewith he served against it, because they ᵀwrought for me, saith the Lord GOD. Is. 10:6-7 ◆ worked

21 In that day will I cause the horn of the house of Israel to bud forth, and I will give thee the opening of the mouth in the midst of them; and they shall know that I *am* the LORD. Ps. 132:17; Ezek. 24:27; 33:22

The Desolation of Egypt and Her Helpers

30 The word of the LORD came again unto me, saying,

2 Son of man, prophesy and say, Thus saith the Lord GOD; Howl ye, Woe worth the day! Is. 13:6; 15:2; Ezek. 21:12

3 For the day *is* near, even the day of the LORD *is* near, a cloudy day; it shall be the time of the heathen. Ezek. 7:7

4 And the sword shall come upon Egypt, and great pain shall be in Ethiopia, when the slain shall fall in Egypt, and they shall take away her multitude, and her foundations shall be broken down. Ezek. 29:8, 19

5 Ethiopia, and Libya, and Lydia, and all the mingled people, and Chub, and the men of the land that is in league, shall fall with them by the sword. Jer. 25:20, 24; Ezek. 27:10

6 Thus saith the LORD; They also that uphold Egypt shall fall; and the pride of her power shall come down: from the tower of Syene shall they fall in it by the sword, saith the Lord GOD. Ezek. 29:10

7 And they shall be desolate in the midst of the countries *that are* desolate, and her cities shall be in the midst of the cities *that are* wasted. Jer. 25:18-26; Ezek. 29:12

8 And they shall know that I *am* the LORD, when I have set a fire in Egypt, and *when* all her helpers shall be destroyed. Ezek. 29:6

9 In that day shall messengers go forth from me in ships to make the careless Ethiopians afraid, and great pain shall come upon them, as in the day of Egypt: for, lo, it cometh. Is. 18:1-2; 23:5; Ezek. 32:9-10

10 Thus saith the Lord GOD; I will also make the multitude of Egypt to cease by the hand of Nebuchadrezzar king of Babylon. Ezek. 29:19

11 He and his people with him, the terrible of the nations, shall be brought to destroy the land: and they shall draw their swords against Egypt, and fill the land with the slain. Ezek. 28:7

12 And I will make the rivers dry, and sell the land into the hand of the wicked: and I will make the land waste, and all that is therein, by the hand of strangers: I the LORD have spoken *it*. Ezek. 29:3

13 Thus saith the Lord GOD; I will also destroy the idols, and I will cause *their* images to cease out of Noph; and there shall be no more a prince of the land of Egypt: and I will put a fear in the land of Egypt. Zech. 10:11

14 And I will make Pathros desolate, and will set fire in Zoan, and will execute judgments in No. Ps. 78:12; Jer. 46:25; Ezek. 29:14

15 And I will pour my fury upon Sin, the strength of Egypt; and I will cut off the multitude of No.

16 And I will set fire in Egypt: Sin shall have great pain, and No shall be ᵀrent ᵀasunder, and Noph *shall have* distresses daily. torn ◆ apart

17 The young men of Aven and of Pi-beseth shall fall by the sword: and these *cities* shall go into captivity.

18 At Tehaphnehes also the day shall be darkened, when I shall break there the yokes of Egypt: and the pomp of her strength shall cease in her: as for her, a cloud shall cover her, and her daughters shall go into captivity. Ezek. 30:3

19 Thus will I execute judgments in Egypt: and they shall know that I *am* the LORD.

The Arm of Egypt Will be Broken

20 And it came to pass in the eleventh year, in the first *month*, in the seventh *day* of the month, *that* the word of the LORD came unto me, saying,   Ezek. 26:1
21 Son of man, I have broken the arm of Pharaoh king of Egypt; and, lo, it shall not be bound up to be healed, to put a roller to bind it, to make it strong to hold the sword.   Jer. 30:13; 46:11; 48:25
22 Therefore thus saith the Lord GOD; Behold, I *am* against Pharaoh king of Egypt, and will break his arms, the strong, and that which was broken; and I will cause the sword to fall out of his hand.   2 Kin. 24:7
23 And I will scatter the Egyptians among the nations, and will disperse them through the countries.   Ezek. 30:17-18
24 And I will strengthen the arms of the king of Babylon, and put my sword in his hand: but I will break Pharaoh's arms, and he shall groan before him with the groanings of a deadly wounded *man*.   Ezek. 30:25
25 But I will strengthen the arms of the king of Babylon, and the arms of Pharaoh shall fall down; and they shall know that I *am* the LORD, when I shall put my sword into the hand of the king of Babylon, and he shall stretch it out upon the land of Egypt.
26 And I will scatter the Egyptians among the nations, and disperse them among the countries; and they shall know that I *am* the LORD.   Ezek. 29:12

Egypt Will be Conquered

31 And it came to pass in the eleventh year, in the third *month*, in the first *day* of the month, *that* the word of the LORD came unto me, saying,   Ezek. 30:20
2 Son of man, speak unto Pharaoh king of Egypt, and to his multitude; Whom art thou like in thy greatness?   Ezek. 29:19
3 Behold, the Assyrian *was* a cedar in Lebanon with fair branches, and with a shadowing shroud, and of an high stature; and his top was among the thick boughs.   Is. 10:33-34
4 The waters made him great, the deep set him up on high with her rivers running round about his plants, and sent out her little rivers unto all the trees of the field.   Ezek. 17:5
5 Therefore his height was exalted above all the trees of the field, and his boughs were multiplied, and his branches became long because of the multitude of waters, when he shot forth.   Dan. 4:11
6 All the fowls of heaven made their nests in his boughs, and under his branches did all the beasts of the field bring forth their young, and under his shadow dwelt all great nations.   Ezek. 17:23; Dan. 4:12, 21
7 Thus was he fair in his greatness, in the length of his branches: for his root was by great waters.
8 The cedars in the garden of God could not hide him: the fir trees were not like his boughs, and the chesnut trees were not like his branches; nor any tree in the garden of God was like unto him in his beauty. Gen. 13:10
9 I have made him fair by the multitude of his branches: so that all the trees of Eden, that *were* in the garden of God, envied him.

31:3–9 From Noble to a Scourge

The rise and fall of the Assyrian Empire is rich in lessons for the nations of earth today. Inspiration has likened the glory of Assyria at the height of her prosperity to a noble tree in the garden of God, towering above the surrounding trees. . . .
But the rulers of Assyria, instead of using their unusual blessings for the benefit of mankind, became the scourge of many lands. *PK 362, 363*

Egypt's Pride

10 Therefore thus saith the Lord GOD; Because thou hast lifted up thyself in height, and he hath shot up his top among the thick boughs, and his heart is lifted up in his height;   Ezek. 28:17
11 I have therefore delivered him into the hand of the mighty one of the heathen; he shall surely deal with him: I have driven him out for his wickedness.   Deut. 18:12
12 And strangers, the terrible of the nations, have cut him off, and have left him: upon the mountains and in all the valleys his branches are fallen, and his boughs are broken by all the rivers of the land; and all the people of the earth are gone down from his shadow, and have left him.   Ezek. 28:7; 30:11; 35:8
13 Upon his ruin shall all the fowls of the heaven remain, and all the beasts of the field shall be upon his branches: Is. 18:6; Ezek. 29:5; 32:4
14 To the end that none of all the trees by the waters exalt themselves for their height, neither shoot up their top among the thick boughs, neither their trees stand up in their height, all that drink water: for they are all delivered unto death, to the ᵀnether parts of the earth, in the midst of the children of men, with them that go down to the pit.   *lower*
15 Thus saith the Lord GOD; In the day when he went down to the grave I caused a mourning: I covered the deep for him, and I restrained the floods thereof, and the great waters were ᵀstayed: and I caused Lebanon to mourn for him, and all the trees of the field fainted for him.   *held back*
16 I made the nations to shake at the sound of his fall, when I cast him down to hell with

them that descend into the pit: and all the trees of Eden, the choice and best of Lebanon, all that drink water, shall be comforted in the nether parts of the earth. Is. 14:8, 15; Ezek. 26:15

17 They also went down into hell with him unto *them that be* slain with the sword; and *they that were* his arm, *that* dwelt under his shadow in the midst of the heathen. Ps. 9:17

18 To whom art thou thus like in glory and in greatness among the trees of Eden? yet shalt thou be brought down with the trees of Eden unto the nether parts of the earth: thou shalt lie in the midst of the uncircumcised with *them that be* slain by the sword. This *is* Pharaoh and all his multitude, saith the Lord GOD. Ezek. 28:10; 32:19, 21

A Lamentation for Pharaoh

32 And it came to pass in the twelfth year, in the twelfth month, in the first *day* of the month, *that* the word of the LORD came unto me, saying, Ezek. 30:20

2 Son of man, take up a lamentation for Pharaoh king of Egypt, and say unto him, Thou art like a young lion of the nations, and thou *art* as a whale in the seas: and thou camest forth with thy rivers, and troubledst the waters with thy feet, and fouledst their rivers. Ezek. 27:2; 29:3; Nah. 2:11-13

3 Thus saith the Lord GOD; I will therefore spread out my net over thee with a company of many people; and they shall bring thee up in my net. Ezek. 12:13

4 Then will I leave thee upon the land, I will cast thee forth upon the open field, and will cause all the fowls of the heaven to remain upon thee, and I will fill the beasts of the whole earth with thee. Is. 18:6

5 And I will lay thy flesh upon the mountains, and fill the valleys with thy height.

6 I will also water with thy blood the land wherein thou swimmest, *even* to the mountains; and the rivers shall be full of thee. Is. 34:3

7 And when I shall put thee out, I will cover the heaven, and make the stars thereof dark; I will cover the sun with a cloud, and the moon shall not give her light. Is. 13:10; Joel 2:31

8 All the bright lights of heaven will I make dark over thee, and set darkness upon thy land, saith the Lord GOD. Gen. 1:14

9 I will also ᵀvex the hearts of many people, when I shall bring thy destruction among the nations, into the countries which thou hast not known. Rev. 18:10-15 ◆ *trouble*

10 Yea, I will make many people amazed at thee, and their kings shall be horribly afraid for thee, when I shall brandish my sword before them; and they shall tremble at *every* moment, every man for his own life, in the day of thy fall. Ezek. 26:16; 27:35

11 For thus saith the Lord GOD; The sword of the king of Babylon shall come upon thee.

12 By the swords of the mighty will I cause thy multitude to fall, the terrible of the nations, all of them: and they shall ᵀspoil the pomp of Egypt, and all the multitude thereof shall be destroyed. Ezek. 28:7; 29:19; 31:11 ◆ *plunder*

13 I will destroy also all the beasts thereof from beside the great waters; neither shall the foot of man trouble them any more, nor the hoofs of beasts trouble them. Ezek. 29:8, 11

14 Then will I make their waters deep, and cause their rivers to run like oil, saith the Lord GOD.

15 When I shall make the land of Egypt desolate, and the country shall be destitute of that whereof it was full, when I shall ᵀsmite all them that dwell therein, then shall they know that I *am* the LORD. Ex. 7:5; 14:4; Ezek. 6:7 ◆ *strike*

16 This *is* the lamentation wherewith they shall lament her: the daughters of the nations shall lament her: they shall lament for her, *even* for Egypt, and for all her multitude, saith the Lord GOD. 2 Sam. 1:17

Egypt Will be Brought Down

17 It came to pass also in the twelfth year, in the fifteenth *day* of the month, *that* the word of the LORD came unto me, saying, Ezek. 32:1

18 Son of man, wail for the multitude of Egypt, and cast them down, *even* her, and the daughters of the famous nations, unto the nether parts of the earth, with them that go down into the pit. Jer. 1:10; Ezek. 31:14; 32:2

19 Whom dost thou pass in beauty? go down, and be thou laid with the uncircumcised. Jer. 9:25-26; Ezek. 31:18; 32:29-30

20 They shall fall in the midst of *them that are* slain by the sword: she is delivered to the sword: draw her and all her multitudes. Ps. 28:3

21 The strong among the mighty shall speak to him out of the midst of hell with them that help him: they are gone down, they lie uncircumcised, slain by the sword. Is. 14:9-10

22 Asshur *is* there and all her company: his graves *are* about him: all of them slain, fallen by the sword: Ezek. 32:26

23 Whose graves are set in the sides of the pit, and her company is round about her grave: all of them slain, fallen by the sword, which caused terror in the land of the living. Ps. 27:13; Ezek. 26:17, 20

24 There *is* Elam and all her multitude round about her grave, all of them slain, fallen by the sword, which are gone down uncircumcised into the ᵀnether parts of the earth, which caused their terror in the land of the living; yet have they borne their shame with them that go down to the pit. Gen. 10:22 ◆ *lower*

25 They have set her a bed in the midst of

the slain with all her multitude: her graves *are* round about him: all of them uncircumcised, slain by the sword: though their terror was caused in the land of the living, yet have they borne their shame with them that go down to the pit: he is put in the midst of *them that be* slain. Ps. 139:8

26 There *is* Meshech, Tubal, and all her multitude: her graves *are* round about him: all of them uncircumcised, slain by the sword, though they caused their terror in the land of the living. Gen. 10:2; Ezek. 27:13; 38:2-3

27 And they shall not lie with the mighty *that are* fallen of the uncircumcised, which are gone down to hell with their weapons of war: and they have laid their swords under their heads, but their iniquities shall be upon their bones, though *they were* the terror of the mighty in the land of the living. Is. 14:18-19

28 Yea, thou shalt be broken in the midst of the uncircumcised, and shalt lie with *them that are* slain with the sword.

29 There *is* Edom, her kings, and all her princes, which with their might are laid by *them that were* slain by the sword: they shall lie with the uncircumcised, and with them that go down to the pit. Jer. 49:7-22

30 There *be* the princes of the north, all of them, and all the Zidonians, which are gone down with the slain; with their terror they are ashamed of their might; and they lie uncircumcised with *them that be* slain by the sword, and bear their shame with them that go down to the pit. Ezek. 28:21; 38:15

31 Pharaoh shall see them, and shall be comforted over all his multitude, *even* Pharaoh and all his army slain by the sword, saith the Lord GOD. Ezek. 14:22; 31:16

32 For I have caused my terror in the land of the living: and he shall be laid in the midst of the uncircumcised with *them that are* slain with the sword, *even* Pharaoh and all his multitude, saith the Lord GOD. Ezek. 32:27

Ezekiel Is a Watchman

33 Again the word of the LORD came unto me, saying,

2 Son of man, speak to the children of thy people, and say unto them, When I bring the sword upon a land, if the people of the land take a man of their coasts, and set him for their watchman: Ezek. 3:11; 33:17, 30

3 If when he seeth the sword come upon the land, he blow the trumpet, and warn the people; Hos. 8:1

4 Then whosoever heareth the sound of the trumpet, and taketh not warning; if the sword come, and take him away, his blood shall be upon his own head. 2 Chr. 25:16; Jer. 6:17; Ezek. 18:13

5 He heard the sound of the trumpet, and took not warning; his blood shall be upon him. But he that taketh warning shall deliver his soul. Ex. 9:19-21

6 But if the watchman see the sword come, and blow not the trumpet, and the people be not warned; if the sword come, and take *any* person from among them, he is taken away in his iniquity; but his blood will I require at the watchman's hand. Ezek. 18:20

7 So thou, O son of man, I have set thee a watchman unto the house of Israel; therefore thou shalt hear the word at my mouth, and warn them from me. Jer. 26:2

8 When I say unto the wicked, O wicked *man*, thou shalt surely die; if thou dost not speak to warn the wicked from his way, that wicked *man* shall die in his iniquity; but his blood will I require at thine hand. Ezek. 18:4

Faithful Watchmen

Ezekiel 33:7–9

The words of the prophet declare the solemn responsibility of those who are appointed as guardians of the church of God, stewards of the mysteries of God. They are to stand as watchmen on the walls of Zion, to sound the note of alarm at the approach of the enemy. Souls are in danger of falling under temptation, and they will perish unless God's ministers are faithful to their trust. If for any reason their spiritual senses become so benumbed that they are unable to discern danger, and through their failure to give warning the people perish, God will require at their hands the blood of those who are lost.

It is the privilege of the watchmen on the walls of Zion to live so near to God, and to be so susceptible to the impressions of His Spirit, that He can work through them to tell men and women of their peril and point them to the place of safety. Faithfully are they to warn them of the sure result of transgression, and faithfully are they to safeguard the interests of the church. At no time may they relax their vigilance. Theirs is a work requiring the exercise of every faculty of the being. In trumpet tones their voices are to be lifted, and never are they to sound one wavering, uncertain note. Not for wages are they to labor, but because they cannot do otherwise, because they realize that there is a woe upon them if they fail to preach the gospel. Chosen of God, sealed with the blood of consecration, they are to rescue men and women from impending destruction. *AA 361, 362*

9 Nevertheless, if thou warn the wicked of his way to turn from it; if he do not turn from his way, he shall die in his iniquity; but thou hast delivered thy soul.   Ezek. 3:19, 21; Acts 13:40

God Shows His Justice

10 Therefore, O thou son of man, speak unto the house of Israel; Thus ye speak, saying, If our ᵀtransgressions and our sins *be* upon us, and we pine away in them, how should we then live? Lev. 26:39 ◆ *violations of the law*

11 Say unto them, *As* I live, saith the Lord GOD, I have no pleasure in the death of the wicked; but that the wicked turn from his way and live: turn ye, turn ye from your evil ways; for why will ye die, O house of Israel?   Is. 49:18; Ezek. 18:23; 2 Pet. 3:9

33:11 God Delights to Rescue Sinners

The Lord seeks to save, not to destroy. He delights in the rescue of sinners. . . . By warnings and entreaties He calls the wayward to cease from their evil-doing and to turn to Him and live. He gives His chosen messengers a holy boldness, that those who hear may fear and be brought to repentance. . . . The messengers of the Lord are never to fear the face of man, but are to stand unflinchingly for the right. *PK 105*

---

12 Therefore, thou son of man, say unto the children of thy people, The righteousness of the righteous shall not deliver him in the day of his ᵀtransgression: as for the wickedness of the wicked, he shall not fall thereby in the day that he turneth from his wickedness; neither shall the righteous be able to live for his *righteousness* in the day that he sinneth.   2 Chr. 7:14; Ezek. 18:21 ◆ *lawlessness*

13 When I shall say to the righteous, *that* he shall surely live; if he trust to his own righteousness, and commit iniquity, all his righteousnesses shall not be remembered; but for his iniquity that he hath committed, he shall die for it.   Ezek. 18:24; Heb. 10:38

14 Again, when I say unto the wicked, Thou shalt surely die; if he turn from his sin, and do that which is lawful and right;   Is. 55:7

15 *If* the wicked restore the pledge, give again that he had robbed, walk in the statutes of life, without committing iniquity; he shall surely live, he shall not die.   Ex. 22:1-4; Ezek. 20:11

16 None of his sins that he hath committed shall be mentioned unto him: he hath done that which is lawful and right; he shall surely live.   Is. 1:18; 43:25; Ezek. 18:22

17 Yet the children of thy people say, The way of the Lord is not equal: but as for them, their way is not equal.   Ezek. 18:25

18 When the righteous turneth from his righteousness, and committeth iniquity, he shall even die thereby.   Ezek. 33:12-13

19 But if the wicked turn from his wickedness, and do that which is lawful and right, he shall live thereby.

20 Yet ye say, The way of the Lord is not equal. O ye house of Israel, I will judge you every one after his ways.   Ezek. 18:25

Ezekiel Receives News of Jerusalem's Fall

21 And it came to pass in the twelfth year of our captivity, in the tenth *month*, in the fifth *day* of the month, *that* one that had escaped out of Jerusalem came unto me, saying, The city is smitten.   2 Kin. 25:10

22 Now the hand of the LORD was upon me in the evening, afore he that was escaped came; and had opened my mouth, until he came to me in the morning; and my mouth was opened, and I was no more ᵀdumb.   Ezek. 1:3; 3:26-27; 24:26-27 ◆ *mute*

23 Then the word of the LORD came unto me, saying,

24 Son of man, they that inhabit those wastes of the land of Israel speak, saying, Abraham was one, and he inherited the land: but we *are* many; the land is given us for inheritance.   Is. 51:2; Ezek. 33:27; Acts 7:5

25 Wherefore say unto them, Thus saith the Lord GOD; Ye eat with the blood, and lift up your eyes toward your idols, and shed blood: and shall ye possess the land?   Gen. 9:4

26 Ye stand upon your sword, ye work abomination, and ye defile every one his neighbour's wife: and shall ye possess the land?   Gen. 27:40

27 Say thou thus unto them, Thus saith the Lord GOD; *As* I live, surely they that *are* in the wastes shall fall by the sword, and him that *is* in the open field will I give to the beasts to be devoured, and they that *be* in the forts and in the caves shall die of the pestilence.   1 Sam. 13:6

28 For I will lay the land most desolate, and the pomp of her strength shall cease; and the mountains of Israel shall be desolate, that none shall pass through.   Ezek. 7:24

29 Then shall they know that I *am* the LORD, when I have laid the land most desolate because of all their abominations which they have committed.   Ezek. 6:7

God's Judgment on the Mockers

30 Also, thou son of man, the children of thy people still are talking against thee by the walls and in the doors of the houses, and speak one to another, every one to his brother, saying, Come, I pray you, and hear what is the word that cometh forth from the LORD.   Is. 29:13

31 And they come unto thee as the people cometh, and they sit before thee *as* my people, and they hear thy words, but they will not do them: for with their mouth they shew much love, *but* their heart goeth after their covetousness. Ps. 78:36-37; Is. 29:13; Ezek. 8:1
32 And, lo, thou *art* unto them as a very lovely song of one that hath a pleasant voice, and can play well on an instrument: for they hear thy words, but they do them not. Mark 6:20

33:30-32 How to Regard the Bible

It is one thing to treat the Bible as a book of good moral instruction, to be heeded so far as is consistent with the spirit of the times and our position in the world; it is another thing to regard it as it really is—the word of the living God, the word that is our life, the word that is to mold our actions, our words, and our thoughts. To hold God's word as anything less than this is to reject it. *Ed 260*

33 And when this cometh to pass, (lo, it will come,) then shall they know that a prophet hath been among them. Jer. 28:9

The Promise of a New Shepherd

34 And the word of the LORD came unto me, saying,
2 Son of man, prophesy against the shepherds of Israel, prophesy, and say unto them, Thus saith the Lord GOD unto the shepherds; Woe *be* to the shepherds of Israel that do feed themselves! should not the shepherds feed the flocks? Ps. 78:71-72; Is. 40:11; Jer. 23:1
3 Ye eat the fat, and ye clothe you with the wool, ye kill them that are fed: *but* ye feed not the flock. Zech. 11:5, 16
4 The diseased have ye not strengthened, neither have ye healed that which was sick, neither have ye bound up *that which was* broken, neither have ye brought again that which was driven away, neither have ye sought that which was lost; but with force and with cruelty have ye ruled them. Ex. 1:13-14

34:2-4 Faithful Undershepherds

Christ, the Chief Shepherd, has entrusted the care of His flock to His ministers as undershepherds; and He bids them have the same interest that He has manifested, and feel the sacred responsibility of the charge He has entrusted to them. He has solemnly commanded them to be faithful, to feed the flock, to strengthen the weak, to revive the fainting, and to shield them from devouring wolves. *PP 191*

5 And they were scattered, because *there is* no shepherd: and they became meat to all the beasts of the field, when they were scattered. Matt. 9:36

6 My sheep wandered through all the mountains, and upon every high hill: yea, my flock was scattered upon all the face of the earth, and none did search or seek *after them*. Ps. 142:4
7 Therefore, ye shepherds, hear the word of the LORD;
8 *As* I live, saith the Lord GOD, surely because my flock became a prey, and my flock became meat to every beast of the field, because *there was* no shepherd, neither did my shepherds search for my flock, but the shepherds fed themselves, and fed not my flock;
9 Therefore, O ye shepherds, hear the word of the LORD;
10 Thus saith the Lord GOD; Behold, I *am* against the shepherds; and I will require my flock at their hand, and cause them to cease from feeding the flock; neither shall the shepherds feed themselves any more; for I will deliver my flock from their mouth, that they may not be meat for them. Jer. 21:13
11 For thus saith the Lord GOD; Behold, I, *even* I, will both search my sheep, and seek them out. Luke 19:10
12 As a shepherd seeketh out his flock in the day that he is among his sheep *that are* scattered; so will I seek out my sheep, and will deliver them out of all places where they have been scattered in the cloudy and dark day. Jer. 13:16; Ezek. 30:3; Zeph. 1:15

34:12 God Loves Every Soul

As the shepherd loves his sheep, and cannot rest if even one be missing, so, in an infinitely higher degree, does God love every outcast soul. Men may deny the claim of His love, they may wander from Him, they may choose another master; yet they are God's, and He longs to recover His own. *COL 187*

13 And I will bring them out from the people, and gather them from the countries, and will bring them to their own land, and feed them upon the mountains of Israel by the rivers, and in all the inhabited places of the country. Ezek. 11:17
14 I will feed them in a good pasture, and upon the high mountains of Israel shall their fold be: there shall they lie in a good fold, and *in* a fat pasture shall they feed upon the mountains of Israel. John 10:9
15 I will feed my flock, and I will cause them to lie down, saith the Lord GOD.
16 I will seek that which was lost, and bring again that which was driven away, and will bind up *that which was* broken, and will strengthen that which was sick: but I will destroy the fat and the strong; I will feed them with judgment. Is. 10:16; 49:26; Ezek. 34:4
17 And *as for* you, O my flock, thus saith the

Lord GOD; Behold, I judge between cattle and cattle, between the rams and the he goats.   Matt. 25:32-33

18 *Seemeth it* a small thing unto you to have eaten up the good pasture, but ye must tread down with your feet the residue of your pastures? and to have drunk of the deep waters, but ye must foul the residue with your feet?   Num. 16:9

19 And *as for* my flock, they eat that which ye have ᵀtrodden with your feet; and they drink that which ye have fouled with your feet.   trampled

20 Therefore thus saith the Lord GOD unto them; Behold, I, *even* I, will judge between the fat cattle and between the lean cattle.

21 Because ye have thrust with side and with shoulder, and pushed all the diseased with your horns, till ye have scattered them abroad;   Deut. 33:17

22 Therefore will I save my flock, and they shall no more be a prey; and I will judge between cattle and cattle.   Ps. 72:12-14

23 And I will set up one shepherd over them, and he shall feed them, *even* my servant David; he shall feed them, and he shall be their shepherd.   Is. 40:11

24 And I the LORD will be their God, and my servant David a prince among them; I the LORD have spoken *it*.   Ezek. 36:28

25 And I will make with them a covenant of peace, and will cause the evil beasts to cease out of the land: and they shall dwell safely in the wilderness, and sleep in the woods.   Lev. 26:6; Is. 11:6-9; Ezek. 37:26

26 And I will make them and the places round about my hill a blessing; and I will cause the shower to come down in his season; there shall be showers of blessing.   Gen. 12:2; Lev. 26:4

34:26 Ministering Gladly to Others

Those who receive are to impart to others. From every direction are coming calls for help. God calls upon men to minister gladly to their fellow men. Immortal crowns are to be won; the kingdom of heaven is to be gained; the world, perishing in ignorance, is to be enlightened. *MH 103*

27 And the tree of the field shall yield her fruit, and the earth shall yield her increase, and they shall be safe in their land, and shall know that I *am* the LORD, when I have broken the bands of their yoke, and delivered them out of the hand of those that served themselves of them.   Lev. 26:4, 13; Jer. 30:8

28 And they shall no more be a prey to the heathen, neither shall the beast of the land devour them; but they shall dwell safely, and none shall make *them* afraid.   Jer. 30:10

29 And I will raise up for them a plant of renown, and they shall be no more consumed with hunger in the land, neither bear the shame of the heathen any more.   Ezek. 36:15, 29

30 Thus shall they know that I the LORD their God *am* with them, and *that* they, *even* the house of Israel, *are* my people, saith the Lord GOD.   Ps. 46:7

31 And ye my flock, the flock of my pasture, *are* men, *and* I *am* your God, saith the Lord GOD.   Ps. 78:52; 80:1; 100:3

Judgment on Edom

35 Moreover the word of the LORD came unto me, saying,

2 Son of man, set thy face against mount Seir, and prophesy against it,   Gen. 32:3

3 And say unto it, Thus saith the Lord GOD; Behold, O mount Seir, I *am* against thee, and

The Infinite Love and Care of Jesus

Ezekiel 34:31

As the shepherd leads his flock over the rocky hills, through forest and wild ravines, to grassy nooks by the riverside; as he watches them on the mountains through the lonely night, shielding from robbers, caring tenderly for the sickly and feeble, his life comes to be one with theirs. A strong and tender attachment unites him to the objects of his care. However large the flock, the shepherd knows every sheep. Every one has its name, and responds to the name at the shepherd's call. . . .

Jesus knows us individually, and is touched with the feeling of our infirmities. He knows us all by name. He knows the very house in which we live, the name of each occupant. He has at times given directions to His servants to go to a certain street in a certain city, to such a house, to find one of His sheep.

Every soul is as fully known to Jesus as if he were the only one for whom the Saviour died. The distress of every one touches His heart. The cry for aid reaches His ear. He came to draw all men unto Himself. He bids them, "Follow Me," and His Spirit moves upon their hearts to draw them to come to Him. Many refuse to be drawn. Jesus knows who they are. He also knows who gladly hear His call, and are ready to come under His pastoral care. He says, "My sheep hear My voice, and I know them, and they follow Me" [John 10:27]. He cares for each one as if there were not another on the face of the earth. *DA 479, 480*

I will stretch out mine hand against thee, and I will make thee most desolate. Jer. 6:12

4 I will lay thy cities waste, and thou shalt be desolate, and thou shalt know that I *am* the LORD. Ezek. 35:9; Mal. 1:3-4

5 Because thou hast had a perpetual hatred, and hast shed *the blood of* the children of Israel by the force of the sword in the time of their calamity, in the time *that their* iniquity *had* an end: Ps. 137:7; Ezek. 21:25, 29

6 Therefore, *as* I live, saith the Lord GOD, I will prepare thee unto blood, and blood shall pursue thee: ᵀsith thou hast not hated blood, even blood shall pursue thee. Is. 63:2-6 ◆ *since*

7 Thus will I make mount Seir most desolate, and cut off from it him that passeth out and him that returneth. Ezek. 29:11

8 And I will fill his mountains with his slain *men*: in thy hills, and in thy valleys, and in all thy rivers, shall they fall that are slain with the sword. Ezek. 31:12; 32:4-5; 39:4-5

9 I will make thee perpetual desolations, and thy cities shall not return: and ye shall know that I *am* the LORD. Ezek. 6:7

10 Because thou hast said, These two nations and these two countries shall be mine, and we will possess it; whereas the LORD was there: Ps. 48:1-3; Ezek. 36:5; 48:35

11 Therefore, *as* I live, saith the Lord GOD, I will even do according to thine anger, and according to thine envy which thou hast used out of thy hatred against them; and I will make myself known among them, when I have judged thee. Ps. 9:16

12 And thou shalt know that I *am* the LORD, *and that* I have heard all thy blasphemies which thou hast spoken against the mountains of Israel, saying, They are laid desolate, they are given us to consume. Ezek. 36:2

13 Thus with your mouth ye have boasted against me, and have multiplied your words against me: I have heard *them*. Dan. 11:36

14 Thus saith the Lord GOD; When the whole earth rejoiceth, I will make thee desolate.

15 As thou didst rejoice at the inheritance of the house of Israel, because it was desolate, so will I do unto thee: thou shalt be desolate, O mount Seir, and all Idumea, *even* all of it: and they shall know that I *am* the LORD. Is. 34:5-6

Blessings for Israel

36 Also, thou son of man, prophesy unto the mountains of Israel, and say, Ye mountains of Israel, hear the word of the LORD:

2 Thus saith the Lord GOD; Because the enemy hath said against you, Aha, even the ancient high places are ours in possession:

3 Therefore prophesy and say, Thus saith the Lord GOD; Because they have made *you* desolate, and swallowed you up on every side, that ye might be a possession unto the residue of the heathen, and ye are taken up in the lips of talkers, and *are* an ᵀinfamy of the people: Ps. 44:13-14 ◆ *evil report*

4 Therefore, ye mountains of Israel, hear the word of the Lord GOD; Thus saith the Lord GOD to the mountains, and to the hills, to the rivers, and to the valleys, to the desolate wastes, and to the cities that are forsaken, which became a prey and derision to the residue of the heathen that *are* round about; Deut. 11:11

5 Therefore thus saith the Lord GOD; Surely in the fire of my jealousy have I spoken against the residue of the heathen, and against all Idumea, which have appointed my land into their possession with the joy of all *their* heart, with despiteful minds, to cast it out for a prey. Ezek. 36:3

6 Prophesy therefore concerning the land of Israel, and say unto the mountains, and to the hills, to the rivers, and to the valleys, Thus saith the Lord GOD; Behold, I have spoken in my jealousy and in my fury, because ye have borne the shame of the heathen: Ps. 123:3-4

7 Therefore thus saith the Lord GOD; I have lifted up mine hand, Surely the heathen that *are* about you, they shall bear their shame. Ezek. 20:5

8 But ye, O mountains of Israel, ye shall shoot forth your branches, and yield your fruit to my people of Israel; for they are at hand to come. Is. 27:6

9 For, behold, I *am* for you, and I will turn unto you, and ye shall be tilled and sown:

10 And I will multiply men upon you, all the house of Israel, *even* all of it: and the cities shall be inhabited, and the wastes shall be builded: Is. 27:6; Jer. 30:19; Ezek. 36:33

11 And I will multiply upon you man and beast; and they shall increase and bring fruit: and I will settle you after your old estates, and will do better *unto you* than at your beginnings: and ye shall know that I *am* the LORD. Mic. 7:14

12 Yea, I will cause men to walk upon you, *even* my people Israel; and they shall possess thee, and thou shalt be their inheritance, and thou shalt no more ᵀhenceforth bereave them *of men*. Jer. 15:7 ◆ *from this time forward*

13 Thus saith the Lord GOD; Because they say unto you, Thou *land* devourest up men, and hast bereaved thy nations; Num. 13:32

14 Therefore thou shalt devour men no more, neither bereave thy nations any more, saith the Lord GOD.

15 Neither will I cause *men* to hear in thee the shame of the heathen any more, neither shalt thou bear the reproach of the people any more, neither shalt thou cause thy nations to fall any more, saith the Lord God.   Ps. 89:50

Israel Was Rejected because of Sin

16 Moreover the word of the Lord came unto me, saying,
17 Son of man, when the house of Israel dwelt in their own land, they defiled it by their own way and by their doings: their way was before me as the uncleanness of a removed woman.   Jer. 2:7
18 Wherefore I poured my fury upon them for the blood that they had shed upon the land, and for their idols *wherewith* they had polluted it: 2 Chr. 34:21
19 And I scattered them among the heathen, and they were dispersed through the countries: according to their way and according to their doings I judged them.   Deut. 28:64
20 And when they entered unto the heathen, whither they went, they profaned my holy name, when they said to them, These *are* the people of the Lord, and are gone forth out of his land.   Is. 52:5; Jer. 33:24; Rom. 2:24
21 But I had pity for mine holy name, which the house of Israel had profaned among the heathen, whither they went.   Ps. 74:18
22 Therefore say unto the house of Israel, Thus saith the Lord God; I do not *this* for your sakes, O house of Israel, but for mine holy name's sake, which ye have profaned among the heathen, whither ye went.   Ezek. 36:32
23 And I will sanctify my great name, which was profaned among the heathen, which ye have profaned in the midst of them; and the heathen shall know that I *am* the Lord, saith the Lord God, when I shall be sanctified in you before their eyes.   Is. 5:16; Ezek. 20:41; 39:7
24 For I will take you from among the heathen, and gather you out of all countries, and will bring you into your own land.   Is. 43:5-6
25 Then will I sprinkle clean water upon you, and ye shall be clean: from all your filthiness, and from all your idols, will I cleanse you.   Ps. 51:7; Is. 4:4; Heb. 10:22

36:25 Necessity of Self-Knowledge

In the whole Satanic force there is not power to overcome one soul who in simple trust casts himself on Christ. . . .

But we must have a knowledge of ourselves, a knowledge that will result in contrition, before we can find pardon and peace. . . . It is only he who knows himself to be a sinner that Christ can save. *COL 157, 158*

---

26 A new heart also will I give you, and a new spirit will I put within you: and I will take away the stony heart out of your flesh, and I will give you an heart of flesh. Zech. 7:12

36:26, 27

36:26 Our Great Need

You feel that sin has separated you from God, that you are in bondage to the power of evil. The more you struggle to escape, the more you realize your helplessness. . . . You long to be forgiven, to be cleansed, to be set free. . . .

You can never hope, by your own efforts, to secure it [Heaven's forgiveness and peace and love in the soul]. But God offers it to you as a gift. . . . It is yours if you will but reach out your hand and grasp it. *SC 49*

---

27 And I will put my spirit within you, and cause you to walk in my statutes, and ye shall keep my judgments, and do *them*. Ezek. 37:14, 24

> The Christian Life   See 2 Corinthians 5:17.

28 And ye shall dwell in the land that I gave to your fathers; and ye shall be my people, and I will be your God.   Ezek. 37:27
29 I will also save you from all your uncleannesses: and I will call for the corn, and will increase it, and lay no famine upon you.
30 And I will multiply the fruit of the tree, and the increase of the field, that ye shall receive no more reproach of famine among the heathen.   Ezek. 34:27
31 Then shall ye remember your own evil ways, and your doings that *were* not good, and shall lothe yourselves in your own sight for your iniquities and for your abominations.   Ezek. 6:9

36:31 Contrast of Our Character With Christ's

The nearer we come to Jesus and the more clearly we discern the purity of His character, the more clearly we shall discern the exceeding sinfulness of sin and the less we shall feel like exalting ourselves. Those whom heaven recognizes as holy ones are the last to parade their own goodness. *COL 160*

---

32 Not for your sakes do I *this*, saith the Lord God, be it known unto you: be ashamed and confounded for your own ways, O house of Israel.   Deut. 9:5
33 Thus saith the Lord God; In the day that I shall have cleansed you from all your iniquities I will also cause *you* to dwell in the cities, and the wastes shall be builded.   Ezek. 36:10
34 And the desolate land shall be tilled, whereas it lay desolate in the sight of all that passed by.
35 And they shall say, This land that was desolate is become like the garden of Eden; and

the waste and desolate and ruined cities *are become* fenced, *and* are inhabited. Is. 51:3; Joel 2:3
36 Then the heathen that are left round about you shall know that I the LORD build the ruined *places, and* plant that that was desolate: I the LORD have spoken *it*, and I will do *it*. Ezek. 17:24
37 Thus saith the Lord GOD; I will yet *for* this be enquired of by the house of Israel, to do *it* for them; I will increase them with men like a flock. Ezek. 14:3
38 As the holy flock, as the flock of Jerusalem in her solemn feasts; so shall the waste cities be filled with flocks of men: and they shall know that I *am* the LORD. John 10:16

The Valley of Dry Bones

37 The hand of the LORD was upon me, and carried me out in the spirit of the LORD, and set me down in the midst of the valley which *was* full of bones, Ezek. 1:3; 8:3; 11:24
2 And caused me to pass by them round about: and, behold, *there were* very many in the open valley; and, lo, *they were* very dry.
3 And he said unto me, Son of man, can these bones live? And I answered, O Lord GOD, thou knowest. 1 Sam. 2:6
4 Again he said unto me, Prophesy upon these bones, and say unto them, O ye dry bones, hear the word of the LORD. Jer. 22:29
5 Thus saith the Lord GOD unto these bones; Behold, I will cause breath to enter into you, and ye shall live: Gen. 2:7; Ps. 104:29-30; Ezek. 37:9-10
6 And I will lay sinews upon you, and will bring up flesh upon you, and cover you with skin, and put breath in you, and ye shall live; and ye shall know that I *am* the LORD. Ezek. 38:23
7 So I prophesied as I was commanded: and as I prophesied, there was a noise, and behold a shaking, and the bones came together, bone to his bone. Jer. 13:5-7
8 And when I beheld, lo, the sinews and the flesh came up upon them, and the skin covered them above: but *there was* no breath in them.
9 Then said he unto me, Prophesy unto the wind, prophesy, son of man, and say to the wind, Thus saith the Lord GOD; Come from the four winds, O breath, and breathe upon these slain, that they may live.
10 So I prophesied as he commanded me, and the breath came into them, and they lived, and stood up upon their feet, an exceeding great army. Rev. 11:11
11 Then he said unto me, Son of man, these bones are the whole house of Israel: behold, they say, Our bones are dried, and our hope is lost: we are cut off for our parts. Ps. 141:7
12 Therefore prophesy and say unto them, Thus saith the Lord GOD; Behold, O my

people, I will open your graves, and cause you to come up out of your graves, and bring you into the land of Israel. Is. 26:19; 66:14; Hos. 13:14
13 And ye shall know that I *am* the LORD, when I have opened your graves, O my people, and brought you up out of your graves,
14 And shall put my spirit in you, and ye shall live, and I shall place you in your own land: then shall ye know that I the LORD have spoken *it*, and performed *it*, saith the LORD. Is. 32:15; Ezek. 36:27; Joel 2:28-29

Uniting the Two Sticks

15 The word of the LORD came again unto me, saying,
16 Moreover, thou son of man, take thee one stick, and write upon it, For Judah, and for the children of Israel his companions: then take another stick, and write upon it, For Joseph, the stick of Ephraim, and *for* all the house of Israel his companions: Num. 17:2-3; 2 Chr. 10:17
17 And join them one to another into one stick; and they shall become one in thine hand. Is. 11:13; Jer. 50:4; Hos. 1:11
18 And when the children of thy people shall speak unto thee, saying, Wilt thou not shew us what thou *meanest* by these? Ezek. 12:9
19 Say unto them, Thus saith the Lord GOD; Behold, I will take the stick of Joseph, which *is* in the hand of Ephraim, and the tribes of Israel his fellows, and will put them with him, *even* with the stick of Judah, and make them one stick, and they shall be one in mine hand. Ezek. 37:16-17
20 And the sticks whereon thou writest shall be in thine hand before their eyes. Ezek. 12:3
21 And say unto them, Thus saith the Lord GOD; Behold, I will take the children of Israel from among the heathen, whither they be gone, and will gather them on every side, and bring them into their own land: Jer. 29:14
22 And I will make them one nation in the land upon the mountains of Israel; and one king shall be king to them all: and they shall be no more two nations, neither shall they be divided into two kingdoms any more at all: Jer. 3:18
23 Neither shall they defile themselves any more with their idols, nor with their detestable things, nor with any of their ᵀtransgressions: but I will save them out of all their dwellingplaces, wherein they have sinned, and will cleanse them: so shall they be my people, and I will be their God. *violations of the law*
24 And David my servant *shall be* king over them; and they all shall have one shepherd: they shall also walk in my judgments, and observe my statutes, and do them. Is. 40:11
25 And they shall dwell in the land that I have given unto Jacob my servant, wherein your fathers have dwelt; and they shall

dwell therein, *even* they, and their children, and their children's children for ever: and my servant David *shall be* their prince for ever. Ezek. 28:25

26 Moreover I will make a covenant of peace with them; it shall be an everlasting covenant with them: and I will place them, and multiply them, and will set my sanctuary in the midst of them for evermore. Is. 55:3; Jer. 30:19; Ezek. 34:25

27 My tabernacle also shall be with them: yea, I will be their God, and they shall be my people. Ezek. 37:23

28 And the heathen shall know that I the LORD do ᵀsanctify Israel, when my sanctuary shall be in the midst of them for evermore. Ex. 31:13; Ezek. 20:12; 36:23 ◆ *make holy*

The Destruction of Gog

38 And the word of the LORD came unto me, saying,

2 Son of man, set thy face against Gog, the land of Magog, the chief prince of Meshech and Tubal, and prophesy against him, Gen. 10:2

3 And say, Thus saith the Lord GOD; Behold, I *am* against thee, O Gog, the chief prince of Meshech and Tubal: Ezek. 13:8

4 And I will turn thee back, and put hooks into thy jaws, and I will bring thee forth, and all thine army, horses and horsemen, all of them clothed with all sorts *of armour, even* a great company *with* bucklers and shields, all of them handling swords: Ezek. 29:4

5 Persia, Ethiopia, and Libya with them; all of them with shield and helmet: Gen. 10:6

6 Gomer, and all his bands; the house of Togarmah of the north quarters, and all his bands: *and* many people with thee. Gen. 10:2-3

7 Be thou prepared, and prepare for thyself, thou, and all thy company that are assembled unto thee, and be thou a guard unto them. Is. 8:9-10

8 After many days thou shalt be visited: in the latter years thou shalt come into the land *that is* brought back from the sword, *and is* gathered out of many people, against the mountains of Israel, which have been always waste: but it is brought forth out of the nations, and they shall dwell safely all of them. Is. 24:22; Jer. 23:6; Ezek. 38:16

9 Thou shalt ascend and come like a storm, thou shalt be like a cloud to cover the land, thou, and all thy bands, and many people with thee. Is. 28:2; Jer. 4:13; Joel 2:2

10 Thus saith the Lord GOD; It shall also come to pass, *that* at the same time shall things come into thy mind, and thou shalt think an evil thought: Ps. 36:4

11 And thou shalt say, I will go up to the land of unwalled villages; I will go to them that are at rest, that dwell safely, all of them

dwelling without walls, and having neither bars nor gates, Zech. 2:4-5

12 To take a ᵀspoil, and to take a prey; to turn thine hand upon the desolate places *that are now* inhabited, and upon the people *that are* gathered out of the nations, which have gotten cattle and goods, that dwell in the midst of the land. Is. 10:6 ◆ *plunder*

13 Sheba, and Dedan, and the merchants of Tarshish, with all the young lions thereof, shall say unto thee, Art thou come to take a spoil? hast thou gathered thy company to take a prey? to carry away silver and gold, to take away cattle and goods, to take a great spoil? Ezek. 27:15

God's Judgment against Gog

14 Therefore, son of man, prophesy and say unto Gog, Thus saith the Lord GOD; In that day when my people of Israel dwelleth safely, shalt thou not know *it*? Ezek. 38:8, 11; Zech. 2:5

15 And thou shalt come from thy place out of the north parts, thou, and many people with thee, all of them riding upon horses, a great company, and a mighty army: Ezek. 38:6; 39:2

16 And thou shalt come up against my people of Israel, as a cloud to cover the land; it shall be in the latter days, and I will bring thee against my land, that the heathen may know me, when I shall be ᵀsanctified in thee, O Gog, before their eyes. Ezek. 38:23 ◆ *made holy*

17 Thus saith the Lord GOD; *Art* thou he of whom I have spoken in old time by my servants the prophets of Israel, which prophesied in those days *many* years that I would bring thee against them? Is. 34:1-6

18 And it shall come to pass at the same time when Gog shall come against the land of Israel, saith the Lord GOD, *that* my fury shall come up in my face.

19 For in my jealousy *and* in the fire of my wrath have I spoken, Surely in that day there shall be a great shaking in the land of Israel; Hag. 2:6-7

20 So that the fishes of the sea, and the fowls of the heaven, and the beasts of the field, and all creeping things that creep upon the earth, and all the men that *are* upon the face of the earth, shall shake at my presence, and the mountains shall be thrown down, and the steep places shall fall, and every wall shall fall to the ground. Hos. 4:3; Nah. 1:4-6

21 And I will call for a sword against him throughout all my mountains, saith the Lord GOD: every man's sword shall be against his brother. Judg. 7:22

22 And I will plead against him with pestilence and with blood; and I will rain upon him, and upon his bands, and upon the many people that *are* with him, an over-

flowing rain, and great hailstones, fire, and ᵀbrimstone.   Ps. 11:6; Is. 66:16; Jer. 25:31 ✦ *sulphur*
23 Thus will I magnify myself, and ᵀsanctify myself; and I will be known in the eyes of many nations, and they shall know that I *am* the LORD.   Ezek. 36:23 ✦ *make holy*

Gog Shall Be Destroyed

39 Therefore, thou son of man, prophesy against Gog, and say, Thus saith the Lord GOD; Behold, I *am* against thee, O Gog, the chief prince of Meshech and Tubal: Ezek. 38:2-3
2 And I will turn thee back, and leave but the sixth part of thee, and will cause thee to come up from the north parts, and will bring thee upon the mountains of Israel: Ezek. 38:15
3 And I will ᵀsmite thy bow out of thy left hand, and will cause thine arrows to fall out of thy right hand. Ps. 76:3; Jer. 21:4-5; Hos. 1:5 ✦ *strike*
4 Thou shalt fall upon the mountains of Israel, thou, and all thy bands, and the people that *is* with thee: I will give thee unto the ravenous birds of every sort, and *to* the beasts of the field to be devoured. Ezek. 33:27
5 Thou shalt fall upon the open field: for I have spoken *it*, saith the Lord GOD.
6 And I will send a fire on Magog, and among them that dwell carelessly in the isles: and they shall know that I *am* the LORD.   Jer. 25:22
7 So will I make my holy name known in the midst of my people Israel; and I will not *let them* pollute my holy name any more: and the heathen shall know that I *am* the LORD, the Holy One in Israel.   Ex. 20:7; Ezek. 38:16, 23

Israel's Victory

8 Behold, it is come, and it is done, saith the Lord GOD; this *is* the day whereof I have spoken.   Ezek. 38:17
9 And they that dwell in the cities of Israel shall go forth, and shall set on fire and burn the weapons, both the shields and the bucklers, the bows and the arrows, and the handstaves, and the spears, and they shall burn them with fire seven years: Josh. 11:6; Ps. 46:9
10 So that they shall take no wood out of the field, neither cut down *any* out of the forests; for they shall burn the weapons with fire: and they shall ᵀspoil those that spoiled them, and rob those that robbed them, saith the Lord GOD.   Is. 14:2; 33:1; Mic. 5:8 ✦ *plunder*
11 And it shall come to pass in that day, *that* I will give unto Gog a place there of graves in Israel, the valley of the passengers on the east of the sea: and it shall stop the *noses* of the passengers: and there shall they bury Gog and all his multitude: and they shall call *it* The valley of Hamon-gog.
12 And seven months shall the house of Israel be burying of them, that they may cleanse the land.   Deut. 21:23; Ezek. 39:14, 16
13 Yea, all the people of the land shall bury *them*; and it shall be to them a renown the day that I shall be glorified, saith the Lord GOD.   Jer. 33:9; Ezek. 28:22; Zeph. 3:19-20
14 And they shall sever out men of continual employment, passing through the land to bury with the passengers those that remain upon the face of the earth, to cleanse it: after the end of seven months shall they search.
15 And the passengers *that* pass through the land, when *any* seeth a man's bone, then shall he set up a sign by it, till the buriers have buried it in the valley of Hamon-gog.
16 And also the name of the city *shall be* Hamonah. Thus shall they cleanse the land.
17 And, thou son of man, thus saith the Lord GOD; Speak unto every feathered fowl, and to every beast of the field, Assemble yourselves, and come; gather yourselves on every side to my sacrifice that I do sacrifice for you, *even* a great sacrifice upon the mountains of Israel, that ye may eat flesh, and drink blood.   Jer. 12:9; Ezek. 39:4; Zeph. 1:7
18 Ye shall eat the flesh of the mighty, and drink the blood of the princes of the earth, of rams, of lambs, and of goats, of bullocks, all of them fatlings of Bashan.   Ps. 22:12; Jer. 50:27
19 And ye shall eat fat till ye be full, and drink blood till ye be drunken, of my sacrifice which I have sacrificed for you.
20 Thus ye shall be filled at my table with horses and chariots, with mighty men, and with all men of war, saith the Lord GOD.
21 And I will set my glory among the heathen, and all the heathen shall see my judgment that I have executed, and my hand that I have laid upon them.   Ex. 9:16
22 So the house of Israel shall know that I *am* the LORD their God from that day and forward.   Jer. 24:7
23 And the heathen shall know that the house of Israel went into captivity for their iniquity: because they ᵀtrespassed against me, therefore hid I my face from them, and gave them into the hand of their enemies: so fell they all by the sword.   Is. 1:15 ✦ *sinned*
24 According to their uncleanness and according to their ᵀtransgressions have I done unto them, and hid my face from them.   Jer. 2:17 ✦ *sins*

Israel Shall Be Restored

25 Therefore thus saith the Lord GOD; Now will I bring again the captivity of Jacob, and have mercy upon the whole house of Israel, and will be jealous for my holy name;
26 After that they have borne their shame, and all their ᵀtrespasses whereby they have

trespassed against me, when they dwelt safely in their land, and none made *them* afraid.   *1 Kin. 4:25* ♦ *sins*

27 When I have brought them again from the people, and gathered them out of their enemies' lands, and am ᵀsanctified in them in the sight of many nations;   *Ezek. 36:23-24* ♦ *made holy*

28 Then shall they know that I *am* the LORD their God, which caused them to be led into captivity among the heathen: but I have gathered them unto their own land, and have left none of them any more there.   *Ezek. 39:22*

29 Neither will I hide my face any more from them: for I have poured out my spirit upon the house of Israel, saith the Lord GOD.   *Is. 32:15; Joel 2:28*

The New Temple of God

40 In the five and twentieth year of our captivity, in the beginning of the year, in the tenth *day* of the month, in the fourteenth year after that the city was smitten, in the selfsame day the hand of the LORD was upon me, and brought me thither.   *Ezek. 1:2-3; 3:14; 33:21*

2 In the visions of God brought he me into the land of Israel, and set me upon a very high mountain, by which *was* as the frame of a city on the south.   *Ezek. 1:1*

3 And he brought me thither, and, behold, *there was* a man, whose appearance *was* like the appearance of brass, with a line of flax in his hand, and a measuring reed; and he stood in the gate.   *Ezek. 1:7; 47:3; Rev. 11:1*

4 And the man said unto me, Son of man, behold with thine eyes, and hear with thine ears, and set thine heart upon all that I shall shew thee; for to the intent that I might shew *them* unto thee *art* thou brought ᵀhither: declare all that thou seest to the house of Israel.   *Is. 21:10; Jer. 26:2; Ezek. 44:5* ♦ *here*

5 And behold a wall on the outside of the house round about, and in the man's hand a measuring reed of six cubits *long* by the cubit and an hand breadth: so he measured the breadth of the building, one reed; and the height, one reed.   *Is. 26:1; Ezek. 42:20*

6 Then came he unto the gate which looketh toward the east, and went up the stairs thereof, and measured the threshold of the gate, *which was* one reed broad; and the other threshold *of the gate, which was* one reed broad.   *Ezek. 8:16*

7 And *every* little chamber *was* one reed long, and one reed broad; and between the little chambers *were* five cubits; and the threshold of the gate by the porch of the gate within *was* one reed.   *Ezek. 40:36*

8 He measured also the porch of the gate within, one reed.

9 Then measured he the porch of the gate, eight cubits; and the posts thereof, two cubits; and the porch of the gate *was* inward.

10 And the little chambers of the gate eastward *were* three on this side, and three on that side; they three *were* of one measure: and the posts had one measure on this side and on that side.

11 And he measured the breadth of the entry of the gate, ten cubits; *and* the length of the gate, thirteen cubits.

12 The space also before the little chambers *was* one cubit *on this side,* and the space *was* one cubit on that side: and the little chambers *were* six cubits on this side, and six cubits on that side.

13 He measured then the gate from the roof of *one* little chamber to the roof of another: the breadth *was* five and twenty cubits, door against door.

14 He made also posts of ᵀthreescore cubits, even unto the post of the court round about the gate.   *Ex. 27:9* ♦ *sixty*

15 And from the face of the gate of the entrance unto the face of the porch of the inner gate *were* fifty cubits.

16 And *there were* narrow windows to the little chambers, and to their posts within the gate round about, and likewise to the arches: and windows *were* round about inward: and upon *each* post *were* palm trees.   *1 Kin. 6:4*

17 Then brought he me into the outward court, and, lo, *there were* chambers, and a pavement made for the court round about: thirty chambers *were* upon the pavement.   *1 Chr. 9:26*

18 And the pavement by the side of the gates over against the length of the gates *was* the lower pavement.

19 Then he measured the breadth from the forefront of the lower gate unto the forefront of the inner court without, an hundred cubits eastward and northward.   *Ezek. 40:23, 27*

20 And the gate of the outward court that looked toward the north, he measured the length thereof, and the breadth thereof.

21 And the little chambers thereof *were* three on this side and three on that side; and the posts thereof and the arches thereof were after the measure of the first gate: the length thereof *was* fifty cubits, and the breadth five and twenty cubits.   *Ezek. 40:29-30*

22 And their windows, and their arches, and their palm trees, *were* after the measure of the gate that looketh toward the east; and they went up unto it by seven steps; and the arches thereof *were* before them.   *Ezek. 40:6, 31, 37*

23 And the gate of the inner court *was* over against the gate toward the north, and toward the east; and he measured from gate to gate an hundred cubits.   *Ezek. 40:19*

24 After that he brought me toward the south, and behold a gate toward the south:

and he measured the posts thereof and the arches thereof according to these measures. *Ezek. 40:6*

25 And *there were* windows in it and in the arches thereof round about, like those windows: the length *was* fifty cubits, and the breadth five and twenty cubits. *Ezek. 40:33*

26 And *there were* seven steps to go up to it, and the arches thereof *were* before them: and it had palm trees, one on this side, and another on that side, upon the posts thereof. *Ezek. 40:6, 16, 22*

27 And *there was* a gate in the inner court toward the south: and he measured from gate to gate toward the south an hundred cubits. *Ezek. 40:19, 23, 32*

28 And he brought me to the inner court by the south gate: and he measured the south gate according to these measures; *Ezek. 40:35*

29 And the little chambers thereof, and the posts thereof, and the arches thereof, according to these measures: and *there were* windows in it and in the arches thereof round about: *it was* fifty cubits long, and five and twenty cubits broad. *Ezek. 40:7, 16, 25*

30 And the arches round about *were* five and twenty cubits long, and five cubits broad. *Ezek. 40:21*

31 And the arches thereof *were* toward the utter court; and palm trees *were* upon the posts thereof: and the going up to it *had* eight steps. *Ezek. 40:22, 26, 34*

32 And he brought me into the inner court toward the east: and he measured the gate according to these measures. *Ezek. 40:28-31*

33 And the little chambers thereof, and the posts thereof, and the arches thereof, *were* according to these measures: and *there were* windows therein and in the arches thereof round about: *it was* fifty cubits long, and five and twenty cubits broad. *Ezek. 40:21*

34 And the arches thereof *were* toward the outward court; and palm trees *were* upon the posts thereof, on this side, and on that side: and the going up to it *had* eight steps.

35 And he brought me to the north gate, and measured *it* according to these measures; *Ezek. 40:32; 44:4; 47:2*

36 The little chambers thereof, the posts thereof, and the arches thereof, and the windows to it round about: the length *was* fifty cubits, and the breadth five and twenty cubits. *Ezek. 40:21*

37 And the posts thereof *were* toward the utter court; and palm trees *were* upon the posts thereof, on this side, and on that side: and the going up to it *had* eight steps.

38 And the chambers and the entries thereof *were* by the posts of the gates, where they washed the burnt offering. *2 Chr. 4:6*

39 And in the porch of the gate *were* two tables on this side, and two tables on that side, to slay thereon the burnt offering and the sin offering and the ᵀtrespass offering. *sin*

40 And at the side without, as one goeth up to the entry of the north gate, *were* two tables; and on the other side, which *was* at the porch of the gate, *were* two tables.

41 Four tables *were* on this side, and four tables on that side, by the side of the gate; eight tables, whereupon they slew *their sacrifices.*

42 And the four tables *were* of ᵀhewn stone for the burnt offering, of a cubit and an half long, and a cubit and an half broad, and one cubit high: whereupon also they laid the instruments wherewith they slew the burnt offering and the sacrifice. *Ezek. 40:39 ◆ cut*

43 And within *were* hooks, an hand broad, fastened round about: and upon the tables *was* the flesh of the offering.

44 And without the inner gate *were* the chambers of the singers in the inner court, which *was* at the side of the north gate; and their ᵀprospect *was* toward the south: one at the side of the east gate *having* the prospect toward the north. *1 Chr. 6:31-32 ◆ face*

45 And he said unto me, This chamber, whose prospect *is* toward the south, *is* for the priests, the keepers of the charge of the house. *Lev. 8:35; 1 Chr. 9:23; Ps. 134:1*

46 And the chamber whose prospect *is* toward the north *is* for the priests, the keepers of the charge of the altar: these *are* the sons of Zadok among the sons of Levi, which come near to the LORD to minister unto him. *1 Kin. 2:35; Ezek. 43:19; 44:15*

47 So he measured the court, an hundred cubits long, and an hundred cubits broad, foursquare; and the altar *that was* before the house. *Ezek. 40:19*

48 And he brought me to the porch of the house, and measured *each* post of the porch, five cubits on this side, and five cubits on that side: and the breadth of the gate *was* three cubits on this side, and three cubits on that side. *1 Kin. 6:3*

49 The length of the porch *was* twenty cubits, and the breadth eleven cubits; and *he brought me* by the steps whereby they went up to it: and *there were* pillars by the posts, one on this side, and another on that side. *1 Kin. 7:15-21*

The Holy Place in the Temple

41 Afterward he brought me to the temple, and measured the posts, six cubits broad on the one side, and six cubits broad on the other side, *which was* the breadth of the tabernacle. *Ezek. 40:2-3*

2 And the breadth of the door *was* ten cubits; and the sides of the door *were* five cubits on the one side, and five cubits on

the other side: and he measured the length thereof, forty cubits: and the breadth, twenty cubits. 　　　1 Kin. 6:2, 17; 2 Chr. 3:3

3 Then went he inward, and measured the post of the door, two cubits; and the door, six cubits; and the breadth of the door, seven cubits.

4 So he measured the length thereof, twenty cubits; and the breadth, twenty cubits, before the temple: and he said unto me, This *is* the most holy *place*. 　Ex. 26:33-34; 1 Kin. 6:20; Heb. 9:3-8

5 After he measured the wall of the house, six cubits; and the breadth of *every* side chamber, four cubits, round about the house on every side.

6 And the side chambers *were* three, one over another, and thirty in order; and they entered into the wall which *was* of the house for the side chambers round about, that they might have hold, but they had not hold in the wall of the house. 　　　　1 Kin. 6:10

7 And *there was* an enlarging, and a winding about still upward to the side chambers: for the winding about of the house went still upward round about the house: therefore the breadth of the house *was still* upward, and so increased *from* the lowest *chamber* to the highest by the midst. 　　　1 Kin. 6:8

8 I saw also the height of the house round about: the foundations of the side chambers *were* a full reed of six great cubits. 　Ezek. 40:5

9 The thickness of the wall, which *was* for the side chamber without, *was* five cubits: and *that* which *was* left *was* the place of the side chambers that *were* within. 　Ezek. 41:11

10 And between the chambers *was* the wideness of twenty cubits round about the house on every side.

11 And the doors of the side chambers *were* toward *the place that was* left, one door toward the north, and another door toward the south: and the breadth of the place that was left *was* five cubits round about. 　Ezek. 41:9

12 Now the building that *was* before the separate place at the end toward the west *was* seventy cubits broad; and the wall of the building *was* five cubits thick round about, and the length thereof ninety cubits. 　Ezek. 41:13-15

13 So he measured the house, an hundred cubits long; and the separate place, and the building, with the walls thereof, an hundred cubits long; 　　　　Ezek. 40:47

14 Also the breadth of the face of the house, and of the separate place toward the east, an hundred cubits.

15 And he measured the length of the building over against the separate place which *was* behind it, and the galleries thereof on the one side and on the other side, an hundred cubits, with the inner temple, and the porches of the court; 　　Ezek. 42:1, 3

16 The door posts, and the narrow windows, and the galleries round about on their three stories, over against the door, cieled with wood round about, and from the ground up to the windows, and the windows *were* covered; 　　　1 Kin. 6:4, 15; Ezek. 40:16

17 To that above the door, even unto the inner house, and without, and by all the wall round about within and without, by measure.

18 And *it was* made with cherubims and palm trees, so that a palm tree *was* between a cherub and a cherub; and *every* cherub had two faces; 　　1 Kin. 7:36; 2 Chr. 3:7; Ezek. 40:16

19 So that the face of a man *was* toward the palm tree on the one side, and the face of a young lion toward the palm tree on the other side: *it was* made through all the house round about. 　　　　　Ezek. 10:14

20 From the ground unto above the door *were* cherubims and palm trees made, and on the wall of the temple.

21 The posts of the temple *were* squared, *and* the face of the sanctuary; the appearance *of the one* as the appearance *of the other*. 　Ezek. 41:1

22 The altar of wood *was* three cubits high, and the length thereof two cubits; and the corners thereof, and the length thereof, and the walls thereof, *were* of wood: and he said unto me, This *is* the table that *is* before the LORD. 　　　Ezek. 23:41; 44:16; Mal. 1:7

23 And the temple and the sanctuary had two doors. 　　　　　　1 Kin. 6:31-35

24 And the doors had two leaves *apiece*, two turning leaves; two *leaves* for the one door, and two leaves for the other *door*. 　1 Kin. 6:34

25 And *there were* made on them, on the doors of the temple, cherubims and palm trees, like as *were* made upon the walls; and *there were* thick planks upon the face of the porch without. 　　　　　Ezek. 41:18

26 And *there were* narrow windows and palm trees on the one side and on the other side, on the sides of the porch, and *upon* the side chambers of the house, and thick planks. 　　　　Ezek. 40:16; 41:16

The Courtyards of the Temple

42 Then he brought me forth into the utter court, the way toward the north: and he brought me into the chamber that *was* over against the separate place, and which *was* before the building toward the north. 　　　Ezek. 40:17, 20; 41:1

2 Before the length of an hundred cubits *was* the north door, and the breadth *was* fifty cubits.

3 Over against the twenty *cubits* which *were* for the inner court, and over against the pavement which *was* for the utter court, *was* gallery against gallery in three *stories*. 　Ezek. 41:10

4 And before the chambers *was* a walk of ten cubits breadth inward, a way of one cubit; and their doors toward the north. Ezek. 46:19
5 Now the upper chambers *were* shorter: for the galleries were higher than these, than the lower, and than the middlemost of the building.
6 For they *were* in three *stories*, but had not pillars as the pillars of the courts: therefore *the building* was ᵀstraitened more than the lowest and the middlemost from the ground. Ezek. 41:6 ◆ shortened
7 And the wall that *was* without over against the chambers, toward the utter court on the forepart of the chambers, the length thereof *was* fifty cubits.
8 For the length of the chambers that *were* in the utter court *was* fifty cubits: and, lo, before the temple *were* an hundred cubits.
9 And from under these chambers *was* the entry on the east side, as one goeth into them from the utter court. Ezek. 44:5; 46:19
10 The chambers *were* in the thickness of the wall of the court toward the east, over against the separate place, and over against the building. Ezek. 42:1, 13
11 And the way before them *was* like the appearance of the chambers which *were* toward the north, as long as they, *and* as broad as they: and all their goings out *were* both according to their fashions, and according to their doors.
12 And according to the doors of the chambers that *were* toward the south *was* a door in the head of the way, *even* the way directly before the wall toward the east, as one entereth into them.
13 Then said he unto me, The north chambers *and* the south chambers, which *are* before the separate place, they *be* holy chambers, where the priests that approach unto the LORD shall eat the most holy things: there shall they lay the most holy things, and the meat offering, and the sin offering, and the ᵀtrespass offering; for the place *is* holy. Lev. 7:6; 10:17; Ezek. 40:46 ◆ sin
14 When the priests enter therein, then shall they not go out of the holy *place* into the utter court, but there they shall lay their garments wherein they minister; for they *are* holy; and shall put on other garments, and shall approach to *those things* which *are* for the people. Ex. 29:4-9; Lev. 8:7; Ezek. 44:19
15 Now when he had made an end of measuring the inner house, he brought me forth toward the gate whose ᵀprospect *is* toward the east, and measured it round about. Ezek. 43:1 ◆ face
16 He measured the east side with the measuring reed, five hundred reeds, with the measuring reed round about. Ezek. 40:3

17 He measured the north side, five hundred reeds, with the measuring reed round about.
18 He measured the south side, five hundred reeds, with the measuring reed.
19 He turned about to the west side, *and* measured five hundred reeds with the measuring reed.
20 He measured it by the four sides: it had a wall round about, five hundred *reeds* long, and five hundred broad, to make a separation between the sanctuary and the profane place. Ezek. 22:26; 40:5; 45:2

God's Glory Again Fills the Temple

43 Afterward he brought me to the gate, *even* the gate that looketh toward the east: Ezek. 40:6; 42:15; 44:1
2 And, behold, the glory of the God of Israel came from the way of the east: and his voice *was* like a noise of many waters: and the earth shined with his glory. Ezek. 11:23; Rev. 1:15; 18:1
3 And *it was* according to the appearance of the vision which I saw, *even* according to the vision that I saw when I came to destroy the city: and the visions *were* like the vision that I saw by the river Chebar; and I fell upon my face. Ezek. 9:1
4 And the glory of the LORD came into the house by the way of the gate whose ᵀprospect *is* toward the east. Ezek. 44:2 ◆ face
5 So the spirit took me up, and brought me into the inner court; and, behold, the glory of the LORD filled the house. Ezek. 8:3
6 And I heard *him* speaking unto me out of the house; and the man stood by me.

The Sin of Israel Had Prevented God's Presence

7 And he said unto me, Son of man, the place of my throne, and the place of the soles of my feet, where I will dwell in the midst of the children of Israel for ever, and my holy name, shall the house of Israel no more defile, *neither* they, nor their kings, by their ᵀwhoredom, nor by the carcases of their kings in their high places. Lev. 26:30 ◆ prostitution
8 In their setting of their threshold by my thresholds, and their post by my posts, and the wall between me and them, they have even defiled my holy name by their abominations that they have committed: wherefore I have consumed them in mine anger.
9 Now let them put away their whoredom, and the carcases of their kings, far from me, and I will dwell in the midst of them for ever. Ezek. 18:30-31; 37:26-28; 43:7
10 Thou son of man, shew the house to the house of Israel, that they may be ashamed of their iniquities: and let them measure the pattern. Ezek. 16:61

11 And if they be ashamed of all that they have done, shew them the form of the house, and the fashion thereof, and the goings out thereof, and the comings in thereof, and all the forms thereof, and all the ordinances thereof, and all the forms thereof, and all the laws thereof: and write it in their sight, that they may keep the whole form thereof, and all the ordinances thereof, and do them.   Ezek. 11:20

12 This is the law of the house; Upon the top of the mountain the whole limit thereof round about shall be most holy. Behold, this is the law of the house.   Ezek. 40:2; 42:20

The Altar in the Temple

13 And these are the measures of the altar after the cubits: The cubit is a cubit and an hand breadth; even the bottom shall be a cubit, and the breadth a cubit, and the border thereof by the edge thereof round about shall be a span: and this shall be the higher place of the altar.   Ex. 27:1-8

14 And from the bottom upon the ground even to the lower settle shall be two cubits, and the breadth one cubit; and from the lesser settle even to the greater settle shall be four cubits, and the breadth one cubit.

15 So the altar shall be four cubits; and from the altar and upward shall be four horns.

16 And the altar shall be twelve cubits long, twelve broad, square in the four squares thereof.   Ex. 27:1

17 And the settle shall be fourteen cubits long and fourteen broad in the four squares thereof; and the border about it shall be half a cubit; and the bottom thereof shall be a cubit about; and his stairs shall look toward the east.   Ex. 20:26; Ezek. 40:6

18 And he said unto me, Son of man, thus saith the Lord GOD; These are the ordinances of the altar in the day when they shall make it, to offer burnt offerings thereon, and to sprinkle blood thereon.   Ex. 40:29

19 And thou shalt give to the priests the Levites that be of the seed of Zadok, which approach unto me, to minister unto me, saith the Lord GOD, a young bullock for a sin offering.   Num. 16:40; Ezek. 40:46; 44:15

20 And thou shalt take of the blood thereof, and put it on the four horns of it, and on the four corners of the [T]settle, and upon the border round about: thus shalt thou cleanse and purge it.   Lev. 8:15 ◆ ledge

21 Thou shalt take the bullock also of the sin offering, and he shall burn it in the appointed place of the house, without the sanctuary.   Ex. 29:14; Lev. 4:12

22 And on the second day thou shalt offer a kid of the goats without blemish for a sin offering; and they shall cleanse the altar, as they did cleanse it with the bullock. Ezek. 43:20

23 When thou hast made an end of cleansing it, thou shalt offer a young [T]bullock without blemish, and a ram out of the flock without blemish.   Ex. 29:1 ◆ bull

24 And thou shalt offer them before the LORD, and the priests shall cast salt upon them, and they shall offer them up for a burnt offering unto the LORD.   Lev. 2:13; Num. 18:19; Mark 9:49-50

25 Seven days shalt thou prepare every day a goat for a sin offering: they shall also prepare a young bullock, and a ram out of the flock, without blemish.   Ex. 29:35-37; Lev. 8:33

26 Seven days shall they purge the altar and purify it; and they shall [T]consecrate themselves.   set apart

27 And when these days are expired, it shall be, that upon the eighth day, and so forward, the priests shall make your burnt offerings upon the altar, and your peace offerings; and I will accept you, saith the Lord GOD. Lev. 9:1

The East Gate Is Sealed Shut

44 Then he brought me back the way of the gate of the outward sanctuary which looketh toward the east; and it was shut.   Ezek. 43:1

2 Then said the LORD unto me; This gate shall be shut, it shall not be opened, and no man shall enter in by it; because the LORD, the God of Israel, hath entered in by it, therefore it shall be shut.   Ezek. 43:2-4

3 It is for the prince; the prince, he shall sit in it to eat bread before the LORD; he shall enter by the way of the porch of that gate, and shall go out by the way of the same.   Gen. 31:54

Those Serving in the Temple

4 Then brought he me the way of the north gate before the house: and I looked, and, behold, the glory of the LORD filled the house of the LORD: and I fell upon my face. Ezek. 1:28

5 And the LORD said unto me, Son of man, mark well, and behold with thine eyes, and hear with thine ears all that I say unto thee concerning all the ordinances of the house of the LORD, and all the laws thereof; and mark well the entering in of the house, with every going forth of the sanctuary.   Deut. 12:32

6 And thou shalt say to the rebellious, even to the house of Israel, Thus saith the Lord GOD; O ye house of Israel, let it suffice you of all your abominations,   Ezek. 3:9

7 In that ye have brought into my sanctuary strangers, uncircumcised in heart, and uncircumcised in flesh, to be in my sanctuary, to pollute it, even my house, when ye offer my bread, the fat and the blood, and they have broken my covenant because of all your abominations.   Gen. 17:14; Lev. 22:25; 26:41

8 And ye have not kept the charge of mine holy things: but ye have set keepers of my charge in my sanctuary for yourselves.

9 Thus saith the Lord GOD; No stranger, uncircumcised in heart, nor uncircumcised in flesh, shall enter into my sanctuary, of any stranger that *is* among the children of Israel.   Ezek. 44:7

10 And the Levites that are gone away far from me, when Israel went astray, which went astray away from me after their idols; they shall even bear their iniquity. Ezek. 48:11

11 Yet they shall be ministers in my sanctuary, *having* charge at the gates of the house, and ministering to the house: they shall slay the burnt offering and the sacrifice for the people, and they shall stand before them to minister unto them. Num. 16:9; 18:6; 2 Chr. 29:34

12 Because they ministered unto them before their idols, and caused the house of Israel to fall into iniquity; therefore have I lifted up mine hand against them, saith the Lord GOD, and they shall bear their iniquity. 2 Kin. 16:10-16

13 And they shall not come near unto me, to do the office of a priest unto me, nor to come near to any of my holy things, in the most holy *place*: but they shall bear their shame, and their abominations which they have committed.   Num. 18:3; 2 Kin. 23:9

14 But I will make them keepers of the charge of the house, for all the service thereof, and for all that shall be done therein.   Num. 18:4

15 But the priests the Levites, the sons of Zadok, that kept the charge of my sanctuary when the children of Israel went astray from me, they shall come near to me to minister unto me, and they shall stand before me to offer unto me the fat and the blood, saith the Lord GOD: Ezek. 40:46

16 They shall enter into my sanctuary, and they shall come near to my table, to minister unto me, and they shall keep my charge.   Num. 18:7-8; Ezek. 41:22; Mal. 1:7

Ordinances for the Priests

17 And it shall come to pass, *that* when they enter in at the gates of the inner court, they shall be clothed with linen garments; and no wool shall come upon them, whiles they minister in the gates of the inner court, and within.   Rev. 19:8

18 They shall have linen bonnets upon their heads, and shall have linen ᵀbreeches upon their ᵀloins; they shall not ᵀgird *themselves* with any thing that causeth sweat. *trousers* ◆ *waist* ◆ *clothe*

19 And when they go forth into the utter court, *even* into the utter court to the people, they shall put off their garments wherein they ministered, and lay them in the holy chambers, and they shall put on other garments;

and they shall not ᵀsanctify the people with their garments. Lev. 6:10-11, 27; Ezek. 46:20 ◆ *make holy*

20 Neither shall they shave their heads, nor suffer their locks to grow long; they shall only ᵀpoll their heads.   Num. 6:5 ◆ *cut hair from*

21 Neither shall any priest drink wine, when they enter into the inner court.   Lev. 10:9

22 Neither shall they take for their wives a widow, nor her that is put away: but they shall take maidens of the seed of the house of Israel, or a widow that had a priest before.   Lev. 21:7, 13-14

23 And they shall teach my people *the difference* between the holy and profane, and cause them to discern between the unclean and the clean.   Lev. 10:10-11; Ezek. 22:26; Hos. 4:6

24 And in controversy they shall stand in judgment; *and* they shall judge it according to my judgments: and they shall keep my laws and my statutes in all mine assemblies; and they shall ᵀhallow my sabbaths.   *render as sacred*

25 And they shall come at no dead person to defile themselves: but for father, or for mother, or for son, or for daughter, for brother, or for sister that hath had no husband, they may defile themselves.

26 And after he is cleansed, they shall reckon unto him seven days.

27 And in the day that he goeth into the sanctuary, unto the inner court, to minister in the sanctuary, he shall offer his sin offering, saith the Lord GOD.   Num. 6:9-11

28 And it shall be unto them for an inheritance: I *am* their inheritance: and ye shall give them no possession in Israel: I *am* their possession.   Num. 18:20; Deut. 10:9; 18:1-2

29 They shall eat the meat offering, and the sin offering, and the ᵀtrespass offering; and every dedicated thing in Israel shall be theirs.   Lev. 27:21, 28; Num. 18:14 ◆ *sin*

30 And the first of all the firstfruits of all *things*, and every ᵀoblation of all, of every *sort* of your oblations, shall be the priest's: ye shall also give unto the priest the first of your dough, that he may cause the blessing to rest in thine house.   Neh. 10:35-37 ◆ *offering*

31 The priests shall not eat of any thing that is dead of itself, or torn, whether it be fowl or beast.   Ex. 22:31; Lev. 22:8; Deut. 14:21

The Portions of Land

45 Moreover, when ye shall divide by lot the land for inheritance, ye shall offer an oblation unto the LORD, an holy portion of the land: the length *shall be* the length of five and twenty thousand *reeds,* and the breadth *shall be* ten thousand. This *shall be* holy in all the borders thereof round about.   Num. 34:13; Ezek. 48:29; Zech. 14:20-21

2 Of this there shall be for the sanctuary five hundred *in length,* with five hundred *in breadth,*

square round about; and fifty cubits round about for the suburbs thereof.   Ezek. 42:16-20

3 And of this measure shalt thou measure the length of five and twenty thousand, and the breadth of ten thousand: and in it shall be the sanctuary *and* the most holy place.   Ezek. 48:10

4 The holy *portion* of the land shall be for the priests the ministers of the sanctuary, which shall come near to minister unto the LORD: and it shall be a place for their houses, and an holy place for the sanctuary.   Num. 16:5

5 And the five and twenty thousand of length, and the ten thousand of breadth, shall also the Levites, the ministers of the house, have for themselves, for a possession for twenty chambers.   Ezek. 48:13

6 And ye shall appoint the possession of the city five thousand broad, and five and twenty thousand long, over against the oblation of the holy *portion*: it shall be for the whole house of Israel.   Ezek. 48:15-18

7 And a *portion shall be* for the prince on the one side and on the other side of the oblation of the holy *portion*, and of the possession of the city, before the oblation of the holy *portion*, and before the possession of the city, from the west side westward, and from the east side eastward: and the length *shall be* over against one of the portions, from the west border unto the east border.   Ezek. 34:24; 48:21

8 In the land shall be his possession in Israel: and my princes shall no more oppress my people; and *the rest of* the land shall they give to the house of Israel according to their tribes.   Josh. 11:23; Ezek. 22:27; 46:18

Honest Weights and Measures

9 Thus saith the Lord GOD; Let it suffice you, O princes of Israel: remove violence and ᵀspoil, and execute judgment and justice, take away your exactions from my people, saith the Lord GOD.   Jer. 22:3 ◆ *plunder*

10 Ye shall have just balances, and a just ephah, and a just bath.   Amos 8:4-6

11 The ephah and the bath shall be of one measure, that the bath may contain the tenth part of an homer, and the ephah the tenth part of an homer: the measure thereof shall be after the homer.   Is. 5:10

12 And the shekel *shall be* twenty gerahs: twenty shekels, five and twenty shekels, fifteen shekels, shall be your maneh.   Ex. 30:13

Rules for Worship

13 This *is* the ᵀoblation that ye shall offer; the sixth part of an ephah of an homer of wheat, and ye shall give the sixth part of an ephah of an homer of barley: *offering*

14 Concerning the ordinance of oil, the bath of oil, *ye shall offer* the tenth part of a bath out of the cor, *which is* an homer of ten baths; for ten baths *are* an homer:

15 And one lamb out of the flock, out of two hundred, out of the fat pastures of Israel; for a meat offering, and for a burnt offering, and for peace offerings, to make reconciliation for them, saith the Lord GOD.   Lev. 1:4; 6:30

16 All the people of the land shall give this oblation for the prince in Israel.   Ex. 30:14-15

17 And it shall be the prince's part *to give* burnt offerings, and meat offerings, and drink offerings, in the feasts, and in the new moons, and in the sabbaths, in all solemnities of the house of Israel: he shall prepare the sin offering, and the meat offering, and the burnt offering, and the peace offerings, to make reconciliation for the house of Israel.   2 Chr. 31:3

18 Thus saith the Lord GOD; In the first *month*, in the first *day* of the month, thou shalt take a young bullock without blemish, and cleanse the sanctuary: Ex. 12:2; Lev. 16:16, 33

19 And the priest shall take of the blood of the sin offering, and put *it* upon the posts of the house, and upon the four corners of the ᵀsettle of the altar, and upon the posts of the gate of the inner court.   Ezek. 43:14, 20 ◆ *ledge*

20 And so thou shalt do the seventh *day* of the month for every one that erreth, and for *him that is* simple: so shall ye reconcile the house.   Lev. 16:20

21 In the first *month*, in the fourteenth day of the month, ye shall have the passover, a feast of seven days; unleavened bread shall be eaten.   Lev. 23:5-8

22 And upon that day shall the prince prepare for himself and for all the people of the land a ᵀbullock *for* a sin offering.   Lev. 4:14 ◆ *bull*

23 And seven days of the feast he shall prepare a burnt offering to the LORD, seven bullocks and seven rams without blemish daily the seven days; and a kid of the goats daily *for* a sin offering.   Lev. 23:8

24 And he shall prepare a meat offering of an ephah for a bullock, and an ephah for a ram, and an hin of oil for an ephah.   Ezek. 46:5-7

25 In the seventh *month*, in the fifteenth day of the month, shall he do the like in the feast of the seven days, according to the sin offering, according to the burnt offering, and according to the meat offering, and according to the oil.   Num. 29:12-38

More Regulations for Worship

46 Thus saith the Lord GOD; The gate of the inner court that looketh toward the east shall be shut the six working days; but on the sabbath it shall be opened, and in the day of the new moon it shall be opened.   Is. 66:23

2 And the prince shall enter by the way of the porch of *that* gate without, and shall stand by the post of the gate, and the priests shall prepare his burnt offering and his peace offerings, and he shall worship at the threshold of the gate: then he shall go forth; but the gate shall not be shut until the evening.   Ezek. 44:3; 46:8

3 Likewise the people of the land shall worship at the door of this gate before the LORD in the sabbaths and in the new moons.

4 And the burnt offering that the prince shall offer unto the LORD in the sabbath day *shall be* six lambs without blemish, and a ram without blemish.   Ezek. 45:17

5 And the meat offering *shall be* an ephah for a ram, and the meat offering for the lambs as he shall be able to give, and an hin of oil to an ephah.   Num. 28:12; Ezek. 45:24; 46:7

6 And in the day of the new moon *it shall be* a young ᵀbullock without blemish, and six lambs, and a ram: they shall be without blemish.   *bull*

7 And he shall prepare a meat offering, an ephah for a bullock, and an ephah for a ram, and for the lambs according as his hand shall attain unto, and an hin of oil to an ephah.   Ezek. 46:5

8 And when the prince shall enter, he shall go in by the way of the porch of *that* gate, and he shall go forth by the way thereof. Ezek. 46:2

9 But when the people of the land shall come before the LORD in the solemn feasts, he that entereth in by the way of the north gate to worship shall go out by the way of the south gate; and he that entereth by the way of the south gate shall go forth by the way of the north gate: he shall not return by the way of the gate whereby he came in, but shall go forth over against it.   Ex. 23:14-17

10 And the prince in the midst of them, when they go in, shall go in; and when they go forth, shall go forth.   1 Chr. 29:20, 22; Ps. 42:4

11 And in the feasts and in the solemnities the meat offering shall be an ephah to a bullock, and an ephah to a ram, and to the lambs as he is able to give, and an hin of oil to an ephah.   Ezek. 46:5, 7

12 Now when the prince shall prepare a voluntary burnt offering or peace offerings voluntarily unto the LORD, *one* shall then open him the gate that looketh toward the east, and he shall prepare his burnt offering and his peace offerings, as he did on the sabbath day: then he shall go forth; and after his going forth *one* shall shut the gate. Ezek. 45:17

13 Thou shalt daily prepare a burnt offering unto the LORD *of* a lamb of the first year without blemish: thou shalt prepare it every morning.   Is. 50:4

14 And thou shalt prepare a meat offering for it every morning, the sixth part of an ephah, and the third part of an hin of oil, to ᵀtemper with the fine flour; a meat offering continually by a perpetual ordinance unto the LORD.   Num. 28:5 ◆ *mix*

15 Thus shall they prepare the lamb, and the meat offering, and the oil, every morning *for* a continual burnt offering.

An Order for the Prince's Inheritance

16 Thus saith the Lord GOD; If the prince give a gift unto any of his sons, the inheritance thereof shall be his sons'; it *shall be* their possession by inheritance.   2 Chr. 21:3

17 But if he give a gift of his inheritance to one of his servants, then it shall be his to the year of liberty; after it shall return to the prince: but his inheritance shall be his sons' for them.   Lev. 25:10

18 Moreover the prince shall not take of the people's inheritance by oppression, to thrust them out of their possession; *but* he shall give his sons inheritance out of his own possession: that my people be not scattered every man from his possession.   1 Kin. 21:19

The Courts for Boiling and Baking

19 After he brought me through the entry, which *was* at the side of the gate, into the holy chambers of the priests, which looked toward the north: and, behold, there *was* a place on the two sides westward.   Ezek. 42:9

20 Then said he unto me, This *is* the place where the priests shall boil the ᵀtrespass offering and the sin offering, where they shall bake the meat offering; that they bear *them* not out into the utter court, to ᵀsanctify the people.   2 Chr. 35:13 ◆ *sin* ◆ *make holy*

21 Then he brought me forth into the utter court, and caused me to pass by the four corners of the court; and, behold, in every corner of the court *there was* a court.

22 In the four corners of the court *there were* courts joined of forty *cubits* long and thirty broad: these four corners *were* of one measure.

23 And *there was* a row *of building* round about in them, round about them four, and *it was* made with boiling places under the rows round about.

24 Then said he unto me, These *are* the places of them that boil, where the ministers of the house shall boil the sacrifice of the people.   Ezek. 46:20

Water Flowing from the Temple

47 Afterward he brought me again unto the door of the house; and, behold, waters issued out from under the threshold of the house eastward: for the forefront of the house *stood toward* the east, and the

waters came down from under from the right side of the house, at the south *side* of the altar.   Ps. 46:4; Joel 3:18; Rev. 22:1

2 Then brought he me out of the way of the gate northward, and led me about the way without unto the utter gate by the way that looketh eastward; and, behold, there ran out waters on the right side.

3 And when the man that had the line in his hand went forth eastward, he measured a thousand cubits, and he brought me through the waters; the waters *were* to the ankles.   Ezek. 40:3

4 Again he measured a thousand, and brought me through the waters; the waters *were* to the knees. Again he measured a thousand, and brought me through; the waters *were* to the ᵀloins.   waist

5 Afterward he measured a thousand; *and it was* a river that I could not pass over: for the waters were risen, waters to swim in, a river that could not be passed over.   Is. 11:9

6 And he said unto me, Son of man, hast thou seen *this*? Then he brought me, and caused me to return to the brink of the river.   Ezek. 40:4

7 Now when I had returned, behold, at the bank of the river *were* very many trees on the one side and on the other.   Ezek. 47:12; Rev. 22:2

8 Then said he unto me, These waters issue out toward the east country, and go down into the desert, and go into the sea: *which being* brought forth into the sea, the waters shall be healed.   Deut. 3:17; 4:49; Josh. 3:16

9 And it shall come to pass, *that* every thing that liveth, which moveth, whithersoever the rivers shall come, shall live: and there shall be a very great multitude of fish, because these waters shall come thither: for they shall be healed; and every thing shall live whither the river cometh.

10 And it shall come to pass, *that* the fishers shall stand upon it from En-gedi even unto En-eglaim; they shall be a *place* to spread forth nets; their fish shall be according to their kinds, as the fish of the great sea, exceeding many.   Num. 34:6

11 But the ᵀmiry places thereof and the ᵀmarishes thereof shall not be healed; they shall be given to salt.   Deut. 29:23 ◆ *muddy* ◆ *marshes*

12 And by the river upon the bank thereof, on this side and on that side, shall grow all trees for meat, whose leaf shall not fade, neither shall the fruit thereof be consumed: it shall bring forth new fruit according to his months, because their waters they issued out of the sanctuary: and the fruit thereof shall be for meat, and the leaf thereof for medicine.   Ps. 1:3; Jer. 17:8; Rev. 22:2

Dividing the Land

13 Thus saith the Lord GOD; This *shall be* the border, whereby ye shall inherit the land according to the twelve tribes of Israel: Joseph *shall have two* portions.   Gen. 48:5

14 And ye shall inherit it, one as well as another: *concerning* the which I lifted up mine hand to give it unto your fathers: and this land shall fall unto you for inheritance.   Gen. 12:7

15 And this *shall be* the border of the land toward the north side, from the great sea, the way of Hethlon, as men go to Zedad;

16 Hamath, Berothah, Sibraim, which *is* between the border of Damascus and the border of Hamath; Hazar-hatticon, which *is* by the coast of Hauran.   Num. 13:21

17 And the border from the sea shall be

God's People to Bless the World

Ezekiel 47:8–12

Wonderful is the work which the Lord designs to accomplish through His church, that His name may be glorified. A picture of this work is given in Ezekiel's vision of the river of healing: "These waters issue out toward the east country, and go down into the desert, and go into the sea: which being brought forth into the sea, the waters shall be healed. And it shall come to pass, that everything that liveth, which moveth, whithersoever the rivers shall come, shall live: . . . and by the river upon the bank thereof, on this side and on that side, shall grow all trees for meat, whose leaf shall not fade, neither shall the fruit thereof be consumed: it shall bring forth new fruit according to his months, because their waters they issued out of the sanctuary: and the fruit thereof shall be for meat, and the leaf thereof for medicine" (Ezekiel 47:8–12).

From the beginning God has wrought through His people to bring blessing to the world. To the ancient Egyptian nation God made Joseph a fountain of life. Through the integrity of Joseph the life of that whole people was preserved. Through Daniel God saved the life of all the wise men of Babylon. And these deliverances are as object lessons; they illustrate the spiritual blessings offered to the world through connection with the God whom Joseph and Daniel worshiped. Everyone in whose heart Christ abides, everyone who will show forth His love to the world, is a worker together with God for the blessing of humanity. As he receives from the Saviour grace to impart to others, from his whole being flows forth the tide of spiritual life. *AA 13*

Hazar-enan, the border of Damascus, and the north northward, and the border of Hamath. And *this is* the north side.   Ezek. 48:1

18 And the east side ye shall measure from Hauran, and from Damascus, and from Gilead, and from the land of Israel *by* Jordan, from the border unto the east sea. And *this is* the east side.   Gen. 13:10

19 And the south side southward, from Tamar *even* to the waters of strife *in* Kadesh, the river to the great sea. And *this is* the south side southward.   Deut. 32:51

20 The west side also *shall be* the great sea from the border, till a man come over against Hamath. This *is* the west side.

21 So shall ye divide this land unto you according to the tribes of Israel.

22 And it shall come to pass, *that* ye shall divide it by lot for an inheritance unto you, and to the strangers that sojourn among you, which shall ᵀbeget children among you: and they shall be unto you as born in the country among the children of Israel; they shall have inheritance with you among the tribes of Israel.   Is. 56:6-7; Eph. 3:6; Col. 3:11 ◆ *bring forth*

23 And it shall come to pass, *that* in what tribe the stranger sojourneth, there shall ye give *him* his inheritance, saith the Lord GOD.

Portions for the Tribes

48 Now these *are* the names of the tribes. From the north end to the coast of the way of Hethlon, as one goeth to Hamath, Hazar-enan, the border of Damascus northward, to the coast of Hamath; for these are his sides east *and* west; a *portion for* Dan.   Ezek. 47:15-17

2 And by the border of Dan, from the east side unto the west side, a *portion for* Asher.

3 And by the border of Asher, from the east side even unto the west side, a *portion for* Naphtali.   Josh. 19:32-39

4 And by the border of Naphtali, from the east side unto the west side, a *portion for* Manasseh.   Josh. 17:1-11

5 And by the border of Manasseh, from the east side unto the west side, a *portion for* Ephraim.   Josh. 17:8-10

6 And by the border of Ephraim, from the east side even unto the west side, a *portion for* Reuben.   Josh. 13:15-21

7 And by the border of Reuben, from the east side unto the west side, a *portion for* Judah.   Josh. 15

8 And by the border of Judah, from the east side unto the west side, shall be the offering which ye shall offer of five and twenty thousand *reeds in* breadth, and *in* length as one of the *other* parts, from the east side unto the west side: and the sanctuary shall be in the midst of it.   Is. 12:6

9 The ᵀoblation that ye shall offer unto the LORD *shall be* of five and twenty thousand in length, and of ten thousand in breadth. *offering*

10 And for them, *even* for the priests, shall be *this* holy oblation; toward the north five and twenty thousand *in length*, and toward the west ten thousand in breadth, and toward the east ten thousand in breadth, and toward the south five and twenty thousand in length: and the sanctuary of the LORD shall be in the midst thereof.   Ezek. 44:28; 45:4

11 *It shall be* for the priests that are ᵀsanctified of the sons of Zadok; which have kept my charge, which went not astray when the children of Israel went astray, as the Levites went astray.   Ezek. 40:46 ◆ *made holy*

12 And *this* oblation of the land that is offered shall be unto them a thing most holy by the border of the Levites.

13 And over against the border of the priests the Levites *shall have* five and twenty thousand in length, and ten thousand in breadth: all the length *shall be* five and twenty thousand, and the breadth ten thousand.

14 And they shall not sell of it, neither exchange, nor alienate the firstfruits of the land: for *it is* holy unto the LORD.   Lev. 27:28

15 And the five thousand, that are left in the breadth over against the five and twenty thousand, shall be a profane *place* for the city, for dwelling, and for suburbs: and the city shall be in the midst thereof.   Ezek. 42:20

16 And these *shall be* the measures thereof; the north side four thousand and five hundred, and the south side four thousand and five hundred, and on the east side four thousand and five hundred, and the west side four thousand and five hundred.   Rev. 21:16

17 And the suburbs of the city shall be toward the north two hundred and fifty, and toward the south two hundred and fifty, and toward the east two hundred and fifty, and toward the west two hundred and fifty.

18 And the residue in length over against the oblation of the holy *portion shall be* ten thousand eastward, and ten thousand westward: and it shall be over against the oblation of the holy *portion*; and the increase thereof shall be for food unto them that serve the city.

19 And they that serve the city shall serve it out of all the tribes of Israel.

20 All the oblation *shall be* five and twenty thousand by five and twenty thousand: ye shall offer the holy oblation foursquare, with the possession of the city.

21 And the residue *shall be* for the prince, on the one side and on the other of the holy oblation, and of the possession of the city, over against the five and twenty thousand of the oblation toward the east

border, and westward over against the five and twenty thousand toward the west border, over against the portions for the prince: and it shall be the holy oblation; and the sanctuary of the house *shall be* in the midst thereof.   Ezek. 48:22

22 Moreover from the possession of the Levites, and from the possession of the city, *being* in the midst *of that* which is the prince's, between the border of Judah and the border of Benjamin, shall be for the prince.

23 As for the rest of the tribes, from the east side unto the west side, Benjamin *shall have* a *portion*.   Josh. 18:21-28

24 And by the border of Benjamin, from the east side unto the west side, Simeon *shall have* a *portion*.   Josh. 19:1-9

25 And by the border of Simeon, from the east side unto the west side, Issachar a *portion*.   Josh. 19:17-23

26 And by the border of Issachar, from the east side unto the west side, Zebulun a *portion*.   Josh. 19:10-16

27 And by the border of Zebulun, from the east side unto the west side, Gad a *portion*.

28 And by the border of Gad, at the south side southward, the border shall be even from Tamar *unto* the waters of strife *in* Kadesh, *and* to the river toward the great sea.

29 This *is* the land which ye shall divide by lot unto the tribes of Israel for inheritance, and these *are* their portions, saith the Lord GOD.

The New City of God

30 And these *are* the goings out of the city on the north side, four thousand and five hundred measures.   Ezek. 48:16

31 And the gates of the city *shall be* after the names of the tribes of Israel: three gates northward; one gate of Reuben, one gate of Judah, one gate of Levi.   Rev. 21:12-13

32 And at the east side four thousand and five hundred: and three gates; and one gate of Joseph, one gate of Benjamin, one gate of Dan.

33 And at the south side four thousand and five hundred measures: and three gates; one gate of Simeon, one gate of Issachar, one gate of Zebulun.

34 At the west side four thousand and five hundred, *with* their three gates; one gate of Gad, one gate of Asher, one gate of Naphtali.

35 *It was* round about eighteen thousand *measures*: and the name of the city from *that* day *shall be*, The LORD *is* there.   Jer. 3:17; 33:16

THE BOOK OF

DANIEL

The stories of Daniel in the lions' den (chapter 6); Shadrach, Meshach, and Abednego in the fiery furnace (chapter 3); and that of a disembodied hand writing on a wall (chapter 5) are familiar to many children who are taught the Bible. But beyond these stories, the Book of Daniel, like the Book of Revelation, is an example of apocalyptic or symbolic literature. More than one hundred prophecies in one chapter alone (chapter 11) have been fulfilled.

Daniel could have easily given in to self-pity when he was taken along with his fellow citizens of Judah to Babylon in 605 B.C.—long before Esther's time. But instead, Daniel focused on this fact: Although the Babylonians flexed their military might at Judah's expense, God is still in control even in desperate times.

Dates

Daniel's life and ministry spanned from the time of his being deported to Babylon (605 B.C.) through the fall of Babylon. He then saw the emergence of a new world power, the Medo-Persians, of whom Darius the Mede was the first king, ruling from 539-536 B.C. He was followed by Cyrus the Persian. Daniel died c. 535 B.C.

The Book of Daniel was probably written after the reign of Cyrus began in about 536 B.C. Some critics, however, have argued for a later writing date (around the time of the Maccabees (second century B.C.). But their arguments stem from disbelief that Daniel could have predicted world events with such accuracy (see chapter 11), and thus someone else must have written the book after the events came to pass. Belief in God's ability to give His servants visions of the future, however, allows us to trust that Daniel himself saw the visions and recorded them.

Another argument in favor of the later writing date stems from Daniel's use of Aramaic in chapters 2—7. While some believed that the Aramaic used comes from a later time period, it actually is an earlier form of Imperial Aramaic.

Author

Daniel is believed to be the author, based on the use of writing in the first person, starting in 7:2. Another point in favor of Daniel as the author comes through 12:4: "But you, Daniel, shut up the words, and seal the book until the time of the end." A quote from 9:27 is attributed to Daniel by Jesus Christ himself in Matthew 24:15.

In the time of Daniel, the southern kingdom of Judah is subordinate to Babylonia. The overthrow of the southern kingdom of Judah came in three stages. In 605 B.C., Nebuchadnezzar conquers King Jehoiakim and carried a small number of hostages to Babylon including Daniel. He then attacked again in 597 B.C., taking ten thousand hostages, including Ezekiel and King Jehoiakim's son, Jehoiachin. In 586 B.C., Nebuchadnezzar destroyed the city and scattered the remainder of the kingdom of Judah.

When the forces of King Nebuchadnezzar of Babylon first invaded Jerusalem, Daniel was among those taken to live in Babylon. Because of their pleasing looks and intelligence, Daniel and his friends Hananiah (Shadrach), Mishael (Meshach), and Azariah (Abed-nego) were tapped for government positions. Although they were given new names reflecting the gods of the Babylonians in order to indoctrinate them in the ways of the Babylonians, Daniel and his friends clung to their belief in the one God of Israel.

Throughout the Book of Daniel and in the Book of Ezekiel (Ezekiel 14:14), Daniel is seen as a man of outstanding character and faith. Like Joseph, Daniel could interpret dreams. His prophetic ability made him a valuable asset during the reigns of Nebuchadnezzar, Belshazzar, Darius, and Cyrus. But beyond interpreting the dreams of kings, Daniel had visions of world events well beyond his time.

Meaning of the Name

The name Daniel is the Greek version of *Daniye'l*, a Hebrew word meaning "God Is My Judge."

Christ in Daniel

Prophecies concerning the Messiah can be found in 2:34, 44; 7:13, 14; 9:25, 27. The kingdom that will break the power of all other kingdoms is that of the kingdom of God—the kingdom that is "an everlasting dominion, which shall not pass away" (7:14). Christ, the

King of kings (Revelation 19:16), is the central figure in that kingdom. His first coming corresponds to the seventy weeks prophecy described in chapter 9.

Overview

The book of Daniel is the last of the major prophets in the Old Testament. It prophesies the passing of eras as kings rise to power only to be conquered by others in addition to revealing the history of the earth through to the end of time when Jesus returns to gather his remnant people. This compact book can be divided into two sections:

(1) *Daniel 1—6, God's Sovereignty in Daniel's Life:* God's promise to allow His people to be conquered by the king of Babylon (Jeremiah 20) comes to pass as the people of Judah find themselves dragged off to Babylonia. But God protects Daniel and his friends as they trust in God for strength to hold on to their integrity in a permissive society with hostile peers. God's sovereignty is apparent in the test of trust in choosing which food to eat (chapter 1), through the interpretation of Nebuchadnezzar's dreams (chapters 2 and 4), in the over-turning of executions (chapters 3 and 6), and in prophesying the dissolution of Belshazzar's kingship (chapter 5).

Nebuchadnezzar's dream of a statue (2:24–45) shows the kingdoms that rose to prominence in the order that ultimately happens on the world stage: the Babylonians (605–539 B.C.), the Medes and Persians (539–331 B.C.), the Greeks (331–168 B.C.), and the Romans (168 B.C.–A.D. 476). These powerful kingdoms, however, are seen as chaff (2:35) in comparison to God's eternal kingdom. As Daniel 2:44 affirms: "And in the days of those kings the God of heaven will set up a kingdom that shall never be destroyed, nor shall this kingdom be left to another people. It shall crush all these kingdoms and bring them to an end, and it shall stand forever."

(2) *Daniel 7—12, God's Sovereignty over History:* The narrative of Daniel's life gives way in favor of Daniel's account of his prophetic visions: the four beasts (chapter 7)—another vision representing the Babylonians, Medes and Persians, the Greeks, and Romans; the ram (the Medes and Persians) and goat (Greece and Alexander the Great) (chapter 8); and in chapter 11, we see the previous visions of Daniel expanded, beginning with Medo-Persia through the end of time. Babylon had already lapsed into history at this point, so it is not expounded upon. The Book of Daniel ends with a prophecy of end-times, when the faithful are resurrected (chapter 12).

Unlocking Daniel

KEY PEOPLE:
Daniel, Shadrach, Meshach, Abed-nego, Nebuchadnezzar, Belshazzar, Darius, Cyrus

KEY EVENTS:
After being taken to Babylonia, Daniel and his three friends propose a diet that honors God (chapter 1); Daniel interprets Nebuchadnezzar's dream and saves the lives of the king's advisors (chapter 2); Shadrach, Meshach, and Abed-nego are thrown in the fiery furnace for their refusal to worship an idol (chapter 3); Nebuchadnezzar is humbled by God (chapter 4); Belshazzar sees a hand writing on the wall, which signals the end of his dominion (chapter 5); Daniel is thrown into a den of lions for his persistence in prayer (chapter 6); Daniel sees a vision of four beasts (chapter 7); Daniel intercedes for his people and is told the meaning of his prophecy of seventy weeks (chapter 9); Daniel's prophecies and visions describe kingdoms to come (chapters 10—11), and end-times events (chapter 12).

KEY WORD:
Sovereignty. The rise and fall of many kingdoms serves as a contrast to the eternal kingdom of the sovereign God of Israel. God is the ultimate mover and shaker who remains in control as conquerors come and go. Although this time of exile was a bleak one for Israel, God still cared for His people.

KEY VERSES:
"Daniel answered and said, Blessed be the name of God for ever and ever: for wisdom and might are his: And he changeth the times and the seasons: he removeth kings, and setteth up kings: he giveth wisdom unto the wise, and knowledge to them that know understanding: He revealeth the deep and secret things: he knoweth what is in the darkness, and the light dwelleth with him" (Daniel 2:20–22).

KEY CHAPTER:
Chapter 9, Daniel intercedes for his people and receives the "seventy-week" prophecy. This prophecy points to the coming of the Messiah and its fulfillment includes Christ's ministry.

Daniel and His Friends Remain Faithful to God

1 In the third year of the reign of Jehoia-kim king of Judah came Nebuchadnez-zar king of Babylon unto Jerusalem, and be-sieged it.   2 Kin. 24:1-2

2 And the Lord gave Jehoiakim king of Judah into his hand, with part of the vessels of the house of God: which he carried into the land of Shinar to the house of his god; and he brought the vessels into the treasure house of his god.   Gen. 11:2; 2 Chr. 36:7; Zech. 5:11

3 And the king spake unto Ashpenaz the master of his eunuchs, that he should bring *certain* of the children of Israel, and of the king's seed, and of the princes;   Is. 39:7

4 Children in whom *was* no blemish, but well favoured, and skilful in all wisdom, and cunning in knowledge, and understanding science, and such as *had* ability in them to stand in the king's palace, and whom they might teach the learning and the tongue of the Chaldeans.   2 Sam. 14:25

1:1–4 Christian Patriots

Among the children of Israel who were carried captive to Babylon at the beginning of the seventy years' captivity were Chris-tian patriots, men who were as true as steel to principle, who would not be corrupted by selfishness, but who would honor God at the loss of all things. In the land of their captivity these men were to carry out God's purpose by giving to heathen nations the blessings that come through a knowledge of Jehovah. They were to be His representatives. *PK 479*

---

5 And the king appointed them a daily pro-vision of the king's meat, and of the wine which he drank: so nourishing them three years, that at the end thereof they might stand before the king.   Dan. 1:19

6 Now among these were of the children of Judah, Daniel, Hananiah, Mishael, and Aza-riah: Ezek. 14:14, 20; Matt. 24:15

7 Unto whom the prince of the eunuchs gave names: for he gave unto Daniel *the name* of Belteshazzar; and to Hananiah, of Shadrach; and to Mishael, of Meshach; and to Azariah, of Abed-nego.   Dan. 2:49; 4:8; 5:12

8 But Daniel purposed in his heart that he would not defile himself with the portion of the king's meat, nor with the wine which he drank: therefore he requested of the prince of the eunuchs that he might not defile him-self.   Ezek. 4:13-14

1:8 Results of Intemperance

Nor dared [Daniel and his three compan-ions] risk the enervating effect of luxury and dissipation on physical, mental, and spiritu-al development. They were acquainted with the history of Nadab and Abihu, the record of whose intemperance and its results had been preserved in the parchments of the Pen-tateuch; and they knew that their own phys-ical and mental power would be injuriously affected by the use of wine. *PK 482*

---

9 Now God had brought Daniel into favour and tender love with the prince of the eu-nuchs.   Gen. 39:21; Ps. 106:46; Prov. 16:7

10 And the prince of the ᵀeunuchs said unto Daniel, I fear my lord the king, who hath ap-pointed your meat and your drink: for why should he see your faces worse liking than the children which *are* of your sort? then shall ye make *me* endanger my head to the king.   *castrated male servants*

11 Then said Daniel to Melzar, whom the

Success Not an Accident

Daniel 1:19, 20

True success in any line of work is not the result of chance or accident or destiny. It is the out-working of God's providences, the reward of faith and discretion, of virtue and perseverance. Fine mental qualities and a high moral tone are not the result of accident. God gives opportunities; suc-cess depends upon the use made of them.

While God was working in Daniel and his companions "to will and to do of His good pleasure," they were working out their own salvation (Philippians 2:13). Herein is revealed the outworking of the divine principle of co-operation, without which no true success can be attained. Human effort avails nothing without divine power; and without human endeavor, divine effort is with many of no avail. To make God's grace our own, we must act our part. His grace is given to work in us to will and to do, but never as a substitute for our effort.

As the Lord co-operated with Daniel and his fellows, so He will co-operate with all who strive to do His will. And by the impartation of His Spirit He will strengthen every true purpose, every noble resolution. Those who walk in the path of obedience will encounter many hindrances. Strong, subtle influences may bind them to the world; but the Lord is able to render futile every agency that works for the defeat of His chosen ones; in His strength they may overcome every temptation, conquer every difficulty. *PK 486, 487*

prince of the eunuchs had set over Daniel, Hananiah, Mishael, and Azariah,

12 Prove thy servants, I ᵀbeseech thee, ten days; and let them give us pulse to eat, and water to drink.   Dan. 1:16 ◆ beg

13 Then let our countenances be looked upon before thee, and the ᵀcountenance of the children that eat of the portion of the king's meat: and as thou seest, deal with thy servants.   appearance

14 So he consented to them in this matter, and proved them ten days.

15 And at the end of ten days their countenances appeared fairer and fatter in flesh than all the children which did eat the portion of the king's meat.   Ex. 23:25

16 Thus Melzar took away the portion of their meat, and the wine that they should drink; and gave them ᵀpulse.   Dan. 1:12 ◆ vegetables

17 As for these four children, God gave them knowledge and skill in all learning and wisdom: and Daniel had understanding in all visions and dreams.   1 Kin. 3:12; Dan. 2:23; James 1:5

18 Now at the end of the days that the king had said he should bring them in, then the prince of the eunuchs brought them in before Nebuchadnezzar.

19 And the king communed with them; and among them all was found none like Daniel, Hananiah, Mishael, and Azariah: therefore stood they before the king.   Gen. 41:46

20 And in all matters of wisdom and understanding, that the king enquired of them, he found them ten times better than all the magicians and astrologers that were in all his realm.   Gen. 31:7

21 And Daniel continued even unto the first year of king Cyrus.   Dan. 6:28; 10:1

Nebuchadnezzar Dreams

2 And in the second year of the reign of Nebuchadnezzar Nebuchadnezzar dreamed dreams, wherewith his spirit was troubled, and his sleep brake from him.   Esth. 6:1; Dan. 4:5

2:1 The Rise and Fall of Kingdoms

Hundreds of years before certain nations came upon the stage of action, the Omniscient One looked down the ages and predicted the rise and fall of the universal kingdoms. God declared to Nebuchadnezzar that the kingdom of Babylon should fall, and a second kingdom would arise, which also would have its period of trial. Failing to exalt the true God, its glory would fade, and a third kingdom would occupy its place. This also would pass away; and a fourth, strong as iron, would subdue the nations of the world. *PK 501*

2 Then the king commanded to call the magicians, and the astrologers, and the sorcerers, and the Chaldeans, for to shew the king his dreams. So they came and stood before the king.   Gen. 41:8; Ex. 7:11; Dan. 1:20

3 And the king said unto them, I have dreamed a dream, and my spirit was troubled to know the dream.   Gen. 40:8

4 Then spake the Chaldeans to the king in Syriack, O king, live for ever: tell thy servants the dream, and we will shew the interpretation.   Ezra 4:7; Dan. 3:9; 5:10

5 The king answered and said to the Chal-

Approval of God Dearer Than Life Itself

Daniel 1:8–21

Daniel and his associates had been trained by their parents to habits of strict temperance. They had been taught that God would hold them accountable for their capabilities, and that they must never dwarf or enfeeble their powers. . . .

Had Daniel so desired, he might have found in his surroundings a plausible excuse for departing from strictly temperate habits. He might have argued that, dependent as he was on the king's favor and subject to his power, there was no other course for him to pursue than to eat of the king's food and drink of his wine; for should he adhere to the divine teaching, he would offend the king and probably lose his position and his life. Should he disregard the commandment of the Lord he would retain the favor of the king and secure for himself intellectual advantages and flattering worldly prospects.

But Daniel did not hesitate. The approval of God was dearer to him than the favor of the most powerful earthly potentate—dearer than life itself. . . .

In reaching this decision, the [four] Hebrew youth did not act presumptuously, but in firm reliance upon God. They did not choose to be singular, but they would be so rather than dishonor God. Should they compromise with wrong in this instance by yielding to the pressure of circumstances, their departure from principle would weaken their sense of right and their abhorrence of wrong. The first wrong step would lead to others, until, their connection with Heaven severed, they would be swept away by temptation. . . .

[Daniel] asked that the matter be tested by a ten days' trial, the Hebrew youth during this time being supplied with simple food, while their companions ate of the king's dainties. . . .

In personal appearance the Hebrew youth showed a marked superiority over their companions. *PK 482–484*

deans, The thing is gone from me: if ye will not make known unto me the dream, with the interpretation thereof, ye shall be cut in pieces, and your houses shall be made a dunghill.   *2 Kin. 10:27; Ezra 6:11; Dan. 3:29*
6 But if ye shew the dream, and the interpretation thereof, ye shall receive of me gifts and rewards and great honour: therefore shew me the dream, and the interpretation thereof.   *Dan. 2:48; 5:7, 29*
7 They answered again and said, Let the king tell his servants the dream, and we will shew the interpretation of it.   *Dan. 2:4*
8 The king answered and said, I know of certainty that ye would gain the time, because ye see the thing is gone from me.   *Eph. 5:16*
9 But if ye will not make known unto me the dream, *there is but* one decree for you: for ye have prepared lying and corrupt words to speak before me, till the time be changed: therefore tell me the dream, and I shall know that ye can shew me the interpretation thereof.   *Esth. 4:11; Is. 41:23; Dan. 2:21*
10 The Chaldeans answered before the king, and said, There is not a man upon the earth that can shew the king's matter: therefore *there is* no king, lord, nor ruler, *that* asked such things at any magician, or astrologer, or Chaldean.
11 And *it is* a rare thing that the king requireth, and there is none other that can shew it before the king, except the gods, whose dwelling is not with flesh.   *Gen. 41:39; Ex. 29:45*
12 For this cause the king was angry and very furious, and commanded to destroy all the wise *men* of Babylon.   *Dan. 3:13*
13 And the decree went forth that the wise *men* should be slain; and they sought Daniel and his fellows to be slain.   *Dan. 1:19-20*

The Dream Is Revealed to Daniel
14 Then Daniel answered with counsel and wisdom to Arioch the captain of the king's guard, which was gone forth to slay the wise *men* of Babylon: *Gen. 37:36*
15 He answered and said to Arioch the king's captain, Why *is* the decree *so* hasty from the king? Then Arioch made the thing known to Daniel.
16 Then Daniel went in, and desired of the king that he would give him time, and that he would shew the king the interpretation.
17 Then Daniel went to his house, and made the thing known to Hananiah, Mishael, and Azariah, his companions:
18 That they would desire mercies of the God of heaven concerning this secret; that Daniel and his fellows should not perish with the rest of the wise *men* of Babylon.   *Is. 37:4*
19 Then was the secret revealed unto Daniel

in a night vision. Then Daniel blessed the God of heaven.   *Num. 12:6*
20 Daniel answered and said, Blessed be the name of God for ever and ever: for wisdom and might are his: *Ps. 113:2; 115:18; 145:1-2*
21 And he changeth the times and the seasons: he removeth kings, and setteth up kings: he giveth wisdom unto the wise, and knowledge to them that know understanding: *Job 12:18; Dan. 2:9; 7:25*

22 He revealeth the deep and secret things: he knoweth what *is* in the darkness, and the light dwelleth with him.   *Job 12:22; Ps. 25:14; Heb. 4:13*
23 I thank thee, and praise thee, O thou God of my fathers, who hast given me wisdom and might, and hast made known unto me now what we desired of thee: for thou hast *now* made known unto us the king's matter.   *Ex. 3:15*
24 Therefore Daniel went in unto Arioch, whom the king had ordained to destroy the wise *men* of Babylon: he went and said thus unto him; Destroy not the wise *men* of Babylon: bring me in before the king, and I will shew unto the king the interpretation.
25 Then Arioch brought in Daniel before the king in haste, and said thus unto him, I have found a man of the captives of Judah, that will make known unto the king the interpretation.   *Dan. 1:6*
26 The king answered and said to Daniel, whose name *was* Belteshazzar, Art thou able to make known unto me the dream which I have seen, and the interpretation thereof?   *Dan. 1:7; 4:8; 5:12*
27 Daniel answered in the presence of the king, and said, The secret which the king hath demanded cannot the wise *men*, the astrologers, the magicians, the ᵀsoothsayers, shew unto the king; *Dan. 2:2 ♦ those who tell future with astrology*
28 But there is a God in heaven that revealeth secrets, and maketh known to the king Nebuchadnezzar what shall be in the latter days. Thy dream, and the visions of thy head upon thy bed, are these;   *Gen. 40:8; 49:1; Dan. 10:14*
29 As for thee, O king, thy thoughts came *into thy mind* upon thy bed, what should come to pass hereafter: and he that revealeth secrets maketh known to thee what shall come to pass.   *Dan. 2:47*
30 But as for me, this secret is not revealed

to me for *any* wisdom that I have more than any living, but for *their* sakes that shall make known the interpretation to the king, and that thou mightest know the thoughts of thy heart.   Gen. 41:16

The Dream

31 Thou, O king, sawest, and behold a great image. This great image, whose brightness *was* excellent, stood before thee; and the form thereof *was* terrible.   Hab. 1:7
32 This image's head *was* of fine gold, his breast and his arms of silver, his belly and his thighs of brass,
33 His legs of iron, his feet part of iron and part of clay.
34 Thou sawest till that a stone was cut out without hands, which smote the image upon his feet *that were* of iron and clay, and brake them to pieces.   Is. 60:12; Dan. 2:44-45; 8:25
35 Then was the iron, the clay, the brass, the silver, and the gold, broken to pieces together, and became like the chaff of the summer threshingfloors; and the wind carried them away, that no place was found for them: and the stone that smote the image became a great mountain, and filled the whole earth.   Ps. 37:10
36 This *is* the dream; and we will tell the interpretation thereof before the king.
37 Thou, O king, *art* a king of kings: for the God of heaven hath given thee a kingdom, power, and strength, and glory.   Ezra 1:2; 7:12
38 And wheresoever the children of men dwell, the beasts of the field and the fowls of the heaven hath he given into thine hand, and hath made thee ruler over them all. Thou *art* this head of gold.   Dan. 4:21-22

2:37, 38 Ruin Through Rejection

Prophecy has traced the rise and fall of the world's great empires—Babylon, Medo-Persia, Greece, and Rome. With each of these, as with nations of less power, history repeated itself. Each had its period of test, each failed, its glory faded, its power departed, and its place was occupied by another.

While the nations rejected God's principles, and in this rejection wrought their own ruin, it was still manifest that the divine, overruling purpose was working through all their movements. *Ed 177*

---

39 And after thee shall arise another kingdom inferior to thee, and another third kingdom of brass, which shall bear rule over all the earth.   Dan. 2:32
40 And the fourth kingdom shall be strong as iron: forasmuch as iron breaketh in pieces and subdueth all *things*: and as iron that breaketh all these, shall it break in pieces and bruise.   Dan. 7:7
41 And whereas thou sawest the feet and toes, part of potters' clay, and part of iron, the kingdom shall be divided; but there shall be in it of the strength of the iron, ᵀforasmuch as thou sawest the iron mixed with miry clay.   *since*
42 And *as* the toes of the feet *were* part of iron, and part of clay, *so* the kingdom shall be partly strong, and partly broken.
43 And whereas thou sawest iron mixed with ᵀmiry clay, they shall mingle themselves with the seed of men: but they shall not cleave one to another, even as iron is not mixed with clay.   *muddy*
44 And in the days of these kings shall the God of heaven set up a kingdom, which shall never be destroyed: and the kingdom shall not be left to other people, *but* it shall break in pieces and consume all these kingdoms, and it shall stand for ever. Is. 60:12; Dan. 4:34; 6:26
45 Forasmuch as thou sawest that the stone was cut out of the mountain without hands, and that it brake in pieces the iron, the brass, the clay, the silver, and the gold; the great God hath made known to the king what shall come to pass hereafter: and the dream *is* certain, and the interpretation thereof sure.   Gen. 41:28, 32; Is. 28:16

2:45 Founded on the Rock

"Other foundation can no man lay than that is laid, which is Jesus Christ" (1 Corinthians 3:11). "Upon this rock," said Jesus, "I will build My church." In the presence of God, and all the heavenly intelligences, in the presence of the unseen army of hell, Christ founded His church upon the living Rock. That Rock is Himself—His own body, for us broken and bruised. Against the church built upon this foundation, the gates of hell shall not prevail. *DA 413*

Daniel's Advancement

46 Then the king Nebuchadnezzar fell upon his face, and worshipped Daniel, and commanded that they should offer an oblation and sweet odours unto him. Ezra 6:10; Acts 10:25
47 The king answered unto Daniel, and said, Of a truth *it is*, that your God *is* a God of gods, and a Lord of kings, and a revealer of secrets, seeing thou couldest reveal this secret.   Deut. 10:17
48 Then the king made Daniel a great man, and gave him many great gifts, and made him ruler over the whole province of Babylon, and chief of the governors over all the wise *men* of Babylon.   Dan. 2:6; 4:9; 5:11
49 Then Daniel requested of the king, and he

set Shadrach, Meshach, and Abed-nego, over the affairs of the province of Babylon: but Daniel *sat* in the gate of the king.   Esth. 2:19

Nebuchadnezzar Dedicates a Golden Image

3 Nebuchadnezzar the king made an image of gold, whose height *was* ᵀthreescore cubits, *and* the breadth thereof six cubits: he set it up in the plain of Dura, in the province of Babylon.   Is. 46:6 ◆ *sixty*
2 Then Nebuchadnezzar the king sent to gather together the princes, the governors, and the captains, the judges, the treasurers, the counsellors, the sheriffs, and all the rulers of the provinces, to come to the dedication of the image which Nebuchadnezzar the king had set up.   Dan. 3:27
3 Then the princes, the governors, and captains, the judges, the treasurers, the counsellors, the sheriffs, and all the rulers of the provinces, were gathered together unto the dedication of the image that Nebuchadnezzar the king had set up; and they stood before the image that Nebuchadnezzar had set up.
4 Then an herald cried aloud, To you it is commanded, O people, nations, and languages,   Dan. 4:1, 14; 6:25
5 *That* at what time ye hear the sound of the cornet, flute, harp, sackbut, psaltery, dulcimer, and all kinds of musick, ye fall down and worship the golden image that Nebuchadnezzar the king hath set up: Dan. 3:10, 15
6 And whoso falleth not down and worshippeth shall the same hour be cast into the midst of a burning fiery furnace.   Jer. 29:22
7 Therefore at that time, when all the people heard the sound of the cornet, flute, harp, sackbut, ᵀpsaltery, and all kinds of musick, all the people, the nations, and the languages, fell down *and* worshipped the golden image that Nebuchadnezzar the king had set up.   *stringed instruments*

The Fiery Furnace

8 Wherefore at that time certain Chaldeans came near, and accused the Jews. Ezra 4:12-16
9 They spake and said to the king Nebuchadnezzar, O king, live for ever.   Dan. 5:10
10 Thou, O king, hast made a decree, that every man that shall hear the sound of the cornet, flute, harp, sackbut, psaltery, and dulcimer, and all kinds of musick, shall fall down and worship the golden image: Dan. 3:4-7
11 And whoso falleth not down and worshippeth, *that* he should be cast into the midst of a burning fiery furnace.
12 There are certain Jews whom thou hast set over the affairs of the province of Babylon, Shadrach, Meshach, and Abed-nego; these men, O king, have not regarded thee: they serve not thy gods, nor worship the golden image which thou hast set up.   Dan. 2:49; 6:13
13 Then Nebuchadnezzar in *his* rage and fury commanded to bring Shadrach, Meshach, and Abed-nego. Then they brought these men before the king.   Dan. 2:12; 3:19

3:14–18 Men of Implicit Trust

From the history of their fathers [the Hebrews] had learned that disobedience to God results in dishonor, disaster, and death; and that the fear of the Lord is the beginning of wisdom, the foundation of all true prosperity. . . . Their faith strengthened as they declared that God would be glorified by delivering them, and with triumphant assurance born of implicit trust in God, they added, "But if not, be it known unto thee, O king, that we will not serve thy gods, nor worship the golden image which thou hast set up" [Daniel 3:18]. *PK 508*

14 Nebuchadnezzar spake and said unto them, *Is it* true, O Shadrach, Meshach, and Abed-nego, do not ye serve my gods, nor worship the golden image which I have set up?   Is. 46:1
15 Now if ye be ready that at what time ye

Nebuchadnezzar's Pride Problem

Daniel 3

The dream of the great image, opening before Nebuchadnezzar events reaching to the close of time, had been given that he might understand the part he was to act in the world's history, and the relation that his kingdom should sustain to the kingdom of heaven. In the interpretation of the dream, he had been plainly instructed regarding the establishment of God's everlasting kingdom. . . .

For a time afterward, Nebuchadnezzar was influenced by the fear of God; but his heart was not yet cleansed from worldly ambition and a desire for self-exaltation. The prosperity attending his reign filled him with pride. In time he ceased to honor God, and resumed his idol worship with increased zeal and bigotry. . . .

Instead of reproducing the image as he had seen it, he would excel the original. His image should not deteriorate in value from the head to the feet, but should be entirely of gold—symbolic throughout [all] of Babylon as an eternal, indestructible, all-powerful kingdom, which should break in pieces all other kingdoms and stand forever. *PK 503, 504*

hear the sound of the cornet, flute, harp, sackbut, psaltery, and dulcimer, and all kinds of musick, ye fall down and worship the image which I have made; *well*: but if ye worship not, ye shall be cast the same hour into the midst of a burning fiery furnace; and who *is* that God that shall deliver you out of my hands?   Ex. 5:2; 2 Kin. 18:35; Dan. 6:20

16 Shadrach, Meshach, and Abed-nego, answered and said to the king, O Nebuchadnezzar, we *are* not careful to answer thee in this matter.

17 If it be *so,* our God whom we serve is able to deliver us from the burning fiery furnace, and he will deliver *us* out of thine hand, O king.   Job 5:19

18 But if not, be it known unto thee, O king, that we will not serve thy gods, nor worship the golden image which thou hast set up.   Is. 51:12-13

19 Then was Nebuchadnezzar full of fury, and the form of his ᵀvisage was changed against Shadrach, Meshach, and Abednego: *therefore* he spake, and commanded that they should heat the furnace one seven times more than it was ᵀwont to be heated.   Dan. 3:13 ◆ appearance ◆ accustomed

20 And he commanded the most mighty men that *were* in his army to bind Shadrach, Meshach, and Abed-nego, *and* to cast *them* into the burning fiery furnace.

21 Then these men were bound in their coats, their ᵀhosen, and their hats, and their *other* garments, and were cast into the midst of the burning fiery furnace.   undergarment

22 Therefore because the king's commandment was urgent, and the furnace exceeding hot, the flame of the fire slew those men that took up Shadrach, Meshach, and Abed-nego.   Ex. 12:33

23 And these three men, Shadrach, Meshach, and Abed-nego, fell down bound into the midst of the burning fiery furnace.

24 Then Nebuchadnezzar the king was ᵀastonied, and rose up in haste, *and* spake, and said unto his counsellors, Did not we cast three men bound into the midst of the fire? They answered and said unto the king, True, O king.   Dan. 6:7 ◆ surprised

3:25 Why the King Recognized Jesus

How did that heathen king [Nebuchadnezzar] know what the Son of God was like? The Hebrew captives filling positions of trust in Babylon had in life and character represented before him the truth. . . . Plainly and simply they had presented the principles of righteousness, thus teaching those around them of the God whom they worshiped. They had told of Christ, the Redeemer to come; and in the form of the fourth in the midst of the fire the king recognized the Son of God. *PK 509*

25 He answered and said, Lo, I see four men loose, walking in the midst of the fire, and they have no hurt; and the form of the fourth is like the Son of God.   Is. 43:2

26 Then Nebuchadnezzar came near to the mouth of the burning fiery furnace, *and* spake, and said, Shadrach, Meshach, and Abed-nego, ye servants of the most high God, come forth, and come ᵀhither. Then Shadrach, Meshach, and Abed-nego, came forth of the midst of the fire.   Dan. 3:17 ◆ here

27 And the princes, governors, and captains, and the king's counsellors, being gathered together, saw these men, upon whose bodies the fire had no power, nor was an hair of their head singed, neither were their coats changed, nor the smell of fire had passed on them.   Is. 43:2; Dan. 3:2-3; Heb. 11:34

28 *Then* Nebuchadnezzar spake, and said, Blessed *be* the God of Shadrach, Meshach, and Abed-nego, who hath sent his angel, and delivered his servants that trusted in him, and have changed the king's word, and yielded their bodies, that they might not serve nor worship any god, except their own God.   Acts 5:19

29 Therefore I make a decree, That every people, nation, and language, which speak any thing amiss against the God of Shadrach, Meshach, and Abed-nego, shall be cut in pieces, and their houses shall be made a dunghill: because there is no other God that can deliver after this sort.   Dan. 2:5

3:29 No Forced Worship

It was right for the king to make public confession, and to seek to exalt the God of heaven above all other gods; but in endeavoring to force his subjects to make a similar confession of faith and to show similar reverence, Nebuchadnezzar was exceeding his right as a temporal sovereign. He had no more right, either civil or moral, to threaten men with death for not worshiping God, than he had to make the decree consigning to the flames all who refused to worship the golden image. God never compels the obedience of man. *PK 510, 511*

30 Then the king promoted Shadrach, Meshach, and Abed-nego, in the province of Babylon.   Dan. 2:49

Nebuchadnezzar Praises God

4 Nebuchadnezzar the king, unto all people, nations, and languages, that dwell in all the earth; Peace be multiplied unto you.   Ezra 4:17; Dan. 3:4; 6:25

2 I thought it good to shew the signs and wonders that the high God hath ᵀwrought toward me.   Dan. 3:26 ◆ made

3 How great *are* his signs! and how mighty

are his wonders! his kingdom *is* an everlasting kingdom, and his dominion *is* from generation to generation. Ps. 77:19; 105:27; Dan. 2:44

Nebuchadnezzar Has Another Dream

4 I Nebuchadnezzar was at rest in mine house, and flourishing in my palace: Is. 47:7-8
5 I saw a dream which made me afraid, and the thoughts upon my bed and the visions of my head troubled me.   Dan. 2:1
6 Therefore made I a decree to bring in all the wise *men* of Babylon before me, that they might make known unto me the interpretation of the dream.   Dan. 2:2
7 Then came in the magicians, the astrologers, the Chaldeans, and the ᵀsoothsayers: and I told the dream before them; but they did not make known unto me the interpretation thereof. Is. 44:25 ◆ *those who tell future with astrology*
8 But at the last Daniel came in before me, whose name *was* Belteshazzar, according to the name of my god, and in whom *is* the spirit of the holy gods: and before him I told the dream, *saying,*   Dan. 1:7; 4:18; 5:14
9 O Belteshazzar, master of the magicians, because I know that the spirit of the holy gods *is* in thee, and no secret troubleth thee, tell me the visions of my dream that I have seen, and the interpretation thereof. Dan. 2:48
10 Thus *were* the visions of mine head in my bed; I saw, and behold a tree in the midst of the earth, and the height thereof *was* great.
11 The tree grew, and was strong, and the height thereof reached unto heaven, and the sight thereof to the end of all the earth:
12 The leaves thereof *were* fair, and the fruit thereof much, and in it *was* meat for all: the beasts of the field had shadow under it, and the fowls of the heaven dwelt in the boughs thereof, and all flesh was fed of it. Ezek. 17:23
13 I saw in the visions of my head upon my bed, and, behold, a watcher and an holy one came down from heaven;Deut. 33:2; Dan. 7:1; 8:13
14 He cried aloud, and said thus, Hew down the tree, and cut off his branches, shake off

his leaves, and scatter his fruit: let the beasts get away from under it, and the fowls from his branches: Ezek. 31:12-13; Dan. 4:23; Matt. 3:10
15 Nevertheless leave the stump of his roots in the earth, even with a band of iron and brass, in the tender grass of the field; and let it be wet with the dew of heaven, and *let* him portion *be* with the beasts in the grass of the earth:
16 Let his heart be changed from man's, and let a beast's heart be given unto him; and let seven times pass over him.   Dan. 4:23, 25
17 This matter *is* by the decree of the watchers, and the demand by the word of the holy ones: to the intent that the living may know that the most High ruleth in the kingdom of men, and giveth it to whomsoever he will, and setteth up over it the basest of men.   1 Sam. 2:8; Jer. 27:5-7; Dan. 4:25

> ### 4:17 Destiny of Men and Nations
>
> The history of nations speaks to us today. To every nation and to every individual God has assigned a place in His great plan. Today men and nations are being tested by the plummet in the hand of Him who makes no mistake. All are by their own choice deciding their destiny, and God is overruling all for the accomplishment of His purposes.
>
> The prophecies which the great I AM has given in His word, uniting link after link in the chain of events, from eternity in the past to eternity in the future, tell us where we are today in the procession of the ages and what may be expected in the time to come. *PK 536*

18 This dream I king Nebuchadnezzar have seen. Now thou, O Belteshazzar, declare the interpretation thereof, ᵀforasmuch as all the wise *men* of my kingdom are not able to make known unto me the interpretation: but thou *art* able; for the spirit of the holy gods *is* in thee.   Gen. 41:8; Dan. 5:8, 15 ◆ *since*

Daniel Interprets the Dream

19 Then Daniel, whose name *was* Belteshazzar, was ᵀastonied for one hour, and

Nebuchadnezzar Transformed

Daniel 4

The once proud monarch had become a humble child of God; the tyrannical, overbearing ruler, a wise and compassionate king. He who had defied and blasphemed the God of heaven, now acknowledged the power of the Most High and earnestly sought to promote the fear of Jehovah and the happiness of his subjects. Under the rebuke of Him who is King of kings and Lord of lords, Nebuchadnezzar had learned at last the lesson which all rulers need to learn—that true greatness consists in true goodness. He acknowledged Jehovah as the living God, saying, "I Nebuchadnezzar praise and extol and honor the King of heaven, all whose works are truth, and His ways judgment: and those that walk in pride He is able to abase" [Daniel 4:37].

God's purpose that the greatest kingdom in the world should show forth His praise was now fulfilled. This public proclamation, in which Nebuchadnezzar acknowledged the mercy and goodness and authority of God, was the last act of his life recorded in sacred history. *PK 521*

his thoughts troubled him. The king spake, and said, Belteshazzar, let not the dream, or the interpretation thereof, trouble thee. Belteshazzar answered and said, My lord, the dream *be* to them that hate thee, and the interpretation thereof to thine enemies.					Dan. 7:28 ◆ *surprised*

20 The tree that thou sawest, which grew, and was strong, whose height reached unto the heaven, and the sight thereof to all the earth;					Dan. 4:10-12

21 Whose leaves *were* fair, and the fruit thereof much, and in it *was* meat for all; under which the beasts of the field dwelt, and upon whose branches the fowls of the heaven had their habitation:

22 It *is* thou, O king, that art grown and become strong: for thy greatness is grown, and reacheth unto heaven, and thy dominion to the end of the earth.					2 Sam. 12:7

23 And whereas the king saw a watcher and an holy one coming down from heaven, and saying, Hew the tree down, and destroy it; yet leave the stump of the roots thereof in the earth, even with a band of iron and brass, in the tender grass of the field; and let it be wet with the dew of heaven, and *let* his portion *be* with the beasts of the field, till seven times pass over him;					Dan. 5:21

24 This *is* the interpretation, O king, and this *is* the decree of the most High, which is come upon my lord the king:					Ps. 107:40

25 That they shall drive thee from men, and thy dwelling shall be with the beasts of the field, and they shall make thee to eat grass as oxen, and they shall wet thee with the dew of heaven, and seven times shall pass over thee, till thou know that the most High ruleth in the kingdom of men, and giveth it to whomsoever he will.					Ps. 83:18; Jer. 27:5; Dan. 4:17

26 And whereas they commanded to leave the stump of the tree roots; thy kingdom shall be sure unto thee, after that thou shalt have known that the heavens do rule.					Dan. 4:15

27 Wherefore, O king, let my counsel be acceptable unto thee, and break off thy sins by righteousness, and thine iniquities by shewing mercy to the poor; if it may be a lengthening of thy tranquillity.					1 Kin. 21:29

Nebuchadnezzar's Temporary Insanity

28 All this came upon the king Nebuchadnezzar.					Num. 23:19

29 At the end of twelve months he walked in the palace of the kingdom of Babylon.

30 The king spake, and said, Is not this great Babylon, that I have built for the house of the kingdom by the might of my power, and for the honour of my majesty?					Is. 37:24-25

31 While the word *was* in the king's mouth, there fell a voice from heaven, *saying*, O king

Nebuchadnezzar, to thee it is spoken; The kingdom is departed from thee.					Luke 12:20

32 And they shall drive thee from men, and thy dwelling *shall be* with the beasts of the field: they shall make thee to eat grass as oxen, and seven times shall pass over thee, until thou know that the most High ruleth in the kingdom of men, and giveth it to whomsoever he will.					Dan. 5:21

33 The same hour was the thing fulfilled upon Nebuchadnezzar: and he was driven from men, and did eat grass as oxen, and his body was wet with the dew of heaven, till his hairs were grown like eagles' *feathers*, and his nails like birds' *claws*.					Dan. 4:25

Nebuchadnezzar Praises God

34 And at the end of the days I Nebuchadnezzar lifted up mine eyes unto heaven, and mine understanding returned unto me, and I blessed the most High, and I praised and honoured him that liveth for ever, whose dominion *is* an everlasting dominion, and his kingdom *is* from generation to generation:					Jer. 10:10; Dan. 12:7; Rev. 4:10

35 And all the inhabitants of the earth *are* reputed as nothing: and he doeth according to his will in the army of heaven, and *among* the inhabitants of the earth: and none can stay his hand, or say unto him, What doest thou?					Job 42:2; Ps. 115:3; 135:6

36 At the same time my reason returned unto me; and for the glory of my kingdom, mine honour and brightness returned unto me; and my counsellors and my lords sought unto me; and I was established in my kingdom, and excellent majesty was added unto me.					Prov. 22:4

37 Now I Nebuchadnezzar praise and ᵀextol and honour the King of heaven, all whose works *are* truth, and his ways judgment: and those that walk in pride he is able to abase.					Ex. 18:11; Deut. 32:4; Job 40:11-12 ◆ *praise*

Belshazzar's Impious Feast

5 Belshazzar the king made a great feast to a thousand of his lords, and drank wine before the thousand.					Esth. 1:3; Is. 22:12, 14

2 Belshazzar, whiles he tasted the wine, commanded to bring the golden and silver vessels which his father Nebuchadnezzar had taken out of the temple which *was* in Jerusalem; that the king, and his princes, his wives, and his concubines, might drink therein.					2 Kin. 24:13; 25:15; Dan. 1:2

3 Then they brought the golden vessels that were taken out of the temple of the house of God which *was* at Jerusalem; and the king, and his princes, his wives, and his concubines, drank in them.

4 They drank wine, and praised the gods of

gold, and of silver, of brass, of iron, of wood, and of stone.   Ps. 135:15-18; Dan. 5:23; Hab. 2:19

The Handwriting on the Wall

5 In the same hour came forth fingers of a man's hand, and wrote over against the candlestick upon the plaister of the wall of the king's palace: and the king saw the part of the hand that wrote.   Dan. 4:31

6 Then the king's countenance was changed, and his thoughts troubled him, so that the joints of his loins were loosed, and his knees smote one against another.   Ps. 69:23; Ezek. 7:17

7 The king cried aloud to bring in the astrologers, the Chaldeans, and the ᵀsoothsayers. And the king spake, and said to the wise men of Babylon, Whosoever shall read this writing, and shew me the interpretation thereof, shall be clothed with scarlet, and have a chain of gold about his neck, and shall be the third ruler in the kingdom.   Dan. 2:6; 5:16, 29

8 Then came in all the king's wise men: but they could not read the writing, nor make known to the king the interpretation thereof.   Gen. 41:8; Dan. 2:27; 4:7

9 Then was king Belshazzar greatly troubled, and his countenance was changed in him, and his lords were ᵀastonied.   Is. 13:6-8; Dan. 2:1

The End of Babylon

10 Now the queen, by reason of the words of the king and his lords, came into the banquet house: and the queen spake and said, O king, live for ever: let not thy thoughts trouble thee, nor let thy ᵀcountenance be changed: Dan. 3:9 ◆ appearance

11 There is a man in thy kingdom, in whom is the spirit of the holy gods; and in the days of thy father light and understanding and wisdom, like the wisdom of the gods, was found in him; whom the king Nebuchadnezzar thy father, the king, I say, thy father, made master of the magicians, astrologers, Chaldeans, and soothsayers;   Gen. 41:11-15

12 Forasmuch as an excellent spirit, and knowledge, and understanding, interpreting of dreams, and shewing of hard sentences, and dissolving of doubts, were found in the same Daniel, whom the king named Belteshazzar: now let Daniel be called, and he will shew the interpretation.   Dan. 1:7; 5:14; 6:3

13 Then was Daniel brought in before the king. And the king spake and said unto Daniel, Art thou that Daniel, which art of the children of the captivity of Judah, whom the king my father brought out of Jewry?   Dan. 2:25

14 I have even heard of thee, that the spirit of the gods is in thee, and that light and understanding and excellent wisdom is found in thee.

15 And now the wise men, the astrologers, have been brought in before me, that they should read this writing, and make known unto me the interpretation thereof: but they could not shew the interpretation of the thing: Dan. 5:7-8

16 And I have heard of thee, that thou canst make interpretations, and dissolve doubts: now if thou canst read the writing, and make known to me the interpretation thereof, thou shalt be clothed with scarlet, and have a chain of gold about thy neck, and shalt be the third ruler in the kingdom.   Gen. 40:8; Dan. 5:7, 29

17 Then Daniel answered and said before the king, Let thy gifts be to thyself, and give thy rewards to another; yet I will read the writing unto the king, and make known to him the interpretation.   2 Kin. 5:16

18 O thou king, the most high God gave Nebuchadnezzar thy father a kingdom, and majesty, and glory, and honour: Dan. 2:37-38

19 And for the majesty that he gave him, all people, nations, and languages, trembled and feared before him: whom he would he slew; and whom he would he kept alive; and whom he would he set up; and whom he would he put down.   Dan. 2:12-13

20 But when his heart was lifted up, and his mind hardened in pride, he was deposed from his kingly throne, and they took his glory from him: Jer. 13:18

21 And he was driven from the sons of men;

Wasted Opportunities

Daniel 5

Through the folly and weakness of Belshazzar, the grandson of Nebuchadnezzar, proud Babylon was soon to fall. Admitted in his youth to a share in kingly authority, Belshazzar gloried in his power and lifted up his heart against the God of heaven. Many had been his opportunities to know the divine will and to understand his responsibility of rendering obedience thereto. He had known of his grandfather's banishment, by the decree of God, from the society of men; and he was familiar with Nebuchadnezzar's conversion and miraculous restoration. But Belshazzar allowed the love of pleasure and self-glorification to efface the lessons that he should never have forgotten. He wasted the opportunities graciously granted him, and neglected to use the means within his reach for becoming more fully acquainted with truth. That which Nebuchadnezzar had finally gained at the cost of untold suffering and humiliation, Belshazzar passed by with indifference. PK 522

and his heart was made like the beasts, and his dwelling *was* with the wild asses: they fed him with grass like oxen, and his body was wet with the dew of heaven; till he knew that the most high God ruled in the kingdom of men, and *that* he appointeth over it whomsoever he will.　Ezek. 17:24; Dan. 4:17, 25

22 And thou his son, O Belshazzar, hast not humbled thine heart, though thou knewest all this;　Ex. 10:3; 2 Chr. 33:23; 36:12

23 But hast lifted up thyself against the Lord of heaven; and they have brought the vessels of his house before thee, and thou, and thy lords, thy wives, and thy concubines, have drunk wine in them; and thou hast praised the gods of silver, and gold, of brass, iron, wood, and stone, which see not, nor hear, nor know: and the God in whose hand thy breath *is*, and whose *are* all thy ways, hast thou not glorified:　Job 12:10; 31:4; Jer. 10:23

24 Then was the part of the hand sent from him; and this writing was written.

25 And this *is* the writing that was written, MENE, MENE, TEKEL, UPHARSIN.

26 This *is* the interpretation of the thing: MENE; God hath numbered thy kingdom, and finished it.　Jer. 27:7

27 TEKEL; Thou art weighed in the balances, and art found wanting.　Job 31:6; Ps. 62:9

5:27 Weighed and Found Wanting

While the man of business is absorbed in the pursuit of gain, while the pleasure lover is seeking indulgence, while the daughter of fashion is arranging her adornments—it may be in that hour the Judge of all the earth will pronounce the sentence: "Thou art weighed in the balances, and art found wanting" (Daniel 5:27). *GC 491*

---

28 PERES; Thy kingdom is divided, and given to the Medes and Persians.　Is. 13:17; 21:2

29 Then commanded Belshazzar, and they clothed Daniel with scarlet, and *put* a chain of gold about his neck, and made a proclamation concerning him, that he should be the third ruler in the kingdom.　Dan. 5:7

30 In that night was Belshazzar the king of the Chaldeans slain.　Jer. 51:31, 39, 57

5:30 Strange Perversity

In that last night of mad folly, Belshazzar and his lords had filled up the measure of their guilt and the guilt of the Chaldean kingdom. No longer could God's restraining hand ward off the impending evil. Through manifold providences, God had sought to teach them reverence for His law. "We would have healed Babylon," He declared of those whose judgment was now reaching unto heaven, "but she is not healed" (Jeremiah 51:9). *PK 530*

---

31 And Darius the Median took the kingdom, *being* about [T]threescore and two years old.　Dan. 6:1; 9:1 ◆ *sixty*

Daniel in the Lions' Den

6 It pleased Darius to set over the kingdom an hundred and twenty princes, which should be over the whole kingdom;　Esth. 1:1

2 And over these three presidents; of whom Daniel *was* first: that the princes might give accounts unto them, and the king should have no damage.　Ezra 4:22

3 Then this Daniel was preferred above the presidents and princes, because an excellent spirit *was* in him; and the king thought to set him over the whole realm.　Esth. 10:3; Dan. 5:12

4 Then the presidents and princes sought to find occasion against Daniel concerning the kingdom; but they could find none occasion nor fault; [T]forasmuch as he *was* faithful, neither was there any error or fault found in him.　Gen. 43:18 ◆ *since*

6:1–4 Faithful and Without Fault

Throughout the reign of successive monarchs, the downfall of the nation, and the establishment of a rival kingdom, such were [Daniel's] wisdom and statesmanship, so perfect his tact, his courtesy, and his genuine goodness of heart, combined with fidelity to principle, that even his enemies were forced to the confession that "they could find none occasion nor fault; forasmuch as he was faithful" (Daniel 6:4). *Ed 56*

---

5 Then said these men, We shall not find any occasion against this Daniel, except we find *it* against him concerning the law of his God.　Acts 24:13-16

6 Then these presidents and princes assembled together to the king, and said thus unto him, King Darius, live for ever.　Neh. 2:3; Dan. 2:4

7 All the presidents of the kingdom, the governors, and the princes, the counsellors, and the captains, have consulted together to establish a royal statute, and to make a firm decree, that whosoever shall ask a petition of any God or man for thirty days, save of thee, O king, he shall be cast into the den of lions.　Ps. 59:3

8 Now, O king, establish the decree, and sign the writing, that it be not changed, according to the law of the Medes and Persians, which altereth not.　Esth. 1:19; Dan. 6:12, 15

9 Wherefore king Darius signed the writing and the decree.　Ps. 118:9

10 Now when Daniel knew that the writing was signed, he went into his house; and his windows being open in his chamber toward Jerusalem, he kneeled upon his knees three

times a day, and prayed, and gave thanks before his God, as he did ^Taforetime.   *before*

11 Then these men assembled, and found Daniel praying and making supplication before his God.   Ps. 37:32-33

12 Then they came near, and spake before the king concerning the king's decree; Hast thou not signed a decree, that every man that shall ask *a petition* of any God or man within thirty days, save of thee, O king, shall be cast into the den of lions? The king answered and said, The thing *is* true, according to the law of the Medes and Persians, which altereth not.   Esth. 1:19; Dan. 3:8-12; 6:8

13 Then answered they and said before the king, That Daniel, which *is* of the children of the captivity of Judah, regardeth not thee, O king, nor the decree that thou hast signed, but maketh his petition three times a day.   Esth. 3:8; Dan. 2:25; 3:12

14 Then the king, when he heard *these* words, was sore displeased with himself, and set *his* heart on Daniel to deliver him: and he laboured till the going down of the sun to deliver him.   Mark 6:26

15 Then these men assembled unto the king, and said unto the king, Know, O king, that the law of the Medes and Persians *is*, That no decree nor statute which the king establisheth may be changed.   Esth. 8:8

16 Then the king commanded, and they brought Daniel, and cast *him* into the den of lions. *Now* the king spake and said unto Daniel, Thy God whom thou servest continually, he will deliver thee.   Job 5:19

17 And a stone was brought, and laid upon the mouth of the den; and the king sealed it with his own ^Tsignet, and with the signet of his lords; that the purpose might not be changed concerning Daniel.   Lam. 3:53 ◆ *identifying seal*

18 Then the king went to his palace, and passed the night fasting: neither were instruments of musick brought before him: and his sleep went from him.   2 Sam. 12:16-17; Esth. 6:1

19 Then the king arose very early in the morning, and went in haste unto the den of lions.

20 And when he came to the den, he cried with a lamentable voice unto Daniel: *and* the king spake and said to Daniel, O Daniel, servant of the living God, is thy God, whom thou servest continually, able to deliver thee from the lions?   Gen. 18:14; Dan. 3:17; 6:16

21 Then said Daniel unto the king, O king, live for ever.   Dan. 2:4; 6:6

22 My God hath sent his angel, and hath shut the lions' mouths, that they have not hurt me: forasmuch as before him innocency was found in me; and also before thee, O king, have I done no hurt. Dan. 3:28; 2 Tim. 4:17; Heb. 11:33

23 Then was the king exceeding glad for him, and commanded that they should take Daniel up out of the den. So Daniel was taken up out of the den, and no manner of hurt was found upon him, because he believed in his God.   1 Chr. 5:20

24 And the king commanded, and they brought those men which had accused Daniel, and they cast *them* into the den of lions, them, their children, and their wives; and the lions had the mastery of them, and brake

all their bones in pieces or ever they came at the bottom of the den.   Deut. 24:16

25 Then king Darius wrote unto all people, nations, and languages, that dwell in all the earth; Peace be multiplied unto you. Ezra 1:1-2

26 I make a decree, That in every dominion of my kingdom men tremble and fear before the God of Daniel: for he *is* the living God, and stedfast for ever, and his kingdom *that* which shall not be destroyed, and his dominion *shall be even* unto the end. Dan. 2:44; 3:29; 4:34

27 He delivereth and rescueth, and he worketh signs and wonders in heaven and in earth, who hath delivered Daniel from the power of the lions.   Dan. 4:2-3

28 So this Daniel prospered in the reign of Darius, and in the reign of Cyrus the Persian.   Is. 44:28–45:1; Dan. 1:21

6:28 An Example to Every Businessman

Daniel, the prime minister of the greatest of earthly kingdoms, was at the same time a prophet of God, receiving the light of heavenly inspiration. A man of like passions as ourselves, the pen of inspiration describes him as without fault. His business transactions, when subjected to the closest scrutiny of his enemies, were found to be without one flaw. He was an example of what every businessman may become when his heart is converted and consecrated, and when his motives are right in the sight of God. *PK 546*

Daniel's Vision of Four Beasts

7 In the first year of Belshazzar king of Babylon Daniel had a dream and visions of his head upon his bed: then he wrote the dream, *and* told the sum of the matters.   Dan. 4:5

2 Daniel spake and said, I saw in my vision by night, and, behold, the four winds of the heaven strove upon the great sea.   Rev. 7:1

3 And four great beasts came up from the sea, diverse one from another. Dan. 7:17; Rev. 13:1

4 The first *was* like a lion, and had eagle's wings: I beheld till the wings thereof were plucked, and it was lifted up from the earth, and made stand upon the feet as a man, and a man's heart was given to it.   Jer. 4:7

5 And behold another beast, a second, like to a bear, and it raised up itself on one side, and *it had* three ribs in the mouth of it between the teeth of it: and they said thus unto it, Arise, devour much flesh.   Dan. 2:39

6 After this I beheld, and lo another, like a leopard, which had upon the back of it four wings of a fowl; the beast had also four heads; and dominion was given to it. Rev. 13:2

7 After this I saw in the night visions, and behold a fourth beast, dreadful and terrible, and strong exceedingly; and it had great iron teeth: it devoured and brake in pieces, and stamped the residue with the feet of it: and it *was* diverse from all the beasts that *were* before it; and it had ten horns.   Rev. 12:3; 13:1

8 I considered the horns, and, behold, there came up among them another little horn, before whom there were three of the first horns plucked up by the roots: and, behold, in this horn *were* eyes like the eyes of man, and a mouth speaking great things.   Ps. 12:3; Rev. 9:7

9 I beheld till the thrones were cast down, and the Ancient of days did sit, whose garment *was* white as snow, and the hair of his head like the pure wool: his throne *was like* the fiery flame, *and* his wheels *as* burning fire.   Ps. 90:2; Dan. 7:22; Rev. 1:14

10 A fiery stream issued and came forth from before him: thousand thousands ministered unto him, and ten thousand times ten thousand stood before him: the judgment was set, and the books were opened.   Deut. 33:2; Ps. 50:3

7:10 The Great Tribunal

Thus was presented to the prophet's vision the great and solemn day when the characters and the lives of men should pass in review before the Judge of all the earth, and to every man should be rendered "according to his works." The Ancient of Days is God the Father. . . . And holy angels as ministers and witnesses, in number "ten thousand times ten thousand, and thousands of thousands," attend this great tribunal [Daniel 7:10]. *GC 479*

11 I beheld then because of the voice of the great words which the horn spake: I beheld *even* till the beast was slain, and his body destroyed, and given to the burning flame.

12 As concerning the rest of the beasts, they had their dominion taken away: yet their lives were prolonged for a season and time.

13 I saw in the night visions, and, behold, *one* like the Son of man came with the clouds of heaven, and came to the Ancient of days, and they brought him near before him.   Matt. 24:30; 26:64; Rev. 1:7

7:13, 14 A Tie Never to Be Broken

By His life and His death, Christ has achieved even more than recovery from the ruin wrought through sin. It was Satan's purpose to bring about an eternal separation between God and man; but in Christ we become more closely united to God than if we had never fallen. In taking our nature, the Saviour has bound Himself to humanity by a tie that is never to be broken. *DA 25*

14 And there was given him dominion, and glory, and a kingdom, that all people, nations, and languages, should serve him: his domin-

ion *is* an everlasting dominion, which shall not pass away, and his kingdom *that* which shall not be destroyed.   Dan. 2:44; 7:27; Rev. 11:15

The Interpretation of the Vision

15 I Daniel was grieved in my spirit in the midst of *my* body, and the visions of my head troubled me.   Dan. 7:28
16 I came near unto one of them that stood by, and asked him the truth of all this. So he told me, and made me know the interpretation of the things.   Rev. 5:5
17 These great beasts, which are four, *are* four kings, *which* shall arise out of the earth.
18 But the saints of the most High shall take the kingdom, and possess the kingdom for ever, even for ever and ever.   Is. 60:12-14
19 Then I would know the truth of the fourth beast, which was diverse from all the others, exceeding dreadful, whose teeth *were of* iron, and his nails *of* brass; *which* devoured, brake in pieces, and stamped the residue with his feet;   Dan. 7:7
20 And of the ten horns that *were* in his head, and *of* the other which came up, and before whom three fell; even *of* that horn that had eyes, and a mouth that spake very great things, whose look *was* more ᵀstout than his fellows.   Dan. 7:8 ◆ strong
21 I beheld, and the same horn made war with the saints, and prevailed against them;   Dan. 8:24
22 Until the Ancient of days came, and judgment was given to the saints of the most High; and the time came that the saints possessed the kingdom.   Dan. 7:18
23 Thus he said, The fourth beast shall be the fourth kingdom upon earth, which shall be diverse from all kingdoms, and shall devour the whole earth, and shall tread it down, and break it in pieces.   Dan. 2:40
24 And the ten horns out of this kingdom *are* ten kings *that* shall arise: and another shall rise after them; and he shall be diverse from the first, and he shall subdue three kings.   Dan. 7:20; Rev. 13:1

7:25 A Catastrophic Change

Says Daniel, of the little horn, the papacy: "He shall think to change times and the law" (Daniel 7:25, R.V.). And Paul styled the same power the "man of sin," who was to exalt himself above God. One prophecy is a complement of the other. Only by changing God's law could the papacy exalt itself above God; whoever should understandingly keep the law as thus changed would be giving supreme honor to that power by which the change was made. *GC 446*

25 And he shall speak *great* words against the most High, and shall wear out the saints of the most High, and think to change times and laws: and they shall be given into his hand until a time and times and the dividing of time.   Dan. 2:21; 12:7; Rev. 12:14
26 But the judgment shall sit, and they shall take away his dominion, to consume and to destroy *it* unto the end.
27 And the kingdom and dominion, and the greatness of the kingdom under the whole heaven, shall be given to the people of the saints of the most High, whose kingdom *is* an everlasting kingdom, and all dominions shall serve and obey him.   Ps. 22:27; 72:11; Dan. 2:44
28 Hitherto *is* the end of the matter. As for me Daniel, my cogitations much troubled me, and my ᵀcountenance changed in me: but I kept the matter in my heart. Luke 2:19 ◆ appearance

Daniel's Vision of the Ram and the Goat

8 In the third year of the reign of king Belshazzar a vision appeared unto me, *even unto* me Daniel, after that which appeared unto me at the first.   Dan. 7:1
2 And I saw in a vision; and it came to pass, when I saw, that I *was* at Shushan *in* the palace, which *is* in the province of Elam; and I saw in a vision, and I was by the river of Ulai.   Gen. 10:22
3 Then I lifted up mine eyes, and saw, and, behold, there stood before the river a ram which had *two* horns: and the *two* horns *were*

The Two Sanctuaries

Daniel 8

Such was the service performed "unto the example and shadow of heavenly things." And what was done in type in the ministration of the earthly sanctuary is done in reality in the ministration of the heavenly sanctuary. After His ascension our Saviour began His work as our high priest. . . .

For eighteen centuries this work of ministration continued in the first apartment of the sanctuary. The blood of Christ, pleaded in behalf of penitent believers, secured their pardon and acceptance with the Father, yet their sins still remained upon the books of record. As in the typical [symbolic] service there was a work of atonement at the close of the year, so before Christ's work for the redemption of men is completed there is a work of atonement for the removal of sin from the sanctuary. *GC 420, 421*

high; but one *was* higher than the other, and the higher came up last.   Dan. 8:20

4 I saw the ram pushing westward, and northward, and southward; so that no beasts might stand before him, neither *was there any* that could deliver out of his hand; but he did according to his will, and became great.   Dan. 11:16

5 And as I was considering, behold, an he goat came from the west on the face of the whole earth, and touched not the ground: and the goat *had* a notable horn between his eyes.   Dan. 8:8, 21; 11:3

6 And he came to the ram that had *two* horns, which I had seen standing before the river, and ran unto him in the fury of his power.

7 And I saw him come close unto the ram, and he was moved with ᵀcholer against him, and smote the ram, and brake his two horns: and there was no power in the ram to stand before him, but he cast him down to the ground, and stamped upon him: and there was none that could deliver the ram out of his hand.   Dan. 7:7 ♦ *anger*

8 Therefore the he goat ᵀwaxed very great: and when he was strong, the great horn was broken; and for it came up four notable ones toward the four winds of heaven.   2 Chr. 26:16

9 And out of one of them came forth a little horn, which waxed exceeding great, toward the south, and toward the east, and toward the pleasant *land*.   Ps. 48:2; Ezek. 20:6; Dan. 11:16

10 And it waxed great, *even* to the host of heaven; and it cast down *some* of the host and of the stars to the ground, and stamped upon them.   Is. 14:13; Dan. 7:7; Rev. 12:4

11 Yea, he magnified *himself* even to the prince of the host, and by him the daily *sacrifice* was taken away, and the place of his sanctuary was cast down. Ezek. 46:14; Dan. 11:31; 12:11

12 And an host was given *him* against the daily *sacrifice* by reason of ᵀtransgression, and it cast down the truth to the ground; and it practised, and prospered.   Is. 59:14 ♦ *lawlessness*

8:14 Cleansing of the Sanctuary

But the most important question remains to be answered: What is the cleansing of the sanctuary? That there was such a service in connection with the earthly sanctuary is stated in the Old Testament Scriptures. But can there be anything in heaven to be cleansed? In Hebrews 9 the cleansing of both the earthly and the heavenly sanctuary is plainly taught. . . .

Once a year, on the great Day of Atonement, the priest entered the most holy place for the cleansing of the sanctuary. The work there performed completed the yearly round of ministration. *GC 417, 419*

---

13 Then I heard one saint speaking, and another saint said unto that certain *saint* which spake, How long *shall be* the vision *concerning* the daily *sacrifice*, and the transgression of desolation, to give both the sanctuary and the host to be ᵀtrodden under foot? Dan. 4:13

14 And he said unto me, Unto two thousand and three hundred days; then shall the sanctuary be cleansed.   Dan. 8:26

Gabriel Comforts Daniel

15 And it came to pass, when I, *even* I Daniel, had seen the vision, and sought for the meaning, then, behold, there stood before me as the appearance of a man.   Dan. 10:16, 18

16 And I heard a man's voice between *the banks of* Ulai, which called, and said, Gabriel, make this *man* to understand the vision.

17 So he came near where I stood: and when he came, I was afraid, and fell upon my face: but he said unto me, Understand, O son of man: for at the time of the end *shall be* the vision.   Dan. 8:19

18 Now as he was speaking with me, I was in a deep sleep on my face toward the ground: but he touched me, and set me upright.

19 And he said, Behold, I will make thee know what shall be in the last end of the ᵀindignation: for at the time appointed the end *shall be*.   Dan. 8:15-17 ♦ *anger*

20 The ram which thou sawest having *two* horns *are* the kings of Media and Persia.

21 And the rough goat *is* the king of Grecia: and the great horn that *is* between his eyes *is* the first king.   Dan. 10:20

22 Now that being broken, whereas four stood up for it, four kingdoms shall stand up out of the nation, but not in his power.

23 And in the latter time of their kingdom, when the ᵀtransgressors are come to the full, a king of fierce ᵀcountenance, and understanding dark sentences, shall stand up.   *those who violate the law* ♦ *appearance*

24 And his power shall be mighty, but not by his own power: and he shall destroy wonderfully, and shall prosper, and practise, and shall destroy the mighty and the holy people.   Dan. 7:25; 8:12; Rev. 17:17

25 And through his policy also he shall cause craft to prosper in his hand; and he shall magnify *himself* in his heart, and by peace shall destroy many: he shall also stand up against the Prince of princes; but he shall be broken without hand.   Job 34:20; Dan. 8:11

26 And the vision of the evening and the morning which was told *is* true: wherefore shut thou up the vision; for it *shall be* for many days.   Dan. 10:1, 14; 12:4

27 And I Daniel fainted, and was sick *certain* days; afterward I rose up, and did the king's

business; and I was astonished at the vision, but none understood *it*.　　Dan. 7:28; Hab. 3:16

8:26 God Reveals His Secrets

"The Lord God will do nothing, but He revealeth His secret unto His servants and prophets." While "the secret things belong unto the Lord our God," "those things which are revealed belong unto us and to our children forever" (Amos 3:7; Deuteronomy 29:29). God has given these things to us, and His blessing will attend the reverent, prayerful study of the prophetic scriptures. *DA 234*

Daniel's Prayer Is Answered

9 In the first year of Darius the son of Ahasuerus, of the seed of the Medes, which was made king over the realm of the Chaldeans;　　Dan. 11:1
2 In the first year of his reign I Daniel understood by books the number of the years, whereof the word of the LORD came to Jeremiah the prophet, that he would accomplish seventy years in the desolations of Jerusalem.　　2 Chr. 36:21; Jer. 29:10; Zech. 7:5
3 And I set my face unto the Lord God, to seek by prayer and supplications, with fasting, and sackcloth, and ashes:

9:3 The Vision Explained

Heaven was bending low to hear the earnest supplication of the prophet. Even before [Daniel] had finished his plea for pardon and restoration, the mighty Gabriel again appeared to him, and called his attention to the vision he had seen prior to the fall of Babylon and the death of Belshazzar. *PK 556*

---

4 And I prayed unto the LORD my God, and made my confession, and said, O Lord, the great and dreadful God, keeping the covenant and mercy to them that love him, and to them that keep his commandments; Deut. 7:9; Neh. 1:5
5 We have sinned, and have committed iniquity, and have done wickedly, and have rebelled, even by departing from thy precepts and from thy judgments:　　Ps. 106:6
6 Neither have we hearkened unto thy

servants the prophets, which spake in thy name to our kings, our princes, and our fathers, and to all the people of the land.
7 O Lord, righteousness *belongeth* unto thee, but unto us confusion of faces, as at this day; to the men of Judah, and to the inhabitants of Jerusalem, and unto all Israel, *that are* near, and *that are* far off, through all the countries whither thou hast driven them, because of their ᵀtrespass that they have ᵀtrespassed against thee. Deut. 4:27 ◆ *sin* ◆ *sinned*
8 O Lord, to us *belongeth* confusion of face, to our kings, to our princes, and to our fathers, because we have sinned against thee.
9 To the Lord our God *belong* mercies and forgivenesses, though we have rebelled against him;　　Ps. 130:4
10 Neither have we obeyed the voice of the LORD our God, to walk in his laws, which he set before us by his servants the prophets.　　2 Kin. 18:12
11 Yea, all Israel have ᵀtransgressed thy law, even by departing, that they might not obey thy voice; therefore the curse is poured upon us, and the oath that *is* written in the law of Moses the servant of God, because we have sinned against him.　　Is. 1:4-6 ◆ *violated*
12 And he hath confirmed his words, which he spake against us, and against our judges that judged us, by bringing upon us a great evil: for under the whole heaven hath not been done as hath been done upon Jerusalem.　　Is. 44:26; Lam. 1:12; Ezek. 5:9
13 As *it is* written in the law of Moses, all this evil is come upon us: yet made we not our prayer before the LORD our God, that we might turn from our iniquities, and understand thy truth.　　Is. 9:13
14 Therefore hath the LORD watched upon the evil, and brought it upon us: for the LORD our God *is* righteous in all his works which he doeth: for we obeyed not his voice.　　Neh. 9:33
15 And now, O Lord our God, that hast brought thy people forth out of the land of Egypt with a mighty hand, and hast gotten thee renown, as at this day; we have sinned, we have done wickedly. Ex. 6:1; 14:18; Neh. 9:10

An Example of Sanctification

Daniel 9

The prophet Daniel was an example of true sanctification. His long life was filled up with noble service for his Master. He was a man "greatly beloved" (Daniel 10:11) of Heaven. Yet instead of claiming to be pure and holy, this honored prophet identified himself with the really sinful of Israel as he pleaded before God in behalf of his people: "We do not present our supplications before Thee for our righteousness, but for Thy great mercies." "We have sinned, we have done wickedly." He declares: "I was speaking, and praying, and confessing my sin and the sin of my people." And when at a later time the Son of God appeared, to give him instruction, Daniel says: "My comeliness was turned in me into corruption, and I retained no strength" (Daniel 9:18, 15, 20; 10:8). *GC 470, 471*

16 O Lord, according to all thy righteousness, I ᵀbeseech thee, let thine anger and thy fury be turned away from thy city Jerusalem, thy holy mountain: because for our sins, and for the iniquities of our fathers, Jerusalem and thy people *are become* a reproach to all *that are* about us. Ps. 31:1; Dan. 9:20; Zech. 8:3 ◆ *beg*

17 Now therefore, O our God, hear the prayer of thy servant, and his supplications, and cause thy face to shine upon thy sanctuary that is desolate, for the Lord's sake. Ps. 80:19

18 O my God, incline thine ear, and hear; open thine eyes, and behold our desolations, and the city which is called by thy name: for we do not present our supplications before thee for our righteousnesses, but for thy great mercies. 2 Kin. 19:16; Is. 37:17; Jer. 25:29

19 O Lord, hear; O Lord, forgive; O Lord, hearken and do; ᵀdefer not, for thine own sake, O my God: for thy city and thy people are called by thy name. Jer. 14:9 ◆ *postpone*

The Seventy Weeks

20 And whiles I *was* speaking, and praying, and confessing my sin and the sin of my people Israel, and presenting my supplication before the Lᴏʀᴅ my God for the holy mountain of my God; Ps. 145:18

21 Yea, whiles I *was* speaking in prayer, even the man Gabriel, whom I had seen in the vision at the beginning, being caused to fly swiftly, touched me about the time of the evening oblation. 1 Kin. 18:36; Dan. 8:16; Luke 1:19

22 And he informed *me*, and talked with me, and said, O Daniel, I am now come forth to give thee skill and understanding. Dan. 8:16

23 At the beginning of thy supplications the commandment came forth, and I am come to shew *thee*; for thou *art* greatly beloved: therefore understand the matter, and consider the vision. Dan. 10:11-12, 19; Matt. 24:15

24 Seventy weeks are determined upon thy people and upon thy holy city, to finish the ᵀtransgression, and to make an end of sins, and to make reconciliation for iniquity, and to bring in everlasting righteousness, and to seal up the vision and prophecy, and to anoint the most Holy. Num. 14:34; Ps. 45:7; Ezek. 4:6

9:24* Seventy Weeks "Cut Off"

The word here translated "determined" literally signifies "cut off." Seventy weeks, representing 490 years, are declared by the angel to be cut off, as specially pertaining to the Jews. But from what were they cut off? As the 2300 days was the only period of time mentioned in chapter 8, it must be the period from which the seventy weeks were cut off; the seventy weeks must therefore be a part of the 2300 days, and the two periods must begin together. *GC 326*

---

25 Know therefore and understand, *that* from the going forth of the commandment to restore and to build Jerusalem unto the Messiah the Prince *shall be* seven weeks, and ᵀthreescore and two weeks: the street shall be built again, and the wall, even in troublous times. Ezra 4:24; Is. 9:6; 55:4 ◆ *sixty*

26 And after threescore and two weeks shall Messiah be cut off, but not for himself: and the people of the prince that shall come shall destroy the city and the sanctuary; and the end thereof *shall be* with a flood, and unto the end of the war desolations are determined. Is. 53:8; Nah. 1:8; Matt. 24:2

27 And he shall confirm the covenant with many for one week: and in the midst of the week he shall cause the sacrifice and the oblation to cease, and for the overspreading of abominations he shall make *it* desolate, even until the consummation, and that determined shall be poured upon the desolate. Matt. 24:15; Mark 13:14; Luke 21:20

An Angel Brings a Message

10 In the third year of Cyrus king of Persia a thing was revealed unto Daniel, whose name was called Belteshazzar; and the thing *was* true, but the time appointed *was* long: and he understood the thing, and had understanding of the vision. Dan. 1:7, 21; 8:26

2 In those days I Daniel was mourning three full weeks. Ezra 9:4-5

3 I ate no pleasant bread, neither came flesh nor wine in my mouth, neither did I anoint myself at all, till three whole weeks were fulfilled. Dan. 6:18

4 And in the four and twentieth day of the first month, as I was by the side of the great river, which *is* Hiddekel; Gen. 2:14

5 Then I lifted up mine eyes, and looked, and behold a certain man clothed in linen, whose ᵀloins *were* girded with fine gold of Uphaz: Jer. 10:9; Ezek. 9:2; Dan. 12:6-7 ◆ *waist*

6 His body also *was* like the ᵀberyl, and his face as the appearance of lightning, and his eyes as lamps of fire, and his arms and his feet like in colour to polished brass, and the voice of his words like the voice of a multitude. Rev. 19:12 ◆ *precious stone*

7 And I Daniel alone saw the vision: for the men that were with me saw not the vision; but a great quaking fell upon them, so that they fled to hide themselves. Ezek. 12:18; Acts 9:7

8 Therefore I was left alone, and saw this great vision, and there remained no strength in me: for my comeliness was turned in me into corruption, and I retained no strength. Dan. 7:28

* For more information on this time prophecy, see pages 1447–1454 of this Bible.

9 Yet heard I the voice of his words: and when I heard the voice of his words, then was I in a deep sleep on my face, and my face toward the ground. Gen. 15:12; Job 4:13; Dan. 8:18
10 And, behold, an hand touched me, which set me upon my knees and *upon* the palms of my hands. Jer. 1:9
11 And he said unto me, O Daniel, a man greatly beloved, understand the words that I speak unto thee, and stand upright: for unto thee am I now sent. And when he had spoken this word unto me, I stood trembling. Ezek. 2:1
12 Then said he unto me, Fear not, Daniel: for from the first day that thou didst set thine heart to understand, and to chasten thyself before thy God, thy words were heard, and I am come for thy words. Dan. 9:20-23; 10:19
13 But the prince of the kingdom of Persia withstood me one and twenty days: but, lo, Michael, one of the chief princes, came to help me; and I remained there with the kings of Persia. Dan. 12:1; Jude 9; Rev. 12:7

10:13 The Effort to Secure Victory

For three weeks Gabriel wrestled with the powers of darkness, seeking to counteract the influences at work on the mind of Cyrus; and before the contest closed, Christ Himself came to Gabriel's aid. "The prince of the kingdom of Persia withstood me one and twenty days," Gabriel declares; "but, lo, Michael, one of the chief princes, came to help me; and I remained there with the kings of Persia" (Daniel 10:13). All that heaven could do in behalf of the people of God was done. The victory was finally gained. *PK 572*

14 Now I am come to make thee understand what shall befall thy people in the latter days: for yet the vision *is* for *many* days. Dan. 2:28; 8:26
15 And when he had spoken such words unto me, I set my face toward the ground, and I became ᵀdumb. Ezek. 24:27 ◆ *mute*
16 And, behold, *one* like the ᵀsimilitude of the sons of men touched my lips: then I opened my mouth, and spake, and said unto him that stood before me, O my lord, by the vision my sorrows are turned upon me, and I have retained no strength. Is. 6:7; Jer. 1:9; Dan. 8:15 ◆ *image*
17 For how can the servant of this my lord talk with this my lord? for as for me, ᵀstraightway there remained no strength in me, neither is there breath left in me. Ex. 24:10-11 ◆ *right away*
18 Then there came again and touched me *one* like the appearance of a man, and he strengthened me, Is. 35:3-4; Dan. 10:16
19 And said, O man greatly beloved, fear not: peace *be* unto thee, be strong, yea, be strong. And when he had spoken unto me, I was strengthened, and said, Let my lord speak; for thou hast strengthened me. Josh. 1:9
20 Then said he, Knowest thou wherefore I come unto thee? and now will I return to fight with the prince of Persia: and when I am gone forth, lo, the prince of Grecia shall come. Dan. 8:21; 10:13
21 But I will shew thee that which is noted in the scripture of truth: and *there is* none that holdeth with me in these things, but Michael your prince. Dan. 10:13; 12:1; Jude 9

10:21 The Angel Gabriel

The words of the angel, "I am Gabriel, that stand in the presence of God" [Luke 1:19], show that he holds a position of high honor in the heavenly courts. . . . Of Gabriel the Saviour speaks in the Revelation, saying that "He sent and signified it by His angel unto His servant John" (Revelation 1:1). . . . Wonderful thought—that the angel who stands next in honor to the Son of God is the one chosen to open the purposes of God to sinful men. *DA 99*

Greece Will Conquer Persia

11 Also I in the first year of Darius the Mede, *even* I, stood to confirm and to strengthen him. Dan. 5:31
2 And now will I shew thee the truth. Behold, there shall stand up yet three kings in Persia; and the fourth shall be far richer than *they* all: and by his strength through his riches he shall stir up all against the realm of Grecia. Dan. 8:26
3 And a mighty king shall stand up, that shall rule with great dominion, and do according to his will. Dan. 8:21; 11:16, 36
4 And when he shall stand up, his kingdom shall be broken, and shall be divided toward the four winds of heaven; and not to his posterity, nor according to his dominion which he ruled: for his kingdom shall be plucked up, even for others beside those. Jer. 12:15; Dan. 8:8, 22

The Northern and Southern Kings

5 And the king of the south shall be strong, and *one* of his princes; and he shall be strong above him, and have dominion; his dominion *shall be* a great dominion. Dan. 11:11
6 And in the end of years they shall join themselves together; for the king's daughter of the south shall come to the king of the north to make an agreement: but she shall not retain the power of the arm; neither shall he stand, nor his arm: but she shall be given up, and they that brought her, and he that ᵀbegat her, and he that strengthened her in *these* times. Dan. 11:7, 13, 15 ◆ *brought forth*
7 But out of a branch of her roots shall *one*

stand up in his estate, which shall come with an army, and shall enter into the fortress of the king of the north, and shall deal against them, and shall prevail:

8 And shall also carry captives into Egypt their gods, with their princes, *and* with their precious vessels of silver and of gold; and he shall continue *more* years than the king of the north. Is. 37:19

9 So the king of the south shall come into *his* kingdom, and shall return into his own land.

10 But his sons shall be stirred up, and shall assemble a multitude of great forces: and *one* shall certainly come, and overflow, and pass through: then shall he return, and be stirred up, *even* to his fortress. Jer. 46:7-8

11 And the king of the south shall be moved with ᵀcholer, and shall come forth and fight with him, *even* with the king of the north: and he shall set forth a great multitude; but the multitude shall be given into his hand. Dan. 8:7 ◆ *anger*

12 *And* when he hath taken away the multitude, his heart shall be lifted up; and he shall cast down *many* ten thousands: but he shall not be strengthened *by it.*

13 For the king of the north shall return, and shall set forth a multitude greater than the former, and shall certainly come after certain years with a great army and with much riches. Dan. 4:16

14 And in those times there shall many stand up against the king of the south: also the robbers of thy people shall exalt themselves to establish the vision; but they shall fall.

15 So the king of the north shall come, and cast up a mount, and take the most fenced cities: and the arms of the south shall not withstand, neither his chosen people, neither *shall there be any* strength to withstand. Jer. 6:6

16 But he that cometh against him shall do according to his own will, and none shall stand before him: and he shall stand in the glorious land, which by his hand shall be consumed. Dan. 8:9; 11:3, 36

17 He shall also set his face to enter with the strength of his whole kingdom, and upright ones with him; thus shall he do: and he shall give him the daughter of women, corrupting her: but she shall not stand on *his side*, neither be for him. 2 Kin. 12:17

18 After this shall he turn his face unto the isles, and shall take many: but a prince for his own behalf shall cause the reproach offered by him to cease; without his own reproach he shall cause *it* to turn upon him. Jer. 2:10; 31:10; Hos. 12:14

19 Then he shall turn his face toward the fort of his own land: but he shall stumble and fall, and not be found. Job 20:8; Ps. 37:36; Ezek. 26:21

20 Then shall stand up in his estate a raiser of taxes *in* the glory of the kingdom: but within few days he shall be destroyed, neither in anger, nor in battle. Is. 60:17

21 And in his estate shall stand up a vile person, to whom they shall not give the honour of the kingdom: but he shall come in peaceably, and obtain the kingdom by flatteries. Dan. 8:25

22 And with the arms of a flood shall they be overflown from before him, and shall be broken; yea, also the prince of the covenant. Dan. 11:10

23 And after the league *made* with him he shall work deceitfully: for he shall come up,

---

These Prophecies Demand Our Attention

Daniel

As we near the close of this world's history, the prophecies recorded by Daniel demand our special attention, as they relate to the very time in which we are living. With them should be linked the teachings of the last book of the New Testament Scriptures. Satan has led many to believe that the prophetic portions of the writings of Daniel and of John the revelator cannot be understood. But the promise is plain that special blessing will accompany the study of these prophecies. "The wise shall understand" (Daniel 12:10), was spoken of the visions of Daniel that were to be unsealed in the latter days; and of the revelation that Christ gave to His servant John for the guidance of God's people all through the centuries, the promise is, "Blessed is he that readeth, and they that hear the words of this prophecy, and keep those things which are written therein" (Revelation 1:3).

From the rise and fall of nations as made plain in the books of Daniel and the Revelation, we need to learn how worthless is mere outward and worldly glory. Babylon, with all its power and magnificence, the like of which our world has never since beheld—power and magnificence which to the people of that day seemed so stable and enduring—how completely has it passed away! . . . And so perishes all that has not God for its foundation. Only that which is bound up with His purpose, and expresses His character, can endure. His principles are the only steadfast things our world knows.

A careful study of the working out of God's purpose in the history of nations and in the revelation of things to come, will help us to estimate at their true value things seen and things unseen, and to learn what is the true aim of life. *PK 547, 548*

and shall become strong with a small people.   *Dan. 8:25*
24 He shall enter peaceably even upon the
fattest places of the province; and he shall
do *that* which his fathers have not done, nor
his fathers' fathers; he shall scatter among
them the prey, and ᵀspoil, and riches: *yea,*
and he shall forecast his devices against the
strong holds, even for a time.   *plunder*
25 And he shall stir up his power and his
courage against the king of the south with a
great army; and the king of the south shall
be stirred up to battle with a very great and
mighty army; but he shall not stand: for they
shall forecast devices against him.
26 Yea, they that feed of the portion of his
meat shall destroy him, and his army shall
overflow: and many shall fall down slain.
27 And both these kings' hearts *shall be* to
do mischief, and they shall speak lies at one
table; but it shall not prosper: for yet the end
shall be at the time appointed.   *Ps. 12:2*
28 Then shall he return into his land with
great riches; and his heart *shall be* against the
holy covenant; and he shall do *exploits,* and
return to his own land.
29 At the time appointed he shall return,
and come toward the south; but it shall not
be as the former, or as the latter.
30 For the ships of Chittim shall come against
him: therefore he shall be grieved, and return,
and have ᵀindignation against the holy covenant: so shall he do; he shall even return, and
have intelligence with them that forsake the
holy covenant.   *Gen. 10:4; Num. 24:24; Is. 23:1 ♦ anger*
31 And arms shall stand on his part, and
they shall pollute the sanctuary of strength,
and shall take away the daily *sacrifice,* and
they shall place the abomination that maketh desolate.   *Dan. 9:27; 12:11; Matt. 24:15*
32 And such as do wickedly against the
covenant shall he corrupt by flatteries: but
the people that do know their God shall be
strong, and do *exploits.*   *Mic. 5:7-9*
33 And they that understand among the
people shall instruct many: yet they shall
fall by the sword, and by flame, by captivity,
and by spoil, *many* days.   *Mal. 2:7*
34 Now when they shall fall, they shall be
ᵀholpen with a little help: but many shall
cleave to them with flatteries.*Matt. 7:15 ♦ helped*
35 And *some* of them of understanding shall
fall, to try them, and to purge, and to make
them white, *even* to the time of the end: because *it is* yet for a time appointed. *Zech. 13:9*
36 And the king shall do according to his
will; and he shall exalt himself, and magnify
himself above every god, and shall speak
marvellous things against the God of gods,
and shall prosper till the indignation be ac-

complished: for that that is determined shall
be done.   *Deut. 10:17; Is. 14:13; 2 Thess. 2:4*
37 Neither shall he regard the God of his fathers, nor the desire of women, nor regard
any god: for he shall magnify himself above
all.
38 But in his estate shall he honour the
God of forces: and a god whom his fathers
knew not shall he honour with gold, and silver, and with precious stones, and pleasant
things.
39 Thus shall he do in the most strong holds
with a strange god, whom he shall acknowledge *and* increase with glory: and he shall
cause them to rule over many, and shall divide the land for gain.
40 And at the time of the end shall the king
of the south push at him: and the king of the
north shall come against him like a whirlwind, with chariots, and with horsemen,
and with many ships; and he shall enter into
the countries, and shall overflow and pass
over.   *Is. 5:28*
41 He shall enter also into the glorious land,
and many *countries* shall be overthrown: but
these shall escape out of his hand, *even*
Edom, and Moab, and the chief of the children of Ammon.   *Jer. 48:47*
42 He shall stretch forth his hand also upon
the countries: and the land of Egypt shall
not escape.
43 But he shall have power over the treasures
of gold and of silver, and over all the precious
things of Egypt: and the Libyans and the Ethiopians *shall be* at his steps.   *2 Chr. 12:3; Nah. 3:9*
44 But tidings out of the east and out of the
north shall trouble him: therefore he shall
go forth with great fury to destroy, and utterly to make away many.
45 And he shall plant the tabernacles of his
palace between the seas in the glorious holy
mountain; yet he shall come to his end, and
none shall help him.

The Words Are Sealed

12 And at that time shall Michael stand
up, the great prince which standeth
for the children of thy people: and there
shall be a time of trouble, such as never was
since there was a nation *even* to that same
time: and at that time thy people shall be delivered, every one that shall be found written
in the book.   *Jer. 30:7; Dan. 10:13; Matt. 24:21*
2 And many of them that sleep in the dust
of the earth shall awake, some to everlasting life, and some to shame *and* everlasting
contempt.   *Is. 26:19; Matt. 25:46; John 5:28-29*

After Death   See Psalm 6:5.

3 And they that be wise shall shine as the
brightness of the ᵀfirmament; and they that

turn many to righteousness as the stars for ever and ever. Dan. 11:33, 35; Matt. 13:43 ◆ *sky*

4 But thou, O Daniel, shut up the words, and seal the book, *even* to the time of the end: many shall run to and fro, and knowledge shall be increased. Dan. 8:17; 12:9; Rev. 22:10

12:4 Daniel and Revelation Linked

In the Revelation all the books of the Bible meet and end. Here is the complement of the book of Daniel. One is a prophecy; the other a revelation. The book that was sealed is not the Revelation, but that portion of the prophecy of Daniel relating to the last days. The angel commanded, "But thou, O Daniel, shut up the words, and seal the book, even to the time of the end" (Daniel 12:4). *AA 585*

5 Then I Daniel looked, and, behold, there stood other two, the one on this side of the bank of the river, and the other on that side of the bank of the river.
6 And *one* said to the man clothed in linen, which *was* upon the waters of the river, How long *shall it be to* the end of these wonders? Ezek. 9:2; Dan. 8:13, 16
7 And I heard the man clothed in linen, which *was* upon the waters of the river, when he held up his right hand and his left hand unto heaven, and sware by him that liveth for ever that *it shall be* for a time, times, and an half; and when he shall have accomplished to scatter the power of the holy people, all these *things* shall be finished. Dan. 7:25; 8:24; Rev. 12:14
8 And I heard, but I understood not: then said I, O my Lord, what *shall be* the end of these *things?*
9 And he said, Go thy way, Daniel: for the words *are* closed up and sealed till the time of the end. Dan. 12:4

10 Many shall be purified, and made white, and tried; but the wicked shall do wickedly: and none of the wicked shall understand; but the wise shall understand. Hos. 14:9; Rev. 22:11

12:10 Last-Day Prophecies

The words of the angel to Daniel relating to the last days were to be understood in the time of the end. . . . The Saviour Himself has given signs of His coming, and He says, "When ye see these things come to pass, know ye that the kingdom of God is nigh at hand." "And take heed to yourselves, lest at any time your hearts be overcharged with surfeiting, and drunkenness, and cares of this life, and so that day come upon you unawares" (Luke 21:31, 34). *DA 234*

11 And from the time *that* the daily *sacrifice* shall be taken away, and the abomination that maketh desolate set up, *there shall be* a thousand two hundred and ninety days. Dan. 9:27
12 Blessed *is* he that waiteth, and cometh to the thousand three hundred and five and thirty days.
13 But go thou thy way till the end *be:* for thou shalt rest, and stand in thy lot at the end of the days. Rev. 14:13

12:13 Limits to Daniel's Understanding

[Daniel's] wonderful prophecies, as recorded by him in chapters 7 to 12 of the book bearing his name, were not fully understood even by the prophet himself; but before his life labors closed, he was given the blessed assurance that "at the end of the days"—in the closing period of this world's history—he would again be permitted to stand in his lot and place. It was not given him to understand all that God had revealed of the divine purpose. *PK 547*

Christ to Gather His Children

Daniel 12

From garrets, from hovels, from dungeons, from scaffolds, from mountains and deserts, from the caves of the earth and the caverns of the sea, Christ will gather His children to Himself. On earth they have been destitute, afflicted, and tormented. Millions have gone down to the grave loaded with infamy because they refused to yield to the deceptive claims of Satan. By human tribunals the children of God have been adjudged the vilest criminals. But the day is near when "God is judge Himself" (Psalm 50:6). Then the decisions of earth shall be reversed. "The rebuke of His people shall He take away" (Isaiah 25:8). White robes will be given to every one of them (Revelation 6:11). And "they shall call them the holy people, the redeemed of the Lord" (Isaiah 62:12). *COL 179, 180*

Hosea Marries a Prostitute

1 The word of the LORD that came unto Hosea, the son of Beeri, in the days of Uzziah, Jotham, Ahaz, *and* Hezekiah, kings of Judah, and in the days of Jeroboam the son of Joash, king of Israel.   Is. 1:1; Amos 1:1; Mic. 1:1

2 The beginning of the word of the LORD by Hosea. And the LORD said to Hosea, Go, take unto thee a wife of whoredoms and children of whoredoms: for the land hath committed great ᵀwhoredom, *departing* from the LORD.
Deut. 31:16; Hos. 2:4-5; 3:1 ◆ *prostitution*

3 So he went and took Gomer the daughter of Diblaim; which conceived, and bare him a son.

4 And the LORD said unto him, Call his name Jezreel; for yet a little *while*, and I will avenge the blood of Jezreel upon the house of Jehu, and will cause to cease the kingdom of the house of Israel.   2 Kin. 10:7-8

5 And it shall come to pass at that day, that I will break the bow of Israel in the valley of Jezreel.   Josh. 17:16

6 And she conceived again, and bare a daughter. And *God* said unto him, Call her name Lo-ruhamah: for I will no more have mercy upon the house of Israel; but I will utterly take them away.   2 Kin. 17:6

7 But I will have mercy upon the house of Judah, and will save them by the LORD their God, and will not save them by bow, nor by sword, nor by battle, by horses, nor by horsemen.   2 Kin. 19:35; Ps. 44:3-6; Zech. 4:6

8 Now when she had weaned Lo-ruhamah, she conceived, and bare a son.

9 Then said *God*, Call his name Lo-ammi: for ye *are* not my people, and I will not be your *God*.

10 Yet the number of the children of Israel shall be as the sand of the sea, which cannot be measured nor numbered; and it shall come to pass, *that in* the place where it was said unto them, Ye *are* not my people, *there* it shall be said unto them, *Ye are* the sons of the living God.   Hos. 1:9

> **1:10 Grace to the Gentiles as Well**
>
> It was God's purpose that His grace should be revealed among the Gentiles as well as among the Israelites. This had been plainly outlined in Old Testament prophecies. *AA 376*

11 Then shall the children of Judah and the children of Israel be gathered together, and appoint themselves one head, and they shall come up out of the land: for great *shall be* the day of Jezreel.   Is. 11:12-13

Israel Is the Lord's Unfaithful Wife

2 Say ye *unto* your brethren, Ammi; and to your *sisters*, Ruhamah.   Hos. 2:23

2 Plead *with* your mother, plead: for she *is* not my wife, neither *am* I her husband: let her therefore put away her whoredoms out of her sight, and her adulteries from between her breasts;   Is. 50:1; Jer. 3:1; Ezek. 23:45

3 Lest I strip her naked, and set her as in the day that she was born, and make her as a wilderness, and set her like a dry land, and slay her with thirst.   Is. 32:13-14

4 And I will not have mercy upon her children; for they *be* the children of ᵀwhoredoms.   Jer. 13:14 ◆ *acts of prostitution*

5 For their mother hath played the harlot: she that conceived them hath done shamefully: for she said, I will go after my lovers, that give *me* my bread and my water, my wool and my flax, mine oil and my drink.   Is. 1:21

God's Judgments against Israel

6 Therefore, behold, I will hedge up thy way with thorns, and make a wall, that she shall not find her paths.   Job 3:23; 19:8

7 And she shall follow after her lovers, but she shall not overtake them; and she shall seek them, but shall not find *them*: then shall she say, I will go and return to my first husband; for then *was it* better with me than now.   Jer. 2:2

8 For she did not know that I gave her corn, and wine, and oil, and multiplied her silver and gold, *which* they prepared for Baal.   Is. 1:3

9 Therefore will I return, and take away my corn in the time thereof, and my wine in the season thereof, and will recover my wool and my flax *given* to cover her nakedness.   Hos. 2:3

10 And now will I discover her lewdness in the sight of her lovers, and none shall deliver her out of mine hand.   Ezek. 23:29

11 I will also cause all her mirth to cease, her feast days, her new moons, and her sabbaths, and all her solemn feasts.   Is. 1:13-14

12 And I will destroy her vines and her fig trees, whereof she hath said, These *are* my rewards that my lovers have given me: and I will make them a forest, and the beasts of the field shall eat them.   Is. 5:5

13 And I will visit upon her the days of Baalim, wherein she burned incense to them, and she decked herself with her earrings and her jewels, and she went after her lovers, and forgat me, saith the LORD.   Judg. 3:7; Jer. 7:9

God's Promises of Reconciliation

14 Therefore, behold, I will allure her, and bring her into the wilderness, and speak comfortably unto her.   Ezek. 20:35-36

15 And I will give her her vineyards from thence, and the valley of Achor for a door of hope: and she shall sing there, as in the days of her youth, and as in the day when she came up out of the land of Egypt.   Josh. 7:26

16 And it shall be at that day, saith the

Lord, *that* thou shalt call me Ishi; and shalt call me no more Baali.   Is. 54:5

17 For I will take away the names of Baalim out of her mouth, and they shall no more be remembered by their name. Ex. 23:13; Josh. 23:7

18 And in that day will I make a covenant for them with the beasts of the field, and *with* the fowls of heaven, and *with* the creeping things of the ground: and I will break the bow and the sword and the battle out of the earth, and will make them to lie down safely.   Is. 2:4; Jer. 23:6; Ezek. 34:25

19 And I will Tbetroth thee unto me for ever; yea, *I* will betroth thee unto me in righteousness, and in judgment, and in lovingkindness, and in mercies.   Jer. 3:14-15 ◆ *promise to marry*

20 I will even betroth thee unto me in faithfulness: and thou shalt know the Lord.

21 And *it* shall come to pass in that day, I will hear, saith the Lord, I will hear the heavens, and they shall hear the earth;   Zech. 8:12

22 And *the* earth shall hear the corn, and the wine, and the oil; and they shall hear Jezreel.   Hos. 1:4

23 And I will sow her unto me in the earth; and I will have mercy upon her that had not obtained mercy; and I will say to *them which were* not my people, Thou *art* my people; and they shall say, *Thou art* my God.   Jer. 31:27

2:14–23 Restored Blessings

In the last days of this earth's history, God's covenant with His commandment-keeping people is to be renewed. . . .

They will free themselves from every entanglement and will stand before the world as monuments of God's mercy. Obedient to the divine requirements, they will be recognized by angels and by men as those that have kept "the commandments of God, and the faith of Jesus" (Revelation 14:12). *PK 299, 300*

Hosea's Adulterous Wife

3 Then said the Lord unto me, Go yet, love a woman beloved of *her* friend, yet an adulteress, according to the love of the Lord toward the children of Israel, who look to other gods, and love flagons of wine.   Jer. 3:20

2 So I bought her to me for fifteen *pieces* of silver, and *for* an homer of barley, and an half homer of barley: Lev. 27:16

3 And I said unto her, Thou shalt abide for me many days; thou shalt not play the harlot, and thou shalt not be for *another* man: so *will* I also *be* for thee.   Deut. 21:13

4 For the children of Israel shall abide many days without a king, and without a prince, and without a sacrifice, and without an

image, and without an ephod, and *without* teraphim: Gen. 31:19; Ex. 28:4; Judg. 17:5

3:4 Wanderers for All Time

The prophecies of judgment delivered by Amos and Hosea were accompanied by predictions of future glory. To the ten tribes, long rebellious and impenitent, was given no promise of complete restoration to their former power in Palestine. Until the end of time, they were to be "wanderers among the nations." *PK 298*

5 Afterward shall the children of Israel return, and seek the Lord their God, and David their king; and shall fear the Lord and his goodness in the latter days.   Is. 2:2

God's Judgments on the Sins of the People

4 Hear the word of the Lord, ye children of Israel: for the Lord hath a controversy with the inhabitants of the land, because *there is* no truth, nor mercy, nor knowledge of God in the land.   Jer. 4:22

2 By swearing, and lying, and killing, and stealing, and committing adultery, they break out, and blood toucheth blood. Hos. 6:9

3 Therefore shall the land mourn, and every one that dwelleth therein shall languish, with the beasts of the field, and with the fowls of heaven; yea, the fishes of the sea also shall be taken away.   Jer. 4:25; Ezek. 38:20; Zeph. 1:3

4 Yet let no man strive, nor reprove another: for thy people *are* as they that strive with the priest.   Deut. 17:12; Amos 5:13

5 Therefore shalt thou fall in the day, and the prophet also shall fall with thee in the night, and I will destroy thy mother.   Jer. 15:8; Hos. 2:2

6 My people are destroyed for lack of knowledge: because thou hast rejected knowledge, I will also reject thee, that thou shalt be no priest to me: seeing thou hast forgotten the law of thy God, I will also forget thy children.   Is. 5:13

4:6 Rejecting Knowledge

Had Israel heeded the messages of the prophets, they would have been spared the humiliation that followed. It was because they had persisted in turning aside from His law that God was compelled to let them go into captivity. . . . "Because thou hast rejected knowledge, I will also reject thee" (Hosea 4:6). . . .

In every age, transgression of God's law has been followed by the same result. *PK 297*

7 As they were increased, so they sinned against me: *therefore* will I change their glory into shame.   1 Sam. 2:30; Hos. 13:6; Mal. 2:9

8 They eat up the sin of my people, and they set their heart on their iniquity. Is. 56:11
9 And there shall be, like people, like priest: and I will punish them for their ways, and reward them their doings. Is. 24:2; Jer. 5:31
10 For they shall eat, and not have enough: they shall commit whoredom, and shall not increase: because they have left off to take heed to the LORD. Lev. 26:26; Mic. 6:14; Hag. 1:6
11 Whoredom and wine and new wine take away the heart. Prov. 20:1; Is. 5:12; 28:7
12 My people ask counsel at their stocks, and their staff declareth unto them: for the spirit of ᵀwhoredoms hath caused *them* to err, and they have gone ᵀa whoring from under their God. Jer. 2:27 ◆ *acts of prostitution* ◆ *giving sex as a prostitute*
13 They sacrifice upon the tops of the mountains, and burn incense upon the hills, under oaks and poplars and elms, because the shadow thereof *is* good: therefore your daughters shall commit whoredom, and your spouses shall commit adultery. Is. 1:29; Jer. 3:6
14 I will not punish your daughters when they commit whoredom, nor your spouses when they commit adultery: for themselves are separated with ᵀwhores, and they sacrifice with harlots: therefore the people *that* doth not understand shall fall. Hos. 4:1 ◆ *prostitutes*
15 Though thou, Israel, play the harlot, *yet* let not Judah offend; and come not ye unto Gilgal, neither go ye up to Bethaven, nor swear, The LORD liveth. Hos. 9:15; 12:11; Amos 4:4
16 For Israel slideth back as a backsliding heifer: now the LORD will feed them as a lamb in a large place.
17 Ephraim *is* joined to idols: let him alone.
18 Their drink is sour: they have committed ᵀwhoredom continually: her rulers *with* shame do love, Give ye. Mic. 3:11 ◆ *prostitution*
19 The wind hath bound her up in her wings, and they shall be ashamed because of their sacrifices. Is. 1:29

The Lord's Verdict against Israel

5 Hear ye this, O priests; and hearken, ye house of Israel; and give ye ear, O house of the king; for judgment *is* toward you, because ye have been a snare on Mizpah, and a net spread upon Tabor. Judg. 4:6; Hos. 6:9; 9:8
2 And the revolters are profound to make slaughter, though I *have been* a rebuker of them all. Is. 29:15; Hos. 6:9; 9:15
3 I know Ephraim, and Israel is not hid from me: for now, O Ephraim, thou committest ᵀwhoredom, *and* Israel is defiled. *prostitution*
4 They will not frame their doings to turn unto their God: for the spirit of ᵀwhoredoms *is* in the midst of them, and they have not known the LORD. Hos. 4:12 ◆ *acts of prostitution*
5 And the pride of Israel doth testify to his face: therefore shall Israel and Ephraim fall

in their iniquity; Judah also shall fall with them. Ezek. 23:31-35; Hos. 7:10
6 They shall go with their flocks and with their herds to seek the LORD; but they shall not find *him*; he hath withdrawn himself from them. Prov. 1:28
7 They have dealt treacherously against the LORD: for they have ᵀbegotten strange children: now shall a month devour them with their portions. Is. 48:8; Jer. 3:20; Hos. 6:7 ◆ *brought forth*

5:7 What Might Have Been

Every principle of justice was set aside; those who should have stood before the nations of earth as the depositaries of divine grace, "dealt treacherously against the Lord" and with one another (Hosea 5:7). *PK 279*

---

8 Blow ye the cornet in Gibeah, *and* the trumpet in Ramah: cry aloud *at* Bethaven, after thee, O Benjamin. 1 Sam. 15:34; Hos. 4:15; 9:9
9 Ephraim shall be desolate in the day of rebuke: among the tribes of Israel have I made known that which shall surely be. Is. 46:10
10 The princes of Judah were like them that remove the bound: *therefore* I will pour out my wrath upon them like water. Deut. 19:14
11 Ephraim *is* oppressed *and* broken in judgment, because he willingly walked after the commandment. Deut. 28:33
12 Therefore *will* I *be* unto Ephraim as a moth, and to the house of Judah as rottenness.
13 When Ephraim saw his sickness, and Judah *saw* his wound, then went Ephraim to the Assyrian, and sent to king Jareb: yet could he not heal you, nor cure you of your wound. Jer. 30:12; Hos. 7:11; 10:6
14 For I *will be* unto Ephraim as a lion, and as a young lion to the house of Judah: I, *even* I, will tear and go away; I will take away, and none shall rescue *him*. Ps. 7:2; 50:22; Mic. 5:8
15 I will go *and* return to my place, till they acknowledge their offence, and seek my face: in their affliction they will seek me early.

Israel Rejected the Lord's Promise

6 Come, and let us return unto the LORD: for he hath torn, and he will heal us; he hath smitten, and he will bind us up.
2 After two days will he revive us: in the third day he will raise us up, and we shall live in his sight. 1 Cor. 15:4
3 Then shall we know, *if* we follow on to know the LORD: his going forth is prepared as the morning; and he shall come unto us as the rain, as the latter *and* former rain unto the earth. Ps. 72:6
4 O Ephraim, what shall I do unto thee? O Judah, what shall I do unto thee? for your goodness *is* as a morning cloud, and as the early dew it goeth away. Ps. 78:34-37; Hos. 11:8; 13:3

6:3 Communion With Heaven

It is in the mount with God—in the secret place of communion—that we are to contemplate His glorious ideal for humanity. In all ages, through the medium of communion with heaven, God has worked out His purpose for His children, by unfolding gradually to their minds the doctrines of grace. His manner of imparting truth is illustrated in the words, "His going forth is prepared as the morning" (Hosea 6:3). *AA 564*

5 Therefore have I ᵀhewed *them* by the prophets; I have slain them by the words of my mouth: and thy judgments *are as* the light *that* goeth forth.   Jer. 1:10; 23:29; Heb. 4:12 ◆ *cut*
6 For I desired mercy, and not sacrifice; and the knowledge of God more than burnt offerings.   Is. 1:11; Matt. 9:13; 12:7
7 But they like men have ᵀtransgressed the covenant: there have they dealt treacherously against me.   Job 31:33; Hos. 5:7; 8:1 ◆ *violated*
8 Gilead *is* a city of them that work iniquity, *and is* polluted with blood.   Hos. 12:11
9 And as troops of robbers wait for a man, *so* the company of priests murder in the way by consent: for they commit lewdness.   Hos. 7:1
10 I have seen an horrible thing in the house of Israel: there *is* the ᵀwhoredom of Ephraim, Israel is defiled.   Jer. 5:30-31; 23:14 ◆ *prostitution*
11 Also, O Judah, he hath set an harvest for thee, when I returned the captivity of my people.   Job 42:10; Jer. 51:33; Joel 3:13

God Reproves Israel for Many Sins

7 When I would have healed Israel, then the iniquity of Ephraim was discovered, and the wickedness of Samaria: for they commit falsehood; and the thief com-

eth in, *and* the troop of robbers spoileth without.   Hos. 4:2
2 And they consider not in their hearts *that* I remember all their wickedness: now their own doings have beset them about; they are before my face.   Jer. 2:19
3 They make the king glad with their wickedness, and the princes with their lies.
4 They *are* all adulterers, as an oven heated by the baker, *who* ceaseth from raising after he hath kneaded the dough, until it be leavened.   Jer. 9:2
5 In the day of our king the princes have made *him* sick with bottles of wine; he stretched out his hand with scorners. Is. 28:1
6 For they have made ready their heart like an oven, whiles they lie in wait: their baker sleepeth all the night; in the morning it burneth as a flaming fire.
7 They are all hot as an oven, and have devoured their judges; all their kings are fallen: *there is* none among them that calleth unto me.   2 Kin. 15:10

7:8, 9 Wanderers Among the Nations

Of Ephraim the prophet testified, "Strangers have devoured his strength, and he knoweth it not: yea, gray hairs are here and there upon him, yet he knoweth not." [The prophet Hosea often referred to Ephraim, a leader in apostasy among the tribes of Israel, as a symbol of the apostate nation.] "Israel hath cast off the thing that is good." "Broken in judgment," unable to discern the disastrous outcome of their evil course, the ten tribes were soon to be "wanderers among the nations" (Hosea 7:9; 8:3; 5:11; 9:17). *PK 280*

8 Ephraim, he hath mixed himself among the people; Ephraim is a cake not turned.

Please Listen; I Desire Mercy

Hosea 6:5–7

There were times when the judgments of Heaven fell very heavily on the rebellious people. "I hewed them by the prophets," God declared; "I have slain them by the words of My mouth: and thy judgments are as the light that goeth forth. For I desired mercy, and not sacrifice; and the knowledge of God more than burnt offerings. But they like men have transgressed the covenant: there have they dealt treacherously against Me" (Hosea 6:5–7).

"Hear the word of the Lord, ye children of Israel," was the message that finally came to them: "Seeing thou hast forgotten the law of thy God, I will also forget thy children. As they were increased, so they sinned against Me: therefore will I change their glory into shame. . . . I will punish them for their ways, and reward them their doings" (Hosea 4:1, 6–9).

The iniquity in Israel during the last half century before the Assyrian captivity was like that of the days of Noah, and of every other age when men have rejected God and have given themselves wholly to evil-doing. The exaltation of nature above the God of nature, the worship of the creature instead of the Creator, has always resulted in the grossest of evils. Thus when the people of Israel, in their worship of Baal and Ashtoreth, paid supreme homage to the forces of nature, they severed their connection with all that is uplifting and ennobling, and fell an easy prey to temptation. With the defenses of the soul broken down, the misguided worshipers had no barrier against sin and yielded themselves to the evil passions of the human heart. *PK 281, 282*

9 Strangers have devoured his strength, and he knoweth *it* not: yea, gray hairs are here and there upon him, yet he knoweth not.   Hos. 8:7
10 And the pride of Israel testifieth to his face: and they do not return to the Lord their God, nor seek him for all this.   Is. 9:13; Hos. 5:5
11 Ephraim also is like a silly dove without heart: they call to Egypt, they go to Assyria.
12 When they shall go, I will spread my net upon them; I will bring them down as the fowls of the heaven; I will chastise them, as their congregation hath heard.   Deut. 28:15-68
13 Woe unto them! for they have fled from me: destruction unto them! because they have ᵀtransgressed against me: though I have redeemed them, yet they have spoken lies against me.   Hos. 9:12; 11:12 ◆ *violated a law*
14 And they have not cried unto me with their heart, when they howled upon their beds: they assemble themselves for corn and wine, *and* they rebel against me.   Amos 2:8
15 Though I have bound *and* strengthened their arms, yet do they imagine mischief against me.   Nah. 1:9
16 They return, *but* not to the most High: they are like a deceitful bow: their princes shall fall by the sword for the rage of their tongue: this *shall be* their derision in the land of Egypt.   Ps. 73:9; 78:57; Hos. 9:3

Destruction Is Threatened

8 *Set* the trumpet to thy mouth. *He shall come* as an eagle against the house of the Lord, because they have ᵀtransgressed my covenant, and ᵀtrespassed against my law.   Deut. 28:49; Jer. 4:13; Hos. 6:7 ◆ *violated* ◆ *sinned*
2 Israel shall cry unto me, My God, we know thee.   Matt. 7:21
3 Israel hath cast off *the thing that is* good: the enemy shall pursue him.
4 They have set up kings, but not by me: they have made princes, and I knew *it* not: of their silver and their gold have they made them idols, that they may be cut off.   Hos. 2:8
5 Thy calf, O Samaria, hath cast *thee* off; mine anger is kindled against them: how long *will it be* ere they attain to innocency?   Jer. 13:27
6 For from Israel *was* it also: the workman made it; therefore it *is* not God: but the calf of Samaria shall be broken in pieces.

8:7 Reaping the Whirlwind

The closing years of the ill-fated kingdom of Israel were marked with violence and bloodshed such as had never been witnessed even in the worst periods of strife and unrest under the house of Ahab. For two centuries and more the rulers of the ten tribes had been sowing the wind; now they were reaping the whirlwind. *PK 279*

7 For they have sown the wind, and they shall reap the whirlwind: it hath no stalk: the bud shall yield no meal: if so be it yield, the strangers shall swallow it up.   Prov. 22:8
8 Israel is swallowed up: now shall they be among the Gentiles as a vessel wherein *is* no pleasure.   Jer. 22:28; 51:34
9 For they are gone up to Assyria, a wild ass alone by himself: Ephraim hath hired lovers.   Jer. 2:24
10 Yea, though they have hired among the nations, now will I gather them, and they shall sorrow a little for the burden of the king of princes.   Ezek. 16:37
11 Because Ephraim hath made many altars to sin, altars shall be unto him to sin. Hos. 12:11
12 I have written to him the great things of my law, *but* they were counted as a strange thing.   Hos. 4:6
13 They sacrifice flesh *for* the sacrifices of mine offerings, and eat *it; but* the Lord accepteth them not; now will he remember their iniquity, and visit their sins: they shall return to Egypt.   Hos. 9:6
14 For Israel hath forgotten his Maker, and buildeth temples; and Judah hath multiplied fenced cities: but I will send a fire upon his cities, and it shall devour the palaces thereof.   Deut. 32:18

Distress and Captivity for Sins and Idolatry

9 Rejoice not, O Israel, for joy, as *other* people: for thou hast gone ᵀa whoring from thy God, thou hast loved a reward upon every cornfloor.   Hos. 10:5 ◆ *giving sex as a prostitute*
2 The floor and the winepress shall not feed them, and the new wine shall fail in her.
3 They shall not dwell in the Lord's land; but Ephraim shall return to Egypt, and they shall eat unclean *things* in Assyria. Lev. 25:23; Ezek. 4:13
4 They shall not offer wine *offerings* to the Lord, neither shall they be pleasing unto him: their sacrifices *shall be* unto them as the bread of mourners; all that eat thereof shall be polluted: for their bread for their soul shall not come into the house of the Lord.   Deut. 26:14; Jer. 6:20; Hos. 8:13
5 What will ye do in the solemn day, and in the day of the feast of the Lord? Is. 10:3; Jer. 5:31
6 For, lo, they are gone because of destruction: Egypt shall gather them up, Memphis shall bury them: the pleasant *places* for their silver, nettles shall possess them: thorns *shall be* in their tabernacles. Is. 5:6; 7:23; Hos. 10:8
7 The days of visitation are come, the days of recompence are come; Israel shall know *it*: the prophet *is* a fool, the spiritual man *is* mad, for the multitude of thine iniquity, and the great hatred.   Is. 10:3; Jer. 10:15; Mic. 7:4
8 The watchman of Ephraim *was* with my

God: *but* the prophet *is* a snare of a ᵀfowler in all his ways, *and* hatred in the house of his God.   Hos. 5:1 ◆ *one who captures birds*

9 They have deeply corrupted *themselves*, as in the days of Gibeah: *therefore* he will remember their iniquity, he will visit their sins.   Is. 31:6; Hos. 8:13; 10:9

> **9:9 Nature Worship**
>
> The first departure from established forms of worship had led to the introduction of grosser forms of idolatry, until finally nearly all the inhabitants of the land had given themselves over to the alluring practices of nature worship. Forgetting their Maker, Israel "deeply corrupted themselves" (Hosea 9:9). *PK 282*

Israel Is Like Rotten Grapes or Figs

10 I found Israel like grapes in the wilderness; I saw your fathers as the firstripe in the fig tree at her first time: *but* they went to Baal-peor, and separated themselves unto *that* shame; and *their* abominations were according as they loved.   Jer. 11:13

11 *As for* Ephraim, their glory shall fly away like a bird, from the birth, and from the womb, and from the conception.   Hos. 4:7

12 Though they bring up their children, yet will I bereave them, *that there shall* not *be* a man *left*: yea, woe also to them when I depart from them!   Deut. 31:17; 1 Sam. 28:15-16; Hos. 7:13

13 Ephraim, as I saw Tyrus, *is* planted in a pleasant place: but Ephraim shall bring forth his children to the murderer.   Ezek. 26

14 Give them, O LORD: what wilt thou give? give them a miscarrying womb and dry breasts.   Luke 23:29

15 All their wickedness *is* in Gilgal: for there I hated them: for the wickedness of their doings I will drive them out of mine house, I will love them no more: all their princes *are* revolters.   Is. 1:23; Hos. 4:15; 12:11

16 Ephraim is smitten, their root is dried up, they shall bear no fruit: yea, though they bring forth, yet will I slay *even* the beloved *fruit* of their womb.   Ezek. 24:21

17 My God will cast them away, because they did not hearken unto him: and they shall be wanderers among the nations.   Hos. 7:13

Israel Is Like a Rotten Vine

10 Israel *is* an empty vine, he bringeth forth fruit unto himself: according to the multitude of his fruit he hath increased the altars; according to the goodness of his land they have made goodly images. 1 Kin. 14:23

2 Their heart is divided; now shall they be found faulty: he shall break down their altars, he shall ᵀspoil their images. 1 Kin. 18:21 ◆ *plunder*

3 For now they shall say, We have no king, because we feared not the LORD; what then should a king do to us?   Hos. 10:7

4 They have spoken words, swearing falsely in making a covenant: thus judgment springeth up as hemlock in the furrows of the field.   2 Kin. 17:3-4; Ezek. 17:13-19; Amos 5:7

5 The inhabitants of Samaria shall fear because of the calves of Beth-aven: for the people thereof shall mourn over it, and the priests thereof *that* rejoiced on it, for the glory thereof, because it is departed from it.   Is. 30:3; Jer. 7:24; Hos. 5:13

6 It shall be also carried unto Assyria *for* a present to king Jareb: Ephraim shall receive shame, and Israel shall be ashamed of his own counsel.   Is. 30:3; Jer. 7:24; Hos. 5:13

7 *As for* Samaria, her king is cut off as the foam upon the water.   Hos. 10:3

8 The high places also of Aven, the sin of Israel, shall be destroyed: the thorn and the thistle shall come up on their altars; and they shall say to the mountains, Cover us; and to the hills, Fall on us.   Hos. 9:6; Luke 23:30; Rev. 6:16

9 O Israel, thou hast sinned from the days of Gibeah: there they stood: the battle in Gibeah against the children of iniquity did not overtake them.   Hos. 9:9

10 *It is* in my desire that I should chastise them; and the people shall be gathered against them, when they shall bind themselves in their two furrows.   Ezek. 5:13

Israel Is Like a Heifer

11 And Ephraim *is as* an heifer *that is* taught, *and* loveth to tread out *the corn*; but I passed over upon her fair neck: I will make Ephraim to ride; Judah shall plow, *and* Jacob shall break his clods.   Deut. 25:4

12 Sow to yourselves in righteousness, reap in mercy; break up your fallow ground: for *it is* time to seek the LORD, till he come and rain righteousness upon you.   Prov. 11:18; Is. 44:3; 45:8

> **10:12 Removing the Weeds**
>
> The garden of the heart must be cultivated. The soil must be broken up by deep repentance for sin. Poisonous, Satanic plants must be uprooted. The soil once overgrown by thorns can be reclaimed only by diligent labor. So the evil tendencies of the natural heart can be overcome only by earnest effort in the name and strength of Jesus. *COL 56*

13 Ye have plowed wickedness, ye have reaped iniquity; ye have eaten the fruit of lies: because thou didst trust in thy way, in the multitude of thy mighty men.   Job 4:8

14 Therefore shall a tumult arise among thy people, and all thy fortresses shall be spoiled, as Shalman spoiled Beth-arbel in

the day of battle: the mother was dashed in pieces upon *her* children.   Hos. 13:16
15 So shall Beth-el do unto you because of your great wickedness: in a morning shall the king of Israel utterly be cut off.   Hos. 10:5

Israel Is Like a Bad Son

11 When Israel *was* a child, then I loved him, and called my son out of Egypt.
2 *As* they called them, so they went from them: they sacrificed unto Baalim, and burned incense to graven images.   Is. 65:7; Jer. 18:15
3 I taught Ephraim also to go, taking them by their arms; but they knew not that I healed them.   Ex. 15:26; Deut. 1:31; Jer. 30:17
4 I drew them with cords of a man, with bands of love: and I was to them as they that take off the yoke on their jaws, and I laid meat unto them.   Lev. 26:13; John 12:32
5 He shall not return into the land of Egypt, but the Assyrian shall be his king, because they refused to return. 2 Kin. 17:13-14; Hos. 7:16; 8:13
6 And the sword shall abide on his cities, and shall consume his branches, and devour *them*, because of their own counsels.   Hos. 13:16
7 And my people are bent to backsliding from me: though they called them to the most High, none at all would exalt *him*. Jer. 8:5

God's Mercy toward His People

8 How shall I give thee up, Ephraim? *how* shall I deliver thee, Israel? how shall I make thee as Admah? *how* shall I set thee as Ze-boim? mine heart is turned within me, my repentings are kindled together.   Gen. 14:8

11:8 Please Let Me Save You

You realize, though it may be but dimly, that you are a cumberer of the ground. Yet in His great mercy God has not cut you down. He does not look coldly upon you. He does not turn away with indifference, or leave you to destruction. Looking upon you He cries, as He cried so many centuries ago concerning Israel, "How shall I give thee up, Ephraim?" . . . (Hosea 11:8). The pitying Saviour is saying concerning you, Spare it this year also, till I shall dig about it and dress it. *COL 217, 218*

---

9 I will not execute the fierceness of mine anger, I will not return to destroy Ephraim: for I *am* God, and not man; the Holy One in the midst of thee: and I will not enter into the city.   Num. 23:19; Is. 12:6; Jer. 30:11
10 They shall walk after the LORD: he shall roar like a lion: when he shall roar, then the children shall tremble from the west. Is. 31:4
11 They shall tremble as a bird out of Egypt, and as a dove out of the land of Assyria: and I will place them in their houses, saith the LORD.   Is. 11:11; 60:8; Hos. 7:11

12 Ephraim ᵀcompasseth me about with lies, and the house of Israel with deceit: but Judah yet ruleth with God, and is faithful with the saints.   *surrounds*

The People Ignored God's Mighty Works

12 Ephraim feedeth on wind, and fol-loweth after the east wind: he daily increaseth lies and desolation; and they do make a covenant with the Assyrians, and oil is carried into Egypt.   Jer. 22:22
2 The LORD hath also a controversy with Judah, and will punish Jacob according to his ways; according to his doings will he ᵀrecompense him.   Hos. 4:1 ◆ *repay*
3 He took his brother by the heel in the womb, and by his strength he had power with God: Gen. 25:26; 32:24-28
4 Yea, he had power over the angel, and pre-vailed: he wept, and made supplication unto him: he found him *in* Beth-el, and there he spake with us;   Gen. 35:15

12:3, 4 A Name Celebrating Victory

Through humiliation, repentance, and self-surrender, this sinful, erring mortal [Jacob] prevailed with the Majesty of heaven. He had fastened his trembling grasp upon the prom-ises of God, and the heart of Infinite Love could not turn away the sinner's plea. As an evidence of his triumph and an encourage-ment to others to imitate his example, his name was changed from one which was a re-minder of his sin, to one that commemorated his victory. *GC 617*

---

5 Even the LORD God of hosts; the LORD *is* his memorial.   Ex. 3:15
6 Therefore turn thou to thy God: keep mercy and judgment, and wait on thy God continually.   Hos. 14:1; Joel 2:13; Mic. 6:8

The People's Sins Provoke God

7 *He is* a merchant, the balances of deceit *are* in his hand: he loveth to oppress.   Prov. 11:1
8 And Ephraim said, Yet I am become rich, I have found me out substance: *in* all my labours they shall find none iniquity in me that *were* sin.   Ps. 62:10; Zech. 11:5; Rev. 3:17
9 And I *that am* the LORD thy God from the land of Egypt will yet make thee to dwell in tabernacles, as in the days of the solemn feast.   Lev. 23:40-43
10 I have also spoken by the prophets, and I have multiplied visions, and used similitudes, by the ministry of the prophets.   2 Kin. 17:13

Gift of Prophecy   See Amos 3:7.

11 *Is there* iniquity *in* Gilead? surely they are vanity: they sacrifice bullocks in Gilgal; yea,

their altars *are* as heaps in the furrows of the fields.   Hos. 4:15; 6:8; 8:11

12 And Jacob fled into the country of Syria, and Israel served for a wife, and for a wife he kept *sheep*.

13 And by a prophet the LORD brought Israel out of Egypt, and by a prophet was he preserved.   Ex. 12:50-51

14 Ephraim provoked *him* to anger most bitterly: therefore shall he leave his blood upon him, and his reproach shall his Lord return unto him.   Ezek. 18:13

Idolatry Will be Punished

13 When Ephraim spake trembling, he exalted himself in Israel; but when he offended in Baal, he died.   Hos. 11:2

2 And now they sin more and more, and have made them molten images of their silver, *and* idols according to their own understanding, all of it the work of the craftsmen: they say of them, Let the men that sacrifice kiss the calves.   Is. 44:17-20

3 Therefore they shall be as the morning cloud, and as the early dew that passeth away, as the chaff *that* is driven with the whirlwind out of the floor, and as the smoke out of the chimney.   Ps. 1:4; 68:2; Hos. 6:4

4 Yet I *am* the LORD thy God from the land of Egypt, and thou shalt know no god but me: for *there is* no saviour beside me.   Is. 45:21-22

5 I did know thee in the wilderness, in the land of great drought.   Deut. 2:7

6 According to their pasture, so were they filled; they were filled, and their heart was exalted; therefore have they forgotten me.

7 Therefore I will be unto them as a lion: as a leopard by the way will I observe *them*:

8 I will meet them as a bear *that is* bereaved of her whelps, and will rend the caul of their heart, and there will I devour them like a lion: the wild beast shall tear them.   2 Sam. 17:8

9 O Israel, thou hast destroyed thyself; but in me *is* thine help.   Deut. 33:26

13:9 Reaping a Bitter Harvest

The Jews had forged their own fetters; they had filled for themselves the cup of vengeance. In the utter destruction that befell them as a nation, and in all the woes that followed them in their dispersion, they were but reaping the harvest which their own hands had sown. *GC 35*

---

10 I will be thy king: where *is any other* that may save thee in all thy cities? and thy judges of whom thou saidst, Give me a king and princes?   1 Sam. 8:5-6; Hos. 8:4; 10:3

11 I gave thee a king in mine anger, and took *him* away in my wrath.   1 Sam. 10:19

12 The iniquity of Ephraim *is* bound up; his sin *is* hid.   Job 14:17

13 The sorrows of a travailing woman shall come upon him: he *is* an unwise son; for he should not stay long in *the place of* the breaking forth of children.   2 Kin. 19:3; Is. 13:8; Mic. 4:9-10

14 I will ransom them from the power of the grave; I will redeem them from death: O death, I will be thy plagues; O grave, I will be thy destruction: repentance shall be hid from mine eyes.   Ps. 49:15

15 Though he be fruitful among *his* brethren, an east wind shall come, the wind of the LORD shall come up from the wilderness, and his spring shall become dry, and his fountain shall be dried up: he shall spoil the treasure of all pleasant vessels.   Gen. 41:52; Ezek. 17:10; 19:12

16 Samaria shall become desolate; for she

Pretentious but Fruitless

Hosea 13:9

Every opportunity and privilege had been granted [Israel], and in return [God] sought their sympathy and co-operation in His work of grace. He longed to see in them self-sacrifice and compassion, zeal for God, and a deep yearning of soul for the salvation of their fellow men. Had they kept the law of God, they would have done the same unselfish work that Christ did. But love to God and man was eclipsed by pride and self-sufficiency. They brought ruin upon themselves by refusing to minister to others. The treasures of truth which God had committed to them, they did not give to the world. . . . Refusing to impart blessing, they would no longer receive it. "O Israel," the Lord says, "thou hast destroyed thyself" (Hosea 13:9).

The warning is for all time. . . . No one can live the law of God without ministering to others. But there are many who do not live out Christ's merciful, unselfish life. Some who think themselves excellent Christians do not understand what constitutes service for God. They plan and study to please themselves. They act only in reference to self. Time is of value to them only as they can gather for themselves. In all the affairs of life this is their object. Not for others but for themselves do they minister. God created them to live in a world where unselfish service must be performed. . . . They observe the forms of worship, but without repentance or faith. In profession they honor the law of God, but obedience is lacking. They say, but do not. . . . He declares that the open sinner is less guilty than is he who professes to serve God, but who bears no fruit to His glory. *DA 583, 584*

hath rebelled against her God: they shall fall by the sword: their infants shall be dashed in pieces, and their women with child shall be ripped up.   2 Kin. 8:12; 15:16; Is. 13:16

The Lord Offers to Forgive

14 O Israel, return unto the LORD thy God; for thou hast fallen by thine iniquity.   Hos. 6:1

2 Take with you words, and turn to the LORD: say unto him, Take away all iniquity, and receive *us* graciously: so will we render the calves of our lips.   Ps. 69:30; Luke 18:13; Heb. 13:15

14:4 Hope, Not Despair

But none who have fallen need give up to despair. Aged men, once honored of God, may have defiled their souls, sacrificing virtue on the altar of lust; but if they repent, forsake sin, and turn to God, there is still hope for them. *PK 84*

---

3 Asshur shall not save us; we will not ride upon horses: neither will we say any more to the work of our hands, *Ye are* our gods: for in thee the fatherless findeth mercy.   Ps. 10:14

4 I will heal their backsliding, I will love them freely: for mine anger is turned away from him.   Zeph. 3:17

5 I will be as the dew unto Israel: he shall grow as the lily, and cast forth his roots as Lebanon.   Job 29:19; Prov. 19:12; Is. 35:2

6 His branches shall spread, and his beauty shall be as the olive tree, and his smell as Lebanon.   Ps. 52:8

7 They that dwell under his shadow shall return; they shall revive *as* the corn, and grow as the vine: the scent thereof *shall be* as the wine of Lebanon.   Ps. 91:1

8 Ephraim *shall say*, What have I to do any more with idols? I have heard *him*, and observed him: I *am* like a green fir tree. From me is thy fruit found.   Job 34:32

9 Who *is* wise, and he shall understand these *things*? prudent, and he shall know them? for the ways of the LORD *are* right, and the just shall walk in them: but the transgressors shall fall therein.   Ps. 107:43; Prov. 10:29; Jer. 9:12

THE BOOK OF

JOEL

"Repent!" This cry may not be a popular idea, but repentance is an essential part of the Christian life. The prophet Joel can teach Christians how to repent and how to think about repentance.

After locusts destroyed the crops of Judah, Joel called elders (1:2), drunkards (1:5), farmers (1:11), and priests (1:13) to heed his message. Later he even called for children, infants, and a couple on their wedding day to repent (2:16)! Repentance may involve fasting, weeping, and mourning (1:13, 14; 2:12), but the most important element in repentance is a heart grief-stricken over sin (2:12).

Dates

Among the prophets, it is most difficult to determine the date of Joel's ministry because he offers no evidence as to the time of his writing. Like Obadiah, Jonah, Nahum, and Habakkuk, the opening verse of Joel lists no kings to establish the time of the prophet's ministry. The political situations described by those prophets or references to them elsewhere in the Old Testament help us to recognize when they ministered, but no other Old Testament book mentions Joel. The absence of discussion of Assyria and Babylon could reveal a date in the ninth century B.C. before they rose to power, or a date in the sixth century B.C. after the collapse of each empire. References to the temple would also fit both dates (1:9, 13–16; 2:15–17). Locust plagues may have been relatively common, so Joel's discussion of the recent locust plague does not settle the issue. Therefore, scholars debate whether Joel ministered in the ninth century before the fall of Israel or in the sixth century after the return from exile.

Those who see Joel ministering in the sixth century B.C. note that he alludes to the Babylonian exile in 3:2, discusses nations more powerful after the exile like the Greeks (3:6) and Sabeans (3:8), and omits remarks about the northern kingdom (Israel), which could mean that it had already succumbed to the Assyrians.

Proponents of a ninth-century B.C. date for Joel counter that 3:2 discusses the exile in future terms. Assyrian records discuss the Greeks in the eighth century. The Sabeans from southwest Arabia also were active in trade during Solomon's reign (1 Kings 10). The lack of reference to the northern kingdom also makes sense because Joel addressed the southern kingdom. Some scholars note that Joel refers to priests instead of a king, which corresponds to Judah's government after its return from exile in the sixth century. However, this would also suit a period from 841–835 B.C., as Athaliah usurped the throne after the death of her son Ahaziah (2 Kings 11:1–3; 2 Chronicles 22:10–12) and Jehoiada the priest protected Joash (also spelled Jehoash), the rightful heir. Jehoiada served as regent when Joash began to reign at the age of seven and guided Joash in the early days of his reign (see 2 Kings 11:21—12:21 and 2 Chronicles 24 for descriptions of Joash's reign). The lack of discussion of idolatry in Joel's prophecy would fit this era, as Israel destroyed the altars and images of Baal under the leadership of Jehoiada the priest (2 Kings 11:17, 18; 2 Chronicles 23:16–21).

While one cannot be certain, the best estimated date seems to be around 620 B.C. for Joel's ministry in Judah.

Author

While there are twelve men named Joel in the Old Testament, none appears to be the prophet who authored this book. The only explicit information the book gives about Joel is the name of his father, Pethuel, a man whose name means "Persuaded of God" and is mentioned nowhere else in the Bible. The frequent remarks about Zion and the temple (1:9, 13, 14; 2:15–17, 23, 32; 3:1, 5, 6, 16, 17, 20, 21) may indicate that Joel lived close to Jerusalem while he served as a prophet to Judah. Since he shows an interest in addressing the priests in this short book (1:13, 14; 2:17), some believe that he was a priest as well as a prophet.

Meaning of the Name

The English name of the book reflects the spelling in the Latin Vulgate of the Hebrew name *Yo'el*, which means, "Yahweh is God." (The Greek form is *Ioel*.) As a preacher of repentance, Joel calls God's people to remember that Yahweh truly is God, sovereign over all the earth.

The best known reference to Joel in the New Testament is in Acts 2:16–21, where Peter quotes Joel 2:28–32 in discussing the coming of the Holy Spirit promised by Jesus in Acts 1:8. This promise from Joel finds fulfillment after Jesus' ascension. Since Jesus is Lord, the promise that "whosoever shall call on the name of the LORD shall be delivered" (Joel 2:32) shows the need to recognize Jesus in whom one finds salvation (Acts 4:9–12) and the promise that confession of Jesus as Lord brings salvation for Jews and Gentiles (Romans 10:9–13). Someday Jesus will judge all nations as described in Joel 3:2, 12 (see Matthew 25:31–46).

Overview

Joel's discussion of the threat of judgment and the promise of salvation at the day of the Lord occurs in two sections:

(1) *Joel 1:1—2:17, The Day of the Lord Will Be a Time of Judgment:* The disaster of the recent locust plague (1:2–12) is a symbol of invasion to come (the Assyrians and Chaldeans), one that should lead the people to repentance (1:13–20).

(2) *Joel 2:1—3:21, The Day of the Lord Will Be a Time of Blessing:* A day will come with destruction even worse than the locust plague upon those who do not repent (2:1–11; 3:1–16). This is the promised day of the Lord. God, however, will have mercy and bestow blessings, one of which is the Holy Spirit, on those who turn to Him (2:18–32; 3:18–21) and respond to the call to repentance (2:12–17).

Unlocking Joel

KEY PEOPLE:
Joel, the people of Judah

KEY EVENTS:
The day of the Lord; a call to repentance; God's judgment and blessing

KEY PHRASE:
Day of the Lord, as the phrase appears five times in the book (1:15; 2:1, 11, 31; 3:14). Three of these references highlight the judgment that comes on this day (1:15; 2:1, 11), illustrated by the recent locust plague (see 1:2–4), while two references describe the provision and protection on this day for those who seek God (2:31; 3:14). Since this day also features judgment upon Israel (2:1–11) as well as all the nations (3:1–16, 19), the prophet issues a call for repentance in preparation of the day of the Lord (1:13, 14; 2:12–17).

KEY VERSES:
"Therefore also now, saith the LORD, turn ye even to me with all your heart, and with fasting, and with weeping, and with mourning: and rend your heart, and not your garments, and turn unto the LORD your God: for he is gracious and merciful, slow to anger, and of great kindness, and repenteth him of the evil" (Joel 2:12, 13).

KEY CHAPTER:
Joel 2, in which the prophet proclaims the judgment that comes with the day of the Lord (2:1–11) and the salvation for those who seek God (2:18–32). He then issues a call to repentance so that the nation can enjoy these blessings (2:12–17).

Judah Is Plagued with Locusts and Famine

1 The word of the LORD that came to Joel the son of Pethuel.   Jer. 1:2

2 Hear this, ye old men, and give ear, all ye inhabitants of the land. Hath this been in your days, or even in the days of your fathers?   Job 8:8; Hos. 5:1; Joel 2:2

3 Tell ye your children of it, and *let* your children *tell* their children, and their children another generation.

4 That which the palmerworm hath left hath the locust eaten; and that which the locust hath left hath the cankerworm eaten; and that which the cankerworm hath left hath the caterpiller eaten.   Ex. 10:4; Amos 4:9

5 Awake, ye drunkards, and weep; and howl, all ye drinkers of wine, because of the new wine; for it is cut off from your mouth.

6 For a nation is come up upon my land, strong, and without number, whose teeth *are* the teeth of a lion, and he hath the cheek teeth of a great lion.   Joel 2:25

7 He hath laid my vine waste, and ᵀbarked my fig tree: he hath made it clean bare, and cast *it* away; the branches thereof are made white.   Is. 5:6 ◆ *removed bark from*

Judah Told to Mourn

8 Lament like a virgin girded with sackcloth for the husband of her youth.   Is. 22:12

9 The meat offering and the drink offering is cut off from the house of the LORD; the priests, the LORD's ministers, mourn.   Hos. 9:4

10 The field is wasted, the land mourneth; for the corn is wasted: the new wine is dried up, the oil ᵀlanguisheth.   Jer. 12:11 ◆ *fails*

11 Be ye ashamed, O ye ᵀhusbandmen; howl, O ye vinedressers, for the wheat and for the barley; because the harvest of the field is perished.   Is. 17:11 ◆ *farmers*

12 The vine is dried up, and the fig tree languisheth; the pomegranate tree, the palm tree also, and the apple tree, *even* all the trees of the field, are withered: because joy is withered away from the sons of men.   Is. 24:11

13 Gird yourselves, and lament, ye priests: howl, ye ministers of the altar: come, lie all night in sackcloth, ye ministers of my God: for the meat offering and the drink offering is withholden from the house of your God.   1 Kin. 21:27; Jer. 4:8; Joel 1:8-9

14 Sanctify ye a fast, call a solemn assembly, gather the elders *and* all the inhabitants of the land *into* the house of the LORD your God, and cry unto the LORD,   Joel 2:15-16

15 Alas for the day! for the day of the LORD is at hand, and as a destruction from the Almighty shall it come.   Jer. 30:7

16 Is not the meat cut off before our eyes, *yea*, joy and gladness from the house of our God?   Deut. 12:6-7

17 The seed is rotten under their clods, the garners are laid desolate, the barns are broken down; for the corn is withered.

18 How do the beasts groan! the herds of cattle are perplexed, because they have no pasture; yea, the flocks of sheep are made desolate.   Jer. 12:4

19 O LORD, to thee will I cry: for the fire hath devoured the pastures of the wilderness, and the flame hath burned all the trees of the field.   Ps. 50:15; Jer. 9:10; Amos 7:4

20 The beasts of the field cry also unto thee: for the rivers of waters are dried up, and the fire hath devoured the pastures of the wilderness.   1 Kin. 17:7; 18:5; Ps. 104:21

1:17-20 Plagues Unmixed With Mercy

These plagues are not universal, or the inhabitants of the earth would be wholly cut off. Yet they will be the most awful scourges that have ever been known to mortals. All the judgments upon men, prior to the close of probation, have been mingled with mercy. The pleading blood of Christ has shielded the sinner from receiving the full measure of his guilt; but in the final judgment, wrath is poured out unmixed with mercy. *GC 628, 629*

The Day of the Lord

2 Blow ye the trumpet in Zion, and sound an alarm in my holy mountain: let all the inhabitants of the land tremble: for the

The World on the Verge of a Crisis

Joel 1:1-3

The present is a time of overwhelming interest to all living. Rulers and statesmen, men who occupy positions of trust and authority, thinking men and women of all classes, have their attention fixed upon the events taking place about us. They are watching the relations that exist among the nations. They observe the intensity that is taking possession of every earthly element, and they recognize that something great and decisive is about to take place—that the world is on the verge of a stupendous crisis.

The Bible, and the Bible only, gives a correct view of these things. Here are revealed the great final scenes in the history of our world, events that already are casting their shadows before, the sound of their approach causing the earth to tremble and men's hearts to fail them for fear. *PK 537*

day of the L ord cometh, for *it is* nigh at hand;   Jer. 4:5; Joel 1:15; 2:15

2:1 God's People Need Reform

To prepare a people to stand in the day of God, a great work of reform was to be accomplished. God saw that many of His professed people were not building for eternity; and in His mercy He was about to send a message of warning to arouse them from their stupor and lead them to make ready for the coming of the Lord. *GC 311*

---

2 A day of darkness and of gloominess, a day of clouds and of thick darkness, as the morning spread upon the mountains: a great people and a strong; there hath not been ever the like, neither shall be any more after it, *even* to the years of many generations.   Dan. 12:1; Joel 1:6; 2:25
3 A fire devoureth before them; and behind them a flame burneth: the land *is* as the garden of Eden before them, and behind them a desolate wilderness; yea, and nothing shall escape them.   Gen. 2:8
4 The appearance of them *is* as the appearance of horses; and as horsemen, so shall they run.   Rev. 9:7
5 Like the noise of chariots on the tops of mountains shall they leap, like the noise of a flame of fire that devoureth the stubble, as a strong people set in battle array.   Is. 5:24; 30:30
6 Before their face the people shall be much pained: all faces shall gather blackness. Is. 13:8
7 They shall run like mighty men; they shall climb the wall like men of war; and they shall march every one on his ways, and they shall not break their ranks: Prov. 30:27
8 Neither shall one thrust another; they shall walk every one in his path: and *when* they fall upon the sword, they shall not be wounded.
9 They shall run to and fro in the city; they shall run upon the wall, they shall climb up upon the houses; they shall enter in at the windows like a thief.   Ex. 10:6; Jer. 9:21; John 10:1
10 The earth shall quake before them; the heavens shall tremble: the sun and the moon shall be dark, and the stars shall withdraw their shining: Ps. 18:7; Is. 13:10; Matt. 24:29
11 And the L ord shall utter his voice before his army: for his camp *is* very great: for *he is* strong that executeth his word: for the day of the L ord *is* great and very terrible; and who can abide it?   Joel 3:16; Mal. 3:2; Rev. 18:8

The Lord Invites His People Back
12 Therefore also now, saith the L ord, turn ye *even* to me with all your heart, and with fasting, and with weeping, and with mourning: Deut. 4:29-30; Jer. 4:1; Hos. 12:6

13 And ᵀrend your heart, and not your garments, and turn unto the L ord your God: for he *is* gracious and merciful, slow to anger, and of great kindness, and repenteth him of the evil.   Job 1:20; Ps. 34:18; Jon. 4:2 ◆ *tear apart*

2:12, 13 One Reason for Fasting

The object of the fast which God calls upon us to keep is not to afflict the body for the sin of the soul, but to aid us in perceiving the grievous character of sin, in humbling the heart before God and receiving His pardoning grace. . . .

It will avail nothing for us to do penance or to flatter ourselves that by our own works we shall merit or purchase an inheritance among the saints. *MB 87*

---

14 Who knoweth *if* he will return and repent, and leave a blessing behind him; *even* a meat offering and a drink offering unto the L ord your God?   Joel 1:9, 13; Hag. 2:19
15 Blow the trumpet in Zion, sanctify a fast, call a solemn assembly: Num. 10:3; 2 Kin. 10:20
16 Gather the people, ᵀsanctify the congregation, assemble the elders, gather the children, and those that suck the breasts: let the bridegroom go forth of his chamber, and the bride out of her closet.   Ex. 19:10 ◆ *make holy*
17 Let the priests, the ministers of the L ord, weep between the porch and the altar, and let them say, Spare thy people, O L ord, and give not thine heritage to reproach, that the heathen should rule over them: wherefore should they say among the people, Where *is* their God?   Ps. 79:10; 115:2; Ezek. 8:16

The Lord Promises Blessings
18 Then will the L ord be jealous for his land, and pity his people. Ps. 103:13; Zech. 1:14; 8:2
19 Yea, the L ord will answer and say unto his people, Behold, I will send you corn, and wine, and oil, and ye shall be satisfied therewith: and I will no more make you a reproach among the heathen: Ezek. 34:29
20 But I will remove far off from you the northern *army*, and will drive him into a land barren and desolate, with his face toward the east sea, and his hinder part toward the utmost sea, and his stink shall come up, and his ill savour shall come up, because he hath done great things.   Deut. 11:24; Is. 34:3; Zech. 14:8
21 Fear not, O land; be glad and rejoice: for the L ord will do great things.   Is. 54:4
22 Be not afraid, ye beasts of the field: for the pastures of the wilderness do spring, for the tree beareth her fruit, the fig tree and the vine do yield their strength.   Ps. 65:12
23 Be glad then, ye children of Zion, and rejoice in the L ord your God: for he hath

given you the former rain moderately, and he will cause to come down for you the rain, the former rain, and the latter rain in the first *month*.   Lev. 26:4; Deut. 11:14; Zech. 10:7

2:23 The Latter Rain

The great work of the gospel is not to close with less manifestation of the power of God than marked its opening. The prophecies which were fulfilled in the outpouring of the former rain at the opening of the gospel are again to be fulfilled in the latter rain at its close. Here are "the times of refreshing" to which the apostle Peter looked forward when he said: "Repent ye therefore, and be converted, that your sins may be blotted out, when the times of refreshing shall come from the presence of the Lord; and He shall send Jesus" (Acts 3:19, 20). *GC 611, 612*

24 And the floors shall be full of wheat, and the fats shall overflow with wine and oil.
25 And I will restore to you the years that the locust hath eaten, the cankerworm, and the caterpiller, and the palmerworm, my great army which I sent among you.   Joel 1:4-7
26 And ye shall eat in plenty, and be satisfied, and praise the name of the LORD your God, that hath dealt wondrously with you: and my people shall never be ashamed.   Lev. 26:5
27 And ye shall know that I *am* in the midst of Israel, and *that* I *am* the LORD your God, and none else: and my people shall never be ashamed.   Lev. 26:11-12; Is. 45:5; Joel 3:17

2:27, 28

The Lord Will Pour Out His Spirit

28 And it shall come to pass afterward, *that* I will pour out my spirit upon all flesh; and your sons and your daughters shall prophesy,

your old men shall dream dreams, your young men shall see visions: Is. 32:15; Ezek. 39:29

Gift of Prophecy   See 1 Corinthians 1:7.

29 And also upon the servants and upon the handmaids in those days will I pour out my spirit.   1 Cor. 12:13; Gal. 3:28
30 And I will shew wonders in the heavens and in the earth, blood, and fire, and pillars of smoke.   Matt. 24:29; Luke 21:11, 25-26

2:30, 31

2:31 The Dark Day

May 19, 1780, stands in history as "The Dark Day." Since the time of Moses no period of darkness of equal density, extent, and duration, has ever been recorded. The description of this event, as given by eyewitnesses, is but an echo of the words of the Lord, recorded by the prophet Joel, twenty-five hundred years previous to their fulfillment: "The sun shall be turned into darkness, and the moon into blood, before the great and terrible day of the Lord come" (Joel 2:31). *GC 308*

31 The sun shall be turned into darkness, and the moon into blood, before the great and the terrible day of the LORD come. Is. 13:9-10; Mal. 4:5

Signs of the End   See Matthew 24:29.

32 And it shall come to pass, *that* whosoever shall call on the name of the LORD shall be delivered: for in mount Zion and in Jerusalem shall be deliverance, as the LORD hath said, and in the remnant whom the LORD shall call.   Is. 11:11; 46:13; Obad. 17

The Lord Will Rescue His People

3 For, behold, in those days, and in that time, when I shall bring again the captivity of Judah and Jerusalem,   Jer. 16:15

The Latter-Day Rain for God's Last-Day Church

Joel 2:23

The outpouring of the Spirit in the days of the apostles was the beginning of the early, or former, rain, and glorious was the result. . . .

But near the close of earth's harvest, a special bestowal of spiritual grace is promised to prepare the church for the coming of the Son of man. This outpouring of the Spirit is likened to the falling of the latter rain; and it is for this added power that Christians are to send their petitions to the Lord of the harvest "in the time of the latter rain." In response, "the Lord shall make bright clouds, and give them showers of rain." "He will cause to come down . . . the rain, the former rain, and the latter rain" (Zechariah 10:1; Joel 2:23).

But unless the members of God's church today have a living connection with the Source of all spiritual growth, they will not be ready for the time of reaping. Unless they keep their lamps trimmed and burning, they will fail of receiving added grace in times of special need.

Those only who are constantly receiving fresh supplies of grace, will have power proportionate to their daily need and their ability to use that power. Instead of looking forward to some future time when, through a special endowment of spiritual power, they will receive a miraculous fitting up for soul winning, they are yielding themselves daily to God, that He may make them vessels meet for His use. Daily they are improving the opportunities for service that lie within their reach. Daily they are witnessing for the Master wherever they may be, whether in some humble sphere of labor in the home, or in a public field of usefulness. *AA 54, 55*

2 I will also gather all nations, and will bring them down into the valley of Jehoshaphat, and will plead with them there for my people and *for* my heritage Israel, whom they have scattered among the nations, and parted my land. Is. 66:16

3 And they have cast lots for my people; and have given a boy for an harlot, and sold a girl for wine, that they might drink. Amos 2:6

4 Yea, and what have ye to do with me, O Tyre, and Zidon, and all the coasts of Palestine? will ye render me a recompence? and if ye ^Trecompense me, swiftly *and* speedily will I return your recompence upon your own head; Is. 34:8 ◆ *repay*

5 Because ye have taken my silver and my gold, and have carried into your temples my goodly pleasant things: 2 Kin. 12:18

6 The children also of Judah and the children of Jerusalem have ye sold unto the Grecians, that ye might remove them far from their border. Ezek. 27:13

7 Behold, I will raise them out of the place whither ye have sold them, and will return your recompence upon your own head: Is. 43:5-6

8 And I will sell your sons and your daughters into the hand of the children of Judah, and they shall sell them to the Sabeans, to a people far off: for the LORD hath spoken *it*.

9 Proclaim ye this among the Gentiles; Prepare war, wake up the mighty men, let all the men of war draw near; let them come up: Is. 8:9-10

10 Beat your plowshares into swords, and your pruninghooks into spears: let the weak say, I *am* strong. Is. 2:4; Mic. 4:3; Zech. 12:8

11 Assemble yourselves, and come, all ye heathen, and gather yourselves together round about: thither cause thy mighty ones to come down, O LORD. Is. 13:3

12 Let the heathen be wakened, and come up to the valley of Jehoshaphat: for there will I sit to judge all the heathen round about. Ps. 96:13; 98:9; Is. 2:4

13 Put ye in the sickle, for the harvest is ripe: come, get you down; for the press is full, the ^Tfats overflow; for their wickedness *is* great. Is. 63:3; Jer. 51:33; Hos. 6:11 ◆ *containers*

14 Multitudes, multitudes in the valley of decision: for the day of the LORD *is* near in the valley of decision. Is. 34:2-8

15 The sun and the moon shall be darkened, and the stars shall withdraw their shining. Joel 2:10

16 The LORD also shall roar out of Zion, and utter his voice from Jerusalem; and the heavens and the earth shall shake: but the LORD *will be* the hope of his people, and the strength of the children of Israel. Ezek. 38:19; Joel 2:10-11

17 So shall ye know that I *am* the LORD your God dwelling in Zion, my holy mountain: then shall Jerusalem be holy, and there shall no strangers pass through her any more. Is. 4:3; 52:1; Joel 2:27

18 And it shall come to pass in that day, *that* the mountains shall drop down new wine, and the hills shall flow with milk, and all the rivers of Judah shall flow with waters, and a fountain shall come forth of the house of the LORD, and shall water the valley of Shittim. Num. 25:1; Is. 30:25; 35:6

19 Egypt shall be a desolation, and Edom shall be a desolate wilderness, for the violence *against* the children of Judah, because they have shed innocent blood in their land. Is. 19:1-15

20 But Judah shall dwell for ever, and Jerusalem from generation to generation. Ezek. 37:25

21 For I will cleanse their blood *that* I have not cleansed: for the LORD dwelleth in Zion. Is. 4:4

God's Presence Shakes the Earth

Joel 3:16

Never since man was created had there been witnessed such a manifestation of divine power as when the law was proclaimed from Sinai. "The earth shook, the heavens also dropped at the presence of God: even Sinai itself was moved at the presence of God, the God of Israel" (Psalm 68:8). Amid the most terrific convulsions of nature the voice of God, like a trumpet, was heard from the cloud. The mountain was shaken from base to summit, and the hosts of Israel, pale and trembling with terror, lay upon their faces upon the earth. He whose voice then shook the earth has declared, "Yet once more I shake not the earth only, but also heaven" (Hebrews 12:26). Says the Scripture, "The Lord shall roar from on high, and utter His voice from His holy habitation;" "and the heavens and the earth shall shake" (Jeremiah 25:30; Joel 3:16). In that great coming day, the heaven itself shall depart "as a scroll when it is rolled together" (Revelation 6:14). And every mountain and island shall be moved out of its place. "The earth shall reel to and fro like a drunkard, and shall be removed like a cottage; and the transgression thereof shall be heavy upon it; and it shall fall, and not rise again" (Isaiah 24:20). PP 340

THE BOOK OF

AMOS

While the people in the northern kingdom of Israel experience economic and political success, many indulge in a luxurious lifestyle (3:15; 6:4–6) at the expense of the poor (4:1; 5:11, 12; 8:4–6), corruption permeates the courts (5:10, 12, 13; 6:12) and the markets (8:4–6), and immorality and idolatry abound (2:7, 8). God sends Amos to tell them that their relationship with God has both good and bad consequences: they are God's chosen people but face special punishment for their sins (3:1, 2). Most of the book denounces Israel's sin and describes its coming judgment (3:1—9:10).

Amos' message challenges contemporary Christians not to become complacent due to economic prosperity but to look to the needs of others, particularly the poor.

Dates

Political and seismological (the study of the earthquakes) markers indicate that Amos ministered around 755 B.C. Since 1:1 states that Amos prophesied during the reigns of Uzziah king of Judah (790–739 B.C.) and Jeroboam II king of Israel (793–753 B.C.), his ministry would fall into the overlap of these kings between 767 and 753 B.C. The earthquake mentioned in 1:1 appears to be the same earthquake Zechariah cited two hundred years later (Zechariah 14:5); Amos spoke two years before this earthquake. Amos' message may also recall a solar eclipse that occurred on June 15, 763 B.C. (see Amos 8:9).

Israel and Judah were at peace with each other and both experienced phases of economic and political success during this period. Amos' message, primarily directed to the northern kingdom, reveals distressing developments in the nation. Immorality and injustice increased during this time of prosperity (2:6–8; 3:1; 4:1; 5:10–12; 8:4–6). The strength of the nation and the weakness of countries like Assyria, Babylon, and Egypt gave Israel a false sense of security that caused them to ignore Amos' words of judgment and exile (3:11; 4:2; 7:11). Although an earthquake came two years later to serve as an initial confirmation of Amos' message (8:8; 9:1, 5), Israel ignored this warning like past warnings (see 4:6–11), and the calamity promised by Amos (2:12–16; 3:14, 15; 5:27; 6:14; 7:9; 9:1–10) occurred with the fall of Israel to the Assyrians in 722 B.C.

Author

Amos is generally believed to be the author. While Isaiah's father had a similar name (Amoz), the name Amos only occurs in this Old Testament book. Because of his humble background—his hometown was the rural village of Tekoa (1:1), located twelve miles south of Jerusalem in the southern kingdom (Judah)—Amos identified himself as a shepherd who also tended sycamore trees, rather than as a prophet (7:14). According to 7:15, this unlikely prophet received a divine commission from God to speak to the northern kingdom (Israel), likely moving to Beth-el (see 7:13) since it housed the king of Israel and featured much idolatry and oppression of the poor. Amos' prophetic message employs metaphors from his former occupation and the natural world (see 2:13; 3:4, 5, 8, 12; 4:1; 5:8, 19; 8:1, 2; 9:9) and also reveals knowledge of international affairs (1:3—2:3) and the Scriptures. Since he was from the southern kingdom and opposed popular practices in Israel, Amos proved to be unpopular among the people of Israel (see 7:10–13).

Meaning of the Name

Derived from the Hebrew word *amas* ("to lift a burden; to carry"), the name Amos means "burden" or "burden-bearer." The English spelling of Amos is a transliteration of the Greek and Latin forms. In his prophetic ministry, Amos carried the burden of declaring God's message of coming judgment to the nation of Israel.

Christ in Amos

God's promise to "raise up the tabernacle of David that is fallen, and close up the breaches thereof" (9:11) was fulfilled in Jesus (see Acts 15:15–17). As the Son of David (see Matthew 1:1), Jesus sits on the throne of David and fulfills God's promise to David to always have a descendant on his throne (see 2 Samuel 7:16). In addition to predicting the restoration of exiled Israel under the Davidic king, Amos points to the inclusion of Gentiles that happens under Jesus (see Amos 9:12).

Amos' message of coming judgment upon the nation of Israel consists of four sections:

(1) *Amos 1:1—2:16, Judgments:* After highlighting judgment upon foreign nations (1:3—2:3), Amos turns to announce judgment upon Judah (2:4, 5) and Israel (2:6–16).

(2) *Amos 3:1—6:14, Sermons:* In three sermons, Amos announces that God will judge Israel for breaking its relationship with Him (3:1–15), refusing to repent after receiving past warnings (4:1–13), and perverting justice and the worship of God (5:1–17). At the conclusion of the third sermon, Amos includes two woes announcing exile for the complacent people (5:18–27; 6:1–14).

(3) *Amos 7:1—9:10, Visions:* The visions of locusts and fire show God relenting on judgment due to the prophet's intercession (7:1–6), but the vision of the plumbline shows that God will not relent (7:7–9). A historical interlude describing the attempt by Amaziah the priest to silence Amos (7:10–17) appears between the third and fourth visions and shows why God will not relent on His punishment: the leaders of the people have rejected God's message. The final two visions, those of the ripe fruit (8:1–14) and God standing by the altar (9:1–10), reveal the certainty of the coming judgment.

(4) *Amos 9:11–15, Promises:* These promises show the restoration of the house of David (9:11, 12) and return of prosperity to the land of Israel (9:13, 14), with the pledge that God will not uproot Israel again (9:15).

Unlocking Amos

KEY PEOPLE:
Amos, Amaziah the priest, Jeroboam II, the people of Israel

KEY EVENTS:
The judgment of the nations; the predicted fall of Israel; the future restoration under the Davidic king

KEY WORD:
Justice, which Amos highlights by noting that God will judge sin and that God desires His people to practice justice and righteousness toward one another. According to Amos, justice is more important than offering sacrifices or celebrating religious feasts (Amos 5:21–24).

KEY VERSES:
"Behold, the days come, saith the Lord GOD, that I will send a famine in the land, not a famine of bread, nor a thirst for water, but of hearing the words of the LORD: and they shall wander from sea to sea, and from the north even to the east, they shall run to and fro to seek the word of the LORD, and shall not find it" (Amos 8:11, 12).

KEY CHAPTER:
Amos 9, which features the promise of certain judgment and of future restoration under the coming Messiah from the line of David.

God's Judgment upon Damascus

1 The words of Amos, who was among the herdmen of Tekoa, which he saw concerning Israel in the days of Uzziah king of Judah, and in the days of Jeroboam the son of Joash king of Israel, two years before the earthquake.   2 Sam. 14:2; Hos. 1:1; Zech. 14:5

2 And he said, The LORD will roar from Zion, and utter his voice from Jerusalem; and the habitations of the shepherds shall mourn, and the top of Carmel shall wither. Is. 42:13; Jer. 12:4

3 Thus saith the LORD; For three transgressions of Damascus, and for four, I will not turn away *the punishment* thereof; because they have threshed Gilead with threshing instruments of iron: Is. 8:4; Amos 1:9; 2:6

4 But I will send a fire into the house of Hazael, which shall devour the palaces of Ben-hadad.   2 Kin. 6:24

5 I will break also the bar of Damascus, and cut off the inhabitant from the plain of Aven, and him that holdeth the sceptre from the house of Eden: and the people of Syria shall go into captivity unto Kir, saith the LORD.   2 Kin. 16:9; Jer. 51:30; Amos 9:7

God's Judgment upon Gaza

6 Thus saith the LORD; For three transgressions of Gaza, and for four, I will not turn away *the punishment* thereof; because they carried away captive the whole captivity, to deliver *them* up to Edom: 1 Sam. 6:17; 2 Chr. 28:18

7 But I will send a fire on the wall of Gaza, which shall devour the palaces thereof:

8 And I will cut off the inhabitant from Ashdod, and him that holdeth the sceptre from Ashkelon, and I will turn mine hand against Ekron: and the remnant of the Philistines shall perish, saith the Lord GOD.   Is. 14:29-31

God's Judgment upon Tyre

9 Thus saith the LORD; For three Ttransgressions of Tyrus, and for four, I will not

turn away *the punishment* thereof; because they delivered up the whole captivity to Edom, and remembered not the brotherly covenant: 1 Kin. 9:11-14 ◆ *violations of a law*

1:8 Refusing to Hear God's Voice

How great is the long-suffering of God toward the wicked! The idolatrous Philistines and backsliding Israel had alike enjoyed the gifts of His providence. Ten thousand unnoticed mercies were silently falling in the pathway of ungrateful, rebellious men. Every blessing spoke to them of the Giver, but they were indifferent to His love. . . . They refused to listen to the voice of God in His created works, and in the warnings, counsels, and reproofs of His word, and thus He was forced to speak to them through judgments. *PP 587, 588*

10 But I will send a fire on the wall of Tyrus, which shall devour the palaces thereof.   Zech. 9:4

God's Judgment upon Edom

11 Thus saith the LORD; For three transgressions of Edom, and for four, I will not turn away *the punishment* thereof; because he did pursue his brother with the sword, and did cast off all pity, and his anger did tear perpetually, and he kept his wrath for ever: Num. 20:14-21; 2 Chr. 28:17; Jer. 49:7-22

12 But I will send a fire upon Teman, which shall devour the palaces of Bozrah.   Jer. 49:7

God's Judgment upon Ammon

13 Thus saith the LORD; For three transgressions of the children of Ammon, and for four, I will not turn away *the punishment* thereof; because they have ripped up the women with child of Gilead, that they might enlarge their border: Jer. 49:1-6; Ezek. 25:2-7; Hos. 13:16

14 But I will kindle a fire in the wall of Rabbah,

God Will Work Through All

Amos 1:1

In giving light to His people anciently, God did not work exclusively through any one class. Daniel was a prince of Judah. Isaiah also was of the royal line. David was a shepherd boy, Amos a herdsman, Zechariah a captive from Babylon, Elisha a tiller of the soil. The Lord raised up as His representatives prophets and princes, the noble and the lowly, and taught them the truths to be given to the world.

To everyone who becomes a partaker of His grace the Lord appoints a work for others. Individually we are to stand in our lot and place, saying, "Here am I; send me" (Isaiah 6:8). Upon the minister of the word, the missionary nurse, the Christian physician, the individual Christian, whether he be merchant or farmer, professional man or mechanic—the responsibility rests upon all. It is our work to reveal to men the gospel of their salvation. Every enterprise in which we engage should be a means to this end.

Those who take up their appointed work will not only be a blessing to others, but they will themselves be blessed. The consciousness of duty well done will have a reflex influence upon their own souls. *MH 148*

and it shall devour the palaces thereof, with shouting in the day of battle, with a ᵀtempest in the day of the whirlwind: *storm*
15 And their king shall go into captivity, he and his princes together, saith the LORD.

God's Judgment upon Moab

2 Thus saith the LORD; For three ᵀtransgressions of Moab, and for four, I will not turn away *the punishment* thereof; because he burned the bones of the king of Edom into lime: Is. 15 ◆ *violations of a law*
2 But I will send a fire upon Moab, and it shall devour the palaces of Kerioth: and Moab shall die with tumult, with shouting, *and* with the sound of the trumpet: Jer. 48:24
3 And I will cut off the judge from the midst thereof, and will slay all the princes thereof with him, saith the LORD.   Jer. 48:7

God's Judgment upon Judah

4 Thus saith the LORD; For three transgressions of Judah, and for four, I will not turn away *the punishment* thereof; because they have despised the law of the LORD, and have not kept his commandments, and their lies caused them to ᵀerr, after the which their fathers have walked: Ezek. 20:13, 16, 24 ◆ *stray*
5 But I will send a fire upon Judah, and it shall devour the palaces of Jerusalem. Jer. 17:27

God's Judgment upon Israel

6 Thus saith the LORD; For three transgressions of Israel, and for four, I will not turn away *the punishment* thereof; because they sold the righteous for silver, and the poor for a pair of shoes;   Joel 3:3
7 That pant after the dust of the earth on the head of the poor, and turn aside the way of the meek: and a man and his father will go in unto the *same* maid, to profane my holy name: Is. 10:2; Ezek. 22:11; Amos 5:12
8 And they lay *themselves* down upon clothes laid to pledge by every altar, and they drink the wine of the condemned *in* the house of their god.   Amos 6:6

2:1–8 The Spirit Resisted

The disobedient and unthankful have great reason for gratitude for God's mercy and long-suffering in holding in check the cruel, malignant power of the evil one. . . . The Spirit of God, persistently resisted, is at last withdrawn from the sinner, and then there is left no power to control the evil passions of the soul, and no protection from the malice and enmity of Satan. *GC 36*

---

9 Yet destroyed I the Amorite before them, whose height *was* like the height of the

cedars, and he *was* strong as the oaks; yet I destroyed his fruit from above, and his roots from beneath.   Mal. 4:1
10 Also I brought you up from the land of Egypt, and led you forty years through the wilderness, to possess the land of the Amorite.   Ex. 12:51
11 And I raised up of your sons for prophets, and of your young men for Nazarites. *Is it* not even thus, O ye children of Israel? saith the LORD.
12 But ye gave the Nazarites wine to drink; and commanded the prophets, saying, Prophesy not.   Is. 30:10
13 Behold, I am pressed under you, as a cart is pressed *that is* full of sheaves.   Is. 1:14
14 Therefore the flight shall perish from the swift, and the strong shall not strengthen his force, neither shall the mighty deliver himself: Jer. 9:23
15 Neither shall he stand that handleth the bow; and *he that is* swift of foot shall not deliver *himself*: neither shall he that rideth the horse deliver himself.
16 And *he that is* courageous among the mighty shall flee away naked in that day, saith the LORD.   Judg. 4:17

The Necessity of God's Judgment against Israel

3 Hear this word that the LORD hath spoken against you, O children of Israel, against the whole family which I brought up from the land of Egypt, saying,   Amos 2:10
2 You only have I known of all the families of the earth: therefore I will punish you for all your iniquities.   Ex. 19:5-6; Deut. 7:6; Rom. 2:9
3 Can two walk together, except they be agreed?

3:3 Unbelieving Companions

No one who fears God can without danger connect himself with one who fears Him not. . . . They are serving two masters, between whom there can be no concord. However pure and correct one's principles may be, the influence of an unbelieving companion will have a tendency to lead away from God. *PP 174*

---

4 Will a lion roar in the forest, when he hath no prey? will a young lion cry out of his den, if he have taken nothing?   Ps. 104:21
5 Can a bird fall in a snare upon the earth, where no ᵀgin *is* for him? shall *one* take up a snare from the earth, and have taken nothing at all?   *trap*
6 Shall a trumpet be blown in the city, and the people not be afraid? shall there be evil in a city, and the LORD hath not done *it*?   Jer. 4:5

3:7 God's Secrets Are Revealed

"The Lord God will do nothing, but He revealeth His secret unto His servants the prophets." While "the secret things belong unto the Lord our God," "those things which are revealed belong unto us and to our children forever" (Amos 3:7; Deuteronomy 29:29). God has given these things to us, and His blessing will attend the reverent, prayerful study of the prophetic scriptures. *DA 234*

3:7

7 Surely the Lord GOD will do nothing, but he revealeth his secret unto his servants the prophets.   *Gen. 6:13; 18:17; John 15:15*

Gift of Prophecy   See Numbers 12:6.

8 The lion hath roared, who will not fear? the Lord GOD hath spoken, who can but prophesy?   *Jer. 20:9*
9 Publish in the palaces at Ashdod, and in the palaces in the land of Egypt, and say, Assemble yourselves upon the mountains of Samaria, and behold the great tumults in the midst thereof, and the oppressed in the midst thereof.   *1 Sam. 5:1; Amos 4:1; 6:1*
10 For they know not to do right, saith the LORD, who store up violence and robbery in their palaces.   *Jer. 4:22*
11 Therefore thus saith the Lord GOD; An adversary *there shall be* even round about the land; and he shall bring down thy strength from thee, and thy palaces shall be spoiled.   *Amos 2:5*
12 Thus saith the LORD; As the shepherd taketh out of the mouth of the lion two legs, or a piece of an ear; so shall the children of Israel be taken out that dwell in Samaria in the corner of a bed, and in Damascus *in* a couch.   *1 Sam. 17:34-37*
13 Hear ye, and testify in the house of Jacob, saith the Lord GOD, the God of hosts,
14 That in the day that I shall visit the ᵀtransgressions of Israel upon him I will also visit the altars of Beth-el: and the horns of the altar shall be cut off, and fall to the ground.   *2 Kin. 23:15* ♦ *sins*
15 And I will smite the winter house with the summer house; and the houses of ivory shall perish, and the great houses shall have an end, saith the LORD.   *Judg. 3:20; 1 Kin. 22:39*

Punishment for the Women of Samaria

4 Hear this word, ye ᵀkine of Bashan, that *are* in the mountain of Samaria, which oppress the poor, which crush the needy, which say to their masters, Bring, and let us drink.   *Ps. 22:12; Ezek. 39:18; Amos 5:11* ♦ *cattle*
2 The Lord GOD hath sworn by his holiness, that, lo, the days shall come upon you, that he will take you away with hooks, and your posterity with fishhooks.   *Ps. 89:35*

3 And ye shall go out at the breaches, every *cow at that which is* before her; and ye shall cast *them* into the palace, saith the LORD.   *Ezek. 12:5*
4 Come to Beth-el, and ᵀtransgress; at Gilgal multiply ᵀtransgression; and bring your sacrifices every morning, *and* your tithes after three years: *Ezek. 20:39* ♦ *violate a law* ♦ *lawlessness*
5 And offer a sacrifice of thanksgiving with leaven, and proclaim *and* publish the free offerings: for this liketh you, O ye children of Israel, saith the Lord GOD.   *Lev. 22:18-21*
6 And I also have given you ᵀcleanness of teeth in all your cities, and want of bread in all your places: yet have ye not returned unto me, saith the LORD.   *Is. 9:13; Jer. 5:3; Hag. 2:17* ♦ *famine*
7 And also I have withholden the rain from you, when *there were* yet three months to the harvest: and I caused it to rain upon one city, and caused it not to rain upon another city: one piece was rained upon, and the piece whereupon it rained not withered.   *Ex. 9:4, 26*
8 So two *or* three cities wandered unto one city, to drink water; but they were not satisfied: yet have ye not returned unto me, saith the LORD.   *1 Kin. 18:5*

4:1-8 Blessings Bestowed; Blessings Removed

God speaks to His people in blessings bestowed; and when these are not appreciated, He speaks to them in blessings removed, that they may be led to see their sins, and return to Him with all the heart. *PP 470*

---

9 I have smitten you with blasting and mildew: when your gardens and your vineyards and your fig trees and your olive trees increased, the palmerworm devoured *them*: yet have ye not returned unto me, saith the LORD.   *Deut. 28:22; Joel 1:4; Hag. 2:17*
10 I have sent among you the pestilence after the manner of Egypt: your young men have I slain with the sword, and have taken away your horses; and I have made the stink of your camps to come up unto your nostrils: yet have ye not returned unto me, saith the LORD.   *Lev. 26:25; Deut. 28:60; 2 Kin. 13:7*

4:6-11 Wholeness for God

No repentance is genuine that does not work reformation. The righteousness of Christ is not a cloak to cover unconfessed and unforsaken sin; it is a principle of life that transforms the character and controls the conduct. Holiness is wholeness for God; it is the entire surrender of heart and life to the indwelling of the principles of heaven. *DA 555, 556*

---

11 I have overthrown *some* of you, as God overthrew Sodom and Gomorrah, and ye were as a firebrand plucked out of the burn-

ing: yet have ye not returned unto me, saith the Lord.   Is. 13:19

12 Therefore thus will I do unto thee, O Israel: *and* because I will do this unto thee, prepare to meet thy God, O Israel.

13 For, lo, he that formeth the mountains, and createth the wind, and declareth unto man what *is* his thought, that maketh the morning darkness, and treadeth upon the high places of the earth, The Lord, The God of hosts, *is* his name.   Amos 5:8; 9:6; Mic. 1:3

A Lamentation for Israel

5 Hear ye this word which I take up against you, *even* a lamentation, O house of Israel.   Jer. 7:29; 9:10; Ezek. 19:1

2 The virgin of Israel is fallen; she shall no more rise: she is forsaken upon her land; *there is* none to raise her up.   Jer. 14:17

3 For thus saith the Lord God; The city that went out *by* a thousand shall leave an hundred, and that which went forth *by* an hundred shall leave ten, to the house of Israel.

An Exhortation to Repentance

4 For thus saith the Lord unto the house of Israel, Seek ye me, and ye shall live: Is. 55:3

5 But seek not Beth-el, nor enter into Gilgal, and pass not to Beer-sheba: for Gilgal shall surely go into captivity, and Beth-el shall come to ᵀnought.   Hos. 4:15; Amos 4:4; 8:14 ◆ *nothing*

6 Seek the Lord, and ye shall live; lest he break out like fire in the house of Joseph, and devour *it*, and *there be* none to quench *it* in Beth-el.   Amos 5:4

7 Ye who turn judgment to wormwood, and leave off righteousness in the earth, Amos 6:12

8 *Seek him* that maketh the seven stars and Orion, and turneth the shadow of death into the morning, and maketh the day dark with night: that calleth for the waters of the sea, and poureth them out upon the face of the earth: The Lord *is* his name: Job 9:9; Ps. 104:20

5:8 Nature Is Not God

God's handiwork in nature is not God Himself in nature. . . . The artistic skill of human beings produces very beautiful workmanship, things that delight the eye, and these things reveal to us something of the thought of the designer; but the thing made is not the maker. . . . So while nature is an expression of God's thought, it is not nature, but the God of nature, that is to be exalted. *MH 413*

9 That strengtheneth the spoiled against the strong, so that the spoiled shall come against the fortress.

10 They hate him that rebuketh in the gate, and they ᵀabhor him that speaketh uprightly.   1 Kin. 22:8; Is. 29:21; Jer. 17:16-17 ◆ *despise*

11 Forasmuch therefore as your treading *is* upon the poor, and ye take from him burdens of wheat: ye have built houses of ᵀhewn stone, but ye shall not dwell in them; ye have planted pleasant vineyards, but ye shall not drink wine of them.   Deut. 28:30; Mic. 6:15 ◆ *cut*

12 For I know your manifold ᵀtransgressions and your mighty sins: they afflict the just, they take a bribe, and they turn aside the poor in the gate *from their right*.   *lawlessness*

5:11, 12 Unseen Auditors

The accounts of every business, the details of every transaction, pass the scrutiny of unseen auditors, agents of Him who never compromises with injustice, never overlooks evil, never palliates wrong. *Ed 144*

13 Therefore the prudent shall keep silence in that time; for it *is* an evil time.   Eccl. 3:7

14 Seek good, and not evil, that ye may live: and so the Lord, the God of hosts, shall be with you, as ye have spoken.   Mic. 3:11

15 Hate the evil, and love the good, and establish judgment in the gate: it may be that the Lord God of hosts will be gracious unto the remnant of Joseph.   Ps. 97:10; Joel 2:14; Rom. 12:9

16 Therefore the Lord, the God of hosts, the Lord, saith thus; Wailing *shall be* in all streets; and they shall say in all the highways, Alas! alas! and they shall call the ᵀhusbandman to mourning, and such as are skilful of lamentation to wailing.   Joel 1:11 ◆ *farmer*

17 And in all vineyards *shall be* wailing: for I will pass through thee, saith the Lord.

18 Woe unto you that desire the day of the Lord! to what end *is* it for you? the day of the Lord *is* darkness, and not light.   Is. 5:19, 30

5:18 As the Midnight Thief

Come when it may, the day of God will come unawares to the ungodly. When life is going on in its unvarying round; when men are absorbed in pleasure, in business, in traffic, in money-making; when religious leaders are magnifying the world's progress and enlightenment, and the people are lulled in a false security—then, as the midnight thief steals within the unguarded dwelling, so shall sudden destruction come upon the careless and ungodly, "and they shall not escape." *GC 38*

19 As if a man did flee from a lion, and a bear met him; or went into the house, and leaned his hand on the wall, and a serpent bit him.   Is. 24:17-18

20 *Shall* not the day of the Lord *be* darkness, and not light? even very dark, and no brightness in it?   Is. 13:10

God Rejects Their Hypocritical Worship

21 I hate, I despise your feast days, and I will not smell in your solemn assemblies.
22 Though ye offer me burnt offerings and your meat offerings, I will not accept *them*: neither will I regard the peace offerings of your fat beasts. Is. 66:3
23 Take thou away from me the noise of thy songs; for I will not hear the melody of thy viols. Amos 6:5
24 But let judgment run down as waters, and righteousness as a mighty stream. Mic. 6:8
25 Have ye offered unto me sacrifices and offerings in the wilderness forty years, O house of Israel? Acts 7:42-43
26 But ye have borne the tabernacle of your Moloch and Chiun your images, the star of your god, which ye made to yourselves.
27 Therefore will I cause you to go into captivity beyond Damascus, saith the Lord, whose name *is* The God of hosts. 2 Kin. 17:6

The Fall of Samaria

6 Woe to them *that are* at ease in Zion, and trust in the mountain of Samaria, *which are* named chief of the nations, to whom the house of Israel came! Is. 32:9-11

6:1 A Degenerating Religion

Unless the church will follow on in [God's] opening providence, accepting every ray of light, performing every duty which may be revealed, religion will inevitably degenerate into the observance of forms, and the spirit of vital godliness will disappear. *GC 316*

2 Pass ye unto Calneh, and see; and from thence go ye to Hamath the great: then go down to Gath of the Philistines: *be they* better than these kingdoms? or their border greater than your border? Gen. 10:10; 2 Kin. 18:34; Nah. 3:8
3 Ye that put far away the evil day, and cause the seat of violence to come near; Is. 56:12
4 That lie upon beds of ivory, and stretch themselves upon their couches, and eat the lambs out of the flock, and the calves out of the midst of the stall; Amos 3:12
5 That chant to the sound of the ᵀviol, *and*

invent to themselves instruments of musick, like David; Is. 5:12 ◆ *stringed musical instrument*
6 That drink wine in bowls, and anoint themselves with the chief ointments: but they are not grieved for the affliction of Joseph.
7 Therefore now shall they go captive with the first that go captive, and the banquet of them that stretched themselves shall be removed. Amos 7:11
8 The Lord God hath sworn by himself, saith the Lord the God of hosts, I ᵀabhor the excellency of Jacob, and hate his palaces: therefore will I deliver up the city with all that is therein. Ps. 47:4 ◆ *despise*
9 And it shall come to pass, if there remain ten men in one house, that they shall die.
10 And a man's uncle shall take him up, and he that burneth him, to bring out the bones out of the house, and shall say unto him that *is* by the sides of the house, *Is there* yet *any* with thee? and he shall say, No. Then shall he say, Hold thy tongue: for we may not make mention of the name of the Lord. 1 Sam. 31:12; Amos 5:13; 8:3
11 For, behold, the Lord commandeth, and he will smite the great house with breaches, and the little house with clefts. 2 Kin. 25:9
12 Shall horses run upon the rock? will *one* plow *there* with oxen? for ye have turned judgment into ᵀgall, and the fruit of righteousness into hemlock: 1 Kin. 21:7-13; Hos. 10:4 ◆ *bitter substance*
13 Ye which rejoice in a thing of ᵀnought, which say, Have we not taken to us horns by our own strength? Is. 28:14-15 ◆ *nothing*
14 But, behold, I will raise up against you a nation, O house of Israel, saith the Lord the God of hosts; and they shall afflict you from the entering in of Hemath unto the river of the wilderness. 1 Kin. 8:65; 2 Kin. 14:25

Famine by Grasshoppers (Locusts)

7 Thus hath the Lord God shewed unto me; and, behold, he formed grasshoppers in the beginning of the shooting up of the latter growth; and, lo, *it was* the latter growth after the king's mowings. Joel 1:4; Amos 4:9; 8:1
2 And it came to pass, *that* when they had made an end of eating the grass of the land,

A Never-Failing Fountain

Amos 5:24

The refreshing water, welling up in a parched and barren land, causing the desert place to blossom, and flowing out to give life to the perishing, is an emblem of the divine grace which Christ alone can bestow, and which is as the living water, purifying, refreshing, and invigorating the soul. He in whom Christ is abiding has within him a never-failing fountain of grace and strength. Jesus cheers the life and brightens the path of all who truly seek Him. His love, received into the heart, will spring up in good works unto eternal life. And not only does it bless the soul in which it springs, but the living stream will flow out in words and deeds of righteousness, to refresh the thirsting around him. *PP 412*

then I said, O Lord GOD, forgive, I beseech thee: by whom shall Jacob arise? for he *is* small.
3 The LORD repented for this: It shall not be, saith the LORD.   Deut. 32:36; Hos. 11:8; Jon. 3:10

Drought by Fire

4 Thus hath the Lord GOD shewed unto me: and, behold, the Lord GOD called to contend by fire, and it devoured the great deep, and did eat up a part.   Is. 66:15-16
5 Then said I, O Lord GOD, cease, I ᵀbeseech thee: by whom shall Jacob arise? for he *is* small.   Ps. 85:4 ◆ *beg*
6 The LORD repented for this: This also shall not be, saith the Lord GOD.

The Plumbline

7 Thus he shewed me: and, behold, the Lord stood upon a wall *made* by a plumbline, with a plumbline in his hand.   2 Kin. 21:13

7:7–11 Incurable Rebellion

From generation to generation the Lord had borne with His wayward children, and even now, in the face of defiant rebellion, He still longed to reveal Himself to them as willing to save. . . .

The evils that had overspread the land had become incurable; and upon Israel was pronounced the dread sentence: "Ephraim is joined to idols: let him alone" (Hosea 4:17). *PK 285*

---

8 And the LORD said unto me, Amos, what seest thou? And I said, A plumbline. Then said the Lord, Behold, I will set a plumbline in the midst of my people Israel: I will not again pass by them any more: Jer. 15:6; Lam. 2:8; Amos 8:2
9 And the high places of Isaac shall be desolate, and the sanctuaries of Israel shall be laid waste; and I will rise against the house of Jeroboam with the sword.   2 Kin. 15:8-10

Amaziah Opposes Amos

10 Then Amaziah the priest of Beth-el sent to Jeroboam king of Israel, saying, Amos hath conspired against thee in the midst of the house of Israel: the land is not able to bear all his words. 1 Kin. 12:31-32; Jer. 26:8-11; 38:4
11 For thus Amos saith, Jeroboam shall die by the sword, and Israel shall surely be led away captive out of their own land.
12 Also Amaziah said unto Amos, O thou seer, go, flee thee away into the land of Judah, and there eat bread, and prophesy there: Matt. 8:34
13 But prophesy not again any more at Beth-el: for it *is* the king's chapel, and it *is* the king's court.   1 Kin. 12:29, 32; Amos 2:12
14 Then answered Amos, and said to Amaziah, I *was* no prophet, neither *was* I a proph-

et's son; but I *was* an herdman, and a gatherer of sycomore fruit: 2 Kin. 2:5
15 And the LORD took me as I followed the flock, and the LORD said unto me, Go, prophesy unto my people Israel.   Ezek. 2:3-4
16 Now therefore hear thou the word of the LORD: Thou sayest, Prophesy not against Israel, and drop not *thy word* against the house of Isaac.   Ezek. 20:46; 21:2; Mic. 2:6
17 Therefore thus saith the LORD; Thy wife shall be an harlot in the city, and thy sons and thy daughters shall fall by the sword, and thy land shall be divided by line; and thou shalt die in a polluted land: and Israel shall surely go into captivity forth of his land.   2 Kin. 17:6

A Basket of Summer Fruit

8 Thus hath the Lord GOD shewed unto me: and behold a basket of summer fruit.   Amos 7:1
2 And he said, Amos, what seest thou? And I said, A basket of summer fruit. Then said the LORD unto me, The end is come upon my people of Israel; I will not again pass by them any more.   Lam. 4:18; Amos 7:8; Mic. 7:1
3 And the songs of the temple shall be howlings in that day, saith the Lord GOD: *there shall be* many dead bodies in every place; they shall cast *them* forth with silence.   Amos 5:23

8:1–3 The Final Plagues

These plagues are not universal, or the inhabitants of the earth would be wholly cut off. Yet they will be the most awful scourges that have ever been known to mortals. All the judgments upon men, prior to the close of probation, have been mingled with mercy. The pleading blood of Christ has shielded the sinner from receiving the full measure of his guilt; but in the final judgment, wrath is poured out unmixed with mercy. *GC 628, 629*

Oppression Is Reproved

4 Hear this, O ye that swallow up the needy, even to make the poor of the land to fail,
5 Saying, When will the new moon be gone, that we may sell corn? and the sabbath, that we may set forth wheat, making the ephah small, and the shekel great, and falsifying the balances by deceit? 2 Kin. 4:23; Hos. 12:7; Mic. 6:10-11
6 That we may buy the poor for silver, and the needy for a pair of shoes; *yea*, and sell the refuse of the wheat?   Amos 2:6
7 The LORD hath sworn by the excellency of Jacob, Surely I will never forget any of their works.   Ps. 10:11; Hos. 8:13; Amos 6:8
8 Shall not the land tremble for this, and every one mourn that dwelleth therein? and it shall rise up wholly as a flood; and it shall

be cast out and drowned, as *by* the flood of Egypt.   Ps. 18:7; Hos. 4:3; Amos 9:5

9 And it shall come to pass in that day, saith the Lord GOD, that I will cause the sun to go down at noon, and I will darken the earth in the clear day: Jer. 15:9; Amos 5:8; Mic. 3:6

10 And I will turn your feasts into mourning, and all your songs into lamentation; and I will bring up sackcloth upon all ᵀloins, and baldness upon every head; and I will make it as the mourning of an only *son*, and the end thereof as a bitter day.   Jer. 6:26; 48:37; Zech. 12:10 ◆ *waists*

A Famine of God's Word

11 Behold, the days come, saith the Lord GOD, that I will send a famine in the land, not a famine of bread, nor a thirst for water, but of hearing the words of the LORD: 1 Sam. 3:1

12 And they shall wander from sea to sea, and from the north even to the east, they shall run to and fro to seek the word of the LORD, and shall not find *it*.

13 In that day shall the fair virgins and young men faint for thirst.   Hos. 2:3

14 They that swear by the sin of Samaria, and say, Thy god, O Dan, liveth; and, The manner of Beer-sheba liveth; even they shall fall, and never rise up again.   Deut. 9:21

The Certainty of the Desolation

9 I saw the Lord standing upon the altar: and he said, Smite the ᵀlintel of the door, that the posts may shake: and cut them in the head, all of them; and I will slay the last of them with the sword: he that fleeth of them shall not flee away, and he that escapeth of them shall not be delivered.   *top of the door frame*

2 Though they dig into hell, thence shall mine hand take them; though they climb up to heaven, thence will I bring them down: Jer. 51:53

3 And though they hide themselves in the top of Carmel, I will search and take them out thence; and though they be hid from my sight in the bottom of the sea, thence will I command the serpent, and he shall bite them: Jer. 16:16

4 And though they go into captivity before their enemies, thence will I command the sword, and it shall slay them: and I will set mine eyes upon them for evil, and not for good.   Lev. 26:33

5 And the Lord GOD of hosts *is* he that toucheth the land, and it shall melt, and all that dwell therein shall mourn: and it shall rise up wholly like a flood; and shall be drowned, as *by* the flood of Egypt. Ps. 46:6; 144:5

6 *It is* he that buildeth his stories in the heaven, and hath founded his troop in the earth; he that calleth for the waters of the sea, and poureth them out upon the face of the earth: The LORD *is* his name.   Ps. 104:3, 13

7 *Are* ye not as children of the Ethiopians unto me, O children of Israel? saith the LORD. Have not I brought up Israel out of the land of Egypt? and the Philistines from Caphtor, and the Syrians from Kir?   Deut. 2:23; Jer. 47:4; Amos 1:5

8 Behold, the eyes of the Lord GOD *are* upon the sinful kingdom, and I will destroy it from off the face of the earth; saving that I will not utterly destroy the house of Jacob, saith the LORD.   Jer. 30:11

9 For, lo, I will command, and I will sift the house of Israel among all nations, like as *corn* is sifted in a sieve, yet shall not the least grain fall upon the earth.

10 All the sinners of my people shall die by the sword, which say, The evil shall not overtake nor ᵀprevent us.   Is. 33:14 ◆ *meet*

9:11, 12 Completing God's Plan

That which God purposed to do for the world through Israel, the chosen nation, He will finally accomplish through His church on earth today. . . .

Today the church of God is free to carry forward to completion the divine plan for the salvation of a lost race. *PK 713, 714*

The One-Soul Audience

Amos 8:11–13

The world is perishing for want of the gospel. There is a famine for the word of God. There are few who preach the word unmixed with human tradition. Though men have the Bible in their hands, they do not receive the blessing that God has placed in it for them. The Lord calls upon His servants to carry His message to the people. . . .

The Lord desires that His word of grace shall be brought home to every soul.

To a great degree this must be accomplished by personal labor. This was Christ's method. His work was largely made up of personal interviews. He had a faithful regard for the one-soul audience. Through that one soul the message was often extended to thousands.

We are not to wait for souls to come to us; we must seek them out where they are. When the word has been preached in the pulpit, the work has but just begun. There are multitudes who will never be reached by the gospel unless it is carried to them. *COL 228, 229*

Restoration Promised

11 In that day will I raise up the tabernacle of David that is fallen, and close up the breaches thereof; and I will raise up his ruins, and I will build it as in the days of old: Ps. 80:12

12 That they may possess the remnant of Edom, and of all the heathen, which are called by my name, saith the LORD that doeth this.   Is. 43:7

13 Behold, the days come, saith the LORD, that the plowman shall overtake the reaper, and the treader of grapes him that soweth seed; and the mountains shall drop sweet wine, and all the hills shall melt.   Joel 3:18

14 And I will bring again the captivity of my people of Israel, and they shall build the waste cities, and inhabit *them*; and they shall plant vineyards, and drink the wine thereof;

they shall also make gardens, and eat the fruit of them.   Is. 61:4; Jer. 30:3, 18

15 And I will plant them upon their land, and they shall no more be pulled up out of their land which I have given them, saith the LORD thy God.   Is. 60:21

9:13–15 A Wise and Beautiful Purpose

In the terrible judgments brought upon the ten tribes the Lord had a wise and merciful purpose. That which He could no longer do through them in the land of their fathers He would seek to accomplish by scattering them among the heathen. His plan for the salvation of all who should choose to avail themselves of pardon through the Saviour of the human race must yet be fulfilled; and in the afflictions brought upon Israel, He was preparing the way for His glory to be revealed to the nations of earth. *PK 292*

THE BOOK OF

OBADIAH

Obadiah prophesied to the nation of Edom, direct descendants of Esau, brother of Jacob, making the two nations "related" by way of ancestry. The sibling rivalry between Jacob and Esau began before their births (Genesis 25:19–23) and continued long after their deaths. Jacob's descendants became the nation of Israel, reflecting the name he received after wrestling with God (32:22–32). Esau's descendants became known as the Edomites, deriving their name from Esau's sale of his birthright for red stew (25:29–34). (*Edom* means "red.")

Obadiah discusses an incident wherein the Edomites not only refused to help their "brother" nation (Obadiah 10) when a foreign nation invaded Jerusalem, but also rejoiced at the disaster coming upon Jerusalem and even aided the attackers (verses 10–14). Because Edom opposed the descendants of Jacob, God sent Obadiah to proclaim their complete destruction (verses 1–9, 15–18), with a promise that Israel would possess the land of Edom (verses 17–21). Hebrews 12:16, 17 shows Esau's inability to change his fate after trading his birthright for a meal. Obadiah shows the inability of Esau's descendants to change their fate after trading their brotherhood with Israel for the spoils of war. Edom has a tumultuous relationship with Israel, refusing to let the nation pass through on its way from Egypt to Canaan (Numbers 20:14–21) and fighting against King Saul (1 Samuel 14:47). The Edomites become servants of Israel during the time of David (2 Samuel 8:14), align with Moab and Ammon to fight against Jehoshaphat of Judah (2 Chronicles 20), gain freedom during the reign of Jehoram of Judah (2 Kings 8:20–22), are recaptured by Amaziah (2 Kings 14:7–10), and reclaim their freedom at the time of Ahaz (2 Kings 16:6). Later, the Assyrians and Babylonians rule over them, and the Nabeatans make the Edomites leave their land in the fifth century B.C.

After settling in southern Palestine and becoming known as the Idumeans, tensions still exist between them and the Israelites. Israel conquers Idumea during the reign of John Hyrcanus I (125 B.C.), so the Idumeans are forced to follow Jewish laws. Herod the Great is an Idumean who serves as king of Judea from 37–4 B.C. The Idumeans join in the ill-fated Jewish rebellion against Rome (A.D. 66–70), culminating with the destruction of Jerusalem in A.D. 70. This occasion also marked the end of the Idumean people as a nation, thus fulfilling the words of Obadiah (verses 10, 18).

Dates

Since the opening verse lists no kings, the events must aid in determining the date. Verses 10–14 describe an attack on Jerusalem that Edom helps join, which could fit a variety of occasions. Since Edom appears to be independent of Judah, it seems unlikely that Obadiah alludes to 926 B.C. when Shishak of Egypt plundered the temple and the palace of Rehoboam (1 Kings 14:25, 26), because Edom was under the control of Judah at this point in history. In addition, the reference to the invading army as "strangers" and "foreigners" (Obadiah 11) renders unlikely a connection to the invasion of Judah under King Jehoash of Israel in 790 B.C. (2 Kings 14:11–16; 2 Chronicles 25).

The invasion by the Philistines and Arabians during the time of Jehoram (848–841 B.C.) is a possibility, as Edom revolted against Judah (2 Kings 8:20–22; 2 Chronicles 21:8–20) shortly before this invasion (2 Chronicles 21:16, 17). These circumstances would put the ministry of Obadiah in the ninth century B.C.

Another possible date is 586 B.C., when Nebuchadnezzar of Babylon destroyed Judah and Jerusalem (2 Kings 24—25), as the other books of the Bible indict the Edomites for participation in this event (Psalm 137:7; Lamentations 4:21, 22). The parallel of Obadiah's condemnation to that of Jeremiah (Jeremiah 49:7–22) and that of Ezekiel (Ezekiel 25:12–14; 35) urges a support of this date.

Author

The book gives little information about Obadiah, as it does not list his father's name or hometown. The Old Testament lists twelve other men named Obadiah; three of them could be the author of this book. These three in chronological order:

(1) A teacher of the law in Judah sent by Jehoshaphat (2 Chronicles 17:7)

(2) An overseer of the repairs to the temple done during the time of Josiah (2 Chronicles 34:12)

(3) A priest who ministered during the time of Nehemiah (Nehemiah 10:5).

While Obadiah *could* be one of these figures, he may be none of them. The lack of information given about Obadiah could show that he was well known by his contemporaries or that he came from an insignificant family. The references to Jerusalem (Obadiah 11) and the people of Judah (verse 12) indicate that Obadiah probably lived in the southern kingdom.

Meaning of the Name

The Hebrew name *Obadyah* translates as "worshiper of Yahweh." The vowels used in the Greek (*Obdiou*) and Latin (*Abdias*) spellings result in a slightly different meaning: "servant of Yahweh."

Christ in Obadiah

The attempt to kill Jesus by Herod the Great (Matthew 2), a descendant of Edom, exemplifies the attack by the Edomites on the Israelites discussed in Obadiah. Also Jesus will be the one to perform the judgment on all nations described in Obadiah 15. The deliverance promised in verse 17 was fulfilled in Christ.

Overview

Consisting of 21 verses, Obadiah is the shortest book of the Old Testament. While other prophets discuss Edom (Isaiah 34:5–15; Jeremiah 49:7–22; Ezekiel 25:12–14; Amos 1:11, 12), this brief prophecy focuses on Edom. Prophets who declare a coming judgment on Israel and Judah end with a note of coming salvation and call for the people to repent, but Obadiah gives no such hope or invitation to the Edomites.

(1) *Obadiah 1–18, Edom Is Judged:* Obadiah enumerates the crimes of Edom toward its brother nation and pronounces a sentence of destruction for its crimes.

(2) *Obadiah 19–21: Israel Is Restored:* Just as there was a reversal of conditions between Esau and Jacob, with the younger brother (Jacob) supplanting the older (Esau), Obadiah points to a reversal among the nations. God will destroy Edom, but will restore Israel. True to Obadiah's word, the nation of Edom no longer exists.

Unlocking Obadiah

KEY PEOPLE:
Obadiah, the people of Edom

KEY EVENTS:
Crimes of Edom during the siege of Jerusalem; the promised destruction of Edom

KEY WORD:
Judgment, as God promises to judge the nation of Edom for the crimes it committed to Israel. It will be destroyed while the nation of Israel will flourish. By avenging the enemies of His people, God fulfills the promise made to Abraham in Genesis 12:3.

KEY VERSE:
"For thy violence against thy brother Jacob shame shall cover thee, and thou shalt be cut off for ever" (verse 10).

The Destruction of Edom

1 The vision of Obadiah. Thus saith the Lord GOD concerning Edom; We have heard a rumour from the LORD, and an ambassador is sent among the heathen, Arise ye, and let us rise up against her in battle. Ezek. 25:12-14

2 Behold, I have made thee small among the heathen: thou art greatly despised. Num. 24:18

3 The pride of thine heart hath deceived thee, thou that dwellest in the clefts of the rock, whose habitation is high; that saith in his heart, Who shall bring me down to the ground? 2 Kin. 14:7; Is. 14:13-15; 16:6

4 Though thou exalt thyself as the eagle, and though thou set thy nest among the stars, thence will I bring thee down, saith the LORD. Hab. 2:9

5 If thieves came to thee, if robbers by night, (how art thou cut off!) would they not have stolen till they had enough? if the grape-gatherers came to thee, would they not leave some grapes? Deut. 24:21

6 How are the things of Esau searched out! how are his hidden things sought up! Jer. 49:10

7 All the men of thy confederacy have brought thee even to the border: the men that were at peace with thee have deceived thee, and prevailed against thee; they that eat thy bread have laid a wound under thee: there is none understanding in him. Ps. 41:9; Jer. 30:14; 49:7

8 Shall I not in that day, saith the LORD, even destroy the wise men out of Edom, and understanding out of the mount of Esau? Job 5:12-14; Is. 29:14

9 And thy mighty men, O Teman, shall be dismayed, to the end that every one of the mount of Esau may be cut off by slaughter. Gen. 36:11

Why Edom Will Be Destroyed

10 For thy violence against thy brother Jacob shame shall cover thee, and thou shalt be cut off for ever. Amos 1:11

11 In the day that thou stoodest on the other side, in the day that the strangers carried away captive his forces, and foreigners entered into his gates, and cast lots upon Jerusalem, even thou wast as one of them. Ps. 137:7

12 But thou shouldest not have looked on the day of thy brother in the day that he became a stranger; neither shouldest thou have rejoiced over the children of Judah in the day of their destruction; neither shouldest thou have spoken proudly in the day of distress. Prov. 17:5; Ezek. 35:15; Mic. 4:11

13 Thou shouldest not have entered into the gate of my people in the day of their calamity; yea, thou shouldest not have looked on their affliction in the day of their calamity, nor have laid hands on their substance in the day of their calamity;

14 Neither shouldest thou have stood in the crossway, to cut off those of his that did escape; neither shouldest thou have delivered up those of his that did remain in the day of distress.

15 For the day of the LORD is near upon all the heathen: as thou hast done, it shall be done unto thee: thy reward shall return upon thine own head. Jer. 50:29; Ezek. 30:3; Hab. 2:8

16 For as ye have drunk upon my holy mountain, so shall all the heathen drink continually, yea, they shall drink, and they shall swallow down, and they shall be as though they had not been. Jer. 49:12

15, 16 The Great Dividing Line

The warfare against God's law, which was begun in heaven, will be continued until the end of time. Every man will be tested. Obedience or disobedience is the question to be decided by the whole world. All will be called to choose between the law of God and the laws of men. Here the dividing line will be drawn. There will be but two classes. Every character will be fully developed; and all will show whether they have chosen the side of loyalty or that of rebellion. DA 763

The First Great Deception

Obadiah 16

The Feast of Tabernacles was not only commemorative but typical [symbolic]. It not only pointed back to the wilderness sojourn, but, as the feast of harvest, it celebrated the ingathering of the fruits of the earth, and pointed forward to the great day of final ingathering, when the Lord of the harvest shall send forth His reapers to gather the tares together in bundles for the fire, and to gather the wheat into His garner. At that time the wicked will all be destroyed. They will become "as though they had not been" (Obadiah 16). And every voice in the whole universe will unite in joyful praise to God. Says the revelator, "Every creature which is in heaven, and on the earth, and under the earth, and such as are in the sea, and all that are in them, heard I saying, Blessing, and honor, and glory, and power, be unto Him that sitteth upon the throne, and unto the Lamb forever and ever" (Revelation 5:13). PP 541

The Salvation and Victory of Jacob

17 But upon mount Zion shall be deliverance, and there shall be holiness; and the house of Jacob shall possess their possessions.   Amos 9:11-15

18 And the house of Jacob shall be a fire, and the house of Joseph a flame, and the house of Esau for stubble, and they shall kindle in them, and devour them; and there shall not be *any* remaining of the house of Esau; for the LORD hath spoken *it*.   Is. 5:24; 10:17; Zech. 12:6

19 And *they of* the south shall possess the mount of Esau; and *they of* the plain the Philistines: and they shall possess the fields of Ephraim, and the fields of Samaria: and Benjamin *shall possess* Gilead.   Jer. 32:44

20 And the captivity of this host of the children of Israel *shall possess* that of the Canaanites, *even* unto Zarephath; and the captivity of Jerusalem, which *is* in Sepharad, shall possess the cities of the south.   Jer. 33:13

21 And saviours shall come up on mount Zion to judge the mount of Esau; and the kingdom shall be the LORD'S.   Ps. 22:28

THE BOOK OF
JONAH

The Book of Jonah has one of the best-known but also one of the most-questioned stories of the Bible. The account of Jonah being swallowed by a great fish and spending three days and three nights in its belly could only happen through the intervention of God.

This surprising story, however, should not obscure two other shocking elements. First is the disobedient prophet who runs away from God to avoid his mission. While everyone and everything else in the story—the storm, the lots, the sailors, the fish, the Ninevites, the plant, the worm, and the wind—obeys God, the one Israelite does not. Second, the city of Nineveh (the capital of Assyria) completely repents. Even the animals wear sackcloth (3:8). While these two points may indeed be shocking, they also point to the fact that God's offer of deliverance is for Jew and Gentile alike.

This story is not primarily about a great fish swallowing a man whole but about God's mercy. He forgives those who repent. This is a message for us to proclaim today.

Dates

The connection to 2 Kings 14:25 situates Jonah's ministry during the reign of Jeroboam II (793–753 B.C.), likely near the beginning, as he had prophesied of the nation's political success under this king. Therefore, Jonah appears to have ministered after Elisha and shortly before Amos and Hosea. In addition to a booming economy, the successes of Israel likely caused a budding nationalistic outlook. Meanwhile, Assyria experienced a slight decline during this period due to weak kings. A pair of plagues (765, 759 B.C.) and a solar eclipse also occurred in this period (763 B.C.) and may have led to anxiety within Assyria. Their reputation for violence, testified by Assyrian records from the ninth and seventh centuries detailing their cruel treatment of captives, caused Israel to see them as a wicked people who were a political threat even if the nation was not as powerful as it once was.

Author

The book does not explicitly name its author, but traditionally it has been ascribed to the prophet appearing in the narrative: Jonah the son of Amittai (1:1). He also appears in 2 Kings 14:25 as the one who prophesied about the restoration of the boundaries of Israel during the reign of Jeroboam II. This reference notes that Jonah came from Gath Hepher, which was three miles north of Nazareth, nullifying the claim made by the Pharisees in John 7:52 that no prophet has come from Galilee. The book shows similarities to the ministries of Elijah and Elisha, as Jonah goes to the Gentiles like Elijah (1 Kings 17:7–24) and Elisha (2 Kings 8:7–15). One Jewish tradition even claims that Jonah is the son of the widow of Zarephath that Elijah raised from the dead (1 Kings 17:17–24).

Some scholars reject the connection of this book to the eighth-century B.C. figure of Jonah and believe that it is a historical fiction written by an anonymous writer between the fifth and third centuries B.C. These scholars marshal a number of reasons for this view:

(1) The book uses Aramaic words.

(2) The tense of its description of Nineveh in 3:3 ("*was* an exceeding great city," italics ours) would make sense after the fall of Nineveh.

(3) The book is in the third person, not first person.

Upon closer examination, however, these arguments are not compelling for these reasons:

(1) The use of Aramaic words is not an indication of a later date, as ancient Near Eastern texts as early as 1500 B.C. use Aramaic words, as do some of the early Old Testament books.

(2) The text of Jonah 3:3 reads "had become," showing the greatness of Nineveh at the time of the story.

(3) The use of the third person and lack of explicit claim that Jonah authored it are arguments from silence and need not prove that Jonah did not write it. There also is no indication that the book is allegorical fiction. In addition, the use of Nineveh would make more sense in the eighth century than the fifth or third century B.C., as the city was destroyed in 612 B.C. Early texts also show God's concern for all the nations (Genesis 9:27; 12:3; Leviticus 19:33, 34, 1 Samuel 2:10; Isaiah 2:2; Joel 2:28–32), so it would address issues in the

eighth century B.C. as well. Jesus' reference to the ministry of Jonah in Matthew 12:39–41 also affirms its historicity.

Meaning of the Name

In Hebrew, *Yonah* means "dove," a term of endearment. The Hellenized form of the word used in the Septuagint is *Ionas*, with *Jonas* the Latin form in the Vulgate.

Christ in Jonah

Jesus makes explicit reference to Jonah in Matthew 12:39–41 (also see Luke 11:29–32). Jonah's three-day stay in the fish prefigures Jesus' three-day stay in the grave. (Three days indicates parts of three days as opposed to three whole days.) In addition, Jesus is greater than Jonah in that He willingly gave up His life for sinners, while Jonah reluctantly went to Nineveh. Jesus' greatness also extends to the larger response to Him, as people from all nations (not just one city) repent at His ministry.

Overview

The four chapters of the book divide into two parts:

(1) *Jonah 1—2, First Call of Jonah:* Jonah receives a call from God to go to Nineveh (1:1, 2) and encounters Gentiles who are more obedient than he is and thereby avert disaster (the sailors in 1:5–16; later, the Ninevites in 3:5–10). Jonah, however, experiences the discipline of God in the form of being trapped in a fish.

(2) *Jonah 3—4, Second Call of Jonah:* Once more, Jonah is sent to Nineveh (3:1, 2). There are contrasts between chapters 2 and 4. While Jonah is grateful to God for sparing his life, he complains about God's decision to spare Nineveh in 4:1–4. The incident concerning the gourd and the worm in 4:5–11 is an object lesson about God's love for Nineveh. The book ends without noting whether Jonah's heart changed.

Unlocking Jonah

KEY PEOPLE:
Jonah, the people of Nineveh

KEY EVENTS:
Jonah's call to Nineveh; Jonah's three days in the fish; revival in Nineveh; Jonah's displeasure; God's lesson to Jonah

KEY WORD:
Revival, because of Jonah's preaching, the people of Nineveh repent. God then withdrew the punishment he had for them.

KEY VERSES:
"They that observe lying vanities forsake their own mercy. But I will sacrifice unto thee with the voice of thanksgiving; I will pay that that I have vowed. Salvation is of the LORD" (Jonah 2:8, 9).

"And he prayed unto the LORD, and said, I pray thee, O LORD, was not this my saying, when I was yet in my country? Therefore I fled before unto Tarshish: for I knew that thou art a gracious God, and merciful, slow to anger, and of great kindness, and repentest thee of the evil" (Jonah 4:2).

KEY CHAPTER:
Jonah 4, where Jonah explains his knowledge that God would relent from judgment if the people of Nineveh repent. The book closes with a question, inviting the reader to adopt the attitude of God (showing mercy) rather than that of Jonah (bitter, unforgiving).

Jonah Tries to Run from God

1 Now the word of the LORD came unto Jonah the son of Amittai, saying, Matt. 16:4
2 Arise, go to Nineveh, that great city, and cry against it; for their wickedness is come up before me. Gen. 10:11; 2 Kin. 19:36; Jon. 3:2
3 But Jonah rose up to flee unto Tarshish from the presence of the LORD, and went down to Joppa; and he found a ship going to Tarshish: so he paid the fare thereof, and went down into it, to go with them unto Tarshish from the presence of the LORD. Gen. 4:16; Josh. 19:46; Acts 9:36

The Storm at Sea

4 But the LORD sent out a great wind into the sea, and there was a mighty ᵀtempest in the sea, so that the ship was like to be broken. Ps. 135:7 ◆ storm
5 Then the mariners were afraid, and cried every man unto his god, and cast forth the wares that were in the ship into the sea, to lighten it of them. But Jonah was gone down into the sides of the ship; and he lay, and was fast asleep. 1 Kin. 18:26; Acts 27:18-19, 38
6 So the shipmaster came to him, and said unto him, What meanest thou, O sleeper? arise, call upon thy God, if so be that God will think upon us, that we perish not. Jon. 3:9
7 And they said every one to his fellow, Come, and let us cast lots, that we may know for whose cause this evil is upon us. So they cast lots, and the lot fell upon Jonah. Prov. 16:33
8 Then said they unto him, Tell us, we pray thee, for whose cause this evil is upon us; What is thine occupation? and whence comest thou? what is thy country? and of what people art thou? Gen. 47:3
9 And he said unto them, I am an Hebrew; and I fear the LORD, the God of heaven, which hath made the sea and the dry land. Gen. 14:13
10 Then were the men exceedingly afraid, and said unto him, Why hast thou done this? For the men knew that he fled from the presence of the LORD, because he had told them. Jon. 1:3

A Great Fish Swallows Jonah

11 Then said they unto him, What shall we do unto thee, that the sea may be calm unto us? for the sea ᵀwrought, and was tempestuous. stirred
12 And he said unto them, Take me up, and cast me forth into the sea; so shall the sea be calm unto you: for I know that for my sake this great tempest is upon you. 2 Sam. 24:17
13 Nevertheless the men rowed hard to bring it to the land; but they could not: for the sea wrought, and was tempestuous against them. Prov. 21:30
14 Wherefore they cried unto the LORD, and said, We ᵀbeseech thee, O LORD, we beseech thee, let us not perish for this man's life, and lay not upon us innocent blood: for thou, O LORD, hast done as it pleased thee. Deut. 21:8; Ps. 107:28; 115:3 ◆ beg
15 So they took up Jonah, and cast him forth into the sea: and the sea ceased from her raging. Ps. 107:29
16 Then the men feared the LORD exceedingly, and offered a sacrifice unto the LORD, and made vows. Gen. 8:20
17 Now the LORD had prepared a great fish to swallow up Jonah. And Jonah was in the belly of the fish three days and three nights. Matt. 12:40; 16:4; Luke 11:30

The Prayer of Jonah

2 Then Jonah prayed unto the LORD his God out of the fish's belly, Job 13:15
2 And said, I cried by reason of mine affliction unto the LORD, and he heard me; out of the belly of hell cried I, and thou heardest my voice. Ps. 34:6; 65:2; 120:1
3 For thou hadst cast me into the deep, in the midst of the seas; and the floods compassed me about: all thy billows and thy waves passed over me. Ps. 42:7; 69:1-2, 14-15
4 Then I said, I am cast out of thy sight; yet I will look again toward thy holy temple. Ps. 5:7

God Tries to Save a Wicked City

Jonah 1:1, 2

In the time of its temporal prosperity Nineveh was a center of crime and wickedness. Inspiration has characterized it as "the bloody city, . . . full of lies and robbery." In figurative language the prophet Nahum compared the Ninevites to a cruel, ravenous lion. "Upon whom," he inquired, "hath not thy wickedness passed continually?" (Nahum 3:1, 19).

Yet Nineveh, wicked though it had become, was not wholly given over to evil. He who "beholdeth all the sons of men" (Psalm 33:13) and "seeth every precious thing" (Job 28:10) perceived in that city many who were reaching out after something better and higher, and who, if granted opportunity to learn of the living God, would put away their evil deeds and worship Him. And so in His wisdom God revealed Himself to them in an unmistakable manner, to lead them, if possible, to repentance. PK 265, 266

5 The waters ᵀcompassed me about, *even* to the soul: the depth closed me round about, the weeds were wrapped about my head.   Ps. 69:1-2 ◆ *surrounded*
6 I went down to the bottoms of the mountains; the earth with her bars *was* about me for ever: yet hast thou brought up my life from corruption, O LORD my God.   Job 33:28
7 When my soul fainted within me I remembered the LORD: and my prayer came in unto thee, into thine holy temple. 2 Chr. 30:27; Ps. 11:4
8 They that observe lying vanities forsake their own mercy.   2 Kin. 17:15; Ps. 31:6; Jer. 10:8
9 But I will sacrifice unto thee with the voice of thanksgiving; I will pay *that* that I have vowed. Salvation *is* of the LORD.   Ps. 3:8; 50:14
10 And the LORD spake unto the fish, and it vomited out Jonah upon the dry *land*. Jon. 1:17

> **2:1–10 Jonah Finally Learns**
>
> At last Jonah had learned that "salvation belongeth unto the Lord" (Psalm 3:8). With penitence and a recognition of the saving grace of God, came deliverance. Jonah was released from the perils of the mighty deep and was cast upon the dry land. *PK 269*

The People of Nineveh Repent

3 And the word of the LORD came unto Jonah the second time, saying,   Jon. 1:1
2 Arise, go unto Nineveh, that great city, and preach unto it the preaching that I bid thee.   Jer. 1:17
3 So Jonah arose, and went unto Nineveh, according to the word of the LORD. Now Nineveh was an exceeding great city of three days' journey.
4 And Jonah began to enter into the city a day's journey, and he cried, and said, Yet forty days, and Nineveh shall be overthrown.
5 So the people of Nineveh believed God, and proclaimed a fast, and put on sackcloth, from the greatest of them even to the least of them.   Luke 11:32
6 For word came unto the king of Nineveh, and he arose from his throne, and he laid his robe from him, and covered *him* with sackcloth, and sat in ashes.   Job 2:8
7 And he caused *it* to be proclaimed and published through Nineveh by the decree of the king and his nobles, saying, Let neither man nor beast, herd nor flock, taste any thing: let them not feed, nor drink water: 2 Chr. 20:3
8 But let man and beast be covered with sackcloth, and cry mightily unto God: yea, let them turn every one from his evil way, and from the violence that *is* in their hands.   Jon. 1:6
9 Who can tell *if* God will turn and repent,

and turn away from his fierce anger, that we perish not?   2 Sam. 12:22

> **3:1–9 A Message Bears Fruit**
>
> The message was not in vain. The cry that rang through the streets of the godless city was passed from lip to lip until all the inhabitants had heard the startling announcement. The Spirit of God pressed the message home to every heart and caused multitudes to tremble because of their sins and to repent in deep humiliation. *PK 270*

10 And God saw their works, that they turned from their evil way; and God repented of the evil, that he had said that he would do unto them; and he did *it* not. Ex. 32:14; Jer. 18:8; Amos 7:6

Jonah's Anger at God's Mercy

4 But it displeased Jonah exceedingly, and he was very angry.   Jon. 4:9
2 And he prayed unto the LORD, and said, I pray thee, O LORD, *was* not this my saying, when I was yet in my country? Therefore I fled before unto Tarshish: for I knew that thou *art* a gracious God, and merciful, slow to anger, and of great kindness, and repentest thee of the evil.   Ps. 86:5
3 Therefore now, O LORD, take, I ᵀbeseech thee, my life from me; for *it is* better for me to die than to live.   1 Kin. 19:4; Job 6:8-9; Eccl. 7:1 ◆ *beg*

> **3:10—4:3 Jonah's Surprising Reaction**
>
> When Jonah learned of God's purpose to spare the city that, notwithstanding its wickedness, had been led to repent in sackcloth and ashes, he should have been the first to rejoice because of God's amazing grace; but instead he allowed his mind to dwell upon the possibility of his being regarded as a false prophet. Jealous of his reputation, he lost sight of the infinitely greater value of the souls in that wretched city. *PK 271*

4 Then said the LORD, Doest thou well to be angry?   Jon. 4:9
5 So Jonah went out of the city, and sat on the east side of the city, and there made him a booth, and sat under it in the shadow, till he might see what would become of the city.   1 Kin. 19:9
6 And the LORD God prepared a gourd, and made *it* to come up over Jonah, that it might be a shadow over his head, to deliver him from his grief. So Jonah was exceeding glad of the gourd.
7 But God prepared a worm when the morning rose the next day, and it smote the gourd that it withered.   Joel 1:12
8 And it came to pass, when the sun did arise, that God prepared a vehement east wind; and the sun beat upon the head of

Jonah, that he fainted, and wished in himself to die, and said, *It is* better for me to die than to live. Ps. 121:6

9 And God said to Jonah, Doest thou well to be angry for the gourd? And he said, I do well to be angry, *even* unto death.

10 Then said the LORD, Thou hast had pity on the gourd, for the which thou hast not laboured, neither madest it grow; which came up in a night, and perished in a night:

11 And should not I spare Nineveh, that great city, wherein are more than sixscore thousand persons that cannot discern between their right hand and their left hand; and *also* much cattle? Jon. 1:2

4:4–11 Warning and Deliverance

Confused, humiliated, and unable to understand God's purpose in sparing Nineveh, Jonah nevertheless had fulfilled the commission given him to warn that great city; and though the event predicted did not come to pass, yet the message of warning was nonetheless from God. And it accomplished the purpose God designed it should. The glory of His grace was revealed among the heathen. *PK 272, 273*

THE BOOK OF

MICAH

God anointed the prophet Micah to deliver a message of God's intense hatred of sin and the immeasurable love He has for His covenant people. Micah's message shows how the rampant injustice in Judah leads to two responses from God, with each response displaying a different characteristic. His hatred of sin appears in the trial scene of chapter 6, where God puts His people on trial for sin, declares them guilty, and assigns them a punishment of destruction and exile. However, God also promises to pardon the sin of His people (7:18–20), using their punishment as a way of purifying His people and drawing them back to Himself.

In addition to extraordinary images of the sin of the people (3:1–4) and the pledged punishment (3:12), this book also contains one of the most elaborate descriptions of a coming time of peace and prosperity when the Messiah will shepherd the people of Israel and rule over the whole world (chapters 4—5). After sending them into captivity, God promises to rescue a remnant of His people from captivity in Babylon (2:12, 13; 4:10) just as He brought them out of Egypt (6:4). This message should cause God's people to mourn over their sin and give thanks for God's grace to His people, living as a people who humbly walk with God by loving justice and mercy (6:8).

Dates

While Micah refers to the northern kingdom in his prophecy (1:6), his ministry primarily concerns the southern kingdom, with 1:1 stating that his ministry occurred during the reigns of three kings of Judah: Jotham (coregent with his father 750–740 B.C.; reigned solely 739–731 B.C.), Ahaz (735–715 B.C.), and Hezekiah (729–686 B.C.). Micah predicts the fall of Samaria (1:6), his ministry begins before Assyria took Israel into captivity in 722 B.C. Also a number of religious changes happened during the time of Hezekiah, in part as a response to Micah's condemnation of the rampant idolatry and immorality in the land (Jeremiah 26:17–19). These factors indicate that Micah likely prophesied from 740 B.C. to 710 B.C., giving him a ministry contemporaneous with Isaiah's ministry to Judah and Hosea's ministry to Israel.

The reigns of these three kings exhibited marked differences. Jotham was the son of Uzziah, (or Azariah, see 2 Kings 15:1–7) who had a successful reign from 790–739 B.C. (2 Chronicles 26), and followed his father's example, even exceeding his father in steadfast devotion to God by not replicating his father's improper entrance into the temple (2 Chronicles 27:2). However, Jotham did not destroy the places of idolatry. In contrast to this pious king, Ahaz was wicked, worshiping idols and sacrificing his sons (2 Chronicles 28). Hezekiah sought to lead the people back to worship of God by repairing the temple and reestablishing proper rituals (2 Chronicles 29—31). Through the power of God he was able to withstand a siege of Jerusalem undertaken by the Assyrians (2 Chronicles 32). The ascension of Assyria during this period under Tiglath-Pileser III (745–727 B.C.), Shalmaneser V (727–722 B.C.), Sargon (722–705 B.C.), and Sennacherib (705–681 B.C.) corresponded with the downfall of Israel, with Assyria conquering Samaria in 722 B.C. Surprisingly, Micah did not predict Judah's being taken captive by the Assyrians but by the Babylonians (4:10), a nation dominated by the Assyrians at this time. This would prove true in 586 B.C.

Author

The opening verse identifies Micah's hometown as Moresheth, likely Moresheth-gath (1:14). This agricultural village was on the border of Judah and Philistia, twenty-five miles southwest of Jerusalem and near the Philistine city of Gath. Micah's ministry to the southern kingdom of Judah likely involved speaking in Jerusalem. The book does not refer to his parentage, suggesting that he may have come from an insignificant family. He lacks the political knowledge shown by Isaiah, a contemporary prophet in Judah, and focuses his complaints on the injustices of the land and the sufferings of the poor at the hands of the rich, similar to the message of the northern prophet Amos. Jeremiah 26:17–19 refers to Micah's ministry, as Hezekiah repented at Micah's ministry; in contrast, Jehoiakim wanted to kill Jeremiah (Jeremiah 26:21).

Micaia is a shortened form of the Hebrew name *Michayahu*, which means, "Who is like Yahweh?" *Michaias* and *Micha* are the respective titles of the book in the Greek and Latin versions. The name of the prophet recalls one of the most memorable passages of the book: "Who is a God like unto thee, that pardoneth iniquity, and passeth by the transgression of the remnant of his heritage? he retaineth not his anger for ever, because he delighteth in mercy" (7:18).

Christ in Micah

One finds references both to Christ's first appearance and His second coming in Micah, a message that came seven hundred years before His birth. In Matthew 2:5, 6, the scribes determine that Jesus' birthplace was Bethlehem as declared in Micah 5:2. Descriptions of the glorious reign of Jesus occur in Micah 2:12, 13; 4:1–8; 5:4, 5.

Overview

Micah has three sections:

(1) *Micah 1—3, Judgment:* The sins of the nation include idolatry (1:5–7; 3:4) and mistreatment of neighbors due to greed and corruption (2:1, 2, 8, 9), with the civil (3:1–3, 9–11) and religious leaders (2:6–11; 3:11) participating in these sins. While there are extended discussions of the judgment to come in the form of destruction and captivity (1:2—2:11; 3:1–12), words of consolation follow these oracles, promising a greater glory for Judah than previously experienced, as well as the forgiveness of sins (2:12, 13).

(2) *Micah 4—5, Restoration:* A message of hope follows the message of judgment. Micah predicts Israel's later restoration and positive influence over other nations (4:2). At that time, peace will prevail. Not so in the present day, with captivity looming and the city of Jerusalem under siege (4:6—5:1). Yet there is still hope, as Micah describes the advent of the Messiah, who will be born in the birthplace of David (5:2; see also Luke 2:4–7).

(3) *Micah 6—7, Repentance:* Chapter 6 resembles a courtroom drama as God pleads His case against His people, with Micah acting as a prosecution witness. Micah's message also points to the heart of true religion that characterizes a repentant life: one should walk with God and practice justice and mercy rather than only offering sacrifices (6:6–8).

Unlocking Micah

KEY PEOPLE:
Micah, the people of Israel and Judah, the promised Messiah

KEY EVENTS:
Exile of Israel and Judah; restoration under the Messiah; birth of the Messiah foretold in Bethlehem

KEY WORDS:
Judgment and *restoration*, as the book graphically describes both the judgment that will come on Judah and the restoration that occurs at the end of the age under the Messiah.

KEY VERSES:
"But thou, Beth-lehem Ephratah, though thou be little among the thousands of Judah, yet out of thee shall he come forth unto me that is to be ruler in Israel; whose goings forth have been from of old, from everlasting" (Micah 5:2).

"He hath shewed thee, O man, what is good; and what doth the LORD require of thee, but to do justly, and to love mercy, and to walk humbly with thy God?" (Micah 6:8).

KEY CHAPTERS:
Micah 6—7, which document God's case against His wayward people (chapter 6), the misery Judah will experience through judgment (7:1–6), and the restoration of Israel that will shock the nations (7:7–17). This restoration will occur because of the forgiving nature of God and the covenant He made with Abraham (7:18–20).

Capital Cities of Israel and Judah to Be Destroyed

1 The word of the LORD that came to Micah the Morasthite in the days of Jotham, Ahaz, *and* Hezekiah, kings of Judah, which he saw concerning Samaria and Jerusalem.   Is. 1:1; Jer. 26:18; Hos. 1:1

2 Hear, all ye people; hearken, O earth, and all that therein is: and let the Lord GOD be witness against you, the Lord from his holy temple.   Ps. 11:4

3 For, behold, the LORD cometh forth out of his place, and will come down, and tread upon the high places of the earth.   Deut. 32:13

4 And the mountains shall be molten under him, and the valleys shall be cleft, as wax before the fire, *and* as the waters *that are* poured down a steep place.   Ps. 97:5; Amos 9:5

5 For the ᵀtransgression of Jacob *is* all this, and for the sins of the house of Israel. What *is* the transgression of Jacob? *is it* not Samaria? and what *are* the high places of Judah? *are they* not Jerusalem?   Amos 8:14 ◆ *sin*

6 Therefore I will make Samaria as an heap of the field, *and* as plantings of a vineyard: and I will pour down the stones thereof into the valley, and I will discover the foundations thereof.   2 Kin. 19:25; Ezek. 13:14; Mic. 3:12

7 And all the ᵀgraven images thereof shall be beaten to pieces, and all the hires thereof shall be burned with the fire, and all the idols thereof will I lay desolate: for she gathered *it* of the hire of an harlot, and they shall return to the hire of an harlot.   *engraved* or *cut out*

8 Therefore I will wail and howl, I will go stripped and naked: I will make a wailing like the dragons, and mourning as the owls.   Job 30:29

9 For her wound *is* incurable; for it is come unto Judah; he is come unto the gate of my people, *even* to Jerusalem.   Is. 8:7-8

10 Declare ye *it* not at Gath, weep ye not at all: in the house of Aphrah roll thyself in the dust.   2 Sam. 1:20

11 Pass ye away, thou inhabitant of Saphir, having thy shame naked: the inhabitant of Zaanan came not forth in the mourning of Beth-ezel; he shall receive of you his standing.   Is. 20:4

12 For the inhabitant of Maroth waited carefully for good: but evil came down from the LORD unto the gate of Jerusalem.   Jer. 14:19

13 O thou inhabitant of Lachish, bind the chariot to the swift beast: she *is* the beginning of the sin to the daughter of Zion: for the ᵀtransgressions of Israel were found in thee.   Josh. 10:3 ◆ *sins*

14 Therefore shalt thou give presents to Moresheth-gath: the houses of Achzib *shall be* a lie to the kings of Israel.   Josh. 15:44; 2 Kin. 16:8

15 Yet will I bring an heir unto thee, O inhabitant of Mareshah: he shall come unto Adullam the glory of Israel.   Josh. 15:44

16 Make thee bald, and ᵀpoll thee for thy delicate children; enlarge thy baldness as the eagle; for they are gone into captivity from thee.   Is. 22:12 ◆ *cut your hair*

Israel's Sins Are Condemned

2 Woe to them that devise iniquity, and work evil upon their beds! when the morning is light, they practise it, because it is in the power of their hand.   Gen. 31:29; Deut. 28:32

2 And they ᵀcovet fields, and take *them* by violence; and houses, and take *them* away: so they oppress a man and his house, even a man and his heritage.   Is. 5:8; Jer. 22:17; Amos 8:4 ◆ *desire*

3 Therefore thus saith the LORD; Behold, against this family do I devise an evil, from which ye shall not remove your necks; neither shall ye go haughtily: for this time *is* evil.   Is. 2:11-12

4 In that day shall *one* take up a parable against you, and lament with a ᵀdoleful lamentation, *and* say, We be utterly spoiled: he hath changed the portion of my people: how hath he removed *it* from me! turning away he hath divided our fields.   Hab. 2:6 ◆ *with howls*

5 Therefore thou shalt have none that shall cast a cord by lot in the congregation of the LORD.   Deut. 32:8

6 Prophesy ye not, *say they to them that* prophesy: they shall not prophesy to them, *that* they shall not take shame.   Is. 30:10; Amos 2:12

7 O *thou that art* named the house of Jacob, is the spirit of the LORD ᵀstraitened? *are* these his doings? do not my words do good to him that walketh uprightly? Ps. 15:2 ◆ *hindered*

8 Even of late my people is risen up as an enemy: ye pull off the robe with the garment from them that pass by securely as men averse from war.   Ps. 120:6-7

9 The women of my people have ye cast out from their pleasant houses; from their children have ye taken away my glory for ever.   Ezek. 39:21

10 Arise ye, and depart; for this *is* not *your* rest: because it is polluted, it shall destroy *you*, even with a sore destruction.   Deut. 12:9; Ps. 106:38

2:10 A Clear, Distinct Voice

Have you wandered far from God? Have you sought to feast upon the fruits of transgression, only to find them turn to ashes upon your lips? And now, your substance spent, your life-plans thwarted, and your hopes dead, do you sit alone and desolate? Now that voice which has long been speaking to your heart but to which you would not listen comes to you distinct and clear. . . . Return to your Father's house. He invites you, saying, "Return unto Me; for I have redeemed thee" (Isaiah 44:22). *COL 205*

11 If a man walking in the spirit and false-hood do lie, *saying,* I will prophesy unto thee of wine and of strong drink; he shall even be the prophet of this people.   Jer. 5:31

Israel Will Be Gathered Again

12 I will surely assemble, O Jacob, all of thee; I will surely gather the remnant of Is-rael; I will put them together as the sheep of Bozrah, as the flock in the midst of their fold: they shall make great noise by reason of *the multitude of* men.   Mic. 4:6-7

13 The breaker is come up before them: they have broken up, and have passed through the gate, and are gone out by it: and their king shall pass before them, and the LORD on the head of them.   Is. 52:12

Israel's Sinful Leaders

3 And I said, Hear, I pray you, O heads of Jacob, and ye princes of the house of Is-rael; *Is it* not for you to know judgment?

2 Who hate the good, and love the evil; who pluck off their skin from off them, and their flesh from off their bones;   Ps. 53:4

3 Who also eat the flesh of my people, and flay their skin from off them; and they break their bones, and chop them in pieces, as for the pot, and as flesh within the caldron.

4 Then shall they cry unto the LORD, but he will not hear them: he will even hide his face from them at that time, as they have behaved themselves ill in their doings. Ps. 18:41; Prov. 1:28

5 Thus saith the LORD concerning the prophets that make my people ^Terr, that bite with their teeth, and cry, Peace; and he that putteth not into their mouths, they even prepare war against him.   Is. 9:15-16 ◆ *stray*

6 Therefore night *shall be* unto you, that ye shall not have a vision; and it shall be dark unto you, that ye shall not ^Tdivine; and the sun shall go down over the prophets, and the day shall be dark over them.   *determine by false magic*

7 Then shall the seers be ashamed, and the di-viners confounded: yea, they shall all cover their lips; for *there is* no answer of God. Is. 44:25

8 But truly I am full of power by the spirit of the LORD, and of judgment, and of might, to declare unto Jacob his ^Ttransgression, and to Israel his sin.   Is. 58:1; Jer. 1:18; 6:11 ◆ *sin*

9 Hear this, I pray you, ye heads of the house of Jacob, and princes of the house of Israel, that ^Tabhor judgment, and pervert all ^Tequity.   Ps. 58:1-2 ◆ *despise* ◆ *uprightness*

10 They build up Zion with blood, and Jeru-salem with iniquity.

11 The heads thereof judge for reward, and the priests thereof teach for hire, and the prophets thereof divine for money: yet will they lean upon the LORD, and say, *Is* not the LORD among us? none evil can come upon us.   Is. 1:23; 48:2; Jer. 6:13

3:9-11 Why Some Hated Jesus

These words faithfully described the cor-rupt and self-righteous inhabitants of Jeru-salem. While claiming to observe rigidly the precepts of God's law, they were transgressing all its principles. They hated Christ because His purity and holiness revealed their iniqui-ty; and they accused Him of being the cause of all the troubles which had come upon them in consequence of their sins. *GC 27*

---

12 Therefore shall Zion for your sake be plowed *as* a field, and Jerusalem shall become heaps, and the mountain of the house as the high places of the forest. Ps. 79:1; Jer. 26:18; Mic. 1:6

The Lord Will Teach the Nations

4 But in the last days it shall come to pass, *that* the mountain of the house of the LORD shall be established in the top of the mountains, and it shall be exalted above the hills; and people shall flow unto it.   Ps. 22:27

2 And many nations shall come, and say, Come, and let us go up to the mountain of the LORD, and to the house of the God of Jacob; and he will teach us of his ways, and we will walk in his paths: for the law shall go forth of Zion, and the word of the LORD from Jerusalem.   Ps. 25:8-9

3 And he shall judge among many people, and rebuke strong nations afar off; and they shall beat their swords into plowshares, and their spears into pruninghooks: nation shall not lift up a sword against nation, neither shall they learn war any more.   Is. 2:4

4 But they shall sit every man under his vine and under his fig tree; and none shall make *them* afraid: for the mouth of the LORD of hosts hath spoken *it.* 1 Kin. 4:25; Is. 1:20; Zech. 3:10

5 For all people will walk every one in the name of his god, and we will walk in the name of the LORD our God for ever and ever.   2 Kin. 17:29; Zech. 10:12

6 In that day, saith the LORD, will I assem-ble her that ^Thalteth, and I will gather her that is driven out, and her that I have af-flicted;   Ps. 147:2; Zeph. 3:19 ◆ *limps*

7 And I will make her that ^Thalted a rem-nant, and her that was cast far off a strong nation: and the LORD shall reign over them in mount Zion from ^Thenceforth, even for ever.   Is. 24:23 ◆ *limped* ◆ *this time forward*

8 And thou, O tower of the flock, the strong hold of the daughter of Zion, unto thee shall it come, even the first dominion; the kingdom shall come to the daughter of Je-rusalem.   Zech. 9:10

4:8 As if Man Had Never Fallen

Satan in his efforts to deceive and tempt our race had thought to frustrate the divine plan in man's creation; but Christ now asks that this plan be carried into effect as if man had never fallen. He asks for His people not only pardon and justification, full and complete, but a share in His glory and a seat upon His throne. *GC 484*

9 Now why dost thou cry out aloud? *is there no king in thee?* is thy counsellor perished? for pangs have taken thee as a woman in travail.   Jer. 8:19

10 Be in pain, and labour to bring forth, O daughter of Zion, like a woman in travail: for now shalt thou go forth out of the city, and thou shalt dwell in the field, and thou shalt go *even* to Babylon; there shalt thou be delivered; there the Lord shall redeem thee from the hand of thine enemies.   2 Kin. 20:18

11 Now also many nations are gathered against thee, that say, Let her be defiled, and let our eye look upon Zion.   Obad. 12

12 But they know not the thoughts of the Lord, neither understand they his counsel: for he shall gather them as the sheaves into the floor.   Is. 55:8

13 Arise and thresh, O daughter of Zion: for I will make thine horn iron, and I will make thy hoofs brass: and thou shalt beat in pieces many people: and I will ᵀconsecrate their gain unto the Lord, and their substance unto the Lord of the whole earth.   Is. 23:18 ♦ *set apart*

The Birth of Christ

5 Now gather thyself in troops, O daughter of troops: he hath laid siege against us: they shall ᵀsmite the judge of Israel with a rod upon the cheek.   Lam. 3:30 ♦ *strike*

2 But thou, Beth-lehem Ephratah, *though* thou be little among the thousands of Judah, *yet* out of thee shall he come forth unto me *that is* to be ruler in Israel; whose goings forth *have been* from of old, from everlasting.   Zech. 9:9; Matt. 2:6; John 7:42

Jesus   See Luke 2:10–16.

3 Therefore will he give them up, until the time *that* she which travaileth hath brought forth: then the remnant of his brethren shall return unto the children of Israel.   Is. 10:20-21

4 And he shall stand and feed in the strength of the Lord, in the majesty of the name of the Lord his God; and they shall abide: for now shall he be great unto the ends of the earth.   Ps. 72:8; Mic. 7:14; Luke 1:32

5 And this *man* shall be the peace, when the Assyrian shall come into our land: and when he shall tread in our palaces, then shall we raise against him seven shepherds, and eight principal men.   Luke 2:14

6 And they shall waste the land of Assyria with the sword, and the land of Nimrod in the entrances thereof: thus shall he deliver *us* from the Assyrian, when he cometh into our land, and when he treadeth within our borders.   Gen. 10:8-11

7 And the remnant of Jacob shall be in the midst of many people as a dew from the Lord, as the showers upon the grass, that tarrieth not for man, nor waiteth for the sons of men.   Mic. 5:3

8 And the remnant of Jacob shall be among the Gentiles in the midst of many people as a lion among the beasts of the forest, as a young lion among the flocks of sheep: who, if he go through, both treadeth down, and teareth in pieces, and none can deliver.   Ps. 50:22

9 Thine hand shall be lifted up upon thine

Christ's First Advent Prophesied

Micah 5:2

The prophecy of Micah designated His birthplace; Daniel specified the time of His advent (Micah 5:2; Daniel 9:25). God committed these prophecies to the Jewish leaders; they were without excuse if they did not know and declare to the people that the Messiah's coming was at hand. Their ignorance was the result of sinful neglect. The Jews were building monuments for the slain prophets of God, while by their deference to the great men of earth they were paying homage to the servants of Satan. Absorbed in their ambitious strife for place and power among men, they lost sight of the divine honors proffered them by the King of heaven.

With profound and reverent interest the elders of Israel should have been studying the place, the time, the circumstances, of the greatest event in the world's history—the coming of the Son of God to accomplish the redemption of man. All the people should have been watching and waiting that they might be among the first to welcome the world's Redeemer. But, lo, at Bethlehem two weary travelers from the hills of Nazareth traverse the whole length of the narrow street to the eastern extremity of the town, vainly seeking a place of rest and shelter for the night. No doors are open to receive them. In a wretched hovel prepared for cattle, they at last find refuge, and there the Saviour of the world is born. *GC 313*

adversaries, and all thine enemies shall be cut off. Is. 26:11

10 And it shall come to pass in that day, saith the LORD, that I will cut off thy horses out of the midst of thee, and I will destroy thy chariots: Hos. 14:3; Zech. 9:10

11 And I will cut off the cities of thy land, and throw down all thy strong holds: Is. 2:12-17

12 And I will cut off witchcrafts out of thine hand; and thou shalt have no *more* ᵀsooth-sayers: *those who tell future with astrology*

13 Thy ᵀgraven images also will I cut off, and thy standing images out of the midst of thee; and thou shalt no more worship the work of thine hands. Ezek. 6:9 ◆ *engraved or cut out*

14 And I will pluck up thy groves out of the midst of thee: so will I destroy thy cities.

15 And I will execute vengeance in anger and fury upon the heathen, such as they have not heard. Ps. 149:7

God's Lawsuit against His People

6 Hear ye now what the LORD saith; Arise, contend thou before the mountains, and let the hills hear thy voice. Ps. 50:1

2 Hear ye, O mountains, the LORD's controversy, and ye strong foundations of the earth: for the LORD hath a controversy with his people, and he will plead with Israel. Is. 1:18

3 O my people, what have I done unto thee? and wherein have I wearied thee? testify against me. Ps. 50:7; Is. 43:22-23; Jer. 2:5

4 For I brought thee up out of the land of Egypt, and redeemed thee out of the house of servants; and I sent before thee Moses, Aaron, and Miriam. Ex. 12:51

5 O my people, remember now what Balak king of Moab consulted, and what Balaam the son of Beor answered him from Shittim unto Gilgal; that ye may know the righteousness of the LORD. Num. 25:1; Josh. 5:9-10; Judg. 5:11

6:6–8 Great Questions Answered

In urging the value of practical godliness, the prophet was only repeating the counsel given Israel centuries before. . . . From age to age these counsels were repeated by the servants of Jehovah to those who were in danger of falling into habits of formalism and of forgetting to show mercy. . . .

We should lose no opportunity of performing deeds of mercy, of tender forethought and Christian courtesy, for the burdened and the oppressed. *PK 326, 327*

---

6 Wherewith shall I come before the LORD, *and* bow myself before the high God? shall I come before him with burnt offerings, with calves of a year old?

7 Will the LORD be pleased with thousands of rams, *or* with ten thousands of rivers of oil?

shall I give my firstborn *for* my ᵀtransgression, the fruit of my body *for* the sin of my soul? 2 Kin. 16:3; Ps. 50:9; Is. 40:16 ◆ *lawlessness*

8 He hath shewed thee, O man, what *is* good; and what doth the LORD require of thee, but to do justly, and to love mercy, and to walk humbly with thy God? Is. 57:15

9 The LORD's voice crieth unto the city, and *the man of* wisdom shall see thy name: hear ye the rod, and who hath appointed it. Is. 30:27

10 Are there yet the treasures of wickedness in the house of the wicked, and the scant measure *that is* abominable? Amos 3:10

11 Shall I count *them* pure with the wicked balances, and with the bag of deceitful weights? Hos. 12:7

12 For the rich men thereof are full of violence, and the inhabitants thereof have spoken lies, and their tongue *is* deceitful in their mouth. Is. 1:23

13 Therefore also will I make *thee* sick in smiting thee, in making *thee* desolate because of thy sins.

14 Thou shalt eat, but not be satisfied; and thy casting down *shall be* in the midst of thee; and thou shalt take hold, but shalt not deliver; and *that* which thou deliverest will I give up to the sword. Hos. 4:10

15 Thou shalt sow, but thou shalt not reap; thou shalt tread the olives, but thou shalt not anoint thee with oil; and sweet wine, but shalt not drink wine. Jer. 12:13; Amos 5:11; Zeph. 1:13

16 For the statutes of Omri are kept, and all the works of the house of Ahab, and ye walk in their counsels; that I should make thee a desolation, and the inhabitants thereof an ᵀhissing: therefore ye shall bear the reproach of my people. Jer. 7:24 ◆ *scorn*

The People Confess Their Sin

7 Woe is me! for I am as when they have gathered the summer fruits, as the grapegleanings of the vintage: *there is* no cluster to eat: my soul desired the firstripe fruit. Is. 24:13

2 The good *man* is perished out of the earth: and *there is* none upright among men: they all lie in wait for blood; they hunt every man his brother with a net. Ps. 12:1

3 That they may do evil with both hands earnestly, the prince asketh, and the judge *asketh* for a reward; and the great *man*, he uttereth his mischievous desire: so they wrap it up. Mic. 3:11

4 The best of them *is* as a brier: the most upright *is sharper* than a thorn hedge: the day of thy watchmen *and* thy visitation cometh; now shall be their perplexity. 2 Sam. 23:6-7; Is. 22:5

5 Trust ye not in a friend, put ye not confidence in a guide: keep the doors of thy mouth from her that lieth in thy bosom. Jer. 9:4

6 For the son dishonoureth the father, the daughter riseth up against her mother, the daughter in law against her mother in law; a man's enemies *are* the men of his own house.   Ezek. 22:7; Matt. 10:21, 35-36

7 Therefore I will look unto the LORD; I will wait for the God of my salvation: my God will hear me.   Is. 25:9

8 Rejoice not against me, O mine enemy: when I fall, I shall arise; when I sit in darkness, the LORD *shall be* a light unto me.   Is. 9:2

7:7, 8 Helpless Yet Invincible

Nothing is apparently more helpless, yet really more invincible, than the soul that feels its nothingness and relies wholly on the merits of the Saviour. By prayer, by the study of His word, by faith in His abiding presence, the weakest of human beings may live in contact with the living Christ, and He will hold them by a hand that will never let go. *MH 182*

9 I will bear the ᵀindignation of the LORD, because I have sinned against him, until he plead my cause, and execute judgment for me: he will bring me forth to the light, *and* I shall behold his righteousness. Ps. 37:6 ◆ *anger*

10 Then *she that is* mine enemy shall see *it*, and shame shall cover her which said unto me, Where is the LORD thy God? mine eyes shall behold her: now shall she be trodden down as the ᵀmire of the streets. Joel 2:17 ◆ *mud*

11 *In* the day that thy walls are to be built, *in* that day shall the decree be far removed.

12 *In* that day *also* he shall come even to thee from Assyria, and *from* the fortified cities, and from the fortress even to the river, and from sea to sea, and *from* mountain to mountain.   Is. 19:23-25

13 Notwithstanding the land shall be desolate because of them that dwell therein, for the fruit of their doings.   Is. 3:10-11

God Comforts His People

14 Feed thy people with thy rod, the flock of thine heritage, which dwell solitarily *in* the wood, in the midst of Carmel: let them feed *in* Bashan and Gilead, as in the days of old.   Ps. 28:9; 95:7; Mic. 5:4

15 According to the days of thy coming out of the land of Egypt will I shew unto him marvellous *things*.   Is. 11:16

16 The nations shall see and be confounded at all their might: they shall lay *their* hand upon *their* mouth, their ears shall be deaf.   Is. 26:11; 52:15

17 They shall lick the dust like a serpent, they shall move out of their holes like worms of the earth: they shall be afraid of the LORD our God, and shall fear because of thee.   Ps. 18:45; 72:9; Is. 49:23

18 Who *is* a God like unto thee, that pardoneth iniquity, and passeth by the ᵀtransgression of the remnant of his heritage? he retaineth not his anger for ever, because he delighteth *in* mercy.   Is. 43:25 ◆ *lawlessness*

19 He will turn again, he will have compassion upon us; he will subdue our iniquities; and thou wilt cast all their sins into the depths of the sea.   Is. 38:17

20 Thou wilt perform the truth to Jacob, *and* the mercy to Abraham, which thou hast sworn unto our fathers from the days of old.

THE BOOK OF

NAHUM

When Jonah preached to the city of Nineveh, its inhabitants repented and God chose to spare them from destruction. But the Assyrians later returned to their brutal ways. Approximately one hundred fifty years later, God proclaimed through Nahum that even though Assyria may have seemed invincible, it would soon be destroyed for its wicked practices. This occurred when Babylon destroyed the city in 612 B.C. At the same time, Judah experienced a spiritual revival under King Josiah (640–609 B.C.).

Dates

Nahum proclaims the fall of Nineveh as a future event (3:7); therefore Nahum wrote sometime before 612 B.C. The vivid description of the fall of Thebes (3:8–10), which occurred in 663 B.C., points to Nahum writing at some time after this event. With this date range in mind (663-612 B.C.), it is acceptable to set Nahum's date around 640 B.C.

After the revival in the early eighth century sparked by Jonah's ministry, Assyria eventually returned to its cruel ways, destroying Samaria in 722 B.C. during the reign of Sargon II. Assyria then set its sights on Judah, as Sennacherib attacked Jerusalem in 701 B.C. Only by turning to God was Hezekiah able to save the city (2 Kings 18—19; 2 Chronicles 32), even though Assyria took some people into exile. Under King Esarhaddon (681–669 B.C.), Judah became subject to Assyria. The early years of the reign of Ashurbanipal (669–627 B.C.) marked the peak of Assyria's power, with the capture of Thebes in 663 B.C. its high point. During the period of Assyria's expansion, the nation was brutal in war, deporting conquered nations from their homelands, torturing leaders before executing them, and evoking fear in all foreign nations. In 652 B.C., Babylon rebelled against Assyrian control and continually fought its former ruling nation. The power of Assyria would decline under the reigns of Ashuretililani, Sinsharishkun, and Ashuruballit II until Babylon destroyed Nineveh in 612 B.C.

Therefore, Assyria was at the height of its influence at the time of Nahum's prophecy. The city had fortifications that would allow it to withstand a twenty-year siege, with walls 100 feet tall, a moat 60 feet deep and 150 feet wide, and towers 200 feet tall overlooking the walls. Three chariots could ride side by side along the top of the city wall. While Nahum's prophecy of its destruction may have been difficult to envision at that time, it would occur less than fifty years later in a manner similar to the description given by Nahum (1:8; 3:15–17), as the Tigris River overflowed, the floodwaters destroyed parts of the immense wall, and the Babylonians invaded by climbing through the holes in the wall, plundering the city and setting it on fire. This indestructible city was lost until its archeological discovery in A.D. 1842, which matched the prophecy that Nineveh would be hidden (3:11).

Author

The only information in the Old Testament about Nahum appears in 1:1, where it identifies his hometown (Elkosh) by calling him an Elkoshite. The location of this city is unknown. Scholars offer at least four possibilities for its location:

(1) A tradition from the sixteenth century A.D. identifies Elkosh as a city in Iraq on the Tigris River north of Nineveh called Al-Qush.

(2) The similarity in consonants between *Elkosh* and *Elkesi* led Jerome to believe Elkosh was Elkesi, a Galilean city near Ramah.

(3) Because *Capernaum* means "City of Nahum" (*Kephar-Nahum*), some think that Elkosh was renamed Capernaum to honor Nahum.

(4) Nahum's reference to the triumph of Judah (1:15; 2:2) leads many to believe Nahum came from a city in southern Judah between Gaza and Jerusalem later called Elcesei. These proposals vary widely, as they place Elkosh in Assyria, the former northern kingdom Israel, or Judah—three drastically different places. Fortunately, the clarity of Nahum's message renders an exact identification unnecessary for understanding his message.

Meaning of the Name

As a shortened form of the name Nehemiah ("Comfort of Yahweh"), the Hebrew name *Nahum* means "comfort," "consolation" or "the comforted one." While the prophet's

message may seem stern, it provided comfort to the people of Judah by proclaiming that God would destroy the cruel Assyrians who had conquered the northern kingdom of Israel and elicited fear in Judah. Rendered *Naoum* in the Greek Bible, the Latin title *Nahum* corresponds to the English title.

Christ in Nahum

Although Nahum's message contains no explicit prophecies concerning the Messiah and focuses on conditions at a point in history more than six hundred years before Jesus, there are similarities between the description of God judging His enemies and delivering His people in Nahum 1:2–8 and the vision of Jesus, the rider on the white horse, in Revelation 19:11–21. The use of Nahum 1:15 (along with Isaiah 52:7) in Romans 10:15 shows that the deliverance of Judah from Assyria symbolizes the deliverance of the believer from sin and the forces of evil that Jesus accomplished on the cross.

Overview

The prophet Obadiah focused on Edom. Likewise, Nahum's message focuses on a foreign nation—Assyria. The Book of Nahum has three sections:

(1) *Nahum 1, God's Anger at Nineveh:* While the Assyrians were prideful of their reputation as conquerors, the seemingly invincible capital city of the Assyrians (Nineveh) is marked by God for destruction. Through Nahum, God describes His character, reiterating the same characteristics discussed with Moses (1:3; see Exodus 34:6). Though God spared the people of Nineveh during Jonah's time, they would be spared no longer. While discussing the fate of Assyria, the primary audience for Nahum's message is Judah. Having watched the Assyrians conquer the northern kingdom (Israel) and threaten to conquer Jerusalem during Hezekiah's reign (2 Kings 18—19; 2 Chronicles 32), the people of Judah well knew the oppression of the Assyrians. But vengeance belongs to God.

(2) *Nahum 2, Nineveh Will Be Destroyed:* Nahum describes in poetic fashion the invasion and destruction of Nineveh. The pride of the Assyrians would be humbled as Nineveh's nobles flee and its treasures are looted.

(3) *Nahum 3, Nineveh's Cruelty Is Ended:* Nahum catalogues the Assyrians' brutality and mentions the capital city of the Egyptians—No Ammon, also called Thebes—a city conquered by the Assyrians. Nineveh's fortifications and fighting forces would be no match for God. Just as the walls of Jericho fell (Joshua 6), so would those of Nineveh. While Nineveh would be utterly destroyed, the kingdom of Judah would be restored.

Unlocking Nahum

KEY PEOPLE:
Nahum, the people of Nineveh

KEY EVENT:
The fall of Nineveh to the Babylonians

KEY PHRASE:
Judgment of Nineveh, as Nahum describes the destruction of this powerful city that would happen at the hands of the Babylonians. It issues a great reminder that the empires, strongholds, and powers of this world that seem indestructible today will eventually fall.

KEY VERSES:
"The LORD is good, a strong hold in the day of trouble; and he knoweth them that trust in him. But with an overrunning flood he will make an utter end of the place thereof, and darkness shall pursue his enemies" (Nahum 1:7, 8).

KEY CHAPTER:
Nahum 1, which presents a glorious vision of God in which He declares that He will judge His enemies but save those who trust in Him. It shows that God is a patient God but also a powerful God (1:3) who can obliterate a strong nation like Assyria with a single blow (1:9).

Who Can Withstand the Lord's Anger?

1 The burden of Nineveh. The book of the vision of Nahum the Elkoshite. Is. 13:1
2 God *is* jealous, and the LORD revengeth; the LORD revengeth, and *is* furious; the LORD will take vengeance on his adversaries, and he reserveth *wrath* for his enemies. Ex. 20:5; Ps. 94:1
3 The LORD *is* slow to anger, and great in power, and will not at all acquit *the wicked*: the LORD hath his way in the whirlwind and in the storm, and the clouds *are* the dust of his feet.

1:3 Even God Has a Limit

The world has become bold in transgression of God's law. Because of His long forbearance, men have trampled upon His authority. They have strengthened one another in oppression and cruelty toward His heritage, saying, "How doth God know? and is there knowledge in the Most High?" (Psalm 73:11). But there is a line beyond which they cannot pass. The time is near when they will have reached the prescribed limit. . . . The Lord will interpose to vindicate His own honor, to deliver His people, and to repress the swellings of unrighteousness. *COL 177, 178*

4 He rebuketh the sea, and maketh it dry, and drieth up all the rivers: Bashan ᵀlanguisheth, and Carmel, and the flower of Lebanon languisheth. Ps. 106:9; Is. 33:9; Matt. 8:26 ◆ *weakens*
5 The mountains quake at him, and the hills melt, and the earth is burned at his presence, yea, the world, and all that dwell therein.
6 Who can stand before his indignation? and who can abide in the fierceness of his anger? his fury is poured out like fire, and the rocks are thrown down by him. Jer. 10:10; Nah. 1:2

Why Does Nineveh Oppose the Lord?

7 The LORD *is* good, a strong hold in the day of trouble; and he knoweth them that trust in him. Ps. 1:6; Jer. 33:11; 2 Tim. 2:19

8 But with an overrunning flood he will make an utter end of the place thereof, and darkness shall pursue his enemies. Is. 8:22
9 What do ye imagine against the LORD? he will make an utter end: affliction shall not rise up the second time. Nah. 1:11

1:9 Sin Ends Forever

The whole universe will have become witnesses to the nature and results of sin. And its utter extermination, which in the beginning would have brought fear to angels and dishonor to God, will now vindicate His love and establish His honor before the universe of beings who delight to do His will, and in whose heart is His law. Never will evil again be manifest. . . . The law of God, which Satan has reproached as the yoke of bondage, will be honored as the law of liberty. *GC 504*

10 For while *they be* folden together *as* thorns, and while they are drunken *as* drunkards, they shall be devoured as stubble fully dry. Mic. 7:4
11 There is *one* come out of thee, that imagineth evil against the LORD, a wicked counsellor. Nah. 1:9

Nineveh Will Fall

12 Thus saith the LORD; Though *they be* quiet, and likewise many, yet thus shall they be cut down, when he shall pass through. Though I have afflicted thee, I will afflict thee no more. Is. 37:36
13 For now will I break his yoke from off thee, and will burst thy bonds in sunder. Is. 9:4; 10:27
14 And the LORD hath given a commandment concerning thee, *that* no more of thy name be sown: out of the house of thy gods will I cut off the ᵀgraven image and the molten image: I will make thy grave; for thou art vile. Ps. 109:13 ◆ *engraved* or *cut out*
15 Behold upon the mountains the feet of

God's Strange Act

Nahum 1:3

God's judgments will be visited upon those who are seeking to oppress and destroy His people. His long forbearance with the wicked emboldens men in transgression, but their punishment is nonetheless certain and terrible because it is long delayed. "The Lord shall rise up as in Mount Perazim, He shall be wroth as in the valley of Gibeon, that He may do His work, His strange work; and bring to pass His act, His strange act" (Isaiah 28:21). To our merciful God the act of punishment is a strange act. "As I live, saith the Lord God, I have no pleasure in the death of the wicked" (Ezekiel 33:11). The Lord is "merciful and gracious, long-suffering, and abundant in goodness and truth, . . . forgiving iniquity and transgression and sin." Yet He will "by no means clear the guilty." "The Lord is slow to anger, and great in power, and will not at all acquit the wicked" (Exodus 34:6, 7; Nahum 1:3). By terrible things in righteousness He will vindicate the authority of His downtrodden law. The severity of the retribution awaiting the transgressor may be judged by the Lord's reluctance to execute justice. The nation with which He bears long, and which He will not smite until it has filled up the measure of its iniquity in God's account, will finally drink the cup of wrath unmixed with mercy. *GC 627*

him that bringeth good tidings, that publisheth peace! O Judah, keep thy solemn feasts, perform thy vows: for the wicked shall no more pass through thee; he is utterly cut off.   Is. 29:7-8; 52:7; Rom. 10:15

An Army Will Conquer Nineveh

2 He that dasheth in pieces is come up before thy face: keep the munition, watch the way, make thy ᵀloins strong, fortify thy power mightily.   Jer. 51:20-23 ◆ waist

2 For the LORD hath turned away the excellency of Jacob, as the excellency of Israel: for the emptiers have emptied them out, and marred their vine branches.   Ps. 80:12-13

3 The shield of his mighty men is made red, the valiant men are in scarlet: the chariots shall be with flaming torches in the day of his preparation, and the fir trees shall be terribly shaken.   Ezek. 23:14-15

4 The chariots shall rage in the streets, they shall justle one against another in the broad ways: they shall seem like torches, they shall run like the lightnings.   Jer. 4:13

5 He shall recount his worthies: they shall stumble in their walk; they shall make haste to the wall thereof, and the defence shall be prepared.   Jer. 46:12

6 The gates of the rivers shall be opened, and the palace shall be dissolved.

7 And Huzzab shall be led away captive, she shall be brought up, and her maids shall lead her as with the voice of doves, ᵀtabering upon their breasts.   Is. 38:14 ◆ beating

8 But Nineveh is of old like a pool of water: yet they shall flee away. Stand, stand, shall they cry; but none shall look back.

9 Take ye the ᵀspoil of silver, take the spoil of gold: for there is none end of the store and glory out of all the pleasant furniture. plunder

10 She is empty, and void, and waste: and the heart melteth, and the knees ᵀsmite together, and much pain is in all loins, and the faces of them all gather blackness.   Ps. 22:14 ◆ strike

11 Where is the dwelling of the lions, and the feedingplace of the young lions, where the lion, even the old lion, walked, and the lion's whelp, and none made them afraid?   Is. 5:29

2:10 My Grace Is Sufficient for You

Before His presence "all faces are turned into paleness;" upon the rejecters of God's mercy falls the terror of eternal despair . . . (Jeremiah 30:6). The righteous cry with trembling: "Who shall be able to stand?" The angels' song is hushed, and there is a period of awful silence. Then the voice of Jesus is heard, saying: "My grace is sufficient for you." The faces of the righteous are lighted up, and joy fills every heart. And the angels strike a note higher and sing again as they draw still nearer to the earth. GC 641

---

12 The lion did tear in pieces enough for his whelps, and strangled for his lionesses, and filled his holes with prey, and his dens with ravin.   Jer. 51:34

13 Behold, I am against thee, saith the LORD of hosts, and I will burn her chariots in the smoke, and the sword shall devour thy young lions: and I will cut off thy prey from the earth, and the voice of thy messengers shall no more be heard.   2 Kin. 19:23; Ps. 46:9; Nah. 3:5

The Miserable Ruin of Nineveh

3 Woe to the bloody city! it is all full of lies and robbery; the prey departeth not;

2 The noise of a whip, and the noise of the rattling of the wheels, and of the pransing horses, and of the jumping chariots.   Judg. 5:22

3 The horseman lifteth up both the bright sword and the glittering spear: and there is a multitude of slain, and a great number of carcases; and there is none end of their corpses; they stumble upon their corpses: Hab. 3:11

4 Because of the multitude of the ᵀwhoredoms of the wellfavoured harlot, the mistress of witchcrafts, that selleth nations through her whoredoms, and families through her witchcrafts.   Is. 47:9, 12-13 ◆ acts of prostitution

5 Behold, I am against thee, saith the LORD of hosts; and I will discover thy skirts upon

---

Nineveh "The Bloody City"

Nahum 3:1–5

In the time of its temporal prosperity Nineveh was a center of crime and wickedness. Inspiration has characterized it as "the bloody city, . . . full of lies and robbery." In figurative language the prophet Nahum compared the Ninevites to a cruel, ravenous lion. "Upon whom," he inquired, "hath not thy wickedness passed continually?" (Nahum 3:1, 19).

Yet Nineveh, wicked though it had become, was not wholly given over to evil. He who "beholdeth all the sons of men" (Psalm 33:13) and "seeth every precious thing" (Job 28:10) perceived in that city many who were reaching out after something better and higher, and who, if granted opportunity to learn of the living God, would put away their evil deeds and worship Him. And so in His wisdom God revealed Himself to them in an unmistakable manner, to lead them, if possible, to repentance. PK 265, 266

thy face, and I will shew the nations thy nakedness, and the kingdoms thy shame.

6 And I will cast abominable filth upon thee, and make thee vile, and will set thee as a gazingstock. Job 9:31

7 And it shall come to pass, *that* all they that look upon thee shall flee from thee, and say, Nineveh is laid waste: who will ᵀbemoan her? whence shall I seek comforters for thee? Is. 51:19; Jer. 15:5; 51:9 ◆ *lament for*

8 Art thou better than populous No, that was situate among the rivers, *that had* the waters round about it, whose rampart *was* the sea, *and* her wall *was* from the sea? Amos 6:2

9 Ethiopia and Egypt *were* her strength, and *it was* infinite; Put and Lubim were thy helpers. Ezek. 27:10

10 Yet *was* she carried away, she went into captivity: her young children also were dashed in pieces at the top of all the streets: and they cast lots for her honourable men, and all her great men were bound in chains. Is. 20:4; Hos. 13:16; Joel 3:3

11 Thou also shalt be drunken: thou shalt be hid, thou also shalt seek strength because of the enemy. Is. 2:10

12 All thy strong holds *shall be like* fig trees with the firstripe figs: if they be shaken, they shall even fall into the mouth of the eater. Rev. 6:13

13 Behold, thy people in the midst of thee *are* women: the gates of thy land shall be set wide open unto thine enemies: the fire shall devour thy bars. Is. 19:16; Jer. 50:37; 51:30

14 Draw thee waters for the siege, fortify thy strong holds: go into clay, and tread the morter, make strong the brickkiln. Nah. 2:1

15 There shall the fire devour thee; the sword shall cut thee off, it shall eat thee up like the cankerworm: make thyself many as the cankerworm, make thyself many as the locusts. Joel 1:4; Nah. 2:13; 3:13

16 Thou hast multiplied thy merchants above the stars of heaven: the cankerworm spoileth, and flieth away.

17 Thy crowned *are* as the locusts, and thy captains as the great grasshoppers, which camp in the hedges in the cold day, *but* when the sun ariseth they flee away, and their place is not known where they *are*. Jer. 51:27

18 Thy shepherds slumber, O king of Assyria: thy nobles shall dwell *in the dust*: thy people is scattered upon the mountains, and no man gathereth *them*. 1 Kin. 22:17; Ps. 76:5-6; Is. 13:14

19 *There is* no healing of thy bruise; thy wound is grievous: all that hear the ᵀbruit of thee shall clap the hands over thee: for upon whom hath not thy wickedness passed continually? Job 27:23; Lam. 2:15; Mic. 1:9 ◆ *news*

THE BOOK OF

HABAKKUK

Faith in God can be difficult in a world in which evil does not seem to be punished and even appears to be rewarded at times. How can God, who is too pure to look on evil, allow evil to continue? The prophet Habakkuk asked this very question of God and received a surprising answer. When he asked God how long He would allow the nation of Judah to reject His law, God declared that He would punish the nation for its sin through the Babylonians (or Chaldeans), a fierce and deplorable people. Rather than satisfying Habakkuk's desire for justice, this answer intensified it, as God seems to reward evil. While God did declare that Babylon would fall, He also called for the prophet to have faith in His actions even when he did not understand them, as "the just shall live by his faith" (2:4).

This private struggle of the prophet with God is a public proclamation to God's people. The questions Habakkuk asked are by no means unique to this prophet or to his time; they continue to plague Christians today. The frankness displayed in the prophet's questions shows we may wrestle with God and ask Him difficult questions. Habakkuk's response—placing his faith and hope in God (3:17–19)—is a model for believers today struggling with the same issues (see 2:2–5). Such a response is not easy but emerges from seeing the power of God that is described in Habakkuk's closing hymn of praise (3:1–19).

Dates

The prediction of a coming invasion by the Babylonians contained in this book (1:6; 2:1; 3:16) and the description of Judah's sins (1:2–4) help determine the date of the book in light of the omission of any references to kings. The list of sins in 1:2–4 leads some scholars to believe that Habakkuk prophesied during the latter part of the reign of Manasseh (697–642 B.C.), Amon (642–640 B.C.), and/or the early part of Josiah's reign (640-609 B.C.).

Most likely Habakkuk's ministry closely followed that of Nahum. Both the Hebrew and Greek cannons situate Habakkuk's writing as subsequent to Nahum, which shows favor to the point of view that his prophecy takes place about 630 B.C.

Habakkuk forewarns his nation of its pending doom at the hands of the idolatrous Babylonians. Because of their sins, the people of Judah fall subject to and will be captured by the iniquitous Babylonians, an enemy of both God and his people.

Author

Habakkuk was a prophet and possibly also a priest (like Jeremiah, Ezekiel, and Zechariah) who helped lead the temple worship, or a Levite musician, as the psalm he composed in chapter 3 is for "the chief singer" (3:19). The only Old Testament references to Habakkuk are in this book (1:1; 3:1), with it giving no indication about his parentage or hometown.

Meaning of the Name

The Hebrew name *Habaqquq* is an uncommon name that derives from a verb meaning "embrace" (*habaq*). Like the meaning of his name ("one who embraces" or "clings"), Habakkuk must cling to God when facing the injustices within the land and the calamity that will come through the Babylonians. His name in Greek is *Amabakouk* and is *Habacuc* in Latin.

Christ in Habakkuk

At the cross, it appeared that the wickedness of the world had triumphed, but the resurrection proves the power of God to defeat evil once and for all. Jesus embodied the words of Habakkuk 2:4 and 3:17–19 by trusting in God on the cross (Matthew 27:38–50). Jesus' name shows Him to be the God who saves—the one about whom Habakkuk speaks in 3:13, 18 (Matthew 1:21).

Overview

The format of Habakkuk differs from the other prophetic books because it primarily consists of a dialogue between God and the prophet, instead of a proclamation from the prophet to the nation. Like the Book of Job and Psalm 73, Habakkuk questions how God can tolerate the injustices seen in the present world and receives an answer from God that

encourages the prophet to place his confidence in the glorious God even in the midst of the horrid present conditions. Thus, the book can be divided into two parts:

(1) *Habakkuk 1—2, Habakkuk Questions:* Habakkuk asks how God can allow injustice in the land of Judah (1:2–4), to which God responds by announcing that the Babylonians will destroy the nation (1:5–11). Habakkuk then questions how God can use an unjust people like the Babylonians to punish a nation more righteous than them (1:12–17) and waits for a response from God (2:1), which God commands Habakkuk to record (2:2, 3). God's answer: the arrogant Babylonians will face judgment but the faithful will live (2:4–20).

(2) *Habakkuk 3, Habakkuk Praises:* Understanding that he is exceeding the limits of decorum by venturing to question divine wisdom and will, Habakkuk repents in all humbleness.

Still deeply concerned about the people of Judah, he pleads that God's mercy will accompany the destruction (3:1, 2). God answers Habakkuk's prayer by revealing to him that He is laboring for the salvation of His faithful and will overthrow their enemy (3:3–16). In closing, Habakkuk confidently affirms God's wisdom in putting His plan into motion so that He can make a success of His people (3:17–19).

Unlocking Habakkuk

KEY PEOPLE:
Habakkuk, the Babylonians

KEY EVENTS:
The fall of Jerusalem to the Babylonians; the destruction of the Babylonians

KEY WORD:
Faith, with the book containing the famous phrase, "the just shall live by his faith" (2:4) quoted by the apostle Paul (see Romans 1:17; Galatians 3:11, 12). Habakkuk must live by faith when he does not understand God's purpose in allowing sin to abound in the land of Judah or sending the wicked Babylonians to punish Judah. Chapter 3 proclaims that one can have faith in God because He is in control of the universe.

KEY VERSE:
"Behold, his soul which is lifted up is not upright in him: but the just shall live by his faith" (Habakkuk 2:4).

KEY CHAPTER:
Habakkuk 3, which is a majestic song of praise to God, proclaiming the power and glory of God demonstrated in the past (3:1–15) and culminating in the declaration of faith in God, even in the midst of calamity: "Although the fig tree shall not blossom, neither shall fruit be in the vines; the labour of the olive shall fail, and the fields shall yield no meat; the flock shall be cut off from the fold, and there shall be no herd in the stalls: Yet I will rejoice in the LORD, I will joy in the God of my salvation" (Habakkuk 3:17, 18).

Habakkuk's Question

1 The burden which Habakkuk the prophet did see. *Nah. 1:1*

2 O LORD, how long shall I cry, and thou wilt not hear! *even* cry out unto thee *of* violence, and thou wilt not save! *Ps. 13:1-2*

3 Why dost thou shew me iniquity, and cause *me* to behold grievance? for spoiling and violence *are* before me: and there are *that* raise up strife and contention. *Ps. 55:9-11*

4 Therefore the law is slacked, and judgment doth never go forth: for the wicked doth ᵀcompass about the righteous; therefore wrong judgment proceedeth. *Ps. 119:126* ◆ *surround*

1:1–4 How Long Shall I Cry?

The prophets had begun to foretell the utter destruction of their fair city, where stood the temple built by Solomon, and where all their earthly hopes of national greatness had centered. . . . In the face of the long-continued persecution of the righteous, and of the apparent prosperity of the wicked, could those who had remained true to God hope for better days?

These anxious questionings were voiced by the prophet Habakkuk. Viewing the situation of the faithful in his day, he expressed the burden of his heart in the inquiry: "O Lord, how long shall I cry, and Thou wilt not hear!" (Habakkuk 1:2). *PK 385*

The Lord's Answer

5 Behold ye among the heathen, and regard, and wonder marvellously: for *I* will work a work in your days, *which* ye will not believe, though it be told *you*. *Is. 29:14; Ezek. 12:22-28*

6 For, lo, I raise up the Chaldeans, *that* bitter and hasty nation, which shall march through the breadth of the land, to possess the dwellingplaces *that are* not theirs. *2 Kin. 24:2*

7 They *are* terrible and dreadful: their judgment and their dignity shall proceed of themselves. *Jer. 39:5-9*

8 Their horses also are swifter than the leopards, and are more fierce than the evening wolves: and their horsemen shall spread themselves, and their horsemen shall come from far; they shall fly as the eagle *that* hasteth to eat. *Deut. 28:49; Jer. 4:13; Zeph. 3:3*

9 They shall come all for violence: their faces shall sup up *as* the east wind, and they shall gather the captivity as the sand.

10 And they shall scoff at the kings, and the princes shall be a scorn unto them: they shall deride every strong hold; for they shall heap dust, and take it. *2 Chr. 36:6*

11 Then shall *his* mind change, and he shall pass over, and offend, *imputing* this his power unto his god.

Another Question from Habakkuk

12 *Art* thou not from everlasting, O LORD my God, mine Holy One? we shall not die. O LORD, thou hast ordained them for judgment; and, O mighty God, thou hast established them for correction. *Deut. 32:4*

1:12 I Rest My Case

Confident that even in this terrible judgment the purpose of God for His people would in some way be fulfilled, Habakkuk bowed in submission. . . . And then, his faith reaching out beyond the forbidding prospect of the immediate future, and laying fast hold on the precious promises that reveal God's love for His trusting children, the prophet added, "We shall not die." With this declaration of faith he rested his case, and that of every believing Israelite, in the hands of a compassionate God. *PK 386*

13 *Thou art* of purer eyes than to behold evil, and canst not look on iniquity: wherefore lookest thou upon them that deal treacherously, *and* holdest thy tongue when the wicked devoureth *the man that is* more righteous than he? *Ps. 34:15-16*

14 And makest men as the fishes of the sea, as the creeping things, *that have* no ruler over them?

15 They take up all of them with the ᵀangle, they catch them in their net, and gather them in their drag: therefore they rejoice and are glad. *Ps. 10:9; Jer. 16:16; Amos 4:2* ◆ *fish hook*

16 Therefore they sacrifice unto their net, and burn incense unto their drag; because by them their portion *is* fat, and their meat plenteous. *Hab. 1:11*

17 Shall they therefore empty their net, and not spare continually to slay the nations?

Habakkuk Awaits the Lord's Answer

2 I will stand upon my watch, and set me upon the tower, and will watch to see what he will say unto me, and what I shall answer when I am reproved. *Ps. 85:8; Is. 21:8*

2:1–4 The Just Shall Live by Faith

The faith that strengthened Habakkuk and all the holy and the just in those days of deep trial was the same faith that sustains God's people today. In the darkest hours, under circumstances the most forbidding, the Christian believer may keep his soul stayed upon the source of all light and power. Day by day, through faith in God, his hope and courage may be renewed. *PK 386, 387*

The Lord's Answer

2 And the LORD answered me, and said, Write the vision, and make *it* plain upon tables, that he may run that readeth it. *Deut. 27:8*

3 For the vision *is* yet for an appointed time, but at the end it shall speak, and not lie: though it tarry, wait for it; because it will surely come, it will not tarry. Ps. 27:14; Dan. 8:19

2:4

4 Behold, his soul *which* is lifted up is not upright in him: but the just shall live by his faith. John 3:36; Rom. 1:17; Heb. 10:38

Faith   See Romans 12:3.

5 Yea also, because he ᵀtransgresseth by wine, *he is* a proud man, neither keepeth at home, who enlargeth his desire as hell, and *is* as death, and cannot be satisfied, but gathereth unto him all nations, and heapeth unto him all people: 2 Kin. 14:10; Prov. 20:1; 27:20 ◆ *violates a law*
6 Shall not all these take up a parable against him, and a taunting proverb against him, and say, Woe to him that increaseth *that which is* not his! how long? and to him that ᵀladeth himself with thick clay! Num. 23:7 ◆ *loads*
7 Shall they not rise up suddenly that shall bite thee, and awake that shall ᵀvex thee, and thou shalt be for booties unto them? *trouble*
8 Because thou hast spoiled many nations, all the remnant of the people shall ᵀspoil thee; because of men's blood, and *for* the violence of the land, of the city, and of all that dwell therein. Is. 33:1; Jer. 27:7; Hab. 2:17 ◆ *plunder*
9 Woe to him that ᵀcoveteth an evil ᵀcovetousness to his house, that he may set his nest on high, that he may be delivered from the power of evil! Jer. 49:16 ◆ *desires* ◆ *strong desire*
10 Thou hast consulted shame to thy house by cutting off many people, and hast sinned *against* thy soul. 2 Kin. 9:26
11 For the stone shall cry out of the wall, and the beam out of the timber shall answer it. Josh. 24:27; Luke 19:40
12 Woe to him that buildeth a town with blood, and stablisheth a city by iniquity!
13 Behold, *is it* not of the LORD of hosts that the people shall labour in the very fire, and the people shall weary themselves for very vanity? Is. 50:11
14 For the earth shall be filled with the knowledge of the glory of the LORD, as the waters cover the sea. Ps. 22:27; 72:19; Is. 11:9
15 Woe unto him that giveth his neighbour drink, that puttest thy bottle to *him*, and makest *him* drunken also, that thou mayest look on their nakedness! Gen. 9:22
16 Thou art filled with shame for glory: drink thou also, and let thy foreskin be uncovered: the cup of the LORD's right hand shall be turned unto thee, and shameful spewing *shall be* on thy glory. Is. 47:3
17 For the violence of Lebanon shall cover thee, and the spoil of beasts, *which* made them afraid, because of men's blood, and for the violence of the land, of the city, and of all that dwell therein. Ps. 55:23; Hab. 2:8; Zech. 11:1
18 What profiteth the ᵀgraven image that the maker thereof hath graven it; the molten image, and a teacher of lies, that the maker of his work trusteth therein, to make ᵀdumb idols? Jer. 10:8 ◆ *engraved* or *cut out* ◆ *mute*
19 Woe unto him that saith to the wood, Awake; to the dumb stone, Arise, it shall teach! Behold, it *is* laid over with gold and silver, and *there is* no breath at all in the midst of it. 1 Kin. 18:26-29; Ps. 135:17; Jer. 10:4
20 But the LORD *is* in his holy temple: let all the earth keep silence before him. Ps. 11:4

2:20 True Reverence

Another precious grace that should be carefully cherished is reverence. True reverence for God is inspired by a sense of His infinite greatness and a realization of His presence. . . . The hour and place of prayer and the services of public worship the child should be taught to regard as sacred because God is there. *Ed 242, 243*

Habakkuk's Prayer

3 A prayer of Habakkuk the prophet upon Shigionoth.

2 O LORD, I have heard thy speech, *and* was afraid: O LORD, revive thy work in the midst

Be Faithful to the End

Habakkuk 2:2–4

We must cherish and cultivate the faith of which prophets and apostles have testified—the faith that lays hold on the promises of God and waits for deliverance in His appointed time and way. The sure word of prophecy will meet its final fulfillment in the glorious advent of our Lord and Saviour Jesus Christ, as King of kings and Lord of lords. The time of waiting may seem long, the soul may be oppressed by discouraging circumstances, many in whom confidence has been placed may fall by the way; but with the prophet who endeavored to encourage Judah in a time of unparalleled apostasy, let us confidently declare, "The Lord is in His holy temple: let all the earth keep silence before Him" (Habakkuk 2:20). Let us ever hold in remembrance the cheering message, "The vision is yet for an appointed time, but at the end it shall speak, and not lie: though it tarry, wait for it; because it will surely come, it will not tarry. . . . The just shall live by his faith" (Habakkuk 2:3, 4). *PK 387, 388*

of the years, in the midst of the years make known; in wrath remember mercy. Ps. 44:1; 85:6

3 God came from Teman, and the Holy One from mount Paran. Selah. His glory covered the heavens, and the earth was full of his praise. Deut. 33:2

4 And *his* brightness was as the light; he had horns *coming* out of his hand: and there *was* the hiding of his power. Job 26:14

5 Before him went the pestilence, and burning coals went forth at his feet. Ex. 12:29-30

6 He stood, and measured the earth: he beheld, and drove Tasunder the nations; and the everlasting mountains were scattered, the perpetual hills did bow: his ways *are* everlasting. Gen. 49:26 ◆ *apart*

7 I saw the tents of Cushan in affliction: *and* the curtains of the land of Midian did tremble. Ex. 15:14-16

8 Was the LORD displeased against the rivers? *was* thine anger against the rivers? *was* thy wrath against the sea, that thou didst ride upon thine horses *and* thy chariots of salvation? Ps. 18:10; 68:17; 114:5

9 Thy bow was made quite naked, *according* to the oaths of the tribes, *even thy* word. Selah. Thou didst cleave the earth with rivers. Ps. 7:12-13

10 The mountains saw thee, *and* they trembled: the overflowing of the water passed by: the deep uttered his voice, *and* lifted up his hands on high. Ps. 93:3; 98:7-8

11 The sun *and* moon stood still in their habitation: at the light of thine arrows they went, *and* at the shining of thy glittering spear.

12 Thou didst march through the land in Tindignation, thou didst thresh the heathen in anger. Jer. 51:33 ◆ *anger*

13 Thou wentest forth for the salvation of thy people, *even* for salvation with thine anointed; thou woundedst the head out of the house of the wicked, by discovering the foundation unto the neck. Selah. Ps. 105:15; 110:6

14 Thou didst strike through with his Tstaves the head of his villages: they came out as a whirlwind to scatter me: their rejoicing *was* as to devour the poor secretly. Ps. 10:8 ◆ *clubs* or *rods*

15 Thou didst walk through the sea with thine horses, *through* the heap of great waters. Ps. 77:19; Hab. 3:8

16 When I heard, my belly trembled; my lips quivered at the voice: rottenness entered into my bones, and I trembled in myself, that I might rest in the day of trouble: when he cometh up unto the people, he will invade them with his troops. Hab. 3:2

17 Although the fig tree shall not blossom, neither *shall* fruit *be* in the vines; the labour of the olive shall fail, and the fields shall yield no meat; the flock shall be cut off from the fold, and *there shall be* no herd in the stalls:

18 Yet I will rejoice in the LORD, I will joy in the God of my salvation. Job 13:15; Is. 61:10

19 The LORD God *is* my strength, and he will make my feet like Thinds' *feet*, and he will make me to walk upon mine high places. To the chief singer on my stringed instruments. Deut. 32:13; 33:29; 2 Sam. 22:34 ◆ *deer's*

THE BOOK OF

ZEPHANIAH

During the reigns of Manasseh and Amon, the people of Judah worshiped other gods, polluted God's holy places, and broke God's law (1:4–6, 8, 9; 3:1–4, 7). They even denied that God would do anything about their actions (1:12). Zephaniah spoke about the coming day of the Lord (1:7, 14) when the wrath of God would come upon Judah (1:3—2:3; 3:1–7) and all the nations of the earth (2:4–15). The prophet also issued a reminder that judgment was not the last word, because after this judgment, God would rejoice over a purified remnant that He would return to the land (3:9–20).

Under the leadership of King Josiah, the nation listened to Zephaniah's call. Their repentance lasted for only a short time, however, as the people forgot Zephaniah's message and experienced the judgment about which Zephaniah spoke when Babylon invaded Judah in 586 B.C.

By speaking about the day of the Lord, Zephaniah also pointed to a coming day in which the wicked will face judgment and the faithful will experience the blessings described in 3:9–20 under the rule of the Messiah. Therefore, Zephaniah's call to seek the Lord (see 2:3) is a message that no one can afford to forget or ignore.

Dates

The opening verse firmly places Zephaniah's ministry during the reign of Josiah (640–609 B.C.). Two factors in the book allow for a more precise date within Josiah's reign:

(1) Zephaniah 2:13 refers to the future destruction of Nineveh. Since this event happened in 612 B.C., Zephaniah prophesied sometime before 612 B.C.

(2) The sins discussed in 1:3–13 and 3:1–7 point to Zephaniah ministering before Josiah's religious reforms in Judah, which began in 628 B.C., the twelfth year of Josiah's rule. These factors indicate that Zephaniah's ministry likely occurred around 630 B.C. This would make him a contemporary of Jeremiah and Habakkuk, who also prophesied during the final years of the southern kingdom.

Josiah's righteous reign came after fifty-five years of wicked rule by Manasseh and Amon (2 Chronicles 33). Josiah took the throne when he was only eight years old and turned from the ways of his father and grandfather when he was sixteen, walking in the ways of God like David (2 Chronicles 34:2, 3). He began to purge Judah of its idols in 628 B.C., breaking carved images like the Asherah poles, demolishing the altars to the god Baal, and burning the bones of priests for other gods on their altars (2 Chronicles 34:3–7). After Hilkiah the priest discovered the book of the law in 622 B.C., Josiah led Judah in a renewal of the covenant and the celebration of the Passover (2 Chronicles 34:14—35:19). While Josiah was greater than any other king in the southern kingdom in his obedience to the law of Moses (see 2 Kings 23:25), even he was not able to save Judah from its coming destruction. After Josiah's death in battle (2 Chronicles 35:20–27), Judah returned to idolatry. The Babylonians destroyed Jerusalem in 586 B.C.

Author

Zephaniah's list of his ancestry to the fourth generation is unusual among the prophets, as other prophets only list one generation (Isaiah 1:1; Jeremiah 1:1; Ezekiel 1:3; Hosea 1:1; Joel 1:1) or two generations (Zechariah 1:1) at the most. The reason for Zephaniah's root tracing stems from the fact that Zephaniah's great-great-grandfather Hizkiah is the same as King Hezekiah of Judah, making Zephaniah the only prophet with royal ancestry. A connection to the leaders of Judah would fit Zephaniah's interest in discussing the sins of the leaders (1:8, 11–13; 3:3, 4) and familiarity with Jerusalem, the capital city (see 1:9, 10; 3:1–7). Zephaniah probably lived in Jerusalem, calling it "this place" (1:4), and may have had access to the court of King Josiah, perhaps influencing the king to make his religious reforms.

Meaning of the Name

The Hebrew name *Tsephan-yah* means "Yahweh Hides" or "Yahweh Has Hidden." Such a meaning may reflect the fact that God "hid" Zephaniah from the wickedness that prevailed

at the time of his birth during the ungodly rule of Manasseh. *Sophnonias* is the title in the Greek and Latin translations.

Christ in Zephaniah

There are no direct messianic prophecies in Zephaniah. The great promises of 3:9–20 find fulfillment in Jesus, as He gathers up the faithful and defeats their enemies, with the whole earth confessing that Jesus is Lord (Philippians 2:9–11). The apostle Paul mentions "the day of the Lord" (described by Zephaniah), but calls it "the day of our Lord Jesus Christ" (1 Corinthians 1:8), noting that it is a day of judgment (Romans 2:16) and rejoicing (Philippians 2:16; 2 Timothy 4:8). When discussing the day of the Lord, Jesus twice alludes to the images of Zephaniah (compare Zephaniah 1:3 with Matthew 13:41, and Zephaniah 1:15 with Matthew 24:29). "The day of the Lord" is the day when God's ire is poured upon nations and the world. When a nation delves so deeply into iniquity that it passes the point of no return, God's final judgment is declared. The biblical "days of the Lord" pronounced upon Israel (Amos 5:18), Judah and Jerusalem (Lamentations 2:22; Ezekiel 13:5; Zephaniah 1:7, 14, 18; 2:2, 3; Zechariah 14:1), Babylon (Isaiah 13:6, 9), Egypt (Jeremiah 46:10; Ezekiel 30:3), Edom and the heathen in general (Obadiah 15) symbolize the greater day of the Lord's judgment yet to come upon the entire world (1 Thessalonians 5:2; 2 Peter 3:10).

Overview

The structure of Zephaniah reveals this emphasis on judgment for sin and joyful restoration that will occur on the day of the Lord. Zephaniah can be divided into two sections:

(1) *Zephaniah 1:1—3:8, Judgment:* Like other prophets (see Isaiah 2:11, 17, 20; Joel 1:15; 2:2; Amos 5:18; 8:9), Zephaniah discusses "the day of the Lord" (1:7–11, 14–18; 2:2). Zephaniah shifts back and forth from discussing judgment on Judah to all the nations of the earth (1:1–3; 2:4–15) to judgment on Judah (1:4—2:3; 3:1–7), and calls Judah to repentance (2:1–3).

(2) *Zephaniah 3:9–20, Salvation:* God has shown His power in the past and will do so again in the future (3:1–15), which gives the prophet confidence even while living through the turbulent last days of the nation of Judah (3:16–19). Zephaniah describes the future blessings of people from all nations (3:9, 10) and the remnant of Judah (3:11–20).

Unlocking Zephaniah

KEY PEOPLE:
Hezekiah, Josiah, the people of Judah

KEY EVENT:
The day of the Lord

KEY PHRASE:
Day of the Lord, which describes an immediate day of judgment for Judah and all the nations as well as a future day when God will judge not only the wicked but also will bless people from all nations (3:9, 10).

KEY VERSE:
"I will also leave in the midst of thee an afflicted and poor people, and they shall trust in the name of the LORD. The remnant of Israel shall not do iniquity, nor speak lies; neither shall a deceitful tongue be found in their mouth: for they shall feed and lie down, and none shall make them afraid" (Zephaniah 3:12, 13).

KEY CHAPTER:
Zephaniah 3, as this chapter features vivid descriptions of the judgment (3:1–8) and restoration that will come on the day of the Lord (3:9–20), in accordance with God's covenant with Israel. Zephaniah 3:17 provides a compelling picture of the love God has for His people: "The LORD thy God in the midst of thee is mighty; he will save, he will rejoice over thee with joy; he will rest in his love, he will joy over thee with singing."

The Lord Will Judge the Earth

1 The word of the LORD which came unto Zephaniah the son of Cushi, the son of Gedaliah, the son of Amariah, the son of Hizkiah, in the days of Josiah the son of Amon, king of Judah.   2 Chr. 34

1:1 More Warnings

Habakkuk was not the only one through whom was given a message of bright hope and of future triumph as well as of present judgment. During the reign of Josiah the word of the Lord came to Zephaniah, specifying plainly the results of continued apostasy, and calling the attention of the true church to the glorious prospect beyond. His prophecies of impending judgment upon Judah apply with equal force to the judgments that are to fall upon an impenitent world at the time of the second advent of Christ. *PK 389*

2 I will utterly consume all *things* from off the land, saith the LORD.   2 Kin. 22:16-17
3 I will consume man and beast; I will consume the fowls of the heaven, and the fishes of the sea, and the stumblingblocks with the wicked; and I will cut off man from off the land, saith the LORD.   Ezek. 7:19

The Lord Will Judge Judah

4 I will also stretch out mine hand upon Judah, and upon all the inhabitants of Jerusalem; and I will cut off the remnant of Baal from this place, *and* the name of the Chemarims with the priests;   Hos. 10:5
5 And them that worship the host of heaven upon the housetops; and them that worship *and* that swear by the LORD, and that swear by Malcham;   1 Kin. 11:33
6 And them that are turned back from the LORD; and *those* that have not sought the LORD, nor enquired for him.   Is. 1:4
7 Hold thy peace at the presence of the Lord GOD: for the day of the LORD *is* at hand: for the LORD hath prepared a sacrifice, he hath bid his guests.   Is. 34:6; Jer. 46:10; Hab. 2:20
8 And it shall come to pass in the day of the LORD's sacrifice, that I will punish the princes, and the king's children, and all such as are clothed with strange apparel.   Is. 24:21
9 In the same day also will I punish all those that leap on the threshold, which fill their masters' houses with violence and deceit.   1 Sam. 5:5
10 And it shall come to pass in that day, saith the LORD, *that there shall be* the noise of a cry from the fish gate, and an howling from the second, and a great crashing from the hills.   2 Kin. 22:14; 2 Chr. 33:14; Neh. 3:3
11 Howl, ye inhabitants of Maktesh, for all the merchant people are cut down; all they that bear silver are cut off.   James 5:1
12 And it shall come to pass at that time, *that* I will search Jerusalem with candles, and punish the men that are settled on their lees: that say in their heart, The LORD will not do good, neither will he do evil.   Jer. 48:11; Ezek. 8:12
13 Therefore their goods shall become a ᵀbooty, and their houses a desolation: they shall also build houses, but not inhabit *them*; and they shall plant vineyards, but not drink the wine thereof.   Deut. 28:30; Amos 5:11 ◆ *plunder*

The Day of the Lord

14 The great day of the LORD *is* near, *it is* near, and hasteth greatly, *even* the voice of the day of the LORD: the mighty man shall cry there bitterly.   Ezek. 7:12; Joel 2:11; Zeph. 1:7
15 That day *is* a day of wrath, a day of trouble

God Will Use All if They Will Surrender

Zephaniah 1:14

In this closing work of the gospel there is a vast field to be occupied; and, more than ever before, the work is to enlist helpers from the common people. Both the youth and those older in years will be called from the field, from the vineyard, and from the workshop, and sent forth by the Master to give His message. Many of these have had little opportunity for education; but Christ sees in them qualifications that will enable them to fulfill His purpose. If they put their hearts into the work, and continue to be learners, He will fit them to labor for Him.

He who knows the depths of the world's misery and despair, knows by what means to bring relief. He sees on every hand souls in darkness, bowed down with sin and sorrow and pain. But He sees also their possibilities; He sees the height to which they may attain. Although human beings have abused their mercies, wasted their talents, and lost the dignity of godlike manhood, the Creator is to be glorified in their redemption. . . .

He will work through those who can see mercy in misery, and gain in loss. When the Light of the world passes by, privilege will be discerned in hardship, order in confusion, success in apparent failure. Calamities will be seen as disguised blessings; woes, as mercies. Laborers from the common people, sharing the sorrows of their fellow men as their Master shared the sorrows of the whole human race, will by faith see Him working with them.

"The great day of the Lord is near, it is near, and hasteth greatly" (Zephaniah 1:14). *Ed 269, 270*

and distress, a day of wasteness and desolation, a day of darkness and gloominess, a day of clouds and thick darkness,   Is. 22:5; Joel 2:2
16 A day of the trumpet and alarm against the fenced cities, and against the high towers.   Is. 2:12-15
17 And I will bring distress upon men, that they shall walk like blind men, because they have sinned against the LORD: and their blood shall be poured out as dust, and their flesh as the dung.   Ps. 83:10
18 Neither their silver nor their gold shall be able to deliver them in the day of the LORD's wrath; but the whole land shall be devoured by the fire of his jealousy: for he shall make even a speedy riddance of all them that dwell in the land.   Ezek. 7:19; Zeph. 1:2-3; 3:8

An Exhortation to Repentance

2 Gather yourselves together, yea, gather together, O nation not desired; 2 Chr. 20:4
2 Before the decree bring forth, *before* the day pass as the chaff, before the fierce anger of the LORD come upon you, before the day of the LORD's anger come upon you. Is. 17:13
3 Seek ye the LORD, all ye meek of the earth, which have ᵀwrought his judgment; seek righteousness, seek meekness: it may be ye shall be hid in the day of the LORD's anger.   Ps. 22:26; 57:1; Amos 5:14-15 ◆ upheld

The Lord Will Judge His People's Enemies

4 For Gaza shall be forsaken, and Ashkelon a desolation: they shall drive out Ashdod at the noon day, and Ekron shall be rooted up.   Amos 1:6-8; Zech. 9:5-7
5 Woe unto the inhabitants of the sea coast, the nation of the Cherethites! the word of the LORD *is* against you; O Canaan, the land of the Philistines, I will even destroy thee, that there shall be no inhabitant.   Josh. 13:3; Ezek. 25:16
6 And the sea coast shall be dwellings *and* cottages for shepherds, and folds for flocks.
7 And the coast shall be for the remnant of the house of Judah; they shall feed thereupon: in the houses of Ashkelon shall they lie down in the evening: for the LORD their God shall visit them, and turn away their captivity.   Zeph. 3:20
8 I have heard the reproach of Moab, and the revilings of the children of Ammon, whereby they have reproached my people, and magnified *themselves* against their border.   Jer. 49:1
9 Therefore *as* I live, saith the LORD of hosts, the God of Israel, Surely Moab shall be as Sodom, and the children of Ammon as Gomorrah, *even* the breeding of nettles, and saltpits, and a perpetual desolation: the residue of my people shall ᵀspoil them,

and the remnant of my people shall possess them.   Deut. 29:23; Is. 11:14; 15 ◆ plunder
10 This shall they have for their pride, because they have reproached and magnified *themselves* against the people of the LORD of hosts.   Is. 16:6; Zeph. 2:8
11 The LORD *will be* terrible unto them: for he will famish all the gods of the earth; and *men* shall worship him, every one from his place, *even* all the isles of the heathen.   Gen. 10:5
12 Ye Ethiopians also, ye *shall be* slain by my sword.   Is. 18
13 And he will stretch out his hand against the north, and destroy Assyria; and will make Nineveh a desolation, *and* dry like a wilderness.   Nah. 3:7
14 And flocks shall lie down in the midst of her, all the beasts of the nations: both the ᵀcormorant and the bittern shall lodge in the upper lintels of it; *their* voice shall sing in the windows; desolation *shall be* in the thresholds: for he shall uncover the cedar work.   Jer. 22:14
15 This *is* the rejoicing city that dwelt carelessly, that said in her heart, I *am*, and *there is* none beside me: how is she become a desolation, a place for beasts to lie down in! every one that passeth by her shall ᵀhiss, *and* wag his hand.   Ezek. 28:2 ◆ whistle

A Sharp Reproof for Jerusalem

3 Woe to her that is filthy and polluted, to the oppressing city!   Jer. 6:6
2 She obeyed not the voice; she received not correction; she trusted not in the LORD; she drew not near to her God.   Ps. 78:22; Jer. 2:30; 5:3
3 Her princes within her *are* roaring lions; her judges *are* evening wolves; they gnaw not the bones till the morrow.   Hab. 1:8
4 Her prophets *are* light *and* treacherous persons: her priests have polluted the sanctuary, they have done violence to the law. Ezek. 22:26
5 The just LORD *is* in the midst thereof; he will not do iniquity: every morning doth he bring his judgment to light, he faileth not; but the unjust knoweth no shame.   Deut. 32:4
6 I have cut off the nations: their towers are desolate; I made their streets waste, that none passeth by: their cities are destroyed, so that there is no man, that there is none inhabitant.
7 I said, Surely thou wilt fear me, thou wilt receive instruction; so their dwelling should not be cut off, howsoever I punished them: but they rose early, *and* corrupted all their doings.   Hos. 9:9

Wait for Israel's Restoration

8 Therefore wait ye upon me, saith the LORD, until the day that I rise up to the prey: for my determination *is* to gather the nations, that I may assemble the kingdoms,

to pour upon them mine ⸆indignation, *even* all my fierce anger: for all the earth shall be devoured with the fire of my jealousy.

9 For then will I turn to the people a pure language, that they may all call upon the name of the LORD, to serve him with one consent.   Ps. 22:27; Is. 19:18; Hab. 2:14

10 From beyond the rivers of Ethiopia my suppliants, *even* the daughter of my dispersed, shall bring mine offering.   Ps. 68:31; Is. 11:11; 18:1

11 In that day shalt thou not be ashamed for all thy doings, wherein thou hast transgressed against me: for then I will take away out of the midst of thee them that rejoice in thy pride, and thou shalt no more be haughty because of my holy mountain.   Is. 54:4

12 I will also leave in the midst of thee an afflicted and poor people, and they shall trust in the name of the LORD. Is. 14:32; 50:10; Nah. 1:7

13 The remnant of Israel shall not do iniquity, nor speak lies; neither shall a deceitful tongue be found in their mouth: for they shall feed and lie down, and none shall make *them* afraid.   Mic. 4:7; Zeph. 2:7; Rev. 14:5

Rejoice at the People's Salvation

14 Sing, O daughter of Zion; shout, O Israel; be glad and rejoice with all the heart, O daughter of Jerusalem.   Is. 12:6

15 The LORD hath taken away thy judgments, he hath cast out thine enemy: the king of Israel, *even* the LORD, *is* in the midst of thee: thou shalt not see evil any more.   Is. 51:22

16 In that day it shall be said to Jerusalem, Fear thou not: *and to* Zion, Let not thine hands be slack.   Is. 35:3-4; Heb. 12:12

17 The LORD thy God in the midst of thee *is* mighty; he will save, he will rejoice over thee with joy; he will rest in his love, he will joy over thee with singing.   Jer. 32:41

3:17 Joy Over One Sinner That Repents

But He waves them back. Not yet; He cannot now receive the coronet of glory and the royal robe. He enters into the presence of His Father. He points to His wounded head, the pierced side, the marred feet; He lifts His hands, bearing the print of nails. . . . He approaches the Father, with whom there is joy over one sinner that repents; who rejoices over one with singing. Before the foundations of the earth were laid, the Father and the Son had united in a covenant to redeem man if he should be overcome by Satan. *DA 834*

---

18 I will gather *them that are* sorrowful for the solemn assembly, *who* are of thee, *to whom* the reproach of it *was* a burden.   Ps. 42:2-4

19 Behold, at that time I will undo all that afflict thee: and I will save her that ⸆halteth, and gather her that was driven out; and I will get them praise and fame in every land where they have been put to shame.   Is. 60:14 ♦ *limps*

20 At that time will I bring you *again*, even in the time that I gather you: for I will make you a name and a praise among all people of the earth, when I turn back your captivity before your eyes, saith the LORD.   Jer. 29:14

THE BOOK OF

HAGGAI

As the old adage goes, "actions speak louder than words." Many claim that obeying God is their greatest priority in life, yet their actions show otherwise. The people of Jerusalem to whom Haggai ministered are perfect examples of people who talk the talk, but don't walk the walk. King Cyrus of Persia had issued a decree allowing Jews to return and rebuild Jerusalem. At first the returning exiles were eager to rebuild Jerusalem and the temple. However, they gave up on this task and sixteen years later, the temple was still not rebuilt (although their houses were, 1:4). Through Haggai, God challenged the people to regain proper priorities and resume work on the temple. Promises also accompany this challenge: God would reward the obedience of the people with blessings that surpass the glory of Israel before the exile (2:6–9, 18–23).

Although a brief book, the message of Haggai is powerful and enduring, reminding Christians of the importance of right priorities. As we continue to walk by faith even through hardships and trials, we can focus on the coming blessings of heaven, which will exceed anything we will experience on earth.

Dates

The book indicates the exact day, month, and year of Darius's reign on which Haggai delivered each message (1:1, 15; 2:1, 10, 18, 20). Remarks made in ancient records concerning astronomical occurrences have allowed scholars to determine the dates of Haggai's preaching August 29, 520 B.C. (1:1), September 21, 520 B.C. (1:15), October 17, 520 B.C. (2:1), and December 18, 520 B.C. (2:10, 20). Zechariah's contemporaneous ministry began between Haggai's second and third messages. Therefore, Haggai ministered during the period when the Jews returned to Jerusalem after being exiled to Babylon, challenging and encouraging this group of returnees to rebuild the temple in Jerusalem.

The decree issued by Cyrus of Persia permitting Jews to return to Jerusalem and rebuild the temple (Ezra 1:2–4; 6:3–5) did not result in a second golden age of Israel. During the fifty years since the fall of Jerusalem, many of those who remembered Jerusalem had died and numerous Jews had followed the instructions of Jeremiah 29:5–7, becoming prosperous in Babylon. Only fifty thousand Jews chose to leave the comforts of Babylon and return at this time (Ezra 2:64, 65). They quickly discovered a land in shambles and controlled by the poor people the Babylonians had left to tend the land (Jeremiah 52:16).

While the returning exiles began work on a new temple, laying its foundations in 536 B.C. (Ezra 3:8–11), the inferiority of the new temple as compared to the old temple (Ezra 3:12, 13) and opposition from the Samaritans (Ezra 4—6), caused them to cease their labors in 534 B.C. In reality, the people used these situations as excuses, neglecting work on the temple while they built new homes for themselves (Haggai 1:2–4). Ironically, the focus on rebuilding their own homes led to poverty rather than prosperity (1:6, 10, 11; 2:17). Only when Haggai and Zechariah called the people to resume work on the temple in 520 B.C., two years after Darius I of Persia assumed the throne, did the people recommence the project (Ezra 4:24—5:2). Under the leadership of Zerubbabel the governor and Joshua the high priest, the people would complete the rebuilding project in 516 B.C. (Ezra 6:15). This new temple, however, lacked some of the important features of the first temple. The Talmud states the major item that this temple lacked was the ark of the covenant, the Shekinah glory, and the Urim and Thummim.

Author

Ezra 5:1 and 6:14 speak of a Haggai who ministered with Zechariah to encourage the people of Jerusalem to rebuild the temple. This book contains the messages that this prophet delivered to the people, listing Haggai's name nine times (1:1, 3, 12, 13; 2:1, 10, 13, 14, 20). Haggai was one of the Jews who returned to Jerusalem under the leadership of Zerubbabel. Some believe Haggai to be an aged man having lived in Jerusalem before its fall in 586 B.C., thereby he would have remembered the first temple (2:3). Whether or not this is true, he is considered to be a link between the new and the old temples.

The Hebrew name *Haggay* ("Festal" or "Festive") has an unknown etymology but likely originates from the word *hag*, which means "festival," and could be an abbreviation of *haggiah* ("festival of Yahweh"). His name may indicate that Haggai was born during a festival, possibly the Feast of Tabernacles since Haggai's second message occurs during this feast (2:1). This book is called *Aggaios* in Greek and *Aggaeus* in Latin.

Christ in Haggai

With the arrival of Jesus, the promise of Haggai 2:9 finds fulfillment, as Jesus brought the glory of God (Hebrews 1:3) and peace into the temple rebuilt during the time of Haggai and extravagantly expanded by Herod the Great. The promise to Zerubbabel in 2:23 also points to Christ, as Zerubbabel was from the line of David and an ancestor of Jesus (Matthew 1:12, 13). The Second Advent of Christ will bring about the judgment and cosmological change in God's promise to "shake the heavens and the earth" and "overthrow the throne of kingdoms" (Haggai 2:21, 22).

Overview

The book consists of Haggai's four sermons, calling for the people to resume construction of the temple after a period of neglect.

(1) *Haggai 1:1–15, Completing the Work:* Haggai confronts the feeble excuses that the people use to rationalize their neglect of the temple, pointing to the poverty that has come upon the land as the reason the temple is still in ruins. The people heed the call of Haggai and restart work on the temple (1:12–15).

(2) *Haggai 2:1–9, Exceeding the Glory:* After noting that the new temple pales in comparison to the first temple, God promises that the glory of the new temple will exceed the glory of the first temple. Christ fulfills this prophecy when He enters the temple (Malachi 3:1; John 2:13–16) that is often called Herod's Temple (Luke 3:1; John 2:20).

(3) *Haggai 2:10–19, Awaiting the Blessings:* Obedience in rebuilding the temple brings blessings just as disobedience in neglecting the temple had brought curses.

(4) *Haggai 2:20–23, Reversing the Curse:* An assurance of restoration for the house of David through Zerubbabel's leadership brings the book of Haggai to a close. Prior demonstrations of God's power, such as the shaking of the earth at Mt. Sinai, reveal that God can and will exercise his authority over all people who counter His will by overthrowing their dominion. God's people are of such great importance to Him that He will not leave any one of His truehearted chosen nation to struggle alone to be ultimately overcome.

Unlocking Haggai

KEY PEOPLE:
Haggai, Zerubbabel, Joshua the high priest, King Darius I, the Jews living in Jerusalem

KEY EVENT:
Construction of the second temple

KEY PHRASE:
Rebuilding the Temple, as the message of Haggai revolves around the call to rebuild the temple and the present and future blessings tied to obeying this command.

KEY VERSES:
"Thus saith the LORD of hosts; Consider your ways. Go up to the mountain, and bring wood, and build the house; and I will take pleasure in it, and I will be glorified, saith the LORD" (Haggai 1:7, 8).

"And I will shake all nations, and the desire of all nations shall come: and I will fill this house with glory, saith the LORD of hosts. The silver is mine, and the gold is mine, saith the LORD of hosts. The glory of this latter house shall be greater than of the former, saith the LORD of hosts: and in this place will I give peace, saith the LORD of hosts" (Haggai 2:7–9).

KEY CHAPTER:
Haggai 2, which gives powerful images of the coming splendor of the new temple, the blessings that come upon obeying the call to rebuild the temple, and the promise of judgment through the Messiah.

A Call to Rebuild the Lord's House

1 In the second year of Darius the king, in the sixth month, in the first day of the month, came the word of the LORD by Haggai the prophet unto Zerubbabel the son of Shealtiel, governor of Judah, and to Joshua the son of Josedech, the high priest, saying,
                                          Ezra 2:2; 3:2, 8
2 Thus speaketh the LORD of hosts, saying, This people say, The time is not come, the time that the LORD's house should be built.

1:2 Hope in a Dark Hour

But even this dark hour was not without hope for those whose trust was in God. The prophets Haggai and Zechariah were raised up to meet the crisis. In stirring testimonies these appointed messengers revealed to the people the cause of their troubles. . . . Had the Israelites honored God, had they shown Him due respect and courtesy, by making the building of His house their first work, they would have invited His presence and blessing. *PK 573, 574*

---

3 Then came the word of the LORD by Haggai the prophet, saying,   Ezra 5:1
4 *Is it* time for you, O ye, to dwell in your cieled houses, and this house *lie* waste?
5 Now therefore thus saith the LORD of hosts; Consider your ways.   Lam. 3:40

1:4–6 Consider Your Ways

"Now therefore thus saith the Lord of hosts; Consider your ways" (Haggai 1:5). Why have you done so little? Why do you feel concern for your own buildings and unconcern for the Lord's building? Where is the zeal you once felt for the restoration of the Lord's house? What have you gained by serving self? The desire to escape poverty has led you to neglect the temple, but this neglect has brought upon you that which you feared. *PK 574*

---

6 Ye have sown much, and bring in little; ye eat, but ye have not enough; ye drink, but ye are not filled with drink; ye clothe you, but there is none warm; and he that earneth wages earneth wages *to put it* into a bag with holes.   Hag. 2:16
7 Thus saith the LORD of hosts; Consider your ways.   Hag. 1:5
8 Go up to the mountain, and bring wood, and build the house; and I will take pleasure in it, and I will be glorified, saith the LORD.   Ps. 132:13-14; Hag. 2:7
9 Ye looked for much, and, lo, *it came* to little; and when ye brought *it* home, I did blow upon it. Why? saith the LORD of hosts. Because of mine house that *is* waste, and ye run every man unto his own house.   Is. 40:7; Hag. 1:4, 6
10 Therefore the heaven over you is ᵀstayed from dew, and the earth is stayed *from* her fruit.   Lev. 26:19 ◆ *held back*
11 And I called for a drought upon the land, and upon the mountains, and upon the corn, and upon the new wine, and upon the oil, and upon *that* which the ground bringeth forth, and upon men, and upon cattle, and upon all the labour of the hands.   Deut. 28:22; 1 Kin. 17:1

The Work on God's House Resumes

12 Then Zerubbabel the son of Shealtiel, and Joshua the son of Josedech, the high priest, with all the remnant of the people, obeyed the voice of the LORD their God, and the words of Haggai the prophet, as the LORD their God had sent him, and the people did fear before the LORD.   Is. 50:10
13 Then spake Haggai the LORD's messenger in the LORD's message unto the people, saying, I *am* with you, saith the LORD.   Ps. 46:11
14 And the LORD stirred up the spirit of Zerubbabel the son of Shealtiel, governor of Judah, and the spirit of Joshua the son of Josedech, the high priest, and the spirit of all the remnant of the people; and they came

---

So Little Could Have Been So Much

Haggai 1:9–12

And then, in words that [the Jews] could not fail to understand, the Lord revealed the cause that had brought them to want: "Ye looked for much, and, lo, it came to little; and when ye brought it home, I did blow upon it. Why? saith the Lord of hosts. Because of Mine house that is waste, and ye run every man unto his own house. Therefore the heaven over you is stayed from dew, and the earth is stayed from her fruit. And I called for a drought upon the land, and upon the mountains, and upon the corn, and upon the new wine, and upon the oil, and upon that which the ground bringeth forth, and upon men, and upon cattle, and upon all the labor of the hands" (Haggai 1:9–11). . . .

The message of counsel and reproof given through Haggai was taken to heart by the leaders and people of Israel. They felt that God was in earnest with them. They dared not disregard the repeated instruction sent them—that their prosperity, both temporal and spiritual, was dependent on faithful obedience to God's commands. Aroused by the warnings of the prophet, Zerubbabel and Joshua, "with all the remnant of the people, obeyed the voice of the Lord their God, and the words of Haggai the prophet" (Haggai 1:12). *PK 574, 575*

and did work in the house of the LORD of hosts, their God,   Ezra 5:2; Hag. 1:1; 2:21

15 In the four and twentieth day of the sixth month, in the second year of Darius the king.   Hag. 1:1

Greater Glory for the Second Temple

2 In the seventh *month*, in the one and twentieth *day* of the month, came the word of the LORD by the prophet Haggai, saying,   Hag. 1:1

2 Speak now to Zerubbabel the son of Shealtiel, governor of Judah, and to Joshua the son of Josedech, the high priest, and to the residue of the people, saying,   Hag. 1:1

3 Who *is* left among you that saw this house in her first glory? and how do ye see it now? *is it* not in your eyes in comparison of it as nothing?   Ezra 3:12

4 Yet now be strong, O Zerubbabel, saith the LORD; and be strong, O Joshua, son of Josedech, the high priest; and be strong, all ye people of the land, saith the LORD, and work: for I *am* with you, saith the LORD of hosts: 2 Sam. 5:10; 1 Chr. 28:20; Zech. 8:9

5 *According to* the word that I covenanted with you when ye came out of Egypt, so my spirit remaineth among you: fear ye not.   Ex. 29:45-46; Neh. 9:20; Zech. 8:13

6 For thus saith the LORD of hosts; Yet once, it *is* a little while, and I will shake the heavens, and the earth, and the sea, and the dry *land*;   Is. 10:25

7 And I will shake all nations, and the desire of all nations shall come: and I will fill this house with glory, saith the LORD of hosts.   1 Kin. 8:11

8 The silver *is* mine, and the gold *is* mine, saith the LORD of hosts.   Is. 60:17

2:8

> Managing God's Gifts   See Psalm 24:1.

9 The glory of this latter house shall be greater than of the former, saith the LORD of hosts: and in this place will I give peace, saith the LORD of hosts.   Is. 9:6-7

The Lord Will Bless

10 In the four and twentieth *day* of the ninth *month*, in the second year of Darius, came the word of the LORD by Haggai the prophet, saying,   Hag. 2:20

11 Thus saith the LORD of hosts; Ask now the priests *concerning* the law, saying,   Lev. 10:10-11

12 If one bear holy flesh in the skirt of his garment, and with his skirt do touch bread, or ᵀpottage, or wine, or oil, or any meat, shall it be holy? And the priests answered and said, No.   Lev. 6:27 ◆ stew

13 Then said Haggai, If *one that is* unclean by a dead body touch any of these, shall it be unclean? And the priests answered and said, It shall be unclean.

14 Then answered Haggai, and said, So *is* this people, and so *is* this nation before me, saith the LORD; and so *is* every work of their hands; and that which they offer there *is* unclean.   Prov. 15:8

2:15–19 Efforts and Offerings

A striking illustration of the results of selfishly withholding even freewill offerings from the cause of God was given in the days of the prophet Haggai. . . .

The Lord has ordained that the diffusion of light and truth in the earth shall be dependent upon the efforts and offerings of those who are partakers of the heavenly gift. *PP 527, 528*

---

15 And now, I pray you, consider from this day and upward, from before a stone

---

Temple Glory

Haggai 2:9, 7

This temple was the most magnificent building which the world ever saw. Yet the Lord had declared by the prophet Haggai, concerning the second temple: "The glory of this latter house shall be greater than of the former." "I will shake all nations, and the Desire of all nations shall come: and I will fill this house with glory, saith the Lord of hosts" (Haggai 2:9, 7). . . .

But the second temple had not equaled the first in magnificence; nor was it hallowed by those visible tokens of the divine presence which pertained to the first temple. . . . The Shekinah no longer abode between the cherubim in the most holy place; the ark, the mercy seat, and the tables of the testimony were not to be found therein. No voice sounded from heaven to make known to the inquiring priest the will of Jehovah.

For centuries the Jews had vainly endeavored to show wherein the promise of God given by Haggai had been fulfilled; yet pride and unbelief blinded their minds to the true meaning of the prophet's words. The second temple was not honored with the cloud of Jehovah's glory, but with the living presence of One in whom dwelt the fullness of the Godhead bodily—who was God Himself manifest in the flesh. The "Desire of all nations" had indeed come to His temple when the Man of Nazareth taught and healed in the sacred courts. In the presence of Christ, and in this only, did the second temple exceed the first in glory. *GC 23, 24*

was laid upon a stone in the temple of the LORD: Ezra 3:10; 4:24; Hag. 1:5

16 Since those *days* were, when *one* came to an heap of twenty *measures*, there were *but* ten: when *one* came to the pressfat for to draw out fifty *vessels* out of the press, there were *but* twenty.   Hag. 1:6

17 I smote you with blasting and with mildew and with hail in all the labours of your hands; yet ye *turned* not to me, saith the LORD.   Deut. 28:22; 1 Kin. 8:37; Jer. 5:3

18 Consider now from this day and upward, from the four and twentieth day of the ninth *month, even* from the day that the foundation of the LORD's temple was laid, consider *it*.   Deut. 32:29; Hag. 2:15; Zech. 8:9

19 Is the seed yet in the barn? yea, as yet the vine, and the fig tree, and the pomegranate, and the olive tree, hath not brought forth: from this day will I bless *you*.   Ps. 128:1-5

God's Promise to Zerubbabel

20 And again the word of the LORD came unto Haggai in the four and twentieth *day* of the month, saying,

21 Speak to Zerubbabel, governor of Judah, saying, I will shake the heavens and the earth;   Ezra 5:2

22 And I will overthrow the throne of kingdoms, and I will destroy the strength of the kingdoms of the heathen; and I will overthrow the chariots, and those that ride in them; and the horses and their riders shall come down, every one by the sword of his brother.   Judg. 7:22; Ps. 46:9; Mic. 5:10

23 In that day, saith the LORD of hosts, will I take thee, O Zerubbabel, my servant, the son of Shealtiel, saith the LORD, and will make thee as a ᵀsignet: for I have chosen thee, saith the LORD of hosts.   Is. 42:1; 43:10 ◆ *identifying seal*

THE BOOK OF

ZECHARIAH

The people of Israel had repeatedly heard God's promise to restore them to their homeland and bless them after allowing them to go into exile. The remnant of Jews who returned from Babylon may have expected these promises to be fulfilled immediately upon their return to Jerusalem. Instead, they still lived under foreign rule and experienced economic hardships in the land, waiting for these promises to come true. They stopped rebuilding the temple in part due to these hardships. The prophet Zechariah exhorted them to rebuild the temple by reminding them of the promises still to come through the ministry of the Messiah. These future promises prompted the people to obey God and complete the temple as they waited for the Messiah to come.

The Messiah has come in Jesus, realizing many of the promises and predictions given by Zechariah. Some of the promises of Zechariah await fulfillment. Just as the people of Zechariah's day waited for the Messiah to come, we today can wait expectantly for His second advent, having assurance that God will keep His promises, just as He has done in the past.

Dates

The book contains the messages Zechariah delivered during two different periods. As noted in the Introduction to Haggai, remarks made in ancient records concerning astronomical occurrences have allowed scholars to also determine the dates of Zechariah's preaching. The dates of Zechariah: 1:1—October/November 520 B.C.; 1:7—February 15, 519 B.C., and 7:1—December 7, 518 B.C.

The first eight chapters occur between 520 and 518 B.C. (1:1, 7; 7:1), this makes Zechariah a younger contemporary of Haggai. As noted in Ezra 5:1 and 6:14, Zechariah's ministry at this time focused on encouraging the people to rebuild the temple during the time of Zerubbabel and Joshua the high priest, resulting in the completion of the temple in 515 B.C.

Author

The son of Berechiah and grandson of Iddo (1:1, 7), Zechariah was a priest (Nehemiah 12:16) like the prophets Ezekiel and Jeremiah. His knowledge and concern with the temple may stem from his priestly work (Zechariah 1:16; 6:9–15; 8:9; 14:16–21). Born in Babylon, Zechariah moved to Jerusalem when his grandfather Iddo returned as part of the group of returnees led by Zerubbabel and Joshua the high priest (Nehemiah 12:4). Zechariah's father may have died when he was young, which may be why Zechariah is the "son of Iddo" in Ezra 5:1 and 6:14. The prophet likely was young when he began his ministry in 520 B.C., perhaps being the "young man" addressed in 2:4. In addition to his ministry described in this book as well as Ezra 5:1 and 6:14, Jewish tradition believes that Zechariah was part of the Great Synagogue, which gathered and protected the Old Testament. According to Matthew 23:35, Zechariah was murdered like another Zechariah (2 Chronicles 24:20, 21).

Although some scholars believe different authors wrote chapters 1—8 and chapters 9—14, both Jewish and Christian tradition hold Zechariah to be the author of the whole book, as the differences in style between these sections reflects the different circumstances at the time of each prophecy.

Meaning of the Name

Twenty-nine Old Testament men have the name *Zekar-yah*, which means "Yahweh Remembers" or "Yahweh Has Remembered." This prophet's message shows that God remembers the covenant He made with His people and will bless them. *Zacharias* is the title in the Greek and Latin versions.

Christ in Zechariah

Zechariah is perhaps one of the most messianic of all the prophets. Jesus is described as the humble king riding a donkey (9:9, 10; Matthew 21:5), the Shepherd–King rejected and sold for thirty pieces of silver (11:4–13; Matthew 27:3–10), the one "whom they have pierced" (12:10; John 19:37), and the shepherd who is struck and whose flock scatters (13:7; Matthew 26:31). Among the other messianic images in this book are the "Branch" (3:8; 6:12,

13), the stone with seven eyes (3:9), the King-Priest (6:13), the cornerstone (10:4), and the fountain cleansing the people from sin (13:1). In addition, the text points to the King who conquers all nations and rules over all the earth (12:8, 9; 14:3–9).

While Zechariah ministered at the same time as Haggai, his message goes into more detail than Haggai, particularly concerning the Messiah and the future promises for Jerusalem. Zechariah is the longest of the minor prophets, with the structure of the book emerging from the different forms used to convey his message.

(1) *Zechariah 1—6, Visions from the Lord:* In a series of visions received at night to encourage the people so they understand that God will restore them and judge the Gentile nations (1:7–17; 6:1–8), to show the means by which God plans to fulfill His purpose (1:18–21);to depict the triumph of God's plan (2:1–13); to reveal Christ's power to conquer the accuser of God's people (3:1–10); to empower Zerubbabel to manage the civil leadership and administration of the Jews and Joshua to provide the religious leadership of the nation (4:1–14); to demonstrate how God will deal with those who rebel and refuse to change their ways (5:1–4); to expel sin from the land (5:5–11).

(2) *Zechariah 7—8, The Word of the Lord:* Zechariah uses four messages to respond to the question posed by a delegation from Bethel regarding whether to continue to practice fasts after rebuilding the temple (7:4, 8; 8:1, 18). In these messages, the people are commanded to show mercy and not simply perform rituals (7:8–10, 8:16, 17), noting the judgment that came for ignoring these commands (7:13, 14) and the promise of restoration that will bring blessings to all nations (see 8:13, 20–23).

(3) *Zechariah 9—14, The Burden of the Word of the Lord:* The first burden (9:1) looks to the coming the Messiah and His rejection by the people (9—11), with the second burden (12:1) describing how God will defeat the nations and cleanse His people and the land through the Messiah, who will rule over all the earth (12—14).

KEY PEOPLE:
Zerubbabel, Joshua the high priest, the promised Messiah, the people in Judah after the exile

KEY EVENTS:
Zachariah's visions; construction of the second temple; advent of the Messiah

KEY WORD:
Prepare, as the different parts of the book point to the need for the people to reorient their actions and their hopes in light of the promise of the coming Messiah. This call includes rebuilding the temple and practicing justice and mercy rather than rituals and fasts (chapters 7—8). The fulfillment of the promises God made to His people occurred through the ministry of the Messiah.

KEY VERSE:
"Rejoice greatly, O daughter of Zion; shout, O daughter of Jerusalem: behold, thy king cometh unto thee: he is just, and having salvation; lowly, and riding upon an ass, and upon a colt the foal of an ass" (Zechariah 9:9).

KEY CHAPTER:
Zechariah 14, in which Zechariah paints a beautiful picture of the final result of restoration for God's people, as God will defend Jerusalem on the day of the last battle, judge the nations, receive worship from all nations, and change Jerusalem into a city of absolute holiness.

Zechariah Exhorts the Jews to Repent

1 In the eighth month, in the second year of Darius, came the word of the LORD unto Zechariah, the son of Berechiah, the son of Iddo the prophet, saying, Ezra 4:24–5:1; Neh. 12:4
2 The LORD hath been sore displeased with your fathers. Jer. 44:6
3 Therefore say thou unto them, Thus saith the LORD of hosts; Turn ye unto me, saith the LORD of hosts, and I will turn unto you, saith the LORD of hosts. Is. 31:6; Jer. 3:22; Mal. 3:7
4 Be ye not as your fathers, unto whom the former prophets have cried, saying, Thus saith the LORD of hosts; Turn ye now from your evil ways, and *from* your evil doings: but they did not hear, nor hearken unto me, saith the LORD. 2 Chr. 36:15-16; Ps. 78:8; 106:6-7
5 Your fathers, where *are* they? and the prophets, do they live for ever?
6 But my words and my statutes, which I commanded my servants the prophets, did they not take hold of your fathers? and they returned and said, Like as the LORD of hosts thought to do unto us, according to our ways, and according to our doings, so hath he dealt with us. Deut. 28:15; Jer. 44:28; Lam. 2:17

The Vision of the Horses

7 Upon the four and twentieth day of the eleventh month, which *is* the month Sebat, in the second year of Darius, came the word of the LORD unto Zechariah, the son of Berechiah, the son of Iddo the prophet, saying,
8 I saw by night, and behold a man riding upon a red horse, and he stood among the myrtle trees that *were* in the bottom; and behind him *were there* red horses, speckled, and white. Is. 41:19; Zech. 6:2-7; Rev. 6:4
9 Then said I, O my lord, what *are* these? And the angel that talked with me said unto me, I will shew thee what these *be*. Zech. 4:4-5

10 And the man that stood among the myrtle trees answered and said, These *are they* whom the LORD hath sent to walk to and fro through the earth. Zech. 1:8, 11; 6:5-8
11 And they answered the angel of the LORD that stood among the myrtle trees, and said, We have walked to and fro through the earth, and, behold, all the earth sitteth still, and is at rest. Zech. 1:10
12 Then the angel of the LORD answered and said, O LORD of hosts, how long wilt thou not have mercy on Jerusalem and on the cities of Judah, against which thou hast had indignation these threescore and ten years?
13 And the LORD answered the angel that talked with me *with* good words *and* comfortable words. Is. 40:1-2

1:13 God's Forbearance With Israel

Because Israel had been chosen to preserve the knowledge of God in the earth, they had ever been the special objects of Satan's enmity. . . . While they were obedient, he could do them no harm. . . . Ensnared by his temptations, they had transgressed the law of God and had been left to become the prey of their enemies.

Yet though they were carried as captives to Babylon, God did not forsake them. He sent His prophets to them with reproofs and warnings, and aroused them to see their guilt. When they humbled themselves before God and returned to Him with true repentance, He sent them messages of encouragement, declaring that He would . . . once more establish them in their own land. *PK 582, 583*

14 So the angel that communed with me said unto me, Cry thou, saying, Thus saith the LORD of hosts; I am jealous for Jerusalem and for Zion with a great jealousy. Joel 2:18

Neglect Leads to Lack

Zechariah 1

This was a time of wonderful opportunity for the Jews. The highest agencies of heaven were working on the hearts of kings, and it was for the people of God to labor with the utmost activity to carry out the decree of Cyrus. They should have spared no effort to restore the temple and its services, and to re-establish themselves in their Judean homes. But in the day of God's power many proved unwilling. The opposition of their enemies was strong and determined, and gradually the builders lost heart. . . .

For over a year the temple was neglected and well-nigh forsaken. The people dwelt in their homes and strove to attain temporal prosperity, but their situation was deplorable. Work as they might they did not prosper. The very elements of nature seemed to conspire against them. Because they had let the temple lie waste, the Lord sent upon their substance a wasting drought. . . .

But even this dark hour was not without hope for those whose trust was in God. The prophets Haggai and Zechariah were raised up to meet the crisis. In stirring testimonies these appointed messengers revealed to the people the cause of their troubles. The lack of temporal prosperity was the result of a neglect to put God's interests first, the prophets declared. Had the Israelites honored God, had they shown Him due respect and courtesy, by making the building of His house their first work, they would have invited His presence and blessing. *PK 572–574*

15 And I am very sore displeased with the heathen *that are* at ease: for I was but a little displeased, and they helped forward the affliction.   Is. 54:8

16 Therefore thus saith the Lord; I am returned to Jerusalem with mercies: my house shall be built in it, saith the Lord of hosts, and a line shall be stretched forth upon Jerusalem.   Zech. 4:9

17 Cry yet, saying, Thus saith the Lord of hosts; My cities through prosperity shall yet be spread abroad; and the Lord shall yet comfort Zion, and shall yet choose Jerusalem.   Is. 14:1; 51:3; Zech. 2:12

The Vision of the Four Horns and the Four Smiths

18 Then lifted I up mine eyes, and saw, and behold four horns.

19 And I said unto the angel that talked with me, What *be* these? And he answered me, These *are* the horns which have scattered Judah, Israel, and Jerusalem.   Zech. 1:21

20 And the Lord shewed me four carpenters.

21 Then said I, What come these to do? And he spake, saying, These *are* the horns which have scattered Judah, so that no man did lift up his head: but these are come to ᵀfray them, to cast out the horns of the Gentiles, which lifted up *their* horn over the land of Judah to scatter it.   Ps. 75:4-5 ◆ *scare*

The Lord Will Choose Jerusalem

2 I lifted up mine eyes again, and looked, and behold a man with a measuring line in his hand.   Ezek. 40:3

2 Then said I, Whither goest thou? And he said unto me, To measure Jerusalem, to see what *is* the breadth thereof, and what *is* the length thereof.   Jer. 31:39

3 And, behold, the angel that talked with me went forth, and another angel went out to meet him,   Zech. 1:19

4 And said unto him, Run, speak to this young man, saying, Jerusalem shall be inhabited *as* towns without walls for the multitude of men and cattle therein: Jer. 1:6

5 For I, saith the Lord, will be unto her a wall of fire round about, and will be the glory in the midst of her.   Is. 4:5

2:1–5 God's Care and Assurances

God had commanded that Jerusalem be rebuilt; the vision of the measuring of the city was an assurance that He would give comfort and strength to His afflicted ones, and fulfill to them the promises of His everlasting covenant. His protecting care, He declared, would be like "a wall of fire round about;" and through them His glory would be revealed to all the sons of men. *PK 581*

---

6 Ho, ho, *come forth*, and flee from the land of the north, saith the Lord: for I have spread you abroad as the four winds of the heaven, saith the Lord.   Ezek. 17:21

7 Deliver thyself, O Zion, that dwellest *with* the daughter of Babylon.   Is. 48:20

8 For thus saith the Lord of hosts; After the glory hath he sent me unto the nations which spoiled you: for he that toucheth you toucheth the ᵀapple of his eye.   Ps. 17:8 ◆ *pupil*

2:8 God Will Deal With Wrongdoers

For the child also who is quick to resent injuries, faith has precious lessons. The disposition to resist evil or to avenge wrong is often prompted by a keen sense of justice and an active, energetic spirit. Let such a child be taught that God is the eternal guardian of right. He has a tender care for the beings whom He has so loved as to give His dearest Beloved to save. He will deal with every wrongdoer. *Ed 256, 257*

---

9 For, behold, I will shake mine hand upon them, and they shall be a ᵀspoil to their servants: and ye shall know that the Lord of hosts hath sent me.   Is. 14:2 ◆ *plunder*

10 Sing and rejoice, O daughter of Zion: for, lo, I come, and I will dwell in the midst of thee, saith the Lord.   Lev. 26:12; Zech. 8:3; 9:9

11 And many nations shall be joined to the Lord in that day, and shall be my people: and I will dwell in the midst of thee, and thou shalt know that the Lord of hosts hath sent me unto thee.

12 And the Lord shall inherit Judah his portion in the holy land, and shall choose Jerusalem again.   Deut. 32:9; Jer. 10:16; Zech. 1:17

13 Be silent, O all flesh, before the Lord: for he is raised up out of his holy habitation.

The Lord Will Send His Servant

3 And he shewed me Joshua the high priest standing before the angel of the Lord, and Satan standing at his right hand to resist him.   Ps. 109:6; Hag. 1:1; Zech. 6:11

2 And the Lord said unto Satan, The Lord rebuke thee, O Satan; even the Lord that hath chosen Jerusalem rebuke thee: *is* not this a brand plucked out of the fire? Amos 4:11; Jude 9

3 Now Joshua was clothed with filthy garments, and stood before the angel.   Is. 64:6

4 And he answered and spake unto those that stood before him, saying, Take away the filthy garments from him. And unto him he said, Behold, I have caused thine iniquity to pass from thee, and I will clothe thee with change of ᵀraiment.   Is. 61:10 ◆ *clothing*

5 And I said, Let them set a fair ᵀmitre upon his head. So they set a fair mitre upon his

head, and clothed him with garments. And the angel of the LORD stood by. Ex. 29:6 ◆ *turban*

> ### 3:4 Our Father's Love
>
> Arise and go to your Father. He will meet you a great way off. If you take even one step toward Him in repentance, He will hasten to enfold you in His arms of infinite love. His ear is open to the cry of the contrite soul. The very first reaching out of the heart after God is known to Him. . . .
>
> Your heavenly Father will take from you the garments defiled by sin. COL 206

6 And the angel of the LORD protested unto Joshua, saying, Zech. 3:1
7 Thus saith the LORD of hosts; If thou wilt walk in my ways, and if thou wilt keep my charge, then thou shalt also judge my house, and shalt also keep my courts, and I will give thee places to walk among these that stand by. Gen. 26:5
8 Hear now, O Joshua the high priest, thou, and thy fellows that sit before thee: for they *are* men wondered at: for, behold, I will bring forth my servant the BRANCH. Is. 11:1; Jer. 23:5
9 For behold the stone that I have laid before Joshua; upon one stone *shall be* seven eyes: behold, I will engrave the graving thereof, saith the LORD of hosts, and I will remove the iniquity of that land in one day. Is. 28:16
10 In that day, saith the LORD of hosts, shall ye call every man his neighbour under the vine and under the fig tree. 1 Kin. 4:25; Is. 36:16

The Lord's House Will be Rebuilt

4 And the angel that talked with me came again, and waked me, as a man that is wakened out of his sleep, Jer. 31:26
2 And said unto me, What seest thou? And

I said, I have looked, and behold a candlestick all *of* gold, with a bowl upon the top of it, and his seven lamps thereon, and seven pipes to the seven lamps, which *are* upon the top thereof: Jer. 52:19; Rev. 1:12; 4:5

> ### 4:2 Golden Oil of Love
>
> It was the golden oil emptied by the heavenly messengers into the golden tubes, to be conducted from the golden bowl into the lamps of the sanctuary, that produced a continuous bright and shining light. It is the love of God continually transferred to man that enables him to impart light. Into the hearts of all who are united to God by faith the golden oil of love flows freely, to shine out again in good works, in real, heartfelt service for God. COL 418, 419

3 And two olive trees by it, one upon the right *side* of the bowl, and the other upon the left *side* thereof. Rev. 11:4
4 So I answered and spake to the angel that talked with me, saying, What *are* these, my lord? Zech. 1:9
5 Then the angel that talked with me answered and said unto me, Knowest thou not what these be? And I said, No, my lord.

> ### 4:6 Christ the Founder of the Church
>
> Human power and human might did not establish the church of God, and neither can they destroy it. Not on the rock of human strength, but on Christ Jesus, the Rock of Ages, was the church founded. . . . God's glorious work, founded on the eternal principles of right, will never come to nought. PK 595, 596

6 Then he answered and spake unto me, saying, This *is* the word of the LORD unto

---

The Accuser—and the Defender

Zechariah 3

In the prophecy of Zechariah is brought to view Satan's accusing work, and the work of Christ in resisting the adversary of His people. . . .

The people of God are here represented as a criminal on trial. Joshua, as high priest, is seeking for a blessing for his people, who are in great affliction. While he is pleading before God, Satan is standing at his right hand as his adversary. He is accusing the children of God, and making their case appear as desperate as possible. He presents before the Lord their evil doings and their defects. He shows their faults and failures, hoping they will appear of such a character in the eyes of Christ that He will render them no help in their great need. Joshua, as the representative of God's people, stands under condemnation, clothed with filthy garments. Aware of the sins of his people, he is weighed down with discouragement. Satan is pressing upon his soul a sense of guiltiness that makes him feel almost hopeless. Yet there he stands as a suppliant, with Satan arrayed against him.

The work of Satan as an accuser began in heaven. This has been his work on earth ever since man's fall, and it will be his work in a special sense as we approach nearer to the close of this world's history. . . .

Every manifestation of God's power for His people arouses the enmity of Satan. Every time God works in their behalf, Satan with his angels works with renewed vigor to compass their ruin. COL 166–168

Zerubbabel, saying, Not by might, nor by power, but by my spirit, saith the LORD of hosts.　　　2 Chr. 32:7-8; Is. 11:2-4; Hos. 1:7

7 Who *art* thou, O great mountain? before Zerubbabel *thou shalt become* a plain: and he shall bring forth the headstone *thereof with* shoutings, *crying*, Grace, grace unto it.

8 Moreover the word of the LORD came unto me, saying,

9 The hands of Zerubbabel have laid the foundation of this house; his hands shall also finish it; and thou shalt know that the LORD of hosts hath sent me unto you.　　Ezra 5:16

10 For who hath despised the day of small things? for they shall rejoice, and shall see the plummet in the hand of Zerubbabel *with* those seven; they *are* the eyes of the LORD, which run to and fro through the whole earth.　　　2 Chr. 16:9; Hag. 2:3; Zech. 3:9

11 Then answered I, and said unto him, What *are* these two olive trees upon the right *side* of the candlestick and upon the left *side* thereof?　　　Zech. 4:3; Rev. 11:4

12 And I answered again, and said unto him, What *be these* two olive branches which through the two golden pipes empty the golden *oil* out of themselves?

13 And he answered me and said, Knowest thou not what these *be*? And I said, No, my lord.　　　Zech. 4:5

14 Then said he, These *are* the two anointed ones, that stand by the Lord of the whole earth.　　　Ex. 29:7

Visions of a Flying Scroll

5 Then I turned, and lifted up mine eyes, and looked, and behold a flying roll.

2 And he said unto me, What seest thou? And I answered, I see a flying roll; the length thereof *is* twenty cubits, and the breadth thereof ten cubits.　　　Zech. 4:2

3 Then said he unto me, This *is* the curse that goeth forth over the face of the whole earth: for every one that stealeth shall be cut off *as* on this side according to it; and every one that sweareth shall be cut off *as* on that side according to it.　　　Ex. 20:15; Is. 24:6; 43:28

5:3 Law Reaches to Secrets and Motives

The righteousness of Christ will not cover one cherished sin. A man may be a lawbreaker in heart; yet if he commits no outward act of transgression, he may be regarded by the world as possessing great integrity. But God's law looks into the secrets of the heart. Every act is judged by the motives that prompt it. Only that which is in accord with the principles of God's law will stand in the judgment. *COL 316*

---

4 I will bring it forth, saith the LORD of hosts, and it shall enter into the house of the thief, and into the house of him that sweareth falsely by my name: and it shall remain in the midst of his house, and shall consume it with the timber thereof and the stones thereof.　　　Lev. 14:34-45

Vision of a Woman in a Basket

5 Then the angel that talked with me went forth, and said unto me, Lift up now thine eyes, and see what *is* this that goeth forth.

6 And I said, What *is* it? And he said, This *is* an ephah that goeth forth. He said moreover, This *is* their resemblance through all the earth.　　　Amos 8:5

7 And, behold, there was lifted up a †talent of lead: and this *is* a woman that sitteth in the midst of the ephah.　　　*weight or sum*

8 And he said, This *is* wickedness. And he cast it into the midst of the ephah; and he cast the weight of lead upon the mouth thereof.

9 Then lifted I up mine eyes, and looked, and, behold, there came out two women, and the wind *was* in their wings; for they had wings like the wings of a stork: and they lifted up the ephah between the earth and the heaven.

10 Then said I to the angel that talked with me, Whither do these bear the ephah?

11 And he said unto me, To build it an house in the land of Shinar: and it shall be established, and set there upon her own base.　　　Gen. 10:10

The Vision of the Four Chariots

6 And I turned, and lifted up mine eyes, and looked, and, behold, there came four chariots out from between two mountains; and the mountains *were* mountains of brass.　　　Dan. 8:22

2 In the first chariot *were* red horses; and in the second chariot black horses;　　Zech. 1:8

3 And in the third chariot white horses; and in the fourth chariot grisled and bay horses.　　　Zech. 1:8; Rev. 6:2, 8

4 Then I answered and said unto the angel that talked with me, What *are* these, my lord?　　　Zech. 1:9

5 And the angel answered and said unto me, These *are* the four spirits of the heavens, which go forth from standing before the Lord of all the earth.　　　Dan. 7:2

6 The black horses which *are* therein go forth into the north country; and the white go forth after them; and the †grisled go forth toward the south country.　Jer. 1:14-15 ◆ *spotted*

7 And the †bay went forth, and sought to go that they might walk to and fro through the earth: and he said, Get you hence, walk to and fro through the earth. So they walked to and fro through the earth. Zech. 1:10 ◆ *brownish-red horses*

8 Then cried he upon me, and spake unto me, saying, Behold, these that go toward the north country have quieted my spirit in the north country.   Ezek. 5:13

Priest and King

9 And the word of the LORD came unto me, saying,   Zech. 1:1
10 Take of *them of* the captivity, *even* of Heldai, of Tobijah, and of Jedaiah, which are come from Babylon, and come thou the same day, and go into the house of Josiah the son of Zephaniah;   Ezra 7:14-16
11 Then take silver and gold, and make crowns, and set *them* upon the head of Joshua the son of Josedech, the high priest;   Ps. 21:3
12 And speak unto him, saying, Thus speaketh the LORD of hosts, saying, Behold the man whose name *is* The BRANCH; and he shall grow up out of his place, and he shall build the temple of the LORD: Is. 4:2; Zech. 3:8

13 Even he shall build the temple of the LORD; and he shall bear the glory, and shall sit and rule upon his throne; and he shall be a priest upon his throne: and the counsel of peace shall be between them both. Ps. 21:5; 110:4
14 And the crowns shall be to Helem, and to Tobijah, and to Jedaiah, and to Hen the son of Zephaniah, for a memorial in the temple of the LORD.   Ex. 12:14
15 And they *that are* far off shall come and build in the temple of the LORD, and ye shall know that the LORD of hosts hath sent me unto you. And *this* shall come to pass, if ye will diligently obey the voice of the LORD your God.   Is. 56:6-8; 60:10; Zech. 3:7

The Words of the Lord's Prophets

7 And it came to pass in the fourth year of king Darius, *that* the word of the LORD came unto Zechariah in the fourth *day* of the ninth month, *even* in Chisleu; Neh. 1:1; Zech. 1:1
2 When they had sent unto the house of God Sherezer and Regemmelech, and their men, to pray before the LORD,   1 Sam. 13:12; Jer. 26:19
3 *And* to speak unto the priests which *were* in the house of the LORD of hosts, and to the prophets, saying, Should I weep in the fifth month, separating myself, as I have done these so many years?   Jer. 52:12-14; Zech. 8:19
4 Then came the word of the LORD of hosts unto me, saying,
5 Speak unto all the people of the land, and to the priests, saying, When ye fasted and mourned in the fifth and seventh *month,* even those seventy years, did ye at all fast unto me, *even* to me?   Zech. 1:12
6 And when ye did eat, and when ye did drink, did not ye eat *for yourselves,* and drink *for yourselves?*   1 Cor. 11:20-21
7 *Should ye* not *hear* the words which the LORD hath cried by the former prophets, when Jerusalem was inhabited and in prosperity, and the cities thereof round about her, when *men* inhabited the south and the plain?   Jer. 17:26

The Cause of Captivity

8 And the word of the LORD came unto Zechariah, saying,

9 Thus speaketh the Lord of hosts, saying, Execute true judgment, and shew mercy and compassions every man to his brother:

10 And oppress not the widow, nor the fatherless, the stranger, nor the poor; and let none of you imagine evil against his brother in your heart.   Ps. 21:11

11 But they refused to hearken, and pulled away the shoulder, and stopped their ears, that they should not hear.   Neh. 9:29; Jer. 8:5

12 Yea, they made their hearts as an ᵀadamant stone, lest they should hear the law, and the words which the Lord of hosts hath sent in his spirit by the former prophets: therefore came a great wrath from the Lord of hosts.   2 Chr. 36:16; Neh. 9:29-30 ◆ hard substance

13 Therefore it is come to pass, that as he cried, and they would not hear; so they cried, and I would not hear, saith the Lord of hosts: Prov. 1:24-28; Is. 1:15; Jer. 11:11

14 But I scattered them with a whirlwind among all the nations whom they knew not. Thus the land was desolate after them, that no man passed through nor returned: for they laid the pleasant land desolate. Deut. 4:27; 28:33

The Restoration of Jerusalem

8 Again the word of the Lord of hosts came to me, saying,

2 Thus saith the Lord of hosts; I was jealous for Zion with great jealousy, and I was jealous for her with great fury.

3 Thus saith the Lord; I am returned unto Zion, and will dwell in the midst of Jerusalem: and Jerusalem shall be called a city of truth; and the mountain of the Lord of hosts the holy mountain.   Zech. 1:16

4 Thus saith the Lord of hosts; There shall yet old men and old women dwell in the streets of Jerusalem, and every man with his staff in his hand for very age.

5 And the streets of the city shall be full of boys and girls playing in the streets thereof.   Jer. 30:19-20

6 Thus saith the Lord of hosts; If it be marvellous in the eyes of the remnant of this people in these days, should it also be marvellous in mine eyes? saith the Lord of hosts.   Jer. 32:17

7 Thus saith the Lord of hosts; Behold, I will save my people from the east country, and from the west country;   Is. 27:12-13

8 And I will bring them, and they shall dwell in the midst of Jerusalem: and they shall be my people, and I will be their God, in truth and in righteousness.   Jer. 4:2; Ezek. 11:20; 36:28

The Jews Are Encouraged to Build

9 Thus saith the Lord of hosts; Let your hands be strong, ye that hear in these days these words by the mouth of the prophets, which were in the day that the foundation of the house of the Lord of hosts was laid, that the temple might be built.   1 Chr. 22:13

10 For before these days there was no hire for man, nor any hire for beast; neither was there any peace to him that went out or came in because of the affliction: for I set all men every one against his neighbour.   Is. 19:2

11 But now I will not be unto the residue of this people as in the former days, saith the Lord of hosts.   Is. 12:1

12 For the seed shall be prosperous; the vine shall give her fruit, and the ground shall give her increase, and the heavens shall give their dew; and I will cause the remnant of this people to possess all these things.   Gen. 27:28

13 And it shall come to pass, that as ye were a curse among the heathen, O house of Judah, and house of Israel; so will I save you, and ye shall be a blessing: fear not, but let your hands be strong.   Zech. 8:9

14 For thus saith the Lord of hosts; As I thought to punish you, when your fathers provoked me to wrath, saith the Lord of hosts, and I repented not: Jer. 4:28; 31:28; Ezek. 24:14

15 So again have I thought in these days to do well unto Jerusalem and to the house of Judah: fear ye not.   Mic. 7:18-20; Zech. 8:13

8:4–15 Christ's Purpose Thwarted

But the bright picture of what Jerusalem might have been fades from the Saviour's sight. He realizes that she now is under the Roman yoke. . . .

Christ came to save Jerusalem with her children; but Pharisaical pride, hypocrisy, jealousy, and malice had prevented Him from accomplishing His purpose. . . .

Jerusalem had been the child of His care, and as a tender father mourns over a wayward son, so Jesus wept over the beloved city. How can I give thee up? . . . When the fast westering sun should pass from sight in the heavens, Jerusalem's day of grace would be ended. DA 577, 578

16 These are the things that ye shall do; Speak ye every man the truth to his neighbour; execute the judgment of truth and peace in your gates: Ps. 15:2; Zech. 7:9; Eph. 4:25

17 And let none of you imagine evil in your hearts against his neighbour; and love no false oath: for all these are things that I hate, saith the Lord.   Prov. 3:29

Many Nations Will Come

18 And the word of the Lord of hosts came unto me, saying,

19 Thus saith the Lord of hosts; The fast of the fourth month, and the fast of the fifth, and the fast of the seventh, and the fast of

the tenth, shall be to the house of Judah joy and gladness, and cheerful feasts; therefore love the truth and peace. Jer. 39:2; Zech. 7:5; 8:16

20 Thus saith the LORD of hosts; *It shall yet come to pass*, that there shall come people, and the inhabitants of many cities; Jer. 16:19

21 And the inhabitants of one *city* shall go to another, saying, Let us go speedily to pray before the LORD, and to seek the LORD of hosts: I will go also.   Zech. 7:2

22 Yea, many people and strong nations shall come to seek the LORD of hosts in Jerusalem, and to pray before the LORD. Is. 25:7

23 Thus saith the LORD of hosts; In those days *it shall come to pass*, that ten men shall take hold out of all languages of the nations, even shall take hold of the skirt of him that is a Jew, saying, We will go with you: for we have heard *that* God *is* with you.   1 Cor. 14:25

The Lord Protects His House

9 The burden of the word of the LORD in the land of Hadrach, and Damascus *shall be* the rest thereof: when the eyes of man, as of all the tribes of Israel, *shall be* toward the LORD.   Jer. 49:23-27

2 And Hamath also shall border thereby; Tyrus, and Zidon, though it be very wise.

3 And Tyrus did build herself a strong hold, and heaped up silver as the dust, and fine gold as the ᵀmire of the streets. Josh. 19:29 ◆ *mud*

4 Behold, the Lord will cast her out, and he will ᵀsmite her power in the sea; and she shall be devoured with fire.   Ezek. 26:17; 28:18 ◆ *strike*

5 Ashkelon shall see *it*, and fear; Gaza also *shall see it*, and be very sorrowful, and Ekron; for her expectation shall be ashamed; and the king shall perish from Gaza, and Ashkelon shall not be inhabited.

6 And a bastard shall dwell in Ashdod, and I will cut off the pride of the Philistines.

7 And I will take away his blood out of his mouth, and his abominations from between his teeth: but he that remaineth, even he, *shall be* for our God, and he shall be as a governor in Judah, and Ekron as a Jebusite.

8 And I will encamp about mine house because of the army, because of him that passeth by, and because of him that returneth: and no oppressor shall pass through them any more: for now have I seen with mine eyes.   Is. 52:1

The Lord Sends His King

9 Rejoice greatly, O daughter of Zion; shout, O daughter of Jerusalem: behold, thy King cometh unto thee: he *is* just, and having salvation; lowly, and riding upon an ass, and upon a colt the foal of an ass.   Is. 9:6-7; Jer. 23:5-6

10 And I will cut off the chariot from Ephraim, and the horse from Jerusalem, and the battle

bow shall be cut off: and he shall speak peace unto the heathen: and his dominion *shall be* from sea *even* to sea, and from the river *even* to the ends of the earth.   Is. 60:12; Hos. 1:7; 2:18

9:9 A Triumphant Procession

Five hundred years before the birth of Christ, the prophet Zechariah thus foretold the coming of the King to Israel. . . .

Never before had the world seen such a triumphal procession. . . . No train of mourning captives, as trophies of kingly valor, made a feature of that scene. But about the Saviour were the glorious trophies of His labors of love for sinful man. There were the captives whom He had rescued from Satan's power, praising God for their deliverance. *DA 569, 572*

11 As for thee also, by the blood of thy covenant I have sent forth thy prisoners out of the pit wherein *is* no water. Ex. 24:8; Is. 42:7; 51:14

God's Promises Victory and Defense

12 Turn you to the strong hold, ye prisoners of hope: even to day do I declare *that* I will render double unto thee;   Is. 61:7

13 When I have bent Judah for me, filled the bow with Ephraim, and raised up thy sons, O Zion, against thy sons, O Greece, and made thee as the sword of a mighty man.   Ps. 45:3

14 And the LORD shall be seen over them, and his arrow shall go forth as the lightning: and the Lord GOD shall blow the trumpet, and shall go with whirlwinds of the south.   Ps. 18:14; Is. 21:1; 27:13

15 The LORD of hosts shall defend them; and they shall devour, and subdue with sling stones; and they shall drink, *and* make a noise as through wine; and they shall be filled like bowls, *and* as the corners of the altar.

16 And the LORD their God shall save them in that day as the flock of his people: for *they shall be as* the stones of a crown, lifted up as an ensign upon his land.   Ps. 100:3; Is. 62:3

9:16 How God Saw Humanity

God looked upon humanity, not as vile and worthless; He looked upon it in Christ, saw it as it might become through redeeming love. He collected all the riches of the universe, and laid them down in order to buy the pearl. And Jesus, having found it, resets it in His own diadem. *COL 118*

17 For how great *is* his goodness, and how great *is* his beauty! corn shall make the young men cheerful, and new wine the maids.

The Lord's People Will Be Victorious

10 Ask ye of the LORD rain in the time of the latter rain; *so* the LORD shall make bright clouds, and give them showers of rain, to every one grass in the field.   Is. 30:23

10:1 Early and Latter Rain

Under the figure of the early and the latter rain, that falls in Eastern lands at seedtime and harvest, the Hebrew prophets foretold the bestowal of spiritual grace in extraordinary measure upon God's church. The outpouring of the Spirit in the days of the apostles was the beginning of the early, or former, rain. . . .

But near the close of earth's harvest, a special bestowal of spiritual grace is promised to prepare the church for the coming of the Son of man. *AA 54, 55*

2 For the idols have spoken vanity, and the ᵀdiviners have seen a lie, and have told false dreams; they comfort in vain: therefore they went their way as a flock, they were troubled, because *there was* no shepherd. Ezek. 34:5; Matt. 9:36 ♦ *false prophets* or *magicians*
3 Mine anger was kindled against the shepherds, and I punished the goats: for the LORD of hosts hath visited his flock the house of Judah, and hath made them as his goodly horse in the battle. Zeph. 2:7
4 Out of him came forth the corner, out of him the nail, out of him the battle bow, out of him every oppressor together. Zech. 9:10
5 And they shall be as mighty *men*, which tread down *their enemies* in the ᵀmire of the streets in the battle: and they shall fight, because the LORD *is* with them, and the riders on horses shall be confounded. Hag. 2:22 ♦ *mud*
6 And I will strengthen the house of Judah, and I will save the house of Joseph, and I will bring them again to place them; for I have mercy upon them: and they shall be as though I had not cast them off: for I *am* the LORD their God, and will hear them. Is. 14:1; Zech. 10:12; 13:9
7 And *they of* Ephraim shall be like a

mighty *man*, and their heart shall rejoice as through wine: yea, their children shall see *it*, and be glad; their heart shall rejoice in the LORD. Zech. 9:15
8 I will ᵀhiss for them, and gather them; for I have redeemed them: and they shall increase as they have increased. Is. 5:26; Jer. 33:22 ♦ *whistle*
9 And I will sow them among the people: and they shall remember me in far countries; and they shall live with their children, and turn again. 1 Kin. 8:47-48; Ezek. 6:9; Hos. 2:23
10 I will bring them again also out of the land of Egypt, and gather them out of Assyria; and I will bring them into the land of Gilead and Lebanon; and *place* shall not be found for them. Hos. 11:11
11 And he shall pass through the sea with affliction, and shall ᵀsmite the waves in the sea, and all the deeps of the river shall dry up: and the pride of Assyria shall be brought down, and the sceptre of Egypt shall depart away. Ezek. 30:13 ♦ *strike*

10:11 Heaven's Arches Ring

The pride of Assyria and its fall are to serve as an object lesson to the end of time. . . .

In the day of final awards, when the righteous Judge of all the earth shall "sift the nations" (Isaiah 30:28), and those that have kept the truth shall be permitted to enter the City of God, heaven's arches will ring with the triumphant songs of the redeemed. *PK 366*

12 And I will strengthen them in the LORD; and they shall walk up and down in his name, saith the LORD. Mic. 4:5; Zech. 10:6

Zechariah to Care for the Sheep

11 Open thy doors, O Lebanon, that the fire may devour thy cedars. Jer. 22:6-7
2 Howl, fir tree; for the cedar is fallen;

The Gospel Closes in Power

Zechariah 10

The great work of the gospel is not to close with less manifestation of the power of God than marked its opening. The prophecies which were fulfilled in the outpouring of the former rain at the opening of the gospel are again to be fulfilled in the latter rain at its close. Here are "the times of refreshing" to which the apostle Peter looked forward [Acts 3:19]. . . .

Servants of God, with their faces lighted up and shining with holy consecration, will hasten from place to place to proclaim the message from heaven. By thousands of voices, all over the earth, the warning will be given. . . .

The message will be carried not so much by argument as by the deep conviction of the Spirit of God. The arguments have been presented. The seed has been sown, and now it will spring up and bear fruit. The publications distributed by missionary workers have exerted their influence, yet many whose minds were impressed have been prevented from fully comprehending the truth or from yielding obedience. Now the rays of light penetrate everywhere, the truth is seen in its clearness, and the honest children of God sever the bands which have held them. Family connections, church relations, are powerless to stay them now. Truth is more precious than all besides. Notwithstanding the agencies combined against the truth, a large number take their stand upon the Lord's side. *GC 611, 612*

because the mighty are spoiled: howl, O ye oaks of Bashan; for the forest of the vintage is come down.

3 *There is* a voice of the howling of the shepherds; for their glory is spoiled: a voice of the roaring of young lions; for the pride of Jordan is spoiled.   Jer. 50:44

4 Thus saith the LORD my God; Feed the flock of the slaughter;   Zech. 11:7

5 Whose possessors slay them, and hold themselves not guilty: and they that sell them say, Blessed *be* the LORD; for I am rich: and their own shepherds pity them not.   Jer. 50:7

6 For I will no more pity the inhabitants of the land, saith the LORD: but, lo, I will deliver the men every one into his neighbour's hand, and into the hand of his king: and they shall ᵀsmite the land, and out of their hand I will not deliver *them*.   Jer. 13:14; Mic. 5:8 ♦ *strike*

7 And I will feed the flock of slaughter, *even* you, O poor of the flock. And I took unto me two ᵀstaves; the one I called Beauty, and the other I called Bands; and I fed the flock.   Is. 11:4; Zech. 11:4, 14 ♦ *clubs* or *rods*

8 Three shepherds also I cut off in one month; and my soul lothed them, and their soul also ᵀabhorred me.   Is. 49:7 ♦ *despised*

9 Then said I, I will not feed you: that that dieth, let it die; and that that is to be cut off, let it be cut off; and let the rest eat every one the flesh of another.   Jer. 43:11

10 And I took my staff, *even* Beauty, and cut it asunder, that I might break my covenant which I had made with all the people. Ps. 89:39

11 And it was broken in that day: and so the poor of the flock that waited upon me knew that it *was* the word of the LORD.   Zeph. 3:12

12 And I said unto them, If ye think good, give *me* my price; and if not, ᵀforbear. So they weighed for my price thirty *pieces* of silver.   Gen. 37:28; Ex. 21:32; Matt. 26:15 ♦ *refuse to act*

11:12 Refusing a Priceless Gift

The priests were greatly rejoiced. These leaders of Israel had been given the privilege of receiving Christ as their Saviour, without money and without price. But they refused the precious gift offered them in the most tender spirit of constraining love. They refused to accept that salvation which is of more value than gold, and bought their Lord for thirty pieces of silver. *DA 564*

---

13 And the LORD said unto me, Cast it unto the potter: a goodly price that I was prised at of them. And I took the thirty *pieces* of silver, and cast them to the potter in the house of the LORD.   Acts 1:18-19

14 Then I cut ᵀasunder mine other staff, *even* Bands, that I might break the brotherhood between Judah and Israel.   Is. 9:21 ♦ *apart*

The Example and Curse of a Foolish Shepherd

15 And the LORD said unto me, Take unto thee yet the instruments of a foolish shepherd.   Is. 6:10-12

16 For, lo, I will raise up a shepherd in the land, *which* shall not visit those that be cut off, neither shall seek the young one, nor heal that that is broken, nor feed that that standeth still: but he shall eat the flesh of the fat, and tear their claws in pieces. Jer. 23:2

17 Woe to the idol shepherd that leaveth the flock! the sword *shall be* upon his arm, and upon his right eye: his arm shall be clean dried up, and his right eye shall be utterly darkened.   Jer. 23:1

The Cup of Trembling

12 The burden of the word of the LORD for Israel, saith the LORD, which stretcheth forth the heavens, and layeth the foundation of the earth, and formeth the spirit of man within him. Is. 42:5; 57:16; Jer. 51:15

2 Behold, I will make Jerusalem a cup of trembling unto all the people round about, when they shall be in the siege both against Judah *and* against Jerusalem. Ps. 75:8; Is. 51:22-23

3 And in that day will I make Jerusalem a burdensome stone for all people: all that burden themselves with it shall be cut in pieces, though all the people of the earth be gathered together against it.   Dan. 2:34-35, 44-45; Matt. 21:44

4 In that day, saith the LORD, I will smite every horse with astonishment, and his rider with madness: and I will open mine eyes upon the house of Judah, and will smite every horse of the people with blindness. Deut. 28:28

5 And the governors of Judah shall say in their heart, The inhabitants of Jerusalem *shall be* my strength in the LORD of hosts their God.

6 In that day will I make the governors of Judah like an hearth of fire among the wood, and like a torch of fire in a ᵀsheaf; and they shall devour all the people round about, on the right hand and on the left: and Jerusalem shall be inhabited again in her own place, *even* in Jerusalem. Obad. 18; Zech. 2:4; 8:3-5 ♦ *bundle of cut grain*

7 The LORD also shall save the tents of Judah first, that the glory of the house of David and the glory of the inhabitants of Jerusalem do not magnify *themselves* against Judah.

8 In that day shall the LORD defend the inhabitants of Jerusalem; and he that is feeble among them at that day shall be as David; and the house of David *shall be* as God, as the angel of the LORD before them.   Mic. 7:8

The Repentance of Jerusalem

9 And it shall come to pass in that day, *that* I will seek to destroy all the nations that come against Jerusalem.

12:8 Results of Pentecost

12:8 Results of Pentecost

What was the result of the outpouring of the Spirit on the Day of Pentecost? The glad tidings of a risen Saviour were carried to the uttermost parts of the inhabited world. As the disciples proclaimed the message of redeeming grace, hearts yielded to the power of this message. The church beheld converts flocking to her from all directions. Backsliders were reconverted. Sinners united with believers in seeking the pearl of great price. Some who had been the bitterest opponents of the gospel became its champions. The prophecy [Zechariah 12:8] was fulfilled. *AA 48*

10 And I will pour upon the house of David, and upon the inhabitants of Jerusalem, the spirit of grace and of supplications: and they shall look upon me whom they have pierced, and they shall mourn for him, as one mourneth for *his* only *son*, and shall be in bitterness for *him*, as one that is in bitterness for *his* firstborn. Jer. 6:26; Ezek. 39:29; Rev. 1:7

12:10 Final Triumph Foreshadowed

The triumphal ride of Christ into Jerusalem was the dim foreshadowing of His coming in the clouds of heaven with power and glory, amid the triumph of angels and the rejoicing of the saints. . . . In prophetic vision Zechariah was shown that day of final triumph; and he beheld also the doom of those who at the first advent had rejected Christ. . . . This scene Christ foresaw when He beheld the city and wept over it. *DA 580*

11 In that day shall there be a great mourning in Jerusalem, as the mourning of Hadadrimmon in the valley of Megiddon.   2 Kin. 23:29
12 And the land shall mourn, every family apart; the family of the house of David apart, and their wives apart; the family of the house of Nathan apart, and their wives apart;   2 Sam. 5:14

13 The family of the house of Levi apart, and their wives apart; the family of Shimei apart, and their wives apart;
14 All the families that remain, every family apart, and their wives apart.

False Prophets Will Be Judged

13 In that day there shall be a fountain opened to the house of David and to the inhabitants of Jerusalem for sin and for uncleanness.   Ps. 51:2
2 And it shall come to pass in that day, saith the LORD of hosts, *that* I will cut off the names of the idols out of the land, and they shall no more be remembered: and also I will cause the prophets and the unclean spirit to pass out of the land.   1 Kin. 22:22
3 And it shall come to pass, *that* when any shall yet prophesy, then his father and his mother that begat him shall say unto him, Thou shalt not live; for thou speakest lies in the name of the LORD: and his father and his mother that begat him shall thrust him through when he prophesieth.   Deut. 13:6-11
4 And it shall come to pass in that day, *that* the prophets shall be ashamed every one of his vision, when he hath prophesied; neither shall they wear a rough garment to deceive: 2 Kin. 1:8
5 But he shall say, I *am* no prophet, I *am* an ᵀhusbandman; for man taught me to keep cattle from my youth.   Amos 7:14 ◆ *farmer*
6 And *one* shall say unto him, What *are* these wounds in thine hands? Then he shall answer, *Those* with which I was wounded *in* the house of my friends.

The Death of Christ Foretold

7 Awake, O sword, against my shepherd, and against the man *that is* my fellow, saith the LORD of hosts: smite the shepherd, and the sheep shall be scattered: and I will turn mine hand upon the little ones.   Is. 40:11; Zech. 11:7

Christ the Water of Life

Zechariah 13

The flowing of the water from the rock in the desert was celebrated by the Israelites, after their establishment in Canaan, with demonstrations of great rejoicing. In the time of Christ this celebration had become a most impressive ceremony. It took place on the occasion of the Feast of Tabernacles, when the people from all the land were assembled at Jerusalem. . . .

The Saviour made use of this symbolic service to direct the minds of the people to the blessings that He had come to bring them. . . . The refreshing water, welling up in a parched and barren land, causing the desert place to blossom, and flowing out to give life to the perishing, is an emblem of the divine grace which Christ alone can bestow, and which is as the living water, purifying, refreshing, and invigorating the soul. . . .

The same beautiful and expressive figures are carried throughout the Bible. . . . In David's song His grace is pictured also as the cool, "still waters," amid green pastures, beside which the heavenly Shepherd leads His flock. . . . To Jeremiah, Christ is "the fountain of living waters;" to Zechariah, "a fountain opened . . . for sin and for uncleaness" (Jeremiah 2:23; Zechariah 13:1). *PP 412, 413*

13:7 Our Substitute and Surety

Of the suffering Saviour Jehovah Himself declared through Zechariah, "Awake, O sword, against My Shepherd, and against the Man that is My Fellow" (Zechariah 13:7). As the substitute and surety for sinful man, Christ was to suffer under divine justice. He was to understand what justice meant. He was to know what it means for sinners to stand before God without an intercessor. *PK 691*

8 And it shall come to pass, *that* in all the land, saith the LORD, two parts therein shall be cut off *and* die; but the third shall be left therein.   Ezek. 5:2-4
9 And I will bring the third part through the fire, and will refine them as silver is refined, and will try them as gold is tried: they shall call on my name, and I will hear them: I will say, It *is* my people: and they shall say, The LORD *is* my God.   Ps. 50:15; Is. 48:10; Zech. 10:6

The Destroyers Will Be Destroyed

14 Behold, the day of the LORD cometh, and thy ᵀspoil shall be divided in the midst of thee.   Is. 13:9 ◆ *plunder*
2 For I will gather all nations against Jerusalem to battle; and the city shall be taken, and the houses rifled, and the women ravished; and half of the city shall go forth into captivity, and the residue of the people shall not be cut off from the city.   Is. 13:16
3 Then shall the LORD go forth, and fight against those nations, as when he fought in the day of battle.   Zech. 12:9
4 And his feet shall stand in that day upon the mount of Olives, which *is* before Jerusalem on the east, and the mount of Olives shall cleave in the midst thereof toward the east and toward the west, *and there shall be* a very great valley; and half of the mountain shall remove toward the north, and half of it toward the south.   Is. 64:1-2; Ezek. 11:23; Mic. 1:3-4

14:4 The Chosen Mount

As the place of His ascension, Jesus chose the spot so often hallowed by His presence while He dwelt among men. Not Mount Zion, the place of David's city, not Mount Moriah, the temple site, was to be thus honored. There Christ had been mocked and rejected. . . . The holy Shekinah, in departing from the first temple, had stood upon the eastern mountain, as if loath to forsake the chosen city; so Christ stood upon Olivet. . . . Upon its summit His feet will rest when He shall come again. *DA 829, 830*

5 And ye shall flee *to* the valley of the mountains; for the valley of the mountains shall reach unto Azal: yea, ye shall flee, like as ye fled from before the earthquake in the

days of Uzziah king of Judah: and the LORD my God shall come, *and* all the saints with thee.   Is. 29:6; 66:15-16; Amos 1:1
6 And it shall come to pass in that day, *that* the light shall not be clear, *nor* dark:
7 But it shall be one day which shall be known to the LORD, not day, nor night: but it shall come to pass, *that* at evening time it shall be light.   Is. 30:26

Living Waters

8 And it shall be in that day, *that* living waters shall go out from Jerusalem; half of them toward the former sea, and half of them toward the hinder sea: in summer and in winter shall it be.   Ezek. 47:1-12
9 And the LORD shall be king over all the earth: in that day shall there be one LORD, and his name one.   Eph. 4:5-6
10 All the land shall be turned as a plain from Geba to Rimmon south of Jerusalem: and it shall be lifted up, and inhabited in her place, from Benjamin's gate unto the place of the first gate, unto the corner gate, and *from* the tower of Hananeel unto the king's winepresses.   Josh. 15:32; 1 Kin. 15:22; Zech. 12:6
11 And *men* shall dwell in it, and there shall be no more utter destruction; but Jerusalem shall be safely inhabited.   Rev. 22:3

14:9-11 All Is Finally Restored

The great plan of redemption results in fully bringing back the world into God's favor. All that was lost by sin is restored. Not only man but the earth is redeemed, to be the eternal abode of the obedient. For six thousand years Satan has struggled to maintain possession of the earth. Now God's original purpose in its creation is accomplished. *PP 342*

12 And this shall be the plague wherewith the LORD will ᵀsmite all the people that have fought against Jerusalem; Their flesh shall consume away while they stand upon their feet, and their eyes shall consume away in their holes, and their tongue shall consume away in their mouth.   *strike*
13 And it shall come to pass in that day, *that* a great tumult from the LORD shall be among them; and they shall lay hold every one on the hand of his neighbour, and his hand shall rise up against the hand of his neighbour.
14 And Judah also shall fight at Jerusalem; and the wealth of all the heathen round about shall be gathered together, gold, and silver, and apparel, in great abundance.   Is. 23:18
15 And so shall be the plague of the horse, of the mule, of the camel, and of the ass, and

of all the beasts that shall be in these tents, as this plague. Zech. 14:12

The Remnant Shall Turn to the Lord

16 And it shall come to pass, *that* every one that is left of all the nations which came against Jerusalem shall even go up from year to year to worship the King, the LORD of hosts, and to keep the feast of tabernacles. Is. 60:6-9

17 And it shall be, *that* whoso will not come up of *all* the families of the earth unto Jerusalem to worship the King, the LORD of hosts, even upon them shall be no rain. Jer. 14:4

18 And if the family of Egypt go not up, and come not, that *have* no *rain*; there shall be the plague, wherewith the LORD will smite the heathen that come not up to keep the feast of tabernacles.

19 This shall be the punishment of Egypt, and the punishment of all nations that come not up to keep the feast of tabernacles.

20 In that day shall there be upon the bells of the horses, HOLINESS UNTO THE LORD; and the pots in the LORD's house shall be like the bowls before the altar. Is. 23:18

21 Yea, every pot in Jerusalem and in Judah shall be holiness unto the LORD of hosts: and all they that sacrifice shall come and take of them, and ᵀseethe therein: and in that day there shall be no more the Canaanite in the house of the LORD of hosts. Neh. 8:10 ◆ cook

THE BOOK OF

MALACHI

As the last of the Old Testament prophets, Malachi stands as a bridge between the Old Testament and the New Testament. Nearly a century after Zechariah's thrilling prophecy of limitless possibilities for the Jewish nation, Malachi portrays a dismal view of escalating spiritual degeneration. He issued a familiar call to the people: return to God by following the covenant and God will return to them (3:6–12). If the people heeded Malachi's message, their obedience was short-lived, for they returned to the religious externalism and immorality Malachi denounced.

After speaking through Malachi, God remained silent for the next four hundred years, sending no prophets to Israel. God was not finished with His people, though. At the end of those four hundred years, He sent John the Baptist as the "Elijah" promised by Malachi (4:5, 6) to "prepare the way" of the Lord (3:1; see also Matthew 3:3). When God came to His people in Jesus Christ, He did not bring the judgment promised but called the people once again to repentance and faith, guaranteeing that He would come again in the final day described in Malachi 4:1, 2. Therefore, God's final call did not come through Malachi but through Jesus, the One to whom the Old and New Testaments both testify (Luke 24:25–27, 44; John 5:39, 46).

Dates

Although no dates appear in the book, a number of other markers indicate the time of Malachi's ministry. The prophet mentions sacrifices in the temple (1:7–10; 3:8), indicating that the temple has already been restored. The use of the Persian term for governor (*pechah*) in 1:8 shows that Malachi ministered when Persia controlled Israel (539–331 B.C.); this term also appears in Nehemiah 5:14; Haggai 1:1, 14; 2:21. Malachi rebukes the corruption of the temple and ceremonial law, which are the same criticisms Nehemiah makes when he returns to Jerusalem for his second governorship.

The list of offenses discussed by Malachi are similar to the problems Nehemiah saw when he came to Jerusalem to rebuild its walls in 444 B.C.: corruption within the priesthood (1:6—2:9; Nehemiah 13:1–9); Sabbath breaking (2:8, 9; 4:4; Nehemiah 10:31; 13:15–22); the presence of foreign wives (2:11; Nehemiah 10:30; 13:27, 28); oppression of the poor (3:5; Nehemiah 5:1–13); and a failure to tithe (3:7–12; Nehemiah 10:37–39; 13:10–13). However, the dating of Nehemiah's second term as governor eludes history. His first term spans from 444–432 B.C., at which point Persia recalls him to resume his duties as cupbearer. We are not told when Nehemiah returns the second time. Malachi likely annunciates his prophecies during the time Nehemiah is away in Persia. This leads to 425 B.C. being the approximate time of Malachi's writing.

Author

The Bible nowhere else mentions a prophet named Malachi, and 1:1 does not give the prophet's lineage or hometown. Because of the meaning of the name, some scholars believe that Malachi is a title rather than a name (see 2:7), making the book anonymous and perhaps equating the author with the messenger described in 3:1. However, the messenger of 3:1 will come in the future and other prophetic books also do not identify the prophet's hometown or father's name (see Obadiah 1; Habakkuk 1:1; Haggai 1:1). Therefore, it seems best to view the author as the prophet Malachi. According to a Jewish tradition, Malachi was part of the Great Synagogue, which gathered and protected the Old Testament.

Meaning of the Name

The name *Mal'aki* means "My Messenger" and likely is an abbreviated version of *Mal'aka* ("Messenger of Yahweh"). In addition to Malachi being a messenger of God as a prophet, his message speaks of a coming messenger (2:7; 3:1). Although the Greek Septuagint translates the prophet's name in 1:1 as "by the hand of his messenger," its title is still *Malachias* and *Maleachi* in the Latin Vulgate.

Malachi's message ushered in a period of four hundred years of silence, as there were no prophets between Malachi and John the Baptist. The closing chapters of Malachi point to John the Baptist (3:1; 4:5, 6; also see Isaiah 40:3), who acted as "Elijah" in preparing the way for Jesus' ministry (Matthew 3:3; 11:10–14; 17:9–13). Malachi also speaks of Jesus' ministry (3:2–5), as Jesus came to the temple. However, the promise of judgment awaits Jesus' second coming.

Overview

God commissions Malachi to serve a somber warning to remind the Jews of their past experience as a nation; he calls them to return to God and the mandates of the covenant relationship. Graciously and unwearyingly, one aspect after another of their apostasy is brought within their preview. Every time they refute any blemish.

God still labors to draw out from them some recognition of their past error, so the book consists of a series of disputes (1:2–5; 1:6—2:9; 2:10–16; 2:17—3:5; 3:6–12; 3:13—4:3), in which God makes a statement, the people ask a question, and then God responds. These disputes reveal important truths about God and the people of Israel. God loves His people (1:2), hates divorce and violence (2:16), does not change (3:6), will bless His people when they return to Him (3:10–12), and will punish the wicked and reward the righteous (3:18—4:2).

(1) *Malachi 1:1–5, Dispute about God's Love:* The people doubt God's love (1:2). Through Malachi, God reminds them how He chose them, just as He chose Jacob over his brother Esau.

(2) *Malachi 1:6—3:15, Disputes about God's Desires:* Malachi speaks out against the contempt shown to God's name with improper sacrifices (1:6–14), the rejection of the covenant God made with the priesthood (2:7–9), marriages to foreign women (2:11), divorce (2:16), calling evil "good" (2:17), questioning God's justice (2:17), withholding tithes (3:9), and the cynical belief that it is futile to serve God (3:14). The priests receive a particularly harsh indictment in this book (1:6—2:9).

(3) *Malachi 3:16—4:6, The Day Is Coming:* In spite of the sin of the people, God once again calls them to repentance through Malachi's ministry (4:4), seeking to help them understand the nature of their rebellion and the results it will cause, and promising to send a messenger to prepare the way for the Lord's judgment (3:1–5; 4:5, 6).

Unlocking Malachi

KEY PEOPLE:
Messiah, priests, the people in Judah, the coming messenger

KEY EVENTS:
Future appearance of "Elijah" (John the Baptist) and the Messiah

KEY WORDS:
Return to God, as Malachi confronts those who have turned their back on the covenant of God due to their disillusionment after the prosperity God promised has not come with the return from exile. He gives two reasons to return to obey God: (1) their disobedience is what causes their lack of blessing; and (2) a day of judgment will come when the wicked will be destroyed and the righteous will experience unimaginable blessings.

KEY VERSES:
"Behold, I will send my messenger, and he shall prepare the way before me: and the Lord, whom ye seek, shall suddenly come to his temple, even the messenger of the covenant, whom ye delight in: behold, he shall come, saith the LORD of hosts" (Malachi 3:1).

"Behold, I will send you Elijah the prophet before the coming of the great and dreadful day of the LORD: and he shall turn the heart of the fathers to the children, and the heart of the children to their fathers, lest I come and smite the earth with a curse" (Malachi 4:5, 6).

KEY CHAPTER:
Malachi 3, a chapter where God outlines both the coming judgment (3:1–5, 18) and the promises of blessings when God's people return to obey Him (3:10–13), reminding the people that it is not *futile* to serve God but futile *not* to serve Him (3:14–18).

God's Complaint against Israel

1 The burden of the word of the LORD to Israel by Malachi. Is. 13:1

1:1 Never Forget the Past

This failure to fulfill the divine purpose was very apparent in Malachi's day. Sternly the Lord's messenger dealt with the evils that were robbing Israel of temporal prosperity and spiritual power. In his rebuke against transgressors the prophet spared neither priests nor people. "The burden of the word of the Lord to Israel" through Malachi was that the lessons of the past be not forgotten and that the covenant made by Jehovah with the house of Israel be kept with fidelity. *PK 705*

2 I have loved you, saith the LORD. Yet ye say, Wherein hast thou loved us? *Was* not Esau Jacob's brother? saith the LORD: yet I loved Jacob, Jer. 31:3

3 And I hated Esau, and laid his mountains and his heritage waste for the dragons of the wilderness. Jer. 49:16-18

4 Whereas Edom saith, We are impoverished, but we will return and build the desolate places; thus saith the LORD of hosts, They shall build, but I will throw down; and they shall call them, The border of wickedness, and, The people against whom the LORD hath ᵀindignation for ever. Is. 9:9-10 ◆ *anger*

5 And your eyes shall see, and ye shall say, The LORD will be magnified from the border of Israel.

Unacceptable Sacrifices

6 A son honoureth *his* father, and a servant his master: if then I *be* a father, where *is* mine honour? and if I *be* a master, where *is* my fear? saith the LORD of hosts unto you, O priests,

that despise my name. And ye say, Wherein have we despised thy name? Ex. 20:12; Is. 1:2

7 Ye offer polluted bread upon mine altar; and ye say, Wherein have we polluted thee? In that ye say, The table of the LORD *is* contemptible. Mal. 1:12

8 And if ye offer the blind for sacrifice, *is it* not evil? and if ye offer the lame and sick, *is it* not evil? offer it now unto thy governor; will he be pleased with thee, or accept thy person? saith the LORD of hosts. Deut. 15:21

9 And now, I pray you, ᵀbeseech God that he will be gracious unto us: this hath been by your means: will he regard your persons? saith the LORD of hosts. Jer. 27:18 ◆ *beg*

10 Who *is there* even among you that would shut the doors for ᵀ*nought*? neither do ye kindle *fire* on mine altar for nought. I have no pleasure in you, saith the LORD of hosts, neither will I accept an offering at your hand. Jer. 6:20 ◆ *nothing*

11 For from the rising of the sun even unto the going down of the same my name *shall be* great among the Gentiles; and in every place incense *shall be* offered unto my name, and a pure offering: for my name *shall be* great among the heathen, saith the LORD of hosts. Is. 66:19-20

12 But ye have profaned it, in that ye say, The table of the LORD *is* polluted; and the fruit thereof, *even* his meat, *is* ᵀcontemptible. *worthless*

13 Ye said also, Behold, what a weariness *is it*! and ye have snuffed at it, saith the LORD of hosts; and ye brought *that which was* torn, and the lame, and the sick; thus ye brought an offering: should I accept this of your hand? saith the LORD. Mic. 6:3

14 But cursed *be* the deceiver, which hath in his flock a male, and voweth, and sacrificeth

The Enemy of Best Is Good

Malachi 1:8

The sanctification set forth in the Scriptures embraces the entire being—spirit, soul, and body. Paul prayed for the Thessalonians that their "whole spirit and soul and body be preserved blameless unto the coming of our Lord Jesus Christ" (1 Thessalonians 5:23). Again he writes to believers: "I beseech you therefore, brethren, by the mercies of God, that ye present your bodies a living sacrifice, holy, acceptable unto God" (Romans 12:1). In the time of ancient Israel every offering brought as a sacrifice to God was carefully examined. If any defect was discovered in the animal presented, it was refused; for God had commanded that the offering be "without blemish." So Christians are bidden to present their bodies, "a living sacrifice, holy, acceptable unto God." In order to do this, all their powers must be preserved in the best possible condition. Every practice that weakens physical or mental strength unfits man for the service of his Creator. And will God be pleased with anything less than the best we can offer? Said Christ: "Thou shalt love the Lord thy God with all thy heart" [Matthew 22:37]. Those who do love God with all the heart will desire to give Him the best service of their life, and they will be constantly seeking to bring every power of their being into harmony with the laws that will promote their ability to do His will. They will not, by the indulgence of appetite or passion, enfeeble or defile the offering which they present to their heavenly Father. *GC 473, 474*

unto the Lord a corrupt thing: for I *am* a great King, saith the Lord of hosts, and my name *is* dreadful among the heathen.   Zech. 14:9

The Priests Neglect Their Covenant

2 And now, O ye priests, this commandment *is* for you.   Mal. 1:6

2 If ye will not hear, and if ye will not lay *it* to heart, to give glory unto my name, saith the Lord of hosts, I will even send a curse upon you, and I will curse your blessings: yea, I have cursed them already, because ye do not lay *it* to heart.   Mal. 3:9

3 Behold, I will corrupt your seed, and spread dung upon your faces, *even* the dung of your solemn feasts; and *one* shall take you away with it.   Nah. 3:6

4 And ye shall know that I have sent this commandment unto you, that my covenant might be with Levi, saith the Lord of hosts.

5 My covenant was with him of life and peace; and I gave them to him *for* the fear wherewith he feared me, and was afraid before my name.   Num. 25:12-13

6 The law of truth was in his mouth, and iniquity was not found in his lips: he walked with me in peace and ᵀequity, and did turn many away from iniquity.   Jer. 23:22 ◆ *uprightness*

7 For the priest's lips should keep knowledge, and they should seek the law at his mouth: for he *is* the messenger of the Lord of hosts.   Lev. 10:11; Deut. 17:8-11; Jer. 18:18

8 But ye are departed out of the way; ye have caused many to stumble at the law; ye have corrupted the covenant of Levi, saith the Lord of hosts.   1 Sam. 2:17; Neh. 13:29; Jer. 18:15

9 Therefore have I also made you ᵀcontemptible and ᵀbase before all the people, according as ye have not kept my ways, but have been partial in the law.   Deut. 1:17 ◆ *worthless* ◆ *meek*

The People Break Marriage Vows

10 Have we not all one father? hath not one God created us? why do we deal treacherously every man against his brother, by profaning the covenant of our fathers?   Is. 63:16; 64:8

2:10 No Distinction of Race With God

No distinction on account of nationality, race, or caste, is recognized by God. He is the Maker of all mankind. All men are of one family by creation, and all are one through redemption. Christ came to demolish every wall of partition, to throw open every compartment of the temple courts, that every soul may have free access to God. His love is so broad, so deep, so full, that it penetrates everywhere. . . . In Christ there is neither Jew nor Greek, bond nor free. *PK 369, 370*

---

11 Judah hath dealt treacherously, and an abomination is committed in Israel and in Jerusalem; for Judah hath profaned the holiness of the Lord which he loved, and hath married the daughter of a strange god.   Ezra 9:1-2

12 The Lord will cut off the man that doeth this, the master and the scholar, out of the tabernacles of Jacob, and him that offereth an offering unto the Lord of hosts.

13 And this have ye done again, covering the altar of the Lord with tears, with weeping, and with crying out, insomuch that he regardeth not the offering any more, or receiveth *it* with good will at your hand.

14 Yet ye say, Wherefore? Because the Lord hath been witness between thee and the

---

Christ Returns When the Work Is Accomplished

Malachi 3:1–5

Those who are living upon the earth when the intercession of Christ shall cease in the sanctuary above are to stand in the sight of a holy God without a mediator. Their robes must be spotless, their characters must be purified from sin by the blood of sprinkling. Through the grace of God and their own diligent effort they must be conquerors in the battle with evil. While the investigative judgment is going forward in heaven, while the sins of penitent believers are being removed from the sanctuary, there is to be a special work of purification, of putting away of sin, among God's people upon earth. This work is more clearly presented in the messages of Revelation 14.

When this work shall have been accomplished, the followers of Christ will be ready for His appearing. "Then shall the offering of Judah and Jerusalem be pleasant unto the Lord, as in the days of old, and as in former years" (Malachi 3:4). Then the church which our Lord at His coming is to receive to Himself will be a "glorious church, not having spot, or wrinkle, or any such thing" (Ephesians 5:27). Then she will look "forth as the morning, fair as the moon, clear as the sun, and terrible as an army with banners" (Song of Solomon 6:10).

Besides the coming of the Lord to His temple, Malachi also foretells His second advent, His coming for the execution of the judgment. . . . [See Malachi 3:5.] Jude refers to the same scene when he says, "Behold, the Lord cometh with ten thousands of His saints, to execute judgment upon all, and to convince all that are ungodly among them of all their ungodly deeds" (Jude 14, 15). This coming, and the coming of the Lord to His temple, are distinct and separate events. *GC 425, 426*

wife of thy youth, against whom thou hast dealt treacherously: yet *is* she thy companion, and the wife of thy covenant.   Is. 54:6

15 And did not he make one? Yet had he the residue of the spirit. And wherefore one? That he might seek a godly seed. Therefore take heed to your spirit, and let none deal treacherously against the wife of his youth.   Matt. 19:4-6

16 For the LORD, the God of Israel, saith that he hateth putting away: for *one* covereth violence with his garment, saith the LORD of hosts: therefore take heed to your spirit, that ye deal not treacherously.   Matt. 5:31-32

17 Ye have wearied the LORD with your words. Yet ye say, Wherein have we wearied *him*? When ye say, Every one that doeth evil *is* good in the sight of the LORD, and he delighteth in them; or, Where *is* the God of judgment?   Is. 43:24; Zeph. 1:12; Mal. 2:14

2:17 Beware of Calling Evil Good

By representing the basest of men as in heaven, and highly exalted there, Satan says to the world: "No matter how wicked you are; no matter whether you believe or disbelieve God and the Bible. Live as you please; heaven is your home." . . . Saith the word of God: "Woe unto them that call evil good, and good evil; that put darkness for light, and light for darkness" (Isaiah 5:20). *GC 557*

The Coming Messenger

3 Behold, I will send my messenger, and he shall prepare the way before me: and the Lord, whom ye seek, shall suddenly come to his temple, even the messenger of the covenant, whom ye delight in: behold, he shall come, saith the LORD of hosts.

2 But who may abide the day of his coming? and who shall stand when he appeareth?

for he *is* like a refiner's fire, and like fullers' soap: Zech. 13:9

3 And he shall sit *as* a refiner and purifier of silver: and he shall purify the sons of Levi, and purge them as gold and silver, that they may offer unto the LORD an offering in righteousness.   Ps. 4:5; Is. 1:25; Dan. 12:10

4 Then shall the offering of Judah and Jerusalem be pleasant unto the LORD, as in the days of old, and as in former years. 2 Chr. 7:1-3

5 And I will come near to you to judgment; and I will be a swift witness against the sorcerers, and against the adulterers, and against false swearers, and against those that oppress the hireling in *his* wages, the widow, and the fatherless, and that turn aside the stranger *from his right*, and fear not me, saith the LORD of hosts. Lev. 19:13; Deut. 24:17; 27:19 ◆ *temporary laborer*

6 For I *am* the LORD, I change not; therefore ye sons of Jacob are not consumed.   Num. 23:19

The Importance of Tithing

7 Even from the days of your fathers ye are gone away from mine ordinances, and have not kept *them*. Return unto me, and I will return unto you, saith the LORD of hosts. But ye said, Wherein shall we return?   Zech. 1:3

8 Will a man rob God? Yet ye have robbed me. But ye say, Wherein have we robbed thee? In tithes and offerings.

3:7,8

Managing God's Gifts   See Matthew 23:23.

9 Ye *are* cursed with a curse: for ye have robbed me, *even* this whole nation.   Mal. 2:2

10 Bring ye all the tithes into the storehouse, that there may be meat in mine house, and prove me now herewith, saith the LORD of hosts, if I will not open you the windows of heaven, and pour you out a blessing, that *there shall* not *be room* enough *to receive it*.   Gen. 7:11

3:10

Managing God's Gifts   See Matthew 6:33.

A Real Christian Loves to Give

Malachi 3:7–10

As God's work extends, calls for help will come more and more frequently. That these calls may be answered, Christians should heed the command, "Bring ye all the tithes into the storehouse, that there may be meat in Mine house" (Malachi 3:10). If professing Christians would faithfully bring to God their tithes and offerings, His treasury would be full. There would then be no occasion to resort to fairs, lotteries, or parties of pleasure to secure funds for the support of the gospel.

Men are tempted to use their means in self-indulgence, in the gratification of appetite, in personal adornment, or in the embellishment of their homes. For these objects many church members do not hesitate to spend freely and even extravagantly. But when asked to give to the Lord's treasury, to carry forward His work in the earth, they demur. Perhaps, feeling that they cannot well do otherwise, they dole out a sum far smaller than they often spend for needless indulgence. They manifest no real love for Christ's service, no earnest interest in the salvation of souls. What marvel that the Christian life of such ones is but a dwarfed, sickly existence!

He whose heart is aglow with the love of Christ will regard it as not only a duty, but a pleasure, to aid in the advancement of the highest, holiest work committed to man—the work of presenting to the world the riches of goodness, mercy, and truth. *AA 338, 339*

11 And I will rebuke the devourer for your sakes, and he shall not destroy the fruits of your ground; neither shall your vine cast her fruit before the time in the field, saith the LORD of hosts.

12 And all nations shall call you blessed: for ye shall be a delightsome land, saith the LORD of hosts.   Is. 61:9

13 Your words have been ᵀstout against me, saith the LORD. Yet ye say, What have we spoken *so much* against thee?   Mal. 2:17 ♦ strong

14 Ye have said, It *is* vain to serve God: and what profit *is it* that we have kept his ordinance, and that we have walked mournfully before the LORD of hosts?   Is. 58:3; Zeph. 1:12

15 And now we call the proud happy; yea, they that work wickedness are set up; yea, *they that* tempt God are even delivered. Mal. 4:1

16 Then they that feared the LORD spake often one to another: and the LORD hearkened, and heard *it*, and a book of remembrance was written before him for them that feared the LORD, and that thought upon his name.   Ps. 56:8

3:18 Character Decides Destiny

Sinners who make a pretension of piety mingle for a time with the true followers of Christ, and the semblance of Christianity is calculated to deceive many; but in the harvest of the world there will be no likeness between good and evil. Then those who have joined the church, but who have not joined Christ, will be manifest. . . .

He will judge every man according to his words and his works. Profession is as nothing in the scale. It is character that decides destiny. *COL 74*

---

17 And they shall be mine, saith the LORD of hosts, in that day when I make up my jewels; and I will spare them, as a man spareth his own son that serveth him.   Ex. 19:5

18 Then shall ye return, and discern between the righteous and the wicked, between him that serveth God and him that serveth him not.   Gen. 18:25

4:1 Sin and Sinners Finally Destroyed

Satan, the root of every sin, and all evil workers, who are his branches, shall be utterly cut off. An end will be made of sin, with all the woe and ruin that have resulted from it. Says the psalmist, "Thou hast destroyed the wicked, thou hast put out their name forever and ever. O thou enemy, destructions are come to a perpetual end" (Psalm 9:5, 6). *PP 341*

God's Judgment on the Wicked

4 For, behold, the day cometh, that shall burn as an oven; and all the proud, yea, and all that do wickedly, shall be stubble: and the day that cometh shall burn them up, saith the LORD of hosts, that it shall leave them neither root nor branch.   Is. 5:24

End of Sin/Hell

2 But unto you that fear my name shall the Sun of righteousness arise with healing in his wings; and ye shall go forth, and grow up as calves of the stall.   Is. 30:26

3 And ye shall tread down the wicked; for they shall be ashes under the soles of your feet in the day that I shall do *this*, saith the LORD of hosts.   Job 40:12

The Spirit and Power of Elijah

Malachi 4:5

Today, in the spirit and power of Elias and of John the Baptist, messengers of God's appointment are calling the attention of a judgment-bound world to the solemn events soon to take place in connection with the closing hours of probation and the appearance of Christ Jesus as King of kings and Lord of lords. Soon every man is to be judged for the deeds done in the body. The hour of God's judgment has come, and upon the members of His church on earth rests the solemn responsibility of giving warning to those who are standing as it were on the very brink of eternal ruin. To every human being in the wide world who will give heed must be made plain the principles at stake in the great controversy being waged, principles upon which hang the destinies of all mankind. . . .

In the visions of the prophets of old the Lord of glory was represented as bestowing special light upon His church in the days of darkness and unbelief preceding His second coming. As the Sun of Righteousness, He was to arise upon His church, "with healing in His wings" (Malachi 4:2). And from every true disciple was to be diffused an influence for life, courage, helpfulness, and true healing. . . .

The days of Noah and of Lot picture the condition of the world just before the coming of the Son of man. . . . Not only is Satan leading the world captive, but his deceptions are leavening the professed churches of our Lord Jesus Christ. The great apostasy will develop into darkness deep as midnight. To God's people it will be a night of trial, a night of weeping, a night of persecution for the truth's sake. But out of that night of darkness God's light will shine. *PK 716, 717*

Remember What God Has Done

4 Remember ye the law of Moses my servant, which I commanded unto him in Horeb for all Israel, *with* the statutes and judgments. Deut. 4:10

5 Behold, I will send you Elijah the prophet before the coming of the great and dreadful day of the LORD: Joel 2:31; Mal. 3:1; Luke 1:17

6 And he shall turn the heart of the fathers to the children, and the heart of the children to their fathers, lest I come and smite the earth with a curse. Is. 11:4 ◆ *strike*

THE NEW TESTAMENT

WORDS OF CHRIST IN RED

THE GOSPEL ACCORDING TO

MATTHEW

"The King is coming!" Such an announcement causes a stir of excitement. The chance of seeing royalty incites people to keep their eyes open—it is the experience of a lifetime. Every effort is made to catch a glimpse or, better yet, reach out to touch the potentate.

Matthew's Gospel is the announcement that the King of kings has come. His Gospel bridges the Old Testament and the New Testament, making the connecting link between the prophecies of the coming Messiah and their fulfillment in Jesus Christ. Matthew repeatedly quotes the Old Testament to show that Jesus is the One who was spoken of by the ancient writers. Matthew was a Jewish man writing to a Jewish audience about their promised King. His book is designed to present overwhelming evidence to support that grand confession. Matthew reinforces Jesus' kingship by showing His genealogy, baptism, messages, miracles, death, and resurrection. They all point to the same inescapable conclusion: Jesus is the eternal King promised from ages past.

The Jews, however, are not looking at the grand plan for eternity; they instead seek freedom from their immediate earthly woes—the twofold Roman oppression of Caesar and Herod. The Jews ardently believe that the Old Testament prophecies regarding the Messiah will present them with both a political relief from this foreign tyranny and hold back all nations from ruling over them. Since Christ does not implement these false expectations, national pride prevents them from recognizing Him as the One about whom the ancient prophets have foretold.

Dates

The likely time frame for the writing of this book is A.D. 58–68. The reasons are as follows: The expressions "unto this day" (27:8) and "until this day" (28:15) indicate a substantial period of time between the events in the book and the time they were written down. The Olivet Discourse (chapters 24—25) provides a dual purpose—that of anticipating the destruction of Jerusalem in A.D. 70, and those things to expect during the last days of earth's history.

Author

Matthew, whose name means "Gift of the Lord," was surnamed Levi (Mark 2:14; Luke 5:27). He was the son of Alphaeus (Mark 2:14) and worked as a tax collector in Capernaum for the Roman government—an unpopular profession among the people of Israel. Yet Jesus called Matthew to follow Him. Matthew readily followed, leaving his former life behind. He was known for inviting large groups of people to his home to meet Jesus. Acts 1:13 details his last recorded appearance in the Bible. Tradition provides the only details of his life after this. The early church believed Matthew, the disciple, to be the author of this Gospel.

Meaning of the Name

Kata Matthaion, "According to Matthew," was the title given to this book from earliest times. Obviously other accounts of Jesus' life were circulating at the time, and this title distinguished Matthew's account. The word "gospel," meaning "good tidings," was added later.

Christ in Matthew

Using more Old Testament references and allusions than any other Gospel writer, Matthew reinforces that Jesus is the Messiah the Old Testament prophets predicted and anticipated, presenting Him as Israel's promised messianic King (Matthew 1:23; 2:2, 6; 3:17; 4:15–17; 21:5, 9; 22:43–45; 26:64; 27:11, 27–37). Jesus entered history to bring redemption and deliverance. The first verse succinctly announces the fulfillment of Israel's hope in the coming Christ: "The book of the generation of Jesus Christ, the son of David, the son of Abraham."

Overview

Matthew, Mark, and Luke are known as the synoptic Gospels. *Synoptic* means "seeing together." Matthew, Mark, and Luke have similarities in form, language, and content.

Matthew's Gospel can be outlined as follows:

(1) *Matthew 1:1—4:11, The King Comes:* The genealogy and witness of John the Baptist

prepare the way for the coming of the King—Jesus. Before beginning His ministry, Jesus is baptized and immediately led away to be tempted.

(2) *Matthew 4:12—7:29, The King Proclaims:* The Sermon on the Mount is the most well-known sermon in the Bible. Jesus expounds on the Law of Moses as He discusses kingdom living.

(3) *Matthew 8:1—11:1, The King Acts:* Matthew presents ten miracles as proof of Jesus' identity as the long-awaited Messiah.

(4) *Matthew 11:2—16:12, The King Opposed:* Opposition from the Pharisees and other teachers of the law increases.

(5) *Matthew 16:13—20:28, The King's Disciples Prepared:* As Jesus resolutely heads toward Jerusalem for the suffering that He knows awaits Him, He reminds His disciples that although He will soon die, He will be raised again (16:21). He also instructs them on the cost of discipleship.

(6) *Matthew 20:29—27:66, The King Rejected:* The parable of the vineyard workers (20:1–16) starts the section on the rejection of Jesus, the "the stone which the builders rejected" (Luke 20:17). As Jesus enters Jerusalem in fulfillment of Zechariah 9:9, the triumphal shouts of "Hosanna" (Matthew 21:9) turn to jeers later in the week as the same crowd seeks His crucifixion (27:22, 23). On the cross, Jesus experiences the final phase of rejection: from God the Father (27:46).

(7) *Matthew 28:1—20, The King Vindicated:* Jesus' resurrection marks "paid in full" to the sin problem and authenticates His status as the Savior of the world.

An important literary device used by Matthew are the similar phrases, "when Jesus had ended" or "made an end" or "finished" (7:28; 11:1; 13:53; 19:1; 26:1), which are used to conclude the five key discourses of the book:

(1) The Sermon on the Mount (5:3—7:27)
(2) Instruction of the Disciples (10:5–42)
(3) Parables of the Kingdom (13:3–52)
(4) Terms of Discipleship (18:3–35)
(5) The Olivet Discourse (24:4—25:46)

Matthew also used the phrase "the kingdom of heaven" more than thirty times, a phrase found in no other New Testament book. He often employed the phrase "that it might be fulfilled which was spoken," which does not appear in the other Gospels.

Unlocking Matthew

KEY PEOPLE:
Jesus, Mary, Joseph, John the Baptist, the disciples, the religious leaders, Caiaphas, Pilate, Mary Magdalene

KEY EVENTS:
The five discourses or sermons of Jesus; the miracles of Jesus; the death and resurrection of Jesus

KEY WORD:
King, for Matthew quoted repeatedly from the Old Testament, hoping to prove that Jesus was the Messiah long promised by the Old Testament prophets. As evidence, Matthew includes events like the wise men's discussion of the sign of the birth of a ruler (a star) and the gifts they brought that were fit for a king (see Matthew 2). Tracing a king's genealogy (Matthew 1) also is a way of proving kingship (see also 1 Chronicles 2—9).

KEY VERSES:
"And Simon Peter answered and said, Thou art the Christ, the Son of the living God. And Jesus answered and said unto him, Blessed art thou, Simon Bar-jona: for flesh and blood hath not revealed it unto thee, but my Father which is in heaven. And I say also unto thee, That thou art Peter, and upon this rock I will build my church; and the gates of hell shall not prevail against it. And I will give unto thee the keys of the kingdom of heaven: and whatsoever thou shalt bind on earth shall be bound in heaven: and whatsoever thou shall loose on earth shall be loosed in heaven" (Matthew 16:16–19).

KEY CHAPTER:
Matthew 12 provides a downward turn as the Pharisees reject Jesus as the Messiah. Jesus then focuses on teaching mainly through parables, instructing His disciples, and reminding them that He would soon die and be resurrected.

The Genealogy of Christ from Abraham to Joseph

1 The book of the generation of Jesus Christ, the son of David, the son of Abraham.   Gen. 22:18; Is. 11:1; Rom. 1:3

2 Abraham ᵀbegat Isaac; and Isaac begat Jacob; and Jacob begat Judas and his brethren;   Gen. 25:26 ◆ *brought forth*

3 And Judas begat Phares and Zara of Thamar; and Phares begat Esrom; and Esrom begat Aram;   Gen. 46:12

4 And Aram begat Aminadab; and Aminadab begat Naasson; and Naasson begat Salmon;

5 And Salmon begat Booz of Rachab; and Booz begat Obed of Ruth; and Obed begat Jesse;   Heb. 11:31

6 And Jesse begat David the king; and David the king begat Solomon of her *that had been the wife* of Urias;   1 Sam. 16:1

7 And Solomon begat Roboam; and Roboam begat Abia; and Abia begat Asa;

8 And Asa begat Josaphat; and Josaphat begat Joram; and Joram begat Ozias;   1 Chr. 3:11

9 And Ozias begat Joatham; and Joatham begat Achaz; and Achaz begat Ezekias;

10 And Ezekias begat Manasses; and Manasses begat Amon; and Amon begat Josias;

11 And Josias begat Jechonias and his brethren, about the time they were carried away to Babylon: Jer. 27:20; Dan. 1:2

12 And after they were brought to Babylon, Jechonias begat Salathiel; and Salathiel begat Zorobabel;   1 Chr. 3:17

13 And Zorobabel begat Abiud; and Abiud begat Eliakim; and Eliakim begat Azor;

14 And Azor begat Sadoc; and Sadoc begat Achim; and Achim begat Eliud;

15 And Eliud begat Eleazar; and Eleazar begat Matthan; and Matthan begat Jacob;

16 And Jacob begat Joseph the husband of Mary, of whom was born Jesus, who is called Christ.   Matt. 27:17

17 So all the generations from Abraham to David *are* fourteen generations; and from David until the carrying away into Babylon *are* fourteen generations; and from the carrying away into Babylon unto Christ *are* fourteen generations.

The Story of Jesus' Birth

18 Now the birth of Jesus Christ was on this wise: When as his mother Mary was ᵀespoused to Joseph, before they came together, she was found with child of the Holy Ghost.   Gen. 3:15 ◆ *engaged to marry*

19 Then Joseph her husband, being a just *man*, and not willing to make her a publick example, was minded to put her away ᵀprivily.   Deut. 22:21-24 ◆ *in secret*

20 But while he thought on these things, behold, the angel of the Lord appeared unto him in a dream, saying, Joseph, thou son of David, fear not to take unto thee Mary thy wife: for that which is conceived in her is of the Holy Ghost.   Matt. 1:18

> **1:21 Saved From Sin**
>
> Satan was exulting that he had succeeded in debasing the image of God in humanity. Then Jesus came to restore in man the image of his Maker. None but Christ can fashion anew the character that has been ruined by sin. He came to expel the demons that had controlled the will. He came to lift us up from the dust, to reshape the marred character after the pattern of His divine character, and to make it beautiful with His own glory. *DA 37, 38*

21 And she shall bring forth a son, and thou shalt call his name JESUS: for he shall save his people from their sins.   Luke 1:31; Acts 4:12; 5:31

Jesus   See Isaiah 53:1–9.

22 Now all this was done, that it might be fulfilled which was spoken of the Lord by the prophet, saying,   Matt. 2:15

23 Behold, a virgin shall be with child, and shall bring forth a son, and they shall call his

The Fullness of the Time

Matthew 1

"When the fullness of the time was come, God sent forth His Son." Providence had directed the movements of nations, and the tide of human impulse and influence, until the world was ripe for the coming of the Deliverer. The nations were united under one government. One language was widely spoken, and was everywhere recognized as the language of literature. From all lands the Jews of the dispersion gathered to Jerusalem to the annual feasts. As these returned to the places of their sojourn, they could spread throughout the world the tidings of the Messiah's coming.

At this time the systems of heathenism were losing their hold upon the people. Men were weary of pageant and fable. They longed for a religion that could satisfy the heart. While the light of truth seemed to have departed from among men, there were souls who were looking for light, and who were filled with perplexity and sorrow. They were thirsting for a knowledge of the living God, for some assurance of a life beyond the grave. *DA 32*

name Emmanuel, which being interpreted is, God with us. _Is. 7:14; 9:6-7; Matt. 28:20_

> **1:23 God With Us**
>
> Since Jesus came to dwell with us, we know that God is acquainted with our trials, and sympathizes with our griefs. Every son and daughter of Adam may understand that our Creator is the friend of sinners. For in every doctrine of grace, every promise of joy, every deed of love, every divine attraction presented in the Saviour's life on earth, we see "God with us." _DA 24_

24 Then Joseph being raised from sleep did as the angel of the Lord had bidden him, and took unto him his wife:

25 And knew her not till she had brought forth her firstborn son: and he called his name JESUS. _Matt. 1:21_

The Wise Men Visit

2 Now when Jesus was born in Bethlehem of Judaea in the days of Herod the king, behold, there came wise men from the east to Jerusalem, _Gen. 25:6; Mic. 5:2; Luke 2:4-7_

2 Saying, Where is he that is born King of the Jews? for we have seen his star in the east, and are come to worship him. _Jer. 23:5; Zech. 9:9_

3 When Herod the king had heard _these things,_ he was troubled, and all Jerusalem with him.

4 And when he had gathered all the chief priests and scribes of the people together, he demanded of them where Christ should be born.

5 And they said unto him, In Bethlehem of Judaea: for thus it is written by the prophet, _Gen. 35:19_

6 And thou Bethlehem, _in_ the land of Juda, art not the least among the princes of Juda: for out of thee shall come a Governor, that shall rule my people Israel. _Mic. 5:2; John 7:42_

> **2:1–6 Wasted Knowledge**
>
> These learned teachers [the priests and rabbis] would not stoop to be instructed by those whom they termed heathen. It could not be, they said, that God had passed them by, to communicate with ignorant shepherds or uncircumcised Gentiles. They determined to show their contempt for the reports that were exciting King Herod and all Jerusalem. They would not even go to Bethlehem to see whether these things were so. And they led the people to regard the interest in Jesus as a fanatical excitement. _DA 62, 63_

7 Then Herod, when he had ᵀprivily called the wise men, enquired of them diligently what time the star appeared. _in secret_

8 And he sent them to Bethlehem, and said,

Go and search diligently for the young child; and when ye have found _him,_ bring me word again, that I may come and worship him also.

9 When they had heard the king, they departed; and, lo, the star, which they saw in the east, went before them, till it came and stood over where the young child was.

10 When they saw the star, they rejoiced with exceeding great joy.

11 And when they were come into the house, they saw the young child with Mary his mother, and fell down, and worshipped him: and when they had opened their treasures, they presented unto him gifts; gold, and frankincense, and myrrh. _Ps. 72:10_

> **2:11 Gifts Fit for the King**
>
> [The magi's] gift was the first that was laid at [Jesus'] feet. And through that gift, what privilege of ministry was theirs! . . . If we have given our hearts to Jesus, we also shall bring our gifts to Him. Our gold and silver, our most precious earthly possessions, our highest mental and spiritual endowments, will be freely devoted to Him who loved us, and gave Himself for us. _DA 65_

12 And being warned of God in a dream that they should not return to Herod, they departed into their own country another way. _Matt. 1:20; 2:22; 27:19_

Escape to Egypt

13 And when they were departed, behold, the angel of the Lord appeareth to Joseph in a dream, saying, Arise, and take the young child and his mother, and flee into Egypt, and be thou there until I bring thee word: for Herod will seek the young child to destroy him. _Acts 5:19_

14 When he arose, he took the young child and his mother by night, and departed into Egypt:

15 And was there until the death of Herod: that it might be fulfilled which was spoken of the Lord by the prophet, saying, Out of Egypt have I called my son. _Ex. 4:22; Num. 24:8; Hos. 11:1_

Herod Slays the Children

16 Then Herod, when he saw that he was mocked of the wise men, was exceeding ᵀwroth, and sent forth, and slew all the children that were in Bethlehem, and in all the coasts thereof, from two years old and under, according to the time which he had diligently enquired of the wise men. _Is. 59:7_ ◆ _angry_

17 Then was fulfilled that which was spoken by Jeremy the prophet, saying,

18 In Rama was there a voice heard, lamentation, and weeping, and great mourning,

The Sermon on the Mount

5 And seeing the multitudes, he went up into a mountain: and when he was set, his disciples came unto him: Matt. 15:29

2 And he opened his mouth, and taught them, saying, Matt. 13:35

The Beatitudes

3 Blessed *are* the poor in spirit: for theirs is the kingdom of heaven. Is. 61:1

5:2, 3 Love Divine

As something strange and new, these words fall upon the ears of the wondering multitude. Such teaching is contrary to all they have ever heard from priest or rabbi. They see in it nothing to flatter their pride or to feed their ambitious hopes. But there is about this new Teacher a power that holds them spellbound. The sweetness of divine love flows from His very presence as the fragrance from a flower. *MB 6*

4 Blessed *are* they that mourn: for they shall be comforted. Is. 61:2-3

5 Blessed *are* the meek: for they shall inherit the earth. Ps. 37:11; Rom. 4:13

6 Blessed *are* they which do hunger and thirst after righteousness: for they shall be filled.

7 Blessed *are* the merciful: for they shall obtain mercy. 2 Sam. 22:26

8 Blessed *are* the pure in heart: for they shall see God. Ps. 24:4; Acts 15:9; Heb. 12:14

9 Blessed *are* the peacemakers: for they shall be called the children of God. Matt. 5:45

10 Blessed *are* they which are persecuted for righteousness' sake: for theirs is the kingdom of heaven. Matt. 5:3

11 Blessed are ye, when *men* shall ᵀrevile you, and persecute *you,* and shall say all manner of evil against you falsely, for my sake. John 15:21; 1 Pet. 4:14 ✦ *attack with words*

12 Rejoice, and be exceeding glad: for great *is* your reward in heaven: for so persecuted they the prophets which were before you. Luke 6:23; Acts 5:41; 1 Thess. 2:15

5:13 Lessons From Salt

Though the wicked know it not, they owe even the blessings of this life to the presence, in the world, of God's people whom they despise and oppress. But if Christians are such in name only, they are like the salt that has lost its savor. They have no influence for good in the world. Through their misrepresentation of God they are worse than unbelievers. *DA 306*

God's People Make a Difference

13 Ye are the salt of the earth: but if the salt have lost his savour, wherewith shall it be

salted? it is thenceforth good for nothing, but to be cast out, and to be ᵀtrodden under foot of men. Lev. 2:13 ✦ *trampled*

14 Ye are the light of the world. A city that is set on an hill cannot be hid. John 8:12

15 Neither do men light a candle, and put it under a bushel, but on a candlestick; and it giveth light unto all that are in the house.

16 Let your light so shine before men, that they may see your good works, and glorify your Father which is in heaven. John 15:8

5:14–16 What Is the True Light?

True character is not shaped from without, and put on; it radiates from within. If we wish to direct others in the path of righteousness, the principles of righteousness must be enshrined in our own hearts. Our profession of faith may proclaim the theory of religion, but it is our practical piety that holds forth the word of truth. The consistent life, the holy conversation, the unswerving integrity, the active, benevolent spirit, the godly example—these are the mediums through which light is conveyed to the world. *DA 307*

Jesus Came to Fulfill the Law

17 Think not that I am come to destroy the law, or the prophets: I am not come to destroy, but to fulfil. Rom. 3:31

18 For verily I say unto you, Till heaven and earth pass, one jot or one ᵀtittle shall in no wise pass from the law, till all be fulfilled. Luke 16:17 ✦ *small point of a Hebrew letter*

God's Law   See John 14:15.

19 Whosoever therefore shall break one of these least commandments, and shall teach men so, he shall be called the least in the kingdom of heaven: but whosoever shall do and teach *them,* the same shall be called great in the kingdom of heaven. Matt. 11:11

20 For I say unto you, That except your righteousness shall exceed *the righteousness* of the scribes and Pharisees, ye shall in no case enter into the kingdom of heaven. Phil. 3:9

Jesus Talks about Anger

21 Ye have heard that it was said by them of old time, Thou shalt not kill; and whosoever shall kill shall be in danger of the judgment: Ex. 20:13; Deut. 5:17; Matt. 5:27

22 But I say unto you, That whosoever is angry with his brother without a cause shall be in danger of the judgment: and whosoever shall say to his brother, Raca, shall be in danger of the council: but whosoever shall say, Thou fool, shall be in danger of hell fire.

23 Therefore if thou bring thy gift to the altar, and there rememberest that thy brother hath ought against thee; Matt. 8:4

24 Leave there thy gift before the altar, and go thy way; first be reconciled to thy brother, and then come and offer thy gift.   Mark 9:50

25 Agree with thine adversary quickly, whiles thou art in the way with him; lest at any time the adversary deliver thee to the judge, and the judge deliver thee to the officer, and thou be cast into prison.   Prov. 25:8

26 Verily I say unto thee, Thou shalt by no means come out thence, till thou hast paid the uttermost farthing.   Matt. 18:34

Jesus Talks about Sexual Sin

27 Ye have heard that it was said by them of old time, Thou shalt not commit adultery: Ex. 20:14; Deut. 5:18

28 But I say unto you, That whosoever looketh on a woman to lust after her hath committed adultery with her already in his heart.   2 Sam. 11:2; Job 31:1; Prov. 6:25

29 And if thy right eye offend thee, pluck it out, and cast *it* from thee: for it is profitable for thee that one of thy members should perish, and not *that* thy whole body should be cast into hell.   Matt. 18:8-9

30 And if thy right hand offend thee, cut it off, and cast *it* from thee: for it is profitable for thee that one of thy members should perish, and not *that* thy whole body should be cast into hell.   Matt. 5:29

31 It hath been said, Whosoever shall put away his wife, let him give her a writing of divorcement: Jer. 3:1

32 But I say unto you, That whosoever shall put away his wife, saving for the cause of fornication, causeth her to commit adultery: and whosoever shall marry her that is divorced committeth adultery.   Luke 16:18; 1 Cor. 7:10-11

Marriage   See Matthew 19:3–9.

5:31, 32

Jesus Talks about Oaths

33 Again, ye have heard that it hath been said by them of old time, Thou shalt not ^Tforswear thyself, but shalt perform unto the Lord thine oaths: Lev. 19:12; Deut. 23:21 ◆ *swear falsely*

34 But I say unto you, Swear not at all; neither by heaven; for it is God's throne: Is. 66:1

35 Nor by the earth; for it is his footstool: neither by Jerusalem; for it is the city of the great King.   Ps. 48:2

36 Neither shalt thou swear by thy head, because thou canst not make one hair white or black.

37 But let your communication be, Yea, yea; Nay, nay: for whatsoever is more than these cometh of evil.   Matt. 13:19; James 5:12

Love Your Enemies

38 Ye have heard that it hath been said, An eye for an eye, and a tooth for a tooth:

39 But I say unto you, That ye resist not evil: but whosoever shall smite thee on thy right cheek, turn to him the other also.   1 Cor. 6:7

40 And if any man will sue thee at the law, and take away thy coat, let him have *thy* ^Tcloke also.   *clothing*

41 And whosoever shall compel thee to go a mile, go with him ^Ttwain.   Matt. 27:32 ◆ *two*

42 Give to him that asketh thee, and from him that would borrow of thee turn not thou away.   Ps. 37:21

43 Ye have heard that it hath been said, Thou shalt love thy neighbour, and hate thine enemy.   Lev. 19:18; Deut. 23:6; Matt. 19:19

44 But I say unto you, Love your enemies, bless them that curse you, do good to them that hate you, and pray for them which despitefully use you, and persecute you; Acts 7:60

45 That ye may be the children of your

The Great Law of Life

Matthew 5:17–19

"Till heaven and earth pass," said Jesus, "one jot or one tittle shall in nowise pass from the law, till all be fulfilled" [Matthew 5:18]. By His own obedience to the law, Christ testified to its immutable character and proved that through His grace it could be perfectly obeyed by every son and daughter of Adam. . . .

Because the law of the Lord is perfect, and therefore changeless, it is impossible for sinful men, in themselves, to meet the standard of its requirement. This was why Jesus came as our Redeemer. It was His mission, by making men partakers of the divine nature, to bring them into harmony with the principles of the law of heaven. When we forsake our sins and receive Christ as our Saviour, the law is exalted. The apostle Paul asks, "Do we then make void the law through faith? God forbid: yea, we establish the law" (Romans 3:31).

The new-covenant promise is, "I will put My laws into their hearts, and in their minds will I write them" (Hebrews 10:16). While the system of types which pointed to Christ as the Lamb of God that should take away the sin of the world was to pass away at His death, the principles of righteousness embodied in the Decalogue are as immutable as the eternal throne. Not one command has been annulled, not a jot or tittle has been changed. Those principles that were made known to man in Paradise as the great law of life will exist unchanged in Paradise restored. When Eden shall bloom on earth again, God's law of love will be obeyed by all beneath the sun. *MB 49–51*

Father which is in heaven: for he maketh his sun to rise on the evil and on the good, and sendeth rain on the just and on the unjust.   *Matt. 5:9*

46 For if ye love them which love you, what reward have ye? do not even the ᵀpublicans the same?   *tax collectors*

47 And if ye salute your brethren only, what do ye more *than others?* do not even the publicans so?   *Matt. 5:20*

48 Be ye therefore perfect, even as your Father which is in heaven is perfect.   *Gen. 17:1; Lev. 19:2*

5:48 What Is Christ Waiting For?

Christ is waiting with longing desire for the manifestation of Himself in His church. When the character of Christ shall be perfectly reproduced in His people, then He will come to claim them as His own. . . .

Were all who profess His name bearing fruit to His glory, how quickly the whole world would be sown with the seed of the gospel. Quickly the last great harvest would be ripened, and Christ would come to gather the precious grain. *COL 69*

Don't Do Good Works for Praise

6 Take heed that ye do not your alms before men, to be seen of them: otherwise ye have no reward of your Father which is in heaven.   *Matt. 6:16; 23:5*

2 Therefore when thou doest *thine* alms, do not sound a trumpet before thee, as the hypocrites do in the synagogues and in the streets, that they may have glory of men. Verily I say unto you, They have their reward.

6:1–4 Real Godliness

Christ's own words make His meaning plain, that in acts of charity the aim should not be to secure praise and honor from men. Real godliness never prompts an effort at display. Those who desire words of praise and flattery, and feed upon them as a sweet morsel, are Christians in name only. . . .

Your prayers, your performance of duty, your benevolence, your self-denial, will not be the theme of your thought or conversation. Jesus will be magnified, self will be hidden, and Christ will appear as all in all. *MB 80, 81*

---

3 But when thou doest ᵀalms, let not thy left hand know what thy right hand doeth: *acts of mercy*

4 That thine alms may be in secret: and thy Father which seeth in secret himself shall reward thee openly.   *Jer. 17:10; Matt. 6:6, 18*

The Lord's Prayer

5 And when thou prayest, thou shalt not be as the hypocrites *are*: for they love to pray standing in the synagogues and in the corners of the streets, that they may be seen of men. Verily I say unto you, They have their reward.   *Matt. 6:2, 16; Mark 11:25*

6 But thou, when thou prayest, enter into thy closet, and when thou hast shut thy door, pray to thy Father which is in secret; and thy Father which seeth in secret shall reward thee openly.   *2 Kin. 4:33*

6:6 Prayer Brings Us Up to Him

In order to have spiritual life and energy, we must have actual intercourse [association] with our heavenly Father. . . . In order to commune with God, we must have something to say to Him concerning our actual life.

Prayer is the opening of the heart to God as to a friend. Not that it is necessary in order to make known to God what we are, but in order to enable us to receive Him. Prayer does not bring God down to us, but brings us up to Him. *SC 93*

---

7 But when ye pray, use not vain repetitions, as the heathen *do*: for they think that they shall be heard for their much speaking.

8 Be not ye therefore like unto them: for your Father knoweth what things ye have need of, before ye ask him.   *Ps. 38:9; 69:17-19*

9 After this manner therefore pray ye: Our Father which art in heaven, Hallowed be thy name.

10 Thy kingdom come. Thy will be done in earth, as *it is* in heaven.   *Matt. 3:2; 4:17; 26:42*

11 Give us this day our daily bread. *Prov. 30:8*

12 And forgive us our debts, as we forgive our debtors.   *Ex. 34:7*

13 And lead us not into temptation, but deliver us from evil: For thine is the kingdom, and the power, and the glory, for ever. Amen.   *Matt. 26:41; John 17:15; 1 Cor. 10:13*

14 For if ye forgive men their trespasses, your heavenly Father will also forgive you: *Mark 11:25; Eph. 4:32; Col. 3:13*

15 But if ye forgive not men their ᵀtrespasses, neither will your Father forgive your trespasses.   *Matt. 18:35* ◆ *sins*

Christian Behavior   See Luke 10:27.

Fasting

16 Moreover when ye fast, be not, as the hypocrites, of a sad ᵀcountenance: for they disfigure their faces, that they may appear unto men to fast. Verily I say unto you, They have their reward.   *Matt. 6:2* ◆ *appearance*

17 But thou, when thou fastest, anoint thine head, and wash thy face;   *Ruth 3:3*

18 That thou appear not unto men to fast, but unto thy Father which is in secret: and

thy Father, which seeth in secret, shall reward thee openly.   Matt. 6:4, 6

True Riches

19 Lay not up for yourselves treasures upon earth, where moth and rust doth corrupt, and where thieves break through and steal: Luke 12:21; 1 Tim. 6:17; Heb. 13:5
20 But lay up for yourselves treasures in heaven, where neither moth nor rust doth corrupt, and where thieves do not break through nor steal: Matt. 19:21; Luke 12:33; 18:22
21 For where your treasure is, there will your heart be also.   Luke 12:34
22 The light of the body is the eye: if therefore thine eye be Tsingle, thy whole body shall be full of light.   *healthy*
23 But if thine eye be evil, thy whole body shall be full of darkness. If therefore the light that is in thee be darkness, how great *is* that darkness!   Matt. 20:15
24 No man can serve two masters: for either he will hate the one, and love the other; or else he will hold to the one, and despise the other. Ye cannot serve God and mammon.

Worry

25 Therefore I say unto you, Take no thought for your life, what ye shall eat, or what ye shall drink; nor yet for your body, what ye shall put on. Is not the life more than meat, and the body than raiment?   Matt. 6:31, 34; Phil. 4:6
26 Behold the fowls of the air: for they sow not, neither do they reap, nor gather into barns; yet your heavenly Father feedeth them. Are ye not much better than they?   Job 38:41; Ps. 147:9; Matt. 10:29-31
27 Which of you by taking thought can add one cubit unto his stature?
28 And why take ye thought for raiment? Consider the lilies of the field, how they grow; they toil not, neither do they spin: Matt. 6:25

29 And yet I say unto you, That even Solomon in all his glory was Tarrayed like one of these.   1 Kin. 10:4-7 ◆ *clothed*
30 Wherefore, if God so clothe the grass of the field, which to day is, and to morrow is cast into the oven, *shall he* not much more *clothe* you, O ye of little faith?   Matt. 14:31; 16:8
31 Therefore take no thought, saying, What shall we eat? or, What shall we drink? or, Wherewithal shall we be clothed?   1 Pet. 5:7
32 (For after all these things do the Gentiles seek:) for your heavenly Father knoweth that ye have need of all these things.   Luke 12:30

6:33 First Things First

We are to engage in no business, follow no pursuit, seek no pleasure, that would hinder the outworking of His righteousness in our character and life. Whatever we do is to be done heartily, as unto the Lord. . . .

If we follow His example, His assurance to us is that all things needful in this life "shall be added." Poverty or wealth, sickness or health, simplicity or wisdom—all are provided for in the promise of His grace. *MB 99*

33 But seek ye first the kingdom of God, and his righteousness; and all these things shall be added unto you.   1 Tim. 4:8

Managing God's Gifts   See Psalm 37:25.

34 Take therefore no thought for the morrow: for the morrow shall take thought for the things of itself. Sufficient unto the day *is* the evil thereof.   Matt. 6:25

Making Judgments

7 Judge not, that ye be not judged. James 4:11
2 For with what judgment ye judge, ye shall be judged: and with what measure ye mete, it shall be measured to you again.
3 And why beholdest thou the mote that is

No In-Between With God

Matthew 6:24

"No man can serve two masters." We cannot serve God with a divided heart. Bible religion is not one influence among many others; its influence is to be supreme, pervading and controlling every other. It is not to be like a dash of color brushed here and there upon the canvas, but it is to pervade the whole life, as if the canvas were dipped into the color, until every thread of the fabric were dyed a deep, unfading hue. . . .

He who desires to know the truth must be willing to accept all that it reveals. He can make no compromise with error. To be wavering and halfhearted in allegiance to truth is to choose the darkness of error and satanic delusion.

Worldly policy and the undeviating principles of righteousness do not blend into each other imperceptibly, like the colors of the rainbow. Between the two a broad, clear line is drawn by the eternal God. The likeness of Christ stands out as distinct from that of Satan as midday in contrast with midnight. And only those who live the life of Christ are His co-workers. If one sin is cherished in the soul, or one wrong practice retained in the life, the whole being is contaminated. The man becomes an instrument of unrighteousness. *DA 312, 313*

in thy brother's eye, but considerest not the beam that is in thine own eye?   John 8:7-9

4 Or how wilt thou say to thy brother, Let me pull out the ᵀmote out of thine eye; and, behold, a beam *is* in thine own eye? *small particle*

5 Thou hypocrite, first cast out the beam out of thine own eye; and then shalt thou see clearly to cast out the mote out of thy brother's eye.

7:1–5 Stay Out of Satan's Trap

Do not think yourself better than other men, and set yourself up as their judge. Since you cannot discern motive, you are incapable of judging another. In criticizing him, you are passing sentence upon yourself; for you show that you are a participant with Satan, the accuser of the brethren. The Lord says, "Examine yourselves, whether ye be in the faith; prove your own selves." This is our work. "If we would judge ourselves, we should not be judged" (2 Corinthians 13:5; 1 Corinthians 11:31). *DA 314*

---

6 Give not that which is holy unto the dogs, neither cast ye your pearls before swine, lest they trample them under their feet, and turn again and ᵀrend you.   Matt. 15:26 ◆ *tear you apart*

Prayer and Good Actions

7 Ask, and it shall be given you; seek, and ye shall find; knock, and it shall be opened unto you: Matt. 21:22; Mark 11:24; John 15:7

8 For every one that asketh receiveth; and he that seeketh findeth; and to him that knocketh it shall be opened.

9 Or what man is there of you, whom if his son ask bread, will he give him a stone?

10 Or if he ask a fish, will he give him a serpent?

11 If ye then, being evil, know how to give good gifts unto your children, how much more shall your Father which is in heaven give good things to them that ask him?

12 Therefore all things whatsoever ye would that men should do to you, do ye even so to them: for this is the law and the prophets.   Lev. 19:18; Luke 6:31; Rom. 13:8-10

13 Enter ye in at the ᵀstrait gate: for wide *is* the gate, and broad *is* the way, that leadeth to destruction, and many there be which go in thereat: *narrow*

14 Because strait *is* the gate, and narrow *is* the way, which leadeth unto life, and few there be that find it.

Beware of False Prophets

15 Beware of false prophets, which come to you in sheep's clothing, but inwardly they are ravening wolves.   Matt. 24:11; Col. 2:8; 1 John 4:1

16 Ye shall know them by their fruits. Do men gather grapes of thorns, or figs of thistles?

17 Even so every good tree bringeth forth good fruit; but a corrupt tree bringeth forth evil fruit.   Matt. 12:33-35

18 A good tree cannot bring forth evil fruit, neither *can* a corrupt tree bring forth good fruit.

19 Every tree that bringeth not forth good fruit is ᵀhewn down, and cast into the fire.   Matt. 3:10; Luke 3:9 ◆ *cut*

20 Wherefore by their fruits ye shall know them.   Matt. 7:16

Gift of Prophecy   See 1 John 4:1–6.

Be Doers of the Word

21 Not every one that saith unto me, Lord, Lord, shall enter into the kingdom of

7:15–20

My Path Is Narrow but Gives Life Eternal

Matthew 7:13, 14

The path which I have set before you, [Jesus] said, is narrow; the gate is difficult of entrance; for the golden rule excludes all pride and self-seeking. There is, indeed, a wider road; but its end is destruction. If you would climb the path of spiritual life, you must constantly ascend; for it is an upward way. You must go with the few; for the multitude will choose the downward path.

In the road to death the whole race may go, with all their worldliness, all their selfishness, all their pride, dishonesty, and moral debasement. There is room for every man's opinions and doctrines, space to follow his inclinations, to do whatever his self-love may dictate. In order to go in the path that leads to destruction, there is no need of searching for the way; for the gate is wide, and the way is broad, and the feet naturally turn into the path that ends in death.

But the way to life is narrow and the entrance strait. If you cling to any besetting sin you will find the way too narrow for you to enter. Your own ways, your own will, your evil habits and practices, must be given up if you would keep the way of the Lord. He who would serve Christ cannot follow the world's opinions or meet the world's standard. Heaven's path is too narrow for rank and riches to ride in state, too narrow for the play of self-centered ambition, too steep and rugged for lovers of ease to climb. Toil, patience, self-sacrifice, reproach, poverty, the contradiction of sinners against Himself, was the portion of Christ, and it must be our portion, if we ever enter the Paradise of God. *MB 138, 139*

heaven; but he that doeth the will of my Father which is in heaven. *Matt. 25:11-12*

22 Many will say to me in that day, Lord, Lord, have we not prophesied in thy name? and in thy name have cast out devils? and in thy name done many wonderful works? *Num. 24:4*

23 And then will I profess unto them, I never knew you: depart from me, ye that work iniquity. *Ps. 6:8; Matt. 25:41; Luke 13:27*

7:21-23 True Sincerity

The test of sincerity is not in words, but in deeds. Christ does not say to any man, What say ye more than others? but, "What do ye more than others?" (Matthew 5:47). Full of meaning are His words, "If ye know these things, happy are ye if ye do them" (John 13:17). Words are of no value unless they are accompanied with appropriate deeds. This is the lesson taught in the parable of the two sons. *COL 272*

24 Therefore whosoever heareth these sayings of mine, and doeth them, I will liken him unto a wise man, which built his house upon a rock: *Luke 6:47-49*

25 And the rain descended, and the floods came, and the winds blew, and beat upon that house; and it fell not: for it was founded upon a rock.

26 And every one that heareth these sayings of mine, and doeth them not, shall be likened unto a foolish man, which built his house upon the sand:

27 And the rain descended, and the floods came, and the winds blew, and beat upon that house; and it fell: and great was the fall of it.

28 And it came to pass, when Jesus had ended these sayings, the people were astonished at his doctrine: *Mark 1:22; 6:2; Luke 4:32*

29 For he taught them as *one* having authority, and not as the scribes.

Jesus Cleanses the Leper

8 When he was come down from the mountain, great multitudes followed him.

2 And, behold, there came a leper and worshipped him, saying, Lord, if thou wilt, thou canst make me clean. *Matt. 15:25; 18:26; John 9:38*

3 And Jesus put forth *his* hand, and touched him, saying, I will; be thou clean. And immediately his leprosy was cleansed.

4 And Jesus saith unto him, See thou tell no man; but go thy way, shew thyself to the priest, and offer the gift that Moses commanded, for a testimony unto them. *Lev. 14:2*

8:4 Jesus Tries to Disarm Prejudice

Every act of Christ's ministry was far-reaching in its purpose. It comprehended more than appeared in the act itself. So in the case of the leper. . . . While He drew the publicans, the heathen, and the Samaritans, He longed to reach the priests and teachers who were shut in by prejudice and tradition. He left untried no means by which they might be reached. In sending the healed leper to the priests, He gave them a testimony calculated to disarm their prejudices. *DA 265*

Jesus Heals the Centurion's Servant

5 And when Jesus was entered into Capernaum, there came unto him a centurion, ᵀbeseeching him, *Luke 7:1-10 ♦ begging*

6 And saying, Lord, my servant lieth at home sick of the ᵀpalsy, grievously tormented. *Matt. 4:24 ♦ paralysis*

7 And Jesus saith unto him, I will come and heal him.

8 The centurion answered and said, Lord, I am not worthy that thou shouldest come under my roof: but speak the word only, and my servant shall be healed. *Ps. 107:20*

9 For I am a man under authority, having soldiers under me: and I say to this *man*, Go, and he goeth; and to another, Come, and he cometh; and to my servant, Do this, and he doeth *it*.

10 When Jesus heard *it*, he marvelled, and said to them that followed, Verily I say unto you, I have not found so great faith, no, not in Israel. *Matt. 15:28*

11 And I say unto you, That many shall come from the east and west, and shall sit down with Abraham, and Isaac, and Jacob, in the kingdom of heaven. *Is. 59:19; Mal. 1:11; Eph. 3:6*

12 But the children of the kingdom shall be cast out into outer darkness: there shall be weeping and gnashing of teeth. *Matt. 25:30*

13 And Jesus said unto the centurion, Go thy way; and as thou hast believed, *so* be it done unto thee. And his servant was healed in the selfsame hour. *Matt. 9:22*

Jesus Heals Peter's Mother-in-law and Others

14 And when Jesus was come into Peter's house, he saw his wife's mother laid, and sick of a fever. *1 Cor. 9:5*

15 And he touched her hand, and the fever left her: and she arose, and ministered unto them.

16 When the even was come, they brought unto him many that were possessed with devils: and he cast out the spirits with *his* word, and healed all that were sick:

17 That it might be fulfilled which was

spoken by Esaias the prophet, saying, Himself took our infirmities, and bare *our* sicknesses.   Is. 53:4; Matt. 1:22

What It Takes to Be a Disciple

18 Now when Jesus saw great multitudes about him, he gave commandment to depart unto the other side.   Mark 4:35; Luke 8:22
19 And a certain scribe came, and said unto him, Master, I will follow thee whithersoever thou goest.
20 And Jesus saith unto him, The foxes have holes, and the birds of the air *have* nests; but the Son of man hath not where to lay *his* head.

8:20 Turning Love to Hatred

Multitudes who desired to exalt Him to the throne today would turn from Him tomorrow. The disappointment of their selfish ambition would turn their love to hatred, and their praise to curses. . . . From the first He had held out to His followers no hope of earthly rewards. . . . Of those now connected with Him there were many who had been attracted by the hope of a worldly kingdom. These must be undeceived. *DA 383*

---

21 And another of his disciples said unto him, Lord, suffer me first to go and bury my father.
22 But Jesus said unto him, Follow me; and let the dead bury their dead.   Matt. 9:9

Jesus Calms the Sea

23 And when he was entered into a ship, his disciples followed him.
24 And, behold, there arose a great ᵀtempest in the sea, insomuch that the ship was covered with the waves: but he was asleep. *storm*
25 And his disciples came to *him*, and awoke him, saying, Lord, save us: we perish.
26 And he saith unto them, Why are ye fearful, O ye of little faith? Then he arose, and rebuked the winds and the sea; and there was a great calm.   Ps. 65:7; 89:9; Matt. 6:30
27 But the men marvelled, saying, What manner of man is this, that even the winds and the sea obey him!   Mark 1:27

Jesus Cures Two Demoniacs

28 And when he was come to the other side into the country of the Gergesenes, there met him two possessed with devils, coming out of the tombs, exceeding fierce, so that no man might pass by that way.   Mark 5:1-20
29 And, behold, they cried out, saying, What have we to do with thee, Jesus, thou Son of God? art thou come hither to torment us before the time?   2 Sam. 16:10; Mark 1:24; Luke 4:34

30 And there was a good way off from them an herd of many swine feeding.
31 So the devils ᵀbesought him, saying, If thou cast us out, suffer us to go away into the herd of swine.   *begged*
32 And he said unto them, Go. And when they were come out, they went into the herd of swine: and, behold, the whole herd of swine ran violently down a steep place into the sea, and perished in the waters.
33 And they that kept them fled, and went their ways into the city, and told every thing, and what was befallen to the possessed of the devils.
34 And, behold, the whole city came out to meet Jesus: and when they saw him, they besought *him* that he would depart out of their coasts.   1 Kin. 17:18; Luke 5:8; Acts 16:39

Jesus Cures a Paralytic

9 And he entered into a ship, and passed over, and came into his own city. Mark 5:21
2 And, behold, they brought to him a man sick of the palsy, lying on a bed: and Jesus seeing their faith said unto the sick of the palsy; Son, be of good cheer; thy sins be forgiven thee.   Matt. 4:24; 8:10; 9:22

9:2 The Foundation of Our Sickness

This lesson should not be overlooked. There are today thousands suffering from physical disease who, like the paralytic, are longing for the message, "Thy sins are forgiven." The burden of sin, with its unrest and unsatisfied desires, is the foundation of their maladies. They can find no relief until they come to the Healer of the soul. The peace which He alone can impart would restore vigor to the mind and health to the body. *MH 77*

---

3 And, behold, certain of the scribes said within themselves, This *man* blasphemeth.
4 And Jesus knowing their thoughts said, Wherefore think ye evil in your hearts?
5 For whether is easier, to say, *Thy* sins be forgiven thee; or to say, Arise, and walk?
6 But that ye may know that the Son of man hath power on earth to forgive sins, (then saith he to the sick of the ᵀpalsy,) Arise, take up thy bed, and go unto thine house. *paralysis*
7 And he arose, and departed to his house.
8 But when the multitudes saw *it*, they marvelled, and glorified God, which had given such power unto men.   Luke 7:16; 17:15

Jesus Calls Matthew to be a Disciple

9 And as Jesus passed forth from thence, he saw a man, named Matthew, sitting at the receipt of custom: and he saith unto him, Follow me. And he arose, and followed him.

9:9 No Hesitation

Matthew "left all, rose up, and followed Him." There was no hesitation, no questioning, no thought of the lucrative business to be exchanged for poverty and hardship. It was enough for him that he was to be with Jesus, that he might listen to His words, and unite with Him in His work. *DA 273*

---

10 And it came to pass, as Jesus sat at meat in the house, behold, many ᵀpublicans and sinners came and sat down with him and his disciples.   *tax collectors*

11 And when the Pharisees saw *it*, they said unto his disciples, Why eateth your Master with publicans and sinners?   Matt. 11:19

12 But when Jesus heard *that*, he said unto them, They that be whole need not a physician, but they that are sick.   Mark 2:17

13 But go ye and learn what *that* meaneth, I will have mercy, and not sacrifice: for I am not come to call the righteous, but sinners to repentance.   Hos. 6:6; Mic. 6:6-8; Matt. 12:7

Jesus Is Questioned about Fasting

14 Then came to him the disciples of John, saying, Why do we and the Pharisees fast ᵀoft, but thy disciples fast not? Matt. 11:2 ♦ *often*

15 And Jesus said unto them, Can the children of the bridechamber mourn, as long as the bridegroom is with them? but the days will come, when the bridegroom shall be taken from them, and then shall they fast.   John 3:29

16 No man putteth a piece of new cloth unto an old garment, for that which is put in to fill it up taketh from the garment, and the ᵀrent is made worse.   *tear*

17 Neither do men put new wine into old bottles: else the bottles break, and the wine runneth out, and the bottles perish: but they put new wine into new bottles, and both are preserved.   Josh. 9:4

Jesus Raises a Dead Girl and Heals a Bleeding Woman

18 While he spake these things unto them, behold, there came a certain ruler, and worshipped him, saying, My daughter is even now dead: but come and lay thy hand upon her, and she shall live.   Mark 5:22-43; Luke 8:41-56

19 And Jesus arose, and followed him, and *so did* his disciples.

20 And, behold, a woman, which was diseased with an issue of blood twelve years, came behind *him*, and touched the hem of his garment: Deut. 22:12; Matt. 14:36; 23:5

21 For she said within herself, If I may but touch his garment, I shall be whole.

22 But Jesus turned him about, and when he saw her, he said, Daughter, be of good comfort; thy faith hath made thee whole. And the woman was made whole from that hour.

23 And when Jesus came into the ruler's house, and saw the minstrels and the people making a noise,   2 Chr. 35:25

24 He said unto them, Give place: for the maid is not dead, but sleepeth. And they laughed him to scorn. John 11:4, 11-13; Acts 20:10

25 But when the people were put forth, he went in, and took her by the hand, and the maid arose.   Mark 9:27

26 And the fame hereof went abroad into all that land.   Matt. 4:24

Jesus Heals Two Blind Men

27 And when Jesus departed thence, two blind men followed him, crying, and saying, *Thou* Son of David, have mercy on us.   Matt. 15:22; 20:30-31; Luke 18:38-39

Principle Is Always Exacting

Matthew 9:9

So it was with the disciples previously called. When Jesus bade Peter and his companions follow Him, immediately they left their boats and nets. Some of these disciples had friends dependent on them for support; but when they received the Saviour's invitation, they did not hesitate, and inquire, How shall I live, and sustain my family? They were obedient to the call; and when afterward Jesus asked them, "When I sent you without purse, and scrip, and shoes, lacked ye anything?" they could answer, "Nothing" (Luke 22:35).

To Matthew in his wealth, and to Andrew and Peter in their poverty, the same test was brought; the same consecration was made by each. At the moment of success, when the nets were filled with fish, and the impulses of the old life were strongest, Jesus asked the disciples at the sea to leave all for the work of the gospel. So every soul is tested as to whether the desire for temporal good or for fellowship with Christ is strongest.

Principle is always exacting. No man can succeed in the service of God unless his whole heart is in the work and he counts all things but loss for the excellency of the knowledge of Christ. No man who makes any reserve can be the disciple of Christ, much less can he be His colaborer. When men appreciate the great salvation, the self-sacrifice seen in Christ's life will be seen in theirs. Wherever He leads the way, they will rejoice to follow. *DA 273*

28 And when he was come into the house, the blind men came to him: and Jesus saith unto them, Believe ye that I am able to do this? They said unto him, Yea, Lord.
29 Then touched he their eyes, saying, According to your faith be it unto you. Matt. 8:13
30 And their eyes were opened; and Jesus ᵀstraitly charged them, saying, See that no man know it.   Matt. 8:4 ◆ with strictness
31 But they, when they were departed, spread abroad his fame in all that country.   Mark 7:36

Jesus Sends a Demon out of a Man
32 As they went out, behold, they brought to him a ᵀdumb man possessed with a devil.   Matt. 4:24 ◆ mute
33 And when the ᵀdevil was cast out, the dumb spake: and the multitudes marvelled, saying, It was never so seen in Israel. false accuser
34 But the Pharisees said, He casteth out devils through the prince of the devils. Luke 11:15

Jesus' Compassion
35 And Jesus went about all the cities and villages, teaching in their synagogues, and preaching the gospel of the kingdom, and healing every sickness and every disease among the people.   Matt. 4:23-24
36 But when he saw the multitudes, he was moved with compassion on them, because they fainted, and were scattered abroad, as sheep having no shepherd. Num. 27:17; Mark 6:34
37 Then saith he unto his disciples, The harvest truly is plenteous, but the labourers are few;   Luke 10:2
38 Pray ye therefore the Lord of the harvest, that he will send forth labourers into his harvest.   2 Thess. 3:1

Jesus Appoints Twelve Disciples
10 And when he had called unto him his twelve disciples, he gave them power against unclean spirits, to cast them out, and to heal all manner of sickness and all manner of disease.   Mark 3:13-15; 6:7-13; Luke 6:13
2 Now the names of the twelve apostles are these; The first, Simon, who is called Peter, and Andrew his brother; James the son of Zebedee, and John his brother; Matt. 4:18; Acts 1:13
3 Philip, and Bartholomew; Thomas, and Matthew the ᵀpublican; James the son of Alphaeus, and Lebbaeus, whose surname was Thaddaeus; Matt. 9:9; Mark 3:18; Acts 1:13 ◆ tax collector
4 Simon the Canaanite, and Judas Iscariot, who also betrayed him.   Matt. 26:14

Jesus Sends Out the Twelve
5 These twelve Jesus sent forth, and commanded them, saying, Go not into the way of the Gentiles, and into any city of the Samaritans enter ye not: 2 Kin. 17:24-41; Luke 9:2; John 4:9

6 But go rather to the lost sheep of the house of Israel.   Jer. 50:6
7 And as ye go, preach, saying, The kingdom of heaven is at hand.   Matt. 3:2; 4:17
8 Heal the sick, cleanse the lepers, raise the dead, cast out devils: freely ye have received, freely give.   Acts 3:6
9 Provide neither gold, nor silver, nor brass in your purses,   Luke 22:35
10 Nor ᵀscrip for your journey, neither two coats, neither shoes, nor yet ᵀstaves: for the workman is worthy of his meat.   sack ◆ clubs
11 And into whatsoever city or town ye shall enter, enquire who in it is worthy; and there abide till ye go thence.
12 And when ye come into an house, salute it.   1 Sam. 25:6
13 And if the house be worthy, let your peace come upon it: but if it be not worthy, let your peace return to you.
14 And whosoever shall not receive you, nor hear your words, when ye depart out of that house or city, shake off the dust of your feet.   Neh. 5:13; Acts 13:51; 18:6
15 Verily I say unto you, It shall be more tolerable for the land of Sodom and Gomorrha in the day of judgment, than for that city.   Matt. 12:36
16 Behold, I send you forth as sheep in the midst of wolves: be ye therefore wise as serpents, and harmless as doves. Gen. 3:1; Luke 10:3
17 But beware of men: for they will deliver you up to the councils, and they will ᵀscourge you in their synagogues;   Mark 13:9 ◆ whip
18 And ye shall be brought before governors and kings for my sake, for a testimony against them and the Gentiles.   Matt. 8:4
19 But when they deliver you up, take no thought how or what ye shall speak: for it shall be given you in that same hour what ye shall speak.   Ex. 4:12
20 For it is not ye that speak, but the Spirit of your Father which speaketh in you.   Acts 4:8
21 And the brother shall deliver up the brother to death, and the father the child: and the children shall rise up against their parents, and cause them to be put to death.
22 And ye shall be hated of all men for my name's sake: but he that endureth to the end shall be saved.   Matt. 24:9, 13; Mark 13:13
23 But when they persecute you in this city, flee ye into another: for ᵀverily I say unto you, Ye shall not have gone over the cities of Israel, till the Son of man be come.   Matt. 16:28 ◆ truly
24 The disciple is not above his master, nor the servant above his lord.   Luke 6:40; John 13:16
25 It is enough for the disciple that he be as his master, and the servant as his lord. If they have called the master of the house Beelzebub, how much more shall they call them of his household? Matt. 9:34; 12:24; Mark 3:22

26 Fear them not therefore: for there is nothing covered, that shall not be revealed; and hid, that shall not be known. Mark 4:22; Luke 8:17
27 What I tell you in darkness, *that* speak ye in light: and what ye hear in the ear, *that* preach ye upon the housetops. Acts 5:20
28 And fear not them which kill the body, but are not able to kill the soul: but rather fear him which is able to destroy both soul and body in hell. Is. 8:12-13
29 Are not two sparrows sold for a ᵀfarthing? and one of them shall not fall on the ground without your Father. *small coin with little value*
30 But the very hairs of your head are all numbered. 1 Sam. 14:45; 2 Sam. 14:11; Luke 21:18
31 Fear ye not therefore, ye are of more value than many sparrows. Matt. 6:26
32 Whosoever therefore shall confess me before men, him will I confess also before my Father which is in heaven. Rev. 3:5
33 But whosoever shall deny me before men, him will I also deny before my Father which is in heaven. Mark 8:38; Luke 9:26; 2 Tim. 2:12
34 Think not that I am come to send peace on earth: I came not to send peace, but a sword.

10:34 The Gospel Is a Message of Peace

Christianity is a system which, received and obeyed, would spread peace, harmony, and happiness throughout the earth. . . . But the world at large are under the control of Satan, Christ's bitterest foe. . . . They hate the purity which reveals and condemns their sins, and they persecute and destroy those who would urge upon them its just and holy claims. It is in this sense—because the exalted truths it brings occasion hatred and strife—that the gospel is called a sword. *GC 47*

35 For I am come to set a man at ᵀvariance against his father, and the daughter against her mother, and the daughter in law against her mother in law. Matt. 10:21 ◆ *conflict*

36 And a man's foes *shall be* they of his own household. Ps. 41:9; 55:13; Mic. 7:6
37 He that loveth father or mother more than me is not worthy of me: and he that loveth son or daughter more than me is not worthy of me. Deut. 33:9; Luke 14:26
38 And he that taketh not his cross, and followeth after me, is not worthy of me. Matt. 16:24; Mark 8:34; Luke 14:27
39 He that findeth his life shall lose it: and he that loseth his life for my sake shall find it. Luke 17:33; John 12:25
40 He that receiveth you receiveth me, and he that receiveth me receiveth him that sent me. Matt. 18:5; Luke 9:48; John 13:20
41 He that receiveth a prophet in the name of a prophet shall receive a prophet's reward; and he that receiveth a righteous man in the name of a righteous man shall receive a righteous man's reward. 3 John 5-8
42 And whosoever shall give to drink unto one of these little ones a cup of cold *water* only in the name of a disciple, verily I say unto you, he shall in no wise lose his reward. Matt. 18:10; 25:40; Heb. 6:10

Jesus Reassures John

11 And it came to pass, when Jesus had made an end of commanding his twelve disciples, he departed thence to teach and to preach in their cities. Matt. 9:35
2 Now when John had heard in the prison the works of Christ, he sent two of his disciples, Matt. 4:12; 9:14; 14:3
3 And said unto him, Art thou he that should come, or do we look for another? Heb. 10:37
4 Jesus answered and said unto them, Go and shew John again those things which ye do hear and see:
5 The blind receive their sight, and the lame walk, the lepers are cleansed, and the deaf hear, the dead are raised up, and the poor have the gospel preached to them. Is. 35:4-6
6 And blessed is *he*, whosoever shall not be offended in me. Is. 8:14-15

How We Deny Christ

Matthew 10:32, 33

He who would confess Christ must have Christ abiding in him. He cannot communicate that which he has not received. The disciples might speak fluently on doctrines, they might repeat the words of Christ Himself; but unless they possessed Christlike meekness and love, they were not confessing Him. A spirit contrary to the spirit of Christ would deny Him, whatever the profession. Men may deny Christ by evilspeaking, by foolish talking, by words that are untruthful or unkind. They may deny Him by shunning life's burdens, by the pursuit of sinful pleasure. They may deny Him by conforming to the world, by uncourteous behavior, by the love of their own opinions, by justifying self, by cherishing doubt, borrowing trouble, and dwelling in darkness. In all these ways they declare that Christ is not in them. And "whosoever shall deny Me before men," He says, "him will I also deny before My Father which is in heaven." *DA 357*

Jesus Speaks about John

7 And as they departed, Jesus began to say unto the multitudes concerning John, What went ye out into the wilderness to see? A reed shaken with the wind?   Eph. 4:14
8 But what went ye out for to see? A man clothed in soft ᵀraiment? behold, they that wear soft *clothing* are in kings' houses.ₐclothing
9 But what went ye out for to see? A prophet? yea, I say unto you, and more than a prophet.   Matt. 14:5; Luke 1:76
10 For this is *he*, of whom it is written, Behold, I send my messenger before thy face, which shall prepare thy way before thee.   Mal. 3:1; Mark 1:2
11 Verily I say unto you, Among them that are born of women there hath not risen a greater than John the Baptist: notwithstanding he that is least in the kingdom of heaven is greater than he.

11:7–11 What God Values Most

[The priests and rulers] were more anxious to gain the admiration of men than to obtain the purity of heart which would win the approval of God. Thus they revealed that their allegiance was not given to God, but to the kingdom of this world.

"But what," said Jesus, "went ye out for to see?" [Matthew 11:7]. . . .

In the estimation of Heaven, what is it that constitutes greatness? . . . It is moral worth that God values. Love and purity are the attributes He prizes most. . . . His unselfish joy in the ministry of Christ presents the highest type of nobility ever revealed in man. *DA 219*

---

12 And from the days of John the Baptist until now the kingdom of heaven suffereth violence, and the violent take it by force.

13 For all the prophets and the law prophesied until John.
14 And if ye will receive *it*, this is Elias, which was for to come.   Mal. 4:5; Mark 9:11-13
15 He that hath ears to hear, let him hear.
16 But whereunto shall I liken this generation? It is like unto children sitting in the markets, and calling unto their fellows,
17 And saying, We have piped unto you, and ye have not danced; we have mourned unto you, and ye have not lamented.
18 For John came neither eating nor drinking, and they say, He hath a devil. Luke 1:15; John 7:20
19 The Son of man came eating and drinking, and they say, Behold a man gluttonous, and aᵀwinebibber, a friend ofᵀpublicans and sinners. But wisdom is justified of her children.   Matt. 9:10-11 ◆ *drinker of wine* ◆ *tax collectors*

Jesus Warns Some Cities

20 Then began he to ᵀupbraid the cities wherein most of his mighty works were done, because they repented not: Ps. 81:11-13 ◆ *scold*
21 Woe unto thee, Chorazin! woe unto thee, Bethsaida! for if the mighty works, which were done in you, had been done in Tyre and Sidon, they would have repented long ago in sackcloth and ashes.   Matt. 15:21
22 But I say unto you, It shall be more tolerable for Tyre and Sidon at the day of judgment, than for you.   Matt. 10:15; 11:24; 12:36
23 And thou, Capernaum, which art exalted unto heaven, shalt be brought down to hell: for if the mighty works, which have been done in thee, had been done in Sodom, it would have remained until this day.   Is. 14:13
24 But I say unto you, That it shall be more tolerable for the land of Sodom in the day of judgment, than for thee.   Matt. 10:15; 11:22

Are You the One?

Matthew 11:2, 3

Like the Saviour's disciples, John the Baptist did not understand the nature of Christ's kingdom. He expected Jesus to take the throne of David; and as time passed, and the Saviour made no claim to kingly authority, John became perplexed and troubled. . . .

In his mission the Baptist had stood as a fearless reprover of iniquity, both in high places and in low. He had dared to face King Herod with the plain rebuke of sin. He had not counted his life dear unto himself, that he might fulfill his appointed work. . . . But Jesus seemed to content Himself with gathering disciples about Him, and healing and teaching the people. . . .

There were hours when the whisperings of demons tortured his spirit, and the shadow of a terrible fear crept over him. Could it be that the long-hoped-for Deliverer had not yet appeared? . . .

But the Baptist did not surrender his faith in Christ. The memory of the voice from heaven and the descending dove, the spotless purity of Jesus, the power of the Holy Spirit that had rested upon John as he came into the Saviour's presence, and the testimony of the prophetic scriptures—all witnessed that Jesus of Nazareth was the Promised One.

John would not discuss his doubts and anxieties with his companions. He determined to send a message of inquiry to Jesus. This he entrusted to two of his disciples, hoping that an interview with the Saviour would confirm their faith, and bring assurance to their brethren. And he longed for some word from Christ spoken directly for himself. *DA 215, 216*

Jesus Calls the Weary to Come

25 At that time Jesus answered and said, I thank thee, O Father, Lord of heaven and earth, because thou hast hid these things from the wise and prudent, and hast revealed them unto babes. Ps. 8:2
26 Even so, Father: for so it seemed good in thy sight.
27 All things are delivered unto me of my Father: and no man knoweth the Son, but the Father; neither knoweth any man the Father, save the Son, and *he* to whomsoever the Son will reveal *him*. Matt. 28:18; John 1:18; 10:15
28 Come unto me, all *ye* that labour and are heavy ¹laden, and I will give you rest. Is. 11:10; John 6:37; 7:37 ◆ *loaded*
29 Take my yoke upon you, and learn of me; for I am meek and lowly in heart: and ye shall find rest unto your souls. Jer. 6:16; Phil. 2:5

11:29 To Be Born From Above

[Jesus] was never elated by applause, nor dejected by censure or disappointment. . . . But many who profess to be His followers have an anxious, troubled heart. . . . They do not make a complete surrender to Him; for they shrink from the consequences that such a surrender may involve. . . .

It is the love of self that brings unrest. When we are born from above, the same mind will be in us that was in Jesus, the mind that led Him to humble Himself that we might be saved. *DA 330, 331*

---

30 For my yoke *is* easy, and my burden is light. 1 John 5:3

Jesus Has Authority over the Sabbath

12 At that time Jesus went on the sabbath day through the corn; and his disciples were an hungred, and began to pluck the ears of corn, and to eat. Deut. 23:25; Luke 6:1-5
2 But when the Pharisees saw *it*, they said unto him, Behold, thy disciples do that which is not lawful to do upon the sabbath day. Ex. 20:9-11; Matt. 12:10; Luke 14:3
3 But he said unto them, Have ye not read what David did, when he was an hungred, and they that were with him; 1 Sam. 21:3-6
4 How he entered into the house of God, and did eat the shewbread, which was not lawful for him to eat, neither for them which were with him, but only for the priests? Ex. 25:30
5 Or have ye not read in the law, how that on the sabbath days the priests in the temple profane the sabbath, and are blameless?
6 But I say unto you, That in this place is *one* greater than the temple. 2 Chr. 6:18; Mal. 3:1
7 But if ye had known what *this* meaneth, I will have mercy, and not sacrifice, ye would not have condemned the guiltless. Hos. 6:6
8 For the Son of man is Lord even of the sabbath day. Matt. 9:6

12:6–8 The Design of the Sabbath

Again Christ reiterated the truth that the sacrifices were in themselves of no value. They were a means, and not an end. Their object was to direct men to the Saviour, and thus to bring them into harmony with God. . . . So with the Sabbath. It was designed to bring men into communion with God; but when the mind was absorbed with wearisome rites, the object of the Sabbath was thwarted. Its mere outward observance was a mockery. *DA 286*

---

9 And when he was departed thence, he went into their synagogue: Luke 6:6-11
10 And, behold, there was a man which had *his* hand withered. And they asked him, saying, Is it lawful to heal on the sabbath days? that they might accuse him. Luke 13:14
11 And he said unto them, What man shall there be among you, that shall have one sheep, and if it fall into a pit on the sabbath day, will he not lay hold on it, and lift *it* out? Luke 14:5
12 How much then is a man better than a sheep? Wherefore it is lawful to do well on the sabbath days. Matt. 6:26
13 Then saith he to the man, Stretch forth thine hand. And he stretched *it* forth; and it was restored whole, like as the other.

The Sabbath   See Mark 2:27.

14 Then the Pharisees went out, and held a council against him, how they might destroy him. John 11:53
15 But when Jesus knew *it*, he withdrew himself from thence: and great multitudes followed him, and he healed them all; Matt. 10:23

Jesus Is God's Servant

16 And charged them that they should not make him known: Matt. 8:4
17 That it might be fulfilled which was spoken by Esaias the prophet, saying,
18 Behold my servant, whom I have chosen; my beloved, in whom my soul is well pleased: I will put my spirit upon him, and he shall shew judgment to the Gentiles. Luke 4:18
19 He shall not strive, nor cry; neither shall any man hear his voice in the streets.
20 A bruised reed shall he not break, and smoking flax shall he not quench, till he send forth judgment unto victory.
21 And in his name shall the Gentiles trust. Is. 11:10

12:11-13

Jesus Is Accused of working with Beelzebub

22 Then was brought unto him one possessed with a ^Tdevil, blind, and ^Tdumb: and he healed him, insomuch that the blind and dumb both spake and saw. *false accuser ◆ mute*
23 And all the people were amazed, and said, Is not this the son of David? John 4:29
24 But when the Pharisees heard *it*, they said, This *fellow* doth not cast out devils, but by Beelzebub the prince of the devils. Matt. 9:34
25 And Jesus knew their thoughts, and said unto them, Every kingdom divided against itself is brought to desolation; and every city or house divided against itself shall not stand:
26 And if Satan cast out Satan, he is divided against himself; how shall then his kingdom stand?
27 And if I by Beelzebub cast out devils, by whom do your children cast *them* out? therefore they shall be your judges.
28 But if I cast out devils by the Spirit of God, then the kingdom of God is come unto you.
29 Or else how can one enter into a strong man's house, and ^Tspoil his goods, except he first bind the strong man? and then he will spoil his house. Is. 49:24 ◆ *plunder*
30 He that is not with me is against me; and he that gathereth not with me scattereth abroad. Mark 9:40; Luke 9:50; 11:23
31 Wherefore I say unto you, All manner of sin and blasphemy shall be forgiven unto men: but the blasphemy *against* the Holy Ghost shall not be forgiven unto men. Is. 1:18
32 And whosoever speaketh a word against the Son of man, it shall be forgiven him: but whosoever speaketh against the Holy Ghost, it shall not be forgiven him, neither in this world, neither in the *world* to come. Matt. 11:19

12:32 It Happens Almost Imperceptibly

It is not God that blinds the eyes of men or hardens their hearts. . . . Often the process is gradual, and almost imperceptible. Light comes to the soul through God's word, through His servants, or by the direct agency of His Spirit; but when one ray of light is disregarded, there is a partial benumbing of the spiritual perceptions, and the second revealing of light is less clearly discerned. So the darkness increases, until it is night in the soul. *DA 322*

---

33 Either make the tree good, and his fruit good; or else make the tree corrupt, and his fruit corrupt: for the tree is known by *his* fruit. Matt. 7:16-20; Luke 6:43-44; John 15:4-7
34 O generation of ^Tvipers, how can ye, being evil, speak good things? for out of the abundance of the heart the mouth speaketh. Matt. 3:7; 23:33; Luke 6:45 ◆ *snakes*

35 A good man out of the good treasure of the heart bringeth forth good things: and an evil man out of the evil treasure bringeth forth evil things. Prov. 10:20-21
36 But I say unto you, That every idle word that men shall speak, they shall give account thereof in the day of judgment. Eccl. 12:14
37 For by thy words thou shalt be justified, and by thy words thou shalt be condemned.

The Sign of Jonah

38 Then certain of the scribes and of the Pharisees answered, saying, Master, we would see a sign from thee. Mark 8:11-12; Luke 11:16; John 2:18
39 But he answered and said unto them, An evil and adulterous generation seeketh after a sign; and there shall no sign be given to it, but the sign of the prophet Jonas: Is. 57:3
40 For as Jonas was three days and three nights in the whale's belly; so shall the Son of man be three days and three nights in the heart of the earth. Jon. 1:17; Matt. 16:21; 17:23
41 The men of Nineveh shall rise in judgment with this generation, and shall condemn it: because they repented at the preaching of Jonas; and, behold, a greater than Jonas *is* here. Is. 54:17; Matt. 12:6, 42
42 The queen of the south shall rise up in the judgment with this generation, and shall condemn it: for she came from the uttermost parts of the earth to hear the wisdom of Solomon; and, behold, a greater than Solomon *is* here.
43 When the unclean spirit is gone out of a man, he walketh through dry places, seeking rest, and findeth none. Ps. 63:1
44 Then he saith, I will return into my house from whence I came out; and when he is come, he findeth *it* empty, swept, and garnished.
45 Then goeth he, and taketh with himself seven other spirits more wicked than himself, and they enter in and dwell there: and the last *state* of that man is worse than the first. Even so shall it be also unto this wicked generation. Mark 5:9

The True Family of Jesus

46 While he yet talked to the people, behold, *his* mother and his brethren stood without, desiring to speak with him. John 2:12; Acts 1:14
47 Then one said unto him, Behold, thy mother and thy brethren stand without, desiring to speak with thee.
48 But he answered and said unto him that told him, Who is my mother? and who are my brethren?
49 And he stretched forth his hand toward his disciples, and said, Behold my mother and my brethren!

50 For whosoever shall do the will of my Father which is in heaven, the same is my brother, and sister, and mother. *John 15:14*

The Parable of the Sower and the Seed

13 The same day went Jesus out of the house, and sat by the sea side.

2 And great multitudes were gathered together unto him, so that he went into a ship, and sat; and the whole multitude stood on the shore. *Luke 5:3*

3 And he spake many things unto them in parables, saying, Behold, a sower went forth to sow; *Matt. 13:10-13*

13:3 Simple but Very Valuable

Because of its simplicity the parable of the sower has not been valued as it should be. From the natural seed cast into the soil, Christ desires to lead our minds to the gospel seed, the sowing of which results in bringing man back to his loyalty to God. *COL 33*

---

4 And when he sowed, some *seeds* fell by the way side, and the fowls came and devoured them up:

5 Some fell upon stony places, where they had not much earth: and ᵀforthwith they sprung up, because they had no deepness of earth: *immediately*

6 And when the sun was up, they were scorched; and because they had no root, they withered away.

7 And some fell among thorns; and the thorns sprung up, and choked them:

8 But other fell into good ground, and brought forth fruit, some an hundredfold, some sixtyfold, some thirtyfold. *Gen. 26:12; Matt. 13:23*

13:4–8 Counting the Cost

"The seed is the word of God." . . .

As the birds are ready to catch up the seed from the wayside, so Satan is ready to catch away the seeds of divine truth from the soul. . . .

It is not because men receive the word immediately, nor because they rejoice in it, that they fall away. . . . But those who in the parable are said to receive the word immediately, do not count the cost. *COL 41–47*

---

9 Who hath ears to hear, let him hear. *Rev. 2:7*

10 And the disciples came, and said unto him, Why speakest thou unto them in parables?

11 He answered and said unto them, Because it is given unto you to know the mysteries of the kingdom of heaven, but to them it is not given. *Matt. 16:17; 19:11; 1 John 2:27*

12 For whosoever hath, to him shall be given, and he shall have more abundance: but who-soever hath not, from him shall be taken away even that he hath. *Matt. 25:29; Luke 8:18; Rev. 2:5*

13 Therefore speak I to them in parables: because they seeing see not; and hearing they hear not, neither do they understand. *Jer. 5:21*

14 And in them is fulfilled the prophecy of Esaias, which saith, By hearing ye shall hear, and shall not understand; and seeing ye shall see, and shall not perceive: *Is. 6:9-10*

15 For this people's heart is ᵀwaxed ᵀgross, and *their* ears are dull of hearing, and their eyes they have closed; lest at any time they should see with *their* eyes, and hear with *their* ears, and should understand with *their* heart, and should be converted, and I should heal them. *Heb. 5:11* ◆ *become* ◆ *dull*

16 But blessed *are* your eyes, for they see: and your ears, for they hear. *Luke 10:23-24; John 20:29*

17 For ᵀverily I say unto you, That many prophets and righteous *men* have desired to see *those things* which ye see, and have not seen *them*; and to hear *those things* which ye hear, and have not heard *them*. *Heb. 11:13* ◆ *truly*

18 Hear ye therefore the parable of the sower.

19 When any one heareth the word of the kingdom, and understandeth *it* not, then cometh the wicked *one*, and catcheth away that which was sown in his heart. This is he which received seed by the way side. *Matt. 4:23; 1 John 2:13-14*

20 But he that received the seed into stony places, the same is he that heareth the word, and anon with joy receiveth it; *Is. 58:2*

21 Yet hath he not root in himself, but ᵀdureth for a while: for when tribulation or persecution ariseth because of the word, by and by he is offended. *Hos. 6:4; Matt. 11:6* ◆ *endures*

22 He also that received seed among the thorns is he that heareth the word; and the care of this world, and the deceitfulness of riches, choke the word, and he becometh unfruitful. *1 Tim. 6:9-10, 17; 2 Tim. 4:10*

23 But he that received seed into the good ground is he that heareth the word, and understandeth *it*; which also beareth fruit, and bringeth forth, some an hundredfold, some sixty, some thirty. *Matt. 13:8; John 15:16; Phil. 1:11*

The Parable of the Tares

24 Another parable put he forth unto them, saying, The kingdom of heaven is likened unto a man which sowed good seed in his field: *Matt. 13:33*

25 But while men slept, his enemy came and sowed ᵀtares among the wheat, and went his way. *weeds*

26 But when the blade was sprung up, and brought forth fruit, then appeared the tares also.

27 So the servants of the householder came and said unto him, Sir, didst not thou sow

13:24–30

good seed in thy field? from whence then hath it tares?

28 He said unto them, An enemy hath done this. The servants said unto him, Wilt thou then that we go and gather them up?

29 But he said, Nay; lest while ye gather up the tares, ye root up also the wheat with them.

30 Let both grow together until the harvest: and in the time of harvest I will say to the reapers, Gather ye together first the tares, and bind them in bundles to burn them: but gather the wheat into my barn. *Matt. 3:12*

> **Signs of the End**   See Matthew 13:39.

Descriptions of the Kingdom of Heaven
31 Another parable put he forth unto them, saying, The kingdom of heaven is like to a grain of mustard seed, which a man took, and sowed in his field: *Matt. 13:24*
32 Which indeed is the least of all seeds: but when it is grown, it is the greatest among herbs, and becometh a tree, so that the birds of the air come and lodge in the branches thereof. *Ezek. 31:6*
33 Another parable spake he unto them; The kingdom of heaven is like unto leaven, which a woman took, and hid in three measures of meal, till the whole was leavened. *Luke 13:21*
34 All these things spake Jesus unto the multitude in parables; and without a parable spake he not unto them: *Mark 4:33-34*
35 That it might be fulfilled which was spoken by the prophet, saying, I will open my mouth in parables; I will utter things which have been kept secret from the foundation of the world. *Ps. 78:2; Rom. 16:25-26; 1 Cor. 2:7*

The Meaning of the Tares
36 Then Jesus sent the multitude away, and went into the house: and his disciples came unto him, saying, Declare unto us the parable of the tares of the field. *Matt. 13:1*
37 He answered and said unto them, He that soweth the good seed is the Son of man;
38 The field is the world; the good seed are the children of the kingdom; but the tares are the children of the wicked *one*; *John 8:44; Acts 13:10*
39 The enemy that sowed them is the devil; the harvest is the end of the world; and the reapers are the angels. *Joel 3:13; Matt. 13:49; 24:3*

> **Signs of the End**   See Mark 4:26–29.

40 As therefore the tares are gathered and burned in the fire; so shall it be in the end of this world.
41 The Son of man shall send forth his angels, and they shall gather out of his kingdom all things that offend, and them which do iniquity; *Matt. 18:7; 24:31*

42 And shall cast them into a furnace of fire: there shall be wailing and gnashing of teeth. *Matt. 8:12; 13:50; 22:13*
43 Then shall the righteous shine forth as the sun in the kingdom of their Father. Who hath ears to hear, let him hear. *Dan. 12:3; Matt. 25:34*

More Descriptions of the Kingdom
44 Again, the kingdom of heaven is like unto treasure hid in a field; the which when a man hath found, he hideth, and for joy thereof goeth and selleth all that he hath, and buyeth that field. *Is. 55:1*

> **13:44 Looking for Buried Treasure**
>
> In the parable the field containing the treasure represents the Holy Scriptures. And the gospel is the treasure. . . .
> The word of God is to be our study. We are to educate our children in the truths found therein. It is an inexhaustible treasure; but men fail to find this treasure because they do not search until it is within their possession. *COL 104, 109*

45 Again, the kingdom of heaven is like unto a merchant man, seeking goodly pearls:
46 Who, when he had found one pearl of great price, went and sold all that he had, and bought it.
47 Again, the kingdom of heaven is like unto a net, that was cast into the sea, and gathered of every kind: *Matt. 4:19*
48 Which, when it was full, they drew to shore, and sat down, and gathered the good into vessels, but cast the bad away.
49 So shall it be at the end of the world: the angels shall come forth, and sever the wicked from among the just, *Matt. 13:39*
50 And shall cast them into the furnace of fire: there shall be wailing and gnashing of teeth. *Matt. 8:12*
51 Jesus saith unto them, Have ye understood all these things? They say unto him, Yea, Lord. *Matt. 13:11*
52 Then said he unto them, Therefore every scribe *which is* instructed unto the kingdom of heaven is like unto a man *that is* an householder, which bringeth forth out of his treasure *things* new and old. *Matt. 12:35*

Christ Is Rejected by His Own Countrymen
53 And it came to pass, *that* when Jesus had finished these parables, he departed thence.
54 And when he was come into his own country, he taught them in their synagogue, insomuch that they were astonished, and said, Whence hath this *man* this wisdom, and *these* mighty works? *Matt. 2:23*

13:39

55 Is not this the carpenter's son? is not his mother called Mary? and his brethren, James, and Joses, and Simon, and Judas?   Mark 6:3
56 And his sisters, are they not all with us? Whence then hath this *man* all these things?
57 And they were offended in him. But Jesus said unto them, A prophet is not without honour, save in his own country, and in his own house.   Matt. 11:6; Luke 4:24; John 4:44
58 And he did not many mighty works there because of their unbelief.

The Death of John the Baptist

14 At that time Herod the tetrarch heard of the fame of Jesus,   Mark 8:15; Luke 3:1
2 And said unto his servants, This is John the Baptist; he is risen from the dead; and therefore mighty works do shew forth themselves in him.   Matt. 16:14
3 For Herod had laid hold on John, and bound him, and put *him* in prison for Herodias' sake, his brother Philip's wife.   Matt. 4:12
4 For John said unto him, It is not lawful for thee to have her.   Lev. 18:16; 20:21
5 And when he would have put him to death, he feared the multitude, because they counted him as a prophet.   Matt. 11:9
6 But when Herod's birthday was kept, the daughter of Herodias danced before them, and pleased Herod.   Gen. 40:20
7 Whereupon he promised with an oath to give her whatsoever she would ask.
8 And she, being before instructed of her mother, said, Give me here John Baptist's head in a ᵀcharger.   *platter*
9 And the king was sorry: nevertheless for the oath's sake, and them which sat with him at meat, he commanded *it* to be given *her*.
10 And he sent, and beheaded John in the prison.   Matt. 17:12
11 And his head was brought in a charger, and given to the damsel: and she brought *it* to her mother.
12 And his disciples came, and took up the body, and buried it, and went and told Jesus.

Jesus Feeds More than Five Thousand

13 When Jesus heard *of it*, he departed thence by ship into a desert place apart: and when the people had heard *thereof*, they followed him on foot out of the cities.   Luke 9:10-17
14 And Jesus went forth, and saw a great multitude, and was moved with compassion toward them, and he healed their sick.   Heb. 4:15
15 And when it was evening, his disciples came to him, saying, This is a desert place, and the time is now past; send the multitude away, that they may go into the villages, and buy themselves ᵀvictuals.   Matt. 15:23   ◆ *food*
16 But Jesus said unto them, They need not depart; give ye them to eat.   2 Kin. 4:42-44
17 And they say unto him, We have here but five loaves, and two fishes.
18 He said, Bring them ᵀhither to me.   *here*
19 And he commanded the multitude to sit down on the grass, and took the five loaves, and the two fishes, and looking up to heaven, he blessed, and brake, and gave the loaves to *his* disciples, and the disciples to the multitude. 1 Sam. 9:13; Luke 24:30; Acts 27:35

14:17-19 A Lesson With Food

The simple food passed round by the hands of the disciples contained a whole treasure of lessons. . . . Christ could have spread before the people a rich repast, but food prepared merely for the gratification of appetite would have conveyed no lesson for their good. Christ taught them in this lesson that the natural provisions of God for man had been perverted. *DA 366, 367*

We Must Discern Our Weakness

Matthew 14:29-31

Jesus read the character of His disciples. He knew how sorely their faith was to be tried. In this incident on the sea He desired to reveal to Peter his own weakness—to show that his safety was in constant dependence upon divine power. . . . It was on the point where he thought himself strong that Peter was weak; and not until he discerned his weakness could he realize his need of dependence upon Christ. . . .

Day by day God instructs His children. By the circumstances of the daily life He is preparing them to act their part upon that wider stage to which His providence has appointed them. It is the issue of the daily test that determines their victory or defeat in life's great crisis.

Those who fail to realize their constant dependence upon God will be overcome by temptation. We may now suppose that our feet stand secure, and that we shall never be moved. We may say with confidence, "I know in whom I have believed; nothing can shake my faith in God and in His word." But Satan is planning to take advantage of our hereditary and cultivated traits of character, and to blind our eyes to our own necessities and defects. Only through realizing our own weakness and looking steadfastly unto Jesus can we walk securely. *DA 382*

20 And they did all eat, and were filled: and they took up of the fragments that remained twelve baskets full.   *Luke 9:17*

21 And they that had eaten were about five thousand men, beside women and children.

Jesus Walks on the Sea

22 And straightway Jesus ᵀconstrained his disciples to get into a ship, and to go before him unto the other side, while he sent the multitudes away.   *compelled*

23 And when he had sent the multitudes away, he went up into a mountain apart to pray: and when the evening was come, he was there alone.   *Luke 6:12*

24 But the ship was now in the midst of the sea, tossed with waves: for the wind was contrary.

25 And in the fourth watch of the night Jesus went unto them, walking on the sea.   *Job 9:8*

26 And when the disciples saw him walking on the sea, they were troubled, saying, It is a spirit; and they cried out for fear. *Luke 24:37*

27 But ᵀstraightway Jesus spake unto them, saying, Be of good cheer; it is I; be not afraid.   *Matt. 9:2 ◆ right away*

28 And Peter answered him and said, Lord, if it be thou, bid me come unto thee on the water.

29 And he said, Come. And when Peter was come down out of the ship, he walked on the water, to go to Jesus.

30 But when he saw the wind boisterous, he was afraid; and beginning to sink, he cried, saying, Lord, save me.

31 And immediately Jesus stretched forth *his* hand, and caught him, and said unto him, O thou of little faith, wherefore didst thou doubt?   *Matt. 6:30*

14:30 Look and Live

When trouble comes upon us, how often we are like Peter! We look upon the waves, instead of keeping our eyes fixed upon the Saviour. Our footsteps slide, and the proud waters go over our souls. Jesus did not bid Peter come to Him that he should perish; He does not call us to follow Him, and then forsake us. . . . "When thou passest through the waters, I will be with thee" (Isaiah 43:2). *DA 382*

---

32 And when they were come into the ship, the wind ceased.

33 Then they that were in the ship came and worshipped him, saying, Of a truth thou art the Son of God.   *Ps. 2:7*

Jesus Heals the Sick

34 And when they were gone over, they came into the land of Gennesaret.   *Mark 6:53-56*

35 And when the men of that place had knowledge of him, they sent out into all that country round about, and brought unto him all that were diseased;

36 And besought him that they might only touch the hem of his garment: and as many as touched were made perfectly whole.

The Religious Leaders Criticize the Disciples

15 Then came to Jesus scribes and Pharisees, which were of Jerusalem, saying,

2 Why do thy disciples transgress the tradition of the elders? for they wash not their hands when they eat bread.   *Luke 11:38*

The Commandments of God or the Traditions of Men

Matthew 15:1–14

[Jesus] answered, "Every plant, which My heavenly Father hath not planted, shall be rooted up." The customs and traditions so highly valued by the rabbis were of this world, not from heaven. However great their authority with the people, they could not endure the testing of God. Every human invention that has been substituted for the commandments of God will be found worthless in that day when "God shall bring every work into judgment, with every secret thing, whether it be good, or whether it be evil" (Ecclesiastes 12:14).

The substitution of the precepts of men for the commandments of God has not ceased. Even among Christians are found institutions and usages that have no better foundation than the traditions of the fathers. Such institutions, resting upon mere human authority, have supplanted those of divine appointment. Men cling to their traditions, and revere their customs, and cherish hatred against those who seek to show them their error. In this day, when we are bidden to call attention to the commandments of God and the faith of Jesus, we see the same enmity as was manifested in the days of Christ. Of the remnant people of God it is written, "The dragon was wroth with the woman, and went to make war with the remnant of her seed, which keep the commandments of God, and have the testimony of Jesus Christ" (Revelation 12:17). . . .

Let all who accept human authority, the customs of the church, or the traditions of the fathers, take heed to the warning conveyed in the words of Christ, "In vain they do worship Me, teaching for doctrines the commandments of men" [Matthew 15:9]. *DA 398*

3 But he answered and said unto them, Why do ye also ᵀtransgress the commandment of God by your tradition?   *violate*

4 For God commanded, saying, Honour thy father and mother: and, He that curseth father or mother, let him die the death. Ex. 20:12; 21:17

5 But ye say, Whosoever shall say to *his* father or *his* mother, *It is* a gift, by whatsoever thou mightest be profited by me;

6 And honour not his father or his mother, *he shall be free*. Thus have ye made the commandment of God of none effect by your tradition.

7 *Ye* hypocrites, well did Esaias prophesy of you, saying,

8 This people draweth nigh unto me with their mouth, and honoureth me with *their* lips; but their heart is far from me.   Is. 29:13

9 But in vain they do worship me, teaching *for* doctrines the commandments of men. Is. 29:13

10 And he called the multitude, and said unto them, Hear, and understand:

11 Not that which goeth into the mouth defileth a man; but that which cometh out of the mouth, this defileth a man.   Acts 10:14-15

12 Then came his disciples, and said unto him, Knowest thou that the Pharisees were offended, after they heard this saying?

15:12 No Compromise

The disciples noted the rage of the spies as their false teaching was exposed. They saw the angry looks, and heard the half-muttered words of dissatisfaction and revenge. Forgetting how often Christ had given evidence that He read the heart as an open book, they told Him of the effect of His words. Hoping that He might conciliate [overcome the distrust or hostility of] the enraged officials, they said to Jesus, "Knowest Thou that the Pharisees were offended, after they heard this saying?" *DA 398*

---

13 But he answered and said, Every plant, which my heavenly Father hath not planted, shall be rooted up.   Is. 60:21; 61:3; John 15:2

14 Let them alone: they be blind leaders of the blind. And if the blind lead the blind, both shall fall into the ditch.   Is. 56:10; Mal. 2:8

15 Then answered Peter and said unto him, Declare unto us this parable.   Matt. 13:36

16 And Jesus said, Are ye also yet without understanding?   Matt. 16:9

17 Do not ye yet understand, that whatsoever entereth in at the mouth goeth into the belly, and is cast out into the draught?   1 Cor. 6:13

18 But those things which proceed out of the mouth come forth from the heart; and they defile the man.   Matt. 12:34

19 For out of the heart proceed evil thoughts, murders, adulteries, fornications, thefts, false witness, blasphemies: Gal. 5:19-21

20 These are *the things* which defile a man: but to eat with unwashen hands defileth not a man.

The Faith of a Canaanite Woman

21 Then Jesus went thence, and departed into the coasts of Tyre and Sidon.

22 And, behold, a woman of Canaan came out of the same coasts, and cried unto him, saying, Have mercy on me, O Lord, *thou* Son of David; my daughter is grievously vexed with a ᵀdevil.   Matt. 9:27; 17:15 ◆ *demon*

23 But he answered her not a word. And his disciples came and ᵀbesought him, saying, Send her away; for she crieth after us.   ◆ *begged*

24 But he answered and said, I am not sent but unto the lost sheep of the house of Israel.   Rom. 15:8

25 Then came she and worshipped him, saying, Lord, help me.   Matt. 8:2

26 But he answered and said, It is not meet to take the children's bread, and to cast *it* to dogs.   Matt. 7:6

27 And she said, Truth, Lord: yet the dogs eat of the crumbs which fall from their masters' table.   Luke 16:21

28 Then Jesus answered and said unto her, O woman, great *is* thy faith: be it unto thee even as thou wilt. And her daughter was made whole from that very hour.   Matt. 8:13

29 And Jesus departed from thence, and came nigh unto the sea of Galilee; and went up into a mountain, and sat down there.   Matt. 4:18

30 And great multitudes came unto him, having with them *those that were* lame, blind, ᵀdumb, maimed, and many others, and cast them down at Jesus' feet; and he healed them: *mute*

31 Insomuch that the multitude wondered, when they saw the dumb to speak, the maimed to be whole, the lame to walk, and the blind to see: and they glorified the God of Israel.   Matt. 9:8, 33; 18:8

Jesus Feeds More than Four Thousand

32 Then Jesus called his disciples *unto him*, and said, I have compassion on the multitude, because they continue with me now three days, and have nothing to eat: and I will not send them away fasting, lest they faint in the way.   Matt. 9:36

33 And his disciples say unto him, Whence should we have so much bread in the wilderness, as to fill so great a multitude?

34 And Jesus saith unto them, How many loaves have ye? And they said, Seven, and a few little fishes.

35 And he commanded the multitude to sit down on the ground.

36 And he took the seven loaves and the fishes, and gave thanks, and brake *them*, and gave to his disciples, and the disciples to the multitude.   Luke 22:19

37 And they did all eat, and were filled: and they took up of the broken *meat* that was left seven baskets full.

38 And they that did eat were four thousand men, beside women and children.

39 And he sent away the multitude, and took ship, and came into the coasts of Magdala.   Mark 8:10

The Pharisees Demand a Sign

16 The Pharisees also with the Sadducees came, and tempting desired him that he would shew them a sign from heaven.   Matt. 16:6; Luke 11:16; John 8:6

2 He answered and said unto them, When it is evening, ye say, *It will be* fair weather: for the sky is red.

3 And in the morning, *It will be* foul weather to day: for the sky is red and ᵀlowring. O *ye* hypocrites, ye can discern the face of the sky; but can ye not *discern* the signs of the times?   Luke 12:56 ◆ *overcast*

4 A wicked and adulterous generation seeketh after a sign; and there shall no sign be given unto it, but the sign of the prophet Jonas. And he left them, and departed.

16:1–4 His Life the Greatest Sign

That which led the Jews to reject the Saviour's work was the highest evidence of His divine character. . . . The highest evidence that He came from God is that His life revealed the character of God. He did the works and spoke the words of God. Such a life is the greatest of all miracles. . . .

The change in human hearts, the transformation of human characters, is a miracle that reveals an ever-living Saviour, working to rescue souls. A consistent life in Christ is a great miracle. *DA 406, 407*

---

5 And when his disciples were come to the other side, they had forgotten to take bread.

6 Then Jesus said unto them, Take heed and beware of the leaven of the Pharisees and of the Sadducees.   Mark 8:15; Luke 12:1; 1 Cor. 5:6-8

7 And they reasoned among themselves, saying, *It is* because we have taken no bread.

8 *Which* when Jesus perceived, he said unto them, O ye of little faith, why reason ye among yourselves, because ye have brought no bread?   Matt. 6:30; 8:26; 14:31

9 Do ye not yet understand, neither remember the five loaves of the five thousand, and how many baskets ye took up?   Matt. 14:17-21

10 Neither the seven loaves of the four thousand, and how many baskets ye took up?   Matt. 15:34-38

11 How is it that ye do not understand that I spake *it* not to you concerning bread, that ye should beware of the leaven of the Pharisees and of the Sadducees?   Matt. 16:6

12 Then understood they how that he bade *them* not beware of the leaven of bread, but of the doctrine of the Pharisees and of the Sadducees.

Peter Declares His Faith

13 When Jesus came into the coasts of Caesarea Philippi, he asked his disciples, saying, Whom do men say that I the Son of man am?   Luke 9:18-20

14 And they said, Some *say that thou art* John the Baptist: some, Elias; and others, Jeremias, or one of the prophets. Mark 6:15; John 1:21

15 He saith unto them, But whom say ye that I am?

16 And Simon Peter answered and said, Thou art the Christ, the Son of the living God.   Ps. 42:2; John 11:27; Acts 14:15

17 And Jesus answered and said unto him, Blessed art thou, Simon Bar-jona: for flesh and blood hath not revealed *it* unto thee, but my Father which is in heaven. John 1:42; Gal. 1:16

18 And I say also unto thee, That thou art Peter, and upon this rock I will build my church; and the gates of hell shall not prevail against it.   Job 38:17; Is. 38:10; John 1:42

16:18 Peter a Stone Not a Rock

The word Peter signifies a stone—a rolling stone. Peter was not the rock upon which the church was founded. The gates of hell did prevail against him when he denied his Lord with cursing and swearing. . . .

That Rock is Himself—His own body, for us broken and bruised. Against the church built upon this foundation, the gates of hell shall not prevail. *DA 413*

---

19 And I will give unto thee the keys of the kingdom of heaven: and whatsoever thou shalt bind on earth shall be bound in heaven: and whatsoever thou shalt loose on earth shall be loosed in heaven.   Is. 22:22; John 20:23

20 Then charged he his disciples that they should tell no man that he was Jesus the Christ.   Matt. 8:4; Mark 8:30; Luke 9:21

Jesus Foretells His Death and Resurrection

21 From that time forth began Jesus to shew unto his disciples, how that he must go unto Jerusalem, and suffer many things of the elders and chief priests and scribes,

and be killed, and be raised again the third day.   Matt. 17:12, 22-23; 27:63

22 Then Peter took him, and began to rebuke him, saying, Be it far from thee, Lord: this shall not be unto thee.

23 But he turned, and said unto Peter, Get thee behind me, Satan: thou art an offence unto me: for thou savourest not the things that be of God, but those that be of men.

What It Means to Follow Jesus

24 Then said Jesus unto his disciples, If any man will come after me, let him deny himself, and take up his cross, and follow me.

25 For whosoever will save his life shall lose it: and whosoever will lose his life for my sake shall find it.   Matt. 10:39

26 For what is a man profited, if he shall gain the whole world, and lose his own soul? or what shall a man give in exchange for his soul?   Ps. 49:7-8

27 For the Son of man shall come in the glory of his Father with his angels; and then he shall reward every man according to his works.   Ps. 62:12; Rom. 2:6; 2 Cor. 5:10

> Christ's Return   See 2 Timothy 4:6–8.

28 Verily I say unto you, There be some standing here, which shall not taste of death, till they see the Son of man coming in his kingdom.   Matt. 10:23

The Transfiguration

17 And after six days Jesus taketh Peter, James, and John his brother, and bringeth them up into an high mountain apart,

2 And was transfigured before them: and his face did shine as the sun, and his ᵀraiment was white as the light.   Ps. 104:2 ◆ clothing

3 And, behold, there appeared unto them Moses and Elias talking with him.

4 Then answered Peter, and said unto Jesus, Lord, it is good for us to be here: if thou wilt, let us make here three tabernacles; one for thee, and one for Moses, and one for Elias.

5 While he yet spake, behold, a bright cloud overshadowed them: and behold a voice out of the cloud, which said, This is my beloved Son, in whom I am well pleased; hear ye him.   Deut. 18:15; Is. 42:1; Matt. 3:17

6 And when the disciples heard it, they fell on their face, and were sore afraid.   2 Pet. 1:18

7 And Jesus came and touched them, and said, Arise, and be not afraid.   Dan. 8:18

8 And when they had lifted up their eyes, they saw no man, save Jesus only.

9 And as they came down from the mountain, Jesus charged them, saying, Tell the vision to no man, until the Son of man be risen again from the dead.   Mark 8:30

10 And his disciples asked him, saying, Why then say the scribes that Elias must first come?   Matt. 11:14

11 And Jesus answered and said unto them, Elias truly shall first come, and restore all things.   Luke 1:16-17

12 But I say unto you, That Elias is come already, and they knew him not, but have done unto him whatsoever they listed. Likewise shall also the Son of man suffer of them.

13 Then the disciples understood that he spake unto them of John the Baptist.

Jesus Heals a Demon-possessed Boy

14 And when they were come to the multitude, there came to him a certain man, kneeling down to him, and saying,

15 Lord, have mercy on my son: for he is lunatick, and sore vexed: for ofttimes he falleth into the fire, and oft into the water.   Matt. 4:24

16 And I brought him to thy disciples, and they could not cure him.

17 Then Jesus answered and said, O faithless and perverse generation, how long shall I be with you? how long shall I suffer you? bring him ᵀhither to me.   John 20:27 ◆ here

18 And Jesus rebuked the ᵀdevil; and he departed out of him: and the child was cured from that very hour.   Matt. 9:22 ◆ demon

19 Then came the disciples to Jesus apart, and said, Why could not we cast him out?

> **17:20 A Faith That Makes Nothing Impossible**
>
> Their faith must be strengthened by fervent prayer and fasting, and humiliation of heart. They must be emptied of self, and be filled with the Spirit and power of God. Earnest, persevering supplication to God in faith—faith that leads to entire dependence upon God, and unreserved consecration to His work—can alone avail to bring men the Holy Spirit's aid in the battle against principalities and powers, the rulers of the darkness of this world, and wicked spirits in high places. *DA 431*

20 And Jesus said unto them, Because of your unbelief: for verily I say unto you, If ye have faith as a grain of mustard seed, ye shall say unto this mountain, Remove hence to yonder place; and it shall remove; and nothing shall be impossible unto you.   Matt. 21:21; Luke 17:6

> Faith   See Romans 10:17.

21 Howbeit this kind goeth not out but by prayer and fasting.   Mark 9:29

Jesus Again Foretells His Death and Resurrection

22 And while they abode in Galilee, Jesus

said unto them, The Son of man shall be betrayed into the hands of men: Matt. 16:21
23 And they shall kill him, and the third day he shall be raised again. And they were exceeding sorry. Matt. 16:21

Paying the Temple Tax

24 And when they were come to Capernaum, they that received tribute *money* came to Peter, and said, Doth not your master pay tribute? Ex. 30:13; 38:26; Mark 9:33
25 He saith, Yes. And when he was come into the house, Jesus prevented him, saying, What thinkest thou, Simon? of whom do the kings of the earth take custom or tribute? of their own children, or of strangers?
26 Peter saith unto him, Of strangers. Jesus saith unto him, Then are the children free.
27 Notwithstanding, lest we should offend them, go thou to the sea, and cast an hook, and take up the fish that first cometh up; and when thou hast opened his mouth, thou shalt find a piece of money: that take, and give unto them for me and thee. 1 Cor. 8:13

> **17:24–27 A Great Principle**
>
> While Jesus made it plain that He was under no obligation to pay the tribute, He entered into no controversy with the Jews in regard to the matter; for they would have misinterpreted His words, and turned them against Him. . . . This lesson would be of great value to His disciples. . . . So far as possible, they were to avoid giving occasion for misinterpretation of their faith. While Christians are not to sacrifice one principle of truth, they should avoid controversy whenever it is possible to do so. *DA 434*

Greatness in the Kingdom

18 At the same time came the disciples unto Jesus, saying, Who is the greatest in the kingdom of heaven? Mark 9:33-37
2 And Jesus called a little child unto him, and set him in the midst of them,
3 And said, Verily I say unto you, Except ye be converted, and become as little children, ye shall not enter into the kingdom of heaven. Ps. 131:2; 1 Cor. 14:20; 1 Pet. 2:2
4 Whosoever therefore shall humble himself as this little child, the same is greatest in the kingdom of heaven. Matt. 23:11-12
5 And whoso shall receive one such little child in my name receiveth me. Matt. 25:40

Causing Others to Sin

6 But whoso shall offend one of these little ones which believe in me, it were better for him that a millstone were hanged about his neck, and *that* he were drowned in the depth of the sea. Mark 9:42
7 Woe unto the world because of offences! for it must needs be that offences come; but woe to that man by whom the offence cometh! Matt. 26:24; Luke 17:1; 1 Cor. 11:19
8 Wherefore if thy hand or thy foot offend thee, cut them off, and cast *them* from thee: it is better for thee to enter into life halt or maimed, rather than having two hands or two feet to be cast into everlasting fire. Matt. 5:29-30
9 And if thine eye offend thee, pluck it out, and cast *it* from thee: it is better for thee to enter into life with one eye, rather than having two eyes to be cast into hell fire. Matt. 5:22
10 Take heed that ye despise not one of these little ones; for I say unto you, That in heaven their angels do always behold the face of my Father which is in heaven. Ps. 34:7; Heb. 1:14

Before Honor Is Humility

Matthew 18:1–5

Very tenderly, yet with solemn emphasis, Jesus tried to correct the evil. He showed what is the principle that bears sway in the kingdom of heaven, and in what true greatness consists, as estimated by the standard of the courts above. . . .

Before honor is humility. To fill a high place before men, Heaven chooses the worker who, like John the Baptist, takes a lowly place before God. The most childlike disciple is the most efficient in labor for God. The heavenly intelligences can co-operate with him who is seeking, not to exalt self, but to save souls. . . .

But when men exalt themselves, feeling that they are a necessity for the success of God's great plan, the Lord causes them to be set aside. . . .

It was not enough for the disciples of Jesus to be instructed as to the nature of His kingdom. What they needed was a change of heart that would bring them into harmony with its principles. . . . The simplicity, the self-forgetfulness, and the confiding love of a little child are the attributes that Heaven values. These are the characteristics of real greatness. . . .

The sincere, contrite soul is precious in the sight of God. He places His own signet upon men, not by their rank, not by their wealth, not by their intellectual greatness, but by their oneness with Christ. *DA 436, 437*

11 For the Son of man is come to save that which was lost.   Luke 19:10

The Lost Sheep

12 How think ye? if a man have an hundred sheep, and one of them be gone astray, doth he not leave the ninety and nine, and goeth into the mountains, and seeketh that which is gone astray?   Luke 15:4-7

13 And if so be that he find it, verily I say unto you, he rejoiceth more of that *sheep*, than of the ninety and nine which went not astray.

14 Even so it is not the will of your Father which is in heaven, that one of these little ones should perish.   John 17:12

Dealing with Believers Who Do Wrong

15 Moreover if thy brother shall trespass against thee, go and tell him his fault between thee and him alone: if he shall hear thee, thou hast gained thy brother.   Lev. 19:17; 1 Cor. 9:19-21

18:15 Dirty Laundry

But it is to the wrongdoer himself that we are to present the wrong. We are not to make it a matter of comment and criticism among ourselves; nor even after it is told to the church, are we at liberty to repeat it to others. A knowledge of the faults of Christians will be only a cause of stumbling to the unbelieving world; and by dwelling upon these things, we ourselves can receive only harm; for it is by beholding that we become changed. *DA 441*

---

16 But if he will not hear *thee, then* take with thee one or two more, that in the mouth of two or three witnesses every word may be established.   Deut. 19:15; John 8:17; 2 Cor. 13:1

17 And if he shall neglect to hear them, tell *it* unto the church: but if he neglect to hear the church, let him be unto thee as an heathen man and a publican.   Matt. 5:46; 6:7; 2 Thess. 3:6

18 Verily I say unto you, Whatsoever ye shall bind on earth shall be bound in heaven: and whatsoever ye shall loose on earth shall be loosed in heaven.   Matt. 16:19; John 20:23

19 Again I say unto you, That if two of you shall agree on earth as touching any thing that they shall ask, it shall be done for them of my Father which is in heaven.   Matt. 7:7

20 For where two or three are gathered together in my name, there am I in the midst of them.   Matt. 28:20

Forgiving Others

21 Then came Peter to him, and said, Lord, how ᵀoft shall my brother sin against me, and I forgive him? till seven times? Matt. 18:15 ◆ *often*

22 Jesus saith unto him, I say not unto thee, Until seven times: but, Until seventy times seven.

23 Therefore is the kingdom of heaven likened unto a certain king, which would take account of his servants.   Matt. 13:24

24 And when he had begun to reckon, one was brought unto him, which owed him ten thousand talents.

25 But ᵀforasmuch as he had not to pay, his lord commanded him to be sold, and his wife, and children, and all that he had, and payment to be made. Lev. 25:39; 2 Kin. 4:1; Neh. 5:5 ◆ *since*

26 The servant therefore fell down, and worshipped him, saying, Lord, have patience with me, and I will pay thee all.   Matt. 8:2

27 Then the lord of that servant was moved with compassion, and loosed him, and forgave him the debt.

28 But the same servant went out, and found one of his fellowservants, which owed him an hundred pence: and he laid hands on him, and took *him* by the throat, saying, Pay me that thou owest.   Matt. 20:2

29 And his fellowservant fell down at his feet, and ᵀbesought him, saying, Have patience with me, and I will pay thee all. *begged*

30 And he would not: but went and cast him into prison, till he should pay the debt.

31 So when his fellowservants saw what

How to Deal With Correcting Errors

Matthew 18:15–17

For evils that we might have checked, we are just as responsible as if we were guilty of the acts ourselves.

But it is to the wrongdoer himself that we are to present the wrong. We are not to make it a matter of comment and criticism among ourselves; nor even after it is told to the church, are we at liberty to repeat it to others. A knowledge of the faults of Christians will be only a cause of stumbling to the unbelieving world; and by dwelling upon these things, we ourselves can receive only harm; for it is by beholding that we become changed. While we seek to correct the errors of a brother, the Spirit of Christ will lead us to shield him, as far as possible, from the criticism of even his own brethren, and how much more from the censure of the unbelieving world. We ourselves are erring, and need Christ's pity and forgiveness, and just as we wish Him to deal with us, He bids us deal with one another. *DA 441*

was done, they were very sorry, and came and told unto their lord all that was done.

32 Then his lord, after that he had called him, said unto him, O thou wicked servant, I forgave thee all that debt, because thou desiredst me:

33 Shouldest not thou also have had compassion on thy fellowservant, even as I had pity on thee? Col. 3:13

34 And his lord was ᵀwroth, and delivered him to the tormentors, till he should pay all that was due unto him. Matt. 5:25-26 ◆ *angered*

35 So likewise shall my heavenly Father do also unto you, if ye from your hearts forgive not every one his brother their trespasses.

Jesus Heals Many

19 And it came to pass, *that* when Jesus had finished these sayings, he departed from Galilee, and came into the coasts of Judaea beyond Jordan; John 10:40

2 And great multitudes followed him; and he healed them there. Matt. 12:15

A Discussion about Divorce

3 The Pharisees also came unto him, tempting him, and saying unto him, Is it lawful for a man to put away his wife for every cause? John 8:6

4 And he answered and said unto them, Have ye not read, that he which made *them* at the beginning made them male and female,

5 And said, For this cause shall a man leave father and mother, and shall cleave to his wife: and they twain shall be one flesh? 1 Cor. 6:16

6 Wherefore they are no more ᵀtwain, but one flesh. What therefore God hath joined together, let not man put ᵀasunder. *two* ◆ *apart*

7 They say unto him, Why did Moses then command to give a writing of divorcement, and to put her away? Deut. 24:1-4; Matt. 5:31

8 He saith unto them, Moses because of the hardness of your hearts suffered you to put away your wives: but from the beginning it was not so. Gen. 2:24

9 And I say unto you, Whosoever shall put away his wife, except *it be* for fornication, and shall marry another, committeth adultery: and whoso marrieth her which is put away doth commit adultery. Luke 16:18; 1 Cor. 7:39

Marriage See 1 Corinthians 7:10, 11.

10 His disciples say unto him, If the case of the man be so with *his* wife, it is not good to marry.

11 But he said unto them, All *men* cannot receive this saying, save *they* to whom it is given. Matt. 13:11; 1 Cor. 7:2, 17

12 For there are some ᵀeunuchs, which were so born from *their* mother's womb: and there are some eunuchs, which were made eunuchs

of men: and there be eunuchs, which have made themselves eunuchs for the kingdom of heaven's sake. He that is able to receive *it*, let him receive *it*. *castrated male servants*

Jesus Blesses Little Children

13 Then were there brought unto him little children, that he should put *his* hands on them, and pray: and the disciples rebuked them.

14 But Jesus said, Suffer little children, and forbid them not, to come unto me: for of such is the kingdom of heaven. Luke 18:16; 1 Cor. 14:20

> **19:14 Mother's Most Important Work**
>
> As the mother teaches her children to obey her because they love her, she is teaching them the first lessons in the Christian life. The mother's love represents to the child the love of Christ, and the little ones who trust and obey their mother are learning to trust and obey the Saviour. *DA 515*

15 And he laid *his* hands on them, and departed thence.

Jesus and the Rich Young Man

16 And, behold, one came and said unto him, Good Master, what good thing shall I do, that I may have eternal life? John 3:15; 1 John 1:2

17 And he said unto him, Why callest thou me good? *there is* none good but one, *that is,* God: but if thou wilt enter into life, keep the commandments. Lev. 18:5; Rom. 10:5; 1 John 4:16

> **19:17 The Law Now and Then**
>
> The character of God is expressed in His law; and in order for you to be in harmony with God, the principles of His law must be the spring of your every action.
>
> Christ does not lessen the claims of the law. In unmistakable language He presents obedience to it as the condition of eternal life—the same condition that was required of Adam before his fall. . . . The requirement under the covenant of grace is just as broad as the requirement made in Eden—harmony with God's law, which is holy, just, and good. *COL 391*

18 He saith unto him, Which? Jesus said, Thou shalt do no murder, Thou shalt not commit adultery, Thou shalt not steal, Thou shalt not bear false witness,

19 Honour thy father and *thy* mother: and, Thou shalt love thy neighbour as thyself. Ex. 20:12; Lev. 19:18; Matt. 22:39

20 The young man saith unto him, All these things have I kept from my youth up: what lack I yet? Phil. 3:6

21 Jesus said unto him, If thou wilt be perfect, go *and* sell that thou hast, and give to the

poor, and thou shalt have treasure in heaven: and come *and* follow me. Luke 12:33; Acts 2:45

22 But when the young man heard that saying, he went away sorrowful: for he had great possessions. Ezek. 33:31

19:20–22 Love of Self Unfits Us

The lover of self is a transgressor of the law. . . . [The rich young ruler] professed to have kept the commandments, but he was destitute of the principle which is the very spirit and life of them all. He did not possess true love for God or man. This want was the want of everything that would qualify him to enter the kingdom of heaven. In his love of self and worldly gain he was out of harmony with the principles of heaven. . . .

He wanted eternal life, but would not receive into the soul that unselfish love which alone is life. *COL 392, 393*

It Is Difficult for the Rich to Enter the Kingdom

23 Then said Jesus unto his disciples, Verily I say unto you, That a rich man shall hardly enter into the kingdom of heaven. Mark 10:23

24 And again I say unto you, It is easier for a camel to go through the eye of a needle, than for a rich man to enter into the kingdom of God. Mark 10:24-25

25 When his disciples heard *it*, they were exceedingly amazed, saying, Who then can be saved?

26 But Jesus beheld *them*, and said unto them, With men this is impossible; but with God all things are possible. Gen. 18:14; Job 42:2

27 Then answered Peter and said unto him, Behold, we have forsaken all, and followed thee; what shall we have therefore?

28 And Jesus said unto them, Verily I say unto you, That ye which have followed me, in the regeneration when the Son of man shall sit in the throne of his glory, ye also shall sit upon twelve thrones, judging the twelve tribes of Israel. Matt. 16:27; 25:31; Rev. 3:21

29 And every one that hath forsaken houses, or brethren, or sisters, or father, or mother, or wife, or children, or lands, for my name's sake, shall receive an hundredfold, and shall inherit everlasting life. Luke 14:26

30 But many *that are* first shall be last; and the last *shall be* first. Matt. 20:16; Mark 10:31; Luke 13:30

The Parable of the Vineyard Workers

20 For the kingdom of heaven is like unto a man *that is* an householder, which went out early in the morning to hire labourers into his vineyard. Song 8:11-12

20:2–7 Where Is Our Confidence?

In the parable [of the laborers in the vineyard] the first laborers agreed to work for a stipulated sum, and they received the amount specified, nothing more. Those later hired believed the master's promise, "Whatsoever is right, that shall ye receive." They showed their confidence in him by asking no question in regard to wages. They trusted to his justice and equity. They were rewarded, not according to the amount of their labor, but according to the generosity of his purpose. *COL 397*

2 And when he had agreed with the labourers for a ᵀpenny a day, he sent them into his vineyard. *daily wage of Roman soldier*

3 And he went out about the third hour, and saw others standing idle in the marketplace,

4 And said unto them; Go ye also into the vineyard, and whatsoever is right I will give you. And they went their way.

Having the Right Spirit

Matthew 20:1–16

So God desires us to trust in Him who justifieth the ungodly. His reward is given not according to our merit but according to His own purpose, "which He purposed in Christ Jesus our Lord" (Ephesians 3:11). "Not by works of righteousness which we have done, but according to His mercy He saved us" (Titus 3:5). And for those who trust in Him He will do "exceeding abundantly above all that we ask or think" (Ephesians 3:20).

Not the amount of labor performed or its visible results but the spirit in which the work is done makes it of value with God. Those who came into the vineyard at the eleventh hour were thankful for an opportunity to work. Their hearts were full of gratitude to the one who had accepted them; and when at the close of the day the householder paid them for a full day's work, they were greatly surprised. They knew they had not earned such wages. And the kindness expressed in the countenance of their employer filled them with joy. They never forgot the goodness of the householder or the generous compensation they had received. Thus it is with the sinner who, knowing his unworthiness, has entered the Master's vineyard at the eleventh hour. His time of service seems so short, he feels that he is undeserving of reward; but he is filled with joy that God has accepted him at all. He works with a humble, trusting spirit, thankful for the privilege of being a co-worker with Christ. This spirit God delights to honor. *COL 397, 398*

5 Again he went out about the sixth and ninth hour, and did likewise.

6 And about the eleventh hour he went out, and found others standing idle, and saith unto them, Why stand ye here all the day idle?

7 They say unto him, Because no man hath hired us. He saith unto them, Go ye also into the vineyard; and whatsoever is right, *that* shall ye receive.

8 So when even was come, the lord of the vineyard saith unto his steward, Call the labourers, and give them *their* hire, beginning from the last unto the first.　　　Lev. 19:13

9 And when they came that *were hired* about the eleventh hour, they received every man a penny.

10 But when the first came, they supposed that they should have received more; and they likewise received every man a penny.

11 And when they had received *it*, they murmured against the ᵀgoodman of the house,　　　　　　　　　　*male leader*

12 Saying, These last have ᵀwrought *but* one hour, and thou hast made them equal unto us, which have borne the burden and heat of the day.　　Luke 12:55 ◆ *worked*

13 But he answered one of them, and said, Friend, I do thee no wrong: didst not thou agree with me for a penny?　　Matt. 22:12; 26:50

14 Take *that* thine *is*, and go thy way: I will give unto this last, even as unto thee.

15 Is it not lawful for me to do what I will with mine own? Is thine eye evil, because I am good?　　　Deut. 15:9; Matt. 6:23; Mark 7:22

16 So the last shall be first, and the first last: for many be called, but few chosen.　Mark 10:31

Jesus Again Foretells His Death and Resurrection

17 And Jesus going up to Jerusalem took the twelve disciples apart in the way, and said unto them,　　　　　　　Mark 10:32-34

18 Behold, we go up to Jerusalem; and the Son of man shall be betrayed unto the chief priests and unto the scribes, and they shall condemn him to death,　　Matt. 16:21; 26:66; 27:1

19 And shall deliver him to the Gentiles to mock, and to scourge, and to crucify *him*: and the third day he shall rise again.　Mark 15:16-20

A Mother's Request

20 Then came to him the mother of Zebedee's children with her sons, worshipping *him*, and desiring a certain thing of him.　　　　　　Matt. 4:21; 8:2; 27:56

21 And he said unto her, What wilt thou? She saith unto him, Grant that these my two sons may sit, the one on thy right hand, and the other on the left, in thy kingdom.　Matt. 19:28

22 But Jesus answered and said, Ye know not what ye ask. Are ye able to drink of the cup that I shall drink of, and to be baptized with the baptism that I am baptized with? They say unto him, We are able.　Luke 22:42; John 18:11

20:20–22 The Importance of Character

In the kingdom of God, position is not gained through favoritism. It is not earned, nor is it received through an arbitrary bestowal. It is the result of character. The crown and the throne are the tokens of a condition attained; they are the tokens of self-conquest through our Lord Jesus Christ. . . .

The one who stands nearest to Christ will be he who on earth has drunk most deeply of the spirit of His self-sacrificing love. *DA 549*

---

23 And he saith unto them, Ye shall drink indeed of my cup, and be baptized with the baptism that I am baptized with: but to sit on my right hand, and on my left, is not mine to give, but *it shall be given to them* for whom it is prepared of my Father.　Acts 12:2; Rev. 1:9

24 And when the ten heard *it*, they were moved with ᵀindignation against the two brethren.　　　　　　　　　　　*anger*

25 But Jesus called them *unto him*, and said, Ye know that the princes of the Gentiles exercise dominion over them, and they that are great exercise authority upon them.　　　　　　　　　Luke 22:25-27

26 But it shall not be so among you: but whosoever will be great among you, let him be your minister;　　　　　　Mark 9:35

27 And whosoever will be chief among you, let him be your servant:

28 Even as the Son of man came not to be ministered unto, but to minister, and to give his life a ransom for many.　1 Tim. 2:6; Heb. 9:28

Jesus Heals Two Blind Men

29 And as they departed from Jericho, a great multitude followed him.　Mark 10:46-52

30 And, behold, two blind men sitting by the way side, when they heard that Jesus passed by, cried out, saying, Have mercy on us, O Lord, *thou* Son of David.　Matt. 21:9

31 And the multitude rebuked them, because they should hold their peace: but they cried the more, saying, Have mercy on us, O Lord, *thou* Son of David.　Matt. 19:13

32 And Jesus stood still, and called them, and said, What will ye that I shall do unto you?

33 They say unto him, Lord, that our eyes may be opened.

34 So Jesus had compassion *on them*, and touched their eyes: and immediately their eyes received sight, and they followed him.

Jesus Rides into Jerusalem

21 And when they drew nigh unto Jerusalem, and were come to Bethphage, unto the mount of Olives, then sent Jesus two disciples,   Matt. 24:3; 26:30; John 8:1

2 Saying unto them, Go into the village over against you, and ᵀstraightway ye shall find an ass tied, and a colt with her: loose *them*, and bring *them* unto me.   *right away*

3 And if any *man* say ought unto you, ye shall say, The Lord hath need of them; and straightway he will send them.

4 All this was done, that it might be fulfilled which was spoken by the prophet, saying,   Matt. 1:22

5 Tell ye the daughter of Sion, Behold, thy King cometh unto thee, meek, and sitting upon an ass, and a colt the foal of an ass.   Gen. 49:10; Is. 62:11; Jer. 23:5-6

6 And the disciples went, and did as Jesus commanded them,

7 And brought the ass, and the colt, and put on them their clothes, and they set *him* thereon.

8 And a very great multitude spread their garments in the way; others cut down branches from the trees, and strawed *them* in the way.   2 Kin. 9:13

9 And the multitudes that went before, and that followed, cried, saying, Hosanna to the Son of David: Blessed *is* he that cometh in the name of the Lord; Hosanna in the highest.

21:8, 9 Everything for Our Benefit

In this one triumphant scene of His earthly life [the triumphal entry into Jerusalem], the Saviour might have appeared escorted by heavenly angels, and heralded by the trump of God; but such a demonstration would have been contrary to the purpose of His mission, contrary to the law which had governed His life. He remained true to the humble lot He had accepted. The burden of humanity He must bear until His life was given for the life of the world. *DA 571*

---

10 And when he was come into Jerusalem, all the city was moved, saying, Who is this?

11 And the multitude said, This is Jesus the prophet of Nazareth of Galilee.   John 6:14

Jesus Drives the Moneychangers out of the Temple

12 And Jesus went into the temple of God, and cast out all them that sold and bought in the temple, and overthrew the tables of the moneychangers, and the seats of them that sold doves,   Lev. 1:14; 5:7; 12:8

13 And said unto them, It is written, My house shall be called the house of prayer; but ye have made it a den of thieves. Is. 56:7; Jer. 7:11

21:12, 13 Second Cleansing Worse Than First

The condition of things was even worse than before. . . . So completely were they controlled by their greed of gain that in the sight of God they were no better than thieves. . . .

The very symbols pointing to the Lamb of God they had made a means of getting gain. . . .

He knew that His efforts to reform a corrupt priesthood would be in vain; nevertheless His work must be done; to an unbelieving people the evidence of His divine mission must be given. *DA 589, 590*

---

14 And the blind and the lame came to him in the temple; and he healed them.

15 And when the chief priests and scribes saw the wonderful things that he did, and the children crying in the temple, and saying, Hosanna to the Son of David; they were sore displeased,   Matt. 21:9

16 And said unto him, Hearest thou what these say? And Jesus saith unto them, Yea; have ye never read, Out of the mouth of babes and sucklings thou hast perfected praise?

17 And he left them, and went out of the city into Bethany; and he lodged there. John 11:1, 18

Jesus Curses the Fig Tree

18 Now in the morning as he returned into the city, he hungered.   Matt. 4:2

19 And when he saw a fig tree in the way, he came to it, and found nothing thereon, but leaves only, and said unto it, Let no fruit grow on thee henceforward for ever. And presently the fig tree withered away.   Luke 13:6-9

20 And when the disciples saw *it*, they marvelled, saying, How soon is the fig tree withered away!

21 Jesus answered and said unto them, Verily I say unto you, If ye have faith, and doubt not, ye shall not only do this *which is done* to the fig tree, but also if ye shall say unto this mountain, Be thou removed, and be thou cast into the sea; it shall be done.   1 Cor. 13:2; James 1:6

22 And all things, whatsoever ye shall ask in prayer, believing, ye shall receive.   John 15:7

Jesus' Authority Is Challenged

23 And when he was come into the temple, the chief priests and the elders of the people came unto him as he was teaching, and said, By what authority doest thou these things? and who gave thee this authority?   Acts 4:7

24 And Jesus answered and said unto them, I also will ask you one thing, which if ye tell me, I in like wise will tell you by what authority I do these things.

25 The baptism of John, whence was it? from heaven, or of men? And they reasoned with themselves, saying, If we shall say,

From heaven; he will say unto us, Why did ye not then believe him?

26 But if we shall say, Of men; we fear the people; for all hold John as a prophet. Mark 6:20
27 And they answered Jesus, and said, We cannot tell. And he said unto them, Neither tell I you by what authority I do these things.

The Parable of the Prodigal Son

28 But what think ye? A *certain* man had two sons; and he came to the first, and said, Son, go work to day in my vineyard.   Matt. 17:25
29 He answered and said, I will not: but afterward he repented, and went.
30 And he came to the second, and said likewise. And he answered and said, I *go*, sir: and went not.
31 Whether of them ᵀtwain did the will of *his* father? They say unto him, The first. Jesus saith unto them, Verily I say unto you, That the publicans and the harlots go into the kingdom of God before you. Luke 7:29, 37-50 ◆ *two*
32 For John came unto you in the way of righteousness, and ye believed him not: but the publicans and the harlots believed him: and ye, when ye had seen *it*, repented not afterward, that ye might believe him. Matt. 11:18

The Parable of the Wicked Husbandmen

33 Hear another parable: There was a certain householder, which planted a vineyard, and hedged it round about, and digged a winepress in it, and built a tower, and let it out to ᵀhusbandmen, and went into a far country: Matt. 25:14-15 ◆ *farmers*
34 And when the time of the fruit drew near, he sent his servants to the husbandmen, that they might receive the fruits of it.

> **21:28–32 What God Has Always Wanted**
>
> As the Lord's vineyard [God's chosen people] were to produce fruit altogether different from that of the heathen nations. . . .
>
> It was the privilege of the Jewish nation to represent the character of God as it had been revealed to Moses. . . . In the purity of their characters, in the holiness of their lives, in their mercy and loving-kindness and compassion, they were to show that "the law of the Lord is perfect, converting the soul" (Psalm 19:7). *COL 285, 286*

35 And the husbandmen took his servants, and beat one, and killed another, and stoned another.   Heb. 11:36-37
36 Again, he sent other servants more than the first: and they did unto them likewise.   Matt. 22:4
37 But last of all he sent unto them his son, saying, They will reverence my son.
38 But when the husbandmen saw the son, they said among themselves, This is the heir; come, let us kill him, and let us seize on his inheritance.
39 And they caught him, and cast *him* out of the vineyard, and slew *him*.   Acts 2:23
40 When the lord therefore of the vineyard cometh, what will he do unto those husbandmen?
41 They say unto him, He will miserably destroy those wicked men, and will let out *his* vineyard unto other husbandmen, which shall render him the fruits in their seasons.   Matt. 21:43; Acts 18:6; 28:28
42 Jesus saith unto them, Did ye never read in the scriptures, The stone which the builders rejected, the same is become the head of

---

A Warning for All Time

Matthew 21:18, 19

"The time of figs was not yet." But in the orchard to which Jesus came, one tree appeared to be in advance of all the others. It was already covered with leaves. It is the nature of the fig tree that before the leaves open, the growing fruit appears. Therefore this tree in full leaf gave promise of well-developed fruit. But its appearance was deceptive. Upon searching its branches, from the lowest bough to the topmost twig, Jesus found "nothing but leaves." It was a mass of pretentious foliage, nothing more. . . .

The warning is for all time. Christ's act in cursing the tree which His own power had created stands as a warning to all churches and to all Christians. No one can live the law of God without ministering to others. . . . Some who think themselves excellent Christians do not understand what constitutes service for God. They plan and study to please themselves. They act only in reference to self. . . . Not for others but for themselves do they minister. God created them to live in a world where unselfish service must be performed. . . . But self is so large that they cannot see anything else. They are not in touch with humanity. Those who thus live for self are like the fig tree, which made every pretension but was fruitless. They observe the forms of worship, but without repentance or faith. In profession they honor the law of God, but obedience is lacking. They say, but do not. In the sentence pronounced on the fig tree Christ demonstrates how hateful in His eyes is this vain pretense. He declares that the open sinner is less guilty than is he who professes to serve God, but who bears no fruit to His glory. *DA 581, 584*

the corner: this is the Lord's doing, and it is marvellous in our eyes? Ps. 118:22-23; Is. 28:16

43 Therefore say I unto you, The kingdom of God shall be taken from you, and given to a nation bringing forth the fruits thereof.

44 And whosoever shall fall on this stone shall be broken: but on whomsoever it shall fall, it will grind him to powder. Is. 8:14-15

45 And when the chief priests and Pharisees had heard his parables, they perceived that he spake of them.

46 But when they sought to lay hands on him, they feared the multitude, because they took him for a prophet. Matt. 21:11, 26

The Parable of the Marriage of the King's Son

22 And Jesus answered and spake unto them again by parables, and said,

2 The kingdom of heaven is like unto a certain king, which made a marriage for his son, Matt. 13:24

3 And sent forth his servants to call them that were bidden to the wedding: and they would not come.

4 Again, he sent forth other servants, saying, Tell them which are bidden, Behold, I have prepared my dinner: my oxen and *my* fatlings *are* killed, and all things *are* ready: come unto the marriage. Matt. 21:36

5 But they made light of *it*, and went their ways, one to his farm, another to his merchandise: Heb. 2:3

6 And the remnant took his servants, and entreated *them* spitefully, and slew *them*.

7 But when the king heard *thereof*, he was ᵀwroth: and he sent forth his armies, and destroyed those murderers, and burned up their city. Luke 19:27 ◆ *angered*

8 Then saith he to his servants, The wedding is ready, but they which were bidden were not worthy. Luke 20:35

9 Go ye therefore into the highways, and as many as ye shall find, bid to the marriage.

10 So those servants went out into the highways, and gathered together all as many as they found, both bad and good: and the wedding was furnished with guests. Matt. 13:47-48

11 And when the king came in to see the guests, he saw there a man which had not on a wedding garment: 2 Kin. 10:22

12 And he saith unto him, Friend, how camest thou in ᵀhither not having a wedding garment? And he was speechless. Matt. 26:50 ◆ *here*

13 Then said the king to the servants, Bind him hand and foot, and take him away, and cast *him* into outer darkness; there shall be weeping and gnashing of teeth. Matt. 13:42

14 For many are called, but few *are* chosen.

A Question about Taxes

15 Then went the Pharisees, and took counsel how they might entangle him in *his* talk. Mark 12:13-17

16 And they sent out unto him their disciples with the Herodians, saying, Master, we know that thou art true, and teachest the way of God in truth, neither carest thou for any *man*: for thou regardest not the person of men. Mark 3:6; 8:15

17 Tell us therefore, What thinkest thou? Is it lawful to give tribute unto Caesar, or not? Luke 2:1

18 But Jesus perceived their wickedness, and said, Why tempt ye me, *ye* hypocrites? John 8:6

19 Shew me the tribute money. And they brought unto him a penny.

20 And he saith unto them, Whose *is* this image and superscription?

21 They say unto him, Caesar's. Then saith he unto them, Render therefore unto Caesar the things which are Caesar's; and unto God the things that are God's. Rom. 13:7

22 When they had heard *these words*, they marvelled, and left him, and went their way. Mark 12:12

Christ Refutes the Sadducees about the Resurrection

23 The same day came to him the Sadducees, which say that there is no resurrection, and asked him, Matt. 3:7

24 Saying, Master, Moses said, If a man die, having no children, his brother shall marry his wife, and raise up seed unto his brother.

25 Now there were with us seven brethren: and the first, when he had married a wife, deceased, and, having no issue, left his wife unto his brother:

26 Likewise the second also, and the third, unto the seventh.

27 And last of all the woman died also.

28 Therefore in the resurrection whose wife shall she be of the seven? for they all had her.

29 Jesus answered and said unto them, Ye do ^Terr, not knowing the scriptures, nor the power of God.   *John 20:9 ◆ stray*

30 For in the resurrection they neither marry, nor are given in marriage, but are as the angels of God in heaven.   *Ps. 103:20*

31 But as touching the resurrection of the dead, have ye not read that which was spoken unto you by God, saying,   *Matt. 21:16*

32 I am the God of Abraham, and the God of Isaac, and the God of Jacob? God is not the God of the dead, but of the living.   *Ex. 3:6*

33 And when the multitude heard *this*, they were astonished at his doctrine.

The Greatest Commandment

34 But when the Pharisees had heard that he had put the Sadducees to silence, they were gathered together.

35 Then one of them, *which was* a lawyer, asked *him a question*, tempting him, and saying,   *Matt. 22:18; Luke 7:30; 14:3*

22:36–40 All or Nothing

Both these commandments ["You shall love the Lord your God with all your heart . . . and your neighbor as yourself"] are an expression of the principle of love. The first cannot be kept and the second broken, nor can the second be kept while the first is broken. . . .

Thus Christ taught His hearers that the law of God is not so many separate precepts, some of which are of great importance, while others are of small importance and may with impunity be ignored. Our Lord presents the first four and the last six commandments as a divine whole, and teaches that love to God will be shown by obedience to all His commandments. *DA 607*

---

36 Master, which *is* the great commandment in the law?

37 Jesus said unto him, Thou shalt love the Lord thy God with all thy heart, and with all thy soul, and with all thy mind.   *Deut. 6:5*

38 This is the first and great commandment.

39 And the second *is* like unto it, Thou shalt love thy neighbour as thyself. *Lev. 19:18; Gal. 5:14*

40 On these two commandments hang all the law and the prophets.   *Matt. 7:12*

God's Law   See 1 John 5:3.

Jesus Silences the Pharisees about the Messiah

41 While the Pharisees were gathered together, Jesus asked them,   *Mark 12:35-37*

42 Saying, What think ye of Christ? whose son is he? They say unto him, The Son of David.   *Matt. 1:1*

43 He saith unto them, How then doth David in spirit call him Lord, saying,   *2 Sam. 23:2*

44 The LORD said unto my Lord, Sit thou on my right hand, till I make thine enemies thy footstool?   *Ps. 110:1; 1 Cor. 15:25; Heb. 1:13*

45 If David then call him Lord, how is he his son?   *Rom. 1:3-4*

46 And no man was able to answer him a word, neither durst any *man* from that day forth ask him any more *questions*.   *Luke 14:6*

Jesus Warns about the Scribes and Pharisees

23 Then spake Jesus to the multitude, and to his disciples,

2 Saying, The scribes and the Pharisees sit in Moses' seat: *Ezra 7:6*

3 All therefore whatsoever they bid you observe, *that* observe and do; but do not ye after their works: for they say, and do not.

4 For they bind heavy burdens and grievous to be borne, and lay *them* on men's shoulders; but they *themselves* will not move them with one of their fingers.   *Luke 11:46; Acts 15:10*

5 But all their works they do for to be seen of men: they make broad their ^Tphylacteries, and enlarge the borders of their garments,   *Ex. 13:9 ◆ small boxes to wear carrying Scriptures*

6 And love the uppermost rooms at feasts, and the chief seats in the synagogues,

7 And greetings in the markets, and to be called of men, Rabbi, Rabbi.   *John 1:38, 49; 3:2*

8 But be not ye called Rabbi: for one is your Master, *even* Christ; and all ye are brethren.   *James 3:1*

9 And call no *man* your father upon the earth: for one is your Father, which is in heaven.   *Mal. 1:6*

10 Neither be ye called masters: for one is your Master, *even* Christ.

11 But he that is greatest among you shall be your servant.

12 And whosoever shall exalt himself shall be ^Tabased; and he that shall humble himself shall be exalted. *Prov. 29:23; Luke 18:14 ◆ brought low*

The Hypocrisy of the Scribes and Pharisees

13 But woe unto you, scribes and Pharisees, hypocrites! for ye shut up the kingdom of heaven against men: for ye neither go in *yourselves*, neither suffer ye them that are entering to go in.   *Matt. 23:27, 29; Luke 11:52*

14 Woe unto you, scribes and Pharisees, hypocrites! for ye devour widows' houses, and for a pretence make long prayer: therefore ye shall receive the greater ^Tdamnation.   *Mark 12:40 ◆ condemnation*

15 Woe unto you, scribes and Pharisees, hypocrites! for ye compass sea and land to make one proselyte, and when he is made, ye make

22:36–40

him twofold more the child of hell than yourselves. Matt. 5:22; Acts 2:10; 13:43

16 Woe unto you, *ye* blind guides, which say,
Whosoever shall swear by the temple, it is
nothing; but whosoever shall swear by the
gold of the temple, he is a debtor! Matt. 5:33-35

17 *Ye* fools and blind: for whether is greater,
the gold, or the temple that sanctifieth the
gold? Matt. 23:19

18 And, Whosoever shall swear by the altar,
it is nothing; but whosoever sweareth by the
gift that is upon it, he is guilty.

19 *Ye* fools and blind: for whether *is* greater,
the gift, or the altar that ^Tsanctifieth the
gift? Ex. 29:37 ◆ *makes holy*

20 Whoso therefore shall swear by the
altar, sweareth by it, and by all things
thereon.

21 And whoso shall swear by the temple,
sweareth by it, and by him that dwelleth
therein. 1 Kin. 8:13; 2 Chr. 6:2; Ps. 26:8

22 And he that shall swear by heaven,
sweareth by the throne of God, and by him
that sitteth thereon. Ps. 11:4; Is. 66:1; Matt. 5:34

23 Woe unto you, scribes and Pharisees,
hypocrites! for ye pay tithe of mint and anise
and cummin, and have omitted the weightier
matters of the law, judgment, mercy, and faith:
these ought ye to have done, and not to leave
the other undone. 1 Sam. 15:22; Mic. 6:8; Luke 11:42

> **Managing God's Gifts** See Numbers 18:21.

24 *Ye* blind guides, which strain at a gnat,
and swallow a camel. Matt. 19:24

> **23:23, 24 Don't Be a Camel Swallower**
>
> Jesus was misunderstood by His broth-
> ers because He was not like them. . . . The
> example of Jesus was to them a continual
> irritation. He hated but one thing in the
> world, and that was sin. He could not wit-
> ness a wrong act without pain which it was
> impossible to disguise. . . . Because the life of
> Jesus condemned evil, He was opposed, both
> at home and abroad. His unselfishness and
> integrity were commented on with a sneer.
> His forbearance and kindness were termed
> cowardice. *DA 88*

25 Woe unto you, scribes and Pharisees,
hypocrites! for ye make clean the outside of
the cup and of the platter, but within they
are full of extortion and excess. Matt. 15:19-20

26 *Thou* blind Pharisee, cleanse first that
which is within the cup and platter, that the
outside of them may be clean also.

27 Woe unto you, scribes and Pharisees,
hypocrites! for ye are like unto whited sepulchres, which indeed appear beautiful outward, but are within full of dead *men's* bones,
and of all uncleanness. Num. 19:16; Acts 23:3

28 Even so ye also outwardly appear righteous unto men, but within ye are full of hypocrisy and iniquity. Matt. 23:5

29 Woe unto you, scribes and Pharisees,
hypocrites! because ye build the tombs of
the prophets, and garnish the sepulchres of
the righteous, Luke 11:47-48

30 And say, If we had been in the days of our
fathers, we would not have been partakers
with them in the blood of the prophets.

31 Wherefore ye be witnesses unto yourselves, that ye are the children of them
which killed the prophets. Acts 7:51-52

> **23:29–31 A Life and Death Lesson**
>
> This should be a lesson to us. It should
> open our eyes to the power of Satan to de-
> ceive the mind that turns from the light of
> truth. Many follow in the track of the Phari-
> sees. They revere those who have died for
> their faith. They wonder at the blindness of
> the Jews in rejecting Christ. . . . But when
> obedience to God requires self-denial and
> humiliation, these very persons stifle their
> convictions, and refuse obedience. Thus they
> manifest the same spirit as did the Pharisees
> whom Christ condemned. *DA 618*

32 Fill ye up then the measure of your fathers. Gen. 15:16

33 *Ye* serpents, *ye* generation of ^Tvipers,
how can ye escape the damnation of
hell? Matt. 3:7; 5:22; 12:34 ◆ *snakes*

Jesus Prophesies the Destruction of Jerusalem

34 Wherefore, behold, I send unto you
prophets, and wise men, and scribes: and
some of them ye shall kill and crucify; and
some of them shall ye ^Tscourge in your synagogues, and persecute *them* from city to
city: Matt. 10:16-17, 23; 13:52 ◆ *whip*

35 That upon you may come all the righteous blood shed upon the earth, from the
blood of righteous Abel unto the blood of
Zacharias son of Barachias, whom ye slew
between the temple and the altar. Gen. 4:8

36 Verily I say unto you, All these things shall
come upon this generation. Matt. 10:23; 24:34

37 O Jerusalem, Jerusalem, *thou* that killest the prophets, and stonest them which
are sent unto thee, how often would I have
gathered thy children together, even as a hen
gathereth her chickens under *her* wings, and
ye would not! Ruth 2:12

38 Behold, your house is left unto you desolate. Jer. 22:5

39 For I say unto you, Ye shall not see
me henceforth, till ye shall say, Blessed *is* he
that cometh in the name of the Lord.

Jesus Tells about the Future

24 And Jesus went out, and departed from the temple: and his disciples came to *him* for to shew him the buildings of the temple.

2 And Jesus said unto them, See ye not all these things? ᵀverily I say unto you, There shall not be left here one stone upon another, that shall not be thrown down.   Luke 19:44 ◆ *truly*

24:1, 2 Jerusalem, a Symbol of the End

The ruin of Jerusalem was a symbol of the final ruin that shall overwhelm the world. The prophecies that received a partial fulfillment in the overthrow of Jerusalem have a more direct application to the last days. We are now standing on the threshold of great and solemn events. A crisis is before us, such as the world has never witnessed. *MB 120, 121*

---

3 And as he sat upon the mount of Olives, the disciples came unto him privately, saying, Tell us, when shall these things be? and what *shall be* the sign of thy coming, and of the end of the world?   Matt. 21:1; Acts 1:7

Signs of the End   See Joel 2:30, 31.

4 And Jesus answered and said unto them, Take heed that no man deceive you.
5 For many shall come in my name, saying, I am Christ; and shall deceive many.   Jer. 14:14
6 And ye shall hear of wars and rumours of wars: see that ye be not troubled: for all *these things* must come to pass, but the end is not yet.   2 Thess. 2:2
7 For nation shall rise against nation, and kingdom against kingdom: and there shall be famines, and pestilences, and earthquakes, in ᵀdivers places.   2 Chr. 15:6; Is. 19:2; Acts 11:28 ◆ *various*
8 All these *are* the beginning of sorrows.
9 Then shall they deliver you up to be afflicted, and shall kill you: and ye shall be hated of all nations for my name's sake.   Matt. 23:34; John 15:19-20; 16:2
10 And then shall many be offended, and shall betray one another, and shall hate one another.   Matt. 10:21
11 And many false prophets shall rise, and shall deceive many.   Matt. 7:15; 24:5, 24
12 And because iniquity shall abound, the love of many shall ᵀwax cold.   *become*
13 But he that shall endure unto the end, the same shall be saved.   Matt. 10:22; Rom. 2:7

24:14 Bringing an End to Sin

Our world is a vast lazar house, a scene of misery that we dare not allow even our thoughts to dwell upon. Did we realize it as it is, the burden would be too terrible. Yet God feels it all. In order to destroy sin and its results He gave His best Beloved, and He has put it in our power, through co-operation with Him, to bring this scene of misery to an end. "This gospel of the kingdom shall be preached in all the world for a witness unto all nations; and then shall the end come" (Matthew 24:14). *Ed 264*

---

14 And this gospel of the kingdom shall be preached in all the world for a witness unto all nations; and then shall the end come.   Rom. 10:18; Col. 1:6, 23

Christ's Return   See Acts 1:9–11.

15 When ye therefore shall see the abomination of desolation, spoken of by Daniel the prophet, stand in the holy place, (whoso readeth, let him understand:)   Dan. 9:27; 12:11
16 Then let them which be in Judaea flee into the mountains:
17 Let him which is on the housetop not come down to take any thing out of his house: Matt. 10:27
18 Neither let him which is in the field return back to take his clothes.

Our Greatest Need

Matthew 23:38

Men cannot with impunity reject the warning which God in mercy sends them. A message was sent from heaven to the world in Noah's day, and their salvation depended upon the manner in which they treated that message. Because they rejected the warning, the Spirit of God was withdrawn from the sinful race, and they perished in the waters of the Flood. In the time of Abraham, mercy ceased to plead with the guilty inhabitants of Sodom, and all but Lot with his wife and two daughters were consumed by the fire sent down from heaven. So in the days of Christ. The Son of God declared to the unbelieving Jews of that generation: "Your house is left unto you desolate" (Matthew 23:38). Looking down to the last days, the same Infinite Power declares, concerning those who "received not the love of the truth, that they might be saved": "For this cause God shall send them strong delusion, that they should believe a lie: that they all might be damned who believed not the truth, but had pleasure in unrighteousness" (2 Thessalonians 2:10–12). As they reject the teachings of His word, God withdraws His Spirit and leaves them to the deceptions which they love. *GC 431*

19 And woe unto them that are with child, and to them that give suck in those days!

20 But pray ye that your flight be not in the winter, neither on the sabbath day:

21 For then shall be great tribulation, such as was not since the beginning of the world to this time, no, nor ever shall be. Dan. 12:1; Joel 2:2

22 And except those days should be shortened, there should no flesh be saved: but for the elect's sake those days shall be shortened. Is. 65:8-9

23 Then if any man shall say unto you, Lo, here *is* Christ, or there; believe *it* not.

24:24 24 For there shall arise false Christs, and false prophets, and shall shew great signs and wonders; insomuch that, if *it were* possible, they shall deceive the very elect. Matt. 24:11

Gift of Prophecy   See Matthew 7:15–20.

25 Behold, I have told you before.

26 Wherefore if they shall say unto you, Behold, he is in the desert; go not forth: behold, *he is* in the secret chambers; believe *it* not. Acts 21:38

27 For as the lightning cometh out of the east, and shineth even unto the west; so shall also the coming of the Son of man be.

28 For wheresoever the carcase is, there will the eagles be gathered together. Luke 17:37

24:29 29 Immediately after the tribulation of those days shall the sun be darkened, and the moon shall not give her light, and the stars shall fall from heaven, and the powers of the heavens shall be shaken: Is. 13:10; Joel 2:10; Amos 8:9

Signs of the End   See Matthew 24:37–39.

24:30-33 30 And then shall appear the sign of the Son of man in heaven: and then shall all the tribes of the earth mourn, and they shall see the Son of man coming in the clouds of heaven with power and great glory. Dan. 7:13; Matt. 24:3; Rev. 1:7

24:30 He Is Coming Soon!

Christ is coming with clouds and with great glory. A multitude of shining angels will attend Him. He will come to raise the dead, and to change the living saints from glory to glory. He will come to honor those who have loved Him, and kept His commandments, and to take them to Himself. He has not forgotten them nor His promise. There will be a relinking of the family chain. . . . A little longer, and He will wipe all tears from our eyes. *DA 632*

31 And he shall send his angels with a great sound of a trumpet, and they shall gather together his elect from the four winds, from one end of heaven to the other. 1 Thess. 4:16

32 Now learn a parable of the fig tree; When his branch is yet tender, and putteth forth leaves, ye know that summer *is* nigh:

33 So likewise ye, when ye shall see all these things, know that it is near, *even* at the doors. James 5:9

Christ's Return   See Matthew 24:14.

34 Verily I say unto you, This generation shall not pass, till all these things be fulfilled. Matt. 16:28; 23:36

24:35 35 Heaven and earth shall pass away, but my words shall not pass away. Ps. 102:26; Is. 40:8

The Bible   See Psalm 119:11.

No One Knows When Jesus Will Return

24:36 36 But of that day and hour knoweth no *man*, no, not the angels of heaven, but my Father only. Matt. 25:13; Mark 13:32; Acts 1:7

Christ's Return   See Matthew 24:30–33.

24:37-39 37 But as the days of Noe *were*, so shall also the coming of the Son of man be. Luke 17:26-27

38 For as in the days that were before the flood they were eating and drinking, marrying and giving in marriage, until the day that Noe entered into the ark, Matt. 22:30

39 And knew not until the flood came, and took them all away; so shall also the coming of the Son of man be. Matt. 24:37

Signs of the End   See 2 Timothy 3:1–5.

40 Then shall two be in the field; the one shall be taken, and the other left.

41 Two *women shall be* grinding at the mill; the one shall be taken, and the other left. Ex. 11:5

24:42-44 42 Watch therefore: for ye know not what hour your Lord doth come. Matt. 25:13; Luke 21:36

43 But know this, that if the ᵀgoodman of the house had known in what watch the thief would come, he would have watched, and would not have suffered his house to be broken up. Luke 12:39 ♦ *male leader*

44 Therefore be ye also ready: for in such an hour as ye think not the Son of man cometh. Matt. 25:10

Christ's Return   See Titus 2:11–13.

45 Who then is a faithful and wise servant, whom his lord hath made ruler over his household, to give them meat in due season? Matt. 25:21, 23, 35-40

46 Blessed *is* that servant, whom his lord when he cometh shall find so doing. Rev. 16:15

47 Verily I say unto you, That he shall make him ruler over all his goods. Matt. 25:21, 23

48 But and if that evil servant shall say in his heart, My lord delayeth his coming;

49 And shall begin to ᵀsmite *his* fellowservants, and to eat and drink with the drunken; *strike*

50 The lord of that servant shall come in a

day when he looketh not for *him,* and in an hour that he is not aware of,

51 And shall cut him [T]asunder, and appoint *him* his portion with the hypocrites: there shall be weeping and gnashing of teeth.   Matt. 8:12 ◆ *apart*

The Parable of the Ten Virgins

25 Then shall the kingdom of heaven be likened unto ten virgins, which took their lamps, and went forth to meet the bridegroom.   Matt. 13:24

2 And five of them were wise, and five *were* foolish.

25:1, 2 Which Class Are You?

The two classes of watchers [the wise and the foolish virgins] represent the two classes who profess to be waiting for their Lord. They are called virgins because they profess a pure faith. By the lamps is represented the word of God. . . . The oil is a symbol of the Holy Spirit.

The class represented by the foolish virgins are not hypocrites. They have a regard for the truth, they have advocated the truth, they are attracted to those who believe the truth; but they have not yielded themselves to the Holy Spirit's working. *COL 406–411*

---

3 They that *were* foolish took their lamps, and took no oil with them:

4 But the wise took oil in their vessels with their lamps.

5 While the bridegroom tarried, they all slumbered and slept.   Matt. 24:48

6 And at midnight there was a cry made, Behold, the bridegroom cometh; go ye out to meet him.

7 Then all those virgins arose, and trimmed their lamps.   Luke 12:35

8 And the foolish said unto the wise, Give us of your oil; for our lamps are gone out.

9 But the wise answered, saying, *Not so;* lest there be not enough for us and you: but go ye rather to them that sell, and buy for yourselves.

10 And while they went to buy, the bridegroom came; and they that were ready went in with him to the marriage: and the door was shut.   Luke 13:25

11 Afterward came also the other virgins, saying, Lord, Lord, open to us.   Matt. 7:21-23

12 But he answered and said, Verily I say unto you, I know you not.   2 Tim. 2:19

13 Watch therefore, for ye know neither the day nor the hour wherein the Son of man cometh.   Matt. 24:42-44

The Parable of the Talents

14 For *the kingdom of heaven is* as a man travelling into a far country, *who* called his own servants, and delivered unto them his goods.   Matt. 21:33; Mark 13:34

15 And unto one he gave five talents, to another two, and to another one; to every

---

As It Was in the Days of Noah . . .

Matthew 24:36–39

The sins that called for vengeance upon the antediluvian world exist today. The fear of God is banished from the hearts of men, and His law is treated with indifference and contempt. . . .

That which is lawful in itself is carried to excess. Appetite is indulged without restraint. Professed followers of Christ are today eating and drinking with the drunken, while their names stand in honored church records. . . . . The issues of the press teem with records of murder—crimes so cold-blooded and causeless that it seems as though every instinct of humanity were blotted out. And these atrocities have become of so common occurrence that they hardly elicit a comment or awaken surprise. . . . The picture which Inspiration has given of the antediluvian world represents too truly the condition to which modern society is fast hastening. . . .

Of the vast population of the earth before the Flood, only eight souls believed and obeyed God's word through Noah. For a hundred and twenty years the preacher of righteousness warned the world of the coming destruction, but his message was rejected and despised. So it will be now. . . .

While God's servants are giving the message that the end of all things is at hand, the world is absorbed in amusements and pleasure seeking. There is a constant round of excitement that causes indifference to God and prevents the people from being impressed by the truths which alone can save them from the coming destruction.

In Noah's day philosophers declared that it was impossible for the world to be destroyed by water; so now there are men of science who endeavor to show that the world cannot be destroyed by fire—that this would be inconsistent with the laws of nature. . . .

When the reasoning of philosophy has banished the fear of God's judgments; when religious teachers are pointing forward to long ages of peace and prosperity, and the world are absorbed in their rounds of business and pleasure, planting and building, feasting and merrymaking, rejecting God's warnings and mocking His messengers—then it is that sudden destruction cometh upon them, and they shall not escape. *PP 101–104*

man according to his several ability; and straightway took his journey.   Matt. 18:24

25:14, 15 Being Faithful in Our Talents

God gives the talents, the powers of the mind; we form the character. It is formed by hard, stern battles with self. . . .

Let no one say, I cannot remedy my defects of character. If you come to this decision, you will certainly fail of obtaining everlasting life. . . . The real difficulty arises from the corruption of an unsanctified heart, and an unwillingness to submit to the control of God. *COL 331*

16 Then he that had received the five talents went and traded with the same, and made *them* other five talents.

17 And likewise he that *had received* two, he also gained other two.

18 But he that had received one went and digged in the earth, and hid his lord's money.

19 After a long time the lord of those servants cometh, and reckoneth with them.   Matt. 25:5

20 And so he that had received five talents came and brought other five talents, saying, Lord, thou deliveredst unto me five talents: behold, I have gained beside them five talents more.

21 His lord said unto him, Well done, *thou* good and faithful servant: thou hast been faithful over a few things, I will make thee ruler over many things: enter thou into the joy of thy lord.   Matt. 24:47; 25:23; Luke 16:10

22 He also that had received two talents came and said, Lord, thou deliveredst unto

me two talents: behold, I have gained two other talents beside them.

23 His lord said unto him, Well done, good and faithful servant; thou hast been faithful over a few things, I will make thee ruler over many things: enter thou into the joy of thy lord.   Matt. 25:21

25:24–26 Set the Standard High

Many whom God has qualified to do excellent work accomplish very little, because they attempt little. Thousands pass through life as if they had no definite object for which to live, no standard to reach. Such will obtain a reward proportionate to their works.

Remember that you will never reach a higher standard than you yourself set. . . . Press with determination in the right direction, and circumstances will be your helpers, not your hindrances. *COL 331, 332*

24 Then he which had received the one talent came and said, Lord, I knew thee that thou art an hard man, reaping where thou hast not sown, and gathering where thou hast not strawed:

25 And I was afraid, and went and hid thy talent in the earth: lo, *there* thou hast *that is* thine.

26 His lord answered and said unto him, *Thou* wicked and slothful servant, thou knewest that I reap where I sowed not, and gather where I have not strawed: Matt. 18:32

27 Thou oughtest therefore to have put my money to the exchangers, and *then* at my

---

Character Not Made but Revealed in a Crisis

Matthew 25:1–13

The two classes of watchers [the wise and the foolish virgins] represent the two classes who profess to be waiting for their Lord. They are called virgins because they profess a pure faith. By the lamps is represented the word of God. . . . The oil is a symbol of the Holy Spirit. . . .

In the parable, all the ten virgins went out to meet the bridegroom. All had lamps and vessels for oil. For a time there was seen no difference between them. So with the church that lives just before Christ's second coming. All have a knowledge of the Scriptures. All have heard the message of Christ's near approach, and confidently expect His appearing. But as in the parable, so it is now. A time of waiting intervenes, faith is tried; and when the cry is heard, "Behold, the Bridegroom cometh; go ye out to meet Him," many are unready. They have no oil in their vessels with their lamps. They are destitute of the Holy Spirit. . . .

The class represented by the foolish virgins are not hypocrites. They have a regard for the truth, they have advocated the truth, they are attracted to those who believe the truth; but they have not yielded themselves to the Holy Spirit's working. . . .

It is in a crisis that character is revealed. . . . It will show whether the soul is sustained by grace. . . .

The ten virgins are watching in the evening of this earth's history. All claim to be Christians. All have a call, a name, a lamp, and all profess to be doing God's service. All apparently wait for Christ's appearing. But five are unready. Five will be found surprised, dismayed, outside the banquet hall. . . .

Saddest of all words that ever fell on mortal ear are those words of doom, "I know you not." *COL 406–413*

coming I should have received mine own with ᵀusury.

interest

28 Take therefore the talent from him, and give *it* unto him which hath ten talents.

29 For unto every one that hath shall be given, and he shall have abundance: but from him that hath not shall be taken away even that which he hath.   Mark 4:25; Luke 8:18

30 And cast ye the unprofitable servant into outer darkness: there shall be weeping and gnashing of teeth.   Matt. 8:12; 13:42; 22:13

The Description of the Last Judgment

31 When the Son of man shall come in his glory, and all the holy angels with him, then shall he sit upon the throne of his glory: Matt. 16:27; 19:28; Mark 8:38

32 And before him shall be gathered all nations: and he shall separate them one from another, as a shepherd divideth *his* sheep from the goats: Matt. 13:49

33 And he shall set the sheep on his right hand, but the goats on the left.   Ps. 45:9

34 Then shall the King say unto them on his right hand, Come, ye blessed of my Father, inherit the kingdom prepared for you from the foundation of the world: Gal. 5:21; James 2:5

35 For I was an hungred, and ye gave me meat: I was thirsty, and ye gave me drink: I was a stranger, and ye took me in: Ezek. 18:7

36 Naked, and ye clothed me: I was sick, and ye visited me: I was in prison, and ye came unto me.   Heb. 10:34; 13:3; James 1:27

37 Then shall the righteous answer him, saying, Lord, when saw we thee an hungred, and fed *thee*? or thirsty, and gave *thee* drink?

38 When saw we thee a stranger, and took *thee* in? or naked, and clothed *thee*?

39 Or when saw we thee sick, or in prison, and came unto thee?

40 And the King shall answer and say unto them, Verily I say unto you, Inasmuch as ye have done *it* unto one of the least of these my brethren, ye have done *it* unto me. Prov. 19:17

41 Then shall he say also unto them on the left hand, Depart from me, ye cursed, into everlasting fire, prepared for the ᵀdevil and his angels: Matt. 3:12; 7:23; 2 Pet. 2:4 ◆ *false accuser*

25:41†

> **End of Sin/Hell**   See Matthew 25:46.

42 For I was an hungred, and ye gave me no meat: I was thirsty, and ye gave me no drink:

43 I was a stranger, and ye took me not in: naked, and ye clothed me not: sick, and in prison, and ye visited me not.

44 Then shall they also answer him, saying, Lord, when saw we thee an hungred, or athirst, or a stranger, or naked, or sick, or in prison, and did not minister unto thee?

45 Then shall he answer them, saying, Verily I say unto you, Inasmuch as ye did *it* not

to one of the least of these, ye did *it* not to me.   Prov. 14:31

46 And these shall go away into everlasting punishment: but the righteous into life eternal.   Dan. 12:2; John 3:36; 5:29

25:46

> **End of Sin/Hell**   See Mark 3:29.

The Plot to Kill Jesus

26 And it came to pass, when Jesus had finished all these sayings, he said unto his disciples,

2 Ye know that after two days is *the feast of the passover*, and the Son of man is betrayed to be crucified.   Mark 14:1-2

3 Then assembled together the chief priests, and the scribes, and the elders of the people, unto the palace of the high priest, who was called Caiaphas,   John 18:24

4 And consulted that they might take Jesus by subtilty, and kill *him*.

5 But they said, Not on the feast *day*, lest there be an uproar among the people.

A Woman Anoints Jesus with Precious Ointment

6 Now when Jesus was in Bethany, in the house of Simon the leper,   Matt. 21:17

7 There came unto him a woman having an alabaster box of very precious ointment, and poured it on his head, as he sat *at meat*.

8 But when his disciples saw *it*, they had ᵀindignation, saying, To what purpose *is* this waste?

anger

9 For this ointment might have been sold for much, and given to the poor.

10 When Jesus understood *it*, he said unto them, Why trouble ye the woman? for she hath ᵀwrought a good work upon me.   *done*

11 For ye have the poor always with you; but me ye have not always.   Deut. 15:11; John 12:8

12 For in that she hath poured this ointment on my body, she did *it* for my burial.

13 Verily I say unto you, Wheresoever this gospel shall be preached in the whole world, *there* shall also this, that this woman hath done, be told for a memorial of her. Matt. 24:14

> **26:10–13 Setting Our Priorities**
>
> Many there are who bring their precious gifts for the dead. As they stand about the cold, silent form, words of love are freely spoken. . . . Had these words been spoken when the weary spirit needed them so much, when the ear could hear and the heart could feel, how precious would have been their fragrance! *DA 560*

Judas Betrays Jesus

14 Then one of the twelve, called Judas Iscariot, went unto the chief priests, Luke 22:3-6
15 And said *unto them*, What will ye give me, and I will deliver him unto you? And they covenanted with him for thirty pieces of silver. Ex. 21:32
16 And from that time he sought opportunity to betray him.

26:14–16 One Little Sin Can Destroy Us

The history of Judas presents the sad ending of a life that might have been honored of God. . . .

Judas had naturally a strong love for money; but he had not always been corrupt enough to do such a deed as this. . . . The love of mammon overbalanced his love for Christ. Through becoming the slave of one vice he gave himself to Satan, to be driven to any lengths in sin. *DA 716*

Jesus and the Disciples Eat the Passover

17 Now the first *day* of the *feast of* unleavened bread the disciples came to Jesus, saying unto him, Where wilt thou that we prepare for thee to eat the passover? Ex. 12:18-20
18 And he said, Go into the city to such a man, and say unto him, The Master saith, My time is at hand; I will keep the passover at thy house with my disciples. John 7:6, 30; 13:1
19 And the disciples did as Jesus had appointed them; and they made ready the passover.
20 Now when the even was come, he sat down with the twelve. Mark 14:17-21
21 And as they did eat, he said, Verily I say unto you, that one of you shall betray me. John 13:21
22 And they were exceeding sorrowful, and began every one of them to say unto him, Lord, is it I?
23 And he answered and said, He that dippeth *his* hand with me in the dish, the same shall betray me. Ps. 41:9; John 13:18
24 The Son of man goeth as it is written of him: but woe unto that man by whom the Son of man is betrayed! it had been good for that man if he had not been born. Luke 24:46
25 Then Judas, which betrayed him, answered and said, Master, is it I? He said unto him, Thou hast said. Matt. 26:64

Jesus Institutes His Holy Supper

26:26-28

26 And as they were eating, Jesus took bread, and blessed *it*, and brake *it*, and gave *it* to the disciples, and said, Take, eat; this is my body. Matt. 14:19

26:26–28 The Reason for Communion

As the Lord's disciples gather about His table, they are not to remember and lament their shortcomings. They are not to dwell upon their past religious experience, whether that experience has been elevating or depressing. They are not to recall the differences between them and their brethren. The preparatory service has embraced all this. . . .

The love of Jesus, with its constraining power, is to be kept fresh in our memory. Christ has instituted this service that it may speak to our senses of the love of God that has been expressed in our behalf. *DA 659, 660*

27 And he took the cup, and gave thanks, and gave *it* to them, saying, Drink ye all of it;
28 For this is my blood of the new ᵀtestament, which is shed for many for the remission of sins. Ex. 24:7-8; Lev. 17:11; Matt. 20:28 ◆ *covenant*

Baptism/Lord's Supper See John 13:12–15.

29 But I say unto you, I will not drink ᵀhenceforth of this fruit of the vine, until that day when I drink it new with you in my Father's kingdom. Matt. 13:43 ◆ *from this time forward*
30 And when they had sung an hymn, they went out into the mount of Olives. Matt. 21:1

Jesus Predicts Peter's Denial

31 Then saith Jesus unto them, All ye shall be offended because of me this night: for it is written, I will ᵀsmite the shepherd, and the sheep of the flock shall be scattered abroad. Zech. 13:7; Matt. 11:6; John 16:32 ◆ *strike*
32 But after I am risen again, I will go before you into Galilee. Matt. 28:10, 16; Mark 16:7
33 Peter answered and said unto him, Though all *men* shall be offended because of thee, *yet* will I never be offended. Luke 22:33
34 Jesus said unto him, Verily I say unto thee, That this night, before the cock crow, thou shalt deny me thrice. Luke 22:34; John 13:38
35 Peter said unto him, Though I should die with thee, yet will I not deny thee. Likewise also said all the disciples. John 13:37

Jesus Prays in Gethsemane

36 Then cometh Jesus with them unto a place called Gethsemane, and saith unto the disciples, Sit ye here, while I go and pray yonder. Matt. 26:39
37 And he took with him Peter and the two sons of Zebedee, and began to be sorrowful and very heavy. Matt. 4:21; 17:1; Mark 5:37
38 Then saith he unto them, My soul is exceeding sorrowful, even unto death: tarry ye here, and watch with me. John 12:27
39 And he went a little further, and fell on his face, and prayed, saying, O my Father,

if it be possible, let this cup pass from me: nevertheless not as I will, but as thou *wilt.*
40 And he cometh unto the disciples, and findeth them asleep, and saith unto Peter, What, could ye not watch with me one hour?
41 Watch and pray, that ye enter not into temptation: the spirit indeed *is* willing, but the flesh *is* weak.   Matt. 6:13
42 He went away again the second time, and prayed, saying, O my Father, if this cup may not pass away from me, except I drink it, thy will be done.   Matt. 26:39

26:36–42 Jesus Loves Me This I Know

Three times has [Jesus] uttered that prayer. Three times has humanity shrunk from the last, crowning sacrifice. But now the history of the human race comes up before the world's Redeemer. He sees that the transgressors of the law, if left to themselves, must perish. . . . He beholds its impending fate, and His decision is made. He will save man at any cost to Himself. He accepts His baptism of blood, that through Him perishing millions may gain everlasting life. . . . And He will not turn from His mission. *DA 690, 693*

---

43 And he came and found them asleep again: for their eyes were heavy.   Luke 9:32
44 And he left them, and went away again, and prayed the third time, saying the same words.   2 Cor. 12:8
45 Then cometh he to his disciples, and saith unto them, Sleep on now, and take *your* rest: behold, the hour is at hand, and the Son of man is betrayed into the hands of sinners.   John 13:1
46 Rise, let us be going: behold, he is at hand that doth betray me.

Jesus Is Betrayed with a Kiss

47 And while he yet spake, lo, Judas, one of the twelve, came, and with him a great multitude with swords and staves, from the chief priests and elders of the people.   Matt. 26:55
48 Now he that betrayed him gave them a sign, saying, Whomsoever I shall kiss, that same is he: hold him fast.
49 And forthwith he came to Jesus, and said, Hail, master; and kissed him.   Matt. 26:25
50 And Jesus said unto him, Friend, wherefore art thou come? Then came they, and laid hands on Jesus, and took him.   Matt. 20:13; 22:12
51 And, behold, one of them which were with Jesus stretched out *his* hand, and drew his sword, and struck a servant of the high priest's, and smote off his ear.   Mark 14:47
52 Then said Jesus unto him, Put up again thy sword into his place: for all they that take the sword shall perish with the sword.   Gen. 9:6

53 Thinkest thou that I cannot now pray to my Father, and he shall presently give me more than twelve legions of angels?   2 Kin. 6:17
54 But how then shall the scriptures be fulfilled, that thus it must be?   Matt. 26:24
55 In that same hour said Jesus to the multitudes, Are ye come out as against a thief with swords and [T] staves for to take me? I sat daily with you teaching in the temple, and ye laid no hold on me.   Mark 12:35 ◆ *clubs* or *rods*
56 But all this was done, that the scriptures of the prophets might be fulfilled. Then all the disciples forsook him, and fled.   Matt. 26:31

Jesus Is Tried before the Jewish Council

57 And they that had laid hold on Jesus led *him* away to Caiaphas the high priest, where the scribes and the elders were assembled.   Matt. 26:3
58 But Peter followed him afar off unto the high priest's palace, and went in, and sat with the servants, to see the end.   John 7:32
59 Now the chief priests, and elders, and all the council, sought false witness against Jesus, to put him to death;
60 But found none: yea, though many false witnesses came, *yet* found they none. At the last came two false witnesses,   Ps. 27:12; 35:11
61 And said, This *fellow* said, I am able to destroy the temple of God, and to build it in three days.   Matt. 27:40
62 And the high priest arose, and said unto him, Answerest thou nothing? what *is it* which these witness against thee?
63 But Jesus held his peace. And the high priest answered and said unto him, I [T]adjure thee by the living God, that thou tell us whether thou be the Christ, the Son of God.   Lev. 5:1; 1 Sam. 14:24; Matt. 16:16 ◆ *appeal to*
64 Jesus saith unto him, Thou hast said: nevertheless I say unto you, Hereafter shall ye see the Son of man sitting on the right hand of power, and coming in the clouds of heaven.   Ps. 110:1; Dan. 7:13; Matt. 16:27
65 Then the high priest [T]rent his clothes, saying, He hath spoken blasphemy; what further need have we of witnesses? behold, now ye have heard his blasphemy.   Matt. 9:3 ◆ *tore*
66 What think ye? They answered and said, He is guilty of death.   John 19:7
67 Then did they spit in his face, and buffeted him; and others smote *him* with the palms of their hands,   Is. 50:6; Matt. 27:30; John 18:22
68 Saying, Prophesy unto us, thou Christ, Who is he that smote thee?   Mark 14:65

Peter Denies Jesus

69 Now Peter sat without in the palace: and a damsel came unto him, saying, Thou also wast with Jesus of Galilee.   Matt. 26:71

70 But he denied before *them* all, saying, I know not what thou sayest.

71 And when he was gone out into the porch, another *maid* saw him, and said unto them that were there, This *fellow* was also with Jesus of Nazareth.

72 And again he denied with an oath, I do not know the man.

73 And after a while came unto *him* they that stood by, and said to Peter, Surely thou also art *one* of them; for thy speech bewrayeth thee.   Judg. 12:6

74 Then began he to curse and to swear, *saying*, I know not the man. And immediately the cock crew.

> **Christian Behavior**   See Ephesians 4:29.

75 And Peter remembered the word of Jesus, which said unto him, Before the cock crow, thou shalt deny me ᵀthrice. And he went out, and wept bitterly. Matt. 26:34; John 13:38 ◆ *three times*

The Death of Judas

27 When the morning was come, all the chief priests and elders of the people took counsel against Jesus to put him to death: Mark 15:1; Luke 22:66; John 18:28

2 And when they had bound him, they led *him* away, and delivered him to Pontius Pilate the governor.   Matt. 20:19; Luke 13:1; Acts 3:13

3 Then Judas, which had betrayed him, when he saw that he was condemned, repented himself, and brought again the thirty pieces of silver to the chief priests and elders,

4 Saying, I have sinned in that I have betrayed the innocent blood. And they said, What *is that* to us? see thou *to that*.

5 And he cast down the pieces of silver in the temple, and departed, and went and hanged himself.   2 Sam. 17:23

6 And the chief priests took the silver pieces, and said, It is not lawful for to put them into the treasury, because it is the price of blood.

7 And they took counsel, and bought with them the potter's field, to bury strangers in.

8 Wherefore that field was called, The field of blood, unto this day.   Matt. 28:15; Acts 1:19

9 Then was fulfilled that which was spoken by Jeremy the prophet, saying, And they took the thirty pieces of silver, the price of him that was valued, whom they of the children of Israel did value;   Zech. 11:12-13

10 And gave them for the potter's field, as the Lord appointed me.

The Trial before Pilate

11 And Jesus stood before the governor: and the governor asked him, saying, Art thou the King of the Jews? And Jesus said unto him, Thou sayest.   Matt. 2:2

12 And when he was accused of the chief priests and elders, he answered nothing.

13 Then said Pilate unto him, Hearest thou not how many things they witness against thee?   Matt. 26:62

14 And he answered him to never a word; insomuch that the governor marvelled greatly.

15 Now at *that* feast the governor was ᵀwont to release unto the people a prisoner, whom they would.   *accustomed to*

16 And they had then a notable prisoner, called Barabbas.

17 Therefore when they were gathered together, Pilate said unto them, Whom will ye that I release unto you? Barabbas, or Jesus which is called Christ?

18 For he knew that for envy they had delivered him.   Prov. 27:4

19 When he was set down on the judgment seat, his wife sent unto him, saying, Have thou nothing to do with that just man: for I have suffered many things this day in a dream because of him.   Matt. 27:24; Luke 23:47; John 19:13

20 But the chief priests and elders persuaded the multitude that they should ask Barabbas, and destroy Jesus.

21 The governor answered and said unto them, Whether of the ᵀtwain will ye that I release unto you? They said, Barabbas.   *two*

22 Pilate saith unto them, What shall I do

26:73, 74

Character Revealed With Scorn

Matthew 26:69–75

Peter had not designed that his real character should be known. . . . If he had been called to fight for his Master, he would have been a courageous soldier; but when the finger of scorn was pointed at him, he proved himself a coward. Many who do not shrink from active warfare for their Lord are driven by ridicule to deny their faith. By associating with those whom they should avoid, they place themselves in the way of temptation. They invite the enemy to tempt them, and are led to say and do that of which under other circumstances they would never have been guilty. The disciple of Christ who in our day disguises his faith through dread of suffering or reproach denies his Lord as really as did Peter in the judgment hall. . . .

It was in sleeping when Jesus bade him watch and pray that Peter had prepared the way for his great sin. All the disciples, by sleeping in that critical hour, sustained a great loss. *DA 712–714*

then with Jesus which is called Christ? *They* all say unto him, Let him be crucified.

23 And the governor said, Why, what evil hath he done? But they cried out the more, saying, Let him be crucified.

27:22, 23 His Blood Be Upon Us

The world is no more in harmony with the principles of Christ today than it was in the days of the apostles. The same hatred that prompted the cry, "Crucify Him! crucify Him!" the same hatred that led to the persecution of the disciples, still works in the children of disobedience. . . . The history of truth has ever been the record of a struggle between right and wrong. The proclamation of the gospel has ever been carried forward in this world in the face of opposition, peril, loss, and suffering. *AA 85*

---

24 When Pilate saw that he could prevail nothing, but *that* rather a tumult was made, he took water, and washed *his* hands before the multitude, saying, I am innocent of the blood of this just person: see ye *to it.*   Deut. 21:6-8; Ps. 26:6; Matt. 27:4

25 Then answered all the people, and said, His blood *be* on us, and on our children.

27:24, 25 The Power of Leadership

They had no king but Caesar. To this the priests and teachers had led the people. For this, with the fearful results that followed, they were responsible. A nation's sin and a nation's ruin were due to the religious leaders. . . .

When Pilate declared himself innocent of the blood of Christ, Caiaphas answered defiantly, "His blood be on us, and on our children." . . .

The people of Israel had made their choice. *DA 738*

Jesus Is Mocked and Crucified

26 Then released he Barabbas unto them: and when he had scourged Jesus, he delivered *him* to be crucified.   Is. 53:5; Luke 23:16; John 19:1

27 Then the soldiers of the governor took Jesus into the common hall, and gathered unto him the whole band *of soldiers.*   Acts 10:1

28 And they stripped him, and put on him a scarlet robe.   Mark 15:17

29 And when they had ᵀplatted a crown of thorns, they put *it* upon his head, and a reed in his right hand: and they bowed the knee before him, and mocked him, saying, Hail, King of the Jews!   Is. 53:3 ◆ *braided*

30 And they spit upon him, and took the reed, and smote him on the head.   Mark 15:19

31 And after that they had mocked him, they took the robe off from him, and put his own ᵀraiment on him, and led him away to crucify *him.*   Is. 53:7 ◆ *clothing*

32 And as they came out, they found a man of Cyrene, Simon by name: him they compelled to bear his cross.   Mark 15:21; Luke 23:26; Acts 2:10

33 And when they were come unto a place called Golgotha, that is to say, a place of a skull,

34 They gave him vinegar to drink mingled with gall: and when he had tasted *thereof,* he would not drink.   Ps. 69:21; Matt. 27:48; Mark 15:23

35 And they crucified him, and parted his garments, casting lots: that it might be fulfilled which was spoken by the prophet, They parted my garments among them, and upon my ᵀvesture did they cast lots. Ps. 22:18 ◆ *clothing*

36 And sitting down they watched him there;   Matt. 27:54

37 And set up over his head his accusation written, THIS IS JESUS THE KING OF THE JEWS.   Mark 15:26

38 Then were there two thieves crucified with him, one on the right hand, and another on the left.   Is. 53:12

39 And they that passed by reviled him, wagging their heads,   Ps. 109:25; Lam. 1:12

40 And saying, Thou that destroyest the temple, and buildest *it* in three days, save thyself. If thou be the Son of God, come down from the cross.   Matt. 4:3, 6; 26:61

41 Likewise also the chief priests mocking *him,* with the scribes and elders, said,

42 He saved others; himself he cannot save. If he be the King of Israel, let him now come down from the cross, and we will believe him.   Matt. 27:37; John 1:49; 12:13

43 He trusted in God; let him deliver him now, if he will have him: for he said, I am the Son of God.   Ps. 22:8

44 The thieves also, which were crucified with him, cast the same in his teeth.

45 Now from the sixth hour there was darkness over all the land unto the ninth hour.   Amos 8:9

46 And about the ninth hour Jesus cried with a loud voice, saying, Eli, Eli, lama sabachthani? that is to say, My God, my God, why hast thou forsaken me? Ps. 22:1; Luke 23:46; Heb. 5:7

27:46 The Burden of Sin Kills

The spotless Son of God took upon Himself the burden of sin. He who had been one with God, felt in His soul the awful separation that sin makes between God and man. This wrung from His lips the anguished cry, "My God, My God, why hast Thou forsaken Me?" (Matthew 27:46). It was the burden of sin, the sense of its terrible enormity, of its separation of the soul from God—it was this that broke the heart of the Son of God. *SC 13*

47 Some of them that stood there, when they heard *that*, said, This *man* calleth for Elias.

48 And ᵀstraightway one of them ran, and took a spunge, and filled *it* with vinegar, and put *it* on a reed, and gave him to drink.   Ps. 69:21; Matt. 27:34; Luke 23:36 ♦ *right away*

49 The rest said, Let be, let us see whether Elias will come to save him.

Jesus Dies and Is Buried

50 Jesus, when he had cried again with a loud voice, yielded up the ghost.   John 19:30

51 And, behold, the veil of the temple was ᵀrent in twain from the top to the bottom; and the earth did quake, and the rocks rent;   Mark 15:38 ♦ *torn*

52 And the graves were opened; and many bodies of the saints which slept arose,

53 And came out of the graves after his resurrection, and went into the holy city, and appeared unto many.   Matt. 4:5

54 Now when the centurion, and they that were with him, watching Jesus, saw the earthquake, and those things that were done, they feared greatly, saying, Truly this was the Son of God.   Matt. 27:36, 43; Mark 15:39

55 And many women were there beholding afar off, which followed Jesus from Galilee, ministering unto him: Luke 8:2-3

56 Among which was Mary Magdalene, and Mary the mother of James and Joses, and the mother of Zebedee's children.   Mark 15:47–16:1

57 When the even was come, there came a rich man of Arimathaea, named Joseph, who also himself was Jesus' disciple: John 19:38-42

58 He went to Pilate, and begged the body of Jesus. Then Pilate commanded the body to be delivered.

59 And when Joseph had taken the body, he wrapped it in a clean linen cloth,

60 And laid it in his own new tomb, which he had ᵀhewn out in the rock: and he rolled a great stone to the door of the sepulchre, and departed.   Matt. 27:66 ♦ *cut*

61 And there was Mary Magdalene, and the other Mary, sitting over against the sepulchre.

62 Now the next day, that followed the day of the preparation, the chief priests and Pharisees came together unto Pilate,   Mark 15:42

63 Saying, Sir, we remember that that deceiver said, while he was yet alive, After three days I will rise again.   Matt. 16:21; 17:23; 20:19

64 Command therefore that the sepulchre be made sure until the third day, lest his disciples come by night, and steal him away, and say unto the people, He is risen from the dead: so the last error shall be worse than the first.   Matt. 28:13

65 Pilate said unto them, Ye have a watch: go your way, make *it* as sure as ye can.

66 So they went, and made the sepulchre sure, sealing the stone, and setting a watch.

Jesus' Resurrection

28 In the end of the sabbath, as it began to dawn toward the first *day* of the week, came Mary Magdalene and the other Mary to see the sepulchre.   Matt. 27:56, 61

2 And, behold, there was a great earthquake: for the angel of the Lord descended from heaven, and came and rolled back the stone from the door, and sat upon it.

At Last, Victory Over Sin and Death

Matthew 28:5, 6

Christ arose from the dead as the first fruits of those that slept. He was the antitype of the wave sheaf, and His resurrection took place on the very day when the wave sheaf was to be presented before the Lord. For more than a thousand years this symbolic ceremony had been performed. From the harvest fields the first heads of ripened grain were gathered, and when the people went up to Jerusalem to the Passover, the sheaf of first fruits was waved as a thank offering before the Lord. Not until this was presented could the sickle be put to the grain, and it be gathered into sheaves. The sheaf dedicated to God represented the harvest. So Christ the first fruits represented the great spiritual harvest to be gathered for the kingdom of God. His resurrection is the type and pledge of the resurrection of all the righteous dead. . . .

During His ministry, Jesus had raised the dead to life. . . . But these were not clothed with immortality. After they were raised, they were still subject to death. But those who came forth from the grave at Christ's resurrection were raised to everlasting life. They ascended with Him as trophies of His victory over death and the grave. These, said Christ, are no longer the captives of Satan; I have redeemed them. I have brought them from the grave as the first fruits of My power, to be with Me where I am, nevermore to see death or experience sorrow. . . .

To the believer, death is but a small matter. Christ speaks of it as if it were of little moment. . . . To the Christian, death is but a sleep, a moment of silence and darkness. . . .

At the Saviour's resurrection a few graves were opened, but at His second coming all the precious dead shall hear His voice, and shall come forth to glorious, immortal life. *DA 785–787*

3 His countenance was like lightning, and his raiment white as snow: Mark 9:3; Acts 1:10

4 And for fear of him the keepers did shake, and became as dead *men*. Rev. 1:17

5 And the angel answered and said unto the women, Fear not ye: for I know that ye seek Jesus, which was crucified. Heb. 1:14

6 He is not here: for he is risen, as he said. Come, see the place where the Lord lay.

7 And go quickly, and tell his disciples that he is risen from the dead; and, behold, he goeth before you into Galilee; there shall ye see him: lo, I have told you. Matt. 26:32; 28:10

8 And they departed quickly from the sepulchre with fear and great joy; and did run to bring his disciples word. Ps. 2:11

Jesus

9 And as they went to tell his disciples, behold, Jesus met them, saying, All hail. And they came and held him by the feet, and worshipped him. Matt. 14:33

10 Then said Jesus unto them, Be not afraid: go tell my brethren that they go into Galilee, and there shall they see me. John 20:17; Rom. 8:29

The Soldiers Are Bribed

11 Now when they were going, behold, some of the watch came into the city, and shewed unto the chief priests all the things that were done. Matt. 27:65-66

12 And when they were assembled with the elders, and had taken counsel, they gave large money unto the soldiers,

13 Saying, Say ye, His disciples came by night, and stole him *away* while we slept.

14 And if this come to the governor's ears, we will persuade him, and secure you. Matt. 27:2

15 So they took the money, and did as they were taught: and this saying is commonly reported among the Jews until this day.

Jesus Gives the Great Commission

16 Then the eleven disciples went away into Galilee, into a mountain where Jesus had appointed them. Matt. 26:32; 28:7, 10

17 And when they saw him, they worshipped him: but some doubted. Matt. 28:9

18 And Jesus came and spake unto them, saying, All power is given unto me in heaven and in earth. Matt. 11:27; Rom. 14:9; Eph. 1:20-22

19 Go ye therefore, and teach all nations, baptizing them in the name of the Father, and of the Son, and of the Holy Ghost: 2 Cor. 13:14

20 Teaching them to observe all things whatsoever I have commanded you: and, lo, I am with you alway, *even* unto the end of the world. Amen. Matt. 1:23; 18:20; Acts 2:42

THE GOSPEL ACCORDING TO

MARK

While the Gospel of Matthew proves beyond a shadow of a doubt that Jesus came to earth as a King—the Messiah promised and foretold throughout the Old Testament—the Gospel of Mark shows that He also came as a servant. The essence of His life was humble service—giving of Himself for the benefit of others. As the apostle Paul mentioned, He "made himself of no reputation, and took upon him the form of a servant, and was made in the likeness of men" (Philippians 2:7).

Mark's Gospel presents Jesus as the ultimate Servant, responding to the will of the Father with the intent of making the most profound statement of servanthood: dying on the cross for the sins of humanity. Even as Jesus is on the way to the cross, Mark shows Him as an active, compassionate, obedient servant who constantly ministers to the physical and spiritual needs of others. By writing about His many works of service, Mark illustrates the power and authority of this unique Servant. Jesus is no less than the Son of God. Mark writes with an evangelistic purpose—to convince his Gentile audience that Jesus is the Christ.

Mark's topical narrative on the life of Christ is the shortest and simplest of the four Gospels. He provides a crisp and fast-moving account of the life of Christ. The miracles of Jesus play a prominent role in the book. Mark highlights eighteen miracles, demonstrating Jesus' power and compassion. Mark shows Jesus' accomplishments and calls us to follow in His steps of servitude, even if suffering is part of the journey.

Dates

Most New Testament scholars agree that Mark's Gospel is the earliest written account of Jesus' life and ministry. Yet some uncertainty exists. The destruction of the temple is mentioned only prophetically (13:2), so it should be dated before A.D. 70, when the prophecy was fulfilled and the temple destroyed by the Romans. The probable date for this book is A.D. 55–65.

Author

The early church attested that Mark wrote this Gospel. Best known by his Latin name *Marcus* (see Colossians 4:10; Philemon 24; 1 Peter 5:13), in Jewish audiences, he was addressed by his Hebrew name John—he is called "John, whose surname was Mark" (Acts 12:12, 25; 15:37). Mark was not one of the original twelve apostles, but he was known around the circle of disciples and later was a companion of Peter and Paul. It is possible that Mark was referring to himself as the "certain young man" who ran naked from the Garden of Gethsemane at Jesus' arrest (Mark 14:51, 52). His mother's home in Jerusalem served as a meeting place for the early believers (Acts 12:12). Mark seems to have had a special relationship with the apostle Peter, who calls him "my son" (1 Peter 5:13). Peter was Mark's primary source of information regarding the life of Jesus.

Surely in his connection with Barnabas as his cousin (Colossians 4:10), Mark was called upon to accompany Barnabas and Paul on their first missionary journey as a minister, or helper (Acts 13:5). Mark left that trip early, which led to an argument between Paul and Barnabas on the second journey as to whether Mark was fit to travel. Barnabas trusted Mark; Paul did not. This led to a split in the missionary effort: Barnabas took Mark and sailed for Cyprus; Paul chose Silas and headed for Syria and Cilicia (Acts 15:36–41). Many years later, however, when Paul was imprisoned, he requested that Timothy bring Mark with him for a visit, signifying reconciliation between Paul and Mark, "Only Luke is with me. Take Mark, and bring him with thee: for he is profitable to me for the ministry" (2 Timothy 4:11).

Meaning of the Name

Kata Markon, "According to Mark," was the ancient title of this book. The word "gospel" was added later.

Christ in Mark

Christ as Servant is the dominate theme of Mark's narrative. Stories telling of Jesus' compassion and concern for the physical and spiritual needs of others are abundant. Jesus

moves purposefully and determinedly toward His final act of service, dying on the cross for the salvation of humanity.

Overview

The Gospel of Mark was written to a Gentile audience, probably the Romans, with a strong evangelistic purpose. Mark's original readers knew little about Old Testament theology or the Jewish language and traditions. In that light, several items that appear in Matthew's Gospel (written to a Jewish audience) are omitted from Mark's account as not pertinent to a non-Jewish audience, such as the genealogy of Jesus, fulfilled prophecy, references to the Jewish law, and certain Jewish customs. When writing an Aramaic word, Mark gave the interpretation for his readers:

♦ 3:17, "Boanerges, which is, The sons of thunder"
♦ 5:41, "Talitha cumi; which is, being interpreted, Damsel, I say unto thee, arise"
♦ 7:34, "Ephphatha, that is, Be opened"
♦ 15:22, "Golgotha, which is, being interpreted, The place of a skull"

The Gospel has two sections:

(1) *Mark 1—10, The Service of the Servant:* The Suffering Servant/Lamb of God described so vividly in Isaiah 53 walks through the pages of Mark's Gospel. The miracles of Jesus are highlighted, but only four parables are presented, thus emphasizing what Jesus did as opposed to what He said. Mark's Gospel is a book of action. (The word "immediately" is used over and over, signifying fast movement throughout the story.)

(2) *Mark 11—16, The Sacrifice of the Servant:* The last eight days of Jesus' earthy life receives the bulk of the discussion in Mark—about forty percent. Mark traces the steady building of hostility and opposition to Jesus as He moves toward the fulfillment of His mission.

Unlocking Mark

KEY PEOPLE:
Jesus, the disciples, Pilate, the Pharisees

KEY EVENTS:
The eighteen miracles reported; signs leading to Jesus' second coming; details of the week leading to Jesus' death; Jesus' burial and resurrection

KEY WORD:
Servant, for Jesus is portrayed as the servant that we can follow, the life of whom we can emulate.

KEY VERSES:
"But so shall it not be among you: but whosoever will be great among you, shall be your minister: And whosoever of you will be the chiefest, shall be servant of all. For even the Son of man came not to be ministered unto, but to minister, and to give his life a ransom for many" (Mark 10:43–45).

KEY CHAPTER:
Mark 8, which details the change of emphasis in Jesus' ministry as Peter confessed to Jesus, "Thou art the Christ" (verse 29). Prior to this point, Jesus had validated His claim as the Messiah; afterward, He prepared His disciples for the arduous road ahead: His arrest, death, and resurrection. This chapter also delineates what it means to become a true follower of Christ.

The Mission of John the Baptist

1 The beginning of the gospel of Jesus Christ, the Son of God;   Matt. 14:33

2 As it is written in the prophets, Behold, I send my messenger before thy face, which shall prepare thy way before thee.   Mal. 3:1

3 The voice of one crying in the wilderness, Prepare ye the way of the Lord, make his paths straight.   Matt. 3:3

4 John did baptize in the wilderness, and preach the baptism of repentance for the ᵀremission of sins.   Luke 1:77 ◆ forgiveness

5 And there went out unto him all the land of Judaea, and they of Jerusalem, and were all baptized of him in the river of Jordan, confessing their sins.   Acts 19:18

6 And John was clothed with camel's hair, and with a girdle of a skin about his loins; and he did eat locusts and wild honey;   Lev. 11:22

7 And preached, saying, There cometh one mightier than I after me, the ᵀlatchet of whose shoes I am not worthy to stoop down and unloose.   Acts 13:25 ◆ sandal strap

8 I indeed have baptized you with water: but he shall baptize you with the Holy Ghost.   Is. 44:3; Joel 2:28; Acts 1:5

John Baptizes Jesus

9 And it came to pass in those days, that Jesus came from Nazareth of Galilee, and was baptized of John in Jordan.   Matt. 2:23

10 And straightway coming up out of the water, he saw the heavens opened, and the Spirit like a dove descending upon him: Is. 64:1

11 And there came a voice from heaven, saying, Thou art my beloved Son, in whom I am well pleased.   Ps. 2:7

Satan Tempts Jesus

12 And immediately the Spirit driveth him into the wilderness.   Matt. 4:1-11

13 And he was there in the wilderness forty days, tempted of Satan; and was with the wild beasts; and the angels ministered unto him.

Calling the First Disciples

14 Now after that John was put in prison, Jesus came into Galilee, preaching the gospel of the kingdom of God,   Matt. 4:12, 23; Luke 3:20

15 And saying, **The time is fulfilled, and the kingdom of God is at hand: repent ye, and believe the gospel.**   Acts 20:21; Gal. 4:4; Eph. 1:10

16 Now as he walked by the sea of Galilee, he saw Simon and Andrew his brother casting a net into the sea: for they were fishers.   Matt. 4:18-22

17 And Jesus said unto them, **Come ye after me, and I will make you to become fishers of men.**

18 And ᵀstraightway they forsook their nets, and followed him.   right away

19 And when he had gone a little further thence, he saw James the son of Zebedee, and John his brother, who also were in the ship mending their nets.

20 And straightway he called them: and they left their father Zebedee in the ship with the hired servants, and went after him.

21 And they went into Capernaum; and straightway on the sabbath day he entered into the synagogue, and taught.   Matt. 4:13, 23

22 And they were astonished at his doctrine: for he taught them as one that had authority, and not as the scribes.   Matt. 7:28-29

Jesus Sends Out an Unclean Spirit

23 And there was in their synagogue a man with an unclean spirit; and he cried out,

24 Saying, Let us alone; what have we to do with thee, thou Jesus of Nazareth? art thou come to destroy us? I know thee who thou art, the Holy One of God.   Luke 4:34; Acts 3:14

25 And Jesus rebuked him, saying, **Hold thy peace, and come out of him.**   Mark 1:34

26 And when the unclean spirit had torn him, and cried with a loud voice, he came out of him.   Mark 9:20

27 And they were all amazed, insomuch that they questioned among themselves, saying, What thing is this? what new doctrine is this? for with authority commandeth he even the unclean spirits, and they do obey him.

28 And immediately his fame spread abroad throughout all the region round about Galilee.

Jesus Heals Peter's Mother-in-law and Many Others

29 And ᵀforthwith, when they were come out of the synagogue, they entered into the house of Simon and Andrew, with James and John.   Matt. 8:14-15 ◆ immediately

30 But Simon's wife's mother lay sick of a fever, and anon they tell him of her.   1 Cor. 9:5

31 And he came and took her by the hand, and lifted her up; and immediately the fever left her, and she ministered unto them.

32 And at even, when the sun did set, they brought unto him all that were diseased, and them that were possessed with devils.

33 And all the city was gathered together at the door.

34 And he healed many that were sick of ᵀdivers diseases, and cast out many devils; and suffered not the devils to speak, because they knew him.   Mark 3:12 ◆ various

35 And in the morning, rising up a great while before day, he went out, and departed into a solitary place, and there prayed.   Luke 6:12

36 And Simon and they that were with him followed after him.

1:35 You Must Hear Him

In all who are under the training of God is to be revealed a life that is not in harmony with the world, its customs, or its practices; and everyone needs to have a personal experience in obtaining a knowledge of the will of God. We must individually hear Him speaking to the heart. When every other voice is hushed, and in quietness we wait before Him, the silence of the soul makes more distinct the voice of God. . . . Here alone can true rest be found. *DA 363*

37 And when they had found him, they said unto him, All *men* seek for thee.   John 12:19
38 And he said unto them, **Let us go into the next towns, that I may preach there also: for therefore came I forth.**
39 And he preached in their synagogues throughout all Galilee, and cast out devils.

Jesus Cleanses a Leper

40 And there came a leper to him, ᵀbeseeching him, and kneeling down to him, and saying unto him, If thou wilt, thou canst make me clean.   Matt. 8:2-4; Mark 10:17; Luke 5:12-14 ◆ *begging*

1:40 "The Stroke," a Symbol of Sin

Of all diseases known in the East the leprosy was most dreaded. Its incurable and contagious character, and its horrible effect upon its victims, filled the bravest with fear. Among the Jews it was regarded as a judgment on account of sin, and hence was called "the stroke," "the finger of God." Deep-rooted, ineradicable, deadly, it was looked upon as a symbol of sin. . . . Even kings and rulers were not exempt. A monarch who was attacked by this terrible disease must yield up the scepter, and flee from society. *DA 262*

41 And Jesus, moved with compassion, put forth *his* hand, and touched him, and saith unto him, **I will; be thou clean.**
42 And as soon as he had spoken, immediately the leprosy departed from him, and he was cleansed.
43 And he ᵀstraitly charged him, and forthwith sent him away;   Matt. 9:30 ◆ *strictly*
44 And saith unto him, **See thou say nothing to any man: but go thy way, shew thyself to the priest, and offer for thy cleansing those things which Moses commanded, for a testimony unto them.**   Matt. 8:4
45 But he went out, and began to publish *it* much, and to ᵀblaze abroad the matter, insomuch that Jesus could no more openly enter into the city, but was without in desert places: and they came to him from every quarter.   Matt. 9:31; Mark 2:13; John 6:2 ◆ *proclaim*

Jesus Heals and Forgives

2 And again he entered into Capernaum after *some* days; and it was noised that he was in the house.   Matt. 9:1
2 And ᵀstraightway many were gathered together, insomuch that there was no room to receive *them*, no, not so much as about the door: and he preached the word unto them.   Mark 1:45 ◆ *right away*
3 And they come unto him, bringing one sick of the palsy, which was borne of four.
4 And when they could not come nigh unto him for the press, they uncovered the roof where he was: and when they had broken *it* up, they let down the bed wherein the sick of the palsy lay.   Luke 5:19
5 When Jesus saw their faith, he said unto the sick of the palsy, **Son, thy sins be forgiven thee.**   Matt. 9:2
6 But there were certain of the scribes sitting there, and reasoning in their hearts,
7 Why doth this *man* thus speak blasphemies? who can forgive sins but God only?   Is. 43:25; Mark 14:64; John 10:36
8 And immediately when Jesus perceived in his spirit that they so reasoned within themselves, he said unto them, **Why reason ye these things in your hearts?**
9 **Whether is it easier to say to the sick of the** ᵀ**palsy,** *Thy* **sins be forgiven thee; or to say, Arise, and take up thy bed, and walk?** *paralysis*
10 **But that ye may know that the Son of man hath power on earth to forgive sins,** (he saith to the sick of the palsy,)
11 **I say unto thee, Arise, and take up thy bed, and go thy way into thine house.**
12 And immediately he arose, took up the bed, and went forth before them all; insomuch that they were all amazed, and glorified God, saying, We never saw it on this fashion.   Matt. 9:8

2:2–12 A Lesson Not to Be Overlooked

The paralytic found in Christ healing for both the soul and the body. The spiritual healing was followed by physical restoration. This lesson should not be overlooked. There are today thousands suffering from physical disease, who, like the paralytic, are longing for the message, "Thy sins are forgiven." The burden of sin, with its unrest and unsatisfied desires, is the foundation of their maladies. . . . The peace which He alone can give, would impart vigor to the mind, and health to the body. *DA 270*

Jesus Chooses Levi (Matthew)

13 And he went forth again by the sea side; and all the multitude resorted unto him, and he taught them.   Mark 1:45

14 And as he passed by, he saw Levi the *son* of Alphaeus sitting at the receipt of custom, and said unto him, Follow me. And he arose and followed him.   Mark 3:18

15 And it came to pass, that, as Jesus sat at meat in his house, many ᵀpublicans and sinners sat also together with Jesus and his disciples: for there were many, and they followed him.   *tax collectors*

16 And when the scribes and Pharisees saw him eat with publicans and sinners, they said unto his disciples, How is it that he eateth and drinketh with publicans and sinners?

2:16 Jesus Looks at the Heart

The calling of Matthew to be one of Christ's disciples excited great indignation. For a religious teacher to choose a publican as one of his immediate attendants was an offense against the religious, social, and national customs. By appealing to the prejudices of the people the Pharisees hoped to turn the current of popular feeling against Jesus. *DA 273*

17 When Jesus heard *it*, he saith unto them, They that are whole have no need of the physician, but they that are sick: I came not to call the righteous, but sinners to repentance.

Questions about Fasting

18 And the disciples of John and of the Pharisees used to fast: and they come and say unto him, Why do the disciples of John and of the Pharisees fast, but thy disciples fast not?   Matt. 6:16

19 And Jesus said unto them, Can the children of the bridechamber fast, while the bridegroom is with them? as long as they have the bridegroom with them, they cannot fast.

20 But the days will come, when the bridegroom shall be taken away from them, and then shall they fast in those days.   Luke 17:22

21 No man also seweth a piece of new cloth on an old garment: else the new piece that filled it up taketh away from the old, and the ᵀrent is made worse.   *tear*

22 And no man putteth new wine into old bottles: else the new wine doth burst the bottles, and the wine is spilled, and the bottles will be marred: but new wine must be put into new bottles.   Josh. 9:4

Jesus Has Authority over the Sabbath

23 And it came to pass, that he went through the corn fields on the sabbath day; and his disciples began, as they went, to pluck the ears of corn.   Matt. 12:1-8

24 And the Pharisees said unto him, Behold, why do they on the sabbath day that which is not lawful?   Ex. 20:10

25 And he said unto them, Have ye never read what David did, when he had need, and was an hungred, he, and they that were with him?   1 Sam. 21:3-6

26 How he went into the house of God in the days of Abiathar the high priest, and did eat the shewbread, which is not lawful to eat but for the priests, and gave also to them which were with him?   Lev. 24:5-9; 1 Sam. 21:1; 2 Sam. 8:17

27 And he said unto them, The sabbath was made for man, and not man for the sabbath: Ex. 23:12; Deut. 5:14; Col. 2:16

The Sabbath   See Luke 14:1-5.

28 Therefore the Son of man is Lord also of the sabbath.   Rev. 1:10

2:23-28 Christ Sets Aside False Teaching

Christ, during His earthly ministry, emphasized the binding claims of the Sabbath; in all His teaching He showed reverence for the institution He Himself had given. In His days the Sabbath had become so perverted that its observance reflected the character of selfish and arbitrary men rather than the character of God. Christ set aside the false teaching by which those who claimed to know God had misrepresented Him. *PK 183*

Jesus Heals on the Sabbath

3 And he entered again into the synagogue; and there was a man there which had a withered hand.   Matt. 12:9-14

2 And they watched him, whether he would heal him on the sabbath day; that they might accuse him.   Luke 6:7; 14:1; 20:20

3 And he saith unto the man which had the withered hand, Stand forth.

4 And he saith unto them, Is it lawful to do good on the sabbath days, or to do evil? to save life, or to kill? But they held their peace.

5 And when he had looked round about on them with anger, being grieved for the hardness of their hearts, he saith unto the man, Stretch forth thine hand. And he stretched *it* out: and his hand was restored whole as the other.   Luke 6:10; Rom. 11:25; Eph. 4:18

6 And the Pharisees went forth, and ᵀstraightway took counsel with the Herodians against him, how they might destroy him.   Matt. 12:14; 22:16; Mark 12:13 ◆ *right away*

7 But Jesus withdrew himself with his disciples to the sea: and a great multitude from Galilee followed him, and from Judaea,   Matt. 4:25; 12:15; Luke 6:17

8 And from Jerusalem, and from Idumaea, and *from* beyond Jordan; and they about Tyre and Sidon, a great multitude, when they had heard what great things he did, came unto him.   Ezek. 35:15

9 And he spake to his disciples, that a small ship should wait on him because of the multitude, lest they should throng him.

10 For he had healed many; insomuch that they pressed upon him for to touch him, as many as had plagues.   Matt. 14:36

11 And unclean spirits, when they saw him, fell down before him, and cried, saying, Thou art the Son of God.   Matt. 4:3

12 And he straitly charged them that they should not make him known.   Matt. 12:16

Jesus Chooses Twelve Apostles

13 And he goeth up into a mountain, and calleth *unto him* whom he would: and they came unto him.

14 And he ordained twelve, that they should be with him, and that he might send them forth to preach,

15 And to have power to heal sicknesses, and to cast out devils:

16 And Simon he surnamed Peter;   John 1:42

17 And James the *son* of Zebedee, and John the brother of James; and he surnamed them Boanerges, which is, The sons of thunder:

18 And Andrew, and Philip, and Bartholomew, and Matthew, and Thomas, and James the *son* of Alphaeus, and Thaddaeus, and Simon the Canaanite,   Matt. 9:9; Acts 1:13

19 And Judas Iscariot, which also betrayed him: and they went into an house.

20 And the multitude cometh together again, so that they could not so much as eat bread.   Mark 6:31

21 And when his friends heard *of it*, they went out to lay hold on him: for they said, He is beside himself.   Mark 3:31; John 10:20; Acts 26:24

Jesus Is Accused of Working with Satan

22 And the scribes which came down from Jerusalem said, He hath Beelzebub, and by the prince of the devils casteth he out devils.   Matt. 9:34; 10:25; 15:1

23 And he called them *unto him*, and said unto them in parables, How can Satan cast out Satan?   Matt. 13:34

24 And if a kingdom be divided against itself, that kingdom cannot stand.

25 And if a house be divided against itself, that house cannot stand.

26 And if Satan rise up against himself, and be divided, he cannot stand, but hath an end.

27 No man can enter into a strong man's house, and ᵀspoil his goods, except he will first bind the strong man; and then he will spoil his house.   Is. 53:12 • *plunder*

28 Verily I say unto you, All sins shall be forgiven unto the sons of men, and blasphemies wherewith soever they shall blaspheme: Matt. 12:31-32

29 But he that shall blaspheme against the Holy Ghost hath never forgiveness, but is in danger of eternal damnation: Matt. 25:46

End of Sin/Hell   See Jude 7.

30 Because they said, He hath an unclean spirit.

Jesus Describes His True Family

31 There came then his brethren and his mother, and, standing without, sent unto him, calling him.   Luke 8:19-21

32 And the multitude sat about him, and they said unto him, Behold, thy mother and thy brethren without seek for thee.

33 And he answered them, saying, Who is my mother, or my brethren?

34 And he looked round about on them which sat about him, and said, Behold my mother and my brethren!

35 For whosoever shall do the will of God, the same is my brother, and my sister, and mother.   Matt. 7:21

The Parable of the Sower

4 And he began again to teach by the sea side: and there was gathered unto him a great multitude, so that he entered into a ship, and sat in the sea; and the whole multitude was by the sea on the land.   Mark 2:13

2 And he taught them many things by parables, and said unto them in his doctrine,

3 Hearken; Behold, there went out a sower to sow:

4 And it came to pass, as he sowed, some fell by the way side, and the fowls of the air came and devoured it up.

5 And some fell on stony ground, where it had not much earth; and immediately it sprang up, because it had no depth of earth:

6 But when the sun was up, it was scorched; and because it had no root, it withered away.   James 1:11

7 And some fell among thorns, and the thorns grew up, and choked it, and it yielded no fruit.   Jer. 4:3

8 And other fell on good ground, and did yield fruit that sprang up and increased; and brought forth, some thirty, and some sixty, and some an hundred.   Gen. 26:12

9 And he said unto them, He that hath ears to hear, let him hear.   Matt. 11:15

10 And when he was alone, they that were about him with the twelve asked of him the parable.   Mark 4:34

11 And he said unto them, Unto you it is given to know the mystery of the kingdom of God: but unto them that are without, all *these* things are done in parables: Col. 4:5; 1 Thess. 4:12

12 That seeing they may see, and not perceive; and hearing they may hear, and not

understand; lest at any time they should be converted, and *their* sins should be forgiven them. Is. 6:9-10

13 And he said unto them, Know ye not this parable? and how then will ye know all parables?

14 The sower soweth the word. Matt. 13:37

15 And these are they by the way side, where the word is sown; but when they have heard, Satan cometh immediately, and taketh away the word that was sown in their hearts.

16 And these are they likewise which are sown on stony ground; who, when they have heard the word, immediately receive it with gladness; Ezek. 33:31-32

17 And have no root in themselves, and so endure but for a time: afterward, when affliction or persecution ariseth for the word's sake, immediately they are offended. Matt. 11:6

18 And these are they which are sown among thorns; such as hear the word,

19 And the cares of this world, and the deceitfulness of riches, and the lusts of other things entering in, choke the word, and it becometh unfruitful. 1 Tim. 6:9-10, 17; 2 Tim. 4:10

20 And these are they which are sown on good ground; such as hear the word, and receive *it*, and bring forth fruit, some thirtyfold, some sixty, and some an hundred. Mark 4:8

4:13–20 He Longs to Enlighten Us

[Jesus] explained the parable to them, as He will make plain His word to all who seek Him in sincerity of heart. Those who study the word of God with hearts open to the enlightenment of the Holy Spirit, will not remain in darkness as to the meaning of the word. . . . All who come to Christ for a clearer knowledge of the truth will receive it. He will unfold to them the mysteries of the kingdom of heaven, and these mysteries will be understood by the heart that longs to know the truth. *COL 35, 36*

A Parable about a Light

21 And he said unto them, Is a candle brought to be put under a bushel, or under a bed? and not to be set on a candlestick? Matt. 5:15; Luke 8:16; 11:33

22 For there is nothing hid, which shall not be ᵀmanifested; neither was any thing kept secret, but that it should come abroad. Luke 8:17 ◆ *made known*

23 If any man have ears to hear, let him hear.

24 And he said unto them, Take heed what ye hear: with what measure ye ᵀmete, it shall be measured to you: and unto you that hear shall more be given. Matt. 7:2 ◆ *measure out*

25 For he that hath, to him shall be given:

and he that hath not, from him shall be taken even that which he hath. Matt. 13:12; Luke 8:18

A Parable about Seeds

26 And he said, So is the kingdom of God, as if a man should cast seed into the ground; Matt. 13:24

27 And should sleep, and rise night and day, and the seed should spring and grow up, he knoweth not how. Eccl. 11:5

28 For the earth bringeth forth fruit of herself; first the blade, then the ear, after that the full corn in the ear.

29 But when the fruit is brought forth, immediately he putteth in the sickle, because the harvest is come. Joel 3:13

Signs of the End   See James 5:7, 8.

Describing the Kingdom of Heaven

30 And he said, Whereunto shall we liken the kingdom of God? or with what comparison shall we compare it?

31 *It is* like a grain of mustard seed, which, when it is sown in the earth, is less than all the seeds that be in the earth:

32 But when it is sown, it groweth up, and becometh greater than all herbs, and shooteth out great branches; so that the fowls of the air may lodge under the shadow of it.

33 And with many such parables spake he the word unto them, as they were able to hear *it*. John 16:12

34 But without a parable spake he not unto them: and when they were alone, he expounded all things to his disciples. Mark 4:10

Jesus Calms the Sea

35 And the same day, when the even was come, he saith unto them, Let us pass over unto the other side. Matt. 8:18

36 And when they had sent away the multitude, they took him even as he was in the ship. And there were also with him other little ships. Mark 3:9

37 And there arose a great storm of wind, and the waves beat into the ship, so that it was now full.

38 And he was in the hinder part of the ship, asleep on a pillow: and they awake him, and say unto him, Master, carest thou not that we perish?

39 And he arose, and rebuked the wind, and said unto the sea, Peace, be still. And the wind ceased, and there was a great calm. Job 38:11

40 And he said unto them, Why are ye so fearful? how is it that ye have no faith?

41 And they feared exceedingly, and said one to another, What manner of man is this, that even the wind and the sea obey him?

4:26-29

Jesus Heals a Man Possessed by Many Demons

5 And they came over unto the other side of the sea, into the country of the Gadarenes.   Matt. 8:28-34

2 And when he was come out of the ship, immediately there met him out of the tombs a man with an unclean spirit,   Mark 1:23

3 Who had *his* dwelling among the tombs; and no man could bind him, no, not with chains:

4 Because that he had been often bound with ᵀfetters and chains, and the chains had been plucked ᵀasunder by him, and the fetters broken in pieces: neither could any *man* tame him.   *chains ◆ apart*

5 And always, night and day, he was in the mountains, and in the tombs, crying, and cutting himself with stones.

6 But when he saw Jesus afar off, he ran and worshipped him,

7 And cried with a loud voice, and said, What have I to do with thee, Jesus, *thou* Son of the most high God? I adjure thee by God, that thou torment me not.   Matt. 4:3; 8:29; Acts 16:17

8 For he said unto him, Come out of the man, *thou* unclean spirit.

9 And he asked him, What *is* thy name? And he answered, saying, My name *is* Legion: for we are many.   Matt. 26:53

10 And he ᵀbesought him much that he would not send them away out of the country. *begged*

11 Now there was there nigh unto the mountains a great herd of swine feeding.

12 And all the devils besought him, saying, Send us into the swine, that we may enter into them.

13 And ᵀforthwith Jesus gave them leave. And the unclean spirits went out, and entered into the swine: and the herd ran violently down a steep place into the sea, (they were about two thousand;) and were choked in the sea.   *immediately*

14 And they that fed the swine fled, and told *it* in the city, and in the country. And they went out to see what it was that was done.

15 And they come to Jesus, and see him that was possessed with the devil, and had the ᵀlegion, sitting, and clothed, and in his right mind: and they were afraid. Mark 5:9 ◆ *large number*

16 And they that saw *it* told them how it befell to him that was possessed with the ᵀdevil, and *also* concerning the swine.   *demon*

17 And they began to pray him to depart out of their coasts.   Acts 16:39

18 And when he was come into the ship, he that had been possessed with the devil prayed him that he might be with him.   Luke 8:38-39

19 Howbeit Jesus suffered him not, but saith unto him, Go home to thy friends, and tell them how great things the Lord hath done for thee, and hath had compassion on thee.   Ps. 66:16

20 And he departed, and began to publish in Decapolis how great things Jesus had done for him: and all *men* did marvel. Matt. 4:25; Mark 7:31

Jesus Raises a Girl from the Dead and Heals a Bleeding Woman

21 And when Jesus was passed over again by ship unto the other side, much people gathered unto him: and he was nigh unto the sea.   Matt. 9:1

The Reason for Crime and Violence

Mark 5:1–8

The encounter with the demoniacs of Gergesa had a lesson for the disciples. It showed the depths of degradation to which Satan is seeking to drag the whole human race, and the mission of Christ to set men free from his power. Those wretched beings, dwelling in the place of graves, possessed by demons, in bondage to uncontrolled passions and loathsome lusts, represent what humanity would become if given up to satanic jurisdiction. . . . Multitudes in every department in life, in the home, in business, and even in the church, are doing this today. It is because of this that violence and crime have overspread the earth, and moral darkness, like the pall of death, enshrouds the habitations of men. . . . The only safeguard against his power is found in the presence of Jesus. Before men and angels Satan has been revealed as man's enemy and destroyer; Christ, as man's friend and deliverer. His Spirit will develop in man all that will ennoble the character and dignify the nature. It will build man up for the glory of God in body and soul and spirit. "For God hath not given us the spirit of fear; but of power, and of love, and of a sound mind" (2 Timothy 1:7). He has called us "to the obtaining of the glory"—character—"of our Lord Jesus Christ;" has called us to be "conformed to the image of His Son" (2 Thessalonians 2:14; Romans 8:29). *DA 341*

22 And, behold, there cometh one of the rulers of the synagogue, Jairus by name; and when he saw him, he fell at his feet, Luke 13:14
23 And besought him greatly, saying, My little daughter lieth at the point of death: *I pray thee*, come and lay thy hands on her, that she may be healed; and she shall live.   Luke 4:40
24 And *Jesus* went with him; and much people followed him, and thronged him. Mark 5:31
25 And a certain woman, which had an issue of blood twelve years,   Lev. 15:25-27
26 And had suffered many things of many physicians, and had spent all that she had, and was nothing bettered, but rather grew worse,
27 When she had heard of Jesus, came in the press behind, and touched his garment.
28 For she said, If I may touch but his clothes, I shall be whole.
29 And straightway the fountain of her blood was dried up; and she felt in *her* body that she was healed of that plague. Mark 3:10
30 And Jesus, immediately knowing in himself that virtue had gone out of him, turned him about in the press, and said, Who touched my clothes?   Luke 6:19
31 And his disciples said unto him, Thou seest the multitude thronging thee, and sayest thou, Who touched me?
32 And he looked round about to see her that had done this thing.
33 But the woman fearing and trembling, knowing what was done in her, came and fell down before him, and told him all the truth.
34 And he said unto her, Daughter, thy faith hath made thee whole; go in peace, and be whole of thy plague.   Matt. 9:22; Luke 7:50; 8:48

5:25–34 Faith That Is Unto Salvation

To the curious crowd pressing about Jesus there was imparted no vital power. But the suffering woman who touched Him in faith received healing. So in spiritual things does the casual contact differ from the touch of faith. To believe in Christ merely as the Saviour of the world can never bring healing to the soul. The faith that is unto salvation is not a mere assent to the truth of the gospel. True faith is that which receives Christ as a personal Saviour. *MH 62*

35 While he yet spake, there came from the ruler of the synagogue's *house certain* which said, Thy daughter is dead: why troublest thou the Master any further?   Mark 5:22
36 As soon as Jesus heard the word that was spoken, he saith unto the ruler of the synagogue, Be not afraid, only believe.   Luke 8:50
37 And he suffered no man to follow him, save Peter, and James, and John the brother of James.   Mark 9:2

38 And he cometh to the house of the ruler of the synagogue, and seeth the tumult, and them that wept and wailed greatly.
39 And when he was come in, he saith unto them, Why make ye this ᵀado, and weep? the damsel is not dead, but sleepeth.   *commotion*
40 And they laughed him to scorn. But when he had put them all out, he taketh the father and the mother of the damsel, and them that were with him, and entereth in where the damsel was lying.
41 And he took the damsel by the hand, and said unto her, Talitha cumi; which is, being interpreted, Damsel, I say unto thee, arise.   Mark 1:31
42 And ᵀstraightway the damsel arose, and walked; for she was *of the age* of twelve years. And they were astonished with a great astonishment.   *right away*
43 And he charged them straitly that no man should know it; and commanded that something should be given her to eat.   Matt. 8:4

Jesus Is Rejected by His Countrymen

6 And he went out from thence, and came into his own country; and his disciples follow him.   Luke 4:16-30
2 And when the sabbath day was come, he began to teach in the synagogue: and many hearing *him* were astonished, saying, From whence hath this *man* these things? and what wisdom *is* this which is given unto him, that even such mighty works are ᵀwrought by his hands?   Matt. 4:23 ♦ *done*
3 Is not this the carpenter, the son of Mary, the brother of James, and Joses, and of Juda, and Simon? and are not his sisters here with us? And they were offended at him. Matt. 11:6
4 But Jesus said unto them, A prophet is not without honour, but in his own country, and among his own kin, and in his own house.   Jer. 11:21; Luke 4:24; John 4:44
5 And he could there do no mighty work, save that he laid his hands upon a few sick folk, and healed *them*.   Gen. 19:22
6 And he marvelled because of their unbelief. And he went round about the villages, teaching.   Matt. 8:10; 9:35; Luke 13:22

Jesus Sends Out the Twelve

7 And he called *unto him* the twelve, and began to send them forth by two and two; and gave them power over unclean spirits;
8 And commanded them that they should take nothing for *their* journey, save a staff only; no ᵀscrip, no bread, no money in *their* purse: *sack*
9 But *be* shod with sandals; and not put on two coats.   Acts 12:8
10 And he said unto them, In what place

soever ye enter into an house, there abide till ye depart from that place.

11 And whosoever shall not receive you, nor hear you, when ye depart thence, shake off the dust under your feet for a testimony against them. Verily I say unto you, It shall be more tolerable for Sodom and Gomorrha in the day of judgment, than for that city.

12 And they went out, and preached that men should repent.   Matt. 4:17

13 And they cast out many devils, and anointed with oil many that were sick, and healed *them*.

The Death of John the Baptist

14 And king Herod heard *of him*; (for his name was spread abroad:) and he said, That John the Baptist was risen from the dead, and therefore mighty works do shew forth themselves in him.   Luke 9:7-9

15 Others said, That it is Elias. And others said, That it is a prophet, or as one of the prophets.   Matt. 16:14; 21:11; Mark 8:28

16 But when Herod heard *thereof*, he said, It is John, whom I beheaded: he is risen from the dead.

17 For Herod himself had sent forth and laid hold upon John, and bound him in prison for Herodias' sake, his brother Philip's wife: for he had married her.   Matt. 11:2

18 For John had said unto Herod, It is not lawful for thee to have thy brother's wife.

19 Therefore Herodias had a quarrel against him, and would have killed him; but she could not:

20 For Herod feared John, knowing that he was a just man and an holy, and observed him; and when he heard him, he did many things, and heard him gladly.   Matt. 14:5; 21:26

21 And when a ᵀconvenient day was come, that Herod on his birthday made a supper to his lords, high captains, and chief *estates* of Galilee;   Gen. 40:20; Esth. 2:18 ◆ *opportune*

22 And when the daughter of the said Herodias came in, and danced, and pleased Herod and them that sat with him, the king said unto the damsel, Ask of me whatsoever thou wilt, and I will give *it* thee.

23 And he sware unto her, Whatsoever thou shalt ask of me, I will give *it* thee, unto the half of my kingdom.   Esth. 5:3, 6; 7:2

24 And she went forth, and said unto her mother, What shall I ask? And she said, The head of John the Baptist.

25 And she came in straightway with haste unto the king, and asked, saying, I will that thou give me by and by in a ᵀcharger the head of John the Baptist.   *platter*

26 And the king was exceeding sorry; *yet* for his oath's sake, and for their sakes which sat with him, he would not reject her.

27 And immediately the king sent an executioner, and commanded his head to be brought: and he went and beheaded him in the prison,

28 And brought his head in a charger, and gave it to the damsel: and the damsel gave it to her mother.

29 And when his disciples heard *of it*, they came and took up his corpse, and laid it in a tomb.

Jesus Feeds More than Five Thousand

30 And the apostles gathered themselves together unto Jesus, and told him all things, both what they had done, and what they had taught.   Matt. 10:2; Luke 9:10; 17:5

31 And he said unto them, Come ye yourselves apart into a desert place, and rest a while: for there were many coming and going, and they had no leisure so much as to eat.   Mark 3:20

32 And they departed into a desert place by ship privately.

33 And the people saw them departing, and many knew him, and ran afoot thither out of all cities, and ᵀoutwent them, and came together unto him.   *went in advance of*

34 And Jesus, when he came out, saw much people, and was moved with compassion toward them, because they were as sheep not having a shepherd: and he began to teach them many things.   Num. 27:17; 1 Kin. 22:17

35 And when the day was now far spent, his disciples came unto him, and said, This is a desert place, and now the time *is* far passed:

36 Send them away, that they may go into the country round about, and into the villages, and buy themselves bread: for they have nothing to eat.   Matt. 15:23

37 He answered and said unto them, Give ye them to eat. And they say unto him, Shall we go and buy two hundred pennyworth of bread, and give them to eat?   2 Kin. 4:42-44

38 He saith unto them, How many loaves have ye? go and see. And when they knew, they say, Five, and two fishes.   Matt. 15:34

39 And he commanded them to make all sit down by companies upon the green grass.

40 And they sat down in ranks, by hundreds, and by fifties.

41 And when he had taken the five loaves and the two fishes, he looked up to heaven, and blessed, and brake the loaves, and gave *them* to his disciples to set before them; and the two fishes divided he among them all.   Matt. 14:19

42 And they did all eat, and were filled.

43 And they took up twelve baskets full of the fragments, and of the fishes.

6:41, 42 God Working Miracles Daily

In the Saviour's miracle of feeding the five thousand is illustrated the working of God's power in the production of the harvest. Jesus draws aside the veil from the world of nature and reveals the creative energy that is constantly exercised for our good. In multiplying the seed cast into the ground, He who multiplied the loaves is working a miracle every day. *Ed 107, 108*

---

44 And they that did eat of the loaves were about five thousand men.

Jesus Walks on the Sea

45 And straightway he ᵀconstrained his disciples to get into the ship, and to go to the other side before unto Bethsaida, while he sent away the people.   Mark 8:22 ♦ *compelled*
46 And when he had sent them away, he departed into a mountain to pray.   Matt. 14:23
47 And when even was come, the ship was in the midst of the sea, and he alone on the land.
48 And he saw them toiling in rowing; for the wind was contrary unto them: and about the fourth watch of the night he cometh unto them, walking upon the sea, and would have passed by them.   Luke 12:38
49 But when they saw him walking upon the sea, they supposed it had been a spirit, and cried out: Luke 24:37
50 For they all saw him, and were troubled. And immediately he talked with them, and saith unto them, **Be of good cheer: it is I; be not afraid.**   Matt. 14:27
51 And he went up unto them into the ship; and the wind ceased: and they were sore

amazed in themselves beyond measure, and wondered.   Mark 4:39
52 For they considered not *the miracle* of the loaves: for their heart was hardened. Mark 3:5
53 And when they had passed over, they came into the land of Gennesaret, and drew to the shore.   Matt. 14:34-36
54 And when they were come out of the ship, ᵀstraightway they knew him,   *right away*
55 And ran through that whole region round about, and began to carry about in beds those that were sick, where they heard he was.   Matt. 4:24
56 And whithersoever he entered, into villages, or cities, or country, they laid the sick in the streets, and besought him that they might touch if it were but the border of his garment: and as many as touched him were made whole.   Num. 15:38-39; Matt. 9:20; Mark 3:10

Jesus Challenges the Pharisees' Traditions

7 Then came together unto him the Pharisees, and certain of the scribes, which came from Jerusalem.   Mark 3:22
2 And when they saw some of his disciples eat bread with defiled, that is to say, with unwashen, hands, they found fault. Acts 10:28
3 For the Pharisees, and all the Jews, except they wash *their* hands ᵀoft, eat not, holding the tradition of the elders.   Mark 7:13 ♦ *often*
4 And *when they come* from the market, except they wash, they eat not. And many other things there be, which they have received to hold, *as* the washing of cups, and pots, brasen vessels, and of tables. Matt. 23:25
5 Then the Pharisees and scribes asked him,

The Greatest Deception of the Human Mind

Mark 7:6–9

Since "the law of the Lord is perfect," every variation from it must be evil. Those who disobey the commandments of God, and teach others to do so, are condemned by Christ. The Saviour's life of obedience maintained the claims of the law; it proved that the law could be kept in humanity, and showed the excellence of character that obedience would develop. All who obey as He did are likewise declaring that the law is "holy, and just, and good" (Romans 7:12). On the other hand, all who break God's commandments are sustaining Satan's claim that the law is unjust, and cannot be obeyed. Thus they second the deceptions of the great adversary, and cast dishonor upon God. They are the children of the wicked one, who was the first rebel against God's law. To admit them into heaven would again bring in the elements of discord and rebellion, and imperil the well-being of the universe. No man who willfully disregards one principle of the law shall enter the kingdom of heaven. . . .

The greatest deception of the human mind in Christ's day was that a mere assent to the truth constitutes righteousness. In all human experience a theoretical knowledge of the truth has been proved to be insufficient for the saving of the soul. It does not bring forth the fruits of righteousness. A jealous regard for what is termed theological truth often accompanies a hatred of genuine truth as made manifest in life. . . .

The same danger still exists. Many take it for granted that they are Christians, simply because they subscribe to certain theological tenets. But they have not brought the truth into practical life. *DA 308, 309*

Why walk not thy disciples according to the tradition of the elders, but eat bread with unwashen hands?

6 He answered and said unto them, Well hath Esaias prophesied of you hypocrites, as it is written, This people honoureth me with *their* lips, but their heart is far from me. Is. 29:13

7 Howbeit in vain do they worship me, teaching *for* doctrines the commandments of men. Matt. 6:7

8 For laying aside the commandment of God, ye hold the tradition of men, *as* the washing of pots and cups: and many other such like things ye do.

9 And he said unto them, Full well ye reject the commandment of God, that ye may keep your own tradition. Mark 7:13

10 For Moses said, Honour thy father and thy mother; and, Whoso curseth father or mother, let him die the death: Ex. 20:12; 21:17

11 But ye say, If a man shall say to his father or mother, *It is* Corban, that is to say, a gift, by whatsoever thou mightest be profited by me; *he shall be free.* Matt. 23:18

12 And ye suffer him no more to do ought for his father or his mother;

13 Making the word of God of none effect through your tradition, which ye have delivered: and many such like things do ye. Mark 7:9

14 And when he had called all the people *unto him*, he said unto them, Hearken unto me every one *of you*, and understand:

15 There is nothing from without a man, that entering into him can defile him: but the things which come out of him, those are they that defile the man.

16 If any man have ears to hear, let him hear.

17 And when he was entered into the house from the people, his disciples asked him concerning the parable. Matt. 15:15

18 And he saith unto them, Are ye so without understanding also? Do ye not perceive, that whatsoever thing from without entereth into the man, *it* cannot defile him;

19 Because it entereth not into his heart, but into the belly, and goeth out into the draught, purging all meats? Acts 10:15

20 And he said, That which cometh out of the man, that defileth the man. James 3:6

21 For from within, out of the heart of men, proceed evil thoughts, adulteries, fornications, murders, Jer. 17:9

22 Thefts, ᵀcovetousness, wickedness, deceit, ᵀlasciviousness, an evil eye, blasphemy, pride, foolishness: Matt. 20:15 ◆ *strong desire* ◆ *lewdness*

23 All these evil things come from within, and defile the man.

Jesus Heals the Syrophenician Woman's Daughter

24 And from thence he arose, and went into the borders of Tyre and Sidon, and entered into an house, and would have no man know *it*: but he could not be hid. Matt. 15:21-28

25 For a *certain* woman, whose young daughter had an unclean spirit, heard of him, and came and fell at his feet:

26 The woman was a Greek, a Syrophenician by nation; and she ᵀbesought him that he would cast forth the devil out of her daughter. *begged*

27 But Jesus said unto her, Let the children first be filled: for it is not meet to take the children's bread, and to cast *it* unto the dogs.

28 And she answered and said unto him, Yes, Lord: yet the dogs under the table eat of the children's crumbs.

29 And he said unto her, For this saying go thy way; the ᵀdevil is gone out of thy daughter. *demon*

30 And when she was come to her house, she found the devil gone out, and her daughter laid upon the bed.

Jesus Heals a Deaf Man

31 And again, departing from the coasts of Tyre and Sidon, he came unto the sea of Galilee, through the midst of the coasts of Decapolis. Matt. 4:25; 15:29-31; Mark 5:20

32 And they bring unto him one that was deaf, and had an impediment in his speech; and they ᵀbeseech him to put his hand upon him. Mark 5:23 ◆ *beg*

33 And he took him aside from the multitude, and put his fingers into his ears, and he spit, and touched his tongue; Mark 8:23

34 And looking up to heaven, he sighed, and saith unto him, Ephphatha, that is, Be opened. Mark 6:41; 8:12; John 11:33

35 And ᵀstraightway his ears were opened, and the string of his tongue was loosed, and he spake plain. Is. 35:5-6 ◆ *right away*

36 And he charged them that they should tell no man: but the more he charged them, so much the more a great deal they published *it*; Matt. 8:4

37 And were beyond measure astonished, saying, He hath done all things well: he maketh both the deaf to hear, and the ᵀdumb to speak. *mute*

Jesus Feeds More than Four Thousand

8 In those days the multitude being very great, and having nothing to eat, Jesus called his disciples *unto him*, and saith unto them, Matt. 15:32-39

2 I have compassion on the multitude, because they have now been with me three days, and have nothing to eat: Matt. 9:36; Mark 6:34

3 And if I send them away fasting to their own houses, they will faint by the way: for ᵀdivers of them came from far.   *various*

4 And his disciples answered him, From whence can a man satisfy these *men* with bread here in the wilderness?

5 And he asked them, How many loaves have ye? And they said, Seven.

6 And he commanded the people to sit down on the ground: and he took the seven loaves, and gave thanks, and brake, and gave to his disciples to set before *them*; and they did set *them* before the people.   John 6:23

7 And they had a few small fishes: and he blessed, and commanded to set them also before *them*.   Matt. 14:19

8 So they did eat, and were filled: and they took up of the broken *meat* that was left seven baskets.   2 Kin. 4:42-44

9 And they that had eaten were about four thousand: and he sent them away.

Jesus Warns about the Pharisees

10 And ᵀstraightway he entered into a ship with his disciples, and came into the parts of Dalmanutha.   Matt. 15:39 ◆ *right away*

11 And the Pharisees came forth, and began to question with him, seeking of him a sign from heaven, tempting him.Matt. 12:38; Luke 11:16

12 And he sighed deeply in his spirit, and saith, Why doth this generation seek after a sign? verily I say unto you, There shall no sign be given unto this generation.   Mark 7:34

> **8:11, 12 Spiritual Renovation Needed Most**
>
> When in the days of Joshua Israel went out to battle with the Canaanites at Beth-horon, the sun had stood still at the leader's command until victory was gained; and many similar wonders had been manifest in [Israel's] history. Some such sign was demanded of Jesus. But these signs were not what the Jews needed. No mere external evidence could benefit them. What they needed was not intellectual enlightenment, but spiritual renovation. *DA 406*

13 And he left them, and entering into the ship again departed to the other side.

14 Now *the disciples* had forgotten to take bread, neither had they in the ship with them more than one loaf.

15 And he charged them, saying, Take heed, beware of the leaven of the Pharisees, and *of* the leaven of Herod.   Mark 12:13

16 And they reasoned among themselves, saying, *It is* because we have no bread.

17 And when Jesus knew *it*, he saith unto them, Why reason ye, because ye have no bread? perceive ye not yet, nei-

ther understand? have ye your heart yet hardened?   Mark 6:52

18 Having eyes, see ye not? and having ears, hear ye not? and do ye not remember?Jer. 5:21

19 When I brake the five loaves among five thousand, how many baskets full of fragments took ye up? They say unto him, Twelve.

20 And when the seven among four thousand, how many baskets full of fragments took ye up? And they said, Seven.

21 And he said unto them, How is it that ye do not understand?   Mark 6:52

Jesus Heals a Blind Man

22 And he cometh to Bethsaida; and they bring a blind man unto him, and ᵀbesought him to touch him.   Matt. 11:21 ◆ *begged*

23 And he took the blind man by the hand, and led him out of the town; and when he had spit on his eyes, and put his hands upon him, he asked him if he saw ought.   Mark 5:23; 7:33

24 And he looked up, and said, I see men as trees, walking.

25 After that he put *his* hands again upon his eyes, and made him look up: and he was restored, and saw every man clearly.

26 And he sent him away to his house, saying, Neither go into the town, nor tell *it* to any in the town.   Matt. 8:4

Peter Declares His Faith

27 And Jesus went out, and his disciples, into the towns of Caesarea Philippi: and by the way he asked his disciples, saying unto them, Whom do men say that I am?   Luke 9:18-20

28 And they answered, John the Baptist: but some *say*, Elias; and others, One of the prophets.   Mal. 4:5

29 And he saith unto them, But whom say ye that I am? And Peter answereth and saith unto him, Thou art the Christ.   John 6:69

30 And he charged them that they should tell no man of him. Matt. 16:20; Mark 9:9; Luke 9:21

Jesus Says He Will Die and Rise Again

31 And he began to teach them, that the Son of man must suffer many things, and be rejected of the elders, and *of* the chief priests, and scribes, and be killed, and after three days rise again.   Matt. 12:40

32 And he spake that saying openly. And Peter took him, and began to rebuke him.

33 But when he had turned about and looked on his disciples, he rebuked Peter, saying, Get thee behind me, Satan: for thou savourest not the things that be of God, but the things that be of men.   Matt. 4:10; Phil. 3:19

What It Means to Follow Jesus

34 And when he had called the people *unto him* with his disciples also, he said unto them, Whosoever will come after me, let

him deny himself, and take up his cross, and follow me.   Matt. 10:38

35 For whosoever will save his life shall lose it; but whosoever shall lose his life for my sake and the gospel's, the same shall save it.   Matt. 10:39

36 For what shall it profit a man, if he shall gain the whole world, and lose his own soul?

37 Or what shall a man give in exchange for his soul?   Ps. 49:7-8

8:35–37 Tipping the Scales for Jesus

Every year millions upon millions of human souls are passing into eternity unwarned and unsaved. . . . Days, weeks, and months are passing; we have one day, one week, one month less in which to do our work. . . .

Put into one scale Jesus, which means eternal treasure, life, truth, heaven, and the joy of Christ in souls redeemed; put into the other every attraction the world can offer. . . . Weigh for time and for eternity. While you are thus engaged, Christ speaks: "What shall it profit a man, if he shall gain the whole world, and lose his own soul?" (Mark 8:36). *COL 373, 374*

---

38 Whosoever therefore shall be ashamed of me and of my words in this adulterous and sinful generation; of him also shall the Son of man be ashamed, when he cometh in the glory of his Father with the holy angels.

The Transfiguration

9 And he said unto them, Verily I say unto you, That there be some of them that stand here, which shall not taste of death, till they have seen the kingdom of God come with power.   Matt. 25:31

2 And after six days Jesus taketh *with him* Peter, and James, and John, and leadeth them up into an high mountain apart by themselves: and he was transfigured before them.

3 And his ᵀraiment became shining, exceeding white as snow; so as no fuller on earth can white them.   Dan. 7:9; Matt. 28:3 ◆ *clothing*

4 And there appeared unto them Elias with Moses: and they were talking with Jesus.

5 And Peter answered and said to Jesus, Master, it is good for us to be here: and let us make three tabernacles; one for thee, and one for Moses, and one for Elias.

6 For he ᵀwist not what to say; for they were sore afraid.   *knew*

7 And there was a cloud that overshadowed them: and a voice came out of the cloud, saying, This is my beloved Son: hear him.

8 And suddenly, when they had looked round about, they saw no man any more, save Jesus only with themselves.

9 And as they came down from the mountain, he charged them that they should tell

no man what things they had seen, till the Son of man were risen from the dead.

10 And they kept that saying with themselves, questioning one with another what the rising from the dead should mean.

11 And they asked him, saying, Why say the scribes that Elias must first come? Matt. 11:14

12 And he answered and told them, Elias verily cometh first, and restoreth all things; and how it is written of the Son of man, that he must suffer many things, and be set at ᵀnought.   Luke 23:11 ◆ *nothing*

13 But I say unto you, That Elias is indeed come, and they have done unto him whatsoever they ᵀlisted, as it is written of him.   Matt. 11:14 ◆ *pleased*

Jesus Heals a Demon-possessed Boy

14 And when he came to *his* disciples, he saw a great multitude about them, and the scribes questioning with them.

15 And ᵀstraightway all the people, when they beheld him, were greatly amazed, and running to *him* saluted him.   *right away*

16 And he asked the scribes, What question ye with them?

17 And one of the multitude answered and said, Master, I have brought unto thee my son, which hath a dumb spirit;   Mark 9:25

18 And wheresoever he taketh him, he teareth him: and he foameth, and gnasheth with his teeth, and pineth away: and I spake to thy disciples that they should cast him out; and they could not.

19 He answereth him, and saith, O faithless generation, how long shall I be with you? how long shall I suffer you? bring him unto me.

9:23 Connecting With Heaven

It is faith that connects us with heaven, and brings us strength for coping with the powers of darkness. In Christ, God has provided means for subduing every sinful trait, and resisting every temptation, however strong. . . . Look not to self, but to Christ. . . . Faith comes by the word of God. Then grasp His promise, "Him that cometh to Me I will in no wise cast out" (John 6:37). Cast yourself at His feet with the cry, "Lord, I believe; help *Thou* mine unbelief" [Mark 9:24]. You can never perish while you do this—never. *DA 429*

---

20 And they brought him unto him: and when he saw him, straightway the spirit tare him; and he fell on the ground, and ᵀwallowed foaming.   Mark 1:26 ◆ *rolled around*

21 And he asked his father, How long is it ago since this came unto him? And he said, Of a child.

22 And ᵀofttimes it hath cast him into the fire, and into the waters, to destroy him: but

if thou canst do any thing, have compassion on us, and help us.   Matt. 9:28 ◆ *often*

23 Jesus said unto him, If thou canst believe, all things *are* possible to him that believeth.   Matt. 17:20

24 And straightway the father of the child cried out, and said with tears, Lord, I believe; help thou mine unbelief.   Luke 17:5

> Faith   See Acts 16:31.

25 When Jesus saw that the people came running together, he rebuked the foul spirit, saying unto him, *Thou* T dumb and deaf spirit, I charge thee, come out of him, and enter no more into him.   Mark 9:15 ◆ *mute*

26 And *the spirit* cried, and rent him sore, and came out of him: and he was as one dead; insomuch that many said, He is dead.

27 But Jesus took him by the hand, and lifted him up; and he arose.   Mark 1:31

28 And when he was come into the house, his disciples asked him privately, Why could not we cast him out?   Mark 7:17

29 And he said unto them, This kind can come forth by nothing, but by prayer and fasting.

Jesus Again Foretells His Death and Resurrection

30 And they departed thence, and passed through Galilee; and he would not that any man should know *it*.

31 For he taught his disciples, and said unto them, The Son of man is delivered into the hands of men, and they shall kill him; and after that he is killed, he shall rise the third day.   Matt. 16:21; Mark 8:31; 9:12

32 But they understood not that saying, and were afraid to ask him.   Luke 2:50; 9:45; 18:34

Greatness in the Kingdom

33 And he came to Capernaum: and being in the house he asked them, What was it that ye disputed among yourselves by the way?   Matt. 17:24

34 But they held their peace: for by the way they had disputed among themselves, who *should be* the greatest.

35 And he sat down, and called the twelve, and saith unto them, If any man desire to be first, *the same* shall be last of all, and servant of all.   Luke 22:26

36 And he took a child, and set him in the midst of them: and when he had taken him in his arms, he said unto them,   Mark 10:16

37 Whosoever shall receive one of such children in my name, receiveth me: and whosoever shall receive me, receiveth not me, but him that sent me.   Luke 10:16

9:33–37 The Lowest Place Is the Highest

Before honor is humility. To fill a high place before men, Heaven chooses the worker who, like John the Baptist, takes a lowly place before God. The most childlike disciple is the most efficient in labor for God. The heavenly intelligences can co-operate with him who is seeking, not to exalt self, but to save souls. . . . From communion with Christ he will go forth to work for those who are perishing in their sins. *DA 436*

Using the Name of Jesus

38 And John answered him, saying, Master, we saw one casting out devils in thy name, and he followeth not us: and we forbad him, because he followeth not us.   Luke 9:49-50

39 But Jesus said, Forbid him not: for there is no man which shall do a miracle in my name, that can lightly speak evil of me.

9:38–40 The Danger of Being Exclusive

None who showed themselves in any way friendly to Christ were to be repulsed. The disciples must not indulge a narrow, exclusive spirit, but must manifest the same far-reaching sympathy which they had seen in their Master. *AA 544*

---

40 For he that is not against us is on our part.

41 For whosoever shall give you a cup of

Jesus Prepares His Disciples

Mark 9:30–32

On the journey through Galilee, Christ had again tried to prepare the minds of His disciples for the scenes before Him. He told them that He was to go up to Jerusalem to be put to death and to rise again. And He added the strange and solemn announcement that He was to be betrayed into the hands of His enemies. The disciples did not even now comprehend His words. Although the shadow of a great sorrow fell upon them, a spirit of rivalry found a place in their hearts. They disputed among themselves which should be accounted greatest in the kingdom. This strife they thought to conceal from Jesus, and they did not, as usual, press close to His side, but loitered behind, so that He was in advance of them as they entered Capernaum. Jesus read their thoughts, and He longed to counsel and instruct them. But for this He awaited a quiet hour, when their hearts should be open to receive His words. *DA 432*

water to drink in my name, because ye belong to Christ, ᵀverily I say unto you, he shall not lose his reward. Matt. 10:42 ◆ truly

Causing Others to Lose Faith

42 And whosoever shall offend one of *these* little ones that believe in me, it is better for him that a millstone were hanged about his neck, and he were cast into the sea. Matt. 18:6
43 And if thy hand offend thee, cut it off: it is better for thee to enter into life maimed, than having two hands to go into hell, into the fire that never shall be quenched: Matt. 3:12; 5:29-30
44 Where their worm dieth not, and the fire is not quenched.
45 And if thy foot offend thee, cut it off: it is better for thee to enter ᵀhalt into life, than having two feet to be cast into hell, into the fire that never shall be quenched: Mark 9:43 ◆ having crippled feet

> **9:43–45 Sin Must Be Put Away**
>
> Every habit or practice that leads into sin and brings dishonor upon Christ must be put away, whatever the sacrifice. The blessing of heaven cannot attend any man in violating the eternal principles of right. One sin cherished is sufficient to work degradation of character and to mislead others. . . .
>
> If to save the body from death, the foot or the hand should be cut off, or even the eye plucked out, how much more earnest should the Christian be to put away sin, which brings death to the soul! *AA 312, 313*

46 Where their worm dieth not, and the fire is not quenched.
47 And if thine eye offend thee, pluck it out: it is better for thee to enter into the kingdom of God with one eye, than having two eyes to be cast into hell fire: Matt. 18:9
48 Where their worm dieth not, and the fire is not quenched. Is. 66:24
49 For every one shall be salted with fire, and every sacrifice shall be salted with salt. Lev. 2:13
50 Salt *is* good: but if the salt have lost his saltness, wherewith will ye season it? Have salt in yourselves, and have peace one with another. Matt. 5:13; Rom. 12:18; 2 Cor. 13:11

> **9:50 Salt Without Savor**
>
> If the salt has lost its savor; if there is only a profession of godliness, without the love of Christ, there is no power for good. The life can exert no saving influence upon the world. . . . You must be partakers of My grace, [Jesus says,] in order to be a savor of life unto life. Then there will be no rivalry, no self-seeking, no desire for the highest place. You will have that love which seeks not her own, but another's wealth. *DA 439*

A Discussion about Divorce

10 And he arose from thence, and cometh into the coasts of Judaea by the farther side of Jordan: and the people resort unto him again; and, as he was ᵀwont, he taught them again. John 10:40 ◆ accustomed to
2 And the Pharisees came to him, and asked him, Is it lawful for a man to put away *his* wife? tempting him. John 8:6
3 And he answered and said unto them, What did Moses command you?
4 And they said, Moses suffered to write a bill of divorcement, and to put *her* away.
5 And Jesus answered and said unto them, For the hardness of your heart he wrote you this precept. Matt. 19:8
6 But from the beginning of the creation God made them male and female. Gen. 1:27; 2 Pet. 3:4
7 For this cause shall a man leave his father and mother, and cleave to his wife; Gen. 2:24
8 And they ᵀtwain shall be one flesh: so then they are no more twain, but one flesh. 1 Cor. 6:16 ◆ two
9 What therefore God hath joined together, let not man put ᵀasunder. apart
10 And in the house his disciples asked him again of the same *matter*.
11 And he saith unto them, Whosoever shall put away his wife, and marry another, committeth adultery against her. Luke 16:18
12 And if a woman shall put away her husband, and be married to another, she committeth adultery. 1 Cor. 7:11

Jesus Blesses the Children

13 And they brought young children to him, that he should touch them: and *his* disciples rebuked those that brought *them*. Matt. 19:13-15

> **10:13–16 Jesus Will Help Weary Mothers**
>
> Let mothers come to Jesus with their perplexities. They will find grace sufficient to aid them in the management of their children. The gates are open for every mother who would lay her burdens at the Saviour's feet. . . . John the Baptist was filled with the Holy Spirit from his birth. If we will live in communion with God, we too may expect the divine Spirit to mold our little ones, even from their earliest moments. *DA 512*

14 But when Jesus saw *it*, he was much displeased, and said unto them, Suffer the little children to come unto me, and forbid them not: for of such is the kingdom of God.
15 Verily I say unto you, Whosoever shall not receive the kingdom of God as a little child, he shall not enter therein. Matt. 18:3
16 And he took them up in his arms, put *his* hands upon them, and blessed them. Mark 9:36

The Danger of Riches

17 And when he was gone forth into the way, there came one running, and kneeled to him, and asked him, Good Master, what shall I do that I may inherit eternal life?   Matt. 19:16-30; Mark 1:40; Luke 18:18-30

18 And Jesus said unto him, Why callest thou me good? *there is* none good but one, *that is,* God.

19 Thou knowest the commandments, Do not commit adultery, Do not kill, Do not steal, Do not bear false witness, Defraud not, Honour thy father and mother.   Ex. 20:12-17

20 And he answered and said unto him, Master, all these have I observed from my youth.

21 Then Jesus beholding him loved him, and said unto him, One thing thou lackest: go thy way, sell whatsoever thou hast, and give to the poor, and thou shalt have treasure in heaven: and come, take up the cross, and follow me.   Luke 12:33

22 And he was sad at that saying, and went away grieved: for he had great possessions.

10:17–22 The Rich Young Ruler

Christ's dealing with the young man is presented as an object lesson. . . . It is obedience to His law, not merely a legal obedience, but an obedience which enters into the life, and is exemplified in the character. God has set His own standard of character for all who would become subjects of His kingdom. . . . All should consider what it means to desire heaven, and yet to turn away because of the conditions laid down. Think of what it means to say "No" to Christ. The ruler said, No, I cannot give You all. Do we say the same? *DA 523*

---

23 And Jesus looked round about, and saith unto his disciples, How hardly shall they that have riches enter into the kingdom of God!

24 And the disciples were astonished at his words. But Jesus answereth again, and saith unto them, Children, how hard is it for them that trust in riches to enter into the kingdom of God!   Ps. 52:7

25 It is easier for a camel to go through the eye of a needle, than for a rich man to enter into the kingdom of God.

26 And they were astonished out of measure, saying among themselves, Who then can be saved?

27 And Jesus looking upon them saith, With men *it is* impossible, but not with God: for with God all things are possible.   Matt. 19:26

28 Then Peter began to say unto him, Lo, we have left all, and have followed thee.

29 And Jesus answered and said, Verily I say unto you, There is no man that hath left house, or brethren, or sisters, or father, or mother, or wife, or children, or lands, for my sake, and the gospel's,   Mark 8:35

30 But he shall receive an hundredfold now in this time, houses, and brethren, and sisters, and mothers, and children, and lands, with persecutions; and in the world to come eternal life.   Matt. 12:32

31 But many *that are* first shall be last; and the last first.   Matt. 19:30; 20:16; Luke 13:30

Jesus Again Foretells His Death and Resurrection

32 And they were in the way going up to Jerusalem; and Jesus went before them: and they were amazed; and as they followed, they were afraid. And he took again the twelve, and began to tell them what things should happen unto him,   Matt. 20:17-19

33 *Saying,* Behold, we go up to Jerusalem; and the Son of man shall be delivered unto the chief priests, and unto the scribes; and they shall condemn him to death, and shall deliver him to the Gentiles: Matt. 27:2

34 And they shall mock him, and shall ᵀscourge him, and shall spit upon him, and shall kill him: and the third day he shall rise again.   Matt. 16:21 ♦ whip

Two Disciples Make a Request

35 And James and John, the sons of Zebedee, come unto him, saying, Master, we would that thou shouldest do for us whatsoever we shall desire.   Matt. 20:20-28

36 And he said unto them, What would ye that I should do for you?   Mark 10:51

37 They said unto him, Grant unto us that we may sit, one on thy right hand, and the other on thy left hand, in thy glory.   Matt. 19:28

38 But Jesus said unto them, Ye know not what ye ask: can ye drink of the cup that I drink of? and be baptized with the baptism that I am baptized with?   Is. 51:22; Luke 12:50

39 And they said unto him, We can. And Jesus said unto them, Ye shall indeed drink of the cup that I drink of; and with the baptism that I am baptized ᵀwithal shall ye be baptized: Acts 12:2; Rev. 1:9 ♦ with

40 But to sit on my right hand and on my left hand is not mine to give; but *it shall be given to them* for whom it is prepared.   Matt. 25:34

41 And when the ten heard *it,* they began to be much displeased with James and John.

42 But Jesus called them *to him,* and saith unto them, Ye know that they which are accounted to rule over the Gentiles exercise lordship over them; and their great ones exercise authority upon them.   Luke 22:25

43 But so shall it not be among you: but whosoever will be great among you, shall be your minister: Mark 9:35

44 And whosoever of you will be the chiefest, shall be servant of all.

45 For even the Son of man came not to be ministered unto, but to minister, and to give his life a ransom for many. Is. 53:10-12; Dan. 9:26

10:35–45 Greatness Means Serving

In the kingdoms of the world, position meant self-aggrandizement. The people were supposed to exist for the benefit of the ruling classes. Influence, wealth, education, were so many means of gaining control of the masses for the use of the leaders. . . .

Christ was establishing a kingdom on different principles. He called men, not to authority, but to service, the strong to bear the infirmities of the weak. Power, position, talent, education, placed their possessor under the greater obligation to serve his fellows. DA 550

Jesus Restores Sight to Bartimaeus

46 And they came to Jericho: and as he went out of Jericho with his disciples and a great number of people, blind Bartimaeus, the son of Timaeus, sat by the highway side begging. Matt. 20:29-34

47 And when he heard that it was Jesus of Nazareth, he began to cry out, and say, Jesus, thou Son of David, have mercy on me.

48 And many charged him that he should hold his peace: but he cried the more a great deal, Thou Son of David, have mercy on me. Matt. 19:13

49 And Jesus stood still, and commanded him to be called. And they call the blind man, saying unto him, Be of good comfort, rise; he calleth thee.

50 And he, casting away his garment, rose, and came to Jesus.

51 And Jesus answered and said unto him, What wilt thou that I should do unto thee? The blind man said unto him, Lord, that I might receive my sight. Mark 10:36

52 And Jesus said unto him, Go thy way; thy faith hath made thee whole. And immediately he received his sight, and followed Jesus in the way. Matt. 9:22; Mark 5:34; Luke 7:50

Jesus Rides in Triumph into Jerusalem

11 And when they came nigh to Jerusalem, unto Bethphage and Bethany, at the mount of Olives, he sendeth forth two of his disciples, Zech. 14:4

2 And saith unto them, Go your way into the village over against you: and as soon as ye be entered into it, ye shall find a colt tied, whereon never man sat; loose him, and bring him.

3 And if any man say unto you, Why do ye this? say ye that the Lord hath need of him; and ᵀstraightway he will send him ᵀhither. right away ◆ here

11:1–11 Reason for Christ's Triumphal Entry

Never before in His earthly life had Jesus permitted such a demonstration. He clearly foresaw the result. It would bring Him to the cross. But it was His purpose thus publicly to present Himself as the Redeemer. He desired to call attention to the sacrifice that was to crown His mission to a fallen world. . . . After such a demonstration as that attending His entry into Jerusalem, all eyes would follow His rapid progress to the final scene. DA 571

4 And they went their way, and found the colt tied by the door without in a place where two ways met; and they loose him.

5 And certain of them that stood there said unto them, What do ye, loosing the colt?

6 And they said unto them even as Jesus had commanded: and they let them go.

7 And they brought the colt to Jesus, and cast their garments on him; and he sat upon him. Matt. 21:4-5

8 And many spread their garments in the way: and others cut down branches off the trees, and strawed them in the way.

9 And they that went before, and they that followed, cried, saying, Hosanna; Blessed is he that cometh in the name of the Lord:

10 Blessed be the kingdom of our father David, that cometh in the name of the Lord: Hosanna in the highest. Luke 2:14

11 And Jesus entered into Jerusalem, and into the temple: and when he had looked round about upon all things, and now the ᵀeventide was come, he went out unto Bethany with the twelve. evening

11:12–14 Christians Without Fruit

Christ's act in cursing the tree which His own power had created stands as a warning to all churches and to all Christians. No one can live the law of God without ministering to others. . . . Some who think themselves excellent Christians do not understand what constitutes service for God. They plan and study to please themselves. They act only in reference to self. . . . Those who thus live for self are like the fig tree, which made every pretension but was fruitless. DA 584

Jesus Curses the Fig Tree

12 And on the morrow, when they were come from Bethany, he was hungry: Matt. 4:2

13 And seeing a fig tree afar off having leaves, he came, if ᵀhaply he might find any thing thereon: and when he came to it, he found nothing but leaves; for the time of figs was not yet. Luke 13:6-9 ◆ maybe

14 And Jesus answered and said unto it, **No man eat fruit of thee hereafter for ever.** And his disciples heard *it*.　　　Matt. 21:19

Jesus Throws the Moneychangers Out of the Temple

15 And they come to Jerusalem: and Jesus went into the temple, and began to cast out them that sold and bought in the temple, and overthrew the tables of the moneychangers, and the seats of them that sold doves;

16 And would not suffer that any man should carry *any* vessel through the temple.

17 And he taught, saying unto them, **Is it not written, My house shall be called of all nations the house of prayer? but ye have made it a den of thieves.**　　Is. 56:7; Jer. 7:11

18 And the scribes and chief priests heard *it*, and sought how they might destroy him: for they feared him, because all the people was astonished at his doctrine. Matt. 7:28; Mark 12:12

19 And when even was come, he went out of the city.　　　Mark 11:11; Luke 21:37

The Fig Tree Dries Up

20 And in the morning, as they passed by, they saw the fig tree dried up from the roots.

21 And Peter calling to remembrance saith unto him, Master, behold, the fig tree which thou cursedst is withered away.

22 And Jesus answering saith unto them, **Have faith in God.**

23 **For** ᵀ**verily I say unto you, That whosoever shall say unto this mountain, Be thou removed, and be thou cast into the sea; and shall not doubt in his heart, but shall believe that those things which he saith shall come to pass; he shall have whatsoever he saith.**　　Matt. 17:20 ◆ *truly*

24 **Therefore I say unto you, What things soever ye desire, when ye pray, believe that ye receive** *them*, **and ye shall have** *them*. 1 John 3:22

25 **And when ye stand praying, forgive, if ye have ought against any: that your Father** also which is in heaven may **forgive you your trespasses.**　　　Col. 3:13

26 **But if ye do not forgive, neither will your Father which is in heaven forgive your** ᵀ**trespasses.**　　　*sins*

Jesus' Authority Is Challenged

27 And they come again to Jerusalem: and as he was walking in the temple, there come to him the chief priests, and the scribes, and the elders,　　　Matt. 21:23-27

28 And say unto him, By what authority doest thou these things? and who gave thee this authority to do these things?　Ex. 2:14

29 And Jesus answered and said unto them, **I will also ask of you one question, and answer me, and I will tell you by what authority I do these things.**

30 **The baptism of John, was** *it* **from heaven, or of men? answer me.**

31 And they reasoned with themselves, saying, If we shall say, From heaven; he will say, Why then did ye not believe him?

32 But if we shall say, Of men; they feared the people: for all *men* counted John, that he was a prophet indeed.　　　Matt. 14:5

33 And they answered and said unto Jesus, We cannot tell. And Jesus answering saith unto them, **Neither do I tell you by what authority I do these things.**

A Parable about a Vineyard

12 And he began to speak unto them by parables. **A** *certain* man planted a vineyard, and set an hedge about *it*, and digged *a place for* the ᵀwinefat, and built a tower, and let it out to husbandmen, and went into a far country.　　Song 8:11-12 ◆ *trough beneath winepress*

2 And at the season he sent to the ᵀhusbandmen a servant, that he might receive from the husbandmen of the fruit of the vineyard.　　　*farmers*

3 And they caught *him*, and beat him, and sent *him* away empty.　　　2 Chr. 36:16

Prayer and Promises

Mark 11:24

Prayer and faith are closely allied, and they need to be studied together. In the prayer of faith there is a divine science; it is a science that everyone who would make his lifework a success must understand. Christ says, "What things soever ye desire, when ye pray, believe that ye receive them, and ye shall have them" (Mark 11:24). He makes it plain that our asking must be according to God's will; we must ask for the things that He has promised, and whatever we receive must be used in doing His will. The conditions met, the promise is unequivocal.

For the pardon of sin, for the Holy Spirit, for a Christlike temper, for wisdom and strength to do His work, for any gift He has promised, we may ask; then we are to believe that we receive, and return thanks to God that we have received.

We need look for no outward evidence of the blessing. The gift is in the promise, and we may go about our work assured that what God has promised He is able to perform, and that the gift, which we already possess, will be realized when we need it most. *Ed 257, 258*

4 And again he sent unto them another servant; and at him they cast stones, and wounded *him* in the head, and sent *him* away shamefully handled.

5 And again he sent another; and him they killed, and many others; beating some, and killing some.

6 Having yet therefore one son, his wellbeloved, he sent him also last unto them, saying, They will reverence my son.   Matt. 3:17

7 But those husbandmen said among themselves, This is the heir; come, let us kill him, and the inheritance shall be ours.

8 And they took him, and killed *him*, and cast *him* out of the vineyard.

9 What shall therefore the lord of the vineyard do? he will come and destroy the husbandmen, and will give the vineyard unto others.   Matt. 21:43

10 And have ye not read this scripture; The stone which the builders rejected is become the head of the corner: Ps. 118:22-23

11 This was the Lord's doing, and it is marvellous in our eyes?

12 And they sought to lay hold on him, but feared the people: for they knew that he had spoken the parable against them: and they left him, and went their way.   Matt. 22:22; Mark 11:18

12:1–12 Repeated Warnings

By many illustrations and repeated warnings, Jesus showed what would be the result to the Jews of rejecting the Son of God. In these words He was addressing all in every age who refuse to receive Him as their Redeemer. Every warning is for them. The desecrated temple, the disobedient son, the false husbandmen, the contemptuous builders, have their counterpart in the experience of every sinner. Unless he repent, the doom which they foreshadowed will be his. *DA 600*

A Question about Paying Tribute to Caesar

13 And they send unto him certain of the Pharisees and of the Herodians, to catch him in *his* words.   Mark 3:6

14 And when they were come, they say unto him, Master, we know that thou art true, and carest for no man: for thou regardest not the person of men, but teachest the way of God in truth: Is it lawful to give tribute to Caesar, or not?

15 Shall we give, or shall we not give? But he, knowing their hypocrisy, said unto them, Why tempt ye me? bring me a †penny, that I may see *it*.   *daily wage of Roman soldier*

16 And they brought *it*. And he saith unto them, Whose *is* this image and superscription? And they said unto him, Caesar's.

17 And Jesus answering said unto them, Render to Caesar the things that are Caesar's, and to God the things that are God's. And they marvelled at him.   Rom. 13:7

12:13–17 Duty to Government and to God

He had rebuked their hypocrisy and presumption, and in doing this He had stated a great principle, a principle that clearly defines the limits of man's duty to the civil government and his duty to God. In many minds a vexed question had been settled. Ever after they held to the right principle. And although many went away dissatisfied, they saw that the principle underlying the question had been clearly set forth, and they marveled at Christ's far-seeing discernment. *DA 602, 603*

A Question about the Resurrection

18 Then come unto him the Sadducees, which say there is no resurrection; and they asked him, saying,   Matt. 22:23-33

19 Master, Moses wrote unto us, If a man's brother die, and leave *his* wife *behind him*, and leave no children, that his brother should take his wife, and raise up seed unto his brother.

20 Now there were seven brethren: and the first took a wife, and dying left no seed.

21 And the second took her, and died, neither left he any seed: and the third likewise.

22 And the seven had her, and left no seed: last of all the woman died also.

23 In the resurrection therefore, when they shall rise, whose wife shall she be of them? for the seven had her to wife.

24 And Jesus answering said unto them, Do ye not therefore err, because ye know not the scriptures, neither the power of God? John 20:9

25 For when they shall rise from the dead, they neither marry, nor are given in marriage; but are as the angels which are in heaven.

12:18–27 Without the Word, Confusion and Darkness

The Sadducees had flattered themselves that they of all men adhered most strictly to the Scriptures. But Jesus showed that they had not known their true meaning. That knowledge must be brought home to the heart by the enlightenment of the Holy Spirit. Their ignorance of the Scriptures and the power of God He declared to be the cause of their confusion of faith and darkness of mind. *DA 605, 606*

26 And as touching the dead, that they rise: have ye not read in the book of Moses, how in the bush God spake unto him, saying,

I *am* the God of Abraham, and the God of Isaac, and the God of Jacob? Luke 20:37
27 He is not the God of the dead, but the God of the living: ye therefore do greatly ᵀerr. *stray*

The Greatest Commandment

28 And one of the scribes came, and having heard them reasoning together, and perceiving that he had answered them well, asked him, Which is the first commandment of all? Matt. 22:34-40
29 And Jesus answered him, The first of all the commandments *is*, Hear, O Israel; The Lord our God is one Lord: Deut. 6:4; Luke 10:27
30 And thou shalt love the Lord thy God with all thy heart, and with all thy soul, and with all thy mind, and with all thy strength: this *is* the first commandment.
31 And the second *is* like, *namely* this, Thou shalt love thy neighbour as thyself. There is none other commandment greater than these. Lev. 19:18
32 And the scribe said unto him, Well, Master, thou hast said the truth: for there is one God; and there is none other but he: Deut. 4:35
33 And to love him with all the heart, and with all the understanding, and with all the soul, and with all the strength, and to love *his* neighbour as himself, is more than all whole burnt offerings and sacrifices. Hos. 6:6; Mic. 6:6-8
34 And when Jesus saw that he answered discreetly, he said unto him, Thou art not far from the kingdom of God. And no man after that durst ask him *any question*. Matt. 22:46

David's Son Is David's Lord

35 And Jesus answered and said, while he taught in the temple, How say the scribes that Christ is the Son of David? Luke 20:41-44
36 For David himself said by the Holy Ghost, The LORD said to my Lord, Sit thou on my right hand, till I make thine enemies thy footstool. 2 Sam. 23:2; Ps. 110:1; 1 Cor. 15:25
37 David therefore himself calleth him Lord; and whence is he *then* his son? And the common people heard him gladly. Rom. 1:3-4
38 And he said unto them in his doctrine, Beware of the scribes, which love to go in long clothing, and *love* salutations in the marketplaces, Luke 11:43
39 And the chief seats in the synagogues, and the uppermost rooms at feasts:
40 Which devour widows' houses, and for a pretence make long prayers: these shall receive greater ᵀdamnation. Luke 20:47 ◆ *condemnation*

Jesus Commends a Poor Widow

41 And Jesus sat over against the treasury, and beheld how the people cast money into the treasury: and many that were rich cast in much. 2 Kin. 12:9; Matt. 27:6; John 8:20
42 And there came a certain poor widow, and she threw in two mites, which make a ᵀfarthing. *small coin with little value*
43 And he called *unto him* his disciples, and saith unto them, Verily I say unto you, That this poor widow hath cast more in, than all they which have cast into the treasury:
44 For all *they* did cast in of their abundance; but she of her want did cast in all that she had, *even* all her living. Luke 8:43

> **12:41–44 Why More Important to God Than How Much**
>
> It is the motive that gives character to our acts, stamping them with ignominy or with high moral worth. . . . The little duties cheerfully done, the little gifts which make no show, and which to human eyes may appear worthless, often stand highest in His sight. . . . The poor widow gave her living to do the little that she did. She deprived herself of food in order to give those two mites to the cause she loved. And she did it in faith, believing that her heavenly Father would not overlook her great need. *DA 615*

Jesus Foretells Future Destruction

13 And as he went out of the temple, one of his disciples saith unto him, Master, see what manner of stones and what buildings *are here*!
2 And Jesus answering said unto him, Seest thou these great buildings? there shall not be left one stone upon another, that shall not be thrown down.
3 And as he sat upon the mount of Olives over against the temple, Peter and James and John and Andrew asked him privately, Matt. 21:1
4 Tell us, when shall these things be? and what *shall be* the sign when all these things shall be fulfilled? Acts 1:6-7
5 And Jesus answering them began to say, Take heed lest any *man* deceive you: Jer. 29:8
6 For many shall come in my name, saying, I am *Christ*; and shall deceive many. Jer. 14:14
7 And when ye shall hear of wars and rumours of wars, be ye not troubled: for *such* things must needs be; but the end *shall* not *be* yet.
8 For nation shall rise against nation, and kingdom against kingdom: and there shall be earthquakes in ᵀdivers places, and there shall be famines and troubles: these *are* the beginnings of sorrows. 2 Chr. 15:6 ◆ *various*
9 But take heed to yourselves: for they shall deliver you up to councils; and in the synagogues ye shall be beaten: and ye shall be brought before rulers and kings for my sake, for a testimony against them. Matt. 10:17-18

10 And the gospel must first be published among all nations. Matt. 24:14

11 But when they shall lead *you*, and deliver you up, take no thought beforehand what ye shall speak, neither do ye premeditate: but whatsoever shall be given you in that hour, that speak ye: for it is not ye that speak, but the Holy Ghost. Matt. 10:19-21

12 Now the brother shall betray the brother to death, and the father the son; and children shall rise up against *their* parents, and shall cause them to be put to death. Matt. 10:21

13 And ye shall be hated of all *men* for my name's sake: but he that shall endure unto the end, the same shall be saved. Matt. 10:22

Great Calamities Shall Befall the Jews

14 But when ye shall see the abomination of desolation, spoken of by Daniel the prophet, standing where it ought not, (let him that readeth understand,) then let them that be in Judaea flee to the mountains: Dan. 9:27; 11:31

15 And let him that is on the housetop not go down into the house, neither enter *therein*, to take any thing out of his house:

16 And let him that is in the field not turn back again for to take up his garment.

17 But woe to them that are with child, and to them that give suck in those days!Luke 23:29

18 And pray ye that your flight be not in the winter.

> **13:4–18 Two Great Crises Predicted**
>
> Jesus did not answer His disciples by taking up separately the destruction of Jerusalem and the great day of His coming. He mingled the description of these two events. Had He opened to His disciples future events as He beheld them, they would have been unable to endure the sight. In mercy to them He blended the description of the two great crises, leaving the disciples to study out the meaning for themselves. *DA 628*

19 For *in* those days shall be affliction, such as was not from the beginning of the creation which God created unto this time, neither shall be. Deut. 4:32; Dan. 9:26; 12:1

20 And except that the Lord had shortened those days, no flesh should be saved: but for the elect's sake, whom he hath chosen, he hath shortened the days. Is. 65:8-9

21 And then if any man shall say to you, Lo, here *is* Christ; or, lo, *he is* there; believe *him* not: Luke 21:8

22 For false Christs and false prophets shall rise, and shall shew signs and wonders, to seduce, if *it were* possible, even the elect. Matt. 24:24

23 But take ye heed: behold, I have foretold you all things. 2 Pet. 3:17

Jesus Foretells the Manner of His Coming

24 But in those days, after that tribulation, the sun shall be darkened, and the moon shall not give her light, Is. 13:10

25 And the stars of heaven shall fall, and the powers that are in heaven shall be shaken. Is. 34:4

26 And then shall they see the Son of man coming in the clouds with great power and glory. Matt. 16:27

27 And then shall he send his angels, and shall gather together his elect from the four winds, from the uttermost part of the earth to the uttermost part of heaven. Deut. 30:4

> **13:26, 27 Only a Little Longer**
>
> Christ is coming with clouds and with great glory. A multitude of shining angels will attend Him. He will come to raise the dead, and to change the living saints from glory to glory. . . . A little longer, and we shall see the King in His beauty. A little longer, and He will wipe all tears from our eyes. A little longer, and He will present us "faultless before the presence of His glory with exceeding joy" (Jude 24). *DA 632*

28 Now learn a parable of the fig tree; When her branch is yet tender, and putteth forth leaves, ye know that summer is near:

29 So ye in like manner, when ye shall see these things come to pass, know that it is nigh, *even* at the doors. James 5:9

30 Verily I say unto you, that this generation shall not pass, till all these things be done. Matt. 24:34

31 Heaven and earth shall pass away: but my words shall not pass away. Matt. 5:18

32 But of that day and *that* hour knoweth no man, no, not the angels which are in heaven, neither the Son, but the Father. Acts 1:7

33 Take ye heed, watch and pray: for ye know not when the time is. Eph. 6:18

> **13:34 "To Each His Work"**
>
> The businessman may conduct his business in a way that will glorify his Master because of his fidelity. If he is a true follower of Christ he will carry his religion into everything that is done and reveal to men the spirit of Christ. The mechanic may be a diligent and faithful representative of Him who toiled in the lowly walks of life among the hills of Galilee. Everyone who names the name of Christ should so work that others, by seeing his good works, may be led to glorify their Creator and Redeemer. *SC 82*

34 *For the Son of man is* as a man taking a far journey, who left his house, and gave authority to his servants, and to every man

his work, and commanded the ^Tporter to watch.

John 10:3 ◆ doorkeeper

35 Watch ye therefore: for ye know not when the master of the house cometh, at even, or at midnight, or at the cockcrowing, or in the morning:

Matt. 24:42

36 Lest coming suddenly he find you sleeping.

Mark 14:40

37 And what I say unto you I say unto all, Watch.

Mark 13:35

The Plot to Kill Jesus

14 After two days was *the feast of* the passover, and of unleavened bread: and the chief priests and the scribes sought how they might take him by craft, and put *him* to death.

Luke 22:1-2

2 But they said, Not on the feast *day*, lest there be an uproar of the people.

A Woman Anoints Jesus' Body

3 And being in Bethany in the house of Simon the leper, as he sat at meat, there came a woman having an alabaster box of ointment of spikenard very precious; and she brake the box, and poured *it* on his head.

4 And there were some that had ^Tindignation within themselves, and said, Why was this waste of the ointment made?

anger

5 For it might have been sold for more than three hundred pence, and have been given to the poor. And they murmured against her.

6 And Jesus said, Let her alone; why trouble ye her? she hath ^Twrought a good work on me.

done

7 For ye have the poor with you always, and whensoever ye will ye may do them good: but me ye have not always.

Deut. 15:11; Matt. 26:11

8 She hath done what she could: she is come aforehand to anoint my body to the burying.

9 Verily I say unto you, Wheresoever this gospel shall be preached throughout the whole world, *this* also that she hath done shall be spoken of for a memorial of her.

Mark 16:15

Judas Plans to Betray Jesus

10 And Judas Iscariot, one of the twelve, went unto the chief priests, to betray him unto them.

Matt. 26:14-16; Luke 22:3-6; John 13:2

11 And when they heard *it*, they were glad, and promised to give him money. And he sought how he might ^Tconveniently betray him.

opportunely

Preparations for the Passover

12 And the first day of unleavened bread, when they killed the passover, his disciples said unto him, Where wilt thou that we go and prepare that thou mayest eat the passover?

Ex. 12:6

13 And he sendeth forth two of his disciples, and saith unto them, Go ye into the city, and there shall meet you a man bearing a pitcher of water: follow him.

14 And wheresoever he shall go in, say ye to the ^Tgoodman of the house, The Master saith, Where is the guestchamber, where I shall eat the passover with my disciples?

John 11:28 ◆ male leader

15 And he will shew you a large upper room furnished *and* prepared: there make ready for us.

Acts 1:13

16 And his disciples went forth, and came into the city, and found as he had said unto them: and they made ready the passover.

17 And in the evening he cometh with the twelve.

Luke 22:14

Jesus Knows Who Will Betray Him

18 And as they sat and did eat, Jesus said, Verily I say unto you, One of you which eateth with me shall betray me.

Ps. 41:9

19 And they began to be sorrowful, and to

Giving While They Are Still Living

Mark 14:3-9

The fragrant gift which Mary had thought to lavish upon the dead body of the Saviour she poured upon His living form. At the burial its sweetness could only have pervaded the tomb; now it gladdened His heart with the assurance of her faith and love. Joseph of Arimathaea and Nicodemus offered not their gift of love to Jesus in His life. With bitter tears they brought their costly spices for His cold, unconscious form. The women who bore spices to the tomb found their errand in vain, for He had risen. But Mary, pouring out her love upon the Saviour while He was conscious of her devotion, was anointing Him for the burial. And as He went down into the darkness of His great trial, He carried with Him the memory of that deed, an earnest of the love that would be His from His redeemed ones forever.

Many there are who bring their precious gifts for the dead. As they stand about the cold, silent form, words of love are freely spoken. Tenderness, appreciation, devotion, all are lavished upon one who sees not nor hears. Had these words been spoken when the weary spirit needed them so much, when the ear could hear and the heart could feel, how precious would have been their fragrance! *DA 560*

say unto him one by one, *Is* it I? and another *said, Is* it I?

20 And he answered and said unto them, *It is one of the twelve, that dippeth with me in the dish.*

John 13:26

21 *The Son of man indeed goeth, as it is written of him: but woe to that man by whom the Son of man is betrayed! good were it for that man if he had never been born.*

Mark 14:49

The Lord's Supper

22 And as they did eat, Jesus took bread, and blessed, and brake *it*, and gave to them, and said, *Take, eat: this is my body.*   Matt. 26:26-29

23 And he took the cup, and when he had given thanks, he gave *it* to them: and they all drank of it.   1 Cor. 10:16

24 And he said unto them, *This is my blood of the new testament, which is shed for many.*

25 *Verily I say unto you, I will drink no more of the fruit of the vine, until that day that I drink it new in the kingdom of God.*

26 And when they had sung an hymn, they went out into the mount of Olives.   Matt. 26:30

Jesus Predicts Peter's Denial

27 And Jesus saith unto them, *All ye shall be offended because of me this night: for it is written, I will smite the shepherd, and the sheep shall be scattered.*   Zech. 13:7; John 16:32

28 *But after that I am risen, I will go before you into Galilee.*   Matt. 28:16

29 But Peter said unto him, Although all shall be offended, yet *will* not I.

30 And Jesus saith unto him, *Verily I say unto thee, That this day, even in this night, before the cock crow twice, thou shalt deny me* ᵀthrice.   Mark 14:66-72 ◆ *three times*

31 But he spake the more ᵀvehemently, If I should die with thee, I will not deny thee in any wise. Likewise also said they all.   *strongly*

14:27–31 Peter Did Not Know Himself

When Peter said he would follow his Lord to prison and to death, he meant it, every word of it; but he did not know himself. Hidden in his heart were elements of evil that circumstances would fan into life. Unless he was made conscious of his danger, these would prove his eternal ruin. . . . Christ's solemn warning was a call to heart searching. Peter needed to distrust himself, and to have a deeper faith in Christ. *DA 673*

Jesus Prays in Gethsemane

32 And they came to a place which was named Gethsemane: and he saith to his disciples, *Sit ye here, while I shall pray.*   Matt. 26:36-46

33 And he taketh with him Peter and James and John, and began to be sore amazed, and to be very heavy;   Mark 5:37

34 And saith unto them, *My soul is exceeding sorrowful unto death: tarry ye here, and watch.*   John 12:27

35 And he went forward a little, and fell on the ground, and prayed that, if it were possible, the hour might pass from him. Mark 14:41

36 And he said, *Abba, Father, all things are possible unto thee; take away this cup from me: nevertheless not what I will, but what thou wilt.*   John 5:30; Gal. 4:6; Phil. 2:8

37 And he cometh, and findeth them sleeping, and saith unto Peter, *Simon, sleepest thou? couldest not thou watch one hour?*

38 *Watch ye and pray, lest ye enter into temptation. The spirit truly is ready, but the flesh is weak.*   Matt. 26:41

39 And again he went away, and prayed, and spake the same words.

40 And when he returned, he found them asleep again, (for their eyes were heavy,) neither ᵀwist they what to answer him. *knew*

41 And he cometh the third time, and saith unto them, *Sleep on now, and take your rest: it is enough, the hour is come; behold, the*

Christ's Supernatural Suffering for Us

Mark 14:32–42

Behold [Jesus] contemplating the price to be paid for the human soul. In His agony He clings to the cold ground, as if to prevent Himself from being drawn farther from God. The chilling dew of night falls upon His prostrate form, but He heeds it not. From His pale lips comes the bitter cry, "O My Father, if it be possible, let this cup pass from Me." Yet even now He adds, "Nevertheless not as I will, but as Thou wilt" [Mark 14:36].

The human heart longs for sympathy in suffering. This longing Christ felt to the very depths of His being. In the supreme agony of His soul He came to His disciples with a yearning desire to hear some words of comfort from those whom He had so often blessed and comforted, and shielded in sorrow and distress. The One who had always had words of sympathy for them was now suffering superhuman agony, and He longed to know that they were praying for Him and for themselves. How dark seemed the malignity of sin! Terrible was the temptation to let the human race bear the consequences of its own guilt, while He stood innocent before God. *DA 687, 688*

Son of man is betrayed into the hands of sinners.   Mark 9:31

42 Rise up, let us go; lo, he that betrayeth me is at hand.

Judas Betrays Jesus with a Kiss

43 And immediately, while he yet spake, cometh Judas, one of the twelve, and with him a great multitude with swords and staves, from the chief priests and the scribes and the elders.   Acts 1:16

44 And he that betrayed him had given them a token, saying, Whomsoever I shall kiss, that same is he; take him, and lead *him* away safely.

45 And as soon as he was come, he goeth ᵀstraightway to him, and saith, Master, master; and kissed him.   *right away*

46 And they laid their hands on him, and took him.

47 And one of them that stood by drew a sword, and smote a servant of the high priest, and cut off his ear.

48 And Jesus answered and said unto them, Are ye come out, as against a thief, with swords and *with* ᵀstaves to take me?   *clubs* or *rods*

49 I was daily with you in the temple teaching, and ye took me not: but the scriptures must be fulfilled.   Mark 12:35

50 And they all forsook him, and fled.

51 And there followed him a certain young man, having a linen cloth cast about *his* naked *body*; and the young men laid hold on him:

52 And he left the linen cloth, and fled from them naked.

The Trial by the Jewish Council

53 And they led Jesus away to the high priest: and with him were assembled all the chief priests and the elders and the scribes.   Matt. 26:57-68

54 And Peter followed him afar off, even into the palace of the high priest: and he sat with the servants, and warmed himself at the fire.   Matt. 26:3; John 18:18

55 And the chief priests and all the council sought for witness against Jesus to put him to death; and found none.

56 For many bare false witness against him, but their witness agreed not together.

57 And there arose certain, and bare false witness against him, saying,   Matt. 26:60-61

58 We heard him say, I will destroy this temple that is made with hands, and within three days I will build another made without hands.

59 But neither so did their witness agree together.

60 And the high priest stood up in the midst, and asked Jesus, saying, Answerest thou nothing? what *is it which* these witness against thee?

61 But he held his peace, and answered nothing. Again the high priest asked him, and said unto him, Art thou the Christ, the Son of the Blessed?   Is. 53:7

62 And Jesus said, I am: and ye shall see the Son of man sitting on the right hand of power, and coming in the clouds of heaven.   Ps. 110:1

63 Then the high priest ᵀrent his clothes, and saith, What need we any further witnesses?   Num. 14:6 ◆ *tore*

64 Ye have heard the blasphemy: what think ye? And they all condemned him to be guilty of death.   Lev. 24:16

65 And some began to spit on him, and to cover his face, and to ᵀbuffet him, and to say unto him, Prophesy: and the servants did strike him with the palms of their hands.   Is. 50:6 ◆ *punch*

14:53-65 What Jesus Endured to Save Us

His love for His Father, and His pledge, made from the foundation of the world, to become the Sin Bearer, led [Jesus] to endure uncomplainingly the coarse treatment of those He came to save. It was a part of His mission to bear, in His humanity, all the taunts and abuse that men could heap upon Him. The only hope of humanity was in this submission of Christ to all that He could endure from the hands and hearts of men. *DA 703*

Peter Denies Jesus

66 And as Peter was beneath in the palace, there cometh one of the maids of the high priest: Mark 14:54

67 And when she saw Peter warming himself, she looked upon him, and said, And thou also wast with Jesus of Nazareth.   Mark 14:54

68 But he denied, saying, I know not, neither understand I what thou sayest. And he went out into the porch; and the cock crew.

69 And a maid saw him again, and began to say to them that stood by, This is *one* of them.

70 And he denied it again. And a little after, they that stood by said again to Peter, Surely thou art *one* of them: for thou art a Galilaean, and thy speech agreeth *thereto*.   Acts 2:7

71 But he began to curse and to swear, *saying*, I know not this man of whom ye speak.

72 And the second time the cock crew. And Peter called to mind the word that Jesus said unto him, Before the cock crow twice, thou shalt deny me thrice. And when he thought thereon, he wept.   Mark 14:30, 68

14:66–72 Peter's Denial and Remorse

The sight of that pale, suffering face, those quivering lips, that look of compassion and forgiveness, pierced [Peter's] heart like an arrow. . . .

Once more he looked at his Master, and saw a sacrilegious hand raised to smite Him in the face. Unable longer to endure the scene, he rushed, heartbroken, from the hall. . . .

At last he found himself in Gethsemane. . . . On the very spot where Jesus had poured out His soul in agony to His Father, Peter fell upon his face, and wished that he might die. *DA 713*

The Trial before Pilate

15 And ᵀstraightway in the morning the chief priests held a consultation with the elders and scribes and the whole council, and bound Jesus, and carried *him* away, and delivered *him* to Pilate.   Matt. 27:1-2 ◆ *right away*

2 And Pilate asked him, Art thou the King of the Jews? And he answering said unto him, Thou sayest *it*.   Matt. 2:2

3 And the chief priests accused him of many things: but he answered nothing.   Is. 53:7

4 And Pilate asked him again, saying, Answerest thou nothing? behold how many things they witness against thee.   John 19:10

5 But Jesus yet answered nothing; so that Pilate marvelled.

6 Now at *that* feast he released unto them one prisoner, whomsoever they desired.   John 18:39

7 And there was *one* named Barabbas, *which lay* bound with them that had made insurrection with him, who had committed murder in the insurrection.

8 And the multitude crying aloud began to desire *him to do* as he had ever done unto them.

9 But Pilate answered them, saying, Will ye that I release unto you the King of the Jews?

10 For he knew that the chief priests had delivered him for envy.

11 But the chief priests moved the people, that he should rather release Barabbas unto them.   Acts 3:14

12 And Pilate answered and said again unto them, What will ye then that I shall do *unto him* whom ye call the King of the Jews?

13 And they cried out again, Crucify him.

14 Then Pilate said unto them, Why, what evil hath he done? And they cried out the more exceedingly, Crucify him.   Luke 23:41

Jesus Is Mocked and Crucified

15 And *so* Pilate, willing to content the people, released Barabbas unto them, and delivered Jesus, when he had ᵀscourged *him*, to be crucified.   Is. 50:6; Matt. 27:26; John 19:1 ◆ *whipped*

16 And the soldiers led him away into the hall, called Praetorium; and they call together the whole band.   John 18:28

17 And they clothed him with purple, and ᵀplatted a crown of thorns, and put it about his *head*,   Luke 23:11 ◆ *braided*

18 And began to salute him, Hail, King of the Jews!

19 And they smote him on the head with a reed, and did spit upon him, and bowing *their* knees worshipped him.   Mark 14:65

20 And when they had mocked him, they took off the purple from him, and put his own clothes on him, and led him out to crucify him.

15:16–20 Jesus Submits to Terrible Abuse

Satan led the cruel mob in its abuse of the Saviour. It was his purpose to provoke Him to retaliation if possible, or to drive Him to perform a miracle to release Himself, and thus break up the plan of salvation. One stain upon His human life, one failure of His humanity to endure the terrible test, and the Lamb of God would have been an imperfect offering, and the redemption of man a failure. *DA 734*

21 And they compel one Simon a Cyrenian, who passed by, coming out of the country, the father of Alexander and Rufus, to bear his cross.   Matt. 27:32; Luke 23:26; Rom. 16:13

22 And they bring him unto the place Golgotha, which is, being interpreted, The place of a skull.   Matt. 27:33-44

23 And they gave him to drink wine mingled with myrrh: but he received *it* not.   Matt. 27:34

24 And when they had crucified him, they parted his garments, casting lots upon them, what every man should take.

25 And it was the third hour, and they crucified him.   Mark 15:33

26 And the superscription of his accusation was written over, THE KING OF THE JEWS.

27 And with him they crucify two thieves; the one on his right hand, and the other on his left.

28 And the scripture was fulfilled, which saith, And he was numbered with the ᵀtransgressors.   *those who violate the law*

29 And they that passed by railed on him, wagging their heads, and saying, Ah, thou that destroyest the temple, and buildest *it* in three days,   Ps. 109:25; Lam. 1:12; Mark 14:58

30 Save thyself, and come down from the cross.

31 Likewise also the chief priests mocking said among themselves with the scribes, He saved others; himself he cannot save.

32 Let Christ the King of Israel descend now from the cross, that we may see and

believe. And they that were crucified with him ᵀreviled him.   Luke 23:39-43 ◆ *verbally attacked*

15:21–32 Jesus Saved Us, Not Himself

Jesus, suffering and dying, heard every word as the priests declared, "He saved others; Himself He cannot save. Let Christ the King of Israel descend now from the cross, that we may see and believe." Christ could have come down from the cross. But it is because He would not save Himself that the sinner has hope of pardon and favor with God. *DA 749*

Jesus Dies

33 And when the sixth hour was come, there was darkness over the whole land until the ninth hour.   Matt. 27:45; Mark 15:25; Luke 23:44-45
34 And at the ninth hour Jesus cried with a loud voice, saying, **Eloi, Eloi, lama sabachthani?** which is, being interpreted, **My God, my God, why hast thou forsaken me?** Ps. 22:1

15:33, 34 Jesus Showed the Value of Even One

Look upon the Saviour uplifted on the cross. Hear that despairing cry, "My God, My God, why hast Thou forsaken Me?" (Mark 15:34). Look upon the wounded head, the pierced side, the marred feet. Remember that Christ risked all. For our redemption, heaven itself was imperiled. At the foot of the cross, remembering that for one sinner Christ would have laid down His life, you may estimate the value of a soul. *COL 196*

---

35 And some of them that stood by, when they heard *it*, said, Behold, he calleth Elias.
36 And one ran and filled a spunge full of vinegar, and put *it* on a reed, and gave him to drink, saying, Let alone; let us see whether Elias will come to take him down.   Ps. 69:21
37 And Jesus cried with a loud voice, and gave up the ghost.   John 19:30
38 And the veil of the temple was rent in twain from the top to the bottom. Luke 23:45
39 And when the centurion, which stood over against him, saw that he so cried out, and gave up the ghost, he said, Truly this man was the Son of God.   Matt. 27:54
40 There were also women looking on afar off: among whom was Mary Magdalene, and Mary the mother of James the less and of Joses, and Salome;   Ps. 38:11
41 (Who also, when he was in Galilee, followed him, and ministered unto him;) and many other women which came up with him unto Jerusalem.   Luke 8:2-3

Jesus Is Buried

42 And now when the even was come, because it was the preparation, that is, the day before the sabbath,

43 Joseph of Arimathaea, an honourable counsellor, which also waited for the kingdom of God, came, and went in boldly unto Pilate, and craved the body of Jesus. Luke 2:25, 38; 23:51
44 And Pilate marvelled if he were already dead: and calling *unto him* the ᵀcenturion, he asked him whether he had been any while dead.   *commander of 100 soldiers*
45 And when he knew *it* of the centurion, he gave the body to Joseph.
46 And he bought fine linen, and took him down, and wrapped him in the linen, and laid him in a sepulchre which was ᵀhewn out of a rock, and rolled a stone unto the door of the sepulchre.   Is. 22:16 ◆ *cut*

15:42–46 From the Cross to the Tomb

Gently and reverently [Joseph of Arimathaea and Nicodemus] removed with their own hands the body of Jesus from the cross. Their tears of sympathy fell fast as they looked upon His bruised and lacerated form. . . . The body, together with the spices brought by Nicodemus, was carefully wrapped in a linen sheet, and the Redeemer was borne to the tomb. There the . . . disciples straightened the mangled limbs, and folded the bruised hands upon the pulseless breast. . . . Then they saw the heavy stone rolled against the entrance of the tomb, and the Saviour was left at rest. *DA 774*

---

47 And Mary Magdalene and Mary *the mother* of Joses beheld where he was laid.   Mark 15:40

Jesus' Resurrection

16 And when the sabbath was past, Mary Magdalene, and Mary the *mother* of James, and Salome, had bought sweet spices, that they might come and anoint him.   Mark 15:40, 47; John 19:25
2 And very early in the morning the first *day* of the week, they came unto the sepulchre at the rising of the sun.   Matt. 28:1
3 And they said among themselves, Who shall roll us away the stone from the door of the sepulchre?

16:1–8 A Living Savior!

He is risen, He is risen! The women [Mary Magdalene, Mary the mother of James, and Salome] repeat the words again and again. No need now for the anointing spices. The Saviour is living, and not dead. They remember now that when speaking of His death He said that He would rise again. What a day is this to the world! *DA 789*

---

4 And when they looked, they saw that the stone was rolled away: for it was very great.

5 And entering into the sepulchre, they saw a young man sitting on the right side, clothed in a long white garment; and they were affrighted. *John 20:11-12*

6 And he saith unto them, Be not ᵀaffrighted: Ye seek Jesus of Nazareth, which was crucified: he is risen; he is not here: behold the place where they laid him.   *scared*

7 But go your way, tell his disciples and Peter that he goeth before you into Galilee: there shall ye see him, as he said unto you.   *Matt. 26:32; Mark 14:28; John 21:1*

8 And they went out quickly, and fled from the sepulchre; for they trembled and were amazed: neither said they any thing to any *man*; for they were afraid.

9 Now when *Jesus* was risen early the first *day* of the week, he appeared first to Mary Magdalene, out of whom he had cast seven devils.   *Mark 15:40*

10 *And* she went and told them that had been with him, as they mourned and wept.

16:15 The Great Commission to Serve

Service to God includes personal ministry. By personal effort we are to co-operate with Him for the saving of the world. . . . All who are ordained unto the life of Christ are ordained to work for the salvation of their fellow men. Their hearts will throb in unison with the heart of Christ. The same longing for souls that He has felt will be manifest in them. Not all can fill the same place in the work, but there is a place and a work for all. *COL 300, 301*

11 And they, when they had heard that he was alive, and had been seen of her, believed not.   *Mark 16:13-14; Luke 24:11*

12 After that he appeared in another form unto two of them, as they walked, and went into the country.   *Luke 24:13-32*

13 And they went and told *it* unto the residue: neither believed they them. *Luke 24:33-35*

14 Afterward he appeared unto the eleven as they sat at meat, and ᵀupbraided them with their unbelief and hardness of heart, because they believed not them which had seen him after he was risen. 1 Cor. 15:5 ◆ *scolded*

15 And he said unto them, **Go ye into all the world, and preach the gospel to every creature.**   *Matt. 28:19; Mark 13:10; Acts 1:8*

16 **He that believeth and is baptized shall be saved; but he that believeth not shall be ᵀdamned.** *Matt. 28:19; John 3:36; 1 Pet. 3:21* ◆ *condemned*

Baptism/Lord's Supper   See Romans 6:3, 4.

17 **And these signs shall follow them that believe; In my name shall they cast out devils; they shall speak with new tongues;**   *Acts 5:16*

18 **They shall take up serpents; and if they drink any deadly thing, it shall not hurt them; they shall lay hands on the sick, and they shall recover.**   *Luke 10:19; Acts 3:16; 5:15-16*

19 So then after the Lord had spoken unto them, he was received up into heaven, and sat on the right hand of God. *Heb. 1:3; 12:2; 1 Pet. 3:22*

16:19, 20 Ascended, but Returning Again

Christ had ascended to heaven in the form of humanity. The disciples had beheld the cloud receive Him. . . . And the angels had assured them that the very One whom they had seen go up into heaven, would come again even as He had ascended. . . . Well might the disciples rejoice in the hope of their Lord's return. *DA 832*

20 And they went forth, and preached every where, the Lord working with *them*, and confirming the word with signs following. Amen.   *Acts 5:12*

THE GOSPEL ACCORDING TO

LUKE

Medical doctors know the human body—what a healthy person is like. For them, the "perfect" person is one who is perfectly healthy, with a regimen geared toward maintaining that health.

Luke, the Gospel writer, was a doctor. With his training and skills, his investigation and attention to detail, he wrote a Gospel describing the perfect man—Jesus Christ. Repeatedly stressed in Luke's narrative is the humanity of Jesus. His humanity made Him the perfect sacrifice for sin. Luke penned the most exhaustive and complete account of Jesus' ancestry, birth, childhood, life, and death. His narrative is built on historical reliability and chronology, thus making his Gospel the longest and most literary of the four. Writing to a Greek audience, Dr. Luke presents Jesus as the fulfillment of the Greek ideal of human perfection. In fact, Luke translates many Aramaic terms using Greek words, to explain Jewish customs and geography to make Jesus more understandable to his Greek audience.

While Luke affirms the divinity of Jesus, the theme of Luke's Gospel is the humanity of Jesus. Jesus is not only the Son of God, He is also the Son of Man. Luke writes to non-Jewish readers, emphasizing how Jesus became fully human, identifying with our human condition. Jesus came to seek and to save all who are lost (19:10). Luke invites his readers to see the humanity of Jesus—through His birth, His childhood, His ministry of compassion and healing, His horrific death, and His glorious resurrection.

Dates

Luke's Gospel was probably written before the destruction of Jerusalem in A.D. 70, and probably during Paul's first Roman imprisonment (about A.D. 61-63).

Acts was written subsequent to Luke's gospel in about A.D. 63. While Luke was not an eyewitness of the life of Jesus, he relied on the testimony of eyewitnesses. Having been with Paul during his Caesarean imprisonment (2 Timothy 4:11), Luke may have traveled to Palestine to gather information from eyewitnesses of Jesus' ministry.

Author

Ancient traditions strongly support Luke as the author of both this Gospel and the Book of Acts. Luke was a doctor by profession (Colossians 4:14), an evangelist by avocation, and a meticulous historian. He also was a Gentile, making him the only Gentile contributor to the New Testament. The reasons verifying his Gentile status are as follows: He is listed by Paul, in Colossians 4:10–14 with two Gentiles (verses 12–14). He had a strong command of the Greek language—he interpreted various Aramaic words for his readers, along with explaining some of the Jewish customs and topography for his non-Jewish readers. He used the phrase "in their proper tongue" in Acts 1:19, implying that he was not Jewish. In addition, Luke wrote this Gospel as a part of a two-volume piece of work—the Gospel of Luke and the Book of Acts—both addressed to his patron/publisher Theophilus.

Luke was a close traveling companion of Paul—in the Book of Acts, starting at 16:10, the words "we" and "us" are used, revealing that Luke was part of the action for several sections of the remainder of the book. Paul referred to him as "Luke, the beloved physician" (Colossians 4:14).

Meaning of the Name

Kata Loukon, "According to Luke," is the ancient title of this book. The name *Luke* appears only three times in the New Testament (Colossians 4:14; 2 Timothy 4:11; Philemon 24 [where he is called Lucas]).

Christ in Luke

Luke repeatedly stresses the humanity of Jesus—giving the details of His birth as a baby and His growing up years. Jesus was the Son of Man who identified with the sorrow and plight of sinful humanity in order to redeem us and give us the priceless gift of salvation.

Luke used Mark's Gospel, written earlier, as a structural basis. His narrative can be outlined as follows:

(1) *Luke 1:1—4:13, Behold the Son of Man:* Luke's Gospel presents the full spectrum of Jesus' life. Jesus is the Son of Man, a title Luke mentions often and one that the prophet Ezekiel used. Only Luke's Gospel contains the birth narratives of Jesus and John the Baptist. John is the forerunner of the Messiah, and is the one whose coming was foretold in Malachi 4:5, 6. Luke also includes details of Jesus' childhood (chapter 2), John's ministry in the wilderness, including Jesus' baptism (chapter 3), and Jesus' temptation (4:1–13). Luke's Gospel also preserves four beautiful hymns (1:46–55, 67–79; 2:14, 29–32).

(2) *Luke 4:14—9:50, The Son of Man Ministers:* The reading of Isaiah 61:1, 2 (Luke 4:18, 19) signals Jesus' fulfillment of that prophecy and the start of His public ministry. Jesus demonstrates His authority through miracles and teachings. Being true to his profession, Luke provides careful details about Jesus' healing of the sick. No other biblical author included or sympathized with as many women as Luke did.

(3) *Luke 9:51—19:27, The Son of Man Rejected:* Opposition mounts as Jesus comes under the radar of the religious leaders. Jesus continues in His ministry to "seek and to save that which was lost" (19:10).

(4) *Luke 19:28—24:53, The Son of Man Crucified and Resurrected:* Jesus arrives in triumph in Jerusalem, is crucified and buried, but rises again triumphantly. Luke alone records the story of Jesus' conversation with some of His disciples on the road to Emmaus—proving to them beyond a doubt that He had risen again.

Unlocking Luke

KEY PEOPLE:
Jesus, Elisabeth, Zacharias, John the Baptist, Mary, the disciples, Herod the Great, Pilate, Mary Magdalene, Jesus' disciples, Martha, Lazarus, Zaccheus

KEY EVENTS:
Jesus' childhood, many parables, and Jesus' one-year ministry through Samaria and Berea leading to His final journey to Jerusalem are all unique to Luke's Gospel.

KEY PHRASE:
Son of Man, for Luke wanted his readers to know that Jesus was not only divine but also human.

KEY VERSE:
"For the Son of Man is come to seek and to save that which was lost" (Luke 19:10).

KEY CHAPTER:
Luke 15, which records three parables for emphasis—the lost coin, the lost sheep, and the lost son—to demonstrate that people, even just one soul, matter to God and He will go to great lengths to draw them into relationship with Him.

Luke's Preface

1 Forasmuch as many have taken in hand to set forth in order a declaration of those things which are most surely believed among us,

2 Even as they delivered them unto us, which from the beginning were eyewitnesses, and ministers of the word; Mark 1:1; John 15:27; Heb. 2:3

3 It seemed good to me also, having had perfect understanding of all things from the very first, to write unto thee in order, most excellent Theophilus, Acts 1:1; 11:4; 24:3

4 That thou mightest know the certainty of those things, wherein thou hast been instructed. John 20:31

The Angel Gabriel Appears to Zacharias

5 There was in the days of Herod, the king of Judaea, a certain priest named Zacharias, of the course of Abia: and his wife *was* of the daughters of Aaron, and her name *was* Elisabeth. 1 Chr. 24:10; Matt. 2:1

6 And they were both righteous before God, walking in all the commandments and ordinances of the Lord blameless. Gen. 7:1; Phil. 2:15;

7 And they had no child, because that Elisabeth was barren, and they both were *now* well stricken in years. Gen. 18:11

8 And it came to pass, that while he executed the priest's office before God in the order of his course, 1 Chr. 24:19; 2 Chr. 8:14; 31:2

9 According to the custom of the priest's office, his lot was to burn incense when he went into the temple of the Lord. Ex. 30:7-8

10 And the whole multitude of the people were praying without at the time of incense. Lev. 16:17; Rev. 8:3

11 And there appeared unto him an angel of the Lord standing on the right side of the altar of incense. Ex. 40:26-27

12 And when Zacharias saw *him*, he was troubled, and fear fell upon him. Judg. 6:22

13 But the angel said unto him, Fear not, Zacharias: for thy prayer is heard; and thy wife Elisabeth shall bear thee a son, and thou shalt call his name John. Acts 10:31

14 And thou shalt have joy and gladness; and many shall rejoice at his birth. Luke 1:58

15 For he shall be great in the sight of the Lord, and shall drink neither wine nor strong drink; and he shall be filled with the Holy Ghost, even from his mother's womb.

16 And many of the children of Israel shall he turn to the Lord their God.

17 And he shall go before him in the spirit and power of Elias, to turn the hearts of the fathers to the children, and the disobedient to the wisdom of the just; to make ready a people prepared for the Lord. Mal. 4:5; Matt. 11:14

18 And Zacharias said unto the angel, Whereby shall I know this? for I am an old man, and my wife well stricken in years. Gen. 15:8; 17:17; Luke 1:34

19 And the angel answering said unto him, I am Gabriel, that stand in the presence of God; and am sent to speak unto thee, and to shew thee these glad tidings. Dan. 8:16; Matt. 18:10

20 And, behold, thou shalt be ᵀdumb, and not able to speak, until the day that these things shall be performed, because thou believest not my words, which shall be fulfilled in their season. Ezek. 3:26 ◆ *mute*

21 And the people waited for Zacharias, and marvelled that he tarried so long in the temple.

22 And when he came out, he could not speak unto them: and they perceived that he had seen a vision in the temple: for he beckoned unto them, and remained speechless. Luke 1:62

23 And it came to pass, that, as soon as the days of his ᵀministration were accomplished, he departed to his own house. 1 Chr. 9:25 ◆ *service*

24 And after those days his wife Elisabeth conceived, and hid herself five months, saying,

25 Thus hath the Lord dealt with me in the days wherein he looked on *me*, to take away my reproach among men. 1 Sam. 1:6; Is. 4:1

The Angel Gabriel Appears to Mary

26 And in the sixth month the angel Gabriel was sent from God unto a city of Galilee, named Nazareth, Matt. 2:23; Luke 1:19

27 To a virgin espoused to a man whose name was Joseph, of the house of David; and the virgin's name *was* Mary. Gen. 3:15; Matt. 1:16

28 And the angel came in unto her, and said, Hail, *thou that art* highly favoured, the Lord *is* with thee: blessed *art* thou among women. Judg. 6:12

29 And when she saw *him*, she was troubled at his saying, and cast in her mind what manner of salutation this should be. Luke 1:12

30 And the angel said unto her, Fear not, Mary: for thou hast found favour with God.

31 And, behold, thou shalt conceive in thy womb, and bring forth a son, and shalt call his name JESUS. Is. 7:14; Matt. 1:21, 25

32 He shall be great, and shall be called the Son of the Highest: and the Lord God shall give unto him the throne of his father David: Ps. 132:11; Mark 5:7; Luke 1:35

33 And he shall reign over the house of Jacob for ever; and of his kingdom there shall be no end. Dan. 2:44; 7:27; Heb. 1:8

34 Then said Mary unto the angel, How shall this be, seeing I know not a man?

35 And the angel answered and said unto her, The Holy Ghost shall come upon thee, and the power of the Highest shall overshadow thee: therefore also that holy thing

which shall be born of thee shall be called the Son of God.   Matt. 1:18

36 And, behold, thy cousin Elisabeth, she hath also conceived a son in her old age: and this is the sixth month with her, who was called barren.

37 For with God nothing shall be impossible.   Gen. 18:14; Jer. 32:17; Matt. 19:26

38 And Mary said, Behold the handmaid of the Lord; be it unto me according to thy word. And the angel departed from her.

Mary Visits Elisabeth

39 And Mary arose in those days, and went into the hill country with haste, into a city of Juda;   Luke 1:65

40 And entered into the house of Zacharias, and saluted Elisabeth.

41 And it came to pass, that, when Elisabeth heard the salutation of Mary, the babe leaped in her womb; and Elisabeth was filled with the Holy Ghost: Luke 1:67

42 And she spake out with a loud voice, and said, Blessed *art* thou among women, and blessed *is* the fruit of thy womb.   Judg. 5:24

43 And whence *is* this to me, that the mother of my Lord should come to me?   John 20:28

44 For, lo, as soon as the voice of thy salutation sounded in mine ears, the babe leaped in my womb for joy.

45 And blessed *is* she that believed: for there shall be a performance of those things which were told her from the Lord.   Luke 1:20

Mary Praises God

46 And Mary said, My soul doth magnify the Lord,   1 Sam. 2:1-10; Ps. 34:2-3; 35:9

47 And my spirit hath rejoiced in God my Saviour.   1 Tim. 1:1; 2:3; Titus 2:10

48 For he hath regarded the low estate of his handmaiden: for, behold, from Thenceforth all generations shall call me blessed.   1 Sam. 1:11; Ps. 138:6 ◆ *this time forward*

49 For he that is mighty hath done to me great things; and holy *is* his name.   Ps. 111:9

50 And his mercy *is* on them that fear him from generation to generation.   Ex. 20:6

51 He hath shewed strength with his arm; he hath scattered the proud in the imagination of their hearts.   Ps. 89:10; 98:1; 118:15

52 He hath put down the mighty from *their* seats, and exalted them of low degree.

53 He hath filled the hungry with good things; and the rich he hath sent empty away.   Ps. 34:10

54 He hath Tholpen his servant Israel, in remembrance of *his* mercy;   Ps. 98:3 ◆ *helped*

55 As he spake to our fathers, to Abraham, and to his seed for ever.   Gen. 17:19

56 And Mary abode with her about three months, and returned to her own house.

The Birth of John

57 Now Elisabeth's full time came that she should be delivered; and she brought forth a son.

58 And her neighbours and her cousins heard how the Lord had shewed great mercy upon her; and they rejoiced with her.

59 And it came to pass, that on the eighth day they came to circumcise the child; and they called him Zacharias, after the name of his father.   Gen. 17:12; Lev. 12:3; Luke 2:21

60 And his mother answered and said, Not *so*; but he shall be called John.   Luke 1:13

61 And they said unto her, There is none of thy kindred that is called by this name.

62 And they made signs to his father, how he would have him called.   Luke 1:22

63 And he asked for a writing table, and wrote, saying, His name is John. And they marvelled all.   Is. 30:8; Luke 1:13, 60

64 And his mouth was opened immediately, and his tongue *loosed*, and he spake, and praised God.   Luke 1:20

65 And fear came on all that dwelt round about them: and all these sayings were noised abroad throughout all the hill country of Judaea.   Luke 1:39; 7:16

66 And all they that heard *them* laid *them* up in their hearts, saying, What manner of child shall this be! And the hand of the Lord was with him.   Gen. 39:2; Luke 2:19; Acts 11:21

The Prophecy of Zacharias

67 And his father Zacharias was filled with the Holy Ghost, and prophesied, saying,   Joel 2:28

68 Blessed *be* the Lord God of Israel; for he hath visited and redeemed his people,

69 And hath raised up an horn of salvation for us in the house of his servant David;

70 As he spake by the mouth of his holy prophets, which have been since the world began:

71 That we should be saved from our enemies, and from the hand of all that hate us;   Ps. 106:10

72 To perform the mercy *promised* to our fathers, and to remember his holy covenant;

73 The oath which he sware to our father Abraham,   Gen. 22:16-18

74 That he would grant unto us, that we being delivered out of the hand of our enemies might serve him without fear, Heb. 9:14

75 In holiness and righteousness before him, all the days of our life.   Eph. 4:24

76 And thou, child, shalt be called the prophet of the Highest: for thou shalt go before the face of the Lord to prepare his ways;   Mal. 3:1; Matt. 3:3; Luke 1:32

77 To give knowledge of salvation unto his people by the Tremission of their sins, *forgiveness*

78 Through the tender mercy of our God; whereby the ᵀdayspring from on high hath visited us,   Num. 24:17; Is. 11:1; Mal. 4:2 ◆ *dawning*
79 To give light to them that sit in darkness and *in* the shadow of death, to guide our feet into the way of peace. Is. 9:2; Matt. 4:16; Acts 26:18
80 And the child grew, and ᵀwaxed strong in spirit, and was in the deserts till the day of his shewing unto Israel.   Matt. 3:1; 11:7 ◆ *became*

Jesus Is Born

2 And it came to pass in those days, that there went out a decree from Caesar Augustus, that all the world should be taxed.   Matt. 24:14; Luke 3:1
2 (*And* this taxing was first made when Cyrenius was governor of Syria.)   Luke 3:1
3 And all went to be taxed, every one into his own city.
4 And Joseph also went up from Galilee, out of the city of Nazareth, into Judaea, unto the city of David, which is called Bethlehem; (because he was of the house and lineage of David:)   John 7:42
5 To be taxed with Mary his ᵀespoused wife, being great with child.   *engaged*
6 And so it was, that, while they were there, the days were accomplished that she should be delivered.
7 And she brought forth her firstborn son, and wrapped him in swaddling clothes, and laid him in a manger; because there was no room for them in the inn.   Matt. 1:25

Angels Announce Jesus' Birth

8 And there were in the same country shepherds abiding in the field, keeping watch over their flock by night.
9 And, lo, the angel of the Lord came upon them, and the glory of the Lord shone round about them: and they were sore afraid.   2 Cor. 3:18
10 And the angel said unto them, Fear not: for, behold, I bring you good tidings of great joy, which shall be to all people.   Gen. 12:3
11 For unto you is born this day in the city of David a Saviour, which is Christ the Lord.   Matt. 1:21; 16:16; Luke 1:43
12 And this *shall be* a sign unto you; Ye shall find the babe wrapped in swaddling clothes, lying in a manger.   1 Sam. 2:34
13 And suddenly there was with the angel a multitude of the heavenly host praising God, and saying,   Gen. 28:12
14 Glory to God in the highest, and on earth peace, good will toward men.   Luke 1:79
15 And it came to pass, as the angels were gone away from them into heaven, the shepherds said one to another, Let us now go even unto Bethlehem, and see this thing

2:10-16

which is come to pass, which the Lord hath made known unto us.
16 And they came with haste, and found Mary, and Joseph, and the babe lying in a manger.   Luke 2:7

Jesus   See Luke 2:40.

17 And when they had seen *it*, they made known abroad the saying which was told them concerning this child.
18 And all they that heard *it* wondered at those things which were told them by the shepherds.
19 But Mary kept all these things, and pondered *them* in her heart.   Gen. 37:11; Luke 1:66; 2:51
20 And the shepherds returned, glorifying and praising God for all the things that they had heard and seen, as it was told unto them.

Jesus' Parents Obey the Law of Moses

21 And when eight days were accomplished for the circumcising of the child, his name was called JESUS, which was so named of the angel before he was conceived in the womb.   Matt. 1:21; Luke 1:31, 59
22 And when the days of her purification according to the law of Moses were accomplished, they brought him to Jerusalem, to present *him* to the Lord;
23 (As it is written in the law of the Lord, Every male that openeth the womb shall be called holy to the Lord;)   Ex. 13:2; Num. 3:13
24 And to offer a sacrifice according to that which is said in the law of the Lord, A pair of turtledoves, or two young pigeons.

Simeon and Anna Prophesy of Jesus

25 And, behold, there was a man in Jerusalem, whose name *was* Simeon; and the same man *was* just and devout, waiting for the consolation of Israel: and the Holy Ghost was upon him.   Mark 15:43; Luke 1:6; 2:38
26 And it was revealed unto him by the Holy Ghost, that he should not see death, before he had seen the Lord's Christ.   John 8:51
27 And he came by the Spirit into the temple: and when the parents brought in the child Jesus, to do for him after the custom of the law,   Luke 2:41
28 Then took he him up in his arms, and blessed God, and said,   Luke 1:64
29 Lord, now lettest thou thy servant depart in peace, according to thy word: Gen. 15:15
30 For mine eyes have seen thy salvation,
31 Which thou hast prepared before the face of all people;
32 A light to lighten the Gentiles, and the glory of thy people Israel.   Is. 9:2; 49:6; 60:19
33 And Joseph and his mother marvelled at those things which were spoken of him.

34 And Simeon blessed them, and said unto Mary his mother, Behold, this *child* is set for the fall and rising again of many in Israel; and for a sign which shall be spoken against;   Matt. 21:44; Acts 28:22; 1 Cor. 1:23

35 (Yea, a sword shall pierce through thy own soul also,) that the thoughts of many hearts may be revealed.

36 And there was one Anna, a prophetess, the daughter of Phanuel, of the tribe of Aser: she was of a great age, and had lived with an husband seven years from her virginity;   Acts 21:9

37 And she *was* a widow of about ᵀfourscore and four years, which departed not from the temple, but served *God* with fastings and prayers night and day.Acts 14:23; 1 Tim. 5:5 ♦ *eighty*

38 And she coming in that instant gave thanks likewise unto the Lord, and spake of him to all them that looked for redemption in Jerusalem.   Luke 1:68; 2:25; 24:21

39 And when they had performed all things according to the law of the Lord, they returned into Galilee, to their own city Nazareth.   Luke 2:4

40 And the child grew, and ᵀwaxed strong in spirit, filled with wisdom: and the grace of God was upon him.   Luke 1:80; 2:52 ♦ *became*

Jesus   See Luke 2:42–49.

Jesus Grows Up

41 Now his parents went to Jerusalem every year at the feast of the passover.   Deut. 16:1-8

42 And when he was twelve years old, they went up to Jerusalem after the custom of the feast.

43 And when they had fulfilled the days, as they returned, the child Jesus tarried behind in Jerusalem; and Joseph and his mother knew not *of it*.

44 But they, supposing him to have been in the company, went a day's journey; and they sought him among *their* kinsfolk and acquaintance.

45 And when they found him not, they turned back again to Jerusalem, seeking him.

46 And it came to pass, that after three days they found him in the temple, sitting in the midst of the ᵀdoctors, both hearing them, and asking them questions.Luke 5:17 ♦ *instructors*

47 And all that heard him were astonished at his understanding and answers.   Matt. 7:28

48 And when they saw him, they were amazed: and his mother said unto him, Son, why hast thou thus dealt with us? behold, thy father and I have sought thee sorrowing.

49 And he said unto them, How is it that ye sought me? ᵀwist ye not that I must be about my Father's business?   John 4:34 ♦ *knew*

Jesus   See John 3:16, 17.

50 And they understood not the saying which he spake unto them.   Luke 18:34

51 And he went down with them, and came to Nazareth, and was subject unto them: but his mother kept all these sayings in her heart.   Mark 6:3; Luke 2:19

52 And Jesus increased in wisdom and stature, and in favour with God and man.   1 Sam. 2:26

The Preaching and Baptism of John

3 Now in the fifteenth year of the reign of Tiberius Caesar, Pontius Pilate being governor of Judaea, and Herod being ᵀtetrarch of Galilee, and his brother Philip tetrarch of Ituraea and of the region of Trachonitis, and Lysanias the tetrarch of Abilene,   Matt. 14:1 ♦ *ruler of one-fourth*

2 Annas and Caiaphas being the high priests, the word of God came unto John the son of Zacharias in the wilderness. Matt. 26:3; John 18:24

3 And he came into all the country about Jordan, preaching the baptism of repentance for the ᵀremission of sins;   Luke 1:77 ♦ *forgiveness*

4 As it is written in the book of the words of Esaias the prophet, saying, The voice of one crying in the wilderness, Prepare ye the way of the Lord, make his paths straight.   Is. 40:3-5

5 Every valley shall be filled, and every mountain and hill shall be brought low; and the crooked shall be made straight, and the rough ways *shall be* made smooth;   Is. 40:4

6 And all flesh shall see the salvation of God.   Is. 40:5

7 Then said he to the multitude that came forth to be baptized of him, O generation of vipers, who hath warned you to flee from the wrath to come?Matt. 12:34; 23:33; 1 Thess. 1:10

8 Bring forth therefore fruits worthy of repentance, and begin not to say within yourselves, We have Abraham to *our* father: for I say unto you, That God is able of these stones to raise up children unto Abraham.   John 8:33

9 And now also the axe is laid unto the root of the trees: every tree therefore which bringeth not forth good fruit is ᵀhewn down, and cast into the fire.   Matt. 7:19 ♦ *cut*

10 And the people asked him, saying, What shall we do then?   Acts 2:37; 16:30

11 He answereth and saith unto them, He that hath two coats, let him impart to him that hath none; and he that hath meat, let him do likewise.   Dan. 4:27

12 Then came also ᵀpublicans to be baptized, and said unto him, Master, what shall we do?   Luke 7:29 ♦ *tax collectors*

13 And he said unto them, Exact no more than that which is appointed you.   Luke 19:8

14 And the soldiers likewise demanded of him, saying, And what shall we do? And he said unto them, Do violence to no man, neither accuse *any* falsely; and be content with your wages.　　　　　　　　　Ex. 23:1

John's Testimony Concerning Christ

15 And as the people were in expectation, and all men mused in their hearts of John, whether he were the Christ, or not;
16 John answered, saying unto *them* all, I indeed baptize you with water; but one mightier than I cometh, the ᵀlatchet of whose shoes I am not worthy to unloose: he shall baptize you with the Holy Ghost and with fire:　　　Matt. 3:11; John 1:26; Acts 1:5 ◆ *sandal strap*
17 Whose fan *is* in his hand, and he will throughly purge his floor, and will gather the wheat into his garner; but the chaff he will burn with fire unquenchable.　Matt. 13:30
18 And many other things in his ᵀexhortation preached he unto the people. *encouragement*
19 But Herod the tetrarch, being reproved by him for Herodias his brother Philip's wife, and for all the evils which Herod had done,　　　　　　　　　Mark 6:17-18
20 Added yet this above all, that he shut up John in prison.

The Baptism of Jesus

21 Now when all the people were baptized, it came to pass, that Jesus also being baptized, and praying, the heaven was opened,　John 1:32
22 And the Holy Ghost descended in a bodily shape like a dove upon him, and a voice came from heaven, which said, Thou art my beloved Son; in thee I am well pleased.　Ps. 2:7

The Ancestors of Jesus

23 And Jesus himself began to be about thirty years of age, being (as was supposed) the son of Joseph, which was *the son* of Heli,　　　　　　　　　Matt. 13:55
24 Which was *the son* of Matthat, which was *the son* of Levi, which was *the son* of Melchi, which was *the son* of Janna, which was *the son* of Joseph,
25 Which was *the son* of Mattathias, which was *the son* of Amos, which was *the son* of Naum, which was *the son* of Esli, which was *the son* of Nagge,
26 Which was *the son* of Maath, which was *the son* of Mattathias, which was *the son* of Semei, which was *the son* of Joseph, which was *the son* of Juda,
27 Which was *the son* of Joanna, which was *the son* of Rhesa, which was *the son* of Zorobabel, which was *the son* of Salathiel, which was *the son* of Neri,　　Matt. 1:12
28 Which was *the son* of Melchi, which was *the son* of Addi, which was *the son* of Cosam,

which was *the son* of Elmodam, which was *the son* of Er,
29 Which was *the son* of Jose, which was *the son* of Eliezer, which was *the son* of Jorim, which was *the son* of Matthat, which was *the son* of Levi,
30 Which was *the son* of Simeon, which was *the son* of Juda, which was *the son* of Joseph, which was *the son* of Jonan, which was *the son* of Eliakim,
31 Which was *the son* of Melea, which was *the son* of Menan, which was *the son* of Mattatha, which was *the son* of Nathan, which was *the son* of David,　　2 Sam. 5:14
32 Which was *the son* of Jesse, which was *the son* of Obed, which was *the son* of Booz, which was *the son* of Salmon, which was *the son* of Naasson,　　　　　　　Ruth 4:18-22
33 Which was *the son* of Aminadab, which was *the son* of Aram, which was *the son* of Esrom, which was *the son* of Phares, which was *the son* of Juda,　　Ruth 4:19-20
34 Which was *the son* of Jacob, which was *the son* of Isaac, which was *the son* of Abraham, which was *the son* of Thara, which was *the son* of Nachor,　　　　　　　Gen. 21:3
35 Which was *the son* of Saruch, which was *the son* of Ragau, which was *the son* of Phalec, which was *the son* of Heber, which was *the son* of Sala,
36 Which was *the son* of Cainan, which was *the son* of Arphaxad, which was *the son* of Sem, which was *the son* of Noe, which was *the son* of Lamech,
37 Which was *the son* of Mathusala, which was *the son* of Enoch, which was *the son* of Jared, which was *the son* of Maleleel, which was *the son* of Cainan,
38 Which was *the son* of Enos, which was *the son* of Seth, which was *the son* of Adam, which was *the son* of God.

The Temptation of Jesus

4 And Jesus being full of the Holy Ghost returned from Jordan, and was led by the Spirit into the wilderness,　Matt. 4:1-11
2 Being forty days tempted of the devil. And in those days he did eat nothing: and when they were ended, he afterward hungered.　　　Ex. 34:28; Deut. 9:9; 1 Kin. 19:8
3 And the ᵀdevil said unto him, If thou be the Son of God, command this stone that it be made bread.　　　　　　*false accuser*
4 And Jesus answered him, saying, It is written, That man shall not live by bread alone, but by every word of God. Deut. 8:3; Luke 4:8, 10
5 And the devil, taking him up into an high mountain, shewed unto him all the kingdoms of the world in a moment of time.
6 And the devil said unto him, All this power will I give thee, and the glory of them:

for that is delivered unto me; and to whomsoever I will I give it.   John 12:31

7 If thou therefore wilt worship me, all shall be thine.

8 And Jesus answered and said unto him, Get thee behind me, Satan: for it is written, Thou shalt worship the Lord thy God, and him only shalt thou serve. Deut. 6:13; Matt. 4:10

9 And he brought him to Jerusalem, and set him on a pinnacle of the temple, and said unto him, If thou be the Son of God, cast thyself down from hence: Matt. 4:5-6

10 For it is written, He shall give his angels charge over thee, to keep thee: Ps. 91:11-12

11 And in *their* hands they shall bear thee up, lest at any time thou ᵀdash thy foot against a stone.   *strike*

12 And Jesus answering said unto him, It is said, Thou shalt not tempt the Lord thy God.   Deut. 6:16

13 And when the devil had ended all the temptation, he departed from him for a season.   John 14:30

Jesus Teaches and Is Rejected in His Hometown

14 And Jesus returned in the power of the Spirit into Galilee: and there went out a fame of him through all the region round about.

15 And he taught in their synagogues, being glorified of all.   Matt. 4:23

16 And he came to Nazareth, where he had been brought up: and, as his custom was, he went into the synagogue on the sabbath day, and stood up for to read. Luke 2:39, 51; Acts 17:2

The Sabbath   See Acts 18:4.

17 And there was delivered unto him the book of the prophet Esaias. And when he had opened the book, he found the place where it was written,

18 The Spirit of the Lord *is* upon me, because he hath anointed me to preach the gospel to the poor; he hath sent me to heal the brokenhearted, to preach deliverance to the captives, and recovering of sight to the blind, to set at liberty them that are bruised,   Ps. 146:7-8; Is. 42:7; Matt. 11:5

19 To preach the acceptable year of the Lord.

20 And he closed the book, and he gave *it* again to the minister, and sat down. And the eyes of all them that were in the synagogue were fastened on him.   Luke 4:17

21 And he began to say unto them, This day is this scripture fulfilled in your ears.

22 And all bare him witness, and wondered at the gracious words which proceeded out of his mouth. And they said, Is not this Joseph's son?   Ps. 45:2; John 6:42

23 And he said unto them, Ye will surely say unto me this proverb, Physician, heal thyself:

whatsoever we have heard done in Capernaum, do also here in thy country.   Matt. 4:13

24 And he said, Verily I say unto you, No prophet is accepted in his own country.

25 But I tell you of a truth, many widows were in Israel in the days of Elias, when the heaven was shut up three years and six months, when great famine was throughout all the land;   1 Kin. 17:1; James 5:17

26 But unto none of them was Elias sent, save unto Sarepta, *a city* of Sidon, unto a woman *that was* a widow.

27 And many lepers were in Israel in the time of Eliseus the prophet; and none of them was cleansed, saving Naaman the Syrian.

28 And all they in the synagogue, when they heard these things, were filled with wrath,

29 And rose up, and thrust him out of the city, and led him unto the brow of the hill whereon their city was built, that they might cast him down headlong.   Num. 15:35

30 But he passing through the midst of them went his way,   John 8:59; 10:39

Jesus Sends Out an Evil Spirit

31 And came down to Capernaum, a city of Galilee, and taught them on the sabbath days.   Matt. 4:13

32 And they were astonished at his doctrine: for his word was with power.   Matt. 7:28-29

33 And in the synagogue there was a man, which had a spirit of an unclean devil, and cried out with a loud voice,

34 Saying, Let *us* alone; what have we to do with thee, *thou* Jesus of Nazareth? art thou come to destroy us? I know thee who thou art; the Holy One of God. Matt. 8:29; James 2:19

35 And Jesus rebuked him, saying, Hold thy peace, and come out of him. And when the devil had thrown him in the midst, he came out of him, and hurt him not.   Matt. 8:26

36 And they were all amazed, and spake among themselves, saying, What a word *is* this! for with authority and power he commandeth the unclean spirits, and they come out.   Luke 4:32

37 And the fame of him went out into every place of the country round about.   Matt. 9:26

Jesus Cures Peter's Mother-in-law and Many Others

38 And he arose out of the synagogue, and entered into Simon's house. And Simon's wife's mother was taken with a great fever; and they besought him for her.   Matt. 8:14-15

39 And he stood over her, and rebuked the fever; and it left her: and immediately she arose and ministered unto them.   Luke 4:35

40 Now when the sun was setting, all they that had any sick with ᵀdivers diseases

brought them unto him; and he laid his hands on every one of them, and healed them.   Matt. 8:16-17 ◆ various

41 And devils also came out of many, crying out, and saying, Thou art Christ the Son of God. And he rebuking *them* suffered them not to speak: for they knew that he was Christ.   Mark 1:34

Spreading the Good News

42 And when it was day, he departed and went into a desert place: and the people sought him, and came unto him, and stayed him, that he should not depart from them.

43 And he said unto them, I must preach the kingdom of God to other cities also: for therefore am I sent.

44 And he preached in the synagogues of Galilee.   Matt. 4:23

A Miraculous Catch of Fish

5 And it came to pass, that, as the people pressed upon him to hear the word of God, he stood by the lake of Gennesaret,   Num. 34:11

2 And saw two ships standing by the lake: but the fishermen were gone out of them, and were washing *their* nets.   Mark 1:19

3 And he entered into one of the ships, which was Simon's, and prayed him that he would thrust out a little from the land. And he sat down, and taught the people out of the ship.

4 Now when he had left speaking, he said unto Simon, Launch out into the deep, and let down your nets for a draught.   John 21:6

5 And Simon answering said unto him, Master, we have toiled all the night, and have taken nothing: nevertheless at thy word I will let down the net.   John 21:3

6 And when they had this done, they inclosed a great multitude of fishes: and their net brake.

7 And they beckoned unto *their* partners, which were in the other ship, that they should come and help them. And they came, and filled both the ships, so that they began to sink.

8 When Simon Peter saw *it*, he fell down at Jesus' knees, saying, Depart from me; for I am a sinful man, O Lord.   Is. 6:5

9 For he was astonished, and all that were with him, at the draught of the fishes which they had taken:

10 And so *was* also James, and John, the sons of Zebedee, which were partners with Simon. And Jesus said unto Simon, Fear not; from ᵀhenceforth thou shalt catch men.   *this time forward*

11 And when they had brought their ships to land, they forsook all, and followed him.

Christ Cleanses the Leper

12 And it came to pass, when he was in a certain city, behold a man full of leprosy: who seeing Jesus fell on *his* face, and ᵀbesought him, saying, Lord, if thou wilt, thou canst make me clean.   Matt. 8:2-4 ◆ begged

13 And he put forth *his* hand, and touched him, saying, I will: be thou clean. And immediately the leprosy departed from him.

14 And he charged him to tell no man: but go, and shew thyself to the priest, and offer for thy cleansing, according as Moses commanded, for a testimony unto them.   Lev. 14:2-32

5:14 Many Times Silence Is Golden

Notwithstanding the caution of Jesus, the man [healed of leprosy] made no further effort to conceal the fact of his cure. . . . He did not understand that every such manifestation made the priests and elders more determined to destroy Jesus. . . . But his act in blazing abroad the matter resulted in hindering the Saviour's work. It caused the people to flock to Him in such multitudes that He was forced for a time to cease His labors. *DA 265*

15 But so much the more went there a fame abroad of him: and great multitudes came together to hear, and to be healed by him of their infirmities.   Matt. 9:26

16 And he withdrew himself into the wilderness, and prayed.   Matt. 14:23; Luke 6:12

Jesus Heals the Paralyzed Man

17 And it came to pass on a certain day, as he was teaching, that there were Pharisees and ᵀdoctors of the law sitting by, which were come out of every town of Galilee, and Judaea, and Jerusalem: and the power of the Lord was *present* to heal them.   Matt. 15:1 ◆ instructors

18 And, behold, men brought in a bed a man which was taken with a palsy: and they sought *means* to bring him in, and to lay *him* before him.   Matt. 9:2-8

19 And when they could not find by what *way* they might bring him in because of the multitude, they went upon the housetop, and let him down through the tiling with *his* ᵀcouch into the midst before Jesus.   Mark 2:4 ◆ mat

20 And when he saw their faith, he said unto him, Man, thy sins are forgiven thee.   Luke 7:48

21 And the scribes and the Pharisees began to reason, saying, Who is this which speaketh blasphemies? Who can forgive sins, but God alone?   Ps. 32:5; Is. 43:25; Matt. 26:65

22 But when Jesus perceived their thoughts, he answering said unto them, What reason ye in your hearts?

23 Whether is easier, to say, Thy sins be forgiven thee; or to say, Rise up and walk?
24 But that ye may know that the Son of man hath power upon earth to forgive sins, (he said unto the sick of the ᵀpalsy,) I say unto thee, Arise, and take up thy couch, and go into thine house.   *paralysis*
25 And immediately he rose up before them, and took up that whereon he lay, and departed to his own house, glorifying God.
26 And they were all amazed, and they glorified God, and were filled with fear, saying, We have seen strange things to day. Matt. 9:8

5:22–26 Recognizing but Not Confessing

The Pharisees were dumb with amazement and overwhelmed with defeat. . . . They were disconcerted and abashed, recognizing, but not confessing, the presence of a superior being. The stronger the evidence that Jesus had power on earth to forgive sins, the more firmly they entrenched themselves in unbelief. From the home of Peter, where they had seen the paralytic restored by His word, they went away to invent new schemes for silencing the Son of God. *DA 270, 271*

Jesus Calls Levi (Matthew)

27 And after these things he went forth, and saw a ᵀpublican, named Levi, sitting at the receipt of custom: and he said unto him, Follow me.   *tax collector*
28 And he left all, rose up, and followed him.   Luke 5:11
29 And Levi made him a great feast in his own house: and there was a great company of ᵀpublicans and of others that sat down with them.   Luke 15:1 ◆ *tax collectors*
30 But their scribes and Pharisees murmured against his disciples, saying, Why do ye eat and drink with publicans and sinners? Acts 23:9
31 And Jesus answering said unto them, They that are whole need not a physician; but they that are sick.   Matt. 9:12-13
32 I came not to call the righteous, but sinners to repentance.   Luke 15:7

New Wine Needs New Wineskins

33 And they said unto him, Why do the disciples of John fast often, and make prayers, and likewise *the disciples* of the Pharisees; but thine eat and drink?   Luke 11:1
34 And he said unto them, Can ye make the children of the bridechamber fast, while the bridegroom is with them?   John 3:29
35 But the days will come, when the bridegroom shall be taken away from them, and then shall they fast in those days.   Luke 17:22
36 And he spake also a parable unto them; No man putteth a piece of a new garment upon an old; if otherwise, then both the new maketh a rent, and the piece that was *taken* out of the new agreeth not with the old.
37 And no man putteth new wine into old bottles; else the new wine will burst the bottles, and be spilled, and the bottles shall perish.   Josh. 9:4
38 But new wine must be put into new bottles; and both are preserved.
39 No man also having drunk old *wine* ᵀstraightway desireth new: for he saith, The old is better.   *right away*

Jesus Has Authority over the Sabbath

6 And it came to pass on the second sabbath after the first, that he went through the corn fields; and his disciples plucked the ears of corn, and did eat, rubbing *them* in *their* hands.   Deut. 23:25; Matt. 12:1-8; Mark 2:23-28
2 And certain of the Pharisees said unto them, Why do ye that which is not lawful to do on the sabbath days?   Matt. 12:2
3 And Jesus answering them said, Have ye not read so much as this, what David did, when himself was an hungred, and they which were with him;   1 Sam. 21:3-6
4 How he went into the house of God, and did take and eat the shewbread, and gave also to them that were with him; which it is not lawful to eat but for the priests alone?
5 And he said unto them, That the Son of man is Lord also of the sabbath.

Principle Is Always Exacting

Luke 5:27, 28

To Matthew in his wealth, and to Andrew and Peter in their poverty, the same test was brought; the same consecration was made by each. At the moment of success, when the nets were filled with fish, and the impulses of the old life were strongest, Jesus asked the disciples at the sea to leave all for the work of the gospel. So every soul is tested as to whether the desire for temporal good or for fellowship with Christ is strongest.

Principle is always exacting. No man can succeed in the service of God unless his whole heart is in the work and he counts all things but loss for the excellency of the knowledge of Christ. No man who makes any reserve can be the disciple of Christ, much less can he be His colaborer. When men appreciate the great salvation, the self-sacrifice seen in Christ's life will be seen in theirs. Wherever He leads the way, they will rejoice to follow. *DA 273*

6:5 The Sabbath a Sign

These words are full of instruction and comfort. Because the Sabbath was made for man, it is the Lord's day. It belongs to Christ. For "all things were made by Him; and without Him was not anything made that was made" (John 1:3). Since He made all things, He made the Sabbath. . . . It points to Him as both the Creator and the Sanctifier. . . . Then the Sabbath is a sign of Christ's power to make us holy. *DA 288*

Jesus Heals on the Sabbath

6 And it came to pass also on another sabbath, that he entered into the synagogue and taught: and there was a man whose right hand was withered.   Matt. 12:9-14

7 And the scribes and Pharisees watched him, whether he would heal on the sabbath day; that they might find an accusation against him.   Mark 3:2

8 But he knew their thoughts, and said to the man which had the withered hand, Rise up, and stand forth in the midst. And he arose and stood forth.   Matt. 9:4

9 Then said Jesus unto them, I will ask you one thing; Is it lawful on the sabbath days to do good, or to do evil? to save life, or to destroy *it*?   Luke 14:3

10 And looking round about upon them all, he said unto the man, Stretch forth thy hand. And he did so: and his hand was restored whole as the other.   Mark 3:5

11 And they were filled with madness; and communed one with another what they might do to Jesus.   Acts 5:33

Jesus Chooses Twelve Disciples

12 And it came to pass in those days, that he went out into a mountain to pray, and continued all night in prayer to God.   Mark 1:35

13 And when it was day, he called *unto him* his disciples: and of them he chose twelve, whom also he named apostles;   Mark 6:7

14 Simon, (whom he also named Peter,) and Andrew his brother, James and John, Philip and Bartholomew,   Acts 1:13

15 Matthew and Thomas, James the *son* of Alphaeus, and Simon called Zelotes, Acts 1:13

16 And Judas *the brother* of James, and Judas Iscariot, which also was the traitor. John 14:22

Jesus Heals Many

17 And he came down with them, and stood in the plain, and the company of his disciples, and a great multitude of people out of all Judaea and Jerusalem, and from the sea coast of Tyre and Sidon, which came to hear him, and to be healed of their diseases;   Matt. 11:21

18 And they that were vexed with unclean spirits: and they were healed.

19 And the whole multitude sought to touch him: for there went virtue out of him, and healed *them* all. Matt. 9:20-21; 14:36; Mark 3:10

Jesus Teaches about Blessings and Curses

20 And he lifted up his eyes on his disciples, and said, Blessed *be ye* poor: for yours is the kingdom of God.   Luke 12:32

21 Blessed *are ye* that hunger now: for ye shall be filled. Blessed *are ye* that weep now: for ye shall laugh.   Matt. 5:4

22 Blessed are ye, when men shall hate you, and when they shall separate you *from their company*, and shall reproach *you*, and cast out your name as evil, for the Son of man's sake.   Matt. 10:22; John 12:42; 16:2

23 Rejoice ye in that day, and leap for joy: for, behold, your reward *is* great in heaven: for in the like manner did their fathers unto the prophets.   2 Chr. 36:16; Matt. 5:12; Rev. 21:7

24 But woe unto you that are rich! for ye have received your consolation.   Matt. 6:2

25 Woe unto you that are full! for ye shall hunger. Woe unto you that laugh now! for ye shall mourn and weep.   Prov. 14:13; Is. 65:13

26 Woe unto you, when all men shall speak well of you! for so did their fathers to the false prophets.   Is. 30:10

Love Your Enemies

27 But I say unto you which hear, Love your enemies, do good to them which hate you,   Prov. 25:21-22; Luke 6:35; 23:34

28 Bless them that curse you, and pray for them which despitefully use you.   1 Pet. 3:9

29 And unto him that [T]smiteth thee on the *one* cheek offer also the other; and him that taketh away thy [T]cloke forbid not *to take thy* coat also.   Is. 50:6 ◆ *strikes* ◆ *cloak*

30 Give to every man that asketh of thee; and of him that taketh away thy goods ask *them* not again.   Prov. 21:26

31 And as ye would that men should do to you, do ye also to them likewise.   Gal. 5:14

32 For if ye love them which love you, what thank have ye? for sinners also love those that love them.

33 And if ye do good to them which do good to you, what thank have ye? for sinners also do even the same.

34 And if ye lend *to them* of whom ye hope to receive, what thank have ye? for sinners also lend to sinners, to receive as much again.

35 But love ye your enemies, and do good, and lend, hoping for nothing again; and your reward shall be great, and ye shall be the children of the Highest: for he is kind unto the unthankful and *to* the evil.   2 Cor. 8:9

36 Be ye therefore merciful, as your Father also is merciful.   Matt. 5:48

Do Not Judge Others

37 Judge not, and ye shall not be judged: condemn not, and ye shall not be condemned: forgive, and ye shall be forgiven: Mark 11:25
38 Give, and it shall be given unto you; good measure, pressed down, and shaken together, and running over, shall men give into your bosom. For with the same measure that ye ᵀmete withal it shall be measured to you again.   Judg. 1:7; Ps. 79:12; Mark 4:24 ◆ measure out
39 And he spake a parable unto them, Can the blind lead the blind? shall they not both fall into the ditch?   Matt. 15:14
40 The disciple is not above his master: but every one that is perfect shall be as his master.
41 And why beholdest thou the mote that is in thy brother's eye, but perceivest not the beam that is in thine own eye?   John 8:7
42 Either how canst thou say to thy brother, Brother, let me pull out the ᵀmote that is in thine eye, when thou thyself beholdest not the beam that is in thine own eye? Thou hypocrite, cast out first the beam out of thine own eye, and then shalt thou see clearly to pull out the mote that is in thy brother's eye.   small particle

An Illustration of Trees and Their Fruit

43 For a good tree bringeth not forth corrupt fruit; neither doth a corrupt tree bring forth good fruit.
44 For every tree is known by his own fruit. For of thorns men do not gather figs, nor of a bramble bush gather they grapes. Matt. 12:33
45 A good man out of the good treasure of his heart bringeth forth that which is good; and an evil man out of the evil treasure of his heart bringeth forth that which is evil: for of the abundance of the heart his mouth speaketh.   Eph. 4:29

Build on the Rock

46 And why call ye me, Lord, Lord, and do not the things which I say?   Mal. 1:6
47 Whosoever cometh to me, and heareth my sayings, and doeth them, I will shew you to whom he is like: James 1:22-25
48 He is like a man which built an house, and digged deep, and laid the foundation on a rock: and when the flood arose, the stream beat ᵀvehemently upon that house, and could not shake it: for it was founded upon a rock.   strongly
49 But he that heareth, and doeth not, is like a man that without a foundation built an house upon the earth; against which the stream did beat vehemently, and immediately it fell; and the ruin of that house was great.

The Centurion's Faith

7 Now when he had ended all his sayings in the audience of the people, he entered into Capernaum.   Matt. 8:5-13
2 And a certain ᵀcenturion's servant, who was dear unto him, was sick, and ready to die.   commander of 100 soldiers
3 And when he heard of Jesus, he sent unto him the elders of the Jews, ᵀbeseeching him that he would come and heal his servant.   Matt. 8:5 ◆ begging
4 And when they came to Jesus, they ᵀbesought him instantly, saying, That he was worthy for whom he should do this: begged
5 For he loveth our nation, and he hath built us a synagogue.
6 Then Jesus went with them. And when he was now not far from the house, the centurion sent friends to him, saying unto him, Lord, trouble not thyself: for I am not worthy that thou shouldest enter under my roof: Luke 8:49
7 Wherefore neither thought I myself worthy to come unto thee: but say in a word, and my servant shall be healed.   Ps. 107:20
8 For I also am a man set under authority, having under me soldiers, and I say unto one, Go, and he goeth; and to another, Come, and he cometh; and to my servant, Do this, and he doeth it.
9 When Jesus heard these things, he marvelled at him, and turned him about, and said unto the people that followed him, I say unto you, I have not found so great faith, no, not in Israel.   Matt. 8:10
10 And they that were sent, returning to the house, found the servant whole that had been sick.

Jesus Raises the Widow's Son from the Dead

11 And it came to pass the day after, that he went into a city called Nain; and many of his disciples went with him, and much people.
12 Now when he came nigh to the gate of the city, behold, there was a dead man carried out, the only son of his mother, and she was a widow: and much people of the city was with her.   Luke 8:42
13 And when the Lord saw her, he had compassion on her, and said unto her, Weep not.   Luke 8:52
14 And he came and touched the bier: and they that bare him stood still. And he said, Young man, I say unto thee, Arise.
15 And he that was dead sat up, and began to speak. And he delivered him to his mother.
16 And there came a fear on all: and they

glorified God, saying, That a great prophet is risen up among us; and, That God hath visited his people. Matt. 9:8; Luke 1:68; 7:39

17 And this rumour of him went forth throughout all Judaea, and throughout all the region round about.

Jesus Reassures John the Baptist

18 And the disciples of John shewed him of all these things.

19 And John calling *unto him* two of his disciples sent *them* to Jesus, saying, Art thou he that should come? or look we for another? Luke 10:1

20 When the men were come unto him, they said, John Baptist hath sent us unto thee, saying, Art thou he that should come? or look we for another?

21 And in that same hour he cured many of *their* infirmities and plagues, and of evil spirits; and unto many *that were* blind he gave sight. Mark 3:10

22 Then Jesus answering said unto them, Go your way, and tell John what things ye have seen and heard; how that the blind see, the lame walk, the lepers are cleansed, the deaf hear, the dead are raised, to the poor the gospel is preached. Is. 29:18-19; 35:5-6; Luke 4:18

23 And blessed is *he*, whosoever shall not be offended in me. Is. 8:14-15

24 And when the messengers of John were departed, he began to speak unto the people concerning John, What went ye out into the wilderness for to see? A reed shaken with the wind? Luke 1:80

25 But what went ye out for to see? A man clothed in soft ᵀraiment? Behold, they which are gorgeously apparelled, and live delicately, are in kings' courts. *clothing*

26 But what went ye out for to see? A prophet? Yea, I say unto you, and much more than a prophet. Luke 1:76

27 This is *he*, of whom it is written, Behold, I send my messenger before thy face, which shall prepare thy way before thee. Mal. 3:1

28 For I say unto you, Among those that are born of women there is not a greater prophet than John the Baptist: but he that is least in the kingdom of God is greater than he.

29 And all the people that heard *him*, and the ᵀpublicans, justified God, being baptized with the baptism of John. Luke 3:12; 7:35 ♦ *tax collectors*

30 But the Pharisees and lawyers rejected the counsel of God against themselves, being not baptized of him. Matt. 22:35

31 And the Lord said, Whereunto then shall I liken the men of this generation? and to what are they like?

32 They are like unto children sitting in the marketplace, and calling one to another, and

saying, We have piped unto you, and ye have not danced; we have mourned to you, and ye have not wept.

33 For John the Baptist came neither eating bread nor drinking wine; and ye say, He hath a ᵀdevil. Matt. 3:4; Mark 1:6; Luke 1:15 ♦ *demon*

34 The Son of man is come eating and drinking; and ye say, Behold a gluttonous man, and a ᵀwinebibber, a friend of publicans and sinners! Luke 15:2 ♦ *drinker of wine*

35 But wisdom is justified of all her children. Prov. 8:32-36

A Sinful Woman Receives Forgiveness

36 And one of the Pharisees desired him that he would eat with him. And he went into the Pharisee's house, and sat down to meat. Luke 11:37

37 And, behold, a woman in the city, which was a sinner, when she knew that *Jesus* sat at meat in the Pharisee's house, brought an alabaster box of ointment,

38 And stood at his feet behind *him* weeping, and began to wash his feet with tears, and did wipe *them* with the hairs of her head, and kissed his feet, and anointed *them* with the ointment.

39 Now when the Pharisee which had bidden him saw *it*, he spake within himself, saying, This man, if he were a prophet, would have known who and what manner of woman *this is* that toucheth him: for she is a sinner. Luke 7:16; 15:2

40 And Jesus answering said unto him, Simon, I have somewhat to say unto thee. And he saith, Master, say on.

41 There was a certain creditor which had two debtors: the one owed five hundred pence, and the other fifty. Matt. 18:28

42 And when they had nothing to pay, he frankly forgave them both. Tell me therefore, which of them will love him most?

43 Simon answered and said, I suppose that *he*, to whom he forgave most. And he said unto him, Thou hast rightly judged.

44 And he turned to the woman, and said unto Simon, Seest thou this woman? I entered into thine house, thou gavest me no water for my feet: but she hath washed my feet with tears, and wiped *them* with the hairs of her head. Gen. 19:2; Judg. 19:21; 1 Tim. 5:10

45 Thou gavest me no kiss: but this woman since the time I came in hath not ceased to kiss my feet. 2 Sam. 15:5

46 My head with oil thou didst not anoint: but this woman hath anointed my feet with ointment. Ps. 23:5; Eccl. 9:8; Dan. 10:3

47 Wherefore I say unto thee, Her sins, which are many, are forgiven; for she loved much: but to whom little is forgiven, *the same* loveth little. 1 John 4:19

48 And he said unto her, Thy sins are for-given.   Matt. 9:2; Mark 2:5

49 And they that sat at meat with him began to say within themselves, Who is this that forgiveth sins also?

50 And he said to the woman, Thy faith hath saved thee; go in peace.   Matt. 9:22; Mark 5:34;

Women Who Supported Jesus

8 And it came to pass afterward, that he went throughout every city and village, preaching and shewing the glad tidings of the kingdom of God: and the twelve *were* with him,   Matt. 4:23

2 And certain women, which had been healed of evil spirits and infirmities, Mary called Magdalene, out of whom went seven devils,   Matt. 27:55-56; Mark 15:40-41; 16:9

3 And Joanna the wife of Chuza Herod's steward, and Susanna, and many others, which ministered unto him of their sub-stance.   Luke 24:10

The Parable of the Sower

4 And when much people were gathered to-gether, and were come to him out of every city, he spake by a parable:

5 A sower went out to sow his seed: and as he sowed, some fell by the way side; and it was ᵀtrodden down, and the fowls of the air devoured it.   *trampled*

6 And some fell upon a rock; and as soon as it was sprung up, it withered away, because it lacked moisture.

7 And some fell among thorns; and the thorns sprang up with it, and choked it. Jer. 4:3

8 And other fell on good ground, and sprang up, and bare fruit an hundredfold. And when he had said these things, he cried, He that hath ears to hear, let him hear.   Gen. 26:12; Matt. 11:15; Rev. 2:7

9 And his disciples asked him, saying, What might this parable be?   Matt. 13:10

10 And he said, Unto you it is given to know the mysteries of the kingdom of God: but to others in parables; that seeing they might not see, and hearing they might not under-stand.   Is. 6:9; Matt. 11:25; Rom. 16:25

11 Now the parable is this: The seed is the word of God.   Matt. 13:19

12 Those by the way side are they that hear; then cometh the ᵀdevil, and taketh away the word out of their hearts, lest they should believe and be saved.   *false accuser*

13 They on the rock *are they*, which, when they hear, receive the word with joy; and these have no root, which for a while believe, and in time of temptation fall away.   Is. 58:2

14 And that which fell among thorns are they, which, when they have heard, go forth, and are choked with cares and riches and

pleasures of *this* life, and bring no fruit to perfection.   1 Tim. 6:9-10

> **8:13 Who Will Not Endure the Test?**
>
> True holiness is wholeness in the service of God. . . .
>
> Love must be the principle of action. Love is the underlying principle of God's govern-ment in heaven and earth, and it must be the foundation of the Christian's character. . . .
>
> The thought of His honor and glory will come before anything else. . . .
>
> This is the religion of Christ. Anything short of it is a deception. . . . The effort to serve both self and Christ makes one a stony-ground hearer, and he will not endure when the test comes upon him. *COL 48–50*

15 But that on the good ground are they, which in an honest and good heart, having heard the word, keep *it*, and bring forth fruit with patience.   Phil. 1:11

16 No man, when he hath lighted a can-dle, covereth it with a vessel, or putteth *it* under a bed; but setteth *it* on a candle-stick, that they which enter in may see the light.   Mark 4:21-22; Luke 11:33

17 For nothing is secret, that shall not be made manifest; neither *any thing* hid, that shall not be known and come abroad.   Matt. 10:26

18 Take heed therefore how ye hear: for who-soever hath, to him shall be given; and who-soever hath not, from him shall be taken even that which he seemeth to have.   Matt. 13:12

Jesus Describes His True Family

19 Then came to him *his* mother and his brethren, and could not come at him for the press.   Matt. 12:46-50

20 And it was told him *by certain* which said, Thy mother and thy brethren stand without, desiring to see thee.

21 And he answered and said unto them, My mother and my brethren are these which hear the word of God, and do it.   James 1:22

Jesus Calms the Sea

22 Now it came to pass on a certain day, that he went into a ship with his disciples: and he said unto them, Let us go over unto the other side of the lake. And they launched forth.

23 But as they sailed he fell asleep: and there came down a storm of wind on the lake; and they were filled *with water*, and were in jeop-ardy.

24 And they came to him, and awoke him, saying, Master, master, we perish. Then he arose, and rebuked the wind and the raging of the water: and they ceased, and there was a calm.   Ps. 65:7

25 And he said unto them, Where is your faith? And they being afraid wondered,

saying one to another, What manner of man is this! for he commandeth even the winds and water, and they obey him.

8:25 We Must Rest in Perfect Peace

When Jesus was awakened to meet the storm, He was in perfect peace. . . . But He rested not in the possession of almighty power. It was not as the "Master of earth and sea and sky" that He reposed in quiet. That power He had laid down, and He says, "I can of Mine own self do nothing" (John 5:30). He trusted in the Father's might. . . .

As Jesus rested by faith in the Father's care, so we are to rest in the care of our Saviour. *DA 336*

Jesus Heals a Demon-possessed Man

26 And they arrived at the country of the Gadarenes, which is over against Galilee.

27 And when he went forth to land, there met him out of the city a certain man, which had devils long time, and ware no clothes, neither abode in *any* house, but in the tombs.

28 When he saw Jesus, he cried out, and fell down before him, and with a loud voice said, What have I to do with thee, Jesus, *thou* Son of God most high? I ᵀbeseech thee, torment me not.   Matt. 8:29 ◆ *beg*

29 (For he had commanded the unclean spirit to come out of the man. For oftentimes it had caught him: and he was kept bound with chains and in ᵀfetters; and he brake the bands, and was driven of the devil into the wilderness.)   *chains*

30 And Jesus asked him, saying, What is thy name? And he said, Legion: because many devils were entered into him.   Matt. 26:53

31 And they besought him that he would not command them to go out into the deep.

32 And there was there an herd of many swine feeding on the mountain: and they ᵀbesought him that he would suffer them to enter into them. And he suffered them.   *begged*

33 Then went the devils out of the man, and entered into the swine: and the herd ran violently down a steep place into the lake, and were choked.

34 When they that fed *them* saw what was done, they fled, and went and told *it* in the city and in the country.

35 Then they went out to see what was done; and came to Jesus, and found the man, out of whom the devils were departed, sitting at the feet of Jesus, clothed, and in his right mind: and they were afraid.   Luke 8:27; 10:39

36 They also which saw *it* told them by what means he that was possessed of the devils was healed.

37 Then the whole multitude of the country of the Gadarenes round about besought him to depart from them; for they were taken with great fear: and he went up into the ship, and returned back again.   Acts 16:39

38 Now the man out of whom the devils were departed besought him that he might be with him: but Jesus sent him away, saying,   Mark 5:18-20

39 Return to thine own house, and shew how great things God hath done unto thee. And he went his way, and published throughout the whole city how great things Jesus had done unto him.   Ps. 66:16

Jesus Raises a Dead Girl and Cures a Bleeding Woman

40 And it came to pass, that, when Jesus was returned, the people *gladly* received him: for they were all waiting for him.   Matt. 9:1

41 And, behold, there came a man named Jairus, and he was a ruler of the synagogue: and he fell down at Jesus' feet, and besought him that he would come into his house: Mark 5:22-43

42 For he had one only daughter, about twelve years of age, and she lay a dying. But as he went the people thronged him.   Luke 7:12

43 And a woman having an issue of blood twelve years, which had spent all her living upon physicians, neither could be healed of any,

44 Came behind *him*, and touched the border of his garment: and immediately her issue of blood ᵀstanched.   Deut. 22:12 ◆ *stopped*

45 And Jesus said, Who touched me? When all denied, Peter and they that were with him said, Master, the multitude throng thee and press *thee*, and sayest thou, Who touched me?

46 And Jesus said, Somebody hath touched me: for I perceive that virtue is gone out of me.   Luke 6:19

47 And when the woman saw that she was not hid, she came trembling, and falling down before him, she declared unto him before all the people for what cause she had touched him, and how she was healed immediately.

48 And he said unto her, Daughter, be of good comfort: thy faith hath made thee whole; go in peace.   Matt. 9:22

49 While he yet spake, there cometh one from the ruler of the synagogue's *house*, saying to him, Thy daughter is dead; trouble not the Master.   Luke 7:6

50 But when Jesus heard *it*, he answered him, saying, Fear not: believe only, and she shall be made whole.   Mark 5:36

8:48 A Most Effectual Testimony

Our confession of His faithfulness is Heaven's chosen agency for revealing Christ to the world. We are to acknowledge His grace as made known through the holy men of old; but that which will be most effectual is the testimony of our own experience. . . . These precious acknowledgments to the praise of the glory of His grace, when supported by a Christ-like life, have an irresistible power that works for the salvation of souls. *DA 347*

51 And when he came into the house, he suffered no man to go in, save Peter, and James, and John, and the father and the mother of the maiden. Mark 14:33
52 And all wept, and bewailed her: but he said, Weep not; she is not dead, but sleepeth. Luke 23:27
53 And they laughed him to scorn, knowing that she was dead.
54 And he put them all out, and took her by the hand, and called, saying, Maid, arise.
55 And her spirit came again, and she arose ᵀstraightway: and he commanded to give her meat. John 11:44 ◆ *right away*
56 And her parents were astonished: but he charged them that they should tell no man what was done. Matt. 8:4

Jesus Sends Out the Twelve

9 Then he called his twelve disciples together, and gave them power and authority over all devils, and to cure diseases.
2 And he sent them to preach the kingdom of God, and to heal the sick. Matt. 3:2
3 And he said unto them, Take nothing for *your* journey, neither ᵀstaves, nor ᵀscrip, neither bread, neither money; neither have two coats apiece. Luke 10:4-12; 22:35 ◆ *clubs* or *rods* ◆ *sack*
4 And whatsoever house ye enter into, there abide, and thence depart.
5 And whosoever will not receive you, when ye go out of that city, shake off the very dust from your feet for a testimony against them. Acts 13:51
6 And they departed, and went through the towns, preaching the gospel, and healing every where.

Herod Wants to Meet Jesus

7 Now Herod the ᵀtetrarch heard of all that was done by him: and he was perplexed, because that it was said of some, that John was risen from the dead; Matt. 14:1-12 ◆ *ruler of one-fourth*
8 And of some, that Elias had appeared; and of others, that one of the old prophets was risen again. Luke 9:19
9 And Herod said, John have I beheaded: but who is this, of whom I hear such things? And he desired to see him. Luke 23:8

Jesus Feeds More than Five Thousand

10 And the apostles, when they were returned, told him all that they had done. And he took them, and went aside privately into a desert place belonging to the city called Bethsaida. Matt. 11:21
11 And the people, when they knew *it*, followed him: and he received them, and spake unto them of the kingdom of God, and healed them that had need of healing.
12 And when the day began to wear away, then came the twelve, and said unto him, Send the multitude away, that they may go into the towns and country round about, and lodge, and get ᵀvictuals: for we are here in a desert place. Matt. 15:23 ◆ *food*
13 But he said unto them, Give ye them to eat. And they said, We have no more but five loaves and two fishes; except we should go and buy meat for all this people. 2 Kin. 4:42-43
14 For they were about five thousand men. And he said to his disciples, Make them sit down by fifties in a company.
15 And they did so, and made them all sit down.
16 Then he took the five loaves and the two fishes, and looking up to heaven, he blessed them, and brake, and gave to the disciples to set before the multitude. Matt. 14:19
17 And they did eat, and were all filled: and there was taken up of fragments that remained to them twelve baskets.

Peter Declares His Faith

18 And it came to pass, as he was alone praying, his disciples were with him: and he asked them, saying, Whom say the people that I am? Matt. 16:13-16
19 They answering said, John the Baptist; but some *say*, Elias; and others *say*, that one of the old prophets is risen again. Luke 9:7-8
20 He said unto them, But whom say ye that I am? Peter answering said, The Christ of God. John 1:49
21 And he straitly charged them, and commanded *them* to tell no man that thing;

Jesus Foretells His Death and Resurrection

22 Saying, The Son of man must suffer many things, and be rejected of the elders and chief priests and scribes, and be slain, and be raised the third day. Luke 24:7

Take Up Your Cross Daily

23 And he said to *them* all, If any *man* will come after me, let him deny himself, and take up his cross daily, and follow me. Matt. 10:38-39
24 For whosoever will save his life shall lose it: but whosoever will lose his life for my sake, the same shall save it. Luke 17:33

25 For what is a man advantaged, if he gain the whole world, and lose himself, or be cast away?

26 For whosoever shall be ashamed of me and of my words, of him shall the Son of man be ashamed, when he shall come in his own glory, and *in his* Father's, and of the holy angels.   Matt. 16:27

27 But I tell you of a truth, there be some standing here, which shall not taste of death, till they see the kingdom of God.   Matt. 16:28

The Transfiguration

28 And it came to pass about an eight days after these sayings, he took Peter and John and James, and went up into a mountain to pray.   Luke 6:12

29 And as he prayed, the fashion of his ᵀcountenance was altered, and his ᵀraiment *was* white *and* ᵀglistering. *appearance ◆ clothing ◆ glistening*

30 And, behold, there talked with him two men, which were Moses and Elias:

31 Who appeared in glory, and spake of his decease which he should accomplish at Jerusalem.

32 But Peter and they that were with him were heavy with sleep: and when they were awake, they saw his glory, and the two men that stood with him.   Dan. 8:18

33 And it came to pass, as they departed from him, Peter said unto Jesus, Master, it is good for us to be here: and let us make three tabernacles; one for thee, and one for Moses, and one for Elias: not knowing what he said.   Mark 9:5-6

34 While he thus spake, there came a cloud, and overshadowed them: and they feared as they entered into the cloud.

35 And there came a voice out of the cloud, saying, This is my beloved Son: hear him.

36 And when the voice was past, Jesus was found alone. And they kept *it* close, and told no man in those days any of those things which they had seen.   Matt. 17:9

Jesus Heals a Demon-possessed Boy

37 And it came to pass, that on the next day, when they were come down from the hill, much people met him.

38 And, behold, a man of the company cried out, saying, Master, I ᵀbeseech thee, look upon my son: for he is mine only child.   Luke 7:12 ◆ *beg*

39 And, lo, a spirit taketh him, and he suddenly crieth out; and it teareth him that he foameth again, and bruising him hardly departeth from him.

40 And I ᵀbesought thy disciples to cast him out; and they could not.   Luke 9:1 ◆ *begged*

41 And Jesus answering said, O faithless and perverse generation, how long shall I be with you, and suffer you? Bring thy son ᵀhither.   Deut. 32:5 ◆ *here*

42 And as he was yet a coming, the devil threw him down, and tare *him*. And Jesus rebuked the unclean spirit, and healed the child, and delivered him again to his father. Luke 7:15

Jesus Again Foretells His Betrayal, Death, and Resurrection

43 And they were all amazed at the mighty power of God. But while they wondered every one at all things which Jesus did, he said unto his disciples,

44 Let these sayings sink down into your ears: for the Son of man shall be delivered into the hands of men.   Luke 9:22

45 But they understood not this saying, and it was hid from them, that they perceived

---

Great Success Depends Upon Self Being Emptied

Luke 9:37–42

The words of Christ pointing to His death had brought sadness and doubt. And the selection of the three disciples to accompany Jesus to the mountain had excited the jealousy of the nine. Instead of strengthening their faith by prayer and meditation on the words of Christ, they had been dwelling on their discouragements and personal grievances. In this state of darkness they had undertaken the conflict with Satan.

In order to succeed in such a conflict they must come to the work in a different spirit. Their faith must be strengthened by fervent prayer and fasting, and humiliation of heart. They must be emptied of self, and be filled with the Spirit and power of God. Earnest, persevering supplication to God in faith—faith that leads to entire dependence upon God, and unreserved consecration to His work—can alone avail to bring men the Holy Spirit's aid in the battle against principalities and powers, the rulers of the darkness of this world, and wicked spirits in high places. . . .

If you have faith like this, you will lay hold upon God's word, and upon all the helpful agencies He has appointed. Thus your faith will strengthen, and will bring to your aid the power of heaven. The obstacles that are piled by Satan across your path, though apparently as insurmountable as the eternal hills, shall disappear before the demand of faith. "Nothing shall be impossible unto you." *DA 431*

it not: and they feared to ask him of that saying. Mark 9:32

Greatness in the Kingdom

46 Then there arose a reasoning among them, which of them should be greatest.

47 And Jesus, perceiving the thought of their heart, took a child, and set him by him,

48 And said unto them, Whosoever shall receive this child in my name receiveth me: and whosoever shall receive me receiveth him that sent me: for he that is least among you all, the same shall be great. Luke 10:16

Using the Name of Jesus

49 And John answered and said, Master, we saw one casting out devils in thy name; and we forbad him, because he followeth not with us. Mark 9:38-40

50 And Jesus said unto him, Forbid *him* not: for he that is not against us is for us. Matt. 12:30

A Samaritan Village Rejects Jesus

51 And it came to pass, when the time was come that he should be received up, he stedfastly set his face to go to Jerusalem, Mark 16:19

52 And sent messengers before his face: and they went, and entered into a village of the Samaritans, to make ready for him. Matt. 10:5; Luke 10:1, 33

53 And they did not receive him, because his face was as though he would go to Jerusalem. John 4:9

54 And when his disciples James and John saw *this*, they said, Lord, wilt thou that we command fire to come down from heaven, and consume them, even as Elias did?

55 But he turned, and rebuked them, and said, Ye know not what manner of spirit ye are of.

56 For the Son of man is not come to destroy men's lives, but to save *them*. And they went to another village.

What It Takes to Follow Jesus

57 And it came to pass, that, as they went in the way, a certain *man* said unto him, Lord, I will follow thee whithersoever thou goest. Luke 9:51

58 And Jesus said unto him, Foxes have holes, and birds of the air *have* nests; but the Son of man hath not where to lay *his* head.

59 And he said unto another, Follow me. But he said, Lord, suffer me first to go and bury my father.

60 Jesus said unto him, Let the dead bury their dead: but go thou and preach the kingdom of God.

61 And another also said, Lord, I will follow thee; but let me first go bid them farewell, which are at home at my house. 1 Kin. 19:20

62 And Jesus said unto him, No man, having put his hand to the plough, and looking back, is fit for the kingdom of God.

Jesus Sends out Seventy Disciples

10 After these things the Lord appointed other seventy also, and sent them two and two before his face into every city and place, whither he himself would come. Num. 11:16; Luke 9:52

Why, Why, Why?

Luke 9:51

To the heart of Christ it was a bitter task to press His way against the fears, disappointment, and unbelief of His beloved disciples. It was hard to lead them forward to the anguish and despair that awaited them at Jerusalem. And Satan was at hand to press his temptations upon the Son of man. Why should He now go to Jerusalem, to certain death? All around Him were souls hungering for the bread of life. On every hand were suffering ones waiting for His word of healing. The work to be wrought by the gospel of His grace was but just begun. And He was full of the vigor of manhood's prime. Why not go forward to the vast fields of the world with the words of His grace, the touch of His healing power? Why not take to Himself the joy of giving light and gladness to those darkened and sorrowing millions? Why leave the harvest gathering to His disciples, so weak in faith, so dull of understanding, so slow to act? Why face death now, and leave the work in its infancy? The foe who in the wilderness had confronted Christ assailed Him now with fierce and subtle temptations. Had Jesus yielded for a moment, had He changed His course in the least particular to save Himself, Satan's agencies would have triumphed, and the world would have been lost.

But Jesus had "steadfastly set His face to go to Jerusalem." The one law of His life was the Father's will. *DA 486*

2 Therefore said he unto them, The harvest truly *is* great, but the labourers *are* few: pray ye therefore the Lord of the harvest, that he would send forth labourers into his harvest.   2 Thess. 3:1

3 Go your ways: behold, I send you forth as lambs among wolves.   Matt. 10:16

4 Carry neither purse, nor ᵀscrip, nor shoes: and salute no man by the way. 2 Kin. 4:29 ◆ *sack*

5 And into whatsoever house ye enter, first say, Peace *be* to this house.   1 Sam. 25:6

6 And if the son of peace be there, your peace shall rest upon it: if not, it shall turn to you again.   Ps. 35:13

7 And in the same house remain, eating and drinking such things as they give: for the labourer is worthy of his hire. Go not from house to house.

8 And into whatsoever city ye enter, and they receive you, eat such things as are set before you: 1 Cor. 10:27

9 And heal the sick that are therein, and say unto them, The kingdom of God is come nigh unto you.   Matt. 3:2; Luke 10:11

10 But into whatsoever city ye enter, and they receive you not, go your ways out into the streets of the same, and say,

11 Even the very dust of your city, which ᵀcleaveth on us, we do wipe off against you: notwithstanding be ye sure of this, that the kingdom of God is come nigh unto you.   Luke 10:9 ◆ *clings*

12 But I say unto you, that it shall be more tolerable in that day for Sodom, than for that city.   Matt. 10:15; 11:24

13 Woe unto thee, Chorazin! woe unto thee, Bethsaida! for if the mighty works had been done in Tyre and Sidon, which have been done in you, they had a great while ago repented, sitting in sackcloth and ashes.   Is. 23; Joel 3:4-8

14 But it shall be more tolerable for Tyre and Sidon at the judgment, than for you. Luke 12:47

15 And thou, Capernaum, which art exalted to heaven, shalt be thrust down to hell.Is. 14:13-15

16 He that heareth you heareth me; and he that despiseth you despiseth me; and he that despiseth me despiseth him that sent me.   Matt. 10:40; John 12:48; 1 Thess. 4:8

17 And the seventy returned again with joy, saying, Lord, even the devils are subject unto us through thy name.   Mark 16:17

18 And he said unto them, I beheld Satan as lightning fall from heaven.   Rev. 9:1

19 Behold, I give unto you power to tread on serpents and scorpions, and over all the power of the enemy: and nothing shall by any means hurt you.Ps. 91:13; Mark 16:18; Acts 28:5

10:16 Results of Rejecting Truth

To reject the Lord's servants is to reject Christ Himself. . . .

With a great show of prudence the rabbis had warned the people against receiving the new doctrines taught by this new teacher; for His theories and practices were contrary to the teachings of the fathers. . . . Thus many rejected the truth that would have proved the saving of the soul.

Our condemnation in the judgment will not result from the fact that we have been in error, but from the fact that we have neglected heaven-sent opportunities for learning what is truth. *DA 489, 490*

20 Notwithstanding in this rejoice not, that the spirits are subject unto you; but rather rejoice, because your names are written in heaven.   Ex. 32:32; Ps. 69:28; Dan. 12:1

21 In that hour Jesus rejoiced in spirit, and said, I thank thee, O Father, Lord of heaven and earth, that thou hast hid these things from the wise and prudent, and hast revealed them unto babes: even so, Father; for so it seemed good in thy sight.   Ps. 8:2

22 All things are delivered to me of my Father: and no man knoweth who the Son is, but the Father; and who the Father is, but the Son, and *he* to whom the Son will reveal *him*.   Matt. 28:18; John 1:18; 10:15

23 And he turned him unto *his* disciples, and said privately, Blessed *are* the eyes which see the things that ye see: Matt. 13:16-17

24 For I tell you, that many prophets and kings have desired to see those things which ye see, and have not seen *them*; and to hear those things which ye hear, and have not heard *them*.   John 8:56

10:25–28 Profession Alone Means Nothing

The lesson is no less needed in the world today than when it fell from the lips of Jesus. Selfishness and cold formality have well-nigh extinguished the fire of love, and dispelled the graces that should make fragrant the character. . . . Unless there is practical self-sacrifice for the good of others, in the family circle, in the neighborhood, in the church, and wherever we may be, then whatever our profession, we are not Christians. *DA 504*

The Good Samaritan

25 And, behold, a certain lawyer stood up, and tempted him, saying, Master, what shall I do to inherit eternal life?   Luke 18:18

26 He said unto him, What is written in the law? how readest thou?

27 And he answering said, Thou shalt love the Lord thy God with all thy heart, and with all thy soul, and with all thy strength, and with all thy mind; and thy neighbour as thyself. *Lev. 19:18; Deut. 6:5; Matt. 19:19*

> **Christian Behavior** See Romans 12:9–19.

28 And he said unto him, Thou hast answered right: this do, and thou shalt live. *Lev. 18:5*
29 But he, willing to justify himself, said unto Jesus, And who is my neighbour? *Luke 16:15*
30 And Jesus answering said, A certain *man* went down from Jerusalem to Jericho, and fell among thieves, which stripped him of his ᵀraiment, and wounded *him*, and departed, leaving *him* half dead. *clothing*
31 And by chance there came down a certain priest that way: and when he saw him, he passed by on the other side.
32 And likewise a Levite, when he was at the place, came and looked *on him*, and passed by on the other side.
33 But a certain Samaritan, as he journeyed, came where he was: and when he saw him, he had compassion *on him*, *Matt. 10:5*
34 And went to *him*, and bound up his wounds, pouring in oil and wine, and set him on his own beast, and brought him to an inn, and took care of him.
35 And on the morrow when he departed, he took out two pence, and gave *them* to the host, and said unto him, Take care of him; and whatsoever thou spendest more, when I come again, I will repay thee.
36 Which now of these three, thinkest thou, was neighbour unto him that fell among the thieves?
37 And he said, He that shewed mercy on him. Then said Jesus unto him, Go, and do thou likewise. *2 Cor. 8:9*

> **10:29–37 Love the Basis of Godliness**
>
> Gospel religion is Christ in the life—a living, active principle. It is the grace of Christ revealed in character and wrought out in good works. The principles of the gospel cannot be disconnected from any department of practical life. Every line of Christian experience and labor is to be a representation of the life of Christ.
>
> Love is the basis of godliness. Whatever the profession, no man has pure love to God unless he has unselfish love for his brother. *COL 384*

Mary and Martha

38 Now it came to pass, as they went, that he entered into a certain village: and a certain woman named Martha received him into her house.

39 And she had a sister called Mary, which also sat at Jesus' feet, and heard his word.
40 But Martha was ᵀcumbered about much serving, and came to him, and said, Lord, dost thou not care that my sister hath left me to serve alone? bid her therefore that she help me. *distracted*
41 And Jesus answered and said unto her, Martha, Martha, thou art careful and troubled about many things: *Matt. 6:25-34*
42 But one thing is needful: and Mary hath chosen that good part, which shall not be taken away from her. *Ps. 27:4*

> **10:38–42 Spiritual Advancement a Must**
>
> The "one thing" that Martha needed was a calm, devotional spirit, a deeper anxiety for knowledge concerning the future, immortal life, and the graces necessary for spiritual advancement. . . . The cause of Christ needs careful, energetic workers. There is a wide field for the Marthas, with their zeal in active religious work. But let them first sit with Mary at the feet of Jesus. Let diligence, promptness, and energy be sanctified by the grace of Christ; then the life will be an unconquerable power for good. *DA 525*

Jesus Teaches How to Pray

11 And it came to pass, that, as he was praying in a certain place, when he ceased, one of his disciples said unto him, Lord, teach us to pray, as John also taught his disciples. *Luke 9:18*

> **11:1 The Mighty Power of Prayer**
>
> The hearts of the listening disciples were deeply moved. They had marked how often [Jesus] spent long hours in solitude in communion with His Father. . . . It was from hours spent with God that He came forth, morning by morning, to bring the light of heaven to men. The disciples had come to connect His hours of prayer with the power of His words and works. *MB 102,103*

2 And he said unto them, When ye pray, say, Our Father which art in heaven, Hallowed be thy name. Thy kingdom come. Thy will be done, as in heaven, so in earth. *Eccl. 5:2*
3 Give us day by day our daily bread. *Prov. 30:8*
4 And forgive us our sins; for we also forgive every one that is indebted to us. And lead us not into temptation; but deliver us from evil. *Matt. 26:41*
5 And he said unto them, Which of you shall have a friend, and shall go unto him at midnight, and say unto him, Friend, lend me three loaves;

6 For a friend of mine in his journey is come to me, and I have nothing to set before him? 7 And he from within shall answer and say, Trouble me not: the door is now shut, and my children are with me in bed; I cannot rise and give thee. 8 I say unto you, Though he will not rise and give him, because he is his friend, yet because of his ᵀimportunity he will rise and give him as many as he needeth. *persistence* 9 And I say unto you, Ask, and it shall be given you; seek, and ye shall find; knock, and it shall be opened unto you. Matt. 21:22 10 For every one that asketh receiveth; and he that seeketh findeth; and to him that knocketh it shall be opened. 11 If a son shall ask bread of any of you that is a father, will he give him a stone? or if *he ask* a fish, will he for a fish give him a serpent? 12 Or if he shall ask an egg, will he offer him a scorpion? 13 If ye then, being evil, know how to give good gifts unto your children: how much more shall *your* heavenly Father give the Holy Spirit to them that ask him? Gen. 8:21; Matt. 7:11

Jesus Is Accused of Working with Beelzebub

14 And he was casting out a ᵀdevil, and it was ᵀdumb. And it came to pass, when the devil was gone out, the dumb spake; and the people wondered. *demon ◆ mute* 15 But some of them said, He casteth out devils through Beelzebub the chief of the devils. Matt. 9:34 16 And others, tempting *him*, sought of him a sign from heaven. 17 But he, knowing their thoughts, said unto them, Every kingdom divided against itself is brought to desolation; and a house *divided* against a house falleth. Matt. 9:4 18 If Satan also be divided against himself, how shall his kingdom stand? because ye say that I cast out devils through Beelzebub. 19 And if I by Beelzebub cast out devils, by whom do your sons cast *them* out? therefore shall they be your judges. 20 But if I with the finger of God cast out devils, no doubt the kingdom of God is come upon you. Ex. 8:19 21 When a strong man armed keepeth his palace, his goods are in peace: 22 But when a stronger than he shall come upon him, and overcome him, he taketh from him all his armour wherein he trusted, and divideth his spoils. Is. 49:24-25 23 He that is not with me is against me: and he that gathereth not with me scattereth. 24 When the unclean spirit is gone out of a man, he walketh through dry places,

seeking rest; and finding none, he saith, I will return unto my house whence I came out. Matt. 12:43-45 25 And when he cometh, he findeth *it* swept and garnished. 26 Then goeth he, and taketh *to him* seven other spirits more wicked than himself; and they enter in, and dwell there: and the last *state* of that man is worse than the first. John 5:14 27 And it came to pass, as he spake these things, a certain woman of the company lifted up her voice, and said unto him, Blessed *is* the womb that bare thee, and the ᵀpaps which thou hast sucked. Luke 1:48 ◆ *breasts* 28 But he said, Yea rather, blessed *are* they that hear the word of God, and keep it.

The Sign of Jonah

29 And when the people were gathered thick together, he began to say, This is an evil generation: they seek a sign; and there shall no sign be given it, but the sign of Jonas the prophet. Mark 8:11-12 30 For as Jonas was a sign unto the Ninevites, so shall also the Son of man be to this generation. Jon. 1:17 31 The queen of the south shall rise up in the judgment with the men of this generation, and condemn them: for she came from the utmost parts of the earth to hear the wisdom of Solomon; and, behold, a greater than Solomon *is* here. 2 Chr. 9:1; Jer. 3:11; Rom. 2:27 32 The men of Nineve shall rise up in the judgment with this generation, and shall condemn it: for they repented at the preaching of Jonas; and, behold, a greater than Jonas *is* here.

Jesus Talks about Light

33 No man, when he hath lighted a candle, putteth *it* in a secret place, neither under a bushel, but on a candlestick, that they which come in may see the light. 34 The light of the body is the eye: therefore when thine eye is ᵀsingle, thy whole body also is full of light; but when *thine eye* is evil, thy body also *is* full of darkness. Matt. 6:22-23 ◆ *healthy* 35 Take heed therefore that the light which is in thee be not darkness. 36 If thy whole body therefore *be* full of light, having no part dark, the whole shall be full of light, as when the bright shining of a candle doth give thee light.

Jesus Rebukes the Hypocrisy of the Religious Leaders

37 And as he spake, a certain Pharisee ᵀbesought him to dine with him: and he went in, and sat down to meat. Luke 7:36 ◆ *begged* 38 And when the Pharisee saw *it*, he

marvelled that he had not first washed before dinner.

39 And the Lord said unto him, Now do ye Pharisees make clean the outside of the cup and the platter; but your inward part is full of ᵀravening and wickedness.   *greed*

40 *Ye fools,* did not he that made that which is without make that which is within also?

41 But rather give ᵀalms of such things as ye have; and, behold, all things are clean unto you.   Luke 12:33; 16:9; Titus 1:15 ◆ *acts of mercy*

42 But woe unto you, Pharisees! for ye tithe mint and rue and all manner of herbs, and pass over judgment and the love of God: these ought ye to have done, and not to leave the other undone.   Mic. 6:8; Matt. 23:23; Luke 18:12

43 Woe unto you, Pharisees! for ye love the uppermost seats in the synagogues, and greetings in the markets. Mark 12:38-39; Luke 20:46

44 Woe unto you, scribes and Pharisees, hypocrites! for ye are as graves which appear not, and the men that walk over *them* are not aware *of them*.

45 Then answered one of the lawyers, and said unto him, Master, thus saying thou reproachest us also.

46 And he said, Woe unto you also, *ye* lawyers! for ye ᵀlade men with burdens grievous to be borne, and ye yourselves touch not the burdens with one of your fingers.   *load*

47 Woe unto you! for ye build the sepulchres of the prophets, and your fathers killed them.   Matt. 23:29-33

48 Truly ye bear witness that ye allow the deeds of your fathers: for they indeed killed them, and ye build their sepulchres.

49 Therefore also said the wisdom of God, I will send them prophets and apostles, and *some* of them they shall slay and persecute:

50 That the blood of all the prophets, which was shed from the foundation of the world, may be required of this generation;

51 From the blood of Abel unto the blood of Zacharias, which perished between the altar and the temple: ᵀverily I say unto you, It shall be required of this generation. Matt. 23:35 ◆ *truly*

52 Woe unto you, lawyers! for ye have taken away the key of knowledge: ye entered not in yourselves, and them that were entering in ye hindered.   Mal. 2:7; Matt. 23:13

53 And as he said these things unto them, the scribes and the Pharisees began to urge *him* ᵀvehemently, and to provoke him to speak of many things: *strongly*

54 Laying wait for him, and seeking to catch something out of his mouth, that they might accuse him.   Matt. 22:15; Mark 12:13

Jesus Encourages His Disciples

12 In the mean time, when there were gathered together an innumerable multitude of people, insomuch that they trode one upon another, he began to say unto his disciples first of all, Beware ye of the leaven of the Pharisees, which is hypocrisy.

2 For there is nothing covered, that shall not be revealed; neither hid, that shall not be known.   Mark 4:22; Luke 8:17

3 Therefore whatsoever ye have spoken in darkness shall be heard in the light; and that which ye have spoken in the ear in closets shall be proclaimed upon the housetops.

4 And I say unto you my friends, Be not afraid of them that kill the body, and after that have no more that they can do.   Jer. 1:8

5 But I will forewarn you whom ye shall fear: Fear him, which after he hath killed hath power to cast into hell; yea, I say unto you, Fear him.   Ps. 9:17

6 Are not five sparrows sold for two farthings, and not one of them is forgotten before God?   Matt. 10:29

7 But even the very hairs of your head are all numbered. Fear not therefore: ye are of more value than many sparrows. 1 Sam. 14:45

8 Also I say unto you, Whosoever shall

A Vital Lesson of Leaven

Luke 12:1

The leaven—something wholly from without—must be put into the meal before the desired change can be wrought in it. So the grace of God must be received by the sinner before he can be fitted for the kingdom of glory. . . . The renewing energy must come from God. The change can be made only by the Holy Spirit. All who would be saved, high or low, rich or poor, must submit to the working of this power.

As the leaven, when mingled with the meal, works from within outward, so it is by the renewing of the heart that the grace of God works to transform the life. No mere external change is sufficient to bring us into harmony with God. There are many who try to reform by correcting this or that bad habit, and they hope in this way to become Christians, but they are beginning in the wrong place. Our first work is with the heart.

A profession of faith and the possession of truth in the soul are two different things. The mere knowledge of truth is not enough. We may possess this, but the tenor of our thoughts may not be changed. The heart must be converted and sanctified. *COL 96, 97*

confess me before men, him shall the Son of man also confess before the angels of God: Luke 15:10

9 But he that denieth me before men shall be denied before the angels of God. Mark 8:38

10 And whosoever shall speak a word against the Son of man, it shall be forgiven him: but unto him that blasphemeth against the Holy Ghost it shall not be forgiven. Matt. 12:31-32; 1 Tim. 1:13; 1 John 5:16

11 And when they bring you unto the synagogues, and *unto* magistrates, and powers, take ye no thought how or what thing ye shall answer, or what ye shall say: Matt. 23:34

12 For the Holy Ghost shall teach you in the same hour what ye ought to say. Luke 21:15

A Parable about Greed

13 And one of the company said unto him, Master, speak to my brother, that he divide the inheritance with me.

14 And he said unto him, Man, who made me a judge or a divider over you? Rom. 2:1

15 And he said unto them, Take heed, and beware of ᵀcovetousness: for a man's life consisteth not in the abundance of the things which he possesseth. 1 Tim. 6:6-10 ◆ *strong desire*

16 And he spake a parable unto them, saying, The ground of a certain rich man brought forth plentifully:

17 And he thought within himself, saying, What shall I do, because I have no room where to ᵀbestow my fruits? *store*

18 And he said, This will I do: I will pull down my barns, and build greater; and there will I bestow all my fruits and my goods.

19 And I will say to my soul, Soul, thou hast much goods laid up for many years; take thine ease, eat, drink, *and* be merry. Eccl. 11:9

20 But God said unto him, *Thou* fool, this night thy soul shall be required of thee: then whose shall those things be, which thou hast provided? Job 27:8; Ps. 39:6; Jer. 17:11

21 So *is* he that layeth up treasure for himself, and is not rich toward God. Luke 12:33

12:16–21 Making the Right Choice

The only thing that would be of value to [the rich man] now he has not secured. In living for self he has rejected that divine love which would have flowed out in mercy to his fellow men. Thus he has rejected life. For God is love, and love is life. This man has chosen the earthly rather than the spiritual, and with the earthly he must pass away. *COL 258*

Do Not Be Anxious

22 And he said unto his disciples, Therefore I say unto you, Take no thought for your life, what ye shall eat; neither for the body, what ye shall put on. Luke 12:29

23 The life is more than meat, and the body *is more* than ᵀraiment. *clothing*

24 Consider the ravens: for they neither sow nor reap; which neither have storehouse nor barn; and God feedeth them: how much more are ye better than the fowls? Job 38:41; Ps. 147:9

25 And which of you with taking thought can add to his stature one cubit?

26 If ye then be not able to do that thing which is least, why take ye thought for the rest?

27 Consider the lilies how they grow: they toil not, they spin not; and yet I say unto you, that Solomon in all his glory was not ᵀarrayed like one of these. *clothed*

28 If then God so clothe the grass, which is to day in the field, and to morrow is cast into the oven; how much more *will he clothe* you, O ye of little faith? Matt. 8:26

29 And seek not ye what ye shall eat, or what ye shall drink, neither be ye of doubtful mind. Matt. 6:31

30 For all these things do the nations of the world seek after: and your Father knoweth that ye have need of these things. Matt. 6:8

31 But rather seek ye the kingdom of God; and all these things shall be added unto you. 1 Kin. 3:11-13

32 Fear not, little flock; for it is your Father's good pleasure to give you the kingdom. Is. 40:11

33 Sell that ye have, and give ᵀalms; provide yourselves bags which ᵀwax not old, a treasure in the heavens that faileth not, where no thief approacheth, neither moth corrupteth. Matt. 19:21; Luke 16:9; 18:22 ◆ *acts of mercy* ◆ *become*

34 For where your treasure is, there will your heart be also. Matt. 6:21

Jesus Will Return Unexpectedly

35 Let your ᵀloins be girded about, and *your* lights burning; Eph. 6:14 ◆ *waist*

36 And ye yourselves like unto men that wait for their lord, when he will return from the wedding; that when he cometh and knocketh, they may open unto him immediately. Rev. 3:20

37 Blessed *are* those servants, whom the lord when he cometh shall find watching: ᵀverily I say unto you, that he shall gird himself, and make them to sit down to meat, and will come forth and serve them. Matt. 24:42 ◆ *truly*

38 And if he shall come in the second watch, or come in the third watch, and find *them* so, blessed are those servants.

39 And this know, that if the ᵀgoodman of the house had known what hour the thief would come, he would have watched, and

not have suffered his house to be broken through. Matt. 24:43-44 ◆ *male leader*
40 Be ye therefore ready also: for the Son of man cometh at an hour when ye think not.
41 Then Peter said unto him, Lord, speakest thou this parable unto us, or even to all? Mark 13:37
42 And the Lord said, Who then is that faithful and wise steward, whom *his* lord shall make ruler over his household, to give *them their* portion of meat in due season? Matt. 24:45
43 Blessed *is* that servant, whom his lord when he cometh shall find so doing.
44 Of a truth I say unto you, that he will make him ruler over all that he hath.
45 But and if that servant say in his heart, My lord delayeth his coming; and shall begin to beat the menservants and maidens, and to eat and drink, and to be drunken;
46 The lord of that servant will come in a day when he looketh not for *him*, and at an hour when he is not aware, and will cut him in sunder, and will appoint him his portion with the unbelievers. Luke 12:40
47 And that servant, which knew his lord's will, and prepared not *himself*, neither did according to his will, shall be beaten with many *stripes*. James 4:17
48 But he that knew not, and did commit things worthy of stripes, shall be beaten with few *stripes*. For unto whomsoever much is given, of him shall be much required: and to whom men have committed much, of him they will ask the more. Lev. 5:17; 1 Tim. 1:13

12:48 Don't Waste God's Talents

We shall individually be held responsible for doing one jot less than we have ability to do. The Lord measures with exactness every possibility for service. The unused capabilities are as much brought into account as are those that are improved. For all that we might become through the right use of our talents God holds us responsible. We shall be judged according to what we ought to have done, but did not accomplish because we did not use our powers to glorify God. *COL 363*

---

49 I am come to send fire on the earth; and what will I, if it be already kindled?
50 But I have a baptism to be baptized with; and how am I ᵀstraitened till it be accomplished! John 19:30 ◆ *hindered*
51 Suppose ye that I am come to give peace on earth? I tell you, Nay; but rather division: Matt. 10:34-36
52 For from ᵀhenceforth there shall be five in one house divided, three against two, and two against three. *this time forward*
53 The father shall be divided against the son, and the son against the father; the

mother against the daughter, and the daughter against the mother; the mother in law against her daughter in law, and the daughter in law against her mother in law. Mic. 7:6

Use Good Judgment
54 And he said also to the people, When ye see a cloud rise out of the west, ᵀstraightway ye say, There cometh a shower; and so it is. *right away*
55 And when *ye see* the south wind blow, ye say, There will be heat; and it cometh to pass.
56 *Ye* hypocrites, ye can discern the face of the sky and of the earth; but how is it that ye do not discern this time? Matt. 16:3
57 Yea, and why even of yourselves judge ye not what is right?
58 When thou goest with thine adversary to the magistrate, *as thou art* in the way, give diligence that thou mayest be delivered from him; lest he ᵀhale thee to the judge, and the judge deliver thee to the officer, and the officer cast thee into prison. Matt. 5:23-26 ◆ *drag*
59 I tell thee, thou shalt not depart thence, till thou hast paid the very last mite. Matt. 18:34

Jesus Preaches Repentance
13 There were present at that season some that told him of the Galilaeans, whose blood Pilate had mingled with their sacrifices.
2 And Jesus answering said unto them, Suppose ye that these Galilaeans were sinners above all the Galilaeans, because they suffered such things? John 9:2; Acts 28:4
3 I tell you, Nay: but, except ye repent, ye shall all likewise perish. Luke 24:47
4 Or those eighteen, upon whom the tower in Siloam fell, and slew them, think ye that they were sinners above all men that dwelt in Jerusalem? Neh. 3:15; John 9:7, 11
5 I tell you, Nay: but, except ye repent, ye shall all likewise perish. Luke 13:3

The Fruitless Fig Tree
6 He spake also this parable; A certain *man* had a fig tree planted in his vineyard; and he came and sought fruit thereon, and found none.
7 Then said he unto the dresser of his vineyard, Behold, these three years I come seeking fruit on this fig tree, and find none: cut it down; why ᵀcumbereth it the ground? Ex. 32:10 ◆ *does it use up*
8 And he answering said unto him, Lord, let it alone this year also, till I shall dig about it, and dung *it*:
9 And if it bear fruit, *well*: and if not, *then* after that thou shalt cut it down.

13:6–9 A Warning to Us

The warning sounds down along the line to us in this generation. Are you, O careless heart, a fruitless tree in the Lord's vineyard? Shall the words of doom erelong be spoken of you? How long have you received His gifts. . . . You have taken the name of Christ, you are outwardly a member of the church which is His body. . . . The sweet graces of His character, "the fruits of the Spirit," are not seen in your life. *COL 216*

Jesus Heals on the Sabbath

10 And he was teaching in one of the synagogues on the sabbath.   Matt. 4:23
11 And, behold, there was a woman which had a spirit of infirmity eighteen years, and was bowed together, and could in no wise lift up *herself*.   Luke 13:16
12 And when Jesus saw her, he called *her to him*, and said unto her, Woman, thou art loosed from thine infirmity.
13 And he laid *his* hands on her: and immediately she was made straight, and glorified God.   Mark 5:23
14 And the ruler of the synagogue answered with ᵀindignation, because that Jesus had healed on the sabbath day, and said unto the people, There are six days in which men ought to work: in them therefore come and be healed, and not on the sabbath day.   Ex. 20:9; Matt. 12:2; Luke 8:41 ◆ *anger*
15 The Lord then answered him, and said, *Thou* hypocrite, doth not each one of you on the sabbath loose his ox or *his* ass from the stall, and lead *him* away to watering? Luke 14:5
16 And ought not this woman, being a daughter of Abraham, whom Satan hath bound, lo, these eighteen years, be loosed from this bond on the sabbath day?   Luke 3:8; 19:9; John 8:44
17 And when he had said these things, all his adversaries were ashamed: and all the people rejoiced for all the glorious things that were done by him.   Ps. 132:18

Parables of Seed and Leaven

18 Then said he, Unto what is the kingdom of God like? and whereunto shall I resemble it?   Luke 13:20
19 It is like a grain of mustard seed, which a man took, and cast into his garden; and it grew, and ᵀwaxed a great tree; and the fowls of the air lodged in the branches of it.   Matt. 17:20 ◆ *became*
20 And again he said, Whereunto shall I liken the kingdom of God?
21 It is like leaven, which a woman took and hid in three measures of meal, till the whole was leavened.   Matt. 13:33; 1 Cor. 5:6

The Narrow Gate

22 And he went through the cities and villages, teaching, and journeying toward Jerusalem.   Mark 6:6; Luke 9:51
23 Then said one unto him, Lord, are there few that be saved? And he said unto them,
24 Strive to enter in at the ᵀstrait gate: for many, I say unto you, will seek to enter in, and shall not be able.   *narrow*

13:24 No Drifting Into Heaven

There is no such thing as a truly converted person living a helpless, useless life. It is not possible for us to drift into heaven. No sluggard can enter there. If we do not strive to gain an entrance into the kingdom, if we do not seek earnestly to learn what constitutes its laws, we are not fitted for a part in it. Those who refuse to co-operate with God on earth would not co-operate with Him in heaven. It would not be safe to take them to heaven. *COL 280*

---

25 When once the master of the house is risen up, and hath shut to the door, and ye begin to stand without, and to knock at the door, saying, Lord, Lord, open unto us; and he shall answer and say unto you, I know you not whence ye are: Matt. 25:10-12; Luke 13:27
26 Then shall ye begin to say, We have eaten and drunk in thy presence, and thou hast taught in our streets.
27 But he shall say, I tell you, I know you not whence ye are; depart from me, all *ye* workers of iniquity. Ps. 6:8; Matt. 25:41; Luke 13:25
28 There shall be weeping and gnashing of teeth, when ye shall see Abraham, and Isaac, and Jacob, and all the prophets, in the kingdom of God, and you *yourselves* thrust out.
29 And they shall come from the east, and *from* the west, and from the north, and *from* the south, and shall sit down in the kingdom of God.
30 And, behold, there are last which shall be first, and there are first which shall be last.   Matt. 19:30; 20:16; Mark 10:31

Jesus Warns Jerusalem

31 The same day there came certain of the Pharisees, saying unto him, Get thee out, and depart hence: for Herod will kill thee.
32 And he said unto them, Go ye, and tell that fox, Behold, I cast out devils, and I do cures to day and to morrow, and the third *day* I shall be perfected.   Heb. 2:10; 5:9
33 Nevertheless I must walk to day, and to morrow, and the *day* following: for it cannot be that a prophet perish out of Jerusalem.   Matt. 21:11
34 O Jerusalem, Jerusalem, which killest the prophets, and stonest them that are

sent unto thee; how often would I have gathered thy children together, as a hen *doth gather* her brood under *her* wings, and ye would not!   Matt. 23:37-39

35 Behold, your house is left unto you desolate: and ᵀverily I say unto you, Ye shall not see me, until *the time* come when ye shall say, Blessed *is* he that cometh in the name of the Lord.   Ps. 118:26; Matt. 21:9 ♦ *truly*

13:34, 35 He's Knocking at Your Heart

Every time you fail to open the door of your heart to Christ, you become more and more unwilling to listen to the voice of Him that speaketh. . . .

We are living in a time when the last message of mercy, the last invitation, is sounding to the children of men. . . . The Holy Spirit is presenting every inducement to constrain you to come. *COL 237*

Jesus Heals a Man on the Sabbath

14:1-5

14 And it came to pass, as he went into the house of one of the chief Pharisees to eat bread on the sabbath day, that they watched him.   Mark 3:2

2 And, behold, there was a certain man before him which had the ᵀdropsy.   *illness with swelling*

3 And Jesus answering spake unto the lawyers and Pharisees, saying, Is it lawful to heal on the sabbath day?   Matt. 12:10

4 And they held their peace. And he took *him*, and healed him, and let him go;

5 And answered them, saying, Which of you shall have an ass or an ox fallen into a pit, and will not ᵀstraightway pull him out on the sabbath day?   Luke 13:15 ♦ *right away*

The Sabbath   See Leviticus 23:32.

6 And they could not answer him again to these things.   Luke 20:40

Jesus Attends a Banquet

7 And he put forth a parable to those which were bidden, when he marked how they chose out the chief rooms; saying unto them,   Luke 11:43

8 When thou art bidden of any *man* to a wedding, sit not down in the highest room; lest a more honourable man than thou be bidden of him;   Prov. 25:6-7

9 And he that bade thee and him come and say to thee, Give this man place; and thou begin with shame to take the lowest room.

10 But when thou art bidden, go and sit down in the lowest room; that when he that bade thee cometh, he may say unto thee, Friend, go up higher: then shalt thou have worship in the presence of them that sit at meat with thee.   Prov. 25:6-7

11 For whosoever exalteth himself shall be ᵀabased; and he that humbleth himself shall be exalted.   Prov. 29:23; Matt. 23:12 ♦ *brought low*

12 Then said he also to him that bade him, When thou makest a dinner or a supper, call not thy friends, nor thy brethren, neither thy kinsmen, nor *thy* rich neighbours; lest they also bid thee again, and a recompence be made thee.

13 But when thou makest a feast, call the poor, the maimed, the lame, the blind:

14 And thou shalt be blessed; for they cannot ᵀrecompense thee: for thou shalt be ᵀrecompensed at the resurrection of the just.   John 5:29; Acts 24:15 ♦ *repay* ♦ *repaid*

A Parable about Heaven's Banquet

15 And when one of them that sat at meat with him heard these things, he said unto him, Blessed *is* he that shall eat bread in the kingdom of God.   Luke 13:29; 22:30; Rev. 19:9

14:16-24 A Lesson for All Time

By the great supper, Christ represents the blessings offered through the gospel. The provision is nothing less than Christ Himself. . . . The love of God had furnished the costly banquet, and had provided inexhaustible resources. . . .

But in order to accept the invitation to the gospel feast, they must make their worldly interests subordinate to the one purpose of receiving Christ and His righteousness. . . .

The lesson is for all time. We are to follow the Lamb of God whithersoever He goeth. *COL 222, 223*

---

16 Then said he unto him, A certain man made a great supper, and bade many:

17 And sent his servant at supper time to say to them that were bidden, Come; for all things are now ready.

18 And they all with one *consent* began to make excuse. The first said unto him, I have bought a piece of ground, and I must needs go and see it: I pray thee have me excused.

19 And another said, I have bought five yoke of oxen, and I go to prove them: I pray thee have me excused.

20 And another said, I have married a wife, and therefore I cannot come.   1 Cor. 7:33

21 So that servant came, and shewed his lord these things. Then the master of the house being angry said to his servant, Go out quickly into the streets and lanes of the city, and bring in hither the poor, and the maimed, and the ᵀhalt, and the blind.   Luke 14:13 ♦ *lame*

22 And the servant said, Lord, it is done as thou hast commanded, and yet there is room.

23 And the lord said unto the servant, Go out into the highways and hedges, and

compel *them* to come in, that my house may be filled.

24 For I say unto you, That none of those men which were bidden shall taste of my supper.   Matt. 21:43

The Cost of Being a Disciple

25 And there went great multitudes with him: and he turned, and said unto them,

26 If any *man* come to me, and hate not his father, and mother, and wife, and children, and brethren, and sisters, yea, and his own life also, he cannot be my disciple. Deut. 33:9

27 And whosoever doth not bear his cross, and come after me, cannot be my disciple.

28 For which of you, intending to build a tower, sitteth not down first, and counteth the cost, whether he have *sufficient* to finish it?   Prov. 24:27

29 Lest ᵀhaply, after he hath laid the foundation, and is not able to finish *it*, all that behold *it* begin to mock him,   *maybe*

30 Saying, This man began to build, and was not able to finish.

31 Or what king, going to make war against another king, sitteth not down first, and consulteth whether he be able with ten thousand to meet him that cometh against him with twenty thousand?   Prov. 20:18

32 Or else, while the other is yet a great way off, he sendeth an ᵀambassage, and desireth conditions of peace.   *delegation*

33 So likewise, whosoever he be of you that forsaketh not all that he hath, he cannot be my disciple.   Luke 14:26

34 Salt *is* good: but if the salt have lost his savour, wherewith shall it be seasoned?

35 It is neither fit for the land, nor yet for the dunghill; *but* men cast it out. He that hath ears to hear, let him hear.   Matt. 11:15

The Lost Sheep

15 Then drew near unto him all the ᵀpublicans and sinners for to hear him.   *tax collectors*

2 And the Pharisees and scribes murmured, saying, This man receiveth sinners, and eateth with them.   Matt. 9:11; Luke 5:30; 7:39

3 And he spake this parable unto them, saying,

4 What man of you, having an hundred sheep, if he lose one of them, doth not leave the ninety and nine in the wilderness, and go after that which is lost, until he find it?   Ezek. 34:11-12

5 And when he hath found *it*, he layeth *it* on his shoulders, rejoicing.

6 And when he cometh home, he calleth together *his* friends and neighbours, saying unto them, Rejoice with me; for I have found my sheep which was lost.   1 Pet. 2:25

7 I say unto you, that likewise joy shall be in heaven over one sinner that repenteth, more than over ninety and nine just persons, which need no repentance.   Luke 5:32

> **15:7 Angels Work on Our Behalf**
>
> It is the work of the angels to come close to the tried, the suffering, the tempted. They labor untiringly in behalf of those for whom Christ died. . . . A report is borne to heaven of every successful effort on our part to dispel the darkness and to spread abroad the knowledge of Christ. As the deed is recounted before the Father, joy thrills through all the heavenly host. *AA 153, 154*

The Lost Coin

8 Either what woman having ten pieces of silver, if she lose one piece, doth not light a candle, and sweep the house, and seek diligently till she find *it*?

9 And when she hath found *it*, she calleth *her* friends and *her* neighbours together, saying, Rejoice with me; for I have found the piece which I had lost.

10 Likewise, I say unto you, there is joy in the presence of the angels of God over one sinner that repenteth.   Heb. 1:14

The Prodigal Son

11 And he said, A certain man had two sons:

12 And the younger of them said to *his* father, Father, give me the portion of goods that falleth *to me*. And he divided unto them *his* living.   Mark 12:44

13 And not many days after the younger son gathered all together, and took his journey into a far country, and there wasted his substance with riotous living.   Luke 15:30

14 And when he had spent all, there arose a mighty famine in that land; and he began to be in want.

15 And he went and joined himself to a citizen of that country; and he sent him into his fields to feed swine.

16 And he would ᵀfain have filled his belly with the husks that the swine did eat: and no man gave unto him.   *desire to*

17 And when he came to himself, he said, How many hired servants of my father's have bread enough and to spare, and I perish with hunger!

18 I will arise and go to my father, and will say unto him, Father, I have sinned against heaven, and before thee,   Luke 15:21

19 And am no more worthy to be called thy son: make me as one of thy hired servants.

20 And he arose, and came to his father. But when he was yet a great way off, his father

saw him, and had compassion, and ran, and fell on his neck, and kissed him.   Gen. 45:14

21 And the son said unto him, Father, I have sinned against heaven, and in thy sight, and am no more worthy to be called thy son.   Ps. 51:4

22 But the father said to his servants, Bring forth the best robe, and put *it* on him; and put a ring on his hand, and shoes on *his* feet: Gen. 41:42; Esth. 3:10; Rev. 6:11

23 And bring ᵀhither the fatted calf, and kill *it*; and let us eat, and be merry: *here*

24 For this my son was dead, and is alive again; he was lost, and is found. And they began to be merry.   Luke 15:32; Eph. 2:1, 5

25 Now his elder son was in the field: and as he came and drew nigh to the house, he heard musick and dancing.

26 And he called one of the servants, and asked what these things meant.

27 And he said unto him, Thy brother is come; and thy father hath killed the fatted calf, because he hath received him safe and sound.

28 And he was angry, and would not go in: therefore came his father out, and ᵀintreated him.   *pled with*

29 And he answering said to *his* father, Lo, these many years do I serve thee, neither ᵀtransgressed I at any time thy commandment: and yet thou never gavest me a kid, that I might make merry with my friends: *violated*

30 But as soon as this thy son was come, which hath devoured thy living with harlots, thou hast killed for him the fatted calf.   Prov. 29:3

31 And he said unto him, Son, thou art ever with me, and all that I have is thine.

32 It was meet that we should make merry, and be glad: for this thy brother was dead, and is alive again; and was lost, and is found.   Luke 15:24

The Parable of the Unfaithful Steward

16 And he said also unto his disciples, There was a certain rich man, which had a steward; and the same was accused unto him that he had wasted his goods.

2 And he called him, and said unto him, How is it that I hear this of thee? give an account of thy stewardship; for thou mayest be no longer steward.

3 Then the steward said within himself, What shall I do? for my lord taketh away from me the stewardship: I cannot dig; to beg I am ashamed.

4 I am resolved what to do, that, when I am put out of the stewardship, they may receive me into their houses.

5 So he called every one of his lord's debtors *unto him*, and said unto the first, How much owest thou unto my lord?

6 And he said, An hundred measures of oil. And he said unto him, Take thy bill, and sit down quickly, and write fifty.

7 Then said he to another, And how much owest thou? And he said, An hundred measures of wheat. And he said unto him, Take thy bill, and write ᵀfourscore.   *eighty*

Your Father Longing to Embrace You

Luke 15:11–32

What a picture [in this story of the prodigal son] of the sinner's state! Although surrounded with the blessings of His love, there is nothing that the sinner, bent on self-indulgence and sinful pleasure, desires so much as separation from God. . . .

Whatever the appearance may be, every life centered in self is squandered. Whoever attempts to live apart from God is wasting his substance. . . .

The love of God still yearns over the one who has chosen to separate from Him, and He sets in operation influences to bring him back to the Father's house. . . .

The young man turns from the swine herds and the husks [pods], and sets his face toward home. Trembling with weakness and faint from hunger, he presses eagerly on his way. He has no covering to conceal his rags; but his misery has conquered pride, and he hurries on to beg a servant's place where he was once a child. . . .

But while he is yet "a great way off" the father discerns his form. Love is of quick sight. . . . He "had compassion, and ran, and fell on his neck" in a long, clinging, tender embrace. . . .

In his restless youth the prodigal looked upon his father as stern and severe. . . . So those who are deceived by Satan look upon God as hard and exacting. . . . His law they regard as a restriction upon men's happiness, a burdensome yoke from which they are glad to escape. But he whose eyes have been opened by the love of Christ will behold God as full of compassion. He does not appear as a tyrannical, relentless being, but as a father longing to embrace his repenting son. . . .

Arise and go to your Father. He will meet you a great way off. If you take even one step toward Him in repentance, He will hasten to enfold you in His arms of infinite love. . . .

And heaven and earth shall unite in the Father's song of rejoicing: "For this My son was dead, and is alive again; he was lost, and is found." COL 200–207

8 And the lord commended the unjust steward, because he had done wisely: for the children of this world are in their generation wiser than the children of light.   John 12:36; Eph. 5:8; 1 Thess. 5:5
9 And I say unto you, Make to yourselves friends of the mammon of unrighteousness; that, when ye fail, they may receive you into everlasting habitations.   Matt. 19:21; Luke 16:11, 13
10 He that is faithful in that which is least is faithful also in much: and he that is unjust in the least is unjust also in much.   Matt. 25:21, 23
11 If therefore ye have not been faithful in the unrighteous ᵀmammon, who will commit to your trust the true *riches*?   riches
12 And if ye have not been faithful in that which is another man's, who shall give you that which is your own?

16:10–12 Don't Skip the Little Things

There are few who realize the influence of the little things of life upon the development of character. Nothing with which we have to do is really small. The varied circumstances that we meet day by day are designed to test our faithfulness and to qualify us for greater trusts. . . . *PP 222, 223*

13 No servant can serve two masters: for either he will hate the one, and love the other; or else he will hold to the one, and despise the other. Ye cannot serve God and mammon.   Matt. 6:24; Luke 16:9
14 And the Pharisees also, who were ᵀcovetous, heard all these things: and they derided him.   Luke 20:47; 23:35 ◆ *greedy*
15 And he said unto them, Ye are they which justify yourselves before men; but God knoweth your hearts: for that which is highly esteemed among men is abomination in the sight of God.   1 Sam. 16:7; Prov. 16:5; Luke 10:29
16 The law and the prophets *were* until John: since that time the kingdom of God is preached, and every man presseth into it.   Matt. 3:2
17 And it is easier for heaven and earth to pass, than one tittle of the law to fail.
18 Whosoever putteth away his wife, and marrieth another, committeth adultery: and whosoever marrieth her that is put away from *her* husband committeth adultery.   Matt. 19:9

The Rich Man and Lazarus

19 There was a certain rich man, which was clothed in purple and fine linen, and fared ᵀsumptuously every day: Esth. 8:15 ◆ *wonderfully*
20 And there was a certain beggar named Lazarus, which was laid at his gate, full of sores,   Acts 3:2
21 And desiring to be fed with the crumbs which fell from the rich man's table: moreover the dogs came and licked his sores.   Matt. 15:27
22 And it came to pass, that the beggar died, and was carried by the angels into Abraham's bosom: the rich man also died, and was buried;   John 13:23
23 And in hell he lift up his eyes, being in torments, and seeth Abraham afar off, and Lazarus in his bosom.   Ps. 9:17
24 And he cried and said, Father Abraham, have mercy on me, and send Lazarus, that he may dip the tip of his finger in water, and cool my tongue; for I am tormented in this flame.   Is. 66:24; Matt. 25:41; Luke 16:30
25 But Abraham said, Son, remember that thou in thy lifetime receivedst thy good things, and likewise Lazarus evil things: but now he is comforted, and thou art tormented.   Ps. 17:14; Luke 6:24
26 And beside all this, between us and you there is a great gulf fixed: so that they which would pass from hence to you cannot; neither can they pass to us, that *would come* from thence.
27 Then he said, I pray thee therefore, father, that thou wouldest send him to my father's house:
28 For I have five brethren; that he may testify unto them, lest they also come into this place of torment.
29 Abraham saith unto him, They have Moses and the prophets; let them hear them.
30 And he said, Nay, father Abraham: but if one went unto them from the dead, they will repent.   Luke 16:24
31 And he said unto him, If they hear not Moses and the prophets, neither will they be persuaded, though one rose from the dead.

Dealing with Others

17 Then said he unto the disciples, It is impossible but that offences will come: but woe *unto him*, through whom they come!   Matt. 18:7; 1 Cor. 11:19
2 It were better for him that a millstone were hanged about his neck, and he cast into the sea, than that he should offend one of these little ones.   Mark 9:42
3 Take heed to yourselves: If thy brother ᵀtrespass against thee, rebuke him; and if he repent, forgive him.   Lev. 19:17 ◆ *sin*
4 And if he trespass against thee seven times in a day, and seven times in a day turn again to thee, saying, I repent; thou shalt forgive him.   Matt. 18:21-22
5 And the apostles said unto the Lord, Increase our faith.   Mark 6:30

Faith See Mark 9:24.

6 And the Lord said, If ye had faith as a grain of mustard seed, ye might say unto this

sycamine tree, Be thou plucked up by the root, and be thou planted in the sea; and it should obey you. Matt. 17:20; Mark 9:23; Luke 13:19

7 But which of you, having a servant plowing or feeding cattle, will say unto him by and by, when he is come from the field, Go and sit down to meat?

8 And will not rather say unto him, Make ready wherewith I may ᵀsup, and ᵀgird thyself, and serve me, till I have eaten and drunken; and afterward thou shalt eat and drink?   Luke 12:37 ◆ *eat a meal* ◆ *equip*

9 Doth he thank that servant because he did the things that were commanded him? I ᵀtrow not.   *think*

10 So likewise ye, when ye shall have done all those things which are commanded you, say, We are unprofitable servants: we have done that which was our duty to do. Job 22:2-3

Jesus Heals Ten Lepers

11 And it came to pass, as he went to Jerusalem, that he passed through the midst of Samaria and Galilee.   Luke 9:51-52

12 And as he entered into a certain village, there met him ten men that were lepers, which stood afar off: Lev. 13:45-46

13 And they lifted up *their* voices, and said, Jesus, Master, have mercy on us.

14 And when he saw *them*, he said unto them, Go shew yourselves unto the priests. And it came to pass, that, as they went, they were cleansed.   Luke 5:14

15 And one of them, when he saw that he was healed, turned back, and with a loud voice glorified God,

16 And fell down on *his* face at his feet, giving him thanks: and he was a Samaritan.

17 And Jesus answering said, Were there not ten cleansed? but where *are* the nine?

18 There are not found that returned to give glory to God, save this stranger.

19 And he said unto him, Arise, go thy way: thy faith hath made thee whole.   Matt. 9:22

The Kingdom of God

20 And when he was demanded of the Pharisees, when the kingdom of God should come, he answered them and said, The kingdom of God cometh not with observation: Luke 19:11

21 Neither shall they say, Lo here! or, lo there! for, behold, the kingdom of God is within you.   Luke 17:23

22 And he said unto the disciples, The days will come, when ye shall desire to see one of the days of the Son of man, and ye shall not see *it*.   Matt. 9:15; Luke 5:35

23 And they shall say to you, See here; or, see there: go not after *them*, nor follow *them*.   Luke 17:21; 21:8

24 For as the lightning, that lighteneth out of the one *part* under heaven, shineth unto the other *part* under heaven; so shall also the Son of man be in his day.   Matt. 24:27

25 But first must he suffer many things, and be rejected of this generation.   Matt. 16:21

26 And as it was in the days of Noe, so shall it be also in the days of the Son of man.   Gen. 7:7-23

27 They did eat, they drank, they married wives, they were given in marriage, until the day that Noe entered into the ark, and the flood came, and destroyed them all.

28 Likewise also as it was in the days of Lot; they did eat, they drank, they bought, they sold, they planted, they builded;

29 But the same day that Lot went out of Sodom it rained fire and ᵀbrimstone from heaven, and destroyed *them* all. 2 Pet. 2:6 ◆ *sulphur*

30 Even thus shall it be in the day when the Son of man is revealed. Matt. 16:27; 24:3; 2 Thess. 1:7

17:28–30 Meeting With Disappointment

Many parents seek to promote the happiness of their children by gratifying their love of amusement. They allow them to engage in sports, and to attend parties of pleasure, and provide them with money to use freely in display and self-gratification. The more the desire for pleasure is indulged, the stronger it becomes. . . .

Many parents who choose a city home for their children, thinking to give them greater advantages, meet with disappointment, and too late repent their terrible mistake. The cities of today are fast becoming like Sodom and Gomorrah. *COL 54*

31 In that day, he which shall be upon the housetop, and his stuff in the house, let him not come down to take it away: and he that is in the field, let him likewise not return back.

32 Remember Lot's wife.   Gen. 19:26

33 Whosoever shall seek to save his life shall lose it; and whosoever shall lose his life shall preserve it.   Matt. 10:39

34 I tell you, in that night there shall be two *men* in one bed; the one shall be taken, and the other shall be left.

35 Two *women* shall be grinding together; the one shall be taken, and the other left.   Ex. 11:5

36 Two *men* shall be in the field; the one shall be taken, and the other left.

37 And they answered and said unto him, Where, Lord? And he said unto them, Wheresoever the body *is*, thither will the eagles be gathered together.   Matt. 24:28

God Will Help His People

18 And he spake a parable unto them *to this end*, that men ought always to pray, and not to faint;   Rom. 12:12; Eph. 6:18; Col. 4:2

2 Saying, There was in a city a judge, which feared not God, neither regarded man: Luke 18:4

3 And there was a widow in that city; and she came unto him, saying, Avenge me of mine adversary.   Is. 1:17

4 And he would not for a while: but afterward he said within himself, Though I fear not God, nor regard man;

5 Yet because this widow troubleth me, I will avenge her, lest by her continual coming she weary me.   Luke 11:8

6 And the Lord said, Hear what the unjust judge saith.

7 And shall not God avenge his own elect, which cry day and night unto him, though he bear long with them?   Ps. 88:1; Rev. 6:10

8 I tell you that he will avenge them speedily. Nevertheless when the Son of man cometh, shall he find faith on the earth?

The Pharisee and the Tax Collector

9 And he spake this parable unto certain which trusted in themselves that they were righteous, and despised others: Prov. 30:12

10 Two men went up into the temple to pray; the one a Pharisee, and the other a ᵀpublican.   Acts 3:1 ♦ *tax collector*

11 The Pharisee stood and prayed thus with himself, God, I thank thee, that I am not as other men *are*, extortioners, unjust, adulterers, or even as this publican.   Matt. 6:5; Rev. 3:17

12 I fast twice in the week, I give tithes of all that I possess.   Mal. 3:8; Matt. 9:14; Luke 11:42

13 And the publican, standing afar off, would not lift up so much as *his* eyes unto heaven, but smote upon his breast, saying, God be merciful to me a sinner.   Ezra 9:6; Jer. 31:18-19

18:13 Faith That Renounces Self-Trust

The prayer of the publican was heard because it showed dependence reaching forth to lay hold upon Omnipotence. Self to the publican appeared nothing but shame. Thus it must be seen by all who seek God. By faith—faith that renounces all self-trust—the needy suppliant is to lay hold upon infinite power. *COL 159*

14 I tell you, this man went down to his house justified *rather* than the other: for every one that exalteth himself shall be ᵀabased; and he that humbleth himself shall be exalted.   Matt. 23:12; Luke 14:11 ♦ *brought low*

Jesus Blesses the Children

15 And they brought unto him also infants, that he would touch them: but when *his* disciples saw *it*, they rebuked them.   Matt. 19:13-15

16 But Jesus called them *unto him*, and said, Suffer little children to come unto me, and forbid them not: for of such is the kingdom of God.

17 Verily I say unto you, Whosoever shall not receive the kingdom of God as a little child shall in no wise enter therein. Mark 10:15

A Rich Young Ruler

18 And a certain ruler asked him, saying, Good Master, what shall I do to inherit eternal life?

19 And Jesus said unto him, Why callest thou me good? none *is* good, save one, *that is*, God.

20 Thou knowest the commandments, Do not commit adultery, Do not kill, Do not

---

To Have Eyes Like the Publican

Luke 18:9–14

No outward observances can take the place of simple faith and entire renunciation of self. But no man can empty himself of self. We can only consent for Christ to accomplish the work. Then the language of the soul will be, Lord, take my heart; for I cannot give it. It is Thy property. Keep it pure, for I cannot keep it for Thee. Save me in spite of myself, my weak, unchristlike self. Mold me, fashion me, raise me into a pure and holy atmosphere, where the rich current of Thy love can flow through my soul. . . .

The nearer we come to Jesus and the more clearly we discern the purity of His character, the more clearly we shall discern the exceeding sinfulness of sin and the less we shall feel like exalting ourselves. Those whom heaven recognizes as holy ones are the last to parade their own goodness. . . .

None of the apostles or prophets ever claimed to be without sin. Men who have lived nearest to God, men who would sacrifice life itself rather than knowingly commit a wrong act, men whom God had honored with divine light and power, have confessed the sinfulness of their own nature. They have put no confidence in the flesh, have claimed no righteousness of their own, but have trusted wholly in the righteousness of Christ. So will it be with all who behold Christ. . . .

Those who are filled with self-esteem and self-love do not feel the need of a living, personal union with Christ. The heart that has not fallen on the Rock is proud of its wholeness. Men want a dignified religion. They desire to walk in a path wide enough to take in their own attributes. COL *159–162*

steal, Do not bear false witness, Honour thy father and thy mother.   Rom. 13:9

21 And he said, All these have I kept from my youth up.   Phil. 3:6

22 Now when Jesus heard these things, he said unto him, Yet lackest thou one thing: sell all that thou hast, and distribute unto the poor, and thou shalt have treasure in heaven: and come, follow me.   Luke 12:33

23 And when he heard this, he was very sorrowful: for he was very rich.   Ezek. 33:31

18:18–23 He Failed the Test

The lover of self is a transgressor of the law. This Jesus desired to reveal to the [rich young ruler], and He gave him a test that would make manifest the selfishness of his heart. He showed him the plague spot in his character. The young man desired no further enlightenment. He had cherished an idol in the soul; the world was his god. . . . In his love of self and worldly gain he was out of harmony with the principles of heaven. COL 392

---

24 And when Jesus saw that he was very sorrowful, he said, How hardly shall they that have riches enter into the kingdom of God!   Prov. 11:28

25 For it is easier for a camel to go through a needle's eye, than for a rich man to enter into the kingdom of God.

26 And they that heard it said, Who then can be saved?

27 And he said, The things which are impossible with men are possible with God.

28 Then Peter said, Lo, we have left all, and followed thee.   Luke 5:11

29 And he said unto them, Verily I say unto you, There is no man that hath left house, or parents, or brethren, or wife, or children, for the kingdom of God's sake,

30 Who shall not receive manifold more in this present time, and in the world to come life everlasting.   Job 42:10

Jesus Again Foretells His Death and Resurrection

31 Then he took unto him the twelve, and said unto them, Behold, we go up to Jerusalem, and all things that are written by the prophets concerning the Son of man shall be accomplished.   Ps. 22; Is. 53; Matt. 20:17-19

32 For he shall be delivered unto the Gentiles, and shall be mocked, and spitefully entreated, and spitted on: Luke 23:11

33 And they shall ᵀscourge him, and put him to death: and the third day he shall rise again.   whip

34 And they understood none of these things: and this saying was hid from them, neither knew they the things which were spoken.   Mark 9:32; Luke 9:45

Jesus Heals a Blind Man

35 And it came to pass, that as he was come nigh unto Jericho, a certain blind man sat by the way side begging: John 9:8

36 And hearing the multitude pass by, he asked what it meant.

37 And they told him, that Jesus of Nazareth passeth by.   Matt. 2:23

38 And he cried, saying, Jesus, thou Son of David, have mercy on me.   Matt. 9:27

39 And they which went before rebuked him, that he should hold his peace: but he cried so much the more, Thou Son of David, have mercy on me.   Luke 18:15

40 And Jesus stood, and commanded him to be brought unto him: and when he was come near, he asked him,

41 Saying, What wilt thou that I shall do unto thee? And he said, Lord, that I may receive my sight.

42 And Jesus said unto him, Receive thy sight: thy faith hath saved thee.   Matt. 9:22

43 And immediately he received his sight, and followed him, glorifying God: and all the people, when they saw it, gave praise unto God.

Zacchaeus Meets Jesus

19 And Jesus entered and passed through Jericho.   Luke 18:35

2 And, behold, there was a man named Zacchaeus, which was the chief among the ᵀpublicans, and he was rich.   tax collectors

3 And he sought to see Jesus who he was; and could not for the press, because he was little of stature.   John 12:21

4 And he ran before, and climbed up into a sycomore tree to see him: for he was to pass that way.   1 Kin. 10:27; 1 Chr. 27:28; Is. 9:10

5 And when Jesus came to the place, he looked up, and saw him, and said unto him, Zacchaeus, make haste, and come down; for to day I must abide at thy house.

6 And he made haste, and came down, and received him joyfully.

7 And when they saw it, they all murmured, saying, That he was gone to be guest with a man that is a sinner.   Matt. 9:11

8 And Zacchaeus stood, and said unto the Lord; Behold, Lord, the half of my goods I give to the poor; and if I have taken any thing from any man by false accusation, I restore him fourfold.   2 Sam. 12:6

9 And Jesus said unto him, This day is salvation come to this house, forsomuch as he also is a son of Abraham.   Luke 13:16; Rom. 4:16; Gal. 3:7

10 For the Son of man is come to seek and to save that which was lost.   Ezek. 34:16

19:8–10 What Constitutes Genuine Repentance?

Before Zacchaeus had looked upon the face of Christ, he had begun the work that made him manifest as a true penitent. . . . He had yielded to the conviction of the Holy Spirit, and had begun to carry out the teaching of the words written for ancient Israel as well as for ourselves. . . .

But no sooner did Zacchaeus yield to the influence of the Holy Spirit than he cast aside every practice contrary to integrity.

No repentance is genuine that does not work reformation. *DA 555*

The Parable of the Pounds

11 And as they heard these things, he added and spake a parable, because he was nigh to Jerusalem, and because they thought that the kingdom of God should immediately appear.   Luke 17:20; Acts 1:6

12 He said therefore, A certain nobleman went into a far country to receive for himself a kingdom, and to return.   Matt. 25:14-30

13 And he called his ten servants, and delivered them ten pounds, and said unto them, Occupy till I come.

14 But his citizens hated him, and sent a message after him, saying, We will not have this *man* to reign over us.

15 And it came to pass, that when he was returned, having received the kingdom, then he commanded these servants to be called unto him, to whom he had given the money, that he might know how much every man had gained by trading.

16 Then came the first, saying, Lord, thy pound hath gained ten pounds.

17 And he said unto him, Well, thou good servant: because thou hast been faithful in a very little, have thou authority over ten cities.   Matt. 25:21; Luke 16:10

18 And the second came, saying, Lord, thy pound hath gained five pounds.

19 And he said likewise to him, Be thou also over five cities.

20 And another came, saying, Lord, behold, *here is* thy pound, which I have kept laid up in a napkin:

21 For I feared thee, because thou art an austere man: thou takest up that thou layedst not down, and reapest that thou didst not sow.

22 And he saith unto him, Out of thine own mouth will I judge thee, *thou* wicked servant. Thou knewest that I was an austere man, taking up that I laid not down, and reaping that I did not sow: 2 Sam. 1:16

23 Wherefore then gavest not thou my money into the bank, that at my coming I might have required mine own with ᵀusury?   *interest charged*

24 And he said unto them that stood by, Take from him the pound, and give *it* to him that hath ten pounds.

25 (And they said unto him, Lord, he hath ten pounds.)

26 For I say unto you, That unto every one which hath shall be given; and from him that hath not, even that he hath shall be taken away from him.   Matt. 13:12; Mark 4:25; Luke 8:18

27 But those mine enemies, which would not that I should reign over them, bring hither, and slay *them* before me.   Matt. 22:7

Jesus Enters Jerusalem in Triumph

28 And when he had thus spoken, he went before, ascending up to Jerusalem.   Luke 9:51

29 And it came to pass, when he was come nigh to Bethphage and Bethany, at the mount called *the mount* of Olives, he sent two of his disciples,   Acts 1:12

30 Saying, Go ye into the village over against *you*; in the which at your entering ye shall

---

Policy Versus Faithfulness

Luke 19:14

Today there is need of the voice of stern rebuke; for grievous sins have separated the people from God. Infidelity is fast becoming fashionable. "We will not have this man to reign over us," is the language of thousands (Luke 19:14). The smooth sermons so often preached make no lasting impression; the trumpet does not give a certain sound. Men are not cut to the heart by the plain, sharp truths of God's word.

There are many professed Christians who, if they should express their real feelings, would say, What need is there of speaking so plainly? They might as well ask, Why need John the Baptist have said to the Pharisees, "O generation of vipers, who hath warned you to flee from the wrath to come?" (Luke 3:7). Why need he have provoked the anger of Herodias by telling Herod that it was unlawful for him to live with his brother's wife? The forerunner of Christ lost his life by his plain speaking. Why could he not have moved along without incurring the displeasure of those who were living in sin?

So men who should be standing as faithful guardians of God's law have argued, till policy has taken the place of faithfulness, and sin is allowed to go unreproved. When will the voice of faithful rebuke be heard once more in the church? *PK 140, 141*

find a colt tied, whereon yet never man sat: loose him, and bring *him* ᵀ*hither*.   here
31 And if any man ask you, Why do ye loose *him*? thus shall ye say unto him, Because the Lord hath need of him.
32 And they that were sent went their way, and found even as he had said unto them.
33 And as they were loosing the colt, the owners thereof said unto them, Why loose ye the colt?
34 And they said, The Lord hath need of him.
35 And they brought him to Jesus: and they cast their garments upon the colt, and they set Jesus thereon.   Matt. 21:7
36 And as he went, they spread their clothes in the way.
37 And when he was come nigh, even now at the descent of the mount of Olives, the whole multitude of the disciples began to rejoice and praise God with a loud voice for all the mighty works that they had seen;
38 Saying, Blessed *be* the King that cometh in the name of the Lord: peace in heaven, and glory in the highest.   Luke 13:35
39 And some of the Pharisees from among the multitude said unto him, Master, rebuke thy disciples.
40 And he answered and said unto them, I tell you that, if these should hold their peace, the stones would immediately cry out.   Hab. 2:11

19:35–40 Everything for a Purpose

The events connected with this triumphal ride would be the talk of every tongue, and would bring Jesus before every mind. After His crucifixion, many would recall these events in their connection with His trial and death. They would be led to search the prophecies, and would be convinced that Jesus was the Messiah; and in all lands converts to the faith would be multiplied. *DA 571*

Jesus Weeps over Jerusalem
41 And when he was come near, he beheld the city, and wept over it,   Luke 13:34-35
42 Saying, If thou hadst known, even thou, at least in this thy day, the things *which belong* unto thy peace! but now they are hid from thine eyes.   Deut. 32:29
43 For the days shall come upon thee, that thine enemies shall cast a trench about thee, and ᵀcompass thee round, and keep thee in on every side,   Ezek. 4:2 ◆ *surround*
44 And shall lay thee even with the ground, and thy children within thee; and they shall not leave in thee one stone upon another; because thou knewest not the time of thy visitation.   Matt. 24:2; Luke 21:6; 1 Pet. 2:12

Jesus Throws Moneychangers from the Temple
45 And he went into the temple, and began to cast out them that sold therein, and them that bought;   Matt. 21:12-13
46 Saying unto them, It is written, My house is the house of prayer: but ye have made it a den of thieves.   Is. 56:7; Jer. 7:11
47 And he taught daily in the temple. But the chief priests and the scribes and the chief of the people sought to destroy him,   Matt. 26:55
48 And could not find what they might do: for all the people were very attentive to hear him.

Jesus' Authority Is Challenged
20 And it came to pass, *that* on one of those days, as he taught the people in the temple, and preached the gospel, the chief priests and the scribes came upon *him* with the elders,
2 And spake unto him, saying, Tell us, by what authority doest thou these things? or who is he that gave thee this authority? Ex.2:14
3 And he answered and said unto them, I will also ask you one thing; and answer me:
4 The baptism of John, was it from heaven, or of men?   Luke 15:18
5 And they reasoned with themselves, saying, If we shall say, From heaven; he will say, Why then believed ye him not?
6 But and if we say, Of men; all the people will stone us: for they be persuaded that John was a prophet.   Matt. 21:26
7 And they answered, that they could not tell whence *it was*.
8 And Jesus said unto them, Neither tell I you by what authority I do these things.

The Parable of the Vineyard
9 Then began he to speak to the people this parable; A certain man planted a vineyard, and let it forth to husbandmen, and went into a far country for a long time. Matt. 21:33-46
10 And at the season he sent a servant to the husbandmen, that they should give him of the fruit of the vineyard: but the husbandmen beat him, and sent *him* away empty.   2 Chr. 36:15-16
11 And again he sent another servant: and they beat him also, and entreated *him* shamefully, and sent *him* away empty.
12 And again he sent a third: and they wounded him also, and cast *him* out.
13 Then said the lord of the vineyard, What shall I do? I will send my beloved son: it may be they will reverence *him* when they see him.   Matt. 3:17
14 But when the ᵀhusbandmen saw him, they reasoned among themselves, saying,

This is the heir: come, let us kill him, that the inheritance may be ours. Rom. 8:17 ✦ farmers
15 So they cast him out of the vineyard, and killed *him*. What therefore shall the lord of the vineyard do unto them?   Heb. 13:12
16 He shall come and destroy these husbandmen, and shall give the vineyard to others. And when they heard *it*, they said, God forbid.   Matt. 21:41; Luke 19:27; Acts 13:46
17 And he beheld them, and said, What is this then that is written, The stone which the builders rejected, the same is become the head of the corner?   Ps. 118:22; Acts 4:11
18 Whosoever shall fall upon that stone shall be broken; but on whomsoever it shall fall, it will grind him to powder.   Is. 8:14-15
19 And the chief priests and the scribes the same hour sought to lay hands on him; and they feared the people: for they perceived that he had spoken this parable against them.   Luke 19:47-48

A Question about Taxes
20 And they watched *him*, and sent forth spies, which should feign themselves just men, that they might take hold of his words, that so they might deliver him unto the power and authority of the governor. Matt. 27:2
21 And they asked him, saying, Master, we know that thou sayest and teachest rightly, neither acceptest thou the person *of any*, but teachest the way of God truly: John 3:2
22 Is it lawful for us to give tribute unto Caesar, or no?
23 But he perceived their craftiness, and said unto them, Why tempt ye me? 1 Cor. 3:19
24 Shew me a ᵀpenny. Whose image and superscription hath it? They answered and said, Caesar's. Matt. 18:28 ✦ daily wage of Roman soldier
25 And he said unto them, Render therefore unto Caesar the things which be Caesar's, and unto God the things which be God's.   Matt. 22:21
26 And they could not take hold of his words before the people: and they marvelled at his answer, and held their peace.   Luke 20:20

A Question about the Resurrection
27 Then came to *him* certain of the Sadducees, which deny that there is any resurrection; and they asked him,   Matt. 16:1
28 Saying, Master, Moses wrote unto us, If any man's brother die, having a wife, and he die without children, that his brother should take his wife, and raise up seed unto his brother.
29 There were therefore seven brethren: and the first took a wife, and died without children.
30 And the second took her to wife, and he died childless.

31 And the third took her; and in like manner the seven also: and they left no children, and died.
32 Last of all the woman died also.
33 Therefore in the resurrection whose wife of them is she? for seven had her to wife.
34 And Jesus answering said unto them, The children of this world marry, and are given in marriage: Luke 16:8
35 But they which shall be accounted worthy to obtain that world, and the resurrection from the dead, neither marry, nor are given in marriage: Acts 5:41
36 Neither can they die any more: for they are equal unto the angels; and are the children of God, being the children of the resurrection.   Matt. 22:30
37 Now that the dead are raised, even Moses shewed at the bush, when he calleth the Lord the God of Abraham, and the God of Isaac, and the God of Jacob.   Ex. 3:2-6
38 For he is not a God of the dead, but of the living: for all live unto him.
39 Then certain of the scribes answering said, Master, thou hast well said.
40 And after that they ᵀdurst not ask him any *question at all*.   Matt. 22:46; Mark 12:34 ✦ dared

David's Son, David's Lord
41 And he said unto them, How say they that Christ is David's son?   Matt. 1:1
42 And David himself saith in the book of Psalms, The LORD said unto my Lord, Sit thou on my right hand,   Ps. 110:1
43 Till I make thine enemies thy footstool.
44 David therefore calleth him Lord, how is he then his son?

Beware of the Scribes
45 Then in the audience of all the people he said unto his disciples,
46 Beware of the scribes, which desire to walk in long robes, and love greetings in the markets, and the highest seats in the synagogues, and the chief rooms at feasts;   Luke 11:43
47 Which devour widows' houses, and for a shew make long prayers: the same shall receive greater ᵀdamnation. Mark 12:40 ✦ condemnation

The Poor Widow's Gift
21 And he looked up, and saw the rich men casting their gifts into the treasury.   Mark 12:41-44
2 And he saw also a certain poor widow casting in thither two mites.   Mark 12:42
3 And he said, Of a truth I say unto you, that this poor widow hath cast in more than they all: 2 Cor. 8:12
4 For all these have of their abundance cast in unto the offerings of God: but she of her

Tpenury hath cast in all the living that she had.

Luke 8:43 ◆ *poverty*

21:1–4 What Makes the Gift Valuable?

The act of the widow who cast two mites—all that she had—into the treasury, is placed on record for the encouragement of those who, struggling with poverty, still desire by their gifts to aid the cause of God. ... To make her offering, the widow had deprived herself of even the necessities of life, trusting God to supply her needs for the morrow. ... Thus He taught that the value of the gift is estimated not by the amount, but by the proportion that is given and the motive that actuates the giver. *AA 342*

Jesus Discusses the Future

5 And as some spake of the temple, how it was adorned with goodly stones and gifts, he said,
6 *As for* these things which ye behold, the days will come, in the which there shall not be left one stone upon another, that shall not be thrown down.
7 And they asked him, saying, Master, but when shall these things be? and what sign *will there be* when these things shall come to pass?

Acts 1:6-7

8 And he said, Take heed that ye be not deceived: for many shall come in my name, saying, I am *Christ*; and the time draweth near: go ye not therefore after them. Jer. 29:8
9 But when ye shall hear of wars and commotions, be not terrified: for these things must first come to pass; but the end *is* not by and by.
10 Then said he unto them, Nation shall rise against nation, and kingdom against kingdom:
11 And great earthquakes shall be in Tdivers places, and famines, and pestilences; and fearful sights and great signs shall there be from heaven. *various*
12 But before all these, they shall lay their hands on you, and persecute *you*, delivering *you* up to the synagogues, and into prisons, being brought before kings and rulers for my name's sake. Acts 8:3
13 And it shall turn to you for a testimony.
14 Settle *it* therefore in your hearts, not to meditate before what ye shall answer:
15 For I will give you a mouth and wisdom, which all your adversaries shall not be able to Tgainsay nor resist. Jer. 1:9 ◆ *speak against*
16 And ye shall be betrayed both by parents, and brethren, and kinsfolks, and friends; and *some* of you shall they cause to be put to death.
17 And ye shall be hated of all *men* for my name's sake. John 15:21
18 But there shall not an hair of your head perish. Matt. 10:30
19 In your patience possess ye your souls.
20 And when ye shall see Jerusalem compassed with armies, then know that the desolation thereof is nigh. Dan. 9:27; Luke 19:43
21 Then let them which are in Judaea flee to the mountains; and let them which are in the midst of it depart out; and let not them that are in the countries enter thereinto.
22 For these be the days of vengeance, that all things which are written may be fulfilled. Is. 34:8
23 But woe unto them that are with child, and to them that give suck, in those days!

Nothing to Fear When We Obey God

Luke 21:20, 21

Not one Christian perished in the destruction of Jerusalem [in A.D. 70]. Christ had given His disciples warning, and all who believed His words watched for the promised sign. ... After the Romans under Cestius had surrounded the city, they unexpectedly abandoned the siege when everything seemed favorable for an immediate attack. ... The promised sign had been given to the waiting Christians, and now an opportunity was offered for all who would, to obey the Saviour's warning. Events were so overruled that neither Jews nor Romans should hinder the flight of the Christians. Upon the retreat of Cestius, the Jews, sallying from Jerusalem, pursued after his retiring army; and while both forces were thus fully engaged, the Christians had an opportunity to leave the city. At this time the country also had been cleared of enemies who might have endeavored to intercept them. At the time of the siege, the Jews were assembled at Jerusalem to keep the Feast of Tabernacles, and thus the Christians throughout the land were able to make their escape unmolested. Without delay they fled to a place of safety—the city of Pella, in the land of Perea, beyond Jordan.

The Jewish forces, pursuing after Cestius and his army, fell upon their rear with such fierceness as to threaten them with total destruction. It was with great difficulty that the Romans succeeded in making their retreat. The Jews escaped almost without loss, and with their spoils returned in triumph to Jerusalem. Yet this apparent success brought them only evil. It inspired them with that spirit of stubborn resistance to the Romans which speedily brought unutterable woe upon the doomed city. *GC 30, 31*

for there shall be great distress in the land, and wrath upon this people.   Luke 23:29

24 And they shall fall by the edge of the sword, and shall be led away captive into all nations: and Jerusalem shall be trodden down of the Gentiles, until the times of the Gentiles be fulfilled. Is. 63:18; Rom. 11:25; Rev. 11:2

25 And there shall be signs in the sun, and in the moon, and in the stars; and upon the earth distress of nations, with perplexity; the sea and the waves roaring;   Is. 13:10

26 Men's hearts failing them for fear, and for looking after those things which are coming on the earth: for the powers of heaven shall be shaken.   Matt. 24:29

27 And then shall they see the Son of man coming in a cloud with power and great glory.   Dan. 7:13

28 And when these things begin to come to pass, then look up, and lift up your heads; for your redemption draweth nigh. Rom. 8:23

29 And he spake to them a parable; Behold the fig tree, and all the trees;

30 When they now shoot forth, ye see and know of your own selves that summer is now nigh at hand.

31 So likewise ye, when ye see these things come to pass, know ye that the kingdom of God is nigh at hand.

32 Verily I say unto you, This generation shall not pass away, till all be fulfilled.   Matt. 24:34

33 Heaven and earth shall pass away: but my words shall not pass away. Ps. 102:26; Is. 40:8

34 And take heed to yourselves, lest at any time your hearts be ᵀovercharged with ᵀsurfeiting, and drunkenness, and cares of this life, and so that day come upon you unawares.   Mark 4:19 ◆ *weighed down* ◆ *excess indulgence*

21:34 The End Is Near

Sad will be the retrospect in that day when men stand face to face with eternity. . . . Men will then see that the righteousness they despised is alone of value. . . .

There will be no future probation in which to prepare for eternity. It is in this life that we are to put on the robe of Christ's righteousness. This is our only opportunity to form characters for the home which Christ has made ready for those who obey His commandments.

The days of our probation are fast closing. The end is near. *COL 318, 319*

---

35 For as a snare shall it come on all them that dwell on the face of the whole earth.

36 Watch ye therefore, and pray always, that ye may be accounted worthy to escape all these things that shall come to pass, and to stand before the Son of man.   Matt. 26:41

37 And in the day time he was teaching in the temple; and at night he went out, and abode in the mount that is called *the mount* of Olives.   Matt. 21:1

38 And all the people came early in the morning to him in the temple, for to hear him.

The Jews Conspire against Jesus

22 Now the feast of unleavened bread drew nigh, which is called the Passover.   Mark 14:1-2

2 And the chief priests and scribes sought how they might kill him; for they feared the people.

3 Then entered Satan into Judas surnamed Iscariot, being of the number of the twelve.

4 And he went his way, and communed with the chief priests and captains, how he might betray him unto them.   Acts 4:1

5 And they were glad, and covenanted to give him money.

6 And he promised, and sought opportunity to betray him unto them in the absence of the multitude.

The Apostles Prepare the Passover

7 Then came the day of unleavened bread, when the passover must be killed.   Ex. 12:18

8 And he sent Peter and John, saying, Go and prepare us the passover, that we may eat.

9 And they said unto him, Where wilt thou that we prepare?

10 And he said unto them, Behold, when ye are entered into the city, there shall a man meet you, bearing a pitcher of water; follow him into the house where he entereth in.

11 And ye shall say unto the goodman of the house, The Master saith unto thee, Where is the guestchamber, where I shall eat the passover with my disciples? John 11:28

12 And he shall shew you a large upper room furnished: there make ready.   Acts 1:13

13 And they went, and found as he had said unto them: and they made ready the passover.

14 And when the hour was come, he sat down, and the twelve apostles with him.

15 And he said unto them, With desire I have desired to eat this passover with you before I suffer:

16 For I say unto you, I will not any more eat thereof, until it be fulfilled in the kingdom of God.   Luke 14:15; 22:30; Rev. 19:9

17 And he took the cup, and gave thanks, and said, Take this, and divide it among yourselves:

18 For I say unto you, I will not drink of the fruit of the vine, until the kingdom of God shall come.   Matt. 26:29; Mark 14:25; Luke 22:16

19 And he took bread, and gave thanks, and brake it, and gave unto them, saying, This is

my body which is given for you: this do in remembrance of me.   1 Cor. 10:16

20 Likewise also the cup after supper, saying, This cup *is* the new testament in my blood, which is shed for you.   Ex. 24:8; Zech. 9:11

22:14–20 Communion, A Constant Lesson

To those who receive the spirit of this service, it can never become a mere ceremonial. Its constant lesson will be, "By love serve one another" (Galatians 5:13). . . . Whenever this ordinance is rightly celebrated, the children of God are brought into a holy relationship, to help and bless each other. They covenant that the life shall be given to unselfish ministry. . . . Those who have communed with Christ in the upper chamber will go forth to minister as He did. *DA 651*

Jesus Knows His Traitor

21 But, behold, the hand of him that betrayeth me *is* with me on the table. Ps. 41:9; John 13:26

22 And truly the Son of man goeth, as it was determined: but woe unto that man by whom he is betrayed!   Acts 2:23

23 And they began to enquire among themselves, which of them it was that should do this thing.

An Argument about Greatness

24 And there was also a strife among them, which of them should be accounted the greatest.   Mark 9:34; Luke 9:46

25 And he said unto them, The kings of the Gentiles exercise lordship over them; and they that exercise authority upon them are called benefactors.   Matt. 20:25-28

26 But ye *shall* not *be* so: but he that is greatest among you, let him be as the younger; and he that is chief, as he that doth serve.   Luke 9:48

27 For whether *is* greater, he that sitteth at meat, or he that serveth? *is* not he that sitteth at meat? but I am among you as he that serveth.   Matt. 20:28; Luke 12:37

28 Ye are they which have continued with me in my temptations.   Heb. 2:18

29 And I appoint unto you a kingdom, as my Father hath appointed unto me;   2 Tim. 2:12

30 That ye may eat and drink at my table in my kingdom, and sit on thrones judging the twelve tribes of Israel. Matt. 8:11; 19:28; Luke 14:15

Jesus Predicts Peter's Denial

31 And the Lord said, Simon, Simon, behold, Satan hath desired *to have* you, that he may sift *you* as wheat: Job 1:6-12; Amos 9:9; 1 Pet. 5:8

32 But I have prayed for thee, that thy faith fail not: and when thou art converted, strengthen thy brethren. John 21:15-17; Rom. 8:34

33 And he said unto him, Lord, I am ready to go with thee, both into prison, and to death.   Matt. 26:33-35

34 And he said, I tell thee, Peter, the cock shall not crow this day, before that thou shalt thrice deny that thou knowest me. Matt. 26:34

22:31–34 Jesus' Love Never Fails

For them all, Peter's experience had a lesson. To self-trust, trial is defeat. . . .

Christ, though foreseeing his sin, had not abandoned him to despair.

If the look that Jesus cast upon him had spoken condemnation instead of pity; if in foretelling the sin He had failed of speaking hope, how dense would have been the darkness that encompassed Peter! . . .

He who could not spare His disciple the anguish, left him not alone to its bitterness. His is a love that fails not nor forsakes. *Ed 88–90*

35 And he said unto them, When I sent you without purse, and scrip, and shoes, lacked ye any thing? And they said, Nothing. Matt. 10:9-10

36 Then said he unto them, But now, he that hath a purse, let him take *it*, and likewise *his* ᵀscrip: and he that hath no sword, let him sell his garment, and buy one.   sack

37 For I say unto you, that this that is written must yet be accomplished in me, And he was reckoned among the ᵀtransgressors: for the things concerning me have an end.   Is. 53:12 ◆ *lawbreakers*

38 And they said, Lord, behold, here *are* two swords. And he said unto them, It is enough.

Jesus Prays in Gethsemane

39 And he came out, and went, as he was wont, to the mount of Olives; and his disciples also followed him. Matt. 21:1; John 18:1-2

40 And when he was at the place, he said unto them, Pray that ye enter not into temptation.   Matt. 6:13; Luke 22:46; 1 Pet. 4:7

41 And he was withdrawn from them about a stone's cast, and kneeled down, and prayed,   Matt. 26:39

42 Saying, Father, if thou be willing, remove this cup from me: nevertheless not my will, but thine, be done.   Matt. 20:22

43 And there appeared an angel unto him from heaven, strengthening him.   Heb. 1:14

44 And being in an agony he prayed more earnestly: and his sweat was as it were great drops of blood falling down to the ground.   Lam. 1:12

45 And when he rose up from prayer, and was come to his disciples, he found them sleeping for sorrow,

46 And said unto them, Why sleep ye? rise and pray, lest ye enter into temptation.

Jesus Is Betrayed with a Kiss

47 And while he yet spake, behold a multitude, and he that was called Judas, one of the twelve, went before them, and drew near unto Jesus to kiss him.

48 But Jesus said unto him, Judas, betrayest thou the Son of man with a kiss?

49 When they which were about him saw what would follow, they said unto him, Lord, shall we ᵀsmite with the sword?   *strike*

50 And one of them smote the servant of the high priest, and cut off his right ear.

51 And Jesus answered and said, Suffer ye thus far. And he touched his ear, and healed him.

52 Then Jesus said unto the chief priests, and captains of the temple, and the elders, which were come to him, Be ye come out, as against a thief, with swords and staves?   Luke 22:4

53 When I was daily with you in the temple, ye stretched forth no hands against me: but this is your hour, and the power of darkness.   John 12:27

Jesus Is Denied by Peter

54 Then took they him, and led *him*, and brought him into the high priest's house. And Peter followed afar off.   Matt. 26:57-58; Mark 14:53

55 And when they had kindled a fire in the midst of the hall, and were set down together, Peter sat down among them.

56 But a certain maid beheld him as he sat by the fire, and earnestly looked upon him, and said, This man was also with him.

57 And he denied him, saying, Woman, I know him not.

58 And after a little while another saw him, and said, Thou art also of them. And Peter said, Man, I am not.

59 And about the space of one hour after another confidently affirmed, saying, Of a truth this *fellow* also was with him: for he is a Galilaean.

60 And Peter said, Man, I know not what thou sayest. And immediately, while he yet spake, the cock crew.

22:61 Bitter Yet Sweet

When the crowing of the cock reminded him of the words of Christ, surprised and shocked at what he had just done he turned and looked at his Master. At that moment Christ looked at Peter, and . . . Peter understood himself. . . . That look of Christ's broke his heart. . . . He was like the publican in his contrition and repentance, and like the publican he found mercy. The look of Christ assured him of pardon.

Now his self-confidence was gone. Never again were the old boastful assertions repeated. *COL 152, 154*

---

61 And the Lord turned, and looked upon Peter. And Peter remembered the word of the Lord, how he had said unto him, Before the cock crow, thou shalt deny me thrice.

62 And Peter went out, and wept bitterly.

The Trial by the Jewish Council

63 And the men that held Jesus mocked him, and smote *him*.   John 18:22

64 And when they had blindfolded him, they struck him on the face, and asked him, saying, Prophesy, who is it that smote thee?

65 And many other things blasphemously spake they against him.

66 And as soon as it was day, the elders of the people and the chief priests and the scribes came together, and led him into their council, saying,   Matt. 27:1; Mark 15:1; Acts 22:5

67 Art thou the Christ? tell us. And he said unto them, If I tell you, ye will not believe:

68 And if I also ask *you*, ye will not answer me, nor let *me* go.   Luke 20:3-7

69 Hereafter shall the Son of man sit on the right hand of the power of God.   Ps. 110:1

70 Then said they all, Art thou then the Son of God? And he said unto them, Ye say that I am.   Matt. 26:64; 27:11; Luke 23:3

71 And they said, What need we any further witness? for we ourselves have heard of his own mouth.

Pilate Questions Jesus

23 And the whole multitude of them arose, and led him unto Pilate.

2 And they began to accuse him, saying, We found this *fellow* perverting the nation, and forbidding to give tribute to Caesar, saying that he himself is Christ a King.   John 19:12

3 And Pilate asked him, saying, Art thou the King of the Jews? And he answered him and said, Thou sayest *it*.   1 Tim. 6:13

4 Then said Pilate to the chief priests and *to* the people, I find no fault in this man.

Jesus Before Herod

5 And they were the more fierce, saying, He stirreth up the people, teaching throughout all Jewry, beginning from Galilee to this place.   Mark 1:14

6 When Pilate heard of Galilee, he asked whether the man were a Galilaean.

7 And as soon as he knew that he belonged unto Herod's jurisdiction, he sent him to Herod, who himself also was at Jerusalem at that time.   Luke 3:1; 13:31

8 And when Herod saw Jesus, he was exceeding glad: for he was desirous to see him of a long *season*, because he had heard many things of him; and he hoped to have seen some miracle done by him.   Matt. 14:1

9 Then he questioned with him in many words; but he answered him nothing.

10 And the chief priests and scribes stood and ᵀvehemently accused him.　　*strongly*

11 And Herod with his men of war set him at ᵀnought, and mocked *him*, and ᵀarrayed him in a gorgeous robe, and sent him again to Pilate.　　*Mark 9:12 ◆ nothing ◆ clothed*

12 And the same day Pilate and Herod were made friends together: for before they were at ᵀenmity between themselves. *Acts 4:27 ◆ hostility*

The Crowd Rejects Jesus

13 And Pilate, when he had called together the chief priests and the rulers and the people,

14 Said unto them, Ye have brought this man unto me, as one that perverteth the people: and, behold, I, having examined *him* before you, have found no fault in this man touching those things whereof ye accuse him:

15 No, nor yet Herod: for I sent you to him; and, lo, nothing worthy of death is done unto him.

16 I will therefore chastise him, and release *him*.　　*Matt. 27:26*

17 (For of necessity he must release one unto them at the feast.)

18 And they cried out all at once, saying, Away with this *man*, and release unto us Barabbas:　　*Acts 3:14*

19 (Who for a certain sedition made in the city, and for murder, was cast into prison.)

20 Pilate therefore, willing to release Jesus, spake again to them.

21 But they cried, saying, Crucify *him*, crucify him.

22 And he said unto them the third time, Why, what evil hath he done? I have found no cause of death in him: I will therefore chastise him, and let *him* go.　　*Luke 23:14*

23 And they were instant with loud voices, requiring that he might be crucified. And the voices of them and of the chief priests prevailed.

24 And Pilate gave sentence that it should be as they required.　　*Ex. 23:2*

25 And he released unto them him that for sedition and murder was cast into prison, whom they had desired; but he delivered Jesus to their will.

Jesus Is Led Away to be Crucified

26 And as they led him away, they laid hold upon one Simon, a Cyrenian, coming out of the country, and on him they laid the cross, that he might bear *it* after Jesus.

27 And there followed him a great company of people, and of women, which also bewailed and lamented him.　　*Luke 8:52*

28 But Jesus turning unto them said, Daughters of Jerusalem, weep not for me, but weep for yourselves, and for your children.

29 For, behold, the days are coming, in the which they shall say, Blessed *are* the barren, and the wombs that never bare, and the paps which never gave suck.　　*Hos. 13:16; Matt. 24:19*

30 Then shall they begin to say to the mountains, Fall on us; and to the hills, Cover us.　　*Is. 2:19; Hos. 10:8; Rev. 6:16*

31 For if they do these things in a green tree, what shall be done in the dry?　　*Prov. 11:31*

"Father, Forgive Them"

Luke 23:34

Heaven viewed with grief and amazement Christ hanging upon the cross, blood flowing from His wounded temples, and sweat tinged with blood standing upon His brow. From His hands and feet the blood fell, drop by drop, upon the rock drilled for the foot of the cross. The wounds made by the nails gaped as the weight of His body dragged upon His hands. His labored breath grew quick and deep, as His soul panted under the burden of the sins of the world. All heaven was filled with wonder when the prayer of Christ was offered in the midst of His terrible suffering— "Father, forgive them; for they know not what they do" (Luke 23:34). Yet there stood men, formed in the image of God, joining to crush out the life of His only-begotten Son. What a sight for the heavenly universe! . . .

Those who mocked Christ as He hung upon the cross were imbued with the spirit of the first great rebel. He filled them with vile and loathsome speeches. He inspired their taunts. But by all this he gained nothing.

Could one sin have been found in Christ, had He in one particular yielded to Satan to escape the terrible torture, the enemy of God and man would have triumphed. Christ bowed His head and died, but He held fast His faith and His submission to God. . . .

Satan saw that his disguise was torn away. His administration was laid open before the unfallen angels and before the heavenly universe. He had revealed himself as a murderer. By shedding the blood of the Son of God, he had uprooted himself from the sympathies of the heavenly beings. Henceforth his work was restricted. . . . The last link of sympathy between Satan and the heavenly world was broken. *DA 760, 761*

32 And there were also two other, malefactors, led with him to be put to death. John 19:18
33 And when they were come to the place, which is called Calvary, there they crucified him, and the malefactors, one on the right hand, and the other on the left. Matt. 27:33-34
34 Then said Jesus, Father, forgive them; for they know not what they do. And they parted his raiment, and cast lots. Ps. 22:18; Matt. 5:44
35 And the people stood beholding. And the rulers also with them derided *him*, saying, He saved others; let him save himself, if he be Christ, the chosen of God. Ps. 22:17
36 And the soldiers also mocked him, coming to him, and offering him vinegar, Ps. 69:21
37 And saying, If thou be the king of the Jews, save thyself.
38 And a superscription also was written over him in letters of Greek, and Latin, and Hebrew, THIS IS THE KING OF THE JEWS. Matt. 27:37; Mark 15:26, 32

The Criminal Believes

39 And one of the ᵀmalefactors which were hanged railed on him, saying, If thou be Christ, save thyself and us. Matt. 27:44 ◆ *evildoers*
40 But the other answering rebuked him, saying, Dost not thou fear God, seeing thou art in the same condemnation?
41 And we indeed justly; for we receive the due reward of our deeds: but this man hath done nothing amiss.
42 And he said unto Jesus, Lord, remember me when thou comest into thy kingdom.
43 And Jesus said unto him, Verily I say unto thee, To day shalt thou be with me in paradise. Is. 53:11; 2 Cor. 5:8; Rev. 2:7

> **23:42, 43 The Difference of One Comma**
>
> I say unto thee today, Thou shalt be with Me in Paradise. Christ did not promise that the thief should be with Him in Paradise that day. He Himself did not go that day to Paradise. He slept in the tomb, and on the morning of the resurrection He said, "I am not yet ascended to My Father" (John 20:17). . . . "Today" while dying upon the cross as a malefactor, Christ assures the poor sinner, Thou shalt be with Me in Paradise. *DA 751*

Jesus Dies on the Cross

44 And it was about the sixth hour, and there was a darkness over all the earth until the ninth hour. Amos 8:9
45 And the sun was darkened, and the veil of the temple was rent in the midst. Ex. 26:31-33
46 And when Jesus had cried with a loud voice, he said, Father, into thy hands I commend my spirit: and having said thus, he gave up the ghost. Ps. 31:5; John 19:30; Acts 7:59

47 Now when the centurion saw what was done, he glorified God, saying, Certainly this was a righteous man. Matt. 27:54
48 And all the people that came together to that sight, beholding the things which were done, smote their breasts, and returned. Luke 18:13
49 And all his acquaintance, and the women that followed him from Galilee, stood afar off, beholding these things. Ps. 38:11; Matt. 27:55-56

Jesus Is Buried

50 And, behold, *there was* a man named Joseph, a counsellor; *and he was* a good man, and a just:
51 (The same had not consented to the counsel and deed of them;) he was of Arimathaea, a city of the Jews: who also himself waited for the kingdom of God. Mark 15:43; Luke 2:25, 38
52 This *man* went unto Pilate, and begged the body of Jesus.
53 And he took it down, and wrapped it in linen, and laid it in a sepulchre that was ᵀhewn in stone, wherein never man before was laid. Is. 53:9 ◆ *cut*
54 And that day was the preparation, and the sabbath drew on. Matt. 27:62; John 19:31
55 And the women also, which came with him from Galilee, followed after, and beheld the sepulchre, and how his body was laid. Luke 23:49
56 And they returned, and prepared spices and ointments; and rested the sabbath day according to the commandment. Mark 16:1

Jesus' Resurrection

24 Now upon the first *day* of the week, very early in the morning, they came unto the sepulchre, bringing the spices which they had prepared, and certain *others* with them. Luke 24:10
2 And they found the stone rolled away from the sepulchre.
3 And they entered in, and found not the body of the Lord Jesus. Luke 24:23
4 And it came to pass, as they were much perplexed thereabout, behold, two men stood by them in shining garments: Mark 16:5
5 And as they were afraid, and bowed down *their* faces to the earth, they said unto them, Why seek ye the living among the dead?
6 He is not here, but is risen: remember how he spake unto you when he was yet in Galilee, Matt. 17:22-23
7 Saying, The Son of man must be delivered into the hands of sinful men, and be crucified, and the third day rise again.
8 And they remembered his words,
9 And returned from the sepulchre, and told all these things unto the eleven, and to all the rest.

10 It was Mary Magdalene, and Joanna, and Mary *the mother* of James, and other *women that were* with them, which told these things unto the apostles. Mark 15:40-41

11 And their words seemed to them as idle tales, and they believed them not. Mark 16:11

12 Then arose Peter, and ran unto the sepulchre; and stooping down, he beheld the linen clothes laid by themselves, and departed, wondering in himself at that which was come to pass.

Jesus Appears on the Road to Emmaus

13 And, behold, two of them went that same day to a village called Emmaus, which was from Jerusalem *about* ^Tthreescore furlongs. sixty

14 And they talked together of all these things which had happened.

15 And it came to pass, that, while they communed *together* and reasoned, Jesus himself drew near, and went with them. Luke 24:36

16 But their eyes were holden that they should not know him. Luke 24:31; John 20:14; 21:4

17 And he said unto them, What manner of communications *are* these that ye have one to another, as ye walk, and are sad?

18 And the one of them, whose name was Cleopas, answering said unto him, Art thou only a stranger in Jerusalem, and hast not known the things which are come to pass there in these days? John 19:25

19 And he said unto them, What things? And they said unto him, Concerning Jesus of Nazareth, which was a prophet mighty in deed and word before God and all the people: Matt. 21:11; Acts 2:22; 7:22

20 And how the chief priests and our rulers delivered him to be condemned to death, and have crucified him. Luke 23:13

21 But we trusted that it had been he which should have redeemed Israel: and beside all this, to day is the third day since these things were done. Luke 1:68; 2:38

22 Yea, and certain women also of our company made us astonished, which were early at the sepulchre;

23 And when they found not his body, they came, saying, that they had also seen a vision of angels, which said that he was alive.

24 And certain of them which were with us went to the sepulchre, and found *it* even so as the women had said: but him they saw not. Luke 24:12

25 Then he said unto them, O fools, and slow of heart to believe all that the prophets have spoken:

26 Ought not Christ to have suffered these things, and to enter into his glory? Zech. 13:7

27 And beginning at Moses and all the prophets, he expounded unto them in all the scriptures the things concerning himself. Gen. 3:15; Is. 7:14; John 1:45

28 And they drew nigh unto the village, whither they went: and he made as though he would have gone further. Mark 6:48

29 But they ^Tconstrained him, saying, Abide with us: for it is toward evening, and the day is far spent. And he went in to tarry with them. compelled

> **24:29 Christ Never Forces**
>
> Had the disciples [on the road to Emmaus] failed to press their invitation, they would not have known that their traveling companion was the risen Lord. Christ never forces His company upon anyone. He interests Himself in those who need Him. . . . But if men are too indifferent to think of the heavenly Guest, or ask Him to abide with them, He passes on. Thus many meet with great loss. *DA 800*

30 And it came to pass, as he sat at meat with them, he took bread, and blessed *it*, and brake, and gave to them. Matt. 14:19; Luke 24:35

31 And their eyes were opened, and they knew him; and he vanished out of their sight. Luke 4:30; 24:16

32 And they said one to another, Did not our heart burn within us, while he talked with us by the way, and while he opened to us the scriptures? Ps. 39:3; Luke 24:45

33 And they rose up the same hour, and returned to Jerusalem, and found the eleven gathered together, and them that were with them,

34 Saying, The Lord is risen indeed, and hath appeared to Simon. 1 Cor. 15:5

35 And they told what things *were done* in the way, and how he was known of them in breaking of bread.

Jesus Appears to the Apostles

36 And as they thus spake, Jesus himself stood in the midst of them, and saith unto them, Peace be unto you. Mark 16:14

37 But they were terrified and affrighted, and supposed that they had seen a spirit.

38 And he said unto them, Why are ye troubled? and why do thoughts arise in your hearts?

39 Behold my hands and my feet, that it is I myself: handle me, and see; for a spirit hath not flesh and bones, as ye see me have.

40 And when he had thus spoken, he shewed them *his* hands and *his* feet.

41 And while they yet believed not for joy, and wondered, he said unto them, Have ye here any meat? John 21:5

42 And they gave him a piece of a broiled fish, and of an honeycomb.

43 And he took *it*, and did eat before them.
44 And he said unto them, These *are* the words which I spake unto you, while I was yet with you, that all things must be fulfilled, which were written in the law of Moses, and *in* the prophets, and *in* the psalms, concerning me. Ps. 72
45 Then opened he their understanding, that they might understand the scriptures,

> **24:44, 45 Now We See**
>
> The disciples began to realize the nature and extent of their work. They were to proclaim to the world the wonderful truths which Christ had entrusted to them. The events of His life, His death and resurrection, the prophecies that pointed to these events, the sacredness of the law of God, the mysteries of the plan of salvation, the power of Jesus for the remission of sins—to all these things they were witnesses, and they were to make them known to the world. *DA 805*

46 And said unto them, Thus it is written, and thus it behoved Christ to suffer, and to rise from the dead the third day: Luke 24:44
47 And that repentance and remission of sins should be preached in his name among all nations, beginning at Jerusalem. Acts 2:38
48 And ye are witnesses of these things.
49 And, behold, I send the promise of my Father upon you: but tarry ye in the city of Jerusalem, until ye be ᵀendued with power from on high. John 14:26; Acts 1:4, 8 ◆ *supplied*
50 And he led them out as far as to Bethany, and he lifted up his hands, and blessed them. Acts 1:12
51 And it came to pass, while he blessed them, he was parted from them, and carried up into heaven. 2 Kin. 2:11
52 And they worshipped him, and returned to Jerusalem with great joy: Matt. 28:9
53 And were continually in the temple, praising and blessing God. Amen.

THE GOSPEL ACCORDING TO

JOHN

"In the beginning." The Gospel writer John is not content to begin his story as Mark with the testimony of John the Baptist, as Luke with the birth narratives of John the Baptist and Jesus, or as Matthew with the genealogy of Jesus beginning with Abraham. No, John starts at the very beginning as Genesis 1:1 does, "In the beginning" when there was just God.

Christian theology cannot go back further than God. The Gospel of John offers a new beginning, brought about by the redemptive work of Christ. In saying, "In the beginning," John describes Jesus as existing from the beginning; in other words, He is the ultimate source of all things.

Whereas the first three Gospels major on events in the life of Jesus, John emphasizes the *meaning* of those events. John's Gospel is not so much biographical as it is a theological argument for the deity of Jesus. John uses every event, "I am" statement, miracle, and title to show us that Jesus is God. He makes the audacious claim by stating the purpose for his writing (and the Bible itself): "But these are written, that ye might believe that Jesus is the Christ, the Son of God; and that believing ye might have life through his name" (20:31). John wants his readers to believe Jesus is God. He writes with a clear, evangelistic purpose.

John, unmistakably, is clear that Jesus is the divine Son of God who deserves our praise and our belief. He offers convincing and compelling proofs that Jesus is our God.

Dates

The probable range for the writing of this Gospel is late in the first century about A.D. 90. It was written after the synoptic Gospels, but before John's three epistles and Revelation. John was the last surviving eyewitness of Jesus' earthly ministry and apostle of the early Christian church. Tradition informs us that John wrote this Gospel in Ephesus.

Author

The disciple "whom Jesus loved" (see 13:23; 19:26; 20:2; 21:7, 20) has long been identified as the author. This disciple is believed to be John, who was one of three men who formed the inner circle of Jesus. Peter, James, and John were often called upon by Jesus to see certain things that the other disciples did not—the Transfiguration, for example (Matthew 17:1–13). John and his brother, James, were the sons of Zebedee and Salome and were called the "sons of thunder" (Mark 3:17) by Jesus because of their fiery temperaments. Having been an ardent follower of John the Baptist along with Andrew, the brother of Simon Peter, John was among the original twelve disciples selected by Jesus (John 1:35–42). He gave great detail to numbers (2:6; 6:13, 19; 21:8, 11) and to names (1:45; 3:1; 11:1; 18:10), which indicated that he was an eyewitness to the events about which he wrote.

Younger than the other disciples, he opens his heart to Jesus with the confiding trust and hero worship of youth. John spends most of his time close to Jesus and surrenders himself more fully to the Master's perfect life. Being that John is the most receptive and teachable, his reflection of Christ's character is deeper and more full than of the other members of the Twelve. It is through this integrity that we see the divine spirit of Christ.

Meaning of the Name

As with the titles of the synoptic Gospels, the title of the fourth Gospel follows the same format: *Kata Ioannen*, "According to John." The word "gospel" was added later. *Ioannes* is derived from the Hebrew name *Johanan*, "Yahweh Has Been Gracious."

Christ in John

Christ is presented as God in this book in a simple yet profound way. To accomplish this purpose, John meticulously recorded seven "I am" statements that Jesus made, attributed only to God: (1) I am the bread of life (6:35, 41, 48, 51); (2) I am the light of the world (8:12; 9:5); (3) I am the door of the sheep (10:7, 9); (4) I am the good shepherd (10:11, 14); (5) I am the resurrection, and the life (11:25); (6) I am the way, the truth, the life (14:6), and (7) I am the true vine (15:1, 5). The words *I am* recall God's revelation of His name, "I AM," to Moses (Exodus 3:14). Note that Jesus did not say He gave bread, but that

He *is* bread. That would be true for the other statements as well—clearly they are claims of His deity.

Furthermore, John recorded seven miracles or signs pointing to Jesus' divine nature: (1) changing water into wine (2:1–11); (2) healing the son of a nobleman (4:46–54); (3) healing a lame man at the pool of Bethesda (5:1–9); (4) feeding the five thousand (6:1–14); (5) walking on water (6:15–21); (6) healing a man born blind (9:1–7); and (7) raising Lazarus from the dead (11:38–44). John's Gospel is sometimes referred to as "The Book of the Seven Signs" because of these seven miracles.

The greatest sign that Jesus is divine was His resurrection from the tomb. John provided a stirring eyewitness account. He was the first disciple to see the empty tomb (20:1–10). He also recorded several post-resurrections appearances by Jesus (20:11—21:23).

Overview

John wrote to communicate that Jesus is God. As an apostle commissioned by Jesus to spread the good news, John wanted people to believe in the Person and the work of Jesus Christ. His Gospel can be divided into five sections:

(1) *John 1:1–18, The Incarnation and Work of the Son of God:* Before He took on flesh, Jesus was with God and "was God" from "the beginning" (1:1). John moves from the work of the preincarnate Christ to the work of John the Baptist (1:6–8) who came "to bear witness of the Light" (1:6). The metaphor of Jesus as the light in contrast to the darkness of the world is one used often in John's Gospel and his epistles (see, for example 1:4–9; 1 John 1:5–7).

(2) *John 1:19—4:54, The Beginning Ministry of the Son of God:* As Jesus begins His public ministry, John makes a strong case for Jesus being the Son of God by providing seven signs of His deity. Two of the seven signs of Jesus' deity (see "Christ in John" above) can be found in this section.

(3) *John 5:1—12:50, The Confrontations of the Son of God:* The One who stated "In the world ye shall have tribulation" (16:33) knew from experience the trouble one can find. As Jesus heals and teaches, the Pharisees and Sadducees begin to oppose Jesus' ministry. Jesus responds to their challenges with miracles and teachings.

(4) *John 13:1—17:26, The Teaching and Intercession of the Son of God:* Unlike the survey approach of the previous twelve chapters, John provides in-depth details of Jesus' last supper and high priestly prayer.

(5) *John 18:1—21:25, The Death and Resurrection of the Son of God:* The crowning jewel of John's Gospel is the account of the death and resurrection of the Lamb of God. During the crucifixion narrative, John includes Jesus' arrangements for the care of His mother since these arrangements affected his own life (19:25–27).

Unlocking John

🔑 **KEY PEOPLE:**
Jesus, John the Baptist, Jesus' disciples (including John), the Pharisees (including Nicodemus), Mary of Bethany, Martha, Lazarus, Jesus' mother, Pilate, Mary Magdalene, the woman at the well, the prodigal son, the good Samaritan, Roman soldiers

🔑 **KEY EVENTS:**
The seven "I am" statements and the seven miracles (see "Christ in John")

🔑 **KEY WORD:**
Believe, because John wanted people to respond in faith intellectually and spiritually about Jesus being God. Belief requires both knowledge and volition.

🔑 **KEY VERSES:**
"He came unto his own, and his own received him not. But as many as received him, to them gave he power to become the sons of God, even to them that believe on his name: which were born, not of blood, nor of the will of the flesh, nor of the will of man, but of God" (John 1:11–13).

"But these are written, that ye might believe that Jesus is the Christ, the Son of God; and that believing ye might have life through his name" (John 20:31).

🔑 **KEY CHAPTER:**
John 3, and especially verse 16, which captures the gospel in its clearest and simplest form: that salvation is a gift from God and is obtainable only through belief. The conversation with Nicodemus and the testimony of John the Baptist clearly explain that being "born again" (verse 7) is the only way to find the "kingdom of God" (verse 5).

The Word Becomes Human

1 In the beginning was the Word, and the Word was with God, and the Word was God. Gen. 1:1; John 17:5; 1 John 1:1-2

2 The same was in the beginning with God.

3 All things were made by him; and without him was not any thing made that was made. John 1:10

Who Is God?   See John 1:14.

4 In him was life; and the life was the light of men. John 5:26; 8:12; 11:25

5 And the light shineth in darkness; and the darkness comprehended it not.

6 There was a man sent from God, whose name *was* John. Mal. 3:1

7 The same came for a witness, to bear witness of the Light, that all *men* through him might believe. John 1:19

8 He was not that Light, but *was sent* to bear witness of that Light. John 1:20

9 *That* was the true Light, which lighteth every man that cometh into the world. Is. 49:6

10 He was in the world, and the world was made by him, and the world knew him not.

11 He came unto his own, and his own received him not. John 3:32

> **1:12 A Transcript of God's Character**
>
> This power is not in the human agent. It is the power of God. When a soul receives Christ, he receives power to live the life of Christ.
>
> God requires perfection of His children. His law is a transcript of His own character, and it is the standard of all character. COL 314, 315

12 But as many as received him, to them gave he power to become the sons of God, *even* to them that believe on his name: Gal. 3:26

Faith   See Hebrews 4:2.

Salvation From Sin   See Ephesians 2:8, 9.

13 Which were born, not of blood, nor of the will of the flesh, nor of the will of man, but of God. James 1:18; 1 Pet. 1:23; 1 John 3:9

14 And the Word was made flesh, and dwelt among us, (and we beheld his glory, the glory as of the only begotten of the Father,) full of grace and truth. John 1:1; Gal. 4:4; 1 Tim. 3:16

Who Is God?   See Colossians 1:15, 16.

John's Testimony concerning Christ

15 John bare witness of him, and cried, saying, This was he of whom I spake, He that cometh after me is preferred before me: for he was before me. Matt. 3:11

16 And of his fulness have all we received, and grace for grace. Eph. 1:23; Col. 1:19

17 For the law was given by Moses, *but* grace and truth came by Jesus Christ. John 1:14

18 No man hath seen God at any time; the only begotten Son, which is in the bosom of the Father, he hath declared *him*. Matt. 11:27

19 And this is the record of John, when the Jews sent priests and Levites from Jerusalem to ask him, Who art thou? John 10:24

20 And he confessed, and denied not; but confessed, I am not the Christ.

21 And they asked him, What then? Art thou Elias? And he saith, I am not. Art thou that prophet? And he answered, No. Matt. 11:14

22 Then said they unto him, Who art thou? that we may give an answer to them that sent us. What sayest thou of thyself?

23 He said, I *am* the voice of one crying in the wilderness, Make straight the way of the Lord, as said the prophet Esaias. Matt. 3:3

24 And they which were sent were of the Pharisees.

25 And they asked him, and said unto him, Why baptizest thou then, if thou be not that Christ, nor Elias, neither that prophet?

26 John answered them, saying, I baptize with water: but there standeth one among you, whom ye know not; Matt. 3:11

27 He it is, who coming after me is preferred before me, whose shoe's latchet I am not worthy to unloose. Matt. 3:11; John 1:15, 30

> **1:19–27 Spirit Removes Pride**
>
> When the Spirit of God, with its marvelous awakening power, touches the soul, it abases human pride. Worldly pleasure and position and power are seen to be worthless. DA 135

28 These things were done in Bethabara beyond Jordan, where John was baptizing.

29 The next day John seeth Jesus coming unto him, and saith, Behold the Lamb of God, which taketh away the sin of the world. Is. 53:7; John 1:36; 1 Pet. 1:19

30 This is he of whom I said, After me cometh a man which is preferred before me: for he was before me. John 1:15, 27

31 And I knew him not: but that he should be made ᵀmanifest to Israel, therefore am I come baptizing with water. Luke 1:17 ◆ *known*

32 And John bare record, saying, I saw the Spirit descending from heaven like a dove, and it abode upon him. Matt. 3:16; Mark 1:10

33 And I knew him not: but he that sent me to baptize with water, the same said unto me, Upon whom thou shalt see the Spirit descending, and remaining on him, the same is he which baptizeth with the Holy Ghost. Matt. 3:11; Luke 3:16; Acts 1:5

34 And I saw, and bare record that this is the Son of God. Matt. 4:3

The First Disciples

35 Again the next day after John stood, and two of his disciples;

36 And looking upon Jesus as he walked, he saith, Behold the Lamb of God! John 1:29

37 And the two disciples heard him speak, and they followed Jesus.

38 Then Jesus turned, and saw them following, and saith unto them, What seek ye? They said unto him, Rabbi, (which is to say, being interpreted, Master,) where dwellest thou? John 1:49; 3:2, 26

39 He saith unto them, Come and see. They came and saw where he dwelt, and abode with him that day: for it was about the tenth hour.

40 One of the two which heard John *speak*, and followed him, was Andrew, Simon Peter's brother.

41 He first findeth his own brother Simon, and saith unto him, We have found the Messias, which is, being interpreted, the Christ. John 4:25

42 And he brought him to Jesus. And when Jesus beheld him, he said, Thou art Simon the son of Jona: thou shalt be called Cephas, which is by interpretation, A stone. John 21:15

43 The day following Jesus would go forth into Galilee, and findeth Philip, and saith unto him, Follow me.

44 Now Philip was of Bethsaida, the city of Andrew and Peter. Matt. 10:3; 11:21; John 12:21

45 Philip findeth Nathanael, and saith unto him, We have found him, of whom Moses in the law, and the prophets, did write, Jesus of Nazareth, the son of Joseph. Matt. 2:23

46 And Nathanael said unto him, Can there any good thing come out of Nazareth? Philip saith unto him, Come and see. John 7:41-42, 52

47 Jesus saw Nathanael coming to him, and saith of him, Behold an Israelite indeed, in whom is no ᵀguile! Ps. 32:2 ◆ *deceit*

48 Nathanael saith unto him, Whence knowest thou me? Jesus answered and said unto him, Before that Philip called thee, when thou wast under the fig tree, I saw thee. John 2:25

49 Nathanael answered and saith unto him, Rabbi, thou art the Son of God; thou art the King of Israel. Zech. 9:9; Matt. 2:2; 27:42

50 Jesus answered and said unto him, Because I said unto thee, I saw thee under the fig tree, believest thou? thou shalt see greater things than these.

51 And he saith unto him, Verily, verily, I say unto you, Hereafter ye shall see heaven open, and the angels of God ascending and descending upon the Son of man. Gen. 28:12; Ezek. 1:1

Jesus Turns Water into Wine

2 And the third day there was a marriage in Cana of Galilee; and the mother of Jesus was there: John 1:43; 4:46; 21:2

2 And both Jesus was called, and his disciples, to the marriage.

3 And when they wanted wine, the mother of Jesus saith unto him, They have no wine.

4 Jesus saith unto her, Woman, what have I to do with thee? mine hour is not yet come.

2:4 Priority of God's Claims

This lesson is also for us. The claims of God are paramount even to the ties of human relationship. No earthly attraction should turn our feet from the path in which He bids us walk. *DA 147*

5 His mother saith unto the servants, Whatsoever he saith unto you, do *it*.

6 And there were set there six waterpots of stone, after the manner of the purifying of the Jews, containing two or three firkins apiece.

7 Jesus saith unto them, Fill the waterpots with water. And they filled them up to the brim.

8 And he saith unto them, Draw out now, and bear unto the governor of the feast. And they bare *it*.

9 When the ruler of the feast had tasted the water that was made wine, and knew not whence it was: (but the servants which drew the water knew;) the governor of the feast called the bridegroom, John 4:46

2:10 Never-Failing Supply

The feast that [Jesus] provides for the soul never fails to give satisfaction and joy. Each new gift increases the capacity of the receiver to appreciate and enjoy the blessings of the Lord. He gives grace for grace. There can be no failure of supply. If you abide in Him, the fact that you receive a rich gift today insures the reception of a richer gift tomorrow. *DA 148*

10 And saith unto him, Every man at the beginning doth set forth good wine; and when men have well drunk, then that which is worse: *but* thou hast kept the good wine until now.

Marriage See 2 Corinthians 6:14.

11 This beginning of miracles did Jesus in Cana of Galilee, and ᵀmanifested forth his glory; and his disciples believed on him. John 1:14; 3:2 ◆ *made known*

Jesus Throws Moneychangers out of the Temple

12 After this he went down to Capernaum, he, and his mother, and his brethren, and

his disciples: and they continued there not many days.   Matt. 4:13; 12:46
13 And the Jews' passover was at hand, and Jesus went up to Jerusalem, Luke 2:41; John 11:55
14 And found in the temple those that sold oxen and sheep and doves, and the changers of money sitting: Mark 11:15
15 And when he had made a ᵀscourge of small cords, he drove them all out of the temple, and the sheep, and the oxen; and poured out the changers' money, and overthrew the tables;   *whip*
16 And said unto them that sold doves, Take these things hence; make not my Father's house an house of merchandise.   Luke 2:49

> **2:14–16 Once Again God's Temple**
>
> Because of sin, humanity ceased to be a temple for God. Darkened and defiled by evil, the heart of man no longer revealed the glory of the Divine One. But by the incarnation of the Son of God, the purpose of Heaven is fulfilled. God dwells in humanity, and through saving grace the heart of man becomes again His temple. *DA 161*

17 And his disciples remembered that it was written, The zeal of thine house hath eaten me up.   Ps. 69:9
18 Then answered the Jews and said unto him, What sign shewest thou unto us, seeing that thou doest these things?   John 6:30
19 Jesus answered and said unto them, Destroy this temple, and in three days I will raise it up.   Matt. 27:40; Mark 14:58; 15:29
20 Then said the Jews, Forty and six years was this temple in building, and wilt thou rear it up in three days?
21 But he spake of the temple of his body.
22 When therefore he was risen from the dead, his disciples remembered that he had said this unto them; and they believed the scripture, and the word which Jesus had said.   Luke 24:7-8; John 12:16; 14:26
23 Now when he was in Jerusalem at the passover, in the feast *day*, many believed in his name, when they saw the miracles which he did.   John 3:2
24 But Jesus did not commit himself unto them, because he knew all *men*,   Matt. 9:4
25 And needed not that any should testify of man: for he knew what was in man.

Jesus and Nicodemus

3 There was a man of the Pharisees, named Nicodemus, a ruler of the Jews:
2 The same came to Jesus by night, and said unto him, Rabbi, we know that thou art a teacher come from God: for no man can do these miracles that thou doest, except God be with him.   Matt. 22:16; Acts 2:22; 10:38

> **3:2 A New Heart Comes First**
>
> Nicodemus had come to the Lord thinking to enter into a discussion with Him, but Jesus laid bare the foundation principles of truth. He said to Nicodemus, It is not theoretical knowledge you need so much as spiritual regeneration. You need not to have your curiosity satisfied, but to have a new heart. You must receive a new life from above before you can appreciate heavenly things. Until this change takes place, making all things new, it will result in no saving good for you to discuss with Me My authority or My mission. *DA 171*

3 Jesus answered and said unto him, Verily, verily, I say unto thee, Except a man be born again, he cannot see the kingdom of God.
4 Nicodemus saith unto him, How can a man be born when he is old? can he enter the second time into his mother's womb, and be born?
5 Jesus answered, Verily, verily, I say unto thee, Except a man be born of water and *of* the Spirit, he cannot enter into the kingdom of God.   Ezek. 36:25-27; Mark 16:16; Acts 2:38
6 That which is born of the flesh is flesh; and that which is born of the Spirit is spirit.
7 Marvel not that I said unto thee, Ye must be born again.   John 3:3

> **3:5–8 Surrender, Then Re-creation**
>
> The blessing comes when by faith the soul surrenders itself to God. Then that power which no human eye can see creates a new being in the image of God. *DA 173*

8 The wind bloweth where it ᵀlisteth, and thou hearest the sound thereof, but canst not tell whence it cometh, and whither it goeth: so is every one that is born of the Spirit.   Ezek. 37:9 ◆ *pleases*

The Christian Life   See Ezekiel 36:26, 27.

9 Nicodemus answered and said unto him, How can these things be?   John 6:52
10 Jesus answered and said unto him, Art thou a master of Israel, and knowest not these things?
11 Verily, verily, I say unto thee, We speak that we do know, and testify that we have seen; and ye receive not our witness. John 1:18
12 If I have told you earthly things, and ye believe not, how shall ye believe, if I tell you *of* heavenly things?
13 And no man hath ascended up to heaven, but he that came down from heaven, *even* the Son of man which is in heaven. Prov. 30:4
14 And as Moses lifted up the serpent in the wilderness, even so must the Son of man be lifted up: John 8:28

15 That whosoever believeth in him should not perish, but have eternal life.   John 3:16

3:16, 17†

16 For God so loved the world, that he gave his only begotten Son, that whosoever believeth in him should not perish, but have everlasting life.   John 1:18; Rom. 5:8; 1 John 4:9-10
17 For God sent not his Son into the world to condemn the world; but that the world through him might be saved. Luke 19:10; John 5:45

†Who Is God?   See 1 John 4:8.

Jesus   See Matthew 1:21.

Salvation From Sin   See Romans 5:8.

18 He that believeth on him is not condemned: but he that believeth not is condemned already, because he hath not believed in the name of the only †begotten Son of God.   Mark 16:16; John 5:24; Rom. 8:1 ◆ brought forth
19 And this is the condemnation, that light is come into the world, and men loved darkness rather than light, because their deeds were evil.   John 1:4; 8:12
20 For every one that doeth evil hateth the light, neither cometh to the light, lest his deeds should be reproved.
21 But he that doeth truth cometh to the light, that his deeds may be made manifest, that they are †wrought in God. 1 John 1:6 ◆ done

John the Baptist and Jesus

22 After these things came Jesus and his disciples into the land of Judaea; and there he tarried with them, and baptized. John 3:26
23 And John also was baptizing in Aenon near to Salim, because there was much water there: and they came, and were baptized.

24 For John was not yet cast into prison.

3:25-28 Avoiding Dissension

Jesus knew that [the Jewish leaders] would spare no effort to create a division between His own disciples and those of John. . . . Wishing to avoid all occasion for misunderstanding or dissension, He quietly ceased His labors, and withdrew to Galilee. We also, while loyal to truth, should try to avoid all that may lead to discord and misapprehension. For whenever these arise, they result in the loss of souls. Whenever circumstances occur that threaten to cause division, we should follow the example of Jesus and of John the Baptist. DA 181

25 Then there arose a question between some of John's disciples and the Jews about purifying.   John 2:6
26 And they came unto John, and said unto him, Rabbi, he that was with thee beyond Jordan, to whom thou barest witness, behold, the same baptizeth, and all men come to him.   John 1:7; 12:19
27 John answered and said, A man can receive nothing, except it be given him from heaven.   1 Cor. 4:7
28 Ye yourselves bear me witness, that I said, I am not the Christ, but that I am sent before him.   Mal. 3:1; John 1:20, 23
29 He that hath the bride is the bridegroom: but the friend of the bridegroom, which standeth and heareth him, rejoiceth greatly because of the bridegroom's voice: this my joy therefore is fulfilled.   Song 5:1; Matt. 9:15
30 He must increase, but I must decrease.

Looking at Scriptures in a New Way

John 3:3-8

[Nicodemus] himself had felt that there was a lack of spirituality among the Jews, that, to a great degree, they were controlled by bigotry and worldly ambition. He had hoped for a better state of things at the Messiah's coming. Yet the heart-searching message of the Baptist had failed to work in him conviction of sin. He was a strict Pharisee, and prided himself on his good works. He was widely esteemed for his benevolence and his liberality in sustaining the temple service, and he felt secure of the favor of God. He was startled at the thought of a kingdom too pure for him to see in his present state. . . .

He felt that he needed no change. Hence his surprise at the Saviour's words. He was irritated by their close application to himself. The pride of the Pharisee was struggling against the honest desire of the seeker after truth. He wondered that Christ should speak to him as He did, not respecting his position as ruler in Israel.

Surprised out of his self-possession, he answered Christ in words full of irony, "How can a man be born when he is old?" Like many others when cutting truth is brought home to the conscience, he revealed the fact that the natural man receiveth not the things of the Spirit of God. . . .

But the Saviour did not meet argument with argument. . . .

Not through controversy and discussion is the soul enlightened. We must look and live. Nicodemus received the lesson, and carried it with him. He searched the Scriptures in a new way, not for the discussion of a theory, but in order to receive life for the soul. He began to see the kingdom of heaven as he submitted himself to the leading of the Holy Spirit. DA 171, 175

31 He that cometh from above is above all: he that is of the earth is earthly, and speaketh of the earth: he that cometh from heaven is above all.   Matt. 28:18; John 6:33; 8:23

32 And what he hath seen and heard, that he testifieth; and no man receiveth his testimony.   John 1:11; 3:11; 8:26

33 He that hath received his testimony hath set to his seal that God is true.

34 For he whom God hath sent speaketh the words of God: for God giveth not the Spirit by measure *unto him*.   Luke 4:18; John 3:17; 5:26

35 The Father loveth the Son, and hath given all things into his hand.   Matt. 28:18; John 5:20

36 He that believeth on the Son hath everlasting life: and he that believeth not the Son shall not see life; but the wrath of God abideth on him.   John 1:12; 3:15-16; 5:24

Jesus Talks with a Samaritan Woman

4 When therefore the Lord knew how the Pharisees had heard that Jesus made and baptized more disciples than John,   John 3:22

2 (Though Jesus himself baptized not, but his disciples,)

3 He left Judaea, and departed again into Galilee.

4 And he must needs go through Samaria.

5 Then cometh he to a city of Samaria, which is called Sychar, near to the parcel of ground that Jacob gave to his son Joseph.   Josh. 24:32

6 Now Jacob's well was there. Jesus therefore, being wearied with *his* journey, sat thus on the well: *and* it was about the sixth hour.   Matt. 4:2

7 There cometh a woman of Samaria to draw water: Jesus saith unto her, Give me to drink.

8 (For his disciples were gone away unto the city to buy meat.)

9 Then saith the woman of Samaria unto him, How is it that thou, being a Jew, askest drink of me, which am a woman of Samaria? for the Jews have no dealings with the Samaritans.   John 8:48

10 Jesus answered and said unto her, If thou knewest the gift of God, and who it is that saith to thee, Give me to drink; thou wouldest have asked of him, and he would have given thee living water.   Jer. 2:13; John 4:14; Rev. 21:6

11 The woman saith unto him, Sir, thou hast nothing to draw with, and the well is deep: from whence then hast thou that living water?

12 Art thou greater than our father Jacob, which gave us the well, and drank thereof himself, and his children, and his cattle?

13 Jesus answered and said unto her, Whosoever drinketh of this water shall thirst again:

14 But whosoever drinketh of the water that I shall give him shall never thirst; but the water that I shall give him shall be in him a well of water springing up into everlasting life.   Is. 49:10; John 6:35, 58

15 The woman saith unto him, Sir, give me this water, that I thirst not, neither come hither to draw.   John 6:34

16 Jesus saith unto her, Go, call thy husband, and come ᵀhither.   *here*

17 The woman answered and said, I have no husband. Jesus said unto her, Thou hast well said, I have no husband:

18 For thou hast had five husbands; and he whom thou now hast is not thy husband: in that saidst thou truly.

19 The woman saith unto him, Sir, I perceive that thou art a prophet.   Luke 7:16

20 Our fathers worshipped in this mountain; and ye say, that in Jerusalem is the place where men ought to worship.   Gen. 12:6-7

21 Jesus saith unto her, Woman, believe me, the hour cometh, when ye shall neither in this mountain, nor yet at Jerusalem, worship the Father.   Mal. 1:11; John 4:23; 1 Tim. 2:8

22 Ye worship ye know not what: we know what we worship: for salvation is of the Jews.

23 But the hour cometh, and now is, when the true worshippers shall worship the Father in spirit and in truth: for the Father seeketh such to worship him.   John 1:17; 5:25; Phil. 3:3

24 God *is* a Spirit: and they that worship him must worship *him* in spirit and in truth.

25 The woman saith unto him, I know that Messias cometh, which is called Christ: when he is come, he will tell us all things.   John 4:29

26 Jesus saith unto her, I that speak unto thee am *he*.

27 And upon this came his disciples, and marvelled that he talked with the woman:

yet no man said, What seekest thou? or, Why talkest thou with her? Luke 7:39

28 The woman then left her waterpot, and went her way into the city, and saith to the men,

29 Come, see a man, which told me all things that ever I did: is not this the Christ? John 4:17-18

30 Then they went out of the city, and came unto him.

4:28–30 Receivers Become Givers

[The Samaritan woman at the well] represents the working of a practical faith in Christ. Every true disciple is born into the kingdom of God as a missionary. He who drinks of the living water becomes a fountain of life. The receiver becomes a giver. The grace of Christ in the soul is like a spring in the desert, welling up to refresh all, and making those who are ready to perish eager to drink of the water of life. *DA 195*

31 In the mean while his disciples prayed him, saying, Master, eat.

32 But he said unto them, I have meat to eat that ye know not of. Job 23:12

33 Therefore said the disciples one to another, Hath any man brought him *ought* to eat?

34 Jesus saith unto them, My meat is to do the will of him that sent me, and to finish his work. John 6:38; 17:4; 19:30

35 Say not ye, There are yet four months, and *then* cometh harvest? behold, I say unto you, Lift up your eyes, and look on the fields; for they are white already to harvest. Matt. 9:37-38

36 And he that reapeth receiveth wages, and gathereth fruit unto life eternal: that both he that soweth and he that reapeth may rejoice together. Rom. 1:13

37 And herein is that saying true, One soweth, and another reapeth. Mic. 6:15

38 I sent you to reap that whereon ye bestowed no labour: other men laboured, and ye are entered into their labours. Acts 8:14-17

39 And many of the Samaritans of that city believed on him for the saying of the woman, which testified, He told me all that ever I did. John 4:5, 29

40 So when the Samaritans were come unto him, they ᵀbesought him that he would tarry with them: and he abode there two days. *begged*

41 And many more believed because of his own word;

42 And said unto the woman, Now we believe, not because of thy saying: for we have heard *him* ourselves, and know that this is indeed the Christ, the Saviour of the world. John 1:29; 2 Cor. 5:19; 1 John 4:14

Jesus Heals a Nobleman's Son

43 Now after two days he departed thence, and went into Galilee. John 4:40

44 For Jesus himself testified, that a prophet hath no honour in his own country. Matt. 13:57

45 Then when he was come into Galilee, the Galilaeans received him, having seen all the things that he did at Jerusalem at the feast: for they also went unto the feast. John 2:23; 3:2

46 So Jesus came again into Cana of Galilee, where he made the water wine. And there was a certain nobleman, whose son was sick at Capernaum. John 2:1-11

47 When he heard that Jesus was come out of Judaea into Galilee, he went unto him, and besought him that he would come down, and heal his son: for he was at the point of death. John 4:3

48 Then said Jesus unto him, Except ye see signs and wonders, ye will not believe.

49 The nobleman saith unto him, Sir, come down ᵀere my child die. *before*

50 Jesus saith unto him, Go thy way; thy son liveth. And the man believed the word that Jesus had spoken unto him, and he went his way. Matt. 8:13

51 And as he was now going down, his servants met him, and told *him*, saying, Thy son liveth.

52 Then enquired he of them the hour when he began to amend. And they said unto him, Yesterday at the seventh hour the fever left him.

53 So the father knew that *it was* at the same hour, in the which Jesus said unto him, Thy son liveth: and himself believed, and his whole house. Acts 11:14

54 This *is* again the second miracle *that* Jesus did, when he was come out of Judaea into Galilee.

Jesus Heals a Lame Man at Bethesda Pool

5 After this there was a feast of the Jews; and Jesus went up to Jerusalem. John 2:13

2 Now there is at Jerusalem by the sheep *market* a pool, which is called in the Hebrew tongue Bethesda, having five porches. Neh. 3:1

3 In these lay a great multitude of impotent folk, of blind, ᵀhalt, withered, waiting for the moving of the water. *having crippled feet*

4 For an angel went down at a certain season into the pool, and troubled the water: whosoever then first after the troubling of the water stepped in was made whole of whatsoever disease he had.

5 And a certain man was there, which had an infirmity thirty and eight years.

6 When Jesus saw him lie, and knew that he had been now a long time *in that case*, he saith unto him, Wilt thou be made whole?

7 The impotent man answered him, Sir, I have no man, when the water is troubled, to put me into the pool: but while I am coming, another steppeth down before me.

8 Jesus saith unto him, Rise, take up thy bed, and walk. Matt. 9:6; Mark 2:11; Luke 5:24

5:8 Acting on Belief

Jesus had given [the lame man] no assurance of divine help. The man might have stopped to doubt, and lost his one chance of healing. But he believed Christ's word, and in acting upon it he received strength. *DA 203*

9 And immediately the man was made whole, and took up his bed, and walked: and on the same day was the sabbath. John 9:14

10 The Jews therefore said unto him that was cured, It is the sabbath day: it is not lawful for thee to carry *thy* bed. Neh. 13:15-21; Jer. 17:21

11 He answered them, He that made me whole, the same said unto me, Take up thy bed, and walk.

12 Then asked they him, What man is that which said unto thee, Take up thy bed, and walk?

13 And he that was healed ᵀwist not who it was: for Jesus had conveyed himself away, a multitude being in *that* place. knew

14 Afterward Jesus findeth him in the temple, and said unto him, Behold, thou art made whole: sin no more, lest a worse thing come unto thee. John 8:11

15 The man departed, and told the Jews that it was Jesus, which had made him whole.

16 And therefore did the Jews persecute Jesus, and sought to slay him, because he had done these things on the sabbath day. John 15:20

Jesus Is One with the Father

17 But Jesus answered them, My Father worketh hitherto, and I work. John 9:4

18 Therefore the Jews sought the more to kill him, because he not only had broken the sabbath, but said also that God was his Father, making himself equal with God. John 10:30, 33

19 Then answered Jesus and said unto them, Verily, verily, I say unto you, The Son can do nothing of himself, but what he seeth the Father do: for what things soever he doeth, these also doeth the Son likewise.

20 For the Father loveth the Son, and sheweth him all things that himself doeth: and he will shew him greater works than these, that ye may marvel. Matt. 3:17; John 3:35; 14:12

21 For as the Father raiseth up the dead, and quickeneth *them*; even so the Son quickeneth whom he will. Deut. 32:39; John 11:25; Rom. 8:11

22 For the Father judgeth no man, but

hath committed all judgment unto the Son: John 5:27; Acts 10:42; 17:31

23 That all *men* should honour the Son, even as they honour the Father. He that honoureth not the Son honoureth not the Father which hath sent him. Luke 10:16; Heb. 1:6; 1 John 2:23

24 Verily, verily, I say unto you, He that heareth my word, and believeth on him that sent me, hath everlasting life, and shall not come into condemnation; but is passed from death unto life. John 3:18, 36; 1 John 3:14

5:24 Promises Contain Power

In every command and in every promise of the word of God is the power, the very life of God, by which the command may be fulfilled and the promise realized. He who by faith receives the word is receiving the very life and character of God. *COL 38*

25 Verily, verily, I say unto you, The hour is coming, and now is, when the dead shall hear the voice of the Son of God: and they that hear shall live. Luke 15:24; John 4:23; 5:28

26 For as the Father hath life in himself; so hath he given to the Son to have life in himself; John 1:4; 11:26; 14:6

27 And hath given him authority to execute judgment also, because he is the Son of man. John 5:22

28 Marvel not at this: for the hour is coming, in the which all that are in the graves shall hear his voice,

29 And shall come forth; they that have done good, unto the resurrection of life; and they that have done evil, unto the resurrection of ᵀdamnation. Acts 24:15 ◆ condemnation

After Death See John 20:17.

30 I can of mine own self do nothing: as I hear, I judge: and my judgment is just; because I seek not mine own will, but the will of the Father which hath sent me. Matt. 26:39

5:30 To Be Like Jesus

So utterly was Christ emptied of self that He made no plans for Himself. He accepted God's plans for Him, and day by day the Father unfolded His plans. So should we depend upon God, that our lives may be the simple outworking of His will. *DA 208*

31 If I bear witness of myself, my witness is not true. John 8:13-14

32 There is another that beareth witness of me; and I know that the witness which he witnesseth of me is true.

33 Ye sent unto John, and he bare witness unto the truth.

34 But I receive not testimony from man: but these things I say, that ye might be saved. 1 John 5:9

35 He was a burning and a shining light: and ye were willing for a season to rejoice in his light.   Matt. 21:26; 2 Pet. 1:19

36 But I have greater witness than *that* of John: for the works which the Father hath given me to finish, the same works that I do, bear witness of me, that the Father hath sent me.   Matt. 11:4; John 10:25; 15:24

37 And the Father himself, which hath sent me, hath borne witness of me. Ye have neither heard his voice at any time, nor seen his shape.   Matt. 3:17; John 1:18; 8:18

38 And ye have not his word abiding in you: for whom he hath sent, him ye believe not.   1 John 2:14

39 Search the scriptures; for in them ye think ye have eternal life: and they are they which testify of me.   Luke 24:27, 44; John 7:52

5:39 Law and Gospel

No man can rightly present the law of God without the gospel, or the gospel without the law. The law is the gospel embodied, and the gospel is the law unfolded. The law is the root, the gospel is the fragrant blossom and fruit which it bears. *COL 128*

40 And ye will not come to me, that ye might have life.   Matt. 23:37

41 I receive not honour from men.   1 Thess. 2:6

42 But I know you, that ye have not the love of God in you.   John 2:25

43 I am come in my Father's name, and ye receive me not: if another shall come in his own name, him ye will receive.   Matt. 24:5

44 How can ye believe, which receive honour one of another, and seek not the honour that *cometh* from God only?   Rom. 2:29

45 Do not think that I will accuse you to the Father: there is *one* that accuseth you, *even* Moses, in whom ye trust.   John 9:28-29

46 For had ye believed Moses, ye would have believed me: for he wrote of me.   Gen. 3:15

47 But if ye believe not his writings, how shall ye believe my words?   Luke 16:29, 31

Jesus Feeds More than Five Thousand

6 After these things Jesus went over the sea of Galilee, which is *the sea* of Tiberias.   Matt. 4:18

2 And a great multitude followed him, because they saw his miracles which he did on them that were diseased.

3 And Jesus went up into a mountain, and there he sat with his disciples.   Luke 9:28; John 6:15

4 And the passover, a feast of the Jews, was nigh.   Ex. 12:6-14; John 2:13; 11:55

5 When Jesus then lifted up *his* eyes, and saw a great company come unto him, he saith unto Philip, Whence shall we buy bread, that these may eat?

6 And this he said to prove him: for he himself knew what he would do.

7 Philip answered him, Two hundred pennyworth of bread is not sufficient for them, that every one of them may take a little.   Mark 6:37

8 One of his disciples, Andrew, Simon Peter's brother, saith unto him,

9 There is a lad here, which hath five barley loaves, and two small fishes: but what are they among so many?

10 And Jesus said, Make the men sit down. Now there was much grass in the place. So the men sat down, in number about five thousand.

11 And Jesus took the loaves; and when he had given thanks, he distributed to the disciples, and the disciples to them that were set down; and likewise of the fishes as much as they would.   John 6:23

6:11 Receiving to Impart

We can impart only that which we receive from Christ; and we can receive only as we impart to others. As we continue imparting, we continue to receive; and the more we impart, the more we shall receive. Thus we may be constantly believing, trusting, receiving, and imparting. *DA 370*

12 When they were filled, he said unto his disciples, Gather up the fragments that remain, that nothing be lost.

13 Therefore they gathered *them* together, and filled twelve baskets with the fragments of the five barley loaves, which remained over and above unto them that had eaten.

14 Then those men, when they had seen the miracle that Jesus did, said, This is of a truth that prophet that should come into the world.   Matt. 11:3; 21:11; John 1:21

15 When Jesus therefore perceived that they would come and take him by force, to make him a king, he departed again into a mountain himself alone.   John 7:3-4; 18:36

Jesus Walks on the Sea

16 And when even was *now* come, his disciples went down unto the sea,

17 And entered into a ship, and went over the sea toward Capernaum. And it was now dark, and Jesus was not come to them.   Mark 6:45

6:16–18 Something Else to Think About

[The disciples'] thoughts were stormy and unreasonable, and the Lord gave them something else to afflict their souls and occupy their minds. God often does this when men create burdens and troubles for themselves. The disciples had no need to make trouble. Already danger was fast approaching. *DA 380*

18 And the sea arose by reason of a great wind that blew.

19 So when they had rowed about five and twenty or thirty furlongs, they see Jesus walking on the sea, and drawing nigh unto the ship: and they were afraid.   Job 9:8

20 But he saith unto them, It is I; be not afraid.

21 Then they willingly received him into the ship: and immediately the ship was at the land whither they went.

Jesus Is the Bread of Life

22 The day following, when the people which stood on the other side of the sea saw that there was none other boat there, save that one whereinto his disciples were entered, and that Jesus went not with his disciples into the boat, but *that* his disciples were gone away alone;

23 (Howbeit there came other boats from Tiberias nigh unto the place where they did eat bread, after that the Lord had given thanks:)

24 When the people therefore saw that Jesus was not there, neither his disciples, they also took shipping, and came to Capernaum, seeking for Jesus.   John 6:17

25 And when they had found him on the other side of the sea, they said unto him, Rabbi, when camest thou ᵀhither?   *here*

26 Jesus answered them and said, Verily, verily, I say unto you, Ye seek me, not because ye saw the miracles, but because ye did eat of the loaves, and were filled.   John 6:24

27 Labour not for the meat which perisheth, but for that meat which endureth unto everlasting life, which the Son of man shall give unto you: for him hath God the Father sealed.

28 Then said they unto him, What shall we do, that we might work the works of God?

29 Jesus answered and said unto them, This is the work of God, that ye believe on him whom he hath sent.   1 John 3:23

30 They said therefore unto him, What sign shewest thou then, that we may see, and believe thee? what dost thou work?

31 Our fathers did eat manna in the desert; as it is written, He gave them bread from heaven to eat.   Neh. 9:15; Ps. 105:40; John 6:49

32 Then Jesus said unto them, Verily, ᵀverily, I say unto you, Moses gave you not that bread from heaven; but my Father giveth you the true bread from heaven.   *truly*

33 For the bread of God is he which cometh down from heaven, and giveth life unto the world.   John 6:50

34 Then said they unto him, Lord, evermore give us this bread.   John 4:15

35 And Jesus said unto them, I am the bread of life: he that cometh to me shall never hunger; and he that believeth on me shall never thirst.   Matt. 11:28

36 But I said unto you, That ye also have seen me, and believe not.   John 6:26

37 All that the Father giveth me shall come to me; and him that cometh to me I will in no wise cast out.   John 6:39; 17:2, 24

38 For I came down from heaven, not to do mine own will, but the will of him that sent me.   John 3:13; 4:34; 5:30

39 And this is the Father's will which hath sent me, that of all which he hath given me I should lose nothing, but should raise it up again at the last day.   John 6:40, 44, 54

40 And this is the will of him that sent me, that every one which seeth the Son, and believeth on him, may have everlasting life: and I will raise him up at the last day.   John 6:54

41 The Jews then murmured at him, because he said, I am the bread which came down from heaven.   John 6:33

42 And they said, Is not this Jesus, the son of Joseph, whose father and mother we know? how is it then that he saith, I came down from heaven?   Luke 4:22

43 Jesus therefore answered and said unto them, Murmur not among yourselves.

44 No man can come to me, except the Father which hath sent me draw him: and I will raise him up at the last day.   Jer. 31:3; John 6:65

45 It is written in the prophets, And they shall be all taught of God. Every man therefore that hath heard, and hath learned of the Father, cometh unto me.   Is. 54:13; Jer. 31:33-34

46 Not that any man hath seen the Father, save he which is of God, he hath seen the Father.   John 1:18; 5:37; 7:29

47 Verily, verily, I say unto you, He that believeth on me hath everlasting life.   John 3:36

48 I am that bread of life.   John 6:51

49 Your fathers did eat manna in the wilderness, and are dead.   John 6:31

50 This is the bread which cometh down from heaven, that a man may eat thereof, and not die.   John 6:33, 51, 58

51 I am the living bread which came down from heaven: if any man eat of this bread, he shall live for ever: and the bread that I will give is my flesh, which I will give for the life of the world.   Matt. 20:28

6:51 Eating the Bread

The Holy Spirit comes to the soul as a Comforter. By the transforming agency of His grace, the image of God is reproduced in the disciple; he becomes a new creature. Love takes the place of hatred, and the heart receives the divine similitude. This is what it means to live "by every word that proceedeth out of the mouth of God" [Deuteronomy 8:3]. This is eating the Bread that comes down from heaven. *DA 391*

52 The Jews therefore strove among themselves, saying, How can this man give us *his* flesh to eat?   John 3:9; 9:16; 10:19

53 Then Jesus said unto them, Verily, verily, I say unto you, Except ye eat the flesh of the Son of man, and drink his blood, ye have no life in you.   John 3:3

54 Whoso eateth my flesh, and drinketh my blood, hath eternal life; and I will raise him up at the last day.   John 6:39-40

55 For my flesh is meat indeed, and my blood is drink indeed.

56 He that eateth my flesh, and drinketh my blood, dwelleth in me, and I in him. 1 John 3:24

57 As the living Father hath sent me, and I live by the Father: so he that eateth me, even he shall live by me.   John 5:26

58 This is that bread which came down from heaven: not as your fathers did eat manna, and are dead: he that eateth of this bread shall live for ever.   John 6:41

59 These things said he in the synagogue, as he taught in Capernaum.   John 6:24

60 Many therefore of his disciples, when they had heard *this*, said, This is an hard saying; who can hear it?   John 6:66

61 When Jesus knew in himself that his disciples murmured at it, he said unto them, Doth this offend you?   John 2:24-25

62 *What* and if ye shall see the Son of man ascend up where he was before?   Mark 16:19

63 It is the spirit that quickeneth; the flesh profiteth nothing: the words that I speak unto you, *they* are spirit, and *they* are life.   John 6:68

64 But there are some of you that believe not. For Jesus knew from the beginning who they were that believed not, and who should betray him.   John 6:61

65 And he said, Therefore said I unto you, that no man can come unto me, except it were given unto him of my Father.   John 6:37

66 From that *time* many of his disciples went back, and walked no more with him. John 6:60

67 Then said Jesus unto the twelve, Will ye also go away?

68 Then Simon Peter answered him, Lord, to whom shall we go? thou hast the words of eternal life.   John 6:63

69 And we believe and are sure that thou art that Christ, the Son of the living God.

70 Jesus answered them, Have not I chosen you twelve, and one of you is a devil? John 13:2

71 He spake of Judas Iscariot *the son* of Simon: for he it was that should betray him, being one of the twelve.

Jesus Teaches at the Feast of Tabernacles

7 After these things Jesus walked in Galilee: for he would not walk in Jewry, because the Jews sought to kill him.   John 4:3

2 Now the Jews' feast of tabernacles was at hand.   Zech. 14:16-19

3 His brethren therefore said unto him, Depart hence, and go into Judaea, that thy disciples also may see the works that thou doest.   Matt. 12:46; John 7:5

4 For *there is* no man *that* doeth any thing in secret, and he himself seeketh to be known openly. If thou do these things, shew thyself to the world.   John 18:20

5 For neither did his brethren believe in him.   Mark 3:21

6 Then Jesus said unto them, My time is not yet come: but your time is alway ready.

7 The world cannot hate you; but me it hateth, because I testify of it, that the works thereof are evil.   John 3:19; 15:18-19

8 Go ye up unto this feast: I go not up yet unto this feast; for my time is not yet full come.   John 7:6

9 When he had said these words unto them, he abode *still* in Galilee.

10 But when his brethren were gone up, then went he also up unto the feast, not openly, but as it were in secret.

11 Then the Jews sought him at the feast, and said, Where is he?   John 11:56

12 And there was much murmuring among the people concerning him: for some said, He is a good man: others said, Nay; but he deceiveth the people.   John 7:40-43

13 Howbeit no man spake openly of him for fear of the Jews.   John 9:22; 19:38; 20:19

14 Now about the midst of the feast Jesus went up into the temple, and taught. John 7:28

15 And the Jews marvelled, saying, How

Food for Body—and Soul

John 6:51–58

To eat the flesh and drink the blood of Christ is to receive Him as a personal Saviour, believing that He forgives our sins, and that we are complete in Him. It is by beholding His love, by dwelling upon it, by drinking it in, that we are to become partakers of His nature. What food is to the body, Christ must be to the soul. Food cannot benefit us unless we eat it, unless it becomes a part of our being. So Christ is of no value to us if we do not know Him as a personal Saviour. A theoretical knowledge will do us no good. We must feed upon Him, receive Him into the heart, so that His life becomes our life. His love, His grace, must be assimilated. *DA 389*

knoweth this man letters, having never learned? Matt. 13:54

16 Jesus answered them, and said, My doctrine is not mine, but his that sent me.

17 If any man will do his will, he shall know of the doctrine, whether it be of God, or *whether* I speak of myself. John 8:31-32, 43

7:17 An Open Heart—and Surrender

Man's advantages for obtaining a knowledge of the truth, however great these may be, will prove of no benefit to him unless the heart is open to receive the truth, and there is a conscientious surrender of every habit and practice that is opposed to its principles. DA 455, 456

18 He that speaketh of himself seeketh his own glory: but he that seeketh his glory that sent him, the same is true, and no unrighteousness is in him. John 5:41

19 Did not Moses give you the law, and *yet* none of you keepeth the law? Why go ye about to kill me? Matt. 12:14; John 1:17; 7:1

20 The people answered and said, Thou hast a ⊤devil: who goeth about to kill thee? John 8:48, 52; 10:20 ◆ demon

21 Jesus answered and said unto them, I have done one work, and ye all marvel.

22 Moses therefore gave unto you circumcision; (not because it is of Moses, but of the fathers;) and ye on the sabbath day circumcise a man. Gen. 17:10-14; Lev. 12:3

23 If a man on the sabbath day receive circumcision, that the law of Moses should not be broken; are ye angry at me, because I have made a man every ⊤whit whole on the sabbath day? bit

24 Judge not according to the appearance, but judge righteous judgment. Deut. 1:16-17

25 Then said some of them of Jerusalem, Is not this he, whom they seek to kill?

26 But, lo, he speaketh boldly, and they say nothing unto him. Do the rulers know indeed that this is the very Christ? John 7:48

27 Howbeit we know this man whence he is: but when Christ cometh, no man knoweth whence he is. John 6:42

28 Then cried Jesus in the temple as he taught, saying, Ye both know me, and ye know whence I am: and I am not come of myself, but he that sent me is true, whom ye know not. John 7:14; 8:26, 42

29 But I know him: for I am from him, and he hath sent me. John 8:55

30 Then they sought to take him: but no man laid hands on him, because his hour was not yet come. John 7:6, 32; 10:39

31 And many of the people believed on him, and said, When Christ cometh, will he do more miracles than these which this *man* hath done? John 12:42

32 The Pharisees heard that the people murmured such things concerning him; and the Pharisees and the chief priests sent officers to take him.

33 Then said Jesus unto them, Yet a little while am I with you, and *then* I go unto him that sent me. John 13:33; 16:5

34 Ye shall seek me, and shall not find *me*: and where I am, *thither* ye cannot come.

35 Then said the Jews among themselves, Whither will he go, that we shall not find him? will he go unto the dispersed among the Gentiles, and teach the Gentiles? Is. 11:12

36 What *manner of* saying is this that he said, Ye shall seek me, and shall not find *me*: and where I am, *thither* ye cannot come? John 7:34

37 In the last day, that great *day* of the feast, Jesus stood and cried, saying, If any man thirst, let him come unto me, and drink. Lev. 23:36; Num. 29:35; Is. 55:1

38 He that believeth on me, as the scripture hath said, out of his belly shall flow rivers of living water. Is. 58:11

7:37, 38 Water for the Thirsty

The cry of Christ to the thirsty soul is still going forth, and it appeals to us with even greater power than to those who heard it in the temple on that last day of the feast. The fountain is open for all. The weary and exhausted ones are offered the refreshing draught of eternal life. DA 454

39 (But this spake he of the Spirit, which they that believe on him should receive: for the Holy Ghost was not yet *given*; because that Jesus was not yet glorified.) Joel 2:28; Acts 2:17, 33

40 Many of the people therefore, when they heard this saying, said, Of a truth this is the Prophet. Matt. 21:11

41 Others said, This is the Christ. But some said, Shall Christ come out of Galilee?

42 Hath not the scripture said, That Christ cometh of the seed of David, and out of the town of Bethlehem, where David was? Mic. 5:2

43 So there was a division among the people because of him. John 7:12; 9:16; 10:19

44 And some of them would have taken him; but no man laid hands on him. John 7:30

The Pharisees Are Angry and Rebuke Nicodemus

45 Then came the officers to the chief priests and Pharisees; and they said unto them, Why have ye not brought him? John 7:32

46 The officers answered, Never man spake like this man.

47 Then answered them the Pharisees, Are ye also deceived?   John 7:12

48 Have any of the rulers or of the Pharisees believed on him?   John 7:26; 12:42; 1 Cor. 1:20

7:47, 48 Commit Your Souls to Christ Only

Many are deceived today in the same way as were the Jews. Religious teachers read the Bible in the light of their own understanding and traditions; and the people do not search the Scriptures for themselves, and judge for themselves as to what is truth; but they yield up their judgment, and commit their souls to their leaders. DA 459

49 But this people who knoweth not the law are cursed.

50 Nicodemus saith unto them, (he that came to Jesus by night, being one of them,)

51 Doth our law judge *any* man, before it hear him, and know what he doeth?   Prov. 18:13

52 They answered and said unto him, Art thou also of Galilee? Search, and look: for out of Galilee ariseth no prophet.   John 1:46; 7:41

53 And every man went unto his own house.

Christ Frees the Woman Taken in Adultery

8 Jesus went unto the mount of Olives.

2 And early in the morning he came again into the temple, and all the people came unto him; and he sat down, and taught them.   Matt. 26:55

3 And the scribes and Pharisees brought unto him a woman taken in adultery; and when they had set her in the midst,

4 They say unto him, Master, this woman was taken in adultery, in the very act.

5 Now Moses in the law commanded us, that such should be stoned: but what sayest thou?   Lev. 20:10

6 This they said, tempting him, that they might have to accuse him. But Jesus stooped down, and with *his* finger wrote on the ground, *as though he heard them* not.   Matt. 19:3

7 So when they continued asking him, he lifted up himself, and said unto them, He that is without sin among you, let him first cast a stone at her.

8:7 Be Careful Before You Accuse

Those who are forward in accusing others, and zealous in bringing them to justice, are often in their own lives more guilty than they. Men hate the sinner, while they love the sin. Christ hates the sin, but loves the sinner. This will be the spirit of all who follow Him. Christian love is slow to censure, quick to discern penitence, ready to forgive, to encourage, to set the wanderer in the path of holiness, and to stay his feet therein. DA 462

8 And again he stooped down, and wrote on the ground.

9 And they which heard *it*, being convicted by *their own* conscience, went out one by one, beginning at the eldest, *even* unto the last: and Jesus was left alone, and the woman standing in the midst.

10 When Jesus had lifted up himself, and saw none but the woman, he said unto her, Woman, where are those thine accusers? hath no man condemned thee?

8:12 Reflected Light

Light was before them. As the moon and the stars of the solar system shine by the reflected light of the sun, so, as far as their teaching is true, do the world's great thinkers reflect the rays of the Sun of Righteousness. Every gem of thought, every flash of the intellect, is from the Light of the world. DA 465

Never Sell Your Conscience

John 7:46–49

The priests and rulers, on first coming into the presence of Christ, had felt . . . deeply moved, and the thought was forced upon them, "Never man spake like this Man." But they had stifled the conviction of the Holy Spirit. Now, enraged that even the instruments of the law [officers of the temple] should be influenced by the hated Galilean, they cried, "Are ye also deceived? Have any of the rulers or of the Pharisees believed on Him? But this people who knoweth not the law are cursed" [John 7:46–49].

Those to whom the message of truth is spoken seldom ask, "Is it true?" but, "By whom is it advocated?" Multitudes estimate it by the numbers who accept it; and the question is still asked, "Have any of the learned men or religious leaders believed?" Men are no more favorable to real godliness now than in the days of Christ. They are just as intently seeking earthly good, to the neglect of eternal riches; and it is not an argument against the truth, that large numbers are not ready to accept it, or that it is not received by the world's great men, or even by the religious leaders.

Again the priests and rulers proceeded to lay plans for arresting Jesus. It was urged that if He were longer left at liberty, He would draw the people away from the established leaders, and the only safe course was to silence Him without delay. DA 459, 460

11 She said, No man, Lord. And Jesus said unto her, Neither do I condemn thee: go, and sin no more. John 3:17; 5:14; 8:15

Jesus Is the Light of the World

12 Then spake Jesus again unto them, saying, I am the light of the world: he that followeth me shall not walk in darkness, but shall have the light of life. Job 33:28; Is. 49:6; John 12:35

13 The Pharisees therefore said unto him, Thou bearest record of thyself; thy record is not true.

14 Jesus answered and said unto them, Though I bear record of myself, *yet* my record is true: for I know whence I came, and whither I go; but ye cannot tell whence I come, and whither I go. John 8:42; 13:3; 16:28

15 Ye judge after the flesh; I judge no man.

16 And yet if I judge, my judgment is true: for I am not alone, but I and the Father that sent me. John 8:29

17 It is also written in your law, that the testimony of two men is true. Deut. 17:6

18 I am one that bear witness of myself, and the Father that sent me beareth witness of me. John 8:58

19 Then said they unto him, Where is thy Father? Jesus answered, Ye neither know me, nor my Father: if ye had known me, ye should have known my Father also. John 7:28; 16:3

20 These words spake Jesus in the treasury, as he taught in the temple: and no man laid hands on him; for his hour was not yet come. Matt. 27:6; Mark 12:41; John 7:30

21 Then said Jesus again unto them, I go my way, and ye shall seek me, and shall die in your sins: whither I go, ye cannot come. John 7:34; 8:24; 13:33

22 Then said the Jews, Will he kill himself? because he saith, Whither I go, ye cannot come.

23 And he said unto them, Ye are from beneath; I am from above: ye are of this world; I am not of this world. John 3:31; 17:14, 16

24 I said therefore unto you, that ye shall die in your sins: for if ye believe not that I am *he*, ye shall die in your sins. John 8:21

25 Then said they unto him, Who art thou? And Jesus saith unto them, Even *the same* that I said unto you from the beginning. John 1:19

26 I have many things to say and to judge of you: but he that sent me is true; and I speak to the world those things which I have heard of him. John 7:28; 8:40; 15:15

27 They understood not that he spake to them of the Father.

28 Then said Jesus unto them, When ye have lifted up the Son of man, then shall ye know that I am *he*, and *that* I do nothing of myself; but as my Father hath taught me, I speak these things. John 3:14; 5:19, 30

29 And he that sent me is with me: the Father hath not left me alone; for I do always those things that please him. John 4:34; 8:16; 16:32

30 As he spake these words, many believed on him. John 7:31

31 Then said Jesus to those Jews which believed on him, If ye continue in my word, *then* are ye my disciples indeed; 2 John 9

32 And ye shall know the truth, and the truth shall make you free. Rom. 8:2; James 2:12

33 They answered him, We be Abraham's seed, and were never in bondage to any man: how sayest thou, Ye shall be made free?

34 Jesus answered them, Verily, verily, I say unto you, Whosoever committeth sin is the servant of sin. John 3:3; Rom. 6:16; 2 Pet. 2:19

35 And the servant abideth not in the house for ever: *but* the Son abideth ever. Gen. 21:10

36 If the Son therefore shall make you free, ye shall be free indeed.

37 I know that ye are Abraham's seed; but ye seek to kill me, because my word hath no place in you. John 7:1

38 I speak that which I have seen with my Father: and ye do that which ye have seen with your father. John 5:19

39 They answered and said unto him, Abraham is our father. Jesus saith unto them, If ye were Abraham's children, ye would do the works of Abraham. John 8:37; Rom. 9:7; Gal. 3:7

40 But now ye seek to kill me, a man that hath told you the truth, which I have heard of God: this did not Abraham. John 8:26

41 Ye do the deeds of your father. Then said they to him, We be not born of fornication; we have one Father, *even* God. Is. 63:16; 64:8; John 8:38

42 Jesus said unto them, If God were your Father, ye would love me: for I proceeded forth and came from God; neither came I of myself, but he sent me. John 3:17; 17:8, 25

43 Why do ye not understand my speech? *even* because ye cannot hear my word. Jer. 6:10

44 Ye are of *your* father the devil, and the lusts of your father ye will do. He was a murderer from the beginning, and abode not in the truth, because there is no truth in him. When he speaketh a lie, he speaketh of his own: for he is a liar, and the father of it. John 8:38

45 And because I tell *you* the truth, ye believe me not.

46 Which of you convinceth me of sin? And if I say the truth, why do ye not believe me?

47 He that is of God heareth God's words: ye therefore hear *them* not, because ye are not of God.

48 Then answered the Jews, and said unto him, Say we not well that thou art a Samaritan, and hast a devil? John 4:9; 7:20; 8:52

49 Jesus answered, I have not a ᵀdevil; but I honour my Father, and ye do dishonour me.

demon

50 And I seek not mine own glory: there is one that seeketh and judgeth.   John 5:41; 8:54

51 Verily, verily, I say unto you, If a man keep my saying, he shall never see death.   Luke 2:26

52 Then said the Jews unto him, Now we know that thou hast a devil. Abraham is dead, and the prophets; and thou sayest, If a man keep my saying, he shall never taste of death.   Heb. 2:9

53 Art thou greater than our father Abraham, which is dead? and the prophets are dead: whom makest thou thyself?   John 4:12

54 Jesus answered, If I honour myself, my honour is nothing: it is my Father that honoureth me; of whom ye say, that he is your God: John 7:39; 8:50; 17:1

55 Yet ye have not known him; but I know him: and if I should say, I know him not, I shall be a liar like unto you: but I know him, and keep his saying.   John 7:28-29; 8:19, 44

56 Your father Abraham rejoiced to see my day: and he saw *it*, and was glad.   Heb. 11:13

8:56 The Great Love of God

This terrible ordeal [offering Isaac as a burnt offering] was imposed upon Abraham that he might see the day of Christ, and realize the great love of God for the world, so great that to raise it from its degradation, He gave His only-begotten Son to a most shameful death. *DA 469*

57 Then said the Jews unto him, Thou art not yet fifty years old, and hast thou seen Abraham?

58 Jesus said unto them, Verily, verily, I say unto you, Before Abraham was, I am. Ex. 3:14

59 Then took they up stones to cast at him: but Jesus hid himself, and went out of the temple, going through the midst of them, and so passed by.   John 11:8

Jesus Heals a Blind Man

9 And as *Jesus* passed by, he saw a man which was blind from *his* birth.

2 And his disciples asked him, saying, Master, who did sin, this man, or his parents, that he was born blind?   Ex. 20:5; Luke 13:2; John 9:34

3 Jesus answered, Neither hath this man sinned, nor his parents: but that the works of God should be made manifest in him.

9:1–3 A Truth Perverted

It was generally believed by the Jews that sin is punished in this life. Every affliction was regarded as the penalty of some wrongdoing, either of the sufferer himself or of his parents. It is true that all suffering results from the transgression of God's law, but this truth had become perverted. Satan, the author of sin and all its results, had led men to look upon disease and death as proceeding from God—as punishment arbitrarily inflicted on account of sin. *DA 471*

4 I must work the works of him that sent me, while it is day: the night cometh, when no man can work.   John 4:34; 12:35

5 As long as I am in the world, I am the light of the world.   John 8:12; 12:46

6 When he had thus spoken, he spat on the ground, and made clay of the ᵀspittle, and he anointed the eyes of the blind man with the clay,   Mark 7:33; 8:23 ◆ spit

7 And said unto him, Go, wash in the pool of Siloam, (which is by interpretation, Sent.) He went his way therefore, and washed, and came seeing.   Is. 35:5; John 9:11; 11:37

The True Children of Abraham

John 8:39–45

The only condition upon which the freedom of man is possible is that of becoming one with Christ. "The truth shall make you free;" and Christ is the truth. . . .

The true children of Abraham would live, as he did, a life of obedience to God. They would not try to kill One who was speaking the truth that was given Him from God. In plotting against Christ, the rabbis were not doing the works of Abraham. A mere lineal descent from Abraham was of no value. Without a spiritual connection with him, which would be manifested in possessing the same spirit, and doing the same works, they were not his children.

This principle bears with equal weight upon a question that has long agitated the Christian world, —the question of apostolic succession. Descent from Abraham was proved, not by name and lineage, but by likeness of character. So the apostolic succession rests not upon the transmission of ecclesiastical authority, but upon spiritual relationship. A life actuated by the apostles' spirit, the belief and teaching of the truth they taught, this is the true evidence of apostolic succession. This is what constitutes men the successors of the first teachers of the gospel. . . .

The fact that Jesus spoke the truth, and that with certainty, was why He was not received by the Jewish leaders. It was the truth that offended these self-righteous men. The truth exposed the fallacy of error; it condemned their teaching and practice, and it was unwelcome. They would rather close their eyes to the truth than humble themselves to confess that they had been in error. They did not love the truth. They did not desire it, even though it was truth. *DA 466, 467*

8 The neighbours therefore, and they which before had seen him that he was blind, said, Is not this he that sat and begged?
9 Some said, This is he: others *said*, He is like him: *but* he said, I am *he*.
10 Therefore said they unto him, How were thine eyes opened?
11 He answered and said, A man that is called Jesus made clay, and anointed mine eyes, and said unto me, Go to the pool of Siloam, and wash: and I went and washed, and I received sight.   *John 9:6-7*
12 Then said they unto him, Where is he? He said, I know not.
13 They brought to the Pharisees him that ᵀaforetime was blind.   *before*
14 And it was the sabbath day when Jesus made the clay, and opened his eyes.   *John 5:9*
15 Then again the Pharisees also asked him how he had received his sight. He said unto them, He put clay upon mine eyes, and I washed, and do see.
16 Therefore said some of the Pharisees, This man is not of God, because he keepeth not the sabbath day. Others said, How can a man that is a sinner do such miracles? And there was a division among them.   *Matt. 12:2; John 7:43; 10:19*
17 They say unto the blind man again, What sayest thou of him, that he hath opened thine eyes? He said, He is a prophet.   *John 4:19*
18 But the Jews did not believe concerning him, that he had been blind, and received his sight, until they called the parents of him that had received his sight.
19 And they asked them, saying, Is this your son, who ye say was born blind? how then doth he now see?
20 His parents answered them and said, We know that this is our son, and that he was born blind:
21 But by what means he now seeth, we know not; or who hath opened his eyes, we know not: he is of age; ask him: he shall speak for himself.
22 These *words* spake his parents, because they feared the Jews: for the Jews had agreed already, that if any man did confess that he was Christ, he should be put out of the synagogue.   *Luke 6:22; John 7:13; 16:2*
23 Therefore said his parents, He is of age; ask him.   *John 9:21*
24 Then again called they the man that was blind, and said unto him, Give God the praise: we know that this man is a sinner.
25 He answered and said, Whether he be a sinner or no, I know not: one thing I know, that, whereas I was blind, now I see.
26 Then said they to him again, What did he to thee? how opened he thine eyes?
27 He answered them, I have told you already, and ye did not hear: wherefore would ye hear *it* again? will ye also be his disciples?
28 Then they reviled him, and said, Thou art his disciple; but we are Moses' disciples.
29 We know that God spake unto Moses: *as for* this *fellow*, we know not from whence he is.   *John 8:14*
30 The man answered and said unto them, Why herein is a marvellous thing, that ye know not from whence he is, and *yet* he hath opened mine eyes.   *John 3:10*
31 Now we know that God heareth not sinners: but if any man be a worshipper of God, and doeth his will, him he heareth.   *Prov. 15:29*
32 Since the world began was it not heard that any man opened the eyes of one that was born blind.
33 If this man were not of God, he could do nothing.   *John 3:2; 9:16*
34 They answered and said unto him, Thou wast altogether born in sins, and dost thou teach us? And they cast him out.   *Is. 66:5*
35 Jesus heard that they had cast him out; and when he had found him, he said unto him, Dost thou believe on the Son of God?   *1 John 5:13*
36 He answered and said, Who is he, Lord, that I might believe on him?   *Rom. 10:14*
37 And Jesus said unto him, Thou hast both seen him, and it is he that talketh with thee.   *John 4:26*
38 And he said, Lord, I believe. And he worshipped him.   *Matt. 28:9*

9:35–38 Now I Really See

The [man born blind] cast himself at the Saviour's feet in worship. Not only had his natural sight been restored, but the eyes of his understanding had been opened. Christ had been revealed to his soul, and he received Him as the Sent of God. *DA 475*

39 And Jesus said, For judgment I am come into this world, that they which see not might see; and that they which see might be made blind.   *Luke 4:18; John 3:19; 2 Cor. 2:16*

9:39–41 Blind by Choice

To all who realized their need, Christ came with infinite help. But the Pharisees would confess no need; they refused to come to Christ, and hence they were left in blindness—a blindness for which they were themselves guilty. Jesus said, "Your sin remaineth." *DA 475*

40 And *some* of the Pharisees which were with him heard these words, and said unto him, Are we blind also?
41 Jesus said unto them, If ye were blind, ye should have no sin: but now ye say, We see; therefore your sin remaineth.   *Prov. 26:12*

Jesus Is the Good Shepherd

10 Verily, ᵀverily, I say unto you, He that entereth not by the door into the sheepfold, but climbeth up some other way, the same is a thief and a robber. *truly*

2 But he that entereth in by the door is the shepherd of the sheep. John 10:14

3 To him the porter openeth; and the sheep hear his voice: and he calleth his own sheep by name, and leadeth them out. John 10:4

4 And when he putteth forth his own sheep, he goeth before them, and the sheep follow him: for they know his voice. John 10:16

5 And a stranger will they not follow, but will flee from him: for they know not the voice of strangers.

6 This parable spake Jesus unto them: but they understood not what things they were which he spake unto them.

7 Then said Jesus unto them again, Verily, verily, I say unto you, I am the door of the sheep. John 10:9

8 All that ever came before me are thieves and robbers: but the sheep did not hear them. Ezek. 34:2

9 I am the door: by me if any man enter in, he shall be saved, and shall go in and out, and find pasture. John 10:1

10:7–9 Thieves of Hope

It is the gospel of the grace of God alone that can uplift the soul. . . . Christ came that He might re-create the image of God in man; and whoever turns men away from Christ is turning them away from the source of true development; he is defrauding them of the hope and purpose and glory of life. He is a thief and a robber. *DA 478*

---

10 The thief cometh not, but for to steal, and to kill, and to destroy: I am come that they might have life, and that they might have *it* more abundantly. John 6:33

11 I am the good shepherd: the good shepherd giveth his life for the sheep. Ezek. 34:23

12 But he that is an hireling, and not the shepherd, whose own the sheep are not, seeth the wolf coming, and leaveth the sheep, and fleeth: and the wolf catcheth them, and scattereth the sheep. Ezek. 34:2-6

13 The ᵀhireling fleeth, because he is an hireling, and careth not for the sheep. *temporary laborer*

10:14 How Well Jesus Knows Us

Jesus knows us individually, and is touched with the feeling of our infirmities. He knows us all by name. He knows the very house in which we live, the name of each occupant. He has at times given directions to His servants to go to a certain street in a certain city, to such a house, to find one of His sheep. *DA 479*

---

14 I am the good shepherd, and know my *sheep,* and am known of mine. Is. 53:11

15 As the Father knoweth me, even so know I the Father: and I lay down my life for the sheep. Is. 53:10; Matt. 11:27; John 10:11

16 And other sheep I have, which are not of this fold: them also I must bring, and they shall hear my voice; and there shall be one fold, *and* one shepherd. Is. 56:8; 1 Pet. 2:25

17 Therefore doth my Father love me, because I lay down my life, that I might take it again. John 10:11

18 No man taketh it from me, but I lay it down of myself. I have power to lay it down, and I have power to take it again. This commandment have I received of my Father. John 10:17; 14:31; 15:10

19 There was a division therefore again among the Jews for these sayings. John 9:16

20 And many of them said, He hath a devil, and is mad; why hear ye him? Mark 3:21; John 7:20

21 Others said, These are not the words of him that hath a ᵀdevil. Can a devil open the eyes of the blind? Ex. 4:11; Ps. 146:8 ◆ *demon*

Many Jews Reject Jesus

22 And it was at Jerusalem the feast of the dedication, and it was winter.

23 And Jesus walked in the temple in Solomon's porch. Acts 3:11; 5:12

24 Then came the Jews round about him, and said unto him, How long dost thou make us to doubt? If thou be the Christ, tell us plainly. John 1:19

25 Jesus answered them, I told you, and ye believed not: the works that I do in my Father's name, they bear witness of me. John 8:58

26 But ye believe not, because ye are not of my sheep, as I said unto you. John 8:47

27 My sheep hear my voice, and I know them, and they follow me: John 10:14, 16

10:27 Fully Known to Jesus

Every soul is as fully known to Jesus as if he were the only one for whom the Saviour died. The distress of every one touches His heart. . . . He bids them, "Follow Me," and His Spirit moves upon their hearts to draw them to come to Him. Many refuse to be drawn. Jesus knows who they are. He also knows who gladly hear His call, and are ready to come under His pastoral care. *DA 480*

---

28 And I give unto them eternal life; and they shall never perish, neither shall any *man* pluck them out of my hand. John 6:37

29 My Father, which gave *them* me, is greater than all; and no *man* is able to pluck *them* out of my Father's hand. John 6:37; 14:28; 17:2

30 I and *my* Father are one. John 14:9

31 Then the Jews took up stones again to stone him.   *John 8:59*

32 Jesus answered them, Many good works have I shewed you from my Father; for which of those works do ye stone me?

33 The Jews answered him, saying, For a good work we stone thee not; but for blasphemy; and because that thou, being a man, makest thyself God.   *Lev. 24:16; John 5:18; 10:30*

34 Jesus answered them, Is it not written in your law, I said, Ye are gods?   *John 12:34*

35 If he called them gods, unto whom the word of God came, and the scripture cannot be broken;

36 Say ye of him, whom the Father hath ᵀsanctified, and sent into the world, Thou blasphemest; because I said, I am the Son of God?   *Jer. 1:5; John 3:17; 5:17-18 ◆ made holy*

37 If I do not the works of my Father, believe me not.   *John 10:25; 15:24*

38 But if I do, though ye believe not me, believe the works: that ye may know, and believe, that the Father *is* in me, and I in him.   *John 10:30; 14:20; 17:21-23*

39 Therefore they sought again to take him: but he escaped out of their hand,   *John 8:59*

40 And went away again beyond Jordan into the place where John at first baptized; and there he abode.   *John 1:28*

41 And many resorted unto him, and said, John did no miracle: but all things that John spake of this man were true.   *John 1:29-30*

42 And many believed on him there.   *John 7:31*

Jesus Raises Lazarus from the Dead

11 Now a certain *man* was sick, *named* Lazarus, of Bethany, the town of Mary and her sister Martha.   *Matt. 21:17*

2 (It was *that* Mary which anointed the Lord with ointment, and wiped his feet with her hair, whose brother Lazarus was sick.) *Mark 14:3*

3 Therefore his sisters sent unto him, saying, Lord, behold, he whom thou lovest is sick.   *John 11:5, 36*

4 When Jesus heard *that*, he said, This sickness is not unto death, but for the glory of God, that the Son of God might be glorified thereby.   *John 9:3; 11:40; 13:31-32*

> **11:1–4 Christ's Greatest Miracle**
>
> It was for Lazarus that the greatest of Christ's miracles was performed. The Saviour blessed all who sought His help; He loves all the human family, but to some He is bound by peculiarly tender associations. His heart was knit by a strong bond of affection to the family at Bethany, and for one of them His most wonderful work was wrought. *DA 524*

5 Now Jesus loved Martha, and her sister, and Lazarus.

6 When he had heard therefore that he was sick, he abode two days still in the same place where he was.

7 Then after that saith he to *his* disciples, Let us go into Judaea again.

8 *His* disciples say unto him, Master, the Jews of late sought to stone thee; and goest thou thither again?   *John 8:59; 10:31*

9 Jesus answered, Are there not twelve hours in the day? If any man walk in the day, he stumbleth not, because he seeth the light of this world.   *John 9:4; 12:35*

10 But if a man walk in the night, he stumbleth, because there is no light in him.

> **11:9, 10 Walking in God's Path**
>
> He who does the will of God, who walks in the path that God has marked out, cannot stumble and fall. The light of God's guiding Spirit gives him a clear perception of his duty, and leads him aright till the close of his work. *DA 527*

11 These things said he: and after that he saith unto them, Our friend Lazarus sleepeth; but I go, that I may awake him out of sleep.

12 Then said his disciples, Lord, if he sleep, he shall do well.

13 Howbeit Jesus spake of his death: but they thought that he had spoken of taking of rest in sleep.

14 Then said Jesus unto them plainly, Lazarus is dead.

After Death   See Psalm 13:3.

15 And I am glad for your sakes that I was not there, to the intent ye may believe; nevertheless let us go unto him.

16 Then said Thomas, which is called Didymus, unto his fellowdisciples, Let us also go, that we may die with him.   *Matt. 10:3; Mark 3:18*

17 Then when Jesus came, he found that he had *lain* in the grave four days already.

18 Now Bethany was nigh unto Jerusalem, about fifteen furlongs off:

19 And many of the Jews came to Martha and Mary, to comfort them concerning their brother.   *Job 2:11; John 11:31*

20 Then Martha, as soon as she heard that Jesus was coming, went and met him: but Mary sat *still* in the house.   *Luke 10:38-42*

21 Then said Martha unto Jesus, Lord, if thou hadst been here, my brother had not died.   *John 11:32, 37*

22 But I know, that even now, whatsoever thou wilt ask of God, God will give *it* thee.

23 Jesus saith unto her, Thy brother shall rise again.

24 Martha saith unto him, I know that he shall rise again in the resurrection at the last day.   *John 5:28-29*

25 Jesus said unto her, I am the resurrection, and the life: he that believeth in me, though he were dead, yet shall he live: 1 Thess. 4:14
26 And whosoever liveth and believeth in me shall never die. Believest thou this?
27 She saith unto him, Yea, Lord: I believe that thou art the Christ, the Son of God, which should come into the world. Matt. 11:3
28 And when she had so said, she went her way, and called Mary her sister secretly, saying, The Master is come, and calleth for thee.
29 As soon as she heard that, she arose quickly, and came unto him.
30 Now Jesus was not yet come into the town, but was in that place where Martha met him.
31 The Jews then which were with her in the house, and comforted her, when they saw Mary, that she rose up hastily and went out, followed her, saying, She goeth unto the grave to weep there. John 11:19
32 Then when Mary was come where Jesus was, and saw him, she fell down at his feet, saying unto him, Lord, if thou hadst been here, my brother had not died. John 11:21
33 When Jesus therefore saw her weeping, and the Jews also weeping which came with her, he groaned in the spirit, and was troubled, Mark 3:5; John 11:38; 12:27
34 And said, Where have ye laid him? They said unto him, Lord, come and see.
35 Jesus wept. Luke 19:41; John 11:33
36 Then said the Jews, Behold how he loved him! John 11:3
37 And some of them said, Could not this man, which opened the eyes of the blind, have caused that even this man should not have died? John 9:6-7
38 Jesus therefore again groaning in himself cometh to the grave. It was a cave, and a stone lay upon it. Is. 22:16; Matt. 27:60; John 11:33
39 Jesus said, Take ye away the stone. Martha, the sister of him that was dead, saith unto him, Lord, by this time he stinketh: for he hath been dead four days. John 11:17

11:39 Slow to Understand

When the Lord is about to do a work, Satan moves upon someone to object. "Take ye away the stone," Christ said. As far as possible, prepare the way for My work. But Martha's positive and ambitious nature asserted itself. She was unwilling that the decomposing body should be brought to view. The human heart is slow to understand Christ's words, and Martha's faith had not grasped the true meaning of His promise. DA 535

40 Jesus saith unto her, Said I not unto thee, that, if thou wouldest believe, thou shouldest see the glory of God? John 11:4, 23-26
41 Then they took away the stone from the place where the dead was laid. And Jesus lifted up his eyes, and said, Father, I thank thee that thou hast heard me. Matt. 11:25; John 17:1
42 And I knew that thou hearest me always: but because of the people which stand by I said it, that they may believe that thou hast sent me. Matt. 26:53; John 3:17; 17:21
43 And when he thus had spoken, he cried with a loud voice, Lazarus, come forth.
44 And he that was dead came forth, bound

Three and One-Half Years Was All the World Could Handle

John 11:47–53

So Caiaphas proposed by the sacrifice of Jesus to save the guilty nation, not from transgression, but in transgression, that they might continue in sin. . . .

At this council Christ's enemies had been deeply convicted. The Holy Spirit had impressed their minds. But Satan strove to gain control of them. He urged upon their notice the grievances they had suffered on account of Christ. How little He had honored their righteousness. He presented a righteousness far greater, which all who would be children of God must possess. Taking no notice of their forms and ceremonies, He had encouraged sinners to go directly to God as a merciful Father, and make known their wants. Thus, in their opinion, He had set aside the priesthood. He had refused to acknowledge the theology of the rabbinical schools. He had exposed the evil practices of the priests, and had irreparably hurt their influence. He had injured the effect of their maxims and traditions, declaring that though they strictly enforced the ritual law, they made void the law of God. All this Satan now brought to their minds.

Satan told them that in order to maintain their authority, they must put Jesus to death. This counsel they followed. The fact that they might lose the power they then exercised, was, they thought, sufficient reason for coming to some decision. With the exception of a few who dared not speak their minds, the Sanhedrin received the words of Caiaphas as the words of God. . . . They regarded themselves as patriots, who were seeking the nation's salvation. . . .

Jesus had now given three years of public labor to the world. His example of self-denial and disinterested benevolence was before them. His life of purity, of suffering and devotion, was known to all. Yet this short period of three years was as long as the world could endure the presence of its Redeemer. DA 540, 541

hand and foot with graveclothes: and his face was bound about with a napkin. Jesus saith unto them, Loose him, and let him go. *John 19:40; 20:7*

The Jewish Council Plots to Kill Jesus

45 Then many of the Jews which came to Mary, and had seen the things which Jesus did, believed on him. *John 2:23; 11:19*
46 But some of them went their ways to the Pharisees, and told them what things Jesus had done.
47 Then gathered the chief priests and the Pharisees a council, and said, What do we? for this man doeth many miracles. *Matt. 5:22*
48 If we let him thus alone, all *men* will believe on him: and the Romans shall come and take away both our place and nation.
49 And one of them, *named* Caiaphas, being the high priest that same year, said unto them, Ye know nothing at all, *Matt. 26:3*
50 Nor consider that it is expedient for us, that one man should die for the people, and that the whole nation perish not. *John 18:14*
51 And this spake he not of himself: but being high priest that year, he prophesied that Jesus should die for that nation; *Ex. 28:30*
52 And not for that nation only, but that also he should gather together in one the children of God that were scattered abroad. *Is. 49:6; John 10:16; 1 John 2:2*
53 Then from that day forth they took counsel together for to put him to death.
54 Jesus therefore walked no more openly among the Jews; but went thence unto a country near to the wilderness, into a city called Ephraim, and there continued with his disciples. *2 Chr. 13:19; John 7:1, 4*
55 And the Jews' passover was nigh at hand: and many went out of the country up to Jerusalem before the passover, to purify themselves. *John 2:13*
56 Then sought they for Jesus, and spake among themselves, as they stood in the temple, What think ye, that he will not come to the feast? *John 7:11*
57 Now both the chief priests and the Pharisees had given a commandment, that, if any man knew where he were, he should shew *it*, that they might take him.

Mary Anoints Jesus

12 Then Jesus six days before the passover came to Bethany, where Lazarus was which had been dead, whom he raised from the dead. *Matt. 21:17; John 11:1, 55*
2 There they made him a supper; and Martha served: but Lazarus was one of them that sat at the table with him. *Luke 10:38-42*
3 Then took Mary a ᵀpound of ointment of spikenard, very costly, and anointed the feet of Jesus, and wiped his feet with her hair: and the house was filled with the odour of the ointment. *John 11:2 ♦ sum of money*
4 Then saith one of his disciples, Judas Iscariot, Simon's *son*, which should betray him, *Matt. 10:4*
5 Why was not this ointment sold for three hundred pence, and given to the poor?
6 This he said, not that he cared for the poor; but because he was a thief, and had the bag, and bare what was put therein. *John 13:29*
7 Then said Jesus, Let her alone: against the day of my burying hath she kept this.

12:3–7 The Broken Box

Kingdoms would rise and fall; the names of monarchs and conquerors would be forgotten; but [Mary's] deed would be immortalized upon the pages of sacred history. Until time should be no more, that broken alabaster box would tell the story of the abundant love of God for a fallen race. *DA 563*

8 For the poor always ye have with you; but me ye have not always.   Deut. 15:11
9 Much people of the Jews therefore knew that he was there: and they came not for Jesus' sake only, but that they might see Lazarus also, whom he had raised from the dead.
10 But the chief priests consulted that they might put Lazarus also to death;   Luke 16:31
11 Because that by reason of him many of the Jews went away, and believed on Jesus.   John 11:45; 12:18

Jesus Rides into Jerusalem

12 On the next day much people that were come to the feast, when they heard that Jesus was coming to Jerusalem,
13 Took branches of palm trees, and went forth to meet him, and cried, Hosanna: Blessed *is* the King of Israel that cometh in the name of the Lord.   Ps. 118:25-26; Rev. 7:9
14 And Jesus, when he had found a young ass, sat thereon; as it is written,
15 Fear not, daughter of Sion: behold, thy King cometh, sitting on an ass's colt. Zech. 9:9
16 These things understood not his disciples at the first: but when Jesus was glorified, then remembered they that these things were written of him, and *that* they had done these things unto him.   John 2:22; 7:39; 12:23

12:12–16 Permitted for a Purpose

Never before in His earthly life had Jesus permitted such a demonstration. He clearly foresaw the result. It would bring Him to the cross. But it was His purpose thus publicly to present Himself as the Redeemer. He desired to call attention to the sacrifice that was to crown His mission to a fallen world. *DA 571*

17 The people therefore that was with him when he called Lazarus out of his grave, and raised him from the dead, bare record.
18 For this cause the people also met him, for that they heard that he had done this miracle.   John 12:11
19 The Pharisees therefore said among themselves, Perceive ye how ye prevail nothing? behold, the world is gone after him.   John 3:26

Some Greeks Desire to See Jesus

20 And there were certain Greeks among them that came up to worship at the feast:
21 The same came therefore to Philip, which was of Bethsaida of Galilee, and desired him, saying, Sir, we would see Jesus.
22 Philip cometh and telleth Andrew: and again Andrew and Philip tell Jesus.
23 And Jesus answered them, saying, The hour is come, that the Son of man should be glorified.   John 13:31-32
24 Verily, ᵀverily, I say unto you, Except a corn of wheat fall into the ground and die, it abideth alone: but if it die, it bringeth forth much fruit.   truly
25 He that loveth his life shall lose it; and he that hateth his life in this world shall keep it unto life eternal. Matt. 10:39; Mark 8:35; Luke 14:26

12:24, 25 Self-Serving = Self-Destruction

The life spent on self is like the grain that is eaten. It disappears, but there is no increase. A man may gather all he can for self; he may live and think and plan for self; but his life passes away, and he has nothing. The law of self-serving is the law of self-destruction. *DA 624*

26 If any man serve me, let him follow me; and where I am, there shall also my servant be: if any man serve me, him will *my* Father honour.   John 14:3; 17:24; 2 Cor. 5:8
27 Now is my soul troubled; and what shall I say? Father, save me from this hour: but for this cause came I unto this hour.   Luke 22:53
28 Father, glorify thy name. Then came there a voice from heaven, *saying*, I have both glorified *it*, and will glorify *it* again. 2 Pet. 1:17
29 The people therefore, that stood by, and heard *it*, said that it thundered: others said, An angel spake to him.
30 Jesus answered and said, This voice came not because of me, but for your sakes.   John 11:42
31 Now is the judgment of this world: now shall the prince of this world be cast out.
32 And I, if I be lifted up from the earth, will draw all *men* unto me.   John 3:14; 6:44; 8:28
33 This he said, signifying what death he should die.   John 18:32; 21:19
34 The people answered him, We have heard out of the law that Christ abideth for ever: and how sayest thou, The Son of man must be lifted up? who is this Son of man?   Is. 9:7
35 Then Jesus said unto them, Yet a little while is the light with you. Walk while ye have the light, lest darkness come upon you: for he that walketh in darkness knoweth not whither he goeth.   John 7:33; 12:46; Eph. 5:8
36 While ye have light, believe in the light, that ye may be the children of light. These

things spake Jesus, and departed, and did hide himself from them. *Luke 16:8*

The Jews Are Generally Blinded

37 But though he had done so many miracles before them, yet they believed not on him:

38 That the saying of Esaias the prophet might be fulfilled, which he spake, Lord, who hath believed our report? and to whom hath the arm of the Lord been revealed? *Is. 53:1; Rom. 10:16*

39 Therefore they could not believe, because that Esaias said again, *John 5:44*

40 He hath blinded their eyes, and hardened their heart; that they should not see with *their* eyes, nor understand with *their* heart, and be converted, and I should heal them. *Is. 6:10*

41 These things said Esaias, when he saw his glory, and spake of him. *Is. 6:1-5*

Many Chief Rulers Believe, but Do Not Confess Him

42 Nevertheless among the chief rulers also many believed on him; but because of the Pharisees they did not confess *him*, lest they should be put out of the synagogue: *John 7:13*

43 For they loved the praise of men more than the praise of God. *John 5:41, 44*

Jesus Calls All to Believe

44 Jesus cried and said, He that believeth on me, believeth not on me, but on him that sent me. *Matt. 10:40; John 5:24; 13:20*

45 And he that seeth me seeth him that sent me.

46 I am come a light into the world, that whosoever believeth on me should not abide in darkness. *John 3:19; 8:12; 9:5*

47 And if any man hear my words, and believe not, I judge him not: for I came not to judge the world, but to save the world. *John 3:17*

48 He that rejecteth me, and receiveth not my words, hath one that judgeth him: the word that I have spoken, the same shall judge him in the last day. *Luke 10:16*

49 For I have not spoken of myself; but the Father which sent me, he gave me a commandment, what I should say, and what I should speak. *John 3:11*

50 And I know that his commandment is life everlasting: whatsoever I speak therefore, even as the Father said unto me, so I speak. *John 6:68*

Jesus Washes the Disciples' Feet

13 Now before the feast of the passover, when Jesus knew that his hour was come that he should depart out of this world unto the Father, having loved his own

which were in the world, he loved them unto the end. *John 12:23; 13:3; 16:28*

2 And supper being ended, the ᵀdevil having now put into the heart of Judas Iscariot, Simon's *son*, to betray him; *Acts 5:3* ♦ *false accuser*

3 Jesus knowing that the Father had given all things into his hands, and that he was come from God, and went to God; *Matt. 11:27*

> **13:4–15 An Unforgettable Example**
>
> This action opened the eyes of the disciples. Bitter shame and humiliation filled their hearts. They understood the unspoken rebuke, and saw themselves in altogether a new light.
>
> So Christ expressed His love for His disciples. Their selfish spirit filled Him with sorrow, but He entered into no controversy with them regarding their difficulty. Instead He gave them an example they would never forget. *DA 644, 645*

4 He riseth from supper, and laid aside his garments; and took a towel, and girded himself. *Luke 12:37*

5 After that he poureth water into a bason, and began to wash the disciples' feet, and to wipe *them* with the towel wherewith he was girded. *Luke 7:44*

6 Then cometh he to Simon Peter: and Peter saith unto him, Lord, dost thou wash my feet?

7 Jesus answered and said unto him, What I do thou knowest not now; but thou shalt know hereafter. *John 12:16*

8 Peter saith unto him, Thou shalt never wash my feet. Jesus answered him, If I wash thee not, thou hast no part with me. *1 Cor. 6:11*

9 Simon Peter saith unto him, Lord, not my feet only, but also *my* hands and *my* head.

10 Jesus saith to him, He that is washed needeth not save to wash *his* feet, but is clean every ᵀwhit: and ye are clean, but not all. *John 15:3* ♦ *bit*

11 For he knew who should betray him; therefore said he, Ye are not all clean. *John 2:25*

12 So after he had washed their feet, and had taken his garments, and was set down again, he said unto them, Know ye what I have done to you? *John 13:7*

13 Ye call me Master and Lord: and ye say well; for *so* I am. *Luke 6:46; 1 Cor. 12:3; Phil. 2:11*

14 If I then, *your* Lord and Master, have washed your feet; ye also ought to wash one another's feet. *1 Pet. 5:5*

15 For I have given you an example, that ye should do as I have done to you. *Matt. 11:29*

13:12-15

Baptism/Lord's Supper   See 1 Corinthians 10:16, 17.

13:12–15 A Consecrated Ordinance

In these words Christ was not merely enjoining the practice of hospitality. More was meant than the washing of the feet of guests to remove the dust of travel. Christ was here instituting a religious service. By the act of our Lord this humiliating ceremony was made a consecrated ordinance. It was to be observed by the disciples, that they might ever keep in mind His lessons of humility and service. *DA 650*

---

16 Verily, verily, I say unto you, The servant is not greater than his lord; neither he that is sent greater than he that sent him. ⠀⠀Luke 6:40
17 If ye know these things, happy are ye if ye do them. ⠀⠀Matt. 7:24-25

Jesus Foretells His Betrayal

18 I speak not of you all: I know whom I have chosen: but that the scripture may be fulfilled, He that eateth bread with me hath lifted up his heel against me. Ps. 41:9; Matt. 26:23
19 Now I tell you before it come, that, when it is come to pass, ye may believe that I am *he*. ⠀⠀John 14:29; 16:4
20 Verily, ᵀverily, I say unto you, He that receiveth whomsoever I send receiveth me; and he that receiveth me receiveth him that sent me. ⠀⠀Luke 10:16 ◆ *truly*
21 When Jesus had thus said, he was troubled in spirit, and testified, and said, Verily, verily, I say unto you, that one of you shall betray me. ⠀⠀Matt. 26:21; Mark 14:18; John 12:27
22 Then the disciples looked one on another, doubting of whom he spake. Luke 22:23
23 Now there was leaning on Jesus' bosom one of his disciples, whom Jesus loved.
24 Simon Peter therefore beckoned to him, that he should ask who it should be of whom he spake.
25 He then lying on Jesus' breast saith unto him, Lord, who is it? ⠀⠀John 21:20
26 Jesus answered, He it is, to whom I shall give a sop, when I have dipped *it*. And when he had dipped the sop, he gave *it* to Judas Iscariot, *the son* of Simon. ⠀⠀Matt. 26:23
27 And after the sop Satan entered into him. Then said Jesus unto him, That thou doest, do quickly. ⠀⠀Luke 22:3; John 13:2
28 Now no man at the table knew for what intent he spake this unto him.
29 For some *of them* thought, because Judas had the bag, that Jesus had said unto him, Buy *those things* that we have need of against the feast; or, that he should give something to the poor. ⠀⠀John 12:5-6
30 He then having received the ᵀsop went immediately out: and it was night. ⠀⠀*small piece*

13:30 Crossing the Line

Night it was to the traitor as he turned away from Christ into the outer darkness.

Until this step was taken, Judas had not passed beyond the possibility of repentance. But when he left the presence of his Lord and his fellow disciples, the final decision had been made. He had passed the boundary line. *DA 654, 655*

Jesus Commands The Disciples to Love

31 Therefore, when he was gone out, Jesus said, Now is the Son of man glorified, and God is glorified in him. John 7:39; 14:13; 1 Pet. 4:11
32 If God be glorified in him, God shall also glorify him in himself, and shall ᵀstraightway glorify him. ⠀⠀John 12:23 ◆ *right away*
33 Little children, yet a little while I am with you. Ye shall seek me: and as I said unto the Jews, Whither I go, ye cannot come; so now I say to you. ⠀⠀John 7:33-34
34 A new commandment I give unto you, That ye love one another; as I have loved you, that ye also love one another. ⠀⠀Lev. 19:18
35 By this shall all *men* know that ye are my disciples, if ye have love one to another.

Jesus Forewarns Peter of His Denial

36 Simon Peter said unto him, Lord, whither goest thou? Jesus answered him, Whither I go, thou canst not follow me now; but thou shalt follow me afterwards. John 13:33; 2 Pet. 1:14
37 Peter said unto him, Lord, why cannot I follow thee now? I will lay down my life for thy sake.
38 Jesus answered him, Wilt thou lay down thy life for my sake? Verily, verily, I say unto thee, The cock shall not crow, till thou hast denied me ᵀthrice. ⠀⠀Mark 14:30 ◆ *three times*

Jesus Promises to Send the Holy Spirit

14 Let not your heart be troubled: ye believe in God, believe also in me.
2 In my Father's house are many mansions: if *it were* not *so*, I would have told you. I go to prepare a place for you. John 13:33, 36; 2 Cor. 5:1
3 And if I go and prepare a place for you, I will come again, and receive you unto myself; that where I am, *there* ye may be also. ⠀⠀Acts 1:11

Christ's Return⠀⠀See Hebrews 9:28.

4 And whither I go ye know, and the way ye know.
5 Thomas saith unto him, Lord, we know not whither thou goest; and how can we know the way? ⠀⠀John 11:16
6 Jesus saith unto him, I am the way, the truth, and the life: no man cometh unto the Father, but by me. ⠀⠀John 1:14; 10:9; Acts 4:12
7 If ye had known me, ye should have

known my Father also: and from henceforth ye know him, and have seen him. *John 8:19*

8 Philip saith unto him, Lord, shew us the Father, and it sufficeth us.

9 Jesus saith unto him, Have I been so long time with you, and yet hast thou not known me, Philip? he that hath seen me hath seen the Father; and how sayest thou *then*, Shew us the Father? *John 12:45; Col. 1:15; Heb. 1:3*

Who Is God?   See John 1:1–3.

10 Believest thou not that I am in the Father, and the Father in me? the words that I speak unto you I speak not of myself: but the Father that dwelleth in me, he doeth the works. *John 5:19; 10:30, 38*

11 Believe me that I *am* in the Father, and the Father in me: or else believe me for the very works' sake. *John 5:36; 10:38*

14:12–14 The Price Paid Was High

The Lord is disappointed when His people place a low estimate upon themselves. He desires His chosen heritage to value themselves according to the price He has placed upon them. God wanted them, else He would not have sent His Son on such an expensive errand to redeem them. He has a use for them, and He is well pleased when they make the very highest demands upon Him, that they may glorify His name. They may expect large things if they have faith in His promises. *DA 668*

12 Verily, ᵀverily, I say unto you, He that believeth on me, the works that I do shall he do also; and greater *works* than these shall he do; because I go unto my Father. *Matt. 21:21* ◆ *truly*

13 And whatsoever ye shall ask in my name, that will I do, that the Father may be glorified in the Son. *Matt. 7:7; John 13:31; 15:16*

14 If ye shall ask any thing in my name, I will do *it*.

14:15 True Love Is the Key

Those who bring their petitions to God, claiming His promise while they do not comply with the conditions, insult Jehovah. They bring the name of Christ as their authority for the fulfillment of the promise, but they do not those things that would show faith in Christ and love for Him. . . .

We present to God His promises, and ask Him to fulfill them, when by so doing He would dishonor His own name. *COL 143*

15 If ye love me, keep my commandments.

God's Law   See John 15:10.

16 And I will pray the Father, and he shall give you another Comforter, that he may abide with you for ever; *John 14:26; 15:26; 1 John 2:1*

17 *Even* the Spirit of truth; whom the world cannot receive, because it seeth him not, neither knoweth him: but ye know him; for he dwelleth with you, and shall be in you. *John 15:26; 16:13; 1 Cor. 2:14*

18 I will not leave you comfortless: I will come to you. *John 14:3*

Who Is God?   See John 15:26.

19 Yet a little while, and the world seeth me no more; but ye see me: because I live, ye shall live also. *John 7:33; 16:16, 22*

20 At that day ye shall know that I *am* in my Father, and ye in me, and I in you. *John 10:38*

21 He that hath my commandments, and keepeth them, he it is that loveth me: and he that loveth me shall be loved of my Father, and I will love him, and will ᵀmanifest myself to him. *John 14:15* ◆ *make known*

22 Judas saith unto him, not Iscariot, Lord, how is it that thou wilt manifest thyself unto us, and not unto the world? *Luke 6:16; Acts 1:13*

23 Jesus answered and said unto him, If a man love me, he will keep my words: and my Father will love him, and we will come unto him, and make our abode with him. *1 John 2:24*

The Gift That Brings All Others

John 14:16-18

Christ has promised the gift of the Holy Spirit to His church, and the promise belongs to us as much as to the first disciples. But like every other promise, it is given on conditions. There are many who believe and profess to claim the Lord's promise; they talk *about* Christ and *about* the Holy Spirit, yet receive no benefit. They do not surrender the soul to be guided and controlled by the divine agencies. We cannot use the Holy Spirit. The Spirit is to use us. Through the Spirit God works in His people "to will and to do of His good pleasure" (Philippians 2:13). But many will not submit to this. They want to manage themselves. This is why they do not receive the heavenly gift. Only to those who wait humbly upon God, who watch for His guidance and grace, is the Spirit given. The power of God awaits their demand and reception. This promised blessing, claimed by faith, brings all other blessings in its train. It is given according to the riches of the grace of Christ, and He is ready to supply every soul according to the capacity to receive. *DA 672*

24 He that loveth me not keepeth not my sayings: and the word which ye hear is not mine, but the Father's which sent me. *John 7:16; 14:10*
25 These things have I spoken unto you, being *yet* present with you.
26 But the Comforter, *which is* the Holy Ghost, whom the Father will send in my name, he shall teach you all things, and bring all things to your remembrance, whatsoever I have said unto you. *John 2:22; 15:26; 16:7*
27 Peace I leave with you, my peace I give unto you: not as the world giveth, give I unto you. Let not your heart be troubled, neither let it be afraid. *John 16:33; Phil. 4:7; Col. 3:15*
28 Ye have heard how I said unto you, I go away, and come *again* unto you. If ye loved me, ye would rejoice, because I said, I go unto the Father: for my Father is greater than I. *John 14:12*
29 And now I have told you before it come to pass, that, when it is come to pass, ye might believe. *John 13:19*
30 Hereafter I will not talk much with you: for the prince of this world cometh, and hath nothing in me. *John 12:31; 2 Cor. 4:4; Heb. 4:15*
31 But that the world may know that I love the Father; and as the Father gave me commandment, even so I do. Arise, let us go hence. *John 10:18*

Jesus Is the Vine

15 I am the true vine, and my Father is the ᵀhusbandman. *Is. 5:1-7 ◆ vinedresser*
2 Every branch in me that beareth not fruit he taketh away: and every *branch* that beareth fruit, he purgeth it, that it may bring forth more fruit. *Matt. 3:10*
3 Now ye are clean through the word which I have spoken unto you. *John 13:10; Eph. 5:26*

4 Abide in me, and I in you. As the branch cannot bear fruit of itself, except it abide in the vine; no more can ye, except ye abide in me. *John 6:56; Gal. 2:20; 1 John 2:6*
5 I am the vine, ye *are* the branches: He that abideth in me, and I in him, the same bringeth forth much fruit: for without me ye can do nothing. *Phil. 4:13*
6 If a man abide not in me, he is cast forth as a branch, and is withered; and men gather them, and cast *them* into the fire, and they are burned. *Matt. 13:41*
7 If ye abide in me, and my words abide in you, ye shall ask what ye will, and it shall be done unto you. *John 14:13*
8 Herein is my Father glorified, that ye bear much fruit; so shall ye be my disciples. *Is. 61:3*

9 As the Father hath loved me, so have I loved you: continue ye in my love. *John 17:26*
10 If ye keep my commandments, ye shall abide in my love; even as I have kept my Father's commandments, and abide in his love. *John 8:29; 14:15; 17:4*

God's Law　See Romans 7:12.

11 These things have I spoken unto you, that my joy might remain in you, and *that* your joy might be full. *John 16:24; 17:13; 1 John 1:4*
12 This is my commandment, That ye love one another, as I have loved you. *1 John 3:23*

13 Greater love hath no man than this, that a man lay down his life for his friends. *Eph. 5:2*
14 Ye are my friends, if ye do whatsoever I command you. *Matt. 12:50; Luke 12:4*
15 Henceforth I call you not servants; for the servant knoweth not what his lord doeth: but I have called you friends; for all things that I have heard of my Father I have made known unto you. *John 8:26*

15:10

16 Ye have not chosen me, but I have chosen you, and ordained you, that ye should go and bring forth fruit, and *that* your fruit should remain: that whatsoever ye shall ask of the Father in my name, he may give it you.   John 6:70; 13:18; 15:19

17 These things I command you, that ye love one another.   John 15:12

> **15:17 Practical Self-Sacrifice**
>
> Many who profess His name have lost sight of the fact that Christians are to represent Christ. Unless there is practical self-sacrifice for the good of others, in the family circle, in the neighborhood, in the church, and wherever we may be, then whatever our profession, we are not Christians. *DA 504*

Comfort in Persecution

18 If the world hate you, ye know that it hated me before *it hated* you. John 7:7; 1 John 3:13

19 If ye were of the world, the world would love his own: but because ye are not of the world, but I have chosen you out of the world, therefore the world hateth you.   John 15:16

20 Remember the word that I said unto you, The servant is not greater than his lord. If they have persecuted me, they will also persecute you; if they have kept my saying, they will keep yours also.   Ezek. 3:7; Matt. 10:24

21 But all these things will they do unto you for my name's sake, because they know not him that sent me.   Matt. 10:22; 24:9; John 16:3

22 If I had not come and spoken unto them, they had not had sin: but now they have no ᵀcloke for their sin.   John 9:41; Rom. 1:20 ◆ *cloke*

23 He that hateth me hateth my Father also.

24 If I had not done among them the works which none other man did, they had not had sin: but now have they both seen and hated both me and my Father.   John 5:36

25 But *this cometh to pass*, that the word might be fulfilled that is written in their law, They hated me without a cause. Ps. 35:19; 69:4

The Work of the Holy Spirit

26 But when the Comforter is come, whom I will send unto you from the Father, *even* the Spirit of truth, which proceedeth from the Father, he shall testify of me: John 14:16-17, 26; 16:7

> **Who Is God?**   See John 16:7, 8.

27 And ye also shall bear witness, because ye have been with me from the beginning.

Sadness Will Turn to Joy

16 These things have I spoken unto you, that ye should not be offended.

2 They shall put you out of the synagogues: yea, the time cometh, that whosoever

killeth you will think that he doeth God service.   John 9:22; 12:42; Acts 26:9-11

3 And these things will they do unto you, because they have not known the Father, nor me.   John 8:19; 15:21; 17:25

4 But these things have I told you, that when the time shall come, ye may remember that I told you of them. And these things I said not unto you at the beginning, because I was with you.   Matt. 9:15; John 13:19; 14:29

5 But now I go my way to him that sent me; and none of you asketh me, Whither goest thou?   John 7:33; 13:36; 16:10

6 But because I have said these things unto you, sorrow hath filled your heart.   John 14:1

7 Nevertheless I tell you the truth; It is expedient for you that I go away: for if I go not away, the Comforter will not come unto you; but if I depart, I will send him unto you.

8 And when he is come, he will reprove the world of sin, and of righteousness, and of judgment: John 8:46

> **Who Is God?**   See John 16:13.

9 Of sin, because they believe not on me;

10 Of righteousness, because I go to my Father, and ye see me no more;   Jer. 23:5-6

11 Of judgment, because the prince of this world is judged.   John 12:31; 14:30; 2 Cor. 4:4

12 I have yet many things to say unto you, but ye cannot bear them now.   Mark 4:33

13 Howbeit when he, the Spirit of truth, is come, he will guide you into all truth: for he shall not speak of himself; but whatsoever he shall hear, *that* shall he speak: and he will shew you things to come.   John 14:17, 26; 15:26

> **Who Is God?**

14 He shall glorify me: for he shall receive of mine, and shall shew *it* unto you. 1 John 4:13-14

15 All things that the Father hath are mine: therefore said I, that he shall take of mine, and shall shew *it* unto you.   John 17:10

16 A little while, and ye shall not see me: and again, a little while, and ye shall see me, because I go to the Father. John 7:33; 16:17-19, 22

17 Then said *some* of his disciples among themselves, What is this that he saith unto us, A little while, and ye shall not see me: and again, a little while, and ye shall see me: and, Because I go to the Father?   John 16:5

18 They said therefore, What is this that he saith, A little while? we cannot tell what he saith.

19 Now Jesus knew that they were desirous to ask him, and said unto them, Do ye enquire among yourselves of that I said, A little while, and ye shall not see me: and again, a little while, and ye shall see me? John 2:24-25

20 Verily, ᵀverily, I say unto you, That ye shall weep and lament, but the world shall rejoice:

and ye shall be sorrowful, but your sorrow shall be turned into joy. Mark 16:10 ◆ *truly*

16:19, 20 Absent, Yet Present

After His ascension He was to be absent in person; but through the Comforter He would still be with [his apostles], and they were not to spend their time in mourning. *DA 277*

---

21 A woman when she is in travail hath sorrow, because her hour is come: but as soon as she is delivered of the child, she remembereth no more the anguish, for joy that a man is born into the world. 1 Thess. 5:3
22 And ye now therefore have sorrow: but I will see you again, and your heart shall rejoice, and your joy no man taketh from you.

Assurance of Answered Prayer

23 And in that day ye shall ask me nothing. Verily, verily, I say unto you, Whatsoever ye shall ask the Father in my name, he will give *it* you. John 16:19
24 Hitherto have ye asked nothing in my name: ask, and ye shall receive, that your joy may be full. John 15:11

16:23, 24 Every Sincere Prayer Heard

The prayer of the humble suppliant [Jesus] presents as His own desire in that soul's behalf. Every sincere prayer is heard in heaven. It may not be fluently expressed; but if the heart is in it, it will ascend to the sanctuary where Jesus ministers, and He will present it to the Father without one awkward, stammering word, beautiful and fragrant with the incense of His own perfection. *DA 667*

---

25 These things have I spoken unto you in proverbs: but the time cometh, when I shall no more speak unto you in proverbs, but I shall shew you plainly of the Father. John 16:2
26 At that day ye shall ask in my name: and I say not unto you, that I will pray the Father for you:
27 For the Father himself loveth you, because ye have loved me, and have believed that I came out from God. John 14:21, 23; 16:30
28 I came forth from the Father, and am come into the world: again, I leave the world, and go to the Father. John 8:14; 13:1, 3
29 His disciples said unto him, Lo, now speakest thou plainly, and speakest no proverb. John 16:25
30 Now are we sure that thou knowest all things, and needest not that any man should ask thee: by this we believe that thou camest forth from God. John 21:17
31 Jesus answered them, Do ye now believe?
32 Behold, the hour cometh, yea, is now come, that ye shall be scattered, every man

to his own, and shall leave me alone: and yet I am not alone, because the Father is with me. Zech. 13:7; Matt. 26:31; John 8:29
33 These things I have spoken unto you, that in me ye might have peace. In the world ye shall have tribulation: but be of good cheer; I have overcome the world. John 14:1, 27; 1 John 4:4

16:33 The Way Already Prepared

By passing over the ground which man must travel, our Lord has prepared the way for us to overcome. It is not His will that we should be placed at a disadvantage in the conflict with Satan. He would not have us intimidated and discouraged by the assaults of the serpent. *DA 122, 123*

Jesus Prays for Himself, His Disciples, and His Church

17 These words spake Jesus, and lifted up his eyes to heaven, and said, Father, the hour is come; glorify thy Son, that thy Son also may glorify thee: John 7:39; 11:41
2 As thou hast given him power over all flesh, that he should give eternal life to as many as thou hast given him. John 6:37; 17:24
3 And this is life eternal, that they might know thee the only true God, and Jesus Christ, whom thou hast sent. 1 John 5:20

17:3 Results of Knowing God

The experimental knowledge of God and of Jesus Christ whom He has sent, transforms man into the image of God. It gives to man the mastery of himself, bringing every impulse and passion of the lower nature under the control of the higher powers of the mind. It makes its possessor a son of God and an heir of heaven. It brings him into communion with the mind of the Infinite, and opens to him the rich treasures of the universe. *COL 114*

---

4 I have glorified thee on the earth: I have finished the work which thou gavest me to do.
5 And now, O Father, glorify thou me with thine own self with the glory which I had with thee before the world was. John 17:24
6 I have ᵀmanifested thy name unto the men which thou gavest me out of the world: thine they were, and thou gavest them me; and they have kept thy word. John 6:37; 17:2, 26 ◆ *made known*
7 Now they have known that all things whatsoever thou hast given me are of thee.
8 For I have given unto them the words which thou gavest me; and they have received *them,* and have known surely that I came out from thee, and they have believed that thou didst send me. John 16:27, 30; 17:14
9 I pray for them: I pray not for the world,

but for them which thou hast given me; for they are thine.   Luke 22:32

10 And all mine are thine, and thine are mine; and I am glorified in them. 2 Thess. 1:10

11 And now I am no more in the world, but these are in the world, and I come to thee. Holy Father, keep through thine own name those whom thou hast given me, that they may be one, as we are.   John 13:1; 17:21-22, 25

12 While I was with them in the world, I kept them in thy name: those that thou gavest me I have kept, and none of them is lost, but the son of [T]perdition; that the scripture might be fulfilled.   John 13:18; 18:9; 2 Thess. 2:3 ◆ destruction

13 And now come I to thee; and these things I speak in the world, that they might have my joy fulfilled in themselves. John 3:29

14 I have given them thy word; and the world hath hated them, because they are not of the world, even as I am not of the world.

15 I pray not that thou shouldest take them out of the world, but that thou shouldest keep them from the evil.

16 They are not of the world, even as I am not of the world.   John 17:14

17 Sanctify them through thy truth: thy word is truth. 2 Sam. 7:28; John 15:3; 2 Thess. 2:13

The Bible

18 As thou hast sent me into the world, even so have I also sent them into the world.   John 20:21

19 And for their sakes I [T]sanctify myself, that they also might be [T]sanctified through the truth.   John 10:36 ◆ make holy ◆ made holy

20 Neither pray I for these alone, but for them also which shall believe on me through their word;

21 That they all may be one; as thou, Father, art in me, and I in thee, that they also may be one in us: that the world may believe that thou hast sent me.   John 10:38; 17:8, 11

22 And the glory which thou gavest me I have given them; that they may be one, even as we are one: John 1:14

17:23 No False Representation

Christians are set as light bearers on the way to heaven. They are to reflect to the world the light shining upon them from Christ....

If we do represent Christ, we shall make His service appear attractive, as it really is. Christians who gather up gloom and sadness to their souls, and murmur and complain, are giving to others a false representation of God and the Christian life. They give the impression that God is not pleased to have His children happy, and in this they bear false witness against our heavenly Father. *SC 115, 116*

23 I in them, and thou in me, that they may be made perfect in one; and that the world may know that thou hast sent me, and hast loved them, as thou hast loved me.   John 16:27

24 Father, I will that they also, whom thou hast given me, be with me where I am; that they may behold my glory, which thou hast given me: for thou lovedst me before the foundation of the world.   John 1:14; 12:26; 17:5

25 O righteous Father, the world hath not known thee: but I have known thee, and these have known that thou hast sent me. John 7:29

26 And I have declared unto them thy name, and will declare it: that the love wherewith thou hast loved me may be in them, and I in them.   John 15:9; 17:6, 23

Who Is God?   See John 14:16-18.

Jesus Is Arrested

18 When Jesus had spoken these words, he went forth with his disciples over the brook Cedron, where was a garden, into the which he entered, and his disciples.   2 Sam. 15:23; Matt. 26:36; Mark 14:32

2 And Judas also, which betrayed him, knew the place: for Jesus [T]ofttimes resorted thither with his disciples.   Luke 21:37; 22:39 ◆ often

3 Judas then, having received a band of men and officers from the chief priests and Pharisees, cometh thither with lanterns and torches and weapons.   Luke 22:47-53; Acts 1:16

4 Jesus therefore, knowing all things that should come upon him, went forth, and said unto them, Whom seek ye?   John 13:1; 18:7

5 They answered him, Jesus of Nazareth. Jesus saith unto them, I am he. And Judas also, which betrayed him, stood with them.

6 As soon then as he had said unto them, I am he, they went backward, and fell to the ground.

7 Then asked he them again, Whom seek ye? And they said, Jesus of Nazareth.   John 18:4

8 Jesus answered, I have told you that I am he: if therefore ye seek me, let these go their way:

9 That the saying might be fulfilled, which he spake, Of them which thou gavest me have I lost none.   John 17:12

10 Then Simon Peter having a sword drew it, and smote the high priest's servant, and cut off his right ear. The servant's name was Malchus.   Mark 14:47

11 Then said Jesus unto Peter, Put up thy sword into the [T]sheath: the cup which my Father hath given me, shall I not drink it?   Matt. 20:22; 26:39, 42 ◆ case for a sword

12 Then the band and the captain and officers of the Jews took Jesus, and bound him,   Matt. 26:57; John 18:3

17:17‡

17:18-26

13 And led him away to Annas first; for he was father in law to Caiaphas, which was the high priest that same year. Matt. 26:3; Luke 3:2
14 Now Caiaphas was he, which gave counsel to the Jews, that it was expedient that one man should die for the people.

Peter Denies Jesus

15 And Simon Peter followed Jesus, and *so did* another disciple: that disciple was known unto the high priest, and went in with Jesus into the palace of the high priest. Mark 14:54; Luke 22:54
16 But Peter stood at the door without. Then went out that other disciple, which was known unto the high priest, and spake unto her that kept the door, and brought in Peter.
17 Then saith the damsel that kept the door unto Peter, Art not thou also *one* of this man's disciples? He saith, I am not.
18 And the servants and officers stood there, who had made a fire of coals; for it was cold: and they warmed themselves: and Peter stood with them, and warmed himself. Mark 14:54; John 18:25

The High Priest Questions Jesus

19 The high priest then asked Jesus of his disciples, and of his doctrine.
20 Jesus answered him, I spake openly to the world; I ever taught in the synagogue, and in the temple, whither the Jews always resort; and in secret have I said nothing. Is. 45:19
21 Why askest thou me? ask them which heard me, what I have said unto them: behold, they know what I said.
22 And when he had thus spoken, one of the officers which stood by struck Jesus with the palm of his hand, saying, Answerest thou the high priest so?
23 Jesus answered him, If I have spoken evil, bear witness of the evil: but if well, why ᵀsmitest thou me? *do you strike*
24 Now Annas had sent him ᵀbound unto Caiaphas the high priest. John 18:13 ◆ *landmark*

Peter Denies Jesus Again

25 And Simon Peter stood and warmed himself. They said therefore unto him, Art not thou also *one* of his disciples? He denied *it*, and said, I am not.
26 One of the servants of the high priest, being *his* ᵀkinsman whose ear Peter cut off, saith, Did not I see thee in the garden with him? John 18:1 ◆ *nearest male blood relative*
27 Peter then denied again: and immediately the cock crew. John 13:38

18:27 Peter's Sorrowful Realization

Peter called to mind his promise of a few short hours before that he would go with his Lord to prison and to death. He remembered his grief when the Saviour told him in the upper chamber that he would deny his Lord thrice that same night. Peter had just declared that he knew not Jesus, but he now realized with bitter grief how well his Lord knew him, and how accurately He had read his heart, the falseness of which was unknown even to himself. *DA 713*

Pilate Questions Jesus

28 Then led they Jesus from Caiaphas unto the hall of judgment: and it was early; and they themselves went not into the judgment hall, lest they should be defiled; but that they might eat the passover. Matt. 27:27; John 18:33; 19:9
29 Pilate then went out unto them, and said, What accusation bring ye against this man?
30 They answered and said unto him, If he were not a ᵀmalefactor, we would not have delivered him up unto thee. *evildoer*
31 Then said Pilate unto them, Take ye him, and judge him according to your law. The Jews therefore said unto him, It is not lawful for us to put any man to death:
32 That the saying of Jesus might be fulfilled, which he spake, signifying what death he should die. Matt. 20:19; 26:2; John 3:14
33 Then Pilate entered into the judgment hall again, and called Jesus, and said unto him, Art thou the King of the Jews? John 19:9
34 Jesus answered him, Sayest thou this thing of thyself, or did others tell it thee of me?
35 Pilate answered, Am I a Jew? Thine own nation and the chief priests have delivered thee unto me: what hast thou done?
36 Jesus answered, My kingdom is not of this world: if my kingdom were of this world, then would my servants fight, that I should not be delivered to the Jews: but now is my kingdom not from hence. Dan. 2:44; 7:14; John 6:15

18:37, 38 Sacrificing Principle

Pilate longed to deliver Jesus. But he saw that he could not do this, and yet retain his own position and honor. Rather than lose his worldly power, he chose to sacrifice an innocent life. How many, to escape loss or suffering, in like manner sacrifice principle. Conscience and duty point one way, and self-interest points another. The current sets strongly in the wrong direction, and he who compromises with evil is swept away into the thick darkness of guilt. *DA 738*

37 Pilate therefore said unto him, Art thou a king then? Jesus answered, Thou sayest that I

am a king. To this end was I born, and for this cause came I into the world, that I should bear witness unto the truth. Every one that is of the truth heareth my voice.   1 John 4:6

38 Pilate saith unto him, What is truth? And when he had said this, he went out again unto the Jews, and saith unto them, I find in him no fault *at all*.   Luke 23:4; John 19:4, 6

39 But ye have a custom, that I should release unto you one at the passover: will ye therefore that I release unto you the King of the Jews?   Matt. 27:15-18

40 Then cried they all again, saying, Not this man, but Barabbas. Now Barabbas was a robber.

Christ Is Mocked and Rejected

19 Then Pilate therefore took Jesus, and ᵀscourged *him*.   Is. 50:6 ◆ *whipped*

2 And the soldiers ᵀplatted a crown of thorns, and put *it* on his head, and they put on him a purple robe,   *braided*

3 And said, Hail, King of the Jews! and they smote him with their hands.   Matt. 27:29

4 Pilate therefore went forth again, and saith unto them, Behold, I bring him forth to you, that ye may know that I find no fault in him.   John 18:38; 19:6

5 Then came Jesus forth, wearing the crown of thorns, and the purple robe. And *Pilate* saith unto them, Behold the man!   John 19:2

6 When the chief priests therefore and officers saw him, they cried out, saying, Crucify *him*, crucify *him*. Pilate saith unto them, Take ye him, and crucify *him*: for I find no fault in him.   John 18:31

7 The Jews answered him, We have a law, and by our law he ought to die, because he made himself the Son of God.   Lev. 24:16; Matt. 26:63-66

8 When Pilate therefore heard that saying, he was the more afraid;

9 And went again into the judgment hall, and saith unto Jesus, Whence art thou? But Jesus gave him no answer.   John 18:33

10 Then saith Pilate unto him, Speakest thou not unto me? knowest thou not that I have power to crucify thee, and have power to release thee?

11 Jesus answered, Thou couldest have no power *at all* against me, except it were given thee from above: therefore he that delivered me unto thee hath the greater sin.   Matt. 27:2; John 9:41; Rom. 13:1

12 And from thenceforth Pilate sought to release him: but the Jews cried out, saying, If thou let this man go, thou art not Caesar's friend: whosoever maketh himself a king speaketh against Caesar.   John 18:33-36

13 When Pilate therefore heard that saying, he brought Jesus forth, and sat down in the judgment seat in a place that is called the Pavement, but in the Hebrew, Gabbatha.   Matt. 27:19

14 And it was the preparation of the passover, and about the sixth hour: and he saith unto the Jews, Behold your King!   Matt. 27:62

15 But they cried out, Away with *him*, away with *him*, crucify him. Pilate saith unto them, Shall I crucify your King? The chief priests answered, We have no king but Caesar.

16 Then delivered he him therefore unto them to be crucified. And they took Jesus, and led *him* away.

Jesus Is Crucified

17 And he bearing his cross went forth into a place called *the place* of a skull, which is called in the Hebrew Golgotha: Luke 14:27; 23:26, 33

18 Where they crucified him, and two other with him, on either side one, and Jesus in the midst.

19 And Pilate wrote a title, and put *it* on the cross. And the writing was, JESUS OF NAZARETH THE KING OF THE JEWS.   Matt. 27:37; Mark 15:26; Luke 23:38

20 This title then read many of the Jews: for the place where Jesus was crucified was nigh to the city: and it was written in Hebrew, *and* Greek, *and* Latin.   John 19:13

21 Then said the chief priests of the Jews to Pilate, Write not, The King of the Jews; but that he said, I am King of the Jews. John 19:14

22 Pilate answered, What I have written I have written.

23 Then the soldiers, when they had crucified Jesus, took his garments, and made four parts, to every soldier a part; and also *his* coat: now the coat was without seam, woven from the top throughout.   Matt. 27:35; Mark 15:24; Luke 23:34

24 They said therefore among themselves, Let us not ᵀrend it, but cast lots for it, whose it shall be: that the scripture might be fulfilled, which saith, They parted my raiment among them, and for my ᵀvesture they did cast lots. These things therefore the soldiers did.   Ps. 22:18; John 19:28, 36-37 ◆ *tear* ◆ *clothing*

19:25–27 Care for Parents

The same spirit will be seen in every disciple of our Lord. Those who follow Christ will feel that it is a part of their religion to respect and provide for their parents. From the heart where His love is cherished, father and mother will never fail of receiving thoughtful care and tender sympathy. *DA 752*

25 Now there stood by the cross of Jesus his mother, and his mother's sister, Mary the *wife* of Cleophas, and Mary Magdalene.   Luke 23:49

26 When Jesus therefore saw his mother, and the disciple standing by, whom he

loved, he saith unto his mother, Woman, behold thy son! John 2:4; 13:23; 20:2

27 Then saith he to the disciple, Behold thy mother! And from that hour that disciple took her unto his own *home.* John 16:32

Jesus Dies on the Cross

19:28-30

28 After this, Jesus knowing that all things were now accomplished, that the scripture might be fulfilled, saith, I thirst. Ps. 69:21

29 Now there was set a vessel full of vinegar: and they filled a spunge with vinegar, and put *it* upon ᵀhyssop, and put *it* to his mouth. Matt. 27:48 ◆ *a bitter herb*

> **19:30 The Universe Forever Secure**
>
> Well, then, might the angels rejoice as they looked upon the Saviour's cross; for though they did not then understand all, they knew that the destruction of sin and Satan was forever made certain, that the redemption of man was assured, and that the universe was made eternally secure. Christ Himself fully comprehended the results of the sacrifice made upon Calvary. To all these He looked forward when upon the cross He cried out, "It is finished." *DA 764*

30 When Jesus therefore had received the vinegar, he said, It is finished: and he bowed his head, and gave up the ghost. Luke 23:46

Jesus See Matthew 28:5–8.

19:31

31 The Jews therefore, because it was the preparation, that the bodies should not remain upon the cross on the sabbath day, (for that sabbath day was an high day,) besought Pilate that their legs might be broken, and *that* they might be taken away. Josh. 8:29; John 19:14

The Sabbath

32 Then came the soldiers, and brake the legs of the first, and of the other which was crucified with him. John 19:18

33 But when they came to Jesus, and saw that he was dead already, they brake not his legs:

> **19:33, 34 An Early Death**
>
> The priests and rulers were amazed to find that Christ was dead. Death by the cross was a lingering process. . . . It was an unheard-of thing for one to die within six hours of crucifixion. The priests wished to make sure of the death of Jesus, and at their suggestion a soldier thrust a spear into the Saviour's side. From the wound thus made, there flowed two copious and distinct streams, one of blood, the other of water. *DA 771, 772*

34 But one of the soldiers with a spear pierced his side, and ᵀforthwith came there out blood and water. 1 John 5:6, 8 ◆ *immediately*

35 And he that saw *it* bare record, and his record is true: and he knoweth that he saith true, that ye might believe. John 15:27; 20:31; 21:24

36 For these things were done, that the scripture should be fulfilled, A bone of him shall not be broken. Ex. 12:46; Num. 9:12; Ps. 34:20

37 And again another scripture saith, They shall look on him whom they pierced. Ps. 22:16

Jesus Is Buried by Joseph and Nicodemus

38 And after this Joseph of Arimathaea, being a disciple of Jesus, but secretly for fear of the Jews, ᵀbesought Pilate that he might take away the body of Jesus: and Pilate gave *him* leave. He came therefore, and took the body of Jesus. *begged*

39 And there came also Nicodemus, which at the first came to Jesus by night, and brought a mixture of myrrh and aloes, about an hundred pound *weight.* Song 4:14

40 Then took they the body of Jesus, and wound it in linen clothes with the spices, as the manner of the Jews is to bury. Luke 24:12

41 Now in the place where he was crucified there was a garden; and in the garden a new sepulchre, wherein was never man yet laid. Luke 23:53

42 There laid they Jesus therefore because of the Jews' preparation *day*; for the sepulchre was nigh at hand. John 19:14, 31, 41

Jesus Is Resurrected

20 The first *day* of the week cometh Mary Magdalene early, when it was yet dark, unto the sepulchre, and seeth the stone taken away from the sepulchre.

2 Then she runneth, and cometh to Simon Peter, and to the other disciple, whom Jesus loved, and saith unto them, They have taken away the Lord out of the sepulchre, and we know not where they have laid him. John 13:23

3 Peter therefore went forth, and that other disciple, and came to the sepulchre. Luke 24:12

4 So they ran both together: and the other disciple did outrun Peter, and came first to the sepulchre.

5 And he stooping down, *and looking in,* saw the linen clothes lying; yet went he not in. John 19:40

6 Then cometh Simon Peter following him, and went into the sepulchre, and seeth the linen clothes lie,

7 And the napkin, that was about his head, not lying with the linen clothes, but wrapped together in a place by itself. John 11:44

8 Then went in also that other disciple, which came first to the sepulchre, and he saw, and believed. John 20:4

20:5–8 An Example for Us

[Peter and John] saw the shroud and the napkin, but they did not find their Lord. Yet even here was testimony that He had risen. The graveclothes were not thrown heedlessly aside, but carefully folded, each in a place by itself. John "saw, and believed." . . .

It was Christ Himself who had placed those graveclothes with such care. . . . In His sight who guides alike the star and the atom, there is nothing unimportant. Order and perfection are seen in all His work. *DA 789*

9 For as yet they knew not the scripture, that he must rise again from the dead.   Luke 24:26
10 Then the disciples went away again unto their own home.

Jesus Appears to Mary Magdalene

11 But Mary stood without at the sepulchre weeping: and as she wept, she stooped down, *and looked* into the sepulchre,
12 And seeth two angels in white sitting, the one at the head, and the other at the feet, where the body of Jesus had lain.
13 And they say unto her, Woman, why weepest thou? She saith unto them, Because they have taken away my Lord, and I know not where they have laid him. John 2:4; 20:2, 15
14 And when she had thus said, she turned herself back, and saw Jesus standing, and knew not that it was Jesus. Matt. 28:9; Mark 16:9
15 Jesus saith unto her, Woman, why weepest thou? whom seekest thou? She, supposing him to be the gardener, saith unto him, Sir, if thou have borne him hence, tell me where thou hast laid him, and I will take him away.
16 Jesus saith unto her, Mary. She turned herself, and saith unto him, Rabboni; which is to say, Master.   John 1:38
17 Jesus saith unto her, Touch me not; for I am not yet ascended to my Father: but go to my brethren, and say unto them, I ascend unto my Father, and your Father; and *to* my God, and your God.

20:17‡

After Death

18 Mary Magdalene came and told the disciples that she had seen the Lord, and *that* he had spoken these things unto her.

Jesus Appears to His Disciples

19 Then the same day at evening, being the first *day* of the week, when the doors were shut where the disciples were assembled for fear of the Jews, came Jesus and stood in the midst, and saith unto them, Peace be unto you.   John 14:27; 20:21, 26
20 And when he had so said, he shewed unto them *his* hands and his side. Then were the disciples glad, when they saw the Lord.   John 16:22; 20:27; 1 John 1:1
21 Then said Jesus to them again, Peace be unto you: as *my* Father hath sent me, even so send I you.   John 13:20
22 And when he had said this, he breathed on *them*, and saith unto them, Receive ye the Holy Ghost: Gen. 2:7

20:22 Spirit Imparts Christ's Life

The Holy Spirit is the breath of spiritual life in the soul. The impartation of the Spirit is the impartation of the life of Christ. It imbues the receiver with the attributes of Christ. *DA 805*

23 Whosoever sins ye [T] remit, they are [T] remitted unto them; *and* whosoever *sins* ye retain, they are retained. 1 Cor. 5:5 ◆ forgive ◆ forgiven

Jesus Appears to Thomas

24 But Thomas, one of the twelve, called Didymus, was not with them when Jesus came.   John 11:16
25 The other disciples therefore said unto him, We have seen the Lord. But he said unto them, Except I shall see in his hands the print of the nails, and put my finger into the print of the nails, and thrust my hand into his side, I will not believe.   Mark 16:11
26 And after eight days again his disciples were within, and Thomas with them: *then* came Jesus, the doors being shut, and stood in the midst, and said, Peace be unto you.

An In-Person Assurance

John 20:17

Jesus refused to receive the homage of His people until He had the assurance that His sacrifice was accepted by the Father. He ascended to the heavenly courts, and from God Himself heard the assurance that His atonement for the sins of men had been ample, that through His blood all might gain eternal life. The Father ratified the covenant made with Christ, that He would receive repentant and obedient men, and would love them even as He loves His Son. Christ was to complete His work, and fulfill His pledge to "make a man more precious than fine gold; even a man than the golden wedge of Ophir" (Isaiah 13:12). All power in heaven and on earth was given to the Prince of Life, and He returned to His followers in a world of sin, that He might impart to them of His power and glory. *DA 790*

27 Then saith he to Thomas, Reach hither thy finger, and behold my hands; and reach hither thy hand, and thrust *it* into my side: and be not faithless, but believing. John 20:25

28 And Thomas answered and said unto him, My Lord and my God. Is. 7:14

29 Jesus saith unto him, Thomas, because thou hast seen me, thou hast believed: blessed *are* they that have not seen, and *yet* have believed. 2 Cor. 5:7; 1 Pet. 1:8

30 And many other signs truly did Jesus in the presence of his disciples, which are not written in this book: John 21:25

31 But these are written, that ye might believe that Jesus is the Christ, the Son of God; and that believing ye might have life through his name. John 3:15-16

Another Miraculous Catch of Fish

21 After these things Jesus shewed himself again to the disciples at the sea of Tiberias; and on this wise shewed he *himself.* John 6:1

2 There were together Simon Peter, and Thomas called Didymus, and Nathanael of Cana in Galilee, and the *sons* of Zebedee, and two other of his disciples. John 1:45–2:1

3 Simon Peter saith unto them, I go a fishing. They say unto him, We also go with thee. They went forth, and entered into a ship immediately; and that night they caught nothing. Luke 5:5

4 But when the morning was now come, Jesus stood on the shore: but the disciples knew not that it was Jesus. John 20:14

5 Then Jesus saith unto them, Children, have ye any meat? They answered him, No.

6 And he said unto them, Cast the net on the right side of the ship, and ye shall find. They cast therefore, and now they were not able to draw it for the multitude of fishes. Luke 5:4-7

> **21:3–6 The Side of Faith**
>
> While [the disciples] were doing His work, He would provide for their needs. And Jesus had a purpose in bidding them cast their net on the right side of the ship. On that side He stood upon the shore. That was the side of faith. If they labored in connection with Him—His divine power combining with their human effort—they could not fail of success. *DA 811*

7 Therefore that disciple whom Jesus loved saith unto Peter, It is the Lord. Now when Simon Peter heard that it was the Lord, he ᵀgirt *his* fisher's coat *unto him*, (for he was naked,) and did cast himself into the sea. John 13:23; 19:26; 20:2 ◆ *wrapped*

8 And the other disciples came in a little ship; (for they were not far from land, but as it were two hundred cubits,) dragging the net with fishes.

9 As soon then as they were come to land, they saw a fire of coals there, and fish laid thereon, and bread.

10 Jesus saith unto them, Bring of the fish which ye have now caught.

11 Simon Peter went up, and drew the net to land full of great fishes, an hundred and fifty and three: and for all there were so many, yet was not the net broken.

12 Jesus saith unto them, Come *and* dine. And none of the disciples durst ask him, Who art thou? knowing that it was the Lord.

13 Jesus then cometh, and taketh bread, and giveth them, and fish likewise. John 21:9

14 This is now the third time that Jesus shewed himself to his disciples, after that he was risen from the dead. John 20:19, 26

Jesus Speaks with Peter

15 So when they had dined, Jesus saith to Simon Peter, Simon, *son* of Jonas, lovest thou me more than these? He saith unto him, Yea, Lord; thou knowest that I love thee. He saith unto him, Feed my lambs. Is. 40:11; Mark 14:29

16 He saith to him again the second time, Simon, *son* of Jonas, lovest thou me? He saith unto him, Yea, Lord; thou knowest that I love thee. He saith unto him, Feed my sheep.

17 He saith unto him the third time, Simon, *son* of Jonas, lovest thou me? Peter was grieved because he said unto him the third time, Lovest thou me? And he said unto him, Lord, thou knowest all things; thou knowest that I love thee. Jesus saith unto him, Feed my sheep. John 13:38; 16:30; 21:15-16

> **21:15–17 The Essential Qualification**
>
> The question that Christ had put to Peter was significant. He mentioned only one condition of discipleship and service. "Lovest thou Me?" He said. This is the essential qualification. Though Peter might possess every other, yet without the love of Christ he could not be a faithful shepherd over the Lord's flock. Knowledge, benevolence, eloquence, gratitude, and zeal are all aids in the good work; but without the love of Jesus in the heart, the work of the Christian minister is a failure. *DA 815*

18 Verily, verily, I say unto thee, When thou wast young, thou girdedst thyself, and walkedst whither thou wouldest: but when thou shalt be old, thou shalt stretch forth thy hands, and another shall gird thee, and carry *thee* whither thou wouldest not. John 13:36

19 This spake he, signifying by what death he should glorify God. And when he had spoken this, he saith unto him, Follow me. 2 Pet. 1:14

20 Then Peter, turning about, seeth the disciple whom Jesus loved following; which also leaned on his breast at supper, and said, Lord, which is he that betrayeth thee? John 20:2; 21:7
21 Peter seeing him saith to Jesus, Lord, and what *shall* this man *do?* Acts 1:6-7
22 Jesus saith unto him, If I will that he tarry till I come, what *is that* to thee? follow thou me. 1 Cor. 4:5; 11:26; Rev. 2:25
23 Then went this saying abroad among the brethren, that that disciple should not die: yet Jesus said not unto him, He shall not die; but, If I will that he tarry till I come, what *is that* to thee?
24 This is the disciple which testifieth of these things, and wrote these things: and we know that his testimony is true. 3 John 12
25 And there are also many other things which Jesus did, the which, if they should be written every one, I suppose that even the world itself could not contain the books that should be written. Amen. Amos 7:10

THE ACTS

OF THE APOSTLES

With the ascension of Jesus, His apostles were left with His instructions to wait until they received the power of the Holy Spirit. They also had received Jesus' Great Commission (Matthew 28:19–20) to take the gospel message throughout the world. Doubtless they felt unequal to the task, but when the Holy Spirit came, everything changed.

The Book of Acts is an account not only of that transformation of the apostles, but of their deeds in spreading the Gospel throughout the Roman world. It is a heroic story, filled with danger and adventure, faith and challenge. These men risked all—especially their lives—to bring the gospel of Jesus to the world.

Dates

The exact date for Acts is uncertain, but modern archaeological discoveries have continued to confirm the historical precision found in Luke's Gospel. The Book of Acts ends with Paul awaiting trial in Rome. It does seem likely, given Luke's tenacity for details, that if he witnessed the trial, he would have included its outcome in this book. Therefore, some feel that Luke completed Acts before the trial's outcome—around A.D. 62.

Acts also gives no information on the persecution of the Christians by Nero (A.D. 64), Paul's death (A.D. 67), or the destruction of Jerusalem by the Romans (A.D. 70). Luke may have had some reason for not including these events, but it seems more likely that he had not witnessed them yet, thus lending credence to a date of A.D. 62.

Author

Luke, a physician-historian, is the acknowledged author both of the Gospel that bears his name and of the Book of Acts. (For more information on Luke, see "Author" in the introduction to the Gospel of Luke.) Luke was noted for his careful investigative procedures (Luke 1:1–4). It is likely he had opportunities to interview the apostles Peter and John in Jerusalem for the information used in Acts 1—12. As a close companion to the apostle Paul, Luke was an eyewitness of many of the events of chapters 13—28. The contents of 15:23–29 and 23:26–30 seem to indicate that Luke may have used other written documents as source material when he wrote the Book of Acts.

Meaning of the Name

The title "Acts" is *Praxeis* in Greek, a title which the Greeks used in their literature as a common heading when outlining the great deeds of notable men. All Greek manuscripts either call the work "Acts" or an expanded form such as "Acts of the Apostles."

Christ in Acts

Jesus is the reason for Acts. Obedient to the command of their Master, the first Christians went forth and shared the message and the power of God with the world. They spoke of Jesus before rulers and commoners, persuading them of the truth of His words from the Scriptures of the Old Testament, the truth of His resurrection, and the testimony of the apostles.

With the power of the Holy Spirit convicting men's hearts, these brave souls bore witness of the truth that Jesus is Lord and Christ (see Peter's sermons in 2:14–40 and 10:34–43). "And we are witnesses of all things which he did both in the land of the Jews, and in Jerusalem; whom they slew and hanged on a tree: him God raised up the third day, and shewed him openly" (10:39–40).

Overview

Acts continues the account Luke began in his Gospel. Jesus has given His disciples the Great Commission (Matthew 28:19–20) and now they must go forth and share His message of the good news of salvation with the world. The Book of Acts contains three thematic divisions that encapsulate the growth of the early church:

(1) *Acts 1:1—8:4, Witness in Jerusalem:* This section covers the time from the ascension of Jesus through the defense of Stephen before the Jewish leaders. Jesus' admonition to "wait for the promise of the Father" (1:4) has yielded the baptism of the Holy Spirit promised in

1:5. Now the disciples (now twelve again, with the addition of Matthias—1:15–26) have the power to carry out the commission. Peter preaches a powerful sermon (2:14–40) that wins three thousand converts. The church is born. Persecution comes swiftly; when Peter and John heal a lame man, they are dragged before the Sanhedrin. The Christian church prays for boldness, gains a reputation for caring and giving, and continues to grow (chapters 3—4). Unfortunately, Ananias and Sapphira lose their lives for lying to the Holy Spirit (chapter 5). Some men are chosen to serve as deacons so that the apostles can focus on preaching. One of those servants, Stephen, becomes the church's first martyr (chapters 6—7).

(2) *Acts 8:5—12:25, Witness in Judea and Samaria:* Philip preaches in Samaria, while Peter preaches and heals (chapter 8). Saul of Tarsus meets the risen Christ on the Damascus Road and receives His commission—to take the gospel to the Gentiles (chapter 9). Peter preaches to Cornelius, a Gentile, and has to defend his actions before the church leaders (chapters 10—11). James, the brother of John, is executed, and Peter is imprisoned but freed by an angel (chapter 12).

(3) *Acts 13—28, Witness to the end of the earth:* Paul takes center stage as Luke chronicles his missionary journeys (13:1—21:16). In Jerusalem, Paul is nearly killed by those opposing his ministry, and later he is tried before Felix, Festus, and Herod Agrippa (chapters 21—24). Upon appealing to Rome, Paul journeys by ship and survives a shipwreck. In Rome, he is placed under house arrest.

Unlocking Acts

KEY PEOPLE:
Jesus, disciples, Matthias, the Holy Spirit, Ananias and Sapphira, Saul/Paul, Peter, Barnabas, Stephen

KEY EVENTS:
The Holy Spirit's arrival at Pentecost; the spread of the gospel in Jerusalem; Stephen's defense before the high priest; Saul's (Paul's) conversion, ministry and missionary journeys

KEY WORD:
Growth. As a seed bursting forth from the ground, so did the church grow by the power of the Holy Spirit and the teachings of the apostles. Acts is the link between the Gospel accounts and the epistles written to the first churches established during the time of Acts. Luke faithfully acknowledges the work of the Holy Spirit in these ministries, giving us the story of the growth of Christianity from an interested, participatory point of view. Acts shows the growth and change of the early church from primarily Jewish adherents to a majority of Gentiles.

KEY VERSES:
"But ye shall receive power, after that the Holy Ghost is come upon you: and ye shall be witnesses unto me both in Jerusalem, and in all Judea, and in Samaria, and unto the uttermost part of the earth" (Acts 1:8).

"And they continued stedfastly in the apostles' doctrine and fellowship, and in breaking of bread, and in prayers. And fear came upon every soul: and many wonders and signs were done by the apostles. And all that believed were together, and had all things common; and sold their possessions and goods, and parted them to all men, as every man had need. And they, continuing daily with one accord in the temple, and breaking bread from house to house, did eat their meat with gladness and singleness of heart, praising God, and having favour with all the people. And the Lord added to the church daily such as should be saved" (Acts 2:42–47).

KEY CHAPTER:
Acts 2, because the anointing of the Holy Spirit at Pentecost gives the believers power to change the world. The Spirit of God transformed the fearful disciples into the most influential force of their day. They left behind an inspiring record of miracles and testimonies of God's grace, power, mercy, and love.

Luke's Introduction

1 The former treatise have I made, O Theophilus, of all that Jesus began both to do and teach,   *Luke 1:3; 24:19*

2 Until the day in which he was taken up, after that he through the Holy Ghost had given commandments unto the apostles whom he had chosen: *John 13:18*

Jesus Ascends to Heaven

3 To whom also he shewed himself alive after his ᵀpassion by many infallible proofs, being seen of them forty days, and speaking of the things pertaining to the kingdom of God: *John 20:26; Acts 13:31; 1 Cor. 15:5-7* ◆ *suffering*

4 And, being assembled together with *them*, commanded them that they should not depart from Jerusalem, but wait for the promise of the Father, which, *saith he*, ye have heard of me.   *Luke 24:49; John 14:16; Acts 2:33*

5 For John truly baptized with water; but ye shall be baptized with the Holy Ghost not many days hence.   *Matt. 3:11; Luke 3:16; Acts 2:1-4*

6 When they therefore were come together, they asked of him, saying, Lord, wilt thou at this time restore again the kingdom to Israel?   *Matt. 17:11*

7 And he said unto them, It is not for you to know the times or the seasons, which the Father hath put in his own power.   *Dan. 2:21*

1:8 The Gospel Commission

Thus Christ gave His disciples their commission. He made full provision for the prosecution of the work, and took upon Himself the responsibility for its success. So long as they obeyed His word, and worked in connection with Him, they could not fail. Go to all nations, He bade them. Go to the farthest part of the habitable globe, but know that My presence will be there. Labor in faith and confidence, for the time will never come when I will forsake you. *DA 822*

---

8 But ye shall receive power, after that the Holy Ghost is come upon you: and ye shall be witnesses unto me both in Jerusalem, and in all Judaea, and in Samaria, and unto the uttermost part of the earth. *Matt. 28:19; Mark 16:15*

1:9–11 The Ascension of Jesus

The same Jesus who had walked and talked and prayed with them; who had broken bread with them; who had been with them in their boats on the lake; and who had that very day toiled with them up the ascent of Olivet— the same Jesus had now gone to share His Father's throne. And the angels had assured them that the very One whom they had seen go up into heaven, would come again even as He had ascended. *DA 832*

---

9 And when he had spoken these things, while they beheld, he was taken up; and a cloud received him out of their sight. *Rev. 1:7*

10 And while they looked stedfastly toward heaven as he went up, behold, two men stood by them in white apparel;   *Luke 24:4; John 20:12*

11 Which also said, Ye men of Galilee, why stand ye gazing up into heaven? this same Jesus, which is taken up from you into heaven, shall so come in like manner as ye have seen him go into heaven.   *Matt. 16:27; Acts 2:7; 13:31*

Christ's Return See 1 Thessalonians 4:16, 17.

The Apostles Devote Themselves to Prayer

12 Then returned they unto Jerusalem from the mount called Olivet, which is from Jerusalem a sabbath day's journey.   *Matt. 21:1*

13 And when they were come in, they went up into an upper room, where abode both Peter, and James, and John, and Andrew, Philip, and Thomas, Bartholomew, and Matthew, James *the son* of Alphaeus, and Simon Zelotes, and Judas *the brother* of James.   *Matt. 10:2-4; Mark 2:14*

14 These all continued with one accord in prayer and supplication, with the women, and Mary the mother of Jesus, and with his brethren.   *Matt. 12:46; Acts 2:42; 6:4*

Matthias Replaces Judas

15 And in those days Peter stood up in the midst of the disciples, and said, (the number of names together were about an hundred and twenty,)

16 Men *and* brethren, this scripture must needs have been fulfilled, which the Holy Ghost by the mouth of David spake before concerning Judas, which was guide to them that took Jesus.   *Matt. 26:47*

17 For he was numbered with us, and had obtained part of this ministry.   *John 6:70-71*

18 Now this man purchased a field with the reward of iniquity; and falling headlong, he burst ᵀasunder in the midst, and all his bowels gushed out.   *Matt. 27:3-10* ◆ *apart*

19 And it was known unto all the dwellers at Jerusalem; insomuch as that field is called in their proper tongue, Aceldama, that is to say, The field of blood.

20 For it is written in the book of Psalms, Let his habitation be desolate, and let no man dwell therein: and his ᵀbishoprick let another take.   *Ps. 69:25* ◆ *office of leadership*

21 Wherefore of these men which have companied with us all the time that the Lord Jesus went in and out among us,   *Num. 27:17*

22 Beginning from the baptism of John, unto that same day that he was taken up from us, must one be ordained to be a witness with us of his resurrection.   *Acts 1:2*

23 And they appointed two, Joseph called Barsabas, who was surnamed Justus, and Matthias.   Acts 15:22

24 And they prayed, and said, Thou, Lord, which knowest the hearts of all *men*, shew whether of these two thou hast chosen,   1 Sam. 16:7; Jer. 17:10; Acts 15:8

25 That he may take part of this ministry and apostleship, from which Judas by ᵀtransgression fell, that he might go to his own place.   *violation of a law*

26 And they gave forth their lots; and the lot fell upon Matthias; and he was numbered with the eleven apostles.   Lev. 16:8

The Apostles Are Filled with the Holy Spirit

2 And when the day of Pentecost was fully come, they were all with one accord in one place.   Acts 20:16; 1 Cor. 16:8

2 And suddenly there came a sound from heaven as of a rushing mighty wind, and it filled all the house where they were sitting.   1 Kin. 19:11; Acts 4:31

2:3, 4 Tongues of Fire

The Holy Spirit, assuming the form of tongues of fire, rested upon those assembled. This was an emblem of the gift then bestowed on the disciples, which enabled them to speak with fluency languages with which they had heretofore been unacquainted. The appearance of fire signified the fervent zeal with which the apostles would labor and the power that would attend their work. *AA 39*

---

3 And there appeared unto them ᵀcloven

tongues like as of fire, and it sat upon each of them.   Matt. 3:11 ♦ *divided*

4 And they were all filled with the Holy Ghost, and began to speak with other tongues, as the Spirit gave them utterance.   Mark 16:17; Acts 1:5; 1 Cor. 12:10

5 And there were dwelling at Jerusalem Jews, devout men, out of every nation under heaven.   Acts 8:2

6 Now when this was noised abroad, the multitude came together, and were confounded, because that every man heard them speak in his own language.

7 And they were all amazed and marvelled, saying one to another, Behold, are not all these which speak Galilaeans?   Acts 1:11; 2:12

8 And how hear we every man in our own tongue, wherein we were born?

9 Parthians, and Medes, and Elamites, and the dwellers in Mesopotamia, and in Judaea, and Cappadocia, in Pontus, and Asia,   Acts 16:6; 18:2; 1 Pet. 1:1

10 Phrygia, and Pamphylia, in Egypt, and in the parts of Libya about Cyrene, and strangers of Rome, Jews and ᵀproselytes,   Acts 13:13 ♦ *converts*

11 Cretes and Arabians, we do hear them speak in our tongues the wonderful works of God.   Ex. 15:11

12 And they were all amazed, and were in doubt, saying one to another, What meaneth this?

13 Others mocking said, These men are full of new wine.   1 Cor. 14:23

Peter Preaches to the Crowd

14 But Peter, standing up with the eleven,

Of One Accord

Acts 2:1

As the disciples waited for the fulfillment of the promise, they humbled their hearts in true repentance and confessed their unbelief. . . . They reproached themselves for their misapprehension of the Saviour. Like a procession, scene after scene of His wonderful life passed before them. As they meditated upon His pure, holy life they felt that no toil would be too hard, no sacrifice too great, if only they could bear witness in their lives to the loveliness of Christ's character. Oh, if they could but have the past three years to live over, they thought, how differently they would act! If they could only see the Master again, how earnestly they would strive to show Him how deeply they loved Him, and how sincerely they sorrowed for having ever grieved Him by a word or an act of unbelief! . . .

Putting away all differences, all desire for the supremacy, they came close together in Christian fellowship. They drew nearer and nearer to God, and as they did this they realized what a privilege had been theirs in being permitted to associate so closely with Christ. Sadness filled their hearts as they thought of how many times they had grieved Him by their slowness of comprehension, their failure to understand the lessons that, for their good, He was trying to teach them.

These days of preparation were days of deep heart searching. The disciples felt their spiritual need and cried to the Lord for the holy unction that was to fit them for the work of soul saving. They did not ask for a blessing for themselves merely. They were weighted with the burden of the salvation of souls. They realized that the gospel was to be carried to the world, and they claimed the power that Christ had promised. *AA 36, 37*

lifted up his voice, and said unto them, Ye men of Judaea, and all *ye* that dwell at Jerusalem, be this known unto you, and hearken to my words: Acts 1:26
15 For these are not drunken, as ye suppose, seeing it is *but* the third hour of the day.
16 But this is that which was spoken by the prophet Joel;
17 And it shall come to pass in the last days, saith God, I will pour out of my Spirit upon all flesh: and your sons and your daughters shall prophesy, and your young men shall see visions, and your old men shall dream dreams: Is. 44:3
18 And on my servants and on my handmaidens I will pour out in those days of my Spirit; and they shall prophesy:
19 And I will shew wonders in heaven above, and signs in the earth beneath; blood, and fire, and vapour of smoke:
20 The sun shall be turned into darkness, and the moon into blood, before that great and notable day of the Lord come: Amos 8:9
21 And it shall come to pass, *that* whosoever shall call on the name of the Lord shall be saved.   Acts 22:16
22 Ye men of Israel, hear these words; Jesus of Nazareth, a man approved of God among you by miracles and wonders and signs, which God did by him in the midst of you, as ye yourselves also know: Matt. 12:28; John 3:2
23 Him, being delivered by the determinate counsel and foreknowledge of God, ye have taken, and by wicked hands have crucified and slain: Luke 22:22; Acts 3:18; 4:28
24 Whom God hath raised up, having loosed the pains of death: because it was not possible that he should be ᵀholden of it.   Acts 2:32; 1 Cor. 6:14; 2 Cor. 4:14 ◆ *held by*
25 For David speaketh concerning him, I foresaw the Lord always before my face, for he is on my right hand, that I should not be moved: Ps. 16:8-11
26 Therefore did my heart rejoice, and my tongue was glad; moreover also my flesh shall rest in hope:
27 Because thou wilt not leave my soul in hell, neither wilt thou suffer thine Holy One to see corruption.   Luke 1:35; Acts 2:31; Rev. 1:18
28 Thou hast made known to me the ways of life; thou shalt make me full of joy with thy ᵀcountenance.   *presence*
29 Men *and* brethren, let me freely speak unto you of the patriarch David, that he is both dead and buried, and his sepulchre is with us unto this day. 1 Kin. 2:10; Acts 7:8-9; 13:36
30 Therefore being a prophet, and knowing that God had sworn with an oath to him, that of the fruit of his ᵀloins, according to the flesh, he would raise up Christ to sit on his throne;   2 Sam. 23:2 ◆ *body*

31 He seeing this before spake of the resurrection of Christ, that his soul was not left in hell, neither his flesh did see corruption.
32 This Jesus hath God raised up, whereof we all are witnesses.   Acts 1:8, 22; 2:24
33 Therefore being by the right hand of God exalted, and having received of the Father the promise of the Holy Ghost, he hath shed forth this, which ye now see and hear.   Mark 16:19
34 For David is not ascended into the heavens: but he saith himself, The LORD said unto my Lord, Sit thou on my right hand,   Ps. 110:1
35 Until I make thy foes thy footstool.
36 Therefore let all the house of Israel know assuredly, that God hath made that same Jesus, whom ye have crucified, both Lord and Christ.

Three Thousand Are Converted

37 Now when they heard *this*, they were pricked in their heart, and said unto Peter and to the rest of the apostles, Men *and* brethren, what shall we do?   Luke 3:10; Acts 5:33; 7:54
38 Then Peter said unto them, Repent, and be baptized every one of you in the name of Jesus Christ for the remission of sins, and ye shall receive the gift of the Holy Ghost.   Luke 24:47

2:38

Baptism/Lord's Supper See 1 Corinthians 12:12, 13.

39 For the promise is unto you, and to your children, and to all that are afar off, *even* as many as the Lord our God shall call. Joel 2:32
40 And with many other words did he testify and exhort, saying, Save yourselves from this ᵀuntoward generation. Matt. 17:17 ◆ *perverse*
41 Then they that gladly received his word were baptized: and the same day there were added *unto them* about three thousand souls.   Acts 2:37

The Apostles Work Miracles

42 And they continued stedfastly in the apostles' doctrine and fellowship, and in breaking of bread, and in prayers.   Acts 1:14; 2:46; 20:7
43 And fear came upon every soul: and many wonders and signs were done by the apostles.
44 And all that believed were together, and had all things common;   Acts 4:32
45 And sold their possessions and goods, and parted them to all *men*, as every man had need.
46 And they, continuing daily with one accord in the temple, and breaking bread from house to house, did eat their meat with gladness and singleness of heart,   Luke 24:53; Acts 5:42; 20:7
47 Praising God, and having favour with all the people. And the Lord added to the church daily such as should be saved.   Acts 11:24

One interest prevailed. One object swallowed up all others. All hearts beat in harmony. The only ambition of the believers was to reveal the likeness of Christ's character, and to labor for the enlargement of His kingdom. . . . The Spirit of Christ animated the whole congregation; for they had found the pearl of great price.

These scenes are to be repeated, and with greater power. The outpouring of the Holy Spirit on the day of Pentecost was the former rain, but the latter rain will be more abundant. . . . Christ is again to be revealed in His fulness by the Holy Spirit's power. *COL 120, 121*

A Lame Man Is Healed

3 Now Peter and John went up together into the temple at the hour of prayer, *being* the ninth *hour*.   Ps. 55:17; Acts 2:46; 10:30
2 And a certain man lame from his mother's womb was carried, whom they laid daily at the gate of the temple which is called Beautiful, to ask alms of them that entered into the temple;   Luke 16:20; John 9:8; Acts 14:8
3 Who seeing Peter and John about to go into the temple asked an ᵀalms.   *act of mercy*
4 And Peter, fastening his eyes upon him with John, said, Look on us.
5 And he gave heed unto them, expecting to receive something of them.
6 Then Peter said, Silver and gold have I none; but such as I have give I thee: In the name of Jesus Christ of Nazareth rise up and walk.   Acts 2:22; 3:16; 4:10
7 And he took him by the right hand, and lifted *him* up: and immediately his feet and ankle bones received strength.
8 And he leaping up stood, and walked, and entered with them into the temple, walking, and leaping, and praising God. Is. 35:6; Acts 14:10
9 And all the people saw him walking and praising God: Acts 4:16
10 And they knew that it was he which sat for alms at the Beautiful gate of the temple: and they were filled with wonder and amazement at that which had happened unto him.   Acts 3:2

3:1–10 The Power of Pentecost

The Jewish leaders had supposed that the work of Christ would end with His death; but, instead of this, they witnessed the marvelous scenes of the Day of Pentecost. They heard the disciples, endowed with a power and energy hitherto unknown, preaching Christ, their words confirmed by signs and wonders. In Jerusalem, the stronghold of Judaism, thousands openly declared their faith in Jesus of Nazareth as the Messiah. *AA 44*

11 And as the lame man which was healed held Peter and John, all the people ran together unto them in the porch that is called Solomon's, greatly wondering.   John 10:23

Peter Speaks to the People

12 And when Peter saw *it*, he answered unto the people, Ye men of Israel, why marvel ye at this? or why look ye so earnestly on us, as though by our own power or holiness we had made this man to walk?
13 The God of Abraham, and of Isaac, and of Jacob, the God of our fathers, hath glorified his Son Jesus; whom ye delivered up, and denied him in the presence of Pilate, when he was determined to let *him* go.   Matt. 22:32
14 But ye denied the Holy One and the Just, and desired a murderer to be granted unto you;   Mark 1:24; Acts 4:27; 7:52
15 And killed the Prince of life, whom God hath raised from the dead; whereof we are witnesses.   John 1:4; Acts 2:24, 32
16 And his name through faith in his name hath made this man strong, whom ye see and know: yea, the faith which is by him hath given him this perfect soundness in the presence of you all.   Deut. 32:4; Acts 3:6
17 And now, brethren, I ᵀwot that through ignorance ye did *it*, as *did* also your rulers.   Luke 23:34; John 16:3; Acts 13:27 ♦ *know*
18 But those things, which God before had shewed by the mouth of all his prophets, that Christ should suffer, he hath so fulfilled.   Acts 26:22-23

3:18 The Deep Things of God

The significance of the Jewish economy is not yet fully comprehended. Truths vast and profound are shadowed forth in its rites and symbols. The gospel is the key that unlocks its mysteries. Through a knowledge of the plan of redemption, its truths are opened to the understanding. Far more than we do, it is our privilege to understand these wonderful themes. We are to comprehend the deep things of God. *COL 133*

19 Repent ye therefore, and be converted, that your sins may be blotted out, when the times of refreshing shall come from the presence of the Lord;   Ps. 51:9; Is. 43:25; Acts 2:38
20 And he shall send Jesus Christ, which before was preached unto you:
21 Whom the heaven must receive until the times of restitution of all things, which God hath spoken by the mouth of all his holy prophets since the world began.   Luke 1:70
22 For Moses truly said unto the fathers, A prophet shall the Lord your God raise up unto you of your brethren, like unto me;

him shall ye hear in all things whatsoever he shall say unto you.   Is. 55:3-4; John 5:24; Acts 7:37

23 And it shall come to pass, *that* every soul, which will not hear that prophet, shall be destroyed from among the people. Deut. 18:19

> **Gift of Prophecy** See 2 Chronicles 36:14–17.

24 Yea, and all the prophets from Samuel and those that follow after, as many as have spoken, have likewise foretold of these days.   1 Sam. 3:20

25 Ye are the children of the prophets, and of the covenant which God made with our fathers, saying unto Abraham, And in thy seed shall all the kindreds of the earth be blessed.   Gen. 12:3; 22:18; Acts 2:39

26 Unto you first God, having raised up his Son Jesus, sent him to bless you, in turning away every one of you from his iniquities.   Acts 3:22

Peter and John Are Arrested and Tried

4 And as they spake unto the people, the priests, and the captain of the temple, and the Sadducees, came upon them, Luke 22:4

2 Being grieved that they taught the people, and preached through Jesus the resurrection from the dead.   Acts 17:18

3 And they laid hands on them, and put *them* in hold unto the next day: for it was now ᵀeventide.   Acts 5:18 ◆ *evening*

4 Howbeit many of them which heard the word believed; and the number of the men was about five thousand.   Acts 2:41

5 And it came to pass on the morrow, that their rulers, and elders, and scribes,   Acts 4:8

6 And Annas the high priest, and Caiaphas, and John, and Alexander, and as many as were of the kindred of the high priest, were gathered together at Jerusalem.   Matt. 26:3

7 And when they had set them in the midst, they asked, By what power, or by what name, have ye done this?   Matt. 21:23

8 Then Peter, filled with the Holy Ghost, said unto them, Ye rulers of the people, and elders of Israel,   Acts 2:4

9 If we this day be examined of the good deed done to the impotent man, by what means he is made whole;   Acts 3:7

10 Be it known unto you all, and to all the people of Israel, that by the name of Jesus Christ of Nazareth, whom ye crucified, whom God raised from the dead, *even* by him doth this man stand here before you whole. Acts 3:6

11 This is the stone which was set at ᵀnought of you builders, which is become the head of the corner.   Is. 28:16 ◆ *nothing*

12 Neither is there salvation in any other: for there is none other name under heaven given among men, whereby we must be saved.   Matt. 1:21; John 3:36; 14:6

> **4:13 Unity in the Spirit**
>
> No longer were [the disciples] ignorant and uncultured. No longer were they a collection of independent units or of discordant and conflicting elements. No longer were their hopes set on worldly greatness. They were of "one accord," of one mind and one soul. Christ filled their thoughts. The advancement of His kingdom was their aim. In mind and character they had become like their Master; and men "took knowledge of them, that they had been with Jesus" (Acts 4:13). *Ed 95*

13 Now when they saw the boldness of Peter and John, and perceived that they were

---

The Meaning of True Repentance

Acts 3:19

Repentance includes sorrow for sin and a turning away from it. We shall not renounce sin unless we see its sinfulness; until we turn away from it in heart, there will be no real change in the life.

There are many who fail to understand the true nature of repentance. Multitudes sorrow that they have sinned and even make an outward reformation because they fear that their wrongdoing will bring suffering upon themselves. But this is not repentance in the Bible sense. They lament the suffering rather than the sin. Such was the grief of Esau when he saw that the birthright was lost to him forever. Balaam, terrified by the angel standing in his pathway with drawn sword, acknowledged his guilt lest he should lose his life; but there was no genuine repentance for sin, no conversion of purpose, no abhorrence of evil. Judas Iscariot, after betraying his Lord, exclaimed, "I have sinned in that I have betrayed the innocent blood" (Matthew 27:4). . . .

These all lamented the results of sin, but did not sorrow for the sin itself.

But when the heart yields to the influence of the Spirit of God, the conscience will be quickened, and the sinner will discern something of the depth and sacredness of God's holy law, the foundation of His government in heaven and on earth. . . . Conviction takes hold upon the mind and heart. The sinner has a sense of the righteousness of Jehovah and feels the terror of appearing, in his own guilt and uncleanness, before the Searcher of hearts. He sees the love of God, the beauty of holiness, the joy of purity; he longs to be cleansed and to be restored to communion with Heaven. *SC 23, 24*

unlearned and ignorant men, they marvelled; and they took knowledge of them, that they had been with Jesus. John 7:15

14 And beholding the man which was healed standing with them, they could say nothing against it.

15 But when they had commanded them to go aside out of the council, they conferred among themselves,

16 Saying, What shall we do to these men? for that indeed a notable miracle hath been done by them *is* ᵀmanifest to all them that dwell in Jerusalem; and we cannot deny it. *made known*

4:16 Bold Witnesses

[Peter and John's] courageous defense appalled the Jewish leaders. They had supposed that the disciples would be overcome with fear and confusion when brought before the Sanhedrin. But, instead, these witnesses spoke as Christ had spoken, with a convincing power that silenced their adversaries. *AA 63, 64*

---

17 But that it spread no further among the people, let us ᵀstraitly threaten them, that they speak ᵀhenceforth to no man in this name. Acts 5:28 ◆ *strictly* ◆ *from this time forward*

18 And they called them, and commanded them not to speak at all nor teach in the name of Jesus. Acts 5:40

19 But Peter and John answered and said unto them, Whether it be right in the sight of God to hearken unto you more than unto God, judge ye. Acts 5:29

4:18, 19 God's Word Final Authority

We are to receive this word as supreme authority. We are to recognize human government as an ordinance of divine appointment, and teach obedience to it as a sacred duty, within its legitimate sphere. But when its claims conflict with the claims of God, we must obey God rather than men. God's word must be recognized as above all human legislation. A "Thus saith the Lord" is not to be set aside for a "Thus saith the church" or a "Thus saith the state." *AA 69*

---

20 For we cannot but speak the things which we have seen and heard. Acts 22:15

21 So when they had further threatened them, they let them go, finding nothing how they might punish them, because of the people: for all *men* glorified God for that which was done.

22 For the man was above forty years old, on whom this miracle of healing was shewed.

The Church Prays for God's Help

23 And being let go, they went to their own company, and reported all that the chief priests and elders had said unto them.

24 And when they heard that, they lifted up their voice to God with one accord, and said, Lord, thou *art* God, which hast made heaven, and earth, and the sea, and all that in them is: Neh. 9:6

25 Who by the mouth of thy servant David hast said, Why did the heathen rage, and the people imagine vain things? Acts 1:16

26 The kings of the earth stood up, and the rulers were gathered together against the Lord, and against his Christ. Luke 4:18

27 For of a truth against thy holy child Jesus, whom thou hast anointed, both Herod, and Pontius Pilate, with the Gentiles, and the people of Israel, were gathered together, Matt. 27:2; Acts 4:30

28 For to do whatsoever thy hand and thy counsel determined before to be done.

29 And now, Lord, behold their threatenings: and grant unto thy servants, that with all boldness they may speak thy word, Acts 14:3

30 By stretching forth thine hand to heal; and that signs and wonders may be done by the name of thy holy child Jesus. Acts 3:6; 4:27

31 And when they had prayed, the place was shaken where they were assembled together; and they were all filled with the Holy Ghost, and they spake the word of God with boldness. Acts 2:2

The Believers Share Their Property

32 And the multitude of them that believed were of one heart and of one soul: neither said any *of them* that ought of the things which he possessed was his own; but they had all things common. 2 Chr. 30:12

33 And with great power gave the apostles witness of the resurrection of the Lord Jesus: and great grace was upon them all. Acts 1:8

34 Neither was there any among them that lacked: for as many as were possessors of lands or houses sold them, and brought the prices of the things that were sold, Acts 2:45

35 And laid *them* down at the apostles' feet: and distribution was made unto every man according as he had need. Acts 2:45; 4:37; 5:2

36 And Joses, who by the apostles was surnamed Barnabas, (which is, being interpreted, The son of consolation,) a Levite, *and* of the country of Cyprus, 1 Cor. 9:6

37 Having land, sold *it*, and brought the money, and laid *it* at the apostles' feet.

Ananias and Sapphira

5 But a certain man named Ananias, with Sapphira his wife, sold a possession,

2 And kept back *part* of the price, his wife also being privy *to it*, and brought a certain part, and laid *it* at the apostles' feet. Acts 4:37

3 But Peter said, Ananias, why hath Satan filled thine heart to lie to the Holy Ghost,

and to keep back *part* of the price of the land?　　　　　　John 13:2, 27; Acts 5:9

4 Whiles it remained, was it not thine own? and after it was sold, was it not in thine own power? why hast thou conceived this thing in thine heart? thou hast not lied unto men, but unto God.　　　　　　　　　Acts 5:3

5 And Ananias hearing these words fell down, and gave up the ghost: and great fear came on all them that heard these things.　　Acts 5:10-11

6 And the young men arose, wound him up, and carried *him* out, and buried *him*. John 19:40

7 And it was about the space of three hours after, when his wife, not knowing what was done, came in.

8 And Peter answered unto her, Tell me whether ye sold the land for so much? And she said, Yea, for so much.

9 Then Peter said unto her, How is it that ye have agreed together to tempt the Spirit of the Lord? behold, the feet of them which have buried thy husband *are* at the door, and shall carry thee out.　　　　　　Acts 5:3-4

10 Then fell she down ᵀstraightway at his feet, and yielded up the ghost: and the young men came in, and found her dead, and, carrying *her* forth, buried *her* by her husband.　　　　　　　　*right away*

11 And great fear came upon all the church, and upon as many as heard these things.　　　　　　　Acts 5:5; 19:17

5:1–11 A Warning Not to Forget

From the stern punishment meted out to those perjurers [Ananias and Sapphira], God would have us learn also how deep is His hatred and contempt for all hypocrisy and deception. In pretending that they had given all, Ananias and Sapphira lied to the Holy Spirit, and, as a result, they lost this life and the life that is to come. . . .

The warning has been given; God has clearly manifested His abhorrence of this sin; and all who give themselves up to hypocrisy and covetousness may be sure that they are destroying their own souls. *AA 75, 76*

The Apostles Work Many Miracles

12 And by the hands of the apostles were many signs and wonders wrought among the people; (and they were all with one accord in Solomon's porch.　　Mark 16:20; John 10:23; Acts 3:11

13 And of the rest ᵀdurst no man join himself to them: but the people magnified them.　　　　Acts 2:47; 4:21 ◆ *dared*

14 And believers were the more added to the Lord, multitudes both of men and women.)　　　　　　　　　Acts 2:47

15 Insomuch that they brought forth the sick into the streets, and laid *them* on beds and couches, that at the least the shadow of Peter passing by might overshadow some of them.

16 There came also a multitude out of the cities round about unto Jerusalem, bringing sick folks, and them which were vexed with unclean spirits: and they were healed every one.　　　　　　　　　Mark 16:17-18

The Apostles Are Again Imprisoned

17 Then the high priest rose up, and all they that were with him, (which is the sect of the Sadducees,) and were filled with ᵀindignation,　　　　　　　　Acts 7:9 ◆ *anger*

18 And laid their hands on the apostles, and put them in the common prison.　　Acts 4:3

19 But the angel of the Lord by night opened the prison doors, and brought them forth, and said,　　　　　　　Acts 8:26

5:19 An Ancient Faith

[The miraculous opening of the prison doors and other such miracles] were not written merely that we might read and wonder, but that the same faith which wrought in God's servants of old might work in us. In no less marked a manner than He wrought then will He work now wherever there are hearts of faith to be channels of His power. *Ed 256*

---

20 Go, stand and speak in the temple to the people all the words of this life.　John 6:63, 68

21 And when they heard *that*, they entered into the temple early in the morning, and taught. But the high priest came, and they that were with him, and called the council together, and all the senate of the children of Israel, and sent to the prison to have them brought.　　　　　　　　John 8:2

22 But when the officers came, and found them not in the prison, they returned, and told,

23 Saying, The prison truly found we shut with all safety, and the keepers standing without before the doors: but when we had opened, we found no man within.

24 Now when the high priest and the captain of the temple and the chief priests heard these things, they doubted of them whereunto this would grow.　　Acts 4:1; 5:26

25 Then came one and told them, saying, Behold, the men whom ye put in prison are standing in the temple, and teaching the people.

26 Then went the captain with the officers, and brought them without violence: for they feared the people, lest they should have been stoned.　　　　　　Acts 5:13

27 And when they had brought them, they set *them* before the council: and the high priest asked them,

28 Saying, Did not we ᵀstraitly command

you that ye should not teach in this name? and, behold, ye have filled Jerusalem with your doctrine, and intend to bring this man's blood upon us.   Matt. 27:25; Acts 7:52 ◆ *strictly*
29 Then Peter and the *other* apostles answered and said, We ought to obey God rather than men.   Acts 4:19
30 The God of our fathers raised up Jesus, whom ye slew and hanged on a tree.   Gal. 3:13
31 Him hath God exalted with his right hand *to be* a Prince and a Saviour, for to give repentance to Israel, and forgiveness of sins.   Luke 2:11; 24:47; Acts 2:33
32 And we are his witnesses of these things; and *so is* also the Holy Ghost, whom God hath given to them that obey him.   John 15:26-27
33 When they heard *that*, they were cut *to the heart*, and took counsel to slay them.   Acts 2:37
34 Then stood there up one in the council, a Pharisee, named Gamaliel, a ᵀdoctor of the law, had in reputation among all the people, and commanded to put the apostles forth a little space;   Luke 2:46; 5:17; Acts 22:3 ◆ *instructor*
35 And said unto them, Ye men of Israel, take heed to yourselves what ye intend to do as touching these men.
36 For before these days rose up Theudas, boasting himself to be somebody; to whom a number of men, about four hundred, joined themselves: who was slain; and all, as many as obeyed him, were scattered, and brought to ᵀnought.   Acts 8:9 ◆ *nothing*
37 After this man rose up Judas of Galilee in the days of the taxing, and drew away much people after him: he also perished; and all, *even* as many as obeyed him, were dispersed.   Luke 2:1-2
38 And now I say unto you, Refrain from these men, and let them alone: for if this counsel or this work be of men, it will come to nought: Lam. 3:37
39 But if it be of God, ye cannot overthrow it; lest ᵀhaply ye be found even to fight against God.   Prov. 21:30 ◆ *maybe*
40 And to him they agreed: and when they had called the apostles, and beaten *them*, they commanded that they should not speak in the name of Jesus, and let them go.   Matt. 10:17
41 And they departed from the presence of the council, rejoicing that they were counted worthy to suffer shame for his name.
42 And daily in the temple, and in every house, they ceased not to teach and preach Jesus Christ.   Acts 2:46; 8:35; 20:20

The Apostles Choose Seven Helpers

6 And in those days, when the number of the disciples was multiplied, there arose a murmuring of the Grecians against the Hebrews, because their widows were neglected in the daily ministration.   Acts 2:41, 47; 4:35
2 Then the twelve called the multitude of the disciples *unto them*, and said, It is not reason that we should leave the word of God, and serve tables.
3 Wherefore, brethren, look ye out among you seven men of honest report, full of the Holy Ghost and wisdom, whom we may appoint over this business.   Deut. 1:13
4 But we will give ourselves continually to prayer, and to the ministry of the word.   Acts 1:14
5 And the saying pleased the whole multitude: and they chose Stephen, a man full of faith and of the Holy Ghost, and Philip, and Prochorus, and Nicanor, and Timon, and Parmenas, and Nicolas a ᵀproselyte of Antioch: Acts 6:3, 8; 11:24 ◆ *convert*

Life-Giving Waters

Acts 5:12–16

The heart that receives the word of God is not as a pool that evaporates, not like a broken cistern that loses its treasure. It is like the mountain stream, fed by unfailing springs, whose cool, sparkling waters leap from rock to rock, refreshing the weary, the thirsty, the heavy-laden. It is like a river constantly flowing and, as it advances, becoming deeper and wider, until its life-giving waters are spread over all the earth. The stream that goes singing on its way leaves behind its gift of verdure and fruitfulness. The grass on its banks is a fresher green, the trees have a richer verdure, the flowers are more abundant. When the earth lies bare and brown under the summer's scorching heat, a line of verdure marks the river's course. . . .

The religion of Christ reveals itself as a vitalizing, pervading principle, a living, working, spiritual energy. When the heart is opened to the heavenly influence of truth and love, these principles will flow forth again like streams in the desert, causing fruitfulness to appear where now are barrenness and dearth.

As those who have been cleansed and sanctified through a knowledge of Bible truth engage heartily in the work of soulsaving, they will become indeed a savor of life unto life. And as daily they drink of the inexhaustible fountain of grace and knowledge, they will find that their own hearts are filled to overflowing with the Spirit of their Master, and that through their unselfish ministry many are benefited physically, mentally, and spiritually. *PK 233, 234*

6 Whom they set before the apostles: and when they had prayed, they laid *their* hands on them. Acts 1:24; 8:17; 1 Tim. 4:14

7 And the word of God increased; and the number of the disciples multiplied in Jerusalem greatly; and a great company of the priests were obedient to the faith. Rom. 1:5

Stephen Is Arrested

8 And Stephen, full of faith and power, did great wonders and miracles among the people.

6:8 Active for Christ

Stephen, the foremost of the seven deacons, was a man of deep piety and broad faith. Though a Jew by birth, he spoke the Greek language and was familiar with the customs and manners of the Greeks. He therefore found opportunity to preach the gospel in the synagogues of the Greek Jews. He was very active in the cause of Christ and boldly proclaimed his faith. *AA 97*

---

9 Then there arose certain of the synagogue, which is called *the synagogue* of the Libertines, and Cyrenians, and Alexandrians, and of them of Cilicia and of Asia, disputing with Stephen. Matt. 27:32

10 And they were not able to resist the wisdom and the spirit by which he spake. Luke 21:15

6:10 Truth Brought to Memory

The servants of Christ were to prepare no set speech to present when brought to trial. Their preparation was to be made day by day in treasuring up the precious truths of God's word, and through prayer strengthening their faith. When they were brought into trial, the Holy Spirit would bring to their remembrance the very truths that would be needed. *DA 355*

---

11 Then they suborned men, which said, We have heard him speak blasphemous words against Moses, and *against* God. Matt. 26:59-60

12 And they stirred up the people, and the elders, and the scribes, and came upon *him*, and caught him, and brought *him* to the council,

13 And set up false witnesses, which said, This man ceaseth not to speak blasphemous words against this holy place, and the law:

14 For we have heard him say, that this Jesus of Nazareth shall destroy this place, and shall change the customs which Moses delivered us. Dan. 9:26

15 And all that sat in the council, looking stedfastly on him, saw his face as it had been the face of an angel. Eccl. 8:1

Stephen Speaks in His Own Defense

7 Then said the high priest, Are these things so?

2 And he said, Men, brethren, and fathers, hearken; The God of glory appeared unto our father Abraham, when he was in Mesopotamia, before he dwelt in Charran, Gen. 11:31

3 And said unto him, Get thee out of thy country, and from thy kindred, and come into the land which I shall shew thee. Gen. 12:1

4 Then came he out of the land of the Chaldaeans, and dwelt in Charran: and from thence, when his father was dead, he removed him into this land, wherein ye now dwell. Gen. 11:31-32; 12:4-5

5 And he gave him none inheritance in it, no, not *so much as* to set his foot on: yet he promised that he would give it to him for a possession, and to his seed after him, when *as yet* he had no child. Gen. 12:7; 13:15; 17:8

6 And God spake on this wise, That his seed should sojourn in a strange land; and that they should bring them into bondage, and entreat *them* evil four hundred years. Gen. 15:13

7 And the nation to whom they shall be in bondage will I judge, said God: and after that shall they come forth, and serve me in this place. Ex. 3:12

8 And he gave him the covenant of circumcision: and so *Abraham* begat Isaac, and circumcised him the eighth day; and Isaac *begat* Jacob; and Jacob *begat* the twelve patriarchs. Gen. 17:9-14

9 And the patriarchs, moved with envy, sold Joseph into Egypt: but God was with him, Gen. 39:2; 45:4; Ps. 105:17

10 And delivered him out of all his afflictions, and gave him favour and wisdom in the sight of Pharaoh king of Egypt; and he made him governor over Egypt and all his house. Gen. 42:6

11 Now there came a dearth over all the land of Egypt and Chanaan, and great affliction: and our fathers found no sustenance.

12 But when Jacob heard that there was corn in Egypt, he sent out our fathers first.

13 And at the second *time* Joseph was made known to his brethren; and Joseph's kindred was made known unto Pharaoh.

14 Then sent Joseph, and called his father Jacob to *him*, and all his kindred, threescore and fifteen souls. Gen. 46:26-27; Ex. 1:5; Deut. 10:22

15 So Jacob went down into Egypt, and died, he, and our fathers, Gen. 46:3-7; 49:33; Ex. 1:6

16 And were carried over into Sychem, and laid in the sepulchre that Abraham bought for a sum of money of the sons of Emmor *the father* of Sychem. Gen. 23:16; Ex. 13:19; Josh. 24:32

17 But when the time of the promise drew nigh, which God had sworn to Abraham, the people grew and multiplied in Egypt, Acts 7:6

18 Till another king arose, which knew not Joseph.   Ex. 1:8
19 The same dealt subtilly with our kindred, and evil entreated our fathers, so that they cast out their young children, to the end they might not live.   Ex. 1:9-22
20 In which time Moses was born, and was exceeding fair, and nourished up in his father's house three months: Heb. 11:23
21 And when he was cast out, Pharaoh's daughter took him up, and nourished him for her own son.
22 And Moses was learned in all the wisdom of the Egyptians, and was mighty in words and in deeds.   Is. 19:11; Dan. 1:4; Luke 24:19
23 And when he was full forty years old, it came into his heart to visit his brethren the children of Israel.   Ex. 2:11-12
24 And seeing one *of them* suffer wrong, he defended *him*, and avenged him that was oppressed, and smote the Egyptian:
25 For he supposed his brethren would have understood how that God by his hand would deliver them: but they understood not.
26 And the next day he shewed himself unto them as they strove, and would have set them at one again, saying, Sirs, ye are brethren; why do ye wrong one to another?
27 But he that did his neighbour wrong thrust him away, saying, Who made thee a ruler and a judge over us?   Acts 7:35
28 Wilt thou kill me, as thou diddest the Egyptian yesterday?
29 Then fled Moses at this saying, and was a stranger in the land of Madian, where he †begat two sons.   *brought forth*
30 And when forty years were expired, there appeared to him in the wilderness of mount Sina an angel of the Lord in a flame of fire in a bush.   Acts 7:35
31 When Moses saw *it*, he wondered at the sight: and as he drew near to behold *it*, the voice of the Lord came unto him,   Ex. 3:3-4
32 *Saying*, I *am* the God of thy fathers, the God of Abraham, and the God of Isaac, and the God of Jacob. Then Moses trembled, and †durst not behold.   Ex. 3:6; Matt. 22:32 ◆ *dared*
33 Then said the Lord to him, Put off thy shoes from thy feet: for the place where thou standest is holy ground.   Ex. 3:5; Josh. 5:15
34 I have seen, I have seen the affliction of my people which is in Egypt, and I have heard their groaning, and am come down to deliver them. And now come, I will send thee into Egypt.   Ex. 3:7-10
35 This Moses whom they refused, saying, Who made thee a ruler and a judge? the same did God send *to be* a ruler and a deliverer by the hand of the angel which appeared to him in the bush.   Ex. 14:19
36 He brought them out, after that he had shewed wonders and signs in the land of Egypt, and in the Red sea, and in the wilderness forty years.   Ex. 12:41; 14:21; 33:1
37 This is that Moses, which said unto the children of Israel, A prophet shall the Lord your God raise up unto you of your brethren, like unto me; him shall ye hear.
38 This is he, that was in the church in the wilderness with the angel which spake to him in the mount Sina, and *with* our fathers: who received the †lively oracles to give unto us: Acts 7:53; Rom. 3:2; Heb. 5:12 ◆ *living*
39 To whom our fathers would not obey, but thrust *him* from them, and in their hearts turned back again into Egypt,   Num. 14:3-4
40 Saying unto Aaron, Make us gods to go before us: for *as for* this Moses, which brought us out of the land of Egypt, we †wot not what is become of him.   Ex. 32:1, 23 ◆ *know*
41 And they made a calf in those days, and offered sacrifice unto the idol, and rejoiced in the works of their own hands.
42 Then God turned, and gave them up to worship the host of heaven; as it is written in the book of the prophets, O ye house of Israel, have ye offered to me slain beasts and sacrifices *by the space of* forty years in the wilderness?   Deut. 4:19; Jer. 19:13; Ezek. 20:39
43 Yea, ye took up the tabernacle of Moloch, and the star of your god Remphan, figures which ye made to worship them: and I will carry you away beyond Babylon.
44 Our fathers had the tabernacle of witness in the wilderness, as he had appointed, speaking unto Moses, that he should make it according to the fashion that he had seen.   Ex. 25:40; 38:21
45 Which also our fathers that came after brought in with Jesus into the possession of the Gentiles, whom God †drave out before the face of our fathers, unto the days of David;   Ps. 44:2 ◆ *drove*
46 Who found favour before God, and desired to find a tabernacle for the God of Jacob.   Ps. 132:1-5
47 But Solomon built him an house. 1 Kin. 8:20
48 Howbeit the most High dwelleth not in temples made with hands; as saith the prophet,   1 Kin. 8:27
49 Heaven *is* my throne, and earth *is* my footstool: what house will ye build me? saith the Lord: or what *is* the place of my rest?
50 Hath not my hand made all these things?
51 Ye stiffnecked and uncircumcised in heart and ears, ye do always resist the Holy Ghost: as your fathers *did*, so *do* ye. Ex. 32:9; Lev. 26:41
52 Which of the prophets have not your fathers persecuted? and they have slain them which shewed before of the coming of the Just One; of whom ye have been now the betrayers and murderers: 1 Kin. 19:10; 2 Chr. 36:16

53 Who have received the law by the disposition of angels, and have not kept *it*. Deut. 33:2

Stephen Is Executed

54 When they heard these things, they were cut to the heart, and they gnashed on him with *their* teeth. Job 16:9; Ps. 35:16; Acts 5:33
55 But he, being full of the Holy Ghost, looked up stedfastly into heaven, and saw the glory of God, and Jesus standing on the right hand of God, Mark 16:19
56 And said, Behold, I see the heavens opened, and the Son of man standing on the right hand of God. Matt. 3:16
57 Then they cried out with a loud voice, and stopped their ears, and ran upon him with one accord,
58 And cast *him* out of the city, and stoned *him*: and the witnesses laid down their clothes at a young man's feet, whose name was Saul. Luke 4:29; Acts 8:1; 22:20

7:58 God's Plan Mightier Than Satan

After the death of Stephen, Saul was elected a member of the Sanhedrin council in consideration of the part he had acted on that occasion. . . . But soon this relentless persecutor was to be employed in building up the church that he was now tearing down. A Mightier than Satan had chosen Saul to take the place of the martyred Stephen, to preach and suffer for His name, and to spread far and wide the tidings of salvation through His blood. *AA 102*

---

59 And they stoned Stephen, calling upon *God*, and saying, Lord Jesus, receive my spirit. Ps. 31:5
60 And he kneeled down, and cried with a loud voice, Lord, lay not this sin to their charge. And when he had said this, he fell asleep. Matt. 5:44; Luke 22:41; Acts 9:40

7:60 A Lasting Memory

The martyrdom of Stephen made a deep impression upon all who witnessed it. The memory of the signet of God upon his face; his words, which touched the very souls of those who heard them, remained in the minds of the beholders, and testified to the truth of that which he had proclaimed. His death was a sore trial to the church, but it resulted in the conviction of Saul, who could not efface from his memory the faith and constancy of the martyr, and the glory that had rested on his countenance. *AA 101*

Saul Persecutes the Believers

8 And Saul was consenting unto his death. And at that time there was a great persecution against the church which was at Jerusalem; and they were all scattered abroad throughout the regions of Judaea and Samaria, except the apostles. Acts 5:33, 40
2 And devout men carried Stephen *to his burial*, and made great lamentation over him.
3 As for Saul, he made havock of the church, entering into every house, and haling men and women committed *them* to prison. 1 Cor. 15:9; Gal. 1:13; Phil. 3:6

Some Samaritans Become Believers

4 Therefore they that were scattered abroad went every where preaching the word. Acts 8:1
5 Then Philip went down to the city of Samaria, and preached Christ unto them. Acts 6:5
6 And the people with one accord gave heed unto those things which Philip spake, hearing and seeing the miracles which he did.
7 For unclean spirits, crying with loud voice, came out of many that were possessed *with them*: and many taken with palsies, and that were lame, were healed. Mark 16:17-18
8 And there was great joy in that city.
9 But there was a certain man, called Simon, which beforetime in the same city used sorcery, and bewitched the people of Samaria, giving out that himself was some great one: Acts 5:36; 13:6
10 To whom they all gave heed, from the least to the greatest, saying, This man is the great power of God. Acts 14:11
11 And to him they had regard, because that of long time he had ᵀbewitched them with sorceries. Gal. 3:1 ◆ *misled*
12 But when they believed Philip preaching the things concerning the kingdom of God, and the name of Jesus Christ, they were baptized, both men and women. Matt. 28:19
13 Then Simon himself believed also: and when he was baptized, he continued with Philip, and wondered, beholding the miracles and signs which were done. Acts 8:6-7
14 Now when the apostles which were at Jerusalem heard that Samaria had received the word of God, they sent unto them Peter and John: Acts 8:1
15 Who, when they were come down, prayed for them, that they might receive the Holy Ghost: Acts 2:38
16 (For as yet he was fallen upon none of them: only they were baptized in the name of the Lord Jesus.) Matt. 28:19; Acts 2:38; 19:2
17 Then laid they *their* hands on them, and they received the Holy Ghost. Acts 6:6; 9:17; 19:6
18 And when Simon saw that through laying on of the apostles' hands the Holy Ghost was given, he offered them money,

8:15 Spirit-Empowered Ministry

It is the absence of the Spirit that makes the gospel ministry so powerless. Learning, talents, eloquence, every natural or acquired endowment, may be possessed; but without the presence of the Spirit of God, no heart will be touched, no sinner be won to Christ. On the other hand, if they are connected with Christ, if the gifts of the Spirit are theirs, the poorest and most ignorant of His disciples will have a power that will tell upon hearts. *COL 328*

19 Saying, Give me also this power, that on whomsoever I lay hands, he may receive the Holy Ghost.
20 But Peter said unto him, Thy money perish with thee, because thou hast thought that the gift of God may be purchased with money.   Dan. 5:17; Matt. 10:8; Acts 2:38
21 Thou hast neither part nor lot in this matter: for thy heart is not right in the sight of God.
22 Repent therefore of this thy wickedness, and pray God, if perhaps the thought of thine heart may be forgiven thee.   Dan. 4:27
23 For I perceive that thou art in the gall of bitterness, and *in* the bond of iniquity.
24 Then answered Simon, and said, Pray ye to the Lord for me, that none of these things which ye have spoken come upon me.   Ex. 8:8
25 And they, when they had testified and preached the word of the Lord, returned to Jerusalem, and preached the gospel in many villages of the Samaritans.

The Ethiopian Eunuch
26 And the angel of the Lord spake unto Philip, saying, Arise, and go toward the south unto the way that goeth down from Jerusalem unto Gaza, which is desert. Acts 5:19; 12:23

8:26 Angel Guidance

An angel guided Philip to the one who was seeking for light and who was ready to receive the gospel, and today angels will guide the footsteps of those workers who will allow the Holy Spirit to sanctify their tongues and refine and ennoble their hearts. *AA 109*

27 And he arose and went: and, behold, a man of Ethiopia, an eunuch of great authority under Candace queen of the Ethiopians, who had the charge of all her treasure, and had come to Jerusalem for to worship,
28 Was returning, and sitting in his chariot read Esaias the prophet.
29 Then the Spirit said unto Philip, Go near, and join thyself to this chariot.   Acts 10:19

30 And Philip ran thither to *him*, and heard him read the prophet Esaias, and said, Understandest thou what thou readest?
31 And he said, How can I, except some man should guide me? And he desired Philip that he would come up and sit with him.
32 The place of the scripture which he read was this, He was led as a sheep to the slaughter; and like a lamb ᵀdumb before his shearer, so opened he not his mouth: Is. 53:7-8 ◆ *mute*
33 In his humiliation his judgment was taken away: and who shall declare his generation? for his life is taken from the earth.
34 And the ᵀeunuch answered Philip, and said, I pray thee, of whom speaketh the prophet this? of himself, or of some other man?   *castrated male servant*
35 Then Philip opened his mouth, and began at the same scripture, and preached unto him Jesus.   Matt. 5:2; Luke 24:27; Acts 18:28
36 And as they went on *their* way, they came unto a certain water: and the eunuch said, See, *here is* water; what doth hinder me to be baptized?   Acts 10:47
37 And Philip said, If thou believest with all thine heart, thou mayest. And he answered and said, I believe that Jesus Christ is the Son of God.
38 And he commanded the chariot to stand still: and they went down both into the water, both Philip and the eunuch; and he baptized him.
39 And when they were come up out of the water, the Spirit of the Lord caught away Philip, that the eunuch saw him no more: and he went on his way rejoicing.   Ezek. 8:3

Baptism/Lord's Supper See Matthew 26:26–28.

40 But Philip was found at Azotus: and passing through he preached in all the cities, till he came to Caesarea.   Acts 10:1

Saul Becomes a Christian
9 And Saul, yet breathing out threatenings and slaughter against the disciples of the Lord, went unto the high priest,
2 And desired of him letters to Damascus to the synagogues, that if he found any of this way, whether they were men or women, he might bring them bound unto Jerusalem.   Acts 9:14; 19:9, 23
3 And as he journeyed, he came near Damascus: and suddenly there shined round about him a light from heaven: Acts 22:6; 1 Cor. 15:8
4 And he fell to the earth, and heard a voice saying unto him, Saul, Saul, why persecutest thou me?   Is. 63:9
5 And he said, Who art thou, Lord? And the Lord said, I am Jesus whom thou persecutest: *it is* hard for thee to kick against the pricks.

6 And he trembling and astonished said, Lord, what wilt thou have me to do? And the Lord *said* unto him, Arise, and go into the city, and it shall be told thee what thou must do.

9:3–6 A Flood of Light

Upon the soul of the stricken Jew [Saul] the image of the Saviour's countenance was imprinted forever. The words spoken struck home to his heart with appalling force. Into the darkened chambers of his mind there poured a flood of light, revealing the ignorance and error of his former life and his present need of the enlightenment of the Holy Spirit. *AA 115*

---

7 And the men which journeyed with him stood speechless, hearing a voice, but seeing no man.   Dan. 10:7; John 12:29; Acts 22:9

8 And Saul arose from the earth; and when his eyes were opened, he saw no man: but they led him by the hand, and brought *him* into Damascus.   Acts 22:11

9 And he was three days without sight, and neither did eat nor drink.   Esth. 4:16

9:9 Lasting Regret

These days of soul agony were to [Saul] as years. Again and again he recalled, with anguish of spirit, the part he had taken in the martyrdom of Stephen. *AA 118*

Saul Is Called to the Gentiles

10 And there was a certain disciple at Damascus, named Ananias; and to him said the Lord in a vision, Ananias. And he said, Behold, I *am here*, Lord.   Acts 10:3

11 And the Lord *said* unto him, Arise, and go into the street which is called Straight, and enquire in the house of Judas for *one* called Saul, of Tarsus: for, behold, he prayeth,   Acts 9:30; 21:39; 22:3

12 And hath seen in a vision a man named Ananias coming in, and putting *his* hand on him, that he might receive his sight.   Mark 5:23

13 Then Ananias answered, Lord, I have heard by many of this man, how much evil he hath done to thy saints at Jerusalem: Acts 8:3

14 And here he hath authority from the chief priests to bind all that call on thy name.   Acts 7:59; 9:21; 22:16

15 But the Lord said unto him, Go thy way: for he is a chosen vessel unto me, to bear my name before the Gentiles, and kings, and the children of Israel: Acts 13:2; Rom. 1:5; Eph. 3:7-8

16 For I will shew him how great things he must suffer for my name's sake.   Cor. 11:23-27

17 And Ananias went his way, and entered into the house; and putting his hands on

him said, Brother Saul, the Lord, *even* Jesus, that appeared unto thee in the way as thou camest, hath sent me, that thou mightest receive thy sight, and be filled with the Holy Ghost.   Acts 2:4

18 And immediately there fell from his eyes as it had been scales: and he received sight Tforthwith, and arose, and was baptized.   Acts 22:16 ◆ *immediately*

19 And when he had received meat, he was strengthened. Then was Saul certain days with the disciples which were at Damascus.   Acts 26:20

20 And Tstraightway he preached Christ in the synagogues, that he is the Son of God.   *right away*

21 But all that heard *him* were amazed, and said; Is not this he that destroyed them which called on this name in Jerusalem, and came Thither for that intent, that he might bring them bound unto the chief priests?   Acts 8:3 ◆ *here*

9:21 Overwhelming Evidence

Paul declared that his change of faith had not been prompted by impulse or fanaticism, but had been brought about by overwhelming evidence. In his presentation of the gospel he sought to make plain the prophecies relating to the first advent of Christ. *AA 125*

---

22 But Saul increased the more in strength, and confounded the Jews which dwelt at Damascus, proving that this is very Christ.   Acts 18:5

The Jews Lay Wait to Kill Saul

23 And after that many days were fulfilled, the Jews took counsel to kill him:

24 But their laying await was known of Saul. And they watched the gates day and night to kill him.   Acts 25:3

25 Then the disciples took him by night, and let *him* down by the wall in a basket.

26 And when Saul was come to Jerusalem, he Tassayed to join himself to the disciples: but they were all afraid of him, and believed not that he was a disciple.   Acts 26:20 ◆ *attempted*

27 But Barnabas took him, and brought *him* to the apostles, and declared unto them how he had seen the Lord in the way, and that he had spoken to him, and how he had preached boldly at Damascus in the name of Jesus.   Acts 4:13, 29, 36

28 And he was with them coming in and going out at Jerusalem.   Acts 1:21

29 And he spake boldly in the name of the Lord Jesus, and disputed against the Grecians: but they went about to slay him.   2 Cor. 11:26

30 *Which* when the brethren knew, they

brought him down to Caesarea, and sent him forth to Tarsus.   Acts 8:40
31 Then had the churches rest throughout all Judaea and Galilee and Samaria, and were edified; and walking in the fear of the Lord, and in the comfort of the Holy Ghost, were multiplied.   Neh. 5:9; Acts 8:1

Peter Heals Aeneas

32 And it came to pass, as Peter passed throughout all *quarters*, he came down also to the saints which dwelt at Lydda.   Acts 9:13
33 And there he found a certain man named Aeneas, which had kept his bed eight years, and was sick of the ᵀpalsy.   *paralysis*
34 And Peter said unto him, Aeneas, Jesus Christ maketh thee whole: arise, and make thy bed. And he arose immediately.   Acts 3:6
35 And all that dwelt at Lydda and Saron saw him, and turned to the Lord.   1 Chr. 5:16

Peter Restores Tabitha to Life

36 Now there was at Joppa a certain disciple named Tabitha, which by interpretation is called Dorcas: this woman was full of good works and almsdeeds which she did.
37 And it came to pass in those days, that she was sick, and died: whom when they had washed, they laid *her* in an upper chamber.   Acts 1:13; 20:8
38 And ᵀforasmuch as Lydda was nigh to Joppa, and the disciples had heard that Peter was there, they sent unto him two men, desiring *him* that he would not delay to come to them.   Acts 9:36 ◆ *since*
39 Then Peter arose and went with them. When he was come, they brought him into the upper chamber: and all the widows stood by him weeping, and shewing the coats and garments which Dorcas made, while she was with them.
40 But Peter put them all forth, and kneeled down, and prayed; and turning *him* to the body said, Tabitha, arise. And she opened her eyes: and when she saw Peter, she sat up.   Matt. 9:25; Acts 7:60

41 And he gave her *his* hand, and lifted her up, and when he had called the saints and widows, presented her alive.   Acts 6:1
42 And it was known throughout all Joppa; and many believed in the Lord.   John 11:45
43 And it came to pass, that he tarried many days in Joppa with one Simon a tanner.   Acts 10:6, 32

Cornelius Has a Vision

10 There was a certain man in Caesarea called Cornelius, a centurion of the band called the Italian *band*,   Acts 8:40; 27:1
2 *A* devout *man*, and one that feared God with all his house, which gave much alms to the people, and prayed to God alway.
3 He saw in a vision evidently about the ninth hour of the day an angel of God coming in to him, and saying unto him, Cornelius.   Acts 3:1; 5:19
4 And when he looked on him, he was afraid, and said, What is it, Lord? And he said unto him, Thy prayers and thine alms are come up for a memorial before God.   Heb. 6:10
5 And now send men to Joppa, and call for *one* Simon, whose surname is Peter:
6 He lodgeth with one Simon a tanner, whose house is by the sea side: he shall tell thee what thou oughtest to do.   Acts 9:43
7 And when the angel which spake unto Cornelius was departed, he called two of his household servants, and a devout soldier of them that waited on him continually;
8 And when he had declared all *these* things unto them, he sent them to Joppa.

Peter Has a Vision

9 On the morrow, as they went on their journey, and drew nigh unto the city, Peter went up upon the housetop to pray about the sixth hour: Ps. 55:17
10 And he became very hungry, and would have eaten: but while they made ready, he fell into a trance,   Acts 22:17

Supernatural Help

Acts 10

Now the Saviour's eye penetrates the future; He beholds the broader fields in which, after His death, the disciples are to be witnesses for Him. His prophetic glance takes in the experience of His servants through all the ages till He shall come the second time. He shows His followers the conflicts they must meet; He reveals the character and plan of the battle. He lays open before them the perils they must encounter, the self-denial that will be required. He desires them to count the cost, that they may not be taken unawares by the enemy. Their warfare is not to be waged against flesh and blood. . . . They are to contend with supernatural forces, but they are assured of supernatural help. All the intelligences of heaven are in this army. And more than angels are in the ranks. The Holy Spirit, the representative of the Captain of the Lord's host, comes down to direct the battle. *DA 352*

The angel, after his interview with Cornelius, went to Peter, in Joppa. . . . It was not for physical food alone that Peter hungered. As from the housetop he viewed the city of Joppa and the surrounding country he hungered for the salvation of his countrymen. He had an intense desire to point out to them from the Scriptures the prophecies relating to the sufferings and death of Christ. *AA 135*

11 And saw heaven opened, and a certain vessel descending unto him, as it had been a great sheet knit at the four corners, and let down to the earth: John 1:51

12 Wherein were all manner of fourfooted beasts of the earth, and wild beasts, and creeping things, and fowls of the air.

13 And there came a voice to him, Rise, Peter; kill, and eat.

14 But Peter said, Not so, Lord; for I have never eaten any thing that is common or unclean.   Lev. 20:25; Ezek. 4:14

15 And the voice *spake* unto him again the second time, What God hath cleansed, *that call not thou common.*   1 Cor. 10:25; Titus 1:15

16 This was done ᵀthrice: and the vessel was received up again into heaven.   *three times*

17 Now while Peter doubted in himself what this vision which he had seen should mean, behold, the men which were sent from Cornelius had made enquiry for Simon's house, and stood before the gate,

This vision conveyed to Peter both reproof and instruction. It revealed to him the purpose of God—that by the death of Christ the Gentiles should be made fellow heirs with the Jews to the blessings of salvation. As yet none of the disciples had preached the gospel to the Gentiles. *AA 135*

18 And called, and asked whether Simon, which was surnamed Peter, were lodged there.

19 While Peter thought on the vision, the Spirit said unto him, Behold, three men seek thee.   Acts 8:29

20 Arise therefore, and get thee down, and go with them, doubting nothing: for I have sent them.   Acts 15:7-9

21 Then Peter went down to the men which were sent unto him from Cornelius; and said, Behold, I am he whom ye seek: what *is* the cause wherefore ye are come?

22 And they said, Cornelius the centurion, a just man, and one that feareth God, and of good report among all the nation of the Jews, was warned from God by an holy angel

to send for thee into his house, and to hear words of thee.   Acts 10:2; 11:14

How carefully the Lord worked to overcome the prejudice against the Gentiles that had been so firmly fixed in Peter's mind by his Jewish training! By the vision of the sheet and its contents He sought to divest the apostle's mind of this prejudice and to teach the important truth that in heaven there is no respect of persons; that Jew and Gentile are alike precious in God's sight; that through Christ the heathen may be made partakers of the blessings and privileges of the gospel. *AA 136*

23 Then called he them in, and lodged *them.* And on the morrow Peter went away with them, and certain brethren from Joppa accompanied him.   Acts 10:45; 11:12

Peter Speaks with Cornelius

24 And the morrow after they entered into Caesarea. And Cornelius waited for them, and had called together his kinsmen and near friends.

25 And as Peter was coming in, Cornelius met him, and fell down at his feet, and worshipped *him.*   Matt. 8:2

26 But Peter took him up, saying, Stand up; I myself also am a man.   Rev. 19:10

27 And as he talked with him, he went in, and found many that were come together.

28 And he said unto them, Ye know how that it is an unlawful thing for a man that is a Jew to keep company, or come unto one of another nation; but God hath shewed me that I should not call any man common or unclean.   John 4:9; 18:28; Acts 15:8-9

29 Therefore came I *unto you* without gainsaying, as soon as I was sent for: I ask therefore for what intent ye have sent for me?

30 And Cornelius said, Four days ago I was fasting until this hour; and at the ninth hour I prayed in my house, and, behold, a man stood before me in bright clothing,   Acts 10:3

31 And said, Cornelius, thy prayer is heard, and thine alms are had in remembrance in the sight of God.   Acts 10:4

32 Send therefore to Joppa, and call ᵀthither Simon, whose surname is Peter; he is lodged in the house of *one* Simon a tanner by the sea side: who, when he cometh, shall speak unto thee.   *here*

33 Immediately therefore I sent to thee; and thou hast well done that thou art come. Now therefore are we all here present before God, to hear all things that are commanded thee of God.

Peter Understands the Vision

34 Then Peter opened *his* mouth, and said, Of a truth I perceive that God is no respecter of persons: Deut. 10:17; 2 Chr. 19:7; Rom. 2:11

35 But in every nation he that feareth him, and worketh righteousness, is accepted with him. Acts 10:2

36 The word which *God* sent unto the children of Israel, preaching peace by Jesus Christ: (he is Lord of all:) Matt. 28:18; Acts 2:36; Rev. 17:14

37 That word, *I say*, ye know, which was published throughout all Judaea, and began from Galilee, after the baptism which John preached;

38 How God anointed Jesus of Nazareth with the Holy Ghost and with power: who went about doing good, and healing all that were oppressed of the ᵀdevil; for God was with him. Luke 4:18 ◆ *false accuser*

39 And we are witnesses of all things which he did both in the land of the Jews, and in Jerusalem; whom they slew and hanged on a tree: Luke 24:48; Acts 1:8; 10:41

40 Him God raised up the third day, and shewed him openly; Acts 2:24

41 Not to all the people, but unto witnesses chosen before of God, *even* to us, who did eat and drink with him after he rose from the dead. John 14:17, 22; Acts 10:39

42 And he commanded us to preach unto the people, and to testify that it is he which was ordained of God *to be* the Judge of ᵀquick and dead. Acts 17:31; 2 Tim. 4:1; 1 Pet. 4:5 ◆ *living*

43 To him give all the prophets witness, that through his name whosoever believeth in him shall receive remission of sins. Acts 15:9

The Holy Ghost Descends

44 While Peter yet spake these words, the Holy Ghost fell on all them which heard the word. Acts 11:15; 15:8

45 And they of the circumcision which believed were astonished, as many as came with Peter, because that on the Gentiles also was poured out the gift of the Holy Ghost.

46 For they heard them speak with tongues, and magnify God. Then answered Peter,

47 Can any man forbid water, that these should not be baptized, which have received the Holy Ghost as well as we? Acts 8:36

48 And he commanded them to be baptized in the name of the Lord. Then prayed they him to tarry certain days. Acts 2:38; 1 Cor. 1:13-17

Gentiles Can Become Christians

11 And the apostles and brethren that were in Judaea heard that the Gentiles had also received the word of God.

2 And when Peter was come up to Jerusalem, they that were of the circumcision contended with him, Acts 10:45

3 Saying, Thou wentest in to men uncircumcised, and didst eat with them. Gal. 2:12

4 But Peter rehearsed *the matter* from the beginning, and expounded *it* by order unto them, saying, Luke 1:3

11:4 The Lessons of Peter's Vision

Peter laid the whole matter before them. He related his experience in regard to the vision and pleaded that it admonished him to observe no longer the ceremonial distinction of circumcision and uncircumcision, nor to look upon the Gentiles as unclean. He told them of the command given him to go to the Gentiles, of the coming of the messengers, of his journey to Caesarea, and of the meeting with Cornelius. *AA 141*

---

5 I was in the city of Joppa praying: and in a trance I saw a vision, A certain vessel descend, as it had been a great sheet, let down from heaven by four corners; and it came even to me: Acts 10:9-32

6 Upon the which when I had fastened mine eyes, I considered, and saw fourfooted beasts of the earth, and wild beasts, and creeping things, and fowls of the air.

7 And I heard a voice saying unto me, Arise, Peter; slay and eat.

8 But I said, Not so, Lord: for nothing common or unclean hath at any time entered into my mouth. Rom. 14:14

9 But the voice answered me again from heaven, What God hath cleansed, *that* call not thou common.

10 And this was done three times: and all were drawn up again into heaven.

11 And, behold, immediately there were three men already come unto the house where I was, sent from Caesarea unto me.

12 And the Spirit bade me go with them, nothing doubting. Moreover these six brethren accompanied me, and we entered into the man's house: Acts 8:29

13 And he shewed us how he had seen an angel in his house, which stood and said unto him, Send men to Joppa, and call for Simon, whose surname is Peter;

14 Who shall tell thee words, whereby thou and all thy house shall be saved. John 4:53

15 And as I began to speak, the Holy Ghost fell on them, as on us at the beginning.

16 Then remembered I the word of the Lord, how that he said, John indeed baptized with water; but ye shall be baptized with the Holy Ghost. Matt. 3:11; Mark 1:8; Acts 1:5

17 Forasmuch then as God gave them the like gift as *he did* unto us, who believed on the Lord Jesus Christ; what was I, that I could withstand God? Acts 10:47

18 When they heard these things, they held their peace, and glorified God, saying, Then hath God also to the Gentiles granted repentance unto life. Acts 5:31; Rom. 10:12-13; 2 Cor. 7:10

11:18 Age-long Custom Abandoned

On hearing this account, the brethren were silenced. Convinced that Peter's course was in direct fulfillment of the plan of God, and that their prejudices and exclusiveness were utterly contrary to the spirit of the gospel, they glorified God, saying, "Then hath God also to the Gentiles granted repentance unto life" [Acts 11:18].

Thus, without controversy, prejudice was broken down, the exclusiveness established by the custom of ages was abandoned, and the way was opened for the gospel to be proclaimed to the Gentiles. *AA 142*

The Church in Antioch

19 Now they which were scattered abroad upon the persecution that arose about Stephen travelled as far as Phenice, and Cyprus, and Antioch, preaching the word to none but unto the Jews only. Acts 4:36
20 And some of them were men of Cyprus and Cyrene, which, when they were come to Antioch, spake unto the Grecians, preaching the Lord Jesus. Matt. 27:32
21 And the hand of the Lord was with them: and a great number believed, and turned unto the Lord. Luke 1:66; Acts 2:47; 9:35
22 Then tidings of these things came unto the ears of the church which was in Jerusalem: and they sent forth Barnabas, that he should go as far as Antioch.
23 Who, when he came, and had seen the grace of God, was glad, and exhorted them all, that with purpose of heart they would cleave unto the Lord. Acts 13:43; 14:22, 26
24 For he was a good man, and full of the Holy Ghost and of faith: and much people was added unto the Lord. Acts 5:14; 6:5; 11:21
25 Then departed Barnabas to Tarsus, for to seek Saul: Acts 9:11
26 And when he had found him, he brought him unto Antioch. And it came to pass, that a whole year they assembled themselves with the church, and taught much people. And the disciples were called Christians first in Antioch. Acts 26:28; 1 Pet. 4:16

Antioch Sends Relief to Judea

27 And in these days came prophets from Jerusalem unto Antioch. Acts 2:17; 13:1; 1 Cor. 12:28
28 And there stood up one of them named Agabus, and signified by the Spirit that there should be great ᵀdearth throughout all the world: which came to pass in the days of Claudius Caesar. Acts 18:2; 21:10 ♦ *famine*

29 Then the disciples, every man according to his ability, determined to send relief unto the brethren which dwelt in Judaea:
30 Which also they did, and sent it to the elders by the hands of Barnabas and Saul.

An Angel Frees Peter from Prison

12 Now about that time Herod the king stretched forth his hands to ᵀvex certain of the church. *trouble*
2 And he killed James the brother of John with the sword. Matt. 20:23
3 And because he saw it pleased the Jews, he proceeded further to take Peter also. (Then were the days of unleavened bread.) Ex. 23:15
4 And when he had apprehended him, he put him in prison, and delivered him to four ᵀquaternions of soldiers to keep him; intending after Easter to bring him forth to the people. Luke 21:12 ♦ *groups of four*
5 Peter therefore was kept in prison: but prayer was made without ceasing of the church unto God for him. 2 Cor. 1:11
6 And when Herod would have brought him forth, the same night Peter was sleeping between two soldiers, bound with two chains: and the keepers before the door kept the prison. Acts 21:33

12:5, 6 Man's Extremity; God's Opportunity

In his cell [Peter] was placed between two soldiers and was bound by two chains, each chain being fastened to the wrist of one of the soldiers. He was unable to move without their knowledge. With the prison doors securely fastened, and a strong guard before them, all chance of rescue or escape through human means was cut off. But man's extremity is God's opportunity. *AA 146*

7 And, behold, the angel of the Lord came upon him, and a light shined in the prison: and he smote Peter on the side, and raised him up, saying, Arise up quickly. And his chains fell off from his hands. 1 Kin. 19:7; Acts 5:19; 16:26

12:7 The Results of Perfect Trust

It is the last night before the proposed execution. A mighty angel is sent from heaven to rescue Peter. . . . He enters the cell, and there lies Peter, sleeping the peaceful sleep of perfect trust.

The light that surrounds the angel fills the cell, but does not rouse the apostle. Not until he feels the touch of the angel's hand and hears a voice saying, "Arise up quickly," does he awaken sufficiently to see his cell illuminated by the light of heaven, and an angel of great glory standing before him. *AA 146, 147*

8 And the angel said unto him, Gird thyself, and bind on thy sandals. And so he did. And

he saith unto him, Cast thy garment about thee, and follow me.

9 And he went out, and followed him; and ᵀwist not that it was true which was done by the angel; but thought he saw a vision.   Ps. 126:1 ✦ knew

10 When they were past the first and the second ward, they came unto the iron gate that leadeth unto the city; which opened to them of his own accord: and they went out, and passed on through one street; and forthwith the angel departed from him.   Acts 5:19; 16:26

11 And when Peter was come to himself, he said, Now I know of a surety, that the Lord hath sent his angel, and hath delivered me out of the hand of Herod, and from all the expectation of the people of the Jews.   Dan. 3:28

12 And when he had considered the thing, he came to the house of Mary the mother of John, whose surname was Mark; where many were gathered together praying.   Col. 4:10

13 And as Peter knocked at the door of the gate, a damsel came to hearken, named Rhoda.

14 And when she knew Peter's voice, she opened not the gate for gladness, but ran in, and told how Peter stood before the gate.   Luke 24:41

15 And they said unto her, Thou art mad. But she constantly affirmed that it was even so. Then said they, It is his angel.   Matt. 18:10

16 But Peter continued knocking: and when they had opened the door, and saw him, they were astonished.

17 But he, beckoning unto them with the hand to hold their peace, declared unto them how the Lord had brought him out of the prison. And he said, Go shew these things unto James, and to the brethren. And he departed, and went into another place.   Acts 13:16; 15:13; 19:33

18 Now as soon as it was day, there was no small stir among the soldiers, what was become of Peter.

19 And when Herod had sought for him, and found him not, he examined the keepers, and commanded that they should be put to death. And he went down from Judaea to Caesarea, and there abode.   Acts 16:27

Herod's Death

20 And Herod was highly displeased with them of Tyre and Sidon: but they came with one accord to him, and, having made Blastus the king's chamberlain their friend, desired peace; because their country was nourished by the king's country.   Ezra 3:7; Ezek. 27:17

21 And upon a set day Herod, ᵀarrayed in royal apparel, sat upon his throne, and made an oration unto them.   clothed

22 And the people gave a shout, saying, It is the voice of a god, and not of a man.

23 And immediately the angel of the Lord smote him, because he gave not God the glory: and he was eaten of worms, and gave up the ghost.   1 Sam. 25:38

12:23 A Mightier Ruler

A moment before [Herod] had been the proud recipient of the praise and worship of that vast throng; now he realized that he was in the hands of a Ruler mightier than himself. AA 151

---

24 But the word of God grew and multiplied.   Acts 6:7; 19:20

25 And Barnabas and Saul returned from Jerusalem, when they had fulfilled their ministry, and took with them John, whose surname was Mark.   Acts 4:36; 11:29-30; 12:12

Paul and Barnabas Go to Cyprus

13 Now there were in the church that was at Antioch certain prophets and teachers; as Barnabas, and Simeon that was called Niger, and Lucius of Cyrene, and Manaen, which had been brought up with Herod the tetrarch, and Saul. Luke 3:1; Acts 4:36; 11:22-27

2 As they ministered to the Lord, and fasted, the Holy Ghost said, Separate me Barnabas and Saul for the work whereunto I have called them.   Acts 9:15

3 And when they had fasted and prayed, and laid their hands on them, they sent them away.   Acts 6:6; 14:23, 26

4 So they, being sent forth by the Holy Ghost, departed unto Seleucia; and from thence they sailed to Cyprus.   Acts 4:36

5 And when they were at Salamis, they preached the word of God in the synagogues of the Jews: and they had also John to their minister.   Acts 13:14

6 And when they had gone through the isle unto Paphos, they found a certain sorcerer, a false prophet, a Jew, whose name was Barjesus: Matt. 7:15

13:8 Powers of Darkness

Not without a struggle does Satan allow the kingdom of God to be built up in the earth. The forces of evil are engaged in unceasing warfare against the agencies appointed for the spread of the gospel, and these powers of darkness are especially active when the truth is proclaimed before men of repute and sterling integrity. AA 167

---

7 Which was with the deputy of the country, Sergius Paulus, a prudent man; who called for Barnabas and Saul, and desired to hear the word of God.   Acts 13:12; 18:12; 19:38

8 But Elymas the sorcerer (for so is his name by interpretation) withstood them, seeking to turn away the deputy from the faith.   Acts 13:6

9 Then Saul, (who also *is called* Paul,) filled with the Holy Ghost, set his eyes on him,   Acts 2:4; 4:8

10 And said, O full of all subtilty and all mischief, *thou* child of the devil, *thou* enemy of all righteousness, wilt thou not cease to pervert the right ways of the Lord?   Hos. 14:9; John 8:44

11 And now, behold, the hand of the Lord *is* upon thee, and thou shalt be blind, not seeing the sun for a season. And immediately there fell on him a mist and a darkness; and he went about seeking some to lead him by the hand.   Ex. 9:3; 1 Sam. 5:11; Ps. 32:4

13:11 God's Miraculous Power

The fact that [Elymas] was obliged to grope about in blindness proved to all that the miracles which the apostles had performed, and which Elymas had denounced as sleight of hand, were wrought by the power of God. The deputy [Sergius Paulus], convinced of the truth of the doctrine taught by the apostles, accepted the gospel. *AA 168*

12 Then the deputy, when he saw what was done, believed, being astonished at the doctrine of the Lord.   Acts 13:7

13 Now when Paul and his company loosed from Paphos, they came to Perga in Pamphylia: and John departing from them returned to Jerusalem.   Acts 2:10

13:13 Young Mark Wavers

It was here that Mark, overwhelmed with fear and discouragement, wavered for a time in his purpose to give himself wholeheartedly to the Lord's work. Unused to hardships, he was disheartened by the perils and privations of the way. He had labored with success under favorable circumstances; but now, amidst the opposition and perils that so often beset the pioneer worker, he failed to endure hardness as a good soldier of the cross. *AA 169, 170*

Paul and Barnabas Go to Antioch in Pisidia

14 But when they departed from Perga, they came to Antioch in Pisidia, and went into the synagogue on the sabbath day, and sat down.   Acts 13:5; 14:19; 16:13

15 And after the reading of the law and the prophets the rulers of the synagogue sent unto them, saying, *Ye* men *and* brethren, if ye have any word of ᵀexhortation for the people, say on.   Mark 5:22; Acts 13:27; 15:21 ◆ *encouragement*

16 Then Paul stood up, and beckoning with

his hand said, Men of Israel, and ye that fear God, give audience.   Acts 10:2; 12:17; 13:26

17 The God of this people of Israel chose our fathers, and exalted the people when they dwelt as strangers in the land of Egypt, and with an high arm brought he them out of it.   Deut. 7:6-8; Ps. 105:23-24

18 And about the time of forty years suffered he their manners in the wilderness.   Deut. 9:7, 21-24; Acts 7:36

19 And when he had destroyed seven nations in the land of Chanaan, he divided their land to them by lot.   Deut. 7:1; Josh. 14:1; Ps. 78:55

20 And after that he gave *unto them* judges about the space of four hundred and fifty years, until Samuel the prophet.   Judg. 2:16

21 And afterward they desired a king: and God gave unto them Saul the son of Cis, a man of the tribe of Benjamin, by the space of forty years.   1 Sam. 10:1

22 And when he had removed him, he raised up unto them David to be their king; to whom also he gave testimony, and said, I have found David the *son* of Jesse, a man after mine own heart, which shall fulfil all my will.   1 Sam. 15:23, 26; 16:1

23 Of this man's seed hath God according to *his* promise raised unto Israel a Saviour, Jesus: Ps. 132:11; Matt. 1:1, 21

24 When John had first preached before his coming the baptism of repentance to all the people of Israel.   Acts 1:22

25 And as John fulfilled his course, he said, Whom think ye that I am? I am not *he*. But, behold, there cometh one after me, whose shoes of *his* feet I am not worthy to loose.   Matt. 3:11; Mark 1:7; Acts 20:24

26 Men *and* brethren, children of the stock of Abraham, and whosoever among you feareth God, to you is the word of this salvation sent.   Acts 4:12

27 For they that dwell at Jerusalem, and their rulers, because they knew him not, nor yet the voices of the prophets which are read every sabbath day, they have fulfilled *them* in condemning *him*.   Luke 24:20; Acts 3:17; 15:21

28 And though they found no cause of death *in him*, yet desired they Pilate that he should be slain.   Matt. 27:22-25

29 And when they had fulfilled all that was written of him, they took *him* down from the tree, and laid *him* in a sepulchre.   Matt. 27:57-60

30 But God raised him from the dead:

31 And he was seen many days of them which came up with him from Galilee to Jerusalem, who are his witnesses unto the people.   Matt. 28:16; Luke 24:48; Acts 1:3

32 And we declare unto you glad tidings, how that the promise which was made unto the fathers,   Acts 26:6; Rom. 4:13

33 God hath fulfilled the same unto us their

children, in that he hath raised up Jesus again; as it is also written in the second psalm, Thou art my Son, this day have I ᵀbegotten thee.   Ps. 2:7; Heb. 5:5 ◆ brought you forth
34 And as concerning that he raised him up from the dead, now no more to return to corruption, he said on this wise, I will give you the sure mercies of David.   Is. 55:3; Rom. 6:9
35 Wherefore he saith also in another psalm, Thou shalt not suffer thine Holy One to see corruption.   Ps. 16:10
36 For David, after he had served his own generation by the will of God, fell on sleep, and was laid unto his fathers, and saw corruption: 1 Kin. 2:10; Acts 2:29; 13:22
37 But he, whom God raised again, saw no corruption.   Acts 13:30
38 Be it known unto you therefore, men and brethren, that through this man is preached unto you the forgiveness of sins: Luke 24:47
39 And by him all that believe are justified from all things, from which ye could not be justified by the law of Moses.   Rom. 8:3; 10:4
40 Beware therefore, lest that come upon you, which is spoken of in the prophets;
41 Behold, ye despisers, and wonder, and perish: for I work a work in your days, a work which ye shall in no wise believe, though a man declare it unto you.   Hab. 1:5

Preaching to the Gentiles

42 And when the Jews were gone out of the synagogue, the Gentiles ᵀbesought that these words might be preached to them the next sabbath.   begged
43 Now when the congregation was broken up, many of the Jews and religious ᵀproselytes followed Paul and Barnabas: who, speaking to them, persuaded them to continue in the grace of God.   Acts 6:5; 11:23; 14:22 ◆ converts
44 And the next sabbath day came almost the whole city together to hear the word of God.
45 But when the Jews saw the multitudes, they were filled with envy, and spake against those things which were spoken by Paul, contradicting and blaspheming.   Acts 18:6
46 Then Paul and Barnabas ᵀwaxed bold, and said, It was necessary that the word of God should first have been spoken to you: but seeing ye put it from you, and judge yourselves unworthy of everlasting life, lo, we turn to the Gentiles.   Acts 3:26; 26:20; 28:28 ◆ became
47 For so hath the Lord commanded us, saying, I have set thee to be a light of the Gentiles, that thou shouldest be for salvation unto the ends of the earth.   Is. 42:6; 49:6; Luke 2:32
48 And when the Gentiles heard this, they were glad, and glorified the word of the Lord: and as many as were ordained to eternal life believed.

49 And the word of the Lord was published throughout all the region.
50 But the Jews stirred up the devout and honourable women, and the chief men of the city, and raised persecution against Paul and Barnabas, and expelled them out of their coasts.   Acts 14:2
51 But they shook off the dust of their feet against them, and came unto Iconium.
52 And the disciples were filled with joy, and with the Holy Ghost.   Acts 2:4

Paul and Barnabas in Iconium

14 And it came to pass in Iconium, that they went both together into the synagogue of the Jews, and so spake, that a great multitude both of the Jews and also of the Greeks believed.   Acts 13:46, 51; 18:4
2 But the unbelieving Jews stirred up the Gentiles, and made their minds evil affected against the brethren.   Acts 13:50
3 Long time therefore abode they speaking boldly in the Lord, which gave testimony unto the word of his grace, and granted signs and wonders to be done by their hands.   Mark 16:20; Acts 20:32; Heb. 2:4
4 But the multitude of the city was divided: and part held with the Jews, and part with the apostles.   Acts 28:24
5 And when there was an assault made both of the Gentiles, and also of the Jews with their rulers, to use them despitefully, and to stone them,   Acts 14:19

14:1–5 The Apostles Opposed

The increasing popularity of the message borne by the apostles, filled the unbelieving Jews with envy and hatred, and they determined to stop the labors of Paul and Barnabas at once. By means of false and exaggerated reports they led the authorities to fear that the entire city was in danger of being incited to insurrection. They declared that large numbers were attaching themselves to the apostles and suggested that it was for secret and dangerous designs. *AA 178*

---

6 They were ware of it, and fled unto Lystra and Derbe, cities of Lycaonia, and unto the region that lieth round about: Matt. 10:23
7 And there they preached the gospel.

Paul and Barnabas in Lystra

8 And there sat a certain man at Lystra, impotent in his feet, being a cripple from his mother's womb, who never had walked:
9 The same heard Paul speak: who stedfastly beholding him, and perceiving that he had faith to be healed,   Matt. 9:28-29
10 Said with a loud voice, Stand upright on thy feet. And he leaped and walked.   Is. 35:6

11 And when the people saw what Paul had done, they lifted up their voices, saying in the speech of Lycaonia, The gods are come down to us in the likeness of men.   Acts 8:10; 28:6

12 And they called Barnabas, Jupiter; and Paul, Mercurius, because he was the chief speaker.   Acts 19:35

13 Then the priest of Jupiter, which was before their city, brought oxen and garlands unto the gates, and would have done sacrifice with the people.   Dan. 2:46

14 *Which* when the apostles, Barnabas and Paul, heard *of*, they rent their clothes, and ran in among the people, crying out,   Matt. 26:65

15 And saying, Sirs, why do ye these things? We also are men of like passions with you, and preach unto you that ye should turn from these vanities unto the living God, which made heaven, and earth, and the sea, and all things that are therein: 1 Sam. 12:21; Jer. 14:22

16 Who in times past suffered all nations to walk in their own ways.   Ps. 81:12; Mic. 4:5

17 Nevertheless he left not himself without witness, in that he did good, and gave us rain from heaven, and fruitful seasons, filling our hearts with food and gladness.

14:18 A Denial Ignored

Notwithstanding the positive denial of the apostles that they were divine, and notwithstanding Paul's endeavors to direct the minds of the people to the true God as the only object worthy of adoration, it was almost impossible to turn the heathen from their intention to offer sacrifice. So firm had been their belief that these men were indeed gods, and so great their enthusiasm, that they were loath to acknowledge their error. *AA 182*

18 And with these sayings scarce restrained they the people, that they had not done sacrifice unto them.

19 And there came thither *certain* Jews from Antioch and Iconium, who persuaded the people, and, having stoned Paul, drew *him* out of the city, supposing he had been dead.   Acts 13:45; 2 Cor. 11:25; 2 Tim. 3:11

20 Howbeit, as the disciples stood round about him, he rose up, and came into the city: and the next day he departed with Barnabas to Derbe.   Acts 14:6

Paul and Barnabas Return to Antioch in Syria

21 And when they had preached the gospel to that city, and had taught many, they returned again to Lystra, and *to* Iconium, and Antioch,   Acts 13:51

22 Confirming the souls of the disciples, *and* ᵀexhorting them to continue in the faith, and that we must through much tribulation enter into the kingdom of God.   John 16:33; Acts 13:43; 2 Tim. 3:12 ◆ *encouraging*

23 And when they had ordained them elders in every church, and had prayed with fasting, they commended them to the Lord, on whom they believed.   Acts 11:30; 20:32; Titus 1:5

24 And after they had passed throughout Pisidia, they came to Pamphylia.   Acts 13:13-14

25 And when they had preached the word in Perga, they went down into Attalia:

26 And thence sailed to Antioch, from whence they had been recommended to the grace of God for the work which they fulfilled.   Acts 11:19; 15:40

27 And when they were come, and had gathered the church together, they rehearsed all that God had done with them, and how he had opened the door of faith unto the Gentiles.   Acts 15:12; 1 Cor. 16:9; 2 Cor. 2:12

28 And there they abode long time with the disciples.   Acts 11:26

Controversy about Moses' Teachings

15 And certain men which came down from Judaea taught the brethren, *and*

Instruments in God's Hands

Acts 15

The work of God in the earth presents, from age to age, a striking similarity in every great reformation or religious movement. The principles of God's dealing with men are ever the same. The important movements of the present have their parallel in those of the past, and the experience of the church in former ages has lessons of great value for our own time.

No truth is more clearly taught in the Bible than that God by His Holy Spirit especially directs His servants on earth in the great movements for the carrying forward of the work of salvation. Men are instruments in the hand of God, employed by Him to accomplish His purposes of grace and mercy. Each has his part to act; to each is granted a measure of light, adapted to the necessities of his time, and sufficient to enable him to perform the work which God has given him to do. But no man, however honored of Heaven, has ever attained to a full understanding of the great plan of redemption, or even to a perfect appreciation of the divine purpose in the work for his own time. Men do not fully understand what God would accomplish by the work which He gives them to do; they do not comprehend, in all its bearings, the message which they utter in His name. *GC 343*

said, Except ye be circumcised after the manner of Moses, ye cannot be saved.   Lev. 12:3

2 When therefore Paul and Barnabas had no small dissension and disputation with them, they determined that Paul and Barnabas, and certain other of them, should go up to Jerusalem unto the apostles and elders about this question.   Acts 15:4, 6-7, 22-23

15:2 A Collective Decision

Finally, the members of the church, fearing that a division among them would be the outcome of continued discussion, decided to send Paul and Barnabas, with some responsible men from the church, to Jerusalem to lay the matter before the apostles and elders. . . . Meanwhile all controversy was to cease until a final decision should be given in general council. This decision was then to be universally accepted by the different churches throughout the country. *AA 190*

---

3 And being brought on their way by the church, they passed through Phenice and Samaria, declaring the conversion of the Gentiles: and they caused great joy unto all the brethren.   Acts 14:27; 21:5; Rom. 15:24

4 And when they were come to Jerusalem, they were received of the church, and of the apostles and elders, and they declared all things that God had done with them.

5 But there rose up certain of the sect of the Pharisees which believed, saying, That it was needful to circumcise them, and to command *them* to keep the law of Moses.   Acts 15:1

The Apostles Consult

6 And the apostles and elders came together for to consider of this matter.   Acts 15:25

7 And when there had been much disputing, Peter rose up, and said unto them, Men *and* brethren, ye know how that a good while ago God made choice among us, that the Gentiles by my mouth should hear the word of the gospel, and believe.   Acts 15:2

8 And God, which knoweth the hearts, bare them witness, giving them the Holy Ghost, even as *he did* unto us;   Acts 1:24; 2:4; 10:47

9 And put no difference between us and them, purifying their hearts by faith.   Acts 11:12

10 Now therefore why tempt ye God, to put a yoke upon the neck of the disciples, which neither our fathers nor we were able to bear?   Is. 7:12; Matt. 23:4; Gal. 5:1

11 But we believe that through the grace of the Lord Jesus Christ we shall be saved, even as they.   Rom. 3:24; 2 Cor. 13:14; Titus 2:11

12 Then all the multitude kept silence, and gave audience to Barnabas and Paul, declaring what miracles and wonders

God had ᵀwrought among the Gentiles by them.   Acts 14:27; 15:4 ♦ *done*

13 And after they had held their peace, James answered, saying, Men *and* brethren, hearken unto me: Acts 12:17

14 Simeon hath declared how God at the first did visit the Gentiles, to take out of them a people for his name.   Is. 43:21

15 And to this agree the words of the prophets; as it is written,

16 After this I will return, and will build again the tabernacle of David, which is fallen down; and I will build again the ruins thereof, and I will set it up: Amos 9:11-12

17 That the residue of men might seek after the Lord, and all the Gentiles, upon whom my name is called, saith the Lord, who doeth all these things.   Is. 43:7

18 Known unto God are all his works from the beginning of the world.

19 Wherefore my sentence is, that we trouble not them, which from among the Gentiles are turned to God: Acts 15:28

20 But that we write unto them, that they abstain from pollutions of idols, and *from* fornication, and *from* things strangled, and *from* blood.   Gen. 9:4; Lev. 3:17; Acts 15:29

21 For Moses of old time hath in every city them that preach him, being read in the synagogues every sabbath day.   Acts 13:15, 27

The Apostles Send Letters with Their Decision

22 Then pleased it the apostles and elders, with the whole church, to send chosen men of their own company to Antioch with Paul and Barnabas; *namely*, Judas surnamed Barsabas, and Silas, chief men among the brethren:

23 And they wrote *letters* by them after this manner; The apostles and elders and brethren *send* greeting unto the brethren which are of the Gentiles in Antioch and Syria and Cilicia: Acts 15:22; 23:26; James 1:1

24 Forasmuch as we have heard, that certain which went out from us have troubled you with words, subverting your souls, saying, *Ye must* be circumcised, and keep the law: to whom we gave no *such* commandment: Acts 15:1; Gal. 1:7; 5:10

25 It seemed good unto us, being assembled with one accord, to send chosen men unto you with our beloved Barnabas and Paul,   Acts 1:14

26 Men that have hazarded their lives for the name of our Lord Jesus Christ.   Acts 14:19

27 We have sent therefore Judas and Silas, who shall also tell *you* the same things by mouth.   Acts 15:22

28 For it seemed good to the Holy Ghost, and to us, to lay upon you no greater burden than these necessary things;   John 16:13

29 That ye abstain from meats offered to idols, and from blood, and from things strangled, and from fornication: from which if ye keep yourselves, ye shall do well. Fare ye well.   Acts 15:20; 21:25; Rev. 2:14

15:28, 29 Dealing With Gentile Converts

James sought to impress the minds of his brethren with the fact that, in turning to God, the Gentiles had made a great change in their lives and that much caution should be used not to trouble them with perplexing and doubtful questions of minor importance, lest they be discouraged in following Christ.

The Gentile converts, however, were to give up the customs that were inconsistent with the principles of Christianity. *AA 195*

30 So when they were dismissed, they came to Antioch: and when they had gathered the multitude together, they delivered the epistle:
31 *Which* when they had read, they rejoiced for the consolation.

15:30, 31 The Spirit Settles the Question

The various points involved in the settlement of the main question at issue seemed to present before the council insurmountable difficulties. But the Holy Spirit had, in reality, already settled this question, upon the decision of which seemed to depend the prosperity, if not the very existence, of the Christian church. *AA 192*

32 And Judas and Silas, being prophets also themselves, exhorted the brethren with many words, and confirmed *them*.   Acts 11:23
33 And after they had tarried *there* a space, they were let go in peace from the brethren unto the apostles.   1 Cor. 16:11; Heb. 11:31
34 Notwithstanding it pleased Silas to abide there still.
35 Paul also and Barnabas continued in Antioch, teaching and preaching the word of the Lord, with many others also.   Acts 13:1

Paul and Barnabas Separate
36 And some days after Paul said unto Barnabas, Let us go again and visit our brethren in every city where we have preached the word of the Lord, *and see* how they do. Acts 13:4, 13, 51
37 And Barnabas determined to take with them John, whose surname was Mark.
38 But Paul thought not good to take him with them, who departed from them from Pamphylia, and went not with them to the work.   Acts 13:13
39 And the contention was so sharp between them, that they departed ᵀasunder one from the other: and so Barnabas took Mark, and sailed unto Cyprus; Acts 4:36 ♦ *apart*

40 And Paul chose Silas, and departed, being recommended by the brethren unto the grace of God.   Acts 14:26
41 And he went through Syria and Cilicia, confirming the churches.   Acts 15:23

Timothy Joins Paul
16 Then came he to Derbe and Lystra: and, behold, a certain disciple was there, named Timotheus, the son of a certain woman, which was a Jewess, and believed; but his father *was* a Greek: Acts 14:6; 17:14; 18:5
2 Which was well reported of by the brethren that were at Lystra and Iconium.
3 Him would Paul have to go forth with him; and took and circumcised him because of the Jews which were in those quarters: for they knew all that his father was a Greek.   Gal. 2:3
4 And as they went through the cities, they delivered them the decrees for to keep, that were ordained of the apostles and elders which were at Jerusalem.   Acts 15:28-29
5 And so were the churches established in the faith, and increased in number daily.   Acts 2:47; 6:7; 9:31

The Macedonian Call
6 Now when they had gone throughout Phrygia and the region of Galatia, and were forbidden of the Holy Ghost to preach the word in Asia,   Acts 18:23; Gal. 1:2; 1 Pet. 1:1
7 After they were come to Mysia, they ᵀassayed to go into Bithynia: but the Spirit suffered them not.   Rom. 8:9 ♦ *attempted*
8 And they passing by Mysia came down to Troas.   Acts 16:11; 2 Cor. 2:12; 2 Tim. 4:13
9 And a vision appeared to Paul in the night; There stood a man of Macedonia, and prayed him, saying, Come over into Macedonia, and help us.   Acts 18:5
10 And after he had seen the vision, immediately we endeavoured to go into Macedonia, assuredly gathering that the Lord had called us for to preach the gospel unto them.

Paul and Silas in Philippi
11 Therefore loosing from Troas, we came with a straight course to Samothracia, and the next *day* to Neapolis;
12 And from thence to Philippi, which is the chief city of that part of Macedonia, *and* a colony: and we were in that city abiding certain days.   Acts 20:6; Phil. 1:1; 1 Thess. 2:2
13 And on the sabbath we went out of the city by a river side, where prayer was wont to be made; and we sat down, and spake unto the women which resorted *thither*.   Acts 13:14
14 And a certain woman named Lydia, a seller of purple, of the city of Thyatira, which worshipped God, heard *us*: whose heart the Lord

opened, that she attended unto the things which were spoken of Paul. Luke 24:45; Rev. 1:11

15 And when she was baptized, and her household, she besought *us*, saying, If ye have judged me to be faithful to the Lord, come into my house, and abide *there*. And she ᵀconstrained us. Gen. 19:3; Acts 11:14; Heb. 13:2 ◆ *compelled*

Paul Frees a Girl of an Evil Spirit

16 And it came to pass, as we went to prayer, a certain damsel possessed with a spirit of divination met us, which brought her masters much gain by soothsaying: 1 Sam. 28:7

17 The same followed Paul and us, and cried, saying, These men are the servants of the most high God, which shew unto us the way of salvation. Dan. 3:26; Mark 5:7

18 And this did she many days. But Paul, being grieved, turned and said to the spirit, I command thee in the name of Jesus Christ to come out of her. And he came out the same hour. Mark 16:17

19 And when her masters saw that the hope of their gains was gone, they caught Paul and Silas, and drew *them* into the marketplace unto the rulers, Acts 8:3; 16:16; 21:30

20 And brought them to the magistrates, saying, These men, being Jews, do exceedingly trouble our city, Acts 28:22

21 And teach customs, which are not lawful for us to receive, neither to observe, being Romans. Esth. 3:8

22 And the multitude rose up together against them: and the magistrates ᵀrent off their clothes, and commanded to beat *them*. 2 Cor. 6:5; 11:23-25; 1 Thess. 2:2 ◆ *tore*

23 And when they had laid many stripes upon them, they cast *them* into prison, charging the jailor to keep them safely:

24 Who, having received such a charge, thrust them into the inner prison, and made their feet fast in the stocks. Job 13:27; 33:11; Jer. 29:26

16:23, 24 God Doesn't Forget His People

Will the Lord forget His people in this trying hour? Did He forget faithful Noah when judgments were visited upon the antediluvian world? Did He forget Lot when the fire came down from Heaven to consume the cities of the plain? Did He forget Joseph surrounded by idolaters in Egypt? Did He forget Elijah when the oath of Jezebel threatened him with the fate of the prophets of Baal? . . . or Daniel in the den of lions? *GC 626*

---

25 And at midnight Paul and Silas prayed, and sang praises unto God: and the prisoners heard them. Job 35:10

26 And suddenly there was a great earthquake, so that the foundations of the prison were shaken: and immediately all the doors

were opened, and every one's bands were loosed. Acts 4:31; 12:7, 10

The Philippian Jailer Believes

27 And the keeper of the prison awaking out of his sleep, and seeing the prison doors open, he drew out his sword, and would have killed himself, supposing that the prisoners had been fled. Acts 12:19

28 But Paul cried with a loud voice, saying, Do thyself no harm: for we are all here.

29 Then he called for a light, and sprang in, and came trembling, and fell down before Paul and Silas,

30 And brought them out, and said, Sirs, what must I do to be saved? Luke 3:10

16:30 No Peace for the Sinner

God does not send messengers to flatter the sinner. He delivers no message of peace to lull the unsanctified into fatal security. He lays heavy burdens upon the conscience of the wrongdoer, and pierces the soul with arrows of conviction. The ministering angels present to him the fearful judgments of God to deepen the sense of need, and prompt the cry, "What must I do to be saved?" *DA 104*

---

31 And they said, Believe on the Lord Jesus Christ, and thou shalt be saved, and thy house. Mark 16:16

16:31

Faith See Romans 5:1.

32 And they spake unto him the word of the Lord, and to all that were in his house.

33 And he took them the same hour of the night, and washed *their* stripes; and was baptized, he and all his, straightway. Acts 16:15

34 And when he had brought them into his house, he set meat before them, and rejoiced, believing in God with all his house. Acts 2:46

35 And when it was day, the magistrates sent the serjeants, saying, Let those men go.

36 And the keeper of the prison told this saying to Paul, The magistrates have sent to let you go: now therefore depart, and go in peace.

37 But Paul said unto them, They have beaten us openly uncondemned, being Romans, and have cast *us* into prison; and now do they thrust us out ᵀprivily? nay ᵀverily; but let them come themselves and fetch us out. Acts 22:25-29 ◆ *in secret* ◆ *truly*

38 And the serjeants told these words unto the magistrates: and they feared, when they heard that they were Romans. Acts 22:29

39 And they came and ᵀbesought them, and brought *them* out, and desired *them* to depart out of the city. Matt. 8:34 ◆ *begged*

40 And they went out of the prison, and entered into *the house of* Lydia: and when

they had seen the brethren, they comforted them, and departed.   Acts 16:14

Paul Preaches at Thessalonica

17 Now when they had passed through Amphipolis and Apollonia, they came to Thessalonica, where was a synagogue of the Jews: Acts 20:4; Phil. 4:16; 1 Thess. 1:1

2 And Paul, as his manner was, went in unto them, and three sabbath days reasoned with them out of the scriptures,   Acts 9:20

3 Opening and alleging, that Christ must needs have suffered, and risen again from the dead; and that this Jesus, whom I preach unto you, is Christ.   Acts 9:22

4 And some of them believed, and consorted with Paul and Silas; and of the devout Greeks a great multitude, and of the chief women not a few.   Acts 14:4

5 But the Jews which believed not, moved with envy, took unto them certain lewd fellows of the baser sort, and gathered a company, and set all the city on an uproar, and assaulted the house of Jason, and sought to bring them out to the people.   Acts 17:13

6 And when they found them not, they drew Jason and certain brethren unto the rulers of the city, crying, These that have turned the world upside down are come ᵀhither also;   Acts 24:5 ◆ here

17:5, 6 Maintaining Courage

Those who today teach unpopular truths need not be discouraged if at times they meet with no more favorable reception, even from those who claim to be Christians, than did Paul and his fellow workers from the people among whom they labored. The messengers of the cross must arm themselves with watchfulness and prayer, and move forward with faith and courage, working always in the name of Jesus. *AA 230*

7 Whom Jason hath received: and these all do contrary to the decrees of Caesar, saying that there is another king, *one* Jesus. Luke 23:2

8 And they troubled the people and the rulers of the city, when they heard these things.

9 And when they had taken security of Jason, and of the other, they let them go.

Paul Preaches at Berea

10 And the brethren immediately sent away Paul and Silas by night unto Berea: who coming *thither* went into the synagogue of the Jews.   Acts 17:13-14

11 These were more noble than those in Thessalonica, in that they received the word with all readiness of mind, and searched the scriptures daily, whether those things were so.   John 5:39

12 Therefore many of them believed; also of honourable women which were Greeks, and of men, not a few.   Acts 13:50

13 But when the Jews of Thessalonica had knowledge that the word of God was preached of Paul at Berea, they came thither also, and stirred up the people.

14 And then immediately the brethren sent away Paul to go as it were to the sea: but Silas and Timotheus abode there still.   Matt. 10:23

Paul Preaches in Athens

15 And they that conducted Paul brought him unto Athens: and receiving a commandment unto Silas and Timotheus for to come to him with all speed, they departed.   1 Thess. 3:1

16 Now while Paul waited for them at Athens, his spirit was stirred in him, when he saw the city wholly given to idolatry.

17 Therefore disputed he in the synagogue with the Jews, and with the devout persons, and in the market daily with them that met with him.

18 Then certain philosophers of the Epicureans, and of the Stoicks, encountered him. And some said, What will this babbler say? other some, He seemeth to be a setter forth of strange gods: because he preached unto them Jesus, and the resurrection.   Acts 4:2

19 And they took him, and brought him unto Areopagus, saying, May we know what this new doctrine, whereof thou speakest, *is?*   Mark 1:27; Acts 17:22

20 For thou bringest certain strange things to our ears: we would know therefore what these things mean.   Hos. 8:12

21 (For all the Athenians and strangers which were there spent their time in nothing else, but either to tell, or to hear some new thing.)

22 Then Paul stood in the midst of Mars' hill, and said, *Ye* men of Athens, I perceive that in all things ye are too superstitious.   Acts 25:19

23 For as I passed by, and beheld your devotions, I found an altar with this inscription, TO THE UNKNOWN GOD. Whom therefore ye ignorantly worship, him declare I unto you.   John 4:22; Acts 17:30; 2 Thess. 2:4

24 God that made the world and all things therein, seeing that he is Lord of heaven and earth, dwelleth not in temples made with hands;   Matt. 11:25; Acts 7:48; 14:15

25 Neither is worshipped with men's hands, as though he needed any thing, seeing he giveth to all life, and breath, and all things;   Job 22:2

Managing God's Gifts See 1 Chronicles 29:12.

26 And hath made of one blood all nations of men for to dwell on all the face of the earth, and hath determined the times

before appointed, and the bounds of their habitation; Mal. 2:10
27 That they should seek the Lord, if haply they might feel after him, and find him, though he be not far from every one of us:
28 For in him we live, and move, and have our being; as certain also of your own poets have said, For we are also his offspring. Dan. 5:23
29 Forasmuch then as we are the offspring of God, we ought not to think that the Godhead is like unto gold, or silver, or stone, ᵀgraven by art and man's device. *engraved or cut out*
30 And the times of this ignorance God winked at; but now commandeth all men every where to repent: Luke 24:47; Rom. 3:25
31 Because he hath appointed a day, in the which he will judge the world in righteousness by *that* man whom he hath ordained; *whereof* he hath given assurance unto all *men*, in that he hath raised him from the dead.
32 And when they heard of the resurrection of the dead, some mocked: and others said, We will hear thee again of this *matter*. Acts 2:13; 17:18; 24:25
33 So Paul departed from among them.
34 Howbeit certain men ᵀclave unto him, and believed: among the which *was* Dionysius the Areopagite, and a woman named Damaris, and others with them. Acts 17:19, 22 ◆ *clung*

Paul in Corinth

18 After these things Paul departed from Athens, and came to Corinth; Acts 19:1
2 And found a certain Jew named Aquila, born in Pontus, lately come from Italy, with his wife Priscilla; (because that Claudius had commanded all Jews to depart from Rome:) and came unto them. 1 Cor. 16:19; 2 Tim. 4:19
3 And because he was of the same craft, he abode with them, and wrought: for by their occupation they were tentmakers. 1 Thess. 2:9

> **18:3 Paul's Vocation**
>
> Before he became a disciple of Christ, Paul had occupied a high position and was not dependent upon manual labor for support. But afterward, when he had used all his means in furthering the cause of Christ, he resorted at times to his trade to gain a livelihood. *AA 347*

4 And he reasoned in the synagogue every sabbath, and persuaded the Jews and the Greeks. Acts 17:17

> The Sabbath See Isaiah 66:23.

5 And when Silas and Timotheus were come from Macedonia, Paul was pressed in the spirit, and testified to the Jews *that* Jesus *was* Christ. Acts 17:3; 18:28; 20:21
6 And when they opposed themselves, and blasphemed, he shook *his* raiment, and said

unto them, Your blood *be* upon your own heads; I *am* clean: from henceforth I will go unto the Gentiles. 2 Sam. 1:16; Ezek. 18:13; 33:4
7 And he departed thence, and entered into a certain *man's* house, named Justus, *one* that worshipped God, whose house joined hard to the synagogue. Acts 16:14; Col. 4:11
8 And Crispus, the chief ruler of the synagogue, believed on the Lord with all his house; and many of the Corinthians hearing believed, and were baptized. Acts 8:12
9 Then spake the Lord to Paul in the night by a vision, Be not afraid, but speak, and hold not thy peace: Acts 23:11
10 For I am with thee, and no man shall set on thee to hurt thee: for I have much people in this city. Matt. 28:20
11 And he continued *there* a year and six months, teaching the word of God among them.

The Jews Attack Paul

12 And when Gallio was the deputy of Achaia, the Jews made insurrection with one accord against Paul, and brought him to the judgment seat, Acts 13:7
13 Saying, This *fellow* persuadeth men to worship God contrary to the law.
14 And when Paul was now about to open *his* mouth, Gallio said unto the Jews, If it were a matter of wrong or wicked lewdness, O *ye* Jews, reason would that I should bear with you:
15 But if it be a question of words and names, and *of* your law, look ye *to it*; for I will be no judge of such *matters*. Acts 23:29
16 And he drave them from the judgment seat.
17 Then all the Greeks took Sosthenes, the chief ruler of the synagogue, and beat *him* before the judgment seat. And Gallio cared for none of those things. 1 Cor. 1:1

Paul's Return to Antioch

18 And Paul *after this* tarried *there* yet a good while, and then took his leave of the brethren, and sailed thence into Syria, and with him Priscilla and Aquila; having shorn *his* head in Cenchrea: for he had a vow. Num. 6:18; Rom. 16:1

> **18:18 Paul's Vital Presence**
>
> If the apostle had at this time been compelled to leave Corinth, the converts to the faith of Jesus would have been placed in a perilous position. The Jews would have endeavored to follow up the advantage gained, even to the extermination of Christianity in that region. *AA 254*

19 And he came to Ephesus, and left them there: but he himself entered into the synagogue, and reasoned with the Jews.

20 When they desired *him* to tarry longer time with them, he consented not;
21 But bade them farewell, saying, I must by all means keep this feast that cometh in Jerusalem: but I will return again unto you, if God will. And he sailed from Ephesus.   Rom. 1:10; 1 Cor. 4:19; James 4:15
22 And when he had landed at Caesarea, and gone up, and saluted the church, he went down to Antioch.   Acts 8:40
23 And after he had spent some time *there*, he departed, and went over *all* the country of Galatia and Phrygia in order, strengthening all the disciples.   Acts 14:22; 15:32; 16:6

Apollos Learns from Priscilla and Aquila

24 And a certain Jew named Apollos, born at Alexandria, an eloquent man, *and* mighty in the scriptures, came to Ephesus. 1 Cor. 1:12; 4:6
25 This man was instructed in the way of the Lord; and being fervent in the spirit, he spake and taught diligently the things of the Lord, knowing only the baptism of John. Rom. 12:11
26 And he began to speak boldly in the synagogue: whom when Aquila and Priscilla had heard, they took him unto *them*, and expounded unto him the way of God more perfectly.
27 And when he was disposed to pass into Achaia, the brethren wrote, ᵀexhorting the disciples to receive him: who, when he was come, helped them much which had believed through grace: Acts 18:18 ♦ *encouraging*
28 For he mightily convinced the Jews, *and that* publickly, shewing by the scriptures that Jesus was Christ.   Acts 9:22; 18:5

> **18:24–28 One Sows, Another Waters**
>
> Later, by God's direction, other workers were brought in, to stand in their lot and place. The seed sown must be watered, and this Apollos was to do. He followed Paul in his work, to give further instruction, and to help the seed sown to develop. He won his way to the hearts of the people, but it was God who gave the increase. It is not human, but divine power, that works transformation of character. *AA 274*

Paul in Ephesus

19 And it came to pass, that, while Apollos was at Corinth, Paul having passed through the upper coasts came to Ephesus: and finding certain disciples,   1 Cor. 1:12
2 He said unto them, Have ye received the Holy Ghost since ye believed? And they said unto him, We have not so much as heard whether there be any Holy Ghost. John 7:39
3 And he said unto them, Unto what then

19:1-7

were ye baptized? And they said, Unto John's baptism.   Acts 18:25
4 Then said Paul, John ᵀverily baptized with the baptism of repentance, saying unto the people, that they should believe on him which should come after him, that is, on Christ Jesus.   John 1:7 ♦ *truly*
5 When they heard *this*, they were baptized in the name of the Lord Jesus. Acts 2:38; 8:12, 16

> **19:3–5 Rebaptism of Some**
>
> When [the Ephesians] received baptism at the hand of John they did not fully comprehend the mission of Jesus as the Sin Bearer. They were holding serious errors. But with clearer light, they gladly accepted Christ as their Redeemer, and with this step of advance came a change in their obligations. As they received a purer faith, there was a corresponding change in their life. In token of this change, and as an acknowledgment of their faith in Christ, they were rebaptized in the name of Jesus. *AA 285*

6 And when Paul had laid *his* hands upon them, the Holy Ghost came on them; and they spake with tongues, and prophesied. Mark 16:17
7 And all the men were about twelve.

> Baptism/Lord's Supper See Matthew 3:16.

The Jews Reject Paul's Teachings

8 And he went into the synagogue, and spake boldly for the space of three months, disputing and persuading the things concerning the kingdom of God.   Acts 1:3; 28:23
9 But when ᵀdivers were hardened, and believed not, but spake evil of that way before the multitude, he departed from them, and separated the disciples, disputing daily in the school of one Tyrannus. Acts 9:2; 14:4; 19:23 ♦ *some*
10 And this continued by the space of two years; so that all they which dwelt in Asia heard the word of the Lord Jesus, both Jews and Greeks.   Acts 16:6; 20:31; 2 Tim. 1:15
11 And God ᵀwrought special miracles by the hands of Paul: Acts 5:12 ♦ *did*
12 So that from his body were brought unto the sick handkerchiefs or aprons, and the diseases departed from them, and the evil spirits went out of them.   Acts 5:15

Many in Ephesus Believe

13 Then certain of the vagabond Jews, exorcists, took upon them to call over them which had evil spirits the name of the Lord Jesus, saying, We ᵀadjure you by Jesus whom Paul preacheth. Matt. 12:27; Mark 9:38; Luke 11:19 ♦ *appeal to*
14 And there were seven sons of *one* Sceva, a Jew, *and* chief of the priests, which did so.
15 And the evil spirit answered and said,

Jesus I know, and Paul I know; but who are ye?

16 And the man in whom the evil spirit was leaped on them, and overcame them, and prevailed against them, so that they fled out of that house naked and wounded.

17 And this was known to all the Jews and Greeks also dwelling at Ephesus; and fear fell on them all, and the name of the Lord Jesus was magnified.   Acts 5:5

19:11–17 Christ's Sacred Name

Thus unmistakable proof was given of the sacredness of the name of Christ, and the peril which they incurred who should invoke it without faith in the divinity of the Saviour's mission. "Fear fell on them all, and the name of the Lord Jesus was magnified" [Acts 19:17]. *AA 288*

18 And many that believed came, and confessed, and shewed their deeds.   Matt. 3:6

19 Many of them also which used ᵀcurious arts brought their books together, and burned them before all *men*: and they counted the price of them, and found *it* fifty thousand *pieces* of silver.   *magic*

20 So mightly grew the word of God and prevailed.   Acts 6:7; 12:24

21 After these things were ended, Paul purposed in the spirit, when he had passed through Macedonia and Achaia, to go to Jerusalem, saying, After I have been there, I must also see Rome.   Acts 18:21; 20:16, 22

22 So he sent into Macedonia two of them that ministered unto him, Timotheus and Erastus; but he himself stayed in Asia for a season.   Acts 13:5; Rom. 16:23; 2 Tim. 4:20

A Riot Erupts

23 And the same time there arose no small stir about that way.   Acts 19:9

24 For a certain *man* named Demetrius, a silversmith, which made silver shrines for Diana, brought no small gain unto the craftsmen;   Acts 16:16

25 Whom he called together with the workmen of like occupation, and said, Sirs, ye know that by this craft we have our wealth.   Acts 16:19

26 Moreover ye see and hear, that not alone at Ephesus, but almost throughout all Asia, this Paul hath persuaded and turned away much people, saying that they be no gods, which are made with hands: Is. 44:10-20; Acts 17:29; 1 Cor. 8:4

27 So that not only this our craft is in danger to be set at ᵀnought; but also that the temple of the great goddess Diana should be despised, and her magnificence should be destroyed, whom all Asia and the world worshippeth.   *nothing*

28 And when they heard *these sayings*, they were full of wrath, and cried out, saying, Great *is* Diana of the Ephesians.

29 And the whole city was filled with confusion: and having caught Gaius and Aristarchus, men of Macedonia, Paul's companions in travel, they rushed with one accord into the theatre.   Acts 20:4; 27:2; Col. 4:10

30 And when Paul would have entered in unto the people, the disciples suffered him not.

31 And certain of the chief of Asia, which were his friends, sent unto him, desiring *him* that he would not adventure himself into the theatre.

32 Some therefore cried one thing, and some another: for the assembly was confused; and the more part knew not wherefore they were come together.   Acts 21:34

33 And they drew Alexander out of the multitude, the Jews putting him forward. And Alexander beckoned with the hand, and would have made his defence unto the people.

34 But when they knew that he was a Jew, all with one voice about the space of two hours cried out, Great *is* Diana of the Ephesians.

35 And when the townclerk had appeased the people, he said, *Ye* men of Ephesus, what man is there that knoweth not how that the city of the Ephesians is a worshipper of the great goddess Diana, and of the *image* which fell down from Jupiter?

36 Seeing then that these things cannot be spoken against, ye ought to be quiet, and to do nothing rashly.

37 For ye have brought hither these men, which are neither robbers of churches, nor yet blasphemers of your goddess.   Rom. 2:22

38 Wherefore if Demetrius, and the craftsmen which are with him, have a matter against any man, the law is open, and there are deputies: let them ᵀimplead one another.   Acts 13:7 ♦ *accuse*

39 But if ye enquire any thing concerning other matters, it shall be determined in a lawful assembly.

40 For we are in danger to be called in question for this day's uproar, there being no cause whereby we may give an account of this concourse.

41 And when he had thus spoken, he dismissed the assembly.

Paul Goes to Macedonia

20 And after the uproar was ceased, Paul called unto *him* the disciples, and embraced *them*, and departed for to go into Macedonia.   Acts 19:21

2 And when he had gone over those parts, and had given them much ᵀexhortation, he came into Greece,   *encouragement*

3 And *there* abode three months. And when the Jews laid wait for him, as he was about to sail into Syria, he purposed to return through Macedonia.   Acts 9:23-24; 20:19; 25:3
4 And there accompanied him into Asia Sopater of Berea; and of the Thessalonians, Aristarchus and Secundus; and Gaius of Derbe, and Timotheus; and of Asia, Tychicus and Trophimus.   Acts 16:1; 19:29; 21:29
5 These going before tarried for us at Troas.

Paul in Troas
6 And we sailed away from Philippi after the days of unleavened bread, and came unto them to Troas in five days; where we abode seven days.   Acts 12:3
7 And upon the first *day* of the week, when the disciples came together to break bread, Paul preached unto them, ready to depart on the morrow; and continued his speech until midnight.   Acts 20:11; 1 Cor. 16:2; Rev. 1:10
8 And there were many lights in the upper chamber, where they were gathered together.   Acts 1:13
9 And there sat in a window a certain young man named Eutychus, being fallen into a deep sleep: and as Paul was long preaching, he sunk down with sleep, and fell down from the third loft, and was taken up dead.
10 And Paul went down, and fell on him, and embracing *him* said, Trouble not yourselves; for his life is in him.   Mark 5:39
11 When he therefore was come up again, and had broken bread, and eaten, and talked a long while, even till break of day, so he departed.   Acts 20:7
12 And they brought the young man alive, and were not a little comforted.

Paul's Trip to Miletus
13 And we went before to ship, and sailed unto Assos, there intending to take in Paul: for so had he appointed, minding himself to go afoot.
14 And when he met with us at Assos, we took him in, and came to Mitylene.
15 And we sailed thence, and came the next *day* over against Chios; and the next *day* we arrived at Samos, and tarried at Trogyllium; and the next *day* we came to Miletus. Acts 20:17
16 For Paul had determined to sail by Ephesus, because he would not spend the time in Asia: for he hasted, if it were possible for him, to be at Jerusalem the day of Pentecost.   Acts 2:1; 19:21; 1 Cor. 16:8

Paul Meets with the Ephesian Elders
17 And from Miletus he sent to Ephesus, and called the elders of the church. Acts 11:30
18 And when they were come to him, he said unto them, Ye know, from the first day that I came into Asia, after what manner I have been with you at all seasons, Acts 18:19; 19:1, 10
19 Serving the Lord with all humility of mind, and with many tears, and temptations, which befell me by the lying in wait of the Jews: Acts 20:3, 31; Rom. 12:11
20 *And* how I kept back nothing that was profitable *unto you*, but have shewed you, and have taught you publickly, and from house to house,   Acts 5:42; 20:27, 31
21 Testifying both to the Jews, and also to the Greeks, repentance toward God, and faith toward our Lord Jesus Christ. Acts 2:38; 11:18; 20:24
22 And now, behold, I go bound in the spirit unto Jerusalem, not knowing the things that shall befall me there:
23 Save that the Holy Ghost witnesseth in

Divine Aid in Service

Acts 20

To the consecrated worker there is wonderful consolation in the knowledge that even Christ during His life on earth sought His Father daily for fresh supplies of needed grace; and from this communion with God He went forth to strengthen and bless others. Behold the Son of God bowed in prayer to His Father! Though He is the Son of God, He strengthens His faith by prayer, and by communion with heaven gathers to Himself power to resist evil and to minister to the needs of men. As the Elder Brother of our race He knows the necessities of those who, compassed with infirmity and living in a world of sin and temptation, still desire to serve Him. He knows that the messengers whom He sees fit to send are weak, erring men; but to all who give themselves wholly to His service He promises divine aid. His own example is an assurance that earnest, persevering supplication to God in faith—faith that leads to entire dependence upon God, and unreserved consecration to His work—will avail to bring to men the Holy Spirit's aid in the battle against sin.

Every worker who follows the example of Christ will be prepared to receive and use the power that God has promised to His church for the ripening of earth's harvest. Morning by morning, as the heralds of the gospel kneel before the Lord and renew their vows of consecration to Him, He will grant them the presence of His Spirit, with its reviving, sanctifying power. As they go forth to the day's duties, they have the assurance that the unseen agency of the Holy Spirit enables them to be "laborers together with God." *AA 56*

every city, saying that bonds and afflictions abide me.   Acts 9:16; 14:22; 21:4

24 But none of these things move me, neither count I my life dear unto myself, so that I might finish my course with joy, and the ministry, which I have received of the Lord Jesus, to testify the gospel of the grace of God.   Acts 1:17; 21:13; 2 Cor. 4:1

25 And now, behold, I know that ye all, among whom I have gone preaching the kingdom of God, shall see my face no more.   Acts 28:31

26 Wherefore I take you to record this day, that I *am* pure from the blood of all *men*.

27 For I have not shunned to declare unto you all the counsel of God.   Luke 7:30; Acts 2:23; 20:20

28 Take heed therefore unto yourselves, and to all the flock, over the which the Holy Ghost hath made you overseers, to feed the church of God, which he hath purchased with his own blood.   Is. 40:11; Mic. 7:14; 1 Cor. 10:32

29 For I know this, that after my departing shall grievous wolves enter in among you, not sparing the flock.   Matt. 7:15; John 10:12; Acts 20:28

> **20:29 Paul's Fears for the Church**
>
> Paul trembled for the church as, looking into the future, he saw the attacks which she must suffer from both external and internal foes. With solemn earnestness he bade his brethren guard vigilantly their sacred trusts. *AA 395*

30 Also of your own selves shall men arise, speaking perverse things, to draw away disciples after them.   1 Tim. 1:19-20

31 Therefore watch, and remember, that by the space of three years I ceased not to warn every one night and day with tears. Heb. 13:17

32 And now, brethren, I commend you to God, and to the word of his grace, which is able to build you up, and to give you an inheritance among all them which are ᵀsanctified.   Acts 14:23; 26:18; Col. 1:12 ♦ *made holy*

33 I have ᵀcoveted no man's silver, or gold, or apparel.   1 Cor. 9:12; 2 Cor. 7:2; 11:9 ♦ *desired*

> **20:33 Paul Not a Wealth Seeker**
>
> Some of the Ephesian brethren were wealthy, but Paul had never sought personal benefit from them. It was no part of his message to call attention to his own wants. *AA 395*

34 Yea, ye yourselves know, that these hands have ministered unto my necessities, and to them that were with me.   Acts 18:3

35 I have shewed you all things, how that so labouring ye ought to support the weak, and to remember the words of the Lord Jesus, how he said, It is more blessed to give than to receive.   Prov. 19:17

> **20:35 Doing Big Things for God**
>
> The apostle Paul in his ministry among the churches was untiring in his efforts to inspire in the hearts of the new converts a desire to do large things for the cause of God. Often he exhorted them to the exercise of liberality. *AA 342*

36 And when he had thus spoken, he kneeled down, and prayed with them all.   Luke 22:41

37 And they all wept sore, and fell on Paul's neck, and kissed him,   Luke 15:20

38 Sorrowing most of all for the words which he spake, that they should see his face no more. And they accompanied him unto the ship.   Acts 15:3

Paul in Tyre

21 And it came to pass, that after we were gotten from them, and had launched, we came with a straight course unto Coos, and the *day* following unto Rhodes, and from thence unto Patara:

2 And finding a ship sailing over unto Phenicia, we went aboard, and set forth.

3 Now when we had discovered Cyprus, we left it on the left hand, and sailed into Syria, and landed at Tyre: for there the ship was to ᵀunlade her burden.   Matt. 4:24 ♦ *unload*

4 And finding disciples, we tarried there seven days: who said to Paul through the Spirit, that he should not go up to Jerusalem.

5 And when we had accomplished those days, we departed and went our way; and they all brought us on our way, with wives and children, till *we were* out of the city: and we kneeled down on the shore, and prayed.   Acts 9:40; 15:3; 20:36

6 And when we had taken our leave one of another, we took ship; and they returned home again.   John 19:27

7 And when we had finished *our* course from Tyre, we came to Ptolemais, and saluted the brethren, and abode with them one day.

Paul in Caesarea

8 And the next *day* we that were of Paul's company departed, and came unto Caesarea: and we entered into the house of Philip the evangelist, which was *one* of the seven; and abode with him.   Acts 6:5; Eph. 4:11; 2 Tim. 4:5

9 And the same man had four daughters, virgins, which did prophesy.   Acts 2:17

10 And as we tarried *there* many days, there came down from Judaea a certain prophet, named Agabus.   Acts 11:28

11 And when he was come unto us, he took Paul's ᵀgirdle, and bound his own hands and feet, and said, Thus saith the Holy Ghost, So shall the Jews at Jerusalem

bind the man that owneth this girdle, and shall deliver *him* into the hands of the Gentiles.   1 Sam. 15:27-28; Jer. 13:1-11; Acts 21:33 ◆ *belt*

12 And when we heard these things, both we, and they of that place, ^Tbesought him not to go up to Jerusalem.   Matt. 16:21-23 ◆ *begged*

13 Then Paul answered, What mean ye to weep and to break mine heart? for I am ready not to be bound only, but also to die at Jerusalem for the name of the Lord Jesus.   Acts 20:24; Phil. 2:17

14 And when he would not be persuaded, we ceased, saying, The will of the Lord be done.   Matt. 6:10

Paul in Jerusalem

15 And after those days we took up our carriages, and went up to Jerusalem.

16 There went with us also *certain* of the disciples of Caesarea, and brought with them one Mnason of Cyprus, an old disciple, with whom we should lodge.

17 And when we were come to Jerusalem, the brethren received us gladly.   Acts 15:4

18 And the *day* following Paul went in with us unto James; and all the elders were present.   Acts 11:30

19 And when he had saluted them, he declared particularly what things God had ^Twrought among the Gentiles by his ministry.   Acts 1:17; 14:27; Rom. 15:18-19 ◆ *done*

20 And when they heard *it*, they glorified the Lord, and said unto him, Thou seest, brother, how many thousands of Jews there are which believe; and they are all zealous of the law.   Acts 22:3; Rom. 10:2; Gal. 1:14

21 And they are informed of thee, that thou teachest all the Jews which are among the Gentiles to forsake Moses, saying that they ought not to circumcise *their* children, neither to walk after the customs.   Acts 21:28

22 What is it therefore? the multitude must needs come together: for they will hear that thou art come.

23 Do therefore this that we say to thee: We have four men which have a vow on them;   Acts 18:18

24 Them take, and purify thyself with them, and be at charges with them, that they may shave *their* heads: and all may know that those things, whereof they were informed concerning thee, are nothing; but *that* thou thyself also walkest orderly, and keepest the law.   Acts 18:18; 21:26; 24:18

25 As touching the Gentiles which believe, we have written *and* concluded that they observe no such thing, save only that they keep themselves from *things* offered to idols, and from blood, and from strangled, and from fornication.   Acts 15:29

26 Then Paul took the men, and the next day purifying himself with them entered into the temple, to signify the accomplishment of the days of purification, until that an offering should be offered for every one of them.   Num. 6:13-20; Acts 24:18

Paul Is Arrested

27 And when the seven days were almost ended, the Jews which were of Asia, when they saw him in the temple, stirred up all the people, and laid hands on him,   Acts 13:50; 24:18

28 Crying out, Men of Israel, help: This is the man, that teacheth all *men* every where against the people, and the law, and this place: and further brought Greeks also into the temple, and hath polluted this holy place.   Acts 21:21; 24:5-6

> **21:28 Reproving Sin Brings Opposition**
>
> Now as in former ages, the presentation of a truth that reproves the sins and errors of the times will excite opposition. . . . As men see that they cannot maintain their position by the Scriptures, many determine to maintain it at all hazards, and with a malicious spirit they assail the character and motives of those who stand in defense of unpopular truth. *GC 458*

29 (For they had seen before with him in the city Trophimus an Ephesian, whom they supposed that Paul had brought into the temple.)   Acts 20:4

30 And all the city was moved, and the people ran together: and they took Paul, and drew him out of the temple: and ^Tforthwith the doors were shut.   Acts 26:21 ◆ *immediately*

31 And as they went about to kill him, tidings came unto the chief captain of the band, that all Jerusalem was in an uproar.

32 Who immediately took soldiers and ^Tcenturions, and ran down unto them: and when they saw the chief captain and the soldiers, they left beating of Paul.   *commanders of 100 soldiers*

33 Then the chief captain came near, and took him, and commanded *him* to be bound with two chains; and demanded who he was, and what he had done.   Acts 12:6; 20:23; 21:11

34 And some cried one thing, some another, among the multitude: and when he could not know the certainty for the tumult, he commanded him to be carried into the castle.   Acts 19:32; 21:37; 23:10

35 And when he came upon the stairs, so it was, that he was borne of the soldiers for the violence of the people.

36 For the multitude of the people followed after, crying, Away with him.   Luke 23:18

37 And as Paul was to be led into the castle, he said unto the chief captain, May I speak

unto thee? Who said, Canst thou speak Greek?

38 Art not thou that Egyptian, which before these days madest an uproar, and leddest out into the wilderness four thousand men that were murderers?   Matt. 24:26

39 But Paul said, I am a man *which am* a Jew of Tarsus, *a city* in Cilicia, a citizen of no mean city: and, I ᵀbeseech thee, suffer me to speak unto the people.   Acts 6:9; 9:11; 22:3 ◆ *beg*

40 And when he had given him licence, Paul stood on the stairs, and beckoned with the hand unto the people. And when there was made a great silence, he spake unto *them* in the Hebrew tongue, saying,   John 5:2; Acts 12:17; 22:2

21:40 A Calm Apostle

In the midst of the tumult the apostle [Paul] was calm and self-possessed. His mind was stayed upon God, and he knew that angels of heaven were about him. He felt unwilling to leave the temple without making an effort to set the truth before his countrymen. *AA 408*

Paul Speaks in His Own Defense

22 Men, brethren, and fathers, hear ye my defence *which I make* now unto you.

2 (And when they heard that he spake in the Hebrew tongue to them, they kept the more silence: and he saith,)   Acts 21:40

3 I am ᵀverily a man *which am* a Jew, born in Tarsus, *a city* in Cilicia, yet brought up in this city at the feet of Gamaliel, *and* taught according to the perfect manner of the law of the fathers, and was zealous toward God, as ye all are this day. Acts 5:34; 9:11; 21:20 ◆ *truly*

4 And I persecuted this way unto the death, binding and delivering into prisons both men and women.   Acts 22:19-20

5 As also the high priest doth bear me witness, and all the estate of the elders: from whom also I received letters unto the brethren, and went to Damascus, to bring them which were there bound unto Jerusalem, for to be punished.   Luke 22:66; Acts 5:21; 9:1-2

6 And it came to pass, that, as I made my journey, and was come nigh unto Damascus about noon, suddenly there shone from heaven a great light round about me.

7 And I fell unto the ground, and heard a voice saying unto me, Saul, Saul, why persecutest thou me?

8 And I answered, Who art thou, Lord? And he said unto me, I am Jesus of Nazareth, whom thou persecutest.

9 And they that were with me saw indeed the light, and were afraid; but they heard not the voice of him that spake to me. Dan. 10:7; Acts 9:7

22:1–21 Paul's Personal Testimony

None could deny the apostle's statements, as the facts that he referred to were well known to many who were still living in Jerusalem. He then spoke of his former zeal in persecuting the disciples of Christ, even unto death; and he narrated the circumstances of his conversion, telling his hearers how his own proud heart had been led to bow to the crucified Nazarene. *AA 409*

10 And I said, What shall I do, Lord? And the Lord said unto me, Arise, and go into Damascus; and there it shall be told thee of all things which are appointed for thee to do.

11 And when I could not see for the glory of that light, being led by the hand of them that were with me, I came into Damascus.

12 And one Ananias, a devout man according to the law, having a good report of all the Jews which dwelt *there*,   Acts 6:3; 10:22

13 Came unto me, and stood, and said unto me, Brother Saul, receive thy sight. And the same hour I looked up upon him.

14 And he said, The God of our fathers hath chosen thee, that thou shouldest know his will, and see that Just One, and shouldest hear the voice of his mouth.   1 Cor. 9:1; 15:8

15 For thou shalt be his witness unto all men of what thou hast seen and heard.   Acts 4:20

16 And now why tarriest thou? arise, and be baptized, and wash away thy sins, calling on the name of the Lord.   1 Cor. 6:11; Heb. 10:22

17 And it came to pass, that, when I was come again to Jerusalem, even while I prayed in the temple, I was in a trance;   2 Cor. 12:1-4

18 And saw him saying unto me, Make haste, and get thee quickly out of Jerusalem: for they will not receive thy testimony concerning me.

19 And I said, Lord, they know that I imprisoned and beat in every synagogue them that believed on thee: Matt. 10:17; Acts 8:3; 22:4

20 And when the blood of thy martyr Stephen was shed, I also was standing by, and consenting unto his death, and kept the ᵀraiment of them that slew him.   Acts 7:58; Rom. 1:32 ◆ *clothing*

21 And he said unto me, Depart: for I will send thee far hence unto the Gentiles. Acts 9:15

22:22 A Fury Born of Exclusivity

Hitherto the people had listened with close attention, but when Paul reached the point in his history where he was appointed Christ's ambassador to the Gentiles, their fury broke forth anew. Accustomed to look upon themselves as the only people favored by God, they were unwilling to permit the despised Gentiles to share the privileges which had hitherto been regarded as exclusively their own. *AA 409, 410*

The Jews Denounce Paul

22 And they gave him audience unto this word, and *then* lifted up their voices, and said, Away with such a *fellow* from the earth: for it is not fit that he should live.   Acts 21:36; 25:24
23 And as they cried out, and cast off *their* clothes, and threw dust into the air,
24 The chief captain commanded him to be brought into the castle, and bade that he should be examined by ᵀscourging; that he might know wherefore they cried so against him.   Acts 21:34 ◆ *whipping*
25 And as they bound him with thongs, Paul said unto the centurion that stood by, Is it lawful for you to ᵀscourge a man that is a Roman, and uncondemned?   Acts 16:37 ◆ *whip*
26 When the centurion heard *that*, he went and told the chief captain, saying, Take heed what thou doest: for this man is a Roman.
27 Then the chief captain came, and said unto him, Tell me, art thou a Roman? He said, Yea.
28 And the chief captain answered, With a great sum obtained I this freedom. And Paul said, But I was *free* born.
29 Then ᵀstraightway they departed from him which should have examined him: and the chief captain also was afraid, after he knew that he was a Roman, and because he had bound him.   *right away*
30 On the morrow, because he would have known the certainty wherefore he was accused of the Jews, he loosed him from *his* bands, and commanded the chief priests and all their council to appear, and brought Paul down, and set him before them. Acts 21:33; 23:28

Paul Before the Jewish Council

23 And Paul, earnestly beholding the council, said, Men *and* brethren, I have lived in all good conscience before God until this day.   Acts 24:16; 2 Cor. 1:12; 2 Tim. 1:3
2 And the high priest Ananias commanded them that stood by him to smite him on the mouth.   1 Kin. 22:24; John 18:22; Acts 24:1
3 Then said Paul unto him, God shall ᵀsmite thee, *thou* whited wall: for sittest thou to judge me after the law, and commandest me to be smitten contrary to the law?   Deut. 25:1-2; John 7:51 ◆ *strike*
4 And they that stood by said, Revilest thou God's high priest?
5 Then said Paul, I ᵀwist not, brethren, that he was the high priest: for it is written, Thou shalt not speak evil of the ruler of thy people.   Ex. 22:28 ◆ *knew*
6 But when Paul perceived that the one part were Sadducees, and the other Pharisees, he cried out in the council, Men *and* brethren, I am a Pharisee, the son of a Pharisee: of

the hope and resurrection of the dead I am called in question.   Acts 24:15, 21; Phil. 3:5
7 And when he had so said, there arose a dissension between the Pharisees and the Sadducees: and the multitude was divided.
8 For the Sadducees say that there is no resurrection, neither angel, nor spirit: but the Pharisees confess both.   Matt. 22:23
9 And there arose a great cry: and the scribes *that were* of the Pharisees' part arose, and strove, saying, We find no evil in this man: but if a spirit or an angel hath spoken to him, let us not fight against God. John 12:29; Acts 22:7
10 And when there arose a great dissension, the chief captain, fearing lest Paul should have been pulled in pieces of them, commanded the soldiers to go down, and to take him by force from among them, and to bring *him* into the castle.   Acts 22:24

23:10 Paul's Anguish

The position which the Jews as God's professed people occupied before an unbelieving world, caused the apostle intense anguish of spirit. How would those heathen officers look upon them?—claiming to be worshipers of Jehovah, and assuming sacred office, yet giving themselves up to the control of blind, unreasoning anger, seeking to destroy even their brethren who dared to differ with them in religious faith, and turning their most solemn deliberative council into a scene of strife and wild confusion. *AA 412*

11 And the night following the Lord stood by him, and said, Be of good cheer, Paul: for as thou hast testified of me in Jerusalem, so must thou bear witness also at Rome.   Matt. 9:2; Acts 18:9; 19:21

23:11 Frustrated by Enmity

Paul had long looked forward to visiting Rome; he greatly desired to witness for Christ there, but had felt that his purposes were frustrated by the enmity of the Jews. He little thought, even now, that it would be as a prisoner that he would go. *AA 413*

Some Jews Plot to Kill Paul

12 And when it was day, certain of the Jews banded together, and bound themselves under a curse, saying that they would neither eat nor drink till they had killed Paul.   Acts 23:14, 21, 30
13 And they were more than forty which had made this conspiracy.
14 And they came to the chief priests and elders, and said, We have bound ourselves under a great curse, that we will eat nothing until we have slain Paul.
15 Now therefore ye with the council signify

to the chief captain that he bring him down unto you to morrow, as though ye would enquire something more perfectly concerning him: and we, or ever he come near, are ready to kill him.

16 And when Paul's sister's son heard of their lying in wait, he went and entered into the castle, and told Paul.   Acts 23:10

17 Then Paul called one of the ᵀcenturions unto *him*, and said, Bring this young man unto the chief captain: for he hath a certain thing to tell him.   *commanders of 100 soldiers*

18 So he took him, and brought *him* to the chief captain, and said, Paul the prisoner called me unto *him*, and prayed me to bring this young man unto thee, who hath something to say unto thee.   Eph. 3:1

19 Then the chief captain took him by the hand, and went *with him* aside privately, and asked *him*, What is that thou hast to tell me?

20 And he said, The Jews have agreed to desire thee that thou wouldest bring down Paul to morrow into the council, as though they would enquire somewhat of him more perfectly.   Acts 23:14-15

21 But do not thou yield unto them: for there lie in wait for him of them more than forty men, which have bound themselves with an oath, that they will neither eat nor drink till they have killed him: and now are they ready, looking for a promise from thee.   Acts 23:12-14

22 So the chief captain *then* let the young man depart, and charged *him, See thou* tell no man that thou hast shewed these things to me.

23 And he called unto *him* two centurions, saying, Make ready two hundred soldiers to go to Caesarea, and horsemen ᵀthreescore and ten, and spearmen two hundred, at the third hour of the night;   *sixty*

24 And provide *them* beasts, that they may set Paul on, and bring *him* safe unto Felix the governor.   Acts 23:26; 24:10; 25:14

25 And he wrote a letter after this manner:

26 Claudius Lysias unto the most excellent governor Felix *sendeth* greeting.   Luke 1:3

27 This man was taken of the Jews, and should have been killed of them: then came I with an army, and rescued him, having understood that he was a Roman.   Acts 22:25-29

28 And when I would have known the cause wherefore they accused him, I brought him forth into their council: Acts 22:30

29 Whom I perceived to be accused of questions of their law, but to have nothing laid to his charge worthy of death or of bonds.   Acts 18:15; 25:25; 26:31

30 And when it was told me how that the Jews laid wait for the man, I sent ᵀstraightway to thee, and gave commandment to his accusers also to say before thee what *they had* against him. Farewell. Acts 23:20 ◆ *right away*

31 Then the soldiers, as it was commanded them, took Paul, and brought *him* by night to Antipatris.

32 On the morrow they left the horsemen to go with him, and returned to the castle:

33 Who, when they came to Caesarea, and delivered the epistle to the governor, presented Paul also before him.

34 And when the governor had read *the letter*, he asked of what province he was. And when he understood that *he was* of Cilicia; Acts 21:39

35 I will hear thee, said he, when thine accusers are also come. And he commanded him to be kept in Herod's judgment hall.   Matt. 27:27

Paul Presents His Case to Felix

24 And after five days Ananias the high priest descended with the elders, and *with* a certain orator *named* Tertullus, who informed the governor against Paul. Acts 23:2

2 And when he was called forth, Tertullus began to accuse *him,* saying, Seeing that by thee we enjoy great quietness, and that very worthy deeds are done unto this nation by thy providence,

3 We accept *it* always, and in all places, most noble Felix, with all thankfulness.   Acts 23:26

4 Notwithstanding, that I be not further tedious unto thee, I pray thee that thou wouldest hear us of thy clemency a few words.

5 For we have found this man *a* pestilent *fellow,* and a mover of sedition among all the Jews throughout the world, and a ringleader of the sect of the Nazarenes: Acts 15:5; 28:22

6 Who also hath gone about to profane the temple: whom we took, and would have judged according to our law.

7 But the chief captain Lysias came *upon us,* and with great violence took *him* away out of our hands,

8 Commanding his accusers to come unto thee: by examining of whom thyself mayest take knowledge of all these things, whereof we accuse him.

9 And the Jews also ᵀassented, saying that these things were so.   *agreed*

10 Then Paul, after that the governor had beckoned unto him to speak, answered, Forasmuch as I know that thou hast been of many years a judge unto this nation, I do the more cheerfully answer for myself:

11 Because that thou mayest understand, that there are yet but twelve days since I went up to Jerusalem for to worship.   Acts 24:1

12 And they neither found me in the temple disputing with any man, neither raising up the people, neither in the synagogues, nor in the city: Acts 25:8; 28:17

13 Neither can they prove the things whereof they now accuse me.   Acts 25:7
14 But this I confess unto thee, that after the way which they call heresy, so worship I the God of my fathers, believing all things which are written in the law and in the prophets: Acts 3:13; 9:2; 24:5
15 And have hope toward God, which they themselves also allow, that there shall be a resurrection of the dead, both of the just and unjust.   Dan. 12:2; John 5:28-29
16 And herein do I exercise myself, to have always a conscience void of offence toward God, and *toward* men.   Acts 23:1
17 Now after many years I came to bring alms to my nation, and offerings.   Acts 11:29; Gal. 2:10
18 Whereupon certain Jews from Asia found me purified in the temple, neither with multitude, nor with tumult.   Acts 26:21
19 Who ought to have been here before thee, and object, if they had ought against me.
20 Or else let these same *here* say, if they have found any evil doing in me, while I stood before the council,
21 Except it be for this one voice, that I cried standing among them, Touching the resurrection of the dead I am called in question by you this day.   Acts 23:6
22 And when Felix heard these things, having more perfect knowledge of *that* way, he deferred them, and said, When Lysias the chief captain shall come down, I will know the uttermost of your matter.
23 And he commanded a centurion to keep Paul, and to let *him* have liberty, and that he should forbid none of his acquaintance to minister or come unto him.   Acts 27:3; 28:16
24 And after certain days, when Felix came with his wife Drusilla, which was a Jewess, he sent for Paul, and heard him concerning the faith in Christ.   Acts 20:21; Gal. 2:16

24:24 Under Conviction

The Jewish princess [Drusilla] well understood the sacred character of that law which she had so shamelessly transgressed, but her prejudice against the Man of Calvary steeled her heart against the word of life. But Felix had never before listened to the truth, and as the Spirit of God sent conviction to his soul, he became deeply agitated. Conscience, now aroused, made her voice heard, and Felix felt that Paul's words were true. *AA 425*

---

25 And as he reasoned of righteousness, ᵀtemperance, and judgment to come, Felix trembled, and answered, Go thy way for this time; when I have a ᵀconvenient season, I will call for thee.   Acts 10:42 ◆ *self-control* ◆ *appropriate*
26 He hoped also that money should have been given him of Paul, that he might loose

him: wherefore he sent for him the oftener, and communed with him.

24:25, 26 Final Opportunity Lost

But instead of permitting his convictions to lead him to repentance, [Felix] sought to dismiss these unwelcome reflections. The interview with Paul was cut short. . . .

A ray of light from heaven had been permitted to shine upon Felix, when Paul reasoned with him concerning righteousness, temperance, and a judgment to come. That was his heaven-sent opportunity to see and to forsake his sins. . . . He had slighted his last offer of mercy. Never was he to receive another call from God. *AA 426, 427*

---

27 But after two years Porcius Festus came into Felix' room: and Felix, willing to shew the Jews a pleasure, left Paul bound.   Acts 12:3

Paul Speaks to Festus

25 Now when Festus was come into the province, after three days he ascended from Caesarea to Jerusalem.   Acts 23:34
2 Then the high priest and the chief of the Jews informed him against Paul, and ᵀbesought him,   Acts 24:1; 25:15 ◆ *begged*
3 And desired favour against him, that he would send for him to Jerusalem, laying wait in the way to kill him.
4 But Festus answered, that Paul should be kept at Caesarea, and that he himself would depart shortly *thither*.
5 Let them therefore, said he, which among you are able, go down with *me*, and accuse this man, if there be any wickedness in him.

25:2–5 A Dilemma

Festus discerned that the question in dispute related wholly to Jewish doctrines, and that, rightly understood, there was nothing in the charges against Paul, could they be proved, that would render him subject to sentence of death, or even to imprisonment. Yet he saw clearly the storm of rage that would be created if Paul were not condemned or delivered into their hands. *AA 429*

---

6 And when he had tarried among them more than ten days, he went down unto Caesarea; and the next day sitting on the judgment seat commanded Paul to be brought.   Matt. 27:19; Acts 25:10, 17
7 And when he was come, the Jews which came down from Jerusalem stood round about, and laid many and grievous complaints against Paul, which they could not prove.   Luke 23:2, 10; Acts 24:13
8 While he answered for himself, Neither against the law of the Jews, neither against

the temple, nor yet against Caesar, have I offended any thing at all. *Acts 24:12; 28:17*
9 But Festus, willing to do the Jews a pleasure, answered Paul, and said, Wilt thou go up to Jerusalem, and there be judged of these things before me? *Acts 12:3; 24:27; 25:20*
10 Then said Paul, I stand at Caesar's judgment seat, where I ought to be judged: to the Jews have I done no wrong, as thou very well knowest.
11 For if I be an offender, or have committed any thing worthy of death, I refuse not to die: but if there be none of these things whereof these accuse me, no man may deliver me unto them. I appeal unto Caesar. *Acts 25:25; 26:32; 28:19*

25:11 Safer With the Heathen

[Paul] knew that he could not look for justice from the people who by their crimes were bringing down upon themselves the wrath of God. He knew that, like the prophet Elijah, he would be safer among the heathen than with those who had rejected light from heaven and hardened their hearts against the gospel. Weary of strife, his active spirit could ill endure the repeated delays and wearing suspense of his trial and imprisonment. *AA 430*

12 Then Festus, when he had conferred with the council, answered, Hast thou appealed unto Caesar? unto Caesar shalt thou go.

King Agrippa Meets Paul
13 And after certain days king Agrippa and Bernice came unto Caesarea to salute Festus.
14 And when they had been there many days, Festus declared Paul's cause unto the king, saying, There is a certain man left in bonds by Felix: *Acts 24:27*
15 About whom, when I was at Jerusalem, the chief priests and the elders of the Jews informed *me*, desiring *to have* judgment against him.
16 To whom I answered, It is not the manner of the Romans to deliver any man to die, before that he which is accused have the accusers face to face, and have licence to answer for himself concerning the crime laid against him. *Acts 25:4-5*
17 Therefore, when they were come ᵀhither, without any delay on the morrow I sat on the judgment seat, and commanded the man to be brought forth. *Acts 25:6 ♦ here*
18 Against whom when the accusers stood up, they brought none accusation of such things as I supposed:
19 But had certain questions against him of their own superstition, and of one Jesus, which was dead, whom Paul affirmed to be alive. *Acts 18:15; 23:29*
20 And because I doubted of such manner of questions, I asked *him* whether he would go to Jerusalem, and there be judged of these matters. *Acts 25:9*
21 But when Paul had appealed to be reserved unto the hearing of Augustus, I commanded him to be kept till I might send him to Caesar.
22 Then Agrippa said unto Festus, I would also hear the man myself. To morrow, said he, thou shalt hear him. *Acts 9:15*
23 And on the morrow, when Agrippa was come, and Bernice, with great pomp, and was entered into the place of hearing, with the chief captains, and principal men of the city, at Festus' commandment Paul was brought forth. *Acts 25:13*
24 And Festus said, King Agrippa, and all men which are here present with us, ye see this man, about whom all the multitude of the Jews have dealt with me, both at Jerusalem, and *also* here, crying that he ought not to live any longer. *Acts 22:22; 25:2-3, 7*
25 But when I found that he had committed nothing worthy of death, and that he himself hath appealed to Augustus, I have determined to send him. *Acts 23:29*
26 Of whom I have no certain thing to write unto my lord. Wherefore I have brought him forth before you, and specially before thee, O king Agrippa, that, after examination had, I might have somewhat to write.
27 For it seemeth to me unreasonable to send a prisoner, and not ᵀwithal to signify the crimes *laid* against him. *together with him*

Hatred Yet to Come

Acts 25:9–12

Thus it was that once more, because of hatred born of bigotry and self-righteousness, a servant of God [Paul] was driven to turn for protection to the heathen. It was this same hatred that forced the prophet Elijah to flee for succor to the widow of Sarepta; and that forced the heralds of the gospel to turn from the Jews to proclaim their message to the Gentiles. And this hatred the people of God living in this age have yet to meet. Among the many of the professing followers of Christ there is the same pride, formalism, and selfishness, the same spirit of oppression, that held so large a place in the Jewish heart. In the future, men claiming to be Christ's representatives will take a course similar to that followed by the priests and rulers in their treatment of Christ and the apostles. *AA 430, 431*

Paul Describes His Life from His Childhood

26 Then Agrippa said unto Paul, Thou art permitted to speak for thyself. Then Paul stretched forth the hand, and answered for himself: Acts 9:15

2 I think myself happy, king Agrippa, because I shall answer for myself this day before thee touching all the things whereof I am accused of the Jews:

3 Especially *because I know* thee to be expert in all customs and questions which are among the Jews: wherefore I ᵀbeseech thee to hear me patiently. Acts 6:14 ◆ beg

4 My manner of life from my youth, which was at the first among mine own nation at Jerusalem, know all the Jews; Gal. 1:13

5 Which knew me from the beginning, if they would testify, that after the most straitest sect of our religion I lived a Pharisee. Acts 22:3; 23:6; 24:5

6 And now I stand and am judged for the hope of the promise made of God unto our fathers: Acts 24:15

7 Unto which *promise* our twelve tribes, instantly serving *God* day and night, hope to come. For which hope's sake, king Agrippa, I am accused of the Jews. Ezra 6:17; James 1:1

8 Why should it be thought a thing incredible with you, that God should raise the dead?

9 I ᵀverily thought with myself, that I ought to do many things contrary to the name of Jesus of Nazareth. Acts 22:8; 1 Tim. 1:13 ◆ truly

10 Which thing I also did in Jerusalem: and many of the saints did I shut up in prison, having received authority from the chief priests; and when they were put to death, I gave my voice against *them*. Acts 8:3; 9:13-14, 21

11 And I punished them oft in every synagogue, and compelled *them* to blaspheme; and being exceedingly mad against them, I persecuted *them* even unto strange cities.

Paul Describes His Conversion

12 Whereupon as I went to Damascus with authority and commission from the chief priests,

13 At midday, O king, I saw in the way a light from heaven, above the brightness of the sun, shining round about me and them which journeyed with me.

14 And when we were all fallen to the earth, I heard a voice speaking unto me, and saying in the Hebrew tongue, Saul, Saul, why persecutest thou me? *it is* hard for thee to kick against the pricks. Acts 21:40

15 And I said, Who art thou, Lord? And he said, I am Jesus whom thou persecutest.

16 But rise, and stand upon thy feet: for I have appeared unto thee for this purpose, to make thee a minister and a witness both of these things which thou hast seen, and of those things in the which I will appear unto thee; Ezek. 2:1; Dan. 10:11; Acts 22:14-15

17 Delivering thee from the people, and *from* the Gentiles, unto whom now I send thee, Jer. 1:8, 19; Acts 9:15

18 To open their eyes, *and* to turn *them* from darkness to light, and *from* the power of Satan unto God, that they may receive forgiveness of sins, and inheritance among them which are ᵀsanctified by faith that is in me. Is. 35:5; Acts 20:32; 1 Pet. 2:9 ◆ made holy

26:18

> Faith See John 1:12.

19 Whereupon, O king Agrippa, I was not disobedient unto the heavenly vision:

20 But shewed first unto them of Damascus, and at Jerusalem, and throughout all the coasts of Judaea, and then to the Gentiles, that they should repent and turn to God, and do works meet for repentance. Matt. 3:8

21 For these causes the Jews caught me in the temple, and went about to kill *me*. Acts 21:27

22 Having therefore obtained help of God, I continue unto this day, witnessing both to small and great, saying none other things than those which the prophets and Moses did say should come: Luke 24:27, 44; Acts 24:14

23 That Christ should suffer, *and* that he should be the first that should rise from the dead, and should shew light unto the people, and to the Gentiles. Luke 2:32; Col. 1:18; Rev. 1:5

Festus Charges Paul with Insanity

24 And as he thus spake for himself, Festus said with a loud voice, Paul, thou art beside thyself; much learning doth make thee mad. 1 Cor. 4:10

25 But he said, I am not mad, most noble Festus; but speak forth the words of truth and soberness. Acts 23:26

26 For the king knoweth of these things, before whom also I speak freely: for I am persuaded that none of these things are hidden from him; for this thing was not done in a corner.

27 King Agrippa, believest thou the prophets? I know that thou believest.

28 Then Agrippa said unto Paul, Almost thou persuadest me to be a Christian. Acts 11:26

> **26:28 Almost Saved; Wholly Lost**
>
> There are some who seem to be always seeking for the heavenly pearl. But they do not make an entire surrender of their wrong habits. They do not die to self that Christ may live in them. Therefore they do not find the precious pearl. They have not overcome unholy ambition and their love for worldly attractions. ... Almost Christians, yet not fully Christians, they seem near the kingdom of heaven, but they cannot enter there. Almost but not wholly saved, means to be not almost but wholly lost. *COL 118*

29 And Paul said, I would to God, that not only thou, but also all that hear me this day, were both almost, and altogether such as I am, except these bonds. *Acts 21:33*
30 And when he had thus spoken, the king rose up, and the governor, and Bernice, and they that sat with them:
31 And when they were gone aside, they talked between themselves, saying, This man doeth nothing worthy of death or of bonds. *Acts 23:29*
32 Then said Agrippa unto Festus, This man might have been set at liberty, if he had not appealed unto Caesar. *Acts 28:18*

Paul Sails for Rome

27 And when it was determined that we should sail into Italy, they delivered Paul and certain other prisoners unto *one* named Julius, a centurion of Augustus' band. *Acts 10:1; 25:12, 25*
2 And entering into a ship of Adramyttium, we launched, meaning to sail by the coasts of Asia; *one* Aristarchus, a Macedonian of Thessalonica, being with us. *Acts 19:29*
3 And the next *day* we touched at Sidon. And Julius courteously entreated Paul, and gave *him* liberty to go unto his friends to refresh himself. *Acts 24:23; 27:43; 28:16*
4 And when we had launched from thence, we sailed under Cyprus, because the winds were contrary. *Acts 4:36*
5 And when we had sailed over the sea of Cilicia and Pamphylia, we came to Myra, *a city* of Lycia. *Acts 6:9*
6 And there the centurion found a ship of Alexandria sailing into Italy; and he put us therein. *Acts 28:11*
7 And when we had sailed slowly many days, and scarce were come over against Cnidus, the wind not suffering us, we sailed under Crete, over against Salmone; *Acts 27:21*
8 And, hardly passing it, came unto a place which is called The fair havens; nigh whereunto was the city *of* Lasea.
9 Now when much time was spent, and when sailing was now dangerous, because the fast was now already past, Paul admonished *them*, *Lev. 16:29-31; 23:27-29; Num. 29:7*
10 And said unto them, Sirs, I perceive that this voyage will be with hurt and much damage, not only of the ᵀlading and ship, but also of our lives. *load*
11 Nevertheless the centurion believed the master and the owner of the ship, more than those things which were spoken by Paul.
12 And because the haven was not ᵀcommodious to winter in, the more part advised to depart thence also, if by any means they might attain to Phenice, *and there* to winter; *which is* an haven of Crete, and lieth toward the south west and north west. *suitable*
13 And when the south wind blew softly, supposing that they had obtained *their* purpose, loosing *thence*, they sailed close by Crete.
14 But not long after there arose against it a tempestuous wind, called Euroclydon.
15 And when the ship was caught, and could not bear up into the wind, we let *her* drive.
16 And running under a certain island which is called Clauda, we had much work to come by the boat:
17 Which when they had taken up, they used helps, undergirding the ship; and, fearing lest they should fall into the quicksands, strake sail, and so were driven. *Acts 27:29*
18 And we being exceedingly tossed with a tempest, the next *day* they lightened the ship; *Jon. 1:5; Acts 27:19, 38*
19 And the third *day* we cast out with our own hands the tackling of the ship.
20 And when neither sun nor stars in many days appeared, and no small ᵀtempest lay on *us*, all hope that we should be saved was then taken away. *storm*
21 But after long abstinence Paul stood forth in the midst of them, and said, Sirs, ye should have hearkened unto me, and not have loosed from Crete, and to have gained this harm and loss.
22 And now I exhort you to be of good cheer: for there shall be no loss of *any man's* life among you, but of the ship. *Acts 27:25, 36*
23 For there stood by me this night the angel of God, whose I am, and whom I serve, *Acts 5:19; 23:11; Rom. 1:9*
24 Saying, Fear not, Paul; thou must be brought before Caesar: and, lo, God hath given thee all them that sail with thee.
25 Wherefore, sirs, be of good cheer: for I believe God, that it shall be even as it was told me. *Rom. 4:20-21*

26 Howbeit we must be cast upon a certain island. Acts 27:17; 28:1

The Shipwreck

27 But when the fourteenth night was come, as we were driven up and down in Adria, about midnight the shipmen deemed that they drew near to some country;

28 And sounded, and found *it* twenty fathoms: and when they had gone a little further, they sounded again, and found *it* fifteen fathoms.

29 Then fearing lest we should have fallen upon rocks, they cast four anchors out of the stern, and wished for the day. Acts 27:17

30 And as the shipmen were about to flee out of the ship, when they had let down the boat into the sea, under colour as though they would have cast anchors out of the foreship, Acts 27:16

31 Paul said to the centurion and to the soldiers, Except these abide in the ship, ye cannot be saved.

32 Then the soldiers cut off the ropes of the boat, and let her fall off.

33 And while the day was coming on, Paul ᵀbesought *them* all to take meat, saying, This day is the fourteenth day that ye have tarried and continued fasting, having taken nothing. *begged*

34 Wherefore I pray you to take *some* meat: for this is for your health: for there shall not an hair fall from the head of any of you. 1 Kin. 1:52; Matt. 10:30; Luke 21:18

35 And when he had thus spoken, he took bread, and gave thanks to God in presence of them all: and when he had broken *it*, he began to eat. Matt. 15:36

36 Then were they all of good cheer, and they also took *some* meat. Acts 27:22

37 And we were in all in the ship two hundred threescore and sixteen souls. Acts 2:41

38 And when they had eaten enough, they lightened the ship, and cast out the wheat into the sea. Jon. 1:5

39 And when it was day, they knew not the land: but they discovered a certain creek with a shore, into the which they were minded, if it were possible, to thrust in the ship. Acts 28:1

40 And when they had taken up the anchors, they committed *themselves* unto the sea, and loosed the rudder bands, and hoised up the mainsail to the wind, and made toward shore.

41 And falling into a place where two seas met, they ran the ship aground; and the forepart stuck fast, and remained unmoveable, but the hinder part was broken with the violence of the waves.

42 And the soldiers' counsel was to kill the prisoners, lest any of them should swim out, and escape.

43 But the centurion, willing to save Paul, kept them from *their* purpose; and commanded that they which could swim should cast *themselves* first *into the sea*, and get to land: Acts 27:3

44 And the rest, some on boards, and some on *broken pieces* of the ship. And so it came to pass, that they escaped all safe to land.

Paul on the Island of Malta

28 And when they were escaped, then they knew that the island was called Melita. Acts 27:26, 39

2 And the barbarous people shewed us no little kindness: for they kindled a fire, and received us every one, because of the present rain, and because of the cold. Acts 28:4

3 And when Paul had gathered a bundle of sticks, and laid *them* on the fire, there came a ᵀviper out of the heat, and fastened on his hand. *snake*

4 And when the barbarians saw the *venomous* beast hang on his hand, they said among themselves, No doubt this man is a murderer,

---

The Results of Paul's Lifework

Acts 28

Who can measure the results to the world of Paul's lifework? Of all those beneficent influences that alleviate suffering, that comfort sorrow, that restrain evil, that uplift life from the selfish and the sensual, and glorify it with the hope of immortality, how much is due to the labors of Paul and his fellow workers, as with the gospel of the Son of God they made their unnoticed journey from Asia to the shores of Europe?

What is it worth to any life to have been God's instrument in setting in motion such influences of blessing? What will it be worth in eternity to witness the results of such a lifework? *Ed 70*

whom, though he hath escaped the sea, yet vengeance suffereth not to live.   Luke 13:2, 4

5 And he shook off the beast into the fire, and felt no harm.   Mark 16:18

6 Howbeit they looked when he should have swollen, or fallen down dead suddenly: but after they had looked a great while, and saw no harm come to him, they changed their minds, and said that he was a god.

7 In the same quarters were possessions of the chief man of the island, whose name was Publius; who received us, and lodged us three days courteously.

8 And it came to pass, that the father of Publius lay sick of a fever and of a bloody flux: to whom Paul entered in, and prayed, and laid his hands on him, and healed him.   Matt. 9:18; Mark 6:5; Acts 9:40

9 So when this was done, others also, which had diseases in the island, came, and were healed:

10 Who also honoured us with many honours; and when we departed, they ᵀladed *us* with such things as were necessary.   *loaded*

Paul's Company Departs for Rome

11 And after three months we departed in a ship of Alexandria, which had wintered in the isle, whose sign was Castor and Pollux.   Acts 27:6

12 And landing at Syracuse, we tarried *there* three days.

13 And from thence we ᵀfetched a compass, and came to Rhegium: and after one day the south wind blew, and we came the next day to Puteoli: *circled around*

14 Where we found brethren, and were desired to tarry with them seven days: and so we went toward Rome.

15 And from thence, when the brethren heard of us, they came to meet us as far as Appii forum, and The three taverns: whom when Paul saw, he thanked God, and took courage.

28:15 The Chained Captive

Suddenly a cry of joy is heard, and a man springs from the passing throng and falls upon the prisoner's neck, embracing him with tears and rejoicing, as a son would welcome a long-absent father. Again and again is the scene repeated as, with eyes made keen by loving expectation, many discern in the chained captive [Paul] the one who at Corinth, at Philippi, at Ephesus, had spoken to them the words of life.

As the warmhearted disciples eagerly flock around their father in the gospel, the whole company is brought to a standstill. *AA 448, 449*

---

16 And when we came to Rome, the ᵀcenturion delivered the prisoners to the captain of the guard: but Paul was suffered to dwell by himself with a soldier that kept him.   Acts 24:23; 27:3 ♦ *commander of 100 soldiers*

Paul in Rome

17 And it came to pass, that after three days Paul called the chief of the Jews together: and when they were come together, he said unto them, Men *and* brethren, though I have committed nothing against the people, or customs of our fathers, yet was I delivered prisoner from Jerusalem into the hands of the Romans.   Acts 6:14; 25:8

18 Who, when they had examined me, would have let *me* go, because there was no cause of death in me.   Acts 26:31-32

19 But when the Jews spake against *it*, I was constrained to appeal unto Caesar; not that I had ought to accuse my nation of.   Acts 26:32

20 For this cause therefore have I called for you, to see *you*, and to speak with *you*: because that for the hope of Israel I am bound with this chain.   Acts 21:33

21 And they said unto him, We neither received letters out of Judaea concerning thee, neither any of the brethren that came shewed or spake any harm of thee.   Acts 22:5

22 But we desire to hear of thee what thou thinkest: for as concerning this sect, we know that every where it is spoken against.   Acts 24:14

23 And when they had appointed him a day, there came many to him into *his* lodging; to whom he expounded and testified the kingdom of God, persuading them concerning Jesus, both out of the law of Moses, and *out of* the prophets, from morning till evening.   Acts 19:8

24 And some believed the things which were spoken, and some believed not. Acts 14:4; 17:4-5

25 And when they agreed not among themselves, they departed, after that Paul had spoken one word, Well spake the Holy Ghost by Esaias the prophet unto our fathers, Matt. 15:7

26 Saying, Go unto this people, and say, Hearing ye shall hear, and shall not understand; and seeing ye shall see, and not perceive:

28:31 Paul Never Faltered

Through his long term of service, Paul had never faltered in his allegiance to his Saviour. Wherever he was—whether before scowling Pharisees, or Roman authorities; before the furious mob at Lystra, or the convicted sinners in the Macedonian dungeon; whether reasoning with the panic-stricken sailors on the shipwrecked vessel, or standing alone before Nero to plead for his life—he had never been ashamed of the cause he was advocating. *AA 500*

27 For the heart of this people is ᵀwaxed ᵀgross, and their ears are dull of hearing, and their eyes have they closed; lest they should see with *their* eyes, and hear with *their* ears, and understand with *their* heart, and should be converted, and I should heal them.   become ◆ dull

28 Be it known therefore unto you, that the salvation of God is sent unto the Gentiles, and *that* they will hear it.   Luke 3:6

29 And when he had said these words, the Jews departed, and had great reasoning among themselves.

30 And Paul dwelt two whole years in his own hired house, and received all that came in unto him,

31 Preaching the kingdom of God, and teaching those things which concern the Lord Jesus Christ, with all confidence, no man forbidding him. Matt. 4:23; Acts 20:25; 28:23

THE EPISTLE OF PAUL THE APOSTLE TO THE

ROMANS

If the four Gospels tell us about the life and work of Jesus, the Epistle of Romans, written by the apostle Paul, helps us wrestle with the meaning of Christ's sacrificial death. Paul lays out his case step-by-step, much like an attorney, convincing his readers—the jury—as to who Christ is, why humankind needs a Savior, and how to live in relationship with Him.

Many argue that Romans is Paul's most theological epistle. Beyond being a theological or doctrinal work, Romans is a guide book on how to apply Christ's work on the cross to daily living. It teaches us about sin, submission, unity, love, and freedom.

Paul's emphasis on freedom, in fact, gives believers hope and encouragement. He uses his own struggle with sin—"For the good that I would I do not: but the evil which I would not, that I do" (7:19)—and reminds us that we can have victory and freedom from sin's power through what Christ has done for us—"There is therefore now no condemnation to them which are in Christ Jesus, who walk not after the flesh, but after the Spirit" (8:1).

If Romans could be summed up in one word, that word would probably be "love." Not only is this love something we can demonstrate between each other, but Paul tells us that the love Christ has for us is like nothing we have ever known: "For I am persuaded, that neither death, nor life, nor angels, nor principalities, nor powers, nor things present, nor things to come, nor height, nor depth, nor any other creature, shall be able to separate us from the love of God, which is in Christ Jesus our Lord" (8:38–39).

Dates

By the time Paul wrote the Epistle to the Romans, the city of Rome was the most important city in the world. He wrote the epistle in A.D. 57–58 while on his third missionary journey, more than likely while in Corinth (Acts 20:3–6).

The number of Christians in Rome at the time Paul wrote the epistle was probably significant, as the church there was well known. However, the majority of the inhabitants were most likely slaves. Indicators that Paul writes from Corinth are his references to Gaius (Romans 16:23; cf. 1 Corinthians 1:14) and Erastus (Romans 16:23; cf. 2 Timothy 4:20). He also commends Phoebe for her service to the church at Cenchrea, which is the eastern seaport of Corinth (Romans 16:1).

Author

Even from early on, the Epistle to the Romans was attributed to Paul. There is very little discussion or debate as to another author of this pivotal New Testament book. Paul dictated this epistle to his scribe, Tertius, who includes his own greeting at the end (16:22).

Some debate has arisen over the last two chapters of the book. Some manuscripts omit 15:1—16:24, and the closing doxology (16:25–27) is included at the end of chapter 14. These variations have resulted in some scholars questioning whether or not these two chapters were part of Paul's original writings—or possibly that Paul had two editions to this epistle.

More debate has taken place over chapter 16, where Paul greets some two dozen people by name in a church he had yet to visit. Some argue that this was a separate letter altogether, while others suggest that chapter 16 may not have been included in some manuscripts because it did not seem particularly relevant. However, people naturally have migrated toward Rome from all over the empire, so it is feasible that these are friends who find their way to the city. In addition, all the earliest manuscripts include chapter 16 as a fundamental element in the Roman epistle.

Meaning of the Name

The title of this letter is *Pros Romaious*, or "To the Romans." Paul wrote the book "to the Romans" in advance of his trip there to give the Romans a sample of his message.

Christ in Romans

In the Epistle to the Romans, Paul presents Christ as the Second Adam, who through His death and resurrection was able to secure justification for all humankind (5:12–21).

Having been substituted for our sins, Christ not only offers us salvation but also the freedom to live as His followers in our fallen world.

Overview

The city of Rome was the center of the Roman empire and one of the greatest cities of the ancient world. With some one million inhabitants, the city was a busy center of activity, worship, pleasure, sports, and art. A church existed in Rome, although Paul had not visited this church prior to writing this letter. The church may have been raised by some who became believers at Pentecost when Peter's speech was heard by people from many nations and cities, including Rome (Acts 2:10). It is also possible that believers from churches that Paul had established in Asia had come to settle in Rome, lead others to Christ, and begin the church there.

The Epistle to the Romans falls into three main parts:

(1) *Romans 1—8, God's Righteousness Revealed:* Paul briefly lays out the story of humankind: from man's sinfulness to God's righteousness to God's love and forgiveness. In addition, Paul talks about how to enjoy the freedom found only in Christ.

(2) *Romans 9—11, God's Righteousness Demonstrated:* Paul gives a shortened recounting of the story of Israel, demonstrating God's righteousness and saving power.

(3) *Romans 12—16, God's Righteousness Applied:* In this section of Romans, Paul gives readers insight as to how their faith could be applied in the world. Having faith in Christ is more than just theological; it is about living in the fullness of Christ in our everyday lives.

Unlocking Romans

KEY PEOPLE:
Jesus, Paul, Phoebe, Tertius

KEY EVENTS:
Since the Epistle to the Romans is more theological than historical, the key events that frame the entire book are Christ's death and resurrection. The framework also includes righteousness by faith, justification, the role of the law in spiritual living, and the behavioral habits of Christians.

KEY WORD:
Righteousness is a key theme in Romans. God's righteousness is available to all who place their faith in Him.

KEY VERSES:
"For I am not ashamed of the gospel of Christ: for it is the power of God unto salvation to every one that believeth; to the Jew first, and also to the Greek. For therein is the righteousness of God revealed from faith to faith: as it is written, The just shall live by faith" (Romans 1:16–17).

"But now the righteousness of God without the law is manifested, being witnessed by the law and the prophets; even the righteousness of God which is by faith of Jesus Christ unto all and upon all them that believe: for there is no difference: for all have sinned, and come short of the glory of God; being justified freely by his grace through the redemption that is in Christ Jesus: whom God hath set forth to be a propitiation through faith in his blood, to declare his righteousness for the remission of sins that are past, through the forbearance of God" (Romans 3:21–25).

KEY CHAPTERS:
Romans 6—8 is one of the most pivotal sections in all of Scripture. In it, Paul describes the struggle with sin, how to achieve victory from it and live in freedom, and how the Holy Spirit can equip us to live faithful lives.

Paul's Greeting

1 Paul, a servant of Jesus Christ, called *to be* an apostle, separated unto the gospel of God,　　Acts 9:15; Rom. 15:16; 1 Cor. 1:1

2 (Which he had promised afore by his prophets in the holy scriptures,)　　Rom. 3:21

3 Concerning his Son Jesus Christ our Lord, which was made of the seed of David according to the flesh;　　Matt. 1:1; John 1:14; Gal. 4:4

4 And declared *to be* the Son of God with power, according to the spirit of holiness, by the resurrection from the dead:　　2 Cor. 13:4

5 By whom we have received grace and apostleship, for obedience to the faith among all nations, for his name:　　Acts 1:25; 6:7; Rom. 16:26

6 Among whom are ye also the called of Jesus Christ:　　Rev. 17:14

7 To all that be in Rome, beloved of God, called *to be* saints: Grace to you and peace from God our Father, and the Lord Jesus Christ.　　2 Cor. 13:14; Eph. 1:2; Col. 1:2

Paul's Desire to Visit Rome

8 First, I thank my God through Jesus Christ for you all, that your faith is spoken of throughout the whole world.　　Rom. 6:17; 16:19

9 For God is my witness, whom I serve with my spirit in the gospel of his Son, that without ceasing I make mention of you always in my prayers;　　Rom. 9:1; 2 Cor. 1:23; 2 Tim. 1:3

10 Making request, if by any means now at length I might have a prosperous journey by the will of God to come unto you.　　Acts 18:21

11 For I long to see you, that I may impart unto you some spiritual gift, to the end ye may be established;　　Rom. 15:23

12 That is, that I may be comforted together with you by the mutual faith both of you and me.　　2 Pet. 1:1

13 Now I would not have you ignorant, brethren, that oftentimes I purposed to come unto you, (but was let ᵀhitherto,) that I might have some fruit among you also, even as among other Gentiles.　　John 4:36 ◆ *up to now*

14 I am debtor both to the Greeks, and to the Barbarians; both to the wise, and to the unwise.

15 So, as much as in me is, I am ready to preach the gospel to you that are at Rome also.

Not Ashamed of the Gospel

16 For I am not ashamed of the gospel of Christ: for it is the power of God unto salvation to every one that believeth; to the Jew first, and also to the Greek.　　Rom. 2:9; 2 Tim. 1:8

17 For therein is the righteousness of God revealed from faith to faith: as it is written, The just shall live by faith.　　Hab. 2:4; Rom. 3:21; Gal. 3:11

1:17 A Mighty Beacon

Through all the ages the great truth of justification by faith has stood as a mighty beacon to guide repentant sinners into the way of life. It was this light that scattered the darkness which enveloped Luther's mind and revealed to him the power of the blood of Christ to cleanse from sin. The same light has guided thousands of sin-burdened souls to the true Source of pardon and peace. *AA 373, 374*

God's Anger at Sinful Humanity

18 For the wrath of God is revealed from heaven against all ungodliness and unrighteousness of men, who hold the truth in unrighteousness;　　Eph. 5:6

19 Because that which may be known of God is ᵀmanifest in them; for God hath shewed *it* unto them.　　Rom. 1:20 ◆ *made known*

20 For the invisible things of him from the creation of the world are clearly seen, being understood by the things that are made, *even* his eternal power and Godhead; so that they are without excuse:　　1 Tim. 1:17

21 Because that, when they knew God, they glorified *him* not as God, neither were thankful; but became vain in their imaginations, and their foolish heart was darkened.　　2 Kin. 17:15; Jer. 2:5; Eph. 4:17-18

22 Professing themselves to be wise, they became fools,　　Jer. 10:14

23 And changed the glory of the uncorruptible God into an image made like to corruptible man, and to birds, and fourfooted beasts, and creeping things. Ps. 106:20; Jer. 2:11; Acts 17:29

24 Wherefore God also gave them up to uncleanness through the lusts of their own hearts, to dishonour their own bodies between themselves:　　1 Thess. 4:4

25 Who changed the truth of God into a lie, and worshipped and served the creature more than the Creator, who is blessed for ever. Amen.　　Is. 44:20; Jer. 13:25; Rom. 9:5

1:25 Soul Defenses Broken Down

Thus when the people of Israel, in their worship of Baal and Ashtoreth, paid supreme homage to the forces of nature, they severed their connection with all that is uplifting and ennobling, and fell an easy prey to temptation. With the defenses of the soul broken down, the misguided worshipers had no barrier against sin and yielded themselves to the evil passions of the human heart. *PK 282*

26 For this cause God gave them up unto vile affections: for even their women did change the natural use into that which is against nature:　　Rom. 1:24

27 And likewise also the men, leaving the natural use of the woman, burned in their

lust one toward another; men with men working that which is unseemly, and receiving in themselves that recompence of their error which was meet.   Lev. 18:22

28 And even as they did not like to retain God in *their* knowledge, God gave them over to a reprobate mind, to do those things which are not ᵀconvenient;   Jer. 6:30 ◆ *appropriate*

1:28 Sinking Lower or Rising Higher

Man will rise no higher than his conceptions of truth, purity, and holiness. If the mind is never exalted above the level of humanity, if it is not uplifted by faith to contemplate infinite wisdom and love, the man will be constantly sinking lower and lower. The worshipers of false gods clothed their deities with human attributes and passions, and thus their standard of character was degraded to the likeness of sinful humanity. They were defiled in consequence. *PP 91*

---

29 Being filled with all unrighteousness, fornication, wickedness, ᵀcovetousness, maliciousness; full of envy, murder, debate, deceit, malignity; whisperers,   2 Cor. 12:20 ◆ *greed*
30 Backbiters, haters of God, despiteful, proud, boasters, inventors of evil things, disobedient to parents,   2 Tim. 3:2
31 Without understanding, covenantbreakers, without natural affection, ᵀimplacable, unmerciful: 2 Tim. 3:3 ◆ *obstinate*
32 Who knowing the judgment of God, that they which commit such things are worthy of death, not only do the same, but have pleasure in them that do them.   Rom. 6:21

God Will Judge Everyone

2 Therefore thou art inexcusable, O man, whosoever thou art that judgest: for wherein thou judgest another, thou condemnest thyself; for thou that judgest doest the same things. 2 Sam. 12:5-7; Luke 6:37; Rom. 2:3

2:1 Motive for Condemning

He who is guilty of wrong is the first to suspect wrong. By condemning another he is trying to conceal or excuse the evil of his own heart. It was through sin that men gained the knowledge of evil; no sooner had the first pair sinned than they began to accuse each other; and this is what human nature will inevitably do when uncontrolled by the grace of Christ. *MB 126*

---

2 But we are sure that the judgment of God is according to truth against them which commit such things.
3 And thinkest thou this, O man, that judgest them which do such things, and doest the same, that thou shalt escape the judgment of God?   Luke 12:14

4 Or despisest thou the riches of his goodness and forbearance and longsuffering; not knowing that the goodness of God leadeth thee to repentance?   Ex. 34:6; Is. 30:18; Rom. 3:25
5 But after thy hardness and ᵀimpenitent heart treasurest up unto thyself wrath against the day of wrath and revelation of the righteous judgment of God;   Deut. 32:34 ◆ *unrepentant*
6 Who will render to every man according to his deeds: Job 34:11; Ps. 62:12; Matt. 16:27
7 To them who by patient continuance in well doing seek for glory and honour and immortality, eternal life: Luke 8:15
8 But unto them that are ᵀcontentious, and do not obey the truth, but obey unrighteousness, ᵀindignation and wrath,   *quarrelsome* ◆ *anger*
9 Tribulation and anguish, upon every soul of man that doeth evil, of the Jew first, and also of the Gentile; Acts 3:26; Rom. 1:16; 1 Pet. 4:17
10 But glory, honour, and peace, to every man that worketh good, to the Jew first, and also to the Gentile: Is. 32:17
11 For there is no respect of persons with God.   Deut. 10:17; 2 Chr. 19:7; Acts 10:34

2:11 All Men Are One to God

No distinction on account of nationality, race, or caste, is recognized by God. He is the Maker of all mankind. All men are of one family by creation, and all are one through redemption. Christ came to demolish every wall of partition, to throw open every compartment of the temple courts, that every soul may have free access to God. His love is so broad, so deep, so full, that it penetrates everywhere. *PK 369, 370*

---

12 For as many as have sinned without law shall also perish without law: and as many as have sinned in the law shall be judged by the law;   1 Cor. 9:21
13 (For not the hearers of the law *are* just before God, but the doers of the law shall be justified.
14 For when the Gentiles, which have not the law, do by nature the things contained in the law, these, having not the law, are a law unto themselves: Rom. 2:12
15 Which shew the work of the law written in their hearts, their conscience also bearing witness, and *their* thoughts the mean while accusing or else excusing one another;)
16 In the day when God shall judge the secrets of men by Jesus Christ according to my gospel.   Acts 10:42; Rom. 16:25; 1 Tim. 1:11
17 Behold, thou art called a Jew, and restest in the law, and makest thy boast of God,   Mic. 3:11; John 5:45; Rom. 2:23
18 And knowest *his* will, and approvest the things that are more excellent, being instructed out of the law;   Phil. 1:10

19 And art confident that thou thyself art a guide of the blind, a light of them which are in darkness,   Matt. 15:14

20 An instructor of the foolish, a teacher of babes, which hast the form of knowledge and of the truth in the law.   2 Tim. 1:13

21 Thou therefore which teachest another, teachest thou not thyself? thou that preachest a man should not steal, dost thou steal?   Ps. 50:16-21

22 Thou that sayest a man should not commit adultery, dost thou commit adultery? thou that [T]abhorrest idols, dost thou commit sacrilege?   Mal. 3:8 ◆ despise

23 Thou that makest thy boast of the law, through breaking the law dishonourest thou God?   John 5:45; Rom. 2:17; 9:4

24 For the name of God is blasphemed among the Gentiles through you, as it is written.   2 Sam. 12:14; Is. 52:5; Ezek. 36:20-23

25 For circumcision [T]verily profiteth, if thou keep the law: but if thou be a breaker of the law, thy circumcision is made uncircumcision.   Jer. 4:4 ◆ truly

26 Therefore if the uncircumcision keep the righteousness of the law, shall not his uncircumcision be counted for circumcision?   Rom. 8:4

27 And shall not uncircumcision which is by nature, if it fulfil the law, judge thee, who by the letter and circumcision dost [T]transgress the law?   Matt. 12:41-42 ◆ violate

28 For he is not a Jew, which is one outwardly; neither is that circumcision, which is outward in the flesh: Matt. 3:9; Gal. 6:15

29 But he is a Jew, which is one inwardly; and circumcision is that of the heart, in the spirit, and not in the letter; whose praise is not of men, but of God.   2 Cor. 10:18; Phil. 3:3; 1 Pet. 3:4

Everyone Is a Sinner

3 What advantage then hath the Jew? or what profit is there of circumcision?

2 Much every way: chiefly, because that unto them were committed the oracles of God.   Ps. 147:19-20; Acts 7:38; Rom. 9:4

3 For what if some did not believe? shall their unbelief make the faith of God without effect?   Rom. 10:16; 2 Tim. 2:13; Heb. 4:2

4 God forbid: yea, let God be true, but every man a liar; as it is written, That thou mightest be justified in thy sayings, and mightest overcome when thou art judged.   Ps. 51:4; 62:9; 116:11

5 But if our unrighteousness commend the righteousness of God, what shall we say? Is God unrighteous who taketh vengeance? (I speak as a man)   Rom. 6:19; 1 Cor. 9:8; Gal. 3:15

6 God forbid: for then how shall God judge the world?   Gen. 18:25

7 For if the truth of God hath more abounded through my lie unto his glory; why yet am I also judged as a sinner?

8 And not rather, (as we be slanderously reported, and as some affirm that we say,) Let us do evil, that good may come? whose [T]damnation is just.   Rom. 6:1, 15 ◆ condemnation

9 What then? are we better than they? No, in no wise: for we have before proved both Jews and Gentiles, that they are all under sin;   Rom. 3:19; Gal. 3:22

10 As it is written, There is none righteous, no, not one: Ps. 14:1-3

11 There is none that understandeth, there is none that seeketh after God.

12 They are all gone out of the way, they are together become unprofitable; there is none that doeth good, no, not one.   Ps. 14:3

13 Their throat is an open sepulchre; with their tongues they have used deceit; the poison of asps is under their lips: Ps. 5:9; Jer. 5:16

14 Whose mouth is full of cursing and bitterness: Ps. 10:7

15 Their feet are swift to shed blood: Prov. 1:16

16 Destruction and misery are in their ways:

17 And the way of peace have they not known: Luke 1:79

18 There is no fear of God before their eyes.

19 Now we know that what things soever the law saith, it saith to them who are under the law: that every mouth may be stopped, and all the world may become guilty before God.

20 Therefore by the deeds of the law there shall no flesh be justified in his sight: for by the law is the knowledge of sin.   Ps. 143:2

3:20

God's Law See James 4:17.

God's Approval Is a Gift

21 But now the righteousness of God without the law is [T]manifested, being witnessed by the law and the prophets; Rom. 1:2, 17 ◆ made known

22 Even the righteousness of God which is by faith of Jesus Christ unto all and upon all them that believe: for there is no difference: Rom. 10:12; Gal. 3:28; Col. 3:11

23 For all have sinned, and come short of the glory of God;   Rom. 3:9

3:23

Salvation From Sin See Romans 5:12–14.

24 Being justified freely by his grace through the redemption that is in Christ Jesus: Rom. 4:16; Col. 1:14

25 Whom God hath set forth to be a propitiation through faith in his blood, to declare his righteousness for the [T]remission of sins that are past, through the forbearance of God;   Acts 17:30; 1 John 2:2; 4:10 ◆ forgiveness

26 To declare, I say, at this time his righteousness: that he might be just, and the justifier of him which believeth in Jesus.

> ### 3:26 Only the Son Could Show Us
>
> None but the Son of God could accomplish our redemption; for only He who was in the bosom of the Father could declare Him. Only He who knew the height and depth of the love of God could make it manifest. Nothing less than the infinite sacrifice made by Christ in behalf of fallen man could express the Father's love to lost humanity. *SC 14*

27 Where *is* boasting then? It is excluded. By what law? of works? Nay: but by the law of faith.　　　　Rom. 2:17, 23; 4:2

28 Therefore we conclude that a man is justified by faith without the deeds of the law.

29 *Is he* the God of the Jews only? *is he* not also of the Gentiles? Yes, of the Gentiles also:

30 Seeing *it is* one God, which shall justify the circumcision by faith, and uncircumcision through faith.　　　　Gal. 3:8, 20

31 Do we then make void the law through faith? God forbid: yea, we establish the law.　　　　Matt. 5:17

> **God's Law** See Romans 6:14, 15.

3:31

Abraham's Faith Was Credited to Him for Righteousness

4 What shall we say then that Abraham our father, as pertaining to the flesh, hath found?　　　　Rom. 4:16

2 For if Abraham were justified by works, he hath *whereof* to glory; but not before God.　　　　1 Cor. 1:31

3 For what saith the scripture? Abraham believed God, and it was counted unto him for righteousness.　　Gen. 15:6; Rom. 4:9; James 2:23

4 Now to him that worketh is the reward not reckoned of grace, but of debt.　　Rom. 11:6

5 But to him that worketh not, but believeth on him that justifieth the ungodly, his faith is counted for righteousness.　　Rom. 3:22

6 Even as David also describeth the blessedness of the man, unto whom God imputeth righteousness without works,

7 *Saying*, Blessed *are* they whose iniquities are forgiven, and whose sins are covered. Ps. 32:1-2

8 Blessed *is* the man to whom the Lord will not [T]impute sin.　　　　*count*

9 *Cometh* this blessedness then upon the circumcision *only*, or upon the uncircumcision also? for we say that faith was reckoned to Abraham for righteousness.　　Rom. 4:3

10 How was it then reckoned? when he was in circumcision, or in uncircumcision? Not in circumcision, but in uncircumcision.

11 And he received the sign of circumcision, a seal of the righteousness of the faith which *he had yet* being uncircumcised: that he might be the father of all them that believe, though they be not circumcised; that righteousness might be imputed unto them also:　Luke 19:9

12 And the father of circumcision to them who are not of the circumcision only, but who also walk in the steps of that faith of our father Abraham, which *he had* being *yet* uncircumcised.

13 For the promise, that he should be the heir of the world, *was* not to Abraham, or to his seed, through the law, but through the righteousness of faith.　　　　Gal. 3:29

14 For if they which are of the law *be* heirs, faith is made void, and the promise made of none effect:

15 Because the law worketh wrath: for where no law is, *there is* no [T]transgression. Rom. 5:13; 1 Cor. 15:56; Gal. 3:10 ◆ *violation of a law*

16 Therefore *it is* of faith, that *it might be* by grace; to the end the promise might be sure

---

The Perfect Law of Love

Romans 3:31

Because the law of the Lord is perfect, and therefore changeless, it is impossible for sinful men, in themselves, to meet the standard of its requirement. This was why Jesus came as our Redeemer. It was His mission, by making men partakers of the divine nature, to bring them into harmony with the principles of the law of heaven. When we forsake our sins and receive Christ as our Saviour, the law is exalted. The apostle Paul asks, "Do we then make void the law through faith? God forbid: yea, we establish the law" (Romans 3:31).

The new-covenant promise is, "I will put My laws into their hearts, and in their minds will I write them" (Hebrews 10:16). While the system of types which pointed to Christ as the Lamb of God that should take away the sin of the world was to pass away at His death, the principles of righteousness embodied in the Decalogue are as immutable as the eternal throne. Not one command has been annulled, not a jot or tittle has been changed. Those principles that were made known to man in Paradise as the great law of life will exist unchanged in Paradise restored. When Eden shall bloom on earth again, God's law of love will be obeyed by all beneath the sun.

"Forever, O Lord, Thy word is settled in heaven." "All His commandments are sure. They stand fast for ever and ever, and are done in truth and uprightness." "Concerning Thy testimonies, I have known of old that Thou hast founded them forever" (Psalms 119:89; 111:7, 8; 119:152). *MB 50, 51*

to all the seed; not to that only which is of the law, but to that also which is of the faith of Abraham; who is the father of us all, Rom. 9:8
17 (As it is written, I have made thee a father of many nations,) before him whom he believed, *even* God, who ᵀquickeneth the dead, and calleth those things which be not as though they were. John 5:21; 1 Cor. 1:28 ♦ *makes alive*
18 Who against hope believed in hope, that he might become the father of many nations, according to that which was spoken, So shall thy seed be.
19 And being not weak in faith, he considered not his own body now dead, when he was about an hundred years old, neither yet the deadness of Sara's womb: Gen. 17:17
20 He staggered not at the promise of God through unbelief; but was strong in faith, giving glory to God;
21 And being fully persuaded that, what he had promised, he was able also to perform. Gen. 18:14; Heb. 11:19

4:21 Gift Is in the Promise

We need look for no outward evidence of the blessing. The gift is in the promise, and we may go about our work assured that what God has promised He is able to perform, and that the gift, which we already possess, will be realized when we need it most. *Ed 258*

22 And therefore it was imputed to him for righteousness. Rom. 4:3
23 Now it was not written for his sake alone, that it was imputed to him; Rom. 15:4
24 But for us also, to whom it shall be imputed, if we believe on him that raised up Jesus our Lord from the dead; Acts 2:24; 1 Pet. 1:21
25 Who was delivered for our offences, and was raised again for our justification.Is. 53:5-6

Peace with God

5 Therefore being justified by faith, we have peace with God through our Lord Jesus Christ: John 14:27

Faith See Acts 26:18.

2 By whom also we have access by faith into this grace wherein we stand, and rejoice in hope of the glory of God. 1 Cor. 15:1; Eph. 2:18
3 And not only *so*, but we glory in tribulations also: knowing that tribulation worketh patience; James 1:2-3
4 And patience, experience; and experience, hope; James 1:12
5 And hope maketh not ashamed; because the love of God is shed abroad in our hearts by the Holy Ghost which is given unto us. Gal. 4:6
6 For when we were yet without strength, in due time Christ died for the ungodly.

7 For scarcely for a righteous man will one die: yet ᵀperadventure for a good man some would even dare to die. *maybe*

5:8 Grace Only for the Unworthy

Grace is an attribute of God exercised toward undeserving human beings. We did not seek for it, but it was sent in search of us. God rejoices to bestow His grace upon us, not because we are worthy, but because we are so utterly unworthy. Our only claim to His mercy is our great need. *MH 161*

8 But God commendeth his love toward us, in that, while we were yet sinners, Christ died for us. Is. 53:6; John 15:13; 1 Pet. 3:18

Salvation From Sin See 1 Corinthians 15:22.

9 Much more then, being now justified by his blood, we shall be saved from wrath through him. Rom. 1:18; 1 Thess. 1:10
10 For if, when we were enemies, we were reconciled to God by the death of his Son, much more, being reconciled, we shall be saved by his life. 2 Cor. 5:18-19
11 And not only *so*, but we also joy in God through our Lord Jesus Christ, by whom we have now received the atonement. Rom. 5:10

A Comparison of Adam and Christ

12 Wherefore, as by one man sin entered into the world, and death by sin; and so death passed upon all men, for that all have sinned: Gen. 2:17; Rom. 6:23; 1 Cor. 15:21-22
13 (For until the law sin was in the world: but sin is not imputed when there is no law. Rom. 4:15
14 Nevertheless death reigned from Adam to Moses, even over them that had not sinned after the ᵀsimilitude of Adam's ᵀtransgression, who is the figure of him that was to come. 1 Cor. 15:45 ♦ *manner* ♦ *sin*

God's Law See Exodus 20:3–17.

Salvation From Sin See Romans 6:23.

15 But not as the offence, so also *is* the free gift. For if through the offence of one many be dead, much more the grace of God, and the gift by grace, *which is* by one man, Jesus Christ, hath abounded unto many. Rom. 5:12
16 And not as *it was* by one that sinned, *so is* the gift: for the judgment *was* by one to condemnation, but the free gift *is* of many offences unto justification.
17 For if by one man's offence death reigned by one; much more they which receive abundance of grace and of the gift of righteousness shall reign in life by one, Jesus Christ.) Rom. 5:12
18 Therefore as by the offence of one *judgment came* upon all men to condemnation; even so

by the righteousness of one *the free gift came* upon all men unto justification of life.
19 For as by one man's disobedience many were made sinners, so by the obedience of one shall many be made righteous.   Phil. 2:8
20 Moreover the law entered, that the offence might abound. But where sin abounded, grace did much more abound: Rom. 6:1

5:20 Ransomed and Exalted

In the place where sin abounded, God's grace much more abounds. The earth itself, the very field that Satan claims as his, is to be not only ransomed but exalted. Our little world, under the curse of sin the one dark blot in His glorious creation, will be honored above all other worlds in the universe of God. *DA 26*

---

21 That as sin hath reigned unto death, even so might grace reign through righteousness unto eternal life by Jesus Christ our Lord.

No Longer Slaves to Sin

6 What shall we say then? Shall we continue in sin, that grace may abound?
2 God forbid. How shall we, that are dead to sin, live any longer therein?   Rom. 7:4; Col. 3:3
3 Know ye not, that so many of us as were baptized into Jesus Christ were baptized into his death?   Matt. 28:19; 1 Cor. 12:13; Gal. 3:27
4 Therefore we are buried with him by baptism into death: that like as Christ was raised up from the dead by the glory of the Father, even so we also should walk in newness of life.   Rom. 7:6; 2 Cor. 5:17; Col. 3:10

Baptism/Lord's Supper See Colossians 2:12.

5 For if we have been planted together in the likeness of his death, we shall be also *in the likeness* of *his* resurrection: Phil. 3:10-11
6 Knowing this, that our old man is crucified with *him*, that the body of sin might be destroyed, that ᵀhenceforth we should not serve sin. Gal. 2:20; 5:24; Eph. 4:22 ◆ *from this time forward*
7 For he that is dead is freed from sin. 1 Pet. 4:1
8 Now if we be dead with Christ, we believe that we shall also live with him: 2 Cor. 13:4
9 Knowing that Christ being raised from the dead dieth no more; death hath no more dominion over him.   Rom. 5:14; Rev. 1:18
10 For in that he died, he died unto sin once: but in that he liveth, he liveth unto God.
11 Likewise reckon ye also yourselves to be dead indeed unto sin, but alive unto God through Jesus Christ our Lord.   Rom. 6:2
12 Let not sin therefore reign in your mortal body, that ye should obey it in the lusts thereof.   Rom. 6:16
13 Neither yield ye your members *as* instruments of unrighteousness unto sin: but yield

yourselves unto God, as those that are alive from the dead, and your members *as* instruments of righteousness unto God.   1 Pet. 2:24
14 For sin shall not have dominion over you: for ye are not under the law, but under grace.   Rom. 6:12

6:14 Humanity United With Divinity

Christ's humanity was united with divinity; He was fitted for the conflict by the indwelling of the Holy Spirit. And He came to make us partakers of the divine nature. So long as we are united to Him by faith, sin has no more dominion over us. God reaches for the hand of faith in us to direct it to lay fast hold upon the divinity of Christ, that we may attain to perfection of character. *DA 123*

---

15 What then? shall we sin, because we are not under the law, but under grace? God forbid.   Rom. 6:1-2

God's Law See Romans 7:22.

16 Know ye not, that to whom ye yield yourselves servants to obey, his servants ye are to whom ye obey; whether of sin unto death, or of obedience unto righteousness?   2 Pet. 2:19
17 But God be thanked, that ye were the servants of sin, but ye have obeyed from the heart that form of doctrine which was delivered you.   Rom. 1:8; 2 Tim. 1:13
18 Being then made free from sin, ye became the servants of righteousness.   John 8:32
19 I speak after the manner of men because of the infirmity of your flesh: for as ye have yielded your members servants to uncleanness and to iniquity unto iniquity; even so now yield your members servants to righteousness unto holiness.   Rom. 3:5; 6:13
20 For when ye were the servants of sin, ye were free from righteousness.
21 What fruit had ye then in those things whereof ye are now ashamed? for the end of those things *is* death.   Rom. 1:32
22 But now being made free from sin, and become servants to God, ye have your fruit unto holiness, and the end everlasting life.   John 8:32; Rom. 6:18; 1 Pet. 2:16

6:23 Only the Gospel Can Free Us

The law reveals to man his sins, but it provides no remedy. While it promises life to the obedient, it declares that death is the portion of the transgressor. The gospel of Christ alone can free him from the condemnation or the defilement of sin. *GC 467, 468*

---

23 For the wages of sin *is* death; but the gift of God *is* eternal life through Jesus Christ our Lord.   Gen. 2:17; Rom. 2:7; 5:12

Salvation From Sin See John 3:16, 17.

We Belong to Christ

7 Know ye not, brethren, (for I speak to them that know the law,) how that the law hath dominion over a man as long as he liveth?

2 For the woman which hath an husband is bound by the law to *her* husband so long as he liveth; but if the husband be dead, she is loosed from the law of *her* husband. 1 Cor. 7:39

3 So then if, while *her* husband liveth, she be married to another man, she shall be called an adulteress: but if her husband be dead, she is free from that law; so that she is no adulteress, though she be married to another man. Matt. 5:32

4 Wherefore, my brethren, ye also are become dead to the law by the body of Christ; that ye should be married to another, *even* to him who is raised from the dead, that we should bring forth fruit unto God. Rom. 7:6; 8:2; Gal. 5:18

5 For when we were in the flesh, the motions of sins, which were by the law, did work in our members to bring forth fruit unto death. Rom. 6:13, 21

6 But now we are delivered from the law, that being dead wherein we were held; that we should serve in newness of spirit, and not *in* the oldness of the letter. Rom. 6:4

Moses' Laws Reveal Sin

7 What shall we say then? *Is* the law sin? God forbid. Nay, I had not known sin, but by the law: for I had not known lust, except the law had said, Thou shalt not covet. Ex. 20:17

8 But sin, taking occasion by the commandment, ᵀwrought in me all manner of ᵀconcupiscence. For without the law sin *was* dead. Rom. 4:15; 7:11; 1 Cor. 15:56 ◆ *made* ◆ *passion*

9 For I was alive without the law once: but when the commandment came, sin revived, and I died.

10 And the commandment, which *was ordained* to life, I found *to be* unto death. Lev. 18:5

11 For sin, taking occasion by the commandment, deceived me, and by it slew *me*.

7:12 God's Law His Character

The Law of God, from its very nature, is unchangeable. It is a revelation of the will and the character of its Author. God is love, and His law is love. Its two great principles are love to God and love to man. . . . The character of God is righteousness and truth; such is the nature of His law. . . . Such a law, being an expression of the mind and will of God, must be as enduring as its Author. GC 467

12 Wherefore the law *is* holy, and the commandment holy, and just, and good. 1 Tim. 1:8

God's Law See 1 John 2:3–6.

13 Was then that which is good made death unto me? God forbid. But sin, that it might appear sin, working death in me by that which is good; that sin by the commandment might become exceeding sinful.

14 For we know that the law is spiritual: but I am carnal, sold under sin. 1 Kin. 21:20

15 For that which I do I allow not: for what I would, that do I not; but what I hate, that do I. Gal. 5:17

16 If then I do that which I would not, I consent unto the law that *it is* good. Rom. 7:12

17 Now then it is no more I that do it, but sin that dwelleth in me. Rom. 7:20

18 For I know that in me (that is, in my flesh,) dwelleth no good thing: for to will is present with me; but *how* to perform that which is good I find not. Gen. 6:5; 8:21; Rom. 7:25

19 For the good that I would I do not: but the evil which I would not, that I do. Rom. 7:15

20 Now if I do that I would not, it is no more I that do it, but sin that dwelleth in me.

21 I find then a law, that, when I would do good, evil is present with me. Rom. 7:23

22 For I delight in the law of God after the inward man: Ps. 1:2; 2 Cor. 4:16; Eph. 3:16

God's Law See Hebrews 8:10.

7:22

23 But I see another law in my members, warring against the law of my mind, and bringing me into captivity to the law of sin which is in my members. Rom. 7:25; Gal. 5:17; James 4:1

24 O wretched man that I am! who shall deliver me from the body of this death? Titus 2:14

25 I thank God through Jesus Christ our Lord. So then with the mind I myself serve the law of God; but with the flesh the law of sin. 1 Cor. 15:57

We Are God's Children

8 *There is* therefore now no condemnation to them which are in Christ Jesus, who walk not after the flesh, but after the Spirit. 1 Cor. 1:30

8:1 Without Sadness or Shame

While the Christian's life will be characterized by humility, it should not be marked with sadness and self-depreciation. It is the privilege of everyone so to live that God will approve and bless him. It is not the will of our heavenly Father that we should be ever under condemnation and darkness. . . . We may go to Jesus and be cleansed, and stand before the law without shame and remorse. *GC 477*

2 For the law of the Spirit of life in Christ Jesus hath made me free from the law of sin and death. John 8:32; Rom. 6:18; 1 Cor. 15:45

3 For what the law could not do, in that it was weak through the flesh, God sending his own

Son in the likeness of sinful flesh, and for sin, condemned sin in the flesh: 2 Cor. 5:21; Heb. 10:14
4 That the righteousness of the law might be fulfilled in us, who walk not after the flesh, but after the Spirit. Gal. 5:16
5 For they that are after the flesh do mind the things of the flesh; but they that are after the Spirit the things of the Spirit. 1 Cor. 2:14

8:5

> **Christian Behavior** See Philippians 4:8.

6 For to be carnally minded *is* death; but to be spiritually minded *is* life and peace. Rom. 6:21
7 Because the carnal mind *is* ᵀenmity against God: for it is not subject to the law of God, neither indeed can be. 1 Cor. 2:14; James 4:4 ◆ *hostility*
8 So then they that are in the flesh cannot please God. Rom. 7:5
9 But ye are not in the flesh, but in the Spirit, if so be that the Spirit of God dwell in you. Now if any man have not the Spirit of Christ, he is none of his. 1 Cor. 3:16; 6:19; Gal. 4:6
10 And if Christ *be* in you, the body *is* dead because of sin; but the Spirit *is* life because of righteousness. Eph. 3:17
11 But if the Spirit of him that raised up Jesus from the dead dwell in you, he that raised up Christ from the dead shall also ᵀquicken your mortal bodies by his Spirit that dwelleth in you. Acts 2:24; Rom. 8:2, 9 ◆ *make alive*
12 Therefore, brethren, we are debtors, not to the flesh, to live after the flesh.
13 For if ye live after the flesh, ye shall die: but if ye through the Spirit do ᵀmortify the deeds of the body, ye shall live. Gal. 6:8 ◆ *destroy*
14 For as many as are led by the Spirit of God, they are the sons of God. Gal. 5:18; Rev. 21:7
15 For ye have not received the spirit of bondage again to fear; but ye have received the Spirit of adoption, whereby we cry, Abba, Father. Mark 14:36; 1 Cor. 2:12; 2 Tim. 1:7
16 The Spirit itself beareth witness with our spirit, that we are the children of God: Eph. 1:13
17 And if children, then heirs; heirs of God, and joint-heirs with Christ; if so be that we suffer with *him*, that we may be also glorified together. Gal. 3:29; 4:7; Titus 3:7
18 For I reckon that the sufferings of this present time *are* not worthy *to be compared* with the glory which shall be revealed in us. 1 Pet. 4:13
19 For the earnest expectation of the creature waiteth for the ᵀmanifestation of the sons of God. 1 John 3:2 ◆ *being made known*
20 For the creature was made subject to vanity, not willingly, but by reason of him who hath subjected *the same* in hope, Gen. 3:17-19; 5:29
21 Because the creature itself also shall be delivered from the bondage of corruption into the glorious liberty of the children of God. 2 Pet. 3:13
22 For we know that the whole creation

groaneth and travaileth in pain together until now. Jer. 12:11
23 And not only *they*, but ourselves also, which have the firstfruits of the Spirit, even we ourselves groan within ourselves, waiting for the adoption, ᵀto wit, the redemption of our body. Rom. 7:24 ◆ *namely*
24 For we are saved by hope: but hope that is seen is not hope: for what a man seeth, why doth he yet hope for? 2 Cor. 4:18; 1 Thess. 5:8
25 But if we hope for that we see not, *then* do we with patience wait for it. 1 Thess. 1:3
26 Likewise the Spirit also helpeth our infirmities: for we know not what we should pray for as we ought: but the Spirit itself maketh intercession for us with groanings which cannot be uttered. Zech. 12:10; Eph. 6:18
27 And he that searcheth the hearts knoweth what *is* the mind of the Spirit, because he maketh intercession for the saints according to *the will of* God. Rom. 8:34
28 And we know that all things work together for good to them that love God, to them who are the called according to *his* purpose. Gal. 1:15

> **8:28 All Things Working for Good**
>
> Study the history of Joseph and of Daniel. The Lord did not prevent the plottings of men who sought to do them harm; but He caused all these devices to work for good to His servants who amidst trial and conflict preserved their faith and loyalty. *MH 487*

Nothing Can Separate Us from God's Love

29 For whom he did foreknow, he also did predestinate *to be* conformed to the image of his Son, that he might be the firstborn among many brethren. Rom. 11:2; 1 Cor. 15:49; Eph. 1:11
30 Moreover whom he did predestinate, them he also called: and whom he called, them he also justified: and whom he justified, them he also glorified. John 17:22; 1 Cor. 6:11; Heb. 9:15
31 What shall we then say to these things? If God *be* for us, who *can be* against us? Num. 14:9; Ps. 118:6; Rom. 4:1
32 He that spared not his own Son, but delivered him up for us all, how shall he not with him also freely give us all things? John 3:16
33 Who shall lay any thing to the charge of God's elect? *It is* God that justifieth. Is. 50:8-9
34 Who *is* he that condemneth? *It is* Christ that died, yea rather, that is risen again, who is even at the right hand of God, who also maketh intercession for us. Mark 16:19; Heb. 7:25
35 Who shall separate us from the love of Christ? *shall* tribulation, or distress, or persecution, or famine, or nakedness, or peril, or sword? 1 Cor. 4:11

36 As it is written, For thy sake we are killed all the day long; we are accounted as sheep for the slaughter. Ps. 44:22; 1 Cor. 15:30
37 Nay, in all these things we are more than conquerors through him that loved us. 1 Cor. 15:57; Gal. 2:20; Rev. 1:5
38 For I am persuaded, that neither death, nor life, nor angels, nor ᵀprincipalities, nor powers, nor things present, nor things to come, Eph. 1:21 ◆ dignitaries
39 Nor height, nor depth, nor any other creature, shall be able to separate us from the love of God, which is in Christ Jesus our Lord. Rom. 5:8

Paul's Concern for the Jews

9 I say the truth in Christ, I lie not, my conscience also bearing me witness in the Holy Ghost, Rom. 1:9; Gal. 1:20; 1 Tim. 2:7
2 That I have great heaviness and continual sorrow in my heart.
3 For I could wish that myself were accursed from Christ for my brethren, my kinsmen according to the flesh: Ex. 32:32; Rom. 11:14; Gal. 1:8
4 Who are Israelites; to whom *pertaineth* the adoption, and the glory, and the covenants, and the giving of the law, and the service *of God*, and the promises; Gen. 17:2; Ex. 4:22
5 Whose *are* the fathers, and of whom as concerning the flesh Christ *came*, who is over all, God blessed for ever. Amen. Rom. 1:3, 25; 11:28
6 Not as though the word of God hath taken none effect. For they *are* not all Israel, which are of Israel: Gal. 6:16
7 Neither, because they are the seed of Abraham, *are they* all children: but, In Isaac shall thy seed be called. Gen. 21:12; Heb. 11:18
8 That is, They which are the children of the flesh, these *are* not the children of God: but the children of the promise are counted for the seed.
9 For this *is* the word of promise, At this time will I come, and Sara shall have a son. Gen. 17:21; 18:10, 14

> **9:10–13 God Chooses None to Be Lost**
>
> There was no arbitrary choice on the part of God by which Esau was shut out from the blessings of salvation. The gifts of His grace through Christ are free to all. There is no election but one's own by which any may perish. . . . As regards man's final salvation, this is the only election brought to view in the word of God. *PP 207, 208*

10 And not only *this*; but when Rebecca also had conceived by one, *even* by our father Isaac; Rom. 5:3
11 (For *the children* being not yet born, neither having done any good or evil, that the purpose of God according to election might

stand, not of works, but of him that calleth;) Rom. 4:17
12 It was said unto her, The elder shall serve the younger.
13 As it is written, Jacob have I loved, but Esau have I hated. Mal. 1:2-3
14 What shall we say then? *Is there* unrighteousness with God? God forbid. Deut. 32:4; 2
15 For he saith to Moses, I will have mercy on whom I will have mercy, and I will have compassion on whom I will have compassion. Ex. 33:19
16 So then *it is* not of him that willeth, nor of him that runneth, but of God that sheweth mercy.
17 For the scripture saith unto Pharaoh, Even for this same purpose have I raised thee up, that I might shew my power in thee, and that my name might be declared throughout all the earth. Ex. 9:16
18 Therefore hath he mercy on whom he will *have mercy*, and whom he will he hardeneth. Ex. 4:21
19 Thou wilt say then unto me, Why doth he yet find fault? For who hath resisted his will? 2 Chr. 20:6; Dan. 4:35; 1 Cor. 15:35
20 Nay but, O man, who art thou that repliest against God? Shall the thing formed say to him that formed *it*, Why hast thou made me thus? Job 33:13; Is. 29:16; Rom. 2:1
21 Hath not the potter power over the clay, of the same lump to make one vessel unto honour, and another unto dishonour? Is. 64:8
22 *What* if God, willing to shew *his* wrath, and to make his power known, endured with much longsuffering the vessels of wrath fitted to destruction: Prov. 16:4; 1 Pet. 2:8; Jude 4
23 And that he might make known the riches of his glory on the vessels of mercy, which he had afore prepared unto glory, Eph. 3:16
24 Even us, whom he hath called, not of the Jews only, but also of the Gentiles?

The Calling of the Gentiles

25 As he saith also in Osee, I will call them my people, which were not my people; and her beloved, which was not beloved. Hos. 2:23
26 And it shall come to pass, *that* in the place where it was said unto them, Ye *are* not my people; there shall they be called the children of the living God.
27 Esaias also crieth concerning Israel, Though the number of the children of Israel be as the sand of the sea, a remnant shall be saved: Is. 10:20-23
28 For he will finish the work, and cut *it* short in righteousness: because a short work will the Lord make upon the earth.
29 And as Esaias said before, Except the Lord of Sabaoth had left us a seed, we had

been as Sodoma, and been made like unto Gomorrha.   Is. 1:9; 13:19; Jer. 50:40

30 What shall we say then? That the Gentiles, which followed not after righteousness, have attained to righteousness, even the righteousness which is of faith.   Phil. 3:9; Heb. 11:7

31 But Israel, which followed after the law of righteousness, hath not attained to the law of righteousness.   Rom. 11:7

32 Wherefore? Because *they sought it* not by faith, but as it were by the works of the law. For they stumbled at that stumblingstone;   1 Pet. 2:8

33 As it is written, Behold, I lay in Sion a stumblingstone and rock of offence: and whosoever believeth on him shall not be ashamed.   Ps. 118:22; Is. 28:16; Rom. 10:11

Those Who Believe Will Be Saved

10 Brethren, my heart's desire and prayer to God for Israel is, that they might be saved.

2 For I bear them record that they have a zeal of God, but not according to knowledge.   Acts 21:20

3 For they being ignorant of God's righteousness, and going about to establish their own righteousness, have not submitted themselves unto the righteousness of God.   Rom. 1:17

4 For Christ *is* the end of the law for righteousness to every one that believeth. Gal. 3:24

5 For Moses describeth the righteousness which is of the law, That the man which doeth those things shall live by them. Neh. 9:29

6 But the righteousness which is of faith speaketh on this wise, Say not in thine heart, Who shall ascend into heaven? (that is, to bring Christ down *from above*:)

7 Or, Who shall descend into the deep? (that is, to bring up Christ again from the dead.)   Heb. 13:20

8 But what saith it? The word is nigh thee, *even* in thy mouth, and in thy heart: that is, the word of faith, which we preach; Deut. 30:14

9 That if thou shalt confess with thy mouth the Lord Jesus, and shalt believe in thine heart that God hath raised him from the dead, thou shalt be saved.   Luke 12:8; Acts 2:24; Phil. 2:11

10 For with the heart man believeth unto righteousness; and with the mouth confession is made unto salvation.

10:11–13 The Role of Our Choice

The blessings of salvation are for every soul. Nothing but his own choice can prevent any man from becoming a partaker of the promise in Christ by the gospel. *DA 403*

---

11 For the scripture saith, Whosoever believeth on him shall not be ashamed. Is. 28:16

12 For there is no difference between the Jew and the Greek: for the same Lord over all is rich unto all that call upon him.   Gal. 3:28

13 For whosoever shall call upon the name of the Lord shall be saved.   Joel 2:32; Acts 2:21

14 How then shall they call on him in whom they have not believed? and how shall they believe in him of whom they have not heard? and how shall they hear without a preacher?   Titus 1:3

15 And how shall they preach, except they be sent? as it is written, How beautiful are the feet of them that preach the gospel of peace, and bring glad tidings of good things!   Is. 52:7; Nah. 1:15; Eph. 6:15

16 But they have not all obeyed the gospel. For Esaias saith, Lord, who hath believed our report?   Is. 53:1; Rom. 3:3; Heb. 4:2

17 So then faith *cometh* by hearing, and hearing by the word of God.   Gal. 3:2

Faith See Luke 17:5.

18 But I say, Have they not heard? Yes verily, their sound went into all the earth, and their words unto the ends of the world.   Ps. 19:4

19 But I say, Did not Israel know? First Moses saith, I will provoke you to jealousy by *them that are* no people, *and* by a foolish nation I will anger you.   Deut. 32:21; Rom. 11:11, 14

20 But Esaias is very bold, and saith, I was found of them that sought me not; I was made ᵀmanifest unto them that asked not after me.   Rom. 9:30 ♦ *made known*

21 But to Israel he saith, All day long I have stretched forth my hands unto a disobedient and gainsaying people.

10:21 Deciding Based on Evidence

God does not compel men to give up their unbelief. Before them are light and darkness, truth and error. It is for them to decide which they will accept. The human mind is endowed with power to discriminate between right and wrong. God designs that men shall not decide from impulse, but from weight of evidence, carefully comparing scripture with scripture. *DA 458*

God's Love for the Jewish People

11 I say then, Hath God cast away his people? God forbid. For I also am an Israelite, of the seed of Abraham, *of* the tribe of Benjamin.   1 Sam. 12:22; 2 Cor. 11:22; Phil. 3:5

2 God hath not cast away his people which he foreknew. Wot ye not what the scripture saith of Elias? how he maketh intercession to God against Israel, saying,   1 Pet. 1:2

3 Lord, they have killed thy prophets, and digged down thine altars; and I am left alone, and they seek my life.

4 But what saith the answer of God unto him? I have reserved to myself seven thousand men, who have not bowed the knee to *the image of* Baal.   1 Kin. 19:18

5 Even so then at this present time also there is a remnant according to the election of grace.   Rom. 9:27

11:5 The Faithful Remnant

At the time of the Saviour's advent there were faithful men and women who had received with gladness the message of John the Baptist, and had thus been led to study anew the prophecies concerning the Messiah. When the early Christian church was founded, it was composed of these faithful Jews who recognized Jesus of Nazareth as the one for whose advent they had been longing. It is to this remnant that Paul refers. *AA 377*

---

6 And if by grace, then *is it* no more of works: otherwise grace is no more grace. But if *it be* of works, then is it no more grace: otherwise work is no more work.

7 What then? Israel hath not obtained that which he seeketh for; but the election hath obtained it, and the rest were blinded

8 (According as it is written, God hath given them the spirit of slumber, eyes that they should not see, and ears that they should not hear;) unto this day.   Deut. 29:4; Is. 29:10; Jer. 5:21

9 And David saith, Let their table be made a snare, and a trap, and a stumblingblock, and a recompence unto them: Ps. 69:22-23

10 Let their eyes be darkened, that they may not see, and bow down their back alway.   Ps. 69:23

11 I say then, Have they stumbled that they should fall? God forbid: but *rather* through their fall salvation *is come* unto the Gentiles, for to provoke them to jealousy.   Rom. 10:19

12 Now if the fall of them *be* the riches of the world, and the diminishing of them the riches of the Gentiles; how much more their fulness?   Rom. 11:25

13 For I speak to you Gentiles, inasmuch as I am the apostle of the Gentiles, I magnify mine office: Acts 9:15

14 If by any means I may provoke to emulation *them which are* my flesh, and might save some of them.   Rom. 9:3; 1 Cor. 7:16; 1 Tim. 4:16

15 For if the casting away of them *be* the reconciling of the world, what *shall* the receiving *of them be*, but life from the dead?

16 For if the firstfruit *be* holy, the lump *is* also *holy*: and if the root *be* holy, so *are* the branches.   Ezek. 44:30

17 And if some of the branches be broken off, and thou, being a wild olive tree, wert graffed in among them, and with them par-

takest of the root and fatness of the olive tree;   Ps. 52:8; Jer. 11:16; Eph. 2:11-13

18 Boast not against the branches. But if thou boast, thou bearest not the root, but the root thee.

19 Thou wilt say then, The branches were broken off, that I might be graffed in.

20 Well; because of unbelief they were broken off, and thou standest by faith. Be not highminded, but fear: Rom. 12:16; 1 Cor. 10:12; 2 Cor. 1:24

21 For if God spared not the natural branches, *take heed* lest he also spare not thee.

22 Behold therefore the goodness and severity of God: on them which fell, severity; but toward thee, goodness, if thou continue in *his* goodness: otherwise thou also shalt be cut off.   John 15:2; 1 Cor. 15:2; Heb. 3:6

23 And they also, if they abide not still in unbelief, shall be graffed in: for God is able to graff them in again.   2 Cor. 3:16

24 For if thou wert cut out of the olive tree which is wild by nature, and wert graffed contrary to nature into a good olive tree: how much more shall these, which be the natural *branches*, be graffed into their own olive tree?

25 For I would not, brethren, that ye should be ignorant of this mystery, lest ye should be wise in your own conceits; that blindness in part is happened to Israel, until the fulness of the Gentiles be come in.   Luke 21:24; Rom. 16:25

26 And so all Israel shall be saved: as it is written, There shall come out of Sion the Deliverer, and shall turn away ungodliness from Jacob: Ps. 14:7; Is. 59:20; Hos. 3:5

27 For this *is* my covenant unto them, when I shall take away their sins.   Is. 27:9; 59:21

28 As concerning the gospel, *they are* enemies for your sakes: but as touching the election, *they are* beloved for the fathers' sakes.   Deut. 10:15; Rom. 9:5

29 For the gifts and calling of God *are* without repentance.   Rom. 8:28

30 For as ye in times past have not believed God, yet have now obtained mercy through their unbelief: Col. 3:7

31 Even so have these also now not believed, that through your mercy they also may obtain mercy.

32 For God hath concluded them all in unbelief, that he might have mercy upon all.

God's Judgments Are Unsearchable

33 O the depth of the riches both of the wisdom and knowledge of God! how unsearchable *are* his judgments, and his ways past finding out!   Rom. 2:4

34 For who hath known the mind of the Lord? or who hath been his counsellor?

> **11:33 Mysteries of the Word**
>
> The word of God, like the character of its divine Author, presents mysteries that can never be fully comprehended by finite beings. ... But we have no reason to doubt God's word because we cannot understand the mysteries of His providence. ... God has given us in the Scriptures sufficient evidence of their divine character, and we are not to doubt His word because we cannot understand all the mysteries of His providence. *SC 106, 107*

35 Or who hath first given to him, and it shall be recompensed unto him again? Job 35:7; 41:11
36 For of him, and through him, and to him, *are* all things: to whom *be* glory for ever. Amen. Rom. 16:27; 1 Cor. 8:6; Eph. 3:21

Dedicate Your Lives to God

12 I beseech you therefore, brethren, by the mercies of God, that ye present your bodies a living sacrifice, holy, acceptable unto God, *which is* your reasonable service.

> **12:2 One Cherished Sin**
>
> Any habit or practice that would lead into sin, and bring dishonor upon Christ, would better be put away, whatever the sacrifice. That which dishonors God cannot benefit the soul. The blessing of heaven cannot attend any man in violating the eternal principles of right. And one sin cherished is sufficient to work the degradation of the character, and to mislead others. *DA 439*

2 And be not conformed to this world: but be ye transformed by the renewing of your mind, that ye may prove what *is* that good, and acceptable, and perfect, will of God. 1 Pet. 1:14
3 For I say, through the grace given unto me, to every man that is among you, not to think *of himself* more highly than he ought

to think; but to think soberly, according as God hath dealt to every man the measure of faith. Rom. 1:5

Faith *See* Matthew 17:20.

4 For as we have many members in one body, and all members have not the same office: 1 Cor. 12:12-14
5 So we, *being* many, are one body in Christ, and every one members one of another. 1 Cor. 10:17; 12:20; Eph. 4:25
6 Having then gifts differing according to the grace that is given to us, whether prophecy, *let us prophesy* according to the proportion of faith; Acts 13:1
7 Or ministry, *let us wait* on *our* ministering: or he that teacheth, on teaching; Acts 13:1
8 Or he that exhorteth, on exhortation: he that giveth, *let him do it* with simplicity; he that ruleth, with diligence; he that sheweth mercy, with cheerfulness. 1 Cor. 12:28; 2 Cor. 9:7; 1 Tim. 5:17
9 *Let* love be without ⊤dissimulation. Abhor that which is evil; cleave to that which is good. Ps. 97:10; 2 Cor. 6:6; 1 Tim. 1:5 ◆ *hypocrisy*
10 *Be* kindly affectioned one to another with brotherly love; in honour preferring one another; Phil. 2:3; Heb. 13:1; 1 Pet. 2:17
11 Not slothful in business; fervent in spirit; serving the Lord; Acts 18:25
12 Rejoicing in hope; patient in tribulation; continuing instant in prayer; Acts 1:14; Heb. 10:36
13 Distributing to the necessity of saints; given to hospitality. 2 Cor. 9:1
14 Bless them which persecute you: bless, and curse not. Matt. 5:44; Luke 6:28; 1 Pet. 3:9
15 Rejoice with them that do rejoice, and weep with them that weep. Heb. 13:3
16 *Be* of the same mind one toward another. Mind not high things, but condescend to men of low estate. Be not wise in your own conceits. Prov. 3:7; Rom. 11:25; 15:5

The Sacrifice, Making It Practical for Today

Romans 12:1

Every morning and evening a lamb of a year old was burned upon the altar, with its appropriate meat offering, thus symbolizing the daily consecration of the nation to Jehovah, and their constant dependence upon the atoning blood of Christ. God expressly directed that every offering presented for the service of the sanctuary should be "without blemish" (Exodus 12:5). The priests were to examine all animals brought as a sacrifice, and were to reject every one in which a defect was discovered. Only an offering "without blemish" could be a symbol of His perfect purity who was to offer Himself as "a lamb without blemish and without spot" (1 Peter 1:19). The apostle Paul points to these sacrifices as an illustration of what the followers of Christ are to become. He says, "I beseech you therefore, brethren, by the mercies of God, that ye present your bodies a living sacrifice, holy, acceptable unto God, which is your reasonable service" (Romans 12:1). We are to give ourselves to the service of God, and we should seek to make the offering as nearly perfect as possible. God will not be pleased with anything less than the best we can offer. Those who love Him with all the heart, will desire to give Him the best service of the life, and they will be constantly seeking to bring every power of their being into harmony with the laws that will promote their ability to do His will. *PP 352, 353*

17 Recompense to no man evil for evil. Provide things honest in the sight of all men.   Prov. 20:22; Matt. 5:39; Rom. 12:19
18 If it be possible, as much as lieth in you, live peaceably with all men. Matt. 5:9; Mark 9:50
19 Dearly beloved, avenge not yourselves, but *rather* give place unto wrath: for it is written, Vengeance *is* mine; I will repay, saith the Lord.   Lev. 19:18; Deut. 32:35; Prov. 24:29

Christian Behavior See 2 Corinthians 9:6, 7.

20 Therefore if thine enemy hunger, feed him; if he thirst, give him drink: for in so doing thou shalt heap coals of fire on his head.   Prov. 25:21-22
21 Be not overcome of evil, but overcome evil with good.   1 Pet. 3:9

12:21 Christ's Method

Under a storm of stinging, faultfinding words, keep the mind stayed upon the word of God. Let mind and heart be stored with God's promises. If you are ill-treated or wrongfully accused, instead of returning an angry answer, repeat to yourself the precious promises:

"Be not overcome of evil, but overcome evil with good" (Romans 12:21). *MH 486*

Obey the Government

13 Let every soul be subject unto the higher powers. For there is no power but of God: the powers that be are ordained of God.   Dan. 2:21; John 19:11; Titus 3:1
2 Whosoever therefore resisteth the power, resisteth the ordinance of God: and they that resist shall receive to themselves damnation.
3 For rulers are not a terror to good works, but to the evil. Wilt thou then not be afraid of the power? do that which is good, and thou shalt have praise of the same:
4 For he is the minister of God to thee for good. But if thou do that which is evil, be afraid; for he beareth not the sword in vain: for he is the minister of God, a revenger to *execute* wrath upon him that doeth evil.
5 Wherefore *ye* must needs be subject, not only for wrath, but also for conscience sake.
6 For for this cause pay ye tribute also: for they are God's ministers, attending continually upon this very thing.
7 Render therefore to all their dues: tribute to whom tribute *is due*; custom to whom custom; fear to whom fear; honour to whom honour.   Matt. 17:25

Love One Another

8 Owe no man any thing, but to love one another: for he that loveth another hath fulfilled the law.   Matt. 7:12; Rom. 13:10; Gal. 5:14

13:7 Allegiance to God and Country

Holding in [Christ's] hand the Roman coin, upon which were stamped the name and image of Caesar, He declared that since they were living under the protection of the Roman power, they should render to that power the support it claimed, so long as this did not conflict with a higher duty. But while peaceably subject to the laws of the land, they should at all times give their first allegiance to God. *DA 602*

9 For this, Thou shalt not commit adultery, Thou shalt not kill, Thou shalt not steal, Thou shalt not bear false witness, Thou shalt not covet; and if *there be* any other commandment, it is briefly comprehended in this saying, namely, Thou shalt love thy neighbour as thyself.   Ex. 20:12-17; Lev. 19:18; Matt. 19:18-19
10 Love worketh no ill to his neighbour: therefore love *is* the fulfilling of the law.   Rom. 13:8

13:10 How to Receive Righteousness

Righteousness is love, and love is the light and the life of God. The righteousness of God is embodied in Christ. We receive righteousness by receiving Him.

Not by painful struggles or wearisome toil, not by gift or sacrifice, is righteousness obtained; but it is freely given to every soul who hungers and thirsts to receive it. *MB 18*

11 And that, knowing the time, that now *it is* high time to awake out of sleep: for now *is* our salvation nearer than when we believed.   Luke 21:28; 1 Cor. 15:34; Eph. 5:14
12 The night is far spent, the day is at hand: let us therefore cast off the works of darkness, and let us put on the armour of light.   2 Cor. 6:7; Eph. 5:11
13 Let us walk honestly, as in the day; not in rioting and drunkenness, not in ᵀchambering and wantonness, not in strife and envying.   Luke 21:34; Gal. 5:21 ♦ *sexual immorality*
14 But put ye on the Lord Jesus Christ, and make not provision for the flesh, to *fulfil* the lusts *thereof*.   Gal. 3:27; Eph. 4:24; 1 Pet. 2:11

The Weaker Believer

14 Him that is weak in the faith receive ye, *but* not to doubtful disputations.
2 For one believeth that he may eat all things: another, who is weak, eateth herbs. Rom. 14:14
3 Let not him that eateth despise him that eateth not; and let not him which eateth not judge him that eateth: for God hath received him.   Luke 18:9
4 Who art thou that judgest another man's servant? to his own master he standeth or

falleth. Yea, he shall be ᵀholden up: for God is able to make him stand.   Rom. 9:20 ◆ held

5 One man esteemeth one day above another: another esteemeth every day *alike*. Let every man be fully persuaded in his own mind.

14:5 Messengers of Mercy

In all matters where principle is involved, "let every man be fully persuaded in his own mind" (Romans 14:5). In Christ's kingdom there is no lordly oppression, no compulsion of manner. The angels of heaven do not come to the earth to rule, and to exact homage, but as messengers of mercy, to co-operate with men in uplifting humanity. *DA 550, 551*

---

6 He that regardeth the day, regardeth *it* unto the Lord; and he that regardeth not the day, to the Lord he doth not regard *it*. He that eateth, eateth to the Lord, for he giveth God thanks; and he that eateth not, to the Lord he eateth not, and giveth God thanks.
7 For none of us liveth to himself, and no man dieth to himself.   2 Cor. 5:15; 1 Thess. 5:10; 1 Pet. 4:2

14:7 Our Unconscious Influence

By our unconscious influence others may be encouraged and strengthened, or they may be discouraged, and repelled from Christ and the truth. *SC 120*

---

8 For whether we live, we live unto the Lord; and whether we die, we die unto the Lord: whether we live therefore, or die, we are the Lord's.   Phil. 1:20
9 For to this end Christ both died, and rose, and revived, that he might be Lord both of the dead and living.   Luke 24:26; Rev. 1:18
10 But why dost thou judge thy brother? or why dost thou set at nought thy brother? for we shall all stand before the judgment seat of Christ.   Rom. 2:16; 1 Cor. 4:5; 2 Cor. 5:10
11 For it is written, *As* I live, saith the Lord, every knee shall bow to me, and every tongue shall confess to God.

12 So then every one of us shall give account of himself to God.   Matt. 12:36; Gal. 6:5; 1 Pet. 4:5

14:13 Avoid Needless Censure

It is always humiliating to have one's errors pointed out. None should make the experience more bitter by needless censure. No one was ever reclaimed by reproach; but many have thus been repelled and have been led to steel their hearts against conviction. A tender spirit, a gentle, winning deportment, may save the erring and hide a multitude of sins. *MH 166*

---

13 Let us not therefore judge one another any more: but judge this rather, that no man put a stumblingblock or an occasion to fall in *his* brother's way.   Matt. 7:1
14 I know, and am persuaded by the Lord Jesus, that *there is* nothing unclean of itself: but to him that esteemeth any thing to be unclean, to him *it is* unclean. Rom. 14:2, 20; 1 Cor. 8:7
15 But if thy brother be grieved with *thy* meat, now walkest thou not charitably. Destroy not him with thy meat, for whom Christ died.   Eph. 5:2
16 Let not then your good be evil spoken of:
17 For the kingdom of God is not meat and drink; but righteousness, and peace, and joy in the Holy Ghost. Rom. 15:13; 1 Cor. 8:8; Gal. 5:22
18 For he that in these things serveth Christ *is* acceptable to God, and approved of men.
19 Let us therefore follow after the things which make for peace, and things wherewith one may edify another. Ps. 34:14; Rom. 12:18; 15:2
20 For meat destroy not the work of God. All things indeed *are* pure; but *it is* evil for that man who eateth with offence.   Rom. 14:14-15
21 *It is* good neither to eat flesh, nor to drink wine, nor *any thing* whereby thy brother stumbleth, or is offended, or is made weak.   1 Cor. 8:13
22 Hast thou faith? have *it* to thyself before God. Happy *is* he that condemneth not himself in that thing which he alloweth.

No Peace in Compromising

Romans 14:19

Jesus Himself never purchased peace by compromise. His heart overflowed with love for the whole human race, but He was never indulgent to their sins. He was too much their friend to remain silent while they were pursuing a course that would ruin their souls—the souls He had purchased with His own blood. He labored that man should be true to himself, true to his higher and eternal interest. The servants of Christ are called to the same work, and they should beware lest, in seeking to prevent discord, they surrender the truth. They are to "follow after the things which make for peace" (Romans 14:19); but real peace can never be secured by compromising principle. And no man can be true to principle without exciting opposition. A Christianity that is spiritual will be opposed by the children of disobedience. . . . Those who are true to God need not fear the power of men nor the enmity of Satan. In Christ their eternal life is secure. Their only fear should be lest they surrender the truth, and thus betray the trust with which God has honored them. *DA 356*

23 And he that doubteth is ^Tdamned if he eat, because *he eateth* not of faith: for whatsoever *is* not of faith is sin.   *condemned*

The Strong Must Bear with the Weak

15 We then that are strong ought to bear the infirmities of the weak, and not to please ourselves. Rom. 14:1; Gal. 6:1-2; 1 Thess. 5:14

> ### 15:1 Angels Help When Most Needed
>
> No soul who believes in Christ, though his faith may be weak, and his steps wavering as those of a little child, is to be lightly esteemed. . . . Angels of glory, that do always behold the face of the Father in heaven, joy in ministering to His little ones. . . . Angels are ever present where they are most needed, with those who have the hardest battle with self to fight, and whose surroundings are the most discouraging. And in this ministry Christ's true followers will cooperate. *DA 440*

2 Let every one of us please *his* neighbour for *his* good to edification.   Rom. 14:19
3 For even Christ pleased not himself; but, as it is written, The reproaches of them that reproached thee fell on me. Ps. 69:9; John 5:30; 6:38
4 For whatsoever things were written ^Taforetime were written for our learning, that we through patience and comfort of the scriptures might have hope.   Rom. 4:23-24 ♦ *before*
5 Now the God of patience and consolation grant you to be likeminded one toward another according to Christ Jesus: 1 Cor. 1:10
6 That ye may with one mind *and* one mouth glorify God, even the Father of our Lord Jesus Christ.   Eph. 1:3

God Gives Unity

7 Wherefore receive ye one another, as Christ also received us to the glory of God.
8 Now I say that Jesus Christ was a minister of the circumcision for the truth of God, to confirm the promises *made* unto the fathers: Matt. 15:24; John 1:11; 2 Cor. 1:20

9 And that the Gentiles might glorify God for *his* mercy; as it is written, For this cause I will confess to thee among the Gentiles, and sing unto thy name.   2 Sam. 22:50; Ps. 18:49; Rom. 3:29
10 And again he saith, Rejoice, ye Gentiles, with his people.   Deut. 32:43
11 And again, Praise the Lord, all ye Gentiles; and ^Tlaud him, all ye people.   Ps. 117:1 ♦ *praise*
12 And again, Esaias saith, There shall be a root of Jesse, and he that shall rise to reign over the Gentiles; in him shall the Gentiles trust.   Is. 11:10; Matt. 12:21; Rev. 5:5
13 Now the God of hope fill you with all joy and peace in believing, that ye may abound in hope, through the power of the Holy Ghost.   Rom. 12:12; 14:17
14 And I myself also am persuaded of you, my brethren, that ye also are full of goodness, filled with all knowledge, able also to admonish one another.   1 Cor. 8:1
15 Nevertheless, brethren, I have written the more boldly unto you in some sort, as putting you in mind, because of the grace that is given to me of God,   Rom. 12:3
16 That I should be the minister of Jesus Christ to the Gentiles, ministering the gospel of God, that the offering up of the Gentiles might be acceptable, being ^Tsanctified by the Holy Ghost.   Acts 9:15; Phil. 2:17 ♦ *made holy*
17 I have therefore whereof I may glory through Jesus Christ in those things which pertain to God.   Heb. 5:1
18 For I will not dare to speak of any of those things which Christ hath not ^Twrought by me, to make the Gentiles obedient, by word and deed,   Acts 15:12; 21:19; Rom. 1:5 ♦ *done*
19 Through mighty signs and wonders, by the power of the Spirit of God; so that from Jerusalem, and round about unto Illyricum, I have fully preached the gospel of Christ.   Acts 22:17-21
20 Yea, so have I strived to preach the gospel, not where Christ was named,

> ## Encouragement and Warning
>
> ### Romans 15:4
>
> Men whom God favored, and to whom He entrusted great responsibilities, were sometimes overcome by temptation and committed sin, even as we at the present day strive, waver, and frequently fall into error. Their lives, with all their faults and follies, are open before us, both for our encouragement and warning. If they had been represented as without fault, we, with our sinful nature, might despair at our own mistakes and failures. But seeing where others struggled through discouragements like our own, where they fell under temptation as we have done, and yet took heart again and conquered through the grace of God, we are encouraged in our striving after righteousness. As they, though sometimes beaten back, recovered their ground, and were blessed of God, so we too may be overcomers in the strength of Jesus. On the other hand, the record of their lives may serve as a warning to us. It shows that God will by no means clear the guilty. He sees sin in His most favored ones, and He deals with it in them even more strictly than in those who have less light and responsibility. *PP 238*

lest I should build upon another man's foundation: 2 Cor. 10:13-16

21 But as it is written, To whom he was not spoken of, they shall see: and they that have not heard shall understand.   Is. 52:15

22 For which cause also I have been much hindered from coming to you.   Rom. 1:13

23 But now having no more place in these parts, and having a great desire these many years to come unto you;   Rom. 15:32

24 Whensoever I take my journey into Spain, I will come to you: for I trust to see you in my journey, and to be brought on my way thitherward by you, if first I be somewhat filled with your *company*.   Acts 15:3; Rom. 1:12; 15:28

25 But now I go unto Jerusalem to minister unto the saints.   Acts 19:21; 20:22; 24:17

26 For it hath pleased them of Macedonia and Achaia to make a certain contribution for the poor saints which are at Jerusalem.

27 It hath pleased them ᵀverily; and their debtors they are. For if the Gentiles have been made partakers of their spiritual things, their duty is also to minister unto them in ᵀcarnal things.   1 Cor. 9:11; Gal. 6:6 ◆ *truly* ◆ *material*

28 When therefore I have performed this, and have sealed to them this fruit, I will come by you into Spain.   Rom. 15:24

29 And I am sure that, when I come unto you, I shall come in the fulness of the blessing of the gospel of Christ.

Paul Requests Prayer

30 Now I ᵀbeseech you, brethren, for the Lord Jesus Christ's sake, and for the love of the Spirit, that ye strive together with me in *your* prayers to God for me;   2 Cor. 1:11; Phil. 2:1 ◆ *beg*

31 That I may be delivered from them that do not believe in Judaea; and that my service which I have for Jerusalem may be accepted of the saints;   Rom. 15:25; 2 Cor. 8:4; 2 Thess. 3:2

32 That I may come unto you with joy by the will of God, and may with you be refreshed.   Acts 18:21

33 Now the God of peace *be* with you all. Amen.   Rom. 16:20; 2 Cor. 13:11; Phil. 4:9

Paul's Farewell

16 I commend unto you Phebe our sister, which is a servant of the church which is at Cenchrea: Acts 18:18; 2 Cor. 3:1

2 That ye receive her in the Lord, as becometh saints, and that ye assist her in whatsoever business she hath need of you: for she hath been a ᵀsuccourer of many, and of myself also.   Phil. 2:29 ◆ *helper*

3 Greet Priscilla and Aquila my helpers in Christ Jesus:

4 Who have for my life laid down their own necks: unto whom not only I give thanks, but also all the churches of the Gentiles.

5 Likewise *greet* the church that is in their house. Salute my wellbeloved Epaenetus, who is the firstfruits of Achaia unto Christ.   1 Cor. 16:15, 19; Col. 4:15

6 Greet Mary, who bestowed much labour on us.   Rom. 16:12

7 Salute Andronicus and Junia, my kinsmen, and my fellowprisoners, who are of note among the apostles, who also were in Christ before me.   Rom. 16:11

8 Greet Amplias my beloved in the Lord.

9 Salute Urbane, our helper in Christ, and Stachys my beloved.

10 Salute Apelles approved in Christ. Salute them which are of Aristobulus' *household*.

11 Salute Herodion my ᵀkinsman. Greet them that be of the *household* of Narcissus, which are in the Lord.   *nearest male blood relative*

12 Salute Tryphena and Tryphosa, who labour in the Lord. Salute the beloved Persis, which laboured much in the Lord.

13 Salute Rufus chosen in the Lord, and his mother and mine.   Mark 15:21

14 Salute Asyncritus, Phlegon, Hermas, Patrobas, Hermes, and the brethren which are with them.

15 Salute Philologus, and Julia, Nereus, and his sister, and Olympas, and all the saints which are with them.   Rom. 16:2

16 Salute one another with an holy kiss. The churches of Christ salute you.   1 Thess. 5:26

Watch Out for Divisions

17 Now I ᵀbeseech you, brethren, mark them which cause divisions and offences contrary to the doctrine which ye have learned; and avoid them.   2 Thess. 3:6 ◆ *beg*

18 For they that are such serve not our Lord Jesus Christ, but their own belly; and by good words and fair speeches deceive the hearts of the simple.   Mic. 3:5; Phil. 3:19; Col. 2:4

19 For your obedience is come abroad unto all *men*. I am glad therefore on your behalf: but yet I would have you wise unto that which is good, and simple concerning evil.   Matt. 10:16; Rom. 1:8; 1 Cor. 14:20

20 And the God of peace shall bruise Satan under your feet shortly. The grace of our Lord Jesus Christ *be* with you. Amen.   Gen. 3:15

Praise and Thanks to God

21 Timotheus my workfellow, and Lucius, and Jason, and Sosipater, my kinsmen, salute you.   Acts 13:1; 17:5; 20:4

22 I Tertius, who wrote *this* epistle, salute you in the Lord.   Gal. 6:11

23 Gaius mine host, and of the whole church, saluteth you. Erastus the ᵀchamberlain of the city saluteth you, and Quartus a brother.   Acts 19:22 ◆ *chief servant*

24 The grace of our Lord Jesus Christ *be* with you all. Amen.

16:25 The Science of All Sciences

The science of redemption is the science of all sciences; the science that is the study of the angels and of all the intelligences of the unfallen worlds . . . the science that enters into the purpose brooded in the mind of the Infinite—"kept in silence through times eternal" (Romans 16:25, R.V.); the science that will be the study of God's redeemed throughout endless ages. . . . As no other study can, it will quicken the mind and uplift the soul. *Ed 126*

25 Now to him that is of power to stablish you according to my gospel, and the preaching of Jesus Christ, according to the revelation of the mystery, which was kept secret since the world began, Rom. 2:16; 1 Cor. 2:7; Eph. 1:9
26 But now is made ᵀmanifest, and by the scriptures of the prophets, according to the commandment of the everlasting God, made known to all nations for the obedience of faith: Rom. 1:5 ◆ *known*
27 To God only wise, *be* glory through Jesus Christ for ever. Amen.   1 Tim. 1:17; 6:16

THE FIRST EPISTLE OF PAUL THE APOSTLE TO THE
CORINTHIANS

As Christians in the twenty-first century, we have a guidebook—the Bible—to look to when we encounter problems, sin, disunity, and a host of other issues that arise while we are on our earthly journeys. The Christians living in Corinth during the time of the writing of 1 Corinthians had no such guidebook yet. Instead, they needed to rely on the visits of Paul and his letters to help them through their various struggles.

Paul felt responsible for the church in Corinth, since he helped found it while on his second missionary journey (Acts 18:1). When Paul wrote 1 Corinthians, the church was struggling with disunity, immorality, and the general difficulty of living as godly believers in a secular culture. Paul encouraged them in unity, helped provide answers to serious spiritual questions, and confronted some members of the community who struggled with sin.

In many ways, the culture of the city of Corinth is not unlike the culture of today. Therefore, Paul's instructions and advice are timeless.

Dates

Paul wrote 1 Corinthians during the end of his third missionary journey while in Ephesus, in the spring of A.D. 57. He wrote in response to a report of members "of the house of Chloe" concerning the lack of unity among the brethren (1:11).

Author

First Corinthians was written by Paul, with almost no debate in favor of any other author. Paul made note of his authorship in the book's first two verses: "Paul, called to be an apostle of Jesus Christ through the will of God, and Sosthenes our brother, unto the church of God which is at Corinth, to them that are sanctified in Christ Jesus, called to be saints, with all that in every place call upon the name of Jesus Christ our Lord, both theirs and ours" (1:1, 2). In addition, in A.D. 95, Clement of Rome wrote to the Corinthian church and mentioned the continuing problems of the church, thus giving early acceptance to Paul's writing of 1 Corinthians.

The apostle Paul is known to have dictated his letters to secretaries. This is true for 1 Corinthians except for the closing remarks, which are written by his "own hand" (16:21). History is uncertain as to why Paul used scribes, but it appears to have been routine for him (Romans 6:22; Colossians 4:18; 2 Thessalonians 3:17). It has been indicated that he may have had poor eyesight or very poor penmanship.

Meaning of the Name

This epistle has long been known as *Pros Korinthious A*, or "to the Corinthians A." The A was a later addition to distinguish this letter from 2 Corinthians.

Christ in 1 Corinthians

It's difficult to read 1 Corinthians and not be able to see Christ in its pages. The believers in Corinth were living in a culture that in many ways was loathsome to everything a believer held true. Many who had renounced their shamelessly immoral ways now have slipped back into their old habits (5:1–13).

In spite of exposure to licentiousness and the rebuke they receive for allowing sin to creep into the church, we can see an empathy and tender mercy that is in the hearts of the genuine co-laborers with Christ. This love always seeks to pick up those who have fallen and return the wandering ones home. Paul not only knew that the love of Christ imparts that converting, heart-conquering power, but he also knew that force and unkindness repels souls. In dealing with the Corinthians, Paul conveyed the comforting solace of Christ's love.

Paul writes, "But of him are ye in Christ Jesus, who of God is made unto us wisdom, and righteousness, and sanctification, and redemption" (1:30). Also, "We have the mind of Christ" (2:16).

First Corinthians gives us a compelling picture of how Christ is relevant to every area of our lives. He has changed everything for us and now we must learn how to live by faith.

Corinth was an important seaport city in ancient Greece, the capital of the province of Achaia. The city's population was about 700,000, with two-thirds of them being slaves. Corinth was a commercial center, with ships arriving from many places around the world. It was also a cosmopolitan religious center, with temples to various gods lining its streets. The most famous of these gods was Aphrodite, goddess of love, whose temple was the most prominent in the city. Worshipers of this goddess made use of the temple's prostitutes (numbering more than a thousand). Indeed, the name of the city became synonymous with debauchery and prostitution.

Wealth, luxury, trade, and a mixed population all contribute to the title "the Paris of antiquity." So understanding the beliefs of the Corinthians emphasizes the wonderful grace of God in overcoming the forces of wickedness to establish a revitalized church in this notorious city.

First Corinthians can be divided into three main parts, each relating to problems Paul addresses:

(1) *1 Corinthians 1—4:* These first four chapters deal with the divisions within the Corinthian church. Paul asserts his role as an apostle as he addresses this issue. He also compares earthly wisdom to that of God (chapters 1—2).

(2) *1 Corinthians 5—6:* Chapter 5 deals with the issue of sexual immorality in the church. This chapter provides information on church discipline. In chapter 6, Paul talks about lawsuits among believers and how their existence among believers is sad evidence of problems within the body of Christ.

(3) *1 Corinthians 7—16:* In the book's final ten chapters, Paul answers questions about a variety of issues, including Christian marriage, freedom, public worship, and the resurrection of believers. Two of the most well-known chapters in this section include chapter 12, which teaches about the body of Christ and the gifts of the spirit, and chapter 13, a treatise on the nature of love. Chapter 15 includes a magnificent narrative on our final victory over sin and receipt of immortality.

Unlocking 1 Corinthians

KEY PEOPLE:
Paul, Jesus, Chloe, Timothy

KEY EVENTS:
Paul's letter covers issues current to his time (disunity in the church, immorality, the true nature of love, spiritual gifts) and the end-times resurrection of believers.

KEY PHRASE:
Living by faith versus living by the flesh is the essential message of 1 Corinthians. Paul teaches believers how Christ is relevant to all aspects of our lives. His message is still relevant today.

KEY VERSES:
"What? know ye not that your body is the temple of the Holy Ghost which is in you, which ye have of God, and ye are not your own? For ye are bought with a price: therefore glorify God in your body, and in your spirit, which are God's" (1 Corinthians 6:19, 20).

"Wherefore let him that thinketh he standeth take heed lest he fall. There hath no temptation taken you but such as is common to man: but God is faithful, who will not suffer you to be tempted above that ye are able; but will with the temptation also make a way to escape, that ye may be able to bear it" (1 Corinthians 10:12, 13).

KEY CHAPTER:
1 Corinthians 13 is one of the most widely read chapters at weddings and in sermons. Paul pens one of the best definitions of love ever written. It's an encouragement and a standard for all believers. Paul demonstrates that true love trumps all the spiritual gifts exercised in the church, and that without love we have nothing.

Paul's Greeting

1 Paul, called *to be* an apostle of Jesus Christ through the will of God, and Sosthenes *our* brother,   Acts 18:17; Rom. 1:1; 2 Cor. 1:1
2 Unto the church of God which is at Corinth, to them that are ᵀsanctified in Christ Jesus, called *to be* saints, with all that in every place call upon the name of Jesus Christ our Lord, both theirs and ours: Acts 18:1; Rom. 1:7; 1 Cor. 1:30 ◆ *made holy*
3 Grace *be* unto you, and peace, from God our Father, and *from* the Lord Jesus Christ.
4 I thank my God always on your behalf, for the grace of God which is given you by Jesus Christ;   Rom. 1:8
5 That in every thing ye are enriched by him, in all utterance, and *in* all knowledge; 2 Cor. 8:7
6 Even as the testimony of Christ was confirmed in you: 1 Tim. 2:6; 2 Tim. 1:8; Rev. 1:2
7 So that ye come behind in no gift; waiting for the coming of our Lord Jesus Christ: Luke 17:30; Phil. 3:20; 2 Pet. 3:12

> **Gift of Prophecy See Revelation 12:17.**

8 Who shall also confirm you unto the end, *that ye may be* blameless in the day of our Lord Jesus Christ.   Phil. 1:6, 10; 1 Thess. 3:13
9 God *is* faithful, by whom ye were called unto the fellowship of his Son Jesus Christ our Lord.   Deut. 7:9; Is. 49:7; 1 John 1:3

Paul Exhorts the Corinthians to Unity

10 Now I ᵀbeseech you, brethren, by the name of our Lord Jesus Christ, that ye all speak the same thing, and *that* there be no divisions among you; but *that* ye be perfectly joined together in the same mind and in the same judgment.   1 Cor. 11:18 ◆ *beg*
11 For it hath been declared unto me of you, my brethren, by them *which are of the house* of Chloe, that there are contentions among you.   1 Cor. 3:3
12 Now this I say, that every one of you saith, I am of Paul; and I of Apollos; and I of Cephas; and I of Christ. John 1:42; 1 Cor. 9:5; 15:5
13 Is Christ divided? was Paul crucified for you? or were ye baptized in the name of Paul?   Matt. 28:19; Acts 2:38; 10:48
14 I thank God that I baptized none of you, but Crispus and Gaius;   Acts 18:8; Rom. 16:23
15 Lest any should say that I had baptized in mine own name.
16 And I baptized also the household of Stephanas: besides, I know not whether I baptized any other.   Acts 16:15; 1 Cor. 16:15, 17
17 For Christ sent me not to baptize, but to preach the gospel: not with wisdom of words, lest the cross of Christ should be made of none effect.   John 4:2; 1 Cor. 2:1, 13
18 For the preaching of the cross is to them that perish foolishness; but unto us which are saved it is the power of God.   1 Cor. 1:21, 23-25

> **1:18 Self-Wisdom Will Fail**
>
> The worldly-wise men who come to Christ as poor lost sinners, will become wise unto salvation; but those who come as distinguished men, extolling their own wisdom, will fail of receiving the light and knowledge that He alone can give. *AA 240*

19 For it is written, I will destroy the wisdom of the wise, and will bring to nothing the understanding of the prudent.   Job 5:12-13; Is. 29:14
20 Where *is* the wise? where *is* the scribe? where *is* the disputer of this world? hath not God made foolish the wisdom of this world?   Job 12:17; Is. 33:18; Rom. 1:22
21 For after that in the wisdom of God the world by wisdom knew not God, it pleased God by the foolishness of preaching to save them that believe.
22 For the Jews require a sign, and the Greeks seek after wisdom:
23 But we preach Christ crucified, unto the Jews a stumblingblock, and unto the Greeks foolishness;   Luke 2:34; 1 Cor. 2:14; Gal. 5:11
24 But unto them which are called, both Jews and Greeks, Christ the power of God, and the wisdom of God.   1 Cor. 1:18, 30; Col. 2:3
25 Because the foolishness of God is wiser than men; and the weakness of God is stronger than men.   1 Cor. 1:18
26 For ye see your calling, brethren, how that not many wise men after the flesh, not many mighty, not many noble, *are called*: 1 Cor. 1:20
27 But God hath chosen the foolish things of the world to confound the wise; and God hath chosen the weak things of the world to confound the things which are mighty; Ps. 8:2

> **1:26, 27 Truth Found With Believers**
>
> As in earlier ages, the special truths for this time are found, not with the ecclesiastical authorities, but with men and women who are not too learned or too wise to believe the word of God. *COL 79*

28 And base things of the world, and things which are despised, hath God chosen, *yea*, and things which are not, to bring to nought things that are: Job 34:24; Rom. 4:17; 1 Cor. 2:6
29 That no flesh should glory in his presence.   Eph. 2:9
30 But of him are ye in Christ Jesus, who of God is made unto us wisdom, and righteousness, and ᵀsanctification, and redemption: Jer. 23:5-6; 1 Cor. 1:2; Eph. 1:7 ◆ *making holy*
31 That, according as it is written, He that glorieth, let him glory in the Lord.   Jer. 9:23-24

Paul Preaches Christ Crucified

2 And I, brethren, when I came to you, came not with excellency of speech or of wisdom, declaring unto you the testimony of God.   1 Cor. 1:17; 2:4, 13
2 For I determined not to know any thing among you, save Jesus Christ, and him crucified.   Gal. 6:14

> **2:1, 2 Christ All and in All**
>
> But to Paul the cross was the one object of supreme interest. Ever since he had been arrested in his career of persecution against the followers of the crucified Nazarene he had never ceased to glory in the cross. . . . He knew by personal experience that when a sinner once beholds the love of the Father, as seen in the sacrifice of His Son, and yields to the divine influence, a change of heart takes place, and henceforth Christ is all and in all. *AA 245*

3 And I was with you in weakness, and in fear, and in much trembling.   2 Cor. 13:4
4 And my speech and my preaching *was* not with enticing words of man's wisdom, but in demonstration of the Spirit and of power: Rom. 15:19; 1 Cor. 1:17; 4:20
5 That your faith should not stand in the wisdom of men, but in the power of God. 2 Cor. 4:7

Maturity in Christ

6 Howbeit we speak wisdom among them that are perfect: yet not the wisdom of this world, nor of the princes of this world, that come to ᵀnought: 1 Cor. 1:28 ◆ *nothing*
7 But we speak the wisdom of God in a mystery, *even* the hidden *wisdom*, which God ordained before the world unto our glory:
8 Which none of the princes of this world knew: for had they known *it*, they would not have crucified the Lord of glory.   Ps. 24:7-10
9 But as it is written, Eye hath not seen, nor ear heard, neither have entered into the heart of man, the things which God hath prepared for them that love him.   Is. 64:4; Matt. 25:34
10 But God hath revealed *them* unto us by his Spirit: for the Spirit searcheth all things, yea, the deep things of God.   John 14:26; Eph. 3:3, 5
11 For what man knoweth the things of a man, save the spirit of man which is in him? even so the things of God knoweth no man, but the Spirit of God.   Prov. 20:27; Jer. 17:9

> **2:12 Just One Way to Find Knowledge**
>
> God intends that even in this life the truths of His word shall be ever unfolding to His people. There is only one way in which this knowledge can be obtained. We can attain to an understanding of God's word only through the illumination of that Spirit by which the word was given. *SC 109*

12 Now we have received, not the spirit of the world, but the spirit which is of God; that we might know the things that are freely given to us of God.
13 Which things also we speak, not in the words which man's wisdom teacheth, but which the Holy Ghost teacheth; comparing spiritual things with spiritual.   1 Cor. 1:17; 2:4
14 But the natural man receiveth not the things of the Spirit of God: for they are foolishness unto him: neither can he know *them*, because they are spiritually discerned.   1 Cor. 1:18; 15:44; Jude 19

> **2:14 Convinced but Not Surrendered**
>
> [The Pharisees] were convinced; they believed Jesus to be the Son of God; but it was not in harmony with their ambitious desires to confess Him. They had not the faith that would have secured for them the heavenly treasure. They were seeking worldly treasure. . . .
>
> For the sake of gaining worldly riches, honor, or power, they place the maxims, traditions, and requirements of men above the requirements of God. From them the treasures of His word are hidden. *COL 106*

15 But he that is spiritual judgeth all things, yet he himself is judged of no man. 1 Cor. 3:1
16 For who hath known the mind of the Lord, that he may instruct him? But we have the mind of Christ.   John 15:15; Rom. 11:34

The Solid Food of Paul's Teaching

3 And I, brethren, could not speak unto you as unto spiritual, but as unto carnal, *even* as unto babes in Christ. Rom. 7:14; 1 Cor. 2:6
2 I have fed you with milk, and not with meat: for ᵀhitherto ye were not able *to bear it*, neither yet now are ye able. John 16:12; 1 Pet. 2:2 ◆ *up to now*
3 For ye are yet carnal: for whereas *there is* among you envying, and strife, and divisions, are ye not carnal, and walk as men? 1 Cor. 1:11
4 For while one saith, I am of Paul; and another, I *am* of Apollos; are ye not carnal?

Paul and Apollos, Fellow Workmen

5 Who then is Paul, and who *is* Apollos, but ministers by whom ye believed, even as the Lord gave to every man?   2 Cor. 6:4
6 I have planted, Apollos watered; but God gave the increase.   Acts 18:4-11
7 So then neither is he that planteth any thing, neither he that watereth; but God that giveth the increase.   Gal. 6:3
8 Now he that planteth and he that watereth are one: and every man shall receive his own reward according to his own labour. Ps. 62:12
9 For we are labourers together with God: ye are God's husbandry, *ye are* God's building.

10 According to the grace of God which is given unto me, as a wise masterbuilder, I have laid the foundation, and another buildeth thereon. But let every man take heed how he buildeth thereupon. Rom. 12:3; 15:20; 1 Cor. 3:11
11 For other foundation can no man lay than that is laid, which is Jesus Christ.   Is. 28:16
12 Now if any man build upon this foundation gold, silver, precious stones, wood, hay, stubble;
13 Every man's work shall be made manifest: for the day shall declare it, because it shall be revealed by fire; and the fire shall try every man's work of what sort it is.   2 Thess. 1:7-10
14 If any man's work abide which he hath built thereupon, he shall receive a reward.   1 Cor. 3:8
15 If any man's work shall be burned, he shall suffer loss: but he himself shall be saved; yet so as by fire.   Jude 23

The Temple of God

3:16, 17

16 Know ye not that ye are the temple of God, and *that* the Spirit of God dwelleth in you?   1 Cor. 6:19; 2 Cor. 6:16

> **3:16 Once Again God's Temple**
>
> From eternal ages it was God's purpose that every created being, from the bright and holy seraph to man, should be a temple for the indwelling of the Creator. Because of sin, humanity ceased to be a temple for God. Darkened and defiled by evil, the heart of man no longer revealed the glory of the Divine One. But by the incarnation of the Son of God, the purpose of Heaven is fulfilled. God dwells in humanity, and through saving grace the heart of man becomes again His temple. *DA 161*

17 If any man defile the temple of God, him shall God destroy; for the temple of God is holy, which *temple* ye are.

Health See 1 Corinthians 6:19, 20.

18 Let no man deceive himself. If any man among you seemeth to be wise in this world, let him become a fool, that he may be wise.   Is. 5:21; Jer. 8:8; Gal. 6:3
19 For the wisdom of this world is foolishness with God. For it is written, He taketh the wise in their own craftiness.   Job 5:13
20 And again, The Lord knoweth the thoughts of the wise, that they are vain.   Ps. 94:11
21 Therefore let no man glory in men. For all things are yours;   Rom. 8:28, 32; 1 Cor. 4:6
22 Whether Paul, or Apollos, or Cephas, or the world, or life, or death, or things present, or things to come; all are yours;
23 And ye are Christ's; and Christ *is* God's.

All Ministers Are Servants of Christ

4 Let a man so account of us, as of the ministers of Christ, and stewards of the mysteries of God.   Rom. 16:25
2 Moreover it is required in stewards, that a man be found faithful.
3 But with me it is a very small thing that I should be judged of you, or of man's judgment: yea, I judge not mine own self.
4 For I know nothing by myself; yet am I not hereby justified: but he that judgeth me is the Lord.   Ps. 143:2
5 Therefore judge nothing before the time, until the Lord come, who both will bring to light the hidden things of darkness, and will make ᵀmanifest the counsels of the hearts: and then shall every man have praise of God.   Rom. 2:1, 16, 29 ◆ *known*
6 And these things, brethren, I have in a figure transferred to myself and *to* Apollos for your sakes; that ye might learn in us not to think *of men* above that which is written, that no one of you be puffed up for one against another.   1 Cor. 1:12
7 For who maketh thee to differ *from another*? and what hast thou that thou didst not receive? now if thou didst receive *it*, why dost thou glory, as if thou hadst not received *it*?   John 3:27; Rom. 12:6; 1 Pet. 4:10
8 Now ye are full, now ye are rich, ye have reigned as kings without us: and I would to God ye did reign, that we also might reign with you.   Rev. 3:17
9 For I think that God hath set forth us the apostles last, as it were appointed to death: for we are made a spectacle unto the world, and to angels, and to men.   Rom. 8:36; Heb. 10:33

> **4:9 City on a Hill**
>
> During ages of spiritual darkness the church of God has been as a city set on a hill. From age to age, through successive generations, the pure doctrines of heaven have been unfolding within its borders. Enfeebled and defective as it may appear, the church is the one object upon which God bestows in a special sense His supreme regard. It is the theater of His grace, in which He delights to reveal His power to transform hearts. *AA 12*

10 We *are* fools for Christ's sake, but ye *are* wise in Christ; we *are* weak, but ye *are* strong; ye *are* honourable, but we *are* despised.   Acts 17:18; 26:24; 1 Cor. 2:3
11 Even unto this present hour we both hunger, and thirst, and are naked, and are ᵀbuffeted, and have no certain dwellingplace;   Matt. 8:20; Rom. 8:35; 2 Cor. 11:23-27 ◆ *beaten*
12 And labour, working with our own hands: being ᵀreviled, we bless; being persecuted, we suffer it: Acts 18:3; 1 Pet. 3:9 ◆ *attacked with words*

13 Being defamed, we intreat: we are made as the filth of the world, *and are* the ᵀoffscouring of all things unto this day.   Lam. 3:45 ◆ scum

Paul as Spiritual Father

14 I write not these things to shame you, but as my beloved sons I warn *you*.   1 Thess. 2:11
15 For though ye have ten thousand instructors in Christ, yet *have ye* not many fathers: for in Christ Jesus I have ᵀbegotten you through the gospel.   Gal. 4:19 ◆ brought you forth
16 Wherefore I ᵀbeseech you, be ye followers of me.   1 Cor. 11:1; Phil. 3:17; 1 Thess. 1:6 ◆ beg

4:16 Lowliest and Highest Duties

One of the greatest of human teachers, Paul cheerfully performed the lowliest as well as the highest duties. When in his service for the Master circumstances seemed to require it, he willingly labored at his trade. Nevertheless, he ever held himself ready to lay aside his secular work, in order to meet the opposition of the enemies of the gospel, or to improve a special opportunity to win souls to Jesus. *AA 354, 355*

17 For this cause have I sent unto you Timotheus, who is my beloved son, and faithful in the Lord, who shall bring you into remembrance of my ways which be in Christ, as I teach every where in every church.   1 Cor. 7:17; 16:10; 1 Tim. 1:2
18 Now some are puffed up, as though I would not come to you.
19 But I will come to you shortly, if the Lord will, and will know, not the speech of them which are puffed up, but the power. Acts 18:21
20 For the kingdom of God *is* not in word, but in power.   1 Cor. 2:4
21 What will ye? shall I come unto you with a rod, or in love, and *in* the spirit of meekness?   2 Cor. 1:23; 13:2, 10

Sexual Sin in the Church

5 It is reported commonly *that there is* fornication among you, and such fornication as is not so much as named among the Gentiles, that one should have his father's wife.   Lev. 18:8; Deut. 22:30; 27:20
2 And ye are puffed up, and have not rather mourned, that he that hath done this deed might be taken away from among you.
3 For I ᵀverily, as absent in body, but present in spirit, have judged already, as though I were present, *concerning* him that hath so done this deed,   Col. 2:5; 1 Thess. 2:17 ◆ truly
4 In the name of our Lord Jesus Christ, when ye are gathered together, and my spirit, with the power of our Lord Jesus Christ, John 20:23
5 To deliver such an one unto Satan for the

destruction of the flesh, that the spirit may be saved in the day of the Lord Jesus.   Job 2:6
6 Your glorying *is* not good. Know ye not that a little leaven leaveneth the whole lump?   1 Cor. 5:2; Gal. 5:9; James 4:16

The Church Must Be Separate

7 Purge out therefore the old leaven, that ye may be a new lump, as ye are unleavened. For even Christ our passover is sacrificed for us:
8 Therefore let us keep the feast, not with old leaven, neither with the leaven of malice and wickedness; but with the unleavened *bread* of sincerity and truth.   Ex. 12:15; Deut. 16:3; Matt. 16:6

5:7, 8 Leaven of Change

But man cannot transform himself by the exercise of his will. He possesses no power by which this change can be effected. The leaven—something wholly from without—must be put into the meal before the desired change can be wrought in it. So the grace of God must be received by the sinner before he can be fitted for the kingdom of glory. *COL 96*

9 I wrote unto you in an epistle not to company with fornicators: Eph. 5:11; 2 Thess. 3:14
10 Yet not altogether with the fornicators of this world, or with the ᵀcovetous, or extortioners, or with idolaters; for then must ye needs go out of the world.   1 Cor. 10:27 ◆ greedy
11 But now I have written unto you not to keep company, if any man that is called a brother be a fornicator, or covetous, or an idolater, or a railer, or a drunkard, or an extortioner; with such an one no not to eat.   Matt. 18:17; Rom. 16:17; 2 Thess. 3:6
12 For what have I to do to judge them also that are without? do not ye judge them that are within?   Mark 4:11
13 But them that are without God judgeth. Therefore put away from among yourselves that wicked person.   Deut. 13:5; 17:7; 21:21

Settling Disputes among Believers

6 Dare any of you, having a matter against another, go to law before the unjust, and not before the saints?
2 Do ye not know that the saints shall judge the world? and if the world shall be judged by you, are ye unworthy to judge the smallest matters?   Dan. 7:22; Matt. 19:28; Rev. 20:4
3 Know ye not that we shall judge angels? how much more things that pertain to this life?

The Millennium See Revelation 20:5.

4 If then ye have judgments of things pertaining to this life, set them to judge who are least esteemed in the church.   1 Cor. 5:12

5 I speak to your shame. Is it so, that there is not a wise man among you? no, not one that shall be able to judge between his brethren? 6 But brother goeth to law with brother, and that before the unbelievers. 7 Now therefore there is utterly a fault among you, because ye go to law one with another. Why do ye not rather take wrong? why do ye not rather *suffer yourselves to* be defrauded?   Prov. 20:22

6:1–7 Christians and the Courts

Christians should not appeal to civil tribunals to settle differences that may arise among church members. Such differences should be settled among themselves, or by the church, in harmony with Christ's instruction. Even though injustice may have been done, the follower of the meek and lowly Jesus will suffer himself "to be defrauded" rather than open before the world the sins of his brethren in the church. *AA 305, 306*

8 Nay, ye do wrong, and defraud, and that *your* brethren.   1 Thess. 4:6

The Wicked Will Not Inherit the Kingdom of God

9 Know ye not that the unrighteous shall not inherit the kingdom of God? Be not deceived: neither fornicators, nor idolaters, nor adulterers, nor effeminate, nor abusers of themselves with mankind,   1 Cor. 15:50
10 Nor thieves, nor ᵀcovetous, nor drunkards, nor revilers, nor extortioners, shall inherit the kingdom of God.   1 Cor. 5:11 ◆ *greedy*

Health

11 And such were some of you: but ye are washed, but ye are ᵀsanctified, but ye are justified in the name of the Lord Jesus, and by the Spirit of our God.   Acts 22:16; Rom. 8:30 ◆ *made holy*

Stay Away from Sexual Sin

12 All things are lawful unto me, but all things are not expedient: all things are lawful for me, but I will not be brought under the power of any.
13 Meats for the belly, and the belly for meats: but God shall destroy both it and them. Now the body *is* not for fornication, but for the Lord; and the Lord for the body.   Matt. 15:17
14 And God hath both raised up the Lord, and will also raise up us by his own power.
15 Know ye not that your bodies are the members of Christ? shall I then take the members of Christ, and make *them* the members of an harlot? God forbid. Rom. 12:5; 1 Cor. 12:27; Eph. 5:30
16 What? know ye not that he which is joined to an harlot is one body? for two, saith he, shall be one flesh. Gen. 2:24; Mark 10:8; Eph. 5:31

17 But he that is joined unto the Lord is one spirit.   John 17:21-23
18 Flee fornication. Every sin that a man doeth is without the body; but he that committeth fornication sinneth against his own body.

6:19, 20 All Are God's Property

All men have been bought with this infinite price. By pouring the whole treasury of heaven into this world, by giving us in Christ all heaven, God has purchased the will, the affections, the mind, the soul, of every human being. Whether believers or unbelievers, all men are the Lord's property. *COL 326*

19 What? know ye not that your body is the temple of the Holy Ghost *which is* in you, which ye have of God, and ye are not your own?   John 2:21; 1 Cor. 3:16; 2 Cor. 6:16
20 For ye are bought with a price: therefore glorify God in your body, and in your spirit, which are God's.   Acts 20:28; Rom. 12:1; 1 Cor. 7:23

Health See Genesis 1:29.

Paul Discusses Marriage

7 Now concerning the things whereof ye wrote unto me: *It is* good for a man not to touch a woman.   1 Cor. 7:8
2 Nevertheless, *to avoid* fornication, let every man have his own wife, and let every woman have her own husband.   1 Cor. 7:9
3 Let the husband render unto the wife due benevolence: and likewise also the wife unto the husband.   Ex. 21:10; 1 Pet. 3:7
4 The wife hath not power of her own body, but the husband: and likewise also the husband hath not power of his own body, but the wife.
5 Defraud ye not one the other, except *it be* with consent for a time, that ye may give yourselves to fasting and prayer; and come together again, that Satan tempt you not for your ᵀincontinency.   Ex. 19:15; 1 Sam. 21:4-5
6 But I speak this by permission, *and* not of commandment.   1 Cor. 7:12, 25; 2 Cor. 8:8
7 For I would that all men were even as I myself. But every man hath his proper gift of God, one after this manner, and another after that.   Matt. 19:11-12; 1 Cor. 9:5; 12:11
8 I say therefore to the unmarried and widows, It is good for them if they abide even as I.   1 Cor. 7:1
9 But if they cannot contain, let them marry: for it is better to marry than to burn. 1 Tim. 5:14

Marriage Vows Are to Be Taken Seriously

10 And unto the married I command, *yet* not I, but the Lord, Let not the wife depart from *her* husband: Mal. 2:14-16; Matt. 5:32; Luke 16:18

6:9, 10 ‡

6:19, 20

7:10, 11

11 But and if she depart, let her remain unmarried, or be reconciled to *her* husband: and let not the husband put away *his* wife.

Marriage See Deuteronomy 6:6–9.

12 But to the rest speak I, not the Lord: If any brother hath a wife that believeth not, and she be pleased to dwell with him, let him not put her away.   1 Cor. 7:6
13 And the woman which hath an husband that believeth not, and if he be pleased to dwell with her, let her not leave him.
14 For the unbelieving husband is ᵀsanctified by the wife, and the unbelieving wife is sanctified by the husband: else were your children unclean; but now are they holy.   *made holy*
15 But if the unbelieving depart, let him depart. A brother or a sister is not under bondage in such *cases*: but God hath called us to peace.   Rom. 14:19; 1 Cor. 14:33
16 For what knowest thou, O wife, whether thou shalt save *thy* husband? or how knowest thou, O man, whether thou shalt save *thy* wife?   Rom. 11:14
17 But as God hath distributed to every man, as the Lord hath called every one, so let him walk. And so ordain I in all churches.   1 Cor. 4:17; 2 Cor. 8:18; 11:28
18 Is any man called being circumcised? let him not become uncircumcised. Is any called in uncircumcision? let him not be circumcised.   Acts 15:5
19 Circumcision is nothing, and uncircumcision is nothing, but the keeping of the commandments of God.   Gal. 5:6; 6:15; Col. 3:11
20 Let every man abide in the same calling wherein he was called.
21 Art thou called *being* a servant? care not for it: but if thou mayest be made free, use *it* rather.
22 For he that is called in the Lord, *being* a servant, is the Lord's freeman: likewise also he that is called, *being* free, is Christ's servant.   Philem. 16; 1 Pet. 2:16

23 Ye are bought with a price; be not ye the servants of men.   Lev. 25:42; 1 Cor. 6:20
24 Brethren, let every man, wherein he is called, therein abide with God.   1 Cor. 7:20

Reasons for Marrying or Remaining Single
25 Now concerning virgins I have no commandment of the Lord: yet I give my judgment, as one that hath obtained mercy of the Lord to be faithful.   1 Cor. 4:2; 7:6
26 I suppose therefore that this is good for the present distress, *I say*, that *it is* good for a man so to be.   Luke 21:23; 1 Cor. 7:1, 8
27 Art thou bound unto a wife? seek not to be loosed. Art thou loosed from a wife? seek not a wife.
28 But and if thou marry, thou hast not sinned; and if a virgin marry, she hath not sinned. Nevertheless such shall have trouble in the flesh: but I spare you.
29 But this I say, brethren, the time *is* short: it remaineth, that both they that have wives be as though they had none;   Rom. 13:11-12
30 And they that weep, as though they wept not; and they that rejoice, as though they rejoiced not; and they that buy, as though they possessed not;
31 And they that use this world, as not abusing *it*: for the fashion of this world passeth away.   Ps. 39:6; 1 Cor. 9:18; 1 John 2:17
32 But I would have you without carefulness. He that is unmarried careth for the things that belong to the Lord, how he may please the Lord: 1 Tim. 5:5
33 But he that is married careth for the things that are of the world, how he may please *his* wife.
34 There is difference *also* between a wife and a virgin. The unmarried woman careth for the things of the Lord, that she may be holy both in body and in spirit: but she that is married careth for the things of the world, how she may please *her* husband.

All Have a Mission

1 Corinthians 7:24

The greater part of our Saviour's life on earth was spent in patient toil in the carpenter's shop at Nazareth. Ministering angels attended the Lord of life as He walked side by side with peasants and laborers, unrecognized and unhonored. He was as faithfully fulfilling His mission while working at His humble trade as when He healed the sick or walked upon the storm-tossed waves of Galilee. So in the humblest duties and lowliest positions of life, we may walk and work with Jesus.

The apostle says, "Let every man, wherein he is called, therein abide with God" (1 Corinthians 7:24). The businessman may conduct his business in a way that will glorify his Master because of his fidelity. If he is a true follower of Christ he will carry his religion into everything that is done and reveal to men the spirit of Christ. The mechanic may be a diligent and faithful representative of Him who toiled in the lowly walks of life among the hills of Galilee. Everyone who names the name of Christ should so work that others, by seeing his good works, may be led to glorify their Creator and Redeemer. *SC 81, 82*

35 And this I speak for your own profit; not that I may cast a snare upon you, but for that which is ᵀcomely, and that ye may attend upon the Lord without distraction. *appropriate*
36 But if any man think that he behaveth himself uncomely toward his virgin, if she pass the flower of *her* age, and need so require, let him do what he will, he sinneth not: let them marry.
37 Nevertheless he that standeth ᵀstedfast in his heart, having no necessity, but hath power over his own will, and hath so decreed in his heart that he will keep his virgin, doeth well.   *steadfast*
38 So then he that giveth *her* in marriage doeth well; but he that giveth *her* not in marriage doeth better.   Heb. 13:4
39 The wife is bound by the law as long as her husband liveth; but if her husband be dead, she is at liberty to be married to whom she will; only in the Lord.   Rom. 7:2-3
40 But she is happier if she so abide, after my judgment: and I think also that I have the Spirit of God.

Food Offered to Idols

8 Now as touching things offered unto idols, we know that we all have knowledge. Knowledge puffeth up, but ᵀcharity edifieth.   Acts 15:29; 1 Cor. 8:4, 7 ◆ *selfless love*
2 And if any man think that he knoweth any thing, he knoweth nothing yet as he ought to know.   1 Cor. 3:18
3 But if any man love God, the same is known of him.   Ex. 33:12, 17; Gal. 4:9
4 As concerning therefore the eating of those things that are offered in sacrifice unto idols, we know that an idol *is* nothing in the world, and that *there is* none other God but one.
5 For though there be that are called gods, whether in heaven or in earth, (as there be gods many, and lords many,)   2 Thess. 2:4
6 But to us *there is but* one God, the Father, of whom *are* all things, and we in him; and one Lord Jesus Christ, by whom *are* all things, and we by him.   Mal. 2:10; John 1:3; Rom. 11:36

Be a Good Example

7 Howbeit *there is* not in every man that knowledge: for some with conscience of the idol unto this hour eat *it* as a thing offered unto an idol; and their conscience being weak is defiled.   Rom. 14:14; 1 Cor. 8:9-10; 10:28-29
8 But meat commendeth us not to God: for neither, if we eat, are we the better; neither, if we eat not, are we the worse.   Rom. 14:17
9 But take heed lest by any means this liberty of yours become a stumblingblock to them that are weak.   Rom. 14:1-2, 20-21; Gal. 5:13
10 For if any man see thee which hast knowledge sit at meat in the idol's temple, shall not the conscience of him which is weak be emboldened to eat those things which are offered to idols;
11 And through thy knowledge shall the weak brother perish, for whom Christ died?   Rom. 14:15; 1 Cor. 8:13
12 But when ye sin so against the brethren, and wound their weak conscience, ye sin against Christ.   Matt. 25:45
13 Wherefore, if meat make my brother to offend, I will eat no flesh while the world standeth, lest I make my brother to offend.   Rom. 14:21; 2 Cor. 11:29

Paul Asserts His Rights

9 Am I not an apostle? am I not free? have I not seen Jesus Christ our Lord? are not ye my work in the Lord?   Acts 9:3, 17; 1 Cor. 3:6
2 If I be not an apostle unto others, yet doubtless I am to you: for the seal of mine apostleship are ye in the Lord.
3 Mine answer to them that do examine me is this,
4 Have we not power to eat and to drink?
5 Have we not power to lead about a sister, a wife, as well as other apostles, and *as* the brethren of the Lord, and Cephas?   Matt. 8:14
6 Or I only and Barnabas, have not we power to ᵀforbear working?   Acts 4:36 ◆ *refuse*

9:7–14 Support of the Priests

The apostle [Paul] here referred to the Lord's plan for the maintenance of the priests who ministered in the temple. Those who were set apart to this holy office were supported by their brethren, to whom they ministered spiritual blessings. *AA 336*

---

7 Who goeth a warfare any time at his own charges? who planteth a vineyard, and eateth not of the fruit thereof? or who feedeth a flock, and eateth not of the milk of the flock?   Deut. 20:6; Prov. 27:18; 1 Tim. 1:18
8 Say I these things as a man? or saith not the law the same also?
9 For it is written in the law of Moses, Thou shalt not muzzle the mouth of the ox that treadeth out the corn. Doth God take care for oxen?   Deut. 25:4; 1 Tim. 5:18
10 Or saith he *it* altogether for our sakes? For our sakes, no doubt, *this* is written: that he that ploweth should plow in hope; and that he that thresheth in hope should be partaker of his hope.   2 Tim. 2:6
11 If we have sown unto you spiritual things, *is it* a great thing if we shall reap your ᵀcarnal things?   Rom. 15:27; Gal. 6:6 ◆ *material*
12 If others be partakers of *this* power over you, *are* not we rather? Nevertheless we have not used this power; but suffer all

things, lest we should hinder the gospel of Christ.   1 Cor. 9:15, 18; 2 Cor. 11:12

13 Do ye not know that they which minister about holy things live *of the things* of the temple? and they which wait at the altar are partakers with the altar?   Lev. 6:26; Num. 5:9-10

14 Even so hath the Lord ordained that they which preach the gospel should live of the gospel.   Matt. 10:10; Luke 10:7; 1 Cor. 9:4

Managing God's Gifts See Malachi 3:10.

15 But I have used none of these things: neither have I written these things, that it should be so done unto me: for *it were* better for me to die, than that any man should make my glorying void.   Acts 18:3

16 For though I preach the gospel, I have nothing to glory of: for necessity is laid upon me; yea, woe is unto me, if I preach not the gospel!   Luke 9:62; Acts 9:15; Rom. 1:14

17 For if I do this thing willingly, I have a reward: but if against my will, a dispensation *of the gospel* is committed unto me. 1 Cor. 3:8; Gal. 2:7

18 What is my reward then? *Verily* that, when I preach the gospel, I may make the gospel of Christ without charge, that I abuse not my power in the gospel.   1 Cor. 7:31

Paul's Work as an Apostle

19 For though I be free from all *men*, yet have I made myself servant unto all, that I might gain the more.   Matt. 18:15; 1 Cor. 9:1; Gal. 5:13

20 And unto the Jews I became as a Jew, that I might gain the Jews; to them that are under the law, as under the law, that I might gain them that are under the law; Acts 16:3; 21:20-26

21 To them that are without law, as without law, (being not without law to God, but under the law to Christ,) that I might gain them that are without law. Rom. 2:12, 14; Gal. 3:2

22 To the weak became I as weak, that I might gain the weak: I am made all things to all *men*, that I might by all means save some.

23 And this I do for the gospel's sake, that I might be partaker thereof with *you*.

Run the Race

24 Know ye not that they which run in a race run all, but one receiveth the prize? So run, that ye may obtain.   Gal. 2:2; Phil. 3:14; Heb. 12:1

25 And every man that striveth for the mastery is temperate in all things. Now they *do it* to obtain a corruptible crown; but we an incorruptible.   1 Tim. 6:12; James 1:12; Rev. 2:10

26 I therefore so run, not as uncertainly; so fight I, not as one that beateth the air:

27 But I keep under my body, and bring *it* into subjection: lest that by any means, when I have preached to others, I myself should be a castaway.   Rom. 8:13

Learn from the Past

10 Moreover, brethren, I would not that ye should be ignorant, how that all our fathers were under the cloud, and all passed through the sea;   Ex. 14:29

2 And were all baptized unto Moses in the cloud and in the sea;

3 And did all eat the same spiritual meat;

4 And did all drink the same spiritual drink: for they drank of that spiritual Rock that followed them: and that Rock was Christ.   Ex. 17:6; Num. 20:11; Ps. 78:15

5 But with many of them God was not well pleased: for they were overthrown in the wilderness.   Num. 26:64-65; Heb. 3:17; Jude 5

Stay Away from Idolatry

6 Now these things were our examples, to the intent we should not lust after evil things, as they also lusted.   Num. 11:4

7 Neither be ye idolaters, as *were* some of them; as it is written, The people sat down to eat and drink, and rose up to play.   Ex. 32:19

8 Neither let us commit fornication, as some of them committed, and fell in one day three and twenty thousand.   Num. 25:1-9

9 Neither let us tempt Christ, as some of them also tempted, and were destroyed of serpents.   Num. 21:5-6

10 Neither murmur ye, as some of them also murmured, and were destroyed of the destroyer.   Ex. 12:23; Num. 16:41; 2 Sam. 24:16

11 Now all these things happened unto them for ensamples: and they are written for our admonition, upon whom the ends of the world are come.   Rom. 13:11

9:25 Battle and a March

The Christian life is a battle and a march. In this warfare there is no release; the effort must be continuous and persevering. It is by unceasing endeavor that we maintain the victory over the temptations of Satan. Christian integrity must be sought with resistless energy and maintained with a resolute fixedness of purpose. *MH 453*

10:11 Reviewing Israel's History

God would have His people in these days review with a humble heart and teachable spirit the trials through which ancient Israel passed, that they may be instructed in their preparation for the heavenly Canaan.

Many look back to the Israelites, and marvel at their unbelief and murmuring, feeling that they themselves would not have been so ungrateful; but when their faith is tested, even by little trials, they manifest no more faith or patience than did ancient Israel. *PP 293*

12 Wherefore let him that thinketh he standeth take heed lest he fall.   Rom. 11:20

13 There hath no temptation taken you but such as is common to man: but God *is* faithful, who will not suffer you to be tempted above that ye are able; but will with the temptation also make a way to escape, that ye may be able to bear *it*.   Jer. 29:11; 1 Cor. 1:9; 2 Pet. 2:9

14 Wherefore, my dearly beloved, flee from idolatry.   1 Cor. 10:7

15 I speak as to wise men; judge ye what I say.   1 Cor. 8:1

10:16, 17

16 The cup of blessing which we bless, is it not the communion of the blood of Christ? The bread which we break, is it not the communion of the body of Christ?   Matt. 26:26-28

17 For we *being* many are one bread, *and* one body: for we are all partakers of that one bread.   Rom. 12:5; 1 Cor. 12:12, 27

Baptism/Lord's Supper See 1 Corinthians 11:23–30.

18 Behold Israel after the flesh: are not they which eat of the sacrifices partakers of the altar?   Rom. 4:1

19 What say I then? that the idol is any thing, or that which is offered in sacrifice to idols is any thing?   1 Cor. 8:4

20 But I *say*, that the things which the Gentiles sacrifice, they sacrifice to devils, and not to God: and I would not that ye should have fellowship with devils.   Rev. 9:20

21 Ye cannot drink the cup of the Lord, and the cup of devils: ye cannot be partakers of the Lord's table, and of the table of devils.

22 Do we provoke the Lord to jealousy? are we stronger than he?   Deut. 32:16, 21; Eccl. 6:10

23 All things are lawful for me, but all things are not expedient: all things are lawful for me, but all things edify not.   1 Cor. 6:12; 8:9

24 Let no man seek his own, but every man another's *wealth*.   1 Cor. 10:33; 13:5; Phil. 2:21

25 Whatsoever is sold in the ᵀshambles, *that* eat, asking no question for conscience sake: 1 Cor. 8:7 ◆ *meat market*

26 For the earth *is* the Lord's, and the fulness thereof.   Ex. 19:5; Ps. 24:1; 50:12

27 If any of them that believe not bid you *to a feast*, and ye be disposed to go; whatsoever is set before you, eat, asking no question for conscience sake.

28 But if any man say unto you, This is offered in sacrifice unto idols, eat not for his sake that shewed it, and for conscience sake: for the earth *is* the Lord's, and the fulness thereof:

29 Conscience, I say, not thine own, but of the other: for why is my liberty judged of another *man's* conscience?   1 Cor. 9:19

30 For if I by grace be a partaker, why am I evil spoken of for that for which I give thanks?

10:31 What Christianity Is Not

A mere profession of faith in Christ, a boastful knowledge of the truth, does not make a man a Christian. A religion that seeks only to gratify the eye, the ear, and the taste, or that sanctions self-indulgence, is not the religion of Christ. *AA 317*

31 Whether therefore ye eat, or drink, or whatsoever ye do, do all to the glory of God.   Col. 3:17; 1 Pet. 4:11

10:31

Health See 1 Corinthians 3:16, 17.

32 Give none offence, neither to the Jews, nor to the Gentiles, nor to the church of God: Acts 20:28; Rom. 14:13; 1 Cor. 8:13

33 Even as I please all *men* in all *things*, not seeking mine own profit, but the *profit* of many, that they may be saved.   1 Cor. 10:24

To Win the Race

1 Corinthians 10:1–12

Paul knew that his warfare against evil would not end so long as life should last. Ever he realized the need of putting a strict guard upon himself, that earthly desires might not overcome spiritual zeal. With all his power he continued to strive against natural inclinations. . . .

It was this singlehearted purpose to win the race for eternal life that Paul longed to see revealed in the lives of the Corinthian believers. He knew that in order to reach Christ's ideal for them, they had before them a life struggle from which there would be no release. He entreated them to strive lawfully, day by day seeking for piety and moral excellence. He pleaded with them to lay aside every weight and to press forward to the goal of perfection in Christ.

Paul pointed the Corinthians to the experiences of ancient Israel, to the blessings that rewarded their obedience, and to the judgments that followed their transgressions. He reminded them of the miraculous way in which the Hebrews were led from Egypt under the protection of the cloud by day and the pillar of fire by night. Thus they were safely conducted through the Red Sea, while the Egyptians, essaying to cross in like manner, were all drowned. By these acts God had acknowledged Israel as His church. . . . The Hebrews, in all their travels, had Christ as a leader. The smitten rock typified Christ, who was to be wounded for men's transgressions, that the stream of salvation might flow to all. *AA 314, 315*

Advice about Worship

11

Be ye followers of me, even as I also *am* of Christ.   1 Cor. 4:16; Phil. 3:17

11:1 Obey Leaders in the Lord

David's power had been given him by God, but to be exercised only in harmony with the divine law. When he commanded that which was contrary to God's law, it became sin to obey. "The powers that be are ordained of God" (Romans 13:1), but we are not to obey them contrary to God's law. The apostle Paul, writing to the Corinthians, sets forth the principle by which we should be governed. He says, "Be ye followers of me, even as I also am of Christ" (1 Corinthians 11:1). *PP 719*

2 Now I praise you, brethren, that ye remember me in all things, and keep the ordinances, as I delivered *them* to you. 1 Cor. 4:17; 2 Thess. 2:15
3 But I would have you know, that the head of every man is Christ; and the head of the woman *is* the man; and the head of Christ *is* God.   Gen. 3:16; 1 Cor. 3:23; Eph. 4:15

11:3 Church Has but One Foundation

The church is built upon Christ as its foundation; it is to obey Christ as its head. It is not to depend upon man, or be controlled by man. Many claim that a position of trust in the church gives them authority to dictate what other men shall believe and what they shall do. This claim God does not sanction. . . . Upon no finite being can we depend for guidance. *DA 414*

4 Every man praying or prophesying, having *his* head covered, dishonoureth his head.
5 But every woman that prayeth or prophesieth with *her* head uncovered dishonoureth her head: for that is even all one as if she were shaven.   Deut. 21:12; Luke 2:36; Acts 21:9
6 For if the woman be not covered, let her also be shorn: but if it be a shame for a woman to be shorn or shaven, let her be covered.
7 For a man indeed ought not to cover *his* head, ᵀforasmuch as he is the image and glory of God: but the woman is the glory of the man.   James 3:9 ◆ *since*
8 For the man is not of the woman; but the woman of the man.   Gen. 2:21-23; 1 Tim. 2:13
9 Neither was the man created for the woman; but the woman for the man.Gen. 2:18
10 For this cause ought the woman to have power on *her* head because of the angels.
11 Nevertheless neither is the man without the woman, neither the woman without the man, in the Lord.   Gal. 3:28
12 For as the woman *is* of the man, even so *is* the man also by the woman; but all things of God.   Rom. 11:36

13 Judge in yourselves: is it comely that a woman pray unto God uncovered?   Luke 12:57
14 Doth not even nature itself teach you, that, if a man have long hair, it is a shame unto him?
15 But if a woman have long hair, it is a glory to her: for *her* hair is given her for a covering.
16 But if any man seem to be contentious, we have no such custom, neither the churches of God.   1 Cor. 7:17; 1 Thess. 2:14; 1 Tim. 6:3-4

Advice about the Lord's Supper

17 Now in this that I declare *unto you* I praise *you* not, that ye come together not for the better, but for the worse.   1 Cor. 11:2
18 For first of all, when ye come together in the church, I hear that there be divisions among you; and I partly believe it. 1 Cor. 1:10-12
19 For there must be also heresies among you, that they which are approved may be made manifest among you. Deut. 13:3; 1 John 2:19
20 When ye come together therefore into one place, *this* is not to eat the Lord's supper.
21 For in eating every one taketh before *other* his own supper: and one is hungry, and another is drunken.   2 Pet. 2:13; Jude 12
22 What? have ye not houses to eat and to drink in? or despise ye the church of God, and shame them that have not? What shall I say to you? shall I praise you in this? I praise *you* not.   1 Cor. 10:32
23 For I have received of the Lord that which also I delivered unto you, That the Lord Jesus the *same* night in which he was betrayed took bread: Matt. 26:26-28; Mark 14:22-24; 1 Cor. 15:3
24 And when he had given thanks, he brake *it*, and said, Take, eat: this is my body, which is broken for you: this do in remembrance of me.
25 After the same manner also *he took* the cup, when he had supped, saying, This cup is the new ᵀtestament in my blood: this do ye, as ᵀoft as ye drink *it*, in remembrance of me.   Luke 22:20; 2 Cor. 3:6 ◆ *covenant* ◆ *often*
26 For as often as ye eat this bread, and drink this cup, ye do shew the Lord's death till he come.   John 21:22

11:23–26 Speaking to Our Senses

Christ has instituted this service that it may speak to our senses of the love of God that has been expressed in our behalf. . . .
The ordinances that point to our Lord's humiliation and suffering are regarded too much as a form. They were instituted for a purpose. Our senses need to be quickened to lay hold of the mystery of godliness. It is the privilege of all to comprehend, far more than we do, the expiatory sufferings of Christ. *DA 660*

27 Wherefore whosoever shall eat this bread, and drink *this* cup of the Lord, unworthily, shall be guilty of the body and blood of the Lord.   Num. 9:10
28 But let a man examine himself, and so let him eat of *that* bread, and drink of *that* cup.   2 Cor. 13:5; Gal. 6:4
29 For he that eateth and drinketh unworthily, eateth and drinketh ^Tdamnation to himself, not discerning the Lord's body.   condemnation
30 For this cause many *are* weak and sickly among you, and many sleep.

Baptism/Lord's Supper

31 For if we would judge ourselves, we should not be judged.   1 John 1:9
32 But when we are judged, we are ^Tchastened of the Lord, that we should not be condemned with the world.   disciplined
33 Wherefore, my brethren, when ye come together to eat, tarry one for another.
34 And if any man hunger, let him eat at home; that ye come not together unto condemnation. And the rest will I set in order when I come.   1 Cor. 4:19; 7:17; 11:21-22

Spiritual Gifts

12 Now concerning spiritual *gifts,* brethren, I would not have you ignorant.   1 Cor. 14:37
2 Ye know that ye were Gentiles, carried away unto these ^Tdumb idols, even as ye were led.   Ps. 115:5; 1 Thess. 1:9; 1 Pet. 4:3 ◆ *mute*
3 Wherefore I give you to understand, that no man speaking by the Spirit of God calleth Jesus accursed: and *that* no man can say that Jesus is the Lord, but by the Holy Ghost.   John 13:13
4 Now there are diversities of gifts, but the same Spirit.   Rom. 12:4-6; Heb. 2:4
5 And there are differences of administrations, but the same Lord.
6 And there are diversities of operations, but it is the same God which worketh all in all.   1 Cor. 15:28
7 But the ^Tmanifestation of the Spirit is given to every man to profit withal.   *being made known*
8 For to one is given by the Spirit the word of wisdom; to another the word of knowledge by the same Spirit;   2 Cor. 8:7
9 To another faith by the same Spirit; to another the gifts of healing by the same Spirit;   Matt. 17:19-20; 1 Cor. 13:2; 2 Cor. 4:13
10 To another the working of miracles; to another prophecy; to another discerning of spirits; to another *divers* kinds of tongues; to another the interpretation of tongues:
11 But all these worketh that one and the selfsame Spirit, dividing to every man severally as he will.   1 Cor. 12:4

The Body and Its Various Members

12 For as the body is one, and hath many members, and all the members of that one body, being many, are one body: so also *is* Christ.   Rom. 12:4-5; 1 Cor. 10:17; 12:27
13 For by one Spirit are we all baptized into one body, whether *we be* Jews or Gentiles, whether *we be* bond or free; and have been all made to drink into one Spirit.   Gal. 3:28; Col. 3:11

Baptism/Lord's Supper See Acts 19:1-7.

14 For the body is not one member, but many.
15 If the foot shall say, Because I am not the hand, I am not of the body; is it therefore not of the body?
16 And if the ear shall say, Because I am not the eye, I am not of the body; is it therefore not of the body?
17 If the whole body *were* an eye, where *were* the hearing? If the whole *were* hearing, where *were* the smelling?
18 But now hath God set the members every one of them in the body, as it hath pleased him.   Rom. 12:3; 1 Cor. 12:11, 28
19 And if they were all one member, where *were* the body?
20 But now *are they* many members, yet but one body.
21 And the eye cannot say unto the hand, I have no need of thee: nor again the head to the feet, I have no need of you.
22 Nay, much more those members of the body, which seem to be more feeble, are necessary:
23 And those *members* of the body, which we think to be less honourable, upon these we ^Tbestow more abundant honour; and our uncomely *parts* have more abundant comeliness.   *give*
24 For our ^Tcomely *parts* have no need: but God hath tempered the body together, having given more abundant honour to that *part* which lacked: *presentable*
25 That there should be no schism in the body; but *that* the members should have the same care one for another.
26 And whether one member suffer, all the members suffer with it; or one member be honoured, all the members rejoice with it.

12:12-26 The Church a Body

By a comparison of the church with the human body, [Paul] aptly illustrated the close and harmonious relationship that should exist among all members of the church of Christ. *AA 317*

The Church, the Body of Christ

27 Now ye are the body of Christ, and members in particular. Rom. 12:5; Eph. 1:23; 4:12
28 And God hath set some in the church, first apostles, secondarily prophets, thirdly teachers, after that miracles, then gifts of healings, helps, governments, diversities of tongues. Eph. 2:20; Heb. 13:17, 24

> **12:28 Duties of Leadership**
>
> Solemn are the responsibilities resting upon those who are called to act as leaders in the church of God on earth. *AA 92*

29 *Are* all apostles? *are* all prophets? *are* all teachers? *are* all workers of miracles?
30 Have all the gifts of healing? do all speak with tongues? do all interpret?
31 But ᵀcovet earnestly the best gifts: and yet shew I unto you a more excellent way.

Love Is the Greatest Gift

13 Though I speak with the tongues of men and of angels, and have not ᵀcharity, I am become *as* sounding brass, or a tinkling cymbal. 2 Cor. 12:4 ◆ *selfless love*
2 And though I have *the gift of* prophecy, and understand all mysteries, and all knowledge; and though I have all faith, so that I could remove mountains, and have not charity, I am nothing. Matt. 17:20; 21:21; 1 Cor. 13:3
3 And though I ᵀbestow all my goods to feed *the poor*, and though I give my body to be burned, and have not charity, it profiteth me nothing. *give*

> **13:1–3 A Profession Without Love**
>
> No matter how high the profession, he whose heart is not filled with love for God and his fellow men is not a true disciple of Christ. . . . In his zeal he might even meet a martyr's death, yet if not actuated by love, he would be regarded by God as a deluded enthusiast or an ambitious hypocrite. *AA 318, 319*

4 Charity suffereth long, *and* is kind; charity envieth not; charity vaunteth not itself, is not puffed up, Prov. 10:12; 1 Cor. 4:6; Col. 3:12
5 Doth not behave itself unseemly, seeketh not her own, is not easily provoked, thinketh no evil; 1 Cor. 10:24; Phil. 2:21
6 Rejoiceth not in iniquity, but rejoiceth in the truth; Rom. 1:32; 2 Thess. 2:12; 2 John 4
7 Beareth all things, believeth all things, hopeth all things, endureth all things.
8 Charity never faileth: but whether *there be* prophecies, they shall fail; whether *there be* tongues, they shall cease; whether *there be* knowledge, it shall vanish away.
9 For we know in part, and we prophesy in part. 1 Cor. 8:2; 13:12

> **13:7 Forward, Even Without Sight**
>
> Often the Christian life is beset by dangers, and duty seems hard to perform. The imagination pictures impending ruin before and bondage or death behind. Yet the voice of God speaks clearly, "Go forward." We should obey this command, even though our eyes cannot penetrate the darkness, and we feel the cold waves about our feet. *PP 290*

10 But when that which is perfect is come, then that which is in part shall be done away.
11 When I was a child, I spake as a child, I understood as a child, I thought as a child: but when I became a man, I put away childish things.
12 For now we see through a ᵀglass, darkly; but then face to face: now I know in part; but then shall I know even as also I am known. Num. 12:8; 2 Cor. 5:7; 1 John 3:2 ◆ *mirror*
13 And now abideth faith, hope, charity, these three; but the greatest of these *is* charity. 1 Cor. 16:14; Gal. 5:6; 1 Pet. 1:21

Speak So As to Be Understood

14 Follow after ᵀcharity, and desire spiritual *gifts*, but rather that ye may prophesy. 1 Cor. 12:1; 14:39; 16:14 ◆ *selfless love*
2 For he that speaketh in an *unknown* tongue speaketh not unto men, but unto God: for no man understandeth *him*; ᵀhowbeit in the spirit he speaketh mysteries. 1 Cor. 13:2 ◆ *however*
3 But he that prophesieth speaketh unto men *to* edification, and ᵀexhortation, and comfort. Rom. 14:19 ◆ *encouragement*
4 He that speaketh in an *unknown* tongue edifieth himself; but he that prophesieth edifieth the church. Mark 16:17

> **Gift of Prophecy** See Ephesians 4:11.

5 I would that ye all spake with tongues, but rather that ye prophesied: for greater *is* he that prophesieth than he that speaketh with tongues, except he interpret, that the church may receive edifying. 1 Cor. 12:10

Interpretation Required

6 Now, brethren, if I come unto you speaking with tongues, what shall I profit you, except I shall speak to you either by revelation, or by knowledge, or by prophesying, or by doctrine? Rom. 6:17; Eph. 1:17
7 And even things without life giving sound, whether pipe or harp, except they give a distinction in the sounds, how shall it be known what is piped or harped?
8 For if the trumpet give an uncertain sound, who shall prepare himself to the battle?
9 So likewise ye, except ye utter by the tongue words easy to be understood, how

shall it be known what is spoken? for ye shall speak into the air.   1 Cor. 9:26

10 There are, it may be, so many kinds of voices in the world, and none of them *is* without signification.

11 Therefore if I know not the meaning of the voice, I shall be unto him that speaketh a ᵀbarbarian, and he that speaketh *shall be* a barbarian unto me.   Acts 28:2 ◆ *non-Greek*

12 Even so ye, ᵀforasmuch as ye are zealous of spiritual *gifts*, seek that ye may excel to the edifying of the church.   1 Cor. 14:26 ◆ *since*

13 Wherefore let him that speaketh in an *unknown* tongue pray that he may interpret.

14 For if I pray in an *unknown* tongue, my spirit prayeth, but my understanding is unfruitful.   1 Cor. 14:2

15 What is it then? I will pray with the spirit, and I will pray with the understanding also: I will sing with the spirit, and I will sing with the understanding also.   Ps. 47:7; Col. 3:16

16 Else when thou shalt bless with the spirit, how shall he that occupieth the room of the unlearned say Amen at thy giving of thanks, seeing he understandeth not what thou sayest?   1 Chr. 16:36; Ps. 106:48; Rev. 5:14

17 For thou ᵀverily givest thanks well, but the other is not edified.   1 Cor. 14:4 ◆ *truly*

18 I thank my God, I speak with tongues more than ye all:

19 Yet in the church I had rather speak five words with my understanding, that *by my voice* I might teach others also, than ten thousand words in an *unknown* tongue.

20 Brethren, be not children in understanding: howbeit in malice be ye children, but in understanding be men.   Ps. 119:99; Matt. 18:3

21 In the law it is written, With *men of* other tongues and other lips will I speak unto this people; and yet for all that will they not hear me, saith the Lord.   Deut. 28:49; Is. 28:11-12

22 Wherefore tongues are for a sign, not to them that believe, but to them that believe not: but prophesying *serveth* not for them that believe not, but for them which believe.

23 If therefore the whole church be come together into one place, and all speak with tongues, and there come in *those that are* unlearned, or unbelievers, will they not say that ye are mad?   Acts 2:13

24 But if all prophesy, and there come in one that believeth not, or *one* unlearned, he is convinced of all, he is judged of all:

25 And thus are the secrets of his heart made ᵀmanifest; and so falling down on *his* face he will worship God, and report that God is in you of a truth.   Is. 45:14; Zech. 8:23 ◆ *known*

Do All Things for Edification

26 How is it then, brethren? when ye come together, every one of you hath a psalm, hath a doctrine, hath a tongue, hath a revelation, hath an interpretation. Let all things be done unto edifying.   Rom. 14:19

27 If any man speak in an *unknown* tongue, *let it be* by two, or at the most *by* three, and *that* by course; and let one interpret.

28 But if there be no interpreter, let him keep silence in the church; and let him speak to himself, and to God.

29 Let the prophets speak two or three, and let the other judge.   1 Cor. 12:10

30 If *any thing* be revealed to another that sitteth by, let the first hold his peace.

31 For ye may all prophesy one by one, that all may learn, and all may be comforted.

32 And the spirits of the prophets are subject to the prophets.   1 John 4:1

33 For God is not *the author* of confusion, but of peace, as in all churches of the saints.

14:33, 40 A Unified Effort

[God] requires that order and system be observed in the conduct of church affairs today no less than in the days of old. He desires His work to be carried forward with thoroughness and exactness so that He may place upon it the seal of His approval. Christian is to be united with Christian, church with church, the human instrumentality cooperating with the divine, every agency subordinate to the Holy Spirit, and all combined in giving to the world the good tidings of the grace of God. *AA 96*

---

34 Let your women keep silence in the churches: for it is not permitted unto them to speak; but *they are commanded* to be under obedience, as also saith the law.   Gen. 3:16;

35 And if they will learn any thing, let them ask their husbands at home: for it is a shame for women to speak in the church.

36 What? came the word of God out from you? or came it unto you only?

37 If any man think himself to be a prophet, or spiritual, let him acknowledge that the things that I write unto you are the commandments of the Lord.   2 Cor. 10:7; 1 John 4:6

38 But if any man be ignorant, let him be ignorant.

39 Wherefore, brethren, ᵀcovet to prophesy, and forbid not to speak with tongues. 1 Cor. 14:1

40 Let all things be done decently and in order.   Col. 2:5

The Gospel of Christ's Resurrection

15 Moreover, brethren, I declare unto you the gospel which I preached unto you, which also ye have received, and wherein ye stand;   Rom. 5:2

2 By which also ye are saved, if ye keep in

memory what I preached unto you, unless ye have believed in vain. Gal. 3:4

3 For I delivered unto you first of all that which I also received, how that Christ died for our sins according to the scriptures; Gal. 1:4

4 And that he was buried, and that he rose again the third day according to the scriptures: Ps. 16:10-11

5 And that he was seen of Cephas, then of the twelve: Mark 16:14; Acts 10:41; 1 Cor. 1:12

6 After that, he was seen of above five hundred brethren at once; of whom the greater part remain unto this present, but some are fallen asleep. Acts 7:60

7 After that, he was seen of James; then of all the apostles. Luke 24:50

8 And last of all he was seen of me also, as of one born out of due time. Acts 9:17; 1 Cor. 9:1

9 For I am the least of the apostles, that am not meet to be called an apostle, because I persecuted the church of God. Acts 8:3

10 But by the grace of God I am what I am: and his grace which *was bestowed* upon me was not in vain; but I laboured more abundantly than they all: yet not I, but the grace of God which was with me. Matt. 10:20; 2 Cor. 3:5; Phil. 2:13

11 Therefore whether *it were* I or they, so we preach, and so ye believed.

The Resurrection of the Dead

12 Now if Christ be preached that he rose from the dead, how say some among you that there is no resurrection of the dead? Acts 23:8

13 But if there be no resurrection of the dead, then is Christ not risen: 1 Thess. 4:14

14 And if Christ be not risen, then *is* our preaching vain, and your faith *is* also vain.

15 Yea, and we are found false witnesses of God; because we have testified of God that he raised up Christ: whom he raised not up, if so be that the dead rise not. Acts 2:24

16 For if the dead rise not, then is not Christ raised:

17 And if Christ be not raised, your faith *is* vain; ye are yet in your sins. Rom. 4:25

18 Then they also which are fallen asleep in Christ are perished. Rev. 14:13

19 If in this life only we have hope in Christ, we are of all men most miserable. 2 Tim. 3:12

20 But now is Christ risen from the dead, *and* become the firstfruits of them that slept. Acts 26:23; 1 Cor. 15:23; 1 Pet. 1:3

21 For since by man *came* death, by man *came* also the resurrection of the dead. John 11:25

22 For as in Adam all die, even so in Christ shall all be made alive.

Salvation From Sin See John 1:12.

23 But every man in his own order: Christ the firstfruits; afterward they that are Christ's at his coming. 1 Cor. 15:20

24 Then *cometh* the end, when he shall have delivered up the kingdom to God, even the Father; when he shall have put down all rule and all authority and power. Is. 9:7; Dan. 7:14, 27

25 For he must reign, till he hath put all enemies under his feet. Ps. 110:1; Matt. 22:44

26 The last enemy *that* shall be destroyed *is* death. 2 Tim. 1:10; Rev. 20:14; 21:4

27 For he hath put all things under his feet. But when he saith all things are put under *him, it is* manifest that he is excepted, which did put all things under him. Ps. 8:6; Matt. 11:27

28 And when all things shall be subdued unto him, then shall the Son also himself be subject unto him that put all things under him, that God may be all in all. 1 Cor. 3:23; 11:3; Phil. 3:21

29 Else what shall they do which are baptized for the dead, if the dead rise not at all? why are they then baptized for the dead?

30 And why stand we in jeopardy every hour?

15:30 A Loyal Soldier to the End

Amidst the constant storm of opposition, the clamor of enemies, and the desertion of friends the intrepid apostle [Paul] almost lost heart. But he looked back to Calvary and with new ardor pressed on to spread the knowledge of the Crucified. He was but treading the blood-stained path that Christ had trodden before him. He sought no discharge from the warfare till he should lay off his armor at the feet of his Redeemer. *AA 297*

31 I protest by your rejoicing which I have in Christ Jesus our Lord, I die daily. 1 Thess. 2:19

32 If after the manner of men I have fought with beasts at Ephesus, what advantageth it me, if the dead rise not? let us eat and drink; for to morrow we die. Is. 22:13; 56:12; Luke 12:19

33 Be not deceived: evil communications corrupt good manners. 1 Cor. 5:6

34 Awake to righteousness, and sin not; for some have not the knowledge of God: I speak *this* to your shame. Rom. 13:11

The Spiritual Body

35 But some *man* will say, How are the dead raised up? and with what body do they come? Ezek. 37:3

36 *Thou* fool, that which thou sowest is not ᵀquickened, except it die: John 12:24 ♦ *made alive*

37 And that which thou sowest, thou sowest not that body that shall be, but bare grain, it may chance of wheat, or of some other *grain*:

38 But God giveth it a body as it hath pleased him, and to every seed his own body.

39 All flesh *is* not the same flesh: but *there is* one *kind of* flesh of men, another flesh

of beasts, another of fishes, *and* another of birds.

40 *There are* also celestial bodies, and bodies terrestrial: but the glory of the celestial *is* one, and the *glory* of the terrestrial *is* another.

41 *There is* one glory of the sun, and another glory of the moon, and another glory of the stars: for *one* star differeth from *another* star in glory.

42 So also *is* the resurrection of the dead. It is sown in corruption; it is raised in incorruption: Dan. 12:3; Matt. 13:43; Rom. 8:21

43 It is sown in dishonour; it is raised in glory: it is sown in weakness; it is raised in power: Col. 3:4

44 It is sown a natural body; it is raised a spiritual body. There is a natural body, and there is a spiritual body.

45 And so it is written, The first man Adam was made a living soul; the last Adam *was made* a quickening spirit.   Gen. 2:7; John 5:21

46 Howbeit that *was* not first which is spiritual, but that which is natural; and afterward that which is spiritual.

47 The first man *is* of the earth, earthy: the second man *is* the Lord from heaven. Gen. 2:7

48 As *is* the earthy, such *are* they also that are earthy: and as *is* the heavenly, such *are* they also that are heavenly.   Phil. 3:20-21

49 And as we have borne the image of the earthy, we shall also bear the image of the heavenly.   Gen. 5:3; Rom. 8:29

50 Now this I say, brethren, that flesh and blood cannot inherit the kingdom of God; neither doth corruption inherit incorruption.   Matt. 16:17

Victory over Death

51 Behold, I shew you a mystery; We shall not all sleep, but we shall all be changed,

52 In a moment, in the twinkling of an eye, at the last trump: for the trumpet shall sound, and the dead shall be raised incorruptible, and we shall be changed. Is. 27:13; Matt. 24:31; John 5:25

> The Millennium See 2 Thessalonians 1:7–9.

53 For this corruptible must put on incorruption, and this mortal *must* put on immortality.   2 Cor. 5:2-4

> **15:51–53 High Calling in Christ**
>
> Glorious is the triumph awaiting the faithful. [Paul], realizing the possibilities before the Corinthian believers, sought to set before them that which uplifts from the selfish and the sensual, and glorifies life with the hope of immortality. Earnestly he exhorted them to be true to their high calling in Christ. *AA 321*

54 So when this corruptible shall have put on incorruption, and this mortal shall have put on immortality, then shall be brought to pass the saying that is written, Death is swallowed up in victory. Is. 25:8; Heb. 2:14-15; Rev. 20:14

55 O death, where *is* thy sting? O grave, where *is* thy victory?   Hos. 13:14

> **15:55 Jesus Sets Them Free**
>
> Satan cannot hold the dead in his grasp when the Son of God bids them live. *DA 320*

56 The sting of death *is* sin; and the strength of sin *is* the law.   Rom. 4:15

57 But thanks *be* to God, which giveth us the victory through our Lord Jesus Christ.

58 Therefore, my beloved brethren, be ye ᵀstedfast, unmoveable, always abounding in the work of the Lord, ᵀforasmuch as ye know that your labour is not in vain in the Lord.   1 Cor. 3:8; 16:10; 2 Pet. 3:14 ◆ *steadfast* ◆ *since*

Collection for the Church in Jerusalem

16 Now concerning the collection for the saints, as I have given order to the churches of Galatia, even so do ye.   Acts 16:6

2 Upon the first *day* of the week let every one of you lay by him in store, as *God* hath prospered him, that there be no gatherings when I come.   Luke 24:1; Acts 20:7; Rev. 1:10

3 And when I come, whomsoever ye shall approve by *your* letters, them will I send to bring your liberality unto Jerusalem.

4 And if it be meet that I go also, they shall go with me.

Paul's Plans

5 Now I will come unto you, when I shall pass through Macedonia: for I do pass through Macedonia.   Acts 19:21; 1 Cor. 4:19

6 And it may be that I will abide, yea, and winter with you, that ye may bring me on my journey whithersoever I go.   Acts 15:3

7 For I will not see you now by the way; but I trust to tarry a while with you, if the Lord permit.   Acts 18:21; 1 Cor. 4:19; James 4:15

8 But I will tarry at Ephesus until Pentecost.

9 For a great door and ᵀeffectual is opened unto me, and *there are* many adversaries.   Acts 14:27 ◆ *effective*

> **16:8, 9 Magnificent, but Corrupt**
>
> Ephesus was not only the most magnificent, but the most corrupt, of the cities of Asia. Superstition and sensual pleasure held sway over her teeming population. Under the shadow of her temples, criminals of every grade found shelter, and the most degrading vices flourished. *AA 286*

15:51, 52

News about Fellow Believers

10 Now if Timotheus come, see that he may be with you without fear: for he worketh the work of the Lord, as I also *do*. Rom. 16:21

11 Let no man therefore despise him: but conduct him forth in peace, that he may come unto me: for I look for him with the brethren. Acts 15:33; 1 Cor. 16:6; 1 Tim. 4:12

12 As touching *our* brother Apollos, I greatly desired him to come unto you with the brethren: but his will was not at all to come at this time; but he will come when he shall have ᵀconvenient time. 1 Cor. 1:12 ◆ *appropriate*

Other Greetings

13 Watch ye, stand fast in the faith, quit you like men, be strong. Gal. 5:1; Eph. 6:10; Phil. 1:27

16:13 We Can Overcome!

Those who put their trust in Christ are not to be enslaved by any hereditary or cultivated habit or tendency. Instead of being held in bondage to the lower nature, they are to rule every appetite and passion. God has not left us to battle with evil in our own finite strength. Whatever may be our inherited or cultivated tendencies to wrong, we can overcome through the power that He is ready to impart. *MH 175, 176*

---

14 Let all your things be done with charity.

15 I beseech you, brethren, (ye know the house of Stephanas, that it is the firstfruits of Achaia, and *that* they have addicted themselves to the ministry of the saints,) Rom. 16:5

16 That ye submit yourselves unto such, and to every one that helpeth with *us*, and laboureth. 1 Thess. 5:12; Heb. 13:17

17 I am glad of the coming of Stephanas and Fortunatus and Achaicus: for that which was lacking on your part they have supplied. 2 Cor. 11:9; Phil. 2:30; Philem. 13

18 For they have refreshed my spirit and yours: therefore acknowledge ye them that are such. 2 Cor. 7:13

19 The churches of Asia salute you. Aquila and Priscilla salute you much in the Lord, with the church that is in their house. Acts 18:2

20 All the brethren greet you. Greet ye one another with an holy kiss. Rom. 16:16

21 The salutation of *me* Paul with mine own hand. Gal. 6:11; Col. 4:18; 2 Thess. 3:17

22 If any man love not the Lord Jesus Christ, let him be Anathema Maran-atha. John 14:21

23 The grace of our Lord Jesus Christ *be* with you. Rom. 16:20

24 My love *be* with you all in Christ Jesus. Amen.

CORINTHIANS

Accomplishing a task is always difficult when you are surrounded by naysayers—those who oppose and distract you from your mission. Every time you think you are making progress, a naysayer utters a negative comment or opposes you in some other way. The apostle Paul understood this type of opposition all too well.

In his first letter to the believers in Corinth, Paul had to deal with various issues surrounding the church community, including immorality, disunity, and the difficulties inherent in living as a believer in a culture radically opposed to the faith. In writing 2 Corinthians, however, Paul faced another significant challenge: defending his ministry against those who questioned his authority as an apostle. The persuasive arguments of these naysayers hindered the Corinthian church from growing and making a broader impact for Christ in the culture. Paul wanted to reset their focus on Jesus.

In this very personal letter, Paul reminds his readers that his authority ultimately comes from God: "For though I should boast somewhat more of our authority, which the Lord hath given us for edification, and not for your destruction, I should not be ashamed" (10:8). Next, Paul responds directly to the opposition he received from the false apostles—those who tried to undermine his mission and authority. He urges the believers at Corinth to stay true to the gospel and the Savior in which they initially believed and to avoid those opposed to Christ.

Second Corinthians teaches us to be wary of those who try to undermine our walk with Christ and to persevere in our faith in Jesus Christ—regardless of what others might claim.

Dates

Second Corinthians was likely written in the summer of A.D. 57 while Paul was in Macedonia.

Author

First and 2 Corinthians were written by Paul. Both books mention early on that Paul is the author of these letters to the church at Corinth. Paul's earlier efforts to resolve the iniquity permeating the Corinthian church had gone without success. As a result, he decides to resolve the issues by sending a young assistant—Titus. Most probably leaving Ephesus for Corinth in the spring of A.D. 57, Titus may well be the courier of 1 Corinthians.

After a missed rendezvous in Troas, Paul and Titus finally meet at Philippi in Macedonia. Joy fills Paul's heart at the good report Titus bears of changes in the erring hearts of Corinth. The people embrace Titus as Paul's representative as well as Paul's loving message of reproof.

Astonished that Titus's work far exceeded his expectations, Paul requests that Titus return to carry on his labors with the Corinthian people. Thus, Paul sends another letter, 2 Corinthians, with Titus. This letter overflows with his joy with the good reports about the changes in their hearts. He also gives them additional spiritual counsel and his plan to visit Corinth upon completion of his work in Macedonia. Bible scholars agree that this particular writing reveals the clearest view of Paul's character, personality, and temperament. His spontaneity is nothing short of genuine.

Meaning of the Name

The title of 2 Corinthians is *Pros Korinthious B*. The *B* was added later to distinguish this letter from 1 Corinthians.

Christ in 2 Corinthians

It's difficult to read 1 and 2 Corinthians and not be able to see Christ in their pages. The believers in Corinth were living in a culture that in many ways was anathema to everything a believer held true. Yet, they were trying to understand how to navigate their daily lives in lieu of the faith in Christ they proclaimed.

Specifically, Paul had to defend his ministry and authority—both of which were given to him by Christ. False teachers, however, tried to dismiss Paul and his ministry to the

believers at Corinth. Paul wanted to make sure the faith of the Corinthian believers was pure and long lasting.

In 2 Corinthians, Christ is represented as the believer's consolation (1:5), triumph (2:14), Lord (4:5), light (4:6), judge (5:10), reconciliation (5:19), substitute (5:21), gift (9:15), owner (10:7), and power (12:9).

Overview

Almost from the beginning, some members divide the Corinthian church over loyalty. Their goal is to undermine Paul's work, authority and apostleship. The opposition charges Paul with inconsistency for not visiting Corinth as he had originally agreed to do, and they squabble over their own perception that he lacks apostolic authority. They accuse him of attempting a cowardly control by sending a letter rather than appearing in person. After following Paul's counsel in 1 Corinthians in disfellowshiping the reprobate (1 Corinthians 5:1–5; 2 Corinthians 2:6), Paul then gives them the tools to win back the offender (2 Corinthians 2:7-10). Second Corinthians can be divided into three main sections.

(1) *2 Corinthians 1—7*: In this first section of the book, Paul defends his ministry against false teachers. Paul describes the comfort a believer can access in times of trouble (1:1–11). No stranger to turmoil (1:8–11), Paul writes from experience. He then describes his delay in visiting the believers before defending his ministry against false teachers (2:4—6:10).

(2) *2 Corinthians 8—9*: Paul encourages believers to be generous and to help others. During his third missionary journey, Paul practiced what he preached, by collecting money for less fortunate believers in Jerusalem.

(3) *2 Corinthians 10—13*: In this last section of the book, Paul defended his authority as an apostle against those who questioned him. Here, we see Paul at his most vulnerable, as he details the "thorn in the flesh" (12:7), a weakness which brought glory to Christ.

Unlocking 2 Corinthians

KEY PEOPLE:
Paul, Timothy, Titus, Corinthians who opposed Paul

KEY EVENTS:
Disorder in the church at Corinth; the opposition to Paul's authority; spiritual counsel

KEY THEME:
Opposition to Paul's ministry, which is the major theme of 2 Corinthians. Paul lays out his credentials in this personal letter and takes on those who would oppose his God ordained authority.

KEY VERSES:
"For we preach not ourselves, but Christ Jesus the Lord; and ourselves your servants for Jesus' sake. For God, who commanded the light to shine out of darkness, hath shined in our hearts, to give the light of the knowledge of the glory of God in the face of Jesus Christ" (2 Corinthians 4:5, 6).

"Therefore if any man be in Christ, he is a new creature: old things are passed away; behold, all things are become new. And all things are of God, who hath reconciled us to himself by Jesus Christ, and hath given to us the ministry of reconciliation; to wit, that God was in Christ, reconciling the world unto himself, not imputing their trespasses unto them; and hath committed unto us the word of reconciliation" (2 Corinthians 5:17–19).

KEY CHAPTERS:
2 Corinthians 8 and 9 form the basis for Christian giving. Paul lays out the case for sacrificial giving and its importance in the life of a believer. Paul affirms: "But this I say, He which soweth sparingly shall reap also sparingly; and he which soweth bountifully shall reap also bountifully. Every man according as he purposeth in his heart, so let him give; not grudgingly, or of necessity: for God loveth a cheerful giver" (2 Corinthians 9:6, 7).

Paul Comforts the Corinthians

1 Paul, an apostle of Jesus Christ by the will of God, and Timothy *our* brother, unto the church of God which is at Corinth, with all the saints which are in all Achaia: Acts 16:1; Eph. 1:1; 2 Tim. 1:1

2 Grace *be* to you and peace from God our Father, and *from* the Lord Jesus Christ. Rom. 1:7

3 Blessed *be* God, even the Father of our Lord Jesus Christ, the Father of mercies, and the God of all comfort; Rom. 15:5-6; Eph. 1:3; 1 Pet. 1:3

4 Who comforteth us in all our tribulation, that we may be able to comfort them which are in any trouble, by the comfort wherewith we ourselves are comforted of God. Is. 51:12

1:4 Paul's Heavy Burden

For some time Paul had been carrying a burden of soul for the churches—a burden so heavy that he could scarcely endure it. False teachers had sought to destroy his influence among the believers and to urge their own doctrines in the place of gospel truth. *AA 325*

5 For as the sufferings of Christ abound in us, so our consolation also aboundeth by Christ.

6 And whether we be afflicted, *it is* for your consolation and salvation, which is ᵀeffectual in the enduring of the same sufferings which we also suffer: or whether we be comforted, *it is* for your consolation and salvation. 2 Tim. 2:10 ◆ *effective*

7 And our hope of you *is* ᵀstedfast, knowing, that as ye are partakers of the sufferings, so *shall ye be* also of the consolation. *steadfast*

8 For we would not, brethren, have you ignorant of our trouble which came to us in Asia, that we were pressed out of measure, above strength, insomuch that we despaired even of life: 1 Cor. 15:32

9 But we had the sentence of death in ourselves, that we should not trust in ourselves, but in God which raiseth the dead: Luke 18:9

10 Who delivered us from so great a death, and doth deliver: in whom we trust that he will yet deliver *us*; Rom. 15:31

11 Ye also helping together by prayer for us, that for the gift *bestowed* upon us by the means of many persons thanks may be given by many on our behalf. Phil. 1:19; Philem. 22

The Sincerity of Paul's Preaching

12 For our rejoicing is this, the testimony of our conscience, that in simplicity and godly sincerity, not with fleshly wisdom, but by the grace of God, we have had our ᵀconversation in the world, and more abundantly to you-ward. Acts 23:1; 1 Cor. 2:13; 2 Cor. 2:17 ◆ *conduct*

13 For we write none other things unto you, than what ye read or acknowledge; and I trust ye shall acknowledge even to the end;

14 As also ye have acknowledged us in part, that we are your rejoicing, even as ye also *are* ours in the day of the Lord Jesus. 1 Cor. 1:8

Why Paul Changed His Plans

15 And in this confidence I was minded to come unto you before, that ye might have a second benefit; Rom. 1:11; 15:29; 1 Cor. 4:19

16 And to pass by you into Macedonia, and to come again out of Macedonia unto you, and of you to be brought on my way toward Judaea. 1 Cor. 16:5-7

17 When I therefore was thus minded, did I use lightness? or the things that I purpose, do I purpose according to the flesh, that with me there should be yea yea, and nay nay?

18 But *as* God *is* true, our word toward you was not yea and nay. 1 Cor. 1:9

19 For the Son of God, Jesus Christ, who was preached among you by us, *even* by me and Silvanus and Timotheus, was not yea and nay, but in him was yea. Acts 18:5; Heb. 13:8

20 For all the promises of God in him *are* yea, and in him Amen, unto the glory of God by us. Rev. 3:14

21 Now he which stablisheth us with you in Christ, and hath anointed us, *is* God; 1 John 2:20

22 Who hath also sealed us, and given the earnest of the Spirit in our hearts. Eph. 1:13-14

1:22 Divine Assistance

The humble worker who obediently responds to the call of God may be sure of receiving divine assistance. To accept so great and holy a responsibility is itself elevating to the character. It calls into action the highest mental and spiritual powers, and strengthens and purifies the mind and heart. *COL 354*

23 Moreover I call God for a record upon my soul, that to spare you I came not as yet unto Corinth. Rom. 1:9; 1 Cor. 4:21; Gal. 1:20

24 Not for that we have dominion over your faith, but are helpers of your joy: for by faith ye stand. Rom. 11:20; 1 Cor. 15:1; 1 Pet. 5:3

Why Paul Did Not Come

2 But I determined this with myself, that I would not come again to you in heaviness. 2 Cor. 1:23

2 For if I make you sorry, who is he then that maketh me glad, but the same which is made sorry by me? 2 Cor. 7:8

3 And I wrote this same unto you, lest, when I came, I should have sorrow from them of whom I ought to rejoice; having confidence in you all, that my joy is *the joy* of you all. 2 Cor. 8:22; Gal. 5:10; Philem. 21

4 For out of much affliction and anguish of heart I wrote unto you with many tears; not that ye should be grieved, but that ye might

know the love which I have more abundantly unto you.   *2 Cor. 7:12*

Forgive the Repentant Person

5 But if any have caused grief, he hath not grieved me, but in part: that I may not overcharge you all.   *Gal. 4:12*
6 Sufficient to such a man *is* this punishment, which *was inflicted* of many.   *1 Cor. 5:4-5*
7 So that ᵀcontrariwise ye *ought* rather to forgive *him*, and comfort *him*, lest perhaps such a one should be swallowed up with overmuch sorrow.   *Eph. 4:32* ◆ *on the contrary*
8 Wherefore I ᵀbeseech you that ye would confirm *your* love toward him.   *beg*
9 For to this end also did I write, that I might know the proof of you, whether ye be obedient in all things.   *2 Cor. 10:6; Phil. 2:22*
10 To whom ye forgive any thing, I *forgive* also: for if I forgave any thing, to whom I forgave *it*, for your sakes *forgave I it* in the person of Christ;   *1 Cor. 5:4*
11 Lest Satan should get an advantage of us: for we are not ignorant of his devices. *1 Pet. 5:8*

Paul's Mission

12 Furthermore, when I came to Troas to *preach* Christ's gospel, and a door was opened unto me of the Lord,   *Acts 14:27; 16:8*
13 I had no rest in my spirit, because I found not Titus my brother: but taking my leave of them, I went from thence into Macedonia.   *2 Cor. 7:5-6*
14 Now thanks *be* unto God, which always causeth us to triumph in Christ, and maketh ᵀmanifest the savour of his knowledge by us in every place.   *Song 1:3* ◆ *known*

> **2:14 Faith, Hope, and New Zeal**
>
> Paul was now full of faith and hope. He felt that Satan was not to triumph over the work of God in Corinth, and in words of praise he poured forth the gratitude of his heart. He and his fellow laborers would celebrate their victory over the enemies of Christ and the truth, by going forth with new zeal to extend the knowledge of the Saviour. *AA 326*

15 For we are unto God a sweet savour of Christ, in them that are saved, and in them that perish: *Ezek. 20:41; 1 Cor. 1:18; Eph. 5:2*

> **2:15 Diffused Fragrance**
>
> Like incense the fragrance of the gospel was to be diffused throughout the world. To those who should accept Christ, the message would be a savor of life unto life; but to those who should persist in unbelief, a savor of death unto death. *AA 326*

16 To the one *we are* the savour of death unto death; and to the other the savour of

life unto life. And who *is* sufficient for these things?   *Luke 2:34; John 9:39; 2 Cor. 3:5-6*
17 For we are not as many, which corrupt the word of God: but as of sincerity, but as of God, in the sight of God speak we in Christ.   *2 Cor. 1:12; 4:2*

The Ministry from Christ

3 Do we begin again to commend ourselves? or need we, as some *others*, epistles of commendation to you, or *letters* of commendation from you? *Acts 18:27; 2 Cor. 12:11*
2 Ye are our epistle written in our hearts, known and read of all men:

> **3:2 Seals of Ministry**
>
> The conversion of sinners and their sanctification through the truth is the strongest proof a minister can have that God has called him to the ministry. The evidence of his apostleship is written upon the hearts of those converted, and is witnessed to by their renewed lives. Christ is formed within, the hope of glory. A minister is greatly strengthened by these seals of his ministry. *AA 328*

3 *Forasmuch as ye are* manifestly declared to be the epistle of Christ ministered by us, written not with ink, but with the Spirit of the living God; not in tables of stone, but in fleshy tables of the heart.   *Ex. 24:12; Jer. 31:33; Ezek. 11:19*
4 And such trust have we through Christ to God-ward: *Eph. 3:12*
5 Not that we are sufficient of ourselves to think any thing as of ourselves; but our sufficiency *is* of God;   *1 Cor. 15:10*
6 Who also hath made us able ministers of the new testament; not of the letter, but of the spirit: for the letter killeth, but the spirit giveth life.   *Jer. 31:31; Luke 22:20; John 6:63*
7 But if the ministration of death, written *and* engraven in stones, was glorious, so that the children of Israel could not stedfastly behold the face of Moses for the glory of his countenance; which *glory* was to be done away: *Ex. 24:12*
8 How shall not the ᵀministration of the spirit be rather glorious?   *service*
9 For if the ministration of condemnation *be* glory, much more doth the ministration of righteousness exceed in glory.   *Heb. 12:18-21*
10 For even that which was made glorious had no glory in this respect, by reason of the glory that excelleth.
11 For if that which is done away *was* glorious, much more that which remaineth *is* glorious.

The New Has Supplanted the Old

12 Seeing then that we have such hope, we use great plainness of speech: *Acts 4:13; 1 Thess. 2:2*

13 And not as Moses, *which* put a vail over his face, that the children of Israel could not stedfastly look to the end of that which is abolished: Ex. 34:33-35

14 But their minds were blinded: for until this day remaineth the same vail untaken away in the reading of the old ᵀtestament; which *vail* is done away in Christ. Acts 13:15 ◆ covenant

15 But even unto this day, when Moses is read, the ᵀvail is upon their heart. veil

16 Nevertheless when it shall turn to the Lord, the vail shall be taken away. Ex. 34:34

17 Now the Lord is that Spirit: and where the Spirit of the Lord *is*, there *is* liberty. Gal. 4:6

3:17 A Strong Bond of Union

Christianity makes a strong bond of union between master and slave, king and subject, the gospel minister and the degraded sinner who has found in Christ cleansing from sin. They have been washed in the same blood, quickened by the same Spirit; and they are made one in Christ Jesus. *AA 460*

18 But we all, with open face beholding as in a glass the glory of the Lord, are changed into the same image from glory to glory, *even* as by the Spirit of the Lord.

Paul Is Never Discouraged

4 Therefore seeing we have this ministry, as we have received mercy, we faint not;

2 But have renounced the hidden things of dishonesty, not walking in craftiness, nor handling the word of God deceitfully; but by ᵀmanifestation of the truth commending ourselves to every man's conscience in the sight of God. Rom. 6:21; 2 Cor. 2:17; 5:11 ◆ being made known

3 But if our gospel be hid, it is hid to them that are lost: 1 Cor. 1:18; 2 Cor. 3:14

4 In whom the god of this world hath blinded the minds of them which believe not, lest the light of the glorious gospel of Christ, who is the image of God, should shine unto them. John 12:31; 2 Cor. 4:6; Heb. 1:3

5 For we preach not ourselves, but Christ Jesus the Lord; and ourselves your servants for Jesus' sake. 1 Cor. 1:23

4:6 Links to the Life of Jesus

Let the glorious conceptions of God possess your mind. Let your life be knit by hidden links to the life of Jesus. He who commanded the light to shine out of darkness is willing to shine in your heart, to give the light of the knowledge of the glory of God in the face of Jesus Christ. . . . Christ will lead you to the threshold of the Infinite. *COL 149*

6 For God, who commanded the light to shine out of darkness, hath shined in our hearts, to give the light of the knowledge of the glory of God in the face of Jesus Christ. Gen. 1:3

7 But we have this treasure in earthen vessels, that the excellency of the power may be of God, and not of us. Lam. 4:2; 2 Cor. 5:1; 2 Tim. 2:20

4:7 Partnership With Jesus

He who called the fisherman of Galilee is still calling men to His service. And He is just as willing to manifest His power through us as through the first disciples. However imperfect and sinful we may be, the Lord holds out to us the offer of partnership with Himself, of apprenticeship to Christ. He invites us to come under the divine instruction, that, uniting with Christ, we may work the works of God. *DA 297*

8 *We are* troubled on every side, yet not distressed; *we are* perplexed, but not in despair;

9 Persecuted, but not forsaken; cast down, but not destroyed; Heb. 13:5

10 Always bearing about in the body the dying of the Lord Jesus, that the life also of Jesus might be made manifest in our body.

11 For we which live are alway delivered unto death for Jesus' sake, that the life also of Jesus might be made manifest in our mortal flesh. Rom. 8:36

12 So then death worketh in us, but life in you. 2 Cor. 13:9

13 We having the same spirit of faith, according as it is written, I believed, and therefore have I spoken; we also believe, and therefore speak; Ps. 116:10; 1 Cor. 12:9; 2 Pet. 1:1

14 Knowing that he which raised up the Lord Jesus shall raise up us also by Jesus, and shall present *us* with you. Eph. 5:27; 1 Thess. 4:14; Jude 24

15 For all things *are* for your sakes, that the abundant grace might through the thanksgiving of many ᵀredound to the glory of God. Rom. 8:28; 2 Cor. 1:11; 8:19 ◆ exceed

16 For which cause we faint not; but though our outward man perish, yet the inward *man* is renewed day by day. Is. 40:31; Rom. 7:22; Col. 3:10

17 For our light affliction, which is but for a moment, worketh for us a far more exceeding *and* eternal weight of glory; Ps. 30:5; Rom. 8:18

18 While we look not at the things which are seen, but at the things which are not seen: for the things which are seen *are* temporal; but the things which are not seen *are* eternal. 2 Cor. 5:7; Heb. 11:1

4:18 Spirit Is Like the Wind

While the wind is itself invisible, it produces effects that are seen and felt. So the work of the Spirit upon the soul will reveal itself in every act of him who has felt its saving power. When the Spirit of God takes possession of the heart, it transforms the life. *DA 173*

Faith Guides Our Lives

5 For we know that if our earthly house of this tabernacle were dissolved, we have a building of God, an house not made with hands, eternal in the heavens. 2 Cor. 4:7

2 For in this we groan, earnestly desiring to be clothed upon with our house which is from heaven: Rom. 8:23; 1 Cor. 15:53-54

3 If so be that being clothed we shall not be found naked.

4 For we that are in *this* tabernacle do groan, being burdened: not for that we would be unclothed, but clothed upon, that mortality might be swallowed up of life. 1 Cor. 15:53-54

5 Now he that hath wrought us for the self-same thing *is* God, who also hath given unto us the earnest of the Spirit. Rom. 8:23; 2 Cor. 1:22

6 Therefore *we are* always confident, knowing that, whilst we are at home in the body, we are absent from the Lord: Heb. 11:13

7 (For we walk by faith, not by sight:)

8 We are confident, *I say*, and willing rather to be absent from the body, and to be present with the Lord.

9 Wherefore we labour, that, whether present or absent, we may be accepted of him.

5:10 Justice and Mercy

The power and authority of the divine government will be employed to put down rebellion; yet all the manifestations of retributive justice will be perfectly consistent with the character of God as a merciful, long-suffering, benevolent being. *GC 541*

10 For we must all appear before the judgment seat of Christ; that every one may receive the things *done* in *his* body, according to that he hath done, whether *it be* good or bad. Matt. 16:27

11 Knowing therefore the terror of the Lord, we persuade men; but we are made manifest unto God; and I trust also are made manifest in your consciences. Job 31:23; Heb. 10:31; Jude 23

Christ's Love Guides Us

12 For we commend not ourselves again unto you, but give you occasion to glory on our behalf, that ye may have somewhat to *answer* them which glory in appearance, and not in heart. 2 Cor. 1:14; 3:1

13 For whether we be beside ourselves, *it is* to God: or whether we be sober, *it is* for your cause. 2 Cor. 11:1, 16-17; 12:6

14 For the love of Christ ᵀconstraineth us; because we thus judge, that if one died for all, then were all dead: Rom. 5:15 ◆ *compels*

5:14 Focus on the Cross

"The love of Christ," said Paul, "constraineth [compels] us" (2 Corinthians 5:14). This was the actuating principle of his conduct; it was his motive power. If ever his ardor in the path of duty flagged for a moment, one glance at the cross caused him to gird up anew the loins of his mind and press forward in the way of self-denial. In his labors for his brethren he relied much upon the manifestation of infinite love in the sacrifice of Christ, with its subduing, constraining power. *MH 500*

15 And *that* he died for all, that they which live should not ᵀhenceforth live unto themselves, but unto him which died for them, and rose again. Rom. 14:7-9 ◆ *from this time forward*

16 Wherefore henceforth know we no man after the flesh: yea, though we have known Christ after the flesh, yet now henceforth know we *him* no more. Phil. 3:7-8

Like a Mountain Stream

2 Corinthians 5:17

To the heart that has become purified, all is changed. Transformation of character is the testimony to the world of an indwelling Christ. The Spirit of God produces a new life in the soul, bringing the thoughts and desires into obedience to the will of Christ; and the inward man is renewed in the image of God. Weak and erring men and women show to the world that the redeeming power of grace can cause the faulty character to develop into symmetry and abundant fruitfulness.

The heart that receives the word of God is not as a pool that evaporates, not like a broken cistern that loses its treasure. It is like the mountain stream, fed by unfailing springs, whose cool, sparkling waters leap from rock to rock, refreshing the weary, the thirsty, the heavy-laden. It is like a river constantly flowing and, as it advances, becoming deeper and wider, until its life-giving waters are spread over all the earth. The stream that goes singing on its way leaves behind its gift of verdure and fruitfulness. The grass on its banks is a fresher green, the trees have a richer verdure, the flowers are more abundant. When the earth lies bare and brown under the summer's scorching heat, a line of verdure marks the river's course.

So it is with the true child of God. The religion of Christ reveals itself as a vitalizing, pervading principle, a living, working, spiritual energy. When the heart is opened to the heavenly influence of truth and love, these principles will flow forth again like streams in the desert, causing fruitfulness to appear where now are barrenness and dearth. *PK 233, 234*

5:17 Exalted From the Depths

Great as is the shame and degradation through sin, even greater will be the honor and exaltation through redeeming love. To human beings striving for conformity to the divine image there is imparted an outlay of heaven's treasure, an excellency of power, that will place them higher than even the angels who have never fallen. *COL 163*

17 Therefore if any man *be* in Christ, *he is* a new creature: old things are passed away; behold, all things are become new.   Gal. 6:15

The Christian Life See Ephesians 4:22–24.

18 And all things *are* of God, who hath reconciled us to himself by Jesus Christ, and hath given to us the ministry of reconciliation;
19 ᵀTo wit, that God was in Christ, reconciling the world unto himself, not imputing their ᵀtrespasses unto them; and hath committed unto us the word of reconciliation.   Is. 43:25 ◆ *Namely* ◆ *sins*
20 Now then we are ambassadors for Christ, as though God did ᵀbeseech *you* by us: we pray *you* in Christ's stead, be ye reconciled to God.   Mal. 2:7; 2 Cor. 6:1; Eph. 6:20 ◆ *beg*
21 For he hath made him *to be* sin for us, who knew no sin; that we might be made the righteousness of God in him.   Rom. 1:17; Gal. 3:13

5:21 An Infinite Fund of Power

He who through His own atonement provided for man an infinite fund of moral power, will not fail to employ this power in our behalf. We may take our sins and sorrows to His feet; for He loves us. His every look and word invites our confidence. *COL 157*

We Are God's Servants

6 We then, *as* workers together *with him*, ᵀbeseech *you* also that ye receive not the grace of God in vain.   1 Cor. 3:9; Heb. 12:15 ◆ *beg*
2 (For he saith, I have heard thee in a time accepted, and in the day of salvation have I succoured thee: behold, now *is* the accepted time; behold, now *is* the day of salvation.)
3 Giving no offence in any thing, that the ministry be not blamed: Rom. 14:13; 1 Cor. 9:12

6:4, 5 Ministers Precious to God

There is nothing more precious in the sight of God than His ministers, who go forth into the waste places of the earth to sow the seeds of truth, looking forward to the harvest. None but Christ can measure the solicitude of His servants as they seek for the lost. He imparts His Spirit to them, and by their efforts souls are led to turn from sin to righteousness. *AA 369, 370*

4 But in all *things* approving ourselves as the ministers of God, in much patience, in afflictions, in necessities, in distresses,   1 Cor. 3:5
5 In stripes, in imprisonments, in tumults, in labours, in watchings, in fastings;   2 Cor. 11:23
6 By pureness, by knowledge, by longsuffering, by kindness, by the Holy Ghost, by love unfeigned,   Rom. 12:9
7 By the word of truth, by the power of God, by the armour of righteousness on the right hand and on the left,   2 Cor. 4:2
8 By honour and dishonour, by evil report and good report: as deceivers, and *yet* true;
9 As unknown, and *yet* well known; as dying, and, behold, we live; as ᵀchastened, and not killed;   Rom. 8:36 ◆ *disciplined*
10 As sorrowful, yet alway rejoicing; as poor, yet making many rich; as having nothing, and *yet* possessing all things. John 16:22; Phil. 4:4

Christians and Their Relationships

11 O *ye* Corinthians, our mouth is open unto you, our heart is enlarged.   Ps. 119:32
12 Ye are not ᵀstraitened in us, but ye are straitened in your own bowels.   *hindered*
13 Now for a recompence in the same, (I speak as unto *my* children,) be ye also enlarged.

6:14 No Union Between Light and Darkness

But there is no union between the Prince of light and the prince of darkness, and there can be no union between their followers. When Christians consented to unite with those who were but half converted from paganism, they entered upon a path which led further and further from the truth. *GC 45*

14 Be ye not unequally yoked together with unbelievers: for what fellowship hath righteousness with unrighteousness? and what communion hath light with darkness? 1 Cor. 5:9

Christian Behavior See Proverbs 6:6–11.

Marriage See Ephesians 5:22–24.

15 And what concord hath Christ with Belial? or what part hath he that believeth with an ᵀinfidel?   *unbeliever*
16 And what agreement hath the temple of God with idols? for ye are the temple of the living God; as God hath said, I will dwell in them, and walk in *them*; and I will be their God, and they shall be my people.   Jer. 31:33
17 Wherefore come out from among them, and be ye separate, saith the Lord, and touch not the unclean *thing*; and I will receive you,
18 And will be a Father unto you, and ye shall be my sons and daughters, saith the Lord Almighty.   Is. 43:6

Paul Was Comforted by the Corinthians

7 Having therefore these promises, dearly beloved, let us cleanse ourselves from all filthiness of the flesh and spirit, perfecting holiness in the fear of God.   *Prov. 8:13*

7:1 Weakening Our Powers

Notwithstanding these inspired declarations, how many professed Christians are enfeebling their powers in the pursuit of gain or the worship of fashion; how many are debasing their godlike manhood by gluttony, by wine drinking, by forbidden pleasure. *GC 474*

2 Receive us; we have wronged no man, we have corrupted no man, we have defrauded no man.   *Acts 20:33*
3 I speak not *this* to condemn *you*: for I have said before, that ye are in our hearts to die and live with *you*.   *2 Cor. 6:11-12*
4 Great *is* my boldness of speech toward you, great *is* my glorying of you: I am filled with comfort, I am exceeding joyful in all our tribulation.   *2 Cor. 1:4*
5 For, when we were come into Macedonia, our flesh had no rest, but we were troubled on every side; without *were* fightings, within *were* fears.   *Deut. 32:25; 2 Cor. 2:13*
6 Nevertheless God, that comforteth those that are cast down, comforted us by the coming of Titus;   *2 Cor. 1:3-4*
7 And not by his coming only, but by the consolation wherewith he was comforted in you, when he told us your earnest desire, your mourning, your fervent mind toward me; so that I rejoiced the more.

7:8, 9 Paul Rejoices

Many had accepted the instruction contained in Paul's letter and had repented of their sins. Their lives were no longer a reproach to Christianity, but exerted a powerful influence in favor of practical godliness.

Filled with joy, the apostle sent another letter to the Corinthian believers, expressing his gladness of heart because of the good work wrought in them. *AA 324*

8 For though I made you sorry with a letter, I do not repent, though I did repent: for I perceive that the same epistle hath made you sorry, though *it were* but for a season.
9 Now I rejoice, not that ye were made sorry, but that ye sorrowed to repentance: for ye were made sorry after a godly manner, that ye might receive damage by us in nothing.   *Acts 20:21*

7:10 Specific Confession

True confession is always of a specific character, and acknowledges particular sins. They may be of such a nature as to be brought before God only; they may be wrongs that should be confessed to individuals who have suffered injury through them; or they may be of a public character, and should then be as publicly confessed. But all confession should be definite and to the point, acknowledging the very sins of which you are guilty. *SC 38*

10 For godly sorrow worketh repentance to salvation not to be repented of: but the sorrow of the world worketh death.   *2 Sam. 12:13*
11 For behold this selfsame thing, that ye sorrowed after a godly sort, what carefulness it ᵀwrought in you, yea, *what* clearing

---

What Does God See in Our Churches Today?

2 Corinthians 7:1

Those who do love God with all the heart will desire to give Him the best service of their life, and they will be constantly seeking to bring every power of their being into harmony with the laws that will promote their ability to do His will. They will not, by the indulgence of appetite or passion, enfeeble or defile the offering which they present to their heavenly Father.

Peter says: "Abstain from fleshly lusts, which war against the soul" (1 Peter 2:11). Every sinful gratification tends to benumb the faculties and deaden the mental and spiritual perceptions, and the word or the Spirit of God can make but a feeble impression upon the heart. Paul writes to the Corinthians: "Let us cleanse ourselves from all filthiness of the flesh and spirit, perfecting holiness in the fear of God" (2 Corinthians 7:1). And with the fruits of the Spirit—"love, joy, peace, long-suffering, gentleness, goodness, faith, meekness"—he classes "temperance" (Galatians 5:22, 23).

Notwithstanding these inspired declarations, how many professed Christians are enfeebling their powers in the pursuit of gain or the worship of fashion; how many are debasing their godlike manhood by gluttony, by wine drinking, by forbidden pleasure. And the church, instead of rebuking, too often encourages the evil by appealing to appetite, to desire for gain or love of pleasure, to replenish her treasury, which love for Christ is too feeble to supply. Were Jesus to enter the churches of today and behold the feasting and unholy traffic there conducted in the name of religion, would He not drive out those desecrators, as He banished the money-changers from the temple? *GC 473, 474*

of yourselves, yea, *what* ᵀindignation, yea, *what* fear, yea, *what* vehement desire, yea, *what* zeal, yea, *what* revenge! In all *things* ye have approved yourselves to be clear in this matter. 2 Cor. 7:7 ◆ worked ◆ anger

12 Wherefore, though I wrote unto you, *I did it* not for his cause that had done the wrong, nor for his cause that suffered wrong, but that our care for you in the sight of God might appear unto you. 2 Cor. 2:9

13 Therefore we were comforted in your comfort: yea, and exceedingly the more joyed we for the joy of Titus, because his spirit was refreshed by you all. 2 Cor. 7:6

14 For if I have boasted any thing to him of you, I am not ashamed; but as we spake all things to you in truth, even so our boasting, which *I made* before Titus, is found a truth. 2 Cor. 7:4

15 And his inward affection is more abundant toward you, whilst he remembereth the obedience of you all, how with fear and trembling ye received him. 2 Cor. 2:9; Phil. 2:12

16 I rejoice therefore that I have confidence in you in all *things*. 2 Cor. 2:3

The Collection for Christians in Jerusalem

8 Moreover, brethren, we do you to ᵀwit of the grace of God bestowed on the churches of Macedonia; Acts 16:9 ◆ know

2 How that in a great trial of affliction the abundance of their joy and their deep poverty abounded unto the riches of their liberality.

3 For to *their* power, I bear record, yea, and beyond *their* power *they were* willing of themselves; 1 Cor. 16:2

4 Praying us with much intreaty that we would receive the gift, and *take upon us* the fellowship of the ministering to the saints.

5 And *this they did*, not as we hoped, but first gave their own selves to the Lord, and unto us by the will of God.

6 Insomuch that we desired Titus, that as he had begun, so he would also finish in you the same grace also. 2 Cor. 8:4, 16-17; 12:18

Paul Urges Generosity

7 Therefore, as ye abound in every *thing, in* faith, and utterance, and knowledge, and *in* all diligence, and *in* your love to us, *see* that ye abound in this grace also. Rom. 15:14; 1 Cor. 1:5

8 I speak not by commandment, but by occasion of the forwardness of others, and to prove the sincerity of your love. 1 Cor. 7:6

9 For ye know the grace of our Lord Jesus Christ, that, though he was rich, yet for your sakes he became poor, that ye through his poverty might be rich. Matt. 20:28; 2 Cor. 6:10; 13:14

10 And herein I give *my* advice: for this is expedient for you, who have begun before, not only to do, but also to be forward a year ago. 1 Cor. 7:25, 40; 2 Cor. 9:2

11 Now therefore perform the doing *of it;* that as *there was* a readiness to will, so *there may be* a performance also out of that which ye have.

12 For if there be first a willing mind, *it is* accepted according to that a man hath, *and* not according to that he hath not. 2 Cor. 9:7

13 For *I mean* not that other men be eased, and ye burdened:

14 But by an equality, *that* now at this time your abundance *may be a supply* for their want, that their abundance also may be *a* supply for your want: that there may be equality: 2 Cor. 9:12

15 As it is written, He that *had gathered* much had nothing over; and he that *had gathered* little had no lack. Ex. 16:18

16 But thanks *be* to God, which put the same earnest care into the heart of Titus for you. Rev. 17:17

17 For indeed he accepted the ᵀexhortation; but being more forward, of his own accord he went unto you. 2 Cor. 8:6 ◆ encouragement

18 And we have sent with him the brother, whose praise *is* in the gospel throughout all the churches; 1 Cor. 7:17; 2 Cor. 12:18

19 And not *that* only, but who was also chosen of the churches to travel with us in this grace, which is administered by us to the glory of the same Lord, and *declaration of* your ready mind: 1 Cor. 16:3-4

20 Avoiding this, that no man should blame us in this abundance which is administered by us:

21 Providing for honest things, not only in the sight of the Lord, but also in the sight of men. Rom. 12:17; 14:18; Phil. 4:8

22 And we have sent with them our brother, whom we have oftentimes proved diligent in many things, but now much more diligent, upon the great confidence which I have in you.

23 Whether *any do enquire* of Titus, *he is* my partner and fellowhelper concerning you: or

our brethren *be enquired of, they are* the messengers of the churches, *and* the glory of Christ.   2 Cor. 8:6; Phil. 2:25; Philem. 17

24 Wherefore shew ye to them, and before the churches, the proof of your love, and of our boasting on your behalf.   2 Cor. 7:14

The Reason to Give

9 For as touching the ministering to the saints, it is ᵀsuperfluous for me to write to you: *more than needed*

2 For I know the forwardness of your mind, for which I boast of you to them of Macedonia, that Achaia was ready a year ago; and your zeal hath provoked very many.

3 Yet have I sent the brethren, lest our boasting of you should be in vain in this behalf; that, as I said, ye may be ready:2 Cor. 8:6

4 Lest ᵀhaply if they of Macedonia come with me, and find you unprepared, we (that we say not, ye) should be ashamed in this same confident boasting.   *maybe*

5 Therefore I thought it necessary to exhort the brethren, that they would go before unto you, and make up beforehand your bounty, whereof ye had notice before, that the same might be ready, as *a matter of* bounty, and not as *of* ᵀcovetousness.   Gen. 33:11 ◆ *greed*

Giving Generously and Cheerfully

6 But this *I say,* He which soweth sparingly shall reap also sparingly; and he which soweth bountifully shall reap also bountifully.

9:6 Receiving by Imparting

The sower multiplies his seed by casting it away. So it is with those who are faithful in distributing God's gifts. By imparting they increase their blessings. God has promised them a sufficiency that they may continue to give. *COL 86*

7 Every man according as he purposeth in his heart, *so let him give*; not grudgingly, or of necessity: for God loveth a cheerful giver.

Christian Behavior See 1 Thessalonians 5:17, 18.

‡Managing God's Gifts

8 And God *is* able to make all grace abound toward you; that ye, always having all sufficiency in all *things*, may abound to every good work:

9 (As it is written, He hath dispersed abroad; he hath given to the poor: his righteousness remaineth for ever.   Ps. 112:9

10 Now he that ministereth seed to the sower both minister bread for *your* food, and multiply your seed sown, and increase the fruits of your righteousness;)Is. 55:10; Hos. 10:12

11 Being enriched in every thing to all bountifulness, which causeth through us thanksgiving to God.   1 Cor. 1:5; 2 Cor. 1:11

9:7–11 Liberality Brings Prosperity

Unselfish liberality threw the early church into a transport of joy; for the believers knew that their efforts were helping to send the gospel message to those in darkness. Their benevolence testified that they had not received the grace of God in vain. What could produce such liberality but the sanctification of the Spirit? In the eyes of believers and unbelievers it was a miracle of grace.

Spiritual prosperity is closely bound up with Christian liberality. *AA 344*

12 For the administration of this service not only supplieth the want of the saints, but is abundant also by many thanksgivings unto God;

13 Whiles by the experiment of this ᵀministration they glorify God for your professed subjection unto the gospel of Christ, and for *your* liberal distribution unto them, and unto all *men*;   Matt. 5:16 ◆ *service*

14 And by their prayer for you, which long after you for the exceeding grace of God in you.

15 Thanks *be* unto God for his unspeakable gift.   John 3:16; 2 Cor. 2:14; Eph. 5:20

Paul's Authority

10 Now I Paul myself beseech you by the meekness and gentleness of Christ, who in presence *am* ᵀbase among you, but being absent am bold toward you: Matt. 11:29 ◆ *meek*

2 But I ᵀbeseech *you*, that I may not be bold when I am present with that confidence, wherewith I think to be bold against some, which think of us as if we walked according to the flesh.   2 Cor. 13:2, 10 ◆ *beg*

3 For though we walk in the flesh, we do not war after the flesh:

4 (For the weapons of our warfare *are* not carnal, but mighty through God to the pulling down of strong holds;)   Jer. 1:10; 1 Cor. 2:5

5 Casting down imaginations, and every high thing that exalteth itself against the knowledge of God, and bringing into captivity every thought to the obedience of Christ;   Is. 2:11-12

10:5 Jesus Can Only Help Us With Our Consent

God wishes us to have the mastery over ourselves. But He cannot help us without our consent and co-operation. The divine Spirit works through the powers and faculties given to man. Of ourselves, we are not able to bring the purposes and desires and inclinations into harmony with the will of God; but if we are "willing to be made willing," the Saviour will accomplish this for us, "Casting down imaginations, and every high thing that exalteth itself against the knowledge of God, and bringing into captivity every thought to the obedience of Christ" (2 Corinthians 10:5). *AA 482, 483*

6 And having in a readiness to revenge all disobedience, when your obedience is fulfilled.

7 Do ye look on things after the outward appearance? If any man trust to himself that he is Christ's, let him of himself think this again, that, as he *is* Christ's, even so *are* we Christ's.　　　John 7:24; 1 Cor. 14:37; 2 Cor. 5:12

8 For though I should boast somewhat more of our authority, which the Lord hath given us for edification, and not for your destruction, I should not be ashamed:　　2 Cor. 13:10

9 That I may not seem as if I would terrify you by letters.

10 For *his* letters, say they, *are* weighty and powerful; but *his* bodily presence *is* weak, and *his* speech contemptible.　　1 Cor. 1:17; Gal. 4:13-14

11 Let such an one think this, that, such as we are in word by letters when we are absent, such *will we be* also in deed when we are present.

Paul's Reason for Boasting

12 For we dare not make ourselves of the number, or compare ourselves with some that commend themselves: but they measuring themselves by themselves, and comparing themselves among themselves, are not wise.　　Prov. 26:12; 27:2; 2 Cor. 3:1

13 But we will not boast of things without *our* measure, but according to the measure of the rule which God hath distributed to us, a measure to reach even unto you. Rom. 15:20

14 For we stretch not ourselves beyond *our* measure, as though we reached not unto you: for we are come as far as to you also in *preaching* the gospel of Christ:　　1 Cor. 4:15

15 Not boasting of things without *our* measure, *that is,* of other men's labours; but having hope, when your faith is increased, that we shall be enlarged by you according to our rule abundantly,　　Rom. 15:20

16 To preach the gospel in the *regions* beyond you, *and* not to boast in another man's line of things made ready to our hand.

10:16 Christ's Footprints Close By

Many feel that it would be a great privilege to visit the scenes of Christ's life on earth, to walk where He trod, to look upon the lake beside which He loved to teach, and the hills and valleys on which His eyes so often rested. But we need not go to Nazareth, to Capernaum, or to Bethany, in order to walk in the steps of Jesus. We shall find His footprints beside the sickbed, in the hovels of poverty, in the crowded alleys of the great city. *DA 640*

17 But he that glorieth, let him glory in the Lord.　　Jer. 9:23-24; 1 Cor. 1:31

18 For not he that commendeth himself is approved, but whom the Lord commendeth.　　Rom. 2:29; 1 Cor. 4:5; 2 Cor. 10:12

Treasure in Earthen Vessels

2 Corinthians 10:12–15

At such a time as this, what is the trend of the education given? To what motive is appeal most often made? To self-seeking. Much of the education given is a perversion of the name. In true education the selfish ambition, the greed for power, the disregard for the rights and needs of humanity, that are the curse of our world, find a counterinfluence. God's plan of life has a place for every human being. Each is to improve his talents to the utmost; and faithfulness in doing this, be the gifts few or many, entitles one to honor. In God's plan there is no place for selfish rivalry. Those who measure themselves by themselves, and compare themselves among themselves, are not wise (2 Corinthians 10:12). Whatever we do is to be done "as of the ability which God giveth" (1 Peter 4:11). It is to be done "heartily, as to the Lord, and not unto men; knowing that of the Lord ye shall receive the reward of the inheritance: for ye serve the Lord Christ" (Colossians 3:23, 24). Precious the service done and the education gained in carrying out these principles. But how widely different is much of the education now given! From the child's earliest years it is an appeal to emulation and rivalry; it fosters selfishness, the root of all evil.

Thus is created strife for supremacy; and there is encouraged the system of "cramming," which in so many cases destroys health and unfits for usefulness. In many others, emulation leads to dishonesty; and by fostering ambition and discontent, it embitters the life and helps to fill the world with those restless, turbulent spirits that are a continual menace to society. *Ed 225, 226*

Paul Contrasts Himself with False Apostles

11 Would to God ye could bear with me a little in *my* folly: and indeed bear with me.   2 Cor. 5:13

2 For I am jealous over you with godly jealousy: for I have ᵀespoused you to one husband, that I may present *you as a* ᵀchaste virgin to Christ.   Is. 54:5 ◆ *given to marry* ◆ *pure*

> ### 11:2 The Marriage Supper
>
> In both the Old and the New Testament, the marriage relation is employed to represent the tender and sacred union that exists between Christ and His people. To the mind of Jesus the gladness of the wedding festivities pointed forward to the rejoicing of that day when He shall bring home His bride to the Father's house, and the redeemed with the Redeemer shall sit down to the marriage supper of the Lamb. *DA 151*

3 But I fear, lest by any means, as the serpent beguiled Eve through his subtilty, so your minds should be corrupted from the simplicity that is in Christ.   Gen. 3:4; Rev. 12:9
4 For if he that cometh preacheth another Jesus, whom we have not preached, or *if* ye receive another spirit, which ye have not received, or another gospel, which ye have not accepted, ye might well bear with *him.*
5 For I suppose I was not a ᵀwhit behind the very chiefest apostles.   *bit*
6 But though *I* be rude in speech, yet not in knowledge; but we have been throughly made manifest among you in all things.   Eph. 3:4
7 Have I committed an offence in ᵀabasing myself that ye might be exalted, because I have preached to you the gospel of God freely?   2 Cor. 12:13 ◆ *bringing low*
8 I robbed other churches, taking wages *of them,* to do you service.
9 And when I was present with you, and wanted, I was chargeable to no man: for that which was lacking to me the brethren which came from Macedonia supplied: and in all *things* I have kept myself from being burdensome unto you, and *so* will I keep *myself.*
10 As the truth of Christ is in me, no man shall stop me of this boasting in the regions of Achaia.   Acts 18:12; Rom. 1:9; 9:1
11 Wherefore? because I love you not? God knoweth.   2 Cor. 12:15
12 But what I do, that I will do, that I may cut off occasion from them which desire occasion; that wherein they glory, they may be found even as we.   1 Cor. 9:12
13 For such *are* false apostles, deceitful workers, transforming themselves into the apostles of Christ.   Gal. 1:7; 2:4; Rev. 2:2

14 And no marvel; for Satan himself is transformed into an angel of light.   Gal. 1:8

> ### 11:14 Deceptions of Spiritualism
>
> Among the most successful agencies of the great deceiver are the delusive teachings and lying wonders of spiritualism. Disguised as an angel of light, he spreads his nets where least suspected. If men would but study the Book of God with earnest prayer that they might understand it, they would not be left in darkness to receive false doctrines. But as they reject the truth they fall a prey to deception. *GC 524*

15 Therefore *it is* no great thing if his ministers also be transformed as the ministers of righteousness; whose end shall be according to their works.   Phil. 3:19
16 I say again, Let no man think me a fool; if otherwise, yet as a fool receive me, that I may boast myself a little.   2 Cor. 11:1
17 That which I speak, I speak *it* not after the Lord, but as it were foolishly, in this confidence of boasting.   1 Cor. 7:12; 2 Cor. 9:4
18 Seeing that many glory after the flesh, I will glory also.
19 For ye suffer fools gladly, seeing ye *yourselves* are wise.   1 Cor. 4:10
20 For ye suffer, if a man bring you into bondage, if a man devour *you,* if a man take *of you,* if a man exalt himself, if a man ᵀsmite you on the face.   Gal. 2:4; 4:3, 9 ◆ *strike*
21 I speak as concerning reproach, as though we had been weak. Howbeit whereinsoever any is bold, (I speak foolishly,) I am bold also.   2 Cor. 10:1-2, 10; 11:17
22 Are they Hebrews? so *am* I. Are they Israelites? so *am* I. Are they the seed of Abraham? so *am* I.   Rom. 9:4; 11:1; Phil. 3:5
23 Are they ministers of Christ? (I speak as a fool) I *am* more; in labours more abundant, in stripes above measure, in prisons more frequent, in deaths ᵀoft.   Acts 9:16; 1 Cor. 15:10 ◆ *often*
24 Of the Jews five times received I forty *stripes* save one.
25 Thrice was I beaten with rods, once was I stoned, thrice I suffered shipwreck, a night and a day I have been in the deep;   Acts 14:19
26 *In* journeyings often, *in* perils of waters, *in* perils of robbers, *in* perils by *mine own* countrymen, *in* perils by the heathen, *in* perils in the city, *in* perils in the wilderness, *in* perils in the sea, *in* perils among false brethren;
27 In weariness and painfulness, in watchings often, in hunger and thirst, in fastings often, in cold and nakedness.   Phil. 4:12; 1 Thess. 2:9
28 Beside those things that are without, that which cometh upon me daily, the care of all the churches.

29 Who is weak, and I am not weak? who is offended, and I burn not?   1 Cor. 8:13
30 If I must needs glory, I will glory of the things which concern mine infirmities.
31 The God and Father of our Lord Jesus Christ, which is blessed for evermore, knoweth that I lie not.   Rom. 9:5
32 In Damascus the governor under Aretas the king kept the city of the Damascenes with a garrison, desirous to apprehend me:
33 And through a window in a basket was I let down by the wall, and escaped his hands.

Paul's Visions and Revelations

12 It is not expedient for me doubtless to glory. I will come to visions and revelations of the Lord.   Gal. 1:12
2 I knew a man in Christ above fourteen years ago, (whether in the body, I cannot tell; or whether out of the body, I cannot tell: God knoweth;) such an one caught up to the third heaven.   Acts 22:17; 2 Cor. 11:11; 1 Thess. 4:17
3 And I knew such a man, (whether in the body, or out of the body, I cannot tell: God knoweth;)
4 How that he was caught up into paradise, and heard unspeakable words, which it is not lawful for a man to utter.   Luke 23:43
5 Of such an one will I glory: yet of myself I will not glory, but in mine infirmities.
6 For though I would desire to glory, I shall not be a fool; for I will say the truth: but now I ᵀforbear, lest any man should think of me above that which he seeth me to be, or that he heareth of me.   2 Cor. 11:16 ◆ refrain
7 And lest I should be exalted above measure through the abundance of the revelations, there was given to me a thorn in the flesh, the messenger of Satan to buffet me, lest I should be exalted above measure. Num. 33:55
8 For this thing I ᵀbesought the Lord ᵀthrice, that it might depart from me. begged ◆ three times
9 And he said unto me, My grace is sufficient for thee: for my strength is made perfect in weakness. Most gladly therefore will I rather glory in my infirmities, that the power of Christ may rest upon me.   Is. 40:29-31; Phil. 4:13
10 Therefore I take pleasure in infirmities, in reproaches, in necessities, in persecutions, in distresses for Christ's sake: for when I am weak, then am I strong. Rom. 5:3; 2 Cor. 6:4; 13:4

12:10 Co-laborers With God

We are to take up the burdens that God appoints, bearing them for His sake, and ever going to Him for rest. Whatever our work, God is honored by wholehearted, cheerful service. He is pleased when we take up our duties with gratitude, rejoicing that we are accounted worthy to be co-laborers with Him. COL 364

Paul Was Not a Burden

11 I am become a fool in glorying; ye have compelled me: for I ought to have been commended of you: for in nothing am I behind the very chiefest apostles, though I be nothing.
12 Truly the signs of an apostle were ᵀwrought among you in all patience, in signs, and wonders, and mighty deeds. done
13 For what is it wherein ye were inferior to other churches, except it be that I myself was not burdensome to you? forgive me this wrong.   1 Cor. 9:12; 2 Cor. 12:14

12:14–21 Paul's Faithful Counsel

With remarkable clearness [Paul] proceeded to answer the various questions brought forward by the church, and to lay down general principles, which, if heeded, would lead them to a higher spiritual plane. They were in peril, and he could not bear the thought of failing at this critical time to reach their hearts. Faithfully he warned them of their dangers and reproved them for their sins. He pointed them again to Christ and sought to kindle anew the fervor of their early devotion. AA 301

Letters to the World

2 Corinthians 13:5

The children of God are called to be representatives of Christ, showing forth the goodness and mercy of the Lord. As Jesus has revealed to us the true character of the Father, so we are to reveal Christ to a world that does not know His tender, pitying love. . . . In every one of His children, Jesus sends a letter to the world. If you are Christ's follower, He sends in you a letter to the family, the village, the street, where you live. Jesus, dwelling in you, desires to speak to the hearts of those who are not acquainted with Him. Perhaps they do not read the Bible, or do not hear the voice that speaks to them in its pages; they do not see the love of God through His works. But if you are a true representative of Jesus, it may be that through you they will be led to understand something of His goodness and be won to love and serve Him.

Christians are set as light bearers on the way to heaven. They are to reflect to the world the light shining upon them from Christ. Their life and character should be such that through them others will get a right conception of Christ and of His service. SC 115

14 Behold, the third time I am ready to come to you; and I will not be burdensome to you: for I seek not yours, but you: for the children ought not to lay up for the parents, but the parents for the children. Prov. 19:14; 1 Cor. 4:14-15

15 And I will very gladly spend and be spent for you; though the more abundantly I love you, the less I be loved. Phil. 2:17; 1 Thess. 2:8

16 But be it so, I did not burden you: nevertheless, being crafty, I caught you with ᵀguile. *deceit*

17 Did I make a gain of you by any of them whom I sent unto you?

18 I desired Titus, and with *him* I sent a brother. Did Titus make a gain of you? walked we not in the same spirit? *walked we* not in the same steps? Rom. 4:12; 2 Cor. 8:6

19 Again, think ye that we excuse ourselves unto you? we speak before God in Christ: but *we do* all things, dearly beloved, for your edifying. Rom. 9:1; 1 Cor. 14:26; 2 Cor. 10:8

Paul's Concern about Their Lifestyles

20 For I fear, lest, when I come, I shall not find you such as I would, and *that* I shall be found unto you such as ye would not: lest *there be* debates, envyings, wraths, strifes, ᵀbackbitings, whisperings, ᵀswellings, tumults: Rom. 1:29 ◆ *slanderings* ◆ *prideful attitudes*

21 *And* lest, when I come again, my God will humble me among you, and *that* I shall bewail many which have sinned already, and have not repented of the uncleanness and fornication and ᵀlasciviousness which they have committed. 1 Cor. 5:1; 2 Cor. 13:2; Gal. 5:19 ◆ *lewdness*

Paul Plans to Visit

13 This *is* the third *time* I am coming to you. In the mouth of two or three witnesses shall every word be established.

2 I told you before, and foretell you, as if I were present, the second time; and being absent now I write to them which ᵀheretofore have sinned, and to all other, that, if I come again, I will not spare: 2 Cor. 1:23 ◆ *before*

3 Since ye seek a proof of Christ speaking in me, which to you-ward is not weak, but is mighty in you. Matt. 10:20

4 For though he was crucified through weakness, yet he liveth by the power of God. For we also are weak in him, but we shall live with him by the power of God toward you. Rom. 1:4; 6:4; 1 Pet. 3:18

5 Examine yourselves, whether ye be in the faith; prove your own selves. Know ye not your own selves, how that Jesus Christ is in you, except ye be reprobates? Rom. 8:10

> **13:5 Faith and Works**
>
> The good tree will produce good fruit. If the fruit is unpalatable and worthless, the tree is evil. So the fruit borne in the life testifies as to the condition of the heart and the excellence of the character. Good works can never purchase salvation, but they are an evidence of the faith that acts by love and purifies the soul. And though the eternal reward is not bestowed because of our merit, yet it will be in proportion to the work that has been done through the grace of Christ. *DA 314*

6 But I trust that ye shall know that we are not reprobates.

7 Now I pray to God that ye do no evil; not that we should appear approved, but that ye should do that which is honest, though we be as reprobates.

8 For we can do nothing against the truth, but for the truth.

9 For we are glad, when we are weak, and ye are strong: and this also we wish, *even* your perfection. 1 Cor. 4:10; 2 Cor. 13:11; 1 Thess. 3:10

10 Therefore I write these things being absent, lest being present I should use sharpness, according to the power which the Lord hath given me to edification, and not to destruction. 2 Cor. 2:3; 10:8; Titus 1:13

11 Finally, brethren, farewell. Be perfect, be of good comfort, be of one mind, live in peace; and the God of love and peace shall be with you. Mark 9:50; Rom. 12:16; 15:33

12 Greet one another with an holy kiss.

13 All the saints salute you.

14 The grace of the Lord Jesus Christ, and the love of God, and the communion of the Holy Ghost, *be* with you all. Amen. Rom. 16:20; Jude 21

THE EPISTLE OF PAUL THE APOSTLE TO THE

GALATIANS

Galatians is a book about commitment and perseverance. It was addressed to believers who had made a commitment to Christ but who, nonetheless, were slipping back into old habits and practices—namely legalism.

Because he was often criticized by those wishing to diminish or deny his authority, Paul begins his letter to the churches in Galatia by reaffirming his credentials. He then reminds the believers that they were saved into freedom in Christ through faith and doing good works and abiding by the Jewish law are not avenues to salvation; instead good works are the result of accepting that freedom in Christ.

His letter is a strong and deliberate attempt to quell those who encouraged the young believers to abandon their newfound freedom to return to their old beliefs. Paul defends the gospel of faith, opposing the gospel of works.

This controversy—a gospel of works versus the gospel of faith—was one of the most difficult and persistent in this early generation of believers. Many new converts were coming out of Jewish backgrounds and needed teaching and help in order to determine how their new faith related to the practices of their old faith.

Paul provided that by showing them the superiority of the gospel and how to rely on the Holy Spirit to help them overcome their struggles. Even though Paul's letter can at times seem extremely straightforward and direct, it was because of his love for these new believers. His commitment to them was not unlike the commitment of a parent to a child—helping the child overcome false beliefs and false teachers in order to give him or her proper direction. And what could be more important than urging them on in their commitment to the Savior?

Dates

Scholars hold two general theories as to the time of Galatians' writing. Some think that this letter is written during Paul's first visit to Corinth because of his use of the words "so soon." The Galatian people "are so soon removed from him that called you into the grace of Christ unto another gospel" (1:6).

Those who believe that Galatians has a later date note that "soon" may well reference a time after his third journey, during his three-month stay in Corinth. This thought is based on the fact that both Galatians and Romans are so much alike in subject matter that Paul very likely composes them at approximately the same time in approximately A.D. 58.

Author

The authorship of Galatians is virtually unchallenged. Paul specifically mentions that he is the author in the first verse. We also read in 5:2, "Behold, I Paul say unto you"—a direct attribute to Paul. Also we read in 6:11 that Paul penned the letter and did not dictate it to a scribe, as he did other books: "Ye see how large a letter I have written unto you with mine own hand."

Meaning of the Name

The epistle of Galatians was known as *Pros Galatas*, which means "To the Galatians." Paul specifically mentions this group of churches in 1:2, when he writes, "And all the brethren which are with me, unto the churches of Galatia." The Galatians were a migratory Celtic people who moved from Gaul to Asia Minor.

Christ in Galatians

Christ frees the believer from sin, thus giving him or her freedom from its power and freedom from the bondage to the law (legalism). Many Galatian believers were coming from a background where adherence to Jewish laws was taken seriously. Paul had to try and reassure these new believers that faith in Christ frees them from bondage not only from sin but also from the laws that they previously believed would make them holy.

Christ is apparent throughout Galatians in that He provides freedom from sin, victory over its power, and the ability to rely on Him for help in any struggle.

Overview

Galatia was a territory in the central part of Asia Minor; it became a Roman province under Caesar Augustus in 25 B.C. This territory includes the cities of Antioch in Pisidia, Iconium, Lystra, and Derbe (cities where Paul ministered, see Acts 13—14).

Paul senses that if apostasy has not already begun in Galatia, it certainly is threatening. The doctrinal controversy is such that Paul's soul is strongly moved to communicate with these people. The disaffection for truth occurs because false teachers give the counsel that it is necessary, even in the new Christianity, to adopt the Jewish customs and beliefs.

While the Judaizing teachers are successful in deceiving a large segment of the membership, it is not apparent how deeply this deception permeated the Galatian churches to lead the members into legalism before Paul's epistle reaches them. The overall tone of the letter gives evidence that a general abandonment of truth is imminent. The misleading teachers work in direct opposition not only to the decisions of the Jerusalem Council but also to Paul's God-given counsel.

The Epistle to the Galatians is organized into three parts to deal with the issue of justification by faith versus the gospel of works.

(1) *Defending the gospel of grace (chapters 1—2):* Paul spends the early part of Galatians defending the gospel of grace the believers had recently accepted, and also defending his authority as an apostle from those who attempted to undermine him.

(2) *The gospel of grace explained (chapters 3—4):* In this section, Paul systematically outlines the gospel of grace, even giving examples with which the believers at Galatia can identify.

(3) *The gospel of grace applied (chapters 5—6):* The final section explains the freedom found in Christ and the gospel of grace. Paul encourages these new believers to "walk in the Spirit" and thus avoid fulfilling the desires of the flesh. Chapter 6 makes practical application of the new principles and glories in the cross.

Unlocking Galatians

KEY PEOPLE:
Paul, Peter, Barnabas, Titus, false teachers

KEY EVENTS:
Paul's trip to Jerusalem; Peter and Paul's meeting in Antioch

KEY PHRASE:
Freedom from the Law, a phrase which encompasses the soul of Galatians. Paul urges the new believers to abide by their freedom in Christ and not to go back to their former beliefs. Christ's death and resurrection, along with the power of the Holy Spirit, gives believers the ability to live in freedom and love.

KEY VERSES:
"I am crucified with Christ: nevertheless I live; yet not I, but Christ liveth in me: and the life which I now live in the flesh I live by the faith of the Son of God, who loved me, and gave himself for me. I do not frustrate the grace of God: for if righteousness come by the law, then Christ is dead in vain" (Galatians 2:20, 21).

"Stand fast therefore in the liberty wherewith Christ hath made us free, and be not entangled again with the yoke of bondage" (Galatians 5:1).

KEY CHAPTER:
Galatians 5, which serves as a reminder for believers not to be "entangled again with the yoke of bondage." Paul urges the believers to put off the sinful nature and to live by the Spirit, thus not only giving us the ability to live in freedom but also to serve others with the love Christ has provided. In this chapter we find a comparison between the fruit of the Spirit and the fruit of the world.

Paul's Greeting

1 Paul, an apostle, (not of men, neither by man, but by Jesus Christ, and God the Father, who raised him from the dead;) Acts 9:6

1:1 Paul's Qualifications

An eloquent speaker and a severe critic, Paul, with his stern purpose and undaunted courage, possessed the very qualifications needed in the early church. *AA 124*

2 And all the brethren which are with me, unto the churches of Galatia: 1 Cor. 16:1; Phil. 4:21
3 Grace *be* to you and peace from God the Father, and *from* our Lord Jesus Christ, 1 Cor. 1:3
4 Who gave himself for our sins, that he might deliver us from this present evil world, according to the will of God and our Father: Matt. 20:28; Rom. 4:25; Phil. 4:20
5 To whom *be* glory for ever and ever. Amen.

Follow the Good News We Brought

6 I marvel that ye are so soon removed from him that called you into the grace of Christ unto another gospel: 2 Cor. 11:4
7 Which is not another; but there be some that trouble you, and would pervert the gospel of Christ. Acts 15:24; Gal. 5:10, 12
8 But though we, or an angel from heaven, preach any other gospel unto you than that which we have preached unto you, let him be accursed. Rom. 9:3; 1 Cor. 16:22
9 As we said before, so say I now again, If any *man* preach any other gospel unto you than that ye have received, let him be accursed.
10 For do I now persuade men, or God? or do I seek to please men? for if I yet pleased men, I should not be the servant of Christ. Rom. 1:1; 1 Cor. 10:33; 1 Thess. 2:4
11 But I certify you, brethren, that the gospel which was preached of me is not after man.
12 For I neither received it of man, neither was I taught *it*, but by the revelation of Jesus Christ.

1:12 Paul's Testimony

In his letter to the Galatian believers Paul briefly reviewed the leading incidents connected with his own conversion and early Christian experience. By this means he sought to show that it was through a special manifestation of divine power that he had been led to see and grasp the great truths of the gospel. *AA 386*

13 For ye have heard of my ᵀconversation in time past in the Jews' religion, how that beyond measure I persecuted the church of God, and wasted it: Acts 8:3; 9:21; 26:4-5 ◆ conduct

14 And profited in the Jews' religion above many my equals in mine own nation, being more exceedingly zealous of the traditions of my fathers. Acts 22:3
15 But when it pleased God, who separated me from my mother's womb, and called *me* by his grace, Is. 49:1, 5; Jer. 1:5
16 To reveal his Son in me, that I might preach him among the heathen; immediately I conferred not with flesh and blood:
17 Neither went I up to Jerusalem to them which were apostles before me; but I went into Arabia, and returned again unto Damascus.
18 Then after three years I went up to Jerusalem to see Peter, and abode with him fifteen days.
19 But other of the apostles saw I none, save James the Lord's brother. Matt. 13:55
20 Now the things which I write unto you, behold, before God, I lie not. Rom. 9:1; 2 Cor. 11:31
21 Afterwards I came into the regions of Syria and Cilicia; Acts 6:9
22 And was unknown by face unto the churches of Judaea which were in Christ:
23 But they had heard only, That he which persecuted us in times past now preacheth the faith which once he destroyed.
24 And they glorified God in me.

Paul Accepted as an Apostle

2 Then fourteen years after I went up again to Jerusalem with Barnabas, and took Titus with *me* also. Gal. 2:3
2 And I went up by revelation, and communicated unto them that gospel which I preach among the Gentiles, but privately to them which were of reputation, lest by any means I should run, or had run, in vain. Acts 15:4; Gal. 2:9; Phil. 2:16
3 But neither Titus, who was with me, being a Greek, was compelled to be circumcised: Acts 16:3
4 And that because of false brethren unawares brought in, who came in privily to spy out our liberty which we have in Christ Jesus, that they might bring us into bondage:
5 To whom we gave place by subjection, no, not for an hour; that the truth of the gospel might continue with you. Gal. 2:14; 4:16; Col. 1:5
6 But of these who seemed to be somewhat, (whatsoever they were, it maketh no matter to me: God accepteth no man's person:) for they who seemed *to be somewhat* in conference added nothing to me: Acts 10:34; 2 Cor. 12:11
7 But contrariwise, when they saw that the gospel of the uncircumcision was committed unto me, as *the gospel* of the circumcision *was* unto Peter; Acts 9:15; Gal. 1:16; 1 Thess. 2:4
8 (For he that ᵀwrought effectually in Peter to the apostleship of the circumcision, the

same was mighty in me toward the Gentiles:) *worked*

9 And when James, Cephas, and John, who seemed to be pillars, perceived the grace that was given unto me, they gave to me and Barnabas the right hands of fellowship; that we *should go* unto the heathen, and they unto the circumcision. *Rom. 12:3*

10 Only *they would* that we should remember the poor; the same which I also was forward to do. *Acts 24:17*

How Peter Was Wrong

11 But when Peter was come to Antioch, I withstood him to the face, because he was to be blamed.

12 For before that certain came from James, he did eat with the Gentiles: but when they were come, he withdrew and separated himself, fearing them which were of the circumcision. *Luke 15:2*

13 And the other Jews ᵀdissembled likewise with him; insomuch that Barnabas also was carried away with their ᵀdissimulation. *deceived ♦ hypocrisy*

14 But when I saw that they walked not uprightly according to the truth of the gospel, I said unto Peter before *them* all, If thou, being a Jew, livest after the manner of Gentiles, and not as do the Jews, why compellest thou the Gentiles to live as do the Jews? *Acts 10:28; Gal. 2:5; 1 Tim. 5:20*

15 We *who are* Jews by nature, and not sinners of the Gentiles, *Eph. 2:3*

16 Knowing that a man is not justified by the works of the law, but by the faith of Jesus Christ, even we have believed in Jesus Christ, that we might be justified by the faith of Christ, and not by the works of the law: for by the works of the law shall no flesh be justified. *Ps. 143:2*

2:16 False Spiritual Guides

To substitute external forms of religion for holiness of heart and life is still as pleasing to the unrenewed nature as it was in the days of these Jewish teachers. Today, as then, there are false spiritual guides, to whose doctrines many listen eagerly. It is Satan's studied effort to divert minds from the hope of salvation through faith in Christ and obedience to the law of God. *AA 387*

---

17 But if, while we seek to be justified by Christ, we ourselves also are found sinners, *is* therefore Christ the minister of sin? God forbid. *Gal. 2:15*

18 For if I build again the things which I destroyed, I make myself a transgressor.

19 For I through the law am dead to the law, that I might live unto God. *Rom. 6:2, 11; 7:4*

20 I am crucified with Christ: nevertheless I live; yet not I, but Christ liveth in me: and the life which I now live in the flesh I live by the faith of the Son of God, who loved me, and gave himself for me. *Rom. 8:37; Gal. 1:4; 5:24*

2:20

The Christian Life See Philippians 2:13.

---

21 I do not frustrate the grace of God: for if righteousness *come* by the law, then Christ is dead in vain. *Gal. 3:21; Heb. 7:11*

God Approves of Those Who Believe

3 O foolish Galatians, who hath ᵀbewitched you, that ye should not obey the truth, before whose eyes Jesus Christ hath been evidently set forth, crucified among you? *misled*

3:1 Real and False Gospel

The men who had attempted to lead [the Galatians] from their belief in the gospel were hypocrites, unholy in heart and corrupt in life. Their religion was made up of a round of ceremonies, through the performance of which they expected to gain the favor of God. They had no desire for a gospel that called for obedience to the word. *AA 386*

---

2 This only would I learn of you, Received ye the Spirit by the works of the law, or by the hearing of faith? *Acts 15:8*

3 Are ye so foolish? having begun in the Spirit, are ye now made perfect by the flesh?

4 Have ye suffered so many things in vain? if *it be* yet in vain. *2 John 8*

5 He therefore that ministereth to you the Spirit, and worketh miracles among you, *doeth he it* by the works of the law, or by the hearing of faith? *1 Cor. 12:10*

Those Who Believe Are Justified

6 Even as Abraham believed God, and it was accounted to him for righteousness. *Gen. 15:6*

7 Know ye therefore that they which are of faith, the same are the children of Abraham. *Gal. 3:9*

3:2–7 Dangerous Influences

In the Galatian churches, open, unmasked error was supplanting the gospel message. Christ, the true foundation of the faith, was virtually renounced for the obsolete ceremonies of Judaism. The apostle saw that if the believers in Galatia were saved from the dangerous influences which threatened them, the most decisive measures must be taken, the sharpest warnings given. *AA 385*

---

8 And the scripture, foreseeing that God would justify the heathen through faith, preached before the gospel unto Abraham, *saying,* In thee shall all nations be blessed.

9 So then they which be of faith are blessed with faithful Abraham.   Rom. 4:16

10 For as many as are of the works of the law are under the curse: for it is written, Cursed *is* every one that continueth not in all things which are written in the book of the law to do them. Deut. 27:26; Jer. 11:3; Ezek. 18:4

11 But that no man is justified by the law in the sight of God, *it is* evident: for, The just shall live by faith.   Hab. 2:4; Rom. 1:17; Gal. 2:16

12 And the law is not of faith: but, The man that doeth them shall live in them.   Lev. 18:5

13 Christ hath redeemed us from the curse of the law, being made a curse for us: for it is written, Cursed *is* every one that hangeth on a tree: Deut. 21:23; Gal. 4:5; 1 Pet. 2:24

14 That the blessing of Abraham might come on the Gentiles through Jesus Christ; that we might receive the promise of the Spirit through faith.   Is. 32:15; Acts 2:33; Gal. 3:2

15 Brethren, I speak after the manner of men; Though *it be* but a man's covenant, yet *if it be* confirmed, no man disannulleth, or addeth thereto.   Heb. 9:17

16 Now to Abraham and his seed were the promises made. He saith not, And to seeds, as of many; but as of one, And to thy seed, which is Christ.   Gen. 12:7

17 And this I say, *that* the covenant, that was confirmed before of God in Christ, the law, which was four hundred and thirty years after, cannot disannul, that it should make the promise of none effect. Gen. 15:13; Ex. 12:40-41

18 For if the inheritance *be* of the law, *it is* no more of promise: but God gave *it* to Abraham by promise.

19 Wherefore then *serveth* the law? It was added because of ᵀtransgressions, till the seed should come to whom the promise was made; *and it was* ordained by angels in the hand of a mediator.   Deut. 5:5; Acts 7:53; Gal. 3:16 ◆ *sins*

20 Now a mediator is not *a mediator* of one, but God is one.   Deut. 6:4; 1 Tim. 2:5; Heb. 8:6

21 *Is* the law then against the promises of God? God forbid: for if there had been a law given which could have given life, ᵀverily righteousness should have been by the law.   Gal. 2:17, 21 ◆ *truly*

22 But the scripture hath concluded all under sin, that the promise by faith of Jesus Christ might be given to them that believe.   Rom. 11:32

23 But before faith came, we were kept under the law, shut up unto the faith which should afterwards be revealed.

24 Wherefore the law was our schoolmaster *to bring us* unto Christ, that we might be justified by faith.   Rom. 10:4; Gal. 2:16; Col. 2:17

25 But after that faith is come, we are no longer under a schoolmaster.

26 For ye are all the children of God by faith in Christ Jesus.   Gal. 4:5-6

27 For as many of you as have been baptized into Christ have put on Christ. Acts 2:38; Rom. 6:3

Baptism/Lord's Supper See Acts 2:38.

28 There is neither Jew nor Greek, there is neither bond nor free, there is neither male nor female: for ye are all one in Christ Jesus.   John 10:16; Gal. 5:6; Col. 3:11

29 And if ye *be* Christ's, then are ye Abraham's seed, and heirs according to the promise.   Rom. 8:17

We Are God's Children

4 Now I say, *That* the heir, as long as he is a child, differeth nothing from a servant, though he be lord of all;

2 But is under tutors and governors until the time appointed of the father.

3 Even so we, when we were children, were in bondage under the elements of the world: Gal. 2:4; 4:9; Col. 2:8

4 But when the fulness of the time was come, God sent forth his Son, made of a woman, made under the law, Gen. 3:15; Mark 1:15; John 1:14

4:4 Satan's Purpose

The fullness of the time had come. Humanity, becoming more degraded through ages of transgression, called for the coming of the Redeemer. Satan had been working to make the gulf deep and impassable between earth and heaven. . . . It was his purpose to wear out the forbearance of God, and to extinguish His love for man, so that He would abandon the world to satanic jurisdiction. *DA 34, 35*

5 To redeem them that were under the law, that we might receive the adoption of sons.

6 And because ye are sons, God hath sent forth the Spirit of his Son into your hearts, crying, Abba, Father.   Rom. 5:5; 8:9; Eph. 4:30

7 Wherefore thou art no more a servant, but a son; and if a son, then an heir of God through Christ.

8 Howbeit then, when ye knew not God, ye did service unto them which by nature are no gods.   1 Cor. 1:21; 8:4; 1 Thess. 4:5

9 But now, after that ye have known God, or rather are known of God, how turn ye again to the weak and beggarly elements, whereunto ye desire again to be in bondage?   Rom. 8:3

10 Ye observe days, and months, and times, and years.   Rom. 14:5

11 I am afraid of you, lest I have bestowed upon you labour in vain.   1 Thess. 3:5

12 Brethren, I beseech you, be as I *am*; for I *am* as ye *are*: ye have not injured me at all.

13 Ye know how through infirmity of the

flesh I preached the gospel unto you at the first. 1 Cor. 2:3

14 And my temptation which was in my flesh ye despised not, nor rejected; but received me as an angel of God, *even* as Christ Jesus. Mal. 2:7; Matt. 10:40; 2 Cor. 5:20

15 Where is then the blessedness ye spake of? for I bear you record, that, if *it had been* possible, ye would have plucked out your own eyes, and have given them to me.

16 Am I therefore become your enemy, because I tell you the truth? Gal. 2:5

17 They zealously affect you, *but* not well; yea, they would exclude you, that ye might affect them.

18 But *it is* good to be zealously affected always in *a* good *thing*, and not only when I am present with you. Gal. 4:13

19 My little children, of whom I travail in birth again until Christ be formed in you,

20 I desire to be present with you now, and to change my voice; for I stand in doubt of you.

21 Tell me, ye that desire to be under the law, do ye not hear the law?

22 For it is written, that Abraham had two sons, the one by a bondmaid, the other by a freewoman. Gen. 16:15

23 But he *who was* of the bondwoman was born after the flesh; but he of the freewoman *was* by promise. Gen. 18:10-14; 21:1-2; Heb. 11:11

24 Which things are an allegory: for these are the two covenants; the one from the mount Sinai, which gendereth to bondage, which is Agar. 1 Cor. 10:11

25 For this Agar is mount Sinai in Arabia, and answereth to Jerusalem which now is, and is in bondage with her children.

26 But Jerusalem which is above is free, which is the mother of us all. Heb. 12:22; Rev. 3:12; 21:2

27 For it is written, Rejoice, *thou* barren that bearest not; break forth and cry, thou that travailest not: for the desolate hath many more children than she which hath an husband.

28 Now we, brethren, as Isaac was, are the children of promise. Gal. 3:29

29 But as then he that was born after the flesh persecuted him *that was born* after the Spirit, even so *it is* now. Gen. 21:9; Gal. 5:11

30 Nevertheless what saith the scripture? Cast out the bondwoman and her son: for the son of the bondwoman shall not be heir with the son of the freewoman. John 8:35

31 So then, brethren, we are not children of the bondwoman, but of the free.

Live in Freedom

5 Stand fast therefore in the liberty wherewith Christ hath made us free, and

be not entangled again with the yoke of bondage. Acts 15:10; 1 Cor. 16:13; Gal. 2:4

2 Behold, I Paul say unto you, that if ye be circumcised, Christ shall profit you nothing. Acts 15:1; 2 Cor. 10:1; Gal. 5:6

3 For I testify again to every man that is circumcised, that he is a debtor to do the whole law. Luke 16:28

4 Christ is become of no effect unto you, whosoever of you are justified by the law; ye are fallen from grace. Rom. 9:31-32; Heb. 12:15

5 For we through the Spirit wait for the hope of righteousness by faith. Rom. 8:23-25

6 For in Jesus Christ neither circumcision availeth any thing, nor uncircumcision; but faith which worketh by love. 1 Thess. 1:3

7 Ye did run well; who did hinder you that ye should not obey the truth? 1 Cor. 9:24

8 This persuasion *cometh* not of him that calleth you. Gal. 1:6

9 A little leaven leaveneth the whole lump.

10 I have confidence in you through the Lord, that ye will be none otherwise minded: but he that troubleth you shall bear his judgment, whosoever he be. 2 Cor. 2:3; Gal. 1:7; 5:12

11 And I, brethren, if I yet preach circumcision, why do I yet suffer persecution? then is the offence of the cross ceased. 1 Cor. 1:23

12 I would they were even cut off which trouble you. Gal. 5:10

13 For, brethren, ye have been called unto liberty; only *use* not liberty for an occasion to the flesh, but by love serve one another.

14 For all the law is fulfilled in one word, *even* in this; Thou shalt love thy neighbour as thyself. Lev. 19:18; Matt. 7:12; 19:18-19

15 But if ye bite and devour one another, take heed that ye be not consumed one of another.

16 *This* I say then, Walk in the Spirit, and ye shall not fulfil the lust of the flesh. Eph. 2:3

17 For the flesh lusteth against the Spirit, and the Spirit against the flesh: and these are contrary the one to the other: so that ye cannot do the things that ye would. Rom. 8:5-8

18 But if ye be led of the Spirit, ye are not under the law. Rom. 8:14

> **5:19–21 Warning Those in Danger**
>
> Warn every soul that is in danger. Leave none to deceive themselves. Call sin by its right name. Declare what God has said in regard to lying, Sabbathbreaking, stealing, idolatry, and every other evil. *DA 806*

19 Now the works of the flesh are manifest, which are *these*; Adultery, fornication, uncleanness, lasciviousness, Matt. 15:18-19

20 Idolatry, witchcraft, hatred, ᵀvariance, emulations, wrath, strife, seditions, heresies,

conflict

21 Envyings, murders, drunkenness, revellings, and such like: of the which I tell you before, as I have also told *you* in time past, that they which do such things shall not inherit the kingdom of God.   Deut. 21:20; Rom. 13:13
22 But the fruit of the Spirit is love, joy, peace, longsuffering, gentleness, goodness, faith,   Rom. 7:4; 1 Cor. 13:13; Eph. 5:9

5:22 Growing and Bearing Fruit

As you receive the Spirit of Christ—the Spirit of unselfish love and labor for others—you will grow and bring forth fruit. The graces of the Spirit will ripen in your character. Your faith will increase, your convictions deepen, your love be made perfect. More and more you will reflect the likeness of Christ in all that is pure, noble, and lovely. *COL 68*

23 Meekness, ᵀtemperance: against such there is no law.   Acts 24:25; 1 Tim. 1:9 ◆ *self-control*
24 And they that are Christ's have crucified the flesh with the affections and lusts.
25 If we live in the Spirit, let us also walk in the Spirit.   Gal. 5:16
26 Let us not be desirous of vain glory, provoking one another, envying one another.

Carry One Another's Burdens

6 Brethren, if a man be overtaken in a fault, ye which are spiritual, restore such an one in the spirit of meekness; considering thyself, lest thou also be tempted.   Heb. 12:13
2 Bear ye one another's burdens, and so fulfil the law of Christ.   John 13:34; Rom. 15:1; 1 Cor. 9:21
3 For if a man think himself to be something, when he is nothing, he deceiveth himself.   Rom. 12:3; 1 Cor. 3:18; 2 Cor. 12:11
4 But let every man prove his own work, and then shall he have rejoicing in himself alone, and not in another.   1 Cor. 11:28
5 For every man shall bear his own burden.

We Will Reap What We Sow

6 Let him that is taught in the word communicate unto him that teacheth in all good things.
7 Be not deceived; God is not mocked: for whatsoever a man soweth, that shall he also reap.   1 Cor. 6:9; 15:33; 2 Cor. 9:6

6:7 Sowing and Reaping

Every seed sown produces a harvest of its kind. So it is in human life. We all need to sow the seeds of compassion, sympathy, and love; for we shall reap what we sow. Every characteristic of selfishness, self-love, self-esteem, every act of self-indulgence, will bring forth a like harvest. He who lives for self is sowing to the flesh, and of the flesh he will reap corruption. *COL 84*

8 For he that soweth to his flesh shall of the flesh reap corruption; but he that soweth to the Spirit shall of the Spirit reap life everlasting.   Job 4:8; Hos. 8:7; James 3:18
9 And let us not be weary in well doing: for in due season we shall reap, if we faint not.   1 Cor. 15:58; Heb. 12:3, 5
10 As we have therefore opportunity, let us do good unto all *men*, especially unto them who are of the household of faith.   John 12:35; Eph. 2:19; Heb. 3:6

6:15 Free in Christ

With unanswerable arguments he set before them their privilege of becoming free men and women in Christ, through whose atoning grace all who make full surrender are clothed with the robe of His righteousness. He took the position that every soul who would be saved must have a genuine, personal experience in the things of God. *AA 388*

Final Teachings

11 Ye see how large a letter I have written unto you with mine own hand.

Glorying in the Cross

Galatians 6:14

Christ's death proves God's great love for man. It is our pledge of salvation. To remove the cross from the Christian would be like blotting the sun from the sky. The cross brings us near to God, reconciling us to Him. With the relenting compassion of a father's love, Jehovah looks upon the suffering that His Son endured in order to save the race from eternal death, and accepts us in the Beloved.

Without the cross, man could have no union with the Father. On it depends our every hope. From it shines the light of the Saviour's love, and when at the foot of the cross the sinner looks up to the One who died to save him, he may rejoice with fullness of joy, for his sins are pardoned. Kneeling in faith at the cross, he has reached the highest place to which man can attain.

Through the cross we learn that the heavenly Father loves us with a love that is infinite. Can we wonder that Paul exclaimed, "God forbid that I should glory, save in the cross of our Lord Jesus Christ" (Galatians 6:14)? It is our privilege also to glory in the cross, our privilege to give ourselves wholly to Him who gave Himself for us. Then, with the light that streams from Calvary shining in our faces, we may go forth to reveal this light to those in darkness. *AA 209, 210*

12 As many as desire to make a fair shew in the flesh, they constrain you to be circumcised; only lest they should suffer persecution for the cross of Christ.   Acts 15:1; 2 Cor. 11:13

13 For neither they themselves who are circumcised keep the law; but desire to have you circumcised, that they may glory in your flesh.

14 But God forbid that I should glory, save in the cross of our Lord Jesus Christ, by whom the world is crucified unto me, and I unto the world.   Rom. 6:6; 1 Cor. 2:2; Phil. 3:3

15 For in Christ Jesus neither circumcision availeth any thing, nor uncircumcision, but a new creature.   1 Cor. 7:19; 2 Cor. 5:17; Gal. 5:6

16 And as many as walk according to this rule, peace *be* on them, and mercy, and upon the Israel of God.   Gal. 3:29

17 From ᵀhenceforth let no man trouble me: for I bear in my body the marks of the Lord Jesus.   2 Cor. 1:5 ◆ *this time forward*

18 Brethren, the grace of our Lord Jesus Christ *be* with your spirit. Amen.   2 Tim. 4:22

EPHESIANS

Many are fascinated and envious of the wealthy. A life of wealth and privilege is very different from that of the average person. But in this letter to the believers at Ephesus, the apostle Paul describes wealth of a different kind—wealth not beyond the reach of anyone.

Paul addressed this letter to believers living in Ephesus and to all believers throughout time. As is similar to his other epistles, Paul instructs and encourages the believers in their faith and struggles.

There was not a particular issue that caused Paul to write to the church at Ephesus. He wrote to help them understand the fullness of the Spirit available to them and also to help them understand the importance of unity.

Once Paul heard about the faith of these new believers, he continually gave "thanks for you, making mention of you in my prayers" (1:16). Paul was excited and encouraged with their new faith and wanted to make sure these believers understood the depth and breadth of the faith which they now proclaimed.

In Ephesians, Paul recounts the situation from which these believers were saved and reminds them that they "are no more strangers and foreigners, but fellowcitizens with the saints, and of the household of God" (2:19).

As such—now that they are heirs of the household of God—Paul expects them to live in a manner worthy of their position and calling. Paul urges them on in love and unity, two main aspects of living in light of their calling.

Finally, Paul encourages the new believers to "put on the whole armor of God" (6:11)—the armor that can protect them (and us) from the snares of the evil one. Paul emphasizes, "We wrestle not against flesh and blood, but against principalities, against powers, against the rulers of the darkness of this world, against spiritual wickedness in high places" (6:12).

Dates

Paul wrote several epistles while in prison in Rome. During his first Roman imprisonment (A.D. 61–63), he wrote Ephesians (most likely in A.D. 62), as well as Colossians and Philemon. He mentions his imprisonment in Ephesians 3:1: "For this cause I Paul, the prisoner of Jesus Christ for you Gentiles" (see also 4:1).

This epistle emerges in troubled times and surroundings that provides the content of this letter. Nero is emperor; licentiousness, luxury and murder are unbridled.

Paul, in the middle of all this confusion, produces one of his most gracious writings on how faith in God alone can restore peace and unity in the hearts of mankind. Many consider Ephesians to stand taller than his other eight epistles.

Author

There is very little debate as to any other author of Ephesians than Paul. He makes his authorship known in the first verse: "Paul, an apostle of Jesus Christ by the will of God, to the saints which are at Ephesus, and to the faithful in Christ Jesus" (1:1). Some critics have attempted to make a case that the book's arguments and style are not typical of Paul's other epistles, but these criticisms overlook Paul's growth and ability to write for specific audiences and particular issues.

Meaning of the Name

The historical title of Ephesians is *Pros Ephesious*, which means "To the Ephesians." Tradition expresses that in all likelihood that after Ephesus, the other churches in the area are also to benefit from its contents.

Christ in Ephesians

Ephesians is centered on the relationship the new believer has in Christ. In fact, the phrase "in Christ" or its equivalent appears nearly three dozen times in this epistle, more than any other New Testament book.

Because of this new relationship with Christ, the believer is in Christ (1:1), chosen in Him (1:4), trusting in Him (1:12), made alive together with Christ (2:5), and given access to God through faith in Christ (3:12).

Overview

Ephesus was one of the five major cities in the Roman Empire, along with Rome, Corinth, Antioch, and Alexandria. Paul visited Ephesus at the end of his second missionary journey (see Acts 18:18–21). During his third missionary journey, he stayed in the city for three years. Acts 19 tells of this ministry, along with the stories of the people burning their books of sorcery, and Paul's run-in with the silversmiths who made silver shrines of the goddess Diana (Artemis)—the center of worship in this city. Her temple was deemed one of the seven wonders of the ancient world. Paul's effective preaching was cutting into their profits and a riot over Paul ensued. After that episode, Paul left the city and headed to Macedonia.

Paul's goal in Ephesians was to remind these believers of their position in Christ and to instruct them as to what was expected of them and available to them in Christ. The letter can be divided into two main sections:

(1) *Ephesians 1—3, The Status of the Christian:* In this section, Paul details the status of every believer—that of a citizen in heaven. We have been saved by grace, adopted into God's family, and sealed by the Holy Spirit. As such, we are co-inheritors with Christ.

(2) *Ephesians 4—6, The Actions of the Christian:* The second half of Ephesians deals specifically with what is expected of believers. How will the individual believer conduct himself or herself in daily life? This section gives dozens of directives to answer that question.

Unlocking Ephesians

KEY PEOPLE:
Paul, Tychicus

KEY EVENTS:
God choosing us before the creation of the world; Christ's death and resurrection; Paul's imprisonment

KEY PHRASE:
Building the Body of Christ, because Paul encouraged new believers in their relationship in Christ so that they could fulfill their calling as members of His church. By helping these believers understand their role as Christ followers, Paul was preparing them to become mature participants in the local church.

KEY VERSES:
"For by grace are ye saved through faith; and that not of yourselves: it is the gift of God: not of works, lest any man should boast. For we are his workmanship, created in Christ Jesus unto good works, which God hath before ordained that we should walk in them" (Ephesians 2:8–10).

"I therefore, the prisoner of the Lord, beseech you that ye walk worthy of the vocation wherewith ye are called, with all lowliness and meekness, with longsuffering, forbearing one another in love; endeavouring to keep the unity of the Spirit in the bond of peace" (Ephesians 4:1–3).

KEY CHAPTER:
In *Ephesians 6,* Paul tells believers that their new relationship with Christ will include spiritual warfare. As such, he instructs them to put on "the whole armour of God" (Ephesians 6:11). By doing so, the believer is fully equipped to live a life of faith in our fallen world. The "armour of God" is the completion of what it means to live "in Christ."

Paul's Greeting

1 Paul, an apostle of Jesus Christ by the will of God, to the saints which are at Ephesus, and to the faithful in Christ Jesus: 2 Cor. 1:1; Col. 1:2

2 Grace *be* to you, and peace, from God our Father, and *from* the Lord Jesus Christ. Rom. 1:7

Thanks for Spiritual Blessings

3 Blessed *be* the God and Father of our Lord Jesus Christ, who hath blessed us with all spiritual blessings in heavenly *places* in Christ: 2 Cor. 1:3; Eph. 2:6; 6:12

4 According as he hath chosen us in him before the foundation of the world, that we should be holy and without blame before him in love: Eph. 2:10; 5:27; Col. 1:22

5 Having predestinated us unto the adoption of children by Jesus Christ to himself, according to the good pleasure of his will, Rom. 8:14-17

6 To the praise of the glory of his grace, wherein he hath made us accepted in the beloved. Matt. 3:17; Eph. 1:12, 14

> ### 1:6 God's Free Grace
>
> We ourselves owe everything to God's free grace. Grace in the covenant ordained our adoption. Grace in the Saviour effected our redemption, our regeneration, and our exaltation to heirship with Christ. Let this grace be revealed to others. *COL 250*

7 In whom we have redemption through his blood, the forgiveness of sins, according to the riches of his grace; Acts 2:38; 20:28; Rom. 3:24

8 Wherein he hath abounded toward us in all wisdom and prudence;

9 Having made known unto us the mystery of his will, according to his good pleasure which he hath purposed in himself: Rom. 8:28

10 That in the dispensation of the fulness of times he might gather together in one all things in Christ, both which are in heaven, and which are on earth; *even* in him: Col. 1:20

11 In whom also we have obtained an inheritance, being ᵀpredestinated according to the purpose of him who worketh all things after the counsel of his own will: Eph. 1:14 ♦ *determined beforehand*

12 That we should be to the praise of his glory, who first trusted in Christ. Eph. 1:6

13 In whom ye also *trusted*, after that ye heard the word of truth, the gospel of your salvation: in whom also after that ye believed, ye were sealed with that holy Spirit of promise, Acts 1:4; 2:33; Eph. 4:30

14 Which is the earnest of our inheritance until the redemption of the purchased possession, unto the praise of his glory. Rom. 8:23

Paul's Prayer for the Ephesians

15 Wherefore I also, after I heard of your faith in the Lord Jesus, and love unto all the saints, Philem. 5

16 Cease not to give thanks for you, making mention of you in my prayers; Rom. 1:8-9

17 That the God of our Lord Jesus Christ, the Father of glory, may give unto you the spirit of wisdom and revelation in the knowledge of him: John 20:17

18 The eyes of your understanding being enlightened; that ye may know what is the hope of his calling, and what the riches of the glory of his inheritance in the saints, Acts 26:18

19 And what *is* the exceeding greatness of his power to us-ward who believe, according to the working of his mighty power, Eph. 3:7; 6:10

20 Which he wrought in Christ, when he raised him from the dead, and set *him* at his own right hand in the heavenly *places*,

21 Far above all ᵀprincipality, and power, and might, and dominion, and every name that is named, not only in this world, but also in that which is to come: Col. 2:10 ♦ *authority*

22 And hath put all *things* under his feet, and gave him *to be* the head over all *things* to the church, 1 Cor. 11:3

23 Which is his body, the fulness of him that filleth all in all. John 1:16

God's Great Love for Us

2 And you *hath he quickened*, who were dead in trespasses and sins; Luke 15:24; Eph. 4:18

2 Wherein in time past ye walked according to the course of this world, according to the prince of the power of the air, the spirit that now worketh in the children of disobedience; John 12:31; Eph. 2:3; 6:12

3 Among whom also we all had our ᵀconversation in times past in the lusts of our flesh, fulfilling the desires of the flesh and of the mind; and were by nature the children of wrath, even as others. Gal. 2:15-16 ♦ *conduct*

4 But God, who is rich in mercy, for his great love wherewith he loved us, Rom. 2:4

5 Even when we were dead in sins, hath ᵀquickened us together with Christ, (by grace ye are saved;) Acts 15:11; Eph. 2:1, 8 ♦ *made alive*

6 And hath raised *us* up together, and made *us* sit together in heavenly *places* in Christ Jesus:

7 That in the ages to come he might shew the exceeding riches of his grace in *his* kindness toward us through Christ Jesus. Titus 3:4

8 For by grace are ye saved through faith; and that not of yourselves: *it is* the gift of God: Mark 16:16; Luke 7:50; Eph. 2:5

9 Not of works, lest any man should boast.

Salvation From Sin See 1 John 5:11–13.

10 For we are his workmanship, created in Christ Jesus unto good works, which God

hath before ordained that we should walk in them.   2 Cor. 5:17; Eph. 1:4; 4:24

2:10 Work That Is Pleasing to God

It is not the length of time we labor but our willingness and fidelity in the work that makes it acceptable to God. In all our service a full surrender of self is demanded. The smallest duty done in sincerity and self-forgetfulness is more pleasing to God than the greatest work when marred with self-seeking. He looks to see how much of the spirit of Christ we cherish, and how much of the likeness of Christ our work reveals. He regards more the love and faithfulness with which we work than the amount we do. *COL 402*

Uniting Jews and Non-Jews

11 Wherefore remember, that ye *being* in time past Gentiles in the flesh, who are called Uncircumcision by that which is called the Circumcision in the flesh made by hands;   1 Cor. 12:2; Eph. 5:8; Col. 2:11
12 That at that time ye were without Christ, being aliens from the commonwealth of Israel, and strangers from the covenants of promise, having no hope, and without God in the world: Gal. 4:8; Col. 1:21; 1 Thess. 4:13
13 But now in Christ Jesus ye who sometimes were far off are made nigh by the blood of Christ.   Is. 57:19; Acts 2:39
14 For he is our peace, who hath made both one, and hath broken down the middle wall of partition *between us;*   Gal. 3:28
15 Having abolished in his flesh the enmity, *even* the law of commandments *contained* in ordinances; for to make in himself of twain one new man, *so* making peace; Col. 2:14, 20; 3:10
16 And that he might reconcile both unto God in one body by the cross, having slain the ᵀenmity thereby: Eph. 2:15 ◆ *hostility*
17 And came and preached peace to you which were afar off, and to them that were nigh.   Ps. 148:14

18 For through him we both have access by one Spirit unto the Father. Rom. 5:2; 1 Cor. 12:13
19 Now therefore ye are no more strangers and foreigners, but fellowcitizens with the saints, and of the household of God; Phil. 3:20

2:19 Heaven-born Love

The word of God is to have a sanctifying effect on our association with every member of the human family. The leaven of truth will not produce the spirit of rivalry, the love of ambition, the desire to be first. True, heaven-born love is not selfish and changeable. It is not dependent on human praise. The heart of him who receives the grace of God overflows with love for God and for those for whom Christ died. *COL 101, 102*

20 And are built upon the foundation of the apostles and prophets, Jesus Christ himself being the chief corner *stone;*   Is. 28:16; Rev. 21:14
21 In whom all the building fitly framed together groweth unto an holy temple in the Lord: 1 Cor. 3:16-17
22 In whom ye also are builded together for an habitation of God through the Spirit.

Paul's Ministry

3 For this cause I Paul, the prisoner of Jesus Christ for you Gentiles,   Eph. 4:1; Philem. 9
2 If ye have heard of the ᵀdispensation of the grace of God which is given me to you-ward: 2 Tim. 1:11 ◆ *arrangement*
3 How that by revelation he made known unto me the mystery; (as I wrote afore in few words,   Acts 22:17, 21; Rom. 16:25
4 Whereby, when ye read, ye may understand my knowledge in the mystery of Christ)   2 Cor. 11:6; Eph. 6:19; Col. 4:3
5 Which in other ages was not made known unto the sons of men, as it is now revealed unto his holy apostles and prophets by the Spirit;   Acts 10:28
6 That the Gentiles should be fellow-heirs, and of the same body, and partakers of his promise in Christ by the gospel:

When Christ Dwells in the Heart

Ephesians 2:8, 9

There are those who profess to serve God, while they rely upon their own efforts to obey His law, to form a right character, and secure salvation. Their hearts are not moved by any deep sense of the love of Christ, but they seek to perform the duties of the Christian life as that which God requires of them in order to gain heaven. Such religion is worth nothing. When Christ dwells in the heart, the soul will be so filled with His love, with the joy of communion with Him, that it will cleave to Him; and in the contemplation of Him, self will be forgotten. Love to Christ will be the spring of action. Those who feel the constraining love of God, do not ask how little may be given to meet the requirements of God; they do not ask for the lowest standard, but aim at perfect conformity to the will of their Redeemer. With earnest desire they yield all and manifest an interest proportionate to the value of the object which they seek. A profession of Christ without this deep love is mere talk, dry formality, and heavy drudgery. *SC 44, 45*

7 Whereof I was made a minister, according to the gift of the grace of God given unto me by the effectual working of his power.

8 Unto me, who am less than the least of all saints, is this grace given, that I should preach among the Gentiles the unsearchable riches of Christ;   Rom. 11:33; 1 Cor. 15:9; Eph. 3:16

9 And to make all *men* see what *is* the fellowship of the mystery, which from the beginning of the world hath been hid in God, who created all things by Jesus Christ: Col. 1:26

10 To the intent that now unto the ᵀprincipalities and powers in heavenly *places* might be known by the church the manifold wisdom of God,   Rom. 11:33; Eph. 1:21; 1 Pet. 1:12 ◆ *authorities*

11 According to the eternal purpose which he purposed in Christ Jesus our Lord: Eph. 1:11

12 In whom we have boldness and access with confidence by the faith of him.   Eph. 2:18

13 Wherefore I desire that ye faint not at my tribulations for you, which is your glory.   Eph. 3:1

Paul's Prayer

14 For this cause I bow my knees unto the Father of our Lord Jesus Christ,

15 Of whom the whole family in heaven and earth is named,   Eph. 1:10

16 That he would grant you, according to the riches of his glory, to be strengthened with might by his Spirit in the inner man; Rom. 7:22

17 That Christ may dwell in your hearts by faith; that ye, being rooted and grounded in love,   John 14:23; Col. 1:23; 2:7

18 May be able to comprehend with all saints what *is* the breadth, and length, and depth, and height;   Eph. 1:15

19 And to know the love of Christ, which passeth knowledge, that ye might be filled with all the fulness of God.   Eph. 1:23

20 Now unto him that is able to do exceeding abundantly above all that we ask or think, according to the power that worketh in us,   Rom. 16:25; Eph. 3:7; Jude 24

21 Unto him *be* glory in the church by Christ Jesus throughout all ages, world without end. Amen.   Rom. 11:36; 1 Pet. 5:11

Christ's Gifts to the Church

4 I therefore, the prisoner of the Lord, beseech you that ye walk worthy of the vocation wherewith ye are called,   Phil. 1:27

2 With all lowliness and meekness, with longsuffering, ᵀforbearing one another in love;   Col. 3:12-13 ◆ *being patient with*

3 Endeavouring to keep the unity of the Spirit in the bond of peace.

4 *There is* one body, and one Spirit, even as ye are called in one hope of your calling; Eph. 1:18

5 One Lord, one faith, one baptism, 1 Cor. 8:6

6 One God and Father of all, who *is* above all, and through all, and in you all. Rom. 11:36

7 But unto every one of us is given grace according to the measure of the gift of Christ.   Matt. 25:15; Rom. 12:3; Eph. 3:2

8 Wherefore he saith, When he ascended up on high, he led captivity captive, and gave gifts unto men.   Judg. 5:12; Ps. 68:18; Col. 2:15

9 (Now that he ascended, what is it but that he also descended first into the lower parts of the earth?   John 3:13

10 He that descended is the same also that ascended up far above all heavens, that he might fill all things.)   Heb. 4:14

11 And he gave some, apostles; and some, prophets; and some, evangelists; and some, pastors and teachers;   Jer. 3:15; Acts 13:1; 21:8

4:11

Gift of Prophecy See Joel 2:27, 28.

12 For the perfecting of the saints, for the work of the ministry, for the edifying of the body of Christ: 1 Cor. 12:27

13 Till we all come in the unity of the faith, and of the knowledge of the Son of God, unto a perfect man, unto the measure of the stature of the fulness of Christ: Eph. 1:23; 4:3, 5

14 That we *henceforth* be no more children, tossed to and fro, and carried about with every wind of doctrine, by the sleight of men, *and* cunning craftiness, whereby they lie in wait to deceive;   Matt. 11:7; 1 Cor. 14:20; James 1:6

A Boundless, Shoreless Sea

Ephesians 3:17–19

Truth in Christ and through Christ is measureless. The student of Scripture looks, as it were, into a fountain that deepens and broadens as he gazes into its depths. Not in this life shall we comprehend the mystery of God's love in giving His Son to be the propitiation for our sins. The work of our Redeemer on this earth is and ever will be a subject that will put to the stretch our highest imagination. Man may tax every mental power in the endeavor to fathom this mystery, but his mind will become faint and weary. The most diligent searcher will see before him a boundless, shoreless sea.

The truth as it is in Jesus can be experienced, but never explained. Its height and breadth and depth pass our knowledge. We may task our imagination to the utmost, and then we shall see only dimly the outlines of a love that is unexplainable, that is as high as heaven, but that stooped to the earth to stamp the image of God on all mankind. *COL 128, 129*

4:11–13 Channels for the Spirit

Learning, talents, eloquence, every natural or acquired endowment, may be possessed; but without the presence of the Spirit of God, no heart will be touched, no sinner be won to Christ. On the other hand, if they are connected with Christ, if the gifts of the Spirit are theirs, the poorest and most ignorant of His disciples will have a power that will tell upon hearts. God makes them the channel for the outworking of the highest influence in the universe. *COL 328*

15 But speaking the truth in love, may grow up into him in all things, which is the head, *even* Christ: Eph. 1:22; 2:21; 4:25

The Christian Life See 2 Peter 3:18.

16 From whom the whole body fitly joined together and compacted by that which every joint supplieth, according to the ᵀeffectual working in the measure of every part, maketh increase of the body unto the edifying of itself in love.   Eph. 1:4; Col. 2:19 ◆ *effective*

4:16 Growing by Receiving

The plants and flowers grow not by their own care or anxiety or effort, but by receiving that which God has furnished to minister to their life. The child cannot, by any anxiety or power of its own, add to its stature. No more can you, by anxiety or effort of yourself, secure spiritual growth. The plant, the child, grows by receiving from its surroundings that which ministers to its life—air, sunshine, and food. What these gifts of nature are to animal and plant, such is Christ to those who trust in Him. *SC 68*

Live as God's People
17 This I say therefore, and testify in the Lord, that ye henceforth walk not as other Gentiles walk, in the vanity of their mind,
18 Having the understanding darkened, being alienated from the life of God through the ignorance that is in them, because of the blindness of their heart: Gal. 4:8; Eph. 2:12; 1 Thess. 4:5
19 Who being past feeling have given themselves over unto ᵀlasciviousness, to work all uncleanness with greediness. 1 Tim. 4:2 ◆ *lewdness*
20 But ye have not so learned Christ;
21 If so be that ye have heard him, and have been taught by him, as the truth is in Jesus: Eph. 1:13
22 That ye put off concerning the former conversation the old man, which is corrupt according to the deceitful lusts; Rom. 6:6; Heb. 3:13
23 And be renewed in the spirit of your mind;   Rom. 12:2; Col. 3:10

24 And that ye put on the new man, which after God is created in righteousness and true holiness.   Rom. 6:4; 13:14; Eph. 2:10

The Christian Life See 1 Peter 1:23.

25 Wherefore putting away lying, speak every man truth with his neighbour: for we are members one of another.   Zech. 8:16; Rom. 12:5
26 Be ye angry, and sin not: let not the sun go down upon your wrath: Ps. 37:8
27 Neither give place to the devil.   James 4:7
28 Let him that stole steal no more: but rather let him labour, working with *his* hands the thing which is good, that he may have to give to him that needeth.   Ex. 20:15
29 Let no corrupt communication proceed out of your mouth, but that which is good to the use of edifying, that it may minister grace unto the hearers.   Col. 4:6

Christian Behavior See Ephesians 5:4.

30 And grieve not the holy Spirit of God, whereby ye are sealed unto the day of redemption.   Is. 63:10; Rom. 8:23; 1 Thess. 5:19
31 Let all bitterness, and wrath, and anger, and clamour, and evil speaking, be put away from you, with all malice: Eccl. 7:9; Col. 3:8, 19
32 And be ye kind one to another, tenderhearted, forgiving one another, even as God for Christ's sake hath forgiven you. Matt. 6:12

Imitate God
5 Be ye therefore followers of God, as dear children;   Matt. 5:48; Eph. 4:32; 1 Pet. 1:15-16
2 And walk in love, as Christ also hath loved us, and hath given himself for us an offering and a sacrifice to God for a sweetsmelling savour.   John 13:34

Flee Fornication
3 But fornication, and all uncleanness, or covetousness, let it not be once named among you, as becometh saints;   1 Cor. 6:18
4 Neither filthiness, nor foolish talking, nor jesting, which are not convenient: but rather giving of thanks.   Eccl. 10:13; Rom. 1:28; Eph. 4:29

Christian Behavior See Proverbs 10:4, 5.

5 For this ye know, that no whoremonger, nor unclean person, nor ᵀcovetous man, who is an idolater, hath any inheritance in the kingdom of Christ and of God.   Gal. 5:21; Col. 3:5 ◆ *greedy*
6 Let no man deceive you with vain words: for because of these things cometh the wrath of God upon the children of disobedience.
7 Be not ye therefore partakers with them.
8 For ye were sometimes darkness, but now *are ye* light in the Lord: walk as children of light: Luke 16:8
9 (For the fruit of the Spirit *is* in all goodness and righteousness and truth;) Rom. 15:14

10 Proving what is acceptable unto the Lord. 1 Thess. 5:21

11 And have no fellowship with the unfruitful works of darkness, but rather reprove *them*. Rom. 13:12

12 For it is a shame even to speak of those things which are done of them in secret.

13 But all things that are reproved are made ᵀmanifest by the light: for whatsoever doth make manifest is light. John 3:20-21 ◆ *known*

14 Wherefore he saith, Awake thou that sleepest, and arise from the dead, and Christ shall give thee light. Is. 26:19; 51:17; 60:1

15 See then that ye walk circumspectly, not as fools, but as wise, Col. 4:5

16 Redeeming the time, because the days are evil. Eccl. 12:1; Eph. 6:13; Col. 4:5

17 Wherefore be ye not unwise, but understanding what the will of the Lord *is*. Rom. 12:2

18 And be not drunk with wine, wherein is excess; but be filled with the Spirit; Prov. 20:1

19 Speaking to yourselves in psalms and hymns and spiritual songs, singing and making melody in your heart to the Lord; Acts 16:25

20 Giving thanks always for all things unto God and the Father in the name of our Lord Jesus Christ; Ps. 34:1; Eph. 5:4; Col. 3:17

Advice to Wives and Husbands

21 Submitting yourselves one to another in the fear of God. Phil. 2:3

22 Wives, submit yourselves unto your own husbands, as unto the Lord. Gen. 3:16

23 For the husband is the head of the wife, even as Christ is the head of the church: and he is the saviour of the body. Eph. 1:22-23

24 Therefore as the church is subject unto Christ, so *let* the wives *be* to their own husbands in every thing. Col. 3:20

Marriage See Ephesians 5:25–30.

25 Husbands, love your wives, even as Christ also loved the church, and gave himself for it; Eph. 5:28; Col. 3:19; 1 Pet. 3:7

26 That he might sanctify and cleanse it with the washing of water by the word, Acts 22:16

27 That he might present it to himself a glorious church, not having spot, or wrinkle, or any such thing; but that it should be holy and without blemish. 2 Cor. 11:2; Eph. 1:4; Col. 1:22

28 So ought men to love their wives as their own bodies. He that loveth his wife loveth himself. Eph. 5:25

29 For no man ever yet hated his own flesh; but nourisheth and cherisheth it, even as the Lord the church:

5:22–30 Marriage a Foretaste of Heaven

Though difficulties, perplexities, and discouragements may arise, let neither husband nor wife harbor the thought that their union is a mistake or a disappointment. Determine to be all that it is possible to be to each other. Continue the early attentions. In every way encourage each other in fighting the battles of life. Study to advance the happiness of each other. . . . Then marriage, instead of being the end of love, will be as it were the very beginning of love. *MH 360*

30 For we are members of his body, of his flesh, and of his bones. 1 Cor. 6:15

Marriage See Ephesians 5:31.

31 For this cause shall a man leave his father and mother, and shall be joined unto his wife, and they two shall be one flesh. Gen. 2:24

Marriage See Ephesians 5:33.

32 This is a great mystery: but I speak concerning Christ and the church.

The True Christian

Ephesians 5:1–17

God's ideal for His children is higher than the highest human thought can reach. . . . The plan of redemption contemplates our complete recovery from the power of Satan. Christ always separates the contrite soul from sin. He came to destroy the works of the devil, and He has made provision that the Holy Spirit shall be imparted to every repentant soul, to keep him from sinning.

The tempter's agency is not to be accounted an excuse for one wrong act. Satan is jubilant when he hears the professed followers of Christ making excuses for their deformity of character. It is these excuses that lead to sin. There is no excuse for sinning. A holy temper, a Christlike life, is accessible to every repenting, believing child of God.

The ideal of Christian character is Christlikeness. As the Son of man was perfect in His life, so His followers are to be perfect in their life. Jesus was in all things made like unto His brethren. He became flesh, even as we are. He was hungry and thirsty and weary. He was sustained by food and refreshed by sleep. He shared the lot of man; yet He was the blameless Son of God. He was God in the flesh. His character is to be ours. The Lord says of those who believe in Him, "I will dwell in them, and walk in them; and I will be their God, and they shall be My people" (2 Corinthians 6:16). *DA 311*

7 With good will doing service, as to the Lord, and not to men:

8 Knowing that whatsoever good thing any man doeth, the same shall he receive of the Lord, whether *he be* bond or free.   Matt. 16:27

9 And, ye masters, do the same things unto them, forbearing threatening: knowing that your Master also is in heaven; neither is there respect of persons with him.   Job 31:13-15

Put on the Armor of God

10 Finally, my brethren, be strong in the Lord, and in the power of his might.   2 Tim. 2:1

11 Put on the whole armour of God, that ye may be able to stand against the wiles of the ᵀdevil.   Rom. 13:12; Eph. 4:14; 6:13 ◆ *false accuser*

6:12, 13 Joy in Persecution

As men seek to come into harmony with God, they will find that the offense of the cross has not ceased. Principalities and powers and wicked spirits in high places are arrayed against all who yield obedience to the law of heaven. Therefore, so far from causing grief, persecution should bring joy to the disciples of Christ, for it is an evidence that they are following in the steps of their Master. *MB 29, 30*

12 For we wrestle not against flesh and blood, but against ᵀprincipalities, against powers, against the rulers of the darkness of this world, against spiritual wickedness in high *places*.   Eph. 1:3, 21; 2:2 ◆ *authorities*

13 Wherefore take unto you the whole armour of God, that ye may be able to withstand in the evil day, and having done all, to stand.   Eph. 5:16

14 Stand therefore, having your loins girt

5:31–33 Marriage a Symbol

Like every other one of God's good gifts entrusted to the keeping of humanity, marriage has been perverted by sin; but it is the purpose of the gospel to restore its purity and beauty. In both the Old and the New Testament the marriage relation is employed to represent the tender and sacred union that exists between Christ and His people, the redeemed ones whom He has purchased at the cost of Calvary. *MB 64*

33 Nevertheless let every one of you in particular so love his wife even as himself; and the wife *see* that she reverence *her* husband.

Marriage See Matthew 5:31, 32.

Advice to Children and Parents

6 Children, obey your parents in the Lord: for this is right.   Prov. 6:20

2 Honour thy father and mother; (which is the first commandment with promise;)

3 That it may be well with thee, and thou mayest live long on the earth.

4 And, ye fathers, provoke not your children to wrath: but bring them up in the nurture and admonition of the Lord. Gen. 18:19; Prov. 22:6

Marriage

Advice to Servants and Masters

5 Servants, be obedient to them that are *your* masters according to the flesh, with fear and trembling, in singleness of your heart, as unto Christ;   1 Cor. 2:3

6 Not with eyeservice, as menpleasers; but as the servants of Christ, doing the will of God from the heart;

Character—Not the Result of Accident

Ephesians 6:12

A noble character is not the result of accident; it is not due to special favors or endowments of Providence. It is the result of self-discipline, of subjection of the lower to the higher nature, of the surrender of self to the service of God and man. . . .

The body is a most important medium through which the mind and the soul are developed for the upbuilding of character. . . . The passions are to be controlled by the will, which is itself to be under the control of God. The kingly power of reason, sanctified by divine grace, is to bear sway in the life. Intellectual power, physical stamina, and the length of life depend upon immutable laws. Through obedience to these laws, man may stand conqueror of himself, conqueror of his own inclinations, conqueror of principalities and powers, of "the rulers of the darkness of this world," and of "spiritual wickedness in high places" (Ephesians 6:12).

In that ancient ritual which is the gospel in symbol, no blemished offering could be brought to God's altar. The sacrifice that was to represent Christ must be spotless. The word of God points to this as an illustration of what His children are to be—"a living sacrifice," "holy and without blemish" (Romans 12:1; Ephesians 5:27). . . .

Though surrounded by temptations to self-indulgence, especially in our large cities, where every form of sensual gratification is made easy and inviting, yet by divine grace their purpose to honor God may remain firm. Through strong resolution and vigilant watchfulness they may withstand every temptation that assails the soul. But only by him who determines to do right because it is right will the victory be gained. *PK 488–490*

about with truth, and having on the breast-plate of righteousness;   Is. 11:5; 59:17; Luke 12:35
15 And your feet shod with the preparation of the gospel of peace;   Is. 52:7; Rom. 10:15
16 Above all, taking the shield of faith, wherewith ye shall be able to quench all the fiery darts of the wicked.
17 And take the helmet of salvation, and the sword of the Spirit, which is the word of God:
18 Praying always with all prayer and supplication in the Spirit, and watching thereunto with all perseverance and supplication for all saints;   Eph. 1:16; Col. 4:2; 1 Tim. 2:1
19 And for me, that utterance may be given unto me, that I may open my mouth boldly, to make known the mystery of the gospel,   Acts 4:29; 2 Cor. 3:12; 1 Thess. 5:25

20 For which I am an ambassador in bonds: that therein I may speak boldly, as I ought to speak.   Acts 28:20; 2 Cor. 5:20; Eph. 3:1

Final Greetings

21 But that ye also may know my affairs, and how I do, Tychicus, a beloved brother and faithful minister in the Lord, shall make known to you all things: Acts 20:4; 2 Tim. 4:12
22 Whom I have sent unto you for the same purpose, that ye might know our affairs, and that he might comfort your hearts.   Col. 4:7-8
23 Peace be to the brethren, and love with faith, from God the Father and the Lord Jesus Christ.   Gal. 5:6; 6:16; 1 Pet. 5:14
24 Grace be with all them that love our Lord Jesus Christ in sincerity. Amen.   Matt. 22:37

THE EPISTLE OF PAUL THE APOSTLE TO THE
PHILIPPIANS

Even though Paul was in prison when he wrote Philippians, the predominant message he wanted to convey to his readers was one of joy. Paul wanted to express his thanks to the believers at Philippi for the gift they sent during his imprisonment; more importantly, however, he wanted to communicate to them that complete joy and unity are only found in Christ.

As with any new endeavor, there will be growing pains, and Paul was concerned that the work of Christ was being hindered by the lack of unity demonstrated within the church at Philippi. Rooted in this call for unity was Paul's encouragement: "Let nothing be done through strife or vainglory; but in lowliness of mind let each esteem other better than themselves" (2:3). Paul wanted them to act in a spirit of humility. By humbling themselves, the believers would not only find unity within their ranks but also the complete joy that is found only in Christ.

Paul's encouragement to the church at Philippi is also a good reminder for believers today: "Be careful for nothing; but in every thing by prayer and supplication with thanksgiving let your requests be made known unto God. And the peace of God, which passeth all understanding, shall keep your hearts and minds through Christ Jesus" (4:6, 7).

Dates

Paul, along with Silas, Timothy, and Luke first visited Philippi in A.D. 50. More than a decade later (probably in A.D. 63), Paul wrote this epistle. Philippians 1:13 and 4:22 suggest the epistle was written from Rome while Paul was imprisoned there.

Author

There is virtually no doubt or debate as to authorship of Philippians. Internal and external evidence both point to Pauline authorship. Paul identifies himself in the book's first verse: "Paul and Timotheus, the servants of Jesus Christ, to all the saints in Christ Jesus which are at Philippi, with the bishops and deacons" (1:1). Paul even mentions his imprisonment (1:7), which is a further indication of his authorship of Philippians.

Meaning of the Name

Philippians is called *Pros Philippesious*, which means "To the Philippians." The church at Philippi was the first founded by Paul while in Macedonia.

Christ in Philippians

Christ is evident throughout Philippians, and serves as the foundation on which Paul built his thesis. In chapter 1, Paul writes, "For to me to live is Christ, and to die is gain" (1:21). In chapter 2, Paul uses Christ as his model for true humility: "Let this mind be in you, which was also in Christ Jesus" (2:5). In chapter 3, Paul used Christ as his example of being transformed: "Who shall change our vile body, that it may be fashioned like unto his glorious body, according to the working whereby he is able even to subdue all things unto himself" (3:21). Finally, in chapter 4, Paul writes: "I can do all things through Christ which strengtheneth me" (4:13).

Overview

The city of Philippi was located in Macedonia (northern Greece). Philip II of Macedon (who was the father of Alexander the Great) took the town, enlarged it, and named it after himself. The city was a military outpost and its people were considered to be Roman citizens.

Acts 16 tells the story of the visit to Philippi. Paul, Silas, and Timothy embarked on Paul's second missionary journey, but the Spirit prevented them from traveling to some locations. Then Paul had a vision of a man from Macedonia calling for help. So Paul and his team traveled there and to the city of Philippi. They met Lydia and others as they met beside the river for worship (the city did not have enough Jewish men to have a synagogue). They also cast a demon out of a slave girl, were thrown into prison, had an earthquake free them, and saw the conversion of the jailer and his family (Acts 16).

The book can be divided into four sections:

(1) *Philippians 1, Joy in Suffering:* Although Paul wrote the epistle while in prison, he was still joyful. His joy—and the joy of his readers and believers throughout the ages—comes from belief and faith in Christ. This joy is evident regardless of our circumstances.

(2) *Philippians 2, Joy in Serving:* Paul explains that true joy comes from being humble and united in spirit. From that unity and humility comes the ability to find joy in service.

(3) *Philippians 3—4:1, Joy in Believing:* Paul encourages the believers to persevere in their faith, overcoming any obstacles. By continuing in the faith, believers can experience true joy.

(4) *Philippians 4:2–23, Joy in Giving:* Paul thanked the believers at Philippi again for their gifts and concern for him. He reminds them that, "I can do all things through Christ which strengtheneth me" (4:13).

Unlocking Philippians

KEY PEOPLE:
Paul, Timothy, Epaphroditus, Euodia, Syntyche

KEY EVENTS:
Paul's imprisonment in Rome; Paul's earlier visit to Philippi; Epaphroditus's visit to Paul to help take care of his needs

KEY PHRASE:
To Live is Christ serves as the centerpiece of the epistle. Paul constantly reminds his readers that Christ is the essence of our lives as believers. This theme resounds throughout the entire book and is reinforced by Paul's admission, "For to me to live is Christ, and to die is gain" (1:21).

KEY VERSES:
"For to me to live is Christ, and to die is gain" (Philippians 1:21).

"I know both how to be abased, and I know how to abound: every where and in all things I am instructed both to be full and to be hungry, both to abound and to suffer need" (Philippians 4:12).

KEY CHAPTER:
Philippians 2, in which Paul writes of Christ's humility. Christ left the grandeur of heaven to come to earth and become human—to suffer, die, and rise again on the third day. This section in Philippians is one of the most powerful and beautifully written in all of Scripture, and serves as a daily reminder of how we are to humble ourselves in order to experience the fullness of joy promised in Christ.

Paul's Greeting

1 Paul and Timotheus, the servants of Jesus Christ, to all the saints in Christ Jesus which are at Philippi, with the bishops and deacons: Acts 20:28; 2 Cor. 1:1; 1 Tim. 3:8

2 Grace *be* unto you, and peace, from God our Father, and *from* the Lord Jesus Christ. Rom. 1:7

Paul's Prayer for the Philippians

3 I thank my God upon every remembrance of you,   Rom. 1:8-9

4 Always in every prayer of mine for you all making request with joy,   Rom. 1:9

5 For your fellowship in the gospel from the first day until now;   Acts 16:12-40

1:6 God Will Finish What He Begins

He desires to restore you to Himself, to see His own purity and holiness reflected in you. And if you will but yield yourself to Him, He that hath begun a good work in you will carry it forward to the day of Jesus Christ. Pray more fervently; believe more fully. *SC 64*

1:6

6 Being confident of this very thing, that he which hath begun a good work in you will perform *it* until the day of Jesus Christ:

The Christian Life See Hebrews 12:2.

7 Even as it is meet for me to think this of you all, because I have you in my heart; inasmuch as both in my bonds, and in the defence and confirmation of the gospel, ye all are partakers of my grace.   Acts 20:23; 2 Cor. 7:3; Eph. 3:1

8 For God is my record, how greatly I long after you all in the bowels of Jesus Christ.

9 And this I pray, that your love may abound yet more and more in knowledge and *in* all judgment;   Col. 1:9; 3:10; 1 Thess. 3:12

10 That ye may approve things that are excellent; that ye may be sincere and without offence till the day of Christ; Rom. 12:2; 1 Cor. 1:8

11 Being filled with the fruits of righteousness, which are by Jesus Christ, unto the glory and praise of God.   John 15:4-5, 8; Col. 1:6

Paul Advances the Gospel

12 But I would ye should understand, brethren, that the things *which happened* unto me have fallen out rather unto the furtherance of the gospel;

13 So that my bonds in Christ are manifest in all the palace, and in all other *places*;   Phil. 1:7

14 And many of the brethren in the Lord, waxing confident by my bonds, are much more bold to speak the word without fear.

15 Some indeed preach Christ even of envy and strife; and some also of good will:

16 The one preach Christ of contention, not sincerely, supposing to add affliction to my bonds: Phil. 1:7

17 But the other of love, knowing that I am set for the defence of the gospel.   Phil. 1:7

18 What then? notwithstanding, every way, whether in pretence, or in truth, Christ is preached; and I therein do rejoice, yea, and will rejoice.

19 For I know that this shall turn to my salvation through your prayer, and the supply of the Spirit of Jesus Christ,   Acts 16:7; Rom. 8:9

20 According to my earnest expectation and *my* hope, that in nothing I shall be ashamed, but *that* with all boldness, as always, *so* now also Christ shall be magnified in my body, whether *it be* by life, or by death.   Rom. 5:5; 8:19; 1 Cor. 6:20

21 For to me to live *is* Christ, and to die *is* gain.   Gal. 2:20

1:21 Paul's Source

Throughout his later ministry, Paul never lost sight of the Source of his wisdom and strength. *AA 128*

22 But if I live in the flesh, this *is* the fruit of my labour: yet what I shall choose I ᵀwot not.   know

23 For I am in a strait betwixt two, having a desire to depart, and to be with Christ; which is far better: Luke 23:43; 2 Cor. 5:8; 2 Tim. 4:6

24 Nevertheless to abide in the flesh *is* more needful for you.

25 And having this confidence, I know that I shall abide and continue with you all for your furtherance and joy of faith;   Phil. 2:24

26 That your rejoicing may be more abundant in Jesus Christ for me by my coming to you again.   2 Cor. 1:14

27 Only let your ᵀconversation be as it becometh the gospel of Christ: that whether I come and see you, or else be absent, I may hear of your affairs, that ye stand fast in one spirit, with one mind striving together for the faith of the gospel; Acts 4:32; Eph. 4:1; Jude 3 ♦ conduct

28 And in nothing terrified by your adversaries: which is to them an evident token of ᵀperdition, but to you of salvation, and that of God.   destruction

29 For unto you it is given in the behalf of Christ, not only to believe on him, but also to suffer for his sake;

1:29 God's Perfect Leading

God never leads His children otherwise than they would choose to be led, if they could see the end from the beginning, and discern the glory of the purpose which they are fulfilling as co-workers with Him. *DA 224, 225*

30 Having the same conflict which ye saw in me, and now hear *to be* in me.   Acts 16:19-40;

The Attitude of Christ

2 If *there be* therefore any consolation in Christ, if any comfort of love, if any fellowship of the Spirit, if any bowels and mercies,   2 Cor. 13:14; Col. 3:12

2 Fulfil ye my joy, that ye be likeminded, having the same love, *being* of one accord, of one mind.   John 3:29; Rom. 12:16; Phil. 4:2

3 *Let* nothing *be done* through strife or vainglory; but in lowliness of mind let each esteem other better than themselves. Rom. 12:10

4 Look not every man on his own things, but every man also on the things of others.

5 Let this mind be in you, which was also in Christ Jesus: Matt. 11:29; Rom. 15:3

> **2:5 Learning in the School of Christ**
>
> We are to enter the school of Christ, to learn from Him meekness and lowliness. Redemption is that process by which the soul is trained for heaven. This training means a knowledge of Christ. It means emancipation from ideas, habits, and practices that have been gained in the school of the prince of darkness. The soul must be delivered from all that is opposed to loyalty to God. *DA 330*

6 Who, being in the form of God, thought it not robbery to be equal with God: John 5:18

7 But made himself of no reputation, and took upon him the form of a servant, and was made in the likeness of men: Is. 42:1; Matt. 20:28

> **2:7 Prepared for the Great Emergency**
>
> From the beginning, God and Christ knew of the apostasy of Satan, and of the fall of man through the deceptive power of the apostate. God did not ordain that sin should exist, but He foresaw its existence, and made provision to meet the terrible emergency. So great was His love for the world, that He covenanted to give His only-begotten Son. *DA 22*

8 And being found in fashion as a man, he humbled himself, and became obedient unto death, even the death of the cross.   Heb. 12:2

9 Wherefore God also hath highly exalted him, and given him a name which is above every name: Is. 52:13; Matt. 28:18; Heb. 2:9

10 That at the name of Jesus every knee should bow, of *things* in heaven, and *things* in earth, and *things* under the earth;   Matt. 28:18

11 And *that* every tongue should confess that Jesus Christ *is* Lord, to the glory of God the Father.   John 13:13; Rom. 14:9; 1 Cor. 12:3

A Christian's Obligations

12 Wherefore, my beloved, as ye have always obeyed, not as in my presence only, but now much more in my absence, work out your own salvation with fear and trembling.

> **2:13 A Divine Principle**
>
> Herein is revealed the outworking of the divine principle of co-operation, without which no true success can be attained. Human effort avails nothing without divine power; and without human endeavor, divine effort is with many of no avail. To make God's grace our own, we must act our part. His grace is given to work in us to will and to do, but never as a substitute for our effort. *PK 486, 487*

13 For it is God which worketh in you both to will and to do of *his* good pleasure.   Heb. 13:21

The Christian Life See Philippians 4:13.

14 Do all things without murmurings and disputings: 1 Cor. 10:10; 1 Pet. 4:9

15 That ye may be blameless and harmless, the sons of God, without rebuke, in the midst of a crooked and perverse nation, among whom ye shine as lights in the world;

16 Holding forth the word of life; that I may rejoice in the day of Christ, that I have not run in vain, neither laboured in vain. Gal. 2:2

Understanding the True Force of the Will

Philippians 2:12–15

The tempted one needs to understand the true force of the will. This is the governing power in the nature of man—the power of decision, of choice. Everything depends on the right action of the will. Desires for goodness and purity are right, so far as they go; but if we stop here, they avail nothing. Many will go down to ruin while hoping and desiring to overcome their evil propensities. They do not yield the will to God. They do not choose to serve Him.

God has given us the power of choice; it is ours to exercise. We cannot change our hearts, we cannot control our thoughts, our impulses, our affections. We cannot make ourselves pure, fit for God's service. But we can *choose* to serve God, we can give Him our will; then He will work in us to will and to do according to His good pleasure. Thus our whole nature will be brought under the control of Christ.

Through the right exercise of the will, an entire change may be made in the life. By yielding up the will to Christ, we ally ourselves with divine power. We receive strength from above to hold us steadfast. A pure and noble life, a life of victory over appetite and lust, is possible to everyone who will unite his weak, wavering human will to the omnipotent, unwavering will of God. *MH 176*

17 Yea, and if I be offered upon the sacrifice and service of your faith, I joy, and rejoice with you all.   Rom. 15:16; 2 Cor. 12:15; 2 Tim. 4:6
18 For the same cause also do ye joy, and rejoice with me.

Timothy and Epaphroditus Will Come

19 But I trust in the Lord Jesus to send Timotheus shortly unto you, that I also may be of good comfort, when I know your state.
20 For I have no man likeminded, who will naturally care for your state.   1 Cor. 16:10
21 For all seek their own, not the things which are Jesus Christ's. 1 Cor. 10:24; 13:5; Phil. 2:4
22 But ye know the proof of him, that, as a son with the father, he hath served with me in the gospel.   1 Cor. 4:17; 2 Cor. 2:9; 1 Tim. 1:2
23 Him therefore I hope to send presently, so soon as I shall see how it will go with me.
24 But I trust in the Lord that I also myself shall come shortly.   Philem. 22
25 Yet I supposed it necessary to send to you Epaphroditus, my brother, and companion in labour, and fellowsoldier, but your messenger, and he that ministered to my wants.
26 For he longed after you all, and was full of heaviness, because that ye had heard that he had been sick.   Phil. 1:8
27 For indeed he was sick nigh unto death: but God had mercy on him; and not on him only, but on me also, lest I should have sorrow upon sorrow.
28 I sent him therefore the more carefully, that, when ye see him again, ye may rejoice, and that I may be the less sorrowful.
29 Receive him therefore in the Lord with all gladness; and hold such in reputation:
30 Because for the work of Christ he was nigh unto death, not regarding his life, to supply your lack of service toward me.   Acts 20:24

Run Straight for the Goal

3 Finally, my brethren, rejoice in the Lord. To write the same things to you, to me indeed *is* not grievous, but for you *it is* safe.
2 Beware of dogs, beware of evil workers, beware of the ᵀconcision.   2 Cor. 11:13 ◆ *circumcision*
3 For we are the circumcision, which worship God in the spirit, and rejoice in Christ Jesus, and have no confidence in the flesh.   Col. 2:11
4 Though I might also have confidence in the flesh. If any other man thinketh that he hath whereof he might trust in the flesh, I more:
5 Circumcised the eighth day, of the stock of Israel, *of* the tribe of Benjamin, an Hebrew of the Hebrews; as touching the law, a Pharisee;
6 Concerning zeal, persecuting the church; touching the righteousness which is in the law, blameless.   Acts 8:3; 22:3-4; 26:9-10

7 But what things were gain to me, those I counted loss for Christ.   Luke 14:33
8 Yea doubtless, and I count all things *but* loss for the excellency of the knowledge of Christ Jesus my Lord: for whom I have suffered the loss of all things, and do count them *but* dung, that I may win Christ,   John 17:3
9 And be found in him, not having mine own righteousness, which is of the law, but that which is through the faith of Christ, the righteousness which is of God by faith: Is. 53:11
10 That I may know him, and the power of his resurrection, and the fellowship of his sufferings, being made conformable unto his death;   Rom. 8:17
11 If by any means I might attain unto the resurrection of the dead.   Acts 26:7
12 Not as though I had already attained, either were already perfect: but I follow after, if that I may apprehend that for which also I am apprehended of Christ Jesus.   1 Cor. 13:10
13 Brethren, I count not myself to have apprehended: but *this* one thing *I do*, forgetting those things which are behind, and reaching forth unto those things which are before,   Ps. 45:10; Luke 9:62; Heb. 6:1
14 I press toward the mark for the prize of the high calling of God in Christ Jesus.   Heb. 3:1

> **3:14 No Divided Service**
>
> He who would build up a strong, symmetrical character, he who would be a well-balanced Christian, must give all and do all for Christ; for the Redeemer will not accept divided service. Daily he must learn the meaning of self-surrender. He must study the word of God, learning its meaning and obeying its precepts. Thus he may reach the standard of Christian excellence. *AA 483*

15 Let us therefore, as many as be perfect, be thus minded: and if in any thing ye be otherwise minded, God shall reveal even this unto you.   John 7:17; 1 Cor. 2:6; Gal. 5:10
16 Nevertheless, whereto we have already attained, let us walk by the same rule, let us mind the same thing.   Gal. 6:16

Imitate Paul

17 Brethren, be followers together of me, and mark them which walk so as ye have us for an ᵀensample.   1 Cor. 4:16; Phil. 4:9; 1 Pet. 5:3 ◆ *example*
18 (For many walk, of whom I have told you often, and now tell you even weeping, *that they are* the enemies of the cross of Christ: Gal. 6:12
19 Whose end *is* destruction, whose God *is their* belly, and *whose* glory *is* in their shame, who mind earthly things.)   Hos. 4:7; Rom. 16:18

20 For our ᵀconversation is in heaven; from whence also we look for the Saviour, the Lord Jesus Christ: Acts 1:11; 1 Cor. 1:7; Eph. 2:19 ◆ conduct
21 Who shall change our vile body, that it may be fashioned like unto his glorious body, according to the working whereby he is able even to subdue all things unto himself. Col. 3:4

Paul's Advice

4 Therefore, my brethren dearly beloved and longed for, my joy and crown, so stand fast in the Lord, my dearly beloved.
2 I ᵀbeseech Euodias, and beseech Syntyche, that they be of the same mind in the Lord. Phil. 2:2-3 ◆ beg
3 And I ᵀintreat thee also, true ᵀyokefellow, help those women which laboured with me in the gospel, with Clement also, and with other my fellowlabourers, whose names are in the book of life. Luke 10:20 ◆ plead with ◆ fellow worker

Rejoice in the Lord

4 Rejoice in the Lord alway: and again I say, Rejoice. Rom. 12:12; Phil. 3:1

> **4:4 No Need for Sadness and Darkness**
>
> While the Christian's life will be characterized by humility, it should not be marked with sadness and self-depreciation. It is the privilege of everyone so to live that God will approve and bless him. It is not the will of our heavenly Father that we should be ever under condemnation and darkness. GC 477

5 Let your moderation be known unto all men. The Lord is at hand. James 5:8-9
6 Be careful for nothing; but in every thing by prayer and supplication with thanksgiving let your requests be made known unto God. Prov. 16:3; Matt. 6:25-33; Eph. 6:18
7 And the peace of God, which passeth all understanding, shall keep your hearts and minds through Christ Jesus. Is. 26:3; John 14:27; Col. 3:15
8 Finally, brethren, whatsoever things are true, whatsoever things are honest, whatsoever things are just, whatsoever things are pure, whatsoever things are lovely, whatsoever things are of good report; if there be any virtue, and if there be any praise, think on these things. Acts 6:3

Christian Behavior See Isaiah 3:16–24.

9 Those things, which ye have both learned, and received, and heard, and seen in me, do: and the God of peace shall be with you. Rom. 15:33; Phil. 3:17; 4:7

Paul Says Thank You

10 But I rejoiced in the Lord greatly, that now at the last your care of me hath flourished again; wherein ye were also careful, but ye lacked opportunity. 2 Cor. 11:9
11 Not that I speak in respect of want: for I have learned, in whatsoever state I am, therewith to be content. Phil. 3:8
12 I know both how to be ᵀabased, and I know how to abound: every where and in all things I am instructed both to be full and to be hungry, both to abound and to suffer need. 2 Cor. 11:27 ◆ brought low

> **4:13 Dependence and Cooperation**
>
> Whenever man accomplishes anything, whether in spiritual or in temporal lines, he should bear in mind that he does it through co-operation with his Maker. There is great necessity for us to realize our dependence on God. COL 82

13 I can do all things through Christ which strengtheneth me. 2 Cor. 12:9-10; Eph. 3:16; 6:10

The Christian Life See Philippians 1:6.

14 Notwithstanding ye have well done, that ye did communicate with my affliction.
15 Now ye Philippians know also, that in the beginning of the gospel, when I departed from Macedonia, no church communicated with me as concerning giving and receiving, but ye only. Phil. 1:5
16 For even in Thessalonica ye sent once and again unto my necessity. 1 Thess. 2:9
17 Not because I desire a gift: but I desire fruit that may abound to your account.
18 But I have all, and abound: I am full, having received of Epaphroditus the things which were sent from you, an odour of a sweet smell, a sacrifice acceptable, wellpleasing to God.
19 But my God shall supply all your need according to his riches in glory by Christ Jesus.

> **4:19 Claim All That God Promises**
>
> Let your heart break for the longing it has for God, for the living God. The life of Christ has shown what humanity can do by being partaker of the divine nature. All that Christ received from God we too may have. Then ask and receive. With the persevering faith of Jacob, with the unyielding persistence of Elijah, claim for yourself all that God has promised. COL 149

20 Now unto God and our Father be glory for ever and ever. Amen. Rom. 11:36; Gal. 1:4-5
21 Salute every saint in Christ Jesus. The brethren which are with me greet you. Gal. 1:2
22 All the saints salute you, chiefly they that are of Caesar's household. 2 Cor. 13:13
23 The grace of our Lord Jesus Christ be with you all. Amen. Rom. 16:20

THE EPISTLE OF PAUL THE APOSTLE TO THE

COLOSSIANS

A harmful heresy threatened the church at Colosse. This heresy—some have referred to it as an early form of Gnosticism—was intent upon devaluing Christ and elevating human practices. Those who promoted it tried to fuse their Christian beliefs with these human-centered practices and beliefs.

Paul lovingly confronted the church with its heresy and reminded them of the fullness found only in Christ. He reminded the believers that Christ existed before the foundation of the world, that all things were created in Him, and that the fullness or completeness of their faith lies with Him—not with anything or anyone else.

Dates

Colossians, Philemon, and Ephesians were most likely written during the same time period—during Paul's first Roman imprisonment. As such, Colossians was most likely written in A.D. 62. The letter was sent with Tychicus and Onesimus (the converted slave Paul writes about in Philemon) to Colosse.

Author

Paul mentions himself by name in this epistle (1:1, 23; 4:18), and the external testimony to his authorship is strong. The epistle's personal information and its similarity with Ephesians and Philemon point to Paul's authorship. Some scholars have challenged Paul's authorship, however, on internal grounds, arguing that the vocabulary was different than that used in Paul's other epistles. Also some concepts and thoughts were believed to be from a later time period. Nevertheless, these challenges are easily answered by Paul's wide use of vocabulary and his obvious knowledge of concepts that were not completely developed until later.

Meaning of the Name

The epistle was called *Pros Kolossaeis*, which means "To the Colossians." Although Paul notes the recipients of the letter in 1:2, he also wanted the letter read to the Laodicean church (4:16).

Christ in Colossians

Colossians is one of the most Christological books in all of Scripture. Paul not only reminds his readers of the supremacy of Christ, but that He also is willing to lead in every aspect of our lives if we allow Him to do so. Living faithfully in Christ means living in such a way that our behavior and attitude reflect our relationship with Christ.

As Christ is the integral component in the Epistle to the Colossians, He forms the basis for our faith; He is the foundation on which our faith is built.

Christ is the one in whom we have redemption (1:14). He is "the image of the invisible God" (1:15), "before all things" (1:17), and "the head of the body" (1:18). All fullness dwells in Him (1:19). He is our reconciler (1:22) in whom "all the treasures of wisdom and knowledge" are hidden (2:3). We share in His resurrection (3:1).

Overview

In Colossians, Paul fights a growing heresy in the church. He turns to Christ—His preeminence and the completeness of salvation He provides—and makes this epistle possibly the most Christ-centered book in all of Scripture.

The city of Colosse was a small city about one hundred miles east of Ephesus. At one time a populous commerce center, Colosse had been eclipsed by the neighboring cities of Laodicea and Hierapolis. Colosse had a large Jewish population, and the church there had been founded by Epaphras (1:7), a man whom Paul had led to Christ. Like his letter to the church in Rome, Paul wrote to the church in Colosse without having been there.

The book can be divided into two parts or two main arguments:

(1) *Colossians 1—2, The Position of Christ:* In order to contest the growing heresy in the church, Paul spends the first two chapters of this epistle on Christ's supremacy, arguing His rightful place in our adoration. Paul writes: "For by him were all things created, that

are in heaven, and that are in earth, visible and invisible, whether they be thrones, or dominions, or principalities, or powers: all things were created by him, and for him: and he is before all things, and by him all things consist. And he is the head of the body, the church: who is the beginning, the firstborn from the dead; that in all things he might have the preeminence" (1:16–18).

(2) *Colossians 3—4, Our Position in Christ:* Since Christ "is before all things" (1:17), submission is the mark of the believer. As Paul explains, "If ye then be risen with Christ, seek those things which are above, where Christ sitteth on the right hand of God" (3:1). Believers are to put to death the things of old and put on the new self.

Unlocking Colossians

KEY PEOPLE:
Paul, Timothy (Timotheus), Tychicus, Onesimus, Aristarchus, Luke, John Mark (Marcus), Barnabas, Epaphras, Laodicean believers

KEY EVENT:
The presence and advancement of a heresy that threatened the church at Colosse

KEY WORD:
Preeminence, the key theme in Paul's epistle. Christ is preeminent over all things and in Him we have everything we need; we are sufficient in Him. Paul is trying to deal with a heresy that elevates human principles at the expense of Christ's fullness and completeness. Paul writes, "If ye be dead with Christ from the rudiments of the world, why, as though living in the world, are ye subject to ordinances" (2:20). Paul does a wonderful job of refuting the claims of this threatening heresy and reassuring the Colossians that everything they need is found in Christ. He died for our sins, rose from the grave, and is able to meet all our needs. He is the "firstborn of every creature" (1:15); thus, we do not need to rely on manmade rules and regulations.

KEY VERSES:
"For in him dwelleth all the fulness of the Godhead bodily. And ye are complete in him, which is the head of all principality and power" (Colossians 2:9, 10).

"If ye then be risen with Christ, seek those things which are above, where Christ sitteth on the right hand of God. Set your affection on things above, not on things on the earth" (Colossians 3:1, 2).

KEY CHAPTER:
Colossians 3, which brings together the three main components in Paul's letter. First, Christ rose from the dead. As believers, we are also risen with Him (3:1–4). Second, since we are new creatures in Christ, we are to put off the old self with all of its sins and shortcomings and put on the new self (3:5–17). Finally, since we have been raised with Christ and have put on the new self, we can also demonstrate holiness in our relationships and in all that we do (3:18–25).

Paul's Greeting

1 Paul, an apostle of Jesus Christ by the will of God, and Timotheus *our* brother,
2 To the saints and faithful brethren in Christ which are at Colosse: Grace *be* unto you, and peace, from God our Father and the Lord Jesus Christ.   Rom. 1:7; Eph. 1:1

Paul's Prayer for the Colossians

3 We give thanks to God and the Father of our Lord Jesus Christ, praying always for you,   Eph. 1:15
4 Since we heard of your faith in Christ Jesus, and of the love *which ye have* to all the saints,   Gal. 5:6
5 For the hope which is laid up for you in heaven, whereof ye heard before in the word of the truth of the gospel;   Acts 23:6
6 Which is come unto you, as *it is* in all the world; and bringeth forth fruit, as *it doth* also in you, since the day ye heard *of it*, and knew the grace of God in truth: John 15:16
7 As ye also learned of Epaphras our dear fellowservant, who is for you a faithful minister of Christ;   Col. 4:12
8 Who also declared unto us your love in the Spirit.   Rom. 15:30
9 For this cause we also, since the day we heard *it*, do not cease to pray for you, and to desire that ye might be filled with the knowledge of his will in all wisdom and spiritual understanding;   Eph. 1:8
10 That ye might walk worthy of the Lord unto all pleasing, being fruitful in every good work, and increasing in the knowledge of God;   Eph. 4:1; 1 Thess. 4:1
11 Strengthened with all might, according to his glorious power, unto all patience and longsuffering with joyfulness;   Eph. 3:16; 4:2

1:9–11 No Limit to Blessings

Thus Paul put into words his desire for the Colossian believers. How high the ideal that these words hold before the follower of Christ! They show the wonderful possibilities of the Christian life and make it plain that there is no limit to the blessings that the children of God may receive. *AA 471*

12 Giving thanks unto the Father, which hath made us meet to be partakers of the inheritance of the saints in light: Acts 20:32

What Christ Has Done

13 Who hath delivered us from the power of darkness, and hath translated *us* into the kingdom of his dear Son: Eph. 1:6; 6:12; 2 Pet. 1:11
14 In whom we have redemption through his blood, *even* the forgiveness of sins: Eph. 1:7
15 Who is the image of the invisible God, the firstborn of every creature: Ps. 89:27; John 1:18

1:15, 16 Perfect Love and Unity

Before the entrance of evil there was peace and joy throughout the universe. All was in perfect harmony with the Creator's will. Love for God was supreme, love for one another impartial. Christ . . . was one with the eternal Father—one in nature, in character, and in purpose—the only being in all the universe that could enter into all the counsels and purposes of God. *GC 493*

16 For by him were all things created, that are in heaven, and that are in earth, visible and invisible, whether *they be* thrones, or dominions, or principalities, or powers: all things were created by him, and for him:

Who Is God? See John 17:18–26.

17 And he is before all things, and by him all things consist.   John 8:58

1:17 God's Hand Always at Work

It is not by inherent power that year by year the earth yields its bounties and continues its march around the sun. The hand of the Infinite One is perpetually at work guiding this planet. It is God's power continually exercised that keeps the earth in position in its rotation. It is God who causes the sun to rise in the heavens. He opens the windows of heaven and gives rain. *MH 416*

18 And he is the head of the body, the church: who is the beginning, the firstborn from the dead; that in all *things* he might have the preeminence.   Acts 26:23; Eph. 1:22-23; Rev. 1:5
19 For it pleased *the Father* that in him should all fulness dwell;   John 1:16; Eph. 1:3; Col. 2:9
20 And, having made peace through the blood of his cross, by him to reconcile all things unto himself; by him, *I say*, whether *they be* things in earth, or things in heaven.
21 And you, that were sometime alienated and enemies in *your* mind by wicked works, yet now hath he reconciled   Eph. 2:12
22 In the body of his flesh through death, to present you holy and unblameable and unreproveable in his sight: Rom. 7:4; Eph. 1:4; 5:27
23 If ye continue in the faith grounded and settled, and *be* not moved away from the hope of the gospel, which ye have heard, *and* which was preached to every creature which is under heaven; whereof I Paul am made a minister;
24 Who now rejoice in my sufferings for you, and fill up that which is behind of the afflictions of Christ in my flesh for his body's sake, which is the church: 2 Tim. 1:8
25 Whereof I am made a minister, according to the dispensation of God which is given to me for you, to fulfil the word of God;

26 *Even* the mystery which hath been hid from ages and from generations, but now is made manifest to his saints: Rom. 16:25-26
27 To whom God would make known what *is* the riches of the glory of this mystery among the Gentiles; which is Christ in you, the hope of glory: 1 Tim. 1:1

1:27 Miracle of Miracles

Souls that have borne the likeness of Satan have been transformed into the image of God. This change is itself the miracle of miracles. A change wrought by the word, it is one of the deepest mysteries of the word. We cannot understand; we can only believe, as declared by the Scriptures, it is "Christ in you, the hope of glory" (Colossians 1:27). *Ed 172*

28 Whom we preach, warning every man, and teaching every man in all wisdom; that we may present every man perfect in Christ Jesus:
29 Whereunto I also labour, striving according to his working, which worketh in me mightily.

Stand Firm in the Faith

2 For I would that ye knew what great conflict I have for you, and *for* them at Laodicea, and *for* as many as have not seen my face in the flesh;   Phil. 1:30; Col. 1:29; Rev. 1:11
2 That their hearts might be comforted, being knit together in love, and unto all riches of the full assurance of understanding, to the acknowledgement of the mystery of God, and of the Father, and of Christ; Rom. 16:25; Col. 1:27; 4:8
3 In whom are hid all the treasures of wisdom and knowledge.   Rom. 11:33
4 And this I say, lest any man should ᵀbeguile you with enticing words. Eph. 5:6 ♦ *deceive*
5 For though I be absent in the flesh, yet am I with you in the spirit, joying and beholding your order, and the stedfastness of your faith in Christ.   1 Cor. 14:40; 1 Thess. 2:17; 1 Pet. 5:9
6 As ye have therefore received Christ Jesus the Lord, *so* walk ye in him: Col. 1:10
7 Rooted and built up in him, and stablished in the faith, as ye have been taught, abounding therein with thanksgiving. Eph. 2:20-22; 3:17
8 Beware lest any man ᵀspoil you through philosophy and vain deceit, after the tradition of men, after the rudiments of the world, and not after Christ. Gal. 4:3; Eph. 5:6; 1 Tim. 6:20 ♦ *cheat*

2:9, 10 Emptied of Self

We can receive of heaven's light only as we are willing to be emptied of self. We cannot discern the character of God, or accept Christ by faith, unless we consent to the bringing into captivity of every thought to the obedience of Christ. To all who do this the Holy Spirit is given without measure. *DA 181*

9 For in him dwelleth all the fulness of the Godhead bodily.   John 1:14; 2 Cor. 5:19; Col. 1:19
10 And ye are complete in him, which is the head of all ᵀprincipality and power: *authority*
11 In whom also ye are circumcised with the circumcision made without hands, in putting off the body of the sins of the flesh by the circumcision of Christ: Rom. 2:29; 6:6; Phil. 3:3
12 Buried with him in baptism, wherein also ye are risen with *him* through the faith of the operation of God, who hath raised him from the dead.   Acts 2:24; Rom. 4:24; 6:3-5

Baptism/Lord's Supper See Galatians 3:27.

13 And you, being dead in your sins and the uncircumcision of your flesh, hath he ᵀquickened together with him, having forgiven you all ᵀtrespasses; Eph. 2:1; James 2:26 ♦ *made alive* ♦ *sins*
14 Blotting out the handwriting of ordinances that was against us, which was contrary to us, and took it out of the way, nailing it to his cross;   Acts 3:19
15 *And* having spoiled principalities and powers, he made a shew of them openly, triumphing over them in it.   Gen. 3:15; Luke 10:18; Eph. 4:8
16 Let no man therefore judge you in meat, or in drink, or in respect of an holyday, or of the new moon, or of the sabbath *days*:   Heb. 9:10
17 Which are a shadow of things to come; but the body *is* of Christ.   Heb. 8:5; 10:1

2:14–17 Ceremonial Versus Moral Law

There are many who try to blend these two systems, using the texts that speak of the ceremonial law to prove that the moral law has been abolished; but this is a perversion of the Scriptures. The distinction between the two systems is broad and clear. The ceremonial system was made up of symbols pointing to Christ, to His sacrifice and His priesthood. This ritual law, with its sacrifices and ordinances, was to be performed by the Hebrews until type met antitype in the death of Christ, the Lamb of God that taketh away the sin of the world. Then all the sacrificial offerings were to cease. *PP 365*

18 Let no man beguile you of your reward in a voluntary humility and worshipping of angels, intruding into those things which he hath not seen, vainly puffed up by his fleshly mind,
19 And not holding the Head, from which all the body by joints and bands having nourishment ministered, and knit together, increaseth with the increase of God.
20 Wherefore if ye be dead with Christ from the rudiments of the world, why, as though living in the world, are ye subject to ordinances,
21 (Touch not; taste not; handle not;
22 Which all are to perish with the using;) after the commandments and doctrines of men?   Is. 29:13; 1 Cor. 6:13; Titus 1:14

2:21 A Habit Difficult to Break

In relation to tea, coffee, tobacco, and alcoholic drinks, the only safe course is to touch not, taste not, handle not. The tendency of tea, coffee, and similar drinks is in the same direction as that of alcoholic liquor and tobacco, and in some cases the habit is as difficult to break as it is for the drunkard to give up intoxicants. *MH 335*

23 Which things have indeed a shew of wisdom in will worship, and humility, and neglecting of the body; not in any honour to the satisfying of the flesh.   *Col. 2:18*

Live as God's People

3 If ye then be risen with Christ, seek those things which are above, where Christ sitteth on the right hand of God.   *Ps. 110:1*
2 Set your affection on things above, not on things on the earth.   *Matt. 16:23*

3:1, 2 No Compromise With Sin

Singleness of purpose, wholehearted devotion to God, is the condition pointed out by the Saviour's words. Let the purpose be sincere and unwavering to discern the truth and to obey it at whatever cost, and you will receive divine enlightenment. Real piety begins when all compromise with sin is at an end. *MB 91*

3 For ye are dead, and your life is hid with Christ in God.   *Rom. 6:2; Col. 2:20*
4 When Christ, *who is* our life, shall appear, then shall ye also appear with him in glory.

3:5–10 Constant Effort Against Evil

At the time of their conversion and baptism the Colossian believers pledged themselves to put away beliefs and practices that had hitherto been a part of their lives, and to be true to their allegiance to Christ. In his letter, Paul reminded them of this, and entreated them not to forget that in order to keep their pledge they must put forth constant effort against the evils that would seek for mastery over them. *AA 475, 476*

5 Mortify therefore your members which are upon the earth; fornication, uncleanness, inordinate affection, evil concupiscence, and covetousness, which is idolatry:
6 For which things' sake the wrath of God cometh on the children of disobedience:
7 In the which ye also walked some time, when ye lived in them.   *Eph. 2:2*
8 But now ye also put off all these; anger, wrath, malice, blasphemy, filthy communication out of your mouth.   *Eph. 4:22, 29; Jude 8*
9 Lie not one to another, seeing that ye have put off the old man with his deeds; *Lev. 19:11*

10 And have put on the new *man*, which is renewed in knowledge after the image of him that created him: *Rom. 12:2; Eph. 2:10*
11 Where there is neither Greek nor Jew, circumcision nor uncircumcision, Barbarian, Scythian, bond *nor* free: but Christ *is* all, and in all.   *Rom. 10:12; 1 Cor. 7:19; Eph. 1:23*
12 Put on therefore, as the elect of God, holy and beloved, bowels of mercies, kindness, humbleness of mind, meekness, longsuffering;
13 Forbearing one another, and forgiving one another, if any man have a quarrel against any: even as Christ forgave you, so also *do* ye.   *Mark 11:25; Eph. 4:2, 32*
14 And above all these things *put on* charity, which is the bond of perfectness.   *1 Cor. 13*
15 And let the peace of God rule in your hearts, to the which also ye are called in one body; and be ye thankful.   *John 14:27*
16 Let the word of Christ dwell in you richly in all wisdom; teaching and admonishing one another in psalms and hymns and spiritual songs, singing with grace in your hearts to the Lord.
17 And whatsoever ye do in word or deed, *do* all in the name of the Lord Jesus, giving thanks to God and the Father by him.
18 Wives, submit yourselves unto your own husbands, as it is fit in the Lord.
19 Husbands, love *your* wives, and be not bitter against them.   *Eph. 5:25*
20 Children, obey *your* parents in all things: for this is well pleasing unto the Lord. *Ex. 20:12*
21 Fathers, provoke not your children *to* anger, lest they be discouraged.   *Eph. 6:4*
22 Servants, obey in all things *your* masters according to the flesh; not with eyeservice, as menpleasers; but in singleness of heart, fearing God: *Col. 3:20*
23 And whatsoever ye do, do *it* heartily, as to the Lord, and not unto men;   *Col. 3:17*
24 Knowing that of the Lord ye shall receive the reward of the inheritance: for ye serve the Lord Christ.   *1 Cor. 7:22*
25 But he that doeth wrong shall receive for the wrong which he hath done: and there is no respect of persons.   *Acts 10:34*

Be Fervent in Prayer

4 Masters, give unto *your* servants that which is just and equal; knowing that ye also have a Master in heaven.

4:2 Prayers That Are Not Just a Form

Speak and act in harmony with your prayers. It will make an infinite difference with you whether trial shall prove your faith to be genuine, or show that your prayers are only a form. *COL 146*

2 Continue in prayer, and watch in the same with thanksgiving; Luke 18:1

3 Withal praying also for us, that God would open unto us a door of utterance, to speak the mystery of Christ, for which I am also in bonds: Acts 14:27; Eph. 6:19-20; Phil. 1:7

4 That I may make it ᵀmanifest, as I ought to speak. Eph. 6:20 ◆ known

5 Walk in wisdom toward them that are without, redeeming the time. Mark 4:11

4:5 Mighty Angelic Power

When unconsciously we are in danger of exerting a wrong influence, the angels will be by our side, prompting us to a better course, choosing our words for us, and influencing our actions. Thus our influence may be a silent, unconscious, but mighty power in drawing others to Christ and the heavenly world. *COL 341, 342*

6 Let your speech *be* alway with grace, seasoned with salt, that ye may know how ye ought to answer every man. Mark 9:50; 1 Pet. 3:15

Final Greetings

7 All my state shall Tychicus declare unto you, *who is* a beloved brother, and a faithful minister and fellowservant in the Lord: Acts 20:4

8 Whom I have sent unto you for the same purpose, that he might know your estate, and comfort your hearts; Eph. 6:22

9 With Onesimus, a faithful and beloved brother, who is *one* of you. They shall make known unto you all things which *are done* here.

10 Aristarchus my fellowprisoner saluteth you, and Marcus, sister's son to Barnabas, (touching whom ye received commandments: if he come unto you, receive him;) Acts 19:29

11 And Jesus, which is called Justus, who are of the circumcision. These only *are my* fellowworkers unto the kingdom of God, which have been a comfort unto me. Acts 11:2

12 Epaphras, who is *one* of you, a servant of Christ, saluteth you, always labouring fervently for you in prayers, that ye may stand perfect and complete in all the will of God. Rom. 15:30; Col. 1:7; Philem. 23

13 For I bear him record, that he hath a great zeal for you, and them *that are* in Laodicea, and them in Hierapolis. Col. 2:1

14 Luke, the beloved physician, and Demas, greet you. 2 Tim. 4:10-11; Philem. 24

4:14 A Shortsighted Exchange

Demas, steadfast for a time, afterward forsook the cause of Christ. In referring to this, Paul wrote, "Demas hath forsaken me, having loved this present world" (2 Timothy 4:10). For worldly gain, Demas bartered every high and noble consideration. How shortsighted the exchange! Possessing only worldly wealth or honor, Demas was poor indeed, however much he might proudly call his own; while Mark, choosing to suffer for Christ's sake, possessed eternal riches, being accounted in heaven an heir of God and a joint heir with His Son. *AA 455*

15 Salute the brethren which are in Laodicea, and Nymphas, and the church which is in his house. Rom. 16:5

16 And when this epistle is read among you, cause that it be read also in the church of the Laodiceans; and that ye likewise read the *epistle* from Laodicea. 1 Thess. 5:27; 2 Thess. 3:14

17 And say to Archippus, Take heed to the ministry which thou hast received in the Lord, that thou fulfil it. Philem. 2

18 The salutation by the hand of me Paul. Remember my bonds. Grace *be* with you. Amen. 1 Cor. 16:21; 1 Tim. 6:21; 2 Tim. 4:22

God Calls Even You to Be a Blessing to Others

Colossians 3:23

With a loving spirit we may perform life's humblest duties "as to the Lord" (Colossians 3:23). If the love of God is in the heart, it will be manifested in the life. The sweet savor of Christ will surround us, and our influence will elevate and bless.

You are not to wait for great occasions or to expect extraordinary abilities before you go to work for God. You need not have a thought of what the world will think of you. If your daily life is a testimony to the purity and sincerity of your faith, and others are convinced that you desire to benefit them, your efforts will not be wholly lost.

The humblest and poorest of the disciples of Jesus can be a blessing to others. They may not realize that they are doing any special good, but by their unconscious influence they may start waves of blessing that will widen and deepen, and the blessed results they may never know until the day of final reward. They do not feel or know that they are doing anything great. They are not required to weary themselves with anxiety about success. They have only to go forward quietly, doing faithfully the work that God's providence assigns, and their life will not be in vain. Their own souls will be growing more and more into the likeness of Christ; they are workers together with God in this life and are thus fitting for the higher work and the unshadowed joy of the life to come. *SC 82, 83*

THESSALONIANS

Expectant parents do their best to prepare for the birth of a child. Providing an environment for growth and health is paramount. The baby's room is equipped with the proper furniture and essentials, clothes and toys are purchased, and the remainder of the house is child-proofed.

Birthing a church is similar to birthing a child. Certain preparations have to be made to help the infant church to grow and thrive. As part of his apostolic ministry, Paul was tasked with facilitating the growth of those under his spiritual wing.

The church at Thessalonica was Paul's baby—one he nurtured through preaching the word (Acts 17:1–9) and now through the written word. In this letter, he offers words of encouragement, edification, and doctrine to assist the fledgling church to mature and to develop.

Just as a baby is thrust from a world of calmness and serenity to a world of chaos and insecurity, so was the church at Thessalonica. Persecution and violence were the norm of the day. Paul wanted the infant church to mature into a vibrant and vital living organism, proclaiming the message of Christ until He returned.

This epistle glows with fervent love for the Thessalonian people. Paul is grateful for Timothy's report of the faithfulness of the Thessalonians as well as for the fact that they highly regard this youthful soul-winner. Paul extols them for their faith, love and hope. He also lets them know that he is most anxious to make a return visit.

Dates

Paul wrote this epistle in A.D. 51. After Paul met Silas and Timothy in Athens (3:1, 2), Paul sent Timothy to Thessalonica while Silas had returned to Macedonia. Paul wrote this epistle in response to Timothy's good report concerning the Thessalonian church.

Author

While Paul the apostle is universally believed to be the author, his authorship was challenged in the nineteenth century. Critics claimed that a lack of doctrinal content made Paul's authorship suspect. This argument is weak on two counts:

(1) The amount of doctrinal teaching varies in each of Paul's letters.

(2) This letter provides the foundational passage on the doctrine of eschatology, the teaching regarding future events.

We learn much of Paul during his stay in Thessalonica. While in Thessalonica, he received two separate offerings from the church at Philippi (one hundred miles away). He ministered extensively to Gentiles who had come out of idolatry (1:9), working "night and day" (2:9) during his time in Thessalonica.

Meaning of the Name

This is the first of Paul's two canonical letters to the church at Thessalonica. It was entitled *Pros Thessalonikeis A*, or "to the Thessalonians I."

Christ in 1 Thessalonians

Christ is portrayed as the believer's hope—both in the present and in the future. The Lord's return is a constant theme throughout this epistle. One of the most complete teachings of Jesus' Second Advent is developed by Paul in 4:13—5:11. When Jesus returns, He will deliver us "from the wrath to come" (1:10), raise believers from the dead (3:13; see also 4:13–18), and sanctify us (5:23).

Overview

Paul wrote from Corinth to encourage the young church at Thessalonica. This city was one of the wealthiest trade centers of the Roman Empire; it sat on the Via Egnatia, a main road from the city of Rome to the eastern parts of the empire and all the way to the Orient. It was the largest city, as well as the capital, of the province of Macedonia, with a population of two hundred thousand. Strategically located, it became the hub for the spreading of the gospel in Macedonia and Greece. The city had a large Jewish population. Many of the

Gentiles who had grown disenchanted with Greek paganism were attracted to the Jewish faith. After Paul was forced out of Thessalonica (Acts 17:9–10), he was concerned about the progress of the believers' faith. He commended them for remaining steadfast, exhorted them to excel, and consoled them concerning their believing loved ones who have died.

First Thessalonians is divided into two major sections:

(1) *1 Thessalonians 1—3, Assessing His Ministry:* Paul commends the faith of the believers at Thessalonica (1:1–10) and defends his ministry in the face of criticism and opposition (2:1—3:5). After Timothy returns from Thessalonica with praise for the growth of the believers, Paul commends them once more (3:6–13).

(2) *1 Thessalonians 4—5, Instructing the Church:* This section has one of the foremost passages of eschatology in the New Testament: 4:13—5:11. To encourage the continued growth of the Thessalonian believers, Paul instructs them about spiritual purity and other aspects of the godly life (4:1–12; 5:12–22), reminds them of the future resurrection of believers (4:13–18), and of the upcoming day of judgment (5:1–11). He concludes with a benediction (5:23–28).

Unlocking 1 Thessalonians

KEY PEOPLE:
Paul, Timothy, Silas, the believers at Thessalonica

KEY THEME:
The Second Advent of Christ

KEY WORD:
Holiness, for Paul challenged his readers to grow in faith and love in light of Christ's return. The believer is set apart for God and is transformed in character as he or she awaits the imminent return of Christ.

KEY VERSES:
"And the Lord make you to increase and abound in love one toward another, and toward all men, even as we do toward you: to the end he may stablish your hearts unblameable in holiness before God, even our Father, at the coming of our Lord Jesus Christ with all his saints" (1 Thessalonians 3:12, 13).

KEY CHAPTER:
1 Thessalonians 4, which contains the description of the future resurrection of believers at the Second Advent of Christ.

Paul's Greeting

1 Paul, and Silvanus, and Timotheus, unto the church of the Thessalonians *which is* in God the Father and *in* the Lord Jesus Christ: Grace *be* unto you, and peace, from God our Father, and the Lord Jesus Christ.   Acts 18:5; Rom. 1:7; 2 Thess. 1:1

Paul's Prayer for the Thessalonians

2 We give thanks to God always for you all, making mention of you in our prayers;
3 Remembering without ceasing your work of faith, and labour of love, and patience of hope in our Lord Jesus Christ, in the sight of God and our Father;   2 Thess. 1:11
4 Knowing, brethren beloved, your election of God.   2 Thess. 2:13
5 For our gospel came not unto you in word only, but also in power, and in the Holy Ghost, and in much assurance; as ye know what manner of men we were among you for your sake.   Col. 2:2
6 And ye became followers of us, and of the Lord, having received the word in much affliction, with joy of the Holy Ghost: Acts 13:52
7 So that ye were ensamples to all that believe in Macedonia and Achaia.
8 For from you sounded out the word of the Lord not only in Macedonia and Achaia, but also in every place your faith to God-ward is spread abroad; so that we need not to speak any thing.   Rom. 1:8; 2 Thess. 1:4; 3:1
9 For they themselves shew of us what manner of entering in we had unto you, and how ye turned to God from idols to serve the living and true God;   Acts 14:15; 1 Cor. 12:2; 1 Thess. 2:1

1:8, 9 True Missionaries

The Thessalonian believers were true missionaries. Their hearts burned with zeal for their Saviour, who had delivered them from fear of "the wrath to come." Through the grace of Christ a marvelous transformation had taken place in their lives, and the word of the Lord, as spoken through them, was accompanied with power. Hearts were won by the truths presented, and souls were added to the number of believers. *AA 256*

---

10 And to wait for his Son from heaven, whom he raised from the dead, *even* Jesus, which delivered us from the wrath to come.   Matt. 3:7; Acts 2:24; 1 Cor. 1:7

Paul Recalls His Visit

2 For yourselves, brethren, know our entrance in unto you, that it was not in vain:
2 But even after that we had suffered before, and were shamefully entreated, as ye know, at Philippi, we were bold in our God

to speak unto you the gospel of God with much contention.   Acts 4:13; 16:22-24; 17:2-9
3 For our exhortation *was* not of deceit, nor of uncleanness, nor in ᵀguile: 2 Cor. 2:17 ♦ *deceit*
4 But as we were allowed of God to be put in trust with the gospel, even so we speak; not as pleasing men, but God, which trieth our hearts.   Rom. 8:27; Gal. 1:10; 2:7
5 For neither at any time used we flattering words, as ye know, nor a cloke of covetousness; God *is* witness: Acts 20:33; Rom. 1:9; 2 Pet. 2:3
6 Nor of men sought we glory, neither of you, nor *yet* of others, when we might have been burdensome, as the apostles of Christ.   John 5:41
7 But we were gentle among you, even as a nurse cherisheth her children: Is. 49:23
8 So being affectionately desirous of you, we were willing to have imparted unto you, not the gospel of God only, but also our own souls, because ye were dear unto us.   2 Cor. 12:15; 1 John 3:16
9 For ye remember, brethren, our labour and travail: for labouring night and day, because we would not be chargeable unto any of you, we preached unto you the gospel of God.
10 Ye *are* witnesses, and God *also*, how holily and justly and unblameably we behaved ourselves among you that believe: 2 Cor. 1:12
11 As ye know how we exhorted and comforted and charged every one of you, as a father *doth* his children,   1 Thess. 2:7
12 That ye would walk worthy of God, who hath called you unto his kingdom and glory.   Eph. 4:1; 1 Thess. 5:24; 1 Pet. 5:10

2:13 Receiving the Word

A knowledge of the truth depends not so much upon strength of intellect as upon pureness of purpose, the simplicity of an earnest, dependent faith. To those who in humility of heart seek for divine guidance, angels of God draw near. The Holy Spirit is given to open to them the rich treasures of the truth. *COL 59*

---

13 For this cause also thank we God without ceasing, because, when ye received the word of God which ye heard of us, ye received *it* not *as* the word of men, but as it is in truth, the word of God, which effectually worketh also in you that believe.   Rom. 10:17; Gal. 4:14; Heb. 4:12

The Bible See Matthew 24:35.

14 For ye, brethren, became followers of the churches of God which in Judaea are in Christ Jesus: for ye also have suffered like things of your own countrymen, even as they *have* of the Jews: Gal. 1:22
15 Who both killed the Lord Jesus, and their own prophets, and have persecuted us; and

they please not God, and are contrary to all men: Esth. 3:8; Matt. 5:12; Acts 2:23
16 Forbidding us to speak to the Gentiles that they might be saved, to fill up their sins alway: for the wrath is come upon them to the uttermost. Gen. 15:16; Matt. 23:32; Acts 13:50
17 But we, brethren, being taken from you for a short time in presence, not in heart, endeavoured the more abundantly to see your face with great desire. 1 Cor. 5:3; Col. 2:5
18 Wherefore we would have come unto you, even I Paul, once and again; but Satan hindered us. Rom. 1:13; 15:22; Phil. 4:16
19 For what *is* our hope, or joy, or crown of rejoicing? *Are* not even ye in the presence of our Lord Jesus Christ at his coming? 2 Cor. 1:14
20 For ye are our glory and joy.

Timothy's Report to Paul

3 Wherefore when we could no longer ᵀforbear, we thought it good to be left at Athens alone; Acts 17:15; 1 Thess. 3:5 ◆ *refuse to act*
2 And sent Timotheus, our brother, and minister of God, and our fellowlabourer in the gospel of Christ, to establish you, and to comfort you concerning your faith:
3 That no man should be moved by these afflictions: for yourselves know that we are appointed thereunto. Acts 9:16; 14:22; 21:13
4 For ᵀverily, when we were with you, we told you before that we should suffer tribulation; even as it came to pass, and ye know. 1 Thess. 2:14 ◆ *truly*
5 For this cause, when I could no longer forbear, I sent to know your faith, lest by some means the tempter have tempted you, and our labour be in vain. Matt. 4:3; 1 Cor. 7:5; Phil. 2:16

3:5 Caring for Converts

The apostle felt that he was to a large extent responsible for the spiritual welfare of those converted under his labors. His desire for them was that they might increase in a knowledge of the only true God, and Jesus Christ, whom He had sent. Often in his ministry he would meet with little companies of men and women who loved Jesus, and bow with them in prayer, asking God to teach them how to maintain a living connection with Him. *AA 262*

---

6 But now when Timotheus came from you unto us, and brought us good tidings of your faith and charity, and that ye have good remembrance of us always, desiring greatly to see us, as we also *to see* you: Acts 18:5; 1 Cor. 11:2
7 Therefore, brethren, we were comforted over you in all our affliction and distress by your faith: 2 Cor. 1:4
8 For now we live, if ye stand fast in the Lord. 1 Cor. 16:13

9 For what thanks can we render to God again for you, for all the joy wherewith we joy for your sakes before our God;
10 Night and day praying exceedingly that we might see your face, and might perfect that which is lacking in your faith? 2 Cor. 13:9
11 Now God himself and our Father, and our Lord Jesus Christ, direct our way unto you.
12 And the Lord make you to increase and abound in love one toward another, and toward all *men*, even as we *do* toward you: Phil. 1:9; 1 Thess. 4:9-10; 2 Thess. 1:3
13 To the end he may stablish your hearts unblameable in holiness before God, even our Father, at the coming of our Lord Jesus Christ with all his saints. Zech. 14:5; 1 Thess. 2:19; 5:23

How Christians Should Live

4 Furthermore then we ᵀbeseech you, brethren, and exhort *you* by the Lord Jesus, that as ye have received of us how ye ought to walk and to please God, *so* ye would abound more and more. Eph. 4:1 ◆ *beg*
2 For ye know what commandments we gave you by the Lord Jesus.
3 For this is the will of God, *even* your ᵀsanctification, that ye should abstain from fornication: Acts 15:29 ◆ *being made holy*
4 That every one of you should know how to possess his vessel in sanctification and honour; 1 Pet. 3:7
5 Not in the lust of concupiscence, even as the Gentiles which know not God: Rom. 1:26
6 That no *man* go beyond and defraud his brother in *any* matter: because that the Lord *is* the avenger of all such, as we also have forewarned you and testified. Rom. 12:19
7 For God hath not called us unto uncleanness, but unto holiness. 1 Thess. 2:3
8 He therefore that despiseth, despiseth not man, but God, who hath also given unto us his holy Spirit. 1 John 3:24

Love One Another

9 But as touching brotherly love ye need not that I write unto you: for ye yourselves are taught of God to love one another. 1 John 3:11
10 And indeed ye do it toward all the brethren which are in all Macedonia: but we beseech you, brethren, that ye increase more and more;
11 And that ye study to be quiet, and to do your own business, and to work with your own hands, as we commanded you; 1 Pet. 4:15
12 That ye may walk honestly toward them that are without, and *that* ye may have lack of nothing. Mark 4:11; Rom. 13:13; Col. 4:5

Comfort About Christians Who Have Died

13 But I would not have you to be ignorant, brethren, concerning them which are asleep,

that ye sorrow not, even as others which
have no hope. Lev. 19:28; Dan. 12:2; Eph. 2:12
14 For if we believe that Jesus died and rose
again, even so them also which sleep in
Jesus will God bring with him. 1 Thess. 4:13

4:13, 14 Asleep in Jesus

As Paul's epistle was opened and read, great joy and consolation was brought to the church by the words revealing the true state of the dead. Paul showed that those living when Christ should come would not go to meet their Lord in advance of those who had fallen asleep in Jesus. . . .

Now they rejoiced in the knowledge that their believing friends would be raised from the grave to live forever in the kingdom of God. The darkness that had enshrouded the resting place of the dead was dispelled. *AA 258, 259*

15 For this we say unto you by the word of
the Lord, that we which are alive *and* remain
unto the coming of the Lord shall not prevent them which are asleep. 1 Kin. 20:35
4:16, 17† 16 For the Lord himself shall descend from
heaven with a shout, with the voice of
the archangel, and with the trump of God:
and the dead in Christ shall rise first:
17 Then we which are alive *and* remain shall
be caught up together with them in the
clouds, to meet the Lord in the air: and so
shall we ever be with the Lord. John 12:26

Christ's Return See Revelation 1:7.

†**The Millennium** See 1 Corinthians 15:51, 52.

18 Wherefore comfort one another with
these words.

Be Ready for Christ's Return

5 But of the times and the seasons, brethren, ye have no need that I write unto
you. Acts 1:7; 1 Thess. 4:9
2 For yourselves know perfectly that the
day of the Lord so cometh as a thief in the
night. 2 Pet. 3:10
3 For when they shall say, Peace and safety;
then sudden destruction cometh upon them,
as travail upon a woman with child; and they
shall not escape. Luke 21:34-35
4 But ye, brethren, are not in darkness,
that that day should overtake you as a
thief. 1 John 2:8
5 Ye are all the children of light, and the
children of the day: we are not of the night,
nor of darkness. Luke 16:8
6 Therefore let us not sleep, as *do* others;
but let us watch and be sober. Luke 22:46

5:1–6 The Day of the Lord

There are in the world today many who close their eyes to the evidences that Christ has given to warn men of His coming. They seek to quiet all apprehension, while at the same time the signs of the end are rapidly fulfilling. . . . Paul teaches that it is sinful to be indifferent to the signs which are to precede the second coming of Christ. Those guilty of this neglect he calls children of the night and of darkness. *AA 260*

7 For they that sleep sleep in the night; and
they that be drunken are drunken in the
night. Acts 2:15; Rom. 13:13; 2 Pet. 2:13
8 But let us, who are of the day, be sober,
putting on the breastplate of faith and
love; and for an helmet, the hope of salvation. Is. 59:17

Heaven at Last!

1 Thessalonians 4:13–17

All come forth from their graves the same in stature as when they entered the tomb. Adam, who stands among the risen throng, is of lofty height and majestic form, in stature but little below the Son of God. He presents a marked contrast to the people of later generations; in this one respect is shown the great degeneracy of the race. But all arise with the freshness and vigor of eternal youth. . . . [Christ] will change our vile bodies and fashion them like unto His glorious body. The mortal, corruptible form, devoid of comeliness, once polluted with sin, becomes perfect, beautiful, and immortal. All blemishes and deformities are left in the grave. Restored to the tree of life in the long-lost Eden, the redeemed will "grow up" (Malachi 4:2) to the full stature of the race in its primeval glory. The last lingering traces of the curse of sin will be removed, and Christ's faithful ones will appear in "the beauty of the Lord our God," in mind and soul and body reflecting the perfect image of their Lord. Oh, wonderful redemption! long talked of, long hoped for, contemplated with eager anticipation, but never fully understood.

The living righteous are changed "in a moment, in the twinkling of an eye" [1 Corinthians 15:52]. At the voice of God they were glorified; now they are made immortal and with the risen saints are caught up to meet their Lord in the air. Angels "gather together His elect from the four winds, from one end of heaven to the other" [Matthew 24:31]. Little children are borne by holy angels to their mothers' arms. Friends long separated by death are united, nevermore to part, and with songs of gladness ascend together to the City of God. *GC 644, 645*

9 For God hath not appointed us to wrath, but to obtain salvation by our Lord Jesus Christ, 1 Thess. 1:10
10 Who died for us, that, whether we wake or sleep, we should live together with him.
11 Wherefore comfort yourselves together, and edify one another, even as also ye do. Eph. 4:29

Honor Leaders

12 And we [T]beseech you, brethren, to know them which labour among you, and are over you in the Lord, and admonish you; 1 Cor. 16:16, 18; Heb. 13:17 ♦ *beg*
13 And to esteem them very highly in love for their work's sake. *And* be at peace among yourselves. Mark 9:50
14 Now we exhort you, brethren, warn them that are unruly, comfort the feeble-minded, support the weak, be patient toward all *men*. Rom. 14:1
15 See that none render evil for evil unto any *man*; but ever follow that which is good, both among yourselves, and to all *men*. Gal. 6:10

Some Practical Precepts

16 Rejoice evermore. Phil. 4:4

17 Pray without ceasing. Eph. 6:18
18 In every thing give thanks: for this is the will of God in Christ Jesus concerning you. Eph. 5:20; Heb. 13:15

> Christian Behavior See 1 Timothy 5:8.

19 Quench not the Spirit. 1 Cor. 14:30; Eph. 4:30
20 Despise not prophesyings. 1 Cor. 11:4
21 Prove all things; hold fast that which is good. Luke 12:57; Acts 17:11; 1 John 4:1

> Gift of Prophecy See 2 Chronicles 20:20.

22 Abstain from all appearance of evil.

Paul's Farewell

23 And the very God of peace [T]sanctify you wholly; and *I pray God* your whole spirit and soul and body be preserved blameless unto the coming of our Lord Jesus Christ. Rom. 15:33; Heb. 4:12 ♦ *make you holy*
24 Faithful *is* he that calleth you, who also will do *it*. 1 Cor. 1:9; 1 Thess. 2:12; 2 Thess. 3:3
25 Brethren, pray for us.
26 Greet all the brethren with an holy kiss.
27 I charge you by the Lord that this epistle be read unto all the holy brethren. Col. 4:16
28 The grace of our Lord Jesus Christ *be* with you. Amen. Rom. 16:20; 2 Thess. 3:18

5:17, 18

5:20, 21

THESSALONIANS

Paul wrote a sequel to his first letter to the believers in Thessalonica to clarify his teaching of the Second Advent of Jesus Christ. The Thessalonian church had misunderstood Paul's teaching regarding the day of the Lord. Thinking God's judgment had already begun, they began to fall prey to false teaching. Some quit their jobs, assuming the end of the world was at hand. Paul wants to rectify any misconceptions and get the believers back on track.

Dates

Second Thessalonians was written in late A.D. 51 or early A.D. 52, while Paul remained in Corinth with Silas (Silvanus—1:1) and Timothy (Timotheus—1:1; see also Acts 18:5). Paul had established the church in Thessalonica, but had to leave quickly because of persecution (see Acts 17:1–9). The bearer of the first letter—1 Thessalonians—may have given Paul an update on the new developments occurring at the church there, thus prompting Paul to write this follow-up letter.

Author

Externally, the evidence regarding Paul's authorship is stronger in this epistle than in his first letter to the believers at Thessalonica. Internally, Paul's claims of authorship in 1:1 and 3:17 are supported by the vocabulary, style, and doctrinal content that are congruent with Paul's other writings.

In the writing of this epistle, we see Paul's character reflected. In his composition, his brotherly love for the new believers (2:13–17), the acclamation of their faith (1:3–5), loving counsel (3:6), and manner in which one should work (3:12) all give evidence as to his authorship.

Meaning of the Name

Paul's second letter had the title *Pros Thessalonikeis B* or "to the Thessalonians II."

Christ in 2 Thessalonians

The return of Christ is the predominant doctrine in the New Testament, and is mentioned more times (318) than any other doctrine. Second Thessalonians is certainly no exception. While 1 Thessalonians focuses on the external framework of Christ's second coming, 2 Thessalonians centers on internal preparation to meet our almighty Maker. Most of the first two chapters deal with this subject. While Christ's return is the joyful hope of believers, it offers terrifying implications for unbelievers (see 1:6–10; 2:8–12).

Overview

The readers of 1 Thessalonians misunderstood Paul's teaching about the return of Christ. Their misunderstanding was due in large part to false teachers who interpreted Paul's words to indicate that Jesus would return within their lifetime. As a result, many of the believers stopped working and were simply waiting for the Lord to suddenly appear. Paul wanted to set the record straight.

Second Thessalonians can be divided into three sections:

(1) 2 *Thessalonians 1, Commendation:* As he did in the first letter, Paul commends the faith of the Thessalonian believers, particularly their perseverance in the face of persecution (1:1–10).

(2) 2 *Thessalonians 2, Clarification:* Here Paul highlights some of the events that will occur before Jesus returns, namely, the arrival of "son of perdition" (2:3), who will lead many astray by miraculous acts fueled by the power of Satan (2:3–12).

(3) 2 *Thessalonians 3, Exhortation:* In this section, Paul addresses the issue of idleness (3:6–15). As the believers eagerly anticipated the return of their Savior, Paul explained that they were to labor for the gospel rather than to lazily wile away their time—thus becoming a burden to others.

KEY PEOPLE:
Paul, Timothy, Silas, the believers at Thessalonica

KEY THEME:
The Second Advent of Christ

KEY PHRASE:
The Day of the Lord refers to Jesus' return. The Thessalonians had misinterpreted Paul's previous teaching, believing the Second Advent of Christ would soon occur. Paul clarified his teaching and exhorted his reader's to follow his example by supporting themselves. Those who failed to follow his instructions were to be disciplined.

KEY VERSES:
"That ye be not soon shaken in mind, or be troubled, neither by spirit, nor by word, nor by letter as from us, as that the day of Christ is at hand. Let no man deceive you by any means: for that day shall not come, except there come a falling away first, and that man of sin be revealed, the son of perdition" (2 Thessalonians 2:2, 3).

KEY CHAPTER:
2 Thessalonians 2, for it corrected the misunderstanding that the day of the Lord—the time of judgment—had already come upon the Thessalonian church. Paul outlined the specific events that would precede that day. Those events had not yet occurred.

Paul's Greeting

1 Paul, and Silvanus, and Timotheus, unto the church of the Thessalonians in God our Father and the Lord Jesus Christ: 2 Cor. 1:19
2 Grace unto you, and peace, from God our Father and the Lord Jesus Christ.   Rom. 1:7

Paul's Prayer for the Thessalonians

3 We are bound to thank God always for you, brethren, as it is meet, because that your faith groweth exceedingly, and the charity of every one of you all toward each other aboundeth;
4 So that we ourselves glory in you in the churches of God for your patience and faith in all your persecutions and tribulations that ye endure: 2 Cor. 7:14; 1 Thess. 2:14, 19
5 *Which is* a ᵀmanifest token of the righteous judgment of God, that ye may be counted worthy of the kingdom of God, for which ye also suffer: Luke 20:35; Acts 14:22 ◆ *known*
6 Seeing *it is* a righteous thing with God to ᵀrecompense tribulation to them that trouble you;   Rev. 6:10 ◆ *repay*
7 And to you who are troubled rest with us, when the Lord Jesus shall be revealed from heaven with his mighty angels,   Rev. 14:13
8 In flaming fire taking vengeance on them that know not God, and that obey not the gospel of our Lord Jesus Christ: Matt. 25:41
9 Who shall be punished with everlasting destruction from the presence of the Lord, and from the glory of his power; Matt. 25:41; Phil. 3:19

> The Millennium See Revelation 20:2, 3.

---

10 When he shall come to be glorified in his saints, and to be admired in all them that believe (because our testimony among you was believed) in that day.   Ps. 89:7; Is. 49:3; John 17:10

1:10 Heaven in Their Hearts

To His faithful followers Christ has been a daily companion and familiar friend. They have lived in close contact, in constant communion with God. . . . In them the light of the knowledge of the glory of God in the face of Jesus Christ has been reflected. Now they rejoice in the undimmed rays of the brightness and glory of the King in His majesty. They are prepared for the communion of heaven; for they have heaven in their hearts. *COL 421*

---

11 Wherefore also we pray always for you, that our God would count you worthy of *this* calling, and fulfil all the good pleasure of *his* goodness, and the work of faith with power: 1 Thess. 1:3; 2 Thess. 1:5
12 That the name of our Lord Jesus Christ may be glorified in you, and ye in him, according to the grace of our God and the Lord Jesus Christ.

Do Not Be Deceived

2 Now we beseech you, brethren, by the coming of our Lord Jesus Christ, and *by* our gathering together unto him,   Mark 13:27
2 That ye be not soon shaken in mind, or be troubled, neither by spirit, nor by word, nor by letter as from us, as that the day of Christ is at hand.   Mark 13:7
3 Let no man deceive you by any means: for *that day shall not come*, except there come a falling away first, and that man of sin be revealed, the son of perdition; Dan. 7:25; John 17:12; Eph. 5:6
4 Who opposeth and exalteth himself above all that is called God, or that is worshipped; so that he as God sitteth in the temple of God, shewing himself that he is God.   Is. 14:13-14
5 Remember ye not, that, when I was yet with you, I told you these things?
6 And now ye know what withholdeth that he might be revealed in his time.
7 For the mystery of iniquity doth already work: only he who now letteth *will let*, until he be taken out of the way.   Rev. 17:5
8 And then shall that Wicked be revealed, whom the Lord shall consume with the spirit of his mouth, and shall destroy with the brightness of his coming: Is. 11:4; Rev. 19:15
9 *Even him*, whose coming is after the working of Satan with all power and signs and lying wonders,   Matt. 24:24; Rev. 18:23; 19:20
10 And with all deceivableness of unrighteousness in them that perish; because they received not the love of the truth, that they might be saved.   1 Cor. 1:18
11 And for this cause God shall send them strong delusion, that they should believe a lie:

2:11 Rejection Leads to Withdrawal

Men cannot with impunity reject the warnings that God in mercy sends them. From those who persist in turning from these warnings, God withdraws His Spirit, leaving them to the deceptions that they love. *AA 266*

---

12 That they all might be ᵀdamned who believed not the truth, but had pleasure in unrighteousness.   Rom. 1:32; 2:8 ◆ *condemned*
13 But we are bound to give thanks alway to God for you, brethren beloved of the Lord, because God hath from the beginning chosen you to salvation through ᵀsanctification of the Spirit and belief of the truth: 1 Thess. 1:4 ◆ *being made holy*
14 Whereunto he called you by our gospel, to the obtaining of the glory of our Lord Jesus Christ.   1 Thess. 1:5; 2:12; 1 Pet. 5:10
15 Therefore, brethren, stand fast, and hold the traditions which ye have been taught, whether by word, or our epistle. 1 Cor. 11:2; 16:13
16 Now our Lord Jesus Christ himself, and God, even our Father, which hath loved us,

and hath given *us* everlasting consolation and good hope through grace, John 3:16; Rev. 1:5

17 Comfort your hearts, and stablish you in every good word and work. 1 Thess. 3:2, 13

2:15–17 No Immediate Deliverance

Thus Paul outlined the baleful work of that power of evil which was to continue through long centuries of darkness and persecution before the second coming of Christ. The Thessalonian believers had hoped for immediate deliverance; now they were admonished to take up bravely and in the fear of God the work before them. *AA 266, 267*

Final Instructions

3 Finally, brethren, pray for us, that the word of the Lord may have *free* course, and be glorified, even as *it is* with you:

2 And that we may be delivered from unreasonable and wicked men: for all *men* have not faith. Deut. 32:20; Rom. 15:31

3 But the Lord is faithful, who shall stablish you, and keep *you* from evil. Matt. 6:13; John 17:15

4 And we have confidence in the Lord touching you, that ye both do and will do the things which we command you. 2 Cor. 2:3; 1 Thess. 4:10

5 And the Lord direct your hearts into the love of God, and into the patient waiting for Christ. 1 Chr. 29:18

6 Now we command you, brethren, in the name of our Lord Jesus Christ, that ye withdraw yourselves from every brother that walketh disorderly, and not after the tradition which he received of us. Rom. 16:17; 1 Cor. 5:4

7 For yourselves know how ye ought to follow us: for we behaved not ourselves disorderly among you; 1 Cor. 4:16

8 Neither did we eat any man's bread for ᵀnought; but ᵀwrought with labour and travail night and day, that we might not be chargeable to any of you: Acts 18:3 ◆ *nothing* ◆ *worked*

9 Not because we have not power, but to make ourselves an ᵀensample unto you to follow us. 1 Cor. 9:4-14 ◆ *example*

10 For even when we were with you, this we commanded you, that if any would not work, neither should he eat. Gen. 3:19; Prov. 13:4

3:8–10 Fanaticism and Extreme Views

In every age Satan has sought to impair the efforts of God's servants by introducing into the church a spirit of fanaticism. . . . Misguided souls have taught that the attainment of true holiness carries the mind above all earthly thoughts and leads men to refrain wholly from labor. Others . . . have taught that it is a sin to work . . . but should devote their lives wholly to spiritual things. The teaching and example of the apostle Paul are a rebuke to such extreme views. *AA 348*

11 For we hear that there are some which walk among you disorderly, working not at all, but are busybodies. 1 Tim. 5:13; 1 Pet. 4:15

12 Now them that are such we command and exhort by our Lord Jesus Christ, that with quietness they work, and eat their own bread.

13 But ye, brethren, be not weary in well doing. 2 Cor. 4:1

14 And if any man obey not our word by this epistle, note that man, and have no company with him, that he may be ashamed. 2 Thess. 3:6

15 Yet count *him* not as an enemy, but admonish *him* as a brother. Matt. 18:15; Gal. 6:1; 1 Thess. 5:14

Paul's Blessing

16 Now the Lord of peace himself give you peace always by all means. The Lord *be* with you all. Num. 6:26; Ruth 2:4; Rom. 15:33

17 The salutation of Paul with mine own hand, which is the token in every epistle: so I write. 1 Cor. 16:21

18 The grace of our Lord Jesus Christ *be* with you all. Amen. Rom. 16:20

Paul, on the Second Coming

2 Thessalonians 3

The instruction that Paul sent the Thessalonians in his first epistle regarding the second coming of Christ, was in perfect harmony with his former teaching. Yet his words were misapprehended by some of the Thessalonian brethren. They understood him to express the hope that he himself would live to witness the Saviour's advent. This belief served to increase their enthusiasm and excitement. Those who had previously neglected their responsibilities and duties, now became more persistent in urging their erroneous views.

In his second letter Paul sought to correct their misunderstanding of his teaching and to set before them his true position. He again expressed his confidence in their integrity, and his gratitude that their faith was strong, and that their love abounded for one another and for the cause of their Master. He told them that he presented them to other churches as an example of the patient, persevering faith that bravely withstands persecution and tribulation, and he carried their minds forward to the time of the second coming of Christ, when the people of God shall rest from all their cares and perplexities. *AA 264*

THE FIRST EPISTLE OF PAUL THE APOSTLE TO

TIMOTHY

Paul writes as a father and mentor to Timothy, a young pastor left behind by Paul in Ephesus to tend the growing number of believers there. This first of two epistles to Timothy reads as a checklist of advice from an aged and experienced apostle. Paul instructs his charge to be watchful of false teachers and those only seeking after profit. He reminds Timothy to not let his youth get in the way of his mission, and to conduct himself as a bearer of the Gospel's truth.

Timothy has several challenges to deal with: false doctrines to be expunged, public worship to be protected, and experienced leadership to be recruited. In all things, Paul reminds Timothy to put God's virtues first: righteousness, godliness, faith, love, perseverance, and gentleness.

Dates

The events referred to in the Pastoral Epistles take place after the Book of Acts, leaving the exact dates of Paul's authorship uncertain. However, it is possible to reconstruct a plausible sequence of events from the writings themselves.

We know that Paul was released from his prison in Rome (Acts 28). His Jewish accusers may have chosen to avoid appearing before Caesar, in which case Paul would likely have been released by default. As Paul promised the Philippians (2:19–23), he sent Timothy to Philippi to give them the good news. Paul went on to Ephesus, allaying the fears of the church members there that they would no longer see him (Acts 20:38). From there, Paul traveled to other churches in Asia, including Colosse (see Philemon 22).

Timothy left Philippi and joined Paul at Ephesus where Paul told him to remain (1 Timothy 1:3) while Paul continued on to Macedonia. Paul likely wrote 1 Timothy at Philippi in Macedonia, when he saw he would be delayed there (3:14, 15).

Author

Paul is recognized as the author of the Pastoral Epistles—1 Timothy, 2 Timothy, and Titus. They are called "pastoral" because Paul wrote to Timothy and Titus, men with pastoral oversight over their respective churches. Paul's authorship of the Pastoral Epistles, however, has been challenged more than any other books attributed to him, an ongoing battle since the early nineteenth century.

One of the reasons that scholars reject Paul's authorship of the Pastoral Epistles is that the word choices are quite atypical of his writing. The diversity in vocabulary is more varied in these letters than in any of Paul's other writings. During his ministry, Paul spends a good deal of time traveling, teaching, giving counsel, and planting churches, so naturally his language skills grow with his experience. Also, Paul has a propensity to use scribes, and those he employs to write these letters may well have exercised some liberty in word choice.

In addition evidence outside the Bible clearly supports Paul's authorship, with only Romans and 1 Corinthians having better extra-biblical support. Polycarp and Clement of Rome, both postapostolic church leaders, allude to the epistles as written by Paul. Irenaeus, Tertullian, Clement of Alexandria, as well as the Muratorian Canon identify Paul as the author of the Pastoral Epistles. Also, the fact that these letters reference historical details outside the context of the book of Acts indicates that they occur following Paul's imprisonment in Rome (Acts 28).

Meaning of the Name

Timothy is translated "Honoring God" or "Honored by God," a name presumably given him by his mother, Eunice. The Greek title for this book is *Pros Timotheon A*, or "to Timothy I."

Christ in 1 Timothy

Jesus is the reason for all the dangers to which Paul and his friends were exposed. Paul reminded Timothy that Jesus "came into the world to save sinners" (1:15) and "gave himself a ransom for all" (2:6) as "the Saviour of all men, specially of those that believe" (4:10). Paul describes Jesus as the "one mediator between God and men" (2:5) and declares that Jesus was "manifest in the flesh, justified in the Spirit, seen of angels, preached unto the

Gentiles, believed on in the world, received up into glory" (3:16). Jesus is the source of all spiritual strength, faith, and love (1:12–14).

The Pastoral Epistles are Paul's last three recorded letters, written near the end of his long and remarkable life. The letters are addressed solely to Timothy and Titus, respectively, the only letters that Paul wrote to individuals. Some would include Philemon in that grouping, but Paul included multiple recipients in that epistle. The epistles to Timothy and Titus were meant to encourage them in their ministry of building up the churches of Ephesus and Crete.

In 1 Timothy, Paul writes to the young pastor while he is at the Ephesian church. His writing is largely instructive, so he counsels Timothy be used of God in a pleasing manner and lead the church to which God has called him. Paul then delivers a most somber responsibility—to preach the Word wholeheartedly, stand firm on its principles, and uphold its doctrine. In this letter Paul gathers together a well developed plan to lead and organize the church.

Paul seems to have felt the closeness of a father to Timothy, more so than any of his other colleagues. However, Timothy has a gentleness of spirit, and Paul thinks that he needs to be more assertive, hence the letter. He lovingly encourages Timothy to be more zealous in his management style. The close bond between the two accounts for the open approach Paul takes in counseling Timothy. Paul's direction to his friend can be categorized into the following points:

(1) *1 Timothy 1, Recognizing False Teaching:* As he begins to warn Timothy about the dangers of false doctrine, Paul contrasts false doctrine with sound doctrine. He also instructs Timothy to stand firm and rebuke the custodians of the false doctrines as necessary.

(2) *1 Timothy 2—3, Conducting Public Worship:* Paul provides advice on the proper conduct in a worship setting as well as tips on the selection of responsible leaders.

(3) *1 Timothy 4, Combating False Teaching:* Paul returns to the subject of false teachers by painting a clearer picture of the actions of these teachers (4:1–3). Godliness is a marked contrast to such behavior (4:6–10). Paul then urges Timothy to continue in his call—preaching and teaching (4:11–16). Throughout this chapter, Paul furnishes his young colleague with practical suggestions on doctrinal studies, to shun conjecture and gossip and above all, to set a godly example.

(4) *1 Timothy 5, Administering Church Discipline:* In this section, Paul gives advice on the proper way to rebuke various members of the church while remaining pure and impartial. He also gives his counsel on church administration among the aged as well as the youthful members, widows and elected leaders.

(5) *1 Timothy 6, Dealing with Miscellaneous Individuals:* Before giving his final charge to Timothy (6:20, 21), Paul dispenses his final counsel concerning Christian slaves, teachers of false doctrine, and the wealthy Christians. Also, Paul admonishes Timothy that he must set an example for the people to whom he ministers (6:11–16).

Unlocking 1 Timothy

KEY PEOPLE:
Paul, Timothy, Zenas, Apollos, Artemas, Tychicus

KEY EVENTS:
Paul leaves Timothy in Ephesus; Paul's instructions to Timothy

KEY WORD:
Leadership, because 1 Timothy is Paul's manual for leadership. Paul exhorts Timothy to be an example to others, exercise the gifts God has given him, and "fight the good fight of faith" (6:12). He provides wise counsel for choosing responsible leaders.

KEY VERSES:
"If I tarry long, that thou mayest know how thou oughtest to behave thyself in the house of God, which is the church of the living God, the pillar and ground of the truth. And without controversy great is the mystery of godliness: God was manifest in the flesh, justified in the Spirit, seen of angels, preached unto the Gentiles, believed on in the world, received up into glory" (1 Timothy 3:15, 16).

🌼 KEY CHAPTER:

In *1 Timothy 3*, Paul outlines the qualifications for those who would lead in the churches. It is clear that moral character is more important to Paul than worldly success. Paul makes the point that true leadership springs from one's walk with God, rather than the achievements made in this world.

Paul's Greeting

1 Paul, an apostle of Jesus Christ by the commandment of God our Saviour, and Lord Jesus Christ, *which is* our hope;   Luke 1:47
2 Unto Timothy, *my* own son in the faith: Grace, mercy, *and* peace, from God our Father and Jesus Christ our Lord.   Rom. 1:7

Warning about False Teachers

3 As I ᵀbesought thee to abide still at Ephesus, when I went into Macedonia, that thou mightest charge some that they teach no other doctrine,   Gal. 1:6-7 ◆ begged
4 Neither give heed to fables and endless genealogies, which minister questions, rather than godly edifying which is in faith: *so do.*   1 Tim. 4:7; 2 Tim. 4:4; Titus 1:14
5 Now the end of the commandment is charity out of a pure heart, and *of* a good conscience, and *of* faith unfeigned: 2 Tim. 1:5; 2:22
6 From which some having swerved have turned aside unto vain jangling;   Titus 1:10
7 Desiring to be teachers of the law; understanding neither what they say, nor whereof they affirm.   1 Tim. 6:4
8 But we know that the law *is* good, if a man use it lawfully;   Rom. 7:16
9 Knowing this, that the law is not made for a righteous man, but for the lawless and disobedient, for the ungodly and for sinners, for unholy and profane, for murderers of fathers and murderers of mothers, for manslayers,   Gal. 5:23
10 For whoremongers, for them that defile themselves with mankind, for menstealers, for liars, for perjured persons, and if there be any other thing that is contrary to sound doctrine;   Lev. 18:22; 1 Tim. 6:3; 2 Tim. 4:3
11 According to the glorious gospel of the blessed God, which was committed to my trust.   2 Cor. 4:4; Gal. 2:7; 1 Tim. 6:15

God's Mercy to Paul

12 And I thank Christ Jesus our Lord, who hath enabled me, for that he counted me faithful, putting me into the ministry; Acts 9:15
13 Who was before a blasphemer, and a persecutor, and injurious: but I obtained mercy, because I did *it* ignorantly in unbelief. Acts 3:17
14 And the grace of our Lord was exceeding abundant with faith and love which is in Christ Jesus.   2 Tim. 1:13
15 This *is* a faithful saying, and worthy of all acceptation, that Christ Jesus came into the world to save sinners; of whom I am chief.   1 Tim. 3:1; 2 Tim. 2:11; Titus 3:8
16 Howbeit for this cause I obtained mercy, that in me first Jesus Christ might shew forth all longsuffering, for a pattern to them which should hereafter believe on him to life everlasting.   1 Tim. 1:13

1:15 Most Forgiven Are Most to Love

We have been great sinners, but Christ died that we might be forgiven. The merits of His sacrifice are sufficient to present to the Father in our behalf. Those to whom He has forgiven most will love Him most, and will stand nearest to His throne to praise Him for His great love and infinite sacrifice. It is when we most fully comprehend the love of God that we best realize the sinfulness of sin. *SC 36*

---

17 Now unto the King eternal, immortal, invisible, the only wise God, *be* honour and glory for ever and ever. Amen.   Matt. 6:13
18 This charge I commit unto thee, son Timothy, according to the prophecies which went before on thee, that thou by them mightest war a good warfare;   1 Tim. 1:2; 4:14; 2 Tim. 4:7
19 Holding faith, and a good conscience; which some having put away concerning faith have made shipwreck;   1 Tim. 1:5
20 Of whom is Hymenaeus and Alexander; whom I have delivered unto Satan, that they may learn not to blaspheme.   Acts 13:45

Guidelines for the Church

2 I exhort therefore, that, first of all, supplications, prayers, intercessions, *and* giving of thanks, be made for all men;
2 For kings, and *for* all that are in authority; that we may lead a quiet and peaceable life in all godliness and honesty.   Ezra 6:10
3 For this *is* good and acceptable in the sight of God our Saviour;   1 Tim. 1:1
4 Who will have all men to be saved, and to come unto the knowledge of the truth.   Ezek. 18:23, 32; 2 Tim. 2:25
5 For *there is* one God, and one mediator between God and men, the man Christ Jesus;   Deut. 6:4; 1 Cor. 8:6; Gal. 3:20
6 Who gave himself a ransom for all, to be testified in due time.   Matt. 20:28; 1 Cor. 1:6
7 Whereunto I am ordained a preacher, and an apostle, (I speak the truth in Christ, *and* lie not;) a teacher of the Gentiles in faith and ᵀverity.   Acts 9:15; Rom. 9:1; 2 Tim. 1:11 ◆ truth
8 I will therefore that men pray every where, lifting up holy hands, without wrath and doubting.   Ps. 134:2

2:9 Our Money Not Our Own

Money is a trust from God. It is not ours to expend for the gratification of pride or ambition. In the hands of God's children it is food for the hungry, and clothing for the naked. . . . You could bring happiness to many hearts by using wisely the means that is now spent for show. Consider the life of Christ. Study His character, and be partakers with Him in His self-denial. *MH 287*

Guidelines for Women

9 In like manner also, that women adorn themselves in modest apparel, with ᵀshamefacedness and sobriety; not with ᵀbroided hair, or gold, or pearls, or costly ᵀarray; *modesty ◆ braided ◆ clothing*
10 But (which becometh women professing godliness) with good works.

Christian Behavior See 1 Peter 3:3, 4.

11 Let the woman learn in silence with all subjection.
12 But I suffer not a woman to teach, nor to usurp authority over the man, but to be in silence. 1 Cor. 14:34
13 For Adam was first formed, then Eve.
14 And Adam was not deceived, but the woman being deceived was in the ᵀtransgression. *Gen. 3:6; 2 Cor. 11:3 ◆ violation of the law*

2:13, 14 Marital Harmony Disrupted

Eve had been the first in transgression. . . . It was by her solicitation that Adam sinned, and she was now placed in subjection to her husband. Had the principles joined in the law of God been cherished by the fallen race, this sentence, though growing out of the results of sin, would have proved a blessing to them; but man's abuse of the supremacy thus given him has too often rendered the lot of woman very bitter and made her life a burden. *PP 58, 59*

15 Notwithstanding she shall be saved in childbearing, if they continue in faith and charity and holiness with sobriety.

Qualifications for Church Leaders

3 This *is* a true saying, If a man desire the office of a ᵀbishop, he desireth a good work. *Acts 1:20; 20:28; 1 Tim. 1:15 ◆ overseer*
2 A bishop then must be blameless, the husband of one wife, vigilant, sober, of good behaviour, given to hospitality, apt to teach;
3 Not given to wine, no striker, not greedy of filthy lucre; but patient, not a brawler, not ᵀcovetous; *Lev. 10:9; 1 Tim. 3:8; Titus 1:7 ◆ greedy*
4 One that ruleth well his own house, having his children in subjection with all gravity; 1 Tim. 3:12
5 (For if a man know not how to rule his own house, how shall he take care of the church of God?) 1 Tim. 3:15
6 Not a novice, lest being lifted up with pride he fall into the condemnation of the ᵀdevil. *1 Tim. 6:4 ◆ false accuser*
7 Moreover he must have a good report of them which are without; lest he fall into reproach and the snare of the devil. 2 Cor. 8:21
8 Likewise *must* the deacons *be* grave, not doubletongued, not given to much wine, not greedy of filthy lucre; Lev. 10:9; Phil. 1:1; Titus 2:3

9 Holding the mystery of the faith in a pure conscience. 1 Tim. 1:5, 19
10 And let these also first be proved; then let them use the office of a ᵀdeacon, being *found* blameless. 1 Tim. 5:22 ◆ *servant*
11 Even so *must their* wives *be* grave, not slanderers, sober, faithful in all things. 1 Tim. 3:2
12 Let the deacons be the husbands of one wife, ruling their children and their own houses well. 1 Tim. 3:2
13 For they that have used the office of a deacon well purchase to themselves a good degree, and great boldness in the faith which is in Christ Jesus. Matt. 25:21

The Purpose of Paul's Writing

14 These things write I unto thee, hoping to come unto thee shortly:
15 But if I tarry long, that thou mayest know how thou oughtest to behave thyself in the house of God, which is the church of the living God, the pillar and ground of the truth. Matt. 16:16
16 And without controversy great is the mystery of godliness: God was manifest in the flesh, justified in the Spirit, seen of angels, preached unto the Gentiles, believed on in the world, received up into glory. Mark 16:19

3:16 Redemption Our Eternal Study

In eternity we shall learn that which, had we received the enlightenment it was possible to obtain here, would have opened our understanding. The themes of redemption will employ the hearts and minds and tongues of the redeemed through the everlasting ages. They will understand the truths which Christ longed to open to His disciples, but which they did not have faith to grasp. Forever and forever new views of the perfection and glory of Christ will appear. *COL 134*

A Prophecy about the Final Days

4 Now the Spirit speaketh expressly, that in the latter times some shall depart from the faith, giving heed to seducing spirits, and doctrines of devils; John 16:13
2 Speaking lies in hypocrisy; having their conscience seared with a hot iron; Eph. 4:19
3 Forbidding to marry, *and commanding* to abstain from meats, which God hath created to be received with thanksgiving of them which believe and know the truth. Gen. 9:3; Rom. 14:6
4 For every creature of God *is* good, and nothing to be refused, if it be received with thanksgiving: Gen. 1:31
5 For it is ᵀsanctified by the word of God and prayer. *made holy*

Guidelines for Serving Christ

6 If thou put the brethren in remembrance of these things, thou shalt be a good minister of Jesus Christ, nourished up in the words of faith and of good doctrine, whereunto thou hast attained. 1 Tim. 1:10

7 But refuse profane and old wives' fables, and exercise thyself *rather* unto godliness.

8 For bodily exercise profiteth little: but godliness is profitable unto all things, having promise of the life that now is, and of that which is to come. Ps. 37:9; Matt. 6:33; 1 Tim. 6:6

9 This *is* a faithful saying and worthy of all acceptation. 1 Tim. 1:15

10 For therefore we both labour and suffer reproach, because we trust in the living God, who is the Saviour of all men, specially of those that believe. 1 Tim. 2:4

11 These things command and teach. 1 Tim. 5:7

12 Let no man despise thy youth; but be thou an example of the believers, in word, in ᵀconversation, in ᵀcharity, in spirit, in faith, in purity. 2 Tim. 2:22; Titus 2:7; 1 Pet. 5:3 ◆ *conduct* ◆ *selfless love*

13 Till I come, give attendance to reading, to ᵀexhortation, to doctrine. *encouragement*

14 Neglect not the gift that is in thee, which was given thee by prophecy, with the laying on of the hands of the ᵀpresbytery. Acts 6:6; 1 Tim. 1:18; 2 Tim. 1:6 ◆ *group of elders*

15 Meditate upon these things; give thyself wholly to them; that thy profiting may appear to all.

16 Take heed unto thyself, and unto the doctrine; continue in them: for in doing this thou shalt both save thyself, and them that hear thee. Titus 2:7

4:15 Ministers Given Wholly to Their Work

It is God's design that such workers shall be freed from unnecessary anxiety, that they may have full opportunity to obey the injunction of Paul to Timothy, "Meditate upon these things; give thyself wholly to them" (1 Timothy 4:15). While they should be careful to exercise sufficiently to keep mind and body vigorous, yet it is not God's plan that they should be compelled to spend a large part of their time at secular employment. *AA 356*

Guidelines for Dealing with Christians

5 Rebuke not an elder, but intreat *him* as a father; *and* the younger men as brethren;

2 The elder women as mothers; the younger as sisters, with all purity.

3 Honour widows that are widows indeed.

4 But if any widow have children or nephews, let them learn first to shew piety at home, and to requite their parents: for that is good and acceptable before God. Gen. 45:10-11; Matt. 15:4-6

5 Now she that is a widow indeed, and desolate, trusteth in God, and continueth in supplications and prayers night and day. Luke 2:37

6 But she that liveth in pleasure is dead while she liveth. Luke 15:24

7 And these things give in charge, that they may be blameless. 1 Tim. 4:11

8 But if any provide not for his own, and specially for those of his own house, he hath denied the faith, and is worse than an ᵀinfidel. Gal. 6:10; 2 Tim. 3:5; Titus 1:16 ◆ *unbeliever*

Christian Behavior See 1 Timothy 6:6–10.

9 Let not a widow be taken into the number under ᵀthreescore years old, having been the wife of one man, 1 Tim. 3:2 ◆ *sixty*

Let Not Satan Deceive You

1 Timothy 4:1, 2

The promise of obedience [some people] appear to fulfill when this involves no sacrifice; but when self-denial and self-sacrifice are required, when they see the cross to be lifted, they draw back. Thus the conviction of duty wears away, and known transgression of God's commandments becomes habit. The ear may hear God's word, but the spiritual perceptive powers have departed. The heart is hardened, the conscience seared.

Do not think that because you do not manifest decided hostility to Christ you are doing Him service. We thus deceive our own souls. . . .

Satan uses the listless, sleepy indolence of professed Christians to strengthen his forces and win souls to his side. Many, who think that though they are doing no actual work for Christ, they are yet on His side, are enabling the enemy to pre-occupy ground and gain advantages. By their failure to be diligent workers for the Master, by leaving duties undone and words unspoken, they have allowed Satan to gain control of souls who might have been won for Christ.

We can never be saved in indolence and inactivity. There is no such thing as a truly converted person living a helpless, useless life. It is not possible for us to drift into heaven. No sluggard can enter there. If we do not strive to gain an entrance into the kingdom, if we do not seek earnestly to learn what constitutes its laws, we are not fitted for a part in it. Those who refuse to co-operate with God on earth would not co-operate with Him in heaven. It would not be safe to take them to heaven. *COL 279, 280*

10 Well reported of for good works; if she have brought up children, if she have lodged strangers, if she have washed the saints' feet, if she have relieved the afflicted, if she have diligently followed every good work. *Luke 7:44; 1 Tim. 6:18; Titus 3:8*

11 But the younger widows refuse: for when they have begun to ᵀwax wanton against Christ, they will marry; *1 Tim. 5:14 ♦ become*

12 Having ᵀdamnation, because they have cast off their first faith. *condemnation*

13 And withal they learn *to be* idle, wandering about from house to house; and not only idle, but tattlers also and busybodies, speaking things which they ought not. *Prov. 20:19*

14 I will therefore that the younger women marry, bear children, guide the house, give none occasion to the adversary to speak reproachfully. *1 Tim. 4:3; 6:1; Titus 2:5*

15 For some are already turned aside after Satan.

16 If any man or woman that believeth have widows, let them relieve them, and let not the church be ᵀcharged; that it may relieve them that are widows indeed. *1 Tim. 5:3-5 ♦ burdened*

Guidelines for the Elders

17 Let the elders that rule well be counted worthy of double honour, especially they who labour in the word and doctrine. *Rom. 12:8*

> **5:17 Honor Those Whom God Honors**
>
> He who has placed upon men the heavy responsibility of leaders and teachers of His people will hold the people accountable for the manner in which they treat His servants. We are to honor those whom God has honored. The judgment visited upon Miriam [see Numbers 12] should be a rebuke to all who yield to jealousy, and murmur against those upon whom God lays the burden of His work. *PP 386*

18 For the scripture saith, Thou shalt not muzzle the ox that treadeth out the corn. And, The labourer *is* worthy of his reward.

19 Against an elder receive not an accusation, but before two or three witnesses. *Deut. 19:15*

20 Them that sin rebuke before all, that others also may fear. *Deut. 13:11*

21 I charge *thee* before God, and the Lord Jesus Christ, and the elect angels, that thou observe these things without preferring one before another, doing nothing by partiality. *1 Tim. 6:13; 2 Tim. 2:14; 4:1*

22 Lay hands suddenly on no man, neither be partaker of other men's sins: keep thyself pure. *Acts 6:6*

23 Drink no longer water, but use a little wine for thy stomach's sake and thine often infirmities. *1 Tim. 3:8*

24 Some men's sins are open beforehand, going before to judgment; and some *men* they follow after.

25 Likewise also the good works *of some* are ᵀmanifest beforehand; and they that are otherwise cannot be hid. *made known*

> **5:24, 25 Do Not Excuse or Conceal Sins**
>
> Satan leads many to believe that God will overlook their unfaithfulness in the minor affairs of life; but the Lord shows in His dealings with Jacob that He will in no wise sanction or tolerate evil. All who endeavor to excuse or conceal their sins, and permit them to remain upon the books of heaven, unconfessed and unforgiven, will be overcome by Satan. *GC 620*

Guidelines for Godly Living

6 Let as many servants as are under the yoke count their own masters worthy of all honour, that the name of God and *his* doctrine be not blasphemed. *Is. 52:5; Rom. 2:24*

2 And they that have believing masters, let them not despise *them*, because they are brethren; but rather do *them* service, because they are faithful and beloved, partakers of the benefit. These things teach and exhort.

3 If any man teach otherwise, and consent not to wholesome words, *even* the words of our Lord Jesus Christ, and to the doctrine which is according to godliness; *1 Tim. 1:3, 10; Titus 1:1*

4 He is proud, knowing nothing, but doting about questions and strifes of words, whereof cometh envy, strife, railings, evil ᵀsurmisings, *1 Tim. 1:4 ♦ suspicions*

5 Perverse disputings of men of corrupt minds, and destitute of the truth, supposing that gain is godliness: from such withdraw thyself.

Godliness Is Great Gain

6 But godliness with contentment is great gain. *Ps. 37:16; 1 Tim. 4:8; Heb. 13:5*

7 For we brought nothing into *this* world, *and it is* certain we can carry nothing out. *Job 1:21*

8 And having food and ᵀraiment let us be therewith content. *Gen. 28:20 ♦ clothing*

9 But they that will be rich fall into temptation and a snare, and *into* many foolish and hurtful lusts, which drown men in destruction and perdition. *Prov. 15:27; Matt. 13:22*

10 For the love of money is the root of all evil: which while some coveted after, they have erred from the faith, and pierced themselves through with many sorrows. *Deut. 16:19*

> **Christian Behavior** See Romans 8:5.

11 But thou, O man of God, flee these things; and follow after righteousness, godliness, faith, love, patience, meekness. *2 Tim. 2:22; 3:17*

12 Fight the good fight of faith, lay hold on eternal life, whereunto thou art also called, and hast professed a good profession before many witnesses. 1 Cor. 9:25-26; Col. 3:15; 1 Tim. 1:18
13 I give thee charge in the sight of God, who quickeneth all things, and *before* Christ Jesus, who before Pontius Pilate witnessed a good confession; Matt. 27:11; John 5:21; 1 Tim. 5:21
14 That thou keep *this* commandment without spot, unrebukeable, until the appearing of our Lord Jesus Christ:
15 Which in his times he shall shew, *who is* the blessed and only Potentate, the King of kings, and Lord of lords; 1 Tim. 1:11, 17; Rev. 17:14

6:15, 16

6:16 In the Light of the Cross

When we study the divine character in the light of the cross we see mercy, tenderness, and forgiveness blended with equity and justice. We see in the midst of the throne One bearing in hands and feet and side the marks of the suffering endured to reconcile man to God. We see a Father, infinite, dwelling in light unapproachable, yet receiving us to Himself through the merits of His Son. *AA 333*

16 Who only hath immortality, dwelling in the light which no man can approach unto; whom no man hath seen, nor can see: to whom *be* honour and power everlasting. Amen. Ps. 104:2; John 1:18; 1 Tim. 1:17

After Death See Genesis 2:7.

17 Charge them that are rich in this world, that they be not highminded, nor trust in uncertain riches, but in the living God, who giveth us richly all things to enjoy;
18 That they do good, that they be rich in good works, ready to distribute, willing to communicate; Rom. 12:8
19 Laying up in store for themselves a good foundation against the time to come, that they may lay hold on eternal life. Luke 16:9
20 O Timothy, keep that which is committed to thy trust, avoiding profane *and* vain babblings, and oppositions of science falsely so called: Col. 2:8
21 Which some professing have erred concerning the faith. Grace *be* with thee. Amen. 2 Tim. 2:18

Selfish Use of Wealth

1 Timothy 6:9, 10, 17–19

The Bible condemns no man for being rich, if he has acquired his riches honestly. Not money, but the love of money, is the root of all evil. It is God who gives men power to get wealth; and in the hands of him who acts as God's steward, using his means unselfishly, wealth is a blessing, both to its possessor and to the world. But many, absorbed in their interest in worldly treasures, become insensible to the claims of God and the needs of their fellow men. They regard their wealth as a means of glorifying themselves. They add house to house, and land to land; they fill their homes with luxuries, while all about them are human beings in misery and crime, in disease and death. Those who thus give their lives to self-serving are developing in themselves, not the attributes of God, but the attributes of the wicked one.

These men are in need of the gospel. They need to have their eyes turned from the vanity of material things to behold the preciousness of the enduring riches. They need to learn the joy of giving, the blessedness of being co-workers with God. *MH 212, 213*

THE SECOND EPISTLE OF PAUL THE APOSTLE TO

TIMOTHY

It is a hard thing when a friend is wrongfully put in prison, so it must have been hard for Timothy to read this second letter from Paul. Still, Paul's words are full of encouragement and instruction, despite the bleakness of the days ahead. He tells Timothy of his continual prayers and love for him, then he reminds Timothy of his godly heritage and his responsibilities.

Paul charges Timothy to remain steadfast in the faith, and that only those who persevere in the things of God will be rewarded by God. There is a warning also of those who would attack Timothy for his teachings, men who would abandon the truth of God's word to seek false doctrines with "itching ears" (4:3). If ever a man had an example to follow, it was Timothy, for Paul remained true to the end despite the knowledge that he would die for what he believed.

Dates

Christianity became an illegal religion when Nero placed blame on the Christians for burning Rome in A.D. 64, giving him the scapegoat he needed to deflect the wrongdoing from himself. Severe persecution awaited anyone who professed the name of Jesus. Paul had been away during Nero's fire, presumably in Spain, and when he returned, he found his enemies in a position of absolute power. They had Paul arrested, and with the penalty of death looming for any Christian, all his supporters remained silent then (1:15), and at Paul's hearing before the Imperial Court (4:16).

Now alone (4:10, 11), Paul finds his situation much more grave than with his first imprisonment at Rome (Acts 28:16–31). Before, he had been under house arrest, where visitors could come and go, and he had the hope of release. Now, the cold walls of a Roman cell surrounded him (2 Timothy 4:13). He was accused of being "an evildoer" (2:9), without hope of freedom despite his successful initial defense (4:6–8, 17, 18).

There, in his cell, Paul wrote this second epistle to Timothy in A.D. 66, hoping that Timothy would reach him by winter (4:21). Timothy likely received Paul's letter at the hands of Tychicus at Ephesus (4:12; see 1:18; 4:19). On the path to Rome, Timothy would have traveled through Troas (4:13) as well as Macedonia. Priscilla and Aquila (4:19) would likely have escaped from Rome (Romans 16:3) to Ephesus after Nero burned it and started the persecutions.

Author

Paul is considered the author of all three Pastoral Letters (1 and 2 Timothy and Titus; see "Author" section of 1 Timothy).

Timothy is named more often by Paul in his letters than anyone else (2 Corinthians; Philippians; Colossians; 1 and 2 Thessalonians; 1 and 2 Timothy; Philemon). Timothy was youthful (1 Timothy 4:12), sickly (5:23), and timid (2 Timothy 1:7). We know that his father was Greek (Acts 16:1) and his mother, Eunice, was Jewish. She and his grandmother, Lois, raised him to know the Hebrew Scriptures (2 Timothy 1:5; 3:15).

It appears that Paul converted Timothy (1 Corinthians 4:17; 1 Timothy 1:2; 2 Timothy 1:2) during his first missionary journey at the town of Lystra (a town in modern-day Turkey; Acts 14:8–20).

Timothy was ordained (1 Timothy 4:14; 2 Timothy 1:6) and served in the role of assistant to Paul in Troas, Berea, Thessalonica, and Corinth (Acts 16—18; 1 Thessalonians 3:1, 2). The young Christian was a gifted teacher who was trustworthy and diligent.

It was during Paul's third missionary journey that Timothy began to serve as his representative, traveling with Paul to Ephesus, Macedonia, and Corinth. He was with Paul when the elder apostle was imprisoned in Rome and Timothy reportedly went to Philippi (Philippians 2:19–23) after Paul's release. Paul left Timothy to supervise matters at Ephesus (1 Timothy 1:3), only writing to him years later when the Romans imprisoned him a second time (2 Timothy 4:9, 21).

Timothy himself was imprisoned and released (Hebrews 13:23), but no reference is made to where the prison was.

Paul's second epistle to Timothy was originally titled *Pros Timotheon B*, or "to Timothy II." When they collected Paul's letters, the "B" was probably the logical means of distinguishing this letter from the previous one.

Christ in 2 Timothy

Again, Paul reminds Timothy that Jesus "was raised from the dead according to my gospel" (2:8). Jesus appeared on earth, where He "abolished death, and hath brought life and immortality to light through the gospel" (1:10). Jesus provides salvation and "eternal glory" (2:10). Anticipating his own death, Paul notes that if believers died with Christ, they will also "live with him" (2:11). All who love Jesus' appearing in the last days will be given a crown of righteousness, like Paul's (4:8).

Overview

Paul, writing from the harshness of a Roman prison cell, knows that this letter will likely be the last communication to his faithful companion. He seeks to challenge and strengthen his spiritual son, Timothy, to remain steadfast in his fulfillment of his God-given task.

Paul calls Timothy a "good soldier of Jesus Christ" (2:3), and indeed the whole of this second epistle has the feeling of a superior officer giving his final commands to a trustworthy junior officer: "stir up" (1:6); "be not thou therefore ashamed" (1:8); "hold fast . . . sound words" (1:13); "be strong" (2:1); "study to shew thyself approved unto God" (2:15); "I charge thee before God" (4:1).

The central message of 2 Timothy is that sure foundation, the Word of God. It can be divided into two sections:

(1) *2 Timothy 1—2, Endure the Current Trials:* Paul urges Timothy to persevere despite the threat of persecution. He reminds Timothy that God has given him, not "the spirit of fear" but one "of power, and of love, and of a sound mind" (1:7). Also, Timothy has the "word of truth" (2:15) to study.

(2) *2 Timothy 3—4, Endure the Future Trials:* In the last two chapters he tells Timothy to be ready to endure through future days of trial. The day will come when apostasy will seem commonplace (3:1–9; 4:3, 4). Persecution, Paul affirms, will occur. Once more Paul reminds Timothy of the Scriptures (3:16, 17) and of his own example (3:10, 11; 4:6–8). The letter concludes with a note of pathos, as Paul mentions that "only Luke is with me" (4:11). The end for Paul was near.

Unlocking 2 Timothy

KEY PEOPLE:
Paul, Timothy, Jesus, Tychicus, Onesiphorus, Priscilla, Aquila, Demas

KEY EVENTS:
Paul's imprisonment; Paul's advice and encouragement to Timothy

KEY WORD:
Endurance is key, because Timothy is facing many problems in Ephesus. Paul calls on him to endure trials for God's holy cause. Paul instructs Timothy on how to handle persecution from secular authorities, as well as disagreements and deception from within the church. Paul speaks as a spiritual father, encouraging Timothy to overcome his timid nature and speak the gospel message with boldness, even if he has to suffer for doing so.

KEY VERSES:
"Thou therefore endure hardness, as a good soldier of Jesus Christ. No man that warreth entangleth himself with the affairs of this life; that he may please him who hath chosen him to be a soldier" (2 Timothy 2:3, 4).

"But continue thou in the things which thou hast learned and hast been assured of, knowing of whom thou hast learned them; and that from a child thou hast known the holy scriptures, which are able to make thee wise unto salvation through faith which is in Christ Jesus. All scripture is given by inspiration of God, and is profitable for doctrine, for reproof, for correction, for instruction in righteousness: that the man of God may be perfect, throughly furnished unto all good works" (2 Timothy 3:14–17).

KEY CHAPTER:

2 Timothy 2 reads like an instruction manual for every pastor and Christian in the ministry. Paul defines an enduring, successful ministry as one that is reproducing (vs. 1, 2), enduring (vs. 3–13), active in studying Scripture (vs. 14–18), and holy (vs. 19–26).

Paul's Greeting

1 Paul, an apostle of Jesus Christ by the will of God, according to the promise of life which is in Christ Jesus,   2 Cor. 1:1; Eph. 3:6
2 To Timothy, *my* dearly beloved son: Grace, mercy, *and* peace, from God the Father and Christ Jesus our Lord.   Rom. 1:7; 1 Tim. 1:2
3 I thank God, whom I serve from *my* forefathers with pure conscience, that without ceasing I have remembrance of thee in my prayers night and day; Acts 23:1; 24:14; Rom. 1:8-9
4 Greatly desiring to see thee, being mindful of thy tears, that I may be filled with joy;   Phil. 1:8; 2 Tim. 4:9, 21
5 When I call to remembrance the unfeigned faith that is in thee, which dwelt first in thy grandmother Lois, and thy mother Eunice; and I am persuaded that in thee also. Ps. 86:16

Paul's Advice for Timothy

6 Wherefore I put thee in remembrance that thou stir up the gift of God, which is in thee by the putting on of my hands.   1 Thess. 5:19
7 For God hath not given us the spirit of fear; but of power, and of love, and of a sound mind.   Luke 24:49; Acts 1:8; Rom. 8:15
8 Be not thou therefore ashamed of the testimony of our Lord, nor of me his prisoner: but be thou partaker of the afflictions of the gospel according to the power of God;   Mark 8:38; Eph. 3:1; 2 Tim. 1:16

1:6–8 Faith Made Strong and Pure

The one great purpose of [Paul's] Christian life had been to serve Him whose name had once filled him with contempt; and from this purpose no opposition or persecution had been able to turn him aside. His faith, made strong by effort and pure by sacrifice, upheld and strengthened him. *AA 500*

---

9 Who hath saved us, and called *us* with an holy calling, not according to our works, but according to his own purpose and grace, which was given us in Christ Jesus before the world began,   Rom. 16:25
10 But is now made ᵀmanifest by the appearing of our Saviour Jesus Christ, who hath abolished death, and hath brought life and immortality to light through the gospel: Rom. 2:7 ◆ *known*
11 Whereunto I am appointed a preacher, and an apostle, and a teacher of the Gentiles.   1 Tim. 2:7
12 For the which cause I also suffer these things: nevertheless I am not ashamed: for I know whom I have believed, and am persuaded that he is able to keep that which I have committed unto him against that day.

1:12 Looking Up to the Throne

Soon the night of trial and suffering would end, and then would dawn the glad morning of peace and perfect day.

The apostle was looking into the great beyond, not with uncertainty or dread, but with joyous hope and longing expectation. As [Paul] stands at the place of martyrdom he sees not the sword of the executioner or the earth so soon to receive his blood; he looks up through the calm blue heaven of that summer day to the throne of the Eternal. *AA 511, 512*

---

13 Hold fast the form of sound words, which thou hast heard of me, in faith and love which is in Christ Jesus.   Rom. 2:20; 1 Tim. 1:14; Titus 1:9
14 That good thing which was committed unto thee keep by the Holy Ghost which dwelleth in us.   Rom. 8:9

News about Paul's Coworkers

15 This thou knowest, that all they which are in Asia be turned away from me; of whom are Phygellus and Hermogenes.   Acts 19:10
16 The Lord give mercy unto the house of Onesiphorus; for he oft refreshed me, and was not ashamed of my chain: Acts 28:20; Eph. 6:20
17 But, when he was in Rome, he sought me out very diligently, and found *me.*
18 The Lord grant unto him that he may find mercy of the Lord in that day: and in how many things he ministered unto me at Ephesus, thou knowest very well. 2 Tim. 1:12

An Exhortation to Perseverance

2 Thou therefore, my son, be strong in the grace that is in Christ Jesus. Eph. 6:10
2 And the things that thou hast heard of me among many witnesses, the same commit thou to faithful men, who shall be able to teach others also.   1 Tim. 1:18
3 Thou therefore endure hardness, as a good soldier of Jesus Christ. 1 Tim. 1:18; 2 Tim. 1:8; 4:5
4 No man that warreth entangleth himself with the affairs of *this* life; that he may please him who hath chosen him to be a soldier.   2 Pet. 2:20
5 And if a man also strive for masteries, *yet* is he not crowned, except he strive lawfully.
6 The ᵀhusbandman that laboureth must be first partaker of the fruits.   *farmer*
7 Consider what I say; and the Lord give thee understanding in all things.
8 Remember that Jesus Christ of the seed of David was raised from the dead according to my gospel: Matt. 1:1; Acts 2:24; Rom. 2:16
9 Wherein I suffer trouble, as an evil doer, *even* unto bonds; but the word of God is not bound.   Phil. 1:7

2:9 Rapid Spread of the Gospel

Rome was at this time the metropolis of the world. The haughty Caesars were giving laws to nearly every nation upon the earth. King and courtier were either ignorant of the humble Nazarene or regarded Him with hatred and derision. And yet in less than two years the gospel found its way from the prisoner's lowly home into the imperial halls. *AA 461, 462*

---

10 Therefore I endure all things for the elect's sakes, that they may also obtain the salvation which is in Christ Jesus with eternal glory.
11 *It is* a faithful saying: For if we be dead with *him*, we shall also live with *him*: Rom. 6:8
12 If we suffer, we shall also reign with *him*: if we deny *him*, he also will deny us: Matt. 10:33
13 If we believe not, *yet* he abideth faithful: he cannot deny himself. Num. 23:19; Rom. 3:3; Titus 1:2
14 Of these things put *them* in remembrance, charging *them* before the Lord that they strive not about words to no profit, *but* to the subverting of the hearers. 1 Tim. 5:21
15 Study to shew thyself approved unto God, a workman that needeth not to be ashamed, rightly dividing the word of truth.
16 But shun profane *and* vain babblings: for they will increase unto more ungodliness.
17 And their word will eat as doth a canker: of whom is Hymenaeus and Philetus;
18 Who concerning the truth have erred, saying that the resurrection is past already; and overthrow the faith of some. 1 Cor. 15:12

The Foundation of the Lord's Work

19 Nevertheless the foundation of God standeth sure, having this seal, The Lord knoweth them that are his. And, Let every one that nameth the name of Christ depart from iniquity. Is. 28:16; Luke 13:27; John 10:14
20 But in a great house there are not only vessels of gold and of silver, but also of wood and of earth; and some to honour, and some to dishonour. 1 Tim. 3:15
21 If a man therefore purge himself from these, he shall be a vessel unto honour, sanctified, and meet for the master's use, *and* prepared unto every good work. Is. 52:11; Eph. 2:10

2:21 Power for Today

Those only who are constantly receiving fresh supplies of grace, will have power proportionate to their daily need and their ability to use that power. Instead of looking forward to some future time when, through a special endowment of spiritual power, they will receive a miraculous fitting up for soul winning, they are yielding themselves daily to God, that He may make them vessels meet for His use. *AA 55*

Guidance for God's Ministers

22 Flee also youthful lusts: but follow righteousness, faith, ᵀcharity, peace, with them that call on the Lord out of a pure heart. 1 Tim. 1:5; 4:12; 6:11 ◆ *selfless love*
23 But foolish and unlearned questions avoid, knowing that they do ᵀgender strifes. Titus 3:9 ◆ *breed*
24 And the servant of the Lord must not strive; but be gentle unto all *men*, apt to teach, patient, 1 Thess. 2:7; 1 Tim. 3:2-3; Titus 3:2
25 In meekness instructing those that oppose themselves; if God ᵀperadventure will give them repentance to the acknowledging of the truth; Acts 8:22; Gal. 6:1; 1 Tim. 2:4 ◆ *maybe*
26 And *that* they may recover themselves out of the snare of the ᵀdevil, who are taken captive by him at his will. 1 Tim. 3:7 ◆ *false accuser*

2:26 Greatest Battle Ever Fought

The warfare against self is the greatest battle that was ever fought. The yielding of self, surrendering all to the will of God, requires a struggle; but the soul must submit to God before it can be renewed in holiness. *SC 43*

Paul Warns of Stressful Times

3 This know also, that in the last days perilous times shall come. Ezek. 38:16
2 For men shall be lovers of their own selves, ᵀcovetous, boasters, proud, blasphemers, disobedient to parents, unthankful, unholy, Phil. 2:21 ◆ *greedy*
3 Without natural affection, trucebreakers, false accusers, incontinent, fierce, despisers of those that are good, Rom. 1:31; 1 Tim. 3:11
4 Traitors, heady, highminded, lovers of pleasures more than lovers of God; 1 Tim. 3:6

3:1-5

3:5 Don't Forget the Past!

How often, in our own day, is the love of pleasure disguised by a "form of godliness"! A religion that permits men, while observing the rites of worship, to devote themselves to selfish or sensual gratification, is as pleasing to the multitudes now as in the days of Israel. And there are still pliant Aarons, who, while holding positions of authority in the church, will yield to the desires of the unconsecrated, and thus encourage them in sin. *PP 317*

---

5 Having a form of godliness, but denying the power thereof: from such turn away. 1 Tim. 5:8

Signs of the End See 2 Peter 3:3, 4.

6 For of this sort are they which creep into houses, and lead captive silly women ᵀladen with sins, led away with ᵀdivers lusts, Titus 3:3 ◆ *loaded* ◆ *various*
7 Ever learning, and never able to come to the knowledge of the truth. 1 Tim. 2:4

8 Now as Jannes and Jambres withstood Moses, so do these also resist the truth: men of corrupt minds, reprobate concerning the faith. Ex. 7:11; 1 Tim. 6:5; Titus 1:16

9 But they shall proceed no further: for their folly shall be ᵀmanifest unto all *men*, as theirs also was. Ex. 7:12; 9:11 ◆ *made known*

Teach the Truth

10 But thou hast fully known my doctrine, manner of life, purpose, faith, longsuffering, ᵀcharity, patience, Phil. 2:22 ◆ *selfless love*

11 Persecutions, afflictions, which came unto me at Antioch, at Iconium, at Lystra; what persecutions I endured: but out of *them* all the Lord delivered me. Ps. 34:19

12 Yea, and all that will live godly in Christ Jesus shall suffer persecution. Acts 14:22

3:12 Principle Never Changes

So it will be with all who will live godly in Christ Jesus. Persecution and reproach await all who are imbued with the Spirit of Christ. The character of the persecution changes with the times, but the principle—the spirit that underlies it—is the same that has slain the chosen of the Lord ever since the days of Abel. *AA 576*

---

13 But evil men and seducers shall ᵀwax worse and worse, deceiving, and being deceived. *become*

14 But continue thou in the things which thou hast learned and hast been assured of, knowing of whom thou hast learned *them*;

15 And that from a child thou hast known the holy scriptures, which are able to make thee wise unto salvation through faith which is in Christ Jesus. 2 Tim. 1:5

16 All scripture *is* given by inspiration of God, and *is* profitable for doctrine, for reproof, for correction, for instruction in righteousness:

The Bible See 2 Peter 1:19–21.

(margin: 3:15, 16†)

17 That the man of God may be perfect, throughly furnished unto all good works.

3:16 Truth Conveyed to Men by God

The testimony is conveyed through the imperfect expression of human language, yet it is the testimony of God; and the obedient, believing child of God beholds in it the glory of a divine power, full of grace and truth.

In His word, God has committed to men the knowledge necessary for salvation. The Holy Scriptures are to be accepted as an authoritative, infallible revelation of His will. They are the standard of character, the revealer of doctrines, and the test of experience. *GC vi, vii*

The Duties of a Minister

4 I charge *thee* therefore before God, and the Lord Jesus Christ, who shall judge the ᵀquick and the dead at his appearing and his kingdom; Acts 10:42; 1 Tim. 5:21; 2 Tim. 2:14 ◆ *living*

2 Preach the word; be instant in season, out of season; reprove, rebuke, exhort with all longsuffering and doctrine. 1 Tim. 4:13; Titus 1:13

3 For the time will come when they will not endure sound doctrine; but after their own lusts shall they heap to themselves teachers, having itching ears; 1 Tim. 1:10

4 And they shall turn away *their* ears from the truth, and shall be turned unto fables.

5 But watch thou in all things, endure afflictions, do the work of an evangelist, make full proof of thy ministry. Acts 21:8; Col. 4:17

4:1–5 Paul's Charge to Timothy

This solemn charge to one so zealous and faithful as was Timothy is a strong testimony to the importance and responsibility of the work of the gospel minister. Summoning Timothy before the bar of God, Paul bids him preach the word, not the sayings and customs of men; to be ready to witness for God whenever opportunity should present itself. *AA 503*

We Are in the Last Days; Take Heed

2 Timothy 3:1–7

Satan has an accurate knowledge of the sins that he has tempted God's people to commit, and he urges his accusations against them, declaring, that by their sins they have forfeited divine protection, and claiming that he has the right to destroy them. He pronounces them just as deserving as himself of exclusion from the favor of God. "Are these," he says, "the people who are to take my place in heaven, and the place of the angels who united with me? They profess to obey the law of God; but have they kept its precepts? Have they not been lovers of self more than lovers of God? Have they not placed their own interests above His service? Have they not loved the things of the world? Look at the sins that have marked their lives. Behold their selfishness, their malice, their hatred of one another. Will God banish me and my angels from His presence, and yet reward those who have been guilty of the same sins? Thou canst not do this, O Lord, in justice. Justice demands that sentence be pronounced against them." *PK 588, 589*

4:6–8

6 For I am now ready to be offered, and the time of my departure is at hand.   Phil. 1:23; 2:17

7 I have fought a good fight, I have finished *my* course, I have kept the faith: Acts 20:24

8 Henceforth there is laid up for me a crown of righteousness, which the Lord, the righteous judge, shall give me at that day: and not to me only, but unto all them also that love his appearing.   Col. 1:5; 2 Tim. 1:12; James 1:12

> Christ's Return See Matthew 24:42–44.

4:7, 8 A Battle and a March

The Christian life is a battle and a march. In this warfare there is no release; the effort must be continuous and persevering. It is by unceasing endeavor that we maintain the victory over the temptations of Satan. . . .

No one will be borne upward without stern, persevering effort in his own behalf. All must engage in this warfare for themselves; no one else can fight our battles. *MH 453*

9 Do thy diligence to come shortly unto me:

10 For Demas hath forsaken me, having loved this present world, and is departed unto Thessalonica; Crescens to Galatia, Titus unto Dalmatia.   Acts 16:6

11 Only Luke is with me. Take Mark, and bring him with thee: for he is profitable to me for the ministry.   Acts 12:12; Col. 4:14; 2 Tim. 1:15

12 And Tychicus have I sent to Ephesus.

13 The ᵀcloke that I left at Troas with Carpus, when thou comest, bring *with thee*, and the books, *but* especially the parchments.   Acts 16:8 ◆ *clothing*

14 Alexander the coppersmith did me much evil: the Lord reward him according to his works: 1 Tim. 1:20

4:10 Unworthy Members

The world has no right to doubt the truth of Christianity because there are unworthy members in the church, nor should Christians become disheartened because of these false brethren. How was it with the early church? Ananias and Sapphira joined themselves to the disciples. Simon Magus was baptized. Demas, who forsook Paul, had been counted a believer. Judas Iscariot was numbered with the apostles. . . . [The Redeemer] has said that false brethren will be found in the church till the close of time. *COL 72, 73*

15 Of whom be thou ware also; for he hath greatly withstood our words.

16 At my first answer no man stood with me, but all *men* forsook me: *I pray God* that it may not be laid to their charge.   Acts 7:60

17 Notwithstanding the Lord stood with me, and strengthened me; that by me the preaching might be fully known, and *that* all the Gentiles might hear: and I was delivered out of the mouth of the lion.   Ps. 22:21; Acts 9:15

18 And the Lord shall deliver me from every evil work, and will preserve *me* unto his heavenly kingdom: to whom *be* glory for ever and ever. Amen.   Ps. 121:7; Rom. 11:36

19 Salute Prisca and Aquila, and the household of Onesiphorus.   Acts 18:2

20 Erastus abode at Corinth: but Trophimus have I left at Miletum sick.   Acts 19:22; 20:4; 21:29

21 Do thy diligence to come before winter. Eubulus greeteth thee, and Pudens, and Linus, and Claudia, and all the brethren.   2 Tim. 4:9

22 The Lord Jesus Christ *be* with thy spirit. Grace *be* with you. Amen.   Gal. 6:18; Col. 4:18

A Most Important Question

2 Timothy 3:12

There is another and more important question that should engage the attention of the churches of today. The apostle Paul declares that "all that will live godly in Christ Jesus shall suffer persecution" (2 Timothy 3:12). Why is it, then, that persecution seems in a great degree to slumber? The only reason is that the church has conformed to the world's standard and therefore awakens no opposition. The religion which is current in our day is not of the pure and holy character that marked the Christian faith in the days of Christ and His apostles. It is only because of the spirit of compromise with sin, because the great truths of the word of God are so indifferently regarded, because there is so little vital godliness in the church, that Christianity is apparently so popular with the world. Let there be a revival of the faith and power of the early church, and the spirit of persecution will be revived, and the fires of persecution will be rekindled. *GC 48*

THE EPISTLE OF PAUL THE APOSTLE TO

TITUS

As with Timothy, Paul recruits Titus, another trustworthy young pastor, to be his representative—this time on the island of Crete. Titus is tasked with setting up the churches on Crete and dealing with the problem of immorality. To aid in this venture, Paul advises Titus to select men of proven godly character to be elders.

Paul makes it clear that the elders are not the only ones who must be of godly character. Men and women, regardless of age, can be reminded of the behaviors that mark members of the body of Christ. Salvation is a journey taken every day. Through Paul's advice to Titus, we can ask ourselves if we're fellow travelers with Christ, walking where He walks, or just along for the ride.

Dates

After leaving Timothy at Ephesus, Paul travels to Crete where he ministers to and leaves Titus to continue his work (1:5). When he learns that Zenas and Apollos will be passing through Crete (3:13), Paul writes this letter. In 3:12, Paul calls for Titus to join him in the Greek city of Nicopolis once his replacement arrives in Crete—Artemas or Tychicus. Paul and Titus likely spend the winter in Nicopolis on the western coast of Greece. Paul likely writes this letter in about A.D. 65.

Crete is an island 156 miles long and varies from 7 to 35 miles wide, located in the Mediterranean Sea south of Turkey. The people of Crete were a challenge for Titus because they were known for their immoral behavior and lying (1:12, 13). Because of their propensity to tell lies, the phrase "to act the Cretan" was coined. This idiom means "to play the liar."

Despite their soiled reputation, we do know that people from Crete were present at Peter's sermon on the Day of Pentecost (Acts 2:11) and may have been converted. This is likely how the gospel message first reached Crete. Paul only had time to visit some of the towns of Crete during his brief stay while on his way to Rome (27:7–13). Paul returned to Crete after his imprisonment to spread the gospel, leaving Titus to continue the work and organize churches (Titus 1:5).

Author

Titus is considered to be one of Paul's Pastoral Epistles, and he is mentioned thirteen times in Paul's writings, making it clear that he is one of Paul's closest friends and companions. Like Timothy, Titus is a convert of Paul, termed "mine own son after the common faith" (1:4). Assuming he is one of the disciples referred to in Acts 11:26, Titus likely was living in Syrian Antioch—a town in present day southern Turkey.

We know that Titus was born Greek and was brought by Paul to Jerusalem (Galatians 2:3), where he became an example of Paul's mission to bring the gospel message to the Gentiles. It is reasonable to conclude that Titus was with Paul on his third missionary journey years later (Acts 18:22), since Paul sent Titus to Corinth on three different occasions (2 Corinthians 2:12, 13; 7:5–7, 13–15; 8:6, 16–24).

There is no record of Titus after that, until Paul reaches Crete and begins his ministry there (Titus 1:5). Titus was with Paul when he was arrested and taken to prison a second time under Nero's Rome, then probably at Paul's request he left for Dalmatia (2 Timothy 4:10).

At different times, Paul referred to Titus as his "partner and fellowhelper" (2 Corinthians 8:23), his "brother" (2:13) and his "son" (Titus 1:4). He praised Titus for his good temperament and enthusiasm (2 Corinthians 7:13–15; 8:16, 17).

Meaning of the Name

The Epistle to Titus was called *Pros Titon* or "To Titus." Titus is also the name of the Roman general who destroyed Jerusalem in A.D. 70 and became emperor after his father Vespasian.

Christ in Titus

Paul reminds Titus that the doctrine he must uphold is "the doctrine of God our Saviour" (2:10). Adherents of this doctrine are instructed to put aside the lusts of this world and live godly before Him, "looking for that blessed hope, and the glorious appearing of the great God and our Saviour Jesus Christ" (2:12, 13). Paul also points out the example of Jesus, who is full of "kindness and love" (3:4), by whom we have access to God's mercy (3:5, 6).

Overview

Paul wrote to Titus after his release from his first Roman imprisonment. His letter came soon after his departure from Crete, doubtless so that the details would be fresh in his mind.

This letter can be divided into two sections:

(1) *Titus 1, Elders:* Paul begins with a doctrinal statement (1:1–3) before mentioning Titus's marching orders: to organize the church and appoint elders (1:5). Paul provides the characteristics of qualified leaders (1:6–9). These characteristics are a marked contrast to those of false teachers (1:10–16).

(2) *Titus 2—3, Order:* Paul stresses the importance of teaching sound doctrine (chapter 2). Paul's words form a code of conduct for Titus and his followers, emphasizing good deeds and honorable behavior among the various groups that made up the churches (chapter 3).

Unlocking Titus

KEY PEOPLE:
Paul, Titus, Artemas, Tychicus

KEY EVENTS:
Titus's mission in Crete; Paul's admonition concerning sound doctrine

KEY WORD:
Conduct, because Paul's letter outlines Titus's responsibilities and the conduct necessary for followers of Christ. The epistle is a means of reinforcing the words Paul doubtless told Titus when he was there, as well as a charge to boldly use his authority as Paul's representative. To improve the people's conduct, the churches must be put in order, false teachers must be refuted, dissenters dealt with, and ungodly behavior replaced with good deeds. He also provides the qualifications for elders in the church, along with the modes of behavior expected of the various groups in the church.

KEY VERSE:
"For this cause left I thee in Crete, that thou shouldest set in order the things that are wanting, and ordain elders in every city, as I had appointed thee" (Titus 1:5).

KEY CHAPTER:
Titus 2 includes Paul's advice for relationships within the church. Paul wanted to be sure that Titus chose people of proper character to help him in his work. The instructions here lay out in detail the qualifications for leaders and tips for godly conduct. "In all things, shewing thyself a pattern of good works" (2:7).

Paul's Greeting

1 Paul, a servant of God, and an apostle of Jesus Christ, according to the faith of God's elect, and the acknowledging of the truth which is after godliness;   Rom. 1:1
2 In hope of eternal life, which God, that cannot lie, promised before the world began;   2 Tim. 1:1, 9; Titus 2:13
3 But hath in due times ᵀmanifested his word through preaching, which is committed unto me according to the commandment of God our Saviour;   1 Tim. 1:1, 11; Titus 2:10 ◆ *made known*
4 To Titus, *mine* own son after the common faith: Grace, mercy, *and* peace, from God the Father and the Lord Jesus Christ our Saviour.   2 Cor. 2:13; 2 Tim. 1:2; 2 Pet. 1:1

1:1–4 Training Younger Workers

The apostle [Paul] made it a part of his work to educate young men for the office of the ministry. He took them with him on his missionary journeys, and thus they gained an experience that later enabled them to fill positions of responsibility. When separated from them, he still kept in touch with their work, and his letters to Timothy and to Titus are evidences of how deep was his desire for their success. *AA 368*

---

5 For this cause left I thee in Crete, that thou shouldest set in order the things that are wanting, and ordain elders in every city, as I had appointed thee: Acts 14:23; 27:7; 1 Tim. 1:3

The Qualifications of Ministers

6 If any be blameless, the husband of one wife, having faithful children not accused of riot or unruly.   1 Tim. 3:2-7
7 For a ᵀbishop must be blameless, as the steward of God; not selfwilled, not soon

angry, not given to wine, no striker, not given to filthy lucre;   Luke 12:42 ◆ *overseer*
8 But a lover of hospitality, a lover of good men, sober, just, holy, temperate;   1 Tim. 3:2
9 Holding fast the faithful word as he hath been taught, that he may be able by sound doctrine both to exhort and to convince the gainsayers.   2 Thess. 2:15; 1 Tim. 1:10; 6:3
10 For there are many unruly and vain talkers and deceivers, specially they of the circumcision: Acts 11:2; 1 Tim. 1:6
11 Whose mouths must be stopped, who subvert whole houses, teaching things which they ought not, for filthy lucre's sake.
12 One of themselves, *even* a prophet of their own, said, The Cretians *are* alway liars, evil beasts, slow bellies.   Acts 17:28
13 This witness is true. Wherefore rebuke them sharply, that they may be sound in the faith;   2 Cor. 13:10; 1 Tim. 5:20; Titus 2:2
14 Not giving heed to Jewish fables, and commandments of men, that turn from the truth.

1:16 To Confess Christ

He who would confess Christ must have Christ abiding in him. He cannot communicate that which he has not received. The disciples might speak fluently on doctrines, they might repeat the words of Christ Himself; but unless they possessed Christlike meekness and love, they were not confessing Him. A spirit contrary to the spirit of Christ would deny Him, whatever the profession. *DA 357*

---

15 Unto the pure all things *are* pure: but unto them that are defiled and unbelieving *is* nothing pure; but even their mind and conscience is defiled.   Rom. 14:14, 20, 23
16 They profess that they know God; but in works they deny *him*, being abominable,

---

Maintaining Church Order

Titus 1:5–9

The same principles of piety and justice that were to guide the rulers among God's people in the time of Moses and of David, were also to be followed by those given the oversight of the newly organized church of God in the gospel dispensation. In the work of setting things in order in all the churches, and ordaining suitable men to act as officers, the apostles held to the high standards of leadership outlined in the Old Testament Scriptures. They maintained that he who is called to stand in a position of leading responsibility in the church "must be blameless . . ." (Titus 1:7).

The order that was maintained in the early Christian church made it possible for them to move forward solidly as a well-disciplined army clad with the armor of God. The companies of believers, though scattered over a large territory, were all members of one body; all moved in concert and in harmony with one another. When dissension arose in a local church, as later it did arise in Antioch and elsewhere, and the believers were unable to come to an agreement among themselves, such matters were not permitted to create a division in the church, but were referred to a general council of the entire body of believers, made up of appointed delegates from the various local churches, with the apostles and elders in positions of leading responsibility. Thus the efforts of Satan to attack the church in isolated places were met by concerted action on the part of all, and the plans of the enemy to disrupt and destroy were thwarted. *AA 95, 96*

and disobedient, and unto every good work reprobate.

1 John 2:4

Guidelines for Christian Living

2 But speak thou the things which become sound doctrine:

1 Tim. 1:10

2 That the aged men be sober, grave, ᵀtemperate, sound in faith, in ᵀcharity, in patience.

1 Tim. 3:11 ♦ *self-controlled* ♦ *selfless love*

3 The aged women likewise, that *they be* in behaviour as becometh holiness, not false accusers, not given to much wine, teachers of good things;

1 Tim. 3:8, 11

4 That they may teach the young women to be sober, to love their husbands, to love their children,

1 Tim. 5:14

5 *To be* discreet, chaste, keepers at home, good, obedient to their own husbands, that the word of God be not blasphemed. Gen. 3:16

6 Young men likewise exhort to be sober minded.

1 Tim. 5:1

7 In all things shewing thyself a pattern of good works: in doctrine *shewing* uncorruptness, gravity, sincerity,

1 Tim. 4:12; 1 Pet. 5:3

8 Sound speech, that cannot be condemned; that he that is of the contrary part may be ashamed, having no evil thing to say of you.

Neh. 5:9; 2 Thess. 3:14; 1 Pet. 2:12

2:8 Proper Habits of Speech

Let the parents themselves be daily learners in the school of Christ. Then by precept and example they can teach their children the use of "sound speech, that cannot be condemned" (Titus 2:8). This is one of the greatest and most responsible of their duties. *COL 338*

9 *Exhort* servants to be obedient unto their own masters, *and* to please *them* well in all *things*; not answering again;

10 Not ᵀpurloining, but shewing all good fidelity; that they may adorn the doctrine of God our Saviour in all things. Matt. 5:16 ♦ *stealing*

11 For the grace of God that bringeth salvation hath appeared to all men,

Acts 11:23

12 Teaching us that, denying ungodliness and worldly lusts, we should live soberly, righteously, and godly, in this present world;

Luke 1:75

13 Looking for that blessed hope, and the glorious appearing of the great God and our Saviour Jesus Christ;

2 Tim. 4:8

Christ's Return See James 5:7, 8.

14 Who gave himself for us, that he might redeem us from all iniquity, and purify unto himself a ᵀpeculiar people, zealous of good works.

Ps. 130:8; Eph. 2:10; Heb. 9:14 ♦ *special*

2:11-13

2:14 Rewards of Good Works

The members of God's church are to be zealous of good works, separating from worldly ambition and walking in the footsteps of Him who went about doing good. With hearts filled with sympathy and compassion, they are to minister to those in need of help, bringing to sinners a knowledge of the Saviour's love. Such work calls for laborious effort, but it brings a rich reward. *AA 109, 110*

15 These things speak, and exhort, and rebuke with all authority. Let no man despise thee.

2 Tim. 4:2

Instructions for Teaching

3 Put them in mind to be subject to ᵀprincipalities and powers, to obey magistrates, to be ready to every good work,

Eccl. 10:4; 2 Tim. 2:21 ♦ *authorities*

2 To speak evil of no man, to be no brawlers, *but* gentle, shewing all meekness unto all men.

Eph. 4:31; 1 Tim. 3:3; 2 Tim. 2:24-25

3:3–5 Pleading Our Helplessness

Do you feel that because you are a sinner you cannot hope to receive blessing from God? Remember that Christ came into the world to save sinners. We have nothing to recommend us to God; the plea that we may urge now and ever is our utterly helpless condition, which makes His redeeming power a necessity. Renouncing all self-dependence, we may look to the cross of Calvary and say:

"In my hand no price I bring;
Simply to Thy cross I cling." *MH 65*

3 For we ourselves also were sometimes foolish, disobedient, deceived, serving ᵀdivers lusts and pleasures, living in malice and envy, hateful, *and* hating one another.

Col. 3:7 ♦ *various*

4 But after that the kindness and love of God our Saviour toward man appeared, Titus 2:10-11

5 Not by works of righteousness which we have done, but according to his mercy he saved us, by the washing of regeneration, and renewing of the Holy Ghost; Rom. 12:2; Eph. 2:4

6 Which he shed on us abundantly through Jesus Christ our Saviour; Joel 2:28; Acts 2:33

7 That being justified by his grace, we should be made heirs according to the hope of eternal life.

Rom. 3:24; 8:17; Titus 1:2

8 *This is* a faithful saying, and these things I will that thou affirm constantly, that they which have believed in God might be careful to maintain good works. These things are good and profitable unto men. 1 Tim. 1:15

9 But avoid foolish questions, and genealogies, and contentions, and strivings about the law; for they are unprofitable and vain.

10 A man that is an heretick after the first and second admonition reject; Rom. 16:17

11 Knowing that he that is such is subverted, and sinneth, being condemned of himself.

12 When I shall send Artemas unto thee, or Tychicus, be diligent to come unto me to Nicopolis: for I have determined there to winter. Acts 20:4

13 Bring Zenas the lawyer and Apollos on their journey diligently, that nothing be wanting unto them. Matt. 22:35; Acts 18:24

14 And let ours also learn to maintain good works for necessary uses, that they be not unfruitful. Phil. 1:11

15 All that are with me salute thee. Greet them that love us in the faith. Grace be with you all. Amen. Col. 4:18

THE EPISTLE OF PAUL THE APOSTLE TO

PHILEMON

Being a believer in Christ causes many changes in our lives and results in new commitments and behaviors. One of these new changes is how Christ's love infiltrates all aspects of our lives—resulting in forgiveness, humility, altruism, and a host of other attributes.

In this short letter to Philemon, who was most likely a prominent member of the Colossian church and a slaveholder, Paul writes with the intent of appealing to Philemon's brotherly love in regard to Philemon's runaway slave Onesimus. With gentleness and love, Paul appeals to Philemon to welcome back Onesimus in the same way he would welcome Paul, as a fellow believer in Christ (verses 8–9).

Onesimus is now a brother in Christ, and Paul urges Philemon, based on their shared faith, to forgive and forget any wrongdoing Onesimus may have committed and to welcome him back with open arms. Paul tells Philemon that he will pay any damages or debts Onesimus owes, thus stepping in to intercede for Onesimus.

Not only does Paul urge Philemon to act with Christ's love, but he is also confident that love will carry the day: "Having confidence in thy obedience I wrote unto thee, knowing that thou wilt also do more than I say" (verse 21).

This letter to Philemon is a reminder to believers that our faith in Christ calls us to a life of love and forgiveness, which Christ demonstrated while living among us.

Dates

Philemon is one of the four Prison Epistles and was written in approximately A.D. 62. The letter was dispatched at the same time as Colossians during Paul's first imprisonment in Rome.

Author

There is very little debate as to any other author besides Paul. Debate has arisen periodically over the centuries, but it has never resulted in serious doubts as to the author of this epistle. Paul mentions himself three times in this short book (verses 1, 9, 19), giving his authorship added support. Church tradition also lends support to Paul's authorship.

Meaning of the Name

The Epistle to Philemon is known as *Pros Philemona*, which means "To Philemon." This is made evident in the book's first verse, when Paul writes, "Paul, a prisoner of Jesus Christ, and Timothy our brother, unto Philemon our dearly beloved, and fellowlabourer" (verse 1). In addition to being addressed to an individual—Philemon—the book is also addressed to a family, a church, and to believers everywhere.

Christ in Philemon

Even in this short book, Paul communicates the truth and beauty of Christ's love and forgiveness. Even though Onesimus is guilty of the offenses against Philemon, Paul records his willingness to intercede for Onesimus, thus taking on the debts he owes. This act by Paul is a wonderful example of how Christ intercedes for us—those who have committed offenses against Him. It also reminds us of His willingness to pay for our debts by His death on the cross.

In addition, the love and forgiveness demonstrated in Philemon encourages believers to respond to others with the same love shown us by Christ.

Overview

Onesimus was a slave in Philemon's household. It appears that he stole something from his master and then escaped to Rome. Under Roman law, Philemon could have punished his slave by death if Onesimus was captured. At some point, Onesimus finds Paul in Rome. Paul converts Onesimus and then sends him back to his master Philemon with this letter from Paul. Philemon lived in Colosse and was one of Paul's converts as well (Colossians 4:9, 17).

Although the epistle to Philemon is the shortest of Paul's epistles, it is one of the finest examples of persuasive writing in the New Testament. Written during Paul's imprisonment, Philemon can be divided into three sections:

(1) *Philemon 1–7, Prayer of Thanksgiving for Philemon:* Paul spends this first section telling Philemon how he thanks God for Philemon's love and faith, "which thou hast toward the Lord Jesus, and toward all saints" (verse 5).

(2) *Philemon 8–16, Petition from Paul Toward Onesimus:* Paul appeals to his brother in Christ, Philemon, to act lovingly toward their mutual friend Onesimus, urging Philemon to forgive him and treat him as the brother in Christ he is.

(3) *Philemon 17–25, Paul's Promise to Philemon:* Paul closes this short, personal letter to Philemon by promising him that he will pay anything owed him by Onesimus.

Unlocking Philemon

KEY PEOPLE:
Paul, Philemon, Onesimus

KEY EVENTS:
Paul's imprisonment; Onesimus's conversion to Christianity; Onesimus's return to Philemon

KEY WORD:
Forgiveness, since Paul asks Philemon to extend the forgiveness he received from Christ to Onesimus, who had recently become a brother in Christ. In the same way Christ calls all of us to respond with the forgiveness He offers to us.

KEY VERSES:
"Not now as a servant, but above a servant, a brother beloved, specially to me, but how much more unto thee, both in the flesh, and in the Lord? If thou count me therefore a partner, receive him as myself" (Philemon 16–17).

KEY CHAPTER:
Philemon is only 25 verses long, but the power of the message Paul communicates is profound and teaches believers to respond to others with love and forgiveness.

Paul's Greeting

1 Paul, a prisoner of Jesus Christ, and Timothy *our* brother, unto Philemon our dearly beloved, and fellowlabourer,   Eph. 3:1
2 And to *our* beloved Apphia, and Archippus our fellowsoldier, and to the church in thy house: Rom. 16:5; Phil. 2:25; Col. 4:17
3 Grace to you, and peace, from God our Father and the Lord Jesus Christ.   Rom. 1:7

Paul's Prayer for Philemon

4 I thank my God, making mention of thee always in my prayers,   Rom. 1:8
5 Hearing of thy love and faith, which thou hast toward the Lord Jesus, and toward all saints;   Eph. 1:15; Col. 1:4
6 That the communication of thy faith may become ᵀeffectual by the acknowledging of every good thing which is in you in Christ Jesus.   *effective*

3–6 Transforming Grace

The apostle [Paul] reminded Philemon that every good purpose and trait of character which he possessed was due to the grace of Christ; this alone made him different from the perverse and the sinful. The same grace could make the debased criminal a child of God and a useful laborer in the gospel. *AA 457*

7 For we have great joy and consolation in thy love, because the bowels of the saints are refreshed by thee, brother.   2 Cor. 7:4, 13; 2 Tim. 1:16

Paul's Advice about Onesimus

8 Wherefore, though I might be much bold in Christ to ᵀenjoin thee that which is ᵀconvenient,   1 Thess. 2:6 ◆ *command* ◆ *appropriate*
9 Yet for love's sake I rather ᵀbeseech *thee*, being such an one as Paul the aged, and now also a prisoner of Jesus Christ.   Eph. 4:1 ◆ *beg*

10–16 Paul's Entreaty

Paul might have urged upon Philemon his duty as a Christian; but he chose rather the language of entreaty. . . .

The apostle asked Philemon, in view of the conversion of Onesimus, to receive the repentant slave as his own child, showing him such affection that he would choose to dwell with his former master, "not now as a servant, but above a servant, a brother beloved" [Philemon 16]. *AA 457*

10 I beseech thee for my son Onesimus, whom I have begotten in my bonds: Gal. 4:19
11 Which in time past was to thee unprofitable, but now profitable to thee and to me:
12 Whom I have sent again: thou therefore receive him, that is, mine own bowels:
13 Whom I would have retained with me, that in thy stead he might have ministered unto me in the bonds of the gospel: 1 Cor. 16:17
14 But without thy mind would I do nothing; that thy benefit should not be as it were of necessity, but willingly.   2 Cor. 9:7
15 For perhaps he therefore departed for a season, that thou shouldest receive him for ever;
16 Not now as a servant, but above a servant, a brother beloved, specially to me, but how much more unto thee, both in the flesh, and in the Lord?   Matt. 23:8; Col. 3:22; 1 Tim. 6:2

17–19 Jesus Pays the Debt

How fitting an illustration of the love of Christ for the repentant sinner! The servant who had defrauded his master had nothing with which to make restitution. The sinner who has robbed God of years of service has no means of canceling the debt. Jesus interposes between the sinner and God, saying, I will pay the debt. Let the sinner be spared; I will suffer in his stead. *AA 458*

Counsel on Slavery

Philemon

Paul's letter to Philemon shows the influence of the gospel upon the relation between master and servant. Slave-holding was an established institution throughout the Roman Empire, and both masters and slaves were found in most of the churches for which Paul labored. . . .

Some masters, more humane than others, were more indulgent toward their servants; but the vast majority of the wealthy and noble, given up without restraint to the indulgence of lust, passion, and appetite, made their slaves the wretched victims of caprice and tyranny. The tendency of the whole system was hopelessly degrading.

It was not the apostle's work to overturn arbitrarily or suddenly the established order of society. To attempt this would be to prevent the success of the gospel. But he taught principles which struck at the very foundation of slavery and which, if carried into effect, would surely undermine the whole system. "Where the Spirit of the Lord is, there is liberty," he declared (2 Corinthians 3:17). When converted, the slave became a member of the body of Christ, and as such was to be loved and treated as a brother, a fellow heir with his master to the blessings of God and the privileges of the gospel. On the other hand, servants were to perform their duties, "not with eyeservice, as men pleasers; but as the servants of Christ, doing the will of God from the heart" (Ephesians 6:6). *AA 459, 460*

17 If thou count me therefore a partner, receive him as myself.   2 Cor. 8:23

18 If he hath wronged thee, or oweth *thee* ought, put that on mine account;

19 I Paul have written *it* with mine own hand, I will repay *it*: albeit I do not say to thee how thou owest unto me even thine own self besides.   Gal. 5:2

20 Yea, brother, let me have joy of thee in the Lord: refresh my bowels in the Lord.

21 Having confidence in thy obedience I wrote unto thee, knowing that thou wilt also do more than I say.   2 Cor. 2:3

22 But withal prepare me also a lodging: for I trust that through your prayers I shall be given unto you.   Acts 28:23; 2 Cor. 1:11; Phil. 2:24

23 There salute thee Epaphras, my fellowprisoner in Christ Jesus;   Rom. 16:7; Col. 1:7; 4:12

24 Marcus, Aristarchus, Demas, Lucas, my fellowlabourers.   Col. 4:10, 14; 2 Tim. 4:10-11

25 The grace of our Lord Jesus Christ *be* with your spirit. Amen.   2 Tim. 4:22

THE EPISTLE TO THE
HEBREWS

One of the common themes in many New Testament books is the danger of apostasy—falling away from God. At the time of the writing of the letter to the Hebrews, many new believers in Christ were coming from Jewish backgrounds. When they became Christ's followers, they were often subject to persecution from their fellow citizens.

With that backdrop, the writer of Hebrews commences to pen a letter to help those who were struggling in their newfound faith. The writer attempts to convince them of Christ's superiority—who He is and what He did. He is over all and above all and thus deserves their worship. The writer uses examples from the Old Testament, examples the readers would be intimately familiar with, to prove that Christ is worthy of their faith.

In addition, the writer reminds the new converts that faith involves growing more like Christ. Regardless of their struggles, believers are called—and equipped in Christ—to become more like Him each day. Faith is not stagnant; it is active and growing.

Dates

Hebrews was most likely written to Jewish Christians because of the book's strong reliance on Old Testament concepts and history, something with which the book's audience would be familiar. In addition, Hebrews does not mention the destruction of Jerusalem, which occurred in A.D. 70. More than likely this epistle was written prior to that date, probably about A.D. 63. Clement of Rome quoted Hebrews in A.D. 95.

Author

Although the message and authority of the book are not questioned, the authorship of Hebrews is not as clear and supported as other books. Eastern and Western churches debated between Paul, Barnabas, Luke, Apollos, or Clement as the book's author. However, from about the fourth century to the late 1800s, most Christians believed Paul to be the author. But this epistle does not bear Paul's usual salutation nor is it directed to a local church.

In approximately A.D. 1930, support favoring Paul's authorship of Hebrews came to light. Discovery of the third century A.D. Chester Beatty Biblical Papyri reveals a listing of his epistles, and Hebrews is clearly placed between Romans and 1 Corinthians. While this fact does not conclusively demonstrate that Paul wrote Hebrews, it does strongly imply that those who played a role in early church history believed that Hebrews should be included as a part of Paul's authorship.

Meaning of the Name

Pros Ebraious, "To Hebrews," is the oldest and most reliable title of the book. The King James titles the book "The Epistle of Paul the Apostle to the Hebrews," but early manuscript evidence does not support this title.

Christ in Hebrews

The epistle to the Hebrews illustrates ways that Christ is superior to all. He is "so much better than the angels" (1:4), because He is "the express image" of God (1:3). Yet He became "a little lower than the angels for the suffering of death, crowned with glory and honour" (2:9). He is superior to Moses, who represents the Law (3:1–6). Christ is described as a high priest "after the order of Melchisedec" (5:6, 10; see also chapter 7). Yet He is vastly superior, since He offered Himself as the perfect sacrifice for sin (see chapters 9—10). Because of His sacrifice, we have a new covenant with God (chapters 8—9). He is "the author and finisher of our faith" (12:2).

Overview

Hebrews can be divided into three sections, each referencing some aspect of Christ's superiority.

(1) *Hebrews 1:1—4:13, Christ's Person:* The writer spends this first section of the book asserting the superiority of Christ to angels, Moses, Old Testament priests, and everyone else. Christ is divine, and therefore, superior to all.

(2) *Hebrews 4:14—10:18, Christ's Work:* Christ validates the law because He was the perfect, definitive sacrifice for our sins. As a greater high priest than Melchisedec (5:5–10), He offers us God's complete forgiveness.

(3) *Hebrews 10:19—13:25, Christ's Life in Us:* This section encourages believers to a walk of faith—the kind exemplified in Hebrews 11.

Unlocking Hebrews

KEY PEOPLE:
Those who were faithful throughout time (chapter 11)

KEY EVENTS:
Christ's death on the cross and His resurrection; the Old Testament legal system and priesthood; the earthly versus heavenly sanctuary; the new covenant

KEY PHRASE:
The Superiority of Christ, which the writer of Hebrews spends a considerable portion of this letter asserting. Christ is superior to everything that has been and will ever be, so our trust and faith in Him is even more deserved and important. The writer is concerned about believers falling away from the faith and moving back into the Judaic system; also he explains how believers can become more Christlike.

KEY VERSES:
"Seeing then that we have a great high priest, that is passed into the heavens, Jesus the Son of God, let us hold fast our profession. For we have not an high priest which cannot be touched with the feeling of our infirmities; but was in all points tempted like as we are, yet without sin. Let us therefore come boldly unto the throne of grace, that we may obtain mercy, and find grace to help in time of need" (Hebrews 4:14–16).

"Wherefore seeing we also are compassed about with so great a cloud of witnesses, let us lay aside every weight, and the sin which doth so easily beset us, and let us run with patience the race that is set before us, looking unto Jesus the author and finisher of our faith; who for the joy that was set before him endured the cross, despising the shame, and is set down at the right hand of the throne of God" (Hebrews 12:1, 2).

KEY CHAPTER:
Hebrews 11, which is known as the faith chapter of Scripture. This chapter defines faith and records the faithful acts of many Old Testament people. "These all died in faith, not having received the promises, but having seen them afar off, and were persuaded of them, and embraced them, and confessed that they were strangers and pilgrims on the earth" (11:13). Even though they didn't see or experience the things promised to them, they were faithful, nonetheless. They will one day receive what God has promised.

God Has Spoken through His Son

1 God, who at sundry times and in ᵀdivers manners spake in time past unto the fathers by the prophets, Joel 2:28 ◆ *various*
2 Hath in these last days spoken unto us by *his* Son, whom he hath appointed heir of all things, by whom also he made the worlds; Matt. 28:18; John 1:3; 1 Cor. 8:6
3 Who being the brightness of *his* glory, and the express image of his person, and upholding all things by the word of his power, when he had by himself purged our sins, sat down on the right hand of the Majesty on high; Mark 16:19; John 1:14; 2 Cor. 4:4

> **1:1–3 Christ in Both Testaments**
>
> Christ as manifested to the patriarchs, as symbolized in the sacrificial service, as portrayed in the law, and as revealed by the prophets, is the riches of the Old Testament. Christ in His life, His death, and His resurrection, Christ as He is manifested by the Holy Spirit, is the treasure of the New Testament. Our Saviour, the outshining of the Father's glory, is both the Old and the New. *COL 126*

Christ Is Superior to the Angels

4 Being made so much better than the angels, as he hath by inheritance obtained a more excellent name than they. Eph. 1:21
5 For unto which of the angels said he at any time, Thou art my Son, this day have I begotten thee? And again, I will be to him a Father, and he shall be to me a Son? 2 Sam. 7:14; Ps. 2:7
6 And again, when he bringeth in the firstbegotten into the world, he saith, And let all the angels of God worship him. Deut. 32:43
7 And of the angels he saith, Who maketh his angels spirits, and his ministers a flame of fire. Ps. 104:4
8 But unto the Son *he saith,* Thy throne, O God, *is* for ever and ever: a sceptre of righteousness *is* the sceptre of thy kingdom.
9 Thou hast loved righteousness, and hated iniquity; therefore God, *even* thy God, hath anointed thee with the oil of gladness above thy fellows. Ps. 45:7; Is. 61:1, 3
10 And, Thou, Lord, in the beginning hast laid the foundation of the earth; and the heavens are the works of thine hands: Ps. 102:25-27
11 They shall perish; but thou remainest; and they all shall ᵀwax old as doth a garment; Is. 34:4 ◆ *become*
12 And as a vesture shalt thou fold them up, and they shall be changed: but thou art the same, and thy years shall not fail. Heb. 13:8
13 But to which of the angels said he at any time, Sit on my right hand, until I make thine enemies thy footstool? Ps. 110:1; Matt. 22:44

14 Are they not all ministering spirits, sent forth to minister for them who shall be heirs of salvation? Ps. 34:7

> **1:14 Invisible Armies**
>
> We need to understand better than we do the mission of the angel visitants. It would be well to consider that in all our work we have the co-operation and care of heavenly beings. Invisible armies of light and power attend the meek and lowly ones who believe and claim the promises of God. Cherubim and seraphim and angels that excel in strength—ten thousand times ten thousand and thousands of thousands—stand at His right hand. *COL 176*

Everything Is Under Christ's Control

2 Therefore we ought to give the more earnest heed to the things which we have heard, lest at any time we should let *them* slip. Prov. 3:21
2 For if the word spoken by angels was ᵀstedfast, and every transgression and disobedience received a just recompence of reward; Acts 7:53; Heb. 10:28, 35 ◆ *steadfast*
3 How shall we escape, if we neglect so great salvation; which at the first began to be spoken by the Lord, and was confirmed unto us by them that heard *him;* Luke 1:2; Heb. 1:2; 12:25
4 God also bearing *them* witness, both with signs and wonders, and with ᵀdivers miracles, and gifts of the Holy Ghost, according to his own will? Eph. 1:5 ◆ *various*

God's New Order and His Gifts to Man

5 For unto the angels hath he not put in subjection the world to come, whereof we speak. Heb. 6:5
6 But one in a certain place testified, saying, What is man, that thou art mindful of him? or the son of man, that thou visitest him? Heb. 4:4
7 Thou madest him a little lower than the angels; thou crownedst him with glory and honour, and didst set him over the works of thy hands:
8 Thou hast put all things in subjection under his feet. For in that he put all in subjection under him, he left nothing *that is* not put under him. But now we see not yet all things put under him. 1 Cor. 15:27
9 But we see Jesus, who was made a little lower than the angels for the suffering of death, crowned with glory and honour; that he by the grace of God should taste death for every man. John 3:16; 8:52; Acts 2:33
10 For it became him, for whom *are* all things, and by whom *are* all things, in bringing many sons unto glory, to make the

captain of their salvation perfect through sufferings.   Luke 24:26, 46; Rom. 11:36

11 For both he that ᵀsanctifieth and they who are sanctified *are* all of one: for which cause he is not ashamed to call them brethren,   Matt. 25:40; John 20:17; Heb. 10:10 ♦ *makes holy*

2:11 Eternally One With Us

Jesus is "not ashamed to call them brethren" (Hebrews 2:11); He is our Sacrifice, our Advocate, our Brother, bearing our human form before the Father's throne, and through eternal ages one with the race He has redeemed—the Son of man. And all this that man might be uplifted from the ruin and degradation of sin that he might reflect the love of God and share the joy of holiness. *SC 14*

12 Saying, I will declare thy name unto my brethren, in the midst of the church will I sing praise unto thee.   Ps. 22:22

13 And again, I will put my trust in him. And again, Behold I and the children which God hath given me.   Ps. 18:2

Christ Shared Man's Mortal Nature

14 Forasmuch then as the children are partakers of flesh and blood, he also himself likewise took part of the same; that through death he might destroy him that had the power of death, that is, the ᵀdevil;   Gen. 3:15; John 1:14; 2 Tim. 1:10 ♦ *false accuser*

15 And deliver them who through fear of death were all their lifetime subject to bondage.   Rom. 8:15

16 For ᵀverily he took not on *him the nature of* angels; but he took on *him* the seed of Abraham.   *truly*

17 Wherefore in all things it behoved him to be made like unto *his* brethren, that he might be a merciful and faithful high priest in things *pertaining* to God, to make reconciliation for the sins of the people.   Dan. 9:24

18 For in that he himself hath suffered being tempted, he is able to ᵀsuccour them that are tempted.   *give help to*

2:18 Never Another Like Him

Christ alone had experience in all the sorrows and temptations that befall human beings. Never another of woman born was so fiercely beset by temptation; never another bore so heavy a burden of the world's sin and pain. Never was there another whose sympathies were so broad or so tender. A sharer in all the experiences of humanity, He could feel not only for, but with, every burdened and tempted and struggling one. *Ed 78*

Christ Is Superior to Moses

3 Wherefore, holy brethren, partakers of the heavenly calling, consider the Apostle and High Priest of our profession, Christ Jesus;   Phil. 3:14

2 Who was faithful to him that appointed him, as also Moses *was faithful* in all his house.   Num. 12:7

3 For this *man* was counted worthy of more glory than Moses, inasmuch as he who hath builded the house hath more honour than the house.

4 For every house is builded by some *man;* but he that built all things *is* God.

5 And Moses ᵀverily *was* faithful in all his house, as a servant, for a testimony of those things which were to be spoken after;   Ex. 14:31; Num. 12:7; Heb. 3:2 ♦ *truly*

6 But Christ as a son over his own house; whose house are we, if we hold fast the confidence and the rejoicing of the hope firm unto the end.   1 Cor. 3:16; 1 Tim. 3:15; Heb. 1:2

3:6 Persisting Through Difficulties

Often men are tempted to falter before the perplexities and obstacles that confront them. But if they will hold the beginning of their confidence steadfast unto the end, God will make the way clear. Success will come to them as they struggle against difficulties. *PK 595*

Warnings against Unbelief

7 Wherefore (as the Holy Ghost saith, To day if ye will hear his voice,   Heb. 3:15

8 Harden not your hearts, as in the provocation, in the day of temptation in the wilderness:

9 When your fathers tempted me, proved me, and saw my works forty years.   Acts 7:36

10 Wherefore I was grieved with that generation, and said, They do alway err in *their* heart; and they have not known my ways.

11 So I sware in my wrath, They shall not enter into my rest.)   Heb. 4:3, 5

12 Take heed, brethren, lest there be in any of you an evil heart of unbelief, in departing from the living God.   Heb. 12:25

13 But exhort one another daily, while it is called To day; lest any of you be hardened through the deceitfulness of sin.   Is. 44:20

14 For we are made partakers of Christ, if we hold the beginning of our confidence ᵀstedfast unto the end;   Heb. 3:6 ♦ *steadfast*

15 While it is said, To day if ye will hear his voice, harden not your hearts, as in the provocation.   Heb. 3:7-8

16 For some, when they had heard, did provoke: ᵀhowbeit not all that came out of Egypt by Moses. Num. 14:2, 30; Deut. 1:38 ♦ *however*

17 But with whom was he grieved forty years? *was it* not with them that had sinned, whose carcases fell in the wilderness?   Num. 14:29
18 And to whom sware he that they should not enter into his rest, but to them that believed not?   Deut. 1:34-35
19 So we see that they could not enter in because of unbelief.   John 3:36

3:19 Delay Not God's Plan

It was not the will of God that Israel should wander forty years in the wilderness; He desired to lead them directly to the land of Canaan and establish them there, a holy, happy people. . . . Because of their backsliding and apostasy they perished in the desert. . . . In like manner, it was not the will of God that the coming of Christ should be so long delayed and His people should remain so many years in this world of sin and sorrow. But unbelief separated them from God. *GC 458*

God's Promise of a Sabbath Rest

4 Let us therefore fear, lest, a promise being left *us* of entering into his rest, any of you should seem to come short of it.   Heb. 12:15
2 For unto us was the gospel preached, as well as unto them: but the word preached did not profit them, not being mixed with faith in them that heard *it*.   1 Thess. 2:13

Faith See James 2:14–26.

3 For we which have believed do enter into rest, as he said, As I have sworn in my wrath, if they shall enter into my rest: although the works were finished from the foundation of the world.   Ps. 95:11; Heb. 3:11

4:3 God's Constant Involvement

As regards this world, God's work of creation is completed. For "the works were finished from the foundation of the world" (Hebrews 4:3). But His energy is still exerted in upholding the objects of His creation. It is not because the mechanism that has once been set in motion continues to act by its own inherent energy that the pulse beats and breath follows breath; but every breath, every pulsation of the heart, is an evidence of the all-pervading care of Him in whom "we live, and move, and have our being" (Acts 17:28). *PP 115*

4 For he spake in a certain place of the seventh *day* on this wise, And God did rest the seventh day from all his works.   Ex. 20:11; 31:17
5 And in this *place* again, If they shall enter into my rest.   Heb. 3:11
6 Seeing therefore it remaineth that some must enter therein, and they to whom it was

first preached entered not in because of unbelief: Heb. 3:18-19
7 Again, he limiteth a certain day, saying in David, To day, after so long a time; as it is said, To day if ye will hear his voice, harden not your hearts.   Ps. 95:7
8 For if Jesus had given them rest, then would he not afterward have spoken of another day.   Josh. 22:4
9 There remaineth therefore a rest to the people of God.
10 For he that is entered into his rest, he also hath ceased from his own works, as God *did* from his.   Rev. 14:13
11 Let us labour therefore to enter into that rest, lest any man fall after the same example of unbelief.   Heb. 3:12
12 For the word of God *is* ᵀquick, and powerful, and sharper than any twoedged sword, piercing even to the dividing ᵀasunder of soul and spirit, and of the joints and marrow, and *is* a discerner of the thoughts and intents of the heart.   Is. 49:2; Jer. 23:29; Eph. 6:17 ♦ *living* ♦ *apart*

The Bible See John 17:17.

13 Neither is there any creature that is not manifest in his sight: but all things *are* naked and opened unto the eyes of him with whom we have to do.   Job 26:6; 34:21; Ps. 33:13-15

4:13 Nothing Escapes God

If we were to cherish an habitual impression that God sees and hears all that we do and say and keeps a faithful record of our words and actions, and that we must meet it all, we would fear to sin. Let the young ever remember that wherever they are, and whatever they do, they are in the presence of God. No part of our conduct escapes observation. . . . Every act, every word, every thought, is as distinctly marked as though there were only one person in the whole world, and the attention of heaven were centered upon him. *PP 217, 218*

14 Seeing then that we have a great high priest, that is passed into the heavens, Jesus the Son of God, let us hold fast *our* profession.   Heb. 1:2-3; 6:20; 8:1
15 For we have not an high priest which cannot be touched with the feeling of our infirmities; but was in all points tempted like as *we are, yet* without sin.   John 8:46; 2 Cor. 5:21; Heb. 7:26
16 Let us therefore come boldly unto the throne of grace, that we may obtain mercy, and find grace to help in time of need.

Christ Is Superior to the Priests

5 For every high priest taken from among men is ordained for men in things *pertaining* to God, that he may offer both gifts and sacrifices for sins: Heb. 2:17; 8:3; 10:11

2 Who can have compassion on the igno-rant, and on them that are out of the way; for that he himself also is ᵀcompassed with infirmity.   Heb. 2:18; 4:15; 7:28 ◆ surrounded

3 And by reason hereof he ought, as for the people, so also for himself, to offer for sins.

4 And no man taketh this honour unto himself, but he that is called of God, as was Aaron.   Ex. 28:1; Num. 16:40; 1 Chr. 23:13

5 So also Christ glorified not himself to be made an high priest; but he that said unto him, Thou art my Son, to day have I ᵀbegot-ten thee.   Ps. 2:7; John 8:54; Heb. 1:5 ◆ brought you forth

6 As he saith also in another place, Thou art a priest for ever after the order of Melchis-edec.   Ps. 110:4; Heb. 7:17, 21

7 Who in the days of his flesh, when he had offered up prayers and supplications with strong crying and tears unto him that was able to save him from death, and was heard in that he feared;   Matt. 27:46, 50; Mark 15:34

8 Though he were a Son, yet learned he obedi-ence by the things which he suffered;   Phil. 2:8

9 And being made perfect, he became the author of eternal salvation unto all them that obey him;   Heb. 2:10

5:7–9 Charged With Heavenly Current

The life of Jesus was a life of constant trust, sustained by continual communion; and His service for heaven and earth was without fail-ure or faltering.

As a man He supplicated the throne of God, till His humanity was charged with a heavenly current that connected humanity with divinity. Receiving life from God, He imparted life to men. *Ed 80, 81*

10 Called of God an high priest after the order of Melchisedec.   Heb. 5:5-6

11 Of whom we have many things to say, and hard to be uttered, seeing ye are dull of hearing.   2 Pet. 3:16

12 For when for the time ye ought to be teachers, ye have need that one teach you again which be the first principles of the oracles of God; and are become such as have need of milk, and not of strong meat.   Acts 7:38; Heb. 6:1; 1 Pet. 2:2

13 For every one that useth milk is unskil-ful in the word of righteousness: for he is a babe.   1 Cor. 14:20

14 But strong meat belongeth to them that are of full age, even those who by reason of use have their senses exercised to discern both good and evil.   Is. 7:15

The Christian Life See Ephesians 4:15.

Warnings against Backsliding

6 Therefore leaving the principles of the doctrine of Christ, let us go on unto per-fection; not laying again the foundation of repentance from dead works, and of faith toward God,   Heb. 9:14

2 Of the doctrine of baptisms, and of laying on of hands, and of resurrection of the dead, and of eternal judgment.   Acts 6:6

3 And this will we do, if God permit. Acts 18:21

4 For it is impossible for those who were once enlightened, and have tasted of the heavenly gift, and were made partakers of the Holy Ghost,   Gal. 3:2; Eph. 2:8; Heb. 10:32

5 And have tasted the good word of God, and the powers of the world to come,   Heb. 2:5

6 If they shall fall away, to renew them again unto repentance; seeing they crucify to themselves the Son of God afresh, and put him to an open shame.   Heb. 10:29

6:6 Wounding Christ Again

The Spirit reveals the ingratitude of the heart that has slighted and grieved the Sav-iour, and brings us in contrition to the foot of the cross. By every sin Jesus is wounded afresh; and as we look upon Him whom we have pierced, we mourn for the sins that have brought anguish upon Him. Such mourning will lead to the renunciation of sin. *DA 300*

7 For the earth which drinketh in the rain that cometh ᵀoft upon it, and bringeth forth herbs meet for them by whom it is dressed, receiveth blessing from God: often

8 But that which beareth thorns and briers is rejected, and is nigh unto cursing; whose end is to be burned.   Gen. 3:17-18

God Will Not Forget You

9 But, beloved, we are persuaded better things of you, and things that accompany salvation, though we thus speak.

10 For God is not unrighteous to forget your work and labour of love, which ye have shewed toward his name, in that ye have ministered to the saints, and do minister.   Prov. 14:31; Matt. 10:42; 1 Thess. 1:3

11 And we desire that every one of you do shew the same diligence to the full assurance of hope unto the end: Rom. 5:2-5; Heb. 3:6, 14

12 That ye be not slothful, but followers of them who through faith and patience inherit the promises.   Heb. 10:36; 13:7; Rev. 13:10

13 For when God made promise to Abra-ham, because he could swear by no greater, he sware by himself,   Luke 1:73

14 Saying, Surely blessing I will bless thee, and multiplying I will multiply thee. Gen. 22:17

15 And so, after he had patiently endured, he obtained the promise.   Heb. 6:12

16 For men ᵀverily swear by the greater: and an oath for confirmation *is* to them an end of all strife.   Ex. 22:11 ◆ *truly*

17 Wherein God, willing more abundantly to shew unto the heirs of promise the immutability of his counsel, confirmed *it* by an oath: Prov. 19:21; Heb. 6:18; 11:9

18 That by two ᵀimmutable things, in which *it was* impossible for God to lie, we might have a strong consolation, who have fled for refuge to lay hold upon the hope set before us: Num. 23:19; Titus 1:2; Heb. 12:1-2 ◆ *unchangeable*

19 Which *hope* we have as an anchor of the soul, both sure and stedfast, and which entereth into that within the veil;   Lev. 16:2, 15

20 Whither the forerunner is for us entered, *even* Jesus, made an high priest for ever after the order of Melchisedec.   Heb. 1:3; 4:14; 5:6

Christ Is Superior to Melchisedec

7 For this Melchisedec, king of Salem, priest of the most high God, who met Abraham returning from the slaughter of the kings, and blessed him;   Gen. 14:18-20; Ps. 76:2

2 To whom also Abraham gave a tenth part of all; first being by interpretation King of righteousness, and after that also King of Salem, which is, King of peace;

3 Without father, without mother, without descent, having neither beginning of days, nor end of life; but made like unto the Son of God; abideth a priest continually. Heb. 7:6

4 Now consider how great this man *was*, unto whom even the patriarch Abraham gave the tenth of the spoils. Gen. 14:20; Acts 2:29; 7:8-9

5 And ᵀverily they that are of the sons of Levi, who receive the office of the priesthood, have a commandment to take tithes of the people according to the law, that is, of their brethren, though they come out of the loins of Abraham: *truly*

6 But he whose descent is not counted from them received tithes of Abraham, and blessed him that had the promises. Gen. 14:19

7 And without all contradiction the less is blessed of the better.

8 And here men that die receive tithes; but there he *receiveth them*, of whom it is witnessed that he liveth.   Heb. 5:6; 6:20; Rev. 1:18

9 And as I may so say, Levi also, who receiveth tithes, payed tithes in Abraham.

10 For he was yet in the loins of his father, when Melchisedec met him.

A New Law and a New Priesthood

11 If therefore perfection were by the Levitical priesthood, (for under it the people received the law,) what further need *was*

there that another priest should rise after the order of Melchisedec, and not be called after the order of Aaron?   Gal. 2:21; Heb. 5:6; 8:7

12 For the priesthood being changed, there is made of necessity a change also of the law.

13 For he of whom these things are spoken pertaineth to another tribe, of which no man gave attendance at the altar.

14 For *it is* evident that our Lord sprang out of Juda; of which tribe Moses spake nothing concerning priesthood. Is. 11:1; Mic. 5:2; Luke 3:33

15 And it is yet far more evident: for that after the ᵀsimilitude of Melchisedec there ariseth another priest,   *manner*

16 Who is made, not after the law of a ᵀcarnal commandment, but after the power of an endless life.   *material*

17 For he testifieth, Thou *art* a priest for ever after the order of Melchisedec. Ps. 110:4

18 For there is verily a disannulling of the commandment going before for the weakness and unprofitableness thereof.   Rom. 8:3; Gal. 4:9

19 For the law made nothing perfect, but the bringing in of a better hope *did*; by the which we draw nigh unto God. Acts 13:39; Heb. 4:16; 9:9

20 And inasmuch as not without an oath *he was made priest*:

21 (For those priests were made without an oath; but this with an oath by him that said unto him, The Lord sware and will not repent, Thou *art* a priest for ever after the order of Melchisedec:)   Ps. 110:4

22 By so much was Jesus made a surety of a better ᵀtestament.   *covenant*

23 And they truly were many priests, because they were not suffered to continue by reason of death:

24 But this *man*, because he continueth ever, hath an unchangeable priesthood.   John 12:34

25 Wherefore he is able also to save them to the uttermost that come unto God by him, seeing he ever liveth to make intercession for them.   John 14:6; Rom. 8:34; Heb. 7:19

> **7:25* Christ Present Through the Spirit**
>
> Though the ministration was to be removed from the earthly to the heavenly temple; though the sanctuary and our great high priest would be invisible to human sight, yet the disciples were to suffer no loss thereby. . . . While Jesus ministers in the sanctuary above, He is still by His Spirit the minister of the church on earth. . . . While He delegates His power to inferior ministers, His energizing presence is still with His church. *DA 166*

26 For such an high priest became us, *who is* holy, harmless, undefiled, separate from

---

* *For more information on the sanctuary, its furniture, and how these things apply to us today, see pages 1438–1446 of this Bible.*

sinners, and made higher than the heavens;   2 Cor. 5:21; Heb. 4:14-15; 8:1

27 Who needeth not daily, as those high priests, to offer up sacrifice, first for his own sins, and then for the people's: for this he did once, when he offered up himself.   Heb. 5:3

28 For the law maketh men high priests which have infirmity; but the word of the oath, which was since the law, *maketh* the Son, who is consecrated for evermore.   Heb. 1:2; 2:10

7:26, 27* Both Priest and Victim

In stooping to take upon Himself humanity, Christ revealed a character the opposite of the character of Satan. But He stepped still lower in the path of humiliation. . . . As the high priest laid aside his gorgeous pontifical robes, and officiated in the white linen dress of the common priest, so Christ took the form of a servant, and offered sacrifice, Himself the priest, Himself the victim. *DA 25*

Christ's Work Is Superior

8 Now of the things which we have spoken *this is* the sum: We have such an high priest, who is set on the right hand of the throne of the Majesty in the heavens;   Heb. 1:3

2 A minister of the sanctuary, and of the true tabernacle, which the Lord pitched, and not man.

3 For every high priest is ordained to offer gifts and sacrifices: wherefore *it is* of necessity that this man have somewhat also to offer.

4 For if he were on earth, he should not be a priest, seeing that there are priests that offer gifts according to the law:

5 Who serve unto the example and shadow of heavenly things, as Moses was admonished of God when he was about to make the tabernacle: for, See, saith he, *that* thou make all things according to the pattern shewed to thee in the mount.   Ex. 25:40; Col. 2:17; Heb. 10:1

8:1-5* The Two Sanctuaries

Here is revealed the sanctuary of the new covenant. The sanctuary of the first covenant was pitched by man, built by Moses; this is pitched by the Lord, not by man. In that sanctuary the earthly priests performed their service; in this, Christ, our great High Priest, ministers at God's right hand. One sanctuary was on earth, the other is in heaven. *GC 413*

The New Covenant Foretold by Jeremiah

6 But now hath he obtained a more excellent ministry, by how much also he is the mediator of a better covenant, which was established upon better promises.   2 Cor. 3:6-11; Heb. 12:24

7 For if that first *covenant* had been faultless, then should no place have been sought for the second.   Heb. 7:11, 18

8 For finding fault with them, he saith, Behold, the days come, saith the Lord, when I will make a new covenant with the house of Israel and with the house of Judah: Jer. 31:31-34

9 Not according to the covenant that I made with their fathers in the day when I took them by the hand to lead them out of the land of Egypt; because they continued not in my covenant, and I regarded them not, saith the Lord.   Deut. 5:2-3

10 For this *is* the covenant that I will make with the house of Israel after those days, saith the Lord; I will put my laws into their mind, and write them in their hearts: and I will be to them a God, and they shall be to me a people: Jer. 31:33; Zech. 8:8; 2 Cor. 3:3

God's Law See James 1:22–25.

Redemption's Heavenly Work

Hebrews 8*

In the temple in heaven, the dwelling place of God, His throne is established in righteousness and judgment. In the most holy place is His law, the great rule of right by which all mankind are tested. The ark that enshrines the tables of the law is covered with the mercy seat, before which Christ pleads His blood in the sinner's behalf. Thus is represented the union of justice and mercy in the plan of human redemption. This union infinite wisdom alone could devise and infinite power accomplish; it is a union that fills all heaven with wonder and adoration. The cherubim of the earthly sanctuary, looking reverently down upon the mercy seat, represent the interest with which the heavenly host contemplate the work of redemption. This is the mystery of mercy into which angels desire to look—that God can be just while He justifies the repenting sinner and renews His intercourse [association] with the fallen race; that Christ could stoop to raise unnumbered multitudes from the abyss of ruin and clothe them with the spotless garments of His own righteousness to unite with angels who have never fallen and to dwell forever in the presence of God. *GC 415*

* For more information on the sanctuary, its furniture, and how these things apply to us today, see pages 1438–1446 of this Bible.

> ### 8:10 The Process of Transformation
>
> The cross reveals the love of God. . . . If we do not resist . . . we shall be led to the foot of the cross in repentance for the sins that have crucified the Saviour. Then the Spirit of God through faith produces a new life in the soul. The thoughts and desires are brought into obedience to the will of Christ. The heart, the mind, are created anew in the image of Him who works in us to subdue all things to Himself. Then the law of God is written in the mind and heart. *DA 176*

11 And they shall not teach every man his neighbour, and every man his brother, saying, Know the Lord: for all shall know me, from the least to the greatest.   Is. 54:13; John 6:45

12 For I will be merciful to their unrighteousness, and their sins and their iniquities will I remember no more.   Rom. 11:27

13 In that he saith, A new *covenant*, he hath made the first old. Now that which decayeth and waxeth old *is* ready to vanish away.

Christ's Sacrifice Is Superior

9 Then ^Tverily the first *covenant* had also ordinances of divine service, and a worldly sanctuary.   Ex. 25:8; Heb. 8:2; 9:10-11 ◆ *truly*

2 For there was a tabernacle made; the first, wherein *was* the candlestick, and the table, and the shewbread; which is called the sanctuary.   Ex. 26:35; 40:4; Lev. 24:5-8

3 And after the second veil, the tabernacle which is called the Holiest of all;   Ex. 26:31-33

4 Which had the golden censer, and the ark of the covenant overlaid round about with gold, wherein *was* the golden pot that had manna, and Aaron's rod that budded, and the tables of the covenant;   Ex. 26:33; 40:3; Num. 17:10

5 And over it the cherubims of glory shadowing the mercyseat; of which we cannot now speak particularly.   Ex. 25:17-22; Lev. 16:2; 1 Kin. 8:6-7

6 Now when these things were thus ordained, the priests went always into the first tabernacle, accomplishing the service of God.   Num. 28:3

7 But into the second *went* the high priest alone once every year, not without blood, which he offered for himself, and *for* the errors of the people: Ex. 30:10; Lev. 16:34

8 The Holy Ghost this signifying, that the way into the holiest of all was not yet made ^Tmanifest, while as the first tabernacle was yet standing: John 14:6; Heb. 3:7 ◆ *known*

9 Which *was* a figure for the time then present, in which were offered both gifts and sacrifices, that could not make him that did the service perfect, as pertaining to the conscience;   Heb. 5:1

10 *Which stood* only in meats and drinks, and ^Tdivers washings, and ^Tcarnal ordinances,

imposed *on them* until the time of reformation.   Col. 2:16 ◆ *various* ◆ *material*

11 But Christ being come an high priest of good things to come, by a greater and more perfect tabernacle, not made with hands, that is to say, not of this building;   2 Cor. 5:1; Heb. 2:17

12 Neither by the blood of goats and calves, but by his own blood he entered in once into the holy place, having obtained eternal redemption *for us*.   Heb. 10:4

13 For if the blood of bulls and of goats, and the ashes of an heifer sprinkling the unclean, ^Tsanctifieth to the purifying of the flesh: *makes holy*

14 How much more shall the blood of Christ, who through the eternal Spirit offered himself without spot to God, purge your conscience from dead works to serve the living God?   Heb. 6:1; 10:22; 1 Pet. 3:18

The Promise of the New Covenant

15 And for this cause he is the mediator of the new testament, that by means of death, for the redemption of the ^Ttransgressions *that were* under the first testament, they which are called might receive the promise of eternal inheritance.   Rom. 8:28 ◆ *violations of the law*

> ### 9:11–15 A New Covenant
>
> Though this covenant was made with Adam and renewed to Abraham, it could not be ratified until the death of Christ. It had existed by the promise of God since the first intimation of redemption had been given; it had been accepted by faith; yet when ratified by Christ, it is called a *new* covenant. The law of God was the basis of this covenant, which was simply an arrangement for bringing men again into harmony with the divine will, placing them where they could obey God's law. *PP 370, 371*

16 For where a ^Ttestament *is*, there must also of necessity be the death of the testator.   *covenant*

17 For a testament *is* of force after men are dead: otherwise it is of no strength at all while the testator liveth.   Gal. 3:15

18 Whereupon neither the first *testament* was dedicated without blood.

19 For when Moses had spoken every precept to all the people according to the law, he took the blood of calves and of goats, with water, and scarlet wool, and ^Thyssop, and sprinkled both the book, and all the people,   Num. 19:6 ◆ *a bitter herb*

20 Saying, This *is* the blood of the testament which God hath enjoined unto you.   Ex. 24:8

21 Moreover he sprinkled with blood both the tabernacle, and all the vessels of the ministry.   Lev. 8:15

22 And almost all things are by the law purged with blood; and without shedding of blood is no ᵀremission. Lev. 17:11 ◆ *forgiveness*
23 *It was* therefore necessary that the patterns of things in the heavens should be purified with these; but the heavenly things themselves with better sacrifices than these. Heb. 8:5; 9:24
24 For Christ is not entered into the holy places made with hands, *which are* the figures of the true; but into heaven itself, now to appear in the presence of God for us: Heb. 8:2
25 Nor yet that he should offer himself often, as the high priest entereth into the holy place every year with blood of others; Heb. 9:7; 10:19
26 For then must he often have suffered since the foundation of the world: but now once in the end of the world hath he appeared to put away sin by the sacrifice of himself. Heb. 1:2; 7:27; 9:12
27 And as it is appointed unto men once to die, but after this the judgment: Gen. 3:19
28 So Christ was once offered to bear the sins of many; and unto them that look for him shall he appear the second time without sin unto salvation. Acts 1:11; Titus 2:13; 1 Pet. 2:24

9:28

Christ's Return See Matthew 24:36.

The Weakness of Sacrifices under the Law

10 For the law having a shadow of good things to come, *and* not the very image of the things, can never with those sacrifices which they offered year by year continually make the comers thereunto perfect. Col. 2:17; Heb. 8:5; 9:11

10:1 Symbols and Fulfillment

Paul endeavored to direct the minds of his hearers to the one great Sacrifice for sin. He pointed to the sacrifices that were shadows of good things to come, and then presented Christ as the antitype [fulfillment] of all those ceremonies—the object to which they pointed as the only source of life and hope for fallen man. *AA 424*

2 For then would they not have ceased to be offered? because that the worshippers once purged should have had no more conscience of sins.
3 But in those *sacrifices there is* a remembrance again *made* of sins every year. Heb. 9:7
4 For *it is* not possible that the blood of bulls and of goats should take away sins. Heb. 10:11
5 Wherefore when he cometh into the world, he saith, Sacrifice and offering thou wouldest not, but a body hast thou prepared me:

6 In burnt offerings and *sacrifices* for sin thou hast had no pleasure.
7 Then said I, Lo, I come (in the volume of the book it is written of me,) to do thy will, O God. Gen. 3:15

10:5–7 Humanity Veiled Christ's Divinity

Christ was about to visit our world, and to become incarnate. He says, "A body hast Thou prepared Me." Had He appeared with the glory that was His with the Father before the world was, we could not have endured the light of His presence. That we might behold it and not be destroyed, the manifestation of His glory was shrouded. His divinity was veiled with humanity—the invisible glory in the visible human form. *DA 23*

8 Above when he said, Sacrifice and offering and burnt offerings and *offering* for sin thou wouldest not, neither hadst pleasure *therein;* which are offered by the law; Heb. 10:5
9 Then said he, Lo, I come to do thy will, O God. He taketh away the first, that he may establish the second. Heb. 10:7
10 By the which will we are sanctified through the offering of the body of Jesus Christ once *for all.* John 17:19
11 And every priest standeth daily ministering and offering oftentimes the same sacrifices, which can never take away sins: Heb. 5:1
12 But this man, after he had offered one sacrifice for sins for ever, sat down on the right hand of God; Heb. 1:3
13 From henceforth expecting till his enemies be made his footstool. Ps. 110:1; Heb. 1:13
14 For by one offering he hath perfected for ever them that are ᵀsanctified. Heb. 10:1
15 *Whereof* the Holy Ghost also is a witness to us: for after that he had said before, Heb. 3:7
16 This *is* the covenant that I will make with them after those days, saith the Lord, I will put my laws into their hearts, and in their minds will I write them; Rom. 11:27
17 And their sins and iniquities will I remember no more. Heb. 8:12
18 Now where ᵀremission of these *is, there is* no more offering for sin. *forgiveness*

We Must Hold Fast to Faith

19 Having therefore, brethren, boldness to enter into the holiest by the blood of Jesus,
20 By a new and living way, which he hath ᵀconsecrated for us, through the veil, that is to say, his flesh; John 10:9; 14:6; Heb. 9:3 ◆ *set apart*
21 And *having* an high priest over the house of God; 1 Tim. 3:15; Heb. 2:17

22 Let us draw near with a true heart in full assurance of faith, having our hearts sprinkled from an evil conscience, and our bodies washed with pure water. Ezek. 36:25; 1 Cor. 6:11
23 Let us hold fast the profession of *our* faith without wavering; (for he *is* faithful that promised;) 1 Cor. 1:9; Heb. 3:6; 11:11

Encourage Each Other
24 And let us consider one another to provoke unto love and to good works: Titus 3:8
25 Not forsaking the assembling of ourselves together, as the manner of some *is*; but exhorting *one another*: and so much the more, as ye see the day approaching. Matt. 18:20; Acts 2:42
26 For if we sin wilfully after that we have received the knowledge of the truth, there remaineth no more sacrifice for sins, Deut. 17:12
27 But a certain fearful looking for of judgment and fiery ᵀindignation, which shall devour the adversaries. Is. 26:11 ◆ anger

---

10:26, 27 Finally, Fully Cut Off From God

God works by the manifestation of His Spirit to reprove and convict the sinner; and if the Spirit's work is finally rejected, there is no more that God can do for the soul. The last resource of divine mercy has been employed. The transgressor has cut himself off from God, and sin has no remedy to cure itself. There is no reserved power by which God can work to convict and convert the sinner. *PP 405*

---

28 He that despised Moses' law died without mercy under two or three witnesses: Heb. 2:2
29 Of how much sorer punishment, suppose ye, shall he be thought worthy, who

hath ᵀtrodden under foot the Son of God, and hath counted the blood of the covenant, wherewith he was sanctified, an unholy thing, and hath done ᵀdespite unto the Spirit of grace? Eph. 4:30; Heb. 2:3; 9:13 ◆ trampled ◆ contempt
30 For we know him that hath said, Vengeance *belongeth* unto me, I will recompense, saith the Lord. And again, The Lord shall judge his people. Deut. 32:35-36; Ps. 50:4; Rom. 12:19
31 *It is* a fearful thing to fall into the hands of the living God. Is. 33:14
32 But call to remembrance the former days, in which, after ye were illuminated, ye endured a great fight of afflictions; Phil. 1:29-30
33 Partly, whilst ye were made a gazingstock both by reproaches and afflictions; and partly, whilst ye became companions of them that were so used. 1 Cor. 4:9; Phil. 4:14; 1 Thess. 2:14
34 For ye had compassion of me in my bonds, and took joyfully the spoiling of your goods, knowing in yourselves that ye have in heaven a better and an enduring substance. 1 Pet. 1:4
35 Cast not away therefore your confidence, which hath great recompence of reward. Heb. 11:26
36 For ye have need of patience, that, after ye have done the will of God, ye might receive the promise. Luke 21:19; Heb. 6:15; 12:1
37 For yet a little while, and he that shall come will come, and will not tarry. Rev. 22:20
38 Now the just shall live by faith: but if *any man* draw back, my soul shall have no pleasure in him. Hab. 2:4; Rom. 1:17; Gal. 3:11
39 But we are not of them who draw back unto ᵀperdition; but of them that believe to the saving of the soul. destruction

---

Understanding Faith Compared to Presumption

Hebrews 11:6

The tempter can never compel us to do evil. He cannot control minds unless they are yielded to his control. The will must consent, faith must let go its hold upon Christ, before Satan can exercise his power upon us. But every sinful desire we cherish affords him a foothold. Every point in which we fail of meeting the divine standard is an open door by which he can enter to tempt and destroy us. And every failure or defeat on our part gives occasion for him to reproach Christ. . . .

We should not present our petitions to God to *prove* whether He will fulfill His word, but *because* He will fulfill it; not to prove that He loves us, but because He loves us. "Without faith it is impossible to please Him: for he that cometh to God must believe that He is, and that He is a rewarder of them that diligently seek Him" (Hebrews 11:6). . . .

But faith is in no sense allied to presumption. Only he who has true faith is secure against presumption. For presumption is Satan's counterfeit of faith. Faith claims God's promises, and brings forth fruit in obedience. Presumption also claims the promises, but uses them as Satan did, to excuse transgression. Faith would have led our first parents to trust the love of God, and to obey His commands. Presumption led them to transgress His law, believing that His great love would save them from the consequence of their sin. It is not faith that claims the favor of Heaven without complying with the conditions on which mercy is to be granted. Genuine faith has its foundation in the promises and provisions of the Scriptures. *DA 125, 126*

Faith Exemplified

11 Now faith is the substance of things hoped for, the evidence of things not seen.   2 Cor. 4:18; 5:7, 17

Faith See Hebrews 11:6.

2 For by it the elders obtained a good report.
3 Through faith we understand that the worlds were framed by the word of God, so that things which are seen were not made of things which do appear.   John 1:3

Faith

4 By faith Abel offered unto God a more excellent sacrifice than Cain, by which he obtained witness that he was righteous, God testifying of his gifts: and by it he being dead yet speaketh.   Gen. 4:10; Matt. 23:35; Heb. 12:24
5 By faith Enoch was translated that he should not see death; and was not found, because God had translated him: for before his translation he had this testimony, that he pleased God.   2 Kin. 2:11
6 But without faith *it is* impossible to please *him*: for he that cometh to God must believe that he is, and *that* he is a rewarder of them that diligently seek him.   1 Chr. 28:9

Faith See Habakkuk 2:4.

7 By faith Noah, being warned of God of things not seen as yet, moved with fear, prepared an ark to the saving of his house; by the which he condemned the world, and became heir of the righteousness which is by faith.   Ezek. 14:14, 20; 1 Pet. 3:20
8 By faith Abraham, when he was called to go out into a place which he should after receive for an inheritance, obeyed; and he went out, not knowing whither he went.   Gen. 12:1-4, 7; Acts 7:2-4
9 By faith he sojourned in the land of promise, as *in* a strange country, dwelling in tabernacles with Isaac and Jacob, the heirs with him of the same promise: Gen. 12:8; 13:3; 18:9
10 For he looked for a city which hath foundations, whose builder and maker *is* God.   Heb. 12:22; 13:14; Rev. 21:2

11:10 Seeing Heaven by Faith

According to the teaching of the Holy Scriptures, the only city that will endure is the city whose builder and maker is God. With the eye of faith man may behold the threshold of heaven, flushed with God's living glory. Through His ministering servants the Lord Jesus is calling upon men to strive with sanctified ambition to secure the immortal inheritance. He urges them to lay up treasure beside the throne of God. *PK 274*

11 Through faith also Sara herself received strength to conceive seed, and was delivered of a child when she was past age, because she judged him faithful who had promised.   Gen. 17:17-19; 18:11-14; Heb. 10:23
12 Therefore sprang there even of one, and him as good as dead, *so many as* the stars of the sky in multitude, and as the sand which is by the sea shore innumerable.   Gen. 15:5
13 These all died in faith, not having received the promises, but having seen them afar off, and were persuaded of *them,* and embraced *them,* and confessed that they were strangers and pilgrims on the earth. Gen. 23:4; 47:9; Ps. 39:12
14 For they that say such things declare plainly that they seek a country.
15 And truly, if they had been mindful of that *country* from whence they came out, they might have had opportunity to have returned.   Gen. 24:6-8
16 But now they desire a better *country,* that is, an heavenly: wherefore God is not ashamed to be called their God: for he hath prepared for them a city.   Ex. 3:6, 15; Heb. 2:11
17 By faith Abraham, when he was tried, offered up Isaac: and he that had received the promises offered up his only begotten *son,*
18 Of whom it was said, That in Isaac shall thy seed be called: Gen. 21:12; Rom. 9:7
19 Accounting that God *was* able to raise *him* up, even from the dead; from whence also he received him in a figure.   Rom. 4:17-21
20 By faith Isaac blessed Jacob and Esau concerning things to come.
21 By faith Jacob, when he was a dying, blessed both the sons of Joseph; and worshipped, *leaning* upon the top of his staff.
22 By faith Joseph, when he died, made mention of the departing of the children of Israel; and gave commandment concerning his bones.   Gen. 50:24-25; Ex. 13:19
23 By faith Moses, when he was born, was hid three months of his parents, because they saw *he was* a proper child; and they were not afraid of the king's commandment.   Ex. 1:16, 22

11:24–27 What Moses Saw by Faith

Moses had been instructed in regard to the final reward to be given to the humble and obedient servants of God, and worldly gain sank to its proper insignificance in comparison. . . . He looked beyond the gorgeous palace, beyond a monarch's crown, to the high honors that will be bestowed on the saints of the Most High in a kingdom untainted by sin. He saw by faith an imperishable crown that the King of heaven would place on the brow of the overcomer. *PP 246*

24 By faith Moses, when he was come to years, refused to be called the son of Pharaoh's daughter;   Ex. 2:10-11

25 Choosing rather to suffer affliction with the people of God, than to enjoy the pleasures of sin for a season; Job 36:21
26 Esteeming the reproach of Christ greater riches than the treasures in Egypt: for he had respect unto the recompence of the reward. Heb. 2:2
27 By faith he forsook Egypt, not fearing the wrath of the king: for he endured, as seeing him who is invisible. Heb. 11:13
28 Through faith he kept the passover, and the sprinkling of blood, lest he that destroyed the firstborn should touch them. Ex. 12:21-30
29 By faith they passed through the Red sea as by dry *land*: which the Egyptians ᵀassaying to do were drowned. *attempting*

11:29 A Test of Faith

God in His providence brought the Hebrews into the mountain fastnesses before the sea, that He might manifest His power in their deliverance and signally humble the pride of their oppressors. He might have saved them in any other way, but He chose this method in order to test their faith and strengthen their trust in Him. *PP 290*

---

30 By faith the walls of Jericho fell down, after they were ᵀcompassed about seven days.
31 By faith the harlot Rahab perished not with them that believed not, when she had received the spies with peace. Josh. 6:22-25
32 And what shall I more say? for the time would fail me to tell of Gedeon, and *of* Barak, and *of* Samson, and *of* Jephthae; *of* David also, and Samuel, and *of* the prophets: 1 Sam. 1:20; 16:1, 13
33 Who through faith subdued kingdoms, ᵀwrought righteousness, obtained promises, stopped the mouths of lions, Judg. 14:5 ♦ *worked*
34 Quenched the violence of fire, escaped the edge of the sword, out of weakness were made strong, waxed valiant in fight, turned to flight the armies of the aliens. Judg. 15:8
35 Women received their dead raised to life again: and others were tortured, not accepting deliverance; that they might obtain a better resurrection:
36 And others had trial of *cruel* mockings and scourgings, yea, moreover of bonds and imprisonment: Gen. 39:20; 1 Kin. 22:27; Jer. 20:2
37 They were stoned, they were sawn ᵀasunder, were tempted, were slain with the sword: they wandered about in sheepskins and goatskins; being destitute, afflicted, tormented; 1 Kin. 19:10; 2 Kin. 1:8; 2 Chr. 24:21 ♦ *apart*
38 (Of whom the world was not worthy:) they wandered in deserts, and *in* mountains, and *in* dens and caves of the earth. 1 Sam. 22:1
39 And these all, having obtained a good report through faith, received not the promise:
40 God having provided some better thing for us, that they without us should not be made perfect. Rev. 6:11

11:36–40 Rejoicing Over Persecution

Christ is acquainted with all that is misunderstood and misrepresented by men. . . .

"When men shall revile you, and persecute you," said Jesus, "rejoice, and be exceeding glad" [Matthew 5:11, 12]. . . .

In every age God's chosen messengers have been reviled and persecuted, yet through their affliction the knowledge of God has been spread abroad. . . . The minds of the people must be agitated; every controversy, every reproach, every effort to restrict liberty of conscience, is God's means of awakening minds that otherwise might slumber. *MB 32, 33*

We Must Persevere in Faith

12 Wherefore seeing we also are ᵀcompassed about with so great a cloud of witnesses, let us lay aside every weight, and the sin which doth so easily beset *us*, and

---

The Cross Our Hope

Hebrews 12:2

If those who today are teaching the word of God, would uplift the cross of Christ higher and still higher, their ministry would be far more successful. If sinners can be led to give one earnest look at the cross, if they can obtain a full view of the crucified Saviour, they will realize the depth of God's compassion and the sinfulness of sin.

Christ's death proves God's great love for man. It is our pledge of salvation. To remove the cross from the Christian would be like blotting the sun from the sky. The cross brings us near to God, reconciling us to Him. With the relenting compassion of a father's love, Jehovah looks upon the suffering that His Son endured in order to save the race from eternal death, and accepts us in the Beloved.

Without the cross, man could have no union with the Father. On it depends our every hope. From it shines the light of the Saviour's love, and when at the foot of the cross the sinner looks up to the One who died to save him, he may rejoice with fullness of joy, for his sins are pardoned. Kneeling in faith at the cross, he has reached the highest place to which man can attain. *AA 209, 210*

let us run with patience the race that is set before us, *surrounded*

12:1, 2 Racing Without Weights

In the epistle to the Hebrews is pointed out the single-hearted purpose that should characterize the Christian's race for eternal life. . . . Envy, malice, evil thinking, evil-speaking, covetousness—these are weights that the Christian must lay aside if he would run successfully the race for immortality. Every habit or practice that leads into sin and brings dishonor upon Christ must be put away, whatever the sacrifice. The blessing of heaven cannot attend any man in violating the eternal principles of right. *AA 312*

2 Looking unto Jesus the author and finisher of *our* faith; who for the joy that was set before him endured the cross, despising the shame, and is set down at the right hand of the throne of God. Is. 53:3; Luke 24:26; Heb. 1:3

The Christian Life

3 For consider him that endured such contradiction of sinners against himself, lest ye be wearied and faint in your minds. Gal. 6:9
4 Ye have not yet resisted unto blood, striving against sin. Heb. 10:32-34
5 And ye have forgotten the ᵀexhortation which speaketh unto you as unto children, My son, despise not thou the chastening of the Lord, nor faint when thou art rebuked of him: Prov. 3:11-12 ◆ *encouragement*
6 For whom the Lord loveth he chasteneth, and ᵀscourgeth every son whom he receiveth. Ps. 119:75; Prov. 3:12; Rev. 3:19 ◆ *whips*
7 If ye endure chastening, God dealeth with you as with sons; for what son is he whom the father ᵀchasteneth not? Prov. 13:24 ◆ *disciplines*
8 But if ye be without chastisement, whereof all are partakers, then are ye bastards, and not sons.
9 Furthermore we have had fathers of our flesh which corrected *us*, and we gave *them* reverence: shall we not much rather be in subjection unto the Father of spirits, and live? Num. 16:22; 27:16; Is. 38:16

12:10　Purpose of Life's Trials

The trials of life are God's workmen, to remove the impurities and roughness from our character. Their hewing, squaring, and chiseling, their burnishing and polishing, is a painful process; it is hard to be pressed down to the grinding wheel. But the stone is brought forth prepared to fill its place in the heavenly temple. Upon no useless material does the Master bestow such careful, thorough work. Only His precious stones are polished after the similitude of a palace. *MB 10*

10 For they ᵀverily for a few days ᵀchastened *us* after their own pleasure; but he for *our* profit, that *we* might be partakers of his holiness. 2 Pet. 1:4 ◆ *truly* ◆ *disciplined*
11 Now no ᵀchastening for the present seemeth to be joyous, but grievous: nevertheless afterward it yieldeth the peaceable fruit of righteousness unto them which are exercised thereby. Is. 32:17 ◆ *disciplining*
12 Wherefore lift up the hands which hang down, and the feeble knees; Job 4:3-4; Is. 35:3
13 And make straight paths for your feet, lest that which is lame be turned out of the way; but let it rather be healed. Prov. 4:26-27; Gal. 6:1
14 Follow peace with all *men*, and holiness, without which no man shall see the Lord:
15 Looking diligently lest any man fail of the grace of God; lest any root of bitterness springing up trouble *you*, and thereby many be defiled; Deut. 29:18; Gal. 5:4; Heb. 3:12
16 Lest there *be* any fornicator, or profane person, as Esau, who for one morsel of meat sold his birthright. Heb. 13:4
17 For ye know how that afterward, when he would have inherited the blessing, he was rejected: for he found no place of repentance, though he sought it carefully with tears.
18 For ye are not come unto the mount that might be touched, and that burned with fire, nor unto blackness, and darkness, and ᵀtempest, Ex. 20:18; Deut. 4:11 ◆ *storm*
19 And the sound of a trumpet, and the voice of words; which *voice* they that heard ᵀintreated that the word should not be spoken to them any more: Deut. 18:16 ◆ *pled*
20 (For they could not endure that which was commanded, And if so much as a beast touch the mountain, it shall be stoned, or thrust through with a dart: Ex. 19:12-13
21 And so terrible was the sight, *that* Moses said, I exceedingly fear and quake:) Ex. 19:16
22 But ye are come unto mount Sion, and unto the city of the living God, the heavenly Jerusalem, and to an innumerable company of angels, Ps. 48:2; Gal. 4:26; Rev. 14:1
23 To the general assembly and church of the firstborn, which are written in heaven, and to God the Judge of all, and to the spirits of just men made perfect, Gen. 18:25; Ex. 4:22; Luke 10:20
24 And to Jesus the mediator of the new covenant, and to the blood of sprinkling, that speaketh better things than *that of* Abel. Gen. 4:10; Heb. 8:6; 11:4
25 See that ye refuse not him that speaketh. For if they escaped not who refused him that spake on earth, much more *shall not* we *escape*, if we turn away from him that *speaketh* from heaven: Heb. 8:5; 11:7
26 Whose voice then shook the earth: but now he hath promised, saying, Yet once

more I shake not the earth only, but also heaven.   Ex. 19:18

27 And this *word*, Yet once more, signifieth the removing of those things that are shaken, as of things that are made, that those things which cannot be shaken may remain.

28 Wherefore we receiving a kingdom which cannot be moved, let us have grace, whereby we may serve God acceptably with reverence and godly fear: Dan. 2:44; Heb. 13:15

29 For our God *is* a consuming fire. Deut. 4:24

The Spirit of Christian Love

13 Let brotherly love continue.   1 Pet. 1:22
2 Be not forgetful to entertain strangers: for thereby some have entertained angels unawares.   Matt. 25:35; Rom. 12:13; 1 Pet. 4:9

> **13:1 God Will Vindicate Us**
>
> Even under false accusation those who are in the right can afford to be calm and considerate. God is acquainted with all that is misunderstood and misinterpreted by men, and we can safely leave our case in His hands. He will as surely vindicate the cause of those who put their trust in Him as He searched out the guilt of Achan [Joshua 7]. Those who are actuated by the spirit of Christ will possess that charity which suffers long and is kind. *PP 520*

3 Remember them that are in bonds, as bound with them; *and* them which suffer adversity, as being yourselves also in the body.   Matt. 25:36; Col. 4:18; Heb. 10:34

4 Marriage *is* honourable in all, and the bed undefiled: but whoremongers and adulterers God will judge.   Gen. 2:24; 1 Cor. 6:9; Gal. 5:19

5 *Let your* conversation *be* without ^Tcovetousness; *and be* content with such things as ye have: for he hath said, I will never leave thee, nor forsake thee.   Deut. 31:6, 8; Josh. 1:5 ♦ *greed*

6 So that we may boldly say, The Lord *is* my helper, and I will not fear what man shall do unto me.   Ps. 56:4

7 Remember them which have the rule over you, who have spoken unto you the word of God: whose faith follow, considering the end of *their* ^Tconversation. Heb. 6:12; 13:17, 24 ♦ *conduct*

8 Jesus Christ the same yesterday, and to day, and for ever.   Mal. 3:6; Heb. 1:12; James 1:17

9 Be not carried about with divers and strange doctrines. For *it is* a good thing that the heart be established with grace; not with meats, which have not profited them that have been occupied therein.   2 Cor. 1:21; Eph. 4:14

10 We have an altar, whereof they have no right to eat which serve the tabernacle.

11 For the bodies of those beasts, whose blood is brought into the sanctuary by the

high priest for sin, are burned without the camp.   Ex. 29:14; Lev. 9:11; 16:27

12 Wherefore Jesus also, that he might ^Tsanctify the people with his own blood, suffered without the gate.   Acts 7:58 ♦ *make the people holy*

13 Let us go forth therefore unto him without the camp, bearing his reproach.   Heb. 11:26

14 For here have we no continuing city, but we seek one to come.   Heb. 12:22

15 By him therefore let us offer the sacrifice of praise to God continually, that is, the fruit of *our* lips giving thanks to his name. Lev. 7:12

16 But to do good and to communicate forget not: for with such sacrifices God is well pleased.   Mic. 6:7-8; Rom. 12:13; Phil. 4:18

17 Obey them that have the rule over you, and submit yourselves: for they watch for your souls, as they that must give account, that they may do it with joy, and not with grief: for that *is* unprofitable for you. Acts 20:28

> **13:17 A True Minister's Work**
>
> The heart of the true minister is filled with an intense longing to save souls. Time and strength are spent, toilsome effort is not shunned; for others must hear the truths that brought to his own soul such gladness and peace and joy. . . . With invitations and pleadings, mingled with the assurances of God's love, he seeks to win souls to Jesus. *AA 371*

18 Pray for us: for we trust we have a good conscience, in all things willing to live honestly.   Acts 23:1; 24:16; 1 Thess. 5:25

19 But I beseech *you* the rather to do this, that I may be restored to you the sooner.

20 Now the God of peace, that brought again from the dead our Lord Jesus, that great shepherd of the sheep, through the blood of the everlasting covenant, Zech. 9:11; John 10:11; Acts 2:24

21 Make you perfect in every good work to do his will, working in you that which is wellpleasing in his sight, through Jesus Christ; to whom *be* glory for ever and ever. Amen.   Phil. 1:11; 2:13; 2 Thess. 2:17

Farewell

22 And I beseech you, brethren, suffer the word of exhortation: for I have written a letter unto you in few words.   Heb. 3:1; 1 Pet. 5:12

23 Know ye that *our* brother Timothy is set at liberty; with whom, if he come shortly, I will see you.   1 Thess. 3:2

24 Salute all them that have the rule over you, and all the saints. They of Italy salute you.   Acts 18:2; Heb. 13:7, 17

25 Grace *be* with you all. Amen.   Col. 4:18

THE EPISTLE OF

JAMES

Faith is exercised every day. For example, when you eat in a restaurant, the food is prepared by someone you don't know and cannot see. It is brought to you by a waiter you don't know. The hope, however, is that the restaurant is sanitary, the plates and cooking utensils are clean, and the cook and food handlers are trustworthy. This same faith is practiced when you drive your car, or visit the doctor, or buy groceries. In fact, in nearly every aspect of life, faith is practiced. Without faith we would be hampered, helpless, and hopeless in life.

Such is true in the spiritual life, as well. Faith is foundational and fundamental. All of the Christian life hinges on faith.

The Epistle of James reminds, informs, and instructs us on matters of faith—faith as it relates to trials, temptations, tests, truth of God's Word, the tongue, wisdom, separation from the world, and submission to God. For the spiritual life to work, faith must work. It is not enough to verbally say one has faith or intellectually claim to have faith; faith must be practically expressed every day in word and deed. Faith without works is dead, and a dead faith is worse than no faith at all.

Dates

The Epistle of James is believed to be one of the first books written in the New Testament. James, according to the Jewish historian Josephus, was martyred in A.D. 62. Scholars have proposed that the writing occurred after A.D. 44. Their reasons are as follows:

(1) James did not mention Gentile Christians and their relationship to Jewish Christians.

(2) Because of the lack of a distinctive theology, other than references, scholars believe that the letter occurred when Christianity was still in the early stages.

(3) The allusions to Christ have such little verbal agreement with the synoptic gospels, and therefore preceded them.

(4) James used the word "synagogue" as well as the word "church," indicating a very simple organization that was patterned after the early synagogue, predating a more formal Christian church organization.

(5) The issues involved in the Council in Jerusalem, which took place in A.D. 49 (Acts 15) are not mentioned.

Author

Four men named James are listed in the New Testament—James, the father of Judas (not Iscariot); James, the son of Alphaeus, one of the twelve disciples; James, the son of Zebedee and brother of John, one of Jesus' intimate disciples; and James, the Lord's half brother, one of the leaders in the Jerusalem church. James is quite a common name in New Testament times because it is the Greek counterpart to the Hebrew name Jacob. The list of the twelve apostles illustrates the commonality of the name (Matthew 10:2, 3; Mark 3:16–19; Luke 6:14–16). As such, sufficient evidence is not readily apparent to identify which James wrote this epistle.

Even though we cannot attribute authorship to any one person, we do know that the creator is well-versed in Greek literary composition. His word choice is rich, and he arranges his material in a Greek literary form of a popular, ethical address.

A few other details can also be surmised about the author. He lives in a land abundant in oil, wine, and figs. He lives near the sea. Salt and bitter springs are close to him. Rain seems to be of great importance, so the land may well be drought-ridden. These points suggest that Palestine is the location from which James records his epistle.

Meaning of the Name

Iakobos (James) is the Greek form of the Hebrew name "Jacob," a common Jewish name in the first century. The early title of this book was *Iakobou Epistole* or "Epistle of James."

James says little about Christ directly but his writings are saturated with allusions to the teaching of Christ. The most prominent are references to the Sermon on the Mount with fifteen indirect references (1:2, 4; 2:13; 4:11; 5:2).

Overview

James is perhaps the most practical book in the New Testament, reading like a "how to" book on living the Christian faith. This epistle has been called the Proverbs of the New Testament because of its pithy style and moralistic and practical teaching. It includes the practical aspects of Christian conduct more than doctrinal issues. Because of its many subjects this epistle is difficult to outline. Here, however, is a general division:

(1) *James 1:1–18, Faith Tests:* James explains the workings of faith under pressure— through trials. Though trials are difficult, they produce endurance in each believer.

(2) *James 1:19—5:6, Faith Characteristics:* The major issue is faith with an emphasis on a working faith. James believed that true saving faith involves actions resulting in a changed life (1:22, 23; 2:14–26). False faith is one that does not work and, therefore, is dead. In other words, a faith that is not demonstrated by loving acts stands on shaky ground. This faith is reflected in our speech as well.

(3) *James 5:7–20, Faith Triumphs:* Believers are encouraged to show endurance in prayer and while waiting for the return of Christ.

Unlocking James

KEY PEOPLE:
No people are mentioned by name other than James and the recipients of his letter, "the twelve tribes which are scattered abroad," indicating that this letter was written to Christians everywhere.

KEY EVENTS:
No events are recorded.

KEY WORD:
Faith, for James indentifies the characteristics of true faith. These characteristics are used as a test for his readers to evaluate the quality of their relationship to Christ. Real faith will produce real changes in a person's conduct and character.

KEY VERSES:
"What doth it profit, my brethren, though a man say he hath faith, and have not works? can faith save him? If a brother or sister be naked, and destitute of daily food, and one of you say unto them, Depart in peace, be ye warmed and filled; notwithstanding ye give them not those things which are needful to the body; what doth it profit? Even so faith, if it hath not works, is dead, being alone" (James 2:14–17).

KEY CHAPTER:
James 1, for it reveals the faith response to tests and temptations. It also discusses the readily available wisdom. Those who seek it should "ask of God, that giveth to all men liberally" (1:5).

Rejoice under Trials

1 James, a servant of God and of the Lord Jesus Christ, to the twelve tribes which are scattered abroad, greeting.   Acts 12:17; 26:7

2 My brethren, count it all joy when ye fall into ᵀdivers temptations;   James 1:12 ◆ *various*

3 Knowing *this*, that the trying of your faith worketh patience.   Heb. 10:36

4 But let patience have *her* perfect work, that ye may be perfect and entire, wanting nothing.   Matt. 5:48

5 If any of you lack wisdom, let him ask of God, that giveth to all *men* liberally, and upbraideth not; and it shall be given him.

6 But let him ask in faith, nothing wavering. For he that wavereth is like a wave of the sea driven with the wind and tossed.   Eph. 4:14

1:5, 6 Expect Great Things

We need to have far less confidence in what man can do and far more confidence in what God can do for every believing soul. He longs to have you reach after Him by faith. He longs to have you expect great things from Him. He longs to give you understanding in temporal as well as in spiritual matters. He can sharpen the intellect. He can give tact and skill. Put your talents into the work, ask God for wisdom, and it will be given you. *COL 146*

7 For let not that man think that he shall receive any thing of the Lord.

8 A double minded man *is* unstable in all his ways.   James 4:8; 2 Pet. 2:14; 3:16

9 Let the brother of low degree rejoice in that he is exalted:

10 But the rich, in that he is made low: because as the flower of the grass he shall pass away.   Ps. 102:11; 1 Cor. 7:31; 1 Pet. 1:24

11 For the sun is no sooner risen with a burning heat, but it withereth the grass, and the flower thereof falleth, and the grace of the fashion of it perisheth: so also shall the rich man fade away in his ways.   Is. 40:7-8

12 Blessed *is* the man that endureth temptation: for when he is tried, he shall receive the crown of life, which the Lord hath promised to them that love him.   1 Cor. 9:25; 2 Tim. 4:8

13 Let no man say when he is tempted, I am tempted of God: for God cannot be tempted with evil, neither tempteth he any man:

14 But every man is tempted, when he is drawn away of his own lust, and enticed.

15 Then when lust hath conceived, it bringeth forth sin: and sin, when it is finished, bringeth forth death.   Job 15:35; Ps. 7:14; Is. 59:4

16 Do not err, my beloved brethren.   James 1:19

17 Every good gift and every perfect gift is from above, and cometh down from the Father of lights, with whom is no variableness, neither shadow of turning.   Num. 23:19; Mal. 3:6

1:17 The Perfect Gift

The heart of God yearns over His earthly children with a love stronger than death. In giving up His Son, He has poured out to us all heaven in one gift. The Saviour's life and death and intercession, the ministry of angels, the pleading of the Spirit, the Father working above and through all, the unceasing interest of heavenly beings—all are enlisted in behalf of man's redemption. *SC 21*

18 Of his own will begat he us with the word of truth, that we should be a kind of firstfruits of his creatures.   John 1:13; 1 Pet. 1:23; Rev. 14:4

19 Wherefore, my beloved brethren, let every man be swift to hear, slow to speak, slow to wrath: Prov. 10:19; 14:29; 16:32

The Perfect Law of God

James 1:25

The tendency of the modern pulpit is to strain out the divine justice from the divine benevolence, to sink benevolence into a sentiment rather than exalt it into a principle. The new theological prism puts asunder what God has joined together. Is the divine law a good or an evil? It is a good. Then justice is good; for it is a disposition to execute the law. From the habit of underrating the divine law and justice, the extent and demerit of human disobedience, men easily slide into the habit of underestimating the grace which has provided an atonement for sin." Thus the gospel loses its value and importance in the minds of men, and soon they are ready practically to cast aside the Bible itself.

Many religious teachers assert that Christ by His death abolished the law, and men are henceforth free from its requirements. There are some who represent it as a grievous yoke, and in contrast to the bondage of the law they present the liberty to be enjoyed under the gospel. . . .

The claim that Christ by His death abolished His Father's law is without foundation. Had it been possible for the law to be changed or set aside, then Christ need not have died to save man from the penalty of sin. The death of Christ, so far from abolishing the law, proves that it is immutable. . . .

The law of God, from its very nature, is unchangeable. It is a revelation of the will and the character of its Author. God is love, and His law is love. Its two great principles are love to God and love to man. "Love is the fulfilling of the law" (Romans 13:10). . . . Such a law, being an expression of the mind and will of God, must be as enduring as its Author. *GC 465–467*

20 For the wrath of man worketh not the righteousness of God.

21 Wherefore lay apart all filthiness and superfluity of naughtiness, and receive with meekness the engrafted word, which is able to save your souls.   1 Cor. 15:2; Eph. 1:13; 4:22

22 But be ye doers of the word, and not hearers only, deceiving your own selves. Rom. 2:13

23 For if any be a hearer of the word, and not a doer, he is like unto a man beholding his natural face in a ᵀglass: mirror

24 For he beholdeth himself, and goeth his way, and ᵀstraightway forgetteth what manner of man he was.   right away

25 But whoso looketh into the perfect law of liberty, and continueth *therein*, he being not a forgetful hearer, but a doer of the work, this man shall be blessed in his deed.   John 13:17

> God's Law

26 If any man among you seem to be religious, and bridleth not his tongue, but deceiveth his own heart, this man's religion *is* vain.   Ps. 34:13

27 Pure religion and undefiled before God and the Father is this, To visit the fatherless and widows in their affliction, *and* to keep himself unspotted from the world.   Is. 1:23

Show No Partiality

2 My brethren, have not the faith of our Lord Jesus Christ, *the Lord* of glory, with respect of persons.   Lev. 19:15; 1 Cor. 2:8; James 2:9

2 For if there come unto your assembly a man with a gold ring, in goodly apparel, and there come in also a poor man in vile raiment;

3 And ye have respect to him that weareth the gay clothing, and say unto him, Sit thou here in a good place; and say to the poor, Stand thou there, or sit here under my footstool:

4 Are ye not then partial in yourselves, and are become judges of evil thoughts? John 7:24

5 Hearken, my beloved brethren, Hath not God chosen the poor of this world rich in faith, and heirs of the kingdom which he hath promised to them that love him?   Matt. 5:3

6 But ye have despised the poor. Do not rich men oppress you, and draw you before the judgment seats?   1 Cor. 11:22

7 Do not they blaspheme that worthy name by the which ye are called?   Acts 11:26

8 If ye fulfil the royal law according to the scripture, Thou shalt love thy neighbour as thyself, ye do well: Lev. 19:18

9 But if ye have respect to persons, ye commit sin, and are convinced of the law as ᵀtransgressors.   *those who violate the law*

10 For whosoever shall keep the whole law, and yet offend in one *point*, he is guilty of all.   Gal. 3:10

11 For he that said, Do not commit adultery, said also, Do not kill. Now if thou commit no adultery, yet if thou kill, thou art become a transgressor of the law.   Ex. 20:13-14

12 So speak ye, and so do, as they that shall be judged by the law of liberty.   James 1:25

13 For he shall have judgment without mercy, that hath shewed no mercy; and mercy rejoiceth against judgment. Prov. 21:13

Faith Is Shown by Deeds

14 What *doth it* profit, my brethren, though a man say he hath faith, and have not works? can faith save him?   James 1:22-25

15 If a brother or sister be naked, and destitute of daily food,   Luke 3:11

16 And one of you say unto them, Depart in peace, be *ye* warmed and filled; notwithstanding ye give them not those things which are needful to the body; what *doth it* profit?

17 Even so faith, if it hath not works, is dead, being alone.   James 2:14

18 Yea, a man may say, Thou hast faith, and I have works: shew me thy faith without thy works, and I will shew thee my faith by my works.   Gal. 5:6

19 Thou believest that there is one God; thou doest well: the devils also believe, and tremble.   Deut. 6:4; Matt. 8:29; Luke 4:34

20 But wilt thou know, O vain man, that faith without works is dead?   James 2:26

21 Was not Abraham our father justified by works, when he had offered Isaac his son upon the altar?   Gen. 22:16-18

22 Seest thou how faith wrought with his works, and by works was faith made perfect?   1 Thess. 1:3

23 And the scripture was fulfilled which saith, Abraham believed God, and it was imputed unto him for righteousness: and he was called the Friend of God.   Gen. 15:6; 2 Chr. 20:7; Is. 41:8
24 Ye see then how that by works a man is justified, and not by faith only.
25 Likewise also was not Rahab the harlot justified by works, when she had received the messengers, and had sent *them* out another way?   Josh. 2:1, 19-21; Heb. 11:31
26 For as the body without the spirit is dead, so faith without works is dead also. James 2:17

> Faith See Hebrews 11:3.

Control the Tongue

3 My brethren, be not many masters, knowing that we shall receive the greater condemnation.   Matt. 23:13
2 For in many things we offend all. If any man offend not in word, the same *is* a perfect man, *and* able also to bridle the whole body.   1 Kin. 8:46; Matt. 12:37; James 1:26
3 Behold, we put bits in the horses' mouths, that they may obey us; and we turn about their whole body.   Ps. 32:9
4 Behold also the ships, which though *they be* so great, and *are* driven of fierce winds, yet are they turned about with a very small helm, whithersoever the governor ᵀlisteth.   *pleases*
5 Even so the tongue is a little member, and boasteth great things. Behold, how great a matter a little fire kindleth!   Ps. 73:8-9
6 And the tongue *is* a fire, a world of iniquity: so is the tongue among our members, that it defileth the whole body, and setteth on fire the course of nature; and it is set on fire of hell.   Prov. 16:27
7 For every kind of beasts, and of birds, and of serpents, and of things in the sea, is tamed, and hath been tamed of mankind:
8 But the tongue can no man tame; *it is* an unruly evil, full of deadly poison.   Ps. 140:3
9 Therewith bless we God, even the Father; and therewith curse we men, which are made after the ᵀsimilitude of God.   1 Cor. 11:7 ◆ *image*
10 Out of the same mouth proceedeth blessing and cursing. My brethren, these things ought not so to be.
11 Doth a fountain send forth at the same place sweet *water* and bitter?
12 Can the fig tree, my brethren, bear olive berries? either a vine, figs? so *can* no fountain both yield salt water and fresh.

Live Wisely

13 Who *is* a wise man and ᵀendued with knowledge among you? let him shew out of a good conversation his works with meekness of wisdom. James 1:21; 2:18; 1 Pet. 2:12 ◆ *supplied*

14 But if ye have bitter envying and strife in your hearts, glory not, and lie not against the truth.   Acts 5:17; 2 Cor. 12:20; James 3:16
15 This wisdom descendeth not from above, but *is* earthly, sensual, devilish.   1 Cor. 3:19
16 For where envying and strife *is*, there *is* confusion and every evil work.   1 Cor. 3:3
17 But the wisdom that is from above is first pure, then peaceable, gentle, *and* easy to be ᵀintreated, full of mercy and good fruits, without partiality, and without hypocrisy.   Luke 6:36; Rom. 12:9; James 2:4 ◆ *dealt with*

> ### 3:17 Purity and Refinement
>
> Into the city of God there will enter nothing that defiles. All who are to be dwellers there will here have become pure in heart. In one who is learning of Jesus, there will be manifest a growing distaste for careless manners, unseemly language, and coarse thought. When Christ abides in the heart, there will be purity and refinement of thought and manner. *MB 24, 25*

18 And the fruit of righteousness is sown in peace of them that make peace.   Prov. 11:18

Stop Coveting

4 From whence *come* wars and fightings among you? *come they* not hence, *even* of your lusts that war in your members?   Rom. 7:23; 1 Pet. 2:11
2 Ye lust, and have not: ye kill, and desire to have, and cannot obtain: ye fight and war, yet ye have not, because ye ask not.
3 Ye ask, and receive not, because ye ask amiss, that ye may consume *it* upon your lusts.   Ps. 18:41; 1 John 3:22; 5:14
4 Ye adulterers and adulteresses, know ye not that the friendship of the world is ᵀenmity with God? whosoever therefore will be a friend of the world is the enemy of God.   John 15:19; Rom. 8:7 ◆ *hostility*

> ### 4:4 The Power of Influence
>
> The followers of Christ are to separate themselves from sinners, choosing their society only when there is opportunity to do them good. We cannot be too decided in shunning the company of those who exert an influence to draw us away from God. While we pray, "Lead us not into temptation," we are to shun temptation, so far as possible. *PP 459*

5 Do ye think that the scripture saith in vain, The spirit that dwelleth in us lusteth to envy?
6 But he giveth more grace. Wherefore he saith, God resisteth the proud, but giveth grace unto the humble.   Job 22:29; Prov. 3:34
7 Submit yourselves therefore to God. Resist the devil, and he will flee from you.

8 Draw nigh to God, and he will draw nigh to you. Cleanse *your* hands, *ye* sinners; and purify *your* hearts, *ye* double minded. Zech. 1:3
9 Be afflicted, and mourn, and weep: let your laughter be turned to mourning, and *your* joy to heaviness.   Luke 6:25
10 Humble yourselves in the sight of the Lord, and he shall lift you up.   Matt. 23:12

Stop Slandering

11 Speak not evil one of another, brethren. He that speaketh evil of *his* brother, and judgeth his brother, speaketh evil of the law, and judgeth the law: but if thou judge the law, thou art not a doer of the law, but a judge.   James 5:9; 1 Pet. 2:1
12 There is one lawgiver, who is able to save and to destroy: who art thou that judgest another?   Is. 33:22; Matt. 10:28; Rom. 14:4

Don't Brag about Future Plans

13 Go to now, ye that say, To day or to morrow we will go into such a city, and continue there a year, and buy and sell, and get gain: Prov. 27:1; James 5:1
14 Whereas ye know not what *shall be* on the morrow. For what *is* your life? It is even a vapour, that appeareth for a little time, and then vanisheth away.   Ps. 39:5; 102:3
15 For that ye *ought* to say, If the Lord will, we shall live, and do this, or that.   Acts 18:21
16 But now ye rejoice in your boastings: all such rejoicing is evil.   1 Cor. 5:6
17 Therefore to him that knoweth to do good, and doeth *it* not, to him it is sin.   Luke 12:47-48

God's Law See 1 John 3:4.

Advice to the Rich

5 Go to now, *ye* rich men, weep and howl for your miseries that shall come upon *you*.   Prov. 11:28
2 Your riches are corrupted, and your garments are motheaten. Job 13:28; Is. 50:9; Matt. 6:19
3 Your gold and silver is ᵀcankered; and the rust of them shall be a witness against you, and shall eat your flesh as it were fire. Ye have heaped treasure together for the last days.   Rom. 2:5 ◆ *decayed*
4 Behold, the hire of the labourers who have reaped down your fields, which is of you kept back by fraud, crieth: and the cries of them which have reaped are entered into the ears of the Lord of sabaoth.   Lev. 19:13; Jer. 22:13
5 Ye have lived in pleasure on the earth, and been ᵀwanton; ye have nourished your hearts, as in a day of slaughter.   Luke 16:19 ◆ *excessive*
6 Ye have condemned *and* killed the just; *and* he doth not resist you.

5:1–6 Oppression and Extortion

The Scriptures describe the condition of the world just before Christ's second coming. James the apostle pictures the greed and oppression that will prevail. . . . [James 5:1–6] is a picture of what exists today. By every species of oppression and extortion, men are piling up colossal fortunes, while the cries of starving humanity are coming up before God. *COL 170*

Be Patient

7 Be patient therefore, brethren, unto the coming of the Lord. Behold, the husbandman waiteth for the precious fruit of the earth,

If They Can Do It, We Can Do It

James 5:17, 18

[A little cloud] was enough. Elijah did not wait for the heavens to gather blackness. In that small cloud he beheld by faith an abundance of rain; and he acted in harmony with his faith, sending his servant quickly to Ahab with the message, "Prepare thy chariot, and get thee down, that the rain stop thee not" [1 Kings 18:44].

It was because Elijah was a man of large faith that God could use him in this grave crisis in the history of Israel. As he prayed, his faith reached out and grasped the promises of Heaven, and he persevered in prayer until his petitions were answered. He did not wait for the full evidence that God had heard him, but was willing to venture all on the slightest token of divine favor. And yet what he was enabled to do under God, all may do in their sphere of activity in God's service; for of the prophet from the mountains of Gilead it is written: "Elias was a man subject to like passions as we are, and he prayed earnestly that it might not rain: and it rained not on the earth by the space of three years and six months" (James 5:17).

Faith such as this is needed in the world today—faith that will lay hold on the promises of God's word and refuse to let go until Heaven hears. Faith such as this connects us closely with Heaven, and brings us strength for coping with the powers of darkness. Through faith God's children have "subdued kingdoms, wrought righteousness, obtained promises, stopped the mouths of lions, quenched the violence of fire, escaped the edge of the sword, out of weakness were made strong, waxed valiant in fight, turned to flight the armies of the aliens" (Hebrews 11:33, 34). And through faith we today are to reach the heights of God's purpose for us. "If thou canst believe, all things are possible to him that believeth" (Mark 9:23). *PK 156, 157*

and hath long patience for it, until he receive the early and latter rain.   Deut. 11:14

8 Be ye also patient; stablish your hearts: for the coming of the Lord draweth nigh.   Phil. 4:5

Christ's Return See 1 John 2:28.

‡Signs of the End

9 Grudge not one against another, brethren, lest ye be condemned: behold, the judge standeth before the door.   Matt. 24:33; 1 Cor. 4:5

10 Take, my brethren, the prophets, who have spoken in the name of the Lord, for an example of suffering affliction, and of patience.

11 Behold, we count them happy which endure. Ye have heard of the patience of Job, and have seen the end of the Lord; that the Lord is very pitiful, and of tender mercy.   Ex. 34:6

Don't Take Oaths

12 But above all things, my brethren, swear not, neither by heaven, neither by the earth, neither by any other oath: but let your yea be yea; and *your* nay, nay; lest ye fall into condemnation.

The Power of Prayer

13 Is any among you afflicted? let him pray. Is any merry? let him sing psalms.   Ps. 50:15

14 Is any sick among you? let him call for the elders of the church; and let them pray over him, anointing him with oil in the name of the Lord: Mark 6:13; 16:18; Acts 14:23

15 And the prayer of faith shall save the sick, and the Lord shall raise him up; and if he have committed sins, they shall be forgiven him.   Is. 33:24

16 Confess *your* faults one to another, and pray one for another, that ye may be healed. The effectual fervent prayer of a righteous man availeth much.   Gen. 18:23-32; 20:17; Matt. 3:6

17 Elias was a man subject to like passions as we are, and he prayed earnestly that it might not rain: and it rained not on the earth by the space of three years and six months.   1 Kin. 17:1; Luke 4:25; Acts 14:15

18 And he prayed again, and the heaven gave rain, and the earth brought forth her fruit.   1 Kin. 18:42-45

5:19, 20 Helping the Erring

Do not put him to shame by exposing his fault to others, nor bring dishonor upon Christ by making public the sin or error of one who bears His name. Often the truth must be plainly spoken to the erring; he must be led to see his error, that he may reform. But you are not to judge or to condemn. . . . In treating the wounds of the soul, there is need of the most delicate touch, the finest sensibility. *DA 440*

Help Those Who Wander

19 Brethren, if any of you do err from the truth, and one convert him;   Matt. 18:15; Gal. 6:1

20 Let him know, that he which converteth the sinner from the error of his way shall save a soul from death, and shall hide a multitude of sins.   Prov. 10:12; Rom. 11:14; 1 Pet. 4:8

THE FIRST EPISTLE OF

PETER

Bad news usually inspires dread in the heart, because we often feel unprepared to handle calamity. Yet Jesus never precludes His followers from knowing about hard times. He also never conceals a difficult message.

Believers are told throughout Scripture that they will be persecuted for their faith. Jesus warned of it just before His crucifixion (John 16:33). This truth has been evident throughout the twenty centuries since Christ walked on the earth. It is this truth that drives the first epistle of Peter.

During the time when Peter wrote this book, the Roman emperor Nero and the Roman authorities tortured and killed Christians. But Peter encouraged perseverance, knowing that faith in Christ gave the believer hope: "Wherein ye greatly rejoice, though now for a season, if need be, ye are in heaviness through manifold temptations" (1:6). Though times were hard, Peter knew that the persecution was temporary and would prove the genuineness of their faith, that it "might be found unto praise and honour and glory at the appearing of Jesus Christ" (1:7).

Believers today also will face persecution. Nonetheless, faith in Christ is our hope of victory as we follow in His footsteps to lead holy lives in an often hostile world.

Dates

The persecution under Nero began around A.D. 64. Peter is taken to Rome at the end of his ministry, where Nero orders his imprisonment about the same time as Paul's second arrest, which was about A.D. 66. Although the precise date that Peter writes his first epistle cannot be verified, it likely is penned in the middle sixties of the first century A.D. Here in Rome, for the first time in their ministries, these two long-serving apostles endure their last days witnessing for Christ in close proximity. Their martyrdom fueled the rapidly spreading fire of Christianity.

Author

The internal evidence in favor of Peter's authorship is strong. Peter makes notes of his authorship in the first verse: "Peter, an apostle of Jesus Christ, to the strangers scattered throughout Pontus, Galatia, Cappadocia, Asia, and Bithynia" (1:1). Certain phrases in this letter also are similar to Peter's sermons in the Book of Acts.

Peter writes this letter from Rome to believers scattered throughout Asia Minor. The majority of the believers at this time are Gentiles; Jewish Christians are in the minority, in which he has a vested interest. However, he does not restrict his remarks to the minority. Peter was the first to baptize Gentiles and to support their equal status in the church.

Nevertheless, critics have challenged Peter's authorship on several grounds. First, the Greek phraseology is too elegant for someone of his educational limitations. Second, the theology resembles Paul's. Third, little reference is made to the life of Christ, which is surprising given how close Peter and Christ were. Fourth, some suggest that Peter had no personal connection to the churches of Asia Minor; however, this remains unproven, especially since he speaks to them directly in 1:1. These challenges are inadequate and easily countered. Nevertheless, none of these objections is irrefutable.

Meaning of the Name

The first sentence of 1 Peter has *Petros apostolos Iesou Christou*, which means, "Peter, an apostle of Jesus Christ." The early title of the book is *Petrou A*, or "Of Peter I."

Christ in 1 Peter

Since Christ suffered in His body, He is to serve as our example of suffering and our hope while living in our fallen world. Peter uses Christ's example of suffering to frame his letter to believers in all places and times. Christ's death and resurrection give us the opportunity to find faith in Him: "Who his own self bare our sins in his own body on the tree, that we, being dead to sins, should live unto righteousness: by whose stripes ye were healed" (2:24).

In writing his first epistle, Peter crafts his message in a pastoral fashion. As thread is woven to produce fabric, he weaves throughout his letter that unsettling times of persecution are ahead. Yet, we are to rejoice in our trials by fire (4:12, 13). Using this tapestry as a backdrop, Peter uses his words to fortify the believers' faith, to impress upon them the necessity of unblemished conduct, to be neighborly, to exhibit allegiance to Christ in living their lives, and to move forward in preparing their hearts to meet their Lord and Savior. To lead the new Christians in achieving these laudable goals, Peter provides detailed advice for servants (2:18), wives (3:1–6), husbands (3:7), elders (5:1–4), and the youth (5:5–9). First Peter can be divided into three parts, each referencing some aspect of the believer's life.

(1) *1 Peter 1:1—2:12, Salvation:* Peter reminds his readers of the salvation they gained through God's grace. Believers are "born again, not of corruptible seed, but of incorruptible, by the word of God, which liveth and abideth for ever" (1:23). Sanctification is the response to salvation (1:13—2:10). "The sincere milk of the word" (2:2) aids in spiritual growth.

(2) *1 Peter 2:13—3:12, Submission:* In this section, Peter tells his readers about the importance of submission—submitting to the King, submitting of wives to husbands, and one to another. Right relationships are a product of submission.

(3) *1 Peter 3:13—5:14, Suffering:* Since Christ suffered in the body, Peter tells his readers that we are to "arm" ourselves with this same attitude. As such, we are to devote our lives to the will of God and not to the evil desires of the flesh.

❧ KEY PEOPLE:
Peter, Silas, Mark

❧ KEY EVENTS:
The persecution under Nero; the dispersion of the Jews throughout Palestine

❧ KEY WORD:
Suffering, which is the message of 1 Peter. When Peter wrote this book, persecution under Nero was just beginning. Knowing that this persecution would only get worse for these believers—and also knowing that the basic trials in life are a constant—Peter wanted to explain how faith in Christ could help a believer through tough times. For Peter, suffering for the cause of Christ was privilege.

❧ KEY VERSES:
"Of which salvation the prophets have enquired and searched diligently, who prophesied of the grace that should come unto you: searching what, or what manner of time the Spirit of Christ which was in them did signify, when it testified beforehand the sufferings of Christ, and the glory that should follow. Unto whom it was revealed, that not unto themselves, but unto us they did minister the things, which are now reported unto you by them that have preached the gospel unto you with the Holy Ghost sent down from heaven; which things the angels desire to look into" (1 Peter 1:10–12).

"Beloved, think it not strange concerning the fiery trial which is to try you, as though some strange thing happened unto you: but rejoice, inasmuch as ye are partakers of Christ's sufferings; that, when his glory shall be revealed, ye may be glad also with exceeding joy" (1 Peter 4:12–13).

❧ KEY CHAPTER:
1 Peter 4, which provides guidance on handling persecution. Since Christ has suffered, He is to be our model (4:1–2). In addition, we are to "rejoice, inasmuch as ye are partakers of Christ's sufferings" (4:13).

God's Many Mercies

1 Peter, an apostle of Jesus Christ, to the strangers scattered throughout Pontus, Galatia, Cappadocia, Asia, and Bithynia,

2 Elect according to the foreknowledge of God the Father, through sanctification of the Spirit, unto obedience and sprinkling of the blood of Jesus Christ: Grace unto you, and peace, be multiplied.   Rom. 11:2; 2 Thess. 2:13

3 Blessed *be* the God and Father of our Lord Jesus Christ, which according to his abundant mercy hath ᵀbegotten us again unto a lively hope by the resurrection of Jesus Christ from the dead, 1 Cor. 15:20; 2 Cor. 1:3; Eph. 1:3 ◆ *brought forth*

4 To an inheritance incorruptible, and undefiled, and that fadeth not away, reserved in heaven for you,   Col. 1:5

5 Who are kept by the power of God through faith unto salvation ready to be revealed in the last time.   Eph. 2:8

6 Wherein ye greatly rejoice, though now for a season, if need be, ye are in heaviness through manifold temptations: Is. 61:3; Rom. 5:2

7 That the trial of your faith, being much more precious than of gold that perisheth, though it be tried with fire, might be found unto praise and honour and glory at the appearing of Jesus Christ: Job 23:10; Prov. 17:3

8 Whom having not seen, ye love; in whom, though now ye see *him* not, yet believing, ye rejoice with joy unspeakable and full of glory: John 20:29; Heb. 11:27

9 Receiving the end of your faith, *even* the salvation of *your* souls.   Rom. 6:22

Salvation Was Prophesied

10 Of which salvation the prophets have enquired and searched diligently, who prophesied of the grace *that should come* unto you: Matt. 13:17; Luke 10:24

11 Searching what, or what manner of time the Spirit of Christ which was in them did signify, when it testified beforehand the sufferings of Christ, and the glory that should follow.   Is. 52:13-14; 53; 2 Pet. 1:21

12 Unto whom it was revealed, that not unto themselves, but unto us they did minister the things, which are now reported unto you by them that have preached the gospel unto you with the Holy Ghost sent down from heaven; which things the angels desire to look into.   John 15:26

Hope in God's Mercy

13 Wherefore gird up the loins of your mind, be sober, and hope to the end for the grace that is to be brought unto you at the revelation of Jesus Christ;   1 Pet. 4:7

14 As obedient children, not fashioning yourselves according to the former lusts in your ignorance: Acts 17:30; Rom. 12:2; 1 Pet. 4:2-3

1:13 Guarding the Soul's Avenues

The apostle [Peter] sought to teach the believers how important it is to keep the mind from wandering to forbidden themes or from spending its energies on trifling subjects. Those who would not fall a prey to Satan's devices, must guard well the avenues of the soul; they must avoid reading, seeing, or hearing that which will suggest impure thoughts. *AA 518*

15 But as he which hath called you is holy, so be ye holy in all manner of conversation;   2 Cor. 7:1; Heb. 12:14; James 3:13

1:15 Living Out God's Love

The grace of Christ is to control the temper and the voice. Its working will be seen in politeness and tender regard shown by brother for brother, in kind, encouraging words. An angel presence is in the home. The life breathes a sweet perfume, which ascends to God as holy incense. Love is manifested in kindness, gentleness, forbearance, and long-suffering. *COL 102*

16 Because it is written, Be ye holy; for I am holy.   Lev. 11:44; 19:2; 20:7

17 And if ye call on the Father, who without respect of persons judgeth according to every man's work, pass the time of your sojourning *here* in fear: Matt. 6:9

18 Forasmuch as ye know that ye were not redeemed with corruptible things, *as* silver and gold, from your vain ᵀconversation *received* by tradition from your fathers; 1 Cor. 6:20 ◆ *conduct*

19 But with the precious blood of Christ, as of a lamb without blemish and without spot: Ex. 12:5; John 1:29; Acts 20:28

20 Who verily was foreordained before the foundation of the world, but was ᵀmanifest in these last times for you, Eph. 1:4 ◆ *made known*

21 Who by him do believe in God, that raised him up from the dead, and gave him glory; that your faith and hope might be in God.   Heb. 2:9

Love Each Other

22 Seeing ye have purified your souls in obeying the truth through the Spirit unto unfeigned love of the brethren, *see that ye* love one another with a pure heart fervently: Rom. 12:9-10; Heb. 13:1; James 4:8

23 Being born again, not of corruptible seed, but of incorruptible, by the word of God, which liveth and abideth for ever.   John 1:13

The Christian Life See 1 Peter 2:1, 2.

24 For all flesh *is* as grass, and all the glory of man as the flower of grass. The grass

withereth, and the flower thereof falleth away: Is. 40:6-8

25 But the word of the Lord endureth for ever. And this is the word which by the gospel is preached unto you.   Is. 40:8

Live as God's Chosen People

2 Wherefore laying aside all malice, and all guile, and hypocrisies, and envies, and all evil speakings,   Eph. 4:31; James 1:21; 4:11

2 As newborn babes, desire the sincere milk of the word, that ye may grow thereby:

> **The Christian Life** See Hebrews 5:12–14.

3 If so be ye have tasted that the Lord *is* gracious.

Christ Is the Cornerstone

4 To whom coming, *as unto* a living stone, ᵀdisallowed indeed of men, but chosen of God, *and* precious,   1 Pet. 2:7 ◆ *rejected*

5 Ye also, as ᵀlively stones, are built up a spiritual house, an holy priesthood, to offer up spiritual sacrifices, acceptable to God by Jesus Christ.   Is. 61:6; Phil. 4:18; 1 Pet. 2:9 ◆ *living*

6 Wherefore also it is contained in the scripture, Behold, I lay in Sion a chief corner stone, elect, precious: and he that believeth on him shall not be confounded.   Is. 28:16; Rom. 9:32-33

7 Unto you therefore which believe *he is* precious: but unto them which be disobedient, the stone which the builders disallowed, the same is made the head of the corner,   Matt. 21:42

8 And a stone of stumbling, and a rock of offence, *even to them* which stumble at the word, being disobedient: whereunto also they were appointed. Is. 8:14; Rom. 9:22; 1 Cor. 1:23

> **2:4–8 Christ: Two Kinds of Stone**
>
> In Isaiah's prophecy, Christ is declared to be both a sure foundation and a stone of stumbling. The apostle Peter, writing by inspiration of the Holy Spirit, clearly shows to whom Christ is a foundation stone, and to whom a rock of offense. *DA 599*

9 But ye *are* a chosen generation, a royal priesthood, an holy nation, a peculiar people; that ye should shew forth the praises of him who hath called you out of darkness into his marvellous light: Deut. 7:6; 10:15; Rev. 1:6

> **2:9 Mission of the Church**
>
> The church is God's appointed agency for the salvation of men. It was organized for service, and its mission is to carry the gospel to the world. From the beginning it has been God's plan that through His church shall be reflected to the world His fullness and His sufficiency. The members of the church, those whom He has called out of darkness into His marvelous light, are to show forth His glory. *AA 9*

10 Which in time past *were* not a people, but *are* now the people of God: which had not obtained mercy, but now have obtained mercy.

11 Dearly beloved, I beseech *you* as strangers and pilgrims, abstain from fleshly lusts, which war against the soul; Lev. 25:23; Rom. 8:13

12 Having your conversation honest among the Gentiles: that, whereas they speak against you as evildoers, they may by *your* good works, which they shall behold, glorify God in the day of visitation. Ps. 50:23; Matt. 5:16

Respect Authority

13 Submit yourselves to every ordinance of man for the Lord's sake: whether it be to the king, as supreme;   Titus 3:1

God's Special People

1 Peter 2:9

In these final hours of probation for the sons of men, when the fate of every soul is so soon to be decided forever, the Lord of heaven and earth expects His church to arouse to action as never before. Those who have been made free in Christ through a knowledge of precious truth, are regarded by the Lord Jesus as His chosen ones, favored above all other people on the face of the earth; and He is counting on them to show forth the praises of Him who hath called them out of darkness into marvelous light. The blessings which are so liberally bestowed are to be communicated to others. The good news of salvation is to go to every nation, kindred, tongue, and people. . . .

The coming of Christ will take place in the darkest period of this earth's history. The days of Noah and of Lot picture the condition of the world just before the coming of the Son of man. The Scriptures, pointing forward to this time, declare that Satan will work with all power and "with all deceivableness of unrighteousness" (2 Thessalonians 2:9, 10). His working is plainly revealed by the rapidly increasing darkness, the multitudinous errors, heresies, and delusions of these last days. Not only is Satan leading the world captive, but his deceptions are leavening the professed churches of our Lord Jesus Christ. The great apostasy will develop into darkness deep as midnight. To God's people it will be a night of trial, a night of weeping, a night of persecution for the truth's sake. But out of that night of darkness God's light will shine. *PK 716, 717*

14 Or unto governors, as unto them that are sent by him for the punishment of evildoers, and for the praise of them that do well.
15 For so is the will of God, that with well doing ye may put to silence the ignorance of foolish men: 1 Pet. 2:12
16 As free, and not using *your* liberty for a ᵀcloke of maliciousness, but as the servants of God.   Rom. 6:22; 1 Cor. 7:22; James 1:25 ♦ *cloak*
17 Honour all *men*. Love the brotherhood. Fear God. Honour the king. Prov. 24:21; Rom. 12:10

> **2:13–17 Always Consider What You Say**
>
> We are not required to defy authorities. Our words, whether spoken or written, should be carefully considered, lest we place ourselves on record as uttering that which would make us appear antagonistic to law and order. We are not to say or do anything that would unnecessarily close up our way. We are to go forward in Christ's name, advocating the truths committed to us. *AA 69*

18 Servants, *be* subject to *your* masters with all fear; not only to the good and gentle, but also to the ᵀfroward.   James 3:17 ♦ *false or perverse*
19 For this *is* thankworthy, if a man for conscience toward God endure grief, suffering wrongfully.   Rom. 13:5
20 For what glory *is it*, if, when ye be buffeted for your faults, ye shall take it patiently? but if, when ye do well, and suffer *for it*, ye take it patiently, this *is* acceptable with God.
21 For even hereunto were ye called: because Christ also suffered for us, leaving us an example, that ye should follow his steps: Matt. 16:24; John 16:33; Acts 14:22
22 Who did no sin, neither was ᵀguile found in his mouth: Is. 53:9; 2 Cor. 5:21; Heb. 4:15 ♦ *deceit*
23 Who, when he was reviled, reviled not again; when he suffered, he threatened not; but committed *himself* to him that judgeth righteously: Is. 53:7; Luke 23:46; Heb. 12:3
24 Who his own self bare our sins in his own body on the tree, that we, being dead to sins, should live unto righteousness: by whose stripes ye were healed.   Rom. 6:2, 11; Heb. 9:28
25 For ye were as sheep going astray; but are now returned unto the Shepherd and Bishop of your souls.   Ps. 119:176; Is. 53:6; Ezek. 34:6

Instructions for Wives and Husbands

3 Likewise, ye wives, *be* in subjection to your own husbands; that, if any obey not the word, they also may without the word be won by the conversation of the wives;
2 While they behold your ᵀchaste conversation *coupled* with fear.   *pure*
3 Whose adorning let it not be that outward *adorning* of plaiting the hair, and of wearing of gold, or of putting on of apparel; Is. 3:18-24

> **3:3, 4 One of Satan's Inventions**
>
> Almost as soon as they come into the world the children are subjected to fashion's influence. They hear more of dress than of their Saviour. . . . The display of dress is treated as of greater importance than the development of character. . . . For fashion's sake they are cheated out of a preparation for the life to come.
>
> It was the adversary of all good who instigated the invention of the ever-changing fashions. He desires nothing so much as to bring grief and dishonor to God by working the misery and ruin of human beings. *MH 291*

4 But *let it be* the hidden man of the heart, in that which is not corruptible, *even the ornament* of a meek and quiet spirit, which is in the sight of God of great price.   Ps. 149:4; Rom. 2:29

> **Christian Behavior** See Matthew 26:73, 74.

5 For after this manner in the old time the holy women also, who trusted in God, adorned themselves, being in subjection unto their own husbands: 1 Tim. 5:5
6 Even as Sara obeyed Abraham, calling him lord: whose daughters ye are, as long as ye do well, and are not afraid with any amazement.   Gen. 18:12
7 Likewise, ye husbands, dwell with *them* according to knowledge, giving honour unto the wife, as unto the weaker vessel, and as being heirs together of the grace of life; that your prayers be not hindered.   Eph. 5:25-28; Col. 3:19

Show Brotherly Love

8 Finally, *be ye* all of one mind, having compassion one of another, love as brethren, *be* pitiful, *be* courteous: Matt. 18:33
9 Not rendering evil for evil, or railing for railing: but ᵀcontrariwise blessing; knowing that ye are thereunto called, that ye should inherit a blessing. Rom. 12:14, 17; 1 Thess. 5:15 ♦ *on the contrary*

> **3:8, 9 When Falsely Accused**
>
> Even under false accusation those who are in the right can afford to be calm and considerate. God is acquainted with all that is misunderstood and misinterpreted by men, and we can safely leave our case in His hands. He will as surely vindicate the cause of those who put their trust in Him as He searched out the guilt of Achan [Joshua 7]. Those who are actuated by the spirit of Christ will possess that charity which suffers long and is kind. *PP 520*

10 For he that will love life, and see good days, let him refrain his tongue from evil, and his lips that they speak no guile: Ps. 34:12-16
11 Let him ᵀeschew evil, and do good; let him seek peace, and ensue it. Ps. 34:14 ♦ *avoid*

12 For the eyes of the Lord *are* over the righteous, and his ears *are open* unto their prayers: but the face of the Lord *is* against them that do evil.
13 And who *is* he that will harm you, if ye be followers of that which is good?   Prov. 16:7
14 But and if ye suffer for righteousness' sake, happy *are ye*: and be not afraid of their terror, neither be troubled; Is. 8:12-13; Matt. 10:28
15 But ᵀsanctify the Lord God in your hearts: and *be* ready always to *give* an answer to every man that asketh you a reason of the hope that is in you with meekness and fear: Is. 29:23; Col. 4:6 ◆ *set apart*
16 Having a good conscience; that, whereas they speak evil of you, as of evildoers, they may be ashamed that falsely accuse your good conversation in Christ.   1 Tim. 1:5; Heb. 13:18
17 For *it is* better, if the will of God be so, that ye suffer for well doing, than for evil doing.   1 Pet. 2:20
18 For Christ also hath once suffered for sins, the just for the unjust, that he might bring us to God, being put to death in the flesh, but quickened by the Spirit: Rom. 4:25; Heb. 9:26
19 By which also he went and preached unto the spirits in prison;   1 Pet. 4:6
20 Which sometime were disobedient, when once the longsuffering of God waited in the days of Noah, while the ark was a preparing, wherein few, that is, eight souls were saved by water.   Gen. 6:3, 5; Heb. 11:7
21 The like figure whereunto *even* baptism doth also now save us (not the putting away of the filth of the flesh, but the answer of a good conscience toward God,) by the resurrection of Jesus Christ: Matt. 28:19; Mark 16:16
22 Who is gone into heaven, and is on the right hand of God; angels and authorities and powers being made subject unto him.

Follow Christ's Example

4 Forasmuch then as Christ hath suffered for us in the flesh, arm yourselves likewise with the same mind: for he that hath suffered in the flesh hath ceased from sin;
2 That he no longer should live the rest of *his* time in the flesh to the lusts of men, but to the will of God.   Mark 3:35
3 For the time past of *our* life may suffice us to have ᵀwrought the will of the Gentiles, when we walked in ᵀlasciviousness, lusts, excess of wine, revellings, banquetings, and abominable idolatries: Is. 28:7 ◆ *done* ◆ *lewdness*
4 Wherein they think it strange that ye run not with *them* to the same excess of riot, speaking evil of *you*:   1 Pet. 2:12; 3:16
5 Who shall give account to him that is ready to judge the quick and the dead.   Acts 10:42
6 For for this cause was the gospel preached also to them that are dead, that

they might be judged according to men in the flesh, but live according to God in the spirit.   1 Pet. 3:19
7 But the end of all things is at hand: be ye therefore sober, and watch unto prayer.

> **4:7 Vital Words for Today**
>
> [Peter's] words were written for the instruction of believers in every age, and they have a special significance for those who live at the time when "the end of all things is at hand." His exhortations and warnings, and his words of faith and courage, are needed by every soul who would maintain his faith. *AA 518*

8 And above all things have fervent ᵀcharity among yourselves: for charity shall cover the multitude of sins.   Prov. 10:12 ◆ *selfless love*

> **4:8 The Love That Can Heal**
>
> Only the love that flows from the heart of Christ can heal. Only he in whom that love flows, even as the sap in the tree or the blood in the body, can restore the wounded soul.
> Love's agencies have wonderful power, for they are divine. The soft answer that "turneth away wrath," the love that "suffereth long, and is kind," the charity that "covereth a multitude of sins" (Proverbs 15:1; 1 Corinthians 13:4, R.V.; 1 Peter 4:8, R.V.). . . . How life would be transformed, and the earth become a very likeness and foretaste of heaven! *Ed 114*

9 Use hospitality one to another without grudging.   Phil. 2:14
10 As every man hath received the gift, *even so* minister the same one to another, as good stewards of the manifold grace of God.   1 Cor. 4:1-2
11 If any man speak, *let him speak* as the oracles of God; if any man minister, *let him do it* as of the ability which God giveth: that God in all things may be glorified through Jesus Christ, to whom be praise and dominion for ever and ever. Amen.   Acts 7:38; Rom. 3:2

Share Christ's Sufferings

12 Beloved, think it not strange concerning the fiery trial which is to try you, as though some strange thing happened unto you:
13 But rejoice, inasmuch as ye are partakers of Christ's sufferings; that, when his glory shall be revealed, ye may be glad also with exceeding joy.   Rom. 8:17; Phil. 3:10; 1 Pet. 5:1
14 If ye be reproached for the name of Christ, happy *are ye*; for the spirit of glory and of God resteth upon you: on their part he is evil spoken of, but on your part he is glorified.   Ps. 89:51; Matt. 5:11; 1 Pet. 3:16

15 But let none of you suffer as a murderer, or *as* a thief, or *as* an evildoer, or as a busybody in other men's matters.   1 Thess. 4:11
16 Yet if *any man suffer* as a Christian, let him not be ashamed; but let him glorify God on this behalf.   Acts 5:41
17 For the time *is come* that judgment must begin at the house of God: and if *it* first *begin* at us, what shall the end *be* of them that obey not the gospel of God?   Jer. 25:29; Ezek. 9:6

4:17 A Serious Work

The judgment of the wicked is a distinct and separate work, and takes place at a later period. "Judgment must begin at the house of God: and if it first begin at us, what shall the end be of them that obey not the gospel?" (1 Peter 4:17). *GC 480*

18 And if the righteous scarcely be saved, where shall the ungodly and the sinner appear?   Prov. 11:31; Luke 23:31
19 Wherefore let them that suffer according to the will of God commit the keeping of their souls *to him* in well doing, as unto a faithful Creator.   Ps. 31:5

Instructions for Spiritual Leaders

5 The elders which are among you I exhort, who am also an elder, and a witness of the sufferings of Christ, and also a partaker of the glory that shall be revealed: Rev. 1:9
2 Feed the flock of God which is among you, taking the oversight *thereof*, not by constraint, but willingly; not for filthy ᵀlucre, but of a ready mind;   1 Tim. 3:8 ♦ *gain*
3 Neither as being lords over *God's* heritage, but being ensamples to the flock.   Ezek. 34:4
4 And when the chief Shepherd shall appear, ye shall receive a crown of glory that fadeth not away.   1 Cor. 9:25; James 1:12; 1 Pet. 1:4

Instructions for Believers

5 Likewise, ye younger, submit yourselves unto the elder. Yea, all *of you* be subject one to another, and be clothed with humility: for God resisteth the proud, and giveth grace to the humble.   Eph. 5:21; James 4:6
6 Humble yourselves therefore under the mighty hand of God, that he may exalt you in due time: James 4:10
7 Casting all your care upon him; for he careth for you.   Ps. 37:5; 55:22

5:6, 7 Strength From Conflict

Through conflict the spiritual life is strengthened. Trials well borne will develop steadfastness of character and precious spiritual graces. The perfect fruit of faith, meekness, and love often matures best amid storm clouds and darkness. *COL 61*

8 Be sober, be vigilant; because your adversary the devil, as a roaring lion, walketh about, seeking whom he may devour:
9 Whom resist ᵀstedfast in the faith, knowing that the same afflictions are accomplished in your brethren that are in the world.   Acts 14:22; Col. 2:5; James 4:7 ♦ *steadfast*

5: 10, 11 To a Church Facing Persecution

Thus Peter wrote to the believers at a time of peculiar trial to the church. Many had already become partakers of Christ's sufferings, and soon the church was to undergo a period of terrible persecution. Within a few brief years many of those who had stood as teachers and leaders in the church were to lay down their lives for the gospel. . . . But none of these things were to bring discouragement to those whose hopes were centered in Christ. *AA 528*

10 But the God of all grace, who hath called us unto his eternal glory by Christ

Bringing Burdens to Jesus

1 Peter 5

The Elder Brother of our race is by the eternal throne. He looks upon every soul who is turning his face toward Him as the Saviour. He knows by experience what are the weaknesses of humanity, what are our wants, and where lies the strength of our temptations; for He was in all points tempted like as we are, yet without sin. He is watching over you, trembling child of God. Are you tempted? He will deliver. Are you weak? He will strengthen. Are you ignorant? He will enlighten. Are you wounded? He will heal. . . . "Come unto Me," is His invitation. Whatever your anxieties and trials, spread out your case before the Lord. Your spirit will be braced for endurance. The way will be opened for you to disentangle yourself from embarrassment and difficulty. The weaker and more helpless you know yourself to be, the stronger will you become in His strength. The heavier your burdens, the more blessed the rest in casting them upon the Burden Bearer. The rest that Christ offers depends upon conditions, but these conditions are plainly specified. They are those with which all can comply. He tells us just how His rest is to be found. *DA 329*

Jesus, after that ye have suffered a while, make you perfect, stablish, strengthen, settle *you*.   1 Cor. 1:9; 2 Cor. 4:17; 2 Thess. 2:17

11 To him *be* glory and dominion for ever and ever. Amen.   1 Pet. 4:11

Farewell

12 By Silvanus, a faithful brother unto you, as I suppose, I have written briefly, exhorting,

and testifying that this is the true grace of God wherein ye stand.   Acts 20:24; 2 Cor. 1:19

13 The *church that is* at Babylon, elected together with *you*, saluteth you; and *so doth* Marcus my son.   Acts 12:12, 25

14 Greet ye one another with a kiss of ᵀcharity. Peace *be* with you all that are in Christ Jesus. Amen.   Rom. 16:16; Eph. 6:23 ◆ *selfless love*

THE SECOND EPISTLE OF

PETER

False teachers—those who teach harmful doctrines and heresies—often use persuasive and compelling arguments, which are difficult to discern from truth.

In this epistle, Peter expresses concern over the influence of these false teachers in the church. He reminds believers of their faith in Christ. Faith is not meant to be stagnant; believers are to grow in their relationship with Christ. By doing so, they will be equipped for the challenges of a fallen world.

Finally, Peter discusses the surety of the return of Christ and the need to be prepared. "Wherefore, beloved, seeing that ye look for such things, be diligent that ye may be found of him in peace, without spot, and blameless" (3:14).

Dates

In 3:1, Peter makes reference to his first letter. Thus we can assume that 2 Peter was written sometime after 1 Peter. Peter wrote this letter in response to the false teachers prevalent at the time, and he also wrote to a wide audience—not to a single church. Since Peter's martyrdom occurred no later than A.D. 67, we can assume 2 Peter was written shortly before that, probably from Rome.

Author

Second Peter was the last book added to the canon of the New Testament. Unlike 1 Peter, this book does not have strong external testimony. Its authorship has been questioned throughout history, mainly because of the differences in the Greek vocabulary and a quote that Jude mentioned in his letter—a letter written after Peter's death. Peter and Jude, however, might have used the same source. As for the vocabulary differences, Peter most likely dictated to different scribes for each letter. By the fourth century, however, 2 Peter became recognized as the authentic work of Peter.

Internally, the book gives a couple clues as to Peter's authorship, one of which occurs in the first verse: "Simon Peter, a servant and an apostle of Jesus Christ, to them that have obtained like precious faith with us through the righteousness of God and our Saviour Jesus Christ." In 3:1, we discover that this is the second letter the author has written—giving the letter credence as 2 Peter.

Meaning of the Name

In the Greek, 2 Peter was entitled *Petrou B,* or "Of Peter II," to distinguish it from 1 Peter.

Christ in 2 Peter

Peter uses the title "Lord" to refer to Christ in 2 Peter. Christ's power has given us "all things that pertain unto life and godliness, through the knowledge of him that hath called us to glory and virtue" (1:3). We have everything we need in Christ in order to combat the challenges the world has to offer, including false teachers and those who deny the Second Coming of Christ.

Overview

Just as in 1 Peter, 2 Peter is pastoral in nature. The author presses his readers to persist in growing in grace and in spiritual knowledge so that God's plan in choosing them to faithfully carry the gospel message is fulfilled. Thus, Second Peter can be divided into three sections:

(1) *2 Peter 1, The Traits of the Godly:* Peter encourages his readers to grow in their faith and to add the following character traits: goodness, knowledge, self-control, perseverance, godliness, and brotherly kindness—a list that accords with the fruit of the Spirit (Galatians 5:22–23). Being a believer means becoming more like Christ each day.

(2) *2 Peter 2, The Advent of False Teachers:* It is quite evident that the readers of Peter's epistle were living in a time of many false teachers and heresies—as many are today. Peter has harsh words for those who teach these false doctrines and for those who fall prey to them.

(3) *2 Peter 3, The Hope of Christ's Return:* In this last, more personal chapter, Peter urges that Christ will again appear. His return "will come as a thief in the night" (3:10). This is a paraphrase of one of Jesus' teachings (see Matthew 24:42, 43). Yet believers must be prepared for His coming, making effort to be "found of him in peace, without spot, and blameless" (2 Peter 3:14).

Unlocking 2 Peter

KEY PEOPLE:
Peter, Paul

KEY EVENTS:
The influence of false prophets and teachers

KEY PHRASE:
False teachers is a key phrase, because Peter warns his readers to be on guard against false teachers. Knowing that the heresies of false teachers would only result in destruction, Peter encouraged his readers to grow in the knowledge of Christ and their faith, which is a good reminder for us today. People will try to convince us of the validity of heresies, and the fate of those who profess these false teachings is certain. In the end, Peter reminds us of the strength and power we have in Christ to overcome these heresies.

KEY VERSES:
"Knowing this first, that no prophecy of the scripture is of any private interpretation. For the prophecy came not in old time by the will of man: but holy men of God spake as they were moved by the Holy Ghost" (2 Peter 1:20, 21).

"The Lord is not slack concerning his promise, as some men count slackness; but is long-suffering to us-ward, not willing that any should perish, but that all should come to repentance. But the day of the Lord will come as a thief in the night; in the which the heavens shall pass away with a great noise, and the elements shall melt with fervent heat, the earth also and the works that are therein shall be burned up. Seeing then that all these things shall be dissolved, what manner of persons ought ye to be in all holy conversation and godliness" (2 Peter 3:9–11).

KEY CHAPTER:
2 Peter 1, which details the path toward true knowledge. This includes the characteristics of godliness that indicate progression: "Add to your faith virtue; and to virtue knowledge; and to knowledge temperance; and to temperance patience; and to patience godliness; and to godliness brotherly kindness; and to brotherly kindness charity" (1:5–7). Peter also includes the source of knowledge—Scripture. This knowledge is in marked contrast to the "cunningly devised fables" (1:16) suggested by the culture and false teachers.

God's Power for Godly Lives

1 Simon Peter, a servant and an apostle of Jesus Christ, to them that have obtained like precious faith with us through the righteousness of God and our Saviour Jesus Christ: Rom. 1:1; 3:21-26; Titus 2:13

2 Grace and peace be multiplied unto you through the knowledge of God, and of Jesus our Lord,   John 17:3

3 According as his divine power hath given unto us all things that *pertain* unto life and godliness, through the knowledge of him that hath called us to glory and virtue: 1 Thess. 2:12

4 Whereby are given unto us exceeding great and precious promises: that by these ye might be partakers of the divine nature, having escaped the corruption that is in the world through lust.   Heb. 12:10; 2 Pet. 2:18-20; 1 John 3:2

1:4 God's Standard Not Ours

The truth is to be planted in the heart. It is to control the mind and regulate the affections. The whole character must be stamped with the divine utterances. Every jot and tittle of the word of God is to be brought into the daily practice.

He who becomes a partaker of the divine nature will be in harmony with God's great standard of righteousness, His holy law. This is the rule by which God measures the actions of men. This will be the test of character in the judgment. *COL 314*

5 And beside this, giving all diligence, add to your faith virtue; and to virtue knowledge;

6 And to knowledge ᵀtemperance; and to temperance patience; and to patience godliness;   Acts 24:25 ◆ *self-control*

7 And to godliness brotherly kindness; and to brotherly kindness charity.   Rom. 12:10

8 For if these things be in you, and abound, they make *you that ye shall* neither *be* barren nor unfruitful in the knowledge of our Lord Jesus Christ.   John 15:2

9 But he that lacketh these things is blind, and cannot see afar off, and hath forgotten that he was purged from his old sins. Eph. 5:26

10 Wherefore the rather, brethren, give diligence to make your calling and election sure: for if ye do these things, ye shall never fall:

1:5–10 Sanctification Is Progressive

The Scriptures plainly show that the work of sanctification is progressive. When in conversion the sinner finds peace with God through the blood of the atonement, the Christian life has but just begun. . . . Peter sets before us the steps by which Bible sanctification is to be attained . . . (2 Peter 1:5–10).

Those who experience the sanctification of the Bible will manifest a spirit of humility. Like Moses, they have had a view of the awful majesty of holiness, and they see their own unworthiness in contrast with the purity and exalted perfection of the Infinite One. *GC 470*

11 For so an entrance shall be ministered unto you abundantly into the everlasting kingdom of our Lord and Saviour Jesus Christ.

12 Wherefore I will not be negligent to put you always in remembrance of these things, though ye know *them*, and be established in the present truth.   Phil. 3:1; 1 John 2:21; Jude 5

13 Yea, I think it meet, as long as I am in this tabernacle, to stir you up by putting *you* in remembrance;   2 Pet. 3:1

14 Knowing that shortly I must put off *this* my tabernacle, even as our Lord Jesus Christ hath shewed me.   Deut. 4:21-22; John 21:18-19; 2 Tim. 4:6

Ladder of Christian Progress

2 Peter 1:2–8

These words are full of instruction, and strike the keynote of victory. The apostle presents before the believers the ladder of Christian progress, every step of which represents advancement in the knowledge of God, and in the climbing of which there is to be no standstill. . . .

God has called His people to glory and virtue, and these will be manifest in the lives of all who are truly connected with Him. . . . It is the glory of God to give His virtue to His children. He desires to see men and women reaching the highest standard; and when by faith they lay hold of the power of Christ, when they plead His unfailing promises, and claim them as their own, when with an importunity that will not be denied they seek for the power of the Holy Spirit, they will be made complete in Him.

Having received the faith of the gospel, the next work of the believer is to add to his character virtue, and thus cleanse the heart and prepare the mind for the reception of the knowledge of God. This knowledge is the foundation of all true education and of all true service. It is the only real safeguard against temptation; and it is this alone that can make one like God in character. Through the knowledge of God and of His Son Jesus Christ, are given to the believer "all things that pertain unto life and godliness." No good gift is withheld from him who sincerely desires to obtain the righteousness of God. *AA 530, 531*

15 Moreover I will endeavour that ye may be able after my decease to have these things always in remembrance.

Listen to God's Words

16 For we have not followed cunningly devised fables, when we made known unto you the power and coming of our Lord Jesus Christ, but were eyewitnesses of his majesty.   1 Tim. 1:4
17 For he received from God the Father honour and glory, when there came such a voice to him from the excellent glory, This is my beloved Son, in whom I am well pleased.   Matt. 3:17; 17:5; Mark 9:7
18 And this voice which came from heaven we heard, when we were with him in the holy mount.   Ex. 3:5; Josh. 5:15; Matt. 17:6
19 We have also a more sure word of prophecy; whereunto ye do well that ye take heed, as unto a light that shineth in a dark place, until the day dawn, and the day star arise in your hearts: Ps. 119:105; Rev. 2:28; 22:16

1:19 Not Left in Mystery

The Bible was designed to be a guide to all who wish to become acquainted with the will of their Maker. God gave to men the sure word of prophecy; angels and even Christ Himself came to make known to Daniel and John the things that must shortly come to pass. Those important matters that concern our salvation were not left involved in mystery. They were not revealed in such a way as to perplex and mislead the honest seeker after truth. *GC 521*

20 Knowing this first, that no prophecy of the scripture is of any private interpretation.   2 Pet. 3:3
21 For the prophecy came not in old time by the will of man: but holy men of God spake *as they were* moved by the Holy Ghost. 2 Sam. 23:2

The Bible See 1 Thessalonians 2:13.

Gift of Prophecy See Matthew 24:24.

Warnings about False Teachers

2 But there were false prophets also among the people, even as there shall be false teachers among you, who privily shall bring in damnable heresies, even denying the Lord that bought them, and bring upon themselves swift destruction.   1 Cor. 6:20; 2 Pet. 2:3
2 And many shall follow their pernicious ways; by reason of whom the way of truth shall be evil spoken of.   Rom. 2:24
3 And through ᵀcovetousness shall they with feigned words make merchandise of you: whose judgment now of a long time lin-

gereth not, and their ᵀdamnation slumbereth not.   Deut. 32:35 ◆ *greed* ◆ *condemnation*
4 For if God spared not the angels that sinned, but cast *them* down to hell, and delivered *them* into chains of darkness, to be reserved unto judgment;   Matt. 25:41; Jude 6; Rev. 20:10
5 And spared not the old world, but saved Noah the eighth *person*, a preacher of righteousness, bringing in the flood upon the world of the ungodly;   Heb. 11:7; 2 Pet. 3:6

2:5 Warnings in Vain

Of the vast population of the earth before the Flood, only eight souls believed and obeyed God's word through Noah. For a hundred and twenty years the preacher of righteousness warned the world of the coming destruction, but his message was rejected and despised. So it will be now. Before the Lawgiver shall come to punish the disobedient, transgressors are warned to repent, and return to their allegiance; but with the majority these warnings will be in vain. *PP 102*

6 And turning the cities of Sodom and Gomorrha into ashes condemned *them* with an overthrow, making *them* an ensample unto those that after should live ungodly;
7 And delivered just Lot, vexed with the filthy conversation of the wicked: Gen. 19:7-8
8 (For that righteous man dwelling among them, in seeing and hearing, vexed *his* righteous soul from day to day with *their* unlawful deeds;)   Ps. 119:136

2:6–8 Limits to Sinning

The flames that consumed the cities of the plain shed their warning light down even to our time. We are taught the fearful and solemn lesson that while God's mercy bears long with the transgressor, there is a limit beyond which men may not go on in sin. When that limit is reached, then the offers of mercy are withdrawn, and the ministration of judgment begins. *PP 162, 165*

9 The Lord knoweth how to deliver the godly out of temptations, and to reserve the unjust unto the day of judgment to be punished: 1 Cor. 10:13; 2 Pet. 3:7
10 But chiefly them that walk after the flesh in the lust of uncleanness, and despise government. Presumptuous *are they*, selfwilled, they are not afraid to speak evil of dignities.   Ex. 22:28; Jude 10, 16
11 Whereas angels, which are greater in power and might, bring not railing accusation against them before the Lord.   Jude 9
12 But these, as natural brute beasts, made to be taken and destroyed, speak evil of the things that they understand not; and shall utterly perish in their own corruption; Jer. 12:3

13 And shall receive the reward of unrighteousness, *as* they that count it pleasure to riot in the day time. Spots *they are* and blemishes, sporting themselves with their own deceivings while they feast with you; Rom. 13:13
14 Having eyes full of adultery, and that cannot cease from sin; beguiling unstable souls: an heart they have exercised with covetous practices; cursed children: Eph. 2:3; 2 Pet. 2:3, 18
15 Which have forsaken the right way, and are gone astray, following the way of Balaam *the son* of Bosor, who loved the wages of unrighteousness; Num. 22:5-7; Jude 11; Rev. 2:14

> **2:15 Satanic Snares**
>
> The sin of covetousness, which God declares to be idolatry, had made [Balaam] a timeserver, and through this one fault Satan gained entire control of him. . . . Many flatter themselves that they can depart from strict integrity for a time, for the sake of some worldly advantage, and that having gained their object, they can change their course when they please. Such are entangling themselves in the snare of Satan, and it is seldom that they escape. *PP 439, 440*

16 But was rebuked for his iniquity: the ᵀdumb ass speaking with man's voice forbad the madness of the prophet. Num. 22:21-33 ◆ *mute*
17 These are wells without water, clouds that are carried with a ᵀtempest; to whom the mist of darkness is reserved for ever. *storm*
18 For when they speak great swelling *words* of vanity, they allure through the lusts of the flesh, *through much* ᵀwantonness, those that were clean escaped from them who live in error. 2 Pet. 1:4 ◆ *indulgence in sexual pleasures*
19 While they promise them liberty, they themselves are the servants of corruption: for of whom a man is overcome, of the same is he brought in bondage. John 8:34; Gal. 5:13
20 For if after they have escaped the pollutions of the world through the knowledge of the Lord and Saviour Jesus Christ, they are again entangled therein, and overcome, the latter end is worse with them than the beginning. 2 Pet. 1:2; 2:18
21 For it had been better for them not to have known the way of righteousness, than, after they have known *it*, to turn from the holy commandment delivered unto them.
22 But it is happened unto them according to the true proverb, The dog *is* turned to his own vomit again; and the sow that was washed to her wallowing in the ᵀmire. Prov. 26:11 ◆ *mud*

Be Ready for Christ's Return

3 This second epistle, beloved, I now write unto you; in *both* which I stir up your pure minds by way of remembrance:

2 That ye may be mindful of the words which were spoken before by the holy prophets, and of the commandment of us the apostles of the Lord and Saviour: Luke 1:70
3 Knowing this first, that there shall come in the last days scoffers, walking after their own lusts, Is. 28:14; 2 Pet. 2:10; Jude 18
4 And saying, Where is the promise of his coming? for since the fathers fell asleep, all things continue as *they were* from the beginning of the creation. Jer. 17:15

> **Signs of the End** See Matthew 13:24–30.

5 For this they willingly are ignorant of, that by the word of God the heavens were of old, and the earth standing out of the water and in the water: Gen. 1:6, 9; Ps. 24:2
6 Whereby the world that then was, being overflowed with water, perished: 2 Pet. 2:5
7 But the heavens and the earth, which are now, by the same word are kept in store, reserved unto fire against the day of judgment and perdition of ungodly men. Matt. 10:15;

God's Patience

8 But, beloved, be not ignorant of this one thing, that one day *is* with the Lord as a thousand years, and a thousand years as one day. Ps. 90:4
9 The Lord is not slack concerning his promise, as some men count slackness; but is longsuffering to us-ward, not willing that any should perish, but that all should come to repentance. Hab. 2:3; 1 Tim. 2:4; Heb. 10:37

> **3:9 Purpose in Affliction**
>
> He does not forget or neglect His children; but He permits the wicked to reveal their true character, that none who desire to do His will may be deceived concerning them. Again, the righteous are placed in the furnace of affliction, that they themselves may be purified; that their example may convince others of the reality of faith and godliness; and also that their consistent course may condemn the ungodly and unbelieving. *GC 48*

10 But the day of the Lord will come as a thief in the night; in the which the heavens shall pass away with a great noise, and the elements shall melt with fervent heat, the earth also and the works that are therein shall be burned up. Matt. 24:35; 2 Pet. 3:7; Rev. 21:1

Live Holy Lives

11 *Seeing* then *that* all these things shall be dissolved, what manner *of persons* ought ye to be in *all* holy ᵀconversation and godliness, 1 Pet. 1:15 ◆ *conduct*
12 Looking for and hasting unto the coming of the day of God, wherein the heavens being

on fire shall be dissolved, and the elements shall melt with fervent heat?   Ps. 50:3; Is. 34:4

3:11, 12 Christ's Character Reproduced

Christ is waiting with longing desire for the manifestation of Himself in His church. When the character of Christ shall be perfectly reproduced in His people, then He will come to claim them as His own. . . .

Were all who profess His name bearing fruit to His glory, how quickly the whole world would be sown with the seed of the gospel. Quickly the last great harvest would be ripened, and Christ would come to gather the precious grain. *COL 69*

13 Nevertheless we, according to his promise, look for new heavens and a new earth, wherein dwelleth righteousness. Is. 65:17; 66:22

The New Earth See Isaiah 35:4–10.

14 Wherefore, beloved, seeing that ye look for such things, be diligent that ye may be found of him in peace, without spot, and blameless.

3:14 Yearning After God

As your soul yearns after God, you will find more and still more of the unsearchable riches of His grace. As you contemplate these riches you will come into possession of them and will reveal the merits of the Saviour's sacrifice, the protection of His righteousness, the fullness of His wisdom, and His power to present you before the Father "without spot, and blameless" (2 Peter 3:14). *AA 567*

15 And account *that* the longsuffering of our Lord *is* salvation; even as our beloved brother Paul also according to the wisdom given unto him hath written unto you;   Acts 15:25
16 As also in all *his* epistles, speaking in them of these things; in which are some things hard to be understood, which they that are unlearned and unstable ᵀwrest, as *they do* also the other scriptures, unto their own destruction.   Heb. 5:11 ◆ *twist*
17 Ye therefore, beloved, seeing ye know *these things* before, beware lest ye also, being led away with the error of the wicked, fall from your own stedfastness.   1 Cor. 10:12

3:18 Deeper and Greater

If you will go to work as Christ designs that His disciples shall, and win souls for Him, you will feel the need of a deeper experience and a greater knowledge in divine things, and will hunger and thirst after righteousness. You will plead with God, and your faith will be strengthened, and your soul will drink deeper drafts at the well of salvation. Encountering opposition and trials will drive you to the Bible and prayer. *SC 80*

18 But grow in grace, and *in* the knowledge of our Lord and Saviour Jesus Christ. To him *be* glory both now and for ever. Amen.   Eph. 4:15; Col. 1:10; 2 Tim. 4:18

The Christian Life See Galatians 2:20.

THE FIRST EPISTLE OF

JOHN

The issue of false teaching has plagued the church for centuries. While these heresies look different in the twenty-first century than they did in the first century, they have the same root: a denial of the gospel of Jesus Christ. Therefore, the apostle John's advice on identifying false teachings is just as important to us, his twenty-first century "spiritual descendants," as they were to his "spiritual children" in the first century.

In his first letter, the apostle describes how the false teachers of his day challenged four essential elements of the gospel.

(1) They denied that they sin (1:8).

(2) They rejected that Jesus is the Son of God who came in the flesh (4:2, 3).

(3) They did not follow God's commandants (2:4).

(4) They hated rather than loved other Christians (2:9). In addition to using these examples to recognize false teaching in today's world, Christians can use them to examine their own beliefs. John wanted his "spiritual children" to take this test so that they may "know that they have eternal life" (5:13). Do you pass this test?

Dates

The New Testament shows John as a leader in the Jerusalem church in the early years after Jesus' ascension (see Acts 8:14; Galatians 2:9) and a prisoner on the island of Patmos at the end of his life (Rev. 1:9). Tradition fills in the gaps between these occasions, as it universally describes John leaving Jerusalem before its destruction in A.D. 70 and ministering in Ephesus. This ministry included oversight of churches around Ephesus, such as the seven churches in Asia Minor addressed in Revelation 2—3. While Paul addressed a particular church in most of his letters, John likely wrote this letter from Ephesus to circulate among the seven churches in Asia Minor. The probable date of composition of this letter is between A.D. 90 and 94, as John appears to have written this letter after his gospel, but before the persecution that occurred at the end of Domitian's reign (A.D. 81—96).

Author

Although the letter does not disclose its author, Greek and Latin church scholars constantly identified the author as the apostle John, the son of Zebedee and the disciple "whom Jesus loved" (see John 13:23; 21:20). Some contemporary scholars interpret a statement of Papias recorded in Eusebius' *Ecclesiastical History* (A.D. 323) making a distinction between John the apostle and John the elder ("presbyter") with the elder as the author of this letter. The wording of Papais, however, does not necessitate such a distinction; they may be the same person. Even if they are different people, numerous factors support the apostle as this letter's author:

(1) The writer asserts he is an eyewitness of Jesus (1:1–4; 4:14).

(2) The authoritative tone of the letter matches what one would expect from an apostle, and his fatherly attitude reflects the apostle's advanced age.

(3) An apostle would be so famous among Christians that he would not need to mention his name.

(4) The simple Greek style, recurring themes, and use of opposing terms (life and death; light and darkness) echoes the fourth gospel.

(5) Several noteworthy parallels in word choice exist in both 1 John and the gospel of John. A few examples are as follows: a) "That your joy may be full" (1 John 1:4; John 16:24); b) "Knoweth not whether he goeth" (1 John 2:11; John 12:35); c) "The spirit of truth" (1 John 4:6; John 14:17); d) "God sent his only begotten Son" (1 John 4:9)/"He gave his only begotten Son" (John 3:16).

(6) The second-century writers Polycarp and Irenaeus believed this letter was by the apostle and were familiar with his teachings and personality, since Polycarp was a disciple of John and Irenaeus was a disciple of Polycarp. Therefore, there is no reason to doubt and every reason to believe that the author of the letter was the apostle John.

As the first of the letters attributed to the apostle John, its Greek name (*Ioannou A*) means "Of John I."

Christ in 1 John

John explains who Jesus is and what He has done. Eighteen times within this short letter, John says that Jesus is God's son, emphasizing that Jesus was divine from His baptism (water) to his death (blood) in 5:6. In addition to being God, Jesus was also fully man (4:2, 3). His death cleanses us from sin (1:5—2:2), destroys the work of the devil (3:8), prompts us to love each other (4:7–21), and allows us to have eternal life (5:12).

Overview

The tone of this letter is extremely pastoral. John showed his immense love for the recipients by addressing them as "little children" (2:1, 28; 3:7, 18; 4:4; 5:21) and "beloved" (2:7; 3:2, 21; 4:1, 7, 11). This concern for the church also led to the harsh words John used for the false teachers threatening the community (2:26).

These false teachers seem to teach an early form of Gnosticism, a heresy that emphasized dualism between spirit and flesh and the belief that the flesh was inherently evil. As a result, these teachers denied that Jesus came in the flesh or made a distinction between Jesus the person and Christ the spirit, maintaining that the "Christ spirit" left the human Jesus before he died. Docetism was a similar idea, as it claimed that Jesus only seemed to be human. (The Greek word *dokeo* means "to seem.") Since the flesh does not matter, Gnostics could adopt a lifestyle of sin and debauchery. Because they thought they possessed special knowledge of the truth (the Greek word *gnosis* means "knowledge"), Gnostics viewed themselves as spiritually superior to others.

First John can be divided into two sections:

(1) *1 John 1:1—2:27, Foundation of Fellowship:* Because of the love of God and the forgiveness He offers, we can have fellowship with God and one another (chapter 1). John warns believers not to love the world (2:15–17) and instead to abide in the truth of God (2:24–27).

(2) *1 John 2:28—5:21, Behaving in Fellowship:* John calls the false teachers "antichrists" (2:18, 22), "children of the devil" (3:10), and "false prophets" (4:1). He then refutes the teachings of these deceivers (3:4–10; 4:2, 3; 5:2–4, 6, 18) and encourages the Christians in the faith that they have heard the truth from the beginning (2:18–27; 3:11). He desires them to have assurance of their salvation (5:13). He exhorts the church to love one another (3:11–19; 4:8–21).

Unlocking 1 John

❦ **KEY PEOPLE:**
Jesus, John, false teachers

❦ **KEY EVENTS:**
The incarnation of Jesus; the death of Jesus

❦ **KEY WORD:**
Fellowship, since John explains throughout the letter of the gift of fellowship with God and with other believers. Jesus' sacrificial death makes fellowship with God possible.

❦ **KEY VERSES:**
"That which we have seen and heard declare we unto you, that ye also may have fellowship with us: and truly our fellowship *is* with the Father, and with his Son Jesus Christ. And these things write we unto you, that your joy may be full" (1 John 1:3, 4).

"He that hath the Son hath life; and he that hath not the Son of God hath not life. These things have I written unto you that believe on the name of the Son of God; that ye may know that ye have eternal life, and that ye may believe on the name of the Son of God" (1 John 5:12, 13).

❦ **KEY CHAPTER:**
1 John 1, which discusses the way to remain in fellowship with God: abiding in Christ. This chapter dovetails with John 15.

John's Reason for Writing

1 That which was from the beginning, which we have heard, which we have seen with our eyes, which we have looked upon, and our hands have handled, of the Word of life; Luke 24:39; John 20:27; Acts 4:20
2 (For the life was manifested, and we have seen *it*, and bear witness, and shew unto you that eternal life, which was with the Father, and was manifested unto us;) John 1:4; 1 John 3:5
3 That which we have seen and heard declare we unto you, that ye also may have fellowship with us: and truly our fellowship *is* with the Father, and with his Son Jesus Christ. 1 Cor. 1:9; Phil. 2:1; 1 John 1:1

1:1–3 John's Eyewitness Testimony

As a witness for Christ, John entered into no controversy, no wearisome contention. He declared what he knew, what he had seen and heard. He had been intimately associated with Christ, had listened to His teachings, had witnessed His mighty miracles. Few could see the beauties of Christ's character as John saw them. For him the darkness had passed away; on him the true light was shining. His testimony in regard to the Saviour's life and death was clear and forcible. *AA 555*

---

4 And these things write we unto you, that your joy may be full. John 15:11

Our Lives Are Living Testimonies

5 This then is the message which we have heard of him, and declare unto you, that God is light, and in him is no darkness at all.
6 If we say that we have fellowship with him, and walk in darkness, we lie, and do not the truth: John 3:19-21; 1 John 1:10; 4:20

1:7–9 Just, Yet the Justifier

We should not try to lessen our guilt by excusing sin. We must accept God's estimate of sin, and that is heavy indeed. Calvary alone can reveal the terrible enormity of sin. If we had to bear our own guilt, it would crush us. But the sinless One has taken our place; though undeserving, He has borne our iniquity. "If we confess our sins," God "is faithful and just to forgive us our sins . . ." (1 John 1:9). Glorious truth!—just to His own law, and yet the Justifier of all that believe in Jesus. *MB 116*

---

7 But if we walk in the light, as he is in the light, we have fellowship one with another, and the blood of Jesus Christ his Son cleanseth us from all sin. Is. 2:5
8 If we say that we have no sin, we deceive ourselves, and the truth is not in us. Job 15:14
9 If we confess our sins, he is faithful and just to forgive us *our* sins, and to cleanse us from all unrighteousness. Ps. 32:5; Prov. 28:13; 1 John 1:7

10 If we say that we have not sinned, we make him a liar, and his word is not in us.

Christ Is Our Advocate

2 My little children, these things write I unto you, that ye sin not. And if any man sin, we have an advocate with the Father, Jesus Christ the righteous: John 13:33; Rom. 8:34
2 And he is the propitiation for our sins: and not for ours only, but also for *the sins of* the whole world. John 4:42; 1 John 4:10, 14

To Know God Is to Obey

3 And hereby we do know that we know him, if we keep his commandments. John 14:15; 15:10
4 He that saith, I know him, and keepeth not his commandments, is a liar, and the truth is not in him. 1 John 1:6, 8

2:3-6

2:3, 4 When Belief Is Presumption

A belief that does not lead to obedience is presumption. . . . Let none cherish the idea that special providences or miraculous manifestations are to be the proof of the genuineness of their work or of the ideas they advocate. When persons will speak lightly of the word of God, and set their impressions, feelings, and exercises above the divine standard, we may know that they have no light in them. *MB 146*

---

5 But whoso keepeth his word, in him verily is the love of God perfected: hereby know we that we are in him. John 14:23; 1 John 3:24; 4:12-13
6 He that saith he abideth in him ought himself also so to walk, even as he walked.

God's Law See Romans 3:31.

7 Brethren, I write no new commandment unto you, but an old commandment which ye had from the beginning. The old commandment is the word which ye have heard from the beginning. Lev. 19:18; 1 John 3:11; 2 John 5-6
8 Again, a new commandment I write unto you, which thing is true in him and in you: because the darkness is past, and the true light now shineth. John 1:9; 13:34; Rom. 13:12
9 He that saith he is in the light, and hateth his brother, is in darkness even until now.
10 He that loveth his brother abideth in the light, and there is none occasion of stumbling in him. 2 Pet. 1:10
11 But he that hateth his brother is in darkness, and walketh in darkness, and knoweth not whither he goeth, because that darkness hath blinded his eyes. John 12:35; 2 Cor. 4:4
12 I write unto you, little children, because your sins are forgiven you for his name's sake. Acts 13:38
13 I write unto you, fathers, because ye have known him *that is* from the beginning.

I write unto you, young men, because ye have overcome the wicked one. I write unto you, little children, because ye have known the Father.   Luke 10:22; John 14:7; 1 John 2:14

14 I have written unto you, fathers, because ye have known him *that is* from the beginning. I have written unto you, young men, because ye are strong, and the word of God abideth in you, and ye have overcome the wicked one.   John 5:38; Eph. 6:10; 1 John 2:13

15 Love not the world, neither the things *that are* in the world. If any man love the world, the love of the Father is not in him.   Matt. 6:24

16 For all that *is* in the world, the lust of the flesh, and the lust of the eyes, and the pride of life, is not of the Father, but is of the world.   Gen. 3:6; Rom. 13:14; Eph. 2:3

2:16 Christians to Be the Light

If all who profess to be followers of Christ were truly sanctified, their means, instead of being spent for needless and even hurtful indulgences, would be turned into the Lord's treasury, and Christians would set an example of temperance, self-denial, and self-sacrifice. Then they would be the light of the world.

The world is given up to self-indulgence. "The lust . . . and the pride of life" [1 John 2:16] control the masses of the people. But Christ's followers have a holier calling. *GC 475*

---

17 And the world passeth away, and the lust thereof: but he that doeth the will of God abideth for ever.   Mark 3:35; 1 Cor. 7:31

Beware of Seducers

18 Little children, it is the last time: and as ye have heard that antichrist shall come, even now are there many antichrists; whereby we know that it is the last time.   Matt. 24:5

19 They went out from us, but they were not of us; for if they had been of us, they would *no doubt* have continued with us: but *they went out*, that they might be made manifest that they were not all of us.   Deut. 13:13; Acts 20:30

Live in Christ

20 But ye have an unction from the Holy One, and ye know all things.   Mark 1:24

21 I have not written unto you because ye know not the truth, but because ye know it, and that no lie is of the truth.   2 Pet. 1:12

22 Who is a liar but he that denieth that Jesus is the Christ? He is antichrist, that denieth the Father and the Son.   1 John 2:18; 4:3; 2 John 7

23 Whosoever denieth the Son, the same hath not the Father: *(but) he that acknowledgeth the Son hath the Father also.*   John 8:19; 1 John 4:15

24 Let that therefore abide in you, which ye have heard from the beginning. If that which ye have heard from the beginning shall remain in you, ye also shall continue in the Son, and in the Father.   John 14:23; 1 John 1:3; 2:7

25 And this is the promise that he hath promised us, *even* eternal life.   1 John 1:2

26 These *things* have I written unto you concerning them that seduce you. 1 John 3:7; 2 John 7

27 But the anointing which ye have received of him abideth in you, and ye need not that any man teach you: but as the same anointing teacheth you of all things, and is truth, and is no lie, and even as it hath taught you, ye shall abide in him.   John 14:26

28 And now, little children, abide in him; that, when he shall appear, we may have confidence, and not be ashamed before him at his coming.   Col. 3:4; 1 John 3:2; 4:17

2:28†

Christ's Return

What Constitutes True Love for God

1 John 2:8–11

It is not the opposition of the world that most endangers the church of Christ. It is the evil cherished in the hearts of believers that works their most grievous disaster and most surely retards the progress of God's cause. There is no surer way of weakening spirituality than by cherishing envy, suspicion, faultfinding, and evil surmising. On the other hand, the strongest witness that God has sent His Son into the world is the existence of harmony and union among men of varied dispositions who form His church. . . .

"A new commandment I give unto you," Christ said, "That ye love one another; as I have loved you, that ye also love one another" (John 13:34). What a wonderful statement; but, oh, how poorly practiced! In the church of God today brotherly love is sadly lacking. Many who profess to love the Saviour do not love one another. Unbelievers are watching to see if the faith of professed Christians is exerting a sanctifying influence upon their lives; and they are quick to discern the defects in character, the inconsistencies in action. Let Christians not make it possible for the enemy to point to them and say, Behold how these people, standing under the banner of Christ, hate one another. . . .

That man only who has unselfish love for his brother has true love for God. . . .

Those who have never experienced the tender, winning love of Christ cannot lead others to the fountain of life. . . . In heaven their fitness as workers is measured by their ability to love as Christ loved and to work as He worked. *AA 549–551*

29 If ye know that he is righteous, ye know that every one that doeth righteousness is born of him.   1 John 3:7; 4:7; 5:1

We Are God's Children

3 Behold, what manner of love the Father hath bestowed upon us, that we should be called the sons of God: therefore the world knoweth us not, because it knew him not.   John 1:12; 3:16; 16:3
2 Beloved, now are we the sons of God, and it doth not yet appear what we shall be: but we know that, when he shall appear, we shall be like him; for we shall see him as he is.   Rom. 8:18, 29; 1 Cor. 13:12
3 And every man that hath this hope in him purifieth himself, even as he is pure. 2 Cor. 7:1
4 Whosoever committeth sin ᵀtransgresseth also the law: for sin is the transgression of the law.   Rom. 3:20; 4:15; 1 John 5:17 ◆ violates

> **God's Law** See Deuteronomy 28:1, 2.

5 And ye know that he was manifested to take away our sins; and in him is no sin.
6 Whosoever abideth in him sinneth not: whosoever sinneth hath not seen him, neither known him.   1 John 2:4; 3:9; 3 John 11
7 Little children, let no man deceive you: he that doeth righteousness is righteous, even as he is righteous.   Rom. 2:13; 1 John 2:26, 29

> **3:5–7 The Fruit of Faith**
>
> We do not earn salvation by our obedience; for salvation is the free gift of God, to be received by faith. But obedience is the fruit of faith. . . . Here is the true test. If we abide in Christ, if the love of God dwells in us, our feelings, our thoughts, our purposes, our actions, will be in harmony with the will of God as expressed in the precepts of His holy law. *SC 61*

8 He that committeth sin is of the ᵀdevil; for the devil sinneth from the beginning. For this purpose the Son of God was manifested, that he might destroy the works of the devil.   Matt. 13:38; John 8:44; 16:11 ◆ *false accuser*
9 Whosoever is born of God doth not commit sin; for his seed remaineth in him: and he cannot sin, because he is born of God.   John 1:13
10 In this the children of God are manifest, and the children of the devil: whosoever doeth not righteousness is not of God, neither he that loveth not his brother. Matt. 13:38

Love One Another

11 For this is the message that ye heard from the beginning, that we should love one another.   John 13:34-35; 1 John 1:5; 2 John 5
12 Not as Cain, *who* was of that wicked one, and slew his brother. And wherefore slew he him? Because his own works were evil, and his brother's righteous.   Heb. 11:4; Jude 11

> **3:12 Light Reveals Sin**
>
> Abel's life of obedience and unswerving faith was to Cain a perpetual reproof. . . . The brighter the heavenly light that is reflected from the character of God's faithful servants, the more clearly the sins of the ungodly are revealed, and the more determined will be their efforts to destroy those who disturb their peace. *PP 74*

13 Marvel not, my brethren, if the world hate you.   John 15:18-19; 17:14
14 We know that we have passed from death unto life, because we love the brethren. He that loveth not *his* brother abideth in death.   Matt. 25:40; John 5:24; 1 John 5:2
15 Whosoever hateth his brother is a murderer: and ye know that no murderer hath eternal life abiding in him.   Matt. 5:21-22

> ### Unparalleled Love
>
> **1 John 3:1**
>
> The price paid for our redemption, the infinite sacrifice of our heavenly Father in giving His Son to die for us, should give us exalted conceptions of what we may become through Christ. As the inspired apostle John beheld the height, the depth, the breadth of the Father's love toward the perishing race, he was filled with adoration and reverence; and, failing to find suitable language in which to express the greatness and tenderness of this love, he called upon the world to behold it. . . . What a value this places upon man! Through transgression the sons of man become subjects of Satan. Through faith in the atoning sacrifice of Christ the sons of Adam may become the sons of God. By assuming human nature, Christ elevates humanity. Fallen men are placed where, through connection with Christ, they may indeed become worthy of the name "sons of God."
>
> Such love is without a parallel. Children of the heavenly King! Precious promise! Theme for the most profound meditation! The matchless love of God for a world that did not love Him! The thought has a subduing power upon the soul and brings the mind into captivity to the will of God. The more we study the divine character in the light of the cross, the more we see mercy, tenderness, and forgiveness blended with equity and justice, and the more clearly we discern innumerable evidences of a love that is infinite and a tender pity surpassing a mother's yearning sympathy for her wayward child. *SC 15*

16 Hereby perceive we the love *of God*, because he laid down his life for us: and we ought to lay down *our* lives for the brethren.

Jesus See John 19:28–30.

17 But whoso hath this world's good, and seeth his brother have need, and shutteth up his bowels *of compassion* from him, how dwelleth the love of God in him? Heb. 13:16; 1 John 4:20
18 My little children, let us not love in word, neither in tongue; but in deed and in truth. 1 John 2:1

3:18 A Constant Inner Impulse

The completeness of Christian character is attained when the impulse to help and bless others springs constantly from within. It is the atmosphere of this love surrounding the soul of the believer that makes him a savor of life unto life and enables God to bless his work. *AA 551*

19 And hereby we know that we are of the truth, and shall assure our hearts before him.
20 For if our heart condemn us, God is greater than our heart, and knoweth all things.
21 Beloved, if our heart condemn us not, *then* have we confidence toward God. Job 22:26
22 And whatsoever we ask, we receive of him, because we keep his commandments, and do those things that are pleasing in his sight. Matt. 21:22; John 8:29; 9:31
23 And this is his commandment, That we should believe on the name of his Son Jesus Christ, and love one another, as he gave us commandment. John 6:29; 13:34; 15:12
24 And he that keepeth his commandments dwelleth in him, and he in him. And hereby we know that he abideth in us, by the Spirit which he hath given us. John 17:21

Test All Teachings

4 Beloved, believe not every spirit, but try the spirits whether they are of God: because many false prophets are gone out into the world. 1 Thess. 5:21; 2 Pet. 2:1; 1 John 2:18
2 Hereby know ye the Spirit of God: Every spirit that confesseth that Jesus Christ is come in the flesh is of God: John 1:14; 1 Cor. 12:3
3 And every spirit that confesseth not that Jesus Christ is come in the flesh is not of God: and this is that *spirit* of antichrist, whereof ye have heard that it should come; and even now already is it in the world. 1 John 2:18, 22; 2 John 7
4 Ye are of God, little children, and have overcome them: because greater is he that is in you, than he that is in the world. John 12:31
5 They are of the world: therefore speak they of the world, and the world heareth them. John 3:31; 8:23; 17:14

4:1 The Word: The Final Standard

Since it was the Spirit of God that inspired the Bible, it is impossible that the teaching of the Spirit should ever be contrary to that of the word.

The Spirit was not given—nor can it ever be bestowed—to supersede the Bible; for the Scriptures explicitly state that the word of God is the standard by which all teaching and experience must be tested. Says the apostle John, "Believe not every spirit, but try the spirits whether they are of God: because many false prophets are gone out into the world" (1 John 4:1). *GC vii*

6 We are of God: he that knoweth God heareth us; he that is not of God heareth not us. Hereby know we the spirit of truth, and the spirit of error. John 10:27; 14:17; 1 Cor. 14:37

Gift of Prophecy See Isaiah 8:20.

God's Love in His People

7 Beloved, let us love one another: for love is of God; and every one that loveth is born of God, and knoweth God. 1 John 2:29
8 He that loveth not knoweth not God; for God is love. 2 Cor. 13:11

Who Is God? See John 14:9.

9 In this was ᵀmanifested the love of God toward us, because that God sent his only begotten Son into the world, that we might live through him. John 3:16; 1 John 4:10; 5:11 ◆ *made known*
10 Herein is love, not that we loved God, but that he loved us, and sent his Son *to be* the propitiation for our sins. 1 Pet. 3:18; 1 John 2:2

4:10 Christ's Measureless Love

In the contemplation of Christ we linger on the shore of a love that is measureless. We endeavor to tell of this love, and language fails us. We consider His life on earth, His sacrifice for us, His work in heaven as our advocate, and the mansions He is preparing for those who love Him, and we can only exclaim, O the height and depth of the love of Christ! *AA 333, 334*

11 Beloved, if God so loved us, we ought also to love one another.
12 No man hath seen God at any time. If we love one another, God dwelleth in us, and his love is perfected in us. John 1:18; 1 Tim. 6:16
13 Hereby know we that we dwell in him, and he in us, because he hath given us of his Spirit. 1 John 3:24
14 And we have seen and do testify that the Father sent the Son *to be* the Saviour of the world. John 4:42

15 Whosoever shall confess that Jesus is the Son of God, God dwelleth in him, and he in God.   Rom. 10:9; 1 John 3:24; 5:5
16 And we have known and believed the love that God hath to us. God is love; and he that dwelleth in love dwelleth in God, and God in him.   1 John 3:24

4:16 Practical Godliness

True sanctification comes through the working out of the principle of love. . . . The life of him in whose heart Christ abides, will reveal practical godliness. The character will be purified, elevated, ennobled, and glorified. Pure doctrine will blend with works of righteousness; heavenly precepts will mingle with holy practices. *AA 560*

17 Herein is our love made perfect, that we may have boldness in the day of judgment: because as he is, so are we in this world.
18 There is no fear in love; but perfect love casteth out fear: because fear hath torment. He that feareth is not made perfect in love.   Rom. 8:15; 2 Tim. 1:7; 1 John 4:12
19 We love him, because he first loved us.
20 If a man say, I love God, and hateth his brother, he is a liar: for he that loveth not his brother whom he hath seen, how can he love God whom he hath not seen? 1 John 2:4; 3:17; 4:12
21 And this commandment have we from him, That he who loveth God love his brother also.   1 John 3:11

We Are God's Children

5 Whosoever believeth that Jesus is the Christ is born of God: and every one that loveth him that ᵀbegat loveth him also that is begotten of him.   1 John 2:29 ◆ *brought forth*
2 By this we know that we love the children of God, when we love God, and keep his commandments.

3 For this is the love of God, that we keep his commandments: and his commandments are not grievous.   John 14:15; 2 John 6

God's Law See Matthew 5:17, 18.

4 For whatsoever is born of God overcometh the world: and this is the victory that overcometh the world, *even* our faith.   John 16:33

5:3, 4 Faith Enables Obedience

Instead of releasing man from obedience, it is faith, and faith only, that makes us partakers of the grace of Christ, which enables us to render obedience. *SC 60, 61*

5 Who is he that overcometh the world, but he that believeth that Jesus is the Son of God?   1 John 4:15
6 This is he that came by water and blood, *even* Jesus Christ; not by water only, but by water and blood. And it is the Spirit that beareth witness, because the Spirit is truth.   John 14:17; 15:26; 16:13
7 For there are three that bear record in heaven, the Father, the Word, and the Holy Ghost: and these three are one.   Deut. 6:4
8 And there are three that bear witness in earth, the Spirit, and the water, and the blood: and these three agree in one.
9 If we receive the witness of men, the witness of God is greater: for this is the witness of God which he hath testified of his Son.   Matt. 3:16-17
10 He that believeth on the Son of God hath the witness in himself: he that believeth not God hath made him a liar; because he believeth not the record that God gave of his Son.   John 3:33; Rom. 8:16; Gal. 4:6
11 And this is the record, that God hath given to us eternal life, and this life is in his Son.   John 1:4; 1 John 2:25; 4:9

5:3

5:11-13

Channels of Blessing

1 John 4:19

Love is the basis of godliness. Whatever the profession, no man has pure love to God unless he has unselfish love for his brother. But we can never come into possession of this spirit by *trying* to love others. What is needed is the love of Christ in the heart. When self is merged in Christ, love springs forth spontaneously. The completeness of Christian character is attained when the impulse to help and bless others springs constantly from within—when the sunshine of heaven fills the heart and is revealed in the countenance.

It is not possible for the heart in which Christ abides to be destitute of love. If we love God because He first loved us, we shall love all for whom Christ died. We cannot come in touch with divinity without coming in touch with humanity; for in Him who sits upon the throne of the universe, divinity and humanity are combined. Connected with Christ, we are connected with our fellow men by the golden links of the chain of love. Then the pity and compassion of Christ will be manifest in our life. We shall not wait to have the needy and unfortunate brought to us. We shall not need to be entreated to feel for the woes of others. It will be as natural for us to minister to the needy and suffering as it was for Christ to go about doing good. *COL 384, 385*

12 He that hath the Son hath life; *and* he that hath not the Son of God hath not life.

5:11, 12 Getting Versus Giving

To live for self is to perish. Covetousness, the desire of benefit for self's sake, cuts the soul off from life. It is the spirit of Satan to get, to draw to self. It is the spirit of Christ to give, to sacrifice self for the good of others. *COL 259*

---

13 These things have I written unto you that believe on the name of the Son of God; that ye may know that ye have eternal life, and that ye may believe on the name of the Son of God.   John 1:12; 20:31; 1 John 3:23

> Salvation From Sin See Revelation 3:20.

Our Confidence in Christ

14 And this is the confidence that we have in him, that, if we ask any thing according to his will, he heareth us: 1 John 3:21-22

15 And if we know that he hear us, whatsoever we ask, we know that we have the petitions that we desired of him.

16 If any man see his brother sin a sin *which is* not unto death, he shall ask, and he shall give him life for them that sin not unto

death. There is a sin unto death: I do not say that he shall pray for it. Jer. 7:16; 14:11; Heb. 6:4-6

5:14, 15 Prayer, Faith, and Promises

Faith is an essential element of prevailing prayer. . . . [Read Hebrews 11:6 and 1 John 5:14, 15.] With the persevering faith of Jacob, with the unyielding persistence of Elijah, we may present our petitions to the Father, claiming all that He has promised. The honor of His throne is staked for the fulfillment of His word. *PK 157, 158*

---

17 All unrighteousness is sin: and there is a sin not unto death.   Is. 1:18; 1 John 3:4; 5:16

18 We know that whosoever is born of God sinneth not; but he that is ᵀbegotten of God keepeth himself, and that wicked one toucheth him not.   1 John 3:9 ◆ *brought forth*

19 *And* we know that we are of God, and the whole world lieth in wickedness.   John 12:31

20 And we know that the Son of God is come, and hath given us an understanding, that we may know him that is true, and we are in him that is true, *even* in his Son Jesus Christ. This is the true God, and eternal life.

21 Little children, keep yourselves from idols. Amen.   1 Cor. 10:7, 14; 1 John 2:1

THE SECOND EPISTLE OF

JOHN

The apostle John is known as the "apostle of love" because of the emphasis on love in his writings. In this brief letter, John models and encourages the love that Christians are to have for each other. He also demonstrates a great concern for knowing the truth. Therefore, he shows the intimate relationship between truth and love.

While Christians are called to love each other, John advises believers to avoid giving hospitality or support to those who do not teach the truth. Such actions promote lies rather than the truth and are actually unloving, because they encourage the self-deception of the false teachers. The loving thing is to deny these teachers support, as this speaks against these teachers who advocate a false gospel and are not Christians.

John's prohibition does not mean that one should not interact with people who are not Christians, but rather that one should not support the beliefs of people who proclaim to be Christians but deny the gospel with their actions. Paul makes a similar point about the immoral behavior of professed Christians in 1 Corinthians 5:9–13. Even the harsh words John uses concerning the false teachers are written with love, as he is "speaking the truth in love" (Ephesians 4:15) and instructs Christians to do the same.

Dates

Second John confronts the same false teachers described in 1 John. Having departed from the community (1 John 2:19), these teachers now seek hospitality from the audience of 2 John (2 John 7–13). Therefore, this letter is probably contemporaneous or slightly later than 1 John, originating from Ephesus between A.D. 90 and A.D. 94. The letter is addressed to "the elect lady and her children" (verse 1). This identification could be literal, referring to a particular woman and her children, or metaphorical, describing a church and its members given that 1 John 2:1 tenderly addresses the believers as "little children." Division exists among scholars, but regardless of one's conclusion, it is clear that John knew the recipients and desired to talk with them "face to face" (verse 12). The audience likely resided in Asia Minor, as John had oversight of churches in this area. Some scholars believe that 2 and 3 John were cover letters for 1 John, providing personal words to the audience alongside of the content of the longer, more general letter. Such an idea, however, remains an unproven hypothesis.

Author

The author of 2 and 3 John only refers to himself as "the elder." Both external and internal evidence indicate that this "elder" was the apostle John. The second-century Christian writers Irenaeus and Clement of Alexandria believed that the apostle wrote these letters. The tone of the letter reflects one with a greater authority than the elder of a local church, particularly if the "elect lady" addressed refers to a congregation rather than an individual (see "Dates").

The vocabulary, style, and themes of 2 and 3 John are exceedingly similar, showing a common authorship of these two letters. In addition, many passages of 2 John have parallels in the fourth gospel and 1 John (for example, compare John 13:34, 35; 1 John 2:7; and 2 John 5), both of which were written by the apostle John. The use of the title "elder" rather than "apostle" is not a reason to question apostolic authorship, as Peter refers to himself as an elder as well (1 Peter 5:1). John may have described himself as "the elder" to indicate his old age, showing his participation in the ministry of Jesus and foundation of the church more than fifty years earlier.

As noted above, writers such as Irenaeus and Clement of Alexandria cited the book and saw it as authoritative due to its apostolic authorship. However, because the letter is brief, reiterates many of the same teachings as 1 John, and was addressed to a particular person or group, it had limited circulation in the early church and rarely appeared in the writings of the early church leaders. Some later writers overlooked its apostolic origin and wondered whether it should be recognized as inspired and part of the canon. Fourth century writers such as Eusebius and Athanasius recalled the testimony of those closest to John's time and recognized it as part of the New Testament because of its apostolic authorship.

Meaning of the Name

The Greek title *Ioannou B* means "Of John II."

Christ in 2 John

Like 1 John, this letter shows the importance and necessity of believing in Jesus' incarnation (verse 7). John also directs attention to the words of Jesus (see John 15:1–17) by highlighting the love commandment that Jesus gave (2 John 5) and the need to abide "in the doctrine of Christ" (verse 9).

Overview

Even in a superficial reading of these thirteen verses, one can see the closeness John shares with his addressee. Within this framework, a theme emerges. The author sends encouragement to walk in the footsteps of Jesus, warns against false teachers and suggests how to deal with deceivers. He writes with a compassionate and loving spirit that exhibits a tight spiritual bond. In addition to its brevity, the similarities between this letter and 1 John can prompt Christians to overlook this book. One can divide this letter into two sections:

(1) *2 John 1–6, God's Commands:* John reiterates key themes from 1 John like truth (verse 4), love (verse 5), and obedience (verse 6).

(2) *2 John 7–13, False Teachers:* Christians are not to receive into their community or offer support to those who claim to teach the gospel but in reality advance heresy. In the ancient world, teachers would often travel from city to city and needed places to stay and places to teach. John warned that opening one's home to a false teacher was the same as giving credence to heresy.

Unlocking 2 John

KEY PEOPLE:
John, Jesus, itinerant false teachers

KEY EVENTS:
Traveling false teachers attempting to seek hospitality from Christians

KEY PHRASE:
Avoid fellowship, as John calls for the community to remain pure in doctrine by not associating with false teachers. The exhortation to love one another does not mean that one should give hospitality to false teachers, as these teachers are not true believers.

KEY VERSES:
"Whosoever transgresseth, and abideth not in the doctrine of Christ, hath not God. He that abideth in the doctrine of Christ, he hath both the Father and the Son. If there come any unto you, and bring not this doctrine, receive him not into *your* house, neither bid him God speed" (2 John 9, 10).

Living in the Truth

1 The elder unto the elect lady and her children, whom I love in the truth; and not I only, but also all they that have known the truth;   *John 8:32*

2 For the truth's sake, which dwelleth in us, and shall be with us for ever.

3 Grace be with you, mercy, *and* peace, from God the Father, and from the Lord Jesus Christ, the Son of the Father, in truth and love.   *Rom. 1:7*

4 I rejoiced greatly that I found of thy children walking in truth, as we have received a commandment from the Father.   *3 John 3-4*

5 And now I beseech thee, lady, not as though I wrote a new commandment unto thee, but that which we had from the beginning, that we love one another.   *John 13:34-35*

6 And this is love, that we walk after his commandments. This is the commandment, That, as ye have heard from the beginning, ye should walk in it.   *1 John 2:24*

Reject False Teachers

7 For many deceivers are entered into the world, who confess not that Jesus Christ is come in the flesh. This is a deceiver and an antichrist.   *1 John 4:1-3*

8 Look to yourselves, that we lose not those things which we have wrought, but that we receive a full reward. *1 Cor. 3:8; Heb. 10:35; Rev. 3:11*

9 Whosoever ᵀtransgresseth, and abideth not in the doctrine of Christ, hath not God. He that abideth in the doctrine of Christ, he hath both the Father and the Son. *violates the law*

10 If there come any unto you, and bring not this doctrine, receive him not into *your* house, neither bid him God speed: *Titus 3:10*

11 For he that biddeth him God speed is partaker of his evil deeds. *Eph. 5:11; 1 Tim. 5:22*

7-11 No Compromise With Evil

We are authorized to hold in the same estimation as did the beloved disciple those who claim to abide in Christ while living in transgression of God's law. There exist in these last days evils similar to those that threatened the prosperity of the early church; and the teachings of the apostle John on these points should be carefully heeded. . . . While we are to love the souls for whom Christ died, we are to make no compromise with evil. *AA 554, 555*

---

12 Having many things to write unto you, I would not *write* with paper and ink: but I trust to come unto you, and speak face to face, that our joy may be full.   *John 15:11*

13 The children of thy elect sister greet thee. Amen.   *2 John*

The Danger of Heresies

2 John 7–11

John was filled with sadness as he saw these poisonous errors creeping into the church. He saw the dangers to which the church was exposed, and he met the emergency with promptness and decision. The epistles of John breathe the spirit of love. It seems as if he wrote with a pen dipped in love. But when he came in contact with those who were breaking the law of God, yet claiming that they were living without sin, he did not hesitate to warn them of their fearful deception. . . .

There exist in these last days evils similar to those that threatened the prosperity of the early church; and the teachings of the apostle John on these points should be carefully heeded. "You must have charity," is the cry heard everywhere, especially from those who profess sanctification. But true charity is too pure to cover an unconfessed sin. *AA 554, 555*

THE THIRD EPISTLE OF

JOHN

While John's first two epistles discuss the danger of false teachers, 3 John addresses the threat of false leaders. Diotrephes had assumed leadership of a church, rejecting John's authority by slandering his name and refusing to accept the teachers John had sent. Diotrephes sought power and opposed anything that may have threatened his influence.

The solution to the problem of false teachers who advocate heresy is to spread the truth of the gospel, and the solution to false leaders who act selfishly is the selflessness of Jesus that all Christians, especially Christian leaders, should imitate (verse 11). John provides examples of this selflessness. Gaius was one such example, as he welcomed the teachers John sent even though he did not know them before (verses 5, 6). The traveling teachers are another example of selflessness, as they labor in the name of Jesus (verse 7). The messenger of this letter, Demetrius, is a third example (verse 12). In addition to imitating the conduct of these true leaders, John teaches Christians to support these leaders with words of respect and acts of kindness (verse 8).

False leaders promote themselves but true leaders glorify the name of Christ and follow His example of servant leadership.

Dates

The similarities in style and theme between 2 and 3 John indicate that John probably wrote them around the same time, likely between A.D. 90 and A.D. 94, when John lived in Ephesus (the most prominent city in the region) and had oversight of the churches in Asia Minor. The situation described in this letter indicates that John sent out itinerant teachers as part of his oversight of the churches of the region. These teachers would stay in the homes of church members while they taught in a particular city. When John received a report from some of the "brethren" that Diotrephes had seized control of a congregation, opposed John's leadership, refused to offer these teachers support, and disfellowshiped those people who accepted these teachers (verses 9, 10), he dispatched Demetrius to bring this letter to Gaius, whose hospitality the brethren had also described in this report (verses 3, 6).

Gaius, Diotrephes, and Demetrius only appear in this letter. The name Diotrephes does not appear anywhere else in the New Testament; it seems unlikely that he was one of the false teachers described in 1 and 2 John since John nowhere denounces his teachings in this letter. Some have suggested that the letter from John that Diotrephes rejected (verse 9) is 1 or 2 John, but it seems more likely that this letter no longer exists—either lost or possibly destroyed by Diotrephes.

The name Gaius was common in the Roman world and is shared by three other figures in the New Testament: (1) a Macedonian who accompanied Paul on his travels (Acts 19:29), (2) a man from Derbe who traveled with Paul from Greece to Syria (20:4), and (3) the Corinthian who was baptized by Paul and hosted the apostle (Romans 16:23; 1 Corinthians 1:14). Since the Gaius of 3 John lived in Asia Minor, he is probably a different person. While Acts describes a silversmith named Demetrius who lived in Ephesus and made idols for Artemis (Acts 19:24, 38), it seems unlikely that the carrier of this letter was this opponent of Paul, particularly since Demetrius was also a common name.

Author

Like 2 John, the author of 3 John identifies himself as "the elder." Because of the similarities between 2 and 3 John, scholars universally believe that the same author wrote both letters. The internal and external evidence indicates that the author is the apostle John.

Meaning of the Name

Because this is the third letter ascribed to the apostle John, the letter received the Greek title of *Ioannou G* "Of John III," (*G* is *gamma*, the third letter of the Greek alphabet).

Christ in 3 John

Although the name Jesus never explicitly appears in this short letter, verse 7 describes messengers who "for his name's sake they went forth," referring to Jesus (for a similar expression, see Acts 5:40, 41). The letter also has an emphasis on the truth, which comes from and exists in Jesus (see John 14:6).

Overview

Among John's letters, this epistle is the most personal, as John openly names and describes three individuals (Gaius, Diotrephes, Demetrius). This straightforward letter opposes the dissidence of Diotrephes. Likely he is an elder in the church who is led from Christianity into Gnosticism. When John admonishes against taking in such teaching, it seems that Diotrephes declines to share the letter with his fellow members (verse 9). John sends other ministers who are denied access to the members. On his own accord, Diotrephes appears to have disfellowshiped anyone who privately listens to these men who speak God's truth.

Even still, John still writes with the same gentle spirit that we see in his other writings. Therein we see John's refined character, which is an inspiration to all readers. One can split this short letter into two sections:

(1) *3 John 1–8, Commendation:* Gaius is a humble and generous servant of Christ, who offered hospitality to the teachers that John sent, recognizing that these teachers are "brethren" even though they are strangers to him (verse 5). His conduct elicits great joy in John (verses 3, 4) and causes John to offer a prayer for Gaius's health and well-being (verse 2).

(2) *3 John 9–14, Condemnation:* In contrast, Diotrephes is an arrogant and self-seeking individual, as he rejects the authority of John and the ministry of the teachers he sent. Diotrephes's opposition to John extends to spreading lies about John and disfellowshiping those who welcome the teachers (verses 9, 10). John noted that he hopes to come to the church to address the problems caused by Diotrephes (verses 10, 14).

Unlocking 3 John

KEY PEOPLE:
John, Gaius, Diotrephes, Demetrius

KEY EVENTS:
Hospitality offered by Gaius; rebellion of Diotrephes

KEY WORD:
Hospitality, as John's commendation of Gaius' hospitality offers an example for Christians to follow. John's rebuke of Diotrephes' inhospitable behavior shows the importance of hospitality. The ministers who labor in fulltime ministry are in particular need of hospitality (3 John 7, 8).

KEY VERSE:
"Beloved, follow not that which is evil, but that which is good. He that doeth good is of God: but he that doeth evil hath not seen God" (2 John 11).

John Commends Gaius

1 The elder unto the wellbeloved Gaius, whom I love in the truth.   1 John 3:18

2 Beloved, I wish above all things that thou mayest prosper and be in health, even as thy soul prospereth.

> Health See Exodus 15:26.

3 For I rejoiced greatly, when the brethren came and testified of the truth that is in thee, even as thou walkest in the truth.   2 John 4

2, 3 Satan Destroys; God Restores

The Saviour in His miracles revealed the power that is continually at work in man's behalf, to sustain and to heal him. . . .

Sickness, suffering, and death are work of an antagonistic power. Satan is the destroyer; God is the restorer. . . .

The desire of God for every human being is expressed in the words, "Beloved, I wish above all things that thou mayest prosper and be in health, even as thy soul prospereth" (3 John 2). *MH 112, 113*

---

4 I have no greater joy than to hear that my children walk in truth.   Gal. 4:19

5 Beloved, thou doest faithfully whatsoever thou doest to the brethren, and to strangers;

6 Which have borne witness of thy †charity before the church: whom if thou bring forward on their journey after a godly sort, thou shalt do well: 1 Thess. 2:12 ◆ *selfless love*

7 Because that for his name's sake they went forth, taking nothing of the Gentiles.

8 We therefore ought to receive such, that we might be fellowhelpers to the truth.

John Criticizes Diotrephes

9 I wrote unto the church: but Diotrephes, who loveth to have the preeminence among them, receiveth us not.

10 Wherefore, if I come, I will remember his deeds which he doeth, †prating against us with malicious words: and not content therewith, neither doth he himself receive the brethren, and forbiddeth them that would, and casteth *them* out of the church.   *gossiping*

11 Beloved, follow not that which is evil, but that which is good. He that doeth good is of God: but he that doeth evil hath not seen God.   Ps. 37:27

John Praises Demetrius

12 Demetrius hath good report of all *men*, and of the truth itself: yea, and we *also* bear record; and ye know that our record is true. John 21:24

13 I had many things to write, but I will not with ink and pen write unto thee: 2 John 12

14 But I trust I shall shortly see thee, and we shall speak face to face. Peace *be* to thee. *Our* friends salute thee. Greet the friends by name.

THE EPISTLE OF

JUDE

Apostasy usually is not instantaneous. Rather, it typically is a long process where one gradually forgets the gospel message and accepts false teachings because often they blend so easily given that an element of truth does exist with the error. Therefore, Jude's letter and call to "contend for the faith which was once delivered unto the saints" (verse 3) is a pre-emptive strike against apostasy. He reveals why apostasy is so dangerous and how to avoid it.

The danger of apostasy stems from the judgment that false teachers will face (verses 14–16). They are like ungodly leaders in the past that God judged; those who accept their teaching will join in the same fate. Christians can avoid this fate by continuing to grow in their faith, praying, studying the Word, remembering the love of God, sharing the good news of salvation, and waiting for Christ to return (verses 20, 21). In addition, Christians should help those who are struggling to maintain their faith (verses 22, 23) and recognize that God has the power to keep them (verses 24, 25). Therefore, the cure for apostasy is to be on guard for false teachers and continue in the Christian faith. Because of the consequences of apostasy, it is imperative that Christians follow this counsel.

Dates

The lack of detailed information presented in the epistle and the dearth of extrabiblical traditions about its author cause the date and location of the letter to remain inexact. Because of its broad nature, the letter probably addressed churches in a region rather than one particular church. These churches likely included Jews and Gentiles. False teachers had crept into these fellowships, promoting immorality, creating factions, and denying the gospel. These individuals are comparable to the false teachers discussed in 2 Peter. In fact, the similarities between 2 Peter 2:1—3:3 and Jude 4–18 are too great merely to be a coincidence. Scholars believe that one of the writers used the other as a source. (The numerous differences between the two works show that one writer did not simply copy the other.) Debate persists over whether Jude used Peter or Peter used Jude—it is possible that they both acquired information from the same third source. Many biblical scholars argue that Jude is written first because it is so brief; Peter then uses Jude as a springboard and simply expands on his thoughts. If 2 Peter is written first and articulates the problem of false teachers well, why would Jude have followed with such a brief letter when the details had already been handily spelled out? Literary studies indicate that typically the shorter pieces are written first. The theory that Jude used Peter seems more likely, as 2 Peter appears older for two reasons:

(1) Second Peter speaks of these apostate teachers coming (2 Peter 2:1, 2; 3:3) while Jude notes that they have come (Jude 4, 11, 12, 17, 18).

(2) In verses 17, 18, Peter issues a warning that mockers of the faith would come and cause division, and Jude notes that this event has already occurred (see 2 Peter 3:3, as well as Paul's words in 1 Timothy 4:11).

If Jude was written prior to 2 Peter, it must have been written prior to A.D. 67, which is probably when Peter was martyred. If Jude is subsequent to 2 Peter, he may have written his letter between A.D. 70 and A.D. 85. The omission of any discussion concerning the fall of Jerusalem in A.D. 70 does not necessitate that Jude wrote before this date.

Author

The only information the author provides about himself occurs in verse 1: "Jude, the servant of Jesus Christ, and brother of James." This Jude does not appear to be the apostle Judas, as the author differentiates himself from the apostles in verse 17. Because people usually referred to themselves as "the son of" rather than "the brother of," Jude's brother James must have been a prominent figure, likely Jesus' brother James, who was a leader of the Jerusalem church (Acts 15:3–12; Galatians 2:9). Matthew 13:55 and Mark 6:3 indicate that Jesus had a brother named Judas, and Jude is a shortened form of this name.

Like James, Jude calls himself a "servant of Jesus" rather than the brother of Jesus (see James 1:1). There is little extrabiblical tradition about Jude, but the New Testament

provides a few details about him. Jude, along with the other brothers of Jesus, did not follow Jesus during His ministry (John 7:1–9) but came into the faith after His Resurrection (Acts 1:14). He probably engaged in missionary activity, as Paul mentions that the "brethren of the Lord" brought their wives with them on their journeys (1 Corinthians 9:5; see also Acts 15:22, 32).

Clear references to the epistle in the last quarter of the second century and possible allusions in earlier texts indicate that the early church saw this letter as authoritative. The Muratorian Canon (approximately A.D. 170), Tertullian, and Origen all held this letter to be Scripture.

Meaning of the Name

Many Jews in the first century were named Judas (Judah in Hebrew). The Greek title *Iouda* ("Of Jude") reflects a shortened form of this name.

Christ in Jude

Jude begins and ends his letter by describing how Jesus preserves those who believe in Him (verses 1, 24). Meanwhile, those who turn God's grace into "lasciviousness" and deny Jesus (verse 4) stand condemned. Therefore, Christians continually need to look to the mercy of Jesus that leads to eternal life (verse 21).

Overview

While this letter is one of the shortest in the New Testament, its intensity is among the highest. In essence, Jude merges the argument of 2 Peter with the style of his brother James, presenting a tightly packed and image-laden argument against the false teachers Peter had predicted. The book contains four sections:

(1) *Jude 1–4, The Problem of False Teaching:* Because false teachers have slipped into the community unnoticed, Jude alters his original plan to write about salvation and instead exhorts his community to vie for the unchanging truth of the gospel.

(2) *Jude 5–16, The Destruction of False Teaching:* The false teachers resemble godless figures from the Old Testament such as Cain, Balaam, and Korah (verse 11) and will face destruction just as Sodom and Gomorrah and the unbelieving Israel in the wilderness did (see verses 5, 7). Jude also includes references to the fallen angels, the archangel Michael, and Enoch in this discussion (verses 6, 8, 9, 14, 15).

(3) *Jude 17–23, The Defense of Truth:* Believers guard against false teachers by devoting themselves to the truth of Christ and by growing in faith.

(4) *Jude 24, 25, The Doxology of the Believer:* God is the one who preserves His people until the last day and receives all glory.

Unlocking Jude

KEY PEOPLE:
Jesus, James, Jude, Michael the archangel, Cain, Balaam, Korah, Enoch

KEY EVENTS:
The death of the generation in the wilderness; the destruction of Sodom and Gomorrah; future judgment; the infiltration of false teachers in the church

KEY PHRASE:
Contend for the faith, as Jude fights against false teachers and exhorts Christians to do the same. Therefore, he both models and commands Christian to contend for their faith.

KEY VERSE:
"Beloved, when I gave all diligence to write unto you of the common salvation, it was needful for me to write unto you, and exhort you that ye should earnestly contend for the faith which was once delivered unto the saints" (Jude 3).

Warnings about False Teachers

1 Jude, the servant of Jesus Christ, and brother of James, to them that are ᵀsanctified by God the Father, and preserved in Jesus Christ, *and* called: Luke 6:16 ◆ *made holy*

2 Mercy unto you, and peace, and love, be multiplied.   1 Pet. 1:2; 2 Pet. 1:2

3 Beloved, when I gave all diligence to write unto you of the common salvation, it was needful for me to write unto you, and exhort *you* that ye should earnestly contend for the faith which was once delivered unto the saints.   Phil. 1:27; 1 Tim. 6:12; Titus 1:4

4 For there are certain men crept in unawares, who were before of old ordained to this condemnation, ungodly men, turning the grace of our God into ᵀlasciviousness, and denying the only Lord God, and our Lord Jesus Christ.   Gal. 2:4; 1 Pet. 2:8; 1 John 2:22 ◆ *lewdness*

5 I will therefore put you in remembrance, though ye once knew this, how that the Lord, having saved the people out of the land of Egypt, afterward destroyed them that believed not.   Ps. 106:26

6 And the angels which kept not their first estate, but left their own habitation, he hath reserved in everlasting chains under darkness unto the judgment of the great day.   Matt. 25:41; Eph. 6:12; 2 Pet. 2:4

6 Evil Angels Judged

Satan also and evil angels are judged by Christ and His people. Says Paul: "Know ye not that we shall judge angels?" (1 Corinthians 6:3). And Jude declares that "the angels which kept not their first estate, but left their own habitation, He hath reserved in everlasting chains under darkness unto the judgment of the great day" (Jude 6). *GC 661*

7 Even as Sodom and Gomorrha, and the cities about them in like manner, giving themselves over to fornication, and going after strange flesh, are set forth for an example, suffering the vengeance of eternal fire.   Deut. 29:23; Hos. 11:8; 2 Pet. 2:6

End of Sin/Hell See Exodus 21:6.

8 Likewise also these *filthy* dreamers defile the flesh, despise dominion, and speak evil of dignities.

9 Yet Michael the ᵀarchangel, when contending with the ᵀdevil he disputed about the body of Moses, ᵀdurst not bring against him a railing accusation, but said, The Lord rebuke thee.   Dan. 10:13, 21; 12:1 ◆ *chief angel* ◆ *false accuser* ◆ *dared*

9 A Satanic Weapon

Christ Himself, when contending with Satan about the body of Moses, "durst not bring against him a railing accusation" (Jude 9). Had He done this, He would have placed Himself on Satan's ground, for accusation is the weapon of the evil one. He is called in Scripture, "the accuser of our brethren" (Revelation 12:10). Jesus would employ none of Satan's weapons. He met him with the words, "The Lord rebuke thee" (Jude 9). *MB 57*

10 But these speak evil of those things which they know not: but what they know naturally, as brute beasts, in those things they corrupt themselves.   2 Pet. 2:12

11 Woe unto them! for they have gone in the way of Cain, and ran greedily after the error of Balaam for reward, and perished in the gainsaying of Core.   Num. 31:16; 2 Pet. 2:15; 1 John 3:12

12 These are spots in your feasts of charity, when they feast with you, feeding themselves without fear: clouds *they are* without water, carried about of winds; trees whose fruit withereth, without fruit, twice dead, plucked up by the roots;   Prov. 25:14; Ezek. 34:8; Matt. 15:13

13 Raging waves of the sea, foaming out their own shame; wandering stars, to whom is reserved the blackness of darkness for ever.   Is. 57:20; Phil. 3:19; 2 Pet. 2:17

The Precious Hope

Jude 14, 15

One of the most solemn and yet most glorious truths revealed in the Bible is that of Christ's second coming to complete the great work of redemption. To God's pilgrim people, so long left to sojourn in "the region and shadow of death," a precious, joy-inspiring hope is given in the promise of His appearing, who is "the resurrection and the life," to "bring home again His banished." The doctrine of the second advent is the very keynote of the Sacred Scriptures. From the day when the first pair turned their sorrowing steps from Eden, the children of faith have waited the coming of the Promised One to break the destroyer's power and bring them again to the lost Paradise. Holy men of old looked forward to the advent of the Messiah in glory, as the consummation of their hope. Enoch, only the seventh in descent from them that dwelt in Eden, he who for three centuries on earth walked with his God, was permitted to behold from afar the coming of the Deliverer. . . . The patriarch Job in the night of his affliction exclaimed with unshaken trust: "I know that my Redeemer liveth, and that He shall stand at the latter day upon the earth: . . . in my flesh shall I see God: whom I shall see for myself, and mine eyes shall behold, and not another" (Job 19:25–27). *GC 299*

14 And Enoch also, the seventh from Adam, prophesied of these, saying, Behold, the Lord cometh with ten thousands of his saints,   Gen. 5:18; Deut. 33:2; Matt. 16:27

15 To execute judgment upon all, and to convince all that are ungodly among them of all their ungodly deeds which they have ungodly committed, and of all their hard *speeches* which ungodly sinners have spoken against him.   1 Sam. 2:3

16 These are murmurers, complainers, walking after their own lusts; and their mouth speaketh great swelling *words*, having men's persons in admiration because of advantage.   Lev. 19:15; 2 Pet. 2:10, 18

17 But, beloved, remember ye the words which were spoken before of the apostles of our Lord Jesus Christ;   2 Pet. 3:2

18 How that they told you there should be mockers in the last time, who should walk after their own ungodly lusts.   Acts 20:29

19 These be they who separate themselves, sensual, having not the Spirit.   1 Cor. 2:14

20 But ye, beloved, building up yourselves on your most holy faith, praying in the Holy Ghost,   1 Cor. 14:4-5; Eph. 6:18; Col. 2:7

21 Keep yourselves in the love of God, looking for the mercy of our Lord Jesus Christ unto eternal life.   Heb. 9:28; 2 Pet. 3:12

22 And of some have compassion, making a difference:

23 And others save with fear, pulling *them* out of the fire; hating even the garment spotted by the flesh.   Amos 4:11; 1 Cor. 3:15; Rev. 3:4

24 Now unto him that is able to keep you from falling, and to present *you* faultless before the presence of his glory with exceeding joy,   2 Cor. 4:14; Col. 1:22; 1 Pet. 4:13

---

24 The Joy of Service

In our life here, earthly, sin-restricted though it is, the greatest joy and the highest education are in service. And in the future state, untrammeled by the limitations of sinful humanity, it is in service that our greatest joy and our highest education will be found—witnessing, and ever as we witness learning anew "the riches of the glory of this mystery;" "which is Christ in you, the hope of glory" (Colossians 1:27). *Ed 309*

---

25 To the only wise God our Saviour, *be* glory and majesty, dominion and power, both now and ever. Amen.   John 5:44; Rom. 11:36; 1 Tim. 1:17

THE REVELATION

OF JESUS CHRIST

Every story describing a climactic battle between good and evil has its root in the book of Revelation, where the final battle between good and evil—Armageddon—plays out. The question of why a good God would allow evil is laid to rest forever as the risen Christ deals with it once and for all.

The Book of Revelation also has a bad news-good news context. The bad news is that Judgment Day is coming, finding many unprepared to meet their Creator. God, who is "merciful and gracious" (Exodus 34:6), has held back His wrath for a long time. Now it will be fully unleashed in response to all-encompassing evil. The good news is that good will triumph. Jesus, the King of kings and the Lamb who was slain, will return in triumph to claim His bride—the church—after a battle to defeat forever Satan and his forces of evil.

Like the Book of Daniel and parts of the Book of Zechariah, Revelation is an apocalyptic book. Seven churches are examined and graded by the risen Christ. John's visions of the outpouring of God's judgment reach a climax at the battle of Armageddon, when the rider on the white horse—the Lamb—rides to victory. Christ's millennial kingdom begins.

How fitting that Revelation ends with a glorious vision of heaven—the prize for a race run well—and a plaintive cry of "Come, Lord Jesus."

Dates

While some scholars would date the book as early as the time of Nero (A.D. 54–68), early Christian writers almost unanimously date Revelation toward the end of John's life, during his exile to the island of Patmos (A.D. 90–95) when Domitian was emperor.

Author

The apostle John is widely considered to be the author of Revelation. In the third century, however, Dionysius, a bishop in Africa, attributed the book to John the Presbyter, rather than the apostle John. But most scholars believe that the apostle John is the author.

Meaning of the Name

In the Greek, the title is *Apokalypsis Ioannou,* or the "Revelation of John." The word *apokalypsis* means "unveiling." End-time events are unveiled through the visions given to the apostle John.

Christ in Revelation

The risen Christ can be seen throughout the Book of Revelation. His revealed truths are given to the apostle John (1:1). He is "the faithful witness, and the first begotten of the dead, and the prince of the kings of the earth" (1:5); the "Alpha and Omega, the beginning and the ending" (1:8; see also 1:11); the Lamb worshiped in heaven (chapter 5); the victorious rider on the white horse who is called "Faithful and True (19:11–16); the "King of Kings, and Lord of Lords" (19:16). He is the One whose return is longed for by every Christian.

Overview

Certain numbers (4, 7, 10, 12) figure heavily in the Book of Revelation. The risen Christ has seven stars in His right hand and points out seven golden lampstands (1:12–20). Seven churches are named (chapters 2—3). Seven lamps are alight around the throne of God (4:5). God's judgment unfolds through seven seals, seven angels with trumpets, seven angels bearing the seven last plagues, (chapters 5—11; 15—16). A beast with ten horns and seven heads rises out of the sea (13:1). A woman has a crown with twelve stars (12:1). The holy city of Jerusalem has twelve gates, each with an angel guarding it (21:12). Four living creatures worship before the throne of God (4:6–11). Four riders—popularly known as the four horsemen of the apocalypse—ride out as the first four of the seven seals (6:1–8). Death and destruction follow in their wake.

All the books of the Bible meet and end in the book of Revelation, and it harmonizes perfectly with the book of Daniel. In Revelation we see unsealed what was sealed in Daniel. Also, Revelation includes references to twenty-eight of the Old Testament books, focusing on the prophecies of Isaiah, Jeremiah, Ezekiel, and Daniel.

Revelation can be divided into two sections:

(1) *Revelation 1—3, Messages for Seven Churches:* The strengths and weaknesses of seven churches—Ephesus, Smyrna, Pergamos, Thyatira, Sardis, Philadelphia, and Laodicea—are discussed as a warning of the coming conquering King.

(2) *Revelation 4—22, A Message for the Whole Church:* God's judgment on the earth unrolls with the opening of seals and the sound of seven trumpets (chapters 6—17). But evil reaches a crescendo with the coming of the beast of the sea (the Antichrist), the false prophet (chapter 13), and minions of the dragon (chapter 12). The final battle between the forces of heaven led by the rider on the white horse (the risen Christ) and the forces of evil ends in a victory for the forces of heaven and the destruction of the Antichrist, the false prophet and their armies (chapter 19). Satan and his angels are bound on earth for 1,000 years while the saints live with Christ in heaven. While in heaven, the saints sit in judgment. When Christ returns to reign on earth, evil is finally eradicated when Satan is cast into the lake of fire along with his demons and followers (chapter 20). The book ends with the blessed hope of all believers: a vision of heaven and the promise of the imminent return of the risen Christ (chapters 21—22).

Unlocking Revelation

KEY PEOPLE:
The risen Christ, John, the leaders of the seven churches (Ephesus, Smyrna, Pergamos, Thyatira, Sardis, Philadelphia, and Laodicea), the woman clothed with the sun, the dragon (Satan), Michael the archangel, the beast from the sea, the beast from the earth, the 144,000, the twenty-four elders and other worshiping believers, Babylon the Great/Mother of Harlots, three angels carrying the message of Revelation 14

KEY EVENTS:
Assessment of the seven churches; seven seals are opened; seven trumpets; the martyrdom of two witnesses; the conflict of the woman and the dragon; sealing of the 144,000; rise of the Antichrist and the false prophet; seven last plagues; fall of Babylon; marriage supper of the Lamb; battle of Armageddon; millennial kingdom of the risen Christ; destruction of Satan and the final judgment of the wicked; vision of new heaven and earth

KEY WORD:
Revelation. The book of Revelation is a book of "unveiled" truths (revelations) about end times.

KEY VERSES:
"Blessed is he that readeth, and they that hear the words of this prophecy, and keep those things which are written therein: for the time is at hand" (1:3).

"And I saw another angel fly in the midst of heaven, having the everlasting gospel to preach unto them that dwell on the earth, and to every nation, and kindred, and tongue, and people, saying with a loud voice, Fear God, and give glory to him; for the hour of his judgment is come: and worship him that made heaven, and earth, and the sea, and the fountains of waters. And there followed another angel, saying, Babylon is fallen, is fallen, that great city, because she made all nations drink of the wine of the wrath of her fornication. And the third angel followed them, saying with a loud voice, If any man worship the beast and his image, and receive his mark in his forehead, or in his hand, the same shall drink of the wine of the wrath of God, which is poured out without mixture into the cup of his indignation; and he shall be tormented with fire and brimstone in the presence of the holy angels, and in the presence of the Lamb: and the smoke of their torment ascendeth up for ever and ever: and they have no rest day nor night, who worship the beast and his image, and whosoever receiveth the mark of his name. Here is the patience of the saints: here are they that keep the commandments of God, and the faith of Jesus" (14:6—12).

"He which testifieth these things saith, Surely I come quickly. Amen. Even so, come, Lord Jesus" (22:20).

KEY CHAPTERS:
Revelation 19—22 show the final conclusion of the history of earth. In Genesis 1, God created the heavens and the earth. In Revelation 21, God creates a new heaven and a new earth. In Genesis 3, sin enters the world. In Revelation 19, sin has now reached its zenith and is handily dealt with by the King of kings and Lord of lords.

John Writes His Revelation

1 The Revelation of Jesus Christ, which God gave unto him, to shew unto his servants things which must shortly come to pass; and he sent and signified *it* by his angel unto his servant John: John 8:26; Rev. 22:6, 16

2 Who bare record of the word of God, and of the testimony of Jesus Christ, and of all things that he saw.   1 Cor. 1:6; Rev. 6:9; 12:17

3 Blessed *is* he that readeth, and they that hear the words of this prophecy, and keep those things which are written therein: for the time *is* at hand.   Luke 11:28; Rom. 13:11

1:3 God Is Not the Author of Confusion

The Bible was designed to be a guide to all who wish to become acquainted with the will of their Maker. God gave to men the sure word of prophecy; angels and even Christ Himself came to make known to Daniel and John the things that must shortly come to pass. Those important matters that concern our salvation were not left involved in mystery. . . . The word of God is plain to all who study it with a prayerful heart. . . . And no church can advance in holiness unless its members are earnestly seeking for truth as for hid treasure. *GC 521, 522*

---

4 John to the seven churches which are in Asia: Grace *be* unto you, and peace, from him which is, and which was, and which is to come; and from the seven Spirits which are before his throne;   Rev. 3:1; 4:5; 5:6

5 And from Jesus Christ, *who is* the faithful witness, *and* the first begotten of the dead, and the prince of the kings of the earth. Unto him that loved us, and washed us from our sins in his own blood,   Col. 1:18; Rev. 3:14; 17:14

6 And hath made us kings and priests unto God and his Father; to him *be* glory and dominion for ever and ever. Amen.   1 Pet. 4:11

7 Behold, he cometh with clouds; and every eye shall see him, and they *also* which pierced him: and all kindreds of the earth shall wail because of him. Even so, Amen.   Dan. 7:13; Zech. 12:10; Matt. 24:30

Christ's Return See Matthew 16:27.

8 I am Alpha and Omega, the beginning and the ending, saith the Lord, which is, and which was, and which is to come, the Almighty.   Is. 41:4; Rev. 21:6; 22:13

9 I John, who also am your brother, and companion in tribulation, and in the kingdom and patience of Jesus Christ, was in the isle that is called Patmos, for the word of God, and for the testimony of Jesus Christ.   Phil. 1:2; Rev. 1:2; 3:10

10 I was in the Spirit on the Lord's day, and heard behind me a great voice, as of a trumpet,   Matt. 22:43; Acts 20:7; Rev. 4:1-2

1:11 The Number Seven

The names of the seven churches are symbolic of the church in different periods of the Christian Era. The number 7 indicates completeness, and is symbolic of the fact that the messages extend to the end of time, while the symbols used reveal the condition of the church at different periods in the history of the world. *AA 585*

---

11 Saying, I am Alpha and Omega, the first and the last: and, What thou seest, write in a book, and send *it* unto the seven churches which are in Asia; unto Ephesus, and unto Smyrna, and unto Pergamos, and unto Thyatira, and unto Sardis, and unto Philadelphia, and unto Laodicea.   Rev. 1:4

Revelation—Revealing the Past, Present, and the Future

Revelation 1:1–3

This revelation was given for the guidance and comfort of the church throughout the Christian dispensation. . . . It is "the revelation of Jesus Christ, which God gave unto Him, to show unto His servants things which must shortly come to pass" (Revelation 1:1). . . .

In the Revelation are portrayed the deep things of God. The very name given to its inspired pages, "the Revelation," contradicts the statement that this is a sealed book. A revelation is something revealed. The Lord Himself revealed to His servant the mysteries contained in this book, and He designs that they shall be open to the study of all. Its truths are addressed to those living in the last days of this earth's history, as well as to those living in the days of John. . . .

Let none think, because they cannot explain the meaning of every symbol in the Revelation, that it is useless for them to search this book in an effort to know the meaning of the truth it contains. . . . Those whose hearts are open to the reception of truth will be enabled to understand its teachings, and will be granted the blessing promised to those who "hear the words of this prophecy, and keep those things which are written therein."

In the Revelation all the books of the Bible meet and end. Here is the complement of the book of Daniel. One is a prophecy; the other a revelation. The book that was sealed is not the Revelation, but that portion of the prophecy of Daniel relating to the last days. The angel commanded, "But thou, O Daniel, shut up the words, and seal the book, even to the time of the end" (Daniel 12:4). *AA 583–585*

12 And I turned to see the voice that spake with me. And being turned, I saw seven golden candlesticks; Ex. 25:37; Zech. 4:2;
13 And in the midst of the seven candlesticks *one* like unto the Son of man, clothed with a garment down to the foot, and girt about the paps with a golden girdle. Dan. 7:13; 10:16
14 His head and *his* hairs *were* white like wool, as white as snow; and his eyes *were* as a flame of fire; Dan. 7:9; 10:6; Rev. 19:12
15 And his feet like unto fine brass, as if they burned in a furnace; and his voice as the sound of many waters. Ezek. 43:2; Dan. 10:6
16 And he had in his right hand seven stars: and out of his mouth went a sharp twoedged sword: and his countenance *was* as the sun shineth in his strength. Is. 49:2; Heb. 4:12
17 And when I saw him, I fell at his feet as dead. And he laid his right hand upon me, saying unto me, Fear not; I am the first and the last: Is. 41:4; 44:6; Rev. 22:13

1:18 He Loves You

Through all our trials we have a never-failing Helper. . . . Though now He is hidden from mortal sight, the ear of faith can hear His voice saying, Fear not; I am with you. . . .

However much a shepherd may love his sheep, he loves his sons and daughters more. Jesus is not only our shepherd; He is our "everlasting Father." . . .

Because we are the gift of His Father, and the reward of His work, Jesus loves us. . . . Reader, He loves you. Heaven itself can bestow nothing greater, nothing better. Therefore trust. *DA 483*

18 I *am* he that liveth, and was dead; and, behold, I am alive for evermore, Amen; and have the keys of hell and of death. Rom. 6:9; Heb. 7:25
19 Write the things which thou hast seen, and the things which are, and the things which shall be hereafter;
20 The mystery of the seven stars which thou sawest in my right hand, and the seven golden candlesticks. The seven stars are the angels of the seven churches: and the seven candlesticks which thou sawest are the seven churches. Zech. 4:2; Rev. 1:16; 2:1

Letter to the Church in Ephesus

2 Unto the angel of the church of Ephesus write; These things saith he that holdeth the seven stars in his right hand, who walketh in the midst of the seven golden candlesticks; Rev. 1:11-13, 16, 20

2:1 No Fear With Christ

Christ is represented as holding the seven stars in His right hand. This assures us that no church faithful to its trust need fear coming to nought, for not a star that has the protection of Omnipotence can be plucked out of the hand of Christ. *AA 586*

2 I know thy works, and thy labour, and thy patience, and how thou canst not bear them which are evil: and thou hast tried them which say they are apostles, and are not, and hast found them liars: 1 John 4:1; Rev. 3:1, 8
3 And hast borne, and hast patience, and for my name's sake hast laboured, and hast not fainted. John 15:21

Never Let Time Make Us Forget

Revelation 2:2–5

At the first the experience of the church at Ephesus was marked with childlike simplicity and fervor. The believers sought earnestly to obey every word of God, and their lives revealed an earnest, sincere love for Christ. They rejoiced to do the will of God because the Saviour was in their hearts as an abiding presence. Filled with love for their Redeemer, their highest aim was to win souls to Him. . . .

The members of the church were united in sentiment and action. Love for Christ was the golden chain that bound them together. . . .

They could not rest till the light which had illumined their minds was shining upon others. Multitudes of unbelievers were made acquainted with the reasons of the Christian's hope. Warm, inspired personal appeals were made to the erring, to the outcast, and to those who, while professing to know the truth, were lovers of pleasure more than lovers of God.

But after a time the zeal of the believers began to wane, and their love for God and for one another grew less. . . . One by one the old standard-bearers fell at their post. . . . In their desire for something novel and startling they attempted to introduce new phases of doctrine, more pleasing to many minds, but not in harmony with the fundamental principles of the gospel. . . .

As these false doctrines were urged, differences sprang up, and the eyes of many were turned from beholding Jesus as the Author and Finisher of their faith. The discussion of unimportant points of doctrine, and the contemplation of pleasing fables of man's invention, occupied time that should have been spent in proclaiming the gospel. . . . Piety was rapidly waning, and Satan seemed about to gain the ascendancy over those who claimed to be followers of Christ. *AA 578–581*

4 Nevertheless I have *somewhat* against thee, because thou hast left thy first love.

5 Remember therefore from whence thou art fallen, and repent, and do the first works; or else I will come unto thee quickly, and will remove thy candlestick out of his place, except thou repent. Rev. 2:16; 3:19

6 But this thou hast, that thou hatest the deeds of the Nicolaitans, which I also hate.

7 He that hath an ear, let him hear what the Spirit saith unto the churches; To him that overcometh will I give to eat of the tree of life, which is in the midst of the paradise of God. Gen. 2:9; Rev. 2:11, 17

Letter to the Church in Smyrna

8 And unto the angel of the church in Smyrna write; These things saith the first and the last, which was dead, and is alive; Rev. 1:11, 17-18

9 I know thy works, and tribulation, and poverty, (but thou art rich) and *I know* the blasphemy of them which say they are Jews, and are not, but *are* the synagogue of Satan. 2 Cor. 6:10; 8:9; Rev. 3:9

10 Fear none of those things which thou shalt suffer: behold, the ᵀdevil shall cast *some* of you into prison, that ye may be tried; and ye shall have tribulation ten days: be thou faithful unto death, and I will give thee a crown of life. Dan. 1:12; Matt. 10:22; James 1:12 ◆ *false accuser*

11 He that hath an ear, let him hear what the Spirit saith unto the churches; He that overcometh shall not be hurt of the second death. Rev. 2:7; 20:6, 14

Letter to the Church in Pergamos

12 And to the angel of the church in Pergamos write; These things saith he which hath the sharp sword with two edges; Rev. 1:11, 16

13 I know thy works, and where thou dwellest, *even* where Satan's seat *is*: and thou holdest fast my name, and hast not denied my faith, even in those days wherein Antipas *was* my faithful martyr, who was slain among you, where Satan dwelleth. Acts 22:20

14 But I have a few things against thee, because thou hast there them that hold the doctrine of Balaam, who taught Balac to cast a stumblingblock before the children of Israel, to eat things sacrificed unto idols, and to commit fornication. Num. 31:16; 2 Pet. 2:15; Rev. 2:20

15 So hast thou also them that hold the doctrine of the Nicolaitans, which thing I hate.

16 Repent; or else I will come unto thee quickly, and will fight against them with the sword of my mouth. 2 Thess. 2:8; Rev. 1:16; 2:5

17 He that hath an ear, let him hear what the Spirit saith unto the churches; To him that overcometh will I give to eat of the hidden manna, and will give him a white stone, and in the stone a new name written, which no man knoweth saving he that receiveth *it*. Is. 65:15; Rev. 2:7, 11

> **2:17 The Bread of Everlasting Life**
>
> The manna, falling from heaven for the sustenance of Israel, was a type of Him who came from God to give life to the world. Said Jesus, "I am that Bread of life. . . . And among the promises of blessing to God's people in the future life it is written, "To him that overcometh will I give to eat of the hidden manna" (Revelation 2:17). PP 297

Letter to the Church in Thyatira

18 And unto the angel of the church in Thyatira write; These things saith the Son of God, who hath his eyes like unto a flame of fire, and his feet *are* like fine brass; Rev. 1:11

19 I know thy works, and charity, and service, and faith, and thy patience, and thy works; and the last *to be* more than the first.

20 Notwithstanding I have a few things against thee, because thou sufferest that woman Jezebel, which calleth herself a prophetess, to teach and to seduce my servants to commit fornication, and to eat things sacrificed unto idols. 1 Kin. 16:31; 2 Kin. 9:7; Rev. 2:14

21 And I gave her space to repent of her fornication; and she repented not. Rom. 2:4-5

22 Behold, I will cast her into a bed, and them that commit adultery with her into great tribulation, except they repent of their deeds. Rev. 17:2

23 And I will kill her children with death; and all the churches shall know that I am he which searcheth the ᵀreins and hearts: and I will give unto every one of you according to your works. Ps. 7:9; Jer. 11:20; Rom. 8:27 ◆ *desires*

24 But unto you I say, and unto the rest in Thyatira, as many as have not this doctrine, and which have not known the depths of Satan, as they speak; I will put upon you none other burden. Acts 15:28

25 But that which ye have *already* hold fast till I come. Rev. 3:11

26 And he that overcometh, and keepeth my works unto the end, to him will I give power over the nations: Rev. 2:7; 3:21; 20:4

27 And he shall rule them with a rod of iron; as the vessels of a potter shall they be broken to ᵀshivers: even as I received of my Father. Is. 30:14; Rev. 12:5; 19:15 ◆ *pieces*

28 And I will give him the morning star.

29 He that hath an ear, let him hear what the Spirit saith unto the churches. Rev. 2:7

Letter to the Church in Sardis

3 And unto the angel of the church in Sardis write; These things saith he that hath the seven Spirits of God, and the seven

stars; I know thy works, that thou hast a name that thou livest, and art dead. 1 Tim. 5:6

2 Be watchful, and strengthen the things which remain, that are ready to die: for I have not found thy works perfect before God.

3 Remember therefore how thou hast received and heard, and hold fast, and repent. If therefore thou shalt not watch, I will come on thee as a thief, and thou shalt not know what hour I will come upon thee. 1 Thess. 5:2; 2 Pet. 3:10

4 Thou hast a few names even in Sardis which have not defiled their garments; and they shall walk with me in white: for they are worthy. Jude 23; Rev. 6:11; 7:9

3:4 His Promise to Our Children

Let the children be taught that as they open their minds to pure, loving thoughts and do loving and helpful deeds, they are clothing themselves with His beautiful garment of character. This apparel will make them beautiful and beloved here, and will hereafter be their title of admission to the palace of the King. His promise is: "They shall walk with Me in white: for they are worthy" (Revelation 3:4). *Ed 249*

5 He that overcometh, the same shall be clothed in white ᵀraiment; and I will not blot out his name out of the book of life, but I will confess his name before my Father, and before his angels. Matt. 10:32; Rev. 13:8; 17:8 ◆ *clothing*

6 He that hath an ear, let him hear what the Spirit saith unto the churches. Rev. 2:7

Letter to the Church in Philadelphia

7 And to the angel of the church in Philadelphia write; These things saith he that is holy, he that is true, he that hath the key of David, he that openeth, and no man shutteth; and shutteth, and no man openeth; Is. 22:22; Matt. 16:19; Rev. 6:10

8 I know thy works: behold, I have set before thee an open door, and no man can shut it: for thou hast a little strength, and hast kept my word, and hast not denied my name. Rev. 2:13

9 Behold, I will make them of the synagogue of Satan, which say they are Jews, and are not, but do lie; behold, I will make them to come and worship before thy feet, and to know that I have loved thee. Is. 49:23; 60:14; Rev. 2:9

10 Because thou hast kept the word of my patience, I also will keep thee from the hour of temptation, which shall come upon all the world, to try them that dwell upon the earth. Matt. 24:14; 2 Pet. 2:9; Rev. 1:9

11 Behold, I come quickly: hold that fast which thou hast, that no man take thy crown.

12 Him that overcometh will I make a pillar in the temple of my God, and he shall go no more out: and I will write upon him the name of my God, and the name of the city of my God, *which is* new Jerusalem, which cometh down out of heaven from my God: and *I will write upon him* my new name. Gal. 2:9; Rev. 21:2

13 He that hath an ear, let him hear what the Spirit saith unto the churches. Rev. 2:7

Letter to the Church in Laodicea

14 And unto the angel of the church of the Laodiceans write; These things saith the Amen, the faithful and true witness, the beginning of the creation of God; 2 Cor. 1:20

15 I know thy works, that thou art neither cold nor hot: I would thou wert cold or hot. Rev. 3:1

16 So then because thou art lukewarm, and neither cold nor hot, I will spue thee out of my mouth.

We Cannot Give What We Don't Have

Revelation 3:15, 16

"I would thou wert cold or hot. So then because thou art lukewarm, and neither cold nor hot, I will spue thee out of My mouth" (Revelation 3:15, 16).

Without a living faith in Christ as a personal Saviour it is impossible to make our influence felt in a skeptical world. We cannot give to others that which we do not ourselves possess. It is in proportion to our own devotion and consecration to Christ that we exert an influence for the blessing and uplifting of mankind. If there is no actual service, no genuine love, no reality of experience, there is no power to help, no connection with heaven, no savor of Christ in the life. Unless the Holy Spirit can use us as agents through whom to communicate to the world the truth as it is in Jesus, we are as salt that has lost its savor and is entirely worthless. By our lack of the grace of Christ we testify to the world that the truth which we claim to believe has no sanctifying power; and thus, so far as our influence goes, we make of no effect the word of God. . . .

When love fills the heart, it will flow out to others, not because of favors received from them, but because love is the principle of action. Love modifies the character, governs the impulses, subdues enmity, and ennobles the affections. This love is as broad as the universe, and is in harmony with that of the angel workers. Cherished in the heart, it sweetens the entire life and sheds its blessing upon all around. *MB 37, 38*

17 Because thou sayest, I am rich, and increased with goods, and have need of nothing; and knowest not that thou art wretched, and miserable, and poor, and blind, and naked:
18 I counsel thee to buy of me gold tried in the fire, that thou mayest be rich; and white raiment, that thou mayest be clothed, and *that* the shame of thy nakedness do not appear; and anoint thine eyes with eyesalve, that thou mayest see. Is. 55:1; Matt. 13:44; Rev. 16:15
19 As many as I love, I rebuke and chasten: be zealous therefore, and repent.   Rev. 2:5

3:19 Thank You, Lord, for My Trials

But when tribulation comes upon us, how many of us are like Jacob! We think it the hand of an enemy; and in the darkness we wrestle blindly until our strength is spent, and we find no comfort or deliverance. . . . [Like Jacob] we also need to learn that trials mean benefit, and not to despise the chastening of the Lord nor faint when we are rebuked of Him.

"Happy is the man whom God correcteth" (Job 5:17). *MB 11, 12*

3:20† 20 Behold, I stand at the door, and knock: if any man hear my voice, and open the door, I will come in to him, and will ᵀsup with him, and he with me.
                              eat a meal

Salvation From Sin

21 To him that overcometh will I grant to sit with me in my throne, even as I also overcame, and am set down with my Father in his throne.   Matt. 19:28; John 16:33; 2 Tim. 2:12

3:21 To Be an Overcomer

The meek "shall inherit the earth." It was through the desire for self-exaltation that sin entered into the world, and our first parents lost the dominion over this fair earth, their kingdom. It is through self-abnegation that Christ redeems what was lost. And He says we are to overcome as He did (Revelation 3:21). *MB 17*

22 He that hath an ear, let him hear what the Spirit saith unto the churches.   Rev. 2:7

The Throne of God in Heaven

4 After this I looked, and, behold, a door *was* opened in heaven: and the first voice which I heard *was* as it were of a trumpet talking with me; which said, Come up ᵀhither, and I will shew thee things which must be hereafter.   Rev. 1:10, 19; 11:12 ♦ *here*
2 And immediately I was in the spirit: and, behold, a throne was set in heaven, and *one* sat on the throne.   Is. 6:1; Ezek. 1:26; Rev. 1:10
3 And he that sat was to look upon like a jasper and a sardine stone: and *there was* a rainbow round about the throne, in sight like unto an emerald.   Ezek. 1:28; 28:13; Rev. 10:1

4:3 God's Promise Has Never Failed

The rainbow spanning the heavens with its arch of light is a token of "the everlasting covenant between God and every living creature" (Genesis 9:16). And the rainbow encircling the throne on high is also a token to God's children of His covenant of peace.

As the bow in the cloud results from the union of sunshine and shower, so the bow above God's throne represents the union of His mercy and His justice. *Ed 115*

4 And round about the throne *were* four and twenty seats: and upon the seats I saw four and twenty elders sitting, clothed in white ᵀraiment; and they had on their heads crowns of gold.   Matt. 19:28; Rev. 4:10; 11:16 ♦ *clothing*
5 And out of the throne proceeded lightnings and thunderings and voices: and *there were* seven lamps of fire burning before the throne, which are the seven Spirits of God.
6 And before the throne *there was* a sea of glass like unto crystal: and in the midst of the throne, and round about the throne, *were* four beasts full of eyes before and behind.   Ezek. 10:12; Rev. 5:6; 15:2
7 And the first beast *was* like a lion, and the second beast like a calf, and the third beast had a face as a man, and the fourth beast *was* like a flying eagle.   Ezek. 1:10; 10:14
8 And the four beasts had each of them six wings about *him*; and *they were* full of eyes within: and they rest not day and night, saying, Holy, holy, holy, Lord God Almighty, which was, and is, and is to come.   Rev. 1:8
9 And when those beasts give glory and honour and thanks to him that sat on the throne, who liveth for ever and ever, Rev. 15:7
10 The four and twenty elders fall down before him that sat on the throne, and worship him that liveth for ever and ever, and cast their crowns before the throne, saying,   Rev. 4:4; 5:8, 14
11 Thou art worthy, O Lord, to receive glory and honour and power: for thou hast created all things, and for thy pleasure they are and were created.   Gen. 1:1; Rev. 5:12; 10:6

The Book Sealed with Seven Seals

5 And I saw in the right hand of him that sat on the throne a book written within and on the backside, sealed with seven seals.   Is. 29:11; Ezek. 2:9-10
2 And I saw a strong angel proclaiming with a loud voice, Who is worthy to open the book, and to loose the seals thereof?
3 And no man in heaven, nor in earth, neither under the earth, was able to open the book, neither to look thereon.   Rev. 5:13

4 And I wept much, because no man was found worthy to open and to read the book, neither to look thereon.

5 And one of the elders saith unto me, Weep not: behold, the Lion of the tribe of Juda, the Root of David, hath prevailed to open the book, and to loose the seven seals thereof.   Is. 11:1, 10; Rom. 15:12

6 And I beheld, and, lo, in the midst of the throne and of the four beasts, and in the midst of the elders, stood a Lamb as it had been slain, having seven horns and seven eyes, which are the seven Spirits of God sent forth into all the earth.   Zech. 4:10; John 1:29

5:5, 6 A Lion and a Lamb

The Saviour is presented before John under the symbols of "the Lion of the tribe of Judah" and of "a Lamb as it had been slain" (Revelation 5:5, 6). These symbols represent the union of omnipotent power and self-sacrificing love. The Lion of Judah, so terrible to the rejectors of His grace, will be the Lamb of God to the obedient and faithful. . . . The arm strong to smite the rebellious will be strong to deliver the loyal. Everyone who is faithful will be saved. *AA 589*

---

7 And he came and took the book out of the right hand of him that sat upon the throne.

8 And when he had taken the book, the four beasts and four *and* twenty elders fell down before the Lamb, having every one of them harps, and golden vials full of odours, which are the prayers of saints. Ps. 141:2; Rev. 4:10; 5:14

9 And they sung a new song, saying, Thou art worthy to take the book, and to open the seals thereof: for thou wast slain, and hast redeemed us to God by thy blood out of every kindred, and tongue, and people, and nation;   Ps. 33:3; 40:3; Rev. 14:6

10 And hast made us unto our God kings and priests: and we shall reign on the earth.   Rev. 1:6; 20:6

11 And I beheld, and I heard the voice of many angels round about the throne and the beasts and the elders: and the number of them was ten thousand times ten thousand, and thousands of thousands;   Dan. 7:10; Heb. 12:22; Rev. 4:4

12 Saying with a loud voice, Worthy is the Lamb that was slain to receive power, and riches, and wisdom, and strength, and honour, and glory, and blessing.   Zech. 13:7

13 And every creature which is in heaven, and on the earth, and under the earth, and such as are in the sea, and all that are in them, heard I saying, Blessing, and honour, and glory, and power, *be* unto him that sitteth upon the throne, and unto the Lamb for ever and ever.   Phil. 2:10

14 And the four beasts said, Amen. And the four *and* twenty elders fell down and worshipped him that liveth for ever and ever.   Rev. 5:8; 19:4

The Lamb Opens Six Seals

6 And I saw when the Lamb opened one of the seals, and I heard, as it were the noise of thunder, one of the four beasts saying, Come and see.   Rev. 5:1

2 And I saw, and behold a white horse: and he that sat on him had a bow; and a crown

---

The Great Reunion

Revelation 5:12, 13

The two Adams are about to meet. The Son of God is standing with outstretched arms to receive the father of our race—the being whom He created, who sinned against his Maker, and for whose sin the marks of the crucifixion are borne upon the Saviour's form. As Adam discerns the prints of the cruel nails, he does not fall upon the bosom of his Lord, but in humiliation casts himself at His feet, crying: "Worthy, worthy is the Lamb that was slain!" . . .

After his expulsion from Eden, Adam's life on earth was filled with sorrow. Every dying leaf, every victim of sacrifice, every blight upon the fair face of nature, every stain upon man's purity, was a fresh reminder of his sin. . . . Faithfully did he repent of his sin and trust in the merits of the promised Saviour, and he died in the hope of a resurrection. The Son of God redeemed man's failure and fall; and now, through the work of the atonement, Adam is reinstated in his first dominion. . . .

The family of Adam take up the strain and cast their crowns at the Saviour's feet as they bow before Him in adoration.

This reunion is witnessed by the angels who wept at the fall of Adam and rejoiced when Jesus, after His resurrection, ascended to heaven, having opened the grave for all who should believe on His name. . . .

The great controversy is ended. Sin and sinners are no more. The entire universe is clean. One pulse of harmony and gladness beats through the vast creation. From Him who created all, flow life and light and gladness, throughout the realms of illimitable space. From the minutest atom to the greatest world, all things, animate and inanimate, in their unshadowed beauty and perfect joy, declare that God is love. *GC 647, 648, 678*

was given unto him: and he went forth conquering, and to conquer.   Zech. 1:8; Rev. 14:14
3 And when he had opened the second seal, I heard the second beast say, Come and see.
4 And there went out another horse *that was* red: and *power* was given to him that sat thereon to take peace from the earth, and that they should kill one another: and there was given unto him a great sword.   Zech. 1:8; 6:2
5 And when he had opened the third seal, I heard the third beast say, Come and see. And I beheld, and lo a black horse; and he that sat on him had a pair of balances in his hand.   Ezek. 4:16; Zech. 6:2, 6
6 And I heard a voice in the midst of the four beasts say, A measure of wheat for a penny, and three measures of barley for a penny; and *see* thou hurt not the oil and the wine.   Rev. 9:4
7 And when he had opened the fourth seal, I heard the voice of the fourth beast say, Come and see.   Rev. 4:7
8 And I looked, and behold a pale horse: and his name that sat on him was Death, and Hell followed with him. And power was given unto them over the fourth part of the earth, to kill with sword, and with hunger, and with death, and with the beasts of the earth.   Jer. 15:2-3; Hos. 13:14; Zech. 6:3
9 And when he had opened the fifth seal, I saw under the altar the souls of them that were slain for the word of God, and for the testimony which they held: Rev. 1:9; 14:18; 20:4
10 And they cried with a loud voice, saying, How long, O Lord, holy and true, dost thou not judge and avenge our blood on them that dwell on the earth? Zech. 1:12; Rev. 3:7; 19:2
11 And white robes were given unto every one of them; and it was said unto them, that they should rest yet for a little season, until their fellowservants also and their brethren, that should be killed as they *were*, should be fulfilled.   Heb. 11:40; Rev. 7:9, 14
12 And I beheld when he had opened the sixth seal, and, lo, there was a great earthquake; and the sun became black as sackcloth of hair, and the moon became as blood;   Matt. 24:29; Rev. 11:13; 16:18
13 And the stars of heaven fell unto the earth, even as a fig tree casteth her untimely figs, when she is shaken of a mighty wind.   Is. 34:4; Matt. 24:29; Rev. 9:1
14 And the heaven departed as a scroll when it is rolled together; and every mountain and island were moved out of their places.   Is. 34:4; 2 Pet. 3:10; Rev. 16:20
15 And the kings of the earth, and the great men, and the rich men, and the chief captains, and the mighty men, and every bondman, and every free man, hid themselves in the dens and in the rocks of the mountains;   Is. 2:10, 19, 21
16 And said to the mountains and rocks, Fall on us, and hide us from the face of him that sitteth on the throne, and from the wrath of the Lamb: Hos. 10:8; Luke 23:30; Rev. 4:2
17 For the great day of his wrath is come; and who shall be able to stand?   Ps. 76:7; Jer. 30:7

6:15–17 No More Scoffing

The derisive jests have ceased. Lying lips are hushed into silence. . . . Nought now is heard but the voice of prayer and the sound of weeping and lamentation. The cry bursts forth from lips so lately scoffing: "The great day of His wrath is come; and who shall be able to stand?" The wicked pray to be buried beneath the rocks of the mountains rather than meet the face of Him whom they have despised and rejected. *GC 642*

The Mark of God's Servants

7 And after these things I saw four angels standing on the four corners of the earth, holding the four winds of the earth, that the wind should not blow on the earth, nor on the sea, nor on any tree.   Jer. 49:36; Dan. 7:2
2 And I saw another angel ascending from the east, having the seal of the living God: and he cried with a loud voice to the four angels, to whom it was given to hurt the earth and the sea,
3 Saying, Hurt not the earth, neither the sea, nor the trees, till we have sealed the servants of our God in their foreheads. Rev. 6:6; 14:1; 22:4
4 And I heard the number of them which were sealed: *and there were* sealed an hundred *and* forty *and* four thousand of all the tribes of the children of Israel.   Rev. 9:16; 14:1, 3
5 Of the tribe of Juda *were* sealed twelve thousand. Of the tribe of Reuben *were* sealed twelve thousand. Of the tribe of Gad *were* sealed twelve thousand.
6 Of the tribe of Aser *were* sealed twelve thousand. Of the tribe of Nepthalim *were* sealed twelve thousand. Of the tribe of Manasses *were* sealed twelve thousand.
7 Of the tribe of Simeon *were* sealed twelve thousand. Of the tribe of Levi *were* sealed twelve thousand. Of the tribe of Issachar *were* sealed twelve thousand.   Gen. 35:23
8 Of the tribe of Zabulon *were* sealed twelve thousand. Of the tribe of Joseph *were* sealed twelve thousand. Of the tribe of Benjamin *were* sealed twelve thousand.

God's People at His Throne

9 After this I beheld, and, lo, a great multitude, which no man could number, of all nations, and kindreds, and people, and tongues,

stood before the throne, and before the Lamb, clothed with white robes, and palms in their hands;   Lev. 23:40; John 12:13; Rev. 5:9

> **7:9 Reward to Those Who Honored Him**
>
> Nearest the throne are those who were once zealous in the cause of Satan, but who, plucked as brands from the burning, have followed their Saviour with deep, intense devotion. Next are those who perfected Christian characters in the midst of falsehood and infidelity, those who honored the law of God when the Christian world declared it void, and the millions, of all ages, who were martyred for their faith. . . . Their warfare is ended, their victory won. They have run the race and reached the prize. *GC 665*

10 And cried with a loud voice, saying, Salvation to our God which sitteth upon the throne, and unto the Lamb.   Ps. 3:8; Rev. 12:10

> **7:10 Salvation Is Alone From God**
>
> The redeemed raise a song of praise that echoes and reechoes through the vaults of heaven: "Salvation to our God which sitteth upon the throne, and unto the Lamb" (Verse 10). . . . In all that shining throng there are none to ascribe salvation to themselves, as if they had prevailed by their own power and goodness. Nothing is said of what they have done or suffered; but the burden of every song, the keynote of every anthem, is: Salvation to our God and unto the Lamb. *GC 665*

11 And all the angels stood round about the throne, and *about* the elders and the four beasts, and fell before the throne on their faces, and worshipped God,   Rev. 4:4, 6, 10
12 Saying, Amen: Blessing, and glory, and wisdom, and thanksgiving, and honour, and power, and might, *be* unto our God for ever and ever. Amen.   Rev. 5:12-14
13 And one of the elders answered, saying unto me, What are these which are ᵀarrayed in white robes? and whence came they?   Rev. 7:9 ◆ *clothed*

> **7:14 It Will Be Worth It All**
>
> In all ages the Saviour's chosen have been educated and disciplined in the school of trial. . . . For Jesus' sake they endured opposition, hatred, calumny. They followed Him through conflicts sore; they endured self-denial and experienced bitter disappointments. By their own painful experience they learned the evil of sin, its power, its guilt, its woe; and they look upon it with abhorrence. . . . They love much because they have been forgiven much. Having been partakers of Christ's sufferings, they are fitted to be partakers with Him of His glory. *GC 649, 650*

14 And I said unto him, Sir, thou knowest. And he said to me, These are they which came out of great tribulation, and have washed their robes, and made them white in the blood of the Lamb.   Zech. 3:3-5; Heb. 9:14; 1 John 1:7
15 Therefore are they before the throne of God, and serve him day and night in his temple: and he that sitteth on the throne shall dwell among them.   Is. 4:5-6; John 1:14; Rev. 22:3
16 They shall hunger no more, neither thirst any more; neither shall the sun light on them, nor any heat.   Ps. 121:6; Is. 49:10
17 For the Lamb which is in the midst of the throne shall feed them, and shall lead them unto living fountains of waters: and God shall wipe away all tears from their eyes.   Is. 25:8; John 10:11; Rev. 21:4

The Lamb Opens the Seventh Seal

8 And when he had opened the seventh seal, there was silence in heaven about the space of half an hour.   Rev. 5:1; 6:1, 3
2 And I saw the seven angels which stood before God; and to them were given seven trumpets.   Rev. 11:15
3 And another angel came and stood at the altar, having a golden ᵀcenser; and there was given unto him much incense, that he should offer *it* with the prayers of all saints upon the golden altar which was before the throne. Heb. 9:4; Rev. 5:8; 9:13 ◆ *holder for burning incense*
4 And the smoke of the incense, *which came* with the prayers of the saints, ascended up before God out of the angel's hand.   Ps. 141:2

> **8:3, 4 A Great Representation**
>
> The incense, ascending with the prayers of Israel, represents the merits and intercession of Christ, His perfect righteousness, which through faith is imputed to His people, and which can alone make the worship of sinful beings acceptable to God. *PP 353*

5 And the angel took the censer, and filled it with fire of the altar, and cast *it* into the earth: and there were voices, and thunderings, and lightnings, and an earthquake. Lev. 16:12; Rev. 4:5
6 And the seven angels which had the seven trumpets prepared themselves to sound.   Rev. 8:2

Four Angels Blow Their Trumpets

7 The first angel sounded, and there followed hail and fire mingled with blood, and they were cast upon the earth: and the third part of trees was burnt up, and all green grass was burnt up.   Ezek. 38:22; Rev. 9:4, 15
8 And the second angel sounded, and as it were a great mountain burning with fire was cast into the sea: and the third part of the sea became blood;   Ex. 7:17-21; Jer. 51:25; Mark 11:23

9 And the third part of the creatures which were in the sea, and had life, died; and the third part of the ships were destroyed. Is. 2:16
10 And the third angel sounded, and there fell a great star from heaven, burning as it were a lamp, and it fell upon the third part of the rivers, and upon the fountains of waters; Is. 14:12; Rev. 9:1; 16:4
11 And the name of the star is called Wormwood: and the third part of the waters became ᵀwormwood; and many men died of the waters, because they were made bitter. Ex. 15:23; Jer. 9:15; 23:15 ◆ *a bitter plant*
12 And the fourth angel sounded, and the third part of the sun was smitten, and the third part of the moon, and the third part of the stars; so as the third part of them was darkened, and the day shone not for a third part of it, and the night likewise. Is. 13:10
13 And I beheld, and heard an angel flying through the midst of heaven, saying with a loud voice, Woe, woe, woe, to the inhabiters of the earth by reason of the other voices of the trumpet of the three angels, which are yet to sound! Rev. 9:12; 11:14; 14:6

Two More Trumpet Blasts

9 And the fifth angel sounded, and I saw a star fall from heaven unto the earth: and to him was given the key of the bottomless pit. Luke 8:31; Rev. 1:18; 8:10
2 And he opened the bottomless pit; and there arose a smoke out of the pit, as the smoke of a great furnace; and the sun and the air were darkened by reason of the smoke of the pit. Gen. 19:28; Joel 2:2, 10
3 And there came out of the smoke locusts upon the earth: and unto them was given power, as the scorpions of the earth have power. Ezek. 2:6
4 And it was commanded them that they should not hurt the grass of the earth, neither any green thing, neither any tree; but only those men which have not the seal of God in their foreheads. Ezek. 9:4; Rev. 6:6; 8:7
5 And to them it was given that they should not kill them, but that they should be tormented five months: and their torment *was* as the torment of a scorpion, when he striketh a man. Rev. 9:3, 10
6 And in those days shall men seek death, and shall not find it; and shall desire to die, and death shall flee from them. Job 7:15-16; Jer. 8:3
7 And the shapes of the locusts *were* like unto horses prepared unto battle; and on their heads *were* as it were crowns like gold, and their faces *were* as the faces of men. Dan. 7:8
8 And they had hair as the hair of women, and their teeth were as *the teeth* of lions. Joel 1:6
9 And they had ᵀbreastplates, as it were breastplates of iron; and the sound of their wings *was* as the sound of chariots of many horses running to battle. Job 39:25 ◆ *pieces of armor*
10 And they had tails like unto scorpions, and there were stings in their tails: and their power *was* to hurt men five months. Rev. 9:3, 5
11 And they had a king over them, *which is* the angel of the bottomless pit, whose name in the Hebrew tongue *is* Abaddon, but in the Greek tongue hath *his* name Apollyon. Eph. 2:2
12 One woe is past; *and*, behold, there come two woes more hereafter. Rev. 11:14
13 And the sixth angel sounded, and I heard a voice from the four horns of the golden altar which is before God,
14 Saying to the sixth angel which had the trumpet, Loose the four angels which are bound in the great river Euphrates.
15 And the four angels were loosed, which were prepared for an hour, and a day, and a month, and a year, for to slay the third part of men. Rev. 8:7
16 And the number of the army of the horsemen *were* two hundred thousand thousand: and I heard the number of them. Ps. 68:17
17 And thus I saw the horses in the vision, and them that sat on them, having breastplates of fire, and of jacinth, and brimstone: and the heads of the horses *were* as the heads of lions; and out of their mouths issued fire and smoke and brimstone. Rev. 9:18
18 By these three was the third part of men killed, by the fire, and by the smoke, and by the ᵀbrimstone, which issued out of their mouths. Rev. 9:15 ◆ *sulphur*
19 For their power is in their mouth, and in their tails: for their tails *were* like unto serpents, and had heads, and with them they do hurt.
20 And the rest of the men which were not killed by these plagues yet repented not of the works of their hands, that they should not worship devils, and idols of gold, and silver, and brass, and stone, and of wood: which neither can see, nor hear, nor walk: Deut. 31:29
21 Neither repented they of their murders, nor of their sorceries, nor of their fornication, nor of their thefts. Rev. 17:2

John Sees an Angel

10 And I saw another mighty angel come down from heaven, clothed with a cloud: and a rainbow *was* upon his head, and his face *was* as it were the sun, and his feet as pillars of fire: Ezek. 1:28; Matt. 17:2; Rev. 1:15-16
2 And he had in his hand a little book open: and he set his right foot upon the sea, and *his* left *foot* on the earth, Rev. 10:5
3 And cried with a loud voice, as *when* a lion roareth: and when he had cried, seven thunders uttered their voices. Is. 31:4

4 And when the seven thunders had uttered their voices, I was about to write: and I heard a voice from heaven saying unto me, Seal up those things which the seven thunders uttered, and write them not.   Dan. 8:26; 12:4, 9
5 And the angel which I saw stand upon the sea and upon the earth lifted up his hand to heaven,   Gen. 14:22; Deut. 32:40; Dan. 12:7
6 And sware by him that liveth for ever and ever, who created heaven, and the things that therein are, and the earth, and the things that therein are, and the sea, and the things which are therein, that there should be time no longer: Rev. 4:11
7 But in the days of the voice of the seventh angel, when he shall begin to sound, the mystery of God should be finished, as he hath declared to his servants the prophets.   Rom. 16:25

John Eats the Book

8 And the voice which I heard from heaven spake unto me again, and said, Go and take the little book which is open in the hand of the angel which standeth upon the sea and upon the earth.
9 And I went unto the angel, and said unto him, Give me the little book. And he said unto me, Take it, and eat it up; and it shall make thy belly bitter, but it shall be in thy mouth sweet as honey. Jer. 15:16; Ezek. 2:8; 3:1-3
10 And I took the little book out of the angel's hand, and ate it up; and it was in my mouth sweet as honey: and as soon as I had eaten it, my belly was bitter.
11 And he said unto me, Thou must prophesy again before many peoples, and nations, and tongues, and kings.   Ezek. 37:4

The Lord's Two Witnesses

11 And there was given me a reed like unto a rod: and the angel stood, saying, Rise, and measure the temple of God, and the altar, and them that worship therein.   Ezek. 42:15-20; Rev. 21:15

11:2, 3 Centuries of Papal Oppression

The periods here mentioned—"forty and two months," and "a thousand two hundred and threescore days"—are the same, alike representing the time in which the church of Christ was to suffer oppression from Rome. The 1260 years of papal supremacy began in A.D. 538, and would therefore terminate in 1798. . . . At that time a French army entered Rome and made the pope a prisoner, and he died in exile. Though a new pope was soon afterward elected, the papal hierarchy has never since been able to wield the power which it before possessed. GC 266

2 But the court which is without the temple leave out, and measure it not; for it is

given unto the Gentiles: and the holy city shall they tread under foot forty and two months.   Dan. 7:25; Luke 21:24; Rev. 12:6
3 And I will give power unto my two witnesses, and they shall prophesy a thousand two hundred and threescore days, clothed in sackcloth.   Gen. 37:34 ♦ sixty
4 These are the two olive trees, and the two candlesticks standing before the God of the earth.   Ps. 52:8; Jer. 11:16
5 And if any man will hurt them, fire proceedeth out of their mouth, and devoureth their enemies: and if any man will hurt them, he must in this manner be killed. 2 Kin. 1:10-12
6 These have power to shut heaven, that it rain not in the days of their prophecy: and have power over waters to turn them to blood, and to smite the earth with all plagues, as often as they will. 1 Kin. 17:1 ♦ strike
7 And when they shall have finished their testimony, the beast that ascendeth out of the bottomless pit shall make war against them, and shall overcome them, and kill them.   Dan. 7:25; Rev. 13:7, 11
8 And their dead bodies shall lie in the street of the great city, which spiritually is called Sodom and Egypt, where also our Lord was crucified.   Jer. 23:14
9 And they of the people and kindreds and tongues and nations shall see their dead bodies three days and an half, and shall not suffer their dead bodies to be put in graves. Ps. 79:2-3
10 And they that dwell upon the earth shall rejoice over them, and make merry, and shall send gifts one to another; because these two prophets tormented them that dwelt on the earth.   Rev. 3:10
11 And after three days and an half the Spirit of life from God entered into them, and they stood upon their feet; and great fear fell upon them which saw them. Gen. 2:7
12 And they heard a great voice from heaven saying unto them, Come up hither. And they ascended up to heaven in a cloud; and their enemies beheld them. 2 Kin. 2:11; Acts 1:9; Rev. 4:1
13 And the same hour was there a great earthquake, and the tenth part of the city fell, and in the earthquake were slain of men seven thousand: and the remnant were affrighted, and gave glory to the God of heaven.   Josh. 7:19; Rev. 6:12; 14:7 ♦ scared

Christ Shall Reign Forever

14 The second woe is past; and, behold, the third woe cometh quickly.   Rev. 8:13; 9:12
15 And the seventh angel sounded; and there were great voices in heaven, saying, The kingdoms of this world are become the kingdoms of our Lord, and of his Christ; and he shall reign for ever and ever.   Dan. 7:14, 27; Rev. 12:10

16 And the four and twenty elders, which sat before God on their seats, fell upon their faces, and worshipped God,   Rev. 4:4, 10

17 Saying, We give thee thanks, O Lord God Almighty, which art, and wast, and art to come; because thou hast taken to thee thy great power, and hast reigned.   Rev. 1:4, 8; 19:6

18 And the nations were angry, and thy wrath is come, and the time of the dead, that they should be judged, and that thou shouldest give reward unto thy servants the prophets, and to the saints, and them that fear thy name, small and great; and shouldest destroy them which destroy the earth.   Rev. 13:10; 19:5; 20:12

19 And the temple of God was opened in heaven, and there was seen in his temple the ark of his testament: and there were lightnings, and voices, and thunderings, and an earthquake, and great hail.   Rev. 4:5; 8:5; 16:21

Two Signs

12 And there appeared a great wonder in heaven; a woman clothed with the sun, and the moon under her feet, and upon her head a crown of twelve stars: Rev. 12:3

2 And she being with child cried, travailing in birth, and pained to be delivered.   Gal. 4:19

3 And there appeared another wonder in heaven; and behold a great red dragon, having seven heads and ten horns, and seven crowns upon his heads.   Is. 27:1; Dan. 7:20; Rev. 17:12

4 And his tail drew the third part of the stars of heaven, and did cast them to the earth: and the dragon stood before the woman which was ready to be delivered, for to devour her child as soon as it was born.   John 8:44

5 And she brought forth a man child, who was to rule all nations with a rod of iron:

and her child was caught up unto God, and *to* his throne.

6 And the woman fled into the wilderness, where she hath a place prepared of God, that they should feed her there a thousand two hundred *and* T threescore days.   Rev. 11:2-3 ◆ *sixty*

12:7–9 The God of Wisdom and Love

Had [Satan] been immediately blotted from existence, [the inhabitants of heaven and of other worlds] would have served God from fear rather than from love. . . .

Satan's rebellion was to be a lesson to the universe through all coming ages, a perpetual testimony to the nature and terrible results of sin. . . .

When it was announced that with all his sympathizers he must be expelled from the abodes of bliss, then the rebel leader boldly avowed his contempt for the Creator's law. GC 499

7 And there was war in heaven: Michael and his angels fought against the dragon; and the dragon fought and his angels,   Dan. 10:13; Jude 9

8 And prevailed not; neither was their place found any more in heaven.

9 And the great dragon was cast out, that old serpent, called the Devil, and Satan, which deceiveth the whole world: he was cast out into the earth, and his angels were cast out with him.   Gen. 3:1; Luke 10:18; John 12:31

Salvation From Sin See Genesis 2:15–17.

10 And I heard a loud voice saying in heaven, Now is come salvation, and strength, and the kingdom of our God, and the power of his Christ: for the accuser of our brethren is cast down, which accused them before our God day and night.   Job 1:9; 2:5; Rev. 11:15

The Importance of the Ark of God

Revelation 11:19

The temple of God was opened in heaven, and there was seen in His temple the ark of His testament" (Revelation 11:19). The ark of God's testament is in the holy of holies, the second apartment of the sanctuary. In the ministration of the earthly tabernacle, which served "unto the example and shadow of heavenly things," this apartment was opened only upon the great Day of Atonement for the cleansing of the sanctuary. Therefore the announcement that the temple of God was opened in heaven and the ark of His testament was seen points to the opening of the most holy place of the heavenly sanctuary in 1844 as Christ entered there to perform the closing work of the atonement. Those who by faith followed their great High Priest as He entered upon His ministry in the most holy place, beheld the ark of His testament. As they had studied the subject of the sanctuary they had come to understand the Saviour's change of ministration, and they saw that He was now officiating before the ark of God, pleading His blood in behalf of sinners.

The ark in the tabernacle on earth contained the two tables of stone, upon which were inscribed the precepts of the law of God. The ark was merely a receptacle for the tables of the law, and the presence of these divine precepts gave to it its value and sacredness. When the temple of God was opened in heaven, the ark of His testament was seen. Within the holy of holies, in the sanctuary in heaven, the divine law is sacredly enshrined—the law that was spoken by God Himself amid the thunders of Sinai and written with His own finger on the tables of stone. GC 433, 434

11 And they overcame him by the blood of the Lamb, and by the word of their testimony; and they loved not their lives unto the death. *Luke 14:26; John 16:33; Rev. 6:9*

12 Therefore rejoice, *ye* heavens, and ye that dwell in them. Woe to the inhabiters of the earth and of the sea! for the devil is come down unto you, having great wrath, because he knoweth that he hath but a short time.

13 And when the dragon saw that he was cast unto the earth, he persecuted the woman which brought forth the man *child*.

14 And to the woman were given two wings of a great eagle, that she might fly into the wilderness, into her place, where she is nourished for a time, and times, and half a time, from the face of the serpent. *Ex. 19:4; Dan. 7:25*

15 And the serpent cast out of his mouth water as a flood after the woman, that he might cause her to be carried away of the flood. *Is. 59:19*

12:17 The Faithful Remnant

Zechariah's vision of Joshua and the Angel applies with peculiar force to the experience of God's people in the closing scenes of the great day of atonement. The remnant church will then be brought into great trial and distress. Those who keep the commandments of God and the faith of Jesus will feel the ire of the dragon and his hosts. Satan numbers the world as his subjects; he has gained control even of many professing Christians. But here is a little company who are resisting his supremacy. *PK 587*

---

16 And the earth helped the woman, and the earth opened her mouth, and swallowed up the flood which the dragon cast out of his mouth.

17 And the dragon was ᵀwroth with the woman, and went to make war with the remnant of her seed, which keep the commandments of God, and have the testimony of Jesus Christ. *Gen. 3:15; Rev. 1:2; 14:12* ◆ *angry*

Gift of Prophecy See Revelation 19:10.

A Beast from the Sea

13 And I stood upon the sand of the sea, and saw a beast rise up out of the sea, having seven heads and ten horns, and upon his horns ten crowns, and upon his heads the name of blasphemy. *Dan. 11:36; Rev. 12:3; 17:3*

2 And the beast which I saw was like unto a leopard, and his feet were as *the feet* of a bear, and his mouth as the mouth of a lion: and the dragon gave him his power, and his seat, and great authority. *Rev. 16:10*

3 And I saw one of his heads as it were wounded to death; and his deadly wound was healed: and all the world wondered after the beast. *Rev. 13:14; 17:8, 13*

4 And they worshipped the dragon which gave power unto the beast: and they worshipped the beast, saying, Who *is* like unto the beast? who is able to make war with him? *Rev. 13:2*

5 And there was given unto him a mouth speaking great things and blasphemies; and power was given unto him to continue forty *and* two months. *Dan. 7:8, 11; 11:36*

The Beast With Lamblike Horns

Revelation 13:11

At this point another symbol is introduced. . . . Both the appearance of this beast and the manner of its rise indicate that the nation which it represents is unlike those presented under the preceding symbols. The great kingdoms that have ruled the world were presented to the prophet Daniel as beasts of prey, rising when "the four winds of the heaven strove upon the great sea" (Daniel 7:2). . . . Winds are a symbol of strife. The four winds of heaven striving upon the great sea represent the terrible scenes of conquest and revolution by which kingdoms have attained to power.

But the beast with lamblike horns was seen "coming up out of the earth." Instead of overthrowing other powers to establish itself, the nation thus represented must arise in territory previously unoccupied and grow up gradually and peacefully. It could not, then, arise among the crowded and struggling nationalities of the Old World—that turbulent sea of "peoples, and multitudes, and nations, and tongues." It must be sought in the Western Continent.

What nation of the New World was in 1798 rising into power, giving promise of strength and greatness, and attracting the attention of the world? . . . One nation, and only one, meets the specifications of this prophecy; it points unmistakably to the United States of America. . . . The beast was seen "coming up out of the earth;" and, according to the translators, the word here rendered "coming up" literally signifies "to grow or spring up as a plant." And, as we have seen, the nation must arise in territory previously unoccupied. . . .

The lamblike horns indicate youth, innocence, and gentleness, fitly representing the character of the United States when presented to the prophet as "coming up" in 1798. . . . Republicanism and Protestantism became the fundamental principles of the nation. These principles are the secret of its power and prosperity. *GC 439–441*

6 And he opened his mouth in blasphemy against God, to blaspheme his name, and his tabernacle, and them that dwell in heaven.   Rev. 12:12
7 And it was given unto him to make war with the saints, and to overcome them: and power was given him over all kindreds, and tongues, and nations.   Dan. 7:21, 25; Rev. 11:7
8 And all that dwell upon the earth shall worship him, whose names are not written in the book of life of the Lamb slain from the foundation of the world.   Phil. 4:3; Rev. 3:5; 17:8
9 If any man have an ear, let him hear. Rev. 2:7
10 He that leadeth into captivity shall go into captivity: he that killeth with the sword must be killed with the sword. Here is the patience and the faith of the saints.   Is. 33:1; Heb. 6:12

13:1–10 Symbols Take on Important Meaning

This symbol, as most Protestants have believed, represents the papacy, which succeeded to the power and seat and authority once held by the ancient Roman empire. . . . This prophecy, which is nearly identical with the description of the little horn of Daniel 7, unquestionably points to the papacy. *GC 439*

A Beast from the Earth

11 And I beheld another beast coming up out of the earth; and he had two horns like a lamb, and he spake as a dragon.
12 And he exerciseth all the power of the first beast before him, and causeth the earth and them which dwell therein to worship the first beast, whose deadly wound was healed.
13 And he doeth great wonders, so that he maketh fire come down from heaven on the earth in the sight of men, 1 Kin. 18:38; Matt. 24:24
14 And deceiveth them that dwell on the earth by *the means of* those miracles which he had power to do in the sight of the beast; saying to them that dwell on the earth, that they should make an image to the beast, which had the wound by a sword, and did live.   Rev. 12:9; 13:8; 19:20

15 And he had power to give life unto the image of the beast, that the image of the beast should both speak, and cause that as many as would not worship the image of the beast should be killed.   Rev. 16:2
16 And he causeth all, both small and great, rich and poor, free and bond, to receive a mark in their right hand, or in their foreheads: Rev. 7:3; 19:5, 18
17 And that no man might buy or sell, save he that had the mark, or the name of the beast, or the number of his name. Rev. 13:16; 14:11; 15:2
18 Here is wisdom. Let him that hath understanding count the number of the beast: for it is the number of a man; and his number *is* Six hundred threescore *and* six.   Rev. 15:2; 17:9

A New Song

14 And I looked, and, lo, a Lamb stood on the mount Sion, and with him an hundred forty *and* four thousand, having his Father's name written in their foreheads.   Ps. 2:6; Rev. 3:12

14:1 Loyalty Now Before Heaven

The vision of the prophet pictures [the hundred and forty-four thousand] as standing on Mount Zion, girt for holy service, clothed in white linen, which is the righteousness of the saints. But all who follow the Lamb in heaven must first have followed Him on earth, not fretfully or capriciously, but in trustful, loving, willing obedience, as the flock follows the shepherd. *AA 591*

2 And I heard a voice from heaven, as the voice of many waters, and as the voice of a great thunder: and I heard the voice of harpers harping with their harps: Rev. 1:15; 5:8; 11:15
3 And they sung as it were a new song before the throne, and before the four beasts, and the elders: and no man could learn that song but the hundred *and* forty *and* four thousand, which were redeemed from the earth.   Rev. 2:17; 5:9; 14:1
4 These are they which were not defiled with women; for they are virgins. These are

The United States Foreseen in Prophecy

Revelation 13:11–15

The prediction that it will speak "as a dragon" and exercise "all the power of the first beast" plainly foretells a development of the spirit of intolerance and persecution that was manifested by the nations represented by the dragon and the leopardlike beast. And the statement that the beast with two horns "causeth the earth and them which dwell therein to worship the first beast" indicates that the authority of this nation is to be exercised in enforcing some observance which shall be an act of homage to the papacy. ...

"Saying to them that dwell on the earth, that *they* should make an image to the beast." Here is clearly presented a form of government in which the legislative power rests with the people, a most striking evidence that the United States is the nation denoted in the prophecy. *GC 442, 443*

they which follow the Lamb whithersoever he goeth. These were redeemed from among men, *being* the firstfruits unto God and to the Lamb.　　　*2 Cor. 11:2; James 1:18; Rev. 3:4*

5 And in their mouth was found no ᵀguile: for they are without fault before the throne of God.　　*Ps. 32:2; Zeph. 3:13; John 1:47 ◆ deceit*

14:5 Preparing to Be With Heavenly Angels

Those who have learned of Christ will "have no fellowship with the unfruitful works of darkness" (Ephesians 5:11). In speech, as in life, they will be simple, straightforward, and true; for they are preparing for the fellowship of those holy ones in whose mouth "was found no guile" (Revelation 14:5). *MB 69*

The Harvest of the Earth

6 And I saw another angel fly in the midst of heaven, having the everlasting gospel to preach unto them that dwell on the earth, and to every nation, and kindred, and tongue, and people,　　　*Rev. 3:10; 8:13; 13:7*

7 Saying with a loud voice, Fear God, and give glory to him; for the hour of his judgment is come: and worship him that made heaven, and earth, and the sea, and the fountains of waters.　　*Rev. 4:11; 11:18; 15:4*

8 And there followed another angel, saying, Babylon is fallen, is fallen, that great city, because she made all nations drink of the wine of the wrath of her fornication.　*Is. 21:9*

9 And the third angel followed them, saying with a loud voice, If any man worship the beast and his image, and receive his mark in his forehead, or in his hand,　　*Rev. 14:11*

10 The same shall drink of the wine of the wrath of God, which is poured out without mixture into the cup of his indignation; and he shall be tormented with fire and brimstone in the presence of the holy angels, and in the presence of the Lamb:　*Ps. 11:6; Is. 51:17*

11 And the smoke of their torment ascendeth up for ever and ever: and they have no rest day nor night, who worship the beast and his image, and whosoever receiveth the mark of his name.　*Is. 34:10; Rev. 18:18; 19:3*

12 Here is the patience of the saints: here *are* they that keep the commandments of God, and the faith of Jesus.　　*Rev. 12:17; 13:10*

13 And I heard a voice from heaven saying unto me, Write, Blessed *are* the dead which

The Beast Power and Its Image

Revelation 13:16–18

But what is the "image to the beast"? and how is it to be formed? . . . .

When the early church became corrupted by departing from the simplicity of the gospel and accepting heathen rites and customs, she lost the Spirit and power of God; and in order to control the consciences of the people, she sought the support of the secular power. The result was the papacy, a church that controlled the power of the state and employed it to further her own ends, especially for the punishment of "heresy." In order for the United States to form an image of the beast, the religious power must so control the civil government that the authority of the state will also be employed by the church to accomplish her own ends.

Whenever the church has obtained secular power, she has employed it to punish dissent from her doctrines. Protestant churches that have followed in the steps of Rome by forming alliance with worldly powers have manifested a similar desire to restrict liberty of conscience. An example of this is given in the long-continued persecution of dissenters by the Church of England. During the sixteenth and seventeenth centuries, thousands of nonconformist ministers were forced to flee from their churches, and many, both of pastors and people, were subjected to fine, imprisonment, torture, and martyrdom.

It was apostasy that led the early church to seek the aid of the civil government, and this prepared the way for the development of the papacy—the beast. Said Paul: "There" shall "come a falling away, . . . and that man of sin be revealed" (2 Thessalonians 2:3). So apostasy in the church will prepare the way for the image [of] the beast.

The Bible declares that before the coming of the Lord there will exist a state of religious deciension similar to that in the first centuries. "In the last days perilous times shall come. For men shall be *lovers of their own selves*, covetous, boasters, proud, blasphemers, disobedient to parents, unthankful, unholy, without natural affection, trucebreakers, false accusers, incontinent, fierce, *despisers of those that are good*, traitors, heady, high-minded, *lovers of pleasures more than lovers of God; having a form of godliness*, but denying the power thereof" (2 Timothy 3:1–5). "Now the Spirit speaketh expressly, that in the latter times some shall depart from the faith, giving heed to seducing spirits, and doctrines of devils" (1 Timothy 4:1). Satan will work "with all power and signs and lying wonders, and with all deceivableness of unrighteousness." And all that "received not the love of the truth, that they might be saved," will be left to accept "strong delusion, that they should believe a lie" (2 Thessalonians 2:9–11). When this state of ungodliness shall be reached, the same results will follow as in the first centuries. *GC 443, 444*

die in the Lord from henceforth: Yea, saith the Spirit, that they may rest from their labours; and their works do follow them.   1 Cor. 15:18

14 And I looked, and behold a white cloud, and upon the cloud *one* sat like unto the Son of man, having on his head a golden crown, and in his hand a sharp sickle.   Dan. 7:13

15 And another angel came out of the temple, crying with a loud voice to him that sat on the cloud, Thrust in thy sickle, and reap: for the time is come for thee to reap; for the harvest of the earth is ripe.   Jer. 51:33; Joel 3:13; Matt. 13:39

16 And he that sat on the cloud thrust in his sickle on the earth; and the earth was reaped.

17 And another angel came out of the temple which is in heaven, he also having a sharp sickle.

18 And another angel came out from the altar, which had power over fire; and cried with a loud cry to him that had the sharp sickle, saying, Thrust in thy sharp sickle, and gather the clusters of the vine of the earth; for her grapes are fully ripe.   Joel 3:13; Rev. 16:8

19 And the angel thrust in his sickle into the earth, and gathered the vine of the earth, and cast *it* into the great winepress of the wrath of God.

20 And the winepress was ᵀtrodden without the city, and blood came out of the winepress, even unto the horse bridles, by the space of a thousand *and* six hundred furlongs.   Lam. 1:15 ◆ *trampled*

Seven Angels with Seven Plagues

15 And I saw another sign in heaven, great and marvellous, seven angels having the seven last plagues; for in them is filled up the wrath of God.   Rev. 21:9

2 And I saw as it were a sea of glass mingled with fire: and them that had gotten the victory over the beast, and over his image, and over his mark, *and* over the number of his name, stand on the sea of glass, having the harps of God.   Rev. 4:6; 5:8; 12:11

3 And they sing the song of Moses the servant of God, and the song of the Lamb, saying, Great and marvellous *are* thy works, Lord God Almighty; just and true *are* thy ways, thou King of saints.   Ps. 111:2; 139:14; 145:17

15:2, 3 John Sees a Perfect Mix

John saw the mercy, the tenderness, and the love of God blending with His holiness, justice, and power. He saw sinners finding a Father in Him of whom their sins had made them afraid. And looking beyond the culmination of the great conflict, he beheld upon Zion "them that had gotten the victory . . . stand on the sea of glass, having the harps of God," and singing "the song of Moses" and the Lamb (Revelation 15:2, 3). *AA 589*

4 Who shall not fear thee, O Lord, and glorify thy name? for *thou* only *art* holy: for all nations shall come and worship before thee; for thy judgments are made ᵀmanifest.   Ps. 86:9; Jer. 10:7 ◆ *known*

5 And after that I looked, and, behold, the temple of the tabernacle of the testimony in heaven was opened: Num. 1:50; Rev. 11:19

15:5 Understanding the Sanctuary a Key

Moses made the earthly sanctuary, "according to the fashion that he had seen." Paul declares that "the tabernacle, and all the vessels of the ministry," when completed, were "the patterns of things in the heavens" (Acts 7:44; Hebrews 9:21, 23). And John says that he saw the sanctuary in heaven. That sanctuary, in which Jesus ministers in our behalf, is the great original, of which the sanctuary built by Moses was a copy. *PP 357*

First Angel of Three Proclaims Message

Revelation 14:6, 7

To prepare a people to stand in the day of God, a great work of reform was to be accomplished. God saw that many of His professed people were not building for eternity, and in His mercy He was about to send a message of warning to arouse them from their stupor and lead them to make ready for the coming of the Lord.

This warning is brought to view in Revelation 14. Here is a threefold message represented as proclaimed by heavenly beings and immediately followed by the coming of the Son of man to reap "the harvest of the earth." The first of these warnings announces the approaching judgment. The prophet beheld an angel flying "in the midst of heaven, having the everlasting gospel to preach unto them that dwell on the earth, and to every nation, and kindred, and tongue, and people, saying with a loud voice, Fear God, and give glory to Him; for the hour of His judgment is come: and worship Him that made heaven, and earth, and the sea, and the fountains of waters" (Revelation 14:6, 7).

This message is declared to be a part of "the everlasting gospel." The work of preaching the gospel has not been committed to angels, but has been entrusted to men. Holy angels have been employed in directing this work, they have in charge the great movements for the salvation of men; but the actual proclamation of the gospel is performed by the servants of Christ upon the earth. *GC 311, 312*

6 And the seven angels came out of the temple, having the seven plagues, clothed in pure and white linen, and having their breasts girded with golden girdles.   Rev. 1:13; 15:1
7 And one of the four beasts gave unto the seven angels seven golden vials full of the wrath of God, who liveth for ever and ever.
8 And the temple was filled with smoke from the glory of God, and from his power; and no man was able to enter into the temple, till the seven plagues of the seven angels were fulfilled.   1 Kin. 8:10-11; 2 Chr. 5:13-14; Is. 6:4

The Angels Pour out Their Bowls

16 And I heard a great voice out of the temple saying to the seven angels, Go your ways, and pour out the vials of the wrath of God upon the earth.   Rev. 15:1, 17
2 And the first went, and poured out his vial upon the earth; and there fell a ᵀnoisome and grievous sore upon the men which had the mark of the beast, and *upon* them which worshipped his image.   Rev. 8:7 ◆ *harmful*
3 And the second angel poured out his vial upon the sea; and it became as the blood of a dead *man*: and every living soul died in the sea.
4 And the third angel poured out his vial upon the rivers and fountains of waters; and they became blood.   Ex. 7:17-20
5 And I heard the angel of the waters say, Thou art righteous, O Lord, which art, and wast, and shalt be, because thou hast judged thus.   Rev. 1:4
6 For they have shed the blood of saints and prophets, and thou hast given them blood to drink; for they are worthy.   Is. 49:26; Rev. 11:18
7 And I heard another out of the altar say, Even so, Lord God Almighty, true and righteous *are* thy judgments.   Rev. 6:9; 14:18; 19:2

16:3-7 The Judgments Finally Come

By condemning the people of God to death, they have as truly incurred the guilt of their blood as if it had been shed by their hands. In like manner Christ declared the Jews of His time guilty of all the blood of holy men which had been shed since the days of Abel; for they possessed the same spirit and were seeking to do the same work with these murderers of the prophets. *GC 628*

8 And the fourth angel poured out his vial upon the sun; and power was given unto him to scorch men with fire.   Rev. 6:12; 8:12; 14:18
9 And men were scorched with great heat, and blasphemed the name of God, which hath power over these plagues: and they repented not to give him glory.   Rev. 2:21; 11:13; 16:21
10 And the fifth angel poured out his ᵀvial upon the seat of the beast; and his kingdom was full of darkness; and they gnawed their tongues for pain,   Rev. 9:2 ◆ *small vessel for liquids*
11 And blasphemed the God of heaven because of their pains and their sores, and repented not of their deeds.   Rev. 16:2, 9, 21
12 And the sixth angel poured out his vial upon the great river Euphrates; and the water thereof was dried up, that the way of the kings of the east might be prepared.   Is. 11:15; 41:25
13 And I saw three unclean spirits like frogs *come* out of the mouth of the dragon, and out of the mouth of the beast, and out of the mouth of the false prophet.   Rev. 19:20; 20:10
14 For they are the spirits of devils, working miracles, *which* go forth unto the kings of the earth and of the whole world, to gather them to the battle of that great day of God Almighty.
15 Behold, I come as a thief. Blessed *is* he that watcheth, and keepeth his garments, lest he walk naked, and they see his shame.   Rev. 3:18

The Most Fearful and Threatening Message to the Human Race

Revelation 14:6-12

The most fearful threatening ever addressed to mortals is contained in the third angel's message. That must be a terrible sin which calls down the wrath of God unmingled with mercy. Men are not to be left in darkness concerning this important matter; the warning against this sin is to be given to the world before the visitation of God's judgments, that all may know why they are to be inflicted, and have opportunity to escape them. Prophecy declares that the first angel would make his announcement to "every nation, and kindred, and tongue, and people." The warning of the third angel, which forms a part of the same threefold message, is to be no less widespread. It is represented in the prophecy as being proclaimed with a loud voice, by an angel flying in the midst of heaven; and it will command the attention of the world.

In the issue of the contest all Christendom will be divided into two great classes—those who keep the commandments of God and the faith of Jesus, and those who worship the beast and his image and receive his mark. Although church and state will unite their power to compel "all, both small and great, rich and poor, free and bond" (Revelation 13:16), to receive "the mark of the beast," yet the people of God will not receive it. The prophet of Patmos beholds "them that had gotten the victory over the beast, and over his image, and over his mark, and over the number of his name, stand on the sea of glass, having the harps of God" and singing the song of Moses and the Lamb (Revelation 15:2, 3). *GC 449, 450*

16 And he gathered them together into a place called in the Hebrew tongue Armageddon.   Judg. 5:19
17 And the seventh angel poured out his vial into the air; and there came a great voice out of the temple of heaven, from the throne, saying, It is done.   Eph. 2:2; Rev. 21:6
18 And there were voices, and thunders, and lightnings; and there was a great earthquake, such as was not since men were upon the earth, so mighty an earthquake, *and* so great.
19 And the great city was divided into three parts, and the cities of the nations fell: and great Babylon came in remembrance before God, to give unto her the cup of the wine of the fierceness of his wrath.   Rev. 17:18; 18:5, 10
20 And every island fled away, and the mountains were not found.   Rev. 6:14; 20:11
21 And there fell upon men a great hail out of heaven, *every stone* about the weight of a talent: and men blasphemed God because of the plague of the hail; for the plague thereof was exceeding great.   Rev. 11:19; 16:9, 11

Babylon the Great

17 And there came one of the seven angels which had the seven vials, and talked with me, saying unto me, Come ᵀhither; I will shew unto thee the judgment of the great whore that sitteth upon many waters: Jer. 51:13; Rev. 19:2; 21:9 ◆ *here*
2 With whom the kings of the earth have committed fornication, and the inhabitants of the earth have been made drunk with the wine of her fornication.   Jer. 51:7; Rev. 14:8; 18:3
3 So he carried me away in the spirit into the wilderness: and I saw a woman sit upon a scarlet coloured beast, full of names of blasphemy, having seven heads and ten horns.   Rev. 12:3, 6, 14
4 And the woman was ᵀarrayed in purple and scarlet colour, and decked with gold and precious stones and pearls, having a golden cup in her hand full of abominations and filthiness of her fornication: Jer. 51:7; Dan. 11:38 ◆ *clothed*
5 And upon her forehead *was* a name written, MYSTERY, BABYLON THE GREAT, THE MOTHER OF HARLOTS AND ABOMINATIONS OF THE EARTH.   2 Thess. 2:7; Rev. 14:8
6 And I saw the woman drunken with the blood of the saints, and with the blood of the martyrs of Jesus: and when I saw her, I wondered with great admiration.   Rev. 16:6

17:1–6 The Meaning of Babylon

The term "Babylon" is derived from "Babel," and signifies confusion. It is employed in Scripture to designate the various forms of false or apostate religion. In Revelation 17 Babylon is represented as a woman—a figure which is used in the Bible as the symbol of a church, a virtuous woman representing a pure church, a vile woman an apostate church. *GC 381*

---

7 And the angel said unto me, Wherefore didst thou marvel? I will tell thee the mystery of the woman, and of the beast that carrieth her, which hath the seven heads and ten horns.
8 The beast that thou sawest was, and is not; and shall ascend out of the bottomless pit, and go into perdition: and they that dwell on the earth shall wonder, whose names were not written in the book of life from the foundation of the world, when they behold the beast that was, and is not, and yet is.   Matt. 25:34; Rev. 11:7; 17:11
9 And here *is* the mind which hath wisdom. The seven heads are seven mountains, on which the woman sitteth.   Rev. 13:18; 17:3
10 And there are seven kings: five are fallen, and one is, *and* the other is not yet come; and when he cometh, he must continue a short space.
11 And the beast that was, and is not, even he is the eighth, and is of the seven, and goeth into ᵀperdition.   Rev. 17:8 ◆ *destruction*
12 And the ten horns which thou sawest are ten kings, which have received no kingdom as yet; but receive power as kings one hour with the beast.   Dan. 7:24
13 These have one mind, and shall give their power and strength unto the beast. Rev. 17:17

Third Angel's Message Bring World to a Test

Revelation 14:9, 10

Fearful is the issue to which the world is to be brought. The powers of earth, uniting to war against the commandments of God, will decree that "all, both small and great, rich and poor, free and bond" (Revelation 13:16), shall conform to the customs of the church by the observance of the false sabbath. All who refuse compliance will be visited with civil penalties, and it will finally be declared that they are deserving of death. On the other hand, the law of God enjoining the Creator's rest day demands obedience and threatens wrath against all who transgress its precepts.

With the issue thus clearly brought before him, whoever shall trample upon God's law to obey a human enactment receives the mark of the beast; he accepts the sign of allegiance to the power which he chooses to obey instead of God. *GC 604*

The Victory of the Lamb

14 These shall make war with the Lamb, and the Lamb shall overcome them: for he is Lord of lords, and King of kings: and they that are with him *are* called, and chosen, and faithful.   1 Tim. 6:15; Rev. 1:5; 16:14

15 And he saith unto me, The waters which thou sawest, where the ᵀwhore sitteth, are peoples, and multitudes, and nations, and tongues.   Rev. 17:1 ◆ prostitute

16 And the ten horns which thou sawest upon the beast, these shall hate the whore, and shall make her desolate and naked, and shall eat her flesh, and burn her with fire.

17 For God hath put in their hearts to fulfil his will, and to agree, and give their kingdom unto the beast, until the words of God shall be fulfilled.   Rev. 10:7

18 And the woman which thou sawest is that great city, which reigneth over the kings of the earth.   Rev. 16:19

17:18 That Great City

Babylon is further declared to be "that great city, which reigneth over the kings of the earth" (Revelation 17:4–6, 18). The power that for so many centuries maintained despotic sway over the monarchs of Christendom is Rome. . . .

Babylon is said to be "the *mother* of harlots." By her *daughters* must be symbolized churches that cling to her doctrines and traditions, and follow her example of sacrificing the truth and the approval of God, in order to form an unlawful alliance with the world. *GC 382, 383*

Babylon Falls

18 And after these things I saw another angel come down from heaven, having great power; and the earth was lightened with his glory.   Ezek. 43:2; Rev. 17:1

2 And he cried mightily with a strong voice, saying, Babylon the great is fallen, is fallen, and is become the habitation of devils, and the hold of every foul spirit, and a cage of every unclean and hateful bird. Is. 14:23; Jer. 51:37

3 For all nations have drunk of the wine of the wrath of her fornication, and the kings of the earth have committed fornication with her, and the merchants of the earth are ᵀwaxed rich through the abundance of her delicacies.   Rev. 14:8; 17:2; 18:9 ◆ become

4 And I heard another voice from heaven, saying, Come out of her, my people, that ye be not partakers of her sins, and that ye receive not of her plagues.   Is. 48:20; Jer. 50:8; 2 Cor. 6:17

5 For her sins have reached unto heaven, and God hath remembered her iniquities.

18:1–5 The Last Message Ever

Revelation 18 points to the time when, as the result of rejecting the threefold warning of Revelation 14:6-12, the church will have fully reached the condition foretold by the second angel, and the people of God still in Babylon will be called upon to separate from her communion. This message is the last that will ever be given to the world; and it will accomplish its work. *GC 390*

6 Reward her even as she rewarded you, and double unto her double according to her works: in the cup which she hath filled fill to her double.   Ps. 137:8; Jer. 50:15, 29

Nature Itself Seems Turned Out of Its Course

Revelation 16:17–21

It is at midnight that God manifests His power for the deliverance of His people. The sun appears, shining in its strength. Signs and wonders follow in quick succession. The wicked look with terror and amazement upon the scene, while the righteous behold with solemn joy the tokens of their deliverance. Everything in nature seems turned out of its course. The streams cease to flow. Dark, heavy clouds come up and clash against each other. In the midst of the angry heavens is one clear space of indescribable glory, whence comes the voice of God like the sound of many waters, saying: "It is done" (Revelation 16:17).

That voice shakes the heavens and the earth. There is a mighty earthquake, "such as was not since men were upon the earth, so mighty an earthquake, and so great" (Verses 17, 18). The firmament appears to open and shut. The glory from the throne of God seems flashing through. . . . The whole earth heaves and swells like the waves of the sea. Its surface is breaking up. Its very foundations seem to be giving way. Mountain chains are sinking. Inhabited islands disappear. The seaports that have become like Sodom for wickedness are swallowed up by the angry waters. Babylon the great has come in remembrance before God, "to give unto her the cup of the wine of the fierceness of His wrath." Great hailstones, every one "about the weight of a talent," are doing their work of destruction (Verses 19, 21). The proudest cities of the earth are laid low. The lordly palaces, upon which the world's great men have lavished their wealth in order to glorify themselves, are crumbling to ruin before their eyes. Prison walls are rent asunder, and God's people, who have been held in bondage for their faith, are set free. *GC 636, 637*

7 How much she hath glorified herself, and lived deliciously, so much torment and sorrow give her: for she saith in her heart, I sit a queen, and am no widow, and shall see no sorrow.   Zeph. 2:15

8 Therefore shall her plagues come in one day, death, and mourning, and famine; and she shall be utterly burned with fire: for strong *is* the Lord God who judgeth her.   Jer. 50:31

Mourning for Babylon

9 And the kings of the earth, who have committed fornication and lived deliciously with her, shall ᵀbewail her, and lament for her, when they shall see the smoke of her burning,   Rev. 17:2; 18:3; 19:3 ♦ *lament*

10 Standing afar off for the fear of her torment, saying, Alas, alas, that great city Babylon, that mighty city! for in one hour is thy judgment come.   Rev. 14:8; 18:8, 19

11 And the merchants of the earth shall weep and mourn over her; for no man buyeth their merchandise any more: Rev. 18:3

12 The merchandise of gold, and silver, and precious stones, and of pearls, and fine linen, and purple, and silk, and scarlet, and all thyine wood, and all manner vessels of ivory, and all manner vessels of most precious wood, and of brass, and iron, and marble,   Rev. 17:4

13 And cinnamon, and odours, and ointments, and frankincense, and wine, and oil, and fine flour, and wheat, and beasts, and sheep, and horses, and chariots, and slaves, and souls of men.   Ezek. 27:13

14 And the fruits that thy soul lusted after are departed from thee, and all things which were dainty and goodly are departed from thee, and thou shalt find them no more at all.

15 The merchants of these things, which were made rich by her, shall stand afar off for the fear of her torment, weeping and wailing,   Ezek. 27:31; Rev. 18:3

16 And saying, Alas, alas, that great city, that was clothed in fine linen, and purple, and scarlet, and decked with gold, and precious stones, and pearls!   Rev. 17:4

17 For in one hour so great riches is come to ᵀnought. And every shipmaster, and all the company in ships, and sailors, and as many as trade by sea, stood afar off,   Rev. 17:16 ♦ *nothing*

18:15–17 Her Time Has Come

Such are the judgments that fall upon Babylon in the day of the visitation of God's wrath. She has filled up the measure of her iniquity; her time has come; she is ripe for destruction. *GC 653*

18 And cried when they saw the smoke of her burning, saying, What *city is* like unto this great city!   Rev. 13:4; 18:9-10

19 And they cast dust on their heads, and cried, weeping and wailing, saying, Alas, alas, that great city, wherein were made rich all that had ships in the sea by reason of her costliness! for in one hour is she made desolate.   Josh. 7:6; Job 2:12; Rev. 18:10

20 Rejoice over her, *thou* heaven, and *ye* holy apostles and prophets; for God hath avenged you on her.   Luke 11:49-50

21 And a mighty angel took up a stone like a great millstone, and cast *it* into the sea, saying, Thus with violence shall that great

The Result of Sacrificing Truth for the Favor of Man

Revelation 18:9–19

When the voice of God turns the captivity of His people, there is a terrible awakening of those who have lost all in the great conflict of life. While probation continued they were blinded by Satan's deceptions, and they justified their course of sin. The rich prided themselves upon their superiority to those who were less favored; but they had obtained their riches by violation of the law of God. . . . They look with terror upon the destruction of the idols which they preferred before their Maker. They have sold their souls for earthly riches and enjoyments, and have not sought to become rich toward God. . . .

The wicked are filled with regret, not because of their sinful neglect of God and their fellow men, but because God has conquered. They lament that the result is what it is; but they do not repent of their wickedness. They would leave no means untried to conquer if they could.

The world see the very class whom they have mocked and derided, and desired to exterminate, pass unharmed through pestilence, tempest, and earthquake. He who is to the transgressors of His law a devouring fire, is to His people a safe pavilion.

The minister who has sacrificed truth to gain the favor of men now discerns the character and influence of his teachings. It is apparent that the omniscient eye was following him as he stood in the desk, as he walked the streets, as he mingled with men in the various scenes of life. Every emotion of the soul, every line written, every word uttered, every act that led men to rest in a refuge of falsehood, has been scattering seed; and now, in the wretched, lost souls around him, he beholds the harvest. *GC 654, 655*

city Babylon be thrown down, and shall be found no more at all.   Jer. 51:63-64

22 And the voice of harpers, and musicians, and of pipers, and trumpeters, shall be heard no more at all in thee; and no craftsman, of whatsoever craft *he be*, shall be found any more in thee; and the sound of a millstone shall be heard no more at all in thee;   Jer. 25:10

23 And the light of a candle shall shine no more at all in thee; and the voice of the bridegroom and of the bride shall be heard no more at all in thee: for thy merchants were the great men of the earth; for by thy sorceries were all nations deceived.   Is. 23:8; Nah. 3:4; Rev. 18:3

24 And in her was found the blood of prophets, and of saints, and of all that were slain upon the earth.   Jer. 51:49; Rev. 16:6; 17:6

The Heavenly Hosts Praise God

19 And after these things I heard a great voice of much people in heaven, saying, Alleluia; Salvation, and glory, and honour, and power, unto the Lord our God: Rev. 11:15; 12:10; 19:6

2 For true and righteous *are* his judgments: for he hath judged the great ᵀwhore, which did corrupt the earth with her fornication, and hath avenged the blood of his servants at her hand.   Deut. 32:43; Ps. 19:9; Rev. 6:10 ◆ *prostitute*

3 And again they said, Alleluia. And her smoke rose up for ever and ever.   Is. 34:10

4 And the four and twenty elders and the four beasts fell down and worshipped God that sat on the throne, saying, Amen; Alleluia.   Ps. 106:48; Rev. 5:14

5 And a voice came out of the throne, saying, Praise our God, all ye his servants, and ye that fear him, both small and great.   Ps. 134:1; 135:1

6 And I heard as it were the voice of a great multitude, and as the voice of many waters, and as the voice of mighty thunderings, saying, Alleluia: for the Lord God ᵀomnipotent reigneth.   Ps. 97:1; Rev. 1:15; 14:2 ◆ *all powerful*

19:7–9 The Wedding Garment: Christ's Character

By the wedding garment in the parable [Matthew 22:1–14] is represented the pure, spotless character which Christ's true followers will possess. To the church it is given "that she should be arrayed in fine linen, clean and white," "not having spot, or wrinkle, or any such thing" (Revelation 19:8; Ephesians 5:27). The fine linen, says the Scripture, "is the righteousness of saints" (Revelation 19:8). It is the righteousness of Christ, His own unblemished character, that through faith is imparted to all who receive Him as their personal Saviour. *COL 310*

7 Let us be glad and rejoice, and give honour to him: for the marriage of the Lamb

is come, and his wife hath made herself ready.   Matt. 22:2; Eph. 5:32; Rev. 21:2

8 And to her was granted that she should be ᵀarrayed in fine linen, clean and white: for the fine linen is the righteousness of saints.   Ps. 45:13-14 ◆ *clothed*

19:8 Christ's Robe for Children and Youth

Let the youth and the little children be taught to choose for themselves that royal robe woven in heaven's loom—the "fine linen, clean and white" (Revelation 19:8), which all the holy ones of earth will wear. This robe, Christ's own spotless character, is freely offered to every human being. But all who receive it will receive and wear it here. *Ed 249*

9 And he saith unto me, Write, Blessed *are* they which are called unto the marriage supper of the Lamb. And he saith unto me, These are the true sayings of God.   Rev. 1:19; 21:5; 22:6

10 And I fell at his feet to worship him. And he said unto me, See *thou do it* not: I am thy fellowservant, and of thy brethren that have the testimony of Jesus: worship God: for the testimony of Jesus is the spirit of prophecy.   Acts 10:25-26; Rev. 12:17; 22:8-9

Gift of Prophecy See 1 Thessalonians 5:20, 21.

11 And I saw heaven opened, and behold a white horse; and he that sat upon him *was* called Faithful and True, and in righteousness he doth judge and make war.   Ps. 96:13; Rev. 3:14

12 His eyes *were* as a flame of fire, and on his head *were* many crowns; and he had a name written, that no man knew, but he himself.   Rev. 1:14; 6:2; 12:3

13 And he *was* clothed with a ᵀvesture dipped in blood: and his name is called The Word of God.   John 1:1 ◆ *robe*

14 And the armies *which were* in heaven followed him upon white horses, clothed in fine linen, white and clean.   Rev. 7:9; 14:20; 19:8

15 And out of his mouth goeth a sharp sword, that with it he should smite the nations: and he shall rule them with a rod of iron: and he treadeth the winepress of the fierceness and wrath of Almighty God.   Is. 11:4; 2 Thess. 2:8

19:16 Christ Will Return as King of Kings

When Christ shall come to the earth again . . . every eye shall see Him, and they also that pierced Him. In the place of a crown of thorns, He will wear a crown of glory—a crown within a crown. In place of that old purple kingly robe, He will be clothed in raiment of whitest white, "so as no fuller on earth can white them" (Mark 9:3). And on His vesture and on His thigh a name will be written, "King of kings, and Lord of lords" (Revelation 19:16). *DA 739*

19:10

16 And he hath on *his* vesture and on his thigh a name written, KING OF KINGS, AND LORD OF LORDS.   Rev. 17:14

17 And I saw an angel standing in the sun; and he cried with a loud voice, saying to all the fowls that fly in the midst of heaven, Come and gather yourselves together unto the supper of the great God;   Jer. 12:9; Rev. 8:13

18 That ye may eat the flesh of kings, and the flesh of captains, and the flesh of mighty men, and the flesh of horses, and of them that sit on them, and the flesh of all *men, both* free and bond, both small and great.   Ezek. 39:18-20

19 And I saw the beast, and the kings of the earth, and their armies, gathered together to make war against him that sat on the horse, and against his army.   Rev. 16:14, 16

20 And the beast was taken, and with him the false prophet that ᵀwrought miracles before him, with which he deceived them that had received the mark of the beast, and them that worshipped his image. These both were cast alive into a lake of fire burning with ᵀbrimstone.   Rev. 14:10; 20:10; 21:8 ◆ *made* ◆ *sulphur*

21 And the remnant were slain with the sword of him that sat upon the horse, which *sword* proceeded out of his mouth: and all the fowls were filled with their flesh.

Satan Is Bound

20 And I saw an angel come down from heaven, having the key of the bottomless pit and a great chain in his hand.   Rev. 1:18

2 And he laid hold on the dragon, that old serpent, which is the Devil, and Satan, and bound him a thousand years,   2 Pet. 2:4; Jude 6

3 And cast him into the bottomless pit, and shut him up, and set a seal upon him, that he should deceive the nations no more, till the thousand years should be fulfilled: and after that he must be loosed a little season.

The Millennium See 1 Corinthians 6:1–3.

20:4, 6 Judgment of the Wicked

During the thousand years between the first and the second resurrection the judgment of the wicked takes place. . . . John in the Revelation says: "I saw thrones, and they sat upon them, and judgment was given unto them" (Revelation 20:4). . . . It is at this time that, as foretold by Paul, "the saints shall judge the world" (1 Corinthians 6:2). In union with Christ they judge the wicked, comparing their acts with the statute book, the Bible, and deciding every case according to the deeds done in the body. *GC 660, 661*

4 And I saw thrones, and they sat upon them, and judgment was given unto them: and *I saw* the souls of them that were beheaded for the witness of Jesus, and for the

word of God, and which had not worshipped the beast, neither his image, neither had received *his* mark upon their foreheads, or in their hands; and they lived and reigned with Christ a thousand years.   Dan. 7:9, 18; Rev. 6:9

20:5 Resurrection of the Wicked

At the close of the thousand years the second resurrection will take place. Then the wicked will be raised from the dead and appear before God for the execution of "the judgment written." Thus the revelator, after describing the resurrection of the righteous, says: "The rest of the dead lived not again until the thousand years were finished" (Revelation 20:5). *GC 661*

5 But the rest of the dead lived not again until the thousand years were finished. This *is* the first resurrection.

The Millennium See Revelation 21:1–5.

6 Blessed and holy *is* he that hath part in the first resurrection: on such the second death hath no power, but they shall be priests of God and of Christ, and shall reign with him a thousand years.   Rev. 1:6; 2:11; 5:10

20:6 Righteous Safe From Second Death

While the earth was wrapped in the fire of destruction, the righteous abode safely in the Holy City. Upon those that had part in the first resurrection, the second death has no power. While God is to the wicked a consuming fire, He is to His people both a sun and a shield. *GC 673*

The Final Judgment

7 And when the thousand years are expired, Satan shall be loosed out of his prison,

8 And shall go out to deceive the nations which are in the four quarters of the earth, Gog and Magog, to gather them together to battle: the number of whom *is* as the sand of the sea.   Rev. 16:14; 20:3, 10

20:7–9 Satan Prepares to Assault the Holy City

[Satan] represents himself to his deluded subjects as a redeemer, assuring them that his power has brought them forth from their graves and that he is about to rescue them from the most cruel tyranny. . . . He proposes to lead them against the camp of the saints and to take possession of the City of God. With fiendish exultation he points to the unnumbered millions who have been raised from the dead and declares that as their leader he is well able to overthrow the city and regain his throne and his kingdom. *GC 663*

9 And they went up on the breadth of the earth, and ᵀcompassed the camp of the saints about, and the beloved city: and fire came down from God out of heaven, and devoured them.   *Ezek. 38:9, 16, 22* ◆ *surrounded*

10 And the ᵀdevil that deceived them was cast into the lake of fire and ᵀbrimstone, where the beast and the false prophet *are*, and shall be tormented day and night for ever and ever.   *Rev. 19:20; 20:2-3, 14-15* ◆ *false accuser* ◆ *sulphur*

> The Millennium

11 And I saw a great white throne, and him that sat on it, from whose face the earth and the heaven fled away; and there was found no place for them.   *Dan. 2:35*

12 And I saw the dead, small and great, stand before God; and the books were opened: and another book was opened, which is *the book* of life: and the dead were judged out of those things which were written in the books, according to their works.   *Dan. 7:10; Matt. 16:27*

20:11, 12 Face-to-Face With Eternity

Solemn will be the day of final decision. . . .

Sad will be the retrospect in that day when men stand face to face with eternity. The whole life will present itself just as it has been. The world's pleasures, riches, and honors will not then seem so important. Men will then see that the righteousness they despised is alone of value. . . . Then they will see the results of their choice. They will have a knowledge of what it means to transgress the commandments of God. *COL 318, 319*

13 And the sea gave up the dead which were in it; and death and hell delivered up the dead which were in them: and they were judged every man according to their works.   *Rev. 6:8; 20:12, 14*

14 And death and hell were cast into the lake of fire. This is the second death.   *1 Cor. 15:26*

15 And whosoever was not found written in the book of life was cast into the lake of fire.   *Matt. 25:41*

20:13, 14 The Final End of Sin and Sinners

Since it is impossible for God, consistently with His justice and mercy, to save the sinner in his sins, He deprives him of the existence which his transgressions have forfeited and of which he has proved himself unworthy. Says an inspired writer: "Yet a little while, and the wicked shall not be: yea, thou shalt diligently consider his place, and it shall not be." . . . (Psalm 37:10). Covered with infamy, they sink into hopeless, eternal oblivion.

Thus will be made an end of sin, with all the woe and ruin which have resulted from it. *GC 544, 545*

A New Heaven and a New Earth

21 And I saw a new heaven and a new earth: for the first heaven and the first earth were passed away; and there was no more sea.   *Is. 66:22; 2 Pet. 3:13; Rev. 20:11*

21:1-5

21:1 No Sign Remains of Sin but One

The fire that consumes the wicked purifies the earth. Every trace of the curse is swept away. No eternally burning hell will keep before the ransomed the fearful consequences of sin.

One reminder alone remains: Our Redeemer will ever bear the marks of His crucifixion. Upon His wounded head, upon His side, His hands and feet, are the only traces of the cruel work that sin has wrought. *GC 674*

2 And I John saw the holy city, new Jerusalem, coming down from God out of heaven, prepared as a bride adorned for her husband.   *Heb. 11:10; Rev. 3:12; 21:10*

3 And I heard a great voice out of heaven saying, Behold, the tabernacle of God *is* with men, and he will dwell with them, and they shall be his people, and God himself shall be with them, *and be* their God.   *2 Cor. 6:16*

21:3 God With Us Forever

Our little world, under the curse of sin the one dark blot in His glorious creation, will be honored above all other worlds in the universe of God. Here, where the Son of God tabernacled in humanity; where the King of glory lived and suffered and died—here, when He shall make all things new, the tabernacle of God shall be with men, "and He will dwell with them, and they shall be His people, and God Himself shall be with them, and be their God." *DA 26*

4 And God shall wipe away all tears from their eyes; and there shall be no more death, neither sorrow, nor crying, neither shall there be any more pain: for the former things are passed away.   *Is. 25:8; 35:10; 1 Cor. 15:26*

5 And he that sat upon the throne said, Behold, I make all things new. And he said unto me, Write: for these words are true and faithful.   *2 Cor. 5:17; Rev. 4:9; 20:11*

> The Millennium See Revelation 20:7–10.

> The New Earth See Revelation 21:10–26.

6 And he said unto me, It is done. I am Alpha and Omega, the beginning and the end. I will give unto him that is athirst of the fountain of the water of life freely.   *John 4:10; Rev. 1:8; 22:13*

7 He that overcometh shall inherit all things; and I will be his God, and he shall be my son.   *Rev. 21:3*

8 But the fearful, and unbelieving, and the abominable, and murderers, and whore-

mongers, and sorcerers, and idolaters, and all liars, shall have their part in the lake which burneth with fire and brimstone: which is the second death.

The New Jerusalem

9 And there came unto me one of the seven angels which had the seven vials full of the seven last plagues, and talked with me, saying, Come ᵀhither, I will shew thee the bride, the Lamb's wife. Rev. 19:7 ◆ here

10 And he carried me away in the spirit to a great and high mountain, and shewed me that great city, the holy Jerusalem, descending out of heaven from God, Rev. 1:10; 17:3; 21:2

> ### 21:9, 10 Holy City Is Christ's Bride
>
> The Holy City, the New Jerusalem, which is the capital and representative of the kingdom, is called "the bride, the Lamb's wife." Said the angel to John: "Come hither, I will show thee the bride, the Lamb's wife." "He carried me away in the spirit," says the prophet, "and showed me that great city, the holy Jerusalem, descending out of heaven from God" (Revelation 21:9, 10). *GC 426, 427*

11 Having the glory of God: and her light *was* like unto a stone most precious, even like a jasper stone, clear as crystal; Rev. 4:6; 22:5

12 And had a wall great and high, *and* had twelve gates, and at the gates twelve angels, and names written thereon, which are *the names* of the twelve tribes of the children of Israel: Ezek. 48:31-34; Rev. 21:25

13 On the east three gates; on the north three gates; on the south three gates; and on the west three gates.

14 And the wall of the city had twelve foundations, and in them the names of the twelve apostles of the Lamb. Heb. 11:10

15 And he that talked with me had a golden reed to measure the city, and the gates thereof, and the wall thereof.

16 And the city lieth foursquare, and the length is as large as the breadth: and he measured the city with the reed, twelve thousand furlongs. The length and the breadth and the height of it are equal.

17 And he measured the wall thereof, an hundred *and* forty *and* four cubits, *according to* the measure of a man, that is, of the angel.

18 And the building of the wall of it was *of* jasper: and the city *was* pure gold, like unto clear glass. Rev. 21:11, 21

19 And the foundations of the wall of the city *were* garnished with all manner of precious stones. The first foundation *was* jasper; the second, sapphire; the third, a chalcedony; the fourth, an emerald; Is. 54:11-12

20 The fifth, sardonyx; the sixth, sardius; the seventh, chrysolite; the eighth, beryl; the ninth, a topaz; the tenth, a ᵀchrysoprasus; the eleventh, a ᵀjacinth; the twelfth, an amethyst. *precious greenish stone* ◆ *precious orange-colored stone*

21 And the twelve gates *were* twelve pearls; every several gate was of one pearl: and the street of the city *was* pure gold, as it were transparent glass. Rev. 17:4; 21:18; 22:2

22 And I saw no temple therein: for the Lord God Almighty and the Lamb are the temple of it. John 4:23

> ### 21:22 Face to Face With Jesus
>
> "I saw no temple therein: for the Lord God Almighty and the Lamb are the temple of it" (Revelation 21:22). The people of God are privileged to hold open communion with the Father and the Son. "Now we see through a glass, darkly" (1 Corinthians 13:12). We behold the image of God reflected, as in a mirror, in the works of nature and in His dealings with men; but then we shall see Him face to face, without a dimming veil between. *GC 676, 677*

23 And the city had no need of the sun, neither of the moon, to shine in it: for the glory of God did lighten it, and the Lamb *is* the light thereof. Is. 60:19-20; Rev. 21:11; 22:5

24 And the nations of them which are saved shall walk in the light of it: and the kings of

---

No More Sin—No More Death

Revelation 21:4

The day is coming when the battle will have been fought, the victory won. The will of God is to be done on earth as it is done in heaven. The nations of the saved will know no other law than the law of heaven. All will be a happy, united family, clothed with the garments of praise and thanksgiving—the robe of Christ's righteousness. All nature, in its surpassing loveliness, will offer to God a tribute of praise and adoration. The world will be bathed in the light of heaven. The light of the moon will be as the light of the sun, and the light of the sun will be sevenfold greater than it is now. The years will move on in gladness. Over the scene the morning stars will sing together, the sons of God will shout for joy, while God and Christ will unite in proclaiming, "There shall be no more sin, neither shall there be any more death." *MH 506*

the earth do bring their glory and honour into it.   Rev. 22:2

25 And the gates of it shall not be shut at all by day: for there shall be no night there.

26 And they shall bring the glory and honour of the nations into it.

The New Earth See Revelation 22:1–5.

27 And there shall in no wise enter into it any thing that defileth, neither *whatsoever* worketh abomination, or *maketh* a lie: but they which are written in the Lamb's book of life.

21:27 Only the Pure Enter the City

Into the city of God there will enter nothing that defiles. All who are to be dwellers there will here have become pure in heart. In one who is learning of Jesus, there will be manifest a growing distaste for careless manners, unseemly language, and coarse thought. When Christ abides in the heart, there will be purity and refinement of thought and manner. *MB 24, 25*

Jesus Is Coming Soon

22 And he shewed me a pure river of water of life, clear as crystal, proceeding out of the throne of God and of the Lamb.

2 In the midst of the street of it, and on either side of the river, *was there* the tree of life, which bare twelve *manner of* fruits, *and* yielded her fruit every month: and the leaves of the tree *were* for the healing of the nations.   Gen. 2:9; Rev. 2:7; 21:21

3 And there shall be no more curse: but the throne of God and of the Lamb shall be in it; and his servants shall serve him: Zech. 14:11

22:1–5

22:3 No More Curse—Only Peace

The earth promised to the meek will not be like this, darkened with the shadow of death and the curse. . . .

There is no disappointment, no sorrow, no sin, no one who shall say, I am sick; there are no burial trains, no mourning, no death, no partings, no broken hearts; but Jesus is there, peace is there. *MB 17*

---

4 And they shall see his face; and his name *shall be* in their foreheads.   Matt. 5:8; 1 Cor. 13:12

5 And there shall be no night there; and they need no candle, neither light of the sun; for the Lord God giveth them light: and they shall reign for ever and ever.   Dan. 7:18, 27; Rom. 5:17

The New Earth See Revelation 22:20.

22:5 No Night—Perpetual Day

In the City of God "there shall be no night." None will need or desire repose. There will be no weariness in doing the will of God and offering praise to His name. We shall ever feel the freshness of the morning and shall ever be far from its close. . . . The light of the sun will be superseded by a radiance which is not painfully dazzling, yet which immeasurably surpasses the brightness of our noontide. . . . The redeemed walk in the sunless glory of perpetual day. *GC 676*

---

6 And he said unto me, These sayings *are* faithful and true: and the Lord God of the holy prophets sent his angel to shew unto his servants the things which must shortly be done.   Rev. 1:1; 19:9; 21:5

7 Behold, I come quickly: blessed *is* he that keepeth the sayings of the prophecy of this book.   Rev. 1:3; 3:11; 22:12

8 And I John saw these things, and heard *them*. And when I had heard and seen, I fell down to worship before the feet of the angel which shewed me these things.   Rev. 1:1; 19:10

9 Then saith he unto me, See *thou do it* not: for I am thy fellowservant, and of thy brethren the prophets, and of them which keep the sayings of this book: worship God.   Rev. 19:10

10 And he saith unto me, Seal not the sayings of the prophecy of this book: for the time is at hand.   Dan. 8:26; Rev. 1:3; 10:4

11 He that is unjust, let him be unjust still: and he which is filthy, let him be filthy still: and he that is righteous, let him be righteous still: and he that is holy, let him be holy still.   Ezek. 3:27; Dan. 12:10; 2 Tim. 3:13

12 And, behold, I come quickly; and my reward *is* with me, to give every man according as his work shall be.   Is. 40:10; 62:11; Rev. 22:7

God Does Not Change for He Is God

Revelation 22:18, 19

Such are the warnings which God has given to guard men against changing in any manner that which He has revealed or commanded. These solemn denunciations apply to all who by their influence lead men to regard lightly the law of God. They should cause those to fear and tremble who flippantly declare it a matter of little consequence whether we obey God's law or not. All who exalt their own opinions above divine revelation, all who would change the plain meaning of Scripture to suit their own convenience, or for the sake of conforming to the world, are taking upon themselves a fearful responsibility. The written word, the law of God, will measure the character of every man and condemn all whom this unerring test shall declare wanting. *GC 268*

22:11, 12 When the Final Decision Is Pronounced

Before the Flood, after Noah entered the ark, God shut him in and shut the ungodly out; but for seven days the people, knowing not that their doom was fixed, continued their careless, pleasure-loving life and mocked the warnings of impending judgment. "So," says the Saviour, "shall also the coming of the Son of man be" (Matthew 24:39). Silently, unnoticed as the midnight thief, will come the decisive hour which marks the fixing of every man's destiny, the final withdrawal of mercy's offer to guilty men. *GC 491*

13 I am Alpha and Omega, the beginning and the end, the first and the last.   Rev. 1:8, 17; 21:6
14 Blessed *are* they that do his commandments, that they may have right to the tree of life, and may enter in through the gates into the city.   John 14:15; Rev. 21:27; 22:2

22:14 Free Access Again to the Tree of Life

Then they that have kept God's commandments shall breathe in immortal vigor beneath the tree of life; and through unending ages the inhabitants of sinless worlds shall behold, in that garden of delight, a sample of the perfect work of God's creation, untouched by the curse of sin—a sample of what the whole earth would have become, had man but fulfilled the Creator's glorious plan. *PP 62*

15 For without *are* dogs, and sorcerers, and whoremongers, and murderers, and idolaters, and whosoever loveth and maketh a lie.
16 I Jesus have sent mine angel to testify unto you these things in the churches. I am

the root and the offspring of David, *and* the bright and morning star.   Matt. 2:2; Rev. 1:1; 5:5
17 And the Spirit and the bride say, Come. And let him that heareth say, Come. And let him that is athirst come. And whosoever will, let him take the water of life freely.   Is. 2:5; Rev. 21:2, 6

22:17 Come, You Who Thirst

The cry of Christ to the thirsty soul is still going forth, and it appeals to us with even greater power than to those who heard it in the temple on that last day of the feast. The fountain is open for all. The weary and exhausted ones are offered the refreshing draught of eternal life. Jesus is still crying, "If any man thirst, let him come unto Me, and drink." *DA 454*

18 For I testify unto every man that heareth the words of the prophecy of this book, If any man shall add unto these things, God shall add unto him the plagues that are written in this book: Deut. 4:2; 12:32; Prov. 30:6
19 And if any man shall take away from the words of the book of this prophecy, God shall take away his part out of the book of life, and out of the holy city, and *from* the things which are written in this book.   Rev. 13:8; 21:2; 22:2
20 He which testifieth these things saith, Surely I come quickly. Amen. Even so, come, Lord Jesus.   Rev. 22:7

The New Earth

21 The grace of our Lord Jesus Christ *be* with you all. Amen.   Rom. 16:20

the root and the offspring of David, and the bright and morning star.

17 And the Spirit and the bride say, Come. And let him that heareth say, Come. And let him that is athirst come. And whosoever will, let him take the water of life freely.

16 For I testify unto every man that heareth the words of the prophecy of this book, If any man shall add unto these things, God shall add unto him the plagues that are written in this book:

19 And if any man shall take away from the words of the book of this prophecy, God shall take away his part out of the book of life, and out of the holy city, and from the things which are written in this book.

20 He which testifieth these things saith, Surely I come quickly. Amen. Even so, come, Lord Jesus.

21 The grace of our Lord Jesus Christ be with you all. Amen.

13 I am Alpha and Omega, the beginning and the end, the first and the last.

14 Blessed are they that do his commandments, that they may have right to the tree of life, and may enter in through the gates into the city.

16 For without are dogs, and sorcerers, and whoremongers, and murderers, and idolaters, and whosoever loveth and maketh a lie.

16 I Jesus have sent mine angel to testify unto you these things in the churches.

ADDITIONAL
STUDY HELPS

Presented Here in Canonical Order

OLD TESTAMENT SCRIPTURE	PROMISE	NEW TESTAMENT FULFILLMENT
And I will put enmity between thee and the woman, and between thy seed and her seed; it shall bruise thy head, and thou shalt bruise his heel. *Genesis 3:15*	**Seed of the woman will become the Savior**	But when the fulness of the time was come, God sent forth his Son, made of a woman, made under the law, to redeem them that were under the law, that we might receive the adoption of sons. *Galatians 4:4–5*
And I will bless them that bless thee, and curse him that curseth thee: and in thee shall all families of the earth be blessed. *Genesis 12:3*	**Abraham's descendant**	The book of the generation of Jesus Christ, the son of David, the son of Abraham. *Matthew 1:1*
And God said, Sarah thy wife shall bear thee a son indeed; and thou shalt call his name Isaac: and I will establish my covenant with him for an everlasting covenant, and with his seed after him. *Genesis 17:19*	**Isaac's descendant**	Which was the son of Jacob, which was the son of Isaac, which was the son of Abraham, which was the son of Thara, which was the son of Nachor. *Luke 3:34*
The sceptre shall not depart from Judah, nor a lawgiver from between his feet, until Shiloh come; and unto him shall the gathering of the people be. *Genesis 49:10*	**From Judah's tribe**	Which was the son of Aminadab, which was the son of Aram, which was the son of Esrom, which was the son of Phares, which was the son of Juda. *Luke 3:33*
The LORD thy God will raise up unto thee a Prophet from the midst of thee, of thy brethren, like unto me; unto him ye shall hearken. *Deuteronomy 18:15*	**Prophet**	And he shall send Jesus Christ, which before was preached unto you: Whom the heaven must receive until the times of restitution of all things, which God hath spoken by the mouth of all his holy prophets since the world began. For Moses truly said unto the fathers, A prophet shall the Lord your God raise up unto you of your brethren, like unto me; him shall ye hear in all things whatsoever he shall say unto you. *Acts 3:20–22*
I shall see him, but not now: I shall behold him, but not nigh: there shall come a Star out of Jacob, and a Sceptre shall rise out of Israel, and shall smite the corners of Moab, and destroy all the children of Sheth. *Numbers 24:17*	**Jacob's descendant**	Abraham begat Isaac; and Isaac begat Jacob; and Jacob begat Judas and his brethren. *Matthew 1:2*
I will declare the decree: the LORD hath said unto me, Thou art my Son; this day have I begotten thee. *Psalm 2:7*	**Called the Son of God**	And lo a voice from heaven, saying, This is my beloved Son, in whom I am well pleased. *Matthew 3:17* (see also *Acts 13:22–23*)

OLD TESTAMENT SCRIPTURE	PROMISE	NEW TESTAMENT FULFILLMENT
Out of the mouth of babes and sucklings hast thou ordained strength because of thine enemies, that thou mightest still the enemy and the avenger. *Psalm 8:2*	Children drawn to him	And when the chief priests and scribes saw the wonderful things that he did, and the children crying in the temple, and saying, Hosanna to the son of David; they were sore displeased, And said unto him, Hearest thou what these say? And Jesus saith unto them, Yea; have ye never read, Out of the mouth of babes and sucklings thou hast perfected praise? *Matthew 21:15–16*
For thou wilt not leave my soul in hell; neither wilt thou suffer thine Holy One to see corruption. *Psalm 16:10*	Resurrected	And he saith unto them, Be not affrighted: Ye seek Jesus of Nazareth, which was crucified: he is risen; he is not here: behold the place where they laid him. But go your way, tell his disciples and Peter that he goeth before you into Galilee: there shall ye see him, as he said unto you. *Mark 16:6–7*
My God, my God, why hast thou forsaken me? why art thou so far from helping me, and from the words of my roaring? *Psalm 22:1*	Forsaken by God	And about the ninth hour Jesus cried with a loud voice, saying, Eli, Eli, lama sabachthani? that is to say, My God, my God, why hast thou forsaken me? *Matthew 27:46*
All they that see me laugh me to scorn: they shoot out the lip, they shake the head, saying, He trusted on the LORD that he would deliver him: let him deliver him, seeing he delighted in him. *Psalm 22:7–8*	Mocked	And the people stood beholding. And the rulers also with them derided him, saying, He saved others; let him save himself, if he be Christ, the chosen of God. *Luke 23:35*
I may tell all my bones: they look and stare upon me. They part my garments among them, and cast lots upon my vesture. *Psalm 22:17–18*	Soldiers gambled for his garments	And they crucified him, and parted his garments, casting lots: that it might be fulfilled which was spoken by the prophet, They parted my garments among them, and upon my vesture did they cast lots. And sitting down they watched him there. *Matthew 27:35–36*
He keepeth all his bones: not one of them is broken. *Psalm 34:20*	No broken bones	Then came the soldiers, and brake the legs of the first, and of the other which was crucified with him. But when they came to Jesus, and saw that he was dead already, they brake not his legs. . . . For these things were done, that the scripture should be fulfilled, A bone of him shall not be broken. *John 19:32–33, 36*
False witnesses did rise up; they laid to my charge things that I knew not. *Psalm 35:11*	Falsely accused	And there arose certain, and bare false witness against him, saying, We heard him say, I will destroy this temple that is made with hands, and within three days I will build another made without hands. *Mark 14:57–58*
Let not them that are mine enemies wrongfully rejoice over me: neither let them wink with the eye that hate me without a cause. *Psalm 35:19*	Hated	If I had not done among them the works which none other man did, they had not had sin: but now have they both seen and hated both me and my Father. But this cometh to pass, that the word might be fulfilled that is written in their law, They hated me without a cause. *John 15:24–25*

OLD TESTAMENT SCRIPTURE	PROMISE	NEW TESTAMENT FULFILLMENT
Yea, mine own familiar friend, in whom I trusted, which did eat of my bread, hath lifted up his heel against me. *Psalm 41:9*	**Betrayed by a friend**	And while he yet spake, behold a multitude, and he that was called Judas, one of the twelve, went before them, and drew near unto Jesus to kiss him. But Jesus said unto him, Judas, betrayest thou the Son of man with a kiss? *Luke 22:47–48*
Thy throne, O God, is for ever and ever: the sceptre of thy kingdom is a right sceptre. Thou lovest righteousness, and hatest wickedness: therefore God, thy God, hath anointed thee with the oil of gladness above thy fellows. *Psalm 45:6–7* Of old hast thou laid the foundation of the earth: and the heavens are the work of thy hands. They shall perish, but thou shalt endure: yea, all of them shall wax old like a garment; as a vesture shalt thou change them, and they shall be changed: But thou art the same, and thy years shall have no end. *Psalm 102:25–27*	**Anointed and eternal**	But unto the Son he saith, Thy throne, O God, is for ever and ever: a sceptre of righteousness is the sceptre of thy kingdom. Thou hast loved righteousness, and hated iniquity; therefore God, even thy God, hath anointed thee with the oil of gladness above thy fellows. And, Thou, Lord, in the beginning hast laid the foundation of the earth; and the heavens are the works of thine hands: They shall perish; but thou remainest; and they all shall wax old as doth a garment; And as a vesture shalt thou fold them up, and they shall be changed: but thou art the same, and thy years shall not fail. *Hebrews 1:8–12*
Thou hast ascended on high, thou hast led captivity captive: thou hast received gifts for men; yea, for the rebellious also, that the LORD God might dwell among them. *Psalm 68:18*	**Ascending to God's right hand**	So then after the Lord had spoken unto them, he was received up into heaven, and sat on the right hand of God. *Mark 16:19* (see also *1 Corinthians 15:4; Ephesians 4:8*)
For the zeal of thine house hath eaten me up; and the reproaches of them that reproached thee are fallen upon me. *Psalm 69:9*	**Zeal for God's house leads to reproach**	And his disciples remembered that it was written, The zeal of thine house hath eaten me up. *John 2:17* (see also *Romans 15:3*)
I will open my mouth in a parable: I will utter dark sayings of old: Which we have heard and known, and our fathers have told us. We will not hide them from their children, shewing to the generation to come the praises of the LORD, and his strength, and his wonderful works that he hath done. *Psalm 78:2–4*	**Taught in parables**	All these things spake Jesus unto the multitude in parables; and without a parable spake he not unto them: That it might be fulfilled which was spoken by the prophet, saying, I will open my mouth in parables; I will utter things which have been kept secret from the foundation of the world. *Matthew 13:34–35*
For my love they are my adversaries: but I give myself unto prayer. *Psalm 109:4*	**Prays for enemies**	Then said Jesus, Father, forgive them; for they know not what they do. *Luke 23:34*
The LORD hath sworn, and will not repent, Thou art a priest for ever after the order of Melchizedek. *Psalm 110:4*	**Priest like Melchizedek**	As he saith also in another place, Thou art a priest for ever after the order of Melchisedec. *Hebrews 5:6*

OLD TESTAMENT SCRIPTURE	PROMISE	NEW TESTAMENT FULFILLMENT
Therefore the Lord himself shall give you a sign; Behold, a virgin shall conceive, and bear a son, and shall call his name Immanuel. *Isaiah 7:14*	Born of a virgin	And in the sixth month the angel Gabriel was sent from God unto a city of Galilee, named Nazareth, to a virgin espoused to a man whose name was Joseph, of the house of David; and the virgin's name was Mary. . . . And the angel said unto her, Fear not, Mary: for thou hast found favour with God. And, behold, thou shalt conceive in thy womb, and bring forth a son, and shalt call his name JESUS. *Luke 1:26–27, 30–31* (see also *Matthew 1:22–23; Luke 2:7*)
Nevertheless the dimness shall not be such as was in her vexation, when at the first he lightly afflicted the land of Zebulun and the land of Naphtali, and afterward did more grievously afflict her by the way of the sea, beyond Jordan, in Galilee of the nations. The people that walked in darkness have seen a great light: they that dwell in the land of the shadow of death, upon them hath the light shined. *Isaiah 9:1–2*	Ministers in Galilee	Now when Jesus had heard that John was cast into prison, he departed into Galilee; and leaving Nazareth, he came and dwelt in Capernaum, which is upon the sea coast, in the borders of Zabulon and Nephthalim: that it might be fulfilled which was spoken by Esaias the prophet, saying, The land of Zabulon, and the land of Nephthalim, by the way of the sea, beyond Jordan, Galilee of the Gentiles; the people which sat in darkness saw great light; and to them which sat in the region and shadow of death light is sprung up. *Matthew 4:12–16*
For unto us a child is born, unto us a son is given: and the government shall be upon his shoulder: and his name shall be called Wonderful, Counsellor, The mighty God, The everlasting Father, The Prince of Peace. Of the increase of his government and peace there shall be no end, upon the throne of David, and upon his kingdom, to order it, and to establish it with judgment and with justice from henceforth even for ever. The zeal of the LORD of hosts will perform this. *Isaiah 9:6–7*	A royal son and heir to David's throne	He shall be great, and shall be called the Son of the Highest: and the Lord God shall give unto him the throne of his father David: And he shall reign over the house of Jacob for ever; and of his kingdom there shall be no end. *Luke 1:32–33* (see also *Matthew 1:1; 3:17; Ephesians 2:14–18*)
And there shall come forth a rod out of the stem of Jesse, and a Branch shall grow out of his roots. . . . And in that day there shall be a root of Jesse, which shall stand for an ensign of the people; to it shall the Gentiles seek: and his rest shall be glorious. *Isaiah 11:1, 10*	Root of Jesse	And Jesus himself began to be about thirty years of age, being (as was supposed) the son of Joseph, which was the son of Heli . . . which was the son of Jesse, which was the son of Obed, which was the son of Booz, which was the son of Salmon, which was the son of Naasson. *Luke 3:23, 32*
And the spirit of the LORD shall rest upon him, the spirit of wisdom and understanding, the spirit of counsel and might, the spirit of knowledge and of the fear of the LORD. *Isaiah 11:2*	Empowered by the Holy Spirit	And the Holy Ghost descended in a bodily shape like a dove upon him, and a voice came from heaven, which said, Thou art my beloved Son; in thee I am well pleased. *Luke 3:22*

OLD TESTAMENT SCRIPTURE	PROMISE	NEW TESTAMENT FULFILLMENT
Therefore thus saith the Lord GOD, Behold, I lay in Zion for a foundation a stone, a tried stone, a precious corner stone, a sure foundation: he that believeth shall not make haste. *Isaiah 28:16*	Chief Cornerstone	Wherefore also it is contained in the scripture, Behold, I lay in Sion a chief corner stone, elect, precious: and he that believeth on him shall not be confounded. *1 Peter 2:6*
The voice of him that crieth in the wilderness, Prepare ye the way of the LORD, make straight in the desert a highway for our God. Every valley shall be exalted, and every mountain and hill shall be made low: and the crooked shall be made straight, and the rough places plain: And the glory of the LORD shall be revealed, and all flesh shall see it together: for the mouth of the LORD hath spoken it. *Isaiah 40:3–5*	The way prepared	In those days came John the Baptist, preaching in the wilderness of Judaea, And saying, Repent ye: for the kingdom of heaven is at hand. For this is he that was spoken of by the prophet Esaias, saying, The voice of one crying in the wilderness, Prepare ye the way of the Lord, make his paths straight. *Matthew 3:1–3*
Behold my servant, whom I uphold; mine elect, in whom my soul delighteth; I have put my spirit upon him: he shall bring forth judgment to the Gentiles. He shall not cry, nor lift up, nor cause his voice to be heard in the street. A bruised reed shall he not break, and the smoking flax shall he not quench: he shall bring forth judgment unto truth. He shall not fail nor be discouraged, till he have set judgment in the earth: and the isles shall wait for his law. *Isaiah 42:1–4*	God's servant	But when Jesus knew it, he withdrew himself from thence: and great multitudes followed him, and he healed them all; and charged them that they should not make him known: That it might be fulfilled which was spoken by Esaias the prophet, saying, Behold my servant, whom I have chosen; my beloved, in whom my soul is well pleased: I will put my spirit upon him, and he shall shew judgment to the Gentiles. He shall not strive, nor cry; neither shall any man hear his voice in the streets. A bruised reed shall he not break, and smoking flax shall he not quench, till he send forth judgment unto victory. And in his name shall the Gentiles trust. *Matthew 12:15–21*
I the LORD have called thee in righteousness, and will hold thine hand, and will keep thee, and give thee for a covenant of the people, for a light of the Gentiles. *Isaiah 42:6*	Initiating a new covenant	Which thou hast prepared before the face of all people; a light to lighten the Gentiles, and the glory of thy people Israel. *Luke 2:31–32* (see also *Hebrews 8:6–13; 9:15*)
I gave my back to the smiters, and my cheeks to them that plucked off the hair: I hid not my face from shame and spitting. *Isaiah 50:6* As many were astonied at thee; his visage was so marred more than any man, and his form more than the sons of men. *Isaiah 52:14*	Abused	Then did they spit in his face, and buffeted him; and others smote him with the palms of their hands. *Matthew 26:67* And they spit upon him, and took the reed, and smote him on the head. *Matthew 27:30*

OLD TESTAMENT SCRIPTURE	PROMISE	NEW TESTAMENT FULFILLMENT
Who hath believed our report? and to whom is the arm of the LORD revealed? For he shall grow up before him as a tender plant, and as a root out of a dry ground: he hath no form nor comeliness; and when we shall see him, there is no beauty that we should desire him. He is despised and rejected of men; a man of sorrows, and acquainted with grief: and we hid as it were our faces from him; he was despised, and we esteemed him not. *Isaiah 53:1–3*	Facing unbelief and rejection	And they cried out all at once, saying, Away with this man, and release unto us Barabbas. *Luke 23:18* He came unto his own, and his own received him not. *John 1:11* (see also *John 7:5; 12:37–38*)
Surely he hath borne our griefs, and carried our sorrows: yet we did esteem him stricken, smitten of God, and afflicted. But he was wounded for our transgressions, he was bruised for our iniquities: the chastisement of our peace was upon him; and with his stripes we are healed. *Isaiah 53:4–5*	Sacrifice	For when we were yet without strength, in due time Christ died for the ungodly. . . . But God commendeth his love toward us, in that, while we were yet sinners, Christ died for us. *Romans 5:6, 8*
He was oppressed, and he was afflicted, yet he opened not his mouth: he is brought as a lamb to the slaughter, and as a sheep before her shearers is dumb, so he openeth not his mouth. *Isaiah 53:7*	Silent when accused	And when he was accused of the chief priests and elders, he answered nothing. Then said Pilate unto him, Hearest thou not how many things they witness against thee? And he answered him to never a word; insomuch that the governor marvelled greatly. *Matthew 27:12–14* (see also *Mark 15:4–5; John 1:29; 1 Peter 1:18–19*)
And he made his grave with the wicked, and with the rich in his death; because he had done no violence, neither was any deceit in his mouth. *Isaiah 53:9*	Buried in a rich man's tomb	When the even was come, there came a rich man of Arimathaea, named Joseph, who also himself was Jesus' disciple: He went to Pilate, and begged the body of Jesus. Then Pilate commanded the body to be delivered. And when Joseph had taken the body, he wrapped it in a clean linen cloth, and laid it in his own new tomb, which he had hewn out in the rock: and he rolled a great stone to the door of the sepulchre, and departed. *Matthew 27:57–60*
Therefore will I divide him a portion with the great, and he shall divide the spoil with the strong; because he hath poured out his soul unto death: and he was numbered with the transgressors; and he bare the sin of many, and made intercession for the transgressors. *Isaiah 53:12*	Crucified with criminals	And with him they crucify two thieves; the one on his right hand, and the other on his left. And the scripture was fulfilled, which saith, And he was numbered with the transgressors. *Mark 15:27–28*

OLD TESTAMENT SCRIPTURE	PROMISE	NEW TESTAMENT FULFILLMENT
The Spirit of the Lord GOD is upon me; because the LORD hath anointed me to preach good tidings unto the meek; he hath sent me to bind up the brokenhearted, to proclaim liberty to the captives, and the opening of the prison to them that are bound; to proclaim the acceptable year of the LORD, and the day of vengeance of our God; to comfort all that mourn. *Isaiah 61:1–2*	**Helping the broken-hearted**	And there was delivered unto him the book of the prophet Esaias. And when he had opened the book, he found the place where it was written, The Spirit of the Lord is upon me, because he hath anointed me to preach the gospel to the poor; he hath sent me to heal the brokenhearted, to preach deliverance to the captives, and recovering of sight to the blind, to set at liberty them that are bruised, To preach the acceptable year of the Lord. . . . And he began to say unto them, This day is this scripture fulfilled in your ears. *Luke 4:17–19, 21*
Thus saith the LORD; A voice was heard in Ramah, lamentation, and bitter weeping; Rahel weeping for her children refused to be comforted for her children, because they were not. *Jeremiah 31:15*	**Children slaughtered**	Then Herod, when he saw that he was mocked of the wise men, was exceeding wroth, and sent forth, and slew all the children that were in Bethlehem, and in all the coasts thereof, from two years old and under, according to the time which he had diligently inquired of the wise men. Then was fulfilled that which was spoken by Jeremiah the prophet, saying, In Rama was there a voice heard, lamentation, and weeping, and great mourning, Rachel weeping for her children, and would not be comforted, because they are not. *Matthew 2:16–18*
Know therefore and understand, that from the going forth of the commandment to restore and to build Jerusalem unto the Messiah the Prince shall be seven weeks, and threescore and two weeks: the street shall be built again, and the wall, even in troublous times. *Daniel 9:25*	**Era of his birth**	And it came to pass in those days, that there went out a decree from Caesar Augustus that all the world should be taxed. (And this taxing was first made when Cyrenius was governor of Syria.) *Luke 2:1–2*
When Israel was a child, then I loved him, and called my son out of Egypt. *Hosea 11:1*	**Flight to Egypt**	When he arose, he took the young child and his mother by night, and departed into Egypt: And was there until the death of Herod: that it might be fulfilled which was spoken of the Lord by the prophet, saying, Out of Egypt have I called my son. *Matthew 2:14–15*
But thou, Bethlehem Ephratah, though thou be little among the thousands of Judah, yet out of thee shall he come forth unto me that is to be ruler in Israel; whose goings forth have been from of old, from everlasting. *Micah 5:2*	**Born in Bethlehem**	And Joseph also went up from Galilee, out of the city of Nazareth, into Judaea, unto the city of David, which is called Bethlehem; (because he was of the house and lineage of David:) to be taxed with Mary his espoused wife, being great with child. . . . And she brought forth her firstborn son, and wrapped him in swaddling clothes, and laid him in a manger; because there was no room for them in the inn. *Luke 2:4–5, 7*

OLD TESTAMENT SCRIPTURE	PROMISE	NEW TESTAMENT FULFILLMENT
Rejoice greatly, O daughter of Zion; shout, O daughter of Jerusalem: behold, thy King cometh unto thee: he is just, and having salvation; lowly, and riding upon an ass, and upon a colt the foal of an ass. *Zechariah 9:9*	Riding on a donkey	All this was done, that it might be fulfilled which was spoken by the prophet, saying, Tell ye the daughter of Sion, Behold, thy King cometh unto thee, meek, and sitting upon an ass, and a colt the foal of an ass. *Matthew 21:4–5*
And I said unto them, If ye think good, give me my price; and if not, forbear. So they weighed for my price thirty pieces of silver. *Zechariah 11:12*	Betrayed for thirty pieces of silver	Then one of the twelve, called Judas Iscariot, went unto the chief priests, and said unto them, What will ye give me, and I will deliver him unto you? And they covenanted with him for thirty pieces of silver. *Matthew 26:14–15*
And I will pour upon the house of David, and upon the inhabitants of Jerusalem, the spirit of grace and of supplications: and they shall look upon me whom they have pierced, and they shall mourn for him, as one mourneth for his only son, and shall be in bitterness for him, as one that is in bitterness for his firstborn. *Zechariah 12:10*	Pierced in the side	But one of the soldiers with a spear pierced his side, and forthwith came there out blood and water. *John 19:34*
Behold, I will send my messenger, and he shall prepare the way before me: and the Lord, whom ye seek, shall suddenly come to his temple, even the messenger of the covenant, whom ye delight in: behold, he shall come, saith the LORD of hosts. *Malachi 3:1*	Forerunner	And when the messengers of John were departed, he began to speak unto the people concerning John, What went ye out into the wilderness for to see? A reed shaken with the wind? . . . This is he, of whom it is written, Behold, I send my messenger before thy face, which shall prepare thy way before thee. *Luke 7:24, 27*
Behold, I will send you Elijah the prophet before the coming of the great and dreadful day of the LORD: And he shall turn the heart of the fathers to the children, and the heart of the children to their fathers, lest I come and smite the earth with a curse. *Malachi 4:5–6*	One like Elijah precedes him	For all the prophets and the law prophesied until John. And if ye will receive it, this is Elias, which was for to come. *Matthew 11:13–14*

Prayers of the Bible

PERSON	PERSON PRAYED FOR/NEED	SCRIPTURE	PERSON	PERSON PRAYED FOR/NEED	SCRIPTURE
Abijah's army	Victory	2 Chronicles 13:14	Jacob	Blessing	Genesis 32:24–30
Abraham	A son	Genesis 15:1–6	Jacob	Deliverance from Esau	Genesis 32:9–12
Abraham	Ishmael	Genesis 17:18–21	Jehoahaz	Victory	2 Kings 13:1–5
Abraham	God to spare Sodom and especially Lot	Genesis 18:20–32	Jehoshaphat	Protection	2 Chronicles 20:5–12, 27
Abraham	Abimelech	Genesis 20:17	Jehoshaphat	Victory	2 Chronicles 18:31
Abraham's servant	Guidance; wife for Isaac	Genesis 24:12–52	Jeremiah	Judah	Jeremiah 42:1–6
Asa	Victory	2 Chronicles 14:11	Jeremiah	Mercy	Jeremiah 14:7–10
Cain	Mercy	Genesis 4:13–15	Jesus	Church	John 17:1–26
Centurion	Sick servant	Matthew 8:5–13	Jesus	Deliverance	Matthew 26:39, 42, 44; 27:46
Christians	Peter	Acts 12:5–12	Jesus	Father's glory	John 12:28
Christians	Kings and others in authority	1 Timothy 2:1–2	Jesus	Forgiveness of enemies	Luke 23:34
Corinthian believers	Paul	2 Corinthians 1:9–11	Jesus	In submission	Luke 23:46
Cornelius	Understanding	Acts 10:1–33	Jesus	Lazarus and those listening	John 11:41–42
Criminal	Salvation	Luke 23:42–43	Jesus	Lord's Prayer	Matthew 6:9–13
Daniel	The Jews	Daniel 9:3–19	Jesus	Praise	Matthew 11:25–26
Daniel	Knowledge	Daniel 2:17–23	Jews	Safe journey	Ezra 8: 21, 23
David	Blessing	2 Samuel 7:18–29	Jonah	Deliverance	Jonah 2:1–10
David	God's help	1 Samuel 23:10–13	Joshua	Help; mercy	Joshua 7:6–9
David	Grace	Psalm 25:16	Leper	Cleansing	Matthew 8:2, 3
David	Guidance	2 Samuel 2:1	Manasseh	Deliverance	2 Chronicles 33:12–13
David	Justice	Psalm 9:17–20	Manoah	Guidance	Judges 13:8–15
Disciples	Boldness	Acts 4:24–31	Moses	Israel	Exodus 32:31–35
Elijah	Drought and rain	James 5:17–18	Moses	Miriam	Numbers 12:11–14
Elijah	Widow's son to be raised	1 Kings 17:20–23	Moses	Pharaoh	Exodus 8:9–13
Elijah	God to defeat Baal	1 Kings 18:36–38	Moses	See Promised Land	Deuteronomy 3:23–25
Elijah	Death	1 Kings 19:4	Moses	Successor	Numbers 27:15–17
Elisha	Blindness; sight	2 Kings 6:17–23	Moses	Water	Exodus 15:24–25
Ezekiel	Undefilement	Ezekiel 4:12–15	Paul	Ephesians	Ephesians 3:14–21
Ezra	Sins of the returning exiles	Ezra 9:6–15	Paul	Grace	2 Corinthians 12:8–9
Gideon	Confirmation of call	Judges 6:36–40	Paul	Healing for Publius's father	Acts 28:8
Habakkuk	Deliverance	Habakkuk 3:1–19	People of Judah	Covenant	2 Chronicles 15:12–15
Habakkuk	Justice	Habakkuk 1:1–4	Peter	Raising of Dorcas	Acts 9:40
Hagar	Consolation	Genesis 21:14–20	Priests	Blessing	2 Chronicles 30:27
Hannah	A son	1 Samuel 1:10–17	Rebekah	Understanding	Genesis 25:22–23
Hezekiah	Deliverance	2 Kings 19:15–19	Reubenites	Victory	1 Chronicles 5:18–20
Hezekiah	Healing from illness	2 Kings 20:1–11	Samson	Water	Judges 15:18–19
Holy Spirit	Believers	Romans 8:26–27	Samson	Strength	Judges 16:29–30
Isaac	Children	Genesis 25:21, 24–26	Samuel	Israel	1 Samuel 7:5–12
			Solomon	Wisdom	1 Kings 3:6–14
Israelites	Deliverance	Exodus 2:23–25	Tax collector	Mercy	Luke 18:13
Jabez	Prosperity	1 Chronicles 4:10	Zechariah	A son	Luke 1:13

The Parables of Jesus Christ

Parable	Matthew	Mark	Luke	Christ's Object Lessons
1. Lamp Under a Basket	5:14–16	4:21, 22	8:16–17; 11:33–36	
2. Wise Man Builds on a Rock	7:24–27		6:47–49	
3. New Cloth on an Old Garment	9:16	2:21	5:36	
4. New Wine in Old Wineskins	9:17	2:22	5:37, 38	
5. The Sower	13:3–23	4:2–20	8:4–15	33–61
6. Tares (Weeds)	13:24–30			70–75
7. Mustard Seed	13:13–32	4:30–32	13:18, 19	
8. Leaven	13:33		13:20, 21	95–102
9. Hidden Treasure	13:44			103–114
10. Pearl of Great Price	13:45, 46			115–121
11. The Dragnet	13:47–50			122, 123
12. Lost Sheep	18:12–14		15:3–7	186–192
13. Unforgiving Servant	18:23–35			243–251
14. Laborers in the Vineyard	20:1–16			
15. Two Sons	21:28–32			272–283
16. Wicked Vinedressers	21:33–45	12:1–12	20:9–19	284–306
17. Wedding Feast	22:2–14			307–319
18. Fig Tree	24:32–44	13:28–32	21:29–33	
19. Wise and Foolish Virgins	25:1–13			405–421
20. Talents	25:14–30			325–365
21. Growing Seed		4:26–29		62–69
22. Absent Householder		13:33–37		
23. Creditor and Two Debtors			7:41–43	
24. Good Samaritan			10:30–37	376–389
25. Friend in Need			11:5–13	139–149
26. Rich Fool			12:16–21	252–259
27. Faithful Servant and Evil Servant			12:35–40	
28. Faithful and Wise Steward			12:42–48	
29. Barren Fig Tree			13:6–9	212–218
30. Great Supper			14:16–24	219–237
31. Building a Tower			14:25–35	
32. Lost Coin			15:8–10	192–197
33. Prodigal Son			15:11–32	198–211
34. Unjust Steward			16:1–13	366–375
35. Rich Man and Lazarus			16:19–31	260–271
36. Unprofitable Servants			17:7–10	
37. Persistent Widow			18:1–8	164–180
38. Pharisee and Tax Collector			18:9–14	150–163
39. Minas			19:11–27	

The Miracles of Jesus Christ

Miracle	Matthew	Mark	Luke	John	Desire of Ages
Cleansing a leper	8:2	1:40	5:12		262–266
Healing a centurion's servant	8:5		7:1		315–318
Healing Peter's mother-in-law	8:14	1:30	4:38		259, 260
Healing the sick at evening	8:16	1:32	4:40		259
Calming a storm	8:23	4:35	8:22		334–337
Casting demons into swine	8:28	5:1	8:26		337–341
Healing the paralytic	9:2	2:3	5:18		267
Raising Jairus's daughter	9:18, 23	5:22, 35	8:40, 49		342, 343
Healing the hemorrhaging woman	9:20	5:25	8:43		343, 347
Healing two blind men	9:27				
Curing a demon-possessed, mute man	9:32				
Healing a man's withered hand	12:9	3:1	6:6		286–289
Curing a demon-possessed, blind and mute man	12:22		11:14		
Feeding the 5,000	14:13	6:30	9:10	6:1	364–371
Walking on the water	14:25	6:48		6:19	379–382
Healing a Gentile woman's daughter	15:21	7:24			399–403
Feeding the 4,000	15:32	8:1			404, 405
Healing an epileptic boy	17:14	9:17	9:38		426–431
Coin in the fish's mouth	17:24				432–434
Healing two blind men	20:30	10:46	18:35		
Withering the fig tree	21:18	11:12			580–588
Casting out an unclean spirit		1:23	4:33		255–258
Healing a deaf and mute man		7:31			
Healing a blind paralytic at Bethsaida		8:22			
Escape from the multitude			4:30		
Amazing catch of fish			5:1		244–251
Raising the widow of Nain's son			7:11		318–320
Healing the infirm, bowed woman			13:11		
Healing a man with dropsy			14:1		
Cleansing ten lepers			17:11		348
Restoring a servant's ear			22:51		696
Water into wine				2:1	144–153
Healing a nobleman's son				4:46	196–200
Healing an infirm man at Bethesda				5:1	201–207
Healing the man born blind				9:1	470–475
Raising Lazarus				11:43	524–536
A second amazing catch of fish				21:1	809–811

NOTE: The following material is drawn from chapters in two different books by E. G. White, whose comments appear throughout this Bible. These two chapters focus on the entrance of sin to planet Earth: Chapter 29 of *The Great Controversy* is entitled "The Origin of Evil"; chapter 1 of *Patriarchs and Prophets* is entitled "Why Was Sin Permitted?"

Sin Is an Intruder

To many minds, the origin of sin and the reason for its existence are a source of great perplexity. They see the work of evil, with its terrible results of woe and desolation, and they question how all this can exist under the sovereignty of One who is infinite in wisdom, in power, and in love. Here is a mystery, of which they find no explanation. And in their uncertainty and doubt, they are blinded to truths plainly revealed in God's Word, and essential to salvation. . . .

It is impossible to explain the origin of sin as to give a reason for its existence. Yet enough may be understood concerning both the origin and the final disposition of sin, to fully make manifest the justice and benevolence of God in all His dealings with evil. Nothing is more plainly taught in Scripture than that God was in nowise responsible for the entrance of sin; that there was no arbitrary withdrawal of divine grace, no deficiency in the divine government, that gave occasion for the uprising of rebellion. Sin is an intruder, for whose presence no reason can be given. It is mysterious, unaccountable; to excuse it, is to defend it. Could excuse for it be found, or cause be shown for its existence, it would cease to be sin. Our only definition of sin is that given in the Word of God; it is "the transgression of the law;" it is the outworking of a principle at war with the great law of love which is the foundation of the divine government.

God Is Love—and His Love Never Changes

"God is love" (1 John 4:16). His nature, His law, is love. It ever has been; it ever will be. "The high and lofty One that inhabiteth eternity," whose "ways are everlasting," changeth not. With Him "is no variableness, neither shadow of turning" (Isaiah 57:15; Habakkuk 3:6; James 1:17).

Every manifestation of creative power is an expression of infinite love. The sovereignty of God involves fullness of blessing to all created beings. . . .

Before the entrance of evil, there was peace and joy throughout the universe. All was in perfect harmony with the Creator's will. Love for God was supreme, love for one another impartial. . . .

The law of love being the foundation of the government of God, the happiness of all created beings depended upon their perfect accord with its great principles of righteousness. God desires from all His creatures the service of love—homage that springs from an intelligent appreciation of His character. He takes no pleasure in a forced allegiance, and to all He grants freedom of will, that they may render Him voluntary service. . . . So long as all created beings acknowledged the allegiance of love, there was perfect harmony throughout the universe of God. It was the joy of the heavenly host to fulfill the purpose of their Creator. They delighted in reflecting His glory and showing forth His praise. And while love to God was supreme, love for one another was confiding and unselfish. There was no note of discord to mar the celestial harmonies.

The history of the great conflict between good and evil, from the time it first began in Heaven to the final overthrow of rebellion and the total eradication of sin, is also a demonstration of God's unchanging love.

God Had a Co-Worker

The Sovereign of the universe was not alone in His work of beneficence. He had an associate—a co-worker who could appreciate His purposes, and could share His joy in giving happiness to created beings. "In the beginning was the Word, and the Word was with God, and the Word was God. The same was in the beginning with God" (John 1:1, 2). Christ, the Word, the only begotten of God, was one with the eternal Father—one in nature, in character, in purpose—the only being that could enter into all the counsels and purposes of God. "His name shall be called Wonderful, Counselor, The mighty God, The everlasting Father, The Prince of Peace" (Isaiah 9:6). His "goings forth have been from of old, from everlasting" (Micah 5:2). And the Son of God declares concerning Himself: "The Lord possessed Me in the beginning of His way, before His works of old. I was set up from everlasting. . . . When He appointed the foundations

of the earth: then I was by Him, as one brought up with Him: and I was daily His delight, rejoicing always before Him" (Proverbs 8:22–30). . . .

Angels are God's ministers, radiant with the light ever flowing from His presence and speeding on rapid wing to execute His will. But the Son, the anointed of God, the "express image of His person," "the brightness of His glory," "upholding all things by the word of His power," holds supremacy over them all (Hebrews 1:3). . . .

What Took Place to Change Things Forever

But a change came over this happy state. There was one who perverted the freedom that God had granted to His creatures. Sin originated with him who, next to Christ, had been most honored of God and was highest in power and glory among the inhabitants of Heaven. Lucifer, "son of the morning," was first of the covering cherubs, holy and undefiled. He stood in the presence of the great Creator, and the ceaseless beams of glory enshrouding the eternal God rested upon him. "Thus saith the Lord God; Thou sealest up the sum, full of wisdom, and perfect in beauty. Thou hast been in Eden the garden of God; every precious stone was thy covering. . . . Thou art the anointed cherub that covereth; and I have set thee so: thou wast upon the holy mountain of God; thou hast walked up and down in the midst of the stones of fire. Thou wast perfect in thy ways from the day that thou wast created, till iniquity was found in thee" (Ezekiel 28:12–15). . . .

The Beginning of Sin

Lucifer might have remained in favor with God, beloved and honored by all the angelic host, exercising his noble powers to bless others and to glorify his Maker. But, says the prophet, "Thine heart was lifted up because of thy beauty, thou hast corrupted thy wisdom by reason of thy brightness" [Ezekiel 28:12–15, 17]. Little by little, Lucifer came to indulge a desire for self-exaltation. "Thou hast set thine heart as the heart of God." "Thou hast said: . . . I will exalt my throne above the stars of God; I will sit also upon the mount of the congregation." "I will ascend above the heights of the clouds; I will be like the Most High" [Ezekiel 28:6; Isaiah 14:13, 14]. Instead of seeking to make God supreme in the affections and allegiance of his creatures, it was Lucifer's endeavor to win their service and homage to himself. And, coveting the honor which the infinite Father had bestowed upon his Son, this prince of angels aspired to power which it was the prerogative of Christ alone to wield.

All Heaven had rejoiced to reflect the Creator's glory and to show forth His praise. And while God was thus honored, all had been peace and gladness. But a note of discord now marred the celestial harmonies. The service and exaltation of self, contrary to the Creator's plan, awakened forebodings of evil in minds to whom God's glory was supreme. The heavenly councils pleaded with Lucifer. The Son of God presented before him the greatness, the goodness, and the justice of the Creator, and the sacred, unchanging nature of His law. God Himself had established the order of Heaven; and in departing from it, Lucifer would dishonor his Maker, and bring ruin upon himself. But the warning, given in infinite love and mercy, only aroused a spirit of resistance. . . .

God Had a Meeting to Set Things Straight

The King of the universe summoned the heavenly hosts before Him, that in their presence He might set forth the true position of His Son and show the relation He sustained to all created beings. The Son of God shared the Father's throne, and the glory of the eternal, self-existent One encircled both. About the throne gathered the holy angels, a vast, unnumbered throng— "ten thousand times ten thousand, and thousands of thousands" (Revelation 5:11), the most exalted angels, as ministers and subjects, rejoicing in the light that fell upon them from the presence of the Deity. Before the assembled inhabitants of Heaven the King declared that none but Christ, the Only Begotten of God, could fully enter into His purposes, and to Him it was committed to execute the mighty counsels of His will. The Son of God had wrought the Father's will in the creation of all the hosts of Heaven; and to Him, as well as to God, their homage and allegiance were due. Christ was still to exercise divine power, in the creation of the earth and its inhabitants. But in all this He would not seek power or exaltation for Himself contrary to God's plan, but would exalt the Father's glory and execute His purposes of beneficence and love.

Lucifer Again Had a Fierce Battle

The angels joyfully acknowledged the supremacy of Christ, and prostrating themselves before Him, poured out their love and adoration. Lucifer bowed with them, but in his heart there was a strange, fierce conflict. Truth, justice, and loyalty were struggling against envy and jealousy. The influence of the holy angels seemed for a time to carry him with them. As songs of praise ascended in melodious strains, swelled by thousands of glad voices, the spirit of evil seemed vanquished; unutterable love thrilled his entire being; his soul went out, in harmony with the sinless worshippers, in love to the Father and the Son. But again he was filled with pride in his own glory. His desire for supremacy returned, and envy of Christ was once more indulged. The high honors conferred upon Lucifer were not appreciated as God's special gift, and therefore, called forth no gratitude to his Creator. He gloried in his brightness and exaltation and aspired to be equal with God. He was beloved and reverenced by the heavenly host, angels delighted to execute his commands, and he was clothed with wisdom and glory above them all. Yet the Son of God was exalted above him, as one in power and authority with the Father. He shared the Father's counsels, while Lucifer did not thus enter into the purposes of God. "Why," questioned this mighty angel, "should Christ have the supremacy? Why is He honored above Lucifer?"

Lucifer Spread the Spirit of Discontent in Secrecy

Leaving his place in the immediate presence of the Father, Lucifer went forth to diffuse the spirit of discontent among the angels. He worked with mysterious secrecy, and for a time concealed his real purpose under an appearance of reverence for God. He began to insinuate doubts concerning the laws that governed heavenly beings, intimating that though laws might be necessary for the inhabitants of the worlds, angels, being more exalted, needed no such restraint, for their own wisdom was a sufficient guide. They were not beings that could bring dishonor to God; all their thoughts were holy; it was no more possible for them than for God Himself to err. The exaltation of the Son of God as equal with the Father was represented as an injustice to Lucifer, who, it was claimed, was also entitled to reverence and honor. If this prince of angels could but attain to his true, exalted position, great good would accrue to the entire host of Heaven; for it was his object to secure freedom for all. But now even the liberty which they had hitherto enjoyed was at an end; for an absolute Ruler had been appointed them, and to His authority all must pay homage. Such were the subtle deceptions that through the wiles of Lucifer were fast obtaining in the heavenly courts.

There had been no change in the position or authority of Christ. Lucifer's envy and misrepresentation and his claims to equality with Christ had made necessary a statement of the true position of the Son of God; but this had been the same from the beginning. Many of the angels were, however, blinded by Lucifer's deceptions.

Lucifer Took Advantage of Love

Taking advantage of the loving, loyal trust reposed in him by the holy beings under his command, he had so artfully instilled into their minds his own distrust and discontent that his agency was not discerned. Lucifer had presented the purposes of God in a false light— misconstruing and distorting them to excite dissent and dissatisfaction. He cunningly drew his hearers on to give utterance to their feelings; then these expressions were repeated by him when it would serve his purpose, as evidence that the angels were not fully in harmony with the government of God. While claiming for himself perfect loyalty to God, he urged that changes in the order and laws of Heaven were necessary for the stability of the divine government. Thus while working to excite opposition to the law of God and to instill his own discontent into the minds of the angels under him, he was ostensibly seeking to remove dissatisfaction and to reconcile disaffected angels to the order of Heaven. While secretly fomenting discord and rebellion, he with consummate craft caused it to appear as his sole purpose to promote loyalty and to preserve harmony and peace.

Lucifer Continued to Sow Seeds of Jealousy

The spirit of dissatisfaction thus kindled was doing its baleful work. While there was no open outbreak, division of feeling imperceptibly grew up among the angels. There were some who looked with favor upon Lucifer's insinuations against the government of God. Although they had heretofore been in perfect harmony with the order which God had established, they were now discontented and unhappy because they could not penetrate His unsearchable

counsels; they were dissatisfied with His purpose in exalting Christ. These stood ready to second Lucifer's demand for equal authority with the Son of God. But angels who were loyal and true maintained the wisdom and justice of the divine decree and endeavored to reconcile this disaffected being to the will of God. Christ was the Son of God; He had been one with Him before the angels were called into existence. He had ever stood at the right hand of the Father; His supremacy, so full of blessing to all who came under its benignant control, had not heretofore been questioned. The harmony of Heaven had never been interrupted; wherefore should there now be discord? The loyal angels could see only terrible consequences from this dissension, and with earnest entreaty they counseled the disaffected ones to renounce their purpose and prove themselves loyal to God by fidelity to His government.

God's Everlasting Grace and Mercy Bore Long With Lucifer

In great mercy, according to His divine character, God bore long with Lucifer. The spirit of discontent and disaffection had never before been known in Heaven. It was a new element, strange, mysterious, unaccountable. Lucifer himself had not at first been acquainted with the real nature of his feelings; for a time he had feared to express the workings and imaginings of his mind; yet he did not dismiss them. He did not see whither he was drifting. But such efforts as infinite love and wisdom only could devise, were made to convince him of his error. His disaffection was proved to be without cause, and he was made to see what would be the result of persisting in revolt. Lucifer was convinced that he was in the wrong. He saw that "the Lord is righteous in all His ways, and holy in all His works" (Psalm 145:17); that the divine statutes are just, and that he ought to acknowledge them as such before all Heaven. Had he done this, he might have saved himself and many angels. He had not at that time fully cast off his allegiance to God. Though he had left his position as covering cherub, yet if he had been willing to return to God, acknowledging the Creator's wisdom, and satisfied to fill the place appointed him in God's great plan, he would have been reinstated in his office. The time had come for a final decision; he must fully yield to the divine sovereignty or place himself in open rebellion. He nearly reached the decision to return, but pride forbade him. It was too great a sacrifice for one who had been so highly honored to confess that he had been in error, that his imaginings were false, and to yield to the authority which he had been working to prove unjust.

A compassionate Creator, in yearning pity for Lucifer and his followers, was seeking to draw them back from the abyss of ruin into which they were about to plunge. But His mercy was misinterpreted. Lucifer pointed to the long-suffering of God as an evidence of his own superiority, an indication that the King of the universe would yet accede to his terms. If the angels would stand firmly with him, he declared, they could yet gain all that they desired. He persistently defended his own course, and fully committed himself to the great controversy against his Maker. Thus it was that Lucifer, "the light bearer," the sharer of God's glory, the attendant of His throne, by transgression became Satan, "the adversary" of God and holy beings and the destroyer of those whom Heaven had committed to his guidance and guardianship.

Lucifer Continued to Reject God's Entreaties

Rejecting with disdain the arguments and entreaties of the loyal angels, he denounced them as deluded slaves. The preference shown to Christ he declared an act of injustice both to himself and to all the heavenly host, and announced that he would no longer submit to this invasion of his rights and theirs. He would never again acknowledge the supremacy of Christ. He had determined to claim the honor which should have been given him, and take command of all who would become his followers; and he promised those who would enter his ranks a new and better government, under which all would enjoy freedom. Great numbers of the angels signified their purpose to accept him as their leader. Flattered by the favor with which his advances were received, he hoped to win all the angels to his side, to become equal with God Himself, and to be obeyed by the entire host of Heaven.

Still the loyal angels urged him and his sympathizers to submit to God; and they set before them the inevitable result should they refuse: He who had created them could overthrow their power and signally punish their rebellious daring. No angel could successfully oppose the law of God, which was as sacred as Himself. They warned all to close their ears against Lucifer's deceptive reasoning, and urged him and his followers to seek the presence of God without delay and confess the error of questioning His wisdom and authority.

Lucifer Continued to Deceive

Many were disposed to heed this counsel, to repent of their disaffection, and seek to be again received into favor with the Father and His Son. But Lucifer had another deception ready. The mighty revolter now declared that the angels who had united with him had gone too far to return; that he was acquainted with the divine law, and knew that God would not forgive. He declared that all who should submit to the authority of Heaven would be stripped of their honor, degraded from their position. For himself, he was determined never again to acknowledge the authority of Christ. The only course remaining for him and his followers, he said, was to assert their liberty, and gain by force the rights which had not been willingly accorded them.

Pride Sealed the Other Angels

So far as Satan himself was concerned, it was true that he had now gone too far to return. But not so with those who had been blinded by his deceptions. To them the counsel and entreaties of the loyal angels opened a door of hope; and had they heeded the warning, they might have broken away from the snare of Satan. But pride, love for their leader, and the desire for unrestricted freedom were permitted to bear sway, and the pleadings of divine love and mercy were finally rejected.

God, in Love, Let Lucifer's Plans Fully Develop

God permitted Satan to carry forward his work until the spirit of disaffection ripened into active revolt. It was necessary for his plans to be fully developed, that their true nature and tendency might be seen by all. Lucifer, as the anointed cherub, had been highly exalted; he was greatly loved by the heavenly beings, and his influence over them was strong. God's government included not only the inhabitants of Heaven, but of all the worlds that He had created; and Lucifer had concluded that if he could carry the angels of Heaven with him in rebellion, he could carry also all the worlds. He had artfully presented his side of the question, employing sophistry and fraud to secure his objects. His power to deceive was very great. By disguising himself in a cloak of falsehood, he had gained an advantage. All his acts were so clothed with mystery that it was difficult to disclose to the angels the true nature of his work. Until fully developed, it could not be made to appear the evil thing it was; his disaffection would not be seen to be rebellion. Even the loyal angels could not fully discern his character or see to what his work was leading. . . .

All the powers of his master-mind were now bent to the work of deception, to secure the sympathy of the angels that had been under his command. Even the fact that Christ had warned and counseled him, was perverted to serve his traitorous designs. To those whose loving trust bound them most closely to him, Satan had represented that he was wrongly judged, that his position was not respected, and that his liberty was to be abridged. From misrepresentation of the words of Christ, he passed to prevarication and direct falsehood, accusing the Son of God of a design to humiliate him before the inhabitants of Heaven. He sought also to make a false issue between himself and the loyal angels. All whom he could not subvert and bring fully to his side, he accused of indifference to the interests of heavenly beings. The very work which he himself was doing, he charged upon those who remained true to God. And to sustain his charge of God's injustice toward him, he resorted to misrepresentation of the words and acts of the Creator. It was his policy to perplex the angels with subtle arguments concerning the purposes of God. Everything that was simple he shrouded in mystery, and by artful perversion cast doubt upon the plainest statements of Jehovah. His high position, in such close connection with the divine administration, gave greater force to his representations, and many were induced to unite with him in rebellion against Heaven's authority.

For Sin to Appear As It Really Is, It Had to Be Fully Developed

Satan had been so highly honored, and all his acts were so clothed with mystery, that it was difficult to disclose to the angels the true nature of his work. Until fully developed, sin would not appear the evil thing it was. Heretofore it had had no place in the universe of God, and holy beings had no conception of its nature and malignity. They could not discern the terrible consequences that would result from setting aside the divine law. Satan had, at first, concealed his work under a specious profession of loyalty to God. He claimed to be seeking to promote the honor of God, the stability of His government, and the good of all the inhabitants of Heaven. While instilling discontent into the minds of the angels under him, he had artfully

made it appear that he was seeking to remove dissatisfaction. When he urged that changes be made in the order and laws of God's government, it was under the pretense that these were necessary in order to preserve harmony in Heaven.

God's Law Versus Satan's Law

In His dealing with sin, God could employ only righteousness and truth. Satan could use what God could not—flattery and deceit. He had sought to falsify the word of God, and had misrepresented his plan of government before the angels, claiming that God was not just in laying laws and rules upon the inhabitants of Heaven; that in requiring submission and obedience from His creatures, He was seeking merely the exaltation of Himself. Therefore it must be demonstrated before the inhabitants of Heaven as well as of all the worlds, that God's government was just, His law perfect. Satan had made it appear that he himself was seeking to promote the good of the universe. The true character of the usurper, and his real object, must be understood by all. He must have time to manifest himself by his wicked works.

The discord which his own course had caused in Heaven, Satan charged upon the law and government of God. All evil he declared to be the result of the divine administration. He claimed that it was his own object to improve upon the statutes of Jehovah. Therefore it was necessary that he should demonstrate the nature of his claims, and show the working out of his proposed changes in the divine law. His own work must condemn him. Satan had claimed from the first that he was not in rebellion. The whole universe must see the deceiver unmasked.

Serving God out of Love and Not out of Fear

Even when it was decided that he could no longer remain in Heaven, infinite wisdom did not destroy Satan. Since the service of love can alone be acceptable to God, the allegiance of His creatures must rest upon a conviction of His justice and benevolence. The inhabitants of Heaven and of other worlds, being unprepared to comprehend the nature or consequences of sin, could not then have seen the justice and mercy of God in the destruction of Satan. Had he been immediately blotted from existence, they would have served God from fear, rather than from love. The influence of the deceiver would not have been fully destroyed, nor would the spirit of rebellion have been utterly eradicated. Evil must be permitted to come to maturity. For the good of the entire universe through ceaseless ages, Satan must more fully develop his principles, that his charges against the divine government might be seen in their true light by all created beings, that the justice and mercy of God and the immutability of His law might forever be placed beyond all question.

Satan's Rebellion a Lesson for All the Universe—for All Time

Satan's rebellion was to be a lesson to the universe through all coming ages—a perpetual testimony to the nature of sin and its terrible results. The working out of Satan's rule, its effects upon both men and angels, would show what must be the fruit of setting aside the divine authority. It would testify that with the existence of God's government is bound up the well-being of all the creatures He has made. Thus the history of this terrible experiment of rebellion was to be a perpetual safeguard to all holy beings, to prevent them from being deceived as to the nature of transgression, to save them from committing sin, and suffering its penalty.

To the very close of the controversy in Heaven, the great usurper continued to justify himself. When it was announced that with all his sympathizers he must be expelled from the abodes of bliss, then the rebel leader boldly avowed his contempt for the Creator's law. He reiterated his claim that angels needed no control, but should be left to follow their own will, which would ever guide them right. He denounced the divine statutes as a restriction of their liberty, and declared that it was his purpose to secure the abolition of law; that, freed from this restraint, the hosts of Heaven might enter upon a more exalted, more glorious state of existence.

Satan Became the Accuser of the Brethren

With one accord, Satan and his host threw the blame of their rebellion wholly upon Christ, declaring that if they had not been reproved, they would never have rebelled. Thus stubborn and defiant in their disloyalty, seeking vainly to overthrow the government of God, yet blasphemously claiming to be themselves the innocent victims of oppressive power, the arch-rebel and all his sympathizers were at last banished from Heaven.

Rebellion from the First to Do Away with the Law of God

The same spirit that prompted rebellion in Heaven, still inspires rebellion on earth. Satan has continued with men the same policy which he pursued with the angels. His spirit now reigns in the children of disobedience. Like him they seek to break down the restraints of the law of God, and promise men liberty through transgression of its precepts. Reproof of sin still arouses the spirit of hatred and resistance. When God's messages of warning are brought home to the conscience, Satan leads men to justify themselves, and to seek the sympathy of others in their course of sin. Instead of correcting their errors, they excite indignation against the reprover, as if he were the sole cause of difficulty. From the days of righteous Abel to our own time, such is the spirit which has been displayed toward those who dare to condemn sin.

By the same misrepresentation of the character of God as he had practiced in Heaven, causing him to be regarded as severe and tyrannical, Satan induced man to sin. And having succeeded thus far, he declared that God's unjust restrictions had led to man's fall, as they had led to his own rebellion.

But the Eternal One himself proclaims His character: "The Lord God, merciful and gracious, long-suffering, and abundant in goodness and truth, keeping mercy for thousands, forgiving iniquity and transgression and sin, and that will by no means clear the guilty" [Exodus 34:6, 7].

God Continues to Show His Infinite Love for Us

In the banishment of Satan from Heaven, God declared His justice, and maintained the honor of His throne. But when man had sinned through yielding to the deceptions of this apostate spirit, God gave an evidence of His love by yielding up His only begotten Son to die for the fallen race. In the atonement the character of God is revealed. The mighty argument of the Cross demonstrates to the whole universe that the course of sin which Lucifer had chosen was in nowise chargeable upon the government of God.

At Last, Satan's Character Is Unmasked

In the contest between Christ and Satan, during the Saviour's earthly ministry, the character of the great deceiver was unmasked. Nothing could so effectually have uprooted Satan from the affections of the heavenly angels and the whole loyal universe as did his cruel warfare upon the world's Redeemer. The daring blasphemy of his demand that Christ should pay him homage, his presumptuous boldness in bearing Him to the mountain summit and the pinnacle of the temple, the malicious intent betrayed in urging Him to cast Himself down from the dizzy height, the unsleeping malice that hunted Him from place to place, inspiring the hearts of priests and people to reject His love, and at the last to cry, "Crucify Him! crucify Him!"—all this excited the amazement and indignation of the universe.

It was Satan that prompted the world's rejection of Christ. The prince of evil exerted all his power and cunning to destroy Jesus; for he saw that the Saviour's mercy and love, His compassion and pitying tenderness, were representing to the world the character of God. Satan contested every claim put forth by the Son of God, and employed men as his agents to fill the Saviour's life with suffering and sorrow. The sophistry and falsehood by which he had sought to hinder the work of Jesus, the hatred manifested through the children of disobedience, his cruel accusations against Him whose life was one of unexampled goodness, all sprung from deep-seated revenge. The pent-up fires of envy and malice, hatred and revenge, burst forth on Calvary against the Son of God, while all Heaven gazed upon the scene in silent horror.

The Victory

When the great sacrifice had been consummated, Christ ascended on high, refusing the adoration of angels until he had presented the request, "I will that they also, whom thou hast given me, be with me where I am" [John 17:24]. Then with inexpressible love and power came forth the answer from the Father's throne, "Let all the angels of God worship him" [Hebrews 1:6]. Not a stain rested upon Jesus. His humiliation ended, His sacrifice completed, there was given unto Him a name that is above every name.

Satan's True Character Revealed—As a Liar and a Murderer

Now the guilt of Satan stood forth without excuse. He had revealed his true character as a liar and a murderer. It was seen that the very same spirit with which he ruled the children of men, who were under his power, he would have manifested had he been permitted to control the

inhabitants of Heaven. He had claimed that the transgression of God's law would bring liberty and exaltation; but it was seen to result in bondage and degradation.

Satan's lying charges against the divine character and government appeared in their true light. He had accused God of seeking merely the exaltation of Himself in requiring submission and obedience from His creatures, and had declared that while the Creator exacted self-denial from all others, He Himself practiced no self-denial, made no sacrifice. Now it was seen that for the salvation of a fallen and sinful race, the Ruler of the universe had made the greatest sacrifice which love could make; for "God was in Christ, reconciling the world unto himself" [2 Corinthians 5:19]. It was seen, also, that while Lucifer had opened the door for the entrance of sin, by his desire for honor and supremacy, Christ had, in order to destroy sin, humbled Himself, and become obedient unto death.

Satan Continued to Make False Claims

God had manifested His abhorrence of the principles of rebellion. All Heaven saw His justice revealed, both in the condemnation of Satan and in the redemption of man. Lucifer had declared that if the law of God was changeless, and its penalty could not be remitted, every transgressor must be forever debarred from the Creator's favor. He had claimed that the sinful race were placed beyond redemption, and were therefore his rightful prey. But the death of Christ was an argument in man's behalf that could not be overthrown. The penalty of the law fell upon Him who was equal with God, and man was free to accept the righteousness of Christ, and by a life of penitence and humiliation to triumph, as the Son of God had triumphed, over the power of Satan. Thus God is just, and yet the justifier of all who believe in Jesus.

Christ Came to Us to Magnify and Make Honorable His Law

But it was not merely to accomplish the redemption of man that Christ came to the earth to suffer and to die. He came to "magnify the law" and to "make it honorable." Not alone that the inhabitants of this world might regard the law as it should be regarded; but it was to demonstrate to all the worlds of the universe that God's law is unchangeable. Could its claims have been set aside, then the Son of God need not have yielded up His life to atone for its transgression. The death of Christ proves it immutable. And the sacrifice to which infinite love impelled the Father and the Son, that sinners might be redeemed, demonstrates to all the universe—what nothing less than this plan of atonement could have sufficed to do—that justice and mercy are the foundation of the law and government of God.

In the End, It Will Be Proved No Cause for Sin Exists

In the final execution of the Judgment it will be seen that no cause for sin exists. When the Judge of all the earth shall demand of Satan, "Why hast thou rebelled against Me, and robbed Me of the subjects of My kingdom?" the originator of evil can render no excuse. Every mouth will be stopped, and all the hosts of rebellion will be speechless.

The Cross of Calvary, while it declares the law immutable, proclaims to the universe that the wages of sin is death. In the Saviour's expiring cry, "It is finished," the death-knell of Satan was rung. The great controversy which had been so long in progress was then decided, and the final eradication of evil was made certain. The Son of God passed through the portals of the tomb, that "through death He might destroy him that had the power of death, that is, the devil" [Hebrews 2:14]. Lucifer's desire for self-exaltation had led him to say, "I will exalt my throne above the stars of God. . . . I will be like the Most High." God declares, "I will bring thee to ashes upon the earth, . . . and never shalt thou be any more" [Isaiah 14:13, 14; Ezekiel 28:18, 19]. When "the day cometh that shall burn as an oven," "all the proud, yea, and all that do wickedly, shall be stubble; and the day that cometh shall burn them up, saith the Lord of hosts, that it shall leave them neither root nor branch" [Malachi 4:1].

The whole universe will have become witnesses to the nature and results of sin. And its utter extermination, which in the beginning would have brought fear to angels and dishonor to God, will now vindicate His love and establish His honor before a universe of beings who delight to do His will, and in whose heart is His law. Never will evil again be manifest. Says the Word of God, "Affliction shall not rise up the second time" [Nahum 1:9]. The law of God, which Satan has reproached as the yoke of bondage, will be honored as the law of liberty. A tested and proved creation will never again be turned from allegiance to Him whose character has been fully manifested before them as fathomless love and infinite wisdom.

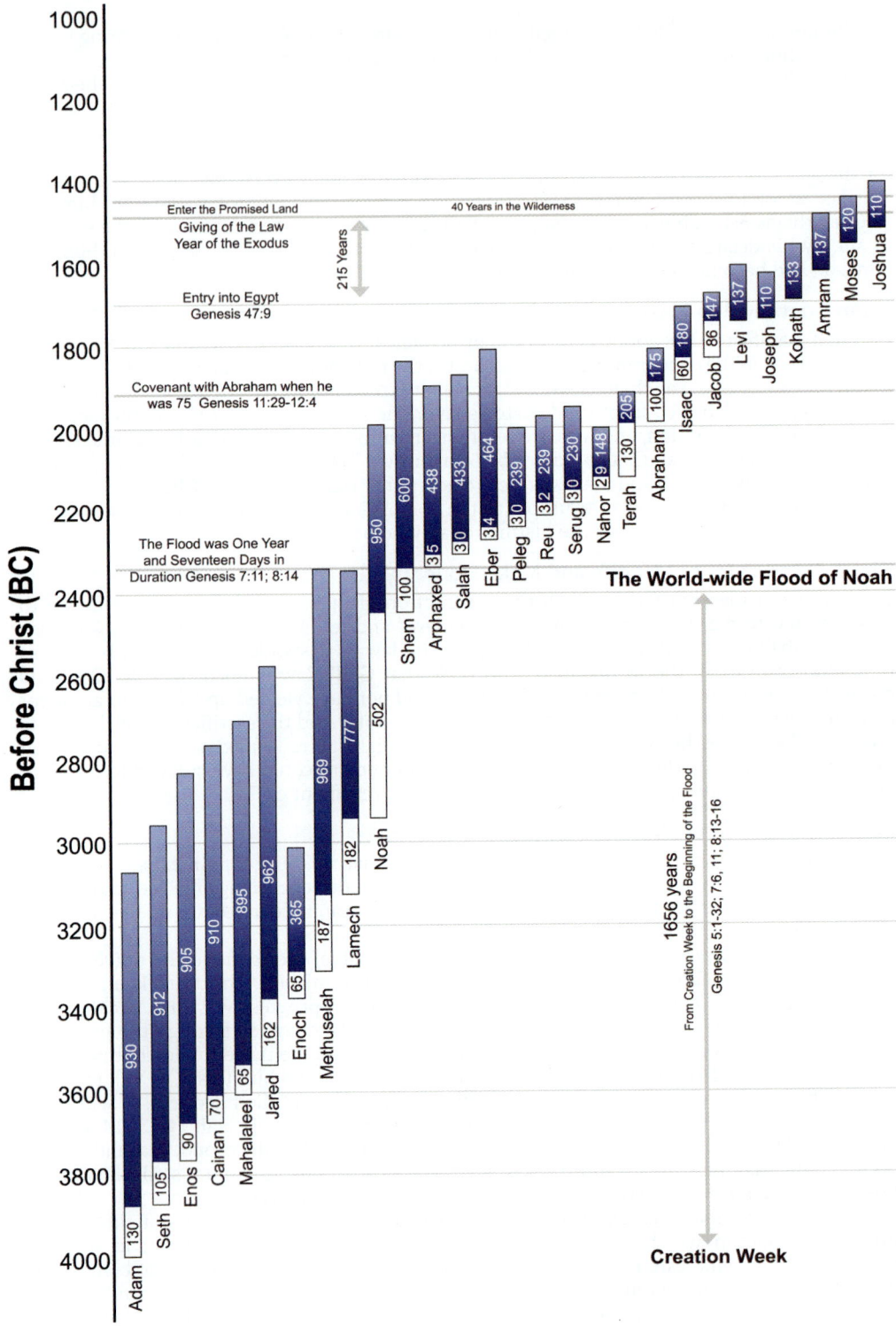

Before Christ (BC)

- Enter the Promised Land
- 40 Years in the Wilderness
- Giving of the Law
- Year of the Exodus
- 215 Years
- Entry into Egypt Genesis 47:9
- Covenant with Abraham when he was 75 Genesis 11:29-12:4
- The Flood was One Year and Seventeen Days in Duration Genesis 7:11; 8:14

The World-wide Flood of Noah

1656 years
From Creation Week to the Beginning of the Flood
Genesis 5:1-32; 7:6, 11; 8:13-16

Creation Week

Adam 130
Seth 105
Enos 90
Cainan 70
Mahalaleel 65
Jared 162
Enoch 65
Methuselah 187
Lamech 182
Noah 502
Shem 100
Arphaxed 35
Salah 30
Eber 34
Peleg 30
Reu 32
Serug 30
Nahor 29
Terah 130
Abraham 100
Isaac 60
Jacob 86
Levi
Joseph 110
Kohath 133
Amram 137
Moses 120
Joshua 110

930, 912, 905, 910, 895, 962, 365, 969, 777, 950, 600, 438, 433, 464, 239, 239, 230, 148, 205, 175, 180, 147, 137

Timeline courtesy of Michael Brown.

1436

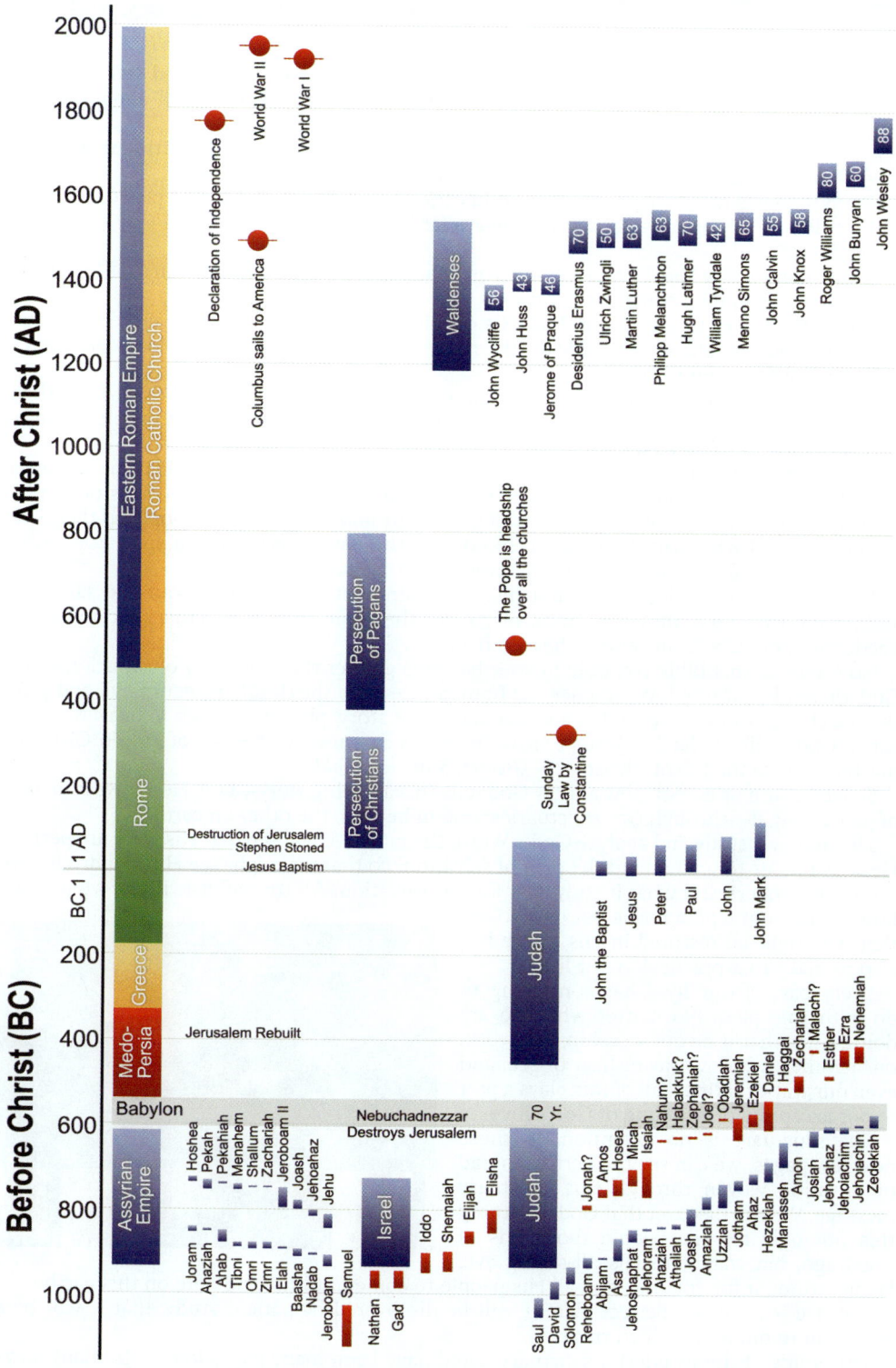

Timeline courtesy of Michael Brown.

Most people have heard of a favorite grade-school activity called "Show and Tell" in which students bring something to class to "show" to their classmates as they "tell" about the item they've brought.

But some of those same students, a dozen or more years later, may be sitting in a college English or writing class and hear their professor insist: "Show—*don't* Tell."

When it comes to sharing a story—whether friend to friend, in print, in a play on stage, or in a movie or TV program—showing is always far better than telling.

Why?

People don't really "get" a story or even an abstract concept, until they can "see" it like an internal movie on the screen of their minds.

In Old Testament times, God did *tell* His people that He had a plan to save them. He told them that Jesus would someday die for them. He told them all the facts about redemption.

But that was not enough.

So God chose to show His people what salvation looked like. He chose to let them experience it through their senses—so they could see, hear, feel, smell, and taste everything He wanted them to understand.

So God commanded His people to build a sanctuary—a place where He could come and dwell with them. God would present His plan of salvation to the people in the form of a story, a play.

Everything about the sanctuary—as well as its daily and yearly services—opened their eyes to some part of what salvation meant. No one in the entire nation was a spectator—every man, woman, and child was actively involved in the drama.

This life-and-death drama was not just entertainment. Everything about the sanctuary and its services illustrated something very real—the great original sanctuary located at the headquarters of God's universe in heaven itself.

No theme of this Bible you hold in your hands is greater than the story of salvation—how God, driven by infinite love, rescues the human race from the deadly power of evil and gives them a chance to live forever. It's a grand, awesome story, played out both in heaven and on earth. God's gift of His Son Jesus to save us is—as captured in the title of Fulton Oursler's masterpiece on the life of Christ—*The Greatest Story Ever Told.*

So let's take a brief look now at how God tells this amazing story—how He shows it instead of just telling it—through two sanctuaries: one in heaven, the other on earth.

The more we study and analyze God's Word, the more we will see that His ways are perfect. He so wants us to understand the plan of salvation, so that we might see His wondrous love for us and understand what it truly cost for our salvation. All through the Bible, we will see how He laid out a plan for us not only to see that we might be restored in His image but also to make that practical in our lives.

Image courtesy www.3dbiblescenes.com

Every part of our lives has something to do with this plan. No matter what we are doing—whether it be our worship, our work, our families, what we say or hear or see, and even our way of eating—all of this plays a part in our accepting or rejecting of God's love.

The sanctuary is no exception. In these next few pages, we can see the perfect thread of salvation woven through this sanctuary message. We will discover that God instituted this not only for His people thousands of years ago, but that with His all-seeing eye, He instituted it for you, me, and all His people to come until the end here on this earth.

Because it is such a perfect plan, it will be discovered by patient study, that it will be a continual reminder for all eternity.

This study of the wonderful sanctuary could have been many pages longer. In many ways we have just scratched the surface. What we want you to see more than anything is that God's plan of restoring His precious people back to His image is found today in the sanctuary.

It is a movement. There is a starting place—and there is an ending place. The question above all else, as you dig deeply into this for yourselves, is where are *you* in His plan of saving you? Don't get bogged down with the minutia in the beginning. Look at the clear simplicity of this picture. Be honest with yourselves, and let the Lord Jesus Christ walk with you on your journey to the perfecting of the saints.

Again, we want you to realize that we did not work to be sure everything is exact in its dimensions and appearance when presenting the sanctuary—although that is also important. We want instead for you to begin by understanding the basics. Don't get hung up on so many details that you will miss the point. Remember that coming to understand the sanctuary is a journey.

Image by Norbert McNulty © Mark & Judy McNulty.

We want to share with you first what the sanctuary was and what the articles of furniture in it represented. We want to let you see in history how you can view and walk through the sanctuary. Then we want to let you see how the sanctuary comes alive in our day and how important it is to know the truth it reveals and follow it.

The sanctuary, courtyard, and the tents and surrounding area are a miniature of the plan of salvation. Let's start with the area outside of the courtyard, which represents the world and sin.

When a person sinned, he or she would take a lamb, still in its first year with no defects, and take it to the courtyard. Can you imagine how it must have felt at first to take a lamb and either carry it or walk it all the way to the courtyard? Think about it—the tents where everyone lived were quite a distance from the courtyard. Many believe that they were at least 2,000 cubits from the sanctuary, which would be about a half mile. See the picture? When they sinned and they wanted to take care of that sin, they would get a lamb with no defects—which represented Christ—and take it to the courtyard. Just imagine stepping out of the camp and into the open space of almost half a mile that surrounded the courtyard.

Just think what the friends and neighbors said. We can almost hear them whispering to each other as sinners took little lambs to the place of slaughter. Perhaps they said, "Oh, what a cute little lamb! I wonder what he did this time."

Just think of all those people walking with their lambs in that vast opening between the camp and the courtyard. It surely had to be a humbling experience.

Upon arriving in the courtyard, this cute little lamb had to be sacrificed. It had done absolutely nothing to cause sin. It was completely innocent of this sin that had been committed.

Inside the courtyard, we see the first piece of furniture—the altar of sacrifice, which is where the second part of the journey began. This altar of sacrifice represented forgiveness. It can only be accomplished through the blood of the lamb. That

Models by GoodSeed International.

Altar of Burnt Offering (Exodus 27:1-8)

is why Jesus is represented as a lamb to take away the sins of the world. Just think—it cost Christ His blood for every time we sin. Having sinned, they watched this little lamb die right in front of them. It must have broken their hearts as it should ours. Remember that it had done absolutely nothing to deserve this terrible sentence. Also, don't forget that the lamb could not have any defects—it had to be a perfect lamb of the first year. It could not be old and ready to die. It was just getting started in life.

As we imagine the life draining from this innocent little lamb, it should remind us of Christ. We can go to the foot of the cross and say, "Please forgive me, Father. I am so sorry for doing this to Your Son. I don't want to do it anymore. By Your grace, I make the decision to turn away from my sin."

Laver (Exodus 30:18)

Models by GoodSeed International.

The next piece of furniture is the laver. This laver had water in it, and the priests used it to wash their feet and hands (Exodus 30:18–20), which represented baptism. In baptism, you are saying, "I don't want this world anymore. I want to follow my Savior." Baptism means a death to your old ways and your selfish thoughts. You are buried under the water to represent a death. That death is the death of your sinfulness.

A significant note is that the laver was made out of bronze. That bronze came from the women's mirrors. What do ladies do with their mirrors? They look at themselves to be sure they look nice and that everything is perfectly arranged. Many times, this can become vanity. But when you come back up from the water of baptism, you are resurrected as a new creature in Christ Jesus and it does not end here either. After the priests had been cleansed at the laver, they entered the sanctuary where there were three pieces of furniture in the first compartment. On the right was the table of showbread. On the left was the gold lampstand. Directly in front was the altar of incense. This entire compartment represents the walk we must have when we've made a commitment to serve our precious Savior. It stands for sanctification.

In the table of showbread we can see many examples of our walk with Christ, but we will share just a few. Jesus said, "I am the living bread" (John 6:51). He then added, "Unless you eat the flesh of the Son of Man and drink His blood, you have no life in you" (verse 53). These words are truly significant and vitally important. We know that bread represents the Word of God. We have to eat and see that God is good. Remember that we are what we eat. As we eat the Word of God and it is assimilated into us, it makes us new creatures in Jesus Christ. It has a changing effect on the human mind. We are starting our journey of life unto life. Another important note is that the table of showbread is on the north side of the sanctuary. Remember the description

Table of Showbread (Exodus 25:23-30)

Models by GoodSeed International.

of Satan in Isaiah? In chapter 14, verse 13, Satan said he would exalt his throne above the stars of God. He also stated where that is—on the farthest sides of the north. Remember that Satan has counterfeited all that God made for us. It is so important that we obey all of God's Word and not just pick and choose what we want, which is just what Satan would have us do.

Gold Lampstand
(Exodus 25:31-40)

Models by GoodSeed International.

The gold lampstand or candlestick on the left side of the Holy Place was made out of one talent of gold. Each of us has one talent in common with everybody else. That talent is the talent of time. Our time is very important. It is quite significant that the lampstand was made from this one talent. We are to give our time to God. For when we have made the commitment to follow Him, we have said that we are no longer going to honor ourselves but that instead we have totally given ourselves to following Christ. When we give ourselves unreservedly, He lights our pathway so we have a clear understanding of His will and how we are to live our lives.

This light that burned with olive oil also represented the Holy Spirit, who gives us light as we read God's Word. The main function of the Holy Spirit is to convict us of sin, righteousness, and judgment. The Holy Spirit works on our conscience. We learn to hear God's voice speaking to us through the Word.

Directly opposite the entryway was the altar of incense. This altar was located next to the curtain or veil that separated the Holy Place from the Most Holy Place. This curtain represented Christ. As we read the Word of God (the table of showbread) and follow our conscience according to this Word (the lampstand), it is a light that shows us Jesus—the Way, the Truth, and the Life. Our sincere prayers go to Jesus as a sweet aroma

rising from the altar of incense. Are we not told that Jesus is within us—the hope of glory (Colossians 1:27)?

This altar of incense never quit burning. It was a sweet fragrance, the Bible says. Is it not a sweet thing when we know that Jesus not only forgives us but that He also continues to guide us in the right direction. He constantly says to us, "Pick up your cross, come and follow Me." Do you hear Him calling you? Can you see that this sanctuary is a movement? We must never stop moving forward. This is sanctification. It is not

Altar of Incense (Exodus 30:1; 37:25; 40:5)

instantaneous but rather, a work of a lifetime. Is it not wonderful that when we stumble, we have a Mediator—Christ?

The veil separating the Holy from the Most Holy was very colorful and had angels woven in it. These angels represented God's ministering spirits for us.

The word *veil* in Hebrew means a screen, divider, or separator that hides. The curtain separated us from a holy God. It shielded mankind from His presence. Because of sin, we would cease to exist if we were to look upon a pure and holy God. Only the high priest— God's chosen mediator—could pass through the veil and enter this sacred dwelling once a year. This special time was called the Day of Atonement.

Behind the veil, the Holy of Holies—the Most Holy Place—was beautiful. Two cherubim— angels—stood over the ark. These angels of God looked down at the mercy seat—the cover of the ark. A number of representations for these angels have been created, but I like this description that comes from *The Great Controversy*, page 415:

Ark of the Testimony (Exodus 25:10-22)

> The cherubim of the earthly sanctuary, looking reverently down upon the mercy seat, represent the interest with which the heavenly host contemplate the work of redemption. This is the mystery of mercy into which angels desire to look—that God can be just while He justifies the repenting sinner and renews His intercourse with the fallen race; that Christ could stoop to raise unnumbered multitudes from the abyss of ruin and clothe them with the spotless garments of His own righteousness to unite with angels who have never fallen and to dwell forever in the presence of God.

Under the cover of the ark were three items: a jar of manna, Aaron's rod that budded, and the two tables of stone on which were written the Ten Commandments, engraved with God's own finger.

Each of these items have so much meaning. The first one we will look at is the jar of manna. This manna came from the Exodus. Remember that manna fell every day of the week except the seventh day—the Sabbath. This manna represented the Word of God. Jesus said, "I am that bread of life" (John 6:48). The manna was to be gathered every morning before the sun came out. If it was not gathered before sunrise, the sun would melt the manna. This is significant. If we do not fill ourselves every morning with the Word of God before we get busy—with our children, our spouses, the workplace, or whatever—we will miss the most important meal of the day. How long do you think you would live without your physical food? God could have rained down manna every evening. Always remember that everything He does means something and is important.

Another principle to understand is that only enough

manna needed to be gathered for one day. If more was gathered than could be eaten for the day, then by the next day, it had already bred worms and smelled rotten. The amount gathered was not measured by a cup or container but by size. A bigger person needed more than a smaller person. This story is found in Exodus, chapter 16, which has vital information for all of us as to God's Word.

One last thing to note about the manna is that on Friday—the preparation day—enough for both Friday and for the Sabbath was to be gathered. Can you imagine the significance of this? For forty years this miracle took place. The manna only lasted for one day—except on the Sabbath. It was not just any day that they wanted to rest but the seventh-day Sabbath. The preparation day was the day preceding the Sabbath—not any other day. Another important thing to understand is that this system was set up not for the Jews only but also for all the Egyptians—the mixed multitudes—that left Egypt with the Jews at the Exodus.

To get the whole picture on this vitally important subject, you need to know a few more details. The Sabbath day was not just a physical rest day. Before the Exodus, the Jews were working seven days a week. The seventh-day Sabbath was a day of oneness with God—symbolizing a rest from sin. The preparation day was just that—preparing to meet God. The Lord gave so many applications so we would not miss this life-and-death principle. In Exodus 21:2, we read that when a Hebrew servant was purchased, he would serve for six years, and then he would go free. He would not have to pay anything for his freedom. Later, in Exodus 23:10, God gave implicit instructions to work the fields for six years and on the seventh year let it rest. God created the earth in six days, and on the seventh day, He rested. Do you get the picture? In Revelation, we know that the millennium is one thousand years and that seven thousand years completes the cycle of sin. God is very particular. He does nothing out of place or less than perfectly. These principles He laid out in signs and symbols so that we would not get confused.

One last point to share concerning the manna—it is inside the ark. God expects us to have the Word in our hearts and minds, not on the outside. This is what will restore us to the image of God. When we just read God's Word and try to put on a Christian face but don't truly love it, other people will pick up on this, and we, in a manner of speaking, breed worms and stink. You know the saying, "I would rather see a sermon than hear one any day."

Photo by Remnant Publications.

The next item in the ark was Aaron's rod that budded. Like the manna, this rod that budded was, and still is, very significant. In Numbers, chapter 16, a story takes place that began with Lucifer. Since then, without God, man has been following in the same footsteps of that great deceiver.

In this story, the main characters are Korah, Dathan, and Abiram. These men, in verse 3, say to Moses and Aaron, "Ye take too much upon you, seeing all the congregation are holy, every one of them, and the LORD is among them." Do you catch what is taking place here? They don't want to listen to Moses or Aaron. They don't like what they have to say. The last sentence says, "Wherefore then lift ye up yourselves above the congregation of the LORD?" In other words, who do you think you are? "Listen," they say to Moses, "we are just as holy as you are. In fact, we have the numbers to prove it." In verse 2, we see that by this statement: "They rose up before Moses, with certain of the children of Israel, two hundred and fifty princes of the assembly, famous in the congregation, men of renown."

Do you see what is going on? They imply to Moses that not only are some of the people here spiritual enough to see this as we do, but that we have with us 250 of the very leaders God appointed to help keep you and Aaron balanced. There is no way that you and your brother are the only spiritual leaders here. We are all holy, every one of the 250, and of course, we are also. What a sad story! Later in verse 19, Korah gathered all the congregation. As you look into this a little deeper, it wasn't that he just brought the congregation but that he brought the *whole* congregation against Moses and Aaron. Satan did the very same thing. He went around and got a third of the angels to go against God in the end.

As the story continues, the earth opened up and swallowed not only these rebellious leaders

but their families also. Can you imagine how that must have looked? It must have been a terrible sight to watch Korah, Dathan, and Abiram, with their families, being swallowed up by the earth. As if this were not enough, the Bible says that fire came out from the Lord and consumed the 250 men. I would think that this certainly would have been enough for the rest of the people to humble themselves and say, "We were wrong. I am glad I am still alive." But in verse 41 of the same chapter (16), we see that the very next day, all the congregation of the children of Israel murmured against Moses and Aaron. Can you believe what they said? That's right: "Ye have killed the people of the LORD." So then God allowed a plague that killed 14,700, and this does not include the ones who had died the previous day.

Now we get back to Aaron's rod that budded. Each leader of the twelve tribes of Israel had a rod, and Moses wrote their names on them. They then took their rods to the tabernacle of meeting. The next day, out of the twelve rods, there was one rod—the rod of Levi, with Aaron's name on it—that not only had budded, but it also actually had almonds on it. In the end, it says in chapter 17, verse 10:

> The LORD said unto Moses, Bring Aaron's rod again before the testimony, to be kept for a token against the rebels; and thou shalt quite take away their murmurings from me, that they die not.

You see, this was a perpetual sign that we don't have a right to make up our own rules or change God's rules. It was out of jealousy that this all began. It began in the mind, so it all comes back to faith and trust. This rod that budded should help us never to forget this story. In the great masterpiece *Patriarchs and Prophets*, we get even more insight:

> In the rebellion of Korah is seen the working out, upon a narrower stage, of the same spirit that led to the rebellion of Satan in heaven. It was pride and ambition that prompted Lucifer to complain of the government of God, and to seek the overthrow of the order which had been established in heaven. Since his fall it has been his object to infuse the same spirit of envy and discontent, the same ambition for position and honor, into the minds of men. He thus worked upon the minds of Korah, Dathan, and Abiram, to arouse the desire for self-exaltation and excite envy, distrust, and rebellion. Satan caused them to reject God as their leader, by rejecting the men of God's appointment. Yet while in their murmuring against Moses and Aaron they blasphemed God, they were so deluded as to think themselves righteous, and to regard those who had faithfully reproved their sins as actuated by Satan.

> Do not the same evils still exist that lay at the foundation of Korah's ruin? Pride and ambition are widespread; and when these are cherished, they open the door to envy, and a striving for supremacy; the soul is alienated from God, and unconsciously drawn into the ranks of Satan. Like Korah and his companions, many, even of the professed followers of Christ, are thinking, planning, and working so eagerly for self-exaltation that in order to gain the sympathy and support of the people they are ready to pervert the truth, falsifying and misrepresenting the Lord's servants, and even charging them with the base and selfish motives that inspire their own hearts. By persistently reiterating falsehood, and that against all evidence, they at last come to believe it to be truth. While endeavoring to destroy the confidence of the people in the men of God's appointment, they really believe that they are engaged in a good work, verily doing God service.

> The Hebrews were not willing to submit to the directions and restrictions of the Lord. They were restless under restraint, and unwilling to receive reproof. This was the secret of their murmuring against Moses. Had they been left free to do as they pleased, there would have been fewer complaints against their leader. All through the history of the church God's servants have had the same spirit to meet.

> It is by sinful indulgence that men give Satan access to their minds, and they go from one stage of wickedness to another. The rejection of light darkens the mind and hardens the heart, so that it is easier for them to take the next step in sin and to reject still clearer light, until at last their habits of wrongdoing become fixed. Sin ceases to appear sinful to them. He who faithfully preaches God's word, thereby condemning their sins, too often incurs their hatred. Unwilling to endure the pain and sacrifice necessary to reform, they turn upon the Lord's servant and denounce his reproofs as uncalled for and severe. Like Korah, they declare that the people are not at fault; it is the reprover that causes all the trouble. And soothing their consciences with this deception, the jealous and disaffected combine to sow discord in the church and weaken the hands of those who would build it up.

Every advance made by those whom God has called to lead in His work has excited suspicion; every act has been misrepresented by the jealous and faultfinding. Thus it was in the time of Luther, of the Wesleys and other reformers. Thus it is today.

Korah would not have taken the course he did had he *known* that all the directions and reproofs communicated to Israel were from God. But he might have known this. God had given overwhelming evidence that He was leading Israel. But Korah and his companions rejected light until they became so blinded that the most striking manifestations of His power were not sufficient to convince them; they attributed them all to human or satanic agency. The same thing was done by the people, who the day after the destruction of Korah and his company came to Moses and Aaron, saying, "Ye have killed the people of the Lord." Notwithstanding they had had the most convincing evidence of God's displeasure at their course, in the destruction of the men who had deceived them, they dared to attribute His judgments to Satan, declaring that through the power of the evil one, Moses and Aaron had caused the death of good and holy men. It was this act that sealed their doom. They had committed the sin against the Holy Spirit, a sin by which man's heart is effectually hardened against the influence of divine grace. "Whosoever speaketh a word against the Son of man," said Christ, "it shall be forgiven him: but whosoever speaketh against the Holy Ghost, it shall not be forgiven him" (Matthew 12:32). These words were spoken by our Saviour when the gracious works which He had performed through the power of God were attributed by the Jews to Beelzebub. It is through the agency of the Holy Spirit that God communicates with man; and those who deliberately reject this agency as satanic, have cut off the channel of communication between the soul and Heaven.

God works by the manifestation of His Spirit to reprove and convict the sinner; and if the Spirit's work is finally rejected, there is no more that God can do for the soul. The last resource of divine mercy has been employed. The transgressor has cut himself off from God, and sin has no remedy to cure itself. There is no reserved power by which God can work to convict and convert the sinner. "Let him alone" (Hosea 4:17) is the divine command. Then "there remaineth no more sacrifice for sins, but a certain fearful looking for of judgment and fiery indignation, which shall devour the adversaries" (Hebrews 10:26, 27). *PP 403–405*

This leaves nothing to the imagination. We can see that the rod that budded was an eternal promise and reminder that trusting in God keeps us connected but rejecting that trust cuts us off from the Lifegiver.

The last item, but certainly not the least, found in the ark of the covenant were the two tables of stone on which the words were written both on the front and the back. This was the law of God and was also very significant.

It was written by God's own finger in stone. This law was of such importance that God allowed no one but Himself to do this vital task. The law was written in stone, which symbolized that it was to last forever. Another item of importance is that Jesus is our chief Cornerstone—our Rock of salvation. Many times, He is represented as a rock—as a stone. Again, this signifies that Christ our Rock will never change. He is the same yesterday, today, and forever! This law was not written on wood or on scrolls. God wrote it on stone to signify that it was perfect and everlasting. There was never any mistake with one of the commandments—it was we who failed in keeping the law of liberty. The law was to keep us free in Christ. It was never to be made a burden.

Image courtesy istockphoto.

In the Book of Revelation, we read about the sanctuary. John in vision saw the ark of the covenant. No matter how hard the world tries to do away with God's law, it can never be abolished or obliterated. We should be so happy about that.

As we take another look back into time, to the very beginning, we see that the great deceiver—Lucifer—wanted to abolish God's law. His whole effort was not only to break God's law himself but to convince the rest of heaven that this law of God was unfair. You can see what happened to him and a third of the angelic host, when they did their own works. Instead of the light-bearer, Lucifer turned into the great deceiver.

Do you know the saying "Misery loves company"? It came from how Satan worked. He was not satisfied to leave well enough alone, but he put his whole mind into deceiving us humans. How did he do this? As we look to the Book of Genesis, we find the answer. In chapter 3, we read that God gave the command not to eat of the tree in the midst of the garden. We see that the devil took advantage of Eve. He lied to her. He broke God's law. Just think—had he not lied to Eve, we would not be in this mess.

This law of God—called the law of love—is liberty to all who obey it. John, in his Gospel, wrote the words of our Lord and Saviour: "If you love Me, keep My commandments." By these words, He is also saying, "If you don't love Me, then forget the law, because it won't do you any good." It is love that motivates us to do the will of God.

So many Christians today say the law was done away with at the cross. This is not at all consistent with Scripture. As Jesus said, "Think not that I am come to destroy the law, or the prophets: I am not come to destroy, but to fulfil" (Matthew 5:17). The sanctuary will tell you the very same thing. Let's take a look at it. In the picture, you see the cross overshadowing the articles of the sanctuary. Where does the crucifixion take place? This is a point never to be forgotten. When we give our hearts to the Lord, we come to the cross. What part of the cross do we come to? You're right—we come to the foot of the cross. It is here that we look to Jesus, the Author and Finisher of our faith. This is where the terrible crucifixion took place. This is where the little lambs that had done nothing wrong were sacrificed. It is because of breaking God's law that we are here. Praise His name, there is a way of escape from our sins.

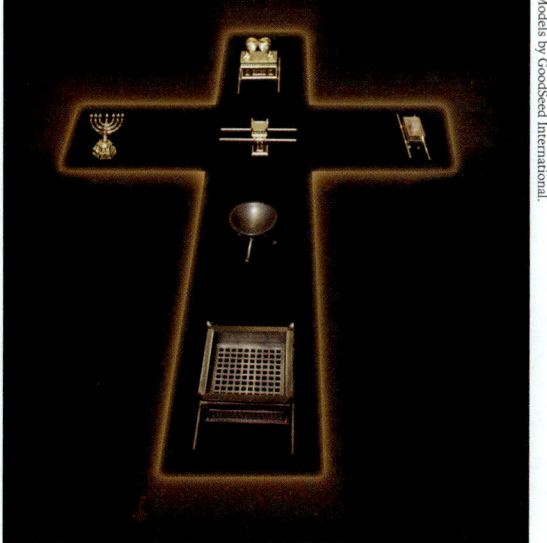

Models by GoodSeed International.

Don't forget this most important and vital key. Our escape is through Jesus. It is not the abolishing of the law that provides an escape. It is the perfect law that Paul tells us is holy, just, and good. James tells us it is the perfect law of liberty. Jesus Himself tells us in the last book of the Bible—where John in vision saw the seven churches—that he who overcomes will be with Me. If this loving law could have been done away with, then there would have been no reason for Jesus to die on the cross. God would have said to Jesus, "No problem, Jesus—this is an easy fix. Let's just do away with this perfect law that I have laid out. Let us bring Satan back up here to heaven, because he was right after all, and we were wrong. There is no reason to keep this law—it is too restraining, too cumbersome, too hard, and most of all, it brings far too much unhappiness."

All at once you begin to reason from cause to effect that if this were the case, then there would be no need for Jesus to be crucified because of our sinfulness. It was because the law will always be the right way of life that it cost Jesus His precious blood and therefore, we have Him as our Saviour.

If you will look at this picture again you will notice that we are just beginning our journey at the foot of the cross. Remember that the sanctuary is a movement. It is a process. Once you give your heart to Jesus and ask Him to take away all your sins, you are at the foot of the cross. Without going back through everything, you can see that the Most Holy Place is at the head of the cross. This is where the ark of the covenant is located. Again, the law is in the ark. Paul wrote these inspired words in Philippians 2:5: "Let this mind be in you, which was also in Christ Jesus." God also says, in Jeremiah 31:33:

> But this shall be the covenant that I will make with the house of Israel; After those days, saith the LORD, I will put my law in their inward parts, and write it in their hearts; and will be their God, and they shall be my people.

In Hebrews 10:16, this very verse is quoted from Jeremiah. God, through the sanctuary, is making these things very clear to us. Can you see how He longs to let the law become spiritual to us? He wants us to be like His Son Jesus. He is speaking to all of us in such a personal way. So let us have this law written in our inmost parts. Let's let the great law of love be formed within us, the hope of glory. Jesus has promised all of us that if we are willing, He will restore the image of God in us. He has the power, let's have the faith—and it will happen.

Prophecies of Daniel

BABYLON
605-539 B.C.

MEDO-PERSIA
539-331 B.C.

GREECE
331-168 B.C.

ROME
168 B.C. - 476 A.D.

LITTLE HORN
538 A.D. - 1798 A.D.

End
Time

Daniel 2—The Great Statue

One night around the year 606 B.C. Nebuchadnezzar—king of Babylon—had a dream. This dream was different from any he had ever had. It was so disturbing to him that he could not even sleep. He called his magicians, astrologers, sorcerers, and the Chaldeans together to tell him the dream.

They could tell that this dream was vitally important to the king. So they told the king to tell them the dream and they would give the interpretation. The king answered and said, "The thing is gone from me: if ye will not make known unto me the dream, with the interpretation thereof, ye shall be cut in pieces, and your houses shall be made a dunghill" (Daniel 2:5).

The king knew that if he told them the dream they would give some explanation for it and then only time would tell if it were true or not. He knew the dream had a very important meaning, and he was not willing to risk an inaccurate interpretation.

As the story in the Book of Daniel continues, the king made a decree to kill all his wise men including Daniel and his companions. Daniel went to the king and asked for a little time. He then went to the house of his companions and they prayed that God might show them the dream and its interpretation. The secret was revealed and Daniel went to the king and told him that the God of heaven had told him the dream and its interpretation.

Daniel began telling the king exactly what he had seen in the dream:

> Thou, O king, sawest, and behold a great image. This great image, whose brightness was excellent, stood before thee; and the form thereof was terrible. This image's head was of fine gold, his breast and his arms of silver, his belly and his thighs of brass, His legs of iron, his feet part of iron and part of clay. Thou sawest till that a stone was cut out without hands, which smote the image upon his feet that were of iron and clay, and brake them to pieces. Then was the iron, the clay, the brass, the silver, and the gold, broken to pieces together, and became like the chaff of the summer threshingfloors; and the wind carried them away, that no place was found for them: and the stone that smote the image became a great mountain, and filled the whole earth (Daniel 2:31–35).

Then Daniel moved on to share with Nebuchadnezzar the meaning of his dream:

> This is the dream; and we will tell the interpretation thereof before the king. Thou, O king, art a king of kings: for the God of heaven hath given thee a kingdom, power, and strength, and glory. And wheresoever the children of men dwell, the beasts of the field and the fowls of the heaven hath he given into thine hand, and hath made thee ruler over them all. Thou art this head of gold. And after thee shall arise another kingdom inferior to thee, and another third kingdom of brass, which shall bear rule over all the earth. And the fourth kingdom shall be strong as iron: forasmuch
> as iron breaketh in pieces and subdueth all things: and as iron that breaketh all these, shall it break in pieces and bruise. And whereas thou sawest the feet and toes, part of potters' clay, and part of iron, the kingdom shall be divided; but there shall be in it of the strength of the iron, forasmuch as thou sawest the iron mixed with miry clay. And

as the toes of the feet were part of iron, and part of clay, so the kingdom shall be partly strong, and partly broken. And whereas thou sawest iron mixed with miry clay, they shall mingle themselves with the seed of men: but they shall not cleave one to another, even as iron is not mixed with clay. And in the days of these kings shall the God of heaven set up a kingdom, which shall never be destroyed: and the kingdom shall not be left to other people, but it shall break in pieces and consume all these kingdoms, and it shall stand for ever. Forasmuch as thou sawest that the stone was cut out of the mountain without hands, and that it brake in pieces the iron, the brass, the clay, the silver, and the gold; the great God hath made known to the king what shall come to pass hereafter: and the dream is certain, and the interpretation thereof sure (Daniel 2:36–45).

In a little more than 300 words, God sketched out the next 2,500 years of human history in this dream—from the time of Babylon to the end of the world history.

Babylon—the Head of Gold

The first of the four kingdoms Nebuchadnezzar saw in his dream—the one in power in his and Daniel's time—was represented by the golden head of the statue. Of course, King Nebuchadnezzar was so certain that his kingdom would last forever that he later ordered to be built a 90-foot-tall copy of the statue he had seen in his dream. Only instead of the statue being divided into different kinds of metal, beginning with the gold head that Daniel said represented Babylon—Nebuchadnezzar ordered that the entire statue be built of gold, showing his certainty that his kingdom would reign forever. How wrong he was!

Through Daniel, God warned Nebuchadnezzar that his unbounded ego would get him into great trouble. But Nebuchadnezzar would have none of it. And in time, just as God had warned, the king went insane and spent seven years crawling around in the pasture eating grass with the cows. At the end of that time, Nebuchadnezzar was humbled, and declared Daniel's God to be the great and only true God.

Medo-Persia—the Chest and Arms of Silver

Just as Daniel prophesied, of course, a time came when the great kingdom of Babylon ended. Daniel lived to see it happen—the silver kingdom replacing the gold. On October 13, 539 B.C., the golden kingdom of Babylon came to an inglorious end. During the reign of Belshazzar, Nebuchadnezzar's proud and arrogant grandson, Cyrus the Mede laid siege to Babylon and overthrew it. The kingdom of Medo-Persia began.

Greece—the Belly and Thighs of Brass

So a new superpower ruled the then-known world. But like the golden kingdom of Babylon that went before it, the reign of Medo-Persia, the silver empire, would not last forever. The brilliant young Greek general, Alexander the Great, defeated Persia's Darius III at the battle of Arbela in 331 B.C. At 23, young Alexander became ruler over the most extensive empire the world had known to that time.

Rome—the Legs of Iron

What great empire came next to overthrow Greece? What nation would then rule during the life of Christ? On June 22, 168 B.C., at the battle of Pydna, the empire of Alexander the Great perished, 155 years after his death. The Roman Empire succeeded the Greeks, thus becoming the fourth world empire, ruling from 168 B.C. to A.D. 476.

Rome was a ruthless nation that ruled with a "rod of iron." Her Caesars called themselves gods and demanded worship and obedience from everyone. Rome ruled the longest and reached the farthest of all empires.

But Rome, too, met an end, but not at the hands of a more powerful kingdom. Just as Daniel predicted, no other world-wide empire succeeded Rome.

Division of Rome—the Feet of Iron and Clay

After more than 600 years in power, God accurately predicted, ancient Rome would not be followed by another world empire but would disintegrate into smaller kingdoms. Through unparalleled luxury, political corruption, and moral decay, Rome lost its stability and strength. It became easy prey for tribes of barbarians that began to invade the empire during the fourth century A.D.

By A.D. 476, Rome had divided into ten parts, listed here with their modern counterparts: Alemanni (Germans), Franks (French), Saxons (English), Visigoths (Spanish), Burgundians (Swiss), Lombards (Italians), Suevi (Portuguese); and the Heruli, Vandals, and Ostrogoths (now extinct). The current nations of Europe developed from these tribes of the divided Roman Empire. Some were strong, some weak.

"Whereas thou sawest iron mixed with miry clay, they shall mingle themselves with the seed of men: but they shall not cleave one to another, even as iron is not mixed with clay" (Daniel 2:43). Many world rulers have tried to unite the nations of Europe, often through royal marriages, mingling themselves "with the seed of men." God's prediction of world empires to the end of time has been remarkably accurate. No effort to unite the divided kingdoms of old Rome—of current Europe—can ever succeed. Charlemagne tried and failed. Charles V and Louis XIV tried and failed. Napoleon Bonaparte tried and failed. Kaiser Wilhelm of Germany in 1914 tried and failed. Later, Hitler tried and failed. And today, efforts continue to bring Europe together, but every such effort fails.

The Great Stone—God's Eternal Kingdom

Daniel ended his explanation of Nebuchadnezzar's dream with these words: "And in the days of these kings shall the God of heaven set up a kingdom, which shall never be destroyed: and the kingdom shall not be left to other people, but it shall break in pieces and consume all these kingdoms, and it shall stand for ever. Forasmuch as thou sawest that the stone was cut out of the mountain without hands, and that it brake in pieces the iron, the brass, the clay, the silver, and the gold; the great God hath made known to the king what shall come to pass hereafter: and the dream is certain, and the interpretation thereof sure" (Daniel 2:44, 45).

Through this dream of a giant metal image that Nebuchadnezzar experienced six centuries before the birth of Christ, God unveiled the course of history to the end of time. All of the kingdoms the king saw—represented by the gold, the silver, the brass, and the iron—have passed into history. Where are we living today? In the days of the kings represented by the ten toes—the nations of Europe today—God will set up a kingdom to end all earthly kingdoms—a kingdom that will last forever. The only event in Bible prophecy yet to take place is the second coming of Jesus Christ and the establishment of His kingdom.

Daniel 7—The Four Beasts

Often in Bible prophecy, we find that God covers the same periods of time, using different symbols. This is true in both of the two key books of the Bible that deal with time prophecies—Daniel and its companion—the Book of Revelation.

So it's not surprising that God would return to this great panoramic view of time from Babylon to the second coming of Christ.

Sure enough, five chapters later, in Daniel 7, God gave Daniel himself a vision at night, and showed him the exact same sweep of time from Babylon to the second coming. This time, though, God gave to Daniel different symbols for the world's kingdoms than Nebuchadnezzar had seen in his dream.

Instead of a statue with different metal sections, God showed Daniel the same kingdoms, but this time, each one was represented by a different animal—or beast. Instead of Babylon being represented by the statue's head of gold, Babylon this time was symbolized by a lion with eagle's wings. According to history, the kingdom of Babylon reigned supreme on earth from 605 B.C. to 539 B.C.

Medo-Persia, rather than the statue's chest and arms of silver, was now a bear with three ribs in its mouth. Medo-Persia ruled from 539 B.C. to 331 B.C.

Greece, instead of the belly and thighs of brass, was now a four-headed leopard with four wings. Interestingly, when Alexander the Great died, his empire was divided between his four top generals. This kingdom ruled from 331 B.C. to 168 B.C.

BABYLON
605-539 B.C.

MEDO-PERSIA
539-331 B.C.

GREECE
331-168 B.C.

ROME
168 B.C. - 476 A.D.

LITTLE HORN
538 A.D.-1798 A.D.

Rome, instead of being the legs of iron, was now a fearsome beast with iron teeth and ten horns. The great kingdom of Rome ruled from 168 B.C. to A.D. 476. When it then ended, the kingdom divided into ten parts. In Daniel 2, those parts were represented by the ten toes of the image. In Daniel 7, they are represented by the ten horns of the fourth beast.

Now, up through this point, the two prophecies run completely parallel to each other. But when the prophecy of Daniel 7 came to Rome, God gave Daniel much more detail than before. The ten horns of the fourth great beast represented the ten pagan, godless fragments of the Roman Empire that became today's nations of Europe.

But Daniel 7 moves the prophetic panorama forward into new territory. Notice Daniel's description of what he saw at this point in his vision of the beasts: "After this I saw in the night visions, and behold a fourth beast, dreadful and terrible, and strong exceedingly; and it had great iron teeth: it devoured and brake in pieces, and stamped the residue with the feet of it: and it was diverse from all the beasts that were before it; and it had ten horns. I considered the horns, and, behold, there came up among them another little horn, before whom there were three of the first horns plucked up by the roots: and, behold, in this horn were eyes like the eyes of man, and a mouth speaking great things" (Daniel 7:7, 8).

Papal Rome—The "Little Horn" Power

So here we have a fearsome ten-horned beast, and a new "little horn" comes up in the midst of the ten and plucks three of them "up by the roots." And, the Bible says, this new little horn has eyes "like the eyes of man" and speaks "great things."

The record of history is the key to identifying this new "little horn" power. And history clearly records that three of those original ten pagan kingdoms into which old Rome splintered were indeed "plucked out by the roots." And all were overthrown by the same power.

When the Roman Empire ended in A.D. 476, a struggle began for control of the ten remaining parts of the empire. On one side were three of the pagan tribes: the Heruli, the Vandals, and the Ostrogoths. On the other side was the Bishop of Rome and the emperors loyal to the Catholic bishop. One by one, the Catholic emperors overthrew these three rebel tribes:

- The Emperor Zeno conquered the Heruli by encouraging the Ostrogoths to invade in A.D. 493.
- The Emperor Justinian sent his General Belisarius to conquer the Vandals in A.D. 534.
- General Belisarius then drove the Ostrogoths out of Rome in A.D. 538.

In A.D. 533, Justinian decreed that the Bishop of Rome was to rule supreme over all the churches. But his decree meant nothing until he and other emperors were able to overthrow the three Arian tribes (Heruli, Vandals, Ostrogoths)—"the three horns" of Daniel 7.

By A.D. 538, this was accomplished, and the era of the little horn's power had begun. The papacy would continue in absolute power for another 1,260 years till the year 1798. (Note: This 1,260-year period is found in Bible prophecy in several places. See Daniel 7:25, Daniel 12:7, Revelation 11:2, Revelation 11:3, Revelation 12:6, Revelation 12:14, and Revelation 13:5.)

When his vision was finished, Daniel asked God for an explanation. Can you imagine if you had just seen a vision like that? With what we've just read, any thinking person would have wanted to know—just as much as Daniel did—what in the world this terrible-looking beast could represent. It was so dreadful looking—so powerful. And it was doing almost unspeakable things. Last but not least, what could this vision mean? Just to read what Daniel saw in his dream would make almost anybody a little afraid. Daniel knew that whatever it was, it was not good.

Another thing we must not let slip through our fingers is that God considered the information in this vision so vitally important that even hundreds of years later, He gave John a similar vision in Revelation 13:5. And it did not stop there. God also gave the same time prophecy in Revelation 11:2, 3; 12:6; and 12:14.

Amazing love! What a wonderful God we serve, that He would not leave us in the dark about something so important that not knowing it could cost us our eternal salvation. Yet many

times, God in His infinite wisdom does not just give us the answers without our own careful study. We are all being tested. Do we love and believe God enough to get into His Word? Are you, reader, diving into His love letter and finding out what He wants you to know? It's all there. Nothing at all is left out that we need for our benefit, safety, and salvation. We just have to dig a little. Let's see what happens next in Daniel 7:19–25:

> Then I would know the truth of the fourth beast, which was diverse from all the others, exceeding dreadful, whose teeth were of iron, and his nails of brass; which devoured, brake in pieces, and stamped the residue with his feet; And of the ten horns that were in his head, and of the other which came up, and before whom three fell; even of that horn that had eyes, and a mouth that spake very great things, whose look was more stout than his fellows. I beheld, and the same horn made war with the saints, and prevailed against them; Until the Ancient of days came, and judgment was given to the saints of the most High; and the time came that the saints possessed the kingdom. Thus he said, The fourth beast shall be the fourth kingdom upon earth, which shall be diverse from all kingdoms, and shall devour the whole earth, and shall tread it down, and break it in pieces. And the ten horns out of this kingdom are ten kings that shall arise: and another shall rise after them; and he shall be diverse from the first, and he shall subdue three kings. And he shall speak great words against the most High, and shall wear out the saints of the most High, and think to change times and laws: and they shall be given into his hand until a time and times and the dividing of time.

Now, in order to fully and fairly identify this "little horn" power as the reign of the papacy, let's allow the Bible itself to provide that identification. We can find at least ten ways in the Word to identify this power:

Ten Ways to Identify the Little Horn

1. It came to power from among the ten divisions of Europe—the ten horns (Daniel 7:8).
2. It came to power after A.D. 476, because the "little horn" succeeded pagan Rome, which fell in that year (Daniel 7:7, 8).
3. It began as "a little horn"—a little power at its beginning (Daniel 7:8).
4. It uprooted three horns—the Heruli, the Vandals, and the Ostrogoths (Daniel 7:8, 24).
5. It has a man at its head (Daniel 7:8; see also 2 Thessalonians 2:3).
6. It is "different" from the others. They were "state" powers, and the little horn was a "church-state" combination (Daniel 7: 24).
7. The little horn would speak great words and blasphemy (Daniel 7:8, 25). The definition of blasphemy from the Bible is to claim to be God and/or to claim to be able to forgive sin. (See Matthew 9:2–6; John 10:30–33.)
8. The little horn would wear out and kill many of God's children. During its 1,260-year reign, the papal persecutions brought the death of millions (Daniel 7: 25).
9. The little horn antichrist would think to change times and law (Daniel 7:25). The Catholic Church notes the changes it made to God's law in its catechism. It removed the second commandment that forbids idolatry, changed the fourth commandment requiring worship on the seventh day of the week, and finally, divided the tenth commandment in two to retain a full ten commandments.
10. The little horn power would rule for "a time and times and the dividing of time"—elsewhere presented in the Bible as 1,260 days or forty-two months of prophetic time. Since a day is equal to a year in Bible prophecy, this power was to rule for 1,260 years. God foretold that it would reign supreme and persecute God's obedient children for 1,260 years.

So in Daniel 2 and Daniel 7, God has given us a sweeping overview of history from the time of Nebuchadnezzar—more than 600 years before Christ's birth—and continuing to the very end of time at the second coming of Jesus.

As we study these two parallel prophecies, we discover exactly where we are today in the stream of time. Yes, we see that we are involved in a great struggle between two systems—truth and error, loyalty and disloyalty, right and wrong, good and evil. But we also are wonderfully encouraged as we realize that we are at the very end of time here on this earth and that the next event yet to happen is the return of Jesus!

We personally hope that you will diligently study these timely and vitally important subjects. Knowing these truths means the difference between life and death. But no one has to be

deceived. Our one and only principle should be no different from that of the disciples in the New Testament, when they said in Acts 5:29, "We ought to obey God rather than men."

Remember the three men who were worthy to be noted in Daniel 3? When the king wanted them to bow down to his image, they said, to put it in a nutshell, "King, we do very much respect you, but we serve the living God. We serve the God of Abraham, Isaac, and Jacob. Our God is able to save us if He wants to. If He would be glorified to keep us from burning up in that fiery furnace, then we are happy and very thankful! If not, it does not make a difference to us. We trust and believe that our God—the only true God—has our best interests in mind."

As you read again this account in the Book of Daniel, you see that these three wise men did not try to be arrogant, nor were they belittling King Nebuchadnezzar. What do you think might have happened, had they tried to be politically correct? They could have played out all kinds of scenarios that might have sounded good and right according to man's thoughts. For example, they could have said, "When the music starts playing, we will look as if we are bowing down, but really, we will just tie our sandals. That way, we are not really worshiping the statue." They could have said, "If we make a scene now, we will throw away everything we have worked so hard for." Another way they could have looked at it might have been: "If we don't bow down, it could save a lot of our friends. Just think—millions of Jews are here, and we don't want to make it bad for the rest of them." By the way, why did no one else stay standing?

You see, it was love for God that kept them from being traditionally or politically correct. And that love meant more to them than even their own lives on this earth.

To go along with the crowd—even a Christian one—just because you don't want to make waves or you think you might be the laughingstock of your family or even your own church, will in the end come down to one final question: Do you love Jesus more than tradition or the approval of the majority? We will be judged by God, and that is the only thing that should matter. We have a more sure word of prophecy. God's Word is always right. Let's not stand up and defend something just because of the majority. Get into those Scriptures and study as never before. As you can see, these end-time prophecies tell us that we are here at the close of history. Time as we have known it will soon be over. It won't get any easier to make hard decisions. In the end, though, the reward is well worth it. Truth will prevail—it will be victorious.

2,300-Day Prophecy

It is so nice to know that God does nothing first unless He reveals it to His prophets. When He does reveal it to us, we need to study to show ourselves approved. He wants us to find out what He is trying to say. God many times gives us more than one place in the Scripture to figure out these puzzles. No man could do this because often the time line is spanning more than one generation.

This prophecy is no exception. We can begin this in the Book of Daniel and find additional information in the Book of Revelation. This is one big reason that we know the Bible comes from God. No man would be able to do this. There are many years—more than five hundred—between Daniel and Revelation. Only the God of heaven Who makes no mistakes and knows the end from the beginning would be able to span such a time period and have everything work like a hand in a glove.

This vitally important study will begin in Daniel 7:9, 10. In a prophetic vision that included the sanctuary in heaven, an angel said to the prophet Daniel:

> I beheld till the thrones were cast down, and the Ancient of days did sit, whose garment was white as snow, and the hair of his head like the pure wool: his throne was like the fiery flame, and his wheels as burning fire. A fiery stream issued and came forth from before him: thousand thousands ministered unto him, and ten thousand times ten thousand stood before him: the judgment was set, and the books were opened.

The yearly cleansing of the sanctuary in the Old Testament was a symbol of the final work of Judgment prior to Christ's second coming.

As you can clearly see, there is a Judgment that takes place. The question here is when does this judgment take place? If you go now to 8:13, 14, you read:

> Then I heard one saint speaking, and another saint said unto that certain saint which spake, How long shall be the vision concerning the daily sacrifice, and the transgression of desolation, to give both the sanctuary and the host to be trodden under foot? And he said unto me, Unto two thousand and three hundred days; then shall the sanctuary be cleansed.

So it's clear that God wanted to share with Daniel just when the real Day of Atonement in heaven would begin: 2,300 days from . . . but when?

The 70-Weeks Prophecy

When the vision Daniel received in chapter 8 was finished, God sent a heavenly angel named Gabriel to explain it to Daniel. But partway through this explanation, Daniel fell ill (Daniel 8:27): "And I Daniel fainted, and was sick certain days; afterward I rose up, and did the king's business; and I was astonished at the vision, but none understood it."

But in the next chapter, after Daniel recovered, Gabriel returned to finish explaining the vision: "And he informed me, and talked with me, and said, O Daniel, I am now come forth to give thee skill and understanding. At the beginning of thy supplications the commandment came forth, and I am come to shew thee; for thou art greatly beloved: therefore understand the matter, and consider the vision" (Daniel 9:22, 23).

It is amazing that many Christians are almost afraid to study prophecy. Or they misinterpret it. When we use the whole Bible to get our information and not tradition, God will send His Holy Spirit and guide us into Truth. Right from the words of the highest Angel those great words—"O Daniel, I am now come forth to give thee skill and understanding"—cannot be refuted. Our Lord wants us desperately to understand what is about to take place on this earth so you and I might be prepared and ready for His coming.

In the next four verses, Gabriel outlined a fascinating time prophecy, explaining it as he went along.

Verse 24

> Seventy weeks are determined upon thy people and upon thy holy city,
> And to finish the transgression,
> And to make an end of sins,
> And to make reconciliation for iniquity,
> And to bring in everlasting righteousness,
> And to seal up the vision and prophecy,
> And to anoint the most Holy.

So out of the long 2,300-day prophecy—part of Daniel's vision in chapter 8—Gabriel said that 70 weeks are "determined" (a word meaning "cut off") from the longer prophecy, for "thy people" (the Jewish nation—the people of Israel). During this 70 weeks, several things would take place. These six tasks could only be fulfilled in and through the work of Jesus, the Messiah. Who else, for example, could possibly make reconciliation for iniquity or bring in everlasting righteousness?

Now, it's important to know about two keys to understanding Bible time prophecies. First, in Bible prophecy, literal time periods are often a symbol of a much longer time period. A twenty-four-hour day, for example, stands for a year (see Numbers 14:34 and Ezekiel 4:6).

A second key important to know is that while our years today have 365 days, in Daniel's time, the Jewish year had only 360 days.

So applying these two keys, we realize that the 2,300 days of Daniel 8:14 are really 2,300 years. In the same way, the 70 weeks here in Daniel 9:24 are actually 490 years (70 weeks x 7 days per week = 490). This means that the first 490 years of the longer 2,300 years are "cut off" or "determined" for several important things to be accomplished.

Verse 25

> Know therefore and understand, that from the going forth of the commandment to restore and to build Jerusalem unto the Messiah the Prince shall be seven weeks, and threescore and two weeks: the street shall be built again, and the wall, even in troublous times.

The first 69 weeks of this 70-week prophecy begin with "the commandment to restore and to build Jerusalem." So if we can learn when this command was given, we will have the starting date for both the 70 weeks—and the longer 2,300 days—from the beginning of which this 70 weeks was "cut off."

History tells us exactly when this command was decreed. This decree, described in Ezra 7:13–26, was sent out by the Persian king Artaxerxes in the year 457 B.C.

Sometimes it is easy to confuse the date or dates of this prophecy because there were two other decrees in Ezra. The first we find in Ezra 1. This decree is missing a vital point of

the prophecy. It only decrees the building of the temple, not Jerusalem. That is a huge difference. The other decree is found in Ezra 6. This decree like the first one talks only of the temple. The third decree in the 7th chapter is the right decree. This decree not only talks of the temple but of restoring the law of God. This third decree is the last decree. The temple is finished. Also when you look at Ezra 9:9, you read that the walls of Jerusalem were to be rebuilt. It was to restore everything.

Gabriel explained that the 69 weeks were the sum of 7 weeks plus 62 weeks. During the first part—the 7 weeks—the angel says, "the street shall be built again, and the wall, even in troublous times." In other words, the 7 weeks would be for the rebuilding of Jerusalem.

The 62 weeks? That would be explained in verse 26.

Verse 26

> And after threescore and two weeks shall Messiah be cut off, but not for himself: and the people of the prince that shall come shall destroy the city and the sanctuary; and the end thereof shall be with a flood, and unto the end of the war desolations are determined.

Sometime after the 62 weeks, Gabriel said, the Messiah would be "cut off"—a reference to Christ's death on the cross.

It's time now to do some "math," and see where we are on the timeline of this prophecy. But first, be careful not to miscalculate, based on the change-over from B.C. dates to A.D. dates. To remember here? There was no "year zero"! B.C. dates counted down to the year 1 B.C. This year was followed immediately—not by a "year 0"—but by the year A.D. 1.

Keep this in mind now, as we move to the next verse.

Image courtesy istockphoto.

Verse 27

> And he shall confirm the covenant with many for one week: and in the midst of the week he shall cause the sacrifice and the oblation to cease, and for the overspreading of abominations he shall make it desolate, even until the consummation, and that determined shall be poured upon the desolate.

The 69 weeks ended in A.D. 27, according to prophecy. But the 70-week prophecy means there is yet one more week. So adding another week (7 years) to A.D. 27, we come to the year A.D. 34.

Now notice that verse 27 says that the Messiah would "confirm the covenant with many for one week." History shows that Jesus began His ministry at His baptism, in the year A.D. 27!

But this verse also says that "in the midst of the week he shall cause the sacrifice and the oblation to cease." The system of sacrifices and offerings, as we've earlier seen, was part of the desert sanctuary. When the symbol met the reality (Christ's sacrifice on the cross), what need would there be after that for the symbolic sacrifices to continue? Christ's very real sacrifice brought that to an end at the cross.

And when did Jesus die on the cross? Again, history shows that He died in the year A.D. 31—precisely in "the midst of the week" as predicted by this prophecy. Remember too that verse 26 said that Jesus would be "cut off" somewhere after the 69th week.

What about the confirming of the covenant "with many for one week"? This refers to the period of time Jesus focused His efforts primarily on His people Israel. But with the stoning of Stephen in A.D. 34, the gospel message now went as well to the Gentiles—non-Jews—that is, to the entire world.

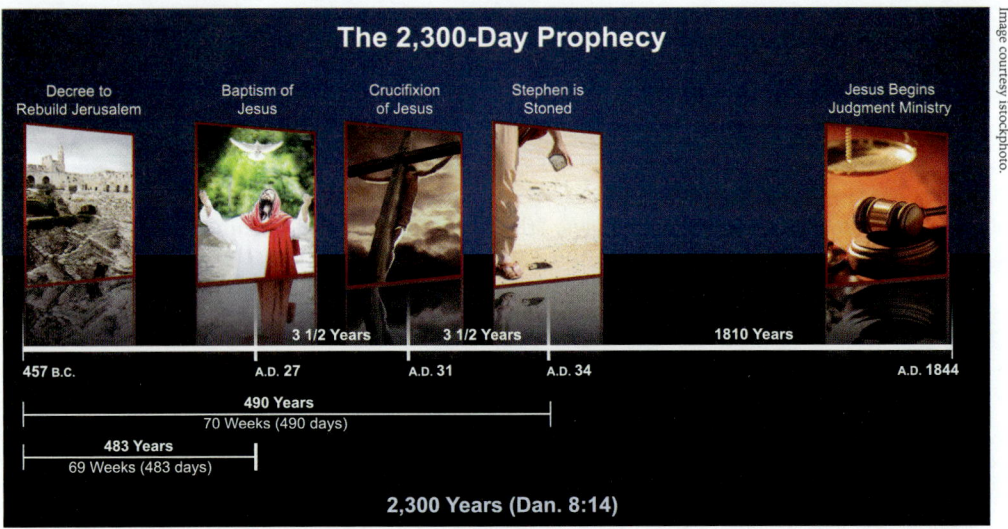

This, then, is in rather abbreviated form an overview of the 70-week prophecy. But to finish the "bigger picture" that began in Daniel 8:14—the larger 2,300-day prophecy about the cleansing of the Sanctuary in heaven—we need to complete the prophecy timeline.

If the first 70 weeks (Part 1 of the 2,300-day prophecy) brought us to the year A.D. 34, then doing a little more math, we subtract the 70 weeks (490 prophetic years) from 2,300 years, and that leaves 1,810 years for Part 2 of the prophecy. All that remains, then, is to add this 1,810 years to the end of the 70 weeks (A.D. 34), and we are brought to the year A.D. 1844.

Daniel's vision of the Bible's longest time prophecy—the 2,300 days—stated clearly in Daniel 8:14: "Unto two thousand and three hundred days; then shall the sanctuary be cleansed." We've now, step by step, established that this 2,300 days (years) ended in the year 1844. And then, the Bible says, the Sanctuary shall be cleansed.

Just as the Old Testament Sanctuary had an annual service called the Day of Atonement, on which day the Sanctuary was symbolically cleansed, this great prophecy tells us that the real Sanctuary in heaven is also cleansed. And when? Beginning in the year 1844.

This means that since that time, Jesus—our High Priest—has been ministering His shed blood in a great courtroom scene in heaven. When His work is done, the Sanctuary will be cleansed, and He will return to this earth at His second coming.

Though we on earth cannot see what is happening in this work of judgment and cleansing in heaven, the Bible has told us that it is happening. It is a solemn time. And just as ancient Israel on that symbolic Day of Atonement spent the day in heart-searching and in putting away their sins, so we who are living in the time of heaven's Day of Atonement should also be searching our hearts and seeking Christ's power to put sin away from our lives.

In heaven, Jesus continues His saving work for us. The great enemy of us all, Satan, has, before the entire universe, accused us each of our sins as reason we shouldn't be saved for eternity (the Bible calls him, "the accuser of our brethren . . . which accused them before our God day and night," Revelation 12:10).

But Satan also has accused Jesus Himself of unfairness—of making a Law that couldn't be kept, of offering mercy and salvation to undeserving sinners. So it's this great judgment going on in heaven, to which the Bible refers in the Book of Revelation 14 (as part of what the Bible calls the "messages of the three angels"): "Fear God, and give glory to him; for the hour of his judgment is come: and worship him that made heaven, and earth, and the sea, and the fountains of waters."

His judgment. So even Jesus is being judged, in the eyes of the onlooking universe and unfallen angels, as to whether He can be both just and merciful.

The Old Testament Sanctuary—as well as the Sanctuary in heaven—do far more than tell us about salvation. They show us how it looks in reality. They illustrate and demonstrate the Bible's greatest theme—how men, women, and children are saved.

This time prophecy is almost completed. The question is are you ready? It will come at the appointed time. God's Word has never failed and it never will. He has done absolutely everything He can to show us and tell us of this endtime judgment. The question for you in the last moments of this earth's history is, Are you willing to not only believe but to make the decision to accept the call? Don't put it off. Tomorrow may be too late. Let us be determined to be on the right side—His side—that we might spend eternity with Jesus and the many others who have accepted His Grace.

Many signs and symbols are contained in the Bible. God had a number of reasons for choosing to use them. Here are a few:

- God knew that if we loved Him, we would search His Word diligently. To understand it as we should, we need to rightly divide the Word of Truth (2 Timothy 2:15). This can only be accomplished by going through many texts—not just one or two.
- Many of the apocalyptic prophecies were given while the prophets were in a hostile foreign land. One reason God cloaked the prophecies in symbols was to protect the messengers.
- When signs and symbols are used, it tends to anchor the things they represent in our memory longer. For instance, if you hear the word *eagle* many times in connection with the United States, you associate the USA with it.

We hope you will get to know your Bible better than ever, and to help you in that effort, we present here a few signs and symbols to get you started.

Animals and Their Parts

- **Bear** = Destructive Power (2 Kings 2:23, 24; Proverbs 28:15)
- **Beast** = Kingdom / Government / Political Power (Daniel 7:17, 23)
- **Blood** = Life (Leviticus 17:11; Deuteronomy 12:23)
- **Dove** = Holy Spirit (Mark 1:10)
- **Dragon** = Satan or His Agency (Revelation 12:7–9)
- **Goat** = Greece (Daniel 8:21)
- **Horn** = King or Kingdom (Daniel 7:24; 8:21, 22; Zechariah 1:18, 19; Revelation 17:12)
  - Strength (Psalm 75:10)
- **Horse** = Strength and Power in Battle (Job 39:19; Psalm 147:10; Proverbs 21:31)
  - Swiftness (Jeremiah 4:13)
  - Stubbornness (Jeremiah 8:4–6)
  - Lust (Jeremiah 5:8)
  - A Form of Trust in the Wrong Way (Psalm 20:7)
- **Lamb** = Jesus / Sacrifice (Isaiah 53:7; John 1:29)
- **Lion** = Powerful King, that is, Babylon (Jeremiah 50:43, 44; Daniel 7:4, 17, 23)
  - Jesus (Revelation 5:4–9)
- **Ram** = Medo-Persia (Daniel 8:20)
- **Serpent** = Satan (Revelation 12:9; 20:2)
- **Wings** = Speed / Protection (Deuteronomy 28:49; Matthew 23:37)
- **Wolf** = False Prophets That Hunt in a Time of Darkness (Matthew 7:15)

Colors

- **Amber** = Glory of God (Ezekiel 1:3, 4; 8:1, 2)
- **Black** = Famine (Revelation 6:5, 6)
- **Blue** = Law, Obedience (Numbers 15:37–41)
  - Royalty (Esther 8:15)
- **Gold** = Holiness, Rulership (Revelation 4:4; 14:14)
  - Spiritual Wealth (Revelation 3:18)
- **Purple** = Royalty (Judges 8:26; Mark 15:17)
- **Red/Scarlet** = Sin / Corruption (Isaiah 1:18; Revelation 17:1–4)
  - War (Nahum 2:3; Revelation 6:4)
- **White** = Purity (Psalm 51:7; Isaiah 1:18)
  - Conquest (Revelation 6:1, 2)

Four Horses of Revelation 6

- **Black Horse** = Famine (Revelation 6:5, 6)
- **Pale Horse** = Death (Revelation 6:7, 8)

- **Red Horse** = War (Revelation 6:4)
- **White Horse** = Conquest (Revelation 6:1, 2)

Metals, Elements, and Natural Objects

- **12 Foundation Stones of New Jerusalem** = Twelve Apostles of Jesus (Revelation 21:14)
- **12 Gates of Pearl, New Jerusalem** = Twelve Tribes of Israel (Revelation 21:12)
- **Ashes** = Mankind Is Like Dust and Ashes (Job 30:19)
- **Brass / Bronze** = Rebels and Slanderers (Isaiah 48:4; Jeremiah 6:28)
  - Earth (Leviticus 26:19)
- **Bread** = Word of God / Jesus (Luke 4:4; John 6:35, 51; 1 Corinthians 11:23, 24)
- **Field** = World (Matthew 13:38; John 4:35)
- **Fig Tree** = A Nation That Should Bear Fruit (Luke 13:6–9)
- **Fire** = Holy Spirit (Luke 3:16)
- **Fruit** = Results of Works / Actions (Galatians 5:22)
- **Gold** = Pure Character / Precious and Rare (Isaiah 13:12; Malachi 3:3)
- **Harvest** = End of World (Matthew 13:39)
- **Honey** = Happy Life (Deuteronomy 8:6–10; Ezekiel 20:6)
- **Mountains** = Political or Religio-Political Powers (Isaiah 2:2, 3; Jeremiah 51:24, 25; Daniel 2:35, 44, 45)
  - Holiness (Jeremiah 31:23)
- **Oil** = Holy Spirit (1 Samuel 16:13; Zechariah 4:2-6; Revelation 4:5)
- **Reapers** = Angels (Matthew 13:39)
- **Rock** = Jesus / Truth (Deuteronomy 32:4; 1 Corinthians 10:4)
- **Seed** = Children of God / Jesus (Romans 9:8; Galatians 3:16)
- **Silver** = Pure Words / Understanding (Psalm 12:6; Proverbs 3:13, 14; 10:20; 25:11)
- **Stars** = Angels (Job 38:7; Revelation 1:16, 20; 12:4, 7–9)
- **Sun** = Jesus (Psalm 84:11; Malachi 4:2; Matthew 17:1, 2)
- **Thorns / Thorny Ground** = Cares of This Life (Mark 4:18, 19)
- **Tree** = Cross / People / Nation (Deuteronomy 21:22, 23; Psalm 37:35; 92:12)
- **Vineyard** = Church That Should Bear Fruit (Luke 20:9–16)
- **Water** = Everlasting Life / Holy Spirit / Cleansing (John 4:14; 7:37–39; Ephesians 5:26; Revelation 22:17)
- **Waters** = Inhabited Area / People / Nations (Revelation 17:15)
- **Winds** = Strife / Commotion / Winds of War (Jeremiah 4:11–13; 25:31–33; 49:36, 37; Zechariah 7:14)

Miscellaneous

- **Angel** = Messenger (Daniel 8:16; 9:21, 22; Luke 1:19, 26; Hebrews 1:13, 14)
- **Arrows** = Bitter Words (Psalm 64:3)
  - False Witness (Proverbs 25:18)
  - Tongue (Jeremiah 9:8)
- **Babel/Babylon** = Confusion / Rebellion / Apostasy (Genesis 10:8–10; 11:6–9; Revelation 17:1–5; 18:2, 3)
- **Clothing / Garments** = Character (Isaiah 59:6; 64:6)
- **Crown** = A Glorious Ruler or Rulership (Proverbs 4:8, 9; 16:31; 27:23, 24; Isaiah 28:5; 62:3)
- **Day** = Literal Year (Numbers 14:34; Ezekiel 4:6)
- **Famine** = Dearth of Truth (Amos 8:11)
- **Healing** = Salvation (Luke 5:23, 24)
- **Jar / Vessel** = Person (Jeremiah 18:1–6; 2 Corinthians 4:7; 2 Timothy 2:21)
- **Lamp** = Word of God (Psalm 119:105)
- **Leprosy / Sickness** = Sin (Leviticus 13:12–17; 2 Kings 5:1–14; Luke 5:12, 13)
- **Mark** = Sign or Seal of Approval or Disapproval (Ezekiel 9:4; Romans 4:11; Revelation 7:2, 3; 13:16, 17; 14:9–11)
  - Ministering Spirits (Hebrews 1:13, 14)
- **Ring** = Authority (Genesis 41:42, 43; Esther 3:10, 11)

- **Seal** = Sign or Seal of Approval or Disapproval (Romans 4:11; Revelation 7:2, 3; 9:4; 20:3)
- **Sword** = Word of God (Ephesians 6:17; Hebrews 4:12)
- **Time** = 360 Days / One Year (Daniel 4:16, 23, 25, 32; 7:25)
- **Times** = 720 Days / Two Years (Daniel 7:25; Revelation 12:14)
- **Trumpet** = Loud Warning of God's Approach (Exodus 19:16, 17; Joshua 6:4, 5; 1 Thessalonians 4:16)
- **White Robes** = Victory / Righteousness (Revelation 3:5; 7:14; 19:8)
- **Wine** = Blood / Covenant / Doctrines (Isaiah 65:8; Joel 2:19; Luke 5:37; 22:17, 20; 1 Corinthians 11:25)

People and Body Parts

- **Eyes** = Spiritual Discernment (Matthew 13:10–17; 1 John 2:11)
- **Feet** = Your Walk / Direction (Genesis 19:2; Joshua 4:18; Psalm 119:105; Hebrews 12:13)
- **Forehead** = Mind (Deuteronomy 6:6–8; Ezekiel 3:4–9; Romans 7:25)
- **Hand** = Deeds / Works / Actions (Ecclesiastes 9:10; Isaiah 59:6)
- **Harlot** = Apostate Church / Religion (Isaiah 1:21–27; Jeremiah 3:1–3, 6–9; Revelation 19:2)
- **Heads** = Major Powers / Rulers / Governments (Revelation 17:3, 9, 10)
- **Thief** = Suddenness of Jesus' Coming (1 Thessalonians 5:2–4; 2 Peter 3:10)
- **Tongue** = Language / Speech (Exodus 4:10; Philippians 2:11)
- **Woman, Corrupt** = Apostate Church (Ezekiel 16:15–58; 23:2–21; Hosea 2:5; 3:1; Revelation 14:4)
- **Woman, Pure** = True Church (Jeremiah 6:2; 2 Corinthians 11:2; Ephesians 5:23–27)

Numbers

- **1** = Oneness of God (Deuteronomy 6:4) / Unity of God's People (John 17:21, 22; Ephesians 4:4–6)
- **2** = The Truth of God's Word; for example, the law and prophets (John 1:45) / Two or Three Witnesses (2 Corinthians 13:1) / A Sword With Two Edges (Hebrews 4:12). [See Mark 6:7 and Revelation 11:3.] The number two is also used 21 times in the books of Daniel and Revelation.
- **3** = The Godhead/Trinity. The angels cry "holy" three times to the triune God (Isaiah 6:3). [See also Matthew 28:19.]
- **4** = Universal Truth, as in the four directions (north, south, east, west) and the four winds (Matthew 24:31; Revelation 7:1; 20:8). A sheet with four corners symbolizes the gospel going to all the Gentiles (Acts 10:11).
- **5** = Teaching. First, there are the five books of Moses. Second, Jesus taught about the five wise virgins (Matthew 25:1–13) and used five barley loaves to feed the 5,000 (Matthew 14:17–21; John 6:1–14).
- **6** = Man, and the Worship of Man, signifying his rebellion, imperfection, works, and disobedience. It is used 273 times in the Bible, including its derivatives (for example, sixth) and another 91 times as "threescore" or "60." Man was created on the sixth day (Genesis 1:26, 31). [See also Exodus 31:15 and Daniel 3:1.] The number is especially significant in the Book of Revelation as "666" identifies the beast. "Here is wisdom. Let him that hath understanding count the number of the beast: for it is the number of a man; and his number is six hundred threescore and six" (Revelation 13:18, KJV).
- **7** = God and His Perfection. The sign of divine worship, completion, obedience, and rest. The "prince" of Bible numbers, it is used 562 times, including its derivatives (for example, seventh, sevens). [See the seventh-day Sabbath in Genesis 2:1–4, Psalm 119:164, and in God's Law in Exodus 20:8–11, for just a few of the examples.] The number seven is also the most common number in biblical prophecy, occurring 42 times in Daniel and Revelation alone. In Revelation, there are seven churches, seven spirits, seven golden candlesticks, seven stars, seven lamps, seven seals, seven

horns, seven eyes, seven angels, seven trumpets, seven thunders, seven thousand slain in a great earthquake, seven heads, seven crowns, seven last plagues, seven golden vials, seven mountains, and seven kings.

- **10** = Law and Restoration. Of course, this includes the Ten Commandments found in Exodus 20. [See also Matthew 25:1 (ten virgins); Luke 17:17 (ten lepers); Luke 15:8 (healing, ten silver coins).]
- **12** = The Church and God's Authority. Jesus had 12 disciples, and there were 12 tribes of Israel. In Revelation 12:1, the 24 elders and 144,000 are multiples of 12. The New Jerusalem city has 12 foundations, 12 gates, 12,000 furlongs, a tree with 12 kinds of fruit 12 times a year eaten by 12 times 12,000 or the 144,000. [See Revelation 21.]
- **40** = One Generation, as well as Times of Testing, and Purification. It rained for 40 days during the flood (Genesis 7:17). Moses spent 40 years in the desert, as did the children of Israel (Numbers 14:33). Jesus fasted for 40 days (Matthew 4:2).
- **50** = Power and Celebration. The Jubilee came after the 49th year (Leviticus 25:10), and Pentecost occurred 50 days after Christ's resurrection (Acts 2).
- **70** = Human Leadership and Judgment. Moses appointed 70 elders (Exodus 24:1), and at Christ's time, the Sanhedrin still had 70 men sit on its council. Jesus sent out 70 disciples (Luke 10:1). Jesus told Peter to forgive 70 times 7 (Matthew 18:21, 22).

Monies, Weights, and Measures

Before 500 B.C., the people of Israel did not use coins. Instead, they used a barter system, or weighed metals (gold, silver) for use as money (see, for example, Genesis 23:16; 2 Samuel 12:30). Coins were mentioned for the first time in Ezra 2:69. During the time of Alexander the Great, Greek coins were more widely in use in Palestine. But after the Maccabean Revolt, Jewish coins were minted.

Some of the monetary units below were named after their weight. Because of the changing values over centuries, exact equivalents are not possible.

The chart below is based on a day's wage based upon a standard unit of $32/per day.

Monies

Unit	Monetary Value	Equivalent	Translation
Jewish			
Talent	Gold—$5,760,000 Silver—$384,000	3,000 shekels; 6,000 bekas	Talent
Shekel	Gold—$1,920 Silver—$128	4 days' wages; 2 bekas; 20 gerahs	Shekel
Beka	Gold—$960 Silver—$64	½ shekel; 10 gerahs	Bekah
Gerah	Gold—$96 Silver—$6.40	⅟₂₀ shekel	Gerah
Persian			Dram
Daric	Gold—$1,280 Silver—$64	2 days' wages; ½ Jewish silver shekel	
Greek			
Tetradrachma	$128	4 drachmas	Piece of money
Didrachma	$64	2 drachmas	Tribute
Drachma	$32	1 day's wage	Piece of silver
Lepton	$.25	½ of a Roman kodrantes	Mite
Roman			
Aureus	$800	25 denarii	
Denarius	$32	1 day's wage	Pence, Penny
Assarius	$2	⅟₁₆ of a denarius	Farthing
Kodrantes	$.50	¼ of an assarius	Farthing

Weights

Unit	Weight	Equivalent	Translation
Jewish			
Talent	c. 75 pounds for common talent c. 150 pounds for royal talent	60 minas; 3,000 shekels	Talent
Mina	1.25 pounds	50 shekels	Mina
Shekel	c. .4 ounce (11.4 grams) for common shekel c. .8 ounce for royal shekel	2 bekahs; 20 gerahs	Shekel
Beka	c. .2 ounce (5.7 grams)	½ shekel; 10 gerahs	Half a shekel
Gerah	c. .02 ounce (.57 grams)	1/20 shekel	Gerah
Pim	.3 ounce	⅔ of a shekel	Quarter
Roman			
Litra	12 ounces	30 shekels	Pound

Length

Unit	Length	Equivalent	Translation
Day's journey	c. 20 miles		Day's journey
Roman mile	4,854 feet	8 stadia	Mile
Sabbath day's journey	3,637 feet	6 stadia	Sabbath day's journey
Stadion	606 feet	⅛ Roman mile	Furlong
Rod	9 feet (but 10.5 feet in Ezekiel)	3 paces; 6 cubits	Measuring reed, reed
Fathom	6 feet	4 cubits	Fathom
Pace	3 feet	⅓ rod; 2 cubits	Pace
Cubit	18 inches	½ pace; 2 spans	Cubit
Span	9 inches	½ cubit; 3 handbreaths	Span
Handbreadth	3 inches	⅓ span; 4 fingers	Handbreadth
Finger	.75 inches	¼ handbreath	Finger

Dry Measures

Unit	Measure	Equivalent	Translation
Homer	6.52 bushes	10 ephahs	Homer
Kor	6.52 bushes	1 homer, 10 ephahs	Cor, Measure
Lethech	3.26 bushes	½ kor	Half homer
Ephah	.65 bushel, 20.8 quarts	⅒ homer	Ephah
Modius	7.68 quarts		Bushel
Seah	7 quarts	⅓ ephah	Measure
Omer	2.08 quarts	⅒ ephah; 1⅘ kab	Omer
Kab	1.16 quarts	4 logs	Cab
Choenix	1 quart		Measure
Xestes	1¹⁄₁₆ pints		Pot
Log	.58 pint	¼ kab	Log

Liquid Measures

Unit	Measure	Equivalent	Translation
Kor	60 gallons	10 baths	Kor
Metretes	10.2 gallons		Gallon
Bath	6 gallons	6 hins	Measure, Bath
Hin	1 gallon	2 kabs	Hin
Kab	2 quarts	4 logs	Kab
Log	1 pint	¼ kab	Log

The Jewish Calendar

The months in the Jewish calendar corresponded to sacred festivals and harvest schedules. The calendar changed with the establishment of the Passover (Exodus 12).

Month	Equivalent	No. of Days	Month of Civil Year	Month of Sacred Year
Tishri	Sept.-Oct.	30	First	Seventh
Heshvan	Oct.-Nov.	29 or 30	Second	Eighth
Chislev	Nov.-Dec.	29 or 30	Third	Ninth
Tebeth	Dec.-Jan.	29	Fourth	Tenth
Shebat	Jan.-Feb.	30	Fifth	Eleventh
Adar	Feb.-Mar.	29 or 30	Sixth	Twelfth
Nisan	Mar.-Apr.	30	Seventh	First
Iyar (Ziv)	Apr.-May	29	Eighth	Second
Sivan	May-June	30	Ninth	Third
Tammuz	June-July	29	Tenth	Fourth
Ab	July-Aug.	30	Eleventh	Fifth
Elul	Aug.-Sept.	29	Twelfth	Sixth

Hours of the Day

Time was measured by the position of the sun. The hours of the day (yôm) were divided into specific watches.

First	Sunset to 9 P.M.
Second	9 P.M. to midnight
Third	Midnight to 3 A.M.
Fourth	3 A.M. to sunrise

First	Sunrise to 9 A.M.
Second	9 A.M. to noon
Third	Noon to 3 P.M.
Fourth	3 P.M. to sunset

Included in the following section are 20 Chain-Reference Bible Topics, exploring some of the most important teachings in God's Word. These studies are not only for our own personal use but are ideal for sharing these truths with others.

Here are a few guidelines on how to use these chain-reference studies:

1. At any time as you proceed through a given topic, you may return to this section for an overview of the topic and for a brief phrase following each verse, describing its key content or major emphasis.
2. In the following example, note what you'll typically find as you arrive in your Bible at the first verse in the study:
    a. In the margin next to the first verse of the first reference, you'll see a "chain-link" symbol. If two chains apply to the verse(s), this symbol appears only once.
    b. In vertical type next to the symbol, you'll see the full range of verses included in this reference. Sometimes, it may be just one verse; other references will include a span of several verses.
    c. In the example below, notice, too, the "dagger" symbol after the range of verses. This dagger, with a single cross-mark, indicates that this is the first verse in the study.
    d. Finally, notice just below the verse of the reference a shaded bar that includes first, the topic under study, and second, the next reference in the "chain" of the study. If there are multiple verses in the chain, this shaded bar will be positioned after the concluding verse in the chain.

> 10 Whatsoever thy hand findeth to do, do *it* with thy might; for *there is* no work, nor device, nor knowledge, nor wisdom, in the grave, whither thou goest.   Ps. 6:5; Rom. 12:11
>
> 9:10†
>
> **Christian Behavior** See Matthew 6:14, 15.

3. When you reach the final reference in the chain, you'll see two cross-marks in the dagger symbol in the margin. The shaded bar below the referenced verse will include just the topic title. This indicates you have reached the end of the study.

> 5 The thoughts of the diligent *tend* only to plenteousness; but of every one *that is* hasty only to want.   Prov. 10:4; 13:4; 28:22
>
> 21:5‡
>
> **Christian Behavior**

May these chain-reference studies prove a great spiritual blessing to you, as well as to those with whom you share them.

1. THE BIBLE

THE AUTHORITY AND SOURCE OF THE BIBLE.

1. 2 Timothy 3:15, 16: All Scripture is given by inspiration of God.
2. 2 Peter 1:19–21: God spoke through holy men in giving the Bible.
3. 1 Thessalonians 2:13: The Word of God is not words of men.
4. Matthew 24:35: God's Word will last forever.

WHAT THE BIBLE DOES FOR US.

5. Psalm 119:11: Keeps us from sin.
6. Psalm 119:105: Lights the path before us.
7. Psalm 119:9: Cleanses us from sin.
8. Hebrews 4:12: Powerful as a sword; reaches deep into our heart.
9. John 17:17: Sanctifies us (makes us like Jesus).

2. WHO IS GOD?

GOD THE FATHER.

1. John 3:16, 17: God the Father gave His Son to save us.
2. 1 John 4:8: God is love—that is His character and essence.
3. John 14:9: While on earth, Jesus revealed the Father.

GOD THE SON.

4. John 1:1–3: Jesus, the Word and Creator, is called God.
5. John 1:14: Jesus the Word came to live among us on earth.
6. Colossians 1:15, 16: Jesus created all things.
7. John 17:18–26: Jesus was in perfect unity with the Father.

GOD THE HOLY SPIRIT.

8. John 14:16–18: Jesus promised the Spirit to take His place on earth.
9. John 15:26: The Spirit reveals Jesus to us.
10. John 16:7, 8: The Spirit convicts of sin.
11. John 16:13: The Spirit guides us into all truth.

3. THE SABBATH

THE SABBATH CREATED AND COMMANDED.

1. Genesis 2:3: God blessed and sanctified the Sabbath at creation.
2. Exodus 20:8–11: The Sabbath is one of the Ten Commandments and is the seventh day of the week.

THE SIGNIFICANCE OF THE SABBATH.

3. Exodus 31:12–17: The Sabbath a sign between God and His people.
4. Ezekiel 20:12: The Sabbath a sign of sanctification (set apart as holy).

THE SABBATH THROUGH HISTORY.

5. Exodus 16:22, 23: Israel kept the Sabbath before Sinai.
6. Luke 4:16: Jesus Himself kept the Sabbath.
7. Acts 18:4: Apostles, Jews, and non-Jews kept the Sabbath.
8. Isaiah 66:23: Sabbath will be kept in the New Earth.

HOW TO ENJOY THE SABBATH.

9. Isaiah 58:13, 14: Set aside week-day pleasures and pursuits.
10. Matthew 12:11–13: Focus on doing good for others.
11. Mark 2:27: God made Sabbath for man, not man for the Sabbath.
12. Luke 14:1–5: What Jesus taught about Sabbath-keeping.

WHEN TO OBSERVE THE SABBATH.

13. Leviticus 23:32: Sabbath celebrated from "evening to evening."
14. John 19:31: Friday is the "day of preparation" just before the Sabbath.

4. MARRIAGE

MARRIAGE: A GIFT FROM GOD.

1. Genesis 2:18–24: The first marriage—a gift of God from Eden.
2. John 2:1–10: Jesus celebrated a marriage with His presence and a miracle.

HOW TO HAVE A SUCCESSFUL MARRIAGE.

3. 2 Corinthians 6:14: Believers should marry believers.
4. Ephesians 5:22–24: How wives should relate to their husbands.
5. Ephesians 5:25–30: How husbands should relate to their wives.
6. Ephesians 5:31: Couples should leave their parents and become one flesh together.
7. Ephesians 5:33: Couples should demonstrate mutual love and respect.

WHAT JESUS TAUGHT ABOUT DIVORCE.

8. Matthew 5:31, 32: Jesus teaches on divorce.
9. Matthew 19:3–9: Further teaching of Jesus on marriage and divorce.
10. 1 Corinthians 7:10, 11: Reconciliation, not divorce, is God's will for a troubled marriage.

FAMILY: PARENTS AND CHILDREN.

11. Deuteronomy 6:6–9: Parents to diligently teach children God's law and will.
12. Proverbs 22:6: Train a child in the right way, and later the child will not depart from it.
13. Ephesians 6:1–4: Children should obey and honor their parents.

5. SALVATION FROM SIN

HOW AND WHEN SIN BEGAN.

1. Ezekiel 28:14–18: Highest angel in heaven chooses self-exaltation; sin begins.
2. Isaiah 14:12–14: Pride leads to Lucifer's fall.
3. Revelation 12:7–9: Lucifer goes to war against God and is cast out of heaven.

THE FIRST MAN AND WOMAN FALL INTO SIN.

4. Genesis 2:15–17: God tests Adam and Eve; states the penalty for failing.
5. Genesis 3:6: Tragically, Adam and Eve fail the test and sin.
6. Genesis 3:19: God restates the penalty for choosing sin and self.

SINCE ADAM, ALL ARE SINNERS UNDER THE PENALTY OF DEATH.

7. Romans 3:23: All have sinned and come short of God's perfect ideal.
8. Romans 5:12–14: Death penalty falls also on all Adam's descendants.
9. Romans 6:23: The wages, or penalty, of sin, is death.

GOD'S PLAN TO SAVE US (HIS PART).

10. John 3:16, 17: God sent His Son Jesus to die in our place.
11. Romans 5:8: Christ did die for us as our Substitute.
12. 1 Corinthians 15:22: Death through Adam, but life through Christ.

HOW WE RECEIVE SALVATION (OUR PART).

13. John 1:12: We receive Jesus as our Savior, by faith.
14. Ephesians 2:8, 9: Salvation is a free gift, which we cannot earn by "being good."
15. 1 John 5:11–13: When by faith we believe in Jesus, we have eternal life.
16. Revelation 3:20: By faith, we invite Jesus into our heart as Savior.

6. FAITH

WHAT FAITH IS AND WHY WE NEED IT.

1. Hebrews 11:1: Believing and trusting in what we don't yet see.
2. Hebrews 11:6: More specifically, believing in Jesus and trusting Him.
3. Habakkuk 2:4: The righteous live by faith.

WHERE FAITH COMES FROM.

4. Romans 12:3: God gives a measure of faith to each of us.
5. Matthew 17:20: Even faith as small as a mustard seed is powerful.

6. Romans 10:17: Faith comes from hearing God speak to us in His Word.
7. Luke 17:5: We can pray and ask God to increase our faith.
8. Mark 9:24: Faith and doubt can exist together.

WHAT FAITH CAN DO.

9. Acts 16:31: Faith is necessary to receive God's salvation.
10. Romans 5:1: We are justified (pardoned and set right with God) by faith.
11. Acts 26:18: We are also sanctified (given power to be like Jesus) by faith.
12. John 1:12: We receive Jesus into our lives and become God's children by faith.
13. Hebrews 4:2: Without faith, God's Word does us no good.
14. James 2:14–26: Real faith shows itself in good works.
15. Hebrews 11:3: We believe in Creation by faith.

7. GOD'S LAW

GOD'S LAW BEFORE MOUNT SINAI.

1. Genesis 26:5: Abraham kept the commandments before Sinai.
2. Exodus 16:24–30: The Sabbath commandment before Sinai.
3. Psalm 111:7–9: God's law is eternal.
4. Romans 5:12–14: Paul shows the law existed from Eden.

GOD'S TEN-COMMANDMENT LAW.

5. Exodus 20:3–17: The law as God gave it at Mt. Sinai.
6. Romans 3:20: The law points out sin.
7. James 4:17: Knowing to do right and not doing it is sin.
8. 1 John 3:4: Sin is transgressing of the law.

THE LAW IN OUR EVERYDAY LIFE.

9. Deuteronomy 28:1, 2: Blessings of obeying God's law.
10. Psalm 19:7–11: Psalmist describes God's law as perfect and wonderful.
11. Jeremiah 31:31–33: God's new covenant: His law inside us, in our minds and hearts.
12. Matthew 22:36–40: Summary of the law: love to God; love to man.
13. 1 John 5:3: God's law is not a burden.

JESUS AND THE LAW.

14. Matthew 5:17, 18: Jesus came not to destroy, but to fulfill the law.
15. John 14:15: If we love Jesus, we will keep His commandments.
16. John 15:10: Jesus kept the commandments.

THE LAW, STILL VALID AFTER JESUS RETURNED TO HEAVEN.

17. Romans 7:12: Paul indicated it was still in effect.
18. 1 John 2:3–6: John indicated it was still in effect.

LAW AND GRACE.

19. Romans 3:31: Law not made void by faith in God's grace.
20. Romans 6:14, 15: We're not under law, but under grace.
21. Romans 7:22: Paul delighted in the law.
22. Hebrews 8:10: How the law can be kept.
23. James 1:22–25: Function of the law to reveal sin not changed after the Cross.

8. JESUS

OLD TESTAMENT PREDICTED COMING OF MESSIAH.

1. Genesis 3:14, 15: A Redeemer promised in Eden.
2. Isaiah 7:14: Savior to be born of a virgin.
3. Isaiah 9:6, 7: Birth of Christ predicted.
4. Micah 5:2: Savior to be born in Bethlehem.

CHRIST'S BIRTH AND EARLY LIFE.

5. Luke 2:10–16: Luke's record of Christ's birth.
6. Luke 2:40: Jesus grew physically and intellectually.
7. Luke 2:42–49: At age 12, Jesus realizes His mission.

CHRIST'S MINISTRY (WHY HE CAME).

8. John 3:16, 17: That we may have everlasting life.
9. Matthew 1:21: To save us from sin.

CHRIST'S DEATH AND RESURRECTION.

10. Isaiah 53:1–9: Christ's death predicted and described.
11. 1 John 3:16: From love for us, Jesus gave His life for us.
12. John 19:28–30: Jesus dies on the cross.
13. Matthew 28:5–8: Jesus is resurrected.

9. THE CHRISTIAN LIFE

BORN AGAIN.

1. John 3:3–8: The necessity and results of the New Birth.
2. Ezekiel 36:26, 27: Old heart, new heart.
3. 2 Corinthians 5:17: Once born again, the old is gone; all things are new.
4. Ephesians 4:22–24: Old man, new man.
5. 1 Peter 1:23: The role of the Word of God in the New Birth.

CHRISTIAN GROWTH.

6. 1 Peter 2:1, 2: New Christians should start with the "milk" of the Word.
7. Hebrews 5:12–14: But don't stay on milk forever.
8. Ephesians 4:15: Grow up in all things, into Christ.
9. 2 Peter 3:18: Grow in grace and in knowing Jesus.

HOW JESUS HELPS US GROW.

10. Galatians 2:20: We live by faith in the Son of God.
11. Philippians 2:13: God works in and through us to will and to do.
12. Philippians 4:13: Through Christ's power in us, we can do all things.

WHAT JESUS BEGINS IN US, HE FINISHES.

13. Philippians 1:6: What Jesus begins in us, He completes.
14. Hebrews 12:2: Jesus is the Author and Finisher of our faith.

10. BAPTISM/LORD'S SUPPER

IMPORTANCE OF BAPTISM.

1. Matthew 3:13–15: Jesus was baptized as an example to us.
2. Mark 16:15, 16: Belief that leads to baptism saves us.

BAPTISM—A SPIRITUAL SYMBOL.

3. Romans 6:3, 4: Death, burial, resurrection.
4. Colossians 2:12: Buried and resurrected by faith.
5. Galatians 3:27: A symbol of a new relationship with Christ.
6. Acts 2:38: We receive the Holy Spirit at baptism.
7. 1 Corinthians 12:12, 13: We become part of Christ's Body at baptism.
8. Acts 19:1–7: On being baptized again after receiving new truth.

BAPTISM IS BY IMMERSION.

9. Matthew 3:16: Jesus came up out of the water.
10. Acts 8:36–39: Philip and the eunuch both went down into the water.

THE LORD'S SUPPER—A SPIRITUAL SYMBOL.

11. Matthew 26:26–28: The record of the original Lord's Supper.
12. John 13:12–15: Before the Lord's Supper came the foot-washing.
13. 1 Corinthians 10:16, 17: The communion service of bread and wine.
14. 1 Corinthians 11:23–30: Jesus established the symbol of the Lord's Supper.

11. CHRISTIAN BEHAVIOR

BASIC PRINCIPLES FOR CHRISTIAN BEHAVIOR.

1. Ecclesiastes 9:10: Whatever you do, do your best.
2. Matthew 6:14, 15: Forgiving others.
3. Luke 10:27: Love others.
4. Romans 12:9–19: Abhor the evil, cling to the good.
5. 2 Corinthians 9:6, 7: Be a cheerful giver.
6. 1 Thessalonians 5:17, 18: Give thanks in everything.
7. 1 Timothy 5:8: Provide for your family.
8. 1 Timothy 6:6–10: Contentment.

BIBLE PRINCIPLES FOR ENTERTAINMENT.

9. Romans 8:5: We either feed the sinful nature or the spiritual nature.
10. Philippians 4:8: The great Bible standard for recreation, amusement, entertainment—
and all our behavior.

BIBLE PRINCIPLES FOR DRESS.

11. Isaiah 3:16–24: God's prophecy about the decorated women of Zion.
12. 1 Timothy 2:9, 10: Modesty and the inward adornment of good works.
13. 1 Peter 3:3, 4: Inner versus outer beauty.

BIBLE PRINCIPLES OF SPEECH.

14. Matthew 26:73, 74: On swearing and bywords.
15. Ephesians 4:29: Let nothing corrupt escape your lips.
16. Ephesians 5:4: Avoid obscenities and foolish talk.

BIBLE PRINCIPLES OF WORK ETHICS.

17. Proverbs 10:4, 5: He who deals with a slack hand becomes poor.
18. Proverbs 14:23: In all labor there is profit.
19. Proverbs 23:4, 5: Don't overwork to be rich.
20. 2 Corinthians 6:14: Don't be unequally yoked.

BIBLE PRINCIPLES OF LAZINESS.

21. Proverbs 6:6–11: Look to the ant for an example.
22. Proverbs 19:15: An idle person will suffer hunger.
23. Proverbs 24:30–34: A little sleep and slumber brings laziness.

BIBLE PRINCIPLES ON AVOIDING GREED.

24. Proverbs 1:19: Greedy for gain.
25. Proverbs 15:27: A greedy person troubles even his own house.
26. Proverbs 21:5: Being hasty leads to poverty.

12. MANAGING GOD'S GIFTS

GOD OWNS EVERYTHING.

1. Psalm 50:10: The cattle on a thousand hills.
2. Haggai 2:8: All the silver and the gold.
3. Psalm 24:1: The world and everything in it.

ALL THAT WE HAVE COMES FROM GOD.

4. Acts 17:25: Life, breath, and all things.
5. 1 Chronicles 29:12: Riches and honor.
6. Deuteronomy 8:11–18: The power to get wealth.

RETURNING A PORTION TO GOD.

7. Leviticus 27:30–32: Tithe is one-tenth of my income.
8. Malachi 3:7, 8: Warning against robbing God of His tithes and offerings.
9. Matthew 23:23: Tithing not to be left undone.

TITHE IS TO BE USED FOR SUPPORT OF THE MINISTRY.

10. Numbers 18:21: Priests received tithe for their services.
11. 1 Corinthians 9:13, 14: Tithe for support of the ministry.

GOD WILL PROVIDE FOR US IF WE PUT HIM FIRST.

12. Malachi 3:10: The great tithing promise.
13. Matthew 6:33: Seek God first, and He will provide.
14. Psalm 37:25: The righteous never have to beg.
15. 2 Corinthians 9:6, 7: God loves a cheerful giver.

13. HEALTH

GOD WANTS US TO BE HEALTHY.

1. 3 John 2: Good health is God's will for us.
2. Exodus 15:26: God promised His people would be disease-free if they followed His instructions.
3. 1 Corinthians 10:31: We should honor and glorify God even in our eating and drinking.

OUR BODIES—THE DWELLING PLACE OF GOD.

4. 1 Corinthians 3:16, 17: We should avoid anything that defiles or destroys God's temple.
5. 1 Corinthians 6:19, 20: Our bodies are not ours—they are God's temples, His dwelling places.

THE IDEAL DIET.

6. Genesis 1:29: Man's original diet: grains, fruits, nuts.
7. Genesis 7:2: Clean and unclean animals enter the ark.
8. Genesis 3:18: Vegetables added to diet after sin entered.
9. Genesis 9:2–4: Flesh food permitted after the Flood.
10. Leviticus 11:1–31: Clean and unclean flesh foods defined.

WARNINGS AGAINST USE OF ALCOHOL.

11. Judges 13:4: Warning against wine and strong drink—1.
12. Proverbs 20:1: Warning against wine and strong drink—2.
13. Proverbs 23:29–32: Results of using intoxicants.
14. 1 Corinthians 6:9, 10: Drunkards will not enter God's kingdom.

14. GIFT OF PROPHECY

GOD'S WAY OF SPEAKING TO MEN.

1. Hosea 12:10: Since man's fall into sin, God speaks to us primarily through His prophets.
2. Amos 3:7: God reveals His secrets to us through His prophets.
3. Numbers 12:6: God speaks to His prophets through visions and dreams.
4. 2 Peter 1:19–21: Prophets speak as they are moved upon by the Holy Spirit.

HOW TO TELL A TRUE PROPHET FROM A FALSE ONE.

5. Matthew 24:24: Warning against false prophets in the last days.
6. Matthew 7:15–20: True prophets are known by their fruit.
7. 1 John 4:1–6: Messages of a true prophet are Christ centered.
8. Isaiah 8:20: Prophet's messages should harmonize with previous prophets, with God's law, and with previous Scripture.
9. Jeremiah 23:16, 17: True prophet reproves sin.
10. Jeremiah 28:9: Predictions of a true prophet must be 100 percent accurate.
11. 1 Corinthians 14:3, 4: A prophet's words edify the church.

THE PROPHETIC GIFT IN THE LAST DAYS.

12. Ephesians 4:11: Prophecy one of the gifts of the Spirit.
13. Joel 2:27, 28: Prophecy to be active in the last days.
14. 1 Corinthians 1:7: God's people who await Christ's return are to lack none of the spiritual gifts.
15. Revelation 12:17: The two identifying marks of God's last, true followers.
16. Revelation 19:10: The testimony of Jesus is the spirit or gift of prophecy.

HOW WE SHOULD RELATE TO THE GIFT OF PROPHECY.

17. 1 Thessalonians 5:20, 21: Do not despise prophesyings.
18. 2 Chronicles 20:20: We prosper as we believe in God's chosen prophets.

WHAT HAPPENS TO US WHEN WE DO NOT OBEY GOD'S PROPHETS?

19. Acts 3:23: Ignoring the prophet's words brings destruction.
20. 2 Chronicles 36:14–17: The tragic results of mocking God's prophets.

15. CHRIST'S RETURN

PROMISES AND PREDICTIONS.

1. John 14:1–3: Jesus Himself promises to return.
2. Hebrews 9:28: Christ coming a second time.

WHEN JESUS IS COMING AGAIN.

3. Matthew 24:36: We don't know the exact day or hour.
4. Matthew 24:30–33: Immediately after all the signs have been fulfilled.
5. Matthew 24:14: Immediately after the gospel reaches the entire world.

THE MANNER OF HIS COMING.

6. Acts 1:9–11: In the same manner as He ascended.
7. 1 Thessalonians 4:16, 17: With a shout, angel voice, and trumpet blast.
8. Revelation 1:7: Every eye will see Him.

WHAT JESUS WILL DO WHEN HE COMES.

9. Matthew 16:27: Reward everyone according to his works.
10. 2 Timothy 4:6–8: Give each saint a crown of righteousness.

HOW TO PREPARE TO MEET JESUS AT HIS COMING.

11. Matthew 24:42–44: Watch and be ready.
12. Titus 2:11–13: Live soberly, righteously, godly.
13. James 5:7, 8: Be patient.
14. 1 John 2:28: Abide in Christ.

16. SIGNS OF THE END

SIGNS THAT THE END IS NEAR.

1. Matthew 24:3: Disciples ask Jesus for signs of the Second Coming.
2. Joel 2:30, 31: Signs in the sun, moon, and stars—1.
3. Matthew 24:29: Signs in the sun, moon, and stars—2.

4. Matthew 24:37–39: Days before the Second Coming like the days before the Flood.
5. 2 Timothy 3:1–5: Intense evil.
6. 2 Peter 3:3, 4: Scoffing at the Second Coming is itself a sign.

THE HARVEST OF BOTH GOOD AND EVIL MUST BE READY TO REAP.

7. Matthew 13:24–30: Parable of the wheat and tares.
8. Matthew 13:39: Harvest is the end of the world, at the Second Coming.
9. Mark 4:26–29: Parable of the harvest at the Second Coming.
10. James 5:7, 8: God waits for the good fruit to ripen.

17. AFTER DEATH

MAN IS MORTAL—GOD IS IMMORTAL.

1. Genesis 3:4: Immortality of man was the devil's first lie.
2. Job 4:17: Man is mortal—1.
3. Ezekiel 18:20: Man is mortal—2.
4. 1 Timothy 6:15, 16: God only has immortality.

MAN DOES NOT HAVE A SOUL—HE IS A SOUL.

5. Genesis 2:7: God breathed into man, and he became a living soul (breath + dust = soul).
6. Ecclesiastes 12:7: At death, the process is reversed.

DEATH IS REFERRED TO AS SLEEP IN THE BIBLE.

7. John 11:11–14: Jesus called death sleep.
8. Psalm 13:3: David called death sleep.
9. Daniel 12:2: Daniel also called death sleep.

THE DEAD ARE TOTALLY UNCONSCIOUS AND UNAWARE.

10. Psalm 6:5: Dead remember nothing and can't give thanks.
11. Psalm 115:17: Dead do not praise God.
12. Psalm 146:3, 4: No one can lay plans after death.
13. Ecclesiastes 9:5, 6: Dead know nothing.

THE DEAD DO NOT GO TO HEAVEN OR HELL AT DEATH.

14. Job 7:9, 10: Dead remain in their graves—1.
15. Job 21:32: Dead remain in their graves—2.
16. John 5:28, 29: Dead are in their graves until the Second Coming.
17. John 20:17: Jesus did not go to heaven at death.

18. THE MILLENNIUM

EVENTS THAT TAKE PLACE AT THE BEGINNING OF THE MILLENNIUM.

1. 1 Thessalonians 4:16, 17: The second coming of Christ; righteous dead resurrected; righteous living caught up to meet them.
2. 1 Corinthians 15:51, 52: Righteous living are changed and caught up to meet Jesus.
3. 2 Thessalonians 1:7–9: Wicked living are slain.
4. Revelation 20:2, 3: Satan bound for 1,000 years.

EVENTS THAT TAKE PLACE DURING THE MILLENNIUM.

5. 1 Corinthians 6:1–3: Righteous in heaven judging the wicked.

EVENTS THAT TAKE PLACE AT THE END OF THE MILLENNIUM.

6. Revelation 20:5: Wicked dead are raised.
7. Revelation 21:1–5: Christ, Holy City, and saints descend to earth.
8. Revelation 20:7–10: Satan and the wicked surround the City; fire destroys them.

19. END OF SIN/HELL

DO THE WICKED SUFFER IN EVERLASTING FIRE?
1. Matthew 25:41: Everlasting fire.
2. Matthew 25:46: Everlasting destruction.
3. Mark 3:29: Eternal damnation.
4. Jude 7: Eternal fire.

HOW IS THE WORD FOREVER USED ELSEWHERE IN THE BIBLE?
5. Exodus 21:6: Slave to serve his master forever.
6. 1 Samuel 1:22: Samuel to abide in the tabernacle forever.
7. Malachi 4:1: Wicked to be totally consumed, with nothing left.

20. THE NEW EARTH

GOD'S FOLLOWERS LOOK FORWARD TO A NEW EARTH.
1. 2 Peter 3:13: God's followers look forward to a new heaven and a new earth.

THE PROPHET ISAIAH DESCRIBES OUR ETERNAL HOME.
2. Isaiah 35:4–10: Isaiah describes the new earth.
3. Isaiah 65:17–25: Isaiah further describes the new earth.

THE PROPHET JOHN ALSO DESCRIBES OUR ETERNAL HOME.
4. Revelation 21:1–5: John describes the new earth.
5. Revelation 21:10–26: John describes the holy city, New Jerusalem.
6. Revelation 22:1–5: John further describes the new earth.
7. Revelation 22:20: Our only response to the prospect of being finally home.

CONCORDANCE

The Concordance includes proper names and significant topics, defined by phrases and Scripture references. Occasionally, a key word applies to more than one Bible person, place, or topic. This is the case with "Abinadab," for whom the Concordance lists four different persons by that name. The second, third, and following occurrences are distinguished by the dash ("———").

AARON

Lineage of, Ex. 6:16–20; Josh. 21:4, 10; 1 Chr. 6:2, 3; 23:13

Marriage of, Ex. 6:23

Children of, Ex. 6:23, 25; 1 Chr. 6:3; 24:1, 2

Descendants of, Ex. 6:23, 25; 1 Chr. 6:3–15, 50–53; 24

Meets Moses in the wilderness and is made spokesman for Moses, Ex. 4:14–16, 27–31; 7:1, 2

Inspiration of, Ex. 12:1; Lev. 10:8; 11:1; 13:1; 15:1; Num. 2:1; 4:1, 17; 18:1; 19:1; 20:12

Commissioned as a deliverer of Israel, Ex. 6:13, 26, 27; Josh. 24:5; 1 Sam. 12:8; Ps. 77:20; 105:26; Mic. 6:4

Summoned to Sinai with Nadab, Abihu, and seventy elders, Ex. 19:24; 24:1, 9, 10

Priesthood of, Ex. 28:1; 29:9; Num. 17; 18:1; Ps. 99:6; Heb. 5:4

Consecration of, to the priesthood, Ex. 28; 29; Lev. 8

Descendants of, ordained priests forever, Ex. 28:40–43; 29:9; Num. 3:3; 18:1; 1 Chr. 23:13; 2 Chr. 26:18

Judges Israel in the absence of Moses, Ex. 24:14

Makes the golden calf, Ex. 32; Deut. 9:20, 21; Acts 7:40

Rod of, buds, Num. 17; Heb. 9:4 preserved, Num. 17; Heb. 9:4

Murmured against, by the people, Ex. 5:20, 21; 16:2–10; Num. 14:2–5, 10; 16:3–11, 41; 20:2; Ps. 106:16

Places pot of manna in the ark, Ex. 16:34

With Hur supports the hands of Moses during battle, Ex. 17:12

His benedictions upon the people, Lev. 9:22; Num. 6:23

Forbidden to mourn the death of his sons, Nadab and Abihu, Lev. 10:6, 19

Intercedes for Miriam, Num. 12:11, 12

Stays the plague by priestly intercession, Num. 16:46–48

Jealous of Moses, Num. 12:1

His presumption, when the rock is smitten, Num. 20:10–12

Not permitted to enter Canaan, Num. 20:12, 23–29

Age of, at death, Ex. 7:7; Num. 33:38, 39

Death and burial of, Num. 20:27, 28; Deut. 10:6; 32:50

Character of, Ps. 106:16

ABEL

Son of Adam; History of, Gen. 4:1–15, 25

References to the death of, Matt. 23:35; Luke 11:51; Heb. 11:4; 12:24; 1 John 3:12

——— A stone, 1 Sam. 6:18

ABHOR

my soul shall
not a . . . . Lev. 26:11
not a us, for thy
name's. . . . . .Jer. 14:21
the God of
hosts, I a . . . . .Amos 6:8
A that which is
evil. . . . . Rom. 12:9

ABHORRED

not despised nor a . . Ps. 22:24
insomuch that
he a . . . . Ps. 106:40
his altar, he hath a . . Lam. 2:7
and their soul
also a . . . . Zech. 11:8

ABIATHAR

High priest; Called Ahimelech in, 2 Sam. 8:17; 1 Chr. 24:3, 6, 31

And Abimelech, 1 Chr. 18:16

Son of Ahimelech, 1 Sam. 22:20

Escapes to David from the vengeance of Saul, who slew the priests in the City of Nob, 1 Sam. 22:20–23; 1 Sam. 6:1—19:24

Consults the ephod for David, 1 Sam. 22:9–12; 30:9–12

Associate high priest with Zadok in the reign of David, 2 Sam. 15:35; 20:25; 1 Kin. 4:4; 1 Chr. 15:11

But called Ahimelech and father of Abiathar, 2 Sam. 8:17; 1 Chr. 18:16

Loyal to David when Absalom

rebelled; leaves Jerusalem with the ark of the covenant, but is directed by David to return with the ark, 2 Sam. 15:24–29

Aids David by sending his son from Jerusalem to David with secret information concerning the counsel of Ahithophel, 2 Sam. 15:35, 36; 17:15–22; 1 Kin. 2:26

Supports Adonijah's pretensions to the throne, 1 Kin. 1:7

Thrust out of office by Solomon, 1 Kin. 2:26, 27; 1 Sam. 2:31–35

ABIDE

a with thee all
night . . . . Lev. 19:13
be able to a his
indignation . . . . . . .Jer. 10:10
LORD, no man
shall a . . . . .Jer. 49:18
children of Israel
shall a . . . . .Hos. 3:4
and who can a it. . . . Joel 2:11
who can a in the
fierceness . . . . .Nah. 1:6
a the day of his
coming . . . . Mal. 3:2
should not a in
darkness . . . . . . .John 12:46
Comforter, that he
may a. . . . . .John 14:16
If a man a not
in me . . . . .John 15:6
If ye a in me, and . . .John 15:7
taught you, ye
shall a . . . . 1 John 2:27

ABIDETH

He that a in this
city. . . . . Jer. 21:9
the wrath of
God a. . . . . .John 3:36
that a in me, and I . .John 15:5
have received of
him a . . . . 1 John 2:27

ABIGAIL

Nabal's wife; Her wisdom and tact, and marriage to David, 1 Sam. 25; 27:3; 2 Sam. 2:2

Mother of Chileab by David, 2 Sam. 3:3; 1 Chr. 3:1

Taken captive and rescued by David, 1 Sam. 30:1–18

——— Sister of David,

and mother of Amasa,
2 Sam. 17:25; 1 Chr. 2:16, 17

ABIHU

Son of Aaron, Ex. 6:23;
Num. 3:2
Summoned by God to Sinai,
Ex. 24:9
Called to the priesthood,
Ex. 28:1
Death of, Lev. 10:1, 2;
Num. 26:61
Died childless, Num. 3:4

ABIJAM

Called also Abijah and Abia;
King of Judah, 1 Kin. 14:31;
15:1; 2 Chr. 12:16
History of, 1 Kin. 15:1–8;
2 Chr. 11:22; 13
Succeeded by Asa, 1 Kin. 15:8;
2 Chr. 14:1

ABIMELECH

King of Gerar, Gen. 20;
21:22–32
——— King of Gerar, Gen. 26
——— Son of Gideon,
Judg. 8:31; 9; 2 Sam. 11:21

ABINADAB

A Levite, in whose house
the ark of God rested
twenty years, 1 Sam. 7:1, 2;
2 Sam. 6:3, 4; 1 Chr. 13:7
——— Son of Jesse,
1 Sam. 16:8; 17:13
——— Called also Ishui, son of
Saul, 1 Sam. 14:49; 31:2
——— Father of one of
Solomon's purveyors,
1 Kin. 4:11

ABISHAI

Son of Zeruiah, David's sister,
1 Chr. 2:16
One of David's chief men,
2 Sam. 23:18
Seeks Saul's life, 1 Sam. 26:6–8
Pursues and kills Abner,
2 Sam. 2:24; 3:30
Defeats the Edomites,
1 Chr. 18:12
Defeats the Ammonites,
2 Sam. 10:10, 14
Seeks the life of Shimei,
2 Sam. 16:9; 19:21
Leads a division of David's
army against Absalom,
2 Sam. 18:2, 5
Overthrows Sheba,
2 Sam. 20:1–22
Saves David from being slain
by a Philistine, 2 Sam. 21:17
Obtains water from the well
of Bethlehem for David,
1 Chr. 11:15–20

ABNER

Son of Ner; Cousin of Saul,
1 Sam. 14:50, 51; 1 Sam. 9:1
Captain of the host,
1 Sam. 14:50; 17:55; 26:5, 14
Dedicated spoils of war to the
tabernacle, 1 Chr. 26:27, 28

Loyalty of, to the house of
Saul, 2 Sam. 2:8–32
Alienation of, from the house
of Saul, 2 Sam. 3:6–21
Murdered by Joab; David's
sorrow for, 2 Sam. 3:27–39

ABODE

where the cloud a . Num. 9:17
of the LORD
they a . . . . Num. 9:20
was, when the
cloud a . . . . Num. 9:21
children of
Israel a . . . . Num. 9:22
the people a in
Kadesh . . . . Num. 20:1
I a in the mount
forty . . . . Deut. 9:9
the beginning,
and a . . . . John 8:44
him, and make
our a . . . . John 14:23
upper room,
where a . . . . Acts 1:13

ABOMINABLE

not make
yourselves a . . . . . Lev. 11:43
detestable and a
things . . . . Jer. 16:18
a flesh into my
mouth . . . . Ezek. 4:14
deny him, being a . Titus 1:16
banquetings,
and a . . . . 1 Pet. 4:3
unbelieving, and
the a . . . . Rev. 21:8

ABOMINATION

earth shall be an a . Lev. 11:41
every a to the
LORD . . . . Deut. 12:31
these things are
an a . . . . Deut. 18:12
is a before the
LORD . . . . Deut. 24:4
molten image,
an a . . . . Deut. 27:15
Chemosh, the a of
Moab . . . . 1 Kin. 11:7
thou hast made
me
an a . . . . Ps. 88:8
false balance is a . . Prov. 11:1
the wicked is an a . Prov. 15:8
both are a to the
LORD . . . . Prov. 17:15
incense is an a
unto . . . . Is. 1:13
mine heritage an a . . . . Jer. 2:7
they had
committed a . . . . . . Jer. 6:15
this a, to cause
Judah . . . . Jer. 32:35
the a that maketh
desolate . . . . Dan. 12:11
a of desolation,
spoken . . . . Matt. 24:15
whatsoever
worketh a . . . . . . Rev. 21:27

ABOMINATIONS

these a have the
men . . . . Lev. 18:27
a the LORD thy
God . . . . Deut. 18:12
strange gods,
with a . . . . Deut. 32:16
to the a of the
heathen . . . . 2 Kin. 16:3
a, and hath done
wickedly . . . . . . 2 Kin. 21:11
delighteth in
their a . . . . Is. 66:3
and with all
thine a . . . . Ezek. 5:11
committed in all
their a . . . . Ezek. 6:9
the evil a of the
house . . . . Ezek. 6:11
upon thee, and
thine a . . . . Ezek. 7:4
thee for all thine a . . Ezek. 7:8
thy ways and
thine a . . . . Ezek. 7:9
the images of
their a . . . . Ezek. 7:20
that cry for all
the a . . . . Ezek. 9:4
hath done all
these a . . . . Ezek. 18:13
man the a of his
eyes . . . . Ezek. 20:7
man cast away
the a . . . . Ezek. 20:8
because of all
your a . . . . Ezek. 44:7
overspreading of a . . Dan. 9:27
and their a were
according . . . . Hos. 9:10

ABRAHAM

Also called Abram; Son of
Terah, Gen. 11:26, 27
Marries Sarah, Gen. 11:29
Lives in Ur, but removes to
Haran, Gen. 11:31; Neh. 9:7;
Acts 7:4
And Canaan, Gen. 12:4, 5, 6;
Acts 7:4
Divine call of, Gen. 12:1–3;
Josh. 24:3; Neh. 9:7; Is. 51:2;
Acts 7:2, 3; Heb. 11:8
Canaan given to, Gen. 12:1, 7;
15:7–21; Ezek. 33:24
Lives in Bethel, Gen. 12:8
Sojourns in Egypt, Gen. 12:10–
20; 26:1
Deferring to Lot, chooses
Hebron, Gen. 13; 14:13;
35:27
Lives in Gerar, Gen. 20;
21:22–34
Defeats Chedorlaomer,
Gen. 14:5–24; Heb. 7:1
Is blessed by Melchizedek,
Gen. 14:18–20; Heb. 7:1–10
God's covenant with,
Gen. 15; 17:1–22; Mic. 7:20;
Luke 1:73; Rom. 4:13; 15:8;
Gal. 3:6–18, 29; 4:22–31;
Heb. 6:13, 14

Called Abraham, Gen. 17:5;
Neh. 9:7
Circumcision of, Gen. 17:10–
14, 23–27
Angels appear to, Gen. 18:1–
16; 22:11, 15; 24:7
His questions about the
destruction of the righteous
and wicked in Sodom,
Gen. 18:23–32
Witnesses the destruction of
Sodom, Gen. 19:27, 28
Ishmael born to, Gen. 16:3, 15
Lives in Gerar; deceives
Abimelech concerning Sarah,
his wife, Gen. 20
Isaac born to, Gen. 21:2, 3;
Gal. 4:22–30
Sends Hagar and Ishmael
away, Gen. 21:10–14;
Gal. 4:22–30
Trial of his faith in the offering
of Isaac, Gen. 22:1–19;
Heb. 11:17; James 2:21
Sarah, his wife, dies,
Gen. 23:1, 2
He purchases a place for her
burial, and buries her in a
cave, Gen. 23:3–20
Marries Keturah, Gen. 25:1
Provides a wife for Isaac,
Gen. 24
Children of, Gen. 16:15; 21:2,
3; 25:1–4; 1 Chr. 1:32–34
Testament of, Gen. 25:5, 6
Wealth of, Gen. 13:2; 24:35;
Is. 51:2
Age of, at different periods,
Gen. 12:4; 16:16; 21:5; 25:7
Death, Gen. 15:15; 25:8–10
In Paradise, Matt. 8:11;
Luke 13:28; 16:22–31
Friend of God, 2 Chr. 20:7;
Is. 41:8; James 2:23
Piety of, Gen. 12:7, 8; 13:4, 18;
18:19; 20:7; 21:33; 22:3–13;
26:5; 2 Chr. 20:7; Neh. 9:7,
8; Is. 41:8; Rom. 4:16–18;
James 2:23
A prophet, Gen. 20:7
Faith of, Gen. 15:6; Rom. 4:1–
22; Gal. 3:6–9; Heb. 11:8–10,
17–19; James 2:21–24
Unselfishness of, Gen. 13:9;
21:25–30
Independence of, in character,
Gen. 14:23; 23:6–16
Ancestors of, idolatrous,
Josh. 24:2
How regarded by his
descendants, Matt. 3:9;
Luke 13:16, 28; 19:9;
John 8:33–40

ABROAD
brought him
forth *a* . . . . Gen. 15:5
thou shalt
spread *a* . . . . Gen. 28:14
a the rage of thy
wrath . . . . Job 40:11

spreadeth *a* the
earth . . . . Is. 44:24
upon the
children *a* . . . . Jer. 6:11
scattered *a*, as
sheep . . . . Matt. 9:36
were all
scattered *a* . . . . Acts 8:1
love of God is
shed *a* . . . . Rom. 5:5

ABSALOM
Also called Abishalom; Son of
David by Maacah, 2 Sam. 3:3;
1 Chr. 3:2
Beauty of, 2 Sam. 14:25
Kills Amnon, 2 Sam. 13:22–29
Flees to Geshur, 2 Sam. 13:37,
38
Is permitted by David
to return to Jerusalem,
2 Sam. 14:1–24
His demagogism, 2 Sam. 15:2–
6, 13
Conspiracy, 2 Sam. 15:17
Death and burial, 2 Sam. 18:9–
17
David's mourning for,
2 Sam. 18:33; 19:1–8
Children of, 2 Sam. 14:27;
18:18; 1 Kin. 15:2;
2 Chr. 11:20
Pillar of, 2 Sam. 18:18

ABUNDANCE
heart, for the *a* . . . Deut. 28:47
and fruit trees in *a* . . Neh. 9:25
but trusted in
the *a* . . . . Ps. 52:7
great *a* of thine
enchantments . . . . . . Is. 47:9
By reason of the *a* Ezek. 26:10
of the *a* of the
heart . . . . Matt. 12:34
have more *a* . . . . . Matt. 13:12
rich through the *a* . . Rev. 18:3

ABUNDANTLY
the water came
out *a* . . . . Num. 20:11
yea, drink *a*,
O beloved . . . . Song 5:1
shall howl,
weeping *a* . . . . Is. 15:3
blossom *a*, and
rejoice . . . . Is. 35:2
God, for he will *a* . . . . Is. 55:7

ACCEPT
humbled, and
they then *a* . . . . . Lev. 26:41
for him will I *a* . . . . . Job 42:8
oblation, I will
not *a* . . . . Jer. 14:12
I will *a* you with
your . . . . Ezek. 20:41

ACCEPTABLE
for it shall not
be *a* . . . . Lev. 22:20
To proclaim the *a*
year . . . . Is. 61:2
offerings are not *a* . . . Jer. 6:20

counsel be *a* unto
thee . . . . Dan. 4:27
sacrifice, holy, *a* . . . Rom. 12:1
good, and *a*, and
perfect . . . . Rom. 12:2
smell, a sacrifice *a* . . Phil. 4:18
a to God by Jesus
Christ . . . . 1 Pet. 2:5

ACCEPTED
a for him to make
atonement . . . . Lev. 1:4
they shall not be *a* . Lev. 22:25
be *a* upon mine
altar . . . . Is. 56:7
willing mind, it
is *a* . . . . 2 Cor. 8:12

ACCOMPLISHED
that her warfare
is *a* . . . . Is. 40:2
seventy years
are *a* . . . . Jer. 25:12
seventy years be *a* . . Jer. 29:10
Lord hath *a* his
fury . . . . Lam. 4:11
shall mine anger
be *a* . . . . Ezek. 5:13
the indignation
be *a* . . . . Dan. 11:36
a to scatter the
power . . . . Dan. 12:7

ACCURSED
is hanged is *a* of
God . . . . Deut. 21:23
a thing, lest ye
make . . . . Josh. 6:18
trespass in the *a*
thing . . . . Josh. 7:1
because they
were *a* . . . . Josh. 7:12

ADAM
The first man. Creation
of, Gen. 1:26–28; 2:7;
1 Cor. 15:45; 1 Tim. 2:13
History of, before he sinned,
Gen. 1:26–30; 2:16–25
Temptation and sin of, Gen. 3;
Job 31:33; Is. 43:27; Hos. 6:7;
Rom. 5:14–21; 1 Tim. 2:14
Subsequent history of,
Gen. 3:20–24; 4:1, 2, 25;
5:1–5
His death, Gen. 5:5
Progenitor of the human race,
Deut. 32:8; Mal. 2:10
Brought sin into the world,
1 Cor. 15:22, 45
Type of Christ, Rom. 5:14
——— A name of Christ,
1 Cor. 15:45, 47
——— A city near the Jordan,
Josh. 3:16

ADONIJAH
Son of David and Haggith,
2 Sam. 3:4; 1 Kin. 1:5, 6;
1 Chr. 3:2
Usurpation of, and downfall,
1 Kin. 1

aid from the king of Assyria,
2 Kin. 16:7–9, 17, 18;
2 Chr. 28:21
Visits Damascus, obtains a
novel pattern of an altar,
which he substitutes for
the altar in the temple in
Jerusalem, and otherwise
perverts the forms of
worship, 2 Kin. 16:10–16
Sundial of, 2 Kin. 20:11;
Is. 38:8
Prophets in the reign of,
Is. 1:1; Hos. 1:1; Mic. 1:1
Prophecies concerning,
Is. 7:13–25
Succeeded by Hezekiah,
2 Kin. 16:20
——— Son of Micah,
1 Chr. 8:35; 9:41, 42

AHAZIAH
King of Judah. Called Azariah
and Jehoahaz, 2 Chr. 21:17;
25:23
History of, 2 Kin. 8:25–29;
9:16–29
Gifts of, to the temple,
2 Kin. 12:18
Brethren of, slain,
2 Kin. 10:13, 14
Succeeded by Athaliah,
2 Chr. 22:10–12
——— King of Israel
History of, 1 Kin. 22:40,
49, 51–53; 2 Kin. 1;
2 Chr. 20:35–37
Succeeded by Jehoram,
2 Kin. 3:1

AHIJAH
Also called Ahiah; Son of Bela,
1 Chr. 8:7
——— Son of Jerahmeel,
1 Chr. 2:25
——— A priest in Shiloh,
probably identical with
Ahimelech, mentioned in,
1 Sam. 22:11
Was priest in Saul's reign,
1 Sam. 14:3, 18
Killed, 1 Sam. 22:11–19
——— One of David's heroes,
1 Chr. 11:36
Also called Eliam,
2 Sam. 23:34
——— A Levite who was
treasurer in the tabernacle,
1 Chr. 26:20
——— Son of Shisha, 1 Kin. 4:3
——— A prophet in Shiloh,
1 Kin. 11:29–39
——— Father of Baasha,
1 Kin. 15:27, 33; 2 Kin. 9:9
——— An Israelite, who
subscribed to the covenant of
Nehemiah, Neh. 10:26

AHIMAAZ
Father-in-law of king Saul,
1 Sam. 14:50
——— Son of Zadok, the
high priest. Loyal to David,

2 Sam. 15:36; 17:17–20;
18:19–33; 1 Chr. 6:8, 9, 53
——— Solomon's son-in-law,
1 Kin. 4:15

AHIMELECH
Also called Ahia. A high priest,
during the reign of David;
Gives shewbread and the
sword of Goliath to David,
1 Sam. 21; Mark 2:26
Killed by the command of
Saul, 1 Sam. 22:9–22
——— A Hittite, and friend of
David, 1 Sam. 26:6

AHITHOPHEL
One of David's counsellors,
2 Sam. 15:12; 1 Chr. 27:33
Joins Absalom, 2 Sam. 15:31,
34; 16:15, 20–23; 17:1–23
Probably referred to by David
in, Ps. 55:12–14
Suicide of, 2 Sam. 17:1–14, 23

AI
A royal city of the Canaanites;
Conquest and destruction of,
Josh. 7:8
Rebuilt, Ezra 2:28
Also called Aija, Neh. 11:31
And Aiath, Is. 10:28
Population of, Josh. 8:25
——— A city of the
Ammonites, Jer. 49:3

AIR
the fowl of the *a* . . . . Gen. 1:26
all fowls of the *a*. . Deut. 28:26
the fowls of the *a* . . Matt. 6:26
the power of the *a* . . . Eph. 2:2

ALEXANDER
Son of Simon who bore the
cross of Jesus, Mark 15:21
——— A relative of the high
priest, present at the defense
of Peter and John, Acts 4:6
——— A Jew of Ephesus,
Acts 19:33
——— A copper-smith,
1 Tim. 1:20; 2 Tim. 4:14

ALEXANDRIA
A city of Egypt, Acts 6:9
Ships of, Acts 27:6; 28:11
Apollos born in, Acts 18:24

ALIVE
are left *a* of you I . . Lev. 26:36
was none left
him *a* . . . . Num. 21:35
inheritance, thou
shalt save *a* . . . . Deut. 20:16
behold, while I
am yet *a* . . . . Deut. 31:27
and I make *a* . . . . . Deut. 32:39
killeth, and
maketh *a* . . . . 1 Sam. 2:6
full line to keep *a* . . 2 Sam. 8:2
are *a* from the
dead . . . . Rom. 6:13
and, behold, I
am *a* . . . . Rev. 1:18
cast *a* into a lake . . . Rev. 19:20

ALMIGHTY
him, I am the *A*
God . . . . Gen. 17:1
unto him, I am
God *A* . . . . Gen. 35:11
Joseph, God *A*
appeared . . . . Gen. 48:3
the name of
God *A* . . . . Ex. 6:3
the arrows of
the *A* . . . . Job 6:4
or doth the *A*
pervert . . . . Job 8:3
destruction from
the *A* . . . . Is. 13:6
destruction from
the *A* . . . . Joel 1:15
is to come, the *A* . . . . Rev. 1:8
holy, holy, Lord
God *A* . . . . Rev. 4:8
works, Lord
God *A* . . . . Rev. 15:3

ALTAR
there builded he
an *a* . . . . Gen. 12:7
there he builded
an *a* . . . . Gen. 12:8
and built there
an *a* . . . . Gen. 13:18
atonement for
the *a* . . . . Ex. 29:37
round about upon
the *a* . . . . Lev. 1:5
memorial of it
upon the *a* . . . . Lev. 2:2
horns of the *a* of
sweet . . . . Lev. 4:7
the horns of the *a* . . . Lev. 4:18
his fat upon the *a* . . . Lev. 4:26
upon the *a*, and
sprinkled . . . . Lev. 8:30
the *a*, and put on
incense . . . . Num. 16:46
mine *a*, to burn
incense . . . . 1 Sam. 2:28
a for Baal in the
house . . . . 1 Kin. 16:32
incense upon
the *a* . . . . 2 Chr. 26:16
accepted upon
mine *a* . . . . Is. 56:7
acceptance on
mine *a* . . . . Is. 60:7
the porch and
the *a* . . . . Ezek. 8:16
the porch and
the *a* . . . . Joel 2:17
the temple and
the *a* . . . . Matt. 23:35
with fire of the *a* . . . . Rev. 8:5

ALTARS
destroy their *a*,
break . . . . Ex. 34:13
shall destroy
their *a* . . . . Deut. 7:5
a, and slain thy
prophets . . . . . . 1 Kin. 19:10
reared up *a* for
Baal . . . . 2 Kin. 21:3

he built *a* in the
  house.......... 2 Kin. 21:4
high places and
  the *a* .... 2 Chr. 31:1
come up on
  their *a* ....Hos. 10:8
yea, their *a* are as ..Hos. 12:11

ALTOGETHER
And mount Sinai
  was *a* .... Ex. 19:18
are *a* brutish and
  foolish ....Jer. 10:8
not leave thee *a*
  unpunished ......Jer. 30:11
thou he that
  shall *a* ....Jer. 49:12

ALWAY
shewbread before
  me *a*............Ex. 25:30
oppressed and
  crushed *a* .....Deut. 28:33
son shall eat
  bread *a* .... 2 Sam. 9:10
may have a
  light *a* .... 1 Kin. 11:36
lo, I am with
  you *a* .... Matt. 28:20
speech be *a* with
  grace .... Col. 4:6

AMALEKITES
A people inhabiting the
  country south of Idumea
  and east of the Red Sea,
  Num. 13:29; 14:25;
  1 Sam. 15:7; 27:8
Defeated by Chedorlaomer,
  Gen. 14:7
Defeated by Joshua, Ex. 17:8,
  13
Defeated by Gideon, Judg. 7
Defeated by Saul,
  1 Sam. 14:47, 48; 15:1–33
Defeated by David,
  1 Sam. 27:8, 9; 30:1–20
Defeated by the Simeonites,
  1 Chr. 4:42, 43
Defeat the Israelites,
  Num. 14:45; Judg. 3:13
Israel commanded to destroy,
  Deut. 25:17–19; 1 Sam. 28:18
Prophecies against, Ex. 17:14,
  16; Num. 24:20

AMASA
Nephew of David,
  2 Sam. 17:25; 1 Chr. 2:17
Joins Absalom, 2 Sam. 17:25
Returns to David, and is
  made captain of the host,
  2 Sam. 19:13
Killed by Joab, 2 Sam. 20:8–12;
  1 Kin. 2:5, 32
———— Son of Hadlai,
  2 Chr. 28:12

AMAZIAH
A Levite, 1 Chr. 6:45
———— King of Judah. History
of, 2 Kin. 14; 2 Chr. 25
———— An idolatrous priest at
Bethel, Amos 7:10–17

———— Father of Joshah,
1 Chr. 4:34

AMMONITES
Descendants of Ben-ammi,
  one of the sons of Lot,
  Gen. 19:38
Character of, Judg. 10:6;
  2 Kin. 23:13; 2 Chr. 20:25;
  Jer. 27:3, 9; Ezek. 25:3, 6;
  Amos 1:13; Zeph. 2:10
Territory of, Num. 21:24;
  Deut. 2:19; Josh. 12:2; 13:10,
  25; Judg. 11:13
Israelites forbidden to disturb,
  Deut. 2:19, 37
Excluded from the
  congregation of Israel,
  Deut. 23:3–6
Confederate with Moabites
  and Amalekites against
  Israel, Judg. 3:12, 13
Defeated by the Israelites,
  Judg. 10:7–18; 11:32,
  33; 12:1–3; 1 Sam. 11;
  2 Sam. 8:12; 10; 11:1; 12:26–
  31; 17:27; 1 Chr. 18:11; 20:1–
  3; 2 Chr. 20; 26:7, 8; 27:5
Conspire against the Jews,
  Neh. 4:7, 8
Solomon takes wives from,
  1 Kin. 11:1; 2 Chr. 12:13;
  Neh. 13:26
Jews intermarry with,
  Ezra 9:12; 10:10–44;
  Neh. 13:23
Kings of Baalis, Jer. 40:14;
  41:10
Kings of Hanun, 2 Sam. 10;
  1 Chr. 19
Kings of Nahash, 1 Sam. 11;
  2 Sam. 10:1, 2; 1 Chr. 19:1, 2
Idols of Milcom, 2 Kin. 23:13
Prophecies concerning,
  Is. 11:14; Jer. 9:25, 26;
  25:15–21; 27:1–11; 49:1–6;
  Ezek. 21:20, 28–32; 25:1–11;
  Dan. 11:41; Amos 1:13–15;
  Zeph. 2:8–11

AMNON
Son of David, 2 Sam. 3:2;
  1 Chr. 3:1
Incest of, and death, 2 Sam. 13
———— Son of Shimon,
  1 Chr. 4:20

AMON
Governor of the city of
  Samaria, 1 Kin. 22:26;
  2 Chr. 18:25
———— King of Judah,
  2 Kin. 21:18–26;
  2 Chr. 33:21–25; Zeph. 1:1;
  Matt. 1:10
———— Ancestor of one of the
  families of the Nethinim,
  Neh. 7:59
Called Ami, Ezra 2:57

AMORITES
Descendants of Canaan,

Gen. 10:15, 16; 1 Chr. 1:13,
  14
Were giants, Amos 2:9
Struck down by Chedorlaomer
  and rescued by Abraham,
  Gen. 14
Territory of, Gen. 14:7;
  Num. 13:29; 21:13;
  Deut. 1:4, 7, 19; 3:8, 9;
  Josh. 5:1; 10:5; 12:2, 3;
  Judg. 1:35, 36; 11:22
Given to descendants of
  Abraham, Gen. 15:21; 48:22;
  Deut. 1:20; 2:26–36; 7:1;
  Josh. 3:10; Judg. 11:23;
  Amos 2:10
Allotted to Reuben, Gad, and
  Manasseh, Num. 32:33–42;
  Josh. 13:15–21
Conquest of, Num. 21:21–30;
  Josh. 10:11
Chiefs of, Josh. 13:21
Wickedness of, Gen. 15:16;
  2 Kin. 21:11; Ezra 9:1
Idolatry of, Judg. 6:10;
  1 Kin. 21:26
Judgments denounced against,
  Ex. 23:24; 33:2; 34:10, 11;
  Deut. 20:17, 18
Hornets sent among,
  Josh. 24:12
Not exterminated, Judg. 1:34–
  36; 3:1–3, 5–8; 1 Sam. 7:14;
  2 Sam. 21:2; 1 Kin. 9:20, 21;
  2 Chr. 8:7
Intermarry with Jews,
  Ezra 9:1, 2; 10:18–44
Kings of, Josh. 10:3–26

AMOS
A prophet, Amos 1:1
Forbidden to prophesy in
  Israel, Amos 7:10–17
Vision of, Amos 8:2

AMRAM
Father of Moses, Ex. 6:18; 20;
  Num. 26:58, 59; 1 Chr. 6:3,
  18; 23:12, 13
Head of one of the branches
  of Levites, Num. 3:19, 27;
  1 Chr. 26:23
Age of, at death, Ex. 6:20
———— Son of Bani, Ezra 10:34
———— Son of Dishon,
  1 Chr. 1:41

ANAKIM
A race of giants, Num. 13:28–
  33; Deut. 1:28; 2:10; 9:2
Defeated by Joshua,
  Josh. 11:21, 22
Defeated by Caleb,
  Josh. 14:12, 15; 15:13, 14;
  Judg. 1:20

ANANIAS
High priest, before whom Paul
  was tried, Acts 23:2–5; 24:1;
  25:2

———— A covetous member
  of church at Jerusalem.

Falsehood and death of,
Acts 5:1–11

——— A Christian in
Damascus, Acts 9:10–18;
22:12–16

ANATHOTH

City of refuge in Benjamin,
Josh. 21:11; 1 Chr. 6:60
Abiathar confined in,
1 Kin. 2:26
Birthplace of Jeremiah, Jer. 1:1;
32:7–12
Birthplace of Abiezer,
2 Sam. 23:27
Birthplace of Jehu, 1 Chr. 12:3
Prophecies against, Jer. 11:21–
23
Inhabitants of, Babylonian
captivity, Ezra 2:23;
Neh. 7:27

——— Son of Becher, 1 Chr. 7:8
——— A Jew, who returned
from Babylon, Neh. 10:19

ANCIENT

The *a* and
honourable . . . . .Is. 9:15
wise, the son of *a* . . . .Is. 19:11
declared this
from *a* . . . . .Is. 45:21
from *a* times the
things . . . . .Is. 46:10
a days, in the
generations . . . . .Is. 51:9
is an *a* nation, a
nation . . . . Jer. 5:15
began at the *a*
men . . . . Ezek. 9:6
the *A* of days did
sit. . . . . .Dan. 7:9
heaven, and came
to the *A* . . . . .Dan. 7:13

ANDREW

An apostle. A fisherman,
Matt. 4:18
Of Bethsaida, John 1:44
A disciple of John, John 1:40
Finds Peter, his brother,
and brings him to Jesus,
John 1:40–42
Call of, Matt. 4:19; Mark 1:16
His name appears in the list of
the apostles in, Matt. 10:2;
Mark 3:18; Luke 6:14
Asks the Master privately
about the destruction of the
temple, Mark 13:3, 4
Tells Jesus of the Greeks
who sought to see him,
John 12:20–22
Reports the number of loaves
at the feeding of the five
thousand, John 6:8
Meets with the disciples
after the Lord's ascension,
Acts 1:13

ANGEL

And the *a* of God,
which . . . . Ex. 14:19

behold, mine *A*
shall . . . . Ex. 32:34
And when the *a*
stretched . . . . . . 2 Sam. 24:16
The *a* of the
Lord encampeth. . . Ps. 34:7
a of his presence
saved . . . . .Is. 63:9
who hath sent
his *a* . . . . .Dan. 3:28
standing before
the *a* . . . . Zech. 3:1
And the *a*
answering . . . . .Luke 1:19
And the *a*
answered. . . . . .Luke 1:35
a of the Lord by
night . . . . Acts 5:19
unto the *a* of the
church . . . . Rev. 3:1
to the *a* of the
church . . . . Rev. 3:7
unto the *a* of the
church . . . . Rev. 3:14
a came and
stood at . . . . Rev. 8:3
the *a* took the
censer . . . . Rev. 8:5
The first *a*
sounded . . . . Rev. 8:7
And the fourth *a*
sounded . . . . Rev. 8:12
And the seventh *a*
sounded . . . . Rev. 11:15
a, saying, Babylon . . Rev. 14:8
Jesus have sent
mine *a* . . . . Rev. 22:16

ANGELS

even thousands
of *a* . . . . Ps. 68:17
shall give his *a*
charge . . . . Ps. 91:11
the Lord, ye
his *a* . . . . Ps. 103:20
Father with his *a* . Matt. 16:27
That in heaven
their *a* . . . . Matt. 18:10
send his *a* with a
great . . . . Matt. 24:31
and all the holy *a* Matt. 25:31
devil and his *a* . . . Matt. 25:41
legions of *a* . . . . . Matt. 26:53
Father with the
holy *a*. . . . . Mark 8:38
tongues of men
and of *a* . . . . .1 Cor. 13:1
it was ordained
by *a* . . . . Gal. 3:19
Spirit, seen of *a* . . 1 Tim. 3:16
little lower than
the *a* . . . . .Heb. 2:9
innumerable
company of *a* . . . .Heb. 12:22
a and authorities
and. . . . . 1 Pet. 3:22
God spared not
the *a* . . . . 2 Pet. 2:4
Father, and before
his *a*. . . . . Rev. 3:5
the earth, and
his *a*. . . . . Rev. 12:9

presence of the
holy *a*. . . . . Rev. 14:10

ANGER

overthrew in his *a* . Deut. 29:23
have provoked me
to *a* . . . . .Deut. 32:21
a of the Lord was
hot. . . . . Judg. 2:14
to provoke him
to *a* . . . . 2 Kin. 17:17
to provoke him
to *a* . . . . 2 Kin. 21:6
why doth thine *a*
smoke . . . . Ps. 74:1
gracious, slow
to *a* . . . . Ps. 103:8
that is slow to *a*
appeaseth . . . . . . Prov. 15:18
the *a* of the Lord
kindled . . . . .Is. 5:25
tread them in
mine *a* . . . . .Is. 63:3
whirlwind, to
render his *a*. . . . . . . .Is. 66:15
Behold, mine *a*
and. . . . . Jer. 7:20
strong arm, even
in *a*. . . . . Jer. 21:5
shall mine *a* be
accomplished . . . . Ezek. 5:13
and accomplish
mine *a* . . . . Ezek. 7:8
to accomplish
my *a* . . . . Ezek. 20:8
merciful, slow
to *a* . . . . Joel 2:13
his *a* did tear
perpetually . . . . . .Amos 1:11
retaineth not his *a* . . Mic. 7:18
fierceness of his *a*. . . .Nah. 1:6

ANGRY

he be *a*, and ye
perish . . . . Ps. 2:12
wilt thou be *a* for . . . . Ps. 79:5
a man stirreth up
strife . . . . Prov. 29:22
though thou
wast *a* . . . . .Is. 12:1
That whosoever
is *a*. . . . . Matt. 5:22
selfwilled, not
soon *a* . . . . Titus 1:7
were *a*, and thy
wrath. . . . . Rev. 11:18

ANGUISH

darkness, dimness
of *a*. . . . . .Is. 8:22
travail, and the *a* . . . . Jer. 4:31
a hath taken
hold of. . . . . Jer. 6:24
Tribulation and *a* . . . Rom. 2:9

ANOINT

upon his head,
and *a* . . . . Ex. 29:7
thou shalt not *a*
thyself . . . . .Deut. 28:40
Lord said,
Arise, *a* . . . . . . .1 Sam. 16:12

mourning apparel,
and *a* . . . . 2 Sam. 14:2
Nimshi shalt
thou *a* . . . . 1 Kin. 19:16
prophecy, and to a . . Dan. 9:24
thou shalt not *a*
thee . . . . Mic. 6:15
a thine eyes with
eyesalve . . . . Rev. 3:18

ANOINTED

the priest that is *a* . . . Lev. 4:3
unleavened
wafers *a* . . . . Lev. 7:12
Aaron's head,
and *a* . . . . Lev. 8:12
the horn of his *a* . . 1 Sam. 2:10
the LORD hath *a*
thee . . . . 1 Sam. 10:1
of oil, and *a* . . . . . 1 Sam. 16:13
slain the
LORD's *a* . . . . 2 Sam. 1:16
tabernacle, and *a*
Solomon . . . . 1 Kin. 1:39
made him king,
and *a* . . . . 2 Kin. 11:12
and against his *a* . . . . . Ps. 2:2
God, thy God,
hath *a* . . . . Ps. 45:7
I shall be *a* with
fresh . . . . Ps. 92:10
LORD to his *a*, to
Cyrus . . . . Is. 45:1
LORD hath *a* me
to preach . . . . Is. 61:1
he hath *a* me to
preach . . . . Luke 4:18
God *a* Jesus of
Nazareth . . . . Acts 10:38

ANOINTING

shalt thou take
the *a* . . . . Ex. 29:7
poured of the *a* oil . . Lev. 8:12
a oil, and of the
blood . . . . Lev. 8:30
a which ye have
received . . . . 1 John 2:27

ANSWER

people shall *a* . . . . Deut. 27:15
a, Because they
forsook . . . . 1 Kin. 9:9
me, but I will
not *a* . . . . Prov. 1:28
was there none
to *a* . . . . Is. 50:2
called, none did *a* . . . . Is. 66:4
Then they shall *a* . . . . Jer. 22:9
I the LORD will *a*
him . . . . Ezek. 14:7
that thou shalt *a* . . . Ezek. 21:7
And the King
shall *a* . . . . Matt. 25:40
know how ye
ought to *a* . . . . Col. 4:6
the *a* of a good
conscience . . . . . . 1 Pet. 3:21

ANTIOCH

A city of Syria; Disciples
first called Christians in,
Acts 11:19–30

The congregation in,
Acts 13:1; 14:26, 27
Barnabas and Paul make
second visit to, Acts 14:26–
28
Dissension within the
congregation of, Acts 15:22;
Acts 15:1–35
Paul and Peter's controversy
at, Gal. 2:11–15
—— A city of Pisidia.
Persecutes Paul, Acts 13:14–
52; 14:19–22; 18:22;
2 Tim. 3:11

APOLLOS

An eloquent Christian convert
at Corinth, Acts 18:24–28;
19:1; 1 Cor. 1:12; 3:4–7
Refuses to return to Rome,
1 Cor. 16:12
Paul writes Titus about,
Titus 3:13

APOSTLE

called to be an *a* . . . . Rom. 1:1
Am I not an *a* . . . . . . 1 Cor. 9:1
Paul, an *a* of Jesus . . 2 Cor. 1:1
the *A* and High
Priest . . . . Heb. 3:1
and an *a* of Jesus
Christ . . . . 2 Pet. 1:1

APOSTLES

things unto the *a* . Luke 24:10
a was surnamed
Barnabas . . . . Acts 4:36
they set before
the *a* . . . . Acts 6:6
Samaria, except
the *a* . . . . Acts 8:1
Then pleased it
the *a* . . . . Acts 15:22
a and elders and
brethren . . . . Acts 15:23
a, and as the
brethren . . . . 1 Cor. 9:5
church, first *a*,
secondarily . . . . 1 Cor. 12:28
such are false *a*,
deceitful . . . . . . 2 Cor. 11:13
the very
chiefest *a* . . . . . 2 Cor. 12:11
the *a* saw I none,
save . . . . Gal. 1:19
a and prophets,
Jesus . . . . Eph. 2:20

APPEARANCE

looketh on the
outward *a* . . . . . 1 Sam. 16:7
a of a sapphire
stone . . . . Ezek. 1:26
As the *a* of the
bow . . . . Ezek. 1:28
was a man,
whose *a* . . . . Ezek. 40:3

APPEARED

the LORD *a* unto
Abram . . . . Gen. 12:7
the LORD *a* to
Abram . . . . Gen. 17:1

And the LORD *a*
unto . . . . Gen. 18:1
And the LORD *a*
unto . . . . Gen. 26:24
Joseph, God
Almighty *a* . . . . . Gen. 48:3
And I *a* unto
Abraham . . . . Ex. 6:3
when the
morning *a* . . . . . . Ex. 14:27
glory of the
LORD *a* . . . . Lev. 9:23
behold, there *a a*
chariot . . . . 2 Kin. 2:11
Moriah, where the
LORD *a* . . . . 2 Chr. 3:1
angel of the
Lord *a* . . . . Matt. 1:20
day of the week,
he *a* . . . . Mark 16:9
The God of
glory *a* . . . . Acts 7:2
even Jesus, that *a* . . Acts 9:17
bringeth salvation
hath *a* . . . . Titus 2:11
And there *a*
another . . . . Rev. 12:3

APPOINT

Israel, and shalt *a* . . Ex. 30:16
I will even *a* over . . Lev. 26:16
And thou shalt *a*
Aaron . . . . Num. 3:10
take your sons,
and *a* . . . . 1 Sam. 8:11
a unto them that
mourn . . . . Is. 61:3
chosen man, that
I may *a* . . . . Jer. 49:19
Jerusalem, to *a*
captains . . . . Ezek. 21:22
gathered together,
and *a* . . . . Hos. 1:11

APPOINTED

the time *a* I will
return . . . . Gen. 18:14
thee, in the time *a* . . Ex. 23:15
they *a* Kedesh in
Galilee . . . . Josh. 20:7
the LORD had *a* to
defeat . . . . 2 Sam. 17:14
the king of
Assyria *a* . . . . . . 2 Kin. 18:14
And he *a*,
according . . . . . . 2 Chr. 8:14
rebellion *a a*
captain . . . . Neh. 9:17
a feasts my soul
hateth . . . . Is. 1:14
I have not *a* the
ordinances . . . . . . Jer. 33:25
Idumea, which
have *a* . . . . Ezek. 36:5
true, but the
time *a* . . . . Dan. 10:1
vision is yet for
an *a* . . . . Hab. 2:3
he hath *a a* day, in . Acts 17:31
city, as I had *a*
thee . . . . Titus 1:5

Son, whom he
hath *a* . . . . .Heb. 1:2
whereunto also
they were *a* . . . . 1 Pet. 2:8

AQUILA AND PRISCILLA
Christians at Corinth,
Acts 18:1–3, 18, 19, 26
Friendship of, for Paul,
Rom. 16:3, 4
Paul sends salutations to,
2 Tim. 4:19

ARABIA
Tribute to Solomon,
2 Chr. 9:14
Tribute to Jehoshaphat,
2 Chr. 17:11
Exports of, Ezek. 27:21
Prophecies against, Is. 21:13;
Jer. 25:24
Paul visits, Gal. 1:17

ARARAT
A district of Armenia,
Jer. 51:27
The ark of Noah came to rest
in the mountains of, Gen. 8:4
Assassins of Sennacherib take
refuge in, Is. 37:38

ARISE
a among you a
prophet . . . . Deut. 13:1
the LORD said, A,
anoint . . . . 1 Sam. 16:12
after thee shall
any *a* . . . . 1 Kin. 3:12
A, O LORD . . . . Ps. 3:7
I *a*, saith the
LORD. . . . . Ps. 12:5
a, pass over to
Chittim . . . . .Is. 23:12
body shall they *a* . . . .Is. 26:19
Kings shall see
and *a* . . . . .Is. 49:7
up thy loins, and *a* . . . Jer. 1:17
trouble they will
say, A . . . . Jer. 2:27
a, if they can save. . . . Jer. 2:28
A, go to Nineveh,
that . . . . Jon. 1:2
A and thresh, O
daughter . . . . Mic. 4:13
the dumb
stone, A . . . . .Hab. 2:19
shall *a* false
Christs . . . . Matt. 24:24
a, and be baptized . Acts 22:16
and the day star *a* . . 2 Pet. 1:19

ARK
thy house into
the *a* . . . . .Gen. 7:1
seat above upon
the *a* . . . . Ex. 25:21
upon the *a* of the
testimony . . . . Ex. 25:22
vail the *a* of the
testimony . . . . Ex. 26:33
which is upon
the *a* . . . . Lev. 16:2
Levi, to bear the *a* . Deut. 10:8

Levi, which bare
the *a* . . . . Deut. 31:9
priests that bear
the *a* . . . . Josh. 3:13
they that bare
the *a* . . . . Josh. 3:15
priests that bare
the *a* . . . . Josh. 3:17
his face before
the *a* . . . . .Josh. 7:6
bring from thence
the *a* . . . . 1 Sam. 4:4
trumpets before
the *a* . . . . 1 Chr. 15:24
house of rest for
the *a* . . . . 1 Chr. 28:2
entered into the *a* . Luke 17:27
golden censer, and
the *a* . . . . .Heb. 9:4
fear, prepared an *a* . .Heb. 11:7
of Noah, while
the *a* . . . . 1 Pet. 3:20
in his temple
the *a* . . . . Rev. 11:19

ARM
a, and with great
judgments. . . . . Ex. 6:6
greatness of
thine *a* . . . . Ex. 15:16
a, and by great
terrors . . . . Deut. 4:34
thy stretched
out *a* . . . . Deut. 9:29
him is an *a* of
flesh. . . . . 2 Chr. 32:8
did their own *a*
save . . . . Ps. 44:3
hand, and his
holy *a* . . . . Ps. 98:1
lighting down of
his *a* . . . . .Is. 30:30
the lambs with
his *a* . . . . .Is. 40:11
put on
strength, O *a* . . . . . .Is. 51:9
made bare his
holy *a* . . . . .Is. 52:10
the *a* of the LORD
revealed. . . . . .Is. 53:1
his glorious *a*,
dividing . . . . .Is. 63:12
strong *a*, even in
anger . . . . Jer. 21:5
and stretched
out *a* . . . . .Jer. 32:17
his *a* is broken,
saith . . . . Jer. 48:25

ARMIES
bring forth mine *a* . . . . Ex. 7:4
of Egypt by their *a* . . Ex. 12:51
defy the *a* of the
living . . . . .1 Sam. 17:26
he hath defied
the *a* . . . . 1 Sam. 17:36

ARMY
a of the Chaldees
pursued. . . . . 2 Kin. 25:5
all the *a* of the
Chaldees . . . . . . 2 Kin. 25:10

king of
Babylon's *a* . . . . Jer. 32:2
king of
Babylon's *a* . . . . Jer. 34:21
Behold,
Pharaoh's *a* . . . . Jer. 37:7
the Chaldeans' *a*
pursued. . . . . Jer. 39:5
a of Pharaoh-
necho king . . . . Jer. 46:2
the wages for
his *a* . . . . Ezek. 29:19
and all thine *a*,
horses . . . . Ezek. 38:4
will in the *a* of
heaven. . . . . .Dan. 4:35
voice before his *a* . . . Joel 2:11
palmerworm, my
great *a* . . . . Joel 2:25

ARNON
A river emptying into the
Dead Sea from the east;
Boundary between Moabites
and Amorites, Num. 21:13,
26; 22:36; Deut. 2:24, 36;
3:8, 16; Josh. 12:1
Fords of, Is. 16:2
Miracles at, Num. 21:14

AROSE
And he *a* and
departed . . . . . . 1 Sam. 20:42
saddled his ass,
and *a* . . . . 2 Sam. 17:23
wrath of the
LORD *a* . . . . 2 Chr. 36:16
Then Job *a*, and
rent . . . . .Job 1:20
Then I *a*, and
went . . . . Ezek. 3:23
Then he *a*, and
rebuked . . . . Matt. 8:26
a certain of the
synagogue . . . . Acts 6:9
there *a* a great cry . . Acts 23:9

ARROWS
For the *a* of the
Almighty . . . . Job 6:4
out his *a*, and
scattered . . . . Ps. 18:14
teeth are spears
and *a* . . . . Ps. 57:4
Whose *a* are sharp . . . .Is. 5:28
Make bright the *a*. . . Jer. 51:11

ASAHEL
Nephew of David, and one of
his captains, 2 Sam. 2:18–24,
32; 3:27; 23:24; 1 Chr. 2:16;
11:26; 27:7
———— A Levite, commissioned
by Jehoshaphat to teach the
law to Judah, 2 Chr. 17:8
———— A Levite, who had
charge of tithes, 2 Chr. 31:13
———— Father of Jonathan,
Ezra 10:15

ASAPH
Father of Joah, 2 Kin. 18:18;
Is. 36:3, 22
———— Son of Berachiah. One

of the three leaders of music
in David's organization
of the tabernacle service,
1 Chr. 15:16–19; 16:5–7;
25:1–9; 2 Chr. 5:12; 35:15;
Neh. 12:46
Apointed to sound the
cymbals in the temple choir,
1 Chr. 15:17, 19; 16:5, 7
A composer of sacred lyrics,
2 Chr. 29:13–30
See titles of, Ps. 50; 73; 74; 75;
76; 77; 78; 79; 80; 81; 82; 83
Descendants of, in the
temple choir, 1 Chr. 25:1–9;
2 Chr. 20:14; 29:13;
Ezra 2:41; 3:10; Neh. 7:44;
11:22
———— A Levite, whose
descendants lived in
Jerusalem after the exile,
1 Chr. 9:15
———— A Kohath Levite,
1 Chr. 26:1
———— Keeper of forests,
Neh. 2:8

ASCEND

causeth the
vapours to *a* . . . . . . Ps. 135:7
If I *a* up into
heaven . . . . Ps. 139:8
thine heart, I
will *a* . . . . Is. 14:13
I will *a* above the . . . . Is. 14:14
them, I *a* unto my
Father . . . . John 20:17

ASCENDED

the smoke
thereof *a* . . . . Ex. 19:18
And they *a* by the
south . . . . Num. 13:22
man hath *a* up to
heaven . . . . John 3:13
for I am not yet *a* . . John 20:17

ASHAMED

said, O my God, I
am *a* . . . . Ezra 9:6
a, let not mine
enemies . . . . Ps. 25:2
let me never be *a* . . . . Ps. 31:1
a and brought to
confusion . . . . Ps. 35:26
shall be *a* of the
oaks . . . . Is. 1:29
afraid and *a* of
Ethiopia . . . . Is. 20:5
confounded, and
the sun *a* . . . . Is. 24:23
a nor confounded
world . . . . Is. 45:17
not be *a* that wait . . . . Is. 49:23
thou shalt not
be *a* . . . . Is. 54:4
a when they had
committed . . . . Jer. 6:15
forsake thee shall
be *a* . . . . Jer. 17:13
Be ye *a*, O ye
husbandmen . . . . . . Joel 1:11

a of me and of my
words . . . . Mark 8:38
I am not *a* of the
gospel . . . . Rom. 1:16
whereof ye are
now *a* . . . . Rom. 6:21
him shall not be *a* . Rom. 9:33
not thou
therefore *a* . . . . . . 2 Tim. 1:8
nevertheless I am
not *a* . . . . 2 Tim. 1:12
be *a* that falsely
accuse . . . . 1 Pet. 3:16

ASHDOD

A city of the Philistines,
Josh. 13:3; 1 Sam. 6:17;
Amos 3:9
Anakim inhabit, Josh. 11:22
Assigned to Judah, Josh. 15:47
Dagon's temple in, where the
ark of the covenant was put
temporarily, 1 Sam. 5
Conquest of, by Uzziah,
2 Chr. 26:6
Conquest by Tartan, Is. 20:1
People of, conspire against the
Jews, Neh. 4:7, 8
Jews intermarry with,
Neh. 13:23, 24
Prophecies concerning,
Jer. 25:20; Amos 1:8; 9;
Zeph. 2:4; Zech. 9:6
Called Azotus, Acts 8:40

ASHER

Son of Jacob, by Zilpah,
Gen. 30:13; 35:26; 49:20;
Ex. 1:4; 1 Chr. 2:2
Descendants of, Gen. 46:17;
Num. 26:44–47
———— Tribe of: Census of, by
families, Num. 1:40, 41;
26:44–47; 1 Chr. 7:40; 12:36
Station of, in camp,
Num. 2:25, 27
Prophecies concerning
By Moses, Deut. 33:24, 25
By John, Rev. 7:6
Allotment to, of land in
Canaan, Josh. 19:24–31;
Ezek. 48:2
Upbraided by Deborah,
Judg. 5:17
Summoned by Gideon,
Judg. 6:35; 7:23
Join Hezekiah, 2 Chr. 30:11
———— A city of Shechem,
Josh. 17:7; 1 Kin. 4:16

ASHES

pans to receive
his *a* . . . . Ex. 27:3
place, where the *a* . . Lev. 4:12
He feedeth on *a* . . . . . Is. 44:20
beauty for *a*, the
oil . . . . Is. 61:3
wallow thyself
in *a* . . . . Jer. 6:26
Gomorrha into *a*
condemned . . . . 2 Pet. 2:6

ASHKELON

Also called Askelon; One of
the five chief cities of the
Philistines, Josh. 13:3
Captured by the people of
Judah, Judg. 1:18
Samson kills thirty men of,
Judg. 14:19
Emerods of, 1 Sam. 6:17
Prophecies concerning,
Jer. 25:20; 47:5, 7; Amos 1:8;
Zeph. 2:4, 7; Zech. 9:5

ASHTAROTH

The capital city of Bashan,
Deut. 1:4; Josh. 9:10
Giants lived at, Josh. 12:4
Allotted to Manasseh,
Josh. 13:31; 1 Chr. 6:71
Possibly identical with
Ashteroth Karnaim,
mentioned in, Gen. 14:5

ASHTORETH

An idol of the Philistines,
Zidonians, and Phoenicians.
Probably identical with queen
of heaven, Jer. 7:18
Worshiped by Israelites,
Judg. 2:13; 10:6; 1 Sam. 7:3,
4; 12:10; 1 Kin. 11:5, 33;
2 Kin. 23:13
Temple of, 1 Sam. 31:10
High places of, at Jerusalem,
destroyed, 2 Kin. 23:13

ASIA

Inhabitants of, in Jerusalem,
at Pentecost, Acts 2:9; 21:27;
24:18
Paul and Silas forbidden by
the Holy Spirit to preach in,
Acts 16:6
Gospel preached in, by Paul,
Acts 19; 20:4
Paul leaves, Acts 20:16
The congregations of,
1 Cor. 16:19; Rev. 1:4, 11

ASKED

men of the place *a* . . Gen. 26:7
people *a*, and he
brought . . . . Ps. 105:40
and the
governor *a* . . . . . . Matt. 27:11
And they *a* him,
What . . . . John 1:21
thou wouldest
have *a* . . . . John 4:10

ASS

thine ox and
thine *a* . . . . Ex. 23:12
thine *a* shall be
violently . . . . Deut. 28:31
sheep, camel
and *a* . . . . 1 Sam. 15:3
a, and arose, and
gat . . . . 2 Sam. 17:23
a his master's crib . . . . Is. 1:3
and riding upon
an *a* . . . . Zech. 9:9

ASSEMBLED

children of
Israel *a* . . . . Josh. 18:1
presidents and
princes *a* . . . . .Dan. 6:6
a for fear of the
Jews . . . . .John 20:19
a whole year
they *a*. . . . . .Acts 11:26

ASSEMBLY

whole *a* of the
congregation. . . . . . . Ex. 12:6
to kill this
whole *a* . . . . Ex. 16:3
it is a solemn *a* . . . . Lev. 23:36
a to the LORD thy
God . . . . .Deut. 16:8
they made a
solemn *a* . . . . .2 Chr. 7:9
the *a* of the
wicked . . . . Ps. 22:16
be feared in the *a* . . . . Ps. 89:7
the *a* of young
men . . . . .Jer. 6:11
a of treacherous
men . . . . Jer. 9:2
Babylon an *a* of
great . . . . Jer. 50:9
be in the *a* of my
people . . . . Ezek. 13:9
fast, call a
solemn *a* . . . . Joel 1:14

ASSYRIA

An empire founded by
Nimrod, Gen. 10:8–12;
Mic. 5:6
It extended from east of the
Tigris, Gen. 2:14; 10:11
Possibly to Egypt, Gen. 25:18
Its armies invade the
land of Israel under Pul,
2 Kin. 15:19; 1 Chr. 5:26
Tiglath, 2 Kin. 15:29;
1 Chr. 5:6, 26
Shalmaneser, 2 Kin. 17:3–6,
24–27; 18:9–12; Jer. 50:17
Sennacherib, 2 Kin. 18:13–
37; 19; 2 Chr. 32; Is. 36; 37
Army of, destroyed by the
angel of the Lord, Is. 37:36
Alliances with, sought by
Judah and Israel, Hos. 5:13
Israelites subject to, Lam. 5:6
Israelites carried captive into,
2 Kin. 17:3–23
Jews carried captive to,
2 Kin. 24; 25; 2 Chr. 36:5–21
Invaded by Pharaoh-necho,
2 Kin. 23:29
Commerce of, Ezek. 27:23
Productiveness of, Is. 36:17
Prophecies concerning,
Is. 7:17–25; 8:4–10; 10:5–34;
14:24–28; 19:23–25; 20;
30:27–33; 31:8, 9; 37:21–35;
Jer. 1:15; Ezek. 31; Jon. 3:1–
4; Nah. 1; 2; 3; Zeph. 2:13–
15; Zech. 10:11
Prophecies of captivity of

Israelites in, Hos. 9:3;
11:5, 11

ASTONISHED

passeth by it shall
be *a* . . . . .1 Kin. 9:8
be *a*, and wag his
head. . . . . .Jer. 18:16
shall be *a* and hiss . . . Jer. 19:8
goeth by it shall
be *a* . . . . .Jer. 49:17
Babylon shall be *a* . . . Jer. 50:13
every moment,
and be *a*. . . . . Ezek. 26:16
which believed
were *a* . . . . .Acts 10:45

ASTONISHMENT

and blindness,
and *a* . . . . Deut. 28:28
become an *a* . . . . . Deut. 28:37
and make them
an *a* . . . . .Jer. 25:9
desolation, and
an *a* . . . . .Jer. 25:11
a desolation, an *a* . . . Jer. 25:18
a curse, and an *a* . . . Jer. 29:18
execration, and
an *a* . . . . .Jer. 42:18
instruction and
an *a* . . . . Ezek. 5:15

ATHALIAH

Wife of Jehoram, king of
Judah, 2 Kin. 8:18, 26; 11:1–
3, 12–16, 20; 2 Chr. 22:10–
12; 23:12–15, 21
——— Son of Jehoram,
1 Chr. 8:26
——— Father of Jeshaiah,
Ezra 8:7

ATONEMENT

thou shalt make
an *a* . . . . .Ex. 29:37
Aaron shall make
an *a* . . . . .Ex. 30:10
thou shalt take
the *a* . . . . Ex. 30:16
accepted for him
to make *a* . . . . Lev. 1:4
priest shall make
an *a* . . . . Lev. 4:20
priest shall make
an *a* . . . . Lev. 4:26
priest that
maketh *a*. . . . . Lev. 7:7
priest shall make
an *a* . . . . Lev. 12:8
altar to make an *a* . Lev. 17:11
congregation, and
make an *a* . . . . . .Num. 16:46
God, and made
an *a* . . . . .Num. 25:13

AVEN

Another name for On,
Ezek. 30:17
——— Beth-aven, Hos. 10:8

AVENGE

Thou shalt not *a*,
nor . . . . Lev. 19:18

that shall *a* the
quarrel. . . . . Lev. 26:25
vengeance, that
he may *a* . . . . .Jer. 46:10
Dearly beloved, *a*
not . . . . .Rom. 12:19
thou not judge
and *a* . . . . Rev. 6:10

AWAKE

A up, my glory . . . . . . Ps. 57:8
A and sing, ye
that . . . . .Is. 26:19
A, *a*, put on
strength . . . . .Is. 51:9
A, *a*, stand up, O
Jerusalem . . . . .Is. 51:17
A, *a* . . . . .Is. 52:1
the earth shall *a* . . . .Dan. 12:2
saith to the
wood, *A*. . . . . .Hab. 2:19
A, O sword,
against. . . . . Zech. 13:7

AZARIAH

Son of Ethan, 1 Chr. 2:8
——— Son of Jehu, 1 Chr. 2:38,
39
——— Son of Zadok, 1 Kin. 4:2
——— Captain of Solomon's
guards, 1 Kin. 4:5
——— A prophet, called Obed,
2 Chr. 15:1, 8
——— A high priest, 1 Chr. 6:9
Also called Amariah,
2 Chr. 19:11
——— Son of Jehoshaphat,
2 Chr. 21:2
——— Son of Jeroham,
2 Chr. 23:1
——— Son of Obed, 2 Chr. 23:3
——— Son of Johanan, possibly
identical with Zechariah, son
of Jehoiada, 1 Chr. 6:10, 11;
2 Chr. 24:20–22
——— Chief of the tribe of
Ephraim, 2 Chr. 28:12
——— A Levite, 1 Chr. 6:36
Called Uzziah, 1 Chr. 6:24
——— High priest in
Hezekiah's reign,
2 Chr. 31:10, 13
Probably identical with Ahitub
mentioned in, 1 Chr. 6:11, 12
——— Son of Hilkiah,
1 Chr. 6:13, 14; 9:11;
Ezra 7:1, 3
——— Son of Hoshaiah,
Jer. 43:2–7
——— Hebrew name of Abed-
nego, Dan. 1:7, 19
——— A captive returned from
Babylon, Neh. 7:7; 10:2
Also called Seraiah, Ezra 2:2

BAAL

An idol of the Phoenicians,
god of the sun; The Israelites
wickedly worshiped in
the time of the judges,
Judg. 2:10–23; 1 Sam. 7:3, 4
By the kingdom of Israel,

2 Kin. 17:16; Jer. 23:13;
Hos. 1; 2; 13:1
Under Ahab, 1 Kin. 16:31–
33; 18:18; 19:18
Under Jehoram, 2 Kin. 3:2
By the Jews, 2 Kin. 21:3;
2 Chr. 22:2–4; 24:7; 28:2;
33:3
Jeremiah expostulates against
the worship of, Jer. 2:8, 23;
7:9
Altars of, destroyed by Gideon,
Judg. 6:25–32
Destroyed by Jehoiada,
2 Kin. 11:18
Destroyed by Josiah,
2 Kin. 23:4, 5
Prophets of, slain by Elijah,
1 Kin. 18:40
All worshipers of, destroyed
by Jehu, 2 Kin. 10:18–25
———— A Benjamite,
1 Chr. 8:30; 9:36
———— A Reubenite, 1 Chr. 5:5
———— A city in the tribe of
Simeon, 1 Chr. 4:33
Called Baalath-beer, Josh. 19:8

BAALAH
A city in the south of Judah,
Josh. 15:29
Apparently identical with
Balah, Josh. 19:3
And Bilhah, 1 Chr. 4:29
———— A mountain in the
territory of the tribe of Judah,
Josh. 15:11
Probably identical with Mount
Jearim, Josh. 15:10

BAANAH
A captain of Ish-bosheth's
army, 2 Sam. 4:2, 5, 6, 9
———— Father of Heleb,
2 Sam. 23:29; 1 Chr. 11:30
———— A chief Jew of the exile,
Ezra 2:2; Neh. 7:7; 10:27
———— Also spelled Baana,
Son of Hushai,
1 Kin. 4:16

BABYLON
City of; Built by Nimrod,
Gen. 10:10
In the land of Shinar,
Gen. 10:10; 11:2
Tower of, Gen. 11:1–9
Capital of the kingdom of
Babylon, 2 Kin. 25:13;
2 Chr. 36:6, 7, 10, 18, 20;
Dan. 4:30
Gates of, Is. 45:1, 2; Jer. 51:58
Walled, Jer. 51:44, 58
Splendor of, Is. 14:4
Peter writes from, 1 Pet. 5:13
Prophecies concerning,
Ps. 87:4; 137:8, 9; Is. 13;
14:4–23; 21:1–10; 46:1, 2;
47; 48:14, 20; Jer. 21:4–10;
25:12–14; 27:1–11; 28:14;
32:28; 34:2, 3; 42:11, 12; 43;
46:13–26; 49:28–30; 50; 51;
Ezek. 21:19; 26; 29:17–20;

30:10; 32:11; Dan. 2:21–38;
4:10–26; 5:25–29; 7;
Hab. 1:5–11; Zech. 2:7–9
Figurative, Rev. 14:8; 16:19;
17; 18

BACK
caused the sea to
go b . . . . Ex. 14:21
and brought b
word . . . . Num. 13:26
he is turned b . . . 1 Sam. 15:11
cast me behind
thy b . . . . 1 Kin. 14:9
the LORD
bringeth b . . . . Ps. 14:7
south, Keep not b . . . . . Is. 43:6
I gave my b to the . . . . Is. 50:6
have turned
their b . . . . Jer. 2:27
Behold, I will
turn b . . . . Jer. 21:4
hath Moab turned
the b . . . . Jer. 48:39
Flee ye, turn b,
dwell . . . . Jer. 49:8
I will turn thee b . . Ezek. 38:4
kept b by fraud,
crieth . . . . James 5:4

BACKSLIDING
which b Israel
hath . . . . Jer. 3:6
whereby b Israel
committed . . . . Jer. 3:8
Turn, O b children . . . Jer. 3:14
Return, ye b
children . . . . Jer. 3:22

BALAAM
Son of Beor; From
Mesopotamia, Deut. 23:4
A soothsayer, Josh. 13:22
A prophet, Num. 24:2–9;
2 Pet. 2:15, 16
Balak sends for, to curse Israel,
Num. 22:5–7; Josh. 24:9;
Neh. 13:2; Mic. 6:5
Anger of, rebuked by his ass,
Num. 22:22–35; 2 Pet. 2:16
Counsel of, an occasion of
Israel's corruption with the
Midianites, Num. 31:16;
Rev. 2:14, 15
Covetousness of, 2 Pet. 2:15;
Jude 11
Death of, Num. 31:8;
Josh. 13:22

BANDS
I have broken
the b . . . . Lev. 26:13
Pharaoh-nechoh
put him in b . . . 2 Kin. 23:33
him b of the
Chaldees . . . . 2 Kin. 24:2
and her hands
as b . . . . Eccl. 7:26
yoke, and burst
thy b . . . . Jer. 2:20
I have broken
the b . . . . Ezek. 34:27

him, and upon
his b . . . . Ezek. 38:22

BAPTISM
the b that I am
baptized . . . . . . Matt. 20:22
Beginning from
the b . . . . Acts 1:22
buried with him
by b . . . . Rom. 6:4
figure whereunto
even b . . . . 1 Pet. 3:21

BAPTIZED
Jesus, when he
was b . . . . Matt. 3:16
drink of, and to
be b . . . . Matt. 20:22
believeth and is b . Mark 16:16
John truly b with
water . . . . Acts 1:5
them, Repent, and
be b . . . . Acts 2:38
received his word
were b . . . . Acts 2:41
was b, and her
household . . . . . . Acts 16:15
and was b, he and
all . . . . Acts 16:33
b, and wash away
thy . . . . Acts 22:16
were b into Jesus
Christ . . . . Rom. 6:3
are we all b . . . . . 1 Cor. 12:13

BARE
Sarah conceived,
and b . . . . Gen. 21:2
Leah conceived,
and b . . . . Gen. 29:32
conceived again,
and b . . . . Gen. 29:33
conceived again,
and b . . . . Gen. 29:34
conceived again,
and b . . . . Gen. 29:35
b him Nadab, and
Abihu . . . . Ex. 6:23
Egyptians, and
how I b . . . . Ex. 19:4
sons of Levi,
which b . . . . Deut. 31:9
they that b the ark . Josh. 3:15
b the ark of the
covenant . . . . Josh. 3:17
The LORD hath
made b . . . . Is. 52:10
and he b the sin of . . . Is. 53:12
he b them, and
carried . . . . Is. 63:9
and thy heels
made b . . . . Jer. 13:22
I have made
Esau b . . . . Jer. 49:10
And all b him
witness . . . . Luke 4:22
own self b our
sins . . . . 1 Pet. 2:24
tree of life,
which b . . . . Rev. 22:2

BARNABAS

Also called Joses; A prophet, Acts 13:1
An apostle, Acts 14:14
A Levite who gave his possessions to be owned in common with other disciples, Acts 4:36, 37
Brings Paul to the apostles, Acts 9:25–27
Accompanies Paul to Jerusalem, Acts 11:30
Returns with Paul to Antioch (of Syria), Acts 12:25
Goes with Paul to Seleucia, Acts 13
Goes with Paul to Iconium, Acts 14:1–7
Called Jupiter (Zeus), Acts 14:12–18
Goes to Derbe, Acts 14:20
Is sent as an emissary to Jerusalem, Acts 15; Gal. 2:1–9
Disaffected toward Paul, Acts 15:36–39
Is reconciled to Paul, 1 Cor. 9:6
Piety of, Acts 11:24
Devotion of, to Jesus, Acts 15:26

BARUCH

An amanuensis (copyist) of Jeremiah, Jer. 32:12–16; 36:4–32; 43:3–6; 45:1, 2
——— Son of Labai, Neh. 3:20; 10:6
——— A descendant of Pharez, Neh. 11:5

BARZILLAI

A friend of David, 2 Sam. 17:27–29; 19:31–39; 1 Kin. 2:7; Ezra 2:61; Neh. 7:63
——— Father of Adriel, 2 Sam. 21:8
——— A priest, Ezra 2:61; Neh. 7:63

BASHAN

A region east of the Jordan River and north of the Arnon River, Gen. 14:5
Og, king of, Josh. 13:12
Allotted to the two and one half tribes, which had their possession east of the Jordan River, Num. 32:33; Deut. 3:10–14; Josh. 12:4–6; 13:29–31; 17:1
Invaded and taken by Hazael, king of Syria, 2 Kin. 10:32, 33
Retaken by Jehoash, 2 Kin. 13:25
Fertility and productiveness of, Is. 33:9; Jer. 50:19; Nah. 1:4
Forests of, famous, Is. 2:13; Ezek. 27:6; Zech. 11:2
Distinguished for its fine cattle, Deut. 32:14; Ps. 22:12;

Ezek. 39:8; Amos 4:1; Mic. 7:14

BASKET

shalt put it in a b . . Deut. 26:2
be thy b and thy store . . . . Deut. 28:5
be thy b and thy store . . . . Deut. 28:17
I said, A b of summer . . . . Amos 8:2

BATH-SHEBA (BATHSHEBA)

Wife of Uriah and later one of the wives of David; Called Bath-shua, 1 Chr. 3:5
Adultery of, 2 Sam. 11:2–5
Solomon's mother, 1 Kin. 1:11–31; 2:13–21; 1 Chr. 3:5

BATTLE

his people, to the b . . . . Num. 21:33
the host of the b . . . . . . Is. 13:4
by the sword in b . . . Jer. 18:21
and rise up to the b . . . . Jer. 49:14
b, against thee, O . . . Jer. 50:42
Betharbel in the day of b . . . . Hos. 10:14
shouting in the day of b . . . . Amos 1:14
b bow shall be cut . Zech. 9:10
the streets in the b . . . . Zech. 10:5

BEAR

ninety years old, b . Gen. 17:17
Sarah thy wife shall b . . . . Gen. 17:19
shalt not avenge, nor b . . . . Lev. 19:18
Kohath shall come to b . . . . Num. 4:15
which she shall b . Deut. 28:57
lion and the b . . . 1 Sam. 17:36
I am weary to b them . . . . Is. 1:14
conceive, and b a son . . . . Is. 7:14
be ye clean, that b . . . Is. 52:11
he shall b their iniquities . . . . Is. 53:11
falsely, and the priests b . . . . Jer. 5:31
sabbath day, and not to b . . . . Jer. 17:27
The son shall not b . . . . Ezek. 18:20
am not worthy to b . . . . Matt. 3:11
ye also shall b witness . . . . John 15:27
vessel unto me, to b . . . . Acts 9:15
steal, Thou shalt not b . . . . Rom. 13:9
ye may be able to b . . . . 1 Cor. 10:13
offered to b the sins . . . . Heb. 9:28

b witness, and shew . . . . 1 John 1:2

BEARETH

And whosoever b ought . . . . Lev. 11:25
you a root that b gall . . . . Deut. 29:18
b, nor any grass groweth . . . . Deut. 29:23
b not fruit he taketh . . . . John 15:2

BEARING

and left b . . . . Gen. 29:35
their camels b spicery . . . . Gen. 37:25
my conscience also b . . . . Rom. 9:1
God also b them witness . . . . Heb. 2:4

BEAST

of every b will I require . . . . Gen. 9:5
Egypt, both man and b . . . . Ex. 12:12
both of man and of b . . . . Ex. 13:2
of a b which thou hast . . . . Ex. 13:12
both of man and b . Lev. 27:28
He giveth to the b . . Ps. 147:9
nor any ravenous b . . . . Is. 35:9
burden to the weary b . . . . Is. 46:1
upon man, and upon b . . . . Jer. 7:20
the heavens and the b . . . . Jer. 9:10
I cut off man and b . . . . Ezek. 14:17
will cut off man and b . . . . Ezek. 25:13
and cut off man and b . . . . Ezek. 29:8
foot of b shall pass . . . . Ezek. 29:11
became meat to every b . . . . Ezek. 34:8
behold a fourth b . . . . Dan. 7:7
night, who worship the b . . . . Rev. 14:11
And the b was taken . . . . Rev. 19:20
not worshipped the b . . . . Rev. 20:4
b and the false prophet . . . . Rev. 20:10

BEASTS

the firstborn of b . . . . Ex. 11:5
and their b . . . . Num. 20:11
and unto the b . . . Deut. 28:26
and the fat of fed b . . . . Is. 1:11
the wild b of the islands . . . . Is. 13:22
idols were upon the b . . . . Is. 46:1
heaven, and for the b . . . . Jer. 7:33

heaven, and for
the *b* . . . . Jer. 16:4
and the *b* of the
field . . . . Jer. 27:6
heaven, and to
the *b* . . . . Jer. 34:20
with the *b* of the
field . . . . Dan. 4:25
diverse from all
the *b* . . . . Dan. 7:7
languish, with
the *b* . . . . Hos. 4:3
a lion among the *b* . . . Mic. 5:8
desolation, a place
for *b* . . . . Zeph. 2:15
fought with *b* at
Ephesus . . . . . . 1 Cor. 15:32
four *b* full of eyes . . . . Rev. 4:6
b, and in the
midst . . . . Rev. 5:6
the book, the
four *b* . . . . Rev. 5:8
the four *b* said,
Amen. . . . . Rev. 5:14

BEAT
round about,
and *b* . . . . Judg. 19:22
shall *b* their swords . . . . Is. 2:4
shall *b* their
swords. . . . . Mic. 4:3
thou shalt *b* in
pieces . . . . Mic. 4:13

BEATEN
b work shalt thou
make . . . . Ex. 25:18
b work shall the
candlestick . . . . Ex. 25:31
b work of pure
gold . . . . Ex. 25:36
part of an hin of *b* . . Ex. 29:40
part of an hin of *b* . Num. 28:5

BEAUTIFUL
ruddy, and withal
of a *b* . . . . 1 Sam. 16:12
B for situation,
the . . . . Ps. 48:2
branch of the
LORD be *b* . . . . Is. 4:2
thy *b* garments, O
Jerusalem . . . . Is. 52:1

BEAUTY
life, to behold
the *b* . . . . Ps. 27:4
worship the
LORD in the *b* . . . . . Ps. 29:2
of *b*, God hath
shined . . . . Ps. 50:2
of kingdoms,
the *b* . . . . Is. 13:19
b that we should
desire. . . . . Is. 53:2
b for ashes, the oil . . . Is. 61:3
The perfection
of *b*. . . . . Lam. 2:15
for the *b* of his
ornament . . . . . . Ezek. 7:20

BED
whosoever
toucheth his *b* . . . Lev. 15:5

and laid him in
the *b* . . . . 2 Chr. 16:14
slumberings upon
the *b* . . . . Job 33:15
if I make my *b* in
hell . . . . Ps. 139:8
thy head upon
thy *b* . . . . Dan. 2:28
thoughts upon
my *b*. . . . . Dan. 4:5
palsy, lying on a *b* . . . Matt. 9:2
honourable in all,
and the *b* . . . . Heb. 13:4

BEER-SHEBA
The most southern city of
Palestine, Judg. 20:1
Named by Abraham, who lived
there, Gen. 21:31–33; 22:19
The place where Isaac lived,
Gen. 26:23
Jacob went out from, toward
Haran, Gen. 28:10
Sacrifices offered at, by Jacob;
when journeying to Egypt,
Gen. 46:1
In the inheritance of Judah,
Josh. 15:20, 28; 2 Sam. 24:7
Afterward assigned to Simeon,
Josh. 19:2, 9; 1 Chr. 4:28
Two sons of Samuel were
judges at, 1 Sam. 8:2
Became a seat of idolatrous
worship, Amos 5:5; 8:14
——— The well of, belonged
to Abraham and Isaac,
Gen. 21:25, 26
——— Wilderness of, Hagar
miraculously sees a well in,
Gen. 21:14–19
An angel fed Elijah in,
1 Kin. 19:5, 7

BEGAN
Spirit of the
LORD *b* . . . . Judg. 13:25
Then Solomon *b*
to build . . . . 2 Chr. 3:1
son of Jozadak,
and *b* . . . . Ezra 5:2
b at the ancient
men . . . . Ezek. 9:6
time Jesus *b* to
preach . . . . Matt. 4:17
that time forth *b*
Jesus . . . . Matt. 16:21
And some *b* to
spit . . . . Mark 14:65
the Holy Ghost,
and *b* . . . . Acts 2:4
since the world *b* . Rom. 16:25
before the world *b* . 2 Tim. 1:9
before the world *b* . . Titus 1:2
the first *b* to be
spoken. . . . . Heb. 2:3

BEGINNING
b God created the
heaven. . . . . Gen. 1:1
And the *b* of his
kingdom . . . . Gen. 10:10
LORD is the *b* of
wisdom . . . . Ps. 111:10

generations from
the *b* . . . . Is. 41:4
the end from the *b* . . . Is. 46:10
And *b* at Moses
and. . . . . Luke 24:27
all nations, *b* at
Jerusalem . . . . . . Luke 24:47
In the *b* was the
Word . . . . John 1:1
was in the *b* with
God . . . . John 1:2
murderer from
the *b* . . . . John 8:44
with me from
the *b* . . . . John 15:27
B from the
baptism. . . . . Acts 1:22
who is the *b*, the
firstborn . . . . Col. 1:18
b, which we have
heard . . . . 1 John 1:1
ye heard from
the *b* . . . . 1 John 3:11
Alpha and
Omega, the *b* . . . . . . Rev. 1:8
true witness, the *b* . . Rev. 3:14
Alpha and
Omega, the *b* . . . . . Rev. 21:6
Alpha and
Omega, the *b* . . . . Rev. 22:13

BEGOTTEN
this day have I *b*
thee . . . . Ps. 2:7
glory as of the
only *b*. . . . . John 1:14
the only *b* Son,
which . . . . John 1:18
gave his only *b*
Son . . . . John 3:16
abundant mercy
hath *b* . . . . 1 Pet. 1:3
b Son into the
world. . . . . 1 John 4:9
that is *b* of God
keepeth . . . . 1 John 5:18
witness, and the
first *b* . . . . Rev. 1:5

BEHELD
up his eyes, and *b* . Gen. 13:10
I *b* till the thrones . . Dan. 7:9
But Jesus *b* them,
and. . . . . Matt. 19:26
b his glory, the
glory . . . . John 1:14
And when Jesus *b*
him . . . . John 1:42
And I *b*, and,
lo, in . . . . Rev. 5:6
I *b* when he had
opened . . . . Rev. 6:12
I *b*, and, lo, a great . . Rev. 7:9

BELIEVED
And the people *b* . . . Ex. 4:31
feared the LORD,
and *b* . . . . Ex. 14:31
fainted, unless I
had *b* . . . . Ps. 27:13
Who hath *b* our
report . . . . Is. 53:1

loved me, and
have *b* ....John 16:27
circumcision
which *b* ....Acts 10:45
Lord, on whom
they *b*...........Acts 14:23
Jews which *b* not,
moved ....Acts 17:5
ministers by
whom ye *b* ....1 Cor. 3:5
have *b* in Jesus
Christ .... Gal. 2:16
ye *b*, ye were
sealed ....Eph. 1:13
unto the
Gentiles, *b*...... 1 Tim. 3:16
I have *b*, and am
persuaded ...... 2 Tim. 1:12
b in God might be
careful .... Titus 3:8

BELIEVETH
b shall not make
haste ....Is. 28:16
That whosoever
b in..............John 3:15
Son, that
whosoever *b* ......John 3:16
b on the Son hath
everlasting ......John 3:36
heareth my word,
and *b* ....John 5:24
seeth the Son,
and *b* ....John 6:40
he that *b* in me,
though..........John 11:25
world, that
whosoever *b* .....John 12:46
to every one
that *b*....... Rom. 1:16

BELIEVING
not faithless,
but *b* ....John 20:27
b ye might have
life ....John 20:31
God of my
fathers, *b*.......Acts 24:14
and peace in *b*.... Rom. 15:13

BELLY
thee in the *b* I
knew .... Jer. 1:5
I heard, my *b*
trembled.........Hab. 3:16
nights in the
whale's *b*....... Matt. 12:40
Christ, but their
own *b*.......... Rom. 16:18
whose God is
their *b* ....Phil. 3:19

BELOVED
drink
abundantly, O *b* ....Song 5:1
wellbeloved a
song of my *b*........Is. 5:1
thou art greatly *b* ...Dan. 9:23
my *b* Son, in
whom I .... Matt. 3:17
my *b* Son, in
whom I .... Matt. 17:5
Thou art my *b* Son ..Luke 3:22

Rome, *b* of God,
called .... Rom. 1:7
Dearly *b*, avenge
not .... Rom. 12:19
is my *b* son, and
faithful ....1 Cor. 4:17
promises, dearly *b* ..2 Cor. 7:1
Wherefore, my *b*
brethren ....James 1:19
Hearken, my *b*
brethren ....James 2:5
Dearly *b*, I
beseech .... 1 Pet. 2:11
B, now are we the
sons........... 1 John 3:2
B, believe not
every .... 1 John 4:1

BEN-HADAD
King of Syria, 1 Kin. 15:18–20;
2 Chr. 16:2–4
——— A king of Syria, who
reigned during the time of
Ahab, son of Ben-hadad I,
1 Kin. 20; 2 Kin. 5; 6; 7;
8:7–15
——— Son of Hazael and king
of Syria, 2 Kin. 13:3, 24, 25;
Amos 1:4

BENAIAH
Son of Jehoiada, commander
of the Cherethites and
Pelethites, 2 Sam. 8:18;
1 Kin. 1:38
A distinguished warrior,
2 Sam. 23:20–23;
1 Chr. 11:22–25; 27:5, 6
Loyal to Solomon, 1 Kin. 1:2;
4:4
——— An Ephraimite, and
distinguished warrior,
2 Sam. 23:30; 1 Chr. 11:31;
27:14
——— A Levitical musician,
1 Chr. 15:18, 20; 16:5
——— A priest, 1 Chr. 15:24;
16:6
——— Son of Jeiel, 2 Chr. 20:14
——— A Levite in time of
Hezekiah, 2 Chr. 31:13
——— A chief of the
Simeonites, 1 Chr. 4:36
——— Father of Pelatiah,
Ezek. 11:1, 13
——— Son of Parosh,
Ezra 10:25
——— Son of Pahath-moab,
Ezra 10:30
——— Son of Bani, Ezra 10:35
——— Son of Nebo, Ezra 10:43

BENEATH
is in the earth *b* .....Ex. 20:4
thou shalt not
be *b* ....Deut. 28:13
above, and in
earth *b*.......... Josh. 2:11
look upon the
earth *b*..............Is. 51:6

BENJAMIN
Son of Jacob by Rachel,
Gen. 35:18, 24; 46:19
Taken into Egypt, Gen. 42; 43;
44; 45
Prophecy concerning,
Gen. 49:27
Descendants of, Gen. 46:21;
Num. 26:38–41
——— Grandson of Benjamin,
1 Chr. 7:10
——— A son of Harim,
Ezra 10:32
Probably identical with the
man mentioned in Neh. 3:23
——— A Jew who assisted
in purifying the wall of
Jerusalem, Neh. 12:34
——— A gate of Jerusalem,
Jer. 20:2; 37:13; 38:7;
Zech. 14:10

BESEECH
we *b* thee, three
days .... Ex. 3:18
O Lord our God,
I *b*............. 2 Kin. 19:19
I *b* thee, O Lord,
remember ...... 2 Kin. 20:3
I *b* thee, thine
eyes .... 2 Chr. 6:40
I *b* thee, O Lord
God ....Neh. 1:5
O Lord, I *b* thee,
let ....Neh. 1:11
I *b* you therefore... Rom. 12:1
prisoner of the
Lord, *b*...........Eph. 4:1
then we *b* you,
brethren ....1 Thess. 4:1
Dearly
beloved, I *b*......1 Pet. 2:11

BESOUGHT
And Moses *b* the
Lord............Ex. 32:11
man of God *b* the
Lord........... 1 Kin. 13:6
he *b* the Lord his
God .... 2 Chr. 33:12
And *b* him greatly . Mark 5:23

BETH-EL
A city north of Jerusalem; The
ancient city adjacent to, and
finally embraced in, Luz,
Josh. 18:13; Judg. 1:23–26
Abraham estblishes an altar at,
Gen. 12:8; 13:3, 4
The place where Jacob saw
the vision of the ladder,
Gen. 28:10–22; 31:13;
Hos. 12:4
Jacob builds an altar at,
Gen. 35:1–15
Deborah dies at, Gen. 35:8
Conquered by Joshua,
Josh. 8:17; Josh. 12:16
Conquered by the household
of Joseph, Judg. 1:22–26
Allotted to Benjamin,
Josh. 18:13, 22

Court of justice held at
 By Deborah, Judg. 4:5
 By Samuel, 1 Sam. 7:16
Tabernacle at, and called
 House of God, Judg. 20:18,
 31; 21:2
Jeroboam institutes idolatrous
 worship at, 1 Kin. 12:25–33;
 2 Kin. 10:29
Idolatry at, Jer. 48:13;
 Amos 4:4
Shalmanezer sends a priest to,
 2 Kin. 17:27, 28
Prophecies against the
 idolatrous altars at,
 1 Kin. 13:1–6, 32;
 2 Kin. 23:4, 15–20;
 Amos 3:14
The school of prophets at,
 2 Kin. 2:3
The young men of, mock
 Elisha, 2 Kin. 2:23, 24
People of, return from
 Babylon, Ezra 2:28; Neh. 7:32
Prophecies against, Amos 5:5
—— A city in the south of
 territory of the tribe of Judah,
 1 Sam. 30:27
—— A mountain, 1 Sam. 13:2

BETH-HORON

Two ancient cities of Canaan,
 near which Joshua defeated
 the Amorites, Josh. 10:10,
 11; 16:3, 5; 18:13;
 1 Sam. 13:18; 1 Chr. 7:24
Solomon builds, 1 Kin. 9:17;
 2 Chr. 8:5
Taken from the tribe of
 Judah by the ten tribes,
 2 Chr. 25:13

BETH-SHEAN

A city of the tribe of
 Manasseh, Josh. 17:11;
 1 Chr. 7:29
Not subdued, Judg. 1:27
Bodies of Saul and his sons
 exposed in, 1 Sam. 31:10, 12
Called Beth-shan,
 1 Sam. 31:10, 12;
 2 Sam. 21:12
District of, under tribute to
 Solomon's commissariat,
 1 Kin. 4:12

BETH-SHEMESH

A priestly city of the tribe
 of Dan, Josh. 21:16;
 1 Sam. 6:15; 1 Chr. 6:59
On the northern border of
 territory of the tribe of Judah,
 Josh. 15:10; 1 Sam. 6:9, 12
In later times transferred
 to the tribe of Judah,
 2 Kin. 14:11
Mentioned in Solomon's
 commission districts,
 1 Kin. 4:9
Amaziah taken prisoner
 at, 2 Kin. 14:11–13;
 2 Chr. 25:21–23

Retaken by the Philistines,
 2 Chr. 28:18
Called Beth-shmesh,
 Josh. 19:41
—— A city near Jerusalem,
 Josh. 19:22
—— A fortified city of
 the territory of the tribe
 of Naphtali, Josh. 19:38;
 Judg. 1:33
—— An idolatrous temple,
 Jer. 43:13

BETHABARA

A city east of the Jordan, called
 Beth-barah, Judg. 7:24
John testifies to Christ's
 messiahship, and baptizes at,
 John 1:28
Jesus at, John 10:39–42

BETHANY

A village on the eastern slope
 of the Mount of Olives,
 John 11:18
Mary, Martha, and Lazarus
 dwell at, Luke 10:38–41
Lazarus dies and is raised to
 life at, John 11
Jesus attends a feast in,
 Matt. 26:6–13; John 12:1–9
The colt of a donkey upon
 which Jesus made his
 triumphal entry into
 Jerusalem, obtained at,
 Mark 11:1–11
Jesus sojourns at, Matt. 21:17;
 Mark 11:11, 12, 19

BETHLEHEM

A city southwest of Jerusalem,
 Judg. 17:7; 19:18
Called Ephratah and Ephrath,
 Gen. 48:7; Ps. 132:6; Mic. 5:2
And Beth-lehem-judah,
 Judg. 17:7–9; 19:1, 18;
 Ruth 1:1; 1 Sam. 17:12
Rachel dies and is buried at,
 Gen. 35:16, 19; 48:7
The city of Boaz, Ruth 1:1, 19;
 2:4; 4
Taken and held by the
 Philistines, 2 Sam. 23:14–16
Jeroboam converts it into
 a military stronghold,
 2 Chr. 11:6
The city of Joseph, Matt. 2:5,
 6; Luke 2:4
Birthplace of Jesus, Mic. 5:2;
 Matt. 2; Luke 2:4, 15
Herod murders the infants of,
 Matt. 2:16–18
—— A town of Zebulun,
 six miles west of Nazareth,
 Josh. 19:15
Israel judged at, Judg. 12:10

BETHSAIDA

A city of Galilee; The city of
 Philip, Andrew, and Peter,
 John 1:44; 12:21
Jesus visits, Mark 6:45

Jesus cures a blind man in,
 Mark 8:22
Jesus prophesies against,
 Matt. 11:21; Luke 10:13
—— Desert of, east of the sea
 of Galilee, Jesus feeds more
 than five thousand people
 in, Matt. 14:13; Mark 6:32;
 Luke 9:10

BEWARE

B that there be
 not . . . . Deut. 15:9
B of false
 prophets . . . . Matt. 7:15
heed, *b* of the
 leaven . . . . Mark 8:15
B lest any man
 spoil. . . . . Col. 2:8

BILHAH

Rachael's servant; Bears
 children by Jacob,
 Gen. 29:29; 30:3, 4; 37:2
Mother of Dan and Naphtali,
 Gen. 30:1–8; 35:25; 46:23–25
Reuben's incest with,
 Gen. 35:22; 49:4
—— A place in the land of
 Simeon, 1 Chr. 4:29
Called Balah, Josh. 19:3
And Baalah, Josh. 15:29

BIND

an ornament,
 and *b* . . . . .Is. 49:18
he hath sent me
 to *b* . . . . .Is. 61:1
mourning for the
 dead, *b* . . . . Ezek. 24:17
smitten, and he
 will *b* . . . . Hos. 6:1
chief priests to *b*. . . . Acts 9:14

BITTER

lives *b* with hard
 bondage . . . . Ex. 1:14
and with *b* herbs
 they . . . . Ex. 12:8
And I find more *b*
 than . . . . .Eccl. 7:26
b, that thou hast
 forsaken . . . . Jer. 2:19
only son, most *b*
 lamentation . . . . Jer. 6:26
end thereof as a *b*. .Amos 8:10

BITTERNESS

afflicted, and she
 is in *b*. . . . . Lam. 1:4
away, and I went
 in *b*. . . . . Ezek. 3:14
son, and shall be
 in *b*. . . . . .Zech. 12:10
b, and wrath, and
 anger . . . . .Eph. 4:31

BLAMELESS

ordinances of the
 Lord *b* . . . . .Luke 1:6
which is in the
 law, *b* . . . . Phil. 3:6
body be
 preserved *b* . . . .1 Thess. 5:23

bishop then must
be *b* . . . . 1 Tim. 3:2
a bishop must
be *b* . . . . Titus 1:7

BLEMISH

be without *b*, a
male . . . . Ex. 12:5
offer a male
without *b* . . . . Lev. 1:3
it a male
without *b* . . . . Lev. 1:10
young bullock
without *b* . . . . Lev. 4:3
b, and one ewe
lamb . . . . Lev. 14:10
whatsoever
hath a *b* . . . . Lev. 22:20
unto you
without *b* . . . . . . Num. 28:19
holy and
without *b* . . . . Eph. 5:27
of a lamb
without *b* . . . . 1 Pet. 1:19

BLESS

b thee, and make
thy . . . . Gen. 12:2
b them that *b* thee . . Gen. 12:3
I will *b* her, and
give . . . . Gen. 17:16
blessing I will *b*
thee . . . . Gen. 22:17
thee, and will *b*
thee . . . . Gen. 26:3
thee, and will *b*
thee . . . . Gen. 26:24
The LORD *b* thee,
and. . . . . Num. 6:24
unto him, and to *b* Deut. 10:8
LORD thy God
may *b* . . . . Deut. 14:29
him, and to *b* . . . . . Deut. 21:5
b thee in the land . . Deut. 28:8
b all the work of
thine . . . . Deut. 28:12
unto him, and
to *b* . . . . 1 Chr. 23:13
Save thy people,
and *b* . . . . Ps. 28:9
LORD will *b* his
people . . . . Ps. 29:11
B the LORD, ye
his . . . . Ps. 103:20
LORD of hosts
shall *b* . . . . Is. 19:25
the nations shall *b* . . . . Jer. 4:2
Love your
enemies, *b*. . . . . . . Matt. 5:44
Jesus, sent him
to *b* . . . . Acts 3:26

BLESSED

of the earth be *b* . . . . Gen. 12:3
of the earth be *b* . . . Gen. 22:18
of the earth be *b* . . . . Gen. 26:4
of the earth be *b* . . . Gen. 28:14
wherefore the
LORD *b* . . . . Ex. 20:11
LORD thy God
hath *b* . . . . Deut. 12:7
B are all they that. . . . Ps. 2:12

B is the man
whom thou . . . . Ps. 65:4
B be the LORD
God of . . . . Ps. 106:48
memory of the
just is *b* . . . . Prov. 10:7
incense, as if he *b* . . . . . Is. 66:3
B art thou, Simon
Barjona . . . . Matt. 16:17
right hand, Come,
ye *b* . . . . Matt. 25:34
B be the Lord
God of . . . . Luke 1:68
is over all, God *b* . . . Rom. 9:5
B be the God and
Father . . . . Eph. 1:3
b hope, and the
glorious . . . . Titus 2:13
B is the man that
endureth . . . . James 1:12
B be the God and
Father . . . . 1 Pet. 1:3
B are they that do . Rev. 22:14

BLESSING

thou shalt be a *b*. . . . Gen. 12:2
in *b* I will bless
thee . . . . Gen. 22:17
b upon thee in thy . Deut. 28:8
the *b*, wherewith
Moses . . . . Deut. 33:1
with Assyria,
even a *b* . . . . Is. 19:24
thy seed, and
my *b*. . . . . Is. 44:3
about my hill a *b* . Ezek. 34:26
repent, and
leave a *b* . . . . Joel 2:14
and ye shall be a *b* . Zech. 8:13
and pour you
out a *b* . . . . Mal. 3:10
but contrariwise *b* . . 1 Pet. 3:9
honour, and glory,
and *b* . . . . Rev. 5:12

BLIND

a gift doth *b* the
eyes . . . . Deut. 16:19
noonday, as the *b*
gropeth . . . . Deut. 28:29
and the eyes of
the *b* . . . . Is. 29:18
Then the eyes of
the *b* . . . . Is. 35:5
To open the *b* eyes . . . Is. 42:7
His watchmen
are *b*. . . . . Is. 56:10
the wall like the *b* . . . Is. 59:10
the *b*, to set at
liberty . . . . Luke 4:18
miserable, and
poor, and *b* . . . . . . Rev. 3:17

BLOOD

Whoso sheddeth
man's *b* . . . . Gen. 9:6
And Moses took
the *b* . . . . Ex. 24:8
shall put some of
the *b* . . . . Lev. 4:7
eateth any
manner of *b* . . . . . Lev. 17:10
hands are full of *b* . . . . Is. 1:15

LORD is filled
with *b* . . . . Is. 34:6
drunk with their *b* . . Jer. 46:10
prey, to shed *b* . . . Ezek. 22:27
pestilence and
with *b* . . . . Ezek. 38:22
and the moon
into *b* . . . . Joel 2:31
purchased with
his own *b* . . . . Acts 20:28
against flesh and *b* . . Eph. 6:12
partakers of flesh
and *b* . . . . Heb. 2:14
year, not
without *b* . . . . Heb. 9:7
shall the *b* of
Christ . . . . Heb. 9:14
sheep, through
the *b* . . . . Heb. 13:20
of the *b* of Jesus
Christ . . . . 1 Pet. 1:2
the *b* of Jesus
Christ . . . . 1 John 1:7
sins in his own *b* . . . . Rev. 1:5
fire mingled
with *b* . . . . Rev. 8:7

BLOODY

thou *b* man, and
thou. . . . . 2 Sam. 16:7
b and deceitful
men . . . . Ps. 55:23
land is full of *b*
crimes . . . . Ezek. 7:23
wilt thou judge
the *b* . . . . Ezek. 22:2

BLOW

shall *b* an alarm . . . Num. 10:9
months, ye
shall *b* . . . . Num. 10:10
priests, did *b*. . . . 1 Chr. 15:24
and say, *B* ye the
trumpet . . . . Jer. 4:5
b the trumpet in
Tekoa . . . . Jer. 6:1
a very grievous *b* . . . Jer. 14:17
B ye the
trumpet in . . . . Joel 2:1

BOAZ

An ancestor of Jesus,
Matt. 1:5; Luke 3:32
History of, Ruth 2; 3; 4
——— One of the bronze pillars
of the temple, 1 Kin. 7:21;
2 Chr. 3:17

BODIES

and their dead *b*
shall. . . . . Jer. 34:20
and yielded their *b* . . Dan. 3:28
quicken your
mortal *b*. . . . . Rom. 8:11
that ye present
your *b* . . . . Rom. 12:1
our *b* washed with
pure . . . . Heb. 10:22

BODY

it were the *b* of
heaven. . . . . Ex. 24:10
the fruit of thy *b*. . . Deut. 28:4
the fruit of thy *b* . . Deut. 28:18

fruit of thine
own *b*.........Deut. 28:53
of thy *b* will I set .. Ps. 132:11
dead *b* shall they
arise..............Is. 26:19
transgression, the
fruit of my *b* .... Mic. 6:7
b, what ye shall
put............. Matt. 6:25
them which kill
the *b* .... Matt. 10:28
b of Jesus, and
wound.........John 19:40
law by the *b* of
Christ .... Rom. 7:4
baptized into
one *b* .... 1 Cor. 12:13
things done in
his *b*............2 Cor. 5:10
is his *b*, the
fulness...........Eph. 1:23
the head of the *b* ... Col. 1:18
In the *b* of his
flesh............. Col. 1:22
are called in one *b* .. Col. 3:15
spirit and soul
and *b* ....1 Thess. 5:23
our sins in his
own *b*.......... 1 Pet. 2:24
the *b* of Moses,
durst ....Jude 9

BONDAGE
bitter with hard *b*.... Ex. 1:14
by reason of the *b*.... Ex. 2:23
b, and I will
redeem .... Ex. 6:6
of the house of *b* .... Ex. 13:3
from the house
of *b*..............Ex. 13:14
of the house of *b* .... Ex. 20:2
house of *b*, to
thrust .... Deut. 13:5
lo, we bring into *b* ...Neh. 5:5
return to their *b* ....Neh. 9:17
received the spirit
of *b*............ Rom. 8:15

BONDMEN
should not be
their *b* ....Lev. 26:13
of the house of *b* ...Deut. 7:8
enemies for *b* and
bondwomen ....Deut. 28:68
my two sons to
be *b* ....2 Kin. 4:1

BONDS
worthy of death
or of *b* ....Acts 23:29
an ambassador
in *b*.............Eph. 6:20
my *b*, and in the
defence ....Phil. 1:7
Remember my *b*.... Col. 4:18

BONES
And the *b* of
Joseph .... Josh. 24:32
b are burned with
heat ....Job 30:30
water, and all
my *b*............. Ps. 22:14

may tell all my *b*. ... Ps. 22:17
like oil into his *b* .. Ps. 109:18
spirit drieth the *b*. Prov. 17:22
and make fat thy *b* ...Is. 58:11
fire shut up in
my *b*..............Jer. 20:9
hath broken his *b*...Jer. 50:17
which was full
of *b*.............. Ezek. 37:1
Son of man,
these *b*........ Ezek. 37:11
b of the king of
Edom............Amos 2:1
into my *b*, and I
trembled ....Hab. 3:16

BOOK
a memorial in a *b* ...Ex. 17:14
took the *b* of the
covenant .... Ex. 24:7
this *b*, that thou
mayest.........Deut. 28:58
not written in
the *b* ....Deut. 28:61
written in this *b* .. 2 Kin. 23:3
blotted out of
the *b* .... Ps. 69:28
the words of the *b* ...Is. 29:18
and note it in a *b* .....Is. 30:8
found written in
the *b* ....Dan. 12:1
words, and seal
the *b* ....Dan. 12:4
The *b* of the
generation........ Matt. 1:1
seest, write in a *b*... Rev. 1:11
b of life, but I will ... Rev. 3:5
prevailed to open
the *b* .... Rev. 5:5
the *b*, the four
beasts .... Rev. 5:8
worthy to take
the *b* .... Rev. 5:9
b of life of the
Lamb .... Rev. 13:8
and another *b* was
opened .... Rev. 20:12
found written in
the *b* .... Rev. 20:15
written in the
Lamb's *b* .... Rev. 21:27

BORDER
And the *b* of the
Canaanites ......Gen. 10:19
uttermost of thy *b*. Num. 20:16
pass through his *b*. Num. 21:23
for the *b* of the
children........Num. 21:24
And Gilead, and
the *b* .... Josh. 13:11
b went up by the
valley........... Josh. 15:8
b compassed from
Baalah .... Josh. 15:10
Zererath, and to
the *b* .... Judg. 7:22
b at the river
Euphrates ...... 2 Sam. 8:3
Philistines, and
unto the *b* ..... 1 Kin. 4:21

might enlarge
their *b* ....Amos 1:13
themselves
against their *b* ....Zeph. 2:8
shall call them,
The *b* .... Mal. 1:4

BORDERS
b of Dor on the
west........... Josh. 11:2
the *b* of Ekron
northward....... Josh. 13:3
destruction within
thy *b* ....Is. 60:18
sea coast, in the *b*.. Matt. 4:13

BORN
generations, he
that is *b*........Gen. 17:12
Shall a child be *b* ..Gen. 17:17
me, because I
have *b* ....Gen. 29:34
be a stranger, or *b* .. Ex. 12:19
stranger, as he
that is *b*........ Lev. 24:16
Behold, a son
shall be *b*...... 1 Chr. 22:9
Man that is *b* of a....Job 14:1
brother is *b* for
adversity .... Prov. 17:17
unto us a child is *b*.....Is. 9:6
is *b* King of the
Jews............. Matt. 2:2
thing which shall
be *b* ....Luke 1:35
b this day in the
city.............Luke 2:11
thee, Except a
man be *b* ....John 3:3
To this end
was I *b*.........John 18:37
Jew named
Aquila, *b* .... Acts 18:2
man which am a
Jew, *b* .... Acts 22:3
b of God doth not
commit .... 1 John 3:9
Christ is *b* of God.. 1 John 5:1
whosoever is *b* of
God .... 1 John 5:18
as soon as it was *b* .. Rev. 12:4

BOSOM
the wife of his *b* .. Deut. 28:54
the husband of
her *b* ....Deut. 28:56
carry them in
his *b*............Is. 40:11
fathers into the *b* ...Jer. 32:18
Son, which is in
the *b* ....John 1:18

BOTTOM
the bullock at
the *b* .... Lev. 4:7
the blood at the *b*... Lev. 4:18
from my sight in
the *b* ....Amos 9:3
that were in the *b*.. Zech. 1:8

BOUGHT
house, or *b* with
money ....Gen. 17:12
father that hath *b*.. Deut. 32:6

sepulchre that
Abraham *b* . . . . Acts 7:16
ye are *b* with a
price . . . . 1 Cor. 6:20
denying the Lord
that *b* . . . . 2 Pet. 2:1

BOUND

king's prisoners
were *b* . . . . Gen. 39:20
of the ephod,
and *b* . . . . Lev. 8:7
Zedekiah, and *b* . . 2 Kin. 25:7
to them that are *b* . . . . Is. 61:1
b of the sea by a
perpetual. . . . . Jer. 5:22
Zedekiah's eyes,
and *b* . . . . Jer. 39:7
her great men
were *b* . . . . Nah. 3:10
had *b* him, they
led . . . . Matt. 27:2
bring them *b* unto
Jerusalem . . . . Acts 9:2
hope of Israel I
am *b* . . . . Acts 28:20
We are *b* to thank
God . . . . 2 Thess. 1:3
b to give thanks
alway . . . . 2 Thess. 2:13
Devil, and Satan,
and *b* . . . . Rev. 20:2

BOW

thee, and
nations *b* . . . . Gen. 27:29
Thou shalt not *b*
down . . . . Ex. 20:5
Thou shalt not *b*
down . . . . Ex. 23:24
in your land, to *b* . . . Lev. 26:1
neither serve
them, nor *b* . . . . . . Josh. 23:7
he breaketh the *b* . . . . Ps. 46:9
shall *b* down to
thee . . . . Is. 49:23
despised thee
shall *b* . . . . Is. 60:14
and ye shall all *b* . . . . . Is. 65:12
Lud, that draw
the *b* . . . . Is. 66:19
tongues like
their *b* . . . . Jer. 9:3
ye that bend the *b* . . Jer. 50:29
They shall hold
the *b* . . . . Jer. 50:42
appearance of
the *b* . . . . Ezek. 1:28
before the Lord,
and *b* . . . . Mic. 6:6
Jerusalem, and
the battle *b* . . . . . . Zech. 9:10
knee should *b*, of
things . . . . Phil. 2:10

BOWED

brethren came,
and *b* . . . . Gen. 42:6
b their heads and
worshipped. . . . . Ex. 4:31
served other gods,
and *b* . . . . Josh. 23:16

And he *b* himself,
and. . . . . 2 Sam. 9:8
upon the house,
they *b*. . . . . 2 Chr. 7:3
haughtiness of
men shall be *b* . . . . . . Is. 2:11
loftiness of man
shall be *b*. . . . . Is. 2:17
I was *b* down at
the . . . . Is. 21:3
b his head, and
gave . . . . John 19:30

BOWELS

thy *b*, and I will
establish . . . . 2 Sam. 7:12
and shed out
his *b*. . . . . 2 Sam. 20:10
the midst of my *b* . . . Ps. 22:14
Wherefore my *b*
shall . . . . Is. 16:11
b of my mother
hath . . . . Is. 49:1
thy *b* and of thy
mercies . . . . Is. 63:15
My *b*, my *b* . . . . Jer. 4:19
fail with tears,
my *b*. . . . . Lam. 2:11

BOZRAH

A city of Edom, Gen. 36:33
Sheep of, Mic. 2:12
Prophecies concerning,
Is. 34:6; 63:1; Jer. 49:13, 22;
Amos 1:12
——— A town of Moab,
Jer. 48:24

BRAKE

places, and *b* . . . . . 2 Kin. 18:4
captain of the
guard, *b* . . . . 2 Kin. 25:10
up into Judah,
and *b* . . . . 2 Chr. 21:17
cities of Judah,
and *b* . . . . 2 Chr. 31:1
house of God,
and *b* . . . . 2 Chr. 36:19
he *b* the whole
staff . . . . Ps. 105:16
people, with fire,
and *b* . . . . Jer. 39:8
Chaldeans *b*, and
carried . . . . Jer. 52:17
troubled, and his
sleep *b* . . . . Dan. 2:1
b in pieces the
iron . . . . Dan. 2:45
devoured and *b* in
pieces . . . . Dan. 7:7
b, and gave the
loaves . . . . Matt. 14:19

BRANCH

a flower in one *b* . . . Ex. 25:33
shall his *b* be cut . . . Job 18:16
b of the Lord be
beautiful . . . . Is. 4:2
stem of Jesse,
and a *B* . . . . Is. 11:1
land for ever,
the *b* . . . . Is. 60:21

David a
righteous *B* . . . . Jer. 23:5
forth my servant
the *B* . . . . Zech. 3:8
whose name is
The *B* . . . . Zech. 6:12
neither root nor *b* . . . . Mal. 4:1
b in me that
beareth . . . . John 15:2
cast forth as a *b* . . . . John 15:6

BRANCHES

b, his bowls, his
knops . . . . Ex. 25:31
And six *b* shall
come . . . . Ex. 25:32
so in the six *b* that . . Ex. 25:33
a knop under
two *b* . . . . Ex. 25:35
Their knops and
their *b* . . . . Ex. 25:36
trees, *b* of palm
trees . . . . Lev. 23:40

BRASEN

brake in pieces
the *b* . . . . 2 Kin. 18:4
bases, and the *b*
sea . . . . 2 Kin. 25:13
iron pillar, and *b* . . . . . Jer. 1:18
bases, and the *b*
sea . . . . Jer. 52:17

BRASS

overlay it with *b* . . . . . Ex. 27:2
thou shalt make
of *b*. . . . . Ex. 27:3
thy head shall
be *b* . . . . Deut. 28:23
took exceeding
much *b* . . . . 2 Sam. 8:8
fetters of *b*, and
carried . . . . 2 Kin. 25:7
And the pillars
of *b*. . . . . 2 Kin. 25:13
pieces the gates
of *b*. . . . . Is. 45:2
Also the pillars
of *b*. . . . . Jer. 52:17
men and vessels
of *b*. . . . . Ezek. 27:13
b, with a line of
flax. . . . . Ezek. 40:3
gold, of *b*, iron,
wood . . . . Dan. 5:23
will make thy
hoofs *b* . . . . Mic. 4:13
sounding *b*, or a
tinkling . . . . 1 Cor. 13:1
feet like unto
fine *b* . . . . Rev. 1:15

BREACH

him in the *b*, to
turn . . . . Ps. 106:23
Lord bindeth up
the *b* . . . . Is. 30:26
broken with a
great *b* . . . . Jer. 14:17
wherein is made
a *b* . . . . Ezek. 26:10

BREAD

face shalt thou
eat *b* . . . . Gen. 3:19
fire, and
unleavened *b* . . . . . . Ex. 12:8
ye eat
unleavened *b* . . . . . Ex. 12:15
shall eat
unleavened *b* . . . . . Ex. 12:18
ye eat
unleavened *b* . . . . . Ex. 12:20
no leavened *b* be
eaten . . . . Ex. 13:3
feast of
unleavened *b* . . . . . Ex. 23:15
eat *b*, nor drink
water . . . . Ex. 34:28
with unleavened *b*
shall . . . . Lev. 6:16
be on the *b* for a
memorial . . . . Lev. 24:7
ye shall eat your *b* . . Lev. 26:5
doth not live by *b* . . . Deut. 8:3
eat *b*, nor drink
water . . . . Deut. 9:18
shalt eat no
leavened *b* . . . . . . Deut. 16:3
feast of
unleavened *b* . . . Deut. 16:16
and fed them
with *b* . . . . 1 Kin. 18:4
people as they
eat *b* . . . . Ps. 14:4
eat of my *b*, hath
lifted . . . . Ps. 41:9
lips, and eat not
the *b* . . . . Ezek. 24:17
to break *b*, Paul
preached . . . . Acts 20:7

BREADTH

thereof, and a
cubit the *b* . . . . Ex. 30:2
and four cubits
the *b* . . . . Deut. 3:11
b of thy land, O
Immanuel . . . . Is. 8:8
fifty cubits, and
the *b* . . . . Ezek. 40:21

BREAK

overthrow them,
and quite *b* . . . . Ex. 23:24
destroy their
altars, *b* . . . . Ex. 34:13
their altars, and *b* . . . Deut. 7:5
Thou shalt *b* them
with . . . . Ps. 2:9
b down the carved
work . . . . Ps. 74:6
b down the wall
thereof. . . . . Is. 5:5
wilderness shall
waters *b* . . . . Is. 35:6
b forth into
singing . . . . Is. 44:23
I will *b* in pieces . . . . . . Is. 45:2
and *b* forth into
singing . . . . Is. 49:13
b forth into
singing . . . . Is. 54:1

and the hills
shall *b* . . . . Is. 55:12
so will I *b* this
people . . . . Jer. 19:11
pluck up, and to *b* . . Jer. 31:28
shall *b* also the
images . . . . Jer. 43:13
or shall he *b* the
covenant . . . . Ezek. 17:15
hand, thou didst *b* . Ezek. 29:7
b in pieces and
consume . . . . Dan. 2:44
I will *b* also the
bar . . . . Amos 1:5
to *b* bread, Paul
preached . . . . Acts 20:7

BREASTPLATE

a *b*, and an ephod . . . . Ex. 28:4
shalt put in the *b* . . . Ex. 28:30
And he put the *b*
upon . . . . Lev. 8:8
on the *b* of
righteousness . . . . . Eph. 6:14

BREATH

nostrils the *b* of
life . . . . Gen. 2:7
host of them by
the *b* . . . . Ps. 33:6
b, they die, and
return . . . . Ps. 104:29
mouth, and with
the *b* . . . . Is. 11:4
the *b* of the Lord . . . Is. 30:33
giveth *b* unto the
people . . . . Is. 42:5
in whose hand
thy *b* . . . . Dan. 5:23
silver, and there is
no *b* . . . . Hab. 2:19

BRETHREN

and Joseph's *b*
came . . . . Gen. 42:6
unto his *b*, I die . . . Gen. 50:24
midst of his *b* . . . 1 Sam. 16:13
rose up with his *b* . . . Neh. 3:1
of these my *b*, ye
have . . . . Matt. 25:40
but go to my *b*,
and. . . . . John 20:17
Jesus, and with
his *b* . . . . Acts 1:14
said, Men, *b*, and
fathers . . . . Acts 7:2
Men and *b*, I am a
Pharisee . . . . Acts 23:6
firstborn among
many *b* . . . . Rom. 8:29
For I would not, *b* Rom. 11:25
beseech you
therefore, *b* . . . . . Rom. 12:1
apostles, and as
the *b* . . . . 1 Cor. 9:5
B, be not children 1 Cor. 14:20
B, if a man be
overtaken . . . . Gal. 6:1
we command
you, *b*. . . . . 2 Thess. 3:6
made like unto
his *b* . . . . Heb. 2:17

Wherefore, my
beloved *b* . . . . . . James 1:19
b, Hath not God
chosen . . . . James 2:5
unfeigned love of
the *b* . . . . 1 Pet. 1:22

BRIDE

ornaments, and
as a *b* . . . . Is. 61:10
the voice of the *b* . . . . Jer. 7:34
the voice of the *b* . . . . Jer. 16:9
the voice of the *b* . . . Jer. 25:10
the voice of the *b* . . . Jer. 33:11
hath the *b* is the
bridegroom . . . . John 3:29
heaven, prepared
as a *b* . . . . Rev. 21:2
the Spirit and
the *b* . . . . Rev. 22:17

BRIDEGROOM

righteousness,
as a *b* . . . . Is. 61:10
the voice of the *b* . . . . Jer. 7:34
the voice of the *b* . . . Jer. 33:11
the bride is the *b* . . . John 3:29

BRIGHTNESS

b shall the moon
give . . . . Is. 60:19
appearance of
the *b* . . . . Ezek. 1:28
with the *b* . . . . . . 2 Thess. 2:8
the *b* of his glory . . . . Heb. 1:3

BRIMSTONE

Gomorrah *b* and
fire . . . . Gen. 19:24
land thereof is *b* . . Deut. 29:23
hailstones, fire,
and *b* . . . . Ezek. 38:22
tormented with
fire and *b* . . . . Rev. 14:10
fire burning
with *b* . . . . Rev. 19:20
lake of fire and *b* . . . Rev. 20:10
burneth with fire
and *b* . . . . Rev. 21:8

BROKEN

of the great deep *b* . . Gen. 7:11
he hath *b* my
covenant . . . . Gen. 17:14
when I have *b* the
staff . . . . Lev. 26:26
the city was *b* . . . . 2 Kin. 25:4
thou hast *b* the
teeth . . . . Ps. 3:7
healeth the *b* in
heart . . . . Ps. 147:3
thou hast *b* the
yoke . . . . Is. 9:4
her gods he hath *b* . . . Is. 21:9
withered, they
shall be *b* . . . . Is. 27:11
staff of this *b* reed . . . Is. 36:6
out cisterns, *b*
cisterns . . . . Jer. 2:13
time I have *b* thy
yoke . . . . Jer. 2:20
daughter of my
people is *b* . . . . . . Jer. 14:17

Coniah a
despised *b* . . . . Jer. 22:28
and his arm is *b*,
saith . . . . Jer. 48:25
confounded,
Merodach is *b* . . . . . . Jer. 50:2
king of Babylon
hath *b* . . . . Jer. 50:17
captives, because I
am *b*. . . . . Ezek. 6:9
covenant that he
hath *b* . . . . Ezek. 17:19
blood, and they
have *b* . . . . Ezek. 44:7

BROOK
and willows of
the *b* . . . . Lev. 23:40
passed over the *b*
Kidron. . . . . 2 Sam. 15:23
the *b* Kishon, and
slew . . . . 1 Kin. 18:40
the *b* Kidron, and
burned. . . . . 2 Kin. 23:6
to Jabin, at the *b* . . . . . Ps. 83:9
disciples over
the *b* . . . . John 18:1

BROTHER
man's *b* will I
require . . . . Gen. 9:5
garments for
Aaron thy *b* . . . . Ex. 28:4
Speak unto Aaron
thy *b* . . . . Lev. 16:2
evil toward his *b*. . Deut. 28:54
Caleb's younger *b*. . . Judg. 3:9
made Zedekiah
his *b*. . . . . 2 Chr. 36:10
one against his *b* . . . . . Is. 19:2
trust ye not in
any *b* . . . . Jer. 9:4
and every man
his *b*. . . . . Jer. 31:34
he did pursue
his *b*. . . . . Amos 1:11
on the day of
thy *b* . . . . Obad. 12
evil against his *b*. . . Zech. 7:10
is angry with his *b* . Matt. 5:22
Zelotes, and Judas
the *b* . . . . Acts 1:13
and Timothy our *b* . . 2 Cor. 1:1
sent Timotheus,
our *b* . . . . 1 Thess. 3:2
b that walketh
disorderly . . . . . . 2 Thess. 3:6
one, and slew
his *b*. . . . . 1 John 3:12
any man see his *b*
sin . . . . 1 John 5:16
am your *b*, and
companion . . . . Rev. 1:9

BROUGHT
he *b* him forth
abroad . . . . Gen. 15:5
When thou hast *b*
forth . . . . Ex. 3:12
of hand the
LORD *b* . . . . Ex. 13:3
of hand the
LORD *b* . . . . Ex. 13:14

thee, which I
have *b* . . . . Ex. 15:26
thy God, which
have *b* . . . . Ex. 20:2
gods, O Israel,
which *b* . . . . 1 Kin. 12:28
Nebuchadnezzar
sent, and *b* . . . . 2 Chr. 36:10
b upon them the
king . . . . 2 Chr. 36:17
the mountains
were *b* . . . . Ps. 90:2
have nourished
and *b* . . . . Is. 1:2
he is *b* as a
lamb to . . . . Is. 53:7
they *b* him up to
Nebuchadnezzar . . . Jer. 39:5
and the heaven,
and *b* . . . . Ezek. 8:3
And he *b* me into
the . . . . Ezek. 8:16
of days, and
they *b*. . . . . Dan. 7:13
upon the evil,
and *b* . . . . Dan. 9:14
Manaen, which
had been *b* . . . . . . Acts 13:1
city in Cilicia,
yet *b*. . . . . Acts 22:3
God of peace,
that *b*. . . . . Heb. 13:20

BUILD
thou shalt *b* an
house. . . . . Deut. 28:30
He shall *b* an
house. . . . . 2 Sam. 7:13
for to *b* the house. 1 Kin. 9:15
then did he *b*
Millo . . . . 1 Kin. 9:24
Solomon *b* an
high place . . . . . . 1 Kin. 11:7
He shall *b* an
house. . . . . 1 Chr. 22:10
in mine heart to *b* 1 Chr. 28:2
hath charged me
to *b* . . . . Ezra 1:2
Jozadak, and
began to *b* . . . . Ezra 5:2
the house that
ye *b* . . . . Is. 66:1
to throw down,
to *b* . . . . Jer. 1:10
and I will *b* them . . . . Jer. 24:6
b thee, and thou
shalt. . . . . Jer. 31:4
b, and to plant,
saith . . . . Jer. 31:28
siege against it,
and *b* . . . . Ezek. 4:2
restore and to *b*
Jerusalem . . . . Dan. 9:25
shall *b* the waste
cities . . . . Amos 9:14
place, and he
shall *b* . . . . Zech. 6:12
return and *b* the
desolate. . . . . Mal. 1:4
rock I will *b* my
church . . . . Matt. 16:18

BUILDED
and there *b* he an
altar . . . . Gen. 12:7
and there he *b* an
altar . . . . Gen. 12:8
which they *b* . . . . Num. 32:38
house that I
have *b* . . . . 1 Kin. 8:27
house, which I
have *b* . . . . 1 Kin. 8:43
elders of the
Jews *b* . . . . Ezra 6:14
they *b* the sheep
gate . . . . Neh. 3:1
the city shall be *b*. . . Jer. 30:18

BUILT
is in Hebron,
and *b* . . . . Gen. 13:18
b for Pharaoh
treasure. . . . . Ex. 1:11
(Now Hebron was
b seven . . . . Num. 13:22
of Sihon be *b*. . . . . Num. 21:27
Then Gideon *b* an
altar . . . . Judg. 6:24
And David *b*
round about . . . . . 2 Sam. 5:9
which Solomon
had *b* . . . . 1 Kin. 9:24
also *b* them high
places . . . . 1 Kin. 14:23
Baal, which he
had *b* . . . . 1 Kin. 16:32
he *b* up again the
high . . . . 2 Kin. 21:3
b altars in the
house. . . . . 2 Kin. 21:4
choicest vine, and *b* . . . Is. 5:2
Jerusalem, Thou
shalt be *b* . . . . Is. 44:28
have *b* the high
places . . . . Jer. 7:31
thou shalt be *b*, O . . . Jer. 31:4
b up a wall,
and, lo . . . . Ezek. 13:10
the street shall
be *b* . . . . Dan. 9:25
b houses of hewn
stone . . . . Amos 5:11
are *b* upon the
foundation . . . . Eph. 2:20
lively stones, are *b* . . 1 Pet. 2:5

BULLOCK
the flesh of the *b* . . . Ex. 29:14
he shall kill the *b* . . . . Lev. 1:5
hath sinned, a
young *b* . . . . Lev. 4:3
he shall bring
the *b* . . . . Lev. 4:4
the blood of the *b*. . . . Lev. 4:7
the *b* for the sin
offering . . . . Lev. 4:8
the skin of the *b* . . . . Lev. 4:11
whole *b* shall he
carry . . . . Lev. 4:12
shall offer a
young *b* . . . . Lev. 4:14
shall do with the *b*. . Lev. 4:20
with oil, for
one *b* . . . . Num. 28:12

hin of wine unto
a *b* . . . . .Num. 28:14
firstling of thy *b* . . Deut. 15:19
firstling of his *b* . . Deut. 33:17
young *b* and seven
rams . . . . 2 Chr. 13:9
eat straw like
the *b* . . . . .Is. 65:25

BULLOCKS
young *b*, and one
ram . . . . .Num. 28:11
seven *b* and seven
rams . . . . .Job 42:8
blood of *b*, or of
lambs. . . . . .Is. 1:11
the *b* with the
bulls . . . . .Is. 34:7
her like fatted *b* . . . . Jer. 46:21
Slay all her *b* . . . . . . Jer. 50:27
sacrifice *b* in
Gilgal. . . . . .Hos. 12:11

BURDEN
b of the sons of
Kohath . . . . .Num. 4:15
bear the *b* of the
people . . . . .Num. 11:17
the yoke of his *b*. . . . . . .Is. 9:4
The *b* of Babylon,
which . . . . .Is. 13:1
The *b* of Moab . . . . . . .Is. 15:1
The *b* of Egypt . . . . . . .Is. 19:1
The *b* of Tyre. . . . . .Is. 23:1
a *b* to the weary
beast . . . . .Is. 46:1
bear no *b* on the
sabbath . . . . .Jer. 17:21
Neither carry
forth a *b* . . . . .Jer. 17:22
to bear a *b*, even
entering. . . . . .Jer. 17:27

BURDENS
them with their *b* . . . . Ex. 1:11
the *b* of the
Egyptians . . . . Ex. 6:6
the *b* of the
Egyptians . . . . Ex. 6:7
ye take from
him *b* . . . . .Amos 5:11

BURIED
thou shalt be *b* in . .Gen. 15:15
died there, and
was *b* . . . . .Num. 20:1
Egypt, *b* they in
Shechem . . . . . .Josh. 24:32
there will I be *b* . . . Ruth 1:17
and died, and
was *b* . . . . 2 Sam. 17:23
b in the city of
David. . . . . 1 Kin. 2:10
b him in his own
sepulchres. . . . . 2 Chr. 16:14
gathered, nor be *b* . . . . Jer. 8:2
neither shall they
be *b* . . . . .Jer. 16:4
are *b* with him by
baptism . . . . .Rom. 6:4

BURN
morning ye shall *b* . . Ex. 12:10

b thereon sweet
incense . . . . Ex. 30:7
even, he shall *b*
incense . . . . Ex. 30:8
the priest shall *b* . . . . Lev. 2:2
are poured out,
and *b* . . . . Lev. 4:12
shall *b* all his fat . . . . Lev. 4:26
b their graven
images. . . . . Deut. 7:5
mine altar, to *b*
incense . . . . 1 Sam. 2:28
children of Israel
did *b* . . . . 2 Kin. 18:4
temple of the
LORD to *b*. . . . . 2 Chr. 26:16
forth like fire,
and *b* . . . . .Jer. 4:4
and it shall *b*, and. . . . Jer. 7:20
son of Hinnom,
to *b* . . . . .Jer. 7:31
Babylon, and he
shall *b* . . . . .Jer. 21:10
Chaldeans, and
they shall *b* . . . . . . Jer. 38:18
shall *b* them, and
carry . . . . Jer. 43:12
own mouth, to *b*
incense . . . . Jer. 44:17
Thou shalt *b* with
fire . . . . Ezek. 5:2
cometh, that
shall *b* . . . . Mal. 4:1
he will *b* up the
chaff. . . . . Matt. 3:12

BURNED
smitten Ziklag,
and *b* . . . . 1 Sam. 30:1
b incense unto
Baal . . . . 2 Kin. 23:5
brook Kidron,
and *b* . . . . 2 Kin. 23:6
gates thereof are *b* . . Neh. 1:3
bones are *b* with
heat . . . . Job 30:30
It is *b* with fire . . . . . Ps. 80:16
desolate, your
cities are *b*. . . . . .Is. 1:7
thou shalt not
be *b* . . . . .Is. 43:2
because they are *b* . . . Jer. 9:10
roofs they have *b*
incense . . . . .Jer. 19:13
city shall not be *b*. . . Jer. 38:17
city to be *b* with
fire . . . . .Jer. 38:23
Chaldeans *b* the
king's. . . . . Jer. 39:8
daughters shall
be *b* . . . . .Jer. 49:2
And *b* the
house of . . . . Jer. 52:13
earth is *b* at his
presence . . . . .Nah. 1:5
fire, and they are *b* . .John 15:6
therein shall be *b* . . 2 Pet. 3:10
brass, as if they *b* . . . Rev. 1:15
be utterly *b* with
fire . . . . Rev. 18:8

BURNING
Israel, bewail
the *b* . . . . Lev. 10:6
consumption, and
the *b* . . . . Lev. 26:16
an extreme *b* . . . .Deut. 28:22
brimstone, and
salt, and *b* . . . . . .Deut. 29:23
made a very
great *b* . . . . 2 Chr. 16:14
mine heart as a *b*
fire . . . . Jer. 20:9
the midst of a *b*
fiery . . . . .Dan. 3:15
his wheels as *b*
fire . . . . .Dan. 7:9
plucked out of
the *b* . . . . .Amos 4:11
and your lights *b* . Luke 12:35
seven lamps of
fire *b* . . . . Rev. 4:5
the smoke of her *b* . . Rev. 18:9
the smoke of her *b* . Rev. 18:18
into a lake of
fire *b* . . . . Rev. 19:20

BURNT
offering be a *b*
sacrifice. . . . . Lev. 1:3
the head of the *b*
offering . . . . Lev. 1:4
altar of the *b*
offering . . . . Lev. 4:7
out shall he be *b* . . . . Lev. 4:12
altar of the *b*
offering . . . . Lev. 4:18
trumpets over
your *b* . . . . Num. 10:10
day, for a
continual *b* . . . . . . Num. 28:3
bring your *b*
offerings . . . . Deut. 12:6
your *b* offerings,
and. . . . . Deut. 12:11
daughters they
have *b* . . . . Deut. 12:31
delight in *b* . . . . .1 Sam. 15:22
And he *b* the
house. . . . . 2 Kin. 25:9
b the house of
God . . . . 2 Chr. 36:19
I am full of the *b*. . . . . .Is. 1:11
their *b* offerings
and. . . . . .Is. 56:7
your *b* offerings
are . . . . Jer. 6:20
when they offer *b*
offering . . . . Jer. 14:12
God more than *b*
offerings . . . . .Hos. 6:6
b offerings, with
calves. . . . . Mic. 6:6
part of trees was *b* . . . Rev. 8:7

BURY
in any wise *b*. . . . .Deut. 21:23
b them in Tophet,
till . . . . Jer. 19:11
up, Memphis
shall *b* . . . . .Hos. 9:6
of the Jews is to *b*. . John 19:40

BUY

and no man
shall *b* . . . . Deut. 28:68
come ye, *b*, and
eat . . . . Is. 55:1
Men shall *b* fields . . . Jer. 32:44
I counsel thee to *b* . . Rev. 3:18

CAESAR

Augustus, Luke 2:1
——— Tiberius, Luke 3:1; 20:22
——— Claudius, Acts 11:28
——— Nero, Phil. 4:22

CAESAREA

A seaport in Palestine; The
home of
Philip, Acts 8:40; 21:8
Cornelius, the centurion,
Acts 10:1, 24
Herod, Acts 12:19–23
Felix, Acts 23:23, 24
Paul conveyed to, by the
disciples to save him from his
enemies, Acts 9:30
By Roman soldiers to be tried
by Felix, Acts 23:23–35

CAIAPHAS

High priest, Luke 3:2
Son-in-law of Annas,
John 18:13
Prophesies concerning Jesus,
John 11:49–51; 18:14
Jesus tried before, Matt. 26:2,
3, 57, 63–65; John 18:24, 28
Peter and other disciples
accused before, Acts 4:1–22

CAIN

Son of Adam, Gen. 4:1
Jealousy and crime of,
Gen. 4:3–15; Heb. 11:4;
1 John 3:12; Jude 11
Sojourns in the land of Nod,
Gen. 4:16
Children and descendants of,
Gen. 4:17, 18
——— A city of Judah,
Josh. 15:57

CAKES

thanksgiving
unleavened *c* . . . . . . Lev. 7:12
the *c*, he shall
offer . . . . Lev. 7:13
flour, and bake
twelve *c* . . . . Lev. 24:5
their dough, to
make *c* . . . . Jer. 7:18

CALEB

One of the two survivors of
the Israelites permitted to
enter the land of promise,
Num. 14:30, 38; 26:63–65;
32:11–13; Deut. 1:34–36;
Josh. 14:6–15
Sent to Canaan as a spy,
Num. 13:6
Brings favorable report,
Num. 13:26–30; 14:6–9
Assists in dividing Canaan,
Num. 34:19

Life of, miraculously saved,
Num. 14:10–12
Leader of the Israelites after
Joshua's death, Judg. 1:11, 12
Age of, Josh. 14:7–10
Inheritance of, Josh. 14:6–15;
15:13–16
Descendants of, 1 Chr. 4:15

CALL

and thou shalt *c*
his . . . . Gen. 17:19
Hermon the
Sidonians *c* . . . . Deut. 3:9
I *c* heaven and
earth . . . . Deut. 4:26
they eat bread,
and *c* . . . . Ps. 14:4
c upon me in the
day . . . . Ps. 50:15
them that *c* upon
thee . . . . Ps. 86:5
c upon me, but I
will . . . . Prov. 1:28
a son, and shall *c* . . . . . Is. 7:14
may be found, *c* ye . . . . Is. 55:6
shall slay thee,
and *c* . . . . Is. 65:15
time they shall *c*
Jerusalem . . . . Jer. 3:17
the city that men *c* . Lam. 2:15
c on my name,
and I . . . . Zech. 13:9
son, and thou
shalt *c* . . . . Matt. 1:21
son, and they
shall *c* . . . . Matt. 1:23
I am not come to *c* . Matt. 9:13
a son, and shalt *c* . . . Luke 1:31
Lord our God
shall *c* . . . . Acts 2:39
not *c* any man
common . . . . Acts 10:28
that in every
place *c* . . . . 1 Cor. 1:2

CALLED

And he *c* the
name of . . . . Gen. 28:19
c a Prophet was
beforetime . . . . . . 1 Sam. 9:9
and he *c* it
Nehushtan . . . . 2 Kin. 18:4
be *c* Wonderful,
Counsellor . . . . Is. 9:6
when I *c*, was
there . . . . Is. 50:2
mine house shall
be *c* . . . . Is. 56:7
be *c* trees of
righteousness . . . . . . Is. 61:3
c, LORD OUR
RIGHTEOUSNESS . Jer. 23:6
be *c* a city of truth . . Zech. 8:3
c the Son of the
Highest . . . . Luke 1:32
be *c* the Son of
God . . . . Luke 1:35
Simeon that was *c*
Niger . . . . Acts 13:1
of Jesus Christ, *c* . . . Rom. 1:1

Rome, beloved of
God, *c* . . . . Rom. 1:7
them who are
the *c* . . . . Rom. 8:28
praises of him
who hath *c* . . . . . . 1 Pet. 2:9
ye are thereunto *c* . . 1 Pet. 3:9
all grace, who
hath *c* . . . . 1 Pet. 5:10
serpent, *c* the
Devil . . . . Rev. 12:9
him are *c*, and
chosen . . . . Rev. 17:14

CALLING

c of assemblies, I . . . . . Is. 1:13
wrought and done
it, *c* . . . . Is. 41:4
wash away thy
sins, *c* . . . . Acts 22:16
us with an holy *c* . . 2 Tim. 1:9

CALVES

counsel, and
made two *c* . . . . 1 Kin. 12:28
sacrificing unto
the *c* . . . . 1 Kin. 12:32
two *c*, and made a
grove . . . . 2 Kin. 17:16
devils, and for
the *c*, and for . . . . 2 Chr. 11:15
fear because of
the *c* . . . . Hos. 10:5
burnt offerings,
with *c* . . . . Mic. 6:6
blood of goats
and *c* . . . . Heb. 9:12

CAMELS

maidservants,
and *c* . . . . Gen. 24:35
their *c* bearing
spicery . . . . Gen. 37:25
c were without
number . . . . Judg. 7:12
of *c* shall cover
thee . . . . Is. 60:6

CAMEST

thou *c* out from
Egypt . . . . Ex. 23:15
the month Abib
thou *c* . . . . Ex. 34:18
for thou *c* forth
out . . . . Deut. 16:3
and before thou *c*
forth . . . . Jer. 1:5
thou *c* forth with
thy . . . . Ezek. 32:2
thou *c* forth from
God . . . . John 16:30

CAMP

the *c* of Israel,
removed . . . . Ex. 14:19
people that was in
the *c* . . . . Ex. 19:16
fire without the *c* . . . Ex. 29:14
turned again into
the *c* . . . . Ex. 33:11
c unto a clean
place . . . . Lev. 4:12
the *c* is to set
forward . . . . Num. 4:15

CANA (col. 1 continued)

they put out of
the c . . . . Num. 5:2
shut out from
the c . . . . Num. 12:14
thing, and make
the c . . . . Josh. 6:18
times in the c of
Dan . . . . Judg. 13:25
man came out of
the c . . . . 2 Sam. 1:2
that bend the
bow, c . . . . Jer. 50:29
set the c also
against . . . . Ezek. 4:2
for his c is very
great . . . . Joel 2:11

CANA

Marriage at, John 2:1–11
Nobleman's son healed at,
John 4:46, 47
Nathanael's home at,
John 21:2

CANAANITES

Eleven nations, descended
from Canaan, Gen. 10:15–19;
Deut. 7:1; 1 Chr. 1:13–16
Territory of, Gen. 10:19;
12:6; 15:18; Ex. 23:31;
Num. 13:29; 34:2–12;
Josh. 1:4; 5:1
Given to the Israelites,
Gen. 12:6, 7; 15:18; 17:8;
Ex. 23:23; Deut. 7:1–3;
32:49; Ps. 135:11, 12
Wickedness of, Gen. 13:13;
Lev. 18:25, 27, 28; 20:23
To be expelled from the land,
Ex. 33:2; 34:11
To be destroyed, Ex. 23:23, 24;
Deut. 19:1; 31:3–5
Not expelled, Josh. 17:12–18;
Judg. 1:1–33; 3:1–3
Defeat the Israelites,
Num. 14:45; Judg. 4:1–3
Defeated by the Israelites,
Num. 21:1–3; Josh. 11:1–16;
Judg. 4:4–24
By the Egyptians, 1 Kin. 9:16
Chariots of, Josh. 17:18
Isaac forbidden by Abraham to
take a wife from, Gen. 28:1
Judah marries a woman of,
Gen. 38:2; 1 Chr. 2:3
The Jews take wives from,
Ezra 9:2
Prophecy concerning,
Gen. 9:25–27

CANDLESTICK

thou shalt
make a c . . . . Ex. 25:31
three branches of
the c . . . . Ex. 25:32
come out of the c . . . Ex. 25:33
c shall be four
bowls . . . . Ex. 25:34
proceed out of
the c . . . . Ex. 25:35
and the c of gold
with . . . . 2 Chr. 13:11

the c, and the
table . . . . Heb. 9:2

CANST

Thou c not see my
face . . . . Ex. 33:20
itch, whereof
thou c . . . . Deut. 28:27
thee, that thou c
make . . . . Dan. 5:16
thou wilt, thou c
make . . . . Matt. 8:2

CAPERNAUM

A city on the shore of the
Sea of Galilee; Jesus chose
as the place of his abode,
Matt. 4:13; Luke 4:31
Miracles of Jesus performed
at, Matt. 9:1–26; 17:24; 27;
Mark 1:21–45; 2; 3:1–6;
Luke 7:1–10; John 4:46–53;
6:17–25, 59
His prophecy against,
Matt. 11:23; Luke 10:15

CAPTAIN

of Pharaoh's,
and c . . . . Gen. 37:36
another, Let us
make a c . . . . Num. 14:4
the c of whose
host . . . . Judg. 4:2
made him head
and c . . . . Judg. 11:11
c over my people
Israel . . . . 1 Sam. 9:16
anointed thee to
be c . . . . 1 Sam. 10:1
commanded him
to be c . . . . 1 Sam. 13:14
Abner the son of
Ner, c . . . . 2 Sam. 2:8
also, if thou be
not c . . . . 2 Sam. 19:13
Abner the son of
Ner, c . . . . 1 Kin. 2:32
c of the guard,
brake . . . . 2 Kin. 25:10
And the c of the
guard . . . . 2 Kin. 25:18
rebellion
appointed a c . . . . . Neh. 9:17
c of the guard left . . . Jer. 39:10
appoint a c against . . Jer. 51:27
silver, took the c . . . . Jer. 52:19
And the c of the
guard . . . . Jer. 52:24
So Nebuzaradan
the c . . . . Jer. 52:26
priests, and the c . . . . Acts 4:1
glory, to make
the c . . . . Heb. 2:10

CAPTAINS

Asa, and sent
the c . . . . 1 Kin. 15:20
the c of the host
separated . . . . . . 1 Chr. 25:1
all the c of the
forces . . . . Jer. 40:7
her wise men,
her c . . . . Jer. 51:57

CAPTIVE

firstborn of the c . . . . Ex. 12:29
carried them c to
Assyria . . . . 2 Kin. 15:29
people of it c to
Kir . . . . 2 Kin. 16:9
of Babylon
brought c . . . . . . 2 Kin. 24:16
is carried away c . . . . Jer. 13:17
be carried away c . . . Jer. 29:14
carried away c to
Babylon . . . . Jer. 40:7
was carried away c . . Jer. 52:27
be led away c . . . . . Luke 21:24

CAPTIVES

even ten
thousand c . . . . 2 Kin. 24:14
that carried
them c . . . . Ps. 106:46
the Ethiopians c,
young . . . . Is. 20:4
proclaim liberty to
the c . . . . Is. 61:1
carry them away c . . Jer. 43:12
thy sons are
taken c . . . . Jer. 48:46
c, because I am
broken . . . . Ezek. 6:9
deliverance to
the c . . . . Luke 4:18

CAPTIVITY

into c unto Sihon
king . . . . Num. 21:29
they shall go
into c . . . . Deut. 28:41
God will turn
thy c . . . . Deut. 30:3
those carried he
into c . . . . 2 Kin. 24:15
his strength into c . . Ps. 78:61
for the c, to the c . . . . Jer. 15:2
c, and I will gather . . Jer. 29:14
c of my people
Israel . . . . Jer. 30:3
the land of their c . . . Jer. 30:10
the c of Jacob's
tents . . . . Jer. 30:18
c to return, saith . . . . Jer. 32:44
cause to return
the c . . . . Jer. 33:11
cause their c to
return . . . . Jer. 33:26
as are for c to c . . . . . Jer. 43:11
into c with his
priests . . . . Jer. 48:7
to turn away thy c . . Lam. 2:14
into c unto Kir,
saith . . . . Amos 1:5
c before their
enemies . . . . Amos 9:4
c of my people of
Israel . . . . Amos 9:14
away, she went
into c . . . . Nah. 3:10

CARCASE

beareth ought of
the c . . . . Lev. 11:25
whoso toucheth
their c . . . . Lev. 11:27
c shall be meat . . . Deut. 28:26

c down from the
tree . . . . Josh. 8:29

CARCASES
images, and cast
your *c* . . . . Lev. 26:30
c shall fall in . . . . . Num. 14:29
whoredoms, until
your *c* . . . . Num. 14:33
tremble, and
their *c* . . . . Is. 5:25
upon the *c* of the
men . . . . Is. 66:24
And the *c* of this
people . . . . Jer. 7:33
their *c* shall be
meat . . . . Jer. 16:4
inheritance with
the *c* . . . . Jer. 16:18

CARMEL
A fertile and picturesque
mountain in Palestine,
Song 7:5; Is. 33:9; 35:2;
Jer. 46:18; 50:19; Amos 1:2
Forests of, 2 Kin. 19:23
Caves of, Amos 9:3; Mic. 7:14
An idolatrous high place
upon which Elijah builds
an altar, and confounds the
worshipers of Baal, putting to
death four hundred and fifty
of its prophets, 1 Kin. 18:17–
46
Elisha's abode in, 2 Kin. 2:25;
4:25
——— A city of Judah,
Josh. 15:55
Saul erects a memorial at,
1 Sam. 15:12
Nabal's possessions at,
1 Sam. 25:2
King Uzziah, who delighted in
agriculture, had vineyards at,
2 Chr. 26:10

CARRIED
c them captive to
Assyria . . . . 2 Kin. 15:29
it, and *c* the
people . . . . 2 Kin. 16:9
Samaria, and *c*
Israel . . . . 2 Kin. 17:6
And he *c* out
thence . . . . 2 Kin. 24:13
And he *c* away all
Jerusalem . . . . . 2 Kin. 24:14
And he *c* away
Jehoiachin . . . . . 2 Kin. 24:15
fetters of brass,
and *c* . . . . 2 Kin. 25:7
So Judah was *c*
away . . . . 2 Kin. 25:21
of Assyria, and
he *c* . . . . 1 Chr. 5:26
brake into it,
and *c* . . . . 2 Chr. 21:17
the froward is *c*
headlong . . . . Job 5:13
borne our griefs,
and *c* . . . . Is. 53:4
he bare them,
and *c* . . . . Is. 63:9

the LORD's flock
is *c* . . . . Jer. 13:17
caused you to be *c* . . Jer. 29:14
c away captive to
Babylon . . . . Jer. 40:7
they shall be *c*
captives . . . . Ezek. 6:9
c me out in the
spirit . . . . Ezek. 37:1
he *c* into the land . . . . Dan. 1:2
Yet was she *c*
away . . . . Nah. 3:10

CARRY
and myrrh, going
to *c* . . . . Gen. 37:25
c us forth out of
Egypt . . . . Ex. 14:11
bullock shall he *c* . . . Lev. 4:12
Thou shalt *c* much
seed . . . . Deut. 28:38
c him out, and
stone . . . . 1 Kin. 21:10
king of Assyria
did *c* . . . . 2 Kin. 18:11
in fetters, to *c* . . . . 2 Chr. 36:6
with his arm,
and *c* . . . . Is. 40:11
and the wind
shall *c* . . . . Is. 41:16
Neither *c* forth a
burden . . . . Jer. 17:22
him with chains,
to *c* . . . . Jer. 39:7
shall burn them,
and *c* . . . . Jer. 43:12

CAST
thine olive shall *c* Deut. 28:40
forsake him, he
will *c* . . . . 1 Chr. 28:9
thee, and *c* thy
law . . . . Neh. 9:26
afflict the people,
and *c* . . . . Ps. 44:2
God, why hast
thou *c* . . . . Ps. 74:1
c fire into thy
sanctuary . . . . Ps. 74:7
thou hast *c* out
the . . . . Ps. 80:8
man *c* away the
abominations . . . . Ezek. 20:8
the sword, and
did *c* . . . . Amos 1:11
was *c* far off a
strong . . . . Mic. 4:7
c out into outer
darkness . . . . Matt. 8:12
shall they *c* out
devils . . . . Mark 16:17
I will in no wise *c* . . . John 6:37
of this world be *c* . . John 12:31
blood, and they
were *c* . . . . Rev. 8:7
great dragon was *c* . . Rev. 12:9
c alive into a lake . . Rev. 19:20
deceived them
was *c* . . . . Rev. 20:10
death and hell
were *c* . . . . Rev. 20:14
book of life was *c* . . Rev. 20:15

CASTING
them with a line, *c* 2 Sam. 8:2
they have defiled
by *c* . . . . Ps. 74:7
profaned his
crown by *c* . . . . . . Ps. 89:39
Andrew his
brother, *c* . . . . Matt. 4:18

CATTLE
air, and over the *c* . . . Gen. 1:26
the firstborn of *c* . . . . Ex. 12:29
thy *c*, nor thy
stranger . . . . Ex. 20:10
of Israel, and the *c* . Num. 3:45
the fruit of thy *c* . . . Deut. 28:4
the fruit of thy *c* . . Deut. 28:51
their *c* and their
tents . . . . Judg. 6:5
to grow for the *c* . . . Ps. 104:14
beasts, and upon
the *c* . . . . Is. 46:1
the voice of the *c* . . . . Jer. 9:10

CAUSED
the LORD *c* the
sea . . . . Ex. 14:21
And Jonathan *c*
David . . . . 1 Sam. 20:17
c thee to rest . . . . . 2 Sam. 7:11
and *c* Solomon to
ride . . . . 1 Kin. 1:38
And they *c* their
sons . . . . 2 Kin. 17:17
divided the sea,
and *c* . . . . Ps. 78:13
have *c* Egypt to
err . . . . Is. 19:14
the place
whence I *c* . . . . . . Jer. 29:14
he hath *c* thine
enemy . . . . Lam. 2:17
Behold, I have *c*
thine . . . . Zech. 3:4
and they *c* great
joy . . . . Acts 15:3

CAUSETH
He *c* the grass to
grow . . . . Ps. 104:14
upon princes,
and *c* . . . . Ps. 107:40
c the vapours to
ascend . . . . Ps. 135:7
he *c* all, both
small . . . . Rev. 13:16

CEASE
prophesied, and
did not *c* . . . . Num. 11:25
He maketh wars
to *c* . . . . Ps. 46:9
c to do evil . . . . Is. 1:16
thereof have I
made to *c* . . . . Is. 21:2
thou shalt *c* to
spoil . . . . Is. 33:1
Then will I cause
to *c* . . . . Jer. 7:34
and let them not *c* . . Jer. 14:17
Behold, I will
cause to *c* . . . . Jer. 16:9

c from yielding
  fruit . . . . Jer. 17:8
of thy songs to *c* . . Ezek. 26:13
cause their images
  to *c* . . . . Ezek. 30:13
the oblation to *c* . . . . Dan. 9:27

CENSER
Used for offering incense,
  Lev. 16:12; Num. 4:14; 16:6,
  7, 16–18, 46; Rev. 8:3
For the temple, made of gold,
  1 Kin. 7:50; 2 Chr. 4:22;
  Heb. 9:4
Those which Korah used
  were converted into plates,
  Num. 16:37–39
Used in idolatrous rites,
  Ezek. 8:11
Symbolical, Rev. 8:3, 5

CHAFF
c which the wind
  driveth . . . . Ps. 1:4
flame consumeth
  the *c* . . . . Is. 5:24
be chased as the *c* . . . . Is. 17:13
passeth away, as
  the *c* . . . . Hos. 13:3
will burn up the *c* . . Matt. 3:12

CHAIN
linen, and put a
  gold *c* . . . . Gen. 41:42
scarlet, and
  have a *c* . . . . Dan. 5:7
a *c* of gold about
  thy . . . . Dan. 5:16
scarlet, and
  put a *c* . . . . Dan. 5:29

CHAINS
in *c* they shall
  come . . . . Is. 45:14
and bound him
  with *c* . . . . Jer. 39:7
men were bound
  in *c* . . . . Nah. 3:10
delivered them
  into *c* . . . . 2 Pet. 2:4

CHAMBERS
the beams of his *c* . . Ps. 104:3
every man in the *c* . Ezek. 8:12
windows to the
  little *c* . . . . Ezek. 40:16
And the little *c*
  thereof . . . . Ezek. 40:21

CHANGE
vesture shalt
  thou *c* . . . . Ps. 102:26
to *c* times and
  laws . . . . Dan. 7:25
clothe thee with *c* . . . Zech. 3:4
I am the LORD, I *c* . . . Mal. 3:6

CHANGED
(their names
  being *c* . . . . Num. 32:38
and they shall be *c* . Ps. 102:26
Hath a nation *c*
  their . . . . Jer. 2:11
have *c* the king's
  word . . . . Dan. 3:28

thy countenance
  be *c* . . . . Dan. 5:10
and my
  countenance *c* . . . . . Dan. 7:28
And *c* the glory of . Rom. 1:23
of the Lord, are *c* . . 2 Cor. 3:18
and they shall be *c* . . Heb. 1:12

CHARGE
Levites shall keep
  the *c* . . . . Num. 1:53
his *c*, and the *c* of . . Num. 3:7
Israel kept the *c* . . . Num. 9:19
son of Nun a *c* . . . Deut. 31:23
c of the LORD our
  God . . . . 2 Chr. 13:11
shall give his
  angels *c* . . . . Ps. 91:11
will I give him a *c* . . . . Is. 10:6
this sin to their *c* . . . Acts 7:60
laid to his *c*
  worthy . . . . Acts 23:29
c I commit unto
  thee . . . . 1 Tim. 1:18
give thee *c* in the . 1 Tim. 6:13
C them that are
  rich . . . . 1 Tim. 6:17
I *c* thee therefore . . 2 Tim. 4:1

CHARIOT
David houghed all
  the *c* . . . . 2 Sam. 8:4
he burneth the
  c in . . . . Ps. 46:9
maketh the clouds
  his *c* . . . . Ps. 104:3
behold, here
  cometh a *c* . . . . Is. 21:9
will cut off the *c* . . . Zech. 9:10

CHARIOTS
and covered the *c* . . . Ex. 14:28
thirty thousand *c* . 1 Sam. 13:5
from him a
  thousand *c* . . . . . . 2 Sam. 8:4
full of horses
  and *c* . . . . 2 Kin. 6:17
With twelve
  hundred *c* . . . . . . 2 Chr. 12:3
Some trust in *c*,
  and . . . . Ps. 20:7
The *c* of God are
  twenty . . . . Ps. 68:17
horses, and trust
  in *c* . . . . Is. 31:1
fire, and with his *c* . . . Is. 66:15
as clouds, and
  his *c* . . . . Jer. 4:13
horses, and upon
  their *c* . . . . Jer. 50:37
horses, and with *c* . Ezek. 26:7
wheels, and of
  the *c* . . . . Ezek. 26:10
and I will burn
  her *c* . . . . Nah. 2:13

CHARITY
c, I am become as
  sounding . . . . 1 Cor. 13:1
mountains, and
  have not *c* . . . . . . 1 Cor. 13:2
exceedingly, and
  the *c* . . . . 2 Thess. 1:3

c out of a pure
  heart . . . . 1 Tim. 1:5

CHERUBIMS
thou shalt make
  two *c* . . . . Ex. 25:18
shall ye make
  the *c* . . . . Ex. 25:19
And the *c* shall
  stretch . . . . Ex. 25:20
from between the
  two *c* . . . . Ex. 25:22
dwelleth between
  the *c* . . . . 1 Sam. 4:4
dwellest between
  the *c* . . . . Ps. 80:1
sitteth between
  the *c* . . . . Ps. 99:1

CHIEF
the head of the *c*
  butler . . . . Gen. 40:20
David's sons
  were *c* . . . . 2 Sam. 8:18
Seraiah the *c*
  priest . . . . 2 Kin. 25:18
priests, and of
  the *c* . . . . 2 Chr. 19:8
rulers hath been *c* . . . Ezra 9:2
the *c* of their
  strength . . . . Ps. 78:51
in their land, the *c* . Ps. 105:36
Seraiah the *c*
  priest . . . . Jer. 52:24
in thy fairs with *c* Ezek. 27:22
province of
  Babylon, and *c* . . . . Dan. 2:48
the elders and *c*
  priests . . . . Matt. 16:21
assembled
  together the *c* . . . . Matt. 26:3
c priests, and
  elders . . . . Matt. 26:59
the *c* priests and
  elders . . . . Matt. 27:1
the *c* priests to
  bind . . . . Acts 9:14
honourable
  women, and the *c* Acts 13:50
Barsabas, and
  Silas, *c* . . . . Acts 15:22
the *c* corner stone . . Eph. 2:20
of whom I am *c* . . 1 Tim. 1:15
And when the *c*
  Shepherd . . . . 1 Pet. 5:4

CHILD
man *c* in your
  generations . . . . . Gen. 17:12
uncircumcised
  man *c* . . . . Gen. 17:14
his heart, Shall a *c* . Gen. 17:17
was his only *c* . . . Judg. 11:34
thine handmaid a
  man *c* . . . . 1 Sam. 1:11
And the *c* Samuel
  ministered . . . . . . 1 Sam. 3:1
their women
  with *c* . . . . 2 Kin. 8:12
c left to himself
  bringeth . . . . Prov. 29:15
unto us a *c* is born . . . . Is. 9:6
not travail with *c* . . . . Is. 54:1

for I am a *c* .... Jer. 1:6
her first *c*, the
voice .... Jer. 4:31
was a *c*, then I
loved .... Hos. 11:1
their women
with *c*.......... Hos. 13:16
virgin shall be
with *c*.......... Matt. 1:23
thou, *c*, shalt be
called .... Luke 1:76
mother, Behold,
this *c* .... Luke 2:34
shall receive this *c* .. Luke 9:48
upon a woman
with *c*......... 1 Thess. 5:3
for to devour her *c* .. Rev. 12:4

CHILDREN
LORD had visited
the *c*............ Ex. 4:31
shalt speak unto
the *c*............ Ex. 19:6
fathers upon the *c* ... Ex. 20:5
commandment
unto the *c* .... Ex. 25:22
the *c* of thy people . Lev. 19:18
Jabbok, even unto
the *c*........... Num. 21:24
thee, and with
thy *c*........... Deut. 4:40
feet, and toward
her *c*.......... Deut. 28:57
the *c* of Israel
assembled....... Josh. 18:1
Then all the *c* of
Israel .... Judg. 20:1
stripes of the *c* ... 2 Sam. 7:14
abomination of
the *c*........... 1 Kin. 11:7
eyelids try, the *c* .... Ps. 11:4
Remember, O
LORD, the *c* ...... Ps. 137:7
nourished and
brought up *c*......... Is. 1:2
c, and their
children's ...... Ezek. 37:25
for the *c* of thy
people .... Dan. 12:1
the *c* of Israel
return .... Hos. 3:5
and kings, and
the *c*........... Acts 9:15
wrath of God
upon the *c*........ Eph. 5:6

CHOOSE
Joshua, *C* us out
men .... Ex. 17:9
love upon you,
nor *c*........... Deut. 7:7
LORD your God
shall *c* .... Deut. 12:5
LORD your God
shall *c* .... Deut. 12:11
LORD shall *c* to
place .... Deut. 16:2
LORD thy God
shall *c* .... Deut. 16:7
place which he
shall *c* .... Deut. 16:16

LORD thy God
shall *c* .... Deut. 26:2
And did I *c* him
out .... 1 Sam. 2:28
yet *c* Israel, and
set .... Is. 14:1
Israel, and he
shall *c* .... Is. 49:7
I also will *c* their...... Is. 66:4

CHOSEN
him whom he
hath *c*.......... Num. 16:5
LORD thy God
hath *c*........... Deut. 7:6
the LORD hath *c*
thee .... Deut. 14:2
whom the LORD
hath *c*......... 1 Sam. 10:24
sake which I
have *c* .... 1 Kin. 11:13
which I have *c*... 1 Kin. 11:36
not Moses his *c*
stood .... Ps. 106:23
gardens that ye
have *c* .... Is. 1:29
Jesurun, whom I
have *c* .... Is. 44:2
a curse unto my *c*.... Is. 65:15
Yea, they have *c*
their............. Is. 66:3
c man, that I may
appoint .... Jer. 49:19
know whom I
have *c* .... John 13:18
c me, but I have *c* .. John 15:16
but I have *c* ...... John 15:19
these two thou
hast *c*......... Acts 1:24
for he is a *c* vessel .. Acts 9:15
brethren, Hath
not God *c* .... James 2:5
But ye are a *c*
generation........ 1 Pet. 2:9
are called, and *c* ... Rev. 17:14

CHRIST
Jesus *C* for the
remission .... Acts 2:38
toward our Lord
Jesus *C* ...... Acts 20:21
servant of Jesus *C* .. Rom. 1:1
and the Lord
Jesus *C* .... Rom. 1:7
preaching of
Jesus *C* .... Rom. 16:25
him are ye in *C*
Jesus .... 1 Cor. 1:30
glorious gospel
of *C* .... 2 Cor. 4:4
if any man be in *C* .2 Cor. 5:17
Jesus *C* neither
circumcision....... Gal. 5:6
C Jesus unto good
works .... Eph. 2:10
walk in love, as *C* .... Eph. 5:2
of our Lord
Jesus *C* .... 1 Thess. 3:13
of our Lord
Jesus *C* .... 2 Thess. 1:8
Jesus *C*, that ye
withdraw....... 2 Thess. 3:6

our Saviour
Jesus *C* .... Titus 2:13
shall the blood
of *C* .... Heb. 9:14
C also hath once
suffered .... 1 Pet. 3:18
resurrection of
Jesus *C* .... 1 Pet. 3:21
his Son Jesus *C* ... 1 John 5:20
And from Jesus *C*,
who .... Rev. 1:5

CHURCH
I will build my *c* .. Matt. 16:18
Lord added to
the *c*............ Acts 2:47
persecution
against the *c* .... Acts 8:1
made havock of
the *c*............. Acts 8:3
with the *c*, and
taught .... Acts 11:26
the *c* that was at
Antioch......... Acts 13:1
elders in every *c* ... Acts 14:23
had gathered the *c* . Acts 14:27
overseers, to feed
the *c*........... Acts 20:28
Unto the *c* of God
which .... 1 Cor. 1:2
some in the *c* ... 1 Cor. 12:28
the *c* may receive
edifying......... 1 Cor. 14:5
brother, unto the *c* ..2 Cor. 1:1
himself a
glorious *c* .... Eph. 5:27
of the body, the *c* ... Col. 1:18
sake, which is
the *c*........... Col. 1:24
c of the living God 1 Tim. 3:15
angel of the *c* in
Sardis .... Rev. 3:1
angel of the *c* in
Philadelphia .... Rev. 3:7
the angel of the *c* ... Rev. 3:14

CHURCHES
John to the
seven *c*........... Rev. 1:4
c which are in
Asia .... Rev. 1:11
Spirit saith unto
the *c*............ Rev. 2:7
Spirit saith unto
the *c*........... Rev. 2:11
Spirit saith unto
the *c*............ Rev. 2:17
c shall know that I .. Rev. 2:23
these things in
the *c*........... Rev. 22:16

CILICIA
A maritime province of Asia
Minor; Jews live in, Acts 6:9
The congregations of,
Acts 15:23, 41; Gal. 1:21
Sea of, Acts 27:5

CIRCUMCISED
days old shall be *c* .Gen. 17:12
foreskin is not *c* ...Gen. 17:14
foreskin shall be *c* .. Lev. 12:3
begat Isaac, and *c*.... Acts 7:8

ye be *c* after the
  manner . . . . Acts 15:1
C the eighth
  day, of . . . . Phil. 3:5

CIRCUMCISION
the covenant of *c* . . . . Acts 7:8
of the *c* which
  believed . . . . Acts 10:45
c is that of the
  heart . . . . Rom. 2:29
and they unto
  the *c* . . . . Gal. 2:9
Jesus Christ
  neither *c* . . . . Gal. 5:6
neither Greek nor
  Jew, *c* . . . . Col. 3:11

CITIES
Pharaoh treasure *c* . . . Ex. 1:11
your *c*, I will send . . Lev. 26:25
desolate, and
  your *c* . . . . Lev. 26:33
Israel took all
  these *c* . . . . Num. 21:25
mightier than
  thyself, *c* . . . . Deut. 9:1
Gozan, and in
  the *c* . . . . 2 Kin. 17:6
answered, Until
  the *c* . . . . Is. 6:11
thy *c* shall be laid . . . . . Jer. 4:7
watch over their *c* . . . . . Jer. 5:6
to cease from
  the *c* . . . . Jer. 7:34
and I will make
  the *c* . . . . Jer. 9:11
Jerusalem, and
  the *c* . . . . Jer. 25:18
Jerusalem, and in
  the *c* . . . . Jer. 32:44
our princes, in
  the *c* . . . . Jer. 44:17
and all the *c*
  thereof. . . . . Jer. 49:13
the neighbour *c*
  thereof. . . . . Jer. 49:18
build the waste *c* . . Amos 9:14
turning the *c* of
  Sodom . . . . 2 Pet. 2:6
Gomorrha, and
  the *c* . . . . Jude 7
c of the nations
  fell . . . . Rev. 16:19

CITY
that *c* was called
  Luz. . . . . Gen. 28:19
flame from the *c* . . Num. 21:28
shalt thou be in
  the *c* . . . . Deut. 28:16
far from the *c*
  Adam . . . . Josh. 3:16
the *c* of Arba the
  father. . . . . Josh. 15:13
And the *c* was
  broken . . . . 2 Kin. 25:4
c of the great King . . . Ps. 48:2
Jerusalem, the
  holy *c* . . . . Is. 52:1
are left in this *c* . . . . Jer. 21:7
face against this *c* . . . Jer. 21:10

princes, then shall
  this *c* . . . . Jer. 38:18
the streets of the *c* . Lam. 2:11
the *c* that men call . Lam. 2:15
thy holy *c*, to
  finish . . . . Dan. 9:24
shall destroy the *c* . . Dan. 9:26
drew him out of
  the *c* . . . . Acts 14:19
born in Tarsus, a *c* . . Acts 22:3
c of the living God . Heb. 12:22
holy *c* shall they
  tread . . . . Rev. 11:2
John saw the
  holy *c* . . . . Rev. 21:2

CLAY
the miry *c*, and set . . . Ps. 40:2
c say to him that
  fashioneth . . . . Is. 45:9
c, and thou our
  potter . . . . Is. 64:8
iron, the brass,
  the *c* . . . . Dan. 2:45

CLEAN
the camp unto a *c*
  place . . . . Lev. 4:12
between unclean
  and *c* . . . . Lev. 10:10
and she shall be *c* . . Lev. 12:8
the man that is *c* . . Num. 9:13
people were
  passed *c* . . . . Josh. 3:17
Who can bring a *c*
  thing . . . . Job 14:4
that he should
  be *c* . . . . Job 15:14
hyssop, and I shall
  be *c* . . . . Ps. 51:7
me a *c* heart, O
  God . . . . Ps. 51:10
Wash you, make
  you *c* . . . . Is. 1:16
be ye *c*, that bear . . . Is. 52:11
unclean and the *c* Ezek. 22:26
will I sprinkle *c*
  water . . . . Ezek. 36:25
thou canst make
  me *c* . . . . Matt. 8:2
I am *c* . . . . Acts 18:6
arrayed in fine
  linen, *c* . . . . Rev. 19:8

CLEANSE
your idols, will I *c* Ezek. 36:25
might sanctify
  and *c* . . . . Eph. 5:26
C your hands, ye
  sinners . . . . James 4:8
our sins, and to *c* . . 1 John 1:9

CLEAVE
shalt thou *c*, and
  swear . . . . Deut. 10:20
shall serve him,
  and *c* . . . . Deut. 13:4
make the
  pestilence *c* . . . . . Deut. 28:21
they shall *c* unto
  thee . . . . Deut. 28:60
c to the house of
  Jacob . . . . Is. 14:1

mount of Olives
  shall *c* . . . . Zech. 14:4
c to that which is . . Rom. 12:9

CLOTHE
thou shalt surely *c* . . . Is. 49:18
ye *c* you, but there . . . Hag. 1:6
thee, and I will *c* . . Zech. 3:4
Wherefore, if God
  so *c* . . . . Matt. 6:30

CLOTHED
with the girdle,
  and *c* . . . . Lev. 8:7
c with shame and
  dishonour . . . . Ps. 35:26
LORD reigneth,
  he is *c* . . . . Ps. 93:1
for he hath *c* me
  with . . . . Is. 61:10
horsemen, all of
  them *c* . . . . Ezek. 38:4
thereof, shall be *c* . . Dan. 5:7
thereof, thou shalt
  be *c* . . . . Dan. 5:16
c Daniel with
  scarlet . . . . Dan. 5:29
And I heard the
  man *c* . . . . Dan. 12:7
Wherewithal shall
  we be *c* . . . . Matt. 6:31
and be *c* with
  humility . . . . 1 Pet. 5:5
unto the Son of
  man, *c* . . . . Rev. 1:13
be *c* in white
  raiment . . . . Rev. 3:5
that thou mayest
  be *c* . . . . Rev. 3:18
heaven, *c* with a
  cloud . . . . Rev. 10:1
threescore days, *c* . . Rev. 11:3

CLOTHES
And Jacob rent
  his *c* . . . . Gen. 37:34
them wash their *c* . . Ex. 19:10
them shall wash
  his *c* . . . . Lev. 11:25
bed shall wash
  his *c* . . . . Lev. 15:5
land, rent their *c* . . Num. 14:6
Joshua rent his *c* . . Josh. 7:6
Saul with his *c*
  rent . . . . 2 Sam. 1:2
took hold on his *c* 2 Sam. 1:11
rent his *c*, and put 1 Kin. 21:27
their *c* rent, and
  told . . . . 2 Kin. 18:37
priest rent his *c* . . Matt. 26:65
swaddling *c*, and
  laid . . . . Luke 2:7
wound it in
  linen *c* . . . . John 19:40
witnesses laid
  down their *c* . . . . . Acts 7:58

CLOUD
pillar of a *c*, to
  lead . . . . Ex. 13:21
the pillar of the *c* . . Ex. 14:19
thee in a thick *c* . . . Ex. 19:9

lightnings, and a
thick *c* . . . . Ex. 19:16
the midst of the *c* . . . Ex. 24:18
a *c* covered the
tent . . . . Ex. 40:34
c upon the mercy
seat . . . . Lev. 16:2
the *c* tarried long . . Num. 9:19
LORD came down
in a *c* . . . . Num. 11:25
face, and that
thy *c* . . . . Num. 14:14
minister because
of the *c* . . . . . . 1 Kin. 8:11
filled with a *c* . . . . 2 Chr. 5:13
let a *c* dwell upon . . . . . Job 3:5
rideth upon a
swift *c* . . . . Is. 19:1
as a thick *c*, thy
transgressions . . . . . Is. 44:22
c in the day of rain . Ezek. 1:28
people of Israel,
as a *c* . . . . Ezek. 38:16
be as the
morning *c* . . . . Hos. 13:3
behold, a bright *c* . . Matt. 17:5
heaven, clothed
with a *c* . . . . Rev. 10:1

CLOUDS
reacheth unto
the *c* . . . . Ps. 36:5
maketh the *c* his
chariot. . . . . Ps. 104:3
also command
the *c*. . . . . Is. 5:6
the heights of
the *c*. . . . . Is. 14:14
up as *c*, and his
chariots . . . . Jer. 4:13
man came with
the *c* . . . . Dan. 7:13
gloominess, a day
of *c* . . . . Joel 2:2
man coming in
the *c*. . . . . Matt. 24:30
and coming in
the *c* . . . . Matt. 26:64
Behold, he
cometh with *c* . . . . . Rev. 1:7

COAST
Jordan, and the *c*
thereof. . . . . Deut. 3:17
with thee in all
thy *c* . . . . Deut. 16:4
down westward to
the *c*. . . . . Josh. 16:3
And the *c* of the
children . . . . Josh. 19:47
restored the *c* of
Israel . . . . 2 Kin. 14:25
the sea *c*, in the
borders . . . . Matt. 4:13

COASTS
thy *c*, but thou
shalt. . . . . Deut. 28:40
Ashdod and the *c*
thereof. . . . . 1 Sam. 5:6
lice in all their *c* . . . Ps. 105:31
them out of
their *c* . . . . Acts 13:50

all the *c* of Judaea . . Acts 26:20

COMEST
from Sidon, as
thou *c* . . . . Gen. 10:19
Egypt, as thou *c* . . . Gen. 13:10
thou be when
thou *c* . . . . Deut. 28:6
thou be when
thou *c* . . . . Deut. 28:19

COMETH
her young one
that *c* . . . . Deut. 28:57
he *c*, for he *c* to
judge . . . . Ps. 96:13
he *c* to judge the
earth . . . . Ps. 98:9
earth, and that
which *c* . . . . Is. 42:5
c from Edom,
with dyed . . . . Is. 63:1
To what purpose *c*
there . . . . Jer. 6:20
he *c*, he shall
smite . . . . Jer. 43:11
thee as the
people *c* . . . . Ezek. 33:31
he *c* up unto the
people . . . . Hab. 3:16
behold, thy King *c* . . Zech. 9:9
behold, the day *c* . . . Mal. 4:1
c after me is
mightier . . . . Matt. 3:11
ashamed, when
he *c* . . . . Mark 8:38
him that *c* to me I . . John 6:37
no man *c* unto the
Father . . . . John 14:6
things *c* the wrath . . . Eph. 5:6
sudden
destruction *c* . . . . 1 Thess. 5:3
c down from the
Father . . . . James 1:17
Lord *c* with ten
thousands . . . . Jude 14
Behold, he *c* with
clouds . . . . Rev. 1:7

COMFORT
daughters rose up
to *c* . . . . Gen. 37:35
mourn with him
and to *c* . . . . Job 2:11
and thy staff
they *c* . . . . Ps. 23:4
bitterly, labour
not to *c* . . . . Is. 22:4
the LORD shall *c*
Zion . . . . Is. 51:3
to *c* all that mourn . . . . Is. 61:2
she hath none to *c* . . Lam. 1:2
they *c* in vain . . . . . Zech. 10:2
Daughter, be of
good *c* . . . . Matt. 9:22
establish you, and
to *c* . . . . 1 Thess. 3:2

COMFORTED
he refused to be *c* . . Gen. 37:35
LORD hath *c* his
people . . . . Is. 49:13

them, and I will
be *c* . . . . Ezek. 5:13
drink water, shall
be *c* . . . . Ezek. 31:16

COMING
company of
prophets *c* . . . . . . 1 Sam. 10:5
withholden thee
from *c* . . . . 1 Sam. 25:26
abide the day of
his *c* . . . . Mal. 3:2
prophet before
the *c* . . . . Mal. 4:5
see the Son of
man *c* . . . . Matt. 16:28
see the Son of
man *c* . . . . Matt. 24:30
hand of power,
and *c* . . . . Matt. 26:64
John seeth Jesus *c* . . John 1:29
shewed before of
the *c* . . . . Acts 7:52
Jesus Christ at
his *c* . . . . 1 Thess. 2:19
the *c* of our Lord
Jesus . . . . 1 Thess. 3:13
the *c* of our Lord
Jesus . . . . 1 Thess. 5:23
brightness of his *c* . 2 Thess. 2:8
city, new
Jerusalem, *c* . . . . . . Rev. 21:2

COMMAND
speak all that I *c* . . . . . . Ex. 7:2
C the children of
Israel . . . . Num. 5:2
I *c* thee this day . . . Deut. 4:40
bring all that I *c* . . Deut. 12:11
I *c* thee this day . . . Deut. 28:1
LORD shall *c* the
blessing . . . . Deut. 28:8
God, which I *c* . . . Deut. 28:13
words which I *c*
thee . . . . Deut. 28:14
I *c* thee this day . . Deut. 28:15
LORD will *c* his
lovingkindness . . . . . Ps. 42:8
I will also *c* the
clouds . . . . Is. 5:6
them all that I *c*
thee . . . . Jer. 1:17
words that I *c* thee . . . Jer. 26:2
sea, thence will I *c* . . Amos 9:3
enemies, thence
will I *c* . . . . Amos 9:4
lo, I will *c*, and I . . . . Amos 9:9
be the Son of
God, *c* . . . . Matt. 4:3
Now we *c* you,
brethren . . . . 2 Thess. 3:6

COMMANDED
days, as I *c* thee . . . . Ex. 23:15
the LORD, which
he *c* . . . . Lev. 10:1
LORD thy God *c*
thee . . . . Deut. 13:5
which I have not *c* . Deut. 17:3
statutes which
he *c* . . . . Deut. 28:45
Moses my
servant *c* . . . . Josh. 1:7

Gomorrha into
  ashes c . . . . 2 Pet. 2:6

CONFESS

I said, I will c my . . . . Ps. 32:5
But this I c unto
  thee . . . . Acts 24:14
C your faults
  one to . . . . James 5:16
c our sins, he is
  faithful . . . . 1 John 1:9
c not that Jesus
  Christ . . . . 2 John 7
life, but I will c . . . . . . Rev. 3:5

CONFIDENCE

of Bethel their c . . . . Jer. 48:13
c of the house of
  Israel . . . . Ezek. 29:16
having c in you all . . 2 Cor. 2:3
Jesus, and have
  no c . . . . Phil. 3:3
we hold fast the c . . . . Heb. 3:6
And this is the c
  that . . . . 1 John 5:14

CONFOUNDED

desired, and ye
  shall be c . . . . Is. 1:29
be c, and the sun
  ashamed . . . . Is. 24:23
be ashamed nor c
  world . . . . Is. 45:17
neither be thou c . . . . Is. 54:4
c by the graven
  image . . . . Jer. 10:14
Moab is c . . . . Jer. 48:20
taken, Bel is c,
  Merodach . . . . Jer. 50:2
horses shall be c . . . Zech. 10:5

CONFUSION

ashamed and
  brought to c . . . . . . Ps. 35:26
for c they shall
  rejoice . . . . Is. 61:7
shame, and our c
  covereth . . . . Jer. 3:25
thee, but unto
  us c . . . . Dan. 9:7
was filled with c . . . Acts 19:29

CONGREGATION

c of Israel shall
  kill . . . . Ex. 12:6
cut off from the c . . Ex. 12:19
tabernacle of the c . . . Lev. 4:7
tabernacle of the c . . Lev. 4:18
tabernacle of the c . . Lev. 6:16
tabernacle of the c . . Lev. 9:23
death, and all
  the c . . . . Lev. 24:16
no wrath upon
  the c . . . . Num. 1:53
tabernacle of the c . . Num. 4:3
tabernacle of the c . Num. 4:15
Aaron, and to all
  the c . . . . Num. 13:26
wroth with all
  the c . . . . Num. 16:22
abundantly, and
  the c . . . . Num. 20:11
that the c of the
  LORD . . . . Num. 27:17

even all the c . . . . . Num. 27:21
whole c of the
  children . . . . Josh. 18:1
and the c was
  gathered . . . . Judg. 20:1
great c, from the
  entering . . . . 1 Kin. 8:65
thy c, which thou
  hast . . . . Ps. 74:2
the mount of the c . . . Is. 14:13

CONSCIENCE

a c void of offence . Acts 24:16
man's c in the
  sight . . . . 2 Cor. 4:2
heart, and of a
  good c . . . . 1 Tim. 1:5
forefathers with
  pure c . . . . 2 Tim. 1:3
to God, purge
  your c . . . . Heb. 9:14
sprinkled from an
  evil c . . . . Heb. 10:22
Having a good c . . . 1 Pet. 3:16
answer of a good c . 1 Pet. 3:21

CONSUME

them, and that I
  may c . . . . Ex. 32:10
mountains, and
  to c . . . . Ex. 32:12
ague, that shall c . . Lev. 26:16
congregation, that
  I may c . . . . Num. 16:45
And thou shalt c
  all . . . . Deut. 7:16
the locust shall c . Deut. 28:38
shall the locust c . Deut. 28:42
but I will c
  them by . . . . Jer. 14:12
the wilderness,
  to c . . . . Ezek. 20:13
break in pieces
  and c . . . . Dan. 2:44
whom the Lord
  shall c . . . . 2 Thess. 2:8

CONSUMED

before the LORD,
  and c . . . . Lev. 9:24
wilderness they
  shall be c . . . . Num. 14:35
from the LORD,
  and c . . . . Num. 16:35
it hath c Ar of
  Moab . . . . Num. 21:28
thee, until he
  have c . . . . Deut. 28:21
the LORD fell,
  and c . . . . 1 Kin. 18:38
from heaven,
  and c . . . . 2 Kin. 1:12
heaven, and c the
  burnt . . . . 2 Chr. 7:1
gates thereof are c . . . Neh. 2:3
thou hast c them,
  but . . . . Jer. 5:3
devoured him,
  and c . . . . Jer. 10:25
those prophets
  be c . . . . Jer. 14:15
shall be c by the
  sword . . . . Jer. 16:4

them, till they
  be c . . . . Jer. 24:10
of Egypt shall be c . . Jer. 44:27
c in the midst of
  thee . . . . Ezek. 5:12
fruit thereof be c . Ezek. 47:12
of Jacob are not c . . . . Mal. 3:6

CONTINUAL

be a c burnt
  offering . . . . Ex. 29:42
day by day, for a c . . Num. 28:3
It is a c burnt
  offering . . . . Num. 28:6
the c burnt
  offering . . . . Num. 28:15

CONTINUALLY

before the LORD c . . Ex. 28:30
before the LORD c . . Lev. 24:8
bread at my
  table c . . . . 2 Sam. 9:7
people
  increased c . . . . 2 Sam. 15:12
c in the room of
  Joab . . . . 2 Sam. 19:13
commanded unto
  them, c . . . . 1 Chr. 23:31
Thus did Job c . . . . . . Job 1:5
night, while they c . . . Ps. 42:3
of God endureth c . . . Ps. 52:1
and hast feared c
  every . . . . Is. 51:13
offered year by
  year c . . . . Heb. 10:1
of praise to God c . . Heb. 13:15

CONTINUE

kingdom shall
  not c . . . . 1 Sam. 13:14
LORD may c his
  word . . . . 1 Kin. 2:4
exhorting them
  to c . . . . Acts 14:22
obtained help of
  God, I c . . . . Acts 26:22
ye c in the faith
  grounded . . . . Col. 1:23
Let brotherly
  love c . . . . Heb. 13:1

CONTINUED

c as long as the
  sun . . . . Ps. 72:17
mountain to pray,
  and c . . . . Luke 6:12
all c with one
  accord . . . . Acts 1:14
and c his speech
  until . . . . Acts 20:7

CONTRARY

they have
  walked c . . . . Lev. 26:40
also have walked c . Lev. 26:41
all do c to the
  decrees . . . . Acts 17:7
is c to sound
  doctrine . . . . 1 Tim. 1:10

CONTROVERSY

recompences for
  the c . . . . Is. 34:8
for the LORD
  hath a c . . . . Hos. 4:1

LORD's *c*, and ye
strong . . . . Mic. 6:2
c great is the
mystery . . . . 1 Tim. 3:16

CONVERSATION
our *c* in times past . . . Eph. 2:3
former *c* the old
man . . . . Eph. 4:22
your *c* be as it
becometh . . . . Phil. 1:27
For our *c* is in
heaven . . . . Phil. 3:20
your *c* be without
covetousness . . . . . Heb. 13:5
gold, from your
vain *c* . . . . 1 Pet. 1:18
Having your *c*
honest . . . . 1 Pet. 2:12
accuse your
good *c* . . . . 1 Pet. 3:16

CONVOCATION
shall be an holy *c* . . . Ex. 12:16
seventh day is an
holy *c* . . . . Lev. 23:8
trumpets, an
holy *c* . . . . Lev. 23:24
shall be an holy *c* . . Lev. 23:36

CORINTH
A city of Achaia; Visited
By Paul, Acts 18;
2 Cor. 12:14; 13:1;
1 Cor. 16:5–7;
2 Cor. 1:16
By Apollos, Acts 19:1
By Titus, 2 Cor. 8:16, 17;
12:18
By Erastus, a Christian of,
Rom. 16:23; 2 Tim. 4:20
The Congregation of
Schism in, 1 Cor. 1:12; 3:4
Immoralities in, 1 Cor. 5; 11
Writes to Paul, 1 Cor. 7:1
Alienation of, from Paul,
2 Cor. 10
Abuse of ordinances in,
1 Cor. 11:22; 14
Heresies in, 1 Cor. 15:12;
2 Cor. 11
Lawsuits in, 1 Cor. 6
Liberality of, 2 Cor. 9
Paul's letters to, 1 Cor. 1:2;
16:21–24; 2 Cor. 1:1, 13

CORN
thee either *c* . . . . . Deut. 28:51
a land of *c* and
wine . . . . Deut. 33:28
and full ears of *c* . . 2 Kin. 4:42
as a shock of *c*
cometh . . . . Job 5:26
c is sifted in a
sieve . . . . Amos 9:9

CORNER
Jerusalem at the *c*. 2 Chr. 26:9
head stone of
the *c* . . . . Ps. 118:22
stone, a precious *c* . . . Is. 28:16
gate, unto the *c*
gate . . . . Zech. 14:10

being the chief *c*
stone . . . . Eph. 2:20

CORNERS
upon the four *c*
thereof. . . . . Ex. 27:2
Judah from the
four *c* . . . . Is. 11:12
utmost *c*, that
dwell . . . . Jer. 9:26
are in the
utmost *c* . . . . Jer. 25:23

COUNSEL
priest, who shall
ask *c* . . . . Num. 27:21
c of Hushai the
Archite . . . . . . 2 Sam. 17:14
Ahithophel saw
that his *c* . . . . . . 2 Sam. 17:23
king took *c*, and
made . . . . 1 Kin. 12:28
and the *c* of the
froward . . . . Job 5:13
walketh not in
the *c* . . . . Ps. 1:1
the *c* of the LORD. Prov. 19:21
Take *c* together,
and. . . . . Is. 8:10
understanding,
the spirit of *c* . . . . . . Is. 11:2
Zoan are fools,
the *c*. . . . . Is. 19:11
deep to hide
their *c* . . . . Is. 29:15
yea, let them
take *c* . . . . Is. 45:21
My *c* shall stand,
and. . . . . Is. 46:10
Great in *c*, and
mighty. . . . . Jer. 32:19
is *c* perished from . . . Jer. 49:7
hear the *c* of the
LORD. . . . . Jer. 49:20
of the people
took *c*. . . . . Matt. 27:1
determinate *c* and
foreknowledge . . . . Acts 2:23
things after the *c* . . . Eph. 1:11
I *c* thee to buy of . . . Rev. 3:18

COUNSELS
walked in their
own *c*. . . . . Ps. 81:12
thy *c* of old are
faithfulness. . . . . Is. 25:1
but walked in
the *c*. . . . . Jer. 7:24
make manifest
the *c*. . . . . 1 Cor. 4:5

COUNTED
northward, which
is *c*. . . . . Josh. 13:3
fruitful field be *c*. . . . Is. 32:15
of the promise
are *c*. . . . . Rom. 9:8
rule well be *c*
worthy. . . . . 1 Tim. 5:17

COUNTENANCE
LORD lift up his *c*. . Num. 6:26
nation of fierce *c*. . Deut. 28:50

his *c*, or on the
height . . . . 1 Sam. 16:7
withal of a
beautiful *c* . . . . . 1 Sam. 16:12
the light of thy *c* . . . . . Ps. 4:6
c doth behold the
upright . . . . Ps. 11:7
the light of thy *c* . . . . Ps. 44:3
the rebuke of thy *c* . . Ps. 80:16
shew of their *c*
doth. . . . . Is. 3:9
thee, nor let thy *c* . . Dan. 5:10
troubled me, and
my *c*. . . . . Dan. 7:28
c was as the sun
shineth . . . . Rev. 1:16

COUNTRIES
c, and I will
perform. . . . . Gen. 26:3
thy seed all
these *c* . . . . Gen. 26:4
the *c* which the
children. . . . . Josh. 14:1
towns, even
three *c* . . . . Josh. 17:11
the gods of the *c*. 2 Kin. 18:35
c whither I have
driven . . . . Jer. 23:3
c whither I had
driven . . . . Jer. 23:8
c, whither I have
driven . . . . Jer. 32:37
gather you out of
the *c*. . . . . Ezek. 20:41
midst of the *c* . . . . Ezek. 29:12
gather them from
the *c*. . . . . Ezek. 34:13
gather you out of
all *c* . . . . Ezek. 36:24
c whither thou
hast . . . . Dan. 9:7

COUNTRY
thee out of thy *c* . . . Gen. 12:1
your own *c*, or a
stranger . . . . Lev. 16:29
the *c* wept with a
loud . . . . 2 Sam. 15:23
c out of mine
hand . . . . 2 Kin. 18:35
cities of the low *c* 2 Chr. 28:18
Your *c* is desolate . . . . . . Is. 1:7
a far *c*, from the
end. . . . . Is. 13:5
a plentiful *c*, to eat . . . . Jer. 2:7
cane from a far *c* . . . . Jer. 6:20
the north *c*, to
make . . . . Jer. 10:22
out of the north *c* . . . Jer. 23:8
Noph, and in the *c* . . Jer. 44:1
sacrifice in the
north *c*. . . . . Jer. 46:10
the remnant of
the *c*. . . . . Jer. 47:4
nations from the
north *c*. . . . . Jer. 50:9
inhabited places
of the *c* . . . . Ezek. 34:13
Jacob fled into
the *c*. . . . . Hos. 12:12
I was yet in my *c* . . . . Jon. 4:2

Levite, and of
the c . . . . Acts 4:36
in a strange c,
dwelling . . . . Heb. 11:9

COURAGE
strong and of a
good c . . . Deut. 31:6
strong and of a
good c . . . . Deut. 31:23
strong and of a
good c . . . . Josh. 1:6
strong and of a
good c . . . . Josh. 1:9
there remain any
more c . . . . Josh. 2:11
be of good c,
and he . . . . Ps. 27:14

COURT
in the c of the
tabernacle . . . . Lev. 6:16
be eaten, in the c . . . Lev. 6:26
of the king in
the c . . . . 2 Chr. 24:21
of dragons,
and a c . . . . Is. 34:13
c of the LORD's
house . . . . Jer. 26:2
was shut up in
the c . . . . Jer. 32:2
Jeremiah into
the c . . . . Jer. 37:21
Hammelech, that
was in the c . . . . Jer. 38:6
c of the LORD's
house . . . . Ezek. 8:16
But the c which is . . Rev. 11:2

COVENANT
day the LORD
made a c . . . . Gen. 15:18
will establish my c . . Gen. 17:7
he hath broken
my c . . . . Gen. 17:14
establish my c . . . . . Gen. 17:19
keep my c, then ye . . . Ex. 19:5
the book of the c . . . . Ex. 24:7
c, which the
LORD hath . . . . Ex. 24:8
of the c, the ten
commandments . . . Ex. 34:28
by an everlasting c . . Lev. 24:8
it is a c of salt for . Num. 18:19
thou shalt make
no c . . . . Deut. 7:2
God, which
keepeth c . . . . Deut. 7:9
remembered for
them his c . . . . Ps. 106:45
make an
everlasting c . . . . Is. 55:3
have forsaken
the c . . . . Jer. 22:9
the c that I will
make . . . . Jer. 31:33
shall confirm the c . . Dan. 9:27
transgressed my c . . . Hos. 8:1
of the c, whom ye
delight . . . . Mal. 3:1
the everlasting c . . . Heb. 13:20

COVER
c thee with his
feathers . . . . Ps. 91:4
the darkness
shall c . . . . Ps. 139:11
LORD, as the
waters c . . . . Is. 11:9
no more c her
slain . . . . Is. 26:21
multitude of
camels shall c . . . . . . Is. 60:6
upon thy feet,
and c . . . . Ezek. 24:17
dust shall c thee . . Ezek. 26:10
Israel, as a cloud
to c . . . . Ezek. 38:16
to the
mountains, C . . . . . Hos. 10:8
LORD, as the
waters c . . . . Hab. 2:14

COVERED
waters returned,
and c . . . . Ex. 14:28
a cloud c the tent . . . Ex. 40:34
grown thick, thou
art c . . . . Deut. 32:15
twain he c his face . . . . . Is. 6:2
mouth, and I
have c . . . . Is. 51:16
salvation, he
hath c . . . . Is. 61:10
thee, and c thy
nakedness . . . . . . Ezek. 16:8
hungry, and hath c . Ezek. 18:7
and hath c . . . . . . Ezek. 18:16

COVERETH
fat that c the
inwards . . . . Ex. 29:13
c the heaven with
clouds . . . . Ps. 147:8
He that c his sins . Prov. 28:13
and our
confusion c . . . . Jer. 3:25

COVERING
high, c the mercy
seat . . . . Ex. 25:20
have made an end
of c . . . . Num. 4:15
that cover with a c . . . . Is. 30:1
precious stone
was thy c . . . . Ezek. 28:13

COVETOUSNESS
of truth, hating c . . . Ex. 18:21
one is given to c . . . . . Jer. 6:13
greatest is given
to c . . . . Jer. 8:10
after their c . . . . . . Ezek. 33:31
concupiscence,
and c . . . . Col. 3:5
conversation be
without c . . . . Heb. 13:5
c shall they with
feigned . . . . 2 Pet. 2:3

CREATED
the beginning
God c . . . . Gen. 1:1
So God c man in
his . . . . Gen. 1:27

the LORD, he
that c . . . . Is. 42:5
LORD that c
thee, O . . . . Is. 43:1
for I have c him
for . . . . Is. 43:7
saith the LORD
that c . . . . Is. 45:18
day that thou
wast c . . . . Ezek. 28:13
workmanship, c in
Christ . . . . Eph. 2:10
after God is c in
righteousness . . . . . Eph. 4:24
image of him
that c . . . . Col. 3:10
thou hast c all
things . . . . Rev. 4:11

CREATURE
Christ, he is a
new c . . . . 2 Cor. 5:17
firstborn of
every c . . . . Col. 1:15
preached to
every c . . . . Col. 1:23
any c that is not
manifest . . . . Heb. 4:13

CREEPING
c thing that
creepeth . . . . Gen. 1:26
c thing that
creepeth . . . . Lev. 11:41
any manner of c
thing . . . . Lev. 11:44
fourfooted beasts,
and c . . . . Rom. 1:23

CRETE
An island in the
Mediterranean Sea; Visited
by Paul, Acts 27:7, 12, 13, 21
Visited by Titus, Titus 1:5
Character of the inhabitants
of, Acts 2:11; Titus 1:12

CROOKED
their c ways, the
LORD . . . . Ps. 125:5
leviathan that c
serpent . . . . Is. 27:1
make the c places
straight . . . . Is. 45:2
midst of a c and
perverse . . . . Phil. 2:15

CROSS
of words, lest
the c . . . . 1 Cor. 1:17
preaching of the c . . 1 Cor. 1:18
the death of the c . . . . Phil. 2:8
endured the c,
despising . . . . Heb. 12:2

CROWN
shalt make unto
it a c . . . . Ex. 30:3
and put the c . . . . 2 Kin. 11:12
hast profaned
his c . . . . Ps. 89:39
the c of your glory . . Jer. 13:18
or joy, or c . . . . . . 1 Thess. 2:19
laid up for me a c . . 2 Tim. 4:8

CRUCIFIED

receive the *c* of
life . . . . James 1:12
ye shall receive a *c* . . 1 Pet. 5:4
give thee a *c* of life . . Rev. 2:10

CRUCIFIED

wicked hands
have *c* . . . . Acts 2:23
that our old man
is *c* . . . . Rom. 6:6
he was *c* through
weakness . . . . 2 Cor. 13:4
I am *c* with Christ . . Gal. 2:20
are Christ's have *c* . . Gal. 5:24

CRYING

rulers of the city, *c* . . Acts 17:6
hearts, *c*, Abba,
Father . . . . Gal. 4:6
supplications with
strong *c* . . . . Heb. 5:7
neither sorrow,
nor *c* . . . . Rev. 21:4

CUBITS

c shall be the
height . . . . Ex. 30:2
c was the length
thereof. . . . . Deut. 3:11
the house,
twenty *c* . . . . 1 Kin. 6:3
thereof was fifty *c* Ezek. 40:21

CUP

portion of their *c* . . . . Ps. 11:6
my *c* runneth over . . . Ps. 23:5
LORD there is a *c* . . . . Ps. 75:8
hand of the LORD
the *c* . . . . Is. 51:17
of thine hand
the *c* . . . . Is. 51:22
wine *c* of this fury . . Jer. 25:15
c have assuredly
drunken. . . . . Jer. 49:12
hath been a
golden *c* . . . . Jer. 51:7
the *c* also shall
pass . . . . Lam. 4:21
c that I shall . . . . . Matt. 20:22
let this *c* pass
from. . . . . Matt. 26:39
Likewise also
the *c* . . . . Luke 22:20
mixture into the *c* . Rev. 14:10
give unto her the *c* . Rev. 16:19
c which she hath
filled . . . . Rev. 18:6

CURSE

I will not again *c* . . . . Gen. 8:21
that bless thee,
and *c* . . . . Gen. 12:3
revile the gods,
nor *c* . . . . Ex. 22:28
east, saying,
Come, *c* . . . . Num. 23:7
camp of Israel a *c* . . Josh. 6:18
c, because the
LORD. . . . . 2 Sam. 16:10
and entered
into a *c* . . . . Neh. 10:29
the people of my *c* . . . Is. 34:5
leave your name
for a *c* . . . . Is. 65:15

proverb, a taunt
and a *c* . . . . Jer. 24:9
an hissing, and a *c* . . Jer. 25:18
make this city a *c* . . . . Jer. 26:6
the earth, to be a *c* . . Jer. 29:18
astonishment,
and a *c* . . . . Jer. 42:18
reproach, a waste,
and a *c* . . . . Jer. 49:13
the *c* is poured
upon . . . . Dan. 9:11
that as ye were a *c* . Zech. 8:13
the earth with a *c* . . . . Mal. 4:6
enemies, bless
them that *c* . . . . . . Matt. 5:44
redeemed us from
the *c* . . . . Gal. 3:13

CURSED

c is the ground for . . Gen. 3:17
c be every one
that . . . . Gen. 27:29
he hath *c* his
father. . . . . Lev. 20:9
C be the man that
maketh . . . . Deut. 27:15
C be he that
setteth . . . . Deut. 27:16
C be he that
removeth . . . . . . Deut. 27:17
C be he that
perverteth . . . . . . Deut. 27:19
C be he that lieth Deut. 27:20
C be he that
confirmeth . . . . . Deut. 27:26
C shalt thou be in Deut. 28:16
C shall be thy
basket . . . . Deut. 28:17
C shall be the
fruit . . . . Deut. 28:18
C shalt thou be
when . . . . Deut. 28:19
he came forth,
and *c* . . . . 2 Sam. 16:5
said Shimei when
he *c* . . . . 2 Sam. 16:7
sinned, and *c*
God in . . . . Job 1:5
Depart from me,
ye *c*. . . . . Matt. 25:41
for it is written, C . . Gal. 3:13

CURSING

send upon thee *c*,
vexation . . . . Deut. 28:20
death, blessing
and *c* . . . . Deut. 30:19
requite me good
for his *c* . . . . . . 2 Sam. 16:12
mouth is full of *c* . . . . Ps. 10:7

CYPRUS

An island, Acts 21:3; 27:4
Barnabas born in, Acts 4:36
Preaching the gospel at,
Acts 11:19, 20
Visited by Barnabas and Saul,
Acts 13:4–12
Barnabas and Mark visit,
Acts 15:39
Mnason, a disciple of,
Acts 21:16

CYRENE

A city in Libya, Acts 2:10
Contained a synagogue,
Acts 6:9
Simon and Lucius belonged to,
Mark 15:21; Acts 11:20; 13:1

DAILY

servants the
prophets, *d* . . . . Jer. 7:25
give him *d* a piece . . Jer. 37:21
time that the *d*
sacrifice . . . . Dan. 12:11
he *d* increaseth
lies . . . . Hos. 12:1
I sat *d* with you
teaching . . . . Matt. 26:55
they, continuing *d* . . Acts 2:46
added to the
church *d* . . . . Acts 2:47
d, as those high
priests . . . . Heb. 7:27

DAMASCUS

An ancient city, Gen. 14:15;
15:2
Capital of Syria, 1 Kin. 20:34;
Is. 7:8; Jer. 49:23–29;
Ezek. 47:16, 17
Laid under tribute to David,
2 Sam. 8:5, 6
Besieged by Rezon,
1 Kin. 11:23, 24
Recovered by Jeroboam,
2 Kin. 14:28
Taken by king of Assyria,
2 Kin. 16:9
Walled, Jer. 49:27; 2 Cor. 11:33
Garrisoned, 2 Cor. 11:32
Luxury in, Amos 3:12
Paul's experiences in,
Acts 9; 22:5–16; 26:12–20;
2 Cor. 11:32; Gal. 1:17
Prophecies concerning,
Is. 8:4; 17:1, 2; Jer. 49:23–29;
Amos 1:3, 5; Zech. 9:1
Wilderness of, 1 Kin. 19:15

DAN

A city of the tribe of Dan; Also
called Laish, and Leshem,
Gen. 14:14; Deut. 34:1;
Judg. 20:1; Jer. 8:16
Captured by the people of
Dan, Josh. 19:47
Idolatry established at,
Judg. 18; 1 Kin. 12:28, 29;
Amos 8:14
Capture by Ben-hadad,
1 Kin. 15:20; 2 Chr. 16:4

DANIEL

A Jewish captive, also called
Belteshazzar; Educated at
king's court, Dan. 1
Interprets visions, Dan. 2; 4; 5
Promotion and executive
authority of, Dan. 2:48, 49;
5:11, 29; 6:2
Conspiracy against, cast into
the lions' den, Dan. 6
Prophecies of, Dan. 4:8, 9; 7;
8; 9; 10; 11; 12; Matt. 24:15

Abstinence of, Dan. 1:8–16
Wisdom of, Ezek. 28:3;
Dan. 1:17
Devoutness of, Ezek. 14:14;
Dan. 2:18; 6; 9; 10; 12
Courage and fidelity of,
Dan. 4:27; 5:17–23; 6:10–23
Worshiped by
Nebuchadnezzar, Dan. 2:6
—— David's son
Also called Chileab,
2 Sam. 3:3; 1 Chr. 3:1
—— A descendant of
Ithamar, and a companion of
Ezra, Ezra 8:2; Neh. 10:6

DARIUS
The Mede, king of Persia,
Dan. 5:31; 6; 9:1
—— King of Persia
Emancipates the Jews, Ezra 5;
6; Hag. 1:1, 15; Zech. 1:1
—— The Persian, Neh. 12:22

DARK
The light shall
be d . . . . Job 18:6
works are in the d . . . Is. 29:15
stumble upon
the d . . . . Jer. 13:16
Israel do in the d . . Ezek. 8:12
the moon shall
be d . . . . Joel 2:10
and maketh the
day d . . . . Amos 5:8
d unto you,
that ye . . . . Mic. 3:6
yet d, unto the
sepulchre . . . . John 20:1
shineth in a d
place . . . . 2 Pet. 1:19

DARKENED
light is d in the
heavens . . . . Is. 5:30
the sun shall be d . . . . Is. 13:10
the moon shall
be d . . . . Joel 3:15
sun be d, and the
moon . . . . Matt. 24:29

DARKNESS
gropeth in d . . . . . Deut. 28:29
shall be silent in d . 1 Sam. 2:9
Let d and the
shadow . . . . Job 3:5
Clouds and d are
round . . . . Ps. 97:2
the land, behold d . . . . Is. 5:30
people that
walked in d . . . . Is. 9:2
them that sit in d . . . . . Is. 42:7
before he cause d . . . Jer. 13:16
A day of d and of
gloominess . . . . Joel 2:2
shall be turned
into d . . . . Joel 2:31
cast out into
outer d . . . . Matt. 8:12
world, and men
loved d . . . . John 3:19
shall not walk in d . . John 8:12

have the light,
lest d . . . . John 12:35
to turn them
from d . . . . Acts 26:18
hidden things of d . . 1 Cor. 4:5
d, but now are ye
light . . . . Eph. 5:8
the rulers of the d . . Eph. 6:12
called you out of d . . 1 Pet. 2:9
them into chains
of d . . . . 2 Pet. 2:4

DASHED
children also shall
be d . . . . Is. 13:16
mother was d in
pieces . . . . Hos. 10:14
infants shall be d . . Hos. 13:16
children also
were d . . . . Nah. 3:10

DAUGHTER
d in law, his son
Abram's . . . . Gen. 11:31
thy son, nor thy d . . . Ex. 20:10
thy d thou shalt
not . . . . Deut. 7:3
maketh his son or
his d . . . . Deut. 18:10
son, and toward
her d . . . . Deut. 28:56
Jezebel the d . . . . 1 Kin. 16:31
make his son or
his d . . . . 2 Kin. 23:10
the spoiling of
the d . . . . Is. 22:4
O d of my people,
gird . . . . Jer. 6:26
the slain of the d . . . . . Jer. 9:1
virgin d of my
people . . . . Jer. 14:17
Thou d that dost
inhabit . . . . Jer. 48:18
The d of
Babylon is . . . . Jer. 51:33
destruction of
the d . . . . Lam. 2:11
head at the d of
Jerusalem . . . . Lam. 2:15
Arise and
thresh, O d . . . . . . Mic. 4:13
Sing and
rejoice, O d . . . . . . Zech. 2:10
Rejoice
greatly, O d . . . . . . Zech. 9:9
D, be of good
comfort . . . . Matt. 9:22
D, thy faith hath
made . . . . Mark 5:34

DAUGHTERS
his d rose up to
comfort . . . . Gen. 37:35
their d unto thy
sons . . . . Ex. 34:16
sons and thy d . . . Num. 18:19
escaped,
and his d . . . . . . Num. 21:29
your sons, and
your d . . . . Deut. 12:12
their sons and
their d . . . . Deut. 12:31
Thy sons and
thy d . . . . Deut. 28:32

shalt beget sons
and d . . . . Deut. 28:41
sons and of thy d . Deut. 28:53
their sons and
their d . . . . 2 Kin. 17:17
have taken of
their d . . . . Ezra 9:2
our sons and
our d . . . . Neh. 5:5
their sons and
their d . . . . Ps. 106:37
sons and of their d . Ps. 106:38
and my d from the
ends . . . . Is. 43:6
their sons and
their d . . . . Jer. 7:31
captives, and thy d . . Jer. 48:46
desolate heap, and
her d . . . . Jer. 49:2
d whom ye have
left . . . . Ezek. 24:21
your sons and
your d . . . . Joel 2:28

DAY
d the Lord made
a covenant . . . . . . Gen. 15:18
until the
fourteenth d . . . . . . Ex. 12:6
first d ye shall put . . Ex. 12:15
seventh d is the
sabbath . . . . Ex. 20:10
you this d, that ye . Deut. 4:26
command thee
this d . . . . Deut. 4:40
command thee
this d . . . . Deut. 28:15
David from that d
forward . . . . 1 Sam. 16:13
d have I begotten
thee . . . . Ps. 2:7
call upon me in
the d . . . . Ps. 50:15
children of Edom
in the d . . . . Ps. 137:7
to pass in that d . . . . Is. 11:11
said in that d, Lo . . . . Is. 25:9
I have this d set
thee . . . . Jer. 1:10
cloud in the d of
rain . . . . Ezek. 1:28
behold, the d
cometh . . . . Mal. 4:1
again the third d . . Matt. 16:21
next d John seeth
Jesus . . . . John 1:29
ye all are this d . . . . Acts 22:3
no rest d nor
night . . . . Rev. 14:11

DAYS
his son many d . . . Gen. 37:34
d shall ye eat
unleavened . . . . . . Ex. 12:15
Six d shalt thou
labour . . . . Ex. 20:9
that thy d may be
long . . . . Ex. 20:12
d, as I
commanded thee . . Ex. 23:15
not prolong
your d . . . . Deut. 4:26

mayest prolong
thy *d* .... Deut. 4:40
thee all the *d* of
thy ....Josh. 1:5
And when thy *d*
be fulfilled ..... 2 Sam. 7:12
In the *d* of Pekah
king .... 2 Kin. 15:29
pass in the last *d* ......Is. 2:2
shall prolong his *d* ...Is. 53:10
carried them all
the *d* .... Is. 63:9
d come, saith the
LORD.............. Jer. 23:5
d Judah shall be
saved .... Jer. 23:6
d, saith the LORD... Jer. 31:33
in the *d* of these
kings ....Dan. 2:44
goodness in the
latter *d*........... Hos. 3:5
tribulation of
those *d*....... Matt. 24:29
Hath in these
last *d* .... Heb. 1:2

DEAD

mourned for
the *d* .... 2 Sam. 14:2
the living to the *d*.....Is. 8:19
Thy *d* men shall
live...............Is. 26:19
and their *d* bodies .. Jer. 34:20
the *d*, bind the
tire............ Ezek. 24:17
raised from the *d* ... Acts 3:15
Judge of quick
and *d* .... Acts 10:42
supposing he had
been *d* .... Acts 14:19
d I am called in
question .... Acts 23:6
should rise from
the *d* .... Acts 26:23
firstborn from
the *d* .... Col. 1:18
conscience from *d*
works ....Heb. 9:14
the *d* our Lord
Jesus ....Heb. 13:20
Christ from the *d* ... 1 Pet. 1:3
d to sins, should
live............. 1 Pet. 2:24
begotten of the *d* .... Rev. 1:5
fell at his feet as *d* .. Rev. 1:17
liveth, and was *d* ... Rev. 1:18
livest, and art *d*...... Rev. 3:1
And I saw the *d*,
small .... Rev. 20:12

DEAD SEA

Lies southeast of Jerusalem;
Called Salt Sea, Gen. 14:3;
Num. 34:12
Sea of the Plain, Deut. 3:17;
4:49; Josh. 3:16
East Sea, Joel 2:20
Former Sea, Zech. 14:8
Prophecy concerning,
Ezek. 47:7–10, 18

DEAL

lamb a tenth *d* of
flour............. Ex. 29:40

tenth *d* of fine
flour........... Lev. 14:21
But thus shall ye *d* .. Deut. 7:5
lest I *d* with you
after .... Job 42:8
shalt make an end
to *d* ....Is. 33:1
servant shall *d*
prudently ....Is. 52:13
happy that *d* very
treacherously ..... Jer. 12:1
will I also *d* in
fury .... Ezek. 8:18

DEALS

tenth *d* of fine
flour........... Lev. 14:10
loaves of two
tenth *d*......... Lev. 23:17
two tenth *d*
shall be .... Lev. 24:5
three tenth *d* of
flour..........Num. 28:12

DEALT

wherefore hast
thou *d* .... Ex. 14:11
d with familiar
spirits .... 2 Kin. 21:6
knewest that
they *d*.........Neh. 9:10
d proudly, and
hearkened ....Neh. 9:29
friends have *d*
treacherously ..... Lam. 1:2
Because that
Edom hath *d*.... Ezek. 25:12
doings, so hath
he *d* .... Zech. 1:6
according as God
hath *d* .... Rom. 12:3

DEATH

ought but *d* part
thee .... Ruth 1:17
measured he to
put to *d* .... 2 Sam. 8:2
into the dust of *d* ... Ps. 22:15
swallow up *d* in
victory ....Is. 25:8
the rich in his *d* ......Is. 53:9
out his soul
unto *d* ....Is. 53:12
as are for *d*, to *d* ..... Jer. 15:2
deliver such as are
for *d*............. Jer. 43:11
but is passed
from *d* ....John 5:24
loosed the pains
of *d*.............. Acts 2:24
wages of sin is *d*... Rom. 6:23
the law of sin
and *d* .... Rom. 8:2
became obedient
unto *d* .... Phil. 2:8
suffering of *d*,
crowned ....Heb. 2:9
d he might
destroy ....Heb. 2:14
God, being put
to *d* ....1 Pet. 3:18
keys of hell and
of *d*........... Rev. 1:18

d and hell were
cast ....Rev. 20:14
more *d*, neither
sorrow .... Rev. 21:4
which is the
second *d* .... Rev. 21:8

DEBIR

King of Eglon, Josh. 10:3–27
——— A town in the
mountains of Judah
Also called Kirjath-sannah,
and Kirjath-sepher, which
signifies a city of books,
Josh. 15:15, 16
Anakim expelled from, by
Joshua, Josh. 11:21
Taken by Othniel, Josh. 15:15–
17, 49; Judg. 1:12, 13
Allotted to the Aaronites,
Josh. 21:15
——— A place near the valley
of Achor, Josh. 15:7

DEBORAH

Nurse to Rebecca, Gen. 24:59
Buried beneath an oak tree
near Beth-el, Gen. 35:8
——— The prophetess, a judge
of Israel, Judg. 4:4, 5; 5:7
Inspires Barak to defeat Sisera,
Judg. 4:6–16
The triumphant song of,
Judg. 5

DECEIT

violence, neither
was any *d* ....Is. 53:9
it speaketh *d*........ Jer. 9:8
of nought, and
the *d* .... Jer. 14:14
covetousness,
wickedness, *d* .... Mark 7:22
philosophy and
vain *d*............ Col. 2:8

DECEITFUL

bloody and *d* men
shall............. Ps. 55:23
The heart is *d*
above............. Jer. 17:9
false apostles, *d*
workers .... 2 Cor. 11:13
to the *d* lusts....... Eph. 4:22

DECEIVE

d every one his
neighbour .... Jer. 9:5
the midst of
you, *d*........... Jer. 29:8
rough garment
to *d* .... Zech. 13:4
shall *d* the very
elect........... Matt. 24:24
and fair
speeches *d*...... Rom. 16:18
no man *d* you
with vain......... Eph. 5:6
we have no sin,
we *d*........... 1 John 1:8

DECEIVED

and whosoever
is *d*............. Prov. 20:1

a *d* heart hath
turned . . . . Is. 44:20
terribleness
hath *d* . . . . Jer. 49:16
be *d* when he hath
spoken . . . . Ezek. 14:9
thine heart hath *d* . . . Obad. 3
Be not *d* . . . . 1 Cor. 6:9
d them that had
received . . . . Rev. 19:20
And the devil
that *d* . . . . Rev. 20:10

DECLARE

I will *d* the decree . . . . . Ps. 2:7
I will *d* thy name
unto . . . . Ps. 22:22
if I would *d* and
speak . . . . Ps. 40:5
d his works with
rejoicing . . . . Ps. 107:22
d their sin as
Sodom . . . . Is. 3:9
voice of singing *d* . . . . Is. 48:20
who shall *d* his
generation . . . . Is. 53:8
they shall *d* my
glory . . . . Is. 66:19
D ye in Judah, and . . . . Jer. 4:5
O ye nations,
and *d* . . . . Jer. 31:10
D ye in Egypt, and . . Jer. 46:14
D ye among the
nations . . . . Jer. 50:2
thy name, and
will *d* . . . . John 17:26
blood, to *d* his
righteousness . . . . Rom. 3:25
have seen and
heard *d* . . . . 1 John 1:3

DECLARED

grievous vision
is *d* . . . . Is. 21:2
that time, and
have *d* . . . . Is. 44:8
hath *d* this from
ancient . . . . Is. 45:21
the Father, he
hath *d* . . . . John 1:18
And I have *d* unto
them . . . . John 17:26
ye are
manifestly *d* . . . . . . 2 Cor. 3:3

DECREE

will declare the *d* . . . . . Ps. 2:7
sea by a
perpetual *d* . . . . Jer. 5:22
matter is by the *d* . . . Dan. 4:17
I make a *d*,
That in . . . . Dan. 6:26

DEEDS

According to
their *d* . . . . Is. 59:18
they overpass
the *d* . . . . Jer. 5:28
light, because
their *d* . . . . John 3:19
the light, lest
his *d* . . . . John 3:20
according to his *d* . . . Rom. 2:6

by the *d* of the law . Rom. 3:20
Spirit do mortify
the *d* . . . . Rom. 8:13

DEEP

fountains of the
great *d* . . . . Gen. 7:11
the night, when *d*
sleep . . . . Job 33:15
D calleth unto *d* at . . . Ps. 42:7
I sink in *d* mire,
where . . . . Ps. 69:2
d sleep, and hath
closed . . . . Is. 29:10
that seek *d* to hide . . . Is. 29:15
he hath made it *d*
and . . . . Is. 30:33
back, dwell *d*, O
inhabitants . . . . Jer. 49:8
me, I was in a *d*
sleep . . . . Dan. 8:18

DEFILE

neither shall ye *d* . . . Lev. 11:44
eat to *d* himself
therewith . . . . Lev. 22:8
Ammon, did the
king *d* . . . . 2 Kin. 23:13
of his eyes, and *d* . . Ezek. 20:7
Neither shall
they *d* . . . . Ezek. 37:23
of Israel no
more *d* . . . . Ezek. 43:7
whoremongers,
for them that *d* . . 1 Tim. 1:10

DEFILED

that ye should
be *d* . . . . Lev. 11:43
him he shall be *d* . . Lev. 13:46
and the land is *d* . . . Lev. 18:27
after wizards, to
be *d* . . . . Lev. 19:31
and whosoever
is *d* . . . . Num. 5:2
thy land be not *d* . Deut. 21:23
after that she is *d* . Deut. 24:4
And he *d* Topheth,
which . . . . 2 Kin. 23:10
he *d* his father's
bed . . . . 1 Chr. 5:1
sanctuary, they
have *d* . . . . Ps. 74:7
temple have
they *d* . . . . Ps. 79:1
d with their own
works . . . . Ps. 106:39
when ye entered,
ye *d* . . . . Jer. 2:7
d the land, and
committed . . . . Jer. 3:9
they have *d* my
land . . . . Jer. 16:18
d as the place of
Tophet . . . . Jer. 19:13
thou hast *d* my
sanctuary . . . . . . Ezek. 5:11
Israel, neither
hath *d* . . . . Ezek. 18:6
hath lewdly *d* his
daughter . . . . Ezek. 22:11

DELIGHT

Lord had a *d* in
thy . . . . Deut. 10:15
great *d* in burnt
offerings . . . . . 1 Sam. 15:22
d myself in thy
statutes . . . . Ps. 119:16
and the scorners *d* . Prov. 1:22
just weight is
his *d* . . . . Prov. 11:1
the upright is
his *d* . . . . Prov. 15:8
I *d* not in the
blood . . . . Is. 1:11
gold, they shall
not *d* . . . . Is. 13:17
Then shalt thou *d*
thyself . . . . Is. 58:14
they have no *d*
in it . . . . Jer. 6:10
these things I *d*,
saith . . . . Jer. 9:24
covenant, whom
ye *d* . . . . Mal. 3:1

DELIGHTETH

feareth the Lord,
that *d* . . . . Ps. 112:1
in whom my
soul *d* . . . . Is. 42:1
for the Lord *d* in
thee . . . . Is. 62:4
ways, and their
soul *d* . . . . Is. 66:3
because he *d* in
mercy . . . . Mic. 7:18

DELIVER

I am come down
to *d* . . . . Ex. 3:8
for I will *d* the
inhabitants . . . . Ex. 23:31
Lord thy God
shall *d* . . . . Deut. 7:2
Lord thy God
shall *d* . . . . Deut. 7:16
can *d* out of my
hand . . . . Deut. 32:39
d you out of the
hand . . . . 1 Sam. 7:3
Lord that he
would *d* . . . . Ps. 22:8
d thee, and thou
shalt . . . . Ps. 50:15
have I no power
to *d* . . . . Is. 50:2
saith the Lord,
to *d* . . . . Jer. 1:19
d up their children . . Jer. 18:21
Lord, I will *d*
Zedekiah . . . . Jer. 21:7
And I will *d*
them to . . . . Jer. 24:9
pestilence, and
will *d* . . . . Jer. 29:18
land of Egypt,
and *d* . . . . Jer. 43:11
midst of Babylon,
and *d* . . . . Jer. 51:6
shall I *d* thee,
Israel . . . . Hos. 11:8

pieces, and none
can d . . . . Mic. 5:8
to d them in the
day . . . . .Zeph. 1:18
d him to the
Gentiles. . . . . . . Matt. 20:19

DELIVERED
and ye shall be d
into . . . . Lev. 26:25
I have d him into
thy . . . . .Num. 21:34
the LORD our
God d . . . . Deut. 2:36
wrote this law,
and d . . . . Deut. 31:9
against Israel, and
he d . . . . Judg. 2:14
children of Israel,
who d. . . . . Judg. 3:9
and the LORD d . . . Judg. 3:10
and the LORD d
them . . . . Judg. 13:1
thou hast d my
soul . . . . Ps. 86:13
covenant, and
be d . . . . Ezek. 17:15
angel, and d his
servants. . . . . .Dan. 3:28
people shall be d . . .Dan. 12:1
All things are d
unto. . . . . Matt. 11:27
d him to Pontius
Pilate . . . . Matt. 27:2
being d by the
determinate . . . . . . Acts 2:23
whom ye d up,
and denied . . . . Acts 3:13
Who was d for
our offences . . . . . Rom. 4:25
and I was d out of 2 Tim. 4:17
down to hell,
and d . . . . .2 Pet. 2:4
was ready to be d . . . Rev. 12:4

DEPART
sceptre shall not d .Gen. 49:10
they d from thy
heart . . . . Deut. 4:9
my mercy shall
not d . . . . .2 Sam. 7:15
to d from evil is
understanding . . . . Job 28:28
of Ephraim shall d . . .Is. 11:13
then shall his
yoke d . . . . .Is. 14:25
D ye, d ye, go ye
out . . . . .Is. 52:11
not d out of thy
mouth . . . . .Is. 59:21
ashamed, and
they that d . . . . . . .Jer. 17:13
that they shall
not d . . . . .Jer. 32:40
on the left
hand, D . . . . Matt. 25:41
d out of this world . .John 13:1
commanded all
Jews to d . . . . Acts 18:2
ready to d on the
morrow . . . . Acts 20:7

he said unto
me, D. . . . . Acts 22:21
of Christ d from
iniquity . . . . 2 Tim. 2:19

DEPARTED
Abram d, as the
LORD . . . . .Gen. 12:4
Nun, a young
man, d . . . . Ex. 33:11
their defence is d . .Num. 14:9
is d out of his
house. . . . . Deut. 24:2
And he arose
and d . . . . .1 Sam. 20:42
David therefore d
thence . . . . .1 Sam. 22:1
heart, which
hath d . . . . Ezek. 6:9
thereof, because it
is d . . . . .Hos. 10:5
he left them,
and d . . . . Matt. 16:4
the sepulchre,
and d . . . . Matt. 27:60
when they d from
Perga . . . . .Acts 13:14
present world,
and is d . . . . 2 Tim. 4:10

DERBE
A city in the region of
Lycaonia; Paul flees to,
Acts 14:6, 20
Visited by Paul and Silas,
Acts 16:1
Gaius born in, Acts 20:4

DERISION
shall have them
in d. . . . . Ps. 2:4
neighbours, a
scorn and a d . . . . . Ps. 44:13
neighbours, a
scorn and d . . . . Ps. 79:4
also shall be in d . . .Jer. 48:26

DESERT
backside of the d . . . . . Ex. 3:1
Philistines, and
from the d . . . . Ex. 23:31
congregation, into
the d . . . . Num. 20:1
found him in a d
land . . . . Deut. 32:10
and streams in
the d . . . . .Is. 35:6
like Eden, and
her d . . . . .Is. 51:3
that dwell in the d . .Jer. 25:24

DESIRE
thy d shall be to
thy . . . . .Gen. 3:16
thy servants,
who d. . . . . .Neh. 1:11
eye hath seen
his d . . . . Ps. 54:7
my d upon mine
enemies. . . . . Ps. 59:10
He will fulfil the d . Ps. 145:19
beauty that we
should d . . . . .Is. 53:2

your strength,
the d . . . . .Ezek. 24:21
his mischievous d. . . Mic. 7:3
things the
angels d . . . . 1 Pet. 1:12

DESIRED
d are they than
gold . . . . Ps. 19:10
One thing have I d . . . Ps. 27:4
things that may
be d . . . . Prov. 8:11
oaks which ye
have d . . . . .Is. 1:29
my soul have I d
thee . . . . .Is. 26:9
For I d mercy, and . . .Hos. 6:6
the Just, and d a
murderer. . . . . Acts 3:14
And d of him
letters . . . . Acts 9:2

DESOLATE
your land shall
be d . . . . Lev. 26:33
she being d shall
sit. . . . . .Is. 3:26
land be utterly d . . . . .Is. 6:11
cry in their d
houses . . . . .Is. 13:22
the children of
the d . . . . .Is. 54:1
any more be
termed D . . . . .Is. 62:4
to make thy land d . . . . Jer. 4:7
whole land shall
be d . . . . Jer. 4:27
the land shall be d . . . Jer. 7:34
cities of Judah d . . . . . Jer. 9:11
make their land d . . . Jer. 18:16
their habitations d . . Jer. 49:20
shall be wholly d . . . Jer. 50:13
all her gates are d. . . Lam. 1:4
my children are d . . Lam. 1:16
and I will make
it d . . . . Ezek. 25:13
he shall make it d . . . Dan. 9:27
abomination that
maketh d . . . . Dan. 12:11
Samaria shall
become d. . . . . Hos. 13:16
return and build
the d . . . . Mal. 1:4

DESOLATION
land shall be a d . . . . Jer. 25:11
thereof, to make
them a d . . . . Jer. 25:18
d, a reproach, a
waste . . . . Jer. 49:13
Edom shall be a d. . . Jer. 49:17
and a perpetual d . . . Zeph. 2:9
d shall be in the
thresholds. . . . . . . Zeph. 2:14
a d, a place for
beasts . . . . Zeph. 2:15
abomination of d,
spoken. . . . . Matt. 24:15

DESOLATIONS
hissing, and
perpetual d . . . . Jer. 25:9

make it
perpetual d . . . . Jer. 25:12
make thee
perpetual d . . . . . . Ezek. 35:9
the end of the
war d . . . . Dan. 9:26

DESPISE

honour, and they
that d . . . . 1 Sam. 2:30
God, thou wilt
not d . . . . Ps. 51:17
but fools d
wisdom . . . . Prov. 1:7
hold to the one,
and d . . . . Matt. 6:24
Take heed that
ye d . . . . Matt. 18:10

DESPISED

land which ye
have d . . . . Num. 14:31
Wherefore hast
thou d . . . . 2 Sam. 12:9
messengers of
God, and d . . . . 2 Chr. 36:16
reproach of men,
and d . . . . Ps. 22:6
LORD of hosts,
and d . . . . Is. 5:24
daughter of Zion,
hath d . . . . Is. 37:22
d and rejected of
men . . . . Is. 53:3
that d thee shall
bow . . . . Is. 60:14
man Coniah a d
broken . . . . Jer. 22:28
oath that he
hath d . . . . Ezek. 17:19
statutes, and
they d . . . . Ezek. 20:13
judgments, but
had d . . . . Ezek. 20:24
hath d the day of
small . . . . Zech. 4:10
that d Moses' law
died . . . . Heb. 10:28

DESTROY

to d you, when I
smite . . . . Ex. 12:13
ye shall d their
altars . . . . Ex. 34:13
them, and
utterly d . . . . Deut. 7:2
rejoice over you
to d . . . . Deut. 28:63
Amalek, and
utterly d . . . . . . 1 Sam. 15:3
against Judah to d . 2 Kin. 24:2
God shall
likewise d . . . . Ps. 52:5
d them, had not
Moses . . . . Ps. 106:23
d in all my holy
mountain . . . . Is. 11:9
LORD shall
utterly d . . . . Is. 11:15
he were ready to d . . . Is. 51:13
pull down, and
to d . . . . Jer. 1:10
and will utterly d . . . . Jer. 25:9

throw down, and
to d . . . . Jer. 31:28
d thy strong holds . . Jer. 48:18
against Babylon,
to d . . . . Jer. 51:11
shed blood, and
to d . . . . Ezek. 22:27
come shall d the
city . . . . Dan. 9:26
d both soul and
body . . . . Matt. 10:28
through death he
might d . . . . Heb. 2:14

DESTROYED

LORD d Sodom
and Gomorrah . . . Gen. 13:10
and I shall be d, I . . Gen. 34:30
shall utterly be d . . Deut. 4:26
be d from before
thee . . . . Deut. 12:30
d, and until thou
perish . . . . Deut. 28:20
thee, until thou
be d . . . . Deut. 28:24
till thou be d . . . . Deut. 28:45
neck, until he
have d . . . . Deut. 28:48
land, until thou
be d . . . . Deut. 28:51
thee, until thou
be d . . . . Deut. 28:61
whom ye utterly d . Josh. 2:10
angel that d the
people . . . . 2 Sam. 24:16
Hezekiah his
father had d . . . . 2 Kin. 21:3
thereof with fire,
and d . . . . 2 Chr. 36:19
shall suddenly
be d . . . . Prov. 29:1
therefore they
have d . . . . Is. 37:19
thee, How art
thou d . . . . Ezek. 26:17
which shall never
be d . . . . Dan. 2:44
which shall not
be d . . . . Dan. 7:14
tempted, and
were d . . . . 1 Cor. 10:9

DESTRUCTION

lifted up to his d . 2 Chr. 26:16
into the pit of d . . . . Ps. 55:23
as a d from the
Almighty . . . . Is. 13:6
the besom of d,
saith . . . . Is. 14:23
raise up a cry of d . . . . Is. 15:5
wasting and d
are in . . . . Is. 59:7
land, wasting
nor d . . . . Is. 60:18
north, and great d . . . . Jer. 6:1
have heard a cry
of d . . . . Jer. 48:5
the earth, for
the d . . . . Lam. 2:11
grave, I will be
thy d . . . . Hos. 13:14
at hand, and as a d . . Joel 1:15

the day of their d . . . Obad. 12
edification, and
not to d . . . . 2 Cor. 13:10
end is d, whose
God . . . . Phil. 3:19
then sudden d
cometh . . . . 1 Thess. 5:3
everlasting d . . . . . 2 Thess. 1:9
which drown men
in d . . . . 1 Tim. 6:9
themselves swift d . . 2 Pet. 2:1

DETERMINED

Seventy weeks
are d . . . . Dan. 9:24
desolations are d . . . Dan. 9:26
consummation,
and that d . . . . . . Dan. 9:27
for that that is d . . . Dan. 11:36
Pilate, when he
was d . . . . Acts 3:13

DETESTABLE

d and abominable
things . . . . Jer. 16:18
sanctuary with all
thy d . . . . Ezek. 5:11
abominations and
of their d . . . . Ezek. 7:20
idols, nor with
their d . . . . Ezek. 37:23

DEVIL

prepared for the d . Matt. 25:41
your father the d . . . John 8:44
being ended, the d . . John 13:2
oppressed of the d . Acts 10:38
death, that is,
the d . . . . Heb. 2:14
d, as a roaring lion . . 1 Pet. 5:8
contending with
the d . . . . Jude 9
behold, the d shall . . Rev. 2:10
serpent, called
the D . . . . Rev. 12:9
And the d that
deceived . . . . Rev. 20:10

DEVILS

sacrifices unto d . . . . Lev. 17:7
places, and for
the d . . . . 2 Chr. 11:15
were possessed
with d . . . . Matt. 4:24
shall they cast
out d . . . . Mark 16:17
whom went
seven d . . . . Luke 8:2
the habitation of d . . Rev. 18:2

DEVOUR

your land,
strangers d . . . . Is. 1:7
d the palaces of
Jerusalem . . . . Jer. 17:27
the sword shall d . . . Jer. 46:10
the sword shall d
round . . . . Jer. 46:14
d the palaces of
Benhadad . . . . Amos 1:4
d the palaces
thereof . . . . Amos 1:10
d the palaces of
Bozrah . . . . Amos 1:12

d the palaces
  thereof. . . . . .Amos 1:14
sword shall *d* thy
  young . . . . .Nah. 2:13
seeking whom he
  may *d* . . . . .1 Pet. 5:8
delivered, for to *d*. . . Rev. 12:4

DEVOURED
from the LORD,
  and *d* . . . . Lev. 10:2
rebel, ye shall be *d* . . . .Is. 1:20
sword hath *d* your
  prophets . . . . .Jer. 2:30
and have *d* the
  land . . . . Jer. 8:16
that found them
  have *d* . . . . Jer. 50:7
king of Assyria
  hath *d* . . . . .Jer. 50:17
Zion, and it
  hath *d* . . . . Lam. 4:11
it *d* and brake in
  pieces . . . . .Dan. 7:7
whole land shall
  be *d* . . . . .Zeph. 1:18
the earth shall
  be *d* . . . . .Zeph. 3:8

DEW
drop down *d* . . . . . Deut. 33:28
d nor rain these
  years . . . . 1 Kin. 17:1
As the *d* of
  Hermon. . . . . Ps. 133:3
thy *d* is as the *d* of . . .Is. 26:19
wet thee with
  the *d* . . . . .Dan. 4:25
the early *d* that
  passeth . . . . .Hos. 13:3
I will be as the *d*. . . .Hos. 14:5

DIBON
Also called Dibon-gad and
  Dimon; A city on the
  northern banks of the Arnon,
  Num. 21:30
Israelites encamp at,
  Num. 33:45
Allotted to Gad and Reuben,
  Num. 32:3, 34; Josh. 13:9, 17
Taken by Moab, Is. 15:2, 9;
  Jer. 48:18, 22
———— A city in the tribe of
  Judah, Neh. 11:25
Probably identical with
  Diminah, Josh. 15:22

DIDST
thou *d* unto Sihon
  king . . . . .Num. 21:34
thou sawest it,
  and *d* . . . . 1 Sam. 19:5
Thou *d* blaspheme
  God . . . . 1 Kin. 21:10
So *d* thou get thee . .Neh. 9:10
wonders that
  thou *d* . . . . .Neh. 9:17
many years *d* thou
  forbear. . . . . .Neh. 9:30
us, what work
  thou *d* . . . . Ps. 44:1

How thou *d* drive
  out . . . . Ps. 44:2
ground, which *d*
  weaken . . . . .Is. 14:12
thou *d* shew
  them no . . . . .Is. 47:6
that thou *d* not lay . . . .Is. 47:7
barren, thou
  that *d*. . . . . .Is. 54:1
thy hand, thou *d*
  break . . . . Ezek. 29:7

DIE
his brethren, I *d* . . .Gen. 50:24
land of Egypt
  shall *d* . . . . Ex. 11:5
that he *d* not . . . . Lev. 16:2
thing, lest they *d* . .Num. 4:15
surely *d* in the
  wilderness . . . . .Num. 26:65
thou diest, will I *d* . Ruth 1:17
thou shalt not *d* . 2 Sam. 12:13
their breath,
  they *d* . . . . Ps. 104:29
dwell therein
  shall *d* . . . . .Is. 51:6
a man that shall *d* . . .Is. 51:12
their worm shall
  not *d* . . . . .Is. 66:24
d of grievous
  deaths . . . . Jer. 16:4
in this city shall *d*. . . . Jer. 21:9
in this city shall *d*. . . . Jer. 38:2
part of thee
  shall *d* . . . . Ezek. 5:12
it, though he
  shall *d* . . . . Ezek. 12:13
sinneth, it shall *d* . . Ezek. 18:4
sinneth, it shall *d* . Ezek. 18:20
ye *d*, O house of
  Israel . . . . Ezek. 18:31
are the dead
  which *d* . . . . Rev. 14:13

DIED
ghost, and *d* in a
  good . . . . .Gen. 25:8
and he *d* in the
  presence . . . . .Gen. 25:18
but Er and Onan *d*
  in . . . . .Gen. 46:12
the king of
  Egypt *d* . . . . Ex. 2:23
was in the river *d* . . . . Ex. 7:21
Would to God we
  had *d* . . . . Ex. 16:3
devoured them,
  and they *d* . . . . Lev. 10:2
d in the land of
  Egypt. . . . . .Num. 14:2
and Miriam *d*
  there . . . . .Num. 20:1
that *d* in the
  plague . . . . .Num. 25:9
fifth rib, that he *d* 2 Sam. 3:27
hanged himself,
  and *d* . . . . .2 Sam. 17:23
stones, that he *d*. 1 Kin. 21:13
So Saul *d* for his
  transgression . . 1 Chr. 10:13
king Uzziah *d* I saw . . . .Is. 6:1

the son of
  Benaiah *d* . . . . . .Ezek. 11:13
yet sinners,
  Christ *d* . . . . Rom. 5:8
is Christ that *d*,
  yea . . . . Rom. 8:34
despised Moses'
  law *d* . . . . .Heb. 10:28
all *d* in faith . . . . . .Heb. 11:13

DIETH
That which *d* of
  itself . . . . Lev. 22:8
of any thing that *d* Deut. 14:21
water, and *d* for
  thirst . . . . .Is. 50:2
eaten of that
  which *d* . . . . Ezek. 4:14

DIFFERENCE
have put no *d* . . . . Ezek. 22:26
And put no *d*
  between . . . . Acts 15:9
for there is no *d* . . . Rom. 3:22
no *d* between the
  Jew . . . . Rom. 10:12

DILIGENTLY
If thou wilt *d*
  hearken . . . . Ex. 15:26
thy soul *d*, lest
  thou. . . . . Deut. 4:9
shalt teach them *d* . . Deut. 6:7
Kedar, and
  consider *d* . . . . Jer. 2:10

DISCIPLES
loaves to his *d*. . . . Matt. 14:19
shew unto his *d* . . Matt. 16:21
then sent Jesus
  two *d* . . . . Matt. 21:1
were shut where
  the *d* . . . . .John 20:19
eight days again
  his *d*. . . . . .John 20:26
the *d* were called
  Christians . . . . Acts 11:26
the souls of the *d* . . Acts 14:22
the week, when
  the *d* . . . . Acts 20:7

DISMAYED
not, neither be *d*. . . Deut. 31:8
neither be thou *d* . . . .Josh. 1:9
dread not, nor
  be *d* . . . . 1 Chr. 22:13
d for the king of
  Assyria . . . . 2 Chr. 32:7
I was *d* at the
  seeing . . . . .Is. 21:3
be not *d* . . . . .Is. 41:10
be not *d* at their
  faces . . . . .Jer. 1:17
neither be *d*, O
  Israel . . . . .Jer. 30:10
their words, nor
  be *d* . . . . Ezek. 2:6

DISOBEDIENT
they were *d*, and
  rebelled . . . . .Neh. 9:26
children, and
  the *d* . . . . .Luke 1:17
abominable, and *d* . Titus 1:16
the word, being *d*. . . 1 Pet. 2:8

DISTRESS

thine enemies
shall *d* . . . . Deut. 28:53
d thee in all thy
gates . . . . Deut. 28:55
d thee in thy . . . . . Deut. 28:57
In my *d* I called
upon . . . . Ps. 18:6
In my *d* I cried
unto . . . . Ps. 120:1
needy in his *d*, a
refuge . . . . Is. 25:4
proudly in the day
of *d*. . . . . Obad. 12

DIVERS

d kinds of spices
prepared . . . . . . 2 Chr. 16:14
d diseases and
torments . . . . Matt. 4:24
d kinds of tongues. 1 Cor. 12:10
d miracles, and
gifts . . . . Heb. 2:4

DIVIDED

the waters were *d*. . . Ex. 14:21
Lord thy God
hath *d* . . . . Deut. 4:19
He *d* the sea, and
caused . . . . Ps. 78:13
and *d* them an
inheritance . . . . Ps. 78:55
the great city
was *d* . . . . Rev. 16:19

DOCTRINE

stock is a *d* of
vanities . . . . Jer. 10:8
apostles' *d* and
fellowship . . . . Acts 2:42
psalm, hath a *d*,
hath . . . . 1 Cor. 14:26
wind of *d*, by the
sleight . . . . Eph. 4:14
contrary to
sound *d* . . . . 1 Tim. 1:10
in the word and *d*. 1 Tim. 5:17
Christ, and to
the *d* . . . . 1 Tim. 6:3
hold the *d* of
Balaam . . . . Rev. 2:14

DOETH

Which *d* great
things . . . . Job 5:9
and whatsoever
he *d* . . . . Ps. 1:3
He that *d* these
things . . . . Ps. 15:5
only *d* wondrous
things . . . . Ps. 72:18
thee, as a bride *d* . . . Is. 49:18
shall he escape
that *d* . . . . Ezek. 17:15
committeth
iniquity, and *d* . . Ezek. 18:24
and he *d*
according . . . . Dan. 4:35
his works which
he *d* . . . . Dan. 9:14
saith the Lord
that *d* . . . . Amos 9:12

d evil hateth the
light . . . . John 3:20
dwelleth in me,
he *d* . . . . John 14:10
not what his
lord *d* . . . . John 15:15
that he *d* God
service . . . . John 16:2
soul of man that *d* . . Rom. 2:9
man which *d*
those things . . . . . Rom. 10:5

DOGS

shall cast it to
the *d* . . . . Ex. 22:31
For *d* have
compassed . . . . Ps. 22:16
they are all
dumb *d* . . . . Is. 56:10
are *d*, and
sorcerers . . . . Rev. 22:15

DOINGS

d of the land of
Egypt . . . . Lev. 18:3
wickedness of
thy *d* . . . . Deut. 28:20
the evil of your *d* . . . . . Is. 1:16
the fruit of their *d* . . . . Is. 3:10
the evil of your *d* . . . . Jer. 4:4
the fruit of his *d* . . . . Jer. 17:10
ways and your *d*
good . . . . Jer. 18:11
the fruit of his *d* . . . . Jer. 32:19
way, and amend
your *d* . . . . Jer. 35:15
themselves ill in
their *d* . . . . Mic. 3:4
our *d*, so hath he
dealt . . . . Zech. 1:6

DOMINION

have *d* over the
fish. . . . . Gen. 1:26
have *d* over the
fish. . . . . Gen. 1:28
have *d* also from
sea . . . . Ps. 72:8
liveth for ever,
whose *d* . . . . Dan. 4:34
d of my kingdom
men . . . . Dan. 6:26
given him *d*, and
glory . . . . Dan. 7:14
the kingdom
and *d* . . . . Dan. 7:27
d shall be from
sea . . . . Zech. 9:10
power, and might,
and *d* . . . . Eph. 1:21
whom be praise
and *d* . . . . 1 Pet. 4:11
him be glory
and *d* . . . . Rev. 1:6

DOOR

he sat in the
tent *d* . . . . Gen. 18:1
heard it in the
tent *d* . . . . Gen. 18:10
on the upper *d*
post . . . . Ex. 12:7

will pass over
the *d* . . . . Ex. 12:23
generations at
the *d* . . . . Ex. 29:42
voluntary will at
the *d* . . . . Lev. 1:3
altar that is by
the *d* . . . . Lev. 1:5
offering, which is
at the *d* . . . . Lev. 4:7
offering, which is
at the *d* . . . . Lev. 4:18
d of her father's
house. . . . . Deut. 22:21
and beat at the *d* . . Judg. 19:22
three keepers of
the *d* . . . . 2 Kin. 25:18
posts of the *d*
moved . . . . Is. 6:4
three keepers of
the *d* . . . . Jer. 52:24
Jerusalem, to
the *d* . . . . Ezek. 8:3
and, behold, at
the *d* . . . . Ezek. 8:16
and behold at
the *d* . . . . Ezek. 11:1
valley of Achor for
a *d* . . . . Hos. 2:15
great stone to
the *d* . . . . Matt. 27:60
opened the *d* of
faith. . . . . Acts 14:27

DOORS

it, and set up
the *d* . . . . Neh. 3:1
the week, when
the *d* . . . . John 20:19
d being shut, and
stood . . . . John 20:26
opened the
prison *d* . . . . Acts 5:19

DOST

Wherefore *d* thou
prophesy . . . . Jer. 32:3
Thou daughter
that *d* . . . . Jer. 48:18
thee, and thou *d*
dwell . . . . Ezek. 2:6
Lord, holy and
true, *d* . . . . Rev. 6:10

DOTH

d thy wrath wax
hot . . . . Ex. 32:11
man *d* not live by
bread . . . . Deut. 8:3
d the Lord thy
God . . . . Deut. 10:12
gift *d* blind the
eyes . . . . Deut. 16:19
Lord thy God *d*
drive . . . . Deut. 18:12
God, he it is
that *d* . . . . Deut. 31:6
Lord, he it is
that *d* . . . . Deut. 31:8
his countenance *d*
behold . . . . Ps. 11:7
why *d* thine anger
smoke . . . . Ps. 74:1

but Israel *d* not
    know . . . . Is. 1:3
fatherless,
    neither *d* . . . . Is. 1:23
stream of
    brimstone, *d* . . . . Is. 30:33
glory for that
    which *d* . . . . Jer. 2:11
Wherefore *d* the
    way . . . . Jer. 12:1
d return from his
    wickedness . . . . Jer. 23:14
what *d* the LORD
    require . . . . Mic. 6:8
morning *d* he
    bring . . . . Zeph. 3:5
forth fruit, as it *d* . . . . Col. 1:6
whereunto even
    baptism *d* . . . . 1 Pet. 3:21
sons of God, and
    it *d* . . . . 1 John 3:2

DOUBLE
flattering lips and
    with a *d* . . . . Ps. 12:2
of the LORD's
    hand *d* . . . . Is. 40:2
iniquity and their
    sin *d* . . . . Jer. 16:18
counted worthy
    of *d* . . . . 1 Tim. 5:17
purify your
    hearts, ye *d* . . . . . . James 4:8
rewarded you,
    and *d* . . . . Rev. 18:6

DRAGON
he shall slay the *d* . . . . Is. 27:1
and wounded
    the *d* . . . . Is. 51:9
Egypt, the great *d* . . Ezek. 29:3
and the *d* stood
    before . . . . Rev. 12:4
the great *d* was
    cast . . . . Rev. 12:9

DRAGONS
desolate houses,
    and *d* . . . . Is. 13:22
the habitation of *d* . . . . Is. 35:7
heaps, and a den
    of *d* . . . . Jer. 9:11
heritage waste for
    the *d* . . . . Mal. 1:3

DRAW
he said, *D* not
    nigh . . . . Ex. 3:5
I will *d* my sword . . . . Ex. 15:9
heathen, and
    will *d* . . . . Lev. 26:33
d toward mount
    Tabor . . . . Judg. 4:6
Forasmuch as this
    people *d* . . . . Is. 29:13
Pul, and Lud,
    that *d* . . . . Is. 66:19
of the flock shall *d* . . Jer. 49:20
I will *d* out a
    sword . . . . Ezek. 5:2
winds, and I will *d* . Ezek. 5:12
earth, will *d* all
    men . . . . John 12:32

us *d* near with a
    true . . . . Heb. 10:22
D nigh to God,
    and . . . . James 4:8

DREAD
Fear and *d* shall
    fall . . . . Ex. 15:16
begin to put the *d* . Deut. 2:25
fear of you and
    the *d* . . . . Deut. 11:25
d not, nor be
    dismayed . . . . . . 1 Chr. 22:13

DREAM
Pharaoh told
    them his *d* . . . . Gen. 41:8
speak unto him in
    a *d* . . . . Num. 12:6
In a *d*, in a vision . . . Job 33:15
thy servants the *d* . . . Dan. 2:4
Thy *d*, and the
    visions . . . . Dan. 2:28
and the *d* is
    certain . . . . Dan. 2:45
I saw a *d* which
    made . . . . Dan. 4:5
before him I told
    the *d* . . . . Dan. 4:8
old men shall *d*
    dreams . . . . Joel 2:28
appeared unto
    him in a *d* . . . . . . Matt. 1:20
old men shall *d*
    dreams . . . . Acts 2:17

DREAMS
dreamer of *d*, and
    giveth . . . . Deut. 13:1
that dreamer of *d* . . Deut. 13:3
that dreamer of *d* . . Deut. 13:5
d, nor by Urim . . . 1 Sam. 28:6
prophesy false *d*,
    saith . . . . Jer. 23:32
neither hearken to
    your *d* . . . . Jer. 29:8
shew the king
    his *d* . . . . Dan. 2:2
men shall dream *d* . . Joel 2:28
have told false *d* . . . Zech. 10:2

DREW
d and lifted up
    Joseph . . . . Gen. 37:28
they *d* nigh unto
    Jerusalem . . . . Matt. 21:1
having stoned
    Paul, *d* . . . . Acts 14:19
tail *d* the third
    part . . . . Rev. 12:4

DRIED
heard how the
    LORD *d* . . . . Josh. 2:10
His roots shall
    be *d* . . . . Job 18:16
My strength is
    d up . . . . Ps. 22:15
the low tree,
    have *d* . . . . Ezek. 17:24
fountain shall be *d* . Hos. 13:15
wine is *d* up, the
    oil . . . . Joel 1:10

DRINK
that the people
    may *d* . . . . Ex. 17:6
eat bread, nor *d*
    water . . . . Ex. 34:28
the *d* offering
    thereof . . . . Num. 28:7
eat bread, nor *d*
    water . . . . Deut. 9:18
shalt neither *d* . . Deut. 28:39
wring them out,
    and *d* . . . . Ps. 75:8
a mocker, strong *d* . Prov. 20:1
and through
    strong *d* . . . . Is. 28:7
thou shalt no
    more *d* . . . . Is. 51:22
D ye, and be
    drunken . . . . Jer. 25:27
heaven, and to
    pour out *d* . . . . . . Jer. 44:17
ye shall not *d*
    wine . . . . Amos 5:11
plant vineyards,
    and *d* . . . . Amos 9:14
wine, but shalt
    not *d* . . . . Mic. 6:15
ye *d*, but ye are
    not . . . . Hag. 1:6
the Lord, and
    shall *d* . . . . Luke 1:15
thee, Give me to *d* . . John 4:10
all made to *d* . . . . 1 Cor. 12:13
made all nations *d* . . Rev. 14:8
shall *d* of the wine . Rev. 14:10

DRIVE
and thou shalt *d*
    them . . . . Ex. 23:31
I will *d* out the
    Canaanite . . . . Ex. 33:2
LORD thy God
    doth *d* . . . . Deut. 18:12
of Judah could
    not *d* . . . . Josh. 15:63
God will no
    more *d* . . . . Josh. 23:13
Benjamin did
    not *d* . . . . Judg. 1:21
Neither did
    Manasseh *d* . . . . . . Judg. 1:27
How thou didst *d*
    out . . . . Ps. 44:2
places whither I
    shall *d* . . . . Jer. 24:9
and that I
    should *d* . . . . Jer. 27:10
shall *d* thee from
    men . . . . Dan. 4:25

DRIVEN
heaven, shouldest
    be *d* . . . . Deut. 4:19
shall be *d* to
    darkness . . . . Is. 8:22
countries whither
    I have *d* . . . . Jer. 23:3
countries whither
    I had *d* . . . . Jer. 23:8
places whither I
    have *d* . . . . Jer. 29:14

nations whither I
   have *d* . . . . .Jer. 29:18
countries, whither
   I have *d* . . . . Jer. 32:37
whither they
   were *d* . . . . Jer. 40:12
nations whither I
   have *d* . . . . Jer. 46:28
the lions have *d*
   him . . . . Jer. 50:17
whither thou
   hast *d*. . . . . .Dan. 9:7
the chaff that is *d* . . . Hos. 13:3

DROUGHT
and scorpions,
   and *d* . . . . Deut. 8:15
is turned into
   the *d* . . . . Ps. 32:4
satisfy thy soul
   in *d*. . . . . .Is. 58:11
careful in the year
   of *d*. . . . . Jer. 17:8

DRUNK
Jerusalem, which
   hast *d*. . . . . .Is. 51:17
satiate and
   made *d*. . . . . Jer. 46:10
concubines,
   have *d* . . . . .Dan. 5:23
And be not *d* with
   wine. . . . . .Eph. 5:18
all nations have *d* . . . Rev. 18:3

DRUNKEN
work thereof,
   as a *d* . . . . .Is. 19:14
d with their own
   blood . . . . .Is. 49:26
thou hast *d* the
   dregs . . . . .Is. 51:17
Drink ye, and be *d* . . Jer. 25:27
Make ye him *d* . . . . . Jer. 48:26
made all the
   earth *d*. . . . . Jer. 51:7
d, and shalt make
   thyself . . . . Lam. 4:21

DRY
made the sea *d*
   land . . . . .Ex. 14:21
sea upon the *d*
   ground. . . . . Ex. 14:22
Israel walked
   upon *d* . . . . Ex. 14:29
LORD stood firm
   on *d* . . . . Josh. 3:17
longeth for thee
   in a *d* . . . . Ps. 63:1
they ran in the *d*
   places . . . . Ps. 105:41
rivers of water
   in a *d* . . . . .Is. 32:2
floods upon the *d*
   ground. . . . . .Is. 44:3
I *d* up the sea, I
   make . . . . .Is. 50:2
a root out of a *d*
   ground. . . . . .Is. 53:2
I will *d* up her sea . . Jer. 51:36
have made the *d*
   tree . . . . Ezek. 17:24

spring shall
   become *d*. . . . . . .Hos. 13:15

DUE
give you rain in *d* . . . Lev. 26:4
foot shall slide
   in *d*. . . . . Deut. 32:35
d season we shall
   reap . . . . Gal. 6:9
hath in *d* times
   manifested . . . . Titus 1:3

DUMB
tongue of the *d*
   sing . . . . .Is. 35:6
her shearers is *d* . . . . . .Is. 53:7
ignorant, they are
   all *d* . . . . .Is. 56:10
speak, and be no
   more *d* . . . . Ezek. 24:27
to make *d* idols . . . . .Hab. 2:18
to the *d* stone,
   Arise . . . . .Hab. 2:19

DUNG
his *d*, shalt thou
   burn. . . . . Ex. 29:14
inwards, and his *d* . . Lev. 4:11
man taketh
   away *d* . . . . 1 Kin. 14:10
as *d* for the earth . . . Ps. 83:10
be as *d* upon the
   face . . . . Jer. 16:4

DUST
formed man of
   the *d* . . . . .Gen. 2:7
for *d* thou art, and . .Gen. 3:19
make thy seed as
   the *d* . . . . .Gen. 13:16
seed shall be as
   the *d* . . . . .Gen. 28:14
powder and *d* . . . . Deut. 28:24
of Israel, and
   put *d* . . . . .Josh. 7:6
poor out of the *d* . . 1 Sam. 2:8
brought me into
   the *d* . . . . Ps. 22:15
return to their *d* . . . Ps. 104:29
d return to the
   earth . . . . .Eccl. 12:7
hide thee in the *d*. . . . .Is. 2:10
blossom shall go
   up as *d*. . . . . .Is. 5:24
ye that dwell in *d* . . . .Is. 26:19
d made fat with
   fatness. . . . . .Is. 34:7
earth, and lick up
   the *d* . . . . .Is. 49:23
d shall be the
   serpent's . . . . .Is. 65:25
d shall cover . . . . . Ezek. 26:10
that sleep in the *d* . .Dan. 12:2
lick the *d* like a
   serpent . . . . Mic. 7:17
they shook off
   the *d* . . . . Acts 13:51

DWELL
not *d* in thy land. . . . Ex. 23:33
sware to make
   you *d* . . . . .Num. 14:30
cause his name
   to *d* . . . . Deut. 12:11

and thou shalt
   not *d* . . . . .Deut. 28:30
world, and they
   that *d*. . . . . Ps. 24:1
unclean lips,
   and I *d* . . . . .Is. 6:5
out as a tent to *d* . . . .Is. 40:22
garment, and they
   that *d*. . . . . .Is. 51:6
I *d* in the high and . . .Is. 57:15
Israel shall *d*
   safely . . . . Jer. 23:6
d in their own
   land . . . . Jer. 23:8
ye shall *d* in the
   land . . . . Jer. 35:15
shall a son of
   man *d* . . . . Jer. 49:18
d in the land . . . . . Ezek. 37:25
but ye shall not *d* . .Amos 5:11
world, and all
   that *d*. . . . . .Nah. 1:5
d in the midst of
   Jerusalem . . . . Zech. 8:3
hath said, I will *d* . .2 Cor. 6:16
blood on them
   that *d*. . . . . Rev. 6:10
that *d* upon the
   earth . . . . Rev. 13:8

DWELLEST
thou that *d*
   between . . . . Ps. 80:1
heart, O thou
   that *d*. . . . . Jer. 49:16
daughter of
   Edom, that *d*. . . . . Lam. 4:21
Son of man,
   thou *d* . . . . Ezek. 12:2

DWELLETH
thy brother that *d*. . Lev. 25:39
LORD of hosts,
   which *d* . . . . 1 Sam. 4:4
d in the secret
   place . . . . Ps. 91:1
LORD of hosts,
   which *d* . . . . .Is. 8:18
d therein shall
   languish . . . . .Hos. 4:3
but the Father
   that *d*. . . . . John 14:10
for he *d* with you . .John 14:17
Spirit of God *d* . . . .1 Cor. 3:16
in him *d* all the
   fulness. . . . . Col. 2:9
commandments *d* 1 John 3:24
one another,
   God *d* . . . . 1 John 4:12

DWELLING
thou in heaven
   thy *d* . . . . 1 Kin. 8:43
people, and on
   his *d*. . . . . 2 Chr. 36:15
pluck thee out of
   thy *d* . . . . Ps. 52:5
the *d* place of thy . . . . Ps. 74:7
from men, and
   thy *d* . . . . .Dan. 4:25
God *d* in Zion, my
   holy . . . . Joel 3:17

hath
immortality, *d* . . 1 Tim. 6:16

DWELT
came unto Haran,
and *d* . . . . .Gen. 11:31
d in the plain of
Mamre. . . . . .Gen. 13:18
And they *d* from
Havilah . . . . .Gen. 25:18
and Israel *d* in all .Num. 21:25
the Amorites,
which *d* . . . . . . .Num. 21:34
possessed it,
and *d* . . . . Josh. 19:47
and *d* among the
people . . . . Judg. 1:16
So David *d* in the
fort. . . . . .2 Sam. 5:9
and Israel *d* . . . . . . 1 Kin. 4:25
king of Syria,
that *d* . . . . 1 Kin. 15:18
(now she *d* in
Jerusalem . . . . . 2 Kin. 22:14
wherein thou
hast *d*. . . . . Ps. 74:2
it be *d* in from
generation. . . . . . . .Is. 13:20
your fathers
have *d* . . . . Ezek. 37:25
rejoicing city
that *d* . . . . .Zeph. 2:15
and *d* in a city
called . . . . Matt. 2:23
Nazareth, he
came and *d* . . . . . Matt. 4:13
was made flesh,
and *d* . . . . .John 1:14
Mesopotamia,
before he *d* . . . . Acts 7:2
which *d* in Asia
heard . . . . Acts 19:10

EAGLE
earth, as swift as
the *e* . . . . Deut. 28:49
shall fly as an *e* . . . . .Jer. 48:40
e, I will bring thee . . Jer. 49:16
fly as the *e*, and
spread . . . . .Jer. 49:22
an *e* against the
house. . . . . Hos. 8:1
fly as the *e* that
hasteth . . . . Hab. 1:8
wings of a great *e* . . Rev. 12:14

EAR
sight, and wilt
give *e* . . . . Ex. 15:26
Give *e*, O ye
heavens . . . . Deut. 32:1
thee, let now
thine *e* . . . . .Neh. 1:11
would they not
give *e* . . . . .Neh. 9:30
O Lord, and
give *e* . . . . Ps. 39:12
Give *e*, O
Shepherd. . . . . Ps. 80:1
and give *e*, O earth. . . . .Is. 1:2
he wakeneth
mine *e* . . . . .Is. 50:4
Incline your *e*, and . . . .Is. 55:3

behold, their *e* is . . . . Jer. 6:10
nor inclined
their *e* . . . . Jer. 7:24
nor inclined
their *e* . . . . Jer. 7:26
not inclined
your *e*. . . . . Jer. 35:15
He that hath an *e* . . . . Rev. 2:7
He that hath an *e* . . . Rev. 2:11
He that hath an *e* . . . Rev. 2:17

EARLY
arose *e* in the
morning . . . . . . 2 Kin. 19:35
rose up *e* in the
morning . . . . .Job 1:5
myself will
awake *e* . . . . Ps. 57:8
e will I seek thee . . . . Ps. 63:1
returned and
enquired *e* . . . . Ps. 78:34
they shall seek
me *e* . . . . Prov. 1:28
will I seek thee *e* . . . . .Is. 26:9
rising up *e* and
speaking . . . . Jer. 7:13
rising up *e*, and
sending . . . . Jer. 26:5
taught them,
rising up *e*. . . . . . . Jer. 32:33
prophets, rising
up *e* . . . . Jer. 35:15
they will seek
me *e* . . . . .Hos. 5:15
as the *e* dew that
passeth . . . . .Hos. 13:3
when Jesus was
risen *e* . . . . Mark 16:9
cometh Mary
Magdalene *e* . . . . . .John 20:1

EARS
rehearse it in the *e* . . Ex. 17:14
barley, and full *e* . . 2 Kin. 4:42
open, and let
thine *e* . . . . 2 Chr. 6:40
openeth the *e* of
men . . . . .Job 33:16
him, even into
his *e* . . . . Ps. 18:6
our *e*, O God, our
fathers . . . . Ps. 44:1
have *e*, but they
hear . . . . Ps. 115:6
fat, and make
their *e* . . . . Is. 6:10
the hearing of
his *e* . . . . Is. 11:3
be opened, and
the *e* . . . . Is. 35:5
which have *e*, and
hear . . . . Jer. 5:21
they cry in mine *e* . . Ezek. 8:18
e to hear, and hear . Ezek. 12:2
and stopped
their *e* . . . . .Zech. 7:11
He that hath *e* to
hear . . . . Matt. 11:15
uncircumcised in
heart and *e* . . . . . . Acts 7:51
e of the Lord of
sabaoth . . . . .James 5:4

EARTH
Judge of all the *e*. . .Gen. 18:25
the nations of
the *e*. . . . . .Gen. 22:18
for all the *e* is
mine . . . . Ex. 19:5
thy days upon
the *e* . . . . Deut. 4:40
the face of the *e* . . . .Deut. 7:6
kingdoms of the *e* Deut. 28:25
end of the *e*, as
swift . . . . Deut. 28:49
the one end of
the *e*. . . . . Deut. 28:64
the meek of the *e* . . . . .Is. 11:4
spreadeth abroad
the *e* . . . . .Is. 44:24
to the end of the *e* . . .Is. 48:20
unto the end of
the *e*. . . . . .Is. 49:6
face toward the *e* . . . .Is. 49:23
wrath the *e* shall
tremble . . . . .Jer. 10:10
the face of the *e* . . . . .Jer. 16:4
and justice in
the *e* . . . . .Jer. 23:5
the kingdoms of
the *e* . . . . .Jer. 24:9
heaven and in *e*. . . Matt. 28:18
the kings of the *e* . . . .Rev. 1:5
all kindreds of
the *e*. . . . . .Rev. 1:7

EARTHQUAKE
there was a great *e* . . Rev. 6:12
lightnings, and
an *e* . . . . Rev. 8:5
great *e*, and the
tenth . . . . Rev. 11:13
an *e*, and great
hail . . . . Rev. 11:19

EAST
e of Bethel, and
pitched . . . . .Gen. 12:8
west, and to the *e*. .Gen. 28:14
back by a strong *e* . . Ex. 14:21
mountains of
the *e* . . . . .Num. 23:7
Chinneroth on
the *e* . . . . Josh. 12:3
children of the *e* . . . . Judg. 6:3
the children of
the *e* . . . . Judg. 6:33
children of the *e*
lay . . . . Judg. 7:12
the *e* side of the
land . . . . Judg. 11:18
spoil them of
the *e* . . . . .Is. 11:14
thy seed from
the *e*. . . . . .Is. 43:5
faces toward the *e* . Ezek. 8:16
the *e* gate of the
Lord. . . . . Ezek. 11:1
when the *e* wind
toucheth . . . . . . Ezek. 17:10
looketh toward
the *e*. . . . . Ezek. 40:6
looketh toward
the *e*. . . . . Ezek. 40:22

followeth after
the *e* . . . . .Hos. 12:1
brethren, an *e*
wind . . . . .Hos. 13:15
Jerusalem on the *e* . Zech. 14:4
his star in the *e* . . . . . Matt. 2:2

EASTWARD
under
Ashdothpisgah *e* . Deut. 3:17
Jordan by Jericho *e* . Josh. 20:8
pitched in
Michmash, *e* . . . . 1 Sam. 13:5
house, which
looketh *e* . . . . Ezek. 11:1

EAT
thy face shalt
thou *e* . . . . .Gen. 3:19
they shall *e* the
flesh. . . . . Ex. 12:8
days shall ye *e*
unleavened . . . . Ex. 12:15
even, ye shall *e*
unleavened . . . . Ex. 12:18
(thou shalt *e*
unleavened . . . . Ex. 23:15
e bread, nor drink. . . Ex. 34:28
And there ye
shall *e* . . . . Deut. 12:7
Thou shalt *e* no
leavened . . . . Deut. 16:3
thou shalt not *e*
thereof. . . . . Deut. 28:31
thou knowest
not *e* . . . . .Deut. 28:33
for the worms
shall *e* . . . . Deut. 28:39
e the fruit of thy . . Deut. 28:51
thou shalt *e* the
fruit . . . . Deut. 28:53
children whom he
shall *e* . . . . Deut. 28:55
for she shall *e*
them . . . . Deut. 28:57
earth, that he
might *e* . . . . Deut. 32:13
e of my bread,
hath . . . . Ps. 41:9
they shall *e* the
fruit . . . . .Is. 3:10
make gardens,
and *e* . . . . .Amos 9:14
overcometh will I
give to *e* . . . . Rev. 2:7

EATEN
thy wife, and
hast *e* . . . . .Gen. 3:17
leavened bread
be *e* . . . . Ex. 13:3
be *e* in the holy
place . . . . Lev. 6:16
place shall it be *e* . . . Lev. 6:26
be *e* in the holy
place . . . . Lev. 7:6
it shall not be *e* . . . . Lev. 11:41
thine house hath *e* . . . Ps. 69:9
I have *e* my
honeycomb . . . . .Song 5:1
thereof, and it
shall be *e* . . . . .Is. 5:5
till now have I
not *e* . . . . Ezek. 4:14

And hath not *e*
upon . . . . Ezek. 18:6
the locust hath *e* . . . . Joel 2:25

EATETH
for whosoever *e*
leavened . . . . .Ex. 12:15
for whosoever *e*
that . . . . Ex. 12:19
e any manner of
blood . . . . Lev. 17:10
e bread with me
hath . . . . .John 13:18
that *e*, *e* to the
Lord . . . . Rom. 14:6

EBENEZER
Name of a memorial stone,
1 Sam. 7:12
Philistines defeat the Israelites
at, 1 Sam. 4
Philistines remove the ark
of the covenant from,
1 Sam. 5:1

EBER
Also called Heber; The
probable founder of the
Hebrew race, Gen. 10:21–25;
11:14; 1 Chr. 1:19, 25;
Luke 3:35
Prophecy concerning,
Num. 24:24
———— A Gadite, called Heber,
1 Chr. 5:13
———— A Benjamite, 1 Chr. 8:12
———— A Benjamite of
Jerusalem, 1 Chr. 8:22
———— A priest, Neh. 12:20

EDEN
The garden of Eden, Gen. 2:8–
17; 3:23, 24; 4:16; Is. 51:3;
Ezek. 28:13; 31:9, 16, 18;
36:35; Joel 2:3
———— A marketplace of costly
merchandise, 2 Kin. 19:12;
Is. 37:12; Ezek. 27:23;
Amos 1:5
———— A Gershonite,
2 Chr. 29:12
———— A Levite, 2 Chr. 31:15

EDGE
smote him with
the *e* . . . . .Num. 21:24
smote it with
the *e* . . . . .Josh. 19:47
smite them with
the *e* . . . . Jer. 21:7
shall fall by the *e* . Luke 21:24

EDOM
Signifies red; A name of Esau,
possibly on account of his
being covered with red hair,
Gen. 25:25, 30; 36:1, 8, 19
———— A name of the land
occupied by the descendants
of Esau
It extended from the Elanitic
Gulf to the Red Sea, and
was also called Idumea,
Gen. 32:3; 36:16, 17, 21;
Jer. 40:11

Noted for its wise men,
Obad. 8
Sins of, Obad. 10–14
Prophecies concerning,
Jer. 25:21–23; 27:1–11;
Dan. 11:41
Figurative of the foes of Zion,
Is. 63:1
Wilderness of, 2 Kin. 3:8

EDOMITES
Also called Edom;
Descendants of Esau, Gen. 36
Kings of, Gen. 36:31–39;
Num. 20:14; 1 Chr. 1:43–50;
Ezek. 32:29; Amos 2:1
Dukes of, Gen. 36:9–43;
Ex. 15:15; 1 Chr. 1:51–54
Land of, Gen. 32:3; Deut. 2:4,
5, 12
Protected by divine command
From desolation by the
Israelites, Deut. 2:4–6
From being held in
abhorrence by the Israelites,
Deut. 23:7
Refuse the Israelites passage
through their country,
Num. 20:18–21
Saul makes war against,
1 Sam. 14:47
David makes conquest
of, 1 Kin. 11:14–16;
1 Chr. 18:11–13
Garrisons, 2 Sam. 8:14
David writes battle songs
concerning his conquest of,
Ps. 60:8, 9; 108:9, 10
Become confederates of
Jehoshaphat, 2 Kin. 3:9, 26
Ruled by a deputy king,
1 Kin. 22:47
The Lord delivers the army
of, into the hands of
Jehoshaphat, 2 Chr. 20:20, 23
Revolt in the days of Joram,
2 Kin. 8:20–22; 2 Chr. 21:8–
10
Amaziah, king of Judah,
invades the territory
of, 2 Kin. 14:5–7, 10;
2 Chr. 25:11, 12; 28:17
Join Babylon in war against
the Israelites, Ezek. 35:5;
Amos 1:9–11; Obad. 11–16
A Jewish prophet in Babylon
denounces, Ps. 137:7;
Ezek. 25:12–14; 35:3–10
Children of the third
generation could be received
into the congregation of
Israel, Deut. 23:8
Prophecies concerning,
Gen. 25:23; 27:29, 37–40;
Num. 24:18; Is. 11:14; 21:11,
12; 34; 63:1–4; Jer. 9:25, 26;
27:1–11; 49:7–22; Lam. 4:21,
22; Ezek. 25:12–14; 32:29,
30; 35; 36:5; Joel 3:19;
Amos 1:11, 12; 9:12;
Obad. 21; Mal. 1:2–5

EHUD

A descendant of Benjamin,
1 Chr. 8:6
Called Ehi, Gen. 46:21
Probably identical with
Ahiram, mentioned in,
Num. 26:38
And Aharah, 1 Chr. 8:1
And Ahoah, 1 Chr. 8:4
And Ahiah, 1 Chr. 8:7
And Aher, 1 Chr. 7:12
—— Son of Bilhan,
1 Chr. 7:10
—— A Benjamite, the
assassin of Eglon, Judg. 3:16

EIGHTH

in the *e* day the
flesh . . . . Lev. 12:3
And on the *e*
day he . . . . Lev. 14:10
e day shall be an
holy . . . . Lev. 23:36
ordained a feast in
the *e* . . . . 1 Kin. 12:32
the *e* year of his
reign . . . . 2 Kin. 24:12
e day they made a
solemn . . . . .2 Chr. 7:9
circumcised him
the *e* . . . . Acts 7:8
Circumcised the *e*
day . . . . Phil. 3:5

EKRON

One of the five chief cities of
the Philistines, Josh. 13:3
Conquered and allotted to
Judah, Josh. 15:11, 45;
Judg. 1:18
Allotted to Dan, Josh. 19:43
The Ark of God taken to,
1 Sam. 5:10
Temple of Baal-zebub at,
2 Kin. 1:2
Prophecies against, Jer. 25:20;
Amos 1:8; Zeph. 2:4;
Zech. 9:5

ELAH

A valley where David killed
Goliath, 1 Sam. 17:2, 19; 21:9
—— An Edomite duke,
Gen. 36:41; 1 Chr. 1:52
—— Son of Caleb, 1 Chr. 4:15
—— Father of Shimei,
1 Kin. 4:18
—— Son and successor
of Baasha, king of Israel,
1 Kin. 16:6–14
—— Father of Hoshea,
2 Kin. 15:30; 17:1
—— A Benjamite chief,
1 Chr. 9:8

ELATH

Also called Eloth; A city
of Idumea, Deut. 2:8;
1 Kin. 9:26; 2 Chr. 8:17
Conquest of, by Uzziah,
2 Chr. 26:2
By the Syrians, 2 Kin. 16:6

ELDERS

thou and the *e* of
Israel . . . . Ex. 3:18
sight of the *e* of
Israel . . . . Ex. 17:6
seventy men of
the *e* . . . . .Num. 11:16
the seventy *e* . . . . .Num. 11:25
unto all the *e* of
Israel . . . . Deut. 31:9
e of Israel, and put . . .Josh. 7:6
Jephthah went
with the *e* . . . . . . Judg. 11:11
mine house, and
the *e* . . . . Ezek. 8:1
of the *e* of Israel . . . Ezek. 20:1
assembly, gather
the *e* . . . . Joel 1:14
the *e* and chief
priests . . . . Matt. 16:21
chief priests and *e* . Matt. 27:1
e by the hands of
Barnabas . . . . .Acts 11:30
had ordained
them *e* . . . . .Acts 14:23
the apostles and *e* . Acts 15:22
e and brethren
send . . . . .Acts 15:23
Let the *e* that rule 1 Tim. 5:17
e saith unto me,
Weep . . . . Rev. 5:5
midst of the *e*,
stood . . . . Rev. 5:6
four and twenty *e*
fell . . . . Rev. 5:8

ELEAZAR (ELEAZER)

Son of Aaron, Ex. 6:23; 28:1
Married a daughter of Putiel,
who bore him Phinehas,
Ex. 6:25
After the death of Nadab and
Abihu is made chief of the
tribe of Levi, Num. 3:32
Duties of, Num. 4:16
Succeeds Aaron as high priest,
Num. 20:26, 28; Deut. 10:6
Assists Moses in the census,
Num. 26:63
With Joshua, divides Palestine,
Num. 34:17
Death and burial of,
Josh. 24:33
Descendants of,
1 Chr. 24:1–19
—— An inhabitant of Kirjath-
jearim who tended the ark
of the covenant for a while,
1 Sam. 7:1, 2
—— A Merarite Levite,
1 Chr. 23:21, 22; 24:28
—— Son of Dodo, and one
of David's distinguished
heroes, 2 Sam. 23:9, 10, 13;
1 Chr. 11:12
—— Son of Phinehas,
Ezra 8:33; Neh. 12:42
—— A returned Israelitish
exile, Ezra 10:25

ELECT

mine *e*, in
whom my . . . . .Is. 42:1
deceive the very *e* . Matt. 24:24
gather together
his *e* . . . . Matt. 24:31
E according to the . . 1 Pet. 1:2

ELI

High priest, 1 Sam. 1:25; 2:11;
1 Kin. 2:27
Judge of Israel, 1 Sam. 4:18
Misjudges and mistakenly
rebukes Hannah, 1 Sam. 1:14
His benediction upon Hannah,
1 Sam. 1:17, 18; 2:20
Officiates when Samuel is
presented at the tabernacle,
1 Sam. 1:24–28
Indulgent to his corrupt sons,
1 Sam. 2:22–25, 29; 3:11–14
His solicitude for the ark,
1 Sam. 4:11–18
Death of, 1 Sam. 4:18
Prophecies of judgments upon
his house, 1 Sam. 2:27–36; 3;
1 Kin. 2:27

ELIAB

A Reubenite, progenitor
of Dathan and Abiram,
Num. 16:1, 12; 26:8, 9;
Deut. 11:6
—— Son of Helon, Num. 1:9;
2:7; 7:24, 29; 10:16
—— Ancestor of Samuel,
1 Chr. 6:27
Also called Elihu, 1 Sam. 1:1
And Eliel, 1 Chr. 6:34
—— Son of Jesse and
eldest brother of David,
1 Sam. 16:6; 17:13, 28;
1 Chr. 2:13
A prince in the tribe of Judah,
1 Chr. 27:16
—— A hero of the tribe of
Gad, 1 Chr. 12:9
—— A Levite, a porter and
musician, 1 Chr. 15:18, 20;
16:5

ELIAKIM

Son of Melea, Luke 3:30
—— Son of Hilkiah, deputy
of Hezekiah, 2 Kin. 18:18;
19:2; Is. 36:3, 11, 22; 37:2
—— Original name of
Jehoiakim, king of Judah,
2 Kin. 23:34; 2 Chr. 36:4
—— Son of Abiud, Matt. 1:13
Probably same as Shechaniah,
1 Chr. 3:21
—— A priest, Neh. 12:41

ELIASHIB

A priest, 1 Chr. 24:12
—— Name of three Israelites
mentioned in, Ezra 10:24,
27, 36
—— High priest, Neh. 3:1;
12:10; 13:4–9, 28

——— Son of Elioenai,
1 Chr. 3:24

ELIHU

A Buzite and one of Job's three
friends, Job 32; 33; 34; 35;
36; 37
——— Son of Tohu, 1 Sam. 1:1
Probably identical with Eliel,
1 Chr. 6:34
And Eliab, 1 Chr. 6:27
——— A Manassite warrior,
who joined David at Ziklag,
1 Chr. 12:20
——— A porter of the temple,
1 Chr. 26:7
——— A chief of the tribe of
Judah, 1 Chr. 27:18
Possibly Eliab, the oldest
brother of David, 1 Sam. 16:6

ELIJAH

The Tishbite, a Gileadite and
prophet, called Elias in the
N. T; Persecuted by Ahab,
1 Kin. 17:2–7; 18:7–10
Escapes to the wilderness,
where he is miraculously fed
by ravens, 1 Kin. 17:1–7
By divine direction goes to
Zarephath, where he is
sustained in the household of
a widow, whose meal and oil
are miraculousiy increased,
1 Kin. 17:8–16
Returns, and sends a message
to Ahab, 1 Kin. 18:1–16
Meets Ahab and directs him
to assemble the prophets of
Baal, 1 Kin. 18:17–20
Derisively challenges the
priests of Baal to offer
sacrifices, 1 Kin. 18:25–29
Kills the prophets of Baal,
1 Kin. 18:40
Escapes to the wilderness
from the fierceness of
Jezebel, 1 Kin. 19:1–18
Fasts for forty days,
1 Kin. 19:8
Despondency and complaints
of, 1 Kin. 19:10, 14
Consolation given to,
1 Kin. 9:11–18
Flees to the wilderness of
Damascus; directed to anoint
Hazael king over Syria, Jehu
king over Israel, and Elisha
to be a prophet in his own
place, 1 Kin. 19:9–21
Personal aspect of, 2 Kin. 1:8
Piety of, 1 Kin. 19:10, 14;
Luke 1:17; Rom. 11:2;
James 5:17
His translation, 2 Kin. 2:11
Appears to Jesus at his
transfiguration, Matt. 17:3, 4;
Mark 9:4; Luke 9:30
Type of John the Baptist,
Matt. 11:14; 16:14; 17:10–12;

Mark 9:12, 13; Luke 1:17;
John 1:21–25
Miracles of
Increases the oil of the
widow of Zarephath,
1 Kin. 17:14–16
Raises the son of the woman
of Zarephath from the dead,
1 Kin. 17:17–24
Causes rain after seven years
of drought, 1 Kin. 18:41–45;
James 5:17, 18
Causes fire to consume the
sacrifice, 1 Kin. 18:24,
36–38
Calls fire down upon the
soldiers of Ahaziah,
2 Kin. 1:10–12; Luke 9:54
Prophecies of
Foretells a drought,
1 Kin. 17:3
The destruction of Ahab and
his house, 1 Kin. 21:17–29;
2 Kin. 9:25–37
The death of Ahaziah,
2 Kin. 1:2–17
The plague sent as a
judgment upon the people
in the time of Jehoram, king
of Israel, 2 Chr. 21:12–15
——— Also called Eliah
A Benjamite chief, 1 Chr. 8:27
——— A post-exile Jew,
Ezra 10:21

ELISHA

Successor to the prophet
Elijah; Elijah instructed to
anoint, 1 Kin. 19:16
Called by Elijah, 1 Kin. 19:19
Ministers unto Elijah,
1 Kin. 19:21
Witnesses Elijah's
transporting, receives a
double portion of his spirit,
2 Kin. 2:1–15; 3:11
Mocked by the young men of
Beth-el, 2 Kin. 2:23, 24
Causes the king to restore the
property of the hospitable
Shunammite woman,
2 Kin. 8:1–6
Instructs that Jehu be anointed
as king of Israel, 2 Kin. 9:1–3
Life of, sought by Jehoram,
2 Kin. 6:31–33
Death of, 2 Kin. 13:14–20
Bones of, restore a dead man
to life, 2 Kin. 13:21
Miracles of
Divides the Jordan,
2 Kin. 2:14
Purifies the waters of Jericho
by casting salt into the
fountain, 2 Kin. 2:19–22
Increases the oil of the
woman whose sons were
to be sold for her debt,
2 Kin. 4:1–7

Raises the son of the
Shunammite woman from
the dead, 2 Kin. 4:18–37
Neutralizes the poison of the
stew, 2 Kin. 4:38–41
Increases the bread to
feed one-hundred men,
2 Kin. 4:42–44
Heals Naaman the leper,
2 Kin. 5:1–19; Luke 4:27
Sends Naaman's leprosy
upon Gehazi as a judgment,
2 Kin. 5:26, 27
Recovers the ax that had
fallen into a stream by
causing it to float, 2 Kin. 6:6
Reveals the counsel of the
king of Syria, 2 Kin. 6:12
Opens the eyes of his servant
to see the hosts of the Lord,
2 Kin. 6:17
Brings blindness upon the
army of Syria, 2 Kin. 6:18
Prophecies of
Foretells
The birth of a son to the
Shunammite woman,
2 Kin. 4:16
Bounty to the starving
people in Samaria,
2 Kin. 7:1
The death of the
unbelieving prince,
2 Kin. 7:2
Seven years of famine
in the land of Canaan,
2 Kin. 8:1–3
The death of Ben-hadad,
king of Syria, 2 Kin. 8:7–10
Elevation of Hazael to the
throne, 2 Kin. 8:11–15
The victory of Jehoash over
Syria, 2 Kin. 13:14–19

ELIZAPHAN

A Levite, Ex. 6:22; Lev. 10:4;
Num. 3:30; 1 Chr. 15:8
——— A prince of Zebulun,
Num. 34:25

ELKANAH

Grandson of Korah, Ex. 6:24;
1 Chr. 6:23
——— Father of Samuel; a
descendant of the preceding,
1 Sam. 1:1, 4, 8, 19, 21, 23;
2:11, 20; 1 Chr. 6:27, 34
——— A Levite, 1 Chr. 6:25, 36
——— A Levite, 1 Chr. 9:16
——— A Levite who joined
David at Ziklag, 1 Chr. 12:6
——— A doorkeeper for the
ark, 1 Chr. 15:23
——— A prince of Ahaz,
2 Chr. 28:7

EN-GEDI

Called Hazezon-tamar; A city
allotted to the tribe of Judah,
Josh. 15:62

shall *e* into our
  habitations . . . . Jer. 21:13
ye shall *e* into
  Egypt . . . . Jer. 42:18
they *e* into the
  land . . . . Ezek. 13:9
shall *e* into thy
  gates . . . . Ezek. 26:10
thee to *e* into life . . Matt. 18:8
e thou into the . . . Matt. 25:21
thee to *e* into life . . Mark 9:43
these things, and
  to *e* . . . . Luke 24:26
by me if any
  man *e* . . . . John 10:9
tribulation *e* . . . . . . Acts 14:22
shall in no wise *e* . . Rev. 21:27
of life, and may *e* . . Rev. 22:14

ENTERED
nobles, and *e* . . . . . Neh. 10:29
but when ye *e*, ye
  defiled . . . . Jer. 2:7
our windows, and
  is *e* . . . . Jer. 9:21
sware unto thee,
  and *e* . . . . Ezek. 16:8
forces, and
  foreigners *e* . . . . Obad. 11
rottenness *e*
  into my . . . . Hab. 3:16
How he *e* into the
  house . . . . Matt. 12:4
I *e* into thine
  house . . . . Luke 7:44
as by one man
  sin *e* . . . . Rom. 5:12
us *e*, even Jesus,
  made . . . . Heb. 6:20
his own blood
  he *e* . . . . Heb. 9:12
e into the holy
  places . . . . Heb. 9:24
which have
  reaped are *e* . . . . . . James 5:4
many deceivers
  are *e* . . . . 2 John 7

ENTERING
and cast it at the *e* . Josh. 8:29
mount Hermon
  unto the *e* . . . . Josh. 13:5
congregation,
  from the *e* . . . . . . 1 Kin. 8:65
there is no house,
  no *e* . . . . Is. 23:1
e of the gates of
  Jerusalem . . . . Jer. 1:15
bear a burden,
  even *e* . . . . Jer. 17:27
havock of the
  church, *e* . . . . Acts 8:3
us what manner
  of *e* . . . . 1 Thess. 1:9

ENVY
The *e* also of
  Ephraim . . . . Is. 11:13
patriarchs, moved
  with *e* . . . . Acts 7:9
were filled with *e* . . Acts 13:45
not, moved with *e* . . Acts 17:5

EPHESUS
Paul visits and preaches in,
  Acts 18:19–21; 19; 20:16–38
Apollos visits and preaches in,
  Acts 18:18–28
Sceva's sons attempt to expel a
  demon in, Acts 19:13–16
Timothy directed by Paul to
  remain at, 1 Tim. 1:3
Paul sends Tychicus to,
  2 Tim. 4:12
Onesiphorus lives at,
  2 Tim. 1:18
The congregation at, Rev. 1:11
Apocalyptic message to,
  Rev. 2:1–7
See Paul's Epistle to the
  Ephesians, Eph. 1

EPHOD
breastplate, and
  an *e* . . . . Ex. 28:4
robe, and put
  the *e* . . . . Lev. 8:7
gods, and made
  an *e* . . . . Judg. 17:5
incense, to wear
  an *e* . . . . 1 Sam. 2:28

EPHRAIM
Second son of Joseph,
  Gen. 41:52
Adopted by Jacob, Gen. 48:5
Blessed before Manasseh;
  prophecies concerning,
  Gen. 48:14–20
Descendants of, Num. 26:35–
  37; 1 Chr. 7:20–27
Mourned for his sons,
  1 Chr. 7:21, 22
——— A tribe of Israel
Prophecy concerning,
  Gen. 49:25, 26; Is. 7;
  9:18–21; 11:13; 28:1; Jer. 31;
  Hos. 5:14; Zech. 9:10; 10:7
Numbered at Mount Sinai
  and in plains of Moab,
  Num. 1:33; 26:37
Position in camp and march,
  Num. 2:18, 24; 10:22
Blessed by Moses,
  Deut. 33:13–17
Territory allotted to, after
  the conquest of Canaan,
  Josh. 16:5–9; 17:9, 10, 15–18;
  1 Chr. 7:28, 29
Failed to expel the Canaanites,
  Josh. 16:10
Captured Beth-el in battle,
  Judg. 1:22–25
Rebuked Gideon for not
  summoning them to join the
  war against the Midianites,
  Judg. 8:1
Joined Gideon against the
  Midianites, Judg. 7:24, 25
Their jealousy of Jephthah,
  Judg. 12:1
Defeated by Jephthah,
  Judg. 12:4–6
Received Ish-bosheth as king,
  2 Sam. 2:9

Jeroboam set up a golden calf
  in Beth-el, 1 Kin. 12:29
Revolted from house of David,
  1 Kin. 12:25; 2 Chr. 10:16
Some of tribe joined Judah
  under Asa, 2 Chr. 15:9
Chastised Ahaz and Judah,
  2 Chr. 28:7
Joined Hezekiah in
  reinstituting the Passover,
  2 Chr. 30:18
Joined in the destruction
  of idolatrous forms in
  Jerusalem, 2 Chr. 31:1
Submitted to the scepter of
  Josiah, 2 Chr. 34:1–6
Envied by other tribes,
  Is. 11:13; Jer. 7:15;
  Ezek. 37:16, 19; Hos. 13:1
Worshiped Baal, Hos. 13:1
Sin of, remembered by God,
  Hos. 13:12
Reallotment of territory, to, by
  Ezekiel, Ezek. 48:5
Name of, applied to the ten
  tribes, 2 Chr. 17:2; 25:6, 7;
  Is. 7:8, 9; 11:12, 13; 17:3;
  Jer. 31:18, 20; Hos. 4:17; 5:3,
  5; 6:4, 10; 8:11; 12:14
Tribe of, called Joseph, Rev. 7:8
——— Mount of
A range of low mountains,
  Josh. 17:15–18
Joshua has his inheritance in,
  Judg. 2:9
Residence of Micah, Judg. 17:8
A place of hiding for Israelites,
  1 Sam. 14:22
Sheba resides in, 2 Sam. 20:21
Noted for rich pastures,
  Jer. 50:19
Prophecy concerning its
  conversion, Jer. 31:6
——— A forest east of the
  Jordan River
Absalom killed in,
  2 Sam. 18:6–17
——— A gate of Jerusalem,
  2 Kin. 14:13; 2 Chr. 25:23;
  Neh. 8:16; 12:39
——— A city in the territory of
  Ephraim, 2 Chr. 13:19
Jesus escapes to, from the
  persecution of Caiaphas,
  John 11:54

EPICUREANS
Referring to those who are
  fastidious in their tastes or
  enjoyments, connoisseurs;
  Reject John the Baptist,
  Matt. 11:18; Luke 7:33
Doctrines propagated by,
  familiar to Solomon,
  Eccl. 2:1–10
To Paul, 1 Cor. 15:32
Dispute with Paul, Acts 17:18

ER
Son of Judah, Gen. 38:3,
  6, 7; 46:12; Num. 26:19;
  1 Chr. 2:3

——— A son of Shelah,
1 Chr. 4:21
——— An ancestor of Jesus,
Luke 3:28

ESAU
Older of the twin sons born to
Isaac and Rebekah; Birth of,
Gen. 25:19–26; 1 Chr. 1:34
Called Edom, Gen. 36:1, 8
A hunter, Gen. 25:27, 28
Beloved by Isaac, Gen. 25:27,
28
Sells his birthright for a
single meal, Gen. 25:29–34;
Mal. 1:2; Rom. 9:13;
Heb. 12:16
Marries a Hittite woman,
Gen. 26:34
His marriage a grief to Isaac
and Rebekah, Gen. 26:35
Polygamy of, Gen. 26:34; 28:9;
36:2, 3
Is defrauded of his father's
blessing by Jacob, Gen. 27;
Heb. 11:20
Meets Jacob on the return
of the latter from Haran,
Gen. 33:1
With Jacob, buries his father,
Gen. 35:29
Descendants of, Gen. 36
Hostility of descendants of,
toward the descendants of
Jacob, Obad. 10–14
Ancestor of Edomites, Jer. 49:8
Mount of Edom, called Mount
of Esau, Obad. 8, 9, 18–21
His name used to denote
his descendants and their
country, Deut. 2:5; Jer. 49:8,
10; Obad. 6
Prophecies concerning,
Obad. 18

ESCAPE
one of them *e* . . . 1 Kin. 18:40
speaketh lies shall
not *e*. . . . . Prov. 19:5
pleaseth God
shall *e* . . . . Eccl. 7:26
will send those
that *e* . . . . Is. 66:19
shall not be able
to *e*. . . . . Jer. 11:11
of Judah shall
not *e*. . . . . Jer. 32:4
and thou shalt
not *e*. . . . . Jer. 38:18
and thou shalt
not *e*. . . . . Jer. 38:23
small number
that *e* . . . . Jer. 44:28
let none thereof *e* . . . Jer. 50:29
e of you shall
remember . . . . Ezek. 6:9
e that doeth such
things . . . . Ezek. 17:15
vipers, how can
ye *e*. . . . . Matt. 23:33

also make a way
to *e*. . . . . 1 Cor. 10:13
and they shall
not *e*. . . . . .1 Thess. 5:3
shall we *e*, if we
neglect. . . . . Heb. 2:3

ESCAPED
given his sons
that *e* . . . . Num. 21:29
and *e* to the cave
Adullam . . . . 1 Sam. 22:1
named
Abiathar, *e*. . . . . 1 Sam. 22:20
that are *e* of Israel . . . . .Is. 4:2
e of the house of
Jacob . . . . Is. 10:20
e of the house of
Judah . . . . Is. 37:31
e, and thou shalt
speak . . . . Ezek. 24:27
violence of fire, *e* . .Heb. 11:34

ESTABLISH
And I will *e* my
covenant . . . . Gen. 17:7
and I will *e* my
covenant . . . . .Gen. 17:19
e thee an holy
people . . . . Deut. 28:9
bowels, and I
will *e* . . . . 2 Sam. 7:12
and I will *e* the
throne . . . . 1 Chr. 22:10
but *e* the just. . . . . Ps. 7:9
order it, and to *e*. . . . . . .Is. 9:7
people, to *e* the
earth . . . . Is. 49:8
gospel of Christ,
to *e*. . . . . .1 Thess. 3:2

ESTABLISHED
which thy hands
have *e* . . . . Ex. 15:17
shall the matter
be *e* . . . . Deut. 19:15
made thee, and *e*
thee . . . . Deut. 32:6
LORD have *e* thy
kingdom . . . . . .1 Sam. 13:13
kingdom shall
be *e* . . . . 2 Sam. 7:16
a rock, and *e* my
goings . . . . Ps. 40:2
e for ever as the
moon. . . . . Ps. 89:37
house shall be *e* . . . . . . .Is. 2:2
he hath *e* it, he
created . . . . Is. 45:18
his power, he
hath *e*. . . . . Jer. 10:12
the LORD shall
be *e* . . . . Mic. 4:1
every word may
be *e* . . . . Matt. 18:16

ESTHER
Also called Hadassah; Niece of
Mordecai, Esth. 2:7, 15
Chosen queen, Esth. 2:17
Tells the king of the plot
against his life, Esth. 2:22
Fasts on account of the decree

to destroy the Israelites;
Accuses Haman to the king;
intercedes for her people,
Esth. 4; 5; 6; 7; 8; 9

ETAM
A village of Simeon,
1 Chr. 4:32
——— A city in Judah,
2 Chr. 11:6
——— A name on the list
of Judah's descendants,
1 Chr. 4:3
——— A rock where Samson
was bound and delivered to
the Philistines, Judg. 15:8,
11–13

ETERNAL
righteous into
life *e* . . . . Matt. 25:46
perish, but have *e*· · ·John 3:15
he should give *e*
life . . . . .John 17:2
And this is life *e* · · · ·John 17:3
immortality, *e* life· · · Rom. 2:7
gift of God is *e* life . Rom. 6:23
King *e*, immortal,
invisible . . . . 1 Tim. 1:17
In hope of *e* life · · · · Titus 1:2
place, having
obtained *e* . . . . . . .Heb. 9:12
the *e* Spirit offered . .Heb. 9:14
receive the
promise of *e* . . . . . .Heb. 9:15
e glory by Christ
Jesus . . . . 1 Pet. 5:10
shew unto you
that *e* . . . . 1 John 1:2
e life, and this life. 1 John 5:11
true God, and *e*
life . . . . 1 John 5:20
vengeance of *e* fire . . . . .Jude 7

ETHIOPIA
A region in Africa, inhabited
by the descendants of Ham;
The inhabitants of, black,
Jer. 13:23
Within the Babylonian empire,
Esth. 1:1
Rivers of, Gen. 10:6; Is. 18:1
Bordered Egypt on the south,
Ezek. 29:10
Was called the land of Cush,
mentioned in, Gen. 10:6;
1 Chr. 1:9; Is. 11:11
Warriors of, 2 Chr. 12:3;
Jer. 46:9; Ezek. 38:5
Defeated by Asa, 2 Chr. 14:9–
15; 16:8
Invaded Syria, 2 Kin. 19:9
Merchandise of, Is. 45:14
Moses marries a woman of,
Num. 12:1
Ebel-melech, at the court of
Babylon, native of
Treats Jeremiah kindly,
Jer. 38:7–13; 39:15–18
Candace, queen of, Acts 8:27
A eunuch from, becomes
a disciple beause of the

preaching of Philip,
Acts 8:27–39
Prophecies concerning the
conversion of, Ps. 68:31;
87:4; Is. 45:14; Dan. 11:43
Desolation of, Is. 18:1–6;
20:2–6; 43:3; Ezek. 30:4–9;
Hab. 3:7; Zeph. 2:12

EUPHRATES
A river in the garden of Eden,
Gen. 2:14
The eastern limit of
the kingdom of Israel,
Gen. 15:18; Ex. 23:31;
Deut. 1:7; 11:24; Josh. 1:4;
2 Sam. 8:3; 1 Kin. 4:21;
1 Chr. 5:9; 18:3
Pharaoh-necho, king of
Egypt, made conquest to,
2 Kin. 24:7; Jer. 46:2–10
On the banks of, Jeremiah
symbolically buries his sash,
Jer. 13:1–7
Casts the scroll containing the
prophecies against Babylon
into, Jer. 51:59–64
Symbolical
The inundations of, of the
extension of the empire of
Assyria, Is. 8:6–8
In the symbolisms of the
Apocalypse, Rev. 9:14;
16:12

EVENING
shall kill it in
the *e* . . . . Ex. 12:6
shall order it
from *e* . . . . Ex. 27:21
and the *e* meat
offering . . . . 2 Kin. 16:15
and every *e* burnt
sacrifices . . . . . . 2 Chr. 13:11
my hands as the *e*
sacrifice . . . . Ps. 141:2
be shut until the *e* . Ezek. 46:2
the vision of the *e* . .Dan. 8:26
fierce than the *e*
wolves . . . . .Hab. 1:8
lie down in the *e* . . . . Zeph. 2:7
the same day at *e* . .John 20:19

EVERLASTING
generations for
an *e* . . . . .Gen. 17:7
Canaan, for an *e*
possession . . . . . . .Gen. 17:8
e to *e*, thou art
God . . . . Ps. 90:2
mighty God, The *e*
Father . . . . .Is. 9:6
e kindness will I
have . . . . .Is. 54:8
I will make an *e*
covenant . . . . .Is. 55:3
living God, and
an *e* . . . . .Jer. 10:10
dominion is an *e*
dominion . . . . .Dan. 7:14
kingdom is an *e*
kingdom . . . . .Dan. 7:27

iniquity, and to
bring in *e* . . . . .Dan. 9:24
from of old,
from *e* . . . . Mic. 5:2
ye cursed, into *e*
fire . . . . Matt. 25:41
go away into *e*
punishment . . . . Matt. 25:46
perish, but have *e* . . .John 3:16
believeth on the
Son hath *e* . . . . . . .John 3:36
springing up
into *e* . . . . .John 4:14
sent me, hath *e*
life . . . . .John 5:24
of *e* life, lo, we
turn . . . . Acts 13:46
honour and
power *e* . . . . 1 Tim. 6:16
blood of the *e*
covenant . . . . . . .Heb. 13:20

EVERMORE
oppressed and
spoiled *e* . . . . . . .Deut. 28:29
are pleasures for *e* . . Ps. 16:11
blessing, even life
for *e* . . . . Ps. 133:3
midst of them
for *e* . . . . .Ezek. 37:26
e, knoweth that I
lie . . . . 2 Cor. 11:31
behold, I am alive
for *e* . . . . Rev. 1:18

EVIL
of man's heart is *e* . .Gen. 8:21
his eye shall be *e* .Deut. 28:54
her eye shall be *e* .Deut. 28:56
behold, I will
bring *e* . . . . 1 Kin. 14:10
to do *e* in the
sight . . . . 2 Kin. 17:17
God, and
eschewed *e* . . . . Job 1:1
heard of all this *e* . . . .Job 2:11
put away the *e* of
your . . . . .Is. 1:16
is an *e* thing and
bitter . . . . Jer. 2:19
e heart, and went
backward . . . . Jer. 7:24
against this city
for *e* . . . . .Jer. 21:10
every man from
his *e* . . . . .Jer. 35:15
well, and saw no *e* . .Jer. 44:17
upon us a great *e* . . .Dan. 9:12
watched upon
the *e* . . . . .Dan. 9:14
repenteth him of
the *e* . . . . Joel 2:13
eyes upon them
for *e* . . . . Amos 9:4
none *e* can come
upon . . . . Mic. 3:11
sprinkled from
an *e* . . . . .Heb. 10:22
rendering *e* for *e* . . . . 1 Pet. 3:9

EVILDOERS
iniquity, a seed of *e* . . . .Is. 1:4

e, that none doth
return . . . . .Jer. 23:14
speak against you
as *e* . . . . 1 Pet. 2:12
evil of you, as of *e* . 1 Pet. 3:16

EXALT
father's God, and
I will *e* . . . . Ex. 15:2
my horn shalt
thou *e* . . . . Ps. 92:10
E ye the Lord
our God . . . . Ps. 99:5
into heaven, I
will *e* . . . . .Is. 14:13
I will *e* thee, I will . . . .Is. 25:1
e himself, and
magnify . . . . .Dan. 11:36
Though thou *e*
thyself . . . . Obad. 4
And whosoever
shall *e* . . . . Matt. 23:12

EXALTED
ever, and they
are *e* . . . . .Job 36:7
righteous shall
be *e* . . . . Ps. 75:10
his horn shall be *e* . . Ps. 112:9
mountains, and
shall be *e* . . . . .Is. 2:2
Lord alone shall
be *e* . . . . .Is. 2:11
Lord alone shall
be *e* . . . . .Is. 2:17
of hosts shall be *e* . . . . .Is. 5:16
prudently, he shall
be *e* . . . . .Is. 52:13
the high tree,
have *e* . . . . .Ezek. 17:24
their heart was *e* . . . .Hos. 13:6
mountains, and it
shall be *e* . . . . Mic. 4:1
himself shall be *e* Matt. 23:12
right hand of
God *e* . . . . Acts 2:33
Him hath God *e*
with . . . . Acts 5:31

EXCEEDING
thy shield, and
thy *e* . . . . .Gen. 15:1
voice of the
trumpet *e* . . . . Ex. 19:16
Talk no more so *e*
proudly . . . . 1 Sam. 2:3
Hadadezer, king
David took *e* . . . . . 2 Sam. 8:8
Israel and Judah
is *e* . . . . Ezek. 9:9
Rejoice, and be *e*
glad . . . . Matt. 5:12
his glory with *e*
joy . . . . Jude 24
plague thereof
was *e* . . . . Rev. 16:21

EXCELLENCY
his *e* on the sky. . .Deut. 33:26
sword of thy *e* . . . .Deut. 33:29
of the Chaldees' *e* . . . .Is. 13:19
e of Carmel and
Sharon . . . . .Is. 35:2

f shall be as
 flames . . . . .Is. 13:8
tears from off all *f* . . . . Is. 25:8
hid as it were
 our *f*. . . . . .Is. 53:3
afraid of their *f* . . . . Jer. 1:8
their *f*, lest I
 confound. . . . . Jer. 1:17
have made their *f*
 harder . . . . Jer. 5:3
Zion with their *f*
 thitherward . . . . Jer. 50:5
the LORD, and
 their *f* . . . . Ezek. 8:16
us confusion of *f* . . . . Dan. 9:7
all loins, and the *f* . .Nah. 2:10

FAIL

eyes shall look,
 and *f* . . . . .Deut. 28:32
not *f* thee, nor
 forsake. . . . . Deut. 31:6
f thee, neither
 forsake. . . . . Deut. 31:8
I will not *f* thee. . . . . .Josh. 1:5
soul, there shall
 not *f*. . . . . .1 Kin. 2:4
spirit of Egypt
 shall *f* . . . . .Is. 19:3
not *f* nor be
 discouraged . . . . .Is. 42:4
the spirit should *f* . . .Is. 57:16
Mine eyes do *f*
 with . . . . Lam. 2:11
ye *f*, they may
 receive. . . . . .Luke 16:9
years shall not *f* . . . .Heb. 1:12
for the time
 would *f* . . . . .Heb. 11:32

FAILETH

flesh and my
 heart *f* . . . . Ps. 73:26
not one *f* . . . . .Is. 40:26
judgment to light,
 he *f* . . . . Zeph. 3:5
heavens that *f*. . . . Luke 12:33

FAINT

inhabitants of the
 land *f*. . . . . .Josh. 2:9
the whole heart *f* . . . . . .Is. 1:5
shall all hands
 be *f*. . . . . .Is. 13:7
shall walk, and
 not *f*. . . . . .Is. 40:31
pray, and not to *f* . . .Luke 18:1
received mercy,
 we *f* . . . . .2 Cor. 4:1
shall reap, if we *f* . . . . Gal. 6:9

FAITH

thy *f* hath made
 thee . . . . Matt. 9:22
thy *f* hath made
 thee . . . . Mark 5:34
woman, Thy *f*
 hath saved . . . . . .Luke 7:50
continue in the *f*. . . Acts 14:22
their hearts by *f* . . . . Acts 15:9
repentance
 toward God, and *f* . Acts 20:21
are sanctified by *f*. . Acts 26:18

that your *f* is
 spoken. . . . . Rom. 1:8
though I have all *f* .1 Cor. 13:2
by the *f* of Jesus
 Christ . . . . Gal. 2:16
flesh I live by the *f* . . Gal. 2:20
but *f* which
 worketh. . . . . Gal. 5:6
ye continue in
 the *f*. . . . . Col. 1:23
ceasing your work
 of *f*. . . . . .1 Thess. 1:3
conscience, and
 of *f*. . . . . 1 Tim. 1:5
full assurance of *f*. .Heb. 10:22
By *f* Noah, being
 warned . . . . .Heb. 11:7
These all died in *f* .Heb. 11:13
finisher of our *f* . . . .Heb. 12:2
this world rich
 in *f*. . . . . .James 2:5

FAITHFUL

God, he is God,
 the *f*. . . . . Deut. 7:9
moon, and as a *f*
 witness . . . . Ps. 89:37
the LORD that is *f* . . . .Is. 49:7
thou good and *f*
 servant . . . . Matt. 25:21
God is *f*, by
 whom ye . . . . .1 Cor. 1:9
beloved son, and *f* .1 Cor. 4:17
but God is *f*, who
 will . . . . 1 Cor. 10:13
a *f* saying, and
 worthy. . . . . 1 Tim. 1:15
This is a *f* saying . . . Titus 3:8
f high priest in
 things . . . . .Heb. 2:17
confess our sins,
 he is *f* . . . . 1 John 1:9
Christ, who is
 the *f*. . . . . Rev. 1:5
be thou *f* unto
 death . . . . Rev. 2:10
saith the Amen,
 the *f*. . . . . Rev. 3:14
and chosen, and *f*. . Rev. 17:14

FALL

Fear and dread
 shall *f* . . . . Ex. 15:16
your enemies
 shall *f* . . . . Lev. 26:8
shall *f* when none
 pursueth . . . . Lev. 26:36
land, to *f* by the
 sword . . . . .Num. 14:3
Your carcases
 shall *f* . . . . .Num. 14:29
Yea, all kings
 shall *f* . . . . Ps. 72:11
their host shall *f*. . . . . .Is. 34:4
drunken, and
 spue, and *f* . . . . . . .Jer. 25:27
f, at the cry the
 noise . . . . .Jer. 49:21
of Babylon shall *f* . . .Jer. 51:44
f by the sword
 round. . . . . Ezek. 5:12

And the slain
 shall *f* . . . . Ezek. 6:7
they of Dedan
 shall *f* . . . . Ezek. 25:13
in league, shall *f*. . . Ezek. 30:5
of his *f*, when I
 cast . . . . Ezek. 31:16
shall *f* by the
 sword . . . . .Hos. 13:16
grain *f* upon the
 earth . . . . .Amos 9:9
and the stars
 shall *f* . . . . Matt. 24:29
shall *f* by the edge . Luke 21:24
be rich *f* into
 temptation . . . . . . 1 Tim. 6:9

FALLEN

be waxen poor,
 and *f* . . . . Lev. 25:35
that your terror
 is *f*. . . . . .Josh. 2:9
whereof they are *f* . . . Ps. 57:6
reproached thee
 are *f*. . . . . Ps. 69:9
for thy harvest is *f* . . . .Is. 16:9
Babylon is *f*, is *f* . . . . . .Is. 21:9
f upon thy
 summer fruits . . . .Jer. 48:32
f, her walls are
 thrown . . . . .Jer. 50:15
of David that is *f* . .Amos 9:11
Babylon is *f*, is *f* . . . . Rev. 14:8
Babylon the great
 is *f*. . . . . Rev. 18:2

FALLETH

night, when deep
 sleep *f* . . . . .Job 33:15
down, as the leaf *f* . . . .Is. 34:4
that goeth out,
 and *f* . . . . .Jer. 21:9
the flower
 thereof *f* . . . . 1 Pet. 1:24

FALSE

Thou shalt not
 bear *f*. . . . . Ex. 20:16
shalt not raise a *f*. . . . Ex. 23:1
thee far from a *f*
 matter . . . . Ex. 23:7
f witnesses are
 risen . . . . Ps. 27:12
A *f* balance is
 abomination . . . . . Prov. 11:1
a *f* vision and
 divination . . . . .Jer. 14:14
that prophesy *f*
 dreams . . . . .Jer. 23:32
seen for thee *f*
 burdens. . . . . Lam. 2:14
and have told *f* . . . .Zech. 10:2
adulterers, and
 against *f* . . . . Mal. 3:5
Beware of *f*
 prophets . . . . Matt. 7:15
Thou shalt not
 bear *f*. . . . . Matt. 19:18
f Christs, and *f*
 prophets . . . . Matt. 24:24
yea, though
 many *f*. . . . . Matt. 26:60

FALSELY

Thou shalt not
bear f . . . . Rom. 13:9
are f apostles,
deceitful . . . . . . 2 Cor. 11:13
But there were f
prophets . . . . 2 Pet. 2:1
because many f
prophets . . . . 1 John 4:1
f prophet that
wrought . . . . Rev. 19:20
beast and the f
prophet . . . . Rev. 20:10

FALSELY

f, neither shalt
thou . . . . Lev. 19:12
prophets
prophesy f . . . . Jer. 5:31
every one
dealeth f . . . . Jer. 6:13
every one
dealeth f . . . . Jer. 8:10
For they
prophesy f . . . . Jer. 29:9
Jeremiah, Thou
speakest f . . . . Jer. 43:2
be ashamed that f
accuse . . . . 1 Pet. 3:16

FAMILIAR

them that have f
spirits . . . . Lev. 19:31
woman that
hath a f . . . . Lev. 20:27
consulter with f
spirits . . . . Deut. 18:11
enchantments,
and dealt with f . 2 Kin. 21:6
a f spirit, to
enquire . . . . 1 Chr. 10:13
dealt with a f
spirit . . . . 2 Chr. 33:6
Yea, mine own f
friend . . . . Ps. 41:9
them that have f
spirits . . . . Is. 8:19

FAMILIES

f of the earth be
blessed . . . . Gen. 12:3
f of the earth be
blessed . . . . Gen. 28:14
after their f . . . . . Num. 26:20
are the f of the
Levites . . . . 1 Chr. 6:19
will call all the f . . . . . Jer. 1:15
upon the f that
call . . . . Jer. 10:25
f of the north,
saith . . . . Jer. 25:9

FAMILY

every man unto
his f . . . . Lev. 25:10
Shelah, the f of . . . Num. 26:20
man, or woman,
or f . . . . Deut. 29:18
a f, and I will
bring . . . . Jer. 3:14

FAMINE

Moreover he
called for a f . . . . . Ps. 105:16

sword, and by
the f . . . . Jer. 14:12
they say, Sword
and f . . . . Jer. 14:15
for the f, to the f . . . . . Jer. 15:2
the sword, and
by f . . . . Jer. 16:4
children to the f . . . . Jer. 18:21
sword, and from
the f . . . . Jer. 21:7
sword, and by
the f . . . . Jer. 21:9
send the sword,
the f . . . . Jer. 24:10
sword, with the f . . . Jer. 29:18
sword, and of
the f . . . . Jer. 32:24
the sword, by
the f . . . . Jer. 38:2
sword and by the f . . Jer. 44:27
month, the f was
sore . . . . Jer. 52:6
pestilence, and
with f . . . . Ezek. 5:12
the sword, by
the f . . . . Ezek. 6:11
months, when
great f . . . . Luke 4:25
and mourning,
and f . . . . Rev. 18:8

FAST

f, I will not hear . . . . Jer. 14:12
ye, Stand f, and
prepare . . . . Jer. 46:14
Sanctify ye a f, call . . Joel 1:14
years, did ye at
all f . . . . Zech. 7:5
Watch ye, stand f
in . . . . 1 Cor. 16:13
affairs, that ye
stand f . . . . Phil. 1:27
if we hold f the
confidence . . . . Heb. 3:6
God, let us hold f . . . Heb. 4:14

FAT

shalt take all the f . . Ex. 29:13
all the f is the
LORD . . . . Lev. 3:16
that ye eat
neither f . . . . Lev. 3:17
all the f of the
bullock . . . . Lev. 4:8
kidneys, and the f . . . Lev. 4:9
shall burn all his f . . Lev. 4:26
f thereof, as the f . . . Lev. 4:35
shalt burn their f . Num. 18:17
But Jeshurun
waxed f . . . . Deut. 32:15
hearken than
the f . . . . 1 Sam. 15:22
strong cities,
and a f . . . . Neh. 9:25
diligent shall be
made f . . . . Prov. 13:4
and the f of fed
beasts . . . . Is. 1:11
heart of this
people f . . . . Is. 6:10
blood, it is made f . . . Is. 34:6

dust made f with
fatness . . . . Is. 34:7
with the f of thy
sacrifices . . . . Is. 43:24
good fold, and
in a f . . . . Ezek. 34:14
offer my bread,
the f . . . . Ezek. 44:7
f and the blood,
saith . . . . Ezek. 44:15

FATHER

unto Abraham
thy f . . . . Gen. 26:3
God of Abraham
thy f . . . . Gen. 28:13
Honour thy f and
thy . . . . Ex. 20:12
will be his f, and . 2 Sam. 7:14
thou the God of
thy f . . . . 1 Chr. 28:9
F, The Prince of
Peace . . . . Is. 9:6
delivered unto me
of my F . . . . . . Matt. 11:27
the glory of his F . Matt. 16:27
ye blessed of my F Matt. 25:34
the F, and of the
Son . . . . Matt. 28:19
throne of his f
David . . . . Luke 1:32
begotten of the F . . John 1:14
of the F, he hath
declared . . . . John 1:18
Ye are of your f
the . . . . John 8:44
and my F are one . . John 10:30
cometh unto the F . John 14:6
the F, even the
Spirit . . . . John 15:26
peace from God
our F . . . . Rom. 1:7
cometh down
from the F . . . . . James 1:17
the F, and was
manifested . . . . . 1 John 1:2

FATHERLESS

stranger, and the f . Deut. 14:29
stranger, and the f . Deut. 16:11
stranger, f, and
widow . . . . Deut. 27:19
A father of the f . . . . Ps. 68:5
oppressed, judge
the f . . . . Is. 1:17
they judge not
the f . . . . Is. 1:23
they may rob the f . . . Is. 10:2
the f, yet they
prosper . . . . Jer. 5:28
the stranger, the f . . . Jer. 7:6
the stranger, the f . . . Jer. 22:3
the widow, nor
the f . . . . Zech. 7:10
the widow, and
the f . . . . Mal. 3:5

FATHERS

thou shalt go to
thy f . . . . Gen. 15:15
LORD God of
your f . . . . Ex. 3:15

the iniquity of
the *f*. . . . . Ex. 20:5
the iniquity of
the *f*. . . . . Ex. 34:7
f, hath the Lord
brought . . . . Deut. 7:8
neither thou nor
thy *f*. . . . . Deut. 28:36
neither thou nor
thy *f*. . . . . Deut. 28:64
shalt sleep with
thy *f*. . . . . 2 Sam. 7:12
Lord God of
their *f* . . . . 2 Chr. 36:15
sojourner, as all
my *f*. . . . . Ps. 39:12
shall be thy
nursing *f*. . . . . .Is. 49:23
inheritance unto
your *f*. . . . . Jer. 3:18
you and to your *f* . . . Jer. 35:15
and our *f*, our
kings . . . . Jer. 44:17
servant, wherein
your *f*. . . . . Ezek. 37:25
take hold of your *f* . . Zech. 1:6
your *f* did, so
do ye . . . . Acts 7:51
prophets have not
your *f*. . . . . Acts 7:52
of the law of the *f*. . . Acts 22:3
Whose are the *f*,
and. . . . . Rom. 9:5

FAVOUR

Lord gave the
people *f*. . . . . Ex. 12:36
find no *f* in his
eyes . . . . Deut. 24:1
nor shew *f* to the
young . . . . Deut. 28:50
because thou
hadst a *f* . . . . Ps. 44:3
will shew them
no *f* . . . . .Is. 27:11
in *f* with God and
man . . . . Luke 2:52
Praising God, and
having *f*. . . . . Acts 2:47

FEAR

a vision, saying, *F*. . .Gen. 15:1
F and dread shall
fall . . . . Ex. 15:16
Thou shalt *f* the
Lord. . . . . Deut. 6:13
Thou shalt *f* the
Lord. . . . . Deut. 10:20
thou mayest *f* . . . .Deut. 28:58
and thou shalt *f*
day . . . . Deut. 28:66
f of thine heart
wherewith . . . . .Deut. 28:67
of a good
courage, *f* . . . . Deut. 31:6
f thee, as do thy
people . . . . 1 Kin. 8:43
Wherefore now
let the *f* . . . . 2 Chr. 19:7
whom shall I *f* . . . . . Ps. 27:1
of the earth, for *f* . . . . .Is. 2:19

f toward me is
taught . . . . .Is. 29:13
F thou not . . . . .Is. 41:10
F not, thou worm
Jacob . . . . .Is. 41:14
f is not in thee,
saith . . . . Jer. 2:19
and shall *f* the
Lord. . . . . Hos. 3:5
and *f* not me,
saith . . . . Mal. 3:5
moved with *f*,
prepared . . . . Heb. 11:7
me, saying unto
me, *F* . . . . Rev. 1:17

FEARED

for he *f* to say, She . .Gen. 26:7
And Moses *f*, and
said . . . . Ex. 2:14
the people *f* the
Lord. . . . . Ex. 14:31
that *f* God, and
eschewed . . . . .Job 1:1
is greatly to be *f* . . . . Ps. 89:7
to be *f* above all
gods. . . . . Ps. 96:4
and hast *f*
continually . . . . .Is. 51:13
treacherous sister
Judah *f*. . . . . Jer. 3:8
death, he *f* the
multitude . . . . Matt. 14:5
heard in that he *f*. . . .Heb. 5:7

FEARFUL

glorious in
holiness, *f*. . . . . . . .Ex. 15:11
f name, THE
Lord THY . . . . .Deut. 28:58
of a *f* heart, Be
strong . . . . .Is. 35:4
But the *f*, and
unbelieving. . . . . . . Rev. 21:8

FEAST

ye shall keep it a *f* . .Ex. 12:14
observe the *f* of
unleavened . . . . Ex. 12:17
thou shalt keep a *f*. . .Ex. 23:14
Thou shalt keep
the *f*. . . . . Ex. 23:15
f of harvest, the
firstfruits. . . . . Ex. 23:16
f of unleavened
bread . . . . Ex. 34:18
month shall be
the *f*. . . . . Lev. 23:34
f of unleavened
bread . . . . Deut. 16:16
time Solomon
held a *f* . . . . 1 Kin. 8:65
Jeroboam
ordained a *f* . . . 1 Kin. 12:32
seven days, and
the *f*. . . . . 2 Chr. 7:9
day of a solemn *f* . . . Lam. 2:7
mirth to cease,
her *f*. . . . . Hos. 2:11
great day of the *f* . . .John 7:37
the *f* of the
passover . . . . John 13:1

f that cometh in
Jerusalem . . . . . . .Acts 18:21

FEASTS

the *f* of the Lord. . . Lev. 23:2
are the *f* of the
Lord. . . . . Lev. 23:4
moons, and on
the set *f*. . . . . . 1 Chr. 23:31
appointed *f* my
soul . . . . .Is. 1:14
wine, are in their *f* . . . .Is. 5:12
come to the
solemn *f* . . . . Lam. 1:4
and all her
solemn *f* . . . . Hos. 2:11
I will turn your *f*. . .Amos 8:10

FED

thee to hunger,
and *f* . . . . Deut. 8:3
fifty in a cave,
and *f* . . . . 1 Kin. 18:4
verily thou shalt
be *f*. . . . . Ps. 37:3
rams, and the fat
of *f* . . . . .Is. 1:11
but the
shepherds *f*. . . . . . Ezek. 34:8

FEEBLE

children is
waxed *f* . . . . 1 Sam. 2:5
our hands wax *f* . . . . .Jer. 6:24
Damascus is
waxed *f* . . . . .Jer. 49:24
all hands shall
be *f*. . . . . Ezek. 21:7
hang down, and
the *f*. . . . . .Heb. 12:12

FEED

f them also, and
lift . . . . Ps. 28:9
brought him to *f*
Jacob . . . . Ps. 78:71
He shall *f* his
flock. . . . . .Is. 40:11
And I will *f* them
that . . . . .Is. 49:26
the earth, and *f*
thee . . . . .Is. 58:14
and the lamb
shall *f* . . . . .Is. 65:25
of Israel that do *f* . . Ezek. 34:2
their own land,
and *f* . . . . Ezek. 34:13
f them, even my
servant . . . . Ezek. 34:23
F thy people with
thy . . . . Mic. 7:14
He saith unto
him, *F* . . . . .John 21:15
He saith unto
him, *F* . . . . .John 21:16
Jesus saith unto
him, *F* . . . . .John 21:17
f the church of
God . . . . Acts 20:28
the throne shall *f* . . . Rev. 7:17
f her there a
thousand. . . . . Rev. 12:6

FEET

fetched, and wash
your *f*. . . . . .Gen. 18:4
his *f*, until Shiloh . .Gen. 49:10
your shoes on
your *f*. . . . . Ex. 12:11
f as it were a
paved. . . . . .Ex. 24:10
f, and toward her
children. . . . . . . .Deut. 28:57
unto Jordan, and
the *f*. . . . . Josh. 3:15
keep the *f* of his
saints. . . . . 1 Sam. 2:9
stood up upon
his *f*. . . . . 1 Chr. 28:2
my hands and
my *f*. . . . . Ps. 22:16
the dust of thy *f*. . . . .Is. 49:23
Their *f* run to evil. . . .Is. 59:7
the soles of thy *f* . . . .Is. 60:14
darkness, and
before your *f*. . . . . .Jer. 13:16
thy shoes upon
thy *f*. . . . . Ezek. 24:17
upon your *f*. . . . . . Ezek. 24:23
stamped with
the *f*. . . . . Ezek. 25:6
city at the *f* of
Gamaliel . . . . Acts 22:3
under your *f* . . . . . Rom. 16:20
f like unto fine
brass . . . . Rev. 1:15
him, I fell at his *f*. . . Rev. 1:17

FELIX

The Roman governor of
Judaea; Paul tried before,
Acts 23:24–35; 24
Trembles under Paul's
preaching, Acts 24:25
Leaves Paul in bonds,
Acts 24:26, 27; 25:14

FELL

Then Abraham *f*
upon . . . . .Gen. 17:17
among them *f* a
lusting. . . . . .Num. 11:4
they *f* upon their
faces . . . . .Num. 16:22
they *f* upon their
faces . . . . .Num. 16:45
And I *f* down
before . . . . .Deut. 9:18
his clothes, and *f* . . . .Josh. 7:6
to David, that he *f* . 2 Sam. 1:2
his own head,
who *f*. . . . . 1 Kin. 2:32
when I saw it, I *f* . . Ezek. 1:28
and I *f* on my face . Ezek. 3:23
hand of the Lord
GOD *f* . . . . Ezek. 8:1
and *f* on his face. . Matt. 26:39
said this, he *f*
asleep . . . . Acts 7:60
when I saw
him, I *f* . . . . Rev. 1:17
and twenty
elders *f* . . . . Rev. 5:8
and twenty
elders *f* . . . . Rev. 5:14

part of the city *f*. . . Rev. 11:13
cities of the
nations *f* . . . . Rev. 16:19
f upon men a
great . . . . Rev. 16:21
beasts *f* down and
worshipped. . . . . . Rev. 19:4

FELLOW

sword against
his *f* . . . . Judg. 7:22
man that is my *f*,
saith . . . . .Zech. 13:7
This *f* said, I am
able . . . . Matt. 26:61
man a pestilent *f* . . . Acts 24:5

FELLOWSHIP

the *f* of his Son
Jesus . . . . .1 Cor. 1:9
the right hands
of *f*. . . . . Gal. 2:9
no *f* with the
unfruitful . . . . .Eph. 5:11
ye also may have *f* . 1 John 1:3
the light, we
have *f*. . . . . 1 John 1:7

FENCED

cities great and *f*. . . .Deut. 9:1
thy high and *f*
walls . . . . .Deut. 28:52
the *f* cities of
Judah. . . . . 2 Kin. 18:13
And he *f* it, and
gathered . . . . .Is. 5:2

FIELD

Jacob came out of
the *f*. . . . . .Gen. 34:7
hast sown in the *f* . .Ex. 23:16
the trees of the *f*. . . . Lev. 26:4
beast, and of the *f* . Lev. 27:28
shalt thou be in
the *f*. . . . . .Deut. 28:16
the *f*, and shalt
gather . . . . .Deut. 28:38
of the fuller's *f* . . 2 Kin. 18:17
his wonders in
the *f*. . . . . Ps. 78:43
wilderness be a
fruitful *f* . . . . .Is. 32:15
the trees of the *f*. . . . .Is. 55:12
the trees of the *f*. . . . Jer. 7:20
the beasts of the *f* . . Jer. 27:6
the trees of the *f*. . Ezek. 17:24
every beast of
the *f*. . . . . Ezek. 34:8
f shall yield her
fruit . . . . Ezek. 34:27
the beasts of the *f* . .Dan. 4:25
the beasts of the *f* . . .Hos. 4:3
the harvest of
the *f*. . . . . Joel 1:11
sake be plowed
as a *f* . . . . Mic. 3:12
the grass of the *f* . . Matt. 6:30

FIELDS

open *f*, or a dead
body. . . . . .Num. 19:16
increase of the *f* . . Deut. 32:13
others, and their *f* . . . Jer. 8:10

Men shall buy *f*
for . . . . .Jer. 32:44
them vineyards
and *f* . . . . .Jer. 39:10
which were in
the *f*. . . . . Jer. 40:7
reaped down
your *f*. . . . . .James 5:4

FIERCE

Turn from thy *f*
wrath. . . . . .Ex. 32:12
A nation of *f*
countenance . . . .Deut. 28:50
his *f* wrath may
turn . . . . 2 Chr. 29:10
f anger, and hath
kindled . . . . Lam. 4:11
f anger, that we
perish . . . . Jon. 3:9
leopards, and are
more *f* . . . . .Hab. 1:8
indignation, even
all my *f* . . . . Zeph. 3:8

FIERY

f serpents, and
scorpions . . . . . . .Deut. 8:15
hand went a *f* law
for . . . . .Deut. 33:2
f flame, and his
wheels. . . . . .Dan. 7:9
A *f* stream issued
and. . . . . .Dan. 7:10

FIFTEENTH

The *f* day of this
seventh . . . . Lev. 23:34
eighth month, on
the *f*. . . . . 1 Kin. 12:32
f to Bilgah, the
sixteenth. . . . . . . 1 Chr. 24:14
the *f* year of the
reign . . . . .Luke 3:1

FIFTY

two hundred and *f*
shekels . . . . Ex. 30:23
hundred and *f*
men. . . . . Ex. 38:26
upward even
until *f* . . . . .Num. 4:3
two hundred and *f*
men . . . . .Num. 16:35
prophets, and hid
them by *f*. . . . . . . 1 Kin. 18:4
consume thee and
thy *f*. . . . . 2 Kin. 1:12
length thereof
was *f* . . . . Ezek. 40:21

FIG

his *f* tree, from
Dan . . . . 1 Kin. 4:25
f from the *f* tree . . . . . .Is. 34:4
firstripe in the *f* . . . .Hos. 9:10
and the *f* tree
languisheth. . . . . . . Joel 1:12
vine and under
his *f*. . . . . Mic. 4:4

FIGHT

The LORD shall *f*
for . . . . .Ex. 14:14
men, and go out, *f* . . .Ex. 17:9

before you, he
shall *f* ....Deut. 1:30
of Dan went up
to *f* ....Josh. 19:47
to *f* with Israel,
thirty ....1 Sam. 13:5
us, and to *f* our
battles ....2 Chr. 32:8
and they shall *f*
every ....Is. 19:2
shall *f* against
thee ....Jer. 1:19
hands, wherewith
ye *f*.............Jer. 21:4
And I myself will *f* ...Jer. 21:5
ye *f* with the
Chaldeans.........Jer. 32:5
the Chaldeans,
that *f* ....Jer. 32:24
f, because the
LORD...........Zech. 10:5
us not *f* against
God ....Acts 23:9
F the good *f* of
faith ....1 Tim. 6:12

FILL

f thine horn with
oil ....1 Sam. 16:1
wings shall *f* the
breadth ....Is. 8:8
blossom and bud,
and *f* ....Is. 27:6
wine, and we
will *f* ....Is. 56:12
I *f* heaven and
earth ....Jer. 23:24
Now the God of
hope *f* ....Rom. 15:13
sufferings for you,
and *f* ....Col. 1:24
which she hath
filled *f* ....Rev. 18:6

FILLED

glory of the LORD
had *f* ....1 Kin. 8:11
till he had *f*
Jerusalem .....2 Kin. 21:16
f Jerusalem with
innocent ....2 Kin. 24:4
then the house
was *f* ....2 Chr. 5:13
was *f* with sweet
odours........2 Chr. 16:14
our mouth *f* with
laughter..........Ps. 126:2
his train *f* the
temple ....Is. 6:1
my loins *f* with
pain ....Is. 21:3
sword of the
LORD is *f* ....Is. 34:6
land, they have *f*
mine ....Jer. 16:18
pasture, so were
they *f*...........Hos. 13:6
drink, but ye are
not *f*.............Hag. 1:6
f with the Holy
Ghost ....Luke 1:15

f with the Holy
Ghost ....Acts 2:4
f with envy, and
spake ....Acts 13:45
city was *f* with
confusion ......Acts 19:29
but be *f* with the
Spirit ....Eph. 5:18
Being *f* with the
fruits ....Phil. 1:11
took the censer,
and *f*............Rev. 8:5
cup which she
hath *f*...........Rev. 18:6

FILTHY

f is man, which
drinketh ....Job 15:16
Take away the *f*
garments.........Zech. 3:4
striker, not greedy
of *f*.............1 Tim. 3:3
striker, not given
to *f*............Titus 1:7

FIND

thy God, thou
shalt *f* ....Deut. 4:29
to pass that she *f* ..Deut. 24:1
nations shalt
thou *f*.........Deut. 28:65
tried me, and
shalt *f* ....Ps. 17:3
Until I *f* out a
place ....Ps. 132:5
but they shall
not *f*...........Prov. 1:28
And I *f* more
bitter ....Eccl. 7:26
and ye shall *f* rest....Jer. 6:16
seek, and ye
shall *f* ....Matt. 7:7
and ye shall *f* rest .Matt. 11:29
in and out, and *f*
pasture ....John 10:9
f no evil in this
man ....Acts 23:9

FINE

in vestures of *f*
linen ....Gen. 41:42
offering shall be
of *f*.............Lev. 2:1
oil, of *f* flour, fried ..Lev. 7:12
tenth deals of *f*
flour............Lev. 14:10
tenth deal of *f*
flour............Lev. 14:21
shall be of *f* flour ..Lev. 23:17
thou shalt take *f*
flour.............Lev. 24:5
a garment of *f*
linen ....Esth. 8:15
yea, above *f* gold .Ps. 119:127
feet like unto *f*
brass ....Rev. 1:15
be arrayed in *f*
linen ....Rev. 19:8

FINGER

written with the *f*...Ex. 31:18
priest shall dip
his *f* ....Lev. 4:6

offering with his *f* ..Lev. 4:34
round about with
his *f* ....Lev. 8:15
dip the tip of his *f* .Luke 16:24
Reach hither thy *f* .John 20:27

FINISHED

they builded,
and *f* ....Ezra 6:14
things shall be *f* ....Dan. 12:7
vinegar, he said, It
is *f* ....John 19:30
f, bringeth forth
death ....James 1:15

FIRE

Gomorrah
brimstone and *f* ..Gen. 19:24
night, roast with *f* ...Ex. 12:8
shall burn with *f* ...Ex. 12:10
on the wood
with *f*...........Lev. 4:12
pass through the *f* . Lev. 18:21
pass through the *f* 2 Kin. 17:17
house burnt he
with *f* ....2 Kin. 25:9
shall burn it
with *f*...........Jer. 21:10
with *f*, and thou
shalt.............Jer. 38:18
men, burned he
with *f*...........Jer. 52:13
part through the *f* . Zech. 13:9
Ghost, and with *f*.. Matt. 3:11
in danger of hell *f*.. Matt. 5:22
everlasting *f*,
prepared ....Matt. 25:41
flaming *f* taking
vengeance ......2 Thess. 1:8
be tormented
with *f*..........Rev. 14:10
alive into a lake
of *f*.............Rev. 19:20
the lake of *f* and
brimstone ....Rev. 20:10
into the lake of *f*... Rev. 20:14
which burneth
with *f*...........Rev. 21:8

FIRSTBORN

the *f* of Ishmael,
Nebajoth........Gen. 25:13
f in the land of
Egypt.............Ex. 11:5
f in the land of
Egypt............Ex. 12:12
LORD smote all
the *f*............Ex. 12:29
the *f*, whatsoever
openeth...........Ex. 13:2
the *f* of thy sons
shalt.............Ex. 22:29
the *f* among the
children........Num. 3:45
f of man shalt
thou...........Num. 18:15
sons of Reuben
the *f* ....1 Chr. 5:1
And smote all
the *f*.............Ps. 78:51
smote also all
the *f*............Ps. 105:36

and Ephraim is
my *f* .... Jer. 31:9
shall I give my *f*
for .... Mic. 6:7
bitterness for his *f* Zech. 12:10
her *f* son, and
wrapped .... Luke 2:7
the *f* among many
brethren .... Rom. 8:29
invisible God,
the *f* .... Col. 1:15
the beginning,
the *f* .... Col. 1:18

FIRSTFRUITS
feast of harvest,
the *f* .... Ex. 23:16
the *f* of thy land
thou .... Ex. 23:19
the *f* of thy land
thou .... Ex. 34:26
bring a sheaf of
the *f* .... Lev. 23:10
the *f* unto the
LORD .... Lev. 23:17
the wheat, the *f* .. Num. 18:12
bread of the *f* .... 2 Kin. 4:42
have the *f* of the
Spirit .... Rom. 8:23

FIRSTLING
matrix, and
every *f* .... Ex. 13:12
surely redeem,
and the *f* .... Num. 18:15
the *f* of a cow .... Num. 18:17
glory is like the *f* . Deut. 33:17

FISH
dominion over
the *f* .... Gen. 1:26
dominion over
the *f* .... Gen. 1:28
f that is in the
river .... Ex. 7:18
f that was in the
river .... Ex. 7:21
f gate, and the
tower .... Neh. 12:39
their *f* stinketh,
because .... Is. 50:2
and they shall *f* .... Jer. 16:16

FLAME
out of Heshbon,
a *f* .... Num. 21:28
f consumeth the
chaff. .... Is. 5:24
f of a devouring
fire .... Is. 30:30
the *f* kindle upon
thee .... Is. 43:2
of Heshbon,
and a *f* .... Jer. 48:45
fiery *f*, and his
wheels .... Dan. 7:9
tormented in
this *f* .... Luke 16:24

FLED
and the
Egyptians *f* .... Ex. 14:27
and the host *f* to
Bethshittah ...... Judg. 7:22

Abiathar, escaped,
and *f* .... 1 Sam. 22:20
I *f* because of
Absalom .... 1 Kin. 2:7
men of war *f* by
night .... 2 Kin. 25:4
did see me
without *f* .... Ps. 31:11
and the beast are *f* ... Jer. 9:10
of war, then they *f* ... Jer. 39:4
turned back, and
are *f* .... Jer. 46:21
f stood under the
shadow .... Jer. 48:45
I *f* before unto
Tarshish .... Jon. 4:2
flee, like as ye *f* .... Zech. 14:5
f unto Lystra and
Derbe .... Acts 14:6
woman *f* into the
wilderness .... Rev. 12:6
earth and the
heaven *f* .... Rev. 20:11

FLEE
Egyptians said,
Let us *f* .... Ex. 14:25
and ye shall *f*
when .... Lev. 26:17
they shall *f*, as
fleeing .... Lev. 26:36
thee one way,
and *f* .... Deut. 28:7
them, and *f* seven
ways .... Deut. 28:25
wicked *f* when no
man .... Prov. 28:1
f unto Zoar, an
heifer .... Is. 15:5
them, and they
shall *f* .... Is. 17:13
and sighing shall *f* ... Is. 35:10
of Babylon, *f* ye
from .... Is. 48:20
gather yourselves
to *f* .... Jer. 6:1
F ye, turn back,
dwell .... Jer. 49:8
f, and fear hath
seized .... Jer. 49:24
F out of the midst ... Jer. 51:6
ye shall *f* to the
valley .... Zech. 14:5
in this city, *f* ye ... Matt. 10:23
F also youthful
lusts .... 2 Tim. 2:22

FLESH
eat the *f* in that
night .... Ex. 12:8
the eighth day
the *f* .... Lev. 12:3
f, shall one man
sin .... Num. 16:22
thine own body,
the *f* .... Deut. 28:53
of the *f* of his
children .... Deut. 28:55
is an arm of *f* .... 2 Chr. 32:8
LORD plead with
all *f* .... Is. 66:16
They sacrifice *f* for .. Hos. 8:13

spirit upon all *f* .... Joel 2:28
for *f* and blood
hath .... Matt. 16:17
the Word was
made *f* .... John 1:14
concerning the *f*
Christ .... Rom. 9:5
law shall no *f* be
justified .... Gal. 2:16
wrestle not
against *f* .... Eph. 6:12
afflictions of
Christ in my *f* ... Col. 1:24
manifest in the *f* . 1 Tim. 3:16
are partakers of *f* ... Heb. 2:14
to death in the *f* ... 1 Pet. 3:18
the filth of the *f* ... 1 Pet. 3:21
strange *f*, are set ...... Jude 7

FLOCK
f of Jethro his
father .... Ex. 3:1
LORD thy God, of
the *f* .... Deut. 16:2
thy people like a *f* ... Ps. 77:20
leadest Joseph
like a *f* .... Ps. 80:1
feed his *f* like a
shepherd .... Is. 40:11
shepherd of his *f* .... Is. 63:11
the LORD's *f* is
carried .... Jer. 13:17
the remnant of
my *f* .... Jer. 23:3
shepherd doth
his *f* .... Jer. 31:10
the young of the *f* .. Jer. 31:12
of the *f* shall draw .. Jer. 49:20
surely because
my *f* .... Ezek. 34:8
lambs out of the *f*. .. Amos 6:4
thy rod, the *f* of
thine .... Mic. 7:14
as a *f*, they were
troubled .... Zech. 10:2
yourselves, and to
all the *f* .... Acts 20:28

FLOCKS
f, and herds, and
silver .... Gen. 24:35
thy kine, and the *f* . Deut. 7:13
herds and of
your *f* .... Deut. 12:6
thy kine, and the *f* . Deut. 28:4
thy kine, and the *f* Deut. 28:18
increase of thy
kine, or *f* ...... Deut. 28:51
All the *f* of Kedar ..... Is. 60:7
goats before the *f* .... Jer. 50:8
shepherds feed
the *f* .... Ezek. 34:2
young lion among
the *f* .... Mic. 5:8

FLOOD
destroying storm,
as a *f* .... Is. 28:2
a *f*, and unto the
end .... Dan. 9:26
the ark, and the *f* . Luke 17:27
righteousness,
bringing in the *f* ... 2 Pet. 2:5

FLOODS

the *f* stood
upright . . . . Ex. 15:8
waters, where
the *f* . . . . Ps. 69:2
f have lifted up, O . . . Ps. 93:3
f upon the dry
ground. . . . . Is. 44:3

FLOUR

lamb a tenth deal
of *f* . . . . Ex. 29:40
shall be of fine *f* . . . . . Lev. 2:1
handful of the *f*
thereof. . . . . Lev. 2:2
oil, of fine *f*, fried . . . Lev. 7:12
tenth deals of
fine *f* . . . . Lev. 14:10
fine *f*, and bake
twelve . . . . Lev. 24:5
part of an ephah
of *f* . . . . Num. 28:5
three tenth deals
of *f* . . . . Num. 28:12

FLOW

all nations shall *f* . . . . . . Is. 2:2
nations shall not *f* . . Jer. 51:44
and the hills
shall *f* . . . . Joel 3:18
and people shall *f* . . . . Mic. 4:1

FLOWER

with a knop
and a *f* . . . . Ex. 25:33
cometh forth
like a *f* . . . . Job 14:2
grass withereth,
the *f* . . . . Is. 40:8
glory of man as
the *f* . . . . 1 Pet. 1:24

FLOWING

large, unto a
land *f* . . . . Ex. 3:8
Jebusites, unto a
land *f* . . . . Ex. 3:17
f with milk and
honey . . . . Ezek. 20:6
f with milk and
honey . . . . Ezek. 20:15

FLY

with twain he did *f* . . . . Is. 6:2
shall *f* upon the
shoulders . . . . Is. 11:14
Behold, he shall *f* . . . Jer. 48:40
up and *f* as the
eagle . . . . Jer. 49:22
shall *f* as the eagle . . . Hab. 1:8
eagle, that she
might *f* . . . . Rev. 12:14

FOLLOW

heart, that he
shall *f* . . . . Ex. 14:4
Thou shalt not *f* a . . . Ex. 23:2
the LORD be
God, *f* . . . . 1 Kin. 18:21
suffered no man
to *f* . . . . Mark 5:37
signs shall *f* . . . . . Mark 16:17
serve me, let
him *f* . . . . John 12:26
f after the things . Rom. 14:19

f that which is
good . . . . 1 Thess. 5:15
f righteousness,
faith . . . . 2 Tim. 2:22
F peace with all
men . . . . Heb. 12:14
that should *f* . . . . . . 1 Pet. 1:11
and their works
do *f* . . . . Rev. 14:13

FOLLY

had wrought *f* in
Israel . . . . Gen. 34:7
hath wrought *f* in
Israel . . . . Deut. 22:21
your *f*, in that ye . . . . . Job 42:8
spirit exalteth *f* . . . Prov. 14:29

FOOD

sight, and good
for *f* . . . . Gen. 2:9
f of the offering
made . . . . Lev. 3:16
master's son may
have *f* . . . . 2 Sam. 9:10
he may bring
forth *f* . . . . Ps. 104:14
giveth *f* to the
hungry. . . . . Ps. 146:7
to the beast his *f* . . . Ps. 147:9
filling our hearts
with *f*. . . . . Acts 14:17

FOOL

f, the spiritual
man . . . . Hos. 9:7
shall say, Thou *f* . . . Matt. 5:22
f, this night thy
soul . . . . Luke 12:20
become a *f* in . . . 2 Cor. 12:11

FOOLISH

requite the
LORD, O *f* . . . . Deut. 32:6
to anger with a *f*
nation . . . . Deut. 32:21
of the *f* women
speaketh . . . . Job 2:10
a *f* son is the
heaviness . . . . Prov. 10:1
For my people is *f* . . . Jer. 4:22
Hear now
this, O *f* . . . . Jer. 5:21
altogether brutish
and *f* . . . . Jer. 10:8
seen vain and *f*
things . . . . Lam. 2:14
f and hurtful lusts . 1 Tim. 6:9

FOOLISHNESS

fools poureth
out *f*. . . . . Prov. 15:2
blasphemy,
pride, *f*. . . . . Mark 7:22
them that perish *f* . 1 Cor. 1:18
for they are *f* unto . 1 Cor. 2:14

FOOLS

but *f* despise
wisdom . . . . Prov. 1:7
scorning, and *f*
hate . . . . Prov. 1:22
the mouth of *f*
poureth . . . . Prov. 15:2

hath no pleasure
in *f*. . . . . Eccl. 5:4
princes of Zoan
are *f*. . . . . Is. 19:11
wayfaring men,
though *f* . . . . Is. 35:8

FOOT

hundred thousand
on *f* . . . . Ex. 12:37
tooth, hand for
hand, *f*. . . . . Deut. 19:21
from the sole of
thy *f*. . . . . Deut. 28:35
set the sole of
her *f*. . . . . Deut. 28:56
shall the sole of
thy *f*. . . . . Deut. 28:65
f shall slide in due Deut. 32:35
thou turn away
thy *f*. . . . . Is. 58:13
and stamp with
thy *f*. . . . . Ezek. 6:11
No *f* of man shall
pass . . . . Ezek. 29:11
thy hand or thy *f*
offend . . . . Matt. 18:8
garment down to
the *f*. . . . . Rev. 1:13
tread under *f* forty . . Rev. 11:2

FOOTSTOOL

LORD, and for
the *f*. . . . . 1 Chr. 28:2
and worship at
his *f*. . . . . Ps. 99:5
thine enemies
thy *f*. . . . . Ps. 110:1
the earth is my *f* . . . . . Is. 66:1

FORASMUCH

f as he hath no
part . . . . Deut. 12:12
f as the LORD
hath . . . . Deut. 17:16
Wherefore the
Lord said, *F*. . . . . . . Is. 29:13
F therefore as
your . . . . Amos 5:11
F then as we are
the . . . . Acts 17:29
F as ye are
manifestly . . . . 2 Cor. 3:3
F then as the
children. . . . . Heb. 2:14
F as ye know
that ye . . . . 1 Pet. 1:18

FORBEAR

whether they
will *f* . . . . Ezek. 2:7
forbeareth, let
him *f* . . . . Ezek. 3:27
F to cry, make no
mourning . . . . . . Ezek. 24:17
longer *f*, I sent . . . 1 Thess. 3:5

FOREHEADS

set a mark upon
the *f*. . . . . Ezek. 9:4
of God in their *f* . . . . . Rev. 9:4
written in their *f* . . . Rev. 14:1
mark upon their *f*. . . Rev. 20:4

FOREST

be counted for a *f* . . . . Is. 32:15
ye mountains, O *f* . . . Is. 44:23
a lion out of the *f* . . . . . Jer. 5:6
the *f*, as a young
lion . . . . Mic. 5:8

FORGET

diligently, lest
thou *f*. . . . . Deut. 4:9
and not *f* thine
handmaid . . . . . . 1 Sam. 1:11
paths of all that *f* . . . . Job 8:13
nations that *f* God . . . Ps. 9:17
f God, lest I tear . . . . Ps. 50:22
I will not *f* thy
word . . . . Ps. 119:16
thou shalt *f* the
shame . . . . Is. 54:4
Can a maid *f* her
ornaments . . . . Jer. 2:32
f your work and
labour . . . . Heb. 6:10
and to
communicate *f* . . . Heb. 13:16

FORGIVE

f, I pray thee, my . . . Ex. 10:17
dwelling place,
and *f* . . . . 1 Kin. 8:39
good, and ready
to *f* . . . . Ps. 86:5
I will *f* their
iniquity . . . . Jer. 31:34
stand praying, *f* . . Mark 11:25
said Jesus,
Father, *f*. . . . . . . Luke 23:34
faithful and just
to *f* . . . . 1 John 1:9

FORGIVEN

them, and it shall
be *f*. . . . . Lev. 4:20
sin, and it shall
be *f*. . . . . Lev. 4:26
thy sins be *f* thee . . . Matt. 9:2
their sins should
be *f*. . . . . Mark 4:12
Christ's sake
hath *f*. . . . . Eph. 4:32

FORGOTTEN

heart, God hath *f* . . . Ps. 10:11
people have *f* me
days . . . . Jer. 2:32
thy lovers have *f*
thee . . . . Jer. 30:14
that shall not be *f*. . . . Jer. 50:5
therefore have
they *f*. . . . . Hos. 13:6

FORM

any man, and his *f* . . . Is. 52:14
he hath no *f* nor
comeliness . . . . Is. 53:2
he put forth the *f* . . . Ezek. 8:3
Hold fast the *f* of . 2 Tim. 1:13

FORMED

the LORD God *f*
man . . . . Gen. 2:7
thou hadst *f* the
earth . . . . Ps. 90:2
that *f* them will
shew . . . . Is. 27:11

f thee, O Israel,
Fear . . . . Is. 43:1
my glory, I have *f* . . . . Is. 43:7
there was no
God *f* . . . . Is. 43:10
This people
have I *f* . . . . Is. 43:21
made thee, and *f*
thee . . . . Is. 44:2
f thee from the
womb . . . . Is. 44:24
f the earth and
made . . . . Is. 45:18
I *f* thee in the
belly. . . . . Jer. 1:5
Shall the thing *f*
say . . . . Rom. 9:20

FORNICATION

strangled, and
from *f* . . . . Acts 15:29
Adultery, *f*,
uncleanness . . . . . . Gal. 5:19
f, uncleanness,
inordinate . . . . Col. 3:5
themselves over
to *f*. . . . . Jude 7
idols, and to
commit *f* . . . . Rev. 2:14
the wrath of her *f*. . . Rev. 14:8
the wrath of her *f*. . . Rev. 18:3
committed *f* and
lived. . . . . Rev. 18:9

FORSAKE

fail thee, nor *f*
thee . . . . Deut. 31:6
fail thee, neither *f* . Deut. 31:8
will *f* me, and
break . . . . Deut. 31:16
fail thee, nor *f*
thee . . . . Josh. 1:5
but if thou *f* him . 1 Chr. 28:9
ye *f* him, he will *f*. 2 Chr. 15:2
against all them
that *f* . . . . Ezra 8:22
of thy father, and *f* . . Prov. 1:8
Let the wicked *f*
his . . . . Is. 55:7
f thee shall be
ashamed . . . . Jer. 17:13
f the idols of
Egypt. . . . . Ezek. 20:8
leave thee, nor *f*
thee . . . . Heb. 13:5

FORSAKEN

whereby thou
hast *f* . . . . Deut. 28:20
f me, and have
worshipped. . . . 1 Kin. 11:33
ye have *f* the
LORD. . . . . 2 Chr. 24:20
God, why hast
thou *f*. . . . . Ps. 22:1
they have *f* the
LORD. . . . . Is. 1:4
no more be
termed F . . . . Is. 62:4
have *f* me the
fountain . . . . Jer. 2:13
thou hast *f* the
LORD. . . . . Jer. 2:17

bitter, that thou
hast *f* . . . . Jer. 2:19
they have *f* the
covenant . . . . Jer. 22:9
LORD hath *f* the
earth . . . . Ezek. 8:12
LORD hath *f* the
earth . . . . Ezek. 9:9
For Demas hath *f*
me . . . . 2 Tim. 4:10

FORTY

mount *f* days
and *f* . . . . Ex. 24:18
LORD *f* days and *f*
nights . . . . Ex. 34:28
the wilderness *f*
years . . . . Num. 14:33
searched the land,
even *f*. . . . . Num. 14:34
f years the LORD
thy . . . . Deut. 2:7
God led thee
these *f* . . . . Deut. 8:2
mount *f* days
and *f* . . . . Deut. 9:9
f days and *f* nights . Deut. 9:18
the Philistines *f*
years . . . . Judg. 13:1
it be inhabited *f*
years . . . . Ezek. 29:11
desolate *f* years. . . Ezek. 29:12
fasted *f* days and *f* . . Matt. 4:2
tread under foot *f*. . . Rev. 11:2
unto him to
continue *f* . . . . Rev. 13:5
with him an
hundred *f* . . . . Rev. 14:1

FOUGHT

him, and *f* with
Amalek . . . . Ex. 17:10
came to Jahaz,
and *f* . . . . Num. 21:23
Amorites, who
had *f* . . . . Num. 21:26
and *f*, then *f* the
kings . . . . Judg. 5:19
Now the
Philistines *f* . . . . 1 Sam. 31:1
Syria went up,
and *f* . . . . 2 Kin. 12:17
their enemy, and
he *f* . . . . Is. 63:10
manner of men I
have *f*. . . . . 1 Cor. 15:32

FOUND

leaven *f* in your
houses. . . . . Ex. 12:19
There shall not
be *f*. . . . . Deut. 18:10
f him in a desert
land . . . . Deut. 32:10
seek him, he will
be *f*. . . . . 1 Chr. 28:9
seek him, he will
be *f*. . . . . 2 Chr. 15:2
good things *f* in
thee . . . . 2 Chr. 19:3
f in the king's
house. . . . . 2 Chr. 21:17
he could not be *f* . . . Ps. 37:36

gladness shall be *f* . . . . Is. 51:3
he may be *f*,
  call ye . . . . Is. 55:6
And I will be *f* of . . . Jer. 29:14
that *f* them have
  devoured . . . . Jer. 50:7
they shall not be *f* . . Jer. 50:20
we have *f*, we
  have . . . . Lam. 2:16
of the gods, was *f* . . . Dan. 5:11
f written in the
  book . . . . Dan. 12:1
f in fashion as a
  man . . . . Phil. 2:8
f unto praise and
  honour . . . . 1 Pet. 1:7
there was *f* no
  place . . . . Rev. 20:11
f written in the
  book . . . . Rev. 20:15

FOUNDATION

LORD, because
  the *f* . . . . Ezra 3:11
hast thou laid
  the *f* . . . . Ps. 102:25
rase it, even to
  the *f* . . . . Ps. 137:7
lay in Zion for a *f* . . . . Is. 28:16
to the temple,
  Thy *f* . . . . Is. 44:28
from the *f* of the
  world . . . . Matt. 25:34
lovedst me before
  the *f* . . . . John 17:24
the *f* of the world . . . . Eph. 1:4
are built upon
  the *f* . . . . Eph. 2:20
the *f* of God
  standeth . . . . 2 Tim. 2:19
Lamb slain from
  the *f* . . . . Rev. 13:8
of life from the *f* . . . . Rev. 17:8

FOUNDATIONS

the *f* also of the
  hills . . . . Ps. 18:7
f of the earth do
  shake . . . . Is. 24:18
heavens, and laid
  the *f* . . . . Is. 51:13
f are fallen, her
  walls . . . . Jer. 50:15
hath devoured
  the *f* . . . . Lam. 4:11
controversy, and
  ye strong *f* . . . . Mic. 6:2

FOUNTAIN

f of Jacob shall . . . Deut. 33:28
the *f* of living
  waters . . . . Jer. 2:13
waters, and mine
  eyes a *f* . . . . Jer. 9:1
forsaken the
  LORD, the *f* . . . . . . Jer. 17:13
become dry, and
  his *f* . . . . Hos. 13:15
with waters,
  and a *f* . . . . Joel 3:18
f of the water of
  life . . . . Rev. 21:6

FOUNTAINS

f of the great deep . . Gen. 7:11
high places, and *f* . . . . Is. 41:18
unto living *f* of
  waters . . . . Rev. 7:17
sea, and the *f* of
  waters . . . . Rev. 14:7

FOURTEENTH

f day of the same
  month . . . . Ex. 12:6
month, on the *f*
  day . . . . Ex. 12:18
In the *f* day of the . . Lev. 23:5
And in the *f*
  day of . . . . Num. 28:16

FOURTH

the third and *f*
  generation . . . . Ex. 20:5
the *f* part of an
  hin . . . . Ex. 29:40
and to the *f*
  generation . . . . Ex. 34:7
the third and *f*
  generation . . . . . . Num. 14:18
the *f* part of an
  hin . . . . Num. 28:5
the *f* part of an
  hin . . . . Num. 28:7
ram, and a *f* part . . Num. 28:14
the *f* month, the
  ninth . . . . Jer. 39:2
Babylon smote in
  the *f* . . . . Jer. 46:2
f month, in the
  ninth . . . . Jer. 52:6
behold a *f* beast,
  dreadful . . . . Dan. 7:7
And the *f* angel
  sounded . . . . Rev. 8:12

FOWLS

be meat unto all *f* Deut. 28:26
shall be meat for
  the *f* . . . . Jer. 7:33
meat for the *f* of
  heaven . . . . Jer. 16:4
for meat unto
  the *f* . . . . Jer. 34:20
field, and with
  the *f* . . . . Hos. 4:3

FREE

truth shall make
  you *f* . . . . John 8:32
being made *f* from
  sin . . . . Rom. 6:22
Jesus hath made
  me *f* . . . . Rom. 8:2
am I not *f* . . . . 1 Cor. 9:1
whether we be
  bond or *f* . . . . . . 1 Cor. 12:13
neither bond nor *f* . . Gal. 3:28
Christ hath made
  us *f* . . . . Gal. 5:1
Scythian, bond
  nor *f* . . . . Col. 3:11

FRIEND

mine own
  familiar *f* . . . . Ps. 41:9
A *f* loveth at all
  times . . . . Prov. 17:17

the flesh of his *f* . . . . . Jer. 19:9
but the *f* of the
  bridegroom . . . . John 3:29
be a *f* of the world . . James 4:4

FRIENDS

Job's three *f* heard . . . Job 2:11
lovers and my *f*
  stand . . . . Ps. 38:11
eat, O *f* . . . . Song 5:1
her *f* have dealt
  treacherously . . . . . Lam. 1:2
Make to
  yourselves *f* . . . . . . Luke 16:9

FRO

the LORD run to
  and *f* . . . . 2 Chr. 16:9
run to and *f*, and
  knowledge . . . . . . Dan. 12:4
run to and *f* . . . . Zech. 4:10
children, tossed to
  and *f* . . . . Eph. 4:14

FRUIT

shall yield their *f* . . . Lev. 26:4
and shewed them
  the *f* . . . . Num. 13:26
be the *f* of thy
  body . . . . Deut. 28:18
The *f* of thy land . . Deut. 28:33
olive shall cast
  his *f* . . . . Deut. 28:40
All thy trees and *f* Deut. 28:42
eat the *f* of thy
  cattle . . . . Deut. 28:51
thou shalt eat
  the *f* . . . . Deut. 28:53
bringeth forth his *f* . . . Ps. 1:3
they shall eat the *f* . . . . Is. 3:10
glorious, and the *f* . . . . . Is. 4:2
field, and upon
  the *f* . . . . Jer. 7:20
to the *f* of his
  doings . . . . Jer. 17:10
to the *f* of his
  doings . . . . Jer. 32:19
gardens, and eat
  the *f* . . . . Amos 9:14
transgression,
  the *f* . . . . Mic. 6:7
and bring forth *f* . . . John 15:16
and bringeth
  forth *f* . . . . Col. 1:6
the *f* of our lips
  giving . . . . Heb. 13:15
fruits, and yielded
  her *f* . . . . Rev. 22:2

FRUITFUL

them, Be *f*, and
  multiply . . . . Gen. 1:28
be *f* and multiply . . Gen. 35:11
A *f* land into
  barrenness . . . . . . Ps. 107:34
vineyard in a very *f* . . . . Is. 5:1
wilderness be a *f*
  field . . . . Is. 32:15
he be *f* among his
  brethren . . . . Hos. 13:15
heaven, and *f*
  seasons . . . . Acts 14:17

Bids David build an altar
on the threshing floor of
Ornan, 2 Sam. 24:18, 19;
1 Chr. 21:18, 19
Assists David in arranging the
temple service, 2 Chr. 29:25
Writings of, 1 Chr. 29:29

GAIUS
A Macedonian, and a
companion of Paul; Seized at
Ephesus, Acts 19:29
———— A man of Derbe;
accompanied Paul from
Macedonia, Acts 20:4
———— A Corinthian, whom
Paul baptized, Rom. 16:23;
1 Cor. 1:14
———— Man to whom John's
third epistle was addressed,
3 John 14

GALATIA
A province of Asia Minor; Its
churches visited by Paul,
Acts 16:6; 18:23
Collection taken in, for
Christians at Jerusalem,
1 Cor. 16:1
Peter's address to, 1 Pet. 1:1
Churches in, Gal. 1:1, 2
See Paul's epistle to Galatians,
Gal. 1

GALILEE
The northern district of
Palestine; A city of refuge in,
Josh. 20:7; 21:32; 1 Chr. 6:76
Cities in, given to Hiram,
1 Kin. 9:11, 12
Taken by king of Assyria,
2 Kin. 15:29
Prophecy concerning, Is. 9:1;
Matt. 4:15
Called Galilee of the Nations,
Is. 9:1
Herod (Antipas), tetrarch of,
Mark 6:21; Luke 3:1; 23:6, 7
Jesus resides in, Matt. 17:22;
19:1; John 7:1, 9
Teaching and miracles of Jesus
in, Matt. 4:23, 25; 15:29–31;
Mark 1:14
People of, receive Jesus,
John 4:45, 53
Disciples were chiefly from,
Acts 1:11; 2:7
Women from, ministered
to Jesus, Matt. 27:55, 56;
Mark 15:41; Luke 23:49, 55
Jesus appeared to his disciples
in, after his resurrection,
Matt. 26:32; 28:7, 10, 16, 17;
Mark 14:28; 16:7; John 21
Routes from, to Judaea,
Judg. 21:19; John 4:3–5
Dialect of, Mark 14:70
Called Gennesaret,
Matt. 14:34; Mark 6:53
Congregations in, Acts 9:31
———— Sea (Lake) of Galilee
Called Sea of Tiberias,
John 21:1

Called Lake of Gennesaret,
Luke 5:1
Called Sea of Chinnereth,
Num. 34:11; Deut. 3:17;
Josh. 13:27
Called Sea of Chinneroth,
Josh. 12:3
Jesus calls disciples on the
shore of, Matt. 4:18–22;
Luke 5:1–11
Jesus teaches from a ship on,
Matt. 13:1–3
Miracles of Jesus on,
Matt. 8:24–32; 14:22–33;
17:27; Mark 4:37–39;
Luke 5:1–9; 8:22–24;
John 21:1–11

GAMALIEL
A celebrated teacher; Speech
of, before the Sanhedrin,
Acts 5:33–40
Paul's teacher, Acts 22:3
———— A captain of the tribe of
Manasseh, Num. 1:10; 2:20;
10:23
Offering of, at dedication of
tabernacle, Num. 7:54–59

GARDEN
the midst of the g. . . . . Gen. 2:9
Gomorrah, even
as the g . . . . Gen. 13:10
is by the king's g . 2 Kin. 25:4
g, my sister, my
spouse . . . . Song 5:1
her desert like
the g . . . . Is. 51:3
be as a watered g . . . Jer. 31:12
king's g, by the
gate . . . . Jer. 39:4
in Eden the g of
God . . . . Ezek. 28:13
the land is as
the g . . . . Joel 2:3
Cedron, where
was a g. . . . . John 18:1

GARMENT
with a g of fine
linen . . . . Esth. 8:15
shall wax old
like a g. . . . . Ps. 102:26
light as with a g . . . . Ps. 104:2
shall wax old
like a g. . . . . Is. 51:6
for mourning,
the g . . . . Is. 61:3
shepherd putteth
on his g . . . . Jer. 43:12
the naked with a g . Ezek. 18:7
naked with a g . . . Ezek. 18:16
days did sit,
whose g . . . . Dan. 7:9
hating even the g
spotted . . . . Jude 23
man, clothed
with a g . . . . Rev. 1:13

GARMENTS
And these are
the g . . . . Ex. 28:4

Aaron, and upon
his g . . . . Lev. 8:30
thy beautiful g, O . . . . . Is. 52:1
put on the g of
vengeance . . . . Is. 59:17
clothed me with
the g . . . . Is. 61:10
from Edom, with
dyed g . . . . Is. 63:1
my g, and I will
stain . . . . Is. 63:3
their broidered g . Ezek. 26:16
heart, and not
your g . . . . Joel 2:13
Take away the
filthy g . . . . Zech. 3:4
clothed him
with g . . . . Zech. 3:5
borders of their g . . Matt. 23:5

GATE
possess the g . . . . . . Gen. 22:17
the g of that city . . Deut. 22:24
aside in the g to
speak . . . . 2 Sam. 3:27
the g between two
walls . . . . 2 Kin. 25:4
courses at every g . 2 Chr. 8:14
Jerusalem at the
corner g . . . . 2 Chr. 26:9
builded the
sheep g . . . . Neh. 3:1
street of the
water g . . . . Neh. 8:16
above the g of
Ephraim . . . . Neh. 12:39
sat in the middle g . . . Jer. 39:3
king's garden, by
the g . . . . Jer. 39:4
door of the
inner g . . . . Ezek. 8:3
the east g of the
LORD . . . . Ezek. 11:1
he stood in the g . . Ezek. 40:3
unto the g which
looketh . . . . Ezek. 40:6
within the g . . . . . Ezek. 40:16
measure of the
first g . . . . Ezek. 40:21
the measure of
the g . . . . Ezek. 40:22
a g in the inner
court . . . . Ezek. 40:27
place, from
Benjamin's g . . . . Zech. 14:10

GATES
that is within
thy g . . . . Ex. 20:10
that is within
your g . . . . Deut. 12:12
stranger that is in
thy g . . . . Deut. 14:21
which are within
thy g . . . . Deut. 14:29
thy g, and the
stranger . . . . Deut. 16:11
thee in all thy g . . Deut. 16:18
thy g, until thy
high . . . . Deut. 28:52
thee in all thy g . . Deut. 28:55

distress thee in
thy g . . . . Deut. 28:57
the g thereof are
burned. . . . . Neh. 1:3
And her g shall
lament . . . . Is. 3:26
him the two
leaved g . . . . Is. 45:1
break in pieces
the g . . . . Is. 45:2
Salvation, and
thy g . . . . Is. 60:18
through, go
through the g . . . . . . Is. 62:10
the entering of
the g . . . . Jer. 1:15
entering in at
the g . . . . Jer. 17:27
all her g are
desolate . . . . Lam. 1:4
and the g of hell
shall . . . . Matt. 16:18
enter in through
the g . . . . Rev. 22:14

GATH
One of the five chief cities of
the Philistines, Josh. 13:3;
1 Sam. 6:17; Amos 6:2;
Mic. 1:10
Anakim, a race of giants,
inhabitants of, Josh. 11:22
Goliath lived in, 1 Sam. 17:4;
1 Chr. 20:5–8
Obed-edom belonged to,
2 Sam. 6:10
The ark of the covenant taken
to, 1 Sam. 5:8
Inhabitants of, called Gittites,
Josh. 13:3
David takes refuge at,
1 Sam. 21:10–15; 27:2–7
Band of Gittites, attached to
David, 2 Sam. 15:18–22
Captured by David, 1 Chr. 18:1
Shimei's servants escape to,
1 Kin. 2:39–41
Fortified by Rehoboam,
2 Chr. 11:8
Captured by Hazael,
2 Kin. 12:17
Recovered by Jehoash,
2 Kin. 13:25
Besieged by Uzziah,
2 Chr. 26:6
Called Methegammah in,
2 Sam. 8:1

GATHER
number, they
shall g . . . . Gen. 34:30
vineyard, and
shalt not g . . . . . . Deut. 28:30
field, and shalt g . . Deut. 28:38
wine, nor g the
grapes . . . . Deut. 28:39
will return and g
thee . . . . Deut. 30:3
outcasts of Israel,
and g . . . . Is. 11:12
he shall g the
lambs . . . . Is. 40:11

the east, and g
thee . . . . Is. 43:5
cry, g together,
and . . . . Jer. 4:5
children of
Benjamin, g . . . . Jer. 6:1
captivity, and I
will g . . . . Jer. 29:14
g the shields . . . . Jer. 51:11
from the people,
and g . . . . Ezek. 20:41
from the people,
and g . . . . Ezek. 34:13
solemn
assembly, g . . . . Joel 1:14
faces of them all g . . Nah. 2:10
determination is
to g . . . . Zeph. 3:8
purge his floor,
and g . . . . Matt. 3:12
reap, nor g into
barns . . . . Matt. 6:26
trumpet, and they
shall g . . . . Matt. 24:31

GATHERED
and was g to his
people . . . . Gen. 25:8
nostrils the
waters were g . . . . . Ex. 15:8
year, when thou
hast g . . . . Ex. 23:16
and when ye are g
together . . . . Lev. 26:25
congregation, that
are g . . . . Num. 14:35
Sihon g all his
people . . . . Num. 21:23
congregation
was g . . . . Judg. 20:1
g together to
Mizpeh . . . . 1 Sam. 7:6
And the
Philistines g . . . . 1 Sam. 13:5
they have g
themselves . . . . Job 16:10
I have g my myrrh
with . . . . Song 5:1
g out the stones
thereof . . . . Is. 5:2
kingdoms of
nations g . . . . Is. 13:4
of Kedar shall be g . . . . Is. 60:7
nations shall be g . . . . Jer. 3:17
g wine and
summer fruits . . . . Jer. 40:12
children of Israel
be g . . . . Hos. 1:11
were g together
praying . . . . Acts 12:12
and had g the
church . . . . Acts 14:27
the baser sort,
and g . . . . Acts 17:5

GAVE
And he g unto
Moses . . . . Ex. 31:18
and g it unto the
seventy . . . . Num. 11:25
he g Joshua the
son . . . . Deut. 31:23

and Joshua g it for Josh. 11:23
son of Jephunneh
he g . . . . Josh. 15:13
and they g
judgment . . . . . 2 Kin. 25:6
he g them all into 2 Chr. 36:17
heavens, and the
Highest g . . . . Ps. 18:13
So I g them up
unto . . . . Ps. 81:12
return unto God
who g . . . . Eccl. 12:7
I g my back to the . . . . Is. 50:6
to the land that I g . . . Jer. 30:3
Hamath, where
he g . . . . Jer. 39:5
thus, he g up the
ghost . . . . Luke 23:46
received him, to
them g . . . . John 1:12
the world, that
he g . . . . John 3:16
tongues, as the
Spirit g . . . . Acts 2:4
who loved me,
and g . . . . Gal. 2:20
Who g himself for
us . . . . Titus 2:14
affrighted, and g
glory . . . . Rev. 11:13

GAVEST
g them bread from
heaven . . . . Neh. 9:15
Thou g also thy
good . . . . Neh. 9:20
therefore g thou
them . . . . Neh. 9:30
leviathan in
pieces, and g . . . . . Ps. 74:14
thine house,
thou g . . . . Luke 7:44
words which
thou g . . . . John 17:8
that thou g me I
have . . . . John 17:12

GAZA
Also called Azzah; A city of
the Philistines, Josh. 13:3;
Jer. 25:20
One of the border cities of the
Canaanites, Gen. 10:19
A city of the Avim and
Anakim, Deut. 2:23;
Josh. 11:22
Allotted to Judah, Josh. 15:47;
Judg. 1:18
A temple of Dagon, situated
at, Judg. 16:23
Samson dies at, Judg. 16:21–
31
On the western boundary of
the kingdom of Israel in the
time of Solomon, 1 Kin. 4:24
Struck by Pharaoh, Jer. 47:1
Prophecies relating to,
Amos 1:6, 7; Zeph. 2:4;
Zech. 9:5
Desert of, Acts 8:26–39
—— A city of the tribe

of Ephraim, Judg. 6:4;
1 Chr. 7:28

GEDALIAH
Governor appointed by
Nebuchadnezzar after
carrying the Jews into
captivity, 2 Kin. 25:22–24
Jeremiah committed to the
care of, Jer. 39:14; 40:5, 6
Warned of the conspiracy of
Ishmael by Johanan, and
the captains of his army,
Jer. 40:13–16
Killed by Ishmael,
2 Kin. 25:25, 26; Jer. 41:1–10
——— A musician,
1 Chr. 25:3, 9
——— A priest, who divorced
his Gentile wife after the
exile, Ezra 10:18
——— Ancestor of Zephaniah,
Zeph. 1:1
——— A prince who caused
imprisonment of Jeremiah,
Jer. 38:1

GEHAZI
Servant of Elisha, 2 Kin. 4:12,
29, 31
Covetousness of, and the
judgment of leprosy upon,
2 Kin. 5:20–27
Mentions to King Jehoram the
miracles of Elisha, his master,
2 Kin. 8:4, 5

GENERATION
before me in
this g . . . . .Gen. 7:1
children of the
third g . . . . .Gen. 50:23
third and fourth g . . . Ex. 20:5
and to the
fourth g . . . . Ex. 34:7
third and fourth g Num. 14:18
and in the g
following. . . . . Ps. 109:13
be dwelt in from g . . .Is. 13:20
shall declare his g. . . . .Is. 53:8
his kingdom is
from g . . . . .Dan. 4:34
book of the g of
Jesus . . . . Matt. 1:1
g of vipers, how . . Matt. 12:34
wicked and
adulterous g . . . . . Matt. 16:4
Ye serpents, ye
g of. . . . . Matt. 23:33
adulterous and
sinful g . . . . Mark 8:38
chosen g, a royal
priesthood . . . . 1 Pet. 2:9

GENERATIONS
after thee in
their g . . . . .Gen. 17:7
according to
their g . . . . .Gen. 25:13
memorial unto
all g . . . . Ex. 3:15
throughout your g . . Ex. 12:14
this day in your g . . . Ex. 12:17

their g on the
behalf . . . . Ex. 27:21
offering
throughout your g . Ex. 29:42
throughout your g . . . Ex. 30:8
throughout your g . . Ex. 30:10
statute for your g . . . Lev. 3:17
throughout your g . . Lev. 10:9
throughout their g . . Lev. 17:7
commandments
to a thousand g . . . Deut. 7:9
done it, calling
the g . . . . .Is. 41:4
ancient days, in
the g . . . . .Is. 51:9
the years of
many g. . . . . .Joel 2:2

GENTILES
to it shall the G
seek . . . . .Is. 11:10
judgment to the G . . . .Is. 42:1
the G, that thou
mayest. . . . . .Is. 49:6
glory among the G . . .Is. 66:19
destroyer of the G . . . . Jer. 4:7
the vanities of
the G . . . . Jer. 14:22
the G in the midst . . . Mic. 5:8
great among the G . . Mal. 1:11
G to mock, and to
scourge . . . . Matt. 20:19
before the G, and
kings . . . . Acts 9:15
hath God also to
the G . . . . Acts 11:18
lo, we turn to
the G . . . . Acts 13:46
will go unto the G . . Acts 18:6
people, and to
the G . . . . Acts 26:23
the fulness of
the G . . . . Rom. 11:25
whether we be
Jews or G . . . . . 1 Cor. 12:13
preach among
the G . . . . Eph. 3:8
preached unto the
G . . . . 1 Tim. 3:16
honest among
the G . . . . .1 Pet. 2:12
is given unto
the G . . . . Rev. 11:2

GERAR
A city of the Philistines,
Gen. 10:19
Abimelech, king of, Gen. 20:1;
26:6
Visited by Abraham, Gen. 20:1
Visited by Isaac, Gen. 26:1;
2 Chr. 14:13, 14
——— A valley, Gen. 26:17–22

GERIZIM
Mount of blessing,
Deut. 11:29; 27:12;
Josh. 8:33
Jotham addresses the
Shechemites from, against
the conspiracy of Abimelech,
Judg. 9:7

Samaritans worship at,
John 4:20

GERSHOM
Son of Moses, Ex. 2:22; 18:3;
1 Chr. 23:15, 16; 26:24
——— A descendant of
Phinehas, Ezra 8:2
——— A Levite, Judg. 18:30

GESHUR
District east of the sources
of the Jordan River; The
inhabitants of, not subdued
by the Israelites, Deut. 3:14;
Josh. 13:2–13; 1 Chr. 2:23
Inhabitants of one of the
villages of, exterminated, and
the spoils taken by David,
1 Sam. 27:8
David marries a princess of,
2 Sam. 3:3; 1 Chr. 3:2
Absalom takes refuge in,
after the murder of Amnon,
2 Sam. 1:3

GEZER
Also called Gazer, Gazara,
Gazera, and Gob; A
Canaanitish royal city
King of, defeats Joshua,
Josh. 10:33; 12:12
Canaanites not all expelled
from, but made to pay
tribute (taxes), Josh. 16:10;
Judg. 1:29
Allotted to the half-tribe of
Ephraim, Josh. 16:3, 10;
1 Chr. 7:28
Assigned to Levites,
Josh. 21:21
Battle with Philistines at,
2 Sam. 21:18; 1 Chr. 20:4
Struck by David, 1 Sam. 27:8
Fortified by Solomon,
1 Kin. 9:15–17; 12:23

GHOST
Holy G, and with
fire . . . . Matt. 3:11
of the Holy G . . . . Matt. 28:19
filled with the
Holy G. . . . . .Luke 1:15
unto her, The
Holy G. . . . . .Luke 1:35
thus, he gave up
the g . . . . Luke 23:46
for the Holy G
was . . . . .John 7:39
Holy G, whom the
Father . . . . .John 14:26
and gave up the g . .John 19:30
baptized with the
Holy G. . . . . Acts 1:5
after that the
Holy G. . . . . Acts 1:8
filled with the
Holy G. . . . . Acts 2:4
Holy G, he hath
shed. . . . . Acts 2:33
gift of the Holy G . . . Acts 2:38
resist the Holy G . . . Acts 7:51

GIBEAH

Nazareth with the
Holy *G* . . . . Acts 10:38
forbidden of the
Holy *G* . . . . Acts 16:6
the Holy *G* hath
made . . . . Acts 20:28
communion of the
Holy *G* . . . . 2 Cor. 13:14
renewing of the
Holy *G* . . . . Titus 3:5
gifts of the Holy *G* . . . Heb. 2:4

GIBEAH

Of Judah, Josh. 15:57
——— Of Saul
Also called Gibeah of
Benjamin
The people's wickedness,
Judg. 19:12–30; Hos. 9:9;
10:9
Destroyed by the Israelites,
Judg. 20
The city of Saul,
1 Sam. 10:26; 15:34; 22:6
The ark of the covenant
conveyed to, by the
Philistines, 1 Sam. 7:1;
2 Sam. 6:3
Deserted, Is. 10:29
——— Another town in
Benjamin, also called
Gibeath, in, Josh. 18:28

GIBEON

A city of the Hivites, Josh. 9:3,
17; 2 Sam. 21:2
The people of, adroitly draw
Joshua into a treaty, Josh. 9
Made servants by the
Israelites, when their sharp
practice was discovered,
Josh. 9:27
The sun stands still over,
during Joshua's battle with
the five confederated kings,
Josh. 10:12–14
Allotted to Benjamin,
Josh. 18:25
Assigned to the Aaronites,
Josh. 21:17
The tabernacle located at,
1 Kin. 3:4; 1 Chr. 16:39;
21:29; 2 Chr. 1:2, 3, 13
Smitten by David, 1 Chr. 14:16
Seven sons of Saul killed at,
to avenge the inhabitants of,
2 Sam. 21:1–9
Solomon worships at, and
offers sacrifices, 1 Kin. 3:4
Has the dream concerning
righteousness, 1 Kin. 3:5; 9:2
Abner slays Asahel at,
2 Sam. 3:30
Ishmael, the son of Nethaniah,
defeated at, by Johanan,
Jer. 41:11–16
——— Pool of, 2 Sam. 2:13;
Jer. 41:12

GIDEON

Call of, by an angel,
Judg. 6:11, 14
His excuses, Judg. 6:15

Promises of the Lord to,
Judg. 6:16
Angel attests the call to, by
miracle, Judg. 6:21–24
He destroys the altar of Baal,
and builds one to the Lord,
Judg. 6:25–27
His prayer tests, Judg. 6:36–40
Leads an army against and
defeats the Midianites,
Judg. 6:33–35; 7; 8:4–12
Reproaches the Ephraimites
for not joining in the
campaign against the
Midianites, Judg. 8:1–3
Avenges himself upon
the people of Succoth,
Judg. 8:14–17
Israel desires to make him
king; he refuses, Judg. 8:22,
23
Makes an ephod which
becomes a snare to the
Israelites, Judg. 8:24–27
Had seventy sons, Judg. 8:30
Death of, Judg. 8:32
Faith of, Heb. 11:32

GIFT

thou shalt take
no *g* . . . . Ex. 23:8
persons, neither
take a *g* . . . . Deut. 16:19
priest, and offer
the *g* . . . . Matt. 8:4
thou knewest
the *g* . . . . John 4:10
the *g* of the Holy
Ghost . . . . Acts 2:38
the *g* of the Holy
Ghost . . . . Acts 10:45
the *g* of God is
eternal . . . . Rom. 6:23
I have the *g* of
prophecy . . . . 1 Cor. 13:2
it is the *g* of God . . . . Eph. 2:8
g of the grace of
God . . . . Eph. 3:7
g, and were made
partakers . . . . Heb. 6:4
good *g* and every
perfect . . . . James 1:17

GIFTS

servants, and
brought *g* . . . . 2 Sam. 8:2
David, and
brought *g* . . . . 2 Sam. 8:6
persons, nor
taking of *g* . . . . . . 2 Chr. 19:7
Seba shall offer *g* . . . Ps. 72:10
one loveth *g*, and
followeth . . . . Is. 1:23
g, and with your
idols . . . . Ezek. 20:39
gave him many
great *g* . . . . Dan. 2:48
divers miracles,
and *g* . . . . Heb. 2:4

GIHON

A river in Egypt, Gen. 2:13

——— Pools near Jerusalem,
1 Kin. 1:33, 38, 45
Hezekiah brings the waters
of the upper pool by an
aqueduct into the city of
Jerusalem, 2 Chr. 32:4, 30;
33:14; Neh. 2:13–15; 3:13–
16; Is. 7:3; 22:9–11; 36:2

GILEAD

A region east of the Jordan
River allotted to the tribes
of Reuben and Gad and
the half tribe of Manasseh,
Num. 32:1–30; Deut. 3:13;
34:1; 2 Kin. 10:33
Reubenites expel the Hagarites
from, 1 Chr. 5:9, 10, 18–22
Ammonites make war against;
defeated by Jephthah,
Judg. 11
The prophet Elijah a native of,
1 Kin. 17:1
David retreats to, at the time
of Absalom's rebellion,
2 Sam. 17:16, 22, 24
Pursued into, by Absalom,
2 Sam. 17:26
Absalom defeated and slain in
the forests of, 2 Sam. 18:9
Hazael, king of Syria, smites
the land of, 2 Kin. 10:32, 33;
Amos 1:3
Invaded by Tiglath-pileser,
king of Syria, 2 Kin. 15:29
A grazing country, Num. 32:1;
1 Chr. 5:9
Exported spices, balm, and
myrrh, Gen. 37:25; Jer. 8:22;
46:11
Figurative
Of prosperity, Jer. 22:6; 50:19
——— A mountain, Judg. 7:3;
Song 4:1; 6:5
Laban overtakes Jacob at,
Gen. 31:21–25
——— A city, Hos. 6:8; 12:11
——— Grandson of Manasseh,
Num. 26:29, 30; 27:1; 36:1;
Josh. 17:1, 3; 1 Chr. 2:21, 23;
7:14, 17
——— Father of Jephthah,
Judg. 11:1, 2
——— A chief of Gad,
1 Chr. 5:14

GILGAL

Place of the first encampment
of the Israelites west of the
Jordan River, Josh. 4:19; 9:6;
10:6, 43; 14:6
Monument erected in, to
commemorate the passage
across the Jordan River
by the people of Israel,
Josh. 4:19–24
Circumcision renewed at,
Josh. 5:2–9
Passover kept at, Josh. 5:10, 11
Manna ceased at, after the
Passover, Josh. 5:12
Quarries at, Judg. 3:19

Eglon, king of Moab, resides and is slain at, Judg. 3:14-26

A judgment seat, where Israel, in that district, came to be judged by Samuel, 1 Sam. 7:16

Saul proclaimed king over all Israel at, 1 Sam. 11:15

An altar built at, and sacrifice offered, 1 Sam. 11:15; 13:4–15; 15:6–23

Agag, king of the Amalekites, slain at, by Samuel, 1 Sam. 15:33

Tribe of Judah assembles at, to proceed to the east side of the Jordan River to conduct King David back after the defeat of Absalom, 2 Sam. 19:14, 15, 40–43

A school of the prophets at, 2 Kin. 4:38–40

Prophecies concerning, Hos. 4:15; 9:15; 12:11; Amos 4:4; 5:5

——— A royal city in Canaan Conquered by Joshua, Josh. 12:23

GIRD
And thou shalt g them . . . . Ex. 29:9
streets they shall g . . . . Is. 15:3
g up thy loins, and . . . Jer. 1:17
daughter of my people, g . . . . Jer. 6:26
daughters of Rabbah, g . . . . Jer. 49:3
G yourselves, and lament . . . . Joel 1:13
Wherefore g up the . . . . 1 Pet. 1:13

GIRDED
loins g, your shoes . . . . Ex. 12:11
him the coat, and g . . . . Lev. 8:7
and he g up his loins . . . . 1 Kin. 18:46
wherewith he hath g . . . . Ps. 93:1
I g thee, though thou . . . . Is. 45:5
your loins be g . . . Luke 12:35

GIRDLE
coat, a mitre, and a g . . . . Ex. 28:4
girded him with the g . . . . Lev. 8:7
hair, and a leathern g . . . . Matt. 3:4
paps with a golden g . . . . Rev. 1:13

GIVE
Unto thy seed will I g . . . . Gen. 12:7
seest, to thee will I g . . . . Gen. 13:15

And I will g unto thee . . . . Gen. 17:8
thy seed, I will g . . . . Gen. 26:3
will g unto thy seed . . . . Gen. 26:4
liest, to thee will I g . . . . Gen. 28:13
I will g thee in commandment . . . . Ex. 25:22
g, every one that passeth . . . . Ex. 30:13
the LORD shall g thee . . . . Deut. 28:65
Hear, O heavens, and g . . . . Is. 1:2
Lord himself shall g . . . . Is. 7:14
I will also g thee . . . . . . Is. 49:6
mourn in Zion, to g . . . . Is. 61:3
the reins, even to g . . . . Jer. 17:10
Behold, I will g the . . . . Ezek. 29:19
to g his life a ransom . . . . Matt. 20:28
the moon shall not g . . . . Matt. 24:29
the Lord God shall g . . . . Luke 1:32
water that I shall g . . . . John 4:14
I g to eat of the tree . . . . Rev. 2:7

GIVETH
LORD thy God g thee . . . . Ex. 20:12
God of your fathers g . . . . Deut. 4:1
LORD thy God g thee . . . . Deut. 4:40
LORD thy God g thee . . . . Deut. 16:18
LORD thy God g thee . . . . Deut. 28:8
He g to the beast his . . . . Ps. 147:9
g breath unto the people . . . . Is. 42:5
saith the LORD, which g . . . . Jer. 31:35
g wisdom unto the wise . . . . Dan. 2:21
kingdom of men, and g . . . . Dan. 4:25
for God g not the Spirit . . . . John 3:34
heaven, and g life . . . John 6:33
All that the Father g . . . . John 6:37
the good shepherd g . . . . . . John 10:11
world g, give I . . . . John 14:27
killeth, but the spirit g . . . . 2 Cor. 3:6
the living God, who g . . . . 1 Tim. 6:17
that g to all men liberally . . . . James 1:5
ability which God g . . . . 1 Pet. 4:11

resisteth the proud, and g . . . . . . 1 Pet. 5:5

GIVING
course in praising and g . . . . Ezra 3:11
covenants, and the g . . . . Rom. 9:4
G thanks always for . . . . Eph. 5:20
fruit of our lips g . . Heb. 13:15
them in like manner, g . . . . Jude 7

GLAD
rejoiced and was g . Esth. 8:15
Israel shall be g . . . . . Ps. 14:7
whereof shall make g . . . . Ps. 46:4
wine that maketh g . . . . Ps. 104:15
wise son maketh a g . . . . . . Prov. 10:1
he that is g at calamities . . . . Prov. 17:5
we will be g and rejoice . . . . Is. 25:9
g, O daughter of Edom . . . . Lam. 4:21
and be exceeding g . . . . . . Matt. 5:12
shew thee these g tidings . . . . Luke 1:19

GLADNESS
joyfulness, and with g . . . . Deut. 28:47
thee with the oil of g . . . . Ps. 45:7
shall obtain joy and g . . . . Is. 35:10
joy and g shall be . . . . . Is. 51:3
voice of g, the voice . . . . Jer. 7:34
voice of g, the voice . . . . Jer. 16:9
voice of g, the voice . . . . Jer. 25:10
voice of g, the voice . . . . Jer. 33:11
hearts with food and g . . . . Acts 14:17

GLORIFIED
redeemed Jacob, and g . . . . Is. 44:23
for he hath g thee . . . . . Is. 55:5
Israel, because he hath g . . . . Is. 60:9
hands, that I may be g . . . . Is. 60:21
that he might be g . . . . Is. 61:3
ways, hast thou not g . . . . Dan. 5:23
and they g God, saying . . . . Luke 7:16
Jesus was not yet g . . . . John 7:39
hath g his Son Jesus . . . . Acts 3:13
peace, and g God, saying . . . . Acts 11:18

that we may be
  also *g* . . . . Rom. 8:17
g through Jesus
  Christ . . . . 1 Pet. 4:11

GLORIFY
thee, and thou
  shalt *g* . . . . Ps. 50:15
and shall *g* thy
  name . . . . Ps. 86:9
altar, and I will *g* . . . . . Is. 60:7
shall behold, *g*
  God . . . . 1 Pet. 2:12

GLORIOUS
like thee, *g* in
  holiness . . . . Ex. 15:11
mayest fear this *g* Deut. 28:58
And blessed be
  his *g* . . . . Ps. 72:19
be beautiful and *g* . . . . . Is. 4:2
his rest shall be *g* . . . . Is. 11:10
his *g* voice to be
  heard . . . . Is. 30:30
g in his apparel,
  travelling . . . . Is. 63:1
Moses with his *g*
  arm . . . . Is. 63:12
light of the *g*
  gospel . . . . 2 Cor. 4:4
present it to
  himself a *g* . . . . . . Eph. 5:27
blessed hope, and
  the *g* . . . . Titus 2:13

GLORY
and the *g* of the
  LORD . . . . 2 Chr. 7:3
will give grace
  and *g* . . . . Ps. 84:11
LORD, and for
  the *g* . . . . Is. 2:19
earth is full of his *g* . . . . Is. 6:3
the *g* of Lebanon
  shall . . . . Is. 35:2
the LORD, and
  shalt *g* . . . . Is. 41:16
neither have seen
  my *g* . . . . Is. 66:19
wise man *g* in his
  wisdom . . . . Jer. 9:23
the likeness of
  the *g* . . . . Ezek. 1:28
him dominion,
  and *g* . . . . Dan. 7:14
be the *g* in the
  midst . . . . Zech. 2:5
in the *g* of his
  Father . . . . Matt. 16:27
enter into his *g* . . . Luke 24:26
beheld his *g*, the *g* . . John 1:14
to whom be *g* for
  ever . . . . Rom. 11:36
God, be honour
  and *g* . . . . 1 Tim. 1:17
received up into *g*. 1 Tim. 3:16
brightness of his *g* . . . Heb. 1:3
death, crowned
  with *g* . . . . Heb. 2:9
his eternal *g* by
  Christ . . . . 1 Pet. 5:10

GOATS
sheep, or from
  the *g* . . . . Ex. 12:5
the *g* for a sin
  offering . . . . . . Num. 28:15
lambs, or of he *g* . . . . . Is. 1:11
blood of lambs
  and *g* . . . . Is. 34:6
he *g* before the
  flocks . . . . Jer. 50:8
blood of *g* and
  calves . . . . Heb. 9:12

GOD
for I the LORD
  thy *G* . . . . Ex. 20:5
the name of thy *G* . Lev. 18:21
G is not a man,
  that . . . . Num. 23:19
unto the LORD
  thy *G* . . . . Deut. 7:6
LORD your *G*
  shall choose . . . . . Deut. 12:5
a *G* of truth and
  without . . . . Deut. 32:4
thou the *G* of thy
  father . . . . 1 Chr. 28:9
the messengers
  of *G* . . . . 2 Chr. 36:16
my *G*, my
  strength . . . . Ps. 18:2
Counsellor, The
  mighty *G* . . . . Is. 9:6
beside me there is
  no *G* . . . . Is. 44:6
Spirit of the
  Lord *G* . . . . Is. 61:1
the *G* of heaven
  set . . . . Dan. 2:44
the Lord *G* shall
  give . . . . Luke 1:32
No man hath
  seen *G* . . . . John 1:18
G so loved the
  world . . . . John 3:16
feed the church
  of *G* . . . . Acts 20:28
and a sacrifice
  to *G* . . . . Eph. 5:2
G, being put to
  death . . . . 1 Pet. 3:18
the paradise of *G* . . . . Rev. 2:7

GODS
g of Egypt I will
  execute . . . . Ex. 12:12
LORD, among
  the *g* . . . . Ex. 15:11
shalt not revile
  the *g* . . . . Ex. 22:28
bow down to
  their *g* . . . . Ex. 23:24
thou serve their *g* . . . Ex. 23:33
thou serve their *g* . . Deut. 7:16
your God is God
  of *g* . . . . Deut. 10:17
done unto their *g* . Deut. 12:31
and serve other *g* . . Deut. 13:13
and served other *g* . Deut. 17:3
thou serve other *g*. Deut. 28:36
shalt serve other *g*. Deut. 28:64

the strange *g* and
  Ashtaroth . . . . . . 1 Sam. 7:3
behold thy *g*, O
  Israel . . . . 1 Kin. 12:28
worshipped
  other *g* . . . . Jer. 22:9
after other *g* to
  serve . . . . Jer. 35:15
God is a God of *g* . . Dan. 2:47
spirit of the holy *g* . . Dan. 5:11
hast praised the *g* . . Dan. 5:23
against the God
  of *g* . . . . Dan. 11:36

GOEST
before Egypt, as
  thou *g* . . . . Gen. 25:18
places whither
  thou *g* . . . . Gen. 28:15
Moses, When
  thou *g* . . . . Ex. 4:21
them, and that
  thou *g* . . . . Num. 14:14
thou be when
  thou *g* . . . . Deut. 28:6
thou be when
  thou *g* . . . . Deut. 28:19
land, whither
  thou *g* . . . . Deut. 28:21
land whither
  thou *g* . . . . Deut. 28:63
whithersoever
  thou *g* . . . . Josh. 1:7
whithersoever
  thou *g* . . . . Josh. 1:9

GOETH
Aaron's heart,
  when he *g* . . . . Ex. 28:30
Whatsoever *g*
  upon the . . . . Lev. 11:42
LORD your God
  which *g* . . . . Deut. 1:30
And *g* down
  westward . . . . Josh. 16:3
every one that *g*
  out . . . . Jer. 5:6
that *g* out, and
  falleth . . . . Jer. 21:9
g forth to the
  Chaldeans . . . . Jer. 38:2
whatsoever
  thing *g* . . . . Jer. 44:17
g by it shall be
  astonished . . . . . . Jer. 49:17
one that *g* by
  Babylon . . . . Jer. 50:13
love, but their
  heart *g* . . . . Ezek. 33:31
knoweth not
  whither he *g* . . . John 12:35

GOINGS
and the *g* out
  thereof . . . . Josh. 16:3
and established
  my *g* . . . . Ps. 40:2
pondereth all
  his *g* . . . . Prov. 5:21
whose *g* forth
  have . . . . Mic. 5:2

GOLD

linen, and put a g . .Gen. 41:42
candlestick of
  pure g . . . . .Ex. 25:31
beaten work of
  pure g . . . . .Ex. 25:36
of silver and g . . . .Num. 22:18
made two calves
  of g . . . . 1 Kin. 12:28
the silver and
  the g . . . . 1 Kin. 15:18
g which Solomon
  king . . . . 2 Kin. 24:13
silver and their g . . . . .Is. 60:9
the carbuncle,
  and g . . . . Ezek. 28:13
and have a chain
  of g . . . . .Dan. 5:7
chain of g about
  thy . . . . .Dan. 5:16
gods of silver,
  and g . . . . .Dan. 5:23
is laid over with g . . .Hab. 2:19
silver nor their g . . .Zeph. 1:18
will try them as g . . Zech. 13:9
and purge them
  as g . . . . Mal. 3:3
g, or silver, or
  stone . . . . Acts 17:29
round about
  with g . . . . .Heb. 9:4
precious than of g . . 1 Pet. 1:7
thee to buy of
  me g . . . . Rev. 3:18

GOLDEN

Babylon hath
  been a g . . . . Jer. 51:7
g censer, and the
  ark . . . . .Heb. 9:4
the paps with a g
  girdle . . . . Rev. 1:13
g vials full of
  odours . . . . Rev. 5:8
altar, having a g
  censer . . . . Rev. 8:3

GOMER

Son of Japheth, Gen. 10:2, 3;
  1 Chr. 1:5, 6
——— A people descended
  from Gomer, Ezek. 38:6
——— Wife (concubine?) of
  Hosea, Hos. 1:3

GOMORRAH

One of the "cities of the
  plain," Gen. 10:19; 13:10
Its king defeated by
  Chedorlaomer, Gen. 14:2,
  8–11
Wickedness of, Gen. 18:20
Destroyed, Gen. 19:24–28;
  Deut. 29:23; 32:32; Is. 1:9,
  10; 13:19; Jer. 23:14; 49:18;
  50:40; Amos 4:11; Zeph. 2:9;
  Matt. 10:15; Mark 6:11;
  Rom. 9:29; 2 Pet. 2:6; Jude 7

GOOD

land unto a g land . . . .Ex. 3:8
shall he not make
  it g . . . . .Num. 23:19

open unto thee
  his g . . . . Deut. 28:12
do you g, and to
  multiply . . . . . . Deut. 28:63
strong and of a g
  courage . . . . Deut. 31:6
strong and of a g
  courage . . . . .Josh. 1:9
thou, Lord, art g . . . . Ps. 86:5
anointed me to
  preach g . . . . .Is. 61:1
for g, saith the
  LORD . . . . Jer. 21:10
for g, and I will
  bring . . . . Jer. 24:6
for the LORD is g . . . Jer. 33:11
thee, O man,
  what is g . . . . Mic. 6:8
Daughter, be of g
  comfort . . . . Matt. 9:22
doing g, and
  healing . . . . Acts 10:38
prove what is
  that g . . . . Rom. 12:2
Christ Jesus
  unto g . . . . Eph. 2:10
people, zealous
  of g . . . . Titus 2:14
g gift and every
  perfect . . . . James 1:17
may by your g
  works . . . . 1 Pet. 2:12
the answer of a g
  conscience . . . . . 1 Pet. 3:21

GOODLY

day the boughs
  of g . . . . Lev. 23:40
countenance,
  and g . . . . 1 Sam. 16:12
g vessels of the
  house . . . . 2 Chr. 36:10
all the g vessels
  thereof. . . . . . . 2 Chr. 36:19

GOODNESS

longsuffering, and
  abundant in g . . . . . Ex. 34:6
believed to see
  the g . . . . Ps. 27:13
with the g of thy
  house. . . . . Ps. 65:4
fruit thereof and
  the g . . . . Jer. 2:7
flow together to
  the g . . . . Jer. 31:12
tremble for all
  the g . . . . Jer. 33:9
the LORD and
  his g . . . . .Hos. 3:5
the riches of his g . . . Rom. 2:4
longsuffering,
  gentleness, g . . . . . Gal. 5:22

GOODS

g, wells digged,
  vineyards . . . . .Neh. 9:25
Soul, thou hast
  much g . . . . Luke 12:19
half of my g I give . .Luke 19:8
and increased
  with g . . . . Rev. 3:17

GOSHEN

A district in Egypt especially
  suitable for herds and
  flocks; Israelites dwelt in,
  Gen. 45:10; 46:28; 47
Exempted from plagues,
  Ex. 8:22; 9:26
——— A town and district
  of the tribe of Judah,
  Josh. 10:41; 11:16; 15:51

GOSPEL

and preaching
  the g . . . . Matt. 4:23
And this g of the
  kingdom . . . . . . Matt. 24:14
me to preach the g . .Luke 4:18
Jesus, to testify
  the g . . . . Acts 20:24
separated unto
  the g . . . . Rom. 1:1
my spirit in the g . . . Rom. 1:9
not ashamed of
  the g . . . . Rom. 1:16
according to my g . . Rom. 2:16
to my g, and the
  preaching . . . . . . Rom. 16:25
but to preach
  the g . . . . .1 Cor. 1:17
hinder the g of
  Christ . . . . .1 Cor. 9:12
light of the
  glorious g . . . . .2 Cor. 4:4
that g which I
  preach . . . . Gal. 2:2
word of truth,
  the g . . . . .Eph. 1:13
the g, ye all are
  partakers . . . . Phil. 1:7
becometh the g of
  Christ . . . . Phil. 1:27
g, which ye have
  heard . . . . Col. 1:23
g of Christ, to
  establish . . . . . . .1 Thess. 3:2
the g of our Lord
  Jesus . . . . .2 Thess. 1:8
afflictions of the g . 2 Tim. 1:8

GOVERNOR

And Joseph was
  the g . . . . .Gen. 42:6
the son of
  Ahikam g . . . . Jer. 40:7
son of Shealtiel, g . . . .Hag. 1:1
thee shall
  come a G . . . . Matt. 2:6
Pontius Pilate
  the g . . . . Matt. 27:2
before the g . . . . . Matt. 27:11
authority of the g . Luke 20:20

GRACE

the LORD will
  give g . . . . Ps. 84:11
Jerusalem, the
  spirit of g . . . . . . Zech. 12:10
full of g and truth . . .John 1:14
gospel of the g . . . .Acts 20:24
G to you and
  peace . . . . Rom. 1:7
say, through the g . Rom. 12:3

The *g* of our Lord
  Jesus . . . . Rom. 16:20
the *g* of our Lord
  Jesus . . . . .2 Cor. 8:9
The *g* of the Lord
  Jesus . . . . 2 Cor. 13:14
the riches of his *g* . . . . Eph. 1:7
all saints, is this *g* . . . Eph. 3:8
partakers of my *g* . . . Phil. 1:7
and knew the *g* of
  God . . . . Col. 1:6
speech be alway
  with *g* . . . . Col. 4:6
g of God should
  taste. . . . . .Heb. 2:9
G unto you, and
  peace . . . . .1 Pet. 1:2
to the end for
  the *g* . . . . .1 Pet. 1:13
proud, and
  giveth *g* . . . . .1 Pet. 5:5
God of all *g*, who
  hath . . . . 1 Pet. 5:10
G be unto you,
  and. . . . . Rev. 1:4

GRACIOUS
God, merciful
  and *g* . . . . Ex. 34:6
upon thee, and
  be *g* . . . . Num. 6:25
ready to pardon, *g* . .Neh. 9:17
compassion, and *g* . . Ps. 86:15
merciful and *g*,
  slow. . . . . Ps. 103:8
g and merciful,
  slow. . . . . Joel 2:13
knew that thou
  art a *g* . . . . Jon. 4:2
wondered at the *g*
  words . . . . .Luke 4:22

GRANTED
and the king *g*
  him . . . . Ezra 7:6
a murderer to be *g* . . Acts 3:14
to the Gentiles *g*
  repentance . . . . . . .Acts 11:18
And to her was *g*
  that . . . . Rev. 19:8

GRAPES
shalt not gather
  the *g* . . . . .Deut. 28:30
wine, nor gather
  the *g* . . . . Deut. 28:39
should bring
  forth *g* . . . . .Is. 5:2
bring forth *g*,
  brought . . . . .Is. 5:4
leave some
  gleaning *g* . . . . .Jer. 49:9
found Israel like *g* . .Hos. 9:10

GRASS
nor any *g* . . . . . . .Deut. 29:23
rain upon the
  mown *g* . . . . .Ps. 72:6
causeth the *g* to
  grow . . . . Ps. 104:14
earth, who
  maketh *g* . . . . Ps. 147:8

g with reeds and
  rushes . . . . .Is. 35:7
g withereth, the
  flower . . . . .Is. 40:8
shall be made as *g* . . .Is. 51:12
make thee to eat *g* . .Dan. 4:25
down on the *g*. . . . Matt. 14:19
all flesh is as *g* . . . . 1 Pet. 1:24
all green *g* was
  burnt . . . . Rev. 8:7
hurt the *g* of the
  earth . . . . Rev. 9:4

GRAVE
the *g* unto my son
  mourning . . . . . . .Gen. 37:35
bone of a man, or
  a *g* . . . . .Num. 19:16
bringeth down to
  the *g* . . . . .1 Sam. 2:6
thy *g* in a full age . . . . Job 5:26
g who shall give
  thee . . . . Ps. 6:5
And he made his *g*
  with . . . . .Is. 53:9
the power of the *g* .Hos. 13:14
deacons be *g*, not
  doubletongued. . . 1 Tim. 3:8

GRAVEN
make unto thee
  any *g* . . . . Ex. 20:4
no idols nor *g*
  image. . . . . Lev. 26:1
groves, and burn
  their *g* . . . . Deut. 7:5
hew down the *g*
  images. . . . . Deut. 12:3
man that maketh
  any *g* . . . . .Deut. 27:15
And he set a *g*
  image. . . . . 2 Kin. 21:7
g images of her
  gods. . . . . .Is. 21:9
my praise to *g*
  images . . . . .Is. 42:8
confounded by
  the *g* . . . . .Jer. 10:14
profiteth the *g*
  image. . . . . .Hab. 2:18
silver, or stone, *g* . .Acts 17:29

GREAT
make of thee a *g*
  nation . . . . .Gen. 12:2
Egypt unto the *g*
  river. . . . . .Gen. 15:18
lords, a *g* God, a
  mighty. . . . . Deut. 10:17
Hath the Lord
  as *g* . . . . .1 Sam. 15:22
g man's house
  burnt . . . . 2 Kin. 25:9
they wrought *g*
  provocations. . . . . .Neh. 9:26
north, the city of
  the *g* . . . . Ps. 48:2
Bozrah, and a *g*
  slaughter. . . . . .Is. 34:6
portion with the *g* . . .Is. 53:12
broken with a *g*
  breach . . . . .Jer. 14:17

earth by thy *g*
  power . . . . Jer. 32:17
houses of the *g*
  men . . . . Jer. 52:13
bringing upon
  us a *g*. . . . . .Dan. 9:12
Michael stand up
  the *g* . . . . .Dan. 12:1
anger, and of *g*
  kindness . . . . Joel 2:13
blood, before
  the *g* . . . . Joel 2:31
g, and shall be
  called . . . . .Luke 1:32
without
  controversy *g* . . 1 Tim. 3:16
the *g* God and our
  Saviour . . . . Titus 2:13
the *g* dragon was
  cast . . . . Rev. 12:9

GREATER
people is *g* and
  taller . . . . Deut. 1:28
Jebusites, seven
  nations *g* . . . . Deut. 7:1
to possess
  nations *g* . . . . Deut. 9:1
nation mightier
  and *g* . . . . Deut. 9:14
The servant is
  not *g* . . . . .John 15:20
for *g* is he that
  prophesieth . . . . .1 Cor. 14:5
things to come, by
  a *g* . . . . .Heb. 9:11
because *g* is he
  that . . . . 1 John 4:4

GREATLY
I will *g* multiply
  thy . . . . .Gen. 3:16
blessed my
  master *g* . . . . . . .Gen. 24:35
whole mount
  quaked *g* . . . . Ex. 19:18
shall he *g* multiply Deut. 17:17
and humbled
  himself *g*. . . . . . 2 Chr. 33:12
Lord, and *g* to be
  praised . . . . Ps. 48:1
God is *g* to be
  feared . . . . Ps. 89:7
Lord is great,
  and *g* . . . . Ps. 96:4
, that delighteth *g* . . Ps. 112:1
I will *g* rejoice in . . . .Is. 61:10
sabbaths they *g*
  polluted. . . . . Ezek. 20:13
vengeance, and
  hath *g* . . . . Ezek. 25:12
Rejoice *g*, O
  daughter . . . . Zech. 9:9
And besought
  him *g*. . . . . Mark 5:23
heareth him,
  rejoiceth *g* . . . . . .John 3:29

GREATNESS
by the *g* of thine
  arm . . . . Ex. 15:16
thy servant thy *g* . . Deut. 3:24

thy *g*, which thou
  hast .... Deut. 9:26
all by names by
  the *g* .... Is. 40:26
travelling in the *g* ..... Is. 63:1
the *g* of thine
  iniquity .... Jer. 13:22
dominion, and
  the *g* .... Dan. 7:27

GREECE
Inhabitants of; Called
  "Gentiles" (non-Jews),
  Mark 7:26; John 7:35;
  Rom. 2:10; 3:9; 1 Cor. 10:32;
  12:13
Desire to see Jesus,
  John 12:20–23
Marry among the Jews,
  Acts 16:1
Accept the Messiah,
  Acts 17:2–4, 12, 34
Persecute the early
  Christians, Acts 6:9–14;
  9:29; 18:17
Gentiles called "Greeks,"
  Rom. 10:12; Gal. 3:28;
  Col. 3:11
Schools of philosophy in
  Athens, Acts 19:9
Philosophy of, 1 Cor. 1:22, 23
Poets of, Acts 17:28
Prophecies concerning,
  Dan. 10:20; Zech. 9:13

GREEN
hills, and under
  every *g* .... Deut. 12:2
hill, and under
  every *g* .... 1 Kin. 14:23
But I am like a *g*
  olive.............. Ps. 52:8
every *g* tree thou
  wanderest .... Jer. 2:20
g tree, and there
  hath .... Jer. 3:6
her leaf shall be *g* .... Jer. 17:8
up the *g* tree ..... Ezek. 17:24
all *g* grass was
  burnt .... Rev. 8:7
earth, neither
  any *g* .... Rev. 9:4

GRIEVED
and the men
  were *g* .... Gen. 34:7
And it *g* Samuel . 1 Sam. 15:11
Ammonite, heard
  of it, it *g* .... Neh. 2:10
but they have
  not *g* .... Jer. 5:3
with anger,
  being *g* .... Mark 3:5
Peter was *g*
  because .... John 21:17

GRIEVOUS
his life shall be *g* ..... Is. 15:4
A *g* vision is
  declared........... Is. 21:2
breach, with a
  very *g* .... Jer. 14:17

shall die of *g*
  deaths .... Jer. 16:4

GROUND
the dust of the *g* ..... Gen. 2:7
return unto the *g* ... Gen. 3:19
not again curse
  the *g* .... Gen. 8:21
which grew upon
  the *g* .... Gen. 19:25
sea upon the dry *g* .. Ex. 14:22
the fruit of thy *g* ... Deut. 28:4
her foot upon
  the *g* .... Deut. 28:56
them down to
  the *g* .... 2 Sam. 8:2
their faces to the *g* .. 2 Chr. 7:3
thy name to the *g* .... Ps. 74:7
shall sit upon
  the *g* .... Is. 3:26
broken unto the *g* .... Is. 21:9
And the parched *g*
  shall................ Is. 35:7
floods upon the
  dry *g* .... Is. 44:3
root out of a dry *g* .... Is. 53:2
the fruit of the *g* ..... Jer. 7:20
them down to
  the *g* .... Lam. 2:2
face toward the *g* ... Dan. 8:18
the *g*, and thy
  children........ Luke 19:44
God, the pillar
  and *g* .... 1 Tim. 3:15

GROVE
And Ahab made a
  g .... 1 Kin. 16:33
calves, and
  made a *g* ...... 2 Kin. 17:16
and made a *g*..... 2 Kin. 21:3
he brought out
  the *g* .... 2 Kin. 23:6

GROVES
and cut down
  their *g* .... Ex. 34:13
g, and burn their
  graven .... Deut. 7:5
served Baalim and
  the *g* .... Judg. 3:7
g, on every high
  hill .... 1 Kin. 14:23
the prophets of
  the *g* .... 1 Kin. 18:19
g, and brake in
  pieces .... 2 Kin. 18:4
hast taken away
  the *g* .... 2 Chr. 19:3
and cut down
  the *g* .... 2 Chr. 31:1

GROW
made the LORD
  God to *g* .... Gen. 2:9
causeth the grass
  to *g*............ Ps. 104:14
who maketh grass
  to *g*............ Ps. 147:8
and a Branch
  shall *g* .... Is. 11:1
For he shall *g* up
  before .... Is. 53:2

he shall *g* as the
  lily .... Hos. 14:5
g up out of his
  place .... Zech. 6:12
truth in love,
  may *g*........... Eph. 4:15
word, that ye
  may *g*.......... 1 Pet. 2:2

GUARD
and captain of
  the *g* .... Gen. 37:36
captain of the *g*,
  brake .... 2 Kin. 25:10
the captain of the
  g............. 2 Kin. 25:18
captain of the *g*
  left .... Jer. 39:10
the captain of
  the *g* .... Jer. 52:19
the captain of
  the *g* .... Jer. 52:24
the captain of
  the *g* .... Jer. 52:26

GUIDE
g thee with mine
  eye .... Ps. 32:8
of water shall he *g* ... Is. 49:10
shadow of death,
  to *g*............. Luke 1:79
Judas, which
  was *g* .... Acts 1:16

GUILTY
means clear the *g* .... Ex. 34:7
he *g*, and shall
  bear .... Lev. 5:17
means clearing
  the *g* .... Num. 14:18
answered and
  said, He is *g* .... Matt. 26:66

HABITATION
will prepare him
  an *h* .... Ex. 15:2
strength unto thy
  holy *h* .... Ex. 15:13
his *h* shall ye seek . Deut. 12:5
God in his holy *h* .... Ps. 68:5
judgment are
  the *h* .... Ps. 97:2
h for the mighty
  God .... Ps. 132:5
shall be an *h* of
  dragons .... Is. 34:13
in the *h* of
  dragons .... Is. 35:7
from the *h* of thy
  holiness.......... Is. 63:15
Jordan against
  the *h* .... Jer. 49:19
LORD, the *h* of
  justice .... Jer. 50:7
the land of their *h* Ezek. 29:14
rock, whose *h* is
  high .... Obad. 3
become the *h* of
  devils .... Rev. 18:2

HABITATIONS
h shall ye eat
  unleavened ...... Ex. 12:20

HAGAR

wailing, and for
the *h* . . . . Jer. 9:10
shall enter into
our *h* . . . . Jer. 21:13
make their *h*
desolate. . . . . Jer. 49:20
h of Jacob, and
hath . . . . Lam. 2:2
and the *h* of the
shepherds . . . . Amos 1:2
into everlasting *h* . . . Luke 16:9

HAGAR

A servant of Abraham and
handmaiden of Sarah; Given
by Sarah to Abraham to be
his wife, Gen. 16
Descendants of, Gen. 25:12–
15; 1 Chr. 5:10, 19–22;
Ps. 83:6
Called Agar, Gal. 4:24, 25

HAIL

there be any
more *h* . . . . Ex. 9:29
h stones and coals . . Ps. 18:13
Fire, and *h* . . . . Ps. 148:8
which as a
tempest of *h* . . . . Is. 28:2
h and fire mingled . . . Rev. 8:7
earthquake, and
great *h* . . . . Rev. 11:19
upon men a
great *h* . . . . Rev. 16:21

HAIR

plucked off the *h* . . . . . Is. 50:6
as snow, and the *h* . . . Dan. 7:9
raiment of
camel's *h* . . . . Matt. 3:4
as sackcloth of *h* . . . . Rev. 6:12

HALF

are numbered, *h* a
shekel . . . . Ex. 30:13
not give less
than *h* . . . . Ex. 30:15
of sweet
cinnamon *h* . . . . Ex. 30:23
man, that is, *h* a
shekel . . . . Ex. 38:26
be *h* an hin of
wine . . . . Num. 28:14
the *h* tribe of
Manasseh . . . . . . 1 Chr. 5:26
live out *h* their
days . . . . Ps. 55:23
time, times, and
an *h* . . . . Dan. 12:7
and *h* of the
mountain . . . . Zech. 14:4
time, and times,
and *h* . . . . Rev. 12:14

HALLOWED

sabbath day, and *h* . . Ex. 20:11
h things of the
children. . . . . Num. 18:8
I have *h* this
house. . . . . 1 Kin. 9:3
house, which I
have *h* . . . . 1 Kin. 9:7

HAM

Son of Noah, Gen. 5:32; 9:18,
24; 1 Chr. 1:4
Provokes his father's wrath
and is cursed by him,
Gen. 9:18–27
His children, Gen. 10:6–20;
1 Chr. 1:8–16
——— Patronymic of the
descendants of Ham,
1 Chr. 4:40; Ps. 78:51;
105:23, 27; 106:22
——— Place where
Chedorlaomer struck down
the Zuzims, Gen. 14:5

HAMAN

Prime minister of Ahasuerus,
Esth. 3:1
Plotted against Esther and the
Jews; thwarted by Esther and
Mordecai
Hanged, Esth. 3; 4; 5; 6; 7; 8; 9

HAMATH

Also called Hemath; A city
of upper Syria, Num. 13:21;
34:8; Josh. 13:5; 1 Kin. 8:65;
Ezek. 47:16
Inhabited by Canaanites,
Gen. 10:18
Prosperity of, Amos 6:2
David receives gifts of gold
and silver from Toi, king of,
2 Sam. 8:9, 10; 1 Chr. 18:3,
9, 10
Conquest of, by Jeroboam,
2 Kin. 14:25, 28
By the Chaldeans,
2 Kin. 25:20, 21
Israelites taken captive to,
Is. 11:11
Prophecy concerning,
Jer. 49:23
Solomon builds store cities in,
2 Chr. 8:4

HAMOR

The father of Shechem; Jacob
buys a piece of property from,
Gen. 33:19; Josh. 24:32;
Judg. 9:28
Murdered by the sons of Jacob,
Gen. 34:26; 49:6
Called Emmor, Acts 7:16

HANANI

Son of Heman, 1 Chr. 25:4, 25
——— A prophet who
rebuked Asa, king of Judah,
2 Chr. 16:7
——— Father of Jehu the
prophet, 1 Kin. 16:1, 7;
2 Chr. 19:2; 20:34
——— A priest, Ezra 10:20
——— A brother of Nehemiah
and keeper of the gates of
Jerusalem, Neh. 1:2; 7:2
——— A priest and musician,
Neh. 12:36

HANANIAH

Son of Heman, 1 Chr. 25:4, 23
——— A captain of Uzziah's
army, 2 Chr. 26:11
——— Father of Zedekiah,
Jer. 36:12
——— A prophet of Gibeon
who uttered false prophecies
in the temple during the
reign of Zedekiah, Jer. 28
——— Grandfather of Irijah,
Jer. 37:13
——— Son of Shashak,
1 Chr. 8:24
——— Son of Zerubbabel,
1 Chr. 3:19, 21
——— Son of Bebai, Ezra 10:28
——— An apothecary and
priest, Neh. 3:8
——— Son of Shelemiah,
Neh. 3:30
——— A keeper of the gates of
Jerusalem, Neh. 7:2
——— One who sealed the
covenant, Neh. 10:23
——— A priest during the time
of Jehoiakim, Neh. 12:12, 41

HAND

deliver them out
of the *h* . . . . Ex. 3:8
stretched out
his *h* . . . . Ex. 14:21
a timbrel in her *h* . . . Ex. 15:20
offerings of your *h* . Deut. 12:6
that ye put your *h* . Deut. 12:7
deliver out of
my *h* . . . . Deut. 32:39
right *h* or to the
left . . . . Josh. 1:7
h, until I make
thine . . . . Ps. 110:1
stretched forth
his *h* . . . . Is. 5:25
Lord shall set
his *h* . . . . Is. 11:11
thee with the
right *h* . . . . Is. 41:10
right *h* I have
holden . . . . Is. 45:1
hast drunk at
the *h* . . . . Is. 51:17
shall prosper in
his *h* . . . . Is. 53:10
and the *h* of the
LORD. . . . . Ezek. 1:3
I will turn mine *h* . . Zech. 13:7
right *h*, Come, ye
blessed . . . . Matt. 25:34
on the left *h*,
Depart . . . . Matt. 25:41
right *h* of the
Majesty . . . . Heb. 1:3
right *h* of the
throne . . . . Heb. 12:2

HANDS

delivered them
into the *h* . . . . Judg. 2:14
the *h* of their
father. . . . . 1 Chr. 25:6
work of his own *h* . . . Ps. 9:16

the work of thy *h* . . Ps. 102:25
h, I will hide mine . . . . Is. 1:15
the reward of
  his *h* . . . . Is. 3:11
planting, the work
  of my *h* . . . . Is. 60:21
strengthen also
  the *h* . . . . Jer. 23:14
the *h* shall be
  cuttings . . . . Jer. 48:37
pass by clap
  their *h* . . . . Lam. 2:15
the palms of their
  h . . . . Matt. 26:67
maimed, than
  having two *h* . . . . . Mark 9:43
into thy *h* I
  commend . . . . . . Luke 23:46
by wicked *h* have
  crucified . . . . Acts 2:23
prayed, they laid
  their *h* . . . . Acts 6:6
h of Barnabas and
  Saul . . . . Acts 11:30
places made
  with *h* . . . . Heb. 9:24
Cleanse your *h*, ye . . James 4:8
looked upon, and
  our *h* . . . . 1 John 1:1
foreheads, or in
  their *h* . . . . Rev. 20:4

HANGED

h is accursed of
  God . . . . Deut. 21:23
household in
  order, and *h* . . . 2 Sam. 17:23
h Haman on the
  gallows . . . . Esth. 7:10
h the shield and
  helmet . . . . Ezek. 27:10

HANNAH

The mother of Samuel;
  Her trials and prayer, and
  promise, 1 Sam. 1:1–18
Samuel born to, dedicated him
  to God, leaves him at the
  temple, 1 Sam. 1:19–28
Her hymn of praise,
  1 Sam. 2:1–10
Visits Samuel at the
  temple from year to year,
  1 Sam. 2:18, 19
Children of, 1 Sam. 2:20, 21

HARAN

Father of Lot and brother of
  Abraham, Gen. 11:26–31
——— Son of Caleb, 1 Chr. 2:46
——— A Levite, 1 Chr. 23:9
——— Also called Charran
A place in Mesopotamia to
  which Terah and Abraham
  migrated, Gen. 11:31; 12:4,
  5; Acts 7:4
Death of Terah at, Gen. 11:32
Abraham leaves, by divine
  command, Gen. 12:1–5
Jacob flees to, Gen. 27:43;
  28:7; 29
Returns from, with Rachel and
  Leah, Gen. 31:17–21

Conquest of, king of Assyria,
  2 Kin. 19:12
Merchants of, Ezek. 27:23
Idolatry in, Josh. 24:2, 14;
  Is. 37:12

HARD

Is any thing too *h* . . Gen. 18:14
lives bitter with *h* . . . . Ex. 1:14
is too *h* for you,
  bring . . . . Deut. 1:17
shewed thy
  people *h* . . . . Ps. 60:3
nothing too *h* for
  thee . . . . Jer. 32:17
there any thing
  too *h* . . . . Jer. 32:27

HARDENED

respite, he *h* his
  heart . . . . Ex. 8:15
LORD *h* Pharaoh's
  heart . . . . Ex. 10:20
the LORD *h* the
  heart . . . . Ex. 14:8
hear, but *h* their
  necks . . . . 2 Kin. 17:14
stiffened his neck,
  and *h* . . . . 2 Chr. 36:13
but *h* their necks . . . Neh. 9:17
the shoulder,
  and *h* . . . . Neh. 9:29
inclined their ear,
  but *h* . . . . Jer. 7:26

HARLOT

wanderest,
  playing the *h* . . . . . . Jer. 2:20
thou hast played
  the *h* . . . . Jer. 3:1
hath played the *h* . . . . . Jer. 3:6
went and played
  the *h* . . . . Jer. 3:8
Israel, play the *h* . . . . Hos. 4:15

HARP

and a pipe,
  and a *h* . . . . 1 Sam. 10:5
prophesied
  with a *h* . . . . 1 Chr. 25:3
awake, psaltery
  and *h* . . . . Ps. 57:8
the timbrel and *h* . . . Ps. 149:3
h for Moab, and
  mine . . . . Is. 16:11

HARPS

should prophesy
  with *h* . . . . 1 Chr. 25:1
psalteries, and *h* . . 1 Chr. 25:6
sound of thy *h* . . . Ezek. 26:13
h, and golden vials . . . Rev. 5:8

HARVEST

feast of *h*, the
  firstfruits . . . . Ex. 23:16
shall reap the *h*
  thereof . . . . Lev. 23:10
all the time of *h* . . . Josh. 3:15
and the time of
  her *h* . . . . Jer. 51:33
h of the field is
  perished . . . . Joel 1:11
the sickle, for
  the *h* . . . . Joel 3:13

HAST

thou *h* obeyed my
  voice . . . . Gen. 22:18
When thou *h*
  brought . . . . Ex. 3:12
which thou *h*
  purchased . . . . Ex. 15:16
labours, which
  thou *h* . . . . Ex. 23:16
doings, whereby
  thou *h* . . . . Deut. 28:20
h thou laid the
  foundation . . . . . . Ps. 102:25
thou *h* broken the
  yoke . . . . Is. 9:4
thou *h* said in
  thine . . . . Is. 14:13
h drunk at the
  hand . . . . Is. 51:17
bitter, that thou *h* . . . Jer. 2:19
a stone, Thou *h*
  brought . . . . Jer. 2:27
thou *h* stricken
  them . . . . Jer. 5:3
for thou *h* made
  all . . . . Jer. 14:22
behold, thou *h*
  made . . . . Jer. 32:17
thou *h* trusted in
  thy . . . . Jer. 48:7
thou *h* defiled my
  sanctuary . . . . Ezek. 5:11
lifted up, and
  thou *h* . . . . Ezek. 28:2
saith unto him,
  Thou *h* . . . . Matt. 26:64
things be, which
  thou *h* . . . . Luke 12:20
believe that
  thou *h* . . . . John 17:21

HASTE

shall eat it in *h* . . . . . Ex. 12:11
land of Egypt in *h* . . Deut. 16:3
come upon them
  make *h* . . . . Deut. 32:35
believeth shall not
  make *h* . . . . Is. 28:16
make *h* to shed
  innocent . . . . Is. 59:7

HATE

generation of
  them that *h* . . . . Ex. 20:5
that *h* you shall
  reign . . . . Lev. 26:17
and love them
  that *h* . . . . 2 Chr. 19:2
with the eye
  that *h* . . . . Ps. 35:19
They that *h* me
  without . . . . Ps. 69:4
love the LORD, *h*
  evil . . . . Ps. 97:10
scorning, and
  fools *h* . . . . Prov. 1:22
the LORD is to *h*
  evil . . . . Prov. 8:13
that *h* me love
  death . . . . Prov. 8:36
excellency of
  Jacob, and *h* . . . . . Amos 6:8

good to them
that *h* . . . . Matt. 5:44
h the one, and
love . . . . Matt. 6:24
ye, when men
shall *h* . . . . .Luke 6:22
man come to me,
and *h* . . . . Luke 14:26

HATED
heard that I was *h* .Gen. 29:33
them that thou
hast *h* . . . . Ezek. 16:37
And I *h* Esau, and
laid. . . . . Mal. 1:3
And ye shall be *h*
of . . . . Matt. 10:22

HATETH
the LORD, which
he *h* . . . . Deut. 12:31
appointed feasts
my soul *h* . . . . .Is. 1:14
doeth evil *h* the
light. . . . . .John 3:20
therefore the
world *h* . . . . .John 15:19

HAZAEL
King of Syria; Anointed king
by Elijah, 1 Kin. 19:15
Conquests by, 2 Kin. 8:28, 29;
9:14; 10:32, 33; 12:17, 18;
13:3, 22; 2 Chr. 22:5, 6
Conspires against, murders,
and succeeds to the throne of
Ben-hadad, 2 Kin. 8:8–15
Death of, 2 Kin. 13:24

HAZOR
A fortified city of Naphtali,
Josh. 11:1, 10, 11, 13;
12:19; 19:36; Judg. 4:2, 17;
1 Sam. 12:9; 2 Kin. 15:29;
Neh. 11:33
——— A city in the south
of Judah, Josh. 15:23;
1 Kin. 9:15
——— A place north of
Jerusalem, Neh. 11:33

HEAD
bruise thy *h*, and
thou. . . . . .Gen. 3:15
h of the burnt
offering . . . . Lev. 1:4
flesh, with his *h* . . . . Lev. 4:11
thy *h* shall be
brass . . . . Deut. 28:23
unto the top of
thy *h* . . . . Deut. 28:35
the *h*, and thou
shalt. . . . . Deut. 28:44
razor come upon
his *h* . . . . .1 Sam. 1:11
poured it upon
his *h* . . . . 1 Sam. 10:1
increased over
our *h* . . . . Ezra 9:6
return upon his
own *h* . . . . Ps. 7:16
lip, they shake
the *h* . . . . Ps. 22:7
a shaking of the *h*. . . Ps. 44:14

h stone of the
corner . . . . Ps. 118:22
the whole *h* is sick . . . . .Is. 1:5
Oh that my *h*
were waters . . . . Jer. 9:1
astonished, and
wag his *h*. . . . . . . .Jer. 18:16
hiss and wag
their *h* . . . . Lam. 2:15
by a lock of
mine *h* . . . . Ezek. 8:3
appoint
themselves one *h* . .Hos. 1:11
is the *h* of the
body. . . . . Col. 1:18

HEADS
bowed their *h* and
worshipped. . . . . Ex. 4:31
Uncover not
your *h* . . . . Lev. 10:6
dust upon their *h* . . .Josh. 7:6
son of Nun, and
the *h* . . . . Josh. 14:1
Thou brakest
the *h* . . . . Ps. 74:14
their *h* shall be
baldness . . . . .Is. 15:2
everlasting joy
upon their *h* . . . . . . .Is. 35:10
their *h* was the
likeness . . . . Ezek. 1:26
your *h*, and your
shoes . . . . Ezek. 24:23
The *h* thereof
judge . . . . Mic. 3:11
be upon your
own *h* . . . . .Acts 18:6
seven *h* and ten
horns . . . . Rev. 12:3

HEAL
I wound, and I *h*. . Deut. 32:39
children, and I
will *h* . . . . Jer. 3:22
he not *h* you, nor
cure . . . . .Hos. 5:13
torn, and he will *h* . . .Hos. 6:1
he hath sent me
to *h* . . . . .Luke 4:18

HEALED
thou canst not
be *h*. . . . . .Deut. 28:27
botch that cannot
be *h* . . . . .Deut. 28:35
convert, and be *h* . . . . .Is. 6:10
his stripes we
are *h*. . . . . .Is. 53:5
have *h* also the
hurt . . . . Jer. 6:14
and he *h* them . . . . Matt. 4:24
that she may be *h*. . Mark 5:23
been *h* of evil
spirits . . . . .Luke 8:2
h on the sabbath
day . . . . Luke 13:14
another, that ye
may be *h* . . . . . . .James 5:16
stripes ye were *h* . . 1 Pet. 2:24

HEAP
stood upright as
an *h* . . . . Ex. 15:8
and rose up upon
an *h* . . . . Josh. 3:16
him a great *h* of
stones . . . . Josh. 7:26
waters to stand as
an *h* . . . . Ps. 78:13
to gather and to *h*. . .Eccl. 2:26
builded upon her
own *h* . . . . Jer. 30:18
shall be a
desolate *h* . . . . Jer. 49:2

HEAPS
laid Jerusalem
on *h* . . . . Ps. 79:1
will make
Jerusalem *h*. . . . . . Jer. 9:11
their altars are
as *h* . . . . .Hos. 12:11
Jerusalem shall
become *h*. . . . . Mic. 3:12

HEAR
he said, *H* now
my words . . . . . . Num. 12:6
H thou in heaven
thy . . . . 1 Kin. 8:43
H ye me, Asa . . . . 2 Chr. 15:2
H my prayer, O
LORD. . . . . Ps. 39:12
H, O heavens, and
give . . . . .Is. 1:2
prayers, I will
not *h* . . . . .Is. 1:15
this people, *H* ye
indeed . . . . .Is. 6:9
with their eyes,
and *h* . . . . .Is. 6:10
h, and your soul
shall . . . . .Is. 55:3
But if ye will not *h* . .Jer. 13:17
whether they
will *h* . . . . Ezek. 2:7
voice, yet will I
not *h* . . . . Ezek. 8:18
and they *h* thy
words . . . . Ezek. 33:31
but he will not *h*. . . . . Mic. 3:4
name, and I will *h* . Zech. 13:9
h ye him . . . . Matt. 17:5
which ye now see
and *h* . . . . .Acts 2:33
h, slow to speak,
slow. . . . . .James 1:19
hath an ear, let
him *h* . . . . Rev. 2:7
hath an ear, let
him *h* . . . . Rev. 2:17

HEARD
h their cry by
reason . . . . Ex. 3:7
they *h* that the
LORD. . . . . Ex. 4:31
make one sound
to be *h* . . . . 2 Chr. 5:13
servant, the
Ammonite, *h* . . . .Neh. 2:10
Job's three
friends *h* . . . . .Job 2:11

he *h* my voice
out of. . . . . Ps. 18:6
h with our ears, O . . . Ps. 44:1
the LORD, and
he *h* . . . . Ps. 120:1
have not *h* my
fame . . . . .Is. 66:19
speaking, but ye *h* . . . Jer. 7:13
For I *h* the
defaming. . . . . .Jer. 20:10
men, *h* that the
king . . . . Jer. 40:7
face, and I *h* a
voice . . . . Ezek. 1:28
And I *h* the man
clothed . . . . .Dan. 12:7
I *h*, my belly
trembled . . . . .Hab. 3:16
When they *h*
these things . . . . . Acts 11:18
since the day ye *h*. . . . Col. 1:6
gospel, which ye
have *h* . . . . Col. 1:23
beginning, which
we have *h* . . . . . . 1 John 1:1
the Lord's day,
and *h* . . . . Rev. 1:10

HEARETH
that *h*, let him
hear . . . . Ezek. 3:27
is he that *h* . . . . . . Matt. 13:22
He that *h* you
h me. . . . . Luke 10:16
h him, rejoiceth
greatly . . . . .John 3:29
h my word, and
believeth . . . . .John 5:24
of the truth *h* my
voice . . . . .John 18:37
according to his
will, he *h* . . . . 1 John 5:14
let him that *h* . . . . . Rev. 22:17

HEARING
reprove after the *h* . . . .Is. 11:3
bowed down at
the *h* . . . . .Is. 21:3
and *h* they may
hear . . . . Mark 4:12
the law, or by
the *h* . . . . Gal. 3:2

HEARKEN
Pharaoh shall
not *h* . . . . Ex. 7:4
thou wilt
diligently *h* . . . . Ex. 15:26
therefore *h*, O
Israel . . . . Deut. 4:1
Thou shalt not *h*
unto. . . . . Deut. 13:3
presumptuously,
and will not *h* . . . Deut. 17:12
thou *h* unto the
commandments. Deut. 28:13
if thou wilt not *h* . Deut. 28:15
said unto
Samuel, H. . . . . . . 1 Sam. 8:7
h than the fat of
rams . . . . 1 Sam. 15:22
that thou
mayest *h* . . . . . . 1 Kin. 8:29

H unto me, O
Jacob . . . . .Is. 48:12
and *h*, ye people,
from. . . . . .Is. 49:1
unto me, I will
not *h* . . . . Jer. 11:11
But if ye will not *h* . . Jer. 17:27
h not ye to your
prophets . . . . Jer. 27:9
deceive you,
neither *h* . . . . Jer. 29:8
me, and would
not *h* . . . . Ezek. 20:8
also, if ye will
not *h* . . . . Ezek. 20:39
brethren, and
fathers, *h* . . . . Acts 7:2
H, my beloved
brethren . . . . .James 2:5

HEARKENED
Because thou
hast *h*. . . . . .Gen. 3:17
Rachel, and
God *h* . . . . .Gen. 30:22
of Israel have
not *h* . . . . Ex. 6:12
hardened his
heart, and *h* . . . . . . Ex. 8:15
times, and have
not *h* . . . . .Num. 14:22
Benhadad *h* unto
king . . . . 1 Kin. 15:20
the king of
Assyria *h* . . . . . . 2 Kin. 16:9
dealt proudly,
and *h* . . . . .Neh. 9:29
not *h* unto my
words . . . . Jer. 6:19
they *h* not, nor
inclined . . . . Jer. 7:24
Yet they *h* not
unto. . . . . Jer. 7:26
but ye have not *h* . . . Jer. 25:4
but ye have not *h* . . . Jer. 26:5
not *h* to receive
instruction . . . . Jer. 32:33
inclined your ear,
nor *h* . . . . Jer. 35:15

HEART
LORD said in
his *h*. . . . . .Gen. 8:21
gladness of *h*. . . . . Deut. 28:47
trembling *h*, and
failing . . . . Deut. 28:65
fear of thine *h*
. wherewith . . . . . Deut. 28:67
LORD looketh on
the *h* . . . . 1 Sam. 16:7
him with a
perfect *h* . . . . 1 Chr. 28:9
h of this people
fat . . . . .Is. 6:10
thine *h*, I will
ascend . . . . .Is. 14:13
My *h* shall cry out . . . .Is. 15:5
and to revive the *h* . . .Is. 57:15
deceit of their *h* . . . .Jer. 14:14
LORD search
the *h* . . . . .Jer. 17:10
pride of thine *h*, O . . Jer. 49:16

h of the mighty
men . . . . Jer. 49:22
whorish *h*, which
hath . . . . Ezek. 6:9
love, but their *h*
goeth . . . . Ezek. 33:31
And rend your *h*,
and. . . . . Joel 2:13
meek and lowly
in *h* . . . . Matt. 11:29
in *h* and ears,
ye do . . . . Acts 7:51
a true *h* in full
assurance . . . . . . .Heb. 10:22

HEARTS
faintness into
their *h* . . . . Lev. 26:36
things, our *h* did
melt. . . . . Josh. 2:11
LORD with all
your *h* . . . . 1 Sam. 7:3
LORD searcheth
all *h* . . . . 1 Chr. 28:9
and their *h*, that
they . . . . .Is. 44:18
write it in their *h* . . . Jer. 31:33
mighty men's *h* in
Moab . . . . Jer. 48:41
time your *h* be
overcharged . . . . Luke 21:34
the *h* of all men,
shew . . . . Acts 1:24
seasons, filling
our *h* . . . . Acts 14:17
them, purifying
their *h* . . . . Acts 15:9
speeches deceive
the *h* . . . . Rom. 16:18
counsels of the *h* . . .1 Cor. 4:5
h, crying, Abba,
Father . . . . Gal. 4:6
with grace in
your *h* . . . . Col. 3:16
stablish your *h*
unblameable. . .1 Thess. 3:13
having our *h* . . . . . .Heb. 10:22
purify your *h*, ye
double . . . . .James 4:8
star arise in
your *h* . . . . .2 Pet. 1:19
searcheth the
reins and *h* . . . . Rev. 2:23

HEAT
tent door in the *h*. . .Gen. 18:1
shadow from
the *h* . . . . .Is. 25:4
the *h* nor sun
smite . . . . .Is. 49:10
h cometh, but her
leaf. . . . . Jer. 17:8
bitterness, in
the *h* . . . . Ezek. 3:14
melt with
fervent *h* . . . . .2 Pet. 3:10

HEATHEN
scatter you among
the *h* . . . . Lev. 26:33
number among
the *h* . . . . Deut. 4:27

_h_, whom the
  Lord cast...... 2 Kin. 16:3
shall give thee
  the _h_ .... Ps. 2:8
didst drive out
  the _h_ .... Ps. 44:2
byword among
  the _h_ .... Ps. 44:14
He cast out the _h_
  also .... Ps. 78:55
O God, the _h_ are
  come .... Ps. 79:1
hast cast out the _h_ ... Ps. 80:8
polluted before
  the _h_ .... Ezek. 20:9
_h_, in whose sight . Ezek. 20:14
in you before
  the _h_ .... Ezek. 20:41
like unto all the _h_.. Ezek. 25:8
_h_, which ye have
  profaned .... Ezek. 36:23
my land, that
  the _h_ .... Ezek. 38:16
reproach, that
  the _h_ .... Joel 2:17
Edom, and of all
  the _h_ ....Amos 9:12
speak peace unto
  the _h_ .... Zech. 9:10
the _h_, saith the
  Lord........... Mal. 1:11
should go unto
  the _h_ .... Gal. 2:9

HEAVE
wave breast and
  the _h_ .... Lev. 7:34
the _h_ offerings ...Num. 18:19
tithes, and _h_
  offerings .... Deut. 12:6
tithes, and the _h_
  offering .... Deut. 12:11

HEAVEN
beginning God
  created the _h_.......Gen. 1:1
_h_, and tell the
  stars.............Gen. 15:5
the Lord out of _h_ .Gen. 19:24
the stars of the _h_ ..Gen. 22:17
as the stars of _h_ ....Gen. 26:4
thing that is in _h_.....Ex. 20:4
thine eyes unto _h_ .. Deut. 4:19
I call _h_ and earth .. Deut. 4:26
And thy _h_ that is
  over ....Deut. 28:23
throne is in _h_ .... Ps. 11:4
And all the host
  of _h_...............Is. 34:4
for the fowls of _h_ .... Jer. 16:4
God of _h_ set up a
  kingdom ....Dan. 2:44
under the whole _h_
  hath.............Dan. 9:12
lo a voice from _h_... Matt. 3:17
shall fall from _h_ .. Matt. 24:29
the clouds of _h_ ... Matt. 26:64
me in _h_ and in
  earth .... Matt. 28:18
creature which is
  under _h_ .... Col. 1:23

God out of _h_,
  prepared .... Rev. 21:2

HEAVENLY
yet your _h_ Father
  feedeth .... Matt. 6:26
for your _h_ Father
  knoweth .... Matt. 6:32
spiritual blessings
  in _h_ .... Eph. 1:3
tasted of the _h_ gift . . . Heb. 6:4
and shadow of _h_
  things .... Heb. 8:5
living God, the _h_
  Jerusalem ....Heb. 12:22

HEAVENS
grown up unto
  the _h_ ....Ezra 9:6
thundered in
  the _h_ .... Ps. 18:13
Lord, is in the _h_ .... Ps. 36:5
_h_ are the work of
  thy.............. Ps. 102:25
Hear, O _h_, and give ....Is. 1:2
darkened in the _h_
  thereof.............Is. 5:30
dissolved, and
  the _h_ ....Is. 34:4
stretcheth out
  the _h_ ....Is. 40:22
that created the _h_.....Is. 42:5
Sing, O ye _h_ ....Is. 44:23
stretcheth forth
  the _h_ ....Is. 44:24
that created the _h_....Is. 45:18
Sing, O _h_...........Is. 49:13
your eyes to the _h_.....Is. 51:6
_h_, and laid the
  foundations ....Is. 51:13
or can the _h_ give
  showers..........Jer. 14:22
the _h_ shall
  tremble .... Joel 2:10
lo, the _h_ were
  opened .... Matt. 3:16
the powers of
  the _h_ .... Matt. 24:29
which the _h_ shall
  pass .... 2 Pet. 3:10

HEAVY
Moses' hands
  were _h_ .... Ex. 17:12
make their ears _h_ .....Is. 6:10
carriages were _h_
  loaden ....Is. 46:1
labour and are _h_
  laden .... Matt. 11:28

HEBREW
Applied to Abraham,
  Gen. 14:13
  And his descendants,
  Gen. 39:14; 40:15; 43:32;
  Ex. 2:6; Deut. 15:12;
  1 Sam. 4:9; 29:3; Jon. 1:9;
  Acts 6:1; 2 Cor. 11:22;
  Phil. 3:5
Used to denote the language
  (Aramaic) of the Jews,
  John 5:2; 19:20; Acts 21:40;
  22:2; 26:14; Rev. 9:11

HEBRON
A city of the territory of the
  tribe of Asher, Josh. 19:28
—— A city of the tribe of
  Judah, south of Jerusalem
When built, Num. 13:22
Fortified, 2 Chr. 11:10
Called Kirjath-arba, Gen. 23:2
Arba, Gen. 35:27; Josh. 15:13
Abraham lived there and Sarah
  died at, Gen. 23:2
Hoham, king of, confederated
  with other kings of the
  Canaanites against Joshua,
  Josh. 10:3–39
Descendants of the Anakim
  live at, Num. 13:22;
  Josh. 11:21
Conquest of, by Caleb,
  Josh. 14:6–15; Judg. 1:10, 20
A city of refuge, Josh. 20:7;
  21:11, 13
David crowned king of Judah
  at, 2 Sam. 2:1–11; 3
David crowned king of Israel
  at, 2 Sam. 5:1–5
The burial place of Sarah,
  Gen. 23:2
The burial place of Abner,
  2 Sam. 3:32
The burial place of Ish-
  bosheth, 2 Sam. 4:12
The conspirators against
  Ish-bosheth hanged at,
  2 Sam. 4:12
Absalom made king at,
  2 Sam. 15:9, 10
Jews of the Babylonian
  captivity lived at, Neh. 11:25
Pool of, 2 Sam. 4:12
—— Son of Kohath, Ex. 6:18;
  Num. 3:19; 1 Chr. 6:2, 18;
  23:12, 19

HEED
Only take _h_ to
  thyself .... Deut. 4:9
_h_ to thyself that
  thou.......... Deut. 12:30
thy children
  take _h_...........1 Kin. 2:4
prosper, if thou
  takest _h_ .... 1 Chr. 22:13
take _h_ and do it... 2 Chr. 19:7
Take ye _h_ every
  one............... Jer. 9:4
Take _h_ to
  yourselves........ Jer. 17:21
and let us not
  give _h_........... Jer. 18:18
Take _h_ that ye
  despise .... Matt. 18:10
_h_, beware of the
  leaven .... Mark 8:15
And take _h_ to
  yourselves....... Luke 21:34
Take _h_ therefore
  unto........... Acts 20:28
well that ye take _h_ . 2 Pet. 1:19

HEIRS

his *h*, saith the
  Lord............Jer. 49:2
if children, then *h* . Rom. 8:17
who shall be *h* of
  salvation.......Heb. 1:14
Isaac and Jacob,
  the *h* ....Heb. 11:9
rich in faith, and *h* . .James 2:5

HELD

time Solomon *h* a
  feast...........1 Kin. 8:65
the river, when
  he *h* ....Dan. 12:7
But Jesus *h* his
  peace ....Matt. 26:63
these things,
  they *h* ....Acts 11:18
testimony which
  they *h* ....Rev. 6:9

HELL

shall be turned
  into *h*...........Ps. 9:17
leave my soul in *h* . . Ps. 16:10
from the lowest *h*. . . Ps. 86:13
I make my bed
  in *h* ....Ps. 139:8
brought down
  to *h* ....Is. 14:15
cast him down
  to *h* ....Ezek. 31:16
be in danger of *h*
  fire ....Matt. 5:22
and body in *h* .... Matt. 10:28
the gates of *h* .... Matt. 16:18
the damnation
  of *h*...........Matt. 23:33
hands to go into *h* . Mark 9:43
cast them down
  to *h* ....2 Pet. 2:4
keys of *h* and of
  death ....Rev. 1:18
death and *h* were
  cast ....Rev. 20:14

HENCEFORTH

you, Ye shall *h*
  return ....Deut. 17:16
h thou shalt have
  wars...........2 Chr. 16:9
with justice from *h*.....Is. 9:7
for *h* there
  shall no...........Is. 52:1
saith the Lord,
  from *h* ....Is. 59:21
mount Zion
  from *h* ....Mic. 4:7
from *h* I will go
  unto............Acts 18:6
H there is laid up . . 2 Tim. 4:8
in the Lord from *h* . Rev. 14:13

HERITAGE

give it you for an *h* .... Ex. 6:8
h of Jacob thy
  father............Is. 58:14
land, and made
  mine *h* ....Jer. 2:7
and give not
  thine *h*..........Joel 2:17

people and for
  my *h*..............Joel 3:2
the flock of
  thine *h* ....Mic. 7:14
the remnant of
  his *h*............Mic. 7:18
h waste for the
  dragons ....Mal. 1:3

HERMON

A mountain in the north of
  Palestine; Called
Sirion, Deut. 3:8, 9; Ps. 29:6
Sion, Deut. 4:48; Ps. 133:3
Shenir, Deut. 3:9; 1 Chr. 5:23;
  Song 4:8

HEROD

King of Judah (Herod the
  Great), Matt. 2
——— Tetrarch of Galilee
  (Herod Antipas), Luke 3:1;
  23:7
Incest of, Matt. 14:3, 4;
  Mark 6:17–19
Beheads John the Baptist,
  Matt. 14:3–11; Mark 6:16–28
Desires to see Jesus, Luke 9:7,
  9; 23:8
Tyranny of, Luke 13:31, 32
Jesus tried by, Luke 23:6–12,
  15; Acts 4:27
——— Son of Aristobulus
  (Herod Agrippa I),
  Acts 12:1–23

HESHBON

A city; Of the Amorites,
  Num. 21:25–35; Deut. 1:4
Built by Reuben, Num. 32:37
Allotted to Gad, Josh. 21:38,
  39
Fish pools at, Song 7:4
Prophecy concerning, Is. 16:8;
  Jer. 48:2, 34, 35; 49:1–3

HEZEKIAH

King of Judah, 2 Kin. 16:20;
  18:1, 2; 1 Chr. 3:13;
  2 Chr. 29:1; Matt. 1:9
Religious zeal of, 2 Chr. 29;
  30; 31
Purges the nation of idolatry,
  2 Kin. 18:4; 2 Chr. 31:1; 33:3
Restores the true forms of
  worship, 2 Chr. 31:2–21
His piety, 2 Kin. 18:3, 5, 6;
  2 Chr. 29:2; 31:20, 21; 32:32;
  Jer. 26:19
Military operations of,
  2 Kin. 18:19; 1 Chr. 4:39–43;
  2 Chr. 32; Is. 36; 37
Sickness and restoration of,
  2 Kin. 20:1–11; 2 Chr. 32:24;
  Is. 38:1–8
His psalm of thanksgiving,
  Is. 38:9–22
His lack of wisdom in
  showing his resources
  to commissioners of
  Babylon, 2 Kin. 20:12–19;
  2 Chr. 32:25, 26, 31; Is. 39

Prospered by God, 2 Kin. 18:7;
  2 Chr. 32:27–30
Conducts the Gihon Brook
  into Jerusalem, 2 Kin. 18:17;
  20:20; 2 Chr. 32:4, 30; 33:14;
  Neh. 2:13–15; 3:13, 16;
  Is. 7:3; 22:9–11; 36:2
Scribes of, Prov. 25:1
Death and burial of,
  2 Kin. 20:21; 2 Chr. 32:33
Prophecies concerning,
  2 Kin. 19:20–34; 20:5, 6,
  16–18; Is. 38:5–8; 39:5–7;
  Jer. 26:18, 19
——— Son of Neariah,
  1 Chr. 3:23
——— One of the exiles,
  Ezra 2:16; Neh. 7:21
Called Hizkijah, Neh. 10:17

HID

And Moses *h* his
  face ....Ex. 3:6
him every whit,
  and *h* ....1 Sam. 3:18
hundred
  prophets, and *h* . 1 Kin. 18:4
iniquity have I
  not *h* ....Ps. 32:5
proud have *h* a
  snare ....Ps. 140:5
falsehood have
  we *h*...............Is. 28:15
prudent men shall
  be *h* ....Is. 29:14
his hand hath he *h* ....Is. 49:2
I *h* not my face
  from...............Is. 50:6
h as it were our
  faces ....Is. 53:3
wrath I *h* my face
  from...............Is. 54:8
are *h* from mine
  eyes ....Is. 65:16
are not *h* from my
  face ....Jer. 16:17
stones that I
  have *h* ....Jer. 43:10
the clean, and
  have *h* ....Ezek. 22:26
be *h* from mine
  eyes ....Hos. 13:14
they be *h* from my
  sight ....Amos 9:3
thou hast *h* these
  things ....Matt. 11:25

HIDE

h it not from me... Josh. 7:19
then the people
  did *h* ....1 Sam. 13:6
apple of the eye, *h* .. Ps. 17:8
trouble he shall *h* .... Ps. 27:5
Thou shalt *h*
  them in ....Ps. 31:20
hands, I will *h*
  mine ....Is. 1:15
sin as Sodom,
  they *h* ....Is. 3:9
that seek deep
  to *h* ....Is. 29:15

HORN

promise, having
no *h* . . . . Eph. 2:12
moved away from
the *h* . . . . Col. 1:23
Christ in you,
the *h* of . . . . Col. 1:27
love, and patience
of *h*. . . . . 1 Thess. 1:3
our *h*, or joy, or
crown . . . . 1 Thess. 2:19
In *h* of eternal life . . Titus 1:2
for that blessed *h* . . Titus 2:13
h firm unto the
end. . . . . Heb. 3:6
a lively *h* by the
resurrection . . . . . . 1 Pet. 1:3
mind, be sober,
and *h* . . . . 1 Pet. 1:13

HORN

fill thine *h* with
oil . . . . 1 Sam. 16:1
the *h* of oil, and
anointed . . . . . . 1 Sam. 16:13
the priest took
an *h* . . . . 1 Kin. 1:39
buckler, and the *h* . . . Ps. 18:2
my *h* shalt thou
exalt. . . . . Ps. 92:10
his *h* shall be
exalted. . . . . Ps. 112:9
The *h* of Moab is
cut . . . . Jer. 48:25
he hath set up
the *h* . . . . Lam. 2:17
them another
little *h* . . . . Dan. 7:8
I will make
thine *h* . . . . Mic. 4:13

HORNS

thou shalt make
the *h* . . . . Ex. 27:2
round about, and
the *h* . . . . Ex. 30:3
atonement upon
the *h* . . . . Ex. 30:10
h of the altar of
sweet. . . . . Lev. 4:7
the blood upon
the *h* . . . . Lev. 4:18
bullock, and his *h* . Deut. 33:17
All the *h* of the
wicked . . . . Ps. 75:10
and it had ten *h* . . . . . Dan. 7:7
I considered the *h* . . Dan. 7:8
the *h* which have
scattered . . . . Zech. 1:19
slain, having
seven *h* . . . . Rev. 5:6
seven heads and
ten *h* . . . . Rev. 12:3

HORSE

h and his rider
hath . . . . Ex. 15:1
riding upon a
red *h* . . . . Zech. 1:8
Ephraim, and
the *h* . . . . Zech. 9:10
and behold a
white *h* . . . . Rev. 19:11

HORSEMEN

chariots, and the *h* . . Ex. 14:28
thousand *h*, and
people . . . . 1 Sam. 13:5
hundred *h*, and
twenty . . . . 2 Sam. 8:4
threescore
thousand *h* . . . . . 2 Chr. 12:3
with a couple of *h* . . . . Is. 21:9
and in *h*, because
they . . . . Is. 31:1
chariots, and
with *h* . . . . Ezek. 26:7
the noise of the *h* . Ezek. 26:10
army, horses
and *h* . . . . Ezek. 38:4
and their *h* shall
spread . . . . Hab. 1:8

HORSES

shall not
multiply *h* . . . . . . Deut. 17:16
chariot *h*, but
reserved . . . . 2 Sam. 8:4
chariot of fire,
and *h* . . . . 2 Kin. 2:11
chariots, and
some in *h* . . . . Ps. 20:7
stay on *h*, and
trust. . . . . Is. 31:1
his *h* are swifter
than . . . . Jer. 4:13
h was heard from
Dan . . . . Jer. 8:16
sword is upon
their *h* . . . . Jer. 50:37
shall ride upon *h* . . . Jer. 50:42
they might give
him *h* . . . . Ezek. 17:15
the north, with *h* . . Ezek. 26:7
abundance of
his *h* . . . . Ezek. 26:10
thine army, *h* and
horsemen . . . . Ezek. 38:4
Their *h* also are
swifter . . . . Hab. 1:8
were there red *h*,
speckled . . . . Zech. 1:8
and the riders
on *h* . . . . Zech. 10:5

HOSHEA

Also called Oshea; The
original name of Joshua,
Num. 13:8, 16; Deut. 32:44
——— A chief of Ephraim,
1 Chr. 27:20
——— King of Israel
Assassinates Pekah and usurps
the throne, 2 Kin. 15:30
The evil reign of, 2 Kin. 17:1, 2
Becomes subject to Assyria,
2 Kin. 17:3
Conspires against Assyria and
is imprisoned, 2 Kin. 17:4
Last king of Israel, 2 Kin. 17:6;
18:9–12; Hos. 10:3, 7
——— A Jewish exile,
Neh. 10:23

HOST

said, This is
God's *h* . . . . Gen. 32:2

and upon all his *h* . . . . Ex. 14:4
horsemen, and all
the *h* . . . . Ex. 14:28
that enter into
the *h* . . . . Num. 4:3
the *h* of heaven,
shouldest . . . . . . Deut. 4:19
moon, or any of
the *h* . . . . Deut. 17:3
throughout all
the *h* . . . . Judg. 7:22
captain of Saul's *h* . 2 Sam. 2:8
Zeruiah was over
the *h* . . . . 2 Sam. 8:16
not captain of
the *h* . . . . 2 Sam. 19:13
Ner, captain of
the *h* . . . . 1 Kin. 2:32
h of heaven, and
served . . . . 2 Kin. 17:16
Hezekiah with a
great *h* . . . . 2 Kin. 18:17
h of heaven, and
served . . . . 2 Kin. 21:3
captains of the *h*
separated . . . . . . 1 Chr. 25:1
heavens, with all
their *h* . . . . Neh. 9:6
hosts mustereth
the *h* . . . . Is. 13:4
And all the *h* of
heaven. . . . . Is. 34:4
incense unto all
the *h* . . . . Jer. 19:13
worship the *h* of
heaven . . . . Zeph. 1:5

HOSTS

O LORD of *h*, if
thou . . . . 1 Sam. 1:11
vineyard of the
LORD of *h* . . . . Is. 5:7
holy, is the LORD
of *h*. . . . . Is. 6:3
zeal of the LORD
of *h* . . . . Is. 9:7
redeemer the
LORD of *h* . . . . Is. 44:6
the Lord GOD of *h* . . . Jer. 2:19
O LORD of *h*, that
judgest . . . . Jer. 11:20
saith the LORD
of *h*. . . . . Jer. 29:8
Praise the LORD
of *h*. . . . . Jer. 33:11
Lord GOD of *h*, a
day . . . . Jer. 46:10
saith the LORD
of *h*. . . . . Jer. 49:7
saith the LORD
of *h*. . . . . Zeph. 2:9
as the LORD of *h*
thought . . . . Zech. 1:6
mountain of the
LORD of *h* . . . . Zech. 8:3
saith the LORD
of *h*. . . . . Zech. 13:7
saith the LORD
of *h*. . . . . Mal. 1:11
messenger of the
LORD of *h* . . . . Mal. 2:7

saith the LORD
of *h*. . . . . Mal. 3:1
saith the LORD
of *h*. . . . . Mal. 3:5
saith the LORD
of *h*. . . . . Mal. 4:1

HOUR
be cast the same *h* . . Dan. 3:15
whole from that *h* . Matt. 9:22
neither the day
nor the *h* . . . . . . Matt. 25:13
that same *h* said
Jesus . . . . Matt. 26:55
mine *h* is not yet
come . . . . John 2:4
for the *h* is
coming . . . . John 5:28
him, because his *h* . . John 7:30
them, saying,
The *h* . . . . John 12:23
Jesus knew that
his *h*. . . . . John 13:1
Behold, the *h*
cometh . . . . John 16:32
said, Father, the *h*. . . John 17:1
about the sixth *h* . . John 19:14
the same *h* of the
night . . . . Acts 16:33
keep thee from
the *h* . . . . Rev. 3:10
h was there a
great . . . . Rev. 11:13
in one *h* is thy
judgment . . . . Rev. 18:10

HOUSE
Egypt, out of the *h* . . . Ex. 20:2
h of the LORD thy
God . . . . Ex. 23:19
thou shalt build
an *h* . . . . Deut. 28:30
He shall build
an *h* . . . . 2 Sam. 7:13
thine *h* and thy
kingdom . . . . 2 Sam. 7:16
treasures of the *h* 2 Kin. 24:13
And he burnt
the *h* . . . . 2 Kin. 25:9
goodly vessels of
the *h* . . . . 2 Chr. 36:10
sword in the *h* . . 2 Chr. 36:17
mountain of the
LORD's *h*. . . . . Is. 2:2
h of the God of
Jacob . . . . Is. 2:3
joyful in my *h* of
prayer . . . . Is. 56:7
will make with
the *h* . . . . Jer. 31:33
of praise into
the *h* . . . . Jer. 33:11
And burned the
h of. . . . . Jer. 52:13
court of the
LORD's *h*. . . . . . . Ezek. 8:16
the *h* of Israel
rebelled. . . . . . . Ezek. 20:13
will pour upon
the *h* . . . . Zech. 12:10
shall reign over
the *h* . . . . Luke 1:33

the saving of his *h* . . Heb. 11:7

HOUSES
door post of the *h*. . . . Ex. 12:7
a token upon
the *h* . . . . Ex. 12:13
leaven out of
your *h* . . . . Ex. 12:15
leaven found in
your *h* . . . . Ex. 12:19
in unto your *h* to
smite . . . . Ex. 12:23
house, and all
the *h* . . . . 2 Kin. 25:9
inhabitant, and
the *h* . . . . Is. 6:11
offence to both
the *h* . . . . Is. 8:14
their *h* shall be
spoiled. . . . . Is. 13:16
desolate *h*, and
dragons . . . . Is. 13:22
the tops of their *h* . . . . Is. 15:3
h on the sabbath
day . . . . Jer. 17:22
And the *h* of
Jerusalem . . . . Jer. 19:13
king's house, and
the *h* . . . . Jer. 39:8
kindle a fire in
the *h* . . . . Jer. 43:12
and the *h* of the
gods. . . . . Jer. 43:13
and all the *h* of
Jerusalem . . . . Jer. 52:13
built *h* of hewn
stone . . . . Amos 5:11

HOWL
H ye . . . . Is. 13:6
Moab shall *h* over
Nebo . . . . Is. 15:2
shall *h*, weeping
abundantly . . . . Is. 15:3
H, ye ships of
Tarshish . . . . Is. 23:1
h, ye
inhabitants of. . . . . . . Is. 23:6
They shall *h*,
saying . . . . Jer. 48:39
h, O ye
vinedressers . . . . . . Joel 1:11
h, ye ministers of . . . Joel 1:13

HUMBLE
wilderness, to *h*
thee . . . . Deut. 8:2
a contrite and *h*
spirit . . . . Is. 57:15
and to the
queen, *H* . . . . Jer. 13:18
he that shall *h*. . . . Matt. 23:12
giveth grace unto
the *h* . . . . James 4:6
giveth grace to
the *h* . . . . 1 Pet. 5:5

HUMBLED
uncircumcised
hearts be *h* . . . . . . Lev. 26:41
he *h* thee, and
suffered. . . . . Deut. 8:3

man, because he
hath *h* . . . . Deut. 22:24
LORD his God,
and *h* . . . . 2 Chr. 33:12
I *h* my soul with
fasting. . . . . Ps. 35:13
of man shall be *h* . . . . . Is. 2:11
fashion as a man,
he *h* . . . . Phil. 2:8

HUNDRED
afflict them four *h* . Gen. 15:13
him that is an *h*
years . . . . Gen. 17:17
an *h* and thirty
years . . . . Gen. 47:9
Kohath were an *h*
thirty . . . . Ex. 6:18
six *h* thousand on
foot . . . . Ex. 12:37
pure myrrh five *h*
shekels . . . . Ex. 30:23
upward, for six *h*
thousand. . . . . Ex. 38:26
you shall chase
an *h* . . . . Lev. 26:8
two *h* and fifty
men . . . . Num. 16:35
I am an *h* and
twenty. . . . . Deut. 31:2
three *h* blew the
trumpets . . . . Judg. 7:22
h horsemen, and
twenty. . . . . 2 Sam. 8:4
gold, four *h* and
twenty. . . . . 1 Kin. 9:28
Obadiah took an *h*
prophets . . . . 1 Kin. 18:4
sinner do evil an *h* . . Eccl. 8:12
fruit thereof two *h* . Song 8:12
two *h* and ninety
days . . . . Dan. 12:11
aloes, about an *h*
pound . . . . John 19:39
prophesy a
thousand two *h* . . . Rev. 11:3
h and threescore
days . . . . Rev. 12:6

HUNGER
whole assembly
with *h* . . . . Ex. 16:3
suffered thee to *h*. . . Deut. 8:3
against thee, in *h* . Deut. 28:48
heaven for their *h*. . . Neh. 9:15
lack, and suffer *h* . . . Ps. 34:10
shall not *h* nor
thirst . . . . Is. 49:10

HUNGRY
they that were *h*
ceased . . . . 1 Sam. 2:5
right hand, and
be *h* . . . . Is. 9:20
the *h*, and hath
covered . . . . Ezek. 18:7
the *h*, and hath
covered . . . . Ezek. 18:16

HUR
An Israelite who assisted in
supporting Moses' hands

during battle, Ex. 17:10, 12;
24:14

———— A son of Caleb, Ex. 31:2;
35:30; 38:22; 1 Chr. 2:19, 20;
2 Chr. 1:5

———— A king of Midian,
Num. 31:8; Josh. 13:21

———— Called Ben Hur,
an officer of Solomon's
commissary, 1 Kin. 4:8

———— Father of Caleb,
1 Chr. 2:50; 4:4

———— A son of Judah,
1 Chr. 4:1

———— A ruler, Neh. 3:9

HURAM
Son of Bela, 1 Chr. 8:5

———— Huram
See Hiram

HURT
rejoice at mine *h*.... Ps. 35:26
shall not *h* nor
destroy ....Is. 11:9
have healed also
the *h* ....Jer. 6:14
other gods to
your *h* ....Jer. 7:6
earth for their *h* .....Jer. 24:9
overcometh shall
not be *h*.........Rev. 2:11
should not *h* the
grass ....Rev. 9:4

HUSBAND
shall be to thy *h* ....Gen. 3:16
my *h* will love me..Gen. 29:32
time will my *h* be
joined ....Gen. 29:34
h hate her, and
write ....Deut. 24:3
Her former *h*,
which ....Deut. 24:4
be evil toward the
h...........Deut. 28:56
thy Maker is
thine *h*...........Is. 54:5
the *h* with the
wife ....Jer. 6:11
her *h* committeth
adultery........ Luke 16:18
For the *h* is the
head...........Eph. 5:23
h of one wife,
vigilant ....1 Tim. 3:2
adorned for her *h* ...Rev. 21:2

IDDO
Father of Ahinadab,
1 Kin. 4:14

———— A descendant of
Gershom, 1 Chr. 6:21

———— A son of Zechariah,
1 Chr. 27:21

———— A prophet, 2 Chr. 9:29;
12:15; 13:22

———— Ancestor of Zechariah,
Ezra 5:1; 6:14; Zech. 1:1, 7

———— A priest, Neh. 12:4, 16

———— The chief of the Jews

established at Casiphia,
Ezra 8:17

IDOLS
make you no *i* nor
graven .... Lev. 26:1
sacrificed unto
the *i*...........Ps. 106:38
and the *i* of Egypt.....Is. 19:1
Nebo stoopeth,
their *i*...........Is. 46:1
her *i* are
confounded........Jer. 50:2
whoring after
their *i*...........Ezek. 6:9
i of the house of
Israel ....Ezek. 18:6
forsake the *i* of
Egypt...........Ezek. 20:8
ye every one his *i*. Ezek. 20:39
also destroy the *i* . Ezek. 30:13
your *i*, will I
cleanse ....Ezek. 36:25
i, nor with their
detestable ......Ezek. 37:23
therein, to make
dumb *i*...........Hab. 2:18
the *i* have spoken
vanity .... Zech. 10:2
the names of the *i* . Zech. 13:2
meats offered to *i*.. Acts 15:29
in sacrifice unto *i*...1 Cor. 8:4
temple of God
with *i*...........2 Cor. 6:16
turned to God
from *i* ....1 Thess. 1:9
i, and to commit
fornication .... Rev. 2:14

IGNORANT
i, they are all
dumb.............Is. 56:10
though Abraham
be *i*............Is. 63:16
i, brethren, that
oftentimes ...... Rom. 1:13
ye should be *i* .... Rom. 11:25

ILLYRICUM
Also called Dalmatia; Visited
By Paul, Rom. 15:19
By Titus, 2 Tim. 4:10

IMAGE
make man in our *i* ..Gen. 1:26
created man in his
own *i*...........Gen. 1:27
i of God made he
man ....Gen. 9:6
thee any graven *i* ....Ex. 20:4
idols nor graven *i*... Lev. 26:1
And he set a
graven *i*........ 2 Kin. 21:7
confounded by
the graven *i*.......Jer. 10:14
seat of the *i* of
jealousy.......... Ezek. 8:3
i which I have
made ....Dan. 3:15
profiteth the
graven *i*.........Hab. 2:18
conformed to the *i* . Rom. 8:29

i from glory to
glory ....2 Cor. 3:18
i of God, should
shine ....2 Cor. 4:4
is the *i* of the
invisible .... Col. 1:15
knowledge after
the *i*...........Col. 3:10
glory, and the
express *i* ....Heb. 1:3
the very *i* of the
things ....Heb. 10:1
i, and whosoever
receiveth .... Rev. 14:11
that worshipped
his *i* ....Rev. 19:20
beast, neither his *i* .. Rev. 20:4

IMAGES
Rachel had stolen
the *i* ....Gen. 31:19
break down their *i* .. Ex. 23:24
altars, break
their *i*...........Ex. 34:13
i, and cast your
carcases .... Lev. 26:30
break down their *i* .. Deut. 7:5
gods, and molten *i* .1 Kin. 14:9
high places, and *i*..1 Kin. 14:23
made them
molten *i*....... 2 Kin. 17:16
places, and brake
the *i* .... 2 Kin. 18:4
graven *i* of her
gods...............Is. 21:9
praise to graven *i* .....Is. 42:8
shall break also
the *i* ....Jer. 43:13
i are broken in
pieces ....Jer. 50:2
but they made
the *i* .... Ezek. 7:20
i to cease out of
Noph ....Ezek. 30:13

IMAGINATION
earth, and that
every *i* ....Gen. 6:5
the *i* of man's
heart ....Gen. 8:21
i of their evil heart... Jer. 3:17
i of their evil heart... Jer. 7:24

INCENSE
an altar to burn *i* ....Ex. 30:1
burn thereon
sweet *i*...........Ex. 30:7
burn *i* upon it, a
perpetual.........Ex. 30:8
the altar of sweet *i*... Lev. 4:7
and put *i* thereon ... Lev. 10:1
men that offered *i* Num. 16:35
come near to
offer *i*.........Num. 16:40
and put on *i* .....Num. 16:46
mine altar, to
burn *i*.........1 Sam. 2:28
of Israel did burn *i* 2 Kin. 18:4
sacrifices and
sweet *i*........ 2 Chr. 13:11
the LORD to
burn *i*........ 2 Chr. 26:16

i is an
  abomination . . . . .Is. 1:13
shall bring gold
  and *i* . . . . .Is. 60:6
he that burneth *i* . . . . .Is. 66:3
cometh there to
  me *i* . . . . .Jer. 6:20
they have burned *i* . .Jer. 19:13
own mouth, to
  burn *i* . . . . .Jer. 44:17
place *i* shall be
  offered . . . . .Mal. 1:11
i, that he should
  offer . . . . Rev. 8:3

INCREASE
usury of him, or *i* . .Lev. 25:36
shall yield her *i* . . . .Lev. 26:4
of thy cattle, the *i* . .Deut. 28:4
of thy land, the *i* . .Deut. 28:18
i of thy kine, or
  flocks . . . . .Deut. 28:51
eat the *i* of the
  fields . . . . .Deut. 32:13
Of the *i* of his
  government . . . . .Is. 9:7
be fruitful and *i* . . . .Jer. 23:3
usury, and hath
  taken *i* . . . . .Ezek. 18:13
shall yield her *i* . . .Ezek. 34:27

INCREASED
for the people *i*
  continually . . . .2 Sam. 15:12
our iniquities are *i* . . .Ezra 9:6
backslidings are *i* . . . . .Jer. 5:6
because thy sins
  were *i* . . . . .Jer. 30:14
knowledge shall
  be *i* . . . . .Dan. 12:4
sayest, I am rich,
  and *i* . . . . Rev. 3:17

INDIGNATION
their hand is
  mine *i* . . . . .Is. 10:5
moment, until
  the *i* . . . . .Is. 26:20
his arm, with the *i* . . .Is. 30:30
able to abide his *i* . . .Jer. 10:10
prosper till the *i* . . .Dan. 11:36
I will bear the *i* of. . . . Mic. 7:9
stand before his *i* . . . .Nah. 1:6
pour upon them
  mine *i* . . . . .Zeph. 3:8
whom the LORD
  hath *i* . . . . .Mal. 1:4
synagogue
  answered with *i* . Luke 13:14
into the cup of
  his *i* . . . . Rev. 14:10

INHABITANT
be wasted
  without *i* . . . . .Is. 6:11
shout, thou *i* of
  Zion . . . . .Is. 12:6
thee, O *i* of the
  earth . . . . .Is. 24:17
waste, without
  an *i* . . . . Jer. 4:7
desolate, without
  an *i* . . . . Jer. 9:11

thee, O *i* of the
  valley . . . . .Jer. 21:13
Damascus, and
  cut off the *i* . . . . . .Amos 1:5
will cut off the *i* . . . .Amos 1:8

INHABITANTS
to stink among
  the *i* . . . . .Gen. 34:30
hold on the *i* of
  Palestina . . . . .Ex. 15:14
i of Canaan shall
  melt . . . . .Ex. 15:15
will deliver the *i* . . . .Ex. 23:31
covenant with
  the *i* . . . . .Ex. 34:15
have withdrawn
  the *i* . . . . .Deut. 13:13
the *i* of the land
  faint . . . . .Josh. 2:9
Jebusites the *i* . . . .Josh. 15:63
i of Dor and her
  towns . . . . .Josh. 17:11
Tishbite, who was
  of the *i* . . . . .1 Kin. 17:1
earth, and the *i*
  thereof. . . . . .Is. 40:22
men of Judah
  and *i* . . . . .Jer. 4:4
Sodom, and the *i*
  thereof. . . . . .Jer. 23:14
land, and against
  the *i* . . . . .Jer. 25:9
purposed against
  the *i* . . . . .Jer. 49:20
she and her *i* . . . . .Ezek. 26:17
And all the *i* of
  Egypt . . . . Ezek. 29:6
all the *i* of the
  earth . . . . .Dan. 4:35
Judah, and to the *i* . . .Dan. 9:7
David, and upon
  the *i* . . . . .Zech. 12:10

INHABITED
Jebusites that *i*
  Jerusalem . . . . Judg. 1:21
It shall never be *i* . . . .Is. 13:20
formed it to be *i* . . . . .Is. 45:18
it shall not be *i* . . . . .Jer. 50:13
destroyed, that
  wast *i* . . . . .Ezek. 26:17
it be *i* forty years . Ezek. 29:11
i places of the
  country . . . . .Ezek. 34:13
be lifted up, and *i* Zech. 14:10

INHERIT
thee this land to *i* . . .Gen. 15:7
thou mayest *i* the
  land . . . . .Gen. 28:4
seed, and they
  shall *i* . . . . .Ex. 32:13
make them *i* the
  throne . . . . .1 Sam. 2:8
they shall *i* the
  land . . . . .Is. 60:21
to them that
  shall *i* . . . . .Jer. 8:10
blessed of my
  Father, *i* . . . . Matt. 25:34
i the kingdom of
  God . . . . .1 Cor. 6:9

i the kingdom of
  God . . . . .1 Cor. 6:10
i the kingdom of
  God . . . . Gal. 5:21
called, that ye
  should *i* . . . . .1 Pet. 3:9
overcometh shall *i* . . Rev. 21:7

INHERITANCE
mountain of
  thine *i* . . . . .Ex. 15:17
Thou shalt have
  no *i* . . . . .Num. 18:20
a people of *i*, as ye Deut. 4:20
people and thine *i* . Deut. 9:29
hath no part nor *i* .Deut. 12:12
hath no part nor *i* .Deut. 14:29
is the lot of his *i* . . .Deut. 32:9
thou divide for
  an *i* . . . . .Josh. 1:6
Joshua gave it for
  an *i* . . . . Josh. 11:23
Israel, distributed
  for *i* . . . . Josh. 14:1
captain over his *i* . 1 Sam. 10:1
heathen for thine *i* . . . .Ps. 2:8
the rod of thine *i* . . . .Ps. 74:2
an *i* by line, and
  made . . . . .Ps. 78:55
come into thine *i* . . . .Ps. 79:1
an *i* unto your
  fathers . . . . .Jer. 3:18
is the rod of his *i* . . .Jer. 10:16
forgiveness of
  sins, and *i* . . . . . . .Acts 26:18
have obtained an *i* . .Eph. 1:11
promise of
  eternal *i* . . . . .Heb. 9:15

INIQUITIES
in the *i* of their
  fathers . . . . .Lev. 26:39
shall ye bear
  your *i* . . . . .Num. 14:34
for our *i* are
  increased. . . . . Ezra 9:6
Thou hast set
  our *i* . . . . Ps. 90:8
shouldest mark
  i, O. . . . . Ps. 130:3
your *i* have ye
  sold . . . . .Is. 50:1
bruised for our *i* . . . . .Is. 53:5
shall bear their *i* . . . . .Is. 53:11
LORD, though
  our *i* . . . . .Jer. 14:7
pine away for
  your *i* . . . . Ezek. 24:23
righteousness,
  and thine *i* . . . . . . .Dan. 4:27
will subdue our *i* . . . Mic. 7:19
of you from his *i* . . . .Acts 3:26

INIQUITY
God, visiting the *i* . . . Ex. 20:5
thousands,
  forgiving *i* . . . . .Ex. 34:7
truth and
  without *i* . . . . .Deut. 32:4
commit *i*, I will
  chasten . . . . .2 Sam. 7:14
is no *i* with the
  LORD. . . . . .2 Chr. 19:7

workers of *i* no
knowledge .... Ps. 14:4
it is *i*, even the
solemn .... Is. 1:13
accomplished,
that her *i* .... Is. 40:2
hath laid on him
the *i* .... Is. 53:6
themselves to
commit *i* .... Jer. 9:5
thine *i* are thy
skirts .... Jer. 13:22
i hid from mine
eyes .... Jer. 16:17
i, and I will
remember .... Jer. 31:34
saith the LORD,
the *i* .... Jer. 50:20
not cut off in her *i* ... Jer. 51:6
so *i* shall not be
your .... Ezek. 18:30
reconciliation for *i* .. Dan. 9:24
multitude of
thine *i* .... Hos. 9:7
thee, that
pardoneth *i* ...... Mic. 7:18
redeem us from
all *i* .... Titus 2:14

INNOCENT

i and righteous
slay .... Ex. 23:7
i blood, to slay
David .... 1 Sam. 19:5
Manasseh shed *i*
blood .... 2 Kin. 21:16
i blood that he
shed .... 2 Kin. 24:4
reward against
the *i* .... Ps. 15:5
And shed *i* blood,
even .... Ps. 106:38
make haste to
shed *i* .... Is. 59:7
widow, and shed
not *i* .... Jer. 7:6
widow, neither
shed *i* .... Jer. 22:3
covetousness, and
for to shed *i* ...... Jer. 22:17

INSTRUCTION

and sealeth their *i* .. Job 33:16
despise wisdom
and *i* .... Prov. 1:7
hearkened to
receive *i* .... Jer. 32:33
reproach and a
taunt, an *i* ...... Ezek. 5:15

INSTRUMENTS

the *i* which I
made .... 1 Chr. 23:5
trumpets and
cymbals and *i* ... 2 Chr. 5:13
Gilead with
threshing *i* .... Amos 1:3
ye your members
as *i* .... Rom. 6:13

INTERPRETATION

we will shew the *i* ... Dan. 2:4

writing, and shew
me the *i* .... Dan. 5:7
i thereof, thou
shalt .... Dan. 5:16
Cephas, which is
by *i* .... John 1:42
another the *i* of
tongues .... 1 Cor. 12:10
revelation, hath
an *i* .... 1 Cor. 14:26

INTREAT

Aaron, and said, I ..... Ex. 8:8
I the LORD (for it .... Ex. 9:28
i the LORD your
God .... Ex. 10:17
unto the man of
God, I .... 1 Kin. 13:6
I *i* thee also, true .... Phil. 4:3

IRON

was a bedstead
of *i* .... Deut. 3:11
out of the *i*
furnace .... Deut. 4:20
under thee shall
be *i* .... Deut. 28:23
shall put a yoke
of *i* .... Deut. 28:48
them with a rod
of *i* .... Ps. 2:9
sunder the bars
of *i* .... Is. 45:2
defenced city, and
an *i* .... Jer. 1:18
brake in pieces
the *i* .... Dan. 2:45
gold, of brass, *i* ..... Dan. 5:23
it had great *i* teeth ... Dan. 7:7
threshing
instruments of *i* ... Amos 1:3
make thine horn *i* .. Mic. 4:13

ISAAC

The miraculous son of
Abraham, Gen. 17:15–19;
18:1–15; 21:1–8; Josh. 24:3;
1 Chr. 1:28; Gal. 4:28;
Heb. 11:11
Ancestor of Jesus, Matt. 1:2
Offered in sacrifice by his
father, Gen. 22:1–19;
Heb. 11:17; James 2:21
Is provided a wife from among
his relatives, Gen. 24; 25:20
Abrahamic covenant
confirmed in, Gen. 26:2–5;
1 Chr. 16:15–19
Lives in the south country
at the well called Lahai-roi,
Gen. 24:62; 25:11
With Ishmael, buries his father
in the cave of Machpelah,
Gen. 25:9
Esau and Jacob born to,
Gen. 25:19–26; Josh. 24:4;
1 Chr. 1:34
Lives in Gerar, Gen. 26:7–11
Prospers, Gen. 26:12–14
Possesses large flocks and
herds, Gen. 26:14
Digs wells, and is defrauded

of them by the herdsmen of
Abimelech, Gen. 26:15, 21
Moves away to the valley of
Gerar, afterward called Beer-
sheba, Gen. 26:22–33
His old age, last blessing upon
his sons, Gen. 27:18–40
Death and burial of,
Gen. 35:27–29; 49:31
His filial obedience, Gen. 22:9
His peaceableness,
Gen. 26:14–22
Was a prophet, Gen. 27:28, 29,
38, 40; Heb. 11:20
His devoutness, Gen. 24:63;
25:21; 26:25; Matt. 8:11;
Luke 13:28
Prophecies concerning,
Gen. 17:16–21; 18:10–14;
21:12; 26:2–5, 24; Ex. 32:13;
1 Chr. 16:16; Rom. 9:7
——— A designation of the ten
tribes, Amos 7:9

ISAIAH

Also called Esaias; Son of
Amos, Is. 1:1
Prophesies in the days of
Uzziah, Jotham, Ahaz, and
Hezekiah, kings of Judah,
Is. 1:1; 6:1; 7:1, 3; 14:27;
20:1; 36:1; 38:1; 39:1
Prophecy at the time of
the invasion by Tartan, of
Assyria, Is. 20:1
Symbolically wears sackcloth,
and walks barefoot as a sign
to Israel, Is. 20:2, 3
Comforts and encourages
Hezekiah and the people
during the siege of Jerusalem
by Rab-shakeh, 2 Kin. 18; 19;
Is. 37:6, 7
Comforts Hezekiah in his
affliction, 2 Kin. 20:1–11;
Is. 38
Performs the miracle of the
returning shadow to confirm
Hezekiah's faith, 2 Kin. 20:8–
11
Reproves Hezekiah's folly
in exhibiting his resources
to the commissioners from
Babylon, 2 Kin. 20:12–19;
Is. 39
Is the chronicler of the times
of Uzziah and Hezekiah,
2 Chr. 26:22; 32:32
Prophecies, Reproofs, and
Exhortations of
Foretells punishment of
the Jews for idolatry, and
reproves self-confidence and
distrust of God, Is. 2:6–20
Foretells the destruction of
the Jews, Is. 3
Promises to the remnant
restoration of divine favour,
Is. 4:2–6; 6
Delineates the ingratitude of
the Jews in the parable of

the vineyard, and reproves
it, Is. 5:1–10

Denounces existing
corruptions, Is. 5:8–30

Foretells the failure of the
plot of the Israelites and
Syrians against Judah,
Is. 7:1–16

Denounces calamities against
Israel and Judah, Is. 7:16–
25; 9:2–6

Foretells prosperity
under Hezekiah, and
the manifestation of the
Messiah, Is. 9:1–7

Denounces vengeance upon
the enemies of Israel,
Is. 9:8–12

Denounces the wickedness
of Israel, and foretells
the judgments of God,
Is. 9:13–21

Denounces judgments
against false prophets,
Is. 10:1–4

Foretells the destruction
of Sennacherib's armies,
Is. 10:5–34

The restoration of Israel
and the triumph of the
Messiah's kingdom, Is. 11

The burden of Babylon,
Is. 13; 14:1–28

Denunciation against the
Philistines, Is. 14:9–32

Burden of Moab, Is. 15; 16

Burden of Damascus, Is. 17

An obscure prophecy,
supposed by some
authorities to be directed
against the Assyrians,
by others against the
Egyptians, and by others
against the Ethiopians,
Is. 18

The burden of Egypt, Is. 19;
20

Denunciations against
Babylon, Is. 21:1–10

Prophecy concerning Seir,
Is. 21:11, 12

Arabia, Is. 21:13–17

Concerning the conquest of
Jerusalem, the captivity of
Shebna, and the promotion
of Eliakim, Is. 22:1–22

The overthrow of Tyre, Is. 23

The judgments upon the
land, but that a remnant of
the Jews would be saved,
Is. 25; 26; 27

Reproves Ephraim for his
wickedness, and foretells the
destruction by Shalmaneser,
Is. 28:1–5

Declares the glory of God
upon the remnant who are
saved, Is. 28:5, 6

Exposes the corruptions in
Jerusalem and exhorts to
repentance, Is. 28:7–29

Foretells the invasion of
Sennacherib, the distress
of the Jews, and the
destruction of the Assyrian
army, Is. 29:1–8

Denounces the hypocrisy of
the Jews, Is. 29:9–17

Promises a reformation,
Is. 29:18–24

Reproves the people for
their confidence in Egypt,
and their contempt of God,
Is. 30:1–17; 31:1–6

Declares the goodness and
longsuffering of God toward
them, Is. 30:18–26; 32; 33;
34; 35

Reproves the Jews for their
spiritual blindness and
infidelity, Is. 42:18–25

Promises ultimate restoration
of the Jews, Is. 43:1–13

Foretells the ultimate
destruction of Babylon,
Is. 43:14–17; 47

Exhorts the people to repent,
Is. 43:22–28

Comforts the Jewish
community with promises,
exposes the folly of idolatry,
and their future deliverance
from captivity by Cyrus,
Is. 44; 45:1–5; 48:20

Foretells the conversion of the
Gentiles and the triumph of
the gospel, Is. 45:5–25

Denounces the evils of
idolatry, Is. 46

Reproves the Jews for
their idolatries and other
wickedness, Is. 48

Exhorts to sanctification,
Is. 56:1–8

Foretells calamities to Judah,
Is. 59:9–12; Is. 57; 58; 59

Foreshadows the person and
the kingdom of the Messiah,
Is. 32

ISH-BOSHETH

Son of Saul; Called Esh-baal
in, 1 Chr. 8:33; 9:39

Made king by Abner,
2 Sam. 2:8–10

Deserted by Abner,
2 Sam. 3:6–12

Restores Michal (David's first
wife) to David, 2 Sam. 3:14–
16

Assassinated, 2 Sam. 4:5–8

Avenged by David, 2 Sam. 4:9–
12

ISHMAEL

Son of Abraham, Gen. 16:11,
15, 16; 1 Chr. 1:28

Prayer of Abraham for,
Gen. 17:18, 20

Circumcised, Gen. 17:23–26

Promised to be the father of

a nation, Gen. 16:11, 12;
17:20; 21:12, 13, 18

Sent away by Abraham,
Gen. 21:6–21

With Isaac buries his father,
Gen. 25:9

Children of, Gen. 25:12–18;
1 Chr. 1:29–31

Daughter of, marries Esau,
Gen. 28:9; 36:2, 3

Death of, Gen. 25:17, 18

—— Father of Zebadiah,
2 Chr. 19:11

—— A son of Azel,
1 Chr. 8:38; 9:44

—— One of the captains of
hundreds, 2 Chr. 23:1

—— A priest of the exile,
Ezra 10:22

—— A son of Nethaniah
Assassinated Gedaliah,
governor of Judah under king
of Babylon, and takes many
Jews captive, 2 Kin. 25:23–
25; Jer. 40:8–16; 41:1–11

Defeated by Johanan, and put
to flight, Jer. 41:12–15

ISHMAELITES

Region occupied by,
Gen. 25:18

Merchants of, buy Joseph,
Gen. 37:25–36; 39:1

Called Midianites, Gen. 37:28,
36; Judg. 8:24, 26

Enemies to Israel, Ps. 83:6

ISLES

the *i* shall bring
presents . . . . Ps. 72:10

and the *i* shall
wait . . . . Is. 42:4

Listen, O *i*,
unto me . . . . Is. 49:1

Surely the *i* shall . . . . . Is. 60:9

Javan, to the *i* afar . . . Is. 66:19

For pass over the *i* . . . Jer. 2:10

the kings of the *i* . . . Jer. 25:22

declare it in the *i* . . . Jer. 31:10

ISRAEL

A name given to Jacob,
Gen. 32:24–32; 2 Kin. 17:34;
Hos. 12:3, 4

—— A name of the Messiah
in prophecy, Is. 49:3

—— The name of the ten
tribes that revolted from the
house (kingdom) of David

Also called Jacob, Hos. 12:2

The list of the kings of Israel,
and the period of time in
which they reigned.

—— Jeroboam, twenty-two
years

—— Nadab, about two years

—— Baasha, twenty-four
years

—— Elah, two years

—— Zimri, seven days

—— Omri, twelve years

—— Ahab, twenty-two years

—— Ahaziah, two years

——— Jehoram, twelve years
——— Jehu, twenty-eight
years
——— Jehoahaz, seventeen
years
——— Jehoash, sixteen years
——— Jeroboam II, forty-one
years
——— Zachariah, six months
——— Shallum, one month
——— Menahem, ten years
——— Pekahiah, two years
——— Pekah, twenty years
——— Hoshea, nine years
History of
War continued between the
two kingdoms all the days
of Rehoboam and Jeroboam,
1 Kin. 14:30
War continued between
Jeroboam and Abijam,
1 Kin. 15:7
War continued between
Baasha and Asa,
1 Kin. 15:16, 32
Famine prevails during the
reign of Ahab, 1 Kin. 18:1–6
Israel, also called Samaria,
invaded by, but defeats,
Ben-hadad, king of Syria,
1 Kin. 20
Moab rebels, 2 Kin. 1:1; 3
Army of Syria invades Israel,
but peacefully withdraws
through the tact of the
prophet Elisha, 2 Kin. 6:8–
23
The city of Samaria besieged,
2 Kin. 6:24–33; 7
The city of Samaria captured,
and the people carried to
Assyria, 2 Kin. 17
The land repopulated,
2 Kin. 17:24
The remnant that remained
after the able-bodied
persons were carried into
captivity affiliated with
the kingdom of Judah,
2 Chr. 30:18–26; 34:6; 35:18
Israel, Prophecies concerning
Of captivity, famine, and
judgments, 1 Kin. 14:15, 16;
17:1; 20:13–28; 2 Kin. 7:1,
2, 17; 8:1; Is. 7:8; 8:4–7;
9:8–21; 17:3–11; 28:1–8;
Hos. 1:1–9; 2:1–13; 4; 8;
9; 10; 11:5, 6; 12:7–14; 13;
Amos 2:6–16; 3; 4; 5; 6; 7;
8; 9
Of restoration, Hos. 2:14–23;
11:9–11; 13:13, 14; 14:8
Of the reunion of the ten
tribes and Judah, Jer. 3:18;
Ezek. 37:16–22

ISSACHAR
A son of Jacob, Gen. 30:18;
Ex. 1:3; 1 Chr. 2:1
Jacob's prophetic benedictions
upon, Gen. 49:14, 15

In the time of David,
1 Chr. 7:2, 5

ITHAMAR
Son of Aaron, Ex. 6:23; 28:1;
1 Chr. 6:3
Entrusted with monies of the
tabernacle, Ex. 38:21
Charged with duties of the
tabernacle, Num. 4:28; 7:8
Forbidden to lament the death
of his brothers, Nadab and
Abihu, Lev. 10:6, 7
Descendants of, 1 Chr. 24:1–
19

JABBOK
A stream on the east of the
Jordan River, the northern
boundary of the possessions
of the Ammonites,
Num. 21:24; Judg. 11:13
Of the Reubenites and
the Gadites, Deut. 3:16;
Josh. 12:2
The northern boundary of the
Amorites, Judg. 11:22

JABESH-GILEAD
A city east of the Jordan River,
Judg. 21:8–15
Beseiged by the Ammonites,
1 Sam. 11:1–11
Saul and his sons buried at,
1 Sam. 31:11–13; 2 Sam. 2:4;
1 Chr. 10:11, 12
Bones of Saul and his sons
removed from, by David,
and buried at Zelah,
2 Sam. 21:12–14

JACHIN
Son of Simeon, Gen. 46:10;
Ex. 6:15; Num. 26:12
Called Jarib, 1 Chr. 4:24
——— A priest, who returned
from the exile to Jerusalem,
1 Chr. 9:10; Neh. 11:10
——— A priest, head of one
of the shifts of priests,
1 Chr. 24:17

JACOB
Son of Isaac, and the twin
brother of Esau, Gen. 25:24–
26; Josh. 24:4; 1 Chr. 1:34;
Acts 7:8
Ancestor of Jesus, Matt. 1:2
Given in answer to prayer,
Gen. 25:21
Obtains Esau's birthright
for just one bowl of stew,
Gen. 25:29–34; Heb. 12:16
Fradulently obtains his
father's blessing, Gen. 27:1–
29; Heb. 11:20
Esau seeks to kill, escapes to
Padan-aram, Gen. 27:41–46;
28:1–5; Hos. 12:12
His vision of the ladder,
Gen. 28:10–22
God confirms the covenant of

Abraham to, Gen. 28:13–22;
35:9–15; 1 Chr. 16:13–18
Sojourns in Haran with his
uncle, Laban, Gen. 29:30;
Hos. 12:12
Serves fourteen years for Leah
and Rachel, Gen. 29:15–30;
Hos. 12:12
Sharp practice of, with the
flocks and herds of Laban,
Gen. 30:32–43
Dissatisfied with Laban's
treatment and returns to the
land of Canaan, Gen. 31
Meets angels of God on the
journey, and calls the place
"Mahanaim," Gen. 32:1, 2
Dreads to meet Esau; sends
him presents; wrestles with
an angel, Gen. 32
Name of, changed to "Israel,"
Gen. 32:28; 35:10
Reconciliation of, with Esau,
Gen. 33:4
Journeys to Succoth,
Gen. 33:17
Journeys to Shalem, where he
purchase a parcel of ground
from Hamor and erects an
altar, Gen. 33:18–20
His daughter, Dinah, is raped,
Gen. 34
Returns to Beth-el, where
he builds an altar, and
erects and dedicates a pillar,
Gen. 35:1–7
Deborah, Rebekah's nurse,
dies, and is buried at Beth-el,
Gen. 35:8
Journeys to Ephrath; Benjamin
is born to; Rachel dies;
and is "buried on the
way to Ephrath, which is
Bethlehem," Gen. 35:16–19;
48:7
Erects a monument at Rachel's
grave, Gen. 35:20
The incest of his son, Reuben,
with his concubine, Bilhah,
Gen. 35:22
List of the names of his twelve
sons, Gen. 35:23–26
Returns to Arbah, the city of
his father, Gen. 35:27
Lives in the land of Canaan,
Gen. 37:1
His partiality for his son,
Joseph, and the consequent
jealousy of his other sons,
Gen. 37:3, 4
Joseph's prophetic dream
concerning, Gen. 37:9–11
His grief over the loss of
Joseph, Gen. 37:34, 35
Sends to Egypt to buy corn
(grain), Gen. 42:1, 2; 43:1–14
His grief over the detention of
Simeon and the demand for
Benjamin to be taken into
Egypt, Gen. 42:36

JEHOAHAZ

Son of Jehu and king of Israel,
2 Kin. 10:35; 13:1–9

——— Also called Shallum
King of Judah and successor
of Josiah, 2 Kin. 23:30, 31;
1 Chr. 3:15; 2 Chr. 36:1;
Jer. 22:11
Wicked reign of, 2 Kin. 23:32
Pharaoh-necho, king of
Egypt, invades the kingdom
of, defeats him, and takes
him away captive to Egypt,
2 Kin. 23:33–35;
2 Chr. 36:3, 4
Prophecies concerning,
Jer. 22:10, 11, 12

JEHOIACHIN

King of Judah and successor
to Jehoiakim, 2 Kin. 24:6–8;
2 Chr. 36:8, 9
Called Jeconiah, 1 Chr. 3:16;
Jer. 24:1
Called Coniah, Jer. 22:24; 37:1
Wicked reign of, 2 Kin. 24:9;
2 Chr. 36:9
Nebuchadnezzar invades
his kingdom, takes
him away captive to
Babylon, 2 Kin. 24:10–16;
2 Chr. 36:10; Esth. 2:6;
Jer. 27:20; 29:1, 2; Ezek. 1:2
Confined in prison for thirty-
seven years, 2 Kin. 25:27
Released from prison by Evil-
merodach, and promoted
above other kings, and
honored until death,
2 Kin. 25:27–30; Jer. 52:31–
34
Prophecies concerning,
Jer. 22:24–30; 28:4
Sons of, 1 Chr. 3:17, 18
Ancestor of Jesus, Matt. 1:12

JEHOIADA

Father of Benaiah, one of
David's officers, 2 Sam. 8:18
——— A high priest
Overthrows Athaliah, the
usurping queen of Judah, and
establishes Jehoash upon the
throne, 2 Kin. 11; 2 Chr. 23
Salutary influence of, over
Jehoash, 2 Kin. 12:2;
2 Chr. 24:2, 22
Directs the repairs of the
temple, 2 Kin. 12:4–16;
2 Chr. 24:4–14
Death of, 2 Chr. 24:4–16
——— A priest who led three-
thousand seven-hundred
priests armed for war,
1 Chr. 12:27
——— Son of Benaiah,
1 Chr. 27:34
——— A returned exile,
Neh. 3:6
——— A priest mentioned
in Jeremiah's letter to the
captive Jews, Jer. 29:26

JEHOIAKIM

Also called Eliakim; King of
Judah, 1 Chr. 3:15
Ancestor of Jesus, Matt. 1:11
Wicked reign and final
overthrow of, 2 Kin. 23:34–
37; 24:1–6; 2 Chr. 36:4–8;
Jer. 22:13–19; 26:22, 23; 36;
Dan. 1:1, 2
Dies, and is succeeded by his
son, Jehoiachin, 2 Kin. 24:6

JEHORAM

King of Judah, 1 Kin. 22:50;
2 Kin. 8:16; 1 Chr. 3:11;
2 Chr. 21:5
Marries Athaliah, whose
wicked counsels influence his
reign for evil, 2 Kin. 8:18, 19;
2 Chr. 21:6–13
Murders his brothers to
strengthen himself in his
sovereignty, 2 Chr. 21:4, 13
Edom revolts from,
2 Kin. 8:20–22; 2 Chr. 21:8–
10
The Philistines and Arabians
invade his territory,
2 Chr. 21:16, 17
Death of, 2 Kin. 8:24;
2 Chr. 21:18–20
Prophecy concerning,
2 Chr. 21:12–15
Ancestor of Jesus, Matt. 1:8
——— A priest commissioned
to go through Israel and
instruct the people in the
law, 2 Chr. 17:8

JEHOSHAPHAT

David's recorder, 2 Sam. 8:16;
20:24; 1 Kin. 4:3;
1 Chr. 18:15
——— One of Solomon's
commissariat officers,
1 Kin. 4:17
——— King of Judah
Succeeds Asa, 1 Kin. 15:24;
22:41; 1 Chr. 3:10;
2 Chr. 17:1; Matt. 1:8
Strengthens himself against
Israel, 2 Chr. 17:2
Inaugurates a system of
public instruction in the law,
2 Chr. 17:7–9
His wise reign, 1 Kin. 22:43;
2 Chr. 17:7–9; 19:3–11
His system of taxation,
2 Chr. 17:11
His military forces and
armaments, 2 Chr. 17:12–19
Joins Ahab in an invasion of
Ramoth-gilead, 1 Kin. 22;
2 Chr. 18
Rebuked by the prophet Jehu,
2 Chr. 19:2
The allied forces of the
Amorites, Moabites, and
other tribes invade his
territory, and are defeated by,
2 Chr. 20
Builds ships for commerce

with Tarshish, ships are
destroyed, 1 Kin. 22:48, 49;
2 Chr. 20:35–37
Joins Jehoram, king of Israel,
in an invasion of the land of
Moab, defeats the Moabites,
2 Kin. 3
Makes valuable gifts to the
temple, 2 Kin. 12:18
Death of, 1 Kin. 22:50;
2 Chr. 21:1
Religious zeal of, 1 Kin. 22:43,
46; 2 Chr. 17:1–9; 19; 20:1–
32; 22:9
Prosperity of, 1 Kin. 22:45, 48
Bequests of, to his children,
1 Chr. 21:2, 3
——— Father of Jehu,
2 Kin. 9:2, 14
——— A priest who assisted
in bringing the ark of the
covenant from Obed-edom,
1 Chr. 15:24
——— A valley
Called The Valley of Decision,
Joel 3:2, 12, 14

JEHOZABAD

Son of Shomer, and one of the
assassins of King Jehoash,
2 Kin. 12:21; 2 Chr. 24:26
——— Son of Obed-edom,
1 Chr. 26:4
——— A Benjamite chief who
commanded One-hundred
and eighty thousand men,
2 Chr. 17:18

JEHU

The prophet who announced
the wrath of Jehovah
against Baasha, king of
Israel, 1 Kin. 16:1, 7, 12;
2 Chr. 19:2; 20:34
——— Son of Nimshi, king
of Israel, 1 Kin. 19:16;
2 Kin. 9:1–14
Religious zeal of, in killing
idolaters, 2 Kin. 9:14–37;
10:1–28; 2 Chr. 22:8, 9
His territory invaded by
Hazael, king of Syria,
2 Kin. 10:32, 33
Prophecies concerning,
1 Kin. 19:17; 2 Kin. 10:30;
15:12; Hos. 1:4
Death of, 2 Kin. 10:35
——— Son of Obed, 1 Chr. 2:38
——— Son of Josibiah,
1 Chr. 4:35
——— A Benjamite, 1 Chr. 12:3

JEPHTHAH

A judge (leader, hero) of
Israel; Illegitimate, and
therefore not entitled to
inherit his father's property,
Judg. 11:1, 2
Escapes the violence of his
half-brothers; lives in the
land of Tob, Judg. 11:3
Recalled from the land of

Tob by the elders of Gilead,
Judg. 11:5
Made captain of the army,
Judg. 11:5–11
Made head of the land of
Gilead, Judg. 11:7–11
His message to the king of the
Ammonites, Judg. 11:12–28
Leads the army of Israel
against the Ammonites,
Judg. 11:29–33
His rash vow concerning his
daughter, Judg. 11:31, 34–40
Falsely accused by the
Ephraimites, Judg. 12:1
Leads the army of the
Gileadites against the
Ephraimites, Judg. 12:4
Leads Israel for six years,
dies, and is buried in Gilead,
Judg. 12:7
Faith of, Heb. 11:32

JEREMIAH
Of Libnah, grandfather of
Jehoahaz, 2 Kin. 23:31;
24:18; Jer. 52:1
————— A chief of Manasseh,
1 Chr. 5:24
————— An Israelite who joined
David at Ziklag, 1 Chr. 12:4
————— Two Gadites who joined
David at Ziklag, 1 Chr. 12:10,
13
————— The prophet, Jer. 1:1
A Rechabite, Jer. 35:3
A priest, Jer. 1:1
Call of, Jer. 1:4–19
Time of his prophecies,
Jer. 3:6; 21:1; 24:1; 25:1–3;
26:1; 28:1; 32:1; 34:1; 45:1;
49:34
Letter to the captives in
Babylon, Jer. 29
Sorrow of, under persecution,
Jer. 15:10, 15; 17:15–18
Conspiracy against, Jer. 11:21–
23; 18:18–23
Foretells the desolation of
Jerusalem, Jer. 19
Pashur, the governor of the
temple, scourges and casts
him into prison, Jer. 20:1–3
Denounces Pashur, Jer. 20:3–6
His melancholy and
complaints against God, in
consequence of persecution,
Jer. 20:7–18
Imprisoned by Zedekiah,
Jer. 32; 33:1; 37:15–21; 38:6–
13; 39:15–18; Lam. 3:53–55
Nebuchadnezzar directs the
release of, Jer. 39:11–14;
40:1–4
Has a friend in Ahikam,
Jer. 26:24
Ebed-melech, the Egyptian,
intercedes to the king for
him, and secures his release,
Jer. 38:7–13
Prophecies of, written by
Baruch, Jer. 36:1–7, 32; 45:1

Prophecies of, destroyed by
Jehoiakim, Jer. 36:8–32
Book of the prophecies of,
delivered to Seraiah, with
a charge from Jeremiah,
Jer. 51:59–64
Zedekiah seeks counsel from
God by, Jer. 21:1, 2; 37:3;
38:14
His intercession asked
By Johanan and all the
people, Jer. 42:1–6
By Zedekiah, Jer. 37:3
Johanan transports Jeremiah
into Egypt, Jer. 43:1–7
Foretells the conquest of Egypt
by Babylon, Jer. 43:8–12
Prophecies of, studied by
Daniel, Dan. 9:2
Celibacy of, Jer. 16:2
Purchases a field, Jer. 32:7–10
Lamentations of
Over Josiah, 2 Chr. 35:25
Over the prosperity of the
wicked, Jer. 12:1–6
Over the desolation of God's
heritage, Jer. 12:7–13
Over Jerusalem, Jer. 4:14–18;
8:18–21; 9:1; 10:19–22
See Book of Lamentations,
Lam. 1
Lives at Mizpah, Jer. 40:6
Prayers of, Jer. 14:7–9;
32:17–25
Zeal of, Jer. 15:16

JERICHO
A city east of Jerusalem
and near the Jordan River,
Num. 22:1; 26:3; Deut. 34:1
Called The City of Palm Trees,
Deut. 34:3
Location of, pleasant,
2 Kin. 2:19
Rahab the harlot lived in,
Josh. 2; Heb. 11:31
Joshua sees the "captain of
the host" of the Lord near,
Josh. 5:13–15
Besieged by Joshua for seven
days; fall and destruction of,
Josh. 6; 24:11
Situated within the territory
allotted to Benjamin,
Josh. 18:12, 21
The Kenites lived at,
Judg. 1:16
King of Moab makes conquest
of, and establishes his capital
at, Judg. 3:13
Rebuilt by Hiel, 1 Kin. 16:34
Company of "the sons of
the prophets," lived at,
2 Kin. 2:4, 5, 15, 18
Captives of Judah, taken by the
king of Israel, released at, on
account of the denunciation
of the prophet Oded,
2 Chr. 28:7–15
Inhabitants of, taken captive to
Babylon, return to, with Ezra

and Nehemiah, Ezra 2:34;
Neh. 7:36
Assist in repairing the walls of
Jerusalem, Neh. 3:2
Blind men healed at, by Jesus,
Matt. 20:29–34; Mark 10:46;
Luke 18:35
Zacchaeus lived at, Luke 19:1–
10
————— Plain of, 2 Kin. 25:5;
Jer. 52:8
————— Waters of, Josh. 16:1
Purified by Elisha, 2 Kin. 2:18–
22

JEROBOAM
First king of Israel after
the revolt; Promoted by
Solomon, 1 Kin. 11:28
Ahijah's prophecy concerning,
1 Kin. 11:29–39; 14:5–16
Flees to Egypt to escape from
Solomon, 1 Kin. 11:26–40
Recalled from Egypt by
the ten tribes on account
of disaffection toward
Rehoboam, and made king,
1 Kin. 12:1–20; 2 Chr. 10:12–
19
Subverts the religion of Moses,
1 Kin. 12:25–33; 13:33,
34; 14:9, 16; 16:2, 26, 31;
2 Chr. 11:14; 13:8, 9
Hand of, paralyzed,
1 Kin. 13:1–10
His wife sent to consult the
prophet Ahijah concerning
her child, 1 Kin. 14:1–18
His wars with Rehoboam,
1 Kin. 14:19, 30; 15:6;
2 Chr. 11:1–4
His war with Abijah,
1 Kin. 15:7; 2 Chr. 13
Death of, 1 Kin. 14:20;
2 Chr. 13:20
————— King of Israel
Successor to Jehoash,
2 Kin. 14:16, 23
Makes conquest of Hamath
and Damascus, 2 Kin. 14:25–
28
Wicked reign of, 2 Kin. 14:24
Prophecies concerning,
Amos 7:7–13
Death of, 2 Kin. 14:29
Genealogies written during his
reign, 1 Chr. 5:17

JERUSALEM
Called Jebus, Josh. 18:28;
Judg. 19:10
Zion, 1 Kin. 8:1; Zech. 9:13
City of David, 2 Sam. 5:7;
Is. 22:9
Salem, Gen. 14:18; Ps. 76:2
Ariel, Is. 29:1
City of God, Ps. 46:4
City of the Great King,
Ps. 48:2
City of Judah, 2 Chr. 25:28
The Perfection of Beauty,

——— A Levite who had charge of the tithes, 2 Chr. 31:15

His descendants returned with Ezra from Babylon, Ezra 2:40; Neh. 7:43

——— Also called Joshua

A priest who accompanied Zerubbabel from Babylon, Ezra 2:2; Neh. 7:7; 12:1

Descendants of, Neh. 12:10

He rebuilt the altar, Ezra 3:2

Rebuilt the temple, Ezra 3:8–13

Contends with those who sought to defeat the rebuilding of the temple, Ezra 4:1–3; 5:1, 2

——— Father of Jozabad, Ezra 8:33

——— Son of Pahath-moab, Ezra 2:6; Neh. 7:11

——— Father of Ezer, Neh. 3:19

——— A Levite who explained the law to the people when Ezra read it aloud, Neh. 8:7; 12:8

——— A Levite who sealed Nehemiah's covenant, Neh. 10:9

——— A city of the tribe of Judah, Neh. 11:26

JESSE

Father of David, Ruth 4:17; 1 Sam. 17:12

Ancestor of Jesus, Matt. 1:5, 6

Samuel visits, under divine command, to select a successor to Saul from his sons, 1 Sam. 16:1–13

Saul asks, to send David to become a member of his court, 1 Sam. 16:19–23

Sons in Saul's army, 1 Sam. 17:13–28

Lives with David in Moab, 1 Sam. 22:3, 4

Descendants of, 1 Chr. 2:13–17

JESUS, THE CHRIST

History of; Genealogy of, Matt. 1:1–17; Luke 3:23–38

Facts before the birth of

The angel Gabriel appears to Mary (at Nazareth), Luke 1:26–38

Mary visits Elisabeth (at Hebron?), Luke 1:39–56

Mary's magnificat (at Hebron?), Luke 1:46–55

An angel appears to Joseph concerning Mary (at Nazareth), Matt. 1:18–25

Birth of (at Bethlehem), Luke 2:1–7

Angels appear to the shepherds (in the vicinity of Bethlehem), Luke 2:8–20

Magi (the wise men

from the east) visit (at Bethlehem), Matt. 2:1–12

Circumcision of (at Bethlehem), Luke 2:21

Is presented in the temple (in Jerusalem), Luke 2:21–38

Flight into and return from Egypt, Matt. 2:13–23

Discussions with the religious experts in the temple area (in Jerusalem), Luke 2:41–52

Is immersed by John in the Jordan River, Matt. 3:13–17; Mark 1:9–11; Luke 3:21–23

Temptation of (in the desert of Judaea), Matt. 1:11; Mark 1:12, 13; Luke 4:1–13

John's testimony concerning him, John 1:1–18

Testimony of John the Baptist concerning (at Bethabara), John 1:19–34

Disciples adhere to, John 1:35–51

Miracle at Cana of Galilee, John 2:1–12

Drives the money-changers from the temple (in Jerusalem), John 2:13–25

Nicodemus comes to Jesus (in Jerusalem), John 3:1–21

His disciples immerse some of the people (at Aenon), John 3:22; John 4:2

Returns to Galilee, Matt. 4:12; Mark 1:14; Luke 4:14; John 4:1–3

Visits Sychar and teaches the Samaritan woman, John 4:4–42

Teaches in Galilee, Matt. 4:17; Mark 1:14; 15; Luke 4:14; 15; John 4:43–45

Heals a nobleman's son of Capernaum (at Cana of Galilee), John 4:46–54

Is rejected by the people of Nazareth; lives at Capernaum, Matt. 4:13–16; Luke 4:16–31

Chooses Peter, Andrew, James, and John as disciples; miracle of the catch of fish (at Capernaum), Matt. 4:18–22; Mark 1:16–20; Luke 5:1–11

Preaches throughout Galilee, Matt. 4:23–25; Mark 1:35–39; Luke 4:42–44

Heals a demoniac (at Capernaum), Mark 1:21–28; Luke 4:31–37

Heals Peter's mother-in-law (at Capernaum), Matt. 8:14–17; Mark 1:29–34; Luke 4:38–41

Heals a leper (in Galilee), Matt. 8:2–4; Mark 1:40–45; Luke 5:12–16

Heals a paralyzed man (at

Capernaum), Matt. 9:2–8; Mark 2:1–12; Luke 5:17–26

Calls Matthew (Capernaum), Matt. 9:9; Mark 2:13, 14; Luke 5:27, 28

Heals an immobile man at the pool of Bethesda on the Sabbath day; is persecuted, and makes his defense, John 5

Defines the law of the Sabbath on the occasion of his disciples plucking the ears of grain (at Capernaum), Matt. 12:1–8; Mark 2:23–28; Luke 6:1–5

Heals a man having a withered hand (at Capernaum), Matt. 12:9–14; Mark 3:1–6; Luke 6:6–11

Withdraws from Capernaum to Lake Galilee, where he heals many, Matt. 12:15–21; Mark 3:7–12

Goes up onto a mountain, and calls and commissions twelve disciples (in Galilee), Matt. 10:2–4; Mark 3:13–19; Luke 6:12–19

Delivers the "Sermon on the Mount" (in Galilee), Matt. 5; 6; 7; Luke 6:20–49

Heals the servant of the centurion (near Capernaum), Matt. 8:5–13; Luke 7:1–10

Raises the widow's son from the dead (at Nain), Luke 7:11–17

Receives the message from John the Baptist (in Galilee), Matt. 11:2–19; Luke 7:18–35

Rebukes the unbelieving cities about Capernaum, Matt. 11:20–30

Anointed by a sinful woman (at Capernaum), Luke 7:36–50

Preaches in the cities of Galilee, Luke 8:1–3

Heals a demoniac, and denounces the scribes and Pharisees (in Galilee), Matt. 12:22–37; Mark 3:19–30; Luke 11:14–26

Replies to the scribes and Pharisees who seek a sign from him (in Galilee), Matt. 12:38–45; Luke 11:16–36

Denounces the Pharisees and other hypocrites (in Galilee), Luke 11:37–54

Discourses to his disciples (in Galilee), Luke 12

Parable of the barren fig tree (in Galilee), Luke 13:6–9

Parable of the sower (at Lake Galilee),

Matt. 13:1–23; Mark 4:1–25; Luke 8:4–18

Parable of the tares and other teachings (in Galilee), Matt. 13:24–53; Mark 4:26–34

Crosses Lake Galilee and quiets the squall, Matt. 8:18–27; Mark 4:35–41; Luke 8:22–25

Miracle of the swine (in Gadara), Matt. 8:28–33; Mark 5:1–21; Luke 8:26–40

Returns to Capernaum, Matt. 9:1; Mark 5:21; Luke 8:40

Eats with tax collectors and sinners, and discourses on fasting (Capernaum), Matt. 9:10–17; Mark 2:15–22; Luke 5:29–39

Raises to life the daughter of Jairus, and heals the woman who has the issue of blood (at Capernaum), Matt. 9:18–26; Mark 5:22–43; Luke 8:41–56

Heals two blind men and casts out an evil spirit from a mute boy (at Capernaum), Matt. 9:27–34

Returns to Nazareth, Matt. 13:53–58; Mark 6:1–6

Teaches in various towns in Galilee, Matt. 9:35–38

Instructs his disciples and empowers them to heal diseases and cast out unclean spirits, Matt. 10; Mark 6:6–13; Luke 9:1–6

Herod (Antipas) falsely supposes him to be John, whom he had beheaded, Matt. 14:1, 2, 6–12; Mark 6:14–16, 21–29; Luke 9:7–9

The twelve apostles return; he goes to the desert, multitudes follow him; he feeds five thousand (at Lake Galilee), Matt. 14:13–21; Mark 6:30–44; Luke 9:10–17; John 6:1–14

Walks on the lake (Lake Galilee), Matt. 14:22–36; Mark 6:45–56; John 6:15–21

Teaches in the synagogue in Capernaum, John 6:22–65

Some disciples forsake him (at Capernaum), John 6:66–71

He justifies his disciples in eating without washing their hands (at Capernaum), Matt. 15:1–20; Mark 7:1–23

Heals the daughter of the Syro-Phoenician woman (near Tyre and Sidon), Matt. 15:21–28; Mark 7:24–30

Heals a deaf man (in the Decapolis region), Matt. 15:29–31; Mark 7:31–37

Feeds more than four-thousand people, Matt. 15:32–39; Mark 8:1–9

Refuses to give a sign to the Pharisees (in the region of Magdala), Matt. 16:1–4; Mark 8:10–12

Cautions his disciples against, the leaven (teachings) of hypocrisy (on Lake Galilee), Matt. 16:4–12; Mark 8:13–21

Heals a blind man (at Bethsaida), Mark 8:22–26

Foretells his own death and resurrection (near Caesarea Philippi), Matt. 16:21–28; Mark 8:31–38; 9:1; Luke 9:22–27

Is transfigured, Matt. 17:1–13; Mark 9:2–13; Luke 9:28–36

Heals a demoniac (near Caesarea Philippi), Matt. 17:14–21; Mark 9:14–29; Luke 9:37–43

Foretells his own death and resurrection (in Galilee), Matt. 17:22, 23; Mark 9:30–32; Luke 9:43–45

Miracle of the temple tax money in the fish's mouth, Matt. 17:24–27

Reproves the ambition of his disciples (at Capernaum), Matt. 18; Mark 9:33–50; Luke 9:46–50

Reproves the intolerance of his disciples, Mark 9:38, 39; Luke 9:49, 50

Journeys to Jerusalem to attend the Feast of Tabernacles, passing through Samaria, Luke 9:51–62; John 7:2–11

Commissions the seventy disciples (in Samaria), Luke 10:1–16

Heals ten lepers (near the border between Samaria and Galilee), Luke 17:11–19

Teaches in Jerusalem at the Feast of Tabernacles, John 7:14–53; 8

Answers a Biblical expert, who tests his wisdom with the question, "What shall I do to inherit eternal life?" by the parable of the Good Samaritan (in Jerusalem), Luke 10:25–37

Hears the report of the seventy disciples (in Jerusalem), Luke 10:17–24

Teaches in the house of Mary, Martha, and Lazarus (in Bethany), Luke 10:38–42

Teaches his disciples to pray, Luke 11:1–13

Heals a blind man, who, because of his faith in Jesus, was excommunicated (in Jerusalem), John 9

Teaches people (in Jerusalem), John 9:39–41; 10:1–21

Teaches in the temple (at Jerusalem) at the Feast of Dedication, John 10:22–39

Goes to Bethabara to escape violence from the rulers (east of the Jordan River), John 10:40–42; 11:3–16

Returns to Bethany and raises Lazarus from the dead, John 11:1–46

Escapes to the town of Ephraim from the conspiracy led by Caiaphas, the high priest (in Judaea), John 11:47–54

Journeys toward Jerusalem to attend the Passover; heals many who are diseased, and teaches the people (in Peraea), Matt. 19:1, 2; Mark 10:1; Luke 13:10–35

Dines with a Pharisee on the Sabbath (in Peraea), Luke 14:1–24

Teaches the multitude the conditions of discipleship (in Peraea), Luke 14:25–35

Enunciates the parables of the lost sheep, of the lost piece of silver, of the prodigal son, and of the unjust steward (in Peraea), Luke 15; 16:1–13

Reproves the hypocrisy of the Pharisees (in Peraea), Luke 16

Enunciates the parable of the rich man and Lazarus (in Peraea), Luke 16:19–31

Teaches his disciples concerning offenses, meekness, and humility (in Peraea), Luke 17:1–10

Teaches the Pharisees concerning the coming of his kingdom (in Peraea), Luke 17:20–37

Enunciates the parables of the unjust judge, and the Pharisee and publican praying in the temple (in Peraea), Luke 18:1–14

Interprets the law concerning marriage and divorce (in Peraea), Matt. 19:3–12; Mark 10:2–12

Blesses little children (in Peraea), Matt. 19:13–15; Mark 10:13–16; Luke 18:15–17

Receives the rich young ruler who asks what he shall do

to inherit eternal life (in Peraea), Matt. 19:16–22; Mark 10:17–22; Luke 18:18–24

Enunciates the parable of the vineyard (in Peraea), Matt. 20:1–16

Foretells his own death and resurrection (in Peraea), Matt. 20:17–19; Mark 10:32–34; Luke 18:31–34

Listens to the mother of James and John in behalf of her sons (in Peraea), Matt. 20:20–28; Mark 10:35–45

Heals two blind men (at Jericho), Matt. 20:29–34; Mark 10:46–50; Luke 18:35–43

Visits Zacchaeus, Luke 19:1–10

Enunciates the parable of the pounds (in Jericho), Luke 19:11–28

Goes to Bethany six days before the Passover, John 12:1–9

Triumphal entry into Jerusalem, while the people throw palm branches on the road in front of him, Matt. 21:1–11; Mark 11:1–11; Luke 19:29–44; John 12:12–19

Enters the temple (in Jerusalem), Matt. 21:12; Mark 11:11; Luke 19:45

Drives the money changers out of the temple (in Jerusalem), Matt. 21:12, 13; Luke 19:45, 46

Heals the sick people in the temple courtyard (in Jerusalem), Matt. 21:14

Teaches daily in the temple courtyard (in Jerusalem), Luke 19:47, 48

Performs the miracle of causing the barren fig tree to wither (just outside Jerusalem), Matt. 21:17–22; Mark 11:12–14, 20–22

Enunciates

    The parable of the two sons (in Jerusalem), Matt. 21:28–31

    The parable of the wicked husbandmen (in Jerusalem), Matt. 21:33–46; Mark 12:1–12; Luke 20:9–19

    The parable of the marriage banquet (in Jerusalem), Matt. 22:1–14; Luke 14:16–24

Tested by the Pharisees and the Herodians, and enunciates the duty of a citizen to his government

(in Jerusalem), Matt. 22:15–22; Mark 12:13–17; Luke 20:20–26

Tested by the Sadducees concerning the resurrection of the dead (in Jerusalem), Matt. 22:23–33; Mark 12:18–27; Luke 20:27–40

Tested by a Biblical expert (in Jerusalem), Matt. 22:34–40; Mark 12:28–34

Exposes the hypocrisies of the scribes and Pharisees (in Jerusalem), Matt. 23; Mark 12:38–40; Luke 20:45–47

Verifies the prophecy of Isaiah concerning the unbelieving Jews, John 12:37–50

Foretells the destruction of the temple, and of Jerusalem (in Jerusalem), Matt. 24; Mark 13; Luke 21:5–36

Laments over Jerusalem (just outside Jerusalem), Matt. 23:37; Luke 19:41–44

Enunciates the parables of the ten virgins and of the talents, Matt. 25:1–30

Foretells the scenes of the day of judgment (on the Mount of Olives), Matt. 25:31–46

Anointed with precious ointment (in Bethany), Matt. 26:6–13; Mark 14:3–9; John 12:1–8

His last Passover meal and his establishment of the Lord's Supper (in Jerusalem), Matt. 26:17–30; Mark 14:12–25; Luke 22:7–20

Washes the disciples' feet (in Jerusalem), John 13:1–17

Foretells his betrayal (in Jerusalem), Matt. 26:23; Mark 14:18–21; Luke 22:21; John 13:18

Accuses Judas of his betrayal (in Jerusalem), Matt. 26:21–25; Mark 14:18–21; Luke 22:21–23; John 13:21–30

Teaches his disciples, and comforts them with promises, and promises the gift of the Holy Spirit (in Jerusalem), John 14; 15; 16

One of his last prayers (in Jerusalem), John 17

Retires to Gethsemane (on the Mount of Olives), Matt. 26:30, 36–46; Mark 14:26, 32–42; Luke 22:39–46; John 18:1

Is betrayed and apprehended (in the garden of Gethsemane), Matt. 26:47–56; Mark 14:43–54, 66–72; Luke 22:47–53; John 18:2–12

Trial of, before Caiaphas (in Jerusalem), Matt. 26:57, 58, 69–75; Mark 14:53, 54, 66–72; Luke 22:54–62; John 18:13–18, 25–27

Tried by the council (in Jerusalem), Matt. 26:59–68; Mark 14:55–65; Luke 22:63–71; John 18:19–21

Led by the council to Pilate (in Jerusalem), Matt. 27:1, 2, 11–14; Mark 15:1–5; Luke 23:1–5; John 18:28–38

Arraigned before Herod Antipas (in Jerusalem), Luke 23:6–12

Tried in front of Pilate (in Jerusalem), Matt. 27:15–26; Mark 15:6–15; Luke 23:13–25; John 18:39, 40; 19:1–16

Mocked by the soldiers (in Jerusalem), Matt. 27:27–31; Mark 15:16–20

Is led away to be crucified (from Jerusalem), Matt. 27:31–34; Mark 15:20–23; Luke 23:26–32; John 19:16, 17

Crucified (just outside Jerusalem), Matt. 27:35–56; Mark 15:24–41; Luke 23:33–49; John 19:18–30

Taken down from the cross and buried (just outside Jerusalem), Matt. 27:57–66; Mark 15:42–47; Luke 23:50–56; John 19:31–42

Arises from the dead (just outside Jerusalem), Matt. 28:2–15; Mark 16:1–11; Luke 24:1–12; John 20:1–18

Is seen by Peter (near Jerusalem), Luke 24:34; 1 Cor. 15:5

Appears to two disciples who journey to the village of Emmaus, Mark 16:12, 13; Luke 24:13–35

Appears in the midst of the disciples, when Thomas was absent (in Jerusalem), Mark 16:14–18; Luke 24:36–49; John 20:19–23

Appears to his disciples, when Thomas was present (in Jerusalem), John 20:26–29

Appears to his disciples at Lake Galilee, Matt. 28:16; John 21:1, 2

Appears to the apostles and more than five hundred

followers on a mountain in Galilee, Matt. 28:16–20; 1 Cor. 15:6

Appears to James and also to all the apostles (in Jerusalem), Acts 1:3–8; 1 Cor. 15:7

Ascends to heaven (near Bethany), Mark 16:19, 20; Luke 24:50–53; Acts 1:9–12

Appears to Paul (on the road to Damascus), Acts 9:3–17; 18:9; 22:14, 18; 23:11; 26:16; 1 Cor. 9:1; 15:8

Appears to the Apostle John (on Patmos Island), Rev. 1:10–18

Miscellaneous Facts concerning

Brothers (physical) of, Matt. 13:55; Mark 6:3; 1 Cor. 9:5; Gal. 1:19

Sisters of, Matt. 13:56; Mark 6:3

Was with the Israelites in the wilderness, 1 Cor. 10:4, 9; Heb. 11:26; Jude 5

Exaltation of, Ps. 2:8, 9; 24:7–10; 68:18; Mark 16:19; Luke 22:69; 24:26; John 7:39; 13:31, 32; 17:5; Acts 2:33, 34; 3:20, 21; 5:31; 7:55, 56; Rom. 8:17, 34; Eph. 1:20; 4:8, 10; Phil. 2:9–11; Col. 2:15; 3:1; 1 Tim. 3:16; Heb. 1:3; 2:9; 4:10, 14; 6:20; 7:26; 8:1; 9:12, 24; 10:12, 13; 12:2; 1 Pet. 3:22

Example, an, Matt. 11:29; 20:28; Mark 10:43–45; Luke 22:26, 27; John 10:4; 13:13–15, 34; 17:14, 18, 21, 22; Rom. 8:29; 13:14; 15:2, 3, 5, 7; 2 Cor. 4:10; 8:9; 10:1; Gal. 3:27; 6:2; Eph. 4:13, 15, 24, 32; 5:2; 6:9; Phil. 2:5–8; Col. 3:10, 11, 13; 1 Thess. 1:6; Heb. 3:1; 12:2–4; 1 Pet. 1:15, 16; 2:21–24; 3:17, 18; 1 John 2:6; 3:1–3, 16; 4:17; Rev. 3:21; 14:4

Mission of, 2 Sam. 23:3, 4; Is. 42:6, 7; 61:1–3; Dan. 9:24, 27; Mic. 5:2; Zech. 13:1; Mal. 3:2, 3; Matt. 1:21; 3:11, 12; 4:23; 5:17; 9:13; 10:34–36; 15:24; 18:11–14; 20:28; Mark 1:38; 2:15–22; 10:45; Luke 1:78, 79; 2:30–32, 34, 35, 38; 4:18, 19, 43; 5:30–32; 8:1; 9:56; 12:49–53; 22:35–38; 24:26, 46, 47; John 3:13–17; 4:25, 34; 6:51; 9:39; 10:10; 12:27, 46, 47; 18:37; Acts 5:31; 10:43; 26:23; Rom. 4:25; 5:6–8; 8:3, 4; 10:4; 14:9, 15; 15:8, 9;

2 Cor. 5:14, 15; Gal. 1:3, 4; 4:4, 5; Eph. 4:10; 1 Tim. 1:15; Heb. 2:9, 14, 15, 18; 9:26; 1 John 3:5, 8; 4:10

Parables of

The wise and foolish builders, Matt. 7:24–27; Luke 6:47–49

Two debtors, Luke 7:41–47

The rich fool, Luke 12:16–21

The servants waiting for their Lord, Luke 12:35–40

The barren fig tree, Luke 13:6–9

The sower, Matt. 13:3–9, 18–23; Mark 4:1–9, 14–20; Luke 8:5–8, 11–15

The tares (darnel), Matt. 13:24–30, 36–43

Seed growing secretly, Mark 4:26–29

The mustard seed, Matt. 13:31, 32; Mark 4:30–32; Luke 13:18, 19

Leaven (yeast), Matt. 13:33; Luke 13:20, 21

The hidden treasure, Matt. 13:44

The pearl of great price, Matt. 13:45, 46

The drag net, Matt. 13:47–50

The unmerciful servant, Matt. 18:23–35

The Good Samaritan, Luke 10:30–37

The friend at midnight, Luke 11:5–8

The Good Shepherd, John 10:1–16

The great supper, Luke 14:15–24

The lost sheep, Matt. 18:12–14; Luke 15:3–7

The lost piece of money (one drachma), Luke 15:8–10

The prodigal son and his older brother, Luke 15:11–32

The unjust steward, Luke 16:1–9

The rich man and Lazarus, Luke 16:19–31

The importunate (unrelenting) widow, Luke 18:1–8

The Pharisee and the publican, Luke 18:9–14

The laborers in the vineyard, Matt. 20:1–16

The pounds, Luke 19:11–27

The two sons, Matt. 21:28–32

The evil sharecroppers, Matt. 21:33–44; Mark 12:1–12; Luke 20:9–18

The marriage of the king's son, Matt. 22:1–14

The fig tree leafing, Matt. 24:32; Mark 13:28, 29

Man taking a far journey, Mark 13:34–37

Ten virgins, Matt. 25:1–13

The talents, Matt. 25:14–30

The vine, John 15:1–5

Perfections of, Ps. 45:2; Is. 11:5; 49:2; 53:9; Ezek. 34:29; Mic. 5:4; Hag. 2:7; Matt. 3:11; 12:41, 42; 27:3, 4; Mark 1:7, 8; Luke 3:16; 23:41; John 1:14, 18; 5:30, 34, 41; 7:18; Acts 13:28; 1 Cor. 1:24; 15:45, 47; 2 Cor. 1:19; 4:4; 5:21; 9:15; Eph. 3:8; Col. 1:19; 2 Thess. 3:3; 2 Tim. 2:13; Heb. 1:3; 2:10; 3:2

Priesthood of

Appointed and called by God, Heb. 3:1, 2; 5:4, 5

After the order of Melchizedek, Ps. 110:4; Heb. 5:6; 6:20; 7:15, 17

Superior to Aaron and the Levitical priests, Heb. 7:11, 16, 22; 8:1, 2, 6

Consecrated with an oath, Heb. 7:20, 21

Has an unchangeable priesthood, Heb. 7:23, 28

Is of unblemished purity, Heb. 7:26, 28

Faithful, Heb. 3:2

Needed no sacrifice for himself, Heb. 7:27

Offered himself as a sacrifice, Heb. 9:14, 26

His sacrifice superior to all others, Heb. 9:13, 14, 23

Offered sacrifice only once, Heb. 7:27

Made reconciliation, Heb. 2:17

Obtained redemption for us, Heb. 9:12

Entered into heaven, Heb. 4:14; 10:12

Sympathizes with saints, Heb. 2:18; 4:15

Intercedes, Heb. 7:25; 9:24

Blesses, Num. 6:23–26; Acts 3:26

On his throne, Zech. 6:13

Appointment of, an encouragement to steadfastness, Heb. 4:14

Typified

Melchizedek, Gen. 14:18–20

Aaron and his sons, Ex. 40:12–15

Promises of, Prophetic, Matt. 19:28, 29; Mark 10:29, 30; Luke 18:29, 30; 22:29, 30; 23:43; 24:49; John 5:25–29; 6:54, 57, 58; 7:39; 12:25, 26;

Death of, at the hand of Jehu,
2 Kin. 9:30–37
Figurative, Rev. 2:20

JEZREEL

A city in the south of the
territory of the tribe of Judah,
Josh. 15:56; 1 Sam. 25:43;
27:3; 29:1, 11
——— A city of the tribe
of Issachar, Josh. 19:18;
2 Sam. 2:9
Ahab's residence in,
1 Kin. 18:45, 46; 21:1
Naboth's vineyard in,
1 Kin. 21:1
Joram's residence in,
2 Kin. 8:29
Jehu kills King Ahab, his wife,
and friends at, 2 Kin. 9:15–
37; 10:11
Prophecies concerning,
Hos. 1:4, 5, 11
——— A valley, Josh. 17:16
Place of Gideon's battle with
the Midianites, Judg. 6:33
Place of the defeat of the
Israelites under Saul and
Jonathan, 1 Sam. 29:1, 11;
31:1–6; 2 Sam. 4:4
——— A descendant of Etam,
1 Chr. 4:3
——— Figurative of the
northern kingdom of Israel,
Hos. 1:4, 5, 11

JOAB

Son of David's sister,
1 Chr. 2:16
Commander of David's
army, 2 Sam. 8:16; 20:23;
1 Chr. 11:6; 18:15; 27:34
Dedicated the plunder of his
battles, 1 Chr. 26:28
Defeated the Jebusites,
1 Chr. 11:6
Defeats and kills Abner,
2 Sam. 2:13–32; 3:27;
1 Kin. 2:5
Destroys all the males in
Edom, 1 Kin. 11:16
Defeats the Ammonites,
2 Sam. 10:7–14; 1 Chr. 19:6–
15
Captures Rabbah, 2 Sam. 11:1,
15–25; 12:26–29;
1 Kin. 20:1, 2
Procures the return of
Absalom to Jerusalem,
2 Sam. 14:1–24
Barley field of, burned by
Absalom, 2 Sam. 14:29–33
Pursues and kills Absalom,
2 Sam. 18
Censures David for lamenting
the death of Absalom,
2 Sam. 19:1–8
Replaced by Amasa as
commander of David's army,
2 Sam. 17:25; 19:13
Kills Amasa, 2 Sam. 20:8–13;
1 Kin. 2:5

Causes Sheba to be put to
death, 2 Sam. 20:16–22
Opposes the numbering of
the people, 2 Sam. 24:3;
1 Chr. 21:3
Numbers the people,
2 Sam. 24:4–9; 1 Chr. 21:4, 5;
27:23, 24
Supports Adonijah as
successor to David,
1 Kin. 1:7; 2:28
Killed by Benaiah, under
Solomon's order, 1 Kin. 2:29–
34
——— A grandson of Kenaz,
1 Chr. 4:14
——— An Israelite (or the
name of two Israelites)
whose descendants returned
from Babylon to Jerusalem,
Ezra 2:6; 8:9; Neh. 7:11
——— "The household of
Joab," 1 Chr. 2:54

JOASH

Son of Becher, 1 Chr. 7:8
——— Keeper of the stores of
oil, 1 Chr. 27:28
——— Father of Gideon,
Judg. 6:11, 29, 31; 7:14; 8:13,
29–32
——— Son of Ahab, king
of Israel, 1 Kin. 22:26;
2 Chr. 18:25
——— Also called Jehoash
(Son of Ahaziah and king of
Judah)
Saved from his grandmother
by Jehosheba, his aunt,
and hidden for six years,
2 Kin. 11:1–3; 2 Chr. 22:11,
12
Anointed king by the priest,
Jehoiada, 2 Kin. 11:12–21;
2 Chr. 23
Righteousness of, under
influence of Jehoiada,
2 Kin. 12:2; 2 Chr. 24:2
Repaired the temple,
2 Kin. 12:4–16; 2 Chr. 24:4–
14, 27
Wickedness of, after
Jehoiada's death,
2 Chr. 24:17–22
Procured peace from Hazael,
king of Syria, by gift of
dedicated treasures from
the temple, 2 Kin. 12:17,
18; 2 Chr. 24:23, 24
Prophecy against,
2 Chr. 24:19, 20
Put Jehoiada's son to
death, 2 Chr. 24:20–22;
Matt. 23:35
Diseases of, 2 Chr. 24:25
Conspired against and
slain, 2 Kin. 12:20, 21;
2 Chr. 24:25, 26
——— A descendant of Shelah,
1 Chr. 4:22

——— One of David's officers,
1 Chr. 12:3

JOB

A man who lived in Uz,
Job 1:1
Righteousness of, Job 1:1, 5, 8;
2:3; Ezek. 14:14, 20
Riches of, Job 1:3
Trial of, by affliction of Satan,
Job 1:13–19; 2:7–10
Fortitude of, Job 1:20–22;
2:10; James 5:11
Visited by Eliphaz, Bildad,
and Zophar as comforters,
Job 2:11–13
Complaints of, and replies by
his three friends to, Job 3; 4;
5; 6; 7; 8; 9; 10; 11; 12; 13;
14; 15; 16; 17; 18; 19; 20; 21;
22; 23; 24; 25; 26; 27; 28; 29;
30; 31; 32; 33; 34; 35; 36; 37
Replied to by God, Job 38; 39;
40; 41
Submission of, to God,
Job 40:3–5; 42:1–6
Later blessings and riches of,
Job 42:10–16
Death of, Job 42:16, 17

JOEL

Son of Samuel, 1 Sam. 8:2;
1 Chr. 6:33; 15:17
Called Vashni, 1 Chr. 6:28
——— A Simeonite, 1 Chr. 4:35
——— A Reubenite,
1 Chr. 5:4, 8
——— A Gadite, 1 Chr. 5:12
——— A Kohathite Levite,
1 Chr. 6:36
——— Descendant of Issachar,
1 Chr. 7:3
——— One of David's valiant
men, 1 Chr. 11:38
Called "Igal, son of Nathan"
2 Sam. 23:36
——— Name of two
Gershonites, 1 Chr. 15:7, 11;
23:8; 26:22
——— Prince of Manasseh,
1 Chr. 27:20
——— A Kohathite who
assisted in the cleansing of
the temple, 2 Chr. 29:12
——— One of Nebo's family,
Ezra 10:43
——— Son of Zichri, Neh. 11:9
——— One of the twelve minor
prophets, probably lived in
the days of Uzziah, Joel 1:1;
Acts 2:16
Declares the terribleness of
God's judgments, Joel 1;
2:1–11
Denounces judgments against
the enemies of God, Joel 3:1–
17
Sets forth the blessings of the
church, Joel 3:18–21

JOHANAN

A Jewish captain,
2 Kin. 25:22–24
Warns Gedaliah against
Ishmael, Jer. 40:13–16
Ishmael defeated by,
Jer. 41:11–15
Sought prayers of Jeremiah,
Jer. 42:2, 3
Disobeyed Jeremiah and took
him to Egypt, Jer. 43:1–7
———— Son of Josiah,
1 Chr. 3:15
———— A son of Elioenai,
1 Chr. 3:24
———— A Levite, 1 Chr. 6:9, 10
———— Two Israelites who
joined David at Ziklag,
1 Chr. 12:4, 12
———— An Ephraimite,
2 Chr. 28:12
———— A returned exile,
Ezra 8:12
———— A priest, Ezra 10:6;
Neh. 12:22, 23
Probably identical with
Jonathan, Neh. 12:11
———— Son of Tobiah the
Ammonite, Neh. 6:18

JOHN

The Apostle; Intimately
associated with Jesus,
John 13:23–26; 21:20
Is present when Jesus
performs the following
miracles
The healing of Peter's
mother-in-law, Matt. 8:14,
15; Mark 1:30, 31;
Luke 4:38, 39
The raising of the daughter of
Jairus, Mark 5:37; Luke 8:51
The two catches of fish,
Luke 5:10; John 21:1–7
The transfiguration,
Matt. 17:1; Mark 9:2;
Luke 9:28
Is present with Jesus in the
garden of Gethsemane,
Matt. 26:37; Mark 14:33;
Luke 22:39
Intolerance of, Mark 9:38;
Luke 9:49, 50, 54–56
Civil ambitions of,
Matt. 20:20–24; Mark 10:35–
41
Prepares the Passover meal,
Matt. 26:18, 19; Mark 14:13–
16; Luke 22:8–13
Present at the trial of Jesus
which took place in front of
the high priest, John 18:15,
16
Present at the crucifixion,
John 19:26, 27
Present at the gravesite of
Jesus, John 20:2–8
Present when Jesus revealed
himself at the Lake Galilee,
John 21
Present with Peter in the

temple courtyard, Acts 3:1–
11
Lives in Jerusalem, Acts 1:13
Is intrusted with the care
of Mary, mother of Jesus,
John 19:26
Imprisoned by the rulers of
the Jews, Acts 4:1–19
Sent by the Jerusalem
congregation with the
commission to Samaria,
Acts 8:14–17
A pillar of the ekklesia (body
of Christ), Gal. 2:9
Writes to the congregations
See the Epistles of John,
1 John 1; 2 John 1; 3 John 1
Writes his apocalyptic vision
from Patmos Island, Rev. 1:9
Prophecy concerning,
Rev. 10:11
———— A relative of Annas the
high priest, Acts 4:6

JONAH

Also called Jonas; A prophet of
Israel, 2 Kin. 14:25
Sent by God to warn the city
of Nineveh, Jon. 1:1, 2
Disobedience and punishment
of, Jon. 1:3–17
Repentance and deliverance of,
Jon. 2; Matt. 12:40
Brought Ninevites to
repentance, Jon. 3;
Matt. 12:41
Displeased with God's mercy
to Nineveh; reproved, Jon. 4
Is a sign, Matt. 16:4;
Luke 11:29, 30

JONATHAN

A Levite of Bethlehem, who
becomes a priest for Micah;
accepts idolatry; joins the
Danites, Judg. 17:7–13;
18:1–30
———— Son of Saul,
1 Sam. 14:49
Victory of, over the
Philistine garrison of Geba,
1 Sam. 13:3, 4, 16
Victory of, over the Philistines
at Michmash, 1 Sam. 14:1–18
Under Saul's curse
pronounced against anyone
who might take food before
Saul was avenged of his
enemies, 1 Sam. 14:24–30,
43
Rescued by the people,
1 Sam. 14:43–45
Love of, for David,
1 Sam. 18:1–4; 19:1–7; 20;
23:16–18
Killed in the battle with the
Philistines, 1 Sam. 31:2, 6;
2 Sam. 21:12–14; 1 Chr. 10:2
Buried by inhabitants of
Jabesh-gilead, 1 Sam. 31:11–
13

Mourned by David,
2 Sam. 1:12, 17–27
Son of, cared for by David,
2 Sam. 4:4; 9; 1 Chr. 8:34
———— Son of Abiathar,
2 Sam. 15:27
Acts as a spy for David,
2 Sam. 15:27, 28; 17:17–22
Informs Adonijah of
Solomon's succession to
David, 1 Kin. 1:42–48
———— Nephew of David, kills
a giant, and becomes one
of David's chief warriors,
2 Sam. 21:21; 1 Chr. 20:7
———— One of David's heroes,
2 Sam. 23:32; 1 Chr. 11:34
———— A son of Jada,
1 Chr. 2:32, 33
———— Secretary of the cabinet
of David, 1 Chr. 27:32
———— Father of Ebed, Ezra 8:6
———— Son of Asahel,
Ezra 10:15
———— Also called Johanan
A descendant of Jeshua,
Neh. 12:11, 22
———— The name of two priests,
Neh. 12:14, 35
———— A scribe, Jer. 37:15, 20;
38:26
———— Son of Kareah, Jer. 40:8

JOPPA

A seaport, Josh. 19:46
Exports from, 2 Chr. 2:16;
Ezra 3:7
Passenger traffic from, Jon. 1:3
Peter performs a miracle at,
Acts 9:36–43
Peter has a vision of a sheet
lowered down from the sky,
at, Acts 10:9–18

JORAM

A son of Toi, 2 Sam. 8:9, 10
Called Hadoram, 1 Chr. 18:10
———— Also called Jehoram
King of Israel, 2 Kin. 1:17; 3:1
King of Syria sends Naaman
to, so that Namaan may be
healed of his leprosy, 2 Kin. 5
Has war with the king of Syria,
2 Kin. 6:8–23; 7; 8:28, 29;
2 Chr. 22:5, 6
Inquires for the particulars
concerning Elisha's miracles,
2 Kin. 8:4, 5
Killed by Jehu, 2 Kin. 9:14–26

JORDAN

A river in Palestine; Empties
into the Dead Sea, Josh. 15:5
Fords of, Gen. 32:10;
Josh. 2:7; Judg. 3:28;
7:24; 8:4; 10:9; 12:5, 6;
2 Sam. 2:29; 17:22, 24;
19:15, 31; 1 Chr. 19:17
Swelling of, at harvest time,
Josh. 3:15; Jer. 12:5
Swelling of, in the early
spring, 1 Chr. 12:15

The waters of, miraculously
separated for the passage
Of the Israelites, Josh. 3; 4;
5:1; Ps. 114:3
Of Elijah, 2 Kin. 2:6–8
Of Elisha, 2 Kin. 2:14
Crossed by a ferry boat,
2 Sam. 19:18
Naaman washes in, for the
healing of his leprosy,
2 Kin. 5:10–14
John the Baptist immerses in,
Matt. 3:6; Mark 1:5
John the Baptist immerses
Jesus in, Matt. 3:13;
Mark 1:9
Plain of, Gen. 13:10–12
Israelites camped in,
Num. 22:1; 26:3, 63
Solomon's foundry in,
1 Kin. 7:46; 2 Chr. 4:17

JOSEPH

Father of Igal, the spy,
Num. 13:7
———— Of the sons of Asaph,
1 Chr. 25:2, 9
———— A returned exile,
Ezra 10:42
———— A priest, Neh. 12:14
———— Husband of Mary,
Matt. 1:18–25; 13:55;
Mark 6:3; Luke 1:27
His genealogy, Matt. 1:1–16;
Luke 3:23–38
An angel appears and testifies
to the innocence of his
betrothed, Matt. 1:19–24
Lives at Nazareth, Luke 2:4
Belongs to the town of
Bethlehem, Luke 2:4
Goes to Bethlehem to be
enrolled, Luke 2:1–4
Jesus born to, Matt. 1:25;
Luke 2:7
Presents Jesus in the temple,
Luke 2:22–39
Returns to Nazareth,
Luke 2:39
Warned in a dream to escape
to Egypt in order to save the
infant's life, Matt. 2:13–15
Warned in a dream to return
to Nazareth, Matt. 2:19–23
Attends the annual feast at
Jerusalem with his family,
Luke 2:42–51
———— Of Arimathaea
Begs for the body of Jesus
for burial in his own tomb,
Matt. 27:57–60; Mark 15:42–
47; Luke 23:50–56;
John 19:38–42
———— Three ancestors of
Joseph, Luke 3:24, 26, 30
———— Also called Barsabas,
surnamed Justus
One of the two persons
nominated in place of Judas,
Acts 1:21, 22, 23
———— A designation of the ten
tribes of Israel, Amos 5:6

JOSHUA

Also called Jehoshua, and
Jehoshuah, and Oshea; Son of
Nun, Num. 13:8; 1 Chr. 7:27
Intimately associated with
Moses, Ex. 24:13; 32:17;
33:11
A religious zealot, Num. 11:28
Sent with others to view the
promised land, Num. 13:8
Makes a favorable report,
Num. 14:6–10
Rewarded for his courage and
fidelity, Num. 14:30, 38;
32:12
Commissioned, ordained,
and charged with the
responsibilites of Moses'
office, Num. 27:18–23;
Deut. 1:38; 3:28; 31:3, 7, 23;
34:9
Divinely inspired, Num. 27:18;
Deut. 34:9; Josh. 1:5, 9; 3:7;
8:8
His life miraculously preserved
when he made a favorable
report about the land,
Num. 14:10
Promises to, Josh. 1:5–9
Leads the people into the land
of Canaan, Josh. 1; 2; 3; 4;
Acts 7:45; Heb. 4:8
Renews circumcision of
the children of Israel; re-
establishes the Passover; has
a vision of the angel of God,
Josh. 5
Besieges and captures Jericho,
Josh. 6
Captures Ai, Josh. 7; 8
Makes a treaty with the
Gibeonites, Josh. 9:3–27
The kings of the six nations of
the Canaanites band together
against him, Josh. 9:1, 2
The six kings make war upon
the Gibeonites; are defeated
and killed, Josh. 10
Defeats seven other kings,
Josh. 10:28–43
Conquers Hazor, Josh. 11
Completes the conquest of the
whole land, Josh. 11:23
List of the kings whom Joshua
struck down, Josh. 12
Allots the land, Josh. 13; 14;
15; 16; 17; 18; 19
Sets the tabernacle up at
Shiloh, Josh. 18:1
Sets apart several cities of
refuge, Josh. 20
Forty-eight cities for the
Levites, Josh. 21
Exhortation of, before his
death, Josh. 23; 24
Survives the Israelites who
refused to enter the promised
land, Num. 26:63–65
His portion of the land,
Josh. 19:49, 50

Death and burial of,
Josh. 24:29, 30
Esteem with which he was
held, Josh. 1:16–18
Faith of, Josh. 6:16
Military genius of, as exhibited
At the defeat of the
Amalekites, Ex. 17:13
At Ai, Josh. 8
At Gibeon, Josh. 10
At Hazor, Josh. 11
Age of, at death, Judg. 2:8
———— An Israelite,
1 Sam. 6:14, 18
———— A governor of Jerusalem,
2 Kin. 23:8
———— Also called Jeshua
The high priest of the
captivity, Ezra 2:2
Assists Zerubbabel in
restoring the temple, Ezra 3;
4:1–6; 5; Hag. 1:1, 12–14; 2:2
Symbolical
Of the restoration of God's
people, Zech. 3; 6:9–15

JOSIAH

King of Judah, 2 Kin. 21:24–
26; 22:1; 1 Chr. 3:14;
2 Chr. 33:25
Ancestor of Jesus, Matt. 1:10,
11
Killed in battle with Pharaoh-
necho, 2 Kin. 23:29, 30;
2 Chr. 35:20–24
Lamentations for, 2 Chr. 35:25
Piety of: exemplified in his
repairing of the temple,
2 Kin. 22:3–7; 2 Chr. 34:1–4
Solicitude when the copy of
the law was discovered and
read to him, 2 Kin. 22:8–20;
2 Chr. 34:14–33
In keeping a solemn Passover,
2 Kin. 23:21–23; 2 Chr. 35:1–
19
Called Josias, Matt. 1:10, 11
Prophecies concerning,
1 Kin. 13:1–3
Destroys the altar and
high places of idolatry,
2 Kin. 23:3–20, 24, 25
———— Son of Zephaniah,
Zech. 6:10

JOTHAM

Son of Gideon, Judg. 9:5, 57
Rebukes the Shechemites with
the parable about the trees,
Judg. 9:7–21
———— Son of Azariah, king of
Judah, 2 Kin. 15:5–7, 32, 38;
1 Chr. 3:12; 2 Chr. 26:21–23;
27
Piety of, 2 Chr. 27
The moral condition of Israel
during his reign, Hos. 4
Ancestor of Jesus, Matt. 1:9
———— Son of Jahdai,
1 Chr. 2:47

JOURNEYED

And they j . . . . Gen. 35:5

children of Israel *j* . . Ex. 12:37
children of Israel *j* . Num. 9:17
of the LORD,
  and *j* . . . . Num. 9:19
of the LORD
  they *j* . . . . Num. 9:20
morning, then
  they *j* . . . . Num. 9:21
their tents, and *j* . . Num. 9:22

JOY

presence is
  fulness of *j* . . . . Ps. 16:11
voice of *j* and
  praise. . . . . Ps. 42:4
for situation, the *j* . . . Ps. 48:2
rejoice even with *j* . . . . Is. 35:2
songs and
  everlasting *j* . . . . Is. 35:10
j and gladness
  shall. . . . . Is. 51:3
with *j*, and be led . . . . Is. 55:12
ashes, the oil of *j* . . . . . Is. 61:3
me a name of *j*, a
  praise. . . . . Jer. 33:9
The voice of *j*, and . . Jer. 33:11
perfection of
  beauty, The *j* . . . . . Lam. 2:15
possession with
  the *j* . . . . Ezek. 36:5
rejoice over thee
  with *j* . . . . Zeph. 3:17
my *j* therefore is
  fulfilled . . . . John 3:29
and your *j* no man
  taketh . . . . John 16:22
finish my course
  with *j* . . . . Acts 20:24
hope, or *j*, or
  crown . . . . 1 Thess. 2:19
the *j* that was set . . . Heb. 12:2
j, and not with
  grief . . . . Heb. 13:17
glory with
  exceeding *j* . . . . Jude 24

JOYFUL

let the hills be *j* . . . . . Ps. 98:8
and be *j*, O earth . . . . Is. 49:13
mountain, and
  make them *j* . . . . Is. 56:7
my soul shall be *j* . . . . Is. 61:10

JUDAH

Son of Jacob, Gen. 35:23
Intercedes for Joseph's life
  when his brothers were
  about to kill him, and
  proposes that they sell him to
  the Ishmaelites, Gen. 37:26,
  27
Takes two wives, Gen. 38:1–6
Lives at Chezib, Gen. 38:5
His incest with his daughter-
  in-law, Gen. 38:12–26
Goes down into Egypt for
  corn (grain), Gen. 43:1–10;
  44:14–34; 46:28
Prophetic benediction of his
  father upon, Gen. 49:8–12
The ancestor of Jesus,
  Matt. 1:2, 3; Rev. 5:5
——— Tribe of

Prophecies concerning,
  Gen. 49:10
Enrollment of the military
  forces of
  At Sinai, Num. 1:26, 27; 2:4
  At Bezek, 1 Sam. 11:8;
    2 Sam. 24:9
  On the plain of Moab,
    Num. 26:22
Place of, in encampments
  and the march, Num. 2:3, 9;
  10:14
By whom commanded,
  Num. 2:3
Moses' benediction upon,
  Deut. 33:7
Commissioned by God to
  lead in the conquest of the
  promised land, Judg. 1:1–3;
  Judg. 1:4–21
Make David king, 2 Sam. 2:1–
  11; 5:4, 5
Rebuked by David for
  lukewarmness toward him
  after Absalom's defeat,
  2 Sam. 19:11–15
Accused by the other tribes of
  stealing the heart of David,
  2 Sam. 19:41–43
Loyal to David at the time of
  the insurrection led by Sheba,
  2 Sam. 20:1, 2
Is accorded the birthright
  forfeited by Reuben,
  1 Chr. 5:1, 2; 28:4; Ps. 60:7
Loyal to the house of David at
  the time of the revolt of the
  ten tribes, 1 Kin. 12:20
Inheritance of, Josh. 15; 18:6;
  19:1, 9
——— Name of two exiled
  priests, Ezra 10:23; Neh. 12:8
——— A Benjamite, Neh. 11:9
——— A prince or priest who
  assisted in the dedication
  of the walls of Jerusalem,
  Neh. 12:34, 36

JUDAS (JUDE)

Surnamed "Iscariot"; Chosen
  as an apostle, Matt. 10:4;
  Mark 3:19; Luke 6:16;
  Acts 1:17
The treasurer of the disciples,
  John 12:6; 13:29
His greed exemplified
By his protest against the
  breaking of the container of
  ointment, John 12:4–6
By his bargaining to betray
  Jesus for a sum of money,
  Matt. 26:14–16; Mark 14:10,
  11; Luke 22:3–6; John 13:2
His apostasy, John 17:12
Betrays the Lord Jesus,
  Matt. 26:47–50; Mark 14:43–
  45; Luke 22:47–49;
  John 18:2–5; Acts 1:16–25
Returns the money to
  the rulers of the Jews,
  Matt. 27:3–10

Hangs himself, Matt. 27:5;
  Acts 1:18
Prophecies concerning,
  Matt. 26:21–25; Mark 14:18–
  21; Luke 22:21–23;
  John 13:18–26; 17:12;
  Acts 1:16, 20; Ps. 41:9; 109:8;
  Zech. 11:12, 13
——— One of the physical
  half-brothers of Jesus,
  Matt. 13:55; Mark 6:3
——— The brother of James
  and probably the writer
  of the Epistle of Jude,
  Luke 6:16; Acts 1:13; Jude 1
——— An apostle, probably
  identical with Lebbaeus, or
  Thaddaeus, John 14:22
——— Of Galilee, who stirred
  up a sedition among the Jews
  soon after the birth of Jesus,
  Acts 5:37
——— A disciple who hosted
  Paul, Acts 9:11
——— Surnamed "Barsabas"
A Christian sent to Antioch of
  Syria with Paul and Barnabas,
  Acts 15:22–32

JUDEA

Also called Judah and Judaea
  (The southern division
  of Palestine); It extended
  from the Jordan River
  and the Dead Sea to the
  Mediterranean Sea, and
  from Shiloh on the north
  to the wilderness on the
  south, Matt. 4:25; Luke 5:17;
  John 4:47, 54
The term applies to all of
  Palestine in, Luke 1:5
It applies to the territory
  east of the Jordan River
  in, Matt. 19:1; Mark 10:1;
  Luke 23:5
——— Wilderness of
Called Beth-arabah, Josh. 15:6,
  61
Assigned to Benjamin,
  Josh. 18:22
John the Baptist preaches in,
  Matt. 3:1; Luke 3:3

JUDGE

the *J* of all the
  earth . . . . Gen. 18:25
shalt thou *j* thy
  neighbour . . . . Lev. 19:15
LORD shall *j* his
  people . . . . Deut. 32:36
fatherless, and a *j* . . . . Ps. 68:5
cometh to *j* the
  earth . . . . Ps. 96:13
cometh to *j* the
  earth . . . . Ps. 98:9
relieve the
  oppressed, *j* . . . . Is. 1:17
they *j* not the
  fatherless . . . . Is. 1:23
j the poor, and
  reprove . . . . Is. 11:4

Judah, and the *k*
thereof. . . . . Jer. 25:18
k of the land of Uz . . Jer. 25:20
And all the *k* of
Tyrus . . . . Jer. 25:22
our fathers, our *k* . . . Jer. 44:17
the spirit of the *k* . . . Jer. 51:11
removeth *k*, and
setteth . . . . Dan. 2:21
the days of these *k* . . Dan. 2:44
gods, and a Lord
of *k* . . . . Dan. 2:47
the Gentiles,
and *k* . . . . Acts 9:15
the prince of the *k* . . . Rev. 1:5
lords, and King
of *k* . . . . Rev. 17:14
written, KING
OF *K* . . . . Rev. 19:16

KIRJATH-JEARIM

Also called Baalah, one
of the four cities of the
Gibeonites; Inhabitants of,
who were not struck down,
on account of the covenant
made by the Israelites with
the Gibeonites, but put
under servitude, Josh. 9:17;
Josh. 9:3–27
In the territory allotted to
Judah, Josh. 15:9, 60; 18:14
The Philistines bring the ark of
the covenant to, 1 Sam. 6:21;
1 Sam. 6
The ark of the covenant
remains for twenty years at,
1 Sam. 7:1, 2; 1 Chr. 13:5, 6
David brings the ark of the
covenant from, 2 Sam. 6:1–
11; 1 Chr. 13:5–8; 2 Chr. 1:4
Inhabitants of, who were
taken into captivity to
Babylon, returned, Ezra 2:25;
Neh. 7:29
Urijah, the prophet, an
inhabitant of, Jer. 26:20

KISH

Father of Saul, 1 Sam. 9:1–3;
10:21; 2 Sam. 21:14
Called Cis, Acts 13:21
——— A Benjamite,
1 Chr. 8:30; 9:36
——— A Levite, 1 Chr. 23:21,
22; 24:29
——— A Levite, 2 Chr. 29:12
——— Great grandfather of
Mordecai, Esth. 2:5

KISHON

Also called Kison (a noted
river of Palestine emptying
into the Mediterranean Sea
near the northern base of
Mount Carmel)
Sisera defeated at, and his
army destroyed in, Judg. 4:7,
13; 5:21; Ps. 83:9
Prophets of Baal destroyed by
Elijah at, 1 Kin. 18:40

KNEES

up upon
Joseph's *k* . . . . Gen. 50:23
smite thee in
the *k* . . . . Deut. 28:35
shall faint, and
all *k* . . . . Ezek. 21:7
melteth, and the *k* . . Nah. 2:10
down, and the
feeble *k* . . . . Heb. 12:12

KNEW

which thy
fathers *k* . . . . Deut. 8:16
them, gods whom
they *k* . . . . Deut. 29:26
they *k* not the
LORD . . . . 1 Sam. 2:12
round about, yet
he *k* . . . . Is. 42:25
k not thee shall
run . . . . Is. 55:5
thee in the
belly I *k* . . . . Jer. 1:5
that handle the
law *k* . . . . Jer. 2:8
made princes,
and I *k* . . . . Hos. 8:4
for I *k* that thou
art . . . . Jon. 4:2
nations whom
they *k* . . . . Zech. 7:14
unto them, I
never *k* . . . . Matt. 7:23
that servant,
which *k* . . . . Luke 12:47
he *k* what was in
man . . . . John 2:25
passover, when
Jesus *k* . . . . John 13:1
be sin for us,
who *k* . . . . 2 Cor. 5:21
ye *k* not God, ye
did . . . . Gal. 4:8
k the grace of God . . . Col. 1:6
us not, because
it *k* . . . . 1 John 3:1

KNOWEST

Israel, whom
thou *k* . . . . Num. 11:16
brother Israel,
Thou *k* . . . . Num. 20:14
nation which
thou *k* . . . . Deut. 28:33
him, Thou *k* the
thing . . . . Josh. 14:6
whose heart
thou *k* . . . . 1 Kin. 8:39
Thou *k* my
downsitting . . . . . . Ps. 139:2
nation that thou *k* . . . Is. 55:5
whose language
thou *k* . . . . Jer. 5:15
thou *k* that I love . . John 21:15
thou *k* that I love . . John 21:16
Lord, thou *k* all
things . . . . John 21:17
Thou, Lord,
which *k* . . . . Acts 1:24
k not that thou art . . Rev. 3:17

KNOWETH

he *k* thy walking
through . . . . Deut. 2:7
us any that *k* how
long . . . . Ps. 74:9
the proud he *k*
afar . . . . Ps. 138:6
For who *k* what is
good . . . . Eccl. 6:12
The ox *k* his owner . . . . Is. 1:3
and who *k* us . . . . . Is. 29:15
understandeth
and *k* . . . . Jer. 9:24
Who *k* if he will
return . . . . Joel 2:14
he *k* them that
trust . . . . Nah. 1:7
the unjust *k* no
shame . . . . Zeph. 3:5
your heavenly
Father *k* . . . . Matt. 6:32
and no man *k* the
Son . . . . Matt. 11:27
As the Father
k me . . . . John 10:15
walketh in
darkness *k* . . . . . John 12:35
him not, neither *k* . John 14:17
for the servant *k*
not . . . . John 15:15
this seal, The
Lord *k* . . . . 2 Tim. 2:19
The Lord *k* how to
deliver . . . . 2 Pet. 2:9
therefore the
world *k* . . . . 1 John 3:1
written, which no
man *k* . . . . Rev. 2:17

KNOWING

father David not *k* 1 Kin. 2:32
And Jesus *k* their
thoughts . . . . Matt. 9:4
k the judgment of
God . . . . Rom. 1:32
not *k* that the
goodness . . . . Rom. 2:4
k that tribulation . . . Rom. 5:3
K this, that our
old . . . . Rom. 6:6
K that a man is
not . . . . Gal. 2:16
k that ye are
thereunto . . . . 1 Pet. 3:9

KNOWLEDGE

workers of
iniquity no *k* . . . . . Ps. 14:4
the beginning of *k* . . Prov. 1:7
scorning, and
fools hate *k* . . . . . Prov. 1:22
the wise useth *k*
aright. . . . . Prov. 15:2
sight wisdom,
and *k* . . . . Eccl. 2:26
might, the spirit
of *k* . . . . Is. 11:2
shall be full of
the *k* . . . . Is. 11:9
by his *k* shall my
righteous. . . . . Is. 53:11

good they have
  no *k* . . . . Jer. 4:22
unto the wise,
  and *k* . . . . Dan. 2:21
run to and fro,
  and *k* . . . . Dan. 12:4
and the *k* of God
  more . . . . Hos. 6:6
be filled with
  the *k* . . . . Hab. 2:14
lips should keep *k* . . . Mal. 2:7
wisdom and *k* of
  God . . . . Rom. 11:33
mysteries, and
  all *k* . . . . 1 Cor. 13:2
increasing in the *k* . . Col. 1:10
which is renewed
  in *k* . . . . Col. 3:10
unto the *k* of the
  truth . . . . 1 Tim. 2:4
have received
  the *k* . . . . Heb. 10:26

KOHATH
Son of Levi, Gen. 46:11;
  Ex. 6:16
Grandfather of Moses, Aaron,
  and Miriam, Num. 26:58, 59
Father of the Kohathites, one
  of the divisions (shifts) of the
  Levites, Ex. 6:18; Num. 3:19,
  27

KORAH
Also spelled Core and Kore; A
  son of Esau, Gen. 36:5,
  14, 18
———— A Korhite Levite,
  Ex. 6:18, 21, 24
Jealous of Moses, leads two-
  hundred and fifty princes
  in an insurrection, and
  is swallowed up in the
  earth, Num. 16; 26:9, 10;
  Deut. 11:6; Ps. 106:17;
  Jude 11
———— Son of Hebron,
  1 Chr. 2:43
———— Son of Kohath, and
  head of the family of sacred
  musicians among the Levites,
  1 Chr. 6:22
See titles to, Ps. 42; 45; 46; 47;
  48; 87; 88

LABAN
Son of Bethuel, Gen. 28:5
Brother of Rebekah,
  Gen. 22:23; 24:15, 29
Receives the servant of
  Abraham, Gen. 24:29–33
Receives Jacob, and gives him
  his daughters in marriage,
  Gen. 29:12–30
Jacob becomes his servant,
  Gen. 29:15–20, 27; 30:27–43
Outwitted by Jacob,
  Gen. 30:37–43; 31:1–21
Pursues Jacob, overtakes
  him at Mount Gilead,
  and covenants with him,
  Gen. 31:22–55

LABOUR
affliction and the *l* . Gen. 31:42
days shalt thou *l* . . . . . Ex. 20:9
house, and from
  his *l* . . . . Neh. 5:13
will weep
  bitterly, *l* . . . . Is. 22:4
saith the LORD,
  The *l* . . . . Is. 45:14
ye that *l* and are
  heavy . . . . Matt. 11:28
according to his
  own *l* . . . . 1 Cor. 3:8
work of faith, and
  l . . . . 1 Thess. 1:3
l in the word and
  doctrine . . . . 1 Tim. 5:17
forget your work
  and *l* . . . . Heb. 6:10

LACHISH
An important city; King of,
  besieges Gibeon, Josh. 10:5
Captured by Joshua,
  Josh. 10:31, 32
Allotted to Judah, Josh. 15:39
Fortified by Rehoboam,
  2 Chr. 11:9
Assassination of Amaziah at,
  2 Kin. 14:19
Besieged by Sennacherib,
  2 Kin. 18:13–17; 19:8;
  2 Chr. 32:9
By Nebuchadnezzar, Jer. 34:7
Prophecy concerning,
  Mic. 1:13

LAID
Dibon, and we
  have *l* . . . . Num. 21:30
of the LORD was *l* . . Ezra 3:11
l Jerusalem on
  heaps . . . . Ps. 79:1
hast thou *l* the
  foundation . . . . . . Ps. 102:25
for it is *l* waste . . . . Is. 23:1
foundation shall
  be *l* . . . . Is. 44:28
the heavens, and *l* . . . Is. 51:13
and the LORD
  hath *l* . . . . Is. 53:6
thy cities shall be *l* . . . . Jer. 4:7
Behold, it is *l* over . . Hab. 2:19
l the pleasant land . Zech. 7:14
I hated Esau, and *l* . . . Mal. 1:3
the temple, and
  ye *l* . . . . Matt. 26:55
And *l* it in his
  own . . . . Matt. 27:60
but no man *l*
  hands . . . . John 7:30
had prayed, they *l* . . . Acts 6:6
and the
  witnesses *l* . . . . Acts 7:58
l to his charge
  worthy . . . . Acts 23:29
Henceforth there
  is *l* . . . . 2 Tim. 4:8
he *l* his right hand . . Rev. 1:17

LAKE
cast alive into a *l* . . Rev. 19:20

the *l* of fire and
  brimstone . . . . Rev. 20:10
were cast into
  the *l* . . . . Rev. 20:14
their part in the *l* . . . Rev. 21:8

LAMB
one *l* thou shalt
  offer . . . . Ex. 29:39
l a tenth deal of
  flour . . . . Ex. 29:40
l thou shalt offer . . . Ex. 29:41
able to bring a *l* . . . . Lev. 12:8
blemish, and one
  ewe *l* . . . . Lev. 14:10
hin for the one *l* . . . Num. 28:7
of an hin unto a *l* Num. 28:14
he is brought
  as a *l* . . . . Is. 53:7
that sacrificeth a *l* . . . Is. 66:3
saith, Behold
  the L . . . . John 1:29
of Christ, as of a *l* . . 1 Pet. 1:19
the elders,
  stood a L . . . . Rev. 5:6
down before the L . . . Rev. 5:8
voice, Worthy is
  the L . . . . Rev. 5:12
the wrath of the L . . Rev. 6:16
L which is in the
  midst . . . . Rev. 7:17
book of life of
  the L . . . . Rev. 13:8
presence of the L . . Rev. 14:10
the song of the L . . . Rev. 15:3
make war with
  the L . . . . Rev. 17:14

LAMBS
two he *l* without
  blemish . . . . Lev. 14:10
l of the first year . . . Num. 28:3
and one ram,
  seven *l* . . . . Num. 28:11
bullocks, or of *l* . . . . . . Is. 1:11
blood of *l* and
  goats . . . . Is. 34:6
shall gather the *l* . . . Is. 40:11
couches, and eat
  the *l* . . . . Amos 6:4
unto him, Feed
  my *l* . . . . John 21:15

LAMECH
Father of Jabal, Jubal, and
  Tubal-Cain, Gen. 4:18–24
———— Son of Methuselah,
  and father of Noah, lived for
  seven-hundred and seventy-
  seven years, Gen. 5:25–31;
  1 Chr. 1:3
Ancestor of Jesus, Luke 3:36

LAMENT
gates shall *l* and
  mourn . . . . Is. 3:26
They shall not *l*
  for . . . . Jer. 22:18
and *l*, ye priests . . . . Joel 1:13
shall bewail her,
  and *l* . . . . Rev. 18:9

LAMENTATION
son, most bitter *l* . . . Jer. 6:26

the wilderness a *l*. . . . Jer. 9:10
Moreover take
  thou up a *l* . . . . . . Ezek. 19:1
take up a *l* for
  thee . . . . Ezek. 26:17
a *l* for Pharaoh
  king . . . . Ezek. 32:2
your songs into *l* . . Amos 8:10

LAMPS
shalt make the
  seven *l*. . . . . Ex. 25:37
l, he shall burn
  incense . . . . Ex. 30:7
Aaron lighteth
  the *l*. . . . . Ex. 30:8
gold with the *l*
  thereof. . . . . 2 Chr. 13:11
and his seven *l*
  thereon . . . . Zech. 4:2
seven *l* of fire
  burning . . . . Rev. 4:5

LAND
will I give this *l* . . . Gen. 12:7
have I given this *l*. . Gen. 15:18
seed after thee,
  the *l*. . . . . Gen. 17:8
Sojourn in this *l*. . . . Gen. 26:3
l whereon thou
  liest . . . . Gen. 28:13
Onan died in the *l* . Gen. 46:12
l unto a good *l* and. . . . Ex. 3:8
l of Egypt this
  night . . . . Ex. 12:12
made the sea dry *l* . . Ex. 14:21
brought thee out
  of the *l*. . . . . Ex. 20:2
l which the LORD
  thy . . . . Ex. 20:12
The fruit of thy *l*. . Deut. 28:33
the fruit of thy *l* . . Deut. 28:51
l thereof is
  brimstone . . . . . . Deut. 29:23
And the *l* was
  subdued . . . . Josh. 18:1
Beersheba, with
  the *l*. . . . . Judg. 20:1
thee up out of
  the *l*. . . . . 1 Kin. 12:28
cut off out of the *l* . . . . Is. 53:8
them against
  this *l* . . . . Jer. 25:9
them upon their *l*. . Amos 9:15

LANDS
their hearts in
  the *l*. . . . . Lev. 26:36
in your enemies' *l* . Lev. 26:39
nations of other *l* . 2 Chr. 13:9
people of those *l*. . . . Ezra 9:2
other men have
  our *l*. . . . . Neh. 5:5
I given all these *l* . . . Jer. 27:6
the glory of all *l* . . Ezek. 20:6
the glory of all *l* . . Ezek. 20:15

LAODICEA
A Phrygian city; Paul's concern
  for, Col. 2:1
Epaphras' zeal for, Col. 4:13
Epistle to the Colossians to be
  read in, Col. 4:15, 16

Message to, through John,
  Rev. 1:11; 3:14–22

LAUGH
the heavens shall *l* . . . . Ps. 2:4
see me *l* me to
  scorn . . . . Ps. 22:7
and fear, and
  shall *l*. . . . . Ps. 52:6
I also will *l* at
  your . . . . Prov. 1:26

LAW
in *l*, his son
  Abram's . . . . Gen. 11:31
Jethro his father
  in *l* . . . . Ex. 3:1
the words of this *l* Deut. 28:58
the book of this *l* . Deut. 28:61
hand went a
  fiery *l* . . . . Deut. 33:2
l, which Moses
  my servant . . . . Josh. 1:7
Moses' father in *l*. . Judg. 1:16
thee, and cast
  thy *l*. . . . . Neh. 9:26
them again unto
  thy *l* . . . . Neh. 9:29
the *l*, and the word . . . . Is. 2:3
LORD, I will put
  my *l*. . . . . Jer. 31:33
violated my *l*. . . . . Ezek. 22:26
transgressed thy *l*. . . Dan. 9:11
trespassed against
  my *l*. . . . . Hos. 8:1
seek the *l* at his
  mouth . . . . Mal. 2:7
perfect manner of
  the *l* . . . . Acts 22:3
For the *l* of the
  Spirit . . . . Rom. 8:2
the works of the *l*. . . Gal. 2:16
l, being made a
  curse . . . . Gal. 3:13
woman, made
  under the *l* . . . . Gal. 4:4

LAY
that I may *l* my
  hand . . . . Ex. 7:4
neither shalt
  thou *l*. . . . . Ex. 22:25
children of the
  east *l* . . . . Judg. 7:12
flesh, and fasted,
  and *l* . . . . 1 Kin. 21:27
life to them that *l*. . Prov. 3:18
And I will *l* it
  waste. . . . . Is. 5:6
l their hand upon
  Edom. . . . . Is. 11:14
Lord GOD,
  Behold, I *l*. . . . . Is. 28:16
dragons, where
  each *l*. . . . . Is. 35:7
the heavens, and *l* . . Is. 51:16
And *l* siege
  against. . . . . Ezek. 4:2
And I will *l* my
  vengeance . . . . . . Ezek. 25:14
their thrones,
  and *l* . . . . Ezek. 26:16

pray thee, come
  and *l* . . . . Mark 5:23
l hands on the
  sick . . . . Mark 16:18
And shall *l* thee
  even. . . . . Luke 19:44
and I *l* down my
  life . . . . John 10:15
loud voice, Lord, *l* . . Acts 7:60
written,
  Behold, I *l* . . . . . . Rom. 9:33
you *l* by him in
  store . . . . 1 Cor. 16:2

LAZARUS
Brother of Mary and Martha;
  Sickness and death of,
  John 11:1–14
Resurrection of,
  John 11:38–44; 12:17, 18
Had dinner with Jesus,
  John 12:1, 2, 9
Plotted against by the chief
  priests, John 12:10, 11

LEAD
pillar of a cloud,
  to *l*. . . . . Ex. 13:21
now go, *l* the
  people . . . . Ex. 32:34
them, and which
  may *l*. . . . . Num. 27:17
whither the LORD
  shall *l*. . . . . Deut. 4:27
the LORD shall *l*
  thee . . . . Deut. 28:37
the king of
  Assyria *l* . . . . Is. 20:4
and shall gently *l* . . . Is. 40:11
mercy on them
  shall *l*. . . . . Is. 49:10
supplications
  will I *l* . . . . Jer. 31:9
l Zedekiah to
  Babylon . . . . Jer. 32:5
Have we not
  power to *l*. . . . . . . 1 Cor. 9:5
feed them, and
  shall *l*. . . . . Rev. 7:17

LEAF
sound of a
  shaken *l*. . . . . Lev. 26:36
l also shall not
  wither . . . . Ps. 1:3
fall down, as the *l*. . . . Is. 34:4
heat cometh, but
  her *l*. . . . . Jer. 17:8

LEAH
The older daughter of Laban,
  Gen. 29:16
Married to Jacob,
  Gen. 29:23–26
Children of, Gen. 29:31–35;
  30:9–13, 17–21
Flees with Jacob, Gen. 31:4,
  14, 17; 33:2–7
"The builder of the house of
  Israel," Ruth 4:11

LEARN
L to do well. . . . . Is. 1:17
shall they *l* war any . . . . Is. 2:4

the world will *l*
righteousness . . . . Is. 26:9
But go ye and *l*
what . . . . Matt. 9:13
yoke upon you,
and *l* . . . . Matt. 11:29
would I *l* of you,
Received . . . . Gal. 3:2

LEAVEN
ye shall put away *l* . . Ex. 12:15
l found in your
houses . . . . Ex. 12:19
not be baken
with *l* . . . . Lev. 6:17
heed, beware of
the *l* . . . . Mark 8:15

LEAVENED
whosoever
eateth *l* . . . . Ex. 12:15
eateth that which
is *l* . . . . Ex. 12:19
shall eat nothing *l* . . Ex. 12:20
no *l* bread be
eaten . . . . Ex. 13:3
Thou shalt eat
no *l* . . . . Deut. 16:3
l bread seen with
thee . . . . : Deut. 16:4

LEBANON
A mountain range; Northern
boundary of the land of
Canaan, Deut. 1:7; 3:25;
11:24; Josh. 1:4; 9:1
Early inhabitants of, Judg. 3:3
Snow of, Jer. 18:14
Streams of, Song 4:15
Cedars of, Judg. 9:15;
2 Kin. 19:23; 2 Chr. 2:8;
Ps. 29:5; 104:16; Is. 2:13;
14:8; Ezek. 27:5
Other trees of, 2 Kin. 19:23;
2 Chr. 2:8
Flower of, Nah. 1:4
Beasts of, Is. 40:16
Fertility and productiveness
of, Hos. 14:5–7
"House of the forest of,"
1 Kin. 7:2–5
Valley of, Josh. 11:17; 12:7
Tower of, Song 7:4
Solomon had storage cities
in, 1 Kin. 9:19
Figurative, Is. 29:17; Jer. 22:6

LED
and he *l* the flock . . . . . Ex. 3:1
in thy mercy
hast *l* . . . . Ex. 15:13
LORD thy God *l*
thee . . . . Deut. 8:2
Who *l* thee
through . . . . Deut. 8:15
l him about, he
instructed . . . . . . Deut. 32:10
with joy, and be *l* . . . . Is. 55:12
That *l* them by the . . . Is. 63:12
thy God, when
he *l* . . . . Jer. 2:17
l the seed of the
house . . . . Jer. 23:8

had bound him,
they *l* . . . . Matt. 27:2
sword, and shall
be *l* . . . . Luke 21:24
And he *l* them out
as . . . . Luke 24:50

LEND
If thou *l* money to . . Ex. 22:25
Thou shalt not *l*
upon . . . . Deut. 23:19
and thou shalt *l*
unto . . . . Deut. 28:12
l to thee, and thou Deut. 28:44

LENGTH
cubits was the *l*
thereof . . . . Deut. 3:11
l of days, and long . . . Prov. 3:2
L of days is in her . . Prov. 3:16
the *l* thereof was
fifty . . . . Ezek. 40:21

LEVI
Son of Jacob, Gen. 29:34;
35:23; 1 Chr. 2:1
Avenges the seduction of
Dinah, Gen. 34; 49:5–7
Jacob's prophecy regarding,
Gen. 49:5–7
His age at death, Ex. 6:16

LIBERTY
year, and
proclaim *l* . . . . Lev. 25:10
brokenhearted, to
proclaim *l* . . . . Is. 61:1
blind, to set at *l* . . . Luke 4:18
been called unto *l* . . . Gal. 5:13
the perfect law
of *l* . . . . James 1:25

LIBNAH
A station of the Israelites in
the desert, Num. 33:20
———— A city of the tribe of
Judah, captured by Joshua,
Josh. 10:29–32, 39; 12:15
Allotted to the priests,
Josh. 21:13; 1 Chr. 6:57
Sennacherib besieged;
his army defeated near,
2 Kin. 19:8, 35; Is. 37:8–36

LIE
land, and ye
shall *l* . . . . Lev. 26:6
man, that he
should *l* . . . . Num. 23:19
another man
shall *l* . . . . Deut. 28:30
and I *l* even
among . . . . Ps. 57:4
lo, they *l* in wait . . . . . Ps. 59:3
the desert shall *l* . . . . Is. 13:21
a *l* in my right
hand . . . . Is. 44:20
We *l* down in our
shame . . . . Jer. 3:25
For they
prophesy a *l* . . . . . . Jer. 27:10
they *l* in a good
fold . . . . Ezek. 34:14
l all night in
sackcloth . . . . Joel 1:13

all *l* in wait for
blood . . . . Mic. 7:2
shall speak, and
not *l* . . . . Hab. 2:3
place for beasts
to *l* . . . . Zeph. 2:15
l, and have told
false . . . . Zech. 10:2
speaketh a *l*, he
speaketh . . . . John 8:44
God, that cannot *l* . . Titus 1:2
truth, and is no *l* . 1 John 2:27
abomination, or
maketh a *l* . . . . . . Rev. 21:27
loveth and
maketh a *l* . . . . . . Rev. 22:15

LIES
he that speaketh *l* . . Prov. 19:5
prophet that
teacheth *l* . . . . Is. 9:15
have made *l* our
refuge . . . . Is. 28:15
like their bow for *l* . . . . Jer. 9:3
tongue to speak *l* . . . . Jer. 9:5
prophets
prophesy *l* . . . . Jer. 14:14
fathers have
inherited *l* . . . . Jer. 16:19
adultery, and walk
in *l* . . . . Jer. 23:14
to err by their *l* . . . . . Jer. 23:32
and that divine *l* . . . Ezek. 13:9
vanity, and
divining *l* . . . . . . Ezek. 22:28
daily increaseth *l* . . . Hos. 12:1
and a teacher of *l* . . . Hab. 2:18
for thou speakest *l* . Zech. 13:3

LIETH
And the man
that *l* . . . . Lev. 20:11
Cursed be he
that *l* . . . . Deut. 27:20
the mountain
that *l* . . . . Josh. 15:8
wilderness of
Judah, which *l* . . . Judg. 1:16
great dragon that *l* . Ezek. 29:3
daughter *l* at the
point . . . . Mark 5:23
the region that *l*
round . . . . Acts 14:6
as *l* in you, live
peaceably . . . . . . Rom. 12:18

LIFE
nostrils the breath
of *l* . . . . Gen. 2:7
time of *l*, and
Sarah . . . . Gen. 18:14
the days of thy *l* . . . . Josh. 1:5
that seek their *l* . . . . Jer. 21:7
minister, and to
give his *l* . . . . . . Matt. 20:28
In him was *l* . . . . . . John 1:4
have everlasting *l* . . John 3:16
hath everlasting *l* . . John 3:36
into everlasting *l* . . . John 4:14
the truth, and
the *l* . . . . John 14:6
repentance unto *l* . . Acts 11:18
of God is eternal *l* . Rom. 6:23

the spirit giveth *l* . . .2 Cor. 3:6
receive the crown
of *l* . . . . .James 1:12
handled, of the
Word of *l* . . . . 1 John 1:1
(For the *l* was
manifested . . . . . . 1 John 1:2
God, and eternal *l* . 1 John 5:20
eat of the tree of *l* . . . Rev. 2:7
book of *l*, but I
will . . . . Rev. 3:5
written in the
book of *l* . . . . Rev. 13:8

LIFT
I have *l* up mine
hand . . . . .Gen. 14:22
The LORD *l* up his
countenance . . . . .Num. 6:26
thou *l* up thine
eyes . . . . Deut. 4:19
wherefore *l* up thy. 2 Kin. 19:4
words of God, to *l* . 1 Chr. 25:5
ashamed and
blush to *l*. . . . . . . .Ezra 9:6
LORD, *l* thou up
the . . . . Ps. 4:6
thine anger, *l* up
thyself . . . . Ps. 7:6
feed them also,
and *l* . . . . Ps. 28:9
floods *l* up their
waves. . . . . Ps. 93:3
nation shall not *l* . . . . . .Is. 2:4
he will *l* up an
ensign . . . . .Is. 5:26
wherefore *l* up thy . . . .Is. 37:4
L up thine eyes
round. . . . . .Is. 49:18
L up your eyes to
the . . . . .Is. 51:6
aloud, spare not, *l* . . . .Is. 58:1
l up a standard for . . .Is. 62:10
L up thine eyes
unto. . . . . Jer. 3:2
the slaughter, to *l*. Ezek. 21:22
nation shall not *l* . . . . Mic. 4:3

LIFTED
And Lot *l* up his
eyes . . . . .Gen. 13:10
drew and *l* up
Joseph . . . . .Gen. 37:28
Moses *l* up his
hand . . . . .Num. 20:11
they *l* up their
voice . . . . 2 Chr. 5:13
strong, his heart
was *l* . . . . 2 Chr. 26:16
for his heart was *l* 2 Chr. 32:25
of my bread,
hath *l*. . . . . Ps. 41:9
as he had *l* up
axes . . . . Ps. 74:5
every one that is *l* . . . .Is. 2:12
throne, high and *l* . . . . .Is. 6:1
So the spirit *l* me . . Ezek. 3:14
and the spirit *l* me . . Ezek. 8:3
mountains,
neither hath *l* . . . . Ezek. 18:6
day that I *l* up
mine . . . . Ezek. 20:6

also I *l* up my
hand . . . . Ezek. 20:15
Because thine
heart is *l* . . . . Ezek. 28:2
Nebuchadnezzar *l* . .Dan. 4:34
But hast *l* up
thyself . . . . .Dan. 5:23
be *l* up, and
inhabited. . . . . . . Zech. 14:10
bread with me
hath *l*. . . . . .John 13:18

LIGHT
shall *l* the lamps
thereof. . . . . Ex. 25:37
servant may have
a *l*. . . . . 1 Kin. 11:36
it had been a *l*
thing . . . . 1 Kin. 16:31
The LORD is my *l*
and. . . . . Ps. 27:1
thine arm, and
the *l*. . . . . Ps. 44:3
and sorrow, and
the *l*. . . . . .Is. 5:30
shall not give
their *l*. . . . . .Is. 13:10
l thing that thou
shouldest . . . . .Is. 49:6
no more thy *l* by
day. . . . . .Is. 60:19
ye look for *l*, he
turn . . . . .Jer. 13:16
not give her *l* . . . . Matt. 24:29
life was the *l* of
men . . . . .John 1:4
I am the *l* of the
world. . . . . .John 8:12
from darkness to *l* . Acts 26:18
bring to *l* the
hidden . . . . .1 Cor. 4:5
l of the glorious
gospel . . . . .2 Cor. 4:4
darkness, but now
are ye *l*. . . . . Eph. 5:8
immortality,
dwelling in the *l*. 1 Tim. 6:16
into his
marvellous *l* . . . . . 1 Pet. 2:9
if we walk in the *l* . 1 John 1:7

LIGHTNINGS
l, and a thick
cloud . . . . Ex. 19:16
shot out *l*, and
discomfited. . . . . . . Ps. 18:14
throne
proceeded *l* . . . . . . Rev. 4:5
thunderings, and *l* . . . Rev. 8:5
there were *l*, and
voices . . . . Rev. 11:19

LIKENESS
image, after our *l* . . .Gen. 1:26
graven image, or
any *l*. . . . . Ex. 20:4
appearance of
the *l*. . . . . Ezek. 1:28
Son in the *l* of
sinful . . . . Rom. 8:3

LIKEWISE
even so will I do *l*. Deut. 12:30

and *l* all the men
that . . . . .2 Sam. 1:11
God shall *l*
destroy . . . . Ps. 52:5
about, and *l*. . . . . .Ezek. 40:16
L also the cup
after . . . . Luke 22:20
blood, he also
himself *l* . . . . .Heb. 2:14
L, ye husbands,
dwell . . . . 1 Pet. 3:7
L, ye younger,
submit. . . . . 1 Pet. 5:5
it, and the night *l* . . . Rev. 8:12

LINE
measured them
with a *l* . . . . 2 Sam. 8:2
over Jerusalem
the *l* . . . . 2 Kin. 21:13
l, and made the
tribes . . . . Ps. 78:55
l of flax in his
hand . . . . Ezek. 40:3

LINEN
fine *l*, and put a
gold . . . . .Gen. 41:42
a garment of fine *l* . Esth. 8:15
the man clothed
in *l* . . . . .Dan. 12:7
Jesus, and wound
it in *l* . . . . .John 19:40
fine *l*, clean and
white . . . . Rev. 19:8

LION
servant slew both
the *l* . . . . 1 Sam. 17:36
No *l* shall be there . . . .Is. 35:9
the *l* shall eat
straw . . . . .Is. 65:25
like a destroying *l*. . . . Jer. 2:30
The *l* is come up
from. . . . . Jer. 4:7
Wherefore a *l*
out of. . . . . Jer. 5:6
like a *l* from the
swelling. . . . . Jer. 49:19
art like a young *l* . . Ezek. 32:2
many people as a *l* . . . Mic. 5:8
mouth of the *l* . . . 2 Tim. 4:17
devil, as a
roaring *l* . . . . 1 Pet. 5:8
L of the tribe of
Juda . . . . Rev. 5:5

LIONS
The young *l* do
lack . . . . Ps. 34:10
My soul is
among *l*. . . . . Ps. 57:4
the *l* have driven
him . . . . Jer. 50:17
devour thy
young *l* . . . . .Nah. 2:13

LIPS
Job sin with his *l* . . . . Job 2:10
with flattering *l*
and. . . . . Ps. 12:2
unclean *l*, and I
dwell . . . . .Is. 6:5
the breath of his *l*. . . . .Is. 11:4

mouth, and with
their *l*. . . . . .Is. 29:13
and cover not
thy *l*. . . . . .Ezek. 24:17
of men touched
my *l*. . . . . .Dan. 10:16
l quivered at the
voice . . . . .Hab. 3:16
For the priest's *l*. . . . . Mal. 2:7
fruit of our *l*
giving . . . . .Heb. 13:15

LIVE
man do, he shall *l*. . . Lev. 18:5
man doth not *l* by
bread . . . . Deut. 8:3
man do, he shall *l*. . .Neh. 9:29
deceitful men
shall not *l* . . . . Ps. 55:23
Thy dead men
shall *l*. . . . . .Is. 26:19
your soul shall *l* . . . . . .Is. 55:3
besiege you, he
shall *l*. . . . . Jer. 21:9
As I *l*, saith the
LORD. . . . . .Jer. 22:24
Chaldeans shall *l* . . . .Jer. 38:2
then thy soul
shall *l*. . . . . .Jer. 38:17
as I *l*, saith the
Lord. . . . . Ezek. 5:11
he shall even *l*. . . . Ezek. 20:13
he shall even *l*. . . . Ezek. 20:21
Syriack, O king, *l* . . . .Dan. 2:4
as I *l*, saith the
LORD. . . . . .Zeph. 2:9
and she shall *l* . . . . Mark 5:23
nevertheless I *l*. . . . . Gal. 2:20
dead to sins,
should *l*. . . . . 1 Pet. 2:24
after should *l*
ungodly. . . . . 2 Pet. 2:6
world, that we
might *l*. . . . . 1 John 4:9

LIVETH
lord, as the
LORD *l* . . . . 1 Sam. 25:26
LORD God of
Israel *l*. . . . . 1 Kin. 17:1
swear, The LORD *l*. . . . Jer. 4:2
The LORD *l*,
which brought . . . . . Jer. 23:8
honoured him
that *l* . . . . .Dan. 4:34
sware by him
that *l* . . . . .Dan. 12:7
swear, The LORD *l*. .Hos. 4:15
l by the power of
God . . . . .2 Cor. 13:4
not I, but Christ *l*. . . Gal. 2:20
he ever *l* to make
intercession . . . . . .Heb. 7:25
I am he that *l*, and . . Rev. 1:18
worshipped him
that *l* . . . . Rev. 5:14

LIVING
man became a *l*
soul . . . . .Gen. 2:7
every thing *l*, as I . . .Gen. 8:21
armies of the *l*
God . . . . .1 Sam. 17:26

armies of the *l*
God . . . . 1 Sam. 17:36
the land of the *l* . . . . . Ps. 52:5
sight shall no
man *l* . . . . Ps. 143:2
for the *l* to the
dead. . . . . .Is. 8:19
the land of the *l* . . . . . .Is. 53:8
the fountain of *l*
waters . . . . Jer. 2:13
true God, he is
the *l* . . . . .Jer. 10:10
Christ, the Son of
the *l* . . . . Matt. 16:16
adjure thee by
the *l* . . . . Matt. 26:63
have given thee *l*
water . . . . .John 4:10
present your
bodies a *l*. . . . . . . Rom. 12:1
temple of the *l*
God . . . . .2 Cor. 6:16
church of the *l*
God . . . . .1 Tim. 3:15
in the *l* God, who
giveth . . . . 1 Tim. 6:17
works to serve
the *l*. . . . . .Heb. 9:14
the city of the *l*
God . . . . .Heb. 12:22
lead them unto *l*
fountains. . . . . Rev. 7:17

LO
and, *l*, Sarah thy
wife . . . . .Gen. 18:10
unto Moses, L, I
come . . . . Ex. 19:9
l, I have given
thee . . . . 1 Kin. 3:12
l, we bring into
bondage . . . . .Neh. 5:5
passed away,
and, *l* . . . . Ps. 37:36
L, this is the man . . . . Ps. 52:7
said in that day, L. . . . .Is. 25:9
L, thou trustest in . . . .Is. 36:6
For, *l*, I will call. . . . . .Jer. 1:15
l, I begin to bring . . . Jer. 25:29
l, the days come,
saith . . . . .Jer. 30:3
l, I will save thee . . . Jer. 30:10
For, *l*, I will
command . . . . Amos 9:9
l, I come, and I
will . . . . Zech. 2:10
and, *l*, the
heavens. . . . . Matt. 3:16
l a voice from
heaven. . . . . Matt. 3:17
l, I am with you
alway. . . . . Matt. 28:20
everlasting life, *l*. . . Acts 13:46
And I beheld,
and, *l*. . . . . Rev. 5:6
sixth seal, and, *l*. . . . Rev. 6:12

LOCUST
the *l* after his kind . Lev. 11:22
for the *l* shall
consume . . . . Deut. 28:38

thy land shall
the *l*. . . . . .Deut. 28:42
l hath eaten, the
cankerworm . . . . . . Joel 2:25

LOINS
come out of thy *l* . .Gen. 35:11
sackcloth upon
his *l*. . . . . .Gen. 37:34
l girded, your
shoes . . . . Ex. 12:11
l, and ran before
Ahab . . . . 1 Kin. 18:46
sackcloth from off
thy *l*. . . . . .Is. 20:2
my *l* filled with
pain . . . . .Is. 21:3
I will loose the *l* . . . . . .Is. 45:1
therefore gird up
thy *l* . . . . Jer. 1:17
cuttings, and
upon the *l* . . . . Jer. 48:37
madest all their *l* . . Ezek. 29:7
sackcloth upon
all *l*. . . . . .Amos 8:10
much pain is in
all *l*. . . . . .Nah. 2:10
Let your *l* be
girded . . . . Luke 12:35
l girt about with
truth . . . . .Eph. 6:14
Wherefore gird up
the *l*. . . . . .1 Pet. 1:13

LONG
that thy days may
be *l*. . . . . .Ex. 20:12
the cloud tarried *l* . Num. 9:19
all the day *l* . . . . . .Deut. 28:32
great plagues, and
of *l*. . . . . .Deut. 28:59
How *l* wilt thou
mourn . . . . .1 Sam. 16:1
that had a *l* time
mourned . . . . . . .2 Sam. 14:2
said, How *l*
halt ye . . . . 1 Kin. 18:21
and as *l* as he
sought . . . . 2 Chr. 26:5
shall be continued
as *l*. . . . . Ps. 72:17
that knoweth
how *l*. . . . . Ps. 74:9
How *l*, ye simple
ones. . . . . Prov. 1:22
length of days,
and *l* . . . . .Prov. 3:2
said I, Lord, how *l* . . . .Is. 6:11
l will it be ere
thou. . . . . Jer. 47:6
children of a
span *l*. . . . . Lam. 2:20
him, though he
bear *l*. . . . . .Luke 18:7
Have I been so *l*
time. . . . . .John 14:9
tarry *l*, that thou . 1 Tim. 3:15
now of a *l* time
lingereth . . . . 2 Pet. 2:3
How *l*, O Lord,
holy . . . . Rev. 6:10

LONGER

ye shall stay no *l*..... Ex. 9:28
could not any *l*
  stand .... Judg. 2:14
to sin, live any *l* .... Rom. 6:2
when I could no *l*
  forbear.........1 Thess. 3:5

LONGSUFFERING

merciful and
  gracious, *l* .... Ex. 34:6
LORD is *l*, and of
  great .... Num. 14:18
compassion, and
  gracious, *l* .... Ps. 86:15
forbearance and *l* ... Rom. 2:4
love, joy, peace, *l* ... Gal. 5:22
but is *l* to us-ward .. 2 Pet. 3:9

LOOKED

Surely the LORD
  hath *l*.......... Gen. 29:32
eyes and *l*, and,
  behold.......... Gen. 37:25
Israel, and that he
  had *l* .... Ex. 4:31
I have *l* upon my
  people .... 1 Sam. 9:16
l that it should
  bring .... Is. 5:2
wherefore, when I *l* .... Is. 5:4
and he *l* for
  judgment .... Is. 5:7
And I *l*, and there..... Is. 63:5
is the day that
  we *l* .... Lam. 2:16
passed by thee,
  and *l* .... Ezek. 16:8
l on the day of thy .. Obad. 12
And I said, I
  have *l*.......... Zech. 4:2
And when he had
  l round .... Mark 3:5
eyes, which we
  have *l*.......... 1 John 1:1
I *l*, and, lo, a
  Lamb........... Rev. 14:1

LOOKETH

for man *l* on the
  outward........ 1 Sam. 16:7
the inner gate
  that *l* .... Ezek. 8:3
unto the gate
  which *l* .... Ezek. 40:6
whosoever *l* on a
  woman .... Matt. 5:28
whoso *l* into the
  perfect......... James 1:25

LORD

L appeared unto
  Abram........... Gen. 12:7
day the *L* made a
  covenant .... Gen. 15:18
like unto
  thee, O *L*........ Ex. 15:11
for I the *L* thy God ... Ex. 20:5
L your God shall
  choose......... Deut. 12:5
The *L* shall cause
  thee .... Deut. 28:25

L shall bring a
  nation .... Deut. 28:49
L shall scatter
  thee .... Deut. 28:64
wrath of the *L*
  arose .... 2 Chr. 36:16
The *L* is my rock,
  and............. Ps. 18:2
L himself shall
  give .... Is. 7:14
zeal of the *L* of
  hosts .... Is. 9:7
saith the *L* the
  King............ Is. 44:6
and the *L* hath
  laid............. Is. 53:6
Spirit of the *L*
  GOD............ Is. 61:1
saith the *L*, that I .... Jer. 23:5
called, THE *L*
  OUR
  RIGHTEOUSNESS . Jer. 23:6
north, saith the *L*.... Jer. 25:9
fellow, saith the *L*.. Zech. 13:7
the *L* God shall
  give .... Luke 1:32

LORDS

the *l* of the high
  places .... Num. 21:28
l, a great God, a
  mighty......... Deut. 10:17
five *l* of the
  Philistines....... Josh. 13:3
the king and his *l* ...Dan. 5:10
thou, and thy *l*,
  thy............ Dan. 5:23
kings, and Lord
  of *l* .... 1 Tim. 6:15
is Lord of *l*, and
  King.......... Rev. 17:14
KINGS, AND
  LORD OF *L*...... Rev. 19:16

LOST

any manner of *l*
  thing .... Ex. 22:9
sought that which
  was *l* .... Ezek. 34:4
salt have *l* his
  saltness .... Mark 9:50
l, but the son of
  perdition ...... John 17:12

LOTS

cast *l* for my
  people .... Joel 3:3
his gates, and
  cast *l* .... Obad. 11
cast *l* for her
  honourable ......Nah. 3:10
raiment, and cast *l*. Luke 23:34

LOUD

trumpet
  exceeding *l* ...... Ex. 19:16
country wept with
  a *l*........... 2 Sam. 15:23
skilfully with a *l* ..... Ps. 33:3
mine ears with a *l* . Ezek. 8:18
cried with a *l*
  voice .... Ezek. 11:13

cried with a *l*
  voice .... Mark 5:7
cried with a *l*
  voice .... Luke 23:46
a *l* voice, Lord, lay .. Acts 7:60
with a *l* voice,
  Worthy .... Rev. 5:12
cried with a *l*
  voice .... Rev. 6:10

LOVE

thou shalt *l* thy
  neighbour ...... Lev. 19:18
mercy with them
  that *l* .... Deut. 7:9
his ways, and to *l*. Deut. 10:12
the ungodly, and *l* 2 Chr. 19:2
his *l* and in his
  pity .... Is. 63:9
and my people *l* to ... Jer. 5:31
mouth they shew
  much *l*........ Ezek. 33:31
justly, and to *l*
  mercy .... Mic. 6:8
unto you, That
  ye *l*.......... John 13:34
world, the world
  would *l* .... John 15:19
good to them
  that *l* .... Rom. 8:28
Thou shalt *l* thy
  neighbour ...... Rom. 13:9
Jesus Christ, and
  the *l* .... 2 Cor. 13:14
which worketh
  by *l*............ Gal. 5:6
And walk in *l*, as
  Christ .... Eph. 5:2
faith, and labour
  of *l* .... 1 Thess. 1:3
promised to them
  that *l* .... James 1:12
promised to them
  that *l* .... James 2:5
Spirit unto
  unfeigned *l* ..... 1 Pet. 1:22
is *l*, not that we
  loved .... 1 John 4:10

LOVED

because the
  LORD *l* .... Deut. 7:8
covenant, because
  he *l*........... 1 Sam. 18:3
again, because
  he *l*........... 1 Sam. 20:17
them that thou
  hast *l* .... Ezek. 16:37
according as they *l* .. Hos. 9:10
was a child,
  then I *l*........ Hos. 11:1
For God so *l* the
  world.......... John 3:16
world, and men *l*
  darkness .... John 3:19
the Father,
  having *l* .... John 13:1
as I have *l* you,
  that .... John 13:34
wherewith thou
  hast *l* .... John 17:26

the Son of God,
who *l* . . . . Gal. 2:20
Christ also hath *l* . . . . Eph. 5:2
l this present
world . . . . 2 Tim. 4:10
not that we *l* . . . . . 1 John 4:10
that *l* us, and
washed . . . . Rev. 1:5

LOVERS
l and my friends
stand . . . . Ps. 38:11
All thy *l* have
forgotten . . . . Jer. 30:14
all her *l* she hath . . . Lam. 1:2
will gather all
thy *l* . . . . Ezek. 16:37

LOVETH
righteous LORD *l*
righteousness . . . . . . Ps. 11:7
For the LORD *l*
judgment . . . . Ps. 37:28
but he that *l* him
chasteneth . . . . . Prov. 13:24
A friend *l* at all
times . . . . Prov. 17:17
one *l* gifts, and
followeth. . . . . Is. 1:23
The Father *l* the
Son . . . . John 3:35
them, he it is
that *l* . . . . John 14:21
the Father
himself *l* . . . . John 16:27
God *l* a cheerful
giver . . . . 2 Cor. 9:7
l him that begat *l* . . 1 John 5:1
idolaters, and
whosoever *l* . . . . . Rev. 22:15

LOVINGKINDNESS
will command
his *l* . . . . Ps. 42:8
according to thy *l* . . . Ps. 51:1
LORD which
exercise *l* . . . . Jer. 9:24
Thou shewest *l*
unto. . . . . Jer. 32:18

LOW
shalt come down
very *l* . . . . Deut. 28:43
cities of the *l*
country . . . . . . 2 Chr. 28:18
proud, and bring
him *l* . . . . Job 40:12
shall bring him *l*. . Prov. 29:23
shall be brought *l* . . . . Is. 2:12
men shall be
made *l* . . . . Is. 2:17
exalted the *l* tree . Ezek. 17:24
set thee in the *l*
parts . . . . Ezek. 26:20
condescend to
men of *l*. . . . . . . Rom. 12:16

LUKE
A disciple; A physician,
Col. 4:14
Wrote to Theophilus,
Luke 1:1–4; Acts 1:1, 2
Accompanies Paul in his tour

of Asia and Macedonia,
Acts 16:10–13; 20:5, 6
To Jerusalem, Acts 21:1–18
To Rome, Acts 27; 28;
2 Tim. 4:11; Philem. 24

LUST
their own hearts' *l* . . Ps. 81:12
looketh on a
woman to *l* . . . . . Matt. 5:28
Not in the *l* of
concupiscence . . 1 Thess. 4:5
in the world, the *l* 1 John 2:16

LUSTS
l of your father ye. . . John 8:44
the affections
and *l* . . . . Gal. 5:24
times past in the *l* . . . Eph. 2:3
foolish and
hurtful *l*. . . . . 1 Tim. 6:9
abstain from
fleshly *l* . . . . 1 Pet. 2:11
l, excess of wine . . . . 1 Pet. 4:3

LYDIA
A woman of Thyatira, who
with her household was
converted through the
preaching of Paul,
Acts 16:14, 15
Entertains Paul and Silas,
Acts 16:15, 40
———— Incorrectly put for Lud,
Ezek. 30:5

LYING
folly in Israel in *l* . . . Gen. 34:7
A proud look, a *l*
tongue. . . . . Prov. 6:17
sleeping, *l* down,
loving . . . . Is. 56:10
Trust ye not in *l*
words . . . . Jer. 7:4
wives, and have
spoken *l*. . . . . Jer. 29:23
By swearing, and *l* . . . Hos. 4:2
sick of the palsy, *l*. . . Matt. 9:2
Wherefore
putting away *l* . . . . Eph. 4:25

LYSTRA
One of two cities of Lycaonia,
to which Paul and Barnabas
fled from persecutions in
Iconium, Acts 14:6–23;
2 Tim. 3:11
Congregation of, elders
ordained for, by Paul and
Barnabas, Acts 14:23
Timothy a resident of,
Acts 16:1–4

MAACHAH
Son of Nahor, Gen. 22:24
———— Also called Maacah
Mother of Absalom,
2 Sam. 3:3; 1 Chr. 3:2
———— Also called Maoch
Father of Achish, 1 Sam. 27:2;
1 Kin. 2:39
———— Also called Michaiah
Mother of Abijam and
grandmother of Asa,

1 Kin. 15:2, 10–13;
2 Chr. 11:20–23; 13:2; 15:16
———— Wife of Machir,
1 Chr. 7:15, 16
———— Concubine of Caleb,
1 Chr. 2:48
———— Wife of Jehiel,
1 Chr. 8:29; 9:35
———— Father of Hanan,
1 Chr. 11:43
———— Father of Shephatiah,
1 Chr. 27:16
———— Also called Maacah and
Maachathi
A small kingdom east
of Bashan, Deut. 3:14;
Josh. 12:5; 2 Sam. 10:6, 8;
1 Chr. 19:6, 7

MACEDONIA
A country in southeastern
Europe; Paul has a vision
concerning, Acts 16:9
Preaches in, at Philippi,
Acts 16:12
Revisits, Acts 20:1–6;
2 Cor. 2:13; 7:5
The congregation in, sends
contributions to the
poor saints in Jerusalem,
Rom. 15:26; 2 Cor. 8:1–5
Timothy visits, Acts 19:22
Disciples in, Acts 19:23; 27:2

MACHIR
One of the sons of Manasseh,
Gen. 50:23
Father of the Machirites,
Num. 26:29; 36:1
The land of Gilead allotted to,
Num. 32:39, 40; Deut. 3:15;
Josh. 13:31
Certain cities of Bashan given
to, Josh. 13:31; 17:1
———— A man of Lo-debar
who took care of Jonathan's
lame son, Mephibosheth,
2 Sam. 9:4, 5; 17:27

MADE
image of God *m*
he man . . . . Gen. 9:6
day the LORD *m* a
covenant . . . . Gen. 15:18
and *m* the sea dry
land . . . . Ex. 14:21
had *m* an end of
communing . . . . . Ex. 31:18
sons have *m* an
end. . . . . Num. 4:15
forsook God
which *m*. . . . . . . Deut. 32:15
m two calves of
gold . . . . 1 Kin. 12:28
king of Israel had
m . . . . 2 Kin. 24:13
the LORD, and *m*
Zedekiah . . . . 2 Chr. 36:10
sin of many,
and *m*. . . . . Is. 53:12
m their faces
harder . . . . Jer. 5:3

the Word was *m*
flesh............John 1:14
the Holy Ghost
hath *m*.........Acts 20:28
Jesus, who of God
is *m*.............1 Cor. 1:30
been all *m* to
drink ....1 Cor. 12:13
hath *m* us able
ministers.........2 Cor. 3:6
hath *m* him to be
sin ....2 Cor. 5:21
his Son, *m* of a
woman ....Gal. 4:4
whereof I Paul
am *m*............Col. 1:23
things, by whom
also he *m*.........Heb. 1:2

MAGICIANS
called for all the *m* ..Gen. 41:8
now the *m* of
Egypt.............Ex. 7:11
commanded to
call the *m* ....Dan. 2:2
made master of
the *m* ....Dan. 5:11

MAGNIFY
and dishonour
that *m* ....Ps. 35:26
foot slippeth,
they *m* ....Ps. 38:16
I *m* myself, and
sanctify ....Ezek. 38:23
exalt himself,
and *m*...........Dan. 11:36

MAGOG
Son of Japheth, Gen. 10:2;
1 Chr. 1:5
Prophecy concerning,
Ezek. 38:2; 39:6
Symbolical of the enemies of
God, Rev. 20:8

MAHANAIM
The place where Jacob had the
vision of angels, Gen. 32:2
The town of, allotted to Gad,
Josh. 13:26, 30
One of the Levitical cities,
Josh. 21:38
Ish-bosheth establishes
himself at, when made king
over Israel, 2 Sam. 2:8–12
David lodges at, at the time
of Absalom's rebellion,
2 Sam. 17:27–29; 1 Kin. 2:8

MAIDSERVANT
firstborn of the *m* ....Ex. 11:5
thy *m*, nor thy
cattle ....Ex. 20:10
manservant, nor
his *m* ....Ex. 20:17
manservant, and
thy *m* ....Deut. 16:11

MAJESTY
is clothed with *m* ....Ps. 93:1
the glory of his *m* .....Is. 2:10
the glory of his *m* .....Is. 2:19
the glory of his *m* .....Is. 2:21

ornament, he set
it in *m* ....Ezek. 7:20
hand of the *M* on
high ....Heb. 1:3
the throne of
the *M* ....Heb. 8:1

MAKE
m of thee a great
nation ....Gen. 12:2
And I will *m* thy
seed ....Gen. 26:4
shall he not *m* it
good ....Num. 23:19
thou shalt *m* no
covenant ....Deut. 7:2
LORD shall *m* the
pestilence ......Deut. 28:21
kill, and I *m* alive .Deut. 32:39
I *m* thine enemies
thy ....Ps. 110:1
yea, when ye *m*
many ....Is. 1:15
M the heart of
this ....Is. 6:10
believeth shall
not *m*............Is. 28:16
and he will *m* her
wilderness ....Is. 51:3
thou shalt *m* his
soul ....Is. 53:10
and I will *m* an
everlasting ....Is. 55:3
holy mountain,
and *m*.............Is. 56:7
destroy them,
and *m*...........Jer. 25:9
covenant that I
will *m*............Jer. 31:33
to *m* an end of
sins ....Dan. 9:24
ceasing I *m*
mention ....Rom. 1:9
m manifest the
counsels ....1 Cor. 4:5
m war with the
Lamb ....Rev. 17:14

MAKER
reproacheth his *M* .Prov. 14:31
forgettest the
LORD thy *m* ......Is. 51:13
thy *M* is thine
husband ....Is. 54:5
m thereof hath
graven ....Hab. 2:18

MAKEST
thou, LORD,
only *m* ....Ps. 4:8
Thou *m* us a
reproach ....Ps. 44:13
Thou *m* us a
byword ....Ps. 44:14
fashioneth it,
What *m* ....Is. 45:9

MAKETH
the priest that *m*
atonement ....Lev. 7:7
blood that *m* an
atonement ......Lev. 17:11

m his son or his
daughter ......Deut. 18:10
LORD killeth,
and *m*............1 Sam. 2:6
He *m* wars to
cease ....Ps. 46:9
m the clouds his
chariot............Ps. 104:3
And wine that *m*
glad ....Ps. 104:15
he *m* lightnings
for ....Ps. 135:7
the earth, who *m*
grass ....Ps. 147:8
wise son *m* a glad
father............Prov. 10:1
hand of the
diligent *m* ......Prov. 10:4
LORD that *m* all
things ....Is. 44:24
my heart *m* a
noise ....Jer. 4:19
revealeth secrets,
and *m*............Dan. 2:28
that *m* desolate
set ....Dan. 12:11
Seek him that *m*
the ....Amos 5:8
And hope *m* not
ashamed .....Rom. 5:5
God, who also *m*
intercession .....Rom. 8:34
worketh
abomination, or *m*. Rev. 21:27
whosoever loveth
and *m*...........Rev. 22:15

MAKING
m their hearts
merry.........Judg. 19:22
LORD is sure, *m*
wise ....Ps. 19:7
twain one new
man, so *m* ....Eph. 2:15
with an
overthrow, *m* .....2 Pet. 2:6

MALACHI
Last of the minor prophets,
Mal. 1:1
Reproves God's people for
their impiety, Mal. 1; 2;
3:7–15
Fortells the coming of the
Messiah, Mal. 3:1–6
The judgments on the wicked
and consolations of the
righteous, Mal. 4:1–3
The coming of the forerunner
of the Messiah, Mal. 4:4–6

MALE
m and female
created ....Gen. 1:27
without
blemish, a *m*.......Ex. 12:5
herd, let him
offer a *m* ....Lev. 1:3
shall bring it a *m* ...Lev. 1:10
Every *m* among
the priests.........Lev. 7:6
every *m* shall
eat it ....Num. 18:10

is neither *m* nor
female . . . . Gal. 3:28

MALES
m shall be the
LORD. . . . . Ex. 13:12
the year all thy *m* . . . . Ex. 23:17
the *m* among the
priests . . . . Lev. 6:29
the firstling *m* . . . . Deut. 15:19
year shall all
thy *m* . . . . Deut. 16:16

MAMRE
A plain near Hebron; Abraham
resides in, Gen. 13:18; 14:13
Entertains three angels, and is
promised a son, Gen. 18:1–15
Isaac lives in, Gen. 35:27
——— An Amorite and
confederate of Abraham,
Gen. 14:13, 24

MAN
Created, Gen. 1:26, 27; 2:7;
5:1, 2; Deut. 4:32; Job 4:17;
10:2, 3, 8, 9; 31:15; 33:4;
35:10; Ps. 8:5; 100:3; 119:73;
138:8; 139:14; Eccl. 7:29;
Is. 17:7; 42:5; 43:7; 45:12;
64:8; Jer. 27:5; Zech. 12:1;
Mal. 2:10; Mark 10:6;
Heb. 2:7
Created in the Image of God,
Gen. 1:26, 27; 9:6; Eccl. 7:29;
1 Cor. 11:7; 15:48, 49;
James 3:9
Design of the Creation of,
Ps. 8:6–8; Prov. 16:4; Is. 43:7
Dominion of, Gen. 1:26, 28;
2:19, 20; 9:2, 3; Jer. 27:6;
28:14; Dan. 2:38; Heb. 2:7, 8
Insignificance of, Job 4:18,
19; 15:14; 22:2–5; 25:4–6;
35:2–8; 38:4, 12, 13; Ps. 8:3,
4; 144:3, 4
Little Lower Than the
Angels, Job 4:18–21; Ps. 8:5;
Heb. 2:7, 8
Spirit, Job 4:19; 32:8; Ps. 31:5;
Prov. 20:27; Eccl. 1:8; 3:21;
12:7; Is. 26:9; Zech. 12:1;
Matt. 4:4; 10:28; 26:41;
Mark 14:38; Luke 22:40;
23:46; 24:39; John 3:3–8;
4:24; Acts 7:59; Rom. 1:9;
2:29; 7:14–25; 1 Cor. 2:11;
6:20; 7:34; 14:14; 2 Cor. 4:6,
7, 16; 5:1–9; Eph. 3:16; 4:4;
1 Thess. 5:23; Heb. 4:12;
James 2:26

MANASSEH
Son of Joseph and Asenath,
Gen. 41:50, 51; 46:20
Adopted by Jacob on his
deathbed, Gen. 48:1, 5–20
Called Manasses, Rev. 7:6
——— Father of Gershom,
Judg. 18:30
——— King of Judah
History of, 2 Kin. 21:1–18;
2 Chr. 33:1–20

——— Two Jews who put away
(divorced) their Gentile
wives after the captivity,
Ezra 10:30, 33

MANIFEST
love him, and
will *m*. . . . . John 14:21
But now is
made *m* . . . . Rom. 16:26
work shall be
made *m* . . . . 1 Cor. 3:13
darkness, and will
make *m* . . . . 1 Cor. 4:5
of the flesh are *m* . . . Gal. 5:19
God was *m* in the
flesh. . . . . 1 Tim. 3:16
creature that is
not *m* . . . . Heb. 4:13

MANIFESTED
hath in due
times *m* . . . . Titus 1:3
(For the life
was *m* . . . . 1 John 1:2
know that he
was *m* . . . . 1 John 3:5
was *m* the love of
God . . . . 1 John 4:9

MANNA
and fed thee
with *m* . . . . Deut. 8:3
fathers did eat *m* . . . John 6:58
golden pot that
had *m*. . . . . Heb. 9:4
eat of the
hidden *m* . . . . Rev. 2:17

MANNER
m, to slay the
righteous. . . . . . . Gen. 18:25
like *m* with their
enchantments. . . . . . Ex. 7:11
no *m* of work shall . . Ex. 12:16
any *m* of creeping
thing . . . . Lev. 11:44
eateth any *m* of
blood . . . . Lev. 17:10
shall die in like *m* . . . . . Is. 51:6
remain after the *m* . . Jer. 30:18
kingdom, and
healing all *m* . . . . . Matt. 4:23
who and what *m*
of woman . . . . Luke 7:39
the spices, as
the *m* . . . . John 19:40
come in like *m*
as ye . . . . Acts 1:11
the *m* of Moses, ye . . Acts 15:1
them after this *m* . . Acts 15:23
And Paul, as his *m* . . Acts 17:2
perfect *m* of the
law. . . . . Acts 22:3
m of men I have
fought . . . . 1 Cor. 15:32
themselves shew
of us what *m* . . . . 1 Thess. 1:9
Behold, what *m* of
love . . . . 1 John 3:1
them in like *m*,
giving . . . . Jude 7

bare twelve *m* of
fruits . . . . Rev. 22:2

MARK
A nephew of Barnabas,
Col. 4:10
A disciple of Jesus, Acts 12:12,
25; 13:5, 13
Paul and Barnabas contend
concerning, Acts 15:36–39
A convert of Peter, 1 Pet. 5:13
Fellow-worker with Paul
at Rome, Col. 4:10, 11;
2 Tim. 4:11; Philem. 24

MARRIED
taken a wife,
and *m*. . . . . Deut. 24:1
m wife, saith the
LORD. . . . . Is. 54:1
thy land shall
be *m* . . . . Is. 62:4
for I am *m* unto
you. . . . . Jer. 3:14
drank, they *m*
wives . . . . Luke 17:27
that ye should
be *m* . . . . Rom. 7:4

MARTHA
Sister of Mary and Lazarus,
John 11:1
Ministers to Jesus,
Luke 10:38–42; John 12:2
Beloved by Jesus, John 11:5

MARVELLOUS
m things without
number . . . . Job 5:9
he hath done *m*
things . . . . Ps. 98:1
god, and shall
speak *m* . . . . Dan. 11:36
darkness into
his *m* . . . . 1 Pet. 2:9

MARY
The mother of Jesus,
Matt. 1:16; Luke 1:26–38;
2:5–19
Visits her cousin, Elisabeth,
Luke 1:39–56
Attends the feast at Jerusalem
with her husband and her
son, starts back on the
return, misses Jesus, seeks
and finds him in the temple
area, Luke 2:48–51
Is present with Jesus at a
marriage feast in Cana of
Galilee, John 2:1–10
Seeks Jesus when he is
teaching in a house,
Matt. 12:46, 47; Mark 3:31;
Luke 8:19
Present at the cross,
John 19:25–27
Is committed to the care of
John, John 19:27
Lives with the disciples in
Jerusalem, Acts 1:14
Prophecies concerning,
Is. 7:14; Luke 2:35
——— Magdalene

Possessed of devils, delivered
by Jesus, Mark 16:9;
Luke 8:2, 3
Present at the crucifixion,
Matt. 27:56; Mark 15:40;
John 20:1, 11–13
Recognizes Jesus after the
resurrection, Matt. 28:8–10;
Mark 16:9; John 20:14–18
——— Sister of Mary the
mother of Jesus, and wife of
Cleophas, John 19:25
Mother of James and Joses,
Matt. 27:56; Mark 15:40;
John 19:25
At the gravesite of Jesus,
Matt. 27:61; Mark 15:47
Assists in preparing the
corpse of Jesus for burial,
Matt. 28:1; Mark 16:1
A witness of the resurrection,
Luke 24:10
——— Sister of Lazarus
Sits at Jesus' feet for
instruction, Luke 10:38–42
Beloved of Jesus, John 11:1, 5
Anoints Jesus, Matt. 26:7–13;
Mark 14:3–9; John 11:2; 12:3
——— Mother of Mark
and sister of Barnabas,
Acts 12:12; Col. 4:10
——— A Christian woman in
Rome, Rom. 16:6

MASTER
Lᴏʀᴅ hath
blessed my *m* . . . .Gen. 24:35
the house of his *m* . .Gen. 39:2
And Joseph's *m*
took . . . . .Gen. 39:20
and spake to
the *m* . . . . Judg. 19:22
said, These have
no *m* . . . . 1 Kin. 22:17
king of Assyria his
m . . . . 2 Kin. 19:4
king of Assyria
his *m* . . . . .Is. 37:4
thy father, made *m* . .Dan. 5:11
Ye call me *M* and
Lord. . . . . .John 13:13
knowing that
your *M*. . . . . Eph. 6:9

MATTANIAH
A Levite of the sons of Asaph,
2 Chr. 20:14; Neh. 12:8
——— Son of Heman, who had
charge of the ninth division
of musicians, 1 Chr. 25:4, 16
——— Descendant of Asaph,
who assisted in purifying the
temple, 2 Chr. 29:13
——— Four Israelites who
divorced their Gentile
wives after the captivity,
Ezra 10:26, 27, 30, 37
——— A Levite, father of
Zaccur, Neh. 13:13

MATTER
far from a false *m* . . . . Ex. 23:7

witnesses, shall
the *m* . . . . .Deut. 19:15
conclusion of the
whole *m*. . . . . . . .Eccl. 12:13
This *m* is by the
decree . . . . .Dan. 4:17
is the end of the *m* . .Dan. 7:28
therefore
understand the *m* . .Dan. 9:23

MAYEST
that thou *m*
inherit . . . . .Gen. 28:4
to the end thou *m*
know . . . . Ex. 8:22
that thou *m* know
how . . . . Ex. 9:29
that thou *m* teach
them . . . . .Ex. 24:12
thou *m* bring in
thither . . . . .Ex. 26:33
thou *m* prolong
thy . . . . .Deut. 4:40
or thou *m* sell it
unto. . . . . .Deut. 14:21
that thou *m*
remember . . . . Deut. 16:3
a stranger thou *m*
lend . . . . .Deut. 23:20
book, that thou *m*
fear . . . . .Deut. 28:58
courageous, that
thou *m* . . . . .Josh. 1:7
thee away, that
thou *m* . . . . .1 Sam. 20:13
that thou *m*
hearken . . . . .1 Kin. 8:29
with thee, that
thou *m*. . . . . Ps. 130:4
profit, if so be
thou *m*. . . . . .Is. 47:12
Gentiles, that
thou *m*. . . . . .Is. 49:6
tarry long, that
thou *m*. . . . . .1 Tim. 3:15
the fire, that
thou *m*. . . . . .Rev. 3:18

MEANS
by no *m* clear the
guilty. . . . . .Ex. 34:7
no *m* clearing the
guilty . . . . .Num. 14:18
bear rule by
their *m*. . . . . Jer. 5:31
saying, I must by
all *m*. . . . . .Acts 18:21
If by any *m* I may
provoke . . . . .Rom. 11:14
m, as the serpent
beguiled . . . . .2 Cor. 11:3
by any *m* I should
run. . . . . Gal. 2:2
testament, that
by *m*. . . . . .Heb. 9:15

MEASURE
correct thee in *m* . . .Jer. 30:11
thereof were after
the *m* . . . . .Ezek. 40:21
trees, were after
the *m* . . . . .Ezek. 40:22

with what *m* ye
mete . . . . Matt. 7:2
not the Spirit
by *m*. . . . . .John 3:34
man the *m* of faith Rom. 12:3
temple leave out,
and *m*. . . . . Rev. 11:2

MEASURED
he smote Moab,
and *m*. . . . . .2 Sam. 8:2
sand of the sea *m* . .Jer. 33:22
sea, which cannot
be *m*. . . . . .Hos. 1:10
mete, it shall be *m* . . Matt. 7:2

MEAT
m offering of the
morning . . . . .Ex. 29:41
will offer a *m*
offering . . . . .Lev. 2:1
remnant of the *m*
offering . . . . .Lev. 2:3
oblation of thy *m*
offering . . . . .Lev. 2:13
fine flour for a *m* . .Lev. 14:10
theirs, every *m*
offering . . . . .Num. 18:9
ephah of flour for
a *m*. . . . . .Num. 28:5
carcase shall be *m* .Deut. 28:26
been my *m* day
and night . . . . Ps. 42:3
also gall for my *m* . . .Ps. 69:21
m to the people
inhabiting . . . . .Ps. 74:14
this people shall
be *m*. . . . . .Jer. 7:33
carcases shall
be *m*. . . . . .Jer. 16:4
bodies shall be
for *m* . . . . .Jer. 34:20
for the *m* offering . . .Joel 1:13
m offering and a
drink . . . . .Joel 2:14
may be *m* in mine
house. . . . . .Mal. 3:10
the life more
than *m* . . . . .Matt. 6:25
saith unto them,
My *m* . . . . .John 4:34
house, did eat
their *m*. . . . . .Acts 2:46

MEDES
Inhabitants of Media;
Israelites distributed among,
when carried to Assyria,
2 Kin. 17:6; 18:11
Palace in the Bablonian
province of, Ezra 6:2
An essential part of the Medo-
Persian Empire, Esth. 1:1, 19
Supremacy of, in the Chaldean
Empire, Dan. 5:28, 31; 9:1;
11:1

MEDITERRANEAN SEA
Mentioned in Scripture as
"the Great Sea," Num. 34:6,
7; Josh. 1:4; 9:1; 15:12, 47;
23:4; Ezek. 47:10, 15, 20;
48:28

Sea of the Philistines,
Ex. 23:31
Sea of Joppa, Ezra 3:7
The hinder sea, Zech. 14:8
The uttermost sea,
Deut. 11:24
The utmost sea, Joel 2:20

MEEK
The *m* shall eat
and. . . . . Ps. 22:26
with equity for
the *m* . . . . Is. 11:4
tidings unto the *m* . . . . Is. 61:1
for I am *m* and
lowly . . . . Matt. 11:29

MEET
I will *m* with thee . . . Ex. 25:22
I will *m* you, to
speak . . . . Ex. 29:42
testimony, where
I will *m* . . . . Ex. 30:6
daughter came
out to *m*. . . . . . . Judg. 11:34
city, that thou
shalt *m*. . . . . 1 Sam. 10:5
he went out to *m*
Asa. . . . . 2 Chr. 15:2
seer went out
to *m* . . . . 2 Chr. 19:2
They *m* with
darkness . . . . Job 5:14
God, and do
works *m* . . . . Acts 26:20
Even as it is *m* for . . . Phil. 1:7
brethren, as it
is *m* . . . . 2 Thess. 1:3

MEGIDDO
Also called Megiddon, and
probably Armageddon;
A city in the territory of
Issachar situated on the
southern edge of the plain
of Esdraelon, Josh. 17:11;
1 Chr. 7:29
Conquest of, by Joshua,
Josh. 12:21
Walled by Solomon,
1 Kin. 9:15
Included in one or Solomon's
commissary districts,
1 Kin. 4:12
Ahaziah dies at, 2 Kin. 9:27
Valley of, Deborah defeats
Sisera in, Judg. 5:19
Josiah killed at, by Pharaoh-
nechoh, 2 Kin. 23:29, 30;
2 Chr. 35:22–24
Prophecy concerning,
Zech. 12:11

MELT
inhabitants of
Canaan shall *m*. . . . Ex. 15:15
things, our hearts
did *m* . . . . Josh. 2:11
heart of the
people *m* . . . . Josh. 14:8
man's heart
shall *m*. . . . . Is. 13:7

heart of Egypt
shall *m* . . . . Is. 19:1
hills *m*, and the
earth . . . . Nah. 1:5
m with fervent
heat . . . . 2 Pet. 3:10

MEMBERS
yielded your *m*
servants. . . . . Rom. 6:19
Christ, and every
one *m* . . . . Rom. 12:5
for we are *m*
one of . . . . Eph. 4:25
Mortify therefore
your *m* . . . . Col. 3:5
tongue among
our *m* . . . . James 3:6

MEMORIAL
is my *m* unto all
generations. . . . . . . Ex. 3:15
be unto you
for a *m* . . . . Ex. 12:14
thine hand, and
for a *m* . . . . Ex. 13:9
m in a book, and
rehearse . . . . Ex. 17:14
priest shall burn
the *m* . . . . Lev. 2:2
a sabbath, a *m* of
blowing. . . . . Lev. 23:24
the bread for a *m* . . . Lev. 24:7
a *m* before your
God . . . . Num. 10:10

MEN
said unto the *m*, I . . . . Josh. 2:9
the rod of *m* . . . . . 2 Sam. 7:14
the mighty *m* of
valour . . . . 2 Kin. 24:14
m of war fled by
night . . . . 2 Kin. 25:4
slew their
young *m* . . . . . . 2 Chr. 36:17
the children of *m* . . . . Ps. 11:4
m may know that
thou. . . . . Ps. 83:18
worm Jacob, and
ye *m* . . . . Is. 41:14
and rejected of *m* . . . . . Is. 53:3
ways of the sons
of *m* . . . . Jer. 32:19
heart of the
mighty *m*. . . . . Jer. 49:22
houses of the
great *m* . . . . Jer. 52:13
the city that *m* call . Lam. 2:15
five and twenty *m*. . Ezek. 8:16
old *m* shall dream
dreams . . . . Joel 2:28
was the light of *m* . . . John 1:4
house, and
haling *m* . . . . Acts 8:3
m of low estate . . . Rom. 12:16
Follow peace with
all *m* . . . . Heb. 12:14
giveth to all *m*
liberally . . . . James 1:5

MENTION
neither make *m* of
the . . . . Josh. 23:7

mother hath he
made *m* . . . . Is. 49:1
said, I will not
make *m* . . . . Jer. 20:9
without ceasing I
make *m* . . . . Rom. 1:9

MEPHIBOSHETH
Son of Saul by Rizpah, whom
David surrendered to the
Gibeonites to be killed,
2 Sam. 21:8, 9
———— Son of Jonathan,
2 Sam. 4:4
Called Merib-baal, 1 Chr. 8:34;
9:40
Was lame, 2 Sam. 4:4
David entertains him at his
table, 2 Sam. 9:1–7; 21:7
Property restored to,
2 Sam. 9:9, 10
His ingratitude to David
at the time of Absolom's
usurpation, 2 Sam. 16:1–4;
19:24–30
Property of, confiscated,
2 Sam. 16:4; 19:29, 30

MERAB
Daughter of King Saul,
1 Sam. 14:49
Betrothed to David by Saul,
1 Sam. 18:17, 18
But given to Adriel for a wife,
1 Sam. 18:19

MERCIES
multitude of thy
tender *m* . . . . Ps. 51:1
multitude of his *m* . Ps. 106:45
the sure *m* of
David. . . . . Is. 55:3
bowels and of
thy *m* . . . . Is. 63:15
lovingkindness,
and in *m* . . . . Hos. 2:19
m of God, that ye
present . . . . Rom. 12:1

MERCIFUL
Lord, The Lord
God, *m*. . . . . Ex. 34:6
pardon, gracious
and *m*. . . . . Neh. 9:17
Be *m* unto me, O
God . . . . Ps. 57:1
The Lord is *m*
and gracious . . . . . Ps. 103:8
gracious and *m*,
slow. . . . . Joel 2:13
gracious God,
and *m*. . . . . Jon. 4:2
a *m* and faithful
high . . . . Heb. 2:17

MERCY
thee from above
the *m* . . . . Ex. 25:22
Keeping *m* for
thousands . . . . Ex. 34:7
with them, nor
shew *m* . . . . Deut. 7:2
my *m* shall not
depart . . . . 2 Sam. 7:15

his *m* endureth . . . 2 Chr. 5:13
for his *m* endureth . . 2 Chr. 7:3
and plenteous
  in *m* . . . . Ps. 86:5
and plenteous
  in *m* . . . . Ps. 86:15
them shall have *m* Prov. 28:13
for he that hath *m* . . . Is. 49:10
people, and will
  have *m* . . . . Is. 49:13
I have *m* on thee,
  saith . . . . Is. 54:8
and he will have *m* . . . . Is. 55:7
have pity, nor
  have *m* . . . . Jer. 21:7
for his *m* endureth . . Jer. 33:11
and I will have *m*
  upon . . . . Hos. 2:23
justly, and to
  love *m* . . . . Mic. 6:8
he delighteth in *m* . . Mic. 7:18
to his *m* he
  saved us . . . . Titus 3:5
abundant *m* hath
  begotten . . . . 1 Pet. 1:3

MESHECH

Also called Mesech; Son of
  Japheth, Gen. 10:2; 1 Chr. 1:5
———— Son of Shem, 1 Chr. 1:17
———— A tribe, Ps. 120:5
———— The Moschi,
  Ezek. 27:13; 32:26; 38:2, 3

MESOPOTAMIA

The country between
  the Tigris River and the
  Euphrates River; Abraham a
  native of, Acts 7:2
Nahor lived in, Gen. 24:10
People who lived in, called
  Syrians, Gen. 25:20
Balaam from, Deut. 23:4
The people of Israel subjected
  to, eight years under the
  judgments of Gog, Judg. 3:8
Delivered from, by Othniel,
  Judg. 3:9, 10
Chariots hired from, by the
  Ammonites, 1 Chr. 19:6, 7
People of, present at Pentecost,
  Acts 2:9

MESSENGERS

Moses sent *m*
  from Kadesh . . . . Num. 20:14
So Ahaz sent *m* to
  Tiglathpileser . . . 2 Kin. 16:7
his *m*, rising up
  betimes . . . . 2 Chr. 36:15
mocked the *m* of
  God . . . . 2 Chr. 36:16
the voice of thy *m* . . . Nah. 2:13

MICAH

An Ephraimite; His robbery
  and idolatry, Judg. 17; 18
———— Head of a family of
  Reuben, 1 Chr. 5:5
———— Also called Micha
Son of Mephibosheth,
  2 Sam. 9:12; 1 Chr. 8:34, 35;
  9:40, 41

———— Also called Michah
A Kohathite, 1 Chr. 23:20;
  24:24, 25
———— Father of Abdon,
  2 Chr. 34:20
———— One of the minor
prophets, Jer. 26:18, 19;
  Mic. 1:1, 14, 15
Denounces the idolatry of his
  times, Mic. 1
The oppressions of the
  covetous, Mic. 2:1–11
Foretells the restoration of
  Israel, Mic. 2:12, 13
The injustice of judges and
  falsehoods of false prophets,
  Mic. 3
Prophesies the coming of the
  Messiah, Mic. 4; 5
Denounces the oppressions

MICHAEL

An Asherite, Num. 13:13
———— Two Gadites,
  1 Chr. 5:13, 14
———— A Gershonite Levite,
  1 Chr. 6:40
———— A descendant of
Issachar, 1 Chr. 7:3
———— A Benjamite, 1 Chr. 8:16
———— A captain of the
thousands of Manasseh
who joined David at Ziklag,
  1 Chr. 12:20
———— Father of Omri,
  1 Chr. 27:18
———— Son of Jehoshaphat
Killed by his brother, Jehoram,
  2 Chr. 21:2–4
———— Father of Zebadiah,
  Ezra 8:8
———— The Archangel
His message to Daniel,
  Dan. 10:13, 21; 12:1
Contention with the devil,
  Jude 9
Fights with the dragon,
  Rev. 12:7

MICHAL

Daughter of Saul; Given to
  David as a reward for killing
  Goliath, 1 Sam. 18:22–28
Rescues David from death,
  1 Sam. 19:9–17
Saul forcibly separates them
  and she is given in marriage
  to Phalti, 1 Sam. 25:44
David recovers, to himself,
  2 Sam. 3:13–16
Ridicules David on account
  of his religious zeal,
  2 Sam. 6:16, 20–23

MICHMASH

A city of the tribe of Benjamin,
  1 Sam. 13:5
People of the captivity return
  to, and dwell in, Ezra 2:27;
  Neh. 11:31
Prophesy concerning the king
  of Assyria storing his baggage
  at, Is. 10:28

Is garrisoned by Saul,
  1 Sam. 13:2
Philistines killed at, by
  Jonathan, 1 Sam. 14:31

MIDIANITES

Descendants of Midian, son
  of Abraham by Keturah,
  Gen. 25:1, 2, 4;
  1 Chr. 1:32, 33
Called Ishmaelites,
  Gen. 37:25, 28; Judg. 8:24
Were merchantmen,
  Gen. 37:28
Buy Joseph and sell him to
  Potiphar, Gen. 37:28, 36
Defeated by the Israelites
  under Phineas
Five of their kings killed
The women taken captive
Cities burned;
And rich spoil taken,
  Num. 31
Defeated by Gideon, Judg. 6;
  7; 8
Owned multitudes of camels,
  and dromedaries, and large
  quantities of gold, Is. 60:6
A snare to the Israelites,
  Num. 25:16–18
Prophecies concerning,
  Is. 60:6; Hab. 3:7

MIDST

anointed him in
  the *m* . . . . 1 Sam. 16:13
is melted in the *m* . . Ps. 22:14
were torn in the *m* . . . . Is. 5:25
of Israel in the *m* . . . . . Is. 12:6
shall melt in
  the *m* . . . . Is. 19:1
perverse spirit in
  the *m* . . . . Is. 19:14
diviners, that be
  in the *m* . . . . Jer. 29:8
m of Babylon, and
  deliver . . . . Jer. 51:6
be consumed in
  the *m* . . . . Ezek. 5:12
shall fall in the *m* . . . Ezek. 6:7
m of the land of
  Egypt . . . . Ezek. 20:8
princes in the *m*
  thereof. . . . . Ezek. 22:27
seat of God, in the
  m . . . . Ezek. 28:2
have profaned in
  the *m* . . . . Ezek. 36:23
in the *m* of the
  week . . . . Dan. 9:27
the glory in the *m* . . . Zech. 2:5
dwell in the *m* of
  Jerusalem . . . . Zech. 8:3
life, which is in
  the *m* . . . . Rev. 2:7
Lamb which is in
  the *m* . . . . Rev. 7:17
In the *m* of the
  street . . . . Rev. 22:2

MIGHTEST

them, that thou *m*
  bring . . . . Neh. 9:29

that thou *m* be
  justified . . . . Ps. 51:4
thou *m* receive thy . . Acts 9:17
them *m* war a
  good warfare . . . 1 Tim. 1:18

MIGHTIER
nations greater
  and *m*. . . . . Deut. 7:1
nations greater
  and *m*. . . . . Deut. 9:1
of thee a nation *m* . Deut. 9:14
m than I, whose
  shoes . . . . Matt. 3:11

MIGHTY
m men of Moab,
  trembling . . . . Ex. 15:15
power, and
  with a *m* . . . . Ex. 32:11
the person of
  the *m* . . . . Lev. 19:15
war, and by a *m*
  hand . . . . Deut. 4:34
a *m* hand, and
  redeemed . . . . Deut. 7:8
broughtest out by
  thy *m* . . . . Deut. 9:29
lords, a great God,
  a *m* . . . . Deut. 10:17
a nation, great, *m* . . Deut. 26:5
all the *m* men of
  valour . . . . 2 Kin. 24:14
and the *m* . . . . . . 2 Kin. 24:15
Wonderful,
  Counsellor, The *m* . . . . Is. 9:6
m wind shall he
  shake . . . . Is. 11:15
Behold, the Lord
  hath a *m* . . . . Is. 28:2
thy Redeemer,
  the *m* . . . . Is. 49:26
in
  righteousness, *m* . . . . Is. 63:1
let the *m* man
  glory . . . . Jer. 9:23
Great in counsel,
  and *m* . . . . Jer. 32:19
m men's hearts in
  Moab . . . . Jer. 48:41
heart of the *m*
  men . . . . Jer. 49:22
city Babylon,
  that *m* . . . . Rev. 18:10

MILETUS
Also called Miletum; A seaport
  in Asia Minor; Paul visits,
  Acts 20:15
And sends to Ephesus for the
  elders of the congregation,
  and addresses them at,
  Acts 20:17–38
Trophimus left sick at,
  2 Tim. 4:20

MILK
land flowing
  with *m* . . . . Ex. 3:8
land flowing
  with *m* . . . . Ex. 3:17
in his mother's *m* . . . Ex. 23:19
in his mother's *m* . . . Ex. 34:26

his mother's *m* . . . Deut. 14:21
my wine with
  my *m* . . . . Song 5:1
them, flowing
  with *m* . . . . Ezek. 20:6
them, flowing
  with *m* . . . . Ezek. 20:15
shall flow with *m* . . . Joel 3:18
desire the
  sincere *m* . . . . 1 Pet. 2:2

MILLO
The house of Millo, possibly a
  clan at Shechem,
  Judg. 9:6, 20
———— A name given to part
  of the citadel of Jerusalem,
  2 Sam. 5:9; 1 Chr. 11:8
King Solomon raises a levy to
  repair, 1 Kin. 9:15, 24; 11:27
Repaired by Hezekiah,
  2 Chr. 32:5
King Joash murdered at,
  2 Kin. 12:20

MIND
bad of mine
  own *m* . . . . Num. 24:13
eyes, and sorrow
  of *m* . . . . Deut. 28:65
and with a
  willing *m* . . . . . . 1 Chr. 28:9
before me, yet
  my *m* . . . . Jer. 15:1
came it into my *m* . . Jer. 32:35
with all thy *m* . . . . Luke 10:27
who hath known
  the *m* . . . . Rom. 11:34
m, that ye may
  prove . . . . Rom. 12:2
Be of the same *m*
  one . . . . Rom. 12:16
flesh and of the *m* . . . Eph. 2:3
spirit, with one *m* . . Phil. 1:27
shame, who *m*
  earthly . . . . Phil. 3:19
m, be sober, and
  hope . . . . 1 Pet. 1:13

MINE
it is *m* . . . . Ex. 13:2
all the earth is *m* . . . . Ex. 19:5
Yea, *m* own
  familiar . . . . Ps. 41:9
hands, I will
  hide *m* . . . . Is. 1:15
doings from
  before *m* . . . . Is. 1:16
m elect, in
  whom my . . . . Is. 42:1
transgressions
  for *m* . . . . Is. 43:25
accepted upon *m*
  altar . . . . Is. 56:7
Behold, *m* anger
  and . . . . Jer. 7:20
m eye shall weep
  sore . . . . Jer. 13:17
Let *m* eyes run
  down . . . . Jer. 14:17
For I will set *m*
  eyes . . . . Jer. 24:6

M eyes do fail
  with . . . . Lam. 2:11
shall *m* eye spare . . Ezek. 5:11
shall *m* anger be
  accomplished . . . . Ezek. 5:13
me by a lock of *m*
  head . . . . Ezek. 8:3
m eye shall not
  spare . . . . Ezek. 8:18
stretch out *m*
  hand . . . . Ezek. 25:13
and I will turn *m*
  hand . . . . Zech. 13:7
written,
  Vengeance is *m* . . Rom. 12:19

MINGLED
tenth deal of
  flour *m* . . . . Ex. 29:40
unleavened
  cakes *m* . . . . Lev. 7:12
a meat offering, *m* . Lev. 14:10
a meat offering, *m* . Num. 28:5
meat offering, *m* . . Num. 28:12
the holy seed
  have *m* . . . . Ezra 9:2
The Lord hath *m*
  a perverse . . . . Is. 19:14
And all the *m*
  people . . . . Jer. 25:20
kings of the *m*
  people . . . . Jer. 25:24
upon all the *m*
  people . . . . Jer. 50:37
the *m* people, and
  Chub . . . . Ezek. 30:5
followed hail and
  fire *m* . . . . Rev. 8:7

MINISTER
rose up, and his *m* . . Ex. 24:13
sons, that he
  may *m* . . . . Ex. 28:4
m unto me in the
  priest's . . . . Ex. 28:41
before the Lord
  to *m* . . . . Deut. 10:8
standeth to *m* . . . . Deut. 17:12
God hath chosen
  to *m* . . . . Deut. 21:5
could not stand
  to *m* . . . . 1 Kin. 8:11
before the Lord,
  to *m* . . . . 1 Chr. 23:13
charges, to praise
  and *m* . . . . 2 Chr. 8:14
of Nebaioth
  shall *m* . . . . Is. 60:7
the Levites that *m* . . Jer. 33:22
ministered unto,
  but to *m* . . . . Matt. 20:28
m grace unto the
  hearers . . . . Eph. 4:29
I Paul am
  made a *m* . . . . Col. 1:23
brother, and *m* of
  God . . . . 1 Thess. 3:2
spirits, sent forth
  to *m* . . . . Heb. 1:14
the saints, and
  do *m* . . . . Heb. 6:10

us they did *m* the
things . . . . 1 Pet. 1:12
if any man *m*, let
him . . . . 1 Pet. 4:11

MINISTERED
thousand
thousands *m* . . . . . .Dan. 7:10
man came not to
be *m* . . . . Matt. 20:28
epistle of Christ *m* . .2 Cor. 3:3
ye have *m* to the
saints . . . . .Heb. 6:10

MINISTERS
howl, ye *m* of the
altar . . . . Joel 1:13
m of the LORD,
weep . . . . Joel 2:17
but *m* by whom ye
believed . . . . .1 Cor. 3:5
hath made us
able *m* . . . . .2 Cor. 3:6

MIRACLES
these *m* that thou
doest . . . . .John 3:2
a sinner do
such *m* . . . . .John 9:16
another the
working of *m* . . 1 Cor. 12:10
m, then gifts of
healings . . . . 1 Cor. 12:28
divers *m*, and gifts . . .Heb. 2:4
prophet that
wrought *m* . . . . . . Rev. 19:20

MIRE
I sink in deep *m*,
where . . . . Ps. 69:2
like the *m* of the
streets . . . . .Is. 10:6
was no water,
but *m* . . . . .Jer. 38:6
their enemies in
the *m* . . . . Zech. 10:5

MIRIAM
Sister of Moses; Watched over
Moses when he was in the
little basket, Ex. 2:4–8
Song of, after the destruction
of Pharaoh and his army,
Ex. 15:20, 21; Mic. 6:4
Jealous of Moses, stricken with
leprosy, healed on account
of the intercession of Moses,
Num. 12; Deut. 24:9
Died and is buried at Kadesh,
Num. 20:1

MISCHIEF
speak, and say,
For *m* . . . . Ex. 32:12
His *m* shall return . . . Ps. 7:16
tongue is *m* and
vanity . . . . Ps. 10:7
their neighbours,
but *m* . . . . Ps. 28:3
thyself in *m*, O
mighty . . . . Ps. 52:1

MIZPAH
A city allotted to the tribe of
Benjamin, Josh. 18:26

The Israelites assemble at,
Judg. 20:1–3
And decree the penalty to be
visited upon the Benjamites
for their maltreatment of
the Levite's concubine,
Judg. 20:10
Assembled by Samuel so that
he could reprove them for
their idolatry, 1 Sam. 7:5
They crown Saul king of Israel
at, 1 Sam. 10:17–25
A judgment seat of Samuel,
1 Sam. 7:16
Walled up by Asa,
1 Kin. 15:22; 2 Chr. 16:6
Temporarily the capitol of the
country after the people of
Israel had been carried away
captive, 2 Kin. 25:23, 25;
Jer. 40:6–15; 41:1–14
Captivity returned to,
Neh. 3:7, 15, 19
——— A valley near Lebanon,
Josh. 11:3, 8
——— A city in Moab
David puts his parents into
the care of the king of,
1 Sam. 22:3, 4
——— A city in the lowlands of
Judah, Josh. 15:38

MOAB
Son of Lot, Gen. 19:37
——— Plains of
Israelites come in, Deut. 2:17,
18
Military forces numbered in,
Num. 26:3, 63
The law rehearsed in, by
Moses, Num. 35; 36;
Deut. 29; 30; 31; 32; 33
The Israelites renew their
covenant in, Deut. 29:1
The land of promise allotted
in, Josh. 13:32

MOABITES
Descendants of Lot through
his son Moab, Gen. 19:37
Called the people of Chemosh,
Num. 21:29
The territory east of the
Jordan River, bounded on the
north by the Arnon River,
Num. 21:13; Judg. 11:18
The people of Israel
commanded not to distress
the Moabites, Deut. 2:9
Refuse passage of Jephthah's
army through their territory,
Judg. 11:17, 18
Balak was king of, Num. 22:4
Calls for Balaam to curse
Israel, Num. 22; 23;
Josh. 24:9; Mic. 6:5
Are a snare to the Israelites,
Num. 25:1–3; Ruth 1:4;
1 Kin. 11:1; 1 Chr. 8:8;
Ezra 9:1, 2; Neh. 13:23
Land of, not given to the

Israelites as a possession,
Deut. 2:9, 29
David takes refuge among,
from Saul, 1 Sam. 22:3, 4
David conquers, 2 Sam. 8:2;
23:20; 1 Chr. 11:22; 18:2–11
Israelites had war with,
2 Kin. 3:5–27; 13:20; 24:2;
2 Chr. 20
Prophecies concerning
judgments upon, Jer. 48

MOLECH
Also called Moloch and
Milcom; An idol of the
Ammonites, Acts 7:43
Worshiped by the wives of
Solomon, and by Solomon,
1 Kin. 11:1–8
Children sacrificed to,
2 Kin. 16:3; 21:6; 23:10;
2 Chr. 28:3; Is. 57:5; Jer. 7:31;
32:35; Ezek. 16:20, 21; 20:26,
31; 23:37, 39

MOLTEN
had made it a *m*
calf . . . . Ex. 32:4
make to
yourselves *m* . . . . . Lev. 19:4
maketh any
graven or *m* . . . . .Deut. 27:15
thee other gods,
and *m* . . . . 1 Kin. 14:9
God, and made
them *m* . . . . 2 Kin. 17:16
formed a god,
or *m* . . . . .Is. 44:10
his *m* image is
falsehood . . . . .Jer. 10:14
m image, and a
teacher . . . . .Hab. 2:18

MOMENT
consume them as
in a *m* . . . . .Num. 16:45
m in one day, the
loss . . . . .Is. 47:9
from thee for a *m* . . . . .Is. 54:8
at every *m* . . . . Ezek. 26:16

MONEY
house, or bought
with *m* . . . . .Gen. 17:12
If thou lend *m* to
any . . . . Ex. 22:25
take the
atonement *m* . . . . . Ex. 30:16
estimation, for
the *m* . . . . .Num. 18:16
usury of *m*, usury
of . . . . .Deut. 23:19
m to usury, nor
taketh . . . . Ps. 15:5
redeemed
without *m* . . . . .Is. 52:3
shall buy fields
for *m* . . . . .Jer. 32:44
thereof divine
for *m* . . . . .Mic. 3:11
bought for a sum
of *m* . . . . .Acts 7:16

love of *m* is the
　root . . . . 1 Tim. 6:10

MONTH
life, in the
　second *m* . . . . Gen. 7:11
day of the same *m* . . . Ex. 12:6
first *m*, on the
　fourteenth . . . . Ex. 12:18
appointed of
　the *m* . . . . Ex. 23:15
the time of the *m*
　Abib . . . . Ex. 34:18
day of the first *m* . . . Lev. 23:5
saying, In the
　seventh *m* . . . . Lev. 23:24
m old shalt thou
　redeem . . . . Num. 18:16
Zin in the first *m* . . Num. 20:1
of every *m* . . . . Num. 28:14
day of the first *m* . Num. 28:16
Observe the *m* of
　Abib . . . . Deut. 16:1
feast in the
　eighth *m* . . . . . . 1 Kin. 12:32
Zedekiah, in the
　fourth *m* . . . . Jer. 39:2
fourth *m*, in the
　ninth . . . . Jer. 52:6
year, in the
　sixth *m* . . . . Ezek. 8:1
m, the tenth
　day of . . . . Ezek. 20:1
king, in the
　sixth *m* . . . . Hag. 1:1
fifth and
　seventh *m* . . . . Zech. 7:5
her fruit every *m* . . . . Rev. 22:2

MONTHS
your *m*, ye shall
　blow . . . . Num. 10:10
your *m* ye shall
　offer . . . . Num. 28:11
month
　throughout
　the *m* . . . . Num. 28:14
six *m*, when great
　famine . . . . Luke 4:25
foot forty and
　two *m* . . . . Rev. 11:2
continue forty and
　two *m* . . . . Rev. 13:5

MOON
the sun, and the *m*　Deut. 4:19
either the sun,
　or *m* . . . . Deut. 17:3
thou, *M*, in the
　valley . . . . Josh. 10:12
the *m*, and as a
　faithful . . . . Ps. 89:37
going forth, and
　the *m* . . . . Is. 13:10
the *m* shall be
　confounded . . . . Is. 24:23
m give light unto
　thee . . . . Is. 60:19
shall thy *m*
　withdraw . . . . Is. 60:20
ordinances of
　the *m* . . . . Jer. 31:35

the sun and the *m*
　shall . . . . Joel 2:10
darkness, and
　the *m* . . . . Joel 2:31
The sun and the *m*
　shall . . . . Joel 3:15
darkened, and
　the *m* . . . . Matt. 24:29
of hair, and the *m* . . . Rev. 6:12
third part of the *m* . . Rev. 8:12
sun, neither of
　the *m* . . . . Rev. 21:23

MORDECAI
A Jewish captive in Persia,
　Esth. 2:5, 6
Foster father of Esther,
　Esth. 2:7
Informs Ahasuerus of a
　conspiracy against his life
　and is rewarded, Esth. 2:21–
　23; 6:1–11
Promoted in Haman's place,
　Esth. 8:1, 2, 15; 10
Intercedes with Ahasuerus
　for the Jews; establishes
　the festival of Purim in
　commemoration of their
　deliverance, Esth. 8; 9

MORNING
came to pass in
　the *m* . . . . Gen. 41:8
remain until the *m* . . Ex. 12:10
strength when
　the *m* . . . . Ex. 14:27
third day in the *m* . . . Ex. 19:16
it from evening
　to *m* . . . . Ex. 27:21
shalt offer in
　the *m* . . . . Ex. 29:39
offering of the *m* . . . . Ex. 29:41
sweet incense
　every *m* . . . . Ex. 30:7
night until the *m* . . Lev. 19:13
thou offer in
　the *m* . . . . Num. 28:4
night until the *m* . . Deut. 16:4
turn in the *m* . . . . . . Deut. 16:7
In the *m* thou
　shalt . . . . Deut. 28:67
he wakeneth *m*
　by *m* . . . . Is. 50:4
m spread upon the
　mountains . . . . Joel 2:2
m, and maketh the
　day . . . . Amos 5:8
m is light, they
　practise . . . . Mic. 2:1
every *m* doth he
　bring . . . . Zeph. 3:5
When the *m* was
　come . . . . Matt. 27:1
the bright and *m*
　star . . . . Rev. 22:16

MORROW
to *m* I will
　stand on . . . . Ex. 17:9
them to day and
　to *m* . . . . Ex. 19:10
m the LORD will
　shew . . . . Num. 16:5

m about this
　time I . . . . 1 Sam. 9:16
to day is, and to *m* . Matt. 6:30
to depart on the *m* . . Acts 20:7
for to *m* we die . . 1 Cor. 15:32
shall be on the *m* . . James 4:14

MOSES
A Levite and son of Amram,
　Ex. 2:1–4; 6:20; Acts 7:20;
　Heb. 11:23
Hidden in a small basket,
　Ex. 2:3
Discovered and adopted by
　the daughter of Pharaoh,
　Ex. 2:5–10
Learned in all the wisdom of
　Egypt, Acts 7:22
His loyalty to his race,
　Heb. 11:24–26
Takes the life of an Egyptian
　taskmaster; flees from
　Egypt; finds refuge among
　the Midianites, Ex. 2:11–22;
　Acts 7:24–29
Joins himself to Jethro, priest
　of Midian; marries his
　daughter Zipporah; has one
　son, Gershom, Ex. 2:15–22
Is a herdsman for Jethro in the
　desert of Horeb, Ex. 3:1
Has the vision of the burning
　bush, Ex. 3:2–6
God reveals to him his
　purpose to deliver the
　Israelites and bring them
　into the land of Canaan,
　Ex. 3:7–10
Commissioned as leader of the
　Israelites, Ex. 3:10–22; 6:13
His rod miraculously turned
　into a serpent, and his hand
　was made leprous, and then
　restored, Ex. 4:1–9, 28
With his wife and sons, he
　leaves Jethro to perform his
　mission in Egypt,
　Ex. 4:18–20
His controversy with his wife
　on account of circumcision,
　Ex. 4:20–26
Meets Aaron in the
　wilderness, Ex. 4:27, 28
With Aaron assembles the
　leaders of Israel, Ex. 4:29–31
Along with Aaron, Moses goes
　before Pharaoh and demands
　the liberties of his people in
　the name of Jehovah, Ex. 5:1
Rejected by Pharaoh;
　hardships of the Israelites
　increased, Ex. 5
Receives comfort and
　assurance from the Lord,
　Ex. 6:1–8
Unbelief of the people, Ex. 6:9
Renews his appeal to Pharaoh,
　Ex. 6:11
Under divine direction brings
　plagues upon the land of
　Egypt, Ex. 7; 8; 9; 10; 11; 12
Secures the deliverance of the

MOTHER

MOUNT

MOUNTAIN

MOUNTAINS
slay them in the *m* . . Ex. 32:12
Aram, out of
  the *m* . . . . Num. 23:7
the north of the *m* . Josh. 11:2
The *m* shall bring
  peace . . . . Ps. 72:3
Before the *m* were
  brought . . . . Ps. 90:2
in the top of the *m* . . . . . Is. 2:2
the chaff of the *m* . . . . Is. 17:13
singing, ye *m*, O
  forest . . . . Is. 44:23
into singing, O *m* . . . . Is. 49:13
the *m* and the hills . . . Is. 55:12
For the *m* will I
  take . . . . Jer. 9:10
stumble upon the
  dark *m* . . . . Jer. 13:16
the cities of the *m* . . Jer. 32:44
feed them upon
  the *m* . . . . Ezek. 34:13
spread upon the *m* . . . . Joel 2:2
in the top of the *m* . . . Mic. 4:1
Hear ye, O *m*, the
  LORD. . . . . Mic. 6:2
The *m* quake at
  him . . . . Nah. 1:5
Esau, and laid
  his *m* . . . . Mal. 1:3
that I could
  remove *m* . . . . 1 Cor. 13:2

MOURN
How long wilt
  thou *m* . . . . 1 Sam. 16:1
m with him and to
  comfort . . . . Job 2:11
shall lament
  and *m* . . . . Is. 3:26
like bears, and *m*
  sore . . . . Is. 59:11
comfort all that *m* . . . . Is. 61:2
m in Zion, to give . . . . . Is. 61:3
ways of Zion do *m* . . Lam. 1:4
shall not *m* nor . . . Ezek. 24:23
Therefore shall
  the land *m* . . . . Hos. 4:3
people thereof
  shall *m* . . . . Hos. 10:5
pierced, and they
  shall *m* . . . . Zech. 12:10
tribes of the
  earth *m* . . . . Matt. 24:30

MOURNING
grave unto my son
  m . . . . .Gen. 37:35
mourner, and put
  on now *m* . . . . . . 2 Sam. 14:2
weeping, and to *m* . . . Is. 22:12
and the days of
  thy *m* . . . . Is. 60:20
the oil of joy for *m* . . . . Is. 61:3
make thee *m*, as
  for . . . . Jer. 6:26
Forbear to cry,
  make no *m* . . . . . Ezek. 24:17
day, death, and *m* . . . Rev. 18:8

MOUTH
put words in
  his *m* . . . . Ex. 4:15

the *m* of the LORD
  doth . . . . Deut. 8:3
LORD by the *m* of
  Jeremiah . . . . Ezra 1:1
the *m* of the LORD
  hath . . . . Is. 1:20
with the rod of
  his *m* . . . . Is. 11:4
m, and with their
  lips. . . . . Is. 29:13
he opened not
  his *m* . . . . Is. 53:7
any deceit in his *m* . . . . Is. 53:9
own *m*, to burn
  incense . . . . Jer. 44:17
have opened
  their *m* . . . . Lam. 2:16
open thy *m*, and
  eat . . . . Ezek. 2:8
abominable flesh
  into my *m* . . . . Ezek. 4:14
m they shew
  much love . . . . . . Ezek. 33:31
the trumpet to
  thy *m* . . . . Hos. 8:1
seek the law at
  his *m* . . . . Mal. 2:7
m of babes and
  sucklings. . . . . . Matt. 21:16
proceeded out of
  his *m* . . . . Luke 4:22
Peter opened
  his *m* . . . . Acts 10:34
delivered out of
  the *m* . . . . 2 Tim. 4:17
m went a sharp
  twoedged . . . . Rev. 1:16

MOVE
I will *m* them to
  jealousy. . . . . Deut. 32:21
the LORD began
  to *m* . . . . Judg. 13:25
serpent, they
  shall *m* . . . . Mic. 7:17
none of these
  things *m* . . . . Acts 20:24

MOVED
They have *m* me
  to jealousy . . . . . Deut. 32:21
things shall never
  be *m* . . . . Ps. 15:5
that it cannot
  be *m* . . . . Ps. 93:1
let the earth be *m* . . . . Ps. 99:1
posts of the door *m* . . . . Is. 6:4
of Egypt shall
  be *m* . . . . Is. 19:1
earth is *m* at the
  noise . . . . Jer. 49:21
multitudes, he
  was *m* . . . . Matt. 9:36
m with envy, sold
  Joseph . . . . Acts 7:9
which believed
  not, *m* . . . . Acts 17:5
settled, and be
  not *m* . . . . Col. 1:23
yet, *m* with fear,
  prepared . . . . .Heb. 11:7

MULTIPLY
Be fruitful, and *m* . . .Gen. 1:28
I will greatly *m*
  thy . . . . .Gen. 3:16
I will *m* thy
  seed as. . . . . .Gen. 22:17
make thy seed
  to *m* . . . . .Gen. 26:4
bless thee, and *m*
  thy . . . . .Gen. 26:24
be fruitful and *m* . .Gen. 35:11
Pharaoh's heart,
  and *m* . . . . Ex. 7:3
I will *m* your seed. . . Ex. 32:13
he shall not *m*
  horses . . . . Deut. 17:16
shall he *m*
  wives to. . . . . Deut. 17:17
you good, and
  to *m* . . . . Deut. 28:63
I *m* the seed of
  David. . . . . Jer. 33:22

MULTITUDE
And the mixt *m*
  that . . . . Num. 11:4
stars of heaven
  for *m* . . . . , Deut. 10:22
stars of heaven
  for *m* . . . . Deut. 28:62
grasshoppers
  for *m* . . . . Judg. 7:12
sea shore in *m*. . . . 1 Sam. 13:5
gone with the *m*, I . . . Ps. 42:4
m of thy tender
  mercies . . . . Ps. 51:1
to the *m* of his
  mercies . . . . Ps. 106:45
what purpose is
  the *m* . . . . .Is. 1:11
The noise of a
  m in . . . . Is. 13:4
with the *m* of thy
  sorceries . . . . .Is. 47:12
m of camels shall
  cover . . . . .Is. 60:6
the *m* of thine
  iniquity . . . . .Jer. 30:14
m, and take her
  spoil. . . . . Ezek. 29:19
man is mad, for
  the *m* . . . . Hos. 9:7
death, he feared
  the *m* . . . . Matt. 14:5
he commanded
  the *m* . . . . Matt. 14:19
m said, This is
  Jesus . . . . Matt. 21:11
pleased the
  whole *m*. . . . . Acts 6:5
shall hide a *m* of
  sins . . . . .James 5:20

MULTITUDES
saw the *m*, he was
  moved . . . . Matt. 9:36
And the *m* that
  went . . . . Matt. 21:9
said Jesus to
  the *m* . . . . Matt. 26:55
the Jews saw
  the *m* . . . . Acts 13:45

NAAMAN
Son of Benjamin, Gen. 46:21
———— Son of Bela, Num. 26:40;
1 Chr. 8:4
———— Son of Ehud, 1 Chr. 8:7
———— A Syrian general,
healed of leprosy by Elisha,
2 Kin. 5:1–23; Luke 4:27

NADAB
Son of Aaron, Ex. 6:23
Called to Mount Sinai with
Moses and Aaron to worship,
Ex. 24:1, 9, 10
Set apart to priesthood,
Ex. 28:1, 4, 40–43
Offers "strange"
(unauthorized) fire to God,
and is destroyed, Lev. 10:1, 2;
Num. 3:4; 26:61
Is buried, Lev. 10:4, 5
His father and brothers
forbidden to mourn,
Lev. 10:6, 7
———— Son and successor of
Jeroboam, 1 Kin. 14:20
His wicked reign; murdered by
Baasha, 1 Kin. 15:25–31
———— Great-grandson of
Jerahmeel, 1 Chr. 2:28, 30
———— A Benjamite,
1 Chr. 8:30; 9:36

NAHASH
An Ammonite king; Defeated
by Saul at Jabesh-gilead,
1 Sam. 11:1–11
Kindness of, to David, and
death, 2 Sam. 10:1, 2;
1 Chr. 19:1, 2
———— Probably identical with
Jesse, 2 Sam. 17:25

NAHOR
Grandfather of Abraham,
Gen. 11:22–26; 1 Chr. 1:26
In the lineage of Christ,
Luke 3:34
———— Brother of Abraham,
Gen. 11:26; Josh. 24:2
Marriage and descendants of,
Gen. 11:27, 29; 22:20–24;
24:15, 24

NAKED
And said, N
came I . . . . .Job 1:21
so, walking n and
barefoot. . . . . .Is. 20:2
Isaiah hath
walked n . . . . .Is. 20:3
captives, young
and old, n . . . . .Is. 20:4
shalt make
thyself n . . . . Lam. 4:21
hath covered the n . Ezek. 18:7
covered the n . . . . Ezek. 18:16
Lest I strip her n. . . . . Hos. 2:3
things are n and
opened . . . . .Heb. 4:13
poor, and blind,
and n . . . . Rev. 3:17

NAKEDNESS
uncovered his
father's n. . . . . Lev. 20:11
thirst, and in n . . .Deut. 28:48
and covered thy n. . Ezek. 16:8
discover thy n . . . . Ezek. 16:37
the shame of thy n . . Rev. 3:18

NAMED
son of Ahitub, n
Abiathar . . . . . . 1 Sam. 22:20
Jew n Aquila, born . . Acts 18:2
as n among the
Gentiles. . . . . .1 Cor. 5:1
every name that
is n . . . . .Eph. 1:21

NAMES
n of the sons of
Ishmael . . . . .Gen. 25:13
Baalmeon,
(their n . . . . .Num. 32:38
gods, and destroy
the n . . . . .Deut. 12:3
calleth them all
by n . . . . .Is. 40:26
will cut off the n . . . Zech. 13:2
n are written in
heaven. . . . . Luke 10:20
fellowlabourers,
whose n. . . . . Phil. 4:3
Thou hast a few n
even. . . . . Rev. 3:4
worship him,
whose n. . . . . Rev. 13:8
whose n were not
written . . . . Rev. 17:8

NAPHTALI
Son of Jacob and Bilhah,
Gen. 30:7, 8; 35:25
Jacob blesses, Gen. 49:21
Sons of, Gen. 46:24;
1 Chr. 7:13
———— Tribe of
Census of, Num. 1:42, 43;
26:48–50
Position assigned to, in
camping and in marching,
Num. 2:25–31; 10:25–27
Moses' benediction on,
Deut. 33:23
Inheritance of, Josh. 19:32–39;
Judg. 1:33; Ezek. 48:3
Defeat Sisera, Judg. 4:6, 10;
5:18
Follow Gideon, Judg. 6:35;
7:23
Help in conveying the ark of
the covenant to Jerusalem,
Ps. 68:27
Military operations of,
1 Chr. 12:34, 40
Against, 1 Kin. 15:20;
2 Kin. 15:29; 2 Chr. 16:4
Prophecies concerning, Is. 9:1,
2; Rev. 7:6

NATHAN
Son of David and Bath-sheba,
2 Sam. 5:14; 1 Chr. 3:5; 14:4
———— A prophet in the time
of David

His message to David
concerning the building of
a temple, 2 Sam. 7:1–17;
1 Chr. 17:1–15
Reproves David for his
adultery with Bath-sheba
and his murder of Uriah,
2 Sam. 12:1–15
Gives Solomon the name
Jedidiah, 2 Sam. 12:25
Assists Bath-sheba in securing
to Solomon, her son, the
succession to the throne,
1 Kin. 1:10–14, 22–27
Assists in anointing Solomon
to be king, 1 Kin. 1:32–45
Kept the chronicles,
1 Chr. 29:29; 2 Chr. 9:29
Assists David in the
organization of the
tabernacle, 2 Chr. 29:25

NATION
of thee a great n . . . .Gen. 12:2
a n and a company
of . . . . .Gen. 35:11
priests, and an
holy n . . . . Ex. 19:6
there a n, great,
mighty. . . . . Deut. 26:5
a n which thou
knowest . . . . . . .Deut. 28:33
over thee,
unto a n. . . . . . . .Deut. 28:36
LORD shall
bring a n . . . . . . .Deut. 28:49
A n of fierce
countenance . . . .Deut. 28:50
anger with a
foolish n . . . . . . .Deut. 32:21
off from being a n. . . . Ps. 83:4
Ah sinful n, a
people . . . . .Is. 1:4
an hypocritical n. . . . . .Is. 10:6
n abhorreth, to a
servant . . . . .Is. 49:7
thou shalt call a n. . . . .Is. 55:5
Hath a n changed
their. . . . . .Jer. 2:11
that n, saith the
LORD. . . . . .Jer. 25:12
since there
was a n . . . . .Dan. 12:1
far off a strong n. . . . . Mic. 4:7
unto one of
another n. . . . . . . .Acts 10:28
priesthood, an
holy n . . . . 1 Pet. 2:9

NATIONS
n of the earth be
blessed . . . . .Gen. 22:18
n of the earth be
blessed . . . . .Gen. 26:4
and a company
of n . . . . .Gen. 35:11
divided unto all n . . Deut. 4:19
himself, above all
the n . . . . .Deut. 14:2
byword, among
all n . . . . .Deut. 28:37

n shalt thou find
　no . . . . Deut. 28:65
the kindreds of
　the *n* . . . . Ps. 22:27
and all *n* shall flow . . . . . Is. 2:2
an ensign for
　the *n* . . . . Is. 11:12
holden, to
　subdue *n* . . . . Is. 45:1
eyes of all the *n* . . . . . Is. 52:10
n, to Tarshish, Pul . . . Is. 66:19
set thee over the *n* . . . Jer. 1:10
tremble, and the *n* . . Jer. 10:10
all these *n* round
　about . . . . Jer. 25:9
Declare ye among
　the *n* . . . . Jer. 50:2
remember me
　among the *n* . . . . . . Ezek. 6:9
and teach all *n*,
　baptizing . . . . . . Matt. 28:19
n, beginning at
　Jerusalem . . . . . . Luke 24:47

NAZARETH
A village in Galilee; Joseph
　and Mary live at, Matt. 2:23;
　Luke 1:26, 27, 56; 2:4, 39, 51
Jesus from, Matt. 21:11;
　Mark 1:24; 10:47; Luke 4:34;
　18:37; 24:19
People of, reject Jesus,
　Luke 4:16–30
Its reputation, John 1:46

NEBO
A city allotted to the tribe
　of Reuben, Num. 32:3, 38;
　1 Chr. 5:8
Prophecies concerning,
　Is. 15:2; Jer. 48:1, 22
——— A mountain range east
　of the Jordan; Moses views
　Canaan from, Deut. 32:49, 50
Dies on, Deut. 34:1
——— A city in territory of the
　tribe of Judah, Ezra 2:29;
　Neh. 7:33
——— The ancestor of certain
　Jews, Ezra 10:43
——— A Babylonian idol,
　Is. 46:1

NECK
chain about his *n* . . Gen. 41:42
iron upon thy *n* . . Deut. 28:48
rebellion, and thy
　stiff *n* . . . . Deut. 31:27
necks, like to
　the *n* . . . . 2 Kin. 17:14
he stiffened his *n* 2 Chr. 36:13
and hardened
　their *n* . . . . Neh. 9:29
reproved
　hardeneth his *n* . . Prov. 29:1
reach even to the *n* . . . . Is. 8:8
cut off a dog's *n* . . . . . . Is. 66:3
but hardened
　their *n* . . . . Jer. 7:26
of gold about
　his *n* . . . . Dan. 5:7
of gold about
　thy *n* . . . . Dan. 5:16

NEEDY
the *n*, now will I
　arise . . . . Ps. 12:5
children of the *n* . . . . . Ps. 72:4
shall deliver the *n* . . . Ps. 72:12
To turn aside
　the *n* . . . . Is. 10:2
a strength to the *n* . . . . Is. 25:4
poor and *n* seek
　water . . . . Is. 41:17
the *n* do they not
　judge . . . . Jer. 5:28

NEHEMIAH
Son of Hachaliah, Neh. 1:1
The cupbearer of Artaxerxes,
　a very trusted position,
　Neh. 1:11; 2:1
Is grieved over the desolation
　of his country, Neh. 1
Is sent by the king to rebuild
　Jerusalem, Neh. 2:1–8
Register of the people whom
　he led from Babylon, Neh. 7
Register of the priests and
　Levites, Neh. 12:1–22
Rebuilds Jerusalem, Neh. 2;
　3; 4; 5; 6
His administration as ruler of
　the people, Neh. 5; 6; 8; 9;
　10; 11; 13
——— Two Jews who returned
　to Jerusalem from exile,
　Ezra 2:2; Neh. 3:16; 7:7

NEIGHBOUR
witness against
　thy *n* . . . . Ex. 20:16
not defraud thy *n* . . Lev. 19:13
shalt thou judge
　thy *n* . . . . Lev. 19:15
thou shalt love
　thy *n* . . . . Lev. 19:18
hath given it
　to a *n* . . . . 1 Sam. 15:28
prophets said
　unto his *n* . . . . . 1 Kin. 20:35
every one with
　his *n* . . . . Ps. 12:2
one against his *n* . . . . . Is. 19:2
his *n*, and trust ye . . . . Jer. 9:4
deceive every one
　his *n* . . . . Jer. 9:5
peaceably to his *n* . . . . Jer. 9:8
man to his *n*,
　Wherefore . . . . Jer. 22:8
more every man
　his *n* . . . . Jer. 31:34
n cities thereof,
　saith . . . . Jer. 49:18
Thou shalt love
　thy *n* . . . . Matt. 19:19
and thy *n* as
　thyself . . . . Luke 10:27
Thou shalt love
　thy *n* . . . . Rom. 13:9
man truth with
　his *n* . . . . Eph. 4:25

NEIGHBOURS
n, and a fear to
　mine . . . . Ps. 31:11

n, a scorn and a
　derision . . . . Ps. 44:13
n, a scorn and
　derision . . . . Ps. 79:4
brethren, and
　his *n* . . . . Jer. 49:10

NET
They have
　prepared a *n* . . . . . . Ps. 57:6
spread a *n* by the
　wayside . . . . Ps. 140:5
My *n* also will I
　spread . . . . Ezek. 12:13
his brother
　with a *n* . . . . Mic. 7:2
brother,
　casting a *n* . . . . . . Matt. 4:18

NIGH
he said, Draw
　not *n* . . . . Ex. 3:5
stranger that
　cometh *n* . . . . Num. 3:10
behold him, but
　not *n* . . . . Num. 24:17
The Lord is *n*
　unto . . . . Ps. 34:18
The Lord is *n*
　unto . . . . Ps. 145:18
cometh, for it is *n* . . . . Joel 2:1
they drew *n* unto
　Jerusalem . . . . Matt. 21:1
Draw *n* to God,
　and . . . . James 4:8

NIGHT
flesh in that *n*,
　roast . . . . Ex. 12:8
land of Egypt
　this *n* . . . . Ex. 12:12
east wind all
　that *n* . . . . Ex. 14:21
abide with thee
　all *n* . . . . Lev. 19:13
out of Egypt by *n* . . Deut. 16:1
shalt fear day
　and *n* . . . . Deut. 28:66
unto the Lord
　all *n* . . . . 1 Sam. 15:11
this house *n* and
　day . . . . 1 Kin. 8:29
men of war fled
　by *n* . . . . 2 Kin. 25:4
daytime, and in
　the *n* . . . . Ps. 42:8
might weep day
　and *n* . . . . Jer. 9:1
run down with
　tears *n* . . . . Jer. 14:17
stars for a light
　by *n* . . . . Jer. 31:35
I saw in the *n*
　visions . . . . Dan. 7:13
Thou fool, this *n*
　thy . . . . Luke 12:20
came to Jesus by *n* . . . John 3:2
angel of the Lord
　by *n* . . . . Acts 5:19
as a thief in the *n* . . 2 Pet. 3:10
no rest day nor *n* . . Rev. 14:11
tormented day
　and *n* . . . . Rev. 20:10

NIGHTS

forty days and
forty n . . . . Ex. 24:18
forty days and
forty n . . . . Ex. 34:28
forty days and
forty n . . . . Deut. 9:9
forty days and
forty n . . . . Deut. 9:18
forty days and
forty n . . . . Matt. 4:2

NINEVEH

Capitol of the Assyrian
Empire, Gen. 10:11, 12
Contained a population of
upwards of one-hundred and
twenty thousand people,
when Jonah preached,
Jon. 4:11
Extent of, Jon. 3:4
Sennacherib in, 2 Kin. 19:36,
37; Is. 37:37, 38
Jonah preaches to, Jon. 1:1,
2; 3
Nahum prophesies against,
Nah. 1; 2; 3
Zephaniah foretells the
desolation of, Zeph. 2:13–15

NINTH

In the n year of
Hoshea . . . . 2 Kin. 17:6
fourth month,
the n . . . . Jer. 39:2
to pass in the n
year . . . . Jer. 52:4
fourth month, in
the n . . . . Jer. 52:6

NOAH

Son of Lamech, Gen. 5:28, 29
Builds an ark (ship) and saves
his family from the great
flood, Gen. 6:14–22; 7; 8;
Matt. 24:38; Luke 17:27;
Heb. 11:7; 1 Pet. 3:20
Builds an altar and offers
sacrifices, Gen. 8:20, 21
Receives the covenant from
God that no flood would
ever again visit the earth; the
rainbow instituted as a token
of the covenant, Gen. 8:20,
22; 9:9–17
Intoxication of, and his curse
upon Canaan, Gen. 9:20–27
His blessing upon Shem and
Japheth, Gen. 9:26, 27
Dies at the age of nine-
hundred and fifty years,
Gen. 9:28, 29
——— A daughter of
Zelophehad, special
legislation in regard to the
inheritance of, Num. 26:33;
27:1–7; 36; Josh. 17:3–7

NOB

A city of the tribe of Benjamin,
Neh. 11:31, 32
Called "the city of the priests,"
1 Sam. 22:19

The home of Ahimelech, the
priest, 1 Sam. 21:1; 22:11
Probable seat of the tabernacle
in Saul's time, 1 Sam. 21:4,
6, 9
Destroyed by Saul,
2 Sam. 22:19
Prophecy concerning, Is. 10:32

NOBLES

brethren, their n . . Neh. 10:29
Make their n like
Oreb . . . . Ps. 83:11
brought down all
their n . . . . Is. 43:14
Babylon slew all
the n . . . . Jer. 39:6

NOISE

skilfully with a
loud n . . . . Ps. 33:3
deep at the n of
thy . . . . Ps. 42:7
Which stilleth
the n . . . . Ps. 65:7
The n of a
multitude . . . . Is. 13:4
who fleeth from
the n . . . . Is. 24:18
my heart
maketh a n . . . . Jer. 4:19
Behold, the n of
the . . . . Jer. 10:22
earth is moved at
the n . . . . Jer. 49:21
shall shake at
the n . . . . Ezek. 26:10
n of thy songs to
cease . . . . Ezek. 26:13
great n, and the
elements . . . . 2 Pet. 3:10

NORTH

east, and to the n . . Gen. 28:14
on the n of the
mountains . . . . . . Josh. 11:2
Chesalon, on
the n . . . . Josh. 15:10
the sides of the n . . . . Ps. 48:2
the sides of the n . . . . . Is. 14:13
say to the n, Give . . . . . Is. 43:6
the n, saith the
LORD. . . . . Jer. 1:15
of the land of
the n . . . . Jer. 3:18
the n, and great
destruction . . . . Jer. 6:1
the n country, to
make . . . . Jer. 10:22
Israel out of the n . . . . Jer. 23:8
the n, saith the
LORD. . . . . Jer. 25:9
the kings of the n . . . Jer. 25:26
n country by the
river . . . . Jer. 46:10
nations from the n . . . Jer. 50:9
looketh toward
the n . . . . Ezek. 8:3
kings, from the n . . Ezek. 26:7
remove toward
the n . . . . Zech. 14:4

NOTWITHSTANDING

N no devoted
thing . . . . Lev. 27:28
N they would not
hear . . . . 2 Kin. 17:14
N the children
rebelled . . . . Ezek. 20:21
N the Lord stood
with . . . . 2 Tim. 4:17

NOUGHT

thou givest him n . . Deut. 15:9
to bring you to n . Deut. 28:63
it shall come to n . . . . . Is. 8:10
sold yourselves
for n . . . . Is. 52:3
divination, and a
thing of n . . . . Jer. 14:14
things, and be set
at n . . . . Mark 9:12
world, that come
to n . . . . 1 Cor. 2:6

NUMBER

a man can n the
dust . . . . Gen. 13:16
if thou be able
to n . . . . Gen. 15:5
and I being few
in n . . . . Gen. 34:30
Israel after their n . . Ex. 30:12
n, from twenty
years . . . . Num. 14:29
shall be left few
in n . . . . Deut. 4:27
because ye were
more in n . . . . Deut. 7:7
shall be left few
in n . . . . Deut. 28:62
camels were
without n . . . . Judg. 7:12
the set feasts, by n
1 Chr. 23:31
and the n of the
workmen. . . . . . . 1 Chr. 25:1
people were
without n . . . . . . 2 Chr. 12:3
The n of the
men of. . . . . Ezra 2:2
marvellous things
without n . . . . Job 5:9
out their host by n . . . Is. 40:26
I n you to the
sword . . . . Is. 65:12
to the n of thy
cities . . . . Jer. 2:28
me days without n . . . Jer. 2:32
a small n that
escape . . . . Jer. 44:28
Yet the n of the
children. . . . . Hos. 1:10

NUMBERED

thy seed also be n . . Gen. 13:16
are n, half a shekel . . Ex. 30:13
be n, from twenty
years . . . . Ex. 38:26
all that were n. . . . Num. 14:29
the priest n . . . . . . Num. 26:64
more than can
be n . . . . Ps. 40:5
he was n with the
transgressors . . . . . . Is. 53:12

heaven cannot
be *n* . . . . Jer. 33:22
be measured nor *n* . . Hos. 1:10

OATH

the *o* which I
sware . . . . Gen. 26:3
o which he had
sworn . . . . Deut. 7:8
an *o*, to walk in
God's . . . . Neh. 10:29
Abraham, and
his *o* . . . . Ps. 105:9
surely mine *o* . . . . Ezek. 17:19
and the *o* that is
written . . . . Dan. 9:11

OBADIAH

The governor of Ahab's house;
Conceals one-hundred
prophets persecuted by
Jezebel in a cave,
1 Kin. 18:3, 4
Meets Elijah and receives
a commission from him,
1 Kin. 18:3–16
———— Head of a family,
1 Chr. 3:21
———— A descendant of Tola,
1 Chr. 7:3
———— Son of Azel, 1 Chr. 8:38;
9:44
———— A Levite, 1 Chr. 9:16
———— A Gadite warrior who
joined David at Ziklag,
1 Chr. 12:9
———— Father of Ishmaiah,
1 Chr. 27:19
———— A prince of Judah who
instructed the people in the
law, 2 Chr. 17:7–9
———— A Levite
One of the overseers in the
repairing of the temple by
Josiah, 2 Chr. 34:12
———— A descendant of Joab
who returned from Babylon,
Ezra 8:9
———— A priest who sealed a
covenant with Nehemiah to
observe God's law, Neh. 10:5
———— A gatekeeper of
Jerusalem, under Nehemiah,
Neh. 12:25
———— A prophet who
prophesied the destruction of
Edom, Obad. 1

OBED

Son of Boaz and grandfather
of David, Ruth 4:17–22;
1 Chr. 2:12; Matt. 1:5;
Luke 3:32
———— Son of Ephlal and
grandson of Zabad,
1 Chr. 2:37, 38
———— One of David's heroes,
1 Chr. 11:47
———— Son of Shemaiah; A
gatekeeper of the temple,
1 Chr. 26:7
———— Father of Azariah,
2 Chr. 23:1

OBED-EDOM

A Korhite Levite; Doorkeeper
of the ark of the covenant,
1 Chr. 15:18, 24; 26:4–8
David leaves the ark of the
covenant with, 2 Sam. 6:10;
1 Chr. 13:13, 14
The ark of the covenant
removed from, 2 Sam. 6:12;
1 Chr. 15:25
Appointed to sound with
harps, 1 Chr. 15:21
Appointed to minister before
the ark of the covenant,
1 Chr. 16:4, 5, 37, 38
———— A doorkeeper of the
temple, 1 Chr. 16:38
———— A conservator of
the vessels of the temple
in the time of Amaziah,
2 Chr. 25:24

OBEY

Lord, that I
should *o* . . . . Ex. 5:2
if ye will *o* my
voice . . . . Ex. 19:5
o his voice, and ye . Deut. 13:4
thou wouldest
not *o* . . . . Deut. 28:62
Behold, to *o* is
better . . . . 1 Sam. 15:22
And refused to *o*,
neither . . . . Neh. 9:17
children of
Ammon shall *o* . . . . Is. 11:14
commanded I
them, saying, O . . . . Jer. 7:23
dominions shall
serve and *o* . . . . . . Dan. 7:27
might not *o* thy
voice . . . . Dan. 9:11
not God, and that
o . . . . 2 Thess. 1:8
O them that have
the . . . . Heb. 13:17

OBEYED

thou hast *o* my
voice . . . . Gen. 22:18
day, and have
not *o* . . . . Jer. 3:25
they *o* not the
voice . . . . Jer. 43:7
for we *o* not his
voice . . . . Dan. 9:14

OBLATION

o of thy meat
offering . . . . Lev. 2:13
every *o* of theirs . . . Num. 18:9
that offereth an *o* . . . . . Is. 66:3
sacrifice and the *o* . . Dan. 9:27

OBSERVE

ye shall *o* the feast . . Ex. 12:17
enchantment,
nor *o* . . . . Lev. 19:26
Ye shall *o* to do
therefore . . . . Deut. 5:32
O the month of
Abib . . . . Deut. 16:1
this day, to *o* . . . . . Deut. 28:13

Lord thy God,
to *o* . . . . Deut. 28:15
If thou wilt not *o* . Deut. 28:58
that thou
mayest *o* . . . . Josh. 1:7
that love him
and *o* . . . . Neh. 1:5
servant of God,
and to *o* . . . . Neh. 10:29
my judgments,
and *o* . . . . Ezek. 37:24
to *o* all things
whatsoever . . . . . Matt. 28:20

OBTAINED

that had not *o*
mercy . . . . Hos. 2:23
o help of God, I
continue . . . . Acts 26:22
also we have *o* an
inheritance . . . . Eph. 1:11
but I *o* mercy,
because . . . . 1 Tim. 1:13
holy place,
having *o* . . . . Heb. 9:12

OFFENCE

and for a rock of *o* . . . . Is. 8:14
conscience void
of *o* . . . . Acts 24:16
stumblingstone
and rock of *o* . . . . . Rom. 9:33
stumbling, and a
rock of *o* . . . . 1 Pet. 2:8

OFFEND

and nothing
shall *o* . . . . Ps. 119:165
adversaries said,
We *o* . . . . Jer. 50:7
yet let not Judah *o* . . Hos. 4:15
thy foot *o* thee,
cut . . . . Matt. 18:8
thy hand *o* thee,
cut . . . . Mark 9:43

OFFER

one lamb thou
shalt *o* . . . . Ex. 29:39
herd, let him *o* a
male . . . . Lev. 1:3
offerings thou
shalt *o* . . . . Lev. 2:13
no more *o* their
sacrifices . . . . Lev. 17:7
that shall ye not *o* . Lev. 22:20
But ye shall *o* an
offering . . . . Lev. 23:8
Seven days ye
shall *o* . . . . Lev. 23:36
of Israel *o* . . . . . . Num. 18:19
fire which ye
shall *o* . . . . Num. 28:3
priest, to *o* upon
mine . . . . 1 Sam. 2:28
O unto God
thanksgiving . . . . . . Ps. 50:14
Sheba and Seba
shall *o* . . . . Ps. 72:10
I will *o* to thee the . Ps. 116:17
when they *o* burnt
offering . . . . Jer. 14:12

OFFERED

my house, when
ye *o* .... Ezek. 44:7
silver, that they
may *o* .... Mal. 3:3
priest, and *o* the
gift .... Matt. 8:4
high priests, to *o* ...Heb. 7:27
let us *o* the
sacrifice ....Heb. 13:15
holy priesthood,
to *o* .... 1 Pet. 2:5

OFFERED

incense thereon,
and *o* .... Lev. 10:1
fifty men that *o*
incense ....Num. 16:35
the LORD shall
be *o* ....Num. 28:15
Giloh, while he *o*
sacrifices ......2 Sam. 15:12
Judah, and he *o*.. 1 Kin. 12:32
if he *o* swine's
blood .... Is. 66:3
incense shall be *o* ...Mal. 1:11
abstain from
meats *o* .... Acts 15:29
those things that
are *o* .... 1 Cor. 8:4
o up prayers and
supplications ......Heb. 5:7
did once, when
he *o* ....Heb. 7:27
without blood,
which he *o* ....Heb. 9:7
the eternal Spirit *o* ..Heb. 9:14
o to bear the sins ...Heb. 9:28
o year by year
continually ....Heb. 10:1
man, after he
had *o* ....Heb. 10:12

OFFERING

blood of the sin *o* ...Ex. 30:10
shekel shall be
the *o* ....Ex. 30:13
head of the
burnt *o* .... Lev. 1:4
remnant of the
meat *o* .... Lev. 2:3
thy meat *o* shalt
thou............. Lev. 2:13
the LORD for a
sin *o*............. Lev. 4:3
altar of the
burnt *o* .. Lev. 4:7
bullock for a sin *o* .. Lev. 4:20
flour for a meat *o* .. Lev. 14:10
ye shall offer an *o*... Lev. 23:8
ye shall offer an *o*.. Lev. 23:36
even an *o* made by
fire .... Lev. 24:7
theirs, every
meat *o* ....Num. 18:9
is the *o* made by
fire ....Num. 28:3
And the drink *o*
thereof...........Num. 28:7
tithes, and the
heave *o* ....Deut. 12:11
make his soul an *o* ...Is. 53:10

name, and a
pure *o* .... Mal. 1:11
the LORD an *o* in
righteousness...... Mal. 3:3
for us an *o* and a
sacrifice.......... Eph. 5:2

OFFERINGS

the *o* of the LORD
made .... Lev. 2:3
all thine *o* thou
shalt.......... Lev. 2:13
sacrifice of peace *o* .. Lev. 4:26
portion of my *o*
made .... Lev. 6:17
the *o* of the LORD
made .... Lev. 24:9
your burnt *o* .....Num. 10:10
heave *o* of the
holy ....Num. 18:19
bring your burnt *o* . Deut. 12:6
burnt *o*, and your
sacrifices ....Deut. 12:11
father all the *o* ... 1 Sam. 2:28
in burnt *o* ...... 1 Sam. 15:22
full of the burnt *o*.....Is. 1:11
burnt *o* and their
sacrifices ....Is. 56:7
burnt *o* are not
acceptable .... Jer. 6:20
to pour out
drink *o*.......... Jer. 7:18
poured out
drink *o*.......... Jer. 19:13
to pour out
drink *o*.......... Jer. 44:17
more than burnt *o* ... Hos. 6:6
sacrifices of
mine *o* .... Hos. 8:13
burnt *o*, with
calves............. Mic. 6:6

OG

King of Bashan; A man of
gigantic stature, Num. 21:33;
Deut. 3:11; Josh. 12:4; 13:12
Defeated and killed by Moses,
Num. 21:33–35; Deut. 1:4;
3:1–7; 29:7; 31:4; Josh. 2:10;
9:10; Ps. 135:10, 11; 136:18–
20
Land of, given to the tribes of
Gad, Reuben, and Manasseh,
Num. 32:33; Deut. 3:8–17;
4:47–49; 29:7, 8; Josh. 12:4–
6; 13:12, 30, 31; 1 Kin. 4:19;
Neh. 9:22; Ps. 136:20, 21

OIL

anointing *o*, and
pour.............. Ex. 29:7
an hin of beaten *o* .. Ex. 29:40
thereof, and of
the *o* .... Lev. 2:2
of the anointing *o*... Lev. 8:30
offering, mingled
with *o* .... Lev. 14:10
an hin of beaten *o* . Num. 28:5
thyself with the *o*. Deut. 28:40
either corn, wine,
or *o* .... Deut. 28:51
of the rock, and *o* Deut. 32:13

Samuel took a vial
of *o*...........1 Sam. 10:1
thine horn with *o* 1 Sam. 16:1
horn of *o*, and
anointed ..... 1 Sam. 16:13
not thyself with *o* 2 Sam. 14:2
anointest my head
with *o* .... Ps. 23:5
anointed thee
with the *o* .... Ps. 45:7
anointed with
fresh *o* .... Ps. 92:10
heart of man,
and *o* .... Ps. 104:15
beauty for ashes,
the *o* ....Is. 61:3
thousands of
rivers of *o* .... Mic. 6:7
anoint thee with *o* .. Mic. 6:15

OLIVES, MOUNT OF

Called Mount of Corruption,
2 Kin. 23:13
East of Jerusalem
The highway to and from
the east passed over it,
2 Sam. 15:30
Jesus' triumphant entry
into Jerusalem by way of,
Matt. 21:1; Mark 11:1;
Luke 19:29, 37
Jesus repairs to, Matt. 24:3;
26:30; Mark 13:3; 14:26;
Luke 21:37; 22:39
Jesus makes his ascension
from, Acts 1:12

OMRI

King of Israel; Was
commander of the army of
Israel, and was proclaimed
king by the army upon news
of the assassination of King
Elah, 1 Kin. 16:16
Defeats his rival, Tibni,
and establishes himself,
1 Kin. 16:17–22
Surrendered cities to king of
Syria, 1 Kin. 20:34
Wicked reign and death of,
1 Kin. 16:23–28
Denounced by Micah,
Mic. 6:16
——— A son of Becher,
grandson of Benjamin,
1 Chr. 7:8
——— A descendant of Pharez,
1 Chr. 9:4
——— Son of Michael, and
ruler of the tribe of Issachar
during the time of David,
1 Chr. 27:18

OPEN

a sword in the *o*
fields ....Num. 19:16
LORD shall *o* unto
thee ....Deut. 28:12
there was no *o*
vision........... 1 Sam. 3:1
thine eyes may
be *o* .... 1 Kin. 8:29

Lord, I pray
  thee, *o* . . . . 2 Kin. 6:17
thee, thine eyes
  be *o* . . . . 2 Chr. 6:40
from on high are *o* . . . Is. 24:18
To *o* the blind eyes . . . . Is. 42:7
loins of kings, to *o* . . . . Is. 45:1
for thine eyes
  are *o* . . . . Jer. 32:19
o thy mouth, and
  eat . . . . Ezek. 2:8
thee, I will *o* thy . . . Ezek. 3:27
appoint captains,
  to *o* . . . . Ezek. 21:22
hosts, if I will
  not *o* . . . . Mal. 3:10
To *o* their eyes,
  and . . . . Acts 26:18
all, with *o* face
  beholding . . . . 2 Cor. 3:18
hath prevailed
  to *o* . . . . Rev. 5:5
to *o* the seals
  thereof . . . . Rev. 5:9

OPENED
windows of
  heaven were *o* . . . . . Gen. 7:11
the Lord *o* the
  eyes . . . . 2 Kin. 6:17
He *o* the rock, and . Ps. 105:41
the blind shall
  be *o* . . . . Is. 35:5
afflicted, yet he *o* . . . . . Is. 53:7
unto thee have I *o* . . Jer. 20:12
thine enemies
  have *o* . . . . Lam. 2:16
shall thy mouth
  be *o* . . . . Ezek. 24:27
and the books
  were *o* . . . . Dan. 7:10
I *o* my mouth, and
  spake . . . . Dan. 10:16
the heavens
  were *o* . . . . Matt. 3:16
the Lord by
  night *o* . . . . Acts 5:19
Then Peter *o* his
  mouth . . . . Acts 10:34
had *o* the door of
  faith . . . . Acts 14:27
things are naked
  and *o* . . . . Heb. 4:13
o the fifth seal, I . . . . . Rev. 6:9
had *o* the sixth
  seal . . . . Rev. 6:12
temple of God
  was *o* . . . . Rev. 11:19
And I saw
  heaven *o* . . . . Rev. 19:11
and the books
  were *o* . . . . Rev. 20:12

OPENETH
firstborn,
  whatsoever *o* . . . . . . Ex. 13:2
the Lord all
  that *o* . . . . Ex. 13:12
thing that *o* the
  matrix . . . . Num. 18:15
he *o* the ears of
  men . . . . Job 33:16

shearers is dumb,
  so he *o* . . . . Is. 53:7
o, and no man
  shutteth . . . . Rev. 3:7

OPHIR
Son of Joktan, Gen. 10:29;
  1 Chr. 1:23
———— A country celebrated for
  its gold and other valuable
  merchandise
Products of, used by Solomon
  and Hiram, 1 Kin. 9:28;
  10:11; 2 Chr. 8:18; 9:10
Jehoshaphat sends ships to,
  which are wrecked at sea,
  1 Kin. 22:48
Gold of, proverbial for its
  fineness, 1 Chr. 29:4;
  Job 22:24; 28:16; Ps. 45:9;
  Is. 13:12

OPHRAH
A city in territory of the tribe
  of Benjamin, Josh. 18:23;
  1 Sam. 13:17
Possibly identical with
  Ephrain, 2 Chr. 13:19
And Ephraim, John 11:54
———— A city in territory of the
  tribe of Manasseh; the home
  of Gideon, Judg. 6:11, 24;
  8:27, 32; 9:5
———— Son of Meonothai,
  1 Chr. 4:14

OPPRESS
vex a stranger,
  nor *o* . . . . Ex. 22:21
feed them that *o*
  thee . . . . Is. 49:26
If ye *o* not the
  stranger . . . . Jer. 7:6
And *o* not the
  widow . . . . Zech. 7:10
those that *o* the
  hireling . . . . Mal. 3:5

OPPRESSED
thou shalt be
  only *o* . . . . Deut. 28:29
thou shalt be
  only *o* . . . . Deut. 28:33
o, a refuge in times . . . Ps. 9:9
judgment, relieve
  the *o* . . . . Is. 1:17
rejoice, O thou *o*
  virgin . . . . Is. 23:12
was *o*, and he was
  afflicted . . . . Is. 53:7
o any, but hath
  restored . . . . Ezek. 18:7
hath *o* any, hath
  not . . . . Ezek. 18:16
healing all that
  were *o* . . . . Acts 10:38

OPPRESSION
For the *o* of the
  poor . . . . Ps. 12:5
If thou seest the *o* . . . Eccl. 5:8
judgment, but
  behold *o* . . . . Is. 5:7

innocent blood,
  and for *o* . . . . Jer. 22:17

ORDAINED
was *o* in mount
  Sinai . . . . Num. 28:6
And Jeroboam *o* a
  feast . . . . 1 Kin. 12:32
kings of Judah
  had *o* . . . . 2 Kin. 23:5
And he *o* him
  priests . . . . 2 Chr. 11:15
For Tophet is *o* of . . . . Is. 30:33
sanctified thee,
  and I *o* . . . . Jer. 1:5
have chosen you,
  and *o* . . . . John 15:16
one be *o* to be a
  witness . . . . Acts 1:22
he which was *o* of
  God . . . . Acts 10:42
they had *o* them
  elders . . . . Acts 14:23
and it was *o* by
  angels . . . . Gal. 3:19
which God hath
  before *o* . . . . Eph. 2:10

ORDER
and his sons
  shall *o* . . . . Ex. 27:21
o before the Lord
  continually . . . . . . Lev. 24:8
his household
  in *o* . . . . 2 Sam. 17:23
to the *o* of the
  king . . . . 1 Chr. 25:2
the king's *o* to
  Asaph . . . . 1 Chr. 25:6
o of David his
  father . . . . 2 Chr. 8:14
o upon the pure
  table . . . . 2 Chr. 13:11
be reckoned up
  in *o* . . . . Ps. 40:5
after the *o* of
  Melchizedek . . . . . . Ps. 110:4
upon his
  kingdom, to *o* . . . . . . Is. 9:7
after the *o* of
  Melchisedec . . . . . . Heb. 5:6
after the *o* of
  Melchisedec . . . . . . Heb. 6:20

ORDINANCE
it a feast by an *o* . . . . Ex. 12:14
generations by
  an *o* . . . . Ex. 12:17
a statute and an *o* . . . Ex. 15:25
to thy sons, by
  an *o* . . . . Num. 18:8
we have kept his *o* . . Mal. 3:14

ORDINANCES
light by day, and
  the *o* . . . . Jer. 31:35
o of heaven and
  earth . . . . Jer. 33:25
statutes, and keep
  mine *o* . . . . Ezek. 11:20
and *o* of the Lord
  blameless . . . . Luke 1:6

commandments
contained in *o*..... Eph. 2:15

OTHNIEL
Son of Kenaz and nephew of
Caleb; Conquers Kirjath-
sepher, and as reward obtains
Caleb's daughter as a wife,
Josh. 15:16–20;
Judg. 1:12, 13
Becomes the deliverer and
leader of Israel, Judg. 3:8–11
Death of, Judg. 3:11
Descendants of,
1 Chr. 4:13, 14

OVERCOMETH
o will I give to eat.... Rev. 2:7
o will I give to eat... Rev. 2:17
He that *o*, the
same .... Rev. 3:5
o will I grant to sit .. Rev. 3:21
He that *o* shall
inherit *o* .... Rev. 21:7

OVERFLOW
where the floods *o* ... Ps. 69:2
he shall *o* and go
over .... Is. 8:8
consumption
decreed shall *o* .....Is. 10:22
rivers, they shall
not *o* ....Is. 43:2
countries, and
shall *o* ....Dan. 11:40
is full, the fats *o* .... Joel 3:13

OVERTAKE
pursue, I will *o*, I .... Ex. 15:9
upon thee, and *o*
thee ....Deut. 28:15
thee, and *o* thee,
till ....Deut. 28:45
neither doth
justice *o* ....Is. 59:9
the plowman
shall *o* ....Amos 9:13

OVERTHREW
And he *o* those
cities ....Gen. 19:25
Zeboim, which
the LORD *o* .....Deut. 29:23
God *o* Sodom and
Gomorrah ....Is. 13:19
God *o* Sodom and
Gomorrah ......Amos 4:11

OVERTHROW
thou shalt
utterly *o* ....Ex. 23:24
ye shall *o* their
altars ....Deut. 12:3
o of Sodom, and
Gomorrah ....Deut. 29:23
to *o* them in the
wilderness ......Ps. 106:26
o of Sodom and
Gomorrah ....Jer. 49:18
o, making them an
ensample.........2 Pet. 2:6

OX
o, for ass, for
sheep ....Ex. 22:9

thine *o* and thine
ass .... Ex. 23:12
Thine *o* shall be
slain...........Deut. 28:31
infant and
suckling, *o*...... 1 Sam. 15:3
The *o* knoweth his
owner ....Is. 1:3
He that killeth
an *o* ....Is. 66:3

PAIN
p as a woman that
travaileth...........Is. 13:8
loins filled with *p* .....Is. 21:3
much *p* is in all
loins ....Nah. 2:10
there be any
more *p*........... Rev. 21:4

PALACES
burnt all the *p*
thereof........ 2 Chr. 36:19
in their pleasant *p* ...Is. 13:22
p, nettles and
brambles..........Is. 34:13
p, to cut off the
children...........Jer. 9:21
devour the *p* of
Jerusalem ....Jer. 17:27
devour the *p* of
Benhadad ....Amos 1:4
devour the *p* of
Bozrah..........Amos 1:12
devour the *p*
thereof.........Amos 1:14
Jacob, and hate
his *p*.............Amos 6:8

PALM
trees, branches
of *p*............ Lev. 23:40
of the city of *p*
trees .... Judg. 1:16
upright as the *p*
tree ....Jer. 10:5
each post were *p*
trees .... Ezek. 40:16

PAMPHYLIA
A province in Asia Minor; Men
of, in Jerusalem, Acts 2:10
Paul goes to, Acts 13:13, 14;
14:24
John, surnamed "Mark," in,
Acts 13:13; 15:38
Sea of, Acts 27:5

PARAN
Desert or wilderness of,
Gen. 21:21; Num. 10:12;
12:16; 13:3, 26; Deut. 1:1
Mountains of, Deut. 33:2;
Hab. 3:3
Israelites encamp in,
Num. 12:16
David takes refuge in,
1 Sam. 25:1
Hadad flees to,
1 Kin. 11:17, 18

PART
mingled with the
fourth *p*.........Ex. 29:40

shalt thou have
any *p*.........Num. 18:20
a tenth *p* of an
ephah ....Num. 28:5
fourth *p* of an hin..Num. 28:7
forasmuch as he
hath no *p*.......Deut. 12:12
he hath no *p* nor
inheritance ....Deut. 14:29
Jephunneh he
gave a *p* .... Josh. 15:13
ought but death *p*
thee .... Ruth 1:17
with fire a third *p*... Ezek. 5:2
p of thee shall die.. Ezek. 5:12
into his hand,
with *p* ....Dan. 1:2
will bring the
third *p* ...... Zech. 13:9
unto the
uttermost *p*....... Acts 1:8
perceived that the
one *p* .... Acts 23:6
blindness in *p* is
happened ..... Rom. 11:25
now I know in *p* . 1 Cor. 13:12
himself likewise
took *p* ....Heb. 2:14
p of trees was
burnt .... Rev. 8:7
earthquake, and
the tenth *p* ...... Rev. 11:13
their *p* in the lake... Rev. 21:8

PARTAKERS
be *p* of this power .1 Cor. 9:12
gospel, ye all are *p* ... Phil. 1:7
children are *p* of
flesh.............Heb. 2:14
Wherefore, holy
brethren, *p* ....Heb. 3:1
gift, and were
made *p*...........Heb. 6:4
people, that ye be
not *p* .... Rev. 18:4

PARTS
and the
uttermost *p*....... Ps. 2:8
Moab, and mine
inward *p* ....Is. 16:11
shout, ye lower
p of............Is. 44:23
inward *p*, and
write ....Jer. 31:33
set thee in the
low *p* ....Ezek. 26:20
comforted in the
nether *p* ...... Ezek. 31:16
cut off for our *p* .. Ezek. 37:11
divided into
three *p* .... Rev. 16:19

PASHUR
A priest, son of Malchiah,
1 Chr. 9:12
An influential man and
ancestor of an influential
family, Ezra 2:38; 10:22;
Neh. 7:41; 10:3; 11:12;
Jer. 21:1; 38:1
——— Son of Immer and
governor of the temple

Beats and imprisons Jeremiah,
Jer. 20:1–6
——— Father of Gedaliah, who
persecuted Jeremiah, Jer. 38:1

PASS
For I will *p*
through . . . . Ex. 12:12
till thy people *p*
over . . . . Ex. 15:16
to *p* on the third
day . . . . Ex. 19:16
let any of thy
seed *p* . . . . Lev. 18:21
suffer Israel to *p* . . Num. 21:23
to *p*, if thou wilt . . Deut. 28:15
to *p*, that as the
LORD . . . . Deut. 28:63
And it came to *p*,
as . . . . 1 Kin. 16:31
their daughters
to *p* . . . . 2 Kin. 17:17
or his daughter
to *p* . . . . 2 Kin. 23:10
to *p* in the last days . . . . Is. 2:2
shall *p* through
Judah . . . . Is. 8:8
come to *p* in that
day . . . . Is. 11:11
come to *p* in that
day . . . . Is. 27:13
p, that like as I
have . . . . Jer. 31:28
p by clap their
hands. . . . . Lam. 2:15
dominion, which
shall not *p* . . . . Dan. 7:14
p afterward, that I . . Joel 2:28
shall no
strangers *p* . . . . . . Joel 3:17
possible, let this
cup *p* . . . . Matt. 26:39

PASSED
p by Midianites
merchantmen . . . . Gen. 37:28
And the LORD *p*
by before . . . . Ex. 34:6
and the people *p*
over . . . . Josh. 3:16
p over on dry
ground. . . . . Josh. 3:17
unto mount Seir,
and *p* . . . . Josh. 15:10
he *p* away, and, lo . . . Ps. 37:36
I *p* by thee, and
looked . . . . Ezek. 16:8
man *p* through
nor returned . . . . . Zech. 7:14
p from death unto
life . . . . John 5:24
the church, they *p* . . Acts 15:3
spirit, when he
had *p* . . . . Acts 19:21
death *p* upon all
men . . . . Rom. 5:12
old things are *p*
away . . . . 2 Cor. 5:17
high priest, that
is *p* . . . . Heb. 4:14
first earth were *p* . . . Rev. 21:1

former things
are *p* . . . . Rev. 21:4

PASSETH
give, every one
that *p* . . . . Ex. 30:13
high, every one
that *p* . . . . 1 Kin. 9:8
as a shadow that *p* . . Ps. 144:4
every one that *p*
thereby . . . . Jer. 18:16
every one that *p*
thereby . . . . Jer. 19:8
the early dew
that *p* . . . . Hos. 13:3
pardoneth
iniquity, and *p* . . . . Mic. 7:18
p by her shall hiss . Zeph. 2:15

PASSOVER
it is the LORD's *p* . . . Ex. 12:11
keep the *p* to the
LORD. . . . . Ex. 12:48
even is the
LORD's *p* . . . . Lev. 23:5
forbeareth to keep
the *p* . . . . Num. 9:13
first month is
the *p* . . . . Num. 28:16
p unto the LORD
thy . . . . Deut. 16:1
p unto the LORD
thy . . . . Deut. 16:2
Gilgal, and kept
the *p* . . . . Josh. 5:10
the *p*, when Jesus
knew . . . . John 13:1
preparation of
the *p* . . . . John 19:14

PAST
judgments, and
his ways *p* . . . . . . Rom. 11:33
told you in time *p* . . Gal. 5:21
in time *p* ye
walked. . . . . Eph. 2:2
conversation in
times *p* . . . . Eph. 2:3

PASTURE
the sheep of thy *p* . . . Ps. 74:1
the people of his *p* . . . Ps. 95:7
the sheep of his *p* . . . Ps. 100:3
p, so were they
filled . . . . Hos. 13:6

PATHS
the *p* of all that
forget. . . . . Job 8:13
set darkness in
my *p* . . . . Job 19:8
will walk in his *p* . . . . . Is. 2:3
destruction are in
their *p* . . . . Is. 59:7
p, where is the
good . . . . Jer. 6:16
will walk in his *p* . . . . Mic. 4:2

PATIENCE
labour of love,
and *p* . . . . 1 Thess. 1:3
ye have need of *p* . . Heb. 10:36
kingdom and *p* of
Jesus . . . . Rev. 1:9

the word of my
p, I . . . . Rev. 3:10

PAUL
Also called Saul, Acts 8:1; 9:1;
13:9
From the tribe of Benjamin,
Rom. 11:1; Phil. 3:5
Personal appearance of,
2 Cor. 10:1, 10; 11:6
Born in the city of Tarsus,
Acts 9:11; 21:39; 22:3
Educated at Jerusalem in the
school of Gamaliel, Acts 22:3;
26:4
A zealous Pharisee, Acts 22:3;
23:6; 26:5; 2 Cor. 11:22;
Gal. 1:14; Phil. 3:5
A Roman citizen, Acts 16:37;
22:25–28
Persecutes the Christians;
present at, and gives consent
to, the stoning of Stephen,
Acts 7:58; 8:1, 3; 9:1; 22:4
Sent to Damascus with letters
for the arrest and return
to Jerusalem of Christians,
Acts 9:1, 2
His vision and conversion,
Acts 9:3–22; 22:4–19;
26:9–15; 1 Cor. 9:1; 15:8;
Gal. 1:13; 1 Tim. 1:12, 13
Is immersed, Acts 9:18; 22:16
Called to be an apostle,
Acts 22:14–21; 26:16–18;
Rom. 1:1; 1 Cor. 1:1; 9:1,
2; 15:9; Gal. 1:1, 15, 16;
Eph. 1:1; Col. 1:1; 1 Tim. 1:1;
2:7; 2 Tim. 1:1, 11;
Titus 1:1, 3
Preaches in Damascus for the
first time, Acts 9:20, 22
Is persecuted by the Jews,
Acts 9:23, 24
Escapes by being let down
from the wall in a basket;
goes to Jerusalem, Acts 9:25,
26; Gal. 1:18, 19
Received by the disciples in
Jerusalem, Acts 9:26–29
Goes to Caesarea, Acts 9:30;
18:22
Sent to the Gentiles,
Acts 13:2, 3, 47, 48;
22:17–21; Rom. 11:13;
15:16; Gal. 1:15–24
Has Barnabas as his
companion, Acts 11:25, 26
Teaches at Antioch (in Syria)
for one year, Acts 11:26
Conveys the contributions of
the Christians in Antioch to
the Christians in Jerusalem,
Acts 11:27–30
Returns with the apostle
John to Antioch (of Syria),
Acts 12:25
Visits Seleucia, Acts 13:4
Visits much of the island of
Cyprus, Acts 13:4
Preaches at Salamis, Acts 13:5
Preaches at Paphos, Acts 13:6

Sergius Paulus, governor of the country, is a convert of, Acts 13:7–12

Contends with Elymas (Bar-Jesus) the sorcerer, Acts 13:6–12

Visits Perga in Pamphylia, Acts 13:13

John (Mark), a companion of, departs for Jerusalem, Acts 13:13

Visits Antioch (in Pisidia), and preaches in the synagogue, Acts 13:14–41

His message received gladly by the Gentiles, Acts 13:42, 49

Persecuted and expelled, Acts 13:50, 51

Visits Iconium, and preaches to the Jews and non-Jews; is persecuted; escapes to Lystra; goes to Derbe, Acts 14:1–6

Heals an immobile man, Acts 14:8–10

The people attempt to worship him, Acts 14:11–18

Is persecuted by certain Jews from Antioch and Iconium, and is stoned, Acts 14:19; 2 Cor. 11:25; 2 Tim. 3:11

Escapes to Derbe, where he preaches the gospel, and returns to Lystra, and to Iconium, and to Antioch, strengthens the souls of the disciples, exhorts them to continue in the faith, and helps to appoint elders, Acts 14:19–23

Re-visits Pisidia, Pamphylia, Perga, Attalia, and Antioch, in Syria, where he lived, Acts 14:24–28

Contends with the Judaizers against their circumcision "theology," Acts 15:1, 2

Refers the question of circumcision to the apostles and elders at Jerusalem, Acts 15:2, 4

He declares to the apostles at Jerusalem the miracles and wonders God had performed among the Gentiles by them, Acts 15:12

Returns to Antioch, accompanied by Barnabas, Judas, and Silas, with letters to the Gentiles, Acts 15:22, 25

Makes his second tour of the congregations, Acts 15:36

Chooses Silas as his companion, and passes through Syria and Cilicia, strengthening the congregations, Acts 15:36–41

Visits Lystra; circumcises Timothy, Acts 16:1–5

Goes through Phrygia and Galatia; is forbidden by the

Holy Spirit to preach in Asia; visits Mysia; attempts to go to Bithynia, but is restrained by the Spirit, Acts 16:6, 7

Goes to Troas, where he has a vision of a man saying, "Come over into Macedonia, and help us;" immediately proceeds to Macedonia, Acts 16:8–10

Visits Samothracia and Neapolis; comes to Philippi, the chief city of Macedonia; visits a place of prayer at the side of the river; preaches the word; the merchant, Lydia, from Thyatira, is converted and immersed, Acts 16:11–15

Reproves the soothsayer; causes the evil spirit to come out of the girl who practises divination, Acts 16:16–18

Persecuted, beaten, and cast into prison with Silas; sings songs of praise in the prison; an earthquake shakes the prison; he preaches to the alarmed jailer, who believes, and is immersed along with his household, Acts 16:19–34

Is released by the civil authorities on the grounds of his being a Roman citizen, Acts 16:35–39; 2 Cor. 6:5; 11:25; 1 Thess. 2:2

Is welcomed at the household of Lydia, Acts 16:40

Visits Amphipolis, Apollonia, and Thessalonica; preaches in the synagogue, Acts 17:1–4

Is persecuted, Acts 17:5–9; 2 Thess. 1:1–4

Escapes to Berea by night; preaches in the synagogue; many honorable women and several men believe, Acts 17:10–12

Persecuted by the Jews who come from Thessalonica; is escorted by some of the brethren to Athens, Acts 17:13–15

Debates on Mars' Hill (at the meeting of the Areopagus Council) with Greeks, Acts 17:16–34

Visits Corinth; lives with Aquila and his wife, Priscilla (Prisca), who were tentmakers; joins in their trade, Acts 18:1–3

Reasons in the synagogue every Sabbath; is rejected by the Jews; turns to the Gentiles; makes his home with Justus; continues there for eighteen months, teaching the word of God, Acts 18:4–11

Persecuted by Jews, drawn before the deputy, charged

with wicked lewdness; accusation dismissed; takes his leave after many days, and sails to Syria, accompanied by Aquila and Priscilla, Acts 18:12–18

Visits Ephesus, where he leaves Aquila and Priscilla; enters into a synagogue, where he reasons with the Jews; starts on his return trip to Jerusalem; visits Caesarea; crosses over the country of Galatia and Phrygia, strengthening the disciples, Acts 18:18–23

Returns to Ephesus; immerses in the name of the Lord Jesus, and lays his hands upon the disciples, who are baptized with the Holy Spirit; preaches in the synagogue; remains in Ephesus for two years; heals the sick people, Acts 19:12

Rebukes the exorcists; casts an evil spirit out of a man, and many believe, bringing their evil books of sorcery to be burned, Acts 19:13–20; 1 Cor. 16:8, 9

Sends Timothy and Erastus into Macedonia, but he himself remains in Asia for a period of time, Acts 19:21, 22

The spread of the gospel through his preaching interferes with the makers of idols; he is persecuted, and a great uproar of the city is created; the town clerk appeases the people; dismisses the accusation against Paul, and disperses the people, Acts 19:23–41; 2 Cor. 1:8; 2 Tim. 4:14

Proceeds to Macedonia after strengthening the congregations in that region; comes into Greece and lives for three months; returns through Macedonia, accompanied by Sopater, Aristarchus, Secundus, Gaius, Timothy, Tychicus, and Trophimus, Acts 20:1–6

Visits Troas; preaches until daybreak; restores to life the young man (Eutychus) who fell from the window, Acts 20:6–12

Visits Assos, Mitylene, Chios, Samos, Trogyllium, and Miletus, hastening to Jerusalem, to be there by Pentecost day, Acts 20:13–16

Sends for the elders of the congregation of Ephesus; relates to them how he had preached in Asia and his temptations and afflictions,

urging repentance toward
God, Acts 20:17–21

Declares he was going bound
in spirit to Jerusalem;
exhorts them to take heed to
themselves and the flock over
whom the Holy Spirit had
made them overseers; kneels
down, prays, and leaves,
Acts 20:22–38

Visits Coos, Rhodes, and
Patara; boards a ship bound
for Tyre, Acts 21:1–3

Waits at Tyre for seven days;
is brought on his way by the
disciples to the outskirts of
the city; kneels down and
prays; boards the ship; comes
to Ptolemais; greets the
brethren, and stays for one
day, Acts 21:4–7

Departs for Caesarea; enters
the house of Philip the
evangelist; is admonished by
the prophet Agabus not to go
to Jerusalem; nevertheless,
he proceeds to Jerusalem,
Acts 21:8–15

Is received by the brethren
gladly; talks about the things
that had been done among
the Gentiles through his
ministry, Acts 21:17–25

Enters the temple courtyard;
the people are stirred up
against him by some Jews
from Asia; an uproar is
created; he is thrust out
of the temple area; the
commander of the Roman
garrison intervenes and
arrests him, Acts 21:26–33

His defense, Acts 21:33–40;
22:1–21

Is confined in the fortress,
Acts 22:24–30

Is brought before the
Sanhedrin; his defense,
Acts 22:30; 23:1–5

Is returned to the fortress,
Acts 23:10

Is encouraged by a vision from
God, promising him that he
will give testimony in Rome,
Acts 23:11

Jewish leaders conspire against
his life, Acts 23:12–15

This plan is thwarted by his
nephew, Acts 23:16–22

Is escorted to Caesarea by a
military guard, Acts 23:23–33

Is confined in Herod's
Judgment Hall in Caesarea,
Acts 23:35

His trial before Governor
Felix, Acts 24

Remains in custody for two
years, Acts 24:27

His trial before Governor
Festus, Acts 25:1–12

Appeals to be heard by Caesar,
Acts 25:10–12

His examination before Herod
Agrippa II, Acts 25:13–27; 26

Is taken to Rome in the
custody of Julius, a centurion,
and a detachment of soldiers;
boards a ship, accompanied
by other prisoners, and sails
by way of the coasts of Asia;
stops at Sidon, and at Myra,
Acts 27:1–5

Transferred to a ship of
Alexandria; sails by way of
Cnidus, Crete, Salamis, and
the Fair Havens, Acts 27:6–8

Predicts misfortune to the
ship; his counsel not heeded,
and the voyage resumes,
Acts 27:9–13

The ship encounters a storm;
Paul encourages and comforts
the officers and crew; the
soldiers advise putting the
prisoners to death; the
centurion interferes, and
all on board (consisting of
two-hundred and seventy-six
persons) survive,
Acts 27:14–44

The ship is wrecked, and all
on board take refuge on the
island of Melita (Malta),
Acts 27:14–44

Kind treatment by the
inhabitants of the island,
Acts 28:1, 2

Is bitten by a viper and
miraculously unharmed,
Acts 28:3–6

Heals the ruler's father and
others, Acts 28:7–10

Is delayed in Melita (Malta)
for three months; proceeds
on the voyage; delays at
Syracuse; sails by Rhegium
and Puteoli, Acts 28:11–13

Meets some brethren who
accompany him to Rome
from Appii Forum; arrives
at Rome; is delivered to
the captain of the guard; is
permitted to live by himself
in custody of a soldier,
Acts 28:14–16

Summons the local Jewish
leadership; states his
position; is kindly received;
expounds the gospel; testifies
to the kingdom of heaven,
Acts 28:17–29

Lives in his own rented house
for two years, preaching and
teaching, Acts 28:30, 31

Supports himself, Acts 18:3;
20:33–35

Sickness of, in Asia,
2 Cor. 1:8–11

His resolute determination

to go to Jerusalem despite
repeated warnings,
Acts 20:22, 23; 21:4, 10–14

Caught up to the third heaven,
2 Cor. 12:1–4

Has "a thorn in the flesh,"
2 Cor. 12:7–9; Gal. 4:13, 14

His independence of character,
1 Thess. 2:9; 2 Thess. 3:8

Persecutions of, 1 Thess. 2:2;
Heb. 10:34

Persecutions endured by,
Acts 9:16, 23–25, 29; 16:19–
25; 20:22–24; 21:13, 27–33;
22:22–24; 23:10, 12–15;
Rom. 8:35–37; 1 Cor. 4:9,
11–13; 2 Cor. 1:8–10; 4:8–12;
6:4, 5, 8–10; 11:23–27,
32, 33; 12:10; Gal. 5:11;
6:17; Phil. 1:30; 2:17, 18;
Col. 1:24; 1 Thess. 2:2, 14,
15; 3:4; 2 Tim. 1:12; 2:9, 10;
3:11, 12; 4:16, 17

PAY

I will *p* my vows
before . . . . Ps. 22:25
and *p* thy vows
unto . . . . Ps. 50:14
hath given will
he *p* . . . . Prov. 19:17
God, defer not
to *p* . . . . Eccl. 5:4

PEACE

to thy fathers in *p* . Gen. 15:15
Solomon, and I
will give *p* . . . . . . 1 Chr. 22:9
hold not thy *p*
at my . . . . Ps. 39:12
Father, The Prince
of *P* . . . . Is. 9:6
his government
and *p* . . . . Is. 9:7
chastisement of
our *p* . . . . Is. 53:5
I cannot hold
my *p* . . . . Jer. 4:19
But Jesus held
his *p* . . . . Matt. 26:63
go in *p*, and be
whole . . . . Mark 5:34
go in *p* . . . . Luke 7:50
P I leave with you . John 14:27
unto them, *P* . . . . . . John 20:19
held their *p*, and
glorified . . . . Acts 11:18
p from God our
Father . . . . Rom. 1:7
God of *p* shall
bruise . . . . Rom. 16:20
shall say, *P* and
safety . . . . 1 Thess. 5:3
Follow *p* with all
men . . . . Heb. 12:14
God of *p*, that
brought . . . . Heb. 13:20
Grace unto you,
and *p* . . . . 1 Pet. 1:2
be unto you,
and *p* . . . . Rev. 1:4

PEKAH

Son of Remaliah; Captain
of the army of Israel,
2 Kin. 15:25

Conspires against and
assassinates King Pekahiah,
2 Kin. 15:25

Is made king of Israel,
2 Kin. 15:27

Victorious in war with Judah,
2 Chr. 28:5, 6

Is plotted against and killed by
Hoshea, 2 Kin. 15:30, 31

Prophecies against, Is. 7:1–16;
8:4–10

PENUEL

Also called Peniel; City built
where Jacob wrestled with
the angel, Gen. 32:31;
Judg. 8:8, 9, 17; 1 Kin. 12:25

——— Chief of Gedor,
1 Chr. 4:4

——— A Benjamite, 1 Chr. 8:25

PEOPLE

gathering of the p . . Gen. 49:10
And the p
believed . . . . Ex. 4:31
unto me above
all p . . . . Ex. 19:5
thy p, but thou
shalt . . . . Lev. 19:18
thou art an holy p . . Deut. 7:6
scatter thee
among all p . . . . . Deut. 28:64
arose against
his p . . . . 2 Chr. 36:16
p, and he hath
stretched . . . . Is. 5:25
heart of this p fat . . . . . Is. 6:10
the remnant of
his p . . . . Is. 11:11
transgression of
my p . . . . Is. 53:8
of prayer for all p . . . . . Is. 56:7
they shall be my p . . Jer. 31:33
be left to other p . . . Dan. 2:44
determined upon
thy p . . . . Dan. 9:24
will say, It is my p . Zech. 13:9
he shall save his p . Matt. 1:21
disease among
the p . . . . Matt. 4:23
a peculiar p,
zealous . . . . Titus 2:14
nation, a
peculiar p . . . . 1 Pet. 2:9

PERCEIVE

Wherefore I p that . . Eccl. 3:22
see ye indeed,
but p . . . . Is. 6:9
may see, and
not p . . . . Mark 4:12
a truth I p that
God . . . . Acts 10:34

PERFECT

me, and be thou p . . Gen. 17:1
Rock, his work
is p . . . . Deut. 32:4

truth and with
a p . . . . 2 Kin. 20:3
serve him with
a p . . . . 1 Chr. 28:9
them whose heart
is p . . . . 2 Chr. 16:9
man was p and
upright . . . . Job 1:1
law of the Lord
is p . . . . Ps. 19:7
more unto the p
day . . . . Prov. 4:18
Be ye therefore p . . Matt. 5:48
p manner of the
law . . . . Acts 22:3
acceptable, and p . . Rom. 12:2
among them that
are p . . . . 1 Cor. 2:6
man p in Christ
Jesus . . . . Col. 1:28
that ye may
stand p . . . . Col. 4:12
of their
salvation p . . . . Heb. 2:10
p tabernacle, not
made . . . . Heb. 9:11
comers
thereunto p . . . . . . Heb. 10:1
good gift and
every p . . . . James 1:17
into the p law of
liberty . . . . James 1:25
make you p,
stablish . . . . 1 Pet. 5:10

PERFORM

countries, and I
will p . . . . Gen. 26:3
soul, to p the
words . . . . 2 Kin. 23:3
soul, to p the
words . . . . 2 Chr. 34:31
Lord of hosts
will p . . . . Is. 9:7
shepherd, and
shall p . . . . Is. 44:28
and p my good
word . . . . Jer. 29:10

PERISH

shall soon
utterly p . . . . Deut. 4:26
A Syrian ready
to p . . . . Deut. 26:5
destroyed, and
until thou p . . . . . Deut. 28:20
thee until thou p . Deut. 28:22
your eyes, until
ye p . . . . Josh. 23:13
to p, all the power . Esth. 8:11
be angry, and ye p . . . Ps. 2:12
they p at the
rebuke . . . . Ps. 80:16
p, but thou shalt
endure . . . . Ps. 102:26
ready to p in the
land . . . . Is. 27:13
serve thee shall p . . . . Is. 60:12
visitation they
shall p . . . . Jer. 10:15
the law shall not p . . Jer. 18:18
out, and ye
should p . . . . Jer. 27:10

p, saith the Lord
God . . . . Amos 1:8
fierce anger, that
we p . . . . Jon. 3:9
not p, but have
eternal . . . . John 3:15
not p, but have
everlasting . . . . . John 3:16
cross is to them
that p . . . . 1 Cor. 1:18
that any should p . . 2 Pet. 3:9

PERISHED

Heshbon is p even
unto . . . . Num. 21:30
Which p at Endor . . . Ps. 83:10
hath gotten are p . . Jer. 48:36
is counsel p from
the . . . . Jer. 49:7
of the field is p . . . . Joel 1:11
The good man is p
out . . . . Mic. 7:2
Balaam for
reward, and p . . . . . Jude 11

PERIZZITES

One of the seven nations in
the land of Canaan, Gen. 13:7

Territory of, given to Abraham,
Gen. 15:20; Ex. 3:8; 23:23

Doomed to destruction,
Deut. 20:17

Not all destroyed; Israelites
intermarry with, Judg. 3:5–7;
Ezra 9:1, 2

PERPETUAL

be theirs for a p
statute . . . . Ex. 29:9
incense upon
it, a p . . . . Ex. 30:8
It shall be a p
statute . . . . Lev. 3:17
made by fire
by a p . . . . Lev. 24:9
bound of the sea
by a p . . . . Jer. 5:22
land desolate,
and a p . . . . Jer. 18:16
an hissing, and p
desolations . . . . . . Jer. 25:9
will make it p
desolations . . . . . Jer. 25:12
thereof shall be p . . Jer. 49:13
the Lord in a p
covenant . . . . Jer. 50:5
shall sleep a p
sleep . . . . Jer. 51:57
saltpits, and a p
desolation . . . . . . Zeph. 2:9

PERSECUTE

And I will p them
with . . . . Jer. 29:18
despitefully use
you, and p . . . . . . Matt. 5:44
p you in this city . Matt. 10:23
me, they will
also p . . . . John 15:20

PERSON

p shall eat thereof . . Ex. 12:48
shalt not respect
the p . . . . Lev. 19:15
shall not regard
the p . . . . Deut. 28:50

p, perceived the
grace . . . . Gal. 2:9
sun, and his feet
as *p* . . . . Rev. 10:1

PISGAH
A ridge or mountain east of
the Jordan River, opposite to
Jericho; The Israelites come
to, Num. 21:20
A boundary of the country
assigned to the Reubenites
and Gadites, Deut. 3:17;
4:49; Josh. 12:3
Balaam prophesies on,
Num. 23:14–24
Moses views Palestine from,
Deut. 3:27; 34:1–4

PIT
the *p*, and sold
Joseph . . . . Gen. 37:28
returned unto
the *p* . . . . Gen. 37:29
go down into
the *p* . . . . Ps. 28:1
out of an
horrible *p* . . . . Ps. 40:2
into the *p* of
destruction . . . . Ps. 55:23
they have
digged a *p* . . . . Ps. 57:6
the sides of the *p* . . . . Is. 14:15
Fear, and the *p*,
and . . . . Is. 24:17
shall fall into
the *p* . . . . Is. 24:18
Fear, and the *p*,
and . . . . Jer. 48:43
shall fall into
the *p* . . . . Jer. 48:44
descend into the *p* . Ezek. 26:20
descend into the *p* . Ezek. 31:16
prisoners out of
the *p* . . . . Zech. 9:11
of the
bottomless *p* . . . . . . Rev. 9:1
of the
bottomless *p* . . . . . Rev. 17:8

PITCHED
east of Bethel,
and *p* . . . . Gen. 12:8
children of
Israel *p* . . . . Num. 9:17
the Kenites, and *p* . Judg. 4:11
and *p* in the valley . Judg. 6:33
land of Moab, and
p . . . . Judg. 11:18
p in Michmash,
eastward . . . . 1 Sam. 13:5
against Jerusalem,
and *p* . . . . Jer. 52:4

PITY
eye shall have
no *p* . . . . Deut. 7:16
thine eye shall
not *p* . . . . Deut. 19:21
hath *p* upon the
poor . . . . Prov. 19:17
his love and in
his *p* . . . . Is. 63:9
have *p*, nor have
mercy . . . . Jer. 21:7

will I have any *p* . . . Ezek. 5:11
neither will I
have *p* . . . . Ezek. 7:9
neither will I
have *p* . . . . Ezek. 8:18
I have *p*, but I will . Ezek. 9:10
did cast off all *p* . . . Amos 1:11

PLACE
name of that *p*
Bethel . . . . Gen. 28:19
called the name of
the *p* . . . . Gen. 32:30
unto the *p* of the
Canaanites . . . . Ex. 3:8
you out from
this *p* . . . . Ex. 13:3
camp unto a
clean *p* . . . . Lev. 4:12
the *p* which the
LORD . . . . Deut. 12:5
be a *p* which the
LORD . . . . Deut. 12:11
LORD thy God in
the *p* . . . . Deut. 16:16
heaven thy
dwelling *p* . . . . . . 1 Kin. 8:43
Solomon build an
high *p* . . . . 1 Kin. 11:7
on his dwelling *p* . 2 Chr. 36:15
one from his
own *p* . . . . Job 2:11
the dwelling *p* of
thy . . . . Ps. 74:7
the high and
holy *p* . . . . Is. 57:15
is the *p* of my rest . . . . Is. 66:1
his *p* to make thy
land . . . . Jer. 4:7
poured out upon
this *p* . . . . Jer. 7:20
the *p* whence I
caused . . . . Jer. 29:14
and in every *p*
incense . . . . Mal. 1:11
give *p* unto wrath . Rom. 12:19

PLACES
p whither thou
goest . . . . Gen. 28:15
lords of the
high *p* . . . . Num. 21:28
ride on the high *p* . . Deut. 32:13
high *p*, and made
priests . . . . 1 Kin. 12:31
built them high *p* . 1 Kin. 14:23
removed the
high *p* . . . . 2 Kin. 18:4
priests for the
high *p* . . . . 2 Chr. 11:15
Dibon, the high *p* . . . . Is. 15:2
make the
crooked *p* . . . . Is. 45:2
comfort all her
waste *p* . . . . Is. 51:3
have built the
high *p* . . . . Jer. 7:31
shall weep in
secret *p* . . . . Jer. 13:17
p whither I shall
drive . . . . Jer. 24:9

p whither I have
driven . . . . Jer. 29:14
all the inhabited *p* . Ezek. 34:13
house as the
high *p* . . . . Mic. 3:12
build the
desolate *p* . . . . Mal. 1:4
blessings in
heavenly *p* . . . . . . Eph. 1:3
wickedness in
high *p* . . . . Eph. 6:12
holy *p* made with
hands . . . . Heb. 9:24

PLAGUE
over you, and
the *p* . . . . Ex. 12:13
that there be no *p* . . Ex. 30:12
the *p* is begun . . . . Num. 16:46
sickness, and
every *p* . . . . Deut. 28:61
be whole of thy *p* . . Mark 5:34
God because of
the *p* . . . . Rev. 16:21

PLAGUES
LORD will make
thy *p* . . . . Deut. 28:59
of all the *p* thereof . . . Jer. 19:8
hiss at all the *p*
thereof . . . . Jer. 49:17
hiss at all her *p* . . . . Jer. 50:13
death, I will be
thy *p* . . . . Hos. 13:14
receive not of
her *p* . . . . Rev. 18:4

PLAIN
and beheld all
the *p* . . . . Gen. 13:10
dwelt in the *p* of
Mamre . . . . Gen. 13:18
cities, and all
the *p* . . . . Gen. 19:25
The *p* also, and
Jordan . . . . Deut. 3:17
p, even the salt
sea . . . . Josh. 3:16
that are in the *p* . . . Josh. 13:17
wilderness upon
the *p* . . . . Josh. 20:8
his tent unto the *p* . Judg. 4:11
unto the sea of
the *p* . . . . 2 Kin. 14:25
the way toward
the *p* . . . . 2 Kin. 25:4
lead me in a *p*
path . . . . Ps. 27:11
rock of the *p*,
saith . . . . Jer. 21:13
out of the way of
the *p* . . . . Jer. 39:4
went forth into
the *p* . . . . Ezek. 3:23
inhabitant from
the *p* . . . . Amos 1:5
a *p* from Geba to
Rimmon . . . . Zech. 14:10

PLAINS
appeared unto
him in the *p* . . . . . . Gen. 18:1
of the *p* south of
Chinneroth . . . . . . Josh. 11:2

overtook him in
the *p* . . . . 2 Kin. 25:5
overtook
Zedekiah in the *p* . . . Jer. 39:5

PLANT
bring them in,
and *p* . . . . Ex. 15:17
thou shalt *p* a
vineyard . . . . Deut. 28:30
Thou shalt *p*
vineyards. . . . . . . Deut. 28:39
Judah his
pleasant *p* . . . . Is. 5:7
hand, that I may *p* . . . Is. 51:16
him as a tender *p* . . . . . Is. 53:2
to build, and to *p* . . . . Jer. 1:10
and I will *p* them . . . . Jer. 24:6
build, and to *p*,
saith . . . . Jer. 31:28
good, and I will *p* . . . Jer. 32:41
p vineyards, and
drink . . . . Amos 9:14
And I will *p* them
upon . . . . Amos 9:15

PLANTED
a tree *p* by the
rivers . . . . Ps. 1:3
the heathen, and *p* . . . Ps. 80:8
stones thereof,
and *p* . . . . Is. 5:2
a tree *p* by the
waters . . . . Jer. 17:8
Yea, behold,
being *p* . . . . Ezek. 17:10
ye have *p* pleasant . Amos 5:11

PLEAD
judge the
fatherless, *p* . . . . Is. 1:17
sword will the
LORD *p* . . . . Is. 66:16
thou, O LORD,
when I *p* . . . . Jer. 12:1
he shall
throughly *p* . . . . . . Jer. 50:34
Behold, I will *p*
thy . . . . Jer. 51:36
And I will *p*
against . . . . Ezek. 38:22
people, and he
will *p* . . . . Mic. 6:2
p my cause, and
execute . . . . Mic. 7:9

PLEASANT
every tree that is *p* . . . Gen. 2:9
Tarshish, and
upon all *p* . . . . Is. 2:16
men of Judah his *p* . . . . Is. 5:7
dragons in their *p* . . . . Is. 13:22
shalt thou plant *p* . . . . Is. 17:10
treasure of all *p*
vessels. . . . . Hos. 13:15
ye have planted *p*
vineyards. . . . . . . Amos 5:11
laid the *p* land
desolate. . . . . Zech. 7:14

PLEASED
it *p* the LORD to
bruise . . . . Is. 53:10

LORD be *p* with
thousands . . . . Mic. 6:7
in whom I am
well *p* . . . . Matt. 3:17
in whom I am
well *p*. . . . . Matt. 17:5
p the whole
multitude . . . . Acts 6:5
Then *p* it the
apostles . . . . Acts 15:22
sacrifices God is
well *p*. . . . . Heb. 13:16

PLEASURE
he hath no *p* in
fools. . . . . Eccl. 5:4
shall perform all
my *p*. . . . . Is. 44:28
I will do all my *p* . . . . Is. 46:10
his days, and the *p* . . . Is. 53:10
vessel wherein is
no *p* . . . . Jer. 22:28
thou hast taken *p* . Ezek. 16:37
Lord GOD, I have
no *p* . . . . Ezek. 33:11
the same, but
have *p* . . . . Rom. 1:32
to do of his
good *p* . . . . Phil. 2:13
things, and for
thy *p* . . . . Rev. 4:11

PLUCK
Then will I *p* them . 2 Chr. 7:20
p thee out of thy
dwelling . . . . Ps. 52:5
hand, yet
would I *p* . . . . Jer. 22:24
plant them, and
not *p* . . . . Jer. 24:6
watched over
them, to *p* . . . . Jer. 31:28

PLUCKED
and ye shall be *p*
from. . . . . Deut. 28:63
cheeks to them
that *p* . . . . Is. 50:6
horns *p* up by the
roots . . . . Dan. 7:8
were as a
firebrand *p* . . . . . . Amos 4:11

POLLUTED
land was *p* with
blood . . . . Ps. 106:38
people, I have *p*
mine . . . . Is. 47:6
land be greatly *p* . . . . . Jer. 3:1
he hath *p* the
kingdom . . . . Lam. 2:2
soul hath not
been *p* . . . . Ezek. 4:14
be *p* before the
heathen . . . . Ezek. 20:9
sabbaths they
greatly *p* . . . . . . Ezek. 20:13
be *p* before the
heathen . . . . Ezek. 20:14
they *p* my
sabbaths . . . . Ezek. 20:21
statutes, and
had *p* . . . . Ezek. 20:24

POOR
p by thee, thou
shalt. . . . . Ex. 22:25
p, nor honour the
person . . . . Lev. 19:15
by thee be
waxen *p*. . . . . Lev. 25:39
oppression of
the *p* . . . . Ps. 12:5
righteousness,
and thy *p*. . . . . Ps. 72:2
the *p* also, and
him . . . . Ps. 72:12
hath given to
the *p* . . . . Ps. 112:9
oppresseth the *p*
reproacheth . . . Prov. 14:31
hath pity upon
the *p* . . . . Prov. 19:17
judge the *p*, and
reprove . . . . Is. 11:4
strength to the *p* . . . . . Is. 25:4
is *p* and of a
contrite . . . . Is. 66:2
souls of the *p*
innocents . . . . Jer. 2:34
children, and of
the *p* . . . . Jer. 40:7
treading is upon
the *p* . . . . Amos 5:11
stranger, nor the *p* . Zech. 7:10
the gospel to the *p* . . Luke 4:18
sakes he became *p* . .2 Cor. 8:9
not God chosen
the *p* . . . . James 2:5
p, and blind, and
naked. . . . . Rev. 3:17

PORTION
p of my offerings
made . . . . Lev. 6:17
LORD's *p* is his
people . . . . Deut. 32:9
be the *p* of their
cup. . . . . Ps. 11:6
my heart, and
my *p*. . . . . Ps. 73:26
for that is his *p* . . . . Eccl. 3:22
will I divide
him a *p* . . . . Is. 53:12
rejoice in their *p*. . . . . Is. 61:7
The *p* of Jacob is
not . . . . Jer. 10:16

POSSESS
and thy seed
shall *p* . . . . Gen. 22:17
and his seed
shall *p* . . . . Num. 14:24
live, and go in
and *p* . . . . Deut. 4:1
go over Jordan
to *p* . . . . Deut. 4:26
whither thou
goest to *p* . . . . . . Deut. 7:1
in to *p* nations
greater. . . . . Deut. 9:1
nations which ye
shall *p* . . . . Deut. 12:2
whither thou
goest to *p* . . . . . Deut. 28:21

whither thou
goest to *p* . . . . . . Deut. 28:63
p the land which
thou . . . . Neh. 9:15
the bittern shall *p*. . . . Is. 34:11
their land they
shall *p* . . . . Is. 61:7
fathers, and they
shall *p* . . . . Jer. 30:3
the kingdom,
and *p* . . . . Dan. 7:18
p the remnant of
Edom . . . . Amos 9:12
of my people
shall *p* . . . . Zeph. 2:9

POSSESSED
sword, and *p* his
land . . . . Num. 21:24
and they *p* his
land . . . . Num. 21:35
of the sword,
and *p* . . . . Josh. 19:47
which were *p* with
devils . . . . Matt. 4:24

POSSESSION
for an
everlasting *p* . . . . . . Gen. 17:8
p, and ye shall
return . . . . Lev. 25:10
the field of his *p* . . . Lev. 27:28
the earth for thy *p* . . . . Ps. 2:8
got not the land
in *p* . . . . Ps. 44:3
will also make
it a *p* . . . . Is. 14:23
places are ours
in *p* . . . . Ezek. 36:2
my land into
their *p* . . . . Ezek. 36:5
of the purchased *p* . . Eph. 1:14

POSTS
side *p* and on the
upper . . . . Ex. 12:7
two side *p*, the
LORD . . . . Ex. 12:23
p within the gate
round . . . . Ezek. 40:16
p thereof and the
arches . . . . Ezek. 40:21

POUR
anointing oil,
and *p* . . . . Ex. 29:7
and he shall *p* oil . . . . Lev. 2:1
shall *p* all the
blood . . . . Lev. 4:7
congregation, and
shall *p* . . . . Lev. 4:18
ye shall *p* it upon . Deut. 12:16
remember these
things, I *p* . . . . Ps. 42:4
For I will *p* water . . . . . Is. 44:3
I will *p* it out
upon . . . . Jer. 6:11
to the famine,
and *p* . . . . Jer. 18:21
to *p* out drink
offerings . . . . Jer. 44:17
Now will I
shortly *p* . . . . Ezek. 7:8

then I said, I
will *p* . . . . Ezek. 20:8
then I said, I
would *p* . . . . Ezek. 20:13
then I said, I
would *p* . . . . Ezek. 20:21
afterward, that I
will *p* . . . . Joel 2:28
p upon them mine
indignation . . . . Zeph. 3:8
I will *p* upon the
house . . . . Zech. 12:10
windows of
heaven, and *p* . . . . . Mal. 3:10

POURED
where the ashes
are *p* . . . . Lev. 4:12
And he *p* of the
anointing . . . . Lev. 8:12
strong wine to
be *p* . . . . Num. 28:7
vial of oil, and *p* . . 1 Sam. 10:1
I am *p* out like
water . . . . Ps. 22:14
Until the spirit
be *p* . . . . Is. 32:15
he hath *p* out his
soul . . . . Is. 53:12
my fury shall be *p* . . . Jer. 7:20
have *p* out drink
offerings . . . . Jer. 19:13
my fury hath
been *p* . . . . Jer. 42:18
troubled, my liver
is *p* . . . . Lam. 2:11
he hath *p* out his
fierce . . . . Lam. 4:11
I have *p* out my
spirit . . . . Ezek. 39:29
therefore the
curse is *p* . . . . Dan. 9:11
determined shall
be *p* . . . . Dan. 9:27
his fury is *p* out
like . . . . Nah. 1:6
Gentiles also
was *p* . . . . Acts 10:45
of God, which is *p* . Rev. 14:10

POWER
seeth that their *p* . Deut. 32:36
or have I no *p* to
deliver . . . . Is. 50:2
earth by thy
great *p* . . . . Jer. 32:17
accomplished to
scatter the *p* . . . . . Dan. 12:7
clouds of heaven
with *p* . . . . Matt. 24:30
hand of *p*, and
coming . . . . Matt. 26:64
them, saying,
All *p* . . . . Matt. 28:18
upon thee, and
the *p* . . . . Luke 1:35
him, to them gave
he *p* . . . . John 1:12
thou hast given
him *p* . . . . John 17:2

hath put in his
own *p* . . . . Acts 1:7
ye shall receive *p* . . . . Acts 1:8
Holy Ghost and
with *p* . . . . Acts 10:38
p of Satan unto
God . . . . Acts 26:18
that is of *p* to
stablish . . . . Rom. 16:25
p of the air, the
spirit . . . . Eph. 2:2
be honour and *p*
everlasting . . . . . 1 Tim. 6:16
to the *p* of God . . . . 2 Tim. 1:8
the word of his *p* . . . . Heb. 1:3
that had the *p* of
death . . . . Heb. 2:14

POWERS
from heaven, and
the *p* . . . . Matt. 24:29
principalities,
against *p* . . . . Eph. 6:12
and *p*, he made a
shew . . . . Col. 2:15
and *p* being made
subject . . . . 1 Pet. 3:22

PRAISE
thy *p*, and he is
thy . . . . Deut. 10:21
made, said David,
to *p* . . . . 1 Chr. 23:5
charges, to *p* and
minister . . . . 2 Chr. 8:14
voice of joy and *p* . . . . Ps. 42:4
P ye the LORD . . . . . Ps. 106:1
P ye the LORD . . . . Ps. 106:48
his *p* endureth for . Ps. 111:10
exalt thee, I will *p* . . . Is. 25:1
my *p* to graven
images . . . . Is. 42:8
mourning, the
garment of *p* . . . . . . Is. 61:3
joy, a *p* and an
honour . . . . Jer. 33:9
P the LORD of
hosts . . . . Jer. 33:11
Nebuchadnezzar *p* . . Dan. 4:37
thou hast
perfected *p* . . . . . Matt. 21:16
whose *p* is not of
men . . . . Rom. 2:29
man have *p* of
God . . . . 1 Cor. 4:5
glory and *p* of God . . Phil. 1:11
sacrifice of *p* to
God . . . . Heb. 13:15
found unto *p* and
honour . . . . 1 Pet. 1:7
Christ, to whom
be *p* . . . . 1 Pet. 4:11

PRAISED
thousand *p* the
LORD . . . . 1 Chr. 23:5
instruments of
musick, and *p* . . . 2 Chr. 5:13
and worshipped,
and *p* . . . . 2 Chr. 7:3

shout, when
they *p* . . . . Ezra 3:11
congregation said,
Amen, and *p* . . . . .Neh. 5:13
and greatly to be *p* . . . Ps. 48:1
High, and I *p* and
honoured . . . . .Dan. 4:34
thou hast *p* the
gods . . . . .Dan. 5:23

PRAISES

holiness, fearful
in *p* . . . . .Ex. 15:11
let them sing *p*
unto: . . . . Ps. 149:3
prayed, and sang *p* . Acts 16:25
p of him who hath
called . . . . 1 Pet. 2:9

PRAY

a little water, I *p* . . . .Gen. 18:4
forgive, I *p* thee . . . . Ex. 10:17
Achan, My son,
give, I *p* . . . . Josh. 7:19
LORD in ceasing
to *p* . . . . 1 Sam. 12:23
I *p* thee, feign
thyself . . . . 2 Sam. 14:2
LORD thy God,
and *p* . . . . 1 Kin. 13:6
LORD, I *p* thee,
open . . . . 2 Kin. 6:17
servant Job shall *p* . . . Job 42:8
of Judah, judge, I *p* . . . . .Is. 5:3
Jeremiah,
saying, P . . . . Jer. 37:3
said, I *p* thee, O
LORD . . . . Jon. 4:2
that hate you,
and *p* . . . . Matt. 5:44
that I cannot
now *p* . . . . Matt. 26:53
I *p* thee, come and . Mark 5:23
into a mountain
to *p* . . . . .Luke 6:12
to *p*, and not to
faint . . . . .Luke 18:1
and I *p* God your
whole . . . . .1 Thess. 5:23
therefore that
men *p* . . . . 1 Tim. 2:8
one to another,
and *p* . . . . .James 5:16
say that he shall *p* . 1 John 5:16

PRAYED

And Elisha *p*, and
said . . . . 2 Kin. 6:17
And he *p* unto the
LORD . . . . Jon. 4:2
p, saying, O my
Father . . . . Matt. 26:39
p, saying, O my
Father . . . . Matt. 26:42
they *p*, and said,
Thou . . . . Acts 1:24
they had *p*, they
laid . . . . Acts 6:6
every church, and
had *p* . . . . .Acts 14:23
midnight Paul and
Silas *p* . . . . Acts 16:25

Jerusalem, even
while I *p* . . . . .Acts 22:17

PRAYER

the *p* which thy
servant . . . . 1 Kin. 8:29
I have heard thy *p* . .1 Kin. 9:3
wherefore lift up
thy *p* . . . . 2 Kin. 19:4
be attent unto
the *p* . . . . 2 Chr. 6:40
to the *p* of thy
servant . . . . .Neh. 1:11
me, and hear my *p* . . . . Ps. 4:1
p returned into
mine . . . . Ps. 35:13
Hear my *p*, O
LORD . . . . Ps. 39:12
and my *p* unto the
God . . . . Ps. 42:8
but the *p* of the
upright . . . . Prov. 15:8
wherefore lift up
thy *p* . . . . .Is. 37:4
joyful in my house
of *p* . . . . .Is. 56:7
for thy *p* is heard . . .Luke 1:13
continued all
night in *p* . . . . . . .Luke 6:12
accord in *p* and
supplication . . . . . Acts 1:14
Praying always
with all *p* . . . . .Eph. 6:18
thing by *p* and
supplication . . . . . . .Phil. 4:6
effectual fervent *p* .James 5:16
sober, and watch
unto *p* . . . . 1 Pet. 4:7

PRAYERS

ye make many *p*, I
will . . . . .Is. 1:15
you always in
my *p* . . . . Rom. 1:9
in *p*, that ye may
stand . . . . Col. 4:12
remembrance of
thee in my *p* . . . . . 2 Tim. 1:3
offered up *p* and
supplications . . . . . .Heb. 5:7
your *p* be not
hindered . . . . 1 Pet. 3:7
odours, which are
the *p* . . . . Rev. 5:8
offer it with the *p* . . . . Rev. 8:3

PREACH

hath anointed me
to *p* . . . . .Is. 61:1
time Jesus began
to *p* . . . . Matt. 4:17
world, and *p* the
gospel . . . . Mark 16:15
hath anointed me
to *p* . . . . .Luke 4:18
he commanded us
to *p* . . . . Acts 10:42
passions with
you, and *p* . . . . . . Acts 14:15
the Holy Ghost
to *p* . . . . Acts 16:6
to baptize, but
to *p* . . . . .1 Cor. 1:17

that gospel
which I *p* . . . . Gal. 2:2
given, that I
should *p* . . . . Eph. 3:8
p, warning every
man . . . . Col. 1:28

PREACHED

kingdom shall
be *p* . . . . Matt. 24:14
of sins should
be *p* . . . . Luke 24:47
break bread,
Paul *p* . . . . Acts 20:7
Illyricum, I have
fully *p* . . . . Rom. 15:19
heathen through
faith, *p* . . . . Gal. 3:8
heard, and which
was *p* . . . . Col. 1:23
Spirit, seen of
angels, *p* . . . . . . 1 Tim. 3:16
that have *p* the
gospel . . . . .1 Pet. 1:12

PREACHING

their synagogues,
and *p* . . . . Matt. 4:23
the *p* of Jesus
Christ . . . . Rom. 16:25
For the *p* of the
cross . . . . .1 Cor. 1:18
me the *p* might be
fully . . . . 2 Tim. 4:17

PRECIOUS

word of the LORD
was *p* . . . . 1 Sam. 3:1
stone, a *p* corner
stone . . . . .Is. 28:16
p stone was thy
covering . . . . Ezek. 28:13
faith, being much
more *p* . . . . 1 Pet. 1:7
the *p* blood of
Christ . . . . 1 Pet. 1:19
obtained like *p*
faith . . . . 2 Pet. 1:1
decked with gold,
and *p* . . . . Rev. 18:16

PREPARE

my God, and I
will *p* . . . . Ex. 15:2
you, and *p* your
hearts . . . . 1 Sam. 7:3
p ye the way of
the . . . . .Is. 62:10
ye, Stand fast,
and *p* . . . . .Jer. 46:14
nations, *p* the
nations . . . . .Jer. 51:27
shall *p* his burnt
offering . . . . Ezek. 46:2
messenger, and he
shall *p* . . . . Mal. 3:1
face of the Lord
to *p* . . . . .Luke 1:76

PREPARED

place which I
have *p* . . . . Ex. 23:20
Sihon be built
and *p* . . . . .Num. 21:27

divers kinds of
  spices p .... 2 Chr. 16:14
land, and hast p
  thine .... 2 Chr. 19:3
gallows that he
  had p .... Esth. 7:10
p a net for my
  steps .... Ps. 57:6
for the king it is p ...Is. 30:33
of thy pipes was p. ..Ezek. 28:13
inherit the
  kingdom p...... Matt. 25:34
everlasting fire, p   Matt. 25:41
make ready a
  people p........Luke 1:17
lord's will, and p . Luke 12:47
moved with fear, p ..Heb. 11:7
hath a place p of
  God .... Rev. 12:6
God out of
  heaven, p........ Rev. 21:2

PRESENCE
and he died in
  the p ....Gen. 25:18
against Naboth, in
  the p .... 1 Kin. 21:13
in thy p is fulness... Ps. 16:11
in the p of mine
  enemies.......... Ps. 23:5
the secret of thy p .. Ps. 31:20
devour it in your p .....Is. 1:7
be moved at his p.....Is. 19:1
angel of his p
  saved ....Is. 63:9
not tremble at
  my p........... Jer. 5:22
burned at his p,
  yea ....Nah. 1:5
stand in the p of
  God ....Luke 1:19
denied him in
  the p .... Acts 3:13
from the p of the
  Lord............Acts 3:19
the p of our Lord
  Jesus ....1 Thess. 2:19
destruction from
  the p ....2 Thess. 1:9
in the p of God for ..Heb. 9:24
faultless before
  the p .... Jude 24
the p of the holy
  angels .... Rev. 14:10

PRESENT
sons of God came
  to p .... Job 1:6
mercies of God,
  that ye p .... Rom. 12:1
And when I was p
  with...........2 Cor. 11:9
p I should use
  sharpness ..... 2 Cor. 13:10
from this p evil
  world .... Gal. 1:4
p it to himself a
  glorious..........Eph. 5:27
death, to p you
  holy .... Col. 1:22
may p every man
  perfect .... Col. 1:28

loved this p world .2 Tim. 4:10
from falling, and
  to p .... Jude 24

PRESERVED
face, and my life
  is p ....Gen. 32:30
the LORD p David
  whithersoever ...2 Sam. 8:6
the LORD p David
  whithersoever ..2 Sam. 8:14
restore the p of
  Israel ....Is. 49:6

PREVAIL
strength shall no
  man p .... 1 Sam. 2:9
not p against thee ...Jer. 1:19
yet can they not p....Jer. 5:22
enticed, and we
  shall p ....Jer. 20:10
of hell shall not p   Matt. 16:18

PREVAILED
with men, and
  hast p.........Gen. 32:28
hand p against
  Chushan-
  rishathaim ...... Judg. 3:10
because the
  enemy p......... Lam. 1:16
Root of David,
  hath p .... Rev. 5:5

PREY
children should
  be a p...........Num. 14:3
spoil of them
  for a p .... Esth. 8:11
the p, and to tread ....Is. 10:6
be unto him
  for a p .... Jer. 21:9
have his life
  for a p .... Jer. 38:2
wolves ravening
  the p .... Ezek. 22:27
spoil, and take
  her p .... Ezek. 29:19
my flock
  became a p ...... Ezek. 34:8
cast it out for a p .. Ezek. 36:5
will cut off thy p....Nah. 2:13
I rise up to the p....Zeph. 3:8

PRIDE
presence from
  the p .... Ps. 31:20
A man's p shall
  bring .... Prov. 29:23
places for your p....Jer. 13:17
p of thine heart, O ..Jer. 49:16
those that walk
  in p.............Dan. 4:37
p of thine heart
  hath .... Obad. 3
eye, blasphemy, p .. Mark 7:22
the eyes, and
  the p .... 1 John 2:16

PRIEST
father in law, the p....Ex. 3:1
If the p that is
  anointed .... Lev. 4:3
And the p shall
  put .... Lev. 4:7

p shall make an
  atonement .... Lev. 4:26
harvest unto the p . Lev. 23:10
before Eleazar
  the p ....Num. 27:21
p, to offer upon
  mine .... 1 Sam. 2:28
commanded
  Hilkiah the p... 2 Kin. 22:12
Seraiah the
  chief p .... 2 Kin. 25:18
Eliashib the
  high p ....Neh. 3:1
repent, Thou
  art a p .... Ps. 110:4
the p and the
  prophet ....Is. 28:7
the p, the son of
  Buzi .... Ezek. 1:3
Josedech, the
  high p .... Hag. 1:1
high p, thou, and
  thy .... Zech. 3:8
shew thyself to
  the p .... Matt. 8:4
And the high p
  answered....... Matt. 26:63
high p in things
  pertaining ....Heb. 2:17
have not an high p ..Heb. 4:15
second went the
  high p ....Heb. 9:7

PRIESTS
of p, and an holy
  nation .... Ex. 19:6
the p shall eat
  thereof............ Lev. 7:6
the p the sons of
  Levi .... Deut. 31:9
p that bare the ark . Josh. 3:15
Abiathar, were
  the p ....2 Sam. 8:17
the p could not
  stand .... 1 Kin. 8:11
places, and
  made p........ 1 Kin. 12:31
the courses of
  the p .... 2 Chr. 8:14
p for the high
  places .... 2 Chr. 11:15
his brethren the p ...Neh. 3:1
thereof, against
  the p ....Jer. 1:18
The p said not,
  Where .... Jer. 2:8
and the p bear
  rule .... Jer. 5:31
captivity with
  his p.......... Jer. 48:7
Her p have
  violated .... Ezek. 22:26
Let the p, the
  ministers....... Joel 2:17
reward, and the p
  thereof........... Mic. 3:11
elders and chief p   Matt. 16:21
daily, as those
  high p ....Heb. 7:27
made us kings
  and p .... Rev. 1:6

PRINCE

as a *p* hast thou
power . . . . .Gen. 32:28
said, Who made
thee a *p* . . . . Ex. 2:14
everlasting Father,
The *P* . . . . .Is. 9:6
p of Tyrus, Thus
saith . . . . Ezek. 28:2
p of the land of
Egypt . . . . Ezek. 30:13
my servant David
a *p* . . . . Ezek. 34:24
David shall be
their *p* . . . . Ezek. 37:25
unto the Messiah
the *P* . . . . .Dan. 9:25
the people of
the *p* . . . . .Dan. 9:26
stand up, the
great *p* . . . . .Dan. 12:1
hands earnestly,
the *p* . . . . Mic. 7:3
the *p* of this world John 12:31
p of this world
cometh . . . . .John 14:30
killed the *P* of life. . . Acts 3:15
right hand to
be a *P*. . . . . Acts 5:31
to the *px* of the
power . . . . Eph. 2:2
the dead, and
the *p* . . . . Rev. 1:5

PRINCES

to set them
among *p* . . . . 1 Sam. 2:8
servants, and
his *p* . . . . 2 Kin. 24:12
Jerusalem, and all
the *p* . . . . 2 Kin. 24:14
yea, the hand of
the *p* . . . . Ezra 9:2
Thy *p* are
rebellious . . . . .Is. 1:23
Surely the *p* of
Zoan . . . . .Is. 19:11
shall see and
arise, *p*. . . . . .Is. 49:7
Judah, against
the *p* . . . . Jer. 1:18
the *p* thereof, to
make . . . . .Jer. 25:18
servants, and
his *p* . . . . .Jer. 25:19
and his *p* will I
give . . . . .Jer. 34:21
king of
Babylon's *p* . . . . . .Jer. 38:17
king of
Babylon's *p* . . . . . .Jer. 38:18
our kings, and
our *p* . . . . .Jer. 44:17
his priests and
his *p* . . . . Jer. 48:7
the *p* of Judah in
Riblah . . . . .Jer. 52:10
kingdom and the
p thereof . . . . Lam. 2:2
p in the midst
thereof. . . . . Ezek. 22:27

among the *p* of
Juda . . . . Matt. 2:6
world, nor of
the *p* . . . . .1 Cor. 2:6

PRISON

put him into the *p* .Gen. 39:20
stood still in the *p* .Neh. 12:39
prisoners from
the *p* . . . . .Is. 42:7
from *p* and from
judgment . . . . .Is. 53:8
the opening of
the *p* . . . . .Is. 61:1
the court of the *p* . . . . Jer. 32:2
the court of the *p* . . .Jer. 37:21
the court of the *p* . . . . Jer. 38:6
John was cast
into *p* . . . . Matt. 4:12
night opened
the *p* . . . . Acts 5:19
committed them
to *p* . . . . Acts 8:3
you into *p*, that ye . . Rev. 2:10

PRISONERS

away the
Egyptians *p* . . . . .Is. 20:4
to bring out the *p* . . . . .Is. 42:7
thy *p* out of the
pit . . . . Zech. 9:11
and the *p* heard
them . . . . Acts 16:25

PROCEED

six branches
that *p* . . . . Ex. 25:35
p out of thy
bowels . . . . .2 Sam. 7:12
p from evil to evil. . . . . Jer. 9:3
corrupt
communication *p* . . Eph. 4:29

PROCLAIM

convocations,
which ye shall *p* . . . Lev. 23:4
fiftieth year, and *p* . Lev. 25:10
p liberty to the
captives . . . . .Is. 61:1
p the acceptable
year . . . . .Is. 61:2

PROFANE

neither shalt
thou *p* . . . . Lev. 18:21
neither shalt
thou *p* . . . . Lev. 19:12
their God, and
not *p* . . . . Lev. 21:6
between the holy
and *p* . . . . Ezek. 22:26

PROFIT

things shall not *p* . . . . .Is. 44:9
p, if so be thou
mayest. . . . . .Is. 47:12
things that do
not *p* . . . . Jer. 2:8
that which doth
not *p* . . . . Jer. 2:11
wherein there is
no *p* . . . . .Jer. 16:19
shall not *p* this
people . . . . Jer. 23:32

and what *p* is it
that . . . . Mal. 3:14
about words to
no *p* . . . . 2 Tim. 2:14

PROMISE

performeth not
this *p* . . . . .Neh. 5:13
the *p* of the Holy
Ghost . . . . Acts 2:33
For the *p* is unto
you. . . . . Acts 2:39
to the end the *p*
might. . . . . Rom. 4:16
the children of
the *p* . . . . Rom. 9:8
to whom the *p*
was made . . . . Gal. 3:19
that holy Spirit
of *p*. . . . . .Eph. 1:13
the covenants of *p* . .Eph. 2:12
receive the *p* of
eternal . . . . .Heb. 9:15
might receive
the *p* . . . . .Heb. 10:36
sojourned in the
land of *p* . . . . .Heb. 11:9
p, as some men
count . . . . .2 Pet. 3:9

PROPHECY

up the vision
and *p* . . . . .Dan. 9:24
whether *p*, let us
prophesy . . . . Rom. 12:6
to another *p* . . . . 1 Cor. 12:10
gift of *p*, and
understand . . . . . .1 Cor. 13:2
more sure word
of *p*. . . . . .2 Pet. 1:19

PROPHESIED

p, and did not
cease . . . . .Num. 11:25
upon him, and
he *p* . . . . .1 Sam. 10:10
hands of Asaph,
which *p* . . . . 1 Chr. 25:2
father Jeduthun,
who *p*. . . . . 1 Chr. 25:3
the prophets *p* by
Baal . . . . Jer. 2:8
to pass, when I *p* . Ezek. 11:13
with tongues,
and *p* . . . . Acts 19:6
but rather that
ye *p* . . . . .1 Cor. 14:5
seventh from
Adam, *p*. . . . . Jude 14

PROPHESY

and they shall *p* . . 1 Sam. 10:5
Jeduthun, who
should *p* . . . . 1 Chr. 25:1
to the prophets, *P* . .Is. 30:10
The prophets *p*
falsely . . . . .Jer. 5:31
thy life, saying, *P*. . . Jer. 11:21
The prophets *p*
lies . . . . .Jer. 14:14
the prophets
that *p* . . . . .Jer. 14:15

p false dreams,
saith . . . . Jer. 23:32
For they *p* a lie
unto . . . . Jer. 27:10
Wherefore dost
thou *p* . . . . Jer. 32:3
Son of man, *p*
against . . . . Ezek. 34:2
daughters shall *p* . . . Joel 2:28
prophets,
saying, P . . . . Amos 2:12
yet *p*, then his
father . . . . Zech. 13:3
to say unto him, P . Mark 14:65
p, and your young
men . . . . Acts 2:17
prophecy, let us *p* . . Rom. 12:6
p a thousand two
hundred . . . . Rev. 11:3

PROPHET
be a *p* among
you, I . . . . Num. 12:6
the words of
that *p* . . . . Deut. 13:3
that *p*, or that
dreamer . . . . Deut. 13:5
called a P was
beforetime . . . . . . 1 Sam. 9:9
p that teacheth
lies . . . . Is. 9:15
the priest and
the *p* . . . . Is. 28:7
I ordained thee a *p* . . . . Jer. 1:5
p even unto the
priest . . . . Jer. 6:13
covetousness,
from the *p* . . . . Jer. 8:10
and Jeremiah
the *p* . . . . Jer. 32:2
priest to the *p*
Jeremiah . . . . Jer. 37:3
p is a fool, the
spiritual . . . . Hos. 9:7
LORD by Haggai
the *p* . . . . Hag. 1:1
send you Elijah
the *p* . . . . Mal. 4:5
is Jesus the *p* of
Nazareth . . . . Matt. 21:11
shalt be called
the *p* . . . . Luke 1:76
man, if he
were a *p* . . . . Luke 7:39
Art thou that *p* . . . . . John 1:21
the false *p* that
wrought . . . . Rev. 19:20
beast and the
false *p* . . . . Rev. 20:10

PROPHETS
behold, a
company of *p* . . 1 Sam. 10:10
his servants the *p* . 2 Kin. 24:2
and misused
his *p* . . . . 2 Chr. 36:16
were the *p* of God
helping . . . . Ezra 5:2
backs, and slew
thy *p* . . . . Neh. 9:26
hath devoured
your *p* . . . . Jer. 2:30

The *p* prophesy
falsely . . . . Jer. 5:31
The *p* prophesy
lies . . . . Jer. 14:14
LORD concerning
the *p* . . . . Jer. 14:15
p of Jerusalem an
horrible . . . . Jer. 23:14
your *p* and your
diviners . . . . Jer. 29:8
servants the *p*,
rising . . . . Jer. 35:15
hire, and the *p*
thereof . . . . Mic. 3:11
my servants the *p* . . . Zech. 1:6
Beware of false *p* . . Matt. 7:15
Moses and all
the *p* . . . . Luke 24:27
p have not your
fathers . . . . Acts 7:52
at Antioch
certain *p* . . . . Acts 13:1
apostles and *p*,
Jesus . . . . Eph. 2:20
because many
false *p* . . . . 1 John 4:1

PROSPER
and thou shalt
not *p* . . . . Deut. 28:29
thou mayest *p*
whithersoever . . . . Josh. 1:7
shalt thou *p*, if
thou . . . . 1 Chr. 22:13
that ye cannot *p* . . 2 Chr. 24:20
whatsoever he
doeth shall *p* . . . . Ps. 1:3
his sins shall
not *p* . . . . Prov. 28:13
of the LORD
shall *p* . . . . Is. 53:10
way of the
wicked *p* . . . . Jer. 12:1
shall reign and *p* . . . . . Jer. 23:5
Chaldeans, ye
shall not *p* . . . . Jer. 32:5
planted, shall it *p* Ezek. 17:10
Shall he *p* . . . . . . Ezek. 17:15
gods, and shall *p*
till . . . . Dan. 11:36

PROUD
thy *p* waves be
stayed . . . . Job 38:11
that is *p*, and
abase . . . . Job 40:11
p, and bring him
low . . . . Job 40:12
high look and a *p*
heart . . . . Ps. 101:5
the *p* he knoweth
afar . . . . Ps. 138:6
The *p* have hid a
snare . . . . Ps. 140:5
one that is *p* and
lofty . . . . Is. 2:12
for she hath
been *p* . . . . Jer. 50:29
now we call the *p*
happy . . . . Mal. 3:15
and all the *p*, yea . . . . Mal. 4:1

God resisteth
the *p* . . . . James 4:6
God resisteth
the *p* . . . . 1 Pet. 5:5

PROVE
humble thee, and
to *p* . . . . Deut. 8:2
p thee, to do thee . . Deut. 8:16
in mine house,
and *p* . . . . Mal. 3:10
mind, that ye
may *p* . . . . Rom. 12:2

PROVERB
astonishment, a *p*. Deut. 28:37
Israel shall be a *p* . . 1 Kin. 9:7
will make it to be
a *p* . . . . 2 Chr. 7:20
p, a taunt and a
curse . . . . Jer. 24:9

PROVINCE
p are in great
affliction . . . . Neh. 1:3
of the people
and *p* . . . . Esth. 8:11
p of Babylon, and
chief . . . . Dan. 2:48
palace, which is in
the *p* . . . . Dan. 8:2

PROVOKE
sight of the
LORD, to *p* . . . . . . Deut. 9:18
I will *p* them to
anger . . . . Deut. 32:21
molten images,
to *p* . . . . 1 Kin. 14:9
p the LORD God
of Israel . . . . 1 Kin. 16:33
sight of the
LORD, to *p* . . . . 2 Kin. 17:17
sight of the
LORD, to *p* . . . . . 2 Kin. 21:6
sight of the
LORD, to *p* . . . . . 2 Chr. 33:6
gods, that they
may *p* . . . . Jer. 7:18

PROVOKED
any of them that *p* . Num. 14:23
They *p* him to
jealousy . . . . Deut. 32:16
they have *p* me to
anger . . . . Deut. 32:21
p the Holy One of
Israel . . . . Is. 1:4

PRUDENT
p men shall be hid . . . Is. 29:14
perished from
the *p* . . . . Jer. 49:7
p, and he shall
know . . . . Hos. 14:9
wise and *p*, and
hast . . . . Matt. 11:25

PUNISH
place to *p* the
inhabitants . . . . Is. 26:21
strong sword
shall *p* . . . . Is. 27:1
accomplished,
that I will *p* . . . . . . Jer. 25:12

I will p Bel in
Babylon . . . . Jer. 51:44

PUNISHMENT
then accept of
the p . . . . Lev. 26:41
turn away the p
thereof. . . . . Amos 1:3
turn away the p
thereof. . . . . Amos 1:9
turn away the p
thereof. . . . . Amos 1:11
into everlasting p Matt. 25:46

PURE
candlestick of p
gold . . . . Ex. 25:31
beaten work of p
gold . . . . Ex. 25:36
thereof, shall be
of p. . . . . Ex. 25:38
Of a talent of p
gold . . . . Ex. 25:39
p gold, the top
thereof. . . . . Ex. 30:3
principal spices,
of p. . . . . Ex. 30:23
a row, upon the p
table . . . . Lev. 24:6
thou shalt put p
frankincense . . . . . . Lev. 24:7
order upon the p
table . . . . 2 Chr. 13:11
head like the p
wool . . . . .Dan. 7:9
my name, and a p
offering . . . . .Mal. 1:11
Blessed are the
p in . . . . Matt. 5:8
p heart, and of a
good . . . . 1 Tim. 1:5
forefathers with p. . 2 Tim. 1:3
bodies washed
with p . . . . .Heb. 10:22
is first p, then
peaceable . . . . . . .James 3:17
with a p heart
fervently . . . . 1 Pet. 1:22

PURPOSE
To what p is the
multitude . . . . .Is. 1:11
To what p cometh
there . . . . Jer. 6:20
according to his p. . Rom. 8:28
the p of him who
worketh. . . . . .Eph. 1:11
to his own p and
grace . . . . 2 Tim. 1:9

PURSUE
not p after the
sons . . . . .Gen. 35:5
I will p, I will
overtake . . . . Ex. 15:9
p thee until thou
perish . . . . Deut. 28:22
thee, and shall p
thee . . . . Deut. 28:45
he did p his
brother . . . . Amos 1:11

PURSUED
of Egypt, and he p . . . Ex. 14:8

Abishai his
brother p . . . . . . 2 Sam. 20:10
army of the
Chaldees p . . . . . 2 Kin. 25:5
the Chaldeans'
army p . . . . Jer. 39:5

QUEEN
make cakes to
the q . . . . Jer. 7:18
king and to the q . . . Jer. 13:18
incense unto the q . . Jer. 44:17
Now the q, by
reason . . . . Dan. 5:10

QUENCHED
shall their fire
be q . . . . Is. 66:24
and shall not be q. . . . Jer. 7:20
it shall not be q . . . Jer. 17:27
that never shall
be q . . . . Mark 9:43

QUICKLY
on incense, and
go q . . . . Num. 16:46
until thou
perish q . . . . Deut. 28:20
And, behold, I
come q . . . . Rev. 22:12
saith, Surely I
come q . . . . Rev. 22:20

RABBAH
Also called Rabbath; A city
east of the Jordan River,
originally belonging to the
Ammonites, Josh. 13:25
Bedstead of the giant named
Og, kept at, Deut. 3:11
Captured by David,
2 Sam. 11:1; 12:26–31;
1 Chr. 20:1–3
Possessed again by the
Ammonites; prophesied
against, Jer. 49:2, 3;
Ezek. 21:20; 25:5; Amos 1:14
——— A city in the territory
of the tribe of Judah,
Josh. 15:60

RACHEL
Daughter of Laban and the
favorite wife of Jacob; Meets
Jacob at a well, Gen. 29:9–12
Jacob serves Laban for an
additional seven years to
obtain her as his wife,
Gen. 29:15–30
Sterility of, Gen. 29:31
Her grief in consequence of
her sterility; gives her maid,
to Jacob in order to obtain
children in her own name,
Gen. 30:1–8, 15, 22–34
Later productiveness of;
becomes the mother of
Joseph, Gen. 30:22–25
Benjamin, Gen. 35:16–18, 24
Steals the household images
(teraphim, legal deed) of
her father, Gen. 31:4, 14–19,
33–35
Her death and burial,

Gen. 35:18–20; 48:7;
1 Sam. 10:2

RAHAB
Also called Rachab (A woman
of Jericho); Assists the spies
of the Israelites, Josh. 2
Is spared when the Israelites
captured Jericho,
Josh. 6:17–25
An ancestor of Joseph of
Nazareth, Matt. 1:5
The faith of, commended,
Heb. 11:31; James 2:25
——— A symbolic name
applied to Egypt, Ps. 87:4;
89:10; Is. 30:7; 51:9

RAIMENT
bread to eat, and r .Gen. 28:20
ass, for sheep,
for r . . . . Ex. 22:9
vessel of wood,
or r . . . . Lev. 11:32
will stain all my r . . . . . Is. 63:3
thee with change
of r . . . . Zech. 3:4
John had his r of
camel's . . . . Matt. 3:4
and the body
than r . . . . Matt. 6:25
parted his r, and
cast . . . . Luke 23:34
blasphemed, he
shook his r . . . . . . Acts 18:6
clothed in white r. . . . Rev. 3:5
and white r, that
thou . . . . Rev. 3:18
clothed in white r. . . . Rev. 4:4

RAIN
give you r in due
season . . . . Lev. 26:4
heaven to give
the r . . . . .Deut. 28:12
make the r of thy
land . . . . .Deut. 28:24
dew nor r these
years . . . . 1 Kin. 17:1
wicked he shall r
snares . . . . Ps. 11:6
r upon the mown
grass . . . . Ps. 72:6
lightnings for
the r. . . . . Ps. 135:7
clouds that they r. . . . . .Is. 5:6
hath been no
latter r . . . . Jer. 3:3
Gentiles that can
cause r. . . . . Jer. 14:22
cloud in the day
of r . . . . Ezek. 1:28
and I will r upon
him . . . . Ezek. 38:22
good, and gave
us r . . . . Acts 14:17

RAISE
Thou shalt not r a . . . Ex. 23:1
r thereon a great
heap. . . . . Josh. 8:29
r up a cry of
destruction . . . . Is. 15:5

be my servant to *r* ....Is. 49:6
LORD, that I will *r* ...Jer. 23:5
king, whom I
  will *r* ....Jer. 30:9
For, lo, I will *r* and ...Jer. 50:9
In that day will I *r* .Amos 9:11
nothing, but
  should *r*.........John 6:39
and I will *r*
  him up..........John 6:40

RAISED

cause have I *r* thee ...Ex. 9:16
they *r* over him a
  great ....Josh. 7:26
the LORD *r* up
  judges ....Judg. 2:16
the LORD, the
  LORD *r* ....Judg. 3:9
which king
  Solomon *r*......1 Kin. 9:15
I have *r* him up in ...Is. 45:13
the LORD hath
  r up ....Jer. 51:11
be killed, and be *r* . Matt. 16:21
Whom God hath
  r up ....Acts 2:24
life, whom God
  hath *r*..........Acts 3:15
r up his Son Jesus ..Acts 3:26
the city, and *r*
  persecution......Acts 13:50
men, in that he
  hath *r*..........Acts 17:31
offences, and
  was *r* ....Rom. 4:25
like as Christ
  was *r* ....Rom. 6:4
who is *r* from the
  dead ....Rom. 7:4
in Christ, when
  he *r* ....Eph. 1:20
from heaven,
  whom he *r* ....1 Thess. 1:10

RAM

bullocks, and
  one *r* ....Num. 28:11
with oil, for one *r* .Num. 28:12
a *r*, and a fourth
  part ....Num. 28:14
bullocks, and
  one *r* ....Num. 28:19

RAMAH

Called Rama, Matt. 2:18
A city allotted to the tribe
  of Benjamin, Josh. 18:25;
  Judg. 19:13
Attempted fortification of,
  by King Baasha; destruction
  of, by Asa, 1 Kin. 15:17–22;
  2 Chr. 16:1–6
People of, return from
  the Babylonian captivity,
  Ezra 2:26; Neh. 7:30; 11:33
Jeremiah imprisoned in,
  Jer. 40:1
Prophecies concerning,
  Is. 10:29; Jer. 31:15; Hos. 5:8;
  Matt. 2:18
——— A city of the territory

of the tribe of Asher,
  Josh. 19:29
——— A city of the territory
  of the tribe of Naphthali,
  Josh. 19:36
——— Also called Ramathaim-
  zophim
A city near Mount Ephraim,
  1 Sam. 1:1; Jude 4, 5
Home of Elkanah, 1 Sam. 1:1,
  19; 2:11
Home of Samuel, 1 Sam. 1:19,
  20; 7:17; 8:4; 15:34; 16:13
David flees to, 1 Sam. 19:18
Samuel dies and was buried in,
  1 Sam. 25:1; 28:3

RAMOTH-GILEAD

Also called Ramah, 2 Kin. 8:2;
  2 Chr. 22:6
A city of the territory of the
  tribe of Gad, and one of the
  cities of refuge, Deut. 4:43;
  Josh. 20:8; 1 Chr. 6:80
One of Solomon's
  commissaries there,
  1 Kin. 4:13
In the possession of the
  Syrians, 1 Kin. 22:3
Besieged by Israel and
  Judah; Ahab killed there,
  1 Kin. 22:29–36; 2 Chr. 18
Recovered by Joram; Joram
  wounded there, 2 Kin. 8:28,
  29; 9:14, 15; 2 Chr. 22:5, 6
Elisha anoints Jehu to be king
  there, 2 Kin. 9:1–6

RAMS

than the fat of *r* . 1 Sam. 15:22
bullock and
  seven *r*........ 2 Chr. 13:9
bullocks and
  seven *r*...........Job 42:8
burnt offerings
  of *r*................Is. 1:11
of the kidneys of *r* ....Is. 34:6
thee, the *r* of
  Nebaioth...........Is. 60:7
and set battering *r* .. Ezek. 4:2
of *r*, or with ten
  thousands........ Mic. 6:7

REACH

your threshing
  shall *r* ....Lev. 26:5
r even to the neck .....Is. 8:8
the mountains
  shall *r* ....Zech. 14:5
saith he to
  Thomas, R ......John 20:27

READ

the covenant,
  and *r* ....Ex. 24:7
Babylon,
  Whosoever shall *r* ..Dan. 5:7
thou canst *r* the
  writing ....Dan. 5:16
have ye never *r*,
  Out ....Matt. 21:16

READY

thy God, A
  Syrian *r* ....Deut. 26:5
God, and had
  made *r*......... 1 Chr. 28:2
a *r* scribe in the
  law................Ezra 7:6
but thou art a
  God *r*...........Neh. 9:17
Lord, art good,
  and *r* ....Ps. 86:5
which were *r* to
  perish ....Is. 27:13
oppressor, as if he
  were *r* ....Is. 51:13
preached unto
  them, *r* ....Acts 20:7
rich in good
  works, *r*........ 1 Tim. 6:18
the woman which
  was *r* ....Rev. 12:4

REAP

r the harvest
  thereof......... Lev. 23:10
wind, and they
  shall *r* ....Hos. 8:7
but thou shalt
  not *r*.............Mic. 6:15
do they *r*, nor
  gather .... Matt. 6:26
of the flesh *r*
  corruption......... Gal. 6:8

REASON

Israel sighed by *r* .... Ex. 2:23
heard their cry
  by *r* .... Ex. 3:7
have I given them
  by *r* ....Num. 18:8
is the *r* of the levy 1 Kin. 9:15
us *r* together,
  saith ....Is. 1:18
By *r* of the
  abundance ..... Ezek. 26:10
Now the queen,
  by *r* ....Dan. 5:10

REBEKAH (REBECCA)

The daughter of Bethuel, the
  grandniece of Abraham,
  Gen. 22:20–23
Becomes Isaac's wife,
  Gen. 24:15–67; 25:20
Mother of Esau and Jacob,
  Gen. 25:21–28
Passes as Isaac's sister,
  Gen. 26:6–11
Displeased with Esau's wives,
  Gen. 26:34, 35
Prompts Jacob to deceive
  Isaac, Gen. 27:5–29
Sends Jacob to Laban, her
  brother, Gen. 27:42–46
Burial place of, Gen. 49:31
Called Rebecca, Rom. 9:10

REBELLED

r against king
  Nebuchadnezzar. 2 Chr. 36:13
disobedient, and *r* ..Neh. 9:26
children, and they
  have *r* ....Is. 1:2

r, and vexed his
holy . . . . .Is. 63:10
r against him in
sending . . . . Ezek. 17:15
But they *r* against. . Ezek. 20:8
the house of
Israel *r*. . . . . Ezek. 20:13
Notwithstanding
the children *r* . . . Ezek. 20:21
for she hath *r*
against. . . . . .Hos. 13:16

REBELLIOUS
day, ye have
been *r* . . . . Deut. 31:27
Thy princes are *r* . . . . .Is. 1:23
they be a *r* house . . . Ezek. 2:6
for they are
most *r* . . . . Ezek. 2:7
thou *r* like that *r* . . . . Ezek. 2:8
for they are a *r*
house. . . . . Ezek. 3:27
the midst of a *r*
house. . . . . Ezek. 12:2

REBUKE
cursing, vexation,
and *r* . . . . Deut. 28:20
at the *r* of thy
countenance . . . . . . Ps. 80:16
nations, and shall *r* . . . .Is. 2:4
but God shall *r*
them . . . . .Is. 17:13
and the *r* of his
people . . . . .Is. 25:8
behold, at my *r* I
dry . . . . .Is. 50:2
wroth with thee,
nor *r* . . . . .Is. 54:9
r with flames of
fire . . . . .Is. 66:15
r strong nations
afar . . . . Mic. 4:3
of God, without *r* . . . Phil. 2:15
said, The Lord *r*
thee . . . . .Jude 9

RECEIVE
mount to *r* the
tables. . . . . Deut. 9:9
we *r* good at the
hand . . . . .Job 2:10
have refused to *r*
correction . . . . Jer. 5:3
be room enough
to *r*. . . . . Mal. 3:10
ye fail, they may *r* . .Luke 16:9
ye believe, which *r* . .John 5:44
believe on him
should *r*. . . . . .John 7:39
the world cannot *r* John 14:17
But ye shall *r*
power . . . . Acts 1:8
sins, and ye shall *r* . . Acts 2:38
r forgiveness of
sins . . . . Acts 26:18
the church may *r*
edifying. . . . . .1 Cor. 14:5
one may *r* the
things . . . . .2 Cor. 5:10
r the promise of
eternal. . . . . .Heb. 9:15
of God, ye might *r* .Heb. 10:36

r the crown of life .James 1:12
ye shall *r* a crown . . . 1 Pet. 5:4
whatsoever we
ask, we *r* . . . . 1 John 3:22
was slain to *r*
power . . . . Rev. 5:12
sins, and that ye *r* . . Rev. 18:4

RECEIVED
she hath *r* of the
LORD. . . . . .Is. 40:2
they *r* no
correction . . . . Jer. 2:30
he was *r* up into
heaven. . . . . Mark 16:19
be *r* up, he
stedfastly . . . . . . .Luke 9:51
as *r* him, to them
gave . . . . .John 1:12
Jesus therefore
had *r* . . . . .John 19:30
exalted, and
having *r*. . . . . Acts 2:33
that gladly *r* his
word . . . . Acts 2:41
ministry, which I
have *r* . . . . Acts 20:24
have *r* grace and
apostleship . . . . Rom. 1:5
ye have not *r* the
spirit . . . . Rom. 8:15
I am full, having *r* . .Phil. 4:18
tradition which
he *r* . . . . .2 Thess. 3:6
world, *r* up into
glory . . . . 1 Tim. 3:16
we have *r* the
knowledge . . . . . .Heb. 10:26
faith, not having *r* .Heb. 11:13
vain
conversation *r* . . . 1 Pet. 1:18
anointing which
ye have *r* . . . . 1 John 2:27
r the mark of the
beast . . . . Rev. 19:20
image, neither
had *r* . . . . Rev. 20:4

RECEIVETH
child in my
name *r* . . . . .Luke 9:48
But the natural
man *r*. . . . . .1 Cor. 2:14
knoweth saving
he that *r* . . . . Rev. 2:17
image, and
whosoever *r* . . . . . Rev. 14:11

RECHAB
Son of Rimmon; Murders Ish-
bosheth, son of Saul; put to
death by David,
2 Sam. 4:5–12
——— Father of Jehonadab,
2 Kin. 10:15, 23; 1 Chr. 2:55;
Jer. 35:6, 8, 16, 19
Ancestor of the Rechabites,
Jer. 35
——— Father of Malchiah,
Neh. 3:14

RECHABITES
A family of Kenites descended

from Rechab, through
Jonadab, 1 Chr. 2:55; Jer. 35:6
Enjoined by Jonadab to drink
no wine, Jer. 35:6
Adhere to the injunction of
abstinence; perpetuation
of the family promised as a
reward, Jer. 35

RECOMPENCE
belongeth
vengeance, and *r* . Deut. 32:35
even God with a *r* . . . .Is. 35:4
render unto
her a *r* . . . . Jer. 51:6
come, the days
of *r*. . . . . .Hos. 9:7

RECOMPENSE
The LORD *r* thy
work . . . . Ruth 2:12
thou, I will *r* evil . Prov. 20:22
I will *r* their
iniquity . . . . .Jer. 16:18
r her according to . . .Jer. 50:29
but I will *r* thy
ways . . . . Ezek. 7:4
thy ways, and
will *r* . . . . Ezek. 7:8
I will *r* thee
according . . . . Ezek. 7:9
pity, but I will *r* . . . Ezek. 9:10
broken, even it
will I *r* . . . . Ezek. 17:19

RECORD
heaven and earth
to *r*. . . . . .Deut. 30:19
I call God for a *r* . . .2 Cor. 1:23
that bear *r* in
heaven. . . . . 1 John 5:7
the *r*, that God
hath . . . . 1 John 5:11

RED
thy bounds from
the *R* . . . . Ex. 23:31
water of the *R* sea . Josh. 2:10
and the wine is *r* . . . . Ps. 75:8
they be *r* like
crimson. . . . . .Is. 1:18
heard in the *R* sea . . Jer. 49:21

REDEEM
bondage, and I
will *r* . . . . Ex. 6:6
shalt thou surely *r*. Num. 18:15
month old shalt
thou *r* . . . . .Num. 18:16
goat, thou shalt
not *r*. . . . . .Num. 18:17
it in our power
to *r*. . . . . .Neh. 5:5
all, that it
cannot *r*. . . . . .Is. 50:2
I will *r* them from .Hos. 13:14
r us from all
iniquity . . . . Titus 2:14

REDEEMED
shall be sold or *r* . . Lev. 27:28
to be *r* from a
month . . . . .Num. 18:16
mighty hand,
and *r* . . . . Deut. 7:8

land of Egypt,
and *r* . . . . Deut. 13:5
which thou hast *r* . . . . Ps. 74:2
but the *r* shall
walk . . . . Is. 35:9
I have *r* thee, I
have . . . . Is. 43:1
for I have *r* thee . . . . . Is. 44:22
the Lord hath *r*
Jacob . . . . Is. 44:23
ye, The Lord
hath *r* . . . . Is. 48:20
and ye shall be *r*
without . . . . Is. 52:3
and in his pity
he *r* . . . . Is. 63:9
hath visited and *r* . . . Luke 1:68
Christ hath *r* us
from . . . . Gal. 3:13
that ye were not *r* . . 1 Pet. 1:18
wast slain, and
hast *r* . . . . Rev. 5:9

REDEEMER
the Lord, and
thy *r* . . . . Is. 41:14
saith the Lord,
your *r* . . . . Is. 43:14
his *r* the Lord of
hosts . . . . Is. 44:6
saith the Lord,
thy *r* . . . . Is. 44:24
saith the Lord,
the R . . . . Is. 49:7
and thy R the
Holy . . . . Is. 54:5
saith the Lord
thy R . . . . Is. 54:8
our father, our *r* . . . . . Is. 63:16

REDEMPTION
sanctification,
and *r* . . . . 1 Cor. 1:30
r through his
blood . . . . Eph. 1:7
unto the day of *r* . . . Eph. 4:30
obtained eternal *r* . . Heb. 9:12
of death, for the *r* . . . Heb. 9:15

REED
staff of this
broken *r* . . . . Is. 36:6
staff of *r* to the
house . . . . Ezek. 29:6
and a measuring *r* . Ezek. 40:3
gate, which was
one *r* . . . . Ezek. 40:6

REFUGE
eternal God is
thy *r* . . . . Deut. 33:27
Lord also will
be a *r* . . . . Ps. 9:9
of Jacob is our *r* . . . . . Ps. 46:7
of Jacob is our *r* . . . . Ps. 46:11
wings will I make
my *r* . . . . Ps. 57:1
God is a *r* for us . . . . . Ps. 62:8
said, Thou art
my *r* . . . . Ps. 142:5
in his distress, a *r* . . . . Is. 25:4
have made lies
our *r* . . . . Is. 28:15

r in the day of
affliction . . . . Jer. 16:19

REFUSED
but he *r* to be
comforted . . . . Gen. 37:35
because I have *r*
him . . . . 1 Sam. 16:7
And the man *r* to
smite . . . . 1 Kin. 20:35
And *r* to obey,
neither . . . . Neh. 9:17
which the
builders *r* . . . . Ps. 118:22
have called, and
ye *r* . . . . Prov. 1:24
have *r* to receive
correction . . . . Jer. 5:3
r to hearken, and
pulled . . . . Zech. 7:11

REGARD
R not them that
have . . . . Lev. 19:31
countenance,
which shall not *r* . Deut. 28:50
they *r* not the
work . . . . Is. 5:12
Lord he doth not *r* . Rom. 14:6

REHOBOAM
Successor to Solomon as king,
1 Kin. 11:43; 2 Chr. 9:31
Refuses to reform abuses,
1 Kin. 12:1–15;
2 Chr. 10:1–15
Ten tribes, under the
leadership of Jeroboam,
successfully revolt
from, 1 Kin. 12:16–24;
2 Chr. 10:16–19; 11:1–4
Builds fortified cities; is
temporarily prosperous,
2 Chr. 11:5–23
Invaded by the king of Egypt
and plundered, 1 Kin. 14:25–
28; 2 Chr. 12:1–12
Death of, 1 Kin. 14:31;
2 Chr. 12:16
Genealogy and descendants of,
1 Chr. 3; Matt. 1
Called Roboam, Matt. 1:7

REHOBOTH
A city built by Asshur,
Gen. 10:11
——— A city of the Edomites,
Gen. 36:37; 1 Chr. 1:48
——— The name given to a
well that was dug by Isaac
and his servants, Gen. 26:22

REIGN
Shalt thou
indeed *r* . . . . Gen. 37:8
that hate you
shall *r* . . . . Lev. 26:17
that I should not *r* . 1 Sam. 8:7
the king that
shall *r* . . . . 1 Sam. 8:11
eighth year of
his *r* . . . . 2 Kin. 24:12
Lord of hosts
shall *r* . . . . Is. 24:23

King shall *r* and
prosper . . . . Jer. 23:5
ninth year of his *r* . . . Jer. 52:4
year of the *r* of
Nebuchadnezzar . . . Dan. 2:1
and the Lord
shall *r* . . . . Mic. 4:7
shall *r* over the
house . . . . Luke 1:33
r, till he hath put 1 Cor. 15:25
suffer, we shall
also *r* . . . . 2 Tim. 2:12
and he shall *r* for . . Rev. 11:15
Christ, and shall *r* . . Rev. 20:6
and they shall *r*
for . . . . Rev. 22:5

REIGNED
king of Canaan,
that *r* . . . . Judg. 4:2
stead thou hast *r* . 2 Sam. 16:8
And Solomon *r*
over . . . . 1 Kin. 4:21
king of Judah,
which *r* . . . . Jer. 22:11
lived and *r* with
Christ . . . . Rev. 20:4

REIGNETH
The Lord *r*, he is
clothed . . . . Ps. 93:1
The Lord *r* . . . . Ps. 99:1
unto Zion, Thy
God *r* . . . . Is. 52:7
Lord God
omnipotent *r* . . . . . Rev. 19:6

REINS
trieth the hearts
and *r* . . . . Ps. 7:9
righteously, that
triest the *r* . . . . Jer. 11:20
heart, I try the *r* . . . . Jer. 17:10
which searcheth
the *r* . . . . Rev. 2:23

REJECTED
they have not *r*
thee . . . . 1 Sam. 8:7
have this day *r* . . 1 Sam. 10:19
thou hast *r* the
word . . . . 1 Sam. 15:23
Saul, seeing I
have *r* . . . . 1 Sam. 16:1
And they *r* his
statutes . . . . 2 Kin. 17:15
despised and *r* of
men . . . . Is. 53:3
nor to my law,
but *r* . . . . Jer. 6:19
because the Lord
hath *r* . . . . Jer. 6:30

REJOICE
God, and ye
shall *r* . . . . Deut. 12:7
And ye shall *r*
before . . . . Deut. 12:12
And thou shalt *r*
before . . . . Deut. 16:11
the Lord will *r* . . Deut. 28:63
enemies
wrongfully *r* . . . . . . Ps. 35:19

that *r* at mine
  hurt . . . . Ps. 35:26
glad and *r* in his
  salvation . . . . Is. 25:9
blossom
  abundantly, and *r* . . . .Is. 35:2
and thou shalt *r* in . . .Is. 41:16
I will greatly *r* in . . . .Is. 61:10
Yea, I will *r* over . . . . Jer. 32:41
caused thine
  enemy to *r* . . . . . . Lam. 2:17
R and be glad, O
  daughter . . . . Lam. 4:21
r over thee with
  joy . . . . .Zeph. 3:17
Sing and *r*, O
  daughter . . . . Zech. 2:10
for they shall *r*,
  and. . . . . Zech. 4:10
R greatly, O
  daughter . . . . Zech. 9:9
R, and be
  exceeding . . . . Matt. 5:12
your heart shall *r* . .John 16:22
Who now *r* in my
  sufferings . . . . Col. 1:24

REJOICED
that as the
  LORD *r* . . . . Deut. 28:63
the city of
  Shushan *r* . . . . Esth. 8:15
If I *r* because my
  wealth . . . . Job 31:25
feet, and *r* in heart . Ezek. 25:6
priests thereof
  that *r* . . . . .Hos. 10:5
shouldest thou
  have *r* . . . . Obad. 12

REJOICING
declare his works
  with *r*. . . . . Ps. 107:22
r city that dwelt
  carelessly . . . . . . .Zeph. 2:15
or crown of *r* . . . .1 Thess. 2:19
the *r* of the hope
  firm . . . . .Heb. 3:6

REMAIN
of it *r* until the
  morning . . . . .Ex. 12:10
first day at even, *r* . Deut. 16:4
His body shall
  not *r*. . . . . .Deut. 21:23
there *r* any more
  courage . . . . Josh. 2:11
nations, these
  that *r* . . . . Josh. 23:7
the palace shall *r* . . .Jer. 30:18
fruit should *r* . . . . .John 15:16

REMAINED
there *r* not so
  much . . . . .Ex. 14:28
Og king of
  Bashan *r* . . . . Deut. 3:11
none *r*, save the
  poorest . . . . 2 Kin. 24:14
Jeremiah *r* in the
  court . . . . .Jer. 37:21

REMAINETH
r of it until the
  morning . . . . Ex. 12:10
There *r* yet the
  youngest . . . . . .1 Sam. 16:11
the LORD, He
  that *r* . . . . Jer. 38:2
every helper that *r* . . . Jer. 47:4
therefore your
  sin *r* . . . . .John 9:41
the truth, there *r* . .Heb. 10:26
for his seed *r* in
  him . . . . 1 John 3:9

REMEMBER
people, *R* this day . . . Ex. 13:3
R the sabbath day . . . Ex. 20:8
R Abraham, Isaac,
  and. . . . . Ex. 32:13
it, and *r* all the
  commandments . Num. 15:39
And thou shalt *r*
  all . . . . Deut. 8:2
thou mayest *r* the
  day . . . . Deut. 16:3
thine handmaid,
  and *r* . . . . .1 Sam. 1:11
beseech thee, O
  LORD, *r* . . . . 2 Kin. 20:3
r the name of the
  LORD. . . . . Ps. 20:7
world shall *r* and
  turn . . . . .Ps. 22:27
I *r* these things, I . . . . Ps. 42:4
R thy
  congregation. . . . . . . Ps. 74:2
R, O LORD, the
  children. . . . . Ps. 137:7
will not *r* thy sins. . . .Is. 43:25
iniquity, and I
  will *r* . . . . Jer. 31:34
escape of you
  shall *r* . . . . Ezek. 6:9
will he *r* their
  iniquity . . . . .Hos. 8:13
he will *r* their
  iniquity . . . . Hos. 9:9
R the word that I
  said . . . . .John 15:20
R my bonds. . . . . . . Col. 4:18

REMEMBERED
God *r* Rachel, and
  God . . . . .Gen. 30:22
groaning, and
  God *r* . . . . Ex. 2:24
and ye shall be *r*
  before . . . . .Num. 10:9
He hath *r* his
  mercy . . . . Ps. 98:3
he *r* for them his
  covenant . . . . Ps. 106:45
Then he *r* the days . . .Is. 63:11
captivity to Edom,
  and *r* . . . . .Amos 1:9
shall no more be *r* . Zech. 13:2

REMEMBRANCE
utterly put out
  the *r*. . . . . .Ex. 17:14
death there is no *r* . . . .Ps. 6:5
evil, to cut off
  the *r*. . . . . Ps. 34:16

I call to *r* my song . . . Ps. 77:6
may be no more
  in *r*. . . . . Ps. 83:4
things to your *r*,
  whatsoever . . . . .John 14:26
shall bring you
  into *r* . . . . .1 Cor. 4:17
without ceasing I
  have *r* . . . . 2 Tim. 1:3
great Babylon
  came in *r* . . . . Rev. 16:19

REMNANT
the *r* of the meat
  offering . . . . Lev. 2:3
Bashan remained
  of the *r* . . . . .Deut. 3:11
bosom, and
  toward the *r* . . . .Deut. 28:54
r of the house of
  Jeroboam . . . . . 1 Kin. 14:10
thy prayer for
  the *r*. . . . . 2 Kin. 19:4
The *r* that are left . . . .Neh. 1:3
us a very small *r*. . . . . . .Is. 1:9
of the sea, yet a *r* . . . .Is. 10:22
time to recover
  the *r*. . . . . .Is. 11:11
an highway for
  the *r*. . . . . .Is. 11:16
thy prayer for
  the *r*. . . . . .Is. 37:4
and Ekron, and
  the *r*. . . . . Jer. 25:20
Philistines, the *r*. . . . . Jer. 47:4
r of thee will I
  scatter . . . . Ezek. 5:10
possess the *r* of
  Edom. . . . . .Amos 9:12
her that halted a *r* . . . Mic. 4:7
And the *r* of Jacob . . . Mic. 5:8
transgression of
  the *r*. . . . . Mic. 7:18
spoil them, and
  the *r*. . . . . Zeph. 2:9
and the *r* were
  affrighted . . . . Rev. 11:13

REMOVE
lie unto you, to *r* . . . Jer. 27:10
the mountain
  shall *r* . . . . Zech. 14:4
R hence to yonder
  place . . . . Matt. 17:20
faith, so that I
  could *r* . . . . .1 Cor. 13:2

REMOVED
And he *r* from
  thence . . . . .Gen. 12:8
Then Abram *r* his
  tent . . . . .Gen. 13:18
the camp of
  Israel, *r* . . . . .Ex. 14:19
shalt be *r* into . . . .Deut. 28:25
He the high
  places . . . . 2 Kin. 18:4
honour me, but
  have *r* . . . . .Is. 29:13
to be *r* into all
  kingdoms . . . . .Jer. 15:4
deliver them to
  be *r* . . . . .Jer. 24:9

deliver them to
be r . . . . .Jer. 29:18

RENDER
which they shall r . Num. 18:9
r his anger with
fury . . . . .Is. 66:15
will r unto her a
recompence . . . . . . .Jer. 51:6
none r evil for evil
1 Thess. 5:15

RENT
And Jacob r his
clothes. . . . . .Gen. 37:34
searched the
land, r . . . . .Num. 14:6
And Joshua r his
clothes. . . . . .Josh. 7:6
LORD hath r the
kingdom . . . . . . 1 Sam. 15:28
clothes r, and
earth . . . . 2 Sam. 1:2
his clothes, and r . 2 Sam. 1:11
those words, that
he r . . . . 1 Kin. 21:27
clothes r, and . . . 2 Kin. 18:37
high priest r his
clothes. . . . . Matt. 26:65

REPENT
fierce wrath, and r . . Ex. 32:12
man, that he
should r. . . . . . . .Num. 23:19
judge his people,
and r . . . . Deut. 32:36
not r, Thou art a
priest . . . . Ps. 110:4
their evil, I will r . . . . Jer. 18:8
R, and turn
yourselves. . . . . . Ezek. 18:30
God will turn
and r . . . . Jon. 3:9
And saying, R ye . . . Matt. 3:2
preach, and to
say, R . . . . Matt. 4:17
them, R, and be
baptized . . . . .Acts 2:38
men every where
to r. . . . . .Acts 17:30
r and turn to God . . Acts 26:20

REPENTANCE
with water unto r . . Matt. 3:11
righteous, but
sinners to r . . . . . . Matt. 9:13
And that r and
remission . . . . . . Luke 24:47
Saviour, for to
give r . . . . .Acts 5:31
Gentiles granted r . Acts 11:18
Greeks, r toward
God . . . . .Acts 20:21
leadeth thee to r . . . . Rom. 2:4
all should come
to r. . . . . .2 Pet. 3:9

REPENTED
the LORD r of the
evil. . . . . .Ex. 32:14
destroy it, the
LORD r . . . . . . .2 Sam. 24:16
his covenant,
and r . . . . Ps. 106:45

r long ago in
sackcloth. . . . . . . Matt. 11:21

REPHAIM
An ancient people of Palestine,
of great stature, Gen. 14:5;
15:20; Deut. 2:11, 20;
3:11, 13; Josh. 12:4; 13:12;
17:15
——— A valley; the boundary
between the territories
of Judah and Benjamin,
Josh. 15:8; 18:16
The battleground of David and
the Philistines, 2 Sam. 5:18,
22; 23:13; 1 Chr. 11:15; 14:9
The productiveness of, Is. 17:5

REPORT
not raise a false r . . . . Ex. 23:1
the r concerning
Egypt. . . . . .Is. 23:5
hath believed
our r . . . . .Is. 53:1
R, say they,
and we. . . . . Jer. 20:10

REPROACH
and taketh away
the r. . . . . .1 Sam. 17:26
master hath sent
to r. . . . . 2 Kin. 19:4
great affliction
and r . . . . .Neh. 1:3
a r of men, and
despised . . . . Ps. 22:6
r among all mine
enemies. . . . . Ps. 31:11
Thou makest
us a r . . . . Ps. 44:13
save me from
the r. . . . . Ps. 57:3
become a r to our
neighbours . . . . Ps. 79:4
master hath sent
to r. . . . . .Is. 37:4
remember the r of
thy . . . . .Is. 54:4
LORD is unto
them a r . . . . Jer. 6:10
their hurt, to
be a r . . . . .Jer. 24:9
an hissing, and a r . . Jer. 29:18
and a curse,
and a r. . . . . Jer. 42:18
r, a waste, and a
curse . . . . Jer. 49:13
r and a taunt, an
instruction . . . . . . Ezek. 5:15
thine heritage to r . . Joel 2:17
I have heard the r. . . Zeph. 2:8
company, and
shall r . . . . .Luke 6:22

REPROVE
and will r the
words . . . . 2 Kin. 19:4
judge the poor,
and r . . . . .Is. 11:4
living God, and
will r . . . . .Is. 37:4
backslidings
shall r . . . . Jer. 2:19

REQUIRE
your lives will I r . . . .Gen. 9:5
LORD thy God r
of thee . . . . .Deut. 10:12
Let the LORD
even r . . . . .1 Sam. 20:16
blood will I r at
thine . . . . Ezek. 3:18
what doth the
LORD r . . . . Mic. 6:8

RESIDUE
Rabmag, with all
the r. . . . . .Jer. 39:3
spoken against
the r. . . . . Ezek. 36:5
pieces, and
stamped the r . . . . .Dan. 7:7
the r of my people . . Zeph. 2:9

RESPECT
thou shalt not r
the . . . . Lev. 19:15
Ye shall not r
persons . . . . .Deut. 1:17
thou shalt not r
persons . . . . .Deut. 16:19
LORD our God,
nor r . . . . 2 Chr. 19:7
high, yet hath he r . . Ps. 138:6
good to have r of
persons . . . . Prov. 24:23
r of persons
judgeth . . . . 1 Pet. 1:17

REST
wash your feet,
and r . . . . .Gen. 18:4
seventh day thou
shalt r . . . . Ex. 23:12
thy foot have r . . . Deut. 28:65
have caused thee
to r. . . . . 2 Sam. 7:11
be a man of r. . . . . 1 Chr. 22:9
build an house
of r. . . . . 1 Chr. 28:2
not enter into
my r . . . . Ps. 95:11
of the LORD
shall r . . . . .Is. 11:2
his r shall be
glorious. . . . . .Is. 11:10
the place of my r . . . . .Is. 66:1
and ye shall find r . . . Jer. 6:16
be in r, and be
quiet . . . . Jer. 30:10
may give r to the
land . . . . Jer. 50:34
cause my fury to r . Ezek. 5:13
I might r in the
day . . . . .Hab. 3:16
he will r in his
love . . . . .Zeph. 3:17
I will give you r . . Matt. 11:28
ye shall find r . . . . Matt. 11:29
have no r day nor
night . . . . Rev. 14:11
Spirit, that they
may r . . . . Rev. 14:13

RESTED
and r the seventh
day. . . . . .Ex. 20:11

cloud *r* in the
wilderness ..... Num. 10:12
that, when the
spirit *r* .... Num. 11:25
the land *r* from
war.......... Josh. 11:23
And the people *r*
themselves ..... 2 Chr. 32:8

RESTORE
father's sake, and
will *r* .... 2 Sam. 9:7
of Jacob, and to *r* ..... Is. 49:6
to *r* and to build
Jerusalem .... Dan. 9:25
And I will *r* to you .. Joel 2:25
which are
spiritual, *r* .... Gal. 6:1

RESTORED
shall not be *r* to
thee .... Deut. 28:31
that my hand may
be *r* .... 1 Kin. 13:6
I *r* that which I
took .... Ps. 69:4
oppressed any,
but hath *r* .... Ezek. 18:7

RESURRECTION
done good, unto
the *r*........... John 5:29
unto her, I am
the *r*........... John 11:25
witness with us of
his *r* .... Acts 1:22
hope and *r* of the
dead........... Acts 23:6
be a *r* of the dead .. Acts 24:15
lively hope by
the *r*........... 1 Pet. 1:3
by the *r* of Jesus
Christ .... 1 Pet. 3:21
part in the first *r* ... Rev. 20:6

RETURN
bread, till thou *r*.... Gen. 3:19
appointed I will *r* .. Gen. 18:14
When thou goest
to *r*.............. Ex. 4:21
people to *r* to
Egypt.......... Deut. 17:16
ye do *r* unto the
Lord.......... 1 Sam. 7:3
His mischief
shall *r* .... Ps. 7:16
the dust *r* to the
earth........ Eccl. 12:7
of the Lord
shall *r* .... Is. 35:10
r unto me .... Is. 44:22
him *r* unto the
Lord........... Is. 55:7
have refused to *r* ..... Jer. 5:3
evildoers, that
none doth *r*....... Jer. 23:14
for they shall *r*
unto.............. Jer. 24:7
in causing you
to *r*.............. Jer. 29:10
For I will cause
to *r*.............. Jer. 33:11
their captivity to *r* .. Jer. 33:26

R ye now every
man .... Jer. 35:15
children of Israel *r* ... Hos. 3:5
let us *r* unto the
Lord............. Hos. 6:1
they shall *r* to
Egypt............ Hos. 8:13

RETURNED
sea, and the sea *r* ... Ex. 14:27
the waters *r*, and
covered .... Ex. 14:28
Abner was *r* to
Hebron .... 2 Sam. 3:27
when he *r* from
smiting .... 2 Sam. 8:13
controversies,
when they *r* ... 2 Chr. 19:8
my prayer *r* into
mine .... Ps. 35:13
r and enquired
early............. Ps. 78:34
Jews *r* out of all
places .... Jer. 40:12
mine
understanding *r* ... Dan. 4:34
ye not *r* unto me,
saith .... Amos 4:11
and they *r* and
said .... Zech. 1:6
passed through
nor *r* .... Zech. 7:14
I am *r* unto Zion,
and.............. Zech. 8:3
Barnabas and
Saul *r*.......... Acts 12:25
departing from
them *r* .... Acts 13:13
now *r* unto the
Shepherd........ 1 Pet. 2:25

REUBEN
Son of Jacob, Gen. 29:32;
1 Chr. 2:1
Brings mandrakes (an
aphrodisiac) to his mother,
Gen. 30:14
Commits incest with one of
his father's concubines, and,
in consequence, forfeits his
birthright, Gen. 35:22; 49:4;
1 Chr. 5:1
Adroitly seeks to save Joseph
from the conspiracy of his
brothers, Gen. 37:21–30;
42:22
Jacob's prophetic benediction
upon, Gen. 49:3, 4
His children, Gen. 46:9;
Ex. 6:14; Num. 16:1;
1 Chr. 5:3–6

REVEALED
of Chittim it is *r*...... Is. 23:1
the Lord shall
be *r* .... Is. 40:5
arm of the Lord *r* .... Is. 53:1
unto thee have I *r*... Jer. 11:20
Persia a thing
was *r* .... Dan. 10:1
prudent, and
hast *r* .... Matt. 11:25

and blood hath
not *r*......... Matt. 16:17
righteousness of
God *r* .... Rom. 1:17
shall that Wicked
be *r* .... 2 Thess. 2:8
Unto whom it
was *r* .... 1 Pet. 1:12

REVELATION
day of wrath and *r* .. Rom. 2:5
to the *r* of the
mystery........ Rom. 16:25
And I went up
by *r* .... Gal. 2:2
at the *r* of Jesus
Christ .... 1 Pet. 1:13

REWARD
exceeding great *r* ... Gen. 15:1
persons, nor
taketh *r* .... Deut. 10:17
work, and a full *r* .. Ruth 2:12
usury, nor taketh *r* ... Ps. 15:5
for the *r* of his
hands.............. Is. 3:11
behold, his *r* is
with .... Is. 40:10
thereof judge for *r* .. Mic. 3:11
judge asketh
for a *r*........... Mic. 7:3
for great is your *r*.. Matt. 5:12
he shall *r* every
man .... Matt. 16:27
shall receive his
own *r*........... 1 Cor. 3:8
error of Balaam
for *r* .... Jude 11
thou shouldest
give *r* .... Rev. 11:18
R her even as she
rewarded.......... Rev. 18:6
r is with me, to
give .... Rev. 22:12

REZIN
A king of Syria who harassed
the southern kingdom
(Judah), 2 Kin. 15:37; 16:5–9
Prophecy against, Is. 7:1–9;
8:4–8; 9:11
——— A returned Babylonian
captive, Ezra 2:48; Neh. 7:50

RIBLAH
A border town of the promised
land, Num. 34:10, 11
King Jehoahaz overthrown in,
by Pharaoh, 2 Kin. 23:33
Headquarters of
Nebuchadnezzar during
the siege of Jerusalem,
2 Kin. 25:6, 20, 21;
Jer. 39:5, 6; 52:9, 26

RICH
wicked, and with
the *r*.............. Is. 53:9
let not the *r* man
glory .... Jer. 9:23
Lord over all is *r*.. Rom. 10:12
r, yet for your
sakes .... 2 Cor. 8:9

be *r* fall into
  temptation . . . . . . 1 Tim. 6:9
Charge them that
  are *r* . . . . 1 Tim. 6:17
r in good works,
  ready . . . . 1 Tim. 6:18
poor of this
  world *r* . . . . .James 2:5
poverty, (but thou
  art *r* . . . . Rev. 2:9
thou sayest, I am *r* . . Rev. 3:17
that thou mayest
  be *r* . . . . Rev. 3:18
the earth are
  waxed *r* . . . . Rev. 18:3

RICHES
not asked, both *r* . 1 Kin. 3:13
abundance of his *r* . . . Ps. 52:7
left hand *r* and
  honour . . . . Prov. 3:16
man glory in his *r* . . . Jer. 9:23
the *r* that he hath . . . Jer. 48:36
of *r*, choke the
  word . . . . Matt. 13:22
despisest thou
  the *r* . . . . Rom. 2:4
depth of the *r* . . . . Rom. 11:33
to the *r* of his
  grace . . . . Eph. 1:7
unsearchable *r* of
  Christ . . . . Eph. 3:8
to the *r* of his
  glory . . . . Eph. 3:16
is the *r* of the
  glory . . . . Col. 1:27
trust in
  uncertain *r* . . . . . 1 Tim. 6:17
receive power,
  and *r* . . . . Rev. 5:12

RIDE
made him *r* on the
  high . . . . Deut. 32:13
caused Solomon
  to *r* . . . . 1 Kin. 1:38
r upon the high
  places . . . . Is. 58:14
sea, and they
  shall *r* . . . . Jer. 50:42

RIGHTEOUS
thee have I seen *r* . . . Gen. 7:1
manner, to slay
  the *r* . . . . Gen. 18:25
innocent and *r*
  slay . . . . Ex. 23:7
the words of the *r* . . . Ex. 23:8
words of the *r* . . . Deut. 16:19
upon two men
  more *r* . . . . 1 Kin. 2:32
the *r* LORD loveth
  righteousness . . . . . . Ps. 11:7
Say ye to the *r*,
  that . . . . .Is. 3:10
my *r* servant
  justify . . . . .Is. 53:11
also shall be all *r* . . . .Is. 60:21
R art thou, O
  LORD. . . . . Jer. 12:1
raise unto
  David a *r* . . . . Jer. 23:5

righteousness of
  the *r*. . . . . Ezek. 18:20
the LORD our
  God is *r* . . . . .Dan. 9:14
call the *r*, but
  sinners . . . . Matt. 9:13
the *r* into life
  eternal . . . . Matt. 25:46
the *r* judgment of
  God . . . . Rom. 2:5
the Lord, the *r*
  judge . . . . 2 Tim. 4:8
Jesus Christ the *r* . . 1 John 2:1
his brother's *r* . . . . 1 John 3:12

RIGHTEOUSNESS
Thou lovest *r*, and . . . Ps. 45:7
judge the world
  with *r* . . . . Ps. 96:13
with *r* shall he
  judge . . . . Ps. 98:9
r, but behold a cry . . . . .Is. 5:7
with *r* shall he
  judge . . . . .Is. 11:4
right hand of my *r* . . .Is. 41:10
called trees of *r* . . . . . .Is. 61:3
robe of *r*, as a
  bridegroom . . . . .Is. 61:10
judgment, and in *r* . . . . Jer. 4:2
called, THE LORD
  OUR *R* . . . . Jer. 23:6
bring in
  everlasting *r* . . . . . .Dan. 9:24
of God, and his *r* . . Matt. 6:33
unto us wisdom,
  and *r* . . . . .1 Cor. 1:30
be made the *r* of
  God . . . . .2 Cor. 5:21
God is created in *r* . . Eph. 4:24
for me a crown
  of *r* . . . . 2 Tim. 4:8
Not by works of *r*
  which . . . . Titus 3:5
became heir of
  the *r* . . . . .Heb. 11:7
should live unto *r* . . 1 Pet. 2:24
fine linen is the *r* . . . Rev. 19:8

RISE
Thou shalt *r* up
  before . . . . Lev. 19:32
and a Sceptre
  shall *r* . . . . Num. 24:17
shall not *r* . . . . . . Deut. 19:15
this people will *r* . Deut. 31:16
of Israel, which *r* . 2 Kin. 16:7
spue, and fall,
  and *r* . . . . Jer. 25:27
and *r* up to the
  battle . . . . Jer. 49:14
until the day
  that I *r* . . . . .Zeph. 3:8
the children
  shall *r* . . . . Matt. 10:21
third day he
  shall *r* . . . . Matt. 20:19
should *r* from the
  dead . . . . Acts 26:23
me, if the dead *r*. 1 Cor. 15:32
dead in Christ
  shall *r* . . . . .1 Thess. 4:16

RISEN
false witnesses
  are *r* . . . . Ps. 27:12
when Jesus was *r*
  early. . . . . Mark 16:9
great prophet is *r* . . .Luke 7:16
yea rather, that
  is *r* . . . . Rom. 8:34

RISING
messengers, *r* up
  betimes . . . . 2 Chr. 36:15
I spake unto
  you, *r* . . . . Jer. 7:13
the prophets,
  daily *r* . . . . Jer. 7:25
r up early, and
  sending . . . . Jer. 26:5
though I taught
  them, *r* . . . . Jer. 32:33
servants the
  prophets, *r* . . . . . Jer. 35:15
from the *r* of the
  sun. . . . . Mal. 1:11
for the fall and *r* . . . .Luke 2:34

RIVER
this land, from
  the *r* . . . . .Gen. 15:18
which are in the *r* . . . . Ex. 7:17
desert unto the *r* . . . Ex. 23:31
brink of the *r* of
  Arnon . . . . .Deut. 2:36
border at the *r*
  Euphrates . . . . . . 2 Sam. 8:3
of Hamath unto
  the *r*. . . . . 1 Kin. 8:65
Habor by the *r* of
  Gozan . . . . 2 Kin. 17:6
Habor by the *r* of
  Gozan . . . . 2 Kin. 18:11
a *r*, the streams
  whereof. . . . . Ps. 46:4
sea, and from
  the *r*. . . . . Ps. 72:8
waters of the *r*,
  strong . . . . .Is. 8:7
his hand over
  the *r*. . . . . .Is. 11:15
her roots by the *r* . . . . Jer. 17:8
north country by
  the *r*. . . . . Jer. 46:10
Chaldeans by
  the *r*. . . . . Ezek. 1:3
which hath said,
  My *r*. . . . . Ezek. 29:3
I was by the *r* of
  Ulai . . . . .Dan. 8:2
the waters of the *r* . .Dan. 12:7
sea, and from
  the *r*. . . . . Zech. 9:10
either side of the *r* . . Rev. 22:2

RIVERS
streams, upon
  their *r* . . . . Ex. 7:19
tree planted by
  the *r*. . . . . Ps. 1:3
r of water in a dry . . . .Is. 32:2
I will open *r* in
  high. . . . . .Is. 41:18
r, they shall not
  overflow . . . . .Is. 43:2

ROAR

the sea, I make
the r . . . . .Is. 50:2
walk by the r of
waters . . . . .Jer. 31:9
the midst of his r . . Ezek. 29:3
camest forth with
thy r . . . . .Ezek. 32:2
of Israel by the r . . Ezek. 34:13
r of Judah shall
flow . . . . .Joel 3:18
ten thousands of r . . . Mic. 6:7
drieth up all the r . . . .Nah. 1:4
r of Ethiopia my
suppliants . . . . . . .Zeph. 3:10

ROAR

Thine enemies
r in . . . . Ps. 74:4
that day they
shall r . . . . .Is. 5:30
We r all like bears . . .Is. 59:11
though they r, yet . . . Jer. 5:22
the waves
thereof r . . . . .Jer. 31:35
their voice shall r . . . Jer. 50:42
Lord will r from
Zion . . . . .Amos 1:2

ROCK

thee there upon
the r . . . . Ex. 17:6
he smote the r . . .Num. 20:11
water out of the r . . Deut. 8:15
R, his work is
perfect . . . . .Deut. 32:4
out of the r . . . . . .Deut. 32:13
lightly esteemed
the R . . . . .Deut. 32:15
flight, except
their R . . . . .Deut. 32:30
any r like our God . 1 Sam. 2:2
The Lord is my r,
and . . . . Ps. 18:2
set me up
upon a r . . . . Ps. 27:5
I cry, O Lord
my r . . . . Ps. 28:1
r, and the waters
gushed . . . . Ps. 105:41
stumbling and
for a r . . . . .Is. 8:14
shadow of a
great r . . . . .Is. 32:2
faces harder
than a r . . . . Jer. 5:3
the clefts of the r . . . Jer. 49:16
r I will build my
church . . . . Matt. 16:18
hewn out in the r Matt. 27:60
stumblingstone
and r . . . . Rom. 9:33
stumbling, and a r . . 1 Pet. 2:8

ROCKS

in r, and in high
places . . . . .1 Sam. 13:6
the holes of the r . . . . .Is. 2:19
the munitions of r . . . .Is. 33:16
the holes of the r . . . Jer. 16:16
like fire, and the r . . . .Nah. 1:6
mountains and r,
Fall . . . . Rev. 6:16

ROD

r that is in mine
hand . . . . Ex. 7:17
Aaron, Take thy r . . . . Ex. 7:19
r of God in mine
hand . . . . Ex. 17:9
r he smote the
rock . . . . .Num. 20:11
chasten him with
the r . . . . .2 Sam. 7:14
break them
with a r . . . . Ps. 2:9
thy r and thy staff . . . . Ps. 23:4
the r of thine
inheritance . . . . Ps. 74:2
The r and reproof
give . . . . Prov. 29:15
his shoulder, the r . . . . .Is. 9:4
O Assyrian, the
r of . . . . .Is. 10:5
a r out of the stem . . . .Is. 11:1
the earth with
the r . . . . .Is. 11:4
and Israel is the r . . . Jer. 10:16
people with thy r . . . Mic. 7:14
manna, and
Aaron's r . . . . Heb. 9:4

ROOM

continually in
the r . . . . .2 Sam. 19:13
be prophet in
thy r . . . . 1 Kin. 19:16
be r enough to
receive . . . . Mal. 3:10
r for them in the
inn . . . . .Luke 2:7
an upper r, where
abode . . . . Acts 1:13

ROOT

a r that beareth
gall . . . . Deut. 29:18
dwelling place,
and r . . . . Ps. 52:5
the chaff, so
their r . . . . .Is. 5:24
shall be a r of
Jesse . . . . .Is. 11:10
tender plant, and
as a r . . . . .Is. 53:2
the kingdoms, to r . . . Jer. 1:10
leave them
neither r . . . . Mal. 4:1
R of David, hath
prevailed . . . . Rev. 5:5
I am the r and the . Rev. 22:16

ROOTS

pluck them up by
the r . . . . 2 Chr. 7:20
grow out of his r . . . . .Is. 11:1
spreadeth out
her r . . . . Jer. 17:8
and cast forth
his r . . . . .Hos. 14:5

ROSE

daughters r up to
comfort . . . . .Gen. 37:35
And Pharaoh r
up in . . . . Ex. 12:30

And Moses r up,
and . . . . Ex. 24:13
came from Sinai,
and r . . . . .Deut. 33:2
from above stood
and r . . . . Josh. 3:16
So Samuel r up,
and . . . . .1 Sam. 16:13
Then r up
Zerubbabel . . . . .Ezra 5:2
Eliashib the high
priest r . . . . .Neh. 3:1
r up early in the
morning . . . . .Job 1:5
Then the high
priest r . . . . Acts 5:17

ROUND

sprinkle the
blood r . . . . Lev. 1:5
Levites shall
pitch r . . . . .Num. 1:53
of their enemies r . . Judg. 2:14
against the city r . 2 Kin. 25:4
from all his
enemies r . . . . . . 1 Chr. 22:9
to them that are r . . . Ps. 44:13
to them that are r . . . . Ps. 79:4
and darkness are r . . . Ps. 97:2
the walls thereof r . . . Jer. 1:15
all these nations r . . . Jer. 25:9
sword shall
devour r . . . . Jer. 46:14
Shout against
her r . . . . .Jer. 50:15
bow, camp against
it r . . . . .Jer. 50:29
of the brightness r . Ezek. 1:28
fall by the sword r . Ezek. 5:12
nations that are r . . Ezek. 5:15
posts within the
gate r . . . . .Ezek. 40:16
her a wall of fire r . . . Zech. 2:5
covenant
overlaid r . . . . Heb. 9:4
of the throne,
and r . . . . Rev. 4:6

RULE

husband, and he
shall r . . . . .Gen. 3:16
r over their
oppressors . . . . .Is. 14:2
and princes shall r . . . .Is. 32:1
and his arm
shall r . . . . .Is. 40:10
the priests bear r . . . . Jer. 5:31
the heathen
should r . . . . Joel 2:17
shall r my people
Israel . . . . Matt. 2:6
the peace of God r . . Col. 3:15
r well be counted
worthy . . . . 1 Tim. 5:17
r over you, and
submit . . . . .Heb. 13:17

RULER

gods, nor curse
the r . . . . Ex. 22:28
the sheep, to be r . 2 Sam. 7:8
gifts, and made
him r . . . . .Dan. 2:48

third *r* in the
kingdom . . . . .Dan. 5:7
shalt be the
third *r* . . . . .Dan. 5:16
third *r* in the
kingdom . . . . .Dan. 5:29
is to be *r* in Israel . . . . Mic. 5:2
And the *r* of the
synagogue . . . . . . Luke 13:14

RULERS
them, to be *r* of
thousands . . . . Ex. 18:21
sons were chief *r* . 2 Sam. 8:18
the princes and *r*
hath . . . . Ezra 9:2
and the *r* take
counsel . . . . Ps. 2:2
your *r*, the seers
hath . . . . Is. 29:10
a servant of *r*,
Kings . . . . Is. 49:7
of his seed to be *r* . . Jer. 33:26
r, and her mighty
men . . . . Jer. 51:57
the prophets the *r* . Acts 13:15
r of the city,
crying . . . . Acts 17:6
powers, against
the *r*. . . . . Eph. 6:12

RUN
r before his
chariots . . . . 1 Sam. 8:11
eyes of the
Lord *r* . . . . 2 Chr. 16:9
r, and not be
weary . . . . Is. 40:31
knew not thee
shall *r* . . . . Is. 55:5
Their feet *r* to evil . . . . Is. 59:7
shall weep sore,
and *r* . . . . Jer. 13:17
Let mine eyes *r*
down . . . . Jer. 14:17
suddenly make
him *r* . . . . Jer. 49:19
r to and fro, and
knowledge . . . . . . .Dan. 12:4
of the Lord,
which *r* . . . . Zech. 4:10
any means I
should *r*. . . . . Gal. 2:2

RUTH
The daughter-in-law of Naomi,
Ruth 1:4
Her devotion to Naomi,
Ruth 1:16, 17; Ruth 1:6–18
Goes to Bethlehem,
Ruth 1:19, 22
Gleaned in the field of Boaz,
Ruth 2:3
Receives kindness from Boaz,
Ruth 2:4–17; 3:15
Under Naomi's instructions
claims from Boaz the duty of
a kinsman, Ruth 3:1–9
Marries Boaz, Ruth 4:9–13
Becomes an ancestor of Jesus,
Ruth 4:13, 21, 22

SABBATH
Remember the *s*
day . . . . Ex. 20:8
s of the Lord thy
God . . . . Ex. 20:10
Lord blessed
the *s* . . . . Ex. 20:11
ye have a *s*, a
memorial . . . . Lev. 23:24
Every *s* he shall
set . . . . Lev. 24:8
kept *s*, to fulfil
threescore . . . . . 2 Chr. 36:21
that keepeth the *s* . . . .Is. 56:6
thy foot from
the *s* . . . . .Is. 58:13
burden on the *s*
day . . . . Jer. 17:21
houses on the *s*
day . . . . Jer. 17:22
to hallow the *s*
day . . . . Jer. 17:27
lawful to do upon
the *s* . . . . Matt. 12:2
healed on the *s*
day . . . . Luke 13:14
keepeth not the *s*
day . . . . John 9:16
on the *s* day, and
sat . . . . Acts 13:14
and three *s* days
reasoned . . . . Acts 17:2

SABBATHS
Verily my *s* ye
shall . . . . Ex. 31:13
father, and keep
my *s* . . . . Lev. 19:3
Lord in the *s* . . . 1 Chr. 23:31
moons and *s*, the
calling . . . . .Is. 1:13
also I gave them
my *s* . . . . Ezek. 20:12
my *s* they greatly
polluted . . . . Ezek. 20:13
they polluted my *s* Ezek. 20:21
my *s*, and I am
profaned . . . . Ezek. 22:26

SACKCLOTH
clothes, and put *s* . .Gen. 37:34
clothes, and put *s* . 1 Kin. 21:27
my clothing was *s* . . Ps. 35:13
themselves with *s* . . . .Is. 15:3
to girding with *s* . . . . .Is. 22:12
people, gird thee
with *s* . . . . Jer. 6:26
and upon the
loins *s* . . . . Jer. 48:37
night in *s*, ye
ministers . . . . Joel 1:13
and I will bring
up *s* . . . . .Amos 8:10
sun became black
as *s* . . . . Rev. 6:12
days, clothed in *s* . . . Rev. 11:3

SACRIFICE
may do *s* unto the
Lord . . . . Ex. 8:8
their gods, and
do *s* . . . . Ex. 34:15

fat of the *s* of
peace . . . . Lev. 4:26
Thou shalt
therefore *s* . . . . . . Deut. 16:2
obey is better
than *s* . . . . 1 Sam. 15:22
The *s* of the
wicked . . . . Prov. 15:8
Lord hath a *s* in
Bozrah . . . . .Is. 34:6
bring the *s* of
praise . . . . Jer. 33:11
God of hosts hath
a *s* . . . . Jer. 46:10
the *s* and the
oblation . . . . .Dan. 9:27
time that the
daily *s* . . . . .Dan. 12:11
desired mercy,
and not *s* . . . . Hos. 6:6
s flesh for the
sacrifices . . . . .Hos. 8:13
have mercy, and
not *s* . . . . Matt. 9:13
a living *s*, holy,
acceptable . . . . Rom. 12:1
offered in *s* unto
idols . . . . 1 Cor. 8:4
a *s* to God for a
sweetsmelling . . . . . Eph. 5:2
sweet smell, a *s*
acceptable . . . . .Phil. 4:18
priests, to offer
up *s* . . . . .Heb. 7:27
us offer the *s* of
praise . . . . .Heb. 13:15

SACRIFICED
he *s* and burnt
incense . . . . 2 Kin. 16:4
Yea, they *s* their
sons . . . . Ps. 106:37
daughters, whom
they *s* . . . . Ps. 106:38
Israel, to eat
things *s* . . . . Rev. 2:14

SACRIFICES
more offer their *s* . . . Lev. 17:7
s of your peace
offerings . . . . . . .Num. 10:10
offerings, and
your *s* . . . . .Deut. 12:6
offerings, and
your *s* . . . . .Deut. 12:11
burnt offerings
and *s* . . . . 1 Sam. 15:22
he offered *s* . . . . . 2 Sam. 15:12
offer all burnt *s* . . 1 Chr. 23:31
offering and the *s* . . .2 Chr. 7:1
burnt *s* and sweet
incense . . . . 2 Chr. 13:11
s of God are a
broken . . . . Ps. 51:17
them sacrifice
the *s* . . . . Ps. 107:22
multitude of
your *s* . . . . .Is. 1:11
offerings and
their *s* . . . . .Is. 56:7
acceptable, nor
your *s* . . . . Jer. 6:20

sacrifice flesh for
the s . . . . .Hos. 8:13
s which they
offered . . . . .Heb. 10:1
s God is well
pleased . . . . .Heb. 13:16
offer up spiritual s . . 1 Pet. 2:5

SADDUCEES
A sect of the Jews; Rebuked by
John the Baptist, Matt. 3:7–9;
Luke 3:7–9
Reject the doctrine of the
resurrection, Matt. 22:23–34;
Mark 12:18–27; Luke 20:27–
40; Acts 23:7, 8
Jesus warns his disciples
against, Matt. 16:6–12
Persecute the apostles,
Acts 4:1–3; 5:17–33

SAFELY
dwell in your
land s . . . . Lev. 26:5
and Israel dwelt s . 1 Kin. 4:25
Israel shall dwell s . . . Jer. 23:6
cause them to
dwell s . . . . .Jer. 32:37

SAINTS
ten thousands of s . Deut. 33:2
the feet of his s . . . . 1 Sam. 2:9
forsaketh not his s . . Ps. 37:28
assembly of the s . . . . Ps. 89:7
shall wear out
the s . . . . .Dan. 7:25
the people of the s . .Dan. 7:27
God, called to be s . . Rom. 1:7
the necessity of s . Rom. 12:13
Jesus, called to
be s . . . . .1 Cor. 1:2
Corinth, with all
the s . . . . .2 Cor. 1:1
of all s, is this
grace . . . . .Eph. 3:8
supplication for
all s . . . . .Eph. 6:18
the s in Christ
Jesus . . . . .Phil. 1:1
Christ with all
his s . . . . .1 Thess. 3:13
ministered to
the s . . . . .Heb. 6:10
thousands of his s . . . Jude 14
are the prayers
of s . . . . Rev. 5:8
s upon the golden
altar . . . . Rev. 8:3
ways, thou King
of s . . . . Rev. 15:3
righteousness of s . . Rev. 19:8

SAKE
the ground for
thy s . . . . .Gen. 3:17
any more for
man's s . . . . .Gen. 8:21
servant
Abraham's s . . . . .Gen. 26:24
Jonathan thy
father's s . . . . 2 Sam. 9:7
David my
servant's s . . . . . 1 Kin. 11:13

s I have sent to
Babylon . . . . .Is. 43:14
transgressions for
mine own s . . . . .Is. 43:25
it for thy name's s . . . Jer. 14:7
us, for thy
name's s . . . . Jer. 14:21
wrought for my
name's s . . . . Ezek. 20:9
wrought for my
name's s . . . . . . Ezek. 20:14
s be plowed as a
field . . . . Mic. 3:12
men for my
name's s . . . . . . Matt. 10:22
the Son of man's s . .Luke 6:22
you for my
name's s . . . . . . .John 15:21
written, For thy s . . Rom. 8:36
Christ's s hath
forgiven . . . . .Eph. 4:32
flesh for his
body's s . . . . Col. 1:24

SALOME
Mother of James and John,
Matt. 27:56; Mark 15:40;
16:1
Asks Jesus to promote her
sons, Matt. 20:20, 21
Present at the crucifixion
of Jesus of Nazareth,
Mark 15:40
Present at the gravesite of
Jesus, Mark 16:1, 2

SALT
thou season
with s . . . . Lev. 2:13
is a covenant of s . Num. 18:19
plain, even the s
sea . . . . Deut. 3:17
is brimstone,
and s . . . . Deut. 29:23
plain, even the s
sea . . . . Josh. 3:16
s, being eighteen
thousand . . . . 2 Sam. 8:13
S is good . . . . Mark 9:50
grace, seasoned
with s . . . . Col. 4:6

SALVATION
see the s of the
LORD . . . . Ex. 14:13
he is become my s . . . Ex. 15:2
the Rock of his s . . Deut. 32:15
my s, and my high
tower . . . . Ps. 18:2
my light and my s . . . . Ps. 27:1
earth have seen
the s . . . . Ps. 98:3
Behold, God is
my s . . . . .Is. 12:2
and rejoice in his s . . . .Is. 25:9
with an
everlasting s . . . . . .Is. 45:17
thou mayest be
my s . . . . .Is. 49:6
but my s shall be
for . . . . .Is. 51:6
that publisheth s . . . . .Is. 52:7

earth shall see
the s . . . . .Is. 52:10
shalt call thy
walls S . . . . .Is. 60:18
garments of s, he
hath . . . . .Is. 61:10
just, and having s . . . Zech. 9:9
power of God
unto s . . . . Rom. 1:16
the gospel of
your s . . . . .Eph. 1:13
shall be heirs of s . . .Heb. 1:14
without sin unto s . .Heb. 9:28

SAMARIA
Country of, Is. 7:9
Foreign colonies distributed
among the cities of, by the
king of Assyria,
2 Kin. 17:24–41; Ezra 4:9, 10
Roads through, from Judaea
into Galilee, Luke 17:11;
John 4:3–8
Jesus travels through,
John 4:1–42
Jesus heals lepers in,
Luke 17:11–19
The Good Samaritan from,
Luke 10:33–35
No dealings between the
Jews and the inhabitants of,
John 4:9
Samaritans were expecting the
Messiah, John 4:25
Disciples made from the
inhabitants of, John 4:39–42;
Acts 8:5–8, 14–17, 25
Jesus forbids the apostles
to preach in the cities of,
Matt. 10:5

SAMUEL
Miraculous birth of,
1 Sam. 1:7–20
Consecrated to God before his
birth, 1 Sam. 1:11, 22, 24–28
His mother's song of
thanksgiving, 1 Sam. 2:1–10
Ministered in the house of
God, 1 Sam. 2:11, 18, 19
Blessed of God, 1 Sam. 2:21;
3:19
His vision concerning the
house of Eli, 1 Sam. 3:1–18
A prophet of the Israelites,
1 Sam. 3:20, 21; 4:1
A judge (leader) of Israel, his
judgment seat at Beth-el,
Gilgal, Mizpeh, and Ramah,
1 Sam. 7:15–17
Organizes the tabernacle
service, 1 Chr. 9:22; 26:28;
2 Chr. 35:18
Israelites repent because of
his reproofs and warnings,
1 Sam. 7:4–6
The Philistines defeated
through his intercession and
sacrifices, 1 Sam. 7:7–14
Makes his corrupt sons judges
in Israel, 1 Sam. 8:1–3

People desire a king; he
protests, 1 Sam. 8:4–22
Anoints Saul to be king of
Israel, 1 Sam. 9:10
Renews the kingdom of Saul,
1 Sam. 11:12–15
Reproves Saul; foretells
that his kingdom will be
established,
1 Sam. 13:11–15; 15
Anoints David to be king,
1 Sam. 16
Shelters David while escaping
from Saul, 1 Sam. 19:18
Death of; the lament for him,
1 Sam. 25:1
Called up by the witch of
Endor, 1 Sam. 28:3–20
His integrity as a judge and
ruler, 1 Sam. 12:1–5; Ps. 99:6;
Jer. 15:1; Heb. 11:32
Chronicles of, 1 Chr. 29:29
Sons of, 1 Chr. 6:28, 33
Called Shemuel, 1 Chr. 6:33

SANCTIFIED
s Aaron, and his
garments . . . . Lev. 8:30
house, which I
have s . . . . 2 Chr. 7:20
priests had s . . . . 2 Chr. 29:34
sanctuary, which
he hath s . . . . 2 Chr. 30:8
they s it, and set . . . . . Neh. 3:1
is holy shall be s . . . . . . Is. 5:16
have commanded
my s . . . . Is. 13:3
I s thee, and I
ordained . . . . Jer. 1:5
and I will be s in . . Ezek. 20:41
and shall be s . . . . Ezek. 28:22
when I shall be s . Ezek. 36:23
be s in thee, O
Gog . . . . Ezek. 38:16
which are s by
faith . . . . Acts 26:18
are s in Christ
Jesus . . . . 1 Cor. 1:2
washed, but ye
are s . . . . 1 Cor. 6:11
are s through the
offering . . . . Heb. 10:10

SANCTIFY
S unto me all the
firstborn . . . . Ex. 13:2
unto the people,
and s . . . . Ex. 19:10
consecrate them,
and s . . . . Ex. 28:41
for the altar, and s . . Ex. 29:37
the LORD that
doth s . . . . Ex. 31:13
anointed him, to s . . Lev. 8:12
ye shall
therefore s . . . . Lev. 11:44
S yourselves
therefore . . . . Lev. 20:7
Thou shalt s him
therefore . . . . Lev. 21:8
flock thou shalt s . Deut. 15:19

s the most holy
things . . . . 1 Chr. 23:13
upright in heart
to s . . . . 2 Chr. 29:34
s my name, and s
the . . . . Is. 29:23
am the LORD
that s . . . . Ezek. 20:12
And I will s my
great . . . . Ezek. 36:23
magnify myself,
and s . . . . Ezek. 38:23
S ye a fast, call a . . . . Joel 1:14
he might s and
cleanse . . . . Eph. 5:26
very God of
peace s . . . . 1 Thess. 5:23

SANCTUARY
S, O Lord, which
thy . . . . Ex. 15:17
let them make
me a s . . . . Ex. 25:8
the shekel of the s . . Ex. 30:13
the shekel of the s . . Ex. 38:26
the vail of the s . . . . . Lev. 4:6
shekel of the s
shalt . . . . Num. 3:47
of covering the s . . . Num. 4:15
shekel of the s . . . . Num. 18:16
s, which he hath
sanctified . . . . . . 2 Chr. 30:8
the house of
their s . . . . 2 Chr. 36:17
cast fire into thy s . . . Ps. 74:7
he shall be for a s . . . . . Is. 8:14
prophet be slain
in the s . . . . Lam. 2:20
thou hast defiled
my s . . . . Ezek. 5:11
and begin at my s . . . Ezek. 9:6
profane my s, the
excellency . . . . . . Ezek. 24:21
set my s in the
midst . . . . Ezek. 37:26
brought into my s
strangers . . . . . . Ezek. 44:7
the city and the s . . . Dan. 9:26
which is called
the s . . . . Heb. 9:2

SAND
heaven, and as
the s . . . . Gen. 22:17
and people as
the s . . . . 1 Sam. 13:5
Israel be as the s . . . . Is. 10:22
the s for the
bound . . . . Jer. 5:22
the s of the sea
measured . . . . Jer. 33:22
Israel shall be as
the s . . . . Hos. 1:10

SARAH
Also called Sarai; Wife of
Abraham, Gen. 11:29–31;
12:5
Near of kin to Abraham,
Gen. 12:10–20; 20:12
Abraham represents her as
his sister, and Abimelech,
king of Gerar, takes her; she

is restored to Abraham by
means of a dream,
Gen. 20:1–14
Is sterile; gives her
handmaiden, Hagar, to
Abraham as a concubine,
Gen. 16:1–3
Her jealousy of Hagar,
Gen. 16:4–6; 21:9–14
Her miraculous conception
of Isaac, Gen. 17:15–21;
18:9–15
Name changed from Sarai to
Sarah, Gen. 17:15
Gives birth to Isaac,
Gen. 21:3, 6–8
Death and burial of, Gen. 23;
25:10
Character of, Heb. 11:11;
1 Pet. 3:5, 6

SAT
he s in the tent
door . . . . Gen. 18:1
s down to eat
bread . . . . Gen. 37:25
firstborn of
Pharaoh that s . . . . Ex. 12:29
we s by the flesh
pots . . . . Ex. 16:3
him, and he s
thereon . . . . Ex. 17:12
children of Belial,
and s . . . . 1 Kin. 21:13
s in the middle
gate . . . . Jer. 39:3
month, as I s in
mine . . . . Ezek. 8:1
of the LORD,
and s . . . . Ezek. 20:1
I s daily with you . Matt. 26:55
heaven, and s . . . . Mark 16:19
sabbath day, and s . Acts 13:14
purged our sins, s . . . Heb. 1:3
for sins for ever, s . . Heb. 10:12
in heaven, and
one s . . . . Rev. 4:2
worshipped God
that s . . . . Rev. 19:4
s upon him was
called . . . . Rev. 19:11
thrones, and
they s . . . . Rev. 20:4
throne, and him
that s . . . . Rev. 20:11

SATAN
before the LORD,
and S . . . . Job 1:6
the LORD, and S
standing . . . . Zech. 3:1
Get thee hence, S . . Matt. 4:10
power of S unto
God . . . . Acts 26:18
peace shall
bruise S . . . . Rom. 16:20
the synagogue
of S . . . . Rev. 2:9
called the Devil,
and S . . . . Rev. 12:9
Devil, and S, and
bound . . . . Rev. 20:2

SCARLET

your sins be as s . . . . . . Is. 1:18
be clothed with s . . . . Dan. 5:7
be clothed with s . . . Dan. 5:16
clothed Daniel
  with s . . . . Dan. 5:29

SCATTER

And I will s you
  among . . . . Lev. 26:33
And the LORD
  shall s . . . . Deut. 4:27
the LORD shall s
  thee . . . . Deut. 28:64
the whirlwind
  shall s . . . . Is. 41:16
third part thou
  shalt s . . . . Ezek. 5:2
remnant of thee
  will I s . . . . Ezek. 5:10
I will s a third part . Ezek. 5:12
have
  accomplished to s . Dan. 12:7

SCATTERED

LORD thy God
  hath s . . . . Deut. 30:3
I saw all Israel s . 1 Kin. 22:17
his army were s . . . 2 Kin. 25:5
out of his arrows,
  and s . . . . Ps. 18:14
thou hast s thine
  enemies . . . . Ps. 89:10
nations whither I
  have s . . . . Jer. 30:11
s Israel will gather . Jer. 31:10
Israel is a s sheep . . . Jer. 50:17
wherein ye have
  been s . . . . Ezek. 20:41
Israel, whom they
  have s . . . . Joel 3:2
have s Judah,
  Israel . . . . Zech. 1:19
I s them with a
  whirlwind . . . . Zech. 7:14
the sheep shall
  be s . . . . Zech. 13:7
were s abroad, as
  sheep . . . . Matt. 9:36
that ye shall be s . . . John 16:32
they were all s
  abroad . . . . Acts 8:1

SCEPTRE

The s shall not
  depart . . . . Gen. 49:10
out of Jacob, and
  a S . . . . Num. 24:17
the s of thy
  kingdom . . . . Ps. 45:6
that holdeth the s . . Amos 1:5

SCORN

see me laugh me
  to s . . . . Ps. 22:7
our
  neighbours, a s . . . . Ps. 44:13
our
  neighbours, a s . . . . . Ps. 79:4
laughed thee to s . . . . Is. 37:22

SCRIBE

Seraiah was the s . 2 Sam. 8:17

household, and
  Shebna the s . . . 2 Kin. 18:18
household, and
  Shebna the s . . . 2 Kin. 18:37
s, and Asahiah a
  servant . . . . 2 Kin. 22:12
a ready s in the
  law . . . . Ezra 7:6
Ezra the priest
  the s . . . . Neh. 8:9

SCRIBES

priests and s . . . . Matt. 16:21
and wise men,
  and s . . . . Matt. 23:34
priests, and the s . . Matt. 26:3
chief priests and s . . Luke 9:22
and the s that
  were . . . . Acts 23:9

SCRIPTURE

Hath not the s
  said . . . . John 7:42
that the s may be
  fulfilled . . . . John 13:18
the s might be
  fulfilled . . . . John 17:12
and brethren,
  this s . . . . Acts 1:16

SEA

the fish of the s . . . . . Gen. 1:26
is upon the s
  shore . . . . Gen. 22:17
his hand over
  the s . . . . Ex. 14:21
s upon the dry
  ground . . . . Ex. 14:22
heaven and earth,
  the s . . . . Ex. 20:11
bounds from the
  Red s . . . . Ex. 23:31
the s of the plain . . Josh. 3:16
on the s shore in
  multitude . . . . . . 1 Sam. 13:5
the roaring of
  the s . . . . Is. 5:30
waters cover the s . . . . Is. 11:9
the islands of
  the s . . . . Is. 11:11
dragon that is in
  the s . . . . Is. 27:1
I dry up the s, I
  make . . . . Is. 50:2
of the s with the
  shepherd . . . . Is. 63:11
which are beyond
  the s . . . . Jer. 25:22
s when the waves
  thereof . . . . Jer. 31:35
heard in the Red s . Jer. 49:21
wast strong in
  the s . . . . Ezek. 26:17
the fishes of the s . . . Hos. 4:3
there was no
  more s . . . . Rev. 21:1

SEAL

subscribe
  evidences, and s . . . Jer. 32:44
righteousness,
  and to s . . . . Dan. 9:24

words, and s the
  book . . . . Dan. 12:4
this s, The Lord
  knoweth . . . . 2 Tim. 2:19
opened the sixth s . . Rev. 6:12

SEALED

closed up and s
  till . . . . Dan. 12:9
believed, ye were s . . Eph. 1:13
God, whereby ye
  are s . . . . Eph. 4:30
on the backside, s . . . . Rev. 5:1

SEARCH

spirit made
  diligent s . . . . Ps. 77:6
found it by
  secret s . . . . Jer. 2:34
I the LORD s the
  heart . . . . Jer. 17:10
did my
  shepherds s . . . . . . Ezek. 34:8

SEAS

are therein, the s . . . . Neh. 9:6
the noise of the s . . . . Ps. 65:7
the midst of the s . . Ezek. 28:2
as a whale in the s . Ezek. 32:2

SEASON

offering shalt
  thou s . . . . Lev. 2:13
you rain in due s . . . . Lev. 26:4
thy land in his s . . Deut. 28:12
cometh in in his s . . . Job 5:26
his fruit in his s . . . . . . Ps. 1:3
and in the night s . . . . Ps. 22:2
to speak a word
  in s . . . . Is. 50:4
come down in
  his s . . . . Ezek. 34:26
wherewith will
  ye s . . . . Mark 9:50
in due s we shall
  reap . . . . Gal. 6:9

SEAT

ends of the
  mercy s . . . . Ex. 25:18
covering the
  mercy s . . . . Ex. 25:20
shalt put the
  mercy s . . . . Ex. 25:21
above the mercy s . . . Ex. 25:22
before the mercy s . . . Ex. 30:6
before the mercy s . . . Lev. 16:2
nor sitteth in the s . . . . Ps. 1:1
s of the image of
  jealousy . . . . Ezek. 8:3
God, I sit in the s . . Ezek. 28:2
the judgment s of
  Christ . . . . 2 Cor. 5:10

SECRET

putteth it in a s
  place . . . . Deut. 27:15
in the s of his
  tabernacle . . . . Ps. 27:5
in the s of thy
  presence . . . . Ps. 31:20
dwelleth in the s
  place . . . . Ps. 91:1
not found it by s
  search . . . . Jer. 2:34

soul shall weep
　in s . . . . Jer. 13:17
hide himself in s
　places . . . . Jer. 23:24
uncovered his s
　places . . . . Jer. 49:10
s that they can
　hide . . . . Ezek. 28:3
couldest reveal
　this s . . . . .Dan. 2:47
s since the world
　began . . . . Rom. 16:25

SEED
woman, and
　between thy s . . . . .Gen. 3:15
Unto thy s will I
　give . . . . .Gen. 12:7
give it, and to
　thy s . . . . .Gen. 13:15
him, So shall thy s . .Gen. 15:5
Unto thy s have I
　given . . . . .Gen. 15:18
and thee and thy s . .Gen. 17:7
thee, and to thy s . . .Gen. 17:8
will multiply thy s .Gen. 22:17
And in thy s shall . .Gen. 22:18
thy s, I will give . . . .Gen. 26:3
And I will make
　thy s . . . . .Gen. 26:4
give it, and to
　thy s . . . . .Gen. 28:13
And thy s shall be .Gen. 28:14
let any of thy s
　pass . . . . Lev. 18:21
unto thee and to
　thy s . . . . .Num. 18:19
carry much s . . . . .Deut. 28:38
thy s, even great
　plagues . . . . .Deut. 28:59
I will set up thy s . 2 Sam. 7:12
spirit upon thy s . . . . . .Is. 44:3
his s, he shall
　prolong . . . . .Is. 53:10

SEEK
spirits, neither s . . . Lev. 19:31
thou shalt s the
　LORD . . . . .Deut. 4:29
ye s, and thither
　thou . . . . Deut. 12:5
if thou s him, he
　will . . . . 1 Chr. 28:9
if ye s him, he . . . . 2 Chr. 15:2
a man to s the
　welfare . . . . .Neh. 2:10
they shall s me
　early . . . . Prov. 1:28
s judgment,
　relieve . . . . .Is. 1:17
shall say unto
　you, S . . . . .Is. 8:19
shall the
　Gentiles s . . . . .Is. 11:10
of Israel, neither s . . . .Is. 31:1
S ye the LORD
　while . . . . .Is. 55:6
hand of those
　that s . . . . Jer. 21:7
hand of them
　that s . . . . Jer. 34:20

s the LORD their
　God . . . . Jer. 50:4
Israel return,
　and s . . . . Hos. 3:5
s the law at his
　mouth . . . . Mal. 2:7
the Lord, whom
　ye s . . . . Mal. 3:1
s ye first the
　kingdom . . . . Matt. 6:33
because I s not
　mine . . . . .John 5:30

SEER
let us go to the s . . . 1 Sam. 9:9
Heman the
　king's s . . . . 1 Chr. 25:5
was wroth with
　the s . . . . 2 Chr. 16:10
son of Hanani
　the s . . . . 2 Chr. 19:2

SEEST
s, to thee will I
　give . . . . .Gen. 13:15
heaven, and when
　thou s . . . . Deut. 4:19
S thou how Ahab
　humbleth . . . . . 1 Kin. 21:29
If thou s the
　oppression . . . . .Eccl. 5:8
and, behold,
　thou s . . . . Jer. 32:24
me, Amos, what s
　thou . . . . .Amos 7:8
unto me, What s
　thou . . . . Zech. 4:2
unto Simon, S
　thou . . . . .Luke 7:44
and, What thou s,
　write . . . . Rev. 1:11

SEETH
and when he s the
　blood . . . . Ex. 12:23
servants, when he
　s . . . . Deut. 32:36
LORD s not as
　man s . . . . 1 Sam. 16:7
and they say,
　Who s . . . . .Is. 29:15
they say, The
　LORD s . . . . Ezek. 8:12
earth, and the
　LORD s . . . . Ezek. 9:9
day John s Jesus
　coming . . . . John 1:29
s the Son, and
　believeth . . . . .John 6:40
receive, because
　it s . . . . .John 14:17

SEND
your cities, I will s . Lev. 26:25
alive of you I
　will s . . . . Lev. 26:36
LORD shall s upon
　thee . . . . Deut. 28:20
which the LORD
　shall s . . . . Deut. 28:48
I will s thee to
　Jesse . . . . 1 Sam. 16:1

I will s him
　against . . . . .Is. 10:6
them, and I will s . . . .Is. 66:19
and s unto Kedar,
　and . . . . Jer. 2:10
Behold, I will s for . .Jer. 16:16
And I will s the
　sword . . . . .Jer. 24:10
Behold, I will s
　and . . . . Jer. 25:9
sword which I
　will s . . . . .Jer. 25:27
Behold, I will s
　and . . . . Jer. 43:10
But I will s a fire . . .Amos 1:12
Behold, I will s my . . . Mal. 3:1
Behold, I will s
　you . . . . Mal. 4:5
he shall s his
　angels . . . . Matt. 24:31
whom the Father
　will s . . . . .John 14:26
come, whom I
　will s . . . . .John 15:26
write in a book,
　and s . . . . Rev. 1:11

SENDING
betimes, and s . . . 2 Chr. 36:15
rising up early,
　and s . . . . Jer. 26:5
rising up early
　and s . . . . .Jer. 35:15
rebelled against
　him in s . . . . Ezek. 17:15
through the flesh,
　God s . . . . Rom. 8:3

SEPARATED
that time the
　LORD s . . . . Deut. 10:8
and Aaron was s,
　that . . . . 1 Chr. 23:13
captains of the
　host s . . . . 1 Chr. 25:1
to Baalpeor, and s . . .Hos. 9:10
to be an apostle, s . . Rom. 1:1

SEPULCHRE
was buried in
　the s . . . . .2 Sam. 17:23
the door of the s . . Matt. 27:60
s, and seeth the
　stone . . . . .John 20:1
Lord out of the s . . . .John 20:2
Sychem, and laid
　in the s . . . . Acts 7:16

SERPENT
pieces the
　brasen s . . . . 2 Kin. 18:4
leviathan the
　piercing s . . . . .Is. 27:1
means, as the s
　beguiled . . . . . . .2 Cor. 11:3
old s, called the
　Devil . . . . Rev. 12:9
the face of the s . . .Rev. 12:14
dragon, that old s . . . Rev. 20:2

SERPENTS
were fiery s, and
　scorpions . . . . . . .Deut. 8:15
s, ye generation . .Matt. 23:33

They shall take
up *s* . . . . Mark 16:18
were destroyed
of *s* . . . . .1 Cor. 10:9

SERVANT
law, which Moses
my *s* . . . . .Josh. 1:7
Thy *s* slew both
the . . . . 1 Sam. 17:36
prayer which thy *s* . 1 Kin. 8:29
Horonite, and
Tobiah the *s* . . . . . .Neh. 2:10
judgment with
thy *s* . . . . Ps. 143:2
Behold my *s*,
whom I . . . . .Is. 42:1
not, O Jacob, my *s* . . . .Is. 44:2
hath redeemed
his *s* . . . . .Is. 48:20
thou shouldest be
my *s* . . . . .Is. 49:6
nation abhorreth,
to a *s* . . . . .Is. 49:7
my *s* shall deal
prudently . . . . .Is. 52:13
my righteous *s*
justify . . . . .Is. 53:11
king of Babylon,
my *s* . . . . Jer. 25:9
feed them, even
my *s* . . . . Ezek. 34:23
God, and my *s*
David. . . . . Ezek. 34:24
And David my *s*
shall. . . . . Ezek. 37:24
given unto Jacob
my *s* . . . . Ezek. 37:25
law of Moses the *s* . .Dan. 9:11
will bring forth
my *s* . . . . Zech. 3:8
Paul, a *s* of Jesus. . . . Rom. 1:1

SERVANTS
and Israel, thy *s* . . . . Ex. 32:13
s of Balak, If . . . . .Num. 22:18
his *s*, when he
seeth . . . . .Deut. 32:36
Moabites became
David's *s* . . . . 2 Sam. 8:2
s to David, and
brought . . . . 2 Sam. 8:6
Edom became
David's *s* . . . . 2 Sam. 8:14
you by my *s* the
prophets . . . . . . 2 Kin. 17:13
which he spake by
his *s* . . . . 2 Kin. 24:2
mother, and his *s* .2 Kin. 24:12
daughters to be *s* . . . .Neh. 5:5
Pharaoh, and on
all his *s* . . . . .Neh. 9:10
thee, and call his *s* . . .Is. 65:15
of Judah, and his *s* . . . Jer. 21:7
of Egypt, and his *s* . . Jer. 25:19
s the prophets,
rising. . . . . Jer. 35:15
tell thy *s* the
dream . . . . .Dan. 2:4
and delivered his *s* . .Dan. 3:28
which I
commanded my *s* . . Zech. 1:6

become *s* to
God, ye . . . . Rom. 6:22
the *s* of Jesus
Christ . . . . Phil. 1:1

SERVE
Egypt, ye shall *s*
God . . . . Ex. 3:12
thyself to them,
nor *s* . . . . Ex. 20:5
if thou *s* their
gods. . . . . Ex. 23:33
worship them,
and *s* . . . . Deut. 4:19
LORD thy God,
and *s* . . . . Deut. 6:13
to *s* the LORD thy
God . . . . Deut. 10:12
him shalt thou *s*,
and. . . . . Deut. 10:20
us go and *s* other
gods. . . . . Deut. 13:13
shalt thou *s* . . . . . Deut. 28:36
thou *s* thine . . . . . Deut. 28:48
thou shalt *s* . . . . . Deut. 28:64
unto the LORD,
and *s* . . . . 1 Sam. 7:3
thy father, and *s* . . 1 Chr. 28:9
after other gods
to *s* . . . . Jer. 35:15
Go ye, *s* ye every
one. . . . . Ezek. 20:39
languages,
should *s* . . . . .Dan. 7:14
all dominions
shall *s* . . . . .Dan. 7:27
only shalt thou *s* . . . Matt. 4:10
my witness,
whom I *s* . . . . Rom. 1:9
from dead works
to *s* . . . . .Heb. 9:14

SERVED
ye shall possess *s* . . Deut. 12:2
s other gods, and
worshipped. . . . . . Deut. 17:3
s other gods, and
worshipped. . . . .Deut. 29:26
s other gods, and
bowed . . . . Josh. 23:16
LORD their God,
and *s* . . . . Judg. 3:7
brought presents,
and *s* . . . . 1 Kin. 4:21
worshipped them,
and *s* . . . . .1 Kin. 9:9
and *s* Baal, and
worshipped. . . . 1 Kin. 16:31
host of heaven,
and *s* . . . . 2 Kin. 17:16
host of heaven,
and *s* . . . . 2 Kin. 21:3
and whom they
have *s*. . . . . Jer. 8:2
worshipped other
gods, and *s* . . . . . . Jer. 22:9
labour wherewith
he *s* . . . . Ezek. 29:20
hand of those
that *s* . . . . Ezek. 34:27

SERVICE
appoint it for the *s* . . Ex. 30:16

congregation, to
do the *s* . . . . Num. 3:7
s of the sons of
Asaph . . . . 1 Chr. 25:1
s of the house of
God . . . . 1 Chr. 25:6
priests to their *s* . . 2 Chr. 8:14
herb for the *s* of
man . . . . Ps. 104:14
that he doeth
God *s* . . . . .John 16:2
law, and the *s* of
God . . . . Rom. 9:4
your reasonable *s* . . Rom. 12:1
knew not God, ye
did *s*. . . . . Gal. 4:8

SET
I will even *s* my
face . . . . Lev. 17:10
And thou shalt *s*
them . . . . Lev. 24:6
And I will *s* my
face . . . . Lev. 26:17
the camp is to *s*
forward . . . . Num. 4:15
thou shalt *s* over
thee . . . . .Deut. 28:36
together at
Shiloh, and *s* . . . . Josh. 18:1
fathers, I will *s* . . .2 Sam. 7:12
he *s* the one in
Bethel . . . . 1 Kin. 12:29
Yet have I *s* my
king . . . . Ps. 2:6
Lord shall *s* his
hand . . . . .Is. 11:11
he shall *s* up an
ensign . . . . .Is. 11:12
And I will *s* a sign . . .Is. 66:19
I have this day *s*
thee . . . . Jer. 1:10
For I have *s* my
face . . . . Jer. 21:10
and publish, and *s* . . . Jer. 50:2
I will *s* up one
shepherd . . . . Ezek. 34:23
the God of
heaven *s* . . . . .Dan. 2:44
the judgment
was *s* . . . . .Dan. 7:10
blind, to *s* at
liberty . . . . .Luke 4:18
the joy that was *s* . . .Heb. 12:2

SETTETH
s light by his
father. . . . . .Deut. 27:16
removeth kings,
and *s* . . . . .Dan. 2:21
whomsoever he
will, and *s* . . . . . . .Dan. 4:17
the holy city, and *s* . . Matt. 4:5
body, and *s* on fire . .James 3:6

SEVENTH
day until the *s* day . . Ex. 12:15
convocation, and
in the *s* . . . . Ex. 12:16
the *s* day is the
sabbath . . . . Ex. 20:10
and rested the *s*
day. . . . . Ex. 20:11

s day thou shalt
  rest . . . . .Ex. 23:12
s day thou shalt
  rest . . . . .Ex. 34:21
the *s* day is the
  sabbath . . . . Lev. 23:3
s day is an holy
  convocation . . . . . . Lev. 23:8
Israel, saying, In
  the *s*. . . . . Lev. 23:24
fifteenth day of
  this *s* . . . . Lev. 23:34
The *s* year, the
  year . . . . Deut. 15:9
s day shall be a
  solemn . . . . Deut. 16:8
to pass in the *s*
  year . . . . Ezek. 20:1
the fifth and *s*
  month . . . . .Zech. 7:5
the *s* from Adam,
  prophesied . . . . Jude 14
And the *s* angel
  sounded . . . . Rev. 11:15

SEVENTY
gave it unto the *s* .Num. 11:25
king of Babylon *s*
  years . . . . .Jer. 25:11
to pass, when *s*
  years . . . . .Jer. 25:12
after *s* years be
  accomplished . . . . .Jer. 29:10
S weeks are
  determined . . . . . .Dan. 9:24
s years, did ye at . . . .Zech. 7:5

SHADOW
the *s* of death
  stain . . . . .Job 3:5
the *s* of thy wings. . . . Ps. 17:8
the *s* of death, I
  will . . . . Ps. 23:4
yea, in the *s* of thy . . . Ps. 57:1
covered with the *s* . . Ps. 80:10
shall abide under
  the *s*. . . . . Ps. 91:1
his days are as a *s*. . . Ps. 144:4
he spendeth as a *s* . .Eccl. 6:12
land of the *s* of
  death . . . . .Is. 9:2
from the
  storm, a *s* . . . . .Is. 25:4
dry place, as the *s*. . . . .Is. 32:2
the *s* of his hand
  hath . . . . .Is. 49:2
covered thee in
  the *s*. . . . . .Is. 51:16
s of death, and
  make . . . . .Jer. 13:16
Orion, and
  turneth the *s*. . . . . .Amos 5:8
and *s* of heavenly
  things . . . . .Heb. 8:5
law having a *s* of
  good . . . . .Heb. 10:1
variableness,
  neither *s* . . . . . . .James 1:17

SHAKE
God *s* out every
  man . . . . .Neh. 5:13

lip, they *s* the
  head. . . . . Ps. 22:7
he ariseth to *s*
  terribly . . . . .Is. 2:19
he ariseth to *s*
  terribly . . . . .Is. 2:21
mighty wind shall
  he *s* . . . . .Is. 11:15
voice unto them, *s* . . . .Is. 13:2
of the earth do *s* . . . . .Is. 24:18
walls shall *s* at . . . Ezek. 26:10
made the nations
  to *s*. . . . . Ezek. 31:16

SHAKEN
the sound of a *s*
  leaf. . . . . Lev. 26:36
promise, even
  thus be he *s* . . . . . .Neh. 5:13
of Jerusalem
  hath *s*. . . . . .Is. 37:22
heavens shall be *s* . .Matt. 24:29

SHAME
them be clothed
  with *s*. . . . . Ps. 35:26
reproach, and
  my *s* . . . . Ps. 69:19
bringeth his
  mother to *s* . . . . . Prov. 29:15
uncovered, to
  the *s*. . . . . .Is. 20:4
face from *s* and
  spitting . . . . .Is. 50:6
shalt not be put
  to *s*. . . . . .Is. 54:4
s ye shall have
  double . . . . .Is. 61:7
lie down in our *s* . . . .Jer. 3:25
turned the back
  with *s*. . . . . .Jer. 48:39
ye have borne
  the *s* . . . . Ezek. 36:6
s and everlasting
  contempt . . . . .Dan. 12:2
themselves unto
  that *s* . . . . .Hos. 9:10
unjust knoweth
  no *s* . . . . .Zeph. 3:5
their *s*, who mind
  earthly. . . . . .Phil. 3:19
cross, despising
  the *s*. . . . . .Heb. 12:2
that the *s* of thy
  nakedness . . . . Rev. 3:18
and they see his *s* . .Rev. 16:15

SHAMMAH
Son of Reuel, Gen. 36:13, 17;
  1 Chr. 1:37
——— David's brother,
  1 Sam. 16:9; 17:13
Called Shimeah, 2 Sam. 13:3,
  32; 21:21
Called Shimma, 1 Chr. 2:13
Called Shimea, 1 Chr. 20:7
——— One of David's
  mighty men, son of Agee,
  2 Sam. 23:11, 12
——— One of David's mighty
  men, 2 Sam. 23:25
Called Shammoth,
  1 Chr. 11:27

——— A Hararite, one of
  David's mighty men,
  2 Sam. 23:33

SHAPHAN
A scribe of King Josiah,
  2 Kin. 22:3–14;
  2 Chr. 34:8–20
Father of Gemariah,
  Jer. 36:10–12
——— The father of Ahikam
  and the grandfather of
  Gedaliah, 2 Kin. 22:12; 25:22;
  2 Chr. 34:20; Jer. 26:24;
  39:14; 40:5, 9, 11; 41:2; 43:6
——— Father of Elasah,
  Jer. 29:3
——— Father of Jaazaniah,
  Ezek. 8:11

SHARON
The maritime slope of
  Palestine north of the city
  of Joppa; David's herds in,
  1 Chr. 27:29
Roses and beauty of, Song 2:1;
  Is. 33:9; 35:2; 65:10
Called Saron, Acts 9:35
——— A place that has not
  been ascertained, 1 Chr. 5:16

SHARP
s razor, working
  deceitfully. . . . . Ps. 52:2
their tongue a *s*
  sword . . . . Ps. 57:4
Whose arrows
  are *s* . . . . .Is. 5:28
mouth went a *s*
  twoedged . . . . Rev. 1:16

SHEBA
Son of Raamah, Gen. 10:7;
  1 Chr. 1:9
——— Son of Joktan,
  Gen. 10:28; 1 Chr. 1:22
——— Son of Jokshan,
  Gen. 25:3; 1 Chr. 1:32
——— A Benjamite who led an
  insurrection against David,
  2 Sam. 20
——— A Gadite, 1 Chr. 5:13
——— A city of the tribe of
  Simeon, Josh. 19:2

SHECHEM
Also called Sichem and
  Sychem, a district in the
  central part of the land of
  Canaan; Abraham lives in,
  Gen. 12:6
The flocks and herds of Jacob
  kept in, Gen. 37:12–14
Joseph buried in, Josh. 24:32
Jacob buried in, Acts 7:16;
  Gen. 50:13
——— Also called Sychar, a city
  of refuge in Mount Ephraim,
  Josh. 20:7; 21:21; Judg. 21:19
Joshua assembled the tribes
  of Israel at, with all their
  elders, chiefs, and judges,
  and presented them before
  the Lord, Josh. 24:1–28

Joshua buried at,
Josh. 24:30–32
Abimelech made king at,
Judg. 8:31; 9
Rehoboam crowned at,
1 Kin. 12:1
Destroyed by Abimelech,
Judg. 9:45
Rebuilt by Jeroboam,
1 Kin. 12:25
Men of, killed by Ishmael,
Jer. 41:5
Jesus visits; disciples made in,
John 4:1–42
———— Son of Hamor; seduces
Jacob's daughter; killed by
Jacob's sons, Gen. 33:19; 34;
Josh. 24:32; Judg. 9:28
Called Sychem, Acts 7:16
———— Ancestor of the
Shechemites, Num. 26:31;
Josh. 17:2
———— Son of Shemidah,
1 Chr. 7:19

SHED
shall his blood
be s . . . . Gen. 9:6
thee from coming
to s . . . . 1 Sam. 25:26
the fifth rib, and s
. . . . 2 Sam. 20:10
Manasseh s
innocent . . . . . . 2 Kin. 21:16
innocent blood
that he s . . . . 2 Kin. 24:4
And s innocent
blood . . . . Ps. 106:38
make haste to s
innocent . . . . Is. 59:7
widow, and s not
innocent . . . . Jer. 7:6
widow, neither s
innocent . . . . Jer. 22:3
for to s innocent
blood . . . . Jer. 22:17
ravening the prey,
to s . . . . Ezek. 22:27
the righteous
blood s . . . . Matt. 23:35
testament, which
is s . . . . Matt. 26:28
my blood, which
is s . . . . Luke 22:20
Holy Ghost, he
hath s . . . . Acts 2:33
love of God is s
abroad . . . . Rom. 5:5

SHEEP
went to shear
his s . . . . Gen. 31:19
the LORD be not
as s . . . . Num. 27:17
flocks of thy s . . . . Deut. 28:18
thy s shall be
given . . . . Deut. 28:31
or flocks of thy s . . Deut. 28:51
suckling, ox and s . 1 Sam. 15:3
builded the s gate . . . . Neh. 3:1
Meah, even unto
the s . . . . Neh. 12:39

the s of thy
pasture . . . . Ps. 74:1
his people, and
the s . . . . Ps. 100:3
like s have gone
astray . . . . Is. 53:6
slaughter, and
as a s . . . . Is. 53:7
Israel is a
scattered s . . . . Jer. 50:17
among the flocks
of s . . . . Mic. 5:8
shepherd, and
the s . . . . Zech. 13:7
scattered abroad,
as s . . . . Matt. 9:36
my life for the s . . . John 10:15
And other s I have . John 10:16
unto him, Feed
my s . . . . John 21:17
shepherd of the s . . Heb. 13:20

SHEKEL
numbered, half a s . . Ex. 30:13
that is, half a s . . . . . Ex. 38:26
the poll, after
the s . . . . Num. 3:47
after the s . . . . Num. 18:16

SHEM
Son of Noah; Preserved in the
ark (ship), Gen. 5:32; 6:10;
7:13; 9:18; 1 Chr. 1:4
His filial conduct,
Gen. 9:23–27
Descendants of, Gen. 10:1, 21–
31; 11:10–29; 1 Chr. 1:17–54
Called Sem, Luke 3:36

SHEMAIAH
A prophet in the time of
Rehoboam; Prevents
Rehoboam from war with
Jeroboam, 1 Kin. 12:22–24;
2 Chr. 11:2–4
Prophesies the punishment of
Rehoboam by Shishak, king
of Egypt, 2 Chr. 12:5, 7
Writes chronicles, 2 Chr. 12:15
———— A descendant of David,
1 Chr. 3:22
———— A Simeonite, 1 Chr. 4:37
———— Son of Joel, 1 Chr. 5:4
Called Shema, 1 Chr. 5:8
———— A Merarite, 1 Chr. 9:14
In charge of the business of
the temple during the time of
Nehemiah, Neh. 11:15, 16
———— Son of Galal, 1 Chr. 9:16
Called Shemmua, Neh. 11:17
———— A chief Levite during
the time of David; assisted
in moving the ark of the
covenant from the house of
Obed-edom, 1 Chr. 15:8, 11
———— A Levite who assisted in
the divisions (shifts) of the
priests, 1 Chr. 24:6
———— A porter of the temple
during the time of David,
1 Chr. 26:4, 6, 7
———— A Levite sent by

Jehoshaphat to instruct the
people in the law, 2 Chr. 17:8
———— A Levite, son of
Jeduthun, 2 Chr. 29:14
———— A Levite, 2 Chr. 31:15
———— A Levite who
contributed largely for
Passover sacrifices,
2 Chr. 35:9
———— A Jew who returned
from Babylon with Ezra,
Ezra 8:13
———— A chief man with Ezra,
Ezra 8:16
———— A priest who put away
(divorced) his Gentile wife,
Ezra 10:21
———— An Israelite who put
away (divorced) his Gentile
wife, Ezra 10:31
———— Keeper of the east gate
of Jerusalem in the time of
Nehemiah, Neh. 3:29
———— A false prophet in the
time of Nehemiah, Neh. 6:10
———— A priest who sealed the
covenant with Nehemiah,
Neh. 10:8
———— A priest with
Zerubbabel, Neh. 12:6, 18
———— A priest, Neh. 12:35
———— The name of three
men who celebrated the
dedication of the new wall of
Jerusalem, Neh. 12:34, 36, 42
———— Father of the prophet
Urijah, Jer. 26:20
———— A false prophet,
Jer. 29:24–32
———— Father of Delaiah,
Jer. 36:12

SHEPHERD
sheep which have
no s . . . . Num. 27:17
that have not a s . 1 Kin. 22:17
Give ear, O S of
Israel . . . . Ps. 80:1
his flock like a s . . . . Is. 40:11
Cyrus, He is my s . . . . Is. 44:28
the sea with the s . . . . Is. 63:11
land of Egypt,
as a s . . . . Jer. 43:12
that s that will
stand . . . . Jer. 49:19
will set up one s . . Ezek. 34:23
all shall have
one s . . . . Ezek. 37:24
because there was
no s . . . . Zech. 10:2
sword, against
my s . . . . Zech. 13:7
sheep having no s . . Matt. 9:36
I am the good s . . . . John 10:11
I am the good s,
and . . . . John 10:14
one fold, and
one s . . . . John 10:16
Jesus, that great s . . Heb. 13:20
returned unto
the S . . . . 1 Pet. 2:25

And when the
chief S . . . . 1 Pet. 5:4

SHEPHERDS
the s make their
fold . . . . Is. 13:20
the s of Israel,
prophesy . . . . Ezek. 34:2
s search for my
flock. . . . . Ezek. 34:8
habitations of
the s . . . . Amos 1:2

SHEW
morrow the LORD
will s . . . . Num. 16:5
covenant with
them, nor s . . . . Deut. 7:2
s favour to the
young . . . . Deut. 28:50
the whole earth,
to s . . . . 2 Chr. 16:9
Thou wilt s me
the . . . . Ps. 16:11
formed them
will s . . . . Is. 27:11
heard, and shall s . . . . Is. 30:30
trumpet, and s my
people . . . . Is. 58:1
mouth they s
much love . . . . . . Ezek. 33:31
dream, and we
will s . . . . Dan. 2:4
this writing, and s . . . Dan. 5:7
but go thy way, s
thyself . . . . Matt. 8:4
forth began Jesus
to s . . . . Matt. 16:21
s great signs and
wonders . . . . Matt. 24:24
s thee these glad
tidings . . . . Luke 1:19
sayest thou
then, S . . . . John 14:9
hearts of all
men, s . . . . Acts 1:24
s light unto the
people . . . . Acts 26:23
that ye should s
forth . . . . 1 Pet. 2:9
bear witness,
and s . . . . 1 John 1:2

SHEWBREAD
set upon the
table s . . . . Ex. 25:30
s also set they . . . 2 Chr. 13:11
and did eat the s . . . Matt. 12:4
the table, and
the s . . . . Heb. 9:2

SHEWED
the LORD s him a
tree . . . . Ex. 15:25
was s thee in the
mount . . . . Ex. 25:40
congregation,
and s . . . . Num. 13:26
have they s
difference . . . . . . Ezek. 22:26
He hath s thee, O
man . . . . Mic. 6:8

s me Joshua the
high . . . . Zech. 3:1
slain them
which s . . . . Acts 7:52
but God hath s me
that . . . . Acts 10:28
But s first unto
them . . . . Acts 26:20
love, which ye
have s. . . . . Heb. 6:10
the pattern s to
thee . . . . Heb. 8:5
mercy, that hath s. . James 2:13

SHEWING
And s mercy unto
thousands . . . . Ex. 20:6
thine iniquities
by s . . . . Dan. 4:27
till the day of his s . . Luke 1:80
the temple of
God, s . . . . 2 Thess. 2:4

SHIELD
I am thy s, and thy . . Gen. 15:1
the s of thy . . . . . . Deut. 33:29
thou, O LORD,
art a s. . . . . Ps. 3:3
God is a sun and s . . Ps. 84:11
truth shall be
thy s. . . . . Ps. 91:4

SHILOH
A name of Jesus, Gen. 49:10
——— City of Ephraim, north
of Beth-el, and on the
highway from Beth-el to
Shechem, Judg. 21:19
Tabernacle located at,
Josh. 18:1–10; Judg. 18:31;
21:19; 1 Sam. 1:3, 9, 21, 24;
2:14; Ps. 78:60; Jer. 7:12
Seat of government during the
time of Joshua, Josh. 21:1, 2
The place of rendezvous for
the tribes, Josh. 22:9, 12;
Judg. 21:12
Eli lived at, 1 Sam. 1:9;
4:12, 13
Eli dies at, 1 Sam. 4:18
Ahijah the prophet lives at,
1 Kin. 14:2
Devoted men from, killed by
Ishmael, Jer. 41:5–9

SHIMEI
Also called Shimi; Son
of Gershon, Ex. 6:17;
Num. 3:18; 1 Chr. 6:17;
23:7, 10
——— A Benjamite
Curses David; David's
magnanimity toward,
2 Sam. 16:5–13; 19:16; 23;
1 Kin. 2:36–46
——— An officer of David,
1 Kin. 1:8
——— One of Solomon's
commissary officers,
1 Kin. 4:18
——— Grandson of Jeconiah,
1 Chr. 3:19

——— Son of Zacchur,
1 Chr. 4:26, 27
——— A Reubenite
Son of Gog, 1 Chr. 5:4
——— A Merarite
Son of Libni, 1 Chr. 6:29
——— A Gershonite
Son of Jahath, 1 Chr. 6:42
——— Father of a family in the
tribe of Benjamin, 1 Chr. 8:21
——— A Levite, 1 Chr. 23:9
——— A leader of singers
during the time of David,
1 Chr. 25:17
——— David's overseer of
vineyards, 1 Chr. 27:27
——— A son of Heman,
2 Chr. 29:14
——— A Levite
Treasurer of tithes and
offerings during the time of
Hezekiah, 2 Chr. 31:12, 13
——— A Levite who put away
(divorced) his Gentile wife,
Ezra 10:23
——— The name of two
Israelites who put away
(divorced) Gentile wives,
Ezra 10:33, 38
——— A Benjamite
Grandfather of Mordecai,
Esth. 2:5
——— The ancestor of a family,
Zech. 12:13

SHINE
LORD make his
face s . . . . Num. 6:25
his fire shall not s. . . . Job 18:5
between the
cherubims, s . . . . . . Ps. 80:1
cause thy face to s . . Ps. 80:3
cause thy face to s . . . Ps. 80:7
cause thy face to s . . Ps. 80:19
make his face to s . . Ps. 104:15
cause her light
to s . . . . Is. 13:10
image of God,
should s. . . . . 2 Cor. 4:4
nation, among
whom ye s. . . . . Phil. 2:15
neither of the
moon, to s . . . . Rev. 21:23

SHIPS
Egypt again with s Deut. 28:68
upon all the s of
Tarshish . . . . Is. 2:16
Howl, ye s of
Tarshish . . . . Is. 23:1
whose cry is in
the s . . . . Is. 43:14
wait for me, and
the s . . . . Is. 60:9

SHOES
loins girded,
your s. . . . . Ex. 12:11
thee, and put on
thy s. . . . . Ezek. 24:17

your heads, and
your s . . . . Ezek. 24:23
mightier than I,
whose s . . . . Matt. 3:11

SHOULDER
and withdrew
the s . . . . .Neh. 9:29
s, the rod of his
oppressor . . . . .Is. 9:4
shall be upon his s . . . . .Is. 9:6
and rend all
their s . . . . Ezek. 29:7
pulled away the s . . Zech. 7:11

SHOULDEST
the host of
heaven, s . . . . Deut. 4:19
servant, that
thou s . . . . 2 Sam. 9:8
king
Jehoshaphat, S . . 2 Chr. 19:2
If thou, LORD, s
mark . . . . Ps. 130:3
light thing that
thou s . . . . .Is. 49:6
art thou, that
thou s . . . . .Is. 51:12
thou s make thy
nest . . . . Jer. 49:16
thou s not have
looked . . . . Obad. 12
that thou s give
reward . . . . Rev. 11:18

SHOUT
Cry out and s,
thou . . . . .Is. 12:6
s, ye lower
parts of . . . . .Is. 44:23
S against her
round . . . . Jer. 50:15
s, O daughter of
Jerusalem . . . . Zech. 9:9

SHOWERS
s that water the
earth . . . . Ps. 72:6
the s have been
withholden . . . . Jer. 3:3
the heavens give s . . Jer. 14:22
shall be s of
blessing . . . . Ezek. 34:26

SHUNAMMITE
A person from the city of
Shunem; Abishag, the girl
who took care of David,
1 Kin. 1:3
Desired by Adonijah as wife,
1 Kin. 2:13–25
——— A woman who gave
hospitality to Elisha, and
whose son he raised to life,
2 Kin. 4:8–37

SHUT
be s out from the
camp . . . . .Num. 12:14
and the LORD
had s . . . . Deut. 32:30
is none s up, or
left . . . . Deut. 32:36
s up and left in
Israel . . . . 1 Kin. 14:10

s up and left in
Israel . . . . 1 Kin. 21:21
I am s up, and I
cannot . . . . Ps. 88:8
their ears heavy,
and s . . . . .Is. 6:10
he hath s their
eyes . . . . .Is. 44:18
gates shall not
be s . . . . .Is. 45:1
the kings shall s
their . . . . .Is. 52:15
as a burning fire s . . . . Jer. 20:9
Jeremiah the
prophet was s . . . . . . Jer. 32:2
king of Judah
had s . . . . Jer. 32:3
wherefore s
thou up . . . . Dan. 8:26
But thou, O
Daniel, s . . . . .Dan. 12:4
when the doors
were s . . . . .John 20:19
the doors being s . . John 20:26

SICK
they were s, my
clothing . . . . Ps. 35:13
the whole head is s . . . .Is. 1:5
healed that which
was s . . . . Ezek. 34:4
brought unto him
all s . . . . Matt. 4:24
brought to him a
man s . . . . Matt. 9:2
hands on the s . . . Mark 16:18

SIDE
strike it on the
two s . . . . Ex. 12:7
two s posts, the
LORD . . . . Ex. 12:23
the one on the
one s . . . . Ex. 17:12
candlestick out of
the one s . . . . Ex. 25:32
other s Jordan,
Sihon . . . . Josh. 2:10
Hinnom unto the
south s . . . . Josh. 15:8
the s of mount
Jearim . . . . Josh. 15:10
other s Jordan by
Jericho . . . . Josh. 20:8
the sand by the
sea s . . . . Judg. 7:12
the east s of the
land . . . . Judg. 11:18
s the river, from
Tiphsah . . . . 1 Kin. 4:24
five on the right s . 1 Kin. 7:49
many, fear on
every s . . . . Jer. 20:10
gather them on
every s . . . . Ezek. 37:21
were three on
this s . . . . Ezek. 40:21
stoodest on the
other s . . . . Obad. 11
thrust it into my s . John 20:27
either s of the
river . . . . Rev. 22:2

SIDES
shall come out of
the s . . . . Ex. 25:32
and the s thereof
round . . . . Ex. 30:3
scourges in your s . Josh. 23:13
mount Zion, on
the s . . . . Ps. 48:2
congregation, in
the s . . . . .Is. 14:13
down to hell, to
the s . . . . .Is. 14:15

SIDON
Also called Zidon; Son
of Canaan, Gen. 10:15;
1 Chr. 1:13
——— A city on the northern
boundary of the Canaanites,
Gen. 10:19
Designated by Jacob as
the border of the tribe of
Zebulun, Gen. 49:13
Was on the northern boundary
of the tribe of Asher,
Josh. 19:28; 2 Sam. 24:6
Belonged to the land of Israel
according to a promise,
Josh. 13:6
Inhabitants of, lived in
security and without a worry,
Judg. 18:7
Israelites failed to make
conquest of, Judg. 1:31; 3:3
The inhabitants of,
contributed cedar for the
first and second temple,
1 Kin. 5:6; 1 Chr. 22:4;
Ezra 3:7
Solomon marries women of,
1 Kin. 11:1
Ahab marries a woman of,
1 Kin. 16:31
People of, come to hear Jesus,
Mark 3:8; Luke 6:17
Inhabitants of, offend Herod
Agrippa I, Acts 12:20–23
Commerce of, Is. 23:2, 4, 12
The sailors of, Ezek. 27:8
Prophecies concerning,
Jer. 25:15–22; 27:3–11;
47:4; Ezek. 28:21–23; 32:30;
Joel 3:4–8
Jesus visits the region of, and
heals the daughter of the
non-Jewish, Syro-Phoenician
woman, Matt. 15:21–28;
Mark 7:24–31
Visited by Paul, Acts 27:3

SIEGE
given thee, in
the s . . . . .Deut. 28:53
left him in the s . . Deut. 28:55
things secretly in
the s . . . . .Deut. 28:57
And lay s
against it . . . . Ezek. 4:2
days of the s are
fulfilled . . . . Ezek. 5:2

SIGHT

s, and wilt give ear . . Ex. 15:26
Moses did so in
  the s . . . . Ex. 17:6
s of the LORD, to
  provoke . . . . Deut. 9:18
shalt be mad for
  the s . . . . Deut. 28:34
s of thine eyes . . . . Deut. 28:67
evil again in the s . . Judg. 13:1
wickedness in
  the s . . . . 1 Kin. 21:25
s of the LORD, to
  provoke . . . . 2 Kin. 17:17
which is good in
  thy s . . . . 2 Kin. 20:3
s of the LORD, to
  provoke . . . . 2 Kin. 21:6
which was evil in
  the s . . . . 2 Kin. 21:16
in thy s shall no
  man . . . . Ps. 143:2
cast them out of
  my s . . . . Jer. 15:1
in whose s I made
  myself . . . . Ezek. 20:9
in whose s I
  brought . . . . Ezek. 20:14
shall be great in
  the s . . . . Luke 1:15
and recovering
  of s . . . . Luke 4:18
unreproveable in
  his s . . . . Col. 1:22
Jesus Christ, in
  the s . . . . 1 Thess. 1:3
manifest in his s . . . Heb. 4:13

SIGN

s unto thee upon
  thine . . . . Ex. 13:9
for it is a s
  between . . . . Ex. 31:13
giveth thee a s . . . . . Deut. 13:1
And the s or the
  wonder . . . . Deut. 13:2
be upon thee for
  a s . . . . Deut. 28:46
shall give you a s . . . . . Is. 7:14
three years for a s . . . . . Is. 20:3
for an
  everlasting s . . . . Is. 55:13
And I will set a s . . . . Is. 66:19
Tekoa, and set
  up a s . . . . Jer. 6:1
and will make him
  a s . . . . Ezek. 14:8
sabbaths, to be a s . Ezek. 20:12
and thou shalt be
  a s . . . . Ezek. 24:27
seeketh after a s . . . Matt. 16:4
s of the Son of
  man . . . . Matt. 24:30
s which shall be
  spoken . . . . Luke 2:34

SIGNS

wherewith thou
  shalt do s . . . . Ex. 4:17
heart, and
  multiply my s . . . . Ex. 7:3
temptations, by s . . Deut. 4:34

shewedst s and
  wonders . . . . Neh. 9:10
their ensigns for s . . . Ps. 74:4
We see not our s . . . . . Ps. 74:9
wrought his s in
  Egypt . . . . Ps. 78:43
are for s and for
  wonders . . . . Is. 8:18
shew great s and
  wonders . . . . Matt. 24:24
And these s shall
  follow . . . . Mark 16:17
witness, both
  with s . . . . Heb. 2:4

SIHON

King of the Amorites; His seat
  of government at Heshbon,
  Num. 21:26
The proverbial chant
  celebrating the victory of
  Sihon over the Moabites,
  Num. 21:26–30
Conquest of his kingdom by
  the Israelites, Num. 21:21–
  25; Deut. 2:24–37; 3:2, 6, 8

SILAS

The short form of the name;
  Also called Silvanus (the long
  form of the name)
Sent to Paul, in Antioch (of
  Syria), from Jerusalem,
  Acts 15:22–34
Becomes Paul's companion,
  Acts 15:40, 41; 2 Cor. 1:19;
  1 Thess. 1:1; 2 Thess. 1:1
Imprisoned with Paul in
  Philippi, Acts 16:19–40
Driven, with Paul, from
  Thessalonica, Acts 17:4–10
Left by Paul at Berea,
  Acts 17:14
Rejoins Paul at Corinth,
  Acts 17:15; 18:5
Carries Peter's letter to Asia
  Minor, 1 Pet. 5:12

SILOAM

Also called Shiloah and
  Siloah; A pool in Jerusalem,
  Neh. 3:15; Is. 8:6
Jesus directs the blind man
  whom he had healed to wash
  in, John 9:1–11
Tower of, in the wall of
  Jerusalem, falls and kills
  eighteen people, Luke 13:4

SILVER

flocks, and herds,
  and s . . . . Gen. 24:35
twenty pieces of s . . Gen. 37:28
house full of s . . . . Num. 22:18
multiply to
  himself s . . . . Deut. 17:17
and ten pieces of s . . Judg. 9:4
bringing gold,
  and s . . . . 1 Kin. 10:22
took all the s . . . . 1 Kin. 15:18
hundred talents
  of s . . . . 2 Kin. 18:14

idols are s and
  gold . . . . Ps. 115:4
fining pot is for s . . Prov. 17:3
shall not regard s . . . . Is. 13:17
sons from far,
  their s . . . . Is. 60:9
Reprobate s shall
  men . . . . Jer. 6:30
praised the gods
  of s . . . . Dan. 5:23
over with gold
  and s . . . . Hab. 2:19
their s nor their
  gold . . . . Zeph. 1:18
will refine them
  as s . . . . Zech. 13:9
and purifier of s . . . . . Mal. 3:3
or s, or stone . . . . . . Acts 17:29
corruptible
  things, as s . . . . . 1 Pet. 1:18

SIMEON

Son of Jacob, Gen. 29:33;
  35:23; Ex. 1:1, 2; 1 Chr. 2:1
With Levi avenges upon the
  Shechemites the seduction of
  Dinah, Gen. 34; 49:5–7
Jacob's denunciation of,
  Gen. 34:30; 49:5–7
Goes down into Egypt to
  buy corn; is imprisoned by
  Joseph, and is detained,
  Gen. 42:24, 36; 43:23
His sons, Gen. 46:10; Ex. 6:15;
  1 Chr. 4:24–37
Descendants of,
  Num. 26:12–14
See Tribe of, below
—— A devout man in
  Jerusalem
Blesses Jesus (when an infant)
  in the temple, Luke 2:25–35
—— An ancestor of Jesus,
  Luke 3:30
—— A disciple
Also called Niger, Acts 13:1

SIMON

One of the twelve apostles; a
  revolutionary and a patriot;
  Called "The Canaanite,"
  (from the Hebrew root
  meaning "religious zeal"
  Matt. 10:4; Mark 3:18
Called "Zelotes," Luke 6:15;
  Acts 1:13
—— A physical half-brother
  of Jesus, Matt. 13:55;
  Mark 6:3
—— A leper
Jesus dines with, Matt. 26:6;
  Mark 14:3
—— A man from the city of
  Cyrene
Compelled to carry Jesus'
  cross, Matt. 27:32;
  Mark 15:21; Luke 23:26
—— A Pharisee
Jesus dines with, Luke 7:36–44
—— The father of Judas
  Iscariot, John 6:71; 12:4;
  13:2, 26

—— A sorcerer (also called Simon Magus)
Converted by Philip
Rebuked by Peter, Acts 8:9–13, 18–24
—— A tanner
Peter lodges with, Acts 9:43; 10:6, 17, 32

SIN

lest they make
  thee *s* . . . . Ex. 23:33
transgression
  and *s* . . . . Ex. 34:7
that is anointed
  do *s* . . . . Lev. 4:3
man *s*, and wilt
  thou . . . . Num. 16:22
and every *s*
  offering . . . . Num. 18:9
this thing became
  a *s* . . . . 1 Kin. 12:30
s, and who made
  Israel . . . . 1 Kin. 14:16
an offering for *s* . . . . . Is. 53:10
and he bare the
  s of . . . . Is. 53:12
will remember
  their *s* . . . . Jer. 31:34
of my body for
  the *s* . . . . Mic. 6:7
which taketh
  away the *s* . . . . John 1:29
the wages of *s* is
  death . . . . Rom. 6:23
free from the law
  of *s* . . . . Rom. 8:2
hath made him to
  be *s* . . . . 2 Cor. 5:21
are, yet without *s* . . . Heb. 4:15
second time
  without *s* . . . . Heb. 9:28
cleanseth us from
  all *s* . . . . 1 John 1:7
unto you, that ye *s* . 1 John 2:1
man see his
  brother *s* . . . . 1 John 5:16

SINAI

Wilderness of; The people
  of Israel journeyed in,
  Num. 10:12
Kept the Passover Festival in,
  Num. 9:1–5
Counted in, Num. 26:64

SING

spake, saying, I
  will *s* . . . . Ex. 15:1
O *s* unto the
  Lord a . . . . Ps. 98:1
let them *s* praises . . . Ps. 149:3
will I *s* to my
  wellbeloved . . . . Is. 5:1
Awake and *s*, ye
  that . . . . Is. 26:19
tongue of the
  dumb *s* . . . . Is. 35:6
S, O ye heavens . . . . . Is. 44:23
S, O heavens . . . . Is. 49:13
S, O barren, thou
  that . . . . Is. 54:1

come and *s* in the
  height . . . . Jer. 31:12
S and rejoice, O
  daughter . . . . Zech. 2:10
s the song of
  Moses . . . . Rev. 15:3

SINGING

even with joy
  and *s* . . . . Is. 35:2
s, ye
  mountains, O . . . . . . Is. 44:23
Chaldeans, with a
  voice of *s* . . . . Is. 48:20
forth into *s*, O
  mountains . . . . Is. 49:13
s, and cry aloud,
  thou . . . . Is. 54:1
s, and all the trees . . . Is. 55:12
spiritual songs, *s* . . . Col. 3:16

SINNED

hath *s*, a young
  bullock . . . . Lev. 4:3
sin, which they
  have *s* . . . . Lev. 4:14
your sins which
  ye *s* . . . . Deut. 9:18
s against the
  Lord . . . . 1 Sam. 7:6
unto Nathan, I
  have *s* . . . . 2 Sam. 12:13
but *s* against thy
  judgments . . . . Neh. 9:29
thee only, have I *s* . . . . Ps. 51:4
have *s* with our
  fathers . . . . Ps. 106:6
s against the
  Lord . . . . Jer. 3:25
we have *s* against
  thee . . . . Jer. 14:7
s against the
  Lord . . . . Jer. 50:7
sin that he hath *s* Ezek. 18:24
have *s*, and will
  cleanse . . . . Ezek. 37:23
God, because we
  have *s* . . . . Dan. 9:11
, because I have *s* . . . . Mic. 7:9
have *s*, and come
  short . . . . Rom. 3:23
for that all have *s* . . Rom. 5:12
the angels that *s* . . . 2 Pet. 2:4

SINNER

the *s* he giveth
  travail . . . . Eccl. 2:26
a *s* do evil an
  hundred . . . . Eccl. 8:12
for she is a *s* . . . . . . Luke 7:39
can a man that
  is a *s*, ... John 9:16

SINNERS

standeth in the
  way of *s* . . . . Ps. 1:1
the righteous,
  but *s* . . . . Matt. 9:13
yet *s*, Christ died . . . Rom. 5:8
the world to
  save *s* . . . . 1 Tim. 1:15
Cleanse your
  hands, ye *s* . . . . . . James 4:8

SINNETH

any sin that he *s* . . Deut. 19:15
the soul that *s*, it . . Ezek. 18:4
soul that *s*, it . . . . . Ezek. 18:20
whosoever is born
  of God *s* . . . . 1 John 5:18

SINS

walk in the *s* of
  Jeroboam . . . . . 1 Kin. 16:31
covereth his *s* . . . . Prov. 28:13
your *s* be as
  scarlet . . . . Is. 1:18
double for all
  her *s* . . . . Is. 40:2
not remember
  thy *s* . . . . Is. 43:25
and the *s* of Judah . . Jer. 50:20
to make an end
  of *s* . . . . Dan. 9:24
and visit their *s* . . . . Hos. 8:13
people from
  their *s* . . . . Matt. 1:21
remission of *s* . . . . Luke 24:47
s, and ye shall
  receive . . . . Acts 2:38
receive
  forgiveness of *s* . . . Acts 26:18
the forgiveness
  of *s* . . . . Eph. 1:7
purged our *s*, sat
  down . . . . Heb. 1:3
offered to bear
  the *s* . . . . Heb. 9:28
once suffered for *s* . 1 Pet. 3:18
If we confess our *s* . 1 John 1:9
propitiation for
  our *s* . . . . 1 John 2:2
propitiation for
  our *s* . . . . 1 John 4:10
washed us from
  our *s* . . . . Rev. 1:5

SISTER

said, She is my *s* . . . Gen. 26:7
the prophetess,
  the *s* . . . . Ex. 15:20
garden, my *s*, my
  spouse . . . . Song 5:1
her treacherous *s*
  Judah . . . . Jer. 3:8
s Judah hath not
  turned . . . . Jer. 3:10
or, Ah *s* . . . . Jer. 22:18
hath humbled
  his *s* . . . . Ezek. 22:11
lead about a *s*, a
  wife . . . . 1 Cor. 9:5

SIT

will not *s* down
  till . . . . 1 Sam. 16:11
unto my Lord, S
  thou . . . . Ps. 110:1
being desolate
  shall *s* . . . . Is. 3:26
I will *s* also upon . . . . Is. 14:13
prison, and them
  that *s* . . . . Is. 42:7
Humble
  yourselves, *s* . . . . . . Jer. 13:18
from thy glory,
  and *s* . . . . Jer. 48:18

SITTETH

said, I am a
God, I s . . . . Ezek. 28:2
cometh, and
they s . . . . Ezek. 33:31
Ancient of days
did s . . . . Dan. 7:9
shall s every man
under . . . . Mic. 4:4
thy fellows that s . . . Zech. 3:8
he shall s as a
refiner . . . . Mal. 3:3
multitude to s . . . . Matt. 14:19
of man shall s . . . . Matt. 19:28
he s upon the
throne . . . . Matt. 25:31
kingdom, and s on
thrones . . . . Luke 22:30
overcometh will I
grant to s . . . . Rev. 3:21

SITTETH

firstborn of
Pharaoh that s . . . . . Ex. 11:5
way of sinners,
nor s . . . . Ps. 1:1
He that s in the
heavens . . . . Ps. 2:4
he s between the
cherubims . . . . Ps. 99:1
that s upon the
circle . . . . Is. 40:22
face of him that s . . . Rev. 6:16

SIXTH

s year, in the s
month . . . . Ezek. 8:1
king, in the s
month . . . . Hag. 1:1
passover, and
about the s . . . . . . John 19:14
had opened the s
seal . . . . Rev. 6:12

SKIN

s, and his dung,
shalt . . . . Ex. 29:14
And the s of the
bullock . . . . Lev. 4:11
wood, or raiment,
or s . . . . Lev. 11:32
My s is black upon . . Job 30:30

SLAIN

you, and ye shall
be s . . . . Lev. 26:17
toucheth one that
is s . . . . Num. 19:16
Thine ox shall
be s . . . . Deut. 28:31
thee, saying, I
have s . . . . 2 Sam. 1:16
thy wife, and
hast s . . . . 2 Sam. 12:9
altars, and s thy
prophets . . . . . . 1 Kin. 19:10
no more cover
her s . . . . Is. 26:21
and the s of the
LORD . . . . Is. 66:16
and night for the s . . . . Jer. 9:1
their young men
be s . . . . Jer. 18:21
And the s shall fall . . Ezek. 6:7

have crucified
and s . . . . Acts 2:23
have s them which
shewed . . . . Acts 7:52
Lamb as it had
been s . . . . Rev. 5:6
thou wast s, and
hast . . . . Rev. 5:9
was s to receive
power . . . . Rev. 5:12
s for the word of
God . . . . Rev. 6:9
s of men seven
thousand . . . . Rev. 11:13
life of the Lamb s . . . Rev. 13:8

SLAUGHTER

Bozrah, and a
great s . . . . Is. 34:6
as a lamb to the s . . . . . Is. 53:7
bow down to the s . . . Is. 65:12
the s, saith the
King . . . . Jer. 48:15
them go down to
the s . . . . Jer. 50:27
s, to lift up the
voice . . . . Ezek. 21:22

SLAY

manner, to s the
righteous . . . . Gen. 18:25
together against
me, and s . . . . Gen. 34:30
innocent and
righteous s . . . . Ex. 23:7
bring them out,
to s . . . . Ex. 32:12
blood himself
shall s . . . . Num. 35:19
s both man and
woman . . . . 1 Sam. 15:3
innocent blood,
to s . . . . 1 Sam. 19:5
young men wilt
thou s . . . . 2 Kin. 8:12
life, to destroy,
to s . . . . Esth. 8:11
his lips shall he s . . . . . Is. 11:4
he shall s the
dragon . . . . Is. 27:1
Lord GOD shall s
thee . . . . Is. 65:15
the forest shall s . . . . . Jer. 5:6
S all her bullocks . . . Jer. 50:27
S utterly old and
young . . . . Ezek. 9:6
sword, and it
shall s . . . . Amos 9:4

SLEEP

Behold, thou shalt
s . . . . Deut. 31:16
fulfilled, and thou
shalt s . . . . 2 Sam. 7:12
night, when
deep s . . . . Job 33:15
down in peace,
and s . . . . Ps. 4:8
deep s, and hath
closed . . . . Is. 29:10
rejoice, and s a
perpetual . . . . Jer. 51:39

s a perpetual s,
and . . . . Jer. 51:57
the wilderness,
and s . . . . Ezek. 34:25
troubled, and his s . . Dan. 2:1
me, I was in a
deep s . . . . Dan. 8:18
that s in the dust . . Dan. 12:2
s in Jesus will . . . 1 Thess. 4:14

SLEW

And he s it . . . . Lev. 8:15
Thy servant s
both . . . . 1 Sam. 17:36
king of Zobah,
David s . . . . 2 Sam. 8:5
s them with the
sword . . . . 1 Kin. 2:32
brook Kishon,
and s . . . . 1 Kin. 18:40
captive to Kir,
and s . . . . 2 Kin. 16:9
s the sons of
Zedekiah . . . . 2 Kin. 25:7
Babylon smote
them, and s . . . . 2 Kin. 25:21
who s their young
men . . . . 2 Chr. 36:17
backs, and s thy
prophets . . . . Neh. 9:26
s them, then they
sought . . . . Ps. 78:34
an ox is as if he s . . . . . Is. 66:3
the king of
Babylon s . . . . Jer. 39:6
the king of
Babylon s . . . . Jer. 52:10
Barachias, whom
ye s . . . . Matt. 23:35
that wicked one,
and s . . . . 1 John 3:12

SLOW

gracious and
merciful, s . . . . Neh. 9:17
merciful and
gracious, s . . . . Ps. 103:8
is s to anger
appeaseth . . . . . . Prov. 15:18
gracious and
merciful, s . . . . Joel 2:13
God, and
merciful, s . . . . Jon. 4:2
hear, s to speak, s . . James 1:19

SMALL

ye shall hear the s . Deut. 1:17
Kidron, and
stamped it s . . . . 2 Kin. 23:6
left unto us a very s . . . . Is. 1:9
Is it a s thing for . . . . . . Is. 7:13
s dust, and the
multitude . . . . Is. 29:5
a s number that
escape . . . . Jer. 44:28
I will make thee s . . . Jer. 49:15
despised the day
of s . . . . Zech. 4:10
witnessing both
to s . . . . Acts 26:22
that fear thy
name, s . . . . Rev. 11:18

And I saw the
   dead, s . . . . Rev. 20:12

SMITE
neither will I
   again s . . . . Gen. 8:21
behold, I will s
   with . . . . Ex. 7:17
this night, and
   will s . . . . Ex. 12:12
I s the land of
   Egypt . . . . Ex. 12:13
will pass through
   to s . . . . Ex. 12:23
thou shalt s the
   rock . . . . Ex. 17:6
thou shalt s them . . . Deut. 7:2
The LORD shall s
   thee . . . . Deut. 28:22
The LORD will s
   thee . . . . Deut. 28:27
The LORD shall s
   thee . . . . Deut. 28:28
The LORD shall s
   thee . . . . Deut. 28:35
and s Amalek, and
   utterly . . . . 1 Sam. 15:3
he shall s the
   earth . . . . Is. 11:4
river, and shall s . . . . . Is. 11:15
the heat nor sun s . . . Is. 49:10
s them with the
   edge . . . . Jer. 21:7
s the land of Egypt . . Jer. 43:11
a third part, and s . . . Ezek. 5:2
melteth, and the
   knees s . . . . Nah. 2:10
s the shepherd,
   and . . . . Zech. 13:7

SMITTEN
be s before thine
   enemies . . . . Deut. 28:25
s me upon the
   cheek . . . . Job 16:10
thou hast s all
   mine . . . . Ps. 3:7
against them, and
   hath s . . . . Is. 5:25
esteem him
   stricken, s . . . . Is. 53:4
In vain have I s
   your . . . . Jer. 2:30
he hath s, and he
   will . . . . Hos. 6:1
part of the sun
   was s . . . . Rev. 8:12

SMOKE
altogether on a s . . . . Ex. 19:18
doth thine anger s . . . Ps. 74:1
was filled with s . . . . Is. 6:4
vanish away like s . . . . Is. 51:6
floor, and as the s . . . Hos. 13:3
chariots in the s . . . . Nah. 2:13
the s of their
   torment . . . . Rev. 14:11
see the s of her
   burning . . . . Rev. 18:9
saw the s of her
   burning . . . . Rev. 18:18

SMOTE
midnight the
   LORD s . . . . Ex. 12:29
his rod he s the
   rock . . . . Num. 20:11
And Israel s him
   with . . . . Num. 21:24
s him, and his
   sons . . . . Num. 21:35
that s him shall
   surely . . . . Num. 35:21
And the men of
   Ai s . . . . Josh. 7:5
and s it with the
   edge . . . . Josh. 19:47
destroyed them,
   and s . . . . 1 Sam. 5:6
quietly, and s . . . . . 2 Sam. 3:27
he s Moab, and
   measured . . . . 2 Sam. 8:2
David s also
   Hadadezer . . . . . . 2 Sam. 8:3
so he s him
   therewith . . . . . 2 Sam. 20:10
cities of Israel,
   and s . . . . 1 Kin. 15:20
the king of
   Babylon s . . . . . . 2 Kin. 25:21
And s all the
   firstborn . . . . Ps. 78:51
He s also all the
   firstborn . . . . Ps. 105:36
stay upon him
   that s . . . . Is. 10:20
Nebuchadrezzar
   king of Babylon s . . . Jer. 46:2
the king of
   Babylon s . . . . Jer. 52:27
s him with the
   palms . . . . Matt. 26:67

SNARE
will surely be a s . . . . Ex. 23:33
will be a s unto
   thee . . . . Deut. 7:16
which were a s
   unto . . . . Ps. 106:36
proud have hid a s . . Ps. 140:5
for a gin and
   for a s . . . . Is. 8:14
s, are upon
   thee, O . . . . Is. 24:17
be taken in the s . . . . . Is. 24:18
be taken in the s . . . . Jer. 48:44
shall be taken in
   my s . . . . Ezek. 12:13
temptation and a s . . 1 Tim. 6:9

SODOM
Also called Sodoma; Situated
   on the plain of the Jordan
   River, Gen. 13:10
The southeastern limit of the
   Canaanites, Gen. 10:19
Lot lived in, Gen. 13:12
King of, joins other kings of
   the nations resisting the
   invasion of Chedorlaomer,
   Gen. 14:1–12
Wickedness of the inhabitants
   of, Gen. 13:13; 19:4–13;
   Deut. 32:32; Is. 3:9;

Jer. 23:14; Lam. 4:6;
   Ezek. 16:46, 48, 49; Jude 7
Abraham's intercession for,
   Gen. 18:16–33
Destroyed on account of the
   wickedness of the people,
   Gen. 19:1–29; Deut. 29:23;
   Is. 13:19; Jer. 49:18; 50:40;
   Lam. 4:6; Amos 4:11;
   Zeph. 2:9; Matt. 10:15;
   Luke 17:29; Rom. 9:29;
   2 Pet. 2:6
Figurative
   Of wickedness, Deut. 23:17;
   32:32; Is. 1:10;
   Ezek. 16:46–56

SOJOURN
S in this land, and . . Gen. 26:3
a stranger shall s . . . Ex. 12:48
the strangers
   that s . . . . Lev. 17:10
a stranger shall s . . . Num. 9:14
not into Egypt to s . . . Jer. 43:2
land of Egypt to s . . . Jer. 44:28

SOLD
of the pit, and s
   Joseph . . . . Gen. 37:28
that s to all the
   people . . . . Gen. 42:6
waxen poor, and
   be s . . . . Lev. 25:39
possession, shall
   be s . . . . Lev. 27:28
ye shall be s . . . . . . Deut. 28:68
except their Rock
   had s . . . . Deut. 32:30
spoiled them, and
   he s . . . . Judg. 2:14
And the LORD s
   them . . . . Judg. 4:2
enchantments,
   and s . . . . 2 Kin. 17:17
it to whom I
   have s . . . . Is. 50:1
the LORD, Ye
   have s . . . . Is. 52:3
harlot, and s a girl . . . Joel 3:3
moved with
   envy, s . . . . Acts 7:9

SOLEMN
it is a s assembly . . Lev. 23:36
gladness, and in
   your s . . . . Num. 10:10
seventh day shall
   be a s . . . . Deut. 16:8
eighth day they
   made a s . . . . 2 Chr. 7:9
iniquity, even
   the s . . . . Is. 1:13
come to the s
   feasts . . . . Lam. 1:4
in the day of a s
   feast . . . . Lam. 2:7
ye a fast, call a s . . . . Joel 1:14

SOLES
place whereon
   the s . . . . Deut. 11:24
pass, as soon as
   the s . . . . Josh. 3:13

at the *s* of thy feet . . . Is. 60:14

the place of the *s* . . . Ezek. 43:7

SOLOMON

Son of David by Bath-sheba, 2 Sam. 12:24; 1 Kin. 1:13, 17, 21

Named Jedidiah, by Nathan the prophet, 2 Sam. 12:24, 25

An ancestor of Joseph, Matt. 1:6

Succeeds David to the throne of Israel, 1 Kin. 1:11–48; 2:12; 1 Chr. 23:1; 28; Eccl. 1:12

Anointed king a second time, 1 Chr. 29:22

His prayer for wisdom, and his vision, 1 Kin. 3:5–14; 2 Chr. 1:7–12

Covenant renewed in a vision after the dedication of the temple, 1 Kin. 9:1–9; 2 Chr. 7:12–22

His rigorous reign, 1 Kin. 2

Builds the temple, 1 Kin. 5; 6; 9:10; 1 Chr. 6:10; 2 Chr. 2; 3; 4; 7:11; Jer. 52:20; Acts 7

Dedicates the temple, 1 Kin. 8; 2 Chr. 6

Renews the courses of the priests and Levites, and the forms of service according to the commandment of Moses and the regulations of David, 2 Chr. 8:12–16; 35:4; Neh. 12:45

Builds his palace, 1 Kin. 3:1; 7:1, 8; 9:10; 2 Chr. 7:11; 8:1; Eccl. 2:4

Builds his house, The Forest of Lebanon, 1 Kin. 7:2–7

Builds another house for Pharaoh's daughter, 1 Kin. 7:8–12; 9:24; 2 Chr. 8:11; Eccl. 2:4

Ivory throne of, 1 Kin. 7:7; 10:18–20

Porches of judgment, 1 Kin. 7:7

Builds Millo (a stronghold), the wall around Jerusalem, the cities of Hazor, Megiddo, Gezer, Beth-horon, Baalath, Tadmor, store cities, and cities for chariots, and for cavalry, 1 Kin. 9:15–19; 2 Chr. 9:25

Provides an armory, 1 Kin. 10:16, 17

Plants vineyards and orchards of all kinds of fruit trees; makes pools, Eccl. 2:4–6

Imports apes and peacocks, 1 Kin. 10:22

Drinking vessels of his houses, 1 Kin. 10:21; 2 Chr. 9:20

Musicians and musical instruments of his court, 1 Kin. 10:12; 2 Chr. 9:11; Eccl. 2:8

The splendor of his court,

1 Kin. 10:5–9, 12; 2 Chr. 9:3–8; Eccl. 2:9; Matt. 6:29; Luke 12:27

Commerce of, 1 Kin. 9:28; 10:11, 12, 22, 28, 29; 2 Chr. 1:16, 17; 8:17, 18; 9:13–22, 28

Presents received by, 1 Kin. 10:10; 2 Chr. 9:9, 23, 24

Is visited by the Queen of Sheba, 1 Kin. 10:1–13; 2 Chr. 9:1–12

Wealth of, 1 Kin. 9; 10:10, 14, 15, 23, 27; 2 Chr. 1:15; 9:1, 9, 13, 24, 27; Eccl. 1:16

Has seven-hundred wives and three-hundred concubines, 1 Kin. 11:3; Deut. 17:17

Their influence over him, 1 Kin. 11:4

Marries one of Pharaoh's daughters, 1 Kin. 3:1

Builds idolatrous temples, 1 Kin. 11:1–8; 2 Kin. 23:13

His idolatry, 1 Kin. 3:3, 4; 2 Kin. 23:13; Neh. 13:26

Extent of his dominions, 1 Kin. 4:21, 24; 8:65; 2 Chr. 7:8; 9:26

Receives tribute (taxes), 1 Kin. 4:21; 9:21; 2 Chr. 8:8

Officers of, 1 Kin. 2:35; 4:1–19; 2 Chr. 8:9, 10

His purveyors, 1 Kin. 4:7–19

Divides his kingdom into subsistence departments; the daily, subsistence rate for his court, 1 Kin. 4:7–23, 27, 28

Military equipment of, 1 Kin. 4:26, 28; 10:16, 17, 26, 28; 2 Chr. 1:14; 9:25; Deut. 17:15, 16

Cedes some inferior cities to Hiram, 1 Kin. 9:10–13; 2 Chr. 8:2

Wisdom and fame of, 1 Kin. 4:29–34; 10:3, 4, 8, 23, 24; 1 Chr. 29:24, 25; 2 Chr. 9:2–7, 22, 23; Eccl. 1:16; Matt. 12:42

Piety of, 1 Kin. 3:5–15; 4:29; 8

Beloved of God, 2 Sam. 12:24

Justice of, illustrated in his judgment of the two prostitutes, 1 Kin. 3:16–28

Oppressions of, 1 Kin. 12:4; 2 Chr. 10:4

Reigns for forty years, 2 Chr. 9:30

Death of, 2 Chr. 9:29–31

Prophecies concerning, 2 Sam. 7:12–16; 1 Kin. 11:9–13; 1 Chr. 17:11–14; 28:6, 7; Ps. 132:11

A "type" of Christ, Ps. 45:2–17

SON

work, thou, nor thy *s* . . . . Ex. 20:10

neither the *s* of man . . . . Num. 23:19

and he shall be my *s* . . . . 2 Sam. 7:14

thou, Solomon my *s* . . . . 1 Chr. 28:9

me, Thou art my *s* . . . . Ps. 2:7

conceive, and bear a *s* . . . . Is. 7:14

is born, unto us a *s* . . . . Is. 9:6

mourneth for his only *s* . . . . Zech. 12:10

s, and thou shalt call . . . . Matt. 1:21

This is my beloved *S* . . . . . . Matt. 3:17

For the *S* of man shall . . . . Matt. 16:27

This is my beloved *S* . . . . . . Matt. 17:5

Even as the *S* of man . . . . Matt. 20:28

Father, and of the *S* . . . . Matt. 28:19

shall be called the *S* . . . . Luke 1:32

the only begotten *S* . . . . John 1:18

Rabbi, thou art the *S* . . . . John 1:49

begotten *S*, that whosoever . . . . John 3:16

his *S* to be the propitiation . . . . 1 John 4:10

that the *S* of God is . . . . 1 John 5:20

SONG

children of Israel this *s* . . . . Ex. 15:1

my strength and *s* . . . Ex. 15:2

their father for *s* . . 1 Chr. 25:6

Sing unto him a new *s* . . . . Ps. 33:3

in the night his *s* . . . . Ps. 42:8

unto the LORD a new *s* . . . . Ps. 98:1

a *s* of my beloved touching . . . . Is. 5:1

strength and my *s* . . . . Is. 12:2

s, saying, Thou art . . . Rev. 5:9

sing the *s* of Moses . . . . Rev. 15:3

SONS

And the *s* of Judah Gen. 46:12

s have made an end . . . . Num. 4:15

thee and for thy *s* . . Num. 18:9

and thy *s* and thy daughters . . . . . . Num. 18:19

he hath given his *s* . . . . Num. 21:29

their *s* and their daughters . . . . . . Deut. 12:31

Thy *s* and thy daughters . . . . . . Deut. 28:32

shalt beget *s* . . . . . Deut. 28:41

thy *s* and of thy daughters . . . . . . Deut. 28:53

king among his *s* . 1 Sam. 16:1

David's *s* were chief . . . . 2 Sam. 8:18

not of the *s* of
　Levi . . . . 1 Kin. 12:31
they caused
　their *s* . . . . 2 Kin. 17:17
slew the *s* of
　Zedekiah . . . . 2 Kin. 25:7
s of men, whose
　teeth . . . . Ps. 57:4
ways of the *s* of
　men . . . . Jer. 32:19
Babylon slew the *s* . . . Jer. 39:6
your *s* and your
　daughters . . . . Joel 2:28
power to become
　the *s* . . . . John 1:12
s of God, and it
　doth . . . . 1 John 3:2

SORCERERS
wise men and
　the *s* . . . . Ex. 7:11
witness against
　the *s* . . . . Mal. 3:5
whoremongers,
　and *s* . . . . Rev. 21:8
dogs, and *s*, and
　whoremongers . . . Rev. 22:15

SORE
legs, with a *s*
　botch . . . . Deut. 28:35
continuance,
　and *s* . . . . Deut. 28:59
And Hezekiah
　wept *s* . . . . 2 Kin. 20:3
stand aloof from
　my *s* . . . . Ps. 38:11
s and great and
　strong . . . . Is. 27:1
bears, and
　mourn *s* . . . . Is. 59:11
mine eye shall
　weep *s* . . . . Jer. 13:17
month, the
　famine was *s* . . . . . . Jer. 52:6
weepeth *s* in the
　night . . . . Lam. 1:2

SORROW
greatly multiply
　thy *s* . . . . Gen. 3:16
in *s* shalt thou eat . . Gen. 3:17
s shall take
　hold on . . . . Ex. 15:14
the eyes, and
　cause *s* . . . . Lev. 26:16
failing of eyes,
　and *s* . . . . Deut. 28:65
behold darkness
　and *s* . . . . Is. 5:30
and gladness,
　and *s* . . . . Is. 35:10
and they shall
　not *s* . . . . Jer. 31:12
rejoice from
　their *s* . . . . Jer. 31:13
s like unto my *s*,
　which . . . . Lam. 1:12
now therefore
　have *s* . . . . John 16:22
more death,
　neither *s* . . . . Rev. 21:4

SORROWS
for I know their *s* . . . . . Ex. 3:7
pangs and *s* shall
　take . . . . Is. 13:8
a man of *s*, and
　acquainted . . . . Is. 53:3
and carried our *s* . . . . . Is. 53:4
vision my *s* are
　turned . . . . Dan. 10:16
through with
　many *s* . . . . 1 Tim. 6:10

SOUGHT
Lord hath *s* him
　a man . . . . 1 Sam. 13:14
he *s* God in the
　days . . . . 2 Chr. 26:5
yea, I *s* him,
　but he . . . . Ps. 37:36
slew them, then
　they *s* . . . . Ps. 78:34
the Lord are
　great, *s* . . . . Ps. 111:2
and whom they
　have *s* . . . . Jer. 8:2
of Israel shall be *s* . . Jer. 50:20
And I *s* for a man
　among . . . . Ezek. 22:30
s for, yet shalt
　thou . . . . Ezek. 26:21
away, neither have
　ye *s* . . . . Ezek. 34:4
Then they *s* to
　take . . . . John 7:30
house of Jason,
　and *s* . . . . Acts 17:5

SOUL
became a living *s* . . . . Gen. 2:7
seventh day, that *s* . . Ex. 12:15
leavened, even
　that *s* . . . . Ex. 12:19
s that eateth blood . Lev. 17:10
and with all thy *s* . . Deut. 4:29
and with all thy *s* . Deut. 10:12
wilt not leave
　my *s* . . . . Ps. 16:10
my *s* trusteth in
　thee . . . . Ps. 57:1
My *s* is among
　lions . . . . Ps. 57:4
appointed feasts
　my *s* . . . . Is. 1:14
elect, in whom
　my *s* . . . . Is. 42:1
thou shalt make
　his *s* . . . . Is. 53:10
the travail of his *s* . . . Is. 53:11
hath poured out
　his *s* . . . . Is. 53:12
hear, and your *s*
　shall . . . . Is. 55:3
rejoice in the
　Lord, my *s* . . . . Is. 61:10
s shall weep in
　secret . . . . Jer. 13:17
deliver every man
　his *s* . . . . Jer. 51:6
for the sin of my *s* . . . Mic. 6:7
fool, this night
　thy *s* . . . . Luke 12:20

SOULS
atonement for
　your *s* . . . . Ex. 30:16
atonement for
　your *s* . . . . Lev. 17:11
s which I have
　made . . . . Is. 57:16
the *s* of the poor
　innocents . . . . Jer. 2:34
find rest for your *s* . . Jer. 6:16
deliver but their
　own *s* . . . . Ezek. 14:14
Behold, all *s* are
　mine . . . . Ezek. 18:4
blood, and to
　destroy *s* . . . . . . Ezek. 22:27
find rest unto
　your *s* . . . . Matt. 11:29
about three
　thousand *s* . . . . . . Acts 2:41
Confirming the
　s of . . . . Acts 14:22
they watch for
　your *s* . . . . Heb. 13:17
s in obeying the
　truth . . . . 1 Pet. 1:22
and Bishop of
　your *s* . . . . 1 Pet. 2:25
s were saved by
　water . . . . 1 Pet. 3:20
under the altar
　the *s* . . . . Rev. 6:9
and I saw the *s* of . . . Rev. 20:4

SOUND
the *s* of a shaken
　leaf . . . . Lev. 26:36
make one *s* to be
　heard . . . . 2 Chr. 5:13
Wherefore my
　bowels shall *s* . . . . . Is. 16:11
heard, O my soul,
　the *s* . . . . Jer. 4:19
land trembled at
　the *s* . . . . Jer. 8:16
of the bride, the *s* . . . Jer. 25:10
mine heart shall *s* . . . Jer. 48:36
and the *s* of thy
　harps . . . . Ezek. 26:13
nations to shake
　at the *s* . . . . Ezek. 31:16
time ye hear the *s* . . . Dan. 3:15
trumpet in Zion,
　and *s* . . . . Joel 2:1
angels with a
　great *s* . . . . Matt. 24:31
is contrary to *s*
　doctrine . . . . 1 Tim. 1:10
fast the form of *s* . 2 Tim. 1:13
his voice as the *s* . . . Rev. 1:15

SOUNDED
The first angel *s* . . . . . Rev. 8:7
the fourth angel *s* . . . Rev. 8:12
angel *s*, and I saw . . . . Rev. 9:1
the seventh
　angel *s* . . . . Rev. 11:15

SOUTH
and to the *s* . . . . Gen. 28:14
ascended by the *s* . Num. 13:22
the plains *s* of
　Chinneroth . . . . . . Josh. 11:2

Hinnom unto the
s side . . . . Josh. 15:8
lieth in the s of
Arad. . . . . Judg. 1:16
invaded the s. . . . . 1 Sam. 30:1
country, and of
the s . . . . 2 Chr. 28:18
the s, Keep not
back . . . . Is. 43:6
the cities of the s . . . Jer. 32:44
toward the s . . . . . Ezek. 40:27
the king of the s
push . . . . Dan. 11:40
of it toward the s . . Zech. 14:4
from Geba to
Rimmon s . . . . . . Zech. 14:10

SOW
ye shall s your
seed . . . . Lev. 26:16
And I will s her
unto. . . . . Hos. 2:23
Thou shalt s, but
thou. . . . . Mic. 6:15
for they s not,
neither. . . . . Matt. 6:26

SOWN
labours, which
thou hast s . . . . Ex. 23:16
burning, that it is
not s. . . . . Deut. 29:23
when Israel had s . . . Judg. 6:3
they have s the
wind . . . . Hos. 8:7

SPARE
that they have,
and s . . . . 1 Sam. 15:3
eye shall not s
children. . . . . Is. 13:18
Cry aloud, s not,
lift . . . . Is. 58:1
he shall not s
them . . . . Jer. 21:7
neither shall mine
eye s. . . . . Ezek. 5:11
mine eye shall
not s. . . . . Ezek. 7:4
mine eye shall
not s. . . . . Ezek. 7:9
mine eye shall
not s. . . . . Ezek. 8:18
mine eye shall
not s. . . . . Ezek. 9:10
S thy people, O
LORD. . . . . Joel 2:17

SPEAKETH
to face, as a man s . . Ex. 33:11
the foolish
women s . . . . Job 2:10
that s like the
piercings . . . . Prov. 12:18
s lies shall not
escape . . . . Prov. 19:5
it s deceit. . . . . Jer. 9:8
abhor him that s
uprightly. . . . . Amos 5:10
s the LORD of
hosts . . . . Zech. 6:12
your Father
which s . . . . Matt. 10:20

the mouth s . . . . . Matt. 12:34
whom God hath
sent s . . . . John 3:34
he s a lie, he s of . . . . John 8:44
prophesieth than
he that s . . . . 1 Cor. 14:5
he being dead
yet s . . . . Heb. 11:4
sprinkling, that s . . Heb. 12:24

SPIRIT
and the S of the
LORD. . . . . 1 Sam. 16:13
I have put my s
upon . . . . Is. 42:1
people upon it,
and s . . . . Is. 42:5
I will pour my s
upon . . . . Is. 44:3
contrite and
humble s . . . . Is. 57:15
The S of the Lord
GOD. . . . . Is. 61:1
of praise for s . . . . . Is. 61:3
will pour out my s . . Joel 2:28
s of grace and of
supplications . . . Zech. 12:10
S of truth, which
proceedeth . . . . . . John 15:26
tongues, as the S
gave . . . . Acts 2:4
whom I serve
with my s . . . . Rom. 1:9
one S are we all
baptized . . . . 1 Cor. 12:13
letter, but of the s. . . 2 Cor. 3:6
filled with the S . . . . Eph. 5:18
S, and watching
thereunto . . . . Eph. 6:18
justified in the S. . 1 Tim. 3:16
the eternal S
offered . . . . Heb. 9:14
quickened by
the S . . . . 1 Pet. 3:18
hear what the S
saith . . . . Rev. 2:7

SPIRITS
that have
familiar s . . . . Lev. 19:31
God, the God of
the s . . . . Num. 16:22
consulter with
familiar s . . . . Deut. 18:11
dealt with
familiar s . . . . . . 2 Kin. 21:6
that have
familiar s . . . . Is. 8:19
that have
familiar s . . . . Is. 19:3
been healed of
evil s . . . . Luke 8:2
rejoice not, that
the s. . . . . Luke 10:20
another
discerning of s . 1 Cor. 12:10
all ministering s . . . . Heb. 1:14
spirit, but try
the s . . . . 1 John 4:1
and from the
seven S . . . . Rev. 1:4

that hath the
seven S . . . . Rev. 3:1
the seven S of
God . . . . Rev. 4:5
the seven S of
God . . . . Rev. 5:6

SPIRITUAL
prophet is a fool,
the s. . . . . Hos. 9:7
s blessings in
heavenly . . . . Eph. 1:3
world, against s
wickedness . . . . . Eph. 6:12
s house, an holy
priesthood . . . . . . 1 Pet. 2:5

SPOIL
will divide the s . . . . Ex. 15:9
women, and to
take the s. . . . . Esth. 8:11
charge, to take
the s. . . . . Is. 10:6
s them of the east. . . Is. 11:14
thou shalt cease
to s . . . . Is. 33:1
shall divide the s . . . Is. 53:12
the evenings
shall s . . . . Jer. 5:6
day that cometh
to s . . . . Jer. 47:4
multitude, and
take her s. . . . . . Ezek. 29:19
he shall s the
treasure. . . . . . . Hos. 13:15
of my people
shall s . . . . Zeph. 2:9
Beware lest any
man s. . . . . Col. 2:8

SPOILED
And they s the
Egyptians . . . . Ex. 12:36
oppressed and s
evermore. . . . . . Deut. 28:29
of spoilers that s. . . Judg. 2:14
hand of those
that s . . . . Judg. 2:16
houses shall be s . . . Is. 13:16
and thou wast
not s. . . . . Is. 33:1
for we are s . . . . Jer. 4:13
righteousness,
and deliver the s. . . Jer. 22:3
Moab is s, and
gone. . . . . Jer. 48:15
Arnon, that Moab
is s . . . . Jer. 48:20
his seed is s, and . . Jer. 49:10
his pledge, hath s. . Ezek. 18:7
pledge, neither
hath s. . . . . Ezek. 18:16
s, as Shalman s
Betharbel . . . . . . Hos. 10:14
the nations
which s . . . . Zech. 2:8

SPOT
year without s day . Num. 28:3
church, not
having s. . . . . Eph. 5:27
without s to God,
purge. . . . . Heb. 9:14

blemish and
without s........ 1 Pet. 1:19

SPREAD

earth, and thou
shalt s ....Gen. 28:14
s a net by the
wayside .... Ps. 140:5
ye s forth your
hands..............Is. 1:15
that s forth the
earth ....Is. 42:5
shall s his royal
pavilion ....Jer. 43:10
s his wings over
Moab ....Jer. 48:40
eagle, and s his
wings..........Jer. 49:22
My net also
will I s .... Ezek. 12:13
I s my skirt over
thee .... Ezek. 16:8
darkness, as the
morning s ....Joel 2:2
their horsemen
shall s ....Hab. 1:8

SPREADETH

alone s out the
heavens............Job 9:8
as a curtain, and s ...Is. 40:22
that s abroad the
earth ....Is. 44:24
waters, and that s....Jer. 17:8

SPRINKLE

bring the blood,
and s .... Lev. 1:5
in the blood, and s ... Lev. 4:6
thou shalt s their .Num. 18:17
shall he s many
nations ....Is. 52:15
I s clean water.... Ezek. 36:25

SPRINKLED

took the blood,
and s .... Ex. 24:8
upon the altar,
and s .... Lev. 8:30
their blood shall
be s ....Is. 63:3
hearts s from an
evil............Heb. 10:22

STAFF

your feet, and
your s.............Ex. 12:11
I have broken
the s........... Lev. 26:26
thy rod and thy s
they .... Ps. 23:4
he brake the
whole s .... Ps. 105:16
his burden, and
the s..............Is. 9:4
mine anger, and
the s..............Is. 10:5
thou trustest in
the s..............Is. 36:6
s of reed to the
house..........Ezek. 29:6

STAND

Behold, I will s
before .... Ex. 17:6

he shall s before
Eleazar ....Num. 27:21
any man be able
to s..............Josh. 1:5
could not any
longer s .... Judg. 2:14
liveth, before
whom I s .... 1 Kin. 17:1
lovers and my
friends s .... Ps. 38:11
made the waters
to s .... Ps. 78:13
and it shall not s......Is. 8:10
Jesse, which
shall s ....Is. 11:10
of our God shall s.....Is. 40:8
My counsel shall s ..Is. 46:10
awake, s up, O
Jerusalem ....Is. 51:17
ye, S fast, and
prepare ....Jer. 46:14
shepherd that
will s ....Jer. 49:19
kingdoms, and it
shall s ....Dan. 2:44
time shall
Michael s........Dan. 12:1
can s before his
indignation ....Nah. 1:6
shall s when he
appeareth .... Mal. 3:2
Galilee, why s ye
gazing .... Acts 1:11
ye, s fast in ..... 1 Cor. 16:13

STANDETH

and that thy
cloud s........Num. 14:14
priest that s to
minister ....Deut. 17:12
the ungodly, nor s .... Ps. 1:1
counsel of the
LORD s .... Ps. 33:11
great prince
which s ....Dan. 12:1
bridegroom,
which s ....John 3:29
foundation of
God s .... 2 Tim. 2:19

STANDING

rear you up a s
image........... Lev. 26:1
where there is
no s .... Ps. 69:2
Joshua the high
priest s.......... Zech. 3:1
you, There be
some s .... Matt. 16:28
shed, I also was s ..Acts 22:20
S afar off for the ...Rev. 18:10

STAR

come a S out of
Jacob ....Num. 24:17
seen his s in the
east .... Matt. 2:2
dawn, and the
day s...........2 Pet. 1:19
bright and
morning s .... Rev. 22:16

STARS

heaven, and tell
the s.............Gen. 15:5
multiply thy seed
as the s ....Gen. 22:17
to multiply as
the s ....Gen. 26:4
seed as the s of
heaven.......... Ex. 32:13
the moon, and
the s .... Deut. 4:19
thee as the s .....Deut. 10:22
s of heaven for
multitude ......Deut. 28:62
For the s of
heaven ....Is. 13:10
throne above the s ...Is. 14:13
s for a light by
night ....Jer. 31:35
be dark, and the s... Joel 2:10
s and Orion, and
turneth ....Amos 5:8
s shall fall from
heaven......... Matt. 24:29
right hand seven s .. Rev. 1:16
God, and the
seven s........... Rev. 3:1
part of the s of
heaven........... Rev. 12:4

STATUTE

he made for
them a s.........Ex. 15:25
it shall be a s for....Ex. 27:21
for a perpetual s .....Ex. 29:9
shall be a
perpetual s .... Lev. 3:17
it shall be a s for....Lev. 10:9
This shall be a s
for .... Lev. 17:7
fire by a
perpetual s .... Lev. 24:9
daughters with
thee, by a s .....Num. 18:19

STATUTES

all his s, I will put ..Ex. 15:26
keep my s, and my
judgments....... Lev. 18:5
Israel, unto the s ...Deut. 4:1
his s, and his
commandments ..Deut. 4:40
s which I
command thee ..Deut. 28:15
commandments
and his s ......Deut. 28:45
and wilt keep my s ..1 Kin. 9:4
eyes, and to keep
my s.......... 1 Kin. 11:33
commandments
and my s ...... 2 Kin. 17:13
rejected his s..... 2 Kin. 17:15
testimonies and
his s .... 2 Kin. 23:3
to fulfil the s .... 1 Chr. 22:13
teach me thy s .... Ps. 119:12
delight myself in
thy s........... Ps. 119:16
word unto Jacob,
his s .... Ps. 147:19
s, and keep mine
ordinances ..... Ezek. 11:20

walked not in
my *s* . . . . Ezek. 20:13
walked not in
my *s* . . . . Ezek. 20:21
judgments, and
observe my *s* . . . . Ezek. 37:24
and my *s*, which I
commanded . . . . . . Zech. 1:6

STAY
s now thine . . . . . 2 Sam. 24:16
and from Judah
the *s* . . . . Is. 3:1
s upon him that
smote . . . . Is. 10:20
s on horses, and
trust . . . . Is. 31:1
the holy city, and *s* . . . Is. 48:2
and I could not *s* . . . . . Jer. 20:9
none can *s* his
hand . . . . Dan. 4:35

STEAL
Thou shalt not *s* . . . . Ex. 20:15
adultery, Thou
shalt not *s* . . . . . . Matt. 19:18
kill, Thou shalt
not *s* . . . . Rom. 13:9
Let him that
stole *s* . . . . Eph. 4:28

STEPHEN
A Christian martyr; Appointed
one of the committee of
seven to oversee the daily
ministration, Acts 6:3, 5, 6
Faith and power of, Acts 6:5,
8–10
False charges against,
Acts 6:11–15
Defense of, Acts 7
Stoned, Acts 7:54–60; 8:1;
22:20
Burial of, Acts 8:2
Gentle and forgiving spirit of,
Acts 7:59, 60

STEPS
and count all my *s* . . . Job 31:4
The *s* of a good
man . . . . Ps. 37:23
prepared a net for
my *s* . . . . Ps. 57:6
unto it by seven *s* Ezek. 40:22

STIFFNECKED
behold, it is a *s*
people . . . . Ex. 32:9
heart, and be no
more *s* . . . . Deut. 10:16
ye not *s*, as your
fathers . . . . 2 Chr. 30:8
Ye *s* and
uncircumcised . . . . Acts 7:51

STIRRED
Jezebel his wife *s* . 1 Kin. 21:25
God of Israel *s* . . . 1 Chr. 5:26
fulfilled, the
LORD *s* . . . . Ezra 1:1
the Jews *s* up the
devout . . . . Acts 13:50

STOCK
fall down to the *s* . . . . Is. 44:19

a *s*, Thou art my
father . . . . Jer. 2:27
the *s* is a doctrine . . . . Jer. 10:8
eighth day, of
the *s* . . . . Phil. 3:5

STONE
be as still as a *s* . . . . . Ex. 15:16
work of a
sapphire *s* . . . . Ex. 24:10
testimony, tables
of *s* . . . . Ex. 31:18
shall *s* them with
stones . . . . Lev. 20:27
congregation shall
certainly *s* . . . . Lev. 24:16
other gods, wood
and *s* . . . . Deut. 28:36
known, even
wood and *s* . . . . Deut. 28:64
The *s* which the
builders . . . . Ps. 118:22
a *s*, a tried *s*, a
precious . . . . Is. 28:16
hands, wood and *s* . . . Is. 37:19
to a *s*, Thou hast
brought . . . . Jer. 2:27
precious *s* was . . . Ezek. 28:13
iron, wood, and *s* . . . Dan. 5:23
built houses of
hewn *s* . . . . Amos 5:11
to the dumb *s*,
Arise . . . . Hab. 2:19
interpretation, A *s* . . John 1:42
the chief corner *s* . . . Eph. 2:20
And a *s* of
stumbling . . . . 1 Pet. 2:8
give him a white *s* . . Rev. 2:17
of heaven, every *s* . . Rev. 16:21

STONED
of the city, and *s* . 1 Kin. 21:13
and *s* him with
stones . . . . 2 Chr. 24:21
of the city, and *s* . . . . Acts 7:58
having *s* Paul,
drew . . . . Acts 14:19

STONES
stone them with *s* . Lev. 20:27
shall stone him
with *s* . . . . Num. 15:35
with *s*, till they
die . . . . Deut. 17:5
shall stone him
with *s* . . . . Deut. 21:21
shall stone her
with *s* . . . . Deut. 22:21
shall stone them
with *s* . . . . Deut. 22:24
him a great heap
of *s* . . . . Josh. 7:26
a great heap of *s* . . . Josh. 8:29
him with *s* . . . . . . 1 Kin. 21:13
and stoned him
with *s* . . . . 2 Chr. 24:21
hail *s* and coals of . . . Ps. 18:13
s thereof, and
planted . . . . Is. 5:2
confusion, and
the *s* . . . . Is. 34:11
gather out the *s* . . . . . Is. 62:10

committed
adultery with *s* . . . . . Jer. 3:9
s that I have hid . . . . Jer. 43:10
precious *s*, and
gold . . . . Ezek. 27:22
these *s* be made
bread . . . . Matt. 4:3
as lively *s*, are
built . . . . 1 Pet. 2:5
gold, and
precious *s* . . . . . . Rev. 18:16

STOOD
behold, the
LORD *s* . . . . Gen. 28:13
before their face,
and *s* . . . . Ex. 14:19
the floods *s*
upright . . . . Ex. 15:8
from above *s* and
rose . . . . Josh. 3:16
spake to the men
that *s* . . . . 1 Sam. 17:26
came and *s* by the
conduit . . . . 2 Kin. 18:17
the king *s* by a
pillar . . . . 2 Kin. 23:3
Then David the
king *s* . . . . 1 Chr. 28:2
the priest, which *s* 2 Chr. 24:20
s still in the
prison . . . . Neh. 12:39
Moses his
chosen *s* . . . . Ps. 106:23
Moses and
Samuel *s* . . . . Jer. 15:1
times ten
thousand *s* . . . . . . Dan. 7:10
spake unto those
that *s* . . . . Zech. 3:4
Jesus *s* before . . . . Matt. 27:11
Jews, came Jesus
and *s* . . . . John 20:19
following the
Lord *s* . . . . Acts 23:11
Notwithstanding
the Lord *s* . . . . . . 2 Tim. 4:17
midst of the
elders, *s* . . . . Rev. 5:6
and the dragon *s*
before . . . . Rev. 12:4

STORE
thy basket and
thy *s* . . . . Deut. 28:17
fathers have laid
up in *s* . . . . 2 Kin. 20:17
in *s*, as God hath
prospered . . . . . . 1 Cor. 16:2
s, reserved unto
fire . . . . 2 Pet. 3:7

STRANGE
thereon, and
offered *s* . . . . Lev. 10:1
jealousy with *s*
gods . . . . Deut. 32:16
put away the *s*
gods . . . . 1 Sam. 7:3
his work, his *s*
work . . . . Is. 28:21
degenerate plant
of a *s* . . . . Jer. 2:21

in a *s* country,
dwelling . . . . Heb. 11:9
s flesh, are set
forth . . . . Jude 7

STRANGER
thy seed shall
be a *s* . . . . Gen. 15:13
wherein thou
art a *s* . . . . Gen. 17:8
with money of
any *s* . . . . Gen. 17:12
s, or born in the
land . . . . Ex. 12:19
thy cattle, nor
thy *s* . . . . Ex. 20:10
shalt neither
vex a *s* . . . . Ex. 22:21
handmaid, and
the *s* . . . . Ex. 23:12
s, as he that is
born . . . . Lev. 24:16
s that is in thy
gates . . . . Deut. 14:21
the *s*, and the
fatherless . . . . . Deut. 14:29
thy gates, and
the *s* . . . . Deut. 16:11
judgment of the *s* . Deut. 27:19
s that is within
thee . . . . Deut. 28:43
the *s* calleth to
thee . . . . 1 Kin. 8:43
for I am a *s* with
thee . . . . Ps. 39:12
oppress not the *s* . . . . . Jer. 7:6
violence to the *s* . . . . . Jer. 22:3
that he became a *s* . . Obad. 12
fatherless, the *s* . . . Zech. 7:10
that turn aside
the *s* . . . . Mal. 3:5

STRANGERS
ye were *s* in the
land . . . . Ex. 22:21
Israel, or of the *s* . . Lev. 17:10
after the gods of
the *s* . . . . Deut. 31:16
we are *s* before
thee . . . . 1 Chr. 29:15
your land, *s* devour . . . . Is. 1:7
the *s* shall be
joined . . . . Is. 14:1
multitude of thy *s* . . . . Is. 29:5
my sanctuary, *s*,
uncircumcised . . . Ezek. 44:7
be it yield, the *s* . . . . . Hos. 8:7
there shall no *s*
pass . . . . Joel 3:17
day that the *s*
carried . . . . Obad. 11
commonwealth of
Israel, and *s* . . . . . . Eph. 2:12
confessed that
they were *s* . . . . . . Heb. 11:13
forgetful to
entertain *s* . . . . Heb. 13:2
I beseech you as *s* . . 1 Pet. 2:11

STREET
s of the water gate . . Neh. 8:16
out of the
bakers' *s* . . . . Jer. 37:21

the *s* shall be built . . Dan. 9:25
the midst of the *s* . . . Rev. 22:2

STREETS
the midst of the *s* . . . . . Is. 5:25
the mire of the *s* . . . . . Is. 10:6
s they shall gird
themselves . . . . Is. 15:3
Judah, and from
the *s* . . . . Jer. 7:34
Judah, and in the *s* . Jer. 44:17
sucklings swoon
in the *s* . . . . Lam. 2:11
the top of all the *s* . . Nah. 3:10
in the mire of
the *s* . . . . Zech. 10:5

STRENGTH
by *s* of hand the
LORD . . . . Ex. 13:3
By *s* of hand the
LORD . . . . Ex. 13:14
LORD is my *s* and
song . . . . Ex. 15:2
by *s* shall no man
prevail . . . . 1 Sam. 2:9
s, in whom I will
trust . . . . Ps. 18:2
My *s* is dried up
like . . . . Ps. 22:15
the LORD is the
s of . . . . Ps. 27:1
made not God
his *s* . . . . Ps. 52:7
the chief of their *s* . . Ps. 78:51
clothed with *s*,
wherewith . . . . Ps. 93:1
chief of all their *s* . . Ps. 105:36
LORD JEHOVAH
is my *s* . . . . Is. 12:2
thou hast been a *s* . . . . Is. 25:4
shall renew their *s* . . . Is. 40:31
Awake, awake,
put on *s* . . . . Is. 51:9
put on thy *s*, O
Zion . . . . Is. 52:1
greatness of his *s* . . . . Is. 63:1
thy zeal and thy *s* . . . Is. 63:15
kingdom, power,
and *s* . . . . Dan. 2:37
sun shineth in
his *s* . . . . Rev. 1:16

STRENGTHEN
he shall *s* thine
heart . . . . Ps. 27:14
I will *s* thee . . . . Is. 41:10
they *s* also the
hands . . . . Jer. 23:14
perfect, stablish, *s* . 1 Pet. 5:10

STRENGTHENED
of his riches, and *s* . . . Ps. 52:7
diseased have ye
not *s* . . . . Ezek. 34:4
his glory, to be *s* . . . . Eph. 3:16
stood with me,
and *s* . . . . 2 Tim. 4:17

STRETCH
I *s* forth mine
hand . . . . Ex. 7:5
Take thy rod,
and *s* . . . . Ex. 7:19

the cherubims
shall *s* . . . . Ex. 25:20
And I will *s* over
Jerusalem . . . . . 2 Kin. 21:13
s out upon it the
line . . . . Is. 34:11
will I *s* out my
hand . . . . Ezek. 6:14
prophet, and I
will *s* . . . . Ezek. 14:9
I will also *s* out
mine . . . . Ezek. 25:13
saith unto the
man, S . . . . Mark 3:5

STRETCHED
redeem you
with a *s* . . . . Ex. 6:6
Moses *s* out his
hand . . . . Ex. 14:21
Moses *s* forth his
hand . . . . Ex. 14:27
mighty hand, and
by a *s* . . . . Deut. 4:34
power and by
thy *s* . . . . Deut. 9:29
angel *s* out his
hand . . . . 2 Sam. 24:16
people, and he
hath *s* . . . . Is. 5:25
away, but his
hand is *s* . . . . Is. 9:21
the heavens, and *s* . . . Is. 42:5
even my hands,
have *s* . . . . Is. 45:12
maker, that hath *s* . . . Is. 51:13
wisdom, and
hath *s* . . . . Jer. 10:12
thy great power
and *s* . . . . Jer. 32:17
And he *s* it out . . . . . Mark 3:5

STRIFE
man stirreth up *s* . Prov. 15:18
man stirreth up *s* . Prov. 29:22
wantonness, not
in *s* . . . . Rom. 13:13
emulations,
wrath, *s* . . . . Gal. 5:20

STRIPES
men, and with
the *s* . . . . 2 Sam. 7:14
with his *s* we are
healed . . . . Is. 53:5
beaten with
many *s* . . . . Luke 12:47
whose *s* ye were
healed . . . . 1 Pet. 2:24

STRONG
back by a *s* east
wind . . . . Ex. 14:21
children of
Ammon was *s* . . . Num. 21:24
s and of a good
courage . . . . Deut. 31:6
s and of a good
courage . . . . Deut. 31:23
thou *s* and very
courageous . . . . Josh. 1:7
s and of a good
courage . . . . Josh. 1:9

s and apt for .... 2 Kin. 24:16
Wine is a
　mocker, s .... Prov. 20:1
sore and great
　and s ....Is. 27:1
wine, and
　through s...........Is. 28:7
because they are
　very s..............Is. 31:1
fearful heart, Be s.....Is. 35:4
the spoil with
　the s................Is. 53:12
outstretched hand
　and with a s ....Jer. 21:5
habitation of the s ..Jer. 49:19
hand of the Lord
　was s ....Ezek. 3:14
city, which wast s Ezek. 26:17
cast far off a s
　nation ....Mic. 4:7
controversy, and
　ye s...............Mic. 6:2
wine nor s drink ....Luke 1:15

STUMBLE
err in vision,
　they s.............Is. 28:7
we s at
　noonday as ....Is. 59:10
feet s upon the
　dark ....Jer. 13:16
wherein they shall
　not s.............Jer. 31:9
which s at the
　word ....1 Pet. 2:8

SUBJECT
Nazareth, and
　was s ....Luke 2:51
that the spirits
　are s .... Luke 10:20
powers being
　made s.........1 Pet. 3:22
Yea, all of you be s .. 1 Pet. 5:5

SUCCOTH
A city which was located
　probably east of the Jordan
　River; Jacob builds a house
　in, Gen. 33:17
Allotted to the tribe of Gad,
　Josh. 13:27
People of, punished by Gideon,
　Judg. 8:5–8, 14–16
Located near the Jordan River,
　1 Kin. 7:46; 2 Chr. 4:17;
　Ps. 60:6; 108:7
——— The first camping
　place of the Israelites after
　leaving the city of Rameses,
　Ex. 12:37; 13:20;
　Num. 33:5, 6

SUDDENLY
and destroy thee s .. Deut. 7:4
hardeneth his
　neck, shall s ..... Prov. 29:1
the spoiler shall s ....Jer. 6:26
I will s make him
　run.............Jer. 49:19
whom ye seek,
　shall s ....Mal. 3:1

SUFFER
door, and will
　not s............Ex. 12:23
shalt thou s the
　salt..............Lev. 2:13
Sihon would not s
　Israel ....Num. 21:23
wilt thou s thine
　Holy............. Ps. 16:10
lions do lack,
　and s .... Ps. 34:10
unto Jerusalem,
　and s ....Matt. 16:21
man, that he
　must s .... Mark 9:12
That Christ
　should s........Acts 26:23
if so be that we s .. Rom. 8:17
but s all things,
　lest.............1 Cor. 9:12
faithful, who will
　not s......... 1 Cor. 10:13
I also s these
　things ....2 Tim. 1:12
s, we shall also
　reign ....2 Tim. 2:12
which thou shalt s .. Rev. 2:10

SUFFERED
humbled thee,
　and s ....Deut. 8:3
he s no man to
　follow .... Mark 5:37
not Christ to
　have s.........Luke 24:26
whom I have s the
　loss ....Phil. 3:8
hath s being
　tempted.........Heb. 2:18
Christ also hath
　once s ....1 Pet. 3:18
after that ye
　have s..........1 Pet. 5:10

SUFFERINGS
now rejoice in
　my s.......... Col. 1:24
perfect through s ...Heb. 2:10
testified
　beforehand the s . 1 Pet. 1:11
a witness of the s ... 1 Pet. 5:1

SUMMER
into the drought
　of s .... Ps. 32:4
shouting for thy s.....Is. 16:9
gathered wine
　and s ....Jer. 40:12
fallen upon thy s
　fruits ....Jer. 48:32

SUN
when thou seest
　the s ....Deut. 4:19
either the s, or
　moon..........Deut. 17:3
continued as long
　as the s ....Ps. 72:17
the Lord God
　is a s............Ps. 84:11
his throne as the s .. Ps. 89:36
after him under
　the s..........Eccl. 6:12

the s shall be
　darkened........... .Is. 13:10
confounded, and
　the s............Is. 24:23
the heat nor s
　smite .... .Is. 49:10
The s shall be no
　more ....Is. 60:19
Thy s shall no
　more ....Is. 60:20
s for a light by day .. Jer. 31:35
they worshipped
　the s...........Ezek. 8:16
the s and the
　moon... Joel 2:10
The s shall be
　turned .... Joel 2:31
The s and the
　moon...........Joel 3:15
the rising of the s... Mal. 1:11
those days shall
　the s........... Matt. 24:29
s shineth in his
　strength .... Rev. 1:16
s became black as
　sackcloth......... Rev. 6:12

SUPPLICATION
thee, they shall
　make s ....Is. 45:14
accord in prayer
　and s ....Acts 1:14
with all prayer
　and s ....Eph. 6:18
thing by prayer
　and s ....Phil. 4:6

SUPPLICATIONS
and with s will I
　lead ....Jer. 31:9
beginning of thy s ..Dan. 9:23
of grace and of s .. Zech. 12:10
offered up prayers
　and s ....Heb. 5:7

SURELY
And s your
　blood of..........Gen. 9:5
S the Lord hath
　looked ....Gen. 29:32
with me, s thou
　hadst ....Gen. 31:42
and God will s
　visit ....Gen. 50:24
Lord said, I
　have s............ Ex. 3:7
shall s be put to
　death ....Ex. 21:17
s be a snare unto
　thee ....Ex. 23:33
shall s be put to
　death ....Lev. 20:10
shall s be put to
　death ....Lev. 20:27
shall s be put to
　death ....Lev. 24:16
s die in the
　wilderness .....Num. 26:65
prolonged, yet s I...Eccl. 8:12
S the princes of
　Zoan ....Is. 19:11
S he hath borne
　our..............Is. 53:4

S the isles shall
wait . . . . Is. 60:9
S the least of the . . . Jer. 49:20
S, because thou
hast . . . . Ezek. 5:11
S in the fire of my . Ezek. 36:5
because it will *s*
come . . . . Hab. 2:3
God of Israel, *S*
Moab . . . . Zeph. 2:9

SWALLOW
of him that
would *s* . . . . Ps. 57:3
s up death in
victory . . . . Is. 25:8
or a *s*, so did I
chatter . . . . Is. 38:14
the strangers
shall *s* . . . . Hos. 8:7

SWARE
I *s* unto Abraham
thy . . . . Gen. 26:3
Jacob *s* by the fear . Gen. 31:53
s to Abraham, to
Isaac . . . . Gen. 50:24
I *s* to make you
dwell . . . . Num. 14:30
he *s* unto thy
fathers . . . . Deut. 7:13
land which I *s* . . . . Deut. 31:23
the land, which I *s* . . Josh. 1:6
Moses *s* on that
day . . . . Josh. 14:9
whom I *s* in my
wrath . . . . Ps. 95:11
yea, I *s* unto thee . . Ezek. 16:8
unto heaven,
and *s* . . . . Dan. 12:7

SWEAR
which I did *s* to
give . . . . Ex. 6:8
And ye shall not *s* . Lev. 19:12
serve him, and
shalt *s* . . . . Deut. 6:13
thou cleave, and *s* Deut. 10:20
gods, nor cause
to *s* . . . . Josh. 23:7
Jonathan caused
David to *s* . . . . . 1 Sam. 20:17
had made him *s*
by God . . . . 2 Chr. 36:13
s by the God of
truth . . . . Is. 65:16
thou shalt *s*, The
LORD . . . . Jer. 4:2
nor *s*, The LORD
liveth . . . . Hos. 4:15
worship and that *s* . . Zeph. 1:5
But I say unto
you, *S* . . . . Matt. 5:34

SWEET
LORD smelled a *s*
savour . . . . Gen. 8:21
waters were
made *s* . . . . Ex. 15:25
offering thereof,
for a *s* . . . . Ex. 29:41
burn thereon *s*
incense . . . . Ex. 30:7

hundred shekels,
and of *s* . . . . Ex. 30:23
made by fire,
of a *s* . . . . Lev. 2:2
made by fire,
of a *s* . . . . Lev. 3:5
made by fire
for a *s* . . . . Lev. 3:16
horns of the altar
of *s* . . . . Lev. 4:7
made by fire, for
a *s* . . . . Num. 18:17
mount Sinai
for a *s* . . . . Num. 28:6
made by fire,
of a *s* . . . . Num. 28:8
burnt sacrifices
and *s* . . . . 2 Chr. 13:11
was filled with *s*
odours . . . . 2 Chr. 16:14
blood, as with *s*
wine . . . . Is. 49:26
Sheba, and the *s*
cane . . . . Jer. 6:20
s savour, when I
bring . . . . Ezek. 20:41
and *s* wine, but
shalt . . . . Mic. 6:15
an odour of a *s*
smell . . . . Phil. 4:18

SWIFT
as *s* as the eagle
flieth . . . . Deut. 28:49
LORD rideth
upon a *s* . . . . Is. 19:1
and I will be a *s*
witness . . . . Mal. 3:5
man be *s* to hear,
slow . . . . James 1:19

SWORD
before you by
the *s* . . . . Lev. 26:8
and will draw
out a *s* . . . . Lev. 26:33
as fleeing from a *s* . Lev. 26:36
the edge of the *s* . . Num. 21:24
burning, and with
the *s* . . . . Deut. 28:22
young men with
the *s* . . . . 2 Chr. 36:17
possession by
their own *s* . . . . Ps. 44:3
their tongue a
sharp *s* . . . . Ps. 57:4
great and strong *s* . . . Is. 27:1
s of the LORD is
filled . . . . Is. 34:6
s will the LORD
plead . . . . Is. 66:16
consumed by the *s* . . Jer. 16:4
pestilence, from
the *s* . . . . Jer. 21:7
for the *s* to the *s* . . . . Jer. 43:11
and the *s* shall
devour . . . . Jer. 46:10
fall by the *s* round . Ezek. 5:12
shall fall by the *s* . Ezek. 25:13
brother with the *s* . Amos 1:11
Awake, O *s*,
against . . . . Zech. 13:7

a sharp
twoedged *s* . . . . Rev. 1:16

SWORDS
beat their *s* into
plowshares . . . . Is. 2:4
of them
handling *s* . . . . . . Ezek. 38:4
beat their *s* into
plowshares . . . . Mic. 4:3
thief with *s* and
staves . . . . Matt. 26:55

SWORN
I *s*, saith the
LORD . . . . Gen. 22:16
oath which he
had *s* . . . . Deut. 7:8
as he hath *s* unto
thee . . . . Deut. 28:9
forasmuch as we
have *s* . . . . 1 Sam. 20:42
thou hadst *s* to
give . . . . Neh. 9:15
The LORD hath *s*,
and . . . . Ps. 110:4
LORD hath *s* in
truth . . . . Ps. 132:11
I have *s* that the
waters . . . . Is. 54:9
For I have *s* by
myself . . . . Jer. 49:13
The Lord GOD
hath *s* . . . . Amos 4:2
The Lord GOD
hath *s* . . . . Amos 6:8

SYNAGOGUE
ruler of the *s*
answered . . . . Luke 13:14
arose certain of
the *s* . . . . Acts 6:9
s on the sabbath
day . . . . Acts 13:14
but are the *s* of
Satan . . . . Rev. 2:9

SYNAGOGUES
teaching in their *s* . Matt. 4:23
scourge you in
their *s* . . . . Matt. 10:17
put you out of
the *s* . . . . John 16:2
Damascus to the *s* . . . Acts 9:2

TABERNACLE
In the *t* of the
congregation . . . . . . Ex. 27:21
at the door of
the *t* . . . . Lev. 1:3
by the door of
the *t* . . . . Lev. 1:5
in the *t* of the
congregation . . . . . . Lev. 4:7
in the *t* of the
congregation . . . . . . Lev. 4:18
the court of the *t* . . . Lev. 6:16
the court of the *t* . . . Lev. 6:26
Aaron went into
the *t* . . . . Lev. 9:23
when ye go into
the *t* . . . . Lev. 10:9
And I will set my *t* . Lev. 26:11

pitch round about
the *t* . . . . Num. 1:53
do the work in
the *t* . . . . Num. 4:3
of Kohath in the *t*. . Num. 4:15
tarried long upon
the *t* . . . . Num. 9:19
Shiloh, and set up
the *t* . . . . Josh. 18:1
the secret of his *t* . . . . Ps. 27:5
t also shall be . . . . Ezek. 37:27
about to make
the *t* . . . . .Heb. 8:5
second veil, the *t* . . . .Heb. 9:3
Behold, the *t* of
God . . . . Rev. 21:3

TABERNACLES

in the feast of *t* . . . Deut. 16:16
holy place of the *t* . . . Ps. 46:4
their strength in
the *t* . . . . Ps. 78:51
country, dwelling
in *t* . . . . .Heb. 11:9

TABLE

shalt set upon
the *t* . . . . Ex. 25:30
row, upon the
pure *t* . . . . Lev. 24:6
shalt eat bread at
my *t* . . . . 2 Sam. 9:7
bread alway at
my *t* . . . . 2 Sam. 9:10
that eat at thy *t* . . . . .1 Kin. 2:7
of gold, and the *t* . 1 Kin. 7:48
eat at Jezebel's *t* . 1 Kin. 18:19
order upon the
pure *t* . . . . 2 Chr. 13:11
Thou preparest a *t* . . . Ps. 23:5
them in a *t*, and
note . . . . .Is. 30:8
eat and drink at
my *t* . . . . Luke 22:30
candlestick, and
the *t* . . . . .Heb. 9:2

TABLES

mount Sinai,
two *t* . . . . Ex. 31:18
he wrote upon
the *t* . . . . Ex. 34:28
mount to receive
the *t* . . . . Deut. 9:9
not in *t* of stone . . . .2 Cor. 3:3

TABOR

A mountain on the border
of the tribe of Issachar,
Josh. 19:22; Judg. 8:18;
Ps. 89:12; Jer. 46:18; Hos. 5:1
The place for assembling
Barak's army, Judg. 4:6, 12,
14
——— A plain ("oak")
of unknown location,
1 Sam. 10:3

TAKETH

him guiltless
that *t* . . . . .Ex. 20:7
persons, nor *t*
reward . . . . .Deut. 10:17

this Philistine,
and *t* . . . . .1 Sam. 17:26
man *t* away dung,
till . . . . 1 Kin. 14:10
He *t* the wise in
their . . . . Job 5:13
money to usury,
nor *t* . . . . Ps. 15:5
Then the devil *t*
him . . . . Matt. 4:5
Lamb of God,
which *t* . . . . .John 1:29
beareth not fruit
he *t* . . . . .John 15:2
and your joy no
man *t* . . . . .John 16:22

TALK

down and *t* with
thee . . . . Num. 11:17
children, and
shalt *t* . . . . Deut. 6:7
me *t* with thee of
thy . . . . Jer. 12:1
Hereafter I will
not *t* . . . . .John 14:30

TALKED

on, and *t*, that,
behold . . . . 2 Kin. 2:11
And the angel
that *t* . . . . Zech. 1:9
unto the angel
that *t* . . . . Zech. 1:19
t to the people,
behold . . . . Matt. 12:46

TAMAR

Wife of the sons of Judah,
Gen. 38:6–24; Ruth 4:12;
1 Chr. 2:4
Called Thamar, Matt. 1:3
——— Daughter of David,
2 Sam. 13:1–32; 1 Chr. 3:9
——— Daughter of Absalom,
2 Sam. 14:27
——— A city of unknown
location, Ezek. 47:19; 48:28

TARSHISH

Son of Javan, Gen. 10:4;
1 Chr. 1:7
——— Also called Tharshish
Probably Spain, Gen. 10:4, 5;
Ps. 72:10; Is. 66:19
Solomon makes valuable
imports from, 1 Kin. 10:22;
2 Chr. 9:21
Commerce and wealth
of, 1 Kin. 10:22; 22:48;
2 Chr. 9:21; 20:36; Ps. 48:7;
Is. 2:16; 23:1–14; 60:9;
Jer. 10:9; Ezek. 27:12, 25;
38:13
Jonah would flee to, Jon. 1:3;
4:2
Prophecies concerning,
Ps. 72:10; Is. 2:16; 23:1–14;
60:9; 66:19
——— Son of Bilhan,
1 Chr. 7:10
——— A Persian prince,
Esth. 1:14

TARSUS

The capitol of Cilicia in Asia
Minor; Paul's birthplace,
Acts 9:11; 21:39; 22:3
Paul sent to, from Jerusalem,
to avoid assassination,
Acts 9:30
Paul brought from, by
Barnabas, Acts 11:25, 26

TASTE

O *t* and see that
the . . . . Ps. 34:8
not *t* of death, till Matt. 16:28
shall never *t* of
death . . . . .John 8:52
grace of God
should *t* . . . . .Heb. 2:9

TAUGHT

the Levites that *t* . . . .Neh. 8:9
fear toward me
is *t* . . . . .Is. 29:13
t their tongue to
speak . . . . Jer. 9:5
shall be all *t* of
God . . . . John 6:45
with the church,
and *t* . . . . Acts 11:26
from Judaea *t* the
brethren . . . . Acts 15:1
of Gamaliel, and *t* . . Acts 22:3
ye have been *t*,
abounding. . . . . Col. 2:7
it hath *t* you, ye . . 1 John 2:27
t Balac to cast a
stumblingblock . . . Rev. 2:14

TEACH

his mouth, and
will *t* . . . . Ex. 4:15
that thou mayest *t* . . Ex. 24:12
judgments,
which I *t* . . . . Deut. 4:1
but *t* them thy
sons . . . . Deut. 4:9
thou shalt *t* them
diligently. . . . . Deut. 6:7
I will *t* you the
good . . . . 1 Sam. 12:23
T me thy way, O
LORD. . . . . Ps. 27:11
t me thy statutes . . Ps. 119:12
will *t* us of his
ways . . . . .Is. 2:3
t no more every
man . . . . Jer. 31:34
the priests
thereof *t* . . . . Mic. 3:11
will *t* us of his
ways . . . . Mic. 4:2
Arise, it shall *t* . . . . .Hab. 2:19
t all nations,
baptizing. . . . . . . Matt. 28:19
shall *t* you all
things . . . . .John 14:26
And *t* customs,
which . . . . .Acts 16:21
in Christ, as I *t* . . . .1 Cor. 4:17
hospitality, apt
to *t* . . . . 1 Tim. 3:2
If any man *t*
otherwise . . . . 1 Tim. 6:3

that any man *t* . . . 1 John 2:27

TEACHING

about all Galilee, *t* . Matt. 4:23
sat daily with
   you *t* . . . . Matt. 26:55
T them to observe
   all . . . . Matt. 28:20
t and
   admonishing one . . Col. 3:16

TEARS

thy peace at my *t* . . . Ps. 39:12
My *t* have been
   my meat . . . . Ps. 42:3
thee with my *t*, O
   Heshbon . . . . Is. 16:9
GOD will wipe
   away *t* . . . . Is. 25:8
eyes a fountain
   of *t* . . . . Jer. 9:1
and run down
   with *t* . . . . Jer. 13:17
eyes run down
   with *t* . . . . Jer. 14:17
the night, and
   her *t* . . . . Lam. 1:2
eyes do fail with *t* . . Lam. 2:11
washed my feet
   with *t* . . . . Luke 7:44
strong crying
   and *t* . . . . Heb. 5:7
shall wipe away
   all *t* . . . . Rev. 7:17
shall wipe away
   all *t* . . . . Rev. 21:4

TEETH

thou hast broken
   the *t* . . . . Ps. 3:7
sons of men,
   whose *t* . . . . Ps. 57:4
hiss and gnash
   the *t* . . . . Lam. 2:16
it had great iron *t* . . . Dan. 7:7
and gnashing of *t* . . Matt. 8:12
gnashing of *t* . . . . Matt. 13:50

TEMAN

Son of Eliphaz, Gen. 36:11
———— Also called Temani and
   Temanites
A people supposed to be
   descended from Teman,
   son of Eliphaz, Gen. 36:34;
   Job 2:11
Prophecies concerning,
   Jer. 49:7; Ezek. 25:13;
   Amos 1:12; Obad. 9; Hab. 3:3

TEMPEST

a *t* of hail and a
   destroying . . . . Is. 28:2
scattering, and *t* . . . . . Is. 30:30
covert from the *t* . . . . . Is. 32:2
of battle, with a *t* . . Amos 1:14

TEMPLE

Israel had made in
   the *t* . . . . 2 Kin. 24:13
t of the LORD to
   burn . . . . 2 Chr. 26:16
LORD is in his
   holy *t* . . . . Ps. 11:4
voice out of his *t* . . . . Ps. 18:6

to enquire in his *t* . . . Ps. 27:4
even of thy holy *t* . . . . Ps. 65:4
thy holy *t* have
   they . . . . Ps. 79:1
train filled the *t* . . . . Is. 6:1
and to the *t*, Thy
   foundation . . . . Is. 44:28
words, saying,
   The *t* . . . . Jer. 7:4
vengeance of his *t* . . Jer. 51:11
at the door of
   the *t* . . . . Ezek. 8:16
suddenly come to
   his *t* . . . . Mal. 3:1
slew between
   the *t* . . . . Matt. 23:35
t, and ye laid no
   hold . . . . Matt. 26:55
t, and breaking
   bread . . . . Acts 2:46
agreement hath
   the *t* . . . . 2 Cor. 6:16
make a pillar in
   the *t* . . . . Rev. 3:12
t leave out, and
   measure . . . . Rev. 11:2
the *t* of God was
   opened . . . . Rev. 11:19

TEMPT

things, that God
   did *t* . . . . Gen. 22:1
wherefore do ye *t*
   the . . . . Ex. 17:2
yea, they that *t*
   God . . . . Mal. 3:15
Neither let us *t*
   Christ . . . . 1 Cor. 10:9

TEMPTATION

lead us not into *t* . . Matt. 6:13
There hath no *t*
   taken . . . . 1 Cor. 10:13
be rich fall into *t* . . 1 Tim. 6:9
man that
   endureth *t* . . . . . . James 1:12
from the hour of *t* . . Rev. 3:10

TEMPTED

they *t* the LORD,
   saying . . . . Ex. 17:7
also *t*, and were
   destroyed . . . . . . 1 Cor. 10:9
suffer you to be *t* 1 Cor. 10:13
lest thou also be *t* . . . Gal. 6:1
tempter have *t* . . . 1 Thess. 3:5
was in all points *t* . . Heb. 4:15

TEN

covenant, the *t*
   commandments . . . Ex. 34:28
put *t* thousand to
   flight . . . . Lev. 26:8
staff of your
   bread, *t* . . . . Lev. 26:26
threescore and *t*
   persons . . . . Deut. 10:22
put *t* thousand to
   flight . . . . Deut. 32:30
t thousands of
   saints . . . . Deut. 33:2
t thousands of
   Ephraim . . . . Deut. 33:17

thee *t* thousand
   men . . . . Judg. 4:6
threescore and *t*
   pieces . . . . Judg. 9:4
t cubits was the
   breadth . . . . 1 Kin. 6:3
men of valour,
   even *t* . . . . 2 Kin. 24:14
and it had *t* horns . . . Dan. 7:7
t thousand times *t* . . Dan. 7:10
rams, or with *t*
   thousands . . . . Mic. 6:7
to pass, that *t*
   men . . . . Zech. 8:23
Lord cometh
   with *t* . . . . Jude 14
tribulation *t* days . . . Rev. 2:10
seven heads and *t*
   horns . . . . Rev. 12:3

TENDER

that the man that
   is *t* . . . . Deut. 28:54
t and delicate
   woman . . . . Deut. 28:56
of thy *t* mercies
   blot . . . . Ps. 51:1
t plant, and as a
   root . . . . Is. 53:2

TENT

and pitched his *t* . . . Gen. 12:8
Abram removed
   his *t* . . . . Gen. 13:18
he sat in the *t*
   door . . . . Gen. 18:1
Sarah heard it in
   the *t* . . . . Gen. 18:10
cloud covered
   the *t* . . . . Ex. 40:34
Kenites, and
   pitched his *t* . . . . . Judg. 4:11
the Arabian
   pitch *t* . . . . Is. 13:20
spreadeth them
   out as a *t* . . . . Is. 40:22

TENTH

lamb a *t* deal of
   flour . . . . Ex. 29:40
t deals of fine
   flour . . . . Lev. 14:10
wave loaves of
   two *t* . . . . Lev. 23:17
two *t* deals
   shall be . . . . Lev. 24:5
a *t* part of an
   ephah . . . . Num. 28:5
three *t* deals of
   flour . . . . Num. 28:12
t month, in the *t*
   day . . . . Jer. 52:4
month, the *t*
   day of . . . . Ezek. 20:1
the *t* part of the
   city . . . . Rev. 11:13

TENTS

Israel pitched
   their *t* . . . . Num. 9:17
they abode in
   their *t* . . . . Num. 9:20
and go unto thy *t* . . Deut. 16:7

cattle and their *t*.... Judg. 6:5
to dwell in their *t*... Ps. 78:55
captivity of
Jacob's *t*......... Jer. 30:18

TERAH
The father of Abraham,
Gen. 11:24–32
Was an idolater, Josh. 24:2
Called Thara, Luke 3:34

TERRIBLE
that great and *t*
wilderness ...... Deut. 8:15
a mighty, and a *t*. . Deut. 10:17
thee these great
and *t* .... Deut. 10:21
great things and *t* 2 Sam. 7:23
heaven, the great
and *t* .... Neh. 1:5
the blast of the *t*...... Is. 25:4
beast, dreadful
and *t* .... Dan. 7:7
is great and very *t* .. Joel 2:11
great and the *t*
day............. Joel 2:31

TERROR
and the *t* of God
was .... Gen. 35:5
appoint over you *t* . Lev. 26:16
land, and that
your *t*........... Josh. 2:9
which cause
their *t* .... Ezek. 26:17

TESTAMENT
of the new *t* ..... Matt. 26:28
This cup is the
new *t* .... Luke 22:20
ministers of the
new *t* .... 2 Cor. 3:6
temple the ark of
his *t* .... Rev. 11:19

TESTIFIED
for thy mouth
hath *t*......... 2 Sam. 1:16
Lord *t* against
Israel .... 2 Kin. 17:13
thy prophets
which *t* .... Neh. 9:26
in the spirit, and *t* .. Acts 18:5
for as thou hast *t* .. Acts 23:11

TESTIFY
Father, he shall *t* . John 15:26
the people, and
to *t*........... Acts 10:42
the Lord Jesus,
to *t*........... Acts 20:24
and do *t* that the
Father .... 1 John 4:14
sent mine angel
to *t*........... Rev. 22:16

TESTIMONY
thou shalt put
the *t*........... Ex. 25:21
upon the ark of
the *t*........... Ex. 25:22
vail the ark of
the *t*........... Ex. 26:33
t, Aaron and his
sons........... Ex. 27:21

by the ark of the *t* ... Ex. 30:6
Sinai, two tables
of *t*........... Ex. 31:18
the tabernacle of *t* . Num. 1:53
the tent of the *t* ... Num. 9:15
and gave him
the *t*........... 2 Kin. 11:12
the *t* of the
Lord is........... Ps. 19:7
commanded,
for a *t*........... Matt. 8:4
therefore
ashamed of the *t* . 2 Tim. 1:8
the *t* of Jesus
Christ .... Rev. 1:9
God, and for the *t* ... Rev. 6:9

THANKSGIVING
he offer it for a *t*.... Lev. 7:12
Offer unto God *t* ... Ps. 50:14
the sacrifices of *t* .. Ps. 107:22
the sacrifice of *t* ... Ps. 116:17
be found
therein, *t*........... Is. 51:3
supplication
with *t*........... Phil. 4:6

THESSALONICA
A city of the Macedonia
area; Paul visits, Acts 17:1;
Phil. 4:16
People of, persecute Paul,
Acts 17:5–8, 11, 13
Men of, accompany Paul,
Acts 20:4; 27:2
Paul writes to Christians in,
1 Thess. 1:1; 2 Thess. 1:1
Demas goes to, 2 Tim. 4:10

THICK
unto thee in a *t*
cloud .... Ex. 19:9
t cloud upon the
mount .... Ex. 19:16
fat, thou art
grown *t* .... Deut. 32:15
as a *t* cloud, thy
transgressions .....Is. 44:22
clouds and of *t*
darkness .... Joel 2:2

THINE
I have put in *t*
hand .... Ex. 4:21
greatness of *t* arm .. Ex. 15:16
thou lift up *t* eyes.. Deut. 4:19
thou settest *t*
hand .... Deut. 28:20
smitten before *t*
enemies........... Deut. 28:25
people, and *t* eyes Deut. 28:32
t eyes which thou
shalt........... Deut. 28:34
for *t* olive shall
cast .... Deut. 28:40
thou serve *t* ..... Deut. 28:48
straitness,
wherewith *t* .... Deut. 28:55
straitness,
wherewith *t* .... Deut. 28:57
fear of *t* heart
wherewith ..... Deut. 28:67
t horn with oil ... 1 Sam. 16:1

t house and thy
kingdom ...... 2 Sam. 7:16
I make *t* enemies
thy .... Ps. 110:1
t heart, I will
ascend .... Is. 14:13
blessing upon *t*
offspring .... Is. 44:3
O Lord, are not *t*
eyes .... Jer. 5:3
for *t* eyes are open .. Jer. 32:19
pride of *t* heart, O .. Jer. 49:16

THIRST
hunger, and in *t* .. Deut. 28:48
the rock for their *t* ..Neh. 9:15
water for their *t* ....Neh. 9:20
my *t* they gave me
vinegar .... Ps. 69:21
shall not hunger
nor *t*........... Is. 49:10
water, and dieth
for *t* .... Is. 50:2
glory, and sit in *t* ... Jer. 48:18
and slay her
with *t*........... Hos. 2:3
him shall never *t* ... John 4:14
saying, If any
man *t*........... John 7:37

THIRTY
an hundred and *t*
years .... Gen. 47:9
Kohath were an
hundred *t* .... Ex. 6:18
t years old and
upward .... Num. 4:3
smote of them
about *t*........... Josh. 7:5
with Israel, *t* ..... 1 Sam. 13:5
talents of silver
and *t* .... 2 Kin. 18:14

THITHER
thou mayest bring
in *t*............. Ex. 26:33
ye seek, and *t*
thou........... Deut. 12:5
And *t* ye shall
bring .... Deut. 12:6
t shall ye brin .... Deut. 12:11
when thou art
come *t* .... 1 Sam. 10:5
t to the hill,
behold........... 1 Sam. 10:10
naked shall I
return *t* .... Job 1:21
And he brought
me *t*........... Ezek. 40:3
came *t* certain
Jews........... Acts 14:19

THOMAS
Called Didymus; One of the
twelve apostles, Matt. 10:3;
Mark 3:18; Luke 6:15
Present at the raising of
Lazarus, John 11:16
Asks Jesus the way to the
Father's house, John 14:5
Absent when Jesus first
appeared to the disciples

after the resurrection,
John 20:24
Skepticism of, John 20:25
Sees Jesus after the
resurrection, John 20:26-29;
21:1, 2
Lives with the other apostles
in Jerusalem, Acts 1:13, 14
Loyalty of, to Jesus,
John 11:16; 20:28

THORNS
in your sides,
and *t* . . . . : Josh. 23:13
quenched as the
fire of *t* . . . . . . Ps. 118:12
come up briers
and *t* . . . . Is. 5:6
be for briers and *t* . . . . Is. 7:23
And *t* shall
come up . . . . Is. 34:13
though briers
and *t* . . . . Ezek. 2:6
received seed
among the *t* . . . . Matt. 13:22

THOUGHT
the evil which he *t* . . Ex. 32:14
a *t* in thy wicked
heart . . . . Deut. 15:9
understandest
my *t* . . . . Ps. 139:2
of the evil that I *t* . . . . Jer. 18:8
the LORD of
hosts *t* . . . . Zech. 1:6
he *t* on these
things . . . . Matt. 1:20
no *t* for your life . . . Matt. 6:25
Therefore take
no *t* . . . . Matt. 6:31

THOUGHTS
imagination of
the *t* . . . . Gen. 6:5
imaginations of
the *t* . . . . 1 Chr. 28:9
standeth for ever,
the *t* . . . . Ps. 33:11
hast done, and
thy *t* . . . . Ps. 40:5
unrighteous man
his *t* . . . . Is. 55:7
their *t* are *t* of
iniquity . . . . Is. 59:7
the fruit of their *t* . . . . Jer. 6:19
me afraid, and
the *t* . . . . Dan. 4:5
not thy *t* trouble
thee . . . . Dan. 5:10
Jesus knowing
their *t* . . . . Matt. 9:4
discerner of the *t* . . . Heb. 4:12

THOUSAND
six hundred *t* on
foot . . . . Ex. 12:37
upward, for six
hundred *t* . . . . Ex. 38:26
put ten *t* to flight . . . Lev. 26:8
commandments
to a *t* . . . . Deut. 7:9
a *t*, and two put
ten . . . . Deut. 32:30

with thee ten *t*
men . . . . Judg. 4:6
Israel, thirty *t*
chariots . . . . 1 Sam. 13:5
David took from
him a *t* . . . . 2 Sam. 8:4
Syrians of Zoba,
twenty *t* . . . . . . 2 Sam. 10:6
valour, even ten *t* . 2 Kin. 24:14
even seven *t*, and
craftsmen . . . . . 2 Kin. 24:16
four *t* were
porters . . . . 1 Chr. 23:5
t thousands
ministered . . . . Dan. 7:10
t two hundred and
ninety . . . . Dan. 12:11
about three *t*
souls . . . . Acts 2:41
prophesy a *t* two
hundred . . . . Rev. 11:3
slain of men
seven *t* . . . . Rev. 11:13
t two hundred and
threescore . . . . Rev. 12:6
reigned with
Christ a *t* . . . . Rev. 20:4
reign with him a *t* . . Rev. 20:6

THOUSANDS
rulers of *t*, and
rulers . . . . Ex. 18:21
shewing mercy
unto *t* . . . . Ex. 20:6
Keeping mercy
for *t* . . . . Ex. 34:7
with ten *t* of
saints . . . . Deut. 33:2
lovingkindness
unto *t* . . . . Jer. 32:18
thousand *t*
ministered . . . . Dan. 7:10
among the *t* of
Judah . . . . Mic. 5:2
LORD be pleased
with *t* . . . . Mic. 6:7
Lord cometh with
ten *t* . . . . Jude 14

THREESCORE
Egypt with *t* and
ten . . . . Deut. 10:22
gave him *t* and ten . . Judg. 9:4
hundred chariots,
and *t* . . . . 2 Chr. 12:3
fulfil *t* and ten
years . . . . 2 Chr. 36:21
seven weeks,
and *t* . . . . Dan. 9:25
after *t* and two
weeks . . . . Dan. 9:26
thousand two
hundred and *t* . . . . . Rev. 11:3
thousand two
hundred and *t* . . . . . Rev. 12:6

THRONE
Pharaoh that sat
on his *t* . . . . Ex. 12:29
stablish the *t* . . . . 2 Sam. 7:13
thy *t* shall be
established . . . . 2 Sam. 7:16

will establish
the *t* . . . . 1 Chr. 22:10
temple, the
LORD's *t* . . . . Ps. 11:4
Thy *t*, O God, is
for . . . . Ps. 45:6
Lord sitting
upon a *t* . . . . Is. 6:1
no end, upon the *t* . . . . Is. 9:7
heaven, I will
exalt my *t* . . . . Is. 14:13
The heaven is
my *t* . . . . Is. 66:1
call Jerusalem
the *t* . . . . Jer. 3:17
t was like the fiery . . . Dan. 7:9
t of his glory, ye . . Matt. 19:28
shall he sit upon
the *t* . . . . Matt. 25:31
t of his father
David . . . . Luke 1:32
hand of the *t* of
God . . . . Heb. 12:2
which are before
his *t* . . . . Rev. 1:4
t, even as I also
overcame . . . . Rev. 3:21
the midst of the *t* . . . . Rev. 5:6
the midst of the *t* . . . Rev. 7:17

THRONES
I beheld till the *t* . . . . Dan. 7:9
sit upon twelve *t* . Matt. 19:28
kingdom, and sit
on *t* . . . . Luke 22:30
I saw *t*, and they
sat . . . . Rev. 20:4

THROWN
his rider hath he *t* . . . Ex. 15:1
fallen, her walls
are *t* . . . . Jer. 50:15
hath *t* down, and
hath . . . . Lam. 2:17
and the rocks are *t* . . Nah. 1:6

THRUST
house of bondage,
to *t* . . . . Deut. 13:5
shall *t* out the
enemy . . . . Deut. 33:27
Draw thy sword,
and *t* . . . . 1 Sam. 31:4
that begat him
shall *t* . . . . Zech. 13:3
hither thy hand,
and *t* . . . . John 20:27
T in thy sharp
sickle . . . . Rev. 14:18

THUNDERINGS
proceeded
lightnings and *t* . . . . Rev. 4:5
were voices, and *t* . . . Rev. 8:5
and voices, and *t* . . Rev. 11:19
voice of mighty *t* . . . Rev. 19:6

TIDINGS
that bringest
good *t* . . . . Is. 40:9
that bringeth
good *t* . . . . Is. 52:7
me to preach
good *t* . . . . Is. 61:1

answer, For the *t* .. Ezek. 21:7
thee these glad *t* .... Luke 1:19

TIME
the *t* appointed I
will .... Gen. 18:14
son asketh thee
in *t* .... Ex. 13:14
commanded thee,
in the *t* .... Ex. 23:15
slide in due *t* ..... Deut. 32:35
t Solomon held a
feast .... 1 Kin. 8:65
t to recover the
remnant .... Is. 11:11
and her *t* is
near to .... Is. 13:22
that *t*, saith the
Lord .... Jer. 50:4
that *t*, saith the
Lord .... Jer. 50:20
t of the Lord's
vengeance .... Jer. 51:6
his hand until a *t* ... Dan. 7:25
t shall Michael
stand .... Dan. 12:1
t, times, and an
half .... Dan. 12:7
t, as they have
behaved .... Mic. 3:4
t forth began
Jesus .... Matt. 16:21
seen God at any *t* ... John 1:18
the *t*, until the
Lord .... 1 Cor. 4:5
the fulness of
the *t* .... Gal. 4:4
told you in *t* past ... Gal. 5:21
t ye were without
Christ .... Eph. 2:12

TIMES
Three *t* thou shalt .. Ex. 23:14
t in the year all
thy .... Ex. 23:17
t into the holy
place .... Lev. 16:2
enchantment, nor
observe *t* .... Lev. 19:26
Three *t* in a year
shall .... Deut. 16:16
an observer of *t* .. Deut. 18:10
began to move
him at *t* .... Judg. 13:25
fire, and
observed *t* ...... 2 Kin. 21:6
oppressed, a
refuge in *t* .... Ps. 9:9
their days, in the *t* ... Ps. 44:1
ancient *t* the
things .... Is. 46:10
And he changeth
the *t* .... Dan. 2:21
t shall pass over
thee .... Dan. 4:25
ten thousand *t* ten .. Dan. 7:10
to change *t* and
laws .... Dan. 7:25
even in
troublous *t* .... Dan. 9:25
a time, *t*, and an
half .... Dan. 12:7

know the *t* or the
seasons .... Acts 1:7
And the *t* of this
ignorance .... Acts 17:30
conversation in *t*
past .... Eph. 2:3

TIMOTHY
also Called Timotheus, the
companion of Paul; Parentage
of, Acts 16:1
Reputation and Christian faith
of, Acts 16:2; 1 Cor. 4:17;
16:10; 2 Tim. 1:5; 3:15
Circumcised; becomes Paul's
companion, Acts 16:3;
1 Thess. 3:2
Left by Paul at Berea,
Acts 17:14
Rejoined Paul at Corinth,
Acts 17:15; 18:5
Sent into Macedonia,
Acts 19:22
Rejoined by Paul; accompanies
Paul to Asia, Acts 20:1–4
Sent salutation to the Romans,
Rom. 16:21
Sent to the Corinthians,
1 Cor. 4:17; 16:10, 11
Preached to the Corinthians,
2 Cor. 1:19
Sent to the Philippians,
Phil. 2:19, 23
Sent to the Thessalonians,
1 Thess. 3:2, 6
Left by Paul in Ephesus,
1 Tim. 1:3
Confined with Paul in Rome,
Phil. 2:19–23; Philem. 1;
Heb. 13:23
His name found with the
postscripts to Philippians,
Philemon, and Hebrews,
ordained bishop of the
Ephesians in postscript to
Second Timothy. Acts as
Paul's amanuesis (scribe),
see the postscript to First
Corinthians and Hebrews.
Joined Paul in the letters
To the Philippians, Phil. 1:1
To the Colossians, Col. 1:1, 2
To the Thessalonians,
1 Thess. 1:1; 2 Thess. 1:1
To Philemon, Philem. 1
Zeal of, Phil. 2:19–22;
1 Tim. 6:12
Power of, 1 Tim. 4:14;
2 Tim. 1:6
Paul's love for, 1 Cor. 4:17;
Phil. 2:22; 1 Tim. 1:2, 18;
2 Tim. 1:2–4
Paul writes to, 1 Tim. 1:1, 2;
2 Tim. 1:1, 2

TIRZAH
A daughter of Zelophehad,
Num. 26:33; 36:11;
Josh. 17:3
Special legislation in
regard to the inheritance

of, Num. 27:1-11; 36;
Josh. 17:3, 4
—— A city of Canaan
Captured by Joshua,
Josh. 12:24
Becomes the residence of
the kings of the northern
kingdom (Israel),
1 Kin. 14:17; 15:21, 33; 16:6,
8, 9, 15, 17, 23
Royal residence moved from,
1 Kin. 16:23, 24
Base of military operations of
Menahem, 2 Kin. 15:14, 16
Beauty of, Song 6:4

TITHES
And he gave him *t*
of .... Gen. 14:20
your *t*, and heave
offerings .... Deut. 12:6
t, and the heave
offering .... Deut. 12:11
Bring ye all the *t*.... Mal. 3:10

TOBIAH
Ancestor of a family of
Babylonian captives,
Ezra 2:60; Neh. 7:62
—— An enemy of the Jews in
the time of Nehemiah
Opposes the rebuilding of the
wall of Jerusalem, Neh. 2:10,
19; 4:3, 7, 8
Conspires to injure and
intimidate Nehemiah,
Neh. 6:1–14, 19
Subverts nobles of Judah,
Neh. 6:17, 18
Allies himself with Eliashib,
the priest, Neh. 13:4–9

TOLD
and Pharaoh *t*
them .... Gen. 41:8
And Moses *t* the
words .... Ex. 19:9
And Samuel *t* him
every .... 1 Sam. 3:18
t us, what work
thou .... Ps. 44:1
have not I *t* thee
from .... Is. 44:8
who hath *t* it from ... Is. 45:21
which had not
been *t* .... Is. 52:15
him I *t* the dream .... Dan. 4:8
morning which
was *t* .... Dan. 8:26
a lie, and have *t*
false .... Zech. 10:2
and *t* them, Elias
verily .... Mark 9:12
which *t* these
things .... Luke 24:10
t you in time past... Gal. 5:21

TONGUE
t thou shalt not
understand ..... Deut. 28:49
t is mischief and
vanity .... Ps. 10:7

t cleaveth to my
jaws .... Ps. 22:15
sin not with my *t* .... Ps. 39:1
Thy *t* deviseth
mischiefs.......... Ps. 52:2
their *t* a sharp
sword .... Ps. 57:4
laughter, and our *t* .. Ps. 126:2
t of the wise is
health .... Prov. 12:18
The *t* of the wise
useth .... Prov. 15:2
utterly destroy
the *t*............. Is. 11:15
the *t* of the dumb
sing .... Is. 35:6
hath given me
the *t*............ Is. 50:4
taught their *t* to
speak .... Jer. 9:5
t is as an arrow
shot .... Jer. 9:8
smite him with
the *t*............. Jer. 18:18
water, and cool
my *t*.......... Luke 16:24
hath a *t*, hath a
revelation ..... 1 Cor. 14:26
t is a fire, a world ... James 3:6
every kindred,
and *t* .... Rev. 5:9

TONGUES
from the strife of *t* .. Ps. 31:20
And they bend
their *t* .... Jer. 9:3
shall speak with
new *t* .... Mark 16:17
t, as the Spirit
gave .... Acts 2:4
divers kinds of *t* . 1 Cor. 12:10
governments,
diversities of *t* . 1 Cor. 12:28
I speak with the *t* .. 1 Cor. 13:1
ye all spake with *t* . 1 Cor. 14:5

TOP
will stand on the *t* ... Ex. 17:9
Hur went up to
the *t*............. Ex. 17:10
pure gold, the *t*
thereof........... Ex. 30:3
foot unto the *t* ... Deut. 28:35
border went up to
the *t*............ Josh. 15:8
established in the *t* .... Is. 2:2
t of Carmel shall
wither .... Amos 1:2
the *t* of Carmel, I ... Amos 9:3
established in
the *t*............. Mic. 4:1
in pieces at the *t*.... Nah. 3:10
with a bowl upon
the *t*........... Zech. 4:2

TOPHET
Also called Topheth; A place
in the valley of the sons of
Hinnom, 2 Kin. 23:10;
Jewish children passed
through the fire to the god
Molech in, 2 Kin. 23:10;

Jer. 7:31, 32; 19:6, 11–14;
32:35
See also, 2 Chr. 28:3; 33:6
Destroyed by Josiah,
2 Kin. 23:10
Horror of, Is. 30:33

TORN
their carcases
were *t* .... Is. 5:25
shall be *t* in pieces .... Jer. 5:6
or is *t* in pieces .... Ezek. 4:14
for he hath *t*, and .... Hos. 6:1

TOUCH
not *t* any holy
thing .... Num. 4:15
t no unclean thing ... Is. 52:11
pressed upon him
for to *t*.......... Mark 3:10
Jesus saith unto
her, *T* .... John 20:17
saith the Lord,
and *t* ....2 Cor. 6:17

TOUCHED
hand, and *t* my
mouth .... Jer. 1:9
t me, and set me
upright .... Dan. 8:18
sons of men *t* my
lips............. Dan. 10:16
priest which
cannot be *t* ...... Heb. 4:15

TOUCHETH
whatsoever *t* the
altar .... Ex. 29:37
whosoever *t* his
bed.............. Lev. 15:5
Whosoever *t* the
dead........... Num. 19:13
And whosoever *t*
one........... Num. 19:16
when the east
wind *t* .... Ezek. 17:10
break out, and
blood *t*.......... Hos. 4:2
that *t* you *t* the
apple .... Zech. 2:8
woman this is
that *t* .... Luke 7:39
and that wicked
one *t* .... 1 John 5:18

TOWER
t of Meah they
sanctified .... Neh. 3:1
fish gate, and
the *t*.......... Neh. 12:39
salvation, and my
high *t*........... Ps. 18:2
vine, and built a *t*...... Is. 5:2

TRANSGRESSED
LORD their God,
but *t*............. 2 Kin. 18:12
he *t* against the
LORD.......... 2 Chr. 26:16
the men that
have *t*........... Is. 66:24
the pastors also *t* ..... Jer. 2:8
whereby ye have *t* Ezek. 18:31
Israel have *t* thy
law............ Dan. 9:11

they have *t* my
covenant .... Hos. 8:1

TRANSGRESSION
forgiving iniquity
and *t* .... Ex. 34:7
forgiving iniquity
and *t* .... Num. 14:18
died for his *t* .... 1 Chr. 10:13
is snared by the *t* . Prov. 12:13
man aboundeth
in *t*........... Prov. 29:22
for the *t* of my
people .... Is. 53:8
my people their *t* ..... Is. 58:1
city, to finish the *t* .. Dan. 9:24
firstborn for my *t* .... Mic. 6:7
and passeth by
the *t*........... Mic. 7:18
is, there is no *t* .... Rom. 4:15

TRANSGRESSIONS
I will confess my *t* ... Ps. 32:5
mercies blot out
my *t*.............. Ps. 51:1
blotteth out thy *t* .... Is. 43:25
thick cloud, thy *t* .... Is. 44:22
wounded for our *t* .... Is. 53:5
because their *t* are .... Jer. 5:6
yourselves from
all your *t* .... Ezek. 18:30
t, whereby ye .... Ezek. 18:31
any of their *t* ..... Ezek. 37:23
For three *t* of
Damascus .... Amos 1:3
For three *t* of
Tyrus .... Amos 1:9
For three *t* of
Edom........... Amos 1:11
of *t*, till the seed.... Gal. 3:19
redemption of
the *t*............ Heb. 9:15

TRAVAIL
Thou knowest all
the *t*.......... Num. 20:14
sinner he giveth *t* ... Eccl. 2:26
of the *t* of his soul ... Is. 53:11
thou that didst
not *t*.............. Is. 54:1
as of a woman in *t* ... Jer. 4:31
as of a woman in *t* ... Jer. 6:24
cometh upon
them, as *t* ...... 1 Thess. 5:3

TREACHEROUS
t dealer dealeth
treacherously ...... Is. 21:2
t sister Judah
feared .... Jer. 3:8
t sister Judah hath ... Jer. 3:10
adulterers, an
assembly of *t* .... Jer. 9:2

TREACHEROUSLY
treacherous dealer
dealeth *t* .... Is. 21:2
and dealest *t*, and..... Is. 33:1
happy that deal
very *t* .... Jer. 12:1
friends have
dealt *t* .... Lam. 1:2

TREAD
that ye shall *t* .... Deut. 11:25

and thou shalt *t*
upon . . . . Deut. 33:29
and *t* down the
wicked . . . . Job 40:12
the prey, and to *t* . . . . . Is. 10:6
upon my
mountains *t* . . . . Is. 14:25
I will *t* them in
mine . . . . Is. 63:3
thou shalt *t* the
olives . . . . Mic. 6:15
mighty men,
which *t* . . . . Zech. 10:5
holy city shall
they *t* . . . . Rev. 11:2

TREASURE
Pharaoh *t* cities,
Pithom . . . . Ex. 1:11
shall be a
peculiar *t* . . . . Ex. 19:5
unto thee his
good *t* . . . . Deut. 28:12
t house of his god . . . Dan. 1:2
t of all pleasant
vessels . . . . Hos. 13:15
which wax not
old, a *t* . . . . Luke 12:33

TREASURES
were left in the *t*. 1 Kin. 15:18
all the *t* of the
house . . . . 2 Kin. 24:13
in thy *t*, thou
shalt . . . . Jer. 48:7
sword is upon
her *t* . . . . Jer. 50:37

TREE
yourselves under
the *t* . . . . Gen. 18:4
under every
green *t* . . . . Deut. 12:2
under every
green *t* . . . . 1 Kin. 14:23
t planted by the
rivers . . . . Ps. 1:3
like a green olive *t* . . . Ps. 52:8
She is a *t* of life. . . Prov. 3:18
fig from the fig *t* . . . . . Is. 34:4
forest, and every *t* . . . Is. 44:23
green *t* thou
wanderest . . . . Jer. 2:20
t, and there hath
played . . . . Jer. 3:6
upright as the
palm *t* . . . . Jer. 10:5
t planted by the
waters . . . . Jer. 17:8
brought down the
high *t* . . . . Ezek. 17:24
and under his fig *t* . . . Mic. 4:4
that hangeth
on a *t* . . . . Gal. 3:13
own body on the *t* . 1 Pet. 2:24
give to eat of the *t* . . . Rev. 2:7
thing, neither
any *t* . . . . Rev. 9:4
t of life, which
bare . . . . Rev. 22:2
right to the *t* of
life . . . . Rev. 22:14

TREES
boughs of goodly *t* . Lev. 23:40
increase, and the *t* . . Lev. 26:4
shalt have olive *t* . Deut. 28:40
thy *t* and fruit . . . . Deut. 28:42
the city of palm *t* . . Judg. 1:16
manner of *t*, of
wine . . . . Neh. 10:37
axes upon the
thick *t* . . . . Ps. 74:5
singing, and all
the *t* . . . . Is. 55:12
be called *t* of
righteousness . . . . Is. 61:3
beast, and upon
the *t* . . . . Jer. 7:20
all the *t* of the
field . . . . Ezek. 17:24
t of Eden, the
choice . . . . Ezek. 31:16
each post were
palm *t* . . . . Ezek. 40:16
arches, and their
palm *t* . . . . Ezek. 40:22
tree, even all the *t* . . Joel 1:12
among the
myrtle *t* . . . . Zech. 1:8
part of *t* was
burnt . . . . Rev. 8:7

TREMBLE
let the people *t* . . . . . . Ps. 99:1
and the hills did *t* . . . . . Is. 5:25
ye not *t* at my
presence . . . . Jer. 5:22
the earth shall *t* . . . . Jer. 10:10
they shall fear
and *t* . . . . Jer. 33:9
kingdom men *t*
and fear . . . . Dan. 6:26
inhabitants of the
land *t* . . . . Joel 2:1
the heavens
shall *t* . . . . Joel 2:10

TREMBLING
mighty men of
Moab, *t* . . . . Ex. 15:15
give thee there a *t* Deut. 28:65
dregs of the cup
of *t* . . . . Is. 51:17
hand the cup of *t* . . . . Is. 51:22
themselves with *t*. Ezek. 26:16

TRESPASS
For all manner
of *t* . . . . Ex. 22:9
offering, and as
the *t* . . . . Lev. 6:17
offering is, so is
the *t* . . . . Lev. 7:7
one lamb for a *t*
offering . . . . Lev. 14:21
fathers, with
their *t* . . . . Lev. 26:40
and every *t*
offering . . . . Num. 18:9
Israel
committed a *t* . . . . . Josh. 7:1
been chief in
this *t* . . . . Ezra 9:2
our head, and
our *t* . . . . Ezra 9:6

great *t* unto this
day . . . . Ezra 9:7
t that he hath
trespassed . . . . . Ezek. 18:24
t that they have
trespassed . . . . Dan. 9:7

TRESPASSED
trespass which
they *t* . . . . Lev. 26:40
trespass that he
hath *t* . . . . Ezek. 18:24
trespass that they
have *t* . . . . Dan. 9:7
my covenant,
and *t* . . . . Hos. 8:1

TRIBE
LORD separated
the *t* . . . . Deut. 10:8
woman, or family,
or *t* . . . . Deut. 29:18
t of Reuben, and
Ramoth . . . . Josh. 20:8
give one *t* to thy
son . . . . 1 Kin. 11:13
will I give one *t* . 1 Kin. 11:36
Gadites, and the
half *t* . . . . 1 Chr. 5:26
t of Benjamin, an
Hebrew . . . . Phil. 3:5
behold, the Lion
of the *t* . . . . Rev. 5:5

TRIBES
choose out of all
your *t* . . . . Deut. 12:5
thee, throughout
thy *t* . . . . Deut. 16:18
divisions by
their *t* . . . . Josh. 11:23
the fathers of
the *t* . . . . Josh. 14:1
of all the *t* of
Israel . . . . 1 Sam. 2:28
t of Israel, will I . . 2 Kin. 21:7
line, and made
the *t* . . . . Ps. 78:55
servant to raise
up the *t* . . . . Is. 49:6
judging the twelve
t . . . . Matt. 19:28
t of the earth
mourn . . . . Matt. 24:30
judging the
twelve *t* . . . . Luke 22:30

TRIBULATION
When thou art
in *t* . . . . Deut. 4:30
Immediately after
the *t* . . . . Matt. 24:29
world ye shall
have *t* . . . . John 16:33
t enter into the
kingdom . . . . Acts 14:22
T and anguish,
upon . . . . Rom. 2:9
and companion
in *t* . . . . Rev. 1:9
know thy works,
and *t* . . . . Rev. 2:9
ye shall have *t* ten . . Rev. 2:10

TRODDEN

whereon thy feet
  have t . . . . Josh. 14:9
thereof, and it
  shall be t . . . . Is. 5:5
I have t the
  winepress . . . . Is. 63:3
Jerusalem shall
  be t . . . . Luke 21:24

TROUBLE

Israel a curse,
  and t . . . . Josh. 6:18
days, and full of t . . . . Job 14:1
refuge in times of t . . . Ps. 9:9
For in the time
  of t . . . . Ps. 27:5
me in the day of t . . . Ps. 50:15
shall come out
  of t . . . . Prov. 12:13
they are a t
  unto me . . . . Is. 1:14
and behold t and
  darkness . . . . Is. 8:22
the time of their t . . . Jer. 2:27
the time of thy t . . . . . Jer. 2:28
time of Jacob's t . . . . . Jer. 30:7
thy thoughts t
  thee . . . . Dan. 5:10
shall be a time of t . . Dan. 12:1
hold in the day
  of t . . . . Nah. 1:7
rest in the day of t . . Hab. 3:16
Jews, do
  exceedingly t . . . . Acts 16:20

TROUBLED

and Levi, Ye
  have t . . . . Gen. 34:30
that his spirit
  was t . . . . Gen. 41:8
thy face, they are t . Ps. 104:29
tears, my bowels
  are t . . . . Lam. 2:11
wherewith his
  spirit was t . . . . Dan. 2:1
visions of my
  head t . . . . Dan. 4:5
cogitations
  much t . . . . Dan. 7:28
flock, they were t . . Zech. 10:2
Now is my soul t . . John 12:27
not your heart
  be t . . . . John 14:27

TRUE

the LORD is the t
  God . . . . Jer. 10:10
which was told
  is t . . . . Dan. 8:26
t, but the time
  appointed . . . . Dan. 10:1
t God, and Jesus
  Christ . . . . John 17:3
righteousness
  and t . . . . Eph. 4:24
intreat thee also, t . . . Phil. 4:3
serve the living
  and t . . . . 1 Thess. 1:9
the figures of the t . . Heb. 9:24
a t heart in full
  assurance . . . . . . Heb. 10:22
him that is t . . . . . 1 John 5:20

holy, he that is t . . . . . Rev. 3:7
faithful and t
  witness . . . . Rev. 3:14
O Lord, holy and t . . Rev. 6:10
t are thy ways,
  thou . . . . Rev. 15:3
called Faithful
  and T . . . . Rev. 19:11
are faithful and t . . . Rev. 22:6

TRUMPET

voice of the t
  exceeding . . . . Ex. 19:16
Gideon, and he
  blew a t . . . . Judg. 6:34
And they blew
  the t . . . . 1 Kin. 1:39
day, that the
  great t . . . . Is. 27:13
thy voice like a t . . . . . Is. 58:1
say, Blow ye the t . . . . Jer. 4:5
t, the alarm of war . . . Jer. 4:19
Jerusalem, and
  blow the t . . . . Jer. 6:1
Set the t to thy
  mouth . . . . Hos. 8:1
Blow ye the t in
  Zion . . . . Joel 2:1
t be blown in the
  city . . . . Amos 3:6
sound of a t . . . . . . Matt. 24:31
great voice, as
  of a t . . . . Rev. 1:10
as it were of a t
  talking . . . . Rev. 4:1

TRUMPETS

memorial of
  blowing of t . . . . . Lev. 23:24
t over your burnt
  offerings . . . . Num. 10:10
hundred blew
  the t . . . . Judg. 7:22
t and cymbals and
  instruments . . . . 2 Chr. 5:13

TRUST

thou art come to t . Ruth 2:12
they that put
  their t . . . . Ps. 2:12
strength, in whom
  I will t . . . . Ps. 18:2
Some t in chariots . . . Ps. 20:7
O my God, I t in
  thee . . . . Ps. 25:2
LORD, do I put
  my t . . . . Ps. 31:1
T in the LORD,
  and . . . . Ps. 37:3
and fear, and
  shall t . . . . Ps. 40:3
I t in the mercy of . . . Ps. 52:8
but I will t in thee . . Ps. 55:23
T in him at all
  times . . . . Ps. 62:8
T not in
  oppression . . . . Ps. 62:10
wings shalt thou t . . . Ps. 91:4
I will t, and not be . . . . Is. 12:2
stay on horses,
  and t . . . . Is. 31:1
Egypt to all that t . . . . . Is. 36:6

T ye not in lying
  words . . . . Jer. 7:4
neighbour, and
  t ye . . . . Jer. 9:4
knoweth them
  that t . . . . Nah. 1:7
t in uncertain
  riches . . . . 1 Tim. 6:17

TRUSTED

I have t in thy
  mercy . . . . Ps. 13:5
He t on the LORD
  that . . . . Ps. 22:8
friend, in
  whom I t . . . . Ps. 41:9
but t in the
  abundance . . . . Ps. 52:7
thou hast t in thy . . . . Jer. 48:7
his servants that t . . Dan. 3:28
t, after that ye
  heard . . . . Eph. 1:13

TRUTH

in goodness and t . . . Ex. 34:6
a God of t and
  without . . . . Deut. 32:4
plenteous in
  mercy and t . . . . . . Ps. 86:15
people with his t . . . Ps. 96:13
his mercy and
  his t . . . . Ps. 98:3
LORD liveth, in t . . . . . Jer. 4:2
thine eyes upon
  the t . . . . Jer. 5:3
not valiant for
  the t . . . . Jer. 9:3
will not speak
  the t . . . . Jer. 9:5
Daniel, and said,
  Of a t . . . . Dan. 2:47
called a city of t . . . . Zech. 8:3
full of grace and t . . . John 1:14
abode not in the t . . John 8:44
the t, and the life . . . John 14:6
Even the Spirit
  of t . . . . John 14:17
the Spirit of t . . . . . John 15:26
lying, speak every
  man t . . . . Eph. 4:25
grace of God in t . . . . Col. 1:6
knowledge of
  the t . . . . 1 Tim. 2:4
souls in obeying
  the t . . . . 1 Pet. 1:22

TURN

he hath spoken
  to t . . . . Deut. 13:5
t not from it to
  the . . . . Josh. 1:7
testified against
  them to t . . . . Neh. 9:26
shall remember
  and t . . . . Ps. 22:27
T us again, O
  God of . . . . Ps. 80:7
T us again, O
  LORD . . . . Ps. 80:19
in the breach, to t . Ps. 106:23
he will not t from . . Ps. 132:11
look for light, he t . . Jer. 13:16

and I will *t* away
your . . . . Jer. 29:14
Repent, and *t*
yourselves . . . . . . Ezek. 18:30
your garments,
and *t* . . . . Joel 2:13
four, I will not *t* . . . . Amos 1:3
four, I will not *t* . . . Amos 1:11
if God will *t* and
repent . . . . Jon. 3:9
and I will *t* mine
hand . . . . Zech. 13:7
fatherless, and
that *t* . . . . Mal. 3:5
everlasting life, lo,
we *t* . . . . Acts 13:46
their eyes, and
to *t* . . . . Acts 26:18
repent and *t* to
God . . . . Acts 26:20

TURNED
shall be *t* to blood . . . Ex. 7:17
And they *t* and
went . . . . Num. 21:33
their enemies,
but *t* . . . . Josh. 7:12
LORD *t* from the
fierceness . . . . Josh. 7:26
for he is *t* back
from . . . . 1 Sam. 15:11
The wicked shall
be *t* . . . . Ps. 9:17
his anger is not *t* . . . . . Is. 5:25
deceived heart
hath *t* . . . . Is. 44:20
we have *t* every
one . . . . Is. 53:6
was *t* to be their
enemy . . . . Is. 63:10
they have *t* their
back . . . . Jer. 2:27
sister Judah hath
not *t* . . . . Jer. 3:10
vision my sorrows
are *t* . . . . Dan. 10:16
mine heart is *t*
within . . . . Hos. 11:8
The sun shall be *t* . . Joel 2:31
t as a plain from
Geba . . . . Zech. 14:10
But Jesus *t* him
about . . . . Matt. 9:22
And he *t* to the
woman . . . . Luke 7:44
have *t* the world
upside . . . . Acts 17:6
ye *t* to God from
idols . . . . 1 Thess. 1:9

TURNETH
And the soul
that *t* . . . . Lev. 20:6
tribe, whose
heart *t* . . . . Deut. 29:18
For the people *t*
not . . . . Is. 9:13
waxed feeble,
and *t* . . . . Jer. 49:24
when the
righteous *t* . . . . . Ezek. 18:24

stars and Orion,
and *t* . . . . Amos 5:8

TURNING
dish, wiping it,
and *t* . . . . 2 Kin. 21:13
hardened his
heart from *t* . . . 2 Chr. 36:13
to bless you, in *t* . . . . Acts 3:26
neither shadow
of *t* . . . . James 1:17
t the cities of
Sodom . . . . 2 Pet. 2:6

TWELVE
fine flour, and
bake *t* . . . . Lev. 24:5
Ishtob *t* thousand
men . . . . 2 Sam. 10:6
With *t* hundred
chariots . . . . 2 Chr. 12:3
shall sit upon *t*
thrones . . . . Matt. 19:28
than *t* legions of
angels . . . . Matt. 26:53
thrones judging
the *t* . . . . Luke 22:30
Jacob begat the *t*
patriarchs . . . . Acts 7:8
bare *t* manner of
fruits . . . . Rev. 22:2

TWENTY
Ishmeelites for *t*
pieces . . . . Gen. 37:28
(a shekel is *t*
gerahs . . . . Ex. 30:13
numbered, from *t*
years . . . . Ex. 38:26
(the shekel is *t*
gerahs . . . . Num. 3:47
number, from *t*
years . . . . Num. 14:29
sanctuary, which
is *t* . . . . Num. 18:16
an hundred and *t*
years . . . . Deut. 31:2
hundred
horsemen, and *t* . . 2 Sam. 8:4
sons and *t* . . . . 2 Sam. 9:10
Zoba, *t* thousand
footmen . . . . 2 Sam. 10:6
hundred and *t*
talents . . . . 1 Kin. 9:28
firstfruits, *t* loaves 2 Kin. 4:42
chariots of God
are *t* . . . . Ps. 68:17
t men, with their
backs . . . . Ezek. 8:16
gate five and *t*
men . . . . Ezek. 11:1
five and *t* . . . . Ezek. 40:21
four and *t* elders
fell . . . . Rev. 5:8
four and *t* elders
fell . . . . Rev. 5:14
the four and *t*
elders . . . . Rev. 19:4

TYCHICUS
An Asian companion of Paul;
Accompanies Paul from
Greece to Asia, Acts 20:4

With Paul in Nicopolis,
Titus 3:12
With Paul in Rome, with
postscripts to Ephesians and
Colossians, Eph. 6:21, 22;
Col. 4:7, 8
Paul's amanuensis (copyist)
in writing to the Ephesians
and Colossians, see the
postscripts to Ephesians and
Colossians
Sent to Ephesus, Eph. 6:21,
22; 2 Tim. 4:12
Sent to Colossae, Col. 4:7, 8

UNAWARES
day come upon
you *u* . . . . Luke 21:34
false brethren *u*
brought . . . . Gal. 2:4
entertained
angels *u* . . . . Heb. 13:2
certain men crept
in *u* . . . . Jude 4

UNCIRCUMCISED
u man child
whose flesh . . . . . . Gen. 17:14
hear me, who am
of *u* . . . . Ex. 6:12
their *u* hearts be
humbled . . . . Lev. 26:41
for who is this *u*
Philistine . . . . . 1 Sam. 17:26
and this *u*
Philistine . . . . . 1 Sam. 17:36
these *u* come and
thrust . . . . 1 Sam. 31:4
come into thee
the *u* . . . . Is. 52:1
behold, their ear
is *u* . . . . Jer. 6:10
these nations
are *u* . . . . Jer. 9:26
sanctuary
strangers, *u* . . . . . . Ezek. 44:7
Ye stiffnecked
and *u* . . . . Acts 7:51

UNCLEAN
his clothes, and
be *u* . . . . Lev. 11:25
is in it shall be *u* . . . Lev. 11:33
ye make
yourselves *u* . . . . . Lev. 11:43
he is *u* . . . . Lev. 13:46
in water, and be *u* . . . Lev. 15:5
of *u* beasts shalt
thou . . . . Num. 18:15
he shall be *u* . . . . . Num. 19:13
grave, shall be *u* . . Num. 19:16
thing out of an *u* . . . . Job 14:4
I am a man of *u*
lips . . . . Is. 6:5
the *u* shall not
pass . . . . Is. 35:8
uncircumcised
and the *u* . . . . Is. 52:1
touch no *u* thing . . . . Is. 52:11
difference
between the *u* . . . Ezek. 22:26
eat *u* things in
Assyria . . . . Hos. 9:3

the *u* spirit to pass   Zech.13:2
any man common
  or *u* . . . . .Acts 10:28
is nothing *u*. . . . . . Rom. 14:14
touch not the *u*
  thing 2 Cor.6:17
u and hateful bird. . . Rev.18:2

UNCLEANNESS
his *u* is yet upon
  him . . . . .Num. 19:13
he hath found
  some *u*. Deut.24:1
Adultery,
  fornication, *u* Gal.5:19
fornication, *u*,
  inordinate Col.3:5

UNDERSTAND
tongue thou shalt
  not *u* . . . . .Deut. 28:49
Hear ye indeed,
  but *u* . . . . .Is. 6:9
with their ears,
  and *u* . . . . .Is. 6:10
me, and *u* that
  I am . . . . .Is. 43:10
that they cannot *u* . . .Is. 44:18
make this man
  to *u* . . . . .Dan. 8:16
therefore *u* the
  matter . . . . .Dan. 9:23
Know therefore
  and *u* . . . . .Dan. 9:25
come to make
  thee *u* . . . . .Dan. 10:14
wise, and he
  shall *u* . . . . .Hos. 14:9
readeth, let him *u* . Matt. 24:15
may hear, and
  not *u* . . . . Mark 4:12
with their eyes,
  nor *u* . . . . .John 12:40
of prophecy, and *u* .1 Cor. 13:2

UNDERSTANDING
thy servant an *u*
  heart . . . . .1 Kin. 3:9
thee a wise and an
  u. . . . . 1 Kin. 3:12
Zechariah, who
  had *u* . . . . 2 Chr. 26:5
depart from evil
  is *u* . . . . .Job 28:28
a good *u* have all
  they . . . . Ps. 111:10
is of great *u* . . . . . . Prov. 14:29
spirit of wisdom
  and *u* Is.11:2
make him of
  quick *u* Is.11:3
is a people of no *u* . . .Is. 27:11
searching of his *u* . . . .Is. 40:28
u to say, I have
  burned. . . . . .Is. 44:19
and they have
  none *u* . . . . .Jer. 4:22
people, and
  without *u* . . . . Jer. 5:21
to them that
  know *u* . . . . .Dan. 2:21

heaven, and
  mine *u* . . . . .Dan. 4:34
father light and *u* . . .Dan. 5:11
the thing, and
  had *u* . . . . .Dan. 10:1
perfect *u* of all
  things . . . . .Luke 1:3
children in *u* . . . . 1 Cor. 14:20
given us an *u*. . . . . 1 John 5:20

UNDERSTOOD
were wise, that
  they *u* . . . . Deut. 32:29
have not known
  nor *u* . . . . .Is. 44:18
and he *u* the thing . .Dan. 10:1
being *u* by the
  things . . . . Rom. 1:20

UNGODLY
Shouldest thou
  help the *u* . . . . . . 2 Chr. 19:2
the counsel of
  the *u* . . . . Ps. 1:1
The *u* are not so . . . . . Ps. 1:4
of the *u* shall
  perish . . . . Ps. 1:6
the teeth of the *u* . . . . Ps. 3:7
after should live *u* . . 2 Pet. 2:6
perdition of *u* men . . 2 Pet. 3:7
condemnation, *u*
  men . . . . .Jude 4

UNJUST
the *u* knoweth no
  shame . . . . .Zeph. 3:5
of the just and *u* . . . Acts 24:15
u, that he might
  bring . . . . .1 Pet. 3:18
u unto the day of
  judgment . . . . .2 Pet. 2:9

UNLEAVENED
roast with fire,
  and *u* . . . . Ex. 12:8
days shall ye eat *u* . . Ex. 12:15
observe the feast
  of *u* . . . . Ex. 12:17
ye shall eat *u*
  bread . . . . Ex. 12:18
habitations shall
  ye eat *u* . . . . Ex. 12:20
the feast of *u*
  bread . . . . Ex. 23:15
feast of *u* bread
  shalt . . . . Ex. 34:18
with *u* bread shall . . Lev. 6:16
sacrifice of
  thanksgiving *u* . . . . Lev. 7:12
days shalt thou
  eat *u* . . . . Deut. 16:3
days thou shalt
  eat *u*. . . . . Deut. 16:8
in the feast of *u*
  bread . . . . Deut. 16:16

UNPUNISHED
calamities shall
  not be *u* . . . . Prov. 17:5
should ye be
  utterly *u* . . . . Jer. 25:29
thee altogether *u* . . .Jer. 30:11

shall altogether
  go *u* . . . . Jer. 49:12

UPPER
and on the *u* door
  post . . . . .Ex. 12:7
conduit of the *u*
  pool . . . . 2 Kin. 18:17
lodge in the *u*
  lintels . . . . .Zeph. 2:14
an *u* room, where
  abode. . . . . .Acts 1:13

UPRIGHT
the floods stood *u* . . . Ex. 15:8
and made you
  go *u* . . . . Lev. 26:13
u in heart to
  sanctify . . . . 2 Chr. 29:34
was perfect and *u* . . . . .Job 1:1
doth behold the *u*. . . . Ps. 11:7
the prayer of the *u* . Prov. 15:8
are *u* as the palm
  tree . . . . Jer. 10:5
touched me, and
  set me *u* . . . . .Dan. 8:18
is none *u* among
  men . . . . Mic. 7:2

UPWARD
twenty years old
  and *u* . . . . Ex. 38:26
thirty years old
  and *u* . . . . Num. 4:3
twenty years old
  and *u* . . . . Num. 14:29
downward, and
  bear fruit *u* . . . . Is. 37:31

UR
Abraham's native place,
  Gen. 11:27, 28
Abraham leaves, Gen. 11:31;
  15:7; Neh. 9:7
——— Father of one of David's
  mighty men, 1 Chr. 11:35

URIAH
One of David's mighty men,
  2 Sam. 23:39; 1 Chr. 11:41
David's adultery with the wife
  of, 2 Sam. 11:2–5; 1 Kin. 15:5
Summoned from seat of war
  by David, 2 Sam. 11:6–13
Noble spirit of, 2 Sam. 11:11
David compasses the death of,
  2 Sam. 11:14–25
David marries the widow of,
  2 Sam. 11:26, 27
Called Urias, Matt. 1:6
——— A priest
The father of Meremoth,
  Ezra 8:33
Called Urijah, Neh. 3:4, 21

URIJAH
A priest in Ahaz; Builds a new
  altar for Ahaz,
  2 Kin. 16:10–16
Probably identical with Uriah,
  witness to a prophecy of
  Isaiah, Is. 8:2
——— A priest
Assistant to Ezra, Neh. 8:4

——— A prophet in the time of
Jehoiakim
Prophesies against Judah,
Jer. 26:20
Fled to Egypt; taken; killed by
Jehoiakim, Jer. 26:21–23

USURY
thou lay upon
him *u* . . . . Ex. 22:25
Take thou no *u* of
him . . . . Lev. 25:36
money to *u*, nor
taketh . . . . Ps. 15:5
upon *u*, neither
hath . . . . Ezek. 18:8
u, and hath taken
increase . . . . Ezek. 18:13

UTTER
if he do not *u* it . . . . . Lev. 5:1
declare ye, tell
this, *u* . . . . .Is. 48:20
LORD shall *u* his
voice . . . . Joel 2:11
roar from Zion,
and *u* . . . . .Amos 1:2

UTTERLY
for I will *u* put out . . Ex. 17:14
but thou shalt *u*
overthrow . . . . Ex. 23:24
ye shall soon *u*
perish . . . . Deut. 4:26
shalt smite them,
and *u* . . . . Deut. 7:2
Ye shall *u* destroy . . Deut. 12:2
Sihon and Og,
whom ye *u* . . . . . . Josh. 2:10
smite Amalek,
and *u* . . . . 1 Sam. 15:3
not able *u* to
destroy . . . . . . 1 Kin. 9:21
man, and the land
be *u* . . . . .Is. 6:11
the LORD shall *u*
destroy . . . . .Is. 11:15
brother will *u*
supplant . . . . Jer. 9:4
round about, and
will *u* . . . . Jer. 25:9
should ye be *u*
unpunished . . . . . . Jer. 25:29
Slay *u* old and
young . . . . Ezek. 9:6
shall it not *u*
wither . . . . Ezek. 17:10
be *u* burned with
fire . . . . Rev. 18:8

UTTERMOST
Kadesh, a city in
the *u* . . . . .Num. 20:16
u sea shall your
coast . . . . .Deut. 11:24
the *u* part of the
heaven . . . . .Neh. 1:9
u parts of the earth . . . Ps. 2:8
the *u* part of the
earth . . . . Acts 1:8
save them to the *u* . .Heb. 7:25

UZZIAH
Called Azariah; King of

Judah, 2 Kin. 14:21; 15:1, 2;
2 Chr. 26:1, 3
Rebuilds Elath, 2 Kin. 14:22;
2 Chr. 26:2
Reigns righteously,
2 Kin. 15:3; 2 Chr. 26:4, 5
Defeats the Philistines,
2 Chr. 26:6, 7
Takes tribute from the
Ammonites
Strengthens the kingdom,
2 Chr. 26:8
Strengthens the fortifications
of Jerusalem, 2 Chr. 26:9
Promotes cattle raising and
agriculture, 2 Chr. 26:10
Military establishment of,
2 Chr. 26:11–15
Is presumptuous in burning
incense; stricken with
leprosy; quarantined,
2 Kin. 15:5; 2 Chr. 26:16–21
Jotham regent during
quarantine of, 2 Kin. 15:5;
2 Chr. 26:21
Death of, 2 Kin. 15:7;
2 Chr. 26:23
History of, written by Isaiah,
2 Chr. 26:22; Is. 1:1
An earthquake occurred
during the reign of,
Amos 1:1; Zech. 14:5
——— Son of Uriel, 1 Chr. 6:24
——— Father of Jehonathan,
1 Chr. 27:25
——— A priest
Puts away (divorced) his
Gentile wife, Ezra 10:21
——— Father of Athaiah,
Neh. 11:4

VAIL
shalt hang up
the *v* . . . . Ex. 26:33
congregation
without the *v* . . . . . Ex. 27:21
LORD, before
the *v* . . . . Lev. 4:6
place within the *v* . . Lev. 16:2

VAIN
LORD thy God
in *v* . . . . Ex. 20:7
sow your seed in *v* . Lev. 26:16
wherewith
Abimelech hired *v* . Judg. 9:4
vanity, and
became *v* . . . . . . 2 Kin. 17:15
oppression, and
become not *v* . . . . . Ps. 62:10
the days of his *v*
life . . . . .Eccl. 6:12
Bring no more *v*
oblations . . . . .Is. 1:13
created it not in *v* . . . .Is. 45:18
In *v* have I
smitten . . . . Jer. 2:30
in *v* shalt thou use . . Jer. 46:11
shall return in *v* . . . . . Jer. 50:9
v and foolish
things . . . . Lam. 2:14
they comfort in *v* . . Zech. 10:2

run, or had run
in *v* . . . . Gal. 2:2
deceive you with *v* . . . Eph. 5:6
philosophy and *v*
deceit . . . . Col. 2:8
labour be in *v* . . .1 Thess. 3:5
gold, from your *v*
conversation . . . . .1 Pet. 1:18

VALLEY
place was called,
The *v* . . . . Josh. 7:26
thou, Moon, in
the *v* . . . . Josh. 10:12
Chinneroth, and
in the *v* . . . . Josh. 11:2
v of the son of
Hinnom . . . . Josh. 15:8
and pitched in
the *v* . . . . Judg. 6:33
lay along in the *v* . . Judg. 7:12
Topheth, which is
in the *v* . . . . 2 Kin. 23:10
gate, and at the *v* . 2 Chr. 26:9
v of the son of
Hinnom . . . . 2 Chr. 33:6
walk through
the *v* . . . . Ps. 23:4
v of the son of
Hinnom . . . . Jer. 7:31
inhabitant of the *v* . .Jer. 21:13
v of the son of
Hinnom . . . . Jer. 32:35
the cities of the *v* . . . Jer. 32:44
the midst of the *v* . . Ezek. 37:1
v of Achor for a
door . . . . .Hos. 2:15
into the *v* of
Jehoshaphat . . . . .Joel 3:2
water the *v* of
Shittim . . . . Joel 3:18
be a very great *v* . . Zech. 14:4
shall flee to the *v* . . Zech. 14:5

VALLEYS
the midst of the *v* . . . .Is. 41:18
the children in
the *v* . . . . .Is. 57:5
v, Thus saith the
Lord . . . . Ezek. 36:6
the *v* shall be cleft . . . Mic. 1:4

VANITY
v, and became
vain . . . . 2 Kin. 17:15
is mischief and *v* . . . . Ps. 10:7
They speak *v*
every . . . . Ps. 12:2
state is
altogether *v* . . . . . . Ps. 39:5
Man is like to *v* . . . . Ps. 144:4
v and vexation of
spirit . . . . .Eccl. 2:26
are *v*, and the
work . . . . .Jer. 10:15
inherited lies, *v* . . . Jer. 16:19
prophets that
see *v* . . . . Ezek. 13:9
untempered
morter, seeing *v* .Ezek. 22:28
surely they are *v* . . .Hos. 12:11
idols have
spoken *v* . . . . Zech. 10:2

VENGEANCE

belongeth *v*, and
  recompence .... Deut. 32:35
day of the
  LORD's *v* .... Is. 34:8
God will come
  with *v* .... Is. 35:4
day of *v* of our
  God .... Is. 61:2
heart, let me see
  thy *v* .... Jer. 11:20
hosts, a day of *v* .... Jer. 46:10
is the *v* of the
  LORD .... Jer. 50:15
time of the
  LORD's *v* .... Jer. 51:6
is the *v* of the
  LORD .... Jer. 51:11
thy cause, and
  take *v* .... Jer. 51:36
Judah by taking *v* . Ezek. 25:12
And I will lay
  my *v* .... Ezek. 25:14
the LORD will
  take *v* .... Nah. 1:2
is written, *V* is
  mine .... Rom. 12:19
flaming fire
  taking *v* .... 2 Thess. 1:8
the *v* of eternal fire .... Jude 7

VERILY

V my sabbaths ye
  shall .... Ex. 31:13
land, and *v* thou
  shalt .... Ps. 37:3
v every man at his .... Ps. 39:5
v I say unto you,
  Till .... Matt. 5:18
V I say unto
  you, It .... Matt. 10:15
v I say unto
  you, Ye .... Matt. 10:23
of a disciple, *v* I .. Matt. 10:42
V I say unto you,
  There .... Matt. 16:28
for *v* I say unto
  you .... Matt. 17:20
Jesus said unto
  them, *V* .... Matt. 19:28
said unto
  them, *V* I ...... Matt. 21:21
unto them, *V* I ... Matt. 25:40
told them, Elias *v* .. Mark 9:12
V, *v*, I say unto
  thee .... John 3:3
V, *v*, I say unto
  you .... John 5:24
unto them, *V*, *v*, I ... John 8:58
I am *v* a man
  which .... Acts 22:3
v, their sound .... Rom. 10:18

VESSEL

every earthen *v*,
  whereinto .... Lev. 11:33
like a potter's *v* ...... Ps. 2:9
breaketh a
  potter's *v* .... Jer. 19:11
a *v* wherein is no
  pleasure .... Jer. 22:28

for he is a
  chosen *v* .... Acts 9:15
unto the weaker *v* .. 1 Pet. 3:7

VESSELS

v of wood, and
  in *v* .... Ex. 7:19
it, with all these *v* .. Ex. 25:39
sanctuary, and all
  the *v* .... Num. 4:15
v of gold which
  Solomon ...... 2 Kin. 24:13
Babylon, with the
  goodly *v* ...... 2 Chr. 36:10
destroyed all the
  goodly *v* ...... 2 Chr. 36:19
clean, that bear
  the *v* .... Is. 52:11
v of brass in thy
  market .... Ezek. 27:13
v of the house of
  God .... Dan. 1:2
have brought
  the *v* .... Dan. 5:23
of all pleasant *v* ... Hos. 13:15

VINE

every man under
  his *v* .... 1 Kin. 4:25
Thou hast
  brought a *v* ...... Ps. 80:8
choicest *v*, and
  built .... Is. 5:2
falleth off from
  the *v* .... Is. 34:4
planted thee a
  noble *v* .... Jer. 2:21
O *v* of Sibmah, I
  will .... Jer. 48:32
The *v* is dried up ... Joel 1:12
every man under
  his *v* .... Mic. 4:4
I am the *v*, ye are ... John 15:5

VINEYARD

thou shalt plant
  a *v* .... Deut. 28:30
beloved touching
  his *v* .... Is. 5:1
betwixt me and
  my *v* .... Is. 5:3
to my *v*, that I have .... Is. 5:4
I will do to my *v* .... Is. 5:5
v of the LORD of
  hosts .... Is. 5:7

VINEYARDS

Thou shalt plant *v* Deut. 28:39
have our lands
  and *v* .... Neh. 5:5
will give her her *v* .. Hos. 2:15
planted pleasant *v* . Amos 5:11
plant *v*, and drink .. Amos 9:14

VIOLENCE

because he had
  done no *v* .... Is. 53:9
V shall no
  more be .... Is. 60:18
do no wrong, do
  no *v* .... Jer. 22:3
oppression, and
  for *v* .... Jer. 22:17
city is full of *v* .... Ezek. 7:23

v, hath given his
  bread .... Ezek. 18:7
spoiled by *v* ...... Ezek. 18:16
Quenched the *v* of
  fire .... Heb. 11:34

VIRGIN

Behold, a *v* shall
  conceive .... Is. 7:14
O thou
  oppressed *v* .... Is. 23:12
The *v*, the
  daughter .... Is. 37:22
v daughter of my
  people .... Jer. 14:17
shalt be built, O *v* ... Jer. 31:4
Behold, a *v*
  shall be .... Matt. 1:23

VISION

unto Abram in a *v* .. Gen. 15:1
in a *v*, and will
  speak .... Num. 12:6
there was no
  open *v* .... 1 Sam. 3:1
In a dream, in a *v* ... Job 33:15
v of Isaiah the son ..... Is. 1:1
A grievous *v* is
  declared .... Is. 21:2
err in *v*, they
  stumble .... Is. 28:7
you a false *v* and
  divination .... Jer. 14:14
and brought me
  in a *v* .... Ezek. 11:24
And I saw in a *v* ..... Dan. 8:2
to understand
  the *v* .... Dan. 8:16
And the *v* of the
  evening .... Dan. 8:26
and consider the *v* .. Dan. 9:23
seal up the *v* and
  prophecy .... Dan. 9:24
understanding of
  the *v* .... Dan. 10:1
O my lord, by
  the *v* .... Dan. 10:16
shall not have a *v* .... Mic. 3:6
v is yet for an
  appointed .... Hab. 2:3

VISIONS

understanding in
  the *v* .... 2 Chr. 26:5
the *v* of God to
  Jerusalem .... Ezek. 8:3
Thy dream, and
  the *v* .... Dan. 2:28
the *v* of my head
  troubled .... Dan. 4:5
the night *v*, and
  behold .... Dan. 7:7
the night *v*, and,
  behold .... Dan. 7:13
young men shall
  see *v* .... Joel 2:28

VISIT

and God will
  surely *v* .... Gen. 50:24
the day when I *v* I .. Ex. 32:34
at the time
  that I *v* .... Jer. 6:15

at Babylon I will *v* . . Jer. 29:10
be until I *v* him,
  saith . . . . Jer. 32:5
time that I will *v* . . . . Jer. 49:8
their iniquity,
  and *v* . . . . Hos. 8:13
iniquity, he will *v* . . . . Hos. 9:9

VISITATION
the time of their *v* . . Jer. 10:15
year of their *v*,
  saith . . . . Jer. 48:44
the time of their *v* . . Jer. 50:27
The days of *v* are
  come . . . . Hos. 9:7
the time of thy *v*. . Luke 19:44
God in the day
  of *v*. . . . . 1 Pet. 2:12

VISITED
LORD had *v* the
  children. . . . . Ex. 4:31
thou hast *v* me in
  the . . . . Ps. 17:3
is the city to be *v* . . . . . Jer. 6:6
for he hath *v* and
  redeemed . . . . .Luke 1:68
from on high
  hath *v* . . . . .Luke 1:78
God hath *v* his
  people . . . . .Luke 7:16

VOICE
thou hast obeyed
  my *v*. . . . . .Gen. 22:18
v of the LORD thy
  God . . . . .Ex. 15:26
if ye will obey
  my *v* . . . . .Ex. 19:5
v of the trumpet
  exceeding . . . . .Ex. 19:16
v of the LORD thy
  God . . . . .Deut. 28:15
v of the LORD thy
  God . . . . .Deut. 28:62
as in obeying
  the *v* . . . . 1 Sam. 15:22
they lifted up
  their *v* . . . . 2 Chr. 5:13
he heard my *v*
  out of. . . . . Ps. 18:6
a *v* of singing
  declare. . . . . .Is. 48:20
thanksgiving, and
  the *v* . . . . .Is. 51:3
v of joy, and the *v* . . . Jer. 33:11
face, and I
  heard a *v* . . . . Ezek. 1:28
ears with a loud *v*. . Ezek. 8:18
might not obey
  thy *v* . . . . .Dan. 9:11
we obeyed not
  his *v*. . . . . .Dan. 9:14
And lo a *v* from
  heaven. . . . . Matt. 3:17
and behold a *v* out . Matt. 17:5
they shall hear
  my *v*. . . . . .John 10:16
great *v*, as of a
  trumpet. . . . . Rev. 1:10

VOICES
thunderings and *v* . . . Rev. 4:5

there were *v*, and
  thunderings . . . . Rev. 8:5
were great *v* in
  heaven. . . . . Rev. 11:15
lightnings, and *v* . . Rev. 11:19

VOW
choice vows
  which ye *v*. . . . . .Deut. 12:11
a *v*, and said, O
  LORD. . . . . 1 Sam. 1:11
When thou
  vowest a *v*. . . . . . . .Eccl. 5:4
for he had a *v* . . . . . Acts 18:18

VOWS
your hand, and
  your *v* . . . . .Deut. 12:6
choice *v* which ye
  vow . . . . .Deut. 12:11
I will pay my *v*
  before . . . . Ps. 22:25
and pay thy *v* unto . . Ps. 50:14

WAGES
w of him that is
  hired . . . . Lev. 19:13
be the *w* for his
  army . . . . Ezek. 29:19
hireling in his *w* . . . . . Mal. 3:5
the *w* of sin is
  death . . . . Rom. 6:23

WAIT
sons, and they
  shall *w* . . . . Num. 3:10
W on the LORD . . . . Ps. 27:14
that *w* upon the
  LORD. . . . . Ps. 37:9
For, lo, they lie
  in *w* . . . . Ps. 59:3
I will *w* upon the
  LORD. . . . . .Is. 8:17
that *w* upon the
  LORD. . . . . .Is. 40:31
and the isles
  shall *w* . . . . .Is. 42:4
not be ashamed
  that *w* . . . . .Is. 49:23
w for light, but
  behold . . . . .Is. 59:9
Surely the isles
  shall *w* . . . . .Is. 60:9
heart he layeth
  his *w* . . . . Jer. 9:8
we will *w* upon
  thee . . . . Jer. 14:22
all lie in *w* for
  blood . . . . Mic. 7:2
though it tarry, *w* . . . . Hab. 2:3
w ye upon me,
  saith . . . . Zeph. 3:8
And to *w* for his
  Son . . . . 1 Thess. 1:10

WALK
w before me,
  and be . . . . .Gen. 17:1
And I will *w*
  among . . . . Lev. 26:12
LORD thy God,
  to *w* . . . . .Deut. 10:12
thy father,
  should *w* . . . . 1 Sam. 2:30

w in the sins of
  Jeroboam . . . . 1 Kin. 16:31
withhold from
  them that *w* . . . . . Ps. 84:11
ways, and we
  will *w*. . . . . .Is. 2:3
spirit to them
  that *w* . . . . .Is. 42:5
neither shall
  they *w* . . . . Jer. 3:17
house of Judah
  shall *w*. . . . . Jer. 3:18
every neighbour
  will *w*. . . . . Jer. 9:4
commit adultery,
  and *w*. . . . . Jer. 23:14
also *w* in my
  judgments. . . . . . Ezek. 37:24
w humbly with
  thy God . . . . Mic. 6:8
followeth me shall
  not *w* . . . . .John 8:12
Let us *w* honestly Rom. 13:13
dwell in them,
  and *w*. . . . . .2 Cor. 6:16
ordained that we
  should *w* . . . . Eph. 2:10
And *w* in love, as
  Christ . . . . Eph. 5:2
if we *w* in the
  light. . . . . 1 John 1:7

WALKED
Israel *w* upon dry
  land . . . . Ex. 14:29
I also have *w*
  contrary. . . . . Lev. 26:41
David thy father *w* . .1 Kin. 9:4
Ammon, and have
  not *w* . . . . 1 Kin. 11:33
But he *w* in the
  way . . . . 2 Kin. 16:3
remember now
  how I have *w* . . . 2 Kin. 20:3
w in their own
  counsels . . . . Ps. 81:12
people that *w* in
  darkness . . . . .Is. 9:2
servant Isaiah
  hath *w* . . . . .Is. 20:3
prophesied by
  Baal, and *w* . . . . Jer. 2:8
inclined their ear,
  but *w*. . . . . Jer. 7:24
they *w* not in my
  statutes . . . . Ezek. 20:13
they *w* not in my
  statutes . . . . Ezek. 20:21
Wherein in time
  past ye *w* . . . . Eph. 2:2
Gentiles, when
  we *w* . . . . 1 Pet. 4:3

WALKETH
Blessed is the
  man that *w* . . . . Ps. 1:1
who *w* upon the
  wings. . . . . Ps. 104:3
that *w* in his ways . . Ps. 128:1
w in darkness
  knoweth . . . . .John 12:35

brother that *w*
  disorderly ...... 2 Thess. 3:6
as a roaring
  lion, *w* .... 1 Pet. 5:8

WALKING
he knoweth thy *w*
  through .... Deut. 2:7
Jesus, *w* by the
  sea .... Matt. 4:18
righteous before
  God, *w* .... Luke 1:6
of dishonesty,
  not *w* .... 2 Cor. 4:2

WALL
the waters
  were a *w* .... Ex. 14:22
the waters
  were a *w* .... Ex. 14:29
pisseth against
  the *w* .... 1 Sam. 25:22
and Millo, and
  the *w* .... 1 Kin. 9:15
pisseth against
  the *w* .... 1 Kin. 14:10
pisseth against
  the *w* .... 1 Kin. 21:21
the turning of
  the *w* .... 2 Chr. 26:9
and brake down
  the *w* .... 2 Chr. 36:19
the *w* of Jerusalem ... Neh. 1:3
break down the *w*
  thereof .... Is. 5:5
storm against
  the *w* .... Is. 25:4
We grope for
  the *w* .... Is. 59:10
a fenced brasen *w* ... Jer. 15:20
kindle a fire in
  the *w* .... Jer. 49:27
yea, the *w* of
  Babylon ...... Jer. 51:44
and one built up
  a *w* .... Ezek. 13:10
built again, and
  the *w* .... Dan. 9:25
send a fire on
  the *w* .... Amos 1:10
kindle a fire in
  the *w* .... Amos 1:14
her a *w* of fire
  round .... Zech. 2:5

WALLS
thy high and
  fenced *w* ...... Deut. 28:52
gate between
  two *w* .... 2 Kin. 25:4
guard, brake
  down the *w* .... 2 Kin. 25:10
thou shalt call
  thy *w* .... Is. 60:18
all the *w* thereof
  round .... Jer. 1:15
pillar, and
  brasen *w* .... Jer. 1:18
Go ye up upon
  her *w* .... Jer. 5:10
the *w*, and I will
  assemble .... Jer. 21:4
betwixt the two *w* ... Jer. 39:4

and brake down
  the *w* .... Jer. 39:8
foundations are
  fallen, her *w* ..... Jer. 50:15
thy *w* shall shake
  at .... Ezek. 26:10

WAR
And if ye go to
  w in .... Num. 10:9
wonders, and
  by *w* .... Deut. 4:34
land rested
  from *w* .... Josh. 11:23
land had rest
  from *w* .... Josh. 14:15
and went out to *w* . Judg. 3:10
strong and apt
  for *w* .... 2 Kin. 24:16
men of *w* fled by
  night .... 2 Kin. 25:4
than butter, but *w* .. Ps. 55:21
shall they learn *w* ...... Is. 2:4
trumpet, the
  alarm of *w* .... Jer. 4:19
back the weapons
  of *w* .... Jer. 21:4
and all the men
  of *w* .... Jer. 39:4
alarm of *w* to be
  heard .... Jer. 49:2
army, thy men
  of *w* .... Ezek. 27:10
the end of the *w*
  desolations ...... Dan. 9:26
shall they learn *w* .... Mic. 4:3
mightest *w* a good
  warfare .... 1 Tim. 1:18
fleshly lusts,
  which *w* .... 1 Pet. 2:11
make *w* with the
  Lamb .... Rev. 17:14
doth judge and
  make *w* .... Rev. 19:11

WASH
w your feet, and
  rest .... Gen. 18:4
morrow, and let
  them *w* .... Ex. 19:10
carcase of them
  shall *w* .... Lev. 11:25
toucheth his bed
  shall *w* .... Lev. 15:5
he *w* his flesh in
  water .... Lev. 16:4
I will *w* mine
  hands .... Ps. 26:6
w me, and I
  shall be .... Ps. 51:7
W you, make you
  clean .... Is. 1:16
w in the pool of
  Siloam .... John 9:7
w away thy sins,
  calling .... Acts 22:16

WASHED
but she hath *w* my
  feet .... Luke 7:44
way therefore,
  and *w* .... John 9:7

but ye are *w*,
  but ye .... 1 Cor. 6:11
conscience, and
  our bodies *w* .... Heb. 10:22
that loved us,
  and *w* .... Rev. 1:5
tribulation, and
  have *w* .... Rev. 7:14

WAST
for out of it *w*
  thou .... Gen. 3:19
Egypt, which thou
  w .... Deut. 28:60
though thou *w*
  angry .... Is. 12:1
spoilest, and
  thou *w* .... Is. 33:1
thou destroyed,
  that *w* .... Ezek. 26:17
day that thou *w*
  created .... Ezek. 28:13
Jerusalem, even
  thou *w* .... Obad. 11
thou *w* slain, and
  hast .... Rev. 5:9

WASTE
and your cities *w* .. Lev. 26:33
we have laid
  them *w* .... Num. 21:30
in the *w* howling
  wilderness ..... Deut. 32:10
And I will lay it *w* ..... Is. 5:6
for it is laid *w*, so ..... Is. 23:1
comfort all her *w*
  places .... Is. 51:3
cities shall be
  laid *w* .... Jer. 4:7
desolation, a
  reproach, a *w* ..... Jer. 49:13
shall build the *w*
  cities .... Amos 9:14
empty, and void,
  and *w* .... Nah. 2:10
and his heritage *w* ... Mal. 1:3

WATCH
them, a leopard
  shall *w* .... Jer. 5:6
I *w* over them, to
  build .... Jer. 31:28
Behold, I will *w*
  over .... Jer. 44:27
W therefore,
  for ye .... Matt. 25:13
W and pray,
  that ye .... Matt. 26:41
W ye, stand
  fast in .... 1 Cor. 16:13
they *w* for your
  souls .... Heb. 13:17
sober, and *w* unto
  prayer .... 1 Pet. 4:7

WATCHED
All my familiars *w* .. Jer. 20:10
that like as I
  have *w* .... Jer. 31:28
Therefore hath
  the LORD *w* ...... Dan. 9:14
And they *w* him,
  and .... Luke 20:20

WATER

there shall
  come *w* . . . . Ex. 17:6
the *w* under the
  earth . . . . Ex. 20:4
bread, nor drink *w* . . Ex. 34:28
bathe himself in *w* . . Lev. 15:5
the *w* came out
  abundantly . . . . . Num. 20:11
poured out like *w* . . . Ps. 22:14
rivers of *w* in a
  dry . . . . Is. 32:2
For I will pour *w*
  upon . . . . Is. 44:3
by the springs
  of *w* . . . . Is. 49:10
w, and dieth for
  thirst . . . . Is. 50:2
arm, dividing
  the *w* . . . . Is. 63:12
that can hold no *w* . . . Jer. 2:13
sprinkle clean *w* . . Ezek. 36:25
baptize you
  with *w* . . . . Matt. 3:11
straightway out of
  the *w* . . . . Matt. 3:16
given thee
  living *w* . . . . John 4:10
whosoever
  drinketh of the *w* . . John 4:14
with the washing
  of *w* . . . . Eph. 5:26
washed with
  pure *w* . . . . Heb. 10:22
of the *w* of life
  freely . . . . Rev. 21:6

WATERS

mine hand upon
  the *w* . . . . Ex. 7:17
dry land, and
  the *w* . . . . Ex. 14:21
and the *w* were a
  wall . . . . Ex. 14:22
w returned, and
  covered . . . . Ex. 14:28
thy nostrils the *w* . . . Ex. 15:8
That the *w* which
  came . . . . Josh. 3:16
he made the *w* to
  stand . . . . Ps. 78:13
chambers in the *w* . . Ps. 104:3
w of the river,
  strong . . . . Is. 8:7
Lord, as the *w*
  cover . . . . Is. 11:9
rushing of many *w* . . Is. 17:13
flood of mighty *w*
  overflowing. . . . . . . Is. 28:2
w break out, and
  streams . . . . Is. 35:6
w, I will be with
  thee . . . . Is. 43:2
fountain of
  living *w* . . . . Jer. 2:13
head were *w*, and
  mine . . . . Jer. 9:1
rivers of *w* in a
  straight . . . . Jer. 31:9
upon the *w* of the
  river. . . . . Dan. 12:7

the sound of
  many *w* . . . . Rev. 1:15
living fountains
  of *w* . . . . Rev. 7:17

WAVES

treadeth upon
  the *w* . . . . Job 9:8
thy proud *w* be
  stayed . . . . Job 38:11
all thy *w* and thy
  billows . . . . Ps. 42:7
w thereof arise,
  thou . . . . Ps. 89:9
floods lift up
  their *w* . . . . Ps. 93:3
the *w* thereof toss . . . Jer. 5:22
sea when the *w*
  thereof. . . . . Jer. 31:35

WAX

my wrath may *w*
  hot . . . . Ex. 32:10
doth thy wrath *w*
  hot . . . . Ex. 32:11
my heart is like *w* . . . Ps. 22:14
w old like a
  garment. . . . . Ps. 102:26
and the earth
  shall *w* . . . . Is. 51:6
yourselves bags
  which *w* . . . . Luke 12:33

WAXED

But Jeshurun *w*
  fat . . . . Deut. 32:15
children is *w*
  feeble. . . . . 1 Sam. 2:5
but David *w*
  stronger . . . . 2 Sam. 3:1
Damascus is *w*
  feeble. . . . . Jer. 49:24
child grew, and *w*
  strong . . . . Luke 1:80
Paul and
  Barnabas *w* . . . . . Acts 13:46
the earth are *w*
  rich . . . . Rev. 18:3

WAYS

walk in all his *w* . . Deut. 10:12
and walk in his *w* . . Deut. 28:9
them, and flee
  seven *w* . . . . Deut. 28:25
not prosper in
  thy *w* . . . . Deut. 28:29
for all his *w* are
  judgment . . . . Deut. 32:4
not walked in
  my *w* . . . . 1 Kin. 11:33
teach us of his *w* . . . . Is. 2:3
w, and their soul
  delighteth . . . . Is. 66:3
walk ye in all
  the *w* . . . . Jer. 7:23
are upon all
  their *w* . . . . Jer. 16:17
according to his *w* . . Jer. 17:10
w of the sons of
  men . . . . Jer. 32:19
thy *w*, and will
  recompense . . . . . . Ezek. 7:8

thy *w* and thine
  abominations . . . . . Ezek. 7:9
w, saith the Lord
  God. . . . . Ezek. 18:30
all thy *w*, hast
  thou . . . . Dan. 5:23
according to
  our *w* . . . . Zech. 1:6
Lord to prepare
  his *w* . . . . Luke 1:76
and his *w* past
  finding. . . . . Rom. 11:33
true are thy *w*,
  thou . . . . Rev. 15:3

WEAK

all knees shall
  be *w* . . . . Ezek. 21:7
was *w* through the
  flesh. . . . . Rom. 8:3
For we also are
  w in . . . . 2 Cor. 13:4
feebleminded,
  support the *w* . . 1 Thess. 5:14

WEARY

I am *w* to bear
  them . . . . Is. 1:14
w men, but will ye . . . Is. 7:13
great rock in a *w*
  land . . . . Is. 32:2
run, and not be *w* . . . Is. 40:31
a burden to the *w*
  beast . . . . Is. 46:1
season to him
  that is *w* . . . . Is. 50:4
I am *w* with
  holding . . . . Jer. 6:11
to speak lies,
  and *w* . . . . Jer. 9:5
bones, and I
  was *w* . . . . Jer. 20:9
And let us not
  be *w* . . . . Gal. 6:9

WEEK

with many for
  one *w* . . . . Dan. 9:27
the *w* cometh
  Mary Magdalene . . John 20:1
first day of the *w* . . John 20:19
first day of the *w* . . . Acts 20:7

WEEP

high places, to *w* . . . Is. 15:2
I will *w* bitterly. . . . . . Is. 22:4
I might *w* day and
  night . . . . Jer. 9:1
soul shall *w* in
  secret. . . . . Jer. 13:17
For these
  things I *w* . . . . . . Lam. 1:16
shall not mourn
  nor *w* . . . . Ezek. 24:23
ministers of the
  Lord, *w* . . . . Joel 2:17
elders saith unto
  me, W . . . . Rev. 5:5

WEEPING

one shall howl, *w*
  abundantly . . . . Is. 15:3
up of Luhith
  with *w* . . . . Is. 15:5

of hosts call to w ....Is. 22:12
and the voice of w ...Is. 65:19
I take up a w and
wailing ....Jer. 9:10
with w, and with
supplications ......Jer. 31:9
Luhith
continual w.......Jer. 48:5
for thee with
the w ....Jer. 48:32
together, going
and w...........Jer. 50:4
w and gnashing of
teeth ....Matt. 8:12

WEPT
Thus his father w
for ....Gen. 37:35
children of Israel
also w ....Num. 11:4
And Hezekiah w
sore ....2 Kin. 20:3
For all the
people w ....Neh. 8:9

WEST
w, and Hai on the
east ....Gen. 12:8
spread abroad to
the w ....Gen. 28:14
Philistines toward
the w ....Is. 11:14
gather thee from
the w ....Is. 43:5

WHATSOEVER
the firstborn, w
openeth...........Ex. 13:2
w toucheth the
altar ....Ex. 29:37
And upon w any
of them ....Lev. 11:32
of them falleth, w. . Lev. 11:33
W goeth upon the
belly............Lev. 11:42
And w man
there be........Lev. 17:10
But w hath a
blemish ....Lev. 22:20
w he doeth shall
prosper ....Ps. 1:3
do w thing goeth
forth ....Jer. 44:17
things w I have
commanded ....Matt. 28:20
w ye shall ask .....John 14:13
remembrance, w I
have............John 14:26
that w ye shall ask John 15:16
And w we ask, we
receive.........1 John 3:22
neither w worketh
abomination .....Rev. 21:27

WHEAT
wine, and of the w Num. 18:12
vinedressers, for
the w ....Joel 1:11
from him burdens
of w ....Amos 5:11
floor, and gather
his w ....Matt. 3:12

WHEELS
off their chariot w ..Ex. 14:25
flint, and their w .....Is. 5:28
horsemen, and of
the w ....Ezek. 26:10
fiery flame, and
his w ....Dan. 7:9

WHEREFORE
W say unto the
children............Ex. 6:6
w the Lord
blessed ....Ex. 20:11
W the Lord God
of Israel ....1 Sam. 2:30
W now let the fear 2 Chr. 19:7
w, when I looked
that ....Is. 5:4
W the Lord said,
Forasmuch ....Is. 29:13
w lift up thy
prayer ....Is. 37:4
W, when I came,
was ....Is. 50:2
W a lion out of the.... Jer. 5:6
W doth the way of
the ....Jer. 12:1
say in thine
heart, W ....Jer. 13:22
his neighbour, W
hath ....Jer. 22:8
w are they cast
out ....Jer. 22:28
W dost thou
prophesy ....Jer. 32:3
W, as I live, saith .. Ezek. 5:11
W putting away
lying ....Eph. 4:25
W in all things it ...Heb. 2:17
W, my beloved
brethren ....James 1:19
W gird up the
loins ....1 Pet. 1:13
And w slew he
him ....1 John 3:12

WHEREOF
to pass, w he
spake ....Deut. 13:2
the itch, w thou
canst ....Deut. 28:27
w I spake unto
thee ....Deut. 28:68
me, the poison w
drinketh ....Job 6:4
river, the
streams w ....Ps. 46:4
w we are
witnesses ....Acts 3:15
w he hath given
assurance ....Acts 17:31
in those things
w ye ....Rom. 6:21
w I Paul am
made a...........Col. 1:23

WHEREON
the land w thou
liest ....Gen. 28:13
the place w thou
standest ....Ex. 3:5
Surely the land w
thy ....Josh. 14:9

w if a man lean, it ....Is. 36:6

WHEREUNTO
land w ye go over
Jordan ....Deut. 4:26
w also they were
appointed ....1 Pet. 2:8
figure w even
baptism........1 Pet. 3:21
w ye do well
that ye ....2 Pet. 1:19

WHEREWITH
the straightness, w
thine ...Deut. 28:53
the straightness, w
thine ....Deut. 28:55
siege and
straitness, w ....Deut. 28:57
fear of thine
heart w ....Deut. 28:67
the blessing, w
Moses ....Deut. 33:1
w Abimelech
hired vain ....Judg. 9:4
his sin w he made
Judah ....2 Kin. 21:16
clothed with
strength, w ....Ps. 93:1
siege and
straitness, w ......Jer. 19:9
your hands, w ye
fight.............Jer. 21:4
w she shall be
called ....Jer. 33:16
w the Lord hath
afflicted ....Lam. 1:12
Egypt for his
labour w ....Ezek. 29:20
W shall I come
before ....Mic. 6:6
lost his
saltness, w ......Mark 9:50
love w thou hast
loved ....John 17:26
vocation w ye are
called ....Eph. 4:1

WHIRLWIND
their wheels
like a w ....Is. 5:28
thing before the w ...Is. 17:13
and the w shall
scatter ....Is. 41:16
w, to render his
anger ....Is. 66:15
chariots shall be
as a w...........Jer. 4:13
they shall reap
the w ....Hos. 8:7
in the day of the w Amos 1:14
scattered them
with a w ....Zech. 7:14

WHITE
apparel of blue
and w ....Esth. 8:15
shall be as w as
snow ....Is. 1:18
garment was w as
snow ....Dan. 7:9
horses, speckled,
and w ....Zech. 1:8

will give him a *w*
  stone .... Rev. 2:17
walk with me in *w* ... Rev. 3:4
be clothed in *w*
  raiment .... Rev. 3:5
w raiment, that
  thou .... Rev. 3:18
robes, and made
  them *w* .... Rev. 7:14
linen, clean and *w* .. Rev. 19:8
opened, and
  behold a *w* ...... Rev. 19:11
I saw a great *w*
  throne .... Rev. 20:11

WHITHERSOEVER
thou mayest
  prosper *w* .... Josh. 1:7
with thee *w* thou
  goest .... Josh. 1:9
LORD preserved
  David *w* .... 2 Sam. 8:6
LORD preserved
  David *w* .... 2 Sam. 8:14

WHOLLY
I *w* followed the
  LORD .... Josh. 14:8
because thou
  hast *w* .... Josh. 14:9
thee a noble
  vine, *w* .... Jer. 2:21
I not leave thee *w* ... Jer. 46:28
inhabited, but it
  shall be *w* .... Jer. 50:13
peace sanctify
  you *w* .... 1 Thess. 5:23

WHOMSOEVER
and giveth it to *w* ... Dan. 4:17
and giveth it to *w* ... Dan. 4:25
to *w* the Son will
  reveal .... Matt. 11:27
but on *w* it shall
  fall .... Matt. 21:44

WHORING
land, and they
  go a *w* .... Ex. 34:15
their daughters go
  a *w* .... Ex. 34:16
they have
  gone a *w* .... Lev. 17:7
which ye use to
  go a *w* .... Num. 15:39
rise up, and
  go a *w* .... Deut. 31:16
works, and
  went a *w* .... Ps. 106:39
eyes, which go a *w* .. Ezek. 6:9

WICKED
righteous with
  the *w* .... Gen. 18:25
thine hand with
  the *w* .... Ex. 23:1
not justify the *w* ..... Ex. 23:7
his saints, and
  the *w* .... 1 Sam. 2:9
the *w* is snared in .... Ps. 9:16
The *w* shall be
  turned .... Ps. 9:17
w he shall rain
  snares .... Ps. 11:6

the assembly of
  the *w* .... Ps. 22:16
but the seed of
  the *w* .... Ps. 37:28
thereof, all the *w* .... Ps. 75:8
of the *w* shall rot .. Prov. 10:7
sacrifice of the *w* .. Prov. 15:8
Woe unto the *w* ...... Is. 3:11
shall he slay the *w* ... Is. 11:4
his grave with
  the *w* .... Is. 53:9
Let the *w* forsake
  his .... Is. 55:7
doth the way of
  the *w* .... Jer. 12:1
wickedness of
  the *w* .... Ezek. 18:20
by *w* hands have
  crucified .... Acts 2:23
Cain, who was of
  that *w* .... 1 John 3:12

WICKEDLY
sinned, in doing *w* Deut. 9:18
abominations, and
  hath done *w* ... 2 Kin. 21:11
iniquity, we have
  done *w* .... Ps. 106:6
do *w*, shall be
  stubble .... Mal. 4:1

WICKEDNESS
no more any
  such *w* .... Deut. 13:11
of the *w* of thy
  doings .... Deut. 28:20
the children of *w*
  afflict .... 2 Sam. 7:10
sell himself to
  work *w* .... 1 Kin. 21:25
he wrought much
  w in .... 2 Kin. 21:6
iniquity, and
  sow *w* .... Job 4:8
let the *w* of the
  wicked .... Ps. 7:9
righteousness,
  and hatest *w* ...... Ps. 45:7
strengthened
  himself in his *w* .... Ps. 52:7
barrenness, for
  the *w* .... Ps. 107:34
Thine own *w* shall
  correct .... Jer. 2:19
whoredoms and
  with thy *w* .... Jer. 3:2
return from his *w* ... Jer. 23:14
and the *w* of the
  wicked .... Ezek. 18:20
for their *w* is great .. Joel 3:13
for their *w* is
  come .... Jon. 1:2
them, The border
  of *w*, The border
  of *w* .... Mal. 1:4
yea, they that
  work *w* .... Mal. 3:15
Thefts,
  covetousness, *w* .. Mark 7:22
spiritual *w* in high .. Eph. 6:12

WIDOW
fatherless, and
  the *w* .... Deut. 14:29

fatherless, and
  the *w* .... Deut. 16:11
fatherless, and *w* . Deut. 27:19
fatherless, plead
  for the *w* .... Is. 1:17
the cause of the *w* .... Is. 1:23
w, and shed not
  innocent .... Jer. 7:6
oppress not the *w* . Zech. 7:10
in his wages,
  the *w* .... Mal. 3:5

WIDOWS
w, is God in his
  holy .... Ps. 68:5
of my people,
  that *w* .... Is. 10:2
children, and be *w* . Jer. 18:21
of a truth, many *w* .. Luke 4:25

WIFE
cleave unto his *w* ... Gen. 2:24
his son Abram's *w* Gen. 11:31
God said, Sarah
  thy *w* .... Gen. 17:19
and, lo, Sarah
  thy *w* .... Gen. 18:10
asked him of
  his *w* .... Gen. 26:7
with another
  man's *w* .... Lev. 20:10
his neighbour's *w* Deut. 22:24
man hath
  taken a *w* .... Deut. 24:1
again to be his *w* .. Deut. 24:4
with his
  father's *w* ...... Deut. 27:20
shalt betroth a *w* . Deut. 28:30
brother, and
  toward the *w* ... Deut. 28:54
to *w* Jezebel the
  daughter ...... 1 Kin. 16:31
Jezebel his *w*
  stirred .... 1 Kin. 21:25
children of the
  married *w* .... Is. 54:1
husband with
  the *w* .... Jer. 6:11
his neighbour's *w* . Ezek. 18:6
unto thee Mary
  thy *w* .... Matt. 1:20
about a sister, a *w* .. 1 Cor. 9:5
husband of one *w*,
  vigilant .... 1 Tim. 3:2

WILD
brought forth *w*
  grapes .... Is. 5:2
brought it forth *w* .... Is. 5:4
w beasts of the
  desert .... Is. 13:21
w beasts of the
  islands .... Is. 13:22

WILDERNESS
the *w* of Zin unto
  Rehob .... Num. 13:21
w of Paran, to
  Kadesh .... Num. 13:26
fall in this *w* ...... Num. 14:29
Israel into the *w* .. Num. 21:23
of Israel in the *w* . Num. 26:64
die in the *w* ...... Num. 26:65

forty years in
the *w* . . . . Deut. 8:2
great and
terrible *w* . . . . Deut. 8:15
w of Judah, which
lieth . . . . Judg. 1:16
w be a fruitful
field . . . . Is. 32:15
w shall waters
break . . . . Is. 35:6
make the
rivers a *w* . . . . Is. 50:2
make her *w* like
Eden . . . . Is. 51:3
habitations of
the *w* . . . . Jer. 9:10
that dwell in
the *w* . . . . Jer. 9:26
against me in
the *w* . . . . Ezek. 20:13
in the *w*, that I
would . . . . Ezek. 20:15
against them in
the *w* . . . . Ezek. 20:21
the *w*, and his
spring . . . . Hos. 13:15
the dragons of
the *w* . . . . Mal. 1:3

WILT

thou *w* diligently
hearken . . . . Ex. 15:26
man sin, and *w*
thou . . . . Num. 16:22
pass, if thou *w* . . . Deut. 28:15
If thou *w* not
observe . . . . Deut. 28:58
of hosts, if thou *w* 1 Sam. 1:11
How long *w* thou
mourn . . . . 1 Sam. 16:1
And if thou *w*
walk . . . . 1 Kin. 9:4
be, if thou *w*
hearken . . . . 1 Kin. 11:38
the evil that
thou *w* . . . . 2 Kin. 8:12
For thou *w* not
leave . . . . Ps. 16:10
Thou *w* shew me
the . . . . Ps. 16:11
w not thou deliver . . Ps. 56:13
w thou be angry
for . . . . Ps. 79:5
If thou *w*
assuredly . . . . Jer. 38:17
But if thou *w*
not go . . . . Jer. 38:18
w thou make a . . . Ezek. 11:13
w thou judge, *w*
thou . . . . Ezek. 22:2
and thou *w* cast
all . . . . Mic. 7:19
Lord, if thou *w*,
thou . . . . Matt. 8:2
will, but as
thou *w* . . . . Matt. 26:39

WIND

God made a *w* to
pass . . . . Gen. 8:1
by a strong east *w* . . Ex. 14:21

chaff which the *w*
driveth . . . . Ps. 1:4
the wings of the *w* . . Ps. 104:3
he bringeth the *w*
out . . . . Ps. 135:7
stormy *w* fulfilling . . Ps. 148:8
mighty *w* shall he
shake . . . . Is. 11:15
mountains before
the *w* . . . . Is. 17:13
hiding place from
the *w* . . . . Is. 32:2
fan them, and
the *w* . . . . Is. 41:16
shalt scatter in
the *w* . . . . Ezek. 5:2
wither, when the
east *w* . . . . Ezek. 17:10
they have sown
the *w* . . . . Hos. 8:7
Ephraim feedeth
on *w* . . . . Hos. 12:1
brethren, an
east *w* . . . . Hos. 13:15
with every *w* of
doctrine . . . . Eph. 4:14

WINDOWS

w of heaven were
opened . . . . Gen. 7:11
for the *w* from on
high . . . . Is. 24:18
our *w*, and is
entered . . . . Jer. 9:21
there were
narrow *w* . . . . Ezek. 40:16
w, and their
arches . . . . Ezek. 40:22
open you the *w* of
heaven . . . . Mal. 3:10

WINDS

scatter into all
the *w* . . . . Ezek. 5:10
the *w*, and I will
draw . . . . Ezek. 5:12
arose, and
rebuked the *w* . . . Matt. 8:26
elect from the
four *w* . . . . Matt. 24:31

WINE

strong *w* to be
poured . . . . Num. 28:7
w, nor gather the
grapes . . . . Deut. 28:39
thee either
corn, *w* . . . . Deut. 28:51
cup, and the *w* is
red . . . . Ps. 75:8
And *w* that
maketh glad . . . . . Ps. 104:15
W is a mocker,
strong . . . . Prov. 20:1
have erred
through *w* . . . . Is. 28:7
Mizpah, and
gathered *w* . . . . . . Jer. 40:12
concubines, have
drunk *w* . . . . Dan. 5:23
ye shall not
drink *w* . . . . Amos 5:11

vineyards, and
drink the *w* . . . . . . Amos 9:14
and sweet *w*, but
shalt . . . . Mic. 6:15
w nor strong
drink . . . . Luke 1:15
be not drunk
with *w* . . . . Eph. 5:18
given to *w*, no
striker . . . . 1 Tim. 3:3
angry, not given
to *w* . . . . Titus 1:7
lusts, excess of *w* . . 1 Pet. 4:3
nations drink of
the *w* . . . . Rev. 14:8
w of the wrath of
God . . . . Rev. 14:10
her the cup of
the *w* . . . . Rev. 16:19

WINGS

bare you on
eagles' *w* . . . . Ex. 19:4
their *w* on high,
covering . . . . Ex. 25:20
whose *w* thou art
come . . . . Ruth 2:12
the shadow of
thy *w* . . . . Ps. 17:8
of thy *w* will I
make . . . . Ps. 57:1
his *w* shalt thou
trust . . . . Ps. 91:4
walketh upon
the *w* . . . . Ps. 104:3
each one had six *w* . . . . Is. 6:2
w shall fill the
breadth . . . . Is. 8:8
shall mount up
with *w* . . . . Is. 40:31
spread his *w* over
Moab . . . . Jer. 48:40
eagle, and spread
his *w* . . . . Jer. 49:22
chickens under
her *w* . . . . Matt. 23:37
each of them
six *w* . . . . Rev. 4:8
two *w* of a great
eagle . . . . Rev. 12:14

WIPE

and I will *w*
Jerusalem . . . . . 2 Kin. 21:13
the Lord GOD
will *w* . . . . Is. 25:8
and God shall *w*
away . . . . Rev. 7:17
And God shall *w*
away . . . . Rev. 21:4

WISDOM

the Lord, that is *w* . . Job 28:28
the beginning
of *w* . . . . Ps. 111:10
but fools
despise *w* . . . . Prov. 1:7
reproof give *w* . . . . Prov. 29:15
good in his
sight *w* . . . . Eccl. 2:26
spirit of *w* and
understanding . . . . . . Is. 11:2
man glory in his *w* . . . Jer. 9:23

Is *w* no more in
 Teman ....Jer. 49:7
giveth *w* unto the
 wise ....Dan. 2:21
understanding
 and *w*...........Dan. 5:11
disobedient to
 the *w* ....Luke 1:17
riches both of
 the *w* .... Rom. 11:33
not with *w* of
 words ....1 Cor. 1:17
is made unto us *w* .1 Cor. 1:30
Howbeit we
 speak *w* ....1 Cor. 2:6
every man in all *w* .. Col. 1:28
you richly in all *w* .. Col. 3:16
any of you lack *w* ...James 1:5
But the *w* that is
 from...........James 3:17
and riches, and *w* ... Rev. 5:12

WISE

Pharaoh also
 called the *w*........ Ex. 7:11
gift blindeth the *w* ... Ex. 23:8
the eyes of the *w* .Deut. 16:19
And ye, in any *w*
 keep............ Josh. 6:18
thence a *w*......2 Sam. 14:2
thee a *w* and an
 understanding .. 1 Kin. 3:12
A *w* son maketh a
 glad .... Prov. 10:1
deceived thereby
 is not *w* .... Prov. 20:1
counsel of the *w*
 counsellors ....Is. 19:11
they are *w* to do
 evil...............Jer. 4:22
Let not the *w* man
 glory .... Jer. 9:23
wisdom unto
 the *w*...........Dan. 2:21
all the *w* men of
 Babylon..........Dan. 2:48
w men of Babylon,
 Whosoever ....Dan. 5:7
these things from
 the *w* ....Matt. 11:25
me I will in no *w*
 cast ....John 6:37
lest ye should
 be *w*.......... Rom. 11:25
not *w* in your own
 conceits........ Rom. 12:16
only *w* God, be
 honour ....1 Tim. 1:17
shall in no *w* enter . Rev. 21:27

WITHHOLDEN

the LORD hath *w*
 thee ....1 Sam. 25:26
showers have
 been *w*............Jer. 3:3
oppressed any,
 hath not *w* .....Ezek. 18:16
drink offering is *w* .. Joel 1:13

WITNESS

be an
 unrighteous *w* .....Ex. 23:1

swearing, and
 is a *w* .... Lev. 5:1
heaven and earth
 to *w* ....Deut. 4:26
One *w* shall not
 rise............Deut. 19:15
countenance
 doth *w* ....Is. 3:9
for a *w* to the
 people ....Is. 55:4
I will be a swift *w*.... Mal. 3:5
all the world for
 a *w* ....Matt. 24:14
bare him *w*, and
 wondered ....Luke 4:22
w, because ye .....John 15:27
ordained to be a *w* .. Acts 1:22
w, in that he did
 good ....Acts 14:17
so must thou
 bear *w* ....Acts 23:11
God is my *w*,
 whom I .... Rom. 1:9
shalt not bear
 false *w* .... Rom. 13:9
also bearing
 them *w* ....Heb. 2:4
and bear *w*, and
 shew .... 1 John 1:2
is the faithful *w* ..... Rev. 1:5
faithful and true *w* .. Rev. 3:14
beheaded for
 the *w* ....Rev. 20:4

WITNESSES

The hands of
 the *w* ....Deut. 17:7
the mouth of
 two *w*..........Deut. 19:15
for false *w* are
 risen .... Ps. 27:12
Ye are my *w*, saith ...Is. 43:10
ye are even my *w* .....Is. 44:8
w in the land of
 Benjamin ....Jer. 32:44
mouth of two or
 three *w* ....Matt. 18:16
false *w* came, yet
 found.........Matt. 26:60
have we of *w*.....Matt. 26:65
and ye shall be *w*
 unto..............Acts 1:8
whereof we are *w*... Acts 3:15
w laid down their
 clothes...........Acts 7:58
profession before
 many *w* ....1 Tim. 6:12
under two or
 three *w* ....Heb. 10:28
power unto my
 two *w*..........Rev. 11:3

WIVES

the sword, that
 our *w* ....Num. 14:3
shall he
 multiply *w*.....Deut. 17:17
w turned away his
 heart .... 1 Kin. 11:4
mother, and the
 king's *w*....... 2 Kin. 24:15

sons also, and
 his *w* ....2 Chr. 21:17
spoiled, and
 their *w*........Is. 13:16
will I give their *w*....Jer. 8:10
let their *w* be
 bereaved ....Jer. 18:21
all thy *w* and thy
 children.........Jer. 38:23
and thy lords,
 thy *w* ....Dan. 5:23

WIZARDS

neither seek
 after *w* .... Lev. 19:31
familiar spirits
 and *w*......... 2 Kin. 21:6
spirit, and with *w*. 2 Chr. 33:6
spirits, and
 unto *w*............Is. 8:19

WOE

W to thee, Moab .Num. 21:29
W unto their soul......Is. 3:9
W unto the
 wicked............Is. 3:11
W unto them that
 are ....Is. 5:22
Then said I, *W*
 is me ....Is. 6:5
W unto them that
 seek ....Is. 29:15
W to them that go
 down ....Is. 31:1
W to thee that
 spoilest ....Is. 33:1
W unto us ....Jer. 4:13
her hands,
 saying, *W* ....Jer. 4:31
W be unto thee, O
 Moab ....Jer. 48:46
w unto them ....Jer. 50:27
W be to the
 shepherds ....Ezek. 34:2
W to them that
 devise .... Mic. 2:1
W unto him that
 saith ....Hab. 2:19
W unto them .... Jude 11

WOMAN

between thee and
 the *w* ....Gen. 3:15
w he said, I will
 greatly...........Gen. 3:16
or *w* that hath a
 familiar .... Lev. 20:27
tender and
 delicate *w* ......Deut. 28:56
you man, or *w*, or
 family ....Deut. 29:18
slay both man
 and *w*..........1 Sam. 15:3
fetched thence a
 wise *w* ....2 Sam. 14:2
pain as a *w* that
 travaileth..........Is. 13:8
pangs of a *w* that
 travaileth..........Is. 21:3
as the heart of a *w* . Jer. 48:41
as the heart of a *w* .. Jer. 49:22
to a menstruous *w* . Ezek. 18:6

whosoever
  looketh on a *w* ... Matt. 5:28
And the *w* was
  made .... Matt. 9:22
and what manner
  of *w* ....Luke 7:39
w, Thy faith hath
  saved ....Luke 7:50
Son, made of a *w*,
  made .... Gal. 4:4
as travail
  upon a *w* ....1 Thess. 5:3
stood before the *w* .. Rev. 12:4
w fled into the
  wilderness .... Rev. 12:6

WOMB
whatsoever
  openeth the *w* ...... Ex. 13:2
the fruit of thy *w* .. Deut. 7:13
unto God from
  the *w* .... Judg. 13:5
mother's *w*, and
  naked............. Job 1:21
the fruit of the *w* ....Is. 13:18
formed thee from
  the *w* ....Is. 44:2
formed thee from
  the *w* ....Is. 44:24
called me from
  the *w* ....Is. 49:1
w I sanctified thee .... Jer. 1:5
from his
  mother's *w* ....Luke 1:15
conceive in thy *w* ...Luke 1:31
conceived in the *w* ..Luke 2:21

WOMEN
and all the *w* went .. Ex. 15:20
of your bread,
  ten *w* .... Lev. 26:26
rip up their *w* .... 2 Kin. 8:12
little ones and *w*... Esth. 8:11
of the foolish *w*
  speaketh .... Job 2:10
Egypt be like
  unto *w* ....Is. 19:16
the *w* come, and
  set ....Is. 27:11
fire, and the *w*
  knead............. Jer. 7:18
men, and *w*, and
  children.......... Jer. 40:7
shall become as *w* .. Jer. 50:37
little children,
  and *w*.......... Ezek. 9:6
pieces, and
  their *w* ....Hos. 13:16
also *w* looking on
  afar .... Mark 15:40
w, which had
  been healed ......Luke 8:2
James, and
  other *w* .... Luke 24:10
w, and Mary the
  mother .... Acts 1:14
haling men and *w*
  committed .... Acts 8:3
they were men
  or *w* .... Acts 9:2
devout and
  honourable *w* .... Acts 13:50

w did change the
  natural.......... Rom. 1:26

WONDERS
thou do all
  those *w* .... Ex. 4:21
multiply my signs
  and my *w* .... Ex. 7:3
in praises,
  doing *w* .... Ex. 15:11
by signs, and by *w* . Deut. 4:34
shewedst signs
  and *w*............Neh. 9:10
thy *w* that thou
  didst ....Neh. 9:17
w in the field of
  Zoan .... Ps. 78:43
for signs and for *w* ....Is. 8:18
great signs and *w* Matt. 24:24
both with signs
  and *w*............Heb. 2:4

WOOD
both in vessels
  of *w* .... Ex. 7:19
shittim *w* shalt
  thou.............. Ex. 30:1
w that is on the
  fire .... Lev. 3:5
and burn him on
  the *w* .... Lev. 4:12
vessel of *w*, or
  raiment .... Lev. 11:32
serve other
  gods, *w* ....Deut. 28:36
known, even *w*
  and stone ......Deut. 28:64
is fire and much *w* ...Is. 30:33
work of men's
  hands, *w* ....Is. 37:19
children gather *w* ....Jer. 7:18
of brass, iron, *w* ....Dan. 5:23
solitarily in the *w*... Mic. 7:14
saith to the *w*,
  Awake ....Hab. 2:19

WORD
these things the *w* ..Gen. 15:1
his *w* shall they ..Num. 27:21
according to my *w* 1 Kin. 17:1
to the *w* of the
  LORD.......... 2 Kin. 24:2
the law, and the *w* .....Is. 2:3
to speak a *w* in
  season ....Is. 50:4
thou shalt say
  this *w*...........Jer. 14:17
and perform my
  good *w*..........Jer. 29:10
The *w* of the
  LORD came...... Ezek. 1:3
w of the LORD by
  Haggai .... Hag. 1:1
beginning was
  the *W*...........John 1:1
the *W* was made
  flesh.............John 1:14
heareth my *w*, and
  believeth ....John 5:24
that the *w* of God
  should .... Acts 13:46
of water by the *w* ...Eph. 5:26
all things by the *w* ...Heb. 1:3

the *w* of God is
  quick ....Heb. 4:12
which stumble at
  the *w* .... 1 Pet. 2:8
have handled, of
  the *W*........... 1 John 1:1
Jesus, and for
  the *w* .... Rev. 20:4

WORDS
and put *w* in his
  mouth .... Ex. 4:15
the *w* which thou
  shalt.............. Ex. 19:6
and perverteth
  the *w* .... Ex. 23:8
concerning all
  these *w* .... Ex. 24:8
upon the tables
  the *w* .... Ex. 34:28
said, Hear now
  my *w* ....Num. 12:6
wise, and pervert
  the *w* ....Deut. 16:19
observe to do all
  the *w* ....Deut. 28:58
to thy *w* .... 1 Kin. 3:12
the *w* of Hezekiah
  king .... 2 Chr. 32:8
and despised
  his *w* .... 2 Chr. 36:16
thou shalt speak
  my *w* .... Ezek. 2:7
and they hear
  thy *w* .... Ezek. 33:31
shall speak
  great *w* ....Dan. 7:25
hath confirmed
  his *w* ....Dan. 9:12
But my *w* and my
  statutes .... Zech. 1:6
wondered at the
  gracious *w*........Luke 4:22
the *w* that I speak .John 14:10
w abide in you, ye ..John 15:7
deceive you with
  vain *w* .... Eph. 5:6

WORK
no manner of *w*
  shall............. Ex. 12:16
labour, and do all
  thy *w* .... Ex. 20:9
w, thou, nor thy
  son.............. Ex. 20:10
shall do no
  servile *w* .... Lev. 23:8
shall do no
  servile *w* .... Lev. 23:36
the *w* of thine
  hand ....Deut. 28:12
Rock, his *w* is
  perfect.......... Deut. 32:4
sell himself to *w*
  wickedness .... 1 Kin. 21:25
is snared in the *w*.... Ps. 9:16
told us, what *w*
  thou.............. Ps. 44:1
according to his *w* .. Ps. 62:12
are the *w* of thy
  hands........... Ps. 102:25

Egypt to err in
  every w . . . . Is. 19:14
my planting,
  the w . . . . Is. 60:21
are the w of thy
  hand . . . . Is. 64:8
counsel, and
  mighty in w . . . . . Jer. 32:19
maker of his w
  trusteth . . . . Hab. 2:18
know that all
  things w . . . . Rom. 8:28
ceasing your w of
  faith . . . . 1 Thess. 1:3
unrighteous to
  forget your w . . . . . Heb. 6:10

WORKETH

Because the law w
  wrath . . . . Rom. 4:15
But all these w
  that . . . . 1 Cor. 12:11
faith which w by
  love . . . . Gal. 5:6
purpose of him
  who w . . . . Eph. 1:11
the spirit that
  now w . . . . Eph. 2:2
whatsoever w
  abomination . . . . . Rev. 21:27

WORKING

a sharp razor, w
  deceitfully . . . . Ps. 52:2
another the w of
  miracles . . . . . . 1 Cor. 12:10
by the effectual w . . . . Eph. 3:7
rather let him
  labour, w . . . . Eph. 4:28

WORKS

nor do after
  their w . . . . Ex. 23:24
are thy
  wonderful w . . . . . . Ps. 40:5
w like unto thy w . . . . Ps. 86:8
w, saith the Lord . . . Jer. 7:13
hast trusted in
  thy w . . . . Jer. 48:7
righteous in all
  his w . . . . Dan. 9:14
according to his w Matt. 16:27
me, he doeth
  the w . . . . John 14:10
turn to God, and
  do w. . . . . Acts 26:20
justified by the w . . . Gal. 2:16
good w, which
  God hath . . . . Eph. 2:10
zealous of good w . Titus 2:14
Not by w of
  righteousness . . . . . Titus 3:5
conscience from
  dead w . . . . Heb. 9:14
may by your
  good w. . . . . 1 Pet. 2:12
earth also and
  the w . . . . 2 Pet. 3:10
his own w were
  evil . . . . 1 John 3:12
according to
  your w . . . . Rev. 2:23

thy w, that thou
  hast . . . . Rev. 3:1
thy w, Lord God
  Almighty . . . . Rev. 15:3

WORLD

All the ends of
  the w . . . . Ps. 22:27
the earth and
  the w . . . . Ps. 90:2
judge the w with
  righteousness . . . . Ps. 96:13
foundation of
  the w . . . . Matt. 25:34
away the sin of
  the w . . . . John 1:29
God so loved
  the w . . . . John 3:16
Son into the w to
  condemn . . . . John 3:17
w, the w would
  love . . . . John 15:19
that the w may
  believe . . . . John 17:21
secret since the w Rom. 16:25
is nothing in
  the w . . . . 1 Cor. 8:4
the god of this w
  hath . . . . 2 Cor. 4:4
believed on in
  the w . . . . 1 Tim. 3:16
are rich in this w . 1 Tim. 6:17
he condemned
  the w . . . . Heb. 11:7
poor of this w rich . James 2:5
gone out into
  the w . . . . 1 John 4:1
kingdoms of
  this w . . . . Rev. 11:15
deceiveth the
  whole w . . . . Rev. 12:9
foundation of
  the w . . . . Rev. 13:8

WORSHIP

For thou shalt
  w no . . . . Ex. 34:14
shouldest be
  driven to w . . . . . . Deut. 4:19
the people went
  to w . . . . 1 Kin. 12:30
the nations
  shall w . . . . Ps. 22:27
w the Lord in the
  beauty . . . . Ps. 29:2
w before thee, O
  Lord . . . . Ps. 86:9
Lord our God,
  and w. . . . . Ps. 99:5
w the Lord in the
  holy . . . . Is. 27:13
princes also
  shall w . . . . Is. 49:7
w in the Lord's
  house. . . . . Jer. 26:2
ye fall down
  and w. . . . . Dan. 3:15
serve nor w any
  god. . . . . Dan. 3:28
w the host of
  heaven . . . . Zeph. 1:5

and men shall w
  him . . . . Zeph. 2:11
east, and are come
  to w . . . . Matt. 2:2
written, Thou
  shalt w . . . . Matt. 4:10
call heresy, so w I. . Acts 24:14
w God in the
  spirit . . . . Phil. 3:3
upon the earth
  shall w . . . . Rev. 13:8
day nor night,
  who w . . . . Rev. 14:11

WORSHIPPED

their heads and w . . . . Ex. 4:31
served other gods,
  and w. . . . . Deut. 17:3
other gods, and
  have w . . . . 1 Kin. 9:9
w Ashtoreth the
  goddess . . . . 1 Kin. 11:33
served Baal,
  and w. . . . . 1 Kin. 16:31
made a grove,
  and w. . . . . 2 Kin. 17:16
w all the host of
  heaven. . . . . 2 Kin. 21:3
the pavement,
  and w. . . . . 2 Chr. 7:3
Lord their God,
  and w. . . . . Jer. 22:9
and they w the
  sun. . . . . Ezek. 8:16
came a leper
  and w. . . . . Matt. 8:2
the ship came and
  w . . . . Matt. 14:33
elders fell down
  and w. . . . . Rev. 5:14
beasts fell down
  and w. . . . . Rev. 19:4
beast, and them
  that w . . . . Rev. 19:20
had not w the
  beast . . . . Rev. 20:4

WORTHY

whose shoes I am
  not w . . . . Matt. 3:11
laid to his
  charge w . . . . Acts 23:29
committed
  nothing w . . . . . . Acts 25:25
commit such
  things are w . . . . . Rom. 1:32
ye walk w of the
  vocation . . . . Eph. 4:1
That ye might
  walk w . . . . Col. 1:10
That ye would
  walk w . . . . 1 Thess. 2:12
faithful saying,
  and w. . . . . 1 Tim. 1:15
rule well be
  counted w . . . . . . 1 Tim. 5:17
Thou art w, O
  Lord . . . . Rev. 4:11
saying, Thou art w . . . Rev. 5:9
with a loud
  voice, W . . . . Rev. 5:12

WOUND

I *w*, and I heal . . . . Deut. 32:39
wounded thee
  with the *w* . . . . Jer. 30:14
and Judah saw
  his *w* . . . . Hos. 5:13
body of Jesus,
  and *w* . . . . John 19:40

WRATH

be no *w* upon the
  congregation . . . . . Num. 1:53
anger, and in
  his *w* . . . . Deut. 29:23
is *w* upon thee
  from . . . . 2 Chr. 19:2
the *w* of the LORD
  arose . . . . 2 Chr. 36:16
when his *w* is
  kindled . . . . Ps. 2:12
to turn away his *w* . Ps. 106:23
of my *w* will I give . . . . Is. 10:6
little *w* I hid my
  face . . . . Is. 54:8
w the earth shall
  tremble . . . . Jer. 10:10
fury, and in
  great *w* . . . . Jer. 21:5
perpetually, and
  he kept his *w* . . . . Amos 1:11
and he
  reserveth *w* . . . . Nah. 1:2
but the *w* of God
  abideth . . . . John 3:36
treasurest up unto
  thyself *w* . . . . Rom. 2:5
give place unto *w* Rom. 12:19
things cometh
  the *w* . . . . Eph. 5:6
to speak, slow
  to *w* . . . . James 1:19
of the wine of
  the *w* . . . . Rev. 14:8
wine of the *w* of
  God . . . . Rev. 14:10
fierceness of his *w* . Rev. 16:19

WRITE

said unto
  Moses, W . . . . Ex. 17:14
w her a bill of
  divorcement . . . . . Deut. 24:1
Now go, *w* it
  before . . . . Is. 30:8
inward parts,
  and *w* . . . . Jer. 31:33
I *w* these things
  being . . . . 2 Cor. 13:10
children, these
  things *w* . . . . 1 John 2:1
What thou
  seest, *w* . . . . Rev. 1:11
church in Sardis *w* . . . Rev. 3:1
in Philadelphia *w* . . . . Rev. 3:7
and I will *w* upon
  him . . . . Rev. 3:12
of the
  Laodiceans *w* . . . . . Rev. 3:14
unto me, W,
  Blessed . . . . Rev. 14:13

WRITING

and put it also
  in *w* . . . . Ezra 1:1
w of the house of
  Israel . . . . Ezek. 13:9
read this *w*, and
  shew . . . . Dan. 5:7
thou canst read
  the *w* . . . . Dan. 5:16

WRITTEN

tables of stone, *w* . . . Ex. 31:18
law that are *w* . . . Deut. 28:58
plague, which is
  not *w* . . . . Deut. 28:61
covenant that
  were *w* . . . . 2 Kin. 23:3
they be *w* in the
  writing . . . . Ezek. 13:9
w in the law of
  Moses . . . . Dan. 9:11
be found *w* in the
  book . . . . Dan. 12:1
is *w*, Thou shalt
  worship . . . . Matt. 4:10
w of the Son of
  man . . . . Mark 9:12
these are *w*,
  that ye . . . . John 20:31
w, Vengeance is
  mine . . . . Rom. 12:19
w, The first man
  Adam . . . . 1 Cor. 15:45
ministered by
  us, *w* . . . . 2 Cor. 3:3
for it is *w*, Cursed . . Gal. 3:13
w, which no man
  knoweth . . . . Rev. 2:17
w in the book of
  life . . . . Rev. 13:8
thigh a name *w*,
  KING . . . . Rev. 19:16
things which
  were *w* . . . . Rev. 20:12
whosoever was
  not found *w* . . . . . Rev. 20:15
w in the Lamb's
  book . . . . Rev. 21:27

WROTE

And he *w* upon
  the tables . . . . Ex. 34:28
And Moses *w* this
  law . . . . Deut. 31:9
Baruch *w* from the
  mouth . . . . Jer. 36:4
And they *w* letters Acts 15:23

WROTH

w, because he had
  wrought . . . . Gen. 34:7
and wilt thou
  be *w* . . . . Num. 16:22
shaken, because
  he was *w* . . . . Ps. 18:7
I was *w* with my
  people . . . . Is. 47:6
w with thee, nor
  rebuke . . . . Is. 54:9
will I be always *w* . . Is. 57:16

WROUGHT

he had *w* folly in
  Israel . . . . Gen. 34:7
hath *w* folly in
  Israel . . . . Deut. 22:21
he *w* much
  wickedness . . . . . 2 Kin. 21:6
he *w* much evil in
  the . . . . 2 Chr. 33:6
thee, and they *w*
  great . . . . Neh. 9:26
w his signs in
  Egypt . . . . Ps. 78:43
Who hath *w* and
  done . . . . Is. 41:4
I *w* for my name's
  sake . . . . Ezek. 20:9
I *w* for my name's
  sake . . . . Ezek. 20:14
Which he *w* in
  Christ . . . . Eph. 1:20
suffice us to
  have *w* . . . . 1 Pet. 4:3
false prophet
  that *w* . . . . Rev. 19:20

YEAR

feast unto me in
  the *y* . . . . Ex. 23:14
y, when thou hast
  gathered . . . . Ex. 23:16
in the *y* all thy
  males . . . . Ex. 23:17
horns of it once in
  a *y* . . . . Ex. 30:10
lamb of the first *y* . . Lev. 14:10
y without spot day Num. 28:3
a *y* shall all thy
  males . . . . Deut. 16:16
In the ninth *y* of
  Hoshea . . . . 2 Kin. 17:6
eighth *y* of his
  reign . . . . 2 Kin. 24:12
y was expired,
  king . . . . 2 Chr. 36:10
first *y* of Cyrus
  king . . . . Ezra 1:1
the *y* that king
  Uzziah . . . . Is. 6:1
vengeance, and
  the *y* . . . . Is. 34:8
proclaim the
  acceptable *y* . . . . . . Is. 61:2
be careful in the *y* . . Jer. 17:8
pass in the sixth *y* . . Ezek. 8:1
pass in the
  seventh *y* . . . . . . Ezek. 20:1
with calves of a *y* . . . Mic. 6:6
y of Darius the
  king . . . . Hag. 1:1
y, not without
  blood . . . . Heb. 9:7

YEARS

Abram was
  ninety *y* . . . . Gen. 17:1
that is an
  hundred *y* . . . . . . Gen. 17:17
Pharaoh, The days
  of the *y* . . . . Gen. 47:9
y of the life of
  Kohath . . . . Ex. 6:18

2 Kin. 24:17, 18; 1 Chr. 3:15;
2 Chr. 36:10; Jer. 37:1
Throws off his allegiance
to Nebuchadnezzar,
2 Kin. 24:20; 2 Chr. 36:13;
Jer. 52:3; Ezek. 17:12–21
Forms an alliance with the
king of Egypt, Ezek. 17:11–18
The allegiance denounced
By Jeremiah, 2 Chr. 36:12;
Jer. 21; 24:8–10; 27:12–22;
32:3–5; 34; 37:7–10, 17;
38:14–28
By Ezekiel, Ezek. 12:10–16;
17:12–21
Imprisons Jeremiah on
account of his denunciations,
Jer. 32:2, 3; 37:15–21;
38:5–28
Seeks the intercession of
Jeremiah with God on his
behalf, Jer. 21:1–3; 37:3;
38:14–27
The evil reign of, 2 Kin. 24:19,
20; 2 Chr. 36:12, 13; Jer. 37:2;
38:5, 19, 24–26; 52:2
Nebuchadnezzar destroys the
city and temple, takes him
captive to Babylon, blinds
his eyes, kills his sons,
2 Kin. 25:1–10; 2 Chr. 36:17–
20; Jer. 1:3; 32:1, 2; 39:1–10;
51:59; 52:4–30
———— Grandson of Jehoiakim,
1 Chr. 3:16
———— A false prophet,
Jer. 29:21–23
———— A prince of Judah,
Jer. 36:12
———— A false prophet
Prophesies to Ahab that he
will be victorious over the
Syrians, instead of being

defeated, 1 Kin. 22:11;
2 Chr. 18:10
Strikes Micaiah, the true
prophet, 1 Kin. 22:24;
2 Chr. 18:23

ZEPHANIAH
A priest in the reign of
Zedekiah, king of Judah;
Sent by the king to Jeremiah
with a message soliciting the
prophet's intercession and
prayers, Jer. 21:1, 2
Shows Jeremiah the false
prophet's letter, Jer. 29:25–29
Taken to Riblah and killed,
2 Kin. 25:18–21; Jer. 52:24–
27
———— A Kohathite, 1 Chr. 6:36
———— A prophet in the days of
Josiah, Zeph. 1:1
———— Father of Josiah,
Zech. 6:10, 14

ZERUBBABEL
Also called Sheshbazzar;
Directs the rebuilding of
the altar and temple after
his return from captivity in
Babylon, Ezra 3:2–8; 4:2, 3;
5:2, 14–16; Hag. 1:12–14
Leads the Emancipated Jews
back from Babylon, Ezra 1:8–
11; 2; Neh. 12
Appoints the Levites to
inaugarate the rebuilding of
the temple, Ezra 3:2–8
Prophecies relating to,
Hag. 2:2; Zech. 4:6–10
Called Zorobabel in the
genealogy of Joseph,
Matt. 1:12; Luke 3:27

ZIKLAG
A city within the territory
allotted to the tribe of Judah,
Josh. 15:31
Re-allotted to the tribe of
Simeon, Josh. 19:5
David lives at, 1 Sam. 27:5, 6;
2 Sam. 1:1; 1 Chr. 12:1
Amalekites destroy, 1 Sam. 30
Inhabited by the returned
exiles of Judah, Neh. 11:28

ZIMRI
A chief of Simeon, Num. 25:6–
8, 14
———— King of Israel,
1 Kin. 16:9–20; 2 Kin. 9:31
———— Son of Zerah, 1 Chr. 2:6
———— A Benjamite,
1 Chr. 8:36; 9:42
———— An unknown place,
Jer. 25:25

ZIPPORAH
Wife of Moses, Ex. 2:16–22
Reproaches Moses, Ex. 4:25,
26
Separates from Moses, is
brought again to him by her
father, Ex. 18:2–6
Miriam and Aaron upbraid
Moses concerning,
Num. 12:1

ZOAR
A city of the Moabites, near
the Jordan River, Gen. 13:10
Territory of, Deut. 34:3;
Is. 15:5; Jer. 48:34
King of, fought against
Chedorlaomer, Gen. 14:2, 8
Not destroyed with Sodom
and Gomorrah, Gen. 19:20–
23, 30

ZIKLAG

A city within the territory allotted to the tribe of Judah. Josh. 15:31.

Re-allotted to the tribe of Simeon. Josh. 19:5.

David lives at. 1 Sam. 27:5-6; 2 Sam. 1:1; 1 Chr. 12:1.

Amalekites destroy. 1 Sam. 30.

Inhabited by returned exiles of Judah. Neh. 11:28.

ZIMRI

A chief of Simeon. Num. 25:8-14.

(King of Israel.)
1 Kin. 16:10-20; 2 Kin. 9:31.

Son of Zerah. 1 Chr. 2:6.

A Benjamite. 1 Chr. 8:36; 9:42.

An unknown place. Jer. 25:25.

ZIPPORAH

Wife of Moses. Ex. 2:16-22.

Reproaches Moses. Ex. 4:25-26.

Separation from Moses, is brought again to join by her father. Ex. 18:2-6.

Miriam and Aaron upbraid Moses concerning. Num. 12:1.

ZOAR

A city of the Moabites, near the Jordan River. Gen. 13:10.

Territory of. Deut. 34:3.

Is. 15:5; Jer. 48:34.

King of, fought against Chedorlaomer. Gen. 14:2, 8.

Not destroyed with Sodom and Gomorrah. Gen. 19:20-23, 30.

---

defeated. 1 Kin. 22:31;
2 Chr. 18:10.

Set as Messiah, the chief prophet. 1 Kin. 22:24;
2 Chr. 18:23.

ZEPHANIAH

A priest in the reign of Zedekiah, King of Judah, sent by the king to Jeremiah with a message soliciting the prophet's intercession and prayers. Jer. 21:1-2.

Shows Jeremiah the false prophet's letter. Jer. 29:25-29.

Taken to Riblah and killed. 2 Chr. 25:18-21; Jer. 52:24.

A Kohathite. 1 Chr. 6:36.

A prophet in the days of Josiah. Zeph. 1:1.

Father of Josiah. Zeph. 6:10-14.

ZERUBBABEL

Also called Sheshbazzar. Begins the rebuilding of the altar and temple after the return from captivity in Babylon. Ezra 2:2; 3:2-8; 4:2-3; 5:2.

Leads the emancipated Jews back from Babylon. Ezra 2:1-2; Neh. 12:1.

Appoints the Levites to inaugurate the rebuilding of the temple. Ezra 3:8-9.

Prophecies relating to. Hag. 2:2; Zech. 4:6-10.

Called Zorobabel in the genealogy of Joseph. Matt. 1:12; Luke 3:27.

---

1 Kin. 24:19; 2 Chr. 3:16.
2 Chr. 36:10, 3:11.

Throws off allegiance to Nebuchadnezzar.
2 Kin. 24:20; 2 Chr. 36:13.
Jer. 34:...; 12:12-21.

Forms an alliance with the king of Egypt. Ezek. 17:11-18.

The allegiance denounced by Ezekiel. 2 Chr. 36:12.
Jer. 24:24; 21:10-12;
34:1-28.

By Ezekiel. Ezek. 12:10-19;
17:11-21.

Hophni's penetration on account of his denunciations. Jer. 32:2-3; 37:15-21.

Seeks the intercession of Jeremiah. Begs help with God on his behalf. Jer. 21:1-3; 37:3-8;
38:14-28.

The evil reign of. 2 Kin. 24:19;
2 Chr. 36:12; Jer. 52:2.
Ezek. 16; 21. Blasphemes.

Nebuchadnezzar destroys the city and carries captive to Babylon, blinds his eyes, kills his sons.
2 Kin. 25:1-10; 2 Chr. 36:17-21; Jer. 32:2; 34:21; 39:1-10;
52:4-30.

Governor of Shechem.
Judg. 9:.

A blasphemer.
Jer. 29:21-23.

A prince of Judah.
Jer. 36:12.

A false prophet. Prophesies to Ahab that he will be victorious over the Syrians, spread of being.

45° N
30° E
45° E

CASPIAN
SEA

BLACK   SEA

CAUCASUS MOUNTAINS

PONTUS MOUNTAINS

• Hattusa
TURKEY
ANATOLIA
Halys R.
• Kanesh
Lake
Tuz

Mount Ararat ▲

Lake
Van

Araxes (Aras) R.

AEGEAN SEA

TAURUS MOUNTAINS

Carchemish •
Alalakh •
Ugarit •
Aleppo •
Ebla •
Hamath •

• Haran

Nineveh •

ZAGROS MOUNTAINS

Lake
Urmia

IRAN

Crete

Cyprus

Byblos •
LEBANON
Sidon •

Tigris River

SYRIA
• Tadmor

• Asshur

MESOPOTAMIA

Euphrates River

Diyala R.

• Mari

Kerkha R.

MEDITERRANEAN SEA

• Damascus

Shechem •
Bethel •
ISRAEL
Gaza •
Zoan
(Tanis) •
Gerar •
Rabbah (Amman) •
Jerusalem •
Hebron •
Dead Sea

SYRIAN
DESERT

Agade •
Babylon •

IRAQ

Beersheba •

Kadesh
Barnea •
• On
(Heliopolis)
Noph •
(Memphis)
SINAI
PENINSULA
JORDAN

Larsa •
• Ur

• Ezion Geber

AN-NAFUD

PERSIAN
GULF

EGYPT

SAHARA

Nile River

RED
SEA

N

SAUDI ARABIA

300 miles
300 kilometers

30° N

15° N

**The World of
the Patriarchs**

☐ Old Babylonian Empire,
c. 1750 B.C.

☐ Egyptian Empire,
c. 1492 B.C.

☐ Hittite Empire,
c. 1350 B.C.

➔ Abraham's route

○ City with uncertain
location

EGYPT Modern name

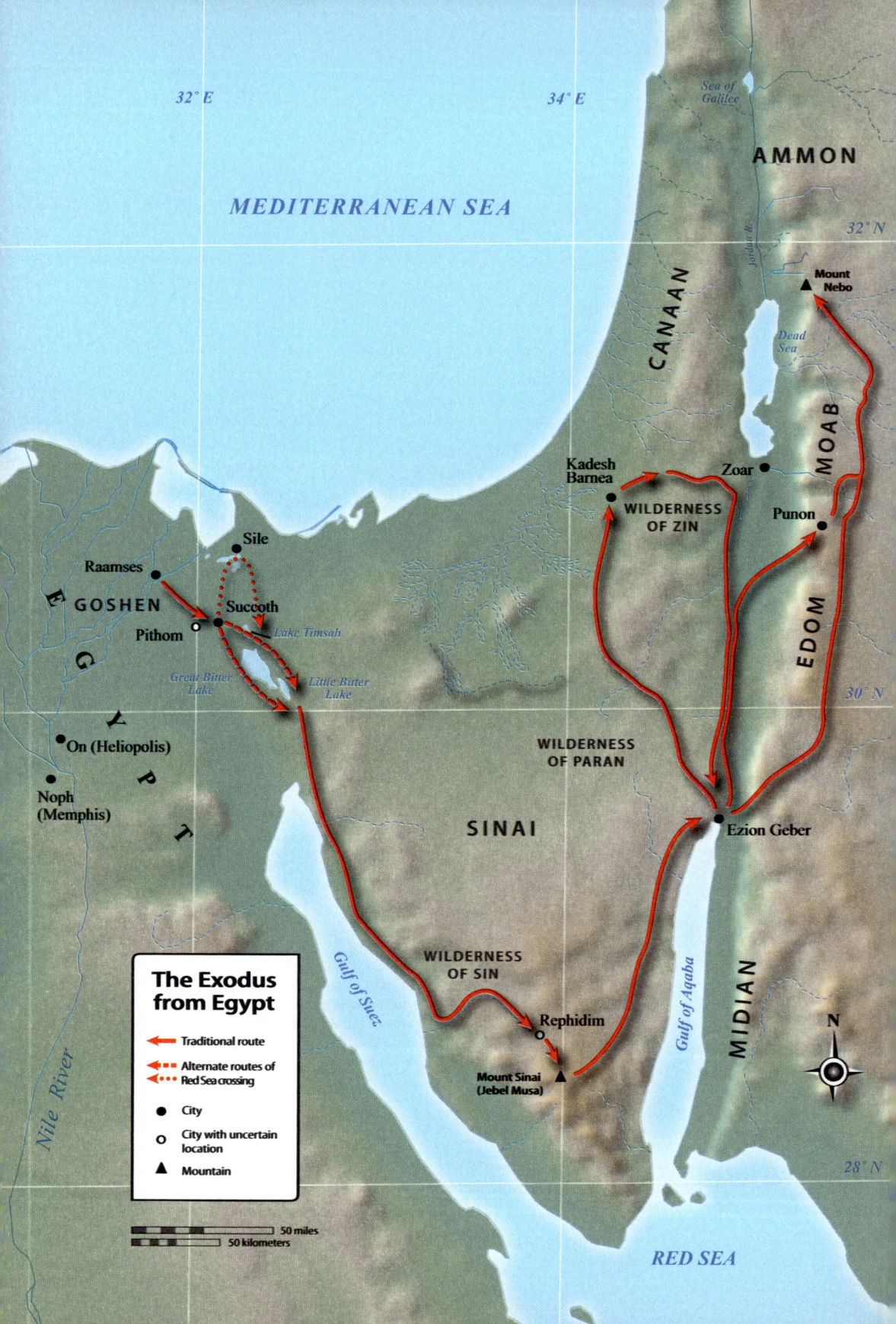

MEDITERRANEAN SEA

AMMON

Sea of
Galilee

Mount
Nebo

Dead
Sea

CANAAN

Kadesh
Barnea
WILDERNESS
OF ZIN

Zoar

MOAB

Punon

Sile

Raamses

GOSHEN

Succoth

Pithom

Lake Timsah

Great Bitter
Lake

Little Bitter
Lake

EDOM

WILDERNESS
OF PARAN

On (Heliopolis)

SINAI

Noph
(Memphis)

Ezion Geber

E
G
Y
P
T

WILDERNESS
OF SIN

**The Exodus
from Egypt**

→ Traditional route

◄--- Alternate routes of
Red Sea crossing

● City

○ City with uncertain
location

▲ Mountain

Rephidim

Mount Sinai
(Jebel Musa)

Gulf of Suez

Gulf of Aqaba

MIDIAN

N

Nile River

50 miles
50 kilometers

RED SEA

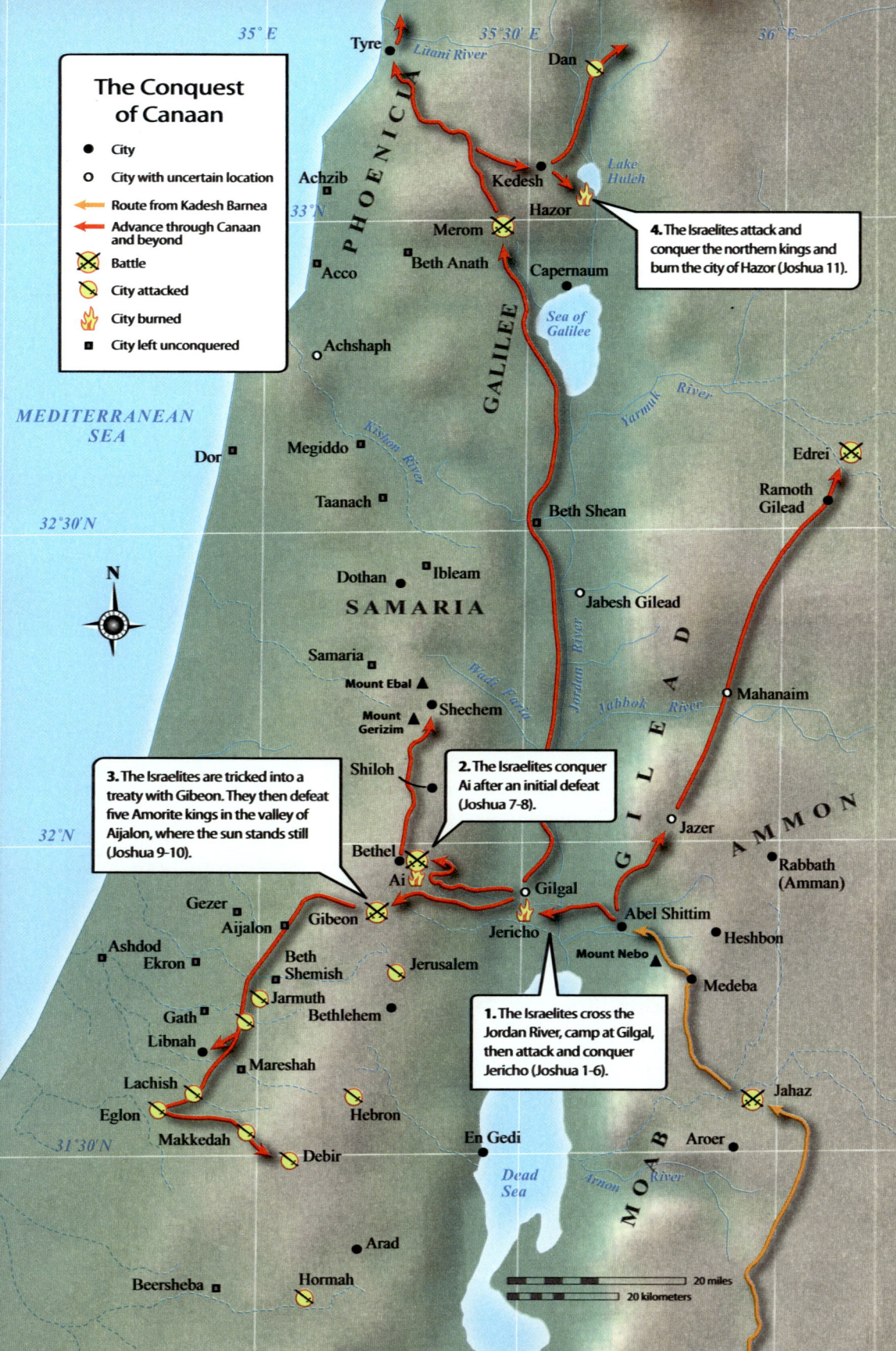

The Conquest of Canaan

- ● City
- ○ City with uncertain location
- → Route from Kadesh Barnea
- → Advance through Canaan and beyond
- ⊗ Battle
- ⊘ City attacked
- 🔥 City burned
- ▣ City left unconquered

4. The Israelites attack and conquer the northern kings and burn the city of Hazor (Joshua 11).

3. The Israelites are tricked into a treaty with Gibeon. They then defeat five Amorite kings in the valley of Aijalon, where the sun stands still (Joshua 9–10).

2. The Israelites conquer Ai after an initial defeat (Joshua 7–8).

1. The Israelites cross the Jordan River, camp at Gilgal, then attack and conquer Jericho (Joshua 1–6).

MEDITERRANEAN SEA

PHOENICIA

GALILEE

SAMARIA

GILEAD

AMMON

MOAB

Litani River
Tyre
Dan
Achzib
Kedesh
Lake Huleh
Hazor
Merom
Beth Anath
Acco
Capernaum
Achshaph
Sea of Galilee
Yarmuk River
Megiddo
Dor
Kishon River
Beth Shean
Taanach
Ramoth Gilead
Edrei
Dothan
Ibleam
Jabesh Gilead
Samaria
Mahanaim
Mount Ebal
Shechem
Wadi Farah
Jordan River
Jabbok River
Mount Gerizim
Shiloh
Jazer
Bethel
Ai
Gilgal
Rabbath (Amman)
Gezer
Gibeon
Jericho
Abel Shittim
Heshbon
Aijalon
Beth Shemish
Jerusalem
Mount Nebo
Ashdod
Ekron
Jarmuth
Bethlehem
Medeba
Gath
Libnah
Mareshah
Lachish
Jahaz
Eglon
Hebron
Makkedah
Debir
En Gedi
Aroer
Arnon River
Dead Sea
Arad
Beersheba
Hormah

N

20 miles
20 kilometers

The Allotments to the Twelve Tribes

- ● City
- ● City of Refuge
- ○ City with uncertain location

MEDITERRANEAN SEA

N

ARAM (Syria)

Litani River

Ijon
Tyre
Dan

ASHER
NAPHTALI
Rehob
Abdon
Kedesh
Hazor
Merom
Lake Huleh

EAST MANASSEH

Mishal
Nahalal
Rimmon
Helkath
ZEBULUN
Daberath
Sea of Galilee
Hammath
Golan
Ashtaroth

Dor
Jokneam
Megiddo
ISSACHAR
Jarmuth
Kishon River
Yarmuk River
Edrei

Taanach
Beth Shean
Ramoth Gilead

Ibleam
Jabesh Gilead
Mahanaim

WEST MANASSEH
Samaria
Mount Ebal ▲ Shechem
Mount Gerizim ▲
Wadi Farah
Jordan River
Jabbok River

Gath Rimmon
Joppa
Shiloh
GAD
Jazer

EPHRAIM
AMMON
Rabbah (Amman)

DAN
Beth Horon
Bethel
Gezer
Gibeon
Geba
Gilgal
Jericho
Abel Shittim
Heshbon

Eltekah
Aijalon
BENJAMIN
Mount Nebo ▲
Bezer
Medeba

Gibbethon
Beth Shemesh
Jerusalem
Bethlehem
REUBEN

Ashkelon
Libnah
Dead Sea

Lachish
Hebron
Jahaz
Aroer

Gaza
Eglon
Juttah
Debir
En Gedi
Eshtemoa
JUDAH
Arnon River

Gerar
MOAB

Ashan
Beersheba
Hormah

SIMEON

EDOM

Zered Brook

20 miles
20 kilometers

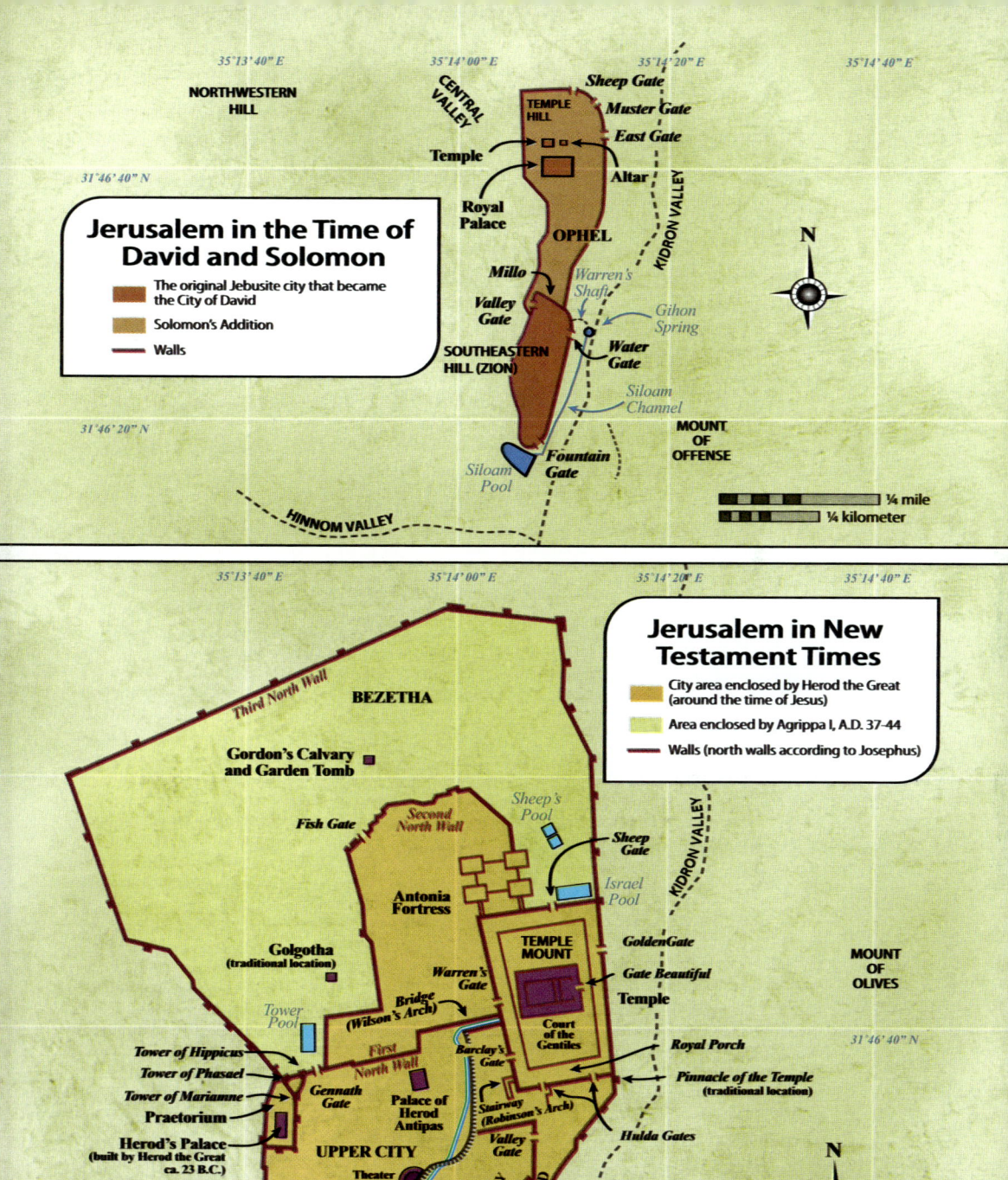

Jerusalem in the Time of David and Solomon

The original Jebusite city that became the City of David

Solomon's Addition

Walls

NORTHWESTERN HILL

CENTRAL VALLEY

TEMPLE HILL

Sheep Gate

Muster Gate

East Gate

Temple

Altar

Royal Palace

OPHEL

KIDRON VALLEY

Millo

Warren's Shaft

Gihon Spring

Valley Gate

Water Gate

SOUTHEASTERN HILL (ZION)

Siloam Channel

MOUNT OF OFFENSE

Siloam Pool

Fountain Gate

HINNOM VALLEY

¼ mile

¼ kilometer

N

Jerusalem in New Testament Times

City area enclosed by Herod the Great (around the time of Jesus)

Area enclosed by Agrippa I, A.D. 37–44

Walls (north walls according to Josephus)

Third North Wall

BEZETHA

Gordon's Calvary and Garden Tomb

Fish Gate

Second North Wall

Sheep's Pool

Sheep Gate

Israel Pool

Antonia Fortress

Golgotha (traditional location)

Warren's Gate

Bridge (Wilson's Arch)

TEMPLE MOUNT

GoldenGate

Gate Beautiful

Temple

Tower Pool

First North Wall

Barclay's Gate

Court of the Gentiles

Royal Porch

Tower of Hippicus

Tower of Phasael

Tower of Mariamne

Praetorium

Gennath Gate

Palace of Herod Antipas

Stairway (Robinson's Arch)

Pinnacle of the Temple (traditional location)

Herod's Palace (built by Herod the Great ca. 23 B.C.)

UPPER CITY

Theater

Valley Gate

Hulda Gates

Herod's Family Tomb

Serpent Pool

High Priest's House

Escarpment

LOWER CITY

TYROPOEON VALLEY

CITY OF DAVID

Gihon Spring

Hezekiah's Tunnel

ESSENE QUARTER

MOUNT OF OLIVES

KIDRON VALLEY

Aqueduct

Essene Gate

Upper Room (traditional location)

Siloam Pool

Water Gate

MOUNT OF OFFENSE

HINNOM VALLEY

¼ mile

¼ kilometer

N

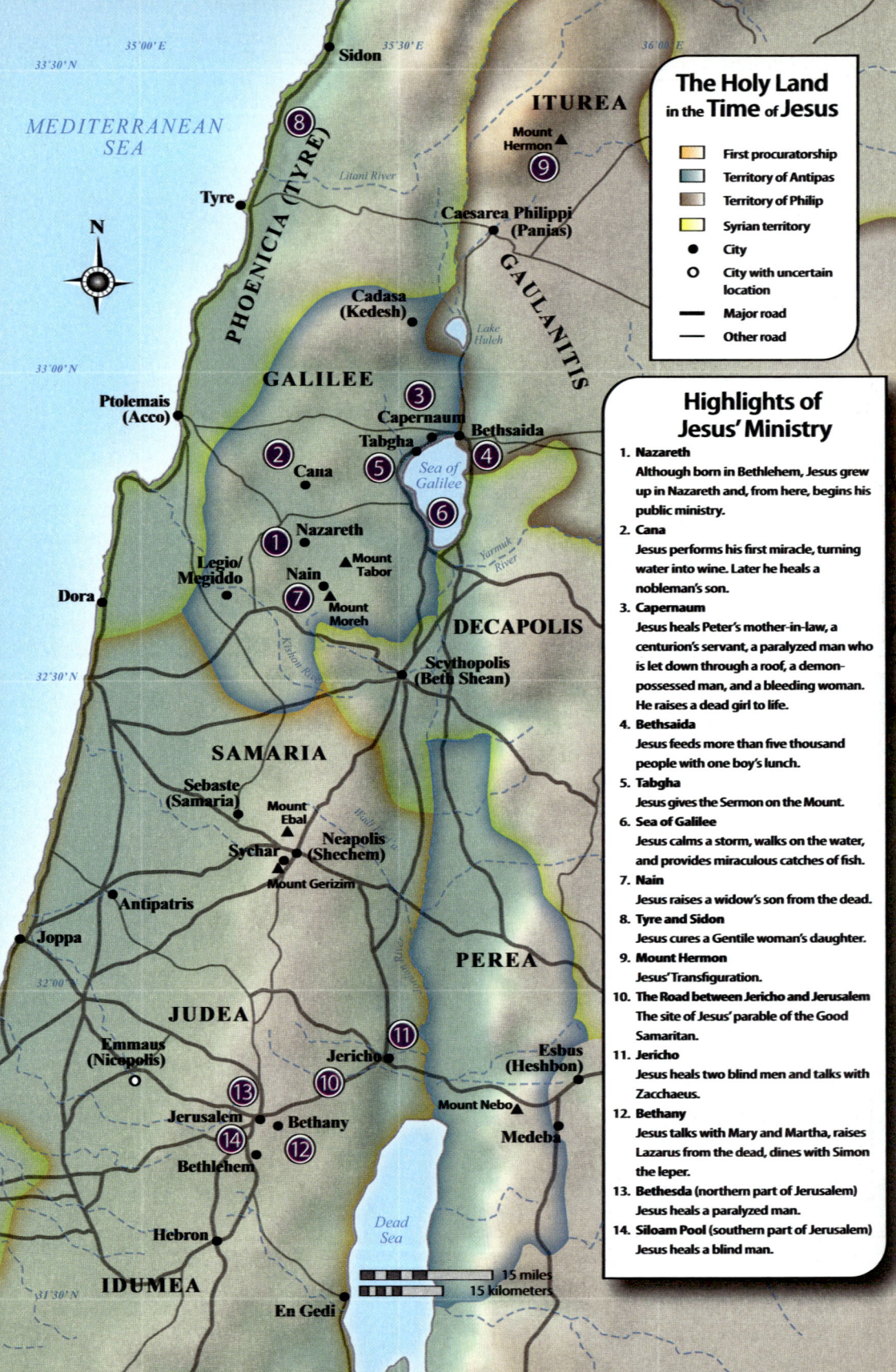

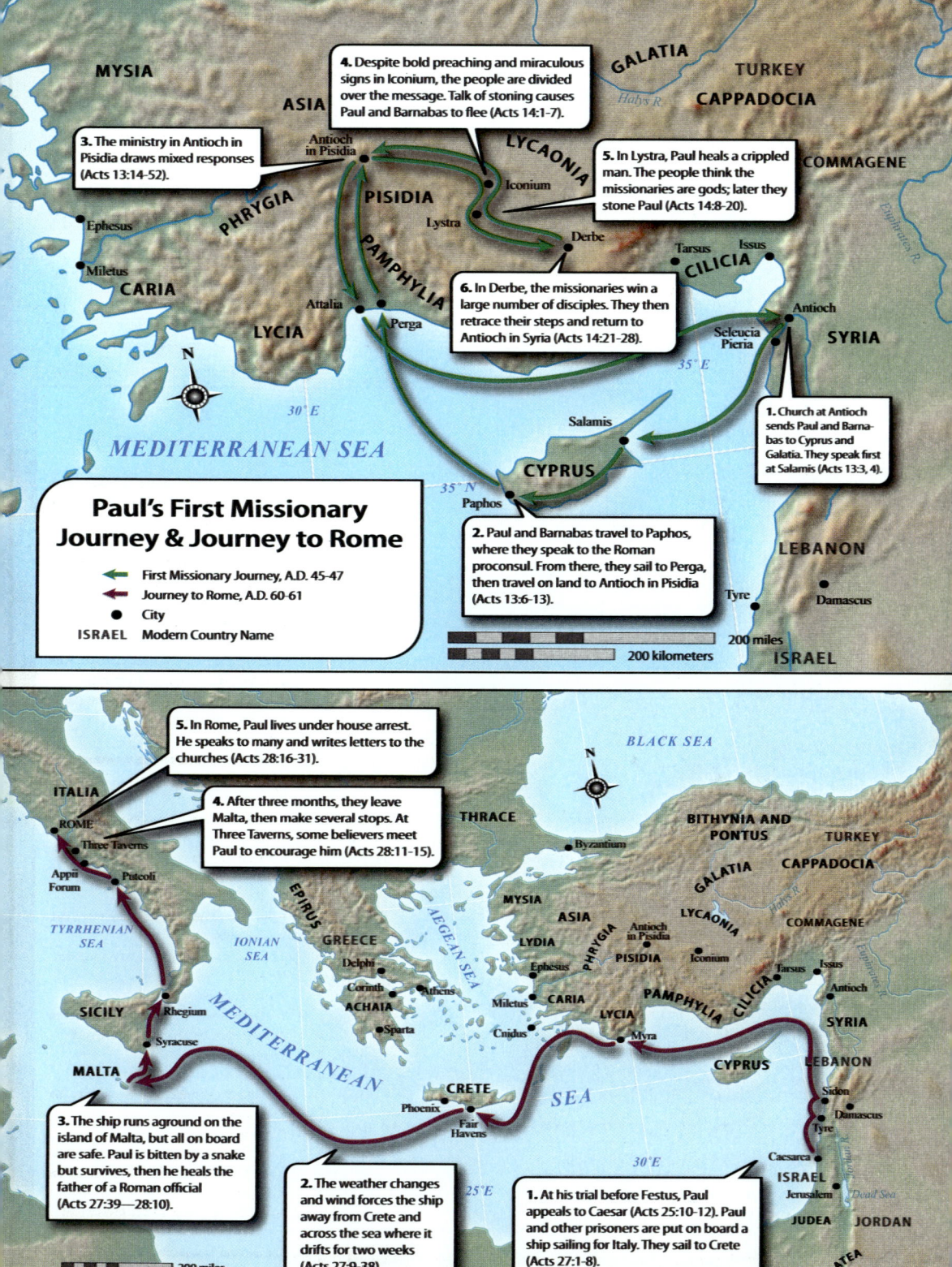

MYSIA

ASIA

GALATIA

TURKEY

Halys R.

CAPPADOCIA

4. Despite bold preaching and miraculous signs in Iconium, the people are divided over the message. Talk of stoning causes Paul and Barnabas to flee (Acts 14:1-7).

3. The ministry in Antioch in Pisidia draws mixed responses (Acts 13:14-52).

LYCAONIA

COMMAGENE

Antioch in Pisidia

5. In Lystra, Paul heals a crippled man. The people think the missionaries are gods; later they stone Paul (Acts 14:8-20).

Euphrates R.

PHRYGIA

PISIDIA

Iconium

• Ephesus

Lystra

Derbe

Tarsus

Issus

• Miletus

PAMPHYLIA

CILICIA

Antioch

CARIA

Attalia

LYCIA

Perga

6. In Derbe, the missionaries win a large number of disciples. They then retrace their steps and return to Antioch in Syria (Acts 14:21-28).

Selucia Pieria

SYRIA

35° E

1. Church at Antioch sends Paul and Barnabas to Cyprus and Galatia. They speak first at Salamis (Acts 13:3, 4).

30° E

Salamis

MEDITERRANEAN SEA

35° N

Paphos

CYPRUS

Paul's First Missionary Journey & Journey to Rome

→ First Missionary Journey, A.D. 45-47
→ Journey to Rome, A.D. 60-61
• City
ISRAEL Modern Country Name

2. Paul and Barnabas travel to Paphos, where they speak to the Roman proconsul. From there, they sail to Perga, then travel on land to Antioch in Pisidia (Acts 13:6-13).

LEBANON

Tyre

• Damascus

200 miles

200 kilometers

ISRAEL

---

5. In Rome, Paul lives under house arrest. He speaks to many and writes letters to the churches (Acts 28:16-31).

BLACK SEA

ITALIA

4. After three months, they leave Malta, then make several stops. At Three Taverns, some believers meet Paul to encourage him (Acts 28:11-15).

THRACE

BITHYNIA AND PONTUS

TURKEY

ROME•

• Three Taverns

Byzantium

GALATIA

CAPPADOCIA

Appii Forum

• Puteoli

TYRRHENIAN SEA

EPIRUS

MYSIA

ASIA

LYCAONIA

COMMAGENE

IONIAN SEA

GREECE

Delphi

AEGEAN SEA

LYDIA

Antioch in Pisidia

PHRYGIA

PISIDIA

Iconium

Tarsus

Issus

Ephesus

Antioch

SICILY

Rhegium

Corinth

ACHAIA

Athens

Miletus

CARIA

PAMPHYLIA

CILICIA

SYRIA

Sparta

Cnidus

LYCIA

Myra

MEDITERRANEAN

Syracuse

MALTA

CRETE

SEA

CYPRUS

LEBANON

Sidon

Phoenix

Fair Havens

Damascus

Tyre

3. The ship runs aground on the island of Malta, but all on board are safe. Paul is bitten by a snake but survives, then he heals the father of a Roman official (Acts 27:39—28:10).

2. The weather changes and wind forces the ship away from Crete and across the sea where it drifts for two weeks (Acts 27:9-38).

30° E

25° E

1. At his trial before Festus, Paul appeals to Caesar (Acts 25:10-12). Paul and other prisoners are put on board a ship sailing for Italy. They sail to Crete (Acts 27:1-8).

Caesarea

ISRAEL

Jerusalem

Dead Sea

JUDEA

JORDAN

NABATEA

200 miles

200 kilometers

EGYPT

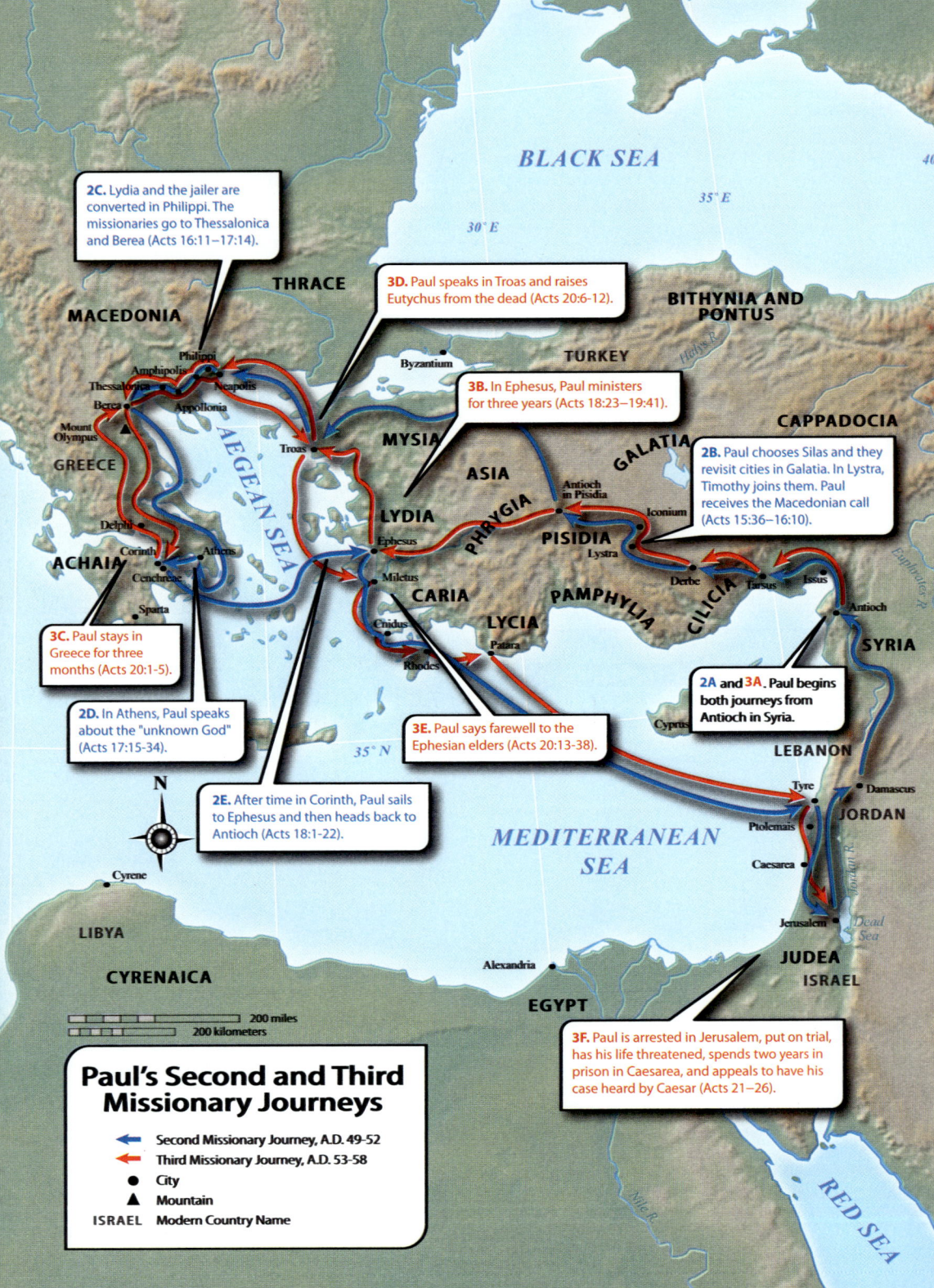

BLACK SEA

40° E
35° E
30° E

THRACE

MACEDONIA

2C. Lydia and the jailer are converted in Philippi. The missionaries go to Thessalonica and Berea (Acts 16:11–17:14).

3D. Paul speaks in Troas and raises Eutychus from the dead (Acts 20:6-12).

BITHYNIA AND PONTUS

Byzantium

TURKEY

CAPPADOCIA

3B. In Ephesus, Paul ministers for three years (Acts 18:23–19:41).

MYSIA

Philippi
Amphipolis
Thessalonica Neapolis
Berea Appollonia
Mount Olympus

GREECE

ASIA

GALATIA

2B. Paul chooses Silas and they revisit cities in Galatia. In Lystra, Timothy joins them. Paul receives the Macedonian call (Acts 15:36–16:10).

Troas

Antioch in Pisidia

PHRYGIA

Iconium

Euphrates R.

AEGEAN SEA

LYDIA

Delphi
Corinth Athens
Cenchreae

ACHAIA

Ephesus

PISIDIA

Lystra

Derbe

Tarsus

Issus

CILICIA

Antioch

SYRIA

Sparta

Miletus

CARIA

PAMPHYLIA

3C. Paul stays in Greece for three months (Acts 20:1-5).

Cnidus

LYCIA

Patara

2A and **3A**. Paul begins both journeys from Antioch in Syria.

Rhodes

2D. In Athens, Paul speaks about the "unknown God" (Acts 17:15-34).

Cyprus

LEBANON

2E. After time in Corinth, Paul sails to Ephesus and then heads back to Antioch (Acts 18:1-22).

3E. Paul says farewell to the Ephesian elders (Acts 20:13-38).

MEDITERRANEAN SEA

Tyre • Damascus
Ptolemais

JORDAN

35° N

Caesarea

Jordan R.

Cyrene

Jerusalem Dead Sea

JUDEA

LIBYA

ISRAEL

CYRENAICA

Alexandria •

200 miles
200 kilometers

EGYPT

3F. Paul is arrested in Jerusalem, put on trial, has his life threatened, spends two years in prison in Caesarea, and appeals to have his case heard by Caesar (Acts 21–26).

Nile R.

RED SEA

Paul's Second and Third Missionary Journeys

⬅ Second Missionary Journey, A.D. 49–52
⬅ Third Missionary Journey, A.D. 53-58
● City
▲ Mountain
ISRAEL Modern Country Name

N